ANDREA BOCELLI — SACRED ARIAS

Y0-BLU-752

Andrea Bocelli. The mention of his voice ignites the passion of millions worldwide. He is an inspiration. Legions of faithful fans can't get enough of him. They eagerly anticipate each and every new album containing the magic that is distinctly Andrea Bocelli.

On his latest album, SACRED ARIAS, Bocelli has recorded some of the most beautiful and inspired music ever written. A combination of timeless melodies, newly discovered gems and the world's favorite "Ave Marias."

Bocelli is a musician with two distinct voices and careers. One is the pop performer singing Italian love songs on the multi-platinum albums *Sogno* and *Romanza*. The other is the classical tenor showcased on the near-platinum *Aria - The Opera Album* and the gold-plus *Viaggio Italiano*. This versatility makes Andrea Bocelli the superstar he is today.

In the all-new Bocelli PBS Special ANDREA BOCELLI - SACRED ARIAS, he is joined by acclaimed Myung-Whun Chung and the Orchestra e coro dell'Accademia Nazionale di Santa Cecilia.

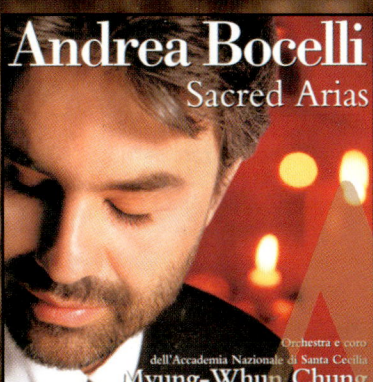

Sacred Arias ~ PPHI 462600

Also Available:
Aria-Opera ~ PPHI 462033

LETTER FROM THE EDITOR

The listings staff here at Schwann has been hard at work making sure that we are up-to-date with new releases in this issue of *Schwann Opus*. Check out the number of new release pages—I'm sure you'll be pleased. And don't pass up the stellar articles in this issue—we interviewed up-and-coming conductor Yuri Temirkanov recently, and he had much to say. He talks about, among other things, his childhood, his relationship with a multitude of orchestras and his thoughts on the best orchestra in the United States.

The past year has seen many new developments for Schwann, and I thought I'd mention one interesting one that you may not yet know about. Last

August, we began publishing a monthly update for classical and jazz retailers—it's called *Schwann Inside*. Each month, this publication lists jazz and classical new releases in the U.S. Because it's so time-sensitive and we need to produce it very quickly, we include fewer details about each release than we do in *Schwann Opus*: composer, piece abbreviation, top artists, catalog number and price. The publication also has notes on our picks for strong-selling releases and other information that's useful to retailers (for example, the February issue had a list of Grammy® Nominees). *Schwann Inside* may not be of direct benefit to you, but, certainly, by informing retailers of what's available, we're helping to make your purchasing experiences more enjoyable. And that harks back to 1949 and the first days of Schwann, when our founder, William Schwann, provided his list of available LPs to other retailers, so that they could find and order product more quickly for their customers.—*Becky Barnhart*

LETTERS TO THE EDITOR

Editor:

I want to express my delight about reading the fine interview with Einojuhani Rautavaara, one of my favorite composers, in the Spring 1999 *Schwann Opus*. I hope that many readers who were not familiar with his name did take note and got to know his majestic music.

A Latvian composer whose star is now rising meteorically is my good friend Peteris Vasks, whose magnificent music is now well-represented in your catalog. During the summer of 1999, my wife and I attended the world premiere of Peteris's Second Symphony in London's Royal Albert Hall, performed with great success by the Bournemouth SO, conducted by Yakov Kreizberg. Peteris was called out for three curtain calls. He recently finished his Fourth String Quartet, commissioned by the Kronos Quartet, which will perform the world premiere of the work in Paris this coming May.

I would be very happy to see an article on Peteris Vasks and his wonderful music in a future issue of *Schwann Opus*.

Dr. Diederik C. D. De Jong
Cincinnati, Ohio

Editor:

The article, "The Decca Legends," by Richard Freed in the Winter 1999-2000 issue of the *Schwann Opus* was more interesting in its omission (by Decca) than in its inclusions. While this is only Decca's first release, with more to come, I wish to comment on a startling omission by Decca with a history that bodes ill for an inclusion in future "Legends."

The Decca recording, Bach, Orchestral Works/Munchinger, Stuttgart Chamber Orchestra, London 458319-2, is not normally available in this country. I located a set for myself in a Washington, D.C. store, and I received a complimentary set for a family member. The store was unsuccessful in getting additional sets beyond only five that it was offered by Decca, and which it quickly sold. (I luckily obtained the last 5-CD set.)

Included in the 5-CD set are the best performance that I have heard (admittedly, an opinion) of the *Brandenburg Concerti* and the Orchestral Suites. But also included in the set are a pair of Crown Jewels: the *Art of the Fugue* and the *Musical Offering*. It is well established that these two works are of unique consequence to classical music. Munchinger's recordings of these works are regarded as unparalleled solutions to the problems that these works present. In brief, the Decca Record Company has a unique treasure in these recordings-modern recordings of the highest sound quality.

I have canvassed many colleagues who are devoted to classical music, and they all agree that this CD set would sell by the thousands in this country. Perhaps Schwann Publications, through its business and musician network, can persuade Decca to release this CD set in this country.

Burton Rothleder
Silver Spring, MD

Letters to the Editor should be addressed to:

**Becky Barnhart
Schwann Publications
1280 Santa Anita Court
Woodland, CA 95776**

**or e-mailed to
schwann@valley-media.com**

Published letters are subject to editing, particularly if they are long or address more than one topic.

THE CLASSICAL MUSIC RESOURCE

VOLUME 11 NUMBER 2

Schwann *opus*

SPRING 2000

SCHWANN PUBLICATIONS
www.schwann.com
1280 Santa Anita Court, Woodland, CA 95776
Tel: 530-669-5077 Fax: 530-669-5184
e-mail: schwann@valley-media.com

Publisher Barney Cohen
Associate Publisher Michael Fallone
Editor/Assistant Publisher Becky Barnhart

LISTINGS
Listings Editor Erin Lynch
Editorial Assistants Becki Clifford
Jeannette Hart
Karen Hustoft
Daryl Loomis
Bryan Redding
Celine Sidebottom
Paul Valencia

EDITORIAL
Features Editor Ted Libbey
Art Director Cheryl Ewasick
Editorial Coordinator Heather Ford
Contributors Lucille Baker-Bolton
Jed Distler
Richard Freed
Herbert Glass
Mike Gray
Heidi Waleson

ADVERTISING SALES
Advertising Manager Eileen Hendren
Tel: 530-661-5461

RETAIL SALES
Sales Manager Ali Crawford
Tel: 530-661-7881

SUBSCRIPTIONS & SINGLE COPIES
800-792-9447
or 530-661-3395 outside U.S.
Fax: 800-999-1794

Schwann Opus (ISSN: 1066-2138) is published quarterly for $59.95 per year by Schwann Publications, 1280 Santa Anita Court, Woodland, CA 95776. Periodicals postage paid at Woodland, CA and at additional mailing offices.
POSTMASTER: Send address changes to Schwann Opus, 1280 Santa Anita Court, Woodland, CA 95776.

© Schwann Publications. All rights reserved. No part of this publication may be reproduced or transmitted in any form or by any means, electronically, optically, or mechanically, including photocopy, recording, or any other information storage or retrieval system, without permission in writing from the publisher. The information contained in this publication is provided for reference uses only. No representations are made as to this publication's completeness or accuracy, although the publisher has made every effort to provide the most up-to-date and useful information possible. The publisher hereby expressly excludes all warranties.

For high-quality article reprints of 100 or more, including electronic reprints, please contact Reprint Management Services at 717-560-2001.
member of

NARM — Give the gift of music.
Member of AFIM

ISBN: 1-57598-074-6
Printed in the USA
Cover Design Cheryl Ewasick
Cover Photography Courtesy of Baltimore Symphony Orchestra

Features

6A ***Yuri Temirkanov*** /Breaking the Russian Stereotype
Herbert Glass

12A ***Mining a Rich Heritage*** /Two Celebratory Box Sets
Jed Distler

Departments

4A Letter from the Editor
18A Record Reviews
33A Music Mart
35A How to Use *Schwann Opus*
1094 Label Addresses

Listings

1 New Releases
50 Composers
927 Collections

PHOTO: BALTIMORE SYMPHONY ORCHESTRA

Breaking the Russian Stereotype

Yuri Temirkanov

by Herbert Glass

Yuri Temirkanov has lately become as familiar a figure in my part of the world, the West Coast—at the head of the touring St. Petersburg Philharmonic and as a guest with the San Francisco Symphony and Los Angeles Philharmonic—as he has with orchestras and their audiences throughout the rest of the U.S. To say nothing of his solid European presence, leading all the usual, glittering suspects in Berlin, Amsterdam, Vienna, Paris, Munich and Dresden.

The atmosphere at a recent Temirkanov/Los Angeles Philharmonic rehearsal was upbeat, to say the least. Launching their first meeting of the season, Temirkanov strode to the podium with a breezy wave of the hand, a bow and a relaxed "good morning" to the players, then calmly set about conducting, as ever without baton, his body language fluid and obviously communicative, virtually the whole of the Mussorgsky-Ravel *Pictures at an Exhibition* without a break. Familiar music to the players, but under the guidance of a man who knows as much about this repertoire as anyone alive. Still, even in the subsequent, by no means grueling polishing of the collaboration, Temirkanov never failed to give the players credit for their knowledge of the music.

When I asked Daniel Rothmuller, the orchestra's associate principal cellist, what it was about Temirkanov that created this collegial atmosphere, he answered, with disarming simplicity, "Hell, we like this guy. We're really comfortable with him. He knows what he's doing and he gets the best out of us without it being a struggle."

It would be impossible to imagine orchestras under Toscanini, Szell, Reiner or Karajan remarking on how "comfortable" those celebrated taskmasters made them. Their closeness was of a decidedly less personal sort. The realities are different today, although stories proliferate about how in recent years some American orchestras had to "tame" (as if they were wild beasts) their European music directors. On the whole, however, the old adversarial relationship is no more: not only because the conductors themselves bring with them a different, more humane attitude, but because today's orchestras have so much more say in determining their own destinies, and the fate of those who lead them, than in earlier times. The autocrat conductor is largely a thing of the past.

But even among a number of respected good-guy conductors on the current scene, Temirkanov stands out, and I got more than an inkling of why when I encountered his offstage persona for the first time, during a long chat in the Los Angeles high-rise apartment that was his temporary home during a guest stint with our orchestra.

Yuri Temirkanov is a slight, taut, wiry man in his early-60s, with an impressive shock of graying brown hair and facial features subtly suggestive of a Central Asian background. And while he obviously speaks some English—he laughs at my wisecracks, perhaps more out of innate courteousness than total comprehension—he communicates with an interviewer in Russian via Marina Stokes, a Russian-born Englishwoman, his astute translator and aide-de-camp of many years' standing.

I had just been informed of Temirkanov's appointment as music director of the Baltimore Symphony Orchestra (he took the reins in January of this year), concurrent with his continuing directorship of the St. Petersburg Philharmonic. Temirkanov arrives in Baltimore as successor to David Zinman, whose decade there brought the orchestra to the kind of prominence that could attract as his successor an international celebrity of Temirkanov's standing.

How did Temirkanov and Baltimore find each other?

"It took some two years for us to come to an agreement. Not because I had any doubts about the orchestra's skills, since I conducted them many times as a guest. It had mainly to do with my apprehensiveness over never having had an American orchestra. A whole new world.

"This was the first orchestra I had encountered that had so much respect and affection for its conductor. Which was

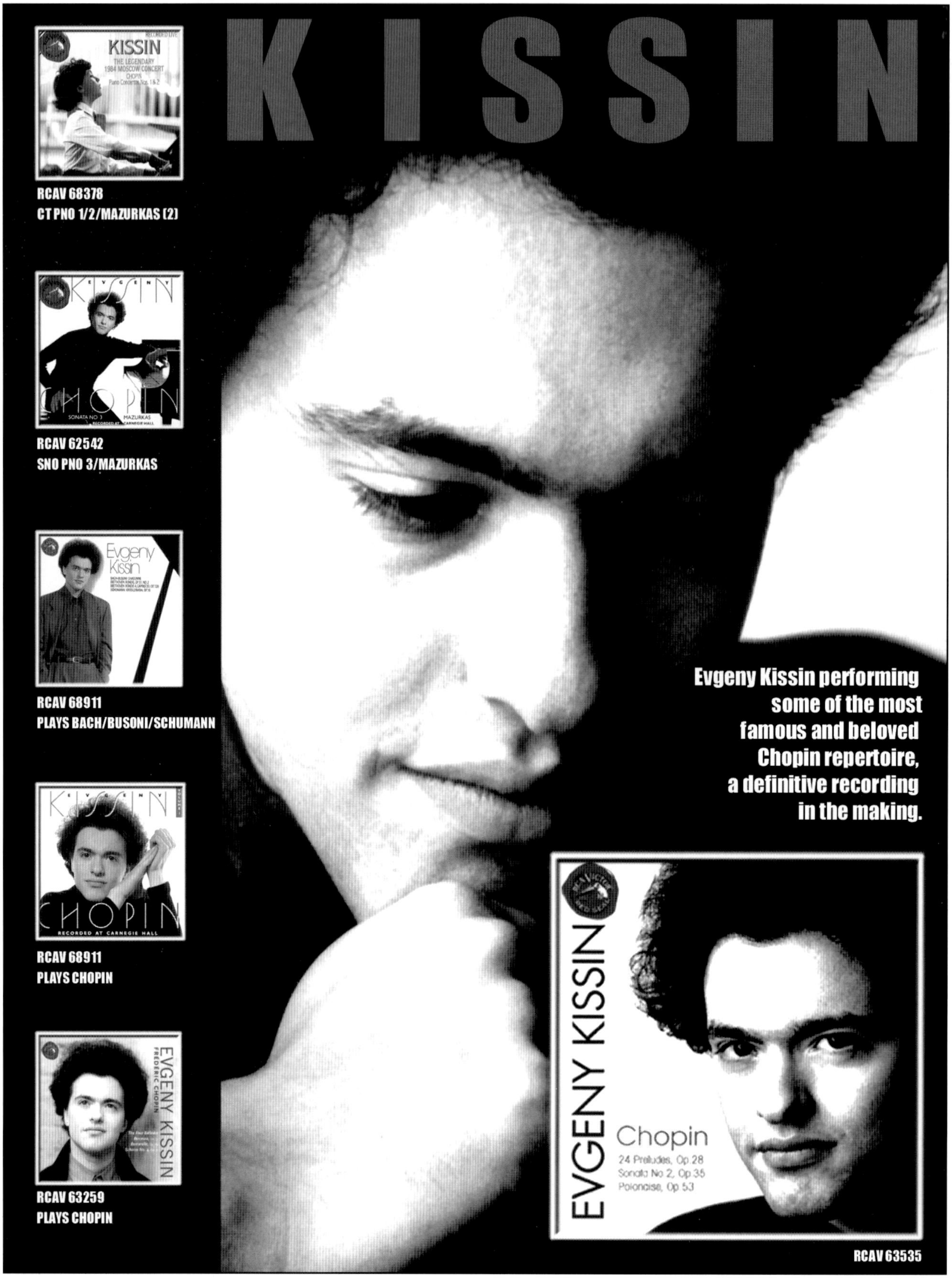

RCAV 68378
CT PNO 1/2/MAZURKAS (2)

RCAV 62542
SNO PNO 3/MAZURKAS

RCAV 68911
PLAYS BACH/BUSONI/SCHUMANN

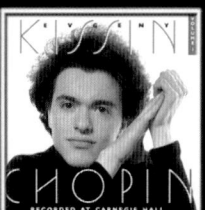
RCAV 68911
PLAYS CHOPIN

RCAV 63259
PLAYS CHOPIN

KISSIN

Evgeny Kissin performing some of the most famous and beloved Chopin repertoire, a definitive recording in the making.

RCAV 63535

all the more unusual because Zinman had already announced he was leaving, a time when people feel they can say things they'd been afraid to express before.

"Why did I take on such a big new responsibility, in a new country, at this time of my life? Well, the situation is such in Russia nowadays that we [the St. Petersburg Philharmonic] have to tour constantly, for money, to survive. And when we tour there's always a compromise over the program, with the promoter, the impresario and others. What people want from a Russian orchestra and Russian conductor is Russian music. So, too much of my work in St. Petersburg is rehearsing for the next tour, which has the effect of limiting the repertoire we can play at home. Baltimore offers me freedom of choice."

Did you feel that it would take longer for a European conductor to achieve as close a relationship with the orchestra as Zinman had? After all, no orchestra player would call you Yuri to your face from day one. And is the language a problem?

"First of all, yes, I don't the speak the language so well. But after a while it made no difficulties with the Royal Philharmonic [of which Temirkanov was for many years principal guest conductor, then principal conductor]. Today the Baltimore Symphony and other American orchestras know me so well that we communicate on other levels. But I wouldn't like them to call me Yuri ever! My profession is being a conductor. The profession demands that we have a friendly relationship. But that doesn't mean musicians come up and slap me on the back. Not because I have any personal dislike for it, but it doesn't further our professional relationship.

"There are players in the St. Petersburg Philharmonic who were my fellow students long ago, and even they wouldn't think of calling me anything but Yuri Hatuevich [the patronymic, the polite Russian form of address] or maestro. As George Orwell said, we are all equal, but some are more equal than others."

When I remind him that it was the pigs who uttered that immortal line in 1984, he bursts out laughing and, somewhat abashed, suggests that we change the subject.
Getting back to the matter of repertoire: Now that the doors have opened wider to him than ever in the United States, I noted that his being stereotyped as a conductor of Russian music extended as well to his guest engagements and of course to his contract with BMG/RCA Victor, which created a small flood of Temirkanov recordings—with the St. Petersburg Philharmonic (mainly), the Royal Philharmonic and the New York Philharmonic.

"Yes, that is unfortunate. Although I'm proud of many of those recordings. But BMG is no longer interested in having conductors under contract. If I am not mistaken the only one they still have under contract is Michael Tilson Thomas, and that is unlikely to last much longer. Very sad.

"But I did not mean earlier to give the impression that even in St. Petersburg we have done nothing but Russian music, although for the obvious reasons the emphasis has been that way in the last years. Until touring became our main means of making a living, we also did our share of Haydn, Mozart, Beethoven, Berlioz, Mahler, and with the Royal Philharmonic I did, in addition to Russian music, Britten, Elgar, Richard Strauss and many others. In coming seasons I will be conducting Danish music—Nielsen, of course, and the fine contemporary composer Poul Ruders— with the Danish National Radio Orchestra [of which Temirkanov is principal guest conductor].

"With Baltimore I want to do much more of the Western classics. In my first weeks there we will play Beethoven, Mahler, Ravel and Debussy, Haydn, as well as Tchaikovsky, Shostakovich and Prokofiev."

Getting into some Temirkanov history, I observe that he hails from an obscure place called the Kabardina-Balkar Republic, situated in the northern Caucasus and bordered on the east by Chechnya. Did his family emigrate there in the 1940s, as did others who sought refuge from the war-torn cities of the north?

"No, I emigrated to Russia. My family is still in Kabardina-Balkar. It's my homeland and it's where I had my earliest musical education. My father, Hatu Temirkanov, was the Minister of Culture in Kabardina and in 1942 he commissioned the Second String Quartet from Prokofiev when the composer was living there [thus his use in the work of Kabardinian folk melodies]. I knew my father only a little while. The Germans executed him when I was four."

When did you begin to study conducting?

"I was studying violin and later viola, which became my instrument, in Leningrad when I was 13, and three years later began conducting studies at the Leningrad Conservatory. But possibly the seed was planted when I was much younger and was taken to hear a brass band in Nalchik [the Kabardinian capital]. I was fascinated by that colorfully dressed man in front of the players, waving his arms at them. I wondered what he was doing. Later I found out, so now I can wave my arms, too."

How did you arrive at the Leningrad—now St. Petersburg—Philharmonic?

"The path was something like this: First, I worked in opera and ballet at the Maly Theater in Leningrad while I was still studying conducting at the Conservatory, then I became an assistant to Evgeny Mravinsky with the Leningrad Philharmonic. At the same time, the second orchestra in the city, the Leningrad Symphony, didn't have a music director, so Mravinsky, who had tremendous influence, suggested to the minister of culture that I be appointed to the job. I was there for ten years, while remaining Mravinsky's assistant. Then I became music director of the Kirov Company, conducting opera and ballet. I should mention that I brought in as my assistant the young Valery Gergiev [now the Kirov's music director], and I am proud to call him my protégé.

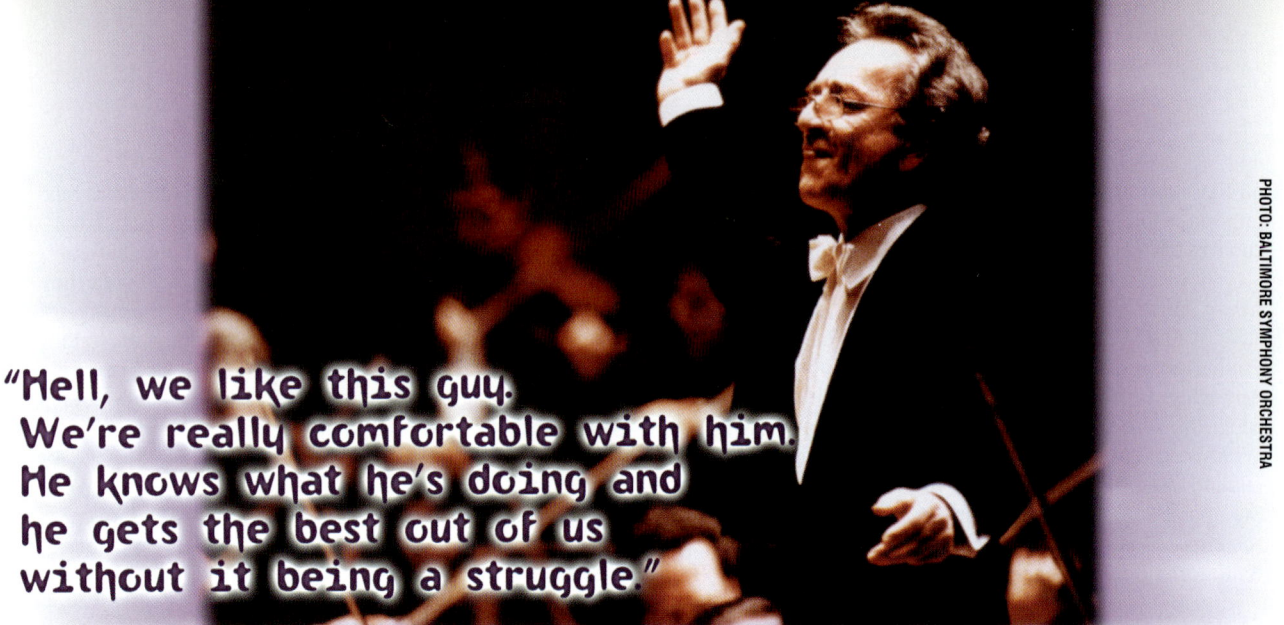

"Hell, we like this guy. We're really comfortable with him. He knows what he's doing and he gets the best out of us without it being a struggle."

"After Mravinsky died in 1988, the members of the Leningrad Philharmonic, which is a democracy, took a vote and named me music director. Which was a great thrill. The best orchestra in Russia, to which all the best players wanted to belong. Not that getting the job was so easy. The government wanted a quick election, to get rid of me, since they were certain I would lose the vote. They wanted someone more friendly to them, and they wanted an ethnic Russian. Actually, I was prepared for that. When I was at the Kirov, I'd get plenty of hate mail. What right do you have to conduct Russian music, you foreigner—*Onegin, Pique Dame*...what could you possibly know of Pushkin? Ethnic hatreds are hardly new in Russia.

"It is ironic that painful things were also said about me in the West. This awful Englishman, this Norman Lebrecht [the "ch" emerges as a guttural snarl] who wrote in this awful book about conductors [*The Maestro Myth: Great Conductors in Pursuit of Power*] that I was a loyal party member, which is why I got the Leningrad Philharmonic job, and then other journalists quoted from that as if it were fact. I was unbelievably offended by this hateful misinformation. The positions I have held...it was unique that I held them without being a party member, which was not easy at all. Many times they tried to persuade me to become a party member, to advance my career.

"I had troubles always with the authorities, above all for taking Jews into the orchestra and having them travel with us when the government did not want them to leave the country. And then Lebrecht writes that I got my jobs because I was a party man...Hah! I hope he doesn't say that Baltimore took me for some political reason."

I asked that Temirkanov tell readers a bit about Mravinsky, to us a somewhat shadowy, near-legendary exemplar of the old-time European podium autocrat, known in the West almost exclusively through his recordings with the Leningrad Philharmonic, to cultists as much "his" orchestra as the NBC Symphony was Toscanini's, or the Berlin Philharmonic Furtwängler's, and for his long association with Shostakovich.

"Frankly, I didn't think highly of him as a musician. A great personality, yes. Tolstoy once said that you can teach almost anyone any profession up to about 95%, but that remaining 5%, which can not be taught, makes all the difference. Mravinsky lacked the 5%. I always have my suspicions about a conductor who rehearses to the final degree every ritenuto or accelerando."

Are you saying that he rehearsed effects, and that he was preoccupied with minor details for want of seeing the big picture?

"Not all of that. He knew how to build a piece. Definitely. He did details and the big picture, but one never felt spontaneity. There was always something about him...the high priest, the concert as a ritual, rather than something living. Rehearsals were of course fascinating, and I was always there. I never came across any conductor who worked so thoroughly, to the point of becoming boring. I can't work like that. I don't have the desire, or the patience.

"The first mistake of the conductor in my opinion is when you come to an orchestra, they play a few bars and you immediately tell them what's wrong and start correcting. But if you play the whole movement, show them on which road you are leading them, they can take it from the beginning again and they'll do what you want mostly by themselves. You don't have to rehearse every sforzando. Even worse, is when you philosophize—when you talk, talk, talk.

"Maybe 180 years ago you had to talk to them about music in general because they were only musicians, but nowadays musicians are broadly educated people. So it irritates them if you give lectures and it adds nothing to the music. I say these things not because I am so intelligent, but because I have had the experience myself, from years of playing in orchestras, for concerts, opera, for films, while pursuing my early education as a conductor."

Could you compare some orchestras with which you've been associated, their sounds, their personalities. What, say, is the great strength of the St. Petersburg Philharmonic?

"With St. Petersburg it is not so much about 'sections,' but of tradition, a tradition going far back into the 19th century. Call it good breeding, which is no longer so easy to find. Part of this breeding, of carrying on a tradition, comes *(continued on page 27)*

BACH, BUSONI AND BIBER

J.S. BACH
VIOLIN SONATAS

HAM 907250

So skillfully does Bach handle the three elements of violin, harpsichord, and gamba testing the relationship between them in every conceivable way, that these pieces might be seen as one of the final and fullest flowerings of the trio sonata form—an apotheosis of the genre. Andrew Manze, whose recent recordings with Richard Egarr and Jaap ter Linden of Violin Sonatas by Pandolfi and Rebel have received acclaim, brings superlative performances for the year 2000.

H. BIBER
MISSA BRUXELLENSIS

AVOX 9808

In the golden age of the Baroque, Biber's Missa Bruxellensis perpetuated a grand tradition of religious music, which florished in a superb and privileged fashion at Salzburg Cathedral. The Missa Bruxellensis is one of the last of Biber's compositions and brilliantly confirms his stature as a true master of sacred music.

F. BUSONI
CT PNO OP. 39

HYP 67143

This has to be the Romantic Piano Concerto for the millennium. The Busoni concerto, with its five movements, choral finale and a length of over 70 minutes, is surely the most grandiose ever written. But this is no over-ambitious monster; Busoni was one of the greatest pianists the world has ever known, but he was also a great intellectual with very strong views on art and culture.

J.S. BACH
HARMONIA MUNDI BACH EDITION

HAM 2908096

This 2 CD set features 144 minutes of highlights from the Harmonia Mundi Bach Edition. Selections include tracks from both reissues and upcoming new releases. Of special note are excerpts from two of the most important new releases in the series: Philippe Herreweghe's penetrating new reading of the St. Matthew Passion, and Andrew Manze's dazzling version of the Violin Sonatas.

J.S. BACH
ST MATTHEW PASSION

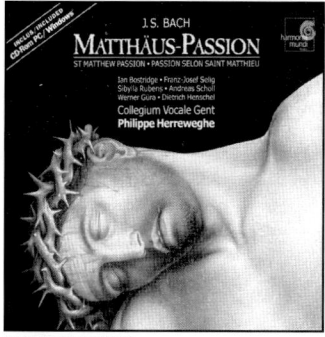

HAM 951676

Johann Sebastian Bach's monumental St. Matthew Passion was first performed on Good Friday on 1727 at the St. Thomas Chruch in Leipzig. It is the single largest composition Bach ever wrote, both in terms of length and in terms of instrumental and vocal forces. This eagerly awaited recording, made shortly after a BBC Prom performance, has the added bonus of a superb CD-ROM.

hyperion   harmonia mundi FRANCE

THIS PAGE, TOP: AARON COPLAND AND LEONARD BERNSTEIN AT THE REHEARSAL FOR THE WORLD PREMIERE OF COPLAND'S *CONNOTATIONS*, PERFORMED BY THE NEW YORK PHILHARMONIC IN 1962; *LOWER LEFT:* IN THEIR FIRST-EVER COLLABORATIVE EFFORT, WYNTON MARSALIS AND THE LINCOLN CENTER JAZZ ORCHESTRA WITH KURT MASUR AND THE NEW YORK PHILHARMONIC IN CELEBRATION OF JAZZ MASTER DUKE ELLINGTON'S 100TH BIRTHDAY; *LOWER RIGHT:* GEORGE GERSHWIN PLAYS HIS "CONCERTO IN F" FOR WALTER DAMROSCH, PREMIERED BY THE NEW YORK PHILHARMONIC. *OPPOSITE PAGE, TOP:* EUGENE ORMANDY AND THE PHILADELPHIA ORCHESTRA AT A RECORDING SESSION IN THE EARLY 1960's; *LOWER RIGHT:* COMPOSER VIRGIL THOMSON WITH MEZZO-SOPRANO BETTY ALLEN, IN PREPARATION FOR THE NEW YORK PHILHARMONIC'S PERFORMANCE OF THOMSON'S *FOUR SAINTS IN THREE ACTS*.

Mining a Rich Heritage: Two Celebratory Box Sets

by jed distler

New York Philharmonic: An American Celebration;
NYP 9904 (10 CDs)

The Philadelphia Orchestra: The Centennial Collection:
Historic Broadcasts and Recordings 1917-1998;
The Philadelphia Orchestra Association (12 CDs)

Over the past decade, collectors have been graced with archival box sets from the New York Philharmonic, The Cleveland Orchestra and the Chicago Symphony. To tie in with their hundredth anniversary this year, the Philadelphia Orchestra lavish similar attention on their rich broadcast and recorded legacy via "The Centennial Collection." The material is culled from live broadcast and concert tapings, along with rare studio recordings that have either been unavailable for years or never before released. The 12 discs are programmed into seven volumes that focus respectively upon the orchestra's music directors (Vols. 1-3), its guest conductors, various composers as conductors, singers as guest artists and instrumental soloists.

Discs one through three focus on the two music directors with whom the "Philadelphia Sound" is synonymous. A 1917 Brahms *Hungarian Dance* No. 5 belies Leopold Stokowski's negative assessment of his pre-electrical recordings. True, the bass line is supplanted by tubas, but the overall orchestral image and quality of execution needs no apology. Released for the first time, a composite Beethoven Fifth Symphony assembled from two incomplete 1931 live performances stems from experimental Bell Laboratories recordings. Some may flinch at Stokowski's exaggerated distention of the motto theme and pronounced rhetorical touches elsewhere, although no stylistic qualms mark Stoki's grandiose, tonally alluring Sibelius Second recorded three decades later. The 82-year-old maestro elicits cleanly contoured section work

Telefunken Legacy

Historic reissue marking the debut of Teldec's new Telefunken Legacy archival series. Originally recorded in 1938 and 1941, this recording of Richard Strauss' "heroic" tone poems serves as a noble tribute to the composer in the 50th anniversary year of his death. Of special mention – the most riveting "Don Juan" ever captured on disc. Carefully restored and remastered with comprehensive annotation.

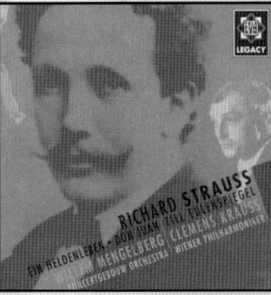

TELC 28409
Clemens Krauss:
Conducts Strauss

TELC 28409
Willem Mengelberg: Conducts
Beethoven Sym 5 & 6 "Pastoral"

Historic reissue marking the debut of Teldec's new Telefunken Legacy archival series. It draws from original recordings from May 4 and December 22, 1937, featuring Mengelberg, noted for the sweep of his Beethoven symphonic interpretations, at the helm. Carefully restored and remastered with comprehensive annotation.

Historic reissue marking the debut of Teldec's new Telefunken Legacy archival series. One of the preeminent coloratura sopranos of this century, "German Nightingale" Erna Sack is presented in the light classics and operetta arias most closely identified with her – music that displays her dazzling pyrotechnics and brilliant high register. Carefully restored and remastered with comprehensive annotation.

TELC 28412
Erna Sack:
Ciribiribin

TELC 28413
Calvet Quartet:
Plays Beethoven

Historic reissue marking the debut of Teldec's new Telefunken Legacy archival series. Featuring the landmark performances (recorded November 23, 1936 and January 19, 1938) of the first Calvet Quartet, formed in 1919 by French violinist Joseph Calvet. Carefully restored and remastered with comprehensive annotation.

Teldec

A collection of this cult-status quartet's most diverse repertoire, from Ravel to Gershwin, and from Shostakovich to Japanese folk song.

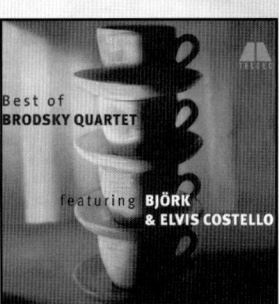

TELC 28404
Brodsky Quartet: Best Of
featuring Björk & Elvis Costello

TELC 21475
John Field:
Piano Concertos Nos. 2 & 3

German pianist Andreas Staier embarks on another recording with Concerto Köln, performing the work of John Field (the "Irish Chopin") on a beautifully restored Broadwood fortepiano, built in 1802.

This 2-CD set pairs tenor Placido Domingo with acclaimed soprano Waltraud Meier for Barenboim's first all-Beethoven recording for Teldec.

TELC 25249
L.V. Beethoven:
Fidelio-Complete Opera

TELC 21472
Vincenzo Bellini:
I Capuleti e i Montecchi

Celebrated mezzo-soprano Jennifer Larmore stars in the trouser role of Romeo in Bellini's bel canto adaptation of Shakespeare's Romeo and Juliet. Lyric soprano Hei-Kyung Hong co-stars as Juliet.

One can sum up the 20th century as the era when American composers came into their own, developing sounds and personalities that could not be mistaken for those of their European counterparts

---

from his responsive musicians. As was his wont, Stoki retools the final bars of Tchaikovsky's *Romeo and Juliet*, and his 1960 studio-led Wagner "Love Music" from *Tristan und Isolde* (never before on CD) is intriguingly spot-lit. Despite its superior sound, Stoki obtained more convincing results in his Philadelphia *Tristan* "Symphonic Syntheses" recorded in the 1930s.

The Eugene Ormandy selections focus on music by his contemporaries. It's good to have the conductor's 1950 studio Schoenberg *Verklärte Nacht* available again, opaque sonics and all. A stately 1977 Rachmaninoff *Isle of the Dead* contrasts well with Ormandy's swifter, long unavailable mono version. More valuable, perhaps, are items otherwise unrecorded by Ormandy: the premiere of Piston's inventive and witty Seventh Symphony, Penderecki's searing *Threnody for the Victims of Hiroshima* and the Shostakovich Sixth Symphony.

In Edgar Varèse's *Arcana*, Ricardo Muti integrates the music's seemingly disjunct sound blocks into an intense, flowing statement. Muti's live Respighi *Pines of Rome* differs little from his excellent EMI studio recording, although the archival tape captures the offstage brass in perfect perspective. Current music director Wolfgang Sawallisch flaunts his considerable keyboard mettle in Beethoven's *Choral Fantasy*, and offers a solid, judiciously paced Brahms *Haydn Variations*, along with one of the finest performances of Martinu's Fourth Symphony you'll ever hear.

Two discs given over to guest conductors yield unusual discoveries. A 1931 selection from the Bell Labs series preserves Fritz Reiner's earliest known recording, a disciplined but frankly run-of-the-mill "Transformation Music" from Act I of Wagner's *Parsifal*. Klaus Tennstedt, by contrast, is heard to better advantage in a lean, quietly authoritative Barber *Adagio for Strings*. In similarly atypical fare, Bruno Walter imbues Debussy's *Afternoon of a Faun* with gentle tempo fluctuation and subtle portamenti. Charles Munch's breezy Ravel *Daphnis et Chloé* Suite No. 2, however, treads familiar ground. While the Philadelphia Orchestra has recorded much Bartók over the years, István Kertész's brilliant dispatch of the *Dance Suite* preserves the short-lived conductor's authoritative manner in a work he did not record commercially. Prefacing Toscanini's well-known 1942 studio account of Berlioz's *Queen Mab* scherzo, we get an eight-minute rehearsal excerpt. The Maestro voices his demands for balance and delicacy in a patient, affectionate tone of voice quite different from the tyrannial outbursts for which he was notorious.

If there is a more eccentric Mahler Fifth in existence than Hermann Scherchen's reading from October 30th, 1964, I haven't heard it. Scherchen makes a huge cut in the scherzo, and turns the second and fifth movements into relay races. At 15 minutes, his Adagietto movement morphs into a vertiable Adagissimo. The orchestra responds amazingly well to their guest conductor's loopy demands. Scherchen's more scrappily executed, and uncut, Vienna Symphony studio recording on Westminster, though, proves that this maverick conductor could play this music straight when he chose. While Scherchen's Philadelphia broadcast remains a fascinating document, its appeal will be limited to specialists.

No question, however, that the rejected 1934 Heifetz/Stokowski Sibelius Concerto deserves its highly anticipated first release here, although the dry ambiance and skewed balances justify the artists' reservations. Pianophiles will welcome Josef Hofmann's 1938 Golden Jubilee broadcast of the Beethoven Fourth Concerto, sonically upgraded from a limited-edition LP incarnation. The aristocratic 1970 Richter/Ormandy Mozart G Major Concerto, K. 453, sounds better here in its official incarnation than previous independent CD and LP releases. One of the collection's finest offerings emerges in the form of violinist Leonid Kogan's noble and undemonstrably meticulous Berg Concerto.

Other concerto items supplant the slender legacies of musicians with tragically foreshortened careers. Michael Rabin's Tchaikovsky Concerto dances with more spontaneity than his familiar commercial recording. A 1945 Brahms D minor Concerto captures William Kapell in excellent form, although I prefer his riskier, more personalized, and poetic (albeit less well-conducted) 1953 New York Philharmonic broadcast. And Jacqueline Du Pré's legion of admirers will certainly want her Saint-Saëns A minor Concerto, stemming from a 1971 concert conducted by her husband Daniel Barenboim. Anneliese Rothenberger and Dietrich Fischer-Dieskau shared the bill with Du Pré on the aforementioned concert, and their second-act duet from Strauss's *Arabella* is one of the high points of disc nine, devoted to vocalists. Two unpublished sides with Dorothy Maynor and Marian Anderson are unearthed, as well as electrifying operatic highlights from 1962-63 gala concerts featuring Franco Corelli, George London, Dame Joan Sutherland and Birgit Nilsson, with Stokowski conducting.

Composer/conductors have long relished the opportunity to lead the Philadelphia Orchestra in their own music. Kodály's zesty 1946 *Peacock Variations* (with Variation 12 omitted) sparkles with authority, as do Stravinsky's 1946 suite from the *Fairy's Kiss* and Virgil Thomson's 1945 commercial recording of *Five Portraits* (fabulously transferred from the original Columbia Masterworks lacquers). Lastly, a 1976 concert featured Aaron Copland sculpting his *Lincoln Portrait* in monumental paragraphs, while Marion Anderson intoned the fallen American president's words to bone-chilling effect. One cannot take leave of this landmark release without praising to the skies Ward Marston's restorations and Barrymore Laurence Scherer's annotations.

As the Philadelphia Orchestra embarks on their second century and the new millennium finds its bearings, one can

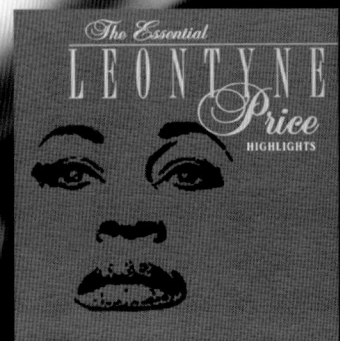

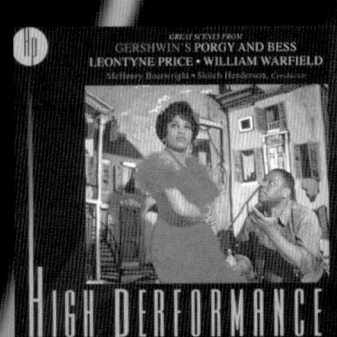

Leontyne Price
RCAV 68152
THE ESSENTIAL LEONTYNE PRICE

Leontyne Price
RCAV 63463
THE ULTIMATE COLLECTION

G. Gershwin
HP 63312
PORGY & BESS-
HIGHLIGHTS

Leontyne PRICE

Leontyne Price
RCAV 68883
VERDI & PUCCINI ARIAS

G. Puccini
RCAV 105
TOSCA-COMPLETE OPERA

G. Verdi
RCAV 39498
AIDA-COMPLETE OPERA

ALSO AVAILABLE:
Placido Domingo	OPERA DUETS	RCAV 62595
Leontyne Price	HER GREATEST ROLES-ESSENTIAL	RCAV 68154
Leontyne Price	ESSENTIAL-SPIRITUAL HYMNS	RCAV 68154

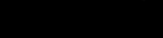

> One measure of the impact of American music on the outside world lies in the fact that out of all the conductors represented here, only four were American born.

sum up the 20th century as the era when American composers came into their own, developing sounds and personalities that could not be mistaken for those of their European counterparts, regardless of style. To celebrate the diverse stylistic landscape of American orchestral music, the New York Philharmonic rings in the third millennium with its latest box set culled from previously unreleased broadcast and archival performances. Nearly 50 compositions are included, encompassing composers from the pioneering Chadwick, MacDowell and Griffes to contemporary beacons like Bolcom, Carter, Crumb, Druckman, Reich, Rouse, Tower and, of course, Copland.

Ten discs are partitioned into a pair of sturdy boxes, each with its own 250-page book, containing detailed notes on the music as well as comments from the performers and composers. Two timelines list the birthdates of every American composer the Philharmonic has performed up to the present. A year-to-year listing of every player in the orchestra allows one to identify, say, principal soloists with a scorecard, so to speak. One measure of the impact of American music on the outside world lies in the fact that out of all the conductors represented here, only four were American born. Yet the performances are never less than idiomatic, and are frequently as inspired as they are historically important.

Thirteen selections, for instance, constitute world premieres, with all the energy and excitement of these special occasions intact. Others showcase conductors in works that they did not record commercially. The latter category accounts for much of the Leonard Bernstein material here: surprising, perhaps, given the conductor's huge discography. High points include a scintillatingly detailed Varèse *Intégrales*, the premiere of Ned Rorem's underrated Third Symphony, and an effective abridgment of Acts III and IV of Virgil Thomson's *Four Saints in Three Acts*. Bernstein's lean, cougar-ish approach to William Schuman's urbanely crafted Sixth Symphony markedly contrasts to the more opulent Ormandy/Philadelphia studio recording. Similarly, a live Roy Harris Third Symphony is charged with unbridled vigor and rough-hewn texturing absent from Bernstein's cleaner Sony and DG studio traversals. As a composer, Bernstein is represented by two moving tributes: Glenn Dicterow's heartfelt reading of the *Serenade*, lovingly partnered by Leonard Slatkin, and a dazzling *Candide Overture*, played without a conductor present, but a conductor in mind.

As with the previous NYP boxes, the earliest recordings make for this set's most interesting and instructive listening. The 1945 premiere of Copland's *Appalachian Spring* in its orchestral version, for instance, is more rhythmically secure and decisive in mood than Koussevitsky's pioneering recording that same year. Rodzinski's rip-roaring Gershwin *An American In Paris* (from a 1944 War Bond concert at Madison Square Garden) proves that strings can sing and swing at the same time. The same can be said for Charles Munch's bristling, vibrant 1948 Bloch *Concerto Grosso* No. 1. Notable too are Howard Hanson's gorgeous yet taut renditions of his own Second Symphony and Griffes's *The White Peacock*, both from a 1946 broadcast. The close miking favored by the CBS radio engineers undoubtedly fuels the overall vivid impression of these airchecks, all stunningly transferred by Seth Winner from the original CBS and Voice of America lacquers. By contrast, the engineering for much of the early to mid-1950s material is less detailed, yet arguably more realistic from the vantage point of a listener in the hall. You get a sense, for instance, of how Guido Cantelli's unpressured, lyrical Copland *El Salón México* sounded from a choice orchestra seat. This is a valuable addition to the conductor's slender recorded output (he perished in a 1956 plane crash), and in vastly better sound than several "underground" issues. Pierre Monteux makes the best possible case for Paul Creston's craggy Second Symphony, but you have to work with the music to divine its considerable virtues. Conversely, Morton Gould's *Dance Variations* pose no problems on first hearing, and disprove any notions that the New York Philharmonic's standards deteriorated under Dimitri Mitropoulos's batonless hands.

Among the recent selections, Pierre Boulez turns in an expectedly sympathetic and laser-clear account of Elliott Carter's *Concerto for Orchestra*: wonderfully played, but not as involved as Bernstein's world-premiere studio recording. On the other hand, Boulez marshals the vast forces required for George Crumb's *Star-Child* with a kind of efficiency that still allows the composer's playful sound world its due. To my ears, the subtle phase shiftings of Steve Reich's *Tehillim* work better within the stripped-down chamber dimensions of the composer's own ensemble than in his relatively static recasting for full orchestra, notwithstanding Zubin Mehta's fine performance. The burnished sonorities and conservative tempos Kurt Masur favors in Brahms and Bruckner are mirrored in his broadly effective Copland *Fanfare for the Comman Man*, in Ives's *Three Places in New England*, and John Adams's *Short Ride in a Fast Machine*. As a encore, Toscanini's 1944 rendition of Sousa's *Stars and Stripes Forever* puts an uplifting button on this collection. One might carp over this or that repertoire choice, but producer Sedgwick Clark has programmed each disc with the same care and consideration that typifies the orchestra's previous boxed compilations. Consumers who may not wish to invest in the whole set should know that each of the two boxes will be made available separately in the future.

In sum, both collections do these respective orchestras proud. One hopes that the Philadelphia Orchestra and New York Philharmonic will continue to mine their rich archives in the future. Dare we hope that the success of these projects might inspire a long-overdue Boston Symphony restrospective?

RECORD REVIEWS

Beethoven: Symphony No. 9 in D minor, Op. 125
Aase Nordmo-Lövberg, Christa Ludwig, Waldemar Kmentt, Hans Hotter; Philharmonia Chorus and Orchestra, Otto Klemperer, cond.
Testament SBT 1177

Otto Klemperer's late-1950s Beethoven symphony cycle long ago achieved the status of a classic for its towering integrity, formal rectitude and granitic tread. The superb sonics, moreover, hold their own in today's digital marketplace. At first glance, this previously unreleased live recording of the Ninth Symphony—recorded in concert on November 15, 1957 by the same forces involved with the studio version taped a fortnight later—might seem superfluous. Not quite. While Klemperer's conception is essentially unchanged, the differences in detail tip the scales in favor of the present performance.

Like many conductors of his generation, Klemperer thrived in front of an audience, and as was often the case, here the "live" environment engenders more animation between the lines, so to speak. The conductor unleashes the transition leading into the scherzo's trio section with more abandon, and imbues the great slow movement with more inflection and transparency. The microphone placement doesn't replicate the resplendency of Walter Legge's Abbey Road production, but one gets a cogent sense of Klemperer's imposing sonorities as they congeal in a large hall. The timpani truly resonate, and the impact of the violins divided left and right is felt as much as heard. Listen, too, to how Klemperer clarifies the motivic interplay in the first movement without the aid of post-production mixing and fancy engineering. In the choral finale, Nordmo-Lövberg and Ludwig dovetail their lines with sensitivity, while Hotter surpasses his studio rendition of the opening recitative. On the other hand, Kmentt's warmly felt solo leading to the incisive fughetta is better controlled in the studio. Top vocal honors, however, go to the thrilling Philharmonia Chorus, appearing in public for the first time.

Klemperer takes both repeats in the scherzo, and eschews that movement's traditional brass amendments (unlike Toscanini and Furtwängler) in favor of the Urtext. In a catalog crowded, from Abendroth to Wand, with excellent Beethoven Ninths, there's always room for long-buried treasure such as this valuable release.—*Jed Distler*

Handel: *Solomon*
Andreas Scholl, Inger Dam-Jensen, Alison Hagley, Susan Bickley, Susan Gritton, Paul Agnew, Peter Harvey; Gabrieli Consort and Players, Paul McCreesh, cond.
DG Archiv 459688-2 [3 CDs]

Current Handel scholarship attempts to place the librettos of his oratorios into the political and social context of 18th-century thought, enabling us to understand the composer's choices with regard to subject matter, dramatic emphases and characterization. Handel's audience was familiar with Old Testament figures and tales, for sermons and political speeches would often draw parallels between biblical characters and current celebrities, and between ancient Hebrew and contemporary British politics. It would have been obvious to them that Solomon was an idealized portrait of King George II, and that the prosperity and concord of the Israelite nation represented the hoped-for peace attained by the Treaty of Aix-la-Chapelle, negotiated in 1748, as Handel was writing this work.

Late 20th-century listeners must perforce come at this material with different expectations. Even to those ignorant of Enlightenment politics and wishing there were more plot and action (as in *Semele* or *Hercules*), *Solomon* is a beautiful and powerful work. Its three acts may be considered a mini-series, highlighting various aspects of Solomon's character and personage, and relating the sensuality and harmony of the natural world to the political environment.

Paul McCreesh and the Gabrieli Consort and Players bring us this first-ever complete recording of *Solomon*, and it is very well done. We hear several arias omitted from John Eliot Gardiner's 1987 account for Philips; in addition, the final choral numbers are restored to their original order, so that the huge and mighty "Praise the Lord with harp and tongue" is not saved up in order to make a loud and splashy finale, but follows directly on the tenor aria in the same key. Consequently the final numbers are allowed to serve as an intimate coda, concluding with the subtle and pointed lines, "The name of the wicked shall quickly be past, But the fame of the just shall eternally last." There are plenty of other improvements on the older recording as well—a much more sensuous conception and sound palate bring forth additional nuances of expression and phrasing, and the splendid choral singing is powerful, warm and supple. The nightingale chorus, "May no rash intruder," allowing Solomon and his queen to retire to their boudoir, becomes a gently stroked royal lullaby, both delicate and luscious.

Where Handel made use of one soprano for the three leading female roles, Archiv's budget has allowed for three, which clarifies the casting and adds to the episodic nature of the work. The vocal soloists are all good, especially Alison Hagley and Susan Bickley as the feuding mothers (First and Second Harlot in the biblically

RECORD REVIEWS

and flashy. As the Queen of Sheba, Susan Gritton sings with ample voice and attractively, and her farewell aria—supported by elegant instrumental playing—is beautifully phrased, but poor diction mars much of her work. Tenor Paul Agnew manages vast sheets of coloratura passages with throaty aerobics, and the commanding bass Peter Harvey shows off his solid top in some high-lying cadenzas.

In the title role, German countertenor Andreas Scholl sounds lovely and does a fair job with the English language, but he does not approach the beauty, power or warm presence of Carolyn Watkinson on the Philips recording. (Handel also preferred a female voice in this role.) Lacking in dramatic flair, Scholl is more effective with the abstract and concert-like Act III masque in praise of music. (Ruth Smith wittily points out in the liner notes that this set piece, offered as a performance for the visiting dignitary from Sheba, clearly denotes Handel's wish for a state-funded arts program.)

Several tempos are disconcertingly brisk (why are early music performances never excessively slow?), and while the solo singers exhibit little distress, the queen's joyous aria "Bless'd the day," and Solomon's sweet and pleased reflection "How green our fertile pastures look," both sound hectic and silly.—*Lucille Baker-Bolton*

The Vivaldi Album
Cecilia Bartoli, Il Giardino Armonico
Decca 466 569-2

Exercising the resurrectionist's art, Cecilia Bartoli has dug up a cache of forgotten Vivaldi operas. One might not want to spend a whole evening listening to a complete one, but the 13 excerpts presented here are certainly intriguing and elegantly performed. "Zeffiretti, che sussurrate," for example, is a thoroughly charming pastorale, poles apart from "Gelido in ogni vena" from *Farnace*, a tremendously dramatic piece of musical scene painting. Bartoli does her best work in such pieces as "Dite, oimè," from *La fida ninfa*, which call on her lyric singing; her voice sounds a little dry and pressured in the big fioratura showstoppers. Il Giardino Armonico does a great deal with instrumental color. The group never recedes into the background, but makes as big a statement as the vocalist does, both through the use of specialty instruments, such as flageolets and psaltery, and interpretive choices, such as deliberately harsh string playing and raucous horns. The program opens with an aria that cribs a passage from the "Spring" concerto of Vivaldi's *The Four Seasons*—a cute touch, just to be sure we know who it is we're dealing with.—*Heidi Waleson*

Brahms: Serenade No.1 in D, Op. 11; Serenade No. 2 in A, Op. 16. Scottish Chamber Orchestra, Sir Charles Mackerras, cond. Telarc CD-80522

Both these works were written during the late 1850s, when the young composer was moving beyond the keyboard to begin fashioning an early version of the monumental Piano Concerto in D minor, Op. 15. In these serenades, however, Brahms keeps his ambitions modest: this is, after all, music intended to soothe, entice and entertain—and do it out-of-doors.

Brahms's fresh-air is more strongly felt in the D major Serenade, where Mackerras encourages his horns to flaunt their rural heritage, and where his small orchestra gives winds and brass rightful parity with the strings. Not all the music of this serenade is equally good, however—the three dance movements are charming, but they flank an Adagio that even Mackerras's performance cannot enliven. No wonder that Toscanini, when he programmed this piece, often presented just the Allegro and the two minuets.

Toscanini always played the A major Serenade complete, and one can see why: this is far more consistent music, unusual in eschewing violins, and hinting at the Brahms of the symphonies to come in both the rhythmic hijinks of the scherzo and rondo and in the pensiveness of the Adagio. As with the First Serenade, this one, too, underwent revision before reaching its final form in the 1870s.

Mackerras's revelatory Brahms symphonies, also on Telarc, gave us a chance to hear the Master as the Meiningen Court Orchestra might have played him—this new CD gives us an even younger composer, eager and talented, paying hommage to Mozart and Haydn, but clearly foretelling of orchestral accomplishments yet to come.

Telarc's sound is superb—but Michael Murray's notes devote ten paragraphs to rehashing biographical information, just one to the works at hand.—*Mike Gray*

Bach: *St. Matthew Passion*
Ian Bostridge, Franz-Josef Selig, Sibylla Rubens, Andreas Scholl, Werner Güra, Dietrich Henschel; Chorus and Orchestra of the Collegium Vocale, Philippe

Platinum

One of the leading classical catalogs encompassing new recordings performed by the world-renowned conductors and artists of the Royal Philharmonic Orchestra

INSD 2891

INSD 2892

INSD 2895

INSD 3603

INSD 2896

INSD 3602

INSD 2894

INSD 2891
This 2-CD collection features excerpts from Beethoven's greatest hits.

INSD 2891
This 2-CD collection presents Mozart's most glorious works of music.

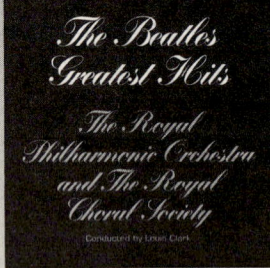
INSD 2891

1 on Billboard's Budget Classical Chart!

RECORD REVIEWS

Herreweghe, cond.
Harmonia Mundi 951676

If you could have only one new Bach recording to celebrate the upcoming Bach anniversary (250 years since his death in 1750), this would have to be it. This is Herreweghe's second recorded traversal of the work, and it is almost operatic in its dramatic intensity. The performance is immensely moving and perfectly paced, right from the magnificent opening chorus—in which the mourning procession still manages to sound like a dance. One determining factor is Ian Bostridge, one of the most theatrical lieder singers around, holding the reins as the tour guide/narrator Evangelist. Herreweghe's complete mastery of the choral idiom goes almost without saying, and it is at its zenith here, matching the crystalline textures, pinpoint balances and flexible tempos of the orchestral playing. The soloists are also part of the texture, fervent without calling unnecessary attention to themselves, and matching their solo instruments with great taste and beauty. Alto Andreas Scholl is the standout among them. Harmonia Mundi has also added an extra treat: a CD-ROM that explores the music, text, and history of the Passion, along with interpretive insights from Herreweghe.
—Heidi Waleson

Beethoven, Krufft, Lachner: Lieder
Christoph Prégardien, tenor;
Andreas Staier, fortepiano
Teldec 3984-21473-2

Christoph Prégardien and Andreas Staier continue their fruitful partnership with a disk introducing some early 19th-century songs by Austrian civil servant Nikolaus von Krufft and Wagner opponent Franz Paul Lachner, in addition to offering Beethoven's well-known song cycle *An die ferne Geliebte*. The poets represented—Schiller, Heine, Matthisson, and others—are familiar to lieder lovers, and several of the texts were later set by Schubert, Brahms and Schumann, as well as by Peter Cornelius and Robert Franz.

The Krufft songs are especially attractive: the grand and expansive "Abend," with its attention-grabbing opening, and the rhythmically lively and harmoniously quirky "Lebenslied" certainly deserve to make their way into the recital repertory. Best of all is the short "Fliess hinab, mein stilles Leben," whose regretful and then resigned text is set in minor and then major keys, over a weird and haunting accompaniment reflecting the title's flowing away of life.

The well-known Beethoven cycle is a perfect jewel, and it hardly matters that there are already many fine recordings available. Staier here is magnificent, setting a firm, beautiful tone, and effecting the many transitions with grace and command, enabling the work to unfold in perfect pace. Fervent and persuasive artistry from both performers produces some magical moments: in the second song, where piano and voice switch parts, the keyboard "singing" and the voice intoning on one note, and the climax in the sixth song, as the poet imagines the beloved singing the very words he has sung.

The Lachner cycle, *Sängerfahrt*, or "Singer's Journey," dates from 1831-32, and is set to texts by Heinrich Heine. Except for the two central songs (which later appear in Schumann's *Dichterliebe*), the texts explore loneliness and betrayal, with prominent themes of night and departure, and there is much use of otherworldly voices. The less successful songs suffer from aimlessness, excessive length and occasional bombast, but there are several gems, especially "Die badende Elfe" (set by Brahms as "Sommerabend"). The poet chances upon a fairy bathing by moonlight; the piano figuration suggests water flowing and splashing, the vocal line is gracious, and Prégardien's ethereal tone creates an atmosphere of wonder and awe.

"Ein Traumbild" introduces death as a dream-vision maid, intent on carrying off the sleeping poet, and the surprise ending (saved by the crowing cock!) is the payoff for the entire song. Similarly, in the ballad "Die Meerfrau," a siren rises from the waves, enticing the poet and clasping him with increasing frenzy and menace. Prégardien's voice reflects the panic gripping the narrator, and in the mermaid's lines he sounds eerie and disembodied. He even transcends the mawkish ending—the creature confesses her wild love for the mortal, while the composer's skill deteriorates correspondingly—by forthright and serious commitment.

Indeed, every piece is approached thoughtfully and performed compellingly. The CD cover shows the two artists dressed alike and posed identically, in what appears to be an airport lounge. Clearly they are comfortably in sync. Both produce gorgeous sounds and handle a broad range of color and dynamics. Prégardien can sound positively massive and baritonal in the powerful moments, and in addition he exploits all the elements of words—the consonants, vowels, diphthongs—to paint eloquently. Most decent singers can make expressive use of vowels, by coloring or lengthening, but here is a rare artist who also manipulates consonants: by caressing and extending, by delaying, by pitching them deliberately. He generously employs all his equipment—voice, brains and heart—and his singing conveys warmth and humanity.
—Lucille Baker-Bolton

NOTABLE

Eleni Karaindrou: *Eternity and a Day*
ECM 465125

This soundtrack is full of stirring and dramatic music that invokes varying emotional responses. It draws you in and keeps your attention through the use of a subtly varying melody that occurs after each section of music. And the unusual horn sections are a call back to other great film scores.—*Erin Lynch*

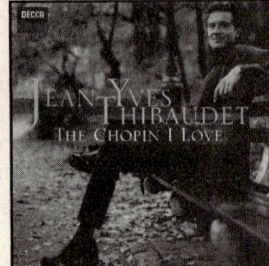

DECC 466357

Chopin's music is perfectly suited to the elegence, refinement and virtuosity of Jean-Yves Thibaudet, who has been very successful performing Chopin in concert, but has never before recorded his works. The recording includes Chopin's most famous and beautiful pieces, such as "G Minor Ballade," the "Minute Waltz," the "Revolutionary Etude," and the "Grand Valse Brillante."

Jean-Yves Thibaudet tour dates:
Jan. 8   La Jolla, CA
Jan. 11   Carmel, CA
Jan. 14   Houston, TX
Jan. 20-23   Newark, NJ
Feb. 10   New York
March 16-18,21   Philadelphia
March 20   Washington, DC
March 26-27   Hawaii
April 6-9   San Francisco
May 4-6   Atlanta
May 17-20   Minneapolis

Also available by Jean-Yves Thibaudet:
Warsaw Concerto
Live In Italy
Paganini Variations & Schumann
Preludes, Books 1&2 (Debussy)
Reflections on Duke
Conversations with Bill Evans
Liszt Transcriptions
Piano Concertos 1&2 (Liszt)
Piano Concertos 1&3 (Rachmaninov)
Piano Concertos 2 (Rachmaninov)
Piano Concertos 4 (Rachmaninov)
Complete Works For Solo Piano
The Piano Concertos and
    Honegger (Ravel)
The Portrait of a Lady (Soundtrack)
Ultimate Romantic Piano Album:
    Dreams of Love

THE CHOPIN I LOVE

DECCA
A UNIVERSAL MUSIC COMPANY
©2000 Decca Records/Universal Classics Group
www.universalclassics.com

Anne-Sophie Mutter's new recording of Vivaldi's THE FOUR SEASONS is an explosion of color, a thrilling performance that showcases the dazzling range of her incomparable artistry. Ms. Mutter was inspired to re-record the world's most popular classical piece after seeing the color-drenched works of a contemporary German artist, Gotthard Grabner. The result is a performance at once sensual and physical, strikingly re-imagined and yet completely fresh and spontaneous.

Also available by Anne-Sophie Mutter:
The Berlin Recital
Carmen-Fantasy
The Great Violin Concertos
Romance
Mutter Modern
Beethoven: The Violin Sonatas
Face To Face with Beethoven
Triple Concerto
Complete Beethoven Edition: String Trios
Berg: Violin Concerto
Brahms: Violin Concerto
Brahms & Mendelssohn: Violin Concerto
Sonata
Brahms: Violin Concerto
Sibelius: Violin Concerto
Tchaikovsky: Violin Concerto
Mozart: Violin Concerto #3 & 5
Mozart: Violin Concertos
Beethoven: Vol. 2 : Concertos
Beethoven Edition Budget Digipack

VIVALDI The Four Seasons
• Le Quattro Stagioni • Die vier Jahreszeiten • Les Quatre Saisons •
ANNE-SOPHIE MUTTER

Deutsche Grammophon
A UNIVERSAL MUSIC COMPANY
©2000 Deutsche Grammophon/Universal Classics Group
www.universalclassics.com

DEUT 463259

CECILIA BARTOLI *the vivaldi album*

Escape to Venice with Cecilia Bartoli! THE VIVALDI ALBUM features extraordinary Vivaldi rarities including vocal arrangements from "The Four Seasons." Cecilia spent months corresponding with musicologists and researching arias from the manuscripts of over a dozen of Vivaldi's greatest operas for this recording.

DECC 466569

Also available by Cecilia Bartoli:
Duets - Cecilia Bartoli and Bryn Terfel
Bartoli Live in Italy
An Italian Songbook
Chant d'Amour - Melodies Francaises
If You Love Me: 18th Century Italian Love Songs
The Impatient Lover: Italian Love Songs
In Paradisum
Cecilia Bartoli: A Portrait
Orfeo ed Euridice
Arias
Portraits
La Clemenza Trio
Mitridate
Requiem
Stabat Mater
Manon Lescaut
Il Turco In Italia
La Cenerentola
La Cenerenrola-Highlights
Heroines
Rossini Arias

DECCA
A UNIVERSAL MUSIC COMPANY
©2000 Decca Records/Universal Classics Group
www.universalclassics.com

Vienna STATE OPERA

G. Verdi
IL TROVATORE - COMPLETE OPERA
RCAV 61951

R. Strauss
ÄGYPTISCHE HELENA - COMPLETE OPERA
RCAV 69429

J. Strauss
DIE FLEDERMAUS - COMPLETE OPERA
RCAV 61949

R. Wagner
PARSIFAL - COMPLETE OPERA
RCAV 61950

R. Strauss
DER ROSENKAVALIER - COMPLETE OPERA
RCA 69431

R. Strauss
SALOME - COMPLETE OPERA
RCAV 69430

RECORD REVIEWS

Sento amor
David Daniels, countertenor
Virgin Veritas 45365

In his first aria recording, David Daniels offered a vibrant tour of the extraordinary music that Handel wrote for castrati. A remarkable singer, he is perhaps uniquely equipped to encompass both the technical and expressive range of that repertory. This second aria recording goes beyond Handel, into Gluck and Mozart. The Mozart selections are a little disappointing, most likely because they are very early works that contain the germ of the operatic greatness that was to come, but are not yet full-fledged. The best aria is "Vadasi...o ciel" from Act III of *Mitridate*, in which the wicked son, Farnace, sees the error of his ways. Daniels gives it an appropriately remorseful air. The two Gluck *Orfeo* arias, including the famous "Che faro," are curiously subdued, as though Daniels were more interested in producing a sweet tone and beautiful legato (which he certainly does) than in expressing despair. Daniels comes alive in the Handel selections from *Tolomeo* (there's a beautiful dying fall at the end of the recitative) and *Partenope*, the opera in which he made a major splash at Glimmerglass in 1998. He is particularly fine in expressing the wrenching pain of "Ch'io parta?" with some exquisitely soft singing, and he tosses off the runs of "Furibondo spira il vento" with his usual breathtaking accuracy and zest. Harry Bicket's leadership of the Orchestra of the Age of Enlightenment is a little square and plain; they had more personality, and more connection with the music and the singer, under Roger Norrington on the earlier recording.—*Heidi Waleson*

Berlioz: Overtures *Les Francs-Juges, Waverley, Le roi Lear, Le Carnaval romain, Béatrice et Bénédict, Le Corsaire, Benvenuto Cellini*
Staatskapelle Dresden,
Sir Colin Davis, cond.
RCA Victor Red Seal 68790

Mozart: Overtures to *Le nozze di Figaro*, K.492; *Bastien und Bastienne*, K.50, *Der Schauspieldirektor*, K.486, *Lucio Silla*, K.135, *Così fan tutte*, K.588, *La finta giardiniera*, K.196, *Die Entführung aus dem Serail*, K.384, *Il ré pastore*, K.208, *Idomeneo*, K.366, *La clemenza di Tito*, K.621, *Don Giovanni*, K.527, *Die Zauberflöte*, K.620.
Staatskapelle Dresden,
Sir Colin Davis, cond.
RCA Victor Red Seal 56698

Davis got his big break substituting for an indisposed Otto Klemperer in a sensational Festival Hall performance of Mozart's *Don Giovanni* in the fall of 1959, but it wasn't until Philips began to record him with the London Symphony Orchestra in the early 1960s that he began to make his mark as one of the most exciting and consistent young conductors then active in Britain.

Davis's Mozart and Beethoven sometimes reminded critics of a more energetic Klemperer, attentive to orchestral balances while rhythmically ever so slightly earth-bound. In Berlioz, however, he drove the LSO to fiery performances of these overtures (on Philips 456 143-2) that were as exciting as they were daring. These new accounts, while not generating the amperage of the older ones, are in many ways more satisfying—here Davis is keenly attentive not just to Berlioz's fire but to his tenderness, leading an orchestra that plays with Central European warmth and grace, if without the ultimate finesse in the brass, and overall coordination, that only a few orchestras anywhere achieve in this music.

Davis's Mozart is equally good, but less essential: despite the name attached to them, only about half of these overtures are first-class music. Purchase only if you're a fan of the conductor, or if you want to hear how this fine old orchestra plays these pieces.

Notes and sound for both discs are splendid—it's a good engineering team that can triumph so successfully over the cavernous acoustics of Dresden's Lukaskirche.—*Mike Gray*

Handel: *L'Allegro, il Penseroso ed il Moderato.*
Susan Gritton, Claron McFadden, Lorna Anderson, Paul Agnew, Neal Davies; The King's Consort & Choir, Robert King, dir.
Hyperion CDA67283/4

En route to inventing the English oratorio, Handel experimented with various theatrical forms treating secular as well as sacred subjects, his friends eagerly suggesting ideas and submitting material. James Harris

Three remarkable virtuosi perform gypsy themes arranged for violin with two guitars.

NON 79505
Nadja Salerno-Sonnenberg
Sergio and Odair Assad

Piazzolla's "Four Seasons" joins the Vivaldi masterwork in performances by violinist Gidon Kremer with his ensemble KremerATA Baltica.

NON 79568
Gidon Kremer/KremerATA Baltica
Eight Seasons

This beautiful collection of enchanting choral music features new compositions based on the Tallis and Pachelbel Canons, as well as songs derived from the ancient Latin mass, plainsong melodies and hymns.

TELC 29053
Libera

An all-star cast of piano soloists – including Héléne Grimaud, Elisabeth Leonskaja, Boris Berezovsky, and Helen Huang – rounds out this 2-CD compilation of the most beautiful slow movements in classical music. The companion release to the best-selling Albinoni's Adagios.

TELC 24679
Piano Adagios

For her first-ever live recording for Warner Classics, Upshaw pays tribute to her "inspiring muse," French soprano Jane Bathori, in songs by Satie, Debussy, Ravel, Milhaud and the world premiere recording of Dutilleux's "San Francisco Night."

TELC 27329
Dawn Upshaw: Hommage á Jane Bathori - The Inspiring Muse

The first recording of this Busoni opera since 1969, with Maestro Nagano at the helm.

ERAT 25501
Ferruccio Busoni
Doktor Faust-Comp Opera

Written in celebration of the 75th birthday of the late Cardinal Basil Hume, Archbishop of Westminster, this mass "for the new millenium" features an English – not Latin – text. The world premiere recording, featuring the Westminster Cathedral Choir, also includes Arvo Pärt's "Beatitudes" and John Tavener's "Funeral Ikos."

TELC 28069
Roxanna Panufnik
Westminster Mass

Finnish maestro Saraste conducts the essential Dutilleux classical works, all of which showcase the French composer's interest in variations (both in time and space). From the Second Symphony (1959) to his study of time, space and movement (1978), this recording portrays Dutilleux as unorthodox and uncompromising.

FNL 25324
Henri Dutilleux
Sym 2/Métaboles/ Timbres, Espace, Mouvement

   FINLANDIA RECORDS

NONESUCH ERATO TELDEC

RECORD REVIEWS

proposed the scheme for combining sections of Milton's two contrasting poems, *L'Allegro* and *Il Penseroso*, and persuaded Charles Jennens (later *Messiah*'s librettist) to pitch the idea to Handel. The project appealed to the composer, with the stipulation that a third section be added, in which the cheerful man and the thoughtful man give way to the moderate man, exemplifying such 18th-century virtues as harmony, balance and reason.

The text—certainly the best Handel ever set—inspired music of great originality. Bells, birdsong, laughter, the chirp of crickets, "the busy hum of men," the sweeping steps of Tragedy, the "even step and musing gait" of a nun, all are evoked in this score, rich in orchestral colors and textures.

In this new recording, Robert King approaches the work with care and earnestness, bringing out the exuberance and joy of *Allegro*'s fairly conventional numbers, and drawing us inward to the hypnotic serenity of *Penseroso*'s more elaborate and luxurious music. King then allows *Moderato* the satisfying and inevitable conclusion (how astute Handel was to require this section!), convincing us of the beauty and wisdom of the middle way.

John Eliot Gardiner's 1980 recording for Erato remains one of his best, and it featured stunning vocal soloists, most notably sopranos Patrizia Kwella, Marie McLaughlin and Jennifer Smith. Hyperion's new offering has many merits, particularly the splendid choral singing (one of the CD's most beautiful moments is the choral reply, "All this company serene, Join to fill thy beauteous train") and superb orchestral solos, especially Rachel Brown's flute contributions to "Sweet bird."

The bulk of the work, however, rests on the vocal soloists and, while King's three sopranos are accomplished musicians, they are not quite up to the Erato team in terms of vocal beauty or musical imagination. Susan Gritton, whose monochromatic singing has begun to suffer a bit from overexposure, continues her wayward disregard for the English language. She sings with security and great range, but in several of her songs it is impossible to make out even one word of text. In contrast, Lorna Anderson, the other *Penseroso* soprano, has a lovely sense of words and phrasing, but a quivery and pressed tone. Claron McFadden attacks *Allegro*'s perky music forthrightly, tenor Paul Agnew transcends his unattractive sound with great theatrical verve, and bass Neal Davies sings his *Allegro* music vigorously and the *Moderato* pieces with elegance.
—Lucille Baker-Bolton

Dvořák: Symphony No. 9 in E minor, Op. 95 (*From the New World*); Polonaise in E-flat; Polonaise from *Rusalka*. Suk: Fairy Tale Suite *Raduz a Mahulena*
Czech Philharmonic Orchestra, Václav Talich, cond.
Biddulph WHL 048

There must be a fascinating story behind these recordings, which derive from a series of thirteen that Talich made for Electrola with the Czech Philharmonic in occupied Prague, between 1940 and 1941. As Rob Cowan's excellent notes point out, the original 78s are superlatively rare, so much so that Czech discographies of both the conductor and orchestra show the Dvořák Ninth, the big item on this CD, as never having been issued. Biddulph published Smetana's *Má Vlast* from this series in 1998 (WHL 049, reviewed by this writer in these pages), and now has issued Dvořák's *New World* Symphony coupled with music by Josef Suk and two small pieces by Dvořák himself. Talich was to record the symphony twice more, upon being reunited with the CPO in 1949, and for Supraphon in 1954, the version that has had the widest circulation on LP and CD since then.

There are two modern models for playing the *New World*: the Toscanini/Szell approach, emphasizing orchestral brilliance and forward momentum, and the songful flexibility and mellowness of the Mittel Europa tradition, exemplified on modern records by Talich's younger colleague and successor at the CPO, Rafael Kubelík.

This performance is clearly in the latter mold, leaning toward the geniality of the composer's G major Symphony while not avoiding the tension implied by the Ninth's minor key. Talich allows the score to breathe without slipping into rhapsodic aimlessness, moving smartly ahead when necessary in the first movement's strenuous development and coda, lingering playfully on the woodwind trills in the trio of the third movement, and downplaying the bombast of the finale.

Two Dvořák polonaises and the Suk suite *Raduz a Mahulena* complete the CD—the Suk leaves no trace in my memory, the polonaises are charming but minor. Buy this CD for the Ninth and for Ward Marston's splendid transfers.—*Mike Gray*

World Premiere Recordings
National Symphony Orchestra (Washington, D.C.),
Hans Kindler cond.
Biddulph WHL-063

In 1940, Victor Records—later known as RCA Victor—began recording a number of supposedly second-string American orchestras, in such cities as Cincinnati, Indianapolis, San Francisco and Washington; the

RECORD REVIEWS

early postwar years saw the addition of Dallas and St. Louis. Needless to say, some of these orchestras had distinguished histories, and some boasted stellar conductors at the time they recorded for Victor: the illustrious Pierre Monteux in San Francisco, Eugene Goossens in Cincinnati, Vladimir Golschmann in St. Louis. For the most part, Victor left the standard repertory to the Philadelphia Orchestra under Eugene Ormandy, the Boston Symphony under Serge Koussevitzky, and the NBC Symphony under Arturo Toscanini, and recorded these other orchestras in less familiar material. Tchaikovsky's first three symphonies, for example, decidedly in the "novelty" category at that time, were recorded by Fabien Sevitzky in Indianapolis (No. 1), Goossens in Cincinnati (No. 2), and Hans Kindler with the National Symphony Orchestra in Washington (No. 3). All of these performances were handsomely recorded and remarkably persuasive—and so remained, even after many others had come along on LP and in stereo.

Sevitzky also recorded Grieg's *Symphonic Dances* and the (then) seldom heard second suite from the *Peer Gynt* music, as well as Tchaikovsky's *Manfred* Symphony and the Kalinnikov First. Goossens gave us the premiere recording of the Walton Violin Concerto, with its dedicatee Jascha Heifetz as soloist, and a reading of Vaughan Williams's *A London Symphony*. Antal Dorati, at the beginning of his orchestra-building career, in Dallas, recorded Glazunov's ballet score *The Seasons*, a still unmatched (even by himself) account of his own *Graduation Ball*, and piano concertos with Arthur Rubinstein and William Kapell. Rubinstein also recorded in St. Louis with Golschmann, whose activity in those years yielded such titles as Schoenberg's *Transfigured Night*, Milhaud's *Suite provençale* and the Sibelius Seventh. Kindler did not record any works with soloists, but, in addition to his striking Tchaikovsky Third, he made well over a dozen "premiere recordings" of brief pieces, most of which have been brought back at last on a Biddulph CD that may well become one of this season's notable "sleepers."

Several of these "premiere recordings" remain even now the only versions of the respective pieces ever recorded. In first position, appropriately enough, is the first recording Kindler and his orchestra made, his own transcription of a toccata attributed to Frescobaldi. Edward Johnson, who did a great deal of research in preparing his sympathetic article on Kindler and the NSO in last fall's *International Classical Record Collector*, provided the comprehensive annotation for this disc, in which he cites one of my own concert notes by way of explaining that Frescobaldi apparently had nothing to do with the piece. Kindler, during his years as a prominent cellist, must have performed the toccata in the well known "arrangement" by his colleague Gaspar Cassadó, who apparently took a leaf from Fritz Kreisler's book and simply composed pieces of his own to which he affixed the names of composers from the 17th and 18th centuries. Regardless of who may or may not have actually composed this piece, it is one of the most attractive things of its kind: a fine workout for the orchestra, blessed with a really memorable tune for its vigorous fugue. Arthur Fiedler used to perform it in Boston, Leonard Slatkin did it with the St. Louis Symphony Youth Orchestra more than 25 years ago and Mstislav Rostropovich, Kindler's latter-day successor (and Slatkin's immediate predecessor) on the NSO podium, programmed it on anniversary occasions, but there have been very few other performances in the last 50 years, and no recording so far since Kindler's own, which projects such exultant vitality and warmth.

While there are collectors for whom the "Frescobaldi" alone would justify investment in the Biddulph CD, there is a good deal more, and much of it is almost as striking. Among the other Kindler arrangements is a sumptuous one of the Fountain Scene from Mussorgsky's *Boris Godunov*. It is based on the Rimsky-Korsakov edition of the score, with the voices eloquently replaced by instruments, and the climax, with its trombones and timpani, is suitably grand. (While the "Frescobaldi"/Kindler score is available in published form, this *Boris* excerpt is not, and apparently survives only in the form of this recording.) Kindler's settings of Handel (the big, beefy overture to the *Chandos Anthem* No. 2, also used in the Concerto grosso, Op. 3, No. 5; here labeled Prelude and Fugue in D minor), Liszt (*Hungarian Rhapsody* No. 6, in a treatment different from Liszt's own), and Dutch folk songs (two from the 16th century, which figured in the NSO's first concert, in 1931) are brilliant, too, as is, in its own way, Morton Gould's lavish arrangement of Lecuona's *Andalucia*, a tune that had been fitted out with words as a popular song, "The Breeze and I."

George Whitefield Chadwick, who only recently has come in for quite a bit of overdue attention, is represented here by *Noel*, the second and most intimate of his four *Symphonic Sketches*. Closer to home, there is music by two Washington composers: one is La Salle Spier, whose transcriptions of two Scriabin etudes rival similar arrangements by Leopold Stokowski (who in fact did orchestrate the first of these himself); the other is Mary Howe, one of the organizers and early supporters of the NSO, whose brief, impressionistic *Stars* is given a most sympathetic statement.

One of the most bizarre programs Kindler or any other conductor ever put together was an NSO concert in January 1942 that opened with Bruckner's Fourth Symphony and continued after intermission with Stravinsky's arrangement of *The Star Spangled Banner*, *The Prelude and Hula* by the young Hawaiian composer Dai-keong Lee, Morton Gould's *Latin American Symphonette* (minus its final movement), and the *Czech Rhapsody* written for the conductor by Jaromir Weinberger, the composer of the opera *Svanda the Bagpiper*, who had settled in our country. Both the Lee and Weinberger pieces incorporate folk tunes, and both are on the Biddulph CD, which ends with Kindler's rousing performance of William Schuman's *American Festival Overture*.

The Schuman is listed on the tray card and in the booklet's track index as "Academic Festival Overture;" also, the *(continued on page 29)*

Yuri Temirkanov: Breaking the Russian Stereotype

(continued from page 10)

from being able to retain the same players over the years. There are still a large number of people here who played under Mravinsky for many years. Perhaps they don't play as well technically as some of the younger members, but they serve as models of dedication to them and help them to grow within the ensemble. They are the glue of the orchestra. Among American orchestras, I have the same feeling of admiration and respect when I am conducting the Chicago Symphony, with its many older players.

"When you ask about characteristics, I should also mention the Royal Philharmonic, possibly the best sightreaders I know of and as a group possessing such a great sense of humor. I not only dislike people who lack humor, I'm rather afraid of them. As regards balance of sections, of uniform strength, the orchestra that immediately comes to mind is the Pittsburgh Symphony. But in general, in Europe it's so easy to say what the handful of truly great orchestras are. We know that the Berlin Philharmonic is always great.... The best in America? How does one say? There are so many, with that huge market, the endless availability of talented players.

"For me, I must add, that the best quality of the very fine, younger American orchestras, not the most famous ones, is that they want to be even better. It is another one of the things that attracted me to the Baltimore Symphony. Some of the established American orchestras are not nearly as good as they used to be and have no idea that they are merely riding on their reputations. Any artist who is self-satisfied is in deep trouble."

Did you work with Shostakovich? One reason I ask is that I'm still trying to find out whether Solomon Volkov was really the voice of Shostakovich in Testimony, *the composer's memoirs "as related to and edited by" Volkov, which remains controversial as regards authorship twenty years after first appearing in print.*

"As soon as a great man dies thousands of people come forward to say that 'I was his best friend,' or 'He shared his deepest secrets with me.' I can only say that I didn't know him that well, having been so much younger than he. We corresponded. He sent me some of his scores and he played some new pieces for me on the piano.

"I have no reason to doubt that Volkov was telling the truth. Some of those stories I heard from Shostakovich himself, and from other people as close to him as Volkov was. Also, while Volkov is himself a talented, intelligent man, I don't think he was capable of producing thoughts that are so...so Shostakovich. I've known Volkov since he was a student and I did see the manuscript before it was published, with Shostakovich's initials on every page."

From Los Angeles, Temirkanov was headed for an all-Russian concert (surprise!) with the Philadelphia Orchestra, and then to present a determinedly non-Russian program with the Santa Cecilia Orchestra of Rome: Beethoven, Elgar and Orff. A relief from the routine, to be sure, and indicative of what Baltimore—and then perhaps other American orchestras, where Temirkanov will continue to appear as a guest conductor—will be hearing in coming seasons.

YURI TEMIRKANOV: A BRIEF, SELECTIVE DISCOGRAPHY

All recordings with the St. Petersburg Philharmonic, except as noted.

Shostakovich: Symphonies Nos. 9 & 5
RCA Victor Red Seal 68548

Sibelius: Symphony No. 2 & Violin Concerto (soloist, Vladimir Spivakov) RCA Victor Red Seal 61701

Rachmaninoff: Symphony No. 2 & *Vocalise*
RCA Victor Red Seal 61281

Prokofiev: Violin Concerto No. 1 (Moscow Philharmonic, soloist David Oistrakh, with other Oistrakh performances of Prokofiev) Praga 250041

Stravinsky: *Petrushka*; Petrov: *The Creation of the World*, ballet suites; Ravel: *Daphnis & Chloé*, Suite No. 2
RCA Victor Gold Seal 32044

Out of print, but worth seeking out: Natalia Gutman performing with the Royal Philharmonic under Temirkanov the two Shostakovich Cello Concertos: RCA Victor Red Seal 7918.

And by all means make room on your shelf for the spectacular BMG videocassette of Sergei Eisenstein's 1938 film *Alexander Nevsky*, its Prokofiev score reconstructed and superbly performed by various Russian choruses and the St. Petersburg Philharmonic under Temirkanov. The score alone is available on CD, as RCA Victor Red Seal 61926.

RECORD REVIEWS

(continued from page 28)

catalogue number, matrix numbers and recording date for the Dutch tunes are repeated for the Scriabin and Lee pieces. These appear to be the only slips in this otherwise faultless production. Mark Obert-Thorn's transfers actually improve on the original sound (we can really hear the drums in the *Boris* excerpt now), and Edward Johnson definitely has all the titles right in his illuminating annotation. Washingtonians will of course be interested in this reissue package as an intriguing souvenir of their city's musical history; but listeners everywhere should be happy to discover (or rediscover) these little-known pieces and the authority, enthusiasm and polish that made them so attractive back in the Forties—and in some cases wonder about the neglect that has been their fate since Kindler's time.—*Richard Freed*

Compact Disc World
Music At Your Fingertips!

1-800-83-MUSIC
6 8 7 4 2

We are a mail order house carrying the largest selection of labels, artists & catagories. Our Director, Ira Hirsch, brings his 30 years of mail order experience to Compact Disc World's mail order operation.

- Classical
- Pop
- Jazz
- Shows
- Soundtracks

- Country
- R & B
- New Age
- Children's
- Languages

- Compact Discs
- Cassettes
- Videos
- Laser Discs
- Accessories

FOR INSTITUTIONS

We specialize in library and other institutional services.

All staff orders at same low discount prices

For library orders S&H free on order of 5 units or more

FOR INDIVIDUALS

We offer fantastic savings and prompt service.

Shipping and handling cost: $5.95 for order of any size

ALL MERCHANDISE GUARANTEED FACTORY FRESH.
All items in this catalog (including Spectrum) always available at great discount prices.
Rapid delivery: all shipments UPS (P.O. Box addresses shipped Parcel Post)

For courteous, knowledgeable and personal service call
1-800-836-8742 or fax 1-800-450-3472
or write:
Compact Disc World, P.O. Box 927, South Plainfield, NJ 07080

AMERIMUSIC, INC.
presents

THE CHIPPENDALE SERIES

When at home with his family, George Washington surrounded himself with music and frequented the theater. Mr. Jimerson recreates historically accurate performances of music familiar to Washington and his family.

Douglas Jimerson
GEORGE WASHINGTON PORTRAIT IN SONG
AMMC 1100

"Tenor Douglas Jimerson's (programs are) meticulously prepared and stylishly sung... There is no other artist doing the kind of work Jimerson does."
– *The Washington Post*

Douglas Jimerson
STEPHEN FOSTER'S AMERICA
AMMC 1003

SOUNDS OF THE CIVIL WAR

Douglas Jimerson
Foster, Gounod, et al...
LINCOLN'S FAVORITE MUSIC
AMMC 1002

Douglas Jimerson
ABRAHAM LINCOLN SINGS ON
AMMC 1001

Douglas Jimerson
ROBERT E. LEE REMEMBERED
AMMC 1004

CONTEMPORARY RECORD SOCIETY

724 Winchester Road
Broomall, Pa. 19008
610-544-5920   fax 610-544-5921

e-mail: crsnews@erols.com
Web page: www.erols.com/crsnews

The **CRS** was established in 1981, to promote both a fellowship in the musical arts, between performing artists, composers, presenters and commercial recordings of participants in this endeavor. **CONTEMPORARY RECORD SOCIETY** offers to members throughout the Globe, in each nations' communities, an opportunity to become culturally enriched by the musical sources available through the **Society**. These services are available to performers, composers, teachers, libraries, educational institutions, amateurs, devotees of music, and prospective sponsors. **CRS** also offers to its participants the opportunity to take an active part in this endeavor, through performances, lectures and recordings, that we present. The intent of the Society is to advance the cause of music in the United States and throughout the world, promoting an association among its constituents. The scope of the Society's repertoire includes the musical masterworks of both well-known and relatively unknown composers of all periods.

CRS may assist as a coordinator in developing government, corporate, foundation, and private funding for the support of performances, commissions, and recordings of its members. Our organization assists in generating public interest and international appreciation of performers and composers, through our presentations at numerous concert halls, cultural centers and in the variety of its commercial recordings available throughout the world. Global distribution is available through international distribution.

The **Society** may provide direct assistance to qualified composers and performing artists, when possible. Such assistance is given to Honorary Recipients, Artist/Composer Recipients and distinguished participants, deemed exceptional by a committee of executive members upon the final approval of the President. The selected participants are guaranteed CRS Recording Grants toward works accepted by the committee.

Membership is available to performing musicians, composers, teachers, libraries, educational institutions, amateurs, devotees of music, and prospective sponsors, hence, anyone seriously interested in music. Special **Honorary Membership** is awarded to sponsors of five hundred dollars or more. Inquire about our special framed autograph letter, from such prestigious personalities as Elliott Carter, Lukas Foss, Norman Dello Joio and Yo Yo Ma, to EXEMPLARY sponsors of our artistic objectives.

MEMBERSHIP APPLICATION FORM:
ANNUAL FEE $40.00 (additional contributions _____)

(Granting categories: $90./Contributing $125./Sustaining $175./Artist-composer $250./guarantor $375./Honorary $500.)

Name_____   Address_____

City/State/Zipcode _____, _____, _____   Category_____,

Telephone/Fax/E-mail _____   _____

AUTHORIZED   SIGNATURE_____

JOIN WITH CRS AND RECEIVE THE SOCIETY NEWS PUBLICATION AND THE OPPORTUNITIES
TO EXPRESS YOUR ARTISTIC ENDEAVOR. JOIN TODAY & BECOME MASTERS OF TOMORROW!

MUSIC MART

It's Back!

Schwann Spectrum, our guide to popular music is reborn! Complete listings of all Rock, Pop, Jazz, Gospel, Soundtrack, World and Children's music available today.

Call to subscribe at 50% off the cover price!

1-800-792-9447

Schwann
PUBLICATIONS

LIVE OPERA PERFORMANCES

Audio/Video Cassette

Over 8,000 selections worldwide. Since 1930.

Free computerized catalog. Personal attention to your special needs.

LIVE OPERA
Box 3141
Steinway Station
L.I.C., NY 11103

http://ourworld.
compuserve.com/
homepages/
handelmania

The Binaural Source

World's only catalog of binaural CDs and cassettes for startling headphone experiences

Most unavailable elsewhere
Classical/Jazz/Nature Sounds/Audio Drama
Loudspeaker compatible

800-934-0442

Box 1727-O
Ross, CA 94957
http://www.binaural.com

THE BINAURAL SOURCE

Back Issues of *Schwann Opus* Now Available.

Call 1-800-792-9447 or
1-530-669-5077

Arizona University Recordings "Music for the Ears of the World"

CDs include:
David Glen Hatch, pianist with the Budapest Symphony Orchestra
William Penn's Award Winning Music for Shakespeare's plays
America's Millennium Tribute to Adolphe Sax., Vols. I & II

www.AURec.com

Do you want to reach music lovers?

Advertise in Schwann's Music Mart.

Reach your audience. More than 12,000 collectors, audiophiles, clubs, societies, libraries, musicians subscribe to Schwann Opus.

To place an ad, fill out the form and send to Schwann Opus Classified
Mail: 1280 Santa Anita Court, Woodland, CA 95776; Fax: 530-669-5184

Your name _____ Company _____
Address _____ Telephone (___) _____
City _____ State _____ Zip _____
Bill my: ❏ Visa ❏ MasterCard ❏ Amex ❏ Payment enclosed: Check/Money order only
Card # _____ Expires _____
Name on card _____ Authorized signature _____
Ad copy _____
_____
_____

Ad Category _____ # of words: _____ ❏ Regular type ❏ Bold type ❏ Mixed (circle bold words)
Run my ad in these issues:
Schwann Opus _____ # of times _____

Music Mart ad specifications and requirements:
REGULAR TYPE, per word: 1x = $2.50, 4x = $2.00.
BOLDFACE TYPE, per word: 1x = $2.75, 4x = $2.25.
DISPLAY ADS, per inch: 1x = $85, 4x = $75 (column width = 2"; advertiser provides artwork).
MINIMUM: 15 words per ad or 1" display ad. No charge for zip code. Address = 1 word; City/State = 1 word; Phone = 1 word. (Post Office Boxes MUST provide permanent street address and telephone number before ad can run.) Indicate "All regular text," "All bold text," or "Mixed text" (circle bold words).

AD CLOSING DATE: Six weeks prior to publication. All ads subject to Publisher acceptance.
PAYMENT: PRE-PAYMENT IN U.S. FUNDS DRAWN ON A U.S. BANK MUST ACCOMPANY ORDER.
DO NOT SEND CASH. Send check, money order, or credit-card information with your order to:
Schwann Opus Classified, 1280 Santa Anita Court, Woodland, CA 95776

Schwann DVD ADVANCE

NOW PREMIERING!
The up-to-date, complete, detailed DVD magazine.

CALL 1-800-792-9447

FEATURING:
MUSIC ON DVD • HONG KONG MOVIES • ANIME

INFORMATION LISTED FOR EACH DVD INCLUDES:

Cover Image	Restored Version	Subtitle Languages	Special Notes
Title	Black & White or Color	Dubbed Languages	Original Language
Director	Running Time	Rating	Package Type
Actors	Sound Quality	Trailers	Studio Name
Year of Production	THX	Music Videos	Catalog Number
Short Description	Aspect	Commentaries	List Price
Director's Cut	Close Caption	Interactive Content	Regional Encoding

Get on the Web!
www.schwann.com

Weekly New Release DVD Picks, Question of the Month, Inside Scoop to Artists and Links to Artist Web sites, Subscriptions and much more!

www.schwann.com is Entertainment Information at Your Fingertips!

HOW TO USE SCHWANN OPUS

Schwann Opus lists currently available CDs and cassettes. The following sample listings demonstrate how to read entries.

COMPOSERS SECTION

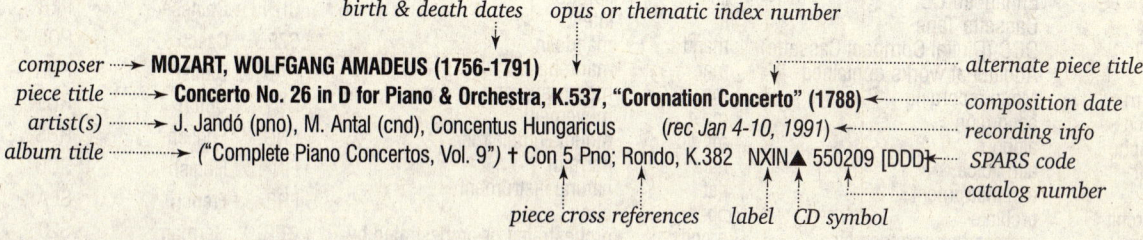

COLLECTIONS SECTION

The COLLECTIONS section lists recordings containing works by six or more composers; or anonymous music falling under a general category, such as Gregorian Chants.

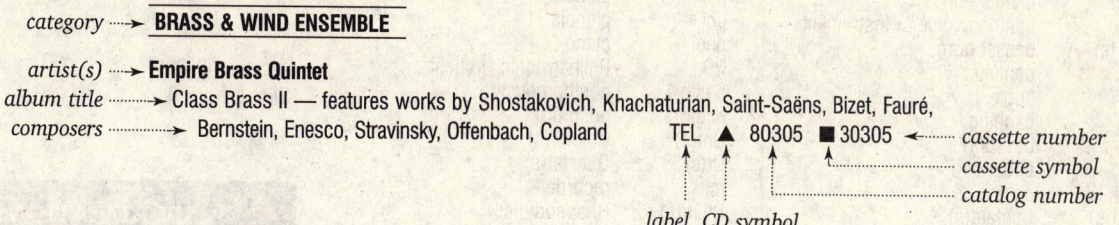

Within the COLLECTIONS section are sub-sections of albums with various artists. These sections list recordings by album title and each listing contains works of various composers performed by various artists.

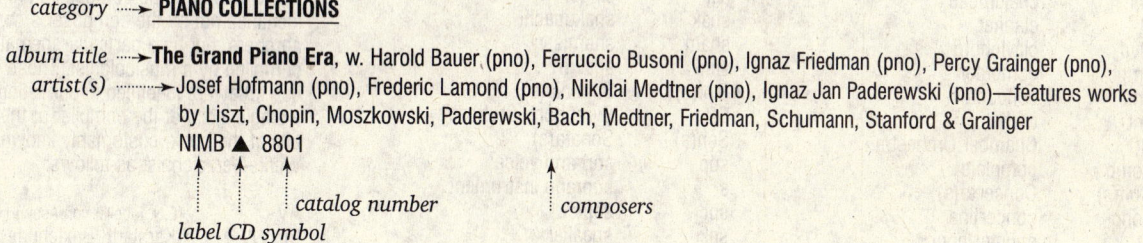

COMPOSER'S NAME

- Composers are listed alphabetically by last name, followed by birth and death dates. When a date is left open, as in (1927- , this indicates that the composer is still living.

PIECE TITLE

- All titles are listed according to the musical form or ensemble. For example: **Concerto for Violin** or **Trio for Piano & Strings**.
- Key signatures are indicated by uppercase letters for major keys, **G**, or by lowercase letters for minor keys, **a**.
- Opus numbers or major thematic index numbers are given when known, followed by the piece numbers from the work which are included (Op. 51/2).
- When an alternate name for a piece exists, it appears after the Opus or catalog number in quotation marks: **"Coronation Concerto"**.
- Dates of composition and revision appear last in parentheses.

ARTIST & RECORDING INFORMATION

- Opera singers are listed from highest vocal range to lowest.
- Most instruments and vocal ranges are abbreviated. See list on next page.
- Language(s) of pieces sung are indicated by an abbreviation in brackets: **[FRE]**. See list on next page.
- If a general piece title is given on the title line, as in **Songs or Music of Brahms**, the specific piece titles will be listed after a dash following the artist information.

- Album titles are listed in parentheses after the artist and recording information. If no title is listed, the piece title is the album title.
- Cross-reference titles are given in abbreviated forms. Each title on the album is listed, though complete information on the additional pieces must be found through cross-referencing. If the source of an additional piece is "Anonymous", "Traditional", or "Narrative" (spoken selection) it cannot be cross-referenced.
- Total CD playing times [TT 1:08:53] are given only in **NEW RELEASES**.

LABEL & FORMAT INFORMATION

- For more information on labels, consult the address list at the back of the Guide.
- Format of the recordings is indicated by a symbol. See list on next page.
- A number appearing before a format symbol indicates number of discs or tapes: 2-▲.
- The inclusion of a list price on a recording should be used as a loose guide to what is easily available in record stores.
- The SPARS Code is a "Consumer Clarification Code" developed by the Society of Professional Audio Recording Studios (SPARS). The three-letter code, in which each letter is either an A (for Analog) or a D (for Digital), appears in a small rectangle on many CD covers. The first letter indicates what kind of tape recorder was originally used; the second, how the mixdown and editing were conducted; and the third, the mastering process.

KEY TO SYMBOLS & ABBREVIATIONS USED IN SCHWANN OPUS

▲	Compact Disc	instr	instrument
△	MD (MiniDisc)	kbd	keyboard(s)
◆	Enhanced CD	lib	libretto
■	Cassette Tape	lt	lute
□	DCC (Digital Compact Cassette)	mand	mandolin
†	Additional works contained	mar	marimba
(m)	Mono recording	mez	mezzo-soprano
acc	accordion	movt	movement
alphn	alphorn	mt dlc	mountain dulcimer
alt	alto voice	nar	narrator
a	alto instrument	nat	natural instrument
archlt	archlute	ob	oboe
arr	arranged or arranged by	orchd	orchestrated or orchestrated by
attrib	attributed	Orch	Orchestra
b	bass instrument	org	organ
b-bar	bass-baritone	Ov(s)	Overture(s)
b.	born	perc	percussion
band	bandoneon	pic	piccolo
bar	baritone voice or instrument	pnl	pianola
bas hn	basset horn	pno	piano
bc	continuo	PO	Philharmonic Orchestra
bgl	bugle	posth	posthumously
bgp	bagpipe	psthn	posthorn
bn	bassoon	Qnt(s)	Quintet(s)
ca	circa	Qt(s)	Quartet(s)
cant	cantor	rcr	recorder
Cant(s)	Cantata(s)	Rhap(s)	Rhapsody(ies)
car	carillons	RSO	Radio Symphony Orchestra
cel	celeste/celesta	sax	saxophone
chit	chitarrone	sels	selections
chl	chalumeau	sgr	singer
cl	clarinet	shak	shakuhachi
clvd	clavichord	sham	shamisen
cmpt	computer	shm	shawm
cnd	conductor	Sinf(s)	Sinfonia(s)
cnt	cornet	SO	Symphony Orchestra
CO	Chamber Orchestra	Son(s)	Sonata(s)
comp	complete	sop	soprano voice
Con(s)	Concerto(s)	s	soprano instrument
conc	concertina	spt	septet
ct	countertenor	spkr	speaker
cta	contralto voice or instrument	strs	strings
ctbn	contrabassoon	sxt	sextet
cym	cymbals	Sym(s)	Symphony(ies)
didj	didjeridu	syn	synthesizer
d.	died	ten	tenor voice
db	double bass	t	tenor instrument
dbl	double	thb	theorbo
Divert(s)	Divertimento(s)	timp	timpani
dlc	dulcimer	tpt	trumpet
dr	drums	trans	transcribed or transcribed by
E hn	English horn	trb	treble voice or instrument
elec	electronics	trbn	trombone
eup	euphonium	trns fl	transverse flute
Fant(s)	Fantasy(ies), Fantasia(s),	va	viola
fid	fiddle	Var(s)	Variation(s)
fl	flute	vc	cello
fl	flourished	vib	vibraphone
flgl	flugelhorn	vih	vihuela
gam	gamelan	vir	virginal
g ar	glass armonica	vl	viol
glock	glockenspiel	vle	violone
gtr	guitar	vn	violin
h-g	hurdy-gurdy	voc	vocalist
ham dlc	hammered dulcimer	w.	with
harm	harmonium	ww	woodwinds
hmc	harmonica	xyl	xylophone
hn	horn	zmz	zoomoozophone
hp	harp		
hpd	harpsichord		

ABBREVIATIONS used to indicate language of vocal recordings

ARM	Armenian	LAT	Latin
BUL	Bulgarian	NOR	Norwegian
CHN	Chinese	PER	Peruvian
CZE	Czech	POL	Polish
DAN	Danish	POR	Portuguese
DUT	Dutch	ROM	Romanian
ENG	English	RUS	Russian
FIN	Finnish	SCO	Scottish
FRE	French	SLA	Slavic
GER	German	SLO	Slovak
GRE	Greek	SPA	Spanish
HEB	Hebrew	SWE	Swedish
HUN	Hungarian	TUR	Turkish
ICE	Icelandic	UKR	Ukrainian
ITA	Italian	WEL	Welsh
JAP	Japanese	YID	Yiddish
KOR	Korean	YUG	Yugoslavian

ABBREVIATIONS used for specialized indices

The works of some composers are usually identified not by the composer's own opus numbers, but by a particular thematic index, compiled by a musicologist. Those in general use today are identified in our listings either by a single initial of the compiler or the title of the book, customarily known as a Werke-Verzeichnis, as follows:

AV.	[E.H. Mueller von Asow] R. Strauss
BuxWV	[Karstadt] Buxtehude
BWV	[Schmieder] J.S. Bach
D.	[Deutsch] Schubert
H.	[Helm] C.P.E. Bach
H.	[Hoboken] Haydn
H.	[Huntington] Sowerby
J.	[Jahns] Weber
K.	[Kirkpatrick] D. Scarlatti
K.	[Köchel] Mozart
L.	[Longo] D. Scarlatti
M.	[Marvin] Soler
M.	[Mohr] Franck
RV.	[Ryom] Vivaldi
S.	[Searle] Liszt
SWV	[Bittinger] Schütz
Sz.	[Szöllösy] Bartók
W.	[Wotquenne] C.P.E. Bach
Z.	[Zimmermann] Purcell

Other abbreviations appearing with composers' works:

WoO	Werk ohne Opuszahl [Work without an Opus number] Beethoven
K.Anh.	Köchel Anhang [Köchel appendix] Mozart

NEW RELEASES

The following is a comprehensive list of recordings released since the last issue. Listings are based on information supplied to us by record companies and distributors. Release information is subject to last-minute changes.

COMPOSERS

ACHRON, JOSEPH (1886-1943)
Hebrew Lullaby for Violin & Piano, Op. 35 (1912)
M. Kramer (vn), S. Over (pno) *(rec St. Silas Church, Kentish Town, London, England, Apr 14-16, 1999)* † Hebrew Melody, Op. 33; Kindersuite Pno, Op. 57; Prelude, Op. 13; Première suite, Op. 21; Son 1 Vn, Op. 29; Stimmungen, Op. 32; Sylphides, Op. 18 [TT 1:17:51] ASVQ ▲ 6235 [DDD] (10.97)
Hebrew Melody for Violin & Piano, Op. 33
M. Kramer (vn), S. Over (pno) *(rec St. Silas Church, Kentish Town, London, England, Apr 14-16, 1999)* † Hebrew Lullaby, Op. 35; Kindersuite Pno, Op. 57; Prelude, Op. 13; Première suite, Op. 21; Son 1 Vn, Op. 29; Stimmungen, Op. 32; Sylphides, Op. 18 [TT 1:17:51] ASVQ ▲ 6235 [DDD] (10.97)
Kindersuite [Children's Suite] (20 pieces) for Piano, Op. 57 (1923)
M. Kramer (vn), S. Over (pno) *(rec St. Silas Church, Kentish Town, London, England, Apr 14-16, 1999)* † Hebrew Lullaby, Op. 35; Hebrew Melody, Op. 33; Prelude, Op. 13; Première suite, Op. 21; Son 1 Vn, Op. 29; Stimmungen, Op. 32; Sylphides, Op. 18 [TT 1:17:51] ASVQ ▲ 6235 [DDD] (10.97)
Les Sylphides for Violin & Piano, Op. 18 (1912)
M. Kramer (vn), S. Over (pno) *(rec St. Silas Church, Kentish Town, London, England, Apr 14-16, 1999)* † Hebrew Lullaby, Op. 35; Hebrew Melody, Op. 33; Kindersuite Pno, Op. 57; Prelude, Op. 13; Première suite, Op. 21; Son 1 Vn, Op. 29; Stimmungen, Op. 32 [TT 1:17:51] ASVQ ▲ 6235 [DDD] (10.97)
Prelude for Violin & Piano, Op. 13 (1910)
M. Kramer (vn), S. Over (pno) *(rec St. Silas Church, Kentish Town, London, England, Apr 14-16, 1999)* † Hebrew Lullaby, Op. 35; Hebrew Melody, Op. 33; Kindersuite Pno, Op. 57; Première suite, Op. 21; Son 1 Vn, Op. 29; Stimmungen, Op. 32; Sylphides, Op. 18 [TT 1:17:51] ASVQ ▲ 6235 [DDD] (10.97)
Première suite en style ancien for Violin & Piano, Op. 21 (ca 1913)
M. Kramer (vn), S. Over (pno) *(rec St. Silas Church, Kentish Town, London, England, Apr 14-16, 1999)* † Hebrew Lullaby, Op. 35; Hebrew Melody, Op. 33; Kindersuite Pno, Op. 57; Prelude, Op. 13; Son 1 Vn, Op. 29; Stimmungen, Op. 32; Sylphides, Op. 18 [TT 1:17:51] ASVQ ▲ 6235 [DDD] (10.97)
Sonata No. 1 for Violin, Op. 29 (ca 1915)
M. Kramer (vn), S. Over (pno) *(rec St. Silas Church, Kentish Town, London, England, Apr 14-16, 1999)* † Hebrew Lullaby, Op. 35; Hebrew Melody, Op. 33; Kindersuite Pno, Op. 57; Prelude, Op. 13; Première suite, Op. 21; Stimmungen, Op. 32; Sylphides, Op. 18 [TT 1:17:51] ASVQ ▲ 6235 [DDD] (10.97)
Stimmungen for Violin and Piano, Op. 32
M. Kramer (vn), S. Over (pno) *(rec St. Silas Church, Kentish Town, London, England, Apr 14-16, 1999)* † Hebrew Lullaby, Op. 35; Hebrew Melody, Op. 33; Kindersuite Pno, Op. 57; Prelude, Op. 13; Première suite, Op. 21; Son 1 Vn, Op. 29; Sylphides, Op. 18 [TT 1:17:51] ASVQ ▲ 6235 [DDD] (10.97)

ADAMS, JOHN (1947-
Short Ride in a Fast Machine (fanfare) for Orchestra (1986)
E. Green (cnd), Univ of Houston Wind Ensemble [arr Odom] *(rec Apr. 21-23, 1996)* † I. Stravinsky:Sacre du printemps (sels); Verdi:Requiem Mass; R. Wagner:Lohengrin (sels) [TT 1:01:44] MRES (Vol. 2) ▲ 2197

ADAMS, RICHARD (dates unknown)
Brutal Reality for Strings & Orchestra
J. Levy (vn), C. Nollaig (vn), D. A. Miller (cnd), Albany SO, Present Music † A. Bloom:Life is Like a Box of Chocolates; E. Chambers:Con Fid; Ince:Fest; J. F. Rogers:Verge ALBA ▲ 354 [DDD] (16.97)

ALABIEV, ALEXANDER (1787-1851)
Quintet in E♭ for Piano & Strings
J. Lagerspetz (pno), A. Mayorov (vn), A. Vinnitsky (vn), A. Yaroshenko (va), A. Rudin (vc) *(rec Small Hall, Moscow Conservatory, Russia, June 1996)* ("Musica Viva") † Arensky:Qnt Pno, Op. 51; Medtner:Qnt Pno [TT 57:33] RD ▲ 30203 [DDD] (16.97)

ALARD, JEAN-DELPHIN (1815-1888)
Duos brillants for 2 Violins, Op. 27
I. Gringolts (vn), A. Bulov (vn)—No. 3 *(rec Länna Church, Sweden, Feb 1999)* † Moszkowski:Suite 2 Vns, Op. 71; Wieniawski:Etude-caprices Vn, Op. 18 [TT 1:06:36] BIS ▲ 1016 [DDD] (17.97)

ALBÉNIZ, ISAAC (1860-1909)
Iberia Suite (in 4 books) for Piano [trans E. Fernandez Arbós for orchestra, 1910-1927] (1906)
W. Kapell (pno)—Book 1/1, "Evocación" *(rec 1945)* † J. S. Bach:Partitas Hpd; Chopin:Son Pno in b, Op. 58; Liszt:Hungarian Rhaps, S.244; Mephisto Waltz 1 Pno, S.514; Sonetti (3) del Petrarca, S.158; S. Prokofiev:Con 3 Pno, Op. 26; S. Rachmaninoff:Con 2 Pno, Op. 18; Rhap on a Theme of Paganini, Op. 43 PPHI (Great Pianists of the 20th Century) ▲ 456853 (22.97)

ALBINONI, TOMASO (1671-1750)
Adagio in g for Organ & Strings [composed by Giazotto on original fragment]
Eroica Trio *(rec St. Stephens Church, CA, July 1999)* † J. S. Bach:Sons & Partitas Vn; Buxtehude:Sons Vns, Op. 2; Loeillet:Sons (12), Op. 2; A. Lotti:Music of Lotti; Vivaldi:Trio Son Vn Vc, RV.83 [TT 56:14] EMIC ▲ 56873 [DDD] (16.97)
Cantatas (12) for Voice & Continuo, Op. 4 (1702)
B. Schlick (mez), D. L. Ragin (ct), N. Selo (vc), R. Shaw (hpd) *(rec Bayerische Rundfunk, Munich, Germany, 1994-97)* [TT 1:33:21] ETC 2-▲ 2027 [DDD] (22.97)
Concertos a cinque (12) for 1 or 2 Oboes & Strings, Op. 9
N. Daniel (ob), Peterborough String Orch—No. 2 in d † V. Bellini:Con Ob; Cimarosa:Con Ob; A. Marcello:Con Ob Strs in d, Op. 1; Vivaldi:Con Ob HYP ▲ 55034 (9.97)
A. Manze (vn), A. Bernardini (ob), F. D. Bruine (ob), C. Hogwood (cnd), Academy of Ancient Music DECC ▲ 458129 (33.97)
S. Schilli (ob), H. Müller-Brühl (cnd), Cologne CO—No. 2 in d *(rec Deutchland Radio, Germany, 1997-98)* ("A Roman Christmas") † A. Corelli:Con grosso, Op. 6/8; A. Marcello:Con Ob Strs in d, Op. 1; A. Scarlatti:Pastorale per nascita di Nostro Signore; Stradella:Son Tpt [TT 1:04:00] NXIN ▲ 8551077 [DDD] (5.97)
Under Ye Gloomy Shade for Soprano & Ensemble
M. Ashton (sop), Concert Royal *(rec St. Mungo's Church, Simonburn, Northumberland, England, Apr 1994)* ("Cantatas from the Georgian Drawing Room") † T. Arne:Cymon & Iphigenia; H. Burgess:Caelia; H. Carey:Belinda & Eurillo; J. Eccles:Love Kindled in a Breast Too Young; N. Pasquali:Pastora; Pepusch:English Cants Book I; Island of Beauty [TT 1:01:32] ORCH ▲ 2927 [DDD] (17.97)

ALESSANDRO, RAFAELE D' (1911-59)
Recitatif and Valse-Impromptu for Oboe & Piano, Op. 20
various artists † Son Fl; Son Giocosa, Op. 6A; Son Ob; Suite Cl, Op. 64 GAAL ▲ 922 [DDD] (18.97)
Sonata for Flute & Piano, Op. 46 (1942)
various artists † Recitatif, Op. 20; Son Fl; Son Giocosa, Op. 6A; Son Ob; Suite Cl, Op. 64 GAAL ▲ 922 [DDD] (18.97)
Sonata for Oboe & Piano, Op. 67 (1949)
various artists † Recitatif, Op. 20; Son Fl; Son Giocosa, Op. 6A; Suite Cl, Op. 64 GAAL ▲ 922 [DDD] (18.97)
Sonatina for Flute Solo, Op. 19
various artists † Recitatif, Op. 20; Son Fl; Son Giocosa, Op. 6A; Son Ob; Suite Cl, Op. 64 GAAL ▲ 922 [DDD] (18.97)
Sonatina Giocosa for Clarinet & Piano, Op. 6A
various artists † Recitatif, Op. 20; Son Fl; Son Ob; Suite Cl, Op. 64 GAAL ▲ 922 [DDD] (18.97)
Suite for Clarinet Solo, Op. 64
various artists † Recitatif, Op. 20; Son Fl; Son Giocosa, Op. 6A; Son Ob GAAL ▲ 922 [DDD] (18.97)

ALLEN, FRED J. (20th cent)
Abide with Me (Chorale Prelude) for Ensemble
Concordia Univ. Wind Sym *(rec Chapel of Our Lord, Concordia University, IL, Mar. 21-23, 1997)* ("Watchman, Tell Us of the Night") † Martyr; Anonymous:Jesus, Jesus, Rest Your Head; Camphouse:Watchman, Tell Us of the Night; J. Curnow:Fanfare Prelude; Nelhybel:Praise to the Lord; C. T. Smith:God of Our Fathers; J. Stamp:Ere the World Began to Be; Vars on Bach Chorale [TT 1:01:07] MRES ▲ 2381
The Martyr for Ensemble
Concordia Univ. Wind Sym *(rec Chapel of Our Lord, Concordia University, IL, Mar. 21-23, 1997)* ("Watchman, Tell Us of the Night") † Abide with Me; Anonymous:Jesus, Jesus, Rest Your Head; Camphouse:Watchman, Tell Us of the Night; J. Curnow:Fanfare Prelude; Nelhybel:Praise to the Lord; C. T. Smith:God of Our Fathers; J. Stamp:Ere the World Began to Be; Vars on Bach Chorale [TT 1:01:07] MRES ▲ 2381

ALYABIEV, ALEXANDER (1787-1851)
Quintet in E♭ for Piano & String Quintet
Em. Gilels (vn), Beethoven String Quartet *(rec 1949)* ("Emil Giles Legacy, Vol. 2") † Son Vn; Trio Pno DHR ▲ 7755 (16.97)
Sonata for Violin & Piano
Em. Gilels (vn), D. Tziganov (vn) *(rec 1951)* ("Emil Giles Legacy, Vol. 2") † Qnt Pno; Trio Pno DHR ▲ 7755 (16.97)
Trio in a for Piano, Violin & Cello
Em. Gilels (vn), D. Tziganov (vn), S. Shirinsky (vc) *(rec 1947)* ("Emil Giles Legacy, Vol. 2") † Qnt Pno; Son Vn DHR ▲ 7755 (16.97)

ANDERSEN, HANS CHRISTIAN (1805-1875)
It's Perfectly True! (recitation) for Voice & Orchestra
V. Bro (nar), J. Wagner (cnd), Odense SO *(rec Odense Concert Hall, Netherlands, May 4-7, 1998)* ("Musical Fairytales") † Fuzzy:Woman with the Eggs; Høffding:Det er ganske vist, Op. 37; S. E. Werner:Most Incredible Thing [TT 59:48] DCAP ▲ 8224099 [DDD] (13.97)

ANDREE, ELFRIDA (1841-1929)
Quintet in e for Piano (1865)
S. Preucil (vn), M. Klein (va), W. Preucil (vc), K. Case (cl), W. Koehler (pno) *(rec Boutell Memorial Hall, Northern Illinois Univ, IL, 1998)* ("Midsummer's Music") † Karg-Elert:Jugend; L. Spohr:Spt Fl [TT 1:08:19] CENT ▲ 2448 [DDD] (16.97)

ANDRIESSEN, JURRIAAN (1925-1996)
Sciarada Spagnuola for Woodwinds
Cumberland Quintet *(rec Tennessee Tech. University, Cookeville, TN, Feb 5-6, 1989)* † A. Jansons:Suite of Old Lettish Dances; Pijper:Sxt Ww; Piston:Qnt Ww; Rameau:Pièces de clavecin; A. Roussel:Divert Ww, Op. 6 [TT 1:00:25] MRES ▲ 20998

ANDRIESSEN, LOUIS (1939-
Trilogy of the Last Day for Voice, Piano, Ensemble & Chorus (1993-97)
Schoenberg Ensemble, R. D. Leeuw (cnd), Asko Ensemble, De Kickers Children's Choir, F. Kol (sop), T. Mukaiyama (pno) [TT 55:53] CV ▲ 79 [DDD] (18.97)

ANGELL, MICHAEL (1964-
Quick 'n Delicious for Trombone (1992)
A. Glendenning (trbn) *(rec U of North Texas Concert Hall, TX)* ("Pathways-New Music for Trombone") † C. Cook:Clowns; B. Hamilton:Wintermute; J. Klein:Pathways; Kleinsasser:Projected Resonance; M. Phillips:T. Rex [TT 1:07:42] MRES ▲ 2645

ANGLEBERT, JEAN-HENRI D' (1635-1691)
Prelude in d for Harpsichord
M. Proud (hpd) *(rec Portola Valley, CA, Nov 1997)* † F. Couperin:Passacaille en rondeau; Marais:Pièces de viole [Book 3] (sels) [TT 1:14:26] CENT ▲ 2429 [DDD] (16.97)

ARENSKY, ANTON (1861-1906)
Quintet in D for Piano & String Quartet, Op. 51 (1900)
J. Lagerspetz (pno), A. Mayorov (vn), A. Vinnitsky (vn), A. Yaroshenko (va), A. Rudin (vc) *(rec Small Hall, Moscow Conservatory, Russia, June 1996)* ("Musica Viva") † Alabiev:Qnt Pno; Medtner:Qnt Pno [TT 57:33] RD ▲ 30203 [DDD] (16.97)

ARNE, THOMAS (1710-1778)
Alfred (opera) [lib. J. Thompson & D. Mallett] (1740)
N. McGegan (cnd), Philharmonia Baroque Orch, Philharmonia Chorus, C. Brandes (sop), J. Smith (sop), J. MacDougall (ten), D. Daniels (sgr) DEHA ▲ 51314 (16.97)
Cymon and Iphigenia (cantata) for Voice & Orchestra
M. Ashton (sop), Concert Royal *(rec St. Mungo's Church, Simonburn, Northumberland, England, Apr 1994)* ("Cantatas from the Georgian Drawing Room") † Albinoni:Under Ye Gloomy Shade; H. Burgess:Caelia; H. Carey:Belinda & Eurillo; J. Eccles:Love Kindled in a Breast Too Young; N. Pasquali:Pastora; Pepusch:English Cants Book I; Island of Beauty [TT 1:01:32] ORCH ▲ 2927 [DDD] (17.97)

ARNOLD, MALCOLM (1921-
Scottish Dances (4) for Orchestra, Op. 59 (1957)
H. Begian (cnd), Univ of Illinois Symphonic Band ("The Begian Years-Vol. 10") † Berlioz:Béatrice et Bénédict (ov); Bilik:Sym Band; A. C. Gomez:Guarany (ov); G. Holst:Hammersmith, Op. 52; Kodály:Galanta Dances; R. Wagner:Lohengrin (sels) [TT 1:15:06] MRES ▲ 1651

ASSAD, SÉRGIO (1952-
Music of Assad
Guitar x 2—Pinote *(rec State University, New York, Purchase, NY, 1998)* ("Catgut Flambo") † P. Bellinati:; E. Granados:Danzas españolas (10) Pno; Goyescas (sels); C. Machado:Music of Machado; H. Rovics:Impressões do Brasil; Sor:Divert Gtrs, Op. 34; Telemann:Music of Telemann MUSC ▲ 21699 (10.97)

ASTORGA, EMANUELE D' (1680-?1757)
Stabat Mater in c for solo Voices, Strings, Continuo & Chorus (?1707)
King's Consort, King's Consort Choir, S. Gritton (sop), S. Fox (sop), S. Bickley (mez), P. Agnew (ten), P. Harvey (bass) † Boccherini:Stabat Mater, G.532 HYP ▲ 67108 (18.97)

ATANASOVA, ELKA (1972-
Transformation for Voice, Violin & Chamber Ensemble
E. Atanasova (sgr), E. Atanasova (vn), A. T. Usseinov (tanbura), A. Gieseler (kbd), F. Accurso (perc) [arr Ivanoff] *(rec Munich, Germany)* † Wedding [TT 53:50] ERD ▲ 91350 [ADD] (17.97)
The Wedding for Voice, Violin & Chamber Ensemble
E. Atanasova (sgr), E. Atanasova (vn), A. T. Usseinov (tanbura), A. Gieseler (kbd), F. Accurso (perc) [arr Ivanoff] *(rec Munich, Germany)* † Transformation [TT 53:50] ERD ▲ 91350 [ADD] (17.97)

ATTAINGNANT, PIERRE (ca 1494-ca 1552)
Dances (6) for Organ
P. Rouet (org) *(rec Org of Moucherel Formentelli Notre-Dame de Mouzon, France, July 1998)* † Anonymous:Estampie; Intabulatura Nova; B. Bartók:Romanian Folk Dances Pno, Sz.56; G. Picchi:Ballo alla polacha; Ballo hongaro; Ballo todescha; Pass'e Mezzo in d; B. Storace:Balleto; Ciaccona in C; Folia; Passacaglia in a; Spagnoletta [TT 1:09:35] PAVA ▲ 7415 [DDD] (10.97)

AURIC, GEORGES (1899-1983)
Les Parents terribles (film music)(sels)
V. Rašková (fl), J. Tchamkerten (ondes martenot), M. Adriano (cnd), Slovak RSO—Image musicale ("Film Music-Vol. 2") † Orphée (sels); Ruy Blas (sels); Thomas l'Imposteur (sels) [TT 1:10:27] MARC ▲ 8225066 (13.97)
Orphée (film music) for Orchestra (sels)
V. Rašková (fl), J. Tchamkerten (ondes martenot), M. Adriano (cnd), Slovak RSO—Suite; Complainte d'Eurydice ("Film Music-Vol. 2") † Parents terribles (sels); Ruy Blas (sels); Thomas l'Imposteur (sels) [TT 1:10:27] MARC ▲ 8225066 (13.97)
Ruy Blas (film music)(sels)
V. Rašková (fl), J. Tchamkerten (ondes martenot), M. Adriano (cnd), Slovak RSO—Suite ("Film Music-Vol. 2") † Orphée (sels); Parents terribles (sels); Thomas l'Imposteur (sels) [TT 1:10:27] MARC ▲ 8225066 (13.97)

AURIC, GEORGES (cont.)

Thomas l'Imposteur (film music)(sels)
V. Rašková (fl), J. Tchamkerten (ondes martenot), M. Adriano (cnd), Slovak RSO—Suite ("Film Music-Vol. 2") † Orphée (sels); Parents terribles (sels); Ruy Blas (sels) [TT 1:10:27] MARC ▲ 8225066 (13.97)

AVSHALOMOV, AARON (1894-1965)

Concerto in D for Violin (1937)
R. Zamuruev (vn), D. Avshalomov (cnd), Moscow SO *(rec Moscow, Russia, May 1997)* ("Orchestral Works-Vol. 2") † Hutungs of Peking; Soul of the Ch'in [TT 1:11:11] MARC ▲ 8225034 [DDD] (13.97)

The Hutungs of Peking for Orchestra
J. Avshalomov (cnd), Moscow SO *(rec Moscow, Russia, May 1997)* ("Orchestral Works-Vol. 2") † Con Vn; Soul of the Ch'in [TT 1:11:11] MARC ▲ 8225034 [DDD] (13.97)

The Soul of the Ch'in (ballet pantomime) for Orchestra (1925-26)
J. Avshalomov (cnd), Moscow SO *(rec Moscow, Russia, May 1997)* ("Orchestral Works-Vol. 2") † Con Vn; Hutungs of Peking [TT 1:11:11] MARC ▲ 8225034 [DDD] (13.97)

BABER, JOSEPH (1937-

Music of Baber
R. Black (ten), M. Taylor (pno)—Longfellow Songs, Op. 2a; Emersonian Hymns, Op. 2b; Cavalier Lyrics, Op. 6; American Songs, Op. 12; Shakespearean Songs, Op. 19; Ere we be young again, Op. 50 *(rec Singletary Center for the Arts, University of KY, KY, Aug 1991)* ("An American Son-The Vocal Works of Joseph Baber-Vol. 1") MRES ▲ 1793

BACH, CARL PHILIPP EMANUEL (1714-1788)

Concerto in d for Flute & Strings, H.484/1 (ca 1747)
M. Schminke (vn), H. Samieian (fl), I. Kocsis (hp), L. Schrettner (cnd), Louis Spohr Sinfonietta † F. Farkas:Aria e Rondo All'ungherese; Partita All'ungherese; Grandjany:Aria in Classic Style, Op. 19; O. Respighi:Adagio con variazioni Vc Pno DI ▲ 920533 (5.97)

Sonatas (5) for Keyboard, H.15-19, W.65/6-10 (1736-38; rev 1743-44)
M. Spányi (clvd)—No. 5 in A, H.19; No. 1 in G, H.15 *(rec Oulu Conservatory of Music, Oulu, Finland, July 1998)* † Son Kbd, H.2; Son Kbd, H.20; Son Kbd, H.21; Sons (4) Kbd, H.3-6 [TT 1:16:43] BIS ▲ 963 [DDD] (17.97)

Sonata in B♭ for Keyboard, H.2, (W.62/1) (1731)
M. Spányi (clvd) *(rec Oulu Conservatory of Music, Oulu, Finland, July 1998)* † Son Kbd, H.20; Son Kbd, H.21; Sons (4) Kbd, H.3-6; Sons (5) Kbd, H.15-19 [TT 1:16:43] BIS ▲ 963 [DDD] (17.97)

Sonata in G for Keyboard, H.20, (W.62/2) (1739)
M. Spányi (clvd) *(rec Oulu Conservatory of Music, Oulu, Finland, July 1998)* † Son Kbd, H.2; Son Kbd, H.21; Sons (4) Kbd, H.3-6; Sons (5) Kbd, H.15-19 [TT 1:16:43] BIS ▲ 963 [DDD] (17.97)

Sonata in g for Keyboard, H.21, (W.65/11) (1739)
M. Spányi (clvd) *(rec Oulu Conservatory of Music, Oulu, Finland, July 1998)* † Son Kbd, H.2; Son Kbd, H.20; Sons (4) Kbd, H.3-6; Sons (5) Kbd, H.15-19 [TT 1:16:43] BIS ▲ 963 [DDD] (17.97)

Sonatas (4) for Keyboard, H.3-6, (W.65/1-4) (1744)
M. Spányi (clvd)—No. 1 in F, H.3 *(rec Oulu Conservatory of Music, Oulu, Finland, July 1998)* † Son Kbd, H.2; Son Kbd, H.20; Son Kbd, H.21; Sons (5) Kbd, H.15-19 [TT 1:16:43] BIS ▲ 963 [DDD] (17.97)

BACH, JOHANN CHRISTIAN (1735-1782)

Music of Bach
A. McDonald (vn), J. Bishop (vn), S. Comberti (vc), A. Halstead (cnd), Hanover Band *(Sym Concertante, C.36b)*, R. Brown (fl), A. Robson (ob), J. Ward (bn), A. Halstead (cnd), Hanover Band *(Sym Concertante, C.37)*, A. McDonald (vn), J. Bishop (vn), A. Halstead (cnd), Hanover Band *(Con Vn, C.76b)*, A. McDonald (vn), J. Bishop (vn), S. Comberti (vc), R. Brown (fl), A. Halstead (cnd), Hanover Band *(Sym Concertante, C.Inc 5) (rec Rosslyn Hill Chapel, Hampstead, England, July 1998)* ("Symphonies Concertantes-Vol. 4") CPO ▲ 999627 [DDD] (14.97)

BACH, JOHANN SEBASTIAN (1685-1750)

Allein Gott in der Höh sei Ehr (chorale) for Organ, BWV 715 (ca 1708)
G. Weinberger (org) *(rec Joachim Wagner Organ, St. Marien, Angermünde, Germany, Sept 1996)* ("Vol. 5") † Allein Gott in der Höh sei Ehr, BWV 716; Allein Gott in der Höh sei Ehr, BWV 717; Gelobet seist du, Jesu Christ, BWV 722; Gelobet seist du, Jesu Christ, BWV 723; Gott durch deine Güte, BWV 724; In dulci jubilo, BWV 729; Nun freut euch, lieben Christen g'mein, BWV 734; Pastorale Org, BWV 590; Preludes & Fugues, BWV 531-552; Trio Org, BWV 583; Wie schön leuchtet der Morgenstern, BWV 739 [TT 1:15:23] CPO ▲ 999654 [DDD] (7.97)

Allein Gott in der Höh sei Ehr (fugue) for Organ, BWV 716
G. Weinberger (org) *(rec Joachim Wagner Organ, St. Marien, Angermünde, Germany, Sept 1996)* ("Vol. 5") † Allein Gott in der Höh sei Ehr, BWV 715; Allein Gott in der Höh sei Ehr, BWV 717; Gelobet seist du, Jesu Christ, BWV 722; Gelobet seist du, Jesu Christ, BWV 723; Gott durch deine Güte, BWV 724; In dulci jubilo, BWV 729; Nun freut euch, lieben Christen g'mein, BWV 734; Pastorale Org, BWV 590; Preludes & Fugues, BWV 531-552; Trio Org, BWV 583; Wie schön leuchtet der Morgenstern, BWV 739 [TT 1:15:23] CPO ▲ 999654 [DDD] (7.97)

Allein Gott in der Höh sei Ehr (chorale) for Organ, BWV 717
G. Weinberger (org) *(rec Joachim Wagner Organ, St. Marien, Angermünde, Germany, Sept 1996)* ("Vol. 5") † Allein Gott in der Höh sei Ehr, BWV 715; Allein Gott in der Höh sei Ehr, BWV 716; Gelobet seist du, Jesu Christ, BWV 722; Gelobet seist du, Jesu Christ, BWV 723; Gott durch deine Güte, BWV 724; In dulci jubilo, BWV 729; Nun freut euch, lieben Christen g'mein, BWV 734; Pastorale Org, BWV 590; Preludes & Fugues, BWV 531-552; Trio Org, BWV 583; Wie schön leuchtet der Morgenstern, BWV 739 [TT 1:15:23] CPO ▲ 999654 [DDD] (7.97)

The Art of the Fugue [Die Kunst der Fuge] for Keyboard, BWV 1080 (ca 1745-50)
Alexander & Daykin Duo CSOC 2-▲ 4203
J. Holloway (vn), J. See (fl), J. T. Linden (cel), D. Moroney (hpd) † Musical Offering, BWV 1079; Wohltemperirte Clavier HAM 7-▲ 2908084 (47.97)
D. Moroney (hpd) HAM ▲ 2951169 (23.97)

The Art of the Fugue (selections)
Quartz Saxophone Quartet—Contrapunctus No. 3 [arr Carpenter] ("Faces") † J. Buckley:Qt Sax; G. Carpenter:Semaine de Bonte; G. Fitkin:Stub; A. Levine:Faces; M. Nyman:Songs for Tony BBCL ▲ 1024 (16.97)

Brandenburg Concertos (6) for Orchestra (1046-51)
Berlin Akademie für Alte Musik † Suites Orch HAM 4-▲ 2908074 (23.97)

Brandenburg Concerto No. 1 in F, BWV 1046 (1717)
R. Friend (vn), R. Winfield (ob), R. Catt (ob), M. Checker (ob), N. Levesley (bn), J. Bryant (hn), C. Hartex (hn), A. Boult (cnd), London PO *(rec 1973)* † Brandenburg Con 2, BWV 1047; Brandenburg Con 3, BWV 1048; Brandenburg Con 4, BWV 1049; Brandenburg Con 5, BWV 1050; Brandenburg Con 6, BWV 1051 RYLC 2-▲ 70569 (10.97)
D. Reed (sax), J. Oviedo (sax), J. Butler (a sax/s sax), D. Goble (a sax/s sax), W. Graves (a sax/s sax), T. Poole (a sax), A. G. Rivard (a sax), T. Oxford (bar sax), K. Russell (a sax/bar sax), T. Yukumoto (b sax), H. Pittel (cnd) [arr Sparks] ("Tex Sax") † Herr Jesu Christ, du höchstes, BWV 334; G. F. Handel:Messiah (choruses); Mussorgsky:Pictures at an Exhibition [TT 1:11:15] MRES ▲ 2280

Brandenburg Concerto No. 2 in F, BWV 1047 (1717-18)
R. Friend (vn), D. Monrow (rcr), R. Winfield (ob), G. Webb (tpt), A. Boult (cnd), London PO *(rec 1973)* † Brandenburg Con 1, BWV 1046; Brandenburg Con 3, BWV 1048; Brandenburg Con 4, BWV 1049; Brandenburg Con 5, BWV 1050; Brandenburg Con 6, BWV 1051 RYLC 2-▲ 70569 (10.97)

Brandenburg Concerto No. 3 in G, BWV 1048 (1711-13)
R. Friend (vn), D. Whittaker (fl), R. Leppard (hpd), A. Boult (cnd), London PO *(rec 1973)* † Brandenburg Con 1, BWV 1046; Brandenburg Con 2, BWV 1047; Brandenburg Con 4, BWV 1049; Brandenburg Con 5, BWV 1050; Brandenburg Con 6, BWV 1051 RYLC 2-▲ 70569 (10.97)

Brandenburg Concerto No. 4 in G, BWV 1049 (ca 1720)
G. Jarvis (vn), D. Monrow (rcr), J. Turner (rcr), A. Boult (cnd), London PO *(rec 1973)* † Brandenburg Con 1, BWV 1046; Brandenburg Con 2, BWV 1047; Brandenburg Con 3, BWV 1048; Brandenburg Con 5, BWV 1050; Brandenburg Con 6, BWV 1051 RYLC 2-▲ 70569 (10.97)

Brandenburg Concerto No. 5 in D, BWV 1050 (1720-21)
R. Friend (vn), D. Whittaker (fl), R. Leppard (hpd), A. Boult (cnd), London PO *(rec 1973)* † Brandenburg Con 1, BWV 1046; Brandenburg Con 2, BWV 1047; Brandenburg Con 3, BWV 1048; Brandenburg Con 4, BWV 1049; Brandenburg Con 6, BWV 1051 RYLC 2-▲ 70569 (10.97)
I. Guetta (elec gtr), Israel String Quartet [arr Guetta] † Con Vns; Con 1 Vn; Easter Oratorio, BWV 249; Sons & Partitas Vn [TT 58:24] JRB ▲ 2003 [DDD] (16.97)

Brandenburg Concerto No. 6 in B♭, BWV 1051 (1708-10)
A. Cameron (vc), W. Webster (db), V. Ameling (hpd), A. Boult (cnd), London PO *(rec 1973)* † Brandenburg Con 1, BWV 1046; Brandenburg Con 2, BWV 1047; Brandenburg Con 3, BWV 1048; Brandenburg Con 4, BWV 1049; Brandenburg Con 5, BWV 1050 RYLC 2-▲ 70569 (10.97)

Cantata No. 8, Liebster Gott, wann werd' ich sterben
P. Herreweghe (cnd), Chapelle Royale, Collegium Vocale † Cant 125; Cant 138; Cant 158; Cant 170; Cant 198; Cant 21; Cant 35; Cant 42; Cant 54; Cant 56; Cant 78; Cant 82 HAM 5-▲ 2908091 (35.97)

BACH, JOHANN SEBASTIAN (cont.)

Cantata No. 21, Ich hatte viel Bekümmernis
P. Herreweghe (cnd), Chapelle Royale, Collegium Vocale † Cant 125; Cant 138; Cant 158; Cant 170; Cant 198; Cant 35; Cant 42; Cant 54; Cant 56; Cant 78; Cant 8; Cant 82 HAM 5-▲ 2908091 (35.97)

Cantata No. 35, Geist und Seele wird verwirret (1726)
A. Scholl (alt), P. Herreweghe (cnd), Chapelle Royale † Cant 125; Cant 138; Cant 158; Cant 170; Cant 198; Cant 21; Cant 42; Cant 54; Cant 56; Cant 78; Cant 8; Cant 82 HAM 5-▲ 2908091 (35.97)
A. Scholl (ct), P. Herreweghe (cnd), Collegium Vocale † Cant 170; Cant 54 HAM ▲ 2951644 (12.97)

Cantata No. 40, Dazu ist erschienen der Sohn Gottes
C. Smith (cnd), Emmanuel Music Orch, Emmanuel Music Chorus † Cant 133; Cant 151; Cant 65 KOCH ▲ 7462 (16.97)

Cantata No. 42, Am Abend aber desselbigen Sabbats
P. Herreweghe (cnd), Chapelle Royale, Collegium Vocale † Cant 125; Cant 138; Cant 158; Cant 170; Cant 198; Cant 21; Cant 35; Cant 54; Cant 56; Cant 78; Cant 8; Cant 82 HAM 5-▲ 2908091 (35.97)

Cantata No. 46, Schauet doch und sehet
M. Suzuki (cnd), Bach Collegium Japan Choir, M. Suzuki (sop), K. Wessel (ct), M. Sakurada (ten), P. Kooij (bass) *(rec Kobe Shoin Women's University, Japan, Sept 1998)* † Cant 136; Cant 138; Cant 95 [TT 1:06:44] BIS ▲ 991 [DDD] (17.97)

Cantata No. 51, Jauchzet Gott in allen Landen
C. Schäfer (sop), R. Goebel (cnd), Musica Antiqua Köln † Cant 202; Cant 210 DEUT ▲ 459621 (16.97)

Cantata No. 54, Widerstehe doch der Sünde
A. Scholl (alt), P. Herreweghe (cnd), Chapelle Royale † Cant 125; Cant 138; Cant 158; Cant 170; Cant 198; Cant 21; Cant 35; Cant 42; Cant 56; Cant 78; Cant 8; Cant 82 HAM 5-▲ 2908091 (35.97)
A. Scholl (ct), P. Herreweghe (cnd), Collegium Vocale † Cant 170; Cant 35 HAM ▲ 2951644 (12.97)

Cantata No. 56, Ich will den Kreuzstab gerne tragen
P. Kooy (bass), P. Herreweghe (cnd), Chapelle Royale † Cant 125; Cant 138; Cant 158; Cant 170; Cant 198; Cant 21; Cant 35; Cant 42; Cant 54; Cant 78; Cant 8; Cant 82 HAM 5-▲ 2908091 (35.97)

Cantata No. 57, Selig ist der Mann
P. Herreweghe (cnd), Collegium Vocale, V. Jezovšek (sop), S. Connolly (alt), M. Padmore (ten), P. Kooy (bass) † Cant 110; Cant 122 HAM ▲ 2951594 (12.97)

Cantata No. 65, Sie werden aus Saba alle kommen
C. Smith (cnd), Emmanuel Music Orch, Emmanuel Music Chorus † Cant 133; Cant 151; Cant 40 KOCH ▲ 7462 (16.97)

Cantata No. 78, Jesu, der du meine Seele
P. Herreweghe (cnd), Chapelle Royale, Collegium Vocale † Cant 125; Cant 138; Cant 158; Cant 170; Cant 198; Cant 21; Cant 35; Cant 42; Cant 54; Cant 56; Cant 8; Cant 82 HAM 5-▲ 2908091 (35.97)

Cantata No. 80, Ein feste Burg ist unser Gott
Collegium Vocale, P. Herreweghe (cnd), La Chapelle Royale, B. Schlick (sop), A. Mellon (sop), G. Lesne (alt), H. Crook (ten), P. Kooy (bass) † Magnificat, BWV 243 HAM ▲ 2951326 (12.97)

Cantata No. 82, Ich habe genug (1727)
P. Kooy (bass), P. Herreweghe (cnd), Chapelle Royale † Cant 125; Cant 138; Cant 158; Cant 170; Cant 198; Cant 21; Cant 35; Cant 42; Cant 54; Cant 56; Cant 78; Cant 8 HAM 5-▲ 2908091 (35.97)

Cantata No. 95, Christus, der ist mein Leben (1723)
M. Suzuki (cnd), Bach Collegium Japan Choir, M. Suzuki (sop), K. Wessel (ct), M. Sakurada (ten), P. Kooij (bass) *(rec Kobe Shoin Women's University, Japan, Sept 1998)* † Cant 136; Cant 138; Cant 46 [TT 1:06:44] BIS ▲ 991 [DDD] (17.97)

Cantata No. 110, Unser Mund sei voll Lachens
P. Herreweghe (cnd), Collegium Vocale, V. Jezovšek (sop), S. Connolly (alt), M. Padmore (ten), P. Kooy (bass) † Cant 122; Cant 57 HAM ▲ 2951594 (12.97)

Cantata No. 122, Das neugebor'ne Kindelein
P. Herreweghe (cnd), Collegium Vocale, V. Jezovšek (sop), S. Connolly (alt), M. Padmore (ten), P. Kooy (bass) † Cant 110; Cant 57 HAM ▲ 2951594 (12.97)

Cantata No. 125, Mit Fried' und Freud' ich fahr' dahin
P. Herreweghe (cnd), Chapelle Royale, Collegium Vocale † Cant 138; Cant 158; Cant 170; Cant 198; Cant 21; Cant 35; Cant 42; Cant 54; Cant 56; Cant 78; Cant 8; Cant 82 HAM 5-▲ 2908091 (35.97)

Cantata No. 133, Ich freue mich in dir
C. Smith (cnd), Emmanuel Music Orch, Emmanuel Music Chorus † Cant 151; Cant 40; Cant 65 KOCH ▲ 7462 (16.97)

Cantata No. 136, Erforsche mich, Gott
M. Suzuki (cnd), Bach Collegium Japan Choir, M. Suzuki (sop), K. Wessel (ct), M. Sakurada (ten), P. Kooij (bass) *(rec Kobe Shoin Women's University, Japan, Sept 1998)* † Cant 138; Cant 46; Cant 95 [TT 1:06:44] BIS ▲ 991 [DDD] (17.97)

Cantata No. 138, Was betrübst du dich, mein Herz
P. Herreweghe (cnd), Chapelle Royale, Collegium Vocale † Cant 125; Cant 158; Cant 170; Cant 198; Cant 21; Cant 35; Cant 42; Cant 54; Cant 56; Cant 78; Cant 8; Cant 82 HAM 5-▲ 2908091 (35.97)
M. Suzuki (cnd), Bach Collegium Japan Choir, M. Suzuki (sop), K. Wessel (ct), M. Sakurada (ten), P. Kooij (bass) *(rec Kobe Shoin Women's University, Japan, Sept 1998)* † Cant 136; Cant 46; Cant 95 [TT 1:06:44] BIS ▲ 991 [DDD] (17.97)

Cantata No. 151, Süsser Trost, mein Jesus kommt
C. Smith (cnd), Emmanuel Music Orch, Emmanuel Music Chorus † Cant 133; Cant 40; Cant 65 KOCH ▲ 7462 (16.97)

Cantata No. 158, Der Friede sei mit dir
P. Kooy (bass), P. Herreweghe (cnd), Chapelle Royale † Cant 125; Cant 138; Cant 170; Cant 198; Cant 21; Cant 35; Cant 42; Cant 54; Cant 56; Cant 78; Cant 8; Cant 82 HAM 5-▲ 2908091 (35.97)

Cantata No. 170, Vergnügte Ruh', beliebte Seelenlust
A. Scholl (alt), P. Herreweghe (cnd), Chapelle Royale † Cant 125; Cant 138; Cant 158; Cant 198; Cant 21; Cant 35; Cant 42; Cant 54; Cant 56; Cant 78; Cant 8; Cant 82 HAM 5-▲ 2908091 (35.97)
A. Scholl (ct), P. Herreweghe (cnd), Collegium Vocale † Cant 35; Cant 54 HAM ▲ 2951644 (12.97)

Cantata No. 198, Lass, Fürstin, lass noch einen Strahl
P. Herreweghe (cnd), Chapelle Royale, Collegium Vocale † Cant 125; Cant 138; Cant 158; Cant 170; Cant 21; Cant 35; Cant 42; Cant 54; Cant 56; Cant 78; Cant 8; Cant 82 HAM 5-▲ 2908091 (35.97)

Cantata No. 201, Der Streit zwischen Phoebus und Pan (?1729)
R. Jacobs (cnd), Berlin Akademie für Alte Musik, Berlin RIAS Chamber Choir † Cant 205; Cant 213 HAM 2-▲ 2951544 (23.97)

Cantata No. 202, Weichet nur, betrübte Schatten, "Wedding Cantata"
C. Schäfer (sop), R. Goebel (cnd), Musica Antiqua Köln † Cant 210; Cant 51 DEUT ▲ 459621 (16.97)

Cantata No. 205, Der zufriedengestellte Aeolus
R. Jacobs (cnd), Berlin Akademie für Alte Musik, Berlin RIAS Chamber Choir † Cant 201; Cant 213 HAM 2-▲ 2951544 (23.97)

Cantata No. 210, O holder Tag, erwünschte Zeit (after 1740)
C. Schäfer (sop), R. Goebel (cnd), Musica Antiqua Köln † Cant 202; Cant 51 DEUT ▲ 459621 (16.97)

Cantata No. 213, Hercules auf dem Scheidewege (1733)
R. Jacobs (cnd), Berlin Akademie für Alte Musik, Berlin RIAS Chamber Choir † Cant 201; Cant 205 HAM 2-▲ 2951544 (23.97)

Canzona in d for Organ, BWV 588 (ca 1715)
P. Hawkins (org) *(rec Greg Harrold Opus 14, 1995, Brentwood, CA)* † Fant & Fugue, BWV 542; Orgelbüchlein; Partite diverse sopra, BWV 767; Preludes & Fugues, BWV 531-552 [TT 1:04:40] ARK ▲ 6170 [DDD] (16.97)

Chorales (18) for Organ, BWV 651-668, "Leipzig Chorales" (ca 1708-17)
L. Rogg (org)—BWV 659, Nun komm, der Heiden Heiland † Cons Org; Fant & Fugue, BWV 542; Passacaglia & Fugue Org, BWV 582; Schübler Chorale Preludes; Toccata & Fugue Org, BWV 565; Toccata, Adagio & Fugue Org, BWV 564 [TT 1:09:10] CSER ▲ 73568 [ADD] (6.97)

Christmas Oratorio, BWV 248 (1734-35)
R. Jacobs (cnd), Berlin Akademie für Alte Musik, R. Jacobs (cnd), RIAS Chamber Choir, D. Röschmann (sop), A. Scholl (ct), K. Häger (bass), W. Güra (sgr) HAM ▲ 2951630 (23.97)

Christmas Oratorio (selections)
G. Oberfrank (cnd), Failoni CO, Hungarian Radio Choir, I. Kertesi (sop), J. Németh (alt), J. Mukk (ten), J. Tóth (bass) [TT 1:11:18] NXIN ▲ 8554508 [DDD] (5.97)

Chromatic Fantasy & Fugue in d for Harpsichord, BWV 903 (ca 1720; rev ca 1730)
S. Bartos (pno) † Goldberg Vars, BWV 988 CSOC ▲ 4176

▲ = CD ♦ = Enhanced CD △ = MD ▮ = Cassette Tape ▯ = DCC

BACH, JOHANN SEBASTIAN (cont.)

Concerto No. 1 in d for Harpsichord & Orchestra, BWV 1052
J. Szigeti (vn), F. Stiedry (cnd), New Friends of Music Orch *(rec 1933-40)* † Mendelssohn (-Bartholdy):Con Vn & Orch, Op. 64; Tartini:Con Vn, D.45 ENT ▲ 99396 (17.97)
Thomas Gabriel Trio [arr Gabriel] *(rec Fürstliche Reitbahn Arolsen, Germany, Aug 7-8, 1998)* ("Bach-Jazz") † Partitas Hpd; Schübler Chorale Preludes [TT 1:02:43] MDG ▲ 6100916 [DDD] (17.97)

Concertos (6) for Organ [arr Bach from concertos by Vivaldi, et al.], BWV 592-597
L. Rogg (org)—BWV 593, No. 2 in a † Chorales Org; Fant & Fugue, BWV 542; Passacaglia & Fugue Org, BWV 582; Schübler Chorale Preludes; Toccata & Fugue Org, BWV 565; Toccata, Adagio & Fugue Org, BWV 564 [TT 1:09:10] CSER ▲ 73568 [ADD] (6.97)

Concerto No. 1 in a for Violin & Orchestra, BWV 1041 (1717-23)
I. Guetta (elec gtr), Israel String Quartet [arr Guetta] † Brandenburg Con 5, BWV 1050; Con Vns; Easter Oratorio, BWV 249; Sons & Partitas Vn [TT 58:24] JRB ▲ 2003 [DDD] (16.97)

Concerto in d for 2 Violins & Orchestra, BWV 1043 (1717-23)
I. Guetta (elec gtr), Israel String Quartet [arr Guetta] † Brandenburg Con 5, BWV 1050; Con 1 Vn; Easter Oratorio, BWV 249; Sons & Partitas Vn [TT 58:24] JRB ▲ 2003 [DDD] (16.97)

Concerto in d for 2 Violins & Orchestra, BWV.1043 (1717-23)
D. Oistrakh (vn), Y. Menuhin (vn) *(rec Atheneum Hall, Bucharest, Romania, Sept 18, 1958)* ("In Memoriam: Rare Broadcast Performances") † B. Bartók:Con 2 Vn, Sz.112; Beethoven:Con Vn; Lalo:Sym espagnole, Op. 21 [TT 1:59:11] MUA 2-▲ 1053 (31.97)
Progetto Avanti ("Baroque Illusions") † J. Pachelbel:Canon & Gigue; A. Templeton:Bach Goes to Town; Vivaldi:Cons Vn Strs, Op. 8/1-4 FNL ▲ 25326 (16.97)

Duets (4) for solo Harpsichord, BWV 802-805
D. Moroney (hpd) † Italian Con, BWV 971; Partita Hpd, BWV 831 HAM ▲ 2951278 (12.97)

Easter Oratorio, BWV 249 (1732-35)
I. Guetta (elec gtr), Israel String Quartet—Adagio [arr Guetta] † Brandenburg Con 5, BWV 1050; Con Vns; Con 1 Vn; Sons & Partitas Vn [TT 58:24] JRB ▲ 2003 [DDD] (16.97)
P. Herreweghe (cnd), Collegium Vocale HAM 4-▲ 2908070 (23.97)

English Suites (6) for Harpsichord, BWV 806-811 (ca 1715)
K. Gilbert (hpd) † French Suites; Partitas Hpd HAM 6-▲ 2908078 (35.97)
P. Ross (pno)—BWV 807, No. 2 in a † French Suites; Partitas Hpd; Toccatas Hpd CSOC ▲ 4201

Fantasia & Fugue in g for Organ, BWV 542 (1708-23)
P. Hawkins (org) *(rec Greg Harrold Opus 14, 1995, Brentwood, CA)* † Canzona; Orgelbüchlein; Partite diverse sopra, BWV 767; Preludes & Fugues, BWV 531-552 [TT 1:04:40] ARK ▲ 6170 [DDD] (16.97)
L. Rogg (org) † Chorales Org; Cons Org; Passacaglia & Fugue Org, BWV 582; Schübler Chorale Preludes; Toccata & Fugue Org, BWV 565; Toccata, Adagio & Fugue Org, BWV 564 [TT 1:09:10] CSER ▲ 73568 [ADD] (6.97)

Fantasia in G for Organ, BWV 572 (ca 1708)
S. Dettra (org) *(rec Cadet Chapel Organ, West Point, NY, Jan 6-7, 1999)* ("Tongues of Fire") † Duruflé:Prélude et fugue, Op. 7; Prélude, Adagio et Choral varié, Op. 4; Grigny:Org Music; Honegger:Fugue & Choral Org; Vierne:Pièces en style libre, Op. 31 [TT 1:13:29] PROO ▲ 7063 [DDD]

French Suites (6) for Harpsichord, BWV 812-817
K. Gilbert (hpd) † English Suites; Partitas Hpd HAM 6-▲ 2908078 (35.97)
A. D. Larrocha (pno)—BWV 817, No. 6 in E † Italian Con, BWV 971; G. F. Handel:Suites de Pièces (8) Hpd, HWV 426-33; J. Haydn:Andante with Vars Pno, H.XVII/6; W. A. Mozart:Rondo in D, K.485; Son 10 Pno, K.330; Son 11 Pno, K.331; Son 18 Pno, K.576; Son 8 Pno, K.310; D. Scarlatti:Sons Kbd PPHI (Great Pianists of the 20th Century) ▲ 456886 (22.97)
M. J. Pires (pno) *(rec 1995)* † Chopin:Nocturnes Pno; W. A. Mozart:Con 14 Pno, K.449; Son 11 Pno, K.331; Son 13 Pno, K.333; Son 16 Pno, K.545; Son 4 Pno, K.282; F. Schubert:Moments musicaux, D.780; R. Schumann:Arabeske Pno, Op. 18 PPHI (Great Pianists of the 20th century) ▲ 456928 (22.97)
P. Ross (pno)—BWV 817, No. 6 in E † English Suites; Partitas Hpd; Toccatas Hpd CSOC ▲ 4201

Fugue in g for Organ, BWV 578, "The little fugue" (ca 1707)
G. Weinberger (org) *(rec Johann Caspar Rommel Organ, Thüringen, Germany, June 1996)* ("Organ Works-Vol. 4") † Fugue on a theme by Corelli, BWV 579; Fugue on a theme by Legrenzi, BWV 574; Orgelbüchlein; Partite diverse sopra, BWV 767; Partite diverse sopra, BWV 770; Prelude Org, BWV 568; Prelude Org, BWV 569 [TT 1:12:19] CPO ▲ 999653 [DDD] (7.97)

Fugue in b on a Theme by Corelli for Organ, BWV 579
G. Weinberger (org) *(rec Nicolaus Seeber Organ,St. Johannes,Thüringen, Germany, June 1996)* ("Organ Works-Vol. 4") † Fugue on a theme by Legrenzi, BWV 574; Fugue Org, BWV 578; Orgelbüchlein; Partite diverse sopra, BWV 767; Partite diverse sopra, BWV 770; Prelude Org, BWV 568; Prelude Org, BWV 569 [TT 1:12:19] CPO ▲ 999653 [DDD] (7.97)

Fugue in c on a Theme by Legrenzi for Organ, BWV 574
G. Weinberger (org) *(rec Johann Caspar Rommel Organ,Thüringen, Germany, June 1996)* ("Organ Works-Vol. 4") † Fugue on a theme by Corelli, BWV 579; Fugue Org, BWV 578; Orgelbüchlein; Partite diverse sopra, BWV 767; Partite diverse sopra, BWV 770; Prelude Org, BWV 568; Prelude Org, BWV 569 [TT 1:12:19] CPO ▲ 999653 [DDD] (7.97)

Gelobet seist du, Jesu Christ (chorale) for Organ, BWV 722
G. Weinberger (org) *(rec Joachim Wagner Organ, St. Marien, Angermünde, Germany, Sept 1996)* ("Vol. 5") † Allein Gott in der Höh sei Ehr, BWV 715; Allein Gott in der Höh sei Ehr, BWV 716; Allein Gott in der Höh sei Ehr, BWV 717; Gelobet seist du, Jesu Christ, BWV 723; Gott durch deine Güte, BWV 724; In dulci jubilo, BWV 729; Nun freut euch, lieben Christen g'mein, BWV 734; Pastorale Org, BWV 590; Preludes & Fugues, BWV 531-552; Trio Org, BWV 583; Wie schön leuchtet der Morgenstern, BWV 739 [TT 1:15:23] CPO ▲ 999654 [DDD] (7.97)

Gelobet seist du, Jesu Christ (chorale) for Organ, BWV 723 (ca 1703-07)
G. Weinberger (org) *(rec Joachim Wagner Organ, St. Marien, Angermünde, Germany, Sept 1996)* ("Vol. 5") † Allein Gott in der Höh sei Ehr, BWV 715; Allein Gott in der Höh sei Ehr, BWV 716; Allein Gott in der Höh sei Ehr, BWV 717; Gelobet seist du, Jesu Christ, BWV 722; Gott durch deine Güte, BWV 724; In dulci jubilo, BWV 729; Nun freut euch, lieben Christen g'mein, BWV 734; Pastorale Org, BWV 590; Preludes & Fugues, BWV 531-552; Trio Org, BWV 583; Wie schön leuchtet der Morgenstern, BWV 739 [TT 1:15:23] CPO ▲ 999654 [DDD] (7.97)

Goldberg Variations for Harpsichord, BWV 988
MUVI ▲ 1130 (17.97)
S. Bartos (pno) † Chromatic Fant & Fugue, BWV 903 CSOC ▲ 4176
R. Hill (hpd) MUA ▲ 4850 (10.97)

Gott durch deine Güte for Organ, BWV 724 (ca 1708)
G. Weinberger (org) *(rec Joachim Wagner Organ, St. Marien, Angermünde, Germany, Sept 1996)* ("Vol. 5") † Allein Gott in der Höh sei Ehr, BWV 715; Allein Gott in der Höh sei Ehr, BWV 716; Allein Gott in der Höh sei Ehr, BWV 717; Gelobet seist du, Jesu Christ, BWV 722; Gelobet seist du, Jesu Christ, BWV 723; In dulci jubilo, BWV 729; Nun freut euch, lieben Christen g'mein, BWV 734; Pastorale Org, BWV 590; Preludes & Fugues, BWV 531-552; Trio Org, BWV 583; Wie schön leuchtet der Morgenstern, BWV 739 [TT 1:15:23] CPO ▲ 999654 [DDD] (7.97)

Herr Jesu Christ, du höchstes (chorale) for Organ, BWV 334
D. Reed (sax), J. Oviedo (sax), J. Butler (a sax/s sax), D. Goble (a sax/s sax), W. Graves (a sax/s sax), T. Poole (a sax), A. G. Rivard (a sax), T. Oxford (bar sax), K. Russell (a sax/bar sax), T. Yukumoto (b sax), H. Pittel (cnd) [arr Rex] ("Tex Sax") † Brandenburg Con 1, BWV 1046; G. F. Handel:Messiah (choruses); Mussorgsky:Pictures at an Exhibition [TT 1:11:15] MRES ▲ 2280

In dulci jubilo (chorale) for Organ, BWV 729 (ca 1708-17)
G. Weinberger (org) *(rec Joachim Wagner Organ, St. Marien, Angermünde, Germany, Sept 1996)* ("Vol. 5") † Allein Gott in der Höh sei Ehr, BWV 715; Allein Gott in der Höh sei Ehr, BWV 716; Allein Gott in der Höh sei Ehr, BWV 717; Gelobet seist du, Jesu Christ, BWV 722; Gelobet seist du, Jesu Christ, BWV 723; Gott durch deine Güte, BWV 724; Nun freut euch, lieben Christen g'mein, BWV 734; Pastorale Org, BWV 590; Preludes & Fugues, BWV 531-552; Trio Org, BWV 583; Wie schön leuchtet der Morgenstern, BWV 739 [TT 1:15:23] CPO ▲ 999654 [DDD] (7.97)

Inventions for Harpsichord
M. Suzuki (hpd) *(rec Kobe Shoin Women's University, Japan, July 1998)* [TT 56:43] BIS ▲ 1009 [DDD] (17.97)

Italian Concerto in F for Harpsichord, BWV 971
A. D. Larrocha (pno) † French Suites; G. F. Handel:Suites de Pièces (8) Hpd, HWV 426-33; J. Haydn:Andante with Vars Pno, H.XVII/6; W. A. Mozart:Rondo in D, K.485; Son 10 Pno, K.330; Son 11 Pno, K.331; Son 18 Pno, K.576; Son 8 Pno, K.310; D. Scarlatti:Sons Kbd PPHI (Great Pianists of the 20th Century) ▲ 456886 (22.97)
D. Moroney (hpd) † Duets Hpd; Partita Hpd, BWV 831 HAM ▲ 2951278 (12.97)

Magnificat in D for solo Voices, Orchestra & Chorus [rev of Magnificat in E♭ without Christmas texts], BWV 243 (ca 1728-31)
Collegium Vocale, P. Herreweghe (cnd), La Chapelle Royale, B. Schlick (sop), A. Mellon (sop), G. Lesne (alt), H. Crook (ten), P. Kooy (bass) † Cant 80 HAM ▲ 2951326 (12.97)

BACH, JOHANN SEBASTIAN (cont.)

Mass in b for Orchestra & Chorus, BWV 232 (ca 1747-49)
P. Herreweghe (cnd), Collegium Vocale Orch, P. Herreweghe (cnd), Collegium Vocale, J. Zomer (sop), V. Gens (sop), A. Scholl (alt), C. Prégardien (ten), P. Kooy (bass), H. Müller-Brachman (bass) HAM ▲ 2951614 (23.97)
R. Shaw (cnd), Robert Shaw Orch, Robert Shaw Chorale, A. Addison (sop), S. Endich (sop), F. Kopleff (cta), M. Walker (ten), A. Berberian (bass) RCAV 2-▲ 63529 (23.97)

A Musical Offering for Chamber Ensemble, BWV 1079 (1747)
J. Holloway (vn), J. See (fl), J. T. Linden (cel), M. Cook (hpd) † Art of the Fugue, BWV 1080; Wohltemperirte Clavier HAM 7-▲ 2908084 (47.97)

Nun freut euch, lieben Christen g'mein for Organ, BWV 734 (ca 1708-17)
G. Weinberger (org) *(rec Joachim Wagner Organ, St. Marien, Angermünde, Germany, Sept 1996)* ("Vol. 5") † Allein Gott in der Höh sei Ehr, BWV 715; Allein Gott in der Höh sei Ehr, BWV 716; Allein Gott in der Höh sei Ehr, BWV 717; Gelobet seist du, Jesu Christ, BWV 722; Gelobet seist du, Jesu Christ, BWV 723; Gott durch deine Güte, BWV 724; In dulci jubilo, BWV 729; Pastorale Org, BWV 590; Preludes & Fugues, BWV 531-552; Trio Org, BWV 583; Wie schön leuchtet der Morgenstern, BWV 739 [TT 1:15:23] CPO ▲ 999654 [DDD] (7.97)

Das Orgelbüchlein for Organ, BWV 599-644 (ca 1713-17)
P. Hawkins (org)—BWV 599, Nun komm der Heiden Heiland; BWV 604, Gelobet seist du, Jesu Christ; BWV 611, Christum wir sollen loben schon; BWV 614, Das alte Jahr vergangen ist; BWV 619, Christe, du Lamm Gottes; BWV 623, Wir danken dir, Herr Jesu Christ; BWV 625, Christ lag in Todesbanden; BWV 626, Jesus Christus, unser Heiland; BWV 633, Liebster Jesu, wir sind hier; BWV 634, Liebster Jesu, wir sind hier; BWV 636, Vater unser im Himmelreich; BWV 641, Wenn wir in höchsten Nöten sein *(rec Greg Harrold Opus 14, 1995, Brentwood, CA)* † Canzona; Fant & Fugue, BWV 542; Partite diverse sopra, BWV 767; Preludes & Fugues, BWV 531-552 [TT 1:04:40] ARK ▲ 6170 [DDD] (16.97)
G. Weinberger (org)—BWV 637, Durch Adams Fall ist ganz verderbt; BWV 638, Es ist das Heil uns kommen her; BWV 639, Ich ruf zu dir, Herr Jesu Christ; BWV 640, In dich hab ich gehoffet, Herr; BWV 641, Wenn wir in höchsten Nöten sein; BWV 642, Wer nur den lieben Gott lasst walten; BWV 643, Alle Menschen müssen sterben; BWV 644, Ach wie nichtig, ach wie flüchtig; BWV 632, Herr Jesu Christ, dich zu uns wend; BWV 633, Liebster Jesu, wir sind hier; BWV 634, Liebster Jesu, wir sind hier; BWV 635, Dies sind die heilgen zehn Gebot; BWV 636, Vater unser im Himmelreich *(rec Johann Caspar Rommel Organ, Thüringen, Germany, June 1996)* ("Organ Works-Vol. 4") † Fugue on a theme by Corelli, BWV 579; Fugue on a theme by Legrenzi, BWV 574; Fugue Org, BWV 578; Partite diverse sopra, BWV 767; Partite diverse sopra, BWV 770; Prelude Org, BWV 568; Prelude Org, BWV 569 [TT 1:12:19] CPO ▲ 999653 [DDD] (7.97)

Partitas (6) for Harpsichord, BWV 825-830 (1726)
K. Gilbert (hpd) † English Suites; French Suites HAM 6-▲ 2908078 (35.97)
W. Kapell (pno)—BWV 828, No. 4 in D *(rec 1952/53)* † I. Albéniz:Iberia Suite; Chopin:Son Pno in b, Op. 58; Liszt:Hungarian Rhaps, S.244; Mephisto Waltz 1 Pno, S.514; Sonetti (3) del Petrarca, S.158; S. Prokofiev:Con 3 Pno, Op. 26; S. Rachmaninoff:Con 2 Pno, Op. 18; Rhap on a Theme of Paganini, Op. 43 PPHI (Great Pianists of the 20th Century) ▲ 456853 (22.97)
N. Krieger (pno)—BWV 826, No. 2 in c † Beethoven:Son 17 Pno, Op. 31/2; Chopin:Études Pno; Nocturnes Pno; W. A. Mozart:Son 10 Pno, K.330 ARII ▲ 491 (17.97)
P. Ross (pno)—BWV 827, No. 3 in a † English Suites; French Suites; Toccatas Hpd CSOC ▲ 4201
Thomas Gabriel Trio—BWV 826, No. 2 in c [arr Gabriel] *(rec Fürstliche Reitbahn Arolsen, Germany, Aug 7-8, 1998)* ("Bach-Jazz") † Con 1 Hpd, BWV 1052; Schübler Chorale Preludes [TT 1:02:43] MDG ▲ 6100916 [DDD] (17.97)

Partita in b for Harpsichord, BWV 831, "Ouvertüre nach französischer Art"
D. Moroney (hpd) † Duets Hpd; Italian Con, BWV 971 HAM ▲ 2951278 (12.97)

Partite diverse sopra Ach, was soll ich Sünder machen for Organ, BWV 770
G. Weinberger (org) *(rec Johann Caspar Rommel Organ, Thüringen, Germany, June 1996)* ("Organ Works-Vol. 4") † Fugue on a theme by Corelli, BWV 579; Fugue on a theme by Legrenzi, BWV 574; Fugue Org, BWV 578; Orgelbüchlein; Partite diverse sopra, BWV 767; Prelude Org, BWV 568; Prelude Org, BWV 569 [TT 1:12:19] CPO ▲ 999653 [DDD] (7.97)

Partite diverse sopra O Gott, du frommer Gott for Organ, BWV 767
P. Hawkins (org) *(rec Greg Harrold Opus 14, 1995, Brentwood, CA)* † Canzona; Fant & Fugue, BWV 542; Orgelbüchlein; Preludes & Fugues, BWV 531-552 [TT 1:04:40] ARK ▲ 6170 [DDD] (16.97)
G. Weinberger (org) *(rec Nicolaus Seeber Organ,St. Johannes,Thüringen, Germany, June 1996)* ("Organ Works-Vol. 4") † Fugue on a theme by Corelli, BWV 579; Fugue on a theme by Legrenzi, BWV 574; Fugue Org, BWV 578; Orgelbüchlein; Partite diverse sopra, BWV 770; Prelude Org, BWV 568; Prelude Org, BWV 569 [TT 1:12:19] CPO ▲ 999653 [DDD] (7.97)

Passacaglia & Fugue in c for Organ, BWV 582
L. Rogg (org) † Chorales Org; Cons Org; Fant & Fugue, BWV 542; Schübler Chorale Preludes; Toccata & Fugue Org, BWV 565; Toccata, Adagio & Fugue Org, BWV 564 [TT 1:09:10] CSER ▲ 73568 [ADD] (6.97)

Pastorale in F for Organ, BWV 590 (ca 1710)
G. Weinberger (org) *(rec Joachim Wagner Organ, St. Marien, Angermünde, Germany, Sept 1996)* ("Vol. 5") † Allein Gott in der Höh sei Ehr, BWV 715; Allein Gott in der Höh sei Ehr, BWV 716; Allein Gott in der Höh sei Ehr, BWV 717; Gelobet seist du, Jesu Christ, BWV 722; Gelobet seist du, Jesu Christ, BWV 723; Gott durch deine Güte, BWV 724; In dulci jubilo, BWV 729; Nun freut euch, lieben Christen g'mein, BWV 734; Preludes & Fugues, BWV 531-552; Trio Org, BWV 583; Wie schön leuchtet der Morgenstern, BWV 739 [TT 1:15:23] CPO ▲ 999654 [DDD] (7.97)

Preludes & Fugues (22) for Organ, BWV 531-552
P. Hawkins (org)—BWV 546, in c *(rec Greg Harrold Opus 14, 1995, Brentwood, CA)* † Canzona; Fant & Fugue, BWV 542; Orgelbüchlein; Partite diverse sopra, BWV 767 [TT 1:04:40] ARK ▲ 6170 [DDD] (16.97)
G. Weinberger (org)—BWV 535, in g; BWV 550, in G; BWV 543, in a *(rec Joachim Wagner Organ, St. Marien, Angermünde, Germany, Sept 1996)* ("Vol. 5") † Allein Gott in der Höh sei Ehr, BWV 715; Allein Gott in der Höh sei Ehr, BWV 716; Allein Gott in der Höh sei Ehr, BWV 717; Gelobet seist du, Jesu Christ, BWV 722; Gelobet seist du, Jesu Christ, BWV 723; Gott durch deine Güte, BWV 724; In dulci jubilo, BWV 729; Nun freut euch, lieben Christen g'mein, BWV 734; Pastorale Org, BWV 590; Trio Org, BWV 583; Wie schön leuchtet der Morgenstern, BWV 739 [TT 1:15:23] CPO ▲ 999654 [DDD] (7.97)

Prelude in G for Organ, BWV 568
G. Weinberger (org) *(rec Nicolaus Seeber Organ,St. Johannes,Thüringen, Germany, June 1996)* ("Organ Works-Vol. 4") † Fugue on a theme by Corelli, BWV 579; Fugue on a theme by Legrenzi, BWV 574; Fugue Org, BWV 578; Orgelbüchlein; Partite diverse sopra, BWV 767; Partite diverse sopra, BWV 770; Prelude Org, BWV 569 [TT 1:12:19] CPO ▲ 999653 [DDD] (7.97)

Prelude in a for Organ, BWV 569 (ca 1709)
G. Weinberger (org) *(rec Johann Caspar Rommel Organ, Thüringen, Germany, June 1996)* ("Organ Works-Vol. 4") † Fugue on a theme by Corelli, BWV 579; Fugue on a theme by Legrenzi, BWV 574; Fugue Org, BWV 578; Orgelbüchlein; Partite diverse sopra, BWV 767; Partite diverse sopra, BWV 770; Prelude Org, BWV 568 [TT 1:12:19] CPO ▲ 999653 [DDD] (7.97)

St. John Passion for SATB solo Voices, Orchestra & Chorus, BWV 245 (1725)
P. Herreweghe (cnd), Collegium Vocale, P. Herreweghe (cnd), La Chapelle Royale, B. Schlick (sop), C. Patriasz (cta), H. Crook (ten), W. Kendall (ten), P. Kooy (bass), P. Lika (bass) HAM 2-▲ 2951264 (23.97)

St. Matthew Passion for solo Voices, Orchestra & Chorus, BWV 244 (1727)
P. Herreweghe (cnd), Ghent Collegium Vocale Orch, Ghent Collegium Vocale, S. Rubens (sop), A. Scholl (ct), I. Bostridge (ten), D. Henschel (bar), F. Selig (bass), W. Güra (sgr) HAM 3-▲ 951676 (52.97)

Schübler Chorale Preludes (6) for Organ, BWV 645-650 (ca 1747)
L. Rogg (org)—BWV 645, No. 1 "Wachet auf, ruft uns Stimme" † Chorales Org; Cons Org; Fant & Fugue, BWV 542; Passacaglia & Fugue Org, BWV 582; Toccata & Fugue Org, BWV 565; Toccata, Adagio & Fugue Org, BWV 564 [TT 1:09:10] CSER ▲ 73568 [ADD] (6.97)
Thomas Gabriel Trio—BWV 645, No. 1 "Wachet auf, ruft uns Stimme" [arr Gabriel] *(rec Fürstliche Reitbahn Arolsen, Germany, Aug 7-8, 1998)* ("Bach-Jazz") † Con 1 Hpd, BWV 1052; Partitas Hpd [TT 1:02:43] MDG ▲ 6100916 [DDD] (17.97)

Sonatas (3) & Partitas (3) for solo Violin, BWV 1001-1006 (1720)
Eroica Trio—BWV 1004, Partita No. 2 in d *(rec St. Stephens Church, CA, July 1999)* † Albinoni:Adagio; Buxtehude:Sons Vns, Op. 2; Loeillet:Sons (12), Op. 2; A. Lotti:Music of Lotti; Vivaldi:Trio Son Vn Vc, RV.83 [TT 56:14] EMIC ▲ 56873 [DDD] (16.97)
I. Guetta (elec gtr), Israel String Quartet—BWV 1005, Son No. 3 in C [arr Guetta-allegro assai only] † Brandenburg Con 5, BWV 1050; Con Vns; Con 1 Vn; Easter Oratorio, BWV 249 [TT 58:24] JRB ▲ 2003 [DDD] (16.97)
J. Martzy (vn) † B. Bartók:Romanian Folk Dances Vn & Pno; Beethoven:Son 8 Vn; G. F. Handel:Son Vn; I. Stravinsky:Duo Concertant; Szymanowski:Notturno e Tarantella, Op. 28 DHR ▲ 7753 (16.97)
F. Platino (gtr)—BWV 1004, Partita No. 2 in d [arr Platino-Chaccone only] *(rec St. John Chrysostom Church, Newmarket, Ontario, Canada, Apr 23-29, 1998)* † A. Barrios:Catedral; Mertz:Elégie; M. Ponce:Sonatina meridional Gtr; J. Rodrigo:Un tiempo fue Itálica famosa; D. Scarlatti:Sons Kbd [TT 57:15] NXIN (Laureate Series) ▲ 8554344 [DDD] (5.97)

NEW RELEASES 3

BACH, JOHANN SEBASTIAN (cont.)

Sonatas (3) & Partitas (3) for solo Violin, BWV 1001-1006 (1720) (cont.)
R. Podger (vn)—BWV 1005, Son No. 3 in C; BWV 1006, Partita No. 3 in E; BWV 1003, Son No. 2 in a CCL ▲ 14498 (18.97)

Sonatas (6) for Flute & Continuo, BWV 1030-1035 [BWV 1031 & 1033 doubtful]
J. Teichmanis (vc), U. Wedemeier (thb), K. Kaiser (fl), S. Kaiser (hpd), B. Lohr (hpd/org)—BWV 1032, No. 3 in A; BWV 1034, No. 5 in e *(rec Oranienburg Nordkirchen, Germany, Feb 1999)* ("Complete Flute Sonatas Vol. 1") † Son Fl & Pno, BWV 1079; Son Fl Vn [TT 1:03:41] MDG ▲ 3090931 [DDD] (17.97)

Sonata for Flute & Piano, BWV 1079, BWV 1079
K. Kaiser (fl), S. Kaiser (hpd) *(rec Oranienburg Nordkirchen, Germany, Feb 1999)* ("Complete Flute Sonatas Vol. 1") † Son Fl Vn; Sons Fl [TT 1:03:41] MDG ▲ 3090931 [DDD] (17.97)

Sonata in G for Flute, Violin & Continuo [constructed on bass of BWV 1021; probably by one of Bach's sons or pupils], BWV 1038
A. Röhrig (vn), J. Teichmanis (vc), K. Kaiser (fl), B. Lohr (hpd) *(rec Oranienburg Nordkirchen, Germany, Feb 1999)* ("Complete Flute Sonatas Vol. 1") † Son Fl & Pno, BWV 1079; Sons Fl [TT 1:03:41] MDG ▲ 3090931 [DDD] (17.97)

Sonatas (3) in G, D & g for Viol & Harpsichord, BWV 1027-1029 (ca 1720)
P. Pandolfo (va da gamba), R. Alessandrini (hpd) HAM ▲ 2955218 (12.97)

Sonatas (6) for Violin & Harpsichord, BWV 1014-1019 (1717-23)
Y. Menuhin (vn), W. Landowska (hpd)—BWV 1016, No. 3 in E *(rec 1932-44)* ("The Bach & Mozart Recordings") † W. A. Mozart:Con 3 Vn, K.216; Con 7 Vn, K.271a ENT ▲ 99400 (17.97)

Suites (6) for solo Cello, BWV 1007-1012 (ca 1720)
J. T. Linden (cel) HAM 2-▲ 2957216 (23.97)
B. Westphal (va) [arr viola] BRID ▲ 9094 (17.97)

Suites (4) for Orchestra [including No. 2 in b for Flute & Strings, BWV 1067], BWV 1066-1069
Berlin Akademie für Alte Musik † Brandenburg Cons HAM 4-▲ 2908074 (23.97)

Suite No. 3 in D for Orchestra, BWV 1068 (ca 1729-31)
W. Furtwängler (cnd), Berlin PO *(rec Berlin, Germany, Oct 1948)* † P. Hindemith:Symphonic Metamorphosis on Themes of Carl Maria vo; H. Pfitzner:Sym in C, Op. 46 [TT 58:15] URAN ▲ 125 (m) [ADD] (15.97)

Toccata, Adagio & Fugue in C for Organ, BWV 564 (1708-17)
L. Rogg (org) † Chorales Org; Cons Org; Fant & Fugue, BWV 542; Passacaglia & Fugue Org, BWV 582; Schübler Chorale Preludes; Toccata & Fugue Org, BWV 565 [TT 1:09:10] CSER ▲ 73568 [ADD] (6.97)

Toccata & Fugue in d for Organ, BWV 565 (before 1708)
H. Begian (cnd), Univ of Illinois Symphonic Band [arr Leidzen] ("The Begian Years-Vol. 6") † P. Hindemith:Symphonic Metamorphosis on Themes of Carl Maria vo; R. Strauss:Don Juan, Op. 20; Rosenkavalier, Op. 59; Tod und Verklärung, Op. 24; R. Wagner:Götterdämmerung (sels) [TT 1:17:22] MRES ▲ 1647
L. Rogg (org) † Chorales Org; Cons Org; Fant & Fugue, BWV 542; Passacaglia & Fugue Org, BWV 582; Schübler Chorale Preludes; Toccata, Adagio & Fugue Org, BWV 564 [TT 1:09:10] CSER ▲ 73568 [ADD] (6.97)

Toccatas (7) for Harpsichord, BWV 910-916 (ca 1738)
P. Ross (pno)—BWV 916, No. 7 in G † English Suites; French Suites; Partitas Hpd CSOC ▲ 4201

Trio in d for Organ, BWV 583
G. Weinberger (org) *(rec Joachim Wagner Organ, St. Marien, Angermünde, Germany, Sept 1996)* ("Vol. 5") † Allein Gott in der Höh sei Ehr, BWV 715; Allein Gott in der Höh sei Ehr, BWV 716; Allein Gott in der Höh sei Ehr, BWV 717; Gelobet seist du, Jesu Christ, BWV 722; Gelobet seist du, Jesu Christ, BWV 723; Gott durch deine Güte, BWV 724; In dulci jubilo, BWV 729; Nun freut euch, lieben Christen g'mein, BWV 734; Pastorale Org, BWV 590; Preludes & Fugues, BWV 531-552; Wie schön leuchtet der Morgenstern, BWV 739 [TT 1:15:23] CPO ▲ 999654 [DDD] (7.97)

Trio Sonatas (6) for Organ, BWV 525-530 (ca 1727)
J. Butt (org) *(rec Greg Harrold Organ, Berkeley, CA)* HAM ▲ 2957055 (12.97)

Verschiedene Canones (14) for Harpsichord, [based on Goldberg Variations], BWV 1087 (1742-46)
M. Beaver (vn), D. Harding (va), B. Epperson (vc) † Goldberg Vars, BWV 988 MUVI ▲ 1130 (17.97)

Wie schön leuchtet der Morgenstern, BWV 739
G. Weinberger (org) *(rec Joachim Wagner Organ, St. Marien, Angermünde, Germany, Sept 1996)* ("Vol. 5") † Allein Gott in der Höh sei Ehr, BWV 715; Allein Gott in der Höh sei Ehr, BWV 716; Allein Gott in der Höh sei Ehr, BWV 717; Gelobet seist du, Jesu Christ, BWV 722; Gelobet seist du, Jesu Christ, BWV 723; Gott durch deine Güte, BWV 724; In dulci jubilo, BWV 729; Nun freut euch, lieben Christen g'mein, BWV 734; Pastorale Org, BWV 590; Preludes & Fugues, BWV 531-552; Trio Org, BWV 583 [TT 1:15:23] CPO ▲ 999654 [DDD] (7.97)

Das wohltemperirte Clavier [The Well-tempered Clavier] [2 books], BWV 846-893 (1722-42)
D. Moroney (hpd) † Art of the Fugue, BWV 1080; Musical Offering, BWV 1079 HAM 7-▲ 2908084 (47.97)

BAINBRIDGE, SIMON (1952-

Ad Ora Incerta (songs) for Voice, Bassoon & Orchestra [text Levi]
S. Bickley (mez), K. Walker (bn), BBC SO *(rec London, England, Dec 15-16, 1997)* † Primo Levi Settings [TT 53:54] NMCC ▲ 59 [DDD] (17.97)

Primo Levi Settings (4) for Mezzo-soprano, Clarinet, Viola & Piano
S. Bickley (mez), Nash Ensemble *(rec London, England, Dec 15-16, 1997)* † Ad Ora Incerta [TT 53:54] NMCC ▲ 59 [DDD] (17.97)

BAINTON, EDGAR (1880-1956)

Symphony No. 2 (1940)
V. Handley (cnd), BBC PO † H. Clifford:Sym 1940; J. Gough:Serenade CHN ▲ 9757 (16.97)

BAKER, DAVID (1931-

Through This Vale of Tears (song cycle) for Tenor, String Quartet & Piano (1986)
Members of Lawrence Conservatory Contemporary Music Ensemble *(rec live, Lawrence Memorial Chapel, Appleton, WI, Jan 15, 1977)* ("A La Par") † T. León:A la Par; W. Logan:; Perkinson:Son 2; Toccata [TT 1:11:49] CRI ▲ 823 [DDD] (16.97)

BALDWIN, DAVID (20th cent)

Concerto for Al's Breakfast for Euphonium & Ensemble
M. A. Craig (eup), J. Staples (pno), J. Stamp (mar), Univ of Pennsylvania Faculty Brass Quintet *(rec U of Pennsylvania Fisher Auditorium, PA, Jan 12-15, 1995)* ("Euphonium...Out On a Limb") † B. Cummings:Spring Suite; J. Curnow:Sym Vars; G. Fritze:Euphonistic Dance; T. R. George:Son Bar Hn, CN 139; S. Romberg:Student Prince (sels) [TT 1:07:52] MRES ▲ 1794

BARATI, GEORGE (1913-1996)

Chant of Darkness for Violin & Orchestra (1993)
J. Herajnová (vn), V. Válek (cnd), Czech RSO † J. D. Goodman:Con Vn; D. L. Post:Sym 1 MASM ▲ 2068 [DDD] (16.97)

BARBER, LESLEY (dates unknown)

Mansfield Park (film music) for Orchestra
various artists RCAV ▲ 63592 (17.97)

BARBER, SAMUEL (1910-1981)

Adagio for Strings [arr from *Quartet for Strings, Op. 11*] (1936)
L. Bernstein (cnd), Los Angeles PO † L. Bernstein:On the Town (sels); On the Waterfront (sym suite); Prelude, Fugue & Riffs; West Side Story (sym dances); A. Copland:Appalachian Spring (suite); G. Gershwin:Rhap in Blue; C. Ives:Unanswered Question DEUT 2-▲ 463465 (17.97)
V. Golschmann (cnd), Symphony of the Air † Essay 2, Op. 17; Hand of Bridge, Op. 35; Music for a Scene from Shelley, Op. 7; Serenade Strs, Op. 1; Stopwatch & an Ordnance Map, Op. 15 VC ▲ 123 (13.97)

Commando March for Band (1943)
E. Green (cnd), Univ of Houston Wind Ensemble *(rec St. Pius V Church, Pasadena, TX, Apr. 21-23, 1995)* † G. Mahler:Sym 3; M. Praetorius:Terpsichore; G. Puccini:Bohème (sels); Turandot (sels); Teike:Conqueror [TT 1:01:39] MRES (Vol. 1) ▲ 1875

Essay No. 2 for Orchestra, Op. 17 (1942)
V. Golschmann (cnd), Symphony of the Air † Adagio Strs; Hand of Bridge, Op. 35; Music for a Scene from Shelley, Op. 7; Serenade Strs, Op. 1; Stopwatch & an Ordnance Map, Op. 15 VC ▲ 123 (13.97)

A Hand of Bridge (opera in 1 act) [lib Spoleto], Op. 35 (1958)
V. Golschmann (cnd), Symphony of the Air † Adagio Strs; Essay 2, Op. 17; Music for a Scene from Shelley, Op. 7; Serenade Strs, Op. 1; Stopwatch & an Ordnance Map, Op. 15 VC ▲ 123 (13.97)

Music for a Scene from Shelley for Orchestra, Op. 7 (1933)
V. Golschmann (cnd), Symphony of the Air † Adagio Strs; Essay 2, Op. 17; Hand of Bridge, Op. 35; Serenade Strs, Op. 1; Stopwatch & an Ordnance Map, Op. 15 VC ▲ 123 (13.97)

Quartet for Strings, Op. 11 (1936)
various artists ("The Philadelphia Connection") † Garfield:Qt Bn; Hoy:Lament; Krantz:Son Vn DTT ▲ 9803 (17.97)

The School for Scandal (overture) for Orchestra, Op. 5 (1931-33)
H. Begian (cnd), Univ of Illinois Symphonic Band [arr Hudson] ("The Begian Years-Vol. 8") † R. R. Bennett:Suite of Old American Dances; Sym Songs; Creston:Anatolia; H. O. Reed:Fiesta Mexicana [TT 1:16:06] MRES ▲ 1649

BARBER, SAMUEL (cont.)

Serenade for String Quartet (or String Orchestra), Op. 1 (1929)
V. Golschmann (cnd), Symphony of the Air † Adagio Strs; Essay 2, Op. 17; Hand of Bridge, Op. 35; Music for a Scene from Shelley, Op. 7; Stopwatch & an Ordnance Map, Op. 15 VC ▲ 123 (13.97)

Sonata for Piano, Op. 26 (1949)
W. Doppmann (pno) † Finney:Son 4 Pno; Griffes:Son Pno; MacDowell:Son 2 Pno, Op. 50 EQLB ▲ 27 (16.97)

A Stopwatch & an Ordnance Map for Orchestra & Chorus, Op. 15 (1940)
V. Golschmann (cnd), Symphony of the Air † Adagio Strs; Essay 2, Op. 17; Hand of Bridge, Op. 35; Music for a Scene from Shelley, Op. 7; Serenade Strs, Op. 1 VC ▲ 123 (13.97)

BARBIREAU, JACQUES (ca 1420-1491)

Choral Music
E. Wickham (cnd), Clerk's Group—Missa Virgo Parens Christi; Kyrie Paschale *(rec Austria)* † Obrecht:Choral Music; Pipelare:Choral Music; J. Pullois:Choral Music ASV ▲ 188 [DDD] (16.97)

BARRIOS, (PIO) AGUSTÍN (1885-1944)

La Catedral for Guitar
F. Platino (gtr) *(rec St. John Chrysostom Church, Newmarket, Ontario, Canada, Apr 23-29, 1998)* † J. S. Bach:Sons & Partitas Vn; Mertz:Elégie; M. Ponce:Sonatina meridional Gtr; J. Rodrigo:Un tiempo fue Itálica famosa; D. Scarlatti:Sons Kbd [TT 57:15] NXIN (Laureate Series) ▲ 8554344 [DDD] (5.97)

BARTÓK, BÉLA (1881-1945)

Allegro barbaro for Piano, Sz.49 (1911)
J. Kalichstein (pno) † Rondos on Folk Tunes, Sz.84; Son Pno, Sz.80; S. Prokofiev:Son 9 Pno, Op. 103 VC ▲ 121 (13.97)

Concerto No. 1 for Violin & Orchestra, Sz.36 (1907-08)
G. Pauk (vn), A. Wit (cnd), National Polish Radio SO *(rec Concert Hall National Polish Radio Symphony, Poland, Dec 13-15, 1997)* † Con 2 Vn, Sz.112 [TT 59:59] NXIN ▲ 8554321 [DDD] (5.97)

Concerto No. 2 for Violin & Orchestra, Sz.112 (1937-38)
Y. Menuhin (vn), E. Ansermet (cnd), Swiss Romande Orch [incl Feb 2, 1978 interview by Maroth] *(rec Atheneum Hall, Bucharest, Romania, Aug 16, 1947)* ("In Memoriam: Rare Broadcast Performances") † J. S. Bach:Con 2 Vns, BWV.1043; Beethoven:Con Vn; Lalo:Sym espagnole, Op. 21 [TT 1:59:11] MUA 2-▲ 1053 (31.97)
G. Pauk (vn), A. Wit (cnd), National Polish Radio SO *(rec Concert Hall National Polish Radio Symphony, Poland, Dec 13-15, 1997)* † Con 1 Vn, Sz.36 [TT 59:59] NXIN ▲ 8554321 [DDD] (5.97)

Hungarian Peasant Songs (15) for Piano, Sz.71 (1914-18; orchd 1933)
W. Corbett-Jones (pno) *(rec Knuth Hall, San Francisco State Univ, CA, Sept 6-7, 1997)* † Busoni:Fant nach J. S. Bach; R. Nixon:Music; Preludes; M. Ravel:Sonatine Pno; F. Schubert:Son Pno, D.959 [TT 1:17:43] CMB ▲ 1119 [DDD] (16.97)
G. Tozer (pno) † Little Pieces, Sz.82; Out of Doors, Sz.81; Romanian Christmas Carols, Sz.57; Romanian Folk Dances Pno, Sz.56; Son Pno, Sz.80 CHN ▲ 9761 (16.97)

Little Pieces (9) for Piano, Sz.82 (1926)
G. Tozer (pno) † Hungarian Peasant Songs, Sz.71; Out of Doors, Sz.81; Romanian Christmas Carols, Sz.57; Romanian Folk Dances Pno, Sz.56; Son Pno, Sz.80 CHN ▲ 9761 (16.97)

Out of Doors [Szabadban] (5 pieces) for Piano, Sz.81 (1926)
G. Tozer (pno) † Hungarian Peasant Songs, Sz.71; Little Pieces, Sz.82; Romanian Christmas Carols, Sz.57; Romanian Folk Dances Pno, Sz.56; Son Pno, Sz.80 CHN ▲ 9761 (16.97)

Romanian Christmas Carols [Román kolinda-dallmok] (20) for Piano, Sz.57 (1915)
G. Tozer (pno) † Hungarian Peasant Songs, Sz.71; Little Pieces, Sz.82; Out of Doors, Sz.81; Romanian Folk Dances Pno, Sz.56; Son Pno, Sz.80 CHN ▲ 9761 (16.97)

Romanian Folk Dances [Román népi táncok] for Piano, Sz.56 (1915; orchd 1917)
J. Bradetich (db), J. R. Bradetich (pno) † E. Bloch:Méditation hébraïque; Boccherini:Sons (34) Vc Bc; G. Fauré:Elégie, Op. 24; V. Monti:Csárdás KLAV ▲ 11100 [DDD] (18.97)
P. Rouet (org) *(rec Org of Moucherel Formentelli Notre-Dame de Mouzon, France, July 1998)* † Anonymous:Estampie; Intabulatura Nova; Attaingnant:Dances; G. Picchi:Ballo alla polacha; Ballo hongaro; Ballo todescha; Pass'e Mezzo in d; B. Storace:Balleto; Ciaccona in C; Folia; Passacaglia in a; Spagnoletta [TT 1:09:35] PAVA ▲ 7415 [DDD] (10.97)
G. Tozer (pno) † Hungarian Peasant Songs, Sz.71; Little Pieces, Sz.82; Out of Doors, Sz.81; Romanian Christmas Carols, Sz.57; Son Pno, Sz.80 CHN ▲ 9761 (16.97)

Romanian Folk Dances for Violin & Piano [arr Székely from Sz.56]
J. Martzy (vn), L. Pommers (pno) † J. S. Bach:Sons & Partitas Vn; Beethoven:Son 8 Vn; G. F. Handel:Son Vn; I. Stravinsky:Duo Concertant; Szymanowski:Notturno e Tarantella, Op. 28 DHR ▲ 7753 (16.97)

Rondos on Folk Tunes (3) [Három rondo népi dallamokkal] for Piano, Sz.84 (1916;1927)
J. Kalichstein (pno) † Allegro barbaro, Sz.49; Son Pno, Sz.80; S. Prokofiev:Son 9 Pno, Op. 103 VC ▲ 121 (13.97)

Sonata for Piano, Sz.80 (1926)
J. Kalichstein (pno) † Allegro barbaro, Sz.49; Rondos on Folk Tunes, Sz.84; S. Prokofiev:Son 9 Pno, Op. 103 VC ▲ 121 (13.97)
G. Tozer (pno) † Hungarian Peasant Songs, Sz.71; Little Pieces, Sz.82; Out of Doors, Sz.81; Romanian Christmas Carols, Sz.57; Romanian Folk Dances Pno, Sz.56 CHN ▲ 9761 (16.97)

Sonata No. 1 for Violin & Piano, Sz.75 (1921)
S. Gawriloff (vn), G. Mishory (pno) † Son 2 Vn & Pno, Sz.76 TUD ▲ 7068 (17.97)
S. Kim (vn), J. Denk (pno) † F. Schubert:Rondo Vn, D.895; R. Strauss:Son Vn DI ▲ 920596 (5.97)

Sonata No. 2 for Violin & Piano, Sz.76 (1922)
S. Gawriloff (vn), G. Mishory (pno) † Son 1 Vn & Pno, Sz.75 TUD ▲ 7068 (17.97)

BAX, ARNOLD (1883-1953)

The Poisoned Fountain for 2 Pianos (1928)
Bradshaw & Buono Piano Duo † Casella:Pupazzetti, Op. 27; Debussy:Danses sacrée et profane; Petite suite Pno; Prélude à l'après-midi d'un faune; M. Ravel:Frontispiece; Ma mère l'oye Suite Pno CSOC ▲ 4171

BEACH, AMY MARCY CHENEY (MRS. H.H.A.) (1867-1944)

Quintet for Piano & String Quartet in f#, Op. 67 (1907)
Ambache Chamber Ensemble † Theme & Vars, Op. 80; Trio Pno, Op. 150 CHN ▲ 9752 (16.97)

Theme & Variations for Flute & String Quartet, Op. 80 (1920)
Ambache Chamber Ensemble † Qnt Pno, Op. 67; Trio Pno, Op. 150 CHN ▲ 9752 (16.97)

Trio in a for Piano, Violin & Cello, Op. 150 (1939)
Ambache Chamber Ensemble † Qnt Pno, Op. 67; Theme & Vars, Op. 80 CHN ▲ 9752 (16.97)

BEAMISH, SALLY (1956-

Concerto for Cello & Orchestra, "River" (1997)
R. Cohen (vc), O. Rudner (cnd), Swedish CO *(rec Örebro Concert Hall, Sweden, Aug 1998)* † Con Va; Tam Lin [TT 1:03:06] BIS ▲ 971 [DDD] (17.97)

Concerto for Viola & Orchestra (1995)
P. Dukes (va), O. Rudner (cnd), Swedish CO *(rec Örebro Concert Hall, Sweden, May 1999)* † Con Vc; Tam Lin [TT 1:03:06] BIS ▲ 971 [DDD] (17.97)

Tam Lin for Oboe & Orchestra (1993)
G. Hunt (ob), O. Rudner (cnd), Swedish CO *(rec Örebro Concert Hall, Sweden, May 1999)* † Con Va; Con Vc [TT 1:03:06] BIS ▲ 971 [DDD] (17.97)

BEECKE, IGNAZ VON (1733-1803)

Quartet in G for Strings, M.11
Arioso String Quartet *(rec July 15-17, 1997)* † Qt Strs, M.16; Qt Strs, M.9 [TT 54:09] CPO ▲ 999509 [DDD] (10.97)

Quartet in B♭ for Strings, M.16
Arioso String Quartet *(rec July 15-17, 1997)* † Qt Strs, M.11; Qt Strs, M.9 [TT 54:09] CPO ▲ 999509 [DDD] (10.97)

Quartet in G for Strings, M.9
Arioso String Quartet *(rec July 15-17, 1997)* † Qt Strs, M.11; Qt Strs, M.16 [TT 54:09] CPO ▲ 999509 [DDD] (10.97)

BEETHOVEN, LUDWIG VAN (1770-1827)

Concerto No. 1 in C for Piano & Orchestra, Op. 15 (1795; rev 1800)
G. Gould (pno), E. MacMillan (cnd), Toronto SO *(rec Toronto, Canada)* † Con 2 Pno, Op. 19 [TT 1:06:35] CBC ▲ 2015 (m) [ADD] (16.97)

Concerto No. 2 in B♭ for Piano & Orchestra, Op. 19 (1793; rev 1794-95 & 1798)
G. Gould (pno), E. MacMillan (cnd), Toronto SO *(rec Toronto, Canada)* † Con 1 Pno, Op. 15 [TT 1:06:35] CBC ▲ 2015 (m) [ADD] (16.97)
J. Lill (pno), A. Gibson (cnd), Scottish National Orch † Con 4 Pno, Op. 58 CFP (Classics for Pleasure) ▲ 72680 (11.97)

Concerto No. 4 in G for Piano & Orchestra, Op. 58 (1805-07)
J. Lill (pno), A. Gibson (cnd), Scottish National Orch † Con 2 Pno, Op. 19 CFP (Classics for Pleasure) ▲ 72680 (11.97)

▲ = CD ♦ = Enhanced CD △ = MD ▮ = Cassette Tape ▯ = DCC

NEW RELEASES

BELLINI, VINCENZO

BEETHOVEN, LUDWIG VAN (cont.)

Concerto No. 5 in E♭ for Piano & Orchestra, Op. 73, "Emperor" (1809)
C. Curzon (pno), P. Boulez (cnd), BBC SO *(rec Royal Festival Hall, England, Feb 17, 1971)* † W. A. Mozart:Con 26 Pno, K.537 [TT 1:11:16] BBC ▲ 4020 [ADD] (17.97)
V. Horowitz (pno), F. Reiner (cnd), RCA Victor SO *(rec 1952)* † Chopin:Études Pno; Barcarolle Pno, Op. 60; Mazurkas Pno; Polonaise 6 Pno, Op. 53; S. Rachmaninoff:Con 3 Pno, Op. 30 PPHI (Great Pianists of the 20th Century) ▲ 456841 (22.97)
A. B. Michelangeli (pno), S. Celibidache (cnd), Paris SO *(rec 1975)* MUA ▲ 4296 (10.97)

Concerto in D for Violin & Orchestra, Op. 61 (1806)
F. Kreisler (vn), J. Barbirolli (cnd), London PO *(rec 1936-37)* † W. A. Mozart:Con 4 Vn, K.218 ENT ▲ 99395 (17.97)
Y. Menuhin (vn), A. Rodzinski (cnd), New York Philharmonic SO *(rec Dec 9, 1945)* ("In Memoriam: Rare Broadcast Performances") † J. S. Bach:Con 2 Vns, BWV.1043; B. Bartók:Con 2 Vn, Sz.112; Lalo:Sym espagnole, Op. 21 [TT 1:59:11] MUA 2-▲ 1053 (31.97)

Consecration of the House for Orchestra, Op. 124 (ca 1822)
H. Rosbaud (cnd), Deutschland Sender Orch † Liszt:Symphonic Poems (13); P. Tchaikovsky:Capriccio italien, Op. 45 GRM2 ▲ 78950 (11.97)

Fidelio (opera in 2 acts) [lib Joseph von Sonnleithner], Op. 72 (1804-05, rev 1806)
M. Halász (cnd), Nicolaus Esterházy Sinfonia, K. Strausz (cnd), Hungarian Radio Chorus, I. Nielsen (sop—Leonore), E. Lienbacher (sop—Marzelline), G. Winbergh (ten—Florestan), H. Pecoraro (ten—Jaquino), A. Titus (bar—Don Pizarro), W. Glashof (bass—Don Fernando), K. Moll (bass—Rocco) *(rec Pheonix Studios, Budapest, Hungary) ([GER] text)* [TT 1:34:49] NXIN (Opera Classics) 2-▲ 8660070 [DDD] (13.97)

Leonore (overture) for Orchestra [3rd version] (1805-06)
W. Furtwängler (cnd), Vienna PO *(rec Germany, July 31, 1948)* † J. Brahms:Sym 4; H. Pfitzner:Sym in C, Op. 46 [TT 1:10:54] ORFE ▲ 525991 (16.97)

Missa Solemnis in D for SATB Soloists, Orchestra & Chorus, Op. 123 (1819-23)
E. Kleiber (cnd), Stockholm PO, Stockholm Phil Chorus, B. Nilsson (sop), L. Tunnel (cta), G. Böckelin (ten), S. Björling (bass) *(rec Stockholm, Sweden, Mar 1948)* † Sym 3 [TT 2:11:34] URAN 2-▲ 124 (m) [ADD] (29.97)
Z. Milanov (sop), K. Thorberg (cta), K. von Pataky (ten), N. Moscona (bass), P. Beard (vn), A. Toscanini (cnd), BBC SO, BBC Choral Society *(rec Queen's Hall, London, England, May 28, 1939)* ("Toscanini") † Sym 7; Cherubini:Anacréon (ov); W. A. Mozart:Sym 35, K.385 [TT 2:22:50] BBC (BBC Legends) ▲ 4016 (m) [ADD] (24.97)

Octet in E♭ for Winds, Op. 103 (?1792-93)
Albion Wind Ensemble † Rondino Ww, WoO 25; C. W. Gluck:Iphigénie en Tauride (sels); J. N. Hummel:Eselshaut; Parthia, S.48 HYP ▲ 55037 (9.97)

Quintet in c for Strings, Op. 104 (1817)
K. Spelina (va), Suk Quartet *(rec Prague, Czech Republic, 1976)* † Qnt Strs, Op. 4 [TT 1:01:55] SUR ▲ 3447 [DDD] (10.97)

Quintet in E♭ for Strings, Op. 4 (1795)
K. Spelina (va), Suk Quartet *(rec Prague, Czech Republic, 1976)* † Qnt Strs, Op. 104 [TT 1:01:55] SUR ▲ 3447 [DDD] (10.97)

Rondino in E♭ for Wind Instruments, WoO 25 (1793)
Albion Wind Ensemble † Octet Ww, Op. 103; C. W. Gluck:Iphigénie en Tauride (sels); J. N. Hummel:Eselshaut; Parthia, S.48 HYP ▲ 55037 (9.97)

Rondo in G for Violin & Piano, WoO 41 (1793-94)
V. Steude (vn), R. Batik (pno) † Son 9 Vn, Op. 47; Vars Vn on Mozart's Se vuol ballare, WoO 40 CAMA ▲ 531 [DDD] (18.97)

Sonata No. 1 in F for Cello & Piano, Op. 5/1 (1796)
J. du Pré (vc), D. Barenboim (pno) *(rec Usher Hall, Edinburgh, England, Aug 1970)* † Son 2 Vc, Op. 5/2; Son 3 Vc, Op. 69; Son 4 Vc; Son 5 Vc; Vars Vc on "Bei Männern", WoO 46; Vars Vc on "Ein Mädchen oder Weibchen", Op. 66; Vars Vc, WoO 45 [TT 2:21:33] EMIC 2-▲ 73332 [ADD] (16.97)

Sonata No. 2 in g for Cello & Piano, Op. 5/2 (1796)
J. du Pré (vc), D. Barenboim (pno) *(rec Usher Hall, Edinburgh, England, Aug 1970)* † Son 1 Vc, Op. 5/1; Son 3 Vc, Op. 69; Son 4 Vc; Son 5 Vc; Vars Vc on "Bei Männern", WoO 46; Vars Vc on "Ein Mädchen oder Weibchen", Op. 66; Vars Vc, WoO 45 [TT 2:21:33] EMIC 2-▲ 73332 [ADD] (16.97)

Sonata No. 3 in A for Cello & Piano, Op. 69 (1807-08)
J. du Pré (vc), D. Barenboim (pno) *(rec Usher Hall, Edinburgh, England, Aug 1970)* † Son 1 Vc, Op. 5/1; Son 2 Vc, Op. 5/2; Son 4 Vc; Son 5 Vc; Vars Vc on "Bei Männern", WoO 46; Vars Vc on "Ein Mädchen oder Weibchen", Op. 66; Vars Vc, WoO 45 [TT 2:21:33] EMIC 2-▲ 73332 [ADD] (16.97)

Sonata No. 4 in C for Cello & Piano, Op. 102/1 (1815)
J. du Pré (vc), D. Barenboim (pno) *(rec Usher Hall, Edinburgh, England, Aug 1970)* † Son 1 Vc, Op. 5/1; Son 2 Vc, Op. 5/2; Son 3 Vc, Op. 69; Son 5 Vc; Vars Vc on "Bei Männern", WoO 46; Vars Vc on "Ein Mädchen oder Weibchen", Op. 66; Vars Vc, WoO 45 [TT 2:21:33] EMIC 2-▲ 73332 [ADD] (16.97)

Sonata No. 5 in D for Cello & Piano, Op. 102/2 (1815)
J. du Pré (vc), D. Barenboim (pno) *(rec Usher Hall, Edinburgh, England, Aug 1970)* † Son 1 Vc, Op. 5/1; Son 2 Vc, Op. 5/2; Son 3 Vc, Op. 69; Son 4 Vc; Vars Vc on "Bei Männern", WoO 46; Vars Vc on "Ein Mädchen oder Weibchen", Op. 66; Vars Vc, WoO 45 [TT 2:21:33] EMIC 2-▲ 73332 [ADD] (16.97)

Sonata in F for Horn & Piano, Op. 17 (1800)
T. Johns (hn), J. Lynch (pno) *(rec Palmerston Place Church, Edinburgh, England, June 1994)* ("Classic & Romantic") † G. Gershwin:Oh, Kay! (sels); P. Hindemith:Son Hn; T. Johns:Holland Park; Saint-Saëns:Romance Hn Pno, Op. 67; Van Heusen:All the Way; K. Weill:Knickerbocker Holiday (sels) [TT 44:52] ORCH ▲ 2918 [ADD] (12.97)

Sonatas (32) for Piano (complete)
D. Barenboim (pno) ("Collectors Edition") DEUT 9-▲ 463127 (60.97)

Sonata No. 2 in A for Piano, Op. 2/2 (1794-95)
M. Horszowski (pno) *(rec Philadelphia, PA, Dec 2, 1977)* † Son 10 Pno, Op. 14/2; Son 30 Pno, Op. 109; Son 5 Pno, Op. 10/1 [TT 1:16:55] ARBT ▲ 119 [ADD] (16.97)

Sonata No. 4 in E♭ for Piano, Op. 7 (1796-97)
A. B. Michelangeli (pno) *(rec 1971)* † J. Brahms:Ballades (4), Op. 10; Vars on a Theme by Paganini, Op. 35; Mompou:Cançons i dansas Pno; R. Schumann:Carnaval, Op. 9 PPHI (Great Pianists of the 20th Century) 2-▲ 456904 (22.97)

Sonata No. 5 in c for Piano, Op. 10/1 (?1795-97)
M. Horszowski (pno) *(rec Philadelphia, PA, Dec 2, 1977)* † Son 10 Pno, Op. 14/2; Son 2 Pno, Op. 2/2; Son 30 Pno, Op. 109 [TT 1:16:55] ARBT ▲ 119 [ADD] (16.97)

Sonata No. 10 in G for Piano, Op. 14/2 (?1799)
M. Horszowski (pno) *(rec Philadelphia, PA, Dec 2, 1977)* † Son 2 Pno, Op. 2/2; Son 30 Pno, Op. 109; Son 5 Pno, Op. 10/1 [TT 1:16:55] ARBT ▲ 119 [ADD] (16.97)

Sonata No. 11 in B♭ for Piano, Op. 22 (1800)
L. Lortie (pno) † Son 12 Pno, Op. 26; Son 19 Pno, Op. 49/1; Son 20 Pno, Op. 49/2 CHN ▲ 9755 (16.97)

Sonata No. 12 in A♭ for Piano, Op. 26, "Funeral March" (1800-01)
L. Lortie (pno) † Son 11 Pno, Op. 22; Son 19 Pno, Op. 49/1; Son 20 Pno, Op. 49/2 CHN ▲ 9755 (16.97)

Sonata No. 17 in d for Piano, Op. 31/2, "Tempest" (1802)
N. Krieger (pno) † J. S. Bach:Partitas Hpd; Chopin:Etudes Pno; Nocturnes Pno; W. A. Mozart:Son 10 Pno, K.330 ARII ▲ 491 (17.97)

Sonata No. 19 in g for Piano, Op. 49/1 (1795-95)
L. Lortie (pno) † Son 11 Pno, Op. 22; Son 12 Pno, Op. 26; Son 20 Pno, Op. 49/2 CHN ▲ 9755 (16.97)

Sonata No. 20 in G for Piano, Op. 49/2 (1795-96)
L. Lortie (pno) † Son 11 Pno, Op. 22; Son 12 Pno, Op. 26; Son 19 Pno, Op. 49/1 CHN ▲ 9755 (16.97)

Sonata No. 23 in f for Piano, Op. 57, "Appassionata" (1804-05)
E. Levy (pno) ("Forgotten Genius") † Son 27 Pno, Op. 90; Son 28 Pno, Op. 101; Son 30 Pno, Op. 109; Son 31 Pno, Op. 110; J. Haydn:Son 32 Kbd, H.XVI/44; Son 46 Kbd, H.XVI/31; Son 50 Kbd, H.XVI/37; Son 51 Kbd, H.XVI/38; W. A. Mozart:Fant Pno, K.397; Strauss (II):Frühlingsstimmen, Op. 410 MRSN 2-▲ 52021 (36.97)

Sonata No. 27 in e for Piano, Op. 90 (1814)
E. Levy (pno) ("Forgotten Genius") † Son 23 Pno, Op. 57; Son 28 Pno, Op. 101; Son 30 Pno, Op. 109; Son 31 Pno, Op. 110; J. Haydn:Son 32 Kbd, H.XVI/44; Son 46 Kbd, H.XVI/31; Son 50 Kbd, H.XVI/37; Son 51 Kbd, H.XVI/38; W. A. Mozart:Fant Pno, K.397; Strauss (II):Frühlingsstimmen, Op. 410 MRSN 2-▲ 52021 (36.97)

Sonata No. 28 in A for Piano, Op. 101 (1816)
E. Levy (pno) ("Forgotten Genius") † Son 23 Pno, Op. 57; Son 27 Pno, Op. 90; Son 30 Pno, Op. 109; Son 31 Pno, Op. 110; J. Haydn:Son 32 Kbd, H.XVI/44; Son 46 Kbd, H.XVI/31; Son 50 Kbd, H.XVI/37; Son 51 Kbd, H.XVI/38; W. A. Mozart:Fant Pno, K.397; Strauss (II):Frühlingsstimmen, Op. 410 MRSN 2-▲ 52021 (36.97)

BEETHOVEN, LUDWIG VAN (cont.)

Sonata No. 29 in B♭ for Piano, Op. 106, "Hammerklavier" (1817-18)
Solomon (pno) † J. Brahms:Intermezzos (3) Pno, Op. 117; Vars & Fugue on a Theme by Handel, Op. 24; Chopin:Ballade 4 Pno, Op. 52; Berceuse, Op. 57; Fantaisie Pno, Op. 49; Polonaise 6 Pno, Op. 53; Liszt:Études de concert (3), S.144; Années de pèlerinage 1, S.160; Hungarian Rhaps, S.244; Trans, Arrs & Paraphrases; W. A. Mozart:Son 13 Pno, K.333 PPHI (Great Pianists of the 20th Century) ▲ 456973 (22.97)

Sonata No. 30 in E for Piano, Op. 109 (1820)
M. Horszowski (pno) *(rec Philadelphia, PA, Dec 2, 1977)* † Son 10 Pno, Op. 14/2; Son 2 Pno, Op. 2/2; Son 5 Pno, Op. 10/1 [TT 1:16:55] ARBT ▲ 119 [ADD] (16.97)
E. Levy (pno) ("Forgotten Genius") † Son 23 Pno, Op. 57; Son 27 Pno, Op. 90; Son 28 Pno, Op. 101; Son 31 Pno, Op. 110; J. Haydn:Son 32 Kbd, H.XVI/44; Son 46 Kbd, H.XVI/31; Son 50 Kbd, H.XVI/37; Son 51 Kbd, H.XVI/38; W. A. Mozart:Fant Pno, K.397; Strauss (II):Frühlingsstimmen, Op. 410 MRSN 2-▲ 52021 (36.97)

Sonata No. 31 in A♭ for Piano, Op. 110 (1821-22)
E. Levy (pno) ("Forgotten Genius") † Son 23 Pno, Op. 57; Son 27 Pno, Op. 90; Son 28 Pno, Op. 101; Son 30 Pno, Op. 109; J. Haydn:Son 32 Kbd, H.XVI/44; Son 46 Kbd, H.XVI/31; Son 50 Kbd, H.XVI/37; Son 51 Kbd, H.XVI/38; W. A. Mozart:Fant Pno, K.397; Strauss (II):Frühlingsstimmen, Op. 410 MRSN 2-▲ 52021 (36.97)

Sonata No. 5 in F for Violin & Piano, Op. 24, "Spring" (1800-01)
F. Kreisler (vn), F. Rupp (pno) *(rec 1936)* † Son 10 Vn, Op. 96; Son 8 Vn; Son 9 Vn, Op. 47; E. Grieg:Son 3 Vn, Op. 45; F. Schubert:Son Vn, D.574 [TT 2:13:17] MPLY 2-▲ 2042 (m) [ADD] (13.97)

Sonata No. 8 in G for Violin & Piano, Op. 30/3 (1801-02)
F. Kreisler (vn), S. Rachmaninoff (pno) *(rec 1928)* † Son 10 Vn, Op. 96; Son 5 Vn, Op. 24; Son 9 Vn, Op. 47; E. Grieg:Son 3 Vn, Op. 45; F. Schubert:Son Vn, D.574 [TT 2:13:17] MPLY 2-▲ 2042 (m) [ADD] (13.97)
J. Martzy (vn), L. Pommers (pno) † J. S. Bach:Sons & Partitas Vn; B. Bartók:Romanian Folk Dances Vn & Pno; G. F. Handel:Son Vn; I. Stravinsky:Duo Concertant; Szymanowski:Notturno e Tarantella, Op. 28 DHR ▲ 7753 (16.97)

Sonata No. 9 in A for Violin & Piano, Op. 47, "Kreutzer" (1802-03)
F. Kreisler (vn), F. Rupp (pno) *(rec 1936)* † Son 10 Vn, Op. 96; Son 5 Vn, Op. 24; Son 8 Vn; E. Grieg:Son 3 Vn, Op. 45; F. Schubert:Son Vn, D.574 [TT 2:13:17] MPLY 2-▲ 2042 (m) [ADD] (13.97)
I. Perlman (vn), M. Argerich (pno) *(rec Saratoga Performing Arts Center, FL, July 30, 1998)* † C. Franck:Son Vn, M.8 [TT 59:57] EMIC ▲ 56815 [DDD] (16.97)
V. Steude (vn), R. Batik (pno) † Rondo Vn, WoO 41; Vars Vn on Mozart's Se vuol ballare, WoO 40 CAMA ▲ 531 [DDD] (18.97)

Sonata No. 10 in G for Violin & Piano, Op. 96 (1812; probably rev 1815)
F. Kreisler (vn), F. Rupp (pno) *(rec 1936)* † Son 5 Vn, Op. 24; Son 8 Vn; Son 9 Vn, Op. 47; E. Grieg:Son 3 Vn, Op. 45; F. Schubert:Son Vn, D.574 [TT 2:13:17] MPLY 2-▲ 2042 (m) [ADD] (13.97)

Songs (3) for Voice & Piano [text Goethe], Op. 83 (1810)
L. D. San (bar), N. Lee (pno)—No. 2, Sehnsucht; No. 1, Wonne der Wehmut *(rec 1983)* † J. Brahms:Songs (5), Op. 72; Songs (7), Op. 48; C. Loewe:Der getreue Eckart, Op. 44/2; Erlkönig, Op. 1/3; F. Schubert:An Schwager Kronos, D.369; Der Musensohn, D.764; Erlkönig, D.328; Ganymed, D.544; Prometheus, D.674; Rastlose Liebe, D.138; Schäfers Klagelied, D.121; R. Schumann:Myrthen, Op. 25; H. Wolf:Gedichte von Goethe [TT 46:47] PAVA ▲ 7122 (10.97)

Symphony No. 3 in E♭, Op. 55, "Eroica" (1803)
B. Nilsson (sop), L. Tunnel (cta), G. Böckelin (ten), S. Björling (bass), E. Kleiber (cnd), Stockholm PO, E. Kleiber (cnd), NBC SO, Stockholm Phil Chorus *(rec New York, NY, Jan 1948)* † Missa Solemnis, Op. 123 [TT 2:11:34] URAN 2-▲ 124 (m) [ADD] (29.97)
Paris Conservatory Société des Concerts Orch, C. Schuricht (cnd), Berlin PO *(rec 1941-46)* † Sym 5 GRM2 ▲ 78951 (11.97)
B. Walter (cnd), Sym of the Air *(rec Carnegie Hall, PA, 1957)* MUA ▲ 4010 (10.97)

Symphony No. 4 in B♭, Op. 60 (1806)
L. Bernstein (cnd), Vienna PO † Sym 6; Sym 9 DEUT 2-▲ 463468 (17.97)
K. Böhm (cnd), Vienna PO *(rec Grosses Festspielhaus, Germany, Aug 17, 1969)* † G. Mahler:Lieder eines fahrenden Gesellen; R. Schumann:Sym 4 [TT 1:19:46] ORFE ▲ 522991 (16.97)
W. Sawallisch (cnd), (Royal) Concertgebouw Orch † Sym 5; Sym 6; Sym 7 [TT 2:26:50] EMIC 2-▲ 73326 [DDD] (16.97)

Symphony No. 5 in c, Op. 67 (1807-08)
Paris Conservatory Société des Concerts Orch, C. Schuricht (cnd), Berlin PO *(rec 1941-46)* † Sym 3 GRM2 ▲ 78951 (11.97)
W. Sawallisch (cnd), (Royal) Concertgebouw Orch † Sym 4; Sym 6; Sym 7 [TT 2:26:50] EMIC 2-▲ 73326 [DDD] (16.97)
L. Stokowski (cnd), All-American Youth SO *(rec 1940-41)* † J. Brahms:Sym 1 MUA ▲ 4857 (10.97)

Symphony No. 6 in F, Op. 68, "Pastorale" (1808)
L. Bernstein (cnd), Vienna PO † Sym 4; Sym 9 DEUT 2-▲ 463468 (17.97)
W. Sawallisch (cnd), (Royal) Concertgebouw Orch † Sym 4; Sym 5; Sym 7 [TT 2:26:50] EMIC 2-▲ 73326 [DDD] (16.97)

Symphony No. 7 in A, Op. 92 (1811-12)
W. Sawallisch (cnd), (Royal) Concertgebouw Orch † Sym 4; Sym 5; Sym 6 [TT 2:26:50] EMIC 2-▲ 73326 [DDD] (16.97)
A. Toscanini (cnd), BBC SO *(rec Queen's Hall, London, England, June 12, 1935)* ("Toscanini") † Missa Solemnis, Op. 123; Cherubini:Anacréon (ov); W. A. Mozart:Sym 35, K.385 [TT 2:22:50] BBC (BBC Legends) ▲ 4016 (m) [ADD] (24.97)
O. Vänskä (cnd), BBC Scottish SO † D. Shostakovich:Sym 3 BBCM ▲ 1005 (13.97)

Symphony No. 9 in d for solo Voices, Orchestra & Chorus, Op. 125, "Choral Symphony" (1822-24)
T. Briem (sop), E. Höngen (cta), P. Anders (ten), R. Watzke (bass), W. Furtwängler (cnd), Berlin PO, Bruno Kittel Choir MUA ▲ 4653 (10.97)
G. Jones (sop), H. Schwarz (cta), R. Kollo (ten), K. Moll (bass), L. Bernstein (cnd), Vienna PO, Vienna Chorus † Sym 4; Sym 6 DEUT 2-▲ 463468 (17.97)
O. Klemperer (cnd), Philharmonia Orch *(rec Royal Festival Hall, England, 1957)* TES ▲ 1177 (17.97)
H. Schymberg (sop), L. Tunell (alt), G. Bäckelin (bass), W. Furtwängler (cnd), Stockholm PO, Musikalist Sällskapet *(rec Stockholm, Sweden, Dec 1943)* MUA ▲ 4002 (10.97)

Variations (12) in F on "Ein Mädchen oder Weibchen" from Mozart's *Die Zauberflöte* for Cello & Piano, Op. 66 (1796)
J. du Pré (vc), D. Barenboim (pno) *(rec Usher Hall, Edinburgh, England, Aug 1970)* † Son 1 Vc, Op. 5/1; Son 2 Vc, Op. 5/2; Son 3 Vc, Op. 69; Son 4 Vc; Son 5 Vc; Vars Vc on "Bei Männern", WoO 46; Vars Vc, WoO 45 [TT 2:21:33] EMIC 2-▲ 73332 [ADD] (16.97)

Variations (12) in G on "See, the Conquering Hero Comes" from Handel's *Judas Maccabaeus* for Cello & Piano, WoO 45 (1796)
J. du Pré (vc), D. Barenboim (pno) *(rec Usher Hall, Edinburgh, England, Aug 1970)* † Son 1 Vc, Op. 5/1; Son 2 Vc, Op. 5/2; Son 3 Vc, Op. 69; Son 4 Vc; Son 5 Vc; Vars Vc on "Bei Männern", WoO 46; Vars Vc on "Ein Mädchen oder Weibchen", Op. 66 [TT 2:21:33] EMIC 2-▲ 73332 [ADD] (16.97)

Variations (7) in E♭ on "Bei Männern" from Mozart's *Die Zauberflöte* for Cello & Piano, WoO 46 (1801)
J. du Pré (vc), D. Barenboim (pno) *(rec Usher Hall, Edinburgh, England, Aug 1970)* † Son 1 Vc, Op. 5/1; Son 2 Vc, Op. 5/2; Son 3 Vc, Op. 69; Son 4 Vc; Son 5 Vc; Vars Vc on "Ein Mädchen oder Weibchen", Op. 66; Vars Vc, WoO 45 [TT 2:21:33] EMIC 2-▲ 73332 [ADD] (16.97)

Variations (12) on Mozart's "Se vuol ballare" for Violin & Piano [from *Le nozze di Figaro*], WoO 40 (1792-93)
V. Steude (vn), R. Batik (pno) † Rondo Vn, WoO 41; Son 9 Vn, Op. 47 CAMA ▲ 531 [DDD] (18.97)

BELLINATI, PAULO (1954-

Music of Bellinati
Guitar x 2—Jongo *(rec State University, New York, Purchase, NY, 1998)* ("Catgut Flambo") † S. Assad:; E. Granados:Danzas españolas (10) Pno; Goyescas (sels); C. Machado:Music of Machado; H. Rovics:Impressões do Brasil; Sor:Divert Gtrs, Op. 34; Telemann:Music of Telemann MUSC ▲ 21699 (10.97)

BELLINI, VINCENZO (1801-1835)

I Capuleti e i Montecchi (opera in 2 acts) [lib Felice Romani after L. Scevola]
P. Bellugi (cnd), Venice Theater Orch, C. Mirandola (cnd), Venice Theater Chorus, K. Ricciarelli (sop—Giulietta), V. Luchetti (ten—Romeo), W. Monachesi (bar—Lorenzo), G. Merighi (sgr—Tebaldi), B. Marangoni (sgr—Capellio) *(rec Venice, Italy, May 16, 1973)* MONM 2-▲ 10604 [ADD] (36.97)

Concerto in E♭ for Oboe & Orchestra (ca 1825)
N. Daniel (ob), Peterborough String Orch † Albinoni:Cons Ob, Op. 9; Cimarosa:Con Ob; A. Marcello:Con Ob Strs in d, Op. 1; Vivaldi:Con Ob HYP ▲ 55034 (9.97)

Il pirata (opera in 2 acts) [Libretto Felice Romani after I.J.S. Taylor]
G. Gavazzeni (cnd), Italian Radio Orch, G. Lazzari (cnd), Italian Radio Chorus, M. Caballé (sop—Imogene), B. Martí (ten—Gualtiero), P. Cappuccilli (bar—Ernesto), R. Raimondi (bass—Goffredo), F. Raffanelli (sop—Adele), G. Baratti (ten—Itulbo) *(rec Rome, Italy, July 1970) ([ENG,ITA] lib text)* [TT 2:22:03] EMIC ▲ 67121 [ADD] (23.97)

NEW RELEASES 5

BELLINI, VINCENZO (cont.)

I puritani (opera in 3 acts) [Libretto C. Pepoli after Ancelot and Xavier]
R. Bonynge (cnd), Teatro Massimo Orchestra, M. Devia (sop), W. Matteuzzi (ten), P. Washington (bass) NUO ▲ 6842 (32.97)

La sonnambula (opera in 2 acts) [text Romani]
R. Cecconi (cnd), Venice Theater Orch, Venice Theater Chorus, J. Anderson (sop—Amina), L. Zannini (mez—Teresa), A. Bertolo (ten—Elvino), G. Surjan (bar—Il conte Rodolfo), G. Antonini (bass—Alessio), P. Dordi (sgr—Lisa), W. Brighi (sgr—Un Notaio) *(rec live, Venice, Italy, Apr 7, 1984)* MONM 2-▲ 10506 (36.97)

BENDA, GEORG ANTON [JIRI ANTONIN] (1722-1795)

Amynts Klagen (cantata) for Voice, Cello & Harpsichord (1779)
M. Fers (sop), R. Pertorini (vc), A. Horváth (hpd) *(rec Hungary, Feb 1998)* † Lieder (20); Spiritual Lieder (3) [TT 57:20] HUN ▲ 31779 [DDD] (16.97)

Lieder (20) for Soprano, Bass, Cello & Harpsichord
M. Fers (sop), I. Kovács (bass), R. Pertorini (vc), A. Horváth (hpd) *(rec Hungary, Feb 1998)* † Amynts Klagen; Spiritual Lieder (3) [TT 57:20] HUN ▲ 31779 [DDD] (16.97)

Spiritual Lieder (3) for Soprano, Cello & Organ
M. Fers (sop), R. Pertorini (vc), A. Horváth (org) *(rec Hungary, Feb 1998)* † Amynts Klagen; Lieder (20) [TT 57:20] HUN ▲ 31779 [DDD] (16.97)

BENDIX, VICTOR (1851-1926)

Sonata in g for Piano, Op. 26 (1901)
P. Seivewright (pno) ROND ▲ 8364 [DDD] (18.97)

BENGUEREL, XAVIER (1931-

Tempo for Guitar & Strings
W. Weigel (gtr), P. Schmelzer (cnd), European Masters Orch † C. Castro:Con Gtr; T. Marco:Con Guadiana DI ▲ 920530 (5.97)

BENNETT, ROBERT RUSSELL (1894-1981)

Suite of Old American Dances for Band (1950)
H. Begian (cnd), Univ of Illinois Symphonic Band ("The Begian Years-Vol. 8") † Sym Songs; S. Barber:School for Scandal, Op. 5; Creston:Anatolia; H. O. Reed:Fiesta Mexicana [TT 1:16:06] MRES ▲ 1649
R. P. Socciarelli (cnd), Trinity Wind Symphony *(rec Ruth Taylor Concert Hall, Trinity University, TX, Apr 16, 1986)* † L. Bernstein:A Musical Toast; H. Fillmore:Men of Ohio; G. Gershwin:Rhap in Blue; Orrego-Salas:Fant; Ticheli:Fortress; R. D. Wetzel:E.W. Scripps [TT 1:04:09] MRES ▲ 595 [DDD]

Symphonic Songs for Wind Band (1958)
H. Begian (cnd), Univ of Illinois Symphonic Band ("The Begian Years-Vol. 8") † Suite of Old American Dances; S. Barber:School for Scandal, Op. 5; Creston:Anatolia; H. O. Reed:Fiesta Mexicana [TT 1:16:06] MRES ▲ 1649

BENSON, WARREN (1924-

Arioso for Tuba (1959)
P. Sinder (tuba) *(rec Michigan St University, MI, 1995)* ("Aerodynamics") † B. Broughton:Son Tb; Gillingham:Divert Hn; C. Ruggiero:Fractured Mambos; W. Schmidt:Tuba Mirum; A. Tcherepnin:Andante Tb; Telemann:Essercizii Musici [TT 1:06:23] MRES ▲ 1701

The Drums of Summer for Ensemble
Meadows Wind Ensemble, Meadows Percussion Ensemble, Meadows Chorale † Messiaen:Oiseaux exotiques; S. Montague:At the White Edge of Phrygia; Varèse:Intégrales GAS ▲ 1017 (16.97)

BENTZON, NIELS VIGGO (1919-

Adagio for Flute & Organ, Op. 414 (1978)
M. Johansen (fl), J. Ramsing (org) *(rec Organ of Poul-Gerhard Andersen 1979, Denmark, Mar 1999)* ("Late 20th Century Pieces-Vol. 2") † Nørholm:Son Fl; M. Olsen:Diptychon; Ørvad:Laminaria; Ramsing:Dodecagon; Rosing-Schow:Twining; S. E. Werner:Secreta [TT 1:01:40] PONT ▲ 5141 (18.97)

Symphony No. 5, Op. 61, "Ellipsen" (1950)
O. Schmidt (cnd), Aarhus SO *(rec Kongreshuset Århus, Netherlands, Mar 4, 1982)* † Sym 7 [TT 1:05:13] DCAP ▲ 8224111 [ADD] (13.97)

Symphony No. 7, Op. 83, "De tre versioner" (c1952)
O. Schmidt (cnd), Aarhus SO *(rec Kongreshuset Århus, Netherlands, Apr 5, 1980)* † Sym 5 [TT 1:05:13] DCAP ▲ 8224111 [ADD] (13.97)

BERG, ALBAN (1885-1935)

Wozzeck (opera in 3 acts) (1914-21)
I. Metzmacher (cnd), Hamburg State PO, S. Kammler (cnd), Hamburg State Opera Chorus, J. Bruns (cnd), Cantilene Children's Choir, R. Spingler (sop—Margret), C. Merritt (ten—Hauptmann), J. Sacher (ten—Andres), B. Skovhus (bar—Wozzeck), F. Olsen (bass—Doktor), K. Rupf (sgr—1. Handwerksbursch), A. Denoke (sgr—Marie), K. Stiefermann (sgr—2. Handwerkbursch), J. Blinkhof (sgr—Tambourmajor), F. Stricker (sgr—Der Narr), F. A. Johnstone (sgr—Soldat) *(rec live, Hamburgische Staatsoper, Germany, Sept-Oct 1998) ([ENG] text)* [TT 1:35:44] EMIC ▲ 56865 [DDD] (32.97)

BERLIOZ, HECTOR (1803-1869)

Béatrice et Bénédict:Overture
H. Begian (cnd), Univ of Illinois Symphonic Band [arr Henning] ("The Begian Years-Vol. 7") † J. Brahms:Vars on a Theme by Haydn; M. Gould:Ballad Band; P. Hindemith:Sym Concert Band; Schoenberg:Theme & Vars Band, Op. 43a; Suppé:Beautiful Galatea (ov); R. Wagner:Lohengrin (preludes) [TT 1:11:58] MRES ▲ 1648
H. Begian (cnd), Univ of Illinois Symphonic Band [arr Paynter] ("The Begian Years-Vol. 10") † M. Arnold:Scottish Dances, Op. 59; Bilik:Sym Band; A. C. Gomez:Guarany (ov); G. Holst:Hammersmith, Op. 52; Kodály:Galanta Dances; R. Wagner:Lohengrin (sels) [TT 1:15:06] MRES ▲ 1651

Benvenuto Cellini:Overture
J. Fournet (cnd), Venice Theater Orch, Venice Theater Chorus *(rec Venice, Italy, Oct 4, 1997)* † Harold en Italie, Op. 16; Herminie; Marche funèbre, Op. 18/3; Mort d'Ophélie, Op. 18/2; Pêcheur, Op. 14bis; Troyens MONM 4-▲ 10124 [DDD] (73.97)

Les francs-juges (Overture) for Orchestra, Op. 3
J. R. Bourgeois (cnd), United States Marine Band [arr Knox for Band] † Grande Symphonie funèbre et triomphale, Op. 15 [TT 50:54] MRES ▲ 3053

Grande Symphonie funèbre et triomphale for Band, Strings & optional Chorus, Op. 15 (1840)
P. Franke (trbn), J. R. Bourgeois (cnd), United States Marine Band † Francs-juges (ov), Op. 3 [TT 50:54] MRES ▲ 3053

Harold en Italie for Viola & Orchestra, Op. 16 (1848)
G. Caussé (va), J. Fournet (cnd), Venice Theater Orch *(rec Venice, Italy, Oct 4, 1997)* † Benvenuto Cellini (ov); Herminie; Marche funèbre, Op. 18/3; Mort d'Ophélie, Op. 18/2; Pêcheur, Op. 14bis; Troyens MONM 4-▲ 10124 [DDD] (73.97)

Herminie (scène lyrique) for Soprano & Orchestra (1828)
J. Fournet (cnd), Venice Theater Orch, Venice Theater Chorus, G. Alperyn (mez) *(rec Venice, Italy, Oct 4, 1997)* † Benvenuto Cellini (ov); Harold en Italie, Op. 16; Marche funèbre, Op. 18/3; Mort d'Ophélie, Op. 18/2; Pêcheur, Op. 14bis; Troyens MONM 4-▲ 10124 [DDD] (73.97)

Marche funèbre (for the final scene of Hamlet), Op. 18/3 (?1848)
J. Fournet (cnd), Venice Theater Orch, Venice Theater Chorus *(rec Venice, Italy, Oct 4, 1997)* † Benvenuto Cellini (ov); Harold en Italie, Op. 16; Herminie; Mort d'Ophélie, Op. 18/2; Pêcheur, Op. 14bis; Troyens MONM 4-▲ 10124 [DDD] (73.97)

La Mort d'Ophélie for Soprano (or Tenor) & Piano [text E. Legouvé after Shakespeare], Op. 18/2 (ca 1847)
J. Fournet (cnd), Venice Theater Orch, Venice Theater Chorus *(rec Venice, Italy, Oct 4, 1997)* † Benvenuto Cellini (ov); Harold en Italie, Op. 16; Herminie; Marche funèbre, Op. 18/3; Pêcheur, Op. 14bis; Troyens MONM 4-▲ 10124 [DDD] (73.97)

Le pêcheur (ballad) for Voice & Orchestra, Op. 14bis (1831-32)
J. Fournet (cnd), Venice Theater Orch, Venice Theater Chorus *(rec Venice, Italy, Oct 4, 1997)* † Benvenuto Cellini (ov); Harold en Italie, Op. 16; Herminie; Marche funèbre, Op. 18/3; Mort d'Ophélie, Op. 18/2; Troyens MONM 4-▲ 10124 [DDD] (73.97)

Les Troyens [The Trojans] (opera in 5 acts) [lib Berlioz after Virgil's *Aenead*] (1856-63)
J. Fournet (cnd), Venice Theater Orch, Venice Theater Chorus, C. C. Pizzutilli (sop—Anna), G. Alperyn (mez—Didon), A. Palombi (ten—Enée), F. Sartori (sgr—Iopas), P. Kahn (sgr—Narbal), N. Agosti (sgr—Ascagne) *(rec Venice, Italy, Oct 4, 1997)* † Benvenuto Cellini (ov); Harold en Italie, Op. 16; Herminie; Marche funèbre, Op. 18/3; Mort d'Ophélie, Op. 18/2; Pêcheur, Op. 14bis MONM 4-▲ 10124 [DDD] (73.97)

BERNERS, LORD (1883-1950) *(Gerald Hugh Tyrwhitt-Wilson Berners, Baronet)*

Fantaisie espagnole for Orchestra (or Piano) (1920)
B. Wordsworth (cnd), Royal Liverpool PO † Fugue; Morceaux; Nicholas Nickleby (film music); Triumph of Neptune OLY ▲ 662 (16.97)

BERNERS, LORD (cont.)

Fugue for Orchestra (1928)
B. Wordsworth (cnd), Royal Liverpool PO † Fant espagnole; Morceaux; Nicholas Nickleby (film music); Triumph of Neptune OLY ▲ 662 (16.97)

Morceaux (3) for Piano 4-Hands [arr of Pieces for Orchestra] (1919)
B. Wordsworth (cnd), Royal Liverpool PO † Fant espagnole; Fugue; Nicholas Nickleby (film music); Triumph of Neptune OLY ▲ 662 (16.97)

Nicholas Nickleby (film music) for Orchestra (1947)
B. Wordsworth (cnd), Royal Liverpool PO † Fant espagnole; Fugue; Morceaux; Triumph of Neptune OLY ▲ 662 (16.97)

The Triumph of Neptune (ballet) for Orchestra (1926)
B. Wordsworth (cnd), Royal Liverpool PO † Fant espagnole; Fugue; Morceaux; Nicholas Nickleby (film music) OLY ▲ 662 (16.97)

BERNSTEIN, LEONARD (1918-1990)

Chichester Psalms for Orchestra & Chorus (1965)
L. Bernstein (cnd), Israel PO, Vienna Boys' Choir soloists, G. Theuring (cnd), Vienna Boys' Choir † Dybbuk; Sym 1; Sym 3 DEUT 2-▲ 463462 (17.97)

Dybbuk (ballet) (1974)

A Musical Toast for Orchestra
E. Carinci (cnd), Trinity Wind Symphony *(rec TMEA Convention, San Antonio, TX, Feb 13, 1987)* † R. R. Bennett:Suite of Old American Dances; H. Fillmore:Men of Ohio; G. Gershwin:Rhap in Blue; Orrego-Salas:Fant; Ticheli:Fortress; R. D. Wetzel:E.W. Scripps [TT 1:04:09] MRES ▲ 595 [DDD]

On the Town (selections)
L. Bernstein (cnd), Israel PO—The Great Lover Displays Himself; Lonely Town; Times Square 1944 † On the Waterfront (sym suite); Prelude, Fugue & Riffs; West Side Story (sym dances); S. Barber:Adagio Strs; A. Copland:Appalachian Spring (suite); G. Gershwin:Rhap in Blue; C. Ives:Unanswered Question DEUT 2-▲ 463465 (17.97)

On the Waterfront:Symphonic Suite (1955)
L. Bernstein (cnd), Israel PO † On the Town (sels); Prelude, Fugue & Riffs; West Side Story (sym dances); S. Barber:Adagio Strs; A. Copland:Appalachian Spring (suite); G. Gershwin:Rhap in Blue; C. Ives:Unanswered Question DEUT 2-▲ 463465 (17.97)

Prelude, Fugue & Riffs for Clarinet & Jazz Ensemble (1949)
L. Bernstein (cnd), Vienna Philharmonic Soloists † On the Town (sels); On the Waterfront (sym suite); West Side Story (sym dances); S. Barber:Adagio Strs; A. Copland:Appalachian Spring (suite); G. Gershwin:Rhap in Blue; C. Ives:Unanswered Question DEUT 2-▲ 463465 (17.97)

Serenade for solo Violin, Strings, Harp & Percussion [after Plato's *Symposium*] (1954)
G. Kremer (vn), L. Bernstein (cnd), New York PO † P. Glass:Con Vn; N. Rorem:Con Vn DEUT (20/21: Music of Our Time) ▲ 445185 (16.97)

Symphony No. 1 for Mezzo-Soprano & Orchestra, "Jeremiah" (1943)
C. Ludwig (mez), L. Bernstein (cnd), Israel PO † Chichester Psalms; Dybbuk; Sym 3 DEUT 2-▲ 463462 (17.97)

Symphony No. 3 for Soprano, Female Speaker, Orchestra, Boys' Choir & Chorus, "Kaddish" (1961-63)
M. Caballé (sop), M. Wager (spkr), L. Bernstein (cnd), Israel PO, Vienna Boys' Choir † Chichester Psalms; Dybbuk; Sym 1 DEUT 2-▲ 463462 (17.97)

West Side Story:Symphonic Dances
L. Bernstein (cnd), Los Angeles PO † On the Town (sels); On the Waterfront (sym suite); Prelude, Fugue & Riffs; S. Barber:Adagio Strs; A. Copland:Appalachian Spring (suite); G. Gershwin:Rhap in Blue; C. Ives:Unanswered Question DEUT 2-▲ 463465 (17.97)

BERWALD, FRANZ (ADOLF) (1796-1868)

Concert Piece for Bassoon & Piano, Op. 2 (1827)
B. R. Stees (bn), P. Hosford (pno) *(rec Molly Grove Chapel, Lansing, MI, May 1993)* ("The Romantic Bassoon") † Hurlstone:Son Bn; F. Mignone:Valsas Bn MRES ▲ 1380

BIBER, CARL HEINRICH VON (1681-1749)

Music of Biber
G. Cassone (tpt), A. Frigé (cnd), Pian e Forte Ensemble—Son 1 Tpts; Son Paschalis; Sons (3) Tpt; Son 2 Tpts *(rec Genoa, Italy, Nov 1998)* † H. I. Biber:Music of Biber DYNC ▲ 234 [DDD] (17.97)

BIBER, HEINRICH IGNAZ FRANZ VON (1644-1704)

Missa Salisburgensis for Voices & Chamber Ensemble
Gabrieli Players, R. Goebel (cnd), Musica Antiqua Köln, P. McCreesh (cnd), Gabrieli Consort *(rec Romsey, Hampshire, England, July 1997)* [TT 1:09:50] PARC ▲ 457611 [DDD] (16.97)

Music of Biber
G. Cassone (tpt), A. Frigé (org), A. Frigé (cnd), Pian e Forte Ensemble—Son à 5 Tpt; Son representativa Vn; Partita 5 Strs & Bc; Son 7 Tpts *(rec Genoa, Italy, Nov 1998)* † C. H. Biber:Music of Biber DYNC ▲ 234 [DDD] (17.97)

Sonata representativa for Violin & Continuo
Berlin Baroque Company *(rec Berlin, Germany, Feb 24-26, 1997)* ("Scherzi Musicali") † J. Fischer:Musical Composition Vns; Fux:Synfonia à 3, K. 331; Marais:Pièces de viole [Book 5]; J. H. Schmelzer:Fechtschule; Music of Schmelzer; Telemann:Getreue Music-Meister [TT 1:07:17] CAPO ▲ 10502 [DDD] (10.97)

BILIK, JERRY H. (1933-

Symphony for Band
H. Begian (cnd), Univ of Illinois Symphonic Band ("The Begian Years-Vol. 10") † M. Arnold:Scottish Dances, Op. 59; Berlioz:Béatrice et Bénédict (ov); A. C. Gomez:Guarany (ov); G. Holst:Hammersmith, Op. 52; Kodály:Galanta Dances; R. Wagner:Lohengrin (sels) [TT 1:15:06] MRES ▲ 1651

BIRO, DANIEL (20th cent)

Music of Biro
J. Chapman (hpd), D. Biro (elec pno)—Imprint; Elegant Enigmas; Notturno o Mattutino SARG ▲ 28028 [DDD] (16.97)

BIZET, GEORGES (1838-1875)

Carmen (opera in 4 acts) [lib Henri Meilhac & Ludovic Halévy] (1873-74)
L. Malajoli (cnd), La Scala Orch, La Scala Chorus, I. A. Tellini (sop), A. Buades (mez), A. Pertile (ten), B. Franci (bar) *(rec 1933)* ENT 2-▲ 1219 (28.97)

Carmen (selections)
E. Rethberg (sop)—Je dis que rien ne m'épouvante (Micaëla's aria) † U. Giordano:Andrea Chénier (sels); W. A. Mozart:Nozze di Figaro (sels); Zauberflöte (sels); G. Puccini:Bohème (sels); Madama Butterfly (sels); Tosca (sels); Strauss (II):Zigeunerbaron (sels); Verdi:Aida (sels); Ballo in maschera (sels); Otello (sels); R. Wagner:Lohengrin (sels); Tannhäuser (sels) NIMB ▲ 7903 [ADD] (11.97)
A. Rothenberger (sop), B. Fassbaender (mez), L. Spiess (ten), W. Annheisser (bar), G. Patanè (cnd), Dresden Staatskapelle, Leipzig Radio Choir, Dresden Philharmonie Children's Chorus [GER] BER ▲ 2030 (10.97)

BLOCH, ERNEST (1880-1959)

Concerto for Violin & Orchestra (1938)
J. Szigeti (vn), C. Munch (cnd), Paris Conservatory Société des Concerts Orch † J. Brahms:Con Vn [TT 1:12:05] SYMP ▲ 1226 (18.97)

In the Night for Piano (1922)
M. Silberstein (pno) † Son Pno; C. Franck:Danse lente, M.22; Prélude, choral et fugue, M.21; V. Giannini:Vars on a Cantus Firmus CSOC ▲ 4208

Méditation hébraïque for Cello & Piano (1924)
J. Bradetich (db), J. R. Bradetich (pno) † B. Bartók:Romanian Folk Dances Pno, Sz.56; Boccherini:Sons (34) Vc Bc; G. Fauré:Elégie, Op. 24; V. Monti:Csárdás KLAV ▲ 11100 [DDD] (18.97)

Sonata for Piano (1935)
M. Silberstein (pno) † In the Night; C. Franck:Danse lente, M.22; Prélude, choral et fugue, M.21; V. Giannini:Vars on a Cantus Firmus CSOC ▲ 4208

BLOOM, ARTHUR (dates unknown)

Life is Like a Box of Chocolates for Strings & Orchestra
J. Levy (vn), C. Nollaig (vn), D. A. Miller (cnd), Albany SO, Present Music † R. Adams:Brutal Reality; E. Chambers:Con Fid; Ince:Fest; J. F. Rogers:Verge ALBA ▲ 354 [DDD] (16.97)

BOCCHERINI, LUIGI (1743-1805)

Quartets (6) for Strings, G.201-206, (Op. 33) (ca. 1782)
Cassado Quartet ("Stradivarius Instruments In the Real Collection") † G. Brunetti:Qnt Strs, Op.1/5; Teixidor:Qt Strs RTVE ▲ 65084 (16.97)

Sonatas (34) for Cello (or Cello duet) & Continuo
J. Bradetich (db), J. R. Bradetich (pno)—G.6 in C † B. Bartók:Romanian Folk Dances Pno, Sz.56; E. Bloch:Méditation hébraïque; G. Fauré:Elégie, Op. 24; V. Monti:Csárdás KLAV ▲ 11100 [DDD] (18.97)

▲ = CD ♦ = Enhanced CD △ = MD ▮ = Cassette Tape ▯ = DCC

BOCCHERINI, LUIGI (cont.)

Stabat Mater for Soprano (or 3 Voices) & Strings, G.532

King's Consort, King's Consort Choir, S. Gritton (sop), S. Fox (sop), S. Bickley (mez), P. Agnew (ten), P. Harvey (bass) † E. D. Astorga:Stabat Mater — HYP ▲ 67108 (18.97)

Symphonies

J. Goritzki (cnd), Neuss German Chamber Academy—Sym in C, G.491, (Op. 7); Sym in C, G.523, (Op. 10/4); Sym in D, G.490; Syms (6), G.503-508, (Op. 12) [Sym in D, G.503; Sym in E♭, G.504; Sym in C, G.505; Sym in d, G.506; Sym in B, G.507; Sym in A, G.508]; Syms (6), G.493-498, (Op. 21) [Sym in B♭, G.493; Sym in E♭, G.494; Sym in C, G.495; Sym in D, G.496; Sym in B♭, G.497; Sym in A, G.498]; Syms (6), G.509-514, (Op. 35) [Sym in D, G.509; Sym in E♭, G.510; Sym in A, G.511; Sym in F, G.512; Sym in E♭, G.513; Sym in B♭, G.514]; Sym in C, G.515, (Op. 37/1); Sym in d, G.517, (Op. 37/3); Sym in A, G.518, (Op. 37/4); Sym in c, G.519, (Op. 41); Sym in D, G.520, (Op. 42); Sym in D, G.522, (Op. 45); Sym in D, G.500 *(rec Historiches Zeughaus, Neuss, Germany, 1993)* — CPO 8-▲ 999401 [DDD] (57.97)

BOCOOK, JAY (1952-

Fanfare and Hymn of Brotherhood for Band

T. G. Leslie (cnd), UNLV Wind Orchestra *(rec Artemus Ham Concert Hall, Las Vegas, NV, 1996)* ("Gawd$illa Eats Las Vegas") † W. Childs:Con Perc; K. L. King:Big Cage; P. Sparke:Celebration; Ticheli:Amazing Grace; Van der Roost:Canterbury Chorale; Whitacre:Gawd$illa Eats Las Vegas [TT 1:03:11] — MRES ▲ 2570

BOITO, ARRIGO (1842-1918)

Mefistofele (selections)

A. Cifrone (sop), M. Mastino (sop), M. Polidori (sop), A. Venturino (sop), A. Gotta (cnd), Compagnia d'Opera Italiana Orchestra—L'altra notte ("Soprano Arias Vol. 3") † W. A. Mozart:Così fan tutte (sels); Don Giovanni (sels); G. Puccini:Bohème (sels); Manon Lescaut (sels); Verdi:Ernani (sels); Trovatore (sels) — BEAU (Cantolopera) ▲ 95042 (16.97)

BOLCOM, WILLIAM (1938-

Capriccio for Cello & Piano (1985)

R. Krishnaswami (vc), M. Salman (pno) † L. Liebermann:Son 1 Vc; D. Stock:Refuge; Vali:Folk Songs Set 12c; Zyman:Son Vc — AMBA ▲ 1022 [DDD] (16.97)

BORNE, FERNAND DE (1862-1929)

Fantasie Brillante on Carmen for Orchestra

J. Bálint (fl), I. Kovács (fl), Budapest Strings *(rec Church of Scottish Mission, Hungary, 1996)* † Briccialdi:Carnival of Venice, Op. 78; A. F. Doppler:Duettino sur des motifs hongrois, Op. 36; Fant pastorale hongroise, Op. 26; Music of Doppler; Rigoletto-Fant, Op. 38 [TT 57:25] — CAPO ▲ 10831 [DDD] (10.97)

BOTTESINI, GIOVANNI (1821-1889)

Elegia for Double Bass & Piano

G. Reinke (db), M. Kapitanova (pno) ("Contrabasso Cantabile") † Melody in e; Rêverie; Paganini:Cantabile, M.S. 109; D. Shostakovich:Gadfly (sels); Taffanel:Meditation — QUER ▲ 9902 (18.97)

Melody in e for Double Bass & String Orchestra

G. Reinke (db), M. Kapitanova (pno) ("Contrabasso Cantabile") † Elegia; Rêverie; Paganini:Cantabile, M.S. 109; D. Shostakovich:Gadfly (sels); Taffanel:Meditation — QUER ▲ 9902 (18.97)

Rêverie for Double Bass & Piano

G. Reinke (db), M. Kapitanova (pno) ("Contrabasso Cantabile") † Elegia; Melody in e; Paganini:Cantabile, M.S. 109; D. Shostakovich:Gadfly (sels); Taffanel:Meditation — QUER ▲ 9902 (18.97)

BOURCIER, TOM (20th cent)

I Saw Elvis for Alto Saxophone & Electric Guitar (1993)

D. Richtmeyer (a sax), M. Zanter (elec gtr) *(rec Krannert Center, Champaign, IL)* ("Light of Sothis") † S. Everett:Proper Behavior; McTee:Etudes; Quate:Light of Sothis; S. A. Wyatt:Counterpoints; Zonn:Midnight Secrets [TT 1:08:19] — MRES ▲ 1806

BRAHMS, JOHANNES (1833-1897)

Academic Festival Overture for Orchestra, Op. 80 (1880)

W. Sawallisch (cnd), London PO † Schicksalslied, Op. 54; Sym 4 [TT 1:07:55] — CSER ▲ 73570 [DDD] (6.97)

Ballades (4) for Piano, Op. 10 (1854)

A. B. Michelangeli (pno) *(rec 1981)* † Vars on a Theme by Paganini, Op. 35; Beethoven:Son 4 Pno, Op. 7; Mompou:Cançons i dansas Pno; R. Schumann:Carnaval, Op. 9 — PPHI (Great Pianists of the 20th Century) 2-▲ 456904 (22.97)

Concerto No. 2 in B♭ for Piano & Orchestra, Op. 83 (1878-81)

E. Fischer (pno), Berlin PO *(rec 1943-54)* † Syms (comp); Vars on a Theme by Haydn — MUA 4-▲ 4941 (30.97)

E. Fischer (pno), W. Furtwängler (cnd), Berlin PO *(rec 1939)* † Furtwängler:Adagio Pno — TES ▲ 1170 (17.97)

S. Richter (pno), G. Georgescu (cnd), George Enescu SO of Bucharest † Vars & Fugue on a Theme by Handel, Op. 24 — DHR (Legendary Treasures) ▲ 7746 (16.97)

Concerto in D for Violin & Orchestra, Op. 77 (1878)

J. Szigeti (vn), H. Harty (cnd), Hallé Orch † E. Bloch:Con Vn [TT 1:12:05] — SYMP ▲ 1226 (18.97)

Ein deutsches Requiem for Soprano, Baritone, Orchestra & Chorus, Op. 45 (1857-68)

S. Matthies (pno), C. Köhn (pno) ("Vol. 4") [TT 1:09:08] — NXIN ▲ 8554115 [DDD] (5.97)

Fantasias (7) for Piano, Op. 116 (1892)

Em. Gilels (pno) *(rec Salzburg Festival, Germany, Aug 17, 1972)* † Debussy:Images (6) Pno; W. A. Mozart:Son 15 Pno, K.533; I. Stravinsky:Scenes (3) Pno [TT 1:12:26] — ORFE ▲ 523991 (16.97)

Hungarian Dances (21) for Orchestra [from Dances for Piano 4-Hands; Nos. 1, 3 & 10 orchd Brahms, 1873]

I. Fischer (cnd), Budapest Festival Orch — PPHI ▲ 462589 (16.97)

A. Toscanini (cnd), NBC SO † Vars on a Theme by Haydn; Mussorgsky:Pictures at an Exhibition; Sibelius:Finlandia, Op. 26; Smetana:Moldau; R. Strauss:Till Eulenspiegels lustige Streiche, Op. 28; Tod und Verklärung, Op. 24; P. Tchaikovsky:Nutcracker Suite, Op. 71a [TT 1:19:11] — RCAV ▲ 59484 (16.97)

Intermezzos (3) for Piano, Op. 117 (1892)

J. Achucarro (pno) *(rec Spain)* † Pieces (4) Pno, Op. 119; Pieces (6) Pno, Op. 118; Vars in f# on Theme of R. Schumann, Op. 9 — ENSA ▲ 9805 [DDD] (16.97)

V. Cliburn (pno)—Intermezzo in E♭; Intermezzo in b♭; Intermezzo in c# *(rec 1970-75)* † Pieces (4) Pno, Op. 119; Pieces (6) Pno, Op. 118; Pieces (7) Pno, Op. 116; Rhaps (2) Pno, Op. 79 — RCAV ▲ 63566 (11.97)

R. Laredo (pno) *(rec Metropolitan Museum of Art, New York City, NY)* ("Such Good Friends") † Pieces (4) Pno, Op. 119; Pieces (6) Pno, Op. 118; Pieces (7) Pno, Op. 116; Mendelssohn (-Bartholdy):Rondo capriccioso, Op. 14; R. Schumann:Fantasiestücke Pno, Op. 12; C. Schumann:Romance, Op. 11 — SACT ▲ 3001 (16.97)

Solomon (pno)—Intermezzo in b♭ *(rec 1944)* † Vars & Fugue on a Theme by Handel, Op. 24; Beethoven:Son 29 Pno, Op. 106; Chopin:Ballade 4 Pno, Op. 52; Berceuse, Op. 57; Fantaisie Pno, Op. 49; Polonaise 6 Pno, Op. 53; Liszt:Etudes de concert (3), S.144; Années de pèlerinage 1, S.160; Hungarian Rhaps, S.244; Trans, Arrs & Paraphrases; W. A. Mozart:Son 13 Pno, K.333 — PPHI (Great Pianists of the 20th Century) ▲ 456973 (22.97)

Motets (2) for 4-6 Voices, Op. 74 (1863-77)

N. Perrin (cnd), Bath Camerata—Warum is das Licht † Songs (5), Op. 104; Bruch:Lieder (7), Op. 71; Schoenberg:Choral Music; R. Schumann:Gedichte, Op. 29; Romanzen und Balladen, Op. 146; H. Wolf:Spanisches Liederbuch (sels) — SOMM ▲ 215 (17.97)

Pieces (7) for Piano, Op. 116

R. Laredo (pno)—Intermezzo in E *(rec Metropolitan Museum of Art, New York City, NY)* ("Such Good Friends") † Intermezzos (3) Pno, Op. 117; Pieces (4) Pno, Op. 119; Pieces (6) Pno, Op. 118; Mendelssohn (-Bartholdy):Rondo capriccioso, Op. 14; R. Schumann:Fantasiestücke Pno, Op. 12; C. Schumann:Romance, Op. 11 — SACT ▲ 3001 (16.97)

Pieces (6) for Piano, Op. 118 (1892)

J. Achucarro (pno) *(rec Spain)* † Intermezzos (3) Pno, Op. 117; Pieces (4) Pno, Op. 119; Vars in f# on Theme of R. Schumann, Op. 9 — ENSA ▲ 9805 [DDD] (16.97)

V. Cliburn (pno)—Ballade in g; Intermezzo in a; Intermezzo in A; Intermezzo in e♭ *(rec 1970-75)* † Intermezzos (3) Pno, Op. 117; Pieces (4) Pno, Op. 119; Pieces (7) Pno, Op. 116; Rhaps (2) Pno, Op. 79 — RCAV ▲ 63566 (11.97)

R. Laredo (pno)—Intermezzo in A *(rec Metropolitan Museum of Art, New York City, NY)* ("Such Good Friends") † Intermezzos (3) Pno, Op. 117; Pieces (4) Pno, Op. 119; Pieces (7) Pno, Op. 116; Mendelssohn (-Bartholdy):Rondo capriccioso, Op. 14; R. Schumann:Fantasiestücke Pno, Op. 12; C. Schumann:Romance, Op. 11 — SACT ▲ 3001 (16.97)

Pieces (4) for Piano, Op. 119 (1892)

J. Achucarro (pno) *(rec Spain)* † Intermezzos (3) Pno, Op. 117; Pieces (6) Pno, Op. 118; Vars in f# on Theme of R. Schumann, Op. 9 — ENSA ▲ 9805 [DDD] (16.97)

V. Cliburn (pno)—Intermezzo in b; Intermezzo in e; Intermezzo in C; Rhapsody in E♭ *(rec 1970-75)* † Intermezzos (3) Pno, Op. 117; Pieces (6) Pno, Op. 118; Pieces (7) Pno, Op. 116; Rhaps (2) Pno, Op. 79 — RCAV ▲ 63566 (11.97)

R. Laredo (pno)—Intermezzo in b *(rec Metropolitan Museum of Art, New York City, NY)* ("Such Good Friends") † Intermezzos (3) Pno, Op. 117; Pieces (6) Pno, Op. 118; Pieces (7) Pno, Op. 116; Mendelssohn (-Bartholdy):Rondo capriccioso, Op. 14; R. Schumann:Fantasiestücke Pno, Op. 12; C. Schumann:Romance, Op. 11 — SACT ▲ 3001 (16.97)

BRAHMS, JOHANNES (cont.)

Pieces (7) for Piano, Op. 116

V. Cliburn (pno)—Capriccio in g; Intermezzo in E *(rec 1970-75)* † Intermezzos (3) Pno, Op. 117; Pieces (4) Pno, Op. 119; Pieces (6) Pno, Op. 118; Rhaps (2) Pno, Op. 79 — RCAV ▲ 63566 (11.97)

Quartet No. 1 in g for Piano & Strings, Op. 25 (1861; orchd Schoenberg, 1937)

R. Schulte (vn), R. Craft (cnd), London Philharmonia [arr Schoenberg] † Schoenberg:Con Vn — KOCH ▲ 7493 (17.97)

Quintet in f for Piano & Strings, Op. 34 (1861-64)

A. Previn (pno), Yale String Quartet *(rec All Saints Church, Tooting, England, Aug 1972)* † Trio 1 Pno, Op. 8; Trio 2 Pno, Op. 87; Trio 3 Pno, Op. 101 [TT 2:13:58] — EMIC 2-▲ 73341 [ADD] (16.97)

Rhapsodies (2) for Piano, Op. 79 (1879)

D. Buechner (pno) † Vars on an Original Theme, Op. 21/1; A. Dvořák:Pieces (4) Pno, Op. 52; Theme with Vars, Op. 36 — CSOC ▲ 4179

V. Cliburn (pno)—No. 1 in b; No. 2 in g *(rec 1970-75)* † Intermezzos (3) Pno, Op. 117; Pieces (4) Pno, Op. 119; Pieces (6) Pno, Op. 118; Pieces (7) Pno, Op. 116 — RCAV ▲ 63566 (11.97)

Schicksalslied for Orchestra & Chorus, Op. 54 (1868-71)

W. Sawallisch (cnd), London PO † Academic Festival Ov, Op. 80; Sym 4 [TT 1:07:55] — CSER ▲ 73570 [DDD] (6.97)

Sonata No. 3 in f for Piano, Op. 5 (1853)

M. Shehori (pno) *(rec Metropolitan Museum of Art, NY, Apr 2, 1977)* ("The New York Recitals-Vol. 1") † Chopin:Nocturnes Pno; Scherzos Pno; M. Ravel:Gaspard de la nuit [TT 1:08:02] — CEMB (Live Concert Series) ▲ 107 [ADD] (15.97)

Songs (6) for Tenor (or Soprano) & Piano, Op. 3 (1852-53)

J. Banse (sop), A. Schmidt (bar), H. Deutsch (pno) *(rec 1996)* ("Complete Edition of the Songs of Johannes Brahms-Vol. 1") † Songs (6), Op. 6; Songs (6), Op. 7; Songs & Romances (8), Op. 14 [TT 57:15] — CPO ▲ 999441 [DDD] (10.97)

Songs (6) for Soprano (or Tenor) & Piano, Op. 6 (1852)

J. Banse (sop), A. Schmidt (bar), H. Deutsch (pno) *(rec 1996)* ("Complete Edition of the Songs of Johannes Brahms-Vol. 1") † Songs (6), Op. 3; Songs (6), Op. 7; Songs & Romances (8), Op. 14 [TT 57:15] — CPO ▲ 999441 [DDD] (10.97)

V. Kasarova (mez), F. Haider (pno)—Der Frühling † Songs (4), Op. 43; Songs (4), Op. 70; Songs (4), Op. 96; Songs (5), Op. 47; Songs (6), Op. 86; F. Schubert:An mein Herz, D.860; Auf dem Wasser zu singen, D.774; Der Jüngling an der Quelle, D.300; Der Wanderer an den Mond, D.870; Fischerweise, D.881b; Im Abendrot, D.799; Im Frühling, D.882; Nacht und Träume, D.827; Romanze zum Drama Rosamunde, D.797; Ständchen, D.889; R. Schumann:Gedichte aus 'Liebesfrühling', Op. 37; Gedichte, Op. 36; Lieder und Gesänge, Op. 77; Myrthen, Op. 25; Zwölf Gedichte, Op. 35 [TT 1:05:20] — RCAV ▲ 68763 (16.97)

Songs (6) for Voice & Piano, Op. 7

J. Banse (sop), A. Schmidt (bar), H. Deutsch (pno) *(rec 1996)* ("Complete Edition of the Songs of Johannes Brahms-Vol. 1") † Songs (6), Op. 3; Songs (6), Op. 6; Songs & Romances (8), Op. 14 [TT 57:15] — CPO ▲ 999441 [DDD] (10.97)

Songs & Romances (8) for Voice & Piano, Op. 14 (1858)

J. Banse (sop), A. Schmidt (bar), H. Deutsch (pno) *(rec 1996)* ("Complete Edition of the Songs of Johannes Brahms-Vol. 1") † Songs (6), Op. 3; Songs (6), Op. 6; Songs (6), Op. 7 [TT 57:15] — CPO ▲ 999441 [DDD] (10.97)

Songs (4) for Voice & Piano, Op. 43 (1864)

V. Kasarova (mez), F. Haider (pno)—Von ewiger Liebe † Songs (4), Op. 70; Songs (4), Op. 96; Songs (5), Op. 47; Songs (6), Op. 6; Songs (6), Op. 86; F. Schubert:An mein Herz, D.860; Auf dem Wasser zu singen, D.774; Der Jüngling an der Quelle, D.300; Der Wanderer an den Mond, D.870; Fischerweise, D.881b; Im Abendrot, D.799; Im Frühling, D.882; Nacht und Träume, D.827; Romanze zum Drama Rosamunde, D.797; Ständchen, D.889; R. Schumann:Gedichte aus 'Liebesfrühling', Op. 37; Gedichte, Op. 36; Lieder und Gesänge, Op. 77; Myrthen, Op. 25; Zwölf Gedichte, Op. 35 [TT 1:05:20] — RCAV ▲ 68763 (16.97)

Songs (5) for Voice & Piano, Op. 47 (1868)

V. Kasarova (mez), F. Haider (pno)—O liebliche Wangen † Songs (4), Op. 43; Songs (4), Op. 70; Songs (4), Op. 96; Songs (6), Op. 6; Songs (6), Op. 86; F. Schubert:An mein Herz, D.860; Auf dem Wasser zu singen, D.774; Der Jüngling an der Quelle, D.300; Der Wanderer an den Mond, D.870; Fischerweise, D.881b; Im Abendrot, D.799; Im Frühling, D.882; Nacht und Träume, D.827; Romanze zum Drama Rosamunde, D.797; Ständchen, D.889; R. Schumann:Gedichte aus 'Liebesfrühling', Op. 37; Gedichte, Op. 36; Lieder und Gesänge, Op. 77; Myrthen, Op. 25; Zwölf Gedichte, Op. 35 [TT 1:05:20] — RCAV ▲ 68763 (16.97)

Songs (7) for Voice & Piano, Op. 48

L. D. San (bar), N. Lee (pno)—Trost in Tränen *(rec 1983)* † Songs (5), Op. 72; Beethoven:Songs (3), Op. 83; C. Loewe:Der getreue Eckart, Op. 44/2; Erlkönig, Op. 1/3; F. Schubert:An Schwager Kronos, D.369; Der Musensohn, D.764; Erlkönig, D.328; Ganymed, D.544; Prometheus, D.674; Rastlose Liebe, D.138; Schäfers Klagelied, D.121; R. Schumann:Myrthen, Op. 25; H. Wolf:Gedichte von Goethe [TT 46:47] — PAVA ▲ 7122 (10.97)

Songs (4) for Voice & Piano, Op. 70 (1877)

V. Kasarova (mez), F. Haider (pno)—Lerchengesang † Songs (4), Op. 43; Songs (4), Op. 96; Songs (5), Op. 47; Songs (6), Op. 6; Songs (6), Op. 86; F. Schubert:An mein Herz, D.860; Auf dem Wasser zu singen, D.774; Der Jüngling an der Quelle, D.300; Der Wanderer an den Mond, D.870; Fischerweise, D.881b; Im Abendrot, D.799; Im Frühling, D.882; Nacht und Träume, D.827; Romanze zum Drama Rosamunde, D.797; Ständchen, D.889; R. Schumann:Gedichte aus 'Liebesfrühling', Op. 37; Gedichte, Op. 36; Lieder und Gesänge, Op. 77; Myrthen, Op. 25; Zwölf Gedichte, Op. 35 [TT 1:05:20] — RCAV ▲ 68763 (16.97)

Songs (5) for Voice & Piano, Op. 72 (1876-77)

L. D. San (bar), N. Lee (pno)—Unüberwindlich *(rec 1983)* † Songs (7), Op. 48; Beethoven:Songs (3), Op. 83; C. Loewe:Der getreue Eckart, Op. 44/2; Erlkönig, Op. 1/3; F. Schubert:An Schwager Kronos, D.369; Der Musensohn, D.764; Erlkönig, D.328; Ganymed, D.544; Prometheus, D.674; Rastlose Liebe, D.138; Schäfers Klagelied, D.121; R. Schumann:Myrthen, Op. 25; H. Wolf:Gedichte von Goethe [TT 46:47] — PAVA ▲ 7122 (10.97)

Songs (6) for Low Voice & Piano, Op. 86 (?1877-79)

V. Kasarova (mez), F. Haider (pno)—Feldeinsamkeit (In Summer Fields) † Songs (4), Op. 43; Songs (4), Op. 70; Songs (4), Op. 96; Songs (5), Op. 47; Songs (6), Op. 6; F. Schubert:An mein Herz, D.860; Auf dem Wasser zu singen, D.774; Der Jüngling an der Quelle, D.300; Der Wanderer an den Mond, D.870; Fischerweise, D.881b; Im Abendrot, D.799; Im Frühling, D.882; Nacht und Träume, D.827; Romanze zum Drama Rosamunde, D.797; Ständchen, D.889; R. Schumann:Gedichte aus 'Liebesfrühling', Op. 37; Gedichte, Op. 36; Lieder und Gesänge, Op. 77; Myrthen, Op. 25; Zwölf Gedichte, Op. 35 [TT 1:05:20] — RCAV ▲ 68763 (16.97)

Songs (4) for Voice & Piano, Op. 96 (1884)

V. Kasarova (mez), F. Haider (pno)—Meerfahrt † Songs (4), Op. 43; Songs (4), Op. 70; Songs (5), Op. 47; Songs (6), Op. 6; Songs (6), Op. 86; F. Schubert:An mein Herz, D.860; Auf dem Wasser zu singen, D.774; Der Jüngling an der Quelle, D.300; Der Wanderer an den Mond, D.870; Fischerweise, D.881b; Im Abendrot, D.799; Im Frühling, D.882; Nacht und Träume, D.827; Romanze zum Drama Rosamunde, D.797; Ständchen, D.889; R. Schumann:Gedichte aus 'Liebesfrühling', Op. 37; Gedichte, Op. 36; Lieder und Gesänge, Op. 77; Myrthen, Op. 25; Zwölf Gedichte, Op. 35 [TT 1:05:20] — RCAV ▲ 68763 (16.97)

Songs (5) for 4-6 Voices, Op. 104 (1886-1888)

N. Perrin (cnd), Bath Camerata—Im Herbst † Motets (2), Op. 74; Bruch:Lieder (7), Op. 71; Schoenberg:Choral Music; R. Schumann:Gedichte, Op. 29; Romanzen und Balladen, Op. 146; H. Wolf:Spanisches Liederbuch (sels) — SOMM ▲ 215 (17.97)

Symphonies (4) (comp)

N. Järvi (cnd), London SO — CHN 4-▲ 9776 (32.97)

Vienna PO, North German RSO, W. Furtwängler (cnd), Berlin PO *(rec 1943-54)* † Con 2 Pno, Op. 83; Vars on a Theme by Haydn — MUA 4-▲ 4941 (30.97)

Symphony No. 1 in c, Op. 68 (1855-1876)

L. Stokowski (cnd), All-American Youth SO *(rec 1940-41)* † Beethoven:Sym 5 — MUA ▲ 4857 (10.97)

Symphony No. 2 in D, Op. 73 (1877)

K. Masur (cnd), Leipzig Gewandhaus Orch *(rec Oct 9, 1989)* ("Wir sind das Volk") † Matthus:Con Tpt; R. Strauss:Till Eulenspiegels lustige Streiche, Op. 28 — QUER ▲ 9918 (35.97)

Symphony No. 3 in F, Op. 90 (1883)

G. Cantelli (cnd), Philharmonia Orch *(rec 1955)* † Mendelssohn (-Bartholdy):Sym 4 — TES ▲ 1173 (17.97)

Symphony No. 4 in e, Op. 98 (1884-85)

W. Furtwängler (cnd), Vienna PO *(rec Germany, Aug 15, 1950)* † Beethoven:Leonore (ov 3); H. Pfitzner:Sym in C, Op. 46 [TT 1:10:54] — ORFE ▲ 525991 (16.97)

W. Sawallisch (cnd), London PO, Ambrosian Singers † Academic Festival Ov, Op. 80; Schicksalslied, Op. 54 [TT 1:07:55] — CSER ▲ 73570 [DDD] (6.97)

Trio in a for Clarinet, Cello & Piano, Op. 114 (1891)

S. Isserlis (vc), M. Collins (cl), S. Hough (pno) † Frühling:Trio Cl, Op. 40; R. Schumann:Kinderszenen Pno, Op. 15; Märchenerzählungen, Op. 132 [TT 1:08:55] — RCAV ▲ 63504 (16.97)

NEW RELEASES 7

BRAHMS, JOHANNES (cont.)

Trio No. 1 in B for Piano, Violin & Cello, Op. 8 (1853-54; rev 1889)
G. Pauk (vn), R. Kirshbaum (vc), P. Frankl (pno) *(rec London, England, Sept 1976)* † Qnt Pno, Op. 34; Trio 2 Pno, Op. 87; Trio 3 Pno, Op. 101 [TT 2:13:58] EMIC 2-▲ 73341 [ADD] (16.97)

Trio No. 2 in C for Piano, Violin & Cello, Op. 87 (1880-82)
G. Pauk (vn), R. Kirshbaum (vc), P. Frankl (pno) *(rec London, England, Sept 1976)* † Qnt Pno, Op. 34; Trio 1 Pno, Op. 8; Trio 3 Pno, Op. 101 [TT 2:13:58] EMIC 2-▲ 73341 [ADD] (16.97)

Trio No. 3 in c for Piano, Violin & Cello, Op. 101 (1886)
G. Pauk (vn), R. Kirshbaum (vc), P. Frankl (pno) *(rec London, England, Sept 1976)* † Qnt Pno, Op. 34; Trio 1 Pno, Op. 8; Trio 2 Pno, Op. 87 [TT 2:13:58] EMIC 2-▲ 73341 [ADD] (16.97)

Variations on a Theme by Haydn for Orchestra, Op. 56a (1873) or 2 Pianos, Op. 56b (1873)
H. Begian (cnd), Univ of Illinois Symphonic Band [arr Hindsley] ("The Begian Years-Vol. 7") † Berlioz:Béatrice et Bénédict (ov); M. Gould:Ballad Band; P. Hindemith:Sym Concert Band; Schoenberg:Theme & Vars Band, Op. 43a; Suppé:Beautiful Galatea (ov); R. Wagner:Lohengrin (preludes) [TT 1:11:58] MRES ▲ 1648
North German RSO *(rec 1943-54)* † Con 2 Pno, Op. 83; Syms (comp) MUA 4-▲ 4941 (30.97)
A. Toscanini (cnd), NBC SO † Hungarian Dances Orch; Mussorgsky:Pictures at an Exhibition; Sibelius:Finlandia, Op. 26; Smetana:Moldau; R. Strauss:Till Eulenspiegels lustige Streiche, Op. 28; Tod und Verklärung, Op. 24; P. Tchaikovsky:Nutcracker Suite, Op. 71a [TT 1:19:11] RCAV ▲ 59484 (16.97)

Variations in f# on a Theme of Robert Schumann for Piano, Op. 9 (1854)
J. Achucarro (pno) *(rec Spain)* † Intermezzos (3) Pno, Op. 117; Pieces (4) Pno, Op. 119; Pieces (6) Pno, Op. 118 ENSA ▲ 9805 [DDD] (16.97)
J. Blancard (pno) † R. Schumann:Faschingsschwank, Op. 26; Kinderszenen Pno, Op. 15; Son 2 Pno, Op. 22 VC ▲ 8212 (13.97)

Variations (11) in D on an Original Theme for Piano, Op. 21/1 (1857)
D. Buechner (pno) † Rhaps (2) Pno, Op. 79; A. Dvořák:Pieces (4) Pno, Op. 52; Theme with Vars, Op. 36 CSOC ▲ 4179

Variations (25) & Fugue in B♭ on a Theme by Handel for Piano, Op. 24 (1861)
S. Richter (pno), G. Georgescu (cnd), George Enescu SO of Bucharest † Con 2 Pno, Op. 83 DHR (Legendary Treasures) ▲ 7746 (16.97)
Solomon (pno) *(rec 1942)* † Intermezzos (3) Pno, Op. 117; Beethoven:Son 29 Pno, Op. 106; Chopin:Ballade 4 Pno, Op. 52; Berceuse, Op. 57; Fantaisie Pno, Op. 49; Polonaise 6 Pno, Op. 53; Liszt:Études de concert (3), S.144; Années de pèlerinage 1, S.160; Hungarian Rhaps, S.244; Trans, Arrs & Paraphrases; W. A. Mozart:Son 13 Pno, K.333 PPHI (Great Pianists of the 20th Century) ▲ 456973 (22.97)

Variations (28) in a on a Theme by Paganini for Piano, Op. 35 (1862-63)
A. B. Michelangeli (pno) *(rec 1948)* † Ballades (4), Op. 10; Beethoven:Son 4 Pno, Op. 7; Mompou:Cançons i dansas Pno; R. Schumann:Carnaval, Op. 9 PPHI (Great Pianists of the 20th Century) 2-▲ 456904 (22.97)

BRANT, HENRY (1913-

Conclusions (2) for Piano
J. McGinn (pno) † Music for a Five & Dime; McGinn:Dream Prologue; Improvisations (3); L. Moss:Racconto; Woollen:Pieces (4) AMCA ▲ 10312 (17.97)

Music for a Five & Dime for Piano
J. McGinn (pno) † Conclusions (2); McGinn:Dream Prologue; Improvisations (3); L. Moss:Racconto; Woollen:Pieces (4) AMCA ▲ 10312 (17.97)

BRIAN, HAVERGAL (1876-1972)

Symphony No. 3 in c#
L. Friend (cnd), BBC SO HYP ▲ 55029 (9.97)

BRICCIALDI, GIULIO (1818-1881)

Carnival of Venice for Flute & Piano, Op. 78
J. Bálint (fl), I. Kovács (fl), Budapest Strings *(rec Church of Scottish Mission, Hungary, Feb-Mar 1996)* † F. D. Borne:Fantasie Brillante on Carmen; A. F. Doppler:Duettino sur des motifs hongrois, Op. 36; Fant pastorale hongroise, Op. 26; Music of Doppler; Rigoletto-Fant, Op. 38 [TT 57:25] CAPO ▲ 10831 [DDD] (10.97)

BRITTEN, BENJAMIN (LORD BRITTEN OF ALDEBURGH) (1913-1976)

Canticle III for Tenor, Horn & Piano, Op. 55, "Still Falls the Rain" (1954)
P. Pears (ten), D. Brain (hn), B. Britten (pno), B. Britten (cnd), London SO ("Britten the performer") † Lachrymae, Op. 48; Our Hunting Fathers, Op. 8; Who are these Children, Op. 84 BBCM ▲ 8014 (17.97)

The Company of Heaven (cantata) (1937)
D. Temple (cnd), National SO, Crouch End Festival Chorus, C. Kinder (sop), H. Nicholl (ten), F. Shaw (spkr), J. Pryce (spkr), P. Knappitt (org), M. Turner (timp) † W. Todd:Burning Road SILC 2-▲ 6021 (18.97)

Concerto in D for Piano & Orchestra, Op. 13 (1938; rev. 1945)
H. Hardenberger (tpt), L. O. Andsnes (pno), P. Järvi (cnd), City of Birmingham SO *(rec Symphony Hall, Birmingham, England, 1997)* † Enescu:Légende Tpt; D. Shostakovich:Con 1 Pno, Op. 35 [TT 1:04:11] EMIC ▲ 56760 [DDD] (16.97)

Insect Pieces (2) for Oboe & Piano [The Grasshopper & The Wasp] (1935)
G. Schmalfuss (ob), M. Watanabe (pno) *(rec Fürtliche Reitbahn Bad Aroseln, Germany, June-Nov 1998)* † Metamorphoses, Op. 49; Phantasy Qt, Op. 2; Temporal Vars [TT 46:18] MDG ▲ 3010925 [DDD] (17.97)

Lachrymae (Reflections on a Song of Dowland) for Viola & Piano [arr for Viola & Strings, 1976], Op. 48
P. Pears (ten), M. Major (va), B. Britten (cnd), London SO ("Britten the performer") † Canticle III, Op. 55; Our Hunting Fathers, Op. 8; Who are these Children, Op. 84 BBCM ▲ 8014 (17.97)

Metamorphoses (6) after Ovid for solo Oboe, Op. 49 (1951)
G. Schmalfuss (ob) *(rec Fürtliche Reitbahn Bad Aroseln, Germany, June-Nov 1998)* † Insect Pieces; Phantasy Qt, Op. 2; Temporal Vars [TT 46:18] MDG ▲ 3010925 [DDD] (17.97)

Nocturne for Tenor, 7 Obbligato Instruments & Strings [after various English poets], Op. 60 (1958)
G. Vishnevskaya (sop), P. Pears (ten), M. Rezhetin (bass), B. Britten (cnd), English CO ("Britten the Performer") † D. Shostakovich:Sym 14 BBC ▲ 8013 (17.97)

On This Island (song cycle) for Soprano (or Tenor) & Piano [text Auden], Op. 11 (1937)
P. Pears (ten), B. Britten (pno) *(rec June 1969)* ("Britten the performer") † F. Schubert:Lieder, Op. 5; H. Wolf:Mörike Lieder BBCM ▲ 8015 (17.97)

Our Hunting Fathers (symphonic cycle) for High Voice & Orchestra [text W. H. Auden], Op. 8 (1936)
P. Pears (ten), B. Britten (cnd), London SO ("Britten the performer") † Canticle III, Op. 55; Lachrymae, Op. 48; Who are these Children, Op. 84 BBCM ▲ 8014 (17.97)

Paul Bunyan (operetta in 2 acts) [lib Auden], Op. 17 (1941)
R. Hickox (cnd), Royal Opera House Orch, Royal Opera House Chorus, S. Gritton (sop), K. Streit (ten), F. Egerton (ten), G. Broadbent (bar), K. Cranham (spkr) CHN 2-▲ 9781 (32.97)

Phantasy Quartet for Oboe, Violin, Viola & Cello, Op. 2 (1932)
G. Schmalfuss (ob), Mannheim String Quartet *(rec Fürtliche Reitbahn Bad Aroseln, Germany, June-Nov 1998)* † Insect Pieces; Metamorphoses, Op. 49; Temporal Vars [TT 46:18] MDG ▲ 3010925 [DDD] (17.97)

Sinfonia da requiem for Orchestra, Op. 20 (1941)
BBC SO † E. Elgar:Froissart, Op. 19; I. Stravinsky:Sacre du printemps BBCM ▲ 1001 (13.97)

Temporal Variations for Oboe & Piano (1936)
G. Schmalfuss (ob), M. Watanabe (pno) *(rec Fürtliche Reitbahn Bad Aroseln, Germany, June-Nov 1998)* † Insect Pieces; Metamorphoses, Op. 49; Phantasy Qt, Op. 2 [TT 46:18] MDG ▲ 3010925 [DDD] (17.97)

Who are these Children for Voice & Orchestra, Op. 84 (1971)
P. Pears (ten), B. Britten (cnd), London SO ("Britten the performer") † Canticle III, Op. 55; Lachrymae, Op. 48; Our Hunting Fathers, Op. 8 BBCM ▲ 8014 (17.97)

BROUGHTON, BRUCE (1945-

Sonata for Tuba & Piano
J. Funderburk (tuba), R. Guy (pno) *(rec Russel Hall Auditorium, Northern Iowa University, IA, 1995-96)* † Capuzzi:Con Db; R. Jones:Dialogs Tuba; J. Koetsier:Sonatina Tuba; A. Lebedev:Con Allegro; Con Tuba; W. A. Mozart:Zauberflöte (sels); R. Vaughan:Concertpiece 1 [TT 57:03] MRES ▲ 2199
P. Sinder (tuba), D. Moriarty (pno) *(rec Michigan St University, MI, 1995)* ("Aerodynamics") † W. Benson:Arioso; Gillingham:Divert Hn; C. Ruggiero:Fractured Mambos; W. Schmidt:Tuba Mirum; A. Tcherepnin:Andante Tb; Telemann:Essercizii Musici [TT 1:06:23] MRES ▲ 1701

BRUCH, MAX (1836-1920)

Concerto No. 1 in g for Violin & Orchestra, Op. 26
Y. Menuhin (vn), L. Ronald (cnd), London SO *(rec Nov 25, 1931)* † E. Elgar:Con Vn [TT 1:12:41] NXIN ▲ 8110902 [AAD] (5.97)

Lieder (7) for Chorus, Op. 71 (1897)
N. Perrin (cnd), Bath Camerata † J. Brahms:Motets (2), Op. 74; Songs (5), Op. 104; Schoenberg:Choral Music; R. Schumann:Gedichte, Op. 29; Romanzen und Balladen, Op. 146; H. Wolf:Spanisches Liederbuch (sels) SOMM ▲ 215 (17.97)

BRUCKNER, ANTON (1824-1896)

Symphony No. 3 in d, "Wagner" (1873-77; recomp W.F. Schalk, 1888-89)
C. Schuricht (cnd), Vienna PO *(rec Dec 1965)* [TT 55:10] PRE ▲ 90409 [ADD]

Symphony No. 7 in E (1881-83)
H. Knappertsbusch (cnd), Vienna PO *(rec Salzburg, Germany, Aug 30, 1949)* PRE ▲ 90408 [AAD]

Symphony No. 8 in c (1884-87; recomp W. J. Schalk, 1889-90)
H. Knappertsbusch (cnd), Berlin PO *(rec 1951)* MUA ▲ 4856 (10.97)

Symphony No. 9 in d [unfinished] (1891-96)
H. Knappertsbusch (cnd), Bavarian State Orch † J. Haydn:Sym 94 MUA ▲ 4896 (10.97)
G. Tintner (cnd), Royal Scottish National Orch [TT 1:00:02] NXIN ▲ 8554268 [DDD] (5.97)

BRUNETTI, GAETANO (Dates unknown)

Quintet in D for Strings, Op.1/5
D. Furnadjev (vc), Cassado Quartet ("Stradivarius Instruments In the Real Collection") † Boccherini:Qts Strs; Teixidor:Qt Strs RTVE ▲ 65084 (16.97)

BRUNI, ANTONIO BARTOLOMEO (1757-1821)

Duo Concertanti (6) for Violin & Viola
A. Cicillini (vn), F. Ammetto (va) *(rec Parma, Italy, Aug 6-7, 1998)* [TT 1:07:08] MONM ▲ 96078 [DDD] (18.97)

BRYANT, STEVEN (1972-

Chester Leaps In for Wind Ensemble
W. Berz (cnd), Rutgers Univ Wind Ensemble *(rec 1998)* ("Dance Rhythms") † R. Hultgren:Bushdance; Masada; Joio:Satiric Dances; Riegger:Dance Rhythms, Op. 58a; Ticheli:Blue Shades; Sun Dance; Yurko:Night Dances [TT 1:01:12] MRES ▲ 2887

BUCKLEY, JOHN (1951-

And Wake the Purple Year for Orchestra (1985)
A. Byrne (pno) *(rec National Concert Hall, Dublin, Ireland, 1995-96)* † Lullabies for Deirdre; Oileáin; Preludes Pno; Silver Apples of the Moon; Winter Music [TT 57:53] MARC (Irish Composer Series) ▲ 8223784 [DDD] (13.97)

Lullabies (3) for Deirdre for Piano (?1989)
A. Byrne (pno) *(rec National Concert Hall, Dublin, Ireland, 1995-96)* † Oileáin; Preludes Pno; Silver Apples of the Moon; Wake the Purple Year; Winter Music [TT 57:53] MARC (Irish Composer Series) ▲ 8223784 [DDD] (13.97)

Oileáin [Islands] for Piano (1979)
A. Byrne (pno) *(rec National Concert Hall, Dublin, Ireland, 1995-96)* † Lullabies for Deirdre; Preludes Pno; Silver Apples of the Moon; Wake the Purple Year; Winter Music [TT 57:53] MARC (Irish Composer Series) ▲ 8223784 [DDD] (13.97)

Preludes (3) for Piano
A. Byrne (pno) *(rec National Concert Hall, Dublin, Ireland, 1995-96)* † Lullabies for Deirdre; Oileáin; Silver Apples of the Moon; Wake the Purple Year; Winter Music [TT 57:53] MARC (Irish Composer Series) ▲ 8223784 [DDD] (13.97)

Quartet for Saxophone
Quartz Saxophone Quartet ("Faces") † J. S. Bach:Art of the Fugue (sels); G. Carpenter:Semaine de Bonte; G. Fitkin:Stub; A. Levine:Faces; M. Nyman:Songs for Tony BBCL ▲ 1024 (16.97)

The Silver Apples of the Moon, the Golden Apples of the Sun for Piano (1994)
A. Byrne (pno) *(rec National Concert Hall, Dublin, Ireland, 1995-96)* † Lullabies for Deirdre; Oileáin; Preludes Pno; Wake the Purple Year; Winter Music [TT 57:53] MARC (Irish Composer Series) ▲ 8223784 [DDD] (13.97)

Winter Music for Piano (1988)
A. Byrne (pno) *(rec National Concert Hall, Dublin, Ireland, 1995-96)* † Lullabies for Deirdre; Oileáin; Preludes Pno; Silver Apples of the Moon; Wake the Purple Year [TT 57:53] MARC (Irish Composer Series) ▲ 8223784 [DDD] (13.97)

BUNTING, EDWARD (1772-1843)

Songs
Baltimore Consort—Girls, Have You Seen George? *(rec Troy Savings Bank Music Hall, NY, May 1999)* ("The Mad Buckgoat") † Anonymous:Bugga Fee Hoosa; Catty Magee; Dwyer's Hornpipe; Kitty Magee; The Goroum; The Kerry Star; The Mad Buckgoat; The Old Woman's Hornpipe; The Pigot Jig; Toss the Feathers; Truagh; Wild Geese; Willie Winkle; Yonder, Westwards, is the Road She Went; Your Old Wig is the Love of My Heart; O Catháin:Songs; Sheedy:Songs; Traditional:Fairy Dance; The Pretty Maid Milking her Cow DOR ▲ 90279 [DDD] (16.97)

BURGESS, HENRY (fl c1738-1765)

Caelia, "Beneath a Sylvian Bower" (cantata) (1749)
M. Ashton (sop), Concert Royal *(rec St. Mungo's Church, Simonburn, Northumberland, England, Apr 1994)* ("Cantatas from the Georgian Drawing Room") † Albinoni:Under Ye Gloomy Shade; T. Arne:Cymon & Iphigenia; H. Carey:Belinda & Eurillo; J. Eccles:Love Kindled in a Breast Too Young; N. Pasquali:Pastora; Pepusch:English Cants Book I; Island of Beauty [TT 1:01:32] ORCH ▲ 2927 [DDD] (17.97)

BURGON, GEOFFREY (1941-

The Calm for Voices & Orchestra
J. Bowman (ct), K. Sillito (vn), M. David (tpt), H. Webb (hpd) *(rec London, England, 1998-99)* † From the Calm; Merciless Beauty; Vision [TT 1:05:25] ASV ▲ 1059 [DDD] (16.97)

From the Calm for Voices
J. Bowman (ct), K. Sillito (vn), M. David (tpt), H. Webb (hpd) *(rec London, England, 1998-99)* † Calm; Merciless Beauty; Vision [TT 1:05:25] ASV ▲ 1059 [DDD] (16.97)

Merciless Beauty (7) for Voices & Orchestra
J. Bowman (ct), G. Burgon (cnd), City of London Sinfonia *(rec London, England, 1998-99)* † Calm; From the Calm; Vision [TT 1:05:25] ASV ▲ 1059 [DDD] (16.97)

A Vision for Voices & Orchestra
N. Jenkins (ten), G. Burgon (cnd), City of London Sinfonia *(rec London, England, 1998-99)* † Calm; From the Calm; Merciless Beauty [TT 1:05:25] ASV ▲ 1059 [DDD] (16.97)

BUSONI, FERRUCCIO (1866-1924)

Bach Transcriptions for solo Piano
M. Perahia (pno)—Wachet auf, ruft uns die Stimme, BWV 645; Nun komm, der Heiden Heiland, BWV 659; Nun freut euch, lieben Christen, BWV 734; Ich ruf zu dir, Herr Jesu Christ, BWV 639 *(rec 1997-98)* † Liszt:Trans, Arrs & Paraphrases; Mendelssohn (-Bartholdy):Lieder ohne Worte [TT 1:05:30] SNYC ▲ 66511 [DDD] (17.97)
J. Slotchiver (pno)—Chaconne in d, BWV 1004 *(rec Academy of Arts & Letters, New York City, NY, Sept 6-7, 1994)* ("Busoni the Visionary") † Elegien Pno; Indianisches Tagebuch 1 [TT 1:12:49] CENT ▲ 2438 [DDD] (16.97)

Chopin Transcriptions for Piano, Op. 22 (1884 [arr 10 vars 1922])
D. Buechner (pno)—Variations & Fugue in Free Form on Chopin's Prelude No. 2 in c for Piano † Toccata Pno; I. Stravinsky:Pétrouchka (sels) CSOC ▲ 4174

Concert for Piano & Orchestra, Op. 31a (1890)
C. Grante (pno), M. Zuccarini (cnd), I Pomeriggi Musicale † Con Pno Strs, Op. 17; Indianische Fant Pno, Op. 44 MUA ▲ 1047 [DDD]

Concerto in d for Piano & String Quartet, Op. 17 (1878)
C. Grante (pno), M. Zuccarini (cnd), I Pomeriggi Musicale † Con Pno Orc, Op. 31a; Indianische Fant Pno, Op. 44 MUA ▲ 1047 [DDD]

Concerto in D for Violin & Orchestra, Op. 35a, K. 243 (1896-7)
J. Szigeti (vn), D. Mitropoulos (cnd), New York Philharmonic SO † Indianische Fant Pno, Op. 44; Sarabande & Cortège, Op. 51 MUA ▲ 1052 (16.97)

Elegien (7) for Piano (1907)
J. Slotchiver (pno) *(rec Academy of Arts & Letters, New York City, NY, Sept 6-7, 1994)* ("Busoni the Visionary") † Bach Trans Pno; Indianisches Tagebuch 1 [TT 1:12:49] CENT ▲ 2438 [DDD] (16.97)

Fantasia nach J. S. Bach for Piano (1909)
W. Corbett-Jones (pno) *(rec Knuth Hall, San Francisco State Univ, CA, Sept 6-7, 1997)* † B. Bartók:Hungarian Peasant Songs, Sz.71; R. Nixon:Music; Preludes; M. Ravel:Sonatine Pno; F. Schubert:Son Pno, D.959 [TT 1:17:43] CMB ▲ 1119 [DDD] (16.97)

Indianische Fantasie for Piano & Orchestra, Op. 44 (1913)
C. Grante (pno), M. Zuccarini (cnd), I Pomeriggi Musicale † Con Pno Orc, Op. 31a; Con Pno Strs, Op. 17 MUA ▲ 1047 [DDD]
E. Petri (pno), D. Mitropoulos (cnd), New York Philharmonic SO † Con Vn; Sarabande & Cortège, Op. 51 MUA ▲ 1052 (16.97)

Indianisches Tagebuch [Book 1] for Piano (1915)
J. Slotchiver (pno) *(rec Academy of Arts & Letters, New York City, NY, Sept 6-7, 1994)* ("Busoni the Visionary") † Bach Trans Pno; Elegien Pno [TT 1:12:49] CENT ▲ 2438 [DDD] (16.97)

Sarabande & Cortège for Orchestra, Op. 51
D. Mitropoulos (cnd), New York Philharmonic SO † Con Vn; Indianische Fant Pno, Op. 44 MUA ▲ 1052 (16.97)

Toccata for Piano (1921)
D. Buechner (pno) † Chopin trans Pno, Op. 22; I. Stravinsky:Pétrouchka (sels) CSOC ▲ 4174

▲ = CD ◆ = Enhanced CD △ = MD ▮ = Cassette Tape ▯ = DCC

NEW RELEASES

CHAUSSON, ERNEST

BUXTEHUDE, DIETRICH (1637-1707)
Canzona in G for Organ, BuxWV 170
L. U. Mortensen (hpd) *(rec Skt. Matthaeus Kirken, Copenhagen, Denmark)* ("Harpsichord Music-Vol. 2") † Canzonetta, BuxWV 171; Courant zimble, BuxWV 245; Fugue; More Palatino, BuxWV 247; Nun lob, mein Seel, den Herren, BuxWV 215; St Kbd; Suite Kbd [TT 52:42] DCAP ▲ 8224117 [DDD] (13.97)
Canzonetta in G for Harpsichord, BuxWV 171
L. U. Mortensen (hpd) *(rec Skt. Matthaeus Kirken, Copenhagen, Denmark)* ("Harpsichord Music-Vol. 2") † Canzona; Courant zimble, BuxWV 245; Fugue; More Palatino, BuxWV 247; Nun lob, mein Seel, den Herren, BuxWV 215; St Kbd; Suite Kbd [TT 52:42] DCAP ▲ 8224117 [DDD] (13.97)
Courant zimble (8 variations) in a for Keyboard, BuxWV 245
L. U. Mortensen (hpd) *(rec Skt. Matthaeus Kirken, Copenhagen, Denmark)* ("Harpsichord Music-Vol. 2") † Canzona; Canzonetta, BuxWV 171; Fugue; More Palatino, BuxWV 247; Nun lob, mein Seel, den Herren, BuxWV 215; St Kbd; Suite Kbd [TT 52:42] DCAP ▲ 8224117 [DDD] (13.97)
Fugue in C for Organ, BuxWV 174, "Gigue Fugue"
L. U. Mortensen (hpd) *(rec Skt. Matthaeus Kirken, Copenhagen, Denmark)* ("Harpsichord Music-Vol. 2") † Canzona; Canzonetta, BuxWV 171; Courant zimble, BuxWV 245; More Palatino, BuxWV 247; Nun lob, mein Seel, den Herren, BuxWV 215; St Kbd; Suite Kbd [TT 52:42] DCAP ▲ 8224117 [DDD] (13.97)
More Palatino (aria & 12 variations) in C for Keyboard, BuxWV 247
L. U. Mortensen (hpd)—Aria *(rec Skt. Matthaeus Kirken, Copenhagen, Denmark)* ("Harpsichord Music-Vol. 2") † Canzona; Canzonetta, BuxWV 171; Courant zimble, BuxWV 245; Fugue; Nun lob, mein Seel, den Herren, BuxWV 215; St Kbd; Suite Kbd [TT 52:42] DCAP ▲ 8224117 [DDD] (13.97)
Nun lob, mein Seel, den Herren (chorale) for Organ, BuxWV 215
L. U. Mortensen (hpd) *(rec Skt. Matthaeus Kirken, Copenhagen, Denmark)* ("Harpsichord Music-Vol. 2") † Canzona; Canzonetta, BuxWV 171; Courant zimble, BuxWV 245; Fugue; More Palatino, BuxWV 247; St Kbd; Suite Kbd [TT 52:42] DCAP ▲ 8224117 [DDD] (13.97)
Sonatas (7) for 2 Violins, Viol & Harpsichord, Op. 2 (BuxWV 259-265)
Eroica Trio *(rec St. Stephens Church, CA, July 1999)* † Albinoni:Adagio; J. S. Bach:Sons & Partitas Vn; Loeillet:Sons (12), Op. 2; A. Lotti:Music of Lotti; Vivaldi:Trio Son Vn Vc, RV.83 [TT 56:14] EMIC ▲ 56873 [DDD] (16.97)
Suite in e for Keyboard, BuxWV 235
L. U. Mortensen (hpd) *(rec Skt. Matthaeus Kirken, Copenhagen, Denmark)* ("Harpsichord Music-Vol. 2") † Canzona; Canzonetta, BuxWV 171; Courant zimble, BuxWV 245; Fugue; More Palatino, BuxWV 247; Nun lob, mein Seel, den Herren, BuxWV 215; St Kbd [TT 52:42] DCAP ▲ 8224117 [DDD] (13.97)
Suite in g for Keyboard, BuxWV 242
L. U. Mortensen (hpd) *(rec Skt. Matthaeus Kirken, Copenhagen, Denmark)* ("Harpsichord Music-Vol. 2") † Canzona; Canzonetta, BuxWV 171; Courant zimble, BuxWV 245; Fugue; More Palatino, BuxWV 247; Nun lob, mein Seel, den Herren, BuxWV 215; Suite Kbd [TT 52:42] DCAP ▲ 8224117 [DDD] (13.97)

BYRD, WILLIAM (1543-1623)
The Battelle (suite) for Band (1591)
W. Berz (cnd), Rutgers Univ Wind Ensemble [trans Jacob] ("Transformations") † Joio:Fants on Haydn; Lampl:Statiphony; Mennin:Canzona; R. Nelson:Courtly Airs & Dances [TT 1:01:31] MRES ▲ 2291

CAGE, JOHN (1912-1992)
For M.C. & D.T. for Piano (1952)
S. Schleiermacher (pno) *(rec Fürstliche Reitbahn Arolsen, Germany, 1998-99)* † For Paul Taylor & Anita Dencks; Haiku (5) Pno; Haiku (7) Pno; Music Walk; Solo Pno; TV Koeln for Pno; Waiting; Water Music; Winter Music; 34' 46.776" [TT 1:56:08] MDG 2-▲ 6130787 [DDD] (32.97)
For Paul Taylor & Anita Dencks for Piano (1957)
S. Schleiermacher (pno) *(rec Fürstliche Reitbahn Arolsen, Germany, 1998-99)* † For M.C. & D.T.; Haiku (5) Pno; Haiku (7) Pno; Music Walk; Solo Pno; TV Koeln for Pno; Waiting; Water Music; Winter Music; 34' 46.776" [TT 1:56:08] MDG 2-▲ 6130787 [DDD] (32.97)
Haiku (5) for Piano (1951)
S. Schleiermacher (pno) *(rec Fürstliche Reitbahn Arolsen, Germany, 1998-99)* † For M.C. & D.T.; For Paul Taylor & Anita Dencks; Haiku (7) Pno; Music Walk; Solo Pno; TV Koeln for Pno; Waiting; Water Music; Winter Music; 34' 46.776" [TT 1:56:08] MDG 2-▲ 6130787 [DDD] (32.97)
Haiku (7) for Piano (1952)
S. Schleiermacher (pno) *(rec Fürstliche Reitbahn Arolsen, Germany, 1998-99)* † For M.C. & D.T.; For Paul Taylor & Anita Dencks; Haiku (5) Pno; Music Walk; Solo Pno; TV Koeln for Pno; Waiting; Water Music; Winter Music; 34' 46.776" [TT 1:56:08] MDG 2-▲ 6130787 [DDD] (32.97)
Music for...for Variable Instruments (1984)
M. Mumelter (vn), W. Yang (vc), W. Bärtschi (pno)—Music for 3 Pnos † C. Ives:Trio KSCH ▲ 367142 (6.97)
Music Walk for Piano (1 or more players) (1958)
S. Schleiermacher (pno) *(rec Fürstliche Reitbahn Arolsen, Germany, 1998-99)* † For M.C. & D.T.; For Paul Taylor & Anita Dencks; Haiku (5) Pno; Haiku (7) Pno; Solo Pno; TV Koeln for Pno; Waiting; Water Music; Winter Music; 34' 46.776" [TT 1:56:08] MDG 2-▲ 6130787 [DDD] (32.97)
Solo for Piano (1958)
artist unknown *(rec Fürstliche Reitbahn Arolsen, Germany, 1998-99)* † For M.C. & D.T.; For Paul Taylor & Anita Dencks; Haiku (5) Pno; Haiku (7) Pno; Music Walk; TV Koeln for Pno; Waiting; Water Music; Winter Music; 34' 46.776" [TT 1:56:08] MDG 2-▲ 6130787 [DDD] (32.97)
Spoken
J. Cage (nar)—Series re Morris Graves; Art is Either a Complaint or Do Something Else; What You Say ("Text Pieces 1-Artist Pieces (spoken)") MODE ▲ 84 (32.97)
34' 46.776" for Piano (1954)
S. Schleiermacher (pno) *(rec Fürstliche Reitbahn Arolsen, Germany, 1998-99)* † For M.C. & D.T.; For Paul Taylor & Anita Dencks; Haiku (5) Pno; Haiku (7) Pno; Music Walk; Solo Pno; TV Koeln for Pno; Waiting; Water Music; Winter Music [TT 1:56:08] MDG 2-▲ 6130787 [DDD] (32.97)
TV Koeln for Piano (1958)
S. Schleiermacher (pno) *(rec Fürstliche Reitbahn Arolsen, Germany, 1998-99)* † For M.C. & D.T.; For Paul Taylor & Anita Dencks; Haiku (5) Pno; Haiku (7) Pno; Music Walk; Solo Pno; Waiting; Water Music; Winter Music; 34' 46.776" [TT 1:56:08] MDG 2-▲ 6130787 [DDD] (32.97)
Waiting for Piano (1952)
S. Schleiermacher (pno) *(rec Fürstliche Reitbahn Arolsen, Germany, 1998-99)* † For M.C. & D.T.; For Paul Taylor & Anita Dencks; Haiku (5) Pno; Haiku (7) Pno; Music Walk; Solo Pno; TV Koeln for Pno; Water Music; Winter Music; 34' 46.776" [TT 1:56:08] MDG 2-▲ 6130787 [DDD] (32.97)
Water Music for Piano (1952)
S. Schleiermacher (pno) *(rec Fürstliche Reitbahn Arolsen, Germany, Feb 8, 1998)* † For M.C. & D.T.; For Paul Taylor & Anita Dencks; Haiku (5) Pno; Haiku (7) Pno; Music Walk; Solo Pno; TV Koeln for Pno; Waiting; Winter Music; 34' 46.776" [TT 1:56:08] MDG 2-▲ 6130787 [DDD] (32.97)
Winter Music for 1, 2, 320 Piano(s) (1957)
S. Schleiermacher (pno) *(rec Fürstliche Reitbahn Arolsen, Germany, 1998-99)* † For M.C. & D.T.; For Paul Taylor & Anita Dencks; Haiku (5) Pno; Haiku (7) Pno; Music Walk; Solo Pno; TV Koeln for Pno; Waiting; Water Music; 34' 46.776" [TT 1:56:08] MDG 2-▲ 6130787 [DDD] (32.97)

CAMPHOUSE, MARK (20th cent)
Watchman, Tell Us of the Night for Symphonic Band
Concordia Univ. Wind Sym *(rec Chapel of Our Lord, Concordia University, IL, Mar. 21-23, 1997)* ("Watchman, Tell Us of the Night") † F. J. Allen:Abide with Me; Martyr; Anonymous:Jesus, Jesus, Rest Your Head; J. Curnow:Fanfare Prelude; Nelhybel:Praise to the Lord; C. T. Smith:God of Our Fathers; J. Stamp:Ere the World Began to Be; Vars on Bach Chorale [TT 1:01:07] MRES ▲ 2381

CAMPRA, ANDRÉ (1660-1744)
Idomenée (lyric tragedy in 5 acts) [lib. Danchet] (1712)
W. Christie (cnd), Les Arts Florissants, M. Saint-Palais (sop), S. Piau (sop), M. Zanetti (sop), A. Pichard (sop), A. Mopin (sop), M. Boyer (mez), J. Fouchécourt (ten), R. Duguay (ten), B. Delétré (bass), J. Sarragosse (bass), J. Corréas (bass) HAM ▲ 2901396 (26.97)

CANNABICH, CHRISTIAN (1731-1798)
Symphony No. 47 (1772)
U. Grodd (cnd), Nicolaus Esterházy Sinfonia *(rec Pheonix Concert Studio, Budapest, Hungary, Feb 21-21, 1998)* † Sym 48; Sym 49; Sym 50; Sym 51; Sym 52 [TT 1:06:17] NXIN ▲ 8554340 [DDD] (5.97)
Symphony No. 48 (1772)
U. Grodd (cnd), Nicolaus Esterházy Sinfonia *(rec Pheonix Concert Studio, Budapest, Hungary, Feb 21-21, 1998)* † Sym 47; Sym 49; Sym 50; Sym 51; Sym 52 [TT 1:06:17] NXIN ▲ 8554340 [DDD] (5.97)
Symphony No. 49 (1772)
U. Grodd (cnd), Nicolaus Esterházy Sinfonia *(rec Pheonix Concert Studio, Budapest, Hungary, Feb 21-21, 1998)* † Sym 47; Sym 48; Sym 50; Sym 51; Sym 52 [TT 1:06:17] NXIN ▲ 8554340 [DDD] (5.97)

CANNABICH, CHRISTIAN (cont.)
Symphony No. 50 (1772)
U. Grodd (cnd), Nicolaus Esterházy Sinfonia *(rec Pheonix Concert Studio, Budapest, Hungary, Feb 21-21, 1998)* † Sym 47; Sym 48; Sym 49; Sym 51; Sym 52 [TT 1:06:17] NXIN ▲ 8554340 [DDD] (5.97)
Symphony No. 51 (1772)
U. Grodd (cnd), Nicolaus Esterházy Sinfonia *(rec Pheonix Concert Studio, Budapest, Hungary, Feb 21-21, 1998)* † Sym 47; Sym 48; Sym 49; Sym 50; Sym 52 [TT 1:06:17] NXIN ▲ 8554340 [DDD] (5.97)
Symphony No. 52 (1772)
U. Grodd (cnd), Nicolaus Esterházy Sinfonia *(rec Pheonix Concert Studio, Budapest, Hungary, Feb 21-21, 1998)* † Sym 47; Sym 48; Sym 49; Sym 50; Sym 51 [TT 1:06:17] NXIN ▲ 8554340 [DDD] (5.97)

CAPLET, ANDRE (1878-1925)
Divertissements (2) for solo Harp (1924)
A. Griffiths (hp)—A la francaise † J. L. Dussek:Son in E for Hp, Op. 34/1; Mortari:Son Prodigio; O. Respighi:Siciliana; Rubbra:Pezzo ostinato, Op. 102; A. Templeton:Siciliana Ob CFP ▲ 72701 (11.97)

CAPUZZI, ANTONIO (1755-1818)
Concerto for Double Bass
J. Funderburk (tuba), O. Skidan (pno) [trans Catelinet] *(rec Russel Hall Auditorium, Northern Iowa University, IA, 1995-96)* † B. Broughton:Son Tb; R. Jones:Dialogs Tuba; J. Koetsier:Sonatina Tuba; A. Lebedev:Con Allegro; Con Tuba; W. A. Mozart:Zauberflöte (sels); R. Vaughan:Concertpiece 1 [TT 57:03] MRES ▲ 2199

CAREY, HENRY (1689-1743)
Belinda and Eurillo, "Regardless of Her Sighing Swain" (cantata) (1732)
M. Ashton (sop), Concert Royal *(rec St. Mungo's Church, Simonburn, Northumberland, England, Apr 1994)* ("Cantatas from the Georgian Drawing Room") † Albinoni:Under Ye Gloomy Shade; T. Arne:Cymon & Iphigenia; H. Burgess:Caelia; J. Eccles:Love Kindled in a Breast Too Young; N. Pasquali:Pastora; Pepusch:English Cants Book I; Island of Beauty [TT 1:01:32] ORCH ▲ 2927 [DDD] (17.97)

CARPENTER, GARY (dates unknown)
Une Semaine de Bonte for Saxophone Quartet
Quartz Saxophone Quartet ("Faces") † J. S. Bach:Art of the Fugue (sels); J. Buckley:Qt Sax; G. Fitkin:Stub; A. Levine:Faces; M. Nyman:Songs for Tony BBCL ▲ 1024 (16.97)

CARTER, ELLIOTT (1908-
Etudes (8) & a Fantasy for Flute, Oboe, Clarinet & Bassoon (1950)
J. B. Yeh (cnd), Chicago Pro Musica *(rec Chicago, IL, 1997-99)* † Pastorale E Hn; Qnt Ww; Son Vc [TT 52:41] CED ▲ 48 [DDD] (16.97)
Pastorale for English Horn (or Viola/Clarinet) & Piano (1940)
J. B. Yeh (cnd), Chicago Pro Musica *(rec Chicago, IL, 1997-99)* † Etudes & Fant; Qnt Ww; Son Vc [TT 52:41] CED ▲ 48 [DDD] (16.97)
Quintet for Woodwinds (1948)
J. B. Yeh (cnd), Chicago Pro Musica *(rec Chicago, IL, 1997-99)* † Etudes & Fant; Pastorale E Hn; Son Vc [TT 52:41] CED ▲ 48 [DDD] (16.97)
Sonata for Cello & Piano (1948)
B. Haffner (vc), J. B. Yeh (cnd), Chicago Pro Musica *(rec Chicago, IL, 1997-99)* † Etudes & Fant; Pastorale E Hn; Qnt Ww [TT 52:41] CED ▲ 48 [DDD] (16.97)

CASELLA, ALFREDO (1883-1947)
Pupazzetti for Piano 4-Hands, Op. 27 (1915; orchd 1920)
Bradshaw & Buono Piano Duo † A. Bax:Poisoned Fountain; Debussy:Danses sacrée et profane; Petite suite Pno; Prélude à l'après-midi d'un faune; M. Ravel:Frontispiece; Ma mère l'oye Suite Pno CSOC ▲ 4171

CASTRO, CARLOS CRUZ DE (1941-
Concierto for Guitar & Strings
W. Weigel (gtr), P. Schmelzer (cnd), European Masters Orch † Benguerel:Tempo Gtr; T. Marco:Con Guadiana DI ▲ 920530 (5.97)

CEREROLS, JOAN (1618-1676)
Choral Music
J. Cabré (cnd), Capilla Peñaflorida—Fuera, que va de invencion; Ha de los hombres; Son tus bellos ojos soles; ¡Ay, qué dolor! *(rec Church of Assumption, Sajazarra, Spain, July 1999)* ("Música Española- Salve Reyna") † Anonymous:Choral Music; J. Hidalgo:Choral Music; Martín y Coll:Choral Music; Patiño:Choral Music; J. G. Salazar:Choral Music GLIS ▲ 5 [DDD] (17.97)

CHABRIER, EMMANUEL (1841-1894)
Cortège burlesque for Piano
A. Tharaud (pno) † España; Prélude et marche française; Souvenir de Brunehaut; Souvenirs de Munich; Sylvia; 3 Valses romantiques ARN ▲ 68450 (16.97)
España for Piano
A. Tharaud (pno), A. Madžar (pno) † Cortège burlesque; Prélude et marche française; Souvenir de Brunehaut; Souvenirs de Munich; Sylvia; 3 Valses romantiques ARN ▲ 68450 (16.97)
Prélude et marche française for Piano
A. Tharaud (pno) † Cortège burlesque; España; Souvenir de Brunehaut; Souvenirs de Munich; Sylvia; 3 Valses romantiques ARN ▲ 68450 (16.97)
Souvenir de Brunehaut for Piano
A. Tharaud (pno) † Cortège burlesque; España; Prélude et marche française; Souvenirs de Munich; Sylvia; 3 Valses romantiques ARN ▲ 68450 (16.97)
Souvenirs de Munich for Piano 4-Hands
A. Tharaud (pno), A. Madžar (pno) † Cortège burlesque; España; Prélude et marche française; Souvenir de Brunehaut; Sylvia; 3 Valses romantiques ARN ▲ 68450 (16.97)
Sylvia for Piano
A. Tharaud (pno), A. Madžar (pno) † Cortège burlesque; España; Prélude et marche française; Souvenir de Brunehaut; Souvenirs de Munich; 3 Valses romantiques ARN ▲ 68450 (16.97)
3 Valses romantiques for 2 Pianos
A. Tharaud (pno), A. Madžar (pno) † Cortège burlesque; España; Prélude et marche française; Souvenir de Brunehaut; Souvenirs de Munich; Sylvia ARN ▲ 68450 (16.97)

CHAMBERS, EVAN (1963-
Concerto for Fiddle, Violin & Orchestra
J. Levy (vn), C. Nollaig (vn), D. A. Miller (cnd), Albany SO, Present Music † R. Adams:Brutal Reality; A. Bloom:Life is Like a Box of Chocolates; Ince:Fest; J. F. Rogers:Verge ALBA ▲ 354 [DDD] (16.97)

CHAMINADE, CÉCILE (1857-1944)
L'Ondine for Piano, Op. 101
A. Muller-Roos (pno) † Muller-Roos:Pieces Pno; C. Schumann:Romances Pno, Op. 21 NSAG ▲ 39 [DDD] (16.97)

CHARPENTIER, JACQUES (1933-
Gavambodi 2 for Saxophone & Piano (1966)
A. Bornkamp (sax), I. Janssen (pno) *(rec Amsterdam, Netherlands, Oct 1989)* † Creston:Son Sax, Op. 19; E. Denisov:Son alt Sax; A. Desenclos:Prélude, cadence et finale; P. Hindemith:Son Hn; F. Schmitt:Légende, Op. 66 [TT 1:06:01] GLOE ▲ 6049 [DDD] (16.97)

CHARPENTIER, MARC-ANTOINE (1645-1704)
Caecilia, Virgo et Martyr
W. Christie (cnd), Les Arts Florissants † Filius Prodigus; Magnificat HAM (Musique d'abord) ▲ 190066 (9.97)
Filius Prodigus
W. Christie (cnd), Les Arts Florissants † Caecilia, Virgo et Martyr; Magnificat HAM (Musique d'abord) ▲ 190066 (9.97)
Magnificat for SATB soloists, Orchestra & Chorus
W. Christie (cnd), Les Arts Florissants † Caecilia, Virgo et Martyr; Filius Prodigus HAM (Musique d'abord) ▲ 190066 (9.97)
Medée (opera in prologue & 5 acts) [lib. Thomas Corneille], H.491 (1693)
W. Christie (cnd), Les Arts Florissants, A. Mellon (sop), J. Feldman (sop), S. Boulin (sop), P. Cantor (ten), G. Ragon (ten), J. Bona (bar) HAM 3-▲ 2901139 (26.97)

CHAUSSON, ERNEST (1855-1899)
Poème for Violin & Orchestra, Op. 25 (1882-90; rev 1893)
V. Repin (vn), K. Nagano (cnd), London SO † Lalo:Sym espagnole, Op. 21; M. Ravel:Tzigane ERAT ▲ 27314 (16.97)
Quartet in A for Piano & Strings, Op. 30 (1897)
B. Kim (vn), P. Neubauer (va), P. Rejto (vc), R. Votapek (pno) *(rec Tuscon, AZ, March 1999)* ("Sixth Annual Tuscon Chamber Music Festival") † G. Fauré:Qt 2 Pno, Op. 45 [TT 1:13:00] ARIZ ▲ 991 (16.97)
Trio in g for Piano, Violin & Cello, Op. 3 (1881)
Wanderer Trio † M. Ravel:Trio Pno LCDM ▲ 2781114 (18.97)

NEW RELEASES 9

CHÁVEZ, CARLOS (1899-1978)

Symphony No. 2, "Sinfonia India" (1935-36)

A. J. Garcia (vn), E. G. Asensio (cnd), RTVE SO, RTVE Sym Chorus ("Musica Iberoamericana") † Ginastera:Estancia, Op. 8; R. Halffter:Con Vn; H. Villa-Lobos:Chôro 10 RTVE ▲ 65029 (16.97)

CHEETHAM, JOHN (1939-

Allusions for Brass Quintet

EKU Brass Quintet *(rec Eastern Kentucky University, Richmond, KY)* ("Menagerie") † A Brass Menagerie; Colloquies; Scherzo; T. R. George:Fanfare 7; Qnt 4 Brass; Qnt 5 Brass [TT 1:03:59] MRES ▲ 2331

A Brass Menagerie for Brass Quintet (1985)

EKU Brass Quintet *(rec Eastern Kentucky University, Richmond, KY)* ("Menagerie") † Allusions; Colloquies; Scherzo; T. R. George:Fanfare 7; Qnt 4 Brass; Qnt 5 Brass [TT 1:03:59] MRES ▲ 2331

Colloquies for Brass Quintet (1992)

EKU Brass Quintet *(rec Eastern Kentucky University, Richmond, KY)* ("Menagerie") † A Brass Menagerie; Allusions; Scherzo; T. R. George:Fanfare 7; Qnt 4 Brass; Qnt 5 Brass [TT 1:03:59] MRES ▲ 2331

Scherzo for Brass Quintet (1962)

EKU Brass Quintet *(rec Eastern Kentucky University, Richmond, KY)* ("Menagerie") † A Brass Menagerie; Allusions; Colloquies; T. R. George:Fanfare 7; Qnt 4 Brass; Qnt 5 Brass [TT 1:03:59] MRES ▲ 2331

CHERUBINI, LUIGI (1760-1842)

Anacréon:Overture

A. Toscanini (cnd), BBC SO *(rec Queens's Hall, London, England, June 3, 1935)* ("Toscanini") † Beethoven:Missa Solemnis, Op. 123; Sym 7; W. A. Mozart:Sym 35, K.385 [TT 2:22:50] BBC (BBC Legends) ▲ 4016 (m) [ADD] (24.97)

Médée (opera in 3 acts) [lib Hoffman] (1797)

V. Gui (cnd), Coro del Teatro alla Scala di Milano, M. Callas (sop), G. Tucci (sop), F. Barbieri (mez), M. Petri (bass), M. Frosini (bass) *(rec live, Firenze, Italy, 1953)* MELO ▲ 20037 [ADD] (31.97)

CHESNOKOV, PAVEL (1877-1944)

Salvation is Created for Chorus

Univ of Georgia Wind Symphony [arr Housenecht] *(rec UGA Performing Arts Center, GA, Mar. 1998)* ("The Riddle of the Sphinx") † A. R. Forte:Riddle of the Sphinx; V. Giannini:Sym 3; Gillingham:Con Per; McTee:Soundings [TT 1:06:25] MRES ▲ 2871

CHILDS, WILLIAM (1957-

Concerto for Percussion (1986)

S. Houghton (perc) *(rec Artemus Ham Concert Hall, Las Vegas, NV, 1996)* ("Gawd$illa Eats Las Vegas") † Bocook:Fanfare & Hymn; K. L. King:Big Cage; P. Sparke:Celebration; Ticheli:Amazing Grace; Van der Roost:Canterbury Chorale; Whitacre:Gawd$illa Eats Las Vegas [TT 1:03:11] MRES ▲ 2570

CHOPIN, FRÉDÉRIC (1810-1849)

Allegro de concert in A for Piano, Op. 46 (1832-41)

N. Magaloff (pno) *(rec 1978)* † Bolero; Ecossaises (3) Pno, Op. 72/3; Intro & Vars in B♭, Op. 12; Mazurkas Pno; Nocturnes Pno; Rondos (4) Pno; Son Pno in c, Op. 4; Tarentelle, Op. 43; J. Haydn:Son 58 Kbd, H.XVI/48; Liszt:Grandes études de Paganini, S.141; R. Schumann:Carnaval, Op. 9 PPHI (Great Pianists of the 20th Century) ▲ 456898 (22.97)

Andante Spianato in G & Grande Polonaise in E♭ for Piano, Op. 22 (1834)

A. Brendel (pno) † Polonaise 4 Pno, Op. 40/2; Polonaise 5 Pno, Op. 44; Polonaise 6 Pno, Op. 53; Polonaises-fant, Op. 61 VC ▲ 127 (13.97)

K. Radziwonowicz (pno) † Études Pno; Con 1 Pno, Op. 11; Con 2 Pno, Op. 21; Fantasy, Op. 13; Intro & Polonaise, Op. 3; Krakowiak, Op. 14; Largo in E♭; Prelude in c#, Op. 45; Preludes (24) Pno, Op. 28; Vars on Mozart, Op. 2; Waltzes Pno TANE ▲ 9909 (24.97)

Ballades (4) for Piano, Opp. 23, 38, 47, 52 (1831-42)

M. Pollini (pno) † Fantaisie Pno, Op. 49; Prelude in c#, Op. 45 DEUT ▲ 459683 (16.97)

Ballade in f for Piano, Op. 52 (1842)

R. Smith (pno) *(rec St George's, Brandon Hill, Bristol, England, Oct 26-28, 1998)* † Barcarolle Pno, Op. 60; Fantaisie Pno, Op. 49; Mazurkas Pno; Nocturnes Pno; Polonaises-fant, Op. 61; Scherzos Pno; Tarentelle, Op. 43 [TT 1:18:59] APR ▲ 5565 [DDD] (18.97)

Solomon (pno) *(rec 1946)* † Berceuse, Op. 57; Fantaisie Pno, Op. 49; Polonaise 6 Pno, Op. 53; Beethoven:Son 29 Pno, Op. 106; J. Brahms:Intermezzos (3) Pno, Op. 117; Vars & Fugue on a Theme by Handel, Op. 24; Liszt:Etudes de concert (3), S.144; Années de pèlerinage 1, S.160; Hungarian Rhaps, S.244; Trans, Arrs & Paraphrases; W. A. Mozart:Son 13 Pno, K.333 PPHI (Great Pianists of the 20th Century) ▲ 456973 (22.97)

Barcarolle in F# for Piano, Op. 60 (1845-46)

V. Horowitz (pno) *(rec 1957)* † Études Pno; Mazurkas Pno; Polonaise 6 Pno, Op. 53; Beethoven:Con 5 Pno, Op. 73; S. Rachmaninoff:Con 3 Pno, Op. 30 PPHI (Great Pianists of the 20th Century) ▲ 456841 (22.97)

M. Pollini (pno) *(rec 1990)* † Études Pno; Berceuse, Op. 57; Con 1 Pno, Op. 11; Nocturnes Pno; Polonaise 5 Pno, Op. 44; Polonaise 6 Pno, Op. 53; Polonaises-fant, Op. 61; Son Pno in b♭, Op. 35 PPHI (Great Pianists of the 20th Century) ▲ 456940 (22.97)

R. Smith (pno) *(rec St George's, Brandon Hill, Bristol, England, Oct 26-28, 1998)* † Ballade 4 Pno, Op. 52; Fantaisie Pno, Op. 49; Mazurkas Pno; Nocturnes Pno; Polonaises-fant, Op. 61; Scherzos Pno; Tarentelle, Op. 43 [TT 1:18:59] APR ▲ 5565 [DDD] (18.97)

Berceuse in D♭ for Piano, Op. 57 (1843-44)

M. Pollini (pno) *(rec 1990)* † Études Pno; Barcarolle Pno, Op. 60; Con 1 Pno, Op. 11; Nocturnes Pno; Polonaise 5 Pno, Op. 44; Polonaise 6 Pno, Op. 53; Polonaises-fant, Op. 61; Son Pno in b♭, Op. 35 PPHI (Great Pianists of the 20th Century) ▲ 456940 (22.97)

Solomon (pno) *(rec 1942)* † Ballade 4 Pno, Op. 52; Fantaisie Pno, Op. 49; Polonaise 6 Pno, Op. 53; Beethoven:Son 29 Pno, Op. 106; J. Brahms:Intermezzos (3) Pno, Op. 117; Vars & Fugue on a Theme by Handel, Op. 24; Liszt:Etudes de concert (3), S.144; Années de pèlerinage 1, S.160; Hungarian Rhaps, S.244; Trans, Arrs & Paraphrases; W. A. Mozart:Son 13 Pno, K.333 PPHI (Great Pianists of the 20th Century) ▲ 456973 (22.97)

Bolero in C/A for Piano, Op. 19 (1833)

N. Magaloff (pno) *(rec 1978)* † Allegro de concert, Op. 46; Ecossaises (3) Pno, Op. 72/3; Intro & Vars in B♭, Op. 12; Mazurkas Pno; Nocturnes Pno; Rondos (4) Pno; Son Pno in c, Op. 4; Tarentelle, Op. 43; J. Haydn:Son 58 Kbd, H.XVI/48; Liszt:Grandes études de Paganini, S.141; R. Schumann:Carnaval, Op. 9 PPHI (Great Pianists of the 20th Century) ▲ 456898 (22.97)

Cantabile in B♭ for Piano (1834)

T. Barto (pno) [Andantino only] † Contredanse; Nocturnes Pno; Preludes (24) Pno, Op. 28 [TT 1:05:19] CSER (Seraphim Classics) ▲ 73571 [DDD] (6.97)

The "Complete Chopin Edition" (the complete works of Chopin in 9 volumes)

M. Argerich (pno) *(Preludes (24) Pno, Op. 28; Prelude in c#, Op. 45; Prelude in A♭, Op. posth.)*, S. Bunin (pno) *(Impromptu in A♭, Op. 29; Impromptu in F#, Op. 36; Impromptu in G♭, Op. 51; Fant-Impromptu, Op. 66)*, M. Pollini (pno) *(Scherzos Pno [No. 1 in b, Op. 20; No. 2 in b♭/D♭, Op. 31; No. 3 in c#, Op. 39; No. 4 in E, Op. 54])*, L. Zilberstein (pno) *(Rondos (4) Pno [Rondo in c, Op. 1; Rondo in F, Op. 5, "a la Mazur"])*, M. Pletnev (pno) *(Intro & Rondo, Op. 16)*, K. Bauer (pno), H. Bung (pno) *(Rondos (4) Pnos [Rondo in C for 2 Pnos, Op. 73])* ("Vol. 6: Preludes/Impromptus/Scherzos/Rondos") DEUT 2-▲ 463063 [DDD] (22.97)

D. Barenboim (pno)—Nocturnes Pno ("Vol. 4: Nocturnes") DEUT 2-▲ 463057 [DDD] (22.97)

M. Pollini (pno) *(Polonaise 1 Pno, Op. 26/1; Polonaise 2 Pno, Op. 26/2; Polonaise 3 Pno, Op. 40/1; Polonaise 4 Pno, Op. 40/2; Polonaise 5 Pno, Op. 44; Polonaise 6 Pno, Op. 53; Polonaises-fant, Op. 61)*, M. Argerich (pno) *(Andante Spianato & Grand Polonaise, Op. 22)*, A. Ugorski (pno) *(Polonaises Pno [No. 8 in d, Op. 71/1; No. 10 in f, Op. 71/3; No. 11 in b♭; No. 12 in G♭; No. 13 in g; No. 14 in B♭; No. 15 in A♭; No. 16 in g#]; Polonaise 9 Pno, Op. 71/2; Bourrées; Galop Marquis; Albumleaf (Feuille d'Album); Cantabile in B♭; Fugue in a; Largo in E♭)* ("Vol. 5: Polonaises") DEUT 2-▲ 463060 [ADD] (22.97)

E. Szmytka (sop), M. Martineau (pno)—Songs Sop ("Vol. 9: Songs") DEUT ▲ 463072 [DDD] (11.97)

L. Zilberstein (pno) *(Son Pno in c, Op. 4; Vars in A, ('Souvenir de Paganini'); Vars brillantes, Op. 12)*, M. Pollini (pno) *(Son Pno in b♭, Op. 35; Son Pno in b, Op. 58)*, T. Vásáry (pno) *(Intro & Vars in E)*, V. Ashkenazy (pno), V. Ashkenazy (pno) *(Intro, Theme & Vars [Vars])*, V. Ashkenazy (pno) *(Var 6 Pno; Allegro de concert, Op. 46)*, A. Ugorski (pno) *(Bolero, Op. 19; Tarentelle, Op. 43)* ("Vol. 7: Sonatas/Variations/Bolero/Tarantella/Allegro de Concert") DEUT 2-▲ 463066 [DDD] (22.97)

L. Zilberstein (pno), J. Luisada (pno)—Mazurkas Pno ("Vol. 3: Mazurkas") DEUT 2-▲ 463054 [DDD] (22.97)

L. Zilberstein (pno), J. Luisada (pno) *(Waltzes Pno)*, Beaux Arts Trio *(Trio, Op. 8)*, M. Rostropovich (vc), M. Argerich (pno) *(Intro & Polonaise, Op. 3; Son Vc, Op. 65)*, A. Bylsma (vc), L. Orkis (pno) *(Grand Duo)* ("Vol. 8: Waltzes/Chamber Music") DEUT 2-▲ 463069 [DDD] (22.97)

K. Zimerman (pno) *(Ballade 1 Pno, Op. 23; Ballade 2 Pno, Op. 38; Ballade 3 Pno, Op. 47; Ballade 4 Pno, Op. 52; Fantaisie Pno, Op, 49)*, A. Ugorski (pno) *(Nouvelles études; Funeral March, Op. 72/2; Ecossaises (3) Pno, Op. 72/3)*, M. Pollini (pno) *(Études Pno; Barcarolle Pno, Op. 60; Berceuse, Op. 57)* ("Vol. 2: Ballades/Etudes") DEUT 2-▲ 463051 [DDD] (22.97)

CHOPIN, FRÉDÉRIC (cont.)

The "Complete Chopin Edition" (the complete works of Chopin in 9 volumes) (cont.)

K. Zimerman (pno), K. Kondrashin (cnd), (Royal) Concertgebouw Orch *(Con 1 Pno, Op. 11)*, K. Zimerman (pno), C. M. Giulini (cnd), Los Angeles PO *(Con 2 Pno, Op. 21; Andante Spianato & Grand Polonaise, Op. 22)*, C. Arrau (pno), E. Inbal (cnd), London Philharmonic SO *(Vars on Mozart, Op. 2)*, C. Arrau (pno), E. Inbal (cnd), London PO *(Fantasy, Op. 13)*, S. Askenase (pno), W. V. Otterloo (cnd), Residentie Orch The Hague *(Krakowiak, Op. 14)* ("Vol. 1: Piano Concertos/Works for Piano & Orches tra") DEUT 2-▲ 463048 [ADD] (22.97)

various artists ("Vols. 1-9") DEUT 9-▲ 463047 (194.97)

Concerto No. 1 in e for Piano & Orchestra, Op. 11 (1830)

M. Horszowski (pno), H. Swarowsky (cnd), Vienna State Opera Orch *(rec Sept 1952)* † Fantaisie Pno, Op. 49; Impromptus (4); Polonaise 4 Pno, Op. 40/2 [TT 1:17:04] RELE ▲ 911023 [ADD] (18.97)

M. Pollini (pno), P. Kletzki (cnd), Philharmonia Orch *(rec 1960)* † Études Pno; Barcarolle Pno, Op. 60; Berceuse, Op. 57; Nocturnes Pno; Polonaise 5 Pno, Op. 44; Polonaise 6 Pno, Op. 53; Polonaises-fant, Op. 61; Son Pno in b♭, Op. 35 PPHI (Great Pianists of the 20th Century) ▲ 456940 (22.97)

K. Radziwonowicz (pno) † Études Pno; Andante Spianato & Grand Polonaise, Op. 22; Con 2 Pno, Op. 21; Fantasy, Op. 13; Intro & Polonaise, Op. 3; Krakowiak, Op. 14; Largo in E♭; Prelude in c#, Op. 45; Preludes (24) Pno, Op. 28; Vars on Mozart, Op. 2; Waltzes Pno TANE ▲ 9909 (24.97)

K. Zimerman (pno), K. Zimerman (cnd), Polish Festival Orch † Con 2 Pno, Op. 21 DEUT ▲ 459684 (17.97)

Concerto No. 2 in f for Piano & Orchestra, Op. 21 (1829-30)

K. Radziwonowicz (pno) † Études Pno; Andante Spianato & Grand Polonaise, Op. 22; Con 1 Pno, Op. 11; Fantasy, Op. 13; Intro & Polonaise, Op. 3; Krakowiak, Op. 14; Largo in E♭; Prelude in c#, Op. 45; Preludes (24) Pno, Op. 28; Vars on Mozart, Op. 2; Waltzes Pno TANE ▲ 9909 (24.97)

K. Zimerman (pno), K. Zimerman (cnd), Polish Festival Orch † Con 1 Pno, Op. 11 DEUT ▲ 459684 (17.97)

Contredanse in G♭ for Piano (?1827)

T. Barto (pno) [Allegretto only] † Cantabile in B♭; Nocturnes Pno; Preludes (24) Pno, Op. 28 [TT 1:05:19] CSER (Seraphim Classics) ▲ 73571 [DDD] (6.97)

Ecossaises (3) in D, G & D♭ for Piano, Op. 72/3 (1826)

N. Magaloff (pno) *(rec 1978)* † Allegro de concert, Op. 46; Bolero; Intro & Vars in B♭, Op. 12; Mazurkas Pno; Nocturnes Pno; Rondos (4) Pno; Son Pno in c, Op. 4; Tarentelle, Op. 43; J. Haydn:Son 58 Kbd, H.XVI/48; Liszt:Grandes études de Paganini, S.141; R. Schumann:Carnaval, Op. 9 PPHI (Great Pianists of the 20th Century) ▲ 456898 (22.97)

Études (24) for Piano, Op. 10 (1829-32) & Op. 25 (1832-36)

V. Horowitz (pno)—No. 4 in c#, Op. 10/4; No. 5 in G♭, Op. 10/5, "Black Keys"; No. 8 in D♭, Op. 10/8; No. 15 in F, Op. 25/3; No. 3 in E, Op. 10/3, "Tristesse"; No. 4 in c#, Op. 10/4; No. 5 in G♭, Op. 10/5, "Black Keys" *(rec 1951)* † Barcarolle Pno, Op. 60; Mazurkas Pno; Polonaise 6 Pno, Op. 53; Beethoven:Con 5 Pno, Op. 73; S. Rachmaninoff:Con 3 Pno, Op. 30 PPHI (Great Pianists of the 20th Century) ▲ 456841 (22.97)

N. Krieger (pno)—No. 13 in A♭, Op. 25/1; No. 12 in c, Op. 10/12, "Revolutionary" † Nocturnes Pno; J. S. Bach:Partitas Hpd; Beethoven:Son 17 Pno, Op. 31/2; W. A. Mozart:Son 10 Pno, K.330 ARII ▲ 491 (17.97)

M. Pollini (pno)—Nos. 1-12, Op. 10 *(rec 1972)* † Barcarolle Pno, Op. 60; Berceuse, Op. 57; Con 1 Pno, Op. 11; Nocturnes Pno; Polonaise 5 Pno, Op. 44; Polonaise 6 Pno, Op. 53; Polonaises-fant, Op. 61; Son Pno in b♭, Op. 35 PPHI (Great Pianists of the 20th Century) ▲ 456940 (22.97)

K. Radziwonowicz (pno) † Andante Spianato & Grand Polonaise, Op. 22; Con 1 Pno, Op. 11; Con 2 Pno, Op. 21; Fantasy, Op. 13; Intro & Polonaise, Op. 3; Krakowiak, Op. 14; Largo in E♭; Prelude in c#, Op. 45; Preludes (24) Pno, Op. 28; Vars on Mozart, Op. 2; Waltzes Pno TANE ▲ 9909 (24.97)

I. Vered (pno)—No. 3 in E, Op. 10/3, "Tristesse"; No. 4 in c#, Op. 10/4; No. 8 in D♭, Op. 10/8; No. 12 in c, Op. 10/12, "Revolutionary" † Liszt:Grandes études de Paganini, S.141; Moszkowski:Etude de virtuosité, Op. 72 CSOC ▲ 4197

Fantaisie in f for Piano, Op. 49 (1841)

M. Horszowski (pno) *(rec live, May 1973)* † Con 1 Pno, Op. 11; Impromptus (4); Polonaise 4 Pno, Op. 40/2 [TT 1:17:04] RELE ▲ 911023 [ADD] (18.97)

M. Pollini (pno) † Ballades (4) Pno; Prelude in c#, Op. 45 DEUT ▲ 459683 (16.97)

R. Smith (pno) *(rec St George's, Brandon Hill, Bristol, England, Oct 26-28, 1998)* † Ballade 4 Pno, Op. 52; Barcarolle Pno, Op. 60; Mazurkas Pno; Nocturnes Pno; Polonaises-fant, Op. 61; Scherzos Pno; Tarentelle, Op. 43 [TT 1:18:59] APR ▲ 5565 [DDD] (18.97)

Solomon (pno) *(rec 1932)* † Ballade 4 Pno, Op. 52; Berceuse, Op. 57; Polonaise 6 Pno, Op. 53; Beethoven:Son 29 Pno, Op. 106; J. Brahms:Intermezzos (3) Pno, Op. 117; Vars & Fugue on a Theme by Handel, Op. 24; Liszt:Études de concert (3), S.144; Années de pèlerinage 1, S.160; Hungarian Rhaps, S.244; Trans, Arrs & Paraphrases; W. A. Mozart:Son 13 Pno, K.333 PPHI (Great Pianists of the 20th Century) ▲ 456973 (22.97)

Fantasy on Polish Airs in A, Op. 13 (1828)

K. Radziwonowicz (pno) † Études Pno; Andante Spianato & Grand Polonaise, Op. 22; Con 1 Pno, Op. 11; Con 2 Pno, Op. 21; Intro & Polonaise, Op. 3; Krakowiak, Op. 14; Largo in E♭; Prelude in c#, Op. 45; Preludes (24) Pno, Op. 28; Vars on Mozart, Op. 2; Waltzes Pno TANE ▲ 9909 (24.97)

Impromptus (4) in A♭, F#, G♭ & c# for Piano, Opp. 29, 36, 51, 66

M. Horszowski (pno) *(rec Sept 1952)* † Con 1 Pno, Op. 11; Fantaisie Pno, Op. 49; Polonaise 4 Pno, Op. 40/2 [TT 1:17:04] RELE ▲ 911023 [ADD] (18.97)

Introduction & Polonaise in C for Cello & Piano, Op. 3, "Polonaise brilliante" (1829-30)

K. Radziwonowicz (pno) † Études Pno; Andante Spianato & Grand Polonaise, Op. 22; Con 1 Pno, Op. 11; Con 2 Pno, Op. 21; Fantasy, Op. 13; Krakowiak, Op. 14; Largo in E♭; Prelude in c#, Op. 45; Preludes (24) Pno, Op. 28; Vars on Mozart, Op. 2; Waltzes Pno TANE ▲ 9909 (24.97)

Introduction & Variations in B♭ on "Je vends des scalpulaines" [from Hérold's Ludovic] for Piano, Op. 12 (1833)

N. Magaloff (pno) *(rec 1978)* † Allegro de concert, Op. 46; Bolero; Ecossaises (3) Pno, Op. 72/3; Mazurkas Pno; Nocturnes Pno; Rondos (4) Pno; Son Pno in c, Op. 4; Tarentelle, Op. 43; J. Haydn:Son 58 Kbd, H.XVI/48; Liszt:Grandes études de Paganini, S.141; R. Schumann:Carnaval, Op. 9 PPHI (Great Pianists of the 20th Century) ▲ 456898 (22.97)

Krakowiak (rondo) in F for Piano & Orchestra, Op. 14 (1828)

K. Radziwonowicz (pno) † Études Pno; Andante Spianato & Grand Polonaise, Op. 22; Con 1 Pno, Op. 11; Con 2 Pno, Op. 21; Fantasy, Op. 13; Intro & Polonaise, Op. 3; Largo in E♭; Prelude in c#, Op. 45; Preludes (24) Pno, Op. 28; Vars on Mozart, Op. 2; Waltzes Pno TANE ▲ 9909 (24.97)

Largo in E♭ for Piano (?1837)

K. Radziwonowicz (pno) † Études Pno; Andante Spianato & Grand Polonaise, Op. 22; Con 1 Pno, Op. 11; Con 2 Pno, Op. 21; Fantasy, Op. 13; Intro & Polonaise, Op. 3; Krakowiak, Op. 14; Prelude in c#, Op. 45; Preludes (24) Pno, Op. 28; Vars on Mozart, Op. 2; Waltzes Pno TANE ▲ 9909 (24.97)

Mazurkas for Piano

V. Horowitz (pno)—No. 21 in c#, Op. 30/4; No. 7 in f, Op. 7/3; No. 27 in e, Op. 41/2; No. 32 in c#, Op. 50/3; No. 17 in b♭, Op. 24/4; No. 19 in b/f#, Op. 30/2; No. 21 in c#, Op. 30/4; No. 20 in D♭, Op. 30/3; No. 38 in f#, Op. 59/3; No. 26 in ç#, Op. 41/1; No. 32 in c#, Op. 50/3; No. 7 in f, Op. 7/3; No. 41 in c#, Op. 63/3; No. 40 in f, Op. 63/2 *(rec 1950)* † Études Pno; Barcarolle Pno, Op. 60; Polonaise 6 Pno, Op. 53; Beethoven:Con 5 Pno, Op. 73; S. Rachmaninoff:Con 3 Pno, Op. 30 PPHI (Great Pianists of the 20th Century) ▲ 456841 (22.97)

N. Magaloff (pno)—No. 10 in B♭, Op. 17/1; No. 11 in e, Op. 17/2; No. 12 in A♭, Op. 17/3; No. 13 in a, Op. 17/4 *(rec 1977)* † Allegro de concert, Op. 46; Bolero; Ecossaises (3) Pno, Op. 72/3; Intro & Vars in B♭, Op. 12; Nocturnes Pno; Rondos (4) Pno; Son Pno in c, Op. 4; Tarentelle, Op. 43; J. Haydn:Son 58 Kbd, H.XVI/48; Liszt:Grandes études de Paganini, S.141; R. Schumann:Carnaval, Op. 9 PPHI (Great Pianists of the 20th Century) ▲ 456898 (22.97)

R. Smith (pno)—No. 13 in a, Op. 17/4 *(rec St George's, Brandon Hill, Bristol, England, Oct 26-28, 1998)* † Ballade 4 Pno, Op. 52; Barcarolle Pno, Op. 60; Fantaisie Pno, Op. 49; Nocturnes Pno; Polonaises-fant, Op. 61; Scherzos Pno; Tarentelle, Op. 43 [TT 1:18:59] APR ▲ 5565 [DDD] (18.97)

Mazurkas (4) for Piano

N. Magaloff (pno)—No. 10 in B♭, Op. 17/1; No. 11 in e, Op. 17/2; No. 12 in A♭, Op. 17/3; No. 13 in a, Op. 17/4 *(rec 1977)* † Allegro de concert, Op. 46; Bolero; Ecossaises (3) Pno, Op. 72/3; Intro & Vars in B♭, Op. 12; Nocturnes Pno; Rondos (4) Pno; Son Pno in c, Op. 4; Tarentelle, Op. 43; J. Haydn:Son 58 Kbd, H.XVI/48; Liszt:Grandes études de Paganini, S.141; R. Schumann:Carnaval, Op. 9 PPHI (Great Pianists of the 20th Century) ▲ 456898 (22.97)

Mazurkas for Piano

V. Horowitz (pno)—No. 21 in c#, Op. 30/4; No. 7 in f, Op. 7/3; No. 27 in e, Op. 41/2; No. 32 in c#, Op. 50/3; No. 17 in b♭, Op. 24/4; No. 19 in b/f#, Op. 30/2; No. 21 in c#, Op. 30/4; No. 20 in D♭, Op. 30/3; No. 38 in f#, Op. 59/3; No. 26 in ç#, Op. 41/1; No. 32 in c#, Op. 50/3; No. 7 in f, Op. 7/3; No. 41 in c#, Op. 63/3; No. 40 in f, Op. 63/2 *(rec live, 1945)* † Études Pno; Barcarolle Pno, Op. 60; Polonaise 6 Pno, Op. 53; Beethoven:Con 5 Pno, Op. 73; S. Rachmaninoff:Con 3 Pno, Op. 30 PPHI (Great Pianists of the 20th Century) ▲ 456841 (22.97)

N. Magaloff (pno)—No. 10 in B♭, Op. 17/1; No. 11 in e, Op. 17/2; No. 12 in A♭, Op. 17/3; No. 13 in a, Op. 17/4 *(rec 1977)* † Allegro de concert, Op. 46; Bolero; Ecossaises (3) Pno, Op. 72/3; Intro & Vars in B♭, Op. 12; Nocturnes Pno; Rondos (4) Pno; Son Pno in c, Op. 4; Tarentelle, Op. 43; J. Haydn:Son 58 Kbd, H.XVI/48; Liszt:Grandes études de Paganini, S.141; R. Schumann:Carnaval, Op. 9 PPHI (Great Pianists of the 20th Century) ▲ 456898 (22.97)

▲ = CD ♦ = Enhanced CD △ = MD ▮ = Cassette Tape ▯ = DCC

AHO, KALEVI (cont.)
Quintet for Alto Saxophone, Bassoon, Viola, Cello & Double Bass (1994)
Lahti SO Chamber Ensemble *(rec Lahti, Finland, 1996-97)* † Qnt Bn — BIS (Complete Aho) ▲ 866 [DDD] (17.97)
Quintet for Bassoon & String Quartet (1977)
Lahti SO Chamber Ensemble *(rec Lahti, Finland, 1996-97)* † Qnt Sax — BIS (Complete Aho) ▲ 866 [DDD] (17.97)
Rejoicing of the Deep Waters (fantasy) for Orchestra (1995)
O. Vänskä (cnd), Lahti SO † Sym 10 — BIS ▲ 856 [DDD] (18.97)
Silence [Hiljaisuus] for Violin & Orchestra (1982)
M. Gräsbeck (vn), O. Vänskä (cnd), Lahti SO † Con Vn; Sym 1 — BIS ▲ 396 [DDD] (17.97)
Symphony No. 1 (1969)
O. Vänskä (cnd), Lahti SO † Con Vn; Silence — BIS ▲ 396 [DDD] (17.97)
Symphony No. 2 (1970; rev 1995)
O. Vänskä (cnd), Lahti SO *(rec Lahti, Finland, Jan 1998)* † Sym 7 — BIS ▲ 936 [DDD] (17.97)
Symphony No. 5 (1975-76)
M. Pommer (cnd), Leipzig RSO † Sym 7 — ODE ▲ 765 [DDD] (17.97)
Symphony No. 7, "Insect Symphony" (1988)
M. Pommer (cnd), Leipzig RSO † Sym 5 — ODE ▲ 765 [DDD] (17.97)
O. Vänskä (cnd), Lahti SO *(rec Lahti, Finland, Jan 1998)* † Sym 2 — BIS ▲ 936 [DDD] (17.97)
Symphony No. 8 for Organ & Orchestra (1993)
H. Ericsson (org), O. Vänskä (cnd), Lahti SO *(rec Lahti, Finland, May 1994)* † Pergamon — BIS ▲ 646 [DDD] (17.97)
Symphony No. 9 for Trombone & Orchestra (1993-94)
C. Lindberg (trbn), O. Vänskä (cnd), Lahti SO *(rec Ristinkirkko, Lahti, Finland, Jan 1995)* † Con Vc — BIS ▲ 706 [DDD] (17.97)
Symphony No. 10 (1996)
O. Vänskä (cnd), Lahti SO † Rejoicing — BIS ▲ 856 [DDD] (18.97)

AIMERIC DE PEGHUILHAN (ca 1175-ca 1230)
Music of Aimeric de Peghuilhan
Sequentia—En amour tob alques en que'm refraing *(rec Abbaye de Fontevraud, France, Dec 1993)* ("Dante & the Troubadours") † Bertran De Born:Rassa, tan creis e monta e poia; A. Daniel:Chanson do'ill mot son plan e prim; Lo ferm voler qu'el cor m'intra; Folquet de Marseille:Tant m'abellis l'amoros pessamens; Guiraut de Bornelh:No posc sifrir c'a la dolor; Peire d'Alvernhe:Dejosta'ls breus jorns — DEHA ▲ 77227 [DDD] (16.97)

AITKEN, HUGH (1924-
Concerto for Violin & Orchestra, "Aspen"
E. Oliveira (vn), G. Schwarz (cnd), Seattle SO † In Praise of Ockeghem; Rameau Remembered — ARTK ▲ 4 (15.97)
Cantatas (8) for solo Voices & Ensemble (1958-87)
J. Hakes (sop), C. Bressler (ten), J. Opalach (b-bar), H. Kwalwasser (vn), Y. Lynch (va), F. Arico (vc), J. Levine (db), K. Kraber (fl), M. Kaplan (ob), T. Taylor (pno) † Fant Pno — CRI ▲ 774 [DDD] (16.97)
Fantasy for Piano (1967)
G. Kirkpatrick (pno) † Cants — CRI ▲ 774 [DDD] (16.97)
In Praise of Ockeghem for String Orchestra
G. Schwarz (cnd), Seattle SO † Con Vn; Rameau Remembered — ARTK ▲ 4 (15.97)
Partita for Violin (1968)
R. Davidovici (vn) † A. Copland:Nocturne; Piston:Sonatina Vn; P. Schoenfield:Country Fiddle Pieces; G. Schuller:Recitative & Rondo — NWW ▲ 334 [DDD] (16.97)
Rameau Remembered for Flute & Orchestra
S. Goff (fl), G. Schwarz (cnd), Seattle SO † Con Vn; In Praise of Ockeghem — ARTK ▲ 4 (15.97)
Rosa de Fuego for Piano (1989)
D. Walsh (pno) † Soledades, Cantata VII; D. Riley:Apparitions; D. E. Thomas:Many Happy Returns; S. Wolfe:Canticle — CRI ▲ 595 [DDD] (17.97)
Soledades, Cantata VII for Soprano & Piano [based on texts by Machado] (1986)
I. Gubrud (sop), M. Garrett (pno) † Rosa de Fuego; D. Riley:Apparitions; D. E. Thomas:Many Happy Returns; S. Wolfe:Canticle — CRI ▲ 595 [DDD] (17.97)

AITKEN, ROBERT (1939-
Berceuse (For Those Who Sleep Before Us) for Flute & Orchestra (1992)
R. Aitken (fl), A. Pauk (cnd), Esprit Orch *(rec Toronto, Canada, Apr 1995)* ("Music for Heaven & Earth") † H. Freedman:Touchings; A. Louie:Music for Heaven & Earth; C. McPhee:Nocturne — CBC (SM 5000) ▲ 5154 [DDD] (16.97)

AKEROYDE, SAMUEL (fl 1684-1706)
Songs
C. LaRue (sop), Baltimore Consort—Jenny, My Blithest Maid ("Ballads") † Anonymous:Geordie; My Heartly Service; The Rebel Soldier; A. Campbell:Gloomy Winter's Now Awa'; T. Ravenscroft:Songs; A. L. Roy:Songs; Traditional:Aupres de ma blonde; Barbara Allen; Charlie's Sweet; Edward; Il a tout dit; In a Garden So Green; J'ai vû le loup; Le matin en me levant; Marlbru s'en va t'en guerre; Mignonne, allons voir si la rose; Soldier Boy for Me; The Fox Went out on a Chilly Night; The True Lover's Farewell; The Wren Song — DOR ▲ 90014 [DDD] (11.97)

ÅKERWALL, MARTIN (1965-
Ergesia for Orchestra (1996)
J. M. Jensen (cnd), Danish Concert Band *(rec 1998-99)* ("Visions from the North") † Almila:Visions from the North; M. Andresen:Con Tpt; V. Brandt:Concertpiece 2 Tpt, Op. 12; J. Gade:Funeral Music; D. W. Jenkins:Con A Sax; Ticheli:Blue Shades — ROND ▲ 8368 (18.97)

AKPABOT, SAMUEL (1940-
Nigerian Dances (3) for Orchestra
R. Cock (cnd), South African Broadcasting Corp National SO *(rec Radio Park, Johannesburg, South Africa, Jan 1995)* † P. L. van Dijk:San Chronicle; San Gloria; Khumalo:African Songs — MARC ▲ 8223832 [DDD] (13.97)

ALAGNA, JEAN PASCAL (20th cent)
Palimpseste for Soprano, Bass Clarinet & Cello
E. Aubert (sop), R. Lay (cnd) ("Jeune ecole de Marseille") † Aue:Monologue; Boeuf:Risées; R. Campo:Anima; Lay:Avec amour; Ombre autour du temps — SONP ▲ 96019 [DDD] (16.97)

ALAIN, ALBERT (1888-1971)
Organ Music (miscellaneous)
B. Mondry (org)—Toccatina; Moderato; Cortège; En Pensant à Boëllmann *(rec Alain Org, Romainmôtier, France, Nov 1996)* † O. Alain:Org Music; Boëllmann:Suite gothique Org, Op. 25 — GALL ▲ 945 [ADD] (18.97)

ALAIN, JEHAN (1911-1940)
Danses (3) for Organ [Joies, Deuils, Luttes], AWV 119 (1937-39)
C. Crozier (org) *(rec Rosales Org, Trinity Church, Portland, OR, May 1993)* ("Things Visible & Invisible") † J. Langlais:Paraphrases grégoriennes; Messiaen:Messe de la Pentecôte — DLS ▲ 3147 [DDD] (14.97)
Deuxième fantaisie for Organ, AWV 91 (1936)
J. Farris (org) † M. Dupré:Vars sur un vieux Noël, Op. 20; Duruflé:Prélude et fugue, Op. 7; C. Franck:Pièces (3) Org, M.35; Vierne:Sym 6 Org, Op. 59; Widor:Sym 6 Org, Op. 42/2 — DLS ▲ 3049 [DDD] (14.97)
Le jardin suspendu for Organ, AWV 63 (1934)
D. Briggs (org) ("Popular Organ Music, Vol. 2") † J. S. Bach:Preludes & Fugues (22) Org, BWV 531-552; Preludes & Fugues, BWV 531-552; P. Cochereau:Boléro on a Theme of Charles Racquet; Dukas:L'Apprenti sorcier; C. Franck:Pièces (3) Org, M.37; P. Tchaikovsky:Nutcracker Suite, Op. 71a — PRIO ▲ 568 [DDD] (16.97)
D. MacDonald (org) *(rec Casavant Org, Basilique Notre-Dame du Cap, Quebec, Canada, Mar 1993)* † Cardy:Éclat Org; Daveluy:Choral Prelude Org; Son 3 Org; Duruflé:Prélude et fugue, Op. 7; C. Franck:Chorales Org, M.38-40; Messiaen:Nativité du Seigneur; Widor:Sym 5 Org, Op. 42/1 — CBC ▲ 1104 [DDD] (16.97)
P. Schumann (org) ("Ensemble Nunc") † Jolivet:Messe pour le jour de la paix; Lohrmann:Allein mit sich; Schnebel:Lamento di guerra — SIGM ▲ 6900 [DDD] (17.97)
Litanies for Organ, Op. 79 (1937)
D. Macomber (org) ("Works of the French Masters") † M. Dupré:Vars sur un vieux Noël, Op. 20; Duruflé:Org Music (misc); Prélude et fugue, Op. 7; Roger-Ducasse:Pastoral Org; Vierne:Carillon de Westminster, Op. 54/6; Widor:Andante sostenuto Org — ARK ▲ 6152 [DDD] (16.97)
Movements (3) for Flute & Piano (1935)
C. Thorspecken (fl), C. Hacke (pno) *(rec Sandhausen, Germany, 1995-96)* ("The Lost Generation") † P. Haas:Suite Pno, Op. 13; Laparra:Suite Fl; Schulhoff:Son Fl; L. Smit:Son Fl — BAYE ▲ 100259 [DDD] (17.97)
Music of Alain
D. Collot (sop), B. Boterf (ten), J. Bona (bar), B. Pasquier (va), P. Muller (vc), F. Gyps (fl), L. Decker (ob), G. Guillard (org), Ludwig String Quartet, G. Guillard (cnd), St. Louis Camerata Vocal Ensemble—Melodies (2) for Sop & Pno; Nuptial Song; Post-Scriptum for 3 Female Voices & Pno; Canticle in Phrygian Mode for 4 Mixed-Voice, Sop &; Invention for Fl, Ob & Cl; Prelude for Str Qnt; Adagio for Str Qnt; Funerals for Str Qnt; March of the Horiaces & the Curiaces for 2 Bugles ("Vocal & Instrumental Works, Vol. 2") † Org Music (misc); O. Alain:Souvenances — ARN ▲ 68321 (16.97)

ALAIN, JEHAN (cont.)
Organ Music (miscellaneous)
F. Bohme (org), F. Werner (org)—Grand Fugue † G. Guami:Org Music; Mieg:Org Music; M. Reger:Org Music (misc colls); P. A. Soler:Cons Kbds — QUER ▲ 9811 (18.97)
G. Bovet (org)—Litanies, Op. 79; Pieces (4) Org [Jules Lemaître]; Monodie; Petite pièce; Vars sur un thème de Clément Janequin; Préludes (2) profane, AWV 57-58; Aria, AWV 120; Prélude & Fugue; Berceuse sur deux notes qui cornent; Ballade en mode phrygien; Grave; Chorals (2) Org; Danses (3) Org, AWV 119 *(rec Romainmôtier Switzerland, Switzerland, Apr 19-21, 1995)* ("L'oeuvre d'orgue de Jehan Alain, Vol 2: Guy Bovet") — GALL ▲ 851 [ADD] (19.97)
S. Farr (org)—Danses (3) Org, AWV 119; Vars sur un thème de Clément Janequin; Chorals (2) Org; Climat; Monodie; Berceuse sur deux notes qui cornent; Première fant, AWV 59; Deuxième fant, AWV 91; Prélude & Fugue; Postlude pour l'office de Complies; Vars sur 'Lucis creator' *(rec Oxford, England)* ("Organ Works") — MER ▲ 84282 [DDD] (16.97)
G. Guillard (org)—Monodie ("Vocal & Instrumental Works, Vol. 2") † Music of Alain; O. Alain:Souvenances — ARN ▲ 68321 (16.97)
E. Lebrun (org)—Litanies, Op. 79; Petite pièce; Jardin suspendu, AWV 63; Deuxième fant, AWV 91; Vars sur un thème de Clément Janequin; Danses (2) à Agni Yavishta, AWV 61; Préludes (2) profane, AWV 57-58; Choral Cistercian; Climat; Monodie; Ballade en mode phrygien; Chorals (2) Org [Choral phrygien]; Suite Org, AWV 86 *(rec June 13-17, 1995)* — NXIN ▲ 8553632 [DDD] (5.97)
E. Lebrun (org)—Danses (3) Org, AWV 119; Intermezzo; Vars sur 'Lucis creator'; Berceuse sur deux notes qui cornent; Grave; Lamento; Première fant, AWV 59; Prélude & Fugue; Chorals (2) Org [Choral dorien]; Aria, AWV 120; Postlude pour l'office de Complies *(rec Church of Saint-Antoine des Quinze-Vingts Paris, France, June 13-17, 1995)* ("Organ Works, Vol. 2") — NXIN ▲ 8553633 [DDD] (5.97)
J. Longhurst (org)—Litanies, Op. 79; Jardin suspendu, AWV 63 *(rec Salt Lake City, UT)* ("Romantic French Fantasies") † Boëllmann:Ronde Française, Op. 37; Suite 2 Org, Op. 27; M. Dupré:Cortège et Litanie, Op. 19/2; C. Franck:Pièces (3) Org, M.35; Vierne:Maestoso; Pièces de fant Org (sels); Widor:Sym 1 Org, Op. 13/1; Sym 4 Org, Op. 13/4; Sym 5 Org, Op. 42/1 — KLAV ▲ 11069 [DDD] (18.97)
Organ Music (complete)
K. Bowyer (org)—Suite Org, AWV 86; Climat; Prélude & Fugue; Chorals (2) Org [Choral dorien; Choral phrygien]; Aria, AWV 120; Vars sur 'Lucis creator'; Berceuse sur deux notes qui cornent; Préludes (2) profane, AWV 57-58 [Premier; Deuxième]; Monodie; Ballade en mode phrygien; Choral Cistercian; Vars sur un thème de Clément Janequin; Jardin suspendu, AWV 63; Litanies, Op. 79; Danses (3) Org, AWV 119; Grave; Petite pièce; Intermezzo; Lamento; Première fant, AWV 59; Deuxième fant, AWV 91; Danses (2) à Agni Yavishta, AWV 61; Complainte à la mode ancienne; Fugue en mode de Fa; Verset-Choral; Pieces (4) Org [Jules Lemaître; Chant donné; Andante; Fantasmagorie]; Postlude pour l'office de Complies *(rec Marcussen Org, St. Augustine Tonbridge, England, 1997)* ("The Complete Works for Organ") — NIMB 2-▲ 5551 [DDD] (23.97)
Y. Rechsteiner (org)—Première fant, AWV 59; Deuxième fant, AWV 91; Jardin suspendu, AWV 63; Danses (2) à Agni Yavishta, AWV 61; Climat; Lamento; Pieces (4) Org [Fantasmagorie; Chant donné]; Choral Cistercian; Vars sur 'Lucis creator'; Postlude pour l'office de Complies; Intermezzo; Suite Org, AWV 86 *(rec Apr 1995)* ("L'intégrale de l'oeuvre d'orgue à l'orgue de la famille Alain: Vol. 1, Yves Rechsteiner") — GALL ▲ 850 [ADD] (19.97)
Variations sur un thème de Clément Janequin
H. Fagius (org) *(rec Nederluleå Church, Gammelstad, Sweden, June 1974)* † Boëllmann:Suite gothique Org, Op. 25; F. Couperin:Pièces d'orgue consistantes en deux Messes; Daquin:Nouveau livre de noëls, Op. 2; M. Dupré:Vars sur un vieux Noël, Op. 20; Duruflé:Prélude et fugue, Op. 7; Saint-Saëns:Fant 1 Org — BIS ▲ 7 [AAD] (17.97)
R. Noehren (org) † J. S. Bach:Org Music (misc colls); Preludes & Fugues, BWV 531-552; J. Brahms:Chorale Preludes Org, Op. 122; Karg-Elert:Fugue, Canzone und Epilog, Op. 85/3; Messiaen:Nativité du Seigneur; Widor:Sym 6 Org, Op. 42/2 — DLS ▲ 3045 [DDD] (14.97)

ALAIN, OLIVIER (1918-1994)
Organ Music
B. Mondry (org)—Suite Org; Chanson de la brune en mer; Pour le 2nd Dimanche après l'Epiphanie *(rec Alain Org, Romainmôtier, France, Nov 1996)* † A. Alain:Org Music (misc); Boëllmann:Suite gothique Org, Op. 25 — GALL ▲ 945 [ADD] (18.97)
Souvenances for Flute & Organ
F. Gyps (fl), G. Guillard (org) ("Vocal & Instrumental Works, Vol. 2") † J. Alain:Music of Alain; Org Music (misc) — ARN ▲ 68321 (16.97)

ALAY, MAURO D' (ca 1687-1757)
Sonatas (6) for Violin & Continuo
M. Cadossi (vn), M. Frezzato (vc), F. S. Pedrini (hpd) [baroque instrs] — TACT ▲ 682901 (16.97)

ALBANESE, GUIDO (1893-1966)
Songs
L. Gentile (sop), M. Gentile (mez), A. Trovarelli (mez), S. Consolini (ten), P. Speca (bar), A. D. Mele (vn), S. Benedetto (sax), R. Rupo (pno)—Aria di Natale; Duettino e coro muto; Passione (M. Gentile); Serenata (Speca); Alzati, o bella (Trovarelli); Mattinata (Speca); Il sogno d'una suora (Trovarelli); Ninna nanna (L. Gentile); Barcarola (Rupo); Madrigale (L. Gentile); Variazioni (L. Gentile); Non so qual io mi voglia (L. Gentile); Io sono un augellin (L. Gentile); Bravo, bene, bis(va bene) (Consolini & Di Bened; Che caviale (Consolini); Ma non sapete chi sono io?; Grappoli di stelle (Consolini); Notte di Capri (Consolini & Di Mele); Una rosa di ferro battuto *(rec Ortona Teatro, Zambra, Italy, 1994)* ("Romanze, Liriche e Canzoni") — BONG ▲ 5054 [DDD] (16.97)

ALBÉNIZ, ISAAC (1860-1909)
Asturias for Piano
O. Chassain (gtr) [arr for solo gtr] *(rec Limoges, France, 1996)* ("Éventail; Masters of the Spanish Guitar") † Córdoba; M. de Falla:Amor brujo (sels); Sombrero de tres picos (suite 2); M. Ponce:Sonatina Meridional; J. Rodrigo:Fandango; Zarabanda lejana; J. Turina:Son Gtr, Op. 61; H. Villa-Lobos:Preludes Gtr — MENO ▲ 1022 [DDD] (20.97)
L'Automne (waltz) for Piano, Op. 170 (ca 1890)
A. Guinovart (pno) † Son 3 Pno, Op. 68; Son 4 Pno, Op. 72; Son 5 Pno, Op. 82 — HMA ▲ 1987007 (9.97)
Azulejos for Piano [completed by Granados 1911]
M. Jones (pno)—No. 1, Prelude † España (Souvenirs); España, Op. 165; Iberia Suite; Navarra; Suite española 1, Op. 47; Vega; E. Granados:Allegro di concierto; Escenas romanticas; Goyescas; Goyescas (sels); Oriental canción variada, intermedio y final; Rapsodia aragonesa Pno; Reverie; Valse de concert — NIMB 4-▲ 5595 [DDD] (31.97)
A. D. Larrocha (pno) † Cantos España, Op. 232; España, Op. 165; Mallorca, Op. 202; Piezas caracteristicas, Op. 92; Pno Music (misc); Suite española 2; Vega — EMIC ▲ 64523 (11.97)
Cantos de España for Piano, Op. 232
(rec Haberdashers' Aske School, England) ("Three Guitars") † E. Granados:Danzas españolas (10) Pno; Valses poeticos — ASV ▲ 2061 [DDD] (12.97)
F. Armbruster (gtr), B. Gräsle (gtr)—Bajo la Palmera [trans Gräsle & Armbruster] † Recuerdos de Viaje, Op. 71; Suite española 1, Op. 47; M. de Falla:Sombrero de tres picos (sels); E. Granados:Danzas españolas (10) Pno — TACE ▲ 20
J. Bream (gtr) ("Music of Spain, Vol. 25") † Mallorca, Op. 202; Suite española 1, Op. 47; E. Granados:Gtr Music — RCAV (Gold Seal) 2-▲ 61608 [AAD] (11.97)
P. Huybregts (pno) *(rec Ghent, Belgium, Dec 1993)* † Pno Music (misc); Suite española 1, Op. 47 — CENT ▲ 2231 [DDD] (16.97)
E. Knardahl (pno) *(rec Salen Church Hall, Scotland, Aug 1991)* † S. Barber:Excursions, Op. 20; G. Gershwin:Preludes Pno; Liszt:Liebesträume, S.541 — SIMX ▲ 1082 [DDD] (18.97)
A. D. Larrocha (pno) † Azulejos; España, Op. 165; Mallorca, Op. 202; Piezas caracteristicas, Op. 92; Pno Music (misc); Suite española 2; Vega — EMIC ▲ 64523 (11.97)
C. M. Ros (gtr), M. G. Ferrer (gtr) † Suite española 1, Op. 47 — OTR ▲ 1026 (18.97)
J. Williams (gtr) † Mallorca, Op. 202; Piezas caracteristicas, Op. 92; Suite española 1, Op. 47; M. de Falla:Sombrero de tres picos (dances); E. Granados:Danzas españolas (10) Pno; La Maja de Goya; J. Rodrigo:Piezas españolas; J. Turina:Danzas andaluzas, Op. 8; Fandanguillo, Op. 36; Homenaje a Tárrega, Op. 69; Ráfaga, Op. 53 — SNYC ▲ 46358 [AAD] (9.97)
Córdoba for Piano
O. Chassain (gtr) [arr for solo gtr] *(rec Limoges, France, 1996)* ("Éventail; Masters of the Spanish Guitar") † Asturias; M. de Falla:Amor brujo (sels); Sombrero de tres picos (suite 2); M. Ponce:Sonatina Meridional; J. Rodrigo:Fandango; Zarabanda lejana; J. Turina:Son Gtr, Op. 61; H. Villa-Lobos:Preludes Gtr — MENO ▲ 1022 [DDD] (20.97)
España (Souvenirs) for Piano (1896)
M. Jones (pno) † Azulejos; España, Op. 165; Iberia Suite; Navarra; Suite española 1, Op. 47; Vega; E. Granados:Allegro di concierto; Escenas romanticas; Goyescas; Goyescas (sels); Oriental canción variada, intermedio y final; Rapsodia aragonesa Pno; Reverie; Valse de concert — NIMB 4-▲ 5595 [DDD] (31.97)
España (6 hojas de album) for Piano, Op. 165 (1890)
E. Bátiz (cnd), Mexican State SO † Iberia Suite — ASV ▲ 888 [DDD] (16.97)

ALBÉNIZ, ISAAC (cont.)

España (6 hojas de album) for Piano, Op. 165 (1890) (cont.)

A. Gerhardt (vc), R. Dokshinsky (pno)—Serenata; Malagueña; Tango [arr Maurice Marechal] *(rec Holy Trinity Church, Weston, Hertfordshire, England, 1998)* † G. Cassadó:Dance du Diable Vert; Lamento de Boabdil; Pendule, la Fileuse et le Galant; Requiebros; Sérénade; M. de Falla:Amor brujo (sels); Amor brujo (Ritual Fire Dance); Vida breve (sels); E. Granados:Colección de Tonadillas; Danzas españolas (10) Pno; Goyescas (sels); A. Piazzolla:Grand Tango; M. Ravel:Alborada del gracioso; Pièce en forme de Habanera EMIC ▲ 73164 [DDD] (6.97)

M. Jones (pno)—Tango † Azulejos; España (Souvenirs); Iberia Suite; Navarra; Suite española 1, Op. 47; Vega; E. Granados:Allegro di concierto; Escenas romanticas; Goyescas; Goyescas (sels); Oriental canción variada, intermedio y final; Rapsodia aragonesa Pno; Reverie; Valse de concert NIMB 4-▲ 5595 [DDD] (31.97)

Katona Twins [arr 2 guitars] † Iberia Suite; Mallorca, Op. 202 CCL ▲ 10397 (18.97)

A. D. Larrocha (pno)—Malagueña † Azulejos; Cantos España, Op. 232; Mallorca, Op. 202; Piezas caracteristicas, Op. 92; Pno Music (misc); Suite española 2; Vega EMIC ▲ 64523 (11.97)

A. B. Michelangeli (pno)—Malagueña *(rec 1939-42)* ("The First HMV Recordings") † Beethoven:Son 3 Pno, Op. 2/3; E. Granados:Andaluza Pno, Op. 37/5; Mompou:Cançons i dansas Pno; D. Scarlatti:Sons Kbd GRM2 ▲ 78698 (13.97)

A. B. Michelangeli (pno)—Malagueña † Beethoven:Son 3 Pno, Op. 2/3; E. Granados:Andaluza Pno, Op. 37/5; E. Grieg:Lyric Pieces; D. Scarlatti:Sons Kbd IMMM (Magic Master series) ▲ 37025 (6.97)

E. Wild (pno)—Malagueña *(rec New York, NY, Oct 12, 1965)* ("Earl Wild Plays Spanish & French Gems") † Iberia Suite; Suite española 1, Op. 47; Debussy:Images (6) Pno; Preludes Pno; Suite bergamasque; M. de Falla:Amor brujo (Ritual Fire Dance); Sombrero de tres picos (sels); E. Granados:Danzas españolas (10) Pno; Goyescas (sels); Mompou:Cançons i dansas Pno; Moszkowski:Caprice Espagnole, Op. 37; M. Ravel:Jeux d'eau; Miroirs IVOR ▲ 70805 [ADD] (16.97)

Guitar Music

Bergerac Duo—Cantos España, Op. 232 [Bajo la Palmera; Córdoba]; Suite española 1, Op. 47 [Castilla]; Recuerdos de Viaje, Op. 71 [Rumores de la caleta]; Iberia Suite [Book 1/1, "Evocación"]; Tango Español; España, Op. 165 [Tango] *(rec Dec 1996)* ("Recital Español") † M. de Falla:Gtr Music THOR ▲ 2347 [DDD] (16.97)

D. Blanco (gtr)—Suite española 1, Op. 47 [Asturias] *(rec Djursholm, Sweden, 1983)* ("Favorite Guitar Music") † S. Myers:Gtr Music; Tárrega:Gtr Music; Recuerdos de la Alhambra; H. Villa-Lobos:Chôro 1; Suite populaire brésilienne; Yocoh:Gtr Music BIS ▲ 233 [DDD] (17.97)

E. Catemario (gtr)—Suite española 1, Op. 47; Suite española 1, Op. 47 *(rec Monteggiori, Italy, Sept 1993)* ("Spanish Guitar Music") † E. Granados:Gtr Music; Moreno Torroba:Sonatina Gtr; Tárrega:Gtr Music AART ▲ 47145 [DDD] (10.97)

G. Garcia (gtr), P. Breiner (cnd), Czech State PO—Suite española 1, Op. 47; Piezas caracteristicas, Op. 92 † J. Rodrigo:Con de Aranjuez NXIN ▲ 550220 [DDD] (5.97)

N. Ruiz (gtr)—Cádiz; Mallorca, Op. 202; Cantos España, Op. 232 [Oriental]; Recuerdos de Viaje, Op. 71 [Rumores de la caleta]; Piezas caracteristicas, Op. 92 [Zambra] *(rec Columbia College, Chicago, IL, 1995)* † Maláts:Serenata Andaluza; Serenata Española; Moreno Torroba:Gtr Music; J. Rodrigo:Por los campos de España CENT ▲ 2279 [DDD] (16.97)

A. Segovia (gtr)—Zambra Ganadina; Torre Bermia; Sevilla † Castelnuovo-Tedesco:Gtr Music; M. Ponce:Gtr Music; Son Mexicana; Sor:Gtr Music; Tansman:Berceuse et Danse; H. Villa-Lobos:Etudes Gtr; Preludes Gtr; S. L. Weiss:Lt Music AURC ▲ 115

Stockholm Guitar Trio—Suite española 1, Op. 47 [Aragon]; Cantos España, Op. 232 [Oriental]; Mallorca, Op. 202 *(rec 1997)* † E. Granados:Danzas españolas (10) Pno; Peterson-Berger:Frösöblomster, Op. 16; M. Ravel:Valses nobles OPU ▲ 19701 [AAD] (16.97)

J. Williams (gtr)—Suite española 1, Op. 47; Cádiz; Cantos España, Op. 232 [Córdoba; Granada; Sevilla]; España, Op. 165 [Tango] ("Echoes of Spain") SNYC ▲ 36679 [DDD] (16.97)

J. Williams (gtr)—Suite española 1, Op. 47; Cantos España, Op. 232 [Córdoba; Granada]; Mallorca, Op. 202 † J. Rodrigo:Con de Aranjuez; Fant para un gentilhombre SNYC ▲ 45648 [DDD] (10.97) ▮ 45648 [DDD] (5.98)

Iberia Suite (in 4 books) for Piano [trans E. Fernandez Arbós for orchestra, 1910-1927] (1906)

E. F. Arbós (cnd), Madrid SO ("Spanish Orchestral Favorites") † Bretón:Dolores (sels); M. de Falla:Sombrero de tres picos (suite 2); E. Granados:Goyescas:Intermezzo; J. Turina:Danzas fantásticas, Op. 22; Procesión del Rocio, Op. 9 VAIA ▲ 1046 (17.97)

C. Arrau (pno)—Book 1/1, "Evocación"; Book 1/2, "El Puerto"; Book 1/3, "El Corpus en Sevilla" *(rec 1946-47)* ("Claudio Arrau") † J. S. Bach:Chromatic Fant & Fugue, BWV 903; Balakirev:Islamey; J. Brahms:Con 1 Pno, Op. 15; Vars on a Theme by Paganini, Op. 35; Liszt:Pno Music (misc) PPHI (Great Pianists of the 20th Century) ▲ 456706 (22.97)

E. Bátiz (cnd), Mexican State SO † España, Op. 165 ASV ▲ 888 [DDD] (16.97)

A. Doráti (cnd), Minneapolis SO † M. de Falla:Vida breve (interlude & dance 1); Mussorgsky:Khovanshchina (orch sels); Smetana:Bartered Bride (orch sels) PPHI ▲ 434388 (11.97)

F. Fennell (cnd), Dallas Wind Sym—Book 1/3, "El Corpus en Sevilla" [arr Cailliet] *(rec June 1992)* ("Trittico") † V. Giannini:Sym 3; E. Grieg:Funeral March in Memory of Rikard Nordraak; Joio:Variants on a Medieval Tune; Nelhybel:Trittico REF ▲ 52 [DDD] (16.97)

G. González (pno) † Suite española 1, Op. 47; Suite española 2 NXIN (Spanish Music Collections) 2-▲ 8554311 [DDD] (15.97)

H. Hiseki (pno) EAM ▲ 10941 [DDD] (33.97)

K. Jean (cnd), Czech-Slovak RSO Bratislava *(rec Sept 1988)* ("Viva España!: Music of Spain") † M. de Falla:Amor brujo (Ritual Fire Dance); Sombrero de tres picos (suite 1); Sombrero de tres picos (suite 2); Vida breve (interlude & dance 1) NXIN ▲ 550174 [DDD] (5.97)

M. Jones (pno) † Azulejos; España (Souvenirs); España, Op. 165; Navarra; Suite española 1, Op. 47; Vega; E. Granados:Allegro di concierto; Escenas romanticas; Goyescas; Goyescas (sels); Oriental canción variada, intermedio y final; Rapsodia aragonesa Pno; Reverie; Valse de concert NIMB 4-▲ 5595 [DDD] (31.97)

Katona Twins [arr 2 gtrs] † España, Op. 165; Mallorca, Op. 202 CCL ▲ 10397 (18.97)

A. D. Larrocha (pno) † E. Granados:Goyescas PLON 2-▲ 448191 (17.97)

A. D. Larrocha (pno) EMIC 2-▲ 64504 (21.97)

A. D. Larrocha (pno) *(rec 1972)* † Navarra; M. P. de Albéniz:Son Pno; E. Granados:Danzas españolas (10) Pno; Goyescas (sels); E. Halffter:Danzas (2) Pno; Mompou:Cançons i dansas Pno; P. A. Soler:Sons Kbd PPHI (Great Pianists of the 20th Century) ▲ 456883 (22.97)

J. López-Cobos (cnd), Cincinnati SO [arr Surinach] *(rec Music Hall, Cincinnati, OH, May 1997)* TEL 2-▲ 80470 (16.97)

P. de Lucia (gtr), J. Bandera (gtr), J. Cañizares (gtr) [arr Lucia] † J. Rodrigo:Con de Aranjuez VERV ▲ 10301 (14.97)

F. Reiner (cnd), Chicago SO *(rec Orchestral Hall, Chicago, IL, Apr 26, 1958)* ("Spain") † Navarra; M. de Falla:Amor brujo; Sombrero de tres picos (sels); Vida breve (interlude & dance 1); E. Granados:Goyescas:Intermezzo RCAV (Living Stereo) ▲ 62586 [ADD/DDD] (11.97)

C. C. Rodríguez (pno)—Book 1/1, "Evocación"; Book 1/2, "El Puerto"; Book 2/2, "Almería"; Book 2/1, "Rondeña"; Book 2/3, "Triana" *(rec Farifax, VA, Dec 1997)* ("España en el Corazón:Portrait of Spain") † M. de Falla:Amor brujo (sels); Vida breve (sels); E. Granados:Danzas españolas (10) Pno; Goyescas (sels); P. A. Soler:Sons Kbd BRIO ▲ 118 [DDD] (16.97)

L. Stokowski (cnd), Philadelphia Orch—Book 1/3, "El Corpus en Sevilla" *(rec 1945-46)* ("Iberia") † Bizet:Carmen (sels); M. de Falla:Amor brujo; Vida breve (sels) PHS ▲ 9276 (17.97)

Y. P. Tortelier (cnd), Philharmonia Orch † M. de Falla:Sombrero de tres picos CHN ▲ 8904 [DDD] (16.97)

E. Wild (pno)—Book 2/3, "Triana" *(rec New York, NY, Oct 12, 1965)* ("Earl Wild Plays Spanish & French Gems") † España, Op. 165; Suite española 1, Op. 47; Debussy:Images (6) Pno; Preludes Pno; Suite bergamasque; M. de Falla:Amor brujo (Ritual Fire Dance); Sombrero de tres picos (sels); E. Granados:Danzas españolas (10) Pno; Goyescas (sels); Mompou:Cançons i dansas Pno; Moszkowski:Caprice Espagnole, Op. 37; M. Ravel:Jeux d'eau; Miroirs IVOR ▲ 70805 [ADD] (16.97)

Mallorca (barcarola) for Piano, Op. 202

J. Bream (gtr) ("Music of Spain, Vol. 25") † Cantos España, Op. 232; Suite española 1, Op. 47; E. Granados:Gtr Music RCAV (Gold Seal) 2-▲ 61608 [AAD] (11.97)

Katona Twins [arr 2 gtrs] † España, Op. 165; Iberia Suite CCL ▲ 10397 (18.97)

N. Kraft (gtr) [arr Kraft] *(rec Cambridge University, England, Jan 1990)* ("Spanish & South American Works for Guitar") † Piezas caracteristicas, Op. 92; Suite española 1, Op. 47; Castelnuovo-Tedesco:Platero y yo, Op. 190; M. de Falla:Homenaje tombeau de Debussy; Sombrero de tres picos (dances); Moreno Torroba:Sonatina Gtr; J. Turina:Homenaje a Tárrega, Op. 69; H. Villa-Lobos:Etudes Gtr CHN ▲ 8857 [DDD] (16.97)

A. D. Larrocha (pno) † Azulejos; Cantos España, Op. 232; España, Op. 165; Piezas caracteristicas, Op. 92; Pno Music (misc); Suite española 2; Vega EMIC ▲ 64523 (11.97)

J. Williams (gtr) † Cantos España, Op. 232; Piezas caracteristicas, Op. 92; Suite española 1, Op. 47; M. de Falla:Sombrero de tres picos (dances); E. Granados:Danzas españolas (10) Pno; La Maja de Goya; J. Rodrigo:Piezas españolas; J. Turina:Danzas andaluzas, Op. 8; Fandanguillo, Op. 36; Homenaje a Tárrega, Op. 69; Ráfága, Op. 53 SNYC ▲ 46358 [AAD] (9.97)

ALBÉNIZ, ISAAC (cont.)

Navarra for Piano [completed by Déodat de Séverac, 1912]

M. Jones (pno) † Azulejos; España (Souvenirs); España, Op. 165; Iberia Suite; Suite española 1, Op. 47; Vega; E. Granados:Allegro di concierto; Escenas romanticas; Goyescas; Goyescas (sels); Oriental canción variada, intermedio y final; Rapsodia aragonesa Pno; Reverie; Valse de concert NIMB 4-▲ 5595 [DDD] (31.97)

A. D. Larrocha (pno) *(rec 1972)* † Iberia Suite; M. P. de Albéniz:Son Pno; E. Granados:Danzas españolas (10) Pno; Goyescas (sels); E. Halffter:Danzas (2) Pno; Mompou:Cançons i dansas Pno; P. A. Soler:Sons Kbd PPHI (Great Pianists of the 20th Century) ▲ 456883 (22.97)

F. Reiner (cnd), Chicago SO [arr Arbós] *(rec Orchestral Hall, Chicago, IL, Apr 26, 1958)* ("Spain") † Iberia Suite; M. de Falla:Amor brujo; Sombrero de tres picos (sels); Vida breve (interlude & dance 1); E. Granados:Goyescas:Intermezzo RCAV (Living Stereo) ▲ 62586 [ADD/DDD] (11.97)

Pepita Jiménez:Suite

S. Chilcott (sop), F. Garrigosa (ten), J. Pons (cnd), Barcelona Teatro Lliure CO HAM ▲ 901537 (18.97)

Piano Music (miscellaneous)

P. Cavazzini (pno)—Iberia Suite [Book 2/3, "Triana"]; Navarra *(rec 1950-60)* ("Un Ritratto") † Cavazzini:Pno Music (misc); Chopin:Pno Music (misc colls); Debussy:Pno Music (misc colls); Liszt:Etudes d'exécution transcendante (6), S.140; Hungarian Rhaps, S.244; Liebesträume, S.541; M. Ravel:Jeux d'eau; D. Scarlatti:Sons Kbd STRV 2-▲ 90005 [ADD] (24.97)

P. Huybregts (pno)—Mallorca, Op. 202; Recuerdos de Viaje, Op. 71; Gavotte; Piezas caracteristicas, Op. 92 [Torre Bermeja] *(rec Ghent, Belgium, Dec 1993)* † Cantos España, Op. 232; Suite española 1, Op. 47 CENT ▲ 2231 [DDD] (16.97)

S. Kowalczuk (hp)—Suite española 1, Op. 47 [Granada]; España, Op. 165 [Malagueña] ("Festival on the Classical Harp") † Albrechtsberger:Partita Hp; Grandjany:Rhap Hp, Op. 10; W. A. Mozart:Adagio & Rondo, K.617; Würtzler:Modern Sketches HUN ▲ 31577 (16.97)

A. D. Larrocha (pno)—Suite española 2 [Zaragoza]; España, Op. 165 [Malagueña] † Azulejos; Cantos España, Op. 232; España, Op. 165; Mallorca, Op. 202; Piezas caracteristicas, Op. 92; Suite española 2; Vega EMIC ▲ 64523 (11.97)

J. Novacek (pno)—Suite española 1, Op. 47 [Asturias; Sevilla]; Tango Español *(rec St. John Vianney Church, Juanita, WA, Aug 1994)* ("Spanish Rhapsody") † Ginastera:Danzas argentinas, Op. 2; E. Granados:Goyescas (sels); Liszt:Rhap espagnole, S.254; M. Ravel:Alborada del gracioso; P. A. Soler:Fandango, M.1A AMBA ▲ 1014 [DDD] (16.97)

E. Rose (va), K. Collier (pno)—Mallorca, Op. 202; España, Op. 165; Recuerdos de Viaje, Op. 71 [Puerta de tierra] *(rec SMU, Dallas, TX, Jan 1995)* ("Spanish Treasures") † M. de Falla:Suite populaire espagnole; M. Ravel:Pièce en forme de Habanera; Sarasate:Vn & Pno Music; Toldrá:Sonnets Vn CENT ▲ 2315 [DDD] (16.97)

A. Ruiz-Pipo (pno) *(Champagne; Automne, Op. 170; España (Souvenirs)), (Sueños, Op. 101; Les saisons, Op. 101; Estudios en los tonos naturales mayores, Op. 65)* KSCH ▲ 315132 [DDD] (16.97)

Piezas (12) caracteristicas for Piano, Op. 92 (1888-9)

N. Kraft (gtr)—Torre Bermeja [arr Kraft] *(rec Cambridge University, England, Jan 1990)* ("Spanish & South American Works for Guitar") † Mallorca, Op. 202; Suite española 1, Op. 47; Castelnuovo-Tedesco:Platero y yo, Op. 190; M. de Falla:Homenaje tombeau de Debussy; Sombrero de tres picos (dances); Moreno Torroba:Sonatina Gtr; J. Turina:Homenaje a Tárrega, Op. 69; H. Villa-Lobos:Etudes Gtr CHN ▲ 8857 [DDD] (16.97)

A. D. Larrocha (pno) † Azulejos; Cantos España, Op. 232; España, Op. 165; Mallorca, Op. 202; Pno Music (misc); Suite española 2; Vega EMIC ▲ 64523 (11.97)

J. Williams (gtr)—Zambra † Cantos España, Op. 232; Mallorca, Op. 202; Suite española 1, Op. 47; M. de Falla:Sombrero de tres picos (dances); E. Granados:Danzas españolas (10) Pno; La Maja de Goya; J. Rodrigo:Piezas españolas; J. Turina:Danzas andaluzas, Op. 8; Fandanguillo, Op. 36; Homenaje a Tárrega, Op. 69; Ráfaga, Op. 53 SNYC ▲ 46358 [AAD] (9.97)

Recuerdos de Viaje for Piano, Op. 71 (1887)

F. Armbruster (gtr), B. Gräsle (gtr)—Rumores de la caleta [trans Gräsle & Armbruster] † Cantos España, Op. 232; Suite española 1, Op. 47; M. de Falla:Sombrero de tres picos (sels); E. Granados:Danzas españolas (10) Pno TACE ▲ 20

A. B. Michelangeli (pno) † Beethoven:Son 3 Pno, Op. 2/3; E. Granados:Andaluza Pno, Op. 37/5; E. Grieg:Lyric Pieces; Mompou:Cançons i dansas Pno; D. Scarlatti:Sons Kbd MTAL ▲ 48010 (6.97)

Sonata No. 3 in A♭ for Piano, Op. 68

A. Guinovart (pno) † Automne; Son 4 Pno, Op. 72; Son 5 Pno, Op. 82 HMA ▲ 1987007 (9.97)

Sonata No. 4 in A♭ for Piano, Op. 72

A. Guinovart (pno) † Automne; Son 3 Pno, Op. 68; Son 5 Pno, Op. 82 HMA ▲ 1987007 (9.97)

Sonata No. 5 in G♭ for Piano, Op. 82

A. Guinovart (pno) † Automne; Son 3 Pno, Op. 68; Son 4 Pno, Op. 72 HMA ▲ 1987007 (9.97)

Suite española No. 1 for Piano, Op. 47 (1886)

F. Armbruster (gtr), B. Gräsle (gtr)—Castilla [trans Gräsle & Armbruster] † Cantos España, Op. 232; Recuerdos de Viaje, Op. 71; M. de Falla:Sombrero de tres picos (sels); E. Granados:Danzas españolas (10) Pno TACE ▲ 20

M. Barrueco (gtr) † J. Turina:Gtr Music EMIC ▲ 66574 [DDD] (11.97)

J. Bream (gtr) ("Music of Spain, Vol. 25") † Cantos España, Op. 232; Mallorca, Op. 202; E. Granados:Gtr Music RCAV (Gold Seal) 2-▲ 61608 [AAD] (11.97)

Falla Trio [arr for 3 gtrs] † W. Boyce:Syms; A. A. Corea:Spain; M. de Falla:Amor brujo (sels); P. A. Soler:Fandango, M.1A ERTO ▲ 42011 (14.97)

G. Fierens (gtr) *(rec London, England)* ("Spanish Guitar Music") † Castelnuovo-Tedesco:Capriccio diabolico Gtr, Op. 85; Son D Gtr, Op. 77; M. Ponce:Preludio, Balletto & Giga; Sor:Grand Solo Gtr, Op. 14; J. Turina:Fandanguillo, Op. 36; H. Villa-Lobos:Preludes Gtr ASLE ▲ 6190 [DDD] (8.97)

G. González (pno) † Iberia Suite; Suite española 2 NXIN (Spanish Music Collections) 2-▲ 8554311 [DDD] (15.97)

P. Huybregts (pno) *(rec Ghent, Belgium, Dec 1993)* † Cantos España, Op. 232; Pno Music (misc) CENT ▲ 2231 [DDD] (16.97)

M. Jones (pno) † Azulejos; España (Souvenirs); España, Op. 165; Iberia Suite; Navarra; Vega; E. Granados:Allegro di concierto; Escenas romanticas; Goyescas; Goyescas (sels); Oriental canción variada, intermedio y final; Rapsodia aragonesa Pno; Reverie; Valse de concert NIMB 4-▲ 5595 [DDD] (31.97)

N. Kraft (gtr)—Sevilla [arr Kraft] *(rec Cambridge University, England, Jan 1990)* ("Spanish & South American Works for Guitar") † Mallorca, Op. 202; Piezas caracteristicas, Op. 92; Castelnuovo-Tedesco:Platero y yo, Op. 190; M. de Falla:Homenaje tombeau de Debussy; Sombrero de tres picos (dances); Moreno Torroba:Sonatina Gtr; J. Turina:Homenaje a Tárrega, Op. 69; H. Villa-Lobos:Etudes Gtr CHN ▲ 8857 [DDD] (16.97)

J. Moser (gtr), F. Rahm (gtr)—Granada; Sevilla ("Musique espagnole pour deux guitares") † Tango Español; A. de Cabezón:Obras de música (sels); Froelicher:Muleta; E. Granados:Goyescas:Intermezzo; Sor:Waltzes Gtrs, Op. 44bis GALL ▲ 881 [DDD] (19.97)

A. Petchersky (pno) † M. de Falla:Fant bética; E. Granados:Allegro di concierto ASVQ ▲ 6079 [ADD] (10.97)

A. Ramírez (gtr)—Asturias *(rec Aug 1991)* † Moreno Torroba:Suite castellana; J. Rodrigo:Gtr Music; Invocación y danza; Por los campos de España; J. Turina:Gtr Music; Son Gtr, Op. 61 DNN ▲ 75357 [DDD] (16.97)

R. Romero (gtr), T. Muska (gtr), F. Corrales (gtr), B. T. King (gtr)—Sevilla ("Las Guitarras de Carmen") † Bizet:Carmen (sels); R. Romero:Gtr Music; Traditional:Amor Torero; Torre Giralda; Zopilote IGO ▲ 212 (16.97)

C. M. Ros (gtr), M. G. Ferrer (gtr) † Cantos España, Op. 232 OTR ▲ 1026 (18.97)

S. Rottersman (gtr) [Leyenda only] ("Sherri Rottersman: The Sensual Guitar") † Anonymous:Renaissance Pieces Lt; J. S. Bach:Sons & Partitas Vn; E. Granados:Danzas españolas (10) Pno; J. Rodrigo:Ecos de Sefarad; Tansman:Mazurka Gtr; Tárrega:Capricho árabe AURR ▲ 23446 [ADD] (16.97)

G. Tinturin (gtr), N. C. Tinturin (pno)—Granada; Sevilla [arr Tinturin] *(rec Hollywood, CA)* † Castelnuovo-Tedesco:Fant Gtr & Pno, Op. 145; Romancero gitano, Op. 152; M. de Falla:Vida breve (sels); Marquina:Espaãna Cañi; M. Ravel:Pièce en forme de Habanera; P. Tinturin:Crazy Quilt of Memories; Latin Rhapsody; Synocpated Nocturne CMB ▲ 1099 (16.97)

E. Wild (pno)—Castilla *(rec New York, NY, Oct 12, 1965)* ("Earl Wild Plays Spanish & French Gems") † España, Op. 165; Iberia Suite; Debussy:Images (6) Pno; Preludes Pno; Suite bergamasque; M. de Falla:Amor brujo (Ritual Fire Dance); Sombrero de tres picos (sels); E. Granados:Danzas españolas (10) Pno; Goyescas (sels); Mompou:Cançons i dansas Pno; Moszkowski:Caprice Espagnole, Op. 37; M. Ravel:Jeux d'eau; Miroirs IVOR ▲ 70805 [ADD] (16.97)

J. Williams (gtr)—Cádiz † Cantos España, Op. 232; Mallorca, Op. 202; Piezas caracteristicas, Op. 92; M. de Falla:Sombrero de tres picos (dances); E. Granados:Danzas españolas (10) Pno; La Maja de Goya; J. Rodrigo:Piezas españolas; J. Turina:Danzas andaluzas, Op. 8; Fandanguillo, Op. 36; Homenaje a Tárrega, Op. 69; Ráfaga, Op. 53 SNYC ▲ 46358 [AAD] (9.97)

Suite española No. 2 for Piano (1889)

G. González (pno) † Iberia Suite; Suite española 1, Op. 47 NXIN (Spanish Music Collections) 2-▲ 8554311 [DDD] (15.97)

A. D. Larrocha (pno)—Zaragoza † Azulejos; Cantos España, Op. 232; España, Op. 165; Mallorca, Op. 202; Piezas caracteristicas, Op. 92; Pno Music (misc); Vega EMIC ▲ 64523 (11.97)

Tango Español for Piano

J. Moser (gtr), F. Rahm (gtr) [arr Tarrago] ("Musique espagnole pour deux guitares") † Suite española 1, Op. 47; A. de Cabezón:Obras de música (sels); Froelicher:Muleta; E. Granados:Goyescas:Intermezzo; Sor:Waltzes Gtrs, Op. 44bis GALL ▲ 881 [DDD] (19.97)

ALBÉNIZ, ISAAC (cont.)
La Vega for Piano (1897)
M. Jones (pno) † Azulejos; España (Souvenirs); España, Op. 165; Iberia Suite; Navarra; Suite española 1, Op. 47; E. Granados:Allegro di concierto; Escenas romanticas; Goyescas; Goyescas (sels); Oriental canción variada, intermedio y final; Rapsodia aragonesa Pno; Reverie; Valse de concert NIMB 4-▲ 5595 [DDD] (31.97)
A. D. Larrocha (pno) † Azulejos; Cantos España, Op. 232; España, Op. 165; Mallorca, Op. 202; Piezas caracteristicas, Op. 92; Pno Music (misc); Suite española 2 EMIC ▲ 64523 (11.97)
ALBÉNIZ, MATEO (ANTONIO) PÉREZ DE (ca 1755-1831)
Sonata in D for Piano
A. D. Larrocha (pno) *(rec 1974)* † I. Albéniz:Iberia Suite; Navarra; E. Granados:Danzas españolas (10) Pno; Goyescas (sels); E. Halffter:Danzas (2) Pno; Mompou:Cançons i dansas Pno; P. A. Soler:Sons Kbd PPHI (Great Pianists of the 20th Century) ▲ 456883 (22.97)
ALBERT, EUGENE D' (1864-1932)
Die Abreise (musical comedy in 1 act) [lib F. von Sporck after A. von Steigentesch] (1898)
L. Schädle (sop—Wife), E. Wohlfahrt (ten—Trott), W. Ferenz (bass—Gilfen), J. Koetsier (cnd), Bavarian RSO *(rec 1964)* CALG (History) ▲ 50964 [ADD] (18.97)
Capriolen for Piano, Op. 32
P. Lane (pno) † Pieces Pno, Op. 5; Serenata; Son Pno, Op. 10 HYP ▲ 66945 (18.97)
Concerto in C for Cello & Orchestra, Op. 20 (1899)
J. Timm (vc), C. P. Flor (cnd), Berlin SO † Con 2 Pno, Op. 12 BER ▲ 9179 (10.97)
Concerto No. 1 in b for Piano & Orchestra, Op. 2 (1884)
J. Banowetz (pno), D. Yablonsky (cnd), Moscow SO *(rec Moscow, Russia, Oct 1996)* † Con 2 Pno, Op. 12; Esther Ov, Op. 8 NXIN ▲ 8553728 [DDD] (5.97)
P. Lane (pno), A. Francis (cnd), BBC Scottish SO ("The Romantic Piano Concerto, Vol. 9") † Con 2 Pno, Op. 12 HYP ▲ 66747 (18.97)
Concerto No. 2 in E for Piano & Orchestra, Op. 12 (1893)
J. Banowetz (pno), D. Yablonsky (cnd), Moscow SO *(rec Moscow, Russia, Oct 1996)* † Con 1 Pno, Op. 2; Esther Ov, Op. 8 NXIN ▲ 8553728 [DDD] (5.97)
P. Lane (pno), A. Francis (cnd), BBC Scottish SO ("The Romantic Piano Concerto, Vol. 9") † Con 1 Pno, Op. 2 HYP ▲ 66747 (18.97)
M. Ponti (pno), P. Cao (cnd), Luxembourg RSO *(rec 1973)* ("The Romantic Piano Concerto, Vol. 4") † Bronsart Von schellendorf:Con Pno, Op. 10; Liszt:Malédiction, S.121; Mosonyi:Con Pno; Raff:Con Pno; Stavenhagen:Con 1 Pno, Op. 4 VB2 2-▲ 5067 [ADD] (9.97)
S. Stöckigt (pno), G. Herbig (cnd), Berlin SO † Con Vc BER ▲ 9179 (10.97)
Esther Overture (lib Grillparzer), Op. 8 (1888)
D. Yablonsky (cnd), Moscow SO *(rec Moscow, Russia, Oct 1996)* † Con 1 Pno, Op. 2; Con 2 Pno, Op. 12 NXIN ▲ 8553728 [DDD] (5.97)
Pieces (8) for Piano, Op. 5
P. Lane (pno) † Capriolen, Op. 32; Serenata; Son Pno, Op. 10 HYP ▲ 66945 (18.97)
Quartets (2) for Strings, Opp. 7 & 11
Sarastro String Quartet PANC ▲ 510097 [DDD] (17.97)
Serenata for Piano
P. Lane (pno) † Capriolen, Op. 32; Pieces Pno, Op. 5; Son Pno, Op. 10 HYP ▲ 66945 (18.97)
Sonata in f# for Piano, Op. 10 (1893)
P. Lane (pno) † Capriolen, Op. 32; Pieces Pno, Op. 5; Serenata HYP ▲ 66945 (18.97)
Tiefland (musikdrama in prologue & 2 acts) [lib Rudolph Lothar] (1903)
H. Kuhse (sop), H. Hoppe (ten), E. Gutstein (bar), T. Adam (b-bar), P. Schmitz (cnd), Dresden Staatskapelle, G. Wüstner (cnd), Dresden State Opera Chorus BER 2-▲ 9108 (21.97)
E. Marton (sop), R. Kollo (ten), B. Weikl (bar), K. Moll (bass), M. Janowski (cnd), Munich RSO AART 2-▲ 47501 (19.97)
Tiefland (selections)
H. de Garmo (bass)—Hüll' in die Mantille dich fester ein *(rec 1917)* † Bizet:Carmen (sels); Leoncavallo:Pagliacci (sels); W. A. Mozart:Don Giovanni (sels); J. Offenbach:Contes d'Hoffmann (sels); Verdi:Otello (sels); R. Wagner:Fliegende Holländer (sels); Meistersinger (sels); Rheingold (sels); Siegfried (sels); Tannhäuser (sels); Walküre (sels) PRE (Lebendige Vergangenheit) ▲ 89175 (m) (16.97)
G. Pistor (ten), E. D. Albert (cnd), Berlin State Opera Orch *(rec 1928)* ("Four German Heldentenors of the Past") † Flotow:Martha (sels); Kienzl:Evangelimann (sels); Verdi:Forza del destino (sels); Otello (sels); Rigoletto (sels); R. Wagner:Lohengrin (sels); Meistersinger (sels); Parsifal (sels); Siegfried (sels); Walküre (sels) PRE ▲ 89975 (m) [AAD] (16.97)
Die toten Augen (opera) [lib H. H. Ewers] (ca 1916)
W. Born (cnd), Stuttgart RSO, M. Schech (sop), L. Paul (mez), H. Plümacher (cta), W. Windgassen (ten), F. Fehringer (ten), E. Czubok (bar) *(rec live, Stuttgart, Germany, 1951) ([GER] text)* MYTO 2-▲ 982185 (34.97)
Waltzes (13) for Piano Duet, Op. 6
T. Korockin (pno), A. Schonhage (pno) † R. Strauss:Sym in f, Op. 12 CPO ▲ 999330 (14.97)
ALBERT, HEINRICH (1870-1950)
Musicalische Kürbs-Hütte (songs) for 3 Voices & Continuo (1645)
Cantus Cologne ("Songs of Love & Death") ARSM ▲ 3026 [DDD] (17.97)
ALBERT, STEPHEN (1941-1992)
Concerto for Cello & Orchestra
Y.-Y. Ma (vc), D. Zinman (cnd), Baltimore SO *(rec Josef Meyerhoff Hall, Baltimore, MD, Mar 1993)* † B. Bartók:Con Va; E. Bloch:Schelomo SNYC ▲ 57961 [DDD] (16.97) ▮ 57961 [DDD] (10.98)
In Concordiam for Violin & Orchestra (1986)
I. Talvi (vn), G. Schwarz (cnd), Seattle SO † TreeStone DLS ▲ 3059 [DDD] (14.97)
Into Eclipse (song cycle) for Tenor & Orchestra [set to a text by Ted Hughes based on Seneca's Oedipus] (1980; rev 1989)
G. Lakes (ten), G. Schwarz (cnd), Juilliard Orch † J. Druckman:Chiaroscuro; Schwantner:Aftertones of Infinity NWW ▲ 381 [DDD] (16.97)
S. Oosting (ten), S. Hodkinson (cnd) *(rec Eastman Theater, NY, Mar 26, 1983)* ("Eastman American Music Series, Vol 1") † C. Rouse:Madrigals; Mitternachtlieder ALBA ▲ 192 [ADD] (16.97)
Symphony RiverRun for Orchestra
M. Rostropovich (cnd), National SO Washington D.C. † To Wake the Dead DLS ▲ 1016 [DDD] (10.97)
To Wake the Dead (song cycle) for Soprano & Ensemble [text from James Joyce's Finnegan's Wake] (1977)
L. Shelton (sop), C. Kendall (cnd) † Sym RiverRun DLS ▲ 1016 [DDD] (10.97)
TreeStone for Soprano, Tenor & Chamber Orchestra (1983-84)
L. Shelton (sop), D. Gordon (ten), G. Schwarz (cnd), New York Chamber SO † In Concordiam DLS ▲ 3059 [DDD] (14.97)
ALBERT, THOMAS (1948-
Devil's Rain for Chamber Ensemble
Relâche Ensemble ("On Edge") † Maze (With Grace); P. A. Epstein:Songs from "Home"; Tenney:Critical Band MODE ▲ 22 (17.97)
A Maze (With Grace) for Chamber Ensemble
Relâche Ensemble ("On Edge") † Devil's Rain; P. A. Epstein:Songs from "Home"; Tenney:Critical Band MODE ▲ 22 (17.97)
ALBERTI, GIUSEPPE MATTEO (1685-1751)
Sonata in D for 2 Trumpets
H. Wobisch (tpt), A. Holler (tpt) *(rec Baumgarten Hall, Vienna, Austria, May 1961)* ("The Virtuoso Trumpet, Vol. 2") † H. I. Biber:Son for 6 Tpts; J. Haydn:Con Tpt; Manfredini:Con for 2 Tpts, Hpd & Strs; L. Mozart:Con Tpt; Torelli:Con for 2 Tpts VC ▲ 2535 [ADD] (13.97)
ALBERTS, ARMENO (1959-
Haké for Gamelan & Tape (1993)
J. Sligter (cnd) *(rec Singelkerk, Amsterdam, Netherlands, Dec 1995)* † Eisma:Mawar Jiwa; T. Leeuw:Gending; Termos:Kendang; Woof:Soundings EMEC ▲ 92062 [DDD]
ALBERTSEN, PER HJORT (1919-
Concerto Piccolo for Violin & String Orchestra
E. Denisova (vn), A. Kornienko (cnd), Collegium Musicum *(rec Pfarrsaal Klagenfurt, Norway, 1997)* † Bjørklund:Cantio Va; Böttcher:Con Ripieno; Divert Concertante Vn; Kleiberg:Dopo NORW ▲ 2926 (17.97)
ALBINONI, TOMASO (1671-1750)
Adagio in g for Organ & Strings [composed by Giazotto on original fragment]
W. Boughton (cnd), English String Orch *(rec Great Hall, Univ of Birmingham, England, May 1985)* ("Orchestral Favorites, Vol. 1") † E. Grieg:Holberg Suite Pno, Op. 40; G. Holst:St. Paul's Suite, Op. 29/2; J. Pachelbel:Canon & Gigue; Warlock:Capriol Suite NIMB ▲ 7019 [DDD] (11.97)

ALBINONI, TOMASO (cont.)
Adagio in g for Organ & Strings [composed by Giazotto on original fragment] (cont.)
M. Bourgue (ob), I Musici † Cons Ob, Op. 9 PPHI (Duo) 2-▲ 456333 (17.97)
M. Braun (vn), R. Kapp (cnd), Philharmonia Virtuosi, New York *(rec NYC, NY)* ("Greatest Hits of 1720") † J. S. Bach:Air on the G String; Anna Magdalena Bach Notebook (sels); Con 1 for 2 Hpds, BWV 1060; Con 5 Hpd, BWV 1056; Campra:Tancrède (sels); A. Corelli:Sonatas (12) for Violin (or Violone) & Continuo Instruments [including No. 12, "La Follia"], Op. 5; G. F. Handel:Suites de Pièces (9) Hpd, HWV 434-42; Mouret:Rondeau; J. Pachelbel:Canon & Gigue SNYC ▲ 34544 [ADD] (9.97)
X. Darasse (org), L. Auriacombe (cnd), Toulouse CO *(rec Chapelle des Italiens Toulouse, France, Jan 1968)* ("Baroque, Vol. 1") † Con in B Tpt; Sinfonie e concerti à 5, Op. 2 EMIC ▲ 65337 [ADD] (9.97)
T. Füri (cnd), Bern Camerata † J. S. Bach:Brandenburg Con 3, BWV 1048; Manfredini:Cons Vns, Op. 3; J. Pachelbel:Canon & Gigue; H. Purcell:Pavane & Chaconne NOVA ▲ 150004 (16.97)
I Musici † W. A. Mozart:Kleine Nachtmusik, K.525; J. Pachelbel:Canon & Gigue PPHI (Digital Classics) ▲ 10606 [DDD] (16.97)
Italian Solisti † J. Pachelbel:Canon & Gigue DNN ▲ 73335 [DDD] (16.97)
H. von Karajan (cnd), Berlin PO † J. S. Bach:Suite 3 Orch, BWV 1068; C. W. Gluck:Orfeo ed Euridice (dance); W. A. Mozart:Serenade 6 Orch, K.239; J. Pachelbel:Canon & Gigue; Vivaldi:Cons Fl, Op. 10/1-6 DEUT ▲ 13309 [DDD] (16.97)
H. von Karajan (cnd), Berlin PO † A. Corelli:Con grosso, Op. 6/8; Vivaldi:Cons Vn Strs, Op. 8/1-4 DEUT ▲ 15301 [ADD] (16.97)
C. Lindberg (trbn), R. Pöntinen (pno) *(rec Danderyd Grammar School, Sweden, June 1986)* ("The Criminal Trombone") † J. S. Bach:Air on the G String; Suite 2 Fl, BWV 1067; W. A. Mozart:Vars "Ah! vous dirai-je, Maman", K.265; G. Rossini:Barbiere di Siviglia (ov); F. Schubert:Son Arpeggione, D.821; R. Schumann:Romances Ob, Op. 94 BIS ▲ 328 [DDD] (17.97)
J. Malgoire (cnd), La Grande Écurie et la Chambre du Roy † J. Pachelbel:Canon & Gigue SNYC ▮ 38482 (3.98) ▲ 38482 (9.97)
N. Marriner (cnd), Academy of St. Martin in the Fields EMIC ▲ 47391 (16.97)
W. Meyer (org), H. von Karajan (cnd), Berlin PO *(rec St. Moritz, Switzerland, Aug 1969)* † Boccherini:Musica notturna, G.324; O. Respighi:Ancient Airs & Dances; Fontane di Roma; Pini di Roma DEUT (The Originals) ▲ 449724 [ADD] (11.97)
New York Harp Ensemble HUN ▲ 12726 (16.97)
Orpheus CO † J. S. Bach:Jesu, bleibet meine Freude; Suite 3 Orch, BWV 1068; A. Corelli:Con grosso, Op. 6/8; G. F. Handel:Solomon (arrival of the queen of Sheba); J. Pachelbel:Canon & Gigue; H. Purcell:Chacony Strs, Z.730; Vivaldi:Cons Vn(s) Strs, Op. 3/1-12 DEUT ▲ 29390 [DDD] (16.97)
J. Paillard (cnd), Jean-François Paillard CO † J. Pachelbel:Canon & Gigue RCAV (Red Seal) ▲ 65468 [DDD] (16.97) ▮ 65468 [DDD] (9.98)
M. Papadopoulos (cnd), City of Oxford Orch *(rec St. Barnabas Church, Oxford, England, May 1994)* ("Baroque Encores") † A. Corelli:Con grosso, Op. 6/8; G. F. Handel:Solomon (arrival of the queen of Sheba); Water Music, HWV 348-50; H. Purcell:Fairy Queen (sels); Torelli:Con for 2 Tpts INMP (Classics) ▲ 1104 (11.97)
J. Williams (cnd), Boston Pops Orch † G. Fauré:Pavane; J. Pachelbel:Canon & Gigue; Satie:Gymnopédies PPHI ▲ 16361 [DDD] (11.97)
A. Wills (org) *(rec Org of Ely Cathedral, England)* ("Full Stops") † H. Purcell:Voluntaries Org, Z.717-720; R. Wagner:Walküre (ride of the Valkyries); Widor:Marche pontificale, Op. 13/1; A. Wills:Vars on Amazing Grace MER ▲ 84305 (16.97)
various artists † J. S. Bach:Brandenburg Con 2, BWV 1047; Brandenburg Con 3, BWV 1048; Brandenburg Con 5, BWV 1050; Jesu, bleibet meine Freude; Suite 2 Fl, BWV 1067; Suite 3 Orch, BWV 1068; G. F. Handel:Messiah (sels); Royal Fireworks Music, HWV 351; Serse (sels); Water Music, HWV 348-50; Mouret:Rondeau; J. Pachelbel:Canon & Gigue; Vivaldi:Con Gtr; Cons Vn Strs, Op. 8/1-4 RCAV ▲ 60840 (10.97) ▮ 60840 (5.98)
various artists † J. S. Bach:Brandenburg Con 2, BWV 1047; Brandenburg Con 3, BWV 1048; Brandenburg Con 5, BWV 1050; Suite 2 Fl, BWV 1067; Suite 3 Orch, BWV 1068; G. F. Handel:Music of Handel; Mouret:Music of Mouret; J. Pachelbel:Canon & Gigue; Vivaldi:Con in D Gtr; Cons Vn Strs, Op. 8/1-4 RCAV ▲ 63501 (11.97)
Cantatas (12) for Voice & Continuo, Op. 4 (1702)
D. L. Ragin (ct), N. Selo (vc), R. Shaw (hpd)—No. 1. Amor, Sorte, Destino; No. 3. Del chiaro rio; No. 5. Lontananza crudel; No. 7. Ove rivoglio il piede; No. 9. Parti, mi lasci; No. 11. Poi che al vago seren ETC ▲ 1204 (17.97)
B. Schlick (sop), N. Selo (vc), R. Shaw (hpd)—No. 1. Amor, Sorte, Destino; No. 3. Del chiaro rio; No. 5. Lontananza crudel; No. 7. Ove rivoglio il piede; No. 9. Parti, mi lasci; No. 11. Poi che al vago seren *(rec Munich, Germany, Nov 1993)* ETC ▲ 1181 [DDD] (17.97)
Concertos à cinque (12) for 3 Violins, 2 Violas, Cello & Continuo, Op. 5
B. Bánfalvi (vn), Budapest Strings CAPO ▲ 10709 (10.97)
Concertos à cinque (12) for 1 or 2 Oboes & Strings, Op. 7
A. Camden (cnd), City of London Sinfonia—No. 12 in C ("The Art of the Oboe") † Cons Ob, Op. 9; V. Bellini:Con Ob; Cimarosa:Con Ob; A. Corelli:Con Ob; G. F. Handel:Cons Ob, HWV 301, 302a & 287; Rondo in G; Suites de Pièces (8) Hpd, HWV 426-33; V. Righini:Con Ob NXIN ▲ 8553991 (5.97)
E. Nepalov (ob), R. Barshaï (cnd), Moscow CO *(rec Great Hall, Moscow Conservatory, Russia, 1965)* † V. Bellini:Con Ob RUS ▲ 10062 [AAD]
P. Nielsen (tpt), South Jutland SO members—No. 3 in B♭ † M. Haydn:Con Tpt, Hns & Strs; L. Mozart:Con Tpt; Torelli:Sinf Tpt, G.9 DANI ▲ 8095 (19.97)
Concertos à cinque (12) for 1 or 2 Oboes & Strings, Op. 9
F. Ayo (vn), H. Holliger (ob), I Musici † Adagio PPHI (Duo) 2-▲ 456333 (17.97)
F. Ayo (vn), H. Holliger (ob), I Musici—No. 1 in B♭; No. 1 in B♭; No. 6 in G; No. 7 in D; No. 10 in F; No. 12 in D PPHI (Baroque Classics) ▲ 26080 (11.97)
A. Camden (cnd), City of London Sinfonia—No. 5 in C; No. 2 in d ("The Art of the Oboe") † Cons Ob, Op. 7; V. Bellini:Con Ob; Cimarosa:Con Ob; A. Corelli:Con Ob; G. F. Handel:Cons Ob, HWV 301, 302a & 287; Rondo in G; Suites de Pièces (8) Hpd, HWV 426-33; V. Righini:Con Ob NXIN ▲ 8553991 (5.97)
A. Camden (ob), J. Girdwood (ob), J. Georgiadis (cnd)—No. 2 in d; No. 3 in F; No. 5 in C; No. 8 in g; No. 9 in C; No. 11 in B♭ *(rec Oct 1992)* NXIN ▲ 550739 [DDD] (5.97)
M. Messiter (ob), Guildhall String Ensemble—No. 2 in d † J. S. Bach:Con Ob; G. F. Handel:Cons Ob, HWV 301, 302a & 287; A. Marcello:Con Ob Strs RCAV (Red Seal) ▲ 60224 [DDD] (16.97)
S. S. Syrinx (pan fl), J. Berlingen (cnd), Normandy Orchestral Ensemble—No. 2 in d [arr Syrinx] *(rec Oct 1994)* † B. Bartók:Romanian Folk Dances Vn & Pno; Cimarosa:Con Fls; Con Ob; C. Stamitz:Con Fl in G, Op. 29; Vivaldi:Con Fls, RV.533 CASC ▲ 65127
M. Wordtmann (sax), N. Kitano (pno)—No. 2 in d *(rec Germany, Apr 1995)* † Debussy:Rapsodie Sax; G. Fauré:Impromptus Pno; Sicilienne, Op. 78; Lully:Music of Lully; R. Noda:Improvisation I; S. Rachmaninoff:Vocalise; M. Ravel:Pièce en forme de Habanera; Tombeau FSM ▲ 97237 [DDD] (15.99)
Concertos à cinque (12) for Strings, Op. 10
J. Corazolla (cnd), Rhenish CO—No. 1 in B♭ ("Symphonies of the Italian Baroque") † A. Corelli:Concerti grossi, Op. 6; Geminiani:Concerti grossi (6) for 2 Vns, Op. 3; Locatelli:Concerti grossi, Op. 1; G. B. Sammartini:Sinf in A; Sym in G; Torelli:Con musicali, Op. 6; Vivaldi:Incoronazione di Dario (sels) ENTE ▲ 92 [DDD] (10.97)
C. Scimone (cnd), Venice Solisti ERAT (Ultima) 2-▲ 18943 (16.97)
Concerto in B for Trumpet & Strings, "San Marco"
M. André (tpt), J. Faerber (cnd), Württemberg CO *(rec Paris, France, June 1978)* ("Baroque, Vol. 1") † Adagio; Sinfonie e concerti à 5, Op. 2 EMIC ▲ 65337 [ADD] (9.97)
H. Pittel (sax), J. Helmer (pno) [arr Pittel] ("Moving Along with Harvey Pittel") † Creston:Son Sax, Op. 19; I. Dahl:Con A Sax; Ibert:Concertino da camera; P. Maurice:Tableaux de Provence; S. Rachmaninoff:Vocalise CRYS ▲ 655 (15.97)
Concertos for Trumpet & Organ
B. Kratzer (tpt), M. Nuber (org)—Con in C Tpt, Op.6/5 *(rec Münster zu Villingen, Germany, Feb 1990)* ("Virtuoso Trumpet Music of the Baroque") † G. B. Martini:Son al'Postcommunio; Toccata; H. Purcell:Cons Tpt & Org; Stradella:Sinf alla Serenata; Telemann:Qnt Tpt; Torelli:Con Tpt; J. G. Walther:Cons Tpt & Org FERM ▲ 20001 [DDD] (16.97)
Concerto in C for Trumpet, Oboes, Bassoon & Strings
R. Roseman (ob), S. Weiner (ob), V. Brewer (ob), R. MacCourt (bn), W. Scribner (bn), G. Schwarz (tpt), E. Brewer (hpd) ("The Age of Splendor") † G. B. Fontana:Sons; Frescobaldi:Canzonas, Capricci & Ricercari; Hertel:Con à cinque VB2 2-▲ 5124 [ADD] (9.97)
A. Vogel (ob), K. Gilad (ob), E. Reed (ob), M. O'Donovan (bn), A. Plog (tpt), O. Burdick (hpd) *(rec St. Augustine Episcopal Church, CA, Sept 1988)* ("The Trumpet in Baroque Chamber Settings") † W. Corbett:Son Tpt; A. Corelli:Son Tpt & Vns; Finger:Son Tpt & Ob; Hertel:Con à cinque; A. Scarlatti:Arias Sop, Tpt & Strs CENT ▲ 2068 [DDD] (16.97)
Flute Music
E. Di Felice (fl), R. Peiretti (hpd), R. Peiretti (cnd), Accademia dei Solinghi—Sons da camera, Op. posth. [No. 2 in a; No. 3 in E; No. 5 in D; No. 6 in B]; Con 1 Fl; Con 2 Fl ("Complete Works for German Flute") STRV ▲ 33377 [DDD] (16.97)

ALBINONI, TOMASO (cont.)

Flute Music (cont.)

A. Ligios (thb), E. Di Felice (fl), P. Erdas (hpd), L'Apothéose Ensemble—Trattenimenti armonici per camera, Op. 6 [No. 4 in d]; Sinfs Fl *(rec Nov 1995)* ("Complete Works for German Flute, Vol. 2") STRV ▲ 33441 (16.97)

Magnificat in g for Soprano, Alto, Tenor, Bass, Chorus & Strings

F. Szekeres (cnd), Budapest Strings † Caldara:Magnificat; G. B. Sammartini:Magnificat in B♭; Vivaldi:Magnificat, RV.610; Magnificat, RV.611 HUN ▲ 31259 [DDD] (16.97)

Music of Albinoni

R. Edlinger (cnd), Capella Istropolitana *(Adagio)*, A. Camden (ob), J. Girdwood (ob), A. Alty (ob), J. Georgiadis (cnd) , J. Georgiadis (cnd), London Virtuosi *(Cons Ob, Op. 9 [No. 5 in C; No. 2 in d; No. 3 in F; No. 9 in C; No. 11 in B♭; No. 8 in g; No. 12 in D; No. 6 in G])*, A. Camden (ob), A. Alty (ob), J. Georgiadis (cnd) , J. Georgiadis (cnd), London Virtuosi *(Cons Ob, Op. 7 [No. 11 in C; No. 6 in D; No. 4 in G; No. 12 in C; No. 2 in C; No. 9 in F; No. 3 in B♭; No. 1 in D])*, A. Camden (ob), A. Alty (ob), J. Georgiadis (cnd) *(Sinf Obs [Adagio])* ("Adagio Albinoni") NXIN ▲ 8552244 [DDD] (5.97)

H. Tims (gtr), H. Visser (gtr), A. Visser (fl), B. Brouwer (hpd)—Trio Sons, Op. 1 [No. 11]; Adagio *(rec 1996)* ("Buon Giorno: Visser Meets Italian Masters") † Cimarosa:Music of Cimarosa; D. Scarlatti:Sons Kbd; Vivaldi:Music of Vivaldi OREA ▲ 5284 [DDD] (11.97)

Sinfonie (6) e concerti (6) à cinque for Strings, Op. 2

R. Leppard (cnd), English CO—No. 6 in g; No. 3 in A *(rec London, England, Dec 1969)* ("Baroque, Vol. 1") † Adagio; Con in B Tpt EMIC ▲ 65337 [ADD] (9.97)

Sonatas (6) for Flute & Continuo [from Sinfonie di vari autori]

C. Piastra (gtr), C. Ferrarini (fl), F. Tasini (hpd) ("The 6 Rediscovered Sonatas") MONM (Il grande barocco Italiano) ▲ 96009 (17.97)

Sonate da chiesa (6) for Violin & Cello (or Continuo), Op. 6/4 (ca 1709)

E. Wallfisch (vn), Locatelli Trio † Trattenimenti armonici per camera, Op. 6 HYP 2-▲ 66831 (36.97)

Trattenimenti armonici per camera (12) for Violin, Violone & Harpsichord, Op. 6 (ca. 1712)

M. Folena (trns fl), Ensemble Barocco Padua Sans Souci—No. 1 in C; No. 2 in D; No. 6 in a; No. 7 in D; No. 8 in e; No. 9 in G *(rec Padova, Italy, 1995)* DYNC ▲ 139 [DDD] (17.97)

E. Wallfisch (vn), Locatelli Trio † Sonate da chiesa, Op. 6/4 HYP 2-▲ 66831 (36.97)

ALBRECHT, MOONYEEN (1936)

Psalms (4) for Flute & Organ

F. Shelly (fl), S. Egler (org) *(rec Wiedemann Recital Hall, Wichita State University, KS)* ("The Dove Descending") † Berlinski:Adagietto; Ochse:Prelude & Fugue Ft & Org; Roush:Dove Descending; B. W. Sanders:Pieces Fl; J. Weaver:Rhapsody; G. Young:Triptych SUMM ▲ 174 [DDD] (16.97)

ALBRECHT, TIMOTHY (20th cent)

Grace Notes (5 sets) for Organ

T. Albrecht (org) *(rec Cassavant Org, Emory Univ, Atlanta, GA, Apr 13, 1996)* ("Grace Notes") † Partita on Nun danket alle Gott ACAD ▲ 20058 [DDD] (16.97)

Partita on Nun danket alle Gott for Organ

T. Albrecht (org) *(rec Cassavant Org, Emory Univ, Atlanta, GA, Apr 13, 1996)* ("Grace Notes") † Grace Notes ACAD ▲ 20058 [DDD] (16.97)

ALBRECHTSBERGER, JOHANN GEORG (1736-1809)

Concertino in E♭ for Trumpet, Strings & Piano (1771)

R. Shermont (vn), J. Cauhape (va), A. Zighera (vc), A. Ghitalla (tpt), J. Weaver (pno) *(rec 1963-64)* † M. Haydn:Con in C Tpt; J. N. Hummel:Con Tpt in E; Molter:Con 3 Tpt CRYS ▲ 760 (15.97)

P. Thibaud (tpt), K. Toyoda (cnd), Gunma SO *(rec Tone-Numata Public Hall, Japan, Sept 1981)* † J. Haydn:Con Tpt; Jolivet:Concertino Tpt CAMA ▲ 168 [DDD] (18.97)

Concerto in E for Jew's Harp, Mandora & Orchestra (1770)

D. Kirsch (mandora), F. Mayr (jew's hp), H. Stadlmair (cnd), Munich CO ORF ▲ 35821 [DDD] (18.97)

Concerto in F for Jew's Harp, Mandora & Orchestra (1771)

D. Kirsch (mandora), F. Mayr (jew's hp), H. Stadlmair (cnd), Munich CO ORF ▲ 35821 [DDD] (18.97)

Missa assumptionis beata Mariae Virginis for SATB Voice, Mixed Voices (4) & Orchestra

F. Schmitt-Bohn (sop), J. Köble (alt), C. Elsner (ten), U. Rausch (bass), R. Hug (cnd) † M. Haydn:Missa Sancti Hieronymi ARSM ▲ 972 [DDD] (17.97)

Partita in F for Harp

S. Kowalczuk (hp) ("Festival on the Classical Harp") † I. Albéniz:Pno Music (misc); Grandjany:Rhap Hp, Op. 10; W. A. Mozart:Adagio & Rondo, K.617; Würtzler:Modern Sketches HUN ▲ 31577 (16.97)

ALBRIGHT, WILLIAM (1944-

Abiding Passions for Woodwind Quintet (1988)

Sierra Wind Quintet *(rec U. of Nevada, Las Vegas, NV)* † B. Childs:Box of Views; Etler:Qnt 2 Ww; M. Powell:Qnt Ww CMB ▲ 1044

Chasm for Organ & Percussion (1985)

P. Decker (org) † Flights of Fancy; H. Bielawa:Undertones; P. Decker:Nightsong & Ostinato Dances ALBA ▲ 140 [DDD] (16.97)

Chromatic Dances (5) for Piano (1976)

T. Warburton (pno) *(rec UNC, Chapel Hill, NC, June 1980)* † Grand Son in Rag; Pianoàgogo; Sphaera CRI ▲ 674 [ADD/DDD] (16.97)

Fancies (4) for Harpsichord (1979)

D. Reed (hpd) ("Eastman American Music Series, Vol. 3") † N. Dinerstein:Love Songs; Hamer:Morning Asanas; Silsbee:Doors ALBA ▲ 251 [ADD] (16.97)

Flights of Fancy (ballet) for Organ (1991-92)

P. Decker (org) † Chasm; H. Bielawa:Undertones; P. Decker:Nightsong & Ostinato Dances ALBA ▲ 140 [DDD] (16.97)

Grand Sonata in Rag for Piano (1968)

T. Warburton (pno) *(rec Duke Univ, Durham, NC, May 1992)* † Chromatic Dances; Pianoàgogo; Sphaera CRI ▲ 674 [ADD/DDD] (16.97)

Jericho: Battle Music for Trumpet & Organ

K. Benjamin (tpt), M. Turnquist (org) ("Clarion: New Music for Trumpet & Organ") † P. Eben:Okna; P. Hamelin:Sonata ben melodico; Nelhybel:Metamorphosis; Starer:Preludes Tpt GOT ▲ 49067 [DDD] (18.97)

Pianoàgogo for Piano (1965-66)

T. Warburton (pno) *(rec UNC, Chapel Hill, NC, June 1980)* † Chromatic Dances; Grand Son in Rag; Sphaera CRI ▲ 674 [ADD/DDD] (16.97)

A Song to David (oratorio in 5 parts) for Voices, Organ & Chorus [set to poetry by Christopher Smart]

H. D. Small (cnd), St. Mark's Cathedral Choir Minneapolis, D. Carbaugh (sop), S. Sacquitne-Druck (mez), R. Penning (ten), J. Bohn (bass), M. Semmes (nar), C. Russell (nar), D. Billmeyer (org) *(rec live, St. Mark's Cathedral, Minneapolis, MN, Apr 28, 1991)* GOT ▲ 49066 [DDD] (17.97)

Sphaera for Piano & Computer Generated Sound (1985)

T. Warburton (pno) *(rec Duke Univ, Durham, NC, May 1992)* † Chromatic Dances; Grand Son in Rag; Pianoàgogo CRI ▲ 674 [ADD/DDD] (16.97)

ALCALAY, LUNA (1928-

Fluchtpunktzeile for Mezzo-Soprano, Baritone & Orchestra

C. Ascher (mez), M. Hemm (bar), C. Kalmar (cnd), Vienna SO ("Und nicht vergessen") † Strofa di Dante; D. Kaufmann:Heiligenlegende; Tod des Trompeters Kirilenko VMM ▲ 3020 [AAD]

Una strofa di Dante for Orchestra & Chorus

B. Maderna (cnd), Austrian RSO, Austrian Radio Chorus ("Und nicht vergessen") † Fluchtpunktzeile; D. Kaufmann:Heiligenlegende; Tod des Trompeters Kirilenko VMM ▲ 3020 [AAD]

ALCORN, MICHAEL (1962-

Making a Song & Dance for Violin, Cello, Clarinet & Piano

Sequenza ("Making a Song & Dance") † Perichoresis; Hellawell:Oh Whistle and I'll Come; Truth or Consequences; Volans:Into Darkness NEU ▲ 45097 [DDD] (16.97)

Perichoresis 1990 for Wind Quintet (1990)

Sequenza ("Making a Song & Dance") † Making a Song & Dance; Hellawell:Oh Whistle and I'll Come; Truth or Consequences; Volans:Into Darkness NEU ▲ 45097 [DDD] (16.97)

ALDANA, MARIO KURI (dates unknown)

Canto Latinoamericano for Orchestra

H. de la Fuente (cnd), Mexican State PO † G. Duran:Nepantla; R. Halffter:Madrugada del panadero, Op. 12a; Jiménez-Mabarak:Sym in 1 Movt; Lavalle-García:Obertura Colonial; Sandi:Theme & Vars CLME ▲ 21006 (13.97)

ALDRIDGE, ROBERT (LIVINGSTON) (1954-

Combo Platter for Soprano Saxophone, Violin & Marimba

S. Leventhal (vn), A. Regni (s sax), N. Zeltsman (mar) ("3 Dark Paintings") † Prisoner of Love; Qt for an Outdoor Festival; Bourland:Dark Paintings; Sax Qnt; Stone Qt MASM ▲ 34 [DDD]

ALDRIDGE, ROBERT (LIVINGSTON) (cont.)

Prisoner of Love for Soprano Saxophone & Piano

A. Regni (s sax), T. O. Sterrett (pno) ("3 Dark Paintings") † Combo Platter; Qt for an Outdoor Festival; Bourland:Dark Paintings; Sax Qnt; Stone Qt MASM ▲ 34 [DDD]

Quartet for an Outdoor Festival for Soprano Saxophone, Violin, Cello & Piano

M. Feldman (vn), B. Lauridsen (vc), A. Regni (s sax), T. O. Sterrett (pno) ("3 Dark Paintings") † Combo Platter; Prisoner of Love; Bourland:Dark Paintings; Sax Qnt; Stone Qt MASM ▲ 34 [DDD]

threedance for Violin & Marimba (1987)

Marimolin † T. O. Lee:Marimolin; L. Mays:Somewhere in Maine; A. Rogers:Shadow-Play; L. Thimmig:Bluefire Crown III; S. Wheeler:Lyric Vars Vn & Mar GMR ▲ 2023 [DDD] (16.97)

ALEXANDER, KATHRYN (1955-

And the Whole Air Is Tremulous for Flute (1985)

D. Stone (fl) ("None but the Lonely Flute") † Babbitt:None but the Lonely; J. Cage:Ryoanji Fl; M. Feldman:Trio Fls; S. L. Mosko:for Morton Feldman; Indigenous Music 2 NWW ▲ 80456 (16.97)

ALEXANDER, WILLIAM (1927-

Cambridge Trio for Oboe, Viola (or Clarinet) & Piano (1984)

C. Englert (ob), J. Russo (cl), L. W. Ignacio (pno) † O. Aubert:Solo de Concours 1; L. Bernstein:Son Cl; Diemer:Vars Pno 4-Hands; J. Fry:Pierrot's Fancy; E. Pellegrini:Divert a tre Bn CRSR ▲ 8949

Salphynx for Orchestra (1992)

R. Stankovský (cnd), Slovak RSO ("MMC New Century, Vol. VII") † E. George:Thanksgiving Ov; Sacco:Flying Saucer Ov; Sketches on Emerson; Wendelburg:Sinf MASM ▲ 2029 [DDD] (16.97)

ALEXIUS, CARL (1928-

Sonatina for Trumpet & Piano (1959)

E. H. Tarr (tpt), E. Westenholz (pno) † Cellier:Thème et variations; G. Gershwin:Rhap in Blue; P. Hindemith:Son Tpt; Martinů:Sonatina Tpt; S. Weiner:Phantasy 1 Tpt, Op. 57; F. Werner:Duo Tpt & Org, Op. 53 BIS ▲ 152 [AAD] (17.97)

ALFONSO EL SABIO (1221-1284)

Cantigas de Santa Maria

A. S. Karlić (cnd), Theatrum Instrumentorum [sels] AART ▲ 47528 (10.97)

Micrologus—A Madre do que livrou (No. 4); Qual é a santivigada (No. 330); Madre de Deus (No. 422); Ben vennas, Mayo (No. 406); Nenbre-sse-te, Madre (No. 421); Quen bõa dona querrá (No. 160); Muito nos faz gran merçee (No. 378); Aver non poderia (No. 403); Ontre toldalas vertudes (No. 323); Rosa des rosas (No. 10); Sabor á Santa Maria (No. 328); Santa Maria valed' ai sennor (No. 279); Quantos me creveren loaran (No. 120); Quen á Santa Maria (No. 138); De todo mal (No. 308); Quantos me creveren loaran (No. 120); Nas mentes senpre tẽer (No. 29) *(rec Ceralto, Italy, Dec 1997)* ("Madre de Deus; Cantigas de Santa Maria") *([ENG,FRE,GER,SPA] text)* OPUS ▲ 30225 [DDD] (18.97)

E. Paniagua (cnd) , Valle de los Caídos Monastery School Children's Choir—Star of the Day; Prologue to the 5 Feasts; Dawn of All Dawns; Nativity of Holy Mary; Virginity; Trinity of Holy Mary; Mother of Jesus Christ; Mother of God; Old Woman & Child; Humanity of Holy Mary; Flower of All Flowers; Annunciation; Ave Maria; The Angels' Greeting; Purification-Candlemas; 7 Gifts; Nun & Gentleman; Assumption; Procession; Day of Judgment; Sybil-Judgement ("The Life of Mary") SNYC 2-▲ 62284 (31.97)

Unicorn Ensemble *(rec Nov 1994)* NXIN ▲ 553133 [DDD] (5.97)

S. Wishart (cnd), Sinfonye—Ben guarda Santa Maria (No. 257); A Virgin mui Groriosa (No. 42); Poder a Santa Maria (No. 185); Santa Maria valed' ai sennor (No. 279); Por nos Virgen Madre (No. 250); Quantos me creveren loaran (No. 120); Os que a Santa Maria (No. 344); Sempr' a Virgen Groriosa (No. 345); Instrumental Improvisation; A que por nos salvar (No. 169); O que mui tarde ou nunca (No. 321); Ontre toldalas vertudes (No. 323) *(rec Cazalla de la Sierra, Seville, Spain)* AL ▲ 105 [DDD]

ALFORD, KENNETH (1881-1945) *(aka Maj. Fredrick Joseph Ricketts)*

Marches

C. R. Mason (cnd), Her Majesty's Royal Marines Band—Musical Switch (2 fants); The Lightning Switch; Colonel Bogey; The Great Little Army; H.M. Jollies; On the Quarterdeck; The Thin Red Line; Voice of the Guns; The Standard of St. George; Cavalry of the Clouds; The Middy; Holyrood; Army of the Nile; Dunedin; The Vanished Army; Old Panama; Eagle Squadron; By Land & Sea; Vedette; The Mad Major CHN (Collect) ▲ 6584 [ADD] (12.97)

ALFVÉN, HUGO (1872-1960)

Bergakungen (ballet pantomime) for Orchestra, Op. 37, "The Mountain King" (1916-23)

E. Svetlanov (cnd), Swedish RSO MSV ▲ 614 [DDD] (16.97)

Bergakungen (selections)

V. Fedoseyev (cnd), Moscow RSO † Berwald:Estrella de Soria (ov); J. M. Kraus:Tragedy of Olympus; M. Kuss:Lyric Poem; Lidholm:Kontakion; Sibelius:Finlandia, Op. 26 CSN ▲ 810011 [DDD] (16.97)

N. Järvi (cnd), Stockholm PO † Gustav II Adolph, Op. 49; Sym 5 BIS ▲ 585 [DDD] (17.97)

S. Westerberg (cnd), Swedish RSO—Shepherd-girl's Dance *(rec Berwald Hall, Stockholm, Sweden, May 7, 1986)* ("Swedish Highlights") † Festspel, Op. 25; Gustav II Adolph, Op. 49; Prodigal Son, Op. 217; Swedish Flag; Swedish Rhap 1, Op. 19; L.-E. Larsson:Pastoralsvit, Op. 19; O. J. Lindblad:Royal Anthem; Söderman:Swedish Festival; Stenhammar:Ett folk, Op. 22; Sången, Op. 44; Traditional:Du Gamla, Du Fria; D. Wirén:Serenade Strs, Op. 11 CAPA ▲ 21340 [DDD] (16.97)

Bergakungen:Suite

N. Järvi (cnd), Royal Stockholm PO *(rec Stockholm Concert Hall, Sweden, Dec 18, 1992)* † Swedish Rhap 1, Op. 19; Swedish Rhap 2, Op. 24; Swedish Rhap 3, Op. 47; Tale from the Archipelago, Op. 20 BIS ▲ 725 [DDD] (17.97)

N. Willén (cnd), Royal Scottish National Orch † Festspel, Op. 25; Swedish Rhap 2, Op. 24; Sym 1 NXIN ▲ 8553962 [DDD] (5.97)

Choral Music

C. H. Ahnsjö (ten), F. Alin (pno), R. Sund (cnd), Orphei Drängar—Hör I Orphei Drängar; Dawn at Sea; Papillon; Gustaf Frödings Funeral; Berceuse; Spring in Roslagen; Sweden's Flag; My Sweetheart; Serenade; Night; Evening; Lullaby; So Take My Heart; Quiet Hours; Scents of Summer; You Are Peaceful Calm; I Long for You; The Forest Sleeps; The Trial; Flowers of Joy; Värmlandsvisan; Oxberg March; Swedish Dance; Fatheads; Herdboy's Song; Andrew Was a Lively Lad; And the Maiden Joins the Ring; In Our Meadow; Swedish Mood *(rec 1993)* BIS ▲ 633 [DDD] (17.97)

Dalecarlian Rhapsody for Orchestra

S. Westerberg (cnd), Stockholm PO † Sym 3 SWES ▲ 1008

A District Fairytale [En Bygdesaga] (suite) for Orchestra, Op. 53 (1944)

H. Frank (cnd), Helsingborg SO *(rec Nov 29, 1982)* † Synnöve Solbakken, Op. 50 STRL ▲ 1012 [ADD] (15.97)

Festspel for Orchestra, Op. 25 (1907)

S. Westerberg (cnd), Swedish RSO *(rec Berwald Hall, Stockholm, Sweden, May 7, 1986)* ("Swedish Highlights") † Bergakungen (sels); Gustav II Adolph, Op. 49; Prodigal Son, Op. 217; Swedish Flag; Swedish Rhap 1, Op. 19; L.-E. Larsson:Pastoralsvit, Op. 19; O. J. Lindblad:Royal Anthem; Söderman:Swedish Festival; Stenhammar:Ett folk, Op. 22; Sången, Op. 44; Traditional:Du Gamla, Du Fria; D. Wirén:Serenade Strs, Op. 11 CAPA ▲ 21340 [DDD] (16.97)

N. Willén (cnd), Royal Scottish National Orch † Bergakungen (suite); Swedish Rhap 2, Op. 24; Sym 1 NXIN ▲ 8553962 [DDD] (5.97)

Gustav II Adolph (incidental music) for Orchestra, Op. 49 (1932)

N. Järvi (cnd), Stockholm PO † Bergakungen (sels); Sym 5 BIS ▲ 585 [DDD] (17.97)

P. Sakari (cnd), Iceland SO † Swedish Rhap 1, Op. 19; Swedish Rhap 2, Op. 24; Swedish Rhap 3, Op. 47; Tale from the Archipelago, Op. 20 CHN ▲ 9313 [DDD] (16.97)

S. Westerberg (cnd), Swedish RSO—Elegy *(rec Berwald Hall, Stockholm, Sweden, May 7, 1986)* ("Swedish Highlights") † Bergakungen (sels); Festspel, Op. 25; Prodigal Son, Op. 217; Swedish Flag; Swedish Rhap 1, Op. 19; L.-E. Larsson:Pastoralsvit, Op. 19; O. J. Lindblad:Royal Anthem; Söderman:Swedish Festival; Stenhammar:Ett folk, Op. 22; Sången, Op. 44; Traditional:Du Gamla, Du Fria; D. Wirén:Serenade Strs, Op. 11 CAPA ▲ 21340 [DDD] (16.97)

Notturno elegiaco for Horn & Piano, Op. 5 (1898)

I. Ølen (hn), G. H. Braaten (pno) *(rec Sweden, 1980-82)* ("The Scandinavian Horn") † N. V. Bentzon:Son Hn; Heise:Fant Piece 2; K. Jeppesen:Little Trio Fl, Hn & Pno; Kvandal:Intro & Allegro, Op. 30; C. Nielsen:Canto serioso, FS.132; S. Olsen:Aubade BIS ▲ 171 [AAD] (17.97)

The Prodigal Son [Den förloarde sonen] (ballet suite) for Piano, Op. 217 (1957)

N. Järvi (cnd), Stockholm PO † Swedish Rhap 3, Op. 47; Sym 3 BIS ▲ 455 [DDD] (17.97)

S. Westerberg (cnd), Swedish RSO—Swedish Polka *(rec Berwald Hall, Stockholm, Sweden, May 7, 1986)* ("Swedish Highlights") † Bergakungen (sels); Festspel, Op. 25; Gustav II Adolph, Op. 49; Swedish Flag; Swedish Rhap 1, Op. 19; L.-E. Larsson:Pastoralsvit, Op. 19; O. J. Lindblad:Royal Anthem; Söderman:Swedish Festival; Stenhammar:Ett folk, Op. 22; Sången, Op. 44; Traditional:Du Gamla, Du Fria; D. Wirén:Serenade Strs, Op. 11 CAPA ▲ 21340 [DDD] (16.97)

Sleeping Forest for Violin

S. Stahlhammer (vn), L. Derwinger (pno) † V. Aulin:Andante Lamentoso; T. Aulin:Character Pieces (2); Four Watercolors; Haquinius:Nocturne; Swedish Dance; Järnefelt:Andante; Rangström:Adagio doloroso; Spring Nights NSAG ▲ 24 [DDD] (16.97)

ALFVÉN, HUGO (cont.)

Songs

J. Björling (ten), N. Grevillius (cnd), Gothenburg SO—Skogen sover, Op. 28/6; Jag längtar dig *(rec Concert Hall Göteborg, Sweden, Aug 5, 1960)* ("Jussi Björling's Last Concert") † Leoncavallo:Pagliacci (sels); G. Puccini:Manon Lescaut (sels); Sibelius:Songs; P. Tchaikovsky:Eugene Onegin (sels); Verdi:Rigoletto (sels); Trovatore (sels); R. Wagner:Lohengrin (sels) MYTO ▲ 953130 (17.97)

The Swedish Flag for Male Chorus (1916)

S. Westerberg (cnd), Swedish Radio Choir *(rec Berwald Hall, Stockholm, Sweden, May 7, 1986)* ("Swedish Highlights") † Bergakungen (sels); Festspel, Op. 25; Gustav II Adolph, Op. 49; Prodigal Son, Op. 217; Swedish Rhap 1, Op. 19; L.-E. Larsson:Pastoralsvit, Op. 19; O. J. Lindblad:Royal Anthem; Söderman:Swedish Festival; Stenhammar:Ett folk, Op. 22; Sången, Op. 44; Traditional:Du Gamla, Du Fria; D. Wirén:Serenade Strs, Op. 11 CAPA ▲ 21340 [DDD] (16.97)

Swedish Rhapsody No. 1 for Orchestra, Op. 19, "Midsommarvaka" (1903)

R. Edlinger (cnd), CSSR State PO Košice *(rec Oct 1988)* † E. Grieg:Lyric Suite, Op. 54/1-4; Norwegian Dances, Op. 35; Symphonic Dances, Op. 64; Sibelius:Karelia Ov, Op. 10; J. S. Svendsen:Norwegian Artists' Carnival, Op. 14 NXIN ▲ 550090 [DDD] (5.97)

N. Järvi (cnd), Royal Stockholm PO *(rec Stockholm Concert Hall, Sweden, Dec 3, 1987)* † Bergakungen (suite); Swedish Rhap 2, Op. 24; Swedish Rhap 3, Op. 47; Tale from the Archipelago, Op. 20 BIS ▲ 725 [DDD] (17.97)

N. Järvi (cnd), Stockholm PO † Sym 2 BIS ▲ 385 [DDD] (17.97)

E. Ormandy (cnd), Philadelphia Orch † Chabrier:España; Enescu:Romanian Rhap 1, Op. 11/1; Liszt:Hungarian Rhaps, S.244; M. Ravel:Rapsodie espagnole SNYC ▲ 38917 (7.97)

E. Ormandy (cnd), Philadelphia Orch ("Famous Rhapsodies") † Chabrier:España; Enescu:Romanian Rhap 1, Op. 11/1; Romanian Rhap 2, Op. 11/2; Liszt:Hungarian Rhaps, S.244 SNYC (Essential Classics) ▲ 60265 (7.97) ▮ 60265 (3.98)

E. Oue (cnd), Minnesota Orch *(rec Minneapolis, MN, Oct 1-3, 1996)* ("Ports of Call") † Borodin:In the Steppes of Central Asia; Chabrier:España; Ibert:Escales; Sibelius:Finlandia, Op. 26; Smetana:Moldau; P. Tchaikovsky:Capriccio italien, Op. 45 REF ▲ 80 (16.97)

P. Sakari (cnd), Iceland SO † Gustav II Adolph, Op. 49; Swedish Rhap 2, Op. 24; Swedish Rhap 3, Op. 47; Tale from the Archipelago, Op. 20 CHN ▲ 9313 [DDD] (16.97)

S. Westerberg (cnd), Swedish RSO *(rec Berwald Hall, Stockholm, Sweden, May 7, 1986)* ("Swedish Highlights") † Bergakungen (sels); Festspel, Op. 25; Gustav II Adolph, Op. 49; Prodigal Son, Op. 217; Swedish Flag; L.-E. Larsson:Pastoralsvit, Op. 19; O. J. Lindblad:Royal Anthem; Söderman:Swedish Festival; Stenhammar:Ett folk, Op. 22; Sången, Op. 44; Traditional:Du Gamla, Du Fria; D. Wirén:Serenade Strs, Op. 11 CAPA ▲ 21340 [DDD] (16.97)

Swedish Rhapsody No. 2 for Orchestra, Op. 24, "Uppsala-rhapsodi" (1907)

N. Järvi (cnd), Royal Stockholm PO *(rec Stockholm Concert Hall, Sweden, Feb 11, 1988)* † Bergakungen (suite); Swedish Rhap 1, Op. 19; Swedish Rhap 3, Op. 47; Tale from the Archipelago, Op. 20 BIS ▲ 725 [DDD] (17.97)

N. Järvi (cnd), Stockholm PO † Sym 1 BIS ▲ 395 (17.97)

P. Sakari (cnd), Iceland SO † Gustav II Adolph, Op. 49; Swedish Rhap 1, Op. 19; Swedish Rhap 3, Op. 47; Tale from the Archipelago, Op. 20 CHN ▲ 9313 [DDD] (16.97)

N. Willén (cnd), Royal Scottish National Orch † Bergakungen (suite); Festspel, Op. 25; Sym 1 NXIN ▲ 8553962 [DDD] (5.97)

Swedish Rhapsody No. 3 for Orchestra, Op. 47, "Dalarhapsodien" (1931)

N. Järvi (cnd), Royal Stockholm PO *(rec Stockholm Concert Hall, Sweden, May 25, 1989)* † Bergakungen (suite); Swedish Rhap 1, Op. 19; Swedish Rhap 2, Op. 24; Tale from the Archipelago, Op. 20 BIS ▲ 725 [DDD] (17.97)

N. Järvi (cnd), Stockholm PO † Prodigal Son, Op. 217; Sym 3 BIS ▲ 455 [DDD] (17.97)

P. Sakari (cnd), Iceland SO † Gustav II Adolph, Op. 49; Swedish Rhap 1, Op. 19; Swedish Rhap 2, Op. 24; Tale from the Archipelago, Op. 20 CHN ▲ 9313 [DDD] (16.97)

Symphony No. 1 in f, Op. 7 (1897)

N. Järvi (cnd), Stockholm PO † Swedish Rhap 2, Op. 24 BIS ▲ 395 (17.97)

N. Willén (cnd), Royal Scottish National Orch † Bergakungen (suite); Festspel, Op. 25; Swedish Rhap 2, Op. 24 NXIN ▲ 8553962 [DDD] (5.97)

Symphony No. 2 in D, Op. 11 (1897-98)

N. Järvi (cnd), Stockholm PO † Swedish Rhap 1, Op. 19 BIS ▲ 385 [DDD] (17.97)

E. Svetlanov (cnd), Swedish RSO MSV ▲ 627 [DDD] (16.97)

Symphony No. 3 in E♭, Op. 23 (1905)

N. Grevillius (cnd), Stockholm PO † Dalecarlian Rhap SWES ▲ 1008

N. Järvi (cnd), Stockholm PO † Prodigal Son, Op. 217; Swedish Rhap 3, Op. 47 BIS ▲ 455 [DDD] (17.97)

Symphony No. 4 for Soprano, Tenor & Orchestra, Op. 39, "Fran havsbandet [From the Seaward Skerries]" (1919)

C. Högman (sop), C. H. Ahnsjö (ten), N. Järvi (cnd), Stockholm PO † Tale from the Archipelago, Op. 20 BIS ▲ 505 [DDD] (17.97)

Symphony No. 5 in a, Op. 54 (1942-53)

N. Järvi (cnd), Stockholm PO † Bergakungen (sels); Gustav II Adolph, Op. 49 BIS ▲ 585 [DDD] (17.97)

Synnöve Solbakken (suite from film music) for Piano (or Orchestra), Op. 50 (1934)

H. Damgaard (cnd), Norrköping SO *(rec Aug 31, 1973)* † District Fairytale, Op. 53 STRL ▲ 1012 [ADD] (15.97)

A Tale from the Archipelago [En skärgårdssägen] (tone poem) for Orchestra, Op. 20 (1904)

N. Järvi (cnd), Royal Stockholm PO *(rec Stockholm Concert Hall, Sweden, Oct 4, 1990)* † Bergakungen (suite); Swedish Rhap 1, Op. 19; Swedish Rhap 2, Op. 24; Swedish Rhap 3, Op. 47 BIS ▲ 725 [DDD] (17.97)

N. Järvi (cnd), Stockholm PO † Sym 4 BIS ▲ 505 [DDD] (17.97)

P. Sakari (cnd), Iceland SO † Gustav II Adolph, Op. 49; Swedish Rhap 1, Op. 19; Swedish Rhap 2, Op. 24; Swedish Rhap 3, Op. 47 CHN ▲ 9313 [DDD] (16.97)

ALI-ZADE, FRANGIZ (1947-

Crossing II for Winds, Strings & Percussion (1993)

F. Ali-zade (glock/vib), La Strimpellata Bern *(rec Bern, Germany, Dec 1996)* ("Crossings") † Dilogie I; From Japanese Poetry; Music for Pno; Watercolours BIS ▲ 827 [DDD] (17.97)

Dilogie I for String Quartet (1988)

La Strimpellata Bern members *(rec Bern, Germany, Dec 1996)* ("Crossings") † Crossing II; From Japanese Poetry; Music for Pno; Watercolours BIS ▲ 827 [DDD] (17.97)

From Japanese Poetry for Soprano, Flute & Keyboard [text Isikawa Takuboku] (1990)

B. Ispir (sop), R. Küffer (fl), F. Ali-zade (cel/vib/pno) *(rec Bern, Germany, Dec 1996)* ("Crossings") † Crossing II; Dilogie I; Music for Pno; Watercolours BIS ▲ 827 [DDD] (17.97)

Mugam Sayagi for String Quartet (1993)

Kronos Quartet ("Night Prayers") † Golijov:K'Vakarat; Gubaidulina:Qt 4 Strs; Kancheli:Night Prayers for Str Qt; Tahmizyan:Cool Wind is Blowing; Yanov-Yanovsky:Lacrymosa NON ▲ 79346 (16.97)

Music for Piano (1989)

F. Ali-zade (pno) *(rec Bern, Germany, Dec 1996)* ("Crossings") † Crossing II; Dilogie I; From Japanese Poetry; Watercolours BIS ▲ 827 [DDD] (17.97)

Watercolours (3) for Soprano, Flute & Prepared Piano [text Nigjar Rafibejli] (1987)

B. Ispir (sop), R. Küffer (fl), F. Ali-zade (prepared pno) *(rec Bern, Germany, Dec 1996)* ("Crossings") † Crossing II; Dilogie I; From Japanese Poetry; Music for Pno BIS ▲ 827 [DDD] (17.97)

ALKAN, CHARLES-VALENTIN (1813-1888)

Chamber Music

Alkan Trio—Grand Duo concertant for Vn & Pno, Op. 21; Sonate de concert, Op. 47; Trio Pno, Op. 30 *(rec June 1991)* MARC ▲ 8223383 [DDD] (13.97)

D. Kang (vn), Y. Chiffoleau (vc), O. Gardon (pno)—Grand Duo concertant for Vn & Pno, Op. 21; Sonate de concert, Op. 47; Trio Pno, Op. 30 TIMP ▲ 1013 [DDD]

Concertos de camera (2) in a & c# for Piano & Chamber Orchestra, Op. 10 (1834)

M. Hamelin (pno), M. Brabbins (cnd), BBC Scottish SO † Henselt:Con Pno, Op. 16; Vars de concert, Op. 11 HYP ▲ 66717 (18.97)

Etudes (12) in major keys for Piano, Op. 35 (1848)

S. McCallum (pno) *(rec Newcastle Conservatorium Hall, England, Dec 1992)* TALP ▲ 55 [DDD] (18.97)

R. Smith (pno)—No. 5, "Allegro barbaro" *(rec London, England, Jan 1977)* † Etudes in minor keys, Op. 39; Petites fants, Op. 41; Preludes Pno, Op. 31 APR 2-▲ 7031 [ADD] (37.97)

Etudes (12) in minor keys for Piano, Op. 39 (1857)

J. Gibbons (pno) † Pno Music ASV 2-▲ 227 [DDD] (31.97)

M.-A. Hamelin (pno)—No. 12, "Le festin d'Esope" † Grande son, Op. 33; Sonatine Pno, Op. 61; Troisième recueil de chants, Op. 65 HYP ▲ 66794 (18.97)

R. Lewenthal (pno)—No. 12, "Le festin d'Esope"; Nos. 4-7, "Symphonie, Mvts 1-4" † Grande son, Op. 33; Troisième recueil de chants, Op. 65; Liszt:Hexaméron Pno, S.392 HP (High Performance) ▲ 63310 (11.97)

S. McCallum (pno) *(rec Sydney, June 1995)* † Preludes Pno, Op. 31; Magnard:Promenades, Op. 7 TALP ▲ 81 [DDD] (18.97)

B. Ringeissen (pno) MARC ▲ 8223285 [DDD] (13.97)

B. Ringeissen (pno) † Pno Music; Sonatine Pno, Op. 61 HMA ▲ 190927 [ADD] (9.97)

ALKAN, CHARLES-VALENTIN (cont.)

Etudes (12) in minor keys for Piano, Op. 39 (1857) (cont.)

M. Salman (pno)—Nos. 4-7, "Symphonie, Mvts 1-4" *(rec Holy Trinity Church, NYC, NY, Feb 1993)* ("The Transcendental Piano") † Beethoven:Son 31 Pno, Op. 110; Liszt:Mephisto Waltz 2 Orch, S.111; Sarabande & Chaconne, S.181 TIT ▲ 220

R. Smith (pno) *(rec London, England, Jan 1977)* † Etudes in major keys, Op. 35; Petites fants, Op. 41; Preludes Pno, Op. 31 APR 2-▲ 7031 [ADD] (37.97)

Grande fantasia on Themes from Mozart's *Don Giovanni* for Piano 4-Hands

Alkan Duo *(rec Milan, Feb 1997)* ("Opera for 4 Hands") † Czerny:Fant elegante, Op. 247/25; Intro & Vars on Donizetti, Op. 398/17; H. Herz:Vars concertanti, Op. 70; Pixis:Fant drammatica; Thalberg:Fant on Rossini, Op. 33 AG ▲ 105 [DDD] (18.97)

Grande sonata [Les quatre âges] for Piano, Op. 33 (1848)

M.-A. Hamelin (pno) † Etudes in minor keys, Op. 39; Sonatine Pno, Op. 61; Troisième recueil de chants, Op. 65 HYP ▲ 66794 (18.97)

R. Lewenthal (pno)—Quasi-Faust † Etudes in minor keys, Op. 39; Troisième recueil de chants, Op. 65; Liszt:Hexaméron Pno, S.392 HP (High Performance) ▲ 63310 (11.97)

P. Réach (pno) † Sonatine Pno, Op. 61 DI ▲ 920362 [DDD] (5.97)

Marches (3) for Piano 4-Hands (1857)

J. Pennetier (pno), H. Sermet (pno) † Petites fants, Op. 41; Pno Music VAL (Musique Française) ▲ 4808 (18.97)

Motifs (49) for Piano, Op. 63, "Esquisses" (1861)

L. Martin (pno) *(rec Dec 1990)* MARC ▲ 8223352 [DDD] (13.97)

Organ Music

L. Martin (org)—Impromptus (4) Pno, Op. 32/1; Deuxième recueil d'impromptus, Op. 32/2; Salut, cendre du pauvre!; Alleluia; Rondeau chromatique; Vars on a theme from Steibelt: Orage; Super flumina Babylonis MARC ▲ 8223657 [DDD] (13.97)

Petites fantaisies (3) for Piano, Op. 41 (1857)

H. Sermet (pno) † Marches; Pno Music VAL (Musique Française) ▲ 4808 (18.97)

R. Smith (pno) *(rec London, England, Jan 1977)* † Etudes in major keys, Op. 35; Etudes in minor keys, Op. 39; Preludes Pno, Op. 31 APR 2-▲ 7031 [ADD] (37.97)

Piano Music

J. Gibbons (pno)—Nocturne in B; Allegro Barbaro; Assez vivement; J'etait endormie, mai mon coeur veillait; Le Staccatissimo; Les Cloches; Les Soupirs; En songe; Gros temps; Barcarolle, Op. 67/6; Le Chanson de la folle au bord de la mer; Le Temps qui n'est plus † Etudes in minor keys, Op. 39 ASV 2-▲ 227 [DDD] (31.97)

J. Pennetier (pno), H. Sermet (pno)—Allegro Barbaro; Deuxième recueil d'impromptus, Op. 32/2 † Marches; Petites fants, Op. 41 VAL (Musique Française) ▲ 4808 (18.97)

B. Ringeissen (pno)—Barcarolle, Op. 67/6; Gigue, Op. 24; Marches [No. 1 in a]; Nocturnes (2) Pno, Op. 57 [No. 2]; Saltarelle, Op. 23 † Etudes in minor keys, Op. 39; Sonatine Pno, Op. 61 HMA ▲ 190927 [ADD] (9.97)

Preludes (25) for Piano, Op. 31

S. McCallum (pno)—No. 8, "La chanson de la folle au bord de la mer" *(rec Sydney, Australia, June 1995)* † Etudes in minor keys, Op. 39; Magnard:Promenades, Op. 7 TALP ▲ 81 [DDD] (18.97)

R. Smith (pno)—No. 8, "La chanson de la folle au bord du mer" *(rec London, England, Jan 1977)* † Etudes in major keys, Op. 35; Etudes in minor keys, Op. 39; Petites fants, Op. 41 APR 2-▲ 7031 [ADD] (37.97)

Sonate de concert for Cello & Piano, Op. 47 (1857)

J. Ehde (vc), C. Dominique (pno) † Debussy:Son Vc; Delius:Son Vc; Messiaen:Quatuor CAPA ▲ 21563 (16.97)

Sonatine for Piano, Op. 61 (1861)

M.-A. Hamelin (pno) † Etudes in minor keys, Op. 39; Grande son, Op. 33; Troisième recueil de chants, Op. 65 HYP ▲ 66794 (18.97)

P. Réach (pno) † Grande son, Op. 33 DI ▲ 920362 [DDD] (5.97)

B. Ringeissen (pno) † Etudes in minor keys, Op. 39; Pno Music HMA ▲ 190927 [ADD] (9.97)

Troisième recueil de chants for Piano, Op. 65

M.-A. Hamelin (pno)—No. 6, "Barcarolle" † Etudes in minor keys, Op. 39; Grande son, Op. 33; Sonatine Pno, Op. 61 HYP ▲ 66794 (18.97)

R. Lewenthal (pno)—No. 6, "Barcarolle" † Etudes in minor keys, Op. 39; Grande son, Op. 33; Liszt:Hexaméron Pno, S.392 HP (High Performance) ▲ 63310 (11.97)

ALLAGA, GÉZA (1841-1913)

Concert Etude in D for Hammered Dulcimer

V. Herencsár (dlc) † Hungarian Con HUN ▲ 31825 [DDD] (16.97)

Hungarian Concerto for Hungarian Hammered Dulcimer

V. Herencsár (dlc) † Concert Etude Dlc HUN ▲ 31825 [DDD] (16.97)

ALLAN, RICHARD VAN (1935- *(aka Alan Philip Jones)*

Cartoon for Wind Orchestra

N. Boddice (cnd), Royal Norwegian Navy Band [plus music by Forde: Boddice; Westby] † P. Graham:Sym Wind Orch; Hardiman:Cry of the Celts DOY ▲ 83 (16.97)

Refrains & Cadenzas for Brass Band

M. P. Parkes (cnd), Grimethorpe Colliery Band ("From Sonnets to Jazz") † P. E. Fletcher:Epic Sym; J. McCabe:Salamander; H. Snell:Fant Cnt; P. Wilby:Jazz; Unholy Sonnets CHN ▲ 4549 (16.97)

ALLEGRI, GREGORIO (1582-1652)

Miserere for Chorus

P. Phillips (cnd), Tallis Scholars † W. Mundy:Vox Patris; Palestrina:Missa "Papae marcelli", R. 12 GIME ▲ 54939 [AAD] (16.97)

P. Phillips (cnd), Tallis Scholars *(rec live, Rome, Italy)* † Palestrina:Missa "Papae marcelli", R. 12; Sacred Music; Stabat mater GIME ▲ 54994 [DDD] (16.97)

P. Phillips (cnd), Tallis Scholars † W. Byrd:Mass 4 Voc; Cornysh:Salve regina; Josquin Desprez:Missa, "L'homme armé sexti toni"; Tallis:Gaude gloriosa Dei Mater; Psalm Tunes; Salvator mundi I GIME ▲ 54999 [AAD/DDD] (16.97)

S. Preston (cnd), Westminster Abbey Choir *(rec All Saints' Church, London, England, Feb 1985)* † Anerio:Vocal Music; Giovannelli:Jubilate Deo; G. B. Nanino:Haec dies; Palestrina:Missa "Papae marcelli", R. 12; Tu es Petrus PARC ▲ 15517 [DDD] (16.97)

J. Summerly (cnd), Oxford Camerata *(rec Dorchester Abbey, Oxon, England, Sept 1991)* † Palestrina:Missa "Papae marcelli", R. 12; Missa Aeterna Christi Munera; Stabat mater NXIN ▲ 8553238 [DDD] (5.97)

D. Warland (cnd), Dale Warland Singers *(rec St. Paul, MN, Aug 1994)* † S. Barber:Agnus Dei; H. Howells:Requiem; F. Martin:Mass for Double Chorus AME ▲ 120 [DDD] (16.97) ▮ 120 [DDD] (10.98)

D. Willcocks (cnd), King's College Choir *(rec 1963)* † Palestrina:Hodie Beata Virgo; Litaniae de Beata Virgine Maria; Magnificat octavi toni; Senex puerum portabat; Stabat mater DECC ▲ 466373 (11.97)

D. Willcocks (cnd), King's College Choir Cambridge ("Great Choral Classics from King's") † J. S. Bach:Cant 41; G. F. Handel:Coronation Anthems for George II, HWV 258-61; Palestrina:Stabat mater; Tallis:Spem in alium; Vivaldi:Gloria (& Intro), RV.588 PLON 2-▲ 452949 (17.97)

Motets

B. Fabre-Garrus (cnd), A Sei Voci—De ore prudentis; Repleti sunt omnes ("Music from the Age of Castratos") † Broschi:Arias; M.-A. Charpentier:Salve regina à 3 voix pareilles, H.23; C. W. Gluck:Orfeo ed Euridice (sels); Vivaldi:Dixit Dominus, RV.594; Montezuma (sels); Nisi Dominus, RV.608 ASTR ▲ 8552 [DDD] (16.97)

B. Fabre-Garrus (cnd), A Sei Voci † Salmo Miserere mei Deus; Vidi tubam magnam ASTR ▲ 8524 (18.97)

Il Salmo Miserere mei Deus for 9 Voices

B. Fabre-Garrus (cnd), A Sei Voci † Motets; Vidi tubam magnam ASTR ▲ 8524 (18.97)

G. Guest (cnd), St. John's College Choir Cambridge ("Allegri-Miserere") † O. de Lassus:Bell'Amfitrit'altera; Palestrina:Veni sponsa Christi CFP (Eminence) ▲ 2180 [DDD] (16.97)

Vidi tubam magnam (mass) for 6 Voices

B. Fabre-Garrus (cnd), A Sei Voci † Motets; Salmo Miserere mei Deus ASTR ▲ 8524 (18.97)

ALLEGRI, LORENZO (ca 1573-1648)

Le suites medicee (sinfonia & 8 suites) for 5-6 Instruments & Continuo, "Il Primo Libro delle Musiche" (ca 1618)

G. L. Lastraioli (cnd) —Suites 1-8 *(rec Bivigliano, Italy, Dec 1997)* DYNC ▲ 218 [DDD] (17.97)

ALLESANDRO, RAFFAELE D' (1911-1959)

Concerto No. 3 for Piano & Orchestra, Op. 70, "Quasi una sinfonia"

K. Kolly (pno), M. Venzago (cnd), Basel SO † Preludes Pno, Op. 30; Sym 1 PANC ▲ 510093 [DDD] (17.97)

Preludes (24) for Piano, Op. 30

K. Kolly (pno) † Con 3 Pno, Op. 70; Sym 1 PANC ▲ 510093 [DDD] (17.97)

Symphony No. 1 in d, Op. 62

M. Venzago (cnd), Basel SO † Con 3 Pno, Op. 70; Preludes Pno, Op. 30 PANC ▲ 510093 [DDD] (17.97)

ALLÚ, MARTÍN SÁNCHEZ (1825-1858)
El peregrino for Piano
P. Cohen (pno) *(rec Auditorio de Cuenca, Spain, Apr 1995)* ("El Último Adiós: Romantic Piano Music from Spain") † Adalid y Gurréa:Ultimo adiós; Lamento; Petits riens; Ocón:Bolero; T. Power:Barcarola Pno; Quesada:Allegro de concierto; Grandes estudios GLSS ▲ 920501 [DDD] (18.97)

ALMEIDA, FRANCISCO ANTONIO DE (ca 1702-1755)
La Giuditta (oratorio) (1726)
L. Lootens (sop—Giuditta), F. Congiu (sop—Achiorre), A. Köhler (ct—Ozia), M. Hill (ten—Oloferne), R. Jacobs (cnd) HMA 2-▲ 1901411 [DDD] (17.97)

ALMEIDA, LAURINDO (1923-1995)
Los Angeles Aquarelle Suite for Guitar Quintet
Los Angeles Guitar Quintet *(rec 1993)* ("Aquarelle") † Beiderbecke:Pno Music; G. Gershwin:Music of Gershwin; Jobim:Gtr Music; W. A. Mozart:Qnt Cl, K.581; Vivaldi:Cons Strs (misc) ERTO ▲ 42016 [ADD] (14.97)
Brazilliance for Guitar
C. Bruinsma (gtr), P. Rueffer (gtr) *(rec Bedford School, England)* ("Brazileira") † D. Milhaud:Scaramouche; A. Piazzolla:Grand Tango; H. Villa-Lobos:A Lenda do Caboclo; Bachiana brasileira 2; Bachiana brasileira 4; Cirandas (16 rondos) Pno; Wüsthoff:Concerto de Samba; A. York:Rosetta Gtr ASV ▲ 2079 [DDD] (12.97)
Concerto No. 1 for Guitar & Orchestra
L. Almeida (gtr), L. Almeida (cnd), Los Angeles CO † Lobiana; Gnattali:Con brasileira 4 ERTO ▲ 42001 (14.97)
Crepusculo em Copacabana
C. Barbosa-Lima (gtr) *(rec Hayward, CA, 1992)* ("Ginastera's Sonata") † A. Barrios:Abejas; Fabiniana Gtr; Ginastera:Son Gtr, Op. 47; Gnattali:Sonatina 1 Gtr; A. Harris:Concertino de California; Lauro:Venezuelan Waltz 3; T. D. Mello:Amor Sem Fim ERTO ▲ 42015 (14.97)
Guitar Music
R. Guthrie (gtr)—Batuque; Crepusculo em Copacabana; Serenata; Brazilliance Gtr *(rec Holy Nativity Episcopal Church, Plano, TX, 1995)* † J. Guimarães:Gtr Music; Lauro:Gtr Music; M. Ponce:Gtr Music; J. Silva:Gtr Music; H. Villa-Lobos:Preludes Gtr ENRE ▲ 9509 [DDD] (16.97)
Lobiana for Guitar & Orchestra
L. Almeida (gtr), L. Almeida (cnd), Los Angeles CO † Con 1 Gtr; Gnattali:Con brasileira 4 ERTO ▲ 42001 (14.97)

ALMENRAEDER, CARL (1786-1843)
Duo for 2 Bassoons, Op. 10/1
O. Eifert (bn), S. Schoenbach (bn) † M. Arnold:Fant Bn, Op. 86; F. Devienne:Duos Concertantes, Op. 3; G. Jacob:Partita Bn; F. Mignone:Son Bns; K. Reiner:Zaznamy; Szelényi:Suite Bns GAS (Silver) ▲ 2007 (7.97)

ALMILA, ATSO (1953-
Te Pa Te Pa for Brass, Op. 26 (1984)
J. Panula (cnd), Scandinavian Brass Ensemble *(rec 1984)* † Danielsson:Suite 3 Brass; E. Grieg:Funeral March in Memory of Rikard Nordraak; Hallberg:Blacksmith's Tune; Holmboe:Con Brass, Op. 157; T. Madsen:Divert Brass & Perc, Op. 47; Per the Fiddler, Norwegian Folk Song BIS ▲ 265 [DDD] (17.97)
Visions from the North for Concert Band
J. M. Jensen (cnd), Danish Concert Band *(rec 1998-99)* ("Visions from the North") † Åkerwall:Ergesia; M. Andresen:Con Tpt; V. Brandt:Concertpiece 2 Tpt, Op. 12; J. Gade:Funeral Music; D. W. Jenkins:Con A Sax; Ticheli:Blue Shades ROND ▲ 8368 (18.97)

ALMODAR, PERE JEAN (16th cent)
Songs
M. Figueras (sop), E. Tiso (sop), M. Arrubarrena (sop), C. Mena (ct), L. Climent (ten), F. Garrigosa (ten), J. Ricart (bar), D. Carnovich (bass), J. Savall (cnd), Capella Reial de Catalunya—Ah, Pelayo que desmayo *(rec Catalogne, Spain, Sept 1995)* ("El Cançoner del Duc de Calabria (1526-1554)") † Anonymous:Instrumental Music; Songs; Carceres:Songs; Flexta:Songs; F. Guerrero:Songs; C. de Morales:Songs ASTR ▲ 8582 [DDD] (18.97)

ALONSO-CRESPO, EDUARDO (1956-
Macbeth (opera in 17 movements) (1994)
E. Alonso-Crespo (cnd), Camerata Lazarte JLR ▲ 1801 (16.97)
Overtures & Dances from Operas for Orchestra
E. Alonso-Crespo (cnd), Cincinnati CO ("New Energy from the Americas") † N. Galbraith:Con 1 Pno ORC ▲ 101 (16.97)

ALOTIN, YARDENA (1930-1994)
Sonatina for Violin & Piano (1970)
M. Boettcher (vn), U. Trede-Boettcher (pno) † Beau:Son Vn; L. Boulanger:D'un matin de printemps Fl; M. Danzi:Son 1 Vn, Op. 1; Dinescu:Echos I; Mendelssohn (-Hensel):Adagio; Zieritz:Triptychion BAYE ▲ 100169 [DDD] (17.97)

ALPAERTS, FLOR (1876-1954)
James Ensor Suite for Orchestra (1929)
A. Rahbari (cnd), Brussels BRTN PO *(rec Magdalena Hall, Brussels, Belgium, Mar 1995)* † Hoedt:Chroniques breves; A. Meulemans:Plinius Fontein DI ▲ 920321 [DDD] (5.97)

ALPHER, DAVID (20th cent)
Atlantic Legend for Viola, Cello & Harpsichord (1983)
M. Gallagher (va), M. Lutzke (vc), J. Newton (hpd) *(rec Jordan Hall, New England Conservatory, Boston, MA, 1998)* ("American Reflections") † Elegy for a Friend; Returnings; Songs of Transcendence; Tribute to Kerouac ONGA ▲ 112 [DDD] (16.97)
Elegy for a Friend for Piano (1997)
D. Alpher (pno) *(rec Jordan Hall, New England Conservatory, Boston, MA, 1998)* ("American Reflections") † Atlantic Legend; Returnings; Songs of Transcendence; Tribute to Kerouac ONGA ▲ 112 [DDD] (16.97)
Returnings for Harp & Piano (1990)
M. Moor (hp), D. Alpher (pno) *(rec Jordan Hall, New England Conservatory, Boston, MA, 1998)* ("American Reflections") † Atlantic Legend; Elegy for a Friend; Songs of Transcendence; Tribute to Kerouac ONGA ▲ 112 [DDD] (16.97)
Songs of Transcendence (6) for Baritone & Piano (1997)
R. Honeysucker (bar), D. Alpher (pno) *(rec Jordan Hall, New England Conservatory, Boston, MA, 1998)* ("American Reflections") † Atlantic Legend; Elegy for a Friend; Returnings; Tribute to Kerouac ONGA ▲ 112 [DDD] (16.97)
Tribute to Kerouac for Clarinet, Tenor Saxophone, Piano & String Bass (1998)
R. Lynam (db), J. Cohler (cl), K. Radnofsky (t sax), D. Alpher (pno) *(rec Jordan Hall, New England Conservatory, Boston, MA, 1998)* ("American Reflections") † Atlantic Legend; Elegy for a Friend; Returnings; Songs of Transcendence ONGA ▲ 112 [DDD] (16.97)

ALT, BERNHARD (1903-1945)
Suite for 4 Double Basses (1933)
Berlin PO Double Bass Quartet *(rec Berlin, Germany, Dec 1978)* † Chihara:Logs; Findeisen:Prelude; Funck:Stricturae Viola di gambicea; E. Hartmann:Quartet; Jorns:Mobile Perpetuum; W. A. Mozart:Ave verum corpus, K.618 CAMA ▲ 2562 [AAD] (18.97)

ALTENA, MAARTEN (1943-
ABCDE for Chamber Ensemble
Altena Ensemble [1996 version] *(rec May 1996)* † Cantus; Trappel; A. Cameron:Leisure; Fuhler:Cinéma; Isadora:En/Of II; Padding:Ballad CV ▲ 69 [DDD] (18.97)
Cantus for Chamber Ensemble
Altena Ensemble *(rec May 1996)* † ABCDE; Trappel; A. Cameron:Leisure; Fuhler:Cinéma; Isadora:En/Of II; Padding:Ballad CV ▲ 69 [DDD] (18.97)
Dowlands for Chamber Ensemble [texts Thomas Wyatt & John Dowland] (1995)
Altena Ensemble *(rec Doopsgezinde Church, Amsterdam, Netherlands, 1995)* ("Working on Time") † R. Ayres:Short Arrs; Bergeijk:Sym joyeuse; Isadora:America Is Waiting; G. van Keulen:Trompeau; H. van der Meulen:Music for a While; Padding:Nicht eilen NMCL ▲ 92063 [DDD] (16.97)
Music of Altena
Altena Ensemble—Punt; 88; Rails; Voices; Quotl *(rec Theater Frascati, Amsterdam, Netherlands, Dec 1988)* † Bergeijk:Scène Rurale; G. Carl:Roscoe Blvd; Hoorn:Music of Hoorn HATH ▲ 6029 [DDD] (15.97)
Altena Ensemble—Slow Motion [1993 version]; Tik; Figuur; Lento; Abcde; Slow Motion [1994 version] ("Muziekpraktijk: Music + Practice") CV ▲ 49 [DDD]
Trappel for Chamber Ensemble
Altena Ensemble *(rec May 1996)* † ABCDE; Cantus; A. Cameron:Leisure; Fuhler:Cinéma; Isadora:En/Of II; Padding:Ballad CV ▲ 69 [DDD] (18.97)

ALTENBURG, JOHANN ERNST (1734-1801)
Concerto in C for 7 Trumpets & Timpani [attrib]
G. Schwarz (tpt), G. Schwarz (cnd) † H. I. Biber:Son Tpts; Telemann:Qnt Tpt; Torelli:Sons à 5 Tpts; Vivaldi:Con Tpts, RV.537 DLS ▲ 3002 [DDD] (14.97)

ALTHANS, MARK (1967-
Valse Excentrique for Orchestra (1992)
R. Black (cnd), Slovak RSO Bratislava † M. Kessler:Con Pno; Leclaire:Haiku; W. T. McKinley:Andante & Scherzo; Rahbee:Tapestry 1; Rendelman:Chorale & Toccata; Stango:Sol' per Dirti Addio MASM ▲ 2009 [DDD] (16.97)

ALVARES, EDUARDO (1959-
Pocema [War-Cry] for 2 Tom-Toms & Voices (1992)
Duo Dialogos *(rec Sao Paolo, Brazil, 1994)* ("Contemporary Percussion Music from Brazil") † Cerqueira:Sketches to Frighten Guido d'Arezzo; Csekö:Volume em sombras; Mannis:Reflexos; Menezes:A dialética da praia; Seincman:A dança do Dibuk GHA ▲ 126033 (17.97)

ALVAREZ, JAVIER (1956-
Metro Chabacano for String Quartet (1991)
Latin American String Quartet † Garrido-Lecca:Qt 2 Strs; Sierra:Memorias Tropicales; Tello:Dansaq II NALB ▲ 51 (16.97)

ALVEZ, FERNANDEZ GABRIEL (1944-
Trio for Piano, Violin & Cello, "Mompou" (1983)
Mompou Trio Madrid † Blanquer:Celista; T. Marco:Trio concertante; J. L. Turina:Trio Pno RTVE ▲ 65014 (16.97)

ALWYN, WILLIAM (1905-1985)
Autumn Legend for English Horn & String Orchestra (1954)
N. Daniel (E hn), R. Hickox (cnd), City of London Sinfonia † Lyra Angelica; Pastoral Fant; Tragic Interlude CHN ▲ 9065 [DDD] (16.97)
Chamber Music
N. Daniel (cnd) —Son Cl; Divert for Fl; Crépuscule for Hp; Son Ob; Son Fl; Son Impromptu ("Chamber Music, Vol. 2") CHN ▲ 9197 [DDD] (16.97)
Concerto for Flute & 8 Instruments
N. Daniel (cnd) † Naiades; Suite Ob Hp; Trio Fl CHN ▲ 9152 [DDD] (16.97)
Concerto grosso No. 1 in B♭ for Chamber Orchestra (1943)
R. Hickox (cnd), City of London Sinfonia † Con grosso 2; Con grosso 3; Con Ob CHN ▲ 8866 [DDD] (16.97)
Concerto grosso No. 2 in G for String Orchestra (1948)
R. Hickox (cnd), City of London Sinfonia † Con grosso 1; Con grosso 3; Con Ob CHN ▲ 8866 [DDD] (16.97)
Concerto grosso No. 3 for Woodwinds, Brass & Strings (1964)
R. Hickox (cnd), City of London Sinfonia † Con grosso 1; Con grosso 2; Con Ob CHN ▲ 8866 [DDD] (16.97)
Concerto for Oboe, String Orchestra & Harp (1944-45)
N. Daniel (E hn), R. Hickox (cnd), City of London Sinfonia † Con grosso 1; Con grosso 2; Con grosso 3 CHN ▲ 8866 [DDD] (16.97)
Concerto No. 1 for Piano (1930)
H. Shelley (pno), R. Hickox (cnd), London SO † Sym 1 CHN ▲ 9155 [DDD] (16.97)
Concerto No. 2 for Piano (1950)
H. Shelley (pno), R. Hickox (cnd), London SO † Sinfonietta; Sym 5 CHN ▲ 9196 (16.97)
Concerto for Violin & Orchestra (1937-39)
L. Mordkovitch (vn), R. Hickox (cnd), London SO † Sym 3 CHN ▲ 9187 [DDD] (16.97)
Derby Day (overture) for Orchestra (1960)
R. Hickox (cnd), London SO † Fanfare for a Joyful Occasion; Magic Island; Ov to a Masque; Sym 2 CHN ▲ 9093 [DDD] (16.97)
Elizabethan Dances (orchestral suite) (1957)
R. Hickox (cnd), London SO † Festival March; Sym 4 CHN ▲ 8902 [DDD] (16.97)
Fanfare for a Joyful Occasion for Brass & Percussion (1948)
R. Hickox (cnd), London SO † Derby Day; Magic Island; Ov to a Masque; Sym 2 CHN ▲ 9093 [DDD] (16.97)
Fantasy-Waltzes for Piano (1956)
J. Ogdon (pno) † Preludes Pno CHN ▲ 8399 [DDD] (16.97)
Festival March for Orchestra (1950)
R. Hickox (cnd), London SO † Elizabethan Dances; Sym 4 CHN ▲ 8902 [DDD] (16.97)
Film Music
R. Hickox (cnd), London SO—Odd Man Out Suite; The History of Mr. Polly Suite; The Fallen Idol Suite; Calypso from The Rake's Progress *(rec Jan 1993)* CHN ▲ 9243 [DDD] (16.97)
Lyra Angelica (concerto) for Harp & String Orchestra (1954)
R. Masters (hp), R. Hickox (cnd), City of London Sinfonia † Autumn Legend; Pastoral Fant; Tragic Interlude CHN ▲ 9065 [DDD] (16.97)
The Magic Island (symphonic prelude) for Orchestra
R. Hickox (cnd), London SO † Derby Day; Fanfare for a Joyful Occasion; Ov to a Masque; Sym 2 CHN ▲ 9093 [DDD] (16.97)
The Moor of Venice (overture) for Orchestra
B. Hurdley (cnd), Williams Fairey Band [arr Wright] *(rec Dewsbury Town Hall, England, Feb 1997)* ("Brass From the Masters, Vol. 1") † E. Elgar:Severn Suite Brass, Op. 87; C. Jenkins:Life Divine; Rubbra:Vars on "The Shining River", Op. 101; R. Simpson:Energy; Vaughan Williams:Vars Brass CHN ▲ 4547 [DDD] (16.97)
Naiades (fantasy sonata) for Flute & Harp (1971)
N. Daniel (cnd) † Con Fl; Suite Ob Hp; Trio Fl CHN ▲ 9152 [DDD] (16.97)
Overture to a Masque for Orchestra (1940)
R. Hickox (cnd), London SO † Derby Day; Fanfare for a Joyful Occasion; Magic Island; Sym 2 CHN ▲ 9093 [DDD] (16.97)
Pastoral Fantasia for Viola & String Orchestra (1939)
S. Tees (va), R. Hickox (cnd), City of London Sinfonia † Autumn Legend; Lyra Angelica; Tragic Interlude CHN ▲ 9065 [DDD] (16.97)
Preludes (12) for Piano (1959)
J. Ogdon (pno) † Fant-Waltzes CHN ▲ 8399 [DDD] (16.97)
Quartet No. 3 for Strings (1984)
London String Quartet † Rhap Pno; Trio Strs CHN ▲ 8440 [DDD] (17.97)
Rhapsody (quartet) for Piano & Strings (1938)
D. Willison (pno), London String Quartet members † Qt 3 Strs; Trio Strs CHN ▲ 8440 [DDD] (17.97)
Sinfonietta for Strings (1976)
R. Hickox (cnd), London SO † Con 2 Pno; Sym 5 CHN ▲ 9196 (16.97)
R. Hickox (cnd), London SO † Syms (comp) CHN 3-▲ 9429 [DDD] (48.97)
Sonata for Clarinet & Piano (1963)
C. West (cl), S. Grace (pno) *(rec Virginia Commonwealth University, Richmond, VA)* † Delmas:Fant italienne; R. Faith:Sea Pieces; Genzmer:Sonatine Cl & Pno; W. Lutoslawski:Dance Preludes Cl & Pno; Muczynski:Time Pieces, Op. 43 KLAV ▲ 11073 [DDD] (18.97)
Suite for Oboe & Harp
N. Daniel (cnd) † Con Fl; Naiades; Trio Fl CHN ▲ 9152 [DDD] (16.97)
Symphonies (5) (complete)
R. Hickox (cnd), London SO † Sinfonietta CHN 3-▲ 9429 [DDD] (48.97)
Symphony No. 1 (1949)
R. Hickox (cnd), London SO † Con 1 Pno CHN ▲ 9155 [DDD] (16.97)
Symphony No. 2 (1953)
R. Hickox (cnd), London SO † Derby Day; Fanfare for a Joyful Occasion; Magic Island; Ov to a Masque CHN ▲ 9093 [DDD] (16.97)
Symphony No. 3 (1955-56)
R. Hickox (cnd), London SO † Con Vn CHN ▲ 9187 [DDD] (16.97)
Symphony No. 4 (1959)
R. Hickox (cnd), London SO † Elizabethan Dances; Festival March CHN ▲ 8902 [DDD] (16.97)
Symphony No. 5, "Hydriotaphia" (1972-73)
R. Hickox (cnd), London SO † Con 2 Pno; Sinfonietta CHN ▲ 9196 (16.97)
Tragic Interlude for 2 Horns, Timpani & String Orchestra (1936)
R. Hickox (cnd), City of London Sinfonia † Autumn Legend; Lyra Angelica; Pastoral Fant CHN ▲ 9065 [DDD] (16.97)
Trio for Flute, Cello & Piano
N. Daniel (cnd) † Con Fl; Naiades; Suite Ob Hp CHN ▲ 9152 [DDD] (16.97)
Trio for Strings (1962)
London String Quartet members † Qt 3 Strs; Rhap Pno CHN ▲ 8440 [DDD] (17.97)

ALYABIEV, ALEXANDER (1787-1851)
Sonata for Violin & Piano
A. Chandler (vn), O. Tverskaya (pno) ("Music in St. Petersburg, Vol. VII") † M. Glinka:Son Va; Trio pathétique
OPUS ▲ 30230 (18.97)
Trio in a for Piano, Violin & Cello
Borodin Trio † P. Tchaikovsky:Trio Pno, Op. 50
CHN ▲ 8975 [DDD] (17.97)
AMBROSE [SAINT AMBROSE] (ca 340-397)
Vocal Music
K. Ruhland (cnd), Munich Capella Antiqua—Aeterne rerum conditor ("Gregorian Chants") † Anonymous:Ad coenam agni providi; Antiphony & Canticum Simeonis; Conditor alme siderum; Cum natus esset Jesus; Kyrie fons bonitatis; Lumen ad Revelationem & Nunc Dimittis; Mittit ad virginem; Nato canunt omnia; O Redemptor sume carmen; Surrexit dominus vere; Te deum laudamus; Langton:Vocal Music
CEHA ▲ 13094 (16.97)
AMIOT, JEAN JOSEPH MARIE (1718-1793)
Divertissements chinois (3) for Chamber Ensemble (ca 1779)
J.-C. Frisch (cnd), Musique des Lumières ("Baroque Concert at the Forbidden City") † T. Pedrini:Sons Vn, Op. 3
ASTR ▲ 128609 (12.97)
AMIRKHANIAN, CHARLES (1945-)
Music of Amirkhanian
C. Amirkhanian (elec)—Chu Lu Lu; Bajanoom; Vers Les Anges; Gold & Spirit; Walking Tune ("Walking Tune")
STKL ▲ 206 [DDD] (16.97)
Politics As Usual for Electronics (1988)
C. Amirkhanian (elec) † ("Auxesis") † Creshevsky:Borrowed Time; Coup d'etat; Private Lives
CENT ▲ 2194 (16.97)
AMIROV, FIKRET (1922-1984)
Azerbaijan Capriccio for Orchestra (1961)
A. De Almeida (cnd), Moscow SO † Shchur, Kyurd Ovsharī; Symphonic Dances
ASV ▲ 1014 (16.97)
Azerbaijan Mugam for Orchestra (1948)
L. Stokowski (cnd), Houston SO (rec Houston Civic Center, TX, 1959) † S. Prokofiev:Peter & the Wolf (suite); Peter & the Wolf, Op. 67; L. Stokowski:Trans Orch
EVC ▲ 9048 [ADD] (13.97)
Pieces (6) for Flute & Piano [Song of the Ashuge; Lullaby; Dance; In the Azerbaijan Mountains; At the Spring; Nocturne]
J. Baxtresser (fl), P. Muzijevic (pno) (rec Bronxville, NY, 1996) ("New York Legends") † Debussy:Prélude à l'après-midi d'un faune; P. Gaubert:Three Water Colours; W. Gieseking:Sonatine Fl; F. Martin:Ballade Fl; Taktakishvili:Son Fl
CAL ▲ 512 [DDD] (15.97)
C. Delafontaine (fl), M. Mourtazine-Chapochnikova (pno) ("Decouvertes Transcaucasiennes") † Gliére:Pieces various instrs, Op. 35; Liadov:Prelude Fl & Pno; S. Rachmaninoff:Vocalise; Taktakishvili:Son Fl
GALL ▲ 894 [DDD] (19.97)
M. Wiesler (fl), R. Pöntinen (pno) † E. Denisov:Pieces Fl; Son Fl; S. Prokofiev:Son Fl; Taktakishvili:Son Fl
BIS ▲ 419 [DDD] (17.97)
Shchur, Kyurd Ovsharī (symphonic mugam) for Orchestra (1948)
A. De Almeida (cnd), Moscow SO † Azerbaijan Capriccio; Symphonic Dances
ASV ▲ 1014 (16.97)
Symphonic Dances for Orchestra (1963)
A. De Almeida (cnd), Moscow SO † Azerbaijan Capriccio; Shchur, Kyurd Ovsharī
ASV ▲ 1014 (16.97)
AMNER, JOHN (1579-1641)
Sacred Music
D. Price (org), P. Trepte (cnd), Parley of Instruments, Ely Cathedral Choir—Te Deum; I Will Sing unto the Lord As Long As I Live; Blessed Be the Lord God; O Ye Little Flock; Magnigicat; Nunc dimitis; Sing, O Heav'ns; Vars. on "O Lord in Thee"; Consider, All Ye Passers by; Hear, O Lord; O Sing unto the Lord ("Cathedral Music")
HYP ▲ 66768 [DDD] (18.97)
AMON, JOHANNES ANDREAS (1763-1825)
Quartet in F for Horn & Strings, Op. 20/1
L. Bergé (hn), Arriaga String Quartet ("Kamermuziek voor hoorn") † F. A. Hoffmeister:Qnt Hn; W. A. Mozart:Qnt Hn; Stich [or stich-Punto]:Qt Hn
EUFO ▲ 1207 [DDD] (19.97)
AMOS, KEITH (1939-)
Salisbury Cathedral for Mixed Chorus
M. Lee (cnd), St. Cecilia Singers (rec Gloucester Cathedral, England, June 1997) ("Over Hill, Over Dale") † Anonymous:Scarborough Fair; She Moved through the Fair; H. Howells:Choral Music; H. Parry:Seven Part Songs; Six Modern Lyrics; Songs of Farewell; J. Sanders:Anthem of the Incarnation; Traditional:Bobby Shaftoe; Dance to Thy Daddy; Frog & the Crow; Vaughan Williams:Shakespeare Songs
PRIO ▲ 620 [DDD] (16.97)
AMRAM, DAVID (1930-)
American Dance Suite for Orchestra (1986)
R. A. Clark (cnd), Manhattan CO † Songs for America; Theme & Vars on Red River Valley; Travels
NPT ▲ 85546 [DDD] (16.97)
Concerto for Bassoon & Orchestra
K. Pasmanick (bn), R. A. Clark (cnd), Manhattan CO (rec SUNY, NY, Oct 1993) ("Three Concertos") † Con Vn; Honor Song for Sitting Bull
NPT ▲ 85601 [DDD] (16.97)
Concerto for Violin & Orchestra
C. Castleman (vn), R. A. Clark (cnd), Manhattan CO (rec SUNY, NY, Oct 1993) ("Three Concertos") † Con Bn; Honor Song for Sitting Bull
NPT ▲ 85601 [DDD] (16.97)
Conversations for Chamber Ensemble (1988)
P. Peace (cnd), Atlanta Chamber Players (rec Atlanta, GA, July 29, 1995) ("Conversations: A 20th Anniversary Salute to American Composers") † A. Copland:Sxt Cl; J. Harbison:Trio Pno & Strs; N. Rorem:Trio Fl
ACAD ▲ 20038 (16.97)
The Final Ingredient (opera of the Holocaust in 1 act) [lib Arnold Weinstein; adapted from play by Reginald Rose]
D. Amram (cnd) (rec Apr 11, 1965)
PREM ▲ 1056 [ADD] (16.97)
Honor Song for Sitting Bull for Cello & Orchestra
N. Rosen (vc), R. A. Clark (cnd), Manhattan CO (rec SUNY, NY, Oct 1993) ("Three Concertos") † Con Bn; Con Vn
NPT ▲ 85601 [DDD] (16.97)
Songs for America (3) for Bass, Woodwind Quintet & String Quintet [based on texts by John F. Kennedy, Robert F. Kennedy & Martin Luther King, Jr.]
J. Courney (bass), R. A. Clark (cnd), Manhattan CO † American Dance Suite; Theme & Vars on Red River Valley; Travels
NPT ▲ 85546 [DDD] (16.97)
Theme & Variations on "Red River Valley" for Flute & Strings
J. Baker (fl), R. A. Clark (cnd), Manhattan CO † American Dance Suite; Songs for America; Travels
NPT ▲ 85546 [DDD] (16.97)
Travels for Trumpet & Orchestra
C. Gekker (tpt), R. A. Clark (cnd), Manhattan CO † American Dance Suite; Songs for America; Theme & Vars on Red River Valley
NPT ▲ 85546 [DDD] (16.97)
AMY, GILBERT (1936-)
Après "...d'un désastre obscur" for Mezzo-Soprano & Small Ensemble (1976)
J. Levy (mez), D. Kawka (cnd), Ensemble Orchestral Contemporain † d'un désastre obscur; Écrits sur toiles; Echoes XIII; Var ajoutée; Vars Fl
2E2M ▲ 1015 (20.97)
...d'un désastre obscur for Mezzo-Soprano & Clarinet (1971)
J. Levy (mez) † Écrits sur toiles; Après d'un désastre obscur; Echoes XIII; Var ajoutée; Vars Fl
2E2M ▲ 1015 (20.97)
Echoes XIII for 13 Instruments (1976)
D. Kawka (cnd), Ensemble Orchestral Contemporain † d'un désastre obscur; Écrits sur toiles; Après d'un désastre obscur; Var ajoutée; Vars Fl
2E2M ▲ 1015 (20.97)
Écrits sur toiles for Reciter & Small Ensemble (1983)
D. Reymond (nar), D. Kawka (cnd), Ensemble Orchestral Contemporain † d'un désastre obscur; Après d'un désastre obscur; Echoes XIII; Var ajoutée; Vars Fl
2E2M ▲ 1015 (20.97)
La Variation ajoutée for Ensemble
D. Kawka (cnd), Ensemble Orchestral Contemporain † d'un désastre obscur; Après d'un désastre obscur; Écrits sur toiles; Echoes XIII; Vars Fl
2E2M ▲ 1015 (20.97)
Variations for Flute, Clarinet, Cello & Piano (1956)
D. Kawka (cnd), Ensemble Orchestral Contemporain † d'un désastre obscur; Après d'un désastre obscur; Écrits sur toiles; Echoes XIII; Var ajoutée
2E2M ▲ 1015 (20.97)
ANCINA, GIOVENALE (1545-1604)
Vocal Music
G. Monaco (cnd), Progetto Musica Vocal Ensemble—Amorosa ero fatta spirituale (rec Mar 1995) ("Sacred Music Connected with St. Philip Neri") † Arascione:Nuove laudi ariose della Beatissime Virgine scelte; Palestrina:Missa "In minoribus", R.84; G. Razzi:Laude spirituale
TACT ▲ 520001 [DDD] (16.97)

ANDERSEN, BO (1963-)
Invocation for solo Flute (1993)
Trio Divertimento member ("New Danish Woodwind Music") † Serenade; J. Bentzon:Sonatina, Op. 7; F. Friis:November; G. Lund:Talks; Tarp:Taffelmusik; F. Weis:Music Fl, Cl & Bn
PLAL ▲ 94 [DAD] (18.97)
Serenade: In fliessender Bewegung for Woodwind Trio (1991)
Trio Divertimento ("New Danish Woodwind Music") † Invocation; J. Bentzon:Sonatina, Op. 7; F. Friis:November; G. Lund:Talks; Tarp:Taffelmusik; F. Weis:Music Fl, Cl & Bn
PLAL ▲ 94 [DAD] (18.97)
ANDERSEN, JOACHIM (1847-1909)
Flute & Piano Music
T. L. Christiansen (fl), P. Salo (pno)—Valse Caprice, Op. 44; Impromptu, Op. 7; Morceaux pour la flûte, Op. 57; Fant on Bellini's Norma; Leichte Stücke, Op. 56; Vortragsstücke, Op. 55 (rec Mar 1991) ("L'Hirondelle")
KPT ▲ 32079 [DDD]
P. Robison (fl), S. Sanders (pno)—Au Bord de la Mer, Op. 9; Babillard, Op. 24/6; Chant Pastorale, Op. 24/1; Alla Mazurka, Op. 24/3; Berceuse, Op. 28/1; Die Mühle, Op. 55/4; Reverie, Op. 24/2; Die Blumen, Op. 56/2; Impromptu, Op. 7; Scherzino, Op. 55/6; Melodie, Op. 52 (rec SUNY, Purchase, NY, Feb 1995) † E. Grieg:Songs
ARA ▲ 6668 [DDD] (16.97)
ANDERSON, ALLEN (1951-)
Charrette for Chamber Ensemble (1984)
D. Palma (cnd) (rec Feb 29, 1988) † Blaustein:Commedia; S. Clement:Chamber Con; D. Rakowski:Imaginary Dances
CRI ▲ 617 [DDD] (17.97)
Drawn from Life for Piano (1992)
A. Karis (pno) ("Drawn from Life") † Qt Strs; Solfeggietti
CRI ▲ 727 [DDD] (16.97)
Quartet for Strings (1990)
Lydian String Quartet ("Drawn from Life") † Drawn from Life; Solfeggietti
CRI ▲ 727 [DDD] (16.97)
Solfeggietti for Piano (1988)
A. Karis (pno) ("Drawn from Life") † Drawn from Life; Qt Strs
CRI ▲ 727 [DDD] (16.97)
ANDERSON, AVRIL (dates unknown)
Songs
Elanara—Los biblicuos; Noches, noches ("Mosaic d'España: Spanish & Sephardic Songs") † R. Gerhard:Songs; E. Granados:Songs; F. Moretti:Songs; Sor:Songs Voice Gtr; Sutton-Anderson:Songs
MER ▲ 84334 [DDD] (16.97)
ANDERSON, BETH (1950-)
Minnesota Swale for Orchestra (1994)
J. E. Suben (cnd), Slovak RSO Bratislava ("New Music for Orchestra") † Bassett:From a Source Evolving; A. Blank:Concertino; Couper:In Memoriam; Matsuo-Hirai V; Retzel:Chansonnier
OPS1 ▲ 156 (12.97)
Net Work for Piano (rev 1984)
M. K. Ernst (pno) ("2 by 3: Music by Women") † Trio: dream; Deussen:Pieces Vn; Trio Pno; Kenessey:Beating Down; Sunburst, Op. 33
NSR ▲ 1015 (15.97)
Trio: dream in d for Violin, Cello & Piano (1980)
T. Lazar (vn), M. Botelho (vc), M. K. Ernst (pno) ("2 by 3: Music by Women") † Net Work; Deussen:Pieces Vn; Trio Pno; Kenessey:Beating Down; Sunburst, Op. 33
NSR ▲ 1015 (15.97)
ANDERSON, EUGENE (1944-)
Baroque 'n Brass for Trumpet & Tuba (1991)
T. Morrison (tpt), S. Pilafian (tuba) (rec Chandler, AZ, Sept 1997) ("Perception") † Con 1 Tuba; Lyri-Tech; Perception of War
DNC ▲ 1027 [DDD] (16.97)
Concerto No. 1 in b for Tuba & Orchestra (1968-70)
S. Pilafian (tuba), T. Russell (cnd), Arizona State University SO (rec Chandler, AZ, Sept 1997) ("Perception") † Baroque 'n Brass; Lyri-Tech; Perception of War
DNC ▲ 1027 [DDD] (16.97)
Lyri-Tech for Tuba (1991)
S. Pilafian (tuba) (rec Chandler, AZ, Sept 1997) ("Perception") † Baroque 'n Brass; Con 1 Tuba; Perception of War
DNC ▲ 1027 [DDD] (16.97)
The Perception of War for Tuba & Orchestra (1973)
S. Pilafian (tuba), T. Russell (cnd), Arizona State University SO (rec Chandler, AZ, Sept 1997) ("Perception") † Baroque 'n Brass; Con 1 Tuba; Lyri-Tech
DNC ▲ 1027 [DDD] (16.97)
ANDERSON, LAURIE (1947-)
Electronic Music
L. Anderson (voc), S. Johnson (tanbura) (New York Social Life), L. Anderson (voc), L. Anderson (vn), S. Johnson (gtr/org) (Time to Go) (rec NYC, NY) ("Women in Electronic Music - 1977") † R. Anderson:Electronic Music; J. M. Beyer:Electronic Music; A. Lockwood:Electronic Music; P. Oliveros:Electronic Music; M. Roberts:Electronic Music; Spiegel:Electronic Music
CRI ▲ 728 [ADD] (16.97)
ANDERSON, LEROY (1908-1975)
Music of Anderson
(Pirate Dance), F. Fennell (cnd) (A Christmas Festival; Suite of Carols; Forgotten Dreams; Sandpaper Ballet; Trumpeter's Lullaby; Penny-Whistle Song; Bugler's Holiday; Irish Suite) † E. Coates:Four Ways Suite; London
MRCR ▲ 34376 (11.97)
M. Abravanel (cnd), Utah SO—Sleigh Ride; Blue Tango; Trumpeter's Lullaby; The Belle of the Ball; Bugler's Holiday; Forgotten Dreams; Syncopated Clock; Plink, Plank, Plunk!; Fiddle Faddle; Sandpaper Ballet; The Typewriter; Sarabande; Song of the Bells; Jazz Pizzicato; Serenata ("Fiddle Faddle")
VC ▲ 4 [ADD] (13.97)
L. Slatkin, St. Louis SO—Belle of the Ball; The Phantom Regiment; The 1st Day of Spring; Sleigh Ride; Plink, Plank, Plunk!; Blue Tango; Forgotten Dreams; Bugler's Holiday; The Penny-Whistle Song; Cl Candy; Horse & Buggy; A Trumpeter's Lullaby; Fiddle Faddle; Jazz Pizzicato; Jazz Legato; The Syncopated Clock; Sandpaper Ballet; The Typewriter; The Waltzing Cat; Promenade; Saraband; Serenata; Balladette; Arietta; Home Stretch (rec Powell Symphony Hall, St. Louis, MO, 1993-95) ("The Typewriter: Leroy Anderson Favorites")
RCAV (Red Seal) ▲ 68048 [DDD] (16.97)
ANDERSON, RUTH (1928-)
Electronic Music
artists unknown—Points (rec Hunter College, NYC, NY) ("Women in Electronic Music - 1977") † L. Anderson:Electronic Music; J. M. Beyer:Electronic Music; A. Lockwood:Electronic Music; P. Oliveros:Electronic Music; M. Roberts:Electronic Music; Spiegel:Electronic Music
CRI ▲ 728 [ADD] (16.97)
I come out of your sleep for Tape
R. Anderson (elec) ("Sinopah") † A. Lockwood:World Rhythms
XIRE ▲ 118 [ADD]
ANDERSON, T. J. [THOMAS JEFFERSON] (1928-)
Chamber Concerto for Orchestra, "Remembrances"
E. London (cnd), Cleveland Chamber SO (rec Drinko Recital Hall, Cleveland, OH) ("The New American Scene II") † D. Baker:Parallel Planes; L. Jenkins:Wonder Lust; W. Logan:Roots, Branches, Shapes & Shades of Green; D. White:Crystal Gazing
ALBA ▲ 303 [DDD] (16.97)
Intermezzos for Clarinet, Tenor Saxophone & Piano (1983)
Videmus † D. Baker:Through This Vale of Tears; D. Fox:Music of Fox; O. Wilson:Sometimes
NWW ▲ 80423 (16.97)
ANDERSON, TOMMY JOE (1947-)
Sonata No. 3 for Alto/Soprano Saxophone & Piano, Op. 30
K. Fischer (sax), R. Zimdars (pno) (rec 1988) † Bassett:Duo Concertante; Heiden:Diversion; L. Nielson:Fants S Sax
ACAD ▲ 20003 (16.97)
ANDERSON, B. TOMMY (20th cent)
Apollo Concerto for solo Percussion & Orchestra
M. Leoson (perc) † Donatoni:Omar; Fukushi:Ground; D. Milhaud:Con Mar; T. Tanaka:Movts Perc; Xenakis:Rebonds Perc
CAPA ▲ 21466 (16.97)
ANDERSSON, RICHARD (1851-1918)
Sonata for Piano, Op. 11 (1878)
S. Lindgren (pno) † Lindegren:Stor sonat, Op. 2
OPU ▲ 19303
ANDREAE, VOLKMAR (1879-1962)
Klavierstücke (6) for Piano, Op. 20 (1911)
C. Aubert-Tackett (pno) † R. Flury:Préludes Pno; P. Müller:Miniatures; Prélude pour la main gauche; Suite Pno, Op. 10
GALL ▲ 942 [DDD] (18.97)
ANDRÉE, ELFRIDA (1841-1929)
Fritiof saga:Suite
G. Sjökvist (cnd), Stockholm SO † Sym 2
STRL ▲ 1016 (15.97)
Music of Andrée
L. Hoel (sop), Y. Larsson (vn), L. Johnson (pno), Stockholm String Quartet—Qnt Pno; Svanen; Visa en Vårmorgon; Polska; En Vacker Höstdag; Son Pno; Öfver Hafvet; Näktergalen; Qt Strs ("Music at Hammersta Castle")
CAPA ▲ 21530 (16.97)

ANDRÉE, ELFRIDA (cont.)
Organ Music (complete)
R. Gustafsson (org) SWES ▲ 1085 (17.97)
Symphony No. 2 in a (1893)
G. Sjökvist (cnd), Stockholm SO † Fritiof saga (suite) STRL ▲ 1016 (15.97)
ANDRES, BERNARD (1941-
Chants d'arreère-saison for Horn & Harp
S. Hermansson (hn), E. Goodman (hp) *(rec Länna Church, Sweden, 1996)* ("Horn & Harp Odyssey") † L. Klein:AOIDOI; E. von Koch:Nocturne; J. Koetsier:Son Hn & Hp, Op. 94; Procaccini:Serenata; J. Singer:Suite Hn BIS ▲ 793 [DDD] (17.97)
Music of Andrès
G. Chevallier (hp), C. Fleischmann (hp) ("Duo de Harpes") † Dalvimare:Hp Music; C. Franck:Prélude, fugue et var, Op. 18; L. Rogg:Irisations; J. Thomas:Grand Duo CASC ▲ 1035 (16.97)
ANDRESEN, MOGENS (1945-
Concertino for Trumpet & Orchestra
K. Christensen (tpt), J. M. Jensen (cnd), Danish Concert Band *(rec 1998-99)* ("Visions from the North") † Åkerwall:Ergesia; Almila:Visions from the North; V. Brandt:Concertpiece 2 Tpt, Op. 12; J. Gade:Funeral Music; D. W. Jenkins:Con A Sax; Ticheli:Blue Shades ROND ▲ 8368 (18.97)
Suite Danica (4 folksong arrangements) for Brass Quintet (1977)
Royal Danish Brass ("Trumpet Concertos, Vol. 5: Danish Concertos") † Holmboe:Chamber Con 11, Op. 44; C. Nielsen:Preludes (29) for Org, Op. 51; Norby:Capriccio Tpt; K. Riisager:Concertino Tpt, Op. 29; Sehested:Spt Cnt ROND ▲ 8351 [ADD] (18.97)
ANDRIESSEN, HENDRIK (1892-1981)
Concerto for Organ & Orchestra (1950)
F. Houbart (org), M. Soustrot (cnd), Het Brabants Chamber Orchestra *(rec Oct 3, 1996)* † H. Badings:Con Hp; Flothuis:Con Fl; Orthel:Scherzo 2 CV ▲ 77 (18.97)
Organ Music
A. D. Klerk (org) *(rec Adema Org, St. Joseph's Church, Haarlem, Netherlands)* ("Complete Organ Works") LDBG 4-▲ 31 (69.97)
ANDRIESSEN, JURRIAAN (1925-1996)
Concertino for Bassoon & Wind Ensemble (1963)
R. Thompson (bn), G. Simon (cnd) ("The Edge of Space") † J. Downey:Edge of Space; G. Jacob:Con Bn CHN ▲ 9278 [DDD] (16.97)
ANDRIESSEN, LOUIS (1939-
Anachrony 1 for Orchestra (1967)
D. Aleven (hp), S. Grotenhuis (cel), N. D. Rooij (pno), N. Heerema (org), A. Cune (vib), H. Williams (cnd), Netherlands Ballet Orch *(rec Amsterdam Music Theater, Netherlands, Oct 1994)* † Anachrony 2; Contra tempus; Ittrospezione 3; Nocturnes CV ▲ 54 [DDD] (19.97)
Anachrony 2 for Oboe & Orchestra (1969)
H. D. Vries (ob), H. Williams (cnd), Netherlands Ballet Orch *(rec Amsterdam Music Theater, Netherlands, Oct 1994)* † Anachrony 1; Contra tempus; Ittrospezione 3; Nocturnes CV ▲ 54 [DDD] (19.97)
Contra tempus for 22 Instruments (1967-68)
G. Bouwhuis (pno), S. Grotenhuis (pno), N. D. Rooij (elec pno), T. Mukaiyama (elec pno) *(rec Amsterdam Music Theater, Netherlands, Oct 1994)* † Anachrony 1; Anachrony 2; Ittrospezione 3; Nocturnes CV ▲ 54 [DDD] (19.97)
Disco for Instrumental Ensemble
California EAR Unit ("Zilver") † Orpheus (ov); Worker's Union; Zilver NALB ▲ 94 (16.97)
Elegie for Double Bass & Piano (1957)
Q. van Regteren Altena (db), P. B. van Henegouwen (pno) ("Characters: 20th-Century Music for Double Bass & Piano") † A. Desenclos:Aria & Rondo; Ginastera:Pampeana 2, Op. 21; P. Hindemith:Son Db; Thilman:Charaktere; A. Wilder:Small Suite OLY ▲ 467 [DDD] (16.97)
Hoketus for 2 Panpipes, 2 Pianos & Electronics (1977)
Hoketus Ensemble † Mausoleum CV ▲ 20 (19.97)
Ittrospezione 3 [Concept 2] for Orchestra (1965)
M. Damsté (db), P. van Bergen (sax), G. Bouwhuis (pno), S. Grotenhuis (pno), H. Williams (cnd), Netherlands Ballet Orch *(rec Amsterdam Music Theater, Netherlands, Oct 1994)* † Anachrony 1; Anachrony 2; Contra tempus; Nocturnes CV ▲ 54 [DDD] (19.97)
De Materie [Matter] (opera in 4 parts) (1984-88)
S. Narucki (sop), J. Doing (ten), C. Oswin (nar), G. Thoma (nar), R. De Leeuw (cnd) , Netherlands Chamber Choir members *(rec Utrecht the Netherlands, Feb 26 & June 29-30, 1994) (D,E lib texts)* NON 2-▲ 79367 (33.97)
Mausoleum for 2 High Baritones & Orchestra
D. Barick (bar), C. van Tassel (bar), R. De Leeuw (cnd) † Hoketus CV ▲ 20 (19.97)
Nocturnes for Soprano & Chamber Orchestra (1959)
L. Emmink (sop), C. McFadden (sop), H. Williams (cnd), Netherlands Ballet Orch *(rec Amsterdam Music Theater, Netherlands, Oct 1994)* † Anachrony 1; Anachrony 2; Contra tempus; Ittrospezione 3 CV ▲ 54 [DDD] (19.97)
Orpheus:Overture
California EAR Unit ("Zilver") † Disco; Worker's Union; Zilver NALB ▲ 94 (16.97)
De Staat [The State] for 4 Women's Voices & 27 Instruments (1972-76)
R. De Leeuw (cnd) NON ▲ 79251 [DDD] (13.97)
De Tijd [Time] [text from St. Augustine's "Confessions"]
R. De Leeuw (cnd) , Netherlands Chamber Choir NON ▲ 79291 (16.97)
Worker's Union (symphonic movement) for Loud Instruments (1975)
California EAR Unit ("Zilver") † Disco; Orpheus (ov); Zilver NALB ▲ 94 (16.97)
Zilver for Instrumental Ensemble (1994)
California EAR Unit ("Zilver") † Disco; Orpheus (ov); Worker's Union NALB ▲ 94 (16.97)
ANERIO, FELICE (1560-1614)
Vocal Music
S. Preston (cnd), Westminster Abbey Choir—Venite ad me omnes *(rec All Saints' Church, London, England, Feb 1985)* † G. Allegri:Miserere; Giovannelli:Jubilate Deo; G. B. Nanino:Haec dies; Palestrina:Missa "Papae marcelli", R. 12; Tu es Petrus PARC ▲ 15517 [DDD] (16.97)
ANFOSSI, PASQUALE (1727-?1797)
La nascita del Redentore (oratorio) [lib G. Terribilini] (1780)
S. Daniel (sop), A. M. Ferrante (sop), L. Petroni (ten), F. Colusso (cnd) MUIM 2-▲ 10018 (36.97)
ANGELI, F. DI ARTA (20th cent)
Frossini (selections)
S. Malakate (sop), A. Agathonos (mez), J. E. Suben (cnd), Slovak RSO—Intermezzo; Elia; Was it August?; The Windmill; Calm, Storm & Sunburst; Frossini at Sunset; Contemplation; Revelries & Distractions; Anguish; Entrance of the Guards & Resignation *(rec Concert Hall of the Slovak Radio, Bratislava, Slovak Republic, Jun 1-3, 1998)* CPS ▲ 8662 (16.97)
Pieces (2) for Orchestra
J. E. Suben (cnd), Slovak RSO Bratislava ("The Orchestra According to the Seven") † Dellaira:Three Rivers; Kenessey:Wintersong, Op. 44; P. Krumm:Con B Cl; Sichel:3 Places in New Jersey; N. Strandberg:Legend of Emmeline Labiche; Van Appledorn:Cycles of Moons & Tides OPS1 ▲ 170 [DDD]
Sta Pestá for Orchestra
J. E. Suben (cnd), Slovak RSO Bratislava *(rec Bratislava, Slovak Republic, June 1996)* ("..and the eagle flies: New American Orchestral Music") † E. Austin:Wilderness Sym; R. Brooks:Landscape...with Grace; Seascape:Ov to Moby Dick CPS ▲ 8634 (16.97)
ANGELO, NUCCIO D' (1955-
Canzoni Lidie (2) for Guitar (1984)
F. Halász (gtr) *(rec Sweden, July 1996)* ("Canzoni") † Magie; L. Berio:Sequenza XI; Petrassi:Nunc; Suoni Notturni; Solbiati:Pezzi Gtr BIS ▲ 823 [DDD] (17.97)
Magie for Guitar (1990)
F. Halász (gtr) *(rec Sweden, July 1996)* ("Canzoni") † Canzoni Lidie; L. Berio:Sequenza XI; Petrassi:Nunc; Suoni Notturni; Solbiati:Pezzi Gtr BIS ▲ 823 [DDD] (17.97)
ANGLEBERT, JEAN-HENRI D' (1635-1691)
Courante in d for Harpsichord, "L'Immortelle"
B. Schenkman (hpd) *(rec Portola Valley, CA, Sept 1997)* † Gaillarde Hpd; Minuet Hpd; Prelude Hpd; Ritounèlle des Fees; Sarabande Hpd; Suite 2 Hpd; Suite 5 Hpd; Tombeau de Monsieur de Chambonnières CENT ▲ 2435 [DDD] (16.97)
Gaillarde in a for Harpsichord
B. M. Willi (hpd) *(rec Aug 1998)* † Suite 1 Hpd; Suite 2 Hpd; Suite 3 Hpd; Suite 4 Hpd; Suite 5 Hpd MPH ▲ 56828 [DDD] (15.97)

ANGLEBERT, JEAN-HENRI D' (cont.)
Gaillarde in C for Harpsichord
B. Schenkman (hpd) *(rec Portola Valley, CA, Sept 1997)* † Courante Hpd; Minuet Hpd; Prelude Hpd; Ritounèlle des Fees; Sarabande Hpd; Suite 2 Hpd; Suite 5 Hpd; Tombeau de Monsieur de Chambonnières CENT ▲ 2435 [DDD] (16.97)
Minuet for Harpsichord, "Dans nos bois"
B. Schenkman (hpd) *(rec Portola Valley, CA, Sept 1997)* † Courante Hpd; Gaillarde Hpd; Prelude Hpd; Ritounèlle des Fees; Sarabande Hpd; Suite 2 Hpd; Suite 5 Hpd; Tombeau de Monsieur de Chambonnières CENT ▲ 2435 [DDD] (16.97)
Pièces de clavecin for Harpsichord
E. Parmentier (hpd)—Prelude Hpd; Passacaglia d'Armide; Tombeau de Monsieur Chambonnières ("17th Century French Harpsichord Music") † Froberger:Hpd Music WILD ▲ 8502 [DDD] (16.97)
Prelude in C for Harpsichord
B. Schenkman (hpd) *(rec Portola Valley, CA, Sept 1997)* † Courante Hpd; Gaillarde Hpd; Minuet Hpd; Ritounèlle des Fees; Sarabande Hpd; Suite 2 Hpd; Suite 5 Hpd; Tombeau de Monsieur de Chambonnières CENT ▲ 2435 [DDD] (16.97)
Ritounèlle des Fees for Harpsichord
B. Schenkman (hpd) *(rec Portola Valley, CA, Sept 1997)* † Courante Hpd; Gaillarde Hpd; Minuet Hpd; Prelude Hpd; Sarabande Hpd; Suite 2 Hpd; Suite 5 Hpd; Tombeau de Monsieur de Chambonnières CENT ▲ 2435 [DDD] (16.97)
Sarabande in F for Harpsichord, "O beau jardin"
B. Schenkman (hpd) *(rec Portola Valley, CA, Sept 1997)* † Courante Hpd; Gaillarde Hpd; Minuet Hpd; Prelude Hpd; Ritounèlle des Fees; Suite 2 Hpd; Suite 5 Hpd; Tombeau de Monsieur de Chambonnières CENT ▲ 2435 [DDD] (16.97)
Sarabande in d for Harpsichord
B. Schenkman (hpd) *(rec Portola Valley, CA, Sept 1997)* † Courante Hpd; Gaillarde Hpd; Minuet Hpd; Prelude Hpd; Ritounèlle des Fees; Suite 2 Hpd; Suite 5 Hpd; Tombeau de Monsieur de Chambonnières CENT ▲ 2435 [DDD] (16.97)
Suite No. 1 in G for Harpsichord
B. M. Willi (hpd)—1st Courante; 2nd Gigue; 3rd Courante *(rec Aug 1998)* † Gaillarde Hpd; Suite 2 Hpd; Suite 3 Hpd; Suite 4 Hpd; Suite 5 Hpd MPH ▲ 56828 [DDD] (15.97)
Suite No. 2 in g for Harpsichord
B. Schenkman (hpd) *(rec Portola Valley, CA, Sept 1997)* † Courante Hpd; Gaillarde Hpd; Minuet Hpd; Prelude Hpd; Ritounèlle des Fees; Sarabande Hpd; Suite 5 Hpd; Tombeau de Monsieur de Chambonnières CENT ▲ 2435 [DDD] (16.97)
B. M. Willi (hpd) *(rec Aug 1998)* † Gaillarde Hpd; Suite 1 Hpd; Suite 3 Hpd; Suite 4 Hpd; Suite 5 Hpd MPH ▲ 56828 [DDD] (15.97)
Suite No. 3 in d for Harpsichord
B. M. Willi (hpd)—2nd Courante; 2nd Sarabande-lentement in d; Variations sur les Folies d'Espagne *(rec Aug 1998)* † Gaillarde Hpd; Suite 1 Hpd; Suite 2 Hpd; Suite 4 Hpd; Suite 5 Hpd MPH ▲ 56828 [DDD] (15.97)
Suite No. 4 in D for Harpsichord
B. M. Willi (hpd)—2nd Courante *(rec Aug 1998)* † Gaillarde Hpd; Suite 1 Hpd; Suite 2 Hpd; Suite 3 Hpd; Suite 5 Hpd MPH ▲ 56828 [DDD] (15.97)
Suite No. 5 in C for Harpsichord
B. Schenkman (hpd) *(rec Portola Valley, CA, Sept 1997)* † Courante Hpd; Gaillarde Hpd; Minuet Hpd; Prelude Hpd; Ritounèlle des Fees; Sarabande Hpd; Suite 2 Hpd; Tombeau de Monsieur de Chambonnières CENT ▲ 2435 [DDD] (16.97)
B. M. Willi (hpd) *(rec Aug 1998)* † Gaillarde Hpd; Suite 1 Hpd; Suite 2 Hpd; Suite 3 Hpd; Suite 4 Hpd MPH ▲ 56828 [DDD] (15.97)
Tombeau de Monsieur de Chambonnières for Harpsichord
B. Schenkman (hpd) *(rec Portola Valley, CA, Sept 1997)* † Courante Hpd; Gaillarde Hpd; Minuet Hpd; Prelude Hpd; Ritounèlle des Fees; Sarabande Hpd; Suite 2 Hpd; Suite 5 Hpd CENT ▲ 2435 [DDD] (16.97)
ANGRISANI, GIOVANNI (18th cent)
Concerto in D for Flute & Strings
G. Petrucci (fl), C. F. Sedazzari (cnd), Schubert Camerata *(rec live, Rome, Italy, July 27, 1995)* ("5 Concertos for Flute & Strings from the Neapolitan School of the 1700's") † Papa:Con Fl; Prota:Con Fl; Sciroli:Con Fl; Servillo:Con 1 Fl BONG ▲ 5553 [ADD] (16.97)
ANGULO, EDUARDO (1954-
De Aires antiguos for Mandolin & Guitar (1994)
Capriccioso Duo ("Duo Capriccioso, Vol. 5") † H. Baumann:Tambourin; Miguel:Back to Sirius; Tober-Vogt:Carnival of Venice; Ueno:Spiral Dance THOR ▲ 2366 [DDD] (16.97)
Paginas en Bronce for 2 guitars
M. Troester (gtr), H. Ahmad (gtr) *(rec Feb 1998)* ("Duettissimo-Masterpieces for Two Guitars") † H. Baumann:Son 2 gtr; P. Bellinati:Jongo; L. Brouwer:Micro piezas Gtr; Gnattali:Schottisch 2 Gtrs; Valse; A. Piazzolla:Lo que vendra; Tango Suite; M. N. Walter:Fusion Tune THOR ▲ 2389 [DDD] (16.97)
Sonata No. 2 for Guitar
M. Tröster (gtr) *(rec Sept 1995)* ("El Decameron Negro") † L. Brouwer:Decameron Negro; Vars on a Theme of Django Reinhardt; A. Piazzolla:Muerte del angel; Pieces (5) Gtr THOR ▲ 2288 [DDD] (16.97)
Die Vögel for Guitar & String Quartet, Op. 21 (1993)
M. Tröster (gtr), Das Sächsische String Quartet *(rec Dresden, Germany, Feb 1994)* ("Guitarrenquintette I") † J. Duarte:Qnt 1 Gtr, Op. 85; B. Hummel:Konzertante Musik, Op. 39 THOR ▲ 2212 [DDD] (17.97)
ANGULO, HECTOR (1933-
Cantos Yoruba de Cuba for Guitar
M. Barrueco (gtr) *(rec London, England, Apr 1998)* ("Cuba!") † Ardévol:Son Gtr; L. Brouwer:Preludio; Rito de los Orishas; Fariñas:Canción Triste; Preludio; E. Lecuona:A la Antigua; Comparsa; Danza Lucumi; Ubieta:New York Rush EMIC ▲ 56757 [DDD] (16.97)
ANGULO, MANUEL (20th cent)
Bisonante for Saxophone & Piano (1983)
Duo Dilemme *(rec Jan 1998)* ("Nouvelle musique pour saxophone et piano") † Charrière:Voix meurtrie; Guerandi:Towards; J. A. Lennon:Distances Within Me; M. Nyman:Shaping the Curve; Visvikis:Mondes irisés DORO ▲ 5011 [DDD] (16.97)
ANHALT, ISTVÁN (1919-1969)
Fantasia for Piano
G. Gould (pno) *(rec 1967)* † Hétu:Vars Pno, Op. 8; Morawetz:Fant Pno; Pentland:Ombres; Valen:Son 2 Pno, Op. 38 SNYC (Glenn Gould Edition) ▲ 52677 [ADD] (16.97)
Sparkskraps for Orchestra (1988)
A. Pauk (cnd), Esprit Orch *(rec Mar 1992)* ("Iridescence") † H. Freedman:Graphic IV; C. P. Harman:Iridescence; A. Pauk:Cosmos; R. M. Schafer:Scorpius CBC (SM 5000) ▲ 5132 [DDD]
ANROOY, PETER VAN (1879-1954)
Piet Hein Rhapsody for Orchestra (1901)
K. Bakels (cnd), Netherlands RSO *(rec 1994-95)* † Dopper:Ciaconna gotica; Sym 7 NMCC ▲ 92060 [DDD] (17.97)
ANTES, JOHN (1740-1811)
Trios (3) for 2 Violins & Cello, Op. 3 (ca 1790)
American Moravian Chamber Ensemble members † J. F. Peter:Qnts Strs NWW 2-▲ 80507 [DDD] (29.97)
ANTHEIL, GEORGE (1900-1959)
Airplane Sonata for Piano (1922)
M. Verbit (pno) † Femme 100 têtes; Pno Music; Son Sauvage; Son 4 Pno ALBA ▲ 146 [DDD] (16.97)
Archipelago (rhumba) for Orchestra (1935)
B. Kolman (cnd), Slovak State PO Košice *(rec House of Arts, Kosice, Slovak Republic, 1995)* † Capital of the World; Sym 5 CENT ▲ 2293 [DDD] (16.97)
Capital of the World (ballet) for Orchestra [after Hemingway] (1953)
B. Kolman (cnd), Slovak State PO Košice *(rec House of Arts, Kosice, Slovak Republic, 1995)* † Archipelago; Sym 5 CENT ▲ 2293 [DDD] (16.97)
J. Levine (cnd), Ballet Theater Orch *(rec 1953-54)* † R. D. Banfield:Combat; W. Schuman:Undertow (choreographic episodes) EMIC ▲ 66548 [ADD] (11.97)
La femme 100 têtes (45 preludes) for Piano (1932-33)
B. Koehlen (pno) ("Piano Pictures") † Satie:Sports et divertissements COLG (deluxe) ▲ 20010 (22.97)
M. Verbit (pno) † Airplane Son; Pno Music; Son Sauvage; Son 4 Pno ALBA ▲ 146 [DDD] (16.97)

▲ = CD ♦ = Enhanced CD △ = MD ▮ = Cassette Tape ▯ = DCC

ANTHEIL, GEORGE (cont.)

Piano Music

B. Koehlen (pno)—Fireworks & the Profane Waltzes; The Golden Bird; Son 2 Pno, "Airplane"; Son 4 Pno, "Jazz"; Mechanisms; Son 3 Pno, "Death of Machines"; Little Shimmy; Son Sauvage; Son 5 Pno; Sonatina for Radio; Sonatina (1932) ("Bad Boy's Piano Music, 1919-32") COLG ▲ 31880 (18.97)

M. Verbit (pno)—Little Shimmy; Tango from the opera "Transatlantic"; Son; Valentine Waltzes † Airplane Son; Femme 100 têtes; Son Sauvage; Son 4 Pno ALBA ▲ 146 [DDD] (16.97)

Sonata No. 4 for Piano (1948)

M. Verbit (pno) † Airplane Son; Femme 100 têtes; Pno Music; Son Sauvage ALBA ▲ 146 [DDD] (16.97)

Sonata Sauvage for Piano (1923)

M. Verbit (pno) † Airplane Son; Femme 100 têtes; Pno Music; Son 4 Pno ALBA ▲ 146 [DDD] (16.97)

Sonata for Trumpet & Piano (1952)

J. Harjanne (tpt), J. Lagerspetz (pno) ("American Trumpet Sonatas") † Joio:Son Tpt; Kennan:Son Tpt; H. Stevens:Son Tpt FNL ▲ 17691 (16.97)

Symphony No. 4, "1942"

E. Goossens (cnd), London SO *(rec Walthamstow Hall, London, England, Mar 1959)* † A. Copland:Statements Orch EVC ▲ 9039 [AAD] (13.97)

Symphony No. 5, "Joyous" (1947-48)

B. Kolman (cnd), Slovak State PO Košice *(rec House of Arts, Kosice, Slovak Republic, 1995)* † Archipelago; Capital of the World CENT ▲ 2293 [DDD] (16.97)

ANTILL, JOHN (1904-1986)

Corroboree:Suite

E. Goossens (cnd), London SO † Ginastera:Estancia (suite); Panambi (suite), Op. 1a; H. Villa-Lobos:Bachiana brasileira 2 EVC ▲ 9007 [AAD] (13.97)

ANTONIOU, THEODORE (1935-

Celebration I for Large Orchestra (1994)

A. Panayotopoulos (cnd), Bulgarian SO † Celebration III; Con-Fant Vn; Prometheus AG ▲ 109 (18.97)

Celebration III for Orchestra & Chorus (1995)

A. Panayotopoulos (cnd), Bulgarian SO, Bulgarian Svetoslav Obretenov Choir † Celebration I; Con-Fant Vn; Prometheus AG ▲ 109 (18.97)

Chorochronos II for Mixed Media Ensemble (1973)

A. Panayotopoulos (cnd), Bulgarian SO Chamber Ensemble † Circle of Thanatos & Genesis; East-West; Ode AG ▲ 153 (18.97)

Circle of Thanatos & Genesis (cantata) (1980)

A. Panayotopoulos (cnd), Bulgarian SO † Chorochronos II; East-West; Ode AG ▲ 153 (18.97)

Concerto-Fantasia for Violin & Chamber Orchestra (1990)

L. Nentchev (vn), A. Panayotopoulos (cnd), Bulgarian SO † Celebration I; Celebration III; Prometheus AG ▲ 109 (18.97)

East-West for Orchestra

A. Panayotopoulos (cnd), Bulgarian SO † Chorochronos II; Circle of Thanatos & Genesis; Ode AG ▲ 153 (18.97)

Ode for Orchestra

A. Panayotopoulos (cnd), Bulgarian SO † Chorochronos II; Circle of Thanatos & Genesis; East-West AG ▲ 153 (18.97)

Prometheus for Baritone & Orchestra (1983)

P. Odajev (bar), A. Panayotopoulos (cnd), Bulgarian SO † Celebration I; Celebration III; Con-Fant Vn AG ▲ 109 (18.97)

APERGHIS, GEORGES (1945-

Récitations for solo Voice (1977-78)

P. Vaillancourt (sop), J. Grégoire (perc) † Scelsi:Canti del Capricorno SNE ▲ 571 (16.97)

APONTE-LEDEE, RAFAEL (1938-

Bagatelas (3) for Guitar (1988)

A. M. Rosado (gtr) *(rec NYC, NY, 1992)* ("We've got (poly)rythm") † R. Cordero:Mensajes para Cuatro Amigos; T. León:Paisanos Semos! Gtr; A. Piazzolla:Pieces (5) Gtr; F. Schwartz:Fronteras Gtr; We've got (poly)rythm Gtr; E. Vásquez:Auzielle-Milonga Gtr; Ofrenda Gtr; Suite Transitorial Gtr ALBA ▲ 87 [DDD] (16.97)

APPLEBAUM, LOUIS (1918-

Harp Music

E. Goodman (hp)—Nightscape *(rec Elora, Ontario, Canada)* † M. Barnes:Hp Music; A. Louie:Hp Music; Mozetich:Hp Music; Pentland:Hp Music; Sharman:Hp Music BIS ▲ 649 [DDD] (17.97)

APPLEBAUM, MARK (1967-

Music of Applebaum

M. Applebaum (duplex mausphon/midi)—Salmagundi; Scrape:Threaded Rods; Bow:Tam Trees; 3 Ictus; Strike:3/2+5:2 Groove; Pluck:Koto; 16 Things; Stroke:Nails; Strike:Dulcimer Groove; S-tog (excerpt) ("Mousetrap Music") INNO ▲ 511 [DDD] (14.97)

APPLETON, JON (1939-

Brush Canyon for Synclavier

J. Appleton (synclavier) *(rec Dartmouth College, Hanover, NH)* ("CDCM Computer Music Series, Vol. 6") † Degitaru Ongaku; D. E. Jones:Still Life in Wood & Metal; Still Life Dancing; P. Moravec:Devices & Desires; C. Wolff:Mayday Materials CENT ▲ 2052 [DDD] (16.97)

Degitaru Ongaku for Synclavier (1983)

J. Appleton (synclavier) *(rec Dartmouth College, Hanover, NH)* ("CDCM Computer Music Series, Vol. 6") † Brush Canyon; D. E. Jones:Still Life in Wood & Metal; Still Life Dancing; P. Moravec:Devices & Desires; C. Wolff:Mayday Materials CENT ▲ 2052 [DDD] (16.97)

ARASCIONE, GIOVANNI (1546-ca 1600)

Nuove laudi ariose della Beatissima Virgine scelte da diversi autori for 4 Voices

G. Monaco (cnd) , Progetto Musica Vocal Ensemble *(rec Santuario di Graglia, Mar 1995)* ("Sacred Music Connected with St. Philip Neri") † Ancina:Vocal Music; Palestrina:Missa "In minoribus", R.84; G. Razzi:Laude spirituale TACT ▲ 520001 [DDD] (16.97)

ARBAN, JEAN-BAPTISTE (1825-1889)

Cavatina & Variations on Verdi's Nabucco for Cornet & Piano

G. Touvron (cnt), N. Cottin (pno) *(rec Feb 1996)* † Fants on Verdi's Operas Cnt LIDI ▲ 105040 [DDD] (16.97)

Fantasie, Theme & Variations on, "The Carnival of Venice"

M. Fisher (eup), M. Lawson (pno) [arr Leidzen] *(rec Boutell Concert Hall, Northern Illinois Univ., IL, 1994)* ("EuFish") † J. Bach:Concert Vars; J. S. Bach:Sons Fl; J. Brahms:Songs; G. Jacob:Fant Eup; Telemann:Son Bn ALBA ▲ 162 [DDD] (16.97)

Fantasies on Verdi's Operas for Cornet & Piano

G. Touvron (cnt), N. Cottin (pno)—Fant 1 on Il Trovatore; Fant brillante on Don Carlos; Fant brillante on I vespri siciliani; Fant on La forza del destino; Fant on Rigoletto; Fant on La traviata *(rec Feb 1996)* † Cavatina & Vars LIDI ▲ 105040 [DDD] (16.97)

Variations on a Theme from Bellini's Norma for Cornet & Piano

H. Hardenberger (cnt), R. Pöntinen (pno) † P. M. Davies:Son Tpt; J. Françaix:Sonatine Tpt & Pno; J. Hartmann:Vars on Rule Britannia; Honegger:Intrada Tpt & Pno; Rabe:Shazam; Tisné:Héraldiques BIS ▲ 287 [DDD] (17.97)

ARBEAU, THOINOT (1520-1595)

Orchésographie [instrumental dances compiled by Arbeau, 1588]

S. Logemann (cnd), New York Renaissance Band ARA ▲ 6514 [DDD] (16.97)

ARCADELT, JACQUES (?1505-1568)

Lamentationes for Voices

E. van Nevel (cnd), Currende ("Polyphony for Passion-Tide") † Clemens Non Papa:Sacred Music; Crecquillon:Lamentationes; O. de Lassus:Sacred Music; Rogier:Sacred Music; Wert:Sacred Music *([ENG,FRE,LAT] text)* EUFO ▲ 1248 [DDD] (18.97)

ARCAS, JULIÁN (1832-1882)

Guitar Music

C. Trepat (gtr)—Bolero; Colección de Tangos † R. Gerhard:Gemini; Son Vc; Trio Pno; José Martinez Palacios:Son Gtr; Llobet:Gtr Music; Tárrega:Gtr Music LAMA ▲ 2021 [DDD] (17.97)

ARCUS, DAVID (20th cent)

Variations on Simple Gifts for Oboe & Orchestra

T. Baskin (ob), Y. Turovsky (cnd), Montreal Musici ("Tranquillity") † J. Christian Bach:Con in c; Boccherini:Con Vc, G.482; D. Shostakovich:Con 2 Pno, Op. 102; I. Stravinsky:Con Str Orch; Vivaldi:Con Rcr, RV.444; Con Strs, RV.158; Con Vcs, RV.531; Cons Fl, Op. 10/1-6; Wassenaer:Concerti Armonici CHN ▲ 8573 [DDD] (16.97)

ARDÉVOL, JOSÉ (1911-1981)

Sonata for Guitar (1948)

M. Barrueco (gtr) *(rec London, England, Apr 1998)* ("Cuba!") † H. Angulo:Cantos Yoruba; L. Brouwer:Preludio; Rito de los Orishas; Fariñas:Canción Triste; Preludio; E. Lecuona:A la Antigua; Comparsa; Danza Lucumi; Ubieta:New York Rush EMIC ▲ 56757 [DDD] (16.97)

AREL, BÜLENT (1919-1990)

Electronic Music

B. Arel (tape)—Stereo Elec Music 2 *(rec Columbia Univ., NYC, NY)* ("Pioneers of Electronic Music") † Davidovsky:Electronic Music; Luening:Electronic Music; P. Smiley:Electronic Music; V. Ussachevsky:Electronic Music; Two Sketches for a Computer Piece CRI ▲ 611 [ADD] (16.97)

Music for a Sacred Service (electronic music) (1961)

B. Arel (elec) *(rec 1961-73)* ("Columbia-Princeton Electronic Music Center") † Out of into; C. Dodge:Earth's Magnetic Field; I. Marshall:Cortez; I. K. Mimaroglu:Prelude 8, "To the Memory of Varèse"; Semegen:Elec Comp 1; A. Shields:Dance Piece 3; Study Voc & Tape NWW ▲ 80521 (16.97)

AREL, BÜLENT (1919-1990)**& DARIA SEMEGEN** (1946-

Out of into (electronic music)

B. Arel (elec), D. Semegen (elec) *(rec 1961-73)* ("Columbia-Princeton Electronic Music Center") † Music for a Sacred Service; C. Dodge:Earth's Magnetic Field; I. Marshall:Cortez; I. K. Mimaroglu:Prelude 8, "To the Memory of Varèse"; Semegen:Elec Comp 1; A. Shields:Dance Piece 3; Study Voc & Tape NWW ▲ 80521 (16.97)

ARENSKY, ANTON (1861-1906)

Caprices (6) for Piano, Op. 43

S. Coombs (pno) † Characteristic Pieces Pno, Op. 36; Pieces (4) Pno, Op. 25; Pieces (6) Pno, Op. 53; Près de la mer, Op. 52; Studies (4) Pno, Op. 41 HYP ▲ 67066 (18.97)

Characteristic Pieces (24) for Piano, Op. 36 (1894)

R. Alston (pno)—Etude *(rec Czech Republic, Nov 1995)* † Con Pno, Op. 2; Pieces (4) Pno, Op. 25; Studies (12) Pno, Op. 74 CENT ▲ 2307 [DDD] (16.97)

S. Coombs (pno)—Nocturne; Le ruisseau dans la forêt; Mazurka; Élégie; Etude † Caprices Pno, Op. 43; Pieces (4) Pno, Op. 25; Pieces (6) Pno, Op. 53; Près de la mer, Op. 52; Studies (4) Pno, Op. 41 HYP ▲ 67066 (18.97)

Children's Suite for Piano 4-Hands, Op. 65

D. Blumenthal (pno), R. Groslot (pno) *(rec Heidelberg, Germany, Aug 1992)* † Suite 1 for 2 Pnos, Op. 15; Suite 2 for 2 Pnos, Op. 23; Suite 3 for 2 Pnos, Op. 33; Suite 4 for 2 Pnos, Op. 62 MARC ▲ 8223497 [DDD] (13.97)

Concerto in f for Piano & Orchestra, Op. 2 (1882)

R. Alston (pno), P. Freeman (cnd), Czech National SO *(rec Czech Republic, Nov 1995)* † Characteristic Pieces Pno, Op. 36; Pieces (4) Pno, Op. 25; Studies (12) Pno, Op. 74 CENT ▲ 2307 [DDD] (16.97)

S. Coombs (pno), J. Maksymiuk (cnd), BBC Scottish SO † Fant on Themes of Ryabinin, Op. 48; Bortkiewicz:Con 1 Pno HYP ▲ 66624 (18.97)

Concerto in a for Violin & Orchestra, Op. 54 (1891)

M. Lubotsky (vn), A. Volmer (cnd), Estonian National SO ("Russian Violin Concertos") † Rimsky-Korsakov:Fant on Russian Themes, Op. 33; P. Tchaikovsky:Con Vn GLOE ▲ 5174 [DDD] (16.97)

S. Stadler (vn), V. Chernushenko (cnd), Leningrad SO *(rec Lenningrad, Russia, 1983)* † D. Shostakovich:Con 1 Vn, Op. 99 CONE (Russian All-Star Orchestra) ▲ 9416 [ADD] (16.97)

A. Trostiansky (vn), Y. Turovsky (cnd), Montreal Musici *(rec 1st Orford International Competition, England)* † Glazunov:Con ballata, Op. 108; Con 1 Pno, Op. 92 CHN ▲ 9528 (16.97)

Egyptian Nights (ballet), Op. 50 (1908)

A. Avramenko (vn), V. Kolpashnikov (vc), D. Yablonsky (cnd), Moscow SO *(rec Moscow, Russia, Mar 1996)* MARC ▲ 8225028 [DDD] (13.97)

Fantasia on Themes of Ryabinin for Piano & Orchestra, Op. 48 (1899)

S. Coombs (pno), J. Maksymiuk (cnd), BBC Scottish SO † Con Pno, Op. 2; Bortkiewicz:Con 1 Pno HYP ▲ 66624 (18.97)

Pieces (4) for Piano, Op. 25

R. Alston (pno)—Etude (on a Chinese Theme) *(rec Czech Republic, Nov 1995)* † Characteristic Pieces Pno, Op. 36; Con Pno, Op. 2; Studies (12) Pno, Op. 74 CENT ▲ 2307 [DDD] (16.97)

S. Coombs (pno) † Caprices Pno, Op. 43; Characteristic Pieces Pno, Op. 36; Pieces (6) Pno, Op. 53; Près de la mer, Op. 52; Studies (4) Pno, Op. 41 HYP ▲ 67066 (18.97)

Pieces (6) for Piano, Op. 53 (1901)

S. Coombs (pno) † Caprices Pno, Op. 43; Characteristic Pieces Pno, Op. 36; Pieces (4) Pno, Op. 25; Près de la mer, Op. 52; Studies (4) Pno, Op. 41 HYP ▲ 67066 (18.97)

Près de la mer (6 esquisses) for Piano, Op. 52

S. Coombs (pno)—No. 4 in G♭: Allegro moderato; No. 5 in e♭: Allegro scherzando † Caprices Pno, Op. 43; Characteristic Pieces Pno, Op. 36; Pieces (4) Pno, Op. 25; Pieces (6) Pno, Op. 53; Studies (4) Pno, Op. 41 HYP ▲ 67066 (18.97)

Quartet No. 1 in G for Strings, Op. 11 (1888)

Lajtha String Quartet *(rec Budapest, Hungary, Jan 1994)* † Qnt Pno, Op. 51; Qt 2 Strs, Op. 35 MARC ▲ 8223811 [DDD] (13.97)

Quartet No. 2 in a for Strings, Op. 35 (1894)

Arensky Ensemble † Borodin:Sxt Strs; P. Tchaikovsky:Souvenir de Florence, Op. 70 MER ▲ 84211 (16.97)

Lajtha String Quartet *(rec Budapest, Hungary, Jan 1994)* † Qnt Pno, Op. 51; Qt 1 Strs, Op. 11 MARC ▲ 8223811 [DDD] (13.97)

Lake Winnipesaukee Chamber Players *(rec Rochester, NY, 1997)* † P. Tchaikovsky:Souvenir de Florence, Op. 70 RUS ▲ 10055 [DDD] (11.97)

Raphael Ensemble † P. Tchaikovsky:Souvenir de Florence, Op. 70 HYP ▲ 66648 (18.97)

Quintet in D for Piano & String Quartet, Op. 51 (1900)

I. Prunyi (pno), Lajtha String Quartet *(rec Budapest, Hungary, Jan 1994)* † Qt 1 Strs, Op. 11; Qt 2 Strs, Op. 35 MARC ▲ 8223811 [DDD] (13.97)

Studies (4) for Piano, Op. 41 (1896)

S. Coombs (pno) † Caprices Pno, Op. 43; Characteristic Pieces Pno, Op. 36; Pieces (4) Pno, Op. 25; Pieces (6) Pno, Op. 53; Près de la mer, Op. 52 HYP ▲ 67066 (18.97)

Studies (12) for Piano, Op. 74 (1905)

R. Alston (pno) *(rec Czech Republic, Nov 1995)* † Characteristic Pieces Pno, Op. 36; Con Pno, Op. 2; Pieces (4) Pno, Op. 25 CENT ▲ 2307 [DDD] (16.97)

Suite No. 1 in F for 2 Pianos, Op. 15

D. Blumenthal (pno), R. Groslot (pno) *(rec Heidelberg, Germany, Aug 1992)* † Children's Suite, Op. 65; Suite 2 for 2 Pnos, Op. 23; Suite 3 for 2 Pnos, Op. 33; Suite 4 for 2 Pnos, Op. 62 MARC ▲ 8223497 [DDD] (13.97)

S. Coombs (pno), I. Munro (pno) † Suite 2 for 2 Pnos, Op. 23; Suite 3 for 2 Pnos, Op. 33; Suite 4 for 2 Pnos, Op. 62 HYP ▲ 66755 (18.97)

Suite No. 2 for 2 Pianos, Op. 23, "Silhouettes" (1892)

D. Blumenthal (pno), R. Groslot (pno) *(rec Heidelberg, Germany, Aug 1992)* † Children's Suite, Op. 65; Suite 1 for 2 Pnos, Op. 15; Suite 3 for 2 Pnos, Op. 33; Suite 4 for 2 Pnos, Op. 62 MARC ▲ 8223497 [DDD] (13.97)

S. Coombs (pno), I. Munro (pno) † Suite 1 for 2 Pnos, Op. 15; Suite 3 for 2 Pnos, Op. 33; Suite 4 for 2 Pnos, Op. 62 HYP ▲ 66755 (18.97)

N. Järvi (cnd), Danish National RSO † A. Scriabin:Sym 3 CHN ▲ 8898 [DDD] (16.97)

Suite No. 3 for 2 Pianos, Op. 33, "Variations"

D. Blumenthal (pno), R. Groslot (pno) *(rec Heidelberg, Germany, Aug 1992)* † Children's Suite, Op. 65; Suite 1 for 2 Pnos, Op. 15; Suite 2 for 2 Pnos, Op. 23; Suite 4 for 2 Pnos, Op. 62 MARC ▲ 8223497 [DDD] (13.97)

S. Coombs (pno), I. Munro (pno) † Suite 1 for 2 Pnos, Op. 15; Suite 2 for 2 Pnos, Op. 23; Suite 4 for 2 Pnos, Op. 62 HYP ▲ 66755 (18.97)

Suite No. 4 for 2 Pianos, Op. 62

D. Blumenthal (pno), R. Groslot (pno) *(rec Heidelberg, Germany, Aug 1992)* † Children's Suite, Op. 65; Suite 1 for 2 Pnos, Op. 15; Suite 2 for 2 Pnos, Op. 23; Suite 3 for 2 Pnos, Op. 33 MARC ▲ 8223497 [DDD] (13.97)

S. Coombs (pno), I. Munro (pno) † Suite 1 for 2 Pnos, Op. 15; Suite 2 for 2 Pnos, Op. 23; Suite 3 for 2 Pnos, Op. 33 HYP ▲ 66755 (18.97)

L. Kinton (pno), J. Anagnoson (pno) MUVI (Musica Viva) ▲ 1036 [DDD] (16.97)

Trio No. 1 in d for Piano, Violin & Cello, Op. 32 (1894)

Borodin Trio † Trio 2 Pno, Op. 73 CHN ▲ 7048 (13.97)

A. Cardenes (vn), J. Solow (vc), M. Golabek (pno) † P. Tchaikovsky:Trio Pno, Op. 50 DLS ▲ 3056 [DDD] (14.97)

Cho Piano Trio † P. Tchaikovsky:Trio Pno, Op. 50 TELO ▲ 9 (16.97)

R. Dubinsky (vn), Turovsky (vc), L. Edlina (pno) † M. Glinka:Trio pathétique CHN ▲ 8477 [DDD] (16.97)

Grumiaux Piano Trio † Smetana:Trio Pno, Op. 15 ECCO ▲ 206292 [DDD] (10.97)

C. Lin (vn), G. Hoffman (vc), Y. Bronfman (pno) *(rec Aug 1992)* † P. Tchaikovsky:Trio Pno, Op. 50 SNYC ▲ 53269 [DDD] (16.97)

Nash Ensemble *(rec 1982)* † Rimsky-Korsakov:Qnt Fl CRD ▲ 3409 [ADD] (17.97)

ARENSKY, ANTON (cont.)
Trio No. 1 in d for Piano, Violin & Cello, Op. 32 (1894) (cont.)
New Arts Trio *(rec Eastman School of Music, Rochester, NY, Jan 1997)* † Trio 2 Pno, Op. 73
FDS ▲ 57930 [DDD] (16.97)
Rembrandt Trio † P. Tchaikovsky:Trio Pno, Op. 50 DOR ▲ 90146 [DDD] (16.97)
R. Stamper (vn), C. Jackson (vc), V. Ashkenazy (pno) *(rec Nov 1990)* † P. Tchaikovsky:Trio Pno, Op. 50
NXIN ▲ 550467 [DDD] (5.97)
Trio No. 2 in f for Piano, Violin & Cello, Op. 73 (1905)
Borodin Trio † Trio 1 Pno, Op. 32 CHN ▲ 7048 (13.97)
New Arts Trio *(rec Eastman School of Music, Rochester, NY, Jan 1997)* † Trio 1 Pno, Op. 32
FDS ▲ 57930 [DDD] (16.97)
Variations on a Theme of Tchaikovsky for String Orchestra [arr from slow movt of Quartet No. 2, Op. 35], Op. 35a (1894)
W. Boughton (cnd), English String Orch *(rec Great Hall Univ of Birmingham, AL, Aug 1991)* ("Orchestral Favorites, Vol. 2") † J. Ireland:Downland Suite; O. Respighi:Ancient Airs & Dances; P. Tchaikovsky:Andante cantabile; W. Walton:Pieces Strs; D. Wirén:Serenade Strs, Op. 11 NIMB ▲ 7020 [DDD] (11.97)
A. Doráti (cnd), Philharmonia Hungarica † P. Tchaikovsky:Sym 1; Sym 2; Sym 3 PPHI 2-▲ 434391 (22.97)
L. Markiz (cnd), Amsterdam New Sinfonietta *(rec 1990)* † P. Tchaikovsky:Andante cantabile; Elegy Strs; Nocturne Vc; Serenade Strs, Op. 48 GLOE ▲ 6021 [DDD] (16.97)
V. Polianski (cnd), Belarussian CO *(rec Belorussia, Russia, 1988)* ("Russian Conducting School: Valery Poliansky") † P. Tchaikovsky:Choral Music; Serenade Strs, Op. 48 RD (Talents of Russia) ▲ 22106 [DDD] (16.97)
E. Schmieder (cnd), I Palpiti CO † J. S. Bach:Air on the G String; F. Schubert:Qt 14 Strs, D.810
TELO ▲ 11 [DDD] (16.97)
J. Somary (cnd), English CO *(rec Conway Hall, London, England, 1972)* ("Russian Favorites for Strings") † Borodin:Nocturne Str Orch; S. Prokofiev:Sym 1; P. Tchaikovsky:Serenade Strs, Op. 48 VC ▲ 37 [AAD] (13.97)
K. Stratton (cnd), Moscow SO ("Slavonic Serenades") † A. Dvořák:Nocturne Strs, Op. 40; Qnt Strs, Op. 77; Glazunov:Suite Strs, Op. 35; Kalinnikov:Chanson triste; J. Suk:Meditation, Op. 35a DORD ▲ 80144 [DDD] (13.97)
G. Varga (cnd), Stuttgart CO *(rec Stuttgart, Germany, 1994)* † M. Glinka:Divert brillante; S. Rachmaninoff:Pieces Vn Pno, Op. 6; P. Tchaikovsky:Serenade Strs, Op. 48 DI ▲ 920323 [DDD] (5.97)

ARGENTO, DOMINICK (1927-
The Andrée Expedition (song cycle) for Baritone & Piano (1983)
B. Nordfors (ten), B. Forsberg (pno) *(rec Sveriges Radio, Stockholm, Sweden)* † Ahlberg:Upp Genom Luften; Munktell:Isjungfrun; Nordholm:Vid Nordpolen; C. A. Strindberg:Luftsegling NSAG ▲ 21 (16.97)
W. Parker (bar), W. Huckaby (pno) *(rec 1988)* † From the Diary of Virginia Woolf CENT ▲ 2092 [DDD] (16.97)
Elizabethan Songs (6) for solo Voice & Piano (or Orchestra) (1958)
B. Bonney (sop), A. Previn (pno) † S. Barber:Hermit Songs, Op. 29; A. Copland:Poems (12) of Emily Dickinson; A. Previn:Sallie Chisum; Vocalise PLON ▲ 455511 (16.97)
F. Urrey (ten), R. A. Clark (cnd), Manhattan CO † Water Bird Talk NPT ▲ 85602 [DDD] (16.97)
Elizabethan Songs (6) for Soprano & Chamber Ensemble (1962)
P. M. Bedi (sop), Rembrandt Chamber Players ("20th Century Baroque: Modern Reflections On Old Instruments") † E. Carter:Son Fl, Ob, Vc & Hpd; M. de Falla:Con Hpd; I. Hurník:Son da camera CED ▲ 11 [DDD] (16.97)
J. Danton (sop), A. Black (vn), J. Bumstead (vc), C. Krueger (fl), J. Harrison (ob), T. Stumpf (hpd), C. T. Brooks (cnd) ("Songs of Innocence") † Songs About Spring; A. Cooke:Nocturnes; Songs of Innocence; Moylan:For a Sleeping Child ALBA ▲ 264 [DDD] (16.97)
From the Diary of Virginia Woolf for Mezzo-Soprano & Piano (1974)
J. Baker (mez), M. Isepp (pno) † Debussy:Songs; Duparc:Songs; G. Fauré:Songs; H. Wolf:Spanisches Liederbuch (Geistliche Lieder) DNC ▲ 1019 [ADD] (16.97)
V. Dupuy (mez) † W. Benson:Songs for the End of the World GAS ▲ 273 (16.97)
L. Maxwell (mez), W. Huckaby (pno) *(rec 1988)* † Andrée Expedition CENT ▲ 2092 [DDD] (16.97)
I Hate & I Love (choral cycle) for Mixed Chorus & Percussion [poems by Gaius Valerius Catullus] (1981)
R. Shaw (cnd), Robert Shaw Festival Singers, T. Sivils (perc), J. Pereira (perc) *(rec Church of St. Pierre, Gramat, France, July 1994)* ("Appear & Inspire") † H. Badings:Chansons bretonnes; B. Britten:Hymn to St. Cecilia, Op. 27; Debussy:Chansons de Charles d'Orléans; F. Poulenc:Soir de neige; M. Ravel:Chansons Chorus
TEL ▲ 80408 [DDD] (16.97)
Letters from Composers (song cycle) for Tenor & Guitar (1968)
P. M. Bedi (sop), J. Kust (gtr) *(rec Mandel Hall, Univ of Chicago, IL, June 1996)* ("To Be Sung Upon the Water") † Songs About Spring; To Be Sung Upon The Water; Vaughan Williams:Along The Field; Vocalises Sop
CED ▲ 29 [DDD] (16.97)
Miss Havisham's Wedding Night (monodrama)
L. Mabbs (sop), S. Watkins (cnd), St. Cecilia Sinfonia † Water Bird Talk KOCH ▲ 7388 (16.97)
Postcard from Morocco (opera in 1 act) [lib John Donahue] (1971)
P. Brunelle (cnd), Minnesota Opera Orch, J. Hardy (mez), V. Sutton (ten), S. Roche (sgr), B. Brandt (sgr), Y. Marshall (sgr), B. Busse (sgr), M. Foreman (sgr) CRI 2-▲ 614 [ADD]
Songs About Spring (song cycle) for Soprano & Orchestra (1950; rev 1954 & 1960)
P. M. Bedi (sop), E. Buccheri (pno) *(rec Mandel Hall, Univ of Chicago, IL, June 1996)* ("To Be Sung Upon the Water") † Letters from Composers; To Be Sung Upon The Water; Vaughan Williams:Along The Field; Vocalises Sop
CED ▲ 29 [DDD] (16.97)
J. Danton (sop), T. Stumpf (pno) ("Songs of Innocence") † Elizabethan Songs Sop & Chamber Ensemble; A. Cooke:Nocturnes; Songs of Innocence; Moylan:For a Sleeping Child ALBA ▲ 264 [DDD] (16.97)
To Be Sung upon the Water for Tenor, Clarinet & Piano [texts Wordsworth] (1972)
P. M. Bedi (sop), L. Combs (cl), E. Buccheri (pno) *(rec Mandel Hall, Univ of Chicago, IL, June 1996)* ("To Be Sung Upon the Water") † Letters from Composers; Songs About Spring; Vaughan Williams:Along The Field; Vocalises Sop CED ▲ 29 [DDD] (16.97)
J. Stewart (ten), C. Russo (cl), D. Hassard (pno) † B. Britten:Canticle II, Op. 51; Sonnets of Michelangelo, Op. 22
PHOE ▲ 129 (15.97)
A Water Bird Talk (monodrama) [after A. Chekhov & J. J. Audubon] (1974)
J. Shirley-Quirk (bar), S. Watkins (cnd), St. Cecilia Sinfonia † Miss Havisham's Wedding Night
KOCH ▲ 7388 (16.97)
V. Sutton (nar), R. A. Clark (cnd), Manhattan CO † Elizabethan Songs Voc & Pno NPT ▲ 85602 [DDD] (16.97)

ARISERINGER, CHARLES (1951-
Concerto for Piano & Chamber Orchestra (1990)
C. Colnot (cnd), San Diego SO, C. Colnot (cnd), Chicago SO members ARUN ▲ 3010 (16.97)
D. Schrader (pno), C. Colnot (cnd), Chicago SO members ("Grand Designs") † Bevelander:Synthecisims 4; Lentini:Music for Brass; D. McCarthy:Harmonizer; E. Mendoza:RainForest; Schwendinger:Chamber Con Pno
CPS (Society of Composers, Inc) ▲ 8639 [DDD] (16.97)

ARIZAGA, RODOLFO (1926-1985)
Passacaglia for Orchestra (1953)
artists unknown *(rec Troy, NY, Jan 1994)* † Bragato:Graciala y Buenos Aires; A. Piazzolla:Suite punta del este; Suite Ob; Tangos Str Orch DOR ▲ 90201 [DDD] (16.97)

ARKAS, NIKOLAI (1853-1909)
Katerina (opera in 3 acts) [after Shevchenko]
K. Simeonov (cnd), Ukrainian Radio Orch, Ukrainian Radio Soloists, Ukrainian Radio Chorus ESTA 2-▮ 2351

ARKHANGELSKY, ALEXANDER (1846-1924)
All Night Vigil for Chorus
A. Rybakova (cnd), Moscow Patriarchal Choir † Hymns of the Russian Orthodox Church
RD ▲ 15004 [AAD] (16.97)
Gospodji Usliži Molitwu for Chorus
Philippopolis Chamber Ensemble [arr Arabadjiev] *(rec Resurrection Church, Plovdiv, Bulgaria, 1994)* ("Liturgical Songs of Praise of the Orthodox Church") † Bortnyansky:Mnogaja leta; Chesnokov:Djertva Vecernaja; Christov:Choral Music; Ljubimov:Blažen Muž; Lomakin:Tebe Poem; Traditional:Dnes Vsjaka Twar; Edin svjat; Lord, have mercy [Prositelna Ektenia]; Nine Otpužtaešti; Our Father [Otče Naš] NOVA ▲ 150149 [DDD] (16.97)
Hymns of the Russian Orthodox Church for Chorus
V. Popov (cnd), Moscow Male Voice Choir ("Spiritual Concert from Russia") † Bortnyansky:Sacred Choral Music; Chesnokov:Sacred Choral Music; Kastalski:Sacred Choral Music KSCH ▲ 315562 (16.97)
A. Rybakova (cnd), Moscow Patriarchal Choir † All Night Vigil RD ▲ 15004 [AAD] (16.97)
Louons la Saint-Vierge
Zagorsk Monastery Monks' Choir *(rec Zagorsk Monastery, France, 1989)* † Anonymous:Chant du Monastère du Désert; Chants rituels Noël; Esprit-Saint tu es là; Heureux soit l'élu du Seigneur; Hymne dédié à Saint-Georges; O douce lumière; Péchés sont pardonés; Que Dieu bénisse mon âme; Sous protection anges; Bortnyansky:Comme les anges; Gloire à Dieu au plus haut des cieux; Ivov:Que ton coeur se réjouisse; Nathaneal (Monk):Just est en toi musique; Znoviev:Dieu est parmi nous AB ▲ 1402 [ADD] (16.97)

ARKHANGELSKY, ALEXANDER (cont.)
Sacred Choral Music
V. Afanasiev (cnd), St. Petersburg Male Choir—Nicene Creed *(rec Maly Hall, St. Petersburg, Russia, Jan 1998)* † Chesnokov:Sacred Choral Music; Shvedov:Sacred Choral Music; Traditional:Along Peterskaya Street; Evening Bell; In a Dark Wood; Like a Nightingale in Flight; O My Field; Polno, polno vam, rebyata; Shchedrik; Steppe, Endless Steppe; Tula Accordian; Twelve Brigands; Vot sluchilasa beda EMIC (Debut) ▲ 73166 [DDD] (6.97)

ARLEN, HAROLD (1905-1986)
Americanegro Suite (concert work) for Soloist, Small Chorus & Piano [incorporating six original spirituals by Arlen] (1940)
P. Howard (pno), Premierospel Quartet PREM ▲ 1004 [DDD] (16.97)
Music of Arlen
S. McNair (sop), D. Finck (db), A. Previn (pno)—Over the Rainbow; Stormy Weather; Between the Devil & the Deep Blue Sea; It Was Written in the Stars; As Long As I Live; That Old Black Magic; The Morning After; A Sleepin' Bee; Ac-cent-tchu-ate the Positive; Goose Never Ba a Peacock; I Wonder What Became of Me; It's Only A Paper Moon - Let's Fall in Love; In the Shade of the Banana Tree; Coconut Sweet; Right as the Rain; I've Got the World on a String - Get Happy; Come Rain or Come Shine; This Time the Dream's on Me; Let's Take a Walk around the Block - Let's Take th; Last Night When We Were Young ("Come Rain or Come Shine") PPHI ▲ 46818 (16.97)
J. Mauceri (cnd), Hollywood Bowl Orch—Free & Easy (blues opera suite): medley of Any Pla; I Had Myself a True Love; 1 for My Baby (& 1 for the Road) ("The Hollywood Bowl on Broadway") † J. Kern:Show Boat (sels); R. Rodgers:Carousel (sels); Slaughter on Tenth Avenue Orch; K. Weill:Songs PPHI ▲ 46404 (16.97)
Piano Music
J. Smith (pno)—Bonbon; Ode; Rhythmic moments † Ellington:Music of Ellington; S. C. Foster:Pno Music; G. Gershwin:Pno Music; O. Levant:Sonatina PREM ▲ 1028 [DDD] (16.97)

ARMANDO, GIBILARO (20th cent)
Concerto for Oboe (or Violin) & Strings, Op. 11 (1939)
P. Oostenrijk (ob), Sonora Hungarica *(rec Amsterdam, Netherlands, Feb 1993)* † Castelnuovo-Tedesco:Con da Camera, Op. 146; Cimarosa:Con Ob; Gibilaro:Fant on British Airs VRDI (Masters) ▲ 32251 [DDD] (13.97)

ARMENGOL, MARIO RUIZ (dates unknown)
Danzas Cubanas for Piano
G. R. Weber (pno)—No. 12; No. 3; No. 10 † R. Castro:Berceuse; Vals Capricho; Vals Caressante; L. G. Jorda:Danzas Nocturnas; M. Ponce:Estrellita; Pno Music CLME ▲ 1 (13.97)
G. R. Weber (pno)—No. 1; No. 7; No. 6; No. 15 † Pno Music; Carrasco:Pno Music; A. Elias:Waltz Pno; M. Ponce:Pno Music; Serratos:Waltz Pno CLME ▲ 2 (13.97)
Piano Music
G. R. Weber (pno)—Prelude Pno; Ay amor, amor; Las Frias Montanas † Danzas Cubanas; Carrasco:Pno Music; A. Elias:Waltz Pno; M. Ponce:Pno Music; Serratos:Waltz Pno CLME ▲ 2 (13.97)
G. R. Weber (pno)—Danzas Cubanas [No. 18]; Nocturne; Waltz Pno; Simplemente Adios † R. Castro:Pno Music; A. Elias:Pno Music; M. Ponce:Pno Music; F. Villanueva:Pno Music CLME ▲ 3 (13.97)

ARMSTRONG, THOMAS (1898-1994)
Choral Music
P. Daniel (cnd), London Philharmonic Choir—Never Weather-beaten Sail; She Is Not Fair; O Mortal Folk; New Year Carol; Sweet Day; With Margerain Gentle *(rec Blackheath Concert, London, England, Feb 1998)* † Fant Qnt; Friends Departed; Passer-by; Sinfonietta Small Orch CHN ▲ 9657 [DDD] (16.97)
Fantasy Quintet for Piano & Strings (1925)
P. Daniel (cnd), London PO *(rec Blackheath Concert, London, England, Feb 1998)* † Choral Music; Friends Departed; Passer-by; Sinfonietta Small Orch CHN ▲ 9657 [DDD] (16.97)
Friends Departed for Chorus & Orchestra
P. Daniel (cnd), London PO, London Philharmonic Choir *(rec Blackheath Concert, London, England, Feb 1998)* † Choral Music; Fant Qnt; Passer-by; Sinfonietta Small Orch CHN ▲ 9657 [DDD] (16.97)
A Passer-by for Baritone, Chorus & Orchestra (1922)
P. Daniel (cnd), London PO, London Philharmonic Choir *(rec Blackheath Concert, London, England, Feb 1998)* † Choral Music; Fant Qnt; Friends Departed; Sinfonietta Small Orch CHN ▲ 9657 [DDD] (16.97)
Sinfonietta for Small Orchestra
P. Daniel (cnd), London PO *(rec Blackheath Concert, London, England, Feb 1998)* † Choral Music; Fant Qnt; Friends Departed; Passer-by CHN ▲ 9657 [DDD] (16.97)

ARNAOUDOV, GHEORGHI (1957-
Borges Fragment (Ritual III) for Cello (1992)
K. Krusteva (vc) † Circle of Rites; Incarnation dans la lumiere; Kyrie; Svarog Ritual GEGA ▲ 187 [DDD] (16.97)
The Circle of Rites for Soprano, Flute & Chamber Ensemble [on ancient Sanskrit texts] (1991-93)
P. Djourov (cnd), Musica Nova Ensemble † Borges Fragment; Incarnation dans la lumiere; Kyrie; Svarog Ritual
GEGA ▲ 187 [DDD] (16.97)
Incarnation dans la lumiere (Ritual II) for Piano (1992)
A. Tosheva (pno) *(rec Sofia, Bulgaria, Jan 1995)* ("The Empire of Light") † "Pan de ciel au milieu du silence"; Partita I; Svarog Ritual ERTO ▲ 42032 [DDD] (16.97)
B. Vodenicharov (pno) † Borges Fragment; Circle of Rites; Kyrie; Svarog Ritual GEGA ▲ 187 [DDD] (16.97)
Kyrie (summe Deus) for Soprano & Chamber Ensemble (1993)
P. Djourov (cnd), Musica Nova Ensemble † Borges Fragment; Circle of Rites; Incarnation dans la lumiere; Svarog Ritual GEGA ▲ 187 [DDD] (16.97)
"Un pan de ciel au milieu du silence" for Piano (1991-94)
A. Tosheva (pno) *(rec Sofia Bulgaria, Jan 1995)* ("The Empire of Light") † Incarnation dans la lumiere; Partita I; Svarog Ritual ERTO ▲ 42032 [DDD] (16.97)
Partita I for Piano (1983)
A. Tosheva (pno) *(rec Sofia Bulgaria, Jan 1995)* ("The Empire of Light") † "Pan de ciel au milieu du silence"; Incarnation dans la lumiere; Svarog Ritual ERTO ▲ 42032 [DDD] (16.97)
Svarog Rituel (Ritual I) for Piano (1991)
A. Tosheva (pno) *(rec Sofia Bulgaria, Jan 1995)* ("The Empire of Light") † "Pan de ciel au milieu du silence"; Incarnation dans la lumiere; Partita I ERTO ▲ 42032 [DDD] (16.97)
B. Vodenicharov (pno) † Borges Fragment; Circle of Rites; Incarnation dans la lumiere; Kyrie
GEGA ▲ 187 [DDD] (16.97)

ARNAUD, LEO (1904-1991)
Bugler's Dream for Orchestra [from Charge!]
M. Mitsumoto (cnd), Cracow RSO *(rec Krakow Poland, Sept 20-22, 1993)* † In Memoriam; Latin American Scenario; Midinette; Symphonie Française; Well Tempered Oboist CMB ▲ 1074 [DDD] (16.97)
Fanfares (3) for for Winds
F. Fennell (cnd) † P. Grainger:Lincolnshire Posy; Vaughan Williams:English Folk Song Suite
TEL ▲ 80099 [DDD] (16.97)
In Memoriam for Flute & String Orchestra
K. Moszynski (fl), M. Mitsumoto (cnd), Cracow RSO *(rec Krakow Poland, Sept 20-22, 1993)* † Bugler's Dream; Latin American Scenario; Midinette; Symphonie Française; Well Tempered Oboist CMB ▲ 1074 [DDD] (16.97)
Latin American Scenario for Orchestra
M. Mitsumoto (cnd), Cracow RSO *(rec Krakow Poland, Sept 20-22, 1993)* † Bugler's Dream; In Memoriam; Midinette; Symphonie Française; Well Tempered Oboist CMB ▲ 1074 [DDD] (16.97)
Midinette for Clarinet & Orchestra
A. Godeck (cl), M. Mitsumoto (cnd), Cracow RSO *(rec Krakow Poland, Sept 20-22, 1993)* † Bugler's Dream; In Memoriam; Latin American Scenario; Symphonie Française; Well Tempered Oboist CMB ▲ 1074 [DDD] (16.97)
Symphonie Française for Orchestra
M. Mitsumoto (cnd), Cracow RSO *(rec Krakow Poland, Sept 20-22, 1993)* † Bugler's Dream; In Memoriam; Latin American Scenario; Midinette; Well Tempered Oboist CMB ▲ 1074 [DDD] (16.97)
Well Tempered Oboist for Oboe & Orchestra
G. Stec (ob), M. Mitsumoto (cnd), Cracow RSO *(rec Krakow Poland, Sept 20-22, 1993)* † Bugler's Dream; In Memoriam; Latin American Scenario; Midinette; Symphonie Française CMB ▲ 1074 [DDD] (16.97)

ARNE, THOMAS (1710-1778)
Artaxerxes (opera) [lib Arne after Metastasio] (1762)
C. Bott (sop), P. Spence (mez), C. Robson (ct), R. Edgar-Wilson (ten), I. Partridge (ten), P. Hyde (sgr), R. Goodman (cnd), Parley of Instruments HYP (The English Orpheus) 2-▲ 67051 (36.97)

ARNE, THOMAS (cont.)

Comus (selections)
E. Kirkby (sop), C. Hogwood (cnd), Academy of Ancient Music—By the rushy-fringed bank; Brightest Lady—Thrice upon thy Finger's Tip † Rosamond (sels); Tempest (sels); G. F. Handel:Alcina (sels); Alessandro Severo (sels); Alexander's Feast (ode), HWV 75; Allegro, il Penseroso ed il Moderato (sels); Ariodante (sels); Hornpipe in D, HWV 356; March; Saul (sels); J. Haydn:Schöpfung (sels); J. F. Lampe:Brittania (sels); Dione (sels); W. A. Mozart:Ah, lo previdi & Ah, t'invola agl'occhi miei, K.272; Ch'io mi scordi di te? & Non temer, amato bene, K.505; Nehmt meinen Dank, ihr holden Gönner!, K.383; Rè pastore (sels); Voi avete un cor fedele, K.217; Zaide (sels) PLON (Double Decker) 2-▲ 458084 [DDD] (17.97)

Favourite Concertos (6) for Keyboard & Orchestra (1787)
P. Nicholson (kbd) † Trio Sons, Op. 3 AMON ▲ 42 [DDD] (16.97)
P. Nicholson (kbd), P. Nicholson (cnd), Parley of Instruments HYP ▲ 66509 (18.97)
R. B. Williams (org), A. Shepherd (cnd), Cantilena CHN 2-▲ 8604 [DDD] (33.97)

Rosamond (selections)
E. Kirkby (sop), C. Hogwood (cnd), Academy of Ancient Music Orch—Rise, Glory, rise † Comus (sels); Tempest (sels); G. F. Handel:Alcina (sels); Alessandro Severo (sels); Alexander's Feast (ode), HWV 75; Allegro, il Penseroso ed il Moderato (sels); Ariodante (sels); Hornpipe in D, HWV 356; March; Saul (sels); J. Haydn:Schöpfung (sels); J. F. Lampe:Brittania (sels); Dione (sels); W. A. Mozart:Ah, lo previdi & Ah, t'involа agl'occhi miei, K.272; Ch'io mi scordi di te? & Non temer, amato bene, K.505; Nehmt meinen Dank, ihr holden Gönner!, K.383; Rè pastore (sels); Voi avete un cor fedele, K.217; Zaide (sels) PLON (Double Decker) 2-▲ 458084 [DDD] (17.97)

Sonata No. 3 in G for Harpsichord
T. Pinnock (spinet) *(rec Victoria & Albert Museum, London, England)* † Anonymous:My Lady Wynkfyld's Rownde; J. Christian Bach:Sons Kbd; W. Byrd:Bells; Queen's Alman; W. Croft:Suite 3 Kbd; G. F. Handel:Harmonious Blacksmith CRD ▲ 3307 [ADD] (17.97)

Sonata No. 5 in B♭ for Harpsichord (1756)
D. Smith (bn), R. Vignoles (pno) [arr Craxton & Mather] *(rec London, England)* † Avison:Son Vn; Dunhill:Lyric Suite Bn & Pno, Op. 96; E. Elgar:Romance Vn, Op. 1; Hurlstone:Son Vn; G. Jacob:Four Sketches Bn; Vaughan Williams:Studies in English Folk-Song ASV ▲ 535 [DDD] (17.97)

Symphonies (4)
A. Shepherd (cnd), Cantilena CHN ▲ 8403 [DDD] (16.97)

Tempest (selections)
E. Kirkby (sop), C. Hogwood (cnd), Academy of Ancient Music—Where the Bee sucks there lurk † Comus (sels); Rosamond (sels); G. F. Handel:Alcina (sels); Alessandro Severo (sels); Alexander's Feast (ode), HWV 75; Allegro, il Penseroso ed il Moderato (sels); Ariodante (sels); Hornpipe in D, HWV 356; March; Saul (sels); J. Haydn:Schöpfung (sels); J. F. Lampe:Brittania (sels); Dione (sels); W. A. Mozart:Ah, lo previdi & Ah, t'invola agl'occhi miei, K.272; Ch'io mi scordi di te? & Non temer, amato bene, K.505; Nehmt meinen Dank, ihr holden Gönner!, K.383; Rè pastore (sels); Voi avete un cor fedele, K.217; Zaide (sels) PLON (Double Decker) 2-▲ 458084 [DDD] (17.97)

Trio Sonatas (7) for 2 Violins & Continuo, Op. 3
London Baroque † C. F. Abel:Sons Vn, Vc & Bc, Op. 9; Avison:Sons AMON ▲ 14 [DDD] (16.97)
Nouveau Quartet [period instrs] † Favourite Cons AMON ▲ 42 [DDD] (16.97)

ARNELL, RICHARD ANTHONY (1917-

Organ Music
A. Sacchetti (org)—Prelude & Fantasia Org, Op. 34 *(rec Chiesa S. Geraldo a Majella, Italy, June 1991)* ("Organ History England from Elgar to Arnell") † B. Britten:Prelude & Fugue on a Theme of Vittoria; E. Elgar:Org Music; Thalben-Ball:Org Music; Vaughan Williams:Org Music AART (Organ History) ▲ 47391 [DDD] (10.97)

ARNESTAD, FINN (1915-1994)

Chamber Music
H. Kraggerud (vn), C. Lindberg (trbn), Oslo Trio—Son solo Vn; Son Trbn; Music for Ww; Sxt; Trio Pno; Son solo Db ("Chamber Interference") NORW ▲ 4987 (17.97)

ARNOLD, CARL (1794-1873)

Grand Sextet for Piano & Strings, Op. 23
D. Styffe (db), E. Steen-Nokleberg (pno), Norwegian String Quartet † F. A. Reissiger:Qnt Strs, Op. 59 NKF ▲ 50035 (16.97)

ARNOLD, DAVID (1963-

Independence Day (film music) for Orchestra (1996)
artists unknown RCAV ▲ 68564 (16.97) ▮ 68564

ARNOLD, MALCOLM (1921-

Concertino for Oboe & Strings, Op. 28a (1993)
N. Daniel (ob), V. Handley (cnd), Bournemouth SO *(rec Dorset, England, June 1996)* † Fant Ob, Op. 90; Sym 9 CONI ▲ 51273 [DDD] (16.97)

Concerto No. 1 for Clarinet & Strings, Op. 20 (1948)
E. Johnson (cl), I. Bolton (cnd), English CO ("Complete Music for Clarinet") † Con 2 Cl, Op. 115; Divert Fl, Op. 37; Fants solo Instrs; Shanties, Op. 4; Son Cl ASV ▲ 922 [DDD] (16.97)

Concerto No. 2 for Clarinet & Chamber Orchestra, Op. 115 (1974)
M. Fröst (cl), L. Shui (cnd), Malmö SO *(rec Malmö, Sweden, 1997)* ("Concertos Dedicated to Benny Goodman") † A. Copland:Con Cl; P. Hindemith:Con Cl BIS ▲ 893 [DDD] (17.97)
E. Johnson (cl), I. Bolton (cnd), English CO ("Complete Music for Clarinet") † Con 1 Cl, Op. 20; Divert Fl, Op. 37; Fants solo Instrs; Shanties, Op. 4; Son Cl ASV ▲ 922 [DDD] (16.97)

Concerto No. 2 for Flute & Chamber Orchestra, Op. 111 (1972)
A. Still (fl), N. Braithwaite (cnd), New Zealand CO † G. Jacob:Con Fl; Musgrave:Orfeo II KOCH ▲ 7140 [DDD]

Concerto for Guitar & Orchestra, Op. 67 (1959)
J. Bream (gtr), M. Arnold (cnd), Melos Ensemble † R. R. Bennett:Con Gtr; J. Rodrigo:Con de Aranjuez RCAV ▲ 61598 (11.97)
M. Conn (gtr), J. Lubbock (cnd), St. John's Smith Square Orch † J. Rodrigo:Con de Aranjuez INMP (Classic) ▲ 2035 (9.97)
E. Fernández (gtr) † M. Giuliani:Con 1 Gtr, Op. 30; M. Ponce:Concierto del sur; J. Rodrigo:Con de Aranjuez; H. Villa-Lobos:Con Gtr; Vivaldi:Con Lt Vns, RV.93 PLON 2-▲ 455364 (17.97)

Concerto for Harmonica & Orchestra, Op. 46 (1954)
T. Reilly (hmc), C. Dumont (cnd), Basel RSO † R. Farnon:Prelude & Dance; J. Moody:Toledo; M. Spivakovsky:Con Hmc; H. Villa-Lobos:Con Hmc CHN ▲ 9248 [DDD] (16.97)

Concerto for 28 Players, Op. 105 (1970)
R. Hickox (cnd), City of London Sinfonia † Little Suite 1 Orch, Op. 53; Little Suite 2 Orch, Op. 78; Little Suite 3 Orch, Op. 142; Vars Ruth Gipps, Op. 122 CHN ▲ 9509 (16.97)

Concerto for 2 Violins & String Orchestra, Op. 77 (1962)
I. Gruppman (pno), V. Gruppman (pno), D. Barra (cnd), San Diego CO *(rec Nov 29, 1991)* † Serenade, Op. 26; Sinf 1 KOCH ▲ 7134 [DDD] (16.97)

Dances for Orchestra
B. Thompson (cnd), Philharmonia Orch *(English Dances)*, B. Thomson (cnd), Philharmonia Orch *(Scottish Dances, Op. 59; Cornish Dances, Op. 91; Irish Dances, Op. 126)* † Solitaire CHN ▲ 8867 [DDD] (16.97)

Divertimento for Flute, Oboe & Clarinet, Op. 37 (1952)
E. Johnson (cl), I. Bolton (cnd), English CO ("Complete Music for Clarinet") † Con 1 Cl, Op. 20; Con 2 Cl, Op. 115; Fants solo Instrs; Shanties, Op. 4; Son Cl ASV ▲ 922 [DDD] (16.97)
Nash Ensemble † Duo fl & vl, Op. 10; Qnt Fl, Op. 7; Qt Ob; Shanties, Op. 4; Son Fl HYP ▲ 66173

Duo for Flute & Viola, Op. 10 (1946)
Nash Ensemble † Divert Fl, Op. 37; Qnt Fl, Op. 7; Qt Ob; Shanties, Op. 4; Son Fl HYP ▲ 66173

Fantasia for Bassoon, Op. 86 (1966)
O. Eifert (bn) † Almenraeder:Duo Bns; F. Devienne:Duos Concertantes, Op. 3; G. Jacob:Partita Bn; F. Mignone:Son Bns; K. Reiner:Zaznamy; Szelényi:Suite Bns GAS (Silver) ▲ 2007 (7.97)
K. Sønstevold (bn) *(rec Nacka, Sweden, Apr 1978)* ("The Virtuoso Bassoon") † Beethoven:Trio Fl, WoO 37; Blomdahl:Liten svit; R. Boutry:Interferences; E. von Koch:Monologue 5; Morthenson:Unisono; Tansman:Sonatine Bn BIS ▲ 122 [AAD] (17.97)

Fantasies for solo Instruments (1965-67)
E. Johnson (cl), I. Bolton (cnd), English CO ("Complete Music for Clarinet") † Con 1 Cl, Op. 20; Con 2 Cl, Op. 115; Divert Fl, Op. 37; Shanties, Op. 4; Son Cl ASV ▲ 922 [DDD] (16.97)
Z. Zuk (hn) [for rcr] ("Horn Expressions") † Jevtic:Dance of Summer; J. Koetsier:Concertino Hn; A. Plog:Nocturne Hn; E. Ristori:Con Hn; K. Turner:Son Hn ZUK ▲ 191122 (10.97)

Fantasy for Brass Band, Op. 114 (1974)
P. Parkes (cnd), Grimethorpe Colliery Band, G. Cutt (cnd) ("Brass for the Masters-Vol. 2") † E. Ball:Kensington Con; Bantock:Frogs; Goffin:Rhaps Brass; G. Holst:Moorside Suite; G. Lloyd:Diversions on a Bass Theme; Vaughan Williams:Henry V CHN ▲ 4553 (16.97)

ARNOLD, MALCOLM (cont.)

Fantasy for Cello, Op. 130 (1987)
J. L. Webber (vc) ("British Cello Music, Vol. I") † B. Britten:Suite 3 Vc, Op. 87; Tema; J. Ireland:Holy Boy; A. Rawsthorne:Son Vc; W. Walton:Passacaglia Vc ASV ▲ 592 (16.97)

Fantasy for Oboe, Op. 90 (1966)
N. Daniel (ob) *(rec Dorset, England, June 1996)* † Con Ob; Sym 9 CONI ▲ 51273 [DDD] (16.97)

Film Music
R. Hickox (cnd), London SO—Bridge on the River Kwai [Suite]; Hobson's Choice (suite); Inn of the Sixth Happiness; Whistle Down the Wind [Suite]; Sound Barrier (rhaps), Op. 38 CHN ▲ 9100 [DDD] (16.97)

Little Suite No. 1 for Orchestra, Op. 53 (1956)
R. Hickox (cnd), City of London Sinfonia † Con Players, Op. 105; Little Suite 2 Orch, Op. 78; Little Suite 3 Orch, Op. 142; Vars Ruth Gipps, Op. 122 CHN ▲ 9509 (16.97)

Little Suite No. 2 for Orchestra, Op. 78 (1962)
R. Hickox (cnd), City of London Sinfonia † Con Players, Op. 105; Little Suite 1 Orch, Op. 53; Little Suite 3 Orch, Op. 142; Vars Ruth Gipps, Op. 122 CHN ▲ 9509 (16.97)

Little Suite No. 3 for Orchestra, Op. 142, "Manx Suite"
R. Hickox (cnd), City of London Sinfonia † Con Players, Op. 105; Little Suite 1 Orch, Op. 53; Little Suite 2 Orch, Op. 78; Vars Ruth Gipps, Op. 122 CHN ▲ 9509 (16.97)

Music of Arnold
J. Junkin (cnd), Dallas Wind Sym—Scottish Dances, Op. 59; Overseas, Op. 70; Little Suite 1 Brass, Op. 80; Tam o'Shanter Ov, Op. 51; Water Music, Op. 82; Padstow Lifeboat, Op. 94; Little Suite 2 Brass, Op. 93; Fanfare for Louis; Duke of Cambridge, Op. 60 *(rec Meyerson Symphony Center, Dallas, TX, June 1995)* REF ▲ 66 [DDD] (16.97)

Overtures
M. Arnold (cnd), London PO—Beckus the Dandipratt, Op. 5; Commonwealth Christmas Ov, Op. 64; Fair Field Ov, Op. 110; Smoke Ov, Op. 21; Sussex Ov, Op. 31 *(rec Oct 1991)* REF ▲ 48 [DDD] (16.97)

Quartet for Oboe & Strings, Op. 61 (1957)
Nash Ensemble † Divert Fl, Op. 37; Duo fl & vl, Op. 10; Qnt Fl, Op. 7; Shanties, Op. 4; Son Fl HYP ▲ 66173

Quartet No. 1 for Strings, Op. 23 (1949)
McCapra String Quartet † Qt 2 Strs, Op. 118 CHN ▲ 9112 [DDD] (17.97)

Quartet No. 2 for Strings, Op. 118 (1975)
McCapra String Quartet † Qt 1 Strs, Op. 23 CHN ▲ 9112 [DDD] (17.97)

Quintet for Brass, Op. 73 (1961)
U. Zaiser (tpt), P. Leiner (tpt), S. Scott (hn), J. Scheerer (trbn), R. Rudolph (tuba) † E. Crespo:Suite Americana 1; V. Ewald:Qnt 1 Brass, Op. 5; Horovitz:Music Hall Suite; J. Koetsier:Qnt Brass, Op. 65 BAYE ▲ 100251 [DDD] (17.97)

Quintet for Flute, Violin, Viola, Horn & Bassoon, Op. 7 (1944)
Nash Ensemble † Divert Fl, Op. 37; Duo fl & vl, Op. 10; Qt Ob; Shanties, Op. 4; Son Fl HYP ▲ 66173

Scottish Dances (4) for Orchestra, Op. 59 (1957)
M. Arnold (cnd), London PO † Vaughan Williams:Job; Wasps EVC ▲ 9006 [AAD] (13.97)
M. Arnold (cnd), London PO † Sym 3 PHOE ▲ 102 [AAD] (15.97)

Serenade for Guitar & Strings, Op. 50 (1955)
O. Assad (gtr), L. Brouwer (cnd), Orquesta de Cordoba *(rec 1997)* † L. Brouwer:Con 6 Gtr; J. Rodrigo:Con de Aranjuez GHA ▲ 126025 [DDD] (17.97)

Serenade for Small Orchestra, Op. 26 (1950)
D. Barra (cnd), San Diego CO *(rec Nov 29, 1991)* † Con Vns, Op. 77; Sinf 1 KOCH ▲ 7134 [DDD] (16.97)

Shanties (3) for Wind Quintet, Op. 4 (1943)
Frö sunda Wind Quintet *(rec Mar 1979)* ("Favorite Music for Wind Quintet") † F. Farkas:Antique Hungarian Dances; Ibert:Pièces brèves Ww; C. Nielsen:Qnt Ww BIS ▲ 136 [AAD] (17.97)
E. Johnson (cl), I. Bolton (cnd), English CO ("Complete Music for Clarinet") † Con 1 Cl, Op. 20; Con 2 Cl, Op. 115; Divert Fl, Op. 37; Fants solo Instrs; Son Cl ASV ▲ 922 [DDD] (16.97)
Nash Ensemble † Divert Fl, Op. 37; Duo fl & vl, Op. 10; Qnt Fl, Op. 7; Qt Ob; Son Fl HYP ▲ 66173

Sinfoniettas No. 1 Orchestra, Op. 48 (1954)
D. Barra (cnd), San Diego CO *(rec Nov 29, 1991)* † Con Vns, Op. 77; Serenade, Op. 26 KOCH ▲ 7134 [DDD] (16.97)

Solitaire (ballet) (1956)
B. Thompson (cnd), Philharmonia Orch † Dances Orch CHN ▲ 8867 [DDD] (16.97)

Sonata for Flute & Piano, Op. 121 (1977)
Nash Ensemble † Divert Fl, Op. 37; Duo fl & vl, Op. 10; Qnt Fl, Op. 7; Qt Ob; Shanties, Op. 4 HYP ▲ 66173

Sonatina for Clarinet & Piano, Op. 29 (1951)
E. Jóhannesson (cl), P. Jenkins (pno) *(rec Cambridge, England, Sept 1991)* ("British Music for Clarinet and Piano") † A. Bliss:Pastoral Cl, Op.posth.; Dunhill:Fant Suite Cl & Pno, Op. 91; H. Ferguson:Short Pieces Cl, Op. 6; Hurlstone:Characteristic Pieces Cl; Stanford:Son Cl; Stoker:Sonatina Cl, Op. 5 CHN ▲ 9079 (16.97)
E. Johnson (cl), I. Bolton (cnd), English CO ("Complete Music for Clarinet") † Con 1 Cl, Op. 20; Con 2 Cl, Op. 115; Divert Fl, Op. 37; Fants solo Instrs; Shanties, Op. 4 ASV ▲ 922 [DDD] (16.97)
P. Meyer (cl), E. Le Sage (pno) *(rec Jan 1996)* ("Clarinet Concordia") † A. Bax:Son Cl; L. Bernstein:Son Cl; A. Copland:Nocturne; Son Vn DNN ▲ 18016 [DDD] (16.97)
G. Peyer (cl), G. Pryor (pno) *(rec Rosslyn Hill Chapel, Hempstead, England, 1982-83)* ("English Music for Clarinet & Piano") † G. Finzi:Bagatelles Cl, Op. 23; P. Harvey:Suite on Themes of Gershwin Clt & Pno; Horovitz:Sonatina Cl; J. Ireland:Fant-Son Cl; A. Richardson:Roundelay CHN ▲ 8549 [DDD] (17.97)
P. Shands (cl), E. Rowley (pno) † V. Babin:Hillandale Waltzes; A. Benjamin:Tombeau; G. Finzi:Bagatelles Cl, Op. 23; W. Lutoslawski:Dance Preludes Cl & Pno RTOP ▲ 116 (16.97)
V. Soames (cl), J. Flinders (pno) ("On the Wings of English Melody") † A. Bliss:Pastoral Cl, Op.posth.; G. Finzi:Bagatelles Cl, Op. 23; J. Ireland:Fant-Son Cl; Stanford:Son Cl; Vaughan Williams:Studies in English Folk-Song CLCL ▲ 25 [DDD] (17.97)

Sonatina for Oboe & Piano, Op. 28 (1951)
J. Rathbun (ob), M. Shapiro (pno) ("Color Factory") † Koechlin:Son Ob; Rathbun:Diversions; V. Ussachevsky:Triskelion DNC ▲ 1028 (16.97)

Symphony No. 1, Op. 22 (1949)
R. Hickox (cnd), London SO † Sym 2 CHN ▲ 9335 [DDD] (16.97)

Symphony No. 2, Op. 40 (1953)
R. Hickox (cnd), London SO † Sym 1 CHN ▲ 9335 [DDD] (16.97)

Symphony No. 3, Op. 63 (1957)
M. Arnold (cnd), London PO † Vaughan Williams:Sym 9 EVC ▲ 9001 [AAD] (13.97)
M. Arnold (cnd), London PO † Scottish Dances, Op. 59 PHOE ▲ 102 [AAD] (15.97)
V. Handley (cnd), Royal Liverpool PO † Sym 4 CONI ▲ 51258 [DDD] (16.97)
R. Hickox (cnd), London SO † Sym 4 CHN ▲ 9290 [DDD] (16.97)
A. Penny (cnd), Irish National SO *(rec National Concert Hall Dublin, Ireland, June 1996)* † Sym 4 NXIN ▲ 8553739 [DDD] (5.97)

Symphony No. 4, Op. 71 (1960)
V. Handley (cnd), Royal Liverpool PO † Sym 3 CONI ▲ 51258 [DDD] (16.97)
R. Hickox (cnd), London SO † Sym 3 CHN ▲ 9290 [DDD] (16.97)
A. Penny (cnd), Irish National SO *(rec National Concert Hall Dublin, Ireland, June 1996)* † Sym 3 NXIN ▲ 8553739 [DDD] (5.97)

Symphony No. 5, Op. 74 (1961)
R. Hickox (cnd), London SO † Sym 6 CHN ▲ 9385 [DDD] (16.97)

Symphony No. 6, Op. 95 (1967)
R. Hickox (cnd), London SO † Sym 5 CHN ▲ 9385 [DDD] (16.97)

Symphony No. 9, Op. 128 (1986)
V. Handley (cnd), Bournemouth SO *(rec Dorset, England, June 1996)* † Con Ob; Fant Ob, Op. 90 CONI ▲ 51273 [DDD] (16.97)
A. Penny (cnd), Irish National SO [incl conversation w/ Arnold & Penny] *(rec National Concert Hall Dublin, Ireland, Sept 1995)* NXIN ▲ 553540 [DDD] (5.97)

Tam o'Shanter Overture for Orchestra, Op. 51 (1955)
P. Daniel (cnd), English Northern Philharmonia *(rec Town Hall, Leeds, England, 1996)* † E. Elgar:Enigma Vars, Op. 36; Pomp & Circumstance, Op. 39; H. Parry:I Was Glad; Jerusalem; W. Walton:Crown Imperial; Orb & Sceptre; H. J. Wood:Fant on British Seas Songs NXIN ▲ 8553981 [DDD] (5.97)
A. Gibson (cnd), Royal Scottish National Orch † MacCunn:Land of the Mountain & the Flood, Op. 8; Mendelssohn (-Bartholdy):Hebriden, Op. 26 CHN ▲ 8379 [DDD] (16.97)

Variations on a Theme of Ruth Gipps for Orchestra, Op. 122 (1977)
R. Hickox (cnd), City of London Sinfonia † Con Players, Op. 105; Little Suite 1 Orch, Op. 53; Little Suite 2 Orch, Op. 78; Little Suite 3 Orch, Op. 142 CHN ▲ 9509 (16.97)

ARPE, MANUEL SECO DE (1958-
Music for Cello & Piano
M. K. Jones (vc), G. Jackson (pno) ("Infrequent Music for Cello & Piano") † M. de Falla:Melodia; Romanza; Tansman:Vc & Pno Music; H. Villa-Lobos:Vc & Pno Music — EMEC ▲ 10 (16.97)
Music of Arpe
Concertus Novo—Vars Little Star, Op. 46; Trio 2 Cl, Op. 18; Hard Edge [Contorno neto], Op. 59; Son Vn, Op. 74 — EMEC ▲ 13 (16.97)

ARRIAGA, JUAN CRISOSTOMO (1806-1826)
Agar (scène biblique-dramatique) for Soprano & Orchestra
A. Denning (sop), J. López-Cobos (cnd), Bilbao SO † Erminia; Nada y mucho; O salutaris; A. Dvořák:Slavonic Dances (comp) — RD 2-▲ 70002 [ADD] (16.97)
Erminia (lyrical dramatic scene) for Soprano & Orchestra [after Tasso]
A. Denning (sop), J. López-Cobos (cnd), Bilbao SO † Agar; Nada y mucho; O salutaris; A. Dvořák:Slavonic Dances (comp) — RD 2-▲ 70002 [ADD] (16.97)
A. R. Taliento (sop), L. Sagrestano (cnd), Hymnus Orch ("Homage to Juan Crisostomo de Arriaga") † Esclavos felices (ov); Stabat mater; Sym in D — FSM ▲ 97774 (15.99)
Los esclavos felices:Overture
C. Mackerras (cnd), Scottish CO † Sym in D; Voříšek:Sym — HYP ▲ 66800 (18.97)
L. Sagrestano (cnd), Hymnus Orch ("Homage to Juan Crisostomo de Arriaga") † Erminia; Stabat mater; Sym in D — FSM ▲ 97774 (15.99)
J. Savall (cnd) † Sym in D — ASTR ▲ 8532 (18.97)
Nada y mucho in F for 2 Violins, Viola, Cello, Double-Bass, Trumpet, Guitar & Piano (1817)
J. López-Cobos (cnd), Bilbao SO † Agar; Erminia; O salutaris; A. Dvořák:Slavonic Dances (comp) — RD 2-▲ 70002 [ADD] (16.97)
O salutaris for 3 Voices & String Quintet
J. López-Cobos (cnd), Bilbao SO † Agar; Erminia; Nada y mucho; A. Dvořák:Slavonic Dances (comp) — RD 2-▲ 70002 [ADD] (16.97)
Quartets (3) for Strings
Guarneri String Quartet — PHLP ▲ 446092
Stabat mater for Small Orchestra & Chorus
L. Sagrestano (cnd), Hymnus Orch, Limburg Collegium Vocale ("Homage to Juan Crisostomo de Arriaga") † Erminia; Esclavos felices (ov); Sym in D — FSM ▲ 97774 (15.99)
Symphony in D
C. Mackerras (cnd), Scottish CO † Esclavos felices (ov); Voříšek:Sym — HYP ▲ 66800 (18.97)
L. Sagrestano (cnd), Hymnus Orch ("Homage to Juan Crisostomo de Arriaga") † Erminia; Esclavos felices (ov); Stabat mater — FSM ▲ 97774 (15.99)
J. Savall (cnd) † Esclavos felices (ov) — ASTR ▲ 8532 (18.97)
artists unknown *(rec 1993)* † F. J. Moreno:Sym in E♭; Nonó:Sym in F; J. Pons:Sym in G — CAPO ▲ 10488 [DDD] (11.97)

ARRIETA, EMILIO (1823-1894)
Marina (zarzuela in 2 acts) [lib. F Camprodón] (1855)
V. P. Pérez (cnd), Tenerife SO, M. Bayo (sop), A. Kraus (ten), J. Pons (bar) — VAL 2-▲ 4854 (36.97)

ARRIEU, CLAUDE (1903-1990)
Quintet for Winds (1955)
Belgian Wind Quintet *(rec Belgian Radio & Television Concert Hall, Belgium, 1988-89)* ("Summer Music") † S. Barber:Summer Music, Op. 31; Beethoven:Qnt Pno, Op. 16; G. Holst:Qnt Ww — DI ▲ 920322 [DDD] (5.97)

ARSENEAULT, RAYNALD (1945-1995)
L'après (l'Infini) for Flute, English Horn, Cello, Piano & Percussion
W. Boudreau (cnd) *(rec Dec 1993)* † L. Berio:Corale; L. Bouchard:Compressions; J. Cage:Daughters of the Lonesome Isle; Xenakis:Eonta — FL ▲ 23111 [DDD] (16.97)

ARUTIUNIAN, ALEXANDER (1920-
Armenian Rhapsody for 2 Pianos (1950)
J. Gordon (perc), Meridian Arts Ensemble *(rec Raphaëlpleinkerk, Amsterdam, Netherlands, Feb 1991)* † J. Bach:Laudes; Etler:Qnt Brass; P. Hindemith:Morgenmusik; W. Lutoslawski:Mini Ov; Taxin:Qnt Brass — CCSC (Winning Artist's Series) ▲ 2191 [DDD] (18.97)
S. Tanyel (pno), J. Brown (pno) † A. Khachaturian:Suite 2 Pnos; D. Shostakovich:Concertino Pnos, Op. 94; Suite Pnos, Op. 6 — CHN ▲ 8466 [DDD] (16.97)
Concertino for Piano & Orchestra (1951)
N. Arutiunian (pno), C. Orbelian (cnd), Moscow CO † Con Vn; Sinfonietta — CHN ▲ 9566 (16.97)
Concerto for Trumpet & Orchestra (1950)
T. Dokshitzer (tpt), G. Rozhdestvensky (cnd), Bolshoi Theater Orch *(rec 1968)* ("Trumpet Rhapsody") † H. I. Biber:Son à 6 Tpt; G. Gershwin:Rhap in Blue; Glazunov:Album Leaf; Glière:Con Coloratura Sop; J. N. Hummel:Con Tpt in E♭, S.49; P. Tchaikovsky:Swan Lake (sels) — RCAV (Gold Seal) ▲ 32045 [ADD] (11.97)
A. Sandoval (tpt), L. Haza (cnd), London SO *(rec 1993)* † J. N. Hummel:Con Tpt in E♭, S.49; L. Mozart:Con Tpt; A. Sandoval:Con Tpt — RCAV (Red Seal) ▲ 62661 [DDD] (16.97)
G. Touvron (tpt) *(rec Jan 1997)* ("Centenary of the Vichy Municipal Wind Band") † J. B. Chance:Vars on a Korean Theme; J. Offenbach:Orphée aux enfers (ov); A. Reed:Hymn Vars; Vivaldi:Con Tpts, RV.537 — LIDI ▲ 301049 [DDD] (16.97)
Concerto for Violin & Orchestra
I. Grubert (vn), C. Orbelian (cnd), Moscow CO † Concertino Pno; Sinfonietta — CHN ▲ 9566 (16.97)
W. Verdehr (vn), K. Trevor (cnd), Bohuslav Martinů PO *(rec 1997-98)* ("Romantic Violin Concertos of the 20th Century") † S. Barber:Con Vn; G. C. Menotti:Con Vn — CRYS ▲ 514 (15.97)
Sinfonietta for Orchestra (1966)
C. Orbelian (cnd), Moscow CO † Con Vn; Concertino Pno — CHN ▲ 9566 (16.97)

ARUTIUNIAN, ALEXANDER (1920- & **ARNO BABADJANYAN** (1921-1983)
Suite for Violin, Clarinet & Piano (1992)
Verdehr Trio ("The Making of a Medium, Vol. 5") † T. C. David:Triple Con; P. Schickele:Serenade for 3; Sculthorpe:Dream Tracks — CRYS ▲ 745 (15.97)

ASCHAFFENBURG, WALTER (1927-
Concerto for Oboe & Orchestra, Op. 25 (1983-86)
E. Zuyeva (ob), E. London (cnd), Russian State SO ("A Hero of Our Time") † E. London:Hero of Our Time; E. J. Miller:Anacrusis — NWW ▲ 80511 [DDD] (16.97)
Conversations (6 pieces) for Piano, Op. 19 (1973)
W. Cosand (pno) *(rec June 1993)* ("20th Century American Piano Music") † D. Cohen:Son Pno; H. Matthews:Preludes; N. Rorem:Etudes Pno — SUMM ▲ 154 [DDD] (16.97)

ASENCIO, VICENTE (1908-1979)
Collectici Intim for Guitar (1970)
D. Azabagić (gtr) † J. M. Fernández:Azaroa; Moreno Torroba:Aires de la Mancha; J. Rodrigo:Invocación y danza; Tárrega:Gtr Music — OTR ▲ 1021 (18.97)
Suite valenciana for solo Guitar
E. Isaac (gtr) † Bogdanović:Son Gtr; F. Hand:Trilogy; W. Heinze:Gtr Music; A. Piazzolla:Acentuado & Romantico — GHA ▲ 126008 (17.97)

ASHLEY, ROBERT (1930-
Atalanta [Acts of God] (opera in 3 episodes) (1982)
T. Buckner (bar), R. Ashley (sgr), J. Humbert (sgr), C. Tatò (sgr), B. G. Tyranny (elec/kbd), P. Shorr (elec) *(rec live, Teatro Olimpico Rome, Italy, 1985) ([ENG] text)* — LOV 2-▲ 3301 [ADD] (16.97)
Automatic Writing for Voices & Electronics (1979)
R. Ashley (voc), M. Johnson (nar), R. Ashley (elec/syn) ("Automatic Writing") † Purposeful Lady Slow Afternoon; She Was a Visitor — LOV ▲ 1002 [AAD] (16.97)
Improvement (opera in 4 acts)
J. La Barbara (sop—Now Eleanor), T. Buckner (bar—Don/Linda's Companion/Mr. Payne), J. Humbert (sgr—Linda), A. X. Neuburg (sgr—Mr. Payne's Mother), A. Klein (sgr—Doctor), R. Ashley (nar) *([ENG] text)* — NON 2-▲ 79289 (24.97)
Outcome Inevitable for Chamber Ensemble (1992)
Relâche Ensemble ("Outcome Inevitable") † F. W.-H. Ho:Contradiction, Please! The Revenge of Charlie Chan; Hovda:Borealis Music; Vierk:Timberline — OOD ▲ 17 [DDD] (16.97)
Purposeful Lady Slow Afternoon for Narrator, Voices & Tape (1968)
M. Ashley (sgr), B. Lloyd (sgr), M. Lucier (sgr), C. Liddell (nar) ("Automatic Writing") † Automatic Writing; She Was a Visitor — LOV ▲ 1002 [AAD] (16.97)

ASHLEY, ROBERT (cont.)
She Was a Visitor for Chorus (1967)
A. Lucier (cnd), Brandeis Univ Chamber Chorus ("Automatic Writing") † Automatic Writing; Purposeful Lady Slow Afternoon — LOV ▲ 1002 [AAD] (16.97)
Superior Seven (concerto) for Flute & Orchestra (1986)
R. Ashley (syn), T. Hamilton (cmpt/syn), B. Held (cmpt) *(rec NYC, NY)* † Tract — NWW ▲ 80460 (16.97)
Tract for Voice & Orchestra (1955)
T. Bruckner (bar), R. Ashley (cmpt/syn), T. Hamilton (syn), N. Reichman (cmpt/syn) *(rec NYC, NY)* † Superior 7 — NWW ▲ 80460 (16.97)
Your Money, My Life, Goodbye [from opera: The ImmortalitySongs] for Voices & Electronic Orchestra [lib. Ashley]
T. Buckner (bar), J. Humbert (sgr), J. La Barbara (sgr), S. Ashley (sgr), R. Ashley (elec) — LOV ▲ 1005 (16.97)

ASHWANDER, DONALD (1929-1994)
Piano Music
D. Ashwander (pno)—Request; Saratoga Rag; Sunday Night, Manhattan; October; Old Streets; Summer Garden; Garden at Night; We Danced † Songs; Traditional Patterns; 3 Unrepentant Ladies — PREM ▲ 1038 [ADD] (16.97)
Songs
S. Moore (sgr), D. Ashwander (pno) *(She Laughed at Him; Turkey & Myrtle, Rilla & Paul; Bar; Chili Billy)*, T. Bogdan (sgr), H. Huff (pno) *(Phases of the Moon; Locust)* † Pno Music; Traditional Patterns; 3 Unrepentant Ladies — PREM ▲ 1038 [ADD] (16.97)
Three Unrepentant Ladies (song cycle) for Voice & Piano
D. Ashwander (pno) † Pno Music; Songs; Traditional Patterns — PREM ▲ 1038 [ADD] (16.97)
Traditional Patterns (suite of 8 pieces) for Piano
D. Ashwander (pno) † Pno Music; Songs; 3 Unrepentant Ladies — PREM ▲ 1038 [ADD] (16.97)

ASHWELL, THOMAS (ca 1745-ca 1510)
Missa Jesu Christe for 6 Voices
S. Darlington (cnd), Christ Church Cathedral Choir ("2 Tudor Masses for the Cardinal") † H. Aston:Missa Videte manus meas — MENO 2-▲ 1030 (23.97)

ASIA, DANIEL (1953-
Miles Mix for Chamber Ensemble
Oberlin Contemporary Chamber Ensemble † Qt 1 Strs; Rivalries; Sand II; Shtay — ALBA ▲ 106 [DDD] (16.97)
Quartet No. 1 for Strings
Rymour String Quartet † Miles Mix; Rivalries; Sand II; Shtay — ALBA ▲ 106 [DDD] (16.97)
Rivalries for Chamber Ensemble
Oberlin Contemporary Chamber Ensemble † Miles Mix; Qt 1 Strs; Sand II; Shtay — ALBA ▲ 106 [DDD] (16.97)
Sand II for Mezzo-Soprano & Chamber Ensemble
M. Feinsinger (mez), Reconnaissance Chamber Ensemble † Miles Mix; Qt 1 Strs; Rivalries; Shtay — ALBA ▲ 106 [DDD] (16.97)
Shtay for Chamber Ensemble
Reconnaissance Chamber Ensemble † Miles Mix; Qt 1 Strs; Rivalries; Sand II — ALBA ▲ 106 [DDD] (16.97)
Symphony No. 2, "Celebration Symphony" (1990)
J. Sedares (cnd), Phoenix SO *(rec May 1993)* † Sym 3 — NWW ▲ 80447 [DDD] (16.97)
Symphony No. 3 (1991)
J. Sedares (cnd), Phoenix SO *(rec May 9, 1993)* † Sym 2 — NWW ▲ 80447 [DDD] (16.97)

ASIOLI, BONIFAZIO (1769-1832)
Sonata in G for Piano, Op. 8/1
V. Pleshakov (pno) *(rec 1970)* — ORIO ▲ 7814 (13.97)

ASMUS, BERND (1959-
malang mujur for Piano & live Electronics (1995)
S. T. Kiebler (pno), B. Asmus (elec), A. Richard (elec) *(rec 1996-97)* ("Recital") † Gavazza:Natura morta con specchio; L. Hiller:Quadrilateral; L. Nono:sofferte onde serene — 2E2M ▲ 1014 [DDD] (20.97)

ASSAD, SERGIO (1952-
Aquarelle for Guitar
E. Isaac (gtr) † Castelnuovo-Tedesco:Caprichos de Goya, Op. 195; B. Lester:Jazz Fugues; J. Rodrigo:Elogio de la guitarra — GHA ▲ 126019 (17.97)
Saga Dos Migrantes for 2 Guitars
S. Assad (gtr), O. Assad (gtr) *(rec Muziekcentrum Frits Phillips, Netherlands, May 1995)* ("Saga Dos Migrantes") † Ginastera:Son 1 Pno, Op. 22; Gismonti:Gtr Music; A. Piazzolla:Music of Piazzolla; H. Villa-Lobos:Bachiana brasileira 4 — NON ▲ 79365 (16.97)
Uarekena for Guitars (1996)
Minneapolis Guitar Quartet † Crittenden:Scottish Fantasy; Funk Pearson:Elassomorph; Kalaniemi:Finnish Pieces; I. Stravinsky:Easy Pieces (5); Torroba:Estampas — ALBA ▲ 339 [DDD] (16.97)

ASTON, HUGH (ca 1485-?1558)
Missa 'Videte manus meas' for 6 Voices
S. Darlington (cnd), Christ Church Cathedral Choir ("2 Tudor Masses for the Cardinal") † Ashwell:Missa Jesu Christe — MENO 2-▲ 1030 (23.97)

ASTORGA, EMANUELE D' (1680-?1757)
Stabat Mater in c for solo Voices, Strings, Continuo & Chorus (?1707)
D. Bostock (cnd) † A. Scarlatti:Stabat Mater — CLSO ▲ 162 (15.97)

ATLI, HEIMIR SVEINSSON (1938-
Pieces (12) from Twenty-One Sounding Minutes for solo Flute
M. Wiesler (fl)—Sounds of Men; Sounds of Women; Sounds of Evening; Sounds of a Museum; Sounds of Snow; Sounds of Heaven; Sounds of Fish; Sounds of the Night; Sounds of Birds; Sounds of Rain; Sounds of Flowers; Sounds of Sound *(rec Furuby Church, Sweden, June 1989)* ("To Manuela") † Hjálmar:Two Etudes Fl; Leifur:Fl Music; Magnús:Fl Music; T. Sigurbjörnsson:Fl Music — BIS ▲ 456 [DDD] (17.97)

ATTERBERG, KURT (1887-1974)
Ballad utan ord [Ballad without Words] for Orchestra, Op. 56 (1957-58)
J. Hirokami (cnd), Norrköping SO † Sym 6; Värmlandrapsodi, Op. 36 — BIS ▲ 553 [DDD] (17.97)
Chamber Music
A. Kiss (vn), E. Pérényi (vn), G. Kertész (vc), D. Spikay (hp), I. Prunyi (pno), S. Falvai (pno)—Son Vc, Op. 27; Höstballader, Op. 15; Valse monotone; Rondeau Rétrospectif, Op. 26; Trio Concertante, Op. 57 ("Chamber Music, Vol. 1") — MARC ▲ 8223404 (13.97)
Concerto in c for Cello & Orchestra, Op. 21 (1922)
W. Thomas-Mifune (vc), K. A. Rickenbacher (cnd), Berlin RSO † Son Vc — KSCH ▲ 315852 (16.97)
Concerto for Horn & Orchestra, Op. 28 (1926)
Hermansson (hn), E. Chivzhel (cnd), Umeå Sinfonietta † G. Jacob:Con Hn; L.-E. Larsson:Concertino Hn, Op. 45/5; M. Reger:Scherzino; Seiber:Notturno Hn — BIS ▲ 376 [DDD] (17.97)
A. Linder (hn), G. Oskamp (cnd), Gothenburg SO † Sym 3 — CAPA ▲ 21364 [AAD/DDD] (16.97)
Quintet in C for Piano, [arr from Sym 6], Op. 31bis
I. Prunyi (pno), New Budapest String Quartet † Son Vc; Suite 1 Orch — MARC ▲ 8223405 [DDD] (13.97)
Sonata in b for Cello & Piano, Op. 27 (1925)
I. Magyari (hn), I. Prunyi (pno) † Qnt Pno; Suite 1 Orch — MARC ▲ 8223405 [DDD] (13.97)
W. Thomas-Mifune (vc), C. Piazzini (pno) † Con Vc — KSCH ▲ 315852 (16.97)
Suite No. 1 for Orchestra, "Orientalisk svit" (1913)
E. Klas (cnd) *(rec 1987)* ("Music at The Royal Dramatic Theatre") † T. Aulin:Mäster Olaf, Op. 22; Stormy Day (ov) — MSV ▲ 618 [DDD] (16.97)
New Budapest String Quartet † Qnt Pno; Son Vc — MARC ▲ 8223405 [DDD] (13.97)
Suite No. 3 for Violin, Viola & Strings, Op. 19/1 (1917)
M. Saulesco (vn), G. Roehr (va), S. Westerberg (cnd), Swedish RSO † Sym 2 — SWES ▲ 1006 (17.97)
Symphony No. 2 in F, Op. 6 (1911-13)
S. Westerberg (cnd), Swedish RSO † Suite 3 — SWES ▲ 1006 (17.97)
Symphony No. 3 (1914-16)
S. Ehrling (cnd), Stockholm PO † Con Hn — CAPA ▲ 21364 [AAD/DDD] (16.97)
Symphony No. 6 in C, Op. 31 (1928)
T. Beecham (cnd), Royal Philharmonic Society Orch † Delius:Walk to the Paradise Garden; E. Grieg:Songs; W. A. Mozart:Sym 34, K.338; Zauberflöte (ov) — DLAB ▲ 7026 (17.97)
J. Hirokami (cnd), Norrköping SO † Ballad utan ord, Op. 56; Värmlandrapsodi, Op. 36 — BIS ▲ 553 [DDD] (17.97)
Symphony No. 7, Op. 45, "Sinfonia romantica" (1942; rev 1972)
M. Jurowski (cnd), Malmö SO † Sym 8 — STRL ▲ 1026 [DDD] (15.97)
Symphony No. 8 in e, Op. 48 (1944)
M. Jurowski (cnd), Malmö SO † Sym 7 — STRL ▲ 1026 [DDD] (15.97)

ATTERBERG, KURT (cont.)

En värmlandrapsodi [A Värmland Rhapsody] for Orchestra, Op. 36 (1933)
J. Hirokami (cnd), Norrköping SO † Ballad utan ord, Op. 56; Sym 6 BIS ▲ 553 [DDD] (17.97)

AUBER, DANIEL-FRANÇOIS (1782-1871)

Le Domino noir (opera in 3 acts) [lib Eugène Scribe]
S. Jo (sop), M. Olmeda (sop), I. Vernet (sop), D. Lamprecht (mez), J. Taillon (mez), B. Ford (ten), P. Power (ten), G. Cachemaille (bar), J. Bastin (bass), R. Bonynge (cnd), English CO, London Voices † Gustave III (ballet) PLON 2-▲ 40646 (32.97)

Fra Diavolo (opera comique in 3 acts) (1830)
K. Elmendorff (cnd), Dresden Opera Orch, Dresden Opera Chorus, I. Beilke (sop—Zerline), M. Schilp (mez—Pamella), L. Fehenberger (ten—Lorenzo), H. Hopf (ten—Fra Diavolo), K. Wessely (ten—Beppo), A. Schellenberg (bar—Lord Kookburn), G. Frick (bass—Matteo), K. Böhme (bass—Giacomo) *(rec live, Dresden, Germany, Nov 14-16, 1944)* PRE 2-▲ 90349 [AAD] (31.97)
H. Termer (sop), G. Neumann (ten), E. Büchner (ten), W. Hauschild (cnd), Berlin RSO BER ▲ 2140 [ADD] (10.97)

Fra Diavolo:Overture
O. Klemperer (cnd), Berlin State Opera Orch *(rec 1929)* ("Otto Klemperer: The Kroll Opera Years, 1926-29") † Beethoven:Coriolan Ov, Op. 62; Debussy:Nocturnes Orch; J. Offenbach:Belle Hélène (ov); M. Ravel:Alborada del gracioso; R. Wagner:Siegfried Idyll IN ▲ 1339 [ADD] (15.97)

Gustave III (ballet music)
R. Bonynge (cnd), English CO, London Voices † Domino noir PLON 2-▲ 40646 (32.97)

La muette de Portici:Overture
C. Cantieri (cnd), London Festival Orch ("Famous Overtures") † M. Glinka:Russlan & Ludmilla (ov); Humperdinck:Hänsel und Gretel (ov); W. A. Mozart:Entführung aus dem Serail (ov); J. Offenbach:Orphée aux enfers (ov); Suppé:Ovs PC ▲ 265013 [DDD] (2.97)
I. Markevitch (cnd), Lamoureux Orch † Berlioz:Sym fantastique, Op. 14; Cherubini:Anacréon (ov) DEUT (The Originals) ▲ 47406 [ADD] (11.97)

Overtures
P. Paray (cnd), Detroit SO—The Bronze Horse; Fra Diavolo; Masaniello † Suppé:Ovs MRCR ▲ 34309 [ADD] (11.97)

Rondo for Cello & Orchestra
M. Ostertag (vc), R. Paternostro (cnd), Berlin RSO † Massenet:Fant Vc & Orc; Popper:Con Vc KSCH ▲ 311039 [DDD] (16.97)

Zerline (selections)
M. Horne (mez), L. Foster (cnd), Monte Carlo PO † Donizetti:Favorita (sels); B. Godard:Vivandiere (sels); Gounod:Sappho (sels); Saint-Saëns:Samson et Dalila (sels) ERAT (Recital) ▲ 98501 (9.97)

AUBERT, LOUIS (1877-1968)

Habanera for Orchestra
P. Coppola (cnd), Paris Conservatory Société des Concerts Orch † E. Chausson:Sym in B♭, Op. 20; G. Fauré:Shylock, Op. 57; G. Pierné:Concertstück Hp, Op. 39; L.-E.-E. Reyer:Sigurd (sels) LYS ▲ 411 (17.97)

Improvisation for 2 Guitars (1960)
Gruber & Maklar Guitar Duo ("Contemporary Works for 2 Guitars") † Absil:Suite for 2 Gtrs, Op. 135; Bogdanović:Son Fant; Bons:Attacca; Jolivet:Sérénade for 2 Gtrs; Smith Brindle:Chaconne & Interludes SIGM ▲ 6800 [DDD] (17.97)

Orchestral Music
L. Segerstam (cnd), Rhineland-Palatinate State PO—Offrande; Cinema:6 Tableaux; Dryade; Feuille d'Images; Tombeau de Chateaubriand *(rec 1989)* MARC ▲ 8223531 [DDD] (13.97)

AUBERT, (PIERRE-FRANÇOIS) OLIVIER (1763-1830)

Solo de Concours No. 1 for Clarinet & Piano
J. Russo (cl), L. W. Ignacio (pno) † W. Alexander:Cambridge Trio; L. Bernstein:Son Cl; Diemer:Vars Pno 4-Hands; J. Fry:Pierrot's Fancy; E. Pellegrini:Divert a tre Bn CRSR ▲ 8949

AUE, THIERRY (1964-

Monologue for Soprano, Clarinets, Cello & Piano
L. Florentin (sop), R. Lay (cnd) ("Jeune ecole de Marseille") † J. P. Alagna:Palimpseste; Boeuf:Risées; R. Campo:Anima; Lay:Avec amour; Ombre autour du temps SONP ▲ 96019 [DDD] (16.97)

AUENBRUGG, MARIANA VON (?-1786)

Sonata in E♭ for Harpsichord
B. Harbach (hpd) ("18th Century Women Composers: Music for Solo Harpsichord, Vol. 1") † Barthélémon:Son Hpd; E. De Gambarini:Pieces Hpd, Op. 2; M. Martinez:Son in A Hpd; Son in E Hpd; M. H. Park:Son Hpd, Op. 4 GAS ▲ 272 [DDD] (16.97)
M. Jakuc (pno) † J. Haydn:Son 49 Kbd, H.XVI/36; Son 50 Kbd, H.XVI/37; M. Martinez:Son in A Hpd; Son in E Hpd TIT ▲ 214

AUFSCHNAITER, BENEDICT ANTON (1665-1742)

Concors discordia (6 suites) for 2 Violins, 2 Violas, Cello & Orchestra, Op. 2 (1695)
M. Gaigg (cnd), L'Orfeo Baroque Orch *(rec Nov 1996)* CPO ▲ 999457 [DDD] (13.97)

AULIN, TOR (1866-1914)

Character Pieces (2) for Violin & Piano
S. Stahlhammer (vn), L. Derwinger (pno) † Four Watercolors; Alfvén:Sleeping Forest; V. Aulin:Andante Lamentoso; Haquinius:Nocturne; Swedish Dance; Järnefelt:Andante; Rangström:Adagio doloroso; Spring Nights NSAG ▲ 24 [DDD] (16.97)

Concerto No. 3 in c for Violin & Orchestra, Op. 14
C. Bergqvist (vn), O. Kamu (cnd), Swedish RSO † Stenhammar:Con 2 Pno, Op. 23 MSV ▲ 622 (16.97)
G. Kulenkampff (vn), T. Mann (cnd), Swedish RSO † Glazunov:Con Vn; E. Grieg:Son 3 Vn, Op. 45 BLUB ▲ 3003 [ADD] (18.97)

Four Watercolors for Violin & Piano (1899)
S. Stahlhammer (vn), L. Derwinger (pno) † Character Pieces (2); Alfvén:Sleeping Forest; V. Aulin:Andante Lamentoso; Haquinius:Nocturne; Swedish Dance; Järnefelt:Andante; Rangström:Adagio doloroso; Spring Nights NSAG ▲ 24 [DDD] (16.97)

Mäster Olaf (incidental music) for Orchestra [for Strindberg's play], Op. 22
E. Klas (cnd) *(rec 1987)* ("Music at The Royal Dramatic Theatre") † Stormy Day (ov); Atterberg:Suite 1 Orch MSV ▲ 618 [DDD] (16.97)
G. W. Nilson (cnd), Örebro SO *(rec 1987)* ("Strindberg in Music") † Rangström:Dithyramb STRL ▲ 1011 [DDD] (15.97)

Sonata in d for Violin & Piano (1892)
P. Enoksson (vn), A. Kilström (pno) † Haquinius:Qt 1 Strs; Peterson-Berger:Pno Music; Stenhammar:Pno Music (misc colls) MSV ▲ 608 [AAD] (16.97)

Stormy Day:Overtures
E. Klas (cnd) *(rec 1987)* ("Music at The Royal Dramatic Theatre") † Mäster Olaf, Op. 22; Atterberg:Suite 1 Orch MSV ▲ 618 [DDD] (16.97)

AULIN, VALBORG (1860-1928)

Andante Lamentoso for Violin & Piano
S. Stahlhammer (vn), L. Derwinger (pno) † Alfvén:Sleeping Forest; T. Aulin:Character Pieces (2); Four Watercolors; Haquinius:Nocturne; Swedish Dance; Järnefelt:Andante; Rangström:Adagio doloroso; Spring Nights NSAG ▲ 24 [DDD] (16.97)

AURIC, GEORGES (1899-1983)

Adieu New York for Piano (1921)
M. Bratke (pno) ("Le Groupe des Six") † Durey:Préludes, Op. 26; Honegger:Pièces brèves; D. Milhaud:Printemps Pno, Op. 25; F. Poulenc:Mouvements perpétuels; Pièces Pno; Tailleferre:Romance Pno OLY ▲ 487 [DDD] (12.97)

Ouverture for Orchestra (1938)
A. Doráti (cnd), London SO *(rec London, England, Aug 1965)* † P. Fetler:Contrasts; J. Françaix:Concertino; D. Milhaud:Boeuf sur le toit, Op. 58; Satie:Parade Orch MRCR ▲ 34335 (11.97)

Trio for Oboe, Clarinet & Bassoon (1936)
Chicago Chamber Musicians *(rec Chicago, IL, 1997)* ("20th Century French Wind Trios") † Canteloube:Rustiques; J. Françaix:Divert Ob, Cl, Bn; Ibert:Pièces (5) en trio; D. Milhaud:Pastorale Ob, Op. 147; Suite d'après Corrette, Op. 161; P. Pierné:Bucolique variée; Tansman:Suite Reed Trio CED ▲ 40 [DDD] (16.97)

Waltz for Piano 4-Hands (1949)
G. Picavet (pno), B. Picavet (pno) † Durey:Carillons; Neige; Honegger:Partita Pno 4-Hands; D. Milhaud:Création du monde, Op. 81; Scaramouche Pnos, Op. 165b; F. Poulenc:Capriccio; Elégie Pnos; Embarquement pour Cythère; Tailleferre:Jeux de plein air ILD ▲ 642129 (11.97)

AUSTIN, ELIZABETH (1938-

An Die Nachgeborenen [To Those Born Later] for solo Voices, Piano & Chorus (1992)
V. Winter (sop), A. Bassermann (sgr), K. Grünenpült (sgr), S. Dotzauer (pno), G. Kegelmann (cnd), Heidelberg-Mannheim State Univ Chamber Choir ("Reflected Light") † Circling; Gathering Threads; Klavier Double; Lighthouse 1; To Begin; Zodiac Suite CPS ▲ 8625 (16.97)

Circling for Cello & Piano (1982)
M. L. Rylands (vc), J. Albee (pno) ("Reflected Light") † An Die Nachgeborenen; Gathering Threads; Klavier Double; Lighthouse 1; To Begin; Zodiac Suite CPS ▲ 8625 (16.97)

Gathering Threads for Clarinet (1990)
M. Lücke (cl) ("Reflected Light") † An Die Nachgeborenen; Circling; Klavier Double; Lighthouse 1; To Begin; Zodiac Suite CPS ▲ 8625 (16.97)

Klavier Double for Piano & Tape (1983)
J. Reed (pno) ("Reflected Light") † An Die Nachgeborenen; Circling; Gathering Threads; Lighthouse 1; To Begin; Zodiac Suite CPS ▲ 8625 (16.97)

Lighthouse 1 for Harpsichord (1989)
U. Trede-Boettcher (hpd) ("Reflected Light") † An Die Nachgeborenen; Circling; Gathering Threads; Klavier Double; To Begin; Zodiac Suite CPS ▲ 8625 (16.97)

To Begin for Brass Quintet (1990)
Constitution Brass ("Reflected Light") † An Die Nachgeborenen; Circling; Gathering Threads; Klavier Double; Lighthouse 1; Zodiac Suite CPS ▲ 8625 (16.97)

Wilderness Symphony for 2 Narrators & Orchestra
M. Liebermann (nar), A. King (nar), S. Kawalla (cnd), Cracow Radio-TV Orch ("..and the eagle flies: New American Orchestral Music") † F. D. Angeli:Sta Pestá; R. Brooks:Landscape...with Grace; Seascape:Ov to Moby Dick CPS ▲ 8634 (16.97)

Zodiac Suite for Piano (1980)
J. Reed (pno) ("Reflected Light") † An Die Nachgeborenen; Circling; Gathering Threads; Klavier Double; Lighthouse 1; To Begin CPS ▲ 8625 (16.97)

AUSTIN, LARRY (1930-

La Barbara:The Name, The Sounds, The Music (1991)
artists unknown ("CDCM Computer Music Series, Vol. 13") † J. La Barbara:Albero della foglie azzure; Pope:Kombination XI; Spiegel:Electronic Music CENT ▲ 2166 (16.97)

Blues Ax for Saxophone & Electronics (1995)
S. Duke (sax), M. Matthews (elec) ("Composer in the Computer Age VIII") † Shin-Edo; Variations CENT (CDCM Computer Music Series) ▲ 2428 [DDD] (16.97)

Montage:Themes & Variations for Violin & Computer Music on Tape (1985)
R. Davidovici (vn), L. Austin (cmpt) *(rec United States of America)* ("The Virtuoso in the Computer Age - I") † A. Braxton:Composition 107 (sels); P. Lansky:As If; J. Melby:Con 1 Fl & Computer; D. Rosenboom:Precipice in Time CENT (CDCM Computer Music Series, Vol 10) ▲ 2110 [DDD] (16.97)

Quadrants: Event/Complex No. 1 for Wind ensemble & Tape (1972; rev 1994)
L. Austin (tape), E. Corporon (cnd), North Texas Wind Sym *(rec Denton, TX, Nov 1997)* † T. Clark:LIGHTFORMS 2: Star Spectra; J. Klein:Dog; J. C. Nelson:rain has a slap and a curve; M. Thompson:Klank; Y. Tseng:Little Ying Yang; Winsor:Passaggio Spaziale CENT ▲ 2407 [DDD] (16.97)

¡Rompido! (computer music on tape) (1993)
L. Austin (cmpt) ("The Composer in the Computer Age VII") † J. Chadabe:Follow; Dashow:Tracce; Lippe:Music Cl; Waschka (li):Visions of Habakkuk CENT (CDCM Computer Music) ▲ 2310 [DDD] (16.97)

Shin-Edo: CityscapeSet for Electronics (1994-96)
M. Matthews (elec) ("Composer in the Computer Age VIII") † Blues Ax; Variations CENT (CDCM Computer Music Series) ▲ 2428 [DDD] (16.97)

Sinfonia Concertante:A Mozartean Episode for Chamber Orchestra & Computer Music Narrative (1988)
L. Austin (cmpt), T. Clark (cnd), Univ of North Texas CO *(rec Univ. of North Texas, Denton, TX, Apr 1987-Jan 1988)* ("Compositions by Larry Austin, Thomas Clark, Jerry Hunt & Phil Winsor") † Son Concertante; T. Clark:Peninsula; J. Hunt:Fluud; Winsor:Dulcimer Dream CENT (CDCM Computer Series, Volume 1) ▲ 2029 (16.97)

Sonata Concertante for Piano & Computer Music on Tape (1988)
A. Wodnicki (pno), L. Austin (tape) *(rec Univ. of North Texas, Denton, TX, Apr 1987-Jan 1988)* ("Compositions by Larry Austin, Thomas Clark, Jerry Hunt & Phil Winsor") † Sinf Concertante; T. Clark:Peninsula; J. Hunt:Fluud; Winsor:Dulcimer Dream CENT (CDCM Computer Series, Volume 1) ▲ 2029 (16.97)

Variations...beyond Pierrot for Soprano, Instruments & Electronics (1993-95)
Thira ("Composer in the Computer Age VIII") † Blues Ax; Shin-Edo CENT (CDCM Computer Music Series) ▲ 2428 [DDD] (16.97)

AVALON, ROBERT (20th cent)

Sextet to Julia de Bourgos for Soprano, Flute, Strings & Piano, Op. 21 (1989)
J. Lattimore (sop), S. Shiragami (vn), D. Strba (vn), D. Garrett (vc), A. Young (fl), R. Avalon (pno) *(rec St Lukes United Methodist Church, Houston, TX, Aug 1998)* † Son Fl; Son Vl, Op. 6 MDG ▲ 6030859 [DDD] (17.97)
J. Lattimore (sop), S. Shiragami (vn), D. Strba (vn), D. Garrett (vc), A. Young (fl), R. Avalon (pno) *(rec St Lukes Methodist Church, Houston, TX, Sept 1998)* † Son Fl; Son Vl, Op. 6 CENT ▲ 2430 [DDD] (16.97)

Sonata for Flute & Piano, Op. 26 (1991)
M. Meisenbach (fl), R. Avalon (pno) *(rec St Lukes United Methodist Church, Houston, TX, Sept 1998)* † Sextet; Son Vl, Op. 6 MDG ▲ 6030859 [DDD] (17.97)
M. Meisenbach (fl), R. Avalon (pno) *(rec St Lukes Methodist Church, Houston, TX, Sept 1998)* † Sextet; Son Vl, Op. 6 CENT ▲ 2430 [DDD] (16.97)

Sonata for Violin & Piano, Op. 6 (1983)
B. Lewis (vn) *(rec St Lukes Methodist Church, Houston, TX, Sept 1998)* † Sextet; Son Fl CENT ▲ 2430 [DDD] (16.97)
B. Lewis (vn), R. Avalon (pno) *(rec St Lukes United Methodist Church, Houston, TX, Sept 1998)* † Sextet; Son Fl MDG ▲ 6030859 [DDD] (17.97)

AVERITT, WILLIAM (1948-

Tripartita for Violin, Clarinet & Piano (1989)
Verdehr Trio ("The Making of a Medium, Vol. 3") † N. Currier:Adagio & Vars; G. Schuller:Trio Setting Vn CRYS ▲ 743 [DDD] (15.97)

AVISON, CHARLES (1709-1770)

Concerti grossi (12) for 4 Violins, Viola, Cello & Harpsichord [after D. Scarlatti] (1744)
R. Goodman (cnd), Brandenburg Consort HYP 2-▲ 66891 (36.97)
J. Lamon (cnd), Tafelmusik SMS (SM 5000) ▲ 5061 [DDD] (16.97)
N. Marriner (cnd), Academy of St. Martin in the Fields PPHI 2-▲ 38806 (17.97)
T. Pinnock (cnd), English Concert † J. Pachelbel:Canon & Gigue; H. Purcell:Chacony Strs, Z.730 PARC ▲ 15518 [DDD] (16.97)

Sonatas (6) for Harpsichord, 2 Violins & Cello, Op. 5
London Baroque † C. F. Abel:Sons Vn, Vc & Bc, Op. 9; T. Arne:Trio Sons, Op. 3 AMON ▲ 14 [DDD] (16.97)

Sonata in F for Violin & Keyboard
D. Smith (bn), R. Vignoles (pno) [arr Arkinson] *(rec London, England)* † T. Arne:Son 5 Hpd; Dunhill:Lyric Suite Bn & Pno, Op. 96; E. Elgar:Romance Vn, Op. 1; Hurlstone:Son Vn; G. Jacob:Four Sketches Bn; Vaughan Williams:Studies in English Folk-Song ASV ▲ 535 [DDD] (17.97)

AVNI, TZVI (1927-

Epitaph (Sonata No. 2) for Piano (1944-79)
D. Holzman (pno) ("Piano Music by Jewish Composers") † Ben-Haim (Frankenburger):Pieces Pno; E. Bloch:Visions & Prophecies; Schoenberg:Pieces (3) Pno, Op. 11; S. Wolpe:Palestinian Notebook ALBA ▲ 283 [DDD] (16.97)

AVSHALOMOV, AARON (1894-1965)

Concerto for Piano & Orchestra
M. Moore (pno), J. Avshalomov (cnd), Portland Youth PO † Peiping Hutungs; J. Avshalomov:Prophecy; Taking of T'ung Kuan CRI ▲ 667 [ADD] (16.97)

Peiping Hutungs (symphonic sketch) for Orchestra
J. Avshalomov (cnd), Portland Youth PO † Con Pno; J. Avshalomov:Prophecy; Taking of T'ung Kuan CRI ▲ 667 [ADD] (16.97)

Songs
D. Avshalomov (va), R. McDonald (pno)—Nocturne/Kwei Fei's Lamnet; Lantern Dance [arr J. Avshalomov] ("Avshalomov: Three Generations") † J. Avshalomov:Evocations; Sonatine Va; D. Avshalomov:Torn Curtain ALBA ▲ 216 [DDD] (16.97)
A. Rogers (mez), L. Barker (pno)—Songs (5) for Alyce; Whimsies (3); Threnos (2); Wonders (3); Biblical Songs (3); From the Chinese; No. 4 w. Melody Wooldridge Avril (fl), Daniel Avsh; 2 Old Birds [w. Marcy Fetchen (cl)]; Who Is My Shepherd; Fed by My Labors; O Time ("24 Songs") ALBA ▲ 249 [DDD] (16.97)

AVSHALOMOV, DAVID (1946-

Torn Curtain for Viola & Piano (1989)
D. Avshalomov (va), R. McDonald (pno) ("Avshalomov: Three Generations") † J. Avshalomov:Evocations; Sonatine Va; A. Avshalomov:Songs ALBA ▲ 216 [DDD] (16.97)

AVSHALOMOV, JACOB (1919-

City upon a Hill for Narrator, Orchestra, Chorus & Liberty Bell [text Blake] (ca 1964)
J. Avshalomov (cnd), Portland Youth PO, Univ of Oregon Choruses, T. L. McCall (nar) [live] † Inscriptions at the City of Brass; Sym, "The Oregon"; Up at Timberline ALBA ▲ 296 [DDD] (16.97)

Evocations for Clarinet (or Viola) & Piano (1947-1953; orchd)
D. Avshalomov (va), R. McDonald (pno) ("Avshalomov: Three Generations") † Sonatine Va; A. Avshalomov:Songs; D. Avshalomov:Torn Curtain ALBA ▲ 216 [DDD] (16.97)

How Long, O Lord (cantata) for Alto, Orchestra & Chorus (ca 1948)
J. Avshalomov (cnd), Portland Youth SO † Phases of the Great Land; R. Harris:Elegy & Dance; R. Ward:Divert Orch CRI ▲ 664 [ADD] (17.97)

Inscriptions at the City of Brass for Female Narrator, Orchestra without Strings & Chorus [text from 1001 Arabian Nights] (1956)
M. Stahl (nar—Sheherezade), J. Avshalomov (cnd), Portland Youth PO, Univ of Oregon Choruses [live] † City upon a Hill; Sym, "The Oregon"; Up at Timberline ALBA ▲ 296 [DDD] (16.97)

Open Sesame! for Orchestra
J. Avshalomov (cnd), Portland Youth SO † Brotons:Obstinacy; B. Johanson:Cretan Rhap; Van Buren:Mementos; Walczyk:Delphic Suite ALBA ▲ 115 [DDD] (16.97)

Phases of the Great Land for Orchestra (ca 1958)
J. Avshalomov (cnd), Portland Youth SO † How Long, O Lord; R. Harris:Elegy & Dance; R. Ward:Divert Orch CRI ▲ 664 [ADD] (17.97)

Praises from the Corners of the Earth for solo Voices, Organ & 3 Percussionists (ca 1964; orchd)
J. Avshalomov (cnd), Portland Youth PO *(rec Portland, OR, Feb 25, 1984)* † Raptures on the Madrigals of Gesualdo; Sym of Songs ALBA ▲ 160 [DDD] (16.97)

Prophecy for Cantor, Chorus & Organ (1948)
C. Matheson (ten), L. Smith (org), J. Dexter (cnd), Mid-America Chorale † Taking of T'ung Kuan; A. Avshalomov:Con Pno; Peiping Hutungs CRI ▲ 667 [ADD] (16.97)

Raptures on the Madrigals of Gesualdo for Voices & Orchestra (1975)
J. Avshalomov (cnd), Portland Youth PO *(rec Portland, OR, May 7, 1989)* † Praises from the Corners of the Earth; Sym of Songs ALBA ▲ 160 [DDD] (16.97)

Sonatine for Viola & Piano (1943)
D. Avshalomov (va), R. McDonald (pno) ("Avshalomov: Three Generations") † Evocations; A. Avshalomov:Songs; D. Avshalomov:Torn Curtain ALBA ▲ 216 [DDD] (16.97)

Symphony of Songs for Orchestra
J. Avshalomov (cnd), Portland Youth PO *(rec Portland, OR, Feb 26, 1994)* † Praises from the Corners of the Earth; Raptures on the Madrigals of Gesualdo ALBA ▲ 160 [DDD] (16.97)

Symphony, "The Oregon" (1962)
J. Avshalomov (cnd), Portland Youth PO [live] † City upon a Hill; Inscriptions at the City of Brass; Up at Timberline ALBA ▲ 296 [DDD] (16.97)

Taking of T'ung Kuan for Orchestra (1948)
I. Buketoff (cnd), Oslo PO † Prophecy; A. Avshalomov:Con Pno; Peiping Hutungs CRI ▲ 667 [ADD] (16.97)

Up at Timberline (suite) for Winds, Brass, Double Bass & Percussion (1987)
J. Avshalomov (cnd), Portland Youth PO [live] † City upon a Hill; Inscriptions at the City of Brass; Sym, "The Oregon" ALBA ▲ 296 [DDD] (16.97)

AYALA, HECTOR (1914-

Serie Americana for Guitar
Y. Kamata (gtr) ("Serie Americana: Guitar Works of Latin America") † Lauro:Suite Venezolano; A. Piazzolla:Pieces (5) Gtr; H. Villa-Lobos:Preludes Gtr CAMA ▲ 453 [DDD] (18.97)

AYRES, RICHARD (1965-

Short Arrangements of Times from My Past (2) for Chamber Ensemble
Altena Ensemble *(rec Doopsgezinde Church, Amsterdam, Netherlands, 1995)* ("Working on Time") † M. Altena:Dowlands; Bergeijk:Sym joyeuse; Isadora:America Is Waiting; G. van Keulen:Trompeau; H. van der Meulen:Music for a While; Padding:Nicht eilen NMCL ▲ 92063 [DDD] (16.97)

Untitled for Trumpet & Piano (1990)
Ives Ensemble members † G. Carl:Claremont Con; Emmerik:Valise; R. Ford:Cross; M. Hamel:There Was Nothing Nobody Could Say; Rijnvos:Gigue et Double CV (Muziepraktijk) ▲ 63 [DDD] (18.97)

AZZAIOLO, FILIPPO (fl 1557-1569)

Instrumental Music
M. Morrow (cnd), Musica Reservata *(Al di dolce ben mio)*, J. Beckett (cnd), Musica Reservata *(Gentil Madonna; Occhio non fu) (rec NY, Oct 1970)* ("16th Century Italian & French Dance Music") † Anonymous:Au joli bois; Bataille; Belle que tiens ma vie; Branle simple 22; Che fa la ramacina; Colognese; Dagdun vetusta; E si son; Fortuna d'un gran; Gagliarda la scarpa; Gagliarda la traditora; Gagliarda Baxela un trato; Gagliarda Zorzi; Giorgio; Hoboeckendans; J'ameroye mieus dormir seulette; Marchese di Saluzzo; Mourisque; Passemeze et gaillarde; Pavana Le forze d'Hercole; Tordion; Dalza:Piva; Janequin:Il estoit une fillette; Passereau:Pourquoy donc; Sermisy:Dance Music; Music of Sermisy BOSK (From the Vault) ▲ 123 [ADD] (15.97)

BAAREN, KEES VAN (1906-1970)

Concertino for Piano & Orchestra (1934)
D. Kuyken (pno), E. Spanjaard (cnd), Netherlands Radio CO ("Piano Concertos in the Netherlands") † Bosmans:Concertino Pno; T. Leeuw:Danses sacrees; L. Smit:Con Pno NMCL ▲ 92044 (16.97)

BABADJANYAN, ARNO (1921-1983)

Heroic Ballade for Piano & Orchestra (1950)
A. Babakhanian (pno), L. Tjeknavorian (cnd), Armenian PO † Nocturne; L. Tjeknavorian:Con Pno, Op. 4 ASV ▲ 984 (16.97)

Music of Babadjanyan
B. Chekmenyov (gtr), A. Tarasov (gtr), A. Babadjanyan (pno), A. Arutiunyan (pno), A. Nikolayev (perc), Y. Silantiev (cnd), All-Union Radio-TV Sym Variety Orch, Y. Silantiev (cnd), Armenian Radio-TV Orch—Nocturne; Prelude & Vagarshapat Dance; Capriccio; Polyphonic Son; Exprompt; Armenian Rhap; Elegy in Commemoration of A. Khachaturyan; 6 Pictures; Melody & Humoresque; Fant on Give Me My Music Back; Fant on Dum spiro spero; Fant on Winer Love; Fant on Call Me; Piece for the Pno & Orch [Dreams] *(rec 1953-83)* ("Russian Violin School: Marina Yashvili") † J. Brahms:Hungarian Dances Pno 4-Hands; Son 2 Vn, Op. 100; M. de Falla:Canciones populares españolas; Paganini:Cantabile, M.S. 109; Moto perpetuo Vn, M.S. 66 RD (Talents of Russia) ▲ 16251 [ADD] (16.97)

Nocturne for Piano
A. Babakhanian (pno) † Heroic Ballade; L. Tjeknavorian:Con Pno, Op. 4 ASV ▲ 984 (16.97)

Piano Music
N. Gavrilova (pno)—Prelude; Vagarshapat Dance; Impromptu; Capriccio *(rec 1976-90)* ("Russian Piano School: Natalia Gavrilova") † S. Rachmaninoff:Preludes Pno; D. Shostakovich:Pno Music; Strauss (II):Pno Trans; Tso Chenhuan:Pno Music RD (Talents of Russia) ▲ 16238 [ADD] (16.97)

Trio for Piano, Violin & Cello (1952)
Bamberg Piano Trio *(rec 1996)* † P. Tchaikovsky:Trio Pno, Op. 50 THOR ▲ 2328 [DDD] (16.97)
Trio Con Brio † Schoenberg:Verklärte Nacht, Op. 4 CLSO ▲ 137 (15.97)

BABBITT, MILTON (1916-

All Set for Jazz Ensemble (1957)
A. Weisberg (cnd) † Rochberg:Serenata d'estate; S. Shifrin:Satires of Circumstance; R. Wernick:Kaddish-Requiem; S. Wolpe:Qt Tpt NON ▲ 79222 (16.97)

Canonical Form for Piano (1983)
M. Goldray (pno) *(rec Princeton, NJ, 1996-97)* † Emblems; Preludes; Tutte le corde CRI ▲ 746 [DDD] (16.97)

Concerto for Piano & Orchestra (1985)
A. Feinberg (pno), C. Wuorinen (cnd), American Composers Orch † Head of the Bed NWW ▲ 346 [DDD] (16.97)

Consortini for Chamber Ensemble (1989)
S. Mosko (cnd) , S. Mosko (cnd), Griffin Music Ensemble † R. Bauer:Along the Way; Geller:Where Silence Reigns GMR ▲ 2032 (16.97)

Cultivated Choruses (3) (1987)
P. Schubert (cnd), New Calliope Singers *(rec NYC, NY, June 1990)* † J. Druckman:Corinna's Going A-Maying; Death Be Not Proud; Faery Beam upon You; Madrigals; Shake off Your Heavy Trance; S. Gerber:Saison en enfer; Gideon:Habitable Earth; Monod:Cantus Contra Cantum IV; M. Wright:Choral Music CRI ▲ 638 [DDD] (16.97)

An Elizabethan Sextette (6 Elizabethan love poems) for Women's Voices in 6 Parts (1978-9)
H. Sollberger (cnd) † Groupwise; Pno Music; Vision & Prayer CRI ▲ 521 [DDD] (16.97)

BABBITT, MILTON (cont.)

Emblems (Ars Emblematica) for Piano (1989)
M. Goldray (pno) *(rec Princeton, NJ, 1996-97)* † Canonical Form; Preludes; Tutte le corde CRI ▲ 746 [DDD] (16.97)

Groupwise (chamber concerto) for Flutes, Piccolo, String Trio & Piano (1983)
D. Shulman (cnd) † Elizabethan Sextette; Pno Music; Vision & Prayer CRI ▲ 521 [DDD] (16.97)

The Head of the Bed for Soprano, Flute, Clarinet, Violin & Cello (1981)
J. Bettina (sop), A. Korf (cnd) † Con Pno NWW ▲ 346 [DDD] (16.97)

The Joy of More Sextets for Violin & Piano (1986)
R. Schulte (vn), A. Feinberg (pno) † Sxts Vn NWW ▲ 364 [DDD] (16.97)

Music of Babbitt
W. Purvis (hn) *(Around the Hn)*, N. Farrell (ten), W. Anderson (gtr) *(4 Cavalier Settings)*, R. Rudich (fl) *(None but the Lonely)*, M. Taylor (a sax), C. Abromovic (pno) *(Whirled Series)*, P. Jarvis (dr) *(Homily)*, T. Kolor (mar) *(Beaten Paths)*, L. Martin (va) *(Play It Again, Sam)*, D. Starobin (gtr), S. Palma (fl) *(Soli e Duettini)*, C. Macomber (vn) *(Melismata)*, M. Babbitt (nar) *(On Having Been & Still Being an American Composer)* ("Soli e Duettini") KOCH 2-▲ 7335 (16.97)

None but the Lonely Flute for solo Flute (1991)
D. Stone (fl) ("None but the Lonely Flute") † K. Alexander:And the Whole Air Is Tremulous; J. Cage:Ryoanji Fl; M. Feldman:Trio Fls; S. L. Mosko:for Morton Feldman; Indigenous Music 2 NWW ▲ 80456 (16.97)

Philomel for Soprano & 4-Track Tape (1964)
B. Beardslee (sop) *(rec General Theological Seminary Chapel, NYC, NY)* † Phonemena Sop & Pno; Phonemena Sop & Tape; Post-Partitions; Reflections NWW ▲ 80466 (16.97)
J. Bettina (sop) ("Electro Acoustic Music: Classics") † Phonemena Sop & Tape; R. Reynolds:Transfigured Wind IV; Varèse:Poeme électronique; Xenakis:Mycenae-Alpha NEU ▲ 45074 [ADD]

Phonemena for Soprano & Piano (1970)
L. Webber (sop), J. Kuderna (pno) *(rec NYC, NY)* † Philomel; Phonemena Sop & Tape; Post-Partitions; Reflections NWW ▲ 80466 (16.97)

Phonemena for Soprano & Tape (1975)
J. Bettina (sop) ("Electro Acoustic Music: Classics") † Philomel; R. Reynolds:Transfigured Wind IV; Varèse:Poeme électronique; Xenakis:Mycenae-Alpha NEU ▲ 45074 [ADD]
J. Heller (sop) ("To the Verge") † L. Berio:Sequenza III; R. Cogan:Polyutterances; T. Stumpf:Lear's Daughters NEU ▲ 45089 (16.97)
L. Webber (sop) *(rec NYC, NY)* † Philomel; Phonemena Sop & Pno; Post-Partitions; Reflections NWW ▲ 80466 (16.97)

Piano Music
A. Feinberg (pno)—About Time; Playing for Time; It Takes 12 to Tango; Minute Waltz; Partitions † Elizabethan Sextette; Groupwise; Vision & Prayer CRI ▲ 521 [DDD] (16.97)
Taub (pno)—Compositions (3) Pno; Duet Pno; Semi-simple Vars; Partitions; Post-Partitions; Tableaux; Reflections; Canonical Form; Lagniappe HAM ▲ 905160 (18.97)

Post-Partitions for Piano (1966)
R. Miller (pno) *(rec NYC, NY)* † Philomel; Phonemena Sop & Pno; Phonemena Sop & Tape; Reflections NWW ▲ 80466 (16.97)

Preludes, Interludes & Postlude for Piano (1991)
M. Goldray (pno) *(rec Princeton, NJ, 1996-97)* † Canonical Form; Emblems; Tutte le corde CRI ▲ 746 [DDD] (16.97)

Quartet No. 4 for Strings (1970)
Juilliard String Quartet † R. Sessions:Qt 2 Strs; S. Wolpe:Qt Strs CRI ▲ 587 [DDD] (16.97)

Reflections for Piano & Tape (1974)
A. Karis (pno) *(rec American Academy of Arts & Letters, NYC, NY, June 1994)* † Davidovsky:Synchronism 6; A. Kreiger:Fant Pno; Primosch:Secret Geometry; J. Yuasa:Towards the Midnight Sun CRI ▲ 707 [DDD] (16.97)
R. Miller (pno) *(rec NYC, NY)* † Philomel; Phonemena Sop & Pno; Phonemena Sop & Tape; Post-Partitions NWW ▲ 80466 (16.97)

Relata I for Orchestra (1965)
P. Zukofsky (cnd), Juilliard Orch † D. Diamond:Sym 5; Persichetti:Night Dances NWW ▲ 80396 [DDD] (16.97)

Sextets for Violin & Piano (1966)
R. Schulte (vn), A. Feinberg (pno) † Joy of More Sextets NWW ▲ 364 [DDD] (16.97)

Soli e Duettini for 2 Guitars (1989)
Anderson/Fader Duo *(rec NY, July 11, 1992)* ("New Music with Guitar, Vol. 5") † Davidovsky:Synchronisms 10; T. Flaherty:Cross-Currents; J. A. Lennon:Zingari; M. Powell:Setting Gtr; R. Reynolds:Behaviour of Mirrors BRID ▲ 9042 [DDD] (17.97)

Transfigured Notes for String Orchestra (1986)
G. Schuller (cnd) *(rec live, Jordan Hall, NEC, Boston, MA, Feb 8, 1991)* † Schoenberg:Verklärte Nacht, Op. 4; I. Stravinsky:Con Str Orch GMR ▲ 2060 (16.97)

Tutte le corde for Piano (1994)
M. Goldray (pno) *(rec Princeton, NJ, 1996-97)* † Canonical Form; Emblems; Preludes CRI ▲ 746 [DDD] (16.97)

Vision & Prayer for Soprano & Synthesized Accompaniment [text by Dylan Thomas] (1961)
B. Beardslee (sop) † Elizabethan Sextette; Groupwise; Pno Music CRI ▲ 521 [DDD] (16.97)

BABELL, WILLIAM (ca 1690-1723)

Concerto in e for Flute & Strings, Op. 3/3
P. Evison (fl), Drottningholm Baroque Ensemble † J. S. Bach:Suite 2 Fl, BWV 1067; Telemann:Qts or trios (6) BIS ▲ 249 [DDD] (17.97)

Concerto in d for Recorder & Strings
S. Reiss (rcr), Hesperus † Graupner:Con Rcr; Naudot:Con Rcr; Telemann:Son Rcr; Vivaldi:Con Rcr, Ob & Vn, RV.94; Con Rcr, RV.444 KOCH ▲ 7454 (16.97)

Concerto in D for Recorder, 2 Violins & Continuo, Op. 3/1
Musica Alta Ripa *(rec June 1997)* ("Londoner's Taste") † W. Boyce:Son 11 Vns; Geminiani:Vars on a Subject; G. F. Handel:Son Rcr; Porpora:Son Vc; G. Sammartini:Con Hpd; R. Valentine:Con Rcr MDG ▲ 3090779 [DDD] (17.97)

Concerto in G for Soprano Recorder, 2 Violins & Continuo, Op. 3/4
T. Perrenoud (rcr), Amsterdam Baroque Soloists ("Sur les Chemins de l'Europe Galante") † Vivaldi:Con Rcr; Con Rcr, RV.441; Cons Rcr CLAV ▲ 509706 (16.97)

Sonata No. 2 in c for Recorder & Continuo (1725)
Trio Basiliensis *(rec Freiburg, Germany, Apr 1996)* ("Concerning Babell & Son") † A. Corelli:Son 5 Va da Gamba, Op. 5; P. A. Fiocco:Son in C; G. F. Handel:Rinaldo (sels); Paisible:Son Rcr in F, Sibley 9; Rosier:Son in g; Steffani:Son in d ARSM ▲ 1167 [DDD] (17.97)

BABIN, VICTOR (1908-1972)

Hillandale Waltzes for Clarinet & Piano (1947)
P. Shands (cl), E. Rowley (pno) † M. Arnold:Son Cl; A. Benjamin:Tombeau; G. Finzi:Bagatelles Cl, Op. 23; W. Lutoslawski:Dance Preludes Cl & Pno RTOP ▲ 116 (16.97)
J. B. Yeh (cnd) [arr Nygren] *(rec May 1993)* † L. Bernstein:Prelude, Fugue & Riffs; M. Gould:Derivations; A. Shaw:Con Cl; I. Stravinsky:Ebony Con REF ▲ 55 [DDD] (16.97)

BACALOV, LUIS ENRIQUE (20th cent)

Il Vangelo Secondo Matthew [The Gospel According to St. Matthew] (film music) for Orchestra [original material incorporating music of Bach, Mozart & Prokofiev] (1966)
L. E. Bacalov (cnd) IMEZ ▲ 132 [AAD] (22.97)

BACARISSE, SALVADOR (1898-1963)

Fantasia andaluza for Harp & Orchestra
A. Ros-Marbá (cnd), Seville Real SO *(rec Central Theater, Seville, Spain, July 1995)* ("The Musical Generation of 1927: Spanish Symphonic Music") † R. Halffter:Don Lindo de Almeria, Op. 7; Pittaluga:Romeria de los Cornudos AL (Musical Heritage of Andalusia) ▲ 118 [DDD] (18.97)

BACCHUS, PETER (1954-

Quartet for Diverse Flutes (1985)
Flute Force *(rec NYC, NY, 1989)* † I. Dahl:Serenade Fls; D. E. Jones:Tibiae; R. Reynolds:Etudes (4) Fl; H. Sollberger:Grand Qt Fls; Trombly:Cantilena CRI ▲ 581 [DDD] (16.97)

BACEWICZ, GRAZYNA (1909-1969)

Concerto No. 7 for Violin & Orchestra (1966)
R. Lasocki (vn), K. Stryja (cnd), Polish National RSO Katowice † K. Meyer:Con Vn; Twardowski:Spanish Fant Vn OLY ▲ 323 [AAD] (16.97)

Partita for Violin & Piano (1955)
A. Belnick (vn), S. Silvansky (pno) *(rec CA, July, 1995)* † Son 3 Vn; Son 4 Vn; Son 5 Vn CMB ▲ 1052 [DDD] (16.97)

Sonata No. 3 for Violin & Piano (1947)
A. Belnick (vn), S. Silvansky (pno) *(rec CA, July, 1995)* † Partita; Son 4 Vn; Son 5 Vn CMB ▲ 1052 [DDD] (16.97)

66 ▲ = CD ♦ = Enhanced CD △ = MD ▮ = Cassette Tape ▯ = DCC

BACH, JOHANN SEBASTIAN (cont.)

Partita in b for Harpsichord, BWV 831, "Ouvertüre nach französischer Art" (cont.)

R. Tureck (pno) *(rec 1957-59)* ("Rosalyn Tureck II") † Duets Hpd; Goldberg Vars, BWV 988; Italian Con, BWV 971 PPHI (Great Pianists of the 20th Century) 2-▲ 456979 (22.97)

B. Verlet (hpd) † Partitas Hpd PPHI 2-▲ 42559 (17.97)

Partita (Suite) in c for Lute, BWV 997 (1737-41)

P. Beier (lt) ("Works for Lute, Vol. 1") † Partita Lt, BWV 1006a; Prelude, Fugue & Allegro Lt, BWV 998 STRV ▲ 33468 (16.97)

J. Gérard (fl), D. Blumenthal (pno) ("Edition Bachakademie, Vol. 121: Chamber Music for Flute") † Partita Fl, BWV 1013; Son Vn; Sons Fl; Trio Son Fl Vn & Hpd, BWV 1038; Trio Son Fls, BWV 1039 HANS 2-▲ 92121 [DDD] (19.97)

K. Heindel (hpd/lt) *(rec Stonington, CT, Oct 26-28, 1993)* ("Aufs Lautenwerk") † Fugue Lt; Partita Lt, BWV 1006a; Prelude, Fugue & Allegro Lt, BWV 998; Suite Lt, BWV 996 DOR ▲ 80126 [DDD] (13.97)

R. Hill (kbd) *(rec Sept 1998)* ("Edition Bachakademie, Vol. 109: Works for the Lute-Harpsichord") † Fant & Fughetta Kbd, BWV 907; Fant & Fughetta Kbd, BWV 908; Prelude Kbd, BWV 921; Prelude Lt, BWV 999; Prelude, Fugue & Allegro Lt, BWV 998; Suite Kbd, BWV 823; Suite Lt, BWV 996 HANS ▲ 92109 [DDD] (11.97)

E. Møldrup (gtr) ("The Guitar Music") † Fugue Lt; Lt Music; Prelude Lt, BWV 999; Prelude, Fugue & Allegro Lt, BWV 998; Sons & Partitas Vn; Suite Lt, BWV 995; Suite Lt, BWV 996 CLSO 2-▲ 171 (15.97)

K. Ragossnig (gtr), P. Graf (fl) ("Transcriptions for Flute & Guitar") † W. A. Mozart:Son 11 Pno, K.331; F. Schubert:Son Arpeggione, D.821 CLAV ▲ 9705 (16.97)

G. Sárközy (lt) *(rec 1980, 1984 & 1991)* ("Johann Sebastian Bach on Viola Bastarda, Lute and Lute-Harpsichord") † Cant 147; Fugue Lt; Prelude, Fugue & Allegro Lt, BWV 998; Sons Vl; Suite Lt, BWV 995; Suite Lt, BWV 996 HUN 2-▲ 31616 [ADD] (32.97)

Tripla Concordia [trans for rcr, hpd & bc] † Trio Sons Org CNTS 2-▲ 9701 (36.97)

Partita in E for Lute, BWV 1006a (1720)

P. Beier (lt) ("Works for Lute, Vol. 1") † Partita Lt, BWV 997; Prelude, Fugue & Allegro Lt, BWV 998 STRV ▲ 33468 (16.97)

K. Heindel (hpd/lt) *(rec Stonington, CT, Oct 26-28, 1993)* ("Aufs Lautenwerk") † Fugue Lt; Partita Lt, BWV 997; Prelude, Fugue & Allegro Lt, BWV 998; Suite Lt, BWV 996 DOR ▲ 80126 [DDD] (13.97)

C. Mathieu (hp) [trans for hp] ("Bach on the Harp") † Italian Con, BWV 971; Partitas Hpd; C.P.E. Bach:Son Hp, H.563 CASC ▲ 1027 (16.97)

Partite diverse sopra Ach, was soll ich Sünder machen for Organ, BWV 770

C. Brembeck (org) *(rec Lahn-Itzgrund Herbst Org, Intzgrund, Germany, Oct 1988)* ("Lahm-Itzgrund Herbst-Orgel") † Chorale Preludes Org; Chorales Org; Fant & Imitatio Org, BWV 563; Org Music (misc colls); Preludes & Fugues, BWV 531-552; Trio Org, BWV 583; J. Lorenz Bach:Prelude & Fugue Org; W. H. Pachelbel:Musicalisches Vergnügen CAPO ▲ 10351 [DDD] (11.97)

C. Herrick (org) *(rec Metzler org, St. Nikolaus Church, Bremgarten, Switzerland, May 1991)* † Canonic Vars on "Von Himmel hoch", BWV 769; Partite diverse sopra, BWV 766; Partite diverse sopra, BWV 767; Partite diverse sopra, BWV 768 HYP ▲ 66455 [DDD] (18.97)

Partite diverse sopra Sei gegrüsset, Jesu gütig for Organ, BWV 768

K. Bowyer (org) ("Complete Works for Organ, Vol. 3") † Cons Org; Preludes & Fugues, BWV 531-552; Trio Org, BWV 585 NIMB ▲ 5290 [DDD] (16.97)

H. Fagius (org) ("Vol. 6") † Chorales (miscellaneous); Fant & Fugue Org, BWV 537; Fant Org, BWV 562; Org Music (comp); Preludes & Fugues, BWV 531-552; Toccata & Fugue Org, BWV 565; Trio Sons Org BIS 2-▲ 397 [DDD] (69.97)

J. Ferrad (org) † Fant Org, BWV 572; Toccata, Adagio & Fugue Org, BWV 564 MOTE ▲ 11971 (17.97)

J. Guillou (org) *(rec Aug 1990)* † Chorales (miscellaneous); Chorales Org; Org Music (misc colls); Orgelbüchlein; Toccata & Fugue Org, BWV 538 DOR ▲ 90149 [DDD] (16.97)

C. Herrick (org) *(rec Metzler org, St. Nikolaus Church, Bremgarten, Switzerland, May 1991)* † Canonic Vars on "Von Himmel hoch", BWV 769; Partite diverse sopra, BWV 766; Partite diverse sopra, BWV 767; Partite diverse sopra, BWV 770 HYP ▲ 66455 [DDD] (18.97)

K. Johannsen (org) ("Edition Bachakademie, Vol. 93: Masterpieces from the Weimar Period") † Chorale Settings (misc); Preludes & Fugues, BWV 531-552 HANS ▲ 92093 [DDD] (11.97)

D. Joyce (org) † Canonic Vars on "Von Himmel hoch", BWV 769; Prelude & Fugue Org, BWV 566; Preludes & Fugues, BWV 531-552; Trio Sons Org TIT ▲ 171 [DDD]

D. Kaufmann (org) *(rec Oct 1962)* ("Chorales from the St. Matthew Passion") † Org Music (misc colls); Orgelbüchlein; St. Matthew Passion (sels) BAYE ▲ 200005 [ADD] (17.97)

T. Koopman (org) † Clavier-Übung III; Org Music (misc colls); Preludes & Fugues, BWV 531-552; Toccata & Fugue Org, BWV 538; Trio Sons Org NOVA ▲ 150036 [DDD] (16.97)

T. Koopman (org) *(rec 1988)* ("Orgelwerke") † Org Music (misc colls); Preludes & Fugues, BWV 531-552; Toccata & Fugue Org, BWV 538; Trio Sons Org NOVA ▲ 150130 [DDD] (69.97)

L. Rogg (org) *(rec Silbermann Org, Arlesheim, Switzerland)* † Allabreve, BWV 589; Canonic Vars on "Von Himmel hoch", BWV 769; Canzona; Chorales Org; Clavier-Übung III; Fant & Fugue Org, BWV 537; Fant & Fugue, BWV 542; Fant Org, BWV 562; Fant Org, BWV 572; Orgelbüchlein; Partite diverse sopra, BWV 766; Partite diverse sopra, BWV 767; Pastorale Org, BWV 590; Prelude & Fugue Org, BWV 566; Preludes & Fugues, BWV 531-552; Schübler Chorale Preludes; Toccata & Fugue Org, BWV 565; Toccata, Adagio & Fugue Org, BWV 564; Trio Org, BWV 583; Trio Sons Org HAM 12-▲ 290772 [ADD] (71.97)

W. Rübsam (org) *(rec Apr 1992)* ("The Art of Fugue, Vol. 2") † Art of the Fugue (sels); Passacaglia & Fugue Org, BWV 582 NXIN ▲ 550704 [DDD] (5.97)

O. Vernet (org) ("The Organ Works, Vol. 2: 1708-1717") † Chorales (miscellaneous); Chorales Org; Fant & Fugue Org, BWV 537; Fant Org, BWV 562; Fant Org, BWV 572; Preludes & Fugues, BWV 531-552; Toccata, Adagio & Fugue Org, BWV 564 LIDI 3-▲ 104046 [DDD]

H. Walcha (org) *(rec St. Laurenskerk Org at St. Laurens Church, Al, Sept 1956, Sept 1962)* † Preludes & Fugues, BWV 531-552; Schübler Chorale Preludes; Toccata & Fugue Org, BWV 565; Trio Sons Org DEUT (The Originals) ▲ 457704 [ADD] (11.97)

Partite diverse sopra Christ, der du bist der helle Tag for Organ, BWV 766

C. Herrick (org) *(rec Metzler org, St. Nikolaus Church, Bremgarten, Switzerland, May 1991)* † Canonic Vars on "Von Himmel hoch", BWV 769; Partite diverse sopra, BWV 767; Partite diverse sopra, BWV 768; Partite diverse sopra, BWV 770 HYP ▲ 66455 [DDD] (18.97)

B. Lagacé (org) *(rec Montreal, Canada, Mar 1996)* ("Toccata in d & Other Early Works") † Chorales (miscellaneous); Org Music (misc colls); Pastorale Org, BWV 590; Prelude & Fugue Org, BWV 566; Toccata & Fugue Org, BWV 565 FL ▲ 23091 [DDD] (16.97)

G. Leonhardt (org) *(rec Amsterdam, Netherlands, 1972-73)* ("Great Organ Works") † Canonic Vars on "Von Himmel hoch", BWV 769; Chorales (miscellaneous); Chorales Org; Fant Org, BWV 562; Fant Org, BWV 572; Fugue on "Meine Seele"; Orgelbüchlein; Partite diverse sopra, BWV 767; Preludes & Fugues, BWV 531-552; Toccata & Fugue Org, BWV 565 SNYC (Seon) 2-▲ 63185 [ADD] (7.97)

L. Rogg (org) *(rec Silbermann Org, Arlesheim, Switzerland)* † Allabreve, BWV 589; Canonic Vars on "Von Himmel hoch", BWV 769; Canzona; Chorales Org; Clavier-Übung III; Fant & Fugue Org, BWV 537; Fant & Fugue, BWV 542; Fant Org, BWV 562; Fant Org, BWV 572; Orgelbüchlein; Partite diverse sopra, BWV 767; Partite diverse sopra, BWV 768; Pastorale Org, BWV 590; Prelude & Fugue Org, BWV 566; Preludes & Fugues, BWV 531-552; Schübler Chorale Preludes; Toccata & Fugue Org, BWV 565; Toccata, Adagio & Fugue Org, BWV 564; Trio Org, BWV 583; Trio Sons Org HAM 12-▲ 290772 [ADD] (71.97)

I. Sokol (org) † Fant Org, BWV 570; Fugue on a theme by Legrenzi, BWV 574; Pedal Exercise Org, BWV 598; Prelude & Fugue Org, BWV 566; Preludes & Fugues, BWV 531-552 PC ▲ 267168 [DDD] (2.97)

O. Vernet (org) ("The Organ Works: Vol. 1, 1700-1708") † Chorales (miscellaneous); Fant & Imitatio Org, BWV 563; Fant Org, BWV 570; Org Music (comp); Partite diverse sopra, BWV 767; Passacaglia & Fugue Org, BWV 582; Prelude Org, BWV 568; Prelude Org, BWV 569; Preludes & Fugues, BWV 531-552; Toccata & Fugue Org, BWV 565 LIDI 3-▲ 104037 (47.97)

Partite diverse sopra O Gott, du frommer Gott for Organ, BWV 767

J. Guillou (org) ("The Organ Works of Bach, Vol. 1") † Fugue on a theme by Corelli, BWV 579; Org Music (comp); Orgelbüchlein; Preludes & Fugues, BWV 531-552; Trio Sons Org DOR ▲ 90111 [DDD] (16.97)

C. Herrick (org) *(rec Metzler org, St. Nikolaus Church, Bremgarten, Switzerland, May 1991)* † Canonic Vars on "Von Himmel hoch", BWV 769; Partite diverse sopra, BWV 766; Partite diverse sopra, BWV 768; Partite diverse sopra, BWV 770 HYP ▲ 66455 [DDD] (18.97)

S. Innocenti (org) *(rec Serassi Org in Church of St. Luborio in Colorno)* † Pastorale Org, BWV 590; G. Böhm:Capriccio; Prelude, Fugue & Postlude Org; Daquin:Nouveau livre de noëls, Op. 2; Frescobaldi:Canzoni alla francese; Toccata VI; Merula:Capricio; Son cromatica LBD ▲ 14 (16.97)

T. Koopman (org) † Fant & Fugue, BWV 542; Toccata & Fugue Org, BWV 565 NOVA ▲ 150005 [DDD] (16.97)

B. Lagacé (org) † Chorale Preludes Org; Fants Hpd; Fugue on a theme by Legrenzi, BWV 574; Preludes & Fugues, BWV 531-552; Toccata, Adagio & Fugue Org, BWV 564; Von Himmel hoch, da komm ich her, BWV 701 FL ▲ 23094 [DDD] (16.97)

BACH, JOHANN SEBASTIAN (cont.)

Partite diverse sopra O Gott, du frommer Gott for Organ, BWV 767 (cont.)

G. Leonhardt (org) *(rec Amsterdam, Netherlands, 1972-73)* ("Great Organ Works") † Canonic Vars on "Von Himmel hoch", BWV 769; Chorales (miscellaneous); Chorales Org; Fant Org, BWV 562; Fant Org, BWV 572; Fugue on "Meine Seele"; Orgelbüchlein; Partite diverse sopra, BWV 766; Preludes & Fugues, BWV 531-552; Toccata & Fugue Org, BWV 565 SNYC (Seon) 2-▲ 63185 [ADD] (7.97)

L. Rogg (org) *(rec Silbermann Org, Arlesheim, Switzerland)* † Allabreve, BWV 589; Canonic Vars on "Von Himmel hoch", BWV 769; Canzona; Chorales Org; Clavier-Übung III; Fant & Fugue Org, BWV 537; Fant & Fugue, BWV 542; Fant Org, BWV 562; Fant Org, BWV 572; Orgelbüchlein; Partite diverse sopra, BWV 766; Partite diverse sopra, BWV 768; Pastorale Org, BWV 590; Prelude & Fugue Org, BWV 566; Preludes & Fugues, BWV 531-552; Schübler Chorale Preludes; Toccata & Fugue Org, BWV 565; Toccata, Adagio & Fugue Org, BWV 564; Trio Org, BWV 583; Trio Sons Org HAM 12-▲ 290772 [ADD] (71.97)

O. Vernet (org) ("The Organ Works: Vol. 1, 1700-1708") † Chorales (miscellaneous); Fant & Imitatio Org, BWV 563; Fant Org, BWV 570; Org Music (comp); Partite diverse sopra, BWV 766; Passacaglia & Fugue Org, BWV 582; Prelude Org, BWV 568; Prelude Org, BWV 569; Preludes & Fugues, BWV 531-552; Toccata & Fugue Org, BWV 565 LIDI 3-▲ 104037 (47.97)

Passacaglia & Fugue in c for Organ, BWV 582

G. D. Agostino (org) *(rec Washington D.C., United States of America, Sept 20-24, 1994)* ("Monuments of Germanic Music") † Org Music (misc colls); Karg-Elert:Pastels, Op. 96; Liszt:Am Grabe Richard Wagners Str Qt, S.135; Consolations (6), S.172; Prelude & Fugue on the name B-A-C-H, S.260; R. Wagner:Meistersinger (ov) CENT ▲ 2246 [DDD] (16.97)

E. P. Biggs (org) † Toccata & Fugue Org, BWV 565; Toccata, Adagio & Fugue Org, BWV 564 SNYC ▲ 42644 [ADD] (11.97)

E. P. Biggs (org) † Pastorale Org, BWV 590; Preludes & Fugues, BWV 531-552; Toccata & Fugue Org, BWV 565; Chopin:Sylphides; Delibes:Coppélia (suite); Sylvia (suite); P. Tchaikovsky:Nutcracker Suite, Op. 71a SNYC (Essential Classics) ▲ 46551 [ADD] (7.97) ▮ 46551 [ADD] (3.98)

K. Bowyer (org) *(rec Sct. Hans Church Odense, Denmark, Mar 13-18, 1997)* ("The Works for Organ, Vol. 9") † Clavier-Übung III; Cons solo Hpd; Org Music (comp) NIMB 2-▲ 5561 [DDD] (23.97)

M. Dupré (org) *(rec Queen's Hall & Alexandra Place orgs, England, June 1929)* ("Bach; The Art of Marcel Dupré") † Cant 29; Clavier-Übung III; Fant & Fugue Org, BWV 537; Orgelbüchlein; Preludes & Fugues, BWV 531-552; Schübler Chorale Preludes; Suite 3 Orch, BWV 1068; Toccata & Fugue Org, BWV 538; Trio Sons Org PHS ▲ 9863 (17.97)

H. Fagius (org) ("Vol. 5") † Org Music (comp); Preludes & Fugues, BWV 531-552; Trio Sons Org BIS 2-▲ 379 [DDD] (69.97)

V. Fox (org) *(rec Dec 20, 1973)* ("Heavy Organ") † Clavier-Übung III; Org Music (misc colls); Toccata & Fugue Org, BWV 538; Toccata & Fugue Org, BWV 565 RCAV (Gold Seal) ▲ 68816 [ADD] (11.97)

A. Heiler (org) *(rec 1964)* † Org Music (misc colls); Preludes & Fugues, BWV 531-552; Toccata & Fugue Org, BWV 565 VC (The Bach Guild) ▲ 2005 [ADD] (13.97)

A. Heiller (org) † Nun komm der Heiden Heiland, BWV 699; Orgelbüchlein; Preludes & Fugues, BWV 531-552; Toccata & Fugue Org, BWV 565 AURC ▲ 145 (5.97)

P. Hurford (org) *(rec Toronto, Canada, 1975; 1977-79)* † Chorales Org; Fant & Fugue Org, BWV 537; Fant & Fugue, BWV 542; Fant Org, BWV 562; Fant Org, BWV 572; Org Music (misc colls); Preludes & Fugues, BWV 531-552; Schübler Chorale Preludes; Toccata & Fugue Org, BWV 538; Toccata & Fugue Org, BWV 565; Toccata, Adagio & Fugue Org, BWV 564 PLON 2-▲ 43485 [ADD] (17.97)

D. Joyce (org) † Org Music (misc colls); Pastorale Org, BWV 590; Preludes & Fugues, BWV 531-552; C. Franck:Prélude, fugue et var, Op. 18; Son Vn, M.8 TIT ▲ 164 [DDD]

H. Kästner (org) *(rec St. Georgenkirche Silbermann Org, Rötha, Germany)* ("Kantors and Organists at St. Thomas, Leipzig") † Preludes & Fugues, BWV 531-552; Calvisius:Unser Leben währet siebnzig Jahr; Kuhnau:Tristis est anima mea; J. H. Schein:Israels Brünnlein CATA ▲ 57619 [AAD] (15.97)

P. Kee (org) ("Piet Kee Plays Bach, Vol. 2") † Fant Org, BWV 572; Org Music (misc colls); Pastorale Org, BWV 590; Preludes & Fugues, BWV 531-552 CHN (Chaconne) ▲ 510 [DDD] (17.97)

T. Koopman (org) *(rec Maassluis Grote Kerk, June 1983)* † Fant Org, BWV 572; Org Music (misc colls); Pastorale Org, BWV 590; Prelude Org, BWV 569; Toccata & Fugue Org, BWV 538; Toccata & Fugue Org, BWV 565 PARC ▲ 47292 [DDD] (9.97)

T. Koopman (org) † Chorales Org; Fant Org, BWV 562; Liebster Jesu, wir sind hier, BWV 730; Liebster Jesu, wir sind hier, BWV 731; Org Music (misc colls); Pastorale Org, BWV 590; Preludes & Fugues, BWV 531-552; Wir glauben all an einen Gott, Vater, BWV 740 NOVA ▲ 150052 [DDD] (16.97)

W. Kraft (org) *(rec 1965)* † Chorales (miscellaneous); Cons Org; Fant Org, BWV 562; Fugue on a theme by Legrenzi, BWV 574; Org Music (misc colls); Orgelbüchlein; Preludes & Fugues, BWV 531-552; Toccata & Fugue Org, BWV 538; Toccata, Adagio & Fugue Org, BWV 564 VB2 2-▲ 5059 [ADD] (9.97)

S. Lautenbacher (vn), D. Vorholz (vn), G. Kehr (cnd), Mainz CO ("The Story of Bach in Words and Music") † Cant 211; Cant 57; Con Vns; Con 2 Vn; Life & Music of Bach; Magnificat, BWV 243; Mass in b, BWV 232; Schübler Chorale Preludes; St. John Passion, BWV 245; Toccata & Fugue Org, BWV 565 MMD (Music Masters) ▲ 8500 [ADD] (3.97) ▮ 8500 [ADD] (2.98)

J. Lippincott (org) *(rec Durham NC, Flentrop Org)* ("Toccatas & Fugues by Bach") † Preludes & Fugues, BWV 531-552; Toccata & Fugue Org, BWV 538; Toccata & Fugue Org, BWV 565; Toccata, Adagio & Fugue Org, BWV 564 GOT ▲ 49093 [DDD] (17.97)

D. Major (org) *(rec Great Org Washington Nat'l Cathedral, DC)* ("Masterworks by Bach") † Chorales Org; Pastorale Org, BWV 590; Preludes & Fugues, BWV 531-552; Toccata & Fugue Org, BWV 538 GOT ▲ 49104 (17.97)

D. Meylan (org) *(rec Porrentruy, Switzerland)* ("Hommage à Albert Schweitzer") CASC ▲ 1047 (16.97)

P. Monteux (cnd), San Francisco SO [arr for orch] ("Vol 1") † Beethoven:Ruinen von Athen (ov); Sym 4; Sym 8 RCAV (Gold Seal; Pierre Monteux Edition) ▲ 61892 (11.97)

A. Newman (org) † Chorales (miscellaneous); Fant & Fugue Org, BWV 537; Jesus, meine Zuversicht, BWV 728; Org Music (misc colls); Orgelbüchlein; Preludes & Fugues, BWV 531-552; Toccata & Fugue Org, BWV 538 VB2 2-▲ 5100 [ADD] (9.97)

A. Newman (org) ("Bach at Lejansk") † Fant & Fugue, BWV 542; Toccata, Adagio & Fugue Org, BWV 564 HEL ▲ 1010 (10.97)

A. Newman (org) ("The Brook & the Well-Spring") † Brandenburg Con 5, BWV 1050; Cant 147; Con 1 Vn; Goldberg Vars, BWV 988; Mass in b, BWV 232; Sons & Partitas Vn; St. John Passion (sels); Wohltemperirte Clavier SNYC (NPR-Milestone of the Millennium) ▲ 60990 [DDD] (11.97)

Oregon Symphony Horns *(rec Sept 1994)* ("Oregon Symphony Horns & Friends") † Cant 140; Music of Bach; Toccata & Fugue Org, BWV 538; Mendelssohn (-Bartholdy):Anthems (6), Op. 79; Psalms (3), Op. 78 CENT ▲ 2344 [DDD] (16.97)

E. Ormandy (cnd), Philadelphia Orch [arr Ormandy] *(rec 1960)* † Brandenburg Con 5, BWV 1050; Cant 140; Toccata & Fugue Org, BWV 565; Toccata, Adagio & Fugue Org, BWV 564; W. F. Bach:Sinf Orch, F.64 SNYC (Masterworks Heritage) 2-▲ 62345 [ADD] (25.97)

R. Pikler (cnd), Sydney SO ("Orchestral Transcriptions by Leopold Stokowski") † Clavier-Übung III; Music of Bach; Toccata & Fugue Org, BWV 565; Toccata, Adagio & Fugue Org, BWV 564 CHN (Collect) ▲ 6532 [ADD] (12.97)

K. Richter (org) *(rec Org of Victoria Hall Geneva)* † Fant & Fugue, BWV 542; Toccata & Fugue Org, BWV 565 PLON (Classic Sound) ▲ 455291 (11.97)

C. Rieger (org) *(rec St. Landolin Ettenheim-Münster)* ("5 Versions of Passacaglia, BWV 582") SIGM ▲ 9300 [DDD] (17.97)

H. Rilling (org), J. E. Hansen (org), H. Otto (org), K. Vad (org) † Cant 147; Org Music (misc colls); Orgelbüchlein; Schübler Chorale Preludes; Toccata & Fugue Org, BWV 565; Trio Org, BWV 583 DNN ▲ 8009 [DDD] (10.97)

L. Rogg (org) *(rec historic org, Alesheim, France)* † Preludes & Fugues, BWV 531-552; Schübler Chorale Preludes; Toccata & Fugue Org, BWV 565 HMA ▲ 190771 (9.97)

B. Römer (org) HANS ▲ 98967 [DDD] (15.97)

W. Rübsam (org) *(rec Apr 1992)* ("The Art of Fugue, Vol. 2") † Art of the Fugue (sels); Partite diverse sopra, BWV 768 NXIN ▲ 550704 [DDD] (5.97)

W. Rübsam (org) ("The Great Organ Works") † Cant 147; Org Music (misc colls); Orgelbüchlein; Preludes & Fugues, BWV 531-552; Toccata & Fugue Org, BWV 565; Toccata, Adagio & Fugue Org, BWV 564 NXIN ▲ 553859 [DDD] (5.97)

M. Sander (org) *(rec Wagner Organ at Nidaros Cathedral, Trondheim, Norway)* ("Pathos und Freude") † Chorales Org; Cons Org; Preludes & Fugues, BWV 531-552; Trio Sons Org FERM ▲ 20028 [DDD] (16.97)

D. Sanger (org) ("Organ Music, Vol. 6") † Cons Org; Org Music (misc colls); Pastorale Org, BWV 590; Schübler Chorale Preludes MER ▲ 84326 [DDD] (16.97)

F. Swann (org) † C. Franck:Chorales Org, M.38-40; M. S. Wright:Intro, Passacaglia & Fugue GOT ▲ 49049 [DDD] (17.97)

A. Toscanini (cnd), NBC SO [orchd] *(rec 1936-47)* ("Baroque & Classic Repertoire") † Brandenburg Con 2, BWV 1047; Toccata & Fugue Org, BWV 565; J. Haydn:Sym 31 IN ▲ 1397 (15.97)

K. van Tricht (org) *(rec Sauer Org Bremen Cathedral, 1987)* † Fant Org, BWV 572 MDG ▲ 3180241 [DDD] (17.97)

BACH, JOHANN SEBASTIAN (cont.)

Passacaglia & Fugue in c for Organ, BWV 582 (cont.)

O. Vernet (org) ("The Organ Works: Vol. 1, 1700-1708") † Chorales (miscellaneous); Fant & Imitatio Org, BWV 563; Fant Org, BWV 570; Org Music (comp); Partite diverse sopra, BWV 766; Partite diverse sopra, BWV 767; Prelude Org, BWV 568; Prelude Org, BWV 569; Preludes & Fugues, BWV 531-552; Toccata & Fugue Org, BWV 565 LIDI 3-▲ 104037 (47.97)

H. Walcha (org) *(rec Great Org, St. Laurenskerk Alkmaar & Strassburg, Germany, 1956-70)* † Canonic Vars on "Von Himmel hoch", BWV 769; Fant Org, BWV 572; Org Music (misc colls); Preludes & Fugues, BWV 531-552; Schübler Chorale Preludes; Toccata & Fugue Org, BWV 538; Toccata & Fugue Org, BWV 565; Trio Sons Org DEUT 2-▲ 453064 [ADD] (17.97)

Pastorale in F for Organ, BWV 590 (ca 1710)

A. Bárta (org) † Chorales (miscellaneous); Chorales Org; Cons Org; Preludes & Fugues, BWV 531-552; Toccata & Fugue Org, BWV 565; Toccata, Adagio & Fugue Org, BWV 564 SUR ▲ 111289 [DDD]

E. P. Biggs (org) † Passacaglia & Fugue Org, BWV 582; Preludes & Fugues, BWV 531-552; Toccata & Fugue Org, BWV 565; Chopin:Sylphides; Delibes:Coppélia (suite); Sylvia (suite); P. Tchaikovsky:Nutcracker Suite, Op. 71a SNYC (Essential Classics) ▲ 46551 [ADD] (7.97) ▮ 46551 [ADD] (3.98)

K. Bowyer (org) *(rec Odense, Denmark)* ("The Works for Organ, Vol. 1") † Cons Org; Org Music (comp); Toccata & Fugue Org, BWV 565; Trio Sons Org NIMB ▲ 5280 (16.97)

J. Guillou (org) *(rec Aug 1990)* ("The Organ Works of Bach, Vol. 5") † Chorales (miscellaneous); Chorales Org; Fugue on a theme by Legrenzi, BWV 574; Org Music (comp); Prelude & Fugue Org, BWV 566; Preludes & Fugues, BWV 531-552; Schübler Chorale Preludes DOR ▲ 90152 [DDD] (16.97)

S. Innocenti (org) *(rec Serassi Org in Church of St. Luborio in Colorno)* † Partite diverse sopra, BWV 767; G. Böhm:Capriccio; Prelude, Fugue & Postlude Org; Daquin:Nouveau livre de noëls, Op. 2; Frescobaldi:Canzoni alla francese; Toccata VI; Merula:Capricio; Son cromatica LBD ▲ 14 (16.97)

D. Joyce (org) † Org Music (misc colls); Passacaglia & Fugue Org, BWV 582; Preludes & Fugues, BWV 531-552; C. Franck:Prélude, fugue et var, Op. 18; Son Vn, M.8 TIT ▲ 164 [DDD]

P. Kee (org) ("Piet Kee Plays Bach, Vol. 2") † Fant Org, BWV 572; Org Music (misc colls); Passacaglia & Fugue Org, BWV 582; Preludes & Fugues, BWV 531-552 CHN (Chaconne) ▲ 510 [DDD] (17.97)

T. Koopman (org) *(rec Maassluis Grote Kerk, June 1983)* † Fant Org, BWV 572; Org Music (misc colls); Passacaglia & Fugue Org, BWV 582; Prelude Org, BWV 569; Toccata & Fugue Org, BWV 538; Toccata & Fugue Org, BWV 565 PARC ▲ 47292 [DDD] (9.97)

T. Koopman (org) † Chorales Org; Fant Org, BWV 562; Liebster Jesu, wir sind hier, BWV 730; Liebster Jesu, wir sind hier, BWV 731; Org Music (misc colls); Passacaglia & Fugue Org, BWV 582; Preludes & Fugues, BWV 531-552; Wir glauben all an einen Gott, Vater, BWV 740 NOVA ▲ 150052 [DDD] (16.97)

B. Lagacé (org) *(rec Church of the Immaculate Conception Montreal, Canada, Mar 1996)* ("Toccata in d & Other Early Works") † Chorales (miscellaneous); Org Music (misc colls); Partite diverse sopra, BWV 766; Prelude & Fugue Org, BWV 566; Toccata & Fugue Org, BWV 565 FL ▲ 23091 [DDD] (16.97)

D. Major (org) *(rec Great Org Washington Nat'l Cathedral, DC)* ("Masterworks by Bach") † Chorales Org; Passacaglia & Fugue Org, BWV 582; Preludes & Fugues, BWV 531-552; Toccata & Fugue Org, BWV 538 GOT ▲ 49104 (17.97)

S. Preston (org) † Canonic Vars on "Von Himmel hoch", BWV 769; Fant Org, BWV 572; Preludes & Fugues, BWV 531-552; Toccata & Fugue Org, BWV 565 PARC ▲ 27668 [DDD] (16.97)

L. Rogg (org) *(rec Silbermann Org, Arlesheim, Switzerland)* † Allabreve, BWV 589; Canonic Vars on "Von Himmel hoch", BWV 769; Canzona; Chorales Org; Clavier-Übung III; Fant & Fugue Org, BWV 537; Fant & Fugue, BWV 542; Fant Org, BWV 562; Fant Org, BWV 572; Orgelbüchlein; Partite diverse sopra, BWV 766; Partite diverse sopra, BWV 767; Partite diverse sopra, BWV 768; Prelude & Fugue Org, BWV 566; Preludes & Fugues, BWV 531-552; Schübler Chorale Preludes; Toccata & Fugue Org, BWV 565; Toccata, Adagio & Fugue Org, BWV 564; Trio Org, BWV 583; Trio Sons Org HAM 12-▲ 290772 [ADD] (71.97)

P. Rouet (org) *(rec Sept 1992)* ("The Complete Toccatas & Fugues for Organ") † Canonic Vars on "Von Himmel hoch", BWV 769; Fant Org, BWV 572; Org Music (misc colls); Preludes & Fugues Org GALL ▲ 720 [DDD]

W. Rübsam (org) † Toccata & Fugue Org, BWV 565 NXIN ▲ 550184 [DDD] (5.97)

D. Sanger (org) ("Organ Music, Vol. 6") † Cons Org; Org Music (misc colls); Passacaglia & Fugue Org, BWV 582; Schübler Chorale Preludes MER ▲ 84326 [DDD] (16.97)

D. Schrader (org) ("The Complete Fantasies, Fantasies & Fugues, & Isolated Fugues for Organ") † Fant & Fugue Org, BWV 537; Fant & Fugue, BWV 542; Fant & Imitatio Org, BWV 563; Fant Org, BWV 562; Fant Org, BWV 570; Fant Org, BWV 572; Org Music (misc colls); Toccata, Adagio & Fugue Org, BWV 564 CED ▲ 12 [DDD] (16.97)

Pedal Exercise in g for Organ, BWV 598

I. Sokol (org) † Fant Org, BWV 570; Fugue on a theme by Legrenzi, BWV 574; Partite diverse sopra, BWV 766; Prelude & Fugue Org, BWV 566; Preludes & Fugues, BWV 531-552 PC ▲ 267168 [DDD] (2.97)

Praeludium in b for Harpsichord, BWV 923

P. Ayrton (hpd) ("Transcriptions & Arrangements of Works by His Contemporaries") † Cons solo Hpd; Cons Org GLOE ▲ 5166 (16.97)

Prelude & Fughetta in d for Keyboard, BWV 899

G. Gould (hpd) ("The Glenn Gould Edition") † Org Music (misc colls); Partitas Hpd; Prelude & Fughetta Kbd, BWV 902a; Preludes & Fugues Hpd; Preludes Hpd; Preludes Kbd SNYC 2-▲ 52597 (31.97)

Prelude & Fughetta in G for Keyboard, BWV 902 (ca 1720)

W. Rübsam (pno) *(rec May 1992)* † Capriccio Departure, BWV 992; Partitas Hpd NXIN ▲ 550692 (5.97)

Prelude & Fughetta in G for Keyboard [variant of BWV 902], BWV 902a (ca 1720)

G. Gould (hpd) ("The Glenn Gould Edition") † Org Music (misc colls); Partitas Hpd; Prelude & Fughetta Kbd, BWV 899; Preludes & Fugues Hpd; Preludes Hpd; Preludes Kbd SNYC 2-▲ 52597 (31.97)

Preludes & Fugues for Harpsichord

J. E. Dähler (hpd)—Preludes Hpd (5) [BWV 939, No. 1 in C; BWV 941, No. 3 in e; BWV 942, No. 4 in a] *(rec Berne Apr. 1968 & Thun, Aug 1971)* † Inventions Hpd; Prelude Lt, BWV 999; Preludes Hpd (5); Preludes Kbd CLAV (Favor Collection) ▲ 170 [ADD] (16.97)

G. Gould (hpd)—Prelude & Fughetta Kbd, BWV 900; Prelude & Fugue Hpd, BWV 895; Prelude & Fughetta Kbd, BWV 902 ("The Glenn Gould Edition") † Org Music (misc colls); Partitas Hpd; Prelude & Fughetta Kbd, BWV 899; Prelude & Fughetta Kbd, BWV 902a; Preludes Hpd; Preludes Kbd SNYC 2-▲ 52597 (31.97)

P. Hantaï (hpd) † Con Fl, Vn & Hpd, BWV 1044; Con 1 Hpd, BWV 1052; Con 3 Hpd, BWV 1054 ASTR ▲ 8523 (18.97)

J. C. Martins (pno)—Prelude & Fughetta Kbd, BWV 899; Prelude & Fugue Hpd, BWV 895; Fugue Kbd, BWV 952; Fughetta, BWV 961; Prelude & Fughetta Kbd, BWV 900 *(rec Sofia Bulgaria, Apr 1997)* ("Complete Keyboard Works, Vol. 15") † Fant & Fugue Hpd, BWV 904; Fant Kbd, BWV 917; Fant Kbd, BWV 918; Fant Kbd, BWV 919; Fugue Kbd, BWV 944; Org Music (misc colls); Prelude & Fugue Hpd, BWV 894; Prelude Kbd, BWV 922 ERTO ▲ 42052 [DDD] (16.97)

Prelude & Fugue in a for Harpsichord, BWV 894 (ca 1708-14)

J. C. Martins (pno) *(rec Sofia, Bulgaria, Apr 1997)* ("Complete Keyboard Works, Vol. 15") † Fant & Fugue Hpd, BWV 904; Fant Kbd, BWV 917; Fant Kbd, BWV 918; Fant Kbd, BWV 919; Fugue Kbd, BWV 944; Org Music (misc colls); Prelude Kbd, BWV 922; Preludes & Fugues Hpd ERTO ▲ 42052 [DDD] (16.97)

Preludes & Fugues (22) for Organ, BWV 531-552

A. Bárta (org)—BWV 541, in G † Chorales (miscellaneous); Chorales Org; Cons Org; Pastorale Org, BWV 590; Toccata & Fugue Org, BWV 565; Toccata, Adagio & Fugue Org, BWV 564 SUR ▲ 111289 [DDD]

E. P. Biggs (org) † Fant Org, BWV 572; Toccata & Fugue Org, BWV 538; Toccata & Fugue Org, BWV 565; Toccata, Adagio & Fugue Org, BWV 564 SNYC ▲ 42643 [ADD] (11.97)

E. P. Biggs (org)—BWV 542, in g; BWV 543, in a; BWV 544, in b; BWV 545, in C † Passacaglia & Fugue Org, BWV 582; Pastorale Org, BWV 590; Toccata & Fugue Org, BWV 565; Chopin:Sylphides; Delibes:Coppélia (suite); Sylvia (suite); P. Tchaikovsky:Nutcracker Suite, Op. 71a SNYC (Essential Classics) ▲ 46551 [ADD] (7.97) ▮ 46551 [ADD] (3.98)

K. Bowyer (org)—BWV 539, in d *(rec Odense, Denmark)* ("The Works for Organ, Volume 5") † Cons Org; Org Music (comp) NIMB ▲ 5400 (16.97)

K. Bowyer (org)—BWV 544, in b; BWV 547, in C; BWV 531, in C ("Works for Organ, Vol. 8") † Cons solo Hpd; Fant & Fugue Org, BWV 537; Fugue on a theme by Legrenzi, BWV 574; Org Music (comp); Toccata & Fugue Org, BWV 538; Trio Son Fls, BWV 1039; Trio Va Kbd, BWV 1027a NIMB 2-▲ 5500 [DDD] (23.97)

K. Bowyer (org)—BWV 534, in f; BWV 543, in a ("Complete Works for Organ, Vol. 3") † Cons Org; Partite diverse sopra, BWV 768; Trio Org, BWV 585 NIMB ▲ 5290 [DDD] (16.97)

K. Bowyer (org)—BWV 532, in D; BWV 536, in A; BWV 541, in G *(rec Odense, Denmark)* ("The Works for Organ, Vol. 2") † Chorales (miscellaneous); Org Music (comp); Trio Sons Org NIMB ▲ 5289 (16.97)

K. Bowyer (org)—Preludes & Fugues, BWV 531-552 [BWV 535, in g] *(rec Odense Denmark, Mar 23-24, 1993)* ("The Works for Organ, Vol. 6") † Org Music (comp); Prelude & Fugue Org, BWV 566; Toccata, Adagio & Fugue Org, BWV 564; Trio Son Org, BWV 584; Trio Sons Org NIMB ▲ 5423 [DDD] (16.97)

BACH, JOHANN SEBASTIAN (cont.)

Preludes & Fugues (22) for Organ, BWV 531-552 (cont.)

C. Brembeck (org)—BWV 549, in c *(rec Lahn-Itzgrund Herbst Org, Intzgrund, Germany, Oct 1988)* ("Lahm-Itzgrund Herbst-Orgel") † Chorale Preludes Org; Chorales Org; Fant & Imitatio Org, BWV 563; Org Music (misc colls); Partite diverse sopra, BWV 770; Trio Org, BWV 583; J. Lorenz Bach:Prelude & Fugue Org; W. H. Pachelbel:Musicalisches Vergnügen CAPO ▲ 10351 [DDD] (11.97)

D. Briggs (org)—BWV 541, in G; BWV 552, in E♭ ("Popular Organ Music, Vol. 2") † J. Alain:Jardin suspendu, AWV 63; P. Cochereau:Boléro on a Theme of Charles Racquet; Dukas:L'Apprenti sorcier; C. Franck:Pièces (3) Org, M.37; P. Tchaikovsky:Nutcracker Suite, Op. 71a PRIO ▲ 568 [DDD] (16.97)

F. Chaffiaud (pno)—BWV 543, in a † Chromatic Fant & Fugue, BWV 903; French Suites; Toccata, Adagio & Fugue Org, BWV 564; Wohltemperirte Clavier MED7 ▲ 141339 [DDD] (18.97)

M. Dupré (org)—BWV 541, in G; BWV 546, in c; BWV 548, in e, "Wedge" *(rec Queen's Hall & Alexandra Place orgs, England, Sept 10, 1930)* ("Bach; The Art of Marcel Dupré") † Cant 29; Clavier-Übung III; Fant & Fugue Org, BWV 537; Orgelbüchlein; Passacaglia & Fugue Org, BWV 582; Schübler Chorale Preludes; Suite 3 Orch, BWV 1068; Toccata & Fugue Org, BWV 538; Trio Sons Org PHS ▲ 9863 (17.97)

M. Eisenberg (org)—BWV 546, in c; BWV 544, in b; BWV 541, in G; BWV 548, in e, "Wedge" † Chorales Org; Org Music (misc colls) CAPO ▲ 10038 [DDD] (11.97)

H. Fagius (org)—BWV 547, in C; BWV 539, in d; BWV 545, in C; BWV 540, in F ("Vol. 7") † Canonic Vars on "Von Himmel hoch", BWV 769; Chorales (miscellaneous); Cons Org; Fugue on a theme by Legrenzi, BWV 574; Fugue Org, BWV 577; Fugue Org, BWV 578; Org Music (comp); Org Music (misc colls); Trio Org, BWV 583 BIS 2-▲ 439 [DDD] (69.97)

H. Fagius (org)—BWV 533, in e; BWV 549, in c; BWV 550, in G ("Vol. 5") † Org Music (comp); Passacaglia & Fugue Org, BWV 582; Trio Sons Org BIS 2-▲ 379 [DDD] (69.97)

H. Fagius (org)—BWV 539, in d; BWV 541, in G ("Vol. 4") BIS 2-▲ 343 (69.97)

H. Fagius (org)—BWV 548, in e, "Wedge"; BWV 544, in b ("Vol. 6") † Chorales (miscellaneous); Fant & Fugue Org, BWV 537; Fant Org, BWV 562; Org Music (comp); Partite diverse sopra, BWV 768; Toccata & Fugue Org, BWV 565; Trio Sons Org BIS 2-▲ 397 [DDD] (69.97)

H. Fagius (org)—BWV 534, in f; BWV 543, in a; BWV 546, in c ("Vol. 9") † Chorales (miscellaneous); Org Music (misc colls); Trio Sons Org BIS ▲ 445 [DDD] (17.97)

H. Fagius (org)—BWV 531, in C; BWV 532, in D; BWV 535, in g; BWV 551, in a *(rec 1728 Cahman Org at Leufsta bruk, Sweden)* ("The Complete Organ Music, Vol. 2") † Chorales (miscellaneous); Cons Org; Org Music (comp); Trio Sons Org BIS 2-▲ 308 [DDD] (69.97)

E. Fischer (pno)—BWV 552, in E♭ [arr Bussoni for pno] *(rec 1933-37)* † Fant & Fugue Hpd, BWV 904; Wohltemperirte Clavier PHS 2-▲ 17 (33.97)

F. Friedrich (org)—BWV 545, in C; BWV 552, in E♭ † Canonic Vars on "Von Himmel hoch", BWV 769; Fant & Fugue Org, BWV 537; Kbd Music (misc); Org Music (misc colls) CAPO ▲ 10036 [DDD] (11.97)

Em. Gilels (pno)—BWV 532, in D *(rec 1968)* † French Suites; Beethoven:Con 4 Pno, Op. 58; Debussy:Images (6) Pno; W. A. Mozart:Con 27 Pno, K.595; M. Ravel:Alborada del gracioso; Jeux d'eau; Tombeau PPHI (Great Pianists of the 20th Century) ▲ 456793 (22.97)

J. Guillou (org)—BWV 548, in e, "Wedge"; BWV 549, in c *(rec Aug 1990)* † Chorales (miscellaneous); Chorales Org; Fant Org, BWV 562 DOR ▲ 90151 [DDD] (16.97)

J. Guillou (org) *(rec Cathedrale de Breda Netherlands, Nov 15-17, 1984)* ("Grandes Toccatas") † Prelude & Fugue Org, BWV 566; Toccata & Fugue Org, BWV 538; Toccata & Fugue Org, BWV 565; Toccata, Adagio & Fugue Org, BWV 564 PVY ▲ 730001 [DDD]

J. Guillou (org)—BWV 539, in d; BWV 547, in C *(rec Aug 1990)* ("The Organ Works of Bach, Vol. 5") † Chorales (miscellaneous); Chorales Org; Fugue on a theme by Legrenzi, BWV 574; Org Music (comp); Pastorale Org, BWV 590; Prelude & Fugue Org, BWV 566; Schübler Chorale Preludes DOR ▲ 90152 [DDD] (16.97)

J. Guillou (org)—BWV 544, in b *(rec Aug 1990)* † Chorales (miscellaneous); Chorales Org; Org Music (misc colls); Orgelbüchlein; Toccata & Fugue Org, BWV 565; Trio Sons Org DOR ▲ 90150 [DDD] (16.97)

J. Guillou (org)—BWV 543, in a; BWV 542, in g ("The Organ Works of Bach, Vol. 1") † Fugue on a theme by Corelli, BWV 579; Org Music (comp); Orgelbüchlein; Partite diverse sopra, BWV 767; Trio Sons Org DOR ▲ 90111 [DDD] (16.97)

F. Hauk (org)—BWV 532, in D *(rec Great Klais Org of Ingolstadt Münster, Germany)* ("Organ Works") † Chorales Org; Org Music (misc colls); Orgelbüchlein; Toccata & Fugue Org, BWV 565; Toccata, Adagio & Fugue Org, BWV 564 INMP ▲ 6600402

A. Heiler (org)—BWV 536, in A; BWV 548, in e, "Wedge" *(rec 1964)* † Org Music (misc colls); Passacaglia & Fugue Org, BWV 582; Toccata & Fugue Org, BWV 565 VC (The Bach Guild) ▲ 2005 [ADD] (13.97)

A. Heiller (org)—BWV 542, in g; BWV 548, in e, "Wedge" † Nun komm der Heiden Heiland, BWV 699; Orgelbüchlein; Passacaglia & Fugue Org, BWV 582; Toccata & Fugue Org, BWV 565 AURC ▲ 145 (5.97)

K. Heindel (org)—BWV 552, in E♭ *(rec Steinfeld Germany, Germany, Oct 5-7, 1992)* ("Bach at Steinfeld") † Cons Org; Org Music (misc colls); Trio Sons Org GAS ▲ 321 (16.97)

C. Herrick (org)—BWV 534, in f; BWV 536, in A; BWV 541, in G; BWV 543, in a; BWV 544, in b; BWV 545, in C; BWV 546, in c; BWV 547, in C; BWV 548, in e, "Wedge"; BWV 552, in E♭ † Fant & Fugue Org, BWV 537; Fant Org, BWV 562; Org Music (misc colls) HYP 2-▲ 66791 (36.97)

D. Higgs (org)—BWV 532, in D; BWV 541, in G † Cons Org; Org Music (misc colls); Trio Sons Org DLS ▲ 3048 [DDD] (14.97)

M. Horszowski (pno)—BWV 543, in a [trans Liszt] *(rec Tuscany, Italy, 1986)* ("Horszowski Bach Recital") † English Suites; Partitas Hpd; Wohltemperirte Clavier ARBT ▲ 113 (m) [ADD] (16.97)

F. Houbart (org)—BWV 534, in f *(rec J.F. Dupont org, Lessay Abbey, France, Oct 1995)* ("The Bach Family & the Organ") † Fant Org, BWV 572; Orgelbüchlein; W. F. Bach:Chorale-Preludes Org, F.38; J. Christoph Bach:Chorales Org; J. M. Bach:Chorales Org; J. B. Bach:Chorales Org; C.P.E. Bach:Fant & Fugue Org, H.103; Sons (4) Org, H.84-87 SOC ▲ 128 (16.97)

P. Hurford (org)—BWV 532, in D; BWV 543, in a; BWV 552, in E♭ *(rec Church of Our Lady of Sorrows Org Toronto, Canada, 1975; 1977-79)* † Chorales Org; Fant & Fugue Org, BWV 537; Fant & Fugue, BWV 542; Fant Org, BWV 562; Fant Org, BWV 572; Org Music (misc colls); Passacaglia & Fugue Org, BWV 582; Schübler Chorale Preludes; Toccata & Fugue Org, BWV 538; Toccata & Fugue Org, BWV 565; Toccata, Adagio & Fugue Org, BWV 564 PLON 2-▲ 43485 [ADD] (17.97)

K. Johannsen (org)—BWV 542, in g; BWV 532, in D; BWV 534, in f ("Edition Bachakademie, Vol. 93: Masterpieces from the Weimar Period") † Chorale Settings (misc); Partite diverse sopra, BWV 768 HANS ▲ 92093 [DDD] (11.97)

J. Johnson (org)—BWV 547, in C; BWV 548, in e, "Wedge" † Org Music (misc colls); Passacaglia & Fugue Org, BWV 582; Pastorale Org, BWV 590; C. Franck:Prélude, fugue et var, Op. 18; Son Vn, M.8 TIT ▲ 164 [DDD]

D. Joyce (org)—BWV 539, in d † Canonic Vars on "Von Himmel hoch", BWV 769; Partite diverse sopra, BWV 768; Prelude & Fugue Org, BWV 566; Trio Sons Org TIT ▲ 171 [DDD]

H. Kaiser (org)—BWV 531, in C † Chorale Preludes Org; F. Couperin:Pièces d'orgue consistantes en deux Messes; P. Hindemith:Sons Org; M. Reger:Org Music (misc colls); Widor:Org Music QUER ▲ 9817 (18.97)

H. Kästner (org)—BWV 547, in C † Org Music (misc colls); Orgelbüchlein; Toccata & Fugue Org, BWV 565 CAPO ▲ 10035 [DDD] (11.97)

H. Kästner (org), G. Lehotka (org)—BWV 542, in g; BWV 552, in E♭ † Chorales (miscellaneous); Clavier-Übung III; Fant & Fugue Org, BWV 561; Fugue Org, BWV 578; Orgelbüchlein; Toccata & Fugue Org, BWV 565 LALI ▲ 15507 [ADD] (3.97)

J. Kauffman (org)—BWV 541, in G ("Pâques") † Org Music (misc colls); Orgelbüchlein; A. Fleury:Org Music; J. Kauffman:Improv; G. Litaize:Liturgical Preludes; Nibelle:Tocatta; Plé:Regina Coeli SKAR ▲ 1957 (18.97)

P. Kee (org)—BWV 533, in e; BWV 546, in c † Chorales (miscellaneous); Orgelbüchlein; Buxtehude:Org Music (misc colls) CHN (Chaconne) ▲ 501 [DDD] (16.97)

P. Kee (org)—BWV 531, in C; BWV 544, in b ("Piet Kee Plays Bach, Vol. 1") † Org Music (misc colls); Orgelbüchlein CHN (Chaconne) ▲ 506 [DDD] (16.97)

P. Kee (org)—BWV 548, in e, "Wedge" ("Piet Kee Plays Bach, Vol. 2") † Fant Org, BWV 572; Org Music (misc colls); Passacaglia & Fugue Org, BWV 582; Pastorale Org, BWV 590 CHN (Chaconne) ▲ 510 [DDD] (17.97)

P. Kee (org)—BWV 534, in f *(rec Gabler org, Weingarten, Benedictine Abbey Basilika, Germany, Oct 1990)* † J. M. Bach:Org Music; Lebègue:Cloches; Murschhauser:Vars on 'Labt uns das Kindelein wiegen'; J. Pachelbel:Ciaccona in d; Ciaccona, POP 16; Fant in g; Prelude in d, POP 256; J. G. Walther:Vars on Jesu meine Freude Org CHN ▲ 520 [DDD] (16.97)

J. Köhler (org), H. Otto (org)—BWV 550, in G; BWV 534, in f; BWV 536, in A *(rec Fraureuth Church Org & Burgk Castle Org in Saxony, Germany)* ("Organ Works on Silbermann Organs, Vol. VIII") † Trio Sons Org BER 2-▲ 9368 (21.97)

D. Kollman-Sperger (org)—BWV 532, in D ("Famous European Organs:Krevese Gansen Orgel") † Org Music (misc colls); Buxtehude:Org Music (misc colls) CAPO ▲ 10506 [DDD] (11.97)

T. Koopman (org)—BWV 533, in e; BWV 547, in C; BWV 548, in e, "Wedge" † Trio Sons Org NOVA ▲ 150078 [DDD] (16.97)

T. Koopman (org)—BWV 543, in a † Clavier-Übung III; Org Music (misc colls); Partite diverse sopra, BWV 768; Toccata & Fugue Org, BWV 538; Trio Sons Org NOVA ▲ 150036 [DDD] (16.97)

BACH, JOHANN SEBASTIAN (cont.)

Preludes & Fugues (22) for Organ, BWV 531-552 (cont.)

T. Koopman (org)—BWV 543, in a *(rec 1988)* ("Orgelwerke") † Org Music (misc colls); Partite diverse sopra, BWV 768; Toccata & Fugue Org, BWV 538; Trio Sons Org NOVA ▲ 150130 [DDD] (69.97)

T. Koopman (org)—BWV 541, in G † Chorales Org; Fant Org, BWV 562; Liebster Jesu, wir sind hier, BWV 730; Liebster Jesu, wir sind hier, BWV 731; Org Music (misc colls); Passacaglia & Fugue Org, BWV 582; Pastorale Org, BWV 590; Wir glauben all an einen Gott, Vater, BWV 740 NOVA ▲ 150052 [DDD] (16.97)

W. Kraft (org)—BWV 550, in G; BWV 539, in d; BWV 540, in F *(rec 1965)* † Chorales (miscellaneous); Cons Org; Fant Org, BWV 562; Fugue on a theme by Legrenzi, BWV 574; Org Music (misc colls); Orgelbüchlein; Passacaglia & Fugue Org, BWV 582; Toccata & Fugue Org, BWV 538; Toccata, Adagio & Fugue Org, BWV 564 VB2 2-▲ 5059 [ADD] (9.97)

B. Lagacé (org)—BWV 533, in e † Chorale Preludes Org; Fants Hpd; Fugue on a theme by Legrenzi, BWV 574; Partite diverse sopra, BWV 767; Toccata, Adagio & Fugue Org, BWV 564; Von Himmel hoch, da komm ich her, BWV 701 FL ▲ 23094 [DDD] (16.97)

B. Lagacé (org)—BWV 544, in b; BWV 548, in e, "Wedge" ("Leipzig Chorales & Other Mature Works") † Chorale Settings (misc) FL 2-▲ 23112 [DDD] (31.97)

B. Lagacé (org)—BWV 545, in C ("Fantasy & Fugue in g & Other Mature Works") † Fant & Fugue Org, BWV 537; Fant & Fugue, BWV 542; Fant Org, BWV 562; Fugue on "Meine Seele"; Trio Org, BWV 583; Trio Sons Org FL ▲ 23096 [DDD] (16.97)

G. Leonhardt (org)—BWV 546, in c; BWV 547, in C; BWV 548, in e, "Wedge" *(rec Amsterdam, Netherlands, 1972-73)* ("Great Organ Works") † Canonic Vars on "Von Himmel hoch", BWV 769; Chorales (miscellaneous); Chorales Org; Fant Org, BWV 562; Fant Org, BWV 572; Fugue on "Meine Seele"; Orgelbüchlein; Partite diverse sopra, BWV 766; Partite diverse sopra, BWV 767; Toccata & Fugue Org, BWV 565 SNYC (Seon) 2-▲ 63185 [ADD] (7.97)

D. Lichti (b-bar), S. Laughton (nat tpt/tpt/nat tpt/), W. O'Meara (org), D. Campion (perc/timp/perc/timp)—BWV 536, in A; BWV 541, in G ("Baroque Banquet") † Music of Bach; J. Clarke:Prince of Denmark's March; P. Franceschini:Son à 7; G. F. Handel:Samson (sels); Suite Tpt & Org; A. Scarlatti:Endimione e Cintia; Telemann:Marches (12), TWV50: 31-42 (comp) OPDR ▲ 9303 [DDD] (16.97)

J. Lippincott (org) *(rec Durham NC, Flentrop Org)* ("Toccatas & Fugues by Bach") † Passacaglia & Fugue Org, BWV 582; Toccata & Fugue Org, BWV 538; Toccata & Fugue Org, BWV 565; Toccata, Adagio & Fugue Org, BWV 564 GOT ▲ 49093 [DDD] (17.97)

M. Lücker (org)—BWV 544, in b; BWV 548, in e, "Wedge" *(rec Sept 1998)* ("Edition Bachakademie, Vol. 100: Late Works from the Leipzig Period") † Canonic Vars on "Von Himmel hoch", BWV 769; Chorales Org; Fant Org, BWV 562; Musical Offering, BWV 1079 HANS ▲ 92100 [DDD] (11.97)

D. Major (org)—BWV 540, in F; BWV 533, in e; BWV 552, in E♭ *(rec Great Org Washington Nat'l Cathedral, DC)* ("Masterworks by Bach") † Chorales Org; Passacaglia & Fugue Org, BWV 582; Pastorale Org, BWV 590; Toccata & Fugue Org, BWV 538 GOT ▲ 49104 (17.97)

R. Marlow (org) *(rec Metzler org, Trinity College, Cambridge, England)* † Prelude & Fugue Org, BWV 566; Toccata & Fugue Org, BWV 538; Toccata & Fugue Org, BWV 565; Toccata, Adagio & Fugue Org, BWV 564 ASV ▲ 6231 (10.97)

M. Murray (org)—BWV 533, in e † M. Dupré:Org Music; C. Franck:Chorales Org, M.38-40; Org Music; Vierne:Meditation & Prelude, Op. 31; Widor:Sym 6 Org, Op. 42/2 TEL ▲ 80169 [DDD] (16.97)

M. Murray (org)—BWV 532, in D; BWV 534, in f; BWV 548, in e, "Wedge" *(rec Kampen; Great Schnitger Org St. Michael's, Zwolle, Germany)* ("Bach at Zwolle") † Chorales Org; Org Music (misc colls); Valet will ich dir geben, BWV 735 TEL ▲ 80385 [DDD] (16.97)

M. Murray (org)—BWV 531, in C; BWV 546, in c; BWV 547, in C; BWV 541, in G ("Bach Organ Blaster") † Cant 29; Cons Org; Fugue Org, BWV 578; Org Music (misc colls); Toccata & Fugue Org, BWV 565 TEL ▲ 80316 [DDD] (16.97)

A. Newman (org)—BWV 533, in e; BWV 534, in f; BWV 539, in d; BWV 542, in g; BWV 543, in a; BWV 544, in b; BWV 545, in C; BWV 547, in C; BWV 552, in E♭ ("24 Preludes & Fugues, Vol. 1") † Chorales (miscellaneous); Orgelbüchlein; Toccata & Fugue Org, BWV 565; Toccata, Adagio & Fugue Org, BWV 564 VB2 2-▲ 5013 [ADD] (9.97)

A. Newman (org)—BWV 532, in D; BWV 541, in G; BWV 548, in e, "Wedge"; BWV 536, in A; BWV 546, in c; BWV 549, in c; BWV 535, in g; BWV 531, in C; BWV 550, in G † Chorales (miscellaneous); Fant & Fugue Org, BWV 537; Jesus, meine Zuversicht, BWV 728; Org Music (misc colls); Orgelbüchlein; Passacaglia & Fugue Org, BWV 582; Toccata & Fugue Org, BWV 538 VB2 2-▲ 5100 [ADD] (9.97)

R. Noehren (org)—BWV 543, in a † Org Music (misc colls); J. Alain:Vars sur un thème de Clément Janequin; J. Brahms:Chorale Preludes Org, Op. 122; Karg-Elert:Fugue, Canzone und Epilog, Op. 85/3; Messiaen:Nativité du Seigneur; Widor:Sym 6 Org, Op. 42/2 DLS ▲ 3045 [DDD] (14.97)

H. Otto (org)—BWV 535, in g; BWV 545, in C † Fant Org, BWV 570; Org Music (misc colls); Schübler Chorale Preludes; Toccata & Fugue Org, BWV 565 DNN ▲ 7004 [DDD]

P. Planyavsky (org)—BWV 547, in C; BWV 552, in E♭ *(rec Fukushima-shi Ongakudo, Japan, Nov 7-8, 1986)* ("Bach: Toccata und fuge in d moll, BWV 565") † Cant 147; Chorales Org; Fugue Org, BWV 578; Org Music (misc colls); Toccata & Fugue Org, BWV 565 CAMA ▲ 197 [DDD] (18.97)

S. Preston (org)—BWV 551, in a; BWV 549, in c *(rec Sainsbury org, St. John's, Smith Square, London, England)* † Org Music (misc colls) DGRM ▲ 453541 [DDD] (18.97)

S. Preston (org)—BWV 547, in C; BWV 548, in e, "Wedge"; BWV 550, in G † Canzona; Preludes & Fugues Org; Toccata & Fugue Org, BWV 565 DGRM ▲ 449212 [DDD]

S. Preston (org)—BWV 532, in D; BWV 552, in E♭ † Canonic Vars on "Von Himmel hoch", BWV 769; Fant Org, BWV 572; Pastorale Org, BWV 590; Toccata & Fugue Org, BWV 565 PARC ▲ 27668 [DDD] (16.97)

G. Ramin (org), H. Kästner (org)—BWV 545, in C; BWV 552, in E♭ *(rec Thomaskirche Sauer Org, Leipzig, Germany)* ("Kantors and Organists at St. Thomas, Leipzig") † Passacaglia & Fugue Org, BWV 582; Calvisius:Unser Leben währet siebnzig Jahr; Kuhnau:Tristis est anima mea; J. H. Schein:Israels Brünnlein CATA ▲ 57619 [AAD] (15.97)

S. Rapp (org)—BWV 531, in C ("New Bach: 21 Newly Published Chorales Attributed to Bach") † Chorale Settings (misc); Chorales (miscellaneous) RAVN ▲ 420 [DDD] (17.97)

G. Ritchie (org)—BWV 546, in c *(rec J. Brombaugh Org Southern Adventist Univ, United States of America)* ("Vol. III: For Music Lovers & Connoisseurs") † Clavier-Übung III; Schübler Chorale Preludes; Trio Sons Org RAVN 2-▲ 400 [DDD] (17.97)

L. Rogg (org) *(rec Silbermann Org, Arlesheim, Switzerland)* † Allabreve, BWV 589; Canonic Vars on "Von Himmel hoch", BWV 769; Canzona; Chorales Org; Clavier-Übung III; Fant & Fugue Org, BWV 537; Fant & Fugue, BWV 542; Fant Org, BWV 562; Fant Org, BWV 572; Orgelbüchlein; Partite diverse sopra, BWV 766; Partite diverse sopra, BWV 767; Partite diverse sopra, BWV 768; Pastorale Org, BWV 590; Prelude & Fugue Org, BWV 566; Schübler Chorale Preludes; Toccata & Fugue Org, BWV 565; Toccata, Adagio & Fugue Org, BWV 564; Trio Org, BWV 583; Trio Sons Org HAM 12-▲ 290772 [ADD] (71.97)

L. Rogg (org) *(rec historic org, Alesheim, France)* † Passacaglia & Fugue Org, BWV 582; Schübler Chorale Preludes; Toccata & Fugue Org, BWV 565 HMA ▲ 190771 (9.97)

W. Rübsam (org)—BWV 536, in A; BWV 541, in G; BWV 542, in g; BWV 544, in b; BWV 546, in c *(rec Nov 1989)* NXIN ▲ 550652 [DDD] (5.97)

W. Rübsam (org)—BWV 552, in E♭ ("The Great Organ Works") † Cant 147; Org Music (misc colls); Orgelbüchlein; Passacaglia & Fugue Org, BWV 582; Toccata & Fugue Org, BWV 565; Toccata, Adagio & Fugue Org, BWV 564 NXIN ▲ 553859 [DDD] (5.97)

M. Sander (org)—BWV 552, in E♭ *(rec Wagner Organ at Nidaros Cathedral, Trondheim, Norway)* ("Pathos und Freude") † Chorales Org; Cons Org; Passacaglia & Fugue Org, BWV 582; Trio Sons Org FERM ▲ 20028 [DDD] (16.97)

D. Sanger (org)—BWV 544, in b ("Complete Organ Music, Vol. 8") † Clavier-Übung III; Fant & Imitatio Org, BWV 563 MER ▲ 84378 (17.97)

D. Schrader (org)—BWV 540, in F; BWV 548, in e, "Wedge" ("The Complete Fantasies, Fantasies & Fugues, & Isolated Fugues for Organ") † Prelude & Fugue Org, BWV 566; Toccata & Fugue Org, BWV 538; Toccata & Fugue Org, BWV 565; Toccata, Adagio & Fugue Org, BWV 564 CED ▲ 6 [DDD] (16.97)

A. Schweitzer (org)—BWV 546, in c; BWV 547, in C; BWV 548, in e, "Wedge" ("Albert Schweitzer Plays Bach, Vol. II") † Chorale Settings (misc) PHS ▲ 9992 [AAD] (17.97)

I. Sokol (org)—BWV 533, in e; BWV 549, in c; BWV 551, in a † Fant Org, BWV 570; Fugue on a theme by Legrenzi, BWV 574; Partite diverse sopra, BWV 766; Pedal Exercise Org, BWV 598; Prelude & Fugue Org, BWV 566 PC ▲ 267168 [DDD] (2.97)

U. Spang-Hanssen (org) † Clavier-Übung III; Duets Hpd CLSO 2-▲ 155 (15.97)

J. Van Landeghem (org)—BWV 543, in a *(rec Apr 1995)* ("Bach-Buxtehude-Mozart-Purcell") † Chorales Org; Schübler Chorale Preludes; St. Matthew Passion (sels); Toccata & Fugue Org, BWV 565; Buxtehude:Passacaglia Org, BuxWV 161; W. A. Mozart:Adagio & Allegro, K.594 PAVA ▲ 7339 [DDD] (10.97)

O. Vernet (org)—BWV 551, in a; BWV 531, in C; BWV 532, in D; BWV 533, in e; BWV 535, in g; BWV 549, in c; BWV 550, in G ("The Organ Works: Vol. 1, 1700-1708") † Chorales (miscellaneous); Fant & Imitatio Org, BWV 563; Fant Org, BWV 570; Org Music (comp); Partite diverse sopra, BWV 766; Partite diverse sopra, BWV 767; Passacaglia & Fugue Org, BWV 582; Prelude Org, BWV 568; Prelude Org, BWV 569; Toccata & Fugue Org, BWV 565 LIDI 3-▲ 104037 (47.97)

BACH, JOHANN SEBASTIAN (cont.)

Preludes & Fugues (22) for Organ, BWV 531-552 (cont.)

O. Vernet (org)—BWV 534, in f; BWV 536, in A; BWV 541, in G; BWV 543, in a ("The Organ Works, Vol. 2: 1708-1717") † Chorales (miscellaneous); Chorales Org; Fant & Fugue Org, BWV 537; Fant Org, BWV 562; Fant Org, BWV 572; Partite diverse sopra, BWV 768; Toccata, Adagio & Fugue Org, BWV 564 LIDI 3-▲ 104046 [DDD]

H. Walcha (org)—BWV 532, in D; BWV 552, in E♭; BWV 540, in F *(rec Great org, St. Laurenskerk Alkmaar & Strassburg, Germany, 1956-70)* † Canonic Vars on "Von Himmel hoch", BWV 769; Fant Org, BWV 572; Org Music (misc colls); Passacaglia & Fugue Org, BWV 582; Schübler Chorale Preludes; Toccata & Fugue Org, BWV 538; Toccata & Fugue Org, BWV 565; Trio Sons Org DEUT 2-▲ 453064 [ADD] (17.97)

H. Walcha (org)—BWV 552, in E♭ *(rec St. Laurenskerk Org at St. Laurens Church, Al, Sept 1956, Sept 1962)* † Partite diverse sopra, BWV 768; Schübler Chorale Preludes; Toccata & Fugue Org, BWV 565; Trio Sons Org DEUT (The Originals) ▲ 457704 [ADD] (11.97)

G. Weinberger (org)—BWV 549, in c; BWV 531, in C; BWV 533, in e; BWV 551, in a *(rec Gottfried-Silbermann org, Dom St. Marien, Freiberg, Germany, Aug 1997)* † Org Music (misc colls) CPO ▲ 999663 [DDD] (14.97)

G. Weinberger (org)—BWV 541, in G; BWV 546, in c *(rec Gottfried Silberman Org, St. Petri, Frieberg, Germany)* † Chorales Org CPO ▲ 999664 (14.97)

Preludes & Fugues (8) for Organ, BWV 553-560, "8 Little Preludes & Fugues"

K. Bowyer (org) ("The Works for Organ, Vol. 4") † Fant & Imitatio Org, BWV 563; Org Music (comp) NIMB ▲ 5377 (16.97)

H. Fagius (org) ("Vol. 3") † Fant & Fugue Org, BWV 561; Trio Org, BWV 585 BIS 2-▲ 329 (69.97)

P. Kee (org) ("Piet Kee Plays Bach, Vol. 3") † Chorale Preludes Org; Chorales Org; Neumeister Collection; Org Music (misc colls); Toccata & Fugue Org, BWV 565 CHN (Chaconne) ▲ 527 [DDD] (16.97)

T. Koopman (org) † Toccata, Adagio & Fugue Org, BWV 564; Trio Sons Org NOVA ▲ 150066 [DDD] (16.97)

M. Lücker (org) ("Edition Bachakademie, Vol. 91: Scales from Weimar") † Fugue on a theme by Corelli, BWV 579; Toccata, Adagio & Fugue Org, BWV 564 HANS ▲ 92091 [DDD] (11.97)

S. Preston (org) † Canzona; Preludes & Fugues, BWV 531-552; Toccata & Fugue Org, BWV 565 DGRM ▲ 449212 [DDD]

P. Rouet (org) *(rec Sept 1992)* ("The Complete Toccatas & Fugues for Organ") † Canonic Vars on "Von Himmel hoch", BWV 769; Fant Org, BWV 572; Org Music (misc colls); Pastorale Org, BWV 590 GALL ▲ 720 [DDD]

Prelude & Fugue in E for Organ, BWV 566 (ca 1708)

K. Bowyer (org) *(rec Odense, Denmark, Mar 23-24, 1993)* ("The Works for Organ, Vol. 6") † Org Music (comp); Preludes & Fugues (22) Org, BWV 531-552; Toccata, Adagio & Fugue Org, BWV 564; Trio Son Org, BWV 584; Trio Sons Org NIMB ▲ 5423 [DDD] (16.97)

H. Fagius (org) ("Vol. 8") † Clavier-Übung III; Cons Org; Trio Sons Org BIS 2-▲ 443 [DDD] (69.97)

J. Guillou (org) *(rec Aug 1990)* ("The Organ Works of Bach, Vol. 5") † Chorales (miscellaneous); Chorales Org; Fugue on a theme by Legrenzi, BWV 574; Org Music (comp); Pastorale Org, BWV 590; Preludes & Fugues, BWV 531-552; Schübler Chorale Preludes DOR ▲ 90152 [DDD] (16.97)

J. Guillou (org) *(rec Cathedrale de Breda, Netherlands, Nov 15-17, 1984)* ("Grandes Toccatas") † Preludes & Fugues, BWV 531-552; Toccata & Fugue Org, BWV 538; Toccata & Fugue Org, BWV 565; Toccata, Adagio & Fugue Org, BWV 564 PVY ▲ 730001 [DDD]

D. Joyce (org) † Canonic Vars on "Von Himmel hoch", BWV 769; Partite diverse sopra, BWV 768; Preludes & Fugues, BWV 531-552; Trio Sons Org TIT ▲ 171 [DDD]

B. Lagacé (org) *(rec Montreal, Canada, Mar 1996)* ("Toccata in d & Other Early Works") † Chorales (miscellaneous); Org Music (misc colls); Partite diverse sopra, BWV 766; Pastorale Org, BWV 590; Toccata & Fugue Org, BWV 565 FL ▲ 23091 [DDD] (16.97)

R. Marlow (org) *(rec Metzler org, Trinity College, Cambridge, England)* † Preludes & Fugues, BWV 531-552; Toccata & Fugue Org, BWV 538; Toccata & Fugue Org, BWV 565; Toccata, Adagio & Fugue Org, BWV 564 ASV ▲ 6231 (10.97)

K. Reymaier (org) *(rec St. Jacobi Church, Hamburg, Germany, Jan 9-10, 1999)* † Buxtehude:Mit Fried und Freud ich fahr dahin, BuxWV 76; Scheidemann:Org Music; Tunder:Org Music; M. Weckmann:Org Music; Org Music (misc) PRIO ▲ 607 [DDD] (16.97)

L. Rogg (org) *(rec Silbermann Org, Arlesheim, Switzerland)* † Allabreve, BWV 589; Canonic Vars on "Von Himmel hoch", BWV 769; Canzona; Chorales Org; Clavier-Übung III; Fant & Fugue Org, BWV 537; Fant & Fugue, BWV 542; Fant Org, BWV 562; Fant Org, BWV 572; Orgelbüchlein; Partite diverse sopra, BWV 766; Partite diverse sopra, BWV 767; Partite diverse sopra, BWV 768; Pastorale Org, BWV 590; Preludes & Fugues, BWV 531-552; Schübler Chorale Preludes; Toccata & Fugue Org, BWV 565; Toccata, Adagio & Fugue Org, BWV 564; Trio Org, BWV 583; Trio Sons Org HAM 12-▲ 290772 [ADD] (71.97)

D. Schrader (org) ("The Complete Fantasies, Fantasies & Fugues, & Isolated Fugues for Organ") † Preludes & Fugues, BWV 531-552; Toccata & Fugue Org, BWV 538; Toccata & Fugue Org, BWV 565; Toccata, Adagio & Fugue Org, BWV 564 CED ▲ 6 [DDD] (16.97)

I. Sokol (org) † Fant Org, BWV 570; Fugue on a theme by Legrenzi, BWV 574; Partite diverse sopra, BWV 766; Pedal Exercise Org, BWV 598; Preludes & Fugues, BWV 531-552 PC ▲ 267168 [DDD] (2.97)

Prelude in G for Organ, BWV 568

O. Vernet (org) ("The Organ Works: Vol. 1, 1700-1708") † Chorales (miscellaneous); Fant & Imitatio Org, BWV 563; Fant Org, BWV 570; Org Music (comp); Partite diverse sopra, BWV 766; Partite diverse sopra, BWV 767; Passacaglia & Fugue Org, BWV 582; Prelude Org, BWV 569; Preludes & Fugues, BWV 531-552; Toccata & Fugue Org, BWV 565 LIDI 3-▲ 104037 (47.97)

Prelude in a for Organ, BWV 569 (ca 1709)

T. Koopman (org) *(rec Maassluis Grote Kerk, Germany, June 1983)* † Fant Org, BWV 572; Org Music (misc colls); Passacaglia & Fugue Org, BWV 582; Pastorale Org, BWV 590; Toccata & Fugue Org, BWV 538; Toccata & Fugue Org, BWV 565 PARC ▲ 47292 [DDD] (9.97)

O. Vernet (org) ("The Organ Works: Vol. 1, 1700-1708") † Chorales (miscellaneous); Fant & Imitatio Org, BWV 563; Fant Org, BWV 570; Org Music (comp); Partite diverse sopra, BWV 766; Partite diverse sopra, BWV 767; Passacaglia & Fugue Org, BWV 582; Prelude Org, BWV 568; Preludes & Fugues, BWV 531-552; Toccata & Fugue Org, BWV 565 LIDI 3-▲ 104037 (47.97)

Prelude, Fugue & Allegro in E♭ for Lute, BWV 998 (ca 1740-45)

M. Barrueco (gtr) [arr for gtr] *(rec 1989)* † Sons & Partitas Vn; Visée:Gtr Pieces (sels) EMIC ▲ 66575 [DDD] (11.97)

P. Beier (lt) ("Works for Lute, Vol. 1") † Partita Lt, BWV 1006a; Partita Lt, BWV 997 STRV ▲ 33468 (16.97)

R. Bluestone (gtr) † Carlevaro:American Preludes; Cimarosa:Sons (50) Kbd; Gomez-Crespo:Norteño, 1940; Mompou:Suite compostelana LINA ▲ 1894 [AAD]

E. M. Dombois (cnd) *(rec Vienna, Austria, Mar & June 1971)* ("The Baroque Lute") † Suite Lt, BWV 995; D. Kellner:Lt Music SNYC ▲ 60372 [ADD] (7.97)

J. Gibbons (hpd) [arr hpd] † Capriccio Departure, BWV 992; Chromatic Fant & Fugue, BWV 903 NON ▲ 79132 [DDD] (9.97)

K. Heindel (hpd/lt) *(rec Stonington, CT, Oct 26-28, 1993)* ("Aufs Lautenwerk") † Fugue Lt; Partita Lt, BWV 1006a; Partita Lt, BWV 997; Suite Lt, BWV 996 DOR ▲ 80126 [DDD] (13.97)

R. Hill (kbd) *(rec Sept 1998)* ("Edition Bachakademie, Vol. 109: Works for the Lute-Harpsichord") † Fant & Fughetta Kbd, BWV 907; Fant & Fughetta Kbd, BWV 908; Partita Lt, BWV 997; Prelude Kbd, BWV 921; Prelude Lt, BWV 999; Suite Kbd, BWV 823; Suite Lt, BWV 996 HANS ▲ 92109 [DDD] (11.97)

A. Laberge (hpd) [arr hpd] *(rec Apr 1996)* † Inventions Hpd FL ▲ 23089 [DDD] (16.97)

E. Møldrup (gtr) ("The Guitar Music") † Fugue Lt; Lt Music; Partita Lt, BWV 997; Prelude Lt, BWV 999; Sons & Partitas Vn; Suite Lt, BWV 995; Suite Lt, BWV 996 CLSO 2-▲ 171 (15.97)

M. Nabeshima (hpd) *(rec Brussels, Belgium, 1991)* ("Bach & His Predecessors") † Froberger:Hpd Music; Kuhnau:Musicalische Vorstellung einiger biblischer Histor DI ▲ 920283 [DDD] (5.97)

S. Richter (pno) *(rec Kempten & Bonn, Germany, 1992-93)* ("Out of Later Years, Vol. 1") † Adagio Clvd, BWV 968; Fant & Fugue Org, BWV 906; Kbd Music (misc); Beethoven:Rondos Pno, Op. 51; J. Brahms:Ballades (4), Op. 10; Fants Pno, Op. 116; Pieces (4) Pno, Op. 119 LV ▲ 471 (17.97)

G. Sárközy (lt) *(rec 1980, 1984 & 1991)* ("Johann Sebastian Bach on Viola Bastarda, Lute and Lute-Harpsichord") † Cant 147; Fugue Lt; Partita Lt, BWV 997; Sons Vl; Suite Lt, BWV 995; Suite Lt, BWV 996 HUN 2-▲ 31616 [ADD] (32.97)

J. Savijoki (lt) *(rec Aug 25-26, 1980)* ("Baroque Suites") BIS ▲ 176 [AAD] (17.97)

Preludes (6) for Harpsichord, BWV 933-938, "Little Preludes"

G. Gould (pno) SNYC ▮ 35891 (10.98)

G. Gould (hpd) ("The Glenn Gould Edition") † Org Music (misc colls); Partitas Hpd; Prelude & Fughetta Kbd, BWV 899; Prelude & Fughetta Kbd, BWV 902a; Preludes & Fugues Hpd; Preludes Kbd SNYC 2-▲ 52597 (31.97)

W. Landowska (hpd) *(rec live, Jan 22, 1950)* ("Landowska Plays Bach") † English Suites; Music of Bach; Partitas Hpd; Prelude Lt, BWV 999; Preludes Hpd (5); Preludes Kbd; Toccatas Hpd PHS ▲ 9489 [AAD] (17.97)

K. McIntosh (hpd) *(rec Ponytracks Farm, May 1992)* † Inventions Hpd GAS ▲ 304 [DDD] (16.97)

J. Payne (hpd) † French Suites; Inventions Hpd BIS 2-▲ 589 [DDD] (69.97)

R. Tureck (pno) *(rec Town Hall New York, 1948)* ("The Young Visionary") † English Suites; Wohltemperirte Clavier VAIA ▲ 1085 (16.97)

BACH, JOHANN SEBASTIAN (cont.)

Preludes (5) for Harpsichord, BWV 939-943, "Little Preludes"

J. E. Dähler (hpd)—BWV 939, No. 1 in C; BWV 941, No. 3 in e; BWV 942, No. 4 in a *(rec Aug 1971)* † Inventions Hpd; Prelude Lt, BWV 999; Preludes Kbd CLAV (Favor Collection) ▲ 170 [ADD] (16.97)

R. Egarr (hpd) *(rec Utrecht, Germany, Sept 1995)* † Anna Magdalena Bach Notebook (sels); Clavier-Büchlein for W. F. Bach; French Suites; Fughetta, BWV 961; Italian Con, BWV 971; Partitas Hpd; Prelude Lt, BWV 999; Preludes Kbd EMIC (Debut) ▲ 69700 [DDD] (6.97)

I. Kipnis (hpd)—BWV 939, No. 1 in C; BWV 941, No. 3 in e; BWV 942, No. 4 in a *(rec May 11, 1965)* † Adagio Clvd, BWV 968; English Suites; Italian Con, BWV 971; Prelude Lt, BWV 999; Preludes Kbd; Wohltemperirte Clavier SNYC ▲ 53263 (7.97) ▮ 53263 (3.98)

W. Landowska (hpd)—BWV 939, No. 1 in C *(rec live, Jan 22, 1950)* ("Landowska Plays Bach") † English Suites; Music of Bach; Partitas Hpd; Prelude Lt, BWV 999; Preludes Hpd; Preludes Kbd; Toccatas Hpd PHS ▲ 9489 [AAD] (17.97)

W. Rübsam (pno) *(rec Valparaiso Indiana, United States of America, Sept-Oct 1994)* † Clavier-Büchlein for W. F. Bach; Preludes Kbd; Wohltemperirte Clavier NXIN ▲ 553097 [DDD] (5.97)

Prelude (fantasia) in c for Keyboard, BWV 921

R. Hill (kbd) *(rec Sept 1998)* ("Edition Bachakademie, Vol. 109: Works for the Lute-Harpsichord") † Fant & Fughetta Kbd, BWV 907; Fant & Fughetta Kbd, BWV 908; Partita Lt, BWV 997; Prelude Lt, BWV 999; Prelude, Fugue & Allegro Lt, BWV 998; Suite Kbd, BWV 823; Suite Lt, BWV 996 HANS ▲ 92109 [DDD] (11.97)

Prelude (fantasia) in a for Keyboard, BWV 922

A. Brendel (pno) † Chorales Org; Chromatic Fant & Fugue, BWV 903; Fant & Fugue Hpd, BWV 904; Italian Con, BWV 971; Orgelbüchlein PPHI ▲ 42400 (9.97)

J. C. Martins (pno) *(rec Sofia, Bulgaria, Apr 1997)* ("Complete Keyboard Works, Vol. 15") † Fant & Fugue Hpd, BWV 904; Fant Kbd, BWV 917; Fant Kbd, BWV 918; Fant Kbd, BWV 919; Fugue Kbd, BWV 944; Org Music (misc colls); Prelude & Fugue Hpd, BWV 894; Preludes & Fugues Hpd ERTO ▲ 42052 [DDD] (16.97)

Preludes (9) for Keyboard (BWV 924-932), "Little Preludes" (ca 1720)

J. E. Dähler (hpd)—BWV 924, No. 1 in C; BWV 925, No. 2 in D; BWV 926, No. 3 in d; BWV 927, No. 4 in F; BWV 928, No. 5 in F; BWV 929, No. 6 in g; BWV 930, No. 7 in g *(rec Aug 1971)* † Inventions Hpd; Prelude Lt, BWV 999; Preludes & Fugues Hpd; Preludes Hpd (5) CLAV (Favor Collection) ▲ 170 [ADD] (16.97)

R. Egarr (hpd)—BWV 930, No. 7 in g; BWV 924, No. 1 in C; BWV 925, No. 2 in D; BWV 926, No. 3 in d; BWV 927, No. 4 in F; BWV 928, No. 5 in F *(rec Utrecht, Germany, Sept 1995)* † Anna Magdalena Bach Notebook (sels); Clavier-Büchlein for W. F. Bach; French Suites; Fughetta, BWV 961; Italian Con, BWV 971; Partitas Hpd; Prelude Lt, BWV 999; Preludes Hpd (5) EMIC (Debut) ▲ 69700 [DDD] (6.97)

G. Gould (hpd)—BWV 924, No. 1 in C; BWV 925, No. 2 in D; BWV 926, No. 3 in d; BWV 927, No. 4 in F; BWV 928, No. 5 in F; BWV 930, No. 7 in g ("The Glenn Gould Edition") † Org Music (misc colls); Partitas Hpd; Prelude & Fughetta Kbd, BWV 899; Prelude & Fughetta Kbd, BWV 902a; Preludes & Fugues Hpd; Preludes Hpd SNYC 2-▲ 52597 (31.97)

I. Kipnis (hpd)—BWV 924, No. 1 in C; BWV 926, No. 3 in d; BWV 927, No. 4 in F; BWV 928, No. 5 in F; BWV 929, No. 6 in g; BWV 930, No. 7 in g; BWV 925, No. 2 in D *(rec May 11, 1965)* † Adagio Clvd, BWV 968; English Suites; Italian Con, BWV 971; Prelude Lt, BWV 999; Preludes Hpd (5); Wohltemperirte Clavier SNYC ▲ 53263 (7.97) ▮ 53263 (3.98)

W. Landowska (hpd)—BWV 924, No. 1 in C *(rec live, Jan 22, 1950)* ("Landowska Plays Bach") † English Suites; Music of Bach; Partitas Hpd; Prelude Lt, BWV 999; Preludes Hpd; Preludes Hpd (5); Toccatas Hpd PHS ▲ 9489 [AAD] (17.97)

W. Rübsam (pno)—BWV 929, No. 6 in g; BWV 924, No. 1 in C; BWV 925, No. 2 in D; BWV 926, No. 3 in d; BWV 927, No. 4 in F; BWV 928, No. 5 in F; BWV 930, No. 7 in g *(rec Valparaiso, IN, Sept-Oct 1994)* † Clavier-Büchlein for W. F. Bach; Preludes Hpd (5); Wohltemperirte Clavier NXIN ▲ 553097 [DDD] (5.97)

Prelude in c for Lute, BWV 999 (ca 1720)

J. E. Dähler (hpd) *(rec Aug 1971)* † Inventions Hpd; Preludes & Fugues Hpd; Preludes Hpd (5); Preludes Kbd CLAV (Favor Collection) ▲ 170 [ADD] (16.97)

R. Egarr (hpd) *(rec Utrecht, Germany, Sept 1995)* † Anna Magdalena Bach Notebook (sels); Clavier-Büchlein for W. F. Bach; French Suites; Fughetta, BWV 961; Italian Con, BWV 971; Partitas Hpd; Preludes Hpd (5); Preludes Kbd EMIC (Debut) ▲ 69700 [DDD] (6.97)

R. Hill (kbd) *(rec Sept 1998)* ("Edition Bachakademie, Vol. 109: Works for the Lute-Harpsichord") † Fant & Fughetta Kbd, BWV 907; Fant & Fughetta Kbd, BWV 908; Partita Lt, BWV 997; Prelude Kbd, BWV 921; Prelude, Fugue & Allegro Lt, BWV 998; Suite Kbd, BWV 823; Suite Lt, BWV 996 HANS ▲ 92109 [DDD] (11.97)

I. Kipnis (hpd) [arr for harp] *(rec May 11, 1965)* † Adagio Clvd, BWV 968; English Suites; Italian Con, BWV 971; Preludes Hpd (5); Preludes Kbd; Wohltemperirte Clavier SNYC ▲ 53263 (7.97) ▮ 53263 (3.98)

W. Landowska (hpd) *(rec live, Jan 22, 1950)* ("Landowska Plays Bach") † English Suites; Music of Bach; Partitas Hpd; Preludes Hpd; Preludes Hpd (5); Preludes Kbd; Toccatas Hpd PHS ▲ 9489 [AAD] (17.97)

J. Lindberg (lt) *(rec Sweden, Mar 9-11, 1986)* ("Baroque Music for Lute & Guitar") † Fugue Lt; Anonymous:Lt & Gtr Music; D. Kellner:Lt & Gtr Music; Roncalli:Lt & Gtr Music; Visée:Lt & Gtr Music; S. L. Weiss:Lt Music *(E, F, G text)* BIS ▲ 327 [DDD] (17.97)

E. Møldrup (gtr) ("The Guitar Music") † Fugue Lt; Lt Music; Partita Lt, BWV 997; Prelude, Fugue & Allegro Lt, BWV 998; Sons & Partitas Vn; Suite Lt, BWV 995; Suite Lt, BWV 996 CLSO 2-▲ 171 (15.97)

A. Segovia (gtr) *(rec 1952-68)* † Sons & Partitas Vn; Suite Lt, BWV 995; Suites Vc MCA1 ▲ 42068 [AAD] (11.97)

F. Trentin (gtr) ("De Bach à Bolling") † Fugue Lt; C. Bolling:Con Gtr; F. Trentin:Gtr Music GALL ▲ 820 [DDD]

D. Yeadon (vc), P. Wispelwey (vc pic), R. Egarr (hpd) [trans Wispelwey in g] † Con 2 Hpd, BWV 1053; Con 5 Hpd, BWV 1056; Italian Con, BWV 971; Sons Vl; Suites Vc; Wohltemperirte Clavier CCL ▲ 14198 (18.97)

various artists ("Bach for Relaxation") † Brandenburg Con 2, BWV 1047; Cant 147; Goldberg Vars, BWV 988; Music of Bach; Musical Offering, BWV 1079; Sons & Partitas Vn; Sons Fl; Sons Vn Hpd; Suites Vc RCAV ▲ 68697 (11.97) ▮ 68697 (5.98)

Psalms (4) for Soprano, Alto & Continuo

S. Ertelthalner (sop), M. Sturm (alt), G. Letzbor (cnd), Ars Antiqua Austria *(rec St. Florian, Mar 1995)* † Cant 182 SYM ▲ 95139 [DDD] (18.97)

Quodlibet for SATB solo Voices & Continuo [fragment], BWV 524 (1707)

T. Koopman (cnd), Amsterdam Baroque Orch, B. Schlick (sop), K. Wessel (alt), C. Prégardien (ten), K. Mertens (bass) *(rec Amsterdam, Netherlands, May 1995)* ("Complete Cantatas, Vol. 2") † Cant 12; Cant 132; Cant 152; Cant 172; Cant 18; Cant 182; Cant 199; Cant 203; Cant 61 ERAT 3-▲ 12598 [DDD] (50.97)

D. Röschmann (sop), A. Köhler (alt), C. Genz (ten), H. Wimmer (bass), R. Goebel (cnd), Cologne Musica Antiqua, Ex Tempore Vocal Ensemble † Cant 201; Cant 206; Cant 207; Cant 36c DGRM 2-▲ 457348 [DDD] (35.97)

Sacred Songs (69) for Voice & Continuo [continuo parts only by Bach, in G.C. Schemellis Musicalisches Gesang-Buch, 1736], BWV 439-507

B. Schlick (sop), K. Mertens (bar), W. Möller (vc), B. V. Asperen (hpd/org) *(rec Mar 6-9, 1995)* CPO 2-▲ 999407 [DDD] (13.97)

St. John Passion for SATB solo Voices, Orchestra & Chorus, BWV 245 (1725)

E. Ameling (sop), H. Watts (cta), P. Pears (ten), H. Prey (bar), T. Krause (bar), K. Münchinger (cnd), Stuttgart CO ("Sacred Masterworks") † Christmas Oratorio, BWV 248; Easter Oratorio, BWV 249; Magnificat, BWV 243; Mass in b, BWV 232; St. Matthew Passion, BWV 244 PLON (Budget Box) 10-▲ 455783 (67.97)

S. Cleobury (cnd), Brandenburg Consort, King's College Choir, C. Bott (sop), M. Chance (alt), J. M. Ainsley (ten—Evangelist), P. Agnew (ten), S. Varcoe (bar—Pilate), S. Richardson (bass—Christus) BRIL 2-▲ 99050 (8.97)

J. E. Gardiner (cnd) , Monteverdi Choir London [GER] PARC 2-▲ 19324 [DDD] (32.97)

A. Giebel (sop), M. Höffgen (cta), E. Haefliger (ten), W. Berry (bass), E. Jochum (cnd), (Royal) Concertgebouw Orch, Netherlands Radio Chorus † Cant 140 PPHI (Duo) 2-▲ 462173 (17.97)

H. Harper (sop), J. Hill (sop), A. Hodgson (cta), R. Tear (ten), P. Pears (ten), R. Burgess (ten), A. Thompson (ten), J. Tobin (ten), J. Shirley-Quirk (bar), G. Howell (bass), B. Britten (cnd), English CO, Wandsworth Boys' School Choir *(rec The Maltings Snape, Apr 1971)* PLON 2-▲ 43859 [ADD] (17.97)

M. Kalmár (sop), J. Hamari (cta), J. Réti (ten—Evangelist), A. Fülöp (ten), G. Melis (bar—Jesus), B. Abel (bass—Pilate), K. Kováts (bass—Peter), G. Lehel (cnd), Franz Liszt CO, Liszt Academy Chamber Chorus *(rec Hungary, 1971)* CLDI 2-▲ 4024 [AAD] (21.97)

P. Kwella (sop), D. James (alt), I. Partridge (ten), W. Kendall (ten), M. George (bar), D. Wilson-Johnson (bar), H. Christophers (cnd), The Sixteen Orch, The Sixteen Chorus [GER] CHN (Chaconne) 2-▲ 507 [DDD] (34.97)

S. Lautenbacher (vn), D. Vorholz (vn), G. Kehr (cnd), Mainz CO ("The Story of Bach in Words and Music") † Cant 211; Cant 57; Con Vns; Con 2 Vn; Life & Music of Bach; Magnificat, BWV 243; Mass in b, BWV 232; Passacaglia & Fugue Org, BWV 582; Schübler Chorale Preludes; Toccata & Fugue Org, BWV 565 MMD (Music Masters) ▲ 8500 [ADD] (3.97) ▮ 8500 [ADD] (2.98)

E. Lear (sop), H. Töpper (mez), E. Haefliger (ten), H. Prey (bar), K. Engen (bass), K. Richter (cnd), Munich Bach Orch, Munich Bach Choir DEUT (2CD) 2-▲ 453007 (17.97)

C. Oleze (sop), M. Groop (alt), M. Schäfer (ten—Evangelist), M. Volle (bass—Peter/Pilate), H. Griepentrog (bass—Christ), K. Beringer (cnd), Munich CO, Windsbach Boys' Choir *(rec Ansbach Germany, Aug 2-3, 1997) (E,G texts)* BAYE ▲ 500007 [DDD] (34.97)

BACH, JOHANN SEBASTIAN (cont.)

St. John Passion for SATB solo Voices, Orchestra & Chorus, BWV 245 (1725) (cont.)

F. Palmer (sop), B. Finnilä (mez), W. Krenn (ten), K. Equiluz (ten), P. Huttenlocher (bar), R. V. Meer (bass), M. Corboz (cnd), Lausanne CO, Lausanne Vocal Ensemble ERAT 2-▲ 45406 (21.97)

H. Rilling (cnd), Stuttgart Bach Collegium, Stuttgart Gächinger Kantorei HANS 3-▲ 98170 [DDD] (15.97)

C. Schäfer (sop), Y. Jänicke (cta), A. Kraus (ten), B. Possemeyer (bar), R. Hagen (bass), E. Weyand (cnd), Stuttgart Hymnus Orch, Stuttgart Hymnus Boys' Choir [GER] *(rec 1990)* HANS 2-▲ 98968 (25.97)

B. Schlick (sop), I. Most (alt), E. Brand (ten), A. Stevenson (ten), P. Lika (bass), P. Langshaw (bass), P. Kuentz (cnd), Paul Kuentz Orch, Paul Kuentz Choir PVY 2-▲ 730051 [DDD] (23.97)

B. Schlick (sop), C. Patriasz (cta), H. Crook (ten), W. Kendall (ten), P. Lika (bass), P. Kooy (bass), P. Herreweghe (cnd), La Chapelle Royale Orch, Ghent Collegium Vocale [GER] HAM 2-▲ 901264 [DDD] (36.97)

M. Suzuki (cnd), Japan Bach Collegium, I. Schmithüsen (sop), Y. Hida (sop—Magd), Y. Mera (ct), G. Türk (ten—Evangelist), M. Sakurada (ten—Diener), P. Kooij (bass—Petrus/Pilatus), C. Urano (bass—Jesus) [version 4, 1749; includes 3 arias from version 2] *(rec Kobe Shoin Women's Univ, Japan, Apr 1998) ([ENG,GER] texts)* BIS 2-▲ 921 [DDD] (34.97)

St. John Passion (selections)

B. Fassbaender (mez), W. Gönnenwein (cnd) , South German Madrigal Choir *(rec Église de Schwaigern, Oct 1969)* ("Baroque, Vol. 2") † Cant 147; Magnificat, BWV 243; Mass in b, BWV 232; St. Matthew Passion (sels) EMIC ▲ 65334 [ADD] (9.97)

M. Forrester (cta), H. Tachezi (hpd/org), A. Janigro (cnd), Zagreb Solisti—Es ist vollbracht *(rec Vienna, Austria, June 1964)* ("Maureen Forrester Sings Bach & Handel") † Cant 169; Cant 53; Cant 54; Christmas Oratorio (sels); St. Matthew Passion (sels); G. F. Handel:Jephtha (sels); Messiah (sels); Samson (sels) VC 2-▲ 64 [AAD] (26.97)

J. E. Gardiner (cnd), English Baroque Soloists, Monteverdi Choir—Die Kriegsknechte aber, da sie Jesum gekreuziget hatten; Lässet uns den nicht zerteilen; Auf dass erfüllet würde die Schrift; Er nahm alles wohl in acht; Ruht wohl, ihr heiligen Gebeine; Ach Herr, lass dein lieb Engelein *(rec Smith Square, London, England, Sept 1989)* † Cant 106; Cant 118; Cant 147; Cant 36c; Cant 62; Christmas Oratorio (sels); Mass in b, BWV 232; St. Matthew Passion (sels) PARC ▲ 39885 [DDD] (16.97)

F. Palmer (sop), B. Finnilä (alt), K. Equiluz (ten—Evangelist), W. Krenn (ten), P. Huttenlocher (bass—Pilate, Peter), R. V. Meer (bass—Jesus), M. Corboz (cnd), Lausanne CO, Lausanne Vocal Ensemble—Herr, unser Herrscher; Die Schar aber und der Oberhauptmann; Von den Stricken; Simon Petrus aber folgete Jesu nach; Ich folge dir; Wer hat dich so geschlagen; Er leugnete aber und sprach; Ach, mein Sinn; Petrus, der nicht denkt zurück, seinen Gott verneinet; Betrachte, meine Seele; Durch dein Gefängnis; Die Juden aber schrieen und sprachen; Lässet uns den nicht zerteilen; Da Pilatus das Wort hörete, fuhrete er Jesum heraus; Weg, weg mit dem; Spricht Pilatus zu ihnen; Wir haben keinen König; Da überantworter er ihn; Eilt, ihr angefocht'nen Seelen; Die Kriegsknechte aber, da sie Jesum gekreuziget hatten; Lässet uns den nicht zerteilen; Und von Stund' an nahm sie der Jünger zu sich; Es ist vollbracht; Und neigte das Haupt und verschied; Mein Herz! Indem die ganze Welt; Ruht wohl, ihr heiligen Gebeine; Ach Herr, lass dein lieb Engelein *(rec Crissier, Switzerland, Oct 1977)* ERAT ▲ 17884 [ADD] (9.97)

H. Rilling (cnd), Stuttgart Bach Collegium, Stuttgart Gächinger Kantorei—Herr, unser Herrscher ("The Brook & the Well-Spring") † Brandenburg Con 5, BWV 1050; Cant 147; Con 1 Vn; Goldberg Vars, BWV 988; Mass in b, BWV 232; Passacaglia & Fugue Org, BWV 582; Sons & Partitas Vn; Wohltemperirte Clavier SNYC (NPR-Milestone of the Millennium) ▲ 60990 [DDD] (11.97)

St. Luke Passion [Passio secundum Lucam], BWV 246

W. Helbich (cnd), Bremen Baroque Orch, Alsfeld Vocal Ensemble, M. Spägele (sop), C. Iven (alt), R. Müller (ten—Evangelist), H. V. Berne (ten), S. Schreckenberger (bass—Jesus), M. Sandmann (bass) *(rec Mar 1996)* ("Apocryphal St. Luke Passion") CPO 2-▲ 999293 [DDD] (13.97)

St. Mark Passion, [most music lost; reconstructed by Dietard Hellmann, Stefan Sutkowski & Tadeusz Maciejewski, 1983], BWV 247

K. Myrlak (ten), B. Jaszkowski (bass), J. Bok (cnd), Warsaw SO, Warsaw Chamber Opera Chorus [GER] BONG 2-▲ 2024 [ADD] (32.97)

G. Webber (cnd), Cambridge Baroque Cantata, Gonville & Caius College Choir Cambridge † R. Keiser:Laudate Pueri Dominum ASV ▲ 237 (31.97)

St. Matthew Passion for solo Voices, Orchestra & Chorus, BWV 244 (1727)

E. Ameling (sop), H. Watts (cta), P. Pears (ten), H. Prey (bar), T. Krause (bar), K. Münchinger (cnd), Stuttgart CO ("Sacred Masterworks") † Christmas Oratorio, BWV 248; Easter Oratorio, BWV 249; Magnificat, BWV 243; Mass in b, BWV 232; St. John Passion, BWV 245 PLON (Budget Box) 10-▲ 455783 (67.97)

B. Bonney (sop), A. Monoyios (sop), A. S. von Otter (mez), M. Chance (ct), H. Crook (ten), A. Rolfe Johnson (ten), O. Bär (bar), A. Schmidt (bar), C. Hauptmann (bass), J. E. Gardiner (cnd) , Monteverdi Choir London [GER] PARC 3-▲ 27648 [DDD] (48.97)

A. Burmeister (mez), P. Schreier (ten), T. Adam (bass), R. Mauersberger (cnd), Leipzig Gewandhaus Orch, Dresden Kreuz Choir, St. Thomas Choir *(rec 1970)* BER 3-▲ 2144 [ADD] (31.97)

P. Esswood (ct), J. Bowman (ct), T. Sutcliffe (ct), K. Equiluz (ten), M. V. Egmond (bass), N. Harnoncourt (cnd), Vienna Concentus Musicus [GER] TELC 3-▲ 42509 [AAD] (32.97)

K. Ferrier (cta), R. Jacques (cnd), Jacques Orch, R. Jacques (cnd), Bach Choir *(rec 1947-48)* † Pergolesi:Stabat mater DLAB ▲ 2005 (33.97)

G. Janowitz (sop), C. Ludwig (mez), P. Schreier (ten), H. Laubenthal (ten), D. Fischer-Dieskau (bar), W. Berry (b-bar), H. von Karajan (cnd), Berlin PO, Berlin German Opera Chorus, Vienna Singverein [GER] DEUT 3-▲ 19789 [ADD] (48.97)

T. Lemnitz (sop), F. Beckmann (alt), K. Erb (ten), G. Hüsch (bar), S. Schulze (bass), G. Ramin (cnd), Leipzig Gewandhaus Orch, St. Thomas Choir [GER] *(rec Mar 1941)* CALG 2-▲ 50859 [AAD] (37.97)

W. Lipp (sop), C. Ludwig (mez), F. Wunderlich (ten—Evangelist), O. Weiner (bar—Jesus), W. Berry (b-bar—Peter), P. Wimberger (b-bar—Pilate), K. Böhm (cnd), Vienna SO, Vienna Boys' Choir, Vienna Gesellschaft Singverein *(rec live Vienna, Apr 18, 1962)* MYTO 2-▲ 973162 (34.97)

F. Lott (sop), A. Hodgson (cta), R. Tear (ten), J. Shirley-Quirk (bar), S. Roberts (bar), D. Willcocks (cnd), Thames CO, Bach Choir [ENG] ASVQ 3-▲ 324 [ADD] (24.97)

M. Marshall (sop), C. Watkinson (cta), K. Equiluz (ten), P. Huttenlocher (bar), G. Faulstich (bar), R. Johnson (bass), M. Corboz (cnd), Lausanne CO, Lausanne Vocal Ensemble ERAT 3-▲ 45375 (32.97)

B. Schlick (sop), R. Jacobs (ct), H. Crook (ten), H. Blochwitz (ten), P. Kooy (bass), U. Cold (bass), P. Herreweghe (cnd), La Chapelle Royale Orch, Ghent Collegium Vocale [GER] HAM 3-▲ 901155 (52.97)

E. Schwarzkopf (sop), C. Ludwig (mez), N. Gedda (ten), D. Fischer-Dieskau (bar), W. Berry (b-bar), O. Klemperer (cnd), Philharmonia Orch EMIC 3-▲ 63058 (31.97)

I. Seefried (sop), A. Fahberg (sop), H. Töpper (mez), E. Haefliger (ten), D. Fischer-Dieskau (bar), K. Engen (bass), M. Proebstl (bass), K. Richter (cnd), Munich Bach Orch, Munich Bach Choir PARC ▲ 39338 [ADD] (34.97)

J. Somary (cnd), English CO, Ambrosian Singers, E. Ameling (sop), B. Finnilä (mez), E. Haefliger (ten), S. McCoy (ten), B. Luxon (bar), B. McDaniel (bar) *(rec 1977)* VC 3-▲ 4060 [ADD] (26.97)

T. Stich-Randall (sop), L. Dutoit (sop—Pilate's Wife/1st Maid), C. Zottl-Holmstädt (alt—1st False Witness/2nd Maid), H. Rössl-Majdan (cta), W. Kmentt (ten), U. Ebrelius (ten—Evangelist), K. Vogel (ten—2nd False Witness), W. Berry (bass—High Priest II/Pilate), H. Braun (bass—Jesus), F. Kummer (bass—High Priest I/Judas), M. Weirich (bass—Peter), A. Heiller (org), M. Wöldike (cnd), Vienna State Opera CO, Vienna Chamber Choir, Shottenstift Boys' Choir *(rec Musikverein Vienna, May-June 1959)* VC (The Bach Guild) 3-▲ 85 [AAD] (39.97)

J. Vincent (sop), I. Durigo (cta), K. Erb (ten), L. van Tulder (ten), H. Schey (bass), W. Ravelli (bass), W. Mengelberg (cnd), (Royal) Concertgebouw Orch, Amsterdam Toonkunst Choir, Zanglust Boys' Choir *(rec live, Apr 2, 1939)* GRM2 3-▲ 78739 (39.97)

J. Zomer (sop), A. Scholl (ct), H. J. Mammel (ten), G. Türk (ten—Evangelist), P. Kooy (bass), G. Smits (bass—Christus), J. van Veldhoven (cnd), Netherlands Bach Society Baroque Orch, Netherlands Bach Society Baroque Choir CCL 3-▲ 11397 (52.97)

St. Matthew Passion (selections)

T. Altmeyer (ten), W. Gönnenwein (cnd) , South German Madrigal Choir *(rec Église de Schwaigern, May-June 1968)* ("Baroque, Vol. 2") † Cant 147; Magnificat, BWV 243; Mass in b, BWV 232; St. John Passion (sels) EMIC ▲ 65334 [ADD] (9.97)

A. Augér (sop), G. Schwarz (cnd), Mostly Mozart Festival Orch—Blute nur, du liebes Herz; Ich will dir mein Herze schenken † Anna Magdalena Bach Notebook (sels); Cant 202; Cant 209; G. F. Handel:Arias DLS ▲ 3026 [DDD] (14.97)

J. Bowman (ct), R. King (cnd), King's Consort—Erbarme dich ("The James Bowman Collection") † Arias; Anonymous:Come tread the paths; T. Ford:Since First I Saw Your Face; G. Gabrieli:O magnum mysterium; G. F. Handel:Music of Handel; H. Purcell:Sacred Music; Songs; Symphonic Poems (misc) HYP ▲ 3 (7.97)

N. Conner (sop), J. Watson (cta), W. Hain (ten), H. Janssen (bar), M. Harrell (bar), L. Alvary (bass), B. Walter (cnd), New York PO, New York Phil Chorus MNER ▲ 20 (15.97)

M. Forrester (cta), H. Tachezi (hpd/org), A. Janigro (cnd), Zagreb Solisti—Du lieber Heiland du; Buss' und Reu'; Erbarme dich *(rec Vienna, Austria, June 1964)* ("Maureen Forrester Sings Bach & Handel") † Cant 169; Cant 53; Cant 54; Christmas Oratorio (sels); St. John Passion (sels); G. F. Handel:Jephtha (sels); Messiah (sels); Samson (sels) VC 2-▲ 64 [AAD] (26.97)

BACH, JOHANN SEBASTIAN (cont.)

St. Matthew Passion (selections) (cont.)

J. E. Gardiner (cnd), English Baroque Soloists, Monteverdi Choir—Kommt, ihr Töchter, helft mir klagen *(rec Fontmell Magna Shaftesbury, Dorset; Blackhea, England, 1988-92)* † Cant 106; Cant 118; Cant 147; Cant 36c; Cant 62; Christmas Oratorio (sels); Mass in b, BWV 232; St. John Passion (sels) PARC ▲ 39885 [DDD] (16.97)

J. E. Gardiner (cnd), English Baroque Soloists, Monteverdi Choir, A. Monoyios (sop), B. Bonney (sop), A. S. von Otter (mez), M. Chance (ct), H. Crook (ten), A. Rolfe Johnson (ten), A. Schmidt (bar), O. Bär (bar), C. Hauptmann (bass) PARC ▲ 29773 [DDD] (16.97)

W. Gönnenwein (cnd), Consortium Musicum, South German Madrigal Choir, T. Zylis-Gara (sop), J. Hamari (mez), N. Gedda (ten), T. Altmeyer (ten—Evangelist), H. Prey (bar), F. Crass (bass—Jesus)—Kommt, ihr Töchter, helft mir klagen; Herzliebster Jesu, was hast du verbrochen; Du lieber Heiland du; Buss' und Reu'; Blute nur, du liebes Herz; Und er nahm den Kelch-Trinket alle daraus; Wiewohl mein Herz in Tränen schwimmt; Ich will dir mein Herze schenken; Da sprach Jesus zu ihnen-Meine Seel ist betrübt; O Schmerz, hier zittert das gequälte Herz; Ich will bei meinem Jesu wachen; Erbarme dich, mein Gott, um meiner Zähren willen; Gebt mir meinen Jesum wieder; Er hat uns allen wohlgetan; Aus Liebe will mein Heiland sterben; O Haupt voll Blut und Wunden; Am Abend, da es kühle war; Mache dich, mein Herze, rein; Wir setzen uns mit Tränen nieder *(rec 1968)* ("Best-Loved Bach") † Brandenburg Con 1, BWV 1046; Brandenburg Con 2, BWV 1047; Brandenburg Con 3, BWV 1048; Con Vns; Con 1 Vn; Con 2 Vn; Suite 1 Orch, BWV 1066; Suite 2 Fl, BWV 1067; Suite 3 Orch, BWV 1068 EMIC 4-▲ 69536 [ADD] (14.97)

K. T. Kanawa (sop), A. S. von Otter (mez), H. Blochwitz (ten), A. Rolfe Johnson (ten), O. Bär (bar), T. Krause (bass), G. Solti (cnd), Chicago SO, Chicago Sym Chorus, Glen Ellyn Children's Chorus [GER] PLON ▲ 25691 [DDD] (16.97)

J. Kowalski (alt), N. Marriner (cnd), Academy of St. Martin in the Fields—Buss' und Reu' ("Jochen Kowalski: Händel & Bach Sacred Arias") † Mass in b, BWV 232; G. F. Handel:Arias; Messiah (sels) CAPO ▲ 10532 [DDD] (11.97)

H. Kreutz (cnd), Gütersloh Bach Choir—O Haupt voll Blut und Wunden *(rec June 1968)* ("Lobe den Herren") † Cant 140; Cant 4; Cant 79; Chorales (miscellaneous) CATA ▲ 57617 [ADD] (15.97)

W. Löffler (vir), D. Kaufmann (org), G. Wilhelm (cnd), Stuttgart Hymnus Boys' Choir—O Haupt voll Blut und Wunden *(rec Oct 1962)* ("Chorales from the St. Matthew Passion") † Org Music (misc colls); Orgelbüchlein; Partite diverse sopra, BWV 768 BAYE ▲ 200005 [ADD] (17.97)

I. Marinov (cnd), Radio Sofia Orch, I. Marinov (cnd), Radio Sofia Chorus—O Haupt voll Blut und Wunden; O Mensch, bewein dein Sünde Gross † Brandenburg Con 3, BWV 1048; Con 1 Vn; Italian Con, BWV 971; Music of Bach; Toccata & Fugue Org, BWV 565 UNIN ▲ 81172 [DDD] (5.97)

B. Mathern (vn), C. Tsan (vc), J. Falala (fl), J. Lecointre (tpt), J. Berlingen (cnd) , St. Eustache Choir ("Music from the Film La Messe in Si Mineur") † Mass in b, BWV 232 DPV ▲ 8906 (15.97)

Neubeuern Chorgemeinschaft members, Tölz Boys' Choir members, E. Z. Guttenberg (cnd), Bach Collegium Munich members—Kommt, ihr Töchter, helft mir klagen † Mass in b, BWV 232; S. Barber:Agnus Dei; Carissimi:Vocal Music (misc); G. F. Handel:Messiah (choruses); W. A. Mozart:Requiem, K.626; S. Rachmaninoff:Vocalise; Verdi:Requiem Mass RCAV ▲ 63450 (11.97)

H. Rilling (cnd), Stuttgart Bach Collegium SNYC (Essential Classics) ▲ 46544 [ADD] (7.97) ▮ 46544 [ADD] (3.98)

E. Schumann (sop)—Aus Liebe will mein Heiland sterben ("Elisabeth Schumann: The Complete Bach Recordings, 1927-1939") † Anna Magdalena Bach Notebook (sels); Cant 159; Cant 202; Mass in b, BWV 232 PHS 2-▲ 9900 [AAD] (33.97)

J. Somary (cnd), English CO, Ambrosian Singers, E. Ameling (sop), B. Finnilä (mez), E. Haefliger (ten), S. McCoy (ten), B. Luxon (bar), B. McDaniel (bar) VC ▲ 4063 [ADD] (13.97)

Swingle Singers—Blute nur, du liebes Herz *(rec 1991)* ("Bach Hits Back/A Cappella Amadeus") † Anna Magdalena Bach Notebook (sels); Brandenburg Con 3, BWV 1048; Cant 140; Cant 208; In dulci jubilo, BWV 729; Inventions Hpd; Music of Bach; Sons & Partitas Vn; Suite 2 Fl, BWV 1067; Wohltemperirte Clavier; W. A. Mozart:Music of Mozart VCL 2-▲ 61472 [DDD] (11.97)

J. Van Landeghem (org)—O Mensch, bewein dein Sünde Gross *(rec Apr 1995)* ("Bach-Buxtehude-Mozart-Purcell") † Chorales Org; Preludes & Fugues, BWV 531-552; Schübler Chorale Preludes; Toccata & Fugue Org, BWV 565; Buxtehude:Passacaglia Org, BuxWV 161; W. A. Mozart:Adagio & Allegro, K.594 PAVA ▲ 7339 [DDD] (10.97)

artists unknown—O Haupt voll Blut und Wunden ("Favourite Bach") † Air on the G String; Anna Magdalena Bach Notebook (sels); Brandenburg Con 2, BWV 1047; Brandenburg Con 3, BWV 1048; Brandenburg Con 4, BWV 1049; Cant 140; Cant 147; Cant 208; Cant 212; Cant 51; Con 1 Hpd, BWV 1052; Con 2 Vn; Suite 2 Fl, BWV 1067; Toccata & Fugue Org, BWV 565; Wohltemperirte Clavier CFP (Favourites) ▲ 4639 (12.97)

Sanctus in D for Orchestra & Chorus, BWV 238

C. Bott (sop), P. Pickett (cnd), New London Consort † Cant 63; Magnificat, BWV 243a DECC ▲ 452920 (16.97)

Schübler Chorale Preludes (6) for Organ, BWV 645-650 (ca 1747)

I. Biret (pno)—BWV 645, No. 1 "Wachet auf, ruft uns Stimme" *(rec 1991)* † Cant 29; Chorales (miscellaneous); Kbd Music (misc); Sons Fl; C. W. Gluck:Orfeo ed Euridice; G. F. Handel:Menuet Pno; Kempff:Pno Music; W. A. Mozart:Pastorale variée, K.Anh.209b MARC ▲ 8223452 [DDD] (13.97)

J. Dimmock (org) ("Complete Organ Works as Published by the Composer") † Clavier-Übung III; Org Music (misc colls) ARK 2-▲ 6161 [DDD] (47.97)

M. Dupré (org)—BWV 645, No. 1 "Wachet auf, ruft uns Stimme" *(rec Queen's Hall & Alexandra Place orgs, England)* ("Bach; The Art of Marcel Dupré") † Cant 29; Clavier-Übung III; Fant & Fugue Org, BWV 537; Orgelbüchlein; Passacaglia & Fugue Org, BWV 582; Preludes & Fugues, BWV 531-552; Suite 3 Orch, BWV 1068; Toccata & Fugue Org, BWV 538; Trio Sons Org PHS ▲ 9863 (17.97)

H. Fagius (org) † Chorales Org BIS 2-▲ 235 [DDD] (69.97)

J. Guillou (org)—BWV 646, No. 2 "Wo soll ich fliehen hin"; BWV 645, No. 1 "Wachet auf, ruft uns Stimme" *(rec Aug 1990)* ("The Organ Works of Bach, Vol. 5") † Chorales (miscellaneous); Chorales Org; Fugue on a theme by Legrenzi, BWV 574; Org Music (comp); Pastorale Org, BWV 590; Prelude & Fugue Org, BWV 566; Preludes & Fugues, BWV 531-552 DOR ▲ 90152 [DDD] (16.97)

C. Herrick (org) *(rec Metzler Org Jesuitenkirche Lucerne)* ("Wachet auf!") † Chorales Org HYP 2-▲ 67071 (36.97)

P. Hurford (org)—BWV 645, No. 1 "Wachet auf, ruft uns Stimme" *(rec Church of Our Lady of Sorrows Org Toronto, Canada, 1975; 1977-79)* † Chorales Org; Fant & Fugue Org, BWV 537; Fant & Fugue, BWV 542; Fant Org, BWV 562; Fant Org, BWV 572; Org Music (misc colls); Passacaglia & Fugue Org, BWV 582; Preludes & Fugues, BWV 531-552; Toccata & Fugue Org, BWV 538; Toccata & Fugue Org, BWV 565; Toccata, Adagio & Fugue Org, BWV 564 PLON 2-▲ 43485 [ADD] (17.97)

R. Köbler (org), A. Eger (org) *(rec Great orgs of Freiberg Cathedral, Germany)* ("Organ Works on Silberman Organs, Vol. 1") † Org Music (misc colls); Orgelbüchlein BER 2-▲ 9361 (21.97)

S. Lautenbacher (vn), D. Vorholz (vn), G. Kehr (cnd), Mainz CO—BWV 645, No. 1 "Wachet auf, ruft uns Stimme" ("The Story of Bach in Words and Music") † Cant 211; Cant 57; Con Vns; Con 2 Vn; Life & Music of Bach; Magnificat, BWV 243; Mass in b, BWV 232; Passacaglia & Fugue Org, BWV 582; St. John Passion, BWV 245; Toccata & Fugue Org, BWV 565 MMD (Music Masters) ▲ 8500 [ADD] (3.97) ▮ 8500 [ADD] (2.98)

J. C. Martins (pno)—BWV 645, No. 1 "Wachet auf, ruft uns Stimme" *(rec NY & Sofia Bulgaria, United States of America, 1986 & 1996)* ("Bach for Christmas") † Cant 147; Music of Bach; Sons & Partitas Vn; Sons Fl; Suite 3 Orch, BWV 1068 COJ ▲ 42040 [DDD] (14.97)

H. Otto (org) † Fant Org, BWV 570; Org Music (misc colls); Preludes & Fugues, BWV 531-552; Toccata & Fugue Org, BWV 565 DNN ▲ 7004 [DDD]

R. Peres (pno)—BWV 645, No. 1 "Wachet auf, ruft uns Stimme" † Cant 147; Orgelbüchlein; Partitas Hpd; Beethoven:Vars Pno on Original Theme, WoO 80; J. Brahms:Intermezzos (3) Pno, Op. 117 PTRY ▲ 2211 (17.97)

H. Rilling (org), J. E. Hansen (org), H. Otto (org), K. Vad (org)—BWV 645, No. 1 "Wachet auf, ruft uns Stimme" † Cant 147; Org Music (misc colls); Orgelbüchlein; Passacaglia & Fugue Org, BWV 582; Toccata & Fugue Org, BWV 565; Trio Org, BWV 583 DNN ▲ 8009 [DDD] (10.97)

G. Ritchie (org) *(rec J. Brombaugh Org Southern Adventist Univ, United States of America)* ("Vol. III: For Music Lovers & Connoisseurs") † Clavier-Übung III; Preludes & Fugues, BWV 531-552; Trio Sons Org RAVN 2-▲ 400 [DDD] (17.97)

L. Rogg (org) *(rec Silbermann Org, Arlesheim, Switzerland)* † Allabreve, BWV 589; Canonic Vars on "Von Himmel hoch", BWV 769; Canzona; Chorales Org; Clavier-Übung III; Fant & Fugue Org, BWV 537; Fant & Fugue, BWV 542; Fant Org, BWV 562; Fant Org, BWV 572; Orgelbüchlein; Partite diverse sopra, BWV 766; Partite diverse sopra, BWV 767; Partite diverse sopra, BWV 768; Pastorale Org, BWV 590; Prelude & Fugue Org, BWV 566; Preludes & Fugues, BWV 531-552; Toccata & Fugue Org, BWV 565; Toccata, Adagio & Fugue Org, BWV 564; Trio Org, BWV 583; Trio Sons Org HAM 12-▲ 290772 [ADD] (71.97)

L. Rogg (org) *(rec historic org, Alesheim, France)* † Passacaglia & Fugue Org, BWV 582; Preludes & Fugues, BWV 531-552; Toccata & Fugue Org, BWV 565 HMA ▲ 190771 (9.97)

D. Sanger (org) ("Organ Music, Vol. 6") † Cons Org; Org Music (misc colls); Passacaglia & Fugue Org, BWV 582; Pastorale Org, BWV 590 MER ▲ 84326 [DDD] (16.97)

BACH, JOHANN SEBASTIAN (cont.)

Schübler Chorale Preludes (6) for Organ, BWV 645-650 (ca 1747) (cont.)

K. Schnorr (org)—BWV 645, No. 1 "Wachet auf, ruft uns Stimme" ("25 Bach Favorites") † Brandenburg Con 1, BWV 1046; Brandenburg Con 2, BWV 1047; Brandenburg Con 3, BWV 1048; Brandenburg Con 4, BWV 1049; Brandenburg Con 5, BWV 1050; Cant 147; Con Hpds (4), BWV 1065; Con Vns; Con 1 for 2 Hpds, BWV 1060; Con 1 Vn; Mass in b, BWV 232; Music of Bach; Sons & Partitas Vn; Suite 2 Fl, BWV 1067; Toccata & Fugue Org, BWV 565; Toccata, Adagio & Fugue Org, BWV 564; Wohltemperirte Clavier VCC ▲ 8817 (3.97)

J. Van Landeghem (org)—BWV 645, No. 1 "Wachet auf, ruft uns Stimme" *(rec Apr 1995)* ("Bach-Buxtehude-Mozart-Purcell") † Chorales Org; Preludes & Fugues, BWV 531-552; St. Matthew Passion (sels); Toccata & Fugue Org, BWV 565; Buxtehude:Passacaglia Org, BuxWV 161; W. A. Mozart:Adagio & Allegro, K.594 PAVA ▲ 7339 [DDD] (10.97)

H. Walcha (org) *(rec Great org, St. Laurenskerk Alkmaar & Strassburg, Germany, 1956-70)* † Canonic Vars on "Von Himmel hoch", BWV 769; Fant Org, BWV 572; Org Music (misc colls); Passacaglia & Fugue Org, BWV 582; Preludes & Fugues, BWV 531-552; Toccata & Fugue Org, BWV 538; Toccata & Fugue Org, BWV 565; Trio Sons Org DEUT 2-▲ 453064 [ADD] (17.97)

H. Walcha (org) *(rec St. Laurenskerk Org at St. Laurens Church, Al, Sept 1956, Sept 1962)* † Partite diverse sopra, BWV 768; Preludes & Fugues, BWV 531-552; Toccata & Fugue Org, BWV 565; Trio Sons Org DEUT (The Originals) ▲ 457704 [ADD] (11.97)

Sinfonias

S. Miassojedov (cnd), Moscow Bach Center Orch—Cant 21 [Sinfonia]; Cant 209 [Sinfonia] † Suite 3 Orch, BWV 1068; Suite 4 Orch, BWV 1069 AART ▲ 47134 (10.97)

T. Pinnock (cnd), English Concert—Cant 42; Cant 52; Cant 110; Cant 174; Cant 249a † Suites Orch ARCV 2-▲ 439780 [DDD] (35.97)

Sonata in C for Keyboard, BWV 966 (ca 1720)

S. Richter (pno) † Capriccio Hpd, BWV 993; Duets Hpd; Italian Con, BWV 971; Son Kbd STRV ▲ 33323 (16.97)

J. Sebestyén (hpd) *(rec 1972)* † Adagio Clvd, BWV 968; Son Kbd; Sons (5) Kbd CLDI ▲ 4021 [ADD] (10.97)

Sonatas (3) & Partitas (3) for solo Violin, BWV 1001-1006 (1720)

M. Barrueco (gtr)—BWV 1004, Partita No. 2 in d [arr for gtr] *(rec 1989)* † Prelude, Fugue & Allegro Lt, BWV 998; Visée:Gtr Pieces (sels) EMIC ▲ 66575 [DDD] (11.97)

W. Baumgratz (org)—BWV 1004, Partita No. 2 in d [Chaconne only; arr Landmann] *(rec July 1997)* ("Works in Romantic Organ Arrangements") † Cant 106; Suite 3 Orch, BWV 1068; Wohltemperirte Clavier; G. F. Handel:Cons (16) Org; Suites de Pièces (8) Hpd, HWV 426-33 MDG ▲ 3200761 [DDD] (17.97)

J. Bream (gtr)—BWV 1004, Partita No. 2 in d [Chaconne only] † Suite Lt, BWV 996 EMIC ▲ 55123 (16.97)

A. Brussilovsky (vn)—BWV 1001, Son No. 1 in g; BWV 1002, Partita No. 1 in b; BWV 1003, Son No. 2 in a ("Vol. 1") SUON ▲ 31001 (16.97)

A. Brussilovsky (vn)—BWV 1004, Partita No. 2 in d; BWV 1005, Son No. 3 in C; BWV 1006, Partita No. 3 in E ("Vol. 2") SUON ▲ 31002 (16.97)

A. Busch (vn), R. Serkin (pno)—BWV 1004, Partita No. 2 in d *(rec 1930 for HMV)* † Beethoven:Son 3 Vn; J. Brahms:Son 2 Vn, Op. 100 PHS ▲ 9942 [AAD] (17.97)

A. Busch (vn), R. Serkin (pno)—BWV 1004, Partita No. 2 in d † J. Brahms:Son 1 Vn, Op. 78; Son 2 Vn, Op. 100 MTAL ▲ 48026 (6.97)

A. Busch (vn), R. Serkin (pno)—BWV 1004, Partita No. 2 in d [Sarabande only] *(rec 1928-37)* ("Busch-Serkin Duo Recordings, Vol. 3") † Son Vn Bc, BWV 1021; Sons Vn Hpd; F. Schubert:Fant Vn, D.934; Vivaldi:Sons Vn APR ▲ 5543 [ADD] (18.97)

P. Casals (vc)—BWV 1003, Son No. 2 in a [Andante only] *(rec 1927-36)* ("Pablo Casals: A Baroque Festival") † English Suites; Music of Bach; Toccata, Adagio & Fugue Org, BWV 564; Boccherini:Con Vc, G.482; Sons Vn, Op. 5; Tartini:Con Vc; G. Valentini:Sons Vn, Op. 8 ENT (Strings) ▲ 99320 (16.97)

A. Delmoni (vn)—BWV 1004, Partita No. 2 in d ("Ysaÿe-Kreisler-Bach: Solo Violin Works") † F. Kreisler:Recitativo & Scherzo-caprice, Op. 6; Ysaÿe:Sons Vn, Op. 27 JMR ▲ 14 (16.97)

Z. Dukic (gtr)—BWV 1001, Son No. 1 in g [trans for gtr] † José Martinez Palacios:Son Gtr; Takemitsu:All in Twilight; Tárrega:Gtr Music OTR ▲ 1023 [DDD] (18.97)

S. Fiorentino (pno)—BWV 1001, Son No. 1 in g [trans Fiorentino] *(rec Berlin, Germany, Oct 1996)* † Partitas Hpd APR ▲ 5558 [DDD] (18.97)

P. Florin (vn)—BWV 1002, Partita No. 1 in b; BWV 1004, Partita No. 2 in d; BWV 1006, Partita No. 3 in E *(rec Falicon, Nice, France, 1989)* TACE ▲ 10

P. Florin (vn)—BWV 1002, Partita No. 1 in b [Presto only] ("Composers & Their Star Signs: Sagitarius") † Art of the Fugue (sels); French Suites; Italian Con, BWV 971; Wohltemperirte Clavier; J. Haydn:Qts (3) Strs, H.III/69-71; Son 60 Kbd, H.XVI/50 TACE ▲ 24

P. Florin (vn)—BWV 1005, Son No. 3 in C; BWV 1001, Son No. 1 in g; BWV 1003, Son No. 2 in a TACE ▲ 47

P. Galbraith (gtr) [arr Galbraith for 8-str gtr in a] DLS 2-▲ 3232 [DDD] (20.97)

S. Gawriloff (vn) [7 vers on 7 vns-Sarabande only] *(rec Cologne, Germany, Dec 1995)* ("What About This, Mr. Paganini?") † A. Dvořák:Romantic Pieces, Op. 75; F. Kreisler:Vars on Tartini; Paganini:Cantabile, M.S. 109; Veracini:Sons Vn (misc); Webern:Pieces Vn, Op. 7 TACE ▲ 36

N. Goluses (gtr)—BWV 1001, Son No. 1 in g; BWV 1003, Son No. 2 in a; BWV 1005, Son No. 3 in C [trans gtr] NXIN ▲ 553193 [DDD] (5.97)

A. Grumiaux (vn) PPHI (Duo) 2-▲ 38736 (17.97)

I. Haendel (vn)—BWV 1001, Son No. 1 in g *(rec live Montreal, Canada, 1968)* ("Vol. 1, Legendary Treasures") † B. Bartók:Son 2 Vn & Pno, Sz.76; W. A. Mozart:Son 26 Vn & Pno, K.378; M. Ravel:Tzigane DHR ▲ 7726 (16.97)

I. Haendel (vn)—BWV 1004, Partita No. 2 in d [Chaconne only] *(rec Abbey Road Studio 1, England, 1994)* † E. Elgar:Con Vn TES ▲ 1146 (17.97)

I. Haendel (vn)—BWV 1004, Partita No. 2 in d [Chaconne only] *(rec Montreal, Canada, 1967)* ("Legendary Treasures, Vol. 2") † Beethoven:Son 7 Vn; C. Champagne:Habanera DHR ▲ 7733 (16.97)

H. Hahn (vn)—Son 3 *(rec Troy New York, June & Dec 1996, Mar 1997)* † Sons & Partitas Vn SNYC ▲ 62793 [DDD] (16.97)

H. Hahn (vn)—BWV 1004, Partita No. 2 in d [Chaconne only] ("The Brook & the Well-Spring") † Brandenburg Con 5, BWV 1050; Cant 147; Con 1 Vn; Goldberg Vars, BWV 988; Mass in b, BWV 232; Passacaglia & Fugue Org, BWV 582; St. John Passion (sels); Wohltemperirte Clavier SNYC (NPR-Milestone of the Millennium) ▲ 60990 [DDD] (11.97)

J. Heifetz (vn)—BWV 1001, Son No. 1 in g; BWV 1004, Partita No. 2 in d *(rec 1935-39)* † J. Brahms:Con Vn & Vc, Op. 102; Glazunov:Con Vn; Saint-Saëns:Intro & Rondo capriccioso, Op. 28; Wieniawski:Con 2 Vn, Op. 22 ENT (Strings) 2-▲ 99312 (32.97)

J. Heifetz (vn), J. Barbirolli (cnd), London PO—BWV 1001, Son No. 1 in g *(rec Dec 11, 1935)* ("Jascha Heifetz: A Profile 1934-1939") † J. Brahms:Con Vn & Vc, Op. 102; Glazunov:Con Vn IN ▲ 1351 [ADD] (15.97)

J. Heifetz (vn), J. Barbirolli (cnd), London SO—BWV 1004, Partita No. 2 in d *(rec London, England, 1935 & 1937)* ("J. Heifetz in the Golden Thirties, Vol. 1") † Saint-Saëns:Havanaise, Op. 83; Intro & Rondo capriccioso, Op. 28; Wieniawski:Con 2 Vn, Op. 22 GRM2 ▲ 78511 [ADD] (13.97)

J. Heifetz (vn), A. Sandor (pno)—BWV 1001, Son No. 1 in g † J. Brahms:Con Vn & Vc, Op. 102; Paganini:Caprices Vn, M.S. 25; Saint-Saëns:Havanaise, Op. 83; Wieniawski:Scherzo-tarantelle, Op. 16 IMMM ▲ 37095 (6.97)

P. Hirschhorn (vn)—BWV 1003, Son No. 2 in a *(rec live, Palais des Beaux-Arts, Brussels, Belgium, June 7, 1967)* † B. Bartók:Son Vn; Geminiani:Sons Vn, Op. 4; P. Hindemith:Son Vn & Pno, Op. 11/1; D. Milhaud:Boeuf sur le toit, Op. 58; M. Ravel:Tzigane; Saint-Saëns:Étude Pno, Op. 52/6 CYPR ▲ 9606 (17.97)

B. Huberman (vn), B. Roubakine (pno)—BWV 1004, Partita No. 2 in d *(rec live, New York, United States of America, 1936-44)* ("Huberman in Recital") † J. Brahms:Son 1 Vn, Op. 78; F. Schubert:Fant Vn, D.934 ARBT ▲ 105 [ADD] (16.97)

M. Huggett (vn) *(rec Dec 1995)* VCL (Veritas) 2-▲ 45205 [DDD] (32.97)

N. Kennedy (vn), K. Tennstedt (cnd), North German RSO—BWV 1003, Son No. 2 in a; BWV 1006, Partita No. 3 in E † Beethoven:Con Vn EMIC ▲ 54574 (16.97)

G. Kessler (gtr), D. Bender (ob)—BWV 1006, Partita No. 3 in E [Gavotte & Rondeau only] *(rec Boston, MA)* ("Trio Sonata - Encore!") † Trio Son for 2 Vns; E. Granados:Danzas españolas (10) Pno; Goyescas:Intermezzo; E. Noda:Tanka Fl, Ob & Gtr; Telemann:Essercizii Musici; Fants (12) Fl, TWV40:2-13; T. Tomkins:Instrumental & Vocal Music; Vivaldi:Con Mands, RV.532; Wooldridge:Partita Ww, Op. 38 *(E text)* BOSK ▲ 114 [DDD] (15.97)

T. Labé (pno)—BWV 1001, Son No. 1 in g; BWV 1004, Partita No. 2 in d; BWV 1006, Partita No. 3 in E; BWV 1003, Son No. 2 in a [arr Rachmaninoff] *(rec June 1993)* † Suites Vc DOR ▲ 80117 [DDD] (13.97)

A. Laberge (hpd)—BWV 1004, Partita No. 2 in d [Chaconne only] *(rec Saint-Benoît-du-Lac Abbey Québec, France, Aug 1989)* ("Harpsichord Transcriptions") FL ▲ 23006 (16.97)

S. Lautenbacher (vn)—BWV 1006, Partita No. 3 in E [Prelude only] ("25 Bach Favorites") † Brandenburg Con 1, BWV 1046; Brandenburg Con 2, BWV 1047; Brandenburg Con 3, BWV 1048; Brandenburg Con 4, BWV 1049; Brandenburg Con 5, BWV 1050; Cant 147; Con Hpds (4), BWV 1065; Con Vns; Con 1 for 2 Hpds, BWV 1060; Con 1 Vn; Mass in b, BWV 232; Music of Bach; Schübler Chorale Preludes; Suite 2 Fl, BWV 1067; Toccata & Fugue Org, BWV 565; Toccata, Adagio & Fugue Org, BWV 564; Wohltemperirte Clavier VCC ▲ 8817 (3.97)

A. Leonard (gtr)—BWV 1003, Son No. 2 in a [trans Andrew Leonard allegro & andante] *(rec Cambridge, MA, May 1996)* ("Music of the Ages") † Suites Vc; J. Dowland:Lt Music; A. Piazzolla:Milonga del angel; Muerte del angel; Sor:Intro & Vars on "Gentil Housard", Op. 27; Intro & Vars on "Malborough", Op. 28; A. York:Sunburst ACTR ▲ 60101 [DDD] (16.97)

BACH, JOHANN SEBASTIAN (cont.)

Sonatas (3) & Partitas (3) for solo Violin, BWV 1001-1006 (1720) (cont.)

H. Lindemann (va)—BWV 1002, Partita No. 1 in b [Chaconne only] † A. Bax:Son Va; J. Brahms:Son 2 Cl; J. N. Hummel:Son Va TACE ▲ 35

J. C. Martins (pno)—BWV 1004, Partita No. 2 in d [Chaconne only; arr Busoni] *(rec NY & Sofia Bulgaria, Bulgaria, 1986 & 1996)* ("Bach for Christmas") † Cant 147; Music of Bach; Schübler Chorale Preludes; Sons Fl; Suite 3 Orch, BWV 1068 COJ ▲ 42040 [DDD] (14.97)

Y. Menuhin (vn)—BWV 1005, Son No. 3 in C BID ▲ 32 [ADD]

A. B. Michelangeli (pno)—BWV 1004, Partita No. 2 in d [Chaconne only] *(rec 1948)* ("The American Debut") † J. Brahms:Vars on a Theme by Paganini, Op. 35; R. Schumann:Con Pno in a, Op. 54 ENPL (Piano Library) ▲ 272 (13.97)

S. Milenkovich (vn) *(rec Genoa, June 1996)* DYNC 2-▲ 164 [DDD] (34.97)

N. Milstein (vn)—BWV 1001, Son No. 1 in g; BWV 1004, Partita No. 2 in d; BWV 1005, Son No. 3 in C; BWV 1002, Partita No. 1 in b; BWV 1006, Partita No. 3 in E [Tempo di Borea only] *(rec Aug 4, 1957)* † Paganini:Caprices Vn, M.S. 25 ORFE (Festspiel Dokumente) ▲ 400951 (16.97)

N. Milstein (vn)—BWV 1002, Partita No. 1 in b; BWV 1004, Partita No. 2 in d; BWV 1006, Partita No. 3 in E *(rec New York, NY, 1954-56)* EMIC (Full Dimensional Sound) ▲ 66870 (m) [ADD] (11.97)

N. Milstein (vn)—BWV 1001, Son No. 1 in g *(rec Coolidge Auditorium, Library of Congress, DC, 1946)* ("Speculum Musicae Plays the New Danes") † Abrahamsen:Winternacht; K. A. Rasmussen:Movements on a Moving Line; Ruders:Bells; B. Sørensen:Deserted Churchyards BRID ▲ 9054 [DDD] (17.97)

N. Milstein (vn) EMIC 2-▲ 64793 (21.97)

N. Milstein (vn) *(rec London; Brent Town Hall Wembley, England, Feb, Apr & Sept 1973)* DEUT (The Originals) 2-▲ 457701 [ADD] (22.97)

N. Milstein (vn)—BWV 1004, Partita No. 2 in d ("The 1953 Library of Congress Recital") † Beethoven:Son 5 Vn, Op. 24; J. Brahms:Son 3 Vn, Op. 108 BRID ▲ 9066 (17.97)

S. Mintz (vn) DEUT 2-▲ 45526 [DDD] (19.97)

E. Møldrup (gtr)—BWV 1004, Partita No. 2 in d [Chaconne only] ("The Guitar Music") † Fugue Lt; Lt Music; Partita Lt, BWV 997; Prelude Lt, BWV 999; Prelude, Fugue & Allegro Lt, BWV 998; Suite Lt, BWV 995; Suite Lt, BWV 996 CLSO 2-▲ 171 (15.97)

F. Moyer (pno)—BWV 1006, Partita No. 3 in E [arr Rachmaninoff for pno] † S. Rachmaninoff:Études-tableaux Pno; Preludes Pno JUP ▲ 106 (13.97)

N. North (lt)—BWV 1001, Son No. 1 in g; BWV 1002, Partita No. 1 in b; BWV 1004, Partita No. 2 in d *(rec July 12-14, 1993)* ("Bach on the Lute, Vol. 1") LINN ▲ 5013 (16.97)

N. North (lt)—BWV 1006, Partita No. 3 in E; BWV 1005, Son No. 3 in C; BWV 1003, Son No. 2 in a *(rec July 12-14, 1993)* ("Bach on the Lute, Vol. 2") LINN ▲ 5029 (16.97)

N. North (lt)—BWV 1004, Partita No. 2 in d [Chaconne only; trans N. North for lt] *(rec Mar 23-26, 1990)* ("Baroque Lute") † S. L. Weiss:Lt Music LINN ▲ 5006 (16.97)

I. Perlman (vn) EMIC 2-▲ 49483 [DDD] (32.97)

R. Podger (vn)—BWV 1001, Son No. 1 in g; BWV 1002, Partita No. 1 in b; BWV 1004, Partita No. 2 in d ("Sonatas & Partitas, Vol. 1") CCL ▲ 12198 (18.97)

G. Poulet (vn) ARN 2-▲ 268296 [DDD] (32.97)

C. Romero (gtr)—BWV 1004, Partita No. 2 in d [trans by Pepe Romero] † Suites Vc; G. Sanz:Suite Española DLS ▲ 1005 [AAD] (10.97)

A. Romero (gtr)—BWV 1004, Partita No. 2 in d [Chaconne only] *(rec Dec 10-15, 1990)* † Cant 147; Suites Vc; Wohltemperirte Clavier TEL ▮ 30288 (8.98) ▲ 80288 (16.97)

A. Romero (gtr)—BWV 1003, Son No. 2 in a [Chaconne only] *(rec Dec 10-15, 1990)* † Cant 147; Suites Vc; Wohltemperirte Clavier TEL ▲ 80288 (16.97) ▮ 30288 (8.98)

A. Rosand (pno/vn) VOXC ▲ 7901 (16.97)

Rosé String Quartet—BWV 1001, Son No. 1 in g [Adagio only] *(rec 1927)* † Air on the G String; Con Vns; Beethoven:Qt 10 Strs, Op. 74; Qt 14 Strs, Op. 131; Qt 4 Strs, Op. 18/4 BID 2-▲ 56 [ADD]

S. Rottersman (gtr)—BWV 1004, Partita No. 2 in d [Chaconne only; tran. A. Segovia] ("Sherri Rottersman: The Sensual Guitar") † I. Albéniz:Suite española 1, Op. 47; Anonymous:Renaissance Pieces Lt; E. Granados:Danzas españolas (10) Pno; J. Rodrigo:Ecos de Sefarad; Tansman:Mazurka Gtr; Tárrega:Capricho árabe AURR ▲ 23446 [ADD] (16.97)

L. St. John (vn)—BWV 1004, Partita No. 2 in d; BWV 1005, Son No. 3 in C ("Works for Violin Solo") WETE ▲ 5180 (16.97)

T. Satoh (lt), T. Satoh (lt)—BWV 1004, Partita No. 2 in d; BWV 1004, Partita No. 2 in d [Chaconne only] *(rec Amsterdam, Netherlands, Feb 1990)* ("Chaconne; Baroque Lute Recital") † Gallot:Folies d'Espagne; T. Satoh:Music of Satoh; Tombeau de Mr. D. Philips; Taxin:Qnt Brass; S. L. Weiss:Lt Music CCL ▲ 490 [DDD]

A. Segovia (gtr)—BWV 1002, Partita No. 1 in b; BWV 1001, Son No. 1 in g; BWV 1006, Partita No. 3 in E; BWV 1004, Partita No. 2 in d [Sarabande, Bourrée & Double only] *(rec 1952-68)* † Prelude Lt, BWV 999; Suite Lt, BWV 995; Suites Vc MCA1 ▲ 42068 [AAD] (11.97)

A. Segovia (gtr)—BWV 1006, Partita No. 3 in E [arr gtr] *(rec May 2, 1927)* ("The Young Segovia, 1927-39") † Suites Vc; Maláts:Impresiones de España; M. Ponce:Gtr Music IN ▲ 1347 [ADD] (15.97)

A. Segovia (gtr)—BWV 1004, Partita No. 2 in d; BWV 1006, Partita No. 3 in E [Gavotte; trans Segovia in E for gtr] *(rec 1947-49)* † Fugue Lt; Suite Lt, BWV 996; Suites Vc; Castelnuovo-Tedesco:Con 1 Gtr, Op. 99; Moreno Torroba:Suite castellana; M. Ponce:Sonatina Meridional; J. Turina:Fandanguillo, Op. 36 URAN ▲ 111 (15.97)

D. Sitkovetsky (vn) ORF 2-▲ 130852 (36.97)

D. Sitkovetsky (vn) *(rec Sept 1997)* ("Edition Bachakademie, Vol. 119") HANS 2-▲ 92119 [DDD] (19.97)

P. Skareng (gtr)—BWV 1001, Son No. 1 in g [trans Per Skareng & Gordon Crosskey] ("El Colibri") † Carlstedt:Swedish Dances; Frumerie:Vars on a Swedish Folk Tune, Op. 69a; M. Giuliani:Rossiniana; Lauro:Gtr Music; Sagreras:El Colibri; Tárrega:Recuerdos de la Alhambra CAPA ▲ 21392 [AAD] (16.97)

R. Smits (gtr)—BWV 1002, Partita No. 1 in b; BWV 1004, Partita No. 2 in d; BWV 1005, Son No. 3 in C *(rec Haarlem The Netherlands, Netherlands, Oct 1993)* † S. L. Weiss:Lt Music ACCE ▲ 93100 [DDD] (17.97)

A. Steinhardt (vn)—BWV 1004, Partita No. 2 in d † Music of Bach TOWN ▲ 7 (17.97)

Swingle Singers—BWV 1003, Son No. 2 in a [Andante only] *(rec 1991)* ("Bach Hits Back/A Cappella Amadeus") † Anna Magdalena Bach Notebook (sels); Brandenburg Con 3, BWV 1048; Cant 140; Cant 208; In dulci jubilo, BWV 729; Inventions Hpd; Music of Bach; St. Matthew Passion (sels); Suite 2 Fl, BWV 1067; Wohltemperirte Clavier; W. A. Mozart:Music of Mozart VCL 2-▲ 61472 [DDD] (11.97)

H. Szeryng (vn) *(rec 1960s)* DEUT (Two-fers) 2-▲ 453004 [ADD] (17.97)

I. Szeverényi (hpd)—BWV 1004, Partita No. 2 in d *(rec 1994)* † Chromatic Fant & Fugue, BWV 903 CLDI ▲ 4004 [DDD] (10.97)

J. Szigeti (vn)—BWV 1002, Partita No. 1 in b; BWV 1006, Partita No. 3 in E *(rec Aug. 1, 1927)* † B. Bartók:Hungarian Folktunes, Sz.66; Romanian Folk Dances Vn & Pno; J. Brahms:Son 3 Pno, Op. 5 BID ▲ 153 [ADD] (16.97)

J. Szigeti (vn)—BWV 1001, Son No. 1 in g; BWV 1006, Partita No. 3 in E; BWV 1003, Son No. 2 in a *(rec New York, NY, Feb 13, 1949)* MUA ▲ 4774 (m) [AAD]

J. Szigeti (vn)—BWV 1001, Son No. 1 in g ("Joseph Szigeti Plays Violin Sonatas") † J. Brahms:Son 3 Vn, Op. 108 IN ▲ 1321 [ADD] (15.97)

J. Szigeti (vn)—BWV 1001, Son No. 1 in g ("A Tribute to Joseph Szigeti") † J. Brahms:Son 3 Vn, Op. 108 GRM2 ▲ 78630 (13.97)

J. Szigeti (vn)—BWV 1001, Son No. 1 in g *(rec 1927-44)* ("Joseph Szigeti: The Great Violin Sonatas") † Beethoven:Son 5 Vn, Op. 24; Son 9 Vn, Op. 47; J. Brahms:Son 3 Vn, Op. 108 ENT (Strings) 2-▲ 99318 (32.97)

J. Szigeti (vn) *(rec July & Oct 1955)* VC 2-▲ 8021 [ADD] (26.97)

M. Tenenbaum (vn)—BWV 1004, Partita No. 2 in d *(rec Performing Arts Center Purchase College, NY, Sept 17, 1997)* ("Musical Evenings with the Captain, Vol. 2") † J. Christian Bach:Sons Hpd Vn, T.325/1; W. A. Mozart:Qt Ob ESSY ▲ 1056 [DDD] (16.97)

L. Tertis (va)—BWV 1004, Partita No. 2 in d [Chaconne only] *(rec 1925)* † A. Bax:Son Va; J. Brahms:Son 2 Cl; Delius:Son 2 Vn PHS ▲ 9918 [AAD] (17.97)

J. Vallières (gtr)—BWV 1005, Son No. 3 in C [Adagio & Fugue only-trans for gtr] ("J. S. Bach: Guitar, Vol. 1") † Suite Lt, BWV 995; Suite Lt, BWV 996; Suites Vc SNE ▲ 599 (16.97)

Vanessa-Mae (vn)—BWV 1006, Partita No. 3 in E ("The Classical Album") † J. Brahms:Scherzo Vn; Bruch:Scottish Fant, Op. 46 ANGL ▲ 55395 (16.97)

E. Wallfisch (vn) HYP (Dyad) 2-▲ 22009 (18.97)

J. Williams (gtr)—BWV 1004, Partita No. 2 in d [Chaconne only] *(rec Warranwood, Victoria, Australia, Apr 30-May 8, 1987)* ("The Baroque Album") † F. Couperin:Pièces de clavecin (sels); Roncalli:Lt & Gtr Music; D. Scarlatti:Sons Kbd; Telemann:Bourree alla Polacca; S. L. Weiss:Fant; Lt Music; Passacaglia *(E text)* SNYC ▲ 44518 [ADD] (16.97)

J. Williams (gtr), K. Sillito (cnd), Academy of St. Martin in the Fields—BWV 1003, Son No. 2 in a [Andante only] † Con 2 Vn; G. F. Handel:Cons (16) Org; A. Marcello:Con Ob Strs SNYC ▲ 39560 [DDD] (16.97)

Y. Zivoni (vn)—Sons 1 in g & 3 in C ("J.S. Bach: Solo Violin Music, Vol. 2") † Sons & Partitas Vn MER ▲ 84283 [DDD] (16.97)

BACH, JOHANN SEBASTIAN (cont.)

Sonatas (3) & Partitas (3) for solo Violin, BWV 1001-1006 (1720) (cont.)

various artists—BWV 1005, Son No. 3 in C; BWV 1001, Son No. 1 in g; BWV 1006, Partita No. 3 in E; BWV 1006, Partita No. 3 in E [Menuet 2] ("Baby Needs Baroque") † Brandenburg Con 1, BWV 1046; French Suites; Goldberg Vars, BWV 988; Inventions Hpd; Son Vn; Suite 2 Fl, BWV 1067; G. F. Handel:Water Music, HWV 348-50; J. Pachelbel:Canon & Gigue; Telemann:Qnt Tpt; Son Fl; Torelli:Son 5 No. 1 in D; Vivaldi:Cons Vn Strs, Op. 8/1-4 DLS ▲ 1609 [DDD] (10.97) ▮ 1609 [DDD] (8.98)

various artists—BWV 1005, Son No. 3 in C; BWV 1001, Son No. 1 in g [Siciliano only] ("Bach for Relaxation") † Brandenburg Con 2, BWV 1047; Cant 147; Goldberg Vars, BWV 988; Music of Bach; Musical Offering, BWV 1079; Prelude Lt, BWV 999; Sons Fl; Sons Vn Hpd; Suites Vc RCAV ▲ 68697 (11.97) ▮ 68697 (5.98)

various artists—BWV 1004, Partita No. 2 in d [excerpt] † Beethoven:Son 9 Vn, Op. 47; Mendelssohn (-Bartholdy):Con Vn & Orch, Op. 64; W. A. Mozart:Con 3 Vn, K.216; Tartini:Son Vn & Pno; P. Tchaikovsky:Con Vn MTAL ▲ 48099 (6.97)

Sonatas (6) for Flute & Continuo, BWV 1030-1035 [BWV 1031 & 1033 doubtful]

J. Adamus (ob), K. Novatná (hpd)—BWV 1030, No. 1 in b [trans for ob & bc as BWV 1030b] ("Baroque Oboe Sonatas") † Son Vn LT ▲ 54 [DDD] (16.97)

P. Alanko (fl), A. Mattila (hpd)—BWV 1031, No. 2 in E♭; BWV 1032, No. 3 in A; BWV 1034, No. 5 in e [w. Jukka Rautasalo (vc)] *(rec Dec 1995)* ("Flute Sonatas, Vol. 1") † Partita Fl, BWV 1013 NXIN ▲ 8553754 [DDD] (5.97)

J. Baxtresser (fl), A. Davis (hpd) ("Baroque Flute") † F. Danzi:Petits Duos, Op. 64; G. F. Handel:Harmonious Blacksmith ICC ▲ 6702272 (9.97)

M. Beaucoudray (fl), W. Christie (hpd) HAM (Suite) ▲ 790065 (12.97)

W. Bennett (fl), G. Malcolm (hpd) ASVQ ▲ 6108 [DDD] (10.97)

I. Biret (pno)—BWV 1031, No. 2 in E♭ [Siciliano only] *(rec 1991)* † Cant 29; Chorales (miscellaneous); Kbd Music (misc); Schübler Chorale Preludes; C. W. Gluck:Orfeo ed Euridice; G. F. Handel:Menuet Pno; Kempff:Pno Music; W. A. Mozart:Pastorale variée, K.Anh.209b MARC ▲ 8223452 [DDD] (13.97)

B. Bogatin (vc), J. Solum (fl), I. Kipnis (hpd) ARA ▲ 6589

R. Canter (ob), P. Nicholson (hpd)—BWV 1030, No. 1 in b; BWV 1031, No. 2 in E♭ *(rec May 1992)* † Sons Vl AMON ▲ 60 [DDD] (16.97)

F. Cooley (tuba), N. C. Nimmo (hpd) ("The Romantic Tuba") † J. Brahms:Ernste Gesänge, Op. 121; A. Russell:Suite Concertante; Zindars:Trigon CRYS ▲ 120 (15.97) ▮ 120 (9.98)

S. Cunningham (vl), J. Galway (fl), P. Moll (hpd)—BWV 1032, No. 3 in A ("Galway Plays Bach, Vol. 2") † Musical Offering, BWV 1079; Partita Fl, BWV 1013; Trio Son Fl Vn & Hpd, BWV 1038; Trio Son Fls, BWV 1039 RCAV (Red Seal) ▲ 68182 [DDD] (16.97)

M. Faust (fl), I. Wjuniski (hpd)—BWV 1030, No. 1 in b; BWV 1031, No. 2 in E♭; BWV 1032, No. 3 in A *(rec May 1991)* † Trio Sons Org GMR ▲ 2036 (16.97)

M. Fisher (eup), M. Lawson (pno)—BWV 1031, No. 2 in E♭ *(rec Northern Illinois Univ., United States of America, June 6-7 & Nov 26-27, 1994)* ("EuFish") † Arban:Fant, Theme & Vars on; J. Bach:Concert Vars; J. Brahms:Songs; G. Jacob:Fant Eup; Telemann:Son Bn ALBA ▲ 162 [DDD] (16.97)

Freiburg Baroque Soloists—BWV 1030, No. 1 in b ("Trio Sonatas In Their Orignal Versions") † Trio Sons (misc); Trio Sons Org ENTE ▲ 53 [ADD] (10.97)

J. Galway (fl), U. Duetschler (hpd)—BWV 1032, No. 3 in A † Con Fl, Vn & Hpd, BWV 1044; Suite 2 Fl, BWV 1067 RCAV (Red Seal) ▲ 60900 (16.97)

J. Gérard (fl), D. Blumenthal (pno) ("Edition Bachakademie, Vol. 121: Chamber Music for Flute") † Partita Fl, BWV 1013; Partita Lt, BWV 997; Son Vn; Trio Son Fl Vn & Hpd, BWV 1038; Trio Son Fls, BWV 1039 HANS 2-▲ 92121 [DDD] (19.97)

I. Goritzki (ob), H. Erhard (hpd) † Art of the Fugue (sels); Trio Sons Org HANS ▲ 98987 [DDD] (15.97)

T. Indermühle (ob), U. Dütschler (hpd)—BWV 1030, No. 1 in b; BWV 1031, No. 2 in E♭; BWV 1032, No. 3 in A [trans for ob & hpd] *(rec Apr 16-20, 1995)* ("6 Oboe Sonatas") † Son Vn; Trio Sons Org CAMA ▲ 404 [DDD] (18.97)

C. K. Kim (fl), E. Picht-Axenfeld (hpd)—BWV 1030, No. 1 in b *(rec Iruma Shimin Kaikan, Japan, May 1979)* ("Baroque Flute Sonatas") † Partita Fl, BWV 1013; C.P.E. Bach:Son Fl, H.562; Telemann:Fants (12) Fl, TWV40:2-13 CAMA ▲ 262 [AAD] (18.97)

W. Kuijken (vl), M. Larrieu (fl), R. Puyana (hpd) † Cant 120; Partita Fl, BWV 1013; Sons Vl PPHI 2-▲ 38809 (17.97)

D. Lipatti (pno)—BWV 1031, No. 2 in E♭ [arr Kempff for pno] *(rec Radio-Genève, Switzerland, July 1950)* † Cant 147; Orgelbüchlein; Partitas Hpd; W. A. Mozart:Son 8 Pno, K.310; D. Scarlatti:Sons Kbd; F. Schubert:Impromptus (4) Pno EMIC (Great Recordings of the Century) ▲ 67003 [ADD] (11.97)

J. C. Martins (pno)—BWV 1031, No. 2 in E♭ [arr Kempff] *(rec NY & Sofia Bulgaria, Bulgaria, 1986 & 1996)* ("Bach for Christmas") † Cant 147; Music of Bach; Schübler Chorale Preludes; Sons & Partitas Vn; Suite 3 Orch, BWV 1068 COJ ▲ 42040 [DDD] (14.97)

P. Meisen (fl), H. Bilgram (hpd)—BWV 1030, No. 1 in b; BWV 1032, No. 3 in A *(rec Polling, Germany, Sept 21-24, 1977)* ("Bach Flute Sonatas") † Partita Fl, BWV 1013 CAMA ▲ 281 [AAD]

M. Petri (rcr), K. Jarrett (hpd) RCAV (Red Seal) ▲ 61274 (16.97)

J. Pinet (fl), G. Soly (hpd)—BWV 1030, No. 1 in b; BWV 1032, No. 3 in A *(rec Oct 1995)* ("Complete Sonatas for Melodic Instrument, Vol. 2") FL ▲ 23061 [DDD] (16.97)

T. Pinnock (hpd) † Son Vn SNYC 2-▲ 39746 (31.97)

B. Re (vl), C. Mendoze (rcr), G. Barbolini (hpd) † A. Corelli:Sons Vn, Op. 5; Vivaldi:Pastor fido, Op. 13/1-6 PVY ▲ 787023 [DDD] (16.97)

D. Russell (gtr) † D. Scarlatti:Sons Kbd GHA ▲ 126006 (17.97)

D. Russell (gtr)—BWV 1034, No. 5 in e [trans Russell] ("The Best of Classical Guitar") † M. de Falla:Amor brujo (sels); Moreno Torroba:Suite castellana; A. Piazzolla:Music of Piazzolla; J. Rodrigo:Tonadilla; D. Scarlatti:Sons Kbd GHA ▲ 126034 (7.97)

D. St. Germain (rcr), M. Chabot (hpd)—BWV 1031, No. 2 in E♭; BWV 1035, No. 6 in E † Son Vn; Telemann:Cons & Suites Fl; Essercizii Musici SNE ▲ 591 (16.97)

H. Sargous (ob), L. Ward (pno)—BWV 1030, No. 1 in b [arr for oboe] ("Architecture & Aria: Three Centuries of Virtuoso Oboe") † A. Mead:Scena; Pasculli:Grand Con Ob; S. Wolpe:Son Ob CRYS ▲ 327 [DDD] (15.97)

J. Savall (vl), S. Preston (fl), T. Pinnock (hpd) † Partita Fl, BWV 1013 CRD 2-▲ 33145 [ADD] (34.97)

H. Schellenberger (ob), M. Süss (hp), K. Stoll (db)—BWV 1033, No. 4 in C; BWV 1031, No. 2 in E♭ *(rec Berlin, Germany)* † Son Vn; C.P.E. Bach:Son Fl, H.562; Son Hp, H.563; Son Ob, H.549 CAMM ▲ 130021 [DDD] (16.97)

B. Schmidt (vn), L. Smirnova (pno) [arr Robert Schumann for pno] ("Bach Interpreted by Schumann") MDG ▲ 3330614 (35.97)

D. Shostac (fl), R. Kato (va), J. Walz (vc), J. Smith (gtr), G. Levant (hp), A. Perry (pno)—BWV 1031, No. 2 in E♭ [Siciliano only] *(rec North Hollywood, CA)* ("The Romantic Flute") † Air on the G String; Arioso Ob; Debussy:Prélude à l'après-midi d'un faune; Suite bergamasque; G. Fauré:Pavane; Sicilienne, Op. 78; Gossec:Tambourin Fl; Marais:Basque; W. A. Mozart:Andante Fl, K.315; Con 21 Pno, K.467; J. Pachelbel:Canon & Gigue XCEL ▲ 30006

M. Springfels (vl), J. See (fl), D. Moroney (hpd) † Partita Fl, BWV 1013; Son Vn; Danielpour:Metamorphosis; Perle:Con 2 Pno HAM 2-▲ 907024 (36.97)

D. Stepner (va/vn), L. Quan (va/vn), L. Jeppesen (vl), J. Gibbons (pno) *(rec Weston, MA, July 1995)* ("Music from Aston Magna") † Canons Goldberg Vars; Musical Offering, BWV 1079 CENT ▲ 2295 [DDD] (16.97)

T. Stone (thb), C. Ferrarini (fl), S. Bassino (bn), F. Tasini (hpd) MONM 2-▲ 96032 (36.97)

L. R. Svendsen (rcr), P. van Duren (hpd/org)—BWV 1031, No. 2 in E♭ ("Barockmusik für Zwei") † Trio Sons Org; Boismortier:Sons Fl, Op. 91; Buxtehude:Magnificat primi toni, BuxWV 204; Frescobaldi:Canzoni for 1-4 Instr; Montalbano:Sinfs; Noordt:Tabulature Book PLAL ▲ 99 [DDD] (18.97)

A. Vanackère (vc), M. Beaucoudray (fl), P. Dubreuil (hpd) † Partita Fl, BWV 1013; Son Vn ARN 2-▲ 268386 (32.97)

M. Verbruggen (rcr), M. Meyerson (hpd)—BWV 1031, No. 2 in E♭ [trans Verbruggen] † Trio Sons Org HAM ▲ 907119 (18.97)

O. Zoboli (ob), A. Cremonesi (hpd)—BWV 1030, No. 1 in b *(rec Apr 4-6, 1995)* ("The Apotheosis of the Oboe") † Geminiani:Son 3 Ob; G. Sammartini:Solos Fl, Op. 13; Telemann:Kleine Kammermusik STRV ▲ 80005 (12.97)

various artists—BWV 1034, No. 5 in e [Andante only] ("Bach for Relaxation") † Brandenburg Con 2, BWV 1047; Cant 147; Goldberg Vars, BWV 988; Music of Bach; Musical Offering, BWV 1079; Prelude Lt, BWV 999; Sons & Partitas Vn; Sons Vn Hpd; Suites Vc RCAV ▲ 68697 (11.97) ▮ 68697 (5.98)

Sonata in G for Flute, Violin & Continuo [constructed on bass of BWV 1021; probably by one of Bach's sons or pupils], BWV 1038

S. Kuijken (vn), B. Kuijken (fl), R. Köhnen (hpd) † C.P.E. Bach:Trio Sons (5) Fl, H.567-571; Telemann:Qts (6) Fl, "Quadri"; Suites (6) Fl ACCE ▲ 58019 [DDD] (17.97)

Sonatas (5) for Keyboard

J. Sebestyén (hpd)—Son Kbd, BWV 965 *(rec 1972)* † Adagio Clvd, BWV 968; Son Kbd CLDI ▲ 4021 [ADD] (10.97)

Sonata in D for Keyboard, BWV 963 (ca 1704)

S. Richter (pno) † Capriccio Hpd, BWV 993; Duets Hpd; Italian Con, BWV 971; Son Kbd STRV ▲ 33323 (16.97)

Sonata in d for Keyboard [doubtful], BWV 964

S. Richter (pno) † Capriccio Hpd, BWV 993; Duets Hpd; Italian Con, BWV 971; Son Kbd STRV ▲ 33323 (16.97)

J. Sebestyén (hpd) *(rec 1972)* † Adagio Clvd, BWV 968; Son Kbd; Sons (5) Kbd CLDI ▲ 4021 [ADD] (10.97)

BACH, JOHANN SEBASTIAN (cont.)

Sonata in d for Keyboard [doubtful], BWV 964 (cont.)

R. Tureck (pno)—Allegro ("A Tribute to the Keyboard Legend") † Anna Magdalena Bach Notebook; English Suites; Goldberg Vars, BWV 988; Italian Con, BWV 971; Partitas Hpd; Wohltemperirte Clavier; Liszt:Grandes études de Paganini, S.141; Mendelssohn (-Bartholdy):Midsummer Night's Dream (sels); F. Schubert:Moments musicaux, D.780 VAIA ▲ 1086 [AAD] (12.97)

Sonatas (3) in G, D & g for Viol & Harpsichord, BWV 1027-1029 (ca 1720)

R. Boothby (vl), S. Ad-El (hpd) CHN ▲ 608 (16.97)

Boston Museum Trio—BWV 1027, No. 1 in G; BWV 1028, No. 2 in D; BWV 1029, No. 3 in g *(rec Waltham, MA, Oct 21-22, 1993)* † Son Vn Bc, BWV 1021; Son Vn Bc, BWV 1023 CENT ▲ 2198 [DDD] (16.97)

A. Bylsma (vc pic), B. V. Asperen (org) † J. C. F. Bach:Son Vc SNYC (Vivarte) ▲ 45945 (16.97)

R. Canter (ob), P. Nicholson (hpd) *(rec May 1992)* † Sons Fl AMON ▲ 60 [DDD] (16.97)

M. Cervera (vl), R. Puyana (hpd) † Cant 120; Partita Fl, BWV 1013; Sons Fl PPHI 2-▲ 38809 (17.97)

L. Dreyfus (vl), K. Haugsand (hpd) SIMX ▲ 1024 [DDD] (18.97)

P. Fournier (vc), M. Hess (pno) *(rec 1959)* ("Hess & Fournier in a New York Sonata Recital") † Beethoven:Son 4 Vc; Vars Vc on "Ein Mädchen oder Weibchen", Op. 66; J. Brahms:Son 2 Vc, Op. 99; W. A. Mozart:Gigue Pno, K.574; Rondo Pno, K.485 RELE ▲ 1895 [ADD]

V. Ghielmi (vl), L. Ghielmi (hpd/pno)—BWV 1028, No. 2 in D; BWV 1027, No. 1 in G; BWV 1029, No. 3 in g *(rec Chiostri della Basilica di San Simplicano Milan, Oct 1997)* ("Sonatas for Viol & Obbligato Harpsichord") † Wohltemperirte Clavier ARSM ▲ 1228 [DDD] (17.97)

R. Gini (vl), L. Alvini (hpd) † Italian Con, BWV 971 TACT ▲ 680201 (16.97)

B. Hoffman (vl), A. Fedi (hpd) *(rec Florence Italy, Jan 1994)* AART ▲ 47252 [DDD] (10.97)

J. H. Jones (cnd), Cambridge Baroque Camerata—BWV 1029, No. 3 in g [arr Duncan Druce] † Brandenburg Cons ITIM 2-▲ 55 [DDD] (31.97)

Y.-Y. Ma (vc), K. Cooper (hpd) SNYC ▲ 37794 [DDD] (11.97)

E. Mainardi (vc), C. Seemann (pno) † M. Reger:Son Vc ORFE ▲ 418971 [ADD] (16.97)

M. Maisky (vc), M. Argerich (pno) DEUT ▲ 15471 [DDD] (16.97)

E. Nyffenegger (vc), G. Wyss (pno) † Francoeur:Sons Vn & Bc; Locatelli:Son Vc; Lully:Passacaglia Vc & Pno DVX ▲ 25206 [ADD] (11.97)

S. Pank (vl), I. Ahlgrimm (hpd) CAPO ▲ 10043 [DDD] (11.97)

J. Rivest (vn), C. Plubeau (vl), G. Soly (hpd)—BWV 1027, No. 1 in G; BWV 1028, No. 2 in D *(rec 1995)* ("Complete Sonatas for Solo Instrument & Harpsichord, Vol. 3") FL ▲ 23062 [DDD] (16.97)

G. Sárközy (va bastarda), P. Ella (hpd), I. Dénes (org) *(rec 1980, 1984 & 1991)* ("Johann Sebastian Bach on Viola Bastarda, Lute and Lute-Harpsichord") † Cant 147; Fugue Lt; Partita Lt, BWV 997; Prelude, Fugue & Allegro Lt, BWV 998; Suite Lt, BWV 995; Suite Lt, BWV 996 HUN 2-▲ 31616 [ADD] (32.97)

J. Starker (vc), G. Sebok (hpd)—BWV 1028, No. 2 in D; BWV 1027, No. 1 in G † Suites Vc MRCR 2-▲ 32756 [ADD] (22.97)

J. Suk (va), Z. Růžičová (hpd) ("The Viola Through the Ages, Vol. 1") † Son Vn PRAG ▲ 250103 (18.97)

R. Verebes (va/vl), M. Lagacé (hpd) *(rec Bourcheville Quebec)* † Chromatic Fant & Fugue, BWV 903 SNE ▲ 564 (16.97)

D. Yeadon (vc), P. Wispelwey (vc pic), R. Egarr (org/pno/hpd)—No. 1 in G; No. 2 in D; BWV 1029, No. 3 in g † Con 2 Hpd, BWV 1053; Con 5 Hpd, BWV 1056; Italian Con, BWV 971; Prelude Lt, BWV 999; Suites Vc; Wohltemperirte Clavier CCL ▲ 14198 (18.97)

Sonatas for Violin & Continuo

E. Wallfisch (vn), R. Tunnicliffe (vc), P. Nicholson (hpd) HYP (Dyad) 2-▲ 22025 (18.97)

Sonata in G for Violin & Continuo, BWV 1021 (ca 1720)

G. Barinova (vn), S. Richter (pno) *(rec 1952)* ("Russian Violin School: Galina Barinova") † Tartini:Son Vn & Bc, Op. 1/10 RD (Talents of Russia) ▲ 16223 [ADD] (16.97)

Boston Museum Trio members *(rec Waltham, MA, Oct 21-22, 1993)* † Son Vn Bc, BWV 1023; Sons Vl CENT ▲ 2198 [DDD] (16.97)

A. Busch (vn), R. Serkin (pno) *(rec 1928-37)* ("Busch-Serkin Duo Recordings, Vol. 3") † Sons & Partitas Vn; Sons Vn Hpd; F. Schubert:Fant Vn, D.934; Vivaldi:Sons Vn APR ▲ 5543 [ADD] (18.97)

A. Busch (vn), R. Serkin (pno) † Beethoven:Son 5 Vn, Op. 24; Son 7 Vn; J. Brahms:Son 1 Vn, Op. 78; Son 2 Vn, Op. 100; R. Schumann:Son 1 Vn, Op. 105 GRM2 ▲ 78820 (26.97)

A. Grumiaux (vn), C. Jaccottet (pno) † Son Vn; Son Vn Bc, BWV 1023; Sons Vn Hpd PPHI ▲ 54011 (17.97)

C. Mackintosh (vn), J. W. Clarke (vc), M. Cole (hpd) ("Complete Violin & Harpsichord Sonatas") † Son Vn Bc, BWV 1023 CHOC (Early Music) 2-▲ 603 (32.97)

Sonata in e for Violin & Continuo, BWV 1023 (1714-17)

Boston Museum Trio members *(rec Waltham, MA, Oct 21-22, 1993)* † Son Vn Bc, BWV 1021; Sons Vl CENT ▲ 2198 [DDD] (16.97)

A. Grumiaux (vn), C. Jaccottet (pno) † Son Vn; Son Vn Bc, BWV 1021; Sons Vn Hpd PPHI ▲ 54011 (17.97)

C. Mackintosh (vn), J. W. Clarke (vc), M. Cole (hpd) ("Complete Violin & Harpsichord Sonatas") † Son Vn Bc, BWV 1021 CHOC (Early Music) 2-▲ 603 (32.97)

I. Stern (vn), A. Zakin (pno) ("Isaac Stern: A Life In Music: Vol. 23") † Son Vn; G. F. Handel:Son Vn; Tartini:Son Vn & Bc, Op. 1/10 SNYC ▲ 68361 [ADD] (10.97)

Sonatas (6) for Violin & Harpsichord, BWV 1014-1019 (1717-23)

E. Blumenstock (vn), J. Butt (hpd) HMA 2-▲ 1907084 (17.97)

A. Busch (vn), R. Serkin (pno)—BWV 1016, No. 3 in E; BWV 1017, No. 4 in c *(rec 1928-37)* ("Busch-Serkin Duo Recordings, Vol. 3") † Son Vn Bc, BWV 1021; Sons & Partitas Vn; F. Schubert:Fant Vn, D.934; Vivaldi:Sons Vn APR ▲ 5543 [ADD] (18.97)

J. Dvořák (cnd), Capella Istropolitana—BWV 1017, No. 4 in c [arr Dvořák] *(rec 1989)* † Cant 140; English Suites; Suite 1 Orch, BWV 1066; Suite 2 Fl, BWV 1067; Wohltemperirte Clavier NXIN ▲ 550244 [DDD] (5.97)

A. Grumiaux (vn), C. Jaccottet (pno) † Son Vn; Son Vn Bc, BWV 1021; Son Vn Bc, BWV 1023 PPHI ▲ 54011 (17.97)

D. Sitkovetsky (vn), R. Hill (hpd) HANS ▲ 98154 [DDD] (15.97)

R. Stallman (fl), E. Swanborn (hpd)—BWV 1014, No. 1 in b; BWV 1015, No. 2 in A; BWV 1016, No. 3 in E; BWV 1017, No. 4 in c; BWV 1019, No. 6 in G [arr Stallman] *(rec Church of the Good Shepherd, NYC, NY, Apr 1995)* VAIA ▲ 1138 [DDD] (16.97)

J. Suk (vn), Z. Růžičová (hpd) *(rec Prague, Czech Republic, May 1998)* LT 2-▲ 60 [DDD] (16.97)

M. Tenenbaum (vn), R. Kapp (pno) ESSY 2-▲ 1066 [DDD] (32.97)

M. Tenenbaum (vn), G. Ranck (hpd) ESSY 2-▲ 1064 (32.97)

R. Terakado (vn), S. Henstra (hpd) DNN 2-▲ 18029 (33.97)

various artists—BWV 1014, No. 1 in b [Andante only] ("Bach for Relaxation") † Brandenburg Con 2, BWV 1047; Cant 147; Goldberg Vars, BWV 988; Music of Bach; Musical Offering, BWV 1079; Prelude Lt, BWV 999; Sons & Partitas Vn; Sons Fl; Suites Vc RCAV ▲ 68697 (11.97) ▮ 68697 (5.98)

Sonata in g for Violin & Harpsichord [doubtful], BWV 1020

J. Adamus (ob), K. Novatná (hpd) [trans for ob & hpd] ("Baroque Oboe Sonatas") † Sons Fl LT ▲ 54 [DDD] (16.97)

M. Beaucoudray (fl), P. Dubreuil (hpd) † Partita Fl, BWV 1013; Sons Fl ARN 2-▲ 268386 (32.97)

M. Faust (fl), I. Wjuniski (hpd) [trans for fl & bc] *(rec May 1991)* GMR ▲ 2037 (16.97)

J. Gérard (fl), D. Blumenthal (pno) ("Edition Bachakademie, Vol. 121: Chamber Music for Flute") † Partita Fl, BWV 1013; Partita Lt, BWV 997; Sons Fl; Trio Son Fl Vn & Hpd, BWV 1038; Trio Son Fls, BWV 1039 HANS 2-▲ 92121 [DDD] (19.97)

A. Grumiaux (vn), C. Jaccottet (pno) † Son Vn; Son Vn Bc, BWV 1021; Son Vn Bc, BWV 1023; Sons Vn Hpd PPHI ▲ 54011 (17.97)

T. Indermühle (ob), U. Dütschler (hpd) [trans for ob & hpd] *(rec Apr 16-20, 1995)* ("6 Oboe Sonatas") † Sons Fl; Trio Sons Org CAMA ▲ 404 [DDD] (18.97)

J. Rampal (fl), T. Pinnock (hpd) [trans for fl & bc] † Sons Fl SNYC 2-▲ 39746 (31.97)

D. St. Germain (rcr), M. Chabot (hpd) † Sons Fl; Telemann:Cons & Suites Fl; Essercizii Musici SNE ▲ 591 (16.97)

H. Schellenberger (ob), M. Süss (hp), K. Stoll (db) *(rec Berlin, Germany)* † Sons Fl; C.P.E. Bach:Son Fl, H.562; Son Hp, H.563; Son Ob, H.549 CAMM ▲ 130021 [DDD] (16.97)

M. Springfels (vl), J. See (fl), D. Moroney (hpd) [trans for fl & bc] † Partita Fl, BWV 1013; Sons Fl; Danielpour:Metamorphosis; Perle:Con 2 Pno HAM 2-▲ 907024 (36.97)

I. Stern (vn), A. Zakin (pno) ("Isaac Stern: A Life In Music: Vol. 23") † Son Vn Bc, BWV 1023; G. F. Handel:Son Vn; Tartini:Son Vn & Bc, Op. 1/10 SNYC ▲ 68361 [ADD] (10.97)

J. Suk (va), Z. Růžičová (hpd) ("The Viola Through the Ages, Vol. 1") † Son Vn; Sons Vl PRAG ▲ 250103 (18.97)

various artists—Adagio ("Baby Needs Baroque") † Brandenburg Con 1, BWV 1046; French Suites; Goldberg Vars, BWV 988; Inventions Hpd; Sons & Partitas Vn; Suite 2 Fl, BWV 1067; G. F. Handel:Water Music, HWV 348-50; J. Pachelbel:Canon & Gigue; Telemann:Qnt Tpt; Son Fl; Torelli:Son 5 No. 1 in D; Vivaldi:Cons Vn Strs, Op. 8/1-4 DLS ▲ 1609 [DDD] (10.97) ▮ 1609 [DDD] (8.98)

BACH, JOHANN SEBASTIAN (cont.)

Sonata in F for Violin & Harpsichord [doubtful], BWV 1022

A. Grumiaux (vn), C. Jaccottet (pno) † Son Vn; Son Vn Bc, BWV 1021; Son Vn Bc, BWV 1023; Sons Vn Hpd PPHI ▲ 54011 (17.97)

J. Suk (va), Z. Růžičová (hpd) ("The Viola Through the Ages, Vol. 1") † Son Vn; Sons Vl PRAG ▲ 250103 (18.97)

Suites (6) for solo Cello, BWV 1007-1012 (ca 1720)

M. Bach (vc) *(rec Germany, Apr 21-22, 1994)* ("The Art of the Curved Bow, Vol. 1") † Schnebel:Inventionen Vc; Mit diesen Händen MODE ▲ 52 [DDD] (17.97)

J. Bárta (vc)—BWV 1007, No. 1 in G; BWV 1008, No. 2 in d; BWV 1009, No. 3 in C SUR ▲ 3241 (16.97)

J. Bárta (vc)—BWV 1010, No. 4 in E♭; BWV 1011, No. 5 in c; BWV 1012, No. 6 in D *(rec July 23-25 & Aug 27, 1996)* SUR ▲ 3242 (16.97)

J. Baumann (vc)—BWV 1012, No. 6 in D ("Works for Violoncello") † W. A. Mozart:Duo Bn Vc, K.292; M. Reger:Suites Vc, Op. 131c CAMA ▲ 373

J. Berger (vc) † Fučik:Marches & Waltzes; Marinarella, Op. 215 ORF ▲ 146852 [DDD] (36.97)

P. Beschi (vc) WNTR 2-▲ 28 (26.97)

P. Beschi (vc)—BWV 1010, No. 4 in E♭; BWV 1011, No. 5 in c; BWV 1012, No. 6 in D WNTR ▲ 27 (16.97)

M. Brunello (vc) *(rec 1993)* AG 2-▲ 160 [DDD] (18.97)

P. Bruns (vc) OPUS 2-▲ 30176 (36.97)

F. Busoni (pno)—BWV 1008, No. 2 in d [arr Busoni for pno] † Chopin:Preludes (24) Pno, Op. 28; Liszt:Études d'exécution transcendante (12), S.139; Grandes études de Paganini, S.141; Polonaises (2) Pno, S.223 NIMB (Grand Piano) ▲ 8810 [DDD] (11.97)

A. Bylsma (cel)—BWV 1007, No. 1 in G; BWV 1008, No. 2 in d; BWV 1009, No. 3 in C *(rec Echig Kirche, Bavaria, Germany, Apr 23-26, 1979)* ("Vol. 1") SNYC ▲ 61811 [ADD] (7.97)

A. Bylsma (cel)—BWV 1010, No. 4 in E♭; BWV 1011, No. 5 in c; BWV 1012, No. 6 in D *(rec Eching Kirche, Bavaria, Germany, May 14-16, 1979)* ("Vol. 2") SNYC ▲ 61812 [ADD] (7.97)

C. Carr (vc) *(rec New England Conservatory Boston, Sept 19 & 23, 1994)* GMR 2-▲ 2054 (32.97)

P. Casals (vc) *(rec 1936-39)* ("Pablo Casals Collection, Vol. 2") GRM2 2-▲ 78627 (26.97)

P. Casals (vc) EMIC 2-▲ 66215 [ADD] (21.97)

P. Casals (vc) *(rec Paris, France, 1938-39)* MPLY 2-▲ 2000 (m) (16.97)

P. Casals (vc) *(rec 1927-39)* ("Pablo Casals Plays Beethoven: The Complete Cello Sonatas") † Beethoven:Vars Vc on "Bei Männern", WoO 46 MPLY 2-▲ 2004 (16.97)

P. Casals (vc)—BWV 1007, No. 1 in G *(rec Paris, France, June 2, 1938)* † Beethoven:Minuets (6) Orch, WoO 10; Son 3 Vc, Op. 69; J. Brahms:Son 2 Vc, Op. 99 EMIC ▲ 67008 (m) [ADD] (11.97)

P. Casals (vc)—BWV 1012, No. 6 in D *(rec London, England, 1936)* ("Pablo Casals Portrait") † Beethoven:Son 4 Vc; J. Brahms:Son 2 Vc, Op. 99 IN ▲ 1308 (15.97)

P. Fournier (vc) DEUT (The Originals) 2-▲ 49711 [ADD] (22.97)

M. Gendron (vc) PPHI (Duo) 2-▲ 42293 (17.97)

Y. Hanani (vc) TOWN 2-▲ 51 (34.97)

K. Kashkashian (vc) *(rec Jan 1991)* ACCE 2-▲ 9171 [DDD] (34.97)

T. Labé (pno)—BWV 1008, No. 2 in d; BWV 1009, No. 3 in C; BWV 1011, No. 5 in c [arr Godowsky] *(rec June 1993)* † Sons & Partitas Vn DOR ▲ 80117 [DDD] (13.97)

A. Leonard (gtr)—BWV 1012, No. 6 in D [trans Andrew Leonard] *(rec Cambridge, MA, May 1996)* ("Music of the Ages") † Sons & Partitas Vn; J. Dowland:Lt Music; A. Piazzolla:Milonga del angel; Muerte del angel; Sor:Intro & Vars on "Gentil Housard", Op. 27; Intro & Vars on "Malborough", Op. 28; A. York:Sunburst ACTR ▲ 60101 [DDD] (16.97)

G. Leonhardt (harmonicord)—BWV 1010, No. 4 in E♭ *(rec 1976-1979)* † Chromatic Fant & Fugue, BWV 903; Fant & Fugue Org, BWV 906; Kbd Music (misc); Suite Lt, BWV 995; Toccatas Hpd SNYC 2-▲ 60375 [ADD] (14.97)

C. Lindberg (trbn)—BWV 1008, No. 2 in d ("Unaccompanied") † Högberg:Su Ba Do Be; C. Lindberg:Vars on Gregorian Chants; J. Sandström:Don Quixote; Telemann:Fants (12) Fl, TWV40:2-13 BIS ▲ 858 [DDD] (17.97)

J. T. Linden (vc) [baroque instr] HAM 2-▲ 907216 (36.97)

Y.-Y. Ma (vc) SNYC 2-▲ 37867 (31.97)

Y.-Y. Ma (vc) *(rec 1994-97)* ("Inspired by Bach") SNYC 2-▲ 63203 [DDD] (31.97)

C. Norton (mar) [arr Norton] *(rec Spence-Thomas Audio Post, Canada, July 1997)* † B. Becker:Cryin' Time; Creston:Concertino Mar, Op. 21; D. McCarthy:Call of Boromir; C. Norton:Forsythian Spring; November Evening ALAB ▲ 201 [DDD]

T. Oxford (b sax)—BWV 1007, No. 1 in G [arr Oxford] *(rec U of Texas, Austin, TX, Jul 1996)* ("Finesse") † P. Bonneau:Caprice in forme de valse; Bozza:Caprice-Improvisation; C. Franck:Son Vn, M.8 EQLB ▲ 22 (16.97)

B. Pergamenschikow (vc) *(rec Heidelberg, Germany, 1998)* ("Edition Bachakademie, Vol. 120") HANS 2-▲ 92120 [DDD] (19.97)

J. du Pré (vc)—BWV 1007, No. 1 in G; BWV 1008, No. 2 in d *(rec Jan 7, 1962)* † J. Brahms:Son 2 Vc, Op. 99; B. Britten:Son Vc; F. Couperin:Nouveaux Concerts; M. de Falla:Suite populaire espagnole; G. F. Handel:Con in g EMIC 2-▲ 73377 [ADD] (16.97)

M. Reynolds (vc) *(rec New York, NY, June 1997)* ECO 2-▲ 7 [DDD]

A. Romero (gtr)—BWV 1007, No. 1 in G [trans for gtr] *(rec Dec 10-15, 1990)* † Cant 147; Sons & Partitas Vn; Wohltemperirte Clavier TEL ▮ 30288 (8.98) ▲ 80288 (16.97)

C. Romero (gtr)—BWV 1009, No. 3 in C [trans by Pepe Romero] † Sons & Partitas Vn; G. Sanz:Suite Española DLS ▲ 1005 [AAD] (10.97)

S. Rowland-Jones (va)—BWV 1010, No. 4 in E♭; BWV 1011, No. 5 in c; BWV 1012, No. 6 in D [trans Rowland-Jones] ("Vol. 2") MER ▲ 84324 (16.97)

A. Segovia (gtr)—BWV 1007, No. 1 in G [arr gtr] *(rec Apr 2, 1935)* ("The Young Segovia, 1927-39") † Sons & Partitas Vn; Maláts:Impresiones de España; M. Ponce:Gtr Music IN ▲ 1347 [ADD] (15.97)

A. Segovia (gtr)—BWV 1009, No. 3 in C [arr Duarte] *(rec 1952-68)* † Prelude Lt, BWV 999; Sons & Partitas Vn; Suite Lt, BWV 995 MCA1 ▲ 42068 [AAD] (11.97)

A. Segovia (gtr)—BWV 1009, No. 3 in C; BWV 1012, No. 6 in D [Prelude; Corrante; trans Segovia in C for gtr] *(rec 1947-49)* † Fugue Lt; Sons & Partitas Vn; Suite Lt, BWV 996; Castelnuovo-Tedesco:Con 1 Gtr, Op. 99; Moreno Torroba:Suite castellana; M. Ponce:Sonatina Meridional; J. Turina:Fandanguillo, Op. 36 URAN ▲ 111 (15.97)

J. Starker (vc) † Sons Vl MRCR 2-▲ 32756 [ADD] (22.97)

J. Starker (vc) *(rec New York City, June 1992)* RCAV (Red Seal) 2-▲ 61436 [DDD] (30.97)

H. Suzuki (vc) DEHA 2-▲ 77387 [DDD] (30.97)

Y. Turovsky (vc) *(rec Aug 1991)* CHN 2-▲ 9034 [DDD] (33.97)

J. Vallières (gtr)—BWV 1009, No. 3 in C [trans J. Valliéres] ("J. S. Bach: Guitar, Vol. 1") † Sons & Partitas Vn; Suite Lt, BWV 995; Suite Lt, BWV 996 SNE ▲ 599 (16.97)

J. Vogler (vc)—BWV 1007, No. 1 in G; BWV 1008, No. 2 in d † M. Reger:Suites Vc, Op. 131c BER ▲ 1175 (16.97)

A. Weisberg (bn)—BWV 1008, No. 2 in d; BWV 1009, No. 3 in C [trans Weisberg for bn] ("Bach & Bassoon") † Partita Fl, BWV 1013 CRYS ▲ 345 (15.97) ▮ 345 (9.98)

J. Williams (gtr)—BWV 1009, No. 3 in C [Bouree only] *(rec NY)* ("John Williams & Friends") † Cant 147; Cons Org; Trio Son for 2 Vns; Daquin:Pièces de clavecin (sels); W. A. Mozart:Adagio Glass Amc, K.356; Son 11 Pno, K.331; H. Purcell:Sons (12) of 3 Parts for 2 Vns, Z.790-801; Telemann:Bourree alla Polacca; Vivaldi:Con Mands, RV.532 SNYC ▲ 35108 [AAD] (16.97)

P. Wispelwey (vc) [baroque instr] CCL 2-▲ 1090 [DDD]

P. Wispelwey (pic) CCL 2-▲ 12298 (18.97)

D. Yeadon (vc), P. Wispelwey (vc pic), R. Egarr (hpd)—BWV 1007, No. 1 in G [trans Wispelwey in D] † Con 2 Hpd, BWV 1053; Con 5 Hpd, BWV 1056; Italian Con, BWV 971; Prelude Lt, BWV 999; Sons Vl; Wohltemperirte Clavier CCL ▲ 14198 (18.97)

various artists—BWV 1012, No. 6 in D [Allemande only] ("Bach for Relaxation") † Brandenburg Con 2, BWV 1047; Cant 147; Goldberg Vars, BWV 988; Music of Bach; Musical Offering, BWV 1079; Prelude Lt, BWV 999; Sons & Partitas Vn; Sons Fl; Sons Vn Hpd RCAV ▲ 68697 (11.97) ▮ 68697 (5.98)

Suite in a for Keyboard, BWV 818 (ca 1722)

I. Grudin-Brandt (clvd) † Suite Kbd, BWV 819 BIS ▲ 142 [AAD] (17.97)

Suite in E♭ for Keyboard, BWV 819 (ca 1722)

I. Grudin-Brandt (clvd) † Suite Kbd, BWV 818 BIS ▲ 142 [AAD] (17.97)

Suite in f for Keyboard, BWV 823 (ca 1708-14)

R. Hill (kbd) *(rec Sept 1998)* ("Edition Bachakademie, Vol. 109: Works for the Lute-Harpsichord") † Fant & Fughetta Kbd, BWV 907; Fant & Fughetta Kbd, BWV 908; Partita Lt, BWV 997; Prelude Kbd, BWV 921; Prelude Lt, BWV 999; Prelude, Fugue & Allegro Lt, BWV 998; Suite Lt, BWV 996 HANS ▲ 92109 [DDD] (11.97)

R. Tureck (pno) ("Bach: The Keyboard Album") † Anna Magdalena Bach Notebook; Aria variata alla maniera italiana, BWV 989; Art of the Fugue, BWV 1080; Inventions Hpd; Italian Con, BWV 971; Kbd Music (misc); Suite Kbd, BWV 824 SNYC (Take Two) 2-▲ 63231 (14.97)

BACH, JOHANN SEBASTIAN (cont.)

Suite in A for Keyboard, BWV 824

R. Tureck (pno) ("Bach: The Keyboard Album") † Anna Magdalena Bach Notebook; Aria variata alla maniera italiana, BWV 989; Art of the Fugue, BWV 1080; Inventions Hpd; Italian Con, BWV 971; Kbd Music (misc); Suite Kbd, BWV 823 SNYC (Take Two) 2-▲ 63231 (14.97)

Suite in g for Lute, BWV 995 (1727-31)

J. Bream (gtr) RCAV (Gold Seal) ▲ 61603 (11.97)

E. M. Dombois (cnd) *(rec Vienna, Austria, Mar & June 1971)* ("The Baroque Lute") † Prelude, Fugue & Allegro Lt, BWV 998; D. Kellner:Lt Music SNYC ▲ 60372 [ADD] (7.97)

V. Drake (hp) [trans for hp] ("Harping on Bach") † French Suites; Partitas Hpd WETE ▲ 5161 [AAD] (16.97)

M. A. Girollet (gtr) [trans M.A. Girollet] ("Baroque Music for Guitar") † J. Dowland:Lt Music; Frescobaldi:Aria detta "La Frescobalda" OTR ▲ 1006 [DDD] (18.97)

G. Kreplin (gtr) *(rec Broad Creek, MD, Spring 1995)* ("Bach in Brazil") † Lauro:Valses Venezolanos; H. Villa-Lobos:Preludes Gtr ASCE ▲ 103 [DDD] (15.97)

G. Leonhardt (harmonicord) *(rec 1976-1979)* † Chromatic Fant & Fugue, BWV 903; Fant & Fugue Org, BWV 906; Kbd Music (misc); Suites Vc; Toccatas Hpd SNYC 2-▲ 60375 [ADD] (14.97)

E. Møldrup (gtr) ("The Guitar Music") † Fugue Lt; Lt Music; Partita Lt, BWV 997; Prelude Lt, BWV 999; Prelude, Fugue & Allegro Lt, BWV 998; Sons & Partitas Vn; Suite Lt, BWV 996 CLSO 2-▲ 171 (15.97)

G. Sárközy (lt) *(rec 1980, 1984 & 1991)* ("Johann Sebastian Bach on Viola Bastarda, Lute and Lute-Harpsichord") † Cant 147; Fugue Lt; Partita Lt, BWV 997; Prelude, Fugue & Allegro Lt, BWV 998; Sons Vl; Suite Lt, BWV 996 HUN 2-▲ 31616 [ADD] (32.97)

A. Segovia (gtr) [Allemande, Sarabande & Gigue only] *(rec 1952-68)* † Prelude Lt, BWV 999; Sons & Partitas Vn; Suites Vc MCA1 ▲ 42068 [AAD] (11.97)

J. Vallières (gtr) ("J. S. Bach: Guitar, Vol. 1") † Sons & Partitas Vn; Suite Lt, BWV 996; Suites Vc SNE ▲ 599 (16.97)

Suite No. 1 in e for Lute, BWV 996 (ca 1708-17)

J. Bream (lt) † Sons & Partitas Vn EMIC ▲ 55123 (16.97)

K. Heindel (hpd/lt) *(rec Stonington, CT, Oct 26-28, 1993)* ("Aufs Lautenwerk") † Fugue Lt; Partita Lt, BWV 1006a; Partita Lt, BWV 997; Prelude, Fugue & Allegro Lt, BWV 998 DOR ▲ 80126 [DDD] (13.97)

R. Hill (kbd) *(rec Sept 1998)* ("Edition Bachakademie, Vol. 109: Works for the Lute-Harpsichord") † Fant & Fughetta Kbd, BWV 907; Fant & Fughetta Kbd, BWV 908; Partita Lt, BWV 997; Prelude Kbd, BWV 921; Prelude Lt, BWV 999; Prelude, Fugue & Allegro Lt, BWV 998; Suite Kbd, BWV 823 HANS ▲ 92109 [DDD] (11.97)

Y. Kondonassis (hp) *(rec Cleveland, OH, June 1994)* ("A New Baroque") † Arioso Ob; Cant 147; Wohltemperirte Clavier; G. F. Handel:Suites de Pièces (8) Hpd, HWV 426-33; J. Pachelbel:Canon & Gigue; D. Scarlatti:Sons Kbd TEL ▲ 80403 [DDD] (16.97)

G. Kreplin (gtr) ("Cathedral") † Mompou:Suite compostelana; R. J. Powell:Mass Gtr ASCE ▲ 104 [DDD] (15.97)

E. Møldrup (gtr) ("The Guitar Music") † Fugue Lt; Lt Music; Partita Lt, BWV 997; Prelude Lt, BWV 999; Prelude, Fugue & Allegro Lt, BWV 998; Sons & Partitas Vn; Suite Lt, BWV 995 CLSO 2-▲ 171 (15.97)

G. Sárközy (lt) *(rec 1980, 1984 & 1991)* ("Johann Sebastian Bach on Viola Bastarda, Lute and Lute-Harpsichord") † Cant 147; Fugue Lt; Partita Lt, BWV 997; Prelude, Fugue & Allegro Lt, BWV 998; Sons Vl; Suite Lt, BWV 995 HUN 2-▲ 31616 [ADD] (32.97)

A. Segovia (gtr) [Sarabande; Bourée; trans Segovia] *(rec 1947-49)* † Fugue Lt; Sons & Partitas Vn; Suites Vc; Castelnuovo-Tedesco:Con 1 Gtr, Op. 99; Moreno Torroba:Suite castellana; M. Ponce:Sonatina Meridional; J. Turina:Fandanguillo, Op. 36 URAN ▲ 111 (15.97)

J. Vallières (gtr) ("J. S. Bach: Guitar, Vol. 1") † Sons & Partitas Vn; Suite Lt, BWV 995; Suites Vc SNE ▲ 599 (16.97)

Suites (4) for Orchestra [including No. 2 in b for Flute & Strings, BWV 1067], BWV 1066-1069

M. Arita (trns fl), A. Manze (cnd), La Stravaganza Cologne [period instrs] *(rec Cologne, Germany, June-Oct 1994)* ("Bach & Handel Suites") † G. F. Handel:Water Music, HWV 348-50 DNN (Classics Exposed) 2-▲ 17015 [DDD] (16.97)

R. Baumgartner (cnd) EUR 3-▲ 69219 [ADD] (13.97)

A. Busch (cnd), Busch Chamber Players † Brandenburg Cons PHS 3-▲ 9263 (49.97)

R. Goodman (cnd), Brandenburg Consort HYP 2-▲ 22002 (18.97)

L. Güttler (tpt), Virtuosi Saxoniae BER ▲ 9002 (10.97)

N. Harnoncourt (cnd), Vienna Concentus Musicus ("Four Orchestral Suites") TELC ▲ 92174 (19.97)

C. Hogwood (cnd), Academy of Ancient Music PLOI 2-▲ 17834 [DDD] (32.97)

C. Hogwood (cnd), Academy of Ancient Music Orch † Con 1 for 2 Hpds, BWV 1060; Con 3 Hpds, BWV 1062 PLON (Double Decker) 2-▲ 458069 (17.97)

O. Klemperer (cnd), Philharmonia Orch † Cherubini:Anacréon (ov); C. W. Gluck:Iphigénie en Aulide (ov); G. F. Handel:Con grosso, HWV 318; Rameau:Gavotte TES ▲ 2131 (33.97)

G. Letzbor (cnd) CHSK ▲ 142 [DDD] (16.97)

W. Malloch (cnd) ("Suites for Dancing") KOCH ▲ 7037 [DDD] (10.97)

N. Marriner (cnd), Academy of St. Martin in the Fields PLON (Jubilee) ▲ 30378 [ADD] (9.97)

P. Pickett (cnd) PLOI ▲ 452000 (32.97)

T. Pinnock (cnd), English Concert † Brandenburg Cons PARC 3-▲ 23492 [ADD/DDD] (29.97)

T. Pinnock (cnd), English Concert † Sinfonias ARCV 2-▲ 439780 [DDD] (35.97)

F. Reiner (cnd), Pittsburgh SO [1 suite] *(rec 1949)* † Brandenburg Cons LYS1 2-▲ 464

J. Rolla (cnd), Franz Liszt CO HUN ▲ 31018 [DDD]

J. Savall (cnd), Capella Reial de Catalunya ASTR 2-▲ 8727 (36.97)

Suite No. 1 in C for Orchestra, BWV 1066 (ca 1717-23)

E. Duvier (cnd), Camerata Romana † Suite 2 Fl, BWV 1067 PC ▲ 267006 [DDD] (2.97)

J. Dvořák (cnd), Capella Istropolitana *(rec 1991)* † Cant 140; English Suites; Sons Vn Hpd; Suite 2 Fl, BWV 1067; Wohltemperirte Clavier NXIN ▲ 550244 [DDD] (5.97)

Y. Menuhin (cnd), Bath Festival Orch *(rec 1959)* ("Best-Loved Bach") † Brandenburg Con 1, BWV 1046; Brandenburg Con 2, BWV 1047; Brandenburg Con 3, BWV 1048; Con Vns; Con 1 Vn; Con 2 Vn; St. Matthew Passion (sels); Suite 2 Fl, BWV 1067; Suite 3 Orch, BWV 1068 EMIC 4-▲ 69536 [ADD] (14.97)

M. Pommer (cnd), Leipzig New Bach Collegium Musicum CAPO ▲ 10011 [DDD] (11.97)

C. Wincenc (fl), H. Rilling (cnd), Oregon Bach Festival CO HANS ▲ 98984 [DDD] (15.97)

artists unknown ("Bach for Book Lovers") † Brandenburg Con 1, BWV 1046; Brandenburg Con 6, BWV 1051; Con 5 Hpd, BWV 1056; Italian Con, BWV 971; Music of Bach; Suite 2 Fl, BWV 1067; Wohltemperirte Clavier PPHI (Set Your Life to Music) ▲ 456497 (9.97) ▮ 456497 (5.98)

Suite No. 2 in b for Flute & Strings, BWV 1067 (late 1730s)

Y. Arnheim (fl), J. Krček (cnd) † J. Christian Bach:Con Bn MER ▲ 84359 (16.97)

G. von Bahr (fl), C. Génetay (cnd), Swedish National Museum CO † Partita Fl, BWV 1013; C.P.E. Bach:Son Fl, H.562; Vivaldi:Con Flautino, RV.443; Con Flautino, RV.444; Con Flautino, RV.445 BIS ▲ 21 (17.97)

W. Bennett (fl), R. Leppard (cnd), English CO ("Sunday Brunch. Vol 2") † Cant 147; Cant 156; Cant 78; Con 5 Hpd, BWV 1056; G. F. Handel:Minuet Vc & Pno; Solomon (arrival of the queen of Sheba); Water Music (sels); A. Marcello:Con Ob Strs in d, Op. 1; Mouret:Suite de symphonies; H. Purcell:Abdelazer (sels); Gordian Knot Unty'd (sels); V. Tommasini:Donne di buon umore (sels); Vivaldi:Con Mand, RV.425; Con Mands, RV.532; Cons Fl, Op. 10/1-6; Cons Vn Strs, Op. 8/1-4 SNYC (Dinner Classics) ▲ 46359 [AAD] (9.97)

Berlin Academy for Early Music † Suite 4 Orch, BWV 1069 HAM ▲ 901579 (18.97)

Caratelli (fl), F. Reiner (cnd), Pittsburgh SO *(rec 1945-46)* ("Reiner, Vol. 4") † Beethoven:Sym 2 LYS ▲ 126 (17.97)

E. Duvier (cnd), Camerata Romana † Suite 1 Orch, BWV 1066 PC ▲ 267006 [DDD] (2.97)

J. Dvořák (cnd), Capella Istropolitana *(rec 1989)* † Cant 140; English Suites; Sons Vn Hpd; Suite 1 Orch, BWV 1066; Wohltemperirte Clavier NXIN ▲ 550244 [DDD] (5.97)

P. Evison (fl), Drottningholm Baroque Ensemble † Babell:Con Fl; Telemann:Qts or trios (6) BIS ▲ 249 [DDD] (17.97)

A. Fiedler (cnd), Boston Pops Orch—Menuet; Badinerie [plus others] † Brandenburg Con 2, BWV 1047; Brandenburg Con 3, BWV 1048; Brandenburg Con 5, BWV 1050; Suite 3 Orch, BWV 1068; Toccata & Fugue Org, BWV 538 RCAV ▲ 60828 (10.97) ▮ 60828 (5.98)

J. Galway (fl), J. Faerber (cnd), Württemberg CO † Con Fl, Vn & Hpd, BWV 1044; Sons Fl RCAV (Red Seal) ▲ 60900 (16.97)

J. Galway (fl), Zagreb Solisti † Con Fl; Con 8 Hpd, BWV 1059; Musical Offering, BWV 1079; Trio Son Fls, BWV 1039 RCAV (Red Seal; Papillon Collection) ▲ 6517 [ADD] (11.97)

R. Goebel (cnd), Cologne Musica Antiqua † Ov Orch; G. F. Handel:Trio Sons, HWV 396-402; J. Pachelbel:Canon & Gigue; Vivaldi:Sons Vns Vl, Op. 1/1-12 PARC (Masters) ▲ 47285 [DDD] (9.97)

R. Kapp (cnd), Philharmonia Virtuosi, New York *(rec NY, United States of America)* ("Greatest Hits of 1721") † Cant 147; Cant 208; J. Clarke:Prince of Denmark's March; A. Corelli:Con Grosso in g 2 Vns, Vla & Vc, Op. 6/8; G. F. Handel:Water Music, HWV 348-50; A. Marcello:Con Ob Strs in c; J. P. A. Martini:Plaisir d'Amour; Vivaldi:Con Mand, RV.425; Con Tpts, RV.537; Cons Vn Strs, Op. 8/1-4 SNYC ▲ 35821 (9.97)

H. von Karajan (cnd), Berlin PO † Brandenburg Cons; Suite 3 Orch, BWV 1068 DEUT 2-▲ 453001 [ADD] (17.97)

BACH, JOHANN SEBASTIAN (cont.)

Suite No. 2 in b for Flute & Strings, BWV 1067 (late 1730s) (cont.)

G. Kehr (cnd), Mainz CO—Badinerie ("25 Bach Favorites") † Brandenburg Con 1, BWV 1046; Brandenburg Con 2, BWV 1047; Brandenburg Con 3, BWV 1048; Brandenburg Con 4, BWV 1049; Brandenburg Con 5, BWV 1050; Cant 147; Con Hpds (4), BWV 1065; Con Vns; Con 1 for 2 Hpds, BWV 1060; Con 1 Vn; Mass in b, BWV 232; Music of Bach; Schübler Chorale Preludes; Sons & Partitas Vn; Toccata & Fugue Org, BWV 565; Toccata, Adagio & Fugue Org, BWV 564; Wohltemperirte Clavier VCC ▲ 8817 (3.97)

C. Lindberg (trbn), R. Pöntinen (pno)—Badinerie *(rec Danderyd Grammar School, Sweden, June 1986)* ("The Criminal Trombone") † Air on the G String; Albinoni:Adagio; W. A. Mozart:Vars "Ah! vous dirai-je, Maman", K.265; G. Rossini:Barbiere di Siviglia (ov); F. Schubert:Son Arpeggione, D.821; R. Schumann:Romances Ob, Op. 94 BIS ▲ 328 [DDD] (17.97)

N. Marriner (cnd), Academy of St. Martin in the Fields † Suite 3 Orch, BWV 1068; Suite 4 Orch, BWV 1069 EMIC (Red Line) ▲ 69879 (6.97)

W. Mengelberg (cnd), (Royal) Concertgebouw Orch ("Willem Mengelberg: A Portrait, 1926-41") † Beethoven:Egmont (ov); Leonore (ov 3); Sym 3; J. Brahms:Academic Festival Ov, Op. 80; Liszt:Préludes, S.97; P. Tchaikovsky:Ov 1812, Op. 49; Sym 6; R. Wagner:Lohengrin (preludes); Tannhäuser (ov); C. M. von Weber:Freischütz (ov); Oberon (ov) GRM2 3-▲ 78637 (39.97)

Y. Menuhin (cnd), Bath Festival Orch *(rec 1959)* ("Best-Loved Bach") † Brandenburg Con 1, BWV 1046; Brandenburg Con 2, BWV 1047; Brandenburg Con 3, BWV 1048; Con Vns; Con 1 Vn; Con 2 Vn; St. Matthew Passion (sels); Suite 1 Orch, BWV 1066; Suite 3 Orch, BWV 1068 EMIC 4-▲ 69536 [ADD] (14.97)

E. Mravinsky (cnd), Leningrad PO *(rec Nov 21, 1961)* † B. Bartók:Music for Strs, Perc & Cel, Sz.106; Debussy:Nocturnes Orch RUS (The Mravinsky Collection) ▲ 11167 [AAD] (12.97)

M. Petri (rcr), Berlin Baroque Soloists † Brandenburg Con 2, BWV 1047; Con Fl, Vn & Hpd, BWV 1044; Telemann:Trios (6) RCAV (Red Seal) ▲ 57130 [DDD] (16.97)

F. Reiner (cnd) *(rec 1939-46)* ("Fritz Reiner Album") † Beethoven:Sym 2; Debussy:Images Orch; Nocturnes Orch; Prélude à l'après-midi d'un faune; R. Wagner:Meistersinger (preludes); Parsifal (preludes) GRM2 2-▲ 78711 (26.97)

R. Smedvig (tpt), J. Ling (cnd), Scottish CO *(rec 1989-92)* † Brandenburg Con 2, BWV 1047; L. Mozart:Con Tpt; Telemann:Qnt Tpt TEL ▲ 80227 [DDD] (16.97)

Swingle Singers—Badinerie *(rec 1991)* ("Bach Hits Back/A Cappella Amadeus") † Anna Magdalena Bach Notebook (sels); Brandenburg Con 3, BWV 1048; Cant 140; Cant 208; In dulci jubilo, BWV 729; Inventions Hpd; Music of Bach; Sons & Partitas Vn; St. Matthew Passion (sels); Wohltemperirte Clavier; W. A. Mozart:Music of Mozart VCL 2-▲ 61472 [DDD] (11.97)

V.I.F Flute Quartet [arr Dahmen] † Art of the Fugue (sels); Fant & Fugue, BWV 542; Frescobaldi:Canzona quatra; Org Music; J. P. Sweelinck:Org Music; Telemann:Musique de Table NCC ▲ 8008 [DDD] (15.99)

J. Válek (fl), J. Suk (cnd), Suk CO † Brandenburg Cons VC 2-▲ 7002 [DDD] (26.97)

R. Wilson (a fl), G. Schwarz (cnd), Los Angeles CO † Brandenburg Con 5, BWV 1050; Brandenburg Con 6, BWV 1051 CSER ▲ 73282 [ADD] (6.97)

artists unknown—Badinerie ("Favourite Bach") † Air on the G String; Anna Magdalena Bach Notebook (sels); Brandenburg Con 2, BWV 1047; Brandenburg Con 3, BWV 1048; Brandenburg Con 4, BWV 1049; Cant 140; Cant 147; Cant 208; Cant 212; Cant 51; Con 1 Hpd, BWV 1052; Con 2 Vn; St. Matthew Passion (sels); Toccata & Fugue Org, BWV 565; Wohltemperirte Clavier CFP (Favourites) ▲ 4639 (12.97)

various artists—Menuet; Badinerie † Brandenburg Con 2, BWV 1047; Brandenburg Con 3, BWV 1048; Brandenburg Con 5, BWV 1050; Suite 3 Orch, BWV 1068; Albinoni:Adagio; G. F. Handel:Music of Handel; Mouret:Music of Mouret; J. Pachelbel:Canon & Gigue; Vivaldi:Con in D Gtr; Cons Vn Strs, Op. 8/1-4 RCAV ▲ 63501 (11.97)

artists unknown ("Bach for Book Lovers") † Brandenburg Con 1, BWV 1046; Brandenburg Con 6, BWV 1051; Con 5 Hpd, BWV 1056; Italian Con, BWV 971; Music of Bach; Suite 1 Orch, BWV 1066; Wohltemperirte Clavier PPHI (Set Your Life to Music) ▲ 456497 (9.97) ▮ 456497 (5.98)

various artists—Menuet † Brandenburg Con 2, BWV 1047; Brandenburg Con 3, BWV 1048; Brandenburg Con 5, BWV 1050; Jesu, bleibet meine Freude; Suite 3 Orch, BWV 1068; Albinoni:Adagio; G. F. Handel:Messiah (sels); Royal Fireworks Music, HWV 351; Serse (sels); Water Music, HWV 348-50; Mouret:Rondeau; J. Pachelbel:Canon & Gigue; Vivaldi:Con Gtr; Cons Vn Strs, Op. 8/1-4 RCAV ▲ 60840 (10.97) ▮ 60840 (5.98)

various artists—Menuet; Polonaise ("Baby Needs Baroque") † Brandenburg Con 1, BWV 1046; French Suites; Goldberg Vars, BWV 988; Inventions Hpd; Son Vn; Sons & Partitas Vn; G. F. Handel:Water Music, HWV 348-50; J. Pachelbel:Canon & Gigue; Telemann:Qnt Tpt; Son Fl; Torelli:Son 5 No. 1 in D; Vivaldi:Cons Vn Strs, Op. 8/1-4 DLS ▲ 1609 [DDD] (10.97) ▮ 1609 [DDD] (8.98)

Suite No. 3 in D for Orchestra, BWV 1068 (ca 1729-31)

("From Authentic to Outrageous") † Brandenburg Con 5, BWV 1050; Cant 140; Fant Org, BWV 562; Mass in b, BWV 232; Musical Offering, BWV 1079; Partitas Hpd; Toccata & Fugue Org, BWV 565 KOCH ▲ 7610 (10.97)

H. Abendroth (cnd), Leipzig Gewandhaus Orch ("Hermann Abendroth:Gewandhaus Kapellmeister 1944-45") † J. Brahms:Tragic Ov, Op. 81; G. F. Handel:Concerti grossi, Op. 6; J. Haydn:Sym 88; Sym 96; W. A. Mozart:Sym 29, K.201; F. Schubert:Sym 3; R. Schumann:Manfred Ov, Op. 115 TAHA 2-▲ 106 (34.97)

W. Baumgratz (org) [arr Karg-Elert] *(rec Sauer org, Bremen Cathedral, Germany, July 1997)* ("Works in Romantic Organ Arrangements") † Cant 106; Sons & Partitas Vn; Wohltemperirte Clavier; G. F. Handel:Cons (16) Org; Suites de Pièces (8) Hpd, HWV 426-33 MDG ▲ 3200761 [DDD] (17.97)

Berlin Academy for Early Music HAM (La Solothèque) ▲ 926002 (5.97)

Berlin Akademie für Alte Musik ("Portrait: Akademie für Alte Musik Berlin") † Brandenburg Con 4, BWV 1049; C.P.E. Bach:Sinfs (4), H.663-66; Boccherini:Sym in D, G.520; G. F. Handel:Radamisto, HWV 12a; Telemann:Musique de Table; Ov in G HAM ▲ 2901673 (7.97)

M. Dupré (org)—Overture [arr Dupré] *(rec Queen's Hall & Alexandra Place orgs, England, June 1928)* ("Bach; The Art of Marcel Dupré") † Cant 29; Clavier-Übung III; Fant & Fugue Org, BWV 537; Orgelbüchlein; Passacaglia & Fugue Org, BWV 582; Preludes & Fugues, BWV 531-552; Schübler Chorale Preludes; Toccata & Fugue Org, BWV 538; Trio Sons Org PHS ▲ 9863 (17.97)

J. Dvořák (cnd), Capella Istropolitana *(rec Jan-Mar 1989)* † Ov Orch NXIN ▲ 550245 [DDD] (5.97)

A. Fiedler (cnd), Boston Pops Orch—"Air on a G String" † Brandenburg Con 2, BWV 1047; Brandenburg Con 3, BWV 1048; Brandenburg Con 5, BWV 1050; Suite 2 Fl, BWV 1067; Toccata & Fugue Org, BWV 538 RCAV ▲ 60828 (10.97) ▮ 60828 (5.98)

W. Furtwängler (cnd), Berlin PO *(rec live, Oct 24, 1948)* † Beethoven:Con Vn MUA ▲ 708 [AAD] (16.97)

G. Gomiero (sop), M. Brunello (vc), Orch Villa-Lobos [trans 12 vcs] † Wohltemperirte Clavier; Jobim:Gtr Music; H. Villa-Lobos:Bachiana brasileira 1; Bachiana brasileira 5 AURC ▲ 403 (5.97)

H. von Karajan (cnd), Berlin PO † Brandenburg Cons; Suite 2 Fl, BWV 1067 DEUT 2-▲ 453001 [ADD] (17.97)

H. von Karajan (cnd), Berlin PO—"Air on a G String" † Albinoni:Adagio; C. W. Gluck:Orfeo ed Euridice (dance); W. A. Mozart:Serenade 6 Orch, K.239; J. Pachelbel:Canon & Gigue; Vivaldi:Cons Fl, Op. 10/1-6 DEUT ▲ 13309 [DDD] (16.97)

N. Marriner (cnd), Academy of St. Martin in the Fields ("Moll Flanders") † Brandenburg Con 3, BWV 1048; G. F. Handel:Water Music, HWV 348-50; Mancina:Moll Flanders; J. Offenbach:Contes d'Hoffmann (sels); Vivaldi:Con Mand, RV.425 PLON ▲ 52485 (16.97)

N. Marriner (cnd), Academy of St. Martin in the Fields † Suite 2 Fl, BWV 1067; Suite 4 Orch, BWV 1069 EMIC (Red Line) ▲ 69879 (6.97)

J. C. Martins (pno) [arr Prado] *(rec NY & Sofia Bulgaria, Bulgaria, 1986 & 1996)* ("Bach for Christmas") † Cant 147; Music of Bach; Schübler Chorale Preludes; Sons & Partitas Vn; Sons Fl COJ ▲ 42040 [DDD] (14.97)

Y. Menuhin (cnd), Bath Festival Orch † Con Vns; Cons Vn (comp) RYLC ▲ 6481

Y. Menuhin (cnd), Bath Festival Orch *(rec 1959)* ("Best-Loved Bach") † Brandenburg Con 1, BWV 1046; Brandenburg Con 2, BWV 1047; Brandenburg Con 3, BWV 1048; Con Vns; Con 1 Vn; Con 2 Vn; St. Matthew Passion (sels); Suite 1 Orch, BWV 1066; Suite 2 Fl, BWV 1067 EMIC 4-▲ 69536 [ADD] (14.97)

S. Miassojedov (cnd), Moscow Bach Center Orch † Sinfonias; Suite 4 Orch, BWV 1069 AART ▲ 47134 (10.97)

Orpheus CO—"Air on a G String" † Jesu, bleibet meine Freude; Albinoni:Adagio; A. Corelli:Con grosso, Op. 6/8; G. F. Handel:Solomon (arrival of the queen of Sheba); J. Pachelbel:Canon & Gigue; H. Purcell:Chacony Strs, Z.730; Vivaldi:Cons Vn(s) Strs, Op. 3/1-12 DEUT ▲ 29390 [DDD] (16.97)

M. Pommer (cnd), Leipzig New Bach Collegium Musicum CAPO ▲ 10012 [DDD] (11.97)

H. Rilling (cnd), Oregon Bach Festival CO HANS ▲ 98978 [DDD] (15.97)

various artists † Brandenburg Con 2, BWV 1047; Brandenburg Con 3, BWV 1048; Brandenburg Con 5, BWV 1050; Suite 2 Fl, BWV 1067; Albinoni:Adagio; G. F. Handel:Music of Handel; Mouret:Music of Mouret; J. Pachelbel:Canon & Gigue; Vivaldi:Con in D Gtr; Cons Vn Strs, Op. 8/1-4 RCAV ▲ 63501 (11.97)

various artists—"Air on a G String" † Brandenburg Con 2, BWV 1047; Brandenburg Con 3, BWV 1048; Brandenburg Con 5, BWV 1050; Jesu, bleibet meine Freude; Suite 2 Fl, BWV 1067; Albinoni:Adagio; G. F. Handel:Messiah (sels); Royal Fireworks Music, HWV 351; Serse (sels); Water Music, HWV 348-50; Mouret:Rondeau; J. Pachelbel:Canon & Gigue; Vivaldi:Con Gtr; Cons Vn Strs, Op. 8/1-4 RCAV ▲ 60840 (10.97) ▮ 60840 (5.98)

Suite No. 4 in D for Orchestra, BWV 1069 (ca 1717-23)

Berlin Academy for Early Music † Suite 2 Fl, BWV 1067 HAM ▲ 901579 (18.97)

N. Marriner (cnd), Academy of St. Martin in the Fields † Suite 2 Fl, BWV 1067; Suite 3 Orch, BWV 1068 EMIC (Red Line) ▲ 69879 (6.97)

BACH, JOHANN SEBASTIAN (cont.)

Suite No. 4 in D for Orchestra, BWV 1069 (ca 1717-23) (cont.)

S. Miassojedov (cnd), Moscow Bach Center Orch † Sinfonias; Suite 3 Orch, BWV 1068 AART ▲ 47134 (10.97)

Toccata, Adagio & Fugue in C for Organ, BWV 564 (1708-17)

A. Bárta (org) † Chorales (miscellaneous); Chorales Org; Cons Org; Pastorale Org, BWV 590; Preludes & Fugues, BWV 531-552; Toccata & Fugue Org, BWV 565 SUR ▲ 111289 [DDD]

E. P. Biggs (org) *(rec 1973)* † Fant Org, BWV 572; Preludes & Fugues, BWV 531-552; Toccata & Fugue Org, BWV 538; Toccata & Fugue Org, BWV 565 SNYC ▲ 42643 [ADD] (11.97)

E. P. Biggs (org) *(rec 1960)* † Passacaglia & Fugue Org, BWV 582; Toccata & Fugue Org, BWV 565 SNYC ▲ 42644 [ADD] (11.97)

K. Bowyer (org) *(rec Odense Denmark, Mar 23-24, 1993)* ("The Works for Organ, Vol. 6") † Org Music (comp); Prelude & Fugue Org, BWV 566; Preludes & Fugues (22) Org, BWV 531-552; Trio Son Org, BWV 584; Trio Sons Org NIMB ▲ 5423 [DDD] (16.97)

P. Casals (vc)—Adagio *(rec 1927-36)* ("Pablo Casals: A Baroque Festival") † English Suites; Music of Bach; Sons & Partitas Vn; Boccherini:Con Vc, G.482; Sons Vn, Op. 5; Tartini:Con Vc; G. Valentini:Sons Vn, Op. 8 ENT (Strings) ▲ 99320 (16.97)

F. Chaffiaud (pno) † Chromatic Fant & Fugue, BWV 903; French Suites; Preludes & Fugues, BWV 531-552; Wohltemperirte Clavier MED7 ▲ 141339 [DDD] (18.97)

J. Ferrad (org) † Fant Org, BWV 572; Partite diverse sopra, BWV 768 MOTE ▲ 11971 (17.97)

J. Guillou (org) *(rec Cathedrale de Breda Netherlands, Nov 15-17, 1984)* ("Grandes Toccatas") † Prelude & Fugue Org, BWV 566; Preludes & Fugues, BWV 531-552; Toccata & Fugue Org, BWV 538; Toccata & Fugue Org, BWV 565 PVY ▲ 730001 [DDD]

F. Hauk (org) *(rec Great Klais Org of Ingolstadt Münster, Germany)* ("Organ Works") † Chorales Org; Org Music (misc colls); Orgelbüchlein; Preludes & Fugues, BWV 531-552; Toccata & Fugue Org, BWV 565 INMP ▲ 6600402

I. Hobson (pno)—Toccata *(rec Letters, NYC, NY, Nov 16-18, 1991)* ("Hobson's Choice") † Chopin:Ballade 4 Pno, Op. 52; P. Grainger:Folk Song Settings; Liszt:Réminiscences de Don Juan Pno, S.418; Mendelssohn (-Bartholdy):Rondo capriccioso, Op. 14; M. Rosenthal:Pno Music; P. Tchaikovsky:Pno Music ARA ▲ 6639 (16.97)

V. Horowitz (pno) [arr Busoni] *(rec 1926)* † V. Horowitz:Moment exotique; Liszt:Trans, Arrs & Paraphrases; S. Rachmaninoff:Preludes Pno INTC ▲ 860864 (13.97)

P. Hurford (org) *(rec Church of Our Lady of Sorrows Org Toronto, Canada, 1975; 1977-79)* † Chorales Org; Fant & Fugue Org, BWV 537; Fant & Fugue, BWV 542; Fant Org, BWV 562; Fant Org, BWV 572; Org Music (misc colls); Passacaglia & Fugue Org, BWV 582; Preludes & Fugues, BWV 531-552; Schübler Chorale Preludes; Toccata & Fugue Org, BWV 538; Toccata & Fugue Org, BWV 565 PLON 2-▲ 43485 [ADD] (17.97)

T. Koopman (org) † Preludes & Fugues Org; Trio Sons Org NOVA ▲ 150066 [DDD] (16.97)

W. Kraft (org)—Adagio ("25 Bach Favorites") † Brandenburg Con 1, BWV 1046; Brandenburg Con 2, BWV 1047; Brandenburg Con 3, BWV 1048; Brandenburg Con 4, BWV 1049; Brandenburg Con 5, BWV 1050; Cant 147; Con Hpds (4), BWV 1065; Con Vns; Con 1 for 2 Hpds, BWV 1060; Con 1 Vn; Mass in b, BWV 232; Music of Bach; Schübler Chorale Preludes; Sons & Partitas Vn; Suite 2 Fl, BWV 1067; Toccata & Fugue Org, BWV 565; Wohltemperirte Clavier VCC ▲ 8817 (3.97)

W. Kraft (org) *(rec 1965)* † Chorales (miscellaneous); Cons Org; Fant Org, BWV 562; Fugue on a theme by Legrenzi, BWV 574; Org Music (misc colls); Orgelbüchlein; Passacaglia & Fugue Org, BWV 582; Preludes & Fugues, BWV 531-552; Toccata & Fugue Org, BWV 538 VB2 2-▲ 5059 [ADD] (9.97)

B. Lagacé (org) † Chorale Preludes Org; Fants Hpd; Fugue on a theme by Legrenzi, BWV 574; Partite diverse sopra, BWV 767; Preludes & Fugues, BWV 531-552; Von Himmel hoch, da komm ich her, BWV 701 FL ▲ 23094 [DDD] (16.97)

J. Lippincott (org) *(rec Durham NC, Flentrop Org)* ("Toccatas & Fugues by Bach") † Passacaglia & Fugue Org, BWV 582; Preludes & Fugues, BWV 531-552; Toccata & Fugue Org, BWV 538; Toccata & Fugue Org, BWV 565 GOT ▲ 49093 [DDD] (17.97)

M. Lücker (org) ("Edition Bachakademie, Vol. 91: Scales from Weimar") † Fugue on a theme by Corelli, BWV 579; Preludes & Fugues Org HANS ▲ 92091 [DDD] (11.97)

A. Marchal (org) *(rec Marchal's home Paris, 1956)* ("The 1956 Zodiac Recordings") ARBT ▲ 111 [ADD] (16.97)

R. Marlow (org) *(rec Metzler org, Trinity College, Cambridge, England)* † Prelude & Fugue Org, BWV 566; Preludes & Fugues, BWV 531-552; Toccata & Fugue Org, BWV 538; Toccata & Fugue Org, BWV 565 ASV ▲ 6231 (10.97)

M. Murray (org) TEL ▲ 80127 [DDD] (16.97)

A. Newman (org) ("24 Preludes & Fugues, Vol. 1") † Chorales (miscellaneous); Orgelbüchlein; Preludes & Fugues, BWV 531-552; Toccata & Fugue Org, BWV 565 VB2 2-▲ 5013 [ADD] (9.97)

A. Newman (org) ("Bach at Lejansk") † Fant & Fugue, BWV 542; Passacaglia & Fugue Org, BWV 582 HEL ▲ 1010 (10.97)

E. Ormandy (cnd), Philadelphia Orch [arr Ormandy] *(rec 1990)* † Brandenburg Con 5, BWV 1050; Cant 140; Passacaglia & Fugue Org, BWV 582; Toccata & Fugue Org, BWV 565; W. F. Bach:Sinf Orch, F.64 SNYC (Masterworks Heritage) 2-▲ 62345 [ADD] (25.97)

R. Pikler (cnd), Sydney SO—Adagio ("Orchestral Transcriptions by Leopold Stokowski") † Clavier-Übung III; Music of Bach; Passacaglia & Fugue Org, BWV 582; Toccata & Fugue Org, BWV 565 CHN (Collect) ▲ 6532 [ADD] (12.97)

L. Rogg (org) *(rec Silbermann Org, Arlesheim, Switzerland)* † Allabreve, BWV 589; Canonic Vars on "Von Himmel hoch", BWV 769; Canzona; Chorales Org; Clavier-Übung III; Fant & Fugue Org, BWV 537; Fant & Fugue, BWV 542; Fant Org, BWV 562; Fant Org, BWV 572; Orgelbüchlein; Partite diverse sopra, BWV 766; Partite diverse sopra, BWV 767; Partite diverse sopra, BWV 768; Pastorale Org, BWV 590; Prelude & Fugue Org, BWV 566; Preludes & Fugues, BWV 531-552; Schübler Chorale Preludes; Toccata & Fugue Org, BWV 565; Trio Org, BWV 583; Trio Sons Org HAM 12-▲ 290772 [ADD] (71.97)

W. Rübsam (org) *(rec Holy Cross College Worcester MA, June 21-22, 1993)* ("Organ Chorales from the Leipzig Manuscript, Vol. 1") NXIN ▲ 550901 [DDD] (5.97)

W. Rübsam (org) ("The Great Organ Works") † Cant 147; Org Music (misc colls); Orgelbüchlein; Passacaglia & Fugue Org, BWV 582; Preludes & Fugues, BWV 531-552; Toccata & Fugue Org, BWV 565 NXIN ▲ 553859 [DDD] (5.97)

D. Schrader (org) ("The Complete Fantasies, Fantasies & Fugues, & Isolated Fugues for Organ") † Prelude & Fugue Org, BWV 566; Preludes & Fugues, BWV 531-552; Toccata & Fugue Org, BWV 538; Toccata & Fugue Org, BWV 565 CED ▲ 6 [DDD] (16.97)

D. Schrader (org) ("The Complete Fantasies, Fantasies & Fugues, & Isolated Fugues for Organ") † Fant & Fugue Org, BWV 537; Fant & Fugue, BWV 542; Fant & Imitatio Org, BWV 563; Fant Org, BWV 562; Fant Org, BWV 570; Fant Org, BWV 572; Org Music (misc colls); Pastorale Org, BWV 590 CED ▲ 12 [DDD] (16.97)

M. Spanyi (org) † Fant & Fugue, BWV 542; Orgelbüchlein; Orgelbüchlein, BWV 599-644 PC ▲ 265031 [DDD] (2.97)

O. Vernet (org) ("The Organ Works, Vol. 2: 1708-1717") † Chorales (miscellaneous); Chorales Org; Fant & Fugue Org, BWV 537; Fant Org, BWV 562; Fant Org, BWV 572; Partite diverse sopra, BWV 768; Preludes & Fugues, BWV 531-552 LIDI 3-▲ 104046 [DDD]

Toccata & Fugue in d for Organ, BWV 538, "Dorian" (1708-17)

E. P. Biggs (org) † Fant Org, BWV 572; Preludes & Fugues, BWV 531-552; Toccata & Fugue Org, BWV 565; Toccata, Adagio & Fugue Org, BWV 564 SNYC ▲ 42643 [ADD] (11.97)

K. Bowyer (org) ("Works for Organ, Vol. 8") † Cons solo Hpd; Fant & Fugue Org, BWV 537; Fugue on a theme by Legrenzi, BWV 574; Org Music (comp); Preludes & Fugues, BWV 531-552; Trio Son Fls, BWV 1039; Trio Va Kbd, BWV 1027a NIMB 2-▲ 5500 [DDD] (23.97)

M. Dupré (org) *(rec Queen's Hall & Alexandra Place orgs, England, Mar 17, 1930)* ("Bach; The Art of Marcel Dupré") † Cant 29; Clavier-Übung III; Fant & Fugue Org, BWV 537; Orgelbüchlein; Passacaglia & Fugue Org, BWV 582; Preludes & Fugues, BWV 531-552; Schübler Chorale Preludes; Suite 3 Orch, BWV 1068; Trio Sons Org PHS ▲ 9863 (17.97)

A. Fiedler (cnd), Boston Pops Orch [arr for orch] † Brandenburg Con 2, BWV 1047; Brandenburg Con 3, BWV 1048; Brandenburg Con 5, BWV 1050; Suite 2 Fl, BWV 1067; Suite 3 Orch, BWV 1068 RCAV ▲ 60828 (10.97) ▮ 60828 (5.98)

V. Fox (org) *(rec live, Carnegie Hall Rodgers Touring Org, United States of America, Dec 20, 1973)* ("Heavy Organ") † Clavier-Übung III; Org Music (misc colls); Passacaglia & Fugue Org, BWV 582; Toccata & Fugue Org, BWV 565 RCAV (Gold Seal) ▲ 68816 [ADD] (11.97)

J. Guillou (org) *(rec Aug 1990)* † Chorales (miscellaneous); Chorales Org; Org Music (misc colls); Orgelbüchlein; Partite diverse sopra, BWV 768 DOR ▲ 90149 [DDD] (16.97)

J. Guillou (org) *(rec Cathedrale de Breda Netherlands, Nov 15-17, 1984)* ("Grandes Toccatas") † Prelude & Fugue Org, BWV 566; Preludes & Fugues, BWV 531-552; Toccata & Fugue Org, BWV 565; Toccata, Adagio & Fugue Org, BWV 564 PVY ▲ 730001 [DDD]

M. Howard (org) *(rec St Michael's Abbey Farnborough, England)* ("J.S. Bach & Aristide Cavaillé-Coll") † Org Music (misc colls) HER ▲ 154 (19.97)

P. Hurford (org) *(rec Church of Our Lady of Sorrows Org Toronto, Canada, 1975; 1977-79)* † Chorales Org; Fant & Fugue Org, BWV 537; Fant & Fugue, BWV 542; Fant Org, BWV 562; Fant Org, BWV 572; Org Music (misc colls); Passacaglia & Fugue Org, BWV 582; Preludes & Fugues, BWV 531-552; Schübler Chorale Preludes; Toccata & Fugue Org, BWV 565; Toccata, Adagio & Fugue Org, BWV 564 PLON 2-▲ 43485 [ADD] (17.97)

BACH, JOHANN SEBASTIAN (cont.)

Toccata & Fugue in d for Organ, BWV 538, "Dorian" (1708-17) (cont.)

T. Koopman (org) *(rec Maassluis Grote Kerk, June 1983)* † Fant Org, BWV 572; Org Music (misc colls); Passacaglia & Fugue Org, BWV 582; Pastorale Org, BWV 590; Prelude Org, BWV 569; Toccata & Fugue Org, BWV 565 PARC ▲ 47292 [DDD] (9.97)

T. Koopman (org) † Clavier-Übung III; Org Music (misc colls); Partite diverse sopra, BWV 768; Preludes & Fugues, BWV 531-552; Trio Sons Org NOVA ▲ 150036 [DDD] (16.97)

T. Koopman (org) *(rec 1988)* ("Orgelwerke") † Org Music (misc colls); Partite diverse sopra, BWV 768; Preludes & Fugues, BWV 531-552; Trio Sons Org NOVA ▲ 150130 [DDD] (69.97)

W. Kraft (org) *(rec 1965)* † Chorales (miscellaneous); Cons Org; Fant Org, BWV 562; Fugue on a theme by Legrenzi, BWV 574; Org Music (misc colls); Orgelbüchlein; Passacaglia & Fugue Org, BWV 582; Preludes & Fugues, BWV 531-552; Toccata, Adagio & Fugue Org, BWV 564 VB2 2-▲ 5059 [ADD] (9.97)

J. Lippincott (org) *(rec Durham NC, Flentrop Org)* ("Toccatas & Fugues by Bach") † Passacaglia & Fugue Org, BWV 582; Preludes & Fugues, BWV 531-552; Toccata & Fugue Org, BWV 565; Toccata, Adagio & Fugue Org, BWV 564 GOT ▲ 49093 [DDD] (17.97)

D. Major (org) *(rec Great Org Washington Nat'l Cathedral, DC)* ("Masterworks by Bach") † Chorales Org; Passacaglia & Fugue Org, BWV 582; Pastorale Org, BWV 590; Preludes & Fugues, BWV 531-552 GOT ▲ 49104 (17.97)

R. Marlow (org) *(rec Metzler org, Trinity College, Cambridge, England)* † Prelude & Fugue Org, BWV 566; Preludes & Fugues, BWV 531-552; Toccata & Fugue Org, BWV 565; Toccata, Adagio & Fugue Org, BWV 564 ASV ▲ 6231 (10.97)

J. Meredith (cnd), Sonos Handbell Ensemble [arr for handbell ensemble] ("Classical Sonos") † W. A. Mozart:Adagio & Rondo, K.617; Son 11 Pno, K.331 WETE ▲ 5182 [DDD] (16.97)

M. Murray (org) † Cons Org; Toccata & Fugue Org, BWV 565 TEL ▲ 80088 [DDD] (16.97)

M. Murray (org) † Chorale Preludes Org; Orgelbüchlein TEL ▲ 80286 [DDD] (16.97)

A. Newman (org) † Chorales (miscellaneous); Fant & Fugue Org, BWV 537; Jesus, meine Zuversicht, BWV 728; Org Music (misc colls); Orgelbüchlein; Passacaglia & Fugue Org, BWV 582; Preludes & Fugues, BWV 531-552 VB2 2-▲ 5100 [ADD] (9.97)

Oregon Symphony Horns *(rec Sept 1994)* ("Oregon Symphony Horns & Friends") † Cant 140; Music of Bach; Passacaglia & Fugue Org, BWV 582; Mendelssohn (-Bartholdy):Anthems (6), Op. 79; Psalms (3), Op. 78 CENT ▲ 2344 [DDD] (16.97)

D. Schrader (org) ("The Complete Fantasies, Fantasies & Fugues, & Isolated Fugues for Organ") † Prelude & Fugue Org, BWV 566; Preludes & Fugues, BWV 531-552; Toccata & Fugue Org, BWV 565; Toccata, Adagio & Fugue Org, BWV 564 CED ▲ 6 [DDD] (16.97)

H. Walcha (org) *(rec Great Org, St. Laurenskerk Alkmaar & Strassberg, Germany, 1956-70)* † Canonic Vars on "Von Himmel hoch", BWV 769; Fant Org, BWV 572; Org Music (misc colls); Passacaglia & Fugue Org, BWV 582; Preludes & Fugues, BWV 531-552; Schübler Chorale Preludes; Toccata & Fugue Org, BWV 565; Trio Sons Org DEUT 2-▲ 453064 [ADD] (17.97)

artists unknown ("Classic Hits: Bach") † Air on the G String; Brandenburg Con 3, BWV 1048; Music of Bach PUBM (Majestic) ▲ 1025 (4.97)

Toccata & Fugue in d for Organ, BWV 565 (before 1708)

A. Bárta (org) † Chorales (miscellaneous); Chorales Org; Cons Org; Pastorale Org, BWV 590; Preludes & Fugues, BWV 531-552; Toccata, Adagio & Fugue Org, BWV 564 SUR ▲ 111289 [DDD]

E. P. Biggs (org) *(rec 1973)* † Fant Org, BWV 572; Preludes & Fugues, BWV 531-552; Toccata & Fugue Org, BWV 538; Toccata, Adagio & Fugue Org, BWV 564 SNYC ▲ 42643 [ADD] (11.97)

E. P. Biggs (org) *(rec 1960)* † Passacaglia & Fugue Org, BWV 582; Toccata, Adagio & Fugue Org, BWV 564 SNYC ▲ 42644 [ADD] (11.97)

E. P. Biggs (org) † Passacaglia & Fugue Org, BWV 582; Pastorale Org, BWV 590; Preludes & Fugues, BWV 531-552; Chopin:Sylphides; Delibes:Coppélia (suite); Sylvia (suite); P. Tchaikovsky:Nutcracker Suite, Op. 71a SNYC (Essential Classics) ▲ 46551 [ADD] (7.97) ▮ 46551 [ADD] (3.98)

K. Bowyer (org) *(rec Odense, Denmark)* ("The Works for Organ, Vol. 1") † Cons Org; Org Music (comp); Pastorale Org, BWV 590; Trio Sons Org NIMB ▲ 5280 (16.97)

A. Davis (org) *(rec Org at Roy Thompson Hall Toronto)* † C. Franck:Prélude, fugue et var, Op. 18; C. Ives:Vars on 'America'; H. Purcell:Cortege Academique; Tpt Tune INMP (IMP Classics) ▲ 6700942 (9.97)

H. Fagius (org) *(rec Sweden, July 8, 1977)* ("Hans Fagius") † Cant 147; Boëllmann:Suite gothique Org, Op. 25; O. Lindberg:Music of Lindberg; Mendelssohn (-Bartholdy):Preludes & Fugues Org, Op. 37; Sons Org, Op. 65; Saint-Saëns:Fant 1 Org; Vierne:Sym 1 Org, Op. 14 *(E, F, G text)* BIS 2-▲ 156 [AAD] (34.97)

H. Fagius (org) ("Vol. 6") † Chorales (miscellaneous); Fant & Fugue Org, BWV 537; Fant Org, BWV 562; Org Music (comp); Partite diverse sopra, BWV 768; Preludes & Fugues, BWV 531-552; Trio Sons Org BIS 2-▲ 397 [DDD] (69.97)

V. Fox (org) † Org Music (misc colls) RCAV (Victrola) ▲ 7736 [ADD] (6.97)

V. Fox (org) *(rec live, Carnegie Hall Rodgers Touring Org, United States of America, Dec 20, 1973)* ("Heavy Organ") † Clavier-Übung III; Org Music (misc colls); Passacaglia & Fugue Org, BWV 582; Toccata & Fugue Org, BWV 538 RCAV (Gold Seal) ▲ 68816 [ADD] (11.97)

J. Guillou (org) *(rec Aug 1990)* † Chorales (miscellaneous); Chorales Org; Org Music (misc colls); Orgelbüchlein; Preludes & Fugues, BWV 531-552; Trio Sons Org DOR ▲ 90150 [DDD] (16.97)

J. Guillou (org) *(rec Cathedrale de Breda Netherlands, Nov 15-17, 1984)* ("Grandes Toccatas") † Prelude & Fugue Org, BWV 566; Preludes & Fugues, BWV 531-552; Toccata & Fugue Org, BWV 538; Toccata, Adagio & Fugue Org, BWV 564 PVY ▲ 730001 [DDD]

F. Hauk (org) *(rec Great Klais Org of Ingolstadt Münster, Germany)* ("Organ Works") † Chorales Org; Org Music (misc colls); Orgelbüchlein; Preludes & Fugues, BWV 531-552; Toccata, Adagio & Fugue Org, BWV 564 INMP ▲ 6600402

A. Heiler (org) *(rec 1964)* † Org Music (misc colls); Passacaglia & Fugue Org, BWV 582; Preludes & Fugues, BWV 531-552 VC (The Bach Guild) ▲ 2005 [ADD] (13.97)

A. Heiller (org) † Nun komm der Heiden Heiland, BWV 699; Orgelbüchlein; Passacaglia & Fugue Org, BWV 582; Preludes & Fugues, BWV 531-552 AURC ▲ 145 (5.97)

D. Hill (org) *(rec Trinity Cathedral Portland, OR, May 1994)* ("There Let the Pealing Organ Blow") † F. Bridge:Adagio Org; C. Franck:Chorales Org, M.38-40; Vierne:Org Music HER ▲ 190 [DDD] (19.97)

P. Hurford (org) ("Great Organ Works") † Fant Org, BWV 572; Strauss (II):Waltzes PLON (Double Decker) 2-▲ 43473 (17.97)

P. Hurford (org) *(rec Toronto, Canada, 1975; 1977-79)* † Chorales Org; Fant & Fugue Org, BWV 537; Fant & Fugue, BWV 542; Fant Org, BWV 562; Fant Org, BWV 572; Org Music (misc colls); Passacaglia & Fugue Org, BWV 582; Preludes & Fugues, BWV 531-552; Schübler Chorale Preludes; Toccata & Fugue Org, BWV 538; Toccata, Adagio & Fugue Org, BWV 564 PLON 2-▲ 43485 [ADD] (17.97)

Ignaz Friedman † Cant 147; Chromatic Fant & Fugue, BWV 903; Fant & Fugue, BWV 542; French Suites; Inventions Hpd; Partitas Hpd; Toccatas Hpd; Wohltemperirte Clavier NIMB (Grand Piano) ▲ 8808 [DDD] (11.97)

H. Kästner (org) † Org Music (misc colls); Orgelbüchlein; Preludes & Fugues, BWV 531-552 CAPO ▲ 10035 [DDD] (11.97)

H. Kästner (org), G. Lehotka (org) † Chorales (miscellaneous); Clavier-Übung III; Fant & Fugue Org, BWV 561; Fugue Org, BWV 578; Orgelbüchlein; Preludes & Fugues, BWV 531-552 LALI ▲ 15507 [ADD] (3.97)

P. Kee (org) ("Piet Kee Plays Bach, Vol. 3") † Chorale Preludes Org; Chorales Org; Neumeister Collection; Org Music (misc colls); Preludes & Fugues Org CHN (Chaconne) ▲ 527 [DDD] (16.97)

C. Keene (pno) [trans Keene based on Tausig & Busoni] † French Suites; Italian Con, BWV 971; Partitas Hpd PROT ▲ 1113 (18.97)

T. Koopman (org) *(rec Maassluis Grote Kerk, June 1983)* † Fant Org, BWV 572; Org Music (misc colls); Passacaglia & Fugue Org, BWV 582; Pastorale Org, BWV 590; Prelude Org, BWV 569; Toccata & Fugue Org, BWV 538 PARC ▲ 47292 [DDD] (9.97)

T. Koopman (org) † Fant & Fugue, BWV 542; Partite diverse sopra, BWV 767 NOVA ▲ 150005 [DDD] (16.97)

W. Kraft (org) ("25 Bach Favorites") † Brandenburg Con 1, BWV 1046; Brandenburg Con 2, BWV 1047; Brandenburg Con 3, BWV 1048; Brandenburg Con 4, BWV 1049; Brandenburg Con 5, BWV 1050; Cant 147; Con Hpds (4), BWV 1065; Con Vns; Con 1 for 2 Hpds, BWV 1060; Con 1 Vn; Mass in b, BWV 232; Music of Bach; Schübler Chorale Preludes; Sons & Partitas Vn; Suite 2 Fl, BWV 1067; Toccata, Adagio & Fugue Org, BWV 564; Wohltemperirte Clavier VCC ▲ 8817 (3.97)

B. Lagacé (org) *(rec Montreal, Canada, Mar 1996)* ("Toccata in d & Other Early Works") † Chorales (miscellaneous); Org Music (misc colls); Partite diverse sopra, BWV 766; Pastorale Org, BWV 590; Prelude & Fugue Org, BWV 566 FL ▲ 23091 [DDD] (16.97)

S. Lautenbacher (vn), D. Vorholz (vn), G. Kehr (cnd), Mainz CO ("The Story of Bach in Words and Music") † Cant 211; Cant 57; Con Vns; Con 2 Vn; Life & Music of Bach; Magnificat, BWV 243; Mass in b, BWV 232; Passacaglia & Fugue Org, BWV 582; Schübler Chorale Preludes; St. John Passion, BWV 245 MMD (Music Masters) ▲ 8500 [ADD] (3.97) ▮ 8500 [ADD] (2.98)

COMPOSERS 101

BACH, JOHANN SEBASTIAN (cont.)

Toccata & Fugue in d for Organ, BWV 565 (before 1708) (cont.)

G. Leonhardt (org) *(rec Amsterdam, Netherlands, 1972-73)* ("Great Organ Works") † Canonic Vars on "Von Himmel hoch", BWV 769; Chorales (miscellaneous); Chorales Org; Fant Org, BWV 562; Fant Org, BWV 572; Fugue on "Meine Seele"; Orgelbüchlein; Partite diverse sopra, BWV 766; Partite diverse sopra, BWV 767; Preludes & Fugues, BWV 531-552 SNYC (Seon) 2-▲ 63185 [ADD] (7.97)

J. Lippincott (org) *(rec Durham NC, Flentrop Org)* ("Toccatas & Fugues by Bach") † Passacaglia & Fugue Org, BWV 582; Preludes & Fugues, BWV 531-552; Toccata & Fugue Org, BWV 538; Toccata, Adagio & Fugue Org, BWV 564 GOT ▲ 49093 [DDD] (17.97)

R. Marlow (org) *(rec Metzler org, Trinity College, Cambridge, England)* † Prelude & Fugue Org, BWV 566; Preludes & Fugues, BWV 531-552; Toccata & Fugue Org, BWV 538; Toccata, Adagio & Fugue Org, BWV 564 ASV ▲ 6231 (10.97)

M. Murray (org) † Cons Org; Toccata & Fugue Org, BWV 538 TEL ▲ 80088 [DDD] (16.97)

M. Murray (org) ("Bach Organ Blaster") † Cant 29; Cons Org; Fugue Org, BWV 578; Org Music (misc colls); Preludes & Fugues, BWV 531-552 TEL ▲ 80316 [DDD] (16.97)

A. Newman (org) ("24 Preludes & Fugues, Vol. 1") † Chorales (miscellaneous); Orgelbüchlein; Preludes & Fugues, BWV 531-552; Toccata, Adagio & Fugue Org, BWV 564 VB2 2-▲ 5013 [ADD] (9.97)

A. Newman (hpd) ("Bach Favorite Organ Works") † Cant 147 SNYC ▲ 62385 [DDD] (4.97)

R. Noehren (org) † Trio Sons Org DLS ▲ 3028 [DDD] (14.97)

E. Ormandy (cnd), Philadelphia Orch [arr Ormandy] *(rec Jan 31, 1960)* † Brandenburg Con 5, BWV 1050; Cant 140; Passacaglia & Fugue Org, BWV 582; Toccata, Adagio & Fugue Org, BWV 564; W. F. Bach:Sinf Orch, F.64 SNYC (Masterworks Heritage) 2-▲ 62345 [ADD] (25.97)

H. Otto (org) † Fant Org, BWV 570; Org Music (misc colls); Preludes & Fugues, BWV 531-552; Schübler Chorale Preludes DNN ▲ 7004 [DDD]

R. Pikler (cnd), Sydney SO ("Orchestral Transcriptions by Leopold Stokowski") † Clavier-Übung III; Music of Bach; Passacaglia & Fugue Org, BWV 582; Toccata, Adagio & Fugue Org, BWV 564 CHN (Collect) ▲ 6532 [ADD] (12.97)

P. Planyavsky (org) *(rec Fukushima-shi Ongakudo, Japan, Nov 7-8, 1986)* ("Bach: Toccata und fuge in d moll, BWV 565") † Cant 147; Chorales Org; Fugue Org, BWV 578; Org Music (misc colls); Preludes & Fugues, BWV 531-552 CAMA ▲ 197 [DDD] (18.97)

S. Preston (org) † Canonic Vars on "Von Himmel hoch", BWV 769; Fant Org, BWV 572; Pastorale Org, BWV 590; Preludes & Fugues, BWV 531-552 PARC ▲ 27668 [DDD] (16.97)

S. Preston (org) † Canzona; Preludes & Fugues Org; Preludes & Fugues, BWV 531-552 DGRM ▲ 449212 [DDD]

K. Richter (org) † Fant & Fugue, BWV 542 DEUT (Musikfest) ▲ 15442 [ADD] (7.97)

K. Richter (org) *(rec Org of Victoria Hall Geneva)* † Fant & Fugue, BWV 542; Passacaglia & Fugue Org, BWV 582 PLON (Classic Sound) ▲ 455291 (11.97)

H. Rilling (org), J. E. Hansen (org), H. Otto (org), K. Vad (org) † Cant 147; Org Music (misc colls); Orgelbüchlein; Passacaglia & Fugue Org, BWV 582; Schübler Chorale Preludes; Trio Org, BWV 583 DNN ▲ 8009 [DDD] (10.97)

L. Rogg (org) *(rec Silbermann Org, Arlesheim, Switzerland)* † Allabreve, BWV 589; Canonic Vars on "Von Himmel hoch", BWV 769; Canzona; Chorales Org; Clavier-Übung III; Fant & Fugue Org, BWV 537; Fant & Fugue, BWV 542; Fant Org, BWV 562; Fant Org, BWV 572; Orgelbüchlein; Partite diverse sopra, BWV 766; Partite diverse sopra, BWV 767; Partite diverse sopra, BWV 768; Pastorale Org, BWV 590; Prelude & Fugue Org, BWV 566; Preludes & Fugues, BWV 531-552; Schübler Chorale Preludes; Toccata, Adagio & Fugue Org, BWV 564; Trio Org, BWV 583; Trio Sons Org HAM 12-▲ 290772 [ADD] (71.97)

L. Rogg (org) *(rec historic org, Alesheim, France)* † Passacaglia & Fugue Org, BWV 582; Preludes & Fugues, BWV 531-552; Schübler Chorale Preludes HMA ▲ 190771 (9.97)

W. Rübsam (org) † Pastorale Org, BWV 590 NXIN ▲ 550184 [DDD] (5.97)

W. Rübsam (org) ("The Great Organ Works") † Cant 147; Org Music (misc colls); Orgelbüchlein; Passacaglia & Fugue Org, BWV 582; Preludes & Fugues, BWV 531-552; Toccata, Adagio & Fugue Org, BWV 564 NXIN ▲ 553859 [DDD] (5.97)

D. Schrader (org) ("The Complete Fantasies, Fantasies & Fugues, & Isolated Fugues for Organ") † Prelude & Fugue Org, BWV 566; Preludes & Fugues, BWV 531-552; Toccata & Fugue Org, BWV 538; Toccata, Adagio & Fugue Org, BWV 564 CED ▲ 6 [DDD] (16.97)

A. Schweitzer (org) ("Albert Schweitzer Plays J. S. Bach: The Legendary 1935 & 1936 Recordings") † Fant & Fugue, BWV 542 GRM2 ▲ 78692 (13.97)

A. Schweitzer (org) *(rec Dec 1935; Oct 1936)* † Fant & Fugue, BWV 542; Fugue Org, BWV 578 MTAL ▲ 48045

J. Sedares (cnd), New Zealand SO ("From Authentic to Outrageous") † Brandenburg Con 5, BWV 1050; Cant 140; Fant Org, BWV 562; Mass in b, BWV 232; Musical Offering, BWV 1079; Partitas Hpd; Suite 3 Orch, BWV 1068 KOCH ▲ 7610 (10.97)

L. Stokowski (cnd), Philadelphia Orch † Dukas:L'Apprenti sorcier; Mussorgsky:Night on Bare Mountain; Saint-Saëns:Danse macabre, Op. 40; Samson et Dalila (Bacchanale); I. Stravinsky:Sacre du printemps MTAL (Leopold Stokowski Conducts) ▲ 48002 (6.97)

Summit Brass † Cant 147; Fugue Org, BWV 578; Music of Bach; G. Gabrieli:Canzoni for Brass Choirs SUMM ▲ 101 [DDD] (16.97)

A. Toscanini (cnd), NBC SO [orchd] *(rec 1936-47)* ("Baroque & Classic Repertoire") † Brandenburg Con 2, BWV 1047; Passacaglia & Fugue Org, BWV 582; J. Haydn:Sym 31 IN ▲ 1397 (15.97)

J. Van Landeghem (org) *(rec Apr 1995)* ("Bach-Buxtehude-Mozart-Purcell") † Chorales Org; Preludes & Fugues, BWV 531-552; Schübler Chorale Preludes; St. Matthew Passion (sels); Buxtehude:Passacaglia Org, BuxWV 161; W. A. Mozart:Adagio & Allegro, K.594 PAVA ▲ 7339 [DDD] (10.97)

O. Vernet (org) ("The Organ Works: Vol. 1, 1700-1708") † Chorales (miscellaneous); Fant & Imitatio Org, BWV 563; Fant Org, BWV 570; Org Music (comp); Partite diverse sopra, BWV 766; Partite diverse sopra, BWV 767; Passacaglia & Fugue Org, BWV 582; Prelude Org, BWV 568; Prelude Org, BWV 569; Preludes & Fugues, BWV 531-552 LIDI 3-▲ 104037 (47.97)

H. Walcha (org) *(rec Great org, St. Laurenskerk Alkmaar & Strassberg, Germany, 1956-70)* † Canonic Vars on "Von Himmel hoch", BWV 769; Fant Org, BWV 572; Org Music (misc colls); Passacaglia & Fugue Org, BWV 582; Preludes & Fugues, BWV 531-552; Schübler Chorale Preludes; Toccata & Fugue Org, BWV 538; Trio Sons Org DEUT 2-▲ 453064 [ADD] (17.97)

H. Walcha (org) *(rec St. Laurenskerk Org at St. Laurens Church, Al, Sept 1956, Sept 1962)* † Partite diverse sopra, BWV 768; Preludes & Fugues, BWV 531-552; Schübler Chorale Preludes; Trio Sons Org DEUT (The Originals) ▲ 457704 [ADD] (11.97)

O. Winter (org) † Brandenburg Con 3, BWV 1048; Con 1 Vn; Italian Con, BWV 971; Music of Bach; St. Matthew Passion (sels) UNIN ▲ 81172 [DDD] (5.97)

artist unknown ("Organ Music from the Island of Ireland") † J. Dexter:Londonderry Air; Kitson:Communion on an Irish Air; C. S. Lang:Tuba Tune, Op. 15; Stanford:Org Music; Widor:Sym 5 Org, Op. 42/1; C. Wood:Preludes Org GILD ▲ 7122 [ADD] (16.97)

artists unknown ("Favourite Bach") † Air on the G String; Anna Magdalena Bach Notebook (sels); Brandenburg Con 2, BWV 1047; Brandenburg Con 3, BWV 1048; Brandenburg Con 4, BWV 1049; Cant 140; Cant 147; Cant 208; Cant 212; Cant 51; Con 1 Hpd, BWV 1052; Con 2 Vn; St. Matthew Passion (sels); Suite 2 Fl, BWV 1067; Wohltemperirte Clavier CFP (Favourites) ▲ 4639 (12.97)

Toccatas (7) for Harpsichord, BWV 910-916 (ca 1738)

G. Gould (pno) *(rec 1963-79)* SNYC 2-▲ 52612 [ADD] (31.97)

C. Haskil (pno)—BWV 914, No. 5 in e ("The Clara Haskil Legacy") † J. Haydn:Son 50 Kbd, H.XVI/37; F. Schubert:Son Pno in B♭, D.960; R. Schumann:Bunte Blätter, Op. 99 TAHA ▲ 291 (17.97)

M. Hess (pno)—BWV 916, No. 7 in G † Cant 147; Chromatic Fant & Fugue, BWV 903; Fant & Fugue, BWV 542; French Suites; Inventions Hpd; Partitas Hpd; Toccata & Fugue Org, BWV 565; Wohltemperirte Clavier NIMB (Grand Piano) ▲ 8808 [DDD] (11.97)

W. Landowska (hpd)—BWV 912, No. 3 in D *(rec live, Jan 22, 1950)* ("Landowska Plays Bach") † English Suites; Music of Bach; Partitas Hpd; Prelude Lt, BWV 999; Preludes Hpd; Preludes Hpd (5); Preludes Kbd PHS ▲ 9489 [AAD] (17.97)

G. Leonhardt (harmonicord)—BWV 912, No. 3 in D; BWV 913, No. 4 in d *(rec 1976-1979)* † Chromatic Fant & Fugue, BWV 903; Fant & Fugue Org, BWV 906; Kbd Music (misc); Suite Lt, BWV 995; Suites Vc SNYC 2-▲ 60375 [ADD] (14.97)

J. C. Martins (pno)—BWV 910, No. 1 in f#; BWV 912, No. 3 in D *(rec Sofia, Bulgaria, Apr 1996)* ("Complete Keyboard Works, Vol. 14") † Adagio Clvd, BWV 968; Aria variata alla maniera italiana, BWV 989; Capriccio Departure, BWV 992; Duets Hpd; Ov Hpd ERTO ▲ 42051 [DDD] (16.97)

J. C. Martins (pno)—BWV 916, No. 7 in G ("The Essential Bach:Selections from the Complete Edition") † Con 1 for 2 Hpds, BWV 1060; Con 1 Pno; Con 2 for 2 Hpds, BWV 1061; Duets Hpd; English Suites; Fant & Fugue Org, BWV 906; French Suites; Fughetta, BWV 961; Goldberg Vars, BWV 988; Inventions Hpd; Italian Con, BWV 971; Partitas Hpd; Wohltemperirte Clavier ERTO ▲ 42054 [DDD] (13.97)

E. Parmentier (hpd) *(rec Schrine Music Museum, Vermillion, SD, June 1994)* WILD ▲ 9402 [DDD] (16.97)

R. Puyana (hpd)—BWV 910, No. 1 in f# ("Puyana Plays Bach") † Cons solo Hpd; Partita Hpd, BWV 831; W. F. Bach:Con 2 Hpds, F.10; J. Christian Bach:Sons & Duets Kbd 4-Hands, T.343/3 MRCR ▲ 434395 [ADD] (11.97)

BACH, JOHANN SEBASTIAN (cont.)

Toccatas (7) for Harpsichord, BWV 910-916 (ca 1738) (cont.)

A. Rangell (pno)—BWV 910, No. 1 in f# † Goldberg Vars, BWV 988; Musical Offering, BWV 1079 DOR ▲ 90138 [DDD] (16.97)

S. Richter (pno)—BWV 913, No. 4 in d; BWV 916, No. 7 in G † Duets Hpd; English Suites; Fant & Fugue Org, BWV 906; French Suites; Italian Con, BWV 971; Partita Hpd, BWV 831 PPHI 3-▲ 38613 (48.97)

Z. Růžičová (hpd) † Chromatic Fant & Fugue, BWV 903; English Suites; French Suites SUR ▲ 111489 [DDD]

A. Schnabel (pno), A. Boult (cnd), London SO—BWV 911, No. 2 in c; BWV 912, No. 3 in D † Chromatic Fant & Fugue, BWV 903; Con 2 for 2 Hpds, BWV 1061; C. M. von Weber:Invitation to the Dance Pno, J.260 URAN ▲ 119 (m) [ADD] (15.97)

C. Tilney (hpd) DOR ▲ 90115 [DDD] (16.97)

J. Vinikour (hpd) MAND ▲ 4936 (18.97)

Trio in d for Organ, BWV 583

C. Brembeck (org) *(rec Intzgrund, Germany, Oct 24-26, 1988)* ("Lahm-Itzgrund Herbst-Orgel") † Chorale Preludes Org; Chorales Org; Fant & Imitatio Org, BWV 563; Org Music (misc colls); Partite diverse sopra, BWV 770; Preludes & Fugues, BWV 531-552; J. Lorenz Bach:Prelude & Fugue Org; W. H. Pachelbel:Musicalisches Vergnügen CAPO ▲ 10351 [DDD] (11.97)

H. Fagius (org) ("Vol. 7") † Canonic Vars on "Von Himmel hoch", BWV 769; Chorales (miscellaneous); Cons Org; Fugue on a theme by Legrenzi, BWV 574; Fugue Org, BWV 577; Fugue Org, BWV 578; Org Music (comp); Org Music (misc colls); Preludes & Fugues, BWV 531-552 BIS 2-▲ 439 [DDD] (69.97)

B. Lagacé (org) ("Fantasy & Fugue in g & Other Mature Works") † Fant & Fugue Org, BWV 537; Fant & Fugue, BWV 542; Fant Org, BWV 562; Fugue on "Meine Seele"; Preludes & Fugues, BWV 531-552; Trio Sons Org FL ▲ 23096 [DDD] (16.97)

H. Rilling (org), J. E. Hansen (org), H. Otto (org), K. Vad (org) † Cant 147; Org Music (misc colls); Orgelbüchlein; Passacaglia & Fugue Org, BWV 582; Schübler Chorale Preludes; Toccata & Fugue Org, BWV 565 DNN ▲ 8009 [DDD] (10.97)

L. Rogg (org) *(rec Silbermann Org, Arlesheim, Switzerland)* † Allabreve, BWV 589; Canonic Vars on "Von Himmel hoch", BWV 769; Canzona; Chorales Org; Clavier-Übung III; Fant & Fugue Org, BWV 537; Fant & Fugue, BWV 542; Fant Org, BWV 562; Fant Org, BWV 572; Orgelbüchlein; Partite diverse sopra, BWV 766; Partite diverse sopra, BWV 767; Partite diverse sopra, BWV 768; Pastorale Org, BWV 590; Prelude & Fugue Org, BWV 566; Preludes & Fugues, BWV 531-552; Schübler Chorale Preludes; Toccata & Fugue Org, BWV 565; Toccata, Adagio & Fugue Org, BWV 564; Trio Sons Org HAM 12-▲ 290772 [ADD] (71.97)

Trio in c for Organ, BWV 585 (ca 1725-27)

K. Bowyer (org) ("Complete Works for Organ, Vol. 3") † Cons Org; Partite diverse sopra, BWV 768; Preludes & Fugues, BWV 531-552 NIMB ▲ 5290 [DDD] (16.97)

H. Fagius (org) ("Vol. 3") † Fant & Fugue Org, BWV 561; Preludes & Fugues Org BIS 2-▲ 329 (69.97)

Trio Sonatas (miscellaneous)

Freiburg Baroque Soloists—Son in C; Son in b ("Trio Sonatas In Their Orignal Versions") † Sons Fl; Trio Sons Org ENTE ▲ 53 [ADD] (10.97)

Trio Sonata in G for Flute, Violin & Harpsichord, [doubtful], BWV 1038

J. Baker (fl), B. Garner (fl) † Trio Son Fls, BWV 1039; Telemann:Essercizii Musici LALI ▲ 14387 (3.97)

W. Forchert (vn), J. Gérard (fl), S. Azzolini (bn), B. Kleiner (hpd) ("Edition Bachakademie, Vol. 121: Chamber Music for Flute") † Partita Fl, BWV 1013; Partita Lt, BWV 997; Son Vn; Sons Fl; Trio Son Fls, BWV 1039 HANS 2-▲ 92121 [DDD] (19.97)

M. Huggett (vn), S. Cunningham (vl), J. Galway (fl), P. Moll (hpd) ("Galway Plays Bach, Vol. 2") † Musical Offering, BWV 1079; Partita Fl, BWV 1013; Sons Fl; Trio Son Fls, BWV 1039 RCAV (Red Seal) ▲ 68182 [DDD] (16.97)

J. Schwarz (vn), E. Potash (vc), J. Solum (fl), I. Kipnis (hpd) [period instrs] † Trio Son Fls, BWV 1039; Telemann:Musique de Table ARA ▲ 6640 [DDD] (16.97)

Trio Sonata in G for 2 Flutes & Continuo, BWV 1039 (ca 1720)

J. Baker (fl), B. Garner (fl) † Trio Son Fl Vn & Hpd, BWV 1038; Telemann:Essercizii Musici LALI ▲ 14387 (3.97)

K. Bowyer (org) ("Works for Organ, Vol. 8") † Cons solo Hpd; Fant & Fugue Org, BWV 537; Fugue on a theme by Legrenzi, BWV 574; Org Music (comp); Preludes & Fugues, BWV 531-552; Toccata & Fugue Org, BWV 538; Trio Va Kbd, BWV 1027a NIMB 2-▲ 5500 [DDD] (23.97)

K. Chung (vn), M. Welsh (vc), J. Galway (fl), P. Moll (hpd) † Con Fl; Con 8 Hpd, BWV 1059; Musical Offering, BWV 1079; Suite 2 Fl, BWV 1067 RCAV (Red Seal; Papillon Collection) ▲ 6517 [ADD] (11.97)

S. Cunningham (vl), J. Galway (fl), J. Galway (fl), P. Moll (hpd) ("Galway Plays Bach, Vol. 2") † Musical Offering, BWV 1079; Partita Fl, BWV 1013; Sons Fl; Trio Son Fl Vn & Hpd, BWV 1038 RCAV (Red Seal) ▲ 68182 [DDD] (16.97)

J. Gérard (fl), D. Formisano (fl), S. Azzolini (bn), B. Kleiner (hpd) ("Edition Bachakademie, Vol. 121: Chamber Music for Flute") † Partita Fl, BWV 1013; Partita Lt, BWV 997; Son Vn; Sons Fl; Trio Son Fl Vn & Hpd, BWV 1038 HANS 2-▲ 92121 [DDD] (19.97)

E. Potash (vc), J. Solum (trns fl), R. Wyton (trns fl), I. Kipnis (hpd) [period instrs] † Trio Son Fl Vn & Hpd, BWV 1038; Telemann:Musique de Table ARA ▲ 6640 [DDD] (16.97)

Trio Sonatas (6) for Organ, BWV 525-530 (ca 1727)

Arion Quartet *(rec Quebec, June 1996)* FL ▲ 23086 [DDD] (16.97)

E. P. Biggs (pedal hpd) *(rec 1966)* SNYC (Essential Classics) ▲ 60290 (7.97) ▮ 60290 (3.98)

D. Bogdanovič (gtr), E. Comparone (hpd) [trans performers for gtr & hpd] ("Bach with Pluck!") ESSY ▲ 1023 [DDD] (16.97)

K. Bowyer (org)—BWV 530, No. 6 in G *(rec Odense Denmark, Mar 23-24, 1993)* ("The Works for Organ, Vol. 6") † Org Music (comp); Prelude & Fugue Org, BWV 566; Preludes & Fugues (22) Org, BWV 531-552; Toccata, Adagio & Fugue Org, BWV 564; Trio Son Org, BWV 584 NIMB ▲ 5423 [DDD] (16.97)

K. Bowyer (org)—BWV 525, No. 1 E♭ *(rec Odense, Denmark)* ("The Works for Organ, Vol. 1") † Cons Org; Org Music (comp); Pastorale Org, BWV 590; Toccata & Fugue Org, BWV 565 NIMB ▲ 5280 (16.97)

K. Bowyer (org)—BWV 529, No. 5 in C *(rec Odense, Denmark)* ("The Works for Organ, Vol. 2") † Chorales (miscellaneous); Org Music (comp); Preludes & Fugues, BWV 531-552 NIMB ▲ 5289 (16.97)

M. Dupré (org)—BWV 525, No. 1 E♭ *(rec Queen's Hall & Alexandra Place orgs, England, June 1928)* ("Bach; The Art of Marcel Dupré") † Cant 29; Clavier-Übung III; Fant & Fugue Org, BWV 537; Orgelbüchlein; Passacaglia & Fugue Org, BWV 582; Preludes & Fugues, BWV 531-552; Schübler Chorale Preludes; Suite 3 Orch, BWV 1068; Toccata & Fugue Org, BWV 538 PHS ▲ 9863 (17.97)

H. Erhard (hpd)—BWV 527, No. 3 in d; BWV 525, No. 1 E♭ † Art of the Fugue (sels); Sons Fl HANS ▲ 98987 [DDD] (15.97)

H. Fagius (org)—BWV 527, No. 3 in d ("Vol. 5") † Org Music (comp); Passacaglia & Fugue Org, BWV 582; Preludes & Fugues, BWV 531-552 BIS 2-▲ 379 [DDD] (69.97)

H. Fagius (org)—BWV 525, No. 1 E♭ *(rec 1728 Cahman Org at Leufsta bruk, Sweden)* ("The Complete Organ Music, Vol. 2") † Chorales (miscellaneous); Cons Org; Org Music (comp); Preludes & Fugues, BWV 531-552 BIS 2-▲ 308 [DDD] (69.97)

H. Fagius (org)—BWV 530, No. 6 in G ("Vol. 9") † Chorales (miscellaneous); Org Music (misc colls); Preludes & Fugues, BWV 531-552 BIS ▲ 445 [DDD] (17.97)

H. Fagius (org)—BWV 529, No. 5 in C ("Vol. 8") † Clavier-Übung III; Cons Org; Prelude & Fugue Org, BWV 566 BIS 2-▲ 443 [DDD] (69.97)

H. Fagius (org)—BWV 528, No. 4 in e ("Vol. 6") † Chorales (miscellaneous); Fant & Fugue Org, BWV 537; Fant Org, BWV 562; Org Music (comp); Partite diverse sopra, BWV 768; Preludes & Fugues, BWV 531-552; Toccata & Fugue Org, BWV 565 BIS 2-▲ 397 [DDD] (69.97)

M. Faust (fl), I. Wjuniski (hpd) *(rec May 1991)* † Sons Fl GMR ▲ 2036 (16.97)

Freiburg Baroque Soloists—BWV 528, No. 4 in e ("Trio Sonatas In Their Orignal Versions") † Sons Fl; Trio Sons (misc) ENTE ▲ 53 [ADD] (10.97)

J. Guillou (org)—BWV 525, No. 1 E♭ ("The Organ Works of Bach, Vol. 1") † Fugue on a theme by Corelli, BWV 579; Org Music (comp); Orgelbüchlein; Partite diverse sopra, BWV 767; Preludes & Fugues, BWV 531-552 DOR ▲ 90111 [DDD] (16.97)

J. Guillou (org)—BWV 526, No. 2 in c *(rec Aug 1990)* † Chorales (miscellaneous); Chorales Org; Org Music (misc colls); Orgelbüchlein; Preludes & Fugues, BWV 531-552; Toccata & Fugue Org, BWV 565 DOR ▲ 90150 [DDD] (16.97)

H. Gurtner (org) *(rec Klosterkirche Muri/AG Org of the Klosterkirche Mur, Germany, May 10-13, 1973)* CLAV 2-▲ 405 [DDD] (27.97)

K. Heindel (org)—BWV 528, No. 4 in e *(rec Steinfeld, Germany, Oct 5-7, 1992)* ("Bach at Steinfeld") † Cons Org; Org Music (misc colls); Preludes & Fugues, BWV 531-552 GAS ▲ 321 (16.97)

D. Higgs (org)—BWV 529, No. 5 in C *(rec Rieger Org Bryn Mawr Presbyterian Church, United States of America)* † Cons Org; Org Music (misc colls); Preludes & Fugues, BWV 531-552 DLS ▲ 3048 [DDD] (14.97)

T. Indermühle (ob), U. Dütschler (hpd)—BWV 527, No. 3 in d; BWV 528, No. 4 in e [trans for ob & hpd] *(rec Apr 16-20, 1995)* ("6 Oboe Sonatas") † Son Vn; Sons Fl CAMA ▲ 404 [DDD] (18.97)

K. Johannsen (org) HANS ▲ 98113 [DDD] (15.97)

J. Johnson (org) † Cons Org TIT ▲ 162 (16.97)

▲ = CD ♦ = Enhanced CD △ = MD ▮ = Cassette Tape ▯ = DCC

BACH, JOHANN SEBASTIAN (cont.)

Trio Sonatas (6) for Organ, BWV 525-530 (ca 1727) (cont.)

D. Joyce (org)—BWV 529, No. 5 in C; BWV 527, No. 3 in d † Canonic Vars on "Von Himmel hoch", BWV 769; Partite diverse sopra, BWV 768; Prelude & Fugue Org, BWV 566; Preludes & Fugues, BWV 531-552 TIT ▲ 171 [DDD]

R. King (cnd), King's Consort [arr for various instr] HYP ▲ 66843 (18.97)

J. Köhler (org), H. Otto (org)—BWV 526, No. 2 in c *(rec Fraureuth Church Org & Burgk Castle Org in Saxony, Germany)* ("Organ Works on Silbermann Organs, Vol. VIII") † Preludes & Fugues, BWV 531-552 BER 2-▲ 9368 (21.97)

T. Koopman (org)—BWV 527, No. 3 in d † Org Music (misc colls); Preludes & Fugues, BWV 531-552 NOVA ▲ 150078 [DDD] (16.97)

T. Koopman (org) † Preludes & Fugues Org; Toccata, Adagio & Fugue Org, BWV 564 NOVA ▲ 150066 [DDD] (16.97)

T. Koopman (org)—BWV 530, No. 6 in G † Clavier-Übung III; Org Music (misc colls); Partite diverse sopra, BWV 768; Preludes & Fugues, BWV 531-552; Toccata & Fugue Org, BWV 538 NOVA ▲ 150036 [DDD] (16.97)

T. Koopman (org)—BWV 530, No. 6 in G *(rec 1988)* ("Orgelwerke") † Org Music (misc colls); Partite diverse sopra, BWV 768; Preludes & Fugues, BWV 531-552; Toccata & Fugue Org, BWV 538 NOVA ▲ 150130 [DDD] (69.97)

B. Lagacé (org)—BWV 525, No. 1 E♭; BWV 526, No. 2 in c ("Fantasy & Fugue in g & Other Mature Works") † Fant & Fugue Org, BWV 537; Fant & Fugue, BWV 542; Fant Org, BWV 562; Fugue on "Meine Seele"; Preludes & Fugues, BWV 531-552; Trio Org, BWV 583 FL ▲ 23096 [DDD] (16.97)

H. Meister (org) MOTE ▲ 11941 (17.97)

R. Noehren (org) † Toccata & Fugue Org, BWV 565 DLS ▲ 3028 [DDD] (14.97)

Palladian Ensemble—BWV 525, No. 1 E♭; BWV 527, No. 3 in d; BWV 529, No. 5 in C; BWV 530, No. 6 in G *(rec Nov 14-17, 1994)* † Duets Hpd; Verschiedene Canones, BWV 1087 LINN ▲ 5036 (16.97)

G. Ritchie (org)—BWV 530, No. 6 in G *(rec J. Brombaugh Org Southern Adventist Univ, United States of America)* ("Vol. III: For Music Lovers & Connoisseurs") † Clavier-Übung III; Preludes & Fugues, BWV 531-552; Schübler Chorale Preludes RAVN 2-▲ 400 [DDD] (17.97)

P. Robison (fl), J. Gibbons (hpd) [trans for fl & hpd] ("Wings of the Morning") ARA ▲ 6694 (16.97)

W. Rübsam (org)—BWV 526, No. 2 in c; BWV 525, No. 1 E♭; BWV 527, No. 3 in d *(rec Nov 1989)* NXIN ▲ 550651 [DDD] (5.97)

W. Rübsam (org)—BWV 528, No. 4 in e; BWV 529, No. 5 in C; BWV 530, No. 6 in G *(rec Nov 1989)* NXIN ▲ 550653 [DDD] (5.97)

M. Sander (org)—BWV 525, No. 1 E♭ *(rec Wagner Organ at Nidaros Cathedral, Trondheim, Norway)* ("Pathos und Freude") † Chorales Org; Cons Org; Passacaglia & Fugue Org, BWV 582; Preludes & Fugues, BWV 531-552 FERM ▲ 20028 [DDD] (16.97)

L. R. Svendsen (rcr), P. van Duren (hpd/org)—BWV 527, No. 3 in d [trans for rcr & bc] ("Barockmusik für Zwei") † Sons Fl; Boismortier:Sons Fl, Op. 91; Buxtehude:Magnificat primi toni, BuxWV 204; Frescobaldi:Canzoni for 1-4 Instr; Montalbano:Sinfs; Noordt:Tabulature Book PLAL ▲ 99 [DDD] (18.97)

Tripla Concordia—BWV 525, No. 1 E♭; BWV 526, No. 2 in c; BWV 529, No. 5 in C [trans for rcr, hpd & bc] † Partita Lt, BWV 997 CNTS 2-▲ 9701 (36.97)

M. Verbruggen (rcr), M. Meyerson (hpd)—BWV 525, No. 1 E♭; BWV 527, No. 3 in d; BWV 529, No. 5 in C; BWV 530, No. 6 in G [trans Verbruggen] † Sons Fl HAM ▲ 907119 (18.97)

H. Walcha (org)—BWV 527, No. 3 in d *(rec Great org, St. Laurenskerk Alkmaar & Strassburg, Germany, 1956-70)* † Canonic Vars on "Von Himmel hoch", BWV 769; Fant Org, BWV 572; Org Music (misc colls); Passacaglia & Fugue Org, BWV 582; Preludes & Fugues, BWV 531-552; Schübler Chorale Preludes; Toccata & Fugue Org, BWV 538; Toccata & Fugue Org, BWV 565 DEUT 2-▲ 453064 [ADD] (17.97)

H. Walcha (org)—BWV 525, No. 1 E♭ *(rec St. Laurenskerk Org at St. Laurens Church, Al, Sept 1956, Sept 1962)* † Partite diverse sopra, BWV 768; Preludes & Fugues, BWV 531-552; Schübler Chorale Preludes; Toccata & Fugue Org, BWV 565 DEUT (The Originals) ▲ 457704 [ADD] (11.97)

Trio Sonata in g for Organ [probably spurious], BWV 584

K. Bowyer (org) *(rec Odense, Denmark, Mar 23-24, 1993)* ("The Works for Organ, Vol. 6") † Org Music (comp); Prelude & Fugue Org, BWV 566; Preludes & Fugues (22) Org, BWV 531-552; Toccata, Adagio & Fugue Org, BWV 564; Trio Sons Org NIMB ▲ 5423 [DDD] (16.97)

Trio Sonata in C for 2 Violins & Continuo, BWV 1037 [doubtful]

G. Kessler (gtr), D. Bender (E hn) *(rec Berklee College of Music, Boston, MA)* ("Trio Sonata - Encore!") † Sons & Partitas Vn; E. Granados:Danzas españolas (10) Pno; Goyescas:Intermezzo; E. Noda:Tanka Fl, Ob & Gtr; Telemann:Essercizii Musici; Fants (12) Fl, TWV40:2-13; T. Tomkins:Instrumental & Vocal Music; Vivaldi:Con Mands, RV.532; Wooldridge:Partita Ww, Op. 38 *(E text)* BOSK ▲ 114 [DDD] (15.97)

J. Schröder (vn), S. Ritchie (vn), A. Fuller (hpd) *(rec June 6-8, 1986)* † Cons Vn (comp); Vivaldi:Cons Vns; Sinf REF ▲ 23 [DDD] (16.97)

J. Williams (gtr), C. Bonell (gtr), K. Marjoram (b chl), B. Gascoigne (mar), M. Pert (vib) *(rec NY)* ("John Williams & Friends") † Cant 147; Cons Org; Suites Vc; Daquin:Pièces de clavecin (sels); W. A. Mozart:Adagio Glass Amc, K.356; Son 11 Pno, K.331; H. Purcell:Sons (12) of 3 Parts for 2 Vns, Z.790-801; Telemann:Bourree alla Polacca; Vivaldi:Con Mands, RV.532 SNYC ▲ 35108 [AAD] (16.97)

Trio Sonatas for Organ

L. Rogg (org) *(rec Silbermann Org, Arlesheim, Switzerland)* † Allabreve, BWV 589; Canonic Vars on "Von Himmel hoch", BWV 769; Canzona; Chorales Org; Clavier-Übung III; Fant & Fugue Org, BWV 537; Fant & Fugue, BWV 542; Fant Org, BWV 562; Fant Org, BWV 572; Orgelbüchlein; Partite diverse sopra, BWV 766; Partite diverse sopra, BWV 767; Partite diverse sopra, BWV 768; Pastorale Org, BWV 590; Prelude & Fugue Org, BWV 566; Preludes & Fugues, BWV 531-552; Schübler Chorale Preludes; Toccata & Fugue Org, BWV 565; Toccata, Adagio & Fugue Org, BWV 564; Trio Org, BWV 583 HAM 12-▲ 290772 [ADD] (71.97)

Trio in G for Viola da Gamba & Keyboard, BWV 1027a (ca 1717-23)

K. Bowyer (org) ("Works for Organ, Vol. 8") † Cons solo Hpd; Fant & Fugue Org, BWV 537; Fugue on a theme by Legrenzi, BWV 574; Org Music (comp); Preludes & Fugues, BWV 531-552; Toccata & Fugue Org, BWV 538; Trio Son Fls, BWV 1039 NIMB 2-▲ 5500 [DDD] (23.97)

Valet will ich dir geben (fantasia) for Organ, BWV 735 (ca 1723)

M. Murray (org) *(rec Kampen; Great Schnitger Org St. Michael's, Zwolle, Germany)* ("Bach at Zwolle") † Chorales Org; Org Music (misc colls); Preludes & Fugues, BWV 531-552 TEL ▲ 80385 [DDD] (16.97)

Verschiedene Canones (14) for Harpsichord, [based on Goldberg Variations], BWV 1087 (1742-46)

Palladian Ensemble *(rec Nov 14-17, 1994)* † Duets Hpd; Trio Sons Org LINN ▲ 5036 (16.97)

Von Himmel hoch, da komm ich her (fughetta) for Organ, BWV 701 (ca 1708)

B. Lagacé (org) † Chorale Preludes Org; Fants Hpd; Fugue on a theme by Legrenzi, BWV 574; Partite diverse sopra, BWV 767; Preludes & Fugues, BWV 531-552; Toccata, Adagio & Fugue Org, BWV 564 FL ▲ 23094 [DDD] (16.97)

Wie schön leuchtet der Morgenstern (chorale) for Organ, BWV 764

C. Herrick (org) *(rec Metzler Org, Pfarrkirche St. Michael, Kaisten, Switzerland)* ("Organ Cornucopia") † Fant Org, BWV 562; Fant Org, BWV 573; Herr Christ, der einig Gottes Sohn, BWV 698; Jesu meine Freude, BWV 753 HYP ▲ 67139 (18.97)

Wir glauben all an einen Gott, Vater for Organ, BWV 740

T. Koopman (org) † Chorales Org; Fant Org, BWV 562; Liebster Jesu, wir sind hier, BWV 730; Liebster Jesu, wir sind hier, BWV 731; Org Music (misc colls); Passacaglia & Fugue Org, BWV 582; Pastorale Org, BWV 590; Preludes & Fugues, BWV 531-552 NOVA ▲ 150052 [DDD] (16.97)

Das wohltemperierte Clavier [The Well-tempered Clavier] [2 books], BWV 846-893 (1722-42)

V. Afanassiev (pno) *(rec Musica Théâtre La Chaux-de-Fonds, Apr 10-14, 1995)* DNN 2-▲ 78834 [DDD] (33.97)

V. Afanassiev (pno) DNN 2-▲ 18008 (33.97)

E. Aldwell (pno) NON 2-▲ 79272 (33.97)

E. Aldwell (pno) NON 2-▲ 79200 (33.97)

S. Assad (gtr), O. Assad (gtr) NON ▲ 79292 (16.97)

H. Bauer (pno), H. Samuel (pno)—Book 1, No. 5 in D, BWV 850 † Cant 147; Chromatic Fant & Fugue, BWV 903; Fant & Fugue, BWV 542; French Suites; Inventions Hpd; Partitas Hpd; Toccata & Fugue Org, BWV 565; Toccatas Hpd NIMB (Grand Piano) ▲ 8808 [DDD] (11.97)

W. Baumgratz (org) [arr Reger] *(rec Sauer org, Bremen Cathedral, Germany, July 1997)* ("Works in Romantic Organ Arrangements") † Cant 106; Sons & Partitas Vn; Suite 3 Orch, BWV 1068; G. F. Handel:Cons (16) Org; Suites de Pièces (8) Hpd, HWV 426-33 MDG ▲ 3200761 [DDD] (17.97)

E. Cavallo (pno) *(rec Genoa, 1995-96)* DYNC 4-▲ 113 [DDD] (34.97)

F. Chaffiaud (pno)—Book 1, No. 22 in b♭, BWV 867; Book 1, No. 1 in C, BWV 846 † Chromatic Fant & Fugue, BWV 903; French Suites; Preludes & Fugues, BWV 531-552; Toccata, Adagio & Fugue Org, BWV 564 MED7 ▲ 141339 [DDD] (18.97)

D. Chorzempa (clvd/hpd/org) PHLP 4-▲ 446690 (71.97)

J. Cload (pno)—Book 1 MER 2-▲ 84384 (32.97)

A. Dudley (cnd) [arr Dudley] *(rec Great Britain & N Ireland)* ("Ancient & Modern") † A. Dudley: ANGL ▲ 56868 (16.97)

BACH, JOHANN SEBASTIAN (cont.)

Das wohltemperierte Clavier [The Well-tempered Clavier] [2 books], BWV 846-893 (1722-42) (cont.)

J. Dvořák (cnd), Capella Istropolitana—Book 1, No. 24 in b, BWV 869 [arr Stokowski] *(rec 1989)* † Cant 140; English Suites; Sons Vn Hpd; Suite 1 Orch, BWV 1066; Suite 2 Fl, BWV 1067 NXIN ▲ 550244 [DDD] (5.97)

S. Feinberg (pno) *(rec 1958-1961)* ("Russian Piano School") RD (Talents of Russia) 4-▲ 16231 [ADD] (63.97)

E. Fischer (pno)—Book 1, No. 4 in c♯, BWV 849; Book 1, No. 12 in f, BWV 857; Book 1, No. 14 in f♯, BWV 859; Book 1, No. 16 in g, BWV 861; Book 1, No. 20 in a, BWV 865; Book 1, No. 22 in b♭, BWV 867; Book 1, No. 23 in B, BWV 868; Book 1, No. 24 in b, BWV 869; Book 2, No. 4 in c♯, BWV 873; Book 2, No. 6 in d, BWV 875; Book 2, No. 9 in E, BWV 878; Book 2, No. 21 in B♭, BWV 890; Book 2, No. 22 in b♭, BWV 891 *(rec 1933-36)* † Chromatic Fant & Fugue, BWV 903; Con 1 Hpd, BWV 1052; Con 4 Hpd, BWV 1055; Con 5 Hpd, BWV 1056; Fant & Fugue Hpd, BWV 904; Busoni:Bach Trans Pno PPHI (Great Pianists of the 20th Century, Vol. 25) 2-▲ 456766 (m) (22.97)

E. Fischer (pno)—Book 1 *(rec 1931-41)* ("Edwin Fischer Plays Bach, Vol. 1") † Chromatic Fant & Fugue, BWV 903 PHS 2-▲ 16 (33.97)

E. Fischer (pno)—Book 2 *(rec 1933-37)* † Fant & Fugue Hpd, BWV 904; Preludes & Fugues, BWV 531-552 PHS 2-▲ 17 (33.97)

E. Fischer (pno) MPLY 3-▲ 2025 (25.97)

E. Freund (pno)—Book 1, No. 2 in c, BWV 847; Book 1, No. 8 in e♭ (d♯), BWV 853 † B. Bartók:Bagatelles Pno, Op. 6; Easy Pieces, Sz.39; For Children, Sz.42; Sketches, Op. 9b; J. Brahms:Fants Pno, Op. 116; Pieces (8) Pno, Op. 76; Kodály:Pieces (9) Pno, Op. 3; Liszt:Pno Music (misc); Mendelssohn (-Bartholdy):Fant "Sonate écossaise", Op. 28 PHS 2-▲ 9193 (33.97)

A. Fuller (hpd)—Book 2, No. 5 in D, BWV 874; Book 2, No. 12 in f, BWV 881 *(rec 1992)* ("Bach For Harpsichord") † Anna Magdalena Bach Notebook (sels); French Suites; Italian Con, BWV 971 REF ▲ 51 [DDD] (16.97)

M. Galling (hpd)—Book 1, No. 1 in C, BWV 846 ("25 Bach Favorites") † Brandenburg Con 1, BWV 1046; Brandenburg Con 2, BWV 1047; Brandenburg Con 3, BWV 1048; Brandenburg Con 4, BWV 1049; Brandenburg Con 5, BWV 1050; Cant 147; Con Hpds (4), BWV 1065; Con Vns; Con 1 for 2 Hpds, BWV 1060; Con 1 Vn; Mass in b, BWV 232; Music of Bach; Schübler Chorale Preludes; Sons & Partitas Vn; Suite 2 Fl, BWV 1067; Toccata & Fugue Org, BWV 565; Toccata, Adagio & Fugue Org, BWV 564 VCC ▲ 8817 (3.97)

V. Ghielmi (vl), L. Ghielmi (hpd/pno/pno)—Book 2, No. 24 in b, BWV 893; Book 1, No. 10 in e, BWV 855; Book 1, No. 4 in c♯, BWV 849 *(rec Oct 1997)* ("Sonatas for Viol & Obbligato Harpsichord") † Sons Vl ARSM ▲ 1228 [DDD] (17.97)

K. Gilbert (hpd) PARC 4-▲ 13439 [DDD] (64.97)

G. Gomiero (sop), M. Brunello (vc), Orch Villa-Lobos—Book 1, No. 8 in e♭ (d♯), BWV 853 [trans 12 vcs] † Suite 3 Orch, BWV 1068; Jobim:Gtr Music; H. Villa-Lobos:Bachiana brasileira 1; Bachiana brasileira 5 AURC ▲ 403 (5.97)

G. Gould (pno) *(rec 1962-65)* ("The Glenn Gould Edition") SNYC 2-▲ 52600 [ADD] (31.97)

G. Gould (pno) *(rec 1966-71)* ("The Glenn Gould Edition") SNYC 2-▲ 52603 [ADD] (31.97)

G. Gould (pno)—Book 2, No. 22 in b♭, BWV 891; Book 2, No. 7 in E♭, BWV 876; Book 2, No. 9 in E, BWV 878; Book 2, No. 14 in f♯, BWV 883 *(rec CBC Concert Hall, Canada, Oct 21, 1952 & Feb 28, 1954)* † Goldberg Vars, BWV 988 CBC (Perspective) ▲ 2007 [ADD] (16.97)

G. Gould (pno)—Book 2, No. 9 in E, BWV 878; Book 2, No. 14 in f♯, BWV 883 *(rec Feb 18, 1970)* SNYC ▲ 52590 [ADD] (16.97)

G. Gould (pno)—Book 2, No. 14 in f♯, BWV 883; Book 2, No. 9 in E, BWV 878 *(rec 1957)* † Goldberg Vars, BWV 988 SNYC (Glenn Gould Edition) ▲ 52594 [ADD] (16.97)

G. Gould (pno)—Book 1, No. 1 in C, BWV 846 *(rec New York City, NY, Sept 1962)* ("Glenn Gould at the Movies") † Art of the Fugue (sels); Brandenburg Con 4, BWV 1049; Con 3 Hpd, BWV 1054; Con 5 Hpd, BWV 1056; English Suites; Goldberg Vars, BWV 988; J. Brahms:Intermezzos (3) Pno, Op. 117; Pieces (6) Pno, Op. 118; A. Scriabin:Pieces (2) Pno, Op. 57; Sibelius:Sonatinas (3) Pno, Op. 67; R. Strauss:Pieces (5) Pno, Op. 3 SNYC ▲ 66531 [DDD] (17.97)

F. Gulda (pno)—Book 1 PPHI 2-▲ 46545 (17.97)

F. Gulda (pno)—Book 2 PPHI 2-▲ 46548 (17.97)

A. Hewitt (pno)—Book 1 HYP 2-▲ 67301 (36.97)

A. Hewitt (pno)—Book 2 HYP 2-▲ 67303 (36.97)

M. Horszowski (pno)—Book 1 *(rec 1979-80)* VC 2-▲ 8046 [ADD] (26.97)

M. Horszowski (pno), M. Horszowski (pno)—Book 1, No. 11 in F, BWV 856; Book 1, No. 12 in f, BWV 857 [Prelude only] *(rec Tuscany, Italy, 1984)* ("Horszowski Bach Recital") † English Suites; Partitas Hpd; Preludes & Fugues, BWV 531-552 ARBT ▲ 113 (m) [ADD] (16.97)

C. Jaccottet (hpd)—Book 1, No. 13 in F♯, BWV 858; Book 1, No. 14 in f♯, BWV 859; Book 1, No. 15 in G, BWV 860; Book 1, No. 16 in g, BWV 861; Book 1, No. 17 in A♭, BWV 862; Book 1, No. 18 in g♯, BWV 863; Book 1, No. 19 in A, BWV 864; Book 1, No. 20 in a, BWV 865; Book 1, No. 21 in B♭, 866; Book 1, No. 22 in b♭, BWV 867; Book 1, No. 23 in B, BWV 868 † Partitas Hpd PC ▲ 265027 [DDD] (2.97)

C. Jaccottet (hpd) PC ▲ 265020 [DDD] (2.97)

J. Jandó (pno) *(rec Budapest Sept. 14-17 & Oct. 13-16, 1999)* NXIN 2-▲ 550970 [DDD] (15.97)

W. Kempff (pno)—Book 1, No. 4 in c♯, BWV 849; Book 1, No. 9 in E, BWV 854; Book 1, No. 10 in e, BWV 855; Book 1, No. 11 in F, BWV 856; Book 1, No. 12 in f, BWV 857; Book 1, No. 13 in F♯, BWV 858; Book 1, No. 14 in f♯, BWV 859; Book 2, No. 3 in C♯, BWV 872; Book 2, No. 6 in d, BWV 875; Book 2, No. 7 in E♭, BWV 876; Book 2, No. 15 in G, BWV 884; Book 2, No. 24 in b, BWV 893 ("Wilhelm Kempff Plays Bach") † Capriccio Departure, BWV 992 DEUT (Double) 2-▲ 39672 (17.97)

I. Kipnis (clvd) *(rec May 11, 1965)* † Adagio Clvd, BWV 968; English Suites; Italian Con, BWV 971; Prelude Lt, BWV 999; Preludes Hpd (5); Preludes Kbd SNYC ▲ 53263 (7.97) ▮ 53263 (3.98)

I. Kipnis (hpd)—Book 1, No. 1 in C, BWV 846 ("The Brook & the Well-Spring") † Brandenburg Con 5, BWV 1050; Cant 147; Con 1 Vn; Goldberg Vars, BWV 988; Mass in b, BWV 232; Passacaglia & Fugue Org, BWV 582; Sons & Partitas Vn; St. John Passion (sels) SNYC (NPR-Milestone of the Millennium) ▲ 60990 [DDD] (11.97)

Y. Kondonassis (hp)—Book 1, No. 1 in C, BWV 846; Book 1, No. 17 in A♭, BWV 862 *(rec Cleveland, OH, June 1994)* ("A New Baroque") † Arioso Ob; Cant 147; Suite Lt, BWV 996; G. F. Handel:Suites de Pièces (8) Hpd, HWV 426-33; J. Pachelbel:Canon & Gigue; D. Scarlatti:Sons Kbd TEL ▲ 80403 [DDD] (16.97)

D. Korevaar (pno)—Book 1 MUSC 2-▲ 82198 [DDD] (21.97)

E. Koroliov (pno)—Book 1, No. 4 in c♯, BWV 849 [Tiel] ("Composers & Their Star Signs: Sagitarius") † Art of the Fugue (sels); French Suites; Italian Con, BWV 971; Sons & Partitas Vn; J. Haydn:Qts (3) Strs, H.III/69-71; Son 60 Kbd, H.XVI/50 TACE ▲ 24

B. Lagacé (org)—Book 1, No. 19 in A, BWV 864; Book 1, No. 13 in F♯, BWV 858; Book 1, No. 14 in f♯, BWV 859; Book 1, No. 15 in G, BWV 860; Book 1, No. 16 in g, BWV 861; Book 1, No. 17 in A♭, BWV 862; Book 1, No. 18 in g♯, BWV 863; Book 1, No. 20 in a, BWV 865; Book 1, No. 21 in B♭, 866; Book 1, No. 22 in b♭, BWV 867; Book 1, No. 23 in B, BWV 868; Book 1, No. 24 in b, BWV 869 ("Well-Tempered Clavier on the Organ I") FL ▲ 23014 [DDD] (16.97)

B. Lagacé (org)—Book 2, No. 8 in e♭ (d♯), BWV 877; Book 2, No. 1 in C, BWV 870; Book 2, No. 2 in c, BWV 871; Book 2, No. 3 in C♯, BWV 872; Book 2, No. 4 in c♯, BWV 873; Book 2, No. 5 in D, BWV 874; Book 2, No. 6 in d, BWV 875; Book 2, No. 7 in E♭, BWV 876; Book 2, No. 9 in E, BWV 878 ("Well-Tempered Clavier on the Organ I") FL ▲ 23015 [DDD] (16.97)

B. Lagacé (org)—Book 1, No. 9 in E, BWV 854; Book 1, No. 1 in C, BWV 846; Book 1, No. 2 in c, BWV 847; Book 1, No. 3 in C♯, BWV 848; Book 1, No. 4 in c♯, BWV 849; Book 1, No. 5 in D, BWV 850; Book 1, No. 6 in d, BWV 851; Book 1, No. 7 in E♭, BWV 852; Book 1, No. 8 in e♭ (d♯), BWV 853; Book 1, No. 12 in f, BWV 857; Book 1, No. 10 in e, BWV 855; Book 1, No. 11 in F, BWV 856 ("Well-Tempered Clavier on the Organ I") FL ▲ 23012 [DDD] (16.97)

B. Lagacé (org)—Book 2, No. 21 in B♭, BWV 890; Book 2, No. 18 in g♯, BWV 887; Book 2, No. 19 in A, BWV 888; Book 2, No. 20 in a BWV 889; Book 2, No. 22 in b♭, BWV 891; Book 2, No. 23 in B, BWV 892; Book 2, No. 24 in b, BWV 893 ("Well-Tempered Clavier on the Organ I") FL ▲ 23017 [DDD] (16.97)

B. Lagacé (org)—Book 2, No. 10 in e, BWV 879; Book 2, No. 11 in F, BWV 880; Book 2, No. 12 in f, BWV 881; Book 2, No. 13 in F♯, BWV 882; Book 2, No. 14 in f♯, BWV 883; Book 2, No. 15 in G, BWV 884; Book 2, No. 16 in g, BWV 885; Book 2, No. 17 in A♭, BWV 886 ("Well-Tempered Clavier on the Organ I") FL ▲ 23016 [DDD] (16.97)

W. Landowska (hpd) RCAV (Red Seal) 2-▲ 6217 [ADD] (30.97)

W. Landowska (hpd)—Book 1 ("Wanda Landowska Portrait") † Chromatic Fant & Fugue, BWV 903; F. Couperin:Pièces de clavecin (sels) ENT (Documents) ▲ 953 [ADD] (13.97)

W. Landowska (hpd) RCAV (Red Seal) 3-▲ 7825 (30.97)

G. Leonhardt (hpd) DEHA 2-▲ 77011 [ADD] (21.97)

T. Lisboa (vc), M. Braga (pno)—Book 1, No. 8 in e♭ (d♯), BWV 853; Book 2, No. 14 in f♯, BWV 883 ("O Violoncello do Villa, Vol. 2") † H. Villa-Lobos:Chôros bis; Son 2 Vc, Op. 66; Trio 1 Pno MER ▲ 84391 (16.97)

J. C. Martins (pno)—Book 1, No. 1 in C, BWV 846; Book 2, No. 1 in C, BWV 870 ("The Essential Bach:Selections from the Complete Edition") † Con 1 for 2 Hpds, BWV 1060; Con 1 Pno; Con 2 for 2 Hpds, BWV 1061; Duets Hpd; English Suites; Fant & Fugue Org, BWV 906; French Suites; Fughetta, BWV 961; Goldberg Vars, BWV 988; Inventions Hpd; Italian Con, BWV 971; Partitas Hpd; Toccatas Hpd ERTO ▲ 42054 [DDD] (13.97)

J. C. Martins (pno) ("Complete Keyboard Works, Vol. 2") ERTO 2-▲ 42019 (22.97)

J. C. Martins (pno), A. Moreira-Lima (pno) ("Bach & Chopin: The Preludes") † Chopin:Preludes (24) Pno, Op. 28 ERTO 2-▲ 42024 (22.97)

D. Moroney (hpd) HMA 4-▲ 1901285 (34.97)

BACH, JOHANN SEBASTIAN (cont.)

Das wohltemperirte Clavier [The Well-tempered Clavier] [2 books], BWV 846-893 (1722-42) (cont.)

H. Neuhaus (pno)—Book 1, No. 18 in g#, BWV 863; Book 1, No. 13 in F#, BWV 858; Book 1, No. 14 in f#, BWV 859; Book 1, No. 15 in G, BWV 860; Book 1, No. 16 in g, BWV 861; Book 1, No. 17 in A♭, BWV 862 *(rec 1951)* † Beethoven:Son 24 Pno, Op. 78; W. A. Mozart:Rondo Pno, K.511; Son Pnos, K.448 RD (Talents of Russia) ▲ 16244 [ADD] (16.97)

T. Nikolayeva (pno)—Book 1, No. 1 in C, BWV 846; Book 1, No. 2 in c, BWV 847; Book 1, No. 4 in c#, BWV 849; Book 1, No. 5 in D, BWV 850; Book 1, No. 6 in d, BWV 851; Book 1, No. 8 in e♭ (d#), BWV 853; Book 1, No. 10 in e, BWV 855; Book 1, No. 11 in F, BWV 856; Book 1, No. 12 in f, BWV 857 *(rec Budapest, Hungary, Mar 18, 1955)* ("Piano Recitals") † Partitas Hpd HUN ▲ 31686 (m) [AAD] (16.97)

J. Ogdon (pno)—Book 1, No. 4 in c#, BWV 849 ("John Ogden: Live in Recital") † Beethoven:Son 30 Pno, Op. 109; G. Lloyd:Road Through Samarkand ALTA ▲ 9072

F. Oubradous (cnd), Oiseau-Lyre Orchestral Ensemble *(rec 1937-1946)* ("Oubradous, Vol. 2") † Brandenburg Con 2, BWV 1047; Musical Offering, BWV 1079 LYS ▲ 412 (17.97)

L. Palmer (hpd)—Book 2, No. 12 in f, BWV 881 *(rec Plano, TX, June 30-July 2, 1994)* ("Harpsichord Music of J.S. Bach") † Italian Con, BWV 971; Kbd Music (misc); Partita Hpd, BWV 831 ENRE (Gold) ▲ 9405 [DDD] (16.97)

M. Pischner (hpd) BER 2-▲ 9291 (21.97)

A. Romero (gtr)—Book 1, No. 1 in C, BWV 846 *(rec Dec 10-15, 1990)* † Cant 147; Sons & Partitas Vn; Suites Vc TEL ▮ 30288 (8.98) ▲ 80288 (16.97)

S. Ross (hpd)—Book 1 *(rec Montreal, Canada, Apr 1980)* PELL 2-▲ 101 [AAD] (32.97)

S. Ross (hpd)—Book 2 *(rec Montreal, Canada, Apr 1980)* PELL 2-▲ 103 [AAD] (32.97)

W. Rübsam (pno)—Book 1, No. 2 in c, BWV 847; Book 1, No. 3 in C#, BWV 848; Book 1, No. 4 in c#, BWV 849; Book 1, No. 5 in D, BWV 850; Book 1, No. 6 in d, BWV 851; Book 1, No. 8 in e♭ (d#), BWV 853; Book 1, No. 9 in E, BWV 854; Book 1, No. 10 in e, BWV 855; Book 1, No. 11 in F, BWV 856; Book 1, No. 12 in f, BWV 857 *(rec Valparaiso, IN, Sept-Oct 1994)* † Clavier-Büchlein for W. F. Bach; Preludes Hpd (5); Preludes Kbd NXIN ▲ 553097 [DDD] (5.97)

F. Say (pno)—Book 1 † French Suites; Italian Con, BWV 971; Busoni:Bach Trans Pno; Liszt:Trans, Arrs & Paraphrases ELEC ▲ 26124 (16.97)

S. Schepkin (pno)—Book 1 ONGA ▲ 113 (24.97)

A. Schiff (pno) PLON 2-▲ 14388 [DDD] (32.97)

A. Schiff (pno) PLON 2-▲ 17236 [DDD] (32.97)

M. Suzuki (hpd) *(rec Japan, May 1996)* ("Complete Keyboard Works, Vol. 1") BIS 2-▲ 813 [DDD] (34.97)

Swingle Singers—Book 1, No. 18 in g#, BWV 863; Book 1, No. 8 in e♭ (d#), BWV 853 *(rec 1991)* ("Bach Hits Back/A Cappella Amadeus") † Anna Magdalena Bach Notebook (sels); Brandenburg Con 3, BWV 1048; Cant 140; Cant 208; In dulci jubilo, BWV 729; Inventions Hpd; Music of Bach; Sons & Partitas Vn; St. Matthew Passion (sels); Suite 2 Fl, BWV 1067; W. A. Mozart:Music of Mozart VCL 2-▲ 61472 [DDD] (11.97)

R. Tureck (pno)—Book 2, No. 11 in F, BWV 880; Book 1, No. 4 in c#, BWV 849; Book 1, No. 10 in e, BWV 855 *(rec live, Town Hall New York, United States of America, 1948)* ("The Young Visionary") † English Suites; Preludes Hpd VAIA ▲ 1085 (16.97)

R. Tureck (pno)—Book 1, No. 21 in B♭, 866 ("The Great Solo Works") † Adagio Clvd, BWV 968; Aria variata alla maniera italiana, BWV 989; Capriccio Departure, BWV 992; Chromatic Fant & Fugue, BWV 903 VAIA ▲ 1041 (17.97)

R. Tureck (pno)—Book 1, No. 21 in B♭, 866 ("A Tribute to the Keyboard Legend") † Anna Magdalena Bach Notebook; English Suites; Goldberg Vars, BWV 988; Italian Con, BWV 971; Partitas Hpd; Son Kbd; Liszt:Grandes études de Paganini, S.141; Mendelssohn (-Bartholdy):Midsummer Night's Dream (sels); F. Schubert:Moments musicaux, D.780 VAIA ▲ 1086 [AAD] (12.97)

R. Tureck (pno) *(rec Great Hall of the Philharmonic, July 5, 1995)* ("Rosalyn Tureck Live in St. Petersburg: All Bach Recital") † Adagio Clvd, BWV 968; Aria variata alla maniera italiana, BWV 989; Capriccio Departure, BWV 992; Chromatic Fant & Fugue, BWV 903; Partitas Hpd VAIA ▲ 1131 [DDD]

V. Viardo (pno)—Book 1, No. 1 in C, BWV 846 *(rec Fort Worth, TX, 1973)* ("The Fourth Cliburn Competition 1973") † Beethoven:Son 28 Pno, Op. 101; Son 32 Pno, Op. 111; Debussy:Estampes; Images (6) Pno; Pour le piano; S. Prokofiev:Visions fugitives, Op. 22; S. Rachmaninoff:Etudes-tableaux Pno; Webern:Vars Pno, Op. 27 VAIA (Retrospective Series, Vol. 7) ▲ 1175 (m) [ADD] (16.97)

G. Walker (pno)—Book 1, No. 5 in D, BWV 850 [Prelude only] † Chopin:Études (24) Pno, Opp. 10 & 25; F. Poulenc:Pièces Pno; R. Schumann:Kreisleriana, Op. 16 ALBA ▲ 252 [DDD] (16.97)

D. Yeadon (vc), P. Wispelwey (vc pic), R. Egarr (hpd)—Book 1, No. 1 in C, BWV 846 [trans Wispelwey in G] † Con 2 Hpd, BWV 1053; Con 5 Hpd, BWV 1056; Italian Con, BWV 971; Prelude Lt, BWV 999; Sons Vl; Suites Vc CCL ▲ 14198 (18.97)

artists unknown—Book 1, No. 1 in C, BWV 846; Book 2, No. 7 in E♭, BWV 876; Book 1, No. 9 in E, BWV 854; Book 1, No. 17 in A♭, BWV 862; Book 2, No. 19 in A, BWV 888; Book 2, No. 21 in B♭, BWV 890 ("Bach for Book Lovers") † Brandenburg Con 1, BWV 1046; Brandenburg Con 6, BWV 1051; Con 5 Hpd, BWV 1056; Italian Con, BWV 971; Music of Bach; Suite 1 Orch, BWV 1066; Suite 2 Fl, BWV 1067 PPHI (Set Your Life to Music) ▲ 456497 (9.97) ▮ 456497 (5.98)

artists unknown—Book 1, No. 1 in C, BWV 846 ("Favourite Bach") † Air on the G String; Anna Magdalena Bach Notebook (sels); Brandenburg Con 2, BWV 1047; Brandenburg Con 3, BWV 1048; Brandenburg Con 4, BWV 1049; Cant 140; Cant 147; Cant 208; Cant 212; Cant 51; Con 1 Hpd, BWV 1052; Con 2 Vn; St. Matthew Passion (sels); Suite 2 Fl, BWV 1067; Toccata & Fugue Org, BWV 565 CFP (Favourites) ▲ 4639 (12.97)

BACH, JOHANN(ES) [HANS] (1604-1673)

Motets

R. Marlow (cnd), Trinity College Choir Cambridge—Sei nun wieder zufrieden meine Seele; Unser Leben ist ein Schatten *(rec Trinity College Chapel, England, July 1995)* ("Bach Family Motets") † J. Ludwig Bach:Motets; J. M. Bach:Motets; J. Christoph Bach:Motets & Cants CONI ▲ 51306 [DDD] (16.97)

BACH, MARIA (1896-1978)

Silhouettes for Orchestra (1937)

M. Müssauer (cnd), Moravian PO *(rec Olomuc Philharmonic, Oct 1994)* ("Frauen Töne, Vol. 1") † Dickenson-Auner:Irish Sym, Op. 16; Müller-Hermann:Heroic Ov, Op. 21; Sym Fant, Op. 25 THOR ▲ 2259 [DDD] (17.97)

BACH, WILHELM FRIEDEMANN (1710-1784)

Cantatas (miscellaneous)

B. Schlick (sop), C. Schubert (cta), W. Jochens (ten), S. Schreckenberger (bass), H. Max (cnd), Das Kleine Konzert, Rhineland Kantorei—Lasset uns ablegen, F.80; Es ist eine Stimme eines Predigers, F.89 ("Kantaten, Volume 1") CAPO ▲ 10425 [DDD] (11.97)

B. Schlick (sop), C. Schubert (cta), W. Jochens (ten), S. Schreckenberger (bass), H. Max (cnd), Das Kleine Konzert, Rhineland Kantorei—Dies ist der Tag, F.85; Erzittert und fallet, F.83 ("Kantaten, Volume 2") CAPO ▲ 10426 [DDD] (11.97)

Chorale-Preludes (7) for Organ, F.38

F. Houbart (org)—Wir danken dir Herr Jesu Christ *(rec J.F. Dupont org, Lessay Abbey, France, Oct 1995)* ("The Bach Family & the Organ") † J. Christoph Bach:Chorales Org; J. M. Bach:Chorales Org; J. B. Bach:Chorales Org; C.P.E. Bach:Fant & Fugue Org, H.103; J. S. Bach:Fant Org, BWV 572; Orgelbüchlein; Preludes & Fugues, BWV 531-552; C.P.E. Bach:Sons (4) Org, H.84-87 SOC ▲ 128 (16.97)

Concertos for Harpsichord

R. Egarr (hpd), C. Medlam (cnd) —Con Kbd, F.41; Con Kbd, F.44; Con Kbd, F.45 HAM ▲ 901558 (18.97)

C. Nediger (hpd), J. Lamon (cnd), Tafelmusik † Sinf Orch, F.64 SNYC (Vivarte) ▲ 62720 (16.97)

Concerto in F for 2 Harpsichords, F.10 (ca 1773)

R. Egarr (hpd), P. Ayrton (hpd) *(rec Mar 1988)* ("Works for 2 Harpsichords") † J. S. Bach:Con 2 for 2 Hpds, BWV 1061a; J. L. Krebs:Con for 2 Hpds; Mattheson:Son for 2 Hpds; Suite for 2 Hpds GLOE ▲ 5179 [DDD] (16.97)

G. Galvez (hpd), R. Puyana (hpd) ("Puyana Plays Bach") † J. S. Bach:Cons solo Hpd; Partita Hpd, BWV 831; J. Christian Bach:Sons & Duets Kbd 4-Hands, T.343/3; J. S. Bach:Toccatas Hpd MRCR ▲ 434395 [ADD] (11.97)

G. Penson (hpd), F. Heyerick (hpd) ("Kammermusik") † Duets Fls, F.54-59; Duets Vas, F.60-62; Trio Sons Fls, F.47-49 RICE 2-▲ 89125 (34.97)

Concerto in E♭ for 2 Harpsichords, Op. 46

C. Hogwood (kbd), C. Rousset (kbd) † J. S. Bach:Art of the Fugue (sels); Con 2 for 2 Hpds, BWV 1061; J. Christian Bach:Duet Kbd; C.P.E. Bach:Kleine Duetten, H.610-13 PLOI ▲ 40649 (16.97)

Duets (6) in e, E♭, E♭, F, f & G for 2 Flutes, F.54-59 (1733-46)

P. Beuckels (trns fl), D. Etienne (trns fl) *(rec 1992)* ("Kammermusik") † Con 2 Hpds, F.10; Duets Vas, F.60-62; Trio Sons Fls, F.47-49 RICE 2-▲ 89125 (34.97)

W. Schulz (fl), H. Schellenberger (ob) *(rec June 28-30, 1993)* SNYC ▲ 58965 [DDD] (16.97)

Duets (3) for 2 Violas, F.60-62

R. Terakado (va), F. Fernandez (va) *(rec 1992)* ("Kammermusik") † Con 2 Hpds, F.10; Duets Fls, F.54-59; Trio Sons Fls, F.47-49 RICE 2-▲ 89125 (34.97)

BACH, WILHELM FRIEDEMANN (cont.)

Keyboard Music

C. Rousset (hpd)—Son Fls, F.48; Fant Hpd; Prelude Kbd, F.29; March Kbd, F.30; Suite Kbd, F.24; Fugues Hpd; Son in g HMA ▲ 1901305 (9.97)

Orchestral Music

H. Haenchen (cnd), C.P.E. Bach CO—Sinf Orch, F.67; Ertönet, ihr seligen Völker, F.88; Sinf Fls, F.65; Sinf Orch, F.64; Wo geht die Lebensreise hin, F.91 [Sinfonia]; O Wunder, wer kann dieses fassen, F.92 [Sinfonia]; Suite Kbd, F.24 BER ▲ 1098 [DDD] (16.97)

Organ Music

U. T. Wegele (org)—Fuge Hpd; Fuge Hpd; Chorale-Preludes Org, F.38 *(rec Basilika Weingarten, Germany, 1993)* † C.P.E. Bach:Org Music; G. A. Homilius:Org Music; J. C. Kittel:Org Music; J. L. Krebs:Org Music TACE ▲ 30

Overture in g for Orchestra [formerly attrib J.S. Bach], BWV 1070

B. Labadie (cnd) *(rec Church of Saint-Isidore, Quebec, Canada, Feb 1996)* ("Music of Bach's Sons") † Sinf Fls, F.65; J. C. F. Bach:Sinf; J. Christian Bach:Sinfs; C.P.E. Bach:Sinfs (3), H.654-56 DOR ▲ 90239 [DDD] (16.97)

Polonaises (12) for Keyboard, F.12-13 (ca 1765)

S. Barrell (clvd) GLOE ▲ 5035 [DDD] (16.97)

Sinfonia in d for 2 Flutes & Strings, F.65

E. Hashimoto (hpd), E. Hashimoto (cnd) *(rec Conservatory of Music, Univ. of Cincinnati, OH)* ("The Bach Boys") † J. C. F. Bach:Sinf; J. Christian Bach:Sinfs; C.P.E. Bach:Sinfs (4), H.663-66; Sinfs (6), H.657-62 KLAV ▲ 11054 [DDD] (18.97)

B. Labadie (cnd) *(rec Church of Saint-Isidore, Quebec, Canada, Feb 1996)* ("Music of Bach's Sons") † Ov; J. C. F. Bach:Sinf; J. Christian Bach:Sinfs; C.P.E. Bach:Sinfs (3), H.654-56 DOR ▲ 90239 [DDD] (16.97)

Sinfonia in D for Orchestra, F.64 (1746-64)

J. Lamon (cnd), Tafelmusik † Cons Hpd SNYC (Vivarte) ▲ 62720 (16.97)

E. Ormandy (cnd), Philadelphia Orch *(rec Mar 17, 1957)* † J. S. Bach:Brandenburg Con 5, BWV 1050; Cant 140; Passacaglia & Fugue Org, BWV 582; Toccata & Fugue Org, BWV 565; Toccata, Adagio & Fugue Org, BWV 564 SNYC (Masterworks Heritage) 2-▲ 62345 [ADD] (25.97)

Sonatas (6) for 2 Flutes

K. Hünteler (fl), M. Schmidt-Casdorff (fl) MDG ▲ 3110844 (17.97)

Sonatas for Harpsichord

C. Mattax (hpd)—Son Kbd, F.7; Son 2 Kbd, F.8; Son Kbd, F.3; Son Kbd, F.9; Son Kbd, F.5; Son 1 Kbd, F.2 *(rec New Brunswick, NJ, Mar 1996)* ("Sonatas for Harpsichord") CENT ▲ 2351 [DDD] (16.97)

Sonata in C for Harpsichord

J. Becker (pno) *(rec Sept 1991)* ("Sonate Facile") † C.P.E. Bach:Sonatas for Viol & Continuo; J. Christian Bach:Sons Kbd; G. A. Benda:Sonatina 1 Pno; Sonatina 2 Pno; Dušeck:Son in F; W. A. Mozart:Son 16 Pno, K.545 CAPO ▲ 10415 [DDD] (11.97)

Trio Sonatas (3) for 2 Flutes & Continuo, F.47-49 (1762)

P. Beuckels (trns fl), D. Etienne (trns fl), G. Penson (hpd) *(rec 1992)* ("Kammermusik") † Con 2 Hpds, F.10; Duets Fls, F.54-59; Duets Vas, F.60-62 RICE 2-▲ 89125 (34.97)

BÄCK, SVEN-ERIK (1919-1994)

Expansive Preludes for Piano (1950)

A. Torger (pno) ("Chamber Music") † Favola; Qnt Strs; Qt 2 Strs; Qt 4 Strs; Son Fl CAPA ▲ 21490 (16.97)

Favola for Clarinet & Percussion (1962)

T. Janson (cl), R. Johansson (perc), S. Arntorp (perc), B. Arsenius (perc), B. Liljequist (perc) ("Chamber Music") † Expansive Preludes; Qnt Strs; Qt 2 Strs; Qt 4 Strs; Son Fl CAPA ▲ 21490 (16.97)

Motets

artists unknown *(Jag är livets bröd; Bedjen, och Eder skall varda givet; Och Ordet vart kött; Icke kommer var och en in I himmelriket; Den stund kommer; Se, vi gå upp till Jerusalem; Han blev lydig intill döden; Jesus, tänk på mig; Transfiguration; Natten är framskriden; Dessa äro de som komma ur den stora bedr; Behold, I Am Making All Things New; Herr, zu wem sollen wir gehen?; Utrannsaka mig), (Vaken för den skull)* PHNS ▲ 10 [AAD] (16.97)

Piano Music

R. Pöntinen (pno)—Expansive Preludes; Impromptu; The Professor's Unfinished; Son alla ricercare; Son in 2 Movts & Epilogue Pno BIS ▲ 354 [DDD] (17.97)

Quartet No. 2 for Strings (1947)

Crafoord String Quartet ("Chamber Music") † Expansive Preludes; Favola; Qnt Strs; Qt 4 Strs; Son Fl CAPA ▲ 21490 (16.97)

Quartet No. 4 for Strings (1984)

Berwald String Quartet ("Chamber Music") † Expansive Preludes; Favola; Qnt Strs; Qt 2 Strs; Son Fl CAPA ▲ 21490 (16.97)

Quintet for Strings, "Exercitier" (1948)

Berwald String Quartet members ("Chamber Music") † Expansive Preludes; Favola; Qt 2 Strs; Qt 4 Strs; Son Fl CAPA ▲ 21490 (16.97)

Sonata for Flute (1949)

M. Wiesler (fl) ("Chamber Music") † Expansive Preludes; Favola; Qnt Strs; Qt 2 Strs; Qt 4 Strs CAPA ▲ 21490 (16.97)

BACKOFEN, JOHANN GEORG (1768-1830)

Concerto in A for 2 Clarinets & Orchestra, Op. 10

N. Bulfone (cl), D. Pacitti (cl), W. Themel (cnd), Udine CO *(rec Oct 14-15, 1995)* † F. Devienne:Sinf concertante Cls, Op. 25; C. Stamitz:Con Cls AG ▲ 39 [DDD] (18.97)

BACON, ERNST (1898-1990)

Piano Music

E. Corbato (pno)—The Lobo Girl; Nuka; Flop-Eared Mule; Maple-Sugaring; Yemassee River; Drip-Drop Rain; Habañera; Pigtown Fling ("Remembering Ansel Adams") † Remembering Ansel Adams; Son Vc; Tumbleweeds Vn CRI ▲ 779 [DDD] (16.97)

Remembering Ansel Adams for Clarinet & Orchestra (1985)

R. Stoltzman (cl), J. Swoboda (cnd), Warsaw PO *(rec Sept 1997)* ("Remembering Ansel Adams") † Pno Music; Son Vc; Tumbleweeds Vn CRI ▲ 779 [DDD] (16.97)

Sonata for Cello & Piano (1948)

B. Greenhouse (vc), M. Pressler (pno) *(rec United States of America, Dec 1964)* ("Remembering Ansel Adams") † Pno Music; Remembering Ansel Adams; Tumbleweeds Vn CRI ▲ 779 [DDD] (16.97)

Songs from Emily Dickinson

H. Boatwright (sop), J. Kirkpatrick (pno), E. Bacon (pno) *(rec 1954-64)* ("Songs of Charles Ives & Ernst Bacon") † C. Ives:Songs CRI ▲ 675 [ADD] (16.97)

Tumbleweeds for Violin & Piano (1979)

D. Bales (vn), A. Sly (pno) ("Remembering Ansel Adams") † Pno Music; Remembering Ansel Adams; Son Vc CRI ▲ 779 [DDD] (16.97)

BADALAMENTI, ANGELO (1937-

The City of Lost Children [La Cité des Enfants Perdus] (film score) (1995)

M. Faithfull (sgr) POIN ▲ 32047 (16.97)

BADINGS, HENK (1907-1987)

Chansons bretonnes (3) for Chorus & Piano (1946)

R. Shaw (cnd), Robert Shaw Festival Singers, N. Mackenzie (pno) *(rec Church of St. Pierre, Gramat, France, July 1994)* ("Appear & Inspire") † D. Argento:I Hate & I Love; B. Britten:Hymn to St. Cecilia, Op. 27; Debussy:Chansons de Charles d'Orléans; F. Poulenc:Soir de neige; M. Ravel:Chansons Chorus TEL ▲ 80408 [DDD] (16.97)

Concerto for Harp & Orchestra (1967)

E. Versney (hp), M. Soustrot (cnd), Het Brabants Chamber Orchestra *(rec Jun 4, 1998)* † H. Andriessen:Con Org; Flothuis:Con Fl; Orthel:Scherzo 2 CV ▲ 77 (18.97)

Concerto for 2 Violins & Orchestra (1954)

H. Krebbers (vn), T. Olof (vn), W. V. Otterloo (cnd), The Hague PO † Dresden:Dansflitsen; Flothuis:Symfonische muziek; Orthel:Sym 2 CV ▲ 26 (19.97)

BAGBY, BENJAMIN (20th cent)

Edda for Vocal Ensemble

Sequentia DEHA ▲ 77381 (16.97)

BAGUER, CARLOS (1768-1808)

Symphony No. 12 in E♭

M. Bamert (cnd), London Mozart Players ("Symphonies") † Sym 13; Sym 16; Sym 18 CHN (Contemporaries of Mozart) ▲ 9456 (16.97)

Symphony No. 13 in E♭

M. Bamert (cnd), London Mozart Players ("Symphonies") † Sym 12; Sym 16; Sym 18 CHN (Contemporaries of Mozart) ▲ 9456 (16.97)

▲ = CD ♦ = Enhanced CD △ = MD ▮ = Cassette Tape ▯ = DCC

BAGUER, CARLOS (cont.)

Symphony No. 16 in G

M. Bamert (cnd), London Mozart Players ("Symphonies") † Sym 12; Sym 13; Sym 18 CHN (Contemporaries of Mozart) ▲ 9456 (16.97)

Symphony No. 18 in B♭

M. Bamert (cnd), London Mozart Players ("Symphonies") † Sym 12; Sym 13; Sym 16 CHN (Contemporaries of Mozart) ▲ 9456 (16.97)

BAILEY, G. (dates unknown)

Diadem of Gold: Overture

P. Parkes (cnd), Black Dyke Mills Band [arr F. Wright] *(rec England)* ("Champions of Brass") † Bantock:Prometheus Unbound; Gregson:Connotations; Langford:Harmonious Vars on a Theme of Handel; W. Mathias:Vivat Regina Bra, Op. 75; Vivat Regina, Op. 75; Vaughan Williams:Vars Brass *([ENG] text)* CHN ▲ 4510 [ADD] (16.97)

BAILLOT, PIERRE (MARIE FRANÇOIS DE SALES) (1771-1842)

Air russe varié for solo Violin, Violin, Viola & Continuo, Op. 11 (1810)

Russian Baroque Ensemble *(rec Nov 1996)* ("Russian Baroque") † M. Berezovsky:Son Vn; Vars on a Russian Folksong; Starzer:Divert Str Qt; Steibelt:Vars on 2 Russian Folksongs; Titz:Qt Strs in G; Son Vn in f# ARNO 2-▲ 51626 [DDD] (9.97)

BAINES, WILLIAM (1899-1922)

Piano Music

E. Parkin (pno)—The Chimes; Paradise Gardens; 7 Preludes; Coloured Leaves; Silverpoints; Idyll [Nocturne]; Tides; The Naiad; Twilight Pieces; Pool-Lights; Etude in f# *(rec Dec 11-12, 1995)* PRIO ▲ 550 [DDD] (16.97)

BAINTON, EDGAR (1880-1956)

Miniature Suite for Piano Duet

A. Goldstone (pno), C. Clemmow (pno) *(rec 1996)* † Bury:Prelude & Fugue; E. Elgar:Serenade Strs, Op. 20; G. Holst:Planets, Op. 32; Sym in F, Op. 8 ALBA ▲ 198 [DDD]

BAIRD, TADEUSZ (1928-1981)

Psychodrama for Orchestra (1972)

W. Michniewski (cnd), Polish National RSO Katowice † Tomorrow OLY ▲ 326 [AAD] (16.97)

Tomorrow [Jutro] (opera) [lib J.S. Sito after Conrad] (1966)

K. Szostek-Radkowa (mez), J. Artysz (bar), E. Pawlak (bass), J. Ostrowski (nar), R. Czajkowski (cnd), Poznan Philharmonic SO [POL] † Psychodrama OLY ▲ 326 [AAD] (16.97)

BAIRSTOW, EDWARD CUTHBERT (1874-1946)

Sonata in E♭ for Organ

J. Scott (org) ("Great European Organs No. 34: John Scott Plays the Organ of St. Paul's Cathedral, London") † E. Elgar:Son Org, Op. 28; J. Harris:Son Org PRIO ▲ 401 [DDD]

BAITZ, RICK (1954-

Kaleidocycles for Synclavier (1985)

R. Baitz (synclavier) *(rec White River Junction, VT)* † M. Bresnick:Lady Neil's Dumpe; S. Lindroth:Syntax; N. B. Rolnick:What Is The Use?; R. Teitelbaum:Golem I CENT (CDCM Computer Music Series, Vol. 2) ▲ 2039 [DDD] (16.97)

BAKER, CLAUDE (1948-

Awaking the Winds for Chamber Ensemble (1993)

D. Dzubay (cnd) *(rec Indiana Univ Bloomington, Apr 1994)* ("New Music from Indiana University, Vol. 1") † Dzubay:Trio; D. W. Freund:Hard Cells; J. Haas:Sussurrando; E. O'Brien:Mysteries of the Horizon IUSM ▲ 5 (16.97)

Nightscenes (4) for Harp (1985/1990)

R. Inglefield (hp) † Omaggi e Fant Db; D. Liptak:Illusions; Songs Bar & Pno GAS ▲ 286 (16.97)

Omaggi e Fantasie for Double Bass & Piano (1984)

M. Cameron (db), D. Liptak (pno) † Nightscenes; D. Liptak:Illusions; Songs Bar & Pno GAS ▲ 286 (16.97)

Omaggi e Fantasie for Tuba & Piano (1980; rev 1987)

D. Randolph (tuba), R. Zimdars (pno) *(rec Georgia State Univ., Atlanta, GA, July & Aug 1991)* ("Contrasts in Contemporary Music") † T. R. George:Son Tuba; H. Stevens:Sonatina Tuba & Pno; J. Takács:Son Capricciosa, Op. 81 ACAD ▲ 20018 (16.97)

BAKER, DAVID (1931-

Concerto for Cello & Jazz Band

E. Laut (vc) ("Cellofire!") † Son solo Vc; Suite Vc & Jazz Trio LISC ▲ 21793 (16.97)

Faces of the Blues for Saxophone Ensemble

Empire Saxophone Quartet ("Classic Saxophone Vol 2") † G. Fauré:Pelléas et Mélisande, Op. 80; S. Galante:Saxounds 111; Kechley:In the Dragon's Garden; W. A. Mozart:Qt in F Ob & Strs, K.370/368b LISC ▲ 9193 (16.97)

Jazz Suite for Clarinet & Orchestra, "3 Ethnic Dances"

A. Balter (cl), A. Balter (cnd), Akron SO *(rec Cleveland, OH, Feb 22, 1993)* ("American Voices: The African-American Composers Project") † W. Banfield:Sym 6; W. Childs:Distant Land TEL ▲ 80409 [DDD] (16.97)

Kosbro for Orchestra (1973; rev 1975)

J. P. Williams (cnd), Bohuslav Martinů PO ("Symphonic Brotherhood: The Music of African-American Composers") † H. T. Burleigh:Young Warrior; Hailstork:Sym 1; G. P. Nash:In Memoriam: Sojourner Truth; J. P. Williams:Is It True?; Meditation from the Easter Celebration ALBA ▲ 104 [DDD] (16.97)

Music of David Baker

artists unknown ("Through the Prism of the Black Experience") † Qnt Jazz Vn; Through This Vale of Tears LISC ▲ 11792 (16.97)

Parallel Planes (3) for Saxophone & Orchestra

H. Smith (sax), E. London (cnd), Cleveland Chamber SO *(rec Drinko Recital Hall, Cleveland, OH)* ("The New American Scene II") † T. J. Anderson:Chamber Con; L. Jenkins:Wonder Lust; W. Logan:Roots, Branches, Shapes & Shades of Green; D. White:Crystal Gazing ALBA ▲ 303 [DDD] (16.97)

Quintet for Jazz Violin & String Quartet (1987)

Jr. (vn), Audubon String Quartet ("Through the Prism of the Black Experience") † Music of; Through This Vale of Tears LISC ▲ 11792 (16.97)

Roots II for Piano Trio

Samaris Piano Trio *(rec Evanston, IL, June 1995 & June 1997)* ("Café Music") † A. Copland:Vitebsk: Study on a Jewish Theme; L. Kirchner:Trio 1 Pno; P. Schoenfield:Café Music NPT ▲ 85642 (16.97)

Singers of Songs/Weavers of Dreams for Cello & 17 Percussion Instruments

J. Starker (vc), G. Gaber (perc) *(rec Indiana Univ Opera House Bloomington, 1980)* ("Starker Plays Baker") † Son Vc LARL ▲ 817 (14.97)

Sonata for Cello & Piano (1973)

J. Starker (vc), A. Planès (pno) *(rec Indiana Univ Opera House Bloomington, 1980)* ("Starker Plays Baker") † Singers of Songs/Weavers of Dreams LARL ▲ 817 (14.97)

Sonata for Clarinet & Piano

M. Eley (cl), L. Desa (pno) *(rec Burbank, CA, May 25, 1995)* ("Welcome Home") † H. T. Burleigh:Songs; T. R. George:Son Cl & Pno; O. Nelson:Son Cl & Pno; J. E. Price:Blues & Dance 1; A. Wilder:Son Cl & Pno ARA ▲ 6703 (16.97)

Sonata for solo Cello

E. Laut (vc) ("Cellofire!") † Con Vc & Jazz Band; Suite Vc & Jazz Trio LISC ▲ 21793 (16.97)

Suite for Cello & Jazz Trio

E. Laut (vc) ("Cellofire!") † Con Vc & Jazz Band; Son solo Vc LISC ▲ 21793 (16.97)

Through This Vale of Tears (song cycle) for Tenor, String Quartet & Piano (1986)

W. Brown (ten), T. Montgomery (pno), Audubon String Quartet ("Through the Prism of the Black Experience") † Music of; Qnt Jazz Vn LISC ▲ 11792 (16.97)

Videmus [ENG] † T. J. Anderson:Intermezzos Cl; D. Fox:Music of Fox; O. Wilson:Sometimes NWW ▲ 80423 (16.97)

BAKER, JEFFREY REID (1947-

Tin Pan Hands for Synthesizer

J. R. Baker (syn)—Andante & Stomp *(rec Huntington, NY, 1987)* ("The Fantastic World of George Gershwin") † G. Gershwin:American in Paris; Con Pno; Preludes Pno; Rhap in Blue JRB ▲ 9003 [DDD] (16.97)

BAKER, MICHAEL CONWAY (1937-

Concerto for Piano & Orchestra

R. Silverman (pno), K. Akiyama (cnd), CBC Vancouver Orch SMS (SM 5000) ▲ 5107 (16.97)

The Flight of Aphrodite for Violin & Chamber Orchestra, Op. 99

M. Davis (vn), T. Russell (cnd), Pro Musica CO *(rec Ohio State Univ. Weigel Hall, 1995)* ("Hope's Journey") † Summit Con, Op. 105; Through the Lions' Gate, Op. 83 SUMM ▲ 182 [DDD] (16.97)

Summit Concerto for Trumpet & Chamber Orchestra, Op. 105

D. Hickman (tpt) ("David Hickman Performs 3 Trumpet Concertos") † Planel:Con Tpt; A. Plog:Con Tpt SUMM ▲ 191 (16.97)

BAKER, MICHAEL CONWAY (cont.)

Summit Concerto for Trumpet & Chamber Orchestra, Op. 105 (cont.)

D. Hickman (tpt), T. Russell (cnd), Pro Musica CO *(rec Ohio State Univ. Weigel Hall, 1995)* ("Hope's Journey") † Flight of Aphrodite, Op. 99; Through the Lions' Gate, Op. 83 SUMM ▲ 182 [DDD] (16.97)

Through the Lions' Gate for Orchestra, Op. 83

B. R. Dunn (cnd), London Sinfonia *(rec London, 1993)* ("Hope's Journey") † Flight of Aphrodite, Op. 99; Summit Con, Op. 105 SUMM ▲ 182 [DDD] (16.97)

Washington Square (ballet)

G. Crum (cnd), London SO SUMM ▲ 165 [DDD] (16.97)

BAKSA, ROBERT (1938-

Earth Elegy for Trumpet & Piano

R. Lee (tpt), M. Vines (pno) *(rec Brooklyn College, Apr 1993 & May 1994)* † Son Tpt; A. Cohen:Song of Myself; Wings of Desire; P. Kirby:Son Tpt CPS ▲ 8620 [DDD] (16.97)

Quintet for Bassoon & Strings (1975-94)

B. Cramer (vn), G. Figueroa (vn), S. Shumway (va), L. Rath (vc), W. Scribner (bn) *(rec Bronx, NY, 1997)* ("For Winds") † Qnt Cl; Son Ob; Son Sax NPT ▲ 85624 [DDD] (16.97)

Quintet for Clarinet & Strings (1973)

B. Cramer (vn), G. Tarack (vn), S. Follari (va), L. Grinhauz (vc), P. Gallo (cl) *(rec Bronx, NY, 1997)* ("For Winds") † Qnt Bn; Son Ob; Son Sax NPT ▲ 85624 [DDD] (16.97)

Sonata for Oboe & Piano (1988)

M. Heller (ob), E. Wright (pno) *(rec Bronx, NY, 1997)* ("For Winds") † Qnt Bn; Qnt Cl; Son Sax NPT ▲ 85624 [DDD] (16.97)

Sonata for Alto Saxophone & Piano (1991)

P. D. Rivera (a sax), P. Zinger (pno) *(rec Bronx, NY, 1997)* ("For Winds") † Qnt Bn; Qnt Cl; Son Ob NPT ▲ 85624 [DDD] (16.97)

Sonata for Trumpet & Piano

R. Lee (tpt), M. Vines (pno) *(rec Brooklyn College, Apr 1993 & May 1994)* † Earth Elegy; A. Cohen:Song of Myself; Wings of Desire; P. Kirby:Son Tpt CPS ▲ 8620 [DDD] (16.97)

BALADA, LEONARDO (1933-

Concerto for Piano & Orchestra (1965)

H. Franklin (pno), R. Strange (cnd) † Son Ww; Torquemada; Transparencies of Chopin's 1st Ballade NWW ▲ 80442 (16.97)

Escenas borrascosas [Thunderous Scenes] (4) for solo Voices, Orchestra & Chorus (1992)

J. P. Izquierdo (cnd), Carnegie Mellon PO, R. Page (cnd), Carnegie Mellon Repertory Chorus, K. Shackleton-Williams (sop—Isabel), N. M. Balach (mez—Beatriz), M. Walley (ten—Colón) *(rec Carnegie Music Hall, Pittsburgh, PA, Apr 7-8, 1994)* † Guernica; Maria Sabina NWW ▲ 80498 (16.97)

Guernica for Orchestra (1966)

J. Mester (cnd), Louisville Orch *(rec Carnegie Music Hall, Pittsburgh, PA)* † Escenas borrascosas; Maria Sabina NWW ▲ 80498 (16.97)

Lament from the Cradle of the Earth for Oboe & Orchestra (1993)

C. K. DeAlmeida (ob), L. Maazel (cnd), Pittsburgh SO *(rec Pittsburgh, PN, May 1996)* † B. Lees:Con Hn; E. T. Zwilich:Con Bn NWW ▲ 80503 [DDD] (16.97)

Maria Sabina (symphonic tragedy in 3 parts) for Narrators, Orchestra & Chorus [text Camilo José Cela] (1969)

J. Mester (cnd), Louisville Orch, R. Spalding (cnd), Univ of Louisville Choir, H. Cortés (nar—Executioner), A. Dunham (nar—Maria Sabina), B. Hardy (nar—Town Crier), G. Helguera (nar—Constable) *(rec Carnegie Music Hall, Pittsburgh, PA, Feb 5, 1973)* † Escenas borrascosas; Guernica NWW ▲ 80498 (16.97)

Sonata for 10 Winds (1980)

American Brass Quintet, Dorian Wind Quintet † Con Pno; Torquemada; Transparencies of Chopin's 1st Ballade NWW ▲ 80442 (16.97)

Steel Symphony for Orchestra (1973)

L. Maazel (cnd), Pittsburgh SO † W. Schuman:Sym 7 NWW ▲ 348 [DDD] (16.97)

Torquemada (cantata) for Chorus (1980)

R. Page (cnd), Carnegie Mellon Concert Choir † Con Pno; Son Ww; Transparencies of Chopin's 1st Ballade NWW ▲ 80442 (16.97)

Transparencies of Chopin's First Ballade for Piano

A. Di Bonaventura (pno) † Con Pno; Son Ww; Torquemada NWW ▲ 80442 (16.97)

BALAKIREV, MILY (1837-1910)

Au jardin in D♭ for Piano (1884)

M. Fingerhut (pno) *(rec Snape, England, July 15/16, 1985)* ("Russian Piano Music") † Polka; Toccata in c#; Borodin:Petite Suite Pno; Scherzo Pno; Cui:Preludes Pno, Op. 64; Mussorgsky:Au village; Kinderscherz; Larme; Souvenir d'enfance; Rimsky-Korsakov:Little Song Pno; Pieces, Op. 11/2; Pieces, Op. 11/3 *([ENG] text)* CHN ▲ 8439 [DDD] (16.97)

Berceuse in D♭ for Piano (1901)

R. Schrade (pno) *(rec Worthington, MA, July 27-28, 1994)* † Islamey; Pno Music; Son in b♭ for Pno CENT ▲ 2236 [DDD] (16.97)

Concerto No. 1 in f# for Piano & Orchestra (1855-56)

M. Binns (pno), D. Lloyd-Jones (cnd), English Northern Philharmonia † Con 2 Pno; Rimsky-Korsakov:Con Pno, Op. 30 HYP ▲ 66640 (18.97)

H. Shelley (pno), V. Sinaisky (cnd), BBC PO † Sym 2; Tamara CHN ▲ 9727 (16.97)

Concerto No. 2 in E♭ for Piano & Orchestra (1861-62)

M. Binns (pno), D. Lloyd-Jones (cnd), English Northern Philharmonia † Con 1 Pno; Rimsky-Korsakov:Con Pno, Op. 30 HYP ▲ 66640 (18.97)

M. Ponti (pno), S. Landau (cnd), Westphalia SO *(rec 1975)* ("The Romantic Piano Concerto, Vol. 5") † H. Goetz:Con 2 Pno, Op. 18; Liapunov:Rhap on Ukranian Themes, Op. 28; Medtner:Con 3 Pno, Op. 60; Sinding:Con Pno VB2 2-▲ 5068 [ADD] (9.97)

Impromptu in E for Violin & Piano

I. Politkovsky (vn), I. Kollegorskaya (pno) *(rec 1957)* ("Igor Politkovsky: Russian Violin School") † A. Dvořák:Zigeunermelodien, Op. 55; S. Rachmaninoff:Romance Vn & Pno, Op. 6/1; A. Rubinstein:Son 1 Vn, Op. 13; S. Taneyev:Son Vn; P. Tchaikovsky:Souvenir d'un lieu cher, Op. 42 RD (Talents of Russia) ▲ 16279 [ADD] (16.97)

Islamey (oriental fantasy) for Piano (1869; rev 1902)

C. Arrau (pno) *(rec 1928)* ("Claudio Arrau") † I. Albéniz:Iberia Suite; J. S. Bach:Chromatic Fant & Fugue, BWV 903; J. Brahms:Con 1 Pno, Op. 15; Vars on a Theme by Paganini, Op. 35; Liszt:Pno Music (misc) PPHI (Great Pianists of the 20th Century) ▲ 456706 (22.97)

S. Barere (pno) ("Simon Barere: Famous Recordings from 1934-1946") † J. S. Bach:Chromatic Fant & Fugue, BWV 903; Liszt:Etudes de concert (3), S.144; Rhap espagnole, S.254; Réminiscences de Don Juan Pno, S.418; R. Schumann:Toccata Pno, Op. 7 ENPL (Piano Library) ▲ 232 (13.97)

S. Barere (pno) *(rec Oct 15, 1935)* † F. Blumenfeld:Etude for the left hand, Op. 36; Chopin:Mazurkas Pno; Waltzes Pno; Glazunov:Etude Pno; Liszt:Pno Music (misc); R. Schumann:Toccata Pno, Op. 7 PHS ▲ 12 [ADD] (17.97)

A. Brendel (pno) *(rec 1955)* † Mussorgsky:Pictures at an Exhibition; I. Stravinsky:Pétrouchka (pno reduction) VOXC ▲ 97203

Y. Bronfman (pno) *(rec Troy, NY, May 21-22, 1998)* † P. Tchaikovsky:Saisons SNYC ▲ 60689 [DDD] (16.97)

A. Gavrilov (pno) † S. Rachmaninoff:Etudes-tableaux Pno; Morceaux de fant, Op. 3; Pno Music (misc colls); Preludes Pno; P. Tchaikovsky:Morceaux (6) Pno, Op. 19 RYLC ▲ 6471

J. Katchen (pno) *(rec 1958)* ("Julius Katchen") † J. Brahms:Son 3 Pno, Op. 5; Vars on an Original Theme, Op. 21/1; Chopin:Ballade 3 Pno, Op. 47; Fantaisie Pno, Op. 49; C. Franck:Prélude, choral et fugue, M.21; Liszt:Hungarian Rhaps, S.244; Mendelssohn (-Bartholdy):Prelude & Fugue Pno; Rondo capriccioso, Op. 14; N. Rorem:Son 2 Pno PPHI (Great Pianists of the 20th Century) ▲ 456856 (22.97)

M. Lewin (pno) *(rec June 1991)* ("Russian Piano Recital") † Paraphrase Pno; Toccata in c#; Glazunov:Theme & Vars, Op. 72; A. Scriabin:Pno Music (misc colls); Son 2 Pno, Op. 19 CENT ▲ 2134 [DDD] (16.97)

V. Leyetchkiss (pno) *(rec Chicago Public Library, IL, July 1991)* † Polka; Borodin:Petite Suite Pno; M. Glinka:Farewell to St Petersburg; Griboyedov:Waltz in e; Waltz in A♭; Kalinnikov:Elegy; Nocturne; Rebikov:Christmas Tree (sels); Mazurka; A. Scriabin:Mazurkas (9) Pno, Op. 25; Pieces (2) Pno, Op. 57 CENT ▲ 2398 (live) [DDD] (16.97)

J. Ogdon (pno) † Liszt:Pno Music (misc); Trans, Arrs & Paraphrases; S. Rachmaninoff:Études-tableaux Pno; Prelude in c#, Op. 3/2; Preludes Pno PPHI (Great Pianists of the 20th Century, Vol. 73) ▲ 456916 (22.97)

E. Ormandy (cnd), Philadelphia Orch [orchd] ("Russian Orchestral Works") † Glière:Red Poppy (suite), Op. 70; Ippolitov-Ivanov:Caucasian Sketches, Op. 10; Kabalevsky:Comedians, Op. 26; A. Khachaturian:Gayane (suites); Masquerade (ballet suite); Mussorgsky:Sorochintsy Fair (orch sels); Rimsky-Korsakov:Orchestral Music SNYC (Essential Classics) ▲ 62647 (7.97) ▮ 62647 (3.98)

R. Schrade (pno) *(rec Worthington, MA, July 27-28, 1994)* † Berceuse; Pno Music; Son in b♭ for Pno CENT ▲ 2236 [DDD] (16.97)

BEETHOVEN, LUDWIG VAN (cont.)

Sonata No. 29 in B♭ for Piano, Op. 106, "Hammerklavier" (1817-18) (cont.)

W. Gieseking (pno) *(rec 1949)* † Son 16 Pno, Op. 31/1; Son 24 Pno, Op. 78; Son 25 Pno, Op. 79; Son 26 Pno, Op. 81a; Son 27 Pno, Op. 90; Son 28 Pno, Op. 101; Son 32 Pno, Op. 111; J. S. Bach:English Suites (6) Hpd, BWV 806-811; French Suites (6) Hpd, BWV 812-817; Inventions Hpd; R. Schumann:Romances Pno, Op. 28; Symphonic Etudes, Op. 13; Waldscenen, Op. 82 MUA 4-▲ 4743 [AAD] (30.97)

R. Goode (pno) † Son 28 Pno, Op. 101; Son 30 Pno, Op. 109; Son 31 Pno, Op. 110; Son 32 Pno, Op. 111; Sons 28-32 Pno NON 2-▲ 79211 [DDD] (33.97)

G. Gould (pno) † Son 24 Pno, Op. 78 SNYC ▲ 52645 (16.97)

F. Guy (pno) † Son 28 Pno, Op. 101 HAM (Les Nouveaux Interprètes) ▲ 911639 (12.97)

I. Hobson (pno) *(rec Rice Univ, Houston, TX, Sept 22-23, 1996)* ("Complete Piano Sonatas, Vol. 8") † Son 28 Pno, Op. 101 ZEPY ▲ 10897 [DDD] (16.97)

M. Horszowski (pno) † Son 28 Pno, Op. 101 RELE ▲ 911021 [ADD] (18.97)

A. Kuerti (pno) *(rec live, 1989)* † Son 14 Pno, Op. 27/2 FL ▲ 23007 [DDD] (16.97)

L. Lortie (pno) ("The Piano Sonatas") † Son 28 Pno, Op. 101 CHN ▲ 9435 (16.97)

J. O'Conor (pno) *(rec Aug 12-13, 1992)* † Son 27 Pno, Op. 90; Son 28 Pno, Op. 101 TEL ▲ 80335 [DDD] (16.97)

D. Rachmanov (pno) † Son 11 Pno, Op. 22 OMCL ▲ 1001 (17.97)

A. Rangell (pno) ("The Late Piano Sonatas, Vol. 1") † Son 28 Pno, Op. 101 DOR ▲ 90143 [DDD] (16.97)

S. Richter (pno) *(rec live London)* STRV ▲ 33313 [ADD] (16.97)

S. Richter (pno) *(rec June 2, 1975)* † Son 27 Pno, Op. 90; Son 28 Pno, Op. 101 PRAG ▲ 254022 [ADD] (18.97)

R. Serkin (pno) † Fant Pno, Op. 77; Son 8 Pno, Op. 13 SNYC (Essential Classics) ▲ 47666 (7.97) ▮ 47666 (3.98)

J. Swann (pno) *(rec Dec 10-14, 1993)* † Son 27 Pno, Op. 90; Son 28 Pno, Op. 101 AKAD ▲ 140 [DDD] (17.97)

E. Wild (pno) † Son 14 Pno, Op. 27/2; Son 8 Pno, Op. 13 CHSK ▲ 120 (16.97)

Sonata No. 30 in E for Piano, Op. 109 (1820)

M. Chung (pno) ("Sonatas & Bagatelles, Vol. 2") † Bagatelles; Son 23 Pno, Op. 57 CCL ▲ 10897 (18.97)

A. Ciccolini (pno) † Son 28 Pno, Op. 101; Son 29 Pno, Op. 106; Son 31 Pno, Op. 110; Son 32 Pno, Op. 111 NUO 2-▲ 6797 (32.97)

A. Ciccolini (pno) *(rec Montebelluna Italy, June 16-17, 1955)* † Son 17 Pno, Op. 31/2; Son 5 Pno, Op. 10/1 BONG ▲ 5582 [DDD] (16.97)

J. Coop (pno) † Son 32 Pno, Op. 111; Vars & Fugue Pno, Op. 35 SKYL ▲ 8802 [AAD] (15.97)

A. Cortot (pno) [Duo-Art pno roll] † Chabrier:Pièces pittoresques; Chopin:Impromptu in G♭, Op. 51; Liszt:Années de pèlerinage 1, S.160; Hungarian Rhaps, S.244; Saint-Saëns:Étude Pno, Op. 52/6 NIMB (Grand Piano) ▲ 8814 [DDD] (11.97)

A. Cortot (pno) [& Pestimo] *(rec Royce Hall, University of California, Los Angeles, CA)* † Son 29 Pno, Op. 106; J. S. Bach:Con 5 Hpd, BWV 1056; Chabrier:Feuillet d'album; Pièces pittoresques; Chopin:Études Pno; Impromptu in G♭, Op. 51; Nocturnes Pno; Preludes (24) Pno, Op. 28; Liszt:Au Bord d'une Source; Trans, Arrs & Paraphrases; A. Scriabin:Etudes (12) Pno, Op. 8 KLAV ▲ 11096 [ADD] (18.97)

E. Fischer (pno) *(rec 1948-54)* ("Edwin Fischer Plays Beethoven") † Son 14 Pno, Op. 27/2; Son 15 Pno, Op. 28; Son 21 Pno, Op. 53; Son 32 Pno, Op. 111 MUA 2-▲ 880 [ADD] (32.97)

J. Golan (pno) ("Time Tracks") † Cardew:Pno Album; A. Curran:For Cornelius Cardew; E. Granados:Goyescas (sels); Nancarrow:Canons for Ursula ALBA ▲ 211 [DDD] (16.97)

R. Goode (pno) † Son 28 Pno, Op. 101; Son 29 Pno, Op. 106; Son 31 Pno, Op. 110; Son 32 Pno, Op. 111; Sons 28-32 Pno NON 2-▲ 79211 [DDD] (33.97)

G. Gould (pno) *(rec NY, NY, 1956)* ("The Glen Gould Legacy Vol. 2") † Con 1 Pno, Op. 15; Con 2 Pno, Op. 19; Son 31 Pno, Op. 110; Son 32 Pno, Op. 111; J. Haydn:Sonatas for Piano SNYC 3-▲ 39036 (m) [ADD] (47.97)

I. Hobson (pno) *(rec Rice Univ, Houston, TX, Sept 6-7, 1996)* ("Complete Piano Sonatas, Vol. 9") † Son 31 Pno, Op. 110; Son 32 Pno, Op. 111 ZEPY ▲ 10997 [DDD] (16.97)

M. Horszowski (pno) *(rec 1949)* † Son 31 Pno, Op. 110; Son 32 Pno, Op. 111 RELE ▲ 911022 [ADD] (18.97)

B. Hungerford (pno) *(rec 1967)* † Son 31 Pno, Op. 110; Son 32 Pno, Op. 111 EC (Everyman) ▲ 5001 [ADD]

A. Klein (pno) † Son 28 Pno, Op. 101; A. Berg:Son Pno, Op. 1 FINE ▲ 9824 (16.97)

S. B. Kovacevich (pno) *(rec 1978)* ("Stephen Kovacevich") † Son 17 Pno, Op. 31/2; Son 18 Pno, Op. 31/3; Son 28 Pno, Op. 101; Son 31 Pno, Op. 110; Son 32 Pno, Op. 111; Son 8 Pno, Op. 13 PPHI (Great Pianists of the 20th Century) ▲ 456877 (22.97)

J. Lill (pno) † Son 31 Pno, Op. 110; Son 32 Pno, Op. 111 ASVQ ▲ 6064 [ADD] (11.97)

Y. Nagai (pno) † Son 14 Pno, Op. 27/2; Son 27 Pno, Op. 90 BIS ▲ 281 [DDD] (17.97)

H. Neuhaus (pno) *(rec 1950)* ("Russian Piano School: Heinrich Neuhaus") † Son 14 Pno, Op. 27/2; Son 17 Pno, Op. 31/2; Son 31 Pno, Op. 110 RD ▲ 16245 [ADD] (16.97)

J. Ogdon (pno) ("John Ogden: Live in Recital") † J. S. Bach:Wohltemperirte Clavier; G. Lloyd:Road Through Samarkand ALTA ▲ 9072

G. Ohlsson (pno) † Son 2 Pno, Op. 2/2; Son 23 Pno, Op. 57 ARA ▲ 6638 [DDD] (16.97)

M. Pollini (pno) † Son 31 Pno, Op. 110; Son 32 Pno, Op. 111 DEUT ▲ 29570 [AAD] (16.97)

A. Rangell (pno) *(rec Mar 1991)* † Son 31 Pno, Op. 110; Son 32 Pno, Op. 111 DOR ▲ 90158 [DDD] (16.97)

S. Richter (pno) *(rec Kieler Schloss Germany, Oct 27, 1992)* † Son 31 Pno, Op. 110; W. A. Mozart:Fant Pno, K.475; Son 14 Pno, K.457 LV ▲ 422 [DDD] (17.97)

S. Richter (pno) *(rec Ohrid Macedonia, July 30, 1971)* ("Sviatoslav Richter Archives Vol. 1") † Son 28 Pno, Op. 101; Son 31 Pno, Op. 110; Son 32 Pno, Op. 111 DHR (Legendary Treasures) ▲ 7718 (16.97)

S. Richter (pno) † Son 31 Pno, Op. 110; Son 32 Pno, Op. 111; J. Brahms:Intermezzos (3) Pno, Op. 117; Pieces (6) Pno, Op. 118 MUA ▲ 1025 [AAD] (16.97)

B. Roberts (pno) *(rec Nimbus Records Wyastone Leys, June 17, 1988)* ("Beethoven: The Last 3 Sonatas") † Son 31 Pno, Op. 110; Son 32 Pno, Op. 111 NIMB ▲ 7709 [DDD] (11.97)

S. Savage (pno) *(rec ABC Ultimo, Jan & July 1995)* † Son 31 Pno, Op. 110; Son 32 Pno, Op. 111 TALP ▲ 76 [DDD] (18.97)

R. Serkin (pno) *(rec June 8, 1976)* ("The Unreleased Studio Recordings") † Son 1 Pno, Op. 2/1; Son 12 Pno, Op. 26; Son 13 Pno, Op. 27/1; Son 16 Pno, Op. 31/1; Son 21 Pno, Op. 53; Son 31 Pno, Op. 110; Son 32 Pno, Op. 111; Son 6 Pno, Op. 10/2 SNYC 3-▲ 64490 [ADD] (33.97)

R. Sherman (pno) *(rec 1993-94)* ("Piano Sonatas, Vol. 1") † Son 1 Pno, Op. 2/1; Son 16 Pno, Op. 31/1; Son 21 Pno, Op. 53; Son 32 Pno, Op. 111; Son 9 Pno, Op. 14/1 GMR 2-▲ 2050 [DDD] (32.97)

R. Silverman (pno) † Son 31 Pno, Op. 110; Son 32 Pno, Op. 111 MARQ ▲ 1901 [DDD]

Sonata No. 31 in A♭ for Piano, Op. 110 (1821-22)

A. Ciccolini (pno) † Son 28 Pno, Op. 101; Son 29 Pno, Op. 106; Son 30 Pno, Op. 109; Son 32 Pno, Op. 111 NUO 2-▲ 6797 (32.97)

A. Ciccolini (pno) † Son 18 Pno, Op. 31/3; Son 7 Pno, Op. 10/3 BONG ▲ 5584 [DDD] (16.97)

E. Del Pueyo (pno) ("Most Beautiful Piano Sonatas") † Son 14 Pno, Op. 27/2; Son 22 Pno, Op. 54; Son 23 Pno, Op. 57; Son 29 Pno, Op. 106; Son 8 Pno, Op. 13 PAVA 2-▲ 7071 (19.97)

E. Fischer (pno) *(rec 1931-38)* † Son 23 Pno, Op. 57; Son 8 Pno, Op. 13 ENPL (Piano Library) ▲ 241 (13.97)

R. Goode (pno) † Son 28 Pno, Op. 101; Son 29 Pno, Op. 106; Son 30 Pno, Op. 109; Son 32 Pno, Op. 111; Sons 28-32 Pno NON 2-▲ 79211 [DDD] (33.97)

G. Gould (pno) *(rec NY, NY, 1956)* ("The Glen Gould Legacy Vol. 2") † Con 1 Pno, Op. 15; Con 2 Pno, Op. 19; Son 30 Pno, Op. 109; Son 32 Pno, Op. 111; J. Haydn:Sonatas for Piano SNYC 3-▲ 39036 (m) [ADD] (47.97)

G. Gould (pno) † Con 2 Pno, Op. 19; A. Berg:Son Pno, Op. 1; J. Haydn:Son 59 Kbd, H.XVI/49; W. A. Mozart:Con 24 Pno, K.491 BIS 2-▲ 323 (34.97)

I. Hobson (pno) *(rec Rice Univ, Houston, TX, Sept 6-7, 1996)* ("Complete Piano Sonatas, Vol. 9") † Son 30 Pno, Op. 109; Son 32 Pno, Op. 111 ZEPY ▲ 10997 [DDD] (16.97)

M. Horszowski (pno) *(rec Jan 29, 1958)* † Son 30 Pno, Op. 109; Son 32 Pno, Op. 111 RELE ▲ 911022 [ADD] (18.97)

B. Hungerford (pno) *(rec 1969)* † Son 30 Pno, Op. 109; Son 32 Pno, Op. 111 EC (Everyman) ▲ 5001 [ADD]

E. Istomin (pno) *(rec White Plains, NY, June 11 & 18, 1991)* † Son 14 Pno, Op. 27/2; Son 21 Pno, Op. 53 REF ▲ 69 [DDD] (16.97)

S. B. Kovacevich (pno) *(rec 1973)* ("Stephen Kovacevich") † Son 17 Pno, Op. 31/2; Son 18 Pno, Op. 31/3; Son 28 Pno, Op. 101; Son 30 Pno, Op. 109; Son 32 Pno, Op. 111; Son 8 Pno, Op. 13 PPHI (Great Pianists of the 20th Century) ▲ 456877 (22.97)

F. Lamond (pno) *(rec 1927-30)* ("Lamond Plays Beethoven, Vol. 2") † Son 17 Pno, Op. 31/2; Son 21 Pno, Op. 53; Son 23 Pno, Op. 57 BPS ▲ 43 [ADD] (16.97)

J. Lill (pno) † Son 30 Pno, Op. 109; Son 32 Pno, Op. 111 ASVQ ▲ 6064 [ADD] (11.97)

H. Neuhaus (pno) *(rec 1947)* ("Russian Piano School: Heinrich Neuhaus") † Son 14 Pno, Op. 27/2; Son 17 Pno, Op. 31/2; Son 30 Pno, Op. 109 RD ▲ 16245 [ADD] (16.97)

M. Pollini (pno) † Son 30 Pno, Op. 109; Son 32 Pno, Op. 111 DEUT ▲ 29570 [AAD] (16.97)

A. Rangell (pno) *(rec Mar 1991)* † Son 30 Pno, Op. 109; Son 32 Pno, Op. 111 DOR ▲ 90158 [DDD] (16.97)

S. Richter (pno) *(rec Kieler Schloss Germany, Oct 27, 1992)* † Son 30 Pno, Op. 109; W. A. Mozart:Fant Pno, K.475; Son 14 Pno, K.457 LV ▲ 422 [DDD] (17.97)

S. Richter (pno) *(rec June 2, 1965)* † Vars Pno on a Waltz by Diabelli, Op. 120 PRAG ▲ 254023 [ADD] (18.97)

BEETHOVEN, LUDWIG VAN (cont.)

Sonata No. 31 in A♭ for Piano, Op. 110 (1821-22) (cont.)

S. Richter (pno) *(rec Tokyo, June 1, 1974)* ("Sviatoslav Richter Archives Vol. 1") † Son 28 Pno, Op. 101; Son 30 Pno, Op. 109; Son 32 Pno, Op. 111 DHR (Legendary Treasures) ▲ 7718 (16.97)

S. Richter (pno) *(rec Munich, May 16, 1992)* ("Richter out of Later Years, Vol. 3: In memoriam Marlene Dietrich") † Chopin:Polonaises-fant, Op. 61; Debussy:Isle joyeuse; J. Haydn:Andante with Vars Pno, H.XVII/6; M. Ravel:Vallée des cloches; A. Scriabin:Mazurkas (2) Pno, Op. 40; Poème-nocturne Pno, Op. 61 LV ▲ 481 (17.97)

S. Richter (pno) † Son 30 Pno, Op. 109; Son 32 Pno, Op. 111; J. Brahms:Intermezzos (3) Pno, Op. 117; Pieces (6) Pno, Op. 118 MUA ▲ 1025 [AAD] (16.97)

B. Roberts (pno) *(rec Nimbus Records Wyastone Leys, Sept 10, 1985)* ("Beethoven: The Last 3 Sonatas") † Son 30 Pno, Op. 109; Son 32 Pno, Op. 111 NIMB ▲ 7709 [DDD] (11.97)

M. Salman (pno) *(rec Holy Trinity Church, NYC, NY, Feb 1993)* ("The Transcendental Piano") † Alkan:Etudes in minor keys, Op. 39; Liszt:Mephisto Waltz 2 Orch, S.111; Sarabande & Chaconne, S.181 TIT ▲ 220

S. Savage (pno) *(rec ABC Ultimo, Jan & July 1995)* † Son 30 Pno, Op. 109; Son 32 Pno, Op. 111 TALP ▲ 76 [DDD] (18.97)

R. Serkin (pno) *(rec Aug 26, 1960)* ("The Unreleased Studio Recordings") † Son 1 Pno, Op. 2/1; Son 12 Pno, Op. 26; Son 13 Pno, Op. 27/1; Son 16 Pno, Op. 31/1; Son 21 Pno, Op. 53; Son 30 Pno, Op. 109; Son 32 Pno, Op. 111; Son 6 Pno, Op. 10/2 SNYC 3-▲ 64490 [ADD] (33.97)

R. Silverman (pno) † Son 30 Pno, Op. 109; Son 32 Pno, Op. 111 MARQ ▲ 1901 [DDD]

D. Tomšič (pno) † Son 23 Pno, Op. 57; Son 26 Pno, Op. 81a KOCH ▲ 7066 [DDD] (10.97)

Sonata No. 32 in c for Piano, Op. 111 (1821-22)

W. Backhaus (pno) *(rec 1954)* ("Wilhelm Backhaus") † Son 17 Pno, Op. 31/2; Son 25 Pno, Op. 79; Son 26 Pno, Op. 81a; Son 8 Pno, Op. 13; J. Brahms:Con 2 Pno, Op. 83; Pieces (4) Pno, Op. 119; Chopin:Etudes Pno; Liszt:Trans, Arrs & Paraphrases; F. Schubert:Impromptus (4); R. Schumann:Fantasiestücke Pno, Op. 12 PPHI (Great Pianists of the 20th Century) ▲ 456718 (22.97)

A. Ciccolini (pno) † Son 28 Pno, Op. 101; Son 29 Pno, Op. 106; Son 30 Pno, Op. 109; Son 31 Pno, Op. 110 NUO 2-▲ 6797 (32.97)

A. Ciccolini (pno) *(rec May 7-8, 1995)* † Son 10 Pno, Op. 14/2; Son 20 Pno, Op. 49/2; Son 9 Pno, Op. 14/1 BONG ▲ 5581 [DDD] (16.97)

J. Coop (pno) † Son 30 Pno, Op. 109; Vars & Fugue Pno, Op. 35 SKYL ▲ 8802 [AAD] (15.97)

A. Fischer (pno) *(rec Hungaroton Studios, 1977-78)* ("Complete Piano Sonatas, Vol. 3") † Son 10 Pno, Op. 14/2; Son 20 Pno, Op. 49/2; Son 7 Pno, Op. 10/3 HUN ▲ 31628 [AAD] (16.97)

E. Fischer (pno) *(rec 1948-54)* ("Edwin Fischer Plays Beethoven") † Son 14 Pno, Op. 27/2; Son 15 Pno, Op. 28; Son 21 Pno, Op. 53; Son 30 Pno, Op. 109 MUA 2-▲ 880 [ADD] (32.97)

W. Gieseking (pno) ("Gieseking, Vol. 2") † Son 28 Pno, Op. 101 HPC1 ▲ 129 (17.97)

W. Gieseking (pno) *(rec 1949)* † Son 16 Pno, Op. 31/1; Son 24 Pno, Op. 78; Son 25 Pno, Op. 79; Son 26 Pno, Op. 81a; Son 27 Pno, Op. 90; Son 28 Pno, Op. 101; Son 29 Pno, Op. 106; J. S. Bach:English Suites (6) Hpd, BWV 806-811; French Suites (6) Hpd, BWV 812-817; Inventions Hpd; R. Schumann:Romances Pno, Op. 28; Symphonic Etudes, Op. 13; Waldscenen, Op. 82 MUA 4-▲ 4743 [AAD] (30.97)

R. Goode (pno) † Son 28 Pno, Op. 101; Son 29 Pno, Op. 106; Son 30 Pno, Op. 109; Son 31 Pno, Op. 110; Sons 28-32 Pno NON 2-▲ 79211 [DDD] (33.97)

G. Gould (pno) *(rec NY, NY, 1956)* ("The Glen Gould Legacy Vol. 2") † Con 1 Pno, Op. 15; Con 2 Pno, Op. 19; Son 30 Pno, Op. 109; Son 31 Pno, Op. 110; J. Haydn:Sonatas for Piano SNYC 3-▲ 39036 (m) [ADD] (47.97)

F. Gulda (pno) † Son 14 Pno, Op. 27/2; Son 15 Pno, Op. 28; Son 17 Pno, Op. 31/2; Son 21 Pno, Op. 53; Son 22 Pno, Op. 54; Son 23 Pno, Op. 57; Son 24 Pno, Op. 78 PLON (Double Decker) 2-▲ 43012 (17.97)

I. Hobson (pno) *(rec Rice Univ, Houston, TX, Sept 6-7, 1996)* ("Complete Piano Sonatas, Vol. 9") † Son 30 Pno, Op. 109; Son 31 Pno, Op. 110 ZEPY ▲ 10997 [DDD] (16.97)

R. Hodgkinson (pno) *(rec Boston, MA)* ("Pétrouchka & Other Prophecies") † Chopin:Scherzos Pno; R. Schumann:Waldscenen, Op. 82; I. Stravinsky:Scenes (3) Pno ONGA ▲ 24111 [DDD] (16.97)

M. Horszowski (pno) *(rec 1949)* † Son 30 Pno, Op. 109; Son 31 Pno, Op. 110 RELE ▲ 911022 [ADD] (18.97)

M. Houstoun (pno)—Maestoso-Allegro con brio ed appassionato *(rec Fort Worth, TX, 1973)* ("The Fourth Cliburn Competition 1973") † Son 28 Pno, Op. 101; J. S. Bach:Wohltemperirte Clavier; Debussy:Estampes; Images (6) Pno; Pour le piano; S. Prokofiev:Visions fugitives, Op. 22; S. Rachmaninoff:Études-tableaux Pno; Webern:Vars Pno, Op. 27 VAIA (Retrospective Series, Vol. 7) ▲ 1175 (m) [ADD] (16.97)

B. Hungerford (pno) *(rec 1967)* † Son 30 Pno, Op. 109; Son 31 Pno, Op. 110 EC (Everyman) ▲ 5001 [ADD]

Y. Kim (pno) *(rec Skywalker Sound Marin County, CA)* † Bagatelle Pno in a, WoO 59; Rondos Pno, Op. 51; Son 17 Pno, Op. 31/2 WETE ▲ 5186 (16.97)

I. Klánský (pno) † Son 14 Pno, Op. 27/2; Son 23 Pno, Op. 57; Son 27 Pno, Op. 90 KPT ▲ 32025 [DDD]

S. B. Kovacevich (pno) *(rec 1973)* ("Stephen Kovacevich") † Son 17 Pno, Op. 31/2; Son 18 Pno, Op. 31/3; Son 28 Pno, Op. 101; Son 30 Pno, Op. 109; Son 31 Pno, Op. 110; Son 8 Pno, Op. 13 PPHI (Great Pianists of the 20th Century) ▲ 456877 (22.97)

J. Lill (pno) † Son 30 Pno, Op. 109; Son 31 Pno, Op. 110 ASVQ ▲ 6064 [ADD] (11.97)

E. Ney (pno) *(rec 1936-38)* ("Elly Ney Plays Beethoven") † Andante Pno, WoO 57; Son 4 Pno, Op. 7; Son 8 Pno, Op. 13; Vars Pno on Paisiello's Nel cor piu non me sento, WoO 70 BPS ▲ 33 [ADD] (16.97)

G. Novaes (pno) ("The Art of Guiomar Novaes, Vol. 1") † Son 14 Pno, Op. 27/2; Son 26 Pno, Op. 81a VC ▲ 8072 (13.97)

M. Pollini (pno) † Son 30 Pno, Op. 109; Son 31 Pno, Op. 110 DEUT ▲ 29570 [AAD] (16.97)

A. Rangell (pno) *(rec Mar 1991)* † Son 30 Pno, Op. 109; Son 31 Pno, Op. 110 DOR ▲ 90158 [DDD] (16.97)

S. Richter (pno) *(rec Tokyo, June 1, 1974)* ("Sviatoslav Richter Archives Vol. 1") † Son 28 Pno, Op. 101; Son 30 Pno, Op. 109; Son 31 Pno, Op. 110 DHR (Legendary Treasures) ▲ 7718 (16.97)

S. Richter (pno) † Son 30 Pno, Op. 109; Son 31 Pno, Op. 110; J. Brahms:Intermezzos (3) Pno, Op. 117; Pieces (6) Pno, Op. 118 MUA ▲ 1025 [AAD] (16.97)

B. Roberts (pno) *(rec Nimbus Records Wyastone Leys, Nov 21, 1985)* ("Beethoven: The Last 3 Sonatas") † Son 30 Pno, Op. 109; Son 31 Pno, Op. 110 NIMB ▲ 7709 [DDD] (11.97)

C. Rosenberger (pno) † Son 23 Pno, Op. 57 DLS ▲ 3009 [DDD] (14.97)

S. Savage (pno) *(rec ABC Ultimo, Jan & July 1995)* † Son 30 Pno, Op. 109; Son 31 Pno, Op. 110 TALP ▲ 76 [DDD] (18.97)

R. Serkin (pno) *(rec Mar 15-16, 1967)* ("The Unreleased Studio Recordings") † Son 1 Pno, Op. 2/1; Son 12 Pno, Op. 26; Son 13 Pno, Op. 27/1; Son 16 Pno, Op. 31/1; Son 21 Pno, Op. 53; Son 30 Pno, Op. 109; Son 31 Pno, Op. 110; Son 6 Pno, Op. 10/2 SNYC 3-▲ 64490 [ADD] (33.97)

R. Sherman (pno) *(rec 1993-94)* ("Piano Sonatas, Vol. 1") † Son 1 Pno, Op. 2/1; Son 16 Pno, Op. 31/1; Son 21 Pno, Op. 53; Son 30 Pno, Op. 109; Son 9 Pno, Op. 14/1 GMR 2-▲ 2050 [DDD] (32.97)

A. Shtarkman (pno) ("Busoni Competition 1995 Winner's Recital") † J. Brahms:Vars on a Theme by Paganini, Op. 35; I. Stravinsky:Scenes (3) Pno DVX ▲ 25219 (11.97)

R. Silverman (pno) † Son 30 Pno, Op. 109; Son 31 Pno, Op. 110 MARQ ▲ 1901 [DDD]

J. Stancul (pno) † Con 5 Pno, Op. 73 DI ▲ 920160 [DDD] (5.97)

J. Stancul (pno) *(rec 1993)* † Cons Pno (comp) DI 3-▲ 94334 [DDD] (17.97)

T. Szász (pno) † Son 21 Pno, Op. 53 BAIN ▲ 6275 [DDD] (16.97)

Sonatas (3) in E♭, f & d for Piano, WoO 47, "Electoral Sonatas" (?1783)

Em. Gilels (pno) ("Sonatas, Vol. 1") † Son 10 Pno, Op. 14/2; Sonatas for Piano (complete); Vars & Fugue Pno, Op. 35 DGRM ▲ 453221 (94.97)

J. Jandó (pno) *(rec Jan 31-Feb 17, 1989)* ("Piano Sonatas, Vol. 10") † Rondos Pno, Op. 51; Son Pno in C, WoO 51; Son 15 Pno, Op. 28; Sonatinas Pno, Anh.5 NXIN ▲ 550255 [DDD] (5.97)

Sonata in D for Piano 4-Hands, Op. 6 (1796-97)

C. Argelli (pno), P. Dirani (pno) ("The Complete Works for Piano 4-Hands") † Grosse Fuge Pnos, Op. 134; Marches Pno 4-Hands, Op. 45; Vars Pno 4-Hands on a Theme by Waldstein, WoO 67; Vars Pno 4-Hands on Ich denke dein, WoO 74 FON ▲ 9326 (13.97)

L. Lortie (pno), H. Mercier (pno) † Son 10 Pno, Op. 14/2; Son 4 Pno, Op. 7; Son 9 Pno, Op. 14/1 CHN ▲ 9347 [DDD] (16.97)

Sonatas (10) for Violin & Piano (complete)

J. Heifetz (vn), E. Bay (pno), B. Smith (pno) *(rec 1947-60)* ("The Heifetz Collection, Vol. 16") RCAV (Gold Seal) 3-▲ 61747 [ADD] (31.97)

G. Kremer (vn), M. Argerich (pno) DGRM 3-▲ 447058 [DDD]

A.-S. Mutter (vn), L. Orkis (pno) DEUT 4-▲ 457619 (64.97)

I. Perlman (vn), V. Ashkenazy (pno) PLON (Jubilee) 4-▲ 21453 [ADD] (38.97)

A. Rosand (vn), E. Flissler (pno) *(rec 1961)* ("Aaron Rosand Plays Beethoven: The Complete Violin Sonatas") VB3 (Legends) 3-▲ 3503 [ADD] (14.97)

I. Stern (vn), E. Istomin (pno) ("Isaac Stern: A Life In Music: Vol. 24") SNYC 3-▲ 64524 [ADD] (32.97)

J. Szigeti (vn), C. Arrau (pno) VC 4-▲ 8060 [ADD] (51.97)

J. Szigeti (vn), C. Arrau (pno) *(rec 1944)* GRM2 3-▲ 78876 (39.97)

BEETHOVEN, LUDWIG VAN (cont.)

Sonata No. 1 in D for Violin & Piano, Op. 12/1 (1797-98)

V. Gluzman (vn), A. Yoffe (pno) *(rec Astoria, NY, Mar 27-28, 1995)* † J. Brahms:Son 3 Vn, Op. 108; P. Hindemith:Son Vn in E KOCH ▲ 7323 [DDD] (16.97)

G. Kremer (vn), M. Argerich (pno) † Son 2 Vn; Son 3 Vn DEUT ▲ 15138 [DDD] (16.97)

T. Nishizaki (vn), J. Jandó (pno) *(rec Feb 18-21 & Sept 2, 1992)* † Son 2 Vn; Son 3 Vn NXIN ▲ 550284 [DDD] (5.97)

R. Terakado (vn), B. Vodenitcharov (pno) † Son 3 Vn; Son 5 Vn, Op. 24 DNN ▲ 18084 (16.97)

Sonata No. 2 in A for Violin & Piano, Op. 12/2 (1797-98)

S. Goldberg (vn), L. Kraus (pno) *(rec 1936-38)* ("Lili Kraus, Vol. 3") † Son 10 Vn, Op: 96; Son 5 Vn, Op. 24; Son 6 Vn; Son 9 Vn, Op. 47 LYS1 2-▲ 444 (34.97)

O. Kagan (vn), S. Richter (pno) *(rec Large Room Conservatory Moscow, Russia, Oct 27 & Nov 6, 1975)* ("Oleg Kagan Edition, Vol. IX") † Son 4 Vn, Op. 23; Son 5 Vn, Op. 24 LV ▲ 145 [ADD] (17.97)

G. Kremer (vn), M. Argerich (pno) † Son 1 Vn; Son 3 Vn DEUT ▲ 15138 [DDD] (16.97)

T. Nishizaki (vn), J. Jandó (pno) *(rec Feb 18-21 & Sept 2, 1992)* † Son 1 Vn; Son 3 Vn NXIN ▲ 550284 [DDD] (5.97)

W. Riessmann (vn), D. Goldmann (pno) † Son 3 Vn; Son 6 Vn PC ▲ 267014 [DDD] (2.97)

Sonata No. 3 in E♭ for Violin & Piano, Op. 12/3 (1797-98)

A. Busch (vn), R. Serkin (pno) *(rec 1930 for HMV)* † J. S. Bach:Sons & Partitas Vn; J. Brahms:Son 2 Vn, Op. 100 PHS ▲ 9942 [AAD] (17.97)

A. Busch (vn), R. Serkin (pno) † Son 23 Pno, Op. 57; R. Schumann:Son 1 Vn, Op. 105 ENPL (The Piano Library) ▲ 189 (13.97)

A. Busch (vn), R. Serkin (pno) *(rec May 5, 1931)* ("The European Busch-Serkin Duo Recordings, Vol. 1") † Son 5 Vn, Op. 24; Son 7 Vn APR ▲ 5541 [ADD] (19.97)

A. Busch (vn), R. Serkin (pno) † Son 5 Vn, Op. 24; Son 9 Vn, Op. 47 PHS ▲ 19 (17.97)

G. Kremer (vn), M. Argerich (pno) † Son 1 Vn; Son 2 Vn DEUT ▲ 15138 [DDD] (16.97)

T. Nishizaki (vn), J. Jandó (pno) *(rec Feb 18-21 & Sept 2, 1992)* † Son 1 Vn; Son 2 Vn NXIN ▲ 550284 [DDD] (5.97)

D. Oistrakh (vn), L. Oborin (pno) † Son 9 Vn, Op. 47 TES ▲ 1115

W. Riessmann (vn), D. Goldmann (pno) † Son 2 Vn; Son 6 Vn PC ▲ 267014 [DDD] (2.97)

W. Schneiderhan (vn), C. Seeman (pno) *(rec June 1964)* † F. Schubert:Son Vn, D.574 ORFE ▲ 473971 (16.97)

R. Terakado (vn), B. Vodenitcharov (pno) † Son 1 Vn; Son 5 Vn, Op. 24 DNN ▲ 18084 (16.97)

Sonata No. 4 in A for Violin & Piano, Op. 23 (1800)

O. Kagan (vn), S. Richter (pno) *(rec Large Room Conservatory Moscow, Russia, Oct 27 & Nov 6, 1975)* ("Oleg Kagan Edition, Vol. IX") † Son 2 Vn; Son 5 Vn, Op. 24 LV ▲ 145 [ADD] (17.97)

G. Kremer (vn), M. Argerich (pno) † Son 5 Vn, Op. 24 DEUT ▲ 19787 [DDD] (16.97)

T. Nishizaki (vn), J. Jandó (pno) *(rec Feb & Sept 1992)* † Son 10 Vn, Op. 96; Vars Vn on Mozart's Se vuol ballare, WoO 40 NXIN ▲ 550285 [DDD] (5.97)

W. Riessmann (vn), D. Goldmann (pno) † Son 7 Vn; Son 8 Vn PC ▲ 267013 [DDD] (2.97)

Sonata No. 5 in F for Violin & Piano, Op. 24, "Spring" (1800-01)

K. Adam (vn), D. Adam (pno) *(rec Vienna, Apr 10-11, 1992)* † Son 9 Vn, Op. 47 CAMA ▲ 266 [DDD] (18.97)

A. Busch (vn), R. Serkin (pno) *(rec May 17, 1933)* ("The European Busch-Serkin Duo Recordings, Vol. 1") † Son 3 Vn; Son 7 Vn APR ▲ 5541 [ADD] (19.97)

A. Busch (vn), R. Serkin (pno) † Son 7 Vn; J. Brahms:Son 1 Vn, Op. 78 MTAL ▲ 48022 (6.97)

A. Busch (vn), R. Serkin (pno) † Son 3 Vn; Son 9 Vn, Op. 47 PHS ▲ 19 (17.97)

A. Busch (vn), R. Serkin (pno) † Son 7 Vn; J. S. Bach:Son Vn Bc, BWV 1021; J. Brahms:Son 1 Vn, Op. 78; Son 2 Vn, Op. 100; R. Schumann:Son 1 Vn, Op. 105 GRM2 ▲ 78820 (26.97)

Z. Francescatti (vn), Casadesus (pno) † Son 10 Vn, Op. 96; Son 9 Vn, Op. 47 SNYC (Essential Classics) ▲ 46342 [ADD] (7.97) ▮ 46342 [ADD] (3.98)

M. Frasca-Colombier (vn), M. Langot (pno) † Son 9 Vn, Op. 47 PVY ▲ 730079 (11.97)

S. Goldberg (vn), L. Kraus (pno) *(rec London, England, 1938-40)* † Son 10 Vn, Op. 96; Son 9 Vn, Op. 47; W. A. Mozart:Duo Vn, K.423; Duo Vn, K.424; Sonatas for Violin & Piano (miscellaneous) MUA 3-▲ 4665 (30.97)

S. Goldberg (vn), L. Kraus (pno) *(rec 1936-38)* ("Lili Kraus, Vol. 3") † Son 10 Vn, Op. 96; Son 2 Vn; Son 6 Vn; Son 9 Vn, Op. 47 LYS1 2-▲ 444 (34.97)

R. Holmes (vn), R. Burnett (pno) † Son 7 Vn AMON ▲ 9 (16.97)

O. Kagan (vn), S. Richter (pno) *(rec Large Room Conservatory Moscow, Russia, Oct 27 & Nov 6, 1975)* ("Oleg Kagan Edition, Vol. IX") † Son 2 Vn; Son 4 Vn, Op. 23 LV ▲ 145 [ADD] (17.97)

F. Kreisler (vn), F. Rupp (pno) *(rec 1936)* † Son 10 Vn, Op. 96; Son 9 Vn, Op. 47 ENT (Strings) ▲ 99340 (16.97)

G. Kremer (vn), M. Argerich (pno) † Son 4 Vn, Op. 23 DEUT ▲ 19787 [DDD] (16.97)

G. Kremer (vn), M. Argerich (pno)—Adagio molto espressivo ("The Complete Beethoven Edition Compactotheque") † Chor auf die verbundeten Fürsten, WoO 95; Glorreiche Augenblick, Op. 136; Leonore (sels); Ländler Pno, WoO 11; Marches Military Band, WoO 18-20; Qt Strs in F, Hess 34; Qt 11 Strs, Op. 95; Qt 16 Strs, Op. 135; Romance Fl, Bn & Pno, Hess 13; Scottish Songs (25), Op. 108; Serenade Str Trio, Op. 8; Son 3 Vc, Op. 69; Son 8 Pno, Op. 13; Spt in E♭, Op. 20; Sym 5; Trio 5 Pno, Op. 70/2; Triumphal March, WoO 2a; Zärtliche Leibe, WoO 123 DEUT ▲ 453811 [ADD/DDD] (11.97)

Y. Menuhin (vn), W. Kempff (pno) ("In Memoriam") † Rondo Vn, WoO 41; Son 7 Vn; Son 9 Vn, Op. 47; P. Tchaikovsky:Con Vn DEUT (2-Fer) 2-▲ 463175 (17.97)

N. Milstein (vn), A. Balsam (pno) ("The 1953 Library of Congress Recital") † J. S. Bach:Sons & Partitas Vn; J. Brahms:Son 3 Vn, Op. 108 BRID ▲ 9066 (17.97)

N. Milstein (vn), R. Firkušný (pno) *(rec 1958-59)* † Son 8 Vn; Son 9 Vn, Op. 47 EMIC ▲ 66874 (m/s) [ADD] (11.97)

T. Nishizaki (vn), J. Jandó (pno) *(rec Apr 1989)* † Son 9 Vn, Op. 47 NXIN ▲ 550283 [DDD] (5.97)

I. Perlman (vn), V. Ashkenazy (pno) † Son 9 Vn, Op. 47 PLON ▲ 10554 [ADD] (16.97)

I. Perlman (vn), V. Ashkenazy (pno) † Son 9 Vn, Op. 47 DECC ▲ 458618 (11.97)

R. Ricci (vn), E. Bagnoli (pno) *(rec live)* † Son 9 Vn, Op. 47; Debussy:Son Vn ONEL ▲ 96010 [ADD] (7.97)

H. Szeryng (vn), A. Rubinstein (pno) ("Basic 100, Vol. 41") † Son 8 Pno, Op. 13; Son 8 Vn; Son 9 Vn, Op. 47 RCAV ▲ 61861 (11.97)

J. Szigeti (vn), C. Arrau (pno) *(rec 1927-44)* ("Joseph Szigeti: The Great Violin Sonatas") † Son 9 Vn, Op. 47; J. S. Bach:Sons & Partitas Vn; J. Brahms:Son 3 Vn, Op. 108 ENT (Strings) 2-▲ 99318 (32.97)

J. Szigeti (vn), A. Schnabel (pno) *(rec live, Apr 1948)* † Son 10 Vn, Op. 96 PHS ▲ 9026 [AAD] (17.97)

J. Szigeti (vn), A. Schnabel (pno) *(rec 1948)* † Son 10 Vn, Op. 96 ENT (Strings) ▲ 99365 (16.97)

R. Terakado (vn), B. Vodenitcharov (pno) † Son 1 Vn; Son 3 Vn DNN ▲ 18084 (16.97)

P. Zukerman (vn), M. Neikrug (pno) † Son 9 Vn, Op. 47 RCAV (Red Seal) ▲ 61561 (16.97)

artists unknown † Sym 7 PC ▲ 265061 [DDD] (2.97)

Sonata No. 6 in A for Violin & Piano, Op. 30/1 (1801-02)

S. Goldberg (vn), L. Kraus (pno) *(rec 1936-38)* ("Lili Kraus, Vol. 3") † Son 10 Vn, Op. 96; Son 2 Vn; Son 5 Vn, Op. 24; Son 9 Vn, Op. 47 LYS1 2-▲ 444 (34.97)

G. Kremer (vn), M. Argerich (pno) † Son 7 Vn; Son 8 Vn DEUT ▲ 45652 [DDD] (16.97)

T. Nishizaki (vn), J. Jandó (pno) *(rec Oct 1989)* † Son 7 Vn; Son 8 Vn NXIN ▲ 550286 [DDD] (5.97)

W. Riessmann (vn), D. Goldmann (pno) † Son 2 Vn; Son 3 Vn PC ▲ 267014 [DDD] (2.97)

Sonata No. 7 in c for Violin & Piano, Op. 30/2 (1801-02)

A. Busch (vn), R. Serkin (pno) *(rec Sept 23, 1932 & May 16, 1933)* ("The European Busch-Serkin Duo Recordings, Vol. 1") † Son 3 Vn; Son 5 Vn, Op. 24 APR ▲ 5541 [ADD] (19.97)

A. Busch (vn), R. Serkin (pno) † Son 5 Vn, Op. 24; J. Brahms:Son 1 Vn, Op. 78 MTAL ▲ 48022 (6.97)

A. Busch (vn), R. Serkin (pno) † Son 5 Vn, Op. 24; J. S. Bach:Son Vn Bc, BWV 1021; J. Brahms:Son 1 Vn, Op. 78; Son 2 Vn, Op. 100; R. Schumann:Son 1 Vn, Op. 105 GRM2 ▲ 78820 (26.97)

O. Charlier (vn), B. Engerer (pno) † Son 8 Vn; Son 9 Vn, Op. 47 HAM ▲ 901580 (18.97)

I. Haendel (vn), J. Newmark (pno) *(rec Montreal, Canada, 1967)* ("Legendary Treasures, Vol. 2") † J. S. Bach:Sons & Partitas Vn; C. Champagne:Habanera DHR ▲ 7733 (16.97)

W. Hink (vn), K. Toyama (pno) *(rec Japan, Oct 6, 1994)* ("Violin Sonatas, Vol. 2") † Son 10 Vn, Op. 96 CAMA ▲ 416 [DDD] (18.97)

R. Holmes (vn), R. Burnett (pno) † Son 5 Vn, Op. 24 AMON ▲ 9 (16.97)

G. Kremer (vn), M. Argerich (pno) † Son 6 Vn; Son 8 Vn DEUT ▲ 45652 [DDD] (16.97)

Y. Menuhin (vn), W. Kempff (pno) ("In Memoriam") † Rondo Vn, WoO 41; Son 5 Vn, Op. 24; Son 9 Vn, Op. 47; P. Tchaikovsky:Con Vn DEUT (2-Fer) 2-▲ 463175 (17.97)

T. Nishizaki (vn), J. Jandó (pno) *(rec Oct 1989)* † Son 6 Vn; Son 8 Vn NXIN ▲ 550286 [DDD] (5.97)

W. Riessmann (vn), D. Goldmann (pno) † Son 4 Vn, Op. 23; Son 8 Vn PC ▲ 267013 [DDD] (2.97)

I. Stern (vn), A. Zakin (pno) *(rec 1945-46)* † Bizet:Carmen Fantasie; Rimsky-Korsakov:Tale of Tsar Saltan (orch sels); Sarasate:Zigeunerweisen, Op. 20; R. Wagner:Fant on *Tristan und Isolde*; Wieniawski:Con 2 Vn, Op. 22 ENT (Strings) ▲ 99387 (14.97)

BEETHOVEN, LUDWIG VAN (cont.)

Sonata No. 8 in G for Violin & Piano, Op. 30/3 (1801-02)

A. Argenta (pno), A. Grumiaux (vn) † Sym 3; J. Brahms:Con Vn; Son 2 Vn, Op. 100; Escudero:Concerto Vasco; M. de Falla:Amor brujo; Smetana:Bartered Bride (orch sels); R. Strauss:Till Eulenspiegels lustige Streiche, Op. 28; P. Tchaikovsky:Sym 4 RTVE 4-▲ 65097 (36.97)

O. Charlier (vn), B. Engerer (pno) † Son 7 Vn; Son 9 Vn, Op. 47 HAM ▲ 901580 (18.97)

R. Holmes (vn), R. Burnett (pno) [1820 Graf fortepno] † Son 9 Vn, Op. 47 AMON ▲ 16 [DDD] (16.97)

F. Kreisler (vn), S. Rachmaninoff (pno) *(rec Mar 1926 for HMV)* † Con Vn; J. Brahms:Con Vn; F. Kreisler:Qt Strs; Scherzo 'in the style of Dittersdorf'; F. Schubert:Fant Vn, D.934; Son Vn, D.574; F. Waxman:Carmen Fant BDR 3-▲ 1 [ADD/DDD]

F. Kreisler (vn), S. Rachmaninoff (pno) † Con Vn BID ▲ 100 (16.97)

F. Kreisler (vn), S. Rachmaninoff (pno) † E. Grieg:Son 3 Vn, Op. 45; F. Kreisler:Vn Pieces; F. Schubert:Son Vn, D.574 MTAL ▲ 48077 (6.97)

F. Kreisler (vn), S. Rachmaninoff (pno) *(rec 1928)* † E. Grieg:Son 3 Vn, Op. 45; F. Schubert:Son Vn, D.574 ENT ▲ 99382 (16.97)

F. Kreisler (vn), F. Rupp (pno) *(rec 1935)* † Son 10 Vn, Op. 96; Son 9 Vn, Op. 47 MTAL ▲ 48011 (6.97)

G. Kremer (vn), M. Argerich (pno) † Son 6 Vn; Son 7 Vn DEUT ▲ 45652 [DDD] (16.97)

N. Milstein (vn), A. Balsam (pno) *(rec 1958-59)* † Son 5 Vn, Op. 24; Son 9 Vn, Op. 47 EMIC ▲ 66874 (m/s) [ADD] (11.97)

N. Milstein (vn), A. Balsam (pno) *(rec 1939-45)* † Mendelssohn (-Bartholdy):Con Vn & Orch, Op. 64 ENT (Strings) ▲ 99368 (16.97)

N. Milstein (vn), A. Balsam (pno) *(rec 1939 & 45)* ("Nathan Milstein, Vol. 1") † Mendelssohn (-Bartholdy):Con Vn & Orch, Op. 64; W. A. Mozart:Son 17 Vn & Pno, K.296 GRM2 ▲ 78875 (13.97)

T. Nishizaki (vn), J. Jandó (pno) *(rec Oct 1989)* † Son 6 Vn; Son 7 Vn NXIN ▲ 550286 [DDD] (5.97)

D. Oistrakh (vn), L. Oborin (pno) *(rec Leningrad, Russia, 1960)* † J. Brahms:Con Vn CONE ▲ 9403 (m) [ADD] (16.97)

W. Riessmann (vn), D. Goldmann (pno) † Son 4 Vn, Op. 23; Son 7 Vn PC ▲ 267013 [DDD] (2.97)

H. Szeryng (vn), A. Rubinstein (pno) ("Basic 100, Vol. 41") † Son 5 Vn, Op. 24; Son 8 Pno, Op. 13; Son 9 Vn, Op. 47 RCAV ▲ 61861 (11.97)

Sonata No. 9 in A for Violin & Piano, Op. 47, "Kreutzer" (1802-03)

K. Adam (vn), D. Adam (pno) *(rec Vienna, Jan 2-4, 1988)* † Son 5 Vn, Op. 24 CAMA ▲ 266 [DDD] (18.97)

A. Busch (vn), R. Serkin (pno) † Son 3 Vn; Son 5 Vn, Op. 24 PHS ▲ 19 (17.97)

O. Charlier (vn), B. Engerer (pno) † Son 7 Vn; Son 8 Vn HAM ▲ 901580 (18.97)

O. Charlier (vn), B. Engerer (pno) HAM (La Solothèque) ▲ 926003 (5.97)

M. Fornaciari (vn), I. Barontini (pno) † Notturno Va; Paganini:Intro & Vars on Nel cor più non mi sento, M.S. 44; Son Va FON ▲ 9320 [DDD]

Z. Francescatti (vn), R. Casadesus (pno) † Son 10 Vn, Op. 96; Son 5 Vn, Op. 24 SNYC (Essential Classics) ▲ 46342 [ADD] (7.97) ▮ 46342 [ADD] (3.98)

M. Frasca-Colombier (vn), M. Langot (pno) † Son 5 Vn, Op. 24 PVY ▲ 730079 (11.97)

S. Goldberg (vn), L. Kraus (pno) *(rec London, England, 1938-40)* † Son 10 Vn, Op. 96; Son 5 Vn, Op. 24; W. A. Mozart:Duo Vn, K.423; Duo Vn, K.424; Sonatas for Violin & Piano (miscellaneous) MUA 3-▲ 4665 (30.97)

S. Goldberg (vn), L. Kraus (pno) *(rec 1936-38)* ("Lili Kraus, Vol. 3") † Son 10 Vn, Op. 96; Son 2 Vn; Son 5 Vn, Op. 24; Son 6 Vn LYS1 2-▲ 444 (34.97)

R. Holmes (vn), R. Burnett (pno) [1820 Graf fortepno] † Son 8 Vn AMON ▲ 16 [DDD] (16.97)

B. Huberman (vn), I. Friedman (pno) [incomplete performance] *(rec London, England, Sept 1930)* ("Huberman Concert & Recital Recordings") † Con Vn; J. S. Bach:Chorales Org; Smetana:From the Homeland ARBT ▲ 115 (m) [AAD] (16.97)

F. Kreisler (vn), F. Rupp (pno) *(rec 1935)* † Son 10 Vn, Op. 96; Son 8 Vn MTAL ▲ 48011 (6.97)

F. Kreisler (vn), F. Rupp (pno) *(rec 1936)* † Son 10 Vn, Op. 96; Son 5 Vn, Op. 24 ENT (Strings) ▲ 99340 (16.97)

G. Kremer (vn), M. Argerich (pno) *(rec Auditorium Stravinski Montreux, Mar 1994)* † Son 10 Vn, Op. 96 DEUT ▲ 47054 [DDD] (16.97)

I. M. Menges (vn), H. Samuel (pno) *(rec 1925-29)* † J. Brahms:Son 2 Vn, Op. 100; Son 3 Vn, Op. 108 MTAL ▲ 48062 (6.97)

Y. Menuhin (vn), W. Kempff (pno) ("In Memoriam") † Rondo Vn, WoO 41; Son 5 Vn, Op. 24; Son 7 Vn; P. Tchaikovsky:Con Vn DEUT (2-Fer) 2-▲ 463175 (17.97)

N. Milstein (vn), A. Balsam (pno) *(rec 1958-59)* † Son 5 Vn, Op. 24; Son 8 Vn EMIC ▲ 66874 (m/s) [ADD] (11.97)

T. Nishizaki (vn), J. Jandó (pno) *(rec Apr 1989)* † Son 5 Vn, Op. 24 NXIN ▲ 550283 [DDD] (5.97)

D. Oistrakh (vn), L. Oborin (pno) † Son 3 Vn TES ▲ 1115

I. Perlman (vn), V. Ashkenazy (pno) † Son 5 Vn, Op. 24 PLON ▲ 10554 [ADD] (16.97)

I. Perlman (vn), V. Ashkenazy (pno) † Son 5 Vn, Op. 24 DECC ▲ 458618 (11.97)

R. Ricci (vn), E. Bagnoli (pno) *(rec live)* † Son 5 Vn, Op. 24; Debussy:Son Vn ONEL ▲ 96010 [ADD] (7.97)

H. Szeryng (vn), A. Rubinstein (pno) ("Basic 100, Vol. 41") † Son 5 Vn, Op. 24; Son 8 Pno, Op. 13; Son 8 Vn RCAV ▲ 61861 (11.97)

J. Szigeti (vn), C. Arrau (pno) *(rec 1927-44)* ("Joseph Szigeti: The Great Violin Sonatas") † Son 5 Vn, Op. 24; J. S. Bach:Sons & Partitas Vn; J. Brahms:Son 3 Vn, Op. 108 ENT (Strings) 2-▲ 99318 (32.97)

J. Szigeti (vn), B. Bartók (pno) *(rec 1940)* † B. Bartók:Rhaps Vn & Pno, Sz.86 & 88; Son 2 Vn & Pno, Sz.76; Debussy:Son Vn VC ▲ 8008 [AAD] (13.97)

J. Thibaud (vn), A. Cortot (pno) *(rec May-June 1929)* † Debussy:Preludes Pno; Son Vn; C. Franck:Son Vn, M.8 ENT (Strings) ▲ 99353 (16.97)

M. Vengerov (vn), A. Markovich (pno) † J. Brahms:Son 2 Vn, Op. 100 ELEC ▲ 74001 (15.97)

D. Zsigmondy (vn), A. Nisse (pno) *(rec 1968-74)* † C. Franck:Son Vn, M.8 CLDI ▲ 4034 [AAD] (10.97)

P. Zukerman (vn), M. Neikrug (pno) † Son 5 Vn, Op. 24 RCAV (Red Seal) ▲ 61561 (16.97)

various artists ["Kreutzer" excerpt] † J. S. Bach:Sons & Partitas Vn; Mendelssohn (-Bartholdy):Con Vn & Orch, Op. 64; W. A. Mozart:Con 3 Vn, K.216; Tartini:Son Vn & Pno; P. Tchaikovsky:Con Vn MTAL ▲ 48099 (6.97)

Sonata No. 10 in G for Violin & Piano, Op. 96 (1812; probably rev 1815)

Z. Francescatti (vn), R. Casadesus (pno) † Son 5 Vn, Op. 24; Son 9 Vn, Op. 47 SNYC (Essential Classics) ▲ 46342 [ADD] (7.97) ▮ 46342 [ADD] (3.98)

S. Goldberg (vn), L. Kraus (pno) *(rec London, England, 1938-40)* † Son 5 Vn, Op. 24; Son 9 Vn, Op. 47; W. A. Mozart:Duo Vn, K.423; Duo Vn, K.424; Sonatas for Violin & Piano (miscellaneous) MUA 3-▲ 4665 (30.97)

S. Goldberg (vn), L. Kraus (pno) *(rec 1936-38)* ("Lili Kraus, Vol. 3") † Son 2 Vn; Son 5 Vn, Op. 24; Son 6 Vn; Son 9 Vn, Op. 47 LYS1 2-▲ 444 (34.97)

W. Hink (vn), K. Toyama (pno) *(rec Japan, Oct 6, 1994)* ("Violin Sonatas, Vol. 2") † Son 7 Vn CAMA ▲ 416 [DDD] (18.97)

F. Kreisler (vn), F. Rupp (pno) *(rec 1935)* † Son 8 Vn; Son 9 Vn, Op. 47 MTAL ▲ 48011 (6.97)

F. Kreisler (vn), F. Rupp (pno) *(rec 1936)* † Son 5 Vn, Op. 24; Son 9 Vn, Op. 47 ENT (Strings) ▲ 99340 (16.97)

G. Kremer (vn), M. Argerich (pno) *(rec Auditorium Stravinski Montreux, Mar 1994)* † Son 9 Vn, Op. 47 DEUT ▲ 47054 [DDD] (16.97)

Y. Menuhin (vn), G. Gould (pno) *(rec Oct 25-26, 1965)* ("Gould Meets Menuhin") † Schoenberg:Phantasy, Op. 47 SNYC ▲ 52688 [ADD] (16.97)

Y. Menuhin (vn), H. Menuhin (pno) *(rec 1947)* † B. Bartók:Son 1 Vn & Pno, Sz.75; J. Brahms:Son 3 Vn, Op. 108 BID ▲ 161 [ADD] (16.97)

T. Nishizaki (vn), J. Jandó (pno) *(rec Feb & Sept 1992)* † Son 4 Vn, Op. 23; Vars Vn on Mozart's Se vuol ballare, WoO 40 NXIN ▲ 550285 [DDD] (5.97)

I. Stern (vn), M. Hess (pno) *(rec 14th Edinburgh Festival, Aug 28, 1960)* ("In Concert 1949-1960") † Con 4 Pno, Op. 58; Con 5 Pno, Op. 73; J. Brahms:Con 2 Pno, Op. 83; Son 2 Vn, Op. 100; W. A. Mozart:Con 12 Pno, K.414; Con 21 Pno, K.467; Con 27 Pno, K.595; F. Schubert:Sonatinas (3) Vn MUA 3-▲ 779 [AAD] (47.97)

J. Szigeti (vn), A. Schnabel (pno) *(rec live, Apr 1948)* † Son 5 Vn, Op. 24 PHS ▲ 9026 [AAD] (17.97)

J. Szigeti (vn), A. Schnabel (pno) *(rec 1948)* † Son 5 Vn, Op. 24 ENT (Strings) ▲ 99365 (16.97)

Sonatina in c for Mandolin & Piano, WoO 43a (1796)

L. Mayer (mand), I. Rohmann (pno) † Adagio Mand, WoO 43b; Andante con vars Mand, WoO 44b; German Dances Vn, WoO 42; National Airs with Vars, Op. 105; Sonatina Mand in C, WoO 44a HUN ▲ 12303 (16.97)

A. Stephens (mand), R. Burnett (pno) *(rec Finchcocks, Goudhurst, Kent, England, March 1991)* ("Music for Mandolin") † Adagio Mand, WoO 43b; Sonatina Mand in C, WoO 44a; Vars Pno on Original Theme, Op. 76; Barbella:Duos (6) Vns; Calace:Suite 3 mand; J. N. Hummel:Son in c Hpd; W. A. Mozart:Die Zufriedenheit, K.349; Komm, liebe Zither, komm, K.351 AMON ▲ 53 [DDD] (16.97)

R. Walz (mand), V. Sofronitzki (pno) *(rec Apr 1998)* ("Works for Mandolin & Fortepiano") † Adagio Mand, WoO 43b; Sonatina Mand in C, WoO 44a; J. N. Hummel:Son Mand, Op. 37a; Neuling:Son Mand, Op. 3 GLOE ▲ 5187 [DDD] (16.97)

Sonatina in C for Mandolin & Piano, WoO 44a (1796)

L. Mayer (mand), I. Rohmann (pno) † Adagio Mand, WoO 43b; Andante con vars Mand, WoO 44b; German Dances Vn, WoO 42; National Airs with Vars, Op. 105; Sonatina Mand in c, WoO 43a HUN ▲ 12303 (16.97)

BEETHOVEN, LUDWIG VAN (cont.)

Sonatina in C for Mandolin & Piano, WoO 44a (1796) (cont.)

A. Stephens (mand), R. Burnett (pno) *(rec Finchcocks, Goudhurst, Kent, England, March 1991)* ("Music for Mandolin") † Adagio Mand, WoO 43b; Sonatina Mand in c, WoO 43a; Vars Pno on Original Theme, Op. 76; Barbella:Duos (6) Vns; Calace:Suite 3 mand; J. N. Hummel:Son in c Hpd; W. A. Mozart:Die Zufriedenheit, K.349; Komm, liebe Zither, komm, K.351 AMON ▲ 53 [DDD] (16.97)

R. Walz (mand), V. Sofronitzki (pno) *(rec Apr 1998)* ("Works for Mandolin & Fortepiano") † Adagio Mand, WoO 43b; Sonatina Mand in c, WoO 43a; J. N. Hummel:Son Mand, Op. 37a; Neuling:Son Mand, Op. 3 GLOE ▲ 5187 [DDD] (16.97)

Sonatinas (2) in G & F for Piano [probably spurious], Anh.5 (?ca 1790-92)

J. Jandó (pno) *(rec Jan 31-Feb 17, 1989)* ("Piano Sonatas, Vol. 10") † Rondos Pno, Op. 51; Son Pno in C, WoO 51; Son 15 Pno, Op. 28; Sons (3) Pno, WoO 47 NXIN ▲ 550255 [DDD] (5.97)

Songs

C. Bartoli (mez), A. Schiff (pno)—La partenza, WoO 124; In questa tomba oscura, WoO 133 *(rec Aug 5-8, 1992)* † Ariettas & Duet, Op. 82; J. Haydn:Arianna a Naxos, H.XXVIb/2; F. Schubert:Songs (misc colls) PLON ▲ 40297 [DDD] (16.97) PPHI ▮ 40297 [DDD] (10.98)

R. DeCormier (cnd) , Robert DeCormier Singers—Assorted Folksongs (12), WoO 157 [No. 9, Highlander's Lament] *(rec 1996)* ("Bobby Burns: Music Celebrating the Poetry of Robert Burns") † Decormier:Jolly Beggars; J. Haydn:Songs; D. Shostakovich:Songs ARA ▲ 6708 [DDD] (16.97)

D. Fischer-Dieskau (bar), H. Klust (pno) TES ▲ 1057 [ADD] (17.97)

K. Flagstad (sop), W. Alme (pno)—Songs (6), Op. 48 [No. 1, "Bitten"; No. 2, "Die Liebe des Nächsten"; No. 3, "Vom Tode"; No. 4, "Die Ehre Gottes aus der Natur"; No. 5, "Gottes Macht und Vorsehnung"; No. 6, "Busslied"]; Songs (3), Op. 83 [No. 1, Wonne der Wehmut]; Andenken, WoO 136; Zärtliche Leibe, WoO 123; An die Hoffnung (II), Op. 94 *(rec Oslo, 1954)* ("Vol. 5: German Lieder, Norwegian Radio 1954") † J. Brahms:Songs; F. Schubert:Ave Maria, Op. 52/6; Songs (misc colls); R. Schumann:Songs; R. Strauss:Songs; H. Wolf:Songs (misc) SIMX 2-▲ 1825 (39.97)

M. Fuchs (sop), M. Müller (sop), H. Rott (mez), E. Leisner (cta), P. Anders (ten), L. Fehenberger (ten), W. Ludwig (ten), K. Schmitt-Walter (bar), A. Schellenberg (bar), H. Hotter (b-bar), H. Alsen (bass), K. Böhme (bass), M. Raucheisen (pno), Raucheisen Trio ("Liederalbum") VOCA (Vocal Archives) 2-▲ 1146 (26.97)

J. Griffett (ten), F. Maier (vn), R. Mandalka (vc), B. Tracey (pno)—Welsh Songs (26), WoO 155 [To the Aeolian Harp]; Scottish Songs (25), Op. 108 [No. 25, Sally in our Alley; No. 10, Sympathy; No. 23, The Shepherd's Song]; Irish Songs (12), WoO 154 [The Soldier in a Foreign Land; The Farewell Song]; Irish Songs (20), WoO 153 [Come, Darby Dear, Easy; The British Light Dragoons] ("Will Ye Go to Flanders: Folksongs of the British Isles") † J. Haydn:Barbara Allen, H.XXXIa/11bis; Blue Bonnets, H.XXXIa/39; Songs ARSM ▲ 1142 [ADD] (17.97)

E. Kirchner (sop), M. D. Vries (sgr), D. Chou (sgr), R. Clemencic (cnd), Alpe Adria Ensemble—Songs of Various Nationality (6), WoO 158c [Non, non, Colette n'est point trompeuse [from Le devin du village]] † W. A. Mozart:Bastien und Bastienne, K.50; J.-J. Rousseau:Devin du village NUO 2-▲ 7106 [DDD] (32.97)

W. Ludwig (ten) *(Der Kuss, Op. 128)*, K. Schmitt-Walter (bar) *(Elegie auf den Tod eines Pudels, WoO 110)*, E. Leisner (cta) *(Sehnsucht (4 settings), WoO 134)*, P. Anders (ten) *(Lied aus der Ferne, WoO 137)*, H. Hotter (b-bar) *(Abendlied unterm gestirnten Himmel, WoO 150) (rec 1942-44)* ("Selected Lieder in Historical Performances") † An die ferne Geliebte, Op. 98; Arias & Duets; Irish Songs (25), WoO 152; Scottish Songs (25), Op. 108 MNER ▲ 69 (m) [ADD] (15.97)

A. Mackay (sop), English Piano Trio—Scottish Songs (25), Op. 108 [No. 5, The Sweetest Lad Was Jamie; No. 14, O How Can I Be Blithe and Glad; No. 21, Jeanie's Distress; No. 20, Faithfu' Johnie; No. 6, Dim, Dim Is My Eye; No. 11, Oh! Thou Art the Lad of My Heart, Willy]; Scottish Songs (12), WoO 156 [No. 5, Cease Your Funning] † Trio 3 Pno, Op. 1/3; Trio 7 Pno, Op. 11 MER ▲ 84253 [DDD] (16.97)

L. D. San (bar), D. Ouziel (pno) ("Lieder") DI ▲ 920276 [DDD] (5.97)

P. Schreier (ten), W. Olbertz (pno)—An die ferne Geliebte, Op. 98; Songs (6), Op. 48; Songs (3), Op. 83 ("Beethoven: Lieder, Vol. 1") BER ▲ 2082 [ADD] (16.97)

F. Wunderlich (ten), H. Giesen (pno)—Adelaide, Op. 46; Resignation, WoO 149; Der Wachtelschlag, WoO 129; Songs (8), Op. 52 [No. 4, Maigesang]; Der Kuss, Op. 128 *(rec Mar 24, 1966)* † F. Schubert:Songs (misc colls); R. Schumann:Dichterliebe, Op. 48 MYTO ▲ 93278 (17.97)

F. Wunderlich (ten), H. Giesen (pno)—Adelaide, Op. 46; Songs (8), Op. 52; Der Wachtelschlag, WoO 129; Resignation, WoO 149; Der Kuss, Op. 128 *(rec Salzburg, Germany, Aug 19, 1965)* † F. Schubert:Songs (misc colls); R. Schumann:Dichterliebe, Op. 48 ORFE (Festspiel Dokumente) ▲ 432961 [ADD] (16.97)

F. Wunderlich (ten), H. Giesen (pno)—Adelaide, Op. 46; Resignation, WoO 149; Songs (8), Op. 52 [No. 4, Maigesang]; Der Kuss, Op. 128 *(rec Hannover, Germany, Mar 24, 1966)* † Christus am Ölberg, Op. 85; Rosenmüller:Lamentationes Jeremiae BELV ▲ 7003 [AAD] (15.97)

F. Wunderlich (ten), H. Giesen (pno)—Zärtliche Leibe, WoO 123; Adelaide, Op. 46; Resignation, WoO 149; Der Kuss, Op. 128 *(rec Hochschule for Music, Munich, Germany, Oct-Nov 1965)* † F. Schubert:Songs (misc colls); R. Schumann:Dichterliebe, Op. 48 DEUT (The Originals) ▲ 449747 [ADD] (11.97)

artists unknown—Songs (6), Op. 48; Songs (8), Op. 52 CPO ▲ 999436 (13.97)

Symphonies (9) (complete)

E. Andor (sop), M. Szirmay (cta), G. Korondi (ten), S. Sólyom-Nagy (bar), J. Ferencsik (cnd), Hungarian State Orch, M. Forrai (cnd), Budapest Chorus *(rec 1969, 1971, 1974-76)* † Egmont (ov) CLDI 6-▲ 4013 [ADD] (60.97)

L. Bernstein (cnd), Vienna PO DEUT 6-▲ 23481 [ADD] (58.97)

H. Doese (sop), M. Schiml (mez), P. Schreier (ten), T. Adam (bass), H. Blomstedt (cnd), Dresden Staatskapelle, Leipzig Radio Chorus, Dresden State Opera Chorus *(rec Lukaskirche Dresden, 1975-80)* BER 5-▲ 2194 [ADD] (41.97)

J. E. Gardiner (cnd), Orch Révolutionnaire et Romantique PARC ▲ 39900 [DDD] (64.97)

J. Glennon (sop), D. Schaechter (mez), A. Janutas (ten), B. Schollum (bar), Y. Menuhin (cnd), Sinfonia Varsovia, Kuanas State Choir Lithuania INMP (IMG) 5-▲ 6800025 (45.97)

C. Hogwood (cnd), Academy of Ancient Music, LSO Chorus PLOI 5-▲ 452551 (33.97)

M. Huggett (cnd), Hanover Band † Coriolan Ov, Op. 62; Egmont (ov); Fidelio (ov); Geschöpfe des Prometheus (ov); König Stephen (ov); Leonore (ov 2); Missa Solemnis, Op. 123; Ruinen von Athen (ov); Weihe des Hauses (ov), Op. 124 NIMB 7-▲ 1760 [DDD] (29.97)

H. von Karajan (cnd), Berlin PO, Vienna Singverein, J. Perry (sop), A. Baltsa (mez), V. Cole (ten), J. Van Dam (bar) † Coriolan Ov, Op. 62; Egmont (ov); Fidelio (ov); Leonore (ov 3) DEUT 6-▲ 39200 [ADD] (96.97)

H. von Karajan (cnd), Philharmonia Orch, Vienna Singverein, E. Schwarzkopf (sop), E. Höngen (cta), E. Haefliger (ten), O. Edelmann (bass) *(rec enna, 1951-55)* † Coriolan Ov, Op. 62; Egmont (ov) EMIC (Studio) 5-▲ 63310 [ADD] (52.97)

H. Kegel (cnd), Dresden PO LALI 5-▲ 15947 [DDD] (16.97) ▮ 79947 [DDD] (12.98)

H. Kegel (cnd), Dresden PO, Berlin Radio Chorus, Leipzig Radio Chorus CAPO 7-▲ 10400 (11.97)

O. Klemperer (cnd), Philharmonia Orch *(rec Vienna, 1960)* † Coriolan Ov, Op. 62; Egmont (ov); Geschöpfe des Prometheus (ov) MUA 5-▲ 886 [ADD] (63.97)

O. Klemperer (cnd), Philharmonia Orch EMIC 7-▲ 68057 (46.97)

J. Krips (cnd), London SO ("The Nine Symphonies") EVC 5-▲ 9010 [AAD] (64.97)

W. Mengelberg (cnd), Concertgebouw Orch † Egmont (ov); Fidelio (ov) GRM2 5-▲ 78032 (57.97)

A. Polizzi (cnd), Prague SO, A. Polizzi (cnd), Budapest SO *(rec 1986 & 1990-94)* ("Symphonies") † R. Wagner:Götterdämmerung (sels) HAM 6-▲ 2905225 (52.97)

E. Schwarzkopf (sop), E. Höngen (mez), H. Hopf (ten), O. Edelmann (bass), W. Furtwängler (cnd), Vienna PO, W. Furtwängler (cnd), Bayreuth Festival Orch, Bayreuth Festival Chorus *(rec 1948-54)* EMIC 5-▲ 63606 (52.97)

G. Szell (cnd), Cleveland Orch † Egmont (ov); Fidelio (ov); König Stephen (ov) SNYC (Essential Classics) 5-▲ 48396 (38.97)

A. Toscanini (cnd), NBC SO, Westminster Choir, J. Novotná (sop), K. Thorborg (mez), J. Peerce (ten), N. Moscona (bass) † Egmont (ov); Fant Pno, Orch & Chorus, Op. 80; Fidelio (ov); Leonore (ov 1), Op. 138; Leonore (ov 2); Leonore (ov 3) GRM2 (The Records of the Century) 5-▲ 78826 (64.97)

W. Weller (cnd), City of Birmingham SO, City of Birmingham Sym Chorus † Sym 10 CHN 5-▲ 7042 (53.97)

I. Wenglor (sop), U. Zollenkopf (cta), H. J. Rotzsch (ten), F. Konwitschny (cnd), Leipzig Gewandhaus Orch, Leipzig Radio Chorus *(rec 1959-61)* † Ovs BER (Eterna) 6-▲ 2005 [ADD] (41.97)

D. Zinman (cnd), Tonhalle Orchestra Zurich ARNO 5-▲ 65410 (22.97)

Symphony No. 1 in C, Op. 21 (1800)

K. Ančerl (cnd), Czech PO † Sym 5 SUR (Czech Philharmonic) ▲ 111937 [AAD]

J. Barbirolli (cnd), Hallé Orch † Con 5 Pno, Op. 73; Egmont (ov); Leonore (ov 3); Sym 5; Sym 8 DLAB (The Barbirolli Society) ▲ 1014 (17.97)

L. Bernstein (cnd), New York PO ("Bernstein: The Royal Edition") † Sym 3 SNYC ▲ 47514 [ADD] (10.97)

H. Blomstedt (cnd), Dresden Staatskapelle *(rec 1975-80)* ("Blomstedt Conducts the Beethoven Symphonies Vol. 1") † Sym 3 BER ▲ 2195 (10.97)

K. Böhm (cnd), Vienna PO † Sym 2; Sym 4; Sym 5 DEUT (Double) 2-▲ 39681 (17.97)

G. Brouwenstijn (sop), K. Meyer (alt), N. Gedda (ten), F. Guthrie (bass), A. Cluytens (cnd), Berlin PO, Choir of St. Hedwigs Cathedral, Berlin † Egmont (ov); Fidelio (ov); Geschöpfe des Prometheus (ov); Sym 2; Sym 3; Sym 4; Sym 5; Sym 6; Sym 7; Sym 8; Sym 9 RYLC 5-▲ 70373 (24.97)

J. Caeyers (cnd), Beethoven Academy *(rec 1995)* † Sym 4 HMA ▲ 1901573 (9.97)

BEETHOVEN, LUDWIG VAN (cont.)

Symphony No. 1 in C, Op. 21 (1800) (cont.)

C. von Dohnányi (cnd), Cleveland Orch † Sym 2 TEL ▲ 80187 [DDD] (16.97)

B. Drahos (cnd), Nicolaus Esterházy Sinfonia *(rec Italian Institute Budapest, June 17-20, 1995)* † Sym 6 NXIN ▲ 553474 [DDD] (5.97)

E. Duvier (cnd), North German PO † Sym 2 PC ▲ 267011 [DDD] (2.97)

J. Ferencsik (cnd), Hungarian PO † Sym 7 LALI ▲ 15904 (3.97)

W. Furtwängler (cnd), Berlin PO *(rec 1954)* † J. Brahms:Sym 4 TAHA ▲ 1025 (17.97)

W. Furtwängler (cnd), Vienna PO *(rec Sept 4, 1953)* † Egmont (ov); Sym 4 MUA ▲ 792 [AAD] (16.97)

C. M. Giulini (cnd), La Scala Orch † Sym 7 SNYC ▲ 48236 [DDD] (11.97)

N. Harnoncourt (cnd), CO of Europe † Sym 3 TELC ▲ 75708 (16.97)

H. von Karajan (cnd), Berlin PO ("Ludwig van Beethoven: Symphonien Nos. 1 & 2 Karajan Gold series") † Sym 2 DEUT ▲ 39001 [DDD] (16.97)

R. Kempe (cnd) † Sym 3; Sym 5 CSER (Seraphim) 2-▲ 68518 (6.97)

O. Klemperer (cnd), Philharmonia Orch *(rec London, England, Oct 1957)* † Sym 6 EMIC (Klemperer Legacy) ▲ 66792 [ADD] (11.97)

J. Krips (cnd), London SO † Sym 5 EVC ▲ 9100 (13.97)

R. Leibowitz (cnd), Royal PO *(rec 1961)* † Sym 3 CHSK ▲ 74 [ADD] (16.97)

P. Maag (cnd), Padova e Veneto CO *(rec Padova Italy, July 13-16, 1994)* † Sym 3 AART ▲ 47246 [DDD] (10.97)

C. Mackerras (cnd), Royal Liverpool PO † Sym 3 CFP ▲ 72846 (11.97)

P. Monteux (cnd), Vienna PO † Sym 3; Sym 6; Sym 8 PLON (Double Decker) 2-▲ 40627 (17.97)

W. Morris (cnd), London SO *(rec May 1988)* † Sym 2 INMP ▲ 929 [DDD]

R. Muti (cnd), Philadelphia Orch † Sym 5 EMIC (Red Line) ▲ 69782 (6.97)

H. Scherchen (cnd), Lugano Radio Orch † Sym 2; Sym 4; Sym 8 TAHA 3-▲ 126 (34.97)

C. Schuricht (cnd), Berlin Municipal Orch *(rec 1941-42)* † Sym 4 IN ▲ 1419 [ADD] (15.97)

G. Schwarz (cnd), Los Angeles CO † Geschöpfe des Prometheus (ov); Sym 8 DLS ▲ 3013 [DDD] (14.97)

G. Szell (cnd), Cleveland Orch † Egmont (ov); Sym 6 SNYC (Essential Classics) ▲ 46532 [ADD] (7.97) ▮ 46532 [ADD] (3.98)

A. Toscanini (cnd), BBC SO *(rec 1937)* ("Toscanini in London, 1935-39, Vol. 5") † Leonore (ov 1), Op. 138; Sym 6 GRM2 ▲ 78615 (13.97)

A. Toscanini (cnd), BBC SO *(rec 1937-39)* † Leonore; Sym 4; Sym 6; J. Brahms:Tragic Ov, Op. 81; W. A. Mozart:Zauberflöte (sels) ENT (Document) 2-▲ 921 [ADD] (26.97)

A. Toscanini (cnd), La Scala Orch *(rec Kunsthaus Lucerne, July 7, 1946)* ("Toscanini in Lucerne") † Egmont (ov); R. Wagner:Ovs, Preludes & Orchestral Sels IN ▲ 1372 (15.97)

A. Toscanini (cnd), La Scala Orch *(rec Lucerne, Switzerland, July 7, 1946)* † Egmont (ov); Sym 9; R. Wagner:Lohengrin (sels); Meistersinger (ov); Meistersinger (sels); Tannhäuser (sels) MUA 2-▲ 1027 [AAD] (31.97)

B. Walter (cnd) *(rec 1940s)* ("The 1st Recordings in America for Columbia") † Sym 6; Sym 8; F. Schubert:Sym 8 GRM2 ▲ 78805 (26.97)

B. Walter (cnd), Columbia SO *(rec Los Angeles, CA, Jan 6-8, 1958)* † Coriolan Ov, Op. 62; Sym 2 SNYC (Bruno Walter Edition, Vol. 2) ▲ 64460 [ADD] (10.97)

B. Walter (cnd), New York PO *(rec 1947)* ("Walter, Vol. 4") † Con Vn LYS ▲ 397 (17.97)

H. Zender (cnd), Saarbrücken RSO ("Hans Zender Edition, Vol. 2") † Con Vn; Sym 6 CPO 2-▲ 999474 (6.97)

D. Zinman (cnd), Tonhalle Orchestra Zurich † Sym 2 ARNO ▲ 63645 (4.97)

Symphony No. 2 in D, Op. 36 (1801-02)

L. Bernstein (cnd), New York PO ("Bernstein: The Royal Edition") † Sym 7 SNYC ▲ 47515 [ADD] (10.97)

L. Bernstein (cnd), New York PO *(rec Manhattan Center, New York City, NY, Jan 1964)* † Sym 7 SNYC (Bernstein Century) ▲ 61835 [ADD] (11.97)

H. Blomstedt (cnd), Dresden Staatskapelle *(rec 1975-80)* ("Blomstedt Conducts the Beethoven Symphonies, Vol. 2") † Sym 4 BER ▲ 2196 (10.97)

K. Böhm (cnd), Vienna PO † Sym 1; Sym 4; Sym 5 DEUT (Double) 2-▲ 39681 (17.97)

G. Brouwenstijn (sop), K. Meyer (alt), N. Gedda (ten), F. Guthrie (bass), A. Cluytens (cnd), Berlin PO, Choir of St. Hedwigs Cathedral, Berlin † Egmont (ov); Fidelio (ov); Geschöpfe des Prometheus (ov); Sym 1; Sym 3; Sym 4; Sym 5; Sym 6; Sym 7; Sym 8; Sym 9 RYLC 5-▲ 70373 (24.97)

C. Cantieri (cnd), London PO † Sym 1 PC ▲ 267011 [DDD] (2.97)

S. Celibidache (cnd), Münchner Philharmoniker *(rec Philharmonie am Gasteig, München, Germany, June 4, 1996)* † Sym 4 EMIC ▲ 56838 [DDD] (16.97)

C. von Dohnányi (cnd), Cleveland Orch † Sym 1 TEL ▲ 80187 [DDD] (16.97)

B. Drahos (cnd), Nicolaus Esterházy Sinfonia *(rec Italian Institute Budapest, June 9-16, 1995)* † Sym 5 NXIN ▲ 8553476 [DDD] (5.97)

R. Edlinger (cnd), Zagreb PO *(rec Sept 1988)* † Sym 5 NXIN ▲ 550177 [DDD] (5.97)

J. Ferencsik (cnd), Hungarian PO † Sym 6 LALI ▲ 15903 (3.97)

C. M. Giulini (cnd), La Scala Orch *(rec Dec 8-11, 1991)* † Sym 8 SNYC ▲ 48238 [DDD] (11.97)

N. Harnoncourt (cnd), CO of Europe † Sym 5 TELC ▲ 75712 (16.97)

H. von Karajan (cnd), Berlin PO ("Ludwig van Beethoven: Symphonien Nos. 1 & 2 Karajan Gold series") † Sym 1 DEUT ▲ 39001 [DDD] (16.97)

H. von Karajan (cnd), Prussian State Orch † Smetana:Moldau IMUS (Magic Master) ▲ 37059 (6.97)

H. Kegel (cnd), Dresden PO † Sym 7 CAPO ▲ 10452 [DDD] (11.97)

O. Klemperer (cnd), Philharmonia Orch *(rec London, England, 1957)* † Sym 5 EMIC (Klemperer Legacy) ▲ 66794 [ADD] (11.97)

S. Koussevitzky (cnd), Boston SO *(rec 1929-39)* ("Koussevitsky Conducts Classical Symphonies") † Sym 8; J. Haydn:Sym 102; Sym 94; W. A. Mozart:Sym 29, K.201; Sym 34, K.338 PHS 2-▲ 9185 (33.97)

J. Krips (cnd), London SO † Sym 6 EVC ▲ 9101 (13.97)

R. Leibowitz (cnd), Royal PO *(rec 1961)* † Leonore (ov 3); Sym 5 CHSK ▲ 17 (16.97)

P. Maag (cnd), Padova e Veneto CO *(rec Vicenza Italy, Feb 1994)* † Sym 4 AART ▲ 47244 [DDD] (10.97)

Y. Menuhin (cnd), Sinfonia Varsovia † Sym 6 ICC ▲ 6702292 (9.97)

P. Monteux (cnd), London SO † Sym 4; Sym 5; Sym 7 PLON (Double Decker) 2-▲ 43479 (17.97)

W. Morris (cnd), London SO *(rec May 1988)* † Sym 1 INMP ▲ 929 [DDD]

F. Reiner (cnd) *(rec 1939-46)* ("Fritz Reiner Album") † J. S. Bach:Suite 2 Fl, BWV 1067; Debussy:Images Orch; Nocturnes Orch; Prélude à l'après-midi d'un faune; R. Wagner:Meistersinger (preludes); Parsifal (preludes) GRM2 2-▲ 78711 (26.97)

F. Reiner (cnd), Pittsburgh SO † W. A. Mozart:Sym 35, K.385; Sym 40, K.550 SNYC (Masterworks Heritage) ▲ 62344 (12.97)

F. Reiner (cnd), Pittsburgh SO *(rec 1945-46)* ("Reiner, Vol. 4") † J. S. Bach:Suite 2 Fl, BWV 1067 LYS ▲ 126 (17.97)

H. Scherchen (cnd), Leipzig Radio Orch † Sym 1; Sym 4; Sym 8 TAHA 3-▲ 126 (34.97)

H. Scherchen (cnd), Vienna SO *(rec 1950-51)* ("The Early Recordings") † Sym 3; Sym 4; J. Haydn:Sym 48; Mendelssohn (-Bartholdy):Lieder ohne Worte; W. A. Mozart:Sym 29, K.201; Sym 35, K.385; Sym 36, K.425; Sym 40, K.550 TAHA 4-▲ 283 (50.97)

C. Schuricht (cnd), Swiss Romande Orch *(rec 1939-46)* ("The Schuricht Heritage, Vol. 1") † Sym 6 LYS ▲ 129 (17.97)

O. Suitner (cnd), Berlin Staatskapelle ("Symphonies, Vol. 1") † Sym 5; Sym 9 DNN (Classics Exposed) 2-▲ 17001 (16.97)

G. Szell (cnd), Cleveland Orch † Sym 5 SNYC (Essential Classics) ▲ 47651 (7.97) ▮ 47651 (3.98)

B. Walter (cnd), Columbia SO *(rec Los Angeles, CA, Jan 5-9, 1959)* † Coriolan Ov, Op. 62; Sym 1 SNYC (Bruno Walter Edition, Vol. 2) ▲ 64460 [ADD] (10.97)

D. Zinman (cnd), Tonhalle Orchestra Zurich † Sym 1 ARNO ▲ 63645 (4.97)

various artists—Larghetto † Con Vn, Vc, Pno, Op. 56; Fidelio (sels); Qt 13 Strs, Op. 130; Son 14 Pno, Op. 27/2; Son 18 Pno, Op. 31/3; Son 5 Pno, Op. 10/1; Son 8 Pno, Op. 13; Sym 6 RCAV ▮ 63328 (5.98) ▲ 63328 (11.97)

Symphony No. 3 in E♭, Op. 55, "Eroica" (1803)

A. Argenta (cnd), Spanish National Orch † Son 8 Vn; J. Brahms:Con Vn; Son 2 Vn, Op. 100; Escudero:Concerto Vasco; M. de Falla:Amor brujo; Smetana:Bartered Bride (orch sels); R. Strauss:Till Eulenspiegels lustige Streiche, Op. 28; P. Tchaikovsky:Sym 4 RTVE 4-▲ 65097 (36.97)

J. Barbirolli (cnd), BBC SO *(rec 1967)* † J. Barbirolli:Elizabethan Suite DLAB (The Barbirolli Society) ▲ 1008 (17.97)

L. Bernstein (cnd), New York PO ("Bernstein: The Royal Edition") † Sym 1 SNYC ▲ 47514 [ADD] (10.97)

L. Bernstein (cnd), Vienna PO ("Leonard Bernstein Edition") † Fidelio (ov) DEUT ▲ 31024 [ADD] (11.97)

H. Blomstedt (cnd), Dresden Staatskapelle *(rec 1975-80)* ("Blomstedt Conducts the Beethoven Symphonies Vol. 1") † Sym 1 BER ▲ 2195 (10.97)

K. Böhm (cnd), Vienna PO † Coriolan Ov, Op. 62; Egmont (ov); Geschöpfe des Prometheus (ov); Sym 9 DEUT (Double) 2-▲ 37368 (17.97)

BEETHOVEN, LUDWIG VAN (cont.)
Symphony No. 3 in E♭, Op. 55, "Eroica" (1803) (cont.)
A. Boult (cnd), London PO *(rec Walthamstow Hall London, June 1956)* † Coriolan Ov, Op. 62; Egmont (ov); Fidelio (ov); Leonore (ov 3); Sym 5; Sym 6; Sym 7 VC 3-▲ 11 [AAD] (39.97)
G. Brouwenstijn (sop), K. Meyer (alt), N. Gedda (ten), F. Guthrie (bass), A. Cluytens (cnd), Berlin PO, Choir of St. Hedwigs Cathedral, Berlin † Egmont (ov); Fidelio (ov); Geschöpfe des Prometheus (ov); Sym 1; Sym 2; Sym 4; Sym 5; Sym 6; Sym 7; Sym 8; Sym 9 RYLC 5-▲ 70373 (24.97)
S. Celibidache (cnd), Münchner Philharmoniker *(rec Philharmonie am Gasteig, München, Germany, April 12-13, 1987)* EMIC ▲ 56839 [ADD] (16.97)
A. Coates (cnd), London SO *(rec 1926)* † W. A. Mozart:Sym 41, K.551 GSE ▲ 785055 (16.97)
C. von Dohnányi (cnd), Cleveland Orch TEL ▲ 80090 [DDD] (16.97)
J. Ferencsik (cnd), Hungarian PO † Sym 8 LALI ▲ 15902 (3.97)
W. Furtwängler (cnd), Berlin PO *(rec Berlin, Dec 8, 1952)* ("Furtwängler Conducts Beethoven: The Finest Post-War Performances") † Leonore (ov 2); Sym 5 MUA 2-▲ 869 [ADD] (31.97)
W. Furtwängler (cnd), Berlin PO ("A Tribute to Furtwängler") † Sym 5; Sym 6; J. Brahms:Sym 2; A. Dvořák:Slavonic Dances (sels); Mendelssohn (-Bartholdy):Hebriden, Op. 26; F. Schubert:Sym 8; Sym 9; R. Schumann:Con Vc; R. Strauss:Till Eulenspiegels lustige Streiche, Op. 28 TAHA 4-▲ 1008 (35.97)
W. Furtwängler (cnd), Berlin PO *(rec June 20, 1950)* TAHA ▲ 1030 (17.97)
W. Furtwängler (cnd), Berlin PO *(rec 1949)* TAHA ▲ 1027 (17.97)
W. Furtwängler (cnd), Berlin PO *(rec live, Dec 7, 1952)* TAHA ▲ 1018 (m) (17.97)
W. Furtwängler (cnd), Lucerne Festival Orch *(rec Aug 26, 1953)* ("Wilhelm Furtwängler at the Lucerne Festival") † Con Vn; Con 1 Pno, Op. 15; Leonore (ov 3); Sym 7; J. Brahms:Con Vn & Vc, Op. 102; Sym 1; R. Schumann:Sym 4; R. Wagner:Lohengrin (preludes) MUA 4-▲ 1018 [ADD] (47.97)
W. Furtwängler (cnd), Vienna PO *(rec Dec 16, 1944)* ("Furtwängler Conducts during the War Years") † Coriolan Ov, Op. 62; Sym 4; Sym 5; Sym 9; E. Grieg:Con Pno, Op. 16 IN 3-▲ 1348 [ADD] (43.97)
W. Furtwängler (cnd), Vienna PO † Coriolan Ov, Op. 62; Leonore (ov 3) GRM2 ▲ 78784 (13.97)
W. Furtwängler (cnd), Vienna PO *(rec Dec 1944)* TAHA ▲ 1031 (17.97)
W. Furtwängler (cnd), Vienna PO *(rec live Vienna, Dec 16, 1944)* † Glazunov:Stenka Razin, Op. 13 RD (Furtwängler) ▲ 25001 [ADD] (16.97)
W. Furtwängler (cnd), Vienna PO *(rec 1944)* ("Wilhelm Furtwängler Wartime Recordings") † Con 4 Pno, Op. 58; Sym 5; Sym 6; Sym 9; J. Brahms:Con 2 Pno, Op. 83; Sym 4; Vars on a Theme by Haydn; R. Strauss:Songs; R. Wagner:Meistersinger (preludes); Tristan und Isolde (prelude & liebestod) TAHA 6-▲ 1034 (50.97)
J. E. Gardiner (cnd), Orch Révolutionnaire et Romantique ("Beethoven the Revolutionary") † Sym 5 PARC ▲ 45944 [DDD] (16.97)
C. M. Giulini (cnd), Los Angeles PO *(rec Shrine Auditorium, Los Angeles, CA, Nov 1978)* † R. Schumann:Manfred Ov, Op. 115 DEUT (The Originals) ▲ 47444 [ADD/DDD] (11.97)
M. Halász (cnd), Czech RSO *(rec Czechoslovak Radio Concert Hall Bratislava, Mar 1988)* ("Famous Symphonies: Beethoven, Tchaikovsky, Brahms, Schubert") † Sym 8; J. Brahms:Academic Festival Ov, Op. 80; Sym 4; Tragic Ov, Op. 81; F. Schubert:Sym 9; P. Tchaikovsky:Francesca da Rimini, Op. 32; Sym 6 NXIN 4-▲ 504012 [DDD] (19.97)
N. Harnoncourt (cnd), CO of Europe † Sym 1 TELC ▲ 75708 (16.97)
J. Israelievitch (vn), G. Herbig (cnd), Toronto SO *(rec Sept 21-22, 1990)* † Romances Vn ANAL ▲ 28201
E. Jochum (cnd), Berlin PO *(rec June 9, 1937)* MTAL ▲ 48065 (6.97)
H. von Karajan (cnd), Berlin PO † Egmont (ov) DEUT ▲ 39002 [DDD] (16.97)
H. von Karajan (cnd), Prussian State Orch *(rec 1944)* KSCH ▲ 315092 [ADD] (16.97)
H. von Karajan (cnd), Prussian State Orch ("The Young Karajan, Vol. 6: The First Recordings") † W. A. Mozart:Sym 40, K.550 GRM2 ▲ 78670 (13.97)
H. von Karajan (cnd), Prussian State Orch *(rec 1944)* † Smetana:Moldau HCO ▲ 37059 (7.97)
R. Kempe (cnd) † Sym 1; Sym 5 CSER (Seraphim) 2-▲ 68518 (6.97)
O. Klemperer (cnd), Philharmonia Orch *(rec London, England, 1956-59)* † Grosse Fuge Str Qt, Op. 133 EMIC (Klemperer Legacy) ▲ 66793 [ADD] (11.97)
H. Knappertsbusch (cnd), Berlin PO *(rec 1943)* ENT (Sirio) ▲ 530028 (13.97)
H. Knappertsbusch (cnd), Munich PO *(rec live, 1953)* TAHA ▲ 294 (17.97)
Z. Košler (cnd), Slovak PO PC ▲ 265094 [DDD] (2.97)
S. Koussevitzky (cnd), Boston SO † Missa Solemnis, Op. 123 PHS 2-▲ 9282 (33.97)
S. Koussevitzky (cnd), London PO *(rec Sept 7, 1934)* ("Koussevitzky: The Complete HMV Recordings") † Sym 5; J. Haydn:Sym 88; W. A. Mozart:Sym 40, K.550; Sibelius:Sym 7 BCS 2-▲ 29 [ADD] (31.97)
J. Krips (cnd), London SO † Sym 8 EVC ▲ 9103 (13.97)
R. Leibowitz (cnd), Royal PO *(rec 1961)* † Sym 1 CHSK ▲ 74 [ADD] (16.97)
J. Levine (cnd), Metropolitan Opera Orch DEUT ▲ 39862 [DDD] (16.97)
P. Maag (cnd), Padova e Veneto CO *(rec Padova Italy, July 13-16, 1994)* † Sym 1 AART ▲ 47246 [DDD] (10.97)
C. Mackerras (cnd), Royal Liverpool PO † Sym 1 CFP ▲ 72846 (11.97)
W. Mengelberg (cnd), New York Philharmonic SO *(rec 1930)* † R. Wagner:Tannhäuser (ov) ENT (Sirio) ▲ 530031 (13.97)
W. Mengelberg (cnd), New York PO ("Willem Mengelberg: A Portrait, 1926-41") † Egmont (ov); Leonore (ov 3); J. S. Bach:Suite 2 Fl, BWV 1067; J. Brahms:Academic Festival Ov, Op. 80; Liszt:Préludes, S.97; P. Tchaikovsky:Ov 1812, Op. 49; Sym 6; R. Wagner:Lohengrin (preludes); Tannhäuser (ov); C. M. von Weber:Freischütz (ov); Oberon (ov) GRM2 3-▲ 78637 (39.97)
P. Monteux (cnd), Vienna PO † Sym 1; Sym 6; Sym 8 PLON (Double Decker) 2-▲ 40627 (17.97)
W. Morris (cnd), London SO † Coriolan Ov, Op. 62 INMP (LSO Classic Masterpieces) ▲ 900 [DDD] (9.97)
K. Münchinger (cnd), Stuttgart RSO INTC (Classical Creations) ▲ 820573 (9.97)
A. Rahbari (cnd), Brussels BRTN PO *(rec Feb 1990)* † Sym 8 NXIN ▲ 550407 [DDD] (5.97)
J. Rescigno (cnd), Orch Métropolitain † Egmont (sels) FL ▲ 23105 [DDD] (16.97)
V. D. Sabata (cnd), London PO † Sym 6; J. Brahms:Sym 4; R. Wagner:Tristan und Isolde (prelude & liebestod) 78'S 2-▲ 78542 (26.97)
J. Savall (cnd), Concert des Nations † Coriolan Ov, Op. 62 FONT ▲ 8557 [DDD] (18.97)
H. Scherchen (cnd), Vienna SO *(rec 1950-51)* ("The Early Recordings") † Sym 2; Sym 4; J. Haydn:Sym 48; Mendelssohn (-Bartholdy):Lieder ohne Worte; W. A. Mozart:Sym 29, K.201; Sym 35, K.385; Sym 36, K.425; Sym 40, K.550 TAHA 4-▲ 283 (50.97)
C. Schuricht (cnd), Berlin PO *(rec 1941)* ("Schuricht Conducts Beethoven") † Sym 5; Sym 6; Sym 7 IN 2-▲ 1404 (m) [ADD] (29.97)
C. Schuricht (cnd), Berlin Staatskapelle *(rec 1937-41)* ("The Schuricht Heritage, Vol. 2") LYS ▲ 130 (17.97)
C. Schuricht (cnd), Paris Conservatory Société des Concerts Orch *(rec 1941)* ("Schuricht Beethoven Recordings, Vol. 3") † Sym 5 GRM2 ▲ 78897 (11.97)
G. Solti (cnd), Chicago SO † Egmont (ov) PLON ▲ 30087 [DDD] (16.97)
W. Steinberg (cnd), Pittsburgh SO *(rec 1954-55)* † Sym 8 EMIC ▲ 67098 (m) [ADD] (11.97)
G. Szell (cnd), Cleveland Orch † Sym 8 SNYC (Essential Classics) ▲ 46328 [ADD] (7.97) ▮ 46328 [ADD] (3.98)
G. Szell (cnd), Czech PO † Egmont (ov) SNYC (Festspiel Dokumente: Salzburger Festspiele) ▲ 68447 (10.97)
P. Tiboris (cnd), Bohuslav Martinů PO *(rec Brno Czech Republic, Nov 28, 1994)* ("All Beethoven") † Coriolan Ov, Op. 62; Leonore (ov 2) ELY ▲ 702 [DDD] (16.97)
A. Titov (cnd), St. Petersburg Conservatory CO † Egmont (ov); Ruinen von Athen (ov) SNYC ▲ 57219 [DDD] (4.97)
A. Toscanini (cnd), NBC SO ("The Toscanini Collection, Vol. 23") † Sym 8 RCAV (Gold Seal) ▲ 60269 (11.97)
A. Toscanini (cnd), NBC SO ("The Toscanini Collection, Vol. 29") † W. A. Mozart:Sym 40, K.550 RCAV (Gold Seal) ▲ 60271 [ADD] (11.97)
A. Toscanini (cnd), NBC SO *(rec 1939)* † Sym 5 GRM2 ▲ 78505 [ADD] (13.97)
A. Toscanini (cnd), NBC SO † Sym 5 ENT (Sirio) ▲ 53001 (13.97)
B. Walter (cnd) ("Bruno Walter: First American Recordings") † G. Mahler:Lieder und Gesänge aus der Jugendzeit; Sym 5 GRM2 2-▲ 78838 (26.97)
B. Walter (cnd), Columbia SO *(rec Los Angeles, CA, Jan 20-25, 1958)* † Sym 8 SNYC (Bruno Walter Edition, Vol. 2) ▲ 64461 [ADD] (10.97)
F. V. Weingartner (cnd), Vienna PO *(rec May 1936)* † Sym 8 PRE ▲ 90113 [ADD] (16.97)
D. Zinman (cnd), Zurich Tonhalle Orch † Sym 4 ARNO ▲ 59214 (4.97)
Symphony No. 4 in B♭, Op. 60 (1806)
H. Abendroth (cnd), Leipzig RSO [rehearsal sels] ("The Art of Hermann Abendroth 1927-41") † Sym 5; J. Brahms:Sym 1; Sym 4; G. F. Handel:Concerti grossi, Op. 6; W. A. Mozart:Serenade 6 Orch, K.239; Serenata notturna, K.239 TAHA 2-▲ 102 (34.97)
J. Barbirolli (cnd), New York PO † Coriolan Ov, Op. 62; W. A. Mozart:Sym 33, K.319 DLAB ▲ 1011 (17.97)
T. Beecham (cnd), London PO ("Beecham & London PO, 1944-45, Vol. 2") † W. A. Mozart:Entführung aus dem Serail (sels); F. Schubert:Sym 6 BCS ▲ 42 (16.97)
L. Bernstein (cnd), New York PO † Egmont (ov); Sym 5 SNYC (Bernstein Century) ▲ 63079 (11.97)
H. Blomstedt (cnd), Dresden Staatskapelle *(rec 1975-80)* ("Blomstedt Conducts the Beethoven Symphonies, Vol. 2") † Sym 2 BER ▲ 2196 (10.97)

BEETHOVEN, LUDWIG VAN (cont.)
Symphony No. 4 in B♭, Op. 60 (1806) (cont.)
K. Böhm (cnd), Vienna PO † Sym 1; Sym 2; Sym 5 DEUT (Double) 2-▲ 39681 (17.97)
G. Brouwenstijn (sop), K. Meyer (alt), N. Gedda (ten), F. Guthrie (bass), A. Cluytens (cnd), Berlin PO, Choir of St. Hedwigs Cathedral, Berlin † Egmont (ov); Fidelio (ov); Geschöpfe des Prometheus (ov); Sym 1; Sym 2; Sym 3; Sym 5; Sym 6; Sym 7; Sym 8; Sym 9 RYLC 5-▲ 70373 (24.97)
J. Caeyers (cnd), Beethoven Academy *(rec 1995)* † Sym 1 HMA ▲ 1901573 (9.97)
S. Celibidache (cnd), Munich PO *(rec live Munich, Mar 19, 1995)* † Sym 5 EMIC (Celibidache Edition) ▲ 56521 [DDD] (16.97)
S. Celibidache (cnd), Münchner Philharmoniker *(rec Philharmonie am Gasteig, München, Germany, April 12-13, 1987)* † Sym 2 EMIC ▲ 56838 [DDD] (16.97)
C. von Dohnányi (cnd), Cleveland Orch † Sym 8 TEL ▲ 80198 [DDD] (16.97)
B. Drahos (cnd), Nicolaus Esterházy Sinfonia *(rec Italian Institute Budapest, Oct 1995)* † Sym 7 NXIN ▲ 8553477 [DDD] (5.97)
R. Edlinger (cnd), Zagreb PO *(rec Sept 1988)* † Sym 7 NXIN ▲ 550180 [DDD] (5.97)
J. Ferencsik (cnd), Hungarian PO † Sym 5 LALI ▲ 15901 (3.97)
W. Furtwängler (cnd), Berlin PO *(rec June 30, 1943)* ("Furtwängler Conducts during the War Years") † Coriolan Ov, Op. 62; Sym 3; Sym 5; Sym 9; E. Grieg:Con Pno, Op. 16 IN 3-▲ 1348 [ADD] (43.97)
W. Furtwängler (cnd), Berlin PO † Coriolan Ov, Op. 62; Sym 5 ENT (Sirio) ▲ 530016 (13.97)
W. Furtwängler (cnd), Vienna PO *(rec Sept 4, 1953)* † Egmont (ov); Sym 1 MUA ▲ 792 [AAD] (16.97)
C. M. Giulini (cnd), La Scala Orch † Sym 5 SNYC ▲ 58921 (16.97)
N. Harnoncourt (cnd), CO of Europe † Sym 7 TELC ▲ 75714 (16.97)
H. Harty (cnd), Hallé Orch *(rec 1927)* † P. Tchaikovsky:Con 1 Pno, Op. 23 PHG ▲ 5015 (14.97)
G. Herbig (cnd), BBC PO † Sym 5 INMP (BBC Radio Classics) ▲ 9123 (13.97)
H. von Karajan (cnd), Berlin PO † Sym 7 DEUT ▲ 39003 (16.97)
H. Kegel (cnd), Dresden PO † Sym 5; Sym 6; Sym 8; Sym 9 CAPO ▲ 10453 [DDD] (11.97)
O. Klemperer (cnd), Bavarian RSO *(rec live, Munich, Germany, 1969)* † Sym 5 EMIC (Klemperer Legacy) ▲ 66865 [ADD] (11.97)
O. Klemperer (cnd), Philharmonia Orch *(rec London, England, 1957)* † Sym 7 EMIC (Klemperer Legacy) ▲ 66795 [ADD] (11.97)
J. Krips (cnd), London SO † Sym 7 EVC ▲ 9102 (13.97)
R. Leibowitz (cnd), Royal PO *(rec May 1961)* † Sym 7 CHSK ▲ 81 [ADD] (16.97)
P. Maag (cnd), Padova e Veneto CO *(rec Vicenza Italy, Feb 1994)* † Sym 2 AART ▲ 47244 [DDD] (10.97)
C. Mackerras (cnd), Royal Liverpool PO † Sym 6 CFP ▲ 72848 (11.97)
P. Monteux (cnd), London SO † Sym 2; Sym 5; Sym 7 PLON (Double Decker) 2-▲ 43479 (17.97)
P. Monteux (cnd), San Francisco SO ("Vol 1") † Ruinen von Athen (ov); Sym 8; J. S. Bach:Passacaglia & Fugue Org, BWV 582 RCAV (Gold Seal; Pierre Monteux Edition) ▲ 61892 (11.97)
E. Mravinsky (cnd), Leningrad PO *(rec 1972-74)* † Glazunov:Raymonda (sels); Liadov:Baba Yaga, Op. 56; W. A. Mozart:Sym 40, K.550; D. Shostakovich:Sym 5; Sym 6 RUS (The Mravinsky Collection) ▲ 10901 [AAD] (12.97)
E. Mravinsky (cnd), Leningrad PO ("Mravinsky in Prague") † S. Prokofiev:Sym 6 PRAG ▲ 256004 (18.97)
C. Munch (cnd), French National Orch *(rec Stockholm, Sweden, Aug 1964)* ("Charles Munch Edition, Vol. 1") † Sym 7; Weihe des Hauses (ov), Op. 124 VAL ▲ 4825 [ADD] (12.97)
H. Scherchen (cnd), Toronto SO † Sym 1; Sym 2; Sym 8 TAHA 3-▲ 126 (34.97)
H. Scherchen (cnd), Vienna SO *(rec 1950-51)* ("The Early Recordings") † Sym 2; Sym 3; J. Haydn:Sym 48; Mendelssohn (-Bartholdy):Lieder ohne Worte; W. A. Mozart:Sym 29, K.201; Sym 35, K.385; Sym 36, K.425; Sym 40, K.550 TAHA 4-▲ 283 (50.97)
C. Schuricht (cnd), Berlin Municipal Orch *(rec 1941-42)* † Sym 1 IN ▲ 1419 [ADD] (15.97)
G. Solti (cnd), Chicago SO † Sym 5 PLON ▲ 21580 [DDD] (16.97)
G. Szell (cnd), Cleveland Orch † König Stephen (ov); Sym 7 SNYC (Essential Classics) ▲ 48158 (7.97) ▮ 48158 (3.98)
A. Toscanini (cnd), BBC SO *(rec 1939)* ("Toscanini in London, 1935-39, Vol. 6") † Geschöpfe des Prometheus (ov); Sym 7 GRM2 ▲ 78616 (13.97)
A. Toscanini (cnd), BBC SO *(rec 1937-39)* † Leonore; Sym 1; Sym 6; J. Brahms:Tragic Ov, Op. 81; W. A. Mozart:Zauberflöte (sels) ENT (Document) 2-▲ 921 [ADD] (26.97)
A. Toscanini (cnd), BBC SO *(rec 1937-39)* † Leonore (ov 1), Op. 138; Sym 6 ARKA (The 78's) ▲ 78521 (13.97)
A. Toscanini (cnd), NBC SO *(rec 1939)* ("Toscanini First Cycle of Beethoven's Complete Symphonies, Vol. 2") † Leonore (ov 1), Op. 138; Sym 7 GRM2 ▲ 78514 [ADD] (13.97)
B. Walter (cnd), Columbia SO *(rec Los Angeles, CA, Feb 8-10, 1958)* † Sym 6 SNYC (Bruno Walter Edition, Vol. 2) ▲ 64462 [ADD] (10.97)
D. Zinman (cnd), Zurich Tonhalle Orch † Sym 3 ARNO ▲ 59214 (4.97)
Symphony No. 5 in c, Op. 67 (1807-08)
H. Abendroth (cnd), Berlin PO ("The Art of Hermann Abendroth 1927-41") † Sym 4; J. Brahms:Sym 1; Sym 4; G. F. Handel:Concerti grossi, Op. 6; W. A. Mozart:Serenade 6 Orch, K.239; Serenata notturna, K.239 TAHA 2-▲ 102 (34.97)
O. Ackermann (cnd), Zurich Tonhalle Orch † Sym 7; A. Dvořák:Con Vc; Sym 9 STRV 2-▲ 12324 [ADD] (25.97)
K. Ančerl (cnd), Czech PO † Sym 1 SUR (Czech Philharmonic) ▲ 111937 [AAD]
V. Ashkenazy (cnd), Philharmonia Orch *(rec Kingsway Hall London, Mar 1981)* † Sym 7 PENG (Penguin Music Classics) ▲ 460603 (11.97)
J. Barbirolli (cnd), Hallé Orch † Con 5 Pno, Op. 73; Egmont (ov); Leonore (ov 3); Sym 1; Sym 8 DLAB (The Barbirolli Society) ▲ 1014 (17.97)
L. Bernstein (cnd), New York PO † F. Schubert:Sym 8 SNYC ▮ 36719 (3.98)
L. Bernstein (cnd), New York PO SNYC ▲ 47645 (7.97)
L. Bernstein (cnd), New York PO † Egmont (ov); Sym 4 SNYC (Bernstein Century) ▲ 63079 (11.97)
L. Bernstein (cnd), Vienna PO ("Leonard Bernstein Edition") † Leonore (ov 3) DEUT ▲ 31049 [ADD] (11.97)
H. Blomstedt (cnd), Dresden Staatskapelle *(rec 1975-80)* ("Blomstedt Conducts the Beethoven Symphonies, Vol. 3") † Sym 6 BER ▲ 2197 (10.97)
K. Böhm (cnd), Vienna PO † Sym 1; Sym 2; Sym 4 DEUT (Double) 2-▲ 39681 (17.97)
A. Boult (cnd), London PO *(rec Walthamstow Hall London, June 1956)* † Coriolan Ov, Op. 62; Egmont (ov); Fidelio (ov); Leonore (ov 3); Sym 3; Sym 6; Sym 7 VC 3-▲ 11 [AAD] (39.97)
G. Brouwenstijn (sop), K. Meyer (alt), N. Gedda (ten), F. Guthrie (bass), A. Cluytens (cnd), Berlin PO, Choir of St. Hedwigs Cathedral, Berlin † Egmont (ov); Fidelio (ov); Geschöpfe des Prometheus (ov); Sym 1; Sym 2; Sym 3; Sym 4; Sym 6; Sym 7; Sym 8; Sym 9 RYLC 5-▲ 70373 (24.97)
S. Celibidache (cnd), Munich PO *(rec live Munich, May 28-31, 1992)* † Sym 4 EMIC (Celibidache Edition) ▲ 56521 [DDD] (16.97)
C. von Dohnányi (cnd), Cleveland Orch † Sym 7 TEL ▲ 80163 [DDD] (16.97)
A. Doráti (cnd), London SO † Geschöpfe des Prometheus (ov); Sym 6 MRCR ▲ 434375 (11.97)
B. Drahos (cnd), Nicolaus Esterházy Sinfonia *(rec Italian Institute Budapest, June 9-16, 1995)* † Sym 2 NXIN ▲ 8553476 [DDD] (5.97)
B. Drahos (cnd), Nicolaus Esterházy Sinfonia *(rec Budapest, June, 1995)* † Sym 6 NXIN ▲ 8554061 [DDD] (5.97)
R. Edlinger (cnd), Zagreb PO *(rec Sept 1988)* † Sym 2 NXIN ▲ 550177 [DDD] (5.97)
R. Edlinger (cnd), Zagreb PO *(rec Sept 1988)* † F. Schubert:Sym 8 NXIN ▲ 550289 [DDD] (5.97)
J. Ferencsik (cnd), Hungarian PO † Sym 4 LALI ▲ 15901 (3.97)
W. Furtwängler (cnd), Berlin PO *(rec Berlin, May 23, 1954)* ("Furtwängler Conducts Beethoven: The Finest Post-War Performances") † Leonore (ov 2); Sym 3 MUA 2-▲ 869 [ADD] (31.97)
W. Furtwängler (cnd), Berlin PO *(rec June 30, 1943)* ("Furtwängler Conducts during the War Years") † Coriolan Ov, Op. 62; Sym 3; Sym 4; Sym 9; E. Grieg:Con Pno, Op. 16 IN 3-▲ 1348 [ADD] (43.97)
W. Furtwängler (cnd), Berlin PO ("A Tribute to Furtwängler") † Sym 3; Sym 6; J. Brahms:Sym 2; A. Dvořák:Slavonic Dances (sels); Mendelssohn (-Bartholdy):Hebriden, Op. 26; F. Schubert:Sym 8; Sym 9; R. Schumann:Con Vc; R. Strauss:Till Eulenspiegels lustige Streiche, Op. 28 TAHA 4-▲ 1008 (35.97)
W. Furtwängler (cnd), Berlin PO † Coriolan Ov, Op. 62; Sym 4 ENT (Sirio) ▲ 530016 (13.97)
W. Furtwängler (cnd), Berlin PO *(rec 1943)* ("Wilhelm Furtwängler Wartime Recordings") † Con 4 Pno, Op. 58; Sym 3; Sym 6; Sym 9; J. Brahms:Con 2 Pno, Op. 83; Sym 4; Vars on a Theme by Haydn; R. Strauss:Songs; R. Wagner:Meistersinger (preludes); Tristan und Isolde (prelude & liebestod) TAHA 6-▲ 1034 (50.97)
W. Furtwängler (cnd), Berlin PO *(rec Paris, France, May 4, 1954)* ("Furtwängler Concert in Paris") † J. Brahms:Vars on a Theme by Haydn; C. M. von Weber:Euryanthe (ov) TAHA ▲ 1023 (34.97)
W. Furtwängler (cnd), Vienna PO *(rec 1952)* † Sym 7 EMIC (Great Recordings of the Century) ▲ 69803 [ADD] (11.97)
W. Furtwängler (cnd), Vienna PO *(rec live Copenhagen, Oct 1, 1950)* † J. Brahms:Alto Rhap, Op. 53 DANR ▲ 301
J. E. Gardiner (cnd), Orch Révolutionnaire et Romantique ("Beethoven the Revolutionary") † Sym 3 PARC ▲ 45944 [DDD] (16.97)
C. M. Giulini (cnd), La Scala Orch † Sym 4 SNYC ▲ 58921 (16.97)

▲ = CD ♦ = Enhanced CD △ = MD ▮ = Cassette Tape ▯ = DCC

BEETHOVEN, LUDWIG VAN (cont.)

Symphony No. 5 in c, Op. 67 (1807-08) (cont.)

C. M. Giulini (cnd), Los Angeles PO † R. Schumann:Sym 3 DEUT (Masters) ▲ 45502 [DDD] (9.97)

G. Gould (pno) [Liszt's solo pno trans] *(rec 1967)* † Sym 6 SNYC (Glenn Gould Edition) ▲ 52636 [ADD] (16.97)

N. Harnoncourt (cnd), CO of Europe † Sym 2 TELC ▲ 75712 (16.97)

G. Herbig (cnd), BBC PO † Sym 4 INMP (BBC Radio Classics) ▲ 9123 (13.97)

H. von Karajan (cnd), Berlin PO—Allegro con brio ("The Complete Beethoven Edition Compactotheque") † Chor auf die verbundeten Fürsten, WoO 95; Glorreiche Augenblick, Op. 136; Leonore (sels); Ländler Pno, WoO 11; Marches Military Band, WoO 18-20; Qt Strs in F, Hess 34; Qt 11 Strs, Op. 95; Qt 16 Strs, Op. 135; Romance Fl, Bn & Pno, Hess 13; Scottish Songs (25), Op. 108; Serenade Str Trio, Op. 8; Son 3 Vc, Op. 69; Son 5 Vn, Op. 24; Son 8 Pno, Op. 13; Spt in E♭, Op. 20; Trio 5 Pno, Op. 70/2; Triumphal March, WoO 2a; Zärtliche Leibe, WoO 123 DEUT ▲ 453811 [ADD/DDD] (11.97)

H. von Karajan (cnd), Berlin PO † Sym 6 DEUT ▲ 39004 (16.97)

H. von Karajan (cnd), Vienna PO *(rec 1948)* † P. Tchaikovsky:Sym 6 GRM2 (Records of the Century) ▲ 78792 (13.97)

H. Kegel (cnd), Dresden PO † Sym 4; Sym 6; Sym 8; Sym 9 CAPO ▲ 10453 [DDD] (11.97)

J. Keilberth (cnd) † Egmont (ov); Leonore (ov 3); Sym 6; Sym 7 TELC (Ultima) 2-▲ 18946 (16.97)

R. Kempe (cnd) † Sym 1; Sym 3 CSER (Seraphim) 2-▲ 68518 (6.97)

C. Kleiber (cnd), Vienna PO † Sym 7 DEUT (The Originals) ▲ 47400 (11.97)

O. Klemperer (cnd), Bavarian RSO *(rec live, Munich, Germany, 1969)* † Sym 4 EMIC (Klemperer Legacy) ▲ 66865 [ADD] (11.97)

O. Klemperer (cnd), Philharmonia Orch *(rec London, England, 1959)* † Sym 2 EMIC (Klemperer Legacy) ▲ 66794 [ADD] (11.97)

O. Klemperer (cnd), Vienna SO *(rec Vienna, 1950)* † Missa Solemnis, Op. 123; Sym 6 VB2 2-▲ 5527 (9.97)

S. Koussevitzky (cnd), London PO *(rec Sept 3-4, 1934)* ("Koussevitzky: The Complete HMV Recordings") † Sym 3; J. Haydn:Sym 88; W. A. Mozart:Sym 40, K.550; Sibelius:Sym 7 BCS 2-▲ 29 [ADD] (31.97)

J. Krips (cnd), London SO † Sym 1 EVC ▲ 9100 (13.97)

R. Leibowitz (cnd), Royal PO *(rec 1961)* † Leonore (ov 3); Sym 2 CHSK ▲ 17 (16.97)

P. Maag (cnd), Padova e Veneto CO *(rec Padova Italy, Feb 5-6, 1995)* † Sym 6 AART ▲ 47247 [DDD] (10.97)

L. Maazel (cnd), Vienna PO † F. Schubert:Sym 8 SNYC ▲ 44783 [DDD] (10.97)

K. Masur (cnd), New York PO † Egmont; Ovs TELC ▲ 77313 (16.97)

W. Mengelberg (cnd), (Royal) Concertgebouw Orch *(rec 1930-38)* † Leonore (ov 3); Sym 8 MTAL ▲ 48056 (6.97)

P. Monteux (cnd), London SO † Sym 2; Sym 4; Sym 7 PLON (Double Decker) 2-▲ 43479 (17.97)

R. Muti (cnd), Philadelphia Orch † Sym 1 EMIC (Red Line) ▲ 69782 (6.97)

A. Nanut (cnd), Ljubljana RSO † Con 1 Pno, Op. 15 PC ▲ 265095 [DDD] (2.97)

A. Nikisch (cnd), Berlin PO † Egmont (ov); Berlioz:Carnaval romain, Op. 9; Liszt:Hungarian Rhaps, S.244; W. A. Mozart:Nozze di Figaro, K.492 SYMP ▲ 1087

E. Ormandy (cnd), Philadelphia Orch † Sym 6; Sym 7; Sym 8 SNYC (Essential Classics Take 2) 2-▲ 63266 (14.97)

S. Ozawa (cnd), Boston SO † Egmont (ov) TEL ▲ 80060 [DDD] (16.97)

F. Reiner (cnd), Chicago SO † Coriolan Ov, Op. 62; Fidelio (ov); F. Schubert:Sym 8 RCAV (Red Seal) ▲ 5403 (16.97)

F. Reiner (cnd), Chicago SO *(rec 1955-59)* † Coriolan Ov, Op. 62; Fidelio (ov); Sym 7 RCAV (Living Stereo) ▲ 68976 (11.97)

A. Rodzinski (cnd), New York PO *(rec live, 1944-45)* † Con Vn; Egmont (ov) IN ▲ 1358 (15.97)

K. Sanderling (cnd), Berlin SO ("The World of Symphony, Vol. 5: Ludwig van Beethoven") † Sym 6 LALI ▲ 15825 [DDD] (3.97)

G. Schuller (cnd) *(rec Manhattan School of Music Myers Recording Studio, Sept 15-16, 1995)* ("Gunther Schuller-Conductor") † J. Brahms:Sym 1 GMR ▲ 2051 (16.97)

C. Schuricht (cnd), Berlin PO *(rec 1946)* ("Schuricht Beethoven Recordings, Vol. 3") † Sym 3 GRM2 ▲ 78897 (11.97)

C. Schuricht (cnd), Paris Conservatory Société des Concerts Orch *(rec 1946)* ("Schuricht Conducts Beethoven") † Sym 3; Sym 6; Sym 7 IN 2-▲ 1404 (m) [ADD] (29.97)

G. Schwarz (cnd), London SO † Con 4 Pno, Op. 58 DLS ▲ 3027 [DDD] (14.97)

G. Solti (cnd), Chicago SO † Sym 4 PLON ▲ 21580 [DDD] (16.97)

W. Steinberg (cnd), Pittsburgh SO † Sym 6 EMIC (Legacy) ▲ 66553 (11.97)

O. Suitner (cnd), Berlin Staatskapelle ("Symphonies, Vol. 1") † Sym 2; Sym 9 DNN (Classics Exposed) 2-▲ 17001 (16.97)

G. Szell (cnd), Cleveland Orch—Allegro con brio *(rec Severance Hall, OH, Oct 1963)* † Bagatelle Pno in a, WoO 59; Con Vn; Con 5 Pno, Op. 73; Fidelio (ov); Minuets (6) Orch, WoO 10; Qt 9 Strs, Op. 59/3; Ruinen von Athen (sels); Son 14 Pno, Op. 27/2; Son 8 Pno, Op. 13; Sym 9 SNYC ▲ 64093 (m) [ADD] (7.97)

G. Szell (cnd), Cleveland Orch † Sym 2 SNYC (Essential Classics) ▲ 47651 (7.97) ▮ 47651 (3.98)

G. Szell (cnd), Vienna PO *(rec Salzburg Festival, Aug 24, 1969)* † Con 3 Pno, Op. 37; Egmont (ov) ORFE (Festspiel Dokumente) ▲ 484981 (16.97)

C. Thielemann (cnd), Philharmonia Orch *(rec London, July 1996)* † Sym 7 PPHI ▲ 449981 [DDD] (16.97)

A. Titov (cnd), St. Petersburg New Philharmony Orch † Coriolan Ov, Op. 62; Geschöpfe des Prometheus (ov); Leonore (ov 2) SNYC ▲ 57220 [DDD] (4.97)

A. Toscanini (cnd), NBC SO ("The Toscanini Collection, Vol. 25") † Egmont (ov); Spt in E♭, Op. 20 RCAV (Gold Seal) ▲ 60270 (11.97)

A. Toscanini (cnd), NBC SO *(rec 1939)* † Sym 3 GRM2 ▲ 78505 [ADD] (13.97)

A. Toscanini (cnd), NBC SO † Sym 3 ENT (Sirio) ▲ 53001 (13.97)

A. Toscanini (cnd), New York Philharmonic SO *(rec Apr 1936)* † Sym 7 MTAL ▲ 48034 (6.97)

B. Walter (cnd), Columbia SO *(rec Los Angeles, CA, Jan 27-30, 1958)* † Sym 7 SNYC (Bruno Walter Edition, Vol. 2) ▲ 64463 [ADD] (10.97)

B. Zander (cnd), Philharmonia Orch *(rec Hampstead, London, England, Oct 1998)* † Sym 7 TEL 2-▲ 80471 [DDD] (16.97)

D. Zinman (cnd), Zurich Tonhalle Orch *(rec 1997)* † Sym 6 ARNO ▲ 49695 [DDD] (4.97)

Symphony No. 6 in F, Op. 68, "Pastorale" (1808)

C. Abbado (cnd), Vienna PO † Sym 8 DEUT (Masters) ▲ 45542 (9.97)

H. Adolph (cnd), South German PO † Sym 8 PC ▲ 265057 [DDD] (2.97)

K. Ančerl (cnd), Toronto SO ("Karl Ančerl in Toronto") † Sym 8; Berlioz:Troyens; Mendelssohn (-Bartholdy):Sym 5; W. A. Mozart:Kleine Nachtmusik, K.525; R. Schumann:Sym 4; Smetana:Moldau TAHA 3-▲ 121 (50.97)

L. Bernstein (cnd), New York PO *(rec New York, May 13, 1963)* † König Stephen (ov); Sym 8 SNYC (Bernstein Century) ▲ 60557 [ADD] (10.97)

H. Blomstedt (cnd), Dresden Staatskapelle *(rec 1975-80)* ("Blomstedt Conducts the Beethoven Symphonies, Vol. 3") † Sym 5 BER ▲ 2197 (10.97)

K. Böhm (cnd), Vienna PO † Fidelio (ov); Leonore (ov 3); Sym 7; Sym 8 DEUT (Double) 2-▲ 37928 (17.97)

K. Böhm (cnd), Vienna PO *(rec Vienna, Austria, May 1971)* † F. Schubert:Sym 5 DEUT ▲ 47433 [ADD] (11.97)

A. Boult (cnd), London PO *(rec Walthamstow Hall London, June 1956)* † Coriolan Ov, Op. 62; Egmont (ov); Fidelio (ov); Leonore (ov 3); Sym 3; Sym 5; Sym 7 VC 3-▲ 11 [AAD] (39.97)

G. Brouwenstijn (sop), K. Meyer (alt), N. Gedda (ten), F. Guthrie (bass), A. Cluytens (cnd), Berlin PO, Choir of St. Hedwigs Cathedral, Berlin † Egmont (ov); Fidelio (ov); Geschöpfe des Prometheus (ov); Sym 1; Sym 2; Sym 3; Sym 4; Sym 5; Sym 7; Sym 8; Sym 9 RYLC 5-▲ 70373 (24.97)

S. Celibidache (cnd), Münchner Philharmoniker *(rec live, Philharmonie am Gasteig, München, Germany, Jan 25, 1993)* † Leonore (ov 3) EMIC ▲ 56840 [DDD] (16.97)

C. von Dohnányi (cnd), Cleveland Orch † Leonore (ov 3) TEL ▲ 80145 [DDD] (16.97)

A. Doráti (cnd), London SO † Geschöpfe des Prometheus (ov); Sym 5 MRCR ▲ 434375 (11.97)

B. Drahos (cnd), Nicolaus Esterházy Sinfonia *(rec Italian Institute Budapest, June 17-20, 1995)* † Sym 1 NXIN ▲ 553474 [DDD] (5.97)

B. Drahos (cnd), Nicolaus Esterházy Sinfonia *(rec Budapest, June, 1995)* † Sym 5 NXIN ▲ 8554061 [DDD] (5.97)

J. Ferencsik (cnd), Hungarian PO † Sym 2 LALI ▲ 15903 (3.97)

W. Furtwängler (cnd), Berlin PO ("Furtwängler Historical Archives 1942-45") † Coriolan Ov, Op. 62; Sym 9; J. Brahms:Con 2 Pno, Op. 83; Sym 1; A. Bruckner:Sym 6; Sym 7; R. Wagner:Tristan und Isolde (prelude & liebestod) TAHA 4-▲ 1004

W. Furtwängler (cnd), Berlin PO ("A Tribute to Furtwängler") † Sym 3; Sym 5; J. Brahms:Sym 2; A. Dvořák:Slavonic Dances (sels); Mendelssohn (-Bartholdy):Hebriden, Op. 26; F. Schubert:Sym 8; Sym 9; R. Schumann:Con Vc; R. Strauss:Till Eulenspiegels lustige Streiche, Op. 28 TAHA 4-▲ 1008 (35.97)

W. Furtwängler (cnd), Berlin PO ("Wilhelm Furtwängler Conducts the Berlin Philharmonic during the 2nd World War") † R. Strauss:Don Juan, Op. 20 GRM2 ▲ 78551 (13.97)

W. Furtwängler (cnd), Berlin PO ("Wilhelm Furtwängler Conducts") † R. Strauss:Don Juan, Op. 20 ENT (Sirio) ▲ 530011 (13.97)

BEETHOVEN, LUDWIG VAN (cont.)

Symphony No. 6 in F, Op. 68, "Pastorale" (1808) (cont.)

W. Furtwängler (cnd), Berlin PO *(rec live, Berlin, Germany, Mar 19, 1944)* ("Furtwängler Conducts Beethoven, Weber & Ravel") † M. Ravel:Daphnis et Chloé (suite 2); C. M. von Weber:Freischütz (ov) RD ▲ 25003 [ADD] (16.97)

W. Furtwängler (cnd), Berlin PO *(rec 1944)* ("Wilhelm Furtwängler Wartime Recordings") † Con 4 Pno, Op. 58; Sym 3; Sym 5; Sym 9; J. Brahms:Con 2 Pno, Op. 83; Sym 4; Vars on a Theme by Haydn; R. Strauss:Songs; R. Wagner:Meistersinger (preludes); Tristan und Isolde (prelude & liebestod) TAHA 6-▲ 1034 (50.97)

W. Furtwängler (cnd), Vienna PO *(rec Dec 1943)* ("Wilhelm Furtwängler dirigiert") † J. Brahms:Vars on a Theme by Haydn PRE ▲ 90199 [ADD] (16.97)

C. M. Giulini (cnd), La Scala Orch † Coriolan Ov, Op. 62; Egmont (ov) SNYC ▲ 53974 (16.97)

G. Gould (pno) [Liszt's solo pno trans] *(rec 1968)* † Sym 5 SNYC (Glenn Gould Edition) ▲ 52636 [ADD] (16.97)

G. Gould (pno) [arr Liszt for pno] *(rec New York, NY, July 30-Aug 1, 1968)* ("The Glenn Gould Silver Jubilee Album") † J. S. Bach:Italian Con, BWV 971; C.P.E. Bach:Sons Kbd; G. Gould:So You Want to Write a Fugue?; D. Scarlatti:Sons Kbd; A. Scriabin:Pieces (2) Pno, Op. 57 SNYC 2-▲ 60686 [ADD/DDD] (31.97)

N. Harnoncourt (cnd), CO of Europe † Sym 8 TELC ▲ 75709 (16.97)

R. Hickox (cnd), Northern Sinfonia of England † Coriolan Ov, Op. 62; Geschöpfe des Prometheus (ov) ASVQ ▲ 6053 [DDD] (11.97)

H. von Karajan (cnd), Berlin PO—Andante molto mosso: By the Brook ("Summer Adagio") † Debussy:Prélude à l'après-midi d'un faune; J. Haydn:Sym 87; G. Holst:Planets, Op. 32; W. A. Mozart:Divert 17 Hns Strs, K.334; Sym 38, K.504; M. Ravel:Rapsodie espagnole; O. Respighi:Fontane di Roma DEUT ▲ 457127 [ADD] (16.97)

H. von Karajan (cnd), Berlin PO *(rec 1977)* † Coriolan Ov, Op. 62; Geschöpfe des Prometheus (ov); Ruinen von Athen (ov) DEUT (Galleria) ▲ 15833 [ADD] (9.97)

H. von Karajan (cnd), Berlin PO † Sym 5 DEUT ▲ 39004 (16.97)

H. Kegel (cnd), Dresden PO ("The World of Symphony, Vol. 5: Ludwig van Beethoven") † Sym 5 LALI ▲ 15825 [DDD] (3.97)

H. Kegel (cnd), Dresden PO † Sym 4; Sym 5; Sym 8; Sym 9 CAPO ▲ 10453 [DDD] (11.97)

J. Keilberth (cnd) † Egmont (ov); Leonore (ov 3); Sym 5; Sym 7 TELC (Ultima) 2-▲ 18946 (16.97)

O. Klemperer (cnd), (Royal) Concertgebouw Orch *(rec live Amsterdam, 1957)* ("From Beethoven to Schubert") † F. Schubert:Sym 8 ENT (Palladio) ▲ 4208 [ADD] (13.97)

O. Klemperer (cnd), Philharmonia Orch *(rec London, England, Oct 1957)* † Sym 1 EMIC (Klemperer Legacy) ▲ 66792 [ADD] (11.97)

O. Klemperer (cnd), Vienna SO *(rec Vienna, 1950)* † Missa Solemnis, Op. 123; Sym 5 VB2 2-▲ 5527 (9.97)

J. Krips (cnd), London SO † Sym 2 EVC ▲ 9101 (13.97)

R. Leibowitz (cnd), Royal PO *(rec Apr 1961)* † Sym 8 CHSK ▲ 69 [ADD] (16.97)

P. Maag (cnd), Padova e Veneto CO *(rec Padova Italy, Feb 5-6, 1995)* † Sym 5 AART ▲ 47247 [DDD] (10.97)

C. Mackerras (cnd), Royal Liverpool PO † Sym 4 CFP ▲ 72848 (11.97)

Y. Menuhin (cnd), Sinfonia Varsovia † Sym 2 ICC ▲ 6702292 (9.97)

D. Mitropoulos (cnd), Minneapolis SO *(rec 1940)* ("D. Mitropouls: From Minneapolis to New York, Vol. 1") † Borodin:Sym 2 GRM2 ▲ 78509 [ADD] (13.97)

D. Mitropoulos (cnd), Minneapolis SO ("Dmitri Mitropoulos: The Minneapolis Years, 1940-45") † Coriolan Ov, Op. 62; Leonore (ov 3); Borodin:Sym 2; Dukas:L'Apprenti sorcier; G. Mahler:Sym 1; R. Schumann:Sym 2; P. Tchaikovsky:Sym 4 GRM2 4-▲ 78646 (52.97)

P. Monteux (cnd), Vienna PO † Sym 1; Sym 3; Sym 8 PLON (Double Decker) 2-▲ 40627 (17.97)

W. Morris (cnd), London SO † Egmont (ov) INMP (LSO Classic Masterpieces) ▲ 912 [DDD] (9.97)

W. Morris (cnd), London SO ("An Evening of Concert Favourites") † Coriolan Ov, Op. 62 INMP (Concert Classics) ▲ 1099 (9.97)

E. Mravinsky (cnd), Leningrad PO—Allegro ma non troppo: Awakening of Cheerful Feelings in the Country *(rec Leningrad Philharmonic Large Hall URSS, Russia, Oct 1982)* ("The Magic of the Symphony") † Bizet:Sym; J. Haydn:Sym 101; Sym 94; W. A. Mozart:Sym 40, K.550; F. Schubert:Sym 8 ERAT ▲ 94682 (9.97)

E. Mravinsky (cnd), Leningrad PO *(rec 1962)* RUS ▲ 11159 (12.97)

K. Münchinger (cnd), Stuttgart RSO ("Classical Creations") INTC ▲ 820574 (9.97)

E. Ormandy (cnd), Philadelphia Orch † Sym 5; Sym 7; Sym 8 SNYC (Essential Classics Take 2) 2-▲ 63266 (14.97)

H. Pfitzner (cnd), Berlin State Opera Orch *(rec 1929-33)* † Sym 8 PRE ▲ 90221 [ADD] (16.97)

S. Pomerantz (cnd), Budapest PO *(rec Italian Institute Budapest, Aug 9-11, 1994)* † Sym 7 DHR ▲ 71116 [DDD] (12.97)

V. D. Sabata (cnd), London PO † Sym 3; J. Brahms:Sym 4; R. Wagner:Tristan und Isolde (prelude & liebestod) 78'S 2-▲ 78542 (26.97)

V. D. Sabata (cnd), St. Cecilia Academy Orch Rome † G. Rossini:Guillaume Tell (ov); Verdi:Traviata (sels); Vespri siciliani (ov) GRM2 (Records of the Century) ▲ 78852 (13.97)

H. Scherchen (cnd), French Radio-TV Orch ("Hermann Scherchen, Vol. 1") † Schoenberg:Vars Orch, Op. 31 STRV ▲ 13592 [AAD] (13.97)

C. Schuricht (cnd), Berlin PO *(rec 1943)* ("Schuricht Conducts Beethoven") † Sym 3; Sym 5; Sym 7 IN 2-▲ 1404 (m) [ADD] (29.97)

C. Schuricht (cnd), Berlin PO *(rec 1943)* † Sym 7 GRM2 ▲ 78890 (14.97)

C. Schuricht (cnd), Swiss Romande Orch *(rec 1939-46)* ("The Schuricht Heritage, Vol. 1") † Sym 2 LYS ▲ 129 (17.97)

G. Schwarz (cnd), 92nd St. Y Chamber SO DLS ▲ 3017 [DDD] (14.97)

G. Solti (cnd), Chicago SO † Sym 8 PLON ▲ 17765 [ADD] (9.97)

G. Solti (cnd), Chicago SO † Leonore (ov 3) PLON ▲ 21773 [DDD] (16.97)

W. Steinberg (cnd), Pittsburgh SO † Sym 5 EMIC (Legacy) ▲ 66553 (11.97)

G. Szell (cnd), Cleveland Orch † Egmont (ov); Sym 1 SNYC (Essential Classics) ▲ 46532 [ADD] (7.97) ▮ 46532 [ADD] (3.98)

A. Toscanini (cnd), BBC SO *(rec 1937)* ("Toscanini in London, 1935-39, Vol. 5") † Leonore (ov 1), Op. 138; Sym 1 GRM2 ▲ 78615 (13.97)

A. Toscanini (cnd), BBC SO *(rec 1937-39)* † Leonore; Sym 1; Sym 4; J. Brahms:Tragic Ov, Op. 81; W. A. Mozart:Zauberflöte (sels) ENT (Document) 2-▲ 921 [ADD] (26.97)

A. Toscanini (cnd), BBC SO *(rec 1937-39)* † Leonore (ov 1), Op. 138; Sym 4 ARKA (The 78's) ▲ 78521 (13.97)

A. Toscanini (cnd), NBC SO *(rec 1938)* ("Toscanini, Vol. 3") † J. Haydn:Sym 98 LYS ▲ 401 (17.97)

B. Walter (cnd) *(rec 1940s)* ("The 1st Recordings in America for Columbia") † Sym 1; Sym 8; F. Schubert:Sym 8 GRM2 ▲ 78805 (26.97)

B. Walter (cnd), Columbia SO *(rec Los Angeles, CA, Jan 13-17, 1958)* † Sym 4 SNYC (Bruno Walter Edition, Vol. 2) ▲ 64462 [ADD] (10.97)

H. Zender (cnd), Saarbrücken RSO ("Hans Zender Edition, Vol. 2") † Con Vn; Sym 1 CPO 2-▲ 999474 (6.97)

D. Zinman (cnd), Zurich Tonhalle Orch *(rec 1997)* † Sym 5 ARNO ▲ 49695 [DDD] (4.97)

various artists—Andante molto mosso: By the Brook [plus others] † Con Vn, Vc, Pno, Op. 56; Fidelio (sels); Qt 13 Strs, Op. 130; Son 14 Pno, Op. 27/2; Son 18 Pno, Op. 31/3; Son 5 Pno, Op. 10/1; Son 8 Pno, Op. 13; Sym 2 RCAV ▮ 63328 (5.98) ▲ 63328 (11.97)

orch unknown † Berlioz:Sym fantastique, Op. 14; A. Dvořák:Sym 9; J. Haydn:Sym 101; W. A. Mozart:Sym 41, K.551 CFP (Unforgettable Classics) ▲ 73418 (11.97)

Symphony No. 7 in A, Op. 92 (1811-12)

C. Abbado (cnd), Vienna PO † Sym 8 DEUT ▲ 23364 [DDD] (16.97)

O. Ackermann (cnd), Zurich Tonhalle Orch † Sym 5; A. Dvořák:Con Vc; Sym 9 STRV 2-▲ 12324 [ADD] (25.97)

V. Ashkenazy (cnd), Philharmonia Orch PLON ▲ 30701 [DDD] (9.97)

V. Ashkenazy (cnd), Philharmonia Orch *(rec Kingsway Hall London, Oct 1983)* † Sym 5 PENG (Penguin Music Classics) ▲ 460603 (11.97)

D. Barenboim (cnd), Berlin PO *(rec West Berlin, Nov 12, 1989)* ("Das Konzert November 1989") † Con 1 Pno, Op. 15 SNYC ▲ 45830 [DDD] (11.97)

L. Bernstein (cnd), Boston SO *(rec live Tanglewood Festival, MA, Aug 19, 1990)* ("Bernstein: The Final Concert") † B. Britten:Peter Grimes (sea interludes & passacaglia) DEUT ▲ 31768 [DDD] (16.97)

L. Bernstein (cnd), New York PO ("Bernstein: The Royal Edition") † Sym 2 SNYC ▲ 47515 [ADD] (10.97)

L. Bernstein (cnd), New York PO *(rec Manhattan Center, New York City, NY, May 1964)* † Sym 2 SNYC (Bernstein Century) ▲ 61835 [ADD] (11.97)

H. Blomstedt (cnd), Dresden Staatskapelle *(rec 1975-80)* ("Blomstedt Conducts the Beethoven Symphonies, Vol. 4") † Sym 8 BER ▲ 2198 (10.97)

K. Böhm (cnd), Vienna PO † Fidelio (ov); Leonore (ov 3); Sym 6; Sym 8 DEUT (Double) 2-▲ 37928 (17.97)

A. Boult (cnd), London PO *(rec Walthamstow Hall London, June 1956)* † Coriolan Ov, Op. 62; Egmont (ov); Fidelio (ov); Leonore (ov 3); Sym 3; Sym 5; Sym 6 VC 3-▲ 11 [AAD] (39.97)

G. Brouwenstijn (sop), K. Meyer (alt), N. Gedda (ten), F. Guthrie (bass), A. Cluytens (cnd), Berlin PO, Choir of St. Hedwigs Cathedral, Berlin † Egmont (ov); Fidelio (ov); Geschöpfe des Prometheus (ov); Sym 1; Sym 2; Sym 3; Sym 4; Sym 5; Sym 6; Sym 8; Sym 9 RYLC 5-▲ 70373 (24.97)

BEETHOVEN, LUDWIG VAN (cont.)
Symphony No. 7 in A, Op. 92 (1811-12) (cont.)

P. Casals (cnd), Marlboro Festival Orch *(rec 1969)* † Sym 8 SNYC ▲ 45893 [ADD] (10.97)

S. Celibidache (cnd), Münchner Philharmoniker *(rec live, Philharmonie am Gasteig, München, Germany, Jan 20, 1989)* † Sym 8 EMIC ▲ 56841 [DDD] (16.97)

C. Davis (cnd), Royal PO † G. Rossini:Ovs; F. Schubert:Sym 9 EMIC (Doubleforte) 2-▲ 69364 (16.97)

C. von Dohnányi (cnd), Cleveland Orch † Sym 5 TEL ▲ 80163 [DDD] (16.97)

A. Doráti (cnd), London SO † Egmont (ov); Leonore (ov 3); Weihe des Hauses (ov), Op. 124 MRCR (Living Presence) ▲ 462958 (11.97)

B. Drahos (cnd), Nicolaus Esterházy Sinfonia *(rec Italian Institute Budapest, Oct 1995)* † Sym 4 NXIN ▲ 8553477 [DDD] (5.97)

R. Edlinger (cnd), Zagreb PO *(rec Sept 1988)* † Sym 4 NXIN ▲ 550180 [DDD] (5.97)

J. Ferencsik (cnd), Hungarian PO † Sym 1 LALI ▲ 15904 (3.97)

W. Furtwängler (cnd), Berlin PO *(rec 1943)* † J. Haydn:Sym 104 IN ▲ 1382 (15.97)

W. Furtwängler (cnd), Berlin PO *(rec live, Berlin, Germany, Oct 31, 1943)* † J. Haydn:Sym 104 RD ▲ 25004 [ADD] (16.97)

W. Furtwängler (cnd), Lucerne Festival Orch *(rec Aug 15, 1951)* ("Wilhelm Furtwängler at the Lucerne Festival") † Con Vn; Con 1 Pno, Op. 15; Leonore (ov 3); Sym 3; J. Brahms:Con Vn & Vc, Op. 102; Sym 1; R. Schumann:Sym 4; R. Wagner:Lohengrin (preludes) MUA 4-▲ 1018 [ADD] (47.97)

W. Furtwängler (cnd), Stockholm PO *(rec Stockholm, Sweden, Nov 13, 1948)* † Leonore (ov 3); Sym 8 MUA ▲ 4793 (live) [AAD] (10.97)

W. Furtwängler (cnd), Vienna PO *(rec 1950)* † Sym 5 EMIC (Great Recordings of the Century) ▲ 69803 [ADD] (11.97)

C. M. Giulini (cnd), La Scala Orch † Sym 1 SNYC ▲ 48236 [DDD] (11.97)

N. Harnoncourt (cnd), CO of Europe † Sym 4 TELC ▲ 75714 (16.97)

H. von Karajan (cnd), Berlin PO † Sym 4 DEUT ▲ 39003 (16.97)

H. von Karajan (cnd), Berlin PO ("The Young Karajan: The 1st Recordings, Vol 3") † A. Dvořák:Sym 9 GRM2 ▲ 78642 (13.97)

H. von Karajan (cnd), Berlin State Orch † Leonore (ov 3); Verdi:Traviata (sels) IMUS (Magic Master) ▲ 37097 (6.97)

H. Kegel (cnd), Dresden PO † Sym 2 CAPO ▲ 10452 [DDD] (11.97)

J. Keilberth (cnd) † Egmont (ov); Leonore (ov 3); Sym 5; Sym 6 TELC (Ultima) 2-▲ 18946 (16.97)

R. Kempe (cnd), Dresden Staatskapelle BER ▲ 9195 (10.97)

C. Kleiber (cnd), Vienna PO † Sym 5 DEUT (The Originals) ▲ 47400 (11.97)

O. Klemperer (cnd), Philharmonia Orch *(rec London, England, 1955)* † Sym 4 EMIC (Klemperer Legacy) ▲ 66795 [ADD] (11.97)

H. Knappertsbusch (cnd) *(rec 1929)* † Liszt:Préludes, S.97; O. Nicolai:Lustigen Weiber von Windsor (ov); R. Wagner:Götterdämmerung (sels) TAHA ▲ 309 (17.97)

J. Krips (cnd), London SO † Sym 4 EVC ▲ 9102 (13.97)

G. Lane (mez), L. Stokowski (cnd), BBC SO † B. Britten:Young Person's Guide to the Orch, Op. 34; M. de Falla:Amor brujo BBC ▲ 4005 (17.97)

R. Leibowitz (cnd), Royal PO *(rec Apr 1961)* † Sym 4 CHSK ▲ 81 [ADD] (16.97)

R. Leppard (cnd), Indianapolis SO † Coriolan Ov, Op. 62; Qt 11 Strs, Op. 95 KOSS ▲ 2215 (18.97)

P. Maag (cnd), Padova e Veneto CO *(rec Padova Italy, June 1994)* † Sym 8 AART ▲ 47245 [DDD] (10.97)

A. Moisan (cnd), Montréal Winds [arr Beethoven for winds] † Spt in E♭, Op. 20 ATMM ▲ 22129 (15.97)

P. Monteux (cnd), London SO † Sym 2; Sym 4; Sym 5 PLON (Double Decker) 2-▲ 43479 (17.97)

W. Morris (cnd), London SO † Sym 8 LSO (LSO) ▲ 6900022 (9.97)

C. Munch (cnd), French National Orch *(rec Maison Radio Paris, France, Dec 1963)* ("Charles Munch Edition, Vol. 1") † Sym 4; Weihe des Hauses (ov), Op. 124 VAL ▲ 4825 [ADD] (12.97)

A. Nanut (cnd), Ljubljana RSO † Son 5 Vn, Op. 24 PC ▲ 265061 [DDD] (2.97)

Netherlands Wind Ensemble [arr for winds] † Octet Ww, Op. 103; Qnt Pno, Op. 16 CHN ▲ 9470 (16.97)

E. Ormandy (cnd), Philadelphia Orch † Sym 5; Sym 6; Sym 8 SNYC (Essential Classics Take 2) 2-▲ 63266 (14.97)

S. Pomerantz (cnd), Budapest PO *(rec Italian Institute Budapest, Aug 9-11, 1994)* † Sym 6 DHR ▲ 71116 [DDD] (12.97)

J. Pritchard (cnd), BBC SO † Fant Pno, Orch & Chorus, Op. 80; Leonore (ov 1), Op. 138 INMP (BBC Radio Classics) ▲ 9132 (13.97)

F. Reiner (cnd), Chicago SO *(rec 1955-59)* † Coriolan Ov, Op. 62; Fidelio (ov); Sym 5 RCAV (Living Stereo) ▲ 68976 (11.97)

T. Schippers (cnd), Venice Theater Orch † S. Barber:Medea's Meditation & Dance of Vengeance, Op. 23e; Constantinidis:Dances from the Greek; Pno Music; R. Strauss:Four Last Songs, AV150; Verdi:Forza del destino (sels) MONM 2-▲ 10010 (36.97)

C. Schuricht (cnd), Berlin PO *(rec 1937)* ("Schuricht Conducts Beethoven") † Sym 3; Sym 5; Sym 6 IN 2-▲ 1404 (m) [ADD] (29.97)

C. Schuricht (cnd), Berlin PO *(rec 1937)* † Sym 6 GRM2 ▲ 78890 (14.97)

G. Solti (cnd), Chicago SO † Sym 8 PLON ▲ 25525 [DDD] (16.97)

W. Steinberg (cnd), Pittsburgh SO *(rec Pittsburgh, PA, Oct 1957)* † Con 5 Pno, Op. 73 EMIC (Full Dimensional Sound) ▲ 66888 [ADD] (11.97)

G. Szell (cnd), Cleveland Orch † König Stephen (ov); Sym 4 SNYC (Essential Classics) ▲ 48158 (7.97) ▮ 48158 (3.98)

C. Thielemann (cnd), Philharmonia Orch *(rec London, July 1996)* † Sym 5 PPHI ▲ 449981 [DDD] (16.97)

A. Toscanini (cnd), BBC SO *(rec 1935)* ("Toscanini in London, 1935-39, Vol. 6") † Geschöpfe des Prometheus (ov); Sym 4 GRM2 ▲ 78616 (13.97)

A. Toscanini (cnd), NBC SO *(rec 1939)* ("Toscanini First Cycle of Beethoven's Complete Symphonies, Vol. 2") † Leonore (ov 1), Op. 138; Sym 4 GRM2 ▲ 78514 [ADD] (13.97)

A. Toscanini (cnd), New York Philharmonic SO *(rec Apr 1936)* † Sym 5 MTAL ▲ 48034 (6.97)

A. Toscanini (cnd), New York Philharmonic SO *(rec 1936)* ("Toscanini Edition, Vol. 1") † R. Wagner:Götterdämmerung (sels); Lohengrin (preludes); Siegfried Idyll GRM2 (Records of the Century) ▲ 78791 (13.97)

A. Toscanini (cnd), New York PO ("The Toscanini Collection, Vol. 64") † J. Haydn:Sym 101; Mendelssohn (-Bartholdy):Midsummer Night's Dream (sels) RCAV (Gold Seal) ▲ 60316 (11.97)

B. Walter (cnd), Columbia SO *(rec Los Angeles, CA, Feb 1-3, 1958)* † Sym 5 SNYC (Bruno Walter Edition, Vol. 2) ▲ 64463 [ADD] (10.97)

B. Zander (cnd), Philharmonia Orch *(rec Hampstead, London, England, Oct 1998)* † Sym 5 TEL 2-▲ 80471 [DDD] (16.97)

D. Zinman (cnd), Zurich Tonhalle Orch † Sym 8 ARNO ▲ 56341 [DDD] (4.97)

Symphony No. 8 in F, Op. 93 (1812)

C. Abbado (cnd), Vienna PO † Sym 7 DEUT ▲ 23364 [DDD] (16.97)

C. Abbado (cnd), Vienna PO † Sym 6 DEUT (Masters) ▲ 45542 (9.97)

H. Adolph (cnd), Slovak PO † Sym 6 PC ▲ 265057 [DDD] (2.97)

K. Ančerl (cnd), Toronto SO ("Karl Ančerl in Toronto") † Sym 6; Berlioz:Troyens; Mendelssohn (-Bartholdy):Sym 5; W. A. Mozart:Kleine Nachtmusik, K.525; R. Schumann:Sym 4; Smetana:Moldau TAHA 3-▲ 121 (50.97)

J. Barbirolli (cnd), Hallé Orch † Con 5 Pno, Op. 73; Egmont (ov); Leonore (ov 3); Sym 1; Sym 5 DLAB (The Barbirolli Society) ▲ 1014 (17.97)

L. Bernstein (cnd), New York PO *(rec New York, Oct 7, 1963)* † König Stephen (ov); Sym 6 SNYC (Bernstein Century) ▲ 60557 [ADD] (10.97)

H. Blomstedt (cnd), Dresden Staatskapelle *(rec 1975-80)* ("Blomstedt Conducts the Beethoven Symphonies, Vol. 4") † Sym 7 BER ▲ 2198 (10.97)

K. Böhm (cnd), Vienna PO † Fidelio (ov); Leonore (ov 3); Sym 6; Sym 7 DEUT (Double) 2-▲ 37928 (17.97)

G. Brouwenstijn (sop), K. Meyer (alt), N. Gedda (ten), F. Guthrie (bass), A. Cluytens (cnd), Berlin PO, Choir of St. Hedwigs Cathedral, Berlin † Egmont (ov); Fidelio (ov); Geschöpfe des Prometheus (ov); Sym 1; Sym 2; Sym 3; Sym 4; Sym 5; Sym 6; Sym 7; Sym 9 RYLC 5-▲ 70373 (24.97)

P. Casals (cnd), Marlboro Festival Orch *(rec 1963)* † Sym 7 SNYC ▲ 45893 [ADD] (10.97)

S. Celibidache (cnd), Münchner Philharmoniker *(rec live, Philharmonie am Gasteig, München, Germany, Jan 4, 1995)* † Sym 7 EMIC ▲ 56841 [DDD] (16.97)

C. von Dohnányi (cnd), Cleveland Orch † Sym 4 TEL ▲ 80198 [DDD] (16.97)

R. Edlinger (cnd), Zagreb PO *(rec Zagreb, Sept 1988)* ("Famous Symphonies: Beethoven, Tchaikovsky, Brahms, Schubert") † Sym 3; J. Brahms:Academic Festival Ov, Op. 80; Sym 4; Tragic Ov, Op. 81; F. Schubert:Sym 9; P. Tchaikovsky:Francesca da Rimini, Op. 32; Sym 6 NXIN 4-▲ 504012 [DDD] (19.97)

J. Ferencsik (cnd), Hungarian PO † Sym 3 LALI ▲ 15902 (3.97)

W. Furtwängler (cnd), Stockholm PO *(rec Stockholm, Sweden, Nov 13, 1948)* † Leonore (ov 3); Sym 7 MUA ▲ 4793 (live) [AAD] (10.97)

C. M. Giulini (cnd), La Scala Orch *(rec Sept 20-22, 1992)* † Sym 2 SNYC ▲ 48238 [DDD] (11.97)

BEETHOVEN, LUDWIG VAN (cont.)
Symphony No. 8 in F, Op. 93 (1812) (cont.)

N. Harnoncourt (cnd), CO of Europe † Sym 6 TELC ▲ 75709 (16.97)

H. von Karajan (cnd), Berlin PO † Coriolan Ov, Op. 62; Fidelio (ov); Leonore (ov 3) DEUT ▲ 39005 [DDD] (16.97)

H. von Karajan (cnd), Vienna PO *(rec 1946)* ("The Young Karajan: The First Recordings, Vol. 7: The Early Recordings with Walter Legge") † W. A. Mozart:German Dances (3), K.605; German Dances (6), K.600; Sym 33, K.319; P. Tchaikovsky:Romeo & Juliet GRM2 ▲ 78691 (13.97)

H. Kegel (cnd), Dresden PO † Sym 4; Sym 5; Sym 6; Sym 9 CAPO ▲ 10453 [DDD] (11.97)

R. Kempe (cnd), Bavarian RSO *(rec 1975)* † P. Tchaikovsky:Sym 5 ORFE ▲ 449961 [ADD] (16.97)

O. Klemperer (cnd), Philharmonia Orch *(rec London, England, 1957-63)* † Coriolan Ov, Op. 62; Leonore (ov 1), Op. 138; Leonore (ov 2); Leonore (ov 3) EMIC (Klemperer Legacy) ▲ 66796 [ADD] (11.97)

H. Knappertsbusch (cnd), Bavarian State Orch *(rec Dec 14, 1959)* † Con 5 Pno, Op. 73 ORFE ▲ 385961 [ADD] (16.97)

S. Koussevitzky (cnd), Boston SO *(rec 1929-39)* ("Koussevitsky Conducts Classical Symphonies") † Sym 2; J. Haydn:Sym 102; Sym 94; W. A. Mozart:Sym 29, K.201; Sym 34, K.338 PHS 2-▲ 9185 (33.97)

J. Krips (cnd), London SO † Sym 3 EVC ▲ 9103 (13.97)

R. Leibowitz (cnd), Royal PO *(rec Apr 1961)* † Sym 6 CHSK ▲ 69 [ADD] (16.97)

P. Maag (cnd), Padova e Veneto CO *(rec Padova Italy, June 1994)* † Sym 7 AART ▲ 47245 [DDD] (10.97)

W. Mengelberg (cnd), (Royal) Concertgebouw Orch *(rec 1930-38)* † Leonore (ov 3); Sym 5 MTAL ▲ 48056 (6.97)

P. Monteux (cnd), San Francisco SO ("Vol 1") † Ruinen von Athen (ov); Sym 4; J. S. Bach:Passacaglia & Fugue Org, BWV 582 RCAV (Gold Seal; Pierre Monteux Edition) ▲ 61892 (11.97)

P. Monteux (cnd), Vienna PO † Sym 1; Sym 3; Sym 6 PLON (Double Decker) 2-▲ 40627 (17.97)

W. Morris (cnd), London SO † Sym 7 LSO (LSO) ▲ 6900022 (9.97)

E. Ormandy (cnd), Philadelphia Orch † Sym 5; Sym 6; Sym 7 SNYC (Essential Classics Take 2) 2-▲ 63266 (14.97)

H. Pfitzner (cnd), Berlin PO *(rec 1929-33)* † Sym 6 PRE ▲ 90221 [ADD] (16.97)

A. Rahbari (cnd), Brussels BRTN PO *(rec Feb 1990)* † Sym 3 NXIN ▲ 550407 [DDD] (5.97)

H. Scherchen (cnd), Stuttgart Radio Orch † Sym 1; Sym 2; Sym 4 TAHA 3-▲ 126 (34.97)

G. Schwarz (cnd), Los Angeles CO † Geschöpfe des Prometheus (ov); Sym 1 DLS ▲ 3013 [DDD] (14.97)

G. Solti (cnd), Chicago SO † Sym 6 PLON ▲ 17765 [ADD] (9.97)

G. Solti (cnd), Chicago SO † Sym 7 PLON ▲ 25525 [DDD] (16.97)

W. Steinberg (cnd), Pittsburgh SO *(rec 1954-55)* † Sym 3 EMIC ▲ 67098 (m) [ADD] (11.97)

G. Szell (cnd), Cleveland Orch † Sym 3 SNYC (Essential Classics) ▲ 46328 [ADD] (7.97) ▮ 46328 [ADD] (3.98)

A. Toscanini (cnd), NBC SO ("The Toscanini Collection, Vol. 23") † Sym 3 RCAV (Gold Seal) ▲ 60269 (11.97)

B. Walter (cnd) *(rec 1940s)* ("The 1st Recordings in America for Columbia") † Sym 1; Sym 6; F. Schubert:Sym 8 GRM2 ▲ 78805 (26.97)

B. Walter (cnd), Columbia SO *(rec Los Angeles, CA, Jan 8-Feb 12, 1958)* † Sym 3 SNYC (Bruno Walter Edition, Vol. 2) ▲ 64461 [ADD] (10.97)

B. Walter (cnd), New York PO *(rec 1938-42)* † A. Corelli:Con grosso, Op. 6/8; G. F. Handel:Concerti grossi, Op. 6 PHG ▲ 5028 (14.97)

F. V. Weingartner (cnd), Vienna PO *(rec Feb 1936)* † Sym 3 PRE ▲ 90113 [AAD] (16.97)

D. Zinman (cnd), Zurich Tonhalle Orch † Sym 7 ARNO ▲ 56341 [DDD] (4.97)

Symphony No. 9 in d for solo Voices, Orchestra & Chorus, Op. 125, "Choral Symphony" (1822-24)

A. Addison (sop), J. Hobson (mez), R. Lewis (ten), D. Bell (bar), G. Szell (cnd), Cleveland Orch, R. Shaw (cnd), Cleveland Orch Chorus—Finale:Presto-Allegro *(rec Cleveland, OH, April 1961)* † Bagatelle Pno in a, WoO 59; Con Vn; Con 5 Pno, Op. 73; Fidelio (ov); Minuets (6) Orch, WoO 10; Qt 9 Strs, Op. 59/3; Ruinen von Athen (sels); Son 14 Pno, Op. 27/2; Son 8 Pno, Op. 13; Sym 5 SNYC ▲ 64093 (m) [ADD] (7.97)

R. Alexander (sop), F. Quivar (cta), G. Lakes (ten), P. Plishka (bass), A. Previn (cnd), Royal PO RCAV (Red Seal) ▲ 60363 (16.97)

L. Amara (sop), J. Alexander (ten), J. Macurdy (bass), E. Ormandy (cnd), Philadelphia Orch, R. P. Condie (cnd), Mormon Tabernacle Choir † Ah, perfido!, Op. 65; Cant on the Death of the Emperor Joseph II, WoO 87; Fant Pno, Orch & Chorus, Op. 80; Meeresstille und glückliche Fahrt, Op. 112 SNYC (Take Two) 2-▲ 63240 (14.97)

E. Andor (sop), M. Szirmay (cta), G. Korondi (ten), S. Solyom-Nagy (bar), J. Ferencsik (cnd), Hungarian PO, Budapest Phil Chorus LALI ▲ 15905 (3.97)

M. Arroyo (sop), R. Sarfaty (mez), N. Di Virgilio (ten), N. Scott (bass), L. Bernstein (cnd), New York PO, Juilliard Chorus † Fidelio (ov) SNYC (Bernstein Century) ▲ 63152 (11.97)

Band of the Life Guards, Band of the Blues and Royals, Pipes and Drums of the Black Watch—Ode to Joy [from 4th movt] [arr D Beat] *(rec Windsor, England, 1997)* ("One Hundred Thousand Welcomes") † Anonymous:A lauidh; Amazing grace; Bluebells of Scotland; Captain Campbell; Ceud mile failte; Colin's cattle; Drummer's call; Festival march; Lochaber broadsword; Lord Lovat's lament; There was a lad born in Kyle; Will ye no come back again?; Fettes:Glendaruel Highlanders; J. MacDonald:79th Farewell to Gibraltar; G. S. Maclennan:Kilworth Hills; Traditional:Blue Bonnets over the Border; Bonnie Lass o' Fyvie; Scotland the Brave BND ▲ 5136 [DDD] (16.97)

E. Berger (sop), G. Pitzinger (cta), W. Ludwig (ten), R. Watzke (bass), W. Furtwängler (cnd), Berlin PO, Bruno Kittel Choir *(rec Queens Hall London, May 1, 1937)* MUA ▲ 818 [ADD] (16.97)

L. Bernstein (cnd), Bavarian Radio Chorus, Berlin Radio Chorus, Dresden Philharmonie Children's Chorus [GER] *(rec Schauspielhaus East Berlin, Dec 25, 1989)* DEUT ▲ 29861 [DDD] (16.97)

L. Bernstein (cnd), Vienna PO [GER] DEUT ▲ 10859 [ADD] (16.97)

H. Blomstedt (cnd), Dresden Staatskapelle *(rec 1975-80)* ("Blomstedt Conducts the Beethoven Symphonies Vol. 5") BER ▲ 2199 (10.97)

H. Blomstedt (cnd), Dresden Staatskapelle, Dresden State Chorus [soloists Edith Wiens, Ute Walther, Reiner Goldberg] LALI ▲ 15826 [DDD] (3.97)

K. Bohm (cnd), Dresden Staatskapelle ("Bohm, Vol. 1") LYS ▲ 403

I. Borkh (sop), R. Siewert (cta), R. Lewis (ten), L. Weber (bass), R. Leibowitz (cnd), Royal PO, Beecham Choral Society [GER] *(rec June 1961)* CHSK ▲ 66 [ADD] (16.97)

V. Bovy (sop), K. Thorborg (mez), J. Peerce (ten), E. Pinza (bass), A. Toscanini (cnd) ("Toscanini, Vol. 4") LYS ▲ 408 (17.97)

T. Briem (sop), E. Höngen (cta), P. Anders (ten), R. Watzke (bass), W. Furtwängler (cnd), Berlin PO, Bruno Kittel Choir *(rec Mar 22, 1942)* ("Furtwängler Conducts during the War Years") † Coriolan Ov, Op. 62; Sym 3; Sym 4; Sym 5; E. Grieg:Con Pno, Op. 16 IN 3-▲ 1348 [ADD] (43.97)

T. Briem (sop), E. Höngen (cta), P. Anders (ten), R. Watzke (bass), W. Furtwängler (cnd), Berlin PO, Bruno Kittel Choir ("Furtwängler Historical Archives 1942-45") † Coriolan Ov, Op. 62; Sym 6; J. Brahms:Con 2 Pno, Op. 83; Sym 1; A. Bruckner:Sym 6; Sym 7; R. Wagner:Tristan und Isolde (prelude & liebestod) TAHA 4-▲ 1004

T. Briem (sop), E. Höngen (cta), P. Anders (ten), R. Watzke (bass), W. Furtwängler (cnd), Berlin PO, Bruno Kittel Choir *(rec 1942)* ("Furtwängler Conducts Beethoven") GRM2 ▲ 78581 (13.97)

G. Brouwenstijn (sop), K. Meyer (mez), N. Gedda (ten), F. Guthrie (bass), A. Cluytens (cnd), Berlin PO, St. Hedwig's Cathedral Choir RYLC ▲ 70098 (8.97)

G. Brouwenstijn (sop), K. Meyer (alt), N. Gedda (ten), F. Guthrie (bass), A. Cluytens (cnd), Berlin PO, Choir of St. Hedwigs Cathedral, Berlin † Egmont (ov); Fidelio (ov); Geschöpfe des Prometheus (ov); Sym 1; Sym 2; Sym 3; Sym 4; Sym 5; Sym 6; Sym 7; Sym 8 RYLC 5-▲ 70373 (24.97)

M. Caniglia (sop), E. Stignani (mez), J. Patzak (ten), H. Hotter (b-bar), H. von Karajan (cnd), Vienna PO, Vienna Singverein *(rec Vienna, 1947)* 78'S (The 78s) ▲ 78544 (13.97)

E. Cundari (sop), N. Rankin (mez), A. Da Costa (ten), W. Wilderman (bass), B. Walter (cnd), Columbia SO, Westminster Sym Choir *(rec Los Angeles, CA, Apr 6, 1954)* SNYC (Bruno Walter Edition, Vol. 2) ▲ 64464 [ADD] (10.97)

P. Curtin (sop), F. Kopleff (cta), J. McCollum (ten), D. Gramm (bass), F. Reiner (cnd), Chicago SO RCAV (Gold Seal) ▲ 61795 (11.97)

A. Davis (sop), R. Cathcart (sgr), R. Betts (sgr), E. Lowenthal (sgr), L. Stokowski (cnd), Philadelphia Orch, Philadelphia Orch Chorus *(rec 1934)* ("Leopold Stokowdki Conducts") † Son 14 Pno, Op. 27/2 MUA ▲ 846 [ADD] (16.97)

A. Davis (sop), R. Cathcart (sgr), R. Betts (sgr), E. Lowenthal (sgr), L. Stokowski (cnd), Philadelphia Orch ("Leopold Stokowski: The Philadelphia Years, Vol. 2") GRM2 ▲ 78577 (13.97)

A. Davis (sop), R. Cathcart (mez), R. Betts (ten), E. Loewenthal (bass), L. Stokowski (cnd), Philadelphia Orch *(rec 1934)* MTAL ▲ 48081 (6.97)

C. von Dohnányi (cnd), Cleveland Orch, Cleveland Orch Chorus [GER] TEL ▮ 30120 [DDD] (8.98) ▲ 80120 [DDD] (16.97)

H. Donath (sop), D. Soffel (cta), S. Jerusalem (ten), P. Lika (bass), S. Celibidache (cnd), Münchner Philharmoniker, J. Schmidhuber (cnd), Philharmonischer Chor München *(rec Philharmonie am Gasteig, München, Germany, March 17, 1989)* EMIC ▲ 56842 [ADD] (16.97)

J. Eaglen (sop), W. Meier (mez), B. Heppner (ten), B. Terfel (b-bar), C. Abbado (cnd), Berlin PO, Eric Ericson Chamber Choir, Swedish Radio Chorus *(rec Salzburg Easter Festival, 1996)* SNYC ▲ 62634 (16.97)

R. Edlinger (cnd), Zagreb PO *(rec Sept 1988)* NXIN ▲ 550181 [DDD] (5.97)

H. Farberman (cnd) —Molto vivace; Presto (scherzo) [arr Farberman] *(rec 1982)* † Berlioz:Sym fantastique, Op. 14; Bizet:Carmen (suite 1); J. Pachelbel:Canon & Gigue ALLO ▲ 8195 (3.97)

▲ = CD ♦ = Enhanced CD △ = MD ▮ = Cassette Tape ▯ = DCC

BEETHOVEN, LUDWIG VAN (cont.)

Symphony No. 9 in d for solo Voices, Orchestra & Chorus, Op. 125, "Choral Symphony" (1822-24) (cont.)

O. Fried (cnd), Berlin State Opera Orch, Bruno Kittel Choir [GER] *(rec 1928 for Polydor)* PHS ▲ 9372 [AAD] (17.97)

W. Furtwängler (cnd), Bayreuth Festival Orch, Bayreuth Festival Chorus, E. Schwarzkopf (sop), E. Höngen (cta), H. Hopf (ten), O. Edelmann (bass) *(rec Bayreuth Festival, Germany, July 29, 1951)* EMIC (Great Recordings of the Century) ▲ 66953 (m) [ADD] (11.97)

W. Furtwängler (cnd), Berlin PO *(rec 1942)* ("Wilhelm Furtwängler Wartime Recordings") † Con 4 Pno, Op. 58; Sym 3; Sym 5; Sym 6; J. Brahms:Con 2 Pno, Op. 83; Sym 4; Vars on a Theme by Haydn; R. Strauss:Songs; R. Wagner:Meistersinger (preludes); Tristan und Isolde (prelude & liebestod) TAHA 6-▲ 1034 (50.97)

W. Furtwängler (cnd), Berlin PO *(rec Berlin, Germany, March 22, 1942)* RD ▲ 25006 [ADD] (16.97)

W. Furtwängler (cnd), Philharmonia Orch *(rec Lucerne, 1954)* TAHA ▲ 1003 (17.97)

G. Gatti (sop), F. Barbieri (mez), G. Prandelli (ten), T. Pasero (bass), A. Toscanini (cnd), La Scala Orch *(rec Milan, Italy, June 24, 1946)* † Egmont (ov); Sym 1; R. Wagner:Lohengrin (sels); Meistersinger (ov); Meistersinger (sels); Tannhäuser (sels) MUA 2-▲ 1027 [AAD] (31.97)

M. Gauci (sop), L. van Deyck (mez), D. George (ten), M. Rosca (bass), A. Rahbari (cnd), Brussels BRTN PO, I. Michiels (cnd), Bruges Cantores Oratorio Choir DI ▲ 920151 [DDD] (5.97)

A. Hargan (sop), U. Walther (cta), E. Büchner (ten), K. Kováts (bass), H. Kegel (cnd), Dresden PO † Sym 4; Sym 5; Sym 6; Sym 8 CAPO ▲ 10453 [DDD] (11.97)

A. Hargen (sop), D. Jones (mez), D. Rendall (ten), G. Howell (bass), W. Morris (cnd), London SO, London Sym Chorus LSO (LSO) ▲ 6900032 (9.97)

N. Harnoncourt (cnd), CO of Europe, Arnold Schoenberg Choir TELC ▲ 75713 (16.97)

L. Helletsgruber (sop), R. Anday (cta), G. Maikl (ten), R. Mayr (bass), F. V. Weingartner (cnd), Vienna PO, Vienna State Opera Chorus 78'S (The 78's) ▲ 78508 [AAD] (13.97)

P. Herreweghe (cnd), Champs Élysées Orch, Collegium Vocale, La Chapelle Royale, M. Diener (sop), P. Lang (mez), E. Wottrich (ten), D. Henschel (bass) HAM ▲ 901687 (18.97)

C. Hogwood (cnd), Academy of Ancient Music [GER] PLOI ▲ 25517 [DDD] (16.97)

G. Janowitz (sop), H. Rössl-Majdan (mez), W. Kmentt (ten), W. Berry (b-bar), H. von Karajan (cnd), Berlin PO, Vienna Singverein † Coriolan Ov, Op. 62 DEUT (The Originals) ▲ 47401 (11.97)

G. Jones (sop), T. Troyanos (mez), J. Thomas (ten), K. Ridderbusch (bass), K. Böhm (cnd), Vienna PO, Vienna State Opera Chorus † Coriolan Ov, Op. 62; Egmont (ov); Geschöpfe des Prometheus (ov); Sym 3 DEUT (Double) 2-▲ 37368 (17.97)

H. von Karajan (cnd), Berlin PO, Vienna Singverein [GER] *(rec 1976)* DEUT (Galleria) ▲ 15832 [ADD] (9.97) ▮ 15832 [ADD] (5.98)

Y. Kenny (sop), S. Walker (mez), P. Power (ten), P. Salomaa (bass), R. Norrington (cnd), London Classical Players, Schütz Choir London VCL (Veritas) ▲ 61378 (11.97)

O. Klemperer (cnd), Philharmonia Orch, Philharmonia Chorus, A. N. Lövberg (sop), C. Ludwig (mez), W. Kmentt (ten), H. Hotter (b-bar) *(rec London, England, 1957)* † Geschöpfe des Prometheus (ov) EMIC (Klemperer Legacy) ▲ 66797 [ADD] (11.97)

J. Krips (cnd), London SO, BBC Phil Chorus, J. Vyvyan (sop), S. Verrett (mez), R. Petrak (ten) EVC ▲ 9104 (13.97)

G. Levine (cnd), Royal PO—Adagio molto e cantabile-Andante moderato-Andante-Adagio *(rec Apr 7, 1994)* ("The Papal Concert to Commemorate the Holocaust") † L. Bernstein:Chichester Psalms; Sym 3; Bruch:Kol Nidrei, Op. 47; F. Schubert:Psalm 92 JUS ▲ 1801 [DDD] ▮ 1801 [DDD]

W. Lipp (sop), U. Boese (mez), F. Wunderlich (ten), F. Crass (bass), O. Klemperer (cnd), Philharmonia Orch, Vienna Singverein *(rec live Vienna Festival, June 14, 1960)* STRV ▲ 10003 [ADD] (13.97)

P. Maag (cnd), Padova e Veneto CO, F. M. Bressan (cnd), Athestis Chorus *(rec Padova Italy, Dec 20, 1994)* AART ▲ 47248 [DDD] (10.97)

L. Maazel (cnd), Cleveland Orch [GER] SNYC ▲ 38868 (16.97)

Z. Macal (cnd), Milwaukee SO, Milwaukee Sym Chorus [soloists: B. Valente, J. Taylor, J. F. West, P. Pl] *(rec July 31, 1989)* KOSS ▲ 1003 [DDD] (17.97)

C. Mackerras (cnd), Liverpool PO, Liverpool Phil Chorus, J. Rodgers (sop), D. Jones (mez), P. Bronder (ten), B. Terfel (b-bar) CFP ▲ 72850 (11.97)

K. Masur (cnd), Leipzig Gewandhaus Orch ("The Complete Symphonies, Vol 3") † Fant Pno, Orch & Chorus, Op. 80; Ovs PPHI 2-▲ 54038 (17.97)

K. Masur (cnd), Leipzig Gewandhaus Orch, Berlin Radio Chorus, Leipzig Radio Chorus, PCD Theo Adam Children's Choir, A. Tomowa-Sintow (sop), A. Burmeister (mez), P. Schreier (ten)—Finale:Presto-Allegro ("Shine: The Complete Classics") † Chopin:Polonaise 6 Pno, Op. 53; Preludes (24) Pno, Op. 28; Liszt:Etudes d'exécution transcendante (6), S.140; Études de concert (3), S.144; Hungarian Rhaps, S.244; S. Rachmaninoff:Con 3 Pno, Op. 30; Prelude in c#, Op. 3/2; Rimsky-Korsakov:Tale of Tsar Saltan (orch sels); R. Schumann:Kinderszenen Pno, Op. 15; Vivaldi:Gloria; Nulla in mundo pax, RV.630 PPHI 2-▲ 456403 (17.97)

Z. Mehta (cnd), New York PO, New York Choral Artists [soloists Margaret Price, Marilyn Horne, Jon Vicker] RCAV (Silver Seal) ▲ 60477 [DDD] (6.97)

E. Moser (sop), R. Lang (cta), P. Schreier (ten), T. Adam (b-bar), K. Masur (cnd), Leipzig Gewandhaus Orch *(rec live, 1981)* BER ▲ 9304 (10.97)

R. Muti (cnd), Philadelphia Orch, J. Flummerfelt (cnd), Westminster Choir, C. Studer (sop), D. Ziegler (mez), P. Seiffert (ten), J. Morris (bass) CSER (Seraphim) ▲ 73284 [DDD] (6.97)

V. Neumann (cnd), Czech PO, Czech Phil Chorus ("Prague Spring Inspiring") † A. Dvořák:Con Vc; Smetana:Má Vlast; P. Tchaikovsky:Con 1 Pno, Op. 23 SUR 3-▲ 546 [AAD]

J. Norman (sop), B. Fassbaender (mez), P. Domingo (ten), W. Berry (b-bar), K. Böhm (cnd), Vienna PO, Vienna State Opera Chorus DEUT (Masters) ▲ 45503 [DDD] (9.97)

J. Novotná (sop), K. Thorborg (mez), J. Peerce (ten), N. Moscona (bass), A. Toscanini (cnd), NBC SO, Westminster Choir *(rec New York City, 1939)* ("Toscanini 1st Cycle of Beethoven's Complete Symphonies, Vol. 3") † Fant Pno, Orch & Chorus, Op. 80 GRM2 ▲ 78524 (13.97)

J. Novotná (sop), K. Thorborg (mez), J. Peerce (ten), N. Moscona (bass), A. Toscanini (cnd), NBC SO, Westminster Choir *(rec 1939)* † Fant Pno, Orch & Chorus, Op. 80 ENT (Sirio) ▲ 530034 (13.97)

J. Novotná (sop), K. Thorborg (mez), J. Peerce (ten), N. Moscona (bass), A. Toscanini (cnd), NBC SO, Westminster Choir *(rec 1939)* ("Toscanini, Vol. 6") LYS ▲ 128 (17.97)

L. Orgonasova (sop), A. S. von Otter (mez), A. Rolfe Johnson (ten), G. Cachemaille (bar), J. E. Gardiner (cnd), Orch Révolutionnaire et Romantique [period instrs] *(rec All Saints' Church London, Oct 1992)* PARC ▲ 47074 [DDD] (16.97)

E. Ormandy (cnd), Philadelphia Orch [GER] SNYC ▲ 37241 [ADD] (9.97)

M. Paloczaj (sop), E. Bandova (alt), P. Kottwald (ten), J. Bacek (bass), E. Duvier (cnd), Slovak PO, Bratislava State Opera Choir PC ▲ 265026 [DDD] (2.97)

H. Papian (sop), R. Donose (mez), M. Fink (ten), C. Otelli (bar), B. Drahos (cnd), Nicolaus Esterházy Sinfonia, Nicolaus Esterházy Sinfonia Chorus *(rec Italian Institute Budapest, Aug 1996)* NXIN ▲ 8553478 [DDD] (5.97)

M. Price (sop), M. Lipovšek (mez), P. Seiffert (ten), J. Rootering (bass), W. Sawallisch (cnd), (Royal) Concertgebouw Orch, Dusseldorf Municipal Choral Society *(rec Concertgebouw, Amsterdam, Netherlands, Dec 1992)* † Con 5 Pno, Op. 73; W. A. Mozart:Con 20 Pno, K.466 EMIC 2-▲ 73329 [DDD] (16.97)

G. Samuel (cnd), Cincinnati PO, CCM Chorus CENT ▲ 2107 (16.97)

E. Schwarzkopf (sop), E. Cavelti (mez), E. Haefliger (ten), O. Edelmann (bass), W. Furtwängler (cnd), Philharmonia Orch, Lucerne Festival Chorus *(rec Aug 22, 1954)* MUA ▲ 790 [ADD] (16.97)

E. Schwarzkopf (sop), E. Höngen (cta), J. Patzak (ten), H. Hotter (b-bar), H. von Karajan (cnd), Vienna PO, Vienna Singverein *(rec 1947)* ("The First Recordings, Vol. 8") GRM2 ▲ 78736 (13.97)

T. Sluys (sop), S. Luger (cta), L. van Tulder (ten), W. Ravelli (bass), W. Mengelberg (cnd), (Royal) Concertgebouw Orch, Toonkunst Chorus *(rec 1938)* MUA ▲ 918 (16.97)

G. Solti (cnd) PLON ▲ 48617 (16.97)

G. Solti (cnd), Chicago SO, Chicago Sym Chorus [soloists P. Lorengar, Y. Minton, S. Burrows, M. Ta] ("The Solti Collection, Vol. 2") PLON (Jubilee) ▲ 30438 [ADD] (11.97)

L. Stokowski (cnd), Philadelphia Orch, A. Davis (sop), E. Loewenthal (bar), R. Cathcart (sgr), R. Betts (sgr) IMMM ▲ 37065 (6.97)

O. Suitner (cnd), Berlin Staatskapelle ("Symphonies, Vol. 1") † Sym 2; Sym 5 DNN (Classics Exposed) 2-▲ 17001 (16.97)

G. Szell (cnd), Cleveland Orch † Fidelio (ov) SNYC (Essential Classics) ▲ 46533 [ADD] (7.97) ▮ 46533 [ADD] (3.98)

M. Teschemacher (sop), E. Höngen (cta), T. Ralf (ten), J. Herrmann (bar), K. Böhm (cnd), Saxon Staatskapelle, Dresden State Opera Chorus *(rec 1941)* IN ▲ 1406 [ADD] (15.97)

P. Tiboris (cnd), Brno State PO, Janáček Opera Chorus [soloists: L. A. Myers, I. Sameth, J. Clark, R. Con] *(rec Dec 1991)* † G. Mahler:Arrangements BRID ▲ 9033 [DDD] (17.97)

A. Toscanini (cnd), NBC SO, Westminster Choir, J. Novotná (sop), K. Thorborg (cta), J. Peerce (ten), N. Moscona (bass) *(rec Carnegie Hall, New York, NY, Dec 2, 1939)* SYMP ▲ 1230 (live) (18.97)

F. V. Weingartner (cnd), Vienna PO, Vienna State Opera Chorus [GER] *(rec 1935)* PHS ▲ 9407 [AAD] (17.97)

D. Zinman (cnd), Tonhalle Orchestra Zurich ARNO ▲ 65411 (4.97)

BEETHOVEN, LUDWIG VAN (cont.)

Symphony No. 10 in E♭ [single movt; realized & compd Dr. Barry Cooper from sketches written 1812-1825, newly identified in 1984]

W. Morris (cnd), London SO [includes "The Story of Beethoven's 10th Symphony"] LSO (London SO) ▲ 6900042 [DDD] (9.97)

W. Weller (cnd), City of Birmingham SO † Con Vn, Vc, Pno, Op. 56 CHN (Collect) ▲ 6501 [DDD] (12.97)

W. Weller (cnd), City of Birmingham SO † Syms (comp) CHN 5-▲ 7042 (53.97)

Tremate, empi, tremate (aria) for Soprano, Tenor, Bass & Orchestra [text Bettoni], Op. 116 (1801-02; rev ?1814)

H. Kuhse (sop), E. Büchner (ten), S. Vogel (bass), A. Apelt (cnd), Dresden Staatskapelle ("Unknown Works, Vol. 1") † Ah, perfido!, Op. 65; Arias & Duets; Con 6 Pno; Contredanses Orch, WoO 14; German Dances Orch, WoO 8; Ländler Vns, WoO 15; Minuets Vns, WoO 9; Mödling Dances, WoO 17; Qt Strs in F, Hess 34; Son 9 Pno, Op. 14/1 BER 3-▲ 9131 [ADD] (31.97)

Trio in G for Flute, Bassoon & Piano, WoO 37 (1786)

S. Milan (fl), S. Azzolini (bn), I. Brown (pno) † Duos Cl, WoO 27; Serenade Fl, Vn & Va, Op. 25 CHN ▲ 9108 [DDD] (16.97)

J. Rampal (fl), P. Hongne (bn), R. Veyron-Lacroix (pno) ("Complete Chamber Music for Flute") † Allegro & Minuet Fls, WoO 26; National Airs with Vars, Op. 107; Serenade Fl, Op. 41; Son Fl, Anh.4; Trio Fls VB2 2-▲ 5000 [ADD] (9.97)

K. Søonstevold (bn), G. V. Bahr (fl), L. Negro (pno) *(rec Nacka, Sweden, June 13, 1976)* ("The Virtuoso Bassoon") † M. Arnold:Fant Bn, Op. 86; Blomdahl:Liten svit; R. Boutry:Interferences; E. von Koch:Monologue 5; Morthenson:Unisono; Tansman:Sonatine Bn BIS ▲ 122 [AAD] (17.97)

Trio in G for 3 Flutes [attrib]

J. Rampal (fl), C. Larde (bn), A. Marion (pno) ("Complete Chamber Music for Flute") † Allegro & Minuet Fls, WoO 26; National Airs with Vars, Op. 107; Serenade Fl, Op. 41; Son Fl, Anh.4; Trio Fl, WoO 37 VB2 2-▲ 5000 [ADD] (9.97)

Trio in C for 2 Oboes & English Horn, Op. 87 (1795)

Consortium Classicum ("Chamber Music for Winds, Vol. 3") † Octet Ww, Op. 103; Rondino Ww, WoO 25 CPO ▲ 999438 [DDD] (14.97)

Consortium Classicum † Allegro & Minuet Fls, WoO 26; Duos Cl, WoO 27; Fidelio (sels); Grenadiersmarsch, Hess 107; Octet Ww, Op. 103; Qnt Ob; Rondino Ww, WoO 25; Spt in E♭, Op. 20; Sxt Ww; Vars Ww on La ci darem la mano, WoO 28 CPO 4-▲ 999658 [DDD] (27.98)

K. Greenbank (ob), M. Zupnik (ob), E. Starr (E hn) † Vars Ww on La ci darem la mano, WoO 28; Triebensee:Trios Obs; Vars on a Theme from Haydn ASLE ▲ 6192 (8.97)

T. Indermühle (ob), D. Carmel (ob), S. Rancourt (E hn) *(rec Vienna, Austria, Feb 24-26, 1996)* † Vars Ww on La ci darem la mano, WoO 28; F. Krommer:Trio Ob; A. Vranicky:Trio Ob CAMA ▲ 481 [DDD] (18.97)

Ricercar Academy ("Music for Winds") † Qnt Ob; Rondino Ww, WoO 25; Sxt Ww; Vars Ww on La ci darem la mano, WoO 28 RICE ▲ 206712 (13.97)

Trio in E♭ for Piano, Clarinet (or Violin) & Cello [arr Beethoven of Septet, Op. 20], Op. 38 (1802-03)

N. Gutman (vc), E. Brunner (cl), E. Wirssaladze (pno) *(rec 1992 & 1994)* ("Oleg Kagan Musikfeste 1992 & 1994") † Duos Cl, WoO 27; Son 3 Vc, Op. 69 LV ▲ 671 [DDD] (17.97)

New Arts Trio *(rec University of Rochester, NY, July 17-18, 1997)* † Trio Pno (from Sym 2), Op. 36b FDS ▲ 57931 [DDD] (16.97)

F. Perrin (vn), P. Feyler (db), T. Ravassard (pno) † F. Kreisler:Vn Pieces; Massenet:Méditation from Thaïs; A. Monti:Czardas GALL ▲ 761 [DDD] (19.97)

Trios (10) for Piano, Violin & Cello (complete)

Fontenay Trio TELC 3-▲ 73281 (29.97)

P. Zukerman (vn), J. D. Pré (vc), D. Barenboim (pno) EMIC (Studio) 3-▲ 63124 [ADD] (31.97)

Trio No. 1 in E♭ for Piano, Violin & Cello, Op. 1/1 (1794-95)

Abegg Trio † Trio 2 Pno, Op. 1/2 TACE ▲ 76

Barcelona Trio HAMP ▲ 3905205 (7.97)

P. Cohen (pno), E. Höbarth (vn), C. Coin (vc) † Son 1 Vc, Op. 5/1; Son 2 Vc, Op. 5/2; Son 3 Vc, Op. 69; Trio 2 Pno, Op. 1/2 HMA 3-▲ 2908030 (26.97)

J. Fuchs (vn), P. Casals (vc), E. Istomin (pno) *(rec Prades France, July 5, 1953)* † F. Schubert:Trio 2 Pno, D.929 SNYC (The Casals Edition) ▲ 58988 [ADD] (10.97)

Guarneri Trio Prague † Allegretto Pno Trio, Hess 48; Trio 2 Pno, Op. 1/2 PRAG ▲ 250120 (18.97)

E. Höbarth (vn), C. Coin (vc), P. Cohen (pno) † Trio 2 Pno, Op. 1/2 HMA ▲ 1901361 (9.97)

London Fortepiano Trio † Trio 2 Pno, Op. 1/2 HYP ▲ 66197 [DDD] (18.97)

Osiris Trio ("Folk Music") † A. Dvořák:Trio 4 Pno, Op. 90; C. Ives:Trio; F. Martin:Trio sur les mélodies populaires irlandaises; V. Novák:Trio Pno, Op. 27; D. Shostakovich:Trio 2 Pno, Op. 67 CCL 2-▲ 13098 (18.97)

I. Stern (vn), L. Rose (vc), E. Istomin (pno) † Trio 2 Pno, Op. 1/2; Trio 3 Pno, Op. 1/3; Trio 8 Pno, WoO 38; Vars Pno Trio on Original Theme, Op. 44 SNYC (Isaac Stern: A Life in Music) 2-▲ 64510 (23.97)

Stuttgart Piano Trio *(rec 1992-93)* ("Beethoven: Piano Trios, Vol. 1") † Trio 2 Pno, Op. 1/2 NXIN ▲ 550946 [DDD] (5.97)

Vienna Piano Trio *(rec June 9-12, 1996)* † Trio 10 Pno, WoO 39; Trio 7 Pno, Op. 11 NIMB ▲ 5508 [DDD] (16.97)

Trio No. 2 in G for Piano, Violin & Cello, Op. 1/2 (1794-95)

Abegg Trio † Trio 1 Pno, Op. 1/1 TACE ▲ 76

P. Cohen (pno), E. Höbarth (vn), C. Coin (vc) † Son 1 Vc, Op. 5/1; Son 2 Vc, Op. 5/2; Son 3 Vc, Op. 69; Trio 1 Pno, Op. 1/1 HMA 3-▲ 2908030 (26.97)

Guarneri Trio Prague † Allegretto Pno Trio, Hess 48; Trio 1 Pno, Op. 1/1 PRAG ▲ 250120 (18.97)

E. Höbarth (vn), C. Coin (vc), P. Cohen (pno) † Trio 1 Pno, Op. 1/1 HMA ▲ 1901361 (9.97)

London Fortepiano Trio † Trio 1 Pno, Op. 1/1 HYP ▲ 66197 [DDD] (18.97)

A. Schneider (vn), P. Casals (vc), E. Istomin (pno) *(rec Perpignan France, Aug 1951)* † F. Schubert:Trio 1 Pno, D.898 SNYC (The Casals Edition) ▲ 58989 [ADD] (10.97)

I. Stern (vn), L. Rose (vc), E. Istomin (pno) † Trio 1 Pno, Op. 1/1; Trio 3 Pno, Op. 1/3; Trio 8 Pno, WoO 38; Vars Pno Trio on Original Theme, Op. 44 SNYC (Isaac Stern: A Life in Music) 2-▲ 64510 (23.97)

Stuttgart Piano Trio *(rec 1992-93)* ("Beethoven: Piano Trios, Vol. 1") † Trio 1 Pno, Op. 1/1 NXIN ▲ 550946 [DDD] (5.97)

Trio No. 3 in c for Piano, Violin & Cello, Op. 1/3 (1794-95)

E. Colomer (cnd), English CO † Con Vn, Vc, Pno, Op. 56 HAM ▲ 1905205 (9.97)

English Piano Trio † Songs; Trio 7 Pno, Op. 11 MER ▲ 84253 [DDD] (16.97)

B. Erichson (vc), G. Zitterbart (pno) † Trio 4 Pno, Op. 70/1 TACE ▲ 77

Guarneri Trio Prague † Trio 7 Pno, Op. 11; Trio 9 Pno, Op. 121a PRAG ▲ 250121 (18.97)

E. Höbarth (vn), C. Coin (vc), P. Cohen (pno) † Trio 10 Pno, WoO 39; Trio 7 Pno, Op. 11 HAM (Suite) ▲ 7901475 (12.97)

Moscow Conservatory Piano Trio ("Great Piano Trios: Brahms & Beethoven") † J. Brahms:Trio 1 Pno, Op. 8 CMH ▲ 8021 (13.97)

I. Stern (vn), L. Rose (vc), E. Istomin (pno) † Trio 1 Pno, Op. 1/1; Trio 2 Pno, Op. 1/2; Trio 8 Pno, WoO 38; Vars Pno Trio on Original Theme, Op. 44 SNYC (Isaac Stern: A Life in Music) 2-▲ 64510 (23.97)

Stuttgart Piano Trio *(rec 1992-93)* ("Beethoven: Piano Trios, Vol. 2") † Allegretto Pno Trio, Hess 48; Trio 8 Pno, WoO 38; Vars Pno Trio on Original Theme, Op. 44 NXIN ▲ 550947 [DDD] (5.97)

Trio Italiano *(rec Padova Italy, May 1994)* ("Piano Trios, Vol 1") † Trio 6 Pno, Op. 97 AART ▲ 47249 [DDD] (10.97)

Vienna Mozart Trio † Smetana:Trio Pno, Op. 15 DI ▲ 920527 (5.97)

Trio No. 4 in D for Piano, Violin & Cello, Op. 70/1, "Ghost" (1808)

Beaux Arts Trio † Trio 6 Pno, Op. 97 PPHI ▲ 12891 [ADD] (16.97)

Beethoven Trio Vienna † Trio 5 Pno, Op. 70/2 CAMA ▲ 253 (18.97)

Borodin Trio ("Beethoven: Piano Trios") † Trio 6 Pno, Op. 97 CHN ▲ 9296 [DDD] (16.97)

B. Erichson (vc), G. Zitterbart (pno) † Trio 3 Pno, Op. 1/3 TACE ▲ 77

Fiesole Trio *(rec 1989-90)* † F. Schubert:Qnt Pno, D.667 FON ▲ 9021 [DDD] (16.97)

J. Fuchs (vn), P. Casals (vc), E. Istomin (pno) *(rec Prades France, July 8-9, 1953)* † Trio 5 Pno, Op. 70/2; Vars Vc, WoO 45 SNYC (The Casals Edition) ▲ 58991 [ADD] (10.97)

Guarneri Trio Prague † Trio 10 Pno, WoO 39; Trio 5 Pno, Op. 70/2 PRAG ▲ 250122 (18.97)

T. Nishizaki (vn), C. Onczay (vc), J. Jandó (pno) *(rec May 27-30, 1991)* † Trio 6 Pno, Op. 97 NXIN ▲ 550442 [DDD] (5.97)

W. Schneiderhan (vn), E. Mainardi (vc), E. Fischer (pno) *(rec 1954)* † J. Brahms:Trio 1 Pno, Op. 8; Trio 2 Pno, Op. 87; Trio 3 Pno, Op. 101; R. Schumann:Trio 1 Pno, Op. 63 ARKA 2-▲ 568 [ADD] (34.97)

A. Schneider (vn), Z. Nelsova (vc), G. Gould (pno) *(rec CBC broadcast, July 18, 1954)* ("Bagatelles, Sonatas & Trios") † Allegretto Pno Trio, WoO 39; Bagatelles; Son 19 Pno, Op. 49/1; Son 28 Pno, Op. 101; Son 4 Pno, Op. 7 CBC ▲ 2013 [ADD] (16.97)

I. Stern (vn), L. Rose (vc), E. Istomin (pno) † Trio 6 Pno, Op. 97 SNYC (Essential Classics) ▲ 53514 (7.97) ▮ 53514 (3.98)

I. Stern (vn), L. Rose (vc), E. Istomin (pno) † Trio 6 Pno, Op. 97; Trio 9 Pno, Op. 121a SNYC (Isaac Stern: A Life in Music) 2-▲ 64513 (23.97)

BEETHOVEN, LUDWIG VAN (cont.)

Trio No. 4 in D for Piano, Violin & Cello, Op. 70/1, "Ghost" (1808) (cont.)

Trio Italiano *(rec Padova Italy, May 1994)* † Trio 5 Pno, Op. 70/2; Vars Pno Trio on Ich bin der Schneider Kakadu, Op. 121a AART ▲ 47251 [DDD] (10.97)

Trio No. 5 in E♭ for Piano, Violin & Cello, Op. 70/2 (1808)

Beethoven Trio Vienna † Trio 4 Pno, Op. 70/1 CAMA ▲ 253 (18.97)

B. Erichson (vc), G. Zitterbart (pno) † Vars Pno Trio on Ich bin der Schneider Kadaku, Op. 121a; Vars Pno Trio on Original Theme, Op. 44 TACE ▲ 78

Guarneri Trio Prague † Trio 10 Pno, WoO 39; Trio 4 Pno, Op. 70/1 PRAG ▲ 250122 (18.97)

W. Kempff (pno), H. Szeryng (vn), P. Fournier (vc)—Allegro ma non troppo ("The Complete Beethoven Edition Compactotheque") † Chor auf die verbundeten Fürsten, WoO 95; Glorreiche Augenblick, Op. 136; Leonore (sels); Ländler Pno, WoO 11; Marches Military Band, WoO 18-20; Qt Strs in F, Hess 34; Qt 11 Strs, Op. 95; Qt 16 Strs, Op. 135; Romance Fl, Bn & Pno, Hess 13; Scottish Songs (25), Op. 108; Serenade Str Trio, Op. 8; Son 3 Vc, Op. 69; Son 5 Vn, Op. 24; Son 8 Pno, Op. 13; Spt in E♭, Op. 20; Sym 5; Triumphal March, WoO 2a; Zärtliche Leibe, WoO 123 DEUT ▲ 453811 [ADD/DDD] (11.97)

A. Schneider (vn), P. Casals (vc), E. Istomin (pno) *(rec Perpignan France, Aug 1951)* † Trio 4 Pno, Op. 70/1; Vars Vc, WoO 45 SNYC (The Casals Edition) ▲ 58991 [ADD] (10.97)

Trio Italiano *(rec Padova Italy, May 1994)* † Trio 4 Pno, Op. 70/1; Vars Pno Trio on Ich bin der Schneider Kakadu, Op. 121a AART ▲ 47251 [DDD] (10.97)

P. Zukerman (vn), J. D. Pré (vc), D. Barenboim (pno) † Son 3 Vc, Op. 69; E. Elgar:Con Vc; J. Haydn:Con 1 Vc EMIC 2-▲ 69707 (21.97)

Trio No. 6 in B♭ for Piano, Violin & Cello, Op. 97, "Archduke" (1810-11)

Bamberg Trio † Trio 9 Pno, Op. 121a PC ▲ 267009 [DDD] (2.97)

Beaux Arts Trio † Trio 4 Pno, Op. 70/1 PPHI ▲ 12891 [ADD] (16.97)

Borodin Trio ("Beethoven: Piano Trios") † Trio 4 Pno, Op. 70/1 CHN ▲ 9296 [DDD] (16.97)

B. Erichson (vc), G. Zitterbart (pno) *(rec Frankfurt, Germany, June 1988)* † Allegretto Pno Trio, Hess 48; Trio 10 Pno, WoO 39; Trio 8 Pno, WoO 38 TACE ▲ 79

H. Holst (vn), A. Pini (vc), Solomon (pno) ("The First HMV Recordings: 1942-43") † J. Brahms:Vars & Fugue on a Theme by Handel, Op. 24; Chopin:Berceuse, Op. 57; Pno Music (misc colls) APR ▲ 5503 [ADD] (19.97)

V. Mullova (vn), H. Schiff (vc), A. Previn (pno) ("Trios") † J. Brahms:Trio 1 Pno, Op. 8 PPHI ▲ 42123 (16.97)

T. Nishizaki (vn), C. Onczay (vc), J. Jandó (pno) *(rec May 27-30, 1991)* † Trio 4 Pno, Op. 70/1 NXIN ▲ 550442 [DDD] (5.97)

I. Perlman (vn), L. Harrell (vc), V. Ashkenazy (pno) † Trio 10 Pno, WoO 39 EMIC ▲ 47010 [DDD] (16.97)

S. Richter (pno) † Qnt Pno, Op. 16; Son 28 Pno, Op. 101 PPHI (Richter: The Authorized Recordings) 2-▲ 38624 (32.97)

A. Sammons (vn), W. H. Squire (vc), W. Murdoch (pno) † Son 23 Pno, Op. 57; Son 8 Pno, Op. 13 PHS ▲ 44 (17.97)

A. Schneider (vn), P. Casals (vc), E. Istomin (pno) *(rec Perpignan France, Aug 1951)* † Trio 7 Pno, Op. 11 SNYC (The Casals Edition) ▲ 58990 [ADD] (10.97)

Solomon (pno) *(rec early 1940s)* † J. Brahms:Intermezzos (3) Pno, Op. 117; Rhaps (2) Pno, Op. 79; Vars & Fugue on a Theme by Handel, Op. 24 ENPL (Piano Library) ▲ 313 (14.97)

I. Stern (vn), L. Rose (vc), E. Istomin (pno) † Trio 4 Pno, Op. 70/1 SNYC (Essential Classics) ▲ 53514 (7.97) ▮ 53514 (3.98)

I. Stern (vn), L. Rose (vc), E. Istomin (pno) † Trio 4 Pno, Op. 70/1; Trio 9 Pno, Op. 121a SNYC (Isaac Stern: A Life in Music) 2-▲ 64513 (23.97)

Stuttgart Piano Trio *(rec Heidelberg, Germany, 1992, 1993)* ("Beethoven Piano Trios, Vol. 4") † Allegretto Pno Trio, WoO 39; Vars Pno Trio on Ich bin der Schneider Kadaku, Op. 121a NXIN ▲ 550949 [DDD] (5.97)

J. Thibaud (vn), P. Casals (vc), A. Cortot (pno) *(rec London, England, 1928)* ("Casals Trio I") † Mendelssohn (-Bartholdy):Trio 1 Pno, Op. 49; F. Schubert:Trio 1 Pno, D.898; R. Schumann:Trio 1 Pno, Op. 63 MPLY 2-▲ 2005 (m) [ADD] (16.97)

Trio Italiano *(rec Padova Italy, May 1994)* ("Piano Trios, Vol 1") † Trio 3 Pno, Op. 1/3 AART ▲ 47249 [DDD] (10.97)

Trio No. 7 in B♭ for Piano, Clarinet (or Violin) & Cello, Op. 11 (1797)

Ambache Chamber Ensemble members *(rec Feb 3-5, 1993)* † Qnt Pno, Op. 16; Son Hn INMP ▲ 6701362 (9.97)

Amici Chamber Ensemble † Chan Ka Nin:Among Friends; Zemlinsky:Trio Cl, Op. 3 SUMM ▲ 151 [DDD] (16.97)

M. Bergman (vc), E. Eban (cl), O. Wolkov (pno) † J. Brahms:Trio Cl MER ▲ 84122 (16.97)

Bonaventura Ensemble *(rec Bavarian Radio, Dec 14-15, 1995)* † J. Brahms:Trio Cl CALG ▲ 50958 [DDD] (19.97)

Classic Trio ("Clarinet Trios") † J. Brahms:Trio Cl; M. Glinka:Trio pathétique ASVQ ▲ 6187 (10.97)

C. Coin (vc), W. Mayer (cl), P. Cohen (pno) HAM (La Solothèque) ▲ 926004 (5.97)

C. Coin (vc), W. Meyer (cl), P. Cohen (pno) † Trio 10 Pno, WoO 39; Trio 3 Pno, Op. 1/3 HAM (Suite) ▲ 7901475 (12.97)

English Piano Trio † Songs; Trio 3 Pno, Op. 1/3 MER ▲ 84253 [DDD] (16.97)

N. Gutman (vc), E. Brunner (cl), E. Wirssaladze (pno) *(rec Wildbad Kreuth, July 3, 1992)* ("Oleg Kagan: Musikfest am Tegernsee") † Son 22 Pno, Op. 54; Son 3 Vc, Op. 69 LV ▲ 622 [DDD] (17.97)

A. Meunier (vc), R. Stolzman (cl), R. Serkin (pno) ("Marlboro Festival 40th Anniversary") † Qnt Pno, Op. 16; Trio 9 Pno, Op. 121a SNYC ▲ 47296 [ADD] (10.97)

P. Moraguès (cl), Guarneri Trio Prague † Trio 3 Pno, Op. 1/3; Trio 9 Pno, Op. 121a PRAG ▲ 250121 (18.97)

Nash Ensemble *(rec 1987-89)* † Spt in E♭, Op. 20; F. Schubert:Octet Ww & Strs, D.803 VCL 2-▲ 61409 [DDD] (11.97)

A. Schneider (vn), P. Casals (vc), E. Istomin (pno) *(rec Perpignan France, Aug 1951)* † Trio 6 Pno, Op. 97 SNYC (The Casals Edition) ▲ 58990 [ADD] (10.97)

Trio Apollon † M. Glinka:Trio pathétique; W. A. Mozart:Trio Cl, K.498; M. Ravel:Pavane pour une infante défunte DI ▲ 920500 [DDD] (5.97)

Vienna Piano Trio *(rec June 9-12, 1996)* † Trio 1 Pno, Op. 1/1; Trio 10 Pno, WoO 39 NIMB ▲ 5508 [DDD] (16.97)

Zurich Piano Trio † Mendelssohn (-Bartholdy):Trio 1 Pno, Op. 49; Rihm:Fremde Szenen III ARSM ▲ 1202 [DDD]

Trio No. 8 in E♭ for Piano, Violin & Cello, WoO 38 (1791)

B. Erichson (vc), G. Zitterbart (pno) *(rec Frankfurt, Germany, June 1988)* † Allegretto Pno Trio, Hess 48; Trio 10 Pno, WoO 39; Trio 6 Pno, Op. 97 TACE ▲ 79

I. Stern (vn), L. Rose (vc), E. Istomin (pno) † Trio 1 Pno, Op. 1/1; Trio 2 Pno, Op. 1/2; Trio 3 Pno, Op. 1/3; Vars Pno Trio on Original Theme, Op. 44 SNYC (Isaac Stern: A Life in Music) 2-▲ 64510 (23.97)

Stuttgart Piano Trio *(rec 1992-93)* ("Beethoven: Piano Trios, Vol. 2") † Allegretto Pno Trio, Hess 48; Trio 3 Pno, Op. 1/3; Vars Pno Trio on Original Theme, Op. 44 NXIN ▲ 550947 [DDD] (5.97)

Trio No. 9 in G for Piano, Violin & Cello, Op. 121a, "Kakadu" (?1813; rev 1816)

Bamberg Trio † Trio 6 Pno, Op. 97 PC ▲ 267009 [DDD] (2.97)

Guarneri Trio Prague † Trio 3 Pno, Op. 1/3; Trio 7 Pno, Op. 11 PRAG ▲ 250121 (18.97)

Y. Horigome (vn), P. Wiley (vc), R. Serkin (pno) ("Marlboro Festival 40th Anniversary") † Qnt Pno, Op. 16; Trio 7 Pno, Op. 11 SNYC ▲ 47296 [ADD] (10.97)

I. Stern (vn), L. Rose (vc), E. Istomin (pno) † Trio 4 Pno, Op. 70/1; Trio 6 Pno, Op. 97 SNYC (Isaac Stern: A Life in Music) 2-▲ 64513 (23.97)

Trio No. 10 in B♭ for Piano, Violin & Cello, WoO 39 (1812)

B. Erichson (vc), G. Zitterbart (pno) *(rec Frankfurt, Germany, June 1988)* † Allegretto Pno Trio, Hess 48; Trio 6 Pno, Op. 97; Trio 8 Pno, WoO 38 TACE ▲ 79

Guarneri Trio Prague † Trio 4 Pno, Op. 70/1; Trio 5 Pno, Op. 70/2 PRAG ▲ 250122 (18.97)

E. Höbarth (vn), C. Coin (vc), P. Cohen (pno) † Trio 3 Pno, Op. 1/3; Trio 7 Pno, Op. 11 HAM (Suite) ▲ 7901475 (12.97)

I. Perlman (vn), L. Harrell (vc), V. Ashkenazy (pno) † Trio 6 Pno, Op. 97 EMIC ▲ 47010 [DDD] (16.97)

Vienna Piano Trio *(rec June 9-12, 1996)* † Trio 1 Pno, Op. 1/1; Trio 7 Pno, Op. 11 NIMB ▲ 5508 [DDD] (16.97)

Trio for Piano, Violin & Cello [arr Beethoven from *Symphony No. 2*], Op. 36b (1805)

Beethoven Trio Vienna † Con Vn, Vc, Pno, Op. 56 CAMA ▲ 252 [DDD] (18.97)

New Arts Trio *(rec University of Rochester, NY, July 17-18, 1997)* † Trio Pno (from Spt, Op. 20), Op. 38 FDS ▲ 57931 [DDD] (16.97)

Trio in E♭ for Strings, Op. 3 (before 1794)

A. Busch (vn), L. H. Bamberger (va), H. Busch (vc) *(rec live, Jan 9, 1944)* ("Busch Quartet Live") † Qt 13 Strs, Op. 130; Qt 9 Strs, Op. 59/3; W. A. Mozart:Trio Pno, K.564 ARBT 2-▲ 112 [ADD] (16.97)

German String Trio ("Early Chamber Music, Vol. 2") † Qt Strs in F, Hess 34; Qt 3 Strs, Op. 18/3; Qt 4 Strs, Op. 18/4; Spt in E♭, Op. 20; Trios Strs, Op. 9 INTC ▲ 885911 (16.97)

A. Grumiaux (vn), G. Janzer (va), E. Czako (vc) † Trios Strs, Op. 9 PPHI (Duo) 2-▲ 456317 (17.97)

L'Archibudelli *(rec Nov 22-25, 1992)* † Serenade Str Trio, Op. 8 SNYC ▲ 53961 [DDD] (16.97)

Leopold Trio † Serenade Str Trio, Op. 8 HYP ▲ 67253 (18.97)

I. Perlman (vn), P. Zukerman (va), L. Harrell (vc) † Serenade Str Trio, Op. 8; Trios Strs, Op. 9 EMIC 2-▲ 54198 (32.97)

BEETHOVEN, LUDWIG VAN (cont.)

Trios (3) for Strings, Op. 9 (1797-98)

Gaede Trio—No. 1 in G † W. A. Mozart:Bach Trans, K.404a; A. Schnittke:Trio Strs TACE ▲ 64 (16.97)

German String Trio ("Early Chamber Music, Vol. 2") † Qt Strs in F, Hess 34; Qt 3 Strs, Op. 18/3; Qt 4 Strs, Op. 18/4; Spt in E♭, Op. 20; Trio Strs, Op. 3 INTC ▲ 885911 (16.97)

A. Grumiaux (vn), G. Janzer (va), E. Czako (vc) † Trio Strs, Op. 3 PPHI (Duo) 2-▲ 456317 (17.97)

L'Archibudelli SNYC (Vivarte) ▲ 48190 (16.97)

La Scala String Trio *(rec Villa Giulini Briosco, Jan 1996)* AG ▲ 40 [DDD] (18.97)

Leopold Trio HYP ▲ 67254 (18.97)

I. Perlman (vn), P. Zukerman (va), L. Harrell (vc) † Serenade Str Trio, Op. 8; Trio Strs, Op. 3 EMIC 2-▲ 54198 (32.97)

Triumphal March [?for Kuffner's *Tarpeja*] in C for Orchestra, WoO 2a (1813)

A. Davis (cnd), BBC SO ("The Complete Beethoven Edition Compactotheque") † Chor auf die verbundeten Fürsten, WoO 95; Glorreiche Augenblick, Op. 136; Leonore (sels); Ländler Pno, WoO 11; Marches Military Band, WoO 18-20; Qt Strs in F, Hess 34; Qt 11 Strs, Op. 95; Qt 16 Strs, Op. 135; Romance Fl, Bn & Pno, Hess 13; Scottish Songs (25), Op. 108; Serenade Str Trio, Op. 8; Son 3 Vc, Op. 69; Son 5 Vn, Op. 24; Son 8 Pno, Op. 13; Spt in E♭, Op. 20; Sym 5; Trio 5 Pno, Op. 70/2; Zärtliche Leibe, WoO 123 DEUT ▲ 453811 [ADD/DDD] (11.97)

K. A. Rickenbacher (cnd), Berlin RSO ("Works for Orchestra & Chorus") † Flamme lodert 1, Op. 121; Flamme lodert 2, Op. 121b; In allen guten Stunden, Op. 122; Leonore Prohaska, WoO 96; Meeresstille und glückliche Fahrt, Op. 112 KSCH ▲ 314852 (16.97)

Variations for Cello & Piano, Op. 66 & WoO 45-46

P. Wispelwey (vc) ("The Complete Performer: Chamber Music Masterpieces") † J. Brahms:Sons Vc (comp); F. Schubert:Qnt in C Strs, D.956; Vivaldi:Sons Vc CCL 4-▲ 697 (36.97)

Variations (12) in F on "Ein Mädchen oder Weibchen" from Mozart's *Die Zauberflöte* for Cello & Piano, Op. 66 (1796)

P. Casals (vc), R. Serkin (pno) *(rec Perpignan France, July 31, 1951)* † Sons Vc (comp); Vars Vc on "Bei Männern", WoO 46 SNYC (The Casals Edition) 2-▲ 58985 [ADD] (23.97)

D. Finckel (vc), W. Han (pno) *(rec Aspen, CO, 1997)* † Sons Vc (comp); Vars Vc on "Bei Männern", WoO 46; Vars Vc, WoO 45 ARLD 2-▲ 19801

P. Fournier (vc), M. Hess (pno) *(rec 1959)* ("Hess & Fournier in a New York Sonata Recital") † Son 4 Vc; J. S. Bach:Sons Vl; J. Brahms:Son 2 Vc, Op. 99; W. A. Mozart:Gigue Pno, K.574; Rondo Pno, K.485 RELE ▲ 1895 [ADD]

P. Fournier (vc), W. Kempff (pno) ("The Music for Cello & Piano") † Sons Vc (comp); Vars Vc on "Bei Männern", WoO 46; Vars Vc, WoO 45 DEUT (2CD) 2-▲ 453013 (17.97)

M. Gendron (vc), J. Françaix (pno) † Sons Vc (comp); Vars Vc on "Bei Männern", WoO 46; Vars Vc, WoO 45 PPHI (Duo) 2-▲ 42565 (17.97)

S. Honigberg (vc), C. Honigberg (pno) *(rec Fort Washington, MD, 1992-96)* ("Complete Works for Cello & Piano") † Sons Vc (comp); Vars Vc on "Bei Männern", WoO 46; Vars Vc, WoO 45 ALBA 2-▲ 268 [DDD] (25.97)

J. Krosnick (vc), G. Kalish (pno) *(rec Recital Hall of the Staller Center SUNY-Stony Broo, May 28-June 1, 1994)* ("Cello Sonatas & Variations") † Sons Vc (comp); Vars Vc on "Bei Männern", WoO 46; Vars Vc, WoO 45 ARA 2-▲ 6656 [DDD] (32.97)

Y.-Y. Ma (vc), E. Ax (pno) † Son 4 Vc; Vars Vc on "Bei Männern", WoO 46; Vars Vc, WoO 45 SNYC ▲ 42121 [DDD] (16.97)

Y.-Y. Ma (vc), E. Ax (pno) † Sons Vc (comp); Vars Vc on "Bei Männern", WoO 46 SNYC 2-▲ 42446 [DDD] (31.97)

M. Maisky (vc), M. Argerich (pno) † Sons Vc (comp); Vars Vc on "Bei Männern", WoO 46; Vars Vc, WoO 45 DGRM 2-▲ 439934 [DDD] (35.97)

J. Metzger (vc), D. Goldmann (pno) † Son 3 Vc, Op. 69; Son 4 Vc; Vars Vc, WoO 45 PC ▲ 267008 [DDD]

R. Metzmacher (vc), E. Steen-Nökleberg (pno) [No. 3] † Son 1 Vc, Op. 5/1; Son 2 Vc, Op. 5/2; Son 3 Vc, Op. 69; Son 4 Vc; Son 5 Vc; Vars Vc, WoO 45 BRIO 2-▲ 100 (16.97)

P. Olefsky (vc), W. Hautzig (pno) ("The Piano & the Cello: Complete Works") † Sons Vc (comp); Vars Vc on "Bei Männern", WoO 46; Vars Vc, WoO 45 AMCU 2-▲ 1001 [DDD] (26.97)

C. Onczay (vc), J. Jandó (pno) *(rec June 25-27, 1991)* † Son 1 Vc, Op. 5/1; Son 2 Vc, Op. 5/2; Vars Vc on "Bei Männern", WoO 46; Vars Vc, WoO 45 NXIN ▲ 550479 (5.97)

P. Pulford (vc), B. McDonald (pno) ("Complete Works for Cello on Historic Instruments") † Sons Vc (comp); Vars Vc on "Bei Männern", WoO 46; Vars Vc, WoO 45 EBS 2-▲ 6030 [DDD] (34.97)

T. Tsutsumi (vc), R. Turini (pno) *(rec May 28-31, 1980)* † Sons Vc (comp); Vars Vc on "Bei Männern", WoO 46 SNYC 2-▲ 53240 [ADD] (14.97)

J. Vogler (vc), B. Camino (pno) ("Vol. 2") † Son 3 Vc, Op. 69; Vars Vc on "Bei Männern", WoO 46; Vars Vc, WoO 45; R. Schumann:Fantasiestücke Cl, Op. 73 BER ▲ 1167 (16.97)

Variations (12) in G on "See, the Conquering Hero Comes" from Handel's *Judas Maccabaeus* for Cello & Piano, WoO 45 (1796)

A. Bylsma (vc), S. Hoogland (pno) ("The Cello & the King of Prussia") † Vars Vc on "Bei Männern", WoO 46; J.-P. Duport:Sons Vc, Op. 2; J.-L. Duport:21 exercicesfaisants suite à l'essai sur l; B. Romberg:Son 1 in E♭ Vc SNYC ▲ 63360 (16.97)

P. Casals (vc), R. Serkin (pno) *(rec Perpignan France, Aug 1951)* † Trio 4 Pno, Op. 70/1; Trio 5 Pno, Op. 70/2 SNYC (The Casals Edition) ▲ 58991 [ADD] (10.97)

C. Coin (vc), P. Cohen (pno) † Son 3 Vc, Op. 69; Vars Vc on "Bei Männern", WoO 46 HMA ▲ 1901180 (9.97)

D. Finckel (vc), W. Han (pno) *(rec Aspen, CO, 1997)* † Sons Vc (comp); Vars Vc on "Bei Männern", WoO 46; Vars Vc on "Ein Mädchen oder Weibchen", Op. 66 ARLD 2-▲ 19801

P. Fournier (vc), W. Kempff (pno) ("The Music for Cello & Piano") † Sons Vc (comp); Vars Vc on "Bei Männern", WoO 46; Vars Vc on "Ein Mädchen oder Weibchen", Op. 66 DEUT (2CD) 2-▲ 453013 (17.97)

M. Gendron (vc), J. Françaix (pno) † Sons Vc (comp); Vars Vc on "Bei Männern", WoO 46; Vars Vc on "Ein Mädchen oder Weibchen", Op. 66 PPHI (Duo) 2-▲ 42565 (17.97)

S. Honigberg (vc), C. Honigberg (pno) † Son 2 Vc, Op. 5/2; Son 3 Vc, Op. 69; Vars Vc on "Bei Männern", WoO 46 ALBA ▲ 116 [DDD] (16.97)

S. Honigberg (vc), C. Honigberg (pno) *(rec Fort Washington, MD, 1992-96)* ("Complete Works for Cello & Piano") † Sons Vc (comp); Vars Vc on "Bei Männern", WoO 46; Vars Vc on "Ein Mädchen oder Weibchen", Op. 66 ALBA 2-▲ 268 [DDD] (25.97)

J. Krosnick (vc), G. Kalish (pno) *(rec Recital Hall of the Staller Center SUNY-Stony Brook, May 28-June 1, 1994)* ("Cello Sonatas & Variations") † Sons Vc (comp); Vars Vc on "Bei Männern", WoO 46; Vars Vc on "Ein Mädchen oder Weibchen", Op. 66 ARA 2-▲ 6656 [DDD] (32.97)

Y.-Y. Ma (vc), E. Ax (pno) † Son 4 Vc; Vars Vc on "Bei Männern", WoO 46; Vars Vc on "Ein Mädchen oder Weibchen", Op. 66 SNYC ▲ 42121 [DDD] (16.97)

M. Maisky (vc), M. Argerich (pno) † Son 3 Vc, Op. 69; Son 4 Vc; Son 5 Vc DEUT ▲ 37514 [DDD] (16.97)

M. Maisky (vc), M. Argerich (pno) † Sons Vc (comp); Vars Vc on "Bei Männern", WoO 46; Vars Vc on "Ein Mädchen oder Weibchen", Op. 66 DGRM 2-▲ 439934 [DDD] (35.97)

J. Metzger (vc), D. Goldmann (pno) † Son 3 Vc, Op. 69; Son 4 Vc; Vars Vc on "Ein Mädchen oder Weibchen", Op. 66 PC ▲ 267008 [DDD]

R. Metzmacher (vc), E. Steen-Nökleberg (pno) [No. 1] † Son 1 Vc, Op. 5/1; Son 2 Vc, Op. 5/2; Son 3 Vc, Op. 69; Son 4 Vc; Son 5 Vc; Vars Vc on "Ein Mädchen oder Weibchen", Op. 66 BRIO 2-▲ 100 (16.97)

P. Olefsky (vc), W. Hautzig (pno) ("The Piano & the Cello: Complete Works") † Sons Vc (comp); Vars Vc on "Bei Männern", WoO 46; Vars Vc on "Ein Mädchen oder Weibchen", Op. 66 AMCU 2-▲ 1001 [DDD] (26.97)

C. Onczay (vc), J. Jandó (pno) *(rec June 25-27, 1991)* † Son 1 Vc, Op. 5/1; Son 2 Vc, Op. 5/2; Vars Vc on "Bei Männern", WoO 46; Vars Vc on "Ein Mädchen oder Weibchen", Op. 66 NXIN ▲ 550479 (5.97)

J. D. Pré (vc), D. Barenboim (pno) † Sons Vc (comp); Vars Vc on "Bei Männern", WoO 46 EMIC 2-▲ 63015 (21.97)

P. Pulford (vc), B. McDonald (pno) ("Complete Works for Cello on Historic Instruments") † Sons Vc (comp); Vars Vc on "Bei Männern", WoO 46; Vars Vc on "Ein Mädchen oder Weibchen", Op. 66 EBS 2-▲ 6030 [DDD] (34.97)

J. Vogler (vc), B. Camino (pno) ("Vol. 2") † Son 3 Vc, Op. 69; Vars Vc on "Bei Männern", WoO 46; Vars Vc on "Ein Mädchen oder Weibchen", Op. 66; R. Schumann:Fantasiestücke Cl, Op. 73 BER ▲ 1167 (16.97)

Variations (7) in E♭ on "Bei Männern" from Mozart's *Die Zauberflöte* for Cello & Piano, WoO 46 (1801)

A. Bylsma (vc), S. Hoogland (pno) ("The Cello & the King of Prussia") † Vars Vc, WoO 45; J.-P. Duport:Sons Vc, Op. 2; J.-L. Duport:21 exercicesfaisants suite à l'essai sur l; B. Romberg:Son 1 in E♭ Vc SNYC ▲ 63360 (16.97)

P. Casals (vc) *(rec 1927-39)* ("Pablo Casals Plays Beethoven: The Complete Cello Sonatas") † J. S. Bach:Suites Vc MPLY 2-▲ 2004 (16.97)

P. Casals (vc), A. Cortot (pno) *(rec 1927 for HMV)* † Minuets (12) Orch, WoO 7; Sons Vc (comp) PHS 2-▲ 9461 [AAD] (33.97)

P. Casals (vc), A. Cortot (pno) *(rec London, June 1927)* ("The Complete Sonatas for Cello & Piano") † Minuets (12) Orch, WoO 7; Sons Vc (comp) ENT (Strings) 2-▲ 99360 (32.97)

P. Casals (vc), A. Cortot (pno) *(rec 1927)* † Vars Pno Trio on Ich bin der Schneider Kakadu, Op. 121a; G. Fauré:Son 1 Vn, Op. 13; J. Haydn:Trio 2 Kbd, H.XV/6 ENT ▲ 99385 (16.97)

P. Casals (vc), R. Serkin (pno) *(rec & Prades France, July 31, 1951 & May 17-20, 1953)* † Sons Vc (comp); Vars Vc on "Ein Mädchen oder Weibchen", Op. 66 SNYC (The Casals Edition) 2-▲ 58985 [ADD] (23.97)

BEETHOVEN, LUDWIG VAN (cont.)

Variations (7) in E♭ on "Bei Männern" from Mozart's *Die Zauberflöte* for Cello & Piano, WoO 46 (1801) (cont.)

C. Coin (vc), P. Cohen (pno) † Son 3 Vc, Op. 69; Vars Vc, WoO 45 HMA ▲ 1901180 (9.97)
D. Finckel (vc), W. Han (pno) *(rec Aspen, CO, 1997)* † Sons Vc (comp); Vars Vc on "Ein Mädchen oder Weibchen", Op. 66; Vars Vc, WoO 45 ARLD 2-▲ 19801
P. Fournier (vc), W. Kempff (pno) ("The Music for Cello & Piano") † Sons Vc (comp); Vars Vc on "Ein Mädchen oder Weibchen", Op. 66; Vars Vc, WoO 45 DEUT (2CD) 2-▲ 453013 (17.97)
M. Gendron (vc), J. Françaix (pno) † Sons Vc (comp); Vars Vc on "Ein Mädchen oder Weibchen", Op. 66; Vars Vc, WoO 45 PPHI (Duo) 2-▲ 42565 (17.97)
B. Hampton (vc), N. Schwartz (pno) *(rec Beverly Hills, 1972)* † Duos Cl, WoO 27; Son Hn ORIO ▲ 7819 (13.97)
S. Honigberg (vc), C. Honigberg (pno) † Son 2 Vc, Op. 5/2; Son 3 Vc, Op. 69; Vars Vc, WoO 45 ALBA ▲ 116 [DDD] (16.97)
S. Honigberg (vc), C. Honigberg (pno) *(rec Fort Washington, MD, 1992-96)* ("Complete Works for Cello & Piano") † Sons Vc (comp); Vars Vc on "Ein Mädchen oder Weibchen", Op. 66; Vars Vc, WoO 45 ALBA 2-▲ 268 [DDD] (25.97)
J. Krosnick (vc), G. Kalish (pno) *(rec Recital Hall of the Staller Center SUNY-Stony Broo, May 28-June 1, 1994)* ("Cello Sonatas & Variations") † Sons Vc (comp); Vars Vc on "Ein Mädchen oder Weibchen", Op. 66; Vars Vc, WoO 45 ARA 2-▲ 6656 [DDD] (32.97)
Y.-Y. Ma (vc), E. Ax (pno) † Son 4 Vc; Vars Vc on "Ein Mädchen oder Weibchen", Op. 66; Vars Vc, WoO 45 SNYC ▲ 42121 [DDD] (16.97)
Y.-Y. Ma (vc), E. Ax (pno) † Sons Vc (comp); Vars Vc on "Ein Mädchen oder Weibchen", Op. 66 SNYC 2-▲ 42446 [DDD] (31.97)
M. Maisky (vc), M. Argerich (pno) † Sons Vc (comp); Vars Vc on "Ein Mädchen oder Weibchen", Op. 66; Vars Vc, WoO 45 DGRM 2-▲ 439934 [DDD] (35.97)
H. Ni (vc), H. Jeanney (pno) *(rec Turku Finland, June 2-4, 1997)* ("Cello Recital") † Mendelssohn (-Bartholdy):Son 2 Vc, Op. 58; Popper:Elfentanz Vc; F. Schubert:Son Arpeggione, D.821; R. Schumann:Fantasiestücke Cl, Op. 73 NXIN ▲ 8554356 [DDD] (5.97)
P. Olefsky (vc), W. Hautzig (pno) ("The Piano & the Cello: Complete Works") † Sons Vc (comp); Vars Vc on "Ein Mädchen oder Weibchen", Op. 66; Vars Vc, WoO 45 AMCU 2-▲ 1001 [DDD] (26.97)
C. Onczay (vc), J. Jandó (pno) *(rec June 25-27, 1991)* † Son 1 Vc, Op. 5/1; Son 2 Vc, Op. 5/2; Vars Vc on "Ein Mädchen oder Weibchen", Op. 66; Vars Vc, WoO 45 NXIN ▲ 550479 (5.97)
J. D. Pré (vc), D. Barenboim (pno) † Sons Vc (comp); Vars Vc, WoO 45 EMIC 2-▲ 63015 (21.97)
P. Pulford (vc), B. McDonald (pno) ("Complete Works for Cello on Historic Instruments") † Sons Vc (comp); Vars Vc on "Ein Mädchen oder Weibchen", Op. 66; Vars Vc, WoO 45 EBS 2-▲ 6030 [DDD] (34.97)
T. Tsutsumi (vc), R. Turini (pno) *(rec May 28-31, 1980)* † Sons Vc (comp); Vars Vc on "Ein Mädchen oder Weibchen", Op. 66 SNYC 2-▲ 53240 [ADD] (14.97)
J. Vogler (vc), B. Camino (pno) ("Vol. 2") † Son 3 Vc, Op. 69; Vars Vc on "Ein Mädchen oder Weibchen", Op. 66; Vars Vc, WoO 45; R. Schumann:Fantasiestücke Cl, Op. 73 BER ▲ 1167 (16.97)

Variations for Piano

A. Brendel (pno)—Vars Pno on Original Theme, Op. 34; Vars & Fugue Pno, Op. 35; Vars Pno on Original Theme, Op. 76 † Pno Music (misc); Son 20 Pno, Op. 49/2; Son 4 Pno, Op. 7 VB3 3-▲ 3017 [ADD] (14.97)

Variations (10) on Salieri's duet "La stessa, le stessissima" for Piano, WoO 73 (1799)

R. Brautigam (pno) *(rec Dec 1992)* † Vars Pno on a Russian Dance, WoO 71; Vars Pno on Ditterdorf's Es war einmal, WoO 66; Vars Pno on Grétry's romance, WoO 72; Vars Pno on Haibel's Menuet, WoO 68; Vars Pno on Paisiello's Nel cor piu non me sento, WoO 70; Vars Pno on Paisiello's Quant' è piu bella, WoO 69; Vars Pno on Winter's Kind willst du ruhig schlafen, WoO 75 GLOE ▲ 5095 [DDD] (16.97)
Y. Kojima (pno) [Anton Walter 1795 fortepiano replica] ("Early Piano Works") † Bagatelles; Son 1 Pno, Op. 2/1; Son 8 Pno, Op. 13 DNN ▲ 18010 (16.97)

Variations (6) in F on an Original Theme for Piano, Op. 34 (1802)

G. Gould (pno) *(rec 1967)* † Bagatelles; Vars & Fugue Pno, Op. 35; Vars Pno on Original Theme, WoO 80 SNYC (Glenn Gould Edition) 2-▲ 52646 [ADD] (31.97)
G. Gould (pno) † Con 3 Pno, Op. 37; Vars & Fugue Pno, Op. 35 CBC (Perspective) ▲ 2004 [ADD] (16.97)
D. Matthews (pno) *(rec Mozart Hall Vienna, Nov 11, 1958)* ("Beethoven, Vol. 2") † Vars & Fugue Pno, Op. 35; Vars Pno on Original Theme, WoO 80 VC ▲ 8074 [ADD] (13.97)
S. Richter (pno) ("The Richter Collection, Vol. 2") † Son 27 Pno, Op. 90; Son 3 Pno, Op. 2/3; Son 4 Pno, Op. 7; Vars & Fugue Pno, Op. 35; Vars Pno on Original Theme, Op. 76; J. Brahms:Son 1 Vn, Op. 78; Chopin:Scherzos Pno; J. Haydn:Son 39 Kbd, H.XVI/24; S. Rachmaninoff:Etudes-tableaux Pno; Preludes Pno; R. Schumann:Bunte Blätter, Op. 99; Symphonic Etudes, Op. 13; D. Shostakovich:Son Vn OLY 5-▲ 5013 [DDD] (64.97)
A. Schnabel (pno) *(rec 1932-38)* ("Schnabel Plays Beethoven, Vol. 3") † Bagatelles PHS 2-▲ 9123 [AAD] (33.97)
A. Schnabel (pno) *(rec 1930s)* † Bagatelle Pno in a, WoO 59; Vars Pno on a Waltz by Diabelli, Op. 120 GRM2 ▲ 78811 (13.97)
A. Schnabel (pno) † Son 11 Pno, Op. 22; Son 12 Pno, Op. 26; Son 13 Pno, Op. 27/1 78'S ▲ 78543 (13.97)
E. Westenholz (pno) † Vars & Fugue Pno, Op. 35; Vars Pno on Original Theme, WoO 80 KPT ▲ 32145 [DDD]

Variations & Fugue in E♭ for Piano, Op. 35, "Eroica" (1802)

C. Arrau (pno) *(rec 1941)* † W. A. Mozart:Son 18 Pno, K.576; Son 5 Pno, K.283; C. M. von Weber:Son 1 Pno, Op. 24 ENPL (Piano Library) ▲ 275 (13.97)
A. Brendel (pno) † Bagatelle Pno in a, WoO 59; Bagatelles PPHI ▲ 12227 [DDD] (16.97)
J. Coop (pno) † Son 30 Pno, Op. 109; Son 32 Pno, Op. 111 SKYL ▲ 8802 [AAD] (15.97)
C. Curzon (pno) † Con 5 Pno, Op. 73 PLON (The Classic Sound) ▲ 452302 (11.97)
B. Gelber (pno) † Vars Pno on Original Theme, WoO 77; Vars Pno on Original Theme, WoO 80 ORF ▲ 40841 [DDD] (18.97)
Em. Gilels (pno) ("Sonatas, Vol. 1") † Son 10 Pno, Op. 14/2; Sonatas for Piano (complete); Sons (3) Pno, WoO 47 DGRM ▲ 453221 (94.97)
G. Gould (pno) *(rec 1970)* † Bagatelles; Vars Pno on Original Theme, Op. 34; Vars Pno on Original Theme, WoO 80 SNYC (Glenn Gould Edition) 2-▲ 52646 [ADD] (31.97)
G. Gould (pno) † Con 3 Pno, Op. 37; Vars Pno on Original Theme, Op. 34 CBC (Perspective) ▲ 2004 [ADD] (16.97)
L. Kraus (pno) *(rec 1939)* † B. Bartók:Romanian Folk Dances Pno, Sz.56; Rondos on Folk Tunes, Sz.84; Chopin:Impromptu in F♯, Op. 36; Preludes (24) Pno, Op. 28; J. Haydn:Andante with Vars Pno, H.XVII/6; F. Schubert:Dances (42), Op. 18; Waltzes, D.969 PHS (Piano Masters) ▲ 55 (17.97)
D. Matthews (pno) *(rec Mozart Hall Vienna, Nov 11, 1958)* ("Beethoven, Vol. 2") † Vars Pno on Original Theme, Op. 34; Vars Pno on Original Theme, WoO 80 VC ▲ 8074 [ADD] (13.97)
R. Pöntinen (pno) † Bagatelles; Son 12 Pno, Op. 26 BIS ▲ 353 [DDD] (17.97)
S. Richter (pno) ("The Richter Collection, Vol. 2") † Son 27 Pno, Op. 90; Son 3 Pno, Op. 2/3; Son 4 Pno, Op. 7; Vars Pno on Original Theme, Op. 34; Vars Pno on Original Theme, Op. 76; J. Brahms:Son 1 Vn, Op. 78; Chopin:Scherzos Pno; J. Haydn:Son 39 Kbd, H.XVI/24; S. Rachmaninoff:Etudes-tableaux Pno; Preludes Pno; R. Schumann:Bunte Blätter, Op. 99; Symphonic Etudes, Op. 13; D. Shostakovich:Son Vn OLY 5-▲ 5013 [DDD] (64.97)
B. Roberts (pno) *(rec Nimbus Records Wyastone Leys, Feb 17 & June 11-12, 1983)* † Vars Pno on a Waltz by Diabelli, Op. 120 NIMB ▲ 7710 [DDD] (11.97)
A. Schnabel (pno) † Vars Pno on a Waltz by Diabelli, Op. 120 78'S ▲ 78546 (13.97)
A. Schnabel (pno) *(rec 1932-38)* † Con 1 Pno, Op. 15 ENPL (The Piano Libary) ▲ 298 (13.97)
E. Westenholz (pno) † Vars Pno on Original Theme, Op. 34; Vars Pno on Original Theme, WoO 80 KPT ▲ 32145 [DDD]
M. Yudina (pno) *(rec 1961)* ("Maria Yudina Plays Beethoven") † Vars Pno on a Waltz by Diabelli, Op. 120 RUS ▲ 15010 [AAD] (12.97)

Variations (6) in D on an Original Theme for Piano, Op. 76 (1809)

S. Richter (pno) ("The Richter Collection, Vol. 2") † Son 27 Pno, Op. 90; Son 3 Pno, Op. 2/3; Son 4 Pno, Op. 7; Vars & Fugue Pno, Op. 35; Vars Pno on Original Theme, Op. 34; J. Brahms:Son 1 Vn, Op. 78; Chopin:Scherzos Pno; J. Haydn:Son 39 Kbd, H.XVI/24; S. Rachmaninoff:Etudes-tableaux Pno; Preludes Pno; R. Schumann:Bunte Blätter, Op. 99; Symphonic Etudes, Op. 13; D. Shostakovich:Son Vn OLY 5-▲ 5013 [DDD] (64.97)
A. Stephens (mand), R. Burnett (pno) *(rec Finchcocks, Goudhurst, Kent, England, March 1991)* ("Music for Mandolin") † Adagio Mand, WoO 43b; Sonatina Mand in c, WoO 43a; Sonatina Mand in C, WoO 44a; Barbella:Duos (6) Vns; Calace:Suite 3 mand; J. N. Hummel:Son in c Hpd; W. A. Mozart:Die Zufriedenheit, K.349; Komm, liebe Zither, komm, K.351 AMON ▲ 53 [DDD] (16.97)
E. Westenholz (pno) † Vars Pno on a Waltz by Diabelli, Op. 120 KPT ▲ 32118 [DDD]

Variations (33) on a Waltz by Diabelli for Piano, Op. 120 (1819; 1822-23)

A. Brendel (pno) *(rec 1964)* ("Alfred Brendel Plays Beethoven, Vol. IV") † Andante Pno, WoO 57; Bagatelle Pno in B♭, WoO 60; Bagatelles; Rondo a capriccio Pno, Op. 129; Rondos Pno, Op. 51 VB2 2-▲ 5112 (9.97)
B. Frith (pno) ASVQ ▲ 6155 [DDD] (10.97)
M. Horszowski (pno) *(rec 1952)* † Son 26 Pno, Op. 81a RELE ▲ 911020 (m) [ADD] (18.97)
W. Kinderman (pno) HYP ▲ 66763 (18.97)
M. Levinas (pno) PVY ▲ 799031 (17.97)

BEETHOVEN, LUDWIG VAN (cont.)

Variations (33) on a Waltz by Diabelli for Piano, Op. 120 (1819; 1822-23) (cont.)

M. Oelbaum (pno) BRID ▲ 9010 [ADD] (17.97)
A. Rangell (pno) *(rec New York City, NY, Apr 1977 (live))* † M. Ravel:Gaspard de la nuit DOR ▲ 93176 [ADD] (16.97)
S. Richter (pno) *(rec May 18, 1986)* † Son 31 Pno, Op. 110 PRAG ▲ 254023 [ADD] (18.97)
S. Richter (pno) *(rec 1959, 1965, 1975 & 1986)* ("Sviatoslav Richter in Prague") PRAG 4-▲ 354022 (36.97)
B. Roberts (pno) *(rec Nimbus Records Wyastone Leys, Feb 17 & June 11-12, 1983)* † Vars & Fugue Pno, Op. 35 NIMB ▲ 7710 [DDD] (11.97)
C. Rosen (pno) INMP (Classics) ▲ 6700112 (9.97)
K. Scherbakov (pno) *(rec East Woodhay Hampshire, England, Nov 12-13, 1997)* † Vars Pno on God Save the King, WoO 78; Vars Pno on Rule Britannia, WoO 79 NXIN ▲ 8554372 [DDD] (5.97)
A. Schnabel (pno) *(rec 1932-37)* ("Schnabel Plays Beethoven") † Bagatelles; Sons 28-32 Pno PHS 3-▲ 9142 [ADD] (49.97)
A. Schnabel (pno) *(rec 1937 for HMV)* PHS ▲ 9378 [AAD] (17.97)
A. Schnabel (pno) *(rec 1930s)* † Bagatelle Pno in a, WoO 59; Vars Pno on Original Theme, Op. 34 GRM2 ▲ 78811 (13.97)
A. Schnabel (pno) † Vars & Fugue Pno, Op. 35 78'S ▲ 78546 (13.97)
G. Sokolov (pno) OPUS ▲ 429106 (18.97)
A. Vieru (pno) † Bagatelles HAM ▲ 901613 (18.97)
E. Westenholz (pno) † Vars Pno on Original Theme, Op. 76 KPT ▲ 32118 [DDD]
M. Yudina (pno) *(rec 1961)* ("Maria Yudina Plays Beethoven") † Vars & Fugue Pno, Op. 35 RUS ▲ 15010 [AAD] (12.97)

Variations in E♭ on an Original Theme for Piano, Violin & Cello, Op. 44

B. Erichson (vc), G. Zitterbart (pno) † Trio 5 Pno, Op. 70/2; Vars Pno Trio on Ich bin der Schneider Kadaku, Op. 121a TACE ▲ 78
I. Stern (vn), L. Rose (vc), E. Istomin (pno) † Trio 1 Pno, Op. 1/1; Trio 2 Pno, Op. 1/2; Trio 3 Pno, Op. 1/3; Trio 8 Pno, WoO 38 SNYC (Isaac Stern: A Life in Music) 2-▲ 64510 (23.97)
Stuttgart Piano Trio *(rec 1992-93)* ("Beethoven: Piano Trios, Vol. 2") † Allegretto Pno Trio, Hess 48; Trio 3 Pno, Op. 1/3; Trio 8 Pno, WoO 38 NXIN ▲ 550947 [DDD] (5.97)

Variations in G on "Ich bin der Schneider Kadaku" from Wenzel Müller's *Die Schwestern von Prag* for Piano, Violin & Cello, Op. 121a (?1803; rev 1816)

B. Erichson (vc), G. Zitterbart (pno) † Trio 5 Pno, Op. 70/2; Vars Pno Trio on Original Theme, Op. 44 TACE ▲ 78
Stuttgart Piano Trio *(rec Heidelberg, Germany, 1992, 1993)* ("Beethoven Piano Trios, Vol. 4") † Allegretto Pno Trio, WoO 39; Trio 6 Pno, Op. 97 NXIN ▲ 550949 [DDD] (5.97)
J. Thibaud (vn), P. Casals (vc), A. Cortot (pno) *(rec 1927)* † Vars Vc on "Bei Männern", WoO 46; G. Fauré:Son 1 Vn, Op. 13; J. Haydn:Trio 2 Kbd, H.XV/6 ENT ▲ 99385 (16.97)
Trio Italiano *(rec Padova, Italy, May 1994)* † Trio 4 Pno, Op. 70/1; Trio 5 Pno, Op. 70/2 AART ▲ 47251 [DDD] (10.97)

Variations (12) in C on Haibel's "Menuet à la Viganò" for Piano, WoO 68 (1795)

R. Brautigam (pno) *(rec Dec 1992)* † Vars Pno on a Russian Dance, WoO 71; Vars Pno on Ditterdorf's Es war einmal, WoO 66; Vars Pno on Grétry's romance, WoO 72; Vars Pno on Paisiello's Nel cor piu non mi sento, WoO 70; Vars Pno on Paisiello's Quant' è piu bella, WoO 69; Vars Pno on Salieri's La stessa, le stessissima, WoO 73; Vars Pno on Winter's Kind willst du ruhig schlafen, WoO 75 GLOE ▲ 5095 [DDD] (16.97)

Variations (9) in A on Paisiello's aria "Quant' è più bello" for Piano, WoO 69 (1795)

R. Brautigam (pno) *(rec Dec 1992)* † Vars Pno on a Russian Dance, WoO 71; Vars Pno on Ditterdorf's Es war einmal, WoO 66; Vars Pno on Grétry's romance, WoO 72; Vars Pno on Haibel's Menuet, WoO 68; Vars Pno on Paisiello's Nel cor piu non me sento, WoO 70; Vars Pno on Salieri's La stessa, le stessissima, WoO 73; Vars Pno on Winter's Kind willst du ruhig schlafen, WoO 75 GLOE ▲ 5095 [DDD] (16.97)

Variations (6) on Paisiello's duet "Nel cor più non mi sento" for Piano, WoO 70 (1795)

R. Brautigam (pno) *(rec Dec 1992)* † Vars Pno on a Russian Dance, WoO 71; Vars Pno on Ditterdorf's Es war einmal, WoO 66; Vars Pno on Grétry's romance, WoO 72; Vars Pno on Haibel's Menuet, WoO 68; Vars Pno on Paisiello's Quant' è piu bella, WoO 69; Vars Pno on Salieri's La stessa, le stessissima, WoO 73; Vars Pno on Winter's Kind willst du ruhig schlafen, WoO 75 GLOE ▲ 5095 [DDD] (16.97)
E. Ney (pno) *(rec 1937-41)* ("Elly Ney: Her Most Famous Recordings") † J. Brahms:Con 2 Pno, Op. 83; F. Schubert:Fant Pno, D.760 PHS ▲ 9170 [ADD] (17.97)
E. Ney (pno) *(rec 1936-38)* ("Elly Ney Plays Beethoven") † Andante Pno, WoO 57; Son 32 Pno, Op. 111; Son 4 Pno, Op. 7; Son 8 Pno, Op. 13 BPS ▲ 33 [ADD] (16.97)

Variations (12) in A on a Russian Dance from Paul Wranitzky's ballet "Das Waldmachen" for Piano, WoO 71 (1796-97)

R. Brautigam (pno) *(rec Dec 1992)* † Vars Pno on Ditterdorf's Es war einmal, WoO 66; Vars Pno on Grétry's romance, WoO 72; Vars Pno on Haibel's Menuet, WoO 68; Vars Pno on Paisiello's Nel cor piu non me sento, WoO 70; Vars Pno on Paisiello's Quant' è piu bella, WoO 69; Vars Pno on Salieri's La stessa, le stessissima, WoO 73; Vars Pno on Winter's Kind willst du ruhig schlafen, WoO 75 GLOE ▲ 5095 [DDD] (16.97)
O. Volkov (pno) † Son 16 Pno, Op. 31/1; Son 3 Pno, Op. 2/3; Vars Pno on Original Theme, WoO 80 BRIO ▲ 115 (16.97)

Variations (8) in C on Grétry's romance "Un fièvre brûlante" for Piano, WoO 72 (?1795)

R. Brautigam (pno) *(rec Dec 1992)* † Vars Pno on a Russian Dance, WoO 71; Vars Pno on Ditterdorf's Es war einmal, WoO 66; Vars Pno on Haibel's Menuet, WoO 68; Vars Pno on Paisiello's Nel cor piu non me sento, WoO 70; Vars Pno on Paisiello's Quant' è piu bella, WoO 69; Vars Pno on Salieri's La stessa, le stessissima, WoO 73; Vars Pno on Winter's Kind willst du ruhig schlafen, WoO 75 GLOE ▲ 5095 [DDD] (16.97)

Variations (7) in F on Winter's "Kind, willst du ruhig schlafen" for Piano, WoO 75 (1799)

R. Brautigam (pno) *(rec Dec 1992)* † Vars Pno on a Russian Dance, WoO 71; Vars Pno on Ditterdorf's Es war einmal, WoO 66; Vars Pno on Grétry's romance, WoO 72; Vars Pno on Haibel's Menuet, WoO 68; Vars Pno on Paisiello's Nel cor piu non me sento, WoO 70; Vars Pno on Paisiello's Quant' è piu bella, WoO 69; Vars Pno on Salieri's La stessa, le stessissima, WoO 73 GLOE ▲ 5095 [DDD] (16.97)

Variations in G on an Original Theme for Piano, WoO 77 (1800)

B. Gelber (pno) † Vars & Fugue Pno, Op. 35; Vars Pno on Original Theme, WoO 80 ORF ▲ 40841 [DDD] (18.97)

Variations (7) in C on "God Save the King" for Piano, WoO 78 (1802-03)

K. Scherbakov (pno) *(rec East Woodhay Hampshire, England, Nov 12-13, 1997)* † Vars Pno on a Waltz by Diabelli, Op. 120; Vars Pno on Rule Britannia, WoO 79 NXIN ▲ 8554372 [DDD] (5.97)

Variations (5) in "Rule, Britannia" in D for Piano, WoO 79 (1803)

K. Scherbakov (pno) *(rec East Woodhay Hampshire, England, Nov 12-13, 1997)* † Vars Pno on a Waltz by Diabelli, Op. 120; Vars Pno on God Save the King, WoO 78 NXIN ▲ 8554372 [DDD] (5.97)

Variations (32) on an Original Theme in c for Piano, WoO 80 (1806)

G. Cascioli (pno) † Bagatelles; Fant Pno, Op. 77; P. Boulez:Incises; G. Ligeti:Études Pno, Book I; Schoenberg:Pieces (5) Pno, Op. 23; Webern:Movt Pno, M112; Son Movt Pno DGRM ▲ 447766 [DDD]
S. Cosma (pno) † J. Brahms:Pieces (8) Pno, Op. 76; Chopin:Mazurkas Pno TOWN ▲ 29 (17.97)
B. Gelber (pno) † Vars & Fugue Pno, Op. 35; Vars Pno on Original Theme, WoO 77 ORF ▲ 40841 [DDD] (18.97)
G. Gould (pno) *(rec 1966)* † Bagatelles; Vars & Fugue Pno, Op. 35; Vars Pno on Original Theme, Op. 34 SNYC (Glenn Gould Edition) 2-▲ 52646 [ADD] (31.97)
S. Hall (pno) † J. S. Bach:Chromatic Fant & Fugue, BWV 903; Liszt:Hungarian Rhaps, S.244; Mendelssohn (-Bartholdy):Rondo capriccioso, Op. 14; D. Scarlatti:Sons Kbd ACAD ▲ 20006 (16.97)
V. Horowitz (pno) † Debussy:Etudes (12) Pno; J. Haydn:Son 62 Kbd, H.XVI/52; D. Scarlatti:Sons Kbd; R. Schumann:Arabeske Pno, Op. 18; Fantasiestücke Pno, Op. 12; Toccata Pno, Op. 7 ENT (Sirio) ▲ 530026 (13.97)
C. Keene (pno) ("C. Keene Plays Variations") † G. F. Handel:Harmonious Blacksmith; Mendelssohn (-Bartholdy):Vars sérieuses, Op. 54; S. Rachmaninoff:Vars on a Theme by Corelli, Op. 42; R. Schumann:Vars on A-B-E-G-G, Op. 1 PROT ▲ 1112 (18.97)
R. Lupu (pno) *(rec 1970)* ("Radu Lupu") † Son 14 Pno, Op. 27/2; J. Brahms:Intermezzos (3) Pno, Op. 117; Theme & Vars Pno; E. Grieg:Con Pno, Op. 16; F. Schubert:Moments musicaux, D.780; Son Pno, D.784; R. Schumann:Kinderszenen Pno, Op. 15 PPHI (Great Pianists of the 20th Century) ▲ 456895 (22.97)
D. Matthews (pno) *(rec Mozart Hall Vienna, Nov 11, 1958)* ("Beethoven, Vol. 2") † Vars & Fugue Pno, Op. 35; Vars Pno on Original Theme, Op. 34 VC ▲ 8074 [ADD] (13.97)
I. Moravec (pno) *(rec 1966)* † Con 4 Pno, Op. 58; Son 27 Pno, Op. 90 VAIA ▲ 1021 [ADD]
M. Perahia (pno) ("The Aldeburgh Recital, 1990") † Liszt:Consolations (6), S.172; Hungarian Rhaps, S.244; S. Rachmaninoff:Etudes-tableaux Pno; R. Schumann:Faschingsschwank, Op. 26 SNYC ▲ 46437 [DDD] (16.97)
R. Peres (pno) † J. S. Bach:Cant 147; Orgelbüchlein; Partitas Hpd; Schübler Chorale Preludes; J. Brahms:Intermezzos (3) Pno, Op. 117 PTRY ▲ 2211 (17.97)
O. Volkov (pno) † Son 16 Pno, Op. 31/1; Son 3 Pno, Op. 2/3; Vars Pno on a Russian Dance, WoO 71 BRIO ▲ 115 (16.97)
E. Westenholz (pno) † Vars & Fugue Pno, Op. 35; Vars Pno on Original Theme, Op. 34 KPT ▲ 32145 [DDD]

BEETHOVEN, LUDWIG VAN (cont.)

Variations (13) in A on Ditterdorf's arietta "Es war einmal ein alter Mann" for Piano, WoO 66 (1792)

R. Brautigam (pno) *(rec Dec 1992)* † Vars Pno on a Russian Dance, WoO 71; Vars Pno on Grétry's romance, WoO 72; Vars Pno on Haibel's Menuet, WoO 68; Vars Pno on Paisiello's Nel cor piu non me sento, WoO 70; Vars Pno on Paisiello's Quant' è piu bella, WoO 69; Vars Pno on Salieri's La stessa, le stessissima, WoO 73; Vars Pno on Winter's Kind willst du ruhig schlafen, WoO 75 GLOE ▲ 5095 [DDD] (16.97)

Variations (8) on a Theme by Count Waldstein for Piano 4-Hands, WoO 67 (?1792)

E. Arciuli (pno), P. Pagny (pno) † Marches Pno 4-Hands, Op. 45; Vars Pno 4-Hands on Ich denke dein, WoO 74; L. Koželuch:Kbd Music STRV ▲ 33464 (16.97)

C. Argelli (pno), P. Dirani (pno) ("The Complete Works for Piano 4-Hands") † Grosse Fuge Pnos, Op. 134; Marches Pno 4-Hands, Op. 45; Son Pno 4-Hands, Op. 6; Vars Pno 4-Hands on Ich denke dein, WoO 74 FON ▲ 9326 (13.97)

Variations in D (song & 6 variations) on "Ich denke dein" for Piano 4-Hands, WoO 74 (1799 & 1803)

E. Arciuli (pno), P. Pagny (pno) † Marches Pno 4-Hands, Op. 45; Vars Pno 4-Hands on a Theme by Waldstein, WoO 67; L. Koželuch:Kbd Music STRV ▲ 33464 (16.97)

C. Argelli (pno), P. Dirani (pno) ("The Complete Works for Piano 4-Hands") † Grosse Fuge Pnos, Op. 134; Marches Pno 4-Hands, Op. 45; Son Pno 4-Hands, Op. 6; Vars Pno 4-Hands on a Theme by Waldstein, WoO 67 FON ▲ 9326 (13.97)

Variations (12) on Mozart's "Se vuol ballare" for Violin & Piano [from *Le nozze di Figaro*], WoO 40 (1792-93)

T. Nishizaki (vn), J. Jandó (pno) *(rec Feb & Sept 1992)* † Son 10 Vn, Op. 96; Son 4 Vn, Op. 23 NXIN ▲ 550285 [DDD] (5.97)

Variations (8) in C on "La ci darem la mano," from Mozart's Don Giovanni for Winds, WoO 28 (?1795)

Consortium Classicum *(rec 1993-94)* ("Chamber Music for Winds, Vol. 2") † Duos Cl, WoO 27; Fidelio (sels) CPO ▲ 999437 [DDD] (14.97)

Consortium Classicum † Allegro & Minuet Fls, WoO 26; Duos Cl, WoO 27; Fidelio (sels); Grenadiersmarsch, Hess 107; Octet Ww, Op. 103; Qnt Ob; Rondino Ww, WoO 25; Spt in E♭, Op. 20; Sxt Ww; Trio Obs & E Hn, Op. 87 CPO 4-▲ 999658 [DDD] (27.98)

B. Goodman (cl), N. Reisenberg (pno) ("Benny Goodman: Clarinet Classics") † B. Bartók:Contrasts, Sz.111; J. Brahms:Son 2 Cl; Debussy:Première rapsodie Cl; W. A. Mozart:Qnt Cl, K.581; C. M. von Weber:Divert assai facile, Op. 38 PHS ▲ 57 (17.97)

K. Greenbank (ob), M. Zupnik (ob), E. Starr (E hn) † Trio Obs & E Hn, Op. 87; Triebensee:Trios Obs; Vars on a Theme from Haydn ASLE ▲ 6192 (8.97)

T. Indermühle (ob), D. Carmel (ob), S. Rancourt (E hn) [trans ob & Eng hn] *(rec Vienna, Austria, Feb 24-26, 1996)* † Trio Obs & E Hn, Op. 87; F. Krommer:Trio Ob; A. Vranicky:Trio Ob CAMA ▲ 481 [DDD] (18.97)

Mayr Ensemble *(rec Sept 1996)* † S. Mayr:Bagatelles Fl; G. Rossini:Semiramide (sels) PHEX ▲ 9608 (16.97)

Ricercar Academy ("Music for Winds") † Qnt Ob; Rondino Ww, WoO 25; Sxt Ww; Trio Obs & E Hn, Op. 87 RICE ▲ 206712 (13.97)

Die Weihe des Hauses [Consecration of the House] (overture) in C for Orchestra [to Meisl's play], Op. 124 (1815)

L. Bernstein (cnd), New York PO *(rec Lincoln Center New York, NY, NY, Oct 9, 1962)* † Con Vn; Leonore (ov 3) SNYC (Bernstein Century) ▲ 63153 [ADD] (10.97)

A. Doráti (cnd), London SO † Egmont (ov); Leonore (ov 3); Sym 7 MRCR (Living Presence) ▲ 462958 (11.97)

M. Huggett (cnd), Hanover Band † Coriolan Ov, Op. 62; Egmont (ov); Fidelio (ov); Geschöpfe des Prometheus (ov); König Stephen (ov); Leonore (ov 2); Missa Solemnis, Op. 123; Ruinen von Athen (ov); Syms (comp) NIMB 7-▲ 1760 [DDD] (29.97)

C. Munch (cnd), French National Orch *(rec 1989)* ("Charles Munch Edition, Vol. 1") † Sym 4; Sym 7 VAL ▲ 4825 [ADD] (12.97)

H. Rosbaud (cnd), Berlin Radio Orch *(rec 1940)* † Liszt:Ce qu'on entend sur la montagne, S.95; P. Tchaikovsky:Capriccio italien, Op. 45 IN ▲ 1401 (15.97)

J. Silverstein (vn), J. Silverstein (cnd), Utah SO † Con Vn PRA ▲ 588 [DDD] (14.97)

Die Weihe des Hauses [Consecration of the House] (incidental music) for solo Voices, Orchestra & Chorus [includes Op. 124, WoO 98 & adaptations from Op. 113]

C. Abbado (cnd), Berlin PO, Berlin Radio Chorus, S. McNair (sop), B. Terfel (b-bar), B. Ganz (nar) *(rec Philharmonie Berlin, Germany, 1993-94)* † Leonore Prohaska, WoO 96 DEUT ▲ 47748 [DDD] (16.97)

Wellington's Victory for Orchestra, Op. 91, "Battle Symphony" (1813)

H. Bongartz (cnd), Leipzig Gewandhaus Orch † Con Vn in C, WoO 5; Rondo Pno & Orch, WoO 6 BER ▲ 2078 [DDD] (10.97)

A. Doráti (cnd), London SO [cannon & musket firing under direction of Gerald C] † P. Tchaikovsky:Ov 1812, Op. 49 MRCR ▲ 34360 (11.97)

E. Kunzel (cnd), Cincinnati SO † Liszt:Battle of the Huns; Hungarian Battle March, S.118 TEL ▲ 80079 [DDD] (16.97)

L. Maazel (cnd), Bavarian RSO ("Symphonic Battle Scenes") † Liszt:Battle of the Huns; P. Tchaikovsky:Capriccio italien, Op. 45; Ov 1812, Op. 49 RCAV (Red Seal) ▲ 68471 (16.97)

E. Ormandy (cnd), Philadelphia Orch † P. Tchaikovsky:Ov 1812, Op. 49 RCAV (Victrola) ▲ 7731 [DDD] (6.97)

Zärtliche Leibe (song) for Voice & Piano [text K. F. Herrosee], WoO 123 (ca 1795)

D. Fischer-Dieskau (bar), J. Demus (pno) ("The Complete Beethoven Edition Compactotheque") † Chor auf die verbundeten Fürsten, WoO 95; Glorreiche Augenblick, Op. 136; Leonore (sels); Ländler Pno, WoO 11; Marches Military Band, WoO 18-20; Qt Strs in F, Hess 34; Qt 11 Strs, Op. 95; Qt 16 Strs, Op. 135; Romance Fl, Bn & Pno, Hess 13; Scottish Songs (25), Op. 108; Serenade Str Trio, Op. 8; Son 3 Vc, Op. 69; Son 5 Vn, Op. 24; Son 8 Pno, Op. 13; Spt in E♭, Op. 20; Sym 5; Trio 5 Pno, Op. 70/2; Triumphal March, WoO 2a DEUT ▲ 453811 [ADD/DDD] (11.97)

BEGLARIAN, EVE (20th cent)

Music of Beglarian

E. Beglarian (voc), M. Lancaster (fl), E. Beglarian (kbd), K. Supové (kbd)—No Man's Land; The Garden of Cyrus; Preciosilla; Disappearance Act; Overstepping *(rec 1990-95)* ("Overstepping") OOD ▲ 33 [DDD] (16.97)

Play Nice for Harp (1997)

E. Panzer (hp) ("Dancing in Place") † Brazelton:Down n Harp n All a Rond o; W. M. Chambers:Moments Hp; Einhorn:New Pages Pnos; Hovda:Dancing in Place; Matamoros:Re: Elizabeth; Panzer:Green Tea with Oranges; Invocation Hp; Syncophony Hp OOD ▲ 56 [DDD] (16.97)

BEHREND, SIEGFRIED (1933-1991)

Serenade for Mandolin & Orchestra

G. Tröster-Weyhofen (mand), G. Vogt (cnd), Bavarian State Youth Plucked Instrument Orch † H. Baumann:Con Capriccioso; A. Starck:Con Mand; Tober-Vogt:Carnival of Venice; Vivaldi:Con Mand, RV.425 THOR ▲ 2146 [DDD] (16.97)

Spielmusik for Guitar & Violin (1952)

Duo 46 ("FM1: Homage to the 50's") † Bartolozzi:; W. Bloch:Son Pno; A. Reiter:Son Pno; Siegl:Son Vn; J. Takács:Divertimento, Op. 61; Truhlács:Zwei Kompositionen, Op. 71a GUPR ▲ 100198

BEHRMAN, DAVID (1937-

Figure in a Clearing for Electronics, Cello & Computer (1977)

D. Gibson (vc), Kim-1 (cmpt), D. Behrman (elec) *(rec State Univ of New York Albany, June 9, 1977)* ("On the Other Ocean") † On the Other Ocean LOV ▲ 1041 [ADD] (16.97)

On the Other Ocean for Electronics, Flute, Bassoon & Computer (1977)

M. Payne (fl), A. Stidfole (bn), Kim-1 (cmpt), D. Behrman (elec) *(rec Oakland, CA, Sep 18, 1977)* ("On the Other Ocean") † Figure in a Clearing LOV ▲ 1041 [ADD] (16.97)

QSRL for Flute and Electronics (1994)

M. Payne (fl), D. Behrman (elec) *(rec Center for Contemporary Music, Mills College, United States of America)* † W. Brooks:Poempiece I; Haubenstock-Ramati:Interpolation mobile; M. Payne:Aeolian Confluence; Hum; Inflections; Trayle:Flaptics CRI ▲ 807 [DDD] (12.97)

Refractive Light for Computer Music System

D. Behrman (cmpt) † Unforseen Events XIRE ▲ 105 [DDD]

Unforseen Events for Mutantrumpet & Electronics

B. Neill (müttertrompette), D. Behrman (elec) † Refractive Light XIRE ▲ 105 [DDD]

BEIDERBECKE, BIX [LEON BISMARCK] (1903-1931)

Piano Music

Los Angeles Guitar Quintet—In a Mist; Candlelights Gtr *(rec 1993)* ("Aquarelle") † L. Almeida:Los Angeles Aquarelle Suite; G. Gershwin:Music of Gershwin; Jobim:Gtr Music; W. A. Mozart:Qnt Cl, K.581; Vivaldi:Cons Strs (misc) ERTO ▲ 42016 [ADD] (14.97)

M. Polad (pno)—In a Mist; Candlelights Gtr; Flashes; In the Dark; Davenport Blues ("Piano Deco, Vol. 1: M. Polad Plays American Music of the 1920's") † R. Bloom:Pno Music; E. Lane:Adirondack Sketches; American Dances; Pno Music PREM ▲ 101 (16.97)

BEKAERT, JACQUES (20th cent)

Distant Harmony for Baritone, Flute, Bass Clarinet & Viola (1987)

T. Buckner (bar), L. Jenkins (va), S. Starin (fl), J. Parran (b cl) † T. Buckner:Inner Journey; Duckworth:Their Song; S. Satoh:Burning Meditation; D. Wessel:Situations for Bar & Synth *([ENG] text)* LOV ▲ 3023 [DDD] (16.97)

BELET, BRIAN (1965-

[Mute]ation for Computer (1994; rev. 1997)

B. Belet (cmpt) *(rec SJSU, San Jose, CA, Dec 1997)* ("Music for Players & Digital Media") † Frengel:Three Short Stories; P. Furman:Synergy; M. Helms:Whispering Modulations; D. Michael:Extensions #1; A. Strange:Shaman: Sisters of Dreamtime; Wyman:Through the Reed CENT ▲ 2404 (live) [DDD] (16.97)

Proportional Preludes (4) for Piano (1991)

J. Mercer (pno) ("Society of Composers, Inc. "Chamber Works"") † C. Delgado:Fugaz; D. Epstein:Vars Pno; Juusela:Ilta Pala(a); Rindfleisch:Tears; Rudajev:Son Vn CPS ▲ 8651 [ADD] (16.97)

BELL, DEREK (dates unknown)

Music of Bell

T. Christoforu (mez), D. Bell (hp), M. Tutoriliva (hp), V. Vatchev (cnd), Vratza PO, G. Robey (cnd), Bulgarian Phil Chorus *(Vars & Musical Quotations)*, P. Belneev (pno), Vratza Philharmonic Wind Quintet *(Divertissement)*, P. Totev (ob), D. Bell (pno) *(Toccata Burlesca)*, D. Bell (hp), M. Tutoriliva (hp), V. Vatchev (cnd), Vratza PO, G. Robey (cnd), Bulgarian Phil Chorus *(Sym 2) (rec Vratza, Bulgaria)* † Douno:Music of Douno ATH ▲ 14 [DDD] (18.97)

BELL, ELIZABETH (1928-

Andromeda for Piano & Orchestra

R. Spindler (pno), S. Kawalla (cnd), Koszalin State PO ("I Am An American Woman") † S. Hershey:Arrival; Mageau:Early Autumn's Dreaming; A. Pierce:Sym 2 VMM (Music from 6 Continents 1994) ▲ 3029 [DDD]

BELL, LARRY (1952-

The Black Cat for Cello & Piano (1987)

R. J. Lurtsema (nar), E. Bartlett (vc), L. Bell (pno) *(rec WGBH-FM, Boston, MA, Apr 11, 1998)* ("River of Ponds") † Caprice; Fantasia on an Imaginary Hymn; River of Ponds NSR ▲ 1018 [DDD] (15.97)

Caprice for Solo Cello (1978)

E. Bartlett (vc) *(rec Unitarian Church, Montclair, United States of America, May 13, 1998)* ("River of Ponds") † Black Cat; Fantasia on an Imaginary Hymn; River of Ponds NSR ▲ 1018 [DDD] (15.97)

Concerto for Piano & Orchestra (1989)

L. Bell (pno), T. Delibozov (cnd), Ruse PO † M. S. Meier:Dawning; H. Reeder:Lark 2; T. Sleeper:Con Bn VMM (Music from 6 Continents 1996) ▲ 3037

Fantasia on an Imaginary Hymn for Viola & Cello (1983)

S. Clarke (va), E. Bartlett (vc) *(rec Unitarian Church, Montclair, United States of America, May 13, 1998)* ("River of Ponds") † Black Cat; Caprice; River of Ponds NSR ▲ 1018 [DDD] (15.97)

River of Ponds for Cello & Piano (1986)

E. Bartlett (vc), L. Bell (pno) *(rec SUNY Purchase Recital Hall, Purchase, NY, May 16, 1998)* ("River of Ponds") † Black Cat; Caprice; Fantasia on an Imaginary Hymn NSR ▲ 1018 [DDD] (15.97)

Sonata for Piano (1990)

L. Bell (pno) *(rec Recital Hall of the Univ at Albany, May 25-26, 1995)* ("New American Romantics: Music for Solo Piano") † Pleskow:Quatrains Pno; Quilling:Son 4 Pno; H. Rovics:Son Pno; Toutant:Small Suite Pno; Van Appledorn:Set of 5 Pno NSR ▲ 1007 [DDD] (15.97)

BELL, WILLIAM HENRY (1873-1946)

A South African Symphony in a (1927)

R. Cock (cnd), South African Broadcasting Corp National SO *(rec Radio Park Johannesburg, Jan 1994 & 1995)* ("South African Orchestral Works") † Fagan:Concert Ov; Ilala MARC ▲ 8223833 [DDD] (13.97)

BELLA, JAN LEVOSLAV (1843-1936)

Notturno for String Quartet (1930)

Moyzes String Quartet *(rec Moyzes Hall of the Slovak Philharmonic Bratislava, June 3 & Dec 4, 1994 & Apr 12, 1995)* † Qt in e Strs; Qt in B Strs MARC ▲ 8223839 [DDD] (13.97)

Quartet in e for Strings (1871)

Moyzes String Quartet *(rec Moyzes Hall of the Slovak Philharmonic Bratislava, June 3 & Dec 4, 1994 & Apr 12, 1995)* † Notturno Str Qt; Qt in B Strs MARC ▲ 8223839 [DDD] (13.97)

Quartet in c for Strings, Op. 25 (1880)

Moyzes String Quartet *(rec Slovak Philharmonic Bratislava, Dec 12, 1993)* † Qnt Strs MARC ▲ 8223658 [DDD] (13.97)

Quartet in B♭ for Strings (1887)

Moyzes String Quartet *(rec Moyzes Hall of the Slovak Philharmonic Bratislava, June 3 & Dec 4, 1994 & Apr 12, 1995)* † Notturno Str Qt; Qt in e Strs MARC ▲ 8223839 [DDD] (13.97)

Quintet in d for Strings (1867-68)

F. Magyar (va), Moyzes String Quartet *(rec Slovak Philharmonic Bratislava, Dec 6, 1993)* † Qt Strs, Op. 25 MARC ▲ 8223658 [DDD] (13.97)

BELLAFRONTE, RAFFAELE (1961-

Dances (4) for Guitar Quartet (1997)

O. Ghiglia (gtr), A. V. Wangenheim (gtr), B. Bunch (gtr), L. Guerra (gtr) *(rec 1998)* ("Chamber Music") † For Five; Hypnós; Indian; Liaisons BONG ▲ 5081 [DDD] (16.97)

For Five for Guitar & String Quartet (1996)

Quintetto Italiamusica *(rec 1998)* ("Chamber Music") † Dances Gtr Qt; Hypnós; Indian; Liaisons BONG ▲ 5081 [DDD] (16.97)

Hypnós for Piano (1996)

C. Trovajoli (pno) *(rec 1998)* ("Chamber Music") † Dances Gtr Qt; For Five; Indian; Liaisons BONG ▲ 5081 [DDD] (16.97)

Indian for English Horn & Piano (1995)

B. Incagnoli (E hn), C. Trovajoli (pno) *(rec 1998)* ("Chamber Music") † Dances Gtr Qt; For Five; Hypnós; Liaisons BONG ▲ 5081 [DDD] (16.97)

Liaisons for Contralto Saxophone, Bass Clarinet & Piano (1997)

F. Paci (b cl), M. Mazzoni (sax), F. Bongelli (pno) *(rec 1998)* ("Chamber Music") † Dances Gtr Qt; For Five; Hypnós; Indian BONG ▲ 5081 [DDD] (16.97)

BELLINATI, PAULO (1954-

Jongo for 2 guitars

M. Troester (gtr), F. Schwichtenberg (gtr) *(rec Feb 1998)* ("Duettissimo-Masterpieces for Two Guitars") † E. Angulo:Paginas en Bronce; H. Baumann:Son 2 gtr; L. Brouwer:Micro piezas Gtr; Gnattali:Schottisch 2 Gtrs; Valse; A. Piazzolla:Lo que vendra; Tango Suite; M. N. Walter:Fusion Tune THOR ▲ 2389 [DDD] (16.97)

BELLINI, VINCENZO (1801-1835)

Adelson e Salvini (opera in 2 acts) [2nd version] [Libretto A.L. Tottola after P. Delamarre]

A. Nafé (mez), F. Previati (bar), A. Licata (cnd), Catania Teatro Massimo Bellini Orch, Catania Teatro Massimo Bellini Chorus *(E,I lib texts)* NUO 2-▲ 7154 [DDD] (32.97)

Arias

L. Aliberti (sop), L. Gardelli (cnd), Munich RSO—Pirata (sels) [Oh! s'io potessi; Col sorriso d'innocenza]; Puritani (sels) [Qui la voce sua soave]; Sonnambula (sels) [Ah, non credea mirarti] ORF ▲ 119841 (18.97)

D. Hvorostovsky (bar), I. Marin (cnd), Philharmonia Orch—Pirata (sels) [Si, vincemmo, e il pregio io sento]; Puritani (sels) [Ah! per sempre] † Donizetti:Arias; G. Rossini:Arias PPHI ▲ 34912 (16.97)

S. Jo (sop), G. Carella (cnd), English CO—Capuleti e i Montecchi (sels) [Eccomi in lieta veste; Oh! quante volte]; Sonnambula (sels) [Care compagne]; Puritani (sels) [Son vergin vezzosa; Qui la voce sua soave] ("Bel Canto") † Donizetti:Arias; L. Ricci:Crispino e la comare (sels); G. Rossini:Arias; Verdi:Arias ERAT ▲ 17580 (16.97)

L. Tetrazzini (sop)—Sonnambula (sels) [Ah, non credea mirarti; Come per me sereno]; Puritani (sels) [Vien, diletto] ("Luisa Tetrazzini Sings Arias from Italian Operas 1907-1914") † Donizetti:Arias; G. Rossini:Arias; Verdi:Arias MNER ▲ 13 [ADD] (15.97)

Ariette da camera (6) for Voice & Piano

J. Aragall (ten), E. Arnaltes (pno)—Vanne, o rosa fortunata; Ma rendi pur contendo; Malinconia, ninfa gentile; Bella Nice, che d'amore; Per pietà, bel'idol mio † Songs; Leoncavallo:Songs; G. Puccini:Songs; G. Rossini:Soirées musicales; Tosti:Songs RTVE ▲ 65026 (16.97)

J. Omilian (sop), S. Frontalini (cnd), Warmia National Orch [ITA] † Sinfs (6) BONG ▲ 2098 [DDD] (16.97)

Beatrice di Tenda (opera in 3 acts) [lib Romani after C. Tedaldi-Fores]

L. Aliberti (sop), M. Thompson (ten), P. Gavanelli (bass), C. Capasso (trbn), F. Luisi (cnd), Berlin German Opera Orch, Berlin German Opera Chorus BER 2-▲ 1042 [DDD] (32.97)

E. Gruberová (sop—Beatrice), V. Kasarova (mez—Agnese), D. Bernardini (ten—Orombello), B. Robinšak (ten—Anichino), I. Morozov (ten—Filippo Maria Viscon), D. Sumegi (bass—Rizzardo), P. Steinberg (cnd), Austrian RSO, Austrian Radio Chorus [ITA] *(rec live Vienna Concert House, Jan 30 & Feb 1, 1992)* NIGC 2-▲ 70560 [DDD] (34.97)

La Fenice, J. Anderson (sop) ODRO 2-▲ 1174 (9.97)

▲ = CD ♦ = Enhanced CD △ = MD ▮ = Cassette Tape ▯ = DCC

BELLINI, VINCENZO (cont.)

Bianca e Fernando (opera in 2 acts) [2nd version of Bianca e Gernando] [Libretto Romani revised from Gilardoni]

Y. O. Shin (sop), G. Kunde (ten), W. Coppola (ten), A. Tomicich (bass), A. Licata (cnd), Catania Teatro Massimo Bellini Orch, Catania Teatro Massimo Bellini Chorus *(E,I lib texts)* NUO 2-▲ 7076 [DDD] (32.97)

Bianca e Fernando (selections)

J. Eaglen (sop), M. Elder (cnd), Orch of the Age of Enlightenment *(rec Abbey Road Studio, England, June 1996)* ("Opera Arias") † Norma (sels); Pirata (sels); R. Wagner:Götterdämmerung (sels); Tristan und Isolde (prelude & liebestod); Walküre (sels) SNYC ▲ 62032 [DDD] (16.97)

I Capuleti e i Montecchi (opera in 2 acts) [lib Felice Romani after L. Scevola]

C. Abbado (cnd) , M. Rinaldi (sop), L. Pavarotti (ten), G. Aragall (ten) ODRO ▲ 1171 (9.97)

E. Guberová (sop—Giulietta), A. Baltsa (mez—Romeo), D. Raffanti (ten—Tebaldo), R. Muti (cnd), Royal Opera House Orch Covent Garden, Royal Opera House Covent Garden Chorus EMIC ▲ 64846 (23.97)

K. Ricciarelli (sop), D. Montague (mez), D. Raffanti (ten), M. Lippi (bass), B. Campanella (cnd), Venice Theater Orch, Venice Theater Chorus [ITA] *(rec 1991)* NUO 2-▲ 7020 [DDD] (32.97)

I Capuleti e i Montecchi (selections)

L. Aliberti (sop), R. Paternostro (cnd), Berlin RSO—Eccomi in lieta veste; Oh! quante volte *(rec Jesus Christ Church, Berlin, Germany, Aug 2-10, 1988)* † Puritani (sels); Donizetti:Anna Bolena (sels); Don Pasquale (sels); Fille du régiment (sels); Torquato Tasso (sels) CAPO ▲ 10246 [DDD] (11.97)

M. Devia (sop), M. Rota (cnd), Swiss-Italian Orch *(rec June 4, 1992)* † Puritani (sels); Sonnambula (sels); G. Charpentier:Louise (sels); Delibes:Lakmé (sels); Donizetti:Lucia di Lammermoor (sels); Gounod:Roméo et Juliette (sels) BONG ▲ 2513 [DDD] (16.97)

V. Kasarova (mez), F. Haider (cnd), Munich RSO, Bavarian Radio Chorus ("Vesselina Kasarova-A Portrait") † Donizetti:Arias; C. W. Gluck:Orfeo ed Euridice (sels); G. F. Handel:Rinaldo (sels); W. A. Mozart:Arias; G. Rossini:Arias RCAV (Red Seal) ▲ 68522 [DDD] (16.97)

L. Pavarotti (ten)—O di Cappelio † Puritani (sels); Donizetti:Elisir d'amore (sels); Lucia di Lammermoor (sels); W. A. Mozart:Idomeneo (sels); G. Puccini:Bohème (sels); Turandot (sels); Verdi:Ballo in maschera (sels); Luisa Miller (sels); Rigoletto (sels) HALM ▲ 30421 (6.97)

L. Pavarotti (ten)—E' serbata a questa acciaro † Puritani (sels); Donizetti:Elisir d'amore (sels); Lucia di Lammermoor (sels); G. Rossini:Stabat Mater; Verdi:Luisa Miller (sels) LALI ▲ 14308 (3.97)

L. Pavarotti (ten), G. Ferrin (bass), A. Giacomotti (bass), C. Abbado (cnd), La Scala Orch, La Scala Chorus—O di Cappelio; E' serbata a questa acciaro *(rec Nov 20, 1969)* ("Pavarotti: The Early Years, Vol. 2") † Puritani (sels); Donizetti:Lucia di Lammermoor (sels); G. Puccini:Turandot (sels); Verdi:Lombardi (sels); Luisa Miller (sels); Rigoletto (sels); Traviata (sels) RCAV (Gold Seal) ▲ 68014 (live) [ADD] (11.97)

K. Ricciarelli (sop), D. Montague (mez), D. Raffanati (ten), D. Raffanti (ten), A. Salvadori (sgr), B. Campanella (cnd), Venice Theater Orch, Venice Theater Chorus NUO ▲ 7183 [DDD] (16.97)

artists unknown ("Romantic Operatic Duets") † Norma (sels); Donizetti:Anna Bolena (sels) GRFM ▲ 289 (10.97)

Concerto in E♭ for Oboe & Orchestra (ca 1825)

A. Camden (cnd), City of London Sinfonia ("The Art of the Oboe") † Albinoni:Cons Ob, Op. 7; Cons Ob, Op. 9; Cimarosa:Con Ob; A. Corelli:Con Ob; G. F. Handel:Cons Ob, HWV 301, 302a & 287; Rondo in G; Suites de Pièces (8) Hpd, HWV 426-33; V. Righini:Con Ob NXIN ▲ 8553991 (5.97)

A. Camden (ob), N. Ward (cnd), City of London Sinfonia *(rec East Finchley, England, Apr 1995)* ("Italian Oboe Concertos") † J. Barbirolli:Con on Themes of Peroglisi; Cimarosa:Con Ob; A. Corelli:Con in A Ob; Fiorillo:Sinf concertante; V. Righini:Con Ob NXIN ▲ 8553433 [DDD] (5.97)

N. Marriner (cnd), Academy of St. Martin in the Fields *(rec 1968)* † Cherubini:Etude 2 PLON 2-▲ 43838 [ADD] (17.97)

E. Nepalov (ob), R. Barshaï (cnd), Moscow CO *(rec Great Hall, Moscow Conservatory, Russia, 1965)* † Albinoni:Cons Ob, Op. 7 RUS ▲ 10062 [AAD]

R. Smedvig (tpt), J. Ling (cnd), Scottish CO † J. Haydn:Con Tpt; J. N. Hummel:Con Tpt in E♭, S.49; Tartini:Con Tpt; Torelli:Con Tpt TEL ▲ 80232 [DDD] (16.97)

Norma (opera in 4 acts) [lib Felice Romani after Soumet]

M. Caballé (sop), F. Cossotto (mez), P. Domingo (ten), R. Raimondi (bass), C. F. Cillario (cnd), London PO, Ambrosian Opera Chorus [ITA] RCAV (Gold Seal) 3-▲ 6502 [ADD] (33.97)

M. Caballé (sop—Norma), M. Zotti (sop—Clotilde), J. Veasey (mez—Adalgisa), J. Vickers (ten—Pollione), G. Sinimberghi (ten—Flavio), A. Ferrin (bass—Oroveso), G. Patanè (cnd), Turin Teatro Regio Orch, Turin Teatro Regio Chorus ODRO 3-▲ 1140 (13.97)

M. Callas (sop), M. Filippeschi (ten), N. Rossi-Lemeni (bass), T. Serafin (cnd), La Scala Orch, La Scala Chorus [1st version] EMIC (Callas Edition) 3-▲ 56271 (47.97)

M. Callas (sop), G. Simionato (mez), K. Baum (ten), G. Picco (cnd), Palacio Bellas Artes Orch, Palacio Bellas Artes Chorus *(rec 1950-51)* ("Maria Callas in Mexico City, Vol. 1") † G. Puccini:Tosca; Verdi:Aida; Traviata; Trovatore MELO (Callas Edition) 10-▲ 20015 [ADD] (155.97)

M. Callas (sop—Norma), E. Vincenzi (sop—Clotilde), C. Ludwig (mez—Adalgisa), F. Corelli (ten—Pollione), P. D. Palma (ten—Flavio), N. Zaccaria (bass—Oroveso), T. Serafin (cnd), La Scala Orch, La Scala Chorus *(rec Teatro alla Scala, Sept 1960) (E,I lib texts)* EMIC (Callas Complete Operas) 3-▲ 66428 [ADD] (34.97)

G. Cigna (sop), E. Stignani (mez), G. Breviario (ten), V. Gui (cnd), EIAR Orch, EIAR Chorus [ITA] *(rec 1936 for Cetra)* PHS 2-▲ 9422 [AAD] (33.97)

G. Cigna (sop), E. Stignani (mez), G. Breviario (ten), T. Pasero (bass), V. Gui (cnd), Turin EIAR Orch, Turin EIAR Chorus *(rec 1937)* GRM2 2-▲ 78583 (26.97)

G. Cigna (sop—Norma), E. Stignani (mez—Adalgisa), A. Perris (mez—Clotilde), G. Breviario (ten—Pollione), E. Renzi (ten—Flavio), T. Pasero (bass—Oroveso), V. Gui (cnd), EIAR Orch, A. Consoli (cnd), EIAR Chorus *(rec Aug-Sept 1937)* ARKA (The 78's) 2-▲ 78010 [ADD] (26.97)

L. Galvano (sop—Clotilde), E. Ross (sop—Norma), F. Cossotto (mez—Adalgisa), M. del Monaco (ten—Pollione), I. Vinco (bass—Oroveso), E. Gracis (cnd), Venice Theater Orch, Venice Theater Chorus *(rec live Venice, Dec 15, 1966)* MONM 2-▲ 10281 [ADD] (54.97)

G. Gavazzeni (cnd), La Scala Orch, La Scala Chorus, M. Caballé (sop—Norma), F. Cossotto (mez—Adalgisa), R. Pallini (mez—Clotilde), G. Raimondi (ten—Pollione), S. Porzano (ten—Flavio), I. Vinco (bass—Oroveso) *(rec live Milan, Italy, 1972) ([ITA] lib text)* MYTO 2-▲ 974168 (34.97)

L. Gencer (sop), F. Cossotto (mez), G. Limarilli (ten), I. Vinco (bass), O. D. Fabriitis (cnd) *(rec Lausanne, 1966)* MYTO 2-▲ 981177 (34.97)

E. Mei (sop), J. Eaglen (sop), V. La Scola (sgr) ODRO 2-▲ 1183 (9.97)

R. Scotto (sop—Norma), A. Murray (mez—Clotilde), T. Troyanos (mez—Adalgisa), G. Giacomini (ten—Pollione), P. Crook (ten—Flavio), P. Plishka (bass—Oroveso), J. Levine (cnd), National PO London, Ambrosian Opera Chorus *(rec London, 1979)* SNYC ▲ 35902 (23.97)

J. Sutherland (sop), M. Caballé (sop), L. Pavarotti (ten), S. Ramey (bass), R. Bonynge (cnd), Welsh National Opera Orch, Welsh National Opera Chorus [ITA] PLON 3-▲ 14476 [DDD] (48.97)

J. Sutherland (sop), M. Horne (mez), J. Alexander (ten), R. Cross (bass), R. Bonynge (cnd), London SO, London Sym Chorus [ITA] PLON 3-▲ 25488 [ADD] (34.97)

Norma (selections)

A. Baltsa (mez), J. Carreras (ten), P. Domingo (cnd), London SO, Tallis Chamber Choir—Va, crudele *(rec Jan-Feb 1991)* † Bizet:Carmen (sels); P. Mascagni:Cavalleria rusticana (sels); Massenet:Werther (sels); Verdi:Traviata (sels); Trovatore (sels) SNYC ▲ 53968 [DDD] (9.97)

M. Caballé (sop) ("The Art of Montserrat Caballé") † Pirata (sels); Donizetti:Lucrezia Borgia (sels); G. Rossini:Donna del lago (sels); Verdi:Arias REPL (Butterfly) ▲ 31 [AAD]

M. Callas (sop) ("Callas & Company") † Pirata (sels); Sonnambula (sels); Donizetti:Lucia di Lammermoor (sels); G. Puccini:Bohème (sels); Tosca (sels); Verdi:Aida (sels); Traviata (sels) EMIC ▲ 56341 (16.97)

M. Callas (sop) *(rec live, 1952-1977)* † Verdi:Macbeth (sels) OMBR ▲ 7005 (17.97)

M. Callas (sop), E. Nicolai (mez), F. Corelli (ten), B. Christoff (bass), A. Votto (cnd), Trieste Teatro Comunale Giuseppe Verdi Orch, Trieste Teatro Comunale Giuseppe Verdi Chorus *(rec Nov 19, 1953)* † Donizetti:Lucia di Lammermoor MYTO 2-▲ 91340 (live) [ADD] (34.97)

C. Deutekom (sop), R. Benzi (cnd), Rotterdam PO *(rec Netherlands, Aug 30, 1975)* ("Cristina Deutekom & José Carreras") † Donizetti:Lucia di Lammermoor (sels); Mercadante:Giuramento (sels); Verdi:Attila (sels); Ernani (sels); Luisa Miller (sels) *(E text)* BELV ▲ 7012 [ADD] (15.97)

J. Eaglen (sop), M. Elder (cnd), Orch of the Age of Enlightenment *(rec Abbey Road Studio, England, Sept 1995)* ("Opera Arias") † Bianca e Fernando (sels); Pirata (sels); R. Wagner:Götterdämmerung (sels); Tristan und Isolde (prelude & liebestod); Walküre (sels) SNYC ▲ 62032 [DDD] (16.97)

T. D. Monte (sop) *(rec 1924-41)* ("Arias & Duets") † Sonnambula (sels); Donizetti:Don Pasquale (sels); Fille du régiment (sels); Linda di Chamounix (sels); Lucia di Lammermoor (sels); W. A. Mozart:Don Giovanni (sels); Nozze di Figaro (sels); G. Rossini:Barbiere di Siviglia (sels); Guillaume Tell (sels); Verdi:Falstaff (sels); Rigoletto (sels); Traviata (sels) ENT (Vocal Archives) ▲ 1191 (13.97)

T. Pasero (bass)—Ite sul colle, o Druidi ("Tancredi Pasero: La Scala Repertoire, Vol. 1 1927-44") † Sonnambula (sels); Boito:Mefistofele (sels); Ponchielli:Gioconda (sels); G. Rossini:Arias; Verdi:Arias VOCA (Vocal Archives) ▲ 1123 (13.97)

BELLINI, VINCENZO (cont.)

Norma (selections) (cont.)

E. Pinza (bass)—Ite sul colle, o Druidi; Deh! Non volerli vittime ("Ezio Pinza: The Early Legendary Recordings") † Puritani (sels); Boito:Mefistofele (sels); Donizetti:Favorita (sels); Lucia di Lammermoor (sels); G. Puccini:Bohème (sels); G. Rossini:Mosè in Egitto (sels); Verdi:Arias VOCA (Vocal Archives) ▲ 1132 (13.97)

K. Pitti (sop), R. Saccani (cnd), Budapest PO, A. Katona (cnd), Hungarian State Opera Chorus—Casta diva † Boito:Mefistofele (sels); A. Catalani:Wally (sels); Leoncavallo:Pagliacci (sels); G. Puccini:Arias; Verdi:Otello (sels); Traviata (sels) *([ITA] text)* HUN ▲ 31801 [DDD] (16.97)

T. Serafin (cnd), La Scala Orch *(rec Milan, Italy, 1954)* ("Opera Rhapsody") † Puritani (sels); Leoncavallo:Pagliacci (sels); P. Mascagni:Cavalleria rusticana (sels); Ponchielli:Gioconda (sels); G. Puccini:Madama Butterfly (sels); Manon Lescaut (sels); Tosca (sels); Verdi:Aida (sels); Ballo in maschera (sels); Forza del destino (sels) EMIC ▲ 66862 [ADD] (11.97)

T. Serafin (cnd), La Scala Orch, La Scala Chorus, M. Callas (sop—Norma), C. Ludwig (mez—Adalgisa), F. Corelli (ten—Pollione), N. Zaccaria (bass—Oroveso)—Guerra, guerra!; Si, fino all'ore estreme *(rec Milan, Italy, Sept 1960)* ("Highlights") EMIC (Maria Callas Edition) ▲ 66662 [ADD] (11.97)

D. Soffel (mez), J. Sutherland (sop), H. Hoffman (ten), R. Bonynge (cnd), Swedish RSO ("Doris Soffel Sings Bel Canto") † Donizetti:Lucrezia Borgia (sels) CAPA ▲ 21601 (16.97)

E. Stignani (mez) † C. W. Gluck:Orfeo ed Euridice (sels); Saint-Saëns:Samson et Dalila (sels); A. Thomas:Mignon (sels); Verdi:Aida (sels); Don Carlos (sels); Forza del destino (sels); Trovatore (sels) PHG (Great Voices) ▲ 5101 (12.97)

E. Stignani (sop), G. Cigna (sop), G. Breviario (ten), E. Renzi (ten), T. Pasero (bass), V. Gui (cnd), Orch of Radio Italiana, Chorus of Radio Italiana OPIT ▲ 54552 (6.97)

J. Sutherland (sop) *(rec 1956-60)* ("Recitals") † Donizetti:Lucia di Lammermoor (sels); G. F. Handel:Alcina (sels); J. Haydn:Arias; W. A. Mozart:Entführung aus dem Serail (sels); Exsultate, jubilate, K.165 BELV ▲ 7001 [ADD] (15.97)

artists unknown ("Romantic Operatic Duets") † Capuleti e i Montecchi (sels); Donizetti:Anna Bolena (sels) GRFM ▲ 289 (10.97)

Norma:Overture

K. Arp (cnd), Southwest German RSO Baden-Baden ("Overtures") † Donizetti:Ovs; G. Rossini:Ovs; Verdi:Ovs & Preludes PVY ▲ 730050 (12.97)

Il pirata (opera in 2 acts) [Libretto Felice Romani after I.J.S. Taylor]

L. Aliberti (sop), J. G. Reyes (ten), R. Frontali (bar), S. Neill (sgr), M. Viotti (cnd), Berlin German Opera Orch, Berlin German Opera Chorus BER 2-▲ 1115 [DDD] (31.97)

Il pirata (selections)

M. Caballé (sop)—Oh! s'io potessi ("The Art of Montserrat Caballé") † Norma (sels); Donizetti:Lucrezia Borgia (sels); G. Rossini:Donna del lago (sels); Verdi:Arias REPL (Butterfly) ▲ 31 [AAD]

M. Callas (sop) ("Callas & Company") † Norma (sels); Sonnambula (sels); Donizetti:Lucia di Lammermoor (sels); G. Puccini:Bohème (sels); Tosca (sels); Verdi:Aida (sels); Traviata (sels) EMIC ▲ 56341 (16.97)

M. Callas (sop), N. Rescigno (cnd), Philharmonia Orch, Philharmonia Chorus—Oh! s'io potessi; Col sorriso d'innocenza *(rec Kingsway Hall London, England, Sept 1958)* ("Mad Scenes") † Donizetti:Anna Bolena (sels); A. Thomas:Hamlet (sels) *(E,F,I lib texts)* EMIC (Callas Edition) ▲ 66459 [ADD] (11.97)

M. Callas (sop), M. Sinclair (cta), A. Young (ten), A. Tonini (cnd), Philharmonia Orch, Philharmonia Chorus—Sorgete, è in me dover; Lo sognai ferito *(rec 1953-69)* ("The EMI Rarities") † Donizetti:Pirata (sels); W. A. Mozart:Don Giovanni (sels); G. Rossini:Arias; Verdi:Arias; C. M. von Weber:Oberon (sels) *(E,I lib texts)* EMIC (Callas Edition) 2-▲ 66468 [ADD] (21.97)

L. Christensen (gtr), M. Kammerling (gtr)—Ov [arr for 2 gtrs] † W. A. Mozart:Clemenza di Tito (ov); G. Rossini:Ovs; Spontini:Vestale (sels) PLAL ▲ 54 (18.97)

J. Eaglen (sop), M. Elder (cnd), Orch of the Age of Enlightenment *(rec Abbey Road Studio, England, 1995-96)* ("Opera Arias") † Bianca e Fernando (sels); Norma (sels); R. Wagner:Götterdämmerung (sels); Tristan und Isolde (prelude & liebestod); Walküre (sels) SNYC ▲ 62032 [DDD] (16.97)

I puritani (opera in 3 acts) [Libretto C. Pepoli after Ancelot and Xavier]

M. Callas (sop), G. Di Stefano (ten), R. Panerai (bar), N. Rossi-Lemeni (bass), T. Serafin (cnd), La Scala Orch, La Scala Chorus EMIC (Callas Edition) 2-▲ 56275 (32.97)

M. Freni (sop), L. Pavarotti (ten), S. Bruscantini (b-bar), R. Muti (cnd), Rome RAI SO, Rome RAI Chorus *(rec Rome, 1969)* ENT (Palladio) 3-▲ 4205 [ADD] (39.97)

M. Freni (sop—Elvira), L. Pavarotti (ten—Arturo), S. Bruscantini (b-bar—Riccardo), B. Giaiotti (bass—Giorgio), R. Muti (cnd), Rome RAI SO, Rome RAI Chorus ODRO 3-▲ 1141 (13.97)

E. Gruberová (sop), K. Lytting (mez), J. Lavender (ten), C. Tuand (ten), E. Kim (bar), F. E. Artegna (bass), D. Siegele (bass), F. Luisi (cnd), Munich RSO, Bavarian Radio Chorus NIGC 3-▲ 70562 (51.97)

J. Sutherland (sop), R. Raimondi (bass), T. Serafin (cnd), Palermo Teatro Massimo Orch, Palermo Teatro Massimo Chorus *(rec 1971)* BELV 2-▲ 7227 (29.97)

I puritani (selections)

L. Aliberti (sop), R. Paternostro (cnd), Berlin RSO—O rendetemi la speme; Vien, diletto; Son vergin vezzosa *(rec Jesus Christ Church, Berlin, Germany, Aug 2-10, 1988)* † Capuleti e i Montecchi (sels); Donizetti:Anna Bolena (sels); Don Pasquale (sels); Fille du régiment (sels); Torquato Tasso (sels) CAPO ▲ 10246 [DDD] (11.97)

M. Callas (sop—Elvira), G. Di Stefano (ten—Arturo), A. Mercuriali (ten—Bruno), R. Panerai (bar—Riccardo), N. Rossi-Lemeni (bass—Giorgio), C. Forti (bass—Valton), T. Serafin (cnd), La Scala Orch, La Scala Chorus—O di Cromvel guerrieri; A te, o cara; Son vergin vezzosa; Ah vieni al tempio; Cinta di fiori; O rendetemi la speme; Qui la voce sua soave; Vien, diletto; Riccardo!..Suoni la tromba; Son già lontani; Fini! Me lassa!; Vieni, fra queste braccia; Credeasi, misera *(rec Milan, Italy, Mar 1953)* ("Highlights") EMIC (Maria Callas Edition) ▲ 66665 [ADD] (11.97)

M. Devia (sop), M. Rota (cnd), Swiss-Italian Orch—Qui la voce sua soave; Vien, diletto *(rec June 4, 1992)* † Capuleti e i Montecchi (sels); Sonnambula (sels); G. Charpentier:Louise (sels); Delibes:Lakmé (sels); Donizetti:Lucia di Lammermoor (sels); Gounod:Roméo et Juliette (sels) BONG ▲ 2513 [DDD] (16.97)

P. Domingo (ten), J. Carreras (ten), L. Pavarotti (ten)—La mia canzon d'amor, Elvira! † Donizetti:Elisir d'amore (sels); Leoncavallo:Pagliacci (sels); P. Mascagni:Cavalleria rusticana (sels); G. Puccini:Bohème (sels); Madama Butterfly (sels); Tosca (sels); Turandot (sels); Verdi:Rigoletto (sels); Traviata (sels); Trovatore (sels) HALM ▲ 30464 (6.97)

M. Freni (sop), L. Pavarotti (ten), G. Antonini (bass), B. Giaiotti (bass), R. Muti (cnd), Rome RAI SO, Rome RAI Chorus *(rec Rome, July 8, 1969)* ("The Great Luciano Pavarotti") † Donizetti:Elisir d'amore (sels); Lucia di Lammermoor (sels); G. Puccini:Bohème (sels); Turandot (sels); G. Rossini:Stabat Mater; Verdi:Luisa Miller (sels); Rigoletto (sels) GDIS ▲ 63202 [ADD] (10.97)

M. Freni (sop), L. Pavarotti (ten), B. Giaiotti (bass), R. Muti (cnd), Rome SO, Rome Sym Chorus—A te, o cara *(rec live Oct 7, 1969)* ("Pavarotti: The Early Years, Vol. 2") † Capuleti e i Montecchi (sels); Donizetti:Lucia di Lammermoor (sels); G. Puccini:Turandot (sels); Verdi:Lombardi (sels); Luisa Miller (sels); Rigoletto (sels); Traviata (sels) RCAV (Gold Seal) ▲ 68014 (live) [ADD] (11.97)

Y. Huang (sop), M. Álvarez (ten), C. Rizzi (cnd), Welsh National Opera Orch, G. Jones (cnd), Welsh National Opera—Act 3, opening scene *(rec Swansea, Wales, Apr 20-22, 28 & May 2, 1998)* † Donizetti:Elisir d'amore (sels); Favorita (sels); Linda di Chamounix (sels); Lucia di Lammermoor (sels); Verdi:Rigoletto (sels); Traviata (sels) *([ENG] lib text)* SNYC ▲ 60721 [DDD] (16.97)

L. Nucci (bar) † Leoncavallo:Pagliacci (sels); Zazà (sels); G. Rossini:Barbiere di Siviglia (sels); Verdi:Arias AG ▲ 184 (18.97)

C. Parmentier (cnd) [arr for mands] ("Opera on Mandolins") † Donizetti:Lucia di Lammermoor (sels); Verdi:Rigoletto (sels); Traviata (sels); Trovatore (sels) PVY ▲ 795042 (16.97)

L. Pavarotti (ten)—Son salvo; Credeasi, misera † Capuleti e i Montecchi (sels); Donizetti:Elisir d'amore (sels); Lucia di Lammermoor (sels); G. Rossini:Stabat Mater; Verdi:Luisa Miller (sels) LALI ▲ 14308 (3.97)

L. Pavarotti (ten)—Credeasi, misera † Capuleti e i Montecchi (sels); Donizetti:Elisir d'amore (sels); Lucia di Lammermoor (sels); W. A. Mozart:Idomeneo (sels); G. Puccini:Bohème (sels); Turandot (sels); Verdi:Ballo in maschera (sels); Luisa Miller (sels); Rigoletto (sels) HALM ▲ 30421 (6.97)

E. Pinza (bass)—Cinta di fiori ("Ezio Pinza: The Early Legendary Recordings") † Norma (sels); Boito:Mefistofele (sels); Donizetti:Favorita (sels); Lucia di Lammermoor (sels); G. Puccini:Bohème (sels); G. Rossini:Mosè in Egitto (sels); Verdi:Arias VOCA (Vocal Archives) ▲ 1132 (13.97)

G. Sabbatini (ten), M. Pertusi (bass), C. Alvarez (bass), L. Albert (sgr)—All'erta!; A te, o cara; Son vergin vezzosa; Ah..Dolor!; Cinta di fiori; O rendetemi la speme; Vien, diletto; Il rival salvar; Suoni la tromba ("Die Puritaner Opera Highlights") LALI ▲ 14208 [DDD] (3.97)

T. Serafin (cnd), La Scala Orch—Sinfonia *(rec Milan, Italy, 1953)* ("Opera Rhapsody") † Norma (sels); Leoncavallo:Pagliacci (sels); P. Mascagni:Cavalleria rusticana (sels); Ponchielli:Gioconda (sels); G. Puccini:Madama Butterfly (sels); Manon Lescaut (sels); Tosca (sels); Verdi:Aida (sels); Ballo in maschera (sels); Forza del destino (sels) EMIC ▲ 66862 [ADD] (11.97)

R. A. Swenson (sop), N. Rescigno (cnd), London PO—O rendetemi la speme *(rec Nov 11-19, 1993)* ("Positively Golden") † Sonnambula (sels); Donizetti:Linda di Chamounix (sels); Lucia di Lammermoor (sels); Gounod:Roméo et Juliette (sels); Meyerbeer:Africaine (sels); Dinorah (sels); Huguenots (sels) EMIC ▲ 54827 [DDD] (16.97)

BELLINI, VINCENZO (cont.)

I puritani (selections) (cont.)

D. Takova (sop), M. Matakiev (cnd), Sofia SO—Qui la voce sua soave ("Opera Recital") † Sonnambula (sels); Delibes:Lakmé (sels); Donizetti:Anna Bolena (sels); Lucia di Lammermoor (sels); W. A. Mozart:Zauberflöte (sels); Rimsky-Korsakov:Golden Cockerel (sels); Verdi:Traviata (sels) GEGA ▲ 105 [DDD] (16.97)

L. Tetrazzini (sop)—Vien, diletto ("Luisa Tetrazzini: The London Recordings, Vol. 1 1907-14") † Sonnambula (sels); Donizetti:Linda di Chamounix (sels); Lucia di Lammermoor (sels); G. Rossini:Barbiere di Siviglia (sels); Semiramide (sels); Verdi:Arias VOCA (Vocal Archives) ▲ 1122 (13.97)

V. Zeani (sop), A. Protti (bar), A. Mongelli (bar), F. M. Prandelli (cnd), Trieste Teatro Communale Giuseppe Verdi Orch—O rendetemi la speme; Qui la voce sua soave *(rec Italy, 1957)* ("Virginia Zeani") † Donizetti:Anna Bolena (sels); Elisir d'amore (sels); Lucia di Lammermoor (sels); F. Lehár:Lustige Witwe (sels); Verdi:Aida (sels); Don Carlos (sels); Forza del destino (sels) *(I text)* BONG (Il Mito Dell'Opera) ▲ 1060 [ADD] (16.97)

Sinfonie (6) for Orchestra (before 1825)

S. Frontalini (cnd), Warmia National Orch † Ariette da camera BONG ▲ 2098 [DDD] (16.97)

Songs

J. Aragall (ten), E. Arnaltes (pno)—Vaga luna, che inargenti; Dolente immagine di figlia mia † Ariette da camera; Leoncavallo:Songs; G. Puccini:Songs; G. Rossini:Soirées musicales; Tosti:Songs RTVE ▲ 65026 (16.97)

C. Bartoli (mez), J. Levine (pno)—Vaga luna, che inargenti; L'abbandono; Ariette da camera [Malinconia, ninfa gentile; Vanne, o rosa fortunata; Per pietà, bel'idol mio]; Il fervido desiderio; Torna, vezzosa Fillide; Dolente immagine di figlia mia; Farfalletta ("An Italian Songbook") † Donizetti:Songs; G. Rossini:Songs PLON ▲ 455513 (17.97) ▮ 455513 (11.98)

D. O'Neill (ten), I. Surgenor (pno) ("Italian Song, Vol. 1") COC ▲ 1507 (16.97)

La sonnambula (opera in 2 acts) [text Romani]

M. Callas (sop), G. Carturan (mez), C. Valletti (ten), G. Modesti (bass), L. Bernstein (cnd), La Scala Orch, La Scala Chorus [ITA] *(rec live, Mar 5, 1955)* † Sonnambula (sels) MYTO 2-▲ 89006 [ADD] (34.97)

M. Callas (sop), E. Ratti (sop), F. Cossotto (mez), N. Monti (ten), N. Zaccaria (bass), A. Votto (cnd), La Scala Orch, La Scala Chorus EMIC (Callas Edition) 2-▲ 56278 (32.97)

M. Callas (sop—Amina), C. Valletti (ten—Elvino), G. Modesti (bass—Conte Rodolfo), L. Bernstein (cnd), La Scala Orch, La Scala Chorus ODRO 2-▲ 1139 (9.97)

M. Devia (sop), L. Canonici (ten), A. Verducci (bass), M. Viotti (cnd), Piacenza SO, Piacenza Chorus [ITA] *(rec live, Nov 1988)* NUO 2-▲ 6764 [DDD] (32.97)

M. C. Nocentini (sop), V. Mosca (mez), G. Morino (ten), G. Furlanetto (bar), P. Ciofi (sgr), E. Ligot (sgr), W. Mikus (sgr), G. Carella (cnd), Italian International Orch NUO 2-▲ 7215 [DDD] (33.97)

L. Orgonasova (sop—Amina), Dilbèr (sop—Lisa), A. Papadjakou (cta—Teresa), R. Giménez (ten—Elvino), I. Micu (ten—Notary), F. E. Artegna (bass—Rodolfo), N. D. Vries (bass—Alessio), A. Zedda (cnd), Netherlands Radio CO, S. Rozin (cnd), Netherlands Radio Chorus *(rec live Amsterdam Concertgebouw, Nov 14, 1992) (I lib text)* NXIN ▲ 660042 [DDD] (14.97)

J. Sutherland (sop), L. Pavarotti (ten), N. Ghiaurov (bass), R. Bonynge (cnd), National PO London [ITA] PLON 2-▲ 17424 [DDD] (32.97)

J. Valásková (sop), P. Mikuláš (bass), J. Galla (bass) ("Bellini: La Sonnambula") OPP 2-▲ 1928

La sonnambula (selections)

J. Anderson (sop), M. A. Martinez (cnd), Emilia Romagna SO—Come per me sereno; Sovra il sen *(rec Parma, Italy, Nov 24, 1984)* ("June Anderson dal Vivo in Concerto") † Donizetti:Lucia di Lammermoor (sels); G. Rossini:Semiramide (sels); Verdi:Battaglia di Legnano (sels); Traviata (sels) BONG ▲ 2504 (16.97)

M. Callas (sop) ("Callas & Company") † Norma (sels); Pirata (sels); Donizetti:Lucia di Lammermoor (sels); G. Puccini:Bohème (sels); Tosca (sels); Verdi:Aida (sels); Traviata (sels) EMIC ▲ 56341 (16.97)

M. Callas (sop), F. Cossotto (mez), N. Monti (ten), N. Zaccaria (bass), A. Votto (cnd), La Scala Orch, La Scala Chorus [ITA] *(rec live, July 4, 1957)* † Sonnambula MYTO 2-▲ 89006 [ADD] (34.97)

M. Callas (sop), T. Serafin (cnd), La Scala Orch—Comapgne, teneri amici; Come per me sereno; Oh! se una volta sola; Ah, non credea mirarti *(rec Teatro alla Scala Milan, Italy, June 1955)* ("Callas at La Scala") † Cherubini:Médée (sels); Spontini:Vestale (sels) *([ENG,ITA] texts)* EMIC (Callas Edition) ▲ 66457 [ADD] (11.97)

M. Devia (sop), M. Rota (cnd), Swiss-Italian Orch—Come per me sereno; Sovra il sen *(rec June 4, 1992)* † Capuleti e i Montecchi (sels); Puritani (sels); G. Charpentier:Louise (sels); Delibes:Lakmé (sels); Donizetti:Lucia di Lammermoor (sels); Gounod:Roméo et Juliette (sels) BONG ▲ 2513 [DDD] (16.97)

Y. Huang (sop), J. Conlon (cnd), London SO—Ah, non credea mirarti *(rec Hampstead London, England, Apr 29-May 5, 1996)* † Donizetti:Arias; G. Puccini:Arias; G. Rossini:Arias; Verdi:Arias SNYC ▲ 62687 [DDD] (16.97)

T. D. Monte (sop) *(rec 1924-41)* ("Arias & Duets") † Norma (sels); Donizetti:Don Pasquale (sels); Fille du régiment (sels); Linda di Chamounix (sels); Lucia di Lammermoor (sels); W. A. Mozart:Don Giovanni (sels); Nozze di Figaro (sels); G. Rossini:Barbiere di Siviglia (sels); Guillaume Tell (sels); Verdi:Falstaff (sels); Rigoletto (sels); Traviata (sels) ENT (Vocal Archives) ▲ 1191 (13.97)

T. Pasero (bass)—Vi ravviso, o luoghi ameni; Tu non sai con quei begli occhi ("Tancredi Pasero: La Scala Repertoire, Vol. 1 1927-44") † Norma (sels); Boito:Mefistofele (sels); Ponchielli:Gioconda (sels); G. Rossini:Arias; Verdi:Arias VOCA (Vocal Archives) ▲ 1123 (13.97)

B. Sayão (sop), F. Cleva (cnd), Metropolitan Opera Orch *(rec 1945)* ("Bidú Sayão") † Debussy:Damoiselle élue; Leoncavallo:Pagliacci (sels); W. A. Mozart:Arias; G. Puccini:Arias; Verdi:Traviata (sels) SNYC (Masterworks Heritage) ▲ 63221 (12.97)

J. Sutherland (sop), T. Serafin (cnd), Royal Opera House Orch Covent Garden, Royal Opera House Covent Garden Chorus *(rec live Covent Garden, England, 1960)* † G. F. Handel:Alcina (sels); J. Haydn:Anima del filosofo, H.XXVIII/13 MYTO 2-▲ 90529 [ADD] (34.97)

R. A. Swenson (sop), N. Rescigno (cnd), London PO—A te dilette tenera madre; Come per me sereno *(rec Nov 11-19, 1993)* ("Positively Golden") † Puritani (sels); Donizetti:Linda di Chamounix (sels); Lucia di Lammermoor (sels); Gounod:Roméo et Juliette (sels); Meyerbeer:Africaine (sels); Dinorah (sels); Huguenots (sels) EMIC ▲ 54827 [DDD] (16.97)

D. Takova (sop), M. Matakiev (cnd), Sofia SO—Oh! se una volta sola ("Opera Recital") † Puritani (sels); Delibes:Lakmé (sels); Donizetti:Anna Bolena (sels); Lucia di Lammermoor (sels); W. A. Mozart:Zauberflöte (sels); Rimsky-Korsakov:Golden Cockerel (sels); Verdi:Traviata (sels) GEGA ▲ 105 [DDD] (16.97)

L. Tetrazzini (sop)—Ah, non credea mirarti; Sovra il sen; Come per me sereno ("Luisa Tetrazzini: The London Recordings, Vol. 1 1907-14") † Puritani (sels); Donizetti:Linda di Chamounix (sels); Lucia di Lammermoor (sels); G. Rossini:Barbiere di Siviglia (sels); Semiramide (sels); Verdi:Arias VOCA (Vocal Archives) ▲ 1122 (13.97)

Zaira (opera in 2 acts) [Libretto Romani] (1829)

K. Ricciarelli (sop), A. Papadjakou (cta), R. Vargas (ten), S. Alaimo (bar), P. Olmi (cnd), Catania Teatro Massimo Bellini Orch, Catania Teatro Massimo Bellini Chorus [ITA] *(rec live, 1990)* NUO 2-▲ 6982 [DDD] (32.97)

R. Scotto (sop—Zaira), M. L. Nave (mez—Nerestano), G. Lamberti (ten—Corasmino), L. Roni (bass—Orosmane), M. Rinaudo (bass—Lusignano), D. Belardinelli (cnd), Catania Teatro Massimo Bellini Orch, Catania Teatro Massimo Bellini Chorus *(rec Catania, Mar 30, 1976)* MYTO 3-▲ 971151 (51.97)

BELLMAN, CARL MICHAEL (1740-1795)

Songs

H. Hagegård (bar), E. Sædén (bar) ("Fredmans Epistles, Vol. 1") PRPI 2-▲ 9131 (34.97)

H. Hagegård (bar), E. Sædén (bar) ("Fredmans Epistles, Vol. 2") PRPI 2-▲ 9133 (34.97)

H. Hagegård (bar), E. Sædén (bar) ("Fredmans Epistles, Vol. 3") PRPI 2-▲ 9135 (34.97)

H. Hagegård (bar), E. Sædén (bar) ("Fredmans Songs, Vol. 1") PRPI ▲ 9146 (17.97)

H. Hagegård (bar), E. Sædén (bar) ("Fredmans Songs, Vol. 2") PRPI ▲ 9147 (17.97)

H. Hagegård (bar), E. Sædén (bar) ("Fredmans Songs, Vol. 3") PRPI 2-▲ 9148 (17.97)

H. Hagegård (bar), E. Sædén (bar) ("The Complete Fredmans Songs") PRPI 4-▲ 9137 (102.97)

H. Hagegård (bar), E. Sædén (bar) ("The Complete Fredmans Epistles") PRPI 6-▲ 9150 (149.97)

H. Wader (sgr), H. Wader (gtr) PLAE ▲ 88790 (17.97)

BELLOLI, AGOSTINO (1778-1870)

Concerto for Hunting Horn & Orchestra

Z. Zuk (hn), J. Stanienda (cnd), Wroclaw CO Leopoldinum ("Il Corno Italiano") † Cherubini:Sons Hn; Mercadante:Con Hn; N. Rota:Castel del Monte; Vivaldi:Con Hns, RV.538; Con Hns, RV.539 ZUK ▲ 160528 (10.97)

BEN-HAIM (FRANKENBURGER), PAUL (1897-1984)

Concerto for Violin & Orchestra (1962)

M. Guttman (vn), D. Shallon (cnd), London PO ("Israeli Violin Concertos") † Sheriff:Con Vn; Zehavi:Con Vn ASV ▲ 1038 (16.97)

Pieces (3) for solo Cello (1973)

S. Honigberg (vc) ("Darkness & Light, Vol. 2") † Castelnuovo-Tedesco:Trio 2 Pno, Op. 70; D. Diamond:Qt 1 Strs; Koffler:Son Pno, Op. 12; Laks:Passacaille; Messiaen:Quatuor ALBA ▲ 229 [DDD] (16.97)

Pieces (5) for Piano

D. Holzman (pno) ("Piano Music by Jewish Composers") † Avni:Epitaph; E. Bloch:Visions & Prophecies; Schoenberg:Pieces (3) Pno, Op. 11; S. Wolpe:Palestinian Notebook ALBA ▲ 283 [DDD] (16.97)

BEN-HAIM (FRANKENBURGER), PAUL (cont.)

Sonatina for Piano (1946)

C. Honigberg (pno) ("Darkness & Light") † Berlinski:From the World of My Father; Perle:Hebrew Melodies; Starer:Elegy for a Woman Who Died Too Young; M. Vainberg:Trio Pno, Op. 24 ALBA ▲ 157 [DDD] (16.97)

Sweet Psalmist of Israel for Orchestra (1958)

L. Bernstein (cnd), New York PO ("Bernstein: The Royal Edition") † E. Bloch:Avodath Hakodesh; L. Foss:Song of Songs SNYC ▲ 47533 [ADD] (23.97)

BENARY, PETER (1931-

Sonata No. 2 for Piano (1996)

H. Sakagami (pno) ("Music in Lucerne, Vol. 1: Solo Piano Music") † Diethelm:Klangfiguren, Op. 244; Eisenmann:Vars Pno, Op. 71; Lauber:Caprices Pno, Op. 44; Schnyder von Wartensee:Scherzi Pno; A. Scriabin:Preludes (24) Pno, Op. 11; Willisegger:Sakura GALL 2-▲ 966 [DDD] (36.97)

BENATZKY, RALPH (1884-1957)

Im weissen Rössl (selections)

H. Brauner (sop), F. Loor (sop), K. Equiluz (ten), K. Terkal (ten), F. Bauer-Theussl (cnd), Vienna Volksoper Orch, Vienna Volksoper Chorus—Aber meine Herrschaften; Im Salzkammergut da kann ma gut lustig sein; Zuschaun kann i net; Im Weissen Rössl; Was kann der Sigismund dafür; Es muss was Wunderbares sein; Die ganze Welt ist himmelblau; Mein Leibeslied muss ein Walzer sein † F. Lehár:Lustige Witwe (sels) PC ▲ 267134 [DDD] (2.97)

F. Loor (sop), H. Brauner (cta), K. Equiluz (ten), K. Terkal (ten), F. Bauer-Theussl (cnd), Vienna Volksoper Orch, Vienna Volksoper Chorus [GER] ("Golden Operetta, Vol. 3") KOCP ▲ 399225 [AAD] (8.97)

A. Rothenberger (sop), M. Schmidt (ten), W. Schmidt-Boelke (cnd), FFB Orch, FFB Chorus † Berté:Dreimäderlhaus (sels); Künneke:Glückliche Reise (sels); Vetter aus Dingsda (sels) EMPE ▲ 86350

BENAUT, [MONSIEUR] (fl 1770-1776)

Mass in C for Organ

C. D. Zeeuw (org) PVY 2-▲ 785032 [DDD] (32.97)

BENDA, FRANZ [FRANTIŠEK] (1709-1786)

Concertos (3) in e, A & a for Flute & Orchestra

A. Adorján (fl), M. Munclinger (cnd) ORF ▲ 151101 [DDD] (18.97)

Concertos (4) in a, e, A & G for Flute & Strings

M. Helasvuo (fl), J. Saraste (cnd), Helsinki CO † C. Stamitz:Con Fl in G, Op. 29 BIS ▲ 268 [DDD] (17.97)

N. McLaren (fl), J. H. Jones (cnd), Cambridge Baroque Camerata [period instrs] ("Rare Baroque Flute Concertos") † Quantz:Con in e Fl; Tartini:Con Fl AMON ▲ 52 [DDD] (16.97)

E. Zukerman (fl), B. Warchal (cnd), Slovak CO † C. Stamitz:Con Fl in D OPP ▲ 2088

E. Zukerman (fl), B. Warchal (cnd), Slovak CO—No. 2 in e ("2") † F. X. Richter:Cons (8) for Fl & Orch; Cons (8) Fl & Orch GZCL ▲ 299 (6.97)

Sonata in A for Cello & Harpsichord

Benda Musicians *(rec Stuttgart, Germany, Feb 1985)* † Trio No. 6; G. A. Benda:Con Hpd & Strs in b; J. G. Benda:Con Vn; G. A. Benda:Trio Sonata ADG ▲ 91004 [DDD] (11.97)

Trio No. 6 in E♭ for Violin, Viola, & Cello

Benda Musicians *(rec Stuttgart, Germany, Feb 1985)* † Son Vc; G. A. Benda:Con Hpd & Strs in b; J. G. Benda:Con Vn; G. A. Benda:Trio Sonata ADG ▲ 91004 [DDD] (11.97)

BENDA, GEORG ANTON [JIŘÍ ANTONÍN] (1722-1795)

Ariadne auf Naxos (melodrama in 1 act) [text J. C. Brandes] (1775)

D. Schortemeier (nar—Theseus), S. Kammer (nar—Ariadne), F. Tiefenbacher (nar—Vox Oreadis), G. Ijac (vn), P. Gülke (cnd), Wuppertal SO, C. Zündorf (cnd), Wupperfeld Chamber Chorus *(rec Sept 2-4 & Oct 22, 1996)* ("Melodrama") † C. Eberwein:Prosperina MDG ▲ 3350740 [DDD] (17.97)

Cephalus & Aurora (instrumental & song cycle) (1789)

E. Kirby (sop), R. Müller (ten), T. Roberts (pno)—Du kleine Blondine; Belise starb; Mein Geliebter hat versprochen; Faulheit, itzo will ich dir; Philint ist still und fleiht die Schonen; Cephalus & Aurore; Ein trunkner Dichter; Wir Arem, denn des Fieberes Kraft; Philint stand vor Babes Thür; Du fehlest mir, wie einsam und wie stille; Das Andenken; Von nonan, O Liebe, lass ich dein Reich; Mein Thrysis!; Ich liebe nur Ismene; Liebe Amor HYP ▲ 66649 (18.97)

Concerto in g for Harpsichord & Strings (1779)

J. Ogg (pno) *(rec Oct 1992)* † Sonatinas Pno; Sons Pno GLOE ▲ 5092 [DDD] (16.97)

R. Plagge (hpd), H. Breuer (cnd), Thüringen Landes SO Gotha *(rec Germany, 1994)* ("Georg Anton Benda (1722-1795)") † Con Va; Sym 1; Sym 7 ESDU ▲ 2027 [DDD] (17.97)

Concerto in b for Harpsichord & Strings

Benda Musicians *(rec Stuttgart, Germany, Feb 1985)* † Trio Sonata; J. G. Benda:Con Vn; F. Benda:Son Vc; Trio No. 6 ADG ▲ 91004 [DDD] (11.97)

Concerto in F for Viola & Orchestra

T. Masurenko (va), H. Breuer (cnd), Thüringen Landas SO Gotha *(rec Germany, 1994)* ("Georg Anton Benda (1722-1795)") † Con Hpd & Strs; Sym 1; Sym 7 ESDU ▲ 2027 [DDD] (17.97)

Medea (melodrama in 1 act) [lib Friedrich Wilhelm Gotter] (1775)

H. Schell (nar), P. Uray (nar), B. Quadlbauer (nar), C. Benda (cnd), Prague CO *(rec Prague, Nov 1994)* † J. G. Benda:Con Vn NXIN ▲ 553346 [DDD] (5.97)

Romeo und Julie (opera in 3 acts) [lib F. W. Gotter after Shakespeare] (1776)

M. Mulder (sop), C. Taha (sop), J. Kueper (ten), A. Näck (bar), T. Pfeifer (nar), H. Breuer (cnd), Thüringen SO CANT 2-▲ 1083 (36.97)

Symphony in B for Orchestra

Czech CO † A. Dvořák:Serenade Strs, Op. 22; Janáček:Suite Str Orch GZCL ▲ 243

Symphony No. 1 in D

H. Breuer (cnd), Thüringen Landes SO Gotha *(rec Germany, 1994)* ("Georg Anton Benda (1722-1795)") † Con Hpd & Strs; Con Va; Sym 7 ESDU ▲ 2027 [DDD] (17.97)

Symphony No. 7 in D, "Der Dorfjahrmarkt"

H. Breuer (cnd), Thüringen Landes SO Gotha *(rec Germany, 1994)* ("Georg Anton Benda (1722-1795)") † Con Hpd & Strs; Con Va; Sym 1 ESDU ▲ 2027 [DDD] (17.97)

Sonatas (6) for Harpsichord (1757)

B. Dobozy (hpd) HUN ▲ 31668 [DDD] (16.97)

Trio Sonata in E for Violins, Cello & Continuo

Benda Musicians *(rec Stuttgart, Germany, Feb 1985)* † Con Hpd & Strs in b; J. G. Benda:Con Vn; F. Benda:Son Vc; Trio No. 6 ADG ▲ 91004 [DDD] (11.97)

Sonatas for Piano

J. Ogg (pno)—No. 1 in B; No. 7 in c; No. 9 in a; No. 13 in E; No. 16 in C *(rec Oct 1992)* † Con Hpd & Strs; Sonatinas Pno GLOE ▲ 5092 [DDD] (16.97)

Sonata No. 9 in a for Piano (ca 1780)

R. Firkušný (pno) *(rec 1972-74)* † J. L. Dussek:Son Pno, Op. 77; A. Dvořák:Humoresques, Op. 101; Mazurkas, Op. 56; Poetic Tone Pictures, Op. 85; Theme with Vars, Op. 36; Smetana:Czech Dances Pno; Tomášek:Eclogues (42) Pno; Voříšek:Impromptus Pno, Op. 7 VB2 2-▲ 5058 [ADD] (9.97)

Sonatas (8) for 2 Violins (or Flutes) & Continuo

J. Suk (vn), S. Ishikawa (vn), J. Vlasankova (vc), J. Hála (hpd) *(rec Czech Republic, August 1995)* ("Baroque Sonatas") † Locatelli:Sons Vn, Op. 8; Tartini:Trio Sons; Trio Sons, Op. 8 LT ▲ 27 [DDD] (16.97)

Sonatinas for Piano

J. Ogg (pno)—No. 3 in a; No. 6 in d; No. 13 in c; No. 21 in F; No. 23 in g; No. 34 in D *(rec Oct 1992)* † Con Hpd & Strs; Sons Pno GLOE ▲ 5092 [DDD] (16.97)

Sonatina No. 1 for Piano

J. Becker (pno) *(rec Sept 1991)* ("Sonate Facile") † Sonatina 2 Pno; W. F. Bach:Son in C Hpd; C.P.E. Bach:Sonatas for Viol & Continuo; J. Christian Bach:Sons Kbd; Dušeck:Son in F; W. A. Mozart:Son 16 Pno, K.545 CAPO ▲ 10415 [DDD] (11.97)

Sonatina No. 2 for Piano

J. Becker (pno) *(rec Sept 1991)* ("Sonate Facile") † Sonatina 1 Pno; W. F. Bach:Son in C Hpd; C.P.E. Bach:Sonatas for Viol & Continuo; J. Christian Bach:Sons Kbd; Dušeck:Son in F; W. A. Mozart:Son 16 Pno, K.545 CAPO ▲ 10415 [DDD] (11.97)

BENDA, JOHANN GEORG [JAN JIŘÍ] (1713-1752)

Concerto in G for Violin & Strings

Benda Musicians *(rec Stuttgart, Germany, Feb 1985)* † G. A. Benda:Con Hpd & Strs in b; F. Benda:Son Vc; Trio No. 6; G. A. Benda:Trio Sonata ADG ▲ 91004 [DDD] (11.97)

C. Benda (vc), C. Benda (cnd), Prague CO [trans for vc & strs] *(rec Prague, Nov 1994)* † G. A. Benda:Medea NXIN ▲ 553346 [DDD] (5.97)

BENEDICT, JULIUS (1804-1885)
La Gitane et l'oiseau for Voice & Flute
C. Hartglass (sop), M. Cabaud-Chiaparin (fl) *(rec Châteaugay Church France, June 1995)* ("Caryn Hartglass") † L. Bernstein:I Hate Music; Mass (sels); Longas:Rossignol et l'Empereur; D. Milhaud:Chansons de Ronsard, Op. 223; Saint-Saëns:Libellule; Rossignol et la rose; R. Strauss:Songs (6), Op. 68 LIDI ▲ 201033 [DDD] (16.97)
BENEJAM, LLUIS (20th cent)
Concerto for Saxophone & Orchestra (1967)
M. Magdalena (fl), J. Harle (sax), R. Casero (trbn), M. Barrera (hp), L. Foster (cnd), Barcelona SO † Brotons:Con Trbn Orch, Op. 70; Montsalvage:Con Capriccio Hp Orch; Serenata a Lydia CLAV ▲ 509808 (16.97)
Moments musicals (3) for Viola & Piano
P. Cortese (va), A. Soler (pno) † Bonet:Sonatina Va; Brotons:Son Va; Lamote De Grignon:Scherzino Va EAM ▲ 7373 [DDD] (17.97)
BENEY, ALAIN (20th cent)
Flashes for Trumpet & Percussion (1974)
E. Sandor (tpt), T. McCutchen (perc) ("The Art of Trumpet & Percussion") † Cirone:Son 2 Perc & Tpt; D. Erb:Diversion; W. Kraft:Encounters III; S. Leonard:Fanfare & Allegro; R. Vogel:Temporal Landscape 6; Voyages ACAD ▲ 20042 [DDD] (16.97)
BENFALL, STEPHEN (1957-
Rough Cut for Percussion Ensemble (1992)
Nova Ensemble ("Mizu to Kori") † Buddle:Just an Inkling for an Angklung; J. Fowler:Echos from an Antique Land; Hille:Mizu to Kori; Smalley:Ceremony I; Travers:Cold Air Rising VOXA ▲ 21 [AAD/ADD] (18.97)
BENGRAF, JOSEPH (ca 1745-1791)
Sacred Music
I. Kertesi (sop), K. Gémes (mez), G. Kállay (ten), Á. Ambrus (bar), Z. Kovács (vc), V. Buza (db), B. Arnóth (bn), I. Ella (org), J. Dobra (cnd), Vienna-Szász CO, Tomkins Vocal Ensemble—Te Deum; O sacrum convivium; Libera me; Gloria [from Missa solemnis in D] † Druschetzky:Missa solemnis HUN ▲ 31609 [DDD] (16.97)
BENGTSON, PETER (20th cent)
Hekas! for Symphonic Winds (1992)
A. V. Beek (cnd) ("Hekas!") † Crusell:Intro, Theme & Vars on a Swedish Air, Op. 12; M. Larsson:Con Trbn; Tykesson:Arabesques BIS ▲ 818 [DDD] (17.97)
The Maids (chamber opera) [text Ragnar Lyth after Jean Genet]
A. Eklund-Tarantino (sop), E. Pilat (mez), G. Söderström (alt), N. Willén (cnd) *(rec 1996)* PHNS ▲ 96 [DDD] (16.97)
BENGTSSON, GUSTAF (1886-1965)
Symphony No. 1 in c, Op. 6 (1907-08)
M. Liljefors (cnd), Gävle SO ("A Romantic Master: Gustaf Bengtsson") † Vadstena Kloster; Vettern STRL ▲ 1008 (15.97)
I Vadstena Kloster (3 tone pictures) for Orchestra (1949)
M. Liljefors (cnd), Gävle SO ("A Romantic Master: Gustaf Bengtsson") † Sym 1; Vettern STRL ▲ 1008 (15.97)
Vettern (symphonic poem) for Orchestra (1950)
M. Liljefors (cnd), Gävle SO ("A Romantic Master: Gustaf Bengtsson") † Sym 1; Vadstena Kloster STRL ▲ 1008 (15.97)
BENJAMIN, ARTHUR (1893-1960)
Concertino for Piano & Orchestra (1927)
L. Crowson (pno), A. Benjamin (cnd), London SO *(rec Walhamstow Assembly Hall London)* † Con quasi una fant EVC ▲ 9029 [AAD] (13.97)
Concerto in G for Oboe & Strings [after Keyboard Sonatas of Cimarosa] (1942)
J. Anderson (ob), S. Wright (cnd), Philharmonia Orch *(rec St. Jude-on-the-Hill Hampstead, England, Jan 5-6, 1989)* † Cimarosa:Con Ob; A. Marcello:Con Ob Strs in d; Vivaldi:Con Ob NIMB ▲ 7027 [DDD] (11.97)
E. Brunner (cl), H. Stadlmair (cnd), Munich CO [arr for cl & strs] † Cimarosa:Con Cl; Donizetti:Concertino Cl; Giampieri:Carnevale di Venezia; Mercadante:Con in B Cl, Op. 101; G. Rossini:Vars Cl TUD ▲ 728 [DDD] (16.97)
Concerto quasi una fantasia for Piano & Orchestra (1949)
L. Crowson (pno), A. Benjamin (cnd), London SO *(rec Walhamstow Assembly Hall London)* † Concertino Pno EVC ▲ 9029 [AAD] (13.97)
Elegy, Waltz & Toccata (sonata) for Viola & Piano (or Orchestra) (1945)
W. Primrose (va), V. Sokoloff (pno) † J. Brahms:Son 1 Cl; Son 2 Cl; R. Harris:Soliloquy & Dance; F. Kreisler:Praeludium & Allegro Va PHS ▲ 9253 (17.97)
Jamaican Rhumba for 2 Pianos (1938)
N. Lester (pno), N. Roldán (pno) *(rec Rosenstock Auditorium, Hood College, Frederick, MD, Oct 1992)* ("Music of the Americas") † Jamaican Street Songs; Aguirre:Huella; A. Copland:Danzón Cubano; R. Cordero:Duo 1954; Guastavino:Pno Music; Joio:Aria & Toccata for 2 Pnos CENT ▲ 2171 [DDD] (16.97)
Jamaican Street Songs (2) for 2 Pianos (1949)
N. Lester (pno), N. Roldán (pno) *(rec Rosenstock Auditorium, Hood College, Frederick, MD, Oct 1992)* ("Music of the Americas") † Jamaican Rhumba; Aguirre:Huella; A. Copland:Danzón Cubano; R. Cordero:Duo 1954; Guastavino:Pno Music; Joio:Aria & Toccata for 2 Pnos CENT ▲ 2171 [DDD] (16.97)
Le tombeau de Ravel for Viola (or Clarinet) & Piano (1958)
P. Shands (cl), E. Rowley (pno) † M. Arnold:Son Cl; V. Babin:Hillandale Waltzes; G. Finzi:Bagatelles Cl, Op. 23; W. Lutoslawski:Dance Preludes Cl & Pno RTOP ▲ 116 (16.97)
BENJAMIN, GEORGE (1960-
At First Light for Chamber Orchestra (1982)
G. Benjamin (cnd), London Sinfonietta † Mind of Winter; Ringed by the Flat Horizon NIMB ▲ 5075 [DDD] (16.97)
A Mind of Winter for Soprano & Chamber Ensemble (1977)
G. Benjamin (cnd), London Sinfonietta † At First Light; Ringed by the Flat Horizon NIMB ▲ 5075 [DDD] (16.97)
Octet for Flute, Clarinet, 4 Strings, Celesta & Percussion (1979)
London Sinfonietta *(rec May 28-29, 1996)* † Sudden Time; Three Inventions; Upon Silence Mez & Strs; Upon Silence Mez & Vls NIMB ▲ 5505 [DDD] (16.97)
Ringed by the Flat Horizon for Chamber Orchestra (1980)
M. Elder (cnd), BBC SO † At First Light; Mind of Winter NIMB ▲ 5075 [DDD] (16.97)
Sudden Time for Orchestra (1989-93)
G. Benjamin (cnd), London PO *(rec Feb 22, 1994)* † Octet; Three Inventions; Upon Silence Mez & Strs; Upon Silence Mez & Vls NIMB ▲ 5505 [DDD] (16.97)
Three Inventions for Chamber Orchestra (1993-5)
J. Wallace (flgl), G. Benjamin (cnd), London Sinfonietta *(rec May 28-29, 1996)* † Octet; Sudden Time; Upon Silence Mez & Strs; Upon Silence Mez & Vls NIMB ▲ 5505 [DDD] (16.97)
Upon Silence for Mezzo-Soprano & 7 Strings (1991)
S. Bickley (mez), London Sinfonietta *(rec May 28-29, 1996)* † Octet; Sudden Time; Three Inventions; Upon Silence Mez & Vls NIMB ▲ 5505 [DDD] (16.97)
Upon Silence for Mezzo-Soprano & 5 Viols (1990)
S. Bickley (mez), Fretwork *(rec July 17, 1994)* † Octet; Sudden Time; Three Inventions; Upon Silence Mez & Strs NIMB ▲ 5505 [DDD] (16.97)
BENNETT, RICHARD RODNEY (1936-
Concerto for Alto Saxophone & Strings
J. Harle (sax), N. Marriner (cnd), Academy of St. Martin in the Fields ("Saxophone Concertos") † Debussy:Rapsodie Sax; Glazunov:Con A Sax, Op. 109; T. Heath:Out of the Cool; Ibert:Concertino da camera; H. Villa-Lobos:Fant Sax EMIC ▲ 72109 [DDD] (6.97)
Concerto for Guitar & Chamber Ensemble
J. Bream (gtr), D. Atherton (cnd), Melos Ensemble † M. Arnold:Con Gtr, Op. 67; J. Rodrigo:Con de Aranjuez RCAV ▲ 61598 (11.97)
Concerto for Piano & Orchestra (1968)
S. B. Kovacevich (pno), A. Gibson (cnd), London SO *(rec 1971)* † B. Bartók:Con 2 Pno, Sz.95; Out of Doors, Sz.81; Sonatina Pno, Sz.55; Beethoven:Son 5 Pno, Op. 10/1; J. Brahms:Pieces (4) Pno, Op. 119; Chopin:Impromptu in G♭, Op. 51; Nocturnes Pno; I. Stravinsky:Con Pno & Ww PPHI (Great Pianists of the 20th Century, Vol. 61) 2-▲ 456880 (22.97)
Concerto for Solo Percussion & Chamber Orchestra
E. Glennie (perc), P. Daniel (cnd), Scottish CO † D. Milhaud:Con Perc, Op. 109; A. Miyoshi:Con Mar; Rosauro:Con Mar RCAV (Red Seal) ▲ 61277 (16.97)
Concerto for Stan Getz for Tenor Saxophone & Orchestra (1990)
J. Harle (sax), B. Wordsworth (cnd), BBC Concert Orch *(rec Golders Green London, Mar 11, 1993)* ("Sax Drive") † S. Myers:Con S Sax; M. Torke:Con Sax PRGO ▲ 43529 (16.97)
Concerto for Violin & Orchestra
V. Gluzman (vn), J. DePreist (cnd), Monte Carlo PO † Diversions; Sym 3 KOCH ▲ 7341 (10.97)
BENNETT, RICHARD RODNEY (cont.)
Crosstalk for 2 Basset Horns
G. Dobrée (bas hn), T. King (bas hn) ("This Green Tide") † A. Cooke:Suite for 3 Cls; Lutyens:This Green Tide; Valediction, Op. 28; J. Mayer:Dance Suite; Raga Music; Pert:Eoastrion, Op. 30; Wellesz:Pieces Cl, Op. 34 CLCL ▲ 12 [AAD] (17.97)
Diversions for Orchestra
J. DePreist (cnd), Monte Carlo PO † Con Vn; Sym 3 KOCH ▲ 7341 (10.97)
Four Piece Suite for 2 Pianos (1974)
R. Markham (pno), D. Nettle (pno) ("Nettle & Markham in America") † L. Bernstein:West Side Story (sels); P. Grainger:Fant on Gershwin's *Porgy & Bess* ICC ▲ 6601042 (16.97)
Impromptus (5) for Guitar (1974)
M. Mangold (gtr) ("English Guitar Music") † Son Gtr; B. Britten:Nocturnal, Op. 70; W. Walton:Bagatelles Gtr MPH ▲ 56824 (15.97)
C. Ogden (gtr) *(rec Wyastone Leys Monmouth, Mar 28-29 & Sept 12-13, 1994)* ("Tippett: The Blue Guitar & Other 20th Century Guitar Classics") † L. Berkeley:Sonatina Gtr, Op. 52/1; B. Britten:Nocturnal, Op. 70; M. Tippett:Blue Gtr; W. Walton:Bagatelles Gtr NIMB ▲ 5390 [DDD] (16.97)
R. Smits (gtr), R. Smits (gtr) *(rec Bcom, Belgium, July 1990)* † A. Barrios:Gtr Music; Burkhart:Passacaglia Gtr; F. Martin:Pièces brèves Gtr; J. Morel:Sonatina Gtr; J. Turina:Son Gtr, Op. 61 ACCE ▲ 8966 [DDD] (17.97)
Partridge Pie for Piano
R. R. Bennett (nar), R. R. Bennett (pno) † Suite for Skip & Sadie; Week of Birthdays; 7 Days a Week; W. Walton:Duets for Children DLS ▮ 6002 [DDD] (7.98)
Quintet for Clarinet & Strings
C. Russo (cl) ("Clarinet alla Cinema") † R. Hyman:Sxt Cl; N. Rota:Trio Cl PREM ▲ 1062 (16.97)
Sermons & Devotions
King's Singers *(rec Salisbury Cathedral, England, Feb 21-23, 1995)* † Górecki:Totus tuus; G. Poole:Wymondham Chants; I. Stravinsky:Blessed Virgin; Our Father; J. Tavener:Music of Tavener; Tormis:Bishop & the Pagan RCAV (Red Seal) ▲ 68255 [DDD] (16.97)
Seven Days a Week for Piano (1962)
R. R. Bennett (nar), R. R. Bennett (pno) † Partridge Pie; Suite for Skip & Sadie; Week of Birthdays; W. Walton:Duets for Children DLS ▮ 6002 [DDD] (7.98)
Sonata after Syrinx for Flute, Viola & Harp
Auréole Trio † Tunes; Maw:Night Thoughts; Qt Fl KOCH ▲ 7355 (16.97)
Sonata for Guitar (1983)
M. Mangold (gtr) ("English Guitar Music") † Impromptus Gtr; B. Britten:Nocturnal, Op. 70; W. Walton:Bagatelles Gtr MPH ▲ 56824 (15.97)
Studies (5) for Piano (1962-64)
S. Cherkassky (pno) *(rec Salzburg, Aug 3, 1968)* † J. S. Bach:Partitas Hpd; J. Brahms:Son 3 Pno, Op. 5; Chopin:Preludes (24) Pno, Op. 28; Liszt:Polonaises (2) Pno, S.223 ORFE (Festspiel Dokumente) 2-▲ 431962 [ADD] (32.97)
Suite for Skip & Sadie for Piano 4-Hands
C. Rosenberger (pno), R. R. Bennett (pno) † Partridge Pie; Week of Birthdays; 7 Days a Week; W. Walton:Duets for Children DLS ▮ 6002 [DDD] (7.98)
Symphony No. 3
J. DePreist (cnd), Monte Carlo PO † Con Vn; Diversions KOCH ▲ 7341 (10.97)
Tunes for the Instruction of Singing Birds (6) for Flute (1981)
Auréole Trio † Son after Syrinx; Maw:Night Thoughts; Qt Fl KOCH ▲ 7355 (16.97)
A Week of Birthdays (music for children) for Piano (1961)
R. R. Bennett (nar), R. R. Bennett (pno) † Partridge Pie; Suite for Skip & Sadie; 7 Days a Week; W. Walton:Duets for Children DLS ▮ 6002 [DDD] (7.98)
BENNETT, ROBERT RUSSELL (1894-1981)
Abraham Lincoln:A Likeness in Symphony Form for Orchestra (1931)
W. T. Stromberg (cnd), Moscow SO *(rec Moscow, Russia, June 1998)* † Sights & Sounds NXIN ▲ 8559004 [DDD] (5.97)
Concerto for Violin & Orchestra (1941)
L. Kaufman (vn), B. Herrmann (cnd), Columbia SO ("Pan-Americana: The Violin Artistry of Louis Kaufman") † Song Son; C. M. Guarnieri:Son 2 Vn; E. Helm:Comment on 2 Spirituals; Mcbride:Aria & Toccata in Swing; D. Milhaud:Saudades do Brasil, Op. 67; W. G. Still:Lenox Ave; Triggs:Danza Braziliana Pnos CMB (Historical) ▲ 1078 [ADD]
Sights & Sounds for Orchestra (1929)
W. T. Stromberg (cnd), Moscow SO *(rec Moscow, Russia, June 1998)* † Abraham Lincoln Sym NXIN ▲ 8559004 [DDD] (5.97)
A Song Sonata for Violin & Piano (1947)
L. Kaufman (vn), T. Saidenberg (pno) ("Pan-Americana: The Violin Artistry of Louis Kaufman") † Con Vn; C. M. Guarnieri:Son 2 Vn; E. Helm:Comment on 2 Spirituals; Mcbride:Aria & Toccata in Swing; D. Milhaud:Saudades do Brasil, Op. 67; W. G. Still:Lenox Ave; Triggs:Danza Braziliana Pnos CMB (Historical) ▲ 1078 [ADD]
Stephen Collins Foster:A Commemoration Symphony [music of Foster arr & orchd Bennett] (1959)
W. Steinberg (cnd), Pittsburgh SO *(rec Pittsburgh; Belock Recording Studio Bayside, NY)* † Symphonic Story of Jerome Kern; I. Berlin:Music of Berlin EVC ▲ 9027 [AAD] (13.97)
Symphonic Songs for Wind Band (1958)
J. P. Paynter (cnd) ("Winds of Change") † H. Brant:Verticals Ascending; Finney:Con A Sax; Persichetti:Pageant, Op. 59; H. Smith:Expansions NWW ▲ 80211 [AAD] (16.97)
A Symphonic Story of Jerome Kern for Orchestra [9 Kern songs arr & orchd Bennett] (1945)
W. Steinberg (cnd), Pittsburgh SO *(rec Pittsburgh; Belock Recording Studio Bayside, NY, NY)* † Stephen Collins Foster:A Commemoration Sym; I. Berlin:Music of Berlin EVC ▲ 9027 [AAD] (13.97)
BENNETT, WILLIAM STERNDALE (1816-1875)
Chamber Trio in A for Piano, Violin & Cello, Op. 26 (1840)
Lengyel Trio † L. Berkeley:Sonatina Vn, Op. 17; B. Britten:Suite Vn, Op. 6 MED7 ▲ 2 [ADD] (18.97)
Piano Music
I. Hobson (pno)—Son in A for Pno, "Die Jungfrau von Orleans,", Op. 46; 3 Romances, Op. 14 ("The London Piano School, Vol. 3") † Chipp:Twilight Fancies; J. B. Cramer:Studio per il Pianoforte (sels); Moscheles:Romance et Tarantelle brilliante, Op. 101; S. Wesley:March & Rondo Pno ARA ▲ 6596 (16.97)
I. Prunyi (pno)—Son in A, Op. 46, "The Maid of Orleans" (1873); Allegro Grazioso, Op.18; 4 Pieces; 3 Musical Sketches, Op. 10; Geneviève; Scherzo, Op. 27 (1845); Rondo Piacevole, Op. 25 *(rec 1992)* ("Piano Works, Vol. 1") † Sterndale-Bennett:Pno Music MARC ▲ 8223512 (13.97)
BENOIT, PETER (1834-1901)
Fantasies (3) for Piano, Op. 18
J. D. Beenhouwer (pno) ("In Flanders' Fields, Vol 15") † Fants (4) Pno, Op. 20; M. De Jong:Nocturne, Op. 53; Pictures, Op. 58; Scherzo-Idyll, Op. 68; J. Jongen:Pieces Pno, Op. 33; Legley:Son 2 Pno, Op. 84; Son 4 Pno, Op. 107; Mortelmans:Minuet Varié; Wielewaalt PHA ▲ 92015 (13.97)
Fantasies (4) for Piano, Op. 20
J. D. Beenhouwer (pno) ("In Flanders' Fields, Vol 15") † Fants Pno, Op. 18; M. De Jong:Nocturne, Op. 53; Pictures, Op. 58; Scherzo-Idyll, Op. 68; J. Jongen:Pieces Pno, Op. 33; Legley:Son 2 Pno, Op. 84; Son 4 Pno, Op. 107; Mortelmans:Minuet Varié; Wielewaalt PHA ▲ 92015 (13.97)
Hoogmis (mass) for solo Voice, Orchestra & Large Chorus
D. George (ten), A. Rahbari (cnd), Brussels BRTN PO, Brussels BRTN Phil Choir, Ars Musica Choir, Koninklijk Chorale Caecilia, Koninklijk Vlaams Choir, Sint Norbertus Choir DI ▲ 920178 [DDD] (5.97)
My Mother Tongue for String Quartet (1889)
R. Morgan (mez), R. Morgan (hp), Gaggini String Quartet † Qt Strs in D; Hoof:Klein Qt Strs; Nietigheden Qt Strs PHA ▲ 92001 (13.97)
Piano Music
F. Gevers (pno)—Fants (2) Pno, Op. 9; Fants Pno, Op. 18; Fants (4) Pno, Op. 20; Mazurkas (2), Op. 4; Mazurkas (2), Op. 8; Scherzandi (2), Op. 3; Scherzando, Op. 21; Tales & Ballads, Op. 34 (sels) TLNT ▲ 291034 (15.97)
Quartet in D for Strings (1858)
R. Morgan (mez), R. Morgan (hp), Gaggini String Quartet † My Mother Tongue; Hoof:Klein Qt Strs; Nietigheden Qt Strs PHA ▲ 92001 (13.97)
Le Roi des Aulnes:Overture
F. Devreese (cnd), Royal Flanders PO *(rec Antwerp Belgium, Apr 1995)* † Symphonic Poem Fl; Symphonic Poem Pno MARC (Anthology of Flemish Music) ▲ 8223827 [DDD] (13.97)
Symphonic Poem for Flute & Orchestra (or Piano) (1866)
G. van Riet (fl), F. Devreese (cnd), Royal Flanders PO *(rec Antwerp Belgium, Apr 1995)* † Roi des Aulnes (ov); Symphonic Poem Pno MARC (Anthology of Flemish Music) ▲ 8223827 [DDD] (13.97)

BRAHMS, JOHANNES (cont.)

Hungarian Dances (21) for Orchestra [from Dances for Piano 4-Hands; Nos. 1, 3 & 10 orchd Brahms, 1873] (cont.)

H. von Karajan (cnd), Berlin PO—No. 1 in g; No. 3 in F; No. 5 in g; No. 6 in D; No. 17 in f#; No. 18 in D; No. 19 in b; No. 20 in e *(rec Jesus-Christus-Kirche Berlin, Germany, Sept 1959)* † A. Dvořák:Scherzo Capriccioso, Op. 66; Slavonic Dances (sels) DEUT ▲ 47434 [ADD] (11.97)

E. Lee (vn), N. Padgett (pno)—No. 1 in g; No. 5 in g; No. 7 in F; No. 17 in f#; No. 21 in e [arr vn & pno] ("In Memory of Rain") † Son 1 Vn, Op. 78 SSCL ▲ 15 (16.97)

G. Prêtre (cnd), Stuttgart RSO FORL ▲ 16770 (16.97)

F. Reiner (cnd), Pittsburgh SO ("Reiner, Vol. 5") † Con 1 Pno, Op. 15 LYS ▲ 127 (17.97)

M. Rossi (cnd), Vienna State Opera Orch VC ▲ 1023 [ADD] (13.97)

J. Sándor (cnd), Hungarian PO LALI ▲ 15501 [DDD] (3.97)

S. Skrowaczewski (cnd), Hallé Orch—No. 1 in g; No. 3 in F; No. 10 in F † Sym 4 ICC ▲ 6700272 (9.97)

S. Skrowaczewski (cnd), Hallé Orch † Academic Festival Ov, Op. 80; Syms (comp); Tragic Ov, Op. 81; Vars on a Theme by Haydn IMPB 4-▲ 3 [DDD]

G. Szell (cnd), Cleveland Orch † Academic Festival Ov, Op. 80; Syms (comp); Tragic Ov, Op. 81; Vars on a Theme by Haydn SNYC (Essential Classics) 3-▲ 48398 (23.97)

M. T. Thomas (cnd), London SO—No. 16 in f † Serenade 2 Orch, Op. 16; Vars on a Theme by Haydn SNYC ▲ 47195 (16.97)

A. Toscanini (cnd), NBC SO—No. 1 in g; No. 17 in f#; No. 20 in e; No. 21 in e ("The Toscanini Collection, Vols. 6-9") † Academic Festival Ov, Op. 80; Con Vn & Vc, Op. 102; Gesäng der Parzen, Op. 89; Liebeslieder Waltzes Pno 4-Hands, Op. 52a; Syms (comp); Tragic Ov, Op. 81; Vars on a Theme by Haydn RCAV (Gold Seal) 4-▲ 60325 [ADD] (40.97)

A. Toscanini (cnd), NBC SO—No. 21 in e; No. 20 in e; No. 21 in e; No. 20 in e ("The Toscanini Collection, Vol. 6") † Academic Festival Ov, Op. 80; Sym 1 RCAV (Gold Seal) ▲ 60257 [ADD] (11.97)

B. Walter (cnd), New York PO *(rec New York City, United States of America, Feb 12, 1951)* † Smetana:Moldau; Strauss (II):Fledermaus (ov); Waltzes; Zigeunerbaron (ov) SNYC (Bruno Walter Edition, Vol. 2) ▲ 64467 [ADD] (10.97)

D. A. Wehr (pno), C. R. Wehr (pno) † Waltzes Pno, Op. 39 CSOC ▲ 4222

Hungarian Dances (10) for Piano [arr Brahms from Nos. 1-10 for Piano 4-Hands] (1872)

W. Backhaus (pno)—No. 7 in F *(rec Berlin, 1934 from HMV 78s)* † Ballades (4), Op. 10; Pno Music (misc colls); Rhaps (2) Pno, Op. 79; Scherzo Pno, Op. 4; Vars on an Original Theme, Op. 21/1 PHS ▲ 9385 [AAD] (17.97)

I. Biret (pno) *(rec 1992)* † Waltzes Pno, Op. 39 NXIN ▲ 550355 [DDD] (5.97)

I. J. Paderewski (pno)—No. 7 in F *(rec 1911-37)* ("Paderewski Portrait") † Chopin:Pno Music (misc colls); Mendelssohn (-Bartholdy):Lieder ohne Worte; A. Rubinstein:Valse-Caprice Pno; R. Schumann:Pno Music (misc colls) IN ▲ 1366 [ADD] (15.97)

I. J. Paderewski (pno)—No. 7 in F *(rec 1911-37)* † Chopin:Études (24) Pno, Opp. 10 & 25; Polonaise 6 Pno, Op. 53; Mendelssohn (-Bartholdy):Lieder ohne Worte; A. Rubinstein:Valse-Caprice Pno; R. Schumann:Fantasiestücke Pno, Op. 12; Nachtstücke, Op. 23 ENPL (The Piano Library) ▲ 182 (13.97)

Hungarian Dances (21) for Piano 4-Hands (1852-69)

A. Brings (pno), G. Chinn (pno) † Waltzes Pno, Op. 39 CENT ▲ 2297 [DDD] (16.97)

A. Busch (vn), B. Seidler-Winkler (pno), R. Serkin (pno)—No. 2 in d; No. 5 in g; No. 20 in e † Son 1 Vn, Op. 78; Son 2 Vn, Op. 100; R. Schumann:Son 1 Vn, Op. 105 PHS ▲ 25 (17.97)

Crommelynck Duo CLAV ▲ 8710 [ADD] (16.97)

Emory Chamber Music Society of Atlanta members—No. 3 in F ("Chamber Music of Johannes Brahms") † Son 2 Cl; Trio Hn, Op. 40 ACAD ▲ 20033 [DDD] (16.97)

S. Kolacny (pno), S. Kolacny (pno)—No. 3 in F; No. 4 in f#; No. 5 in g ("Dances & Variations for Piano Duo") † Liebeslieder Waltzes, Op. 52; Vars on a Theme by Haydn; Waltzes Pno, Op. 39 EUFO ▲ 1238 [DDD] (18.97)

H. Moreno (pno), N. Capelli (pno) *(rec Florence Italy, Aug 1993)* † Academic Festival Ov, Op. 80 AART ▲ 47136 [DDD] (10.97)

A.-S. Mutter (vn), L. Orkis (pno)—No. 2 in d; No. 5 in g [arr vn & pno] ("The Berlin Recital") † Scherzo Vn; Debussy:Beau soir; Son Vn; C. Franck:Son Vn, M.8; W. A. Mozart:Son 21 Vn & Pno, K.304 DEUT ▲ 45826 [DDD] (16.97)

H. Peter (pno), V. Stenzl (pno)—No. 20 in e; No. 2 in d; No. 3 in F; No. 4 in f#; No. 5 in g; No. 6 in D; No. 5 in g *(rec live)* † Serenade 1 Orch, Op. 11; Vars in E♭ on Theme of R. Schumann Pno 4-Hands, Op. 23 ARSM ▲ 1130 [DDD] (17.97)

Shirim [sel unknown; arr Shirim] *(rec Carlisle, MA, Oct 31 & Dec 6, 1997)* ("Klezmer Nutcracker") † Chopin:Preludes (24) Pno, Op. 28; Enescu:Romanian Rhap 1, Op. 11/1; G. Mahler:Sym 1; Satie:Gnossiennes; Gymnopédies; P. Tchaikovsky:Nutcracker Suite, Op. 71a; Traditional:Russian Bulgar; Turk in America NPT ▲ 85640 (16.97)

Tal & Groethuysen Duo *(rec Nov 15-17, 1992)* † Waltzes Pno, Op. 39 SNYC ▲ 53285 [DDD] (11.97)

M. Yashvili (vn), T. Schpiller (pno)—No. 1 in g; No. 7 in F; No. 16 in f; No. 17 in f# [arr Joachim vn & pno] *(rec 1975)* ("Russian Violin School: Marina Yashvili") † Son 2 Vn, Op. 100; Babadjanyan:Music of Babadjanyan; M. de Falla:Canciones populares españolas; Paganini:Cantabile, M.S. 109; Moto perpetuo Vn, M.S. 66 RD (Talents of Russia) ▲ 16251 [ADD] (16.97)

Intermezzos (3) for Piano, Op. 117 (1892)

P. Badura-Skoda (pno) † Pieces (4) Pno, Op. 119; Pieces (6) Pno, Op. 118 VAL ▲ 6115 [AAD] (18.97)

V. Cliburn (pno)—Intermezzo in E♭; Intermezzo in b♭ † Con 2 Pno, Op. 83; Pieces (4) Pno, Op. 119 RCAV (Gold Seal) ▲ 7942 [ADD] (11.97)

C. Curzon (pno)—Intermezzo in E♭ † Pieces (4) Pno, Op. 119; Son 3 Pno, Op. 5; F. Schubert:Son Pno, D.960 PLON (The Classic Sound) ▲ 48578 (11.97)

E. Erdmann (pno) *(rec 1920-33)* ("Eduard Erdmann:The Telefunken, Polydor & Parlophone Recordings 1920-1933") † Beethoven:Bagatelles; Con 3 Pno, Op. 37; Debussy:Preludes Pno; J. Haydn:Son Kbd ENPL (Piano Library) ▲ 215 (13.97)

E. Erdmann (pno) *(rec 1928-45)* ("Erdmann: The Vinyl Recordings") † Beethoven:Con 3 Pno, Op. 37; Debussy:Preludes Pno; J. Haydn:Son Kbd; F. Schubert:German Dances Pno, D.790; R. Schumann:Intro & Allegro appassionato, Op. 92 BAYE 2-▲ 200044 (34.97)

D. Goldmann (pno)—Intermezzo in E♭; Intermezzo in b♭ † Con 2 Pno, Op. 83 PC ▲ 267126 [DDD] (2.97)

G. Gould (pno)—Intermezzo in E♭ *(rec New York City, NY, Sept 1960)* ("Glenn Gould at the Movies") † Pieces (6) Pno, Op. 118; J. S. Bach:Art of the Fugue (sels); Brandenburg Con 4, BWV 1049; Con 3 Hpd, BWV 1054; Con 5 Hpd, BWV 1056; English Suites; Goldberg Vars, BWV 988; Wohltemperirte Clavier; A. Scriabin:Pieces (2) Pno, Op. 57; Sibelius:Sonatinas (3) Pno, Op. 67; R. Strauss:Pieces (5) Pno, Op. 3 SNYC ▲ 66531 [DDD] (17.97)

M. Hess (pno) *(rec 1928-46)* † Beethoven:Con 3 Pno, Op. 37; F. Schubert:Son Pno, D.664 ENPL (The Piano Library) ▲ 290 (13.97)

V. Horowitz (pno)—Intermezzo in b♭ † Con 2 Pno, Op. 83; Liszt:Album d'un voyageur, S.156; Années de pèlerinage 2, S.161; Hungarian Rhaps, S.244; F. Schubert:Impromptus (4) Pno RCAV (Gold Seal) ▲ 60523 [ADD] (11.97)

V. Kastelsky (pno) *(rec 1981-84)* ("Russian Piano School: Kastelsky Plays Performs Brahms") † Fants Pno, Op. 116; Pieces (4) Pno, Op. 119; Pieces (6) Pno, Op. 118 RD (Talents of Russia) ▲ 16340 [ADD] (17.97)

P. Katin (pno) ("A Brahms Recital") † Fants Pno, Op. 116; Rhaps (2) Pno, Op. 79; Vars & Fugue on a Theme by Handel, Op. 24 OLY ▲ 263 [DDD] (16.97)

W. Kempff (pno) *(rec 1950)* ("Wilhlem Kempff") † Ballades (4), Op. 10; Fants Pno, Op. 116; Pieces (4) Pno, Op. 119; Pieces (6) Pno, Op. 118; Pieces (8) Pno, Op. 76; R. Schumann:Arabeske Pno, Op. 18; Kreisleriana, Op. 16 PPHI (Great Pianists of the 20th Century) ▲ 456862 (22.97)

A. Kubalek (pno) ("Piano Music of Brahms, Vol. 1") † Son 3 Pno, Op. 5; Waltzes Pno, Op. 39 DOR ▲ 90141 [DDD] (16.97)

A. Kuerti (pno), J. Rescigno (cnd), Orch Metropolitan *(rec Ottawa, Canada, May 1998)* † Con 1 Pno, Op. 15; Con 2 Pno, Op. 83 FL 2-▲ 23139 [DDD] (31.97)

M. Lapšanský (pno) ("Peter & the Wolf") † A. Dvořák:Suite Pno, Op. 98; S. Prokofiev:Peter & the Wolf, Op. 67 SUR ▲ 3174 (16.97)

R. Lupu (pno) † Pieces (4) Pno, Op. 119; Pieces (6) Pno, Op. 118; Rhaps (2) Pno, Op. 79 PLON ▲ 17599 [ADD] (16.97)

R. Lupu (pno) *(rec 1971)* ("Radu Lupu") † Theme & Vars Pno; Beethoven:Son 14 Pno, Op. 27/2; Vars Pno on Original Theme, WoO 80; E. Grieg:Con Pno, Op. 16; F. Schubert:Moments musicaux, D.780; Son Pno, D.784; R. Schumann:Kinderszenen Pno, Op. 15 PPHI (Great Pianists of the 20th Century) ▲ 456895 (22.97)

M. Mares (pno) † Sons Cl NOVA ▲ 150137 (16.97)

I. Moravec (pno)—Intermezzo in b♭ *(rec 1970)* † Beethoven:Bagatelle Pno in a, WoO 59; Bagatelles; W. A. Mozart:Fant Pno, K.475; Son 14 Pno, K.457; Son 17 Pno, K.570 VAIA ▲ 1096 (17.97)

D. Paperno (pno)—Intermezzo in c# *(rec 1980-95)* ("Paperno Live") † J. Haydn:Sonatas for Piano; Liszt:Années de pèlerinage 2, S.161; Trans, Arrs & Paraphrases; Medtner:Forgotten Melodies 1, Op. 38; S. Rachmaninoff:Moments musicaux, Op. 16; R. Schumann:Bunte Blätter, Op. 99; P. Tchaikovsky:Dumka CED ▲ 44 [DDD] (16.97)

R. Peres (pno) † J. S. Bach:Cant 147; Orgelbüchlein; Partitas Hpd; Schübler Chorale Preludes; Beethoven:Vars Pno on Original Theme, WoO 80 PTRY ▲ 2211 (17.97)

I. Pogorelich (pno) † Pieces (8) Pno, Op. 76; Rhaps (2) Pno, Op. 79 DEUT ▲ 37460 [DDD] (16.97)

BRAHMS, JOHANNES (cont.)

Intermezzos (3) for Piano, Op. 117 (1892) (cont.)

A. Pratt (pno) *(rec live, Dec 1995)* ("Live from South Africa") † J. S. Bach:Chromatic Fant & Fugue, BWV 903; Busoni:Bach Transcriptions Pno; C. Franck:Prélude, fugue et var, Op. 18; S. Rachmaninoff:Moments musicaux, Op. 16; Preludes Pno EMIC ▲ 55293 (16.97)

S. Richter (pno)—Intermezzo in E♭; Intermezzo in b♭ † Pieces (6) Pno, Op. 118; Beethoven:Son 30 Pno, Op. 109; Son 31 Pno, Op. 110; Son 32 Pno, Op. 111 MUA ▲ 1025 [AAD] (16.97)

P. Rösel (pno) ("Piano Works") † Ballades (4), Op. 10; Pieces (4) Pno, Op. 119; Rhaps (2) Pno, Op. 79; Scherzo Pno, Op. 4 BER ▲ 2095 (10.97)

A. Rubinstein (pno) *(rec 1958)* † Con 2 Pno, Op. 83; Fants Pno, Op. 116; Rhaps (2) Pno, Op. 79 RCAV (Gold Seal) ▲ 61442 (11.97)

A. Schnabel (pno) *(rec London, England, 1946-47)* ("The 1946-47 HMV Solo Recordings") † Fants Pno, Op. 116; Rhaps (2) Pno, Op. 79; W. A. Mozart:Rondo Pno, K.511; Son 12 Pno, K.332; R. Schumann:Kinderszenen Pno, Op. 15; C. M. von Weber:Invitation to the Dance Pno, J.260 APR ▲ 5526 (mono) [ADD] (18.97)

Solomon (pno)—Intermezzo in b♭ *(rec early 1940s)* † Rhaps (2) Pno, Op. 79; Vars & Fugue on a Theme by Handel, Op. 24; Beethoven:Trio 6 Pno, Op. 97 ENPL (Piano Library) ▲ 313 (14.97)

Solomon (pno)—Intermezzo in E♭ *(rec 1956)* † Fants Pno, Op. 116; Rhaps (2) Pno, Op. 79; J. S. Bach:Italian Con, BWV 971; Beethoven:Son 14 Pno, Op. 27/2; Son 3 Pno, Op. 2/3 APR 2-▲ 7030 [ADD] (38.97)

I. Tiegerman (pno)—Intermezzo in b♭ *(rec 1965)* ("The Lost Legend of Cairo: Radio & Private Recordings") † Con 2 Pno, Op. 83; Pieces (6) Pno, Op. 118; Pieces (8) Pno, Op. 76; Chopin:Ballade 4 Pno, Op. 52; Nocturnes Pno; Preludes (24) Pno, Op. 28; Scherzos Pno; Son Pno in b, Op. 58; G. Fauré:Nocturnes Pno; J. Field:Nocturnes Pno; C. Franck:Symphonic Vars, M.46; Saint-Saëns:Con 5 Pno, Op. 103; Tiegerman:Meditation Pno ARBT 2-▲ 116 (32.97)

N. Zaslav (pno)—Intermezzo in b♭; Intermezzo in E♭ *(rec Monterey, CA, 1996-97)* ("The Intimate Brahms") † Ballades (4), Op. 10; Fants Pno, Op. 116; Pieces (4) Pno, Op. 119; Pieces (6) Pno, Op. 118; Pieces (8) Pno, Op. 76 MUA ▲ 1031 [DDD] (16.97)

Kleine Hochzeitskantate (1874)

G. Jena (cnd), North German Radio Chorus ("The Complete Brahms Edition, Vol. 7:Choral Works") † Ave Maria, Op. 12; Begräbnisgesang, Op. 13; Canons (13), Op. 113; Dem dunkeln Schoss der heil'gen Erde; Deutsche Volkslieder (26); Fest- und Gedenksprüche, Op. 109; Geistliches Lied, Op. 30; Grausam erweiset sich Amor an mir, Op. 113/2; Marienlieder (7), Op. 22; Mir lächelt kein Frühling; Motets (2), Op. 29; Motets (2), Op. 74; Motets (3), Op. 110; O wie sanft; Psalm 13, Op. 27; Sacred Choruses (3), Op. 37; Songs (3), Op. 42; Songs (4), Op. 17; Songs (5), Op. 104; Songs (5), Op. 41; Songs (7), Op. 62; Songs & Romances (12), Op. 44; Songs & Romances (6), Op. 93a; Spruch; Tafellied, Op. 93b; Töne, lindernder Klang; Wann?; Zu Rauch DGRM 4-▲ 449646

Liebeslieder Waltzes (18) for Soprano, Alto, Tenor, Bass & Piano 4-Hands, Op. 52 (1868-69)

Crommelynck Duo † Neue Liebeslieder Waltzes Pno 4-Hands, Op.65a; Souvenir de la Russie; Vars in E♭ on Theme of R. Schumann Pno 4-Hands, Op. 23 CLAV ▲ 8711 [ADD] (16.97)

R. Follman (sop), L. D. Mills (mez), R. MacNeil (ten), P. Atherton (b-bar), S. McCune (pno), T. Fleischer (pno), W. Hall (cnd), Master Chorale of Orange County *(rec Chapman University, Salmon Recital Hall, Orange, CA)* † Duets (3), Op. 20; Duets (4), Op. 61; Qts (3) SATB, Op. 31; Qts (3) SATB, Op. 64; R. Schumann:Mädchenlieder, Op. 103; Spanische Liebeslieder, Op. 138; Spanisches Liederspiel, Op. 74; Zweistimmige Lieder, Op. 43 KLAV ▲ 11092 [DDD] (18.97)

W. Hauschild (cnd) , Leipzig Radio Chorus—O wie sanfr die Quelle † Choral Music; Songs (3), Op. 42; Songs (4), Op. 43 ORF 4-▲ 26972 [DDD] (36.97)

S. Kolacny (pno), S. Kolacny (pno) ("Dances & Variations for Piano Duo") † Hungarian Dances Pno 4-Hands; Vars on a Theme by Haydn; Waltzes Pno, Op. 39 EUFO ▲ 1238 [DDD] (18.97)

E. Mathis (sop), B. Fassbaender (mez), P. Schreier (ten), D. Fischer-Dieskau (bar), W. Sawallisch (pno), K. Engel (pno) [GER] † Neue Liebeslieder Waltzes, Op. 65; Qts (3) SATB, Op. 64 DEUT ▲ 23133 [DDD] (16.97)

G. Parker (pno), N. Parrella (pno), J. Flummerfeldt (cnd), Westminster Choir—Nein, es ist nicht Auszukommen; Schlosser auf; Vögelein durchrauscht die Luft; Sieh, wie ist die Welle klar; Nachtigall, sie singt so choön *(rec Westminster Choir College of Rider Univ. Princeton, NJ, May 14-16, 1995)* ("Singing for Pleasure") † Motets (2), Op. 74; Neue Liebeslieder Waltzes, Op. 65; Qts (3) SATB, Op. 64; Zigeunerlieder, Op. 103 DLS ▲ 3193 [DDD] (14.97)

Liebeslieder Waltzes (18) for Piano 4-Hands [arr from Op. 52], Op. 52a (1874)

A. Balsam (pno), J. Kahn (pno) [GER] *(rec Studio 8-H broadcast, Nov 27, 1948)* ("The Toscanini Collection, Vols. 6-9") † Academic Festival Ov, Op. 80; Con Vn & Vc, Op. 102; Gesäng der Parzen, Op. 89; Hungarian Dances Orch; Syms (comp); Tragic Ov, Op. 81; Vars on a Theme by Haydn RCAV (Gold Seal) 4-▲ 60325 [ADD] (40.97)

A. Balsam (pno), J. Kahn (pno), W. Preston (cnd) [GER] ("The Toscanini Collection, Vol. 9") † Gesäng der Parzen, Op. 89; Sym 4 RCAV (Gold Seal) ▲ 60260 [ADD] (11.97)

K. Brett (sop), C. Robbin (mez), B. Butterfield (ten), R. Braun (bar), S. Ralls (pno), B. Ubukata (pno) *(rec CBC Toronto, Dec 7-9, 1993)* ("The Aldeburgh Connection") † J. Greer:All Around the Circle; R. Schumann:Spanische Liebeslieder, Op. 138 CBC (Musica Viva) ▲ 1077 [DDD] (16.97)

B. Hoene (sop), G. Pohl (cta), A. Ude (ten), S. Lorenz (bar), K. Bässler (pno), D. Zechlin (pno), W. Hauschild (cnd), Berlin RSO † Neue Liebeslieder Waltzes, Op. 65 BER ▲ 9269 (10.97)

E. Höngen (cta), I. Seefried (sop), H. Meyer-Welfing (ten), H. Hotter (b-bar), H. V. Nordberg (pno), F. Wührer (pno) *(rec Nov 1947)* † B. Marcello:Mio bel foco; F. Schubert:Songs (misc colls); R. Schumann:Gesänge, Op. 31; Liederkreis, Op. 39; Myrthen, Op. 25; R. Wagner:Wesendonck Songs; H. Wolf:Gedichte von Goethe; Gedichte von Mörike PRE ▲ 90356 (m) (16.97)

C. Ivaldi (pno), N. Lee (pno), Lieder Vocal Quartet † Qts (3) SATB, Op. 31; Qts (3) SATB, Op. 64; Qts (4) SATB, Op. 92; Qts (6) SATB, Op. 112 ARN ▲ 68392 (16.97)

N. Mackenzie (pno), J. Wustman (pno), Robert Shaw Festival Singers [GER] *(rec Aug 6-7, 1992)* † Neue Liebeslieder Waltzes, Op. 65 TEL ▲ 80326 [DDD] (16.97)

B. Valente (sop), M. Kleinman (cta), W. Conner (ten), M. Singher (bar), R. Serkin (pno), L. Fleisher (pno) [GER] † Ernste Gesänge, Op. 121; F. Schubert:Der Hirt auf dem Felsen, D.965 SNYC (Essential Classics) ▲ 48176 (7.97) ▮ 48176 (3.98)

Life & Music of Brahms

J. Perlea (cnd), Bamberg SO—Con 1 Pno, Op. 15; Con 2 Pno, Op. 83; Songs (5), Op. 106 [Ständchen]; Con Vn, Op. 77; Pieces (8) Pno, Op. 76 [Capriccio in b]; Hungarian Dances Pno 4-Hands [No. 1 in g; No. 5 in g; No. 6 in D]; Songs (5), Op. 49 [Wiegenlied (Lullaby)]; Vars on a Theme by Paganini, Op. 35; Vars on a Theme by Haydn; Rinaldo, Op. 50; Waltzes Pno, Op. 39 [No. 15 in A♭]; Liebeslieder Waltzes, Op. 52 [Rede, Mädchen, allzu liebes]; Academic Festival Ov, Op. 80; Qnt Cl, Op. 115; Tragic Ov, Op. 81 ("The Story of Brahms in Words and Music") MMD (Music Masters) ▲ 8513 [ADD] (3.97) ▮ 8513 [ADD/DDD] (2.98)

Marienlieder (7) for Chorus, Op. 22 (1859)

C. Davis (cnd), Bavarian RSO, Bavarian Radio Chorus † Alto Rhap, Op. 53; Gesäng der Parzen, Op. 89; Nänie, Op. 82; Schicksalslied, Op. 54 RCAV (Red Seal) ▲ 61201 (16.97)

G. Jena (cnd), North German Radio Chorus ("The Complete Brahms Edition, Vol. 7:Choral Works") † Ave Maria, Op. 12; Begräbnisgesang, Op. 13; Canons (13), Op. 113; Dem dunkeln Schoss der heil'gen Erde; Deutsche Volkslieder (26); Fest- und Gedenksprüche, Op. 109; Geistliches Lied, Op. 30; Grausam erweiset sich Amor an mir, Op. 113/2; Kleine Hochzeitskantate; Mir lächelt kein Frühling; Motets (2), Op. 29; Motets (2), Op. 74; Motets (3), Op. 110; O wie sanft; Psalm 13, Op. 27; Sacred Choruses (3), Op. 37; Songs (3), Op. 42; Songs (4), Op. 17; Songs (5), Op. 104; Songs (5), Op. 41; Songs (7), Op. 62; Songs & Romances (12), Op. 44; Songs & Romances (6), Op. 93a; Spruch; Tafellied, Op. 93b; Töne, lindernder Klang; Wann?; Zu Rauch DGRM 4-▲ 449646

M. Lipovšek (mez)—Marias Wallfahrt † Deutsche Volkslieder (26); Deutsche Volkslieder (49), WoO 33; Romances & Songs (5), Op. 84; Songs; Songs (5), Op. 49; Songs & Romances (6); Songs & Romances (8), Op. 14; Zigeunerlieder, Op. 103 *(E,F,G texts)* ORF ▲ 441971 [DDD] (18.97)

G. Ratzinger (cnd), Regensburg Cathedral Choir † F. Schubert:Deutsche Messe ARSM ▲ 929 [DDD] (17.97)

Mir lächelt kein Frühling (canon) for 4 Female Voices

G. Jena (cnd), North German Radio Chorus ("The Complete Brahms Edition, Vol. 7:Choral Works") † Ave Maria, Op. 12; Begräbnisgesang, Op. 13; Canons (13), Op. 113; Dem dunkeln Schoss der heil'gen Erde; Deutsche Volkslieder (26); Fest- und Gedenksprüche, Op. 109; Geistliches Lied, Op. 30; Grausam erweiset sich Amor an mir, Op. 113/2; Kleine Hochzeitskantate; Marienlieder (7), Op. 22; Motets (2), Op. 29; Motets (2), Op. 74; Motets (3), Op. 110; O wie sanft; Psalm 13, Op. 27; Sacred Choruses (3), Op. 37; Songs (3), Op. 42; Songs (4), Op. 17; Songs (5), Op. 104; Songs (5), Op. 41; Songs (7), Op. 62; Songs & Romances (12), Op. 44; Songs & Romances (6), Op. 93a; Spruch; Tafellied, Op. 93b; Töne, lindernder Klang; Wann?; Zu Rauch DGRM 4-▲ 449646

Missa Canonica for Chorus (1856)

Cologne Chamber Choir, P. Neumann (org)—Kyrie † Fugue Org; R. Schumann:Mass MDG ▲ 3320598 [DDD] (17.97)

P. Conte (cnd), St. Clement's Choir Philadelphia *(rec Paoli, PA, June 1994 & Jan 1995)* ("The Romantic Mass: Choral Works by Rheinberger & Brahms") † Geistliches Lied, Op. 30; Rheinberger:Geistliche Gesänge, Op. 69; Mass; Omnes de Saba DORD ▲ 80137 [DDD] (13.97)

Motets

M. Morley (org), R. Jones (cnd), St. Bride's Choir—Fest- und Gedenksprüche, Op. 109; Ave Maria, Op. 12; Motets (2), Op. 74; Motets (2), Op. 29; Psalm 13, Op. 27; Motets (3), Op. 110; Geistliches Lied, Op. 30 NXIN ▲ 8553877 (5.97)

BRAHMS, JOHANNES (cont.)

Motets (2), Op. 29 (?1860)

G. Jena (cnd), North German Radio Chorus ("The Complete Brahms Edition, Vol. 7:Choral Works") † Ave Maria, Op. 12; Begräbnisgesang, Op. 13; Canons (13), Op. 113; Dem dunkeln Schoss der heil'gen Erde; Deutsche Volkslieder (26); Fest- und Gedenksprüche, Op. 109; Geistliches Lied, Op. 30; Grausam erweiset sich Amor an mir, Op. 113/2; Kleine Hochzeitskantate; Marienlieder (7), Op. 22; Mir lächelt kein Frühling; Motets (2), Op. 74; Motets (3), Op. 110; O wie sanft; Psalm 13, Op. 27; Sacred Choruses (3), Op. 37; Songs (3), Op. 42; Songs (4), Op. 17; Songs (5), Op. 104; Songs (5), Op. 41; Songs (7), Op. 62; Songs & Romances (12), Op. 44; Songs & Romances (6), Op. 93a; Spruch; Tafellied, Op. 93b; Töne, lindernder Klang; Wann?; Zu Rauch DGRM 4-▲ 449646

Motets (3) for 4-8 Voices, Op. 110

G. Jena (cnd), North German Radio Chorus ("The Complete Brahms Edition, Vol. 7:Choral Works") † Ave Maria, Op. 12; Begräbnisgesang, Op. 13; Canons (13), Op. 113; Dem dunkeln Schoss der heil'gen Erde; Deutsche Volkslieder (26); Fest- und Gedenksprüche, Op. 109; Geistliches Lied, Op. 30; Grausam erweiset sich Amor an mir, Op. 113/2; Kleine Hochzeitskantate; Marienlieder (7), Op. 22; Mir lächelt kein Frühling; Motets (2), Op. 29; Motets (2), Op. 74; O wie sanft; Psalm 13, Op. 27; Sacred Choruses (3), Op. 37; Songs (3), Op. 42; Songs (4), Op. 17; Songs (5), Op. 104; Songs (5), Op. 41; Songs (7), Op. 62; Songs & Romances (12), Op. 44; Songs & Romances (6), Op. 93a; Spruch; Tafellied, Op. 93b; Töne, lindernder Klang; Wann?; Zu Rauch DGRM 4-▲ 449646

Motets (2) for 4-6 Voices, Op. 74 (1863-77)

J. Flummerfeldt (cnd), Westminster Choir *(rec Westminster Choir College of Rider Univ. Princeton, NJ, May 14-16, 1995)* ("Singing for Pleasure") † Liebeslieder Waltzes, Op. 52; Neue Liebeslieder Waltzes, Op. 65; Qts (3) SATB, Op. 64; Zigeunerlieder, Op. 103 DLS ▲ 3193 [DDD] (14.97)

G. Jena (cnd), North German Radio Chorus ("The Complete Brahms Edition, Vol. 7:Choral Works") † Ave Maria, Op. 12; Begräbnisgesang, Op. 13; Canons (13), Op. 113; Dem dunkeln Schoss der heil'gen Erde; Deutsche Volkslieder (26); Fest- und Gedenksprüche, Op. 109; Geistliches Lied, Op. 30; Grausam erweiset sich Amor an mir, Op. 113/2; Kleine Hochzeitskantate; Marienlieder (7), Op. 22; Mir lächelt kein Frühling; Motets (2), Op. 29; Motets (3), Op. 110; O wie sanft; Psalm 13, Op. 27; Sacred Choruses (3), Op. 37; Songs (3), Op. 42; Songs (4), Op. 17; Songs (5), Op. 104; Songs (5), Op. 41; Songs (7), Op. 62; Songs & Romances (12), Op. 44; Songs & Romances (6), Op. 93a; Spruch; Tafellied, Op. 93b; Töne, lindernder Klang; Wann?; Zu Rauch DGRM 4-▲ 449646

F. Näf (cnd), Basel Madrigalists ("Da Pacem") † H. Eisler:Gegen den Krieg, Op. 51; Josquin Desprez:Missa, "Da Pacem"; Resinarius:Verleih uns Frieden genädiglich; H. Schütz:Verleih uns Frieden, SWV 372 MUSS ▲ 6124 [DDD] (17.97)

Music of Brahms

P. Gulda (pno) *(Qnt Pno, Op. 34)*, LaSalle Qt *(Qt 1 Strs, Op. 51/1)*, K. Leister (cl) *(Qnt Cl, Op. 115 [Adagio])*, T. Vásáry (pno) *(Trio 1 Pno, Op. 8; Qt 3 Pno, Op. 60; Qt 2 Pno, Op. 26 [Poco adagio])* ("Intimate Conversations") † Son 1 Cl; Son 3 Vn, Op. 108 PPHI (Night Moods) ▲ 453905 [DDD] (9.97)

H. Knappertsbusch (cnd), Berlin PO *(rec 1942)* † Beethoven:Music of; Liszt:Music of Liszt TAHA 2-▲ 311 (34.97)

artists unknown—Songs (5), Op. 49 [Wiegenlied (Lullaby)]; Con 2 Pno, Op. 83; Con Vn, Op. 77 [Adagio]; Con Vn & Vc, Op. 102; Qnt Cl, Op. 115 [Adagio]; Qt 3 Pno, Op. 60 [Andante]; Trio 3 Pno, Op. 101 [Andante grazioso] (3) Pno, Op. 117 [Intermezzo in E♭]; Fants Pno, Op. 116 [Intermezzo in E]; Waltzes Pno, Op. 39 [No. 15 in A♭]; Son 3 Vn, Op. 108 [Adagio] ("Brahms at Bedtime") † Son 3 Vn, Op. 108; Songs; Vars & Fugue on a Theme by Handel, Op. 24 PPHI (Set Your Life to Music) ▲ 54966 (9.97) ▮ 54966 (5.98)

artists unknown—Qnt Cl, Op. 115 [Adagio]; Son 1 Cl, Op. 120/1 [Allegro grazioso]; Trio 3 Pno, Op. 101 [Andante grazioso]; Son 2 Cl, Op. 120/2 [Andante con moto-Allegro non troppo]; Deutsche Volkslieder (49), WoO 33 [Schwesterlein, Schwesterlein]; Son 2 Vn, Op. 100 [Allegretto grazioso (quasi Andante)]; Qnt Pno, Op. 34; Qt 1 Strs, Op. 51/1; Trio Cl, Op. 114 [Andante grazioso] ("Brahms for Book Lovers") † Serenade 1 Orch, Op. 11; Son 2 Vn, Op. 100 PPHI (Set Your Life to Music) ▲ 462561 (9.97) ▮ 462561 (5.98)

artists unknown ("The Book Lover's Companion") † J. S. Bach:Music of Bach; Beethoven:Music of PPHI (Set Your Life to Music) 3-▲ 462773 (29.97)

Nänie for Orchestra & Chorus, Op. 82 (1880-81)

C. Abbado (cnd), Berlin PO, Berlin Radio Chorus † Sym 4; Vars on a Theme by Haydn DEUT ▲ 35349 [DDD] (16.97)

C. Abbado (cnd), Berlin PO, Berlin Radio Chorus, Ernst Senff Chorus † Academic Festival Ov, Op. 80; Alto Rhap, Op. 53; Gesäng der Parzen, Op. 89; Schicksalslied, Op. 54; Syms (comp); Tragic Ov, Op. 81; Vars on a Theme by Haydn DGRM 4-▲ 435683 [DDD]

C. Davis (cnd), Bavarian RSO, Bavarian Radio Chorus † Alto Rhap, Op. 53; Gesäng der Parzen, Op. 89; Marienlieder (7), Op. 22; Schicksalslied, Op. 54 RCAV (Red Seal) ▲ 61201 (16.97)

B. Haitink (cnd), Bavarian RSO, Bavarian Radio Chorus [GER] † Alto Rhap, Op. 53; Begräbnisgesang, Op. 13; Gesäng der Parzen, Op. 89 ORF ▲ 25821 [DDD] (18.97)

R. Shaw (cnd), Atlanta SO, Atlanta Sym Chorus [GER] † Alto Rhap, Op. 53; Gesäng der Parzen, Op. 89; Schicksalslied, Op. 54 TEL ▲ 80176 [DDD] (16.97)

G. Sinopoli (cnd), Czech PO, Prague Phil Chorus ("The Complete Brahms Edition, Vol. 8:Works for Chorus & Orchestra") † Alto Rhap, Op. 53; Deutsches Requiem, Op. 45; Gesäng der Parzen, Op. 89; Rinaldo, Op. 50; Schicksalslied, Op. 54; Triumphlied, Op. 55 DGRM 3-▲ 449651

Neue Liebeslieder Waltzes (15) for SATB & Piano 4-Hands, Op. 65 (1877)

J. Flummerfeldt (cnd), Westminster Choir, N. Parrella (pno)—No. 15 *(rec Westminster Choir College of Rider Univ. Princeton, NJ, May 14-16, 1995)* ("Singing for Pleasure") † Liebeslieder Waltzes, Op. 52; Motets (2), Op. 74; Qts (3) SATB, Op. 64; Zigeunerlieder, Op. 103 DLS ▲ 3193 [DDD] (14.97)

B. Hoene (sop), G. Pohl (cta), A. Ude (ten), S. Lorenz (bar), K. Bässler (pno), D. Zechlin (pno), W. Hauschild (cnd), Berlin RSO † Liebeslieder Waltzes Pno 4-Hands, Op. 52a BER ▲ 9269 (10.97)

N. Mackenzie (pno), J. Wustman (pno), Robert Shaw Festival Singers [GER] *(rec Aug 6-7, 1992)* † Liebeslieder Waltzes Pno 4-Hands, Op. 52a TEL ▲ 80326 [DDD] (16.97)

E. Mathis (sop), B. Fassbaender (mez), P. Schreier (ten), D. Fischer-Dieskau (bar), W. Sawallisch (pno), K. Engel (pno) [GER] † Liebeslieder Waltzes, Op. 52; Qts (3) SATB, Op. 64 DEUT ▲ 23133 [DDD] (16.97)

S. Matthies (pno), C. Köhn (pno) *(rec Clara Wieck Auditorium Sandhausen, Sept 4-9, 1995)* ("Four Hand Piano Music, Vol. 1") † Souvenir de la Russie; Vars in E♭ on Theme of R. Schumann Pno 4-Hands, Op. 23; Waltzes Pno, Op. 39 NXIN ▲ 8553139 [DDD] (5.97)

Neue Liebeslieder Waltzes (15) for Piano 4-Hands, Op.65a (1877)

Crommelynck Duo † Liebeslieder Waltzes, Op. 52; Souvenir de la Russie; Vars in E♭ on Theme of R. Schumann Pno 4-Hands, Op. 23 CLAV ▲ 8711 [ADD] (16.97)

B. Eden (pno), A. Tamir (pno) † Vars on a Theme by Haydn CRD ▲ 3413 [ADD] (17.97)

O wie sanft (canon) for Female Chorus [text Daumer]

G. Jena (cnd), North German Radio Chorus ("The Complete Brahms Edition, Vol. 7:Choral Works") † Ave Maria, Op. 12; Begräbnisgesang, Op. 13; Canons (13), Op. 113; Dem dunkeln Schoss der heil'gen Erde; Deutsche Volkslieder (26); Fest- und Gedenksprüche, Op. 109; Geistliches Lied, Op. 30; Grausam erweiset sich Amor an mir, Op. 113/2; Kleine Hochzeitskantate; Marienlieder (7), Op. 22; Mir lächelt kein Frühling; Motets (2), Op. 29; Motets (2), Op. 74; Motets (3), Op. 110; Psalm 13, Op. 27; Sacred Choruses (3), Op. 37; Songs (3), Op. 42; Songs (4), Op. 17; Songs (5), Op. 104; Songs (5), Op. 41; Songs (7), Op. 62; Songs & Romances (12), Op. 44; Songs & Romances (6), Op. 93a; Spruch; Tafellied, Op. 93b; Töne, lindernder Klang; Wann?; Zu Rauch DGRM 4-▲ 449646

Organ Music [11 Chorale Preludes, Op. 122; Fugue in a♭; Chorale Prelude & Fugue; 2 Preludes & Fugues] (complete)

K. Bowyer (org) [plus others] *(rec Org of Odense Cathedral Denmark, Denmark)* NIMB ▲ 5262 [DDD] (16.97)

R. Innig (org) ("Complete Organ Works") MDG ▲ 3170137 (17.97)

J. van Oortmerssen (org) [plus others] BIS ▲ 479 [DDD] (17.97)

R. Parkins (org) *(rec Chapel of Duke Univ Durham, NC, Jan 4-5, 1994)* NXIN ▲ 550824 [DDD] (5.97)

H. Schäffer (org) MOTE ▲ 10711 [DDD] (18.97)

Piano Music (miscellaneous collections)

W. Backhaus (pno)—Pieces (8) Pno, Op. 76 [Intermezzo in a; Capriccio in C]; Intermezzos (3) Pno, Op. 117 [Intermezzo in E♭; Intermezzo in b♭]; Pieces (6) Pno, Op. 118 *(rec London & Berlin, England, 1933 & 1935 from HMV 78s)* † Ballades (4), Op. 10; Hungarian Dances Pno; Rhaps (2) Pno, Op. 79; Scherzo Pno, Op. 4; Vars on an Original Theme, Op. 21/1 PHS ▲ 9385 [AAD] (17.97)

W. Backhaus (pno)—Ballades (4), Op. 10 [Ballade in d, "Edward"; Ballade in D]; Waltzes Pno, Op. 39 [No. 1 in B; No. 2 in E; No. 12 in E; No. 13 in B; No. 14 in g#; No. 15 in A♭; No. 16 in c#]; Pieces (8) Pno, Op. 76 [Intermezzo in a; Capriccio in C]; Pieces (6) Pno, Op. 118; Songs (4), Op. 70 [Im garten am Seegestade; Lerchengesang]; Hungarian Dances Pno 4-Hands [No. 6 in D; No. 7 in F]; Intermezzos (3) Pno, Op. 117 [Intermezzo in E♭; Intermezzo in b♭]; Vars on an Original Theme, Op. 21/1 ("Wilhelm Backhaus: The Recordings, 1933-39") ENPL (The Piano Library) ▲ 192 (13.97)

W. Backhaus (pno)—Intermezzos (3) Pno, Op. 117 [Intermezzo in E♭; Intermezzo in b♭]; Pieces (8) Pno, Op. 76 [Intermezzo in a; Capriccio in C]; Pieces (6) Pno, Op. 118 *(rec 1933-39)* ("Great Recordings of the Thirties") † Ballades (4), Op. 10; Rhaps (2) Pno, Op. 79; Vars on an Original Theme, Op. 21/1 GRM2 ▲ 78507 [ADD] (13.97)

BRAHMS, JOHANNES (cont.)

Piano Music (miscellaneous collections) (cont.)

W. Backhaus (pno)—Ballades (4), Op. 10 [Ballade in d, "Edward"; Ballade in D]; Hungarian Dances Pno 4-Hands [No. 6 in D; No. 7 in F]; Intermezzos (3) Pno, Op. 117 [Intermezzo in E♭; Intermezzo in b♭]; Pieces (8) Pno, Op. 76 [Intermezzo in a; Capriccio in C]; Pieces (6) Pno, Op. 118 [Intermezzo in a; Intermezzo in A; Ballade in g; Romance in F; Intermezzo in e♭]; Romanzen aus Tieck's Magelone, Op. 33 [Romanze in F]; Rhaps (2) Pno, Op. 79; Scherzo Pno, Op. 4; Vars on an Original Theme, Op. 21/1; Waltzes Pno, Op. 39 [No. 1 in B; No. 2 in E; No. 15 in A♭] *(rec 1933-35)* MTAL ▲ 48042 (6.97)

H. Bauer (pno), A. Rubenstein (pno) *(Intermezzos (3) Pno, Op. 117 [Intermezzo in E♭]) (rec 1915-30)*, H. Bauer (pno), M. Hess (pno), A. Rubenstein (pno) *(Pieces (4) Pno, Op. 119 [Intermezzo in e; Intermezzo in C; Rhapsody in E♭]) (rec 1915-30)*, C. Friedberg (pno) *(Ballades (4), Op. 10 [Ballade in b; Ballade in B]) (rec 1915-30)*, A. Rubinstein (pno) *(Rhaps (2) Pno, Op. 79 [No. 1 in b]; Pieces (8) Pno, Op. 76 [Capriccio in b]) (rec 1915-30)*, W. Backhaus (pno), M. Hess (pno) *(Vars on a Theme by Paganini, Op. 35)* † Son 3 Pno, Op. 5; Vars on a Theme by Paganini, Op. 35 NIMB (Grand Piano) ▲ 8806 [DDD] (11.97)

P. Berkowitz (pno)—Fants Pno, Op. 116; Intermezzos (3) Pno, Op. 117; Pieces (6) Pno, Op. 118 ("Piano Music, Vol. 1") MER ▲ 84287 (16.97)

I. Biret (pno)—Theme & Vars Pno; Gavotte in A by Gluck; Gigues (2) [Gigue in a; Gigue in b]; Sarabandes (2) Pno [No. 2 in b; No. 1 in a]; Kleine Klavierstück; Rákoczy March; Study on Impromptu in E♭ [after Schubert], D.935/2 NXIN ▲ 550958 [DDD] (5.97)

A. Brendel (pno), H. Holliger (cnd), Berlin PO, H. Holliger (cnd), London SO—Ballades (4), Op. 10; Con 1 Pno, Op. 15; Con 2 Pno, Op. 83 ("The Art of Arthur Brendel") † Beethoven:Pno Music (misc); J. Haydn:Pno Music; Liszt:Pno Music (misc); W. A. Mozart:Pno Music (misc colls); F. Schubert:Allegretto Pno, D.915; Pno Music (misc colls); R. Schumann:Pno Music (misc colls) PPHI 25-▲ 46920 (294.62)

L. Edlina (pno) *(Pieces (8) Pno, Op. 76 [Intermezzo in A♭; Intermezzo in B♭; Intermezzo in a; Capriccio in f#; Capriccio in b]; Fants Pno, Op. 116 [Intermezzo in a; Intermezzo in E; Intermezzo in e]; Intermezzos (3) Pno, Op. 117; Pieces (6) Pno, Op. 118 [Intermezzo in a; Intermezzo in A; Intermezzo in f; Intermezzo in e♭]), (Pieces (4) Pno, Op. 119 [Intermezzo in C])* ("The Complete Intermezzos") CHN ▲ 8467 [DDD] (16.97)

J. Fennimore (pno)—Rhaps (2) Pno, Op. 79 [No. 1 in b]; Pieces (6) Pno, Op. 118 [Intermezzo in e♭]; Pieces (8) Pno, Op. 76 [Capriccio in b] *(rec Kiggins Hall, Emma Willard School, Troy, NY, Sept 1992)* ("Joseph Fennimore in Concert II") † J. Fennimore:Romance 4 Pno; Son 3 Pno; E. Granados:Goyescas (sels) ALBA ▲ 161 [DDD] (16.97)

W. Kempff (pno)—Con 2 Pno, Op. 83; Intermezzos (3) Pno, Op. 117; Pieces (6) Pno, Op. 118; Pieces (4) Pno, Op. 119 DEUT ▲ 37249 [ADD] (9.97)

A. Rubinstein (pno)—Intermezzos (3) Pno, Op. 117 [Intermezzo in c#]; Pieces (6) Pno, Op. 118 [Intermezzo in A; Intermezzo in e♭]; Pieces (4) Pno, Op. 119 [Intermezzo in e; Intermezzo in C] *(rec Hollywood, United States of America, Aug 3, 5 & 7, 1953)* † Sons Vc (comp) RCAV (Gold Seal) ▲ 62592 (11.97)

D. Varsi (pno), S. B. Kovacevich (pno), A. Harasiewicz (pno)—Rhaps (2) Pno, Op. 79; Fants Pno, Op. 116; Intermezzos (3) Pno, Op. 117; Pieces (6) Pno, Op. 118; Pieces (4) Pno, Op. 119; Vars & Fugue on a Theme by Handel, Op. 24; Vars on a Theme by Paganini, Op. 35 ("The Late Piano Music") PPHI (Duo) 2-▲ 42589 (17.97)

Piano Music (complete)

M. Jones (pno) NIMB 6-▲ 1788 (29.97)

Pieces (8) for Piano, Op. 76 (1878)

S. Cosma (pno)—Capriccio in f#; Capriccio in c# † Beethoven:Vars Pno on Original Theme, WoO 80; Chopin:Mazurkas Pno TOWN ▲ 29 (17.97)

E. Freund (pno) † Fants Pno, Op. 116; J. S. Bach:Wohltemperirte Clavier; B. Bartók:Bagatelles Pno, Op. 6; Easy Pieces, Sz.39; For Children, Sz.42; Sketches, Op. 9b; Kodály:Pieces (9) Pno, Op. 3; Liszt:Pno Music (misc); Mendelssohn (-Bartholdy):Fant "Sonate écossaise", Op. 28 PHS 2-▲ 9193 (33.97)

R. Goode (pno) † Fants Pno, Op. 116; Pieces (4) Pno, Op. 119 NON ▲ 79154 [DDD] (16.97)

W. Kempff (pno) † Ballades (4), Op. 10; Con 1 Pno, Op. 15; Rhaps (2) Pno, Op. 79; Scherzo Pno, Op. 4; Son 3 Pno, Op. 5 DEUT (Double) 2-▲ 37374 (17.97)

W. Kempff (pno) *(rec 1953)* ("Wilhelm Kempff") † Ballades (4), Op. 10; Fants Pno, Op. 116; Intermezzos (3) Pno, Op. 117; Pieces (4) Pno, Op. 119; Pieces (6) Pno, Op. 118; R. Schumann:Arabeske Pno, Op. 18; Kreisleriana, Op. 16 PPHI (Great Pianists of the 20th Century) ▲ 456862 (22.97)

H. Neuhaus (pno) *(rec 1947-52)* ("Russian Piano School: Neuhaus") † Pieces (4) Pno, Op. 119; R. Schumann:Kreisleriana, Op. 16 RD (Talents of Russia) ▲ 16246 [ADD] (16.97)

M. Perahia (pno)—Capriccio in b † Pieces (4) Pno, Op. 119; Rhaps (2) Pno, Op. 79; Son 3 Pno, Op. 5 SNYC ▲ 47181 (16.97)

I. Pogorelich (pno)—Capriccio in f# † Intermezzos (3) Pno, Op. 117; Rhaps (2) Pno, Op. 79 DEUT ▲ 37460 [DDD] (16.97)

S. Richter (pno)—Capriccio in C † Fants Pno, Op. 116; Pieces (4) Pno, Op. 119; Pieces (6) Pno, Op. 118; S. Prokofiev:Son 6 Pno, Op. 82; C. M. von Weber:Son 3 Pno, Op. 49 AURC ▲ 127 (5.97)

A. Rubinstein (pno)—Capriccio in b † Con 1 Pno, Op. 15; Rhaps (2) Pno, Op. 79 RCAV (Gold Seal) ▲ 61263 (11.97)

A. Rubinstein (pno)—Capriccio in b *(rec 1928-47)* † Songs (5), Op. 49; Liszt:Liebesträume, S.541; F. Schubert:Impromptus (4) Pno; R. Schumann:Arabeske Pno, Op. 18; Kinderszenen Pno, Op. 15; Myrthen, Op. 25; Romances Pno, Op. 28; P. Tchaikovsky:Con 1 Pno, Op. 23 GRM2 ▲ 78783 (13.97)

I. Tiegerman (pno)—Capriccio in b *(rec 1965)* ("The Lost Legend of Cairo: Radio & Private Recordings") † Con 2 Pno, Op. 83; Intermezzos (3) Pno, Op. 117; Pieces (6) Pno, Op. 118; Chopin:Ballade 4 Pno, Op. 52; Nocturnes Pno; Preludes (24) Pno, Op. 28; Scherzos Pno; Son Pno in b, Op. 58; G. Fauré:Nocturnes Pno; J. Field:Nocturnes Pno; C. Franck:Symphonic Vars, M.46; Saint-Saëns:Con 5 Pno, Op. 103; Tiegerman:Meditation Pno ARBT 2-▲ 116 (32.97)

N. Zaslav (pno)—Intermezzo in A♭; Capriccio in f#; Capriccio in C; Intermezzo in B♭; Intermezzo in A; Intermezzo in a *(rec Monterey, CA, 1996-97)* ("The Intimate Brahms") † Ballades (4), Op. 10; Fants Pno, Op. 116; Intermezzos (3) Pno, Op. 117; Pieces (4) Pno, Op. 119; Pieces (6) Pno, Op. 118 MUA ▲ 1031 [DDD] (16.97)

Pieces (6) for Piano, Op. 118 (1892)

M. Anderson (pno) *(rec Wyastone Leys Monmouth, Nov 25-27, 1996)* † Pieces (4) Pno, Op. 119; Vars on a Hungarian Song, Op. 21/2; Vars on an Original Theme, Op. 21/1 NIMB ▲ 5521 [DDD] (16.97)

E. Ax (pno) † Rhaps (2) Pno, Op. 79; Vars & Fugue on a Theme by Handel, Op. 24 SNYC ▲ 48046 (16.97)

P. Badura-Skoda (pno) † Intermezzos (3) Pno, Op. 117; Pieces (4) Pno, Op. 119 VAL ▲ 6115 [AAD] (18.97)

V. Cliburn (pno) † Fants Pno, Op. 116; Rhaps (2) Pno, Op. 79; Beethoven:Con 3 Pno, Op. 37 RCAV (Gold Seal) ▲ 60419 [ADD] (11.97)

J. Coop (pno)—Intermezzo in A *(rec Toronto, Canada)* ("The Romantic Piano") † Waltzes (16) Pno, Op. 39; Chopin:Etudes (24) Pno, Opp. 10 & 25; Mazurkas Pno; Nocturnes Pno; Debussy:Isle joyeuse; Suite bergamasque; Liszt:Études de concert (3), S.144; Liebesträume, S.541; Mendelssohn (-Bartholdy):Pno Music (misc); S. Rachmaninoff:Etudes-tableaux Pno, Opp. 33 & 39; Preludes (23) Pno, Opp. 23 & 32; R. Schumann:Kinderszenen Pno, Op. 15 MUVI ▲ 1015 [DDD] (16.97)

L. Edlina (pno)—Intermezzo in A ("Daydreams") † Chorale Preludes Org, Op. 122; Fants Pno, Op. 116; Beethoven:Son 1 Pno, Op. 2/1; Son 14 Pno, Op. 27/2; Chopin:Etudes Pno; J. Field:Nocturnes Pno; Liszt:Études de concert (3), S.144; Hungarian Rhaps, S.244; R. Schumann:Albumblätter, Op. 124; Vivaldi:Cons Vn Strs, Op. 8/1-4 CHN ▲ 6537 [DDD] (12.97)

G. Gould (pno)—Intermezzo in e♭ *(rec New York City, NY, Sept 1960)* ("Glenn Gould at the Movies") † Intermezzos (3) Pno, Op. 117; J. S. Bach:Art of the Fugue (sels); Brandenburg Con 4, BWV 1049; Con 3 Hpd, BWV 1054; Con 5 Hpd, BWV 1056; English Suites; Goldberg Vars, BWV 988; Wohltemperirte Clavier; A. Scriabin:Pieces (2) Pno, Op. 57; Sibelius:Sonatinas (3) Pno, Op. 67; R. Strauss:Pieces (5) Pno, Op. 3 SNYC ▲ 66531 [DDD] (17.97)

V. Kastelsky (pno) *(rec 1981-84)* ("Russian Piano School: Kastelsky Plays Performs Brahms") † Fants Pno, Op. 116; Intermezzos (3) Pno, Op. 117; Pieces (4) Pno, Op. 119 RD (Talents of Russia) ▲ 16340 [ADD] (17.97)

W. Kempff (pno) *(rec 1953)* ("Wilhelm Kempff") † Ballades (4), Op. 10; Fants Pno, Op. 116; Intermezzos (3) Pno, Op. 117; Pieces (4) Pno, Op. 119; Pieces (8) Pno, Op. 76; R. Schumann:Arabeske Pno, Op. 18; Kreisleriana, Op. 16 PPHI (Great Pianists of the 20th Century) ▲ 456862 (22.97)

A. Kubalek (pno) *(rec Apr 1991)* ("Piano Music of Brahms, Vol. 2") † Fants Pno, Op. 116; Pieces (4) Pno, Op. 119; Rhaps (2) Pno, Op. 79 DOR ▲ 90159 [DDD] (16.97)

Y. Lefébure (pno)—Intermezzo in e♭ *(rec Paris, France, Feb-Oct 1971)* † Pieces (4) Pno, Op. 119; B. Bartók:Mikrokosmos, Sz.107; J. Haydn:Son Kbd; Liszt:Ballade 2, S.171; Lugubre gondola [2nd ver] Pno, S.200/2; Trans, Arrs & Paraphrases; Rameau:Nouvelles suites; F. Schubert:Son Pno, D.958 SOC ▲ 159 (16.97)

R. Lupu (pno) † Intermezzos (3) Pno, Op. 117; Pieces (4) Pno, Op. 119; Rhaps (2) Pno, Op. 79 PLON ▲ 17599 [ADD] (16.97)

S. Richter (pno)—Ballade in g † Fants Pno, Op. 116; Pieces (4) Pno, Op. 119; Pieces (8) Pno, Op. 76; S. Prokofiev:Son 6 Pno, Op. 82; C. M. von Weber:Son 3 Pno, Op. 49 AURC ▲ 127 (5.97)

S. Richter (pno) † Intermezzos (3) Pno, Op. 117; Beethoven:Son 30 Pno, Op. 109; Son 31 Pno, Op. 110; Son 32 Pno, Op. 111 MUVI ▲ 1025 [ADD] (16.97)

R. Silverman (pno) † Rhaps (2) Pno, Op. 79; Vars on a Hungarian Song, Op. 21/2 MUVI (Musica Viva) ▲ 1028 (16.97)

▲ = CD ♦ = Enhanced CD △ = MD ▮ = Cassette Tape ▯ = DCC

BRAHMS, JOHANNES (cont.)

Pieces (6) for Piano, Op. 118 (1892) (cont.)

I. Tiegerman (pno)—Romance in F *(rec Cairo, Egypt, ca 1955)* ("The Lost Legend of Cairo: Radio & Private Recordings") † Con 2 Pno, Op. 83; Intermezzos (3) Pno, Op. 117; Pieces (8) Pno, Op. 76; Chopin:Ballade 4 Pno, Op. 52; Nocturnes Pno; Preludes (24) Pno, Op. 28; Scherzos Pno; Son Pno in b, Op. 58; G. Fauré:Nocturnes Pno; J. Field:Nocturnes Pno; C. Franck:Symphonic Vars, M.46; Saint-Saëns:Con 5 Pno, Op. 103; Tiegerman:Meditation Pno ARBT 2-▲ 116 (32.97)

R. Votapek (pno)—Intermezzo in a; Intermezzo in A; Ballade in g *(rec Fort Worth, TX, 1962 & 1966)* ("The 1st & 2nd Cliburn Competitions 1962-66") † A. Copland:Son Pno; MacDowell:Son 2 Pno, Op. 50; Son 3 Pno, Op. 57; S. Prokofiev:Con 2 Pno, Op. 16; D. Scarlatti:Sons Kbd VAIA (Retrospective, Vol 4) ▲ 1156 (m) [ADD]

N. Zaslav (pno)—Romance in F; Intermezzo in A; Intermezzo in e♭ *(rec Monterey, CA, 1996-97)* ("The Intimate Brahms") † Ballades (4), Op. 10; Fants Pno, Op. 116; Intermezzos (3) Pno, Op. 117; Pieces (4) Pno, Op. 119; Pieces (8) Pno, Op. 76 MUA ▲ 1031 [DDD] (16.97)

Pieces (4) for Piano, Op. 119 (1892)

M. Anderson (pno) *(rec Wyastone Leys Monmouth, Nov 25-27, 1996)* † Pieces (6) Pno, Op. 118; Vars on a Hungarian Song, Op. 21/2; Vars on an Original Theme, Op. 21/1 NIMB ▲ 5521 [DDD] (16.97)

W. Backhaus (pno)—Intermezzo in C *(rec 1954)* ("Wilhelm Backhaus") † Con 2 Pno, Op. 83; Beethoven:Son 17 Pno, Op. 31/2; Son 25 Pno, Op. 79; Son 26 Pno, Op. 81a; Son 32 Pno, Op. 111; Son 8 Pno, Op. 13; Chopin:Etudes Pno; Liszt:Trans, Arrs & Paraphrases; F. Schubert:Impromptus (4); R. Schumann:Fantasiestücke Pno, Op. 12 PPHI (Great Pianists of the 20th Century) ▲ 456718 (22.97)

P. Badura-Skoda (pno) † Intermezzos (3) Pno, Op. 117; Pieces (6) Pno, Op. 118 VAL ▲ 6115 [AAD] (18.97)

V. Cliburn (pno)—Intermezzo in e; Intermezzo in b † Con 2 Pno, Op. 83; Intermezzos (3) Pno, Op. 117 RCAV (Gold Seal) ▲ 7942 [ADD] (11.97)

C. Curzon (pno)—Intermezzo in C † Intermezzos (3) Pno, Op. 117; Son 3 Pno, Op. 5; F. Schubert:Son Pno, D.960 PLON (The Classic Sound) ▲ 48578 (11.97)

R. Goode (pno) † Fants Pno, Op. 116; Pieces (8) Pno, Op. 76 NON ▲ 79154 [DDD] (16.97)

M. Hess (pno) *(rec Univ of Illinois, Mar 17-18, 1949)* ("Live Recordings, Vol. 1") † Chopin:Fantaisie Pno, Op. 49; D. Scarlatti:Sons Kbd; F. Schubert:Dances (42), Op. 18; Dances Pno (misc); Son Pno, D.960 APR (Musique-Vérité) ▲ 5520 [ADD] (18.97)

V. Kastelsky (pno) *(rec 1981-84)* ("Russian Piano School: Kastelsky Plays Performs Brahms") † Fants Pno, Op. 116; Intermezzos (3) Pno, Op. 117; Pieces (6) Pno, Op. 118 RD (Talents of Russia) ▲ 16340 [ADD] (17.97)

W. Kempff (pno) *(rec 1954)* ("Wilhelm Kempff") † Ballades (4), Op. 10; Fants Pno, Op. 116; Intermezzos (3) Pno, Op. 117; Pieces (6) Pno, Op. 118; Pieces (8) Pno, Op. 76; R. Schumann:Arabeske Pno, Op. 18; Kreisleriana, Op. 16 PPHI (Great Pianists of the 20th Century) ▲ 456862 (22.97)

S. B. Kovacevich (pno) *(rec 1983)* † B. Bartók:Con 2 Pno, Sz.95; Out of Doors, Sz.81; Sonatina Pno, Sz.55; Beethoven:Son 5 Pno, Op. 10/1; R. R. Bennett:Con Pno; Chopin:Impromptu in G♭, Op. 51; Nocturnes Pno; I. Stravinsky:Con Pno & Ww PPHI (Great Pianists of the 20th Century, Vol. 61) 2-▲ 456880 (22.97)

A. Kubalek (pno) *(rec Apr 1991)* ("Piano Music of Brahms, Vol. 2") † Fants Pno, Op. 116; Pieces (6) Pno, Op. 118; Rhaps (2) Pno, Op. 79 DOR ▲ 90159 [DDD] (16.97)

K. Lechner (pno) † Con 2 Pno, Op. 83 VRDI (Masters) ▲ 32211 (13.97)

Y. Lefébure (pno)—Intermezzo in b *(rec Paris, France, Feb-Oct 1971)* † Pieces (6) Pno, Op. 118; B. Bartók:Mikrokosmos, Sz.107; J. Haydn:Son Kbd; Liszt:Ballade 2, S.171; Lugubre gondola [2nd ver] Pno, S.200/2; Trans, Arrs & Paraphrases; Rameau:Nouvelles suites; F. Schubert:Son Pno, D.958 SOC ▲ 159 (16.97)

R. Lupu (pno) † Intermezzos (3) Pno, Op. 117; Pieces (6) Pno, Op. 118; Rhaps (2) Pno, Op. 79 PLON ▲ 17599 [ADD] (16.97)

H. Neuhaus (pno) *(rec 1947-52)* ("Russian Piano School: Neuhaus") † Pieces (8) Pno, Op. 76; R. Schumann:Kreisleriana, Op. 16 RD (Talents of Russia) ▲ 16246 [ADD] (16.97)

G. Oppitz (pno) † Son 3 Pno, Op. 5 ORF ▲ 20821 [ADD] (18.97)

J. F. Osorio (pno) *(rec SUNY Purchase, New York, United States of America, Feb 2, 1999)* † Fants Pno, Op. 116; Son 3 Pno, Op. 5 ARTK ▲ 5 (15.97)

M. Perahia (pno) † Pieces (8) Pno, Op. 76; Rhaps (2) Pno, Op. 79; Son 3 Pno, Op. 5 SNYC ▲ 47181 (16.97)

S. Richter (pno) *(rec Kempten & Bonn Germany, Germany, 1992-93)* ("Out of Later Years, Vol. 1") † Ballades (4), Op. 10; Fants Pno, Op. 116; J. S. Bach:Adagio Clvd, BWV 968; Fant & Fugue Org, BWV 906; Kbd Music (misc); Prelude, Fugue & Allegro Lt, BWV 998; Beethoven:Rondos Pno, Op. 51 LV ▲ 471 (17.97)

S. Richter (pno)—Rhapsody in E♭ † Fants Pno, Op. 116; Pieces (6) Pno, Op. 118; Pieces (8) Pno, Op. 76; S. Prokofiev:Son 6 Pno, Op. 82; C. M. von Weber:Son 3 Pno, Op. 49 AURC ▲ 127 (5.97)

P. Rösel (pno) ("Piano Works") † Ballades (4), Op. 10; Intermezzos (3) Pno, Op. 117; Rhaps (2) Pno, Op. 79; Scherzo Pno, Op. 4 BER ▲ 2095 (10.97)

N. Zaslav (pno)—Intermezzo in b; Intermezzo in e *(rec Monterey, CA, 1996-97)* ("The Intimate Brahms") † Ballades (4), Op. 10; Fants Pno, Op. 116; Intermezzos (3) Pno, Op. 117; Pieces (6) Pno, Op. 118; Pieces (8) Pno, Op. 76 MUA ▲ 1031 [DDD] (16.97)

Poems (5), Op. 19

I. Danz (cta), A. Eckels (pno)—An eine Äolsharfe † Deutsche Volkslieder (49), WoO 33; Songs (4), Op. 96; Songs (5), Op. 49; Songs (5), Op. 71; Songs (5), Op. 72; Songs (6), Op. 85; Songs (6), Op. 86; Songs (8), Op. 59 HANS (Vocal Series) ▲ 98150 (15.97)

Psalm 13 for 3 Female Voices & Organ or Piano, Op. 27 (1859)

G. Jena (cnd), North German Radio Chorus ("The Complete Brahms Edition, Vol. 7:Choral Works") † Ave Maria, Op. 12; Begräbnisgesang, Op. 13; Canons (13), Op. 113; Dem dunkeln Schoss der heil'gen Erde; Deutsche Volkslieder (26); Fest- und Gedenksprüche, Op. 109; Geistliches Lied, Op. 30; Grausam erweiset sich Amor an mir, Op. 113/2; Kleine Hochzeitskantate; Marienlieder (7), Op. 22; Mir lächelt kein Frühling; Motets (2), Op. 29; Motets (2), Op. 74; Motets (3), Op. 110; O wie sanft; Sacred Choruses (3), Op. 37; Songs (3), Op. 42; Songs (4), Op. 17; Songs (5), Op. 104; Songs (5), Op. 41; Songs (7), Op. 62; Songs & Romances (12), Op. 44; Songs & Romances (6), Op. 93a; Spruch; Tafellied, Op. 93b; Töne, lindernder Klang; Wann?; Zu Rauch DGRM 4-▲ 449646

Quartets (3) in g, A & c for Piano & Strings Opp. 25, 26 & 60 (complete)

V. Aller (pno), Hollywood String Quartet members *(rec Hollywood & Melrose Studio Hollywood, Jan-June 1956)* † Qnt Pno, Op. 34; Qt 2 Strs, Op. 51/2; R. Schumann:Qnt Pno, Op. 44 TES 3-▲ 3063 [ADD] (49.97)

Clementi Quartet *(rec Mesquite Performing Arts Center Texas, Apr 1996)* ENRE 2-▲ 9611 [DDD] (26.97)

Eastman Quartet *(rec 1968)* VB2 2-▲ 5052 [ADD] (9.97)

R. Golani (va), Borodin Trio CHN 2-▲ 8809 [DDD] (33.97)

I. Stern (vn), J. Laredo (va), Y.-Y. Ma (vc), E. Ax (pno) SNYC 2-▲ 45846 [DDD] (31.97)

I. Stern (vn), J. Laredo (va), Y.-Y. Ma (vc), E. Ax (pno) † Trio 1 Pno, Op. 8; Trio 2 Pno, Op. 87; Trio 3 Pno, Op. 101 SNYC (Isaac Stern: A Life in Music) 3-▲ 64520 (32.97)

W. Trampler (va), Beaux Arts Trio ("Brahms: Complete Piano Quartets") † Trio Pno in A PPHI ▲ 54017 (17.97)

Quartet No. 1 in g for Piano & Strings, Op. 25 (1861; orchd Schoenberg, 1937)

Amabile Piano Quartet † F. Bridge:Phantasie Qt Pno; J. Turina:Qt Pno SUMM ▲ 199 (16.97)

P. Csaba (vn), M. Hirvikangas (va), F. Helmerson (vc), R. Gothóni (pno) † Qt 3 Pno, Op. 60 ODE ▲ 843 (17.97)

Em. Gilels (pno), Amadeus String Quartet † Ballades (4), Op. 10 DEUT (The Originals) ▲ 47407 [ADD] (11.97)

N. Järvi (cnd), London SO † Vars & Fugue on a Theme by Handel, Op. 24 CHN ▲ 8825 [DDD] (16.97)

P. Kolmós (vn), G. Németh (va), K. Botvay (vc), C. Szabó (pno) *(rec 1972-74)* † Qt 2 Pno, Op. 26; Qt 3 Pno, Op. 60 HUN 2-▲ 11597 [ADD] (16.97)

Menuhin Festival Piano Quartet † Qt 2 Pno, Op. 26; Qt 3 Pno, Op. 60 CLAV 2-▲ 509701 (27.97)

R. Pasquier (vn), B. Pasquier (va), R. Pidoux (vc), J. Pennetier (pno) † Son 3 Vn, Op. 108 HAM ▲ 7901062 (12.97)

M. Perahia (pno), Amadeus String Quartet members SNYC ▲ 42361 [DDD] (16.97)

A. Rubenstein (pno), Pro Arte String Quartet *(rec 1932 & 1936)* ("Arthur Rubenstein Plays Brahms Chamber Music") † Son 1 Vc, Op. 38; Son 3 Vn, Op. 108 ENPL (Piano Library) ▲ 233 (13.97)

A. Rubinstein (pno), Guarneri String Quartet members † Qt 3 Pno, Op. 60 RCAV (Gold Seal) ▲ 5677 [ADD] (11.97)

A. Rubinstein (pno), Pro Arte String Quartet members *(rec 1932)* † Qt 2 Pno, Op. 26 BID ▲ 27 [ADD]

A. Schneider (vn), W. Trampler (va), L. Parnas (vc), S. Brown (pno) ("Brahms: The Three Piano Quartets") † Qt 2 Pno, Op. 26; Qt 3 Pno, Op. 60 VC 2-▲ 97 [AAD] (26.97)

Schubert Ensemble of London † Mendelssohn (-Bartholdy):Qt 2 Pno, Op. 2 ASVQ ▲ 6194 (10.97)

Viardot † Jost:Ritual Returning QUER ▲ 9813

Vienna Piano Quartet † W. A. Mozart:Qt Pno, K.478 PLAL ▲ 108 (18.97)

Quartet No. 2 in A for Piano & Strings, Op. 26 (1861-62)

P. Kolmós (vn), G. Németh (va), K. Botvay (vc), I. Lantos (pno) *(rec 1972-74)* † Qt 1 Pno, Op. 25; Qt 3 Pno, Op. 60 HUN 2-▲ 11597 [ADD] (16.97)

Menuhin Festival Piano Quartet † Qt 1 Pno, Op. 25; Qt 3 Pno, Op. 60 CLAV 2-▲ 509701 (27.97)

A. Rubinstein (pno), Busch String Quartet members *(rec 1932)* † Qt 1 Pno, Op. 25 BID ▲ 27 [ADD]

A. Schneider (vn), W. Trampler (va), L. Parnas (vc), S. Brown (pno) ("Brahms: The Three Piano Quartets") † Qt 1 Pno, Op. 25; Qt 3 Pno, Op. 60 VC 2-▲ 97 [AAD] (26.97)

Schubert Ensemble of London † Mendelssohn (-Bartholdy):Qt 1 Pno, Op. 1 ASV ▲ 6199 (10.97)

R. Serkin (pno), Busch String Quartet members *(rec 1932-41)* † A. Dvořák:Qt 10 Strs, Op. 51 ENT ▲ 99378 (16.97)

BRAHMS, JOHANNES (cont.)

Quartet No. 2 in A for Piano & Strings, Op. 26 (1861-62) (cont.)

S. Staples (vn), G. Walther (va), N. Rosen (vc), C. O'Riley (pno) *(rec St. Francis Auditorium Santa Fe, NM, July 20, 21, 24 & 25, 1997)* ("Encore: The Best of the 1997 Santa Fe Chamber Music Festival") † Mendelssohn (-Bartholdy):Sxt STPH ▲ 11 (16.97)

Quartet No. 3 in c for Piano & Strings, Op. 60 (1855-75)

Apple Hill Chamber Players *(rec Apr 22-23, 1991)* † A. Dvořák:Trio 1 Pno, Op. 21 CENT ▲ 2158 [DDD] (16.97)

P. Csaba (vn), M. Hirvikangas (va), F. Helmerson (vc), R. Gothóni (pno) † Qt 1 Pno, Op. 25 ODE ▲ 843 (17.97)

P. Kolmós (vn), G. Németh (va), K. Botvay (vc), S. Falvai (pno) *(rec 1972-74)* † Qt 1 Pno, Op. 25; Qt 2 Pno, Op. 26 HUN 2-▲ 11597 [ADD] (16.97)

Menuhin Festival Piano Quartet † Qt 1 Pno, Op. 25; Qt 2 Pno, Op. 26 CLAV 2-▲ 509701 (27.97)

A. Rubinstein (pno), Guarneri String Quartet members † Qt 1 Pno, Op. 25 RCAV (Gold Seal) ▲ 5677 [ADD] (11.97)

A. Schneider (vn), W. Trampler (va), L. Parnas (vc), S. Brown (pno) ("Brahms: The Three Piano Quartets") † Qt 1 Pno, Op. 25; Qt 2 Pno, Op. 26 VC 2-▲ 97 [AAD] (26.97)

Schubert Ensemble London † Mendelssohn (-Bartholdy):Qt 3 Pno, Op. 3 ASVQ ▲ 6198 (10.97)

I. Stern (vn), J. Laredo (va), Y.-Y. Ma (vc), E. Ax (pno) † Con Vn & Vc, Op. 102 SNYC ▲ 42387 [DDD] (16.97)

Quartets for SATB Vocal Quartet & Piano (miscellaneous)

A. Planès (pno), M. Creed (cnd), Berlin RIAS Chamber Choir † Zigeunerlieder, Op. 103 HAM ▲ 901593 (18.97)

Quartets (3) for SATB Vocal Quartet & Piano, Op. 31 (1859)

R. Follman (sop), L. D. Mills (mez), R. MacNeil (ten), P. Atherton (b-bar), S. McCune (pno), T. Fleischer (pno), W. Hall (cnd), Master Chorale of Orange County—Wechsellied zum Tanze; Neckereien *(rec Chapman University, Salmon Recital Hall, Orange, CA)* † Duets (3), Op. 20; Duets (4), Op. 61; Liebeslieder Waltzes, Op. 52; Qts (3) SATB, Op. 64; R. Schumann:Mädchenlieder, Op. 103; Spanische Liebeslieder, Op. 138; Spanisches Liederspiel, Op. 74; Zweistimmige Lieder, Op. 43 KLAV ▲ 11092 [DDD] (18.97)

C. Ivaldi (pno), N. Lee (pno), Lieder Vocal Quartet † Liebeslieder Waltzes Pno 4-Hands, Op. 52a; Qts (3) SATB, Op. 64; Qts (4) SATB, Op. 92; Qts (6) SATB, Op. 112 ARN ▲ 68392 (16.97)

Quartets (3) for SATB Vocal Quartet & Piano, Op. 64 (1862-74)

J. Flummerfeldt (cnd), Westminster Choir, G. Parker (pno), N. Parrella (pno) *(rec Westminster Choir College of Rider Univ. Princeton, NJ, May 14-16, 1995)* ("Singing for Pleasure") † Liebeslieder Waltzes, Op. 52; Motets (2), Op. 74; Neue Liebeslieder Waltzes, Op. 65; Zigeunerlieder, Op. 103 DLS ▲ 3193 [DDD] (14.97)

R. Follman (sop), L. D. Mills (mez), R. MacNeil (ten), P. Atherton (b-bar), S. McCune (pno), T. Fleischer (pno), W. Hall (cnd), Master Chorale of Orange County—Fragen *(rec Chapman University, Salmon Recital Hall, Orange, CA)* † Duets (3), Op. 20; Duets (4), Op. 61; Liebeslieder Waltzes, Op. 52; Qts (3) SATB, Op. 31; R. Schumann:Mädchenlieder, Op. 103; Spanische Liebeslieder, Op. 138; Spanisches Liederspiel, Op. 74; Zweistimmige Lieder, Op. 43 KLAV ▲ 11092 [DDD] (18.97)

C. Ivaldi (pno), N. Lee (pno), Lieder Vocal Quartet † Liebeslieder Waltzes Pno 4-Hands, Op. 52a; Qts (3) SATB, Op. 31; Qts (4) SATB, Op. 92; Qts (6) SATB, Op. 112 ARN ▲ 68392 (16.97)

E. Mathis (sop), B. Fassbaender (mez), P. Schreier (ten), D. Fischer-Dieskau (bar), W. Sawallisch (pno), K. Engel (pno) [GER] † Liebeslieder Waltzes, Op. 52; Neue Liebeslieder Waltzes, Op. 65 DEUT ▲ 23133 [DDD] (16.97)

C. Piazzini (pno), W. Seeliger (cnd), Darmstadt Concert Choir ("Choral Songs of the Romantic Period") † Mendelssohn (-Bartholdy):Choruses, Op. 88; R. Schumann:Romanzen und Balladen, Op. 67; H. Wolf:Fröhliche Fahrt, Op. 17/1; Grablied; Im stillen Friedhof ENTE ▲ 80 [ADD] (10.97)

Quartets (4) for SATB Vocal Quartet & Piano, Op. 92 (1877; 1884)

C. Ivaldi (pno), N. Lee (pno), Lieder Vocal Quartet † Liebeslieder Waltzes Pno 4-Hands, Op. 52a; Qts (3) SATB, Op. 31; Qts (3) SATB, Op. 64; Qts (6) SATB, Op. 112 ARN ▲ 68392 (16.97)

Quartets (6) for SATB Vocal Quartet & Piano, Op. 112 (1888-91)

H. M. Beuerle (cnd), Anton Webern Choir Freiburg ("Secular Choral Songs a Cappella & with Piano") † Songs; Songs (5), Op. 104; Zigeunerlieder, Op. 103 ARSM ▲ 1136 [DDD] (17.97)

C. Ivaldi (pno), N. Lee (pno), Lieder Vocal Quartet † Liebeslieder Waltzes Pno 4-Hands, Op. 52a; Qts (3) SATB, Op. 31; Qts (3) SATB, Op. 64; Qts (4) SATB, Op. 92 ARN ▲ 68392 (16.97)

Quartets (3) in c, a & c for Strings, Op. 51/1 & 2 & Op. 67 (complete)

Alban Berg String Quartet † A. Dvořák:Qt 13 Strs, Op. 106 TELC 2-▲ 95503 (16.97)

Amadeus String Quartet *(rec Beethovensaal Hanover, Germany, Sept 1959 & Jan 1960)* † A. Dvořák:Qt 12 Strs, Op. 96 DEUT (The Originals) 2-▲ 457707 [ADD] (22.97)

Bartók String Quartet *(rec 1971-74)* † Qnt 1 Strs, Op. 88; Qnt 2 Strs, Op. 111; Sextet Strs, Op. 18; Sextet Strs, Op. 36 HUN 3-▲ 11591 [ADD]

Danish String Quartet KPT 2-▲ 32033 [DDD]

Juilliard String Quartet † Qnt Cl; Qt 1 Strs, Op. 51/1; Qt 2 Strs, Op. 51/2; Qt 3 Strs, Op. 67 SNYC 2-▲ 66285 (31.97)

New Budapest String Quartet † Qnt Pno, Op. 34 HYP (Dyad) 2-▲ 22018 (18.97)

Quartetto Italiano † Sons Cl PPHI (Duo) 2-▲ 456320 (17.97)

Sine Nomine String Quartet *(rec Jan 14-17, 1993)* ("The Three String Quartets") CLAV 2-▲ 9404 [DDD]

Quartet No. 1 in c for Strings, Op. 51/1 (ca 1865-73)

Borodin String Quartet *(rec Berlin, Jan 1993)* † Qt 3 Strs, Op. 67 TELC ▲ 90889 [DDD] (16.97)

Busch String Quartet † Qt 2 Strs, Op. 51/2; M. Reger:Son Vn Pno, Op. 84; R. Schumann:Son 1 Vn, Op. 105 BID ▲ 165 [ADD] (16.97)

Cleveland String Quartet *(rec Sept 20-24, 1993)* † Qt 2 Strs, Op. 51/2 TEL ▲ 80346 [DDD] (16.97)

Colorado String Quartet † Qt 2 Strs, Op. 51/2 PACD ▲ 96007 [DDD] (15.97)

Juilliard String Quartet † Qnt Cl; Qt 2 Strs, Op. 51/2; Qt 3 Strs, Op. 67; Qts Strs (comp) SNYC 2-▲ 66285 (31.97)

Quatuor Ludwig † Qt 2 Strs, Op. 51/2 NXIN ▲ 8554271 [DDD] (5.97)

Rubio String Quartet *(rec Utrecht, Germany, May 1998)* † Qt 2 Strs, Op. 51/2 GLOE ▲ 5164 [DDD] (16.97)

Skampa String Quartet † A. Dvořák:Qt 12 Strs, Op. 96 SUR ▲ 3380 (16.97)

artists unknown † Qt 2 Strs, Op. 51/2; W. A. Mozart:Qnt Cl, K.581; C. M. von Weber:Qnt Cl SNYC ▲ 69270 [DDD] (4.97)

Quartet No. 2 in a for Strings, Op. 51/2 (ca 1865-73)

Busch String Quartet † Qt 1 Strs, Op. 51/1; M. Reger:Son Vn Pno, Op. 84; R. Schumann:Son 1 Vn, Op. 105 BID ▲ 165 [ADD] (16.97)

Cleveland String Quartet *(rec Sept 20-24, 1993)* † Qt 1 Strs, Op. 51/1 TEL ▲ 80346 [DDD] (16.97)

Colorado String Quartet † Qt 1 Strs, Op. 51/1 PACD ▲ 96007 [DDD] (15.97)

Hollywood String Quartet *(rec Hollywood, Jan 28-30, 1952)* † Qnt Pno, Op. 34; Qts Pno (comp); R. Schumann:Qnt Pno, Op. 44 TES 3-▲ 3063 [ADD] (49.97)

Juilliard String Quartet † Qnt Cl; Qt 1 Strs, Op. 51/1; Qt 3 Strs, Op. 67; Qts Strs (comp) SNYC 2-▲ 66285 (31.97)

Leipzig String Quartet † Qnt Cl MDG ▲ 3070719 (17.97)

Lindsay String Quartet † Mendelssohn (-Bartholdy):Qt 6 Strs, Op. 80 ASVQ ▲ 6173 (10.97)

Quatuor Ludwig † Qt 1 Strs, Op. 51/1 NXIN ▲ 8554271 [DDD] (5.97)

Rubio String Quartet *(rec Utrecht, Germany, May 1998)* † Qt 1 Strs, Op. 51/1 GLOE ▲ 5164 [DDD] (16.97)

Simi String Quartet *(rec Music Centre Tbilisi, Sept 1994)* † Qt 1 Strs, Op. 51/1; W. A. Mozart:Qnt Cl, K.581; C. M. von Weber:Qnt Cl SNYC ▲ 69270 [DDD] (4.97)

Quartet No. 3 in B♭ for Strings, Op. 67 (1876)

Borodin String Quartet *(rec Berlin, Jan 1993)* † Qt 1 Strs, Op. 51/1 TELC ▲ 90889 [DDD] (16.97)

Flonzaley String Quartet *(rec Mar 1928)* † Qnt Pno, Op. 34; Mendelssohn (-Bartholdy):Qt 1 Strs, Op. 12; F. Schubert:Qt 15 Strs, D.887; R. Schumann:Qnt Pno, Op. 44; Qts Strs, Op. 41 BID 2-▲ 72 [ADD]

Gaggini String Quartet † P. Hindemith:Qt 1 Strs, Op. 10 CYPR ▲ 2616 (17.97)

Juilliard String Quartet † Qnt Cl; Qt 1 Strs, Op. 51/1; Qt 2 Strs, Op. 51/2; Qts Strs (comp) SNYC 2-▲ 66285 (31.97)

Manfred String Quartet † R. Schumann:Qnt Pno, Op. 44 PVY ▲ 798012 (16.97)

Primrose String Quartet *(rec 1941)* † J. Haydn:7 Last Words of Christ on the Cross; R. Schumann:Qnt Pno, Op. 44; Smetana:Qt 1 Strs BID 2-▲ 52 [ADD]

Shanghai String Quartet *(rec Church of the Ascension New York, NY)* ("The Shanghai Quartet Plays Brahms") † Qnt 1 Strs, Op. 88 DLS ▲ 3198 [DDD] (14.97)

Smetana String Quartet † F. Schubert:Qnt in C Strs, D.956 TES ▲ 1120 (17.97)

Quintet in b for Clarinet & Strings, Op. 115 (1891)

Y. Bashmet (va) [trans Y. Bashmet] *(rec London, England, Mar 21-22, 1998)* † D. Shostakovich:Qt 13 Strs, Op. 138 SNYC ▲ 60550 [DDD] (16.97)

Berlin Philharmonic Octet members ("The Complete Quintets") † Qnt Pno, Op. 34; Qnt 1 Strs, Op. 88; Qnt 2 Strs, Op. 111 PPHI (Duo) 2-▲ 46172 (17.97)

D. Campbell (cl), Bingham String Quartet † W. A. Mozart:Qnt Cl, K.581 OLY ▲ 637 (16.97)

E. Daniels (cl), Composers String Quartet † C. M. von Weber:Qnt Cl REF ▲ 40 [DDD] (16.97)

C. Draper (cl), Léner String Quartet *(rec 1928 for Columbia Records)* † W. A. Mozart:Qnt Cl, K.581 PHS ▲ 9903 [AAD] (17.97)

K. Fagéus (b cl), Zetterqvist String Quartet † W. A. Mozart:Qnt Cl, K.581 OPU ▲ 19301

T. Friedli (cl), Sine Nomine String Quartet *(rec Salle de la Foundation Tibor Varga Sion, Switzerland, 1995-96)* ("Complete Quintets, Vol 1") † Qnt Pno, Op. 34 CLAV ▲ 9608 [DDD] (16.97)

BRAHMS, JOHANNES (cont.)

Quintet in b for Clarinet & Strings, Op. 115 (1891) (cont.)

R. Kell (cl), Busch String Quartet † Trio Hn, Op. 40 PHS ▲ 7 [ADD] (17.97)

R. Kell (cl), Fine Arts String Quartet ("The Great Clarinet Quintets") † W. A. Mozart:Qnt Cl, K.581 BOSK ▲ 135 [AAD] (15.97)

T. King (cl), Gabrieli String Quartet † Trio Cl HYP ▲ 66107 (18.97)

B. Kovčs (cl), Bartók String Quartet † Qnt Pno, Op. 34 HUN ▲ 11596

K. Leister (cl), Amadeus String Quartet † Qnt Pno, Op. 34; Qnt 1 Strs, Op. 88; Qnt 2 Strs, Op. 111; Sextet Strs, Op. 18; Sextet Strs, Op. 36 DEUT 3-▲ 19875 [ADD] (34.97)

K. Leister (cl), Brandis String Quartet *(rec Berlin-Lichterfelde, June 30-July 2, 1996)* † Qnt 1 Strs, Op. 88 NIMB ▲ 5515 [DDD] (16.97)

K. Leister (cl), Leipzig String Quartet † Qt 2 Strs, Op. 51/2 MDG ▲ 3070719 (17.97)

K. Leister (cl), Vienna String Quartet—Adagio ("Leister Plays Adagio") † Bärmann:Adagio Cl & Str Qt; Crusell:Qts Cl; W. A. Mozart:Qnt Cl, K.581; M. Reger:Qnt Cl; C. M. von Weber:Qnt Cl CAMA (After Hours Classics) ▲ 424 [DDD] (15.97)

K. Leister (cl), Vermeer String Quartet ORF ▲ 68831 [DDD] (18.97)

Melos Ensemble *(rec 1964-70)* † Beethoven:Duos Cl, WoO 27; March Cls, WoO 29; Qnt Pno, Op. 16; Rondino Ww, WoO 25; Sxt Hns; W. A. Mozart:Qnt Pno, K.452; R. Schumann:Fantasiestücke Cl, Op. 73; Märchenerzählungen, Op. 132 EMIC 2-▲ 72643 [ADD] (16.97)

A. Moccia (vn), A. Chamorro (vn), J. Vasseur (va), A. Zwistra (vc), J. Veilhan (cl) † Krehl:Qnt Cl K617 ▲ 7084 (18.97)

C. Neidich (cl), Juilliard String Quartet † Qt 1 Strs, Op. 51/1; Qt 2 Strs, Op. 51/2; Qt 3 Strs, Op. 67; Qts Strs (comp) SNYC 2-▲ 66285 (31.97)

D. Oistrakh (vn), P. Bondarenko (vn), M. Terian (va), S. Knushevitsky (vc), V. Sorokin (cl) ("David Oistrakh Collection, Vol. 2") † W. A. Mozart:Qnt Cl, K.581 DHR (Legendary Treasures) ▲ 7702 (16.97)

C. Onczay (vc), J. Balogh (cl), Danubius String Quartet *(rec Oct 16-18, 1991)* † Trio Cl NXIN ▲ 550391 [DDD] (5.97)

M. Portal (cl), Melos String Quartet † Qnt 2 Strs, Op. 111 HAM ▲ 901349 (18.97)

K. Puddy (cl), Delmé String Quartet † A. Dvořák:Qt 12 Strs, Op. 96 INMP (IMP Classics) ▲ 6700972 [DDD] (9.97)

D. Shifrin (cl), Chamber Music Northwest † Qnt 2 Strs, Op. 111 DLS ▲ 3066 [DDD] (14.97)

D. Shifrin (cl), Emerson String Quartet † W. A. Mozart:Qnt Cl, K.581 DEUT ▲ 459641 (16.97)

P. Woudenberg (cl), Schoenberg String Quartet † M. Reger:Qnt Cl KSCH ▲ 311502 (16.97)

Quintet in f for Piano & Strings, Op. 34 (1861-64)

V. Aller (pno), Hollywood String Quartet members *(rec Hollywood, Mar 30-31, 1954)* † Qt 2 Strs, Op. 51/2; Qts Pno (comp); R. Schumann:Qnt Pno, Op. 44 TES 3-▲ 3063 [ADD] (49.97)

L. Artymiw (pno), American String Quartet *(rec Tuscon Winter Chamber Festival, Mar 10, 1995)* † N. Rorem:Santa Fe Songs ARIZ ▲ 95102 [DDD] (16.97)

H. Bauer (pno), Flonzaley String Quartet *(rec Dec 1925)* † Qt 3 Strs, Op. 67; Mendelssohn (-Bartholdy):Qt 1 Strs, Op. 12; F. Schubert:Qt 15 Strs, D.887; R. Schumann:Qnt Pno, Op. 44; Qts Strs, Op. 41 BID 2-▲ 72 [ADD]

P. Bianconi (pno), Sine Nomine String Quartet *(rec Salle de la Foundation Tibor Varga Sion, Switzerland, 1995-96)* ("Complete Quintets, Vol 1") † Qnt Cl CLAV ▲ 9608 [DDD] (16.97)

M. Duchemin (pno), Laval String Quartet ("Piano Chamber Music") † Mendelssohn (-Bartholdy):Trio 1 Pno, Op. 49 SNE ▲ 2035 (16.97)

C. Eschenbach (pno), Amadeus String Quartet † Qnt Cl; Qnt 1 Strs, Op. 88; Qnt 2 Strs, Op. 111; Sextet Strs, Op. 18; Sextet Strs, Op. 36 DEUT 3-▲ 19875 [ADD] (34.97)

P. Frankl (pno), Lindsay String Quartet † R. Schumann:Qnt Pno, Op. 44 ASV ▲ 728 [DDD] (16.97)

G. Gould (pno), Montreal String Quartet † R. Schumann:Qt Pno in E♭, Op. 47 SNYC ▲ 52684 (16.97)

W. Hass (pno), Berlin Philharmonic Octet members ("The Complete Quintets") † Qnt Cl; Qnt 1 Strs, Op. 88; Qnt 2 Strs, Op. 111 PPHI (Duo) 2-▲ 46172 (17.97)

J. Jandó (pno), Kodály String Quartet *(rec Feb 1990)* † R. Schumann:Qnt Pno, Op. 44 NXIN ▲ 550406 [DDD] (5.97)

P. Komen (pno), Rubio String Quartet *(rec Dec 1997)* † R. Schumann:Qnt Pno, Op. 44 GLOE ▲ 5177 [DDD] (16.97)

P. Lane (pno), New Budapest String Quartet † Qts Strs (comp) HYP (Dyad) 2-▲ 22018 (18.97)

J. E. Merrett (bass), C. Curzon (pno), Amadeus String Quartet † F. Schubert:Qnt Pno, D.667 BBC ▲ 4009 (17.97)

Nash Ensemble *(rec Nov 25-27, 1991)* † Trio Hn, Op. 40 CRD ▲ 3489 [DDD] (17.97)

L. Natochenny (pno), Penderecki String Quartet † F. Schubert:Son Pno, D.959 MARQ ▲ 187 (16.97)

D. Ránki (pno), Bartók String Quartet † Qnt Cl HUN ▲ 11596

P. Rybar (vn), C. Dahinden (vn), H. Wigand (va), A. Tusa (vc), C. Haskil (pno) † Sextet Strs, Op. 36; Busoni:Son 2 Vn, Op. 36a DORO 2-▲ 4007 [ADD] (32.97)

G. Saarinen (pno), Orford String Quartet † Vars & Fugue on a Theme by Handel, Op. 24 DHR ▲ 71129 (16.97)

R. Serkin (pno), Busch String Quartet *(rec 1938)* † R. Schumann:Qnt Pno, Op. 44 PHS ▲ 9275 (17.97)

G. Szell (pno), Budapest String Quartet *(rec Coolidge Auditorium Library of Congress, Oct 11, 1945)* † F. Schubert:Qnt Pno, D.667 BRID ▲ 9062 (17.97)

Quintet No. 1 in F for Strings, Op. 88 (1882)

C. Aronowitz (va), Amadeus String Quartet † Qnt Cl; Qnt Pno, Op. 34; Qnt 2 Strs, Op. 111; Sextet Strs, Op. 18; Sextet Strs, Op. 36 DEUT 3-▲ 19875 [ADD] (34.97)

Berlin Philharmonic Octet members ("The Complete Quintets") † Qnt Cl; Qnt Pno, Op. 34; Qnt 2 Strs, Op. 111 PPHI (Duo) 2-▲ 46172 (17.97)

G. Caussé (va), Hagen String Quartet † Qnt 2 Strs, Op. 111 DGRM ▲ 453420 [DDD]

B. Dean (va), Brandis String Quartet *(rec Berlin-Lichterfelde, June 26-28, 1996)* † Qnt Cl NIMB ▲ 5515 [DDD] (16.97)

G. Konrád (va), Bartók String Quartet *(rec 1971-74)* † Qnt 2 Strs, Op. 111; Qts Strs (comp); Sextet Strs, Op. 18; Sextet Strs, Op. 36 HUN 3-▲ 11591 [ADD]

R. Oleg (va), Sine Nomine String Quartet ("Complete Quintets, Vol 2") † Qnt 2 Strs, Op. 111 CLAV ▲ 9609 (16.97)

Raphael Ensemble ("String Quintets") † Qnt 2 Strs, Op. 111 HYP ▲ 66804 (18.97)

A. Steinhardt (va), Shanghai String Quartet *(rec Church of the Ascension New York, NY)* ("The Shanghai Quartet Plays Brahms") † Qt 3 Strs, Op. 67 DLS ▲ 3198 [DDD] (14.97)

W. Trampler (va), Juilliard String Quartet † Qnt 2 Strs, Op. 111 SNYC ▲ 68476 (16.97)

Vienna Philharmonia Quintet *(rec Vienna, Austria, 1997)* † Qnt 2 Strs, Op. 111 CAMA ▲ 534 [DDD] (18.97)

Quintet No. 2 in G for Strings, Op. 111 (1890)

C. Aronowitz (va), Amadeus String Quartet † Qnt Cl; Qnt Pno, Op. 34; Qnt 1 Strs, Op. 88; Sextet Strs, Op. 18; Sextet Strs, Op. 36 DEUT 3-▲ 19875 [ADD] (34.97)

Berlin Philharmonic Octet members ("The Complete Quintets") † Qnt Cl; Qnt Pno, Op. 34; Qnt 1 Strs, Op. 88 PPHI (Duo) 2-▲ 46172 (17.97)

G. Caussé (va), Hagen String Quartet † Qnt 1 Strs, Op. 88 DGRM ▲ 453420 [DDD]

G. Caussé (va), Melos String Quartet † Qnt Cl HAM ▲ 901349 (18.97)

B. Dean (va), Brandis String Quartet *(rec Berlin, Feb 23-26, 1996)* † A. Bruckner:Qnt Strs NIMB ▲ 5488 [DDD] (16.97)

G. Konrád (va), Bartók String Quartet *(rec 1971-74)* † Qnt 1 Strs, Op. 88; Qts Strs (comp); Sextet Strs, Op. 18; Sextet Strs, Op. 36 HUN 3-▲ 11591 [ADD]

R. Oleg (va), Sine Nomine String Quartet ("Complete Quintets, Vol 2") † Qnt 1 Strs, Op. 88 CLAV ▲ 9609 (16.97)

Raphael Ensemble ("String Quintets") † Qnt 1 Strs, Op. 88 HYP ▲ 66804 (18.97)

Tiramisu Ensemble ("Brahms & His Friends, Vol. 4") † Herzogenberg:Qnt Strs, Op. 77 DVX ▲ 29608 (16.97)

W. Trampler (va), Chamber Music Northwest † Qnt Cl DLS ▲ 3066 [DDD] (14.97)

W. Trampler (va), Juilliard String Quartet † Qnt 1 Strs, Op. 88 SNYC ▲ 68476 (16.97)

S. Végh (cnd), Salzburg Mozarteum Camerata Academia—Adagio ("Sándor Végh Portrait") † B. Bartók:Divert Strs, Sz.113; Beethoven:Qt 14 Strs, Op. 131; J. Haydn:7 Last Words of Christ on the Cross CAPO ▲ 14860 [DDD] (6.97)

Vienna Philharmonia Quintet *(rec Vienna, Austria, 1997)* † Qnt 1 Strs, Op. 88 CAMA ▲ 534 [DDD] (18.97)

Rhapsodies (2) for Piano, Op. 79 (1879)

V. Afanassiev (pno) † Ballades (4), Op. 10; Fants Pno, Op. 116 DNN ▲ 78906 [DDD] (16.97)

M. Argerich (pno) *(rec 1960 & 1971)* ("Début Recital") † Chopin:Barcarolle Pno, Op. 60; Liszt:Hungarian Rhaps, S.244; Son Pno, S.178; S. Prokofiev:Toccata Pno, Op. 11; M. Ravel:Jeux d'eau DEUT (The Originals) ▲ 47430 [ADD] (11.97)

E. Ax (pno) † Pieces (6) Pno, Op. 118; Vars & Fugue on a Theme by Handel, Op. 24 SNYC ▲ 48046 (16.97)

W. Backhaus (pno) *(rec London, 1933 from HMV 78s)* † Ballades (4), Op. 10; Hungarian Dances Pno; Pno Music (misc colls); Scherzo Pno, Op. 4; Vars on an Original Theme, Op. 21/1 PHS ▲ 9385 [AAD] (17.97)

W. Backhaus (pno) *(rec 1933-39)* ("Great Recordings of the Thirties") † Ballades (4), Op. 10; Pno Music (misc colls); Vars on an Original Theme, Op. 21/1 GRM2 ▲ 78507 [ADD] (13.97)

V. Cliburn (pno) † Fants Pno, Op. 116; Pieces (6) Pno, Op. 118; Beethoven:Con 3 Pno, Op. 37 RCAV (Gold Seal) ▲ 60419 [ADD] (11.97)

W. Gieseking (pno) *(rec 1924-55)* ("Gieseking: A Retrospective, Vol. 3") † Casella:Son Pno, Op. 28; Chopin:Nocturnes (21) Pno; Polonaise 6 Pno, Op. 53; W. A. Mozart:Con 9 Pno, K.271; M. Ravel:Jeux d'eau PHS ▲ 9038 (17.97)

BRAHMS, JOHANNES (cont.)

Rhapsodies (2) for Piano, Op. 79 (1879) (cont.)

W. Gieseking (pno) ("Walter Gieseking: The Homochord Recordings, 1923-25") † J. S. Bach:Partitas Hpd; Chopin:Polonaise 6 Pno, Op. 53; Debussy:Images (6) Pno; Liszt:Hungarian Rhaps, S.244; M. Ravel:Jeux d'eau ENPL (Piano Library) ▲ 203 (13.97)

P. Katin (pno) ("A Brahms Recital") † Fants Pno, Op. 116; Intermezzos (3) Pno, Op. 117; Vars & Fugue on a Theme by Handel, Op. 24 OLY ▲ 263 [DDD] (16.97)

W. Kempff (pno) † Ballades (4), Op. 10; Con 1 Pno, Op. 15; Pieces (8) Pno, Op. 76; Scherzo Pno, Op. 4; Son 3 Pno, Op. 5 DEUT (Double) 2-▲ 37374 (17.97)

W. Kempff (pno) ("Wilhelm Kempff III") † Beethoven:Rondos Pno, Op. 51; Son 11 Pno, Op. 22; Son 2 Pno, Op. 2/2; G. Fauré:Nocturnes Pno; W. A. Mozart:Con 8 Pno, K.246; Vars on "Unser dummer Pöbel", K.455; F. Schubert:Son Pno, D.840; R. Schumann:Romances Pno, Op. 28 PPHI (Great Pianists of the 20th Century) 2-▲ 456868 (22.97)

A. Kubalek (pno) *(rec Apr 1991)* ("Piano Music of Brahms, Vol. 2") † Fants Pno, Op. 116; Pieces (4) Pno, Op. 119; Pieces (6) Pno, Op. 118 DOR ▲ 90159 [DDD] (16.97)

A. Laplante (pno) *(rec Boston, MA, Dec 1994)* † Son 3 Pno, Op. 5 FL ▲ 23011 [DDD] (16.97)

R. Lupu (pno) † Intermezzos (3) Pno, Op. 117; Pieces (4) Pno, Op. 119; Pieces (6) Pno, Op. 118 PLON ▲ 17599 [ADD] (16.97)

D. Paperno (pno)—No. 2 in g ("Recordings of a Moscow Pianist") † Chopin:Son Pno in b♭, Op. 35; E. Grieg:Ballade Pno, Op. 24; Liszt:Polonaises (2) Pno, S.223; Rhap espagnole, S.254; Venezia e Napoli, S.159 CED ▲ 37 [ADD] (16.97)

M. Perahia (pno)—No. 2 in g † Pieces (4) Pno, Op. 119; Pieces (8) Pno, Op. 76; Son 3 Pno, Op. 5 SNYC ▲ 47181 (16.97)

I. Pogorelich (pno) † Intermezzos (3) Pno, Op. 117; Pieces (8) Pno, Op. 76 DEUT ▲ 37460 [DDD] (16.97)

P. Rösel (pno) ("Piano Works") † Ballades (4), Op. 10; Intermezzos (3) Pno, Op. 117; Pieces (4) Pno, Op. 119; Scherzo Pno, Op. 4 BER ▲ 2095 (10.97)

A. Rubinstein (pno)—No. 2 in g *(rec 1958)* † Con 2 Pno, Op. 83; Fants Pno, Op. 116; Intermezzos (3) Pno, Op. 117 RCAV (Gold Seal) ▲ 61442 (11.97)

A. Rubinstein (pno) † Con 1 Pno, Op. 15; Pieces (8) Pno, Op. 76 RCAV (Gold Seal) ▲ 61263 (11.97)

Salzburg Mozarteum Camerata Academica † Schoenberg:Verklärte Nacht, Op. 4 CAPO ▲ 10427 [DDD] (11.97)

A. Schnabel (pno) *(rec London, England, 1946-47)* ("The 1946-47 HMV Solo Recordings") † Fants Pno, Op. 116; Intermezzos (3) Pno, Op. 117; W. A. Mozart:Rondo Pno, K.511; Son 12 Pno, K.332; R. Schumann:Kinderszenen Pno, Op. 15; C. M. von Weber:Invitation to the Dance Pno, J.260 APR ▲ 5526 (mono) [ADD] (18.97)

R. Silverman (pno) † Pieces (6) Pno, Op. 118; Vars on a Hungarian Song, Op. 21/2 MUVI (Musica Viva) ▲ 1028 (16.97)

R. Slenczynska (pno)—No. 1 in b *(rec St. Louis, MO, Apr 8, 1984)* ("Slenczynska in Concert") † Chopin:Son Pno in b, Op. 58; A. Copland:Midsummer Nocturne; J. Haydn:Sonatas for Piano; S. Rachmaninoff:Prelude in c♯, Op. 3/2; Preludes Pno IVOR ▲ 70902 [DDD] (16.97)

Solomon (pno)—No. 2 in g *(rec early 1940s)* † Intermezzos (3) Pno, Op. 117; Vars & Fugue on a Theme by Handel, Op. 24; Beethoven:Trio 6 Pno, Op. 97 ENPL (Piano Library) ▲ 313 (14.97)

Solomon (pno) *(rec 1956)* † Fants Pno, Op. 116; Intermezzos (3) Pno, Op. 117; J. S. Bach:Italian Con, BWV 971; Beethoven:Son 14 Pno, Op. 27/2; Son 3 Pno, Op. 2/3 APR 2-▲ 7030 [ADD] (38.97)

Rhapsody for Alto, Male Chorus & Orchestra [text Goethe], Op. 53 (1863-68)

L. West (cta), H. Knappertsbusch (cnd), Vienna PO *(rec Vienna, Germany, 1957)* † Academic Festival Ov, Op. 80; Con Vn & Vc, Op. 102; Con 2 Pno, Op. 83; Sym 2; Sym 3; Sym 4; Tragic Ov, Op. 81; Vars on a Theme by Haydn MELO 4-▲ 40039 (m) [ADD] (62.97)

Rinaldo (cantata) for Tenor & 4 Male Voices & Orchestra, Op. 50 (1863-68)

G. Sinopoli (cnd), Czech PO, Prague Phil Chorus, R. Kollo (ten) ("The Complete Brahms Edition, Vol. 8:Works for Chorus & Orchestra") † Alto Rhap, Op. 53; Deutsches Requiem, Op. 45; Gesäng der Parzen, Op. 89; Nänie, Op. 82; Schicksalslied, Op. 54; Triumphlied, Op. 55 DGRM 3-▲ 449651

Romances & Songs (5) for Voice & Piano, Op. 84 (1881)

M. Lipovšek (mez) † Deutsche Volkslieder (26); Deutsche Volkslieder (49), WoO 33; Marienlieder (7), Op. 22; Songs; Songs (5), Op. 49; Songs & Romances (6); Songs & Romances (8), Op. 14; Zigeunerlieder, Op. 103 *(E,F,G texts)* ORF ▲ 441971 [DDD] (18.97)

Romanzen (cycle of 15 songs) aus Tieck's *Magelone* for Voice & Piano, Op. 33 (1861)

D. Fischer-Dieskau (bar), S. Richter (pno) *(rec July 1970)* ORFE (Festspiel Dokumente) ▲ 490981 (16.97)

W. Grönroos (bar), R. Gothóni (pno) *(rec Nacka Aula Nacka Sweden, July 26-27, 1976)* † Duets (4), Op. 28; Ernste Gesänge, Op. 121; Vars on an Original Theme, Op. 21/1 BIS ▲ 70 [AAD] (17.97)

W. Holzmair (bar), W. Quadflieg (spkr), G. Wyss (pno) [GER] TUD 2-▲ 761 [DDD] (32.97)

H. Prey (bar), A. Prey (nar), H. Deutsch (pno) [GER] ORF 2-▲ 116842 [DDD] (36.97)

Sacred Choruses (3) for 4 Female Voices, Op. 37

G. Jena (cnd), North German Radio Chorus ("The Complete Brahms Edition, Vol. 7:Choral Works") † Ave Maria, Op. 12; Begräbnisgesang, Op. 13; Canons (13), Op. 113; Dem dunkeln Schoss der heil'gen Erde; Deutsche Volkslieder (26); Fest- und Gedenksprüche, Op. 109; Geistliches Lied, Op. 30; Grausam erweiset sich Amor an mir, Op. 113/2; Kleine Hochzeitskantate; Marienlieder (7), Op. 22; Mir lächelt kein Frühling; Motets (2), Op. 29; Motets (2), Op. 74; Motets (3), Op. 110; O wie sanft; Psalm 13, Op. 27; Songs (3), Op. 42; Songs (4), Op. 17; Songs (5), Op. 104; Songs (5), Op. 41; Songs (7), Op. 62; Songs & Romances (12), Op. 44; Songs & Romances (6), Op. 93a; Spruch; Tafellied, Op. 93b; Töne, lindernder Klang; Wann?; Zu Rauch DGRM 4-▲ 449646

Scherzo in e♭ for Piano, Op. 4 (1851)

W. Backhaus (pno) *(rec London, 1933 from HMV 78s)* † Ballades (4), Op. 10; Hungarian Dances Pno; Pno Music (misc colls); Rhaps (2) Pno, Op. 79; Vars on an Original Theme, Op. 21/1 PHS ▲ 9385 [AAD] (17.97)

W. Kempff (pno) † Ballades (4), Op. 10; Con 1 Pno, Op. 15; Pieces (8) Pno, Op. 76; Rhaps (2) Pno, Op. 79; Son 3 Pno, Op. 5 DEUT (Double) 2-▲ 37374 (17.97)

P. Rösel (pno) ("Piano Works") † Ballades (4), Op. 10; Intermezzos (3) Pno, Op. 117; Pieces (4) Pno, Op. 119; Rhaps (2) Pno, Op. 79 BER ▲ 2095 (10.97)

Scherzo in c for Violin & Piano [from the *F.A.E. Sonata*] (1853)

L. Bobesco (vn), J. Genty (pno) † Sons Vn (comp) TLNT ▲ 291002 [ADD] (15.97)

S. Elbæk (vn), M. Mogensen (pno) † Sons Vn (comp) KPT ▲ 32177 [DDD]

C. Feige (vn), S. Redaelli (pno) † Sons Vn (comp) STRV ▲ 33498 (16.97)

J. Laredo (vn), J. Pommier (pno) *(rec 1982-83)* † Sons Vc (comp); Sons Vn (comp) VCL 2-▲ 61415 [DDD] (11.97)

A.-S. Mutter (vn), L. Orkis (pno) ("The Berlin Recital") † Hungarian Dances Pno 4-Hands; Debussy:Beau soir; Son Vn; C. Franck:Son Vn, M.8; W. A. Mozart:Son 21 Vn & Pno, K.304 DEUT ▲ 45826 [DDD] (16.97)

Vanessa-Mae (vn) ("The Classical Album") † J. S. Bach:Sons & Partitas Vn; Bruch:Scottish Fant, Op. 46 ANGL ▲ 55395 (16.97)

V. Vassilev (vn), P. Tan-Nicholson (pno) † Sons Vn (comp) HAM (Les Nouveaux Interprètes) ▲ 911576 (12.97)

B. Westphal (va), U. Oppens (pno) [trans Westphal for va & pno] † Sons Cl BRID ▲ 9021 [DDD] (17.97)

Schicksalslied for Orchestra & Chorus, Op. 54 (1868-71)

C. Abbado (cnd), Berlin PO, Berlin Radio Chorus, Ernst Senff Chorus † Academic Festival Ov, Op. 80; Alto Rhap, Op. 53; Gesäng der Parzen, Op. 89; Nänie, Op. 82; Syms (comp); Tragic Ov, Op. 81; Vars on a Theme by Haydn DGRM 4-▲ 435683 [DDD]

C. Abbado (cnd), Berlin PO, Ernst Senff Chorus [GER] † Sym 3; Tragic Ov, Op. 81 DEUT ▲ 29765 [DDD] (16.97)

M. Anderson (cta), P. Monteux (cnd), San Francisco SO [arr for voc & orch] ("Vol 3") † Sym 2; G. Mahler:Kindertotenlieder RCAV (Gold Seal) ▲ 61891 (11.97)

C. Davis (cnd), Bavarian RSO, Bavarian Radio Chorus † Alto Rhap, Op. 53; Gesäng der Parzen, Op. 89; Marienlieder (7), Op. 22; Nänie, Op. 82 RCAV (Red Seal) ▲ 61201 (16.97)

K. Masur (cnd), New York PO, Westminster Sym Choir † Sym 4 TELC ▲ 13695 (16.97)

H. Rilling (cnd), Stuttgart Bach Collegium, Gächinger Kantorei HANS (Exclusive) ▲ 98122 [DDD] (15.97)

R. Shaw (cnd), Atlanta SO, Atlanta Sym Chorus [GER] † Alto Rhap, Op. 53; Gesäng der Parzen, Op. 89; Nänie, Op. 82 TEL ▲ 80176 [DDD] (16.97)

G. Sinopoli (cnd), Czech PO, Prague Phil Chorus ("The Complete Brahms Edition, Vol. 8:Works for Chorus & Orchestra") † Alto Rhap, Op. 53; Deutsches Requiem, Op. 45; Gesäng der Parzen, Op. 89; Nänie, Op. 82; Rinaldo, Op. 50; Triumphlied, Op. 55 DGRM 3-▲ 449651

Serenade No. 1 in D for Orchestra, Op. 11 (1857-58)

C. Abbado (cnd), Berlin PO ("Complete Brahms Edition, Vol. 1:Orchestral Works") † Academic Festival Ov, Op. 80; Hungarian Dances Orch; Serenade 2 Orch, Op. 16; Syms (comp); Tragic Ov, Op. 81; Vars on a Theme by Haydn DGRM 5-▲ 449601 (64.97)

H. Abendroth (cnd), Berlin RSO *(rec Mar, 1953)* † R. Schumann:Sym 1; Sym 4; P. Tchaikovsky:Vars on a Rococo Theme, Op. 33; R. Wagner:Wesendonck Songs MUA 2-▲ 1038 [AAD] (31.97)

D. Avalos (cnd), Philharmonia Orch † Hungarian Dances Orch; Serenade 2 Orch, Op. 16 ASVQ ▲ 6216 (10.97)

J. Bělohlávek (cnd), Czech PO ("Serenades") † Serenade 2 Orch, Op. 16; Fibich:Fall of Arkona (ov); Komenský, Op. 34; Toman & the Wood Nymph, Op. 49; Záboj, Slavoj & Luděk, Op. 37; A. Roussel:Evocations; J. Suk:Praga; Summer's Tale, Op. 29 SUR ▲ 111823 [AAD]

▲ = CD ♦ = Enhanced CD △ = MD ▮ = Cassette Tape ▯ = DCC

BRAHMS, JOHANNES (cont.)

Serenade No. 1 in D for Orchestra, Op. 11 (1857-58) (cont.)

G. Bertini (cnd), Vienna SO † Serenade 2 Orch, Op. 16 ORF ▲ 8101 [ADD] (18.97)

D. Bostock (cnd), Bohemia CO † Serenade 2 Orch, Op. 16 CLSO ▲ 196 (15.97)

L. Botstein (cnd), American SO, Chelsea Chamber Ensemble [1st version for nonet; reconstrd Alan Boustead] *(rec Feb 24, 1993)* VC ▲ 8049 [DDD] (13.97)

A. Boult (cnd), London PO † Academic Festival Ov, Op. 80; Alto Rhap, Op. 53; Serenade 2 Orch, Op. 16; Tragic Ov, Op. 81; Vars on a Theme by Haydn EMIC (Doublefforte) 2-▲ 68655 (16.97)

D. Joeres (cnd), West German Sinfonia *(rec German Radio Cologne, June 1992)* † Serenade 2 Orch, Op. 16 INMP ▲ 2046 (9.97)

I. Kertész (cnd), Vienna PO † Sym 3; Sym 4 PLON 2-▲ 48200 (17.97)

Y. Levi (cnd), Atlanta SO *(rec 1993)* † Vars on a Theme by Haydn TEL ▲ 80349 [DDD] (16.97)

M. Lipovšek (mez), L. Hager (cnd), Luxembourg Radio-TV SO, L. Hager (cnd), Luxembourg RSO, Friedrich von Spee Male Voice Choir *(rec Feb-Mar 1983)* † Alto Rhap, Op. 53 FORL ▲ 16671 [DDD] (16.97)

S. Matthies (pno), C. Köhn (pno) † Serenade 2 Orch, Op. 16 NXIN ▲ 8553726 [DDD] (5.97)

R. Muti (cnd), La Scala Orch *(rec July 8-12, 1993)* † E. Elgar:In the South, Op. 50 SNYC ▲ 57973 [DDD] (16.97)

H. Peter (pno), V. Stenzl (pno) [arr J. Brahms for pno 4-hands] *(rec live)* † Hungarian Dances Pno 4-Hands; Vars in E♭ on Theme of R. Schumann Pno 4-Hands, Op. 23 ARSM ▲ 1130 [DDD] (17.97)

A. Rahbari (cnd), Belgian Radio-TV Orch *(rec June 1990)* † Sym 1 NXIN ▲ 550280 [DDD] (5.97)

A. Rahbari (cnd), Brussels BRTN PO *(rec Brussels, June 1990)* † P. Tchaikovsky:Serenade Strs, Op. 48 NXIN ▲ 8553227 [DDD] (5.97)

G. Schwarz (cnd), Los Angeles CO NON ▲ 79065 [DDD] (16.97)

M. T. Thomas (cnd), London SO † Academic Festival Ov, Op. 80; Tragic Ov, Op. 81 SNYC ▲ 45932 [DDD] (16.97)

I. M. Witoschynskyj (pno) *(rec Mar 15-17, 1996)* ("Clara Schumann & Her Family") † Bargiel:Bagatelles, Op. 4; Characteristic Pieces, Op. 1; Fant Pieces, Op. 9; R. Schumann:Albumblätter, Op. 124; Liederkreis, Op. 39; C. Schumann:Pièces fugitives, Op. 15; Romances Pno, Op. 21; Songs; R. Schumann:Studies Canon Form, Op. 56 MDG ▲ 6040729 [DDD] (17.97)

artists unknown—Menuetto I & II ("Brahms for Book Lovers") † Music of Brahms; Son 2 Vn, Op. 100 PPHI (Set Your Life to Music) ▲ 462561 (9.97) ▮ 462561 (5.98)

Serenade No. 2 in A for Orchestra, Op. 16 (1858-59)

C. Abbado (cnd), Berlin PO ("Complete Brahms Edition, Vol. 1:Orchestral Works") † Academic Festival Ov, Op. 80; Hungarian Dances Orch; Serenade 1 Orch, Op. 11; Syms (comp); Tragic Ov, Op. 81; Vars on a Theme by Haydn DGRM 5-▲ 449601 (64.97)

D. Avalos (cnd), Philharmonia Orch † Hungarian Dances Orch; Serenade 1 Orch, Op. 11 ASVQ ▲ 6216 (10.97)

J. Bělohlávek (cnd), Czech PO ("Serenades") † Serenade 1 Orch, Op. 11; Fibich:Fall of Arkona (ov); Komenský, Op. 34; Toman & the Wood Nymph, Op. 49; Záboj, Slavoj & Luděk, Op. 37; A. Roussel:Evocations; J. Suk:Praga; Summer's Tale, Op. 29 SUR ▲ 111823 [AAD]

L. Bernstein (cnd), New York PO ("Bernstein: The Royal Edition") † Sym 1 SNYC ▲ 47536 [ADD] (10.97)

G. Bertini (cnd), Vienna SO † Serenade 1 Orch, Op. 11 ORF ▲ 8101 [ADD] (18.97)

D. Bostock (cnd), Bohemia CO † Serenade 1 Orch, Op. 11 CLSO ▲ 196 (15.97)

A. Boult (cnd), London PO † Academic Festival Ov, Op. 80; Alto Rhap, Op. 53; Serenade 1 Orch, Op. 11; Tragic Ov, Op. 81; Vars on a Theme by Haydn EMIC (Doublefforte) 2-▲ 68655 (16.97)

D. Joeres (cnd), West German Sinfonia *(rec German Radio Cologne)* † Serenade 1 Orch, Op. 11 INMP ▲ 2046 (9.97)

I. Kertész (cnd), Vienna PO † Sym 1; Sym 2; Vars on a Theme by Haydn PLON 2-▲ 48197 (17.97)

S. Matthies (pno), C. Köhn (pno) † Serenade 1 Orch, Op. 11 NXIN ▲ 8553726 [DDD] (5.97)

A. Rahbari (cnd), Belgian Radio-TV Orch *(rec Mar 1990)* † Sym 2 NXIN ▲ 550279 [DDD] (5.97)

L. Slatkin (cnd), St. Louis SO † Academic Festival Ov, Op. 80; Vars on a Theme by Haydn RCAV (Red Seal) ▲ 7920 [DDD] (16.97)

M. T. Thomas (cnd), London SO † Hungarian Dances Orch; Vars on a Theme by Haydn SNYC ▲ 47195 (16.97)

A. Toscanini (cnd), NBC SO ("The Toscanini Collection, Vol. 26") † Sym 1 RCAV (Gold Seal) ▲ 60277 (11.97)

Sextet in B♭ for Strings, Op. 18 (1858-60)

Academy of St. Martin in the Fields Chamber Ensemble † Sextet Strs, Op. 36 CHN ▲ 9151 [DDD] (16.97)

C. Aronowitz (va), A. Pleeth (vc), Amadeus String Quartet † Qnt Cl; Qnt Pno, Op. 34; Qnt 1 Strs, Op. 88; Qnt 2 Strs, Op. 111; Sextet Strs, Op. 36 DEUT 3-▲ 19875 [ADD] (34.97)

A. Bylsma (vc), Smithsonian Chamber Players, L'Archibudelli † Sextet Strs, Op. 36 SNYC (Vivarte) ▲ 68252 (16.97)

A. Hobday (va), A. Pini (vc), Pro Arte String Quartet *(rec 1935)* † F. Schubert:Qnt in C Strs, D.956 BID ▲ 93

G. Konrád (va), E. Banda (vc), Bartók String Quartet *(rec 1971-74)* † Qnt 1 Strs, Op. 88; Qnt 2 Strs, Op. 111; Qts Strs (comp); Sextet Strs, Op. 36 HUN 3-▲ 11591 [ADD]

Les Musiciens † Trio 3 Pno, Op. 101; Mendelssohn (-Bartholdy):Son 1 Vc, Op. 45; Son 2 Vc, Op. 58; F. Schubert:Ländler Pno; Son Arpeggione, D.821; Waltzes Pno HMA 3-▲ 290882 (17.97)

C. Lin (vn), I. Stern (vn), J. Laredo (va), M. Tree (va), Y.-Y. Ma (vc), S. Robinson (vc) † Sextet Strs, Op. 36; Theme & Vars Pno SNYC 2-▲ 45820 (31.97)

Parnassus Trio [arr Theodor Kirchner for pno trio] ("Complete Piano Trios, Vol. 2") † Trio 2 Pno, Op. 87 MDG ▲ 3030656 (17.97)

R. Pasquier (vn), R. Oleg (vn), J. Dupouy (va), B. Pasquier (va), R. Pidoux (vc), E. Péclard (vc) HAM ▲ 1901073 (9.97)

Raphael Ensemble † Sextet Strs, Op. 36 HYP ▲ 66276 (18.97)

N. Salerno-Sonnenberg (vn), B. Kim (vn), M. Kawasaki (va), R. Sasaki (va), M. Lidström (vc), E. Kim (vc) *(rec Harris Concert Hall Aspen, June 30-July 3, 1997)* ("Night & Day: Music from the Aspen Festival") † Borodin:Qt 2 Strs; F. Kreisler:Qt Strs; Strauss (II):Fledermaus (ov) EMIC ▲ 56481 [DDD] (16.97)

I. Stern (vn), A. Schneider (vn), M. Katims (va), M. Thomas (va), P. Casals (vc), M. Foley (vc) *(rec 1952)* SNYC (Portrait) ▲ 44851 [ADD] (10.97)

I. Stern (vn), A. Schneider (vn), M. Katims (va), M. Thomas (va), P. Casals (vc), M. Foley (vc) *(rec Prades France, June 23-July 3, 1952)* † Trio 1 Pno, Op. 8 SNYC (The Casals Edition) ▲ 58994 [ADD] (10.97)

Stuttgart String Sextet *(rec Nov 1989)* † Sextet Strs, Op. 36 NXIN ▲ 550436 [DDD] (5.97)

Trio Stradivari [arr T. Kirchner for pno trio] *(rec Genoa, Dec 1995)* † Sextet Strs, Op. 36 DYNC ▲ 158 [DDD] (17.97)

Vienna String Sextet † R. Strauss:Capriccio (sels) CAMA ▲ 93 [DDD] (18.97)

Sextet in G for Strings, Op. 36 (1864-65)

Academy of St. Martin in the Fields Chamber Ensemble † Sextet Strs, Op. 18 CHN ▲ 9151 [DDD] (16.97)

C. Aronowitz (va), A. Pleeth (vc), Amadeus String Quartet † Qnt Cl; Qnt Pno, Op. 34; Qnt 1 Strs, Op. 88; Qnt 2 Strs, Op. 111; Sextet Strs, Op. 18 DEUT 3-▲ 19875 [ADD] (34.97)

A. Bylsma (vc), Smithsonian Chamber Players, L'Archibudelli † Sextet Strs, Op. 18 SNYC (Vivarte) ▲ 68252 (16.97)

P. Carmirelli (vn), J. Toth (vn), P. Naegele (va), C. Levine (va), F. Arico (vc), D. Reichenberger (vc) † Trio Hn, Op. 40 SNYC ▲ 46249 [ADD] (10.97)

A. Kavafian (vn), V. Holek (vn), C. Phelps (va), J. Klusoň (va), M. Kaňka (vc), P. Rejto (vc) *(rec Tucson, AZ, Mar 1996)* ("The 3rd Tucson Winter Chamber Music Festival, Vol. 2") † A. Dvořák:Qnt Pno, Op. 81 ARIZ ▲ 96102 [DDD] (16.97)

A. Kavafian (vn), B. Kim (vn), C. Phelps (va), R. Kelly (va), P. Rejto (vc), C. Karr (vc) *(rec Tuscon Winter Chamber Festival, Mar 11, 1994)* † D. Shostakovich:Trio 2 Pno, Op. 67 ARIZ ▲ 94101 [DDD] (16.97)

G. Konrád (va), E. Banda (vc), Bartók String Quartet *(rec 1971-74)* † Qnt 1 Strs, Op. 88; Qnt 2 Strs, Op. 111; Qts Strs (comp); Sextet Strs, Op. 18 HUN 3-▲ 11591 [ADD]

C. Lin (vn), I. Stern (vn), J. Laredo (va), M. Tree (va), Y.-Y. Ma (vc), S. Robinson (vc) † Sextet Strs, Op. 18; Theme & Vars Pno SNYC 2-▲ 45820 (31.97)

Parnassus Trio [arr T. Kirchner for pno trio] ("Complete Piano Trios, Vol 1") † Trio 1 Pno, Op. 8 MDG ▲ 3030655 (17.97)

Raphael Ensemble † Sextet Strs, Op. 18 HYP ▲ 66276 (18.97)

P. Rybar (vn), C. Dahinden (vn), H. Wigand (va), O. Kromer (va), R. Jucker (vc), A. Tusa (vc) † Qnt Pno, Op. 34; Busoni:Son 2 Vn, Op. 36a DORO 2-▲ 4007 [ADD] (32.97)

Stuttgart String Sextet *(rec Nov 1989)* † Sextet Strs, Op. 18 NXIN ▲ 550436 [DDD] (5.97)

Trio Stradivari [arr T. Kirchner for pno trio] *(rec Genoa, Dec 1995)* † Sextet Strs, Op. 18 DYNC ▲ 158 [DDD] (17.97)

Sonatas (2) in e & F for Cello & Piano, Opp. 38 (1862-65) & 99 (1885)

A. Bylsma (vc), L. Orkis (pno) † R. Schumann:Stücke im Volkston, Op. 102 SNYC (Vivarte) ▲ 68249 (16.97)

A. Diaz (vc), S. Sanders (pno) *(rec 1991)* † A. Dvořák:Silent Woods Vc & Pno, Op. 68/5 DOR ▲ 90165 [DDD] (16.97)

P. Fournier (vc), J. Fonda (pno) † E. Grieg:Son Vc STRV ▲ 33320 [ADD] (16.97)

M. Fukačová (vc), I. Klánský (pno) † Son Vc in D KPT ▲ 32027 [DDD]

K. Georgian (vc), P. Gililov (pno) ("Complete Cello Sonatas") † Son Vc in D BNT ▲ 14

C. Henkel (vc), E. Westenholz (pno) BIS ▲ 192 (17.97)

BRAHMS, JOHANNES (cont.)

Sonatas (2) in e & F for Cello & Piano, Opp. 38 (1862-65) & 99 (1885) (cont.)

S. Isserlis (vc), B. Evans (pno) HYP ▲ 66159 [DDD] (18.97)

M. Kliegel (vc), K. Merscher (pno) *(rec Nov 1992)* † Son Vc in D NXIN ▲ 550656 [DDD] (5.97)

Y.-Y. Ma (vc), E. Ax (pno) † Son 3 Vn, Op. 108 SNYC ▲ 48191 [DDD] (16.97) COL △ 48191 [DDD]

G. Piatigorsky (vc), A. Rubinstein (pno) *(rec American Legion Hall Hollywood, Oct 11, 1966)* † Pno Music (misc colls) RCAV (Gold Seal) ▲ 62592 (11.97)

J. D. Pré (vc), D. Barenboim (pno) EMIC (Studio) ▲ 63298 [ADD] (11.97)

N. Rosen (vc), D. Stevenson (pno) ("Rosen Plays Brahms") † Mendelssohn (-Bartholdy):Lied Vc; R. Schumann:Fantasiestücke Cl, Op. 73 JMR ▲ 5 [DDD] (16.97)

L. Rose (vc), J. Pommier (pno) *(rec 1982-83)* † Scherzo Vn; Sons Vn (comp) VCL 2-▲ 61415 [DDD] (11.97)

M. Rostropovich (vc), R. Serkin (pno) DEUT ▲ 10510 [DDD] (16.97)

H. Schiff (vc), G. Oppitz (pno) PPHI ▲ 456402 (16.97)

C. Starck (vc), C. Eschenbach (pno) *(rec Paris, Oct 1989)* ("The 2 Cello Sonatas") CLAV ▲ 9005 [DDD] (16.97)

P. Wispelwey (vc) ("The Complete Performer: Chamber Music Masterpieces") † Beethoven:Vars Vc; F. Schubert:Qnt in C Strs, D.956; Vivaldi:Sons Vc CCL 4-▲ 697 (36.97)

P. Wispelwey (vc), P. Komen (pno) *(rec Sept 1992)* CCL ▲ 5493 [DDD] (18.97)

D. Yablonski (vc), O. Yablonskaya (pno) DI ▲ 920186 [DDD] (5.97)

Sonata No. 1 in e for Cello & Piano, Op. 38 (1862-65)

P. Bruns (vc), O. Tverskaya (pno) † Son 2 Vc, Op. 99 OPUS ▲ 30144 (18.97)

K. B. Dinitzen (vc), E. Westenholz (pno) † R. Schumann:Adagio & Allegro Hn, Op. 70; R. Strauss:Son Vc, Op. 6 KPT ▲ 32172 [DDD]

E. Feuermann (vc), T. Van der Pas (pno) *(rec 1934)* † A. Dvořák:Con Vc; F. Schubert:Son Arpeggione, D.821 ENT (Strings) ▲ 99328 (16.97)

E. Feuermann (vc), T. Van der Pas (pno) ("Heifetz & Feuermann Play Brahms") † Con Vn & Vc, Op. 102; Son 2 Vn, Op. 100 PHS ▲ 9293 (17.97)

A. Gerhard (vc), M. Groh (pno) † Son Vc in D; Son 2 Vc, Op. 99 HAM (Les Nouveaux Interprétes) ▲ 911641 (12.97)

C. Hermann (vc), S. Sasaki (pno) ("Brahms & His Friends, Vol. 2") † Herzogenberg:Duo Vc; Röntgen:Son Vc, Op. 3; R. Schumann:Adagio & Allegro Hn, Op. 70 DVX ▲ 29407 (16.97)

R. Metzmacher (vc), E. Steen-Nökleberg (pno) † Son 2 Vc, Op. 99 BRIO ▲ 101 (16.97)

G. Piatigorsky (vc), I. Newton (pno), A. Rubinstein (pno), Solomon (pno) † Beethoven:Son 1 Vc, Op. 5/1; Son 2 Vc, Op. 5/2; Son 3 Vc, Op. 69; Son 4 Vc; Son 5 Vc TES ▲ 2158 (33.97)

G. Piatigorsky (vc), A. Rubenstein (pno) *(rec 1932 & 1936)* ("Arthur Rubenstein Plays Brahms Chamber Music") † Qt 1 Pno, Op. 25; Son 3 Vn, Op. 108 ENPL (Piano Library) ▲ 233 (13.97)

G. Piatigorsky (vc), A. Rubinstein (pno) *(rec 1936 from HMV DB 2952-54)* † Beethoven:Son 2 Vc, Op. 5/2; R. Schumann:Con Vc PHS ▲ 9447 [AAD] (18.97)

J. Starker (vc), G. Sebok (pno) † Son 2 Vc, Op. 99; Mendelssohn (-Bartholdy):Son 2 Vc, Op. 58 MRCR ▲ 34377 (11.97)

J. Vogler (vc), B. Canino (pno) *(rec Hamburg, Germany, Dec 1997)* † Songs (5), Op. 105; Songs (5), Op. 49; Songs (5), Op. 71; Songs (5), Op. 94; Songs (6), Op. 3; Songs (6), Op. 86; F. Schubert:Son Arpeggione, D.821 BER ▲ 1179 [DDD] (16.97)

Sonata No. 2 in F for Cello & Piano, Op. 99 (1885)

P. Bruns (vc), O. Tverskaya (pno) † Son 1 Vc, Op. 38 OPUS ▲ 30144 (18.97)

P. Casals (vc), M. Horszowski (pno) *(rec 1936 for HMV)* † Con Vn & Vc, Op. 102 PHS ▲ 9363 [AAD] (17.97)

P. Casals (vc), M. Horszowski (pno) *(rec 1936)* ("Pablo Casals Portrait") † J. S. Bach:Suites Vc; Beethoven:Son 4 Vc IN ▲ 1308 (15.97)

P. Casals (vc), M. Horszowski (pno) *(rec 1936-45)* † Bruch:Kol Nidrei, Op. 47; E. Elgar:Con Vc ENT (Strings) ▲ 99329 (16.97)

P. Casals (vc), M. Horszowski (pno) † Boccherini:Sons (34) Vc Bc; P. Casals:Trans MTAL ▲ 48030 (6.97)

P. Casals (vc), M. Horszowski (pno) ("The Great Concerto Recordings") † Con Vn & Vc, Op. 102; Bruch:Kol Nidrei, Op. 47; A. Dvořák:Con Vc; E. Elgar:Con Vc MPLY 2-▲ 2006 (16.97)

P. Casals (vc), M. Horszowski (pno) *(rec London, England, Nov 28, 1936)* † J. S. Bach:Suites Vc; Beethoven:Minuets (6) Orch, WoO 10; Son 3 Vc, Op. 69 EMIC ▲ 67008 (m) [ADD] (11.97)

P. Fournier (vc), M. Hess (pno) *(rec 1959)* ("Hess & Fournier in a New York Sonata Recital") † J. S. Bach:Sons Vl; Beethoven:Son 4 Vc; Vars Vc on "Ein Mädchen oder Weibchen", Op. 66; W. A. Mozart:Gigue Pno, K.574; Rondo Pno, K.485 RELE ▲ 1895 [ADD]

A. Gerhard (vc), M. Groh (pno) † Son Vc in D; Son 1 Vc, Op. 38 HAM (Les Nouveaux Interprétes) ▲ 911641 (12.97)

P. Hörr (vc), S. Sasaki (pno) † Herzogenberg:Legenden, Op. 62; G. Jenner:Son Vc DVX ▲ 29106 [DDD] (16.97)

R. Metzmacher (vc), E. Steen-Nökleberg (pno) † Son 1 Vc, Op. 38 BRIO ▲ 101 (16.97)

J. du Pré (vc), E. Lush (pno) *(rec Mar 17, 1963)* † J. S. Bach:Suites Vc; B. Britten:Son Vc; F. Couperin:Nouveaux Concerts; M. de Falla:Suite populaire espagnole; G. F. Handel:Con in g EMIC 2-▲ 73377 [ADD] (16.97)

J. Starker (vc), G. Sebok (pno) † Son 1 Vc, Op. 38; Mendelssohn (-Bartholdy):Son 2 Vc, Op. 58 MRCR ▲ 34377 (11.97)

Sonata in D for Cello & Piano [arr from *Sonata No. 1 in G for Violin, Op. 78*, not by Brahms], "Regenlieder"

M. Fukačová (vc), I. Klánský (pno) † Sons Vc (comp) KPT ▲ 32027 [DDD]

K. Georgian (vc), P. Gililov (pno) ("Complete Cello Sonatas") † Sons Vc (comp) BNT ▲ 14

A. Gerhard (vc), M. Groh (pno) † Son 1 Vc, Op. 38; Son 2 Vc, Op. 99 HAM (Les Nouveaux Interprétes) ▲ 911641 (12.97)

S. Heled (vc), J. Zak (pno) † Magnard:Son Vc CLSO (Simca Heled Collection) ▲ 243 (15.97)

M. Kliegel (vc), K. Merscher (pno) *(rec Nov 1992)* † Sons Vc (comp) NXIN ▲ 550656 [DDD] (5.97)

Phillips-Blumenthal Duo † J. Haydn:Qts (6) Strs, H.III/31-36, Op. 20; Mendelssohn (-Bartholdy):Vars concertantes, Op. 17 GAS (Silver) ▲ 2006 [DDD] (7.97)

Sonatas (2) in f & E♭ for Clarinet (or Viola) & Piano, Op. 120/1 & 2 (1894)

Amici Chamber Ensemble members *(rec Toronto, Canada, Dec 10-11, 1996 & Jan 3-4, 1997)* ("In Brahms' Apartment") † Trio Cl SUMM ▲ 219 [DDD] (16.97)

A. Carbonare (cl), A. Dindo (pno) *(rec Milan, Oct 1994)* † Trio Cl AG ▲ 8 [DDD] (18.97)

A. Hacker (cl), R. Burnett (pno) [period instrs] † Trio Cl AMON ▲ 37 [DDD] (16.97)

P. Hatch (va), M. Wagemans (pno) *(rec Elder Forest, CA)* PROD ▲ 6215 [DDD] (17.97)

P. Hörr (vc), J. Alexander (pno) [trans Hörr for vc & pno] ("Brahms & His Friends, Vol. 5") † R. Schumann:Fantasiestücke Cl, Op. 73 DVX ▲ 29609 (16.97)

N. Imai (va), R. Vignoles (pno) † R. Schumann:Märchenbilder, Op. 113 CHN ▲ 8550 [DDD] (16.97)

D. Klöcker (cl), W. Genuit (pno) † Trio Hn, Op. 40 AART ▲ 47368 (10.97)

D. Klöcker (cl), C. Tanski (pno) *(rec Oct 8-10, 1996 & Jan 29, 1997)* † Ernste Gesänge, Op. 121 MDG ▲ 3010765 [DDD] (17.97)

K. Leister (cl), F. Bognár (pno) † Trio Cl NIMB ▲ 5600 [DDD] (16.97)

K. Leister (cl), D. Levine (pno) ("Complete Clarinet Sonatas") CAMA ▲ 75 [DDD]

K. Leister (cl), G. Oppitz (pno) ORF ▲ 86841 (18.97)

G. Peyer (cl), G. Pryor (pno) CHN ▲ 8563 [DDD] (16.97)

K. Pfister (sax), G. Wyss (pno) [trans for sax & pno] † R. Schumann:Adagio & Allegro Hn, Op. 70; Fantasiestücke Cl, Op. 73 GALL ▲ 931 [DDD] (18.97)

G. Pieterson (cl), H. Menuhin (pno) † Qts Strs (comp) PPHI (Duo) 2-▲ 456320 (17.97)

J. Rubenstein (vn), D. Ouziel (pno) [trans Brahms for vn & pno] *(rec Brussels, Belgium, 1997)* † FAE Son Vn; Sons Vn (comp) PAVA 2-▲ 7398 [DDD] (21.97)

C. Schiller (va), M. Mares (pno) † Intermezzos (3) Pno, Op. 117 NOVA ▲ 150137 (16.97)

P. Schmidl (cl), B. Canino (pno) † A. Berg:Pieces Cl, Op. 5; R. Schumann:Fantasiestücke Cl, Op. 73 CAMA ▲ 454 [DDD] (18.97)

D. Shifrin (cl), C. Rosenberger (pno) † R. Schumann:Fantasiestücke Cl, Op. 73 DLS ▲ 3025 [DDD] (14.97)

P. Silverthorne (va), J. Jacobson (pno) † Songs (2), Op. 91 MER ▲ 84190 (16.97)

V. Soames (cl), J. Higgins (pno) ("Music for Clarinet") † Trio Cl CLCL ▲ 16 [DDD] (17.97)

R. Stoltzman (cl), R. Goode (pno) RCAV (Gold Seal) ▲ 60036 [DDD] (11.97)

M. Tanamura (va), T. Hironaka (pno) ("Brahms: Complete Viola Sonatas") † A. Dietrich:Allegro Vn CAMA ▲ 377

N. Thomsen (cl), E. Westenholz (pno) † N. W. Gade:Fantasistykker, Op. 43 KPT ▲ 32078 [DDD]

G. Tirincanti (cl), M. Deoriti (pno) † Trio Cl STRV ▲ 27 [DDD] (16.97)

B. Westphal (va), U. Oppens (pno) † Scherzo Vn BRID ▲ 9021 [DDD] (17.97)

H. Wright (cl), P. Serkin (pno) *(rec Aug 1992)* † R. Schumann:Fantasiestücke Cl, Op. 73 BOST ▲ 1005 (15.97)

P. Zukerman (va), D. Barenboim (pno) † Sons Vn (comp) DEUT (2-Fers) 2-▲ 453121 [ADD] (17.97)

P. Zukerman (va), M. Neikrug (pno) † Songs (2), Op. 91 RCAV (Red Seal) ▲ 61276 (16.97)

BRAHMS, JOHANNES (cont.)

Sonata No. 1 in f for Clarinet (or Viola) & Piano, Op. 120/1 (1894)

L. Aabo (cl), S. Balshem (pno) *(rec Aarhus Denmark, July 1995)* † M. Reger:Son Cl; Winding:Fants Cl, Op. 19 ROND ▲ 8348 [DDD]

J. Cohler (cl), J. Gordon (pno) *(rec May 29-30, 1992)* ("Cohler on Clarinet") † Bärmann:Qnt 3 Cl & Str Qt, Op. 23; S. Sargon:Deep Ellum Nights; C. M. von Weber:Grand Duo Concertant, J.204 ONGA ▲ 101 [DDD] (16.97)

V. Hagen (va), P. Gulda (pno) † Son 2 Cl; Songs (2), Op. 91 DGRM ▲ 453421 [DDD]

H. D. Klaus (cl), N. Barrett (pno) *(rec England, May 1997)* † Son 2 Cl; H. Gál:Son Cl CAMM ▲ 130052 [DDD] (16.97)

K. Leister (cl)—Andante un poco adagio ("Intimate Conversations") † Music of Brahms; Son 3 Vn, Op. 108 PPHI (Night Moods) ▲ 453905 [DDD] (9.97)

H. Lindemann (va), B. Martin (pno) ("Hommage a Primrose") † J. Joachim:Vars on a Theme Va, Op. 10; Paganini:Caprices Vn, M.S. 25; S. Rachmaninoff:Vocalise; T. A. Vitali:Chaconne Vn; Wieniawski:Etude-caprices Vn, Op. 18 TACE ▲ 45

W. Ludwig (bn), A. Epperson (pno) [trans for bn & pno] † S. Prokofiev:Son Fl; R. Schumann:Fantasiestücke Cl, Op. 73 CENT ▲ 2130 (16.97)

P. Meyer (cl), F. Duchable (pno)—Vivace *(rec Corseaux, Switzerland, Oct 1989)* ("The Magic of the Clarinet") † Son 2 Cl; Bruch:Pieces Cl, Op. 83; Debussy:Première rapsodie Cl; W. A. Mozart:Con Cl, K.622; C. M. von Weber:Con 1 Cl, Op. 73; Con 2 Cl, Op. 74; Grand Duo Concertant, J.204 ERAT ▲ 94679 (9.97)

M. Portal (cl), G. Pludermacher (pno) † Son 2 Cl HMA ▲ 190904 (9.97)

W. Primrose (va), W. Kapell (pno) † Son 2 Cl; A. Benjamin:Elegy, Waltz & Toccata; R. Harris:Soliloquy & Dance; F. Kreisler:Praeludium & Allegro Va PHS ▲ 9253 (17.97)

W. Primrose (va), W. Kappell (pno) *(rec May 1946)* † Alto Rhap, Op. 53; Son 2 Cl; Songs; Songs (2), Op. 91 BID ▲ 150 [AAD] (16.97)

W. Strehle (va), K. Wisniewska (pno) † A. Dvořák:Sonatina Vn, Op. 100; P. Hindemith:Duet Va & Vc; Son Va; Trauermusik NIMB ▲ 5473 [DDD] (16.97)

L. Verney (va), N. Angelich (pno) † Son 2 Cl HAM (Les Nouveaux Interprètes) ▲ 911565 (12.97)

Wallfisch Duo ("Duo Wallfisch at Prades Festival") † Mendelssohn (-Bartholdy):Son Va; R. Schumann:Märchenbilder, Op. 113 BAYE ▲ 200050 [AAD] (17.97)

artists unknown—Allegro grazioso *(rec United States of America)* ("Brahms for Book Lovers") † Music of Brahms; Son 1 Vn, Op. 78; Son 2 Vn, Op. 100; Trio 3 Pno, Op. 101 PPHI (Set Your Life to Music) ▮ 462561 (5.98) ▲ 462561 (9.97)

Sonata No. 2 in E♭ for Clarinet (or Viola) & Piano, Op. 120/2 (1894)

G. Amann (cl), R. Hoffmann (pno) *(rec July 1996)* ("German Works for Clarinet & Piano") † N. Burgmüller:Duo Cl & Pno, Op. 15; P. Hindemith:Son Cl; C. M. von Weber:Grand Duo Concertant, J.204 LAVE ▲ 100245 [DDD] (17.97)

J. Cohler (cl) ("More Cohler on Clarinet") † D. Milhaud:Sonatina Cl, Op. 100; F. Poulenc:Son Cl & Pno; R. Schumann:Fantasiestücke Cl, Op. 73; I. Stravinsky:Pieces Cl ONGA ▲ 102 (16.97)

Emory Chamber Music Society of Atlanta members ("Chamber Music of Johannes Brahms") † Hungarian Dances Pno 4-Hands; Trio Hn, Op. 40 ACAD ▲ 20033 [DDD] (16.97)

B. Goodman (cl), N. Reisenberg (pno) ("Benny Goodman: Clarinet Classics") † B. Bartók:Contrasts, Sz.111; Beethoven:Vars Ww on La ci darem la mano, WoO 28; Debussy:Première rapsodie Cl; W. A. Mozart:Qnt Cl, K.581; C. M. von Weber:Divert assai facile, Op. 38 PHS ▲ 57 (17.97)

V. Hagen (va), P. Gulda (pno) † Son 1 Cl; Songs (2), Op. 91 DGRM ▲ 453421 [DDD]

H. D. Klaus (cl), N. Barrett (pno) *(rec England, May 1997)* † Son 1 Cl; H. Gál:Son Cl CAMM ▲ 130052 [DDD] (16.97)

H. Lindemann (va), B. Martin (pno) † J. S. Bach:Sons & Partitas Vn; A. Bax:Son Va; J. N. Hummel:Son Va TACE ▲ 35

P. Meyer (cl), F. Duchable (pno)—Allegro amabile; Allegro amabile *(rec Corseaux, Switzerland, Oct 1989)* ("The Magic of the Clarinet") † Son 1 Cl; Bruch:Pieces Cl, Op. 83; Debussy:Première rapsodie Cl; W. A. Mozart:Con Cl, K.622; C. M. von Weber:Con 1 Cl, Op. 73; Con 2 Cl, Op. 74; Grand Duo Concertant, J.204 ERAT ▲ 94679 (9.97)

M. Portal (cl), G. Pludermacher (pno) † Son 1 Cl HMA ▲ 190904 (9.97)

W. Primrose (va), G. Moore (pno) † Son 1 Cl; A. Benjamin:Elegy, Waltz & Toccata; R. Harris:Soliloquy & Dance; F. Kreisler:Praeludium & Allegro Va PHS ▲ 9253 (17.97)

W. Primrose (va), G. Moore (pno) *(rec Sept 1937)* † Alto Rhap, Op. 53; Son 1 Cl; Songs; Songs (2), Op. 91 BID ▲ 150 [AAD] (16.97)

L. Tertis (va), H. Cohen (pno) *(rec 1933)* † J. S. Bach:Sons & Partitas Vn; A. Bax:Son Va; Delius:Son 2 Vn PHS ▲ 9918 [AAD] (17.97)

L. Verney (va), N. Angelich (pno) † Son 1 Cl HAM (Les Nouveaux Interprètes) ▲ 911565 (12.97)

Sonata No. 1 in C for Piano, Op. 1 (1852-53)

I. Biret (pno) *(rec Nov 1989)* † Son 2 Pno, Op. 2 NXIN ▲ 550351 [DDD] (5.97)

S. Richter (pno) † Son 2 Pno, Op. 2 PRAG ▲ 254059 (18.97)

A. Ugorski (pno) † Son 2 Pno, Op. 2; Son 3 Pno, Op. 5; Studies (5) Pno; Vars & Fugue on a Theme by Handel, Op. 24 DGRM 2-▲ 449182 [DDD]

Sonata No. 2 in f# for Piano, Op. 2 (1852)

I. Biret (pno) *(rec Nov 1989)* † Son 1 Pno, Op. 1 NXIN ▲ 550351 [DDD] (5.97)

H. Grimaud (pno) † R. Schumann:Kreisleriana, Op. 16 DNN ▲ 73336 [DDD] (16.97)

F. F. Guy (pno) ("Veiled Symphonies") † Son 3 Pno, Op. 5 MER ▲ 84351 [DDD] (16.97)

B. Petrushansky (pno) † Ballades (4), Op. 10; Vars in f# on Theme of R. Schumann, Op. 9 AG ▲ 185 (18.97)

S. Richter (pno) † Son 1 Pno, Op. 1 PRAG ▲ 254059 (18.97)

A. Ugorski (pno) † Son 1 Pno, Op. 1; Son 3 Pno, Op. 5; Studies (5) Pno; Vars & Fugue on a Theme by Handel, Op. 24 DGRM 2-▲ 449182 [DDD]

Sonata No. 3 in f for Piano, Op. 5 (1853)

M. Anderson (pno) *(rec Nimbus Foundation Concert Hall, Nov 17-19, 1993)* † Liszt:Années de pèlerinage 2, S.161; R. Schumann:Toccata Pno, Op. 7 NIMB ▲ 5422 [DDD] (16.97)

S. Cherkassky (pno) *(rec Salzburg, Aug 3, 1968)* † J. S. Bach:Partitas Hpd; R. R. Bennett:Studies Pno; Chopin:Preludes (24) Pno, Op. 28; Liszt:Polonaises (2) Pno, S.223 ORFE (Festspiel Dokumente) 2-▲ 431962 [ADD] (32.97)

J. C. Cocarelli (pno) *(rec Fort Worth, TX, 1989)* ("Van Cliburn Retrospective Series, Vol. 6") † S. Barber:Son Pno, Op. 26; Chopin:Scherzos Pno; J. Haydn:Sonatas for Piano; Liszt:Etudes d'exécution transcendante (12), S.139; W. A. Mozart:Son 10 Pno, K.330; R. Schumann:Son 2 Pno, Op. 22 VAIA ▲ 1158 [DDD]

C. Curzon (pno) † Intermezzos (3) Pno, Op. 117; Pieces (4) Pno, Op. 119; F. Schubert:Son Pno, D.960 PLON (The Classic Sound) ▲ 48578 (11.97)

E. Fischer (pno) *(rec 1915-30)* † Pno Music (misc colls); Vars on a Theme by Paganini, Op. 35 NIMB (Grand Piano) ▲ 8806 [DDD] (11.97)

W. Gieseking (pno) *(rec 1939-56)* ("Gieseking Plays Brahms") † Con 2 Pno, Op. 83 ARBT ▲ 103 [ADD] (16.97)

W. Gieseking (pno) *(rec live, 1947)* ("Gieseking, Vol. 1") † Trio 1 Pno, Op. 8 HPC1 ▲ 128 (17.97)

F. F. Guy (pno) ("Veiled Symphonies") † Son 2 Pno, Op. 2 MER ▲ 84351 [DDD] (16.97)

J. Katchen (pno) *(rec 1949)* ("Julius Katchen") † Vars on an Original Theme, Op. 21/1; Balakirev:Islamey; Chopin:Ballade 3 Pno, Op. 47; Fantaisie Pno, Op. 49; C. Franck:Prélude, choral et fugue, M.21; Liszt:Hungarian Rhaps, S.244; Mendelssohn (-Bartholdy):Prelude & Fugue Pno; Rondo capriccioso, Op. 14; N. Rorem:Son 2 Pno PPHI (Great Pianists of the 20th Century) ▲ 456856 (22.97)

W. Kempff (pno) † Ballades (4), Op. 10; Con 1 Pno, Op. 15; Pieces (8) Pno, Op. 76; Rhaps (2) Pno, Op. 79; Scherzo Pno, Op. 4 DEUT (Double) 2-▲ 37374 (17.97)

Z. Kocsis (pno) HUN ▲ 12601 [DDD] (16.97)

A. Kubalek (pno) ("Piano Music of Brahms, Vol. 1") † Intermezzos (3) Pno, Op. 117; Waltzes Pno, Op. 39 DOR ▲ 90141 [DDD] (16.97)

A. Kuerti (pno) † Vars & Fugue on a Theme by Handel, Op. 24 PPR ▲ 224512 (16.97)

A. Laplante (pno) *(rec Boston, MA, Dec 1994)* † Rhaps (2) Pno, Op. 79 FL ▲ 23011 [DDD] (16.97)

D. Lively (pno) † Ballades (4), Op. 10 DI ▲ 920123 [DDD] (5.97)

G. Oppitz (pno) † Pieces (4) Pno, Op. 119 ORF ▲ 20821 [ADD] (18.97)

J. F. Osorio (pno) *(rec SUNY Purchase, New York, United States of America, Feb 2, 1999)* † Fants Pno, Op. 116; Pieces (4) Pno, Op. 119 ARTK ▲ 5 (15.97)

M. Perahia (pno) † Pieces (4) Pno, Op. 119; Pieces (8) Pno, Op. 76; Rhaps (2) Pno, Op. 79 SNYC ▲ 47181 (16.97)

G. Sokolov (pno) † Ballades (4), Op. 10 OPUS ▲ 30103 (18.97)

Solomon (pno) *(rec London, 1952)* † Liszt:Études de concert (3), S.144; Album d'un voyageur, S.156; Rákóczy March Orch, S.117; R. Schumann:Carnaval, Op. 9 TES ▲ 1084 (17.97)

J. Szigeti (vn), E. Petri (pno) *(rec Dec. 8, 1937)* † J. S. Bach:Sons & Partitas Vn; B. Bartók:Hungarian Folktunes, Sz.66; Romanian Folk Dances Vn & Pno BID ▲ 153 [ADD] (16.97)

A. Ugorski (pno) † Son 1 Pno, Op. 1; Son 2 Pno, Op. 2; Studies (5) Pno; Vars & Fugue on a Theme by Handel, Op. 24 DGRM 2-▲ 449182 [DDD]

BRAHMS, JOHANNES (cont.)

Sonata for 2 Pianos [arr Brahms from *Quintet in f for Piano & Strings, Op. 34*], Op. 34b (1864)

V. Afanassiev (pno), V. Suchanov (pno) *(rec Musica-Théâtre La Chaux-de-Fonds, Oct 31-Nov 2, 1994)* † Souvenir de la Russie DNN ▲ 78976 [DDD] (16.97)

M. Argerich (pno), A. Rabinovitch (pno) *(rec Berlin, Apr 1993)* † Vars on a Theme by Haydn; Waltzes Pno, Op. 39 TELC ▲ 92257 [DDD] (16.97)

S. Matthies (pno), C. Köhn (pno) *(rec Sandhausen, Germany, Nov 9-11, 1996)* ("4-Hand Piano Music Vol. 3") † Vars on a Theme by Haydn NXIN ▲ 8553654 [DDD] (5.97)

Mendelssohn Duo *(rec Apr 1997)* † Waltzes Pno, Op. 39 RD ▲ 30105 [DDD] (16.97)

A. Paratore (pno), J. Paratore (pno) † Vars on a Theme by Haydn FWIN ▲ 3009 (16.97)

M. Turkovič (bn), K. Engel (pno) [arr bn & pno] † Ibert:Carignane Bn & Pno; Saint-Saëns:Son Bn; R. Schumann:Romances Ob, Op. 94 CAMA ▲ 66 (18.97)

Sonatas (3) for Violin & Piano, Opp. 78, 100 & 108 (complete)

L. Ambartsumian (vn), E. Rivkin (pno) *(rec Mar 1996)* ACAD ▲ 20055 [DDD] (16.97)

B. Belkin (vn), M. Dalberto (pno) *(rec La Chaux-de-Fonds Switzerland, May 24-29, 1994)* DNN ▲ 78962 [DDD] (16.97)

L. Bobesco (vn), J. Genty (pno) † Scherzo Vn TLNT ▲ 291002 [ADD] (15.97)

S. Elbæk (vn), M. Mogensen (pno) † Scherzo Vn KPT ▲ 32177 [DDD]

C. Feige (vn), S. Redaelli (pno) † Scherzo Vn STRV ▲ 33498 (16.97)

P. Frank (vn), P. Serkin (pno) PLON ▲ 455643 (16.97)

O. Krysa (vn), T. Tchekina (pno) *(rec Moscow Conservatory Small Hall, Jan 1996)* ("The Violin Sonatas") RUS ▲ 10019 [DDD] (11.97)

J. Laredo (vn), J. Pommier (pno) *(rec 1982-83)* † Scherzo Vn; Sons Vc (comp) VCL 2-▲ 61415 [DDD] (11.97)

V. Mullova (vn), P. Anderszewski (pno) ("Complete Violin Sonatas") PPHI ▲ 446709 (16.97)

A.-S. Mutter (vn), A. Weissenberg (pno) EMIC ▲ 72093 [DDD] (6.97)

M. Nicolas (vn), A. Bonatta (pno) VAL ▲ 4709 [DDD]

K. Osostowicz (vn), S. Tomes (pno) HYP ▲ 66465 (18.97)

I. Perlman (vn), D. Barenboim (pno) SNYC ▲ 45819 [DDD] (16.97)

R. Ricci (vn), C. Höfer (pno) *(rec Mozarteum Akademie, Salzburg, Austria, Jun 3, 1996)* ("The Salzburg Series: Brahms") ONEL (Essential Performance Reference) ▲ 10001 [DDD] (7.97)

A. Rosand (vn), H. Sung (pno) *(rec Philadelphia, Jan 1992)* VOXC ▲ 7535 [DDD] (5.97)

J. Rubenstein (vn), D. Ouziel (pno) *(rec Brussels, Belgium, 1997)* † FAE Son Vn; Sons Cl PAVA 2-▲ 7398 [DDD] (21.97)

K. Smietana (vn), C. Palmer (pno) *(rec Feb 1997)* ("The 3 Violin Sonatas") † Son 1 Vn, Op. 78; Son 2 Vn, Op. 100; Son 3 Vn, Op. 108 ASVQ ▲ 6227 [DDD] (10.97)

N. E. Sparf (vn), E. Westenholz (pno) BIS ▲ 212 [AAD] (17.97)

I. Stern (vn), Y. Bronfman (pno) *(rec Dec 18-19, 1991)* SNYC ▲ 53107 [DDD] (16.97)

I. Stern (vn), A. Zakin (pno) ("Isaac Stern: A Life In Music: Vol. 26") SNYC ▲ 64531 [ADD] (10.97)

J. Suk (vn), P. Badura-Skoda (pno) LT ▲ 47 [DDD] (16.97)

V. Vassilev (vn), P. Tan-Nicholson (pno) † Scherzo Vn HAM (Les Nouveaux Interprètes) ▲ 911576 (12.97)

N. Wakabayashi (vn), K. Sturrock (pno) INMP ▲ 1050 [DDD] (11.97)

P. Zukerman (vn), D. Barenboim (pno) † Sons Cl DEUT (2-Fers) 2-▲ 453121 [ADD] (17.97)

Sonata No. 1 in G for Violin & Piano, Op. 78 (1878-79)

A. Busch (vn), B. Seidler-Winkler (pno), R. Serkin (pno) † Hungarian Dances Pno 4-Hands; Son 2 Vn, Op. 100; R. Schumann:Son 1 Vn, Op. 105 PHS ▲ 25 (17.97)

A. Busch (vn), R. Serkin (pno) *(rec 1931)* ("Rudolf Serkin Plays Brahms") † Con 1 Pno, Op. 15 ENPL (Piano Library) ▲ 237 (13.97)

A. Busch (vn), R. Serkin (pno) † Son 2 Vn, Op. 100; J. S. Bach:Sons & Partitas Vn MTAL ▲ 48026 (6.97)

A. Busch (vn), R. Serkin (pno) † Beethoven:Son 5 Vn, Op. 24; Son 7 Vn MTAL ▲ 48022 (6.97)

A. Busch (vn), R. Serkin (pno) † Son 2 Vn, Op. 100; J. S. Bach:Son Vn Bc, BWV 1021; Beethoven:Son 5 Vn, Op. 24; Son 7 Vn; R. Schumann:Son 1 Vn, Op. 105 GRM2 ▲ 78820 (26.97)

K. Chung (vn), P. Frankl (pno) *(rec Bristol, England, Sept 1995)* † Son 2 Vn, Op. 100; Son 3 Vn, Op. 108 EMIC ▲ 56203 [DDD] (16.97)

A. Delmoni (vn), Y. Funahashi (pno) † Beach:Son Vn JMR ▲ 2 (16.97)

B. Huberman (vn), B. Roubakine (pno) *(rec live New York, 1936-44)* ("Huberman in Recital") † J. S. Bach:Sons & Partitas Vn; F. Schubert:Fant Vn, D.934 ARBT ▲ 105 [ADD] (16.97)

O. Kagan (vn), S. Richter (pno) ("The Richter Collection, Vol. 2") † Beethoven:Son 27 Pno, Op. 90; Son 3 Pno, Op. 2/3; Son 4 Pno, Op. 7; Vars & Fugue Pno, Op. 35; Vars Pno on Original Theme, Op. 34; Vars Pno on Original Theme, Op. 76; Chopin:Scherzos Pno; J. Haydn:Son 39 Kbd, H.XVI/24; S. Rachmaninoff:Etudes-tableaux Pno; Preludes Pno; R. Schumann:Bunte Blätter, Op. 99; Symphonic Etudes, Op. 13; D. Shostakovich:Son Vn OLY 5-▲ 5013 [DDD] (64.97)

O. Kagan (vn), S. Richter (pno) *(rec Tchaikovsky Conservatory, Moscow, Russia, May 13, 1988)* † D. Shostakovich:Son Vn LV ▲ 183 (17.97)

E. Lee (vn), N. Padgett (pno) ("In Memory of Rain") † Hungarian Dances Orch SSCL ▲ 15 (16.97)

L. Maazel (vn), H. Franklin (pno) † R. Strauss:Son Vn CMRE ▲ 981002 (16.97)

M. Maisky (vc), P. Gililov (pno) [arr Klengel for vc] ("Songs without Words") † Songs DGRM ▲ 453424 [DDD] (18.97)

I. Perlman (vn), V. Ashkenazy (pno) *(rec London, England, Apr 20-23, 1983)* † Son 2 Vn, Op. 100; Son 3 Vn, Op. 108 EMIC (Great Recordings of the Century) ▲ 66945 [DDD] (11.97)

L. Pollet (fl), B. Vogt (pno) [trans Paul Klengel in D for vc & pno; adapted for] ("Poetic License") † Debussy:Epigraphes antiques (6) Pno; G. F. Handel:Sons Vn & Kbd, Op. 1 TIT ▲ 216 (16.97)

K. Smietana (vn), C. Palmer (pno) *(rec Bristol, England, Feb 10-12, 1997)* ("The 3 Violin Sonatas") † Son 2 Vn, Op. 100; Son 3 Vn, Op. 108; Sons Vn (comp) ASVQ ▲ 6227 [DDD] (10.97)

artists unknown ("Brahms for Book Lovers") † Music of Brahms; Son 1 Cl; Son 2 Vn, Op. 100; Trio 3 Pno, Op. 101 PPHI (Set Your Life to Music) ▮ 462561 (5.98) ▲ 462561 (9.97)

Sonata No. 2 in A for Violin & Piano, Op. 100 (1886)

A. Argenta (pno), A. Grumiaux (vn) † Con Vn; Beethoven:Son 8 Vn; Sym 3; Escudero:Concerto Vasco; M. de Falla:Amor brujo; Smetana:Bartered Bride (orch sels); R. Strauss:Till Eulenspiegels lustige Streiche, Op. 28; P. Tchaikovsky:Sym 4 RTVE 4-▲ 65097 (36.97)

A. Busch (vn), B. Seidler-Winkler (pno), R. Serkin (pno) † Hungarian Dances Pno 4-Hands; Son 1 Vn, Op. 78; R. Schumann:Son 1 Vn, Op. 105 PHS ▲ 25 (17.97)

A. Busch (vn), R. Serkin (pno) *(rec 1932 for HMV)* † J. S. Bach:Sons & Partitas Vn; Beethoven:Son 3 Vn PHS ▲ 9942 [AAD] (17.97)

A. Busch (vn), R. Serkin (pno) † Son 1 Vn, Op. 78; J. S. Bach:Sons & Partitas Vn MTAL ▲ 48026 (6.97)

A. Busch (vn), R. Serkin (pno) † Son 1 Vn, Op. 78; J. S. Bach:Son Vn Bc, BWV 1021; Beethoven:Son 5 Vn, Op. 24; Son 7 Vn; R. Schumann:Son 1 Vn, Op. 105 GRM2 ▲ 78820 (26.97)

K. Chung (vn), P. Frankl (pno) *(rec Bristol, England, Sept 1995)* † Son 1 Vn, Op. 78; Son 3 Vn, Op. 108 EMIC ▲ 56203 [DDD] (16.97)

L. Combs (cl), D. Sobol (pno) [cl & pno trans Kent Kennan] † S. Prokofiev:Son 2 Vn SUMM ▲ 125 [DDD] (16.97)

J. Heifetz (vn), E. Bay (pno) *(rec New York, Jan 31, 1936)* ("The Heifetz Collection, Volume 4, 1935-1939") † Con Vn; G. Fauré:Son 1 Vn, Op. 13; S. Prokofiev:Con 2 Vn, Op. 63; Saint-Saëns:Havanaise, Op. 83; Intro & Rondo capriccioso, Op. 28; Sarasate:Zigeunerweisen, Op. 20 RCAV (Gold Seal) 2-▲ 61735 [ADD] (21.97)

J. Heifetz (vn), E. Bay (pno) ("Heifetz & Feuermann Play Brahms") † Con Vn & Vc, Op. 102; Son 1 Vc, Op. 38 PHS ▲ 9293 (17.97)

I. M. Menges (vn), A. D. Greef (pno) *(rec 1925-29)* † Son 3 Vn, Op. 108; Beethoven:Son 9 Vn, Op. 47 MTAL ▲ 48062 (6.97)

D. Oistrakh (vn), S. Richter (pno) *(rec Aug 1972)* † S. Prokofiev:Son 1 Vn, Op. 80 ORFE (Festspiel Dokumente) ▲ 489981 (16.97)

I. Perlman (vn), V. Ashkenazy (pno) *(rec London, England, Apr 20-23, 1983)* † Son 1 Vn, Op. 78; Son 3 Vn, Op. 108 EMIC (Great Recordings of the Century) ▲ 66945 [DDD] (11.97)

K. Smietana (vn), C. Palmer (pno) *(rec Bristol, England, Feb 10-12, 1997)* ("The 3 Violin Sonatas") † Son 1 Vn, Op. 78; Son 3 Vn, Op. 108; Sons Vn (comp) ASVQ ▲ 6227 [DDD] (10.97)

A. Spalding (vn), A. Benoist (pno) ("The Art of the Violin, Vol. 3") † C. Franck:Son Vn, M.8; G. F. Handel:Son Vn; R. Schumann:Klavierstücke, Op. 85; Tartini:Son Vn & Pno ACLR ▲ 42 (17.97)

I. Stern (vn), M. Hess (pno) *(rec 14th Edinburgh Festival, Aug 28, 1960)* ("In Concert 1949-1960") † Con 2 Pno, Op. 83; Beethoven:Con 4 Pno, Op. 58; Con 5 Pno, Op. 73; Son 10 Vn, Op. 96; W. A. Mozart:Con 12 Pno, K.414; Con 21 Pno, K.467; Con 27 Pno, K.595; F. Schubert:Sonatinas (3) Vn MUA 3-▲ 779 [AAD] (47.97)

M. Vengerov (vn), A. Markovich (pno) † Beethoven:Son 9 Vn, Op. 47 ELEC ▲ 74001 (15.97)

M. Yashvili (vn), I. Chernyshov (pno) *(rec 1991)* ("Russian Violin School: Marina Yashvili") † Hungarian Dances Pno 4-Hands; Babadjanyan:Music of Babadjanyan; M. de Falla:Canciones populares españolas; Paganini:Cantabile, M.S. 109; Moto perpetuo Vn, M.S. 66 RD (Talents of Russia) ▲ 16251 [ADD] (16.97)

190 ▲ = CD ♦ = Enhanced CD △ = MD ▮ = Cassette Tape ▯ = DCC

BRAHMS, JOHANNES (cont.)

Sonata No. 2 in A for Violin & Piano, Op. 100 (1886) (cont.)

artists unknown—Andante tranquillo - vivace; Allegretto grazioso (quasi Andante) ("Brahms for Book Lovers") † Music of Brahms; Serenade 1 Orch, Op. 11 PPHI (Set Your Life to Music) ▲ 462561 (9.97) ■ 462561 (5.98)

artists unknown—Andante tranquillo - vivace; Allegretto grazioso (quasi Andante) ("Brahms for Book Lovers") † Music of Brahms; Son 1 Cl; Son 1 Vn, Op. 78; Trio 3 Pno, Op. 101 PPHI (Set Your Life to Music) ■ 462561 (5.98) ▲ 462561 (9.97)

Sonata No. 3 in d for Violin & Piano, Op. 108 (1886-88)

Y. Bushkov (vn), L. Blok (pno) † W. A. Mozart:Sons Vn & Pno (misc) DI ▲ 920124 [DDD] (5.97)

K. Chung (vn), P. Frankl (pno) *(rec Bristol, England, Sept 1995)* † Son 1 Vn, Op. 78; Son 2 Vn, Op. 100 EMIC ▲ 56203 [DDD] (16.97)

M. Elman (vn), W. Rosé (pno) *(rec Nov 1947)* † Balakirev:Songs; A. Dvořák:Slavonic Fant; Hubay:Hejre Kati, Op. 32/4; Mendelssohn (-Bartholdy):Con Vn & Orch, Op. 64; Lieder ohne Worte; Smetana:From the Homeland BID ▲ 160 [ADD] (16.97)

B. Gianneo (vn), E. Murano (pno) † L. Gianneo:Music of Gianneo DI ▲ 920268 [DDD] (5.97)

V. Gluzman (vn), A. Yoffe (pno) *(rec Astoria, NY, Mar 27-28, 1995)* † Beethoven:Son 1 Vn; P. Hindemith:Son Vn in E KOCH ▲ 7323 [DDD] (16.97)

O. Kagan (vn), V. Lobanov (pno) *(rec Apr 1989)* † Songs (2), Op. 91 LV ▲ 661 [ADD/DDD] (17.97)

P. Kochansky (vn), A. Rubenstein (pno) *(rec 1932 & 1936)* ("Arthur Rubenstein Plays Brahms Chamber Music") † Qt 1 Pno, Op. 25; Son 1 Vc, Op. 38 ENPL (Piano Library) ▲ 233 (13.97)

G. Kremer (vn), V. Afanassiev (pno)—Adagio ("Intimate Conversations") † Music of Brahms; Son 1 Cl PPHI (Night Moods) ▲ 453905 [DDD] (9.97)

Y.-Y. Ma (vc), E. Ax (pno) [trans for vc & pno] † Sons Vc (comp) SNYC ▲ 48191 [DDD] (16.97) COL △ 48191 [DDD]

I. M. Menges (vn), A. D. Greef (pno) *(rec 1925-29)* † Son 2 Vn, Op. 100; Beethoven:Son 9 Vn, Op. 47 MTAL ▲ 48062 (6.97)

Y. Menuhin (vn), H. Menuhin (pno) *(rec 1947)* † B. Bartók:Son 1 Vn & Pno, Sz.75; Beethoven:Son 10 Vn, Op. 96 BID ▲ 161 [ADD] (16.97)

N. Milstein (vn), A. Balsam (pno) *(rec Library of Congress, Mar 13, 1953)* ("The 1953 Library of Congress Recital") † J. S. Bach:Sons & Partitas Vn; Beethoven:Son 5 Vn, Op. 24 BRID ▲ 9066 (17.97)

G. Neveu (vn), J. Neveu (pno) [also includes 2 interviews w. Neveu] ("Tribute to Ginette Neveu") † Con Vn; Beethoven:Con Vn TAHA 3-▲ 355 (50.97)

R. Pasquier (vn), J. Pennetier (pno) † Qt 1 Pno, Op. 25 HAM ▲ 7901062 (12.97)

I. Perlman (vn), V. Ashkenazy (pno) *(rec London, England, Apr 20-23, 1983)* † Son 1 Vn, Op. 78; Son 2 Vn, Op. 100 EMIC (Great Recordings of the Century) ▲ 66945 [DDD] (11.97)

K. Smietana (vn), C. Palmer (pno) *(rec Bristol, England, Feb 10-12, 1997)* ("The 3 Violin Sonatas") † Son 1 Vn, Op. 78; Son 2 Vn, Op. 100; Sons Vn (comp) ASVQ ▲ 6227 [DDD] (10.97)

H. Szeryng (vn), M. Katz (pno) *(rec June 1973)* ("A Legendary Collaboration") † C. Franck:Son Vn, M.8 CEMB (Historic Series) ▲ 105 [ADD] (15.97)

J. Szigeti (vn), E. Petri (pno) ("Joseph Szigeti Plays Violin Sonatas") † J. S. Bach:Sons & Partitas Vn IN ▲ 1321 [ADD] (15.97)

J. Szigeti (vn), E. Petri (pno) ("A Tribute to Joseph Szigeti") † J. S. Bach:Sons & Partitas Vn GRM2 ▲ 78630 (13.97)

J. Szigeti (vn), E. Petri (pno) *(rec 1927-44)* ("Joseph Szigeti: The Great Violin Sonatas") † J. S. Bach:Sons & Partitas Vn; Beethoven:Son 5 Vn, Op. 24; Son 9 Vn, Op. 47 ENT (Strings) 2-▲ 99318 (32.97)

E. Zimbalist (vn), H. Kaufman (pno) *(rec 1930)* † Con Vn DHR ▲ 7739 (16.97)

artists unknown—Adagio; Adagio ("Brahms at Bedtime") † Music of Brahms; Songs; Vars & Fugue on a Theme by Handel, Op. 24 PPHI (Set Your Life to Music) ▲ 54966 (9.97) ■ 54966 (5.98)

Songs

T. Allen (bar), G. Parsons (pno)—Songs (4), Op. 96 [Wir wandelten]; Songs (7), Op. 48 [Der Gang zum Liebchen]; Songs (6), Op. 97 [Komm bald; Nachtigall]; Songs (5), Op. 107 [Salamander]; Songs (4), Op. 70 [Serenade]; Songs (5), Op. 71 [Geheimnis; Minnelied (Lovesong)]; Songs (8), Op. 57 [Von waldbekräntzer Höhe]; Songs (8), Op. 59 [Dein blaues Auge]; Songs (9), Op. 32; Songs (9), Op. 63 [Junge Lieder I in F#; Heimweh II]; Songs (4), Op. 46 [Die Kränze; Magyarisch; An die Nachtigall; Die Schale der Vegessenheit]; Songs (6), Op. 85 [In Waldeseinamkeit]; Songs (6), Op. 86 [Feldeinsamkeit (In Summer Fields)]; Songs (5), Op. 106 [Ständchen]; Songs (4), Op. 43 [Von ewiger Liebe; Die Mainacht]; Songs (5), Op. 47 [Botschaft] *(rec 1989-91)* † Songs (5), Op. 49; H. Wolf:Gedichte von Goethe; Gedichte von Mörike VCL 2-▲ 61418 [DDD] (11.97)

M. Anderson (cta), E. Ormandy (cnd), Philadelphia Orch—Poems (5), Op. 19 [Der Schmied]; Songs (8), Op. 59 [Dein blaues Auge]; Songs (5), Op. 105 [Immer leiser wird mein Schlummer] *(rec 1939 for HMV)* † Alto Rhap, Op. 53; Sibelius:Songs PHS ▲ 9405 [AAD] (17.97)

M. Anderson (cta), E. Ormandy (cnd), Philadelphia Orch—Songs (8), Op. 59 [Dein blaues Auge]; Songs (5), Op. 105 [Immer leiser wird mein Schlummer]; Poems (5), Op. 19 [Der Schmied] *(rec Jan 1939)* † Alto Rhap, Op. 53; Son 1 Cl; Son 2 Cl; Songs (2), Op. 91 BID ▲ 150 [AAD] (16.97)

J. DeGaetani (mez), L. Dutton (va), L. Luvisi (pno)—Songs (5), Op. 72 [O kühler Wald; Verzagen]; Songs (2), Op. 91 [Geistliches Wiegenlied] *(rec Aspen Music Festival, July 7, 1983)* ("Jan DeGaetani In Concert, Vol. 2") † Gypsy Songs (8); R. Schumann:Frauenliebe und -leben, Op. 42 BRID ▲ 9025 [ADD] (17.97)

K. Erb (ten), B. Seidler-Winkler (pno)—Songs (4), Op. 70 [Lerchengesang]; Songs (9), Op. 63 [Heimweh II]; Songs (5), Op. 72 [O kühler Wald] ("Liederabend") † Beethoven:Adelaide, Op. 46; Der Wachtelschlag, WoO 129; Liszt:Es muss ein Wunderbares sein, S.314; F. Schubert:Songs (misc colls); R. Schumann:Songs; H. Wolf:Gedichte von Mörike ENT (Vocal Archives) ▲ 1185 [ADD] (13.97)

B. Fassbaender (mez), H. Komatsu (bar), K. Moll (bass), C. Garben (pno)—Duets (4) [Die Nonne und der Ritter]; Duets (4), Op. 28 [Vor der Tür; Es rauschet das Wasser; Der Jäger und sein Liebchen] *(rec Nov 1989)* ("Romantic Duets") † P. Cornelius:Songs; Liszt:Songs; Mendelssohn (-Bartholdy):Songs; A. Rubinstein:Songs; R. Schumann:Songs HMA ▲ 1905210 [DDD] (9.97)

D. Fischer-Dieskau (bar), H. Höll (pno)—Poems (5), Op. 19 [An eine Äolsharfe]; Songs (9), Op. 32 [Nicht mehr zu dir zu gehen; Der Strom, der neben mir verrauschte; Wehe, so willst du mich wieder; Wie bist du, meine Königin]; Songs (7), Op. 48 [Der Gang zum Liebchen]; Songs (5), Op. 49 [Abenddämmerung]; Songs (8), Op. 59 [Auf dem See]; Songs (9), Op. 69 [Tambourliedchen]; Songs (4), Op. 70 [Serenade; Abendregen]; Songs (5), Op. 71 [Es liebt sich so lieblich im Lenze; Geheimnis]; Songs (5), Op. 72 [Unüberwindlich]; Songs (6), Op. 86 [Therese; Feldeinsamkeit (In Summer Fields)]; Songs (7), Op. 95 [Bei dir sind meine Gedanken]; Songs (4), Op. 96 [Es schauen die Blumen; Meerfahrt]; Songs (5), Op. 105 [Auf dem Kirchhofe]; Songs (5), Op. 107 [Maienkätzchen] † Songs (9), Op. 32 BAYE ▲ 100006 [DDD] (17.97)

M. Fisher (eup), M. Lawson (pno)—Duets (4), Op. 28 [Es rauschet das Wasser; Der Jäger und sein Liebchen]; Duets (3), Op. 20 [Weg der Liebe I]; Ballads & Romances, Op. 75 [So lass uns wandern] *(rec Boutell Concert Hall Northern Illinois Univ., June 6-7 & Nov 26-27, 1994)* ("EuFish") † Arban:Fant, Theme & Vars on; J. Bach:Concert Vars; J. S. Bach:Sons Fl; G. Jacob:Fant Eup; Telemann:Son Bn ALBA ▲ 162 [DDD] (16.97)

K. Flagstad (sop), W. Alme (pno)—Romanzen aus Tieck's Magelone, Op. 33 [Sind es Schmerzen; Ruhe, Süssliebchen; Muss es eine Trennung geben; Wie froh und frisch]; Songs (8), Op. 59 [Dein blaues Auge]; Songs (6), Op. 86 [Therese]; Songs (4), Op. 46 [An die Nachtigall]; Songs (9), Op. 32 [Wie bist du, meine Königin] *(rec Oslo, 1954)* ("Vol. 5: German Lieder, Norwegian Radio 1954") † Beethoven:Songs; F. Schubert:Ave Maria, Op. 52/6; Songs (misc colls); R. Schumann:Songs; R. Strauss:Songs; H. Wolf:Songs (misc) SIMX 2-▲ 1825 (39.97)

M. Groop (mez), A. Lubimov (pno)—Deutsche Volkslieder (26) [Da untem im Tale; In stiller Nacht]; Deutsche Volkslieder (49), WoO 33 [Och Moder, ich well en Ding hanl; Verstohlen geht der Mond auf]; Songs (9), Op. 69 [Die Liebsten Schwur]; Songs (5), Op. 72 [Alte Liebe]; Songs (5), Op. 105 [Wie Melodien zieht es mir; Immer leiser wird mein Schlummer; Auf dem Kirchhofe]; Songs (8), Op. 59 [Dein blaues Auge]; Songs (4), Op. 43 [Von ewiger Liebe; Die Mainacht]; Romances & Songs (5), Op. 84 [Vergebliches Ständchen] *(rec Järvenpää Hall, Feb 1997)* † Songs (2), Op. 91; Songs (5), Op. 49; Songs (6), Op. 86; Zigeunerlieder, Op. 103 ODE ▲ 896 [DDD] (17.97)

E. Grümmer (sop), G. Moore (pno)—Songs (8), Op. 59 [Regenlied]; Songs (7), Op. 95 [Das Mädchen]; Songs (5), Op. 71 [Geheimnis]; Songs (5), Op. 107 [Mädchenlied] † Songs (5), Op. 49; E. Grieg:Peer Gynt (sels); F. Schubert:Songs (misc colls); Verdi:Arias; Otello (sels) TES ▲ 1086 (17.97)

A. Kipnis (bass), E. V. Wolff (pno)—Deutsche Volkslieder (26) [In stiller Nacht]; Songs (8), Op. 58 [Blinde Kuh]; Songs (5), Op. 106 [Ein Wanderer]; Songs (5), Op. 49 [Am Sonntag Morgen]; Songs (8), Op. 59 [Dein blaues Auge]; Songs (7), Op. 48 [Der Gang zum Liebchen]; Songs & Romances (8), Op. 14 [Vor dem Fenster]; Songs (5), Op. 71 [Geheimnis] ("Lieder, Part 1") † Songs (5), Op. 49 VOCA (Vocal Archives) ▲ 1160 (13.97)

T. Körber (pno), H. M. Beuerle (cnd), Anton Webern Choir Freiburg—Deutsche Volkslieder (26) [In stiller Nacht; Die Wollust in den Maien; Von edler Art; Mit Lust tät ich ausreiten; Abschiedslied] ("Secular Choral Songs a Cappella & with Piano") † Qts (6) SATB, Op. 112; Songs (5), Op. 104; Zigeunerlieder, Op. 103 ARSM ▲ 1136 [DDD] (17.97)

BRAHMS, JOHANNES (cont.)

Songs (cont.)

L. Lehmann (sop), P. Ulanowsky (pno)—Songs (4), Op. 96 [Wir wandelten]; Songs (4), Op. 46 [An die Nachtigall]; Deutsche Volkslieder (26) [Erlaube mir, feins Mädchen; Da untem im Tale]; Deutsche Volkslieder (49), WoO 33 [Feinsliebchen du sollst mir nicht]; Songs (4), Op. 43 [Die Mainacht]; Songs (5), Op. 49 [Am Sonntag Morgen]; Songs (5), Op. 47 [O liebliche Wangen]; Songs (5), Op. 105 [Auf dem Kirchhofe] ("26 Lieder") † Songs (9), Op. 32; R. Schumann:Songs; R. Strauss:Songs; H. Wolf:Songs (misc) GSE ▲ 785057

M. Lipovšek (mez), Folkwang Guitar Duo—Songs (7), Op. 48 [Der Gang zum Liebchen]; Songs (6), Op. 85 [Mädchenlied]; Songs & Romances (8), Op. 14 [Ständchen] † Deutsche Volkslieder (26); Deutsche Volkslieder (49), WoO 33; Marienlieder (7), Op. 22; Romances & Songs (5), Op. 84; Songs (5), Op. 49; Songs & Romances (6); Songs & Romances (8), Op. 14; Zigeunerlieder, Op. 103 ORF ▲ 441971 [DDD] (18.97)

K. McMillan (bar), M. McMahon (pno)—Songs (4), Op. 96 [Der Tod, das ist die kühle Nacht; Es schauen die Blumen; Meerfahrt] *(rec Canada)* ("Lieder on Poems of Heinrich Heine") † Liszt:Songs; Mendelssohn (-Bartholdy):Songs; F. Schubert:Schwanengesang, D.957; R. Schumann:Dichterliebe, Op. 48 MUVI ▲ 1052 [DDD] (16.97)

M. Maisky (vc), P. Gililov (pno)—Songs (8), Op. 59 [Nachklang]; Songs (9), Op. 32 [Nicht mehr zu dir zu gehen]; Songs (5), Op. 94 [Sapphische Ode]; Songs (5), Op. 105 [Wie Melodien zieht es mir; Immer leiser wird mein Schlummer]; Ernste Gesänge, Op. 121 [Denn es gehet dem Menschen; Ich wandte mich und sahe; O Tod, o Tod wie bitter bist du]; Songs (6), Op. 86 [Über die Heide]; Songs (6), Op. 3 [Liebestreu]; Songs (4), Op. 70 [Lerchengesang] ("Songs without Words") † Son 1 Vn, Op. 78 DGRM ▲ 453424 [DDD] (18.97)

E. Mathis (sop), B. Fassbaender (mez), P. Schreier (ten), D. Fischer-Dieskau (bar), W. Sawallisch (pno), K. Engel (pno), G. Kahl (pno)—Geistliches Lied, Op. 30; Duets (4), Op. 28; Qts (3) SATB, Op. 31; Liebeslieder Waltzes, Op. 52; Duets (4), Op. 61; Duets (5), Op. 66; Qts (3) SATB, Op. 64; Neue Liebeslieder Waltzes, Op. 65; Ballads & Romances, Op. 75; Qts (4) SATB, Op. 92; Zigeunerlieder, Op. 103; Qts (6) SATB, Op. 112; Deutsche Volkslieder (49), WoO 33 ("The Complete Brahms Edition, Vol. 4:Vocal Ensembles") DGRM 4-▲ 449641

J. Norman (sop), D. Fischer-Dieskau (bar), D. Barenboim (pno)—Songs (2), Op. 91; Songs (6), Op. 3; Songs (6), Op. 6; Songs (6), Op. 7; Songs (4), Op. 17; Songs (9), Op. 69; Songs (4), Op. 70; Songs (5), Op. 71; Songs (5), Op. 72; Songs & Romances (8), Op. 14; Poems (5), Op. 19; Songs (9), Op. 32; Songs (8), Op. 57; Songs (8), Op. 58; Songs (8), Op. 59; Songs (9), Op. 63; Romanzen aus Tieck's Magelone, Op. 33; Romances & Songs (5), Op. 84; Songs (4), Op. 46; Songs (5), Op. 47; Songs (7), Op. 48; Songs (5), Op. 49; Songs (6), Op. 85; Songs (6), Op. 86; Songs (5), Op. 94; Songs (7), Op. 95; Songs (6), Op. 97; Songs (4), Op. 96; Songs (5), Op. 105; Songs (5), Op. 106; Songs (5), Op. 107; Mondnacht; Regenlied; Songs of Ophelia; Zigeunerlieder, Op. 103; Ernste Gesänge, Op. 121 ("The Complete Brahms Edition, Vol. 5:Lieder") DGRM 7-▲ 449633

A. S. von Otter (mez), B. Forsberg (pno)—Songs (6), Op. 97 [Dort in den Weiden]; Romances & Songs (5), Op. 84 [Vergebliches Ständchen]; Songs (4), Op. 43 [Die Mainacht; Von ewiger Liebe]; Songs (8), Op. 57 [Ach, wende diesen Blick]; Songs (5), Op. 72 [O kühler Wald]; Songs (9), Op. 63 [Junge Lieder I in F#]; Songs (9), Op. 32 [Wie rafft ich mich auf in der Nacht]; Songs (5), Op. 47 [Sonntag]; Songs (5), Op. 49 [Wiegenlied (Lullaby)]; Songs (2), Op. 91 [Gestillte Sehnsucht; Geistliches Wiegenlied] † Gypsy Songs (8) DEUT ▲ 29727 [DDD] (16.97)

J. Patzak (ten), M. Raucheisen (pno)—Songs (4), Op. 46 [An die Nachtigall]; Songs (9), Op. 63 [An die Tauben]; Songs (6), Op. 6 [Nachtigallen schwingen] *(rec 1943-44)* † W. A. Mozart:Songs; F. Schubert:Songs (misc colls); R. Strauss:Songs; H. Wolf:Songs (misc colls) PRE ▲ 90347 (m) (16.97)

M. Pedrotti (bar), S. Ralls (pno)—Songs (5), Op. 72 [Alte Liebe]; Songs (4), Op. 46 [An die Nachtigall]; Songs (5), Op. 105 [Immer leiser wird mein Schlummer; Wie Melodien zieht es mir] † Songs (6), Op. 86; Duparc:Songs; Morawetz:Songs; R. Strauss:Songs; P. Tchaikovsky:Songs MUVI (Musica Viva) ▲ 1051 [DDD] (16.97)

D. Pereira (vc), D. Bollard (pno)—Songs (5), Op. 105 [Wie Melodien zieht es mir]; Songs (5), Op. 94 [Sapphische Ode]; Songs (6), Op. 3 [Liebestreu]; Songs (5), Op. 71 [Minnelied (Lovesong)] ("Cello Rhapsody") † Songs (5), Op. 49; Songs (6), Op. 86; M. de Falla:Suite populaire espagnole; Ginastera:Pampeana 2, Op. 21; J. Nin:Songs; R. Schumann:Stücke im Volkston, Op. 102; D. Shostakovich:Ballet Suite 2 TALP ▲ 78 [DDD] (18.97)

L. Popp (sop), G. Parsons (pno)—Songs (9), Op. 69 [Mädchenfluch]; Songs (7), Op. 95 [Vorschneller Schwur]; Songs (6), Op. 85 [Mädchenlied]; Songs (5), Op. 107 [Mädchenlied; Das Mädchen spricht]; Songs (6), Op. 7 [Die Trauernde]; Songs & Romances (8), Op. 14 [Sehnsucht]; Deutsche Volkslieder (49), WoO 33 [Wie komm'ich denn zu Tür herein; Es steht ein Lind]; Deutsche Volkslieder (26) [In stiller Nacht]; Songs (8), Op. 59 [Regenlied] *(rec Munich, 1983)* ("Lieder") † G. Mahler:Lieder und Gesänge aus der Jugendzeit AART ▲ 47367 [DDD] (10.97)

C. Prégardien (ten), T. Hoppstock (gtr) ("Lieder on Love & Death") † F. Schubert:Songs (misc); L. Spohr:Songs SIGM ▲ 9500 (17.97)

C. Robbin (mez), M. McMahon (pno)—Songs (8), Op. 58 [Blinde Kuh]; Songs (4), Op. 43 [Die Mainacht; Von ewiger Liebe]; Songs (5), Op. 49 [Am Sonntag Morgen] † F. Schubert:Songs (misc colls) MARQ ▲ 113 (16.97)

I. Seefried (sop), E. Werba (pno)—Deutsche Volkslieder (49), WoO 33 [Feinsliebchen du sollst mir nicht]; Deutsche Volkslieder (26) [In stiller Nacht; Da untem im Tale]; Songs (6), Op. 7 [Die Trauernde] *(rec Aug 18, 1960)* † R. Schumann:Frauenliebe und -leben, Op. 42; Liederkreis, Op. 39; Myrthen, Op. 25; Songs ORFE (Festspiel Dokumente) ▲ 398951 (16.97)

D. Soffel (mez), C. Spencer (pno)—Songs (6), Op. 3; Mondnacht; Songs (2), Op. 91; Songs (8), Op. 59 [Regenlied]; Songs of Ophelia; Ernste Gesänge, Op. 121 ("Brahms Lieder, Vol. 1") † Zigeunerlieder, Op. 103 ARSM ▲ 1190 (17.97)

N. Stutzmann (cta), I. Södergren (pno)—Poems (5), Op. 19 [An eine Äolsharfe]; Songs (9), Op. 32 [Wie rafft ich mich auf in der Nacht]; Songs (4), Op. 43 [Von ewiger Liebe; Die Mainacht]; Songs (5), Op. 47 [Botschaft]; Songs (7), Op. 48 [Der Gang zum Liebchen]; Songs (8), Op. 57 [Unbewegte laue Luft]; Songs (9), Op. 63 [Junge Lieder I in F#; Heimweh II]; Songs (5), Op. 72 [Verzagen]; Romances & Songs (5), Op. 84 [Vergebliches Ständchen]; Songs (5), Op. 94 [Sapphische Ode]; Songs (5), Op. 105 [Wie Melodien zieht es mir; Immer leiser wird mein Schlummer]; Songs (5), Op. 107 [Mädchenlied]; Ernste Gesänge, Op. 121 *(rec July 1996)* ("Lieder") † Songs (5), Op. 106 RCAV (Red Seal) ▲ 68660 [DDD] (16.97)

S. Walker (mez), R. Vignoles (pno)—Gypsy Songs (8); Marienlieder (7), Op. 22; Songs (2), Op. 91 † A. Dvořák:Zigeunermelodien, Op. 55 MER ▲ 84232 [DDD] (16.97)

artists unknown—As Melodies Were Passing By ("Brahms at Bedtime") † Music of Brahms; Son 3 Vn, Op. 108; Vars & Fugue on a Theme by Handel, Op. 24 PPHI (Set Your Life to Music) ▲ 54966 (9.97) ■ 54966 (5.98)

Songs (6) for Tenor (or Soprano) & Piano, Op. 3 (1852-53)

J. Vogler (vc), B. Canino (pno) *(rec Hamburg, Germany, Dec 1997)* † Son 1 Vc, Op. 38; Songs (5), Op. 105; Songs (5), Op. 49; Songs (5), Op. 71; Songs (5), Op. 94; Songs (6), Op. 86; F. Schubert:Son Arpeggione, D.821 BER ▲ 1179 [DDD] (16.97)

Songs & Romances (8) for Voice & Piano, Op. 14 (1858)

M. Lipovšek (mez), Folkwang Guitar Duo—Vor dem Fenster; Ständchen † Deutsche Volkslieder (26); Deutsche Volkslieder (49), WoO 33; Marienlieder (7), Op. 22; Romances & Songs (5), Op. 84; Songs; Songs (5), Op. 49; Songs & Romances (6); Zigeunerlieder, Op. 103 *(E,F,G texts)* ORF ▲ 441971 [DDD] (18.97)

Songs (4) for 3 Female Voices, 2 Horns & Harp, Op. 17

G. Jena (cnd), North German Radio Chorus ("The Complete Brahms Edition, Vol. 7:Choral Works") † Ave Maria, Op. 12; Begräbnisgesang, Op. 13; Canons (13), Op. 113; Dem dunkeln Schoss der heil'gen Erde; Deutsche Volkslieder (26); Fest- und Gedenksprüche, Op. 109; Geistliches Lied, Op. 30; Grausam erweiset sich Amor an mir, Op. 113/2; Kleine Hochzeitskantate; Marienlieder (7), Op. 22; Mir lächelt kein Frühling; Motets (2), Op. 29; Motets (2), Op. 74; Motets (3), Op. 110; O wie sanft; Psalm 13, Op. 27; Sacred Choruses (3), Op. 37; Songs (3), Op. 42; Songs (5), Op. 104; Songs (5), Op. 41; Songs (7), Op. 62; Songs & Romances (12), Op. 44; Songs & Romances (6), Op. 93a; Spruch; Tafellied, Op. 93b; Töne, lindernder Klang; Wann?; Zu Rauch DGRM 4-▲ 449646

London Sym Chorus, F. Lloyd (hn), S. Sterling (hn), R. Masters (hp) *(rec 1989-90)* † Alto Rhap, Op. 53; Berlioz:Captive, Op. 12; Mélodies, Op. 2; Nuits d'été, Op. 7; Zaïde, Op. 19/1; Mendelssohn (-Bartholdy):Infelice, Op. 94; Psalm 42, Op. 42; O. Respighi:Sensitiva VCL 2-▲ 61469 [DDD] (11.97)

Songs (9) for Voice & Piano, Op. 32 (1864)

D. Fischer-Dieskau (bar), H. Höll (pno)—Wie rafft ich mich auf in der Nacht; Nicht mehr zu dir zu gehen; Der Strom, der neben mir verrauschte; Wehe, so willst du mich wieder; Wie bist du, meine Königin † Songs BAYE ▲ 100006 [DDD] (17.97)

L. Lehmann (sop), P. Ulanowsky (pno)—Wie bist du, meine Königin ("26 Lieder") † Songs; R. Schumann:Songs; R. Strauss:Songs; H. Wolf:Songs (misc) GSE ▲ 785057

H. Schlusnus (bar), F. Rupp (pno)—Wie bist du, meine Königin *(rec 1919-27)* † Songs (6), Op. 86; Beethoven:Adelaide, Op. 46; F. Schubert:Songs (misc colls); R. Schumann:Dichterliebe, Op. 48; R. Strauss:Songs; H. Wolf:Songs (misc) PRE (Lebendige Vergangenheit) ▲ 89188 (m) (16.97)

Songs (5) for 4 Male Voices, Op. 41 (1861-62)

G. Jena (cnd), North German Radio Chorus ("The Complete Brahms Edition, Vol. 7:Choral Works") † Ave Maria, Op. 12; Begräbnisgesang, Op. 13; Canons (13), Op. 113; Dem dunkeln Schoss der heil'gen Erde; Deutsche Volkslieder (26); Fest- und Gedenksprüche, Op. 109; Geistliches Lied, Op. 30; Grausam erweiset sich Amor an mir, Op. 113/2; Kleine Hochzeitskantate; Marienlieder (7), Op. 22; Mir lächelt kein Frühling; Motets (2), Op. 29; Motets (2), Op. 74; Motets (3), Op. 110; O wie sanft; Psalm 13, Op. 27; Sacred Choruses (3), Op. 37; Songs (3), Op. 42; Songs (4), Op. 17; Songs (5), Op. 104; Songs (7), Op. 62; Songs & Romances (12), Op. 44; Songs & Romances (6), Op. 93a; Spruch; Tafellied, Op. 93b; Töne, lindernder Klang; Wann?; Zu Rauch DGRM 4-▲ 449646

BRAHMS, JOHANNES (cont.)

Songs (3) for 6 Voices, Op. 42 (1859-61)

W. Hauschild (cnd) , Leipzig Radio Chorus † Choral Music; Liebeslieder Waltzes, Op. 52; Songs (4), Op. 43 ORF 4-▲ 26972 [DDD] (36.97)

G. Jena (cnd), North German Radio Chorus ("The Complete Brahms Edition, Vol. 7:Choral Works") † Ave Maria, Op. 12; Begräbnisgesang, Op. 13; Canons (13), Op. 113; Dem dunkeln Schoss der heil'gen Erde; Deutsche Volkslieder (26); Fest- und Gedenksprüche, Op. 109; Geistliches Lied, Op. 30; Grausam erweiset sich Amor an mir, Op. 113/2; Kleine Hochzeitskantate; Marienlieder (7), Op. 22; Mir lächelt kein Frühling; Motets (2), Op. 29; Motets (2), Op. 74; Motets (3), Op. 110; O wie sanft; Psalm 13, Op. 27; Sacred Choruses (3), Op. 37; Songs (4), Op. 17; Songs (5), Op. 104; Songs (5), Op. 41; Songs (7), Op. 62; Songs & Romances (12), Op. 44; Songs & Romances (6), Op. 93a; Spruch; Tafellied, Op. 93b; Töne, lindernder Klang; Wann?; Zu Rauch DGRM 4-▲ 449646

Songs (4) for Voice & Piano, Op. 43 (1864)

W. Hauschild (cnd) , Leipzig Radio Chorus—Die Mainacht † Choral Music; Liebeslieder Waltzes, Op. 52; Songs (3), Op. 42 ORF 4-▲ 26972 [DDD] (36.97)

Songs & Romances (12) for 4 Female Voices, Op. 44 (1859-66)

G. Jena (cnd), North German Radio Chorus ("The Complete Brahms Edition, Vol. 7:Choral Works") † Ave Maria, Op. 12; Begräbnisgesang, Op. 13; Canons (13), Op. 113; Dem dunkeln Schoss der heil'gen Erde; Deutsche Volkslieder (26); Fest- und Gedenksprüche, Op. 109; Geistliches Lied, Op. 30; Grausam erweiset sich Amor an mir, Op. 113/2; Kleine Hochzeitskantate; Marienlieder (7), Op. 22; Mir lächelt kein Frühling; Motets (2), Op. 29; Motets (2), Op. 74; Motets (3), Op. 110; O wie sanft; Psalm 13, Op. 27; Sacred Choruses (3), Op. 37; Songs (3), Op. 42; Songs (4), Op. 17; Songs (5), Op. 104; Songs (5), Op. 41; Songs (7), Op. 62; Songs & Romances (6), Op. 93a; Spruch; Tafellied, Op. 93b; Töne, lindernder Klang; Wann?; Zu Rauch DGRM 4-▲ 449646

Songs (5) for Voice & Piano, Op. 49 (1868)

T. Allen (bar), G. Parsons (pno)—Wiegenlied (Lullaby); Am Sonntag Morgen *(rec 1989-91)* † Songs; H. Wolf:Gedichte von Goethe; Gedichte von Mörike VCL 2-▲ 61418 [DDD] (11.97)

I. Danz (cta), A. Eckels (pno)—Wiegenlied (Lullaby) † Deutsche Volkslieder (49), WoO 33; Poems (5), Op. 19; Songs (4), Op. 96; Songs (5), Op. 71; Songs (5), Op. 72; Songs (6), Op. 85; Songs (6), Op. 86; Songs (8), Op. 59 HANS (Vocal Series) ▲ 98150 (15.97)

M. Groop (mez), A. Lubimov (pno)—Wiegenlied (Lullaby) [plus others] *(rec Järvenpää Hall, Germany, Feb 1997)* † Songs; Songs (2), Op. 91; Songs (6), Op. 86; Zigeunerlieder, Op. 103 ODE ▲ 896 [DDD] (17.97)

E. Grümmer (sop), G. Moore (pno)—Wiegenlied (Lullaby) † Songs; E. Grieg:Peer Gynt (sels); F. Schubert:Songs (misc colls); Verdi:Arias; Otello (sels) TES ▲ 1086 (17.97)

A. Kipnis (bass), E. V. Wolff (pno)—Wiegenlied (Lullaby); Am Sonntag Morgen ("Lieder, Part 1") † Songs VOCA (Vocal Archives) ▲ 1160 (13.97)

M. Lipovšek (mez), Folkwang Guitar Duo—Am Sonntag Morgen † Deutsche Volkslieder (26); Deutsche Volkslieder (49), WoO 33; Marienlieder (7), Op. 22; Romances & Songs (5), Op. 84; Songs; Songs & Romances (6); Songs & Romances (8), Op. 14; Zigeunerlieder, Op. 103 ORF ▲ 441971 [DDD] (18.97)

D. Pereira (vc), D. Bollard (pno)—Wiegenlied (Lullaby) ("Cello Rhapsody") † Songs; Songs (6), Op. 86; M. de Falla:Suite populaire espagnole; Ginastera:Pampeana 2, Op. 21; J. Nin:Songs; R. Schumann:Stücke im Volkston, Op. 102; D. Shostakovich:Ballet Suite 2 TALP ▲ 78 [DDD] (18.97)

A. Rubenstein (pno)—Wiegenlied (Lullaby) *(rec 1928-47)* † Pieces (8) Pno, Op. 76; Liszt:Liebesträume, S.541; F. Schubert:Impromptus (4) Pno; R. Schumann:Arabeske Pno, Op. 18; Kinderszenen Pno, Op. 15; Myrthen, Op. 25; Romances Pno, Op. 28; P. Tchaikovsky:Con 1 Pno, Op. 23 GRM2 ▲ 78783 (13.97)

J. Vogler (vc), B. Canino (pno) *(rec Hamburg, Germany, Dec 1997)* † Son 1 Vc, Op. 38; Songs (5), Op. 105; Songs (5), Op. 71; Songs (5), Op. 94; Songs (6), Op. 3; Songs (6), Op. 86; F. Schubert:Son Arpeggione, D.821 BER ▲ 1179 [DDD] (16.97)

Songs (8) for Voice & Piano, Op. 59 (1873)

I. Danz (cta), A. Eckels (pno)—Dämmrung senkte sich von oben; Regenlied; Nachklang † Deutsche Volkslieder (49), WoO 33; Poems (5), Op. 19; Songs (4), Op. 96; Songs (5), Op. 49; Songs (5), Op. 71; Songs (5), Op. 72; Songs (6), Op. 85; Songs (6), Op. 86 HANS (Vocal Series) ▲ 98150 (15.97)

Songs (7) for 4-6 Voices, Op. 62 (1874)

G. Jena (cnd), North German Radio Chorus ("The Complete Brahms Edition, Vol. 7:Choral Works") † Ave Maria, Op. 12; Begräbnisgesang, Op. 13; Canons (13), Op. 113; Dem dunkeln Schoss der heil'gen Erde; Deutsche Volkslieder (26); Fest- und Gedenksprüche, Op. 109; Geistliches Lied, Op. 30; Grausam erweiset sich Amor an mir, Op. 113/2; Kleine Hochzeitskantate; Marienlieder (7), Op. 22; Mir lächelt kein Frühling; Motets (2), Op. 29; Motets (2), Op. 74; Motets (3), Op. 110; O wie sanft; Psalm 13, Op. 27; Sacred Choruses (3), Op. 37; Songs (3), Op. 42; Songs (4), Op. 17; Songs (5), Op. 104; Songs (5), Op. 41; Songs & Romances (12), Op. 44; Songs & Romances (6), Op. 93a; Spruch; Tafellied, Op. 93b; Töne, lindernder Klang; Wann?; Zu Rauch DGRM 4-▲ 449646

Songs (5) for Voice & Piano, Op. 71 (1877)

I. Danz (cta), A. Eckels (pno)—Geheimnis; Es liebt sich so lieblich im Lenze † Deutsche Volkslieder (49), WoO 33; Poems (5), Op. 19; Songs (4), Op. 96; Songs (5), Op. 49; Songs (5), Op. 72; Songs (6), Op. 85; Songs (6), Op. 86; Songs (8), Op. 59 HANS (Vocal Series) ▲ 98150 (15.97)

J. Vogler (vc), B. Canino (pno)—Minnelied (Lovesong) *(rec Hamburg, Germany, Dec 1997)* † Son 1 Vc, Op. 38; Songs (5), Op. 105; Songs (5), Op. 49; Songs (5), Op. 94; Songs (6), Op. 3; Songs (6), Op. 86; F. Schubert:Son Arpeggione, D.821 BER ▲ 1179 [DDD] (16.97)

Songs (5) for Voice & Piano, Op. 72 (1876-77)

I. Danz (cta), A. Eckels (pno)—Alte Liebe; Verzagen † Deutsche Volkslieder (49), WoO 33; Poems (5), Op. 19; Songs (4), Op. 96; Songs (5), Op. 49; Songs (5), Op. 71; Songs (6), Op. 85; Songs (6), Op. 86; Songs (8), Op. 59 HANS (Vocal Series) ▲ 98150 (15.97)

Songs (6) for Voice & Piano, Op. 85 (1878)

I. Danz (cta), A. Eckels (pno)—Sommerabend; Mondenschein † Deutsche Volkslieder (49), WoO 33; Poems (5), Op. 19; Songs (4), Op. 96; Songs (5), Op. 49; Songs (5), Op. 71; Songs (5), Op. 72; Songs (6), Op. 86; Songs (8), Op. 59 HANS (Vocal Series) ▲ 98150 (15.97)

Songs (6) for Low Voice & Piano, Op. 86 (?1877-79)

I. Danz (cta), A. Eckels (pno)—Feldeinsamkeit (In Summer Fields) † Deutsche Volkslieder (49), WoO 33; Poems (5), Op. 19; Songs (4), Op. 96; Songs (5), Op. 49; Songs (5), Op. 71; Songs (5), Op. 72; Songs (6), Op. 85; Songs (8), Op. 59 HANS (Vocal Series) ▲ 98150 (15.97)

M. Groop (mez), A. Lubimov (pno)—Feldeinsamkeit (In Summer Fields) *(rec Järvenpää Hall, Germany, Feb 1997)* † Songs; Songs (2), Op. 91; Songs (5), Op. 49; Zigeunerlieder, Op. 103 ODE ▲ 896 [DDD] (17.97)

M. Müller (sop), I. Newton (pno)—Feldeinsamkeit (In Summer Fields) *(rec 1937)* † Zigeunerlieder, Op. 103; G. Puccini:Bohème (sels); M. Reger:Schlichte Weisen, Op. 76; F. Schubert:Songs (misc colls); R. Wagner:Fliegende Holländer (sels); Lohengrin (sels); Tannhäuser (sels); Walküre (sels); Wesendonck Songs; C. M. von Weber:Freischütz (sels) PRE 2-▲ 89235 (m) (31.97)

M. Pedrotti (bar), S. Ralls (pno)—Feldeinsamkeit (In Summer Fields) † Songs; Duparc:Songs; Morawetz:Songs; R. Strauss:Songs; P. Tchaikovsky:Songs MUVI (Musica Viva) ▲ 1051 [DDD] (16.97)

D. Pereira (vc), D. Bollard (pno)—Feldeinsamkeit (In Summer Fields) ("Cello Rhapsody") † Songs; Songs (5), Op. 49; M. de Falla:Suite populaire espagnole; Ginastera:Pampeana 2, Op. 21; J. Nin:Songs; R. Schumann:Stücke im Volkston, Op. 102; D. Shostakovich:Ballet Suite 2 TALP ▲ 78 [DDD] (18.97)

H. Schlusnus (bar), F. Rupp (pno)—Feldeinsamkeit (In Summer Fields) *(rec 1919-27)* † Songs (9), Op. 32; Beethoven:Adelaide, Op. 46; F. Schubert:Songs (misc colls); R. Schumann:Dichterliebe, Op. 48; R. Strauss:Songs; H. Wolf:Songs (misc) PRE (Lebendige Vergangenheit) ▲ 89188 (m) (16.97)

J. Vogler (vc), B. Canino (pno)—Feldeinsamkeit (In Summer Fields) *(rec Hamburg, Germany, Dec 1997)* † Son 1 Vc, Op. 38; Songs (5), Op. 105; Songs (5), Op. 49; Songs (5), Op. 71; Songs (5), Op. 94; Songs (6), Op. 3; F. Schubert:Son Arpeggione, D.821 BER ▲ 1179 [DDD] (16.97)

Songs (2) for Alto, Viola & Piano, Op. 91 (1864-84)

M. Anderson (cta), W. Primrose (va), F. Rupp (pno) *(rec June 1941)* † Alto Rhap, Op. 53; Son 1 Cl; Son 2 Cl; Songs BID ▲ 150 [AAD] (16.97)

J. Baker (mez), C. Aronowitz (va), A. Previn (pno) † Duets (4), Op. 28; Ernste Gesänge, Op. 121; E. Chausson:Poème de l'amour et de la mer, Op. 19; M. Ravel:Shéhérazade Mez; R. Schumann:Frauenliebe und -leben, Op. 42 EMIC (Doublefforte) 2-▲ 68667 (16.97)

B. Fink (cta), J. Richter (va), P. Jiřikovský (pno) ("Gypsy Songs") † Gypsy Songs (8); Songs (5), Op. 94; A. Dvořák:Songs from the Dvůr Králové Ms, Op. 7; Zigeunermelodien, Op. 55 STMA ▲ 43 [DDD] (18.97)

M. Groop (mez), I. Angervo (va), A. Lubimov (pno) *(rec Järvenpää Hall, Feb 1997)* † Songs; Songs (5), Op. 49; Songs (6), Op. 86; Zigeunerlieder, Op. 103 ODE ▲ 896 [DDD] (17.97)

M. Horne (mez), P. Zukerman (va), M. Neikrug (pno) [GER] † Sons Cl RCAV (Red Seal) ▲ 61276 (16.97)

T. Masur (sop), Y. Bashmet (va), V. Lobanov (pno) *(rec May 1996)* † Son 3 Vn, Op. 108 LV ▲ 661 [ADD/DDD] (17.97)

I. Vermillion (mez), P. Gulda (pno) † Son 1 Cl; Son 2 Cl DGRM ▲ 453421 [DDD]

S. Walker (mez), P. Silverthorne (va), J. Jacobson (pno) [GER] † Sons Cl MER ▲ 84190 (16.97)

BRAHMS, JOHANNES (cont.)

Songs & Romances (6) for 4 Voices, Op. 93a (1883-84)

G. Jena (cnd), North German Radio Chorus ("The Complete Brahms Edition, Vol. 7:Choral Works") † Ave Maria, Op. 12; Begräbnisgesang, Op. 13; Canons (13), Op. 113; Dem dunkeln Schoss der heil'gen Erde; Deutsche Volkslieder (26); Fest- und Gedenksprüche, Op. 109; Geistliches Lied, Op. 30; Grausam erweiset sich Amor an mir, Op. 113/2; Kleine Hochzeitskantate; Marienlieder (7), Op. 22; Mir lächelt kein Frühling; Motets (2), Op. 29; Motets (2), Op. 74; Motets (3), Op. 110; O wie sanft; Psalm 13, Op. 27; Sacred Choruses (3), Op. 37; Songs (3), Op. 42; Songs (4), Op. 17; Songs (5), Op. 104; Songs (5), Op. 41; Songs (7), Op. 62; Songs & Romances (12), Op. 44; Spruch; Tafellied, Op. 93b; Töne, lindernder Klang; Wann?; Zu Rauch DGRM 4-▲ 449646

Songs (5) for Low Voice & Piano, Op. 94 (?1884)

B. Fink (cta), P. Jiřikovský (pno) ("Gypsy Songs") † Gypsy Songs (8); Songs (2), Op. 91; A. Dvořák:Songs from the Dvůr Králové Ms, Op. 7; Zigeunermelodien, Op. 55 STMA ▲ 43 [DDD] (18.97)

D. Lichti (b-bar), J. Fialkowska (pno) *(rec Waterloo, Ontario, Canada, Mar 8-10, 1997)* ("Daniel Lichti Sings Brahms & Schumann") † Ernste Gesänge, Op. 121; R. Schumann:Gedichte, Op. 35 *([ENG,FRE,GER] text)* ODRE ▲ 9311 (16.97)

J. Vogler (vc), B. Canino (pno)—Sapphische Ode *(rec Hamburg, Germany, Dec 1997)* † Son 1 Vc, Op. 38; Songs (5), Op. 105; Songs (5), Op. 49; Songs (5), Op. 71; Songs (6), Op. 3; Songs (6), Op. 86; F. Schubert:Son Arpeggione, D.821 BER ▲ 1179 [DDD] (16.97)

Songs (4) for Voice & Piano, Op. 96 (1884)

I. Danz (cta), A. Eckels (pno)—Der Tod, das ist die kühle Nacht; Es schauen die Blumen; Es schauen die Blumen; Meerfahrt † Deutsche Volkslieder (49), WoO 33; Poems (5), Op. 19; Songs (5), Op. 49; Songs (5), Op. 71; Songs (5), Op. 72; Songs (6), Op. 85; Songs (6), Op. 86; Songs (8), Op. 59 HANS (Vocal Series) ▲ 98150 (15.97)

Songs (5) for 4-6 Voices, Op. 104 (1888)

H. M. Beuerle (cnd), Anton Webern Choir Freiburg ("Secular Choral Songs a Cappella & with Piano") † Qts (6) SATB, Op. 112; Songs; Zigeunerlieder, Op. 103 ARSM ▲ 1136 [DDD] (17.97)

G. Jena (cnd), North German Radio Chorus ("The Complete Brahms Edition, Vol. 7:Choral Works") † Ave Maria, Op. 12; Begräbnisgesang, Op. 13; Canons (13), Op. 113; Dem dunkeln Schoss der heil'gen Erde; Deutsche Volkslieder (26); Fest- und Gedenksprüche, Op. 109; Geistliches Lied, Op. 30; Grausam erweiset sich Amor an mir, Op. 113/2; Kleine Hochzeitskantate; Marienlieder (7), Op. 22; Mir lächelt kein Frühling; Motets (2), Op. 29; Motets (2), Op. 74; Motets (3), Op. 110; O wie sanft; Psalm 13, Op. 27; Sacred Choruses (3), Op. 37; Songs (3), Op. 42; Songs (4), Op. 17; Songs (5), Op. 41; Songs (7), Op. 62; Songs & Romances (12), Op. 44; Songs & Romances (6), Op. 93a; Spruch; Tafellied, Op. 93b; Töne, lindernder Klang; Wann?; Zu Rauch DGRM 4-▲ 449646

M. Piquemal (cnd), Michel Piquemal Vocal Ensemble *(rec Apr 1990)* † Vocal Qts; Brian:Vocal Qts ARN ▲ 68132 [DDD] (16.97)

Songs (5) for Low Voice & Piano, Op. 105 (1886)

H. Hagegård (bar), W. Jones (pno) † Ernste Gesänge, Op. 121; Sibelius:Songs; Stenhammar:Songs RCAV (Red Seal) ▲ 68097 (16.97)

J. Vogler (vc), B. Canino (pno) *(rec Hamburg, Germany, Dec 1997)* † Son 1 Vc, Op. 38; Songs (5), Op. 49; Songs (5), Op. 71; Songs (5), Op. 94; Songs (6), Op. 3; Songs (6), Op. 86; F. Schubert:Son Arpeggione, D.821 BER ▲ 1179 [DDD] (16.97)

Songs (5) for Voice & Piano, Op. 106 (1886)

N. Stutzmann (cta), I. Södergren (pno)—Ständchen *(rec July 1996)* ("Lieder") † Songs RCAV (Red Seal) ▲ 68660 [DDD] (16.97)

Songs & Romance (6) for Chorus (1883-84)

M. Lipovšek (mez)—Der bucklichte Fiedler † Deutsche Volkslieder (26); Deutsche Volkslieder (49), WoO 33; Marienlieder (7), Op. 22; Romances & Songs (5), Op. 84; Songs; Songs (5), Op. 49; Songs & Romances (8), Op. 14; Zigeunerlieder, Op. 103 *(E,F,G texts)* ORF ▲ 441971 [DDD] (18.97)

Souvenir de la Russie (5 pieces) for Piano 4-Hands

V. Afanassiev (pno), V. Suchanov (pno) *(rec Musica-Théâtre La Chaux-de-Fonds, Oct 31-Nov 2, 1994)* † Son for 2 Pnos, Op. 34b DNN ▲ 78976 [DDD] (16.97)

Crommelynck Duo † Liebeslieder Waltzes, Op. 52; Neue Liebeslieder Waltzes Pno 4-Hands, Op.65a; Vars in E♭ on Theme of R. Schumann Pno 4-Hands, Op. 23 CLAV ▲ 8711 [ADD] (16.97)

S. Matthies (pno), C. Köhn (pno) *(rec Clara Wieck Auditorium Sandhausen, Sept 4-9, 1995)* ("Four Hand Piano Music, Vol. 1") † Neue Liebeslieder Waltzes, Op. 65; Vars in E♭ on Theme of R. Schumann Pno 4-Hands, Op. 23; Waltzes Pno, Op. 39 NXIN ▲ 8553139 [DDD] (5.97)

Spruch (canon) for Voice & Viola [text H. von Fallersleben] (1856-58)

G. Jena (cnd), North German Radio Chorus ("The Complete Brahms Edition, Vol. 7:Choral Works") † Ave Maria, Op. 12; Begräbnisgesang, Op. 13; Canons (13), Op. 113; Dem dunkeln Schoss der heil'gen Erde; Deutsche Volkslieder (26); Fest- und Gedenksprüche, Op. 109; Geistliches Lied, Op. 30; Grausam erweiset sich Amor an mir, Op. 113/2; Kleine Hochzeitskantate; Marienlieder (7), Op. 22; Mir lächelt kein Frühling; Motets (2), Op. 29; Motets (2), Op. 74; Motets (3), Op. 110; O wie sanft; Psalm 13, Op. 27; Sacred Choruses (3), Op. 37; Songs (3), Op. 42; Songs (4), Op. 17; Songs (5), Op. 104; Songs (5), Op. 41; Songs (7), Op. 62; Songs & Romances (12), Op. 44; Songs & Romances (6), Op. 93a; Tafellied, Op. 93b; Töne, lindernder Klang; Wann?; Zu Rauch DGRM 4-▲ 449646

Studies (5) for Piano (1879)

A. Ugorski (pno)—Chaconne after J.S. Bach in g † Son 1 Pno, Op. 1; Son 2 Pno, Op. 2; Son 3 Pno, Op. 5; Vars & Fugue on a Theme by Handel, Op. 24 DGRM 2-▲ 449182 [DDD]

Symphonies (4) (complete)

A. Doráti (cnd), London SO *(Sym 1, Op. 68; Sym 3, Op. 90; Sym 4, Op. 98)*, A. Doráti (cnd), Minneapolis SO *(Sym 2, Op. 73)* MRCR ▲ 34380 (22.97)

F. V. Weingartner (cnd), London PO *(Sym 3, Op. 90)*, F. V. Weingartner (cnd), London SO *(Sym 4, Op. 98) (rec 1938)* CENT ▲ 2128 (16.97)

Symphonies (4) (comp)

C. Abbado (cnd), Berlin PO † Academic Festival Ov, Op. 80; Alto Rhap, Op. 53; Gesäng der Parzen, Op. 89; Nänie, Op. 82; Schicksalslied, Op. 54; Tragic Ov, Op. 81; Vars on a Theme by Haydn DGRM 4-▲ 435683 [DDD]

M. Abravanel (cnd), Utah SO *(rec Mormon Tabernacle Salt Lake City, May 17-24, 1976)* ("Orchestral Works") † Academic Festival Ov, Op. 80; Tragic Ov, Op. 81; Vars on a Theme by Haydn VC 3-▲ 1719 [AAD] (39.97)

L. Bernstein (cnd), Vienna PO † Academic Festival Ov, Op. 80; Tragic Ov, Op. 81; Vars on a Theme by Haydn DEUT 4-▲ 15570 [DDD] (38.97)

N. Harnoncourt (cnd), Berlin PO † Academic Festival Ov, Op. 80; Tragic Ov, Op. 81; Vars on a Theme by Haydn TELC 3-▲ 13136 (50.97)

E. Jochum (cnd), Berlin PO DEUT (The Originals) 2-▲ 49715 [ADD] (22.97)

H. von Karajan (cnd), Berlin PO † Tragic Ov, Op. 81; Vars on a Theme by Haydn DEUT 3-▲ 27602 [DDD] (48.97)

H. von Karajan (cnd), Berlin PO ("Complete Brahms Edition, Vol. 1:Orchestral Works") † Academic Festival Ov, Op. 80; Hungarian Dances Orch; Serenade 1 Orch, Op. 11; Serenade 2 Orch, Op. 16; Tragic Ov, Op. 81; Vars on a Theme by Haydn DGRM 5-▲ 449601 (64.97)

H. von Karajan (cnd), Berlin PO *(rec Berlin Philharmonie, Germany, Oct 1977-Feb 1978)* DEUT (2-Fers) 2-▲ 453097 [ADD] (17.97)

R. Kubelík (cnd), Bavarian RSO ORF 3-▲ 70833 [DDD] (54.97)

G. Lehel (cnd), Budapest SO *(rec Italian Cultural Institute Budapest, Sept 1982)* † Academic Festival Ov, Op. 80; Tragic Ov, Op. 81; Vars on a Theme by Haydn CLDI 3-▲ 4038 [ADD/DDD] (10.97)

C. Mackerras (cnd), Scottish CO *(rec Edinburgh Scotland, Jan 6-11 & 27-30, 1997)* † Academic Festival Ov, Op. 80; Vars on a Theme by Haydn TEL 3-▲ 80450 [DDD] (38.97)

E. Marturet (cnd), Berlin SO † Academic Festival Ov, Op. 80; Tragic Ov, Op. 81; Vars on a Theme by Haydn VRDI 4-▲ 6814 (20.97)

K. Sanderling (cnd), Dresden Staatskapelle † Tragic Ov, Op. 81; Vars on a Theme by Haydn EUR 3-▲ 69220 [ADD] (13.97)

W. Sawallisch (cnd), Vienna SO PPHI (Duo) 2-▲ 38757 (17.97)

S. Skrowaczewski (cnd), Hallé Orch † Academic Festival Ov, Op. 80; Hungarian Dances Orch; Tragic Ov, Op. 81; Vars on a Theme by Haydn IMPB 4-▲ 3 [DDD]

H. Swarowsky (cnd), Grosses SO *(rec 1970)* CALG ▲ 704031 [ADD] (18.97)

G. Szell (cnd), Cleveland Orch † Academic Festival Ov, Op. 80; Hungarian Dances Orch; Tragic Ov, Op. 81; Vars on a Theme by Haydn SNYC (Essential Classics) 3-▲ 48398 (23.97)

A. Toscanini (cnd), NBC SO *(rec Studio 8-H broadcast)* ("The Toscanini Collection, Vols. 6-9") † Academic Festival Ov, Op. 80; Con Vn & Vc, Op. 102; Gesäng der Parzen, Op. 89; Hungarian Dances Orch; Liebeslieder Waltzes Pno 4-Hands, Op. 52a; Tragic Ov, Op. 81; Vars on a Theme by Haydn RCAV (Gold Seal) 4-▲ 60325 [ADD] (40.97)

F. V. Weingartner (cnd), London PO, F. V. Weingartner (cnd), London SO *(rec 1938-40)* GRM2 2-▲ 78764 (26.97)

Symphony No. 1 in c, Op. 68 (1855-1876)

C. Abbado (cnd), Berlin PO, Berlin Radio Chorus † Gesäng der Parzen, Op. 89 DEUT ▲ 431790 [DDD] (16.97)

H. Abendroth (cnd), Bavarian State Orch ("Edition Hermann Abendroth Vol 2") † Kalinnikov:Sym 1; G. Mahler:Sym 8; R. Schumann:Sym 1; Strauss (II):An der schönen blauen Donau, Op. 314; Kaiser-Walzer, Op. 437; Ovs TAHA 2-▲ 120 (17.97)

BRAHMS, JOHANNES (cont.)

Symphony No. 1 in c, Op. 68 (1855-1876) (cont.)

H. Abendroth (cnd), Berlin PO ("The Art of Hermann Abendroth 1927-41") † Sym 4; Beethoven:Sym 4; Sym 5; G. F. Handel:Concerti grossi, Op. 6; W. A. Mozart:Serenade 6 Orch, K.239; Serenata notturna, K.239 TAHA 2-▲ 102 (34.97)

H. Abendroth (cnd), Berlin PO *(rec 1941)* † Tragic Ov, Op. 81 IN ▲ 1391 (15.97)

H. Abendroth (cnd), London SO *(rec England, Mar 1928)* † Sym 3 BCS ▲ 52 [ADD] (16.97)

G. Albrecht (cnd), Czech PO † A. Dvořák:Carnival, Op. 92; In Nature's Realm, Op. 91; Othello, Op. 93 SUR (Czech PO Centennial) ▲ 111995

K. Ančerl (cnd), Czech PO † Tragic Ov, Op. 81 SUR (Czech Philharmonic) ▲ 111941 [AAD]

A. Augér (sop), F. Gerihsen (bar), S. Celibidache (cnd), Munich PO, J. Schmidhuber (cnd), Munich Phil Chorus, J. Schmidhuber (cnd), Munich Bach Choir Members *(rec live, Lukaskirche, Munich, Germany, July 2, 1981)* † Deutsches Requiem, Op. 45 EMIC 2-▲ 56843 [ADD] (32.97)

J. Barbirolli (cnd), Vienna PO † Tragic Ov, Op. 81 RYLC ▲ 6433

J. Bělohlávek (cnd), Czech PO † Vars on a Theme by Haydn SUR ▲ 111989

L. Bernstein (cnd), New York PO ("Bernstein: The Royal Edition") † Serenade 2 Orch, Op. 16 SNYC ▲ 47536 [ADD] (10.97)

L. Bernstein (cnd), Vienna PO † Academic Festival Ov, Op. 80 DEUT (Leonard Bernstein Edition) ▲ 31029 [DDD] (11.97)

L. Bernstein (cnd), Vienna PO † Beethoven:Coriolan Ov, Op. 62; Egmont (ov) DEUT (Masters) ▲ 45505 [DDD] (9.97)

K. Böhm (cnd), Vienna PO † F. Schubert:Sym 8 MTAL ▲ 48051 (6.97)

K. Böhm (cnd), Vienna PO *(rec 1940)* ("Böhm, Vol. 4") † F. Schubert:Sym 8 LYS ▲ 407 (17.97)

K. Böhm (cnd), Vienna PO † F. Schubert:Sym 8 HCO ▲ 37008 (7.97)

K. Böhm (cnd), Vienna PO † F. Schubert:Sym 8 IMMM ▲ 37008 (6.97)

W. Furtwängler (cnd) *(rec Nov 17-20, 1947)* † Con 2 Pno, Op. 83; Sym 2 GRM2 2-▲ 78751 (26.97)

W. Furtwängler (cnd), Berlin PO ("Furtwängler Historical Archives 1942-45") † Con 2 Pno, Op. 83; Beethoven:Coriolan Ov, Op. 62; Sym 6; Sym 9; A. Bruckner:Sym 6; Sym 7; R. Wagner:Tristan und Isolde (prelude & liebestod) TAHA 4-▲ 1004

W. Furtwängler (cnd), Berlin PO *(rec live, May 18, 1953)* † I. Stravinsky:Baiser de la fée TAHA ▲ 1019 (m) (17.97)

W. Furtwängler (cnd), Lucerne Festival Orch *(rec France, Aug 1947)* ("Furtwangler: Concert in Lucerne") † Beethoven:Con 1 Pno, Op. 15; Leonore (ov 3) TAHA 2-▲ 1028

W. Furtwängler (cnd), Lucerne Festival Orch *(rec Aug 27, 1947)* ("Wilhelm Furtwängler at the Lucerne Festival") † Con Vn & Vc, Op. 102; Beethoven:Con Vn; Con 1 Pno, Op. 15; Leonore (ov 3); Sym 3; Sym 7; R. Schumann:Sym 4; R. Wagner:Lohengrin (preludes) MUA 4-▲ 1018 [ADD] (47.97)

W. Furtwängler (cnd), North German RSO ("Furtwängler Concert in Hamburg 1951") † Vars on a Theme by Haydn TAHA ▲ 1001 (17.97)

W. Furtwängler (cnd), Vienna PO *(rec 1952)* † Vars on a Theme by Haydn TES ▲ 1142 (17.97)

J. Horenstein (cnd), London SO *(rec 1962)* † R. Wagner:Tannhäuser (orch sels) CHSK ▲ 19 (16.97)

E. Jochum (cnd), London PO † Academic Festival Ov, Op. 80; Sym 2; Sym 3; Tragic Ov, Op. 81 EMIC (Doublefforte) 2-▲ 69515 (16.97)

H. von Karajan (cnd), (Royal) Concertgebouw Orch ("The Young Karajan: The First Recordings, Vol. 5") † W. A. Mozart:Sym 35, K.385; Strauss (II):Zigeunerbaron (ov) GRM2 ▲ 78663 (13.97)

H. von Karajan (cnd), Berlin PO DEUT ▲ 23141 [DDD] (16.97)

H. von Karajan (cnd), Berlin PO *(rec 1963 & 1973)* † R. Schumann:Sym 1 DEUT (The Originals) ▲ 47408 [ADD] (11.97)

H. von Karajan (cnd), Berlin PO *(rec 1941-43)* † Strauss (II):Künstlerleben, Op. 316; Waltzes HCO ▲ 37027 (7.97)

H. von Karajan (cnd), Concertgebouw Orch † Strauss (II):Kaiser-Walzer, Op. 437; Künstlerleben, Op. 316 IMUS (Magic Master) ▲ 37075 (6.97)

I. Kertész (cnd), Vienna PO † Serenade 2 Orch, Op. 16; Sym 2; Vars on a Theme by Haydn PLON 2-▲ 48197 (17.97)

C. Mackerras (cnd), Scottish CO † Academic Festival Ov, Op. 80 TEL ▲ 80463 (16.97)

N. Marriner (cnd), Academy of St. Martin in the Fields † Sym 2 HANS 2-▲ 98186 (15.97)

K. Masur (cnd), New York PO † Tragic Ov, Op. 81 TELC ▲ 90883 (16.97)

W. Mengelberg (cnd), Concertgebouw Orch † Academic Festival Ov, Op. 80 GRM2 (Records of the Century) ▲ 78853 (13.97)

P. Monteux (cnd), (Royal) Concertgebouw Orch ("The Art of Pierre Monteux") † Con Vn; Sym 3; Tragic Ov, Op. 81; Berlioz:Sym fantastique, Op. 14; Sibelius:Con Vn; I. Stravinsky:Pétrouchka TAHA 4-▲ 175 (67.97)

E. Ormandy (cnd), Philadelphia Orch † Academic Festival Ov, Op. 80; Sym 2; Tragic Ov, Op. 81; Vars & Fugue on a Theme by Handel, Op. 24; Vars on a Theme by Haydn SNYC (Essential Classics Take 2) 2-▲ 63287 (14.97)

W. Primrose (va), G. Moore (pno)—Andante sostenuto *(rec 1937)* † H. G. Casadesus:Con Va; W. A. Mozart:Sinf concertante Vn, K.364 PHS ▲ 9045 [AAD] (17.97)

A. Rahbari (cnd), Belgian Radio-TV Orch *(rec June 1990)* † Serenade 1 Orch, Op. 11 NXIN ▲ 550280 [DDD] (5.97)

A. Scholz (cnd), South German PO † Vars on a Theme by Haydn PC ▲ 267127 [DDD] (2.97)

G. Schuller (cnd) *(rec Manhattan School of Music Myers Recording Studio, Dec 22-23, 1995)* ("Gunther Schuller-Conductor") † Beethoven:Sym 5 GMR ▲ 2051 (16.97)

S. Skrowaczewski (cnd), Hallé Orch † Academic Festival Ov, Op. 80 INMP ▲ 2014 (9.97)

W. Steinberg (cnd), Pittsburgh SO *(rec Syria Mosque, Pittsburgh, United States of America, Apr 17, 1956)* † P. Tchaikovsky:Con Vn EMIC ▲ 67101 [ADD] (11.97)

H. Swarowsky (cnd), South German PO † Academic Festival Ov, Op. 80; Con Vn & Vc, Op. 102; Con 2 Pno, Op. 83; Sym 4 INTC ▲ 885924 (16.97)

G. Szell (cnd), Cleveland Orch † Vars on a Theme by Haydn SNYC (Essential Classics) ▲ 46534 [ADD] (7.97) ▮ 46534 [ADD] (3.98)

A. Toscanini (cnd), NBC SO *(rec live, Dec 25, 1937)* ("Toscanini's First Concert with the N.B.C. Symphony Orchestra") † W. A. Mozart:Sym 40, K.550 MYTO ▲ 89009 [ADD] (17.97)

A. Toscanini (cnd), NBC SO ("The Toscanini Collection, Vol. 6") † Academic Festival Ov, Op. 80; Hungarian Dances Orch RCAV (Gold Seal) ▲ 60257 [ADD] (11.97)

A. Toscanini (cnd), NBC SO ("The Toscanini Collection, Vol. 26") † Serenade 2 Orch, Op. 16 RCAV (Gold Seal) ▲ 60277 (11.97)

A. Toscanini (cnd), NBC SO ("Christmas 1937: Toscanini's 1st NBC Concert") † W. A. Mozart:Sym 40, K.550; Vivaldi:Cons Vn(s) Strs, Op. 3/1-12 RY (The Radio Years) ▲ 13 (16.97)

B. Walter (cnd), Columbia SO † Academic Festival Ov, Op. 80; Vars on a Theme by Haydn SNYC (Bruno Walter: The Edition) ▲ 64470 (10.97)

B. Walter (cnd), Vienna PO *(rec Vienna, 1937)* ("Bruno Walter in Vienna, Vol. 1: The Last Recordings in Europe before WW II") † Beethoven:Leonore (ov 3) GRM2 ▲ 78517 [ADD] (13.97)

B. Walter (cnd), Vienna PO † Beethoven:Leonore (ov 3) ENT (Sirio) ▲ 53005 (13.97)

F. V. Weingartner (cnd), London SO *(rec London, 1939)* † Sym 2 78'S (The 78's) ▲ 78512 [ADD] (13.97)

artists unknown † Tragic Ov, Op. 81 SNYC ▲ 62288 [DDD] (4.97)

Symphony No. 2 in D, Op. 73 (1877)

C. Abbado (cnd), Berlin PO † Alto Rhap, Op. 53 DEUT ▲ 27643 [DDD] (16.97)

J. Barbirolli (cnd), Vienna PO † Sym 3 RYLC ▲ 6434 (8.97)

R. Barshaï (cnd), Cologne RSO *(rec Philharmonie Köln, Germany)* † Sym 4 LARL 2-▲ 903 (22.97)

J. Bělohlávek (cnd), Czech PO † Academic Festival Ov, Op. 80; Tragic Ov, Op. 81 SUR ▲ 111990

L. Bernstein (cnd), Vienna PO † Academic Festival Ov, Op. 80 DEUT (Masters) ▲ 45506 [DDD] (9.97)

K. Böhm (cnd), Vienna PO ("Karl Böhm, Vol. 2") † M. Reger:Vars & Fugue on a Theme by Mozart, Op. 132 LYS ▲ 405 (17.97)

S. Celibidache (cnd), Münchner Philharmoniker *(rec live, Philharmonie am Gasteig, Munich, Germany, June 8, 1991)* † Sym 3; Sym 4 EMIC 2-▲ 56846 [ADD/DDD] (32.97)

W. Damrosch (cnd), New York SO *(rec Jan 1928)* † Sym 4 BCS ▲ 53 [ADD] (16.97)

W. Furtwängler (cnd) *(rec Jan 28, 1945)* † Con 2 Pno, Op. 83; Sym 1 GRM2 2-▲ 78751 (26.97)

W. Furtwängler (cnd), Berlin PO—Adagio non troppo ("A Tribute to Furtwängler") † Beethoven:Sym 3; Sym 5; Sym 6; A. Dvořák:Slavonic Dances (sels); Mendelssohn (-Bartholdy):Hebriden, Op. 26; F. Schubert:Sym 8; Sym 9; R. Schumann:Con Vc; R. Strauss:Till Eulenspiegels lustige Streiche, Op. 28 TAHA 4-▲ 1008 (35.97)

W. Furtwängler (cnd), London PO *(rec live, Kingsway Hall, England, March 22, 1948)* † Con Vn DLAB ▲ 5024 (15.97)

N. Järvi (cnd), Moscow PO *(rec Moscow Conservatory Great Hall, Apr 1966)* ("Neeme Järvi: The Early Recordings, Vol. 1") † Sym 3 MELD ▲ 40719 [ADD] (6.97)

E. Jochum (cnd), London PO † Academic Festival Ov, Op. 80; Sym 1; Sym 3; Tragic Ov, Op. 81 EMIC (Doublefforte) 2-▲ 69515 (16.97)

H. von Karajan (cnd), Berlin PO † Sym 3 DEUT ▲ 29153 [ADD] (7.97)

I. Kertész (cnd), Vienna PO † Serenade 2 Orch, Op. 16; Sym 1; Vars on a Theme by Haydn PLON 2-▲ 48197 (17.97)

BRAHMS, JOHANNES (cont.)

Symphony No. 2 in D, Op. 73 (1877) (cont.)

H. Knappertsbusch (cnd), Berlin PO, H. Knappertsbusch (cnd), Vienna PO † Sym 3; J. S. Bach:Music of Bach; A. Bruckner:Sym 4; W. A. Mozart:Music of Mozart TAHA 3-▲ 320 (50.97)

H. Knappertsbusch (cnd), Dresden Staatskapelle ("Dresden Staatskapelle 450th Anniversary Recordings") † Sym 3; J. Haydn:Sym 94; R. Strauss:Tod und Verklärung, Op. 24 TAHA 2-▲ 303 (34.97)

H. Knappertsbusch (cnd), Munich PO *(rec München, Germany, 1959)* † Academic Festival Ov, Op. 80; Con Vn & Vc, Op. 102; Con 2 Pno, Op. 83; Rhap Alt, Op. 53; Sym 3; Sym 4; Tragic Ov, Op. 81; Vars on a Theme by Haydn MELO 4-▲ 40039 (m) [ADD] (62.97)

H. Knappertsbusch (cnd), Swiss Romande Orch † Liszt:Préludes, S.97 GRM2 (Records of the Century) ▲ 78845 (13.97)

C. Mackerras (cnd), Scottish CO † Vars on a Theme by Haydn TEL ▲ 80464 (16.97)

N. Marriner (cnd), Academy of St. Martin in the Fields † Sym 1 HANS 2-▲ 98186 (15.97)

K. Masur (cnd), New York PO † Academic Festival Ov, Op. 80 TELC ▲ 77291 (16.97)

Z. Mehta (cnd), Israel PO *(rec live Tel-Aviv, Dec 26, 1996)* ("Israel Philharmonic 60th Anniversary Gala Concert") † J. S. Bach:Con Vns; Halvorsen:Passacaglia & Sarabande con variazioni; W. A. Mozart:Serenade 6 Orch, K.239; C. M. von Weber:Oberon (ov) RCAV (Red Seal) 2-▲ 68768 [DDD] (16.97)

W. Mengelberg (cnd), Amsterdam Concertgebouw Orch *(rec Apr 4, 1940)* † Sym 4 BCS ▲ 57 [ADD] (16.97)

W. Mengelberg (cnd), Concertgebouw Orch † Sym 3; Sym 4; Tragic Ov, Op. 81 TAHA ▲ 274 (34.97)

P. Monteux (cnd), San Francisco SO ("Vol 3") † Schicksalslied, Op. 54; G. Mahler:Kindertotenlieder RCAV (Gold Seal) ▲ 61891 (11.97)

C. Munch (cnd), French National Orch ("Charles Munch Edition 3") † R. Schumann:Sym 4 VAL ▲ 4827 (12.97)

E. Ormandy (cnd), Philadelphia Orch † Academic Festival Ov, Op. 80; Sym 1; Tragic Ov, Op. 81; Vars & Fugue on a Theme by Handel, Op. 24; Vars on a Theme by Haydn SNYC (Essential Classics Take 2) 2-▲ 63287 (14.97)

A. Rahbari (cnd), Belgian Radio-TV Orch *(rec Mar 1990)* † Serenade 2 Orch, Op. 16 NXIN ▲ 550279 [DDD] (5.97)

A. Scholz (cnd), South German PO † Sym 3 PC ▲ 267157 [DDD] (2.97)

S. Skrowaczewski (cnd), Hallé Orch † Tragic Ov, Op. 81 INMP ▲ 857 [DDD] (11.97)

S. Skrowaczewski (cnd), Hallé Orch † Tragic Ov, Op. 81 ICC ▲ 6700982 (9.97)

H. Swarowsky (cnd), South German PO—Adagio non troppo ("Music for Meditation, Vol. 3") † Debussy:Syrinx Fl; Valse romantique Pno; Lalo:Rapsodie norvégienne; M. Reger:Con Vn; Rimsky-Korsakov:Scheherazade, Op. 35; I. Stravinsky:Firebird (sels) ECL ▲ 507 (2.97)

G. Szell (cnd), Cleveland Orch † Sym 3 SNYC (Essential Classics) ▲ 47652 (7.97) ▮ 47652 (3.98)

A. Toscanini (cnd), BBC SO *(rec 1935-39)* ("Toscanini in London, Vol. 2") † Sym 4 GRM2 ▲ 78612 (13.97)

A. Toscanini (cnd), BBC SO *(rec 1938)* † Sym 4 GRM2 (Records of the Century) ▲ 78851 (13.97)

B. Walter (cnd), Columbia SO † Sym 3 SNYC (Bruno Walter: The Edition) ▲ 64471 (10.97)

F. V. Weingartner (cnd), London PO *(rec London, 1940)* † Sym 1 78'S (The 78's) ▲ 78512 [ADD] (13.97)

orch unknown † Mendelssohn (-Bartholdy):Hebriden, Op. 26 SNYC ▲ 62287 [DDD] (4.97)

Symphony No. 3 in F, Op. 90 (1883)

C. Abbado (cnd), Berlin PO † Schicksalslied, Op. 54; Tragic Ov, Op. 81 DEUT ▲ 29765 [DDD] (16.97)

J. Barbirolli (cnd), Vienna PO † Sym 2 RYLC ▲ 6434 (8.97)

J. Bělohlávek (cnd), Czech PO † Sym 4 SUR ▲ 111991

L. Bernstein (cnd), Vienna PO † Vars on a Theme by Haydn DEUT (Masters) ▲ 45507 [DDD] (9.97)

G. Cantelli (cnd), New York PO ("Guido Cantelli, Vol. 1") † B. Bartók:Music for Strs, Perc & Cel, Sz.106 STRV ▲ 13591 [AAD] (13.97)

S. Celibidache (cnd), Münchner Philharmoniker *(rec live, Herkulesaal der Münchner Residenz, Germany, June 20, 1979)* † Sym 2; Sym 4 EMIC 2-▲ 56846 [ADD/DDD] (32.97)

B. Eden (pno), A. Tamir (pno) [2-pno version] † Vars in E♭ on Theme of R. Schumann Pno 4-Hands, Op. 23 CRD ▲ 3414 (17.97)

N. Järvi (cnd), Moscow PO *(rec Moscow Conservatory Great Hall, Apr 1966)* ("Neeme Järvi: The Early Recordings, Vol. 1") † Sym 2 MELD ▲ 40719 [ADD] (6.97)

E. Jochum (cnd), London PO † Academic Festival Ov, Op. 80; Sym 1; Sym 2; Tragic Ov, Op. 81 EMIC (Doublefforte) 2-▲ 69515 (16.97)

H. von Karajan (cnd), Berlin PO † Sym 2 DEUT ▲ 29153 [ADD] (7.97)

H. von Karajan (cnd), Berlin PO † Sym 4 DEUT ▲ 31593 [ADD] (9.97)

H. von Karajan (cnd), Berlin PO *(rec 1977)* † Sym 4 DEUT (Galleria) ▲ 37645 [ADD] (9.97)

I. Kertész (cnd), Vienna PO † Serenade 1 Orch, Op. 11; Sym 4 PLON 2-▲ 48200 (17.97)

H. Knappertsbusch (cnd), Berlin PO ("Original Recordings from 1906 to 1943") † Verdi:Aida (sels); R. Wagner:Götterdämmerung (sels); Rienzi (ov) GRM2 ▲ 78522 (13.97)

H. Knappertsbusch (cnd), Berlin PO, H. Knappertsbusch (cnd), Vienna PO † Sym 2; J. S. Bach:Music of Bach; A. Bruckner:Sym 4; W. A. Mozart:Music of Mozart TAHA 3-▲ 320 (50.97)

H. Knappertsbusch (cnd), Dresden Staatskapelle ("Dresden Staatskapelle 450th Anniversary Recordings") † Sym 2; J. Haydn:Sym 94; R. Strauss:Tod und Verklärung, Op. 24 TAHA 2-▲ 303 (34.97)

H. Knappertsbusch (cnd), Vienna PO *(rec Salzburg, Germany, 1958)* † Academic Festival Ov, Op. 80; Con Vn & Vc, Op. 102; Con 2 Pno, Op. 83; Rhap Alt, Op. 53; Sym 2; Sym 4; Tragic Ov, Op. 81; Vars on a Theme by Haydn MELO 4-▲ 40039 (m) [ADD] (62.97)

S. Koussevitzky (cnd), Boston SO *(rec 1938)* ("Koussevitzky Conducts Brahms") † Sym 4 PHS ▲ 9237 (17.97)

C. Krauss (cnd), Vienna PO *(rec Jan & Mar 1930)* † Sym 1 BCS ▲ 52 [ADD] (16.97)

T. Lønskov (pno), R. Llambias (pno) [original 2 pno version] *(rec Sept 1992)* † Vars on a Theme by Haydn KPT ▲ 32148 [DDD]

C. Mackerras (cnd), Scottish CO † Academic Festival Ov, Op. 80; Sym 4 TEL ▲ 80465 (16.97)

N. Marriner (cnd), Academy of St. Martin in the Fields † Sym 4 HANS (Academy) ▲ 98187 (15.97)

K. Masur (cnd), New York PO † Vars on a Theme by Haydn TELC ▲ 90862 (16.97)

W. Mengelberg (cnd), (Royal) Concertgebouw Orch *(rec 1932)* ("Mengelberg 1928-32 Columbia Recordings") † P. Tchaikovsky:Romeo & Juliet; Sym 4; Sym 5 GSE 2-▲ 785048 (32.97)

W. Mengelberg (cnd), Concertgebouw Orch † Sym 2; Sym 4; Tragic Ov, Op. 81 TAHA ▲ 274 (34.97)

W. Mengelberg (cnd), Concertgebouw Orch *(rec 1931)* ("Art of Mengelberg, Vol. 1") † C. Franck:Sym in d, M.48 GRM2 ▲ 78866 (11.97)

N. Milstein (vn), E. Leinsdorf (cnd), Philharmonia Orch *(rec Abbey Road, London, England, June 23-4, 1960)* † Con Vn EMIC ▲ 67021 [ADD] (11.97)

D. Mitropoulos (cnd), (Royal) Concertgebouw Orch *(rec live Salzburg Festival, Aug 1958)* † R. Strauss:Also sprach Zarathustra, Op. 30 ORFE ▲ 458971 [ADD] (16.97)

P. Monteux (cnd), (Royal) Concertgebouw Orch ("The Art of Pierre Monteux") † Con Vn; Sym 1; Tragic Ov, Op. 81; Berlioz:Sym fantastique, Op. 14; Sibelius:Con Vn; I. Stravinsky:Pétrouchka TAHA 4-▲ 175 (67.97)

R. Muti (cnd), Philadelphia Orch † Alto Rhap, Op. 53 PPHI (Digital Classics) ▲ 26253 [DDD] (16.97)

J. V. Nes (cta), B. Haitink (cnd), Boston SO, Tanglewood Festival Chorus † Alto Rhap, Op. 53 PPHI ▲ 42120 (16.97)

R. Norrington (cnd), London Classical Players † Sym 4 EMIC ▲ 56118

A. Rahbari (cnd), Belgian Radio-TV Orch *(rec 1989)* † Vars on a Theme by Haydn NXIN ▲ 550278 [DDD] (5.97)

F. Reiner (cnd), Chicago SO † F. Schubert:Sym 5 RCAV (Gold Seal) ▲ 61793 (11.97)

H. Scherchen (cnd), Swiss-Italian RSO ("Hermann Scherchen in Lugano Vol 1") † A. Dvořák:Con Vc TAHA ▲ 116 (17.97)

A. Scholz (cnd), South German PO † Sym 2 PC ▲ 267157 [DDD] (2.97)

S. Skrowaczewski (cnd), Hallé Orch † Vars on a Theme by Haydn INMP (Classic) ▲ 2039 (9.97)

L. Stokowski (cnd), Houston SO *(rec Civic Center Houston)* † Sym 4 EVC ▲ 9016 [AAD] (13.97)

L. Stokowski (cnd), Philadelphia Orch † Sym 4 78'S ▲ 78549 (13.97)

G. Szell (cnd), Cleveland Orch † Sym 2 SNYC (Essential Classics) ▲ 47652 (7.97) ▮ 47652 (3.98)

E. Van Beinum (cnd), London PO *(rec 1946-49)* ("Van Beinum, Vol. 2") † Mendelssohn (-Bartholdy):Con Vn & Orch, Op. 64; Hebriden, Op. 26 LYS ▲ 471 (17.97)

B. Walter (cnd), Columbia SO † Sym 2 SNYC (Bruno Walter: The Edition) ▲ 64471 (10.97)

F. V. Weingartner (cnd), London PO *(rec London, 1938)* † Academic Festival Ov, Op. 80; Sym 4 78'S (The 78's) ▲ 78516 [ADD] (13.97)

artists unknown † Liszt:Préludes, S.97 SNYC ▲ 62302 [DDD] (4.97)

Symphony No. 4 in e, Op. 98 (1884-85)

C. Abbado (cnd), Berlin PO † Nänie, Op. 82; Vars on a Theme by Haydn DEUT ▲ 35349 [DDD] (16.97)

H. Abendroth (cnd), London SO ("The Art of Hermann Abendroth 1927-41") † Sym 1; Beethoven:Sym 4; Sym 5; G. F. Handel:Concerti grossi, Op. 6; W. A. Mozart:Serenade 6 Orch, K.239; Serenata notturna, K.239 TAHA 2-▲ 102 (34.97)

H. Abendroth (cnd), London SO *(rec Mar 1927)* † Sym 2 BCS ▲ 53 [ADD] (16.97)

V. Ashkenazy (cnd), Cleveland Orch PLON ▲ 36853 [DDD] (16.97)

J. Barbirolli (cnd), Vienna PO † Academic Festival Ov, Op. 80; Vars on a Theme by Haydn RYLC ▲ 6435

J. Bělohlávek (cnd), Czech PO † Sym 3 SUR ▲ 111991

BRAHMS, JOHANNES (cont.)

Symphony No. 4 in e, Op. 98 (1884-85) (cont.)

L. Bernstein (cnd), New York PO ("Bernstein: The Royal Edition") † Academic Festival Ov, Op. 80; Tragic Ov, Op. 81 SNYC ▲ 47538 [ADD] (10.97)
L. Bernstein (cnd), Vienna PO † Tragic Ov, Op. 81 DEUT (Masters) ▲ 45508 [DDD] (9.97)
K. Böhm (cnd), Saxon State Orch *(rec 1938-39)* ("Karl Böhm Conducts Brahms & Reger") † M. Reger:Vars & Fugue on a Theme by Mozart, Op. 132 IN ▲ 1387 [AAD] (15.97)
S. Celibidache (cnd), Berlin PO *(rec 1945-46)* ("The Unknown Recordings") † Beethoven:Egmont (ov); Leonore (ov 3); Glière:Con Coloratura Sop; J. Haydn:Sym 96 GRM2 2-▲ 78774 (26.97)
S. Celibidache (cnd), Berlin PO *(rec live Berlin, 1945-46)* † Beethoven:Leonore (ov 3); Glière:Con Coloratura Sop MYTO (Historic) ▲ 81009 (17.97)
S. Celibidache (cnd), Münchner Philharmoniker *(rec live, Herkulesaal der Münchner Residenz, Germany, March 16, 1985)* † Sym 2; Sym 3 EMIC 2-▲ 56846 [ADD/DDD] (32.97)
W. Furtwängler (cnd), Berlin PO *(rec live, 1942-43)* † Vars on a Theme by Haydn GRM2 ▲ 78594 (13.97)
W. Furtwängler (cnd), Berlin PO *(rec 1942)* † Vars on a Theme by Haydn MTAL ▲ 48059 (6.97)
W. Furtwängler (cnd), Berlin PO *(rec 1948)* † Beethoven:Sym 1 TAHA ▲ 1025 (17.97)
W. Furtwängler (cnd), Berlin PO *(rec 1943)* ("Wilhelm Furtwängler Wartime Recordings") † Con 2 Pno, Op. 83; Vars on a Theme by Haydn; Beethoven:Con 4 Pno, Op. 58; Sym 3; Sym 5; Sym 6; Sym 9; R. Strauss:Songs; R. Wagner:Meistersinger (preludes); Tristan und Isolde (prelude & liebestod) TAHA 6-▲ 1034 (50.97)
W. Furtwängler (cnd), Berlin PO † Vars on a Theme by Haydn HCO ▲ 37049 (7.97)
H. Haenchen (cnd), Netherlands PO † Tragic Ov, Op. 81 LALI ▲ 14001 [DDD] (3.97)
E. Jochum (cnd), London PO † Deutsches Requiem, Op. 45 EMIC (Doubleforte) 2-▲ 69518 (16.97)
H. von Karajan (cnd), Berlin PO † Sym 3 DEUT ▲ 31593 [ADD] (9.97)
H. von Karajan (cnd), Berlin PO *(rec 1977)* † Sym 3 DEUT (Galleria) ▲ 37645 [ADD] (9.97)
R. Kempe (cnd), BBC SO *(rec 1976)* † F. Schubert:Sym 5 BBC ▲ 4003 (17.97)
I. Kertész (cnd), Vienna PO † Serenade 1 Orch, Op. 11; Sym 3 PLON 2-▲ 48200 (17.97)
C. Kleiber (cnd), Vienna PO *(rec Musikverein Vienna, Austria, Mar 1980)* DEUT (The Originals) ▲ 457706 [DDD] (11.97)
H. Knappertsbusch (cnd), Cologne RSO *(rec Köln, Germany, 1953)* † Academic Festival Ov, Op. 80; Con Vn & Vc, Op. 102; Con 2 Pno, Op. 83; Rhap Alt, Op. 53; Sym 2; Sym 3; Tragic Ov, Op. 81; Vars on a Theme by Haydn MELO 4-▲ 40039 (m) [ADD] (62.97)
S. Koussevitzky (cnd), Boston SO *(rec 1945)* ("Koussevitzky Conducts Brahms") † Sym 3 PHS ▲ 9237 (17.97)
C. Mackerras (cnd), Scottish CO † Academic Festival Ov, Op. 80; Sym 3 TEL ▲ 80465 (16.97)
N. Marriner (cnd), Academy of St. Martin in the Fields † Sym 3 HANS (Academy) ▲ 98187 (15.97)
K. Masur (cnd), New York PO † Schicksalslied, Op. 54 TELC ▲ 13695 (16.97)
W. Mengelberg (cnd), Amsterdam Concertgebouw Orch *(rec Nov 30, 1938)* † Sym 2 BCS ▲ 57 [ADD] (16.97)
W. Mengelberg (cnd), Concertgebouw Orch † Sym 2; Sym 3; Tragic Ov, Op. 81 TAHA ▲ 274 (34.97)
E. Mravinsky (cnd), Leningrad PO *(rec 1961)* ("The Mvravinsky Collection") † Sibelius:Swan of Tuonela; C. M. von Weber:Oberon (ov) RUS ▲ 10907 [AAD] (12.97)
R. Norrington (cnd), London Classical Players † Sym 3 EMIC ▲ 56118
A. Rahbari (cnd), Belgian Radio-TV PO *(rec Belgian RTV Concert Hall Brussels, Apr 27-May 5, 1989)* ("Famous Symphonies: Beethoven, Tchaikovsky, Brahms, Schubert") † Academic Festival Ov, Op. 80; Tragic Ov, Op. 81; Beethoven:Sym 3; Sym 8; F. Schubert:Sym 9; P. Tchaikovsky:Francesca da Rimini, Op. 32; Sym 6 NXIN 4-▲ 504012 [DDD] (19.97)
A. Rahbari (cnd), Belgian Radio-TV PO † Academic Festival Ov, Op. 80; Tragic Ov, Op. 81 NXIN ▲ 550281 [DDD] (5.97)
F. Reiner (cnd), Royal PO *(rec 1962)* † Beethoven:Egmont (ov) CHSK ▲ 6 (16.97)
F. Reiner (cnd), Royal PO CHGR ▲ 906 [DDD] (29.97)
V. D. Sabata (cnd), Berlin PO † Beethoven:Sym 3; Sym 6; R. Wagner:Tristan und Isolde (prelude & liebestod) 78'S 2-▲ 78542 (26.97)
A. Scholz (cnd), South German PO † Academic Festival Ov, Op. 80; Tragic Ov, Op. 81 PC ▲ 267156 [DDD] (2.97)
S. Skrowaczewski (cnd), Hallé Orch † Hungarian Dances Orch ICC ▲ 6700272 (9.97)
W. Steinberg (cnd), Pittsburgh SO *(rec Syria Mosque Pittsburgh)* † Sym 3 EVC ▲ 9016 [AAD] (13.97)
V. Stenzl (pno), H. Stenzl (pno) [arr for 2 pnos] ARSM ▲ 1232 (17.97)
L. Stokowski (cnd), London SO, L. Stokowski (cnd), London Sym Chorus, M. Price (sop), B. Fassbaender (mez) † G. Mahler:Sym 2 RCAV ▲ 62606 (21.97)
L. Stokowski (cnd), Philadelphia Orch † Sym 3 78'S ▲ 78549 (13.97)
H. Swarowsky (cnd), South German PO † Academic Festival Ov, Op. 80; Con Vn & Vc, Op. 102; Con 2 Pno, Op. 83; Sym 1 INTC ▲ 885924 (16.97)
G. Szell (cnd), Cleveland Orch † Academic Festival Ov, Op. 80; Tragic Ov, Op. 81 SNYC (Essential Classics) ▲ 46330 [ADD] (7.97) ▮ 46330 [ADD] (3.98)
A. Toscanini (cnd), BBC SO *(rec 1935-39)* ("Toscanini in London, Vol. 2") † Sym 2 GRM2 ▲ 78612 (13.97)
A. Toscanini (cnd), BBC SO *(rec 1935-37)* † Tragic Ov, Op. 81; R. Wagner:Parsifal (orch sels) 78'S (The 78s) ▲ 78537 (13.97)
A. Toscanini (cnd), BBC SO *(rec 1935)* † Sym 2 GRM2 (Records of the Century) ▲ 78851 (13.97)
A. Toscanini (cnd), NBC SO ("The Toscanini Collection, Vol. 9") † Gesäng der Parzen, Op. 89; Liebeslieder Waltzes Pno 4-Hands, Op. 52a RCAV (Gold Seal) ▲ 60260 [ADD] (11.97)
B. Walter (cnd), BBC SO *(rec May 1934)* ("Bruno Walter in London") † Beethoven:Fidelio (ov); W. A. Mozart:Sym 39, K.543 GRM2 ▲ 78560 (13.97)
B. Walter (cnd), Columbia SO † Tragic Ov, Op. 81 SNYC (Bruno Walter: The Edition) ▲ 64472 (10.97)
F. V. Weingartner (cnd), London SO † Mendelssohn (-Bartholdy):Sym 3 ENT (Sirio) ▲ 530015 (13.97)
F. V. Weingartner (cnd), London SO *(rec London, 1938)* † Academic Festival Ov, Op. 80; Sym 3 78'S (The 78's) ▲ 78516 [ADD] (13.97)
various artists [excerpt; plus others] † J. S. Bach:Air on the G String; Beethoven:Con Vn; Con 3 Pno, Op. 37; H. Pfitzner:Palestrina (sels); Smetana:Moldau; P. Tchaikovsky:Ov 1812, Op. 49 MTAL ▲ 48096 (6.97)

Tafellied for 6 Voices & Piano, Op. 93b (1884)

G. Jena (cnd), North German Radio Chorus ("The Complete Brahms Edition, Vol. 7:Choral Works") † Ave Maria, Op. 12; Begräbnisgesang, Op. 13; Canons (13), Op. 113; Dem dunkeln Schoss der heil'gen Erde; Deutsche Volkslieder (26); Fest- und Gedenksprüche, Op. 109; Geistliches Lied, Op. 30; Grausam erweiset sich Amor an mir, Op. 113/2; Kleine Hochzeitskantate; Marienlieder (7), Op. 22; Mir lächelt kein Frühling; Motets (2), Op. 29; Motets (2), Op. 74; Motets (3), Op. 110; O wie sanft; Psalm 13, Op. 27; Sacred Choruses (3), Op. 37; Songs (3), Op. 42; Songs (4), Op. 17; Songs (5), Op. 104; Songs (5), Op. 41; Songs (7), Op. 62; Songs & Romances (12), Op. 44; Songs & Romances (6), Op. 93a; Spruch; Töne, lindernder Klang; Wann?; Zu Rauch DGRM 4-▲ 449646

Theme & Variations in d for Piano [arr Brahms from slow movt of *Sextet for Strings, Op. 18*] (1860)

E. Ax (pno) † Sextet Strs, Op. 18; Sextet Strs, Op. 36 SNYC 2-▲ 45820 (31.97)
M. Boriskin (pno) *(rec Univ of Iowa, IA, Feb 24-27, 1990)* † Vars & Fugue on a Theme by Handel, Op. 24; Vars on a Hungarian Song, Op. 21/2; Vars on an Original Theme, Op. 21/1 MUA ▲ 4726 [DDD] (10.97)
I. Hobson (pno) ("The Complete Variations of Johannes Brahms") † Vars Pno (comp) ARA 2-▲ 6654 [DDD] (32.97)
R. Lupu (pno) *(rec 1981)* ("Radu Lupu") † Intermezzos (3) Pno, Op. 117; Beethoven:Son 14 Pno, Op. 27/2; Vars Pno on Original Theme, WoO 80; E. Grieg:Con Pno, Op. 16; F. Schubert:Moments musicaux, D.780; Son Pno, D.784; R. Schumann:Kinderszenen Pno, Op. 15 PPHI (Great Pianists of the 20th Century) ▲ 456895 (22.97)

Töne, lindernder Klang (canon) for Chorus

G. Jena (cnd), North German Radio Chorus ("The Complete Brahms Edition, Vol. 7:Choral Works") † Ave Maria, Op. 12; Begräbnisgesang, Op. 13; Canons (13), Op. 113; Dem dunkeln Schoss der heil'gen Erde; Deutsche Volkslieder (26); Fest- und Gedenksprüche, Op. 109; Geistliches Lied, Op. 30; Grausam erweiset sich Amor an mir, Op. 113/2; Kleine Hochzeitskantate; Marienlieder (7), Op. 22; Mir lächelt kein Frühling; Motets (2), Op. 29; Motets (2), Op. 74; Motets (3), Op. 110; O wie sanft; Psalm 13, Op. 27; Sacred Choruses (3), Op. 37; Songs (3), Op. 42; Songs (4), Op. 17; Songs (5), Op. 104; Songs (5), Op. 41; Songs (7), Op. 62; Songs & Romances (12), Op. 44; Songs & Romances (6), Op. 93a; Spruch; Tafellied, Op. 93b; Wann?; Zu Rauch DGRM 4-▲ 449646

Tragic Overture in d for Orchestra, Op. 81 (1880; rev 1881)

C. Abbado (cnd), Berlin PO † Schicksalslied, Op. 54; Sym 3 DEUT ▲ 29765 [DDD] (16.97)
C. Abbado (cnd), Berlin PO † Academic Festival Ov, Op. 80; Alto Rhap, Op. 53; Gesäng der Parzen, Op. 89; Nänie, Op. 82; Schicksalslied, Op. 54; Syms (comp); Vars on a Theme by Haydn DGRM 4-▲ 435683 [DDD]
H. Abendroth (cnd), Leipzig Gewandhaus Orch ("Hermann Abendroth:Gewandhaus Kapellmeister 1944-45") † J. S. Bach:Suite 3 Orch, BWV 1068; G. F. Handel:Concerti grossi, Op. 6; J. Haydn:Sym 88; Sym 96; W. A. Mozart:Sym 29, K.201; F. Schubert:Sym 3; R. Schumann:Manfred Ov, Op. 115 TAHA 2-▲ 106 (34.97)
H. Abendroth (cnd), Leipzig Gewandhaus Orch *(rec 1945)* † Sym 1 IN ▲ 1391 (15.97)
M. Abravanel (cnd), Utah SO *(rec Mormon Tabernacle Salt Lake City, May 17-24, 1976)* ("Orchestral Works") † Academic Festival Ov, Op. 80; Syms (comp); Vars on a Theme by Haydn VC 3-▲ 1719 [AAD] (39.97)
K. Ančerl (cnd), Czech PO † Sym 1 SUR (Czech Philharmonic) ▲ 111941 [AAD]
J. Barbirolli (cnd), Vienna PO † Sym 1 RYLC ▲ 6433

BRAHMS, JOHANNES (cont.)

Tragic Overture in d for Orchestra, Op. 81 (1880; rev 1881) (cont.)

J. Barbirolli (cnd), Vienna PO *(rec Vienna, Austria, 1967)* ("Piano Concertos & Overtures") † Academic Festival Ov, Op. 80; Con 1 Pno, Op. 15; Con 2 Pno, Op. 83; Vars on a Theme by Haydn EMIC 2-▲ 72649 [ADD] (16.97)
J. Bělohlávek (cnd), Czech PO † Academic Festival Ov, Op. 80; Sym 2 SUR ▲ 111990
L. Bernstein (cnd), New York PO ("Bernstein: The Royal Edition") † Academic Festival Ov, Op. 80; Sym 4 SNYC ▲ 47538 [ADD] (10.97)
L. Bernstein (cnd), Vienna PO † Academic Festival Ov, Op. 80; Syms (comp); Vars on a Theme by Haydn DEUT 4-▲ 15570 [DDD] (38.97)
L. Bernstein (cnd), Vienna PO † Sym 4 DEUT (Masters) ▲ 45508 [DDD] (9.97)
K. Böhm (cnd), Vienna PO *(rec Musikverein Vienna, Austria, Feb 1977)* † Con 1 Pno, Op. 15; Con 2 Pno, Op. 83; Vars on a Theme by Haydn DEUT 2-▲ 453067 [ADD] (17.97)
A. Boult (cnd), London SO † Academic Festival Ov, Op. 80; Alto Rhap, Op. 53; Serenade 1 Orch, Op. 11; Serenade 2 Orch, Op. 16; Vars on a Theme by Haydn EMIC (Doubleforte) 2-▲ 68655 (16.97)
H. Haenchen (cnd), Netherlands PO † Sym 4 LALI ▲ 14001 [DDD] (3.97)
B. Haitink (cnd), (Royal) Concertgebouw Orch † Academic Festival Ov, Op. 80; Con 1 Pno, Op. 15; Con 2 Pno, Op. 83; Vars on a Theme by Haydn PPHI 2-▲ 38320 (17.97)
N. Harnoncourt (cnd), Berlin PO † Academic Festival Ov, Op. 80; Syms (comp); Vars on a Theme by Haydn TELC 3-▲ 13136 (50.97)
E. Jochum (cnd), London PO † Academic Festival Ov, Op. 80; Sym 1; Sym 2; Sym 3 EMIC (Doubleforte) 2-▲ 69515 (16.97)
H. von Karajan (cnd), Berlin PO † Syms (comp); Vars on a Theme by Haydn DEUT 3-▲ 27602 [DDD] (48.97)
H. von Karajan (cnd), Berlin PO ("Complete Brahms Edition, Vol. 1:Orchestral Works") † Academic Festival Ov, Op. 80; Hungarian Dances Orch; Serenade 1 Orch, Op. 11; Serenade 2 Orch, Op. 16; Syms (comp); Vars on a Theme by Haydn DGRM 5-▲ 449601 (64.97)
H. Knappertsbusch (cnd), Vienna PO *(rec Vienna, Germany, 1957)* † Academic Festival Ov, Op. 80; Con Vn & Vc, Op. 102; Con 2 Pno, Op. 83; Rhap Alt, Op. 53; Sym 2; Sym 3; Sym 4; Vars on a Theme by Haydn MELO 4-▲ 40039 (m) [ADD] (62.97)
V. Kojian (cnd), Utah SO † Liszt:Dante Sym, S.109 CIT ▲ 88102 [DDD] (15.97)
J. Krips (cnd), Philharmonia Orch *(rec London, England, June 22 1963)* ("Testament") † Academic Festival Ov, Op. 80; Vars on a Theme by Haydn; R. Strauss:Rosenkavalier (suite); I. Stravinsky:Firebird Suite 2 TES ▲ 1122 [ADD] (17.97)
G. Lehel (cnd), Budapest SO *(rec Italian Cultural Institute Budapest, Sept 1982)* † Academic Festival Ov, Op. 80; Syms (comp); Vars on a Theme by Haydn CLDI 3-▲ 4038 [ADD/DDD] (10.97)
E. Marturet (cnd), Berlin SO † Academic Festival Ov, Op. 80; Syms (comp); Vars on a Theme by Haydn VRDI 4-▲ 6814 (20.97)
K. Masur (cnd), New York PO † Sym 1 TELC ▲ 90883 (16.97)
W. Mengelberg (cnd), Concertgebouw Orch † Sym 2; Sym 3; Sym 4 TAHA ▲ 274 (34.97)
P. Monteux (cnd), (Royal) Concertgebouw Orch ("The Art of Pierre Monteux") † Con Vn; Sym 1; Sym 3; Berlioz:Sym fantastique, Op. 14; Sibelius:Con Vn; I. Stravinsky:Pétrouchka TAHA 4-▲ 175 (67.97)
A. Previn (cnd), Royal PO † Con 1 Pno, Op. 15 TEL ▲ 80252 [DDD] (16.97)
A. Rahbari (cnd), Belgian Radio-TV PO *(rec Belgian RTV Concert Hall Brussels, Apr 27-May 5, 1989)* ("Famous Symphonies: Beethoven, Tchaikovsky, Brahms, Schubert") † Academic Festival Ov, Op. 80; Sym 4; Beethoven:Sym 3; Sym 8; F. Schubert:Sym 9; P. Tchaikovsky:Francesca da Rimini, Op. 32; Sym 6 NXIN 4-▲ 504012 [DDD] (19.97)
A. Rahbari (cnd), Belgian Radio-TV PO † Academic Festival Ov, Op. 80; Sym 4 NXIN ▲ 550281 [DDD] (5.97)
K. Sanderling (cnd), Dresden Staatskapelle † Syms (comp); Vars on a Theme by Haydn EUR 3-▲ 69220 [ADD] (13.97)
W. Sawallisch (cnd), Bavarian State Orch † Beethoven:Leonore (ov 2) ORF ▲ 161871 [DDD] (18.97)
U. Schneider (cnd), Nuremberg SO † Academic Festival Ov, Op. 80; Sym 4 PC ▲ 267156 [DDD] (2.97)
S. Skrowaczewski (cnd), Hallé Orch † Sym 2 INMP ▲ 857 [DDD] (11.97)
S. Skrowaczewski (cnd), Hallé Orch † Academic Festival Ov, Op. 80; Hungarian Dances Orch; Syms (comp); Vars on a Theme by Haydn IMPB 4-▲ 3 [DDD]
S. Skrowaczewski (cnd), Hallé Orch † Sym 2 ICC ▲ 6700982 (9.97)
L. Stokowski (cnd), National PO London † Academic Festival Ov, Op. 80; Sym 1; Sym 2; Vars & Fugue on a Theme by Handel, Op. 24; Vars on a Theme by Haydn SNYC (Essential Classics Take 2) 2-▲ 63287 (14.97)
G. Szell (cnd), Cleveland Orch † Academic Festival Ov, Op. 80; Sym 4 SNYC (Essential Classics) ▲ 46330 [ADD] (7.97) ▮ 46330 [ADD] (3.98)
G. Szell (cnd), Cleveland Orch † Academic Festival Ov, Op. 80; Hungarian Dances Orch; Syms (comp); Vars on a Theme by Haydn SNYC (Essential Classics) 3-▲ 48398 (23.97)
M. T. Thomas (cnd), London SO † Academic Festival Ov, Op. 80; Serenade 1 Orch, Op. 11 SNYC ▲ 45932 [DDD] (16.97)
A. Toscanini (cnd), BBC SO *(rec 1935-39)* ("Toscanini in London, Vol. 1") † R. Wagner:Faust Ov; Götterdämmerung (sels); Parsifal (good friday music); Parsifal (preludes) GRM2 ▲ 78611 (13.97)
A. Toscanini (cnd), BBC SO *(rec 1937-39)* † Beethoven:Leonore; Sym 1; Sym 4; Sym 6; W. A. Mozart:Zauberflöte (sels) ENT (Document) 2-▲ 921 [ADD] (26.97)
A. Toscanini (cnd), BBC SO *(rec 1935-37)* † Sym 4; R. Wagner:Parsifal (orch sels) 78'S (The 78s) ▲ 78537 (13.97)
A. Toscanini (cnd), NBC SO *(rec Studio 8-H broadcast)* ("The Toscanini Collection, Vols. 6-9") † Academic Festival Ov, Op. 80; Con Vn & Vc, Op. 102; Gesäng der Parzen, Op. 89; Hungarian Dances Orch; Liebeslieder Waltzes Pno 4-Hands, Op. 52a; Syms (comp); Vars on a Theme by Haydn RCAV (Gold Seal) 4-▲ 60325 [ADD] (40.97)
B. Walter (cnd), Columbia SO † Con Vn & Vc, Op. 102 SNYC ▲ 37237 [ADD] (9.97)
B. Walter (cnd), Columbia SO † Sym 4 SNYC (Bruno Walter: The Edition) ▲ 64472 (10.97)
artists unknown † Sym 1 SNYC ▲ 62288 [DDD] (4.97)

Trio in a for Clarinet, Cello & Piano, Op. 114 (1891)

Amici Chamber Ensemble *(rec Toronto, Canada, Dec 10-11, 1996 & Jan 3-4, 1997)* ("In Brahms' Apartment") † Sons Cl SUMM ▲ 219 [DDD] (16.97)
Bekova Sisters † Trio Hn, Op. 40; Trio 3 Pno, Op. 101 CHN ▲ 9400 (16.97)
M. Bergman (vc), E. Eban (cl), A. Volkov (pno) † Beethoven:Trio 7 Pno, Op. 11 MER ▲ 84122 (16.97)
Bonaventura Ensemble *(rec Bavarian Radio, Dec 18-19, 1995)* † Beethoven:Trio 7 Pno, Op. 11 CALG ▲ 50958 [DDD] (19.97)
M. Boni (vc), G. Tirincanti (cl), M. Deoriti (pno) † Sons Cl STRV ▲ 27 [DDD] (16.97)
Chalumeau Trio † M. Glinka:Trio pathétique; Komma:Trio Cl BAYE ▲ 800877 (17.97)
J. W. Clarke (vc), A. Hacker (cl), R. Burnett (pno) [period instrs] † Sons Cl AMON ▲ 37 [DDD] (16.97)
Classic Trio ("Clarinet Trios") † Beethoven:Trio 7 Pno, Op. 11; M. Glinka:Trio pathétique ASVQ ▲ 6187 (10.97)
Danish Trio † Zemlinsky:Trio Cl, Op. 3 PLAL ▲ 52
M. Decimo (vc), A. Carbonare (cl), A. Dindo (pno) *(rec Milan, Oct 1994)* † Sons Cl AG ▲ 8 [DDD] (18.97)
R. Drinkall (vc), C. West (cl), D. Baker (pno) ("Clarinet Trios") † Indy:Trio Cl, Op. 29; Muczynski:Fant Trio, Op. 26 KLAV ▲ 11088 [DDD] (18.97)
Ensemble Kontraste † Rabl:Qt Cl; Zemlinsky:Trio Cl, Op. 3 THOR ▲ 2368 [DDD] (16.97)
K. Georgian (vc), T. King (cl), C. Benson (pno) † Qnt Cl HYP ▲ 66107 (18.97)
C. Henkel (vc), D. Klöcker (cl), C. Tanski (pno) † Trio Hn, Op. 40 MDG ▲ 3010595 [DDD] (19.97)
R. Hosford (cl), Florestan Trio members † Trio Hn, Op. 40; Trio 1 Pno, Op. 8; Trio 2 Pno, Op. 87; Trio 3 Pno, Op. 101 HYP 2-▲ 67251 (36.97)
K. Leister (cl), W. Boettcher (vc), F. Bognár (pno) † Sons Cl NIMB ▲ 5600 [DDD] (16.97)
C. Onczay (vc), J. Balogh (cl), J. Jandó (pno) *(rec Oct 16-18, 1991)* † Qnt Cl NXIN ▲ 550391 [DDD] (5.97)
Paideia Trio ("In the Shadow of Brahms") † P. Juon:Trio Miniatures Cl; Zemlinsky:Trio Cl, Op. 3 TACE ▲ 58
J. Potter (vc), V. Soames (cl), J. Higgins (pno) ("Music for Clarinet") † Sons Cl CLCL ▲ 16 [DDD] (17.97)
Transatlantic Trio † Indy:Trio Cl, Op. 29 4TAY ▲ 4008 (17.97)
Y. Turovsky (vc), J. Campbell (cl), L. Edlina (pno) † Trio Hn, Op. 40 CHN ▲ 8606 [DDD] (16.97)

Trio in E♭ for Horn, Violin & Piano, Op. 40 (1865)

Algae Trio *(rec Apr 1993)* † Beethoven:Son Hn; Cherubini:Sons Hn; R. Schumann:Adagio & Allegro Hn, Op. 70 PAVA ▲ 7295 [DDD] (10.97)
Bekova Sisters † Trio Cl; Trio 3 Pno, Op. 101 CHN ▲ 9400 (16.97)
A. Brusch (vn), A. Brain (hn), R. Serkin (pno) *(rec 1933)* † G. Fauré:Qt 2 Pno, Op. 45 ENT (Strings) ▲ 99302 (16.97)
A. Busch (vn), A. Brain (hn), R. Serkin (pno) † Qnt Cl PHS ▲ 7 [ADD] (17.97)
A. Busch (vn), A. Brain (hn), R. Serkin (pno) † W. A. Mozart:Divert 17 Hns Strs, K.334 MTAL ▲ 48021 (6.97)
S. Chase (vn), L. Greer (nat hn), S. Lubin (pno) † Beethoven:Son Hn; Krufft:Son Hn in F HAM ▲ 907037 (18.97)
A. Clark (nat hn), Ensemble Galant *(rec Highgate, London, England, Sept 1997)* † Beethoven:Son Hn; Sxt Hns; W. A. Mozart:Duos Hns, K.487; Qnt Hn EMIC (Debut) ▲ 72822 [DDD] (6.97)
R. Dubinsky (vn), M. Thompson (hn), L. Edlina (pno) † Trio Cl CHN ▲ 8606 [DDD] (16.97)
Emory Chamber Music Society of Atlanta members ("Chamber Music of Johannes Brahms") † Hungarian Dances Pno 4-Hands; Son 2 Cl ACAD ▲ 20033 [DDD] (16.97)

▲ = CD ♦ = Enhanced CD △ = MD ▮ = Cassette Tape ▯ = DCC

BRAHMS, JOHANNES (cont.)

Trio in E♭ for Horn, Violin & Piano, Op. 40 (1865) (cont.)

J. Kantorow (vn), H. Joulain (hn), M. Jude (pno) † R. Schumann:Andante & Vars Hn HAM (Les Nouveaux Interprètes) ▲ 911559 (12.97)
J. Kantorow (vn), H. Joulain (hn), M. Jude (pno) HAM (La Solothèque) ▲ 926006 (5.97)
M. Kaplan (vn), D. Jolley (hn), D. Golub (pno) † Trio 1 Pno, Op. 8 ARA ▲ 6607 (16.97)
B. Langbein (vn), B. Tuckwell (hn), M. Jones (pno) *(rec Apr 1987)* † D. Banks:Trio Hn; Koechlin:Petites Pièces, Op. 32 TUD ▲ 771 [DDD] (16.97)
Nash Ensemble *(rec Nov 25-27, 1991)* † Qnt Pno, Op. 34 CRD ▲ 3489 [DDD] (17.97)
I. Perlman (vn), B. Tuckwell (hn), V. Ashkenazy (pno) † C. Franck:Son Vn, M.8 PLON (Classic Sound) ▲ 452887 (11.97)
D. Phillips (vn), W. Purvis (hn), R. Goode (pno) † G. Ligeti:Trio Hn, Vn & Pno BRID ▲ 9012 [DDD] (17.97)
J. Stanienda (vn), Z. Zuk (hn), P. Folkert (pno) † D. Banks:Trio Hn; L. Berkeley:Trio Vn, Op. 44 ZUK ▲ 310
S. Stirling (hn), Florestan Trio members † Trio Cl; Trio 1 Pno, Op. 8; Trio 2 Pno, Op. 87; Trio 3 Pno, Op. 101 HYP 2-▲ 67251 (36.97)
D. Streicher (vn), S. Weigle (hn), C. Tanski (pno) † Trio Cl MDG ▲ 3010595 [DDD] (19.97)
J. Suk (vn), P. Damm (hn), W. Genuit (pno) † Sons Cl AART ▲ 47368 (10.97)
M. Tree (vn), M. Bloom (hn), R. Serkin (pno) † Sextet Strs, Op. 36 SNYC ▲ 46249 [ADD] (10.97)
Trio Apollon † R. Schumann:Märchenerzählungen, Op. 132 DI ▲ 920363 [DDD] (5.97)

Trios (6) for Piano, Opp. 8, 40, 87, 101, 114 & posth. (complete)

Beaux Arts Trio ("Brahms:The Complete Trios") PPHI 2-▲ 38365 (17.97)

Trio No. 1 in B for Piano, Violin & Cello, Op. 8 (1853-54; rev 1889)

Bamberg Trio † Trio 2 Pno, Op. 87 PC ▲ 267016 [DDD] (2.97)
Bekova Sisters ("The Bekova Sisters") † Trio 2 Pno, Op. 87 CHN (New Direction) ▲ 9340 [DDD] (16.97)
Borodin Trio † Trio 2 Pno, Op. 87; Trio 3 Pno, Op. 101 CHN 2-▲ 8334 [DDD] (33.97)
Copenhagen Trio † Trio 2 Pno, Op. 87; Trio 3 Pno, Op. 101 KPT 2-▲ 32090
Florestan Trio † Trio Cl; Trio Hn, Op. 40; Trio 2 Pno, Op. 87; Trio 3 Pno, Op. 101 HYP 2-▲ 67251 (36.97)
W. Gieseking (pno), G. Taschner (vn), L. Hoelscher (vc) *(rec live, 1947)* ("Gieseking, Vol. 1") † Son 3 Pno, Op. 5 HPC1 ▲ 128 (17.97)
Jerusalem Trio † Trio 2 Pno, Op. 87 DHR ▲ 71132 (16.97)
M. Kaplan (vn), C. Carr (vc), D. Golub (pno) † Trio Hn, Op. 40 ARA ▲ 6607 (16.97)
J. Laredo (vn), S. Robinson (vc), J. Kalichstein (pno) † Trio 2 Pno, Op. 87; Trio 3 Pno, Op. 101; A. Dvořák:Trio 4 Pno, Op. 90; Mendelssohn (-Bartholdy):Trio 1 Pno, Op. 49; Trio 2 Pno, Op. 66 VB3 3-▲ 3029 [DDD] (14.97)
Moscow Conservatory Piano Trio ("Great Piano Trios: Brahms & Beethoven") † Beethoven:Trio 3 Pno, Op. 1/3 CMH ▲ 8021 (13.97)
V. Mullova (vn), H. Schiff (vc), A. Previn (pno) ("Trios") † Beethoven:Trio 6 Pno, Op. 97 PPHI ▲ 42123 (16.97)
E. Ney (pno) ("The Art of the Piano, Vol. 1") † M. Reger:Suite Vn Pno, Op. 103a; F. Schubert:Son Arpeggione, D.821; R. Schumann:Kinderszenen Pno, Op. 15 ACLR ▲ 39 (17.97)
Parnassus Trio ("Complete Piano Trios, Vol 1") † Sextet Strs, Op. 36 MDG ▲ 3030655 (17.97)
Parnassus Trio [1st version, 1854] *(rec Dec 11-13, 1995)* ("Complete Piano Trios, Vol. 3") † Trio 3 Pno, Op. 101 MDG ▲ 3030657 (17.97)
M. J. Pires (pno), A. Dumay (vn), J. Wang (vc) † Trio 2 Pno, Op. 87 DGRM ▲ 447055 [DDD]
Pro Arte Piano Trio † Trio 3 Pno, Op. 101 BIS ▲ 98 [AAD] (17.97)
Rembrandt Trio *(rec Apr 1991)* † A. Dvořák:Trio 4 Pno, Op. 90 DOR ▲ 90160 [DDD] (16.97)
Röhn Trio † Trio 2 Pno, Op. 87 CALG ▲ 50932
W. Schneiderhan (vn), E. Mainardi (vc), E. Fischer (pno) *(rec 1954)* † Trio 2 Pno, Op. 87; Trio 3 Pno, Op. 101; Beethoven:Trio 4 Pno, Op. 70/1; R. Schumann:Trio 1 Pno, Op. 63 ARKA 2-▲ 568 [ADD] (34.97)
Solomon Trio ("Piano Trios") † Trio Pno in A; Trio 2 Pno, Op. 87; Trio 3 Pno, Op. 101 IMAS 2-▲ 94 (26.97)
I. Stern (vn), P. Casals (vc), M. Hess (pno) *(rec Prades France, June 23-July 3, 1952)* † Sextet Strs, Op. 18 SNYC (The Casals Edition) ▲ 58994 [ADD] (10.97)
I. Stern (vn), L. Rose (vc), E. Istomin (pno) † Qts Pno (comp); Trio 2 Pno, Op. 87; Trio 3 Pno, Op. 101 SNYC (Isaac Stern: A Life in Music) 3-▲ 64520 (32.97)
Vienna Piano Trio *(rec Mar 1993)* ("Brahms: Piano Trios") † Trio 2 Pno, Op. 87 NXIN ▲ 550746 [DDD] (5.97)
H. Wang (pno), S. Wang (vn), B. Myers (vc) ("Gems of the Gemini Piano Trio") † H. Isaac:Easter Mass AWPR ▲ 4247 (17.97)

Trio No. 2 in C for Piano, Violin & Cello, Op. 87 (1880-82)

Bamberg Trio † Trio 1 Pno, Op. 8 PC ▲ 267016 [DDD] (2.97)
Bekova Sisters ("The Bekova Sisters") † Trio 1 Pno, Op. 8 CHN (New Direction) ▲ 9340 [DDD] (16.97)
Borodin Trio † Trio 1 Pno, Op. 8; Trio 3 Pno, Op. 101 CHN 2-▲ 8334 [DDD] (33.97)
Copenhagen Trio † Trio 1 Pno, Op. 8; Trio 3 Pno, Op. 101 KPT 2-▲ 32090
Florestan Trio † Trio Cl; Trio Hn, Op. 40; Trio 1 Pno, Op. 8; Trio 3 Pno, Op. 101 HYP 2-▲ 67251 (36.97)
Jerusalem Trio † Trio 1 Pno, Op. 8 DHR ▲ 71132 (16.97)
J. Laredo (vn), S. Robinson (vc), J. Kalichstein (pno) † Trio 1 Pno, Op. 8; Trio 3 Pno, Op. 101; A. Dvořák:Trio 4 Pno, Op. 90; Mendelssohn (-Bartholdy):Trio 1 Pno, Op. 49; Trio 2 Pno, Op. 66 VB3 3-▲ 3029 [DDD] (14.97)
Myra Hess Trio ("Myra Hess: A Vignette") † J. Haydn:Son 50 Kbd, H.XVI/37; W. A. Mozart:Con 21 Pno, K.467; F. Schubert:Rosamunde (sels); Son Pno, D.664; Trio 1 Pno, D.898 APR 2-▲ 7012 [AAD] (38.97)
Parnassus Trio ("Complete Piano Trios, Vol. 2") † Sextet Strs, Op. 18 MDG ▲ 3030656 (17.97)
M. J. Pires (pno), A. Dumay (vn), J. Wang (vc) † Trio 1 Pno, Op. 8 DGRM ▲ 447055 [DDD]
Pro Arte Piano Trio † Trio Pno in A BIS ▲ 99 [AAD] (17.97)
Röhn Trio † Trio 1 Pno, Op. 8 CALG ▲ 50932
W. Schneiderhan (vn), E. Mainardi (vc), E. Fischer (pno) *(rec 1954)* † Trio 1 Pno, Op. 8; Trio 3 Pno, Op. 101; Beethoven:Trio 4 Pno, Op. 70/1; R. Schumann:Trio 1 Pno, Op. 63 ARKA 2-▲ 568 [ADD] (34.97)
Solomon Trio ("Piano Trios") † Trio Pno in A; Trio 1 Pno, Op. 8; Trio 3 Pno, Op. 101 IMAS 2-▲ 94 (26.97)
I. Stern (vn), L. Rose (vc), E. Istomin (pno) † Qts Pno (comp); Trio 1 Pno, Op. 8; Trio 3 Pno, Op. 101 SNYC (Isaac Stern: A Life in Music) 3-▲ 64520 (32.97)
J. Szigeti (vn), P. Casals (vc), M. Hess (pno) *(rec Prades, June 16, 1952)* † Mendelssohn (-Bartholdy):Trio 1 Pno, Op. 49 SNYC ▲ 66571 [ADD] (10.97)
Vienna Piano Trio *(rec Mar 1993)* ("Brahms: Piano Trios") † Trio 1 Pno, Op. 8 NXIN ▲ 550746 [DDD] (5.97)

Trio No. 3 in c for Piano, Violin & Cello, Op. 101 (1886)

Bekova Sisters † Trio Cl; Trio Hn, Op. 40 CHN ▲ 9400 (16.97)
Borodin Trio † Trio 1 Pno, Op. 8; Trio 2 Pno, Op. 87 CHN 2-▲ 8334 [DDD] (33.97)
Copenhagen Trio † Trio 1 Pno, Op. 8; Trio 2 Pno, Op. 87 KPT 2-▲ 32090
Florestan Trio † Trio Cl; Trio Hn, Op. 40; Trio 1 Pno, Op. 8; Trio 2 Pno, Op. 87 HYP 2-▲ 67251 (36.97)
J. Laredo (vn), S. Robinson (vc), J. Kalichstein (pno) † Trio 1 Pno, Op. 8; Trio 2 Pno, Op. 87; A. Dvořák:Trio 4 Pno, Op. 90; Mendelssohn (-Bartholdy):Trio 1 Pno, Op. 49; Trio 2 Pno, Op. 66 VB3 3-▲ 3029 [DDD] (14.97)
Les Musiciens † Sextet Strs, Op. 18; Mendelssohn (-Bartholdy):Son 1 Vc, Op. 45; Son 2 Vc, Op. 58; F. Schubert:Ländler Pno; Son Arpeggione, D.821; Waltzes Pno HMA 3-▲ 290882 (17.97)
Parnassus Trio *(rec Dec. 11-13, 1995)* ("Complete Piano Trios, Vol. 3") † Trio 1 Pno, Op. 8 MDG ▲ 3030657 (17.97)
Pro Arte Piano Trio † Trio 1 Pno, Op. 8 BIS ▲ 98 [AAD] (17.97)
Röhn Trio ("Piano Trios, Vol. 2") † Trio Pno in A CALG ▲ 50985 [DDD] (18.97)
W. Schneiderhan (vn), E. Mainardi (vc), E. Fischer (pno) *(rec 1954)* † Trio 1 Pno, Op. 8; Trio 2 Pno, Op. 87; Beethoven:Trio 4 Pno, Op. 70/1; R. Schumann:Trio 1 Pno, Op. 63 ARKA 2-▲ 568 [ADD] (34.97)
Solomon Trio ("Piano Trios") † Trio Pno in A; Trio 1 Pno, Op. 8; Trio 2 Pno, Op. 87 IMAS 2-▲ 94 (26.97)
I. Stern (vn), L. Rose (vc), E. Istomin (pno) † Qts Pno (comp); Trio 1 Pno, Op. 8; Trio 2 Pno, Op. 87 SNYC (Isaac Stern: A Life in Music) 3-▲ 64520 (32.97)
Vienna Piano Trio *(rec Sept 30-Oct 3, 1993)* † Trio Pno in A NXIN ▲ 550747 [DDD] (5.97)
artists unknown—Andante grazioso ("Brahms for Book Lovers") † Music of Brahms; Son 1 Cl; Son 1 Vn, Op. 78; Son 2 Vn, Op. 100 PPHI (Set Your Life to Music) ▮ 462561 (5.98) ▲ 462561 (9.97)

Trio in A for Piano, Violin & Cello, Op. posth. [attrib]

Beaux Arts Trio ("Brahms: Complete Piano Quartets") † Qts Pno (comp) PPHI ▲ 54017 (17.97)
Pro Arte Piano Trio † Trio 2 Pno, Op. 87 BIS ▲ 99 [AAD] (17.97)
Röhn Trio ("Piano Trios, Vol. 2") † Trio 3 Pno, Op. 101 CALG ▲ 50985 [DDD] (18.97)
Solomon Trio ("Piano Trios") † Trio 1 Pno in A; Trio 1 Pno, Op. 8; Trio 3 Pno, Op. 101 IMAS 2-▲ 94 (26.97)
Vienna Piano Trio *(rec Sept 30-Oct 3, 1993)* † Trio 3 Pno, Op. 101 NXIN ▲ 550747 [DDD] (5.97)

Triumphlied for Baritone, Orchestra & Chorus, Op. 55 (1870-71)

G. Sinopoli (cnd), Czech PO, Prague Phil Chorus, W. Brendel (bar) ("The Complete Brahms Edition, Vol. 8:Works for Chorus & Orchestra") † Alto Rhap, Op. 53; Deutsches Requiem, Op. 45; Gesäng der Parzen, Op. 89; Nänie, Op. 82; Rinaldo, Op. 50; Schicksalslied, Op. 54 DGRM 3-▲ 449651

Variations on a Theme by Haydn for Orchestra, Op. 56a (1873) or 2 Pianos, Op. 56b (1873)

C. Abbado (cnd), Berlin PO † Nänie, Op. 82; Sym 4 DEUT ▲ 35349 [DDD] (16.97)

BRAHMS, JOHANNES (cont.)

Variations on a Theme by Haydn for Orchestra, Op. 56a (1873) or 2 Pianos, Op. 56b (1873) (cont.)

C. Abbado (cnd), Berlin PO † Academic Festival Ov, Op. 80; Alto Rhap, Op. 53; Gesäng der Parzen, Op. 89; Nänie, Op. 82; Schicksalslied, Op. 54; Syms (comp); Tragic Ov, Op. 81 DGRM 4-▲ 435683 [DDD]
C. Abbado (cnd), Dresden Staatskapelle † Hungarian Dances Orch DEUT ▲ 31594 [ADD] (9.97)
M. Abravanel (cnd), Utah SO *(rec Mormon Tabernacle Salt Lake City, May 17-24, 1976)* ("Orchestral Works") † Academic Festival Ov, Op. 80; Syms (comp); Tragic Ov, Op. 81 VC 3-▲ 1719 [AAD] (39.97)
M. Argerich (pno), A. Rabinovitch (pno) *(rec Berlin, Apr 1993)* † Son for 2 Pnos, Op. 34b; Waltzes Pno, Op. 39 TELC ▲ 92257 [DDD] (16.97)
J. Barbirolli (cnd), Vienna PO † Academic Festival Ov, Op. 80; Sym 4 RYLC ▲ 6435
J. Barbirolli (cnd), Vienna PO *(rec Vienna, Austria, 1967)* ("Piano Concertos & Overtures") † Academic Festival Ov, Op. 80; Con 1 Pno, Op. 15; Con 2 Pno, Op. 83; Tragic Ov, Op. 81 EMIC 2-▲ 72649 [ADD] (16.97)
J. Bělohlávek (cnd), Czech PO † Sym 1 SUR ▲ 111989
L. Bernstein (cnd), New York PO ("Bernstein: The Royal Edition") † Con 2 Pno, Op. 83 SNYC ▲ 47539 [ADD] (10.97)
L. Bernstein (cnd), Vienna PO † Academic Festival Ov, Op. 80; Syms (comp); Tragic Ov, Op. 81 DEUT 4-▲ 15570 [DDD] (38.97)
L. Bernstein (cnd), Vienna PO † Sym 3 DEUT (Masters) ▲ 45507 [DDD] (9.97)
K. Böhm (cnd), Vienna PO *(rec Musikverein Vienna, Austria, Feb 1977)* † Con 1 Pno, Op. 15; Con 2 Pno, Op. 83; Tragic Ov, Op. 81 DEUT 2-▲ 453067 [ADD] (17.97)
A. Boult (cnd), London PO † Academic Festival Ov, Op. 80; Alto Rhap, Op. 53; Serenade 1 Orch, Op. 11; Serenade 2 Orch, Op. 16; Tragic Ov, Op. 81 EMIC (Doubleforte) 2-▲ 68655 (16.97)
S. Celibidache (cnd), Munich PO *(rec live, Herkulessaal der Münchner Residenz, Germany, Oct 16, 1980)* † R. Schumann:Sym 2 EMIC ▲ 56849 [ADD/DDD] (16.97)
A. Dorati (cnd), London SO † Hungarian Dances Orch; Enescu:Romanian Rhap 2, Op. 11/2 MRCR ▲ 34326 [ADD] (11.97)
B. Eden (pno), A. Tamir (pno) [arr 2 pnos] † Neue Liebeslieder Waltzes Pno 4-Hands, Op.65a CRD ▲ 3413 [ADD] (17.97)
W. Furtwängler (cnd), Berlin PO *(rec live, 1942-43)* † Sym 4 GRM2 ▲ 78594 (13.97)
W. Furtwängler (cnd), Berlin PO *(rec 1943)* † Sym 4 MTAL ▲ 48059 (6.97)
W. Furtwängler (cnd), Berlin PO *(rec 1943)* ("Wilhelm Furtwängler Wartime Recordings") † Con 2 Pno, Op. 83; Sym 4; Beethoven:Con 4 Pno, Op. 58; Sym 3; Sym 5; Sym 6; Sym 9; R. Strauss:Songs; R. Wagner:Meistersinger (preludes); Tristan und Isolde (prelude & liebestod) TAHA 6-▲ 1034 (50.97)
W. Furtwängler (cnd), Berlin PO *(rec Paris, France, May 4, 1954)* ("Furtwängler Concert in Paris") † Beethoven:Sym 5; C. M. von Weber:Euryanthe (ov) TAHA ▲ 1023 (34.97)
W. Furtwängler (cnd), Berlin PO † Sym 4 HCO ▲ 37049 (7.97)
W. Furtwängler (cnd), North German RSO ("Furtwängler Concert in Hamburg 1951") † Sym 1 TAHA ▲ 1001 (17.97)
W. Furtwängler (cnd), Vienna PO *(rec Dec 1943)* ("Wilhelm Furtwängler dirigiert") † Beethoven:Sym 6 PRE ▲ 90199 [ADD] (16.97)
W. Furtwängler (cnd), Vienna PO *(rec 1947)* † Sym 1 TES ▲ 1142 (17.97)
B. Haitink (cnd), (Royal) Concertgebouw Orch † Academic Festival Ov, Op. 80; Con 1 Pno, Op. 15; Con 2 Pno, Op. 83; Tragic Ov, Op. 81 PPHI 2-▲ 38320 (17.97)
N. Harnoncourt (cnd), Berlin PO † Academic Festival Ov, Op. 80; Syms (comp); Tragic Ov, Op. 81 TELC 3-▲ 13136 (50.97)
M. Horvat (cnd), Austrian RSO † Sym 1 PC ▲ 267127 [DDD] (2.97)
H. von Karajan (cnd), Berlin PO † Syms (comp); Tragic Ov, Op. 81 DEUT 3-▲ 27602 [DDD] (48.97)
H. von Karajan (cnd), Berlin PO ("Complete Brahms Edition, Vol. 1:Orchestral Works") † Academic Festival Ov, Op. 80; Hungarian Dances Orch; Serenade 1 Orch, Op. 11; Serenade 2 Orch, Op. 16; Syms (comp); Tragic Ov, Op. 81 DGRM 5-▲ 449601 (64.97)
I. Kertész (cnd), Vienna PO † Serenade 2 Orch, Op. 16; Sym 1; Sym 2 PLON 2-▲ 48197 (17.97)
H. Knappertsbusch (cnd), Vienna PO *(rec Wien, Germany, 1957)* † Academic Festival Ov, Op. 80; Con Vn & Vc, Op. 102; Con 2 Pno, Op. 83; Rhap Alt, Op. 53; Sym 2; Sym 3; Sym 4; Tragic Ov, Op. 81 MELO 4-▲ 40039 (m) [ADD] (62.97)
Z. Kocsis (pno), D. Ránki (pno) [arr 2 pnos] † W. A. Mozart:Son Pnos, K.448; M. Ravel:Ma mère l'oye Suite Pno HUN ▲ 11646
S. Kolacny (pno), S. Kolacny (pno) ("Dances & Variations for Piano Duo") † Hungarian Dances Pno 4-Hands; Liebeslieder Waltzes, Op. 52; Waltzes Pno, Op. 39 EUFO ▲ 1238 [DDD] (18.97)
J. Krips (cnd), Philharmonia Orch *(rec London, England, June 1 1963)* ("Testament") † Academic Festival Ov, Op. 80; Tragic Ov, Op. 81; R. Strauss:Rosenkavalier (suite); I. Stravinsky:Firebird Suite 2 TES ▲ 1122 [ADD] (17.97)
Y. Levi (cnd), Atlanta SO *(rec 1993)* † Serenade 1 Orch, Op. 11 TEL ▲ 80349 [DDD] (16.97)
T. Lønskov (pno), R. Llambias (pno) *(rec Sept 1992)* † Sym 3 KPT ▲ 32148 [DDD]
C. Mackerras (cnd), Scottish CO *(rec Edinburgh Scotland, Jan 6-11 & 27-30, 1997)* † Academic Festival Ov, Op. 80; Syms (comp) TEL 3-▲ 80450 [DDD] (38.97)
C. Mackerras (cnd), Scottish CO † Sym 2 TEL ▲ 80464 (16.97)
E. Marturet (cnd), Berlin SO † Academic Festival Ov, Op. 80; Syms (comp); Tragic Ov, Op. 81 VRDI 4-▲ 6814 (20.97)
K. Masur (cnd), New York PO † Sym 3 TELC ▲ 90862 (16.97)
S. Matthies (pno), C. Köhn (pno) *(rec Sandhausen, Germany, Nov 9-11, 1996)* ("4-Hand Piano Music Vol. 3") † Son for 2 Pnos, Op. 34b NXIN ▲ 8553654 [DDD] (5.97)
P. Monteux (cnd), London SO † J. Haydn:Sym 101; Sym 94 PLON (Classic Sound) ▲ 452893 (11.97)
G. Németh (cnd), Hungarian State Orch *(rec Budapest, Feb 1977)* † Academic Festival Ov, Op. 80; Syms (comp); Tragic Ov, Op. 81 CLDI 3-▲ 4038 [ADD/DDD] (10.97)
E. Ormandy (cnd), Philadelphia Orch [plus others] † Sym 1 SNYC (Essential Classics) ▲ 46534 [ADD] (7.97) ▮ 46534 [ADD] (3.98)
E. Ormandy (cnd), Philadelphia Orch † Academic Festival Ov, Op. 80; Sym 1; Sym 2; Tragic Ov, Op. 81; Vars & Fugue on a Theme by Handel, Op. 24 SNYC (Essential Classics Take 2) 2-▲ 63287 (14.97)
A. Paratore (pno), J. Paratore (pno) † Son for 2 Pnos, Op. 34b FWIN ▲ 3009 (16.97)
A. Previn (cnd), Royal PO † Con 2 Pno, Op. 83 TEL ▲ 80197 [DDD] (16.97)
W. Proost (cnd), San Remo SO ("Classical Music around the World, Vol. 3: Germany") † Beethoven:Con 4 Pno, Op. 58; Egmont (ov) GALL ▲ 891 [DDD] (18.97)
A. Rahbari (cnd), Belgian Radio-TV PO *(rec 1989)* † Sym 3 NXIN ▲ 550278 [DDD] (5.97)
J. Rogers (pno), J. Morrison (pno) *(rec Morrow, GA, United States of America, June 8-9, 1993)* ("A Virtuoso Duo-Piano Showcase") † J. Costa:Flying Fingers 2 Pnos; E. von Dohnányi:Suite en valse 2 Pnos, Op. 39a; J. B. Duvernoy:Feu roulant, Op. 256; W. Lutosławski:Vars Theme Paganini 2 Pnos; H. Stover:Rag Pastorale & Carillon ACAD ▲ 20023 (16.97)
L. Rogg (org) [trans L. Rogg for org] *(rec Victoria Hall Geneva, Switzerland)* † C. Franck:Chorales Org, M.38-40; Vierne:Sym 1 Org, Op. 14; Widor:Sym 5 Org, Op. 42/1 CASC ▲ 1028 (16.97)
K. Sanderling (cnd), Dresden Staatskapelle † Syms (comp); Tragic Ov, Op. 81 EUR 3-▲ 69220 [ADD] (13.97)
S. Skrowaczewski (cnd), Hallé Orch † Sym 3 INMP (Classic) ▲ 2039 (9.97)
S. Skrowaczewski (cnd), Hallé Orch † Academic Festival Ov, Op. 80; Hungarian Dances Orch; Syms (comp); Tragic Ov, Op. 81 IMPB 4-▲ 3 [DDD]
L. Slatkin (cnd), St. Louis SO † Academic Festival Ov, Op. 80; Serenade 2 Orch, Op. 16 RCAV (Red Seal) ▲ 7920 [DDD] (16.97)
G. Solti (cnd) *(rec Carnegie Hall New York City, June 21, 1994)* ("Sir Georg Solti: Carnegie Hall Project") † Smetana:Bartered Bride (ov); R. Strauss:Don Juan, Op. 20; R. Wagner:Meistersinger (ov) PLON ▲ 44458 [DDD] (16.97)
G. Solti (pno), M. Perahia (pno) † B. Bartók:Son 2 Pnos & Perc, Sz.110 SNYC ▲ 42625 [DDD] (16.97)
G. Szell (cnd), Cleveland Orch † Academic Festival Ov, Op. 80; Hungarian Dances Orch; Syms (comp); Tragic Ov, Op. 81 SNYC (Essential Classics) 3-▲ 48398 (23.97)
M. T. Thomas (cnd), London SO † Hungarian Dances Orch; Serenade 2 Orch, Op. 16 SNYC ▲ 47195 (16.97)
A. Toscanini (cnd), NBC SO *(rec Studio 8-H broadcast)* ("The Toscanini Collection, Vols. 6-9") † Academic Festival Ov, Op. 80; Con Vn & Vc, Op. 102; Gesäng der Parzen, Op. 89; Hungarian Dances Orch; Liebeslieder Waltzes Pno 4-Hands, Op. 52a; Syms (comp); Tragic Ov, Op. 81 RCAV (Gold Seal) 4-▲ 60325 [ADD] (40.97)
A. Toscanini (cnd), New York Philharmonic SO † J. Haydn:Sym 101; W. A. Mozart:Sym 35, K.385 MTAL ▲ 48049 (6.97)
A. Toscanini (cnd), New York PO ("The Toscanini Collection, Vol. 65") † Dukas:L'Apprenti sorcier; Mendelssohn (-Bartholdy):Midsummer Night's Dream (sels); W. A. Mozart:Sym 35, K.385; R. Wagner:Siegfried Idyll RCAV (Gold Seal) ▲ 60317 (11.97)
A. Toscanini (cnd), New York PO *(rec 1928-36)* ("Toscanini Edition, Vol. 4") † Dukas:L'Apprenti sorcier; C. W. Gluck:Orfeo ed Euridice (dance); Mendelssohn (-Bartholdy):Midsummer Night's Dream (sels); G. Rossini:Barbiere di Siviglia (ov); Italiana in Algeri (ov); Semiramide (ov); Verdi:Traviata (sels) GRM2 ▲ 78817 (13.97)

BRAHMS, JOHANNES (cont.)

Variations on a Theme by Haydn for Orchestra, Op. 56a (1873) or 2 Pianos, Op. 56b (1873) (cont.)

B. Walter (cnd), Columbia SO † Academic Festival Ov, Op. 80; Sym 1 SNYC (Bruno Walter: The Edition) ▲ 64470 (10.97)

B. Walter (cnd), New York PO *(rec 1953)* † G. Mahler:Sym 1 SNYC (Masterworks Heritage) ▲ 63328 [ADD] (12.97)

various artists [excerpt] † B. Bartók:Con Orch, Sz.116; G. Holst:Planets, Op. 32; W. A. Mozart:Con 3 Vn, K.216; R. Strauss:Also sprach Zarathustra, Op. 30; Salome (dance of the 7 veils) MTAL ▲ 48095 (6.97)

Variations (8 sets) for Piano, Opp. 9, 21/1 & 2, 23, 24, 35 & 56b (complete)

I. Hobson (pno), C. Hobson (pno) [w. C. Hobson on Opp. 23 & 56b] *(rec Urbana, IL, Nov 1-3, 1993, Feb 14 & 17 & Mar 28-29, 1994)* ("The Complete Variations of Johannes Brahms") † Theme & Vars Pno ARA 2-▲ 6654 [DDD] (32.97)

Variations in f# on a Theme of Robert Schumann for Piano, Op. 9 (1854)

I. Biret (pno) *(rec Nov 1989)* † Vars & Fugue on a Theme by Handel, Op. 24; Vars on a Theme by Paganini, Op. 35 NXIN ▲ 550350 [DDD] (5.97)

I. Janssen (pno) *(rec Nov 1992)* † Vars & Fugue on a Theme by Handel, Op. 24; Vars on a Theme by Paganini, Op. 35 GLOE ▲ 5096 [DDD] (16.97)

V. Jochum (pno) ("Theme & Variations") † R. Schumann:Bunte Blätter, Op. 99; Impromptus on a Theme by Clara Wieck, Op. 5; C. Schumann:Romance varié, Op. 3; Vars on a Theme by Robert Schumann, Op. 20 TUD ▲ 7028 (16.97)

L. Lortie (pno) † R. Schumann:Blumenstück, Op. 19; Bunte Blätter, Op. 99 CHN ▲ 9289 [DDD] (16.97)

J. F. Osorio (pno) ("Ballades & Variations") † Ballades (4), Op. 10; Vars & Fugue on a Theme by Handel, Op. 24 ASVQ ▲ 6161 [DDD] (10.97)

B. Petrushansky (pno) † Ballades (4), Op. 10; Son 2 Pno, Op. 2 AG ▲ 185 (18.97)

Variations (11) in D on an Original Theme for Piano, Op. 21/1 (1857)

M. Anderson (pno) *(rec Wyastone Leys Monmouth, Nov 25-27, 1996)* † Pieces (4) Pno, Op. 119; Pieces (6) Pno, Op. 118; Vars on a Hungarian Song, Op. 21/2 NIMB ▲ 5521 [DDD] (16.97)

W. Backhaus (pno) *(rec Berlin, 1935 from HMV 78s)* † Ballades (4), Op. 10; Hungarian Dances Pno; Pno Music (misc colls); Rhaps (2) Pno, Op. 79; Scherzo Pno, Op. 4 PHS ▲ 9385 [AAD] (17.97)

W. Backhaus (pno) *(rec 1933-39)* ("Great Recordings of the Thirties") † Ballades (4), Op. 10; Pno Music (misc colls); Rhaps (2) Pno, Op. 79 GRM2 ▲ 78507 [ADD] (13.97)

M. Boriskin (pno) *(rec Univ of Iowa, IA, Feb 24-27, 1990)* † Theme & Vars Pno; Vars & Fugue on a Theme by Handel, Op. 24; Vars on a Hungarian Song, Op. 21/2 MUA ▲ 4726 [DDD] (10.97)

J. Katchen (pno) *(rec 1962)* ("Julius Katchen") † Son 3 Pno, Op. 5; Balakirev:Islamey; Chopin:Ballade 3 Pno, Op. 47; Fantaisie Pno, Op. 49; C. Franck:Prélude, choral et fugue, M.21; Liszt:Hungarian Rhaps, S.244; Mendelssohn (-Bartholdy):Prelude & Fugue Pno; Rondo capriccioso, Op. 14; N. Rorem:Son 2 Pno PPHI (Great Pianists of the 20th Century) ▲ 456856 (22.97)

K. Lifschitz (pno) *(rec Wigmore Hall London)* ("London Debut Recital Live") † Vars on a Hungarian Song, Op. 21/2; F. Couperin:Pièces de clavecin (sels); S. Rachmaninoff:Preludes Pno DNN ▲ 78773 (16.97)

L. Negro (pno) *(rec Nacka Aula Nacka Sweden, Dec 20-22, 1976)* † Duets (4), Op. 28; Ernste Gesänge, Op. 121; Romanzen aus Tieck's Magelone, Op. 33 BIS ▲ 70 [AAD] (17.97)

Variations (13) on a Hungarian Song for Piano, Op. 21/2 (1853)

M. Anderson (pno) *(rec Wyastone Leys Monmouth, Nov 25-27, 1996)* † Pieces (4) Pno, Op. 119; Pieces (6) Pno, Op. 118; Vars on an Original Theme, Op. 21/1 NIMB ▲ 5521 [DDD] (16.97)

M. Boriskin (pno) *(rec Univ of Iowa, IA, Feb 24-27, 1990)* † Theme & Vars Pno; Vars & Fugue on a Theme by Handel, Op. 24; Vars on an Original Theme, Op. 21/1 MUA ▲ 4726 [DDD] (10.97)

K. Lifschitz (pno) *(rec Wigmore Hall London)* ("London Debut Recital Live") † Vars on an Original Theme, Op. 21/1; F. Couperin:Pièces de clavecin (sels); S. Rachmaninoff:Preludes Pno DNN ▲ 78773 (16.97)

R. Silverman (pno) † Pieces (6) Pno, Op. 118; Rhaps (2) Pno, Op. 79 MUVI (Musica Viva) ▲ 1028 (16.97)

Variations in E♭ on a Theme by Robert Schumann for Piano 4-Hands, Op. 23 (1861)

Crommelynck Duo † Liebeslieder Waltzes, Op. 52; Neue Liebeslieder Waltzes Pno 4-Hands, Op.65a; Souvenir de la Russie CLAV ▲ 8711 [ADD] (16.97)

B. Eden (pno), A. Tamir (pno) † Sym 3 CRD ▲ 3414 (17.97)

P. Komen (pno), P. Verhagen (pno) *(rec Nov 1998)* † A. Dietrich:Son Pno 4-Hands, Op. 19; H. Goetz:Son Pno 4-Hands, Op. 17; R. Schumann:Bilder aus Osten, Op. 66 GLOE ▲ 5188 [DDD] (16.97)

S. Matthies (pno), C. Köhn (pno) *(rec Clara Wieck Auditorium Sandhausen, Sept 4-9, 1995)* ("Four Hand Piano Music, Vol. 1") † Neue Liebeslieder Waltzes, Op. 65; Souvenir de la Russie; Waltzes Pno, Op. 39 NXIN ▲ 8553139 [DDD] (5.97)

H. Peter (pno), V. Stenzl (pno) *(rec live)* † Hungarian Dances Pno 4-Hands; Serenade 1 Orch, Op. 11 ARSM ▲ 1130 [DDD] (17.97)

Variations (25) & Fugue in B♭ on a Theme by Handel for Piano, Op. 24 (1861)

C. Arrau (pno) † Chopin:Songs Sop; Liszt:Études de concert (2), S.145; Mephisto Waltz 1 Pno, S.514; M. Ravel:Gaspard de la nuit AURC ▲ 118 (5.97)

E. Ax (pno) † Pieces (6) Pno, Op. 118; Rhaps (2) Pno, Op. 79 SNYC ▲ 48046 (16.97)

I. Biret (pno) *(rec Nov 1989)* † Vars in f# on Theme of R. Schumann, Op. 9; Vars on a Theme by Paganini, Op. 35 NXIN ▲ 550350 [DDD] (5.97)

M. Boriskin (pno) *(rec Univ of Iowa, IA, Feb 24-27, 1990)* † Theme & Vars Pno; Vars on a Hungarian Song, Op. 21/2; Vars on an Original Theme, Op. 21/1 MUA ▲ 4726 [DDD] (10.97)

V. Cliburn (pno) † Con 1 Pno, Op. 15 RCAV (Gold Seal) ▲ 60357 [ADD] (11.97)

A. Cohen (pno) † R. Schumann:Arabeske Pno, Op. 18; Fant Pno, Op. 17 VOXC ▲ 7539 (5.97)

P. Egon (pno) *(rec 1936-51)* ("Petri Egon, Vol. 3") † Busoni:Albumblätter Pno; Elegien Pno; Chopin:Nocturnes Pno PHS ▲ 9078 [AAD] (17.97)

L. Fleisher (pno) *(rec 1956)* † Con 1 Pno, Op. 15; Con 2 Pno, Op. 83; Waltzes Pno, Op. 39 SNYC (Masterworks Heritage) 2-▲ 63225

J. Gilad (pno) *(rec Highgate, London, England, Oct 1997)* † Beethoven:Son 28 Pno, Op. 101; W. A. Mozart:Son 18 Pno, K.576 EMIC (Debut) ▲ 72823 [DDD] (6.97)

S. Gorodnitzki (pno) *(rec New York City, NY, June 8-10, 1953)* † Vars on a Theme by Paganini, Op. 35; Chopin:Polonaise 3 Pno, Op. 40/1; Debussy:Preludes Pno; Liszt:Consolations (6), S.172; Trans, Arrs & Paraphrases EMIC ▲ 67018 [ADD] (11.97)

I. Janssen (pno) *(rec Nov 1992)* † Vars in f# on Theme of R. Schumann, Op. 9; Vars on a Theme by Paganini, Op. 35 GLOE ▲ 5096 [DDD] (16.97)

N. Järvi (cnd), London SO [Edmund Rubbra's 1938 orch] † Qt 1 Pno, Op. 25 CHN ▲ 8825 [DDD] (16.97)

P. Katin (pno) ("A Brahms Recital") † Fants Pno, Op. 116; Intermezzos (3) Pno, Op. 117; Rhaps (2) Pno, Op. 79 OLY ▲ 263 [DDD] (16.97)

A. Kuerti (pno) † Son 3 Pno, Op. 5 PPR ▲ 224512 (16.97)

B. Moiseiwitsch (pno) *(rec 1930-43)* ("A Portrait, Part 2") † Chopin:Barcarolle Pno, Op. 60; Polonaise 6 Pno, Op. 53; Liszt:Hungarian Rhaps, S.244; Liebesträume, S.541; Légendes, S.175; C. M. von Weber:Invitation to the Dance Pno, J.260 ENPL (Piano Library) ▲ 265 (13.97)

E. Ormandy (cnd), Philadelphia Orch [arr Rubbra] † Academic Festival Ov, Op. 80; Sym 1; Sym 2; Tragic Ov, Op. 81; Vars on a Theme by Haydn SNYC (Essential Classics Take 2) 2-▲ 63287 (14.97)

J. F. Osorio (pno) ("Ballades & Variations") † Ballades (4), Op. 10; Vars in f# on Theme of R. Schumann, Op. 9 ASVQ ▲ 6161 [DDD] (10.97)

E. Petri (pno) *(rec 1937-38)* † P. Tchaikovsky:Con 1 Pno, Op. 23 ENPL (The Piano Library) ▲ 286 (13.97)

G. Saarinen (pno) † Qnt Pno, Op. 34 DHR ▲ 71129 (16.97)

Solomon (pno) [10 vars] ("The First HMV Recordings: 1942-43") † Beethoven:Trio 6 Pno, Op. 97; Chopin:Berceuse, Op. 57; Pno Music (misc colls) APR ▲ 5503 [ADD] (19.97)

Solomon (pno) *(rec early 1940s)* † Intermezzos (3) Pno, Op. 117; Rhaps (2) Pno, Op. 79; Beethoven:Trio 6 Pno, Op. 97 ENPL (Piano Library) ▲ 313 (14.97)

A. Ugorski (pno) † Son 1 Pno, Op. 1; Son 2 Pno, Op. 2; Son 3 Pno, Op. 5; Studies (5) Pno DGRM 2-▲ 449182 [DDD]

M. Yudina (pno) *(rec 1947)* † F. Schubert:Son Pno, D.960 HPC1 ▲ 123 (17.97)

artists unknown [Var 5] ("Brahms at Bedtime") † Music of Brahms; Son 3 Vn, Op. 108; Songs PPHI (Set Your Life to Music) ▲ 54966 (9.97) ▮ 54966 (5.98)

Variations (28) in a on a Theme by Paganini for Piano, Op. 35 (1862-63)

C. Arrau (pno) *(rec 1974)* ("Claudio Arrau") † Con 1 Pno, Op. 15; I. Albéniz:Iberia Suite; J. S. Bach:Chromatic Fant & Fugue, BWV 903; Balakirev:Islamey; Liszt:Pno Music (misc) PPHI (Great Pianists of the 20th Century) ▲ 456706 (22.97)

G. Bachauer (pno) *(rec New York, Feb 20 & 26, 1963)* † Con 2 Pno, Op. 83; Beethoven:Son 9 Pno, Op. 14/1; Liszt:Hungarian Rhaps, S.244 MRCR ▲ 34340 (11.97)

W. Backhaus (pno) ("Wilhelm Backhaus Plays Brahms") † Con 2 Pno, Op. 83 ENPL (Piano Library) ▲ 213 (13.97)

BRAHMS, JOHANNES (cont.)

Variations (28) in a on a Theme by Paganini for Piano, Op. 35 (1862-63) (cont.)

W. Backhaus (pno) *(rec Berlin, Germany, 1916)* † Chopin:Études Pno; Polonaise 3 Pno, Op. 40/1; Liszt:Hungarian Rhaps, S.244; A. Rubinstein:Album of Popular Dances, Op. 82; Soirées à Saint-Pétersbourg; F. Schubert:Qnt Pno, D.667 BPS ▲ 38 [ADD] (16.97)

W. Backhaus (pno) *(rec Nov 1929)* † Con 1 Pno, Op. 15 MPLY ▲ 2028 (m) (13.97)

W. Backhaus (pno), M. Hess (pno)—Book I:1; Book I:3; Book I:7; Book I:12; *(rec 1915-30)* † Pno Music (misc colls); Son 3 Pno, Op. 5 NIMB (Grand Piano) ▲ 8806 [DDD] (11.97)

I. Biret (pno) *(rec Nov 1989)* † Vars & Fugue on a Theme by Handel, Op. 24; Vars in f# on Theme of R. Schumann, Op. 9 NXIN ▲ 550350 [DDD] (5.97)

E. Brancart (pno) † Liszt:Grandes études de Paganini, S.141 DI ▲ 920423 [DDD] (5.97)

S. Cherkassky (pno) † Mussorgsky:Pictures at an Exhibition; S. Rachmaninoff:Vars on a Theme by Corelli, Op. 42 NIMB ▲ 7706 (11.97)

S. Gorodnitzki (pno) *(rec New York City, NY, June 8-10, 1953)* † Vars & Fugue on a Theme by Handel, Op. 24; Chopin:Polonaise 3 Pno, Op. 40/1; Debussy:Preludes Pno; Liszt:Consolations (6), S.172; Trans, Arrs & Paraphrases EMIC ▲ 67018 [ADD] (11.97)

I. Janssen (pno) *(rec Nov 1992)* † Vars & Fugue on a Theme by Handel, Op. 24; Vars in f# on Theme of R. Schumann, Op. 9 GLOE ▲ 5096 [DDD] (16.97)

E. Kissin (pno) † Beethoven:Son 14 Pno, Op. 27/2; C. Franck:Prélude, choral et fugue, M.21 RCAV (Red Seal) ▲ 68910 [DDD] (16.97)

V. Krpan (pno) † Con Vn PC ▲ 267155 [DDD] (2.97)

V. Merzhanov (pno) *(rec 1951)* † Liszt:Études d'exécution transcendante (6), S.140 RD ▲ 16209 [AAD] (16.97)

A. B. Michelangeli (pno) *(rec 1960-73)* ("Michelangeli in Recital") † Ballades (4), Op. 10; Busoni:Chaconne Pno; Chopin:Fantaisie Pno, Op. 49; Waltzes Pno; M. Ravel:Gaspard de la nuit; R. Schumann:Carnaval, Op. 9 MUA 2-▲ 817 [AAD] (31.97)

A. B. Michelangeli (pno) *(rec 1948)* ("The American Debut") † J. S. Bach:Sons & Partitas Vn; R. Schumann:Con Pno in a, Op. 54 ENPL (Piano Library) ▲ 272 (13.97)

M. Raekallio (pno) † I. Friedman:Studies on a Theme by Paganini, Op. 47b; Liszt:Études d'exécution transcendante (6), S.140 ODE ▲ 777 [DDD] (17.97)

M. Shehori (pno) † Beethoven:Son 3 Pno, Op. 2/3; D. Scarlatti:Sons Kbd CEMB ▲ 99 [DDD] (15.97)

A. Shtarkman (pno) ("Busoni Competition 1995 Winner's Recital") † Beethoven:Son 32 Pno, Op. 111; I. Stravinsky:Scenes (3) Pno DVX ▲ 25219 (11.97)

A. Simon (pno) † Liszt:Grandes études de Paganini, S.141; Paganini:Caprice d'adieux; Caprices Vn, M.S. 25; Con 2 Vn, M.S. 48; S. Rachmaninoff:Rhap on a Theme of Paganini, Op. 43; R. Schumann:Studien nach Capricen von Paganini, Op. 3 VB3 3-▲ 3020 [ADD] (14.97)

J. Thibaudet (pno) *(rec London, England, July 1994)* † R. Schumann:Arabeske Pno, Op. 18; Symphonic Etudes, Op. 13 PLON ▲ 44338 [DDD] (16.97)

L. Vassiliadis (pno) † R. Schumann:Carnaval, Op. 9 DI ▲ 920257 [DDD] (5.97)

A. Walachowski (pno), I. Walachowski (pno) ("Klavierduo Walachowski") † Chopin:Rondos (4) Pnos; W. A. Mozart:Andante & Vars, K.501; M. Ravel:Valse; P. Tchaikovsky:Sleeping Beauty, Op. 66 ARS ▲ 368359 [DDD] (15.99)

E. Wild (pno) † Ballades (4), Op. 10; Liszt:Études d'exécution transcendante (6), S.140 VC ▲ 118 (13.97)

Vocal Quartets

M. Piquemal (cnd), Michel Piquemal Vocal Ensemble—Qts (6) SATB, Op. 112 [Sehnsucht; Nächtens]; Qts (3) SATB, Op. 64; Qts (4) SATB, Op. 92; Geistliches Lied, Op. 30 *(rec Apr 1990)* † Songs (5), Op. 104; Brian:Vocal Qts ARN ▲ 68132 [DDD] (16.97)

Waltzes (16) for Piano (or Piano 4-Hands), Op. 39 (1865)

C. Aebersold (pno), R. Neiweem (pno) *(rec Chicago, IL)* † Con 1 Pno, Op. 15 SUMM ▲ 184 [DDD] (16.97)

M. Argerich (pno), A. Rabinovitch (pno) *(rec Berlin, Apr 1993)* † Son for 2 Pnos, Op. 34b; Vars on a Theme by Haydn TELC ▲ 92257 [DDD] (16.97)

I. Biret (pno) *(rec 1992)* † Hungarian Dances Pno NXIN ▲ 550355 [DDD] (5.97)

A. Brings (pno), G. Chinn (pno) † Hungarian Dances Pno 4-Hands CENT ▲ 2297 [DDD] (16.97)

J. Coop (pno)—Waltzes Pno, Op. 39 [No. 15 in A♭] *(rec Toronto, Canada)* ("The Romantic Piano") † Pieces (6) Pno, Op. 118; Chopin:Etudes (24) Pno, Opp. 10 & 25; Mazurkas Pno; Nocturnes Pno; Debussy:Isle joyeuse; Suite bergamasque; Liszt:Études de concert (3), S.144; Liebesträume, S.541; Mendelssohn (-Bartholdy):Pno Music (misc); S. Rachmaninoff:Études-tableaux Pno, Opp. 33 & 39; Preludes (23) Pno, Opp. 23 & 32; R. Schumann:Kinderszenen Pno, Op. 15 MUVI ▲ 1015 [DDD] (16.97)

L. Fleisher (pno) *(rec 1956)* † Con 1 Pno, Op. 15; Con 2 Pno, Op. 83; Vars & Fugue on a Theme by Handel, Op. 24 SNYC (Masterworks Heritage) 2-▲ 63225

D. Joeres (pno) *(rec Mar 1993)* † A. Dvořák:Waltzes Pno, Op. 54; F. Schubert:German Dances Pno, D.820; Waltzes, D.969 INMP ▲ 6701742 (9.97)

A. Kitain (pno) *(rec 1936-39)* † Chopin:Études Pno; Ballade 2 Pno, Op. 38; Ballade 3 Pno, Op. 47; Mazurkas Pno; Scherzos Pno; Liszt:Pno Music (misc); R. Schumann:Toccata Pno, Op. 7 ENPL (Piano Library) ▲ 221 (13.97)

S. Kolacny (pno), S. Kolacny (pno) ("Dances & Variations for Piano Duo") † Hungarian Dances Pno 4-Hands; Liebeslieder Waltzes, Op. 52; Vars on a Theme by Haydn EUFO ▲ 1238 [DDD] (18.97)

A. Kubalek (pno) ("Piano Music of Brahms, Vol. 1") † Intermezzos (3) Pno, Op. 117; Son 3 Pno, Op. 5 DOR ▲ 90141 [DDD] (16.97)

S. Matthies (pno), C. Köhn (pno) *(rec Clara Wieck Auditorium Sandhausen, Sept 4-9, 1995)* ("Four Hand Piano Music, Vol. 1") † Neue Liebeslieder Waltzes, Op. 65; Souvenir de la Russie; Vars in E♭ on Theme of R. Schumann Pno 4-Hands, Op. 23 NXIN ▲ 8553139 [DDD] (5.97)

Mendelssohn Duo *(rec Apr 1997)* † Son for 2 Pnos, Op. 34b RD ▲ 30105 [DDD] (16.97)

A. Serdar (pno) *(rec Highgate, London, England, Mar 1997)* † Busoni:Bach Transcriptions Pno; Chopin:Andante Spianato & Grand Polonaise, Op. 22; Galuppi:Son 5 Kbd; Mendelssohn (-Bartholdy):Vars sérieuses, Op. 54 EMIC (Debut) ▲ 72821 [DDD] (6.97)

Tal & Groethuysen Duo *(rec Nov 15-17, 1992)* † Hungarian Dances Pno 4-Hands SNYC ▲ 53285 [DDD] (11.97)

D. A. Wehr (pno), C. R. Wehr (pno) † Hungarian Dances Orch CSOC ▲ 4222

artists unknown—No. 15 in A♭ ("Brahms at Bedtime") † Music of Brahms; Son 3 Vn, Op. 108; Vars & Fugue on a Theme by Handel, Op. 24 PPHI (Set Your Life to Music) ▮ 54966 (5.98) ▲ 54966 (9.97)

Wann? (canon) for Female Chorus [text Uhlnad]

G. Jena (cnd), North German Radio Chorus ("The Complete Brahms Edition, Vol. 7:Choral Works") † Ave Maria, Op. 12; Begräbnisgesang, Op. 13; Canons (13), Op. 113; Dem dunkeln Schoss der heil'gen Erde; Deutsche Volkslieder (26); Fest- und Gedenksprüche, Op. 109; Geistliches Lied, Op. 30; Grausam erweiset sich Amor an mir, Op. 113/2; Kleine Hochzeitskantate; Marienlieder (7), Op. 22; Mir lächelt kein Frühling; Motets (2), Op. 29; Motets (2), Op. 74; Motets (3), Op. 110; O wie sanft; Psalm 13, Op. 27; Sacred Choruses (3), Op. 37; Songs (3), Op. 42; Songs (4), Op. 17; Songs (5), Op. 104; Songs (5), Op. 41; Songs (7), Op. 62; Songs & Romances (12), Op. 44; Songs & Romances (6), Op. 93a; Spruch; Tafellied, Op. 93b; Töne, lindernder Klang; Zu Rauch DGRM 4-▲ 449646

Zigeunerlieder (11) for SATB Vocal Quartet, Op. 103 (1887)

H. M. Beuerle (cnd), Anton Webern Choir Freiburg ("Secular Choral Songs a Cappella & with Piano") † Qts (6) SATB, Op. 112; Songs; Songs (5), Op. 104 ARSM ▲ 1136 [DDD] (17.97)

J. C. Conlon (cnd), Pacific Northwest Chamber Chorus † Castelnuovo-Tedesco:Romancero gitano, Op. 152; F. Schubert:Songs (misc colls) AMBA ▲ 1015 (16.97)

J. Flummerfeldt (cnd), Westminster Choir, G. Parker (pno), N. Parrella (pno)—Brauner Bursche; Röslein dreie; Kommt dir manchmal in den Sinn; Horch, der Wind; Weit und breit schaut niemand *(rec Westminster Choir College of Rider Univ. Princeton, NJ, May 14-16, 1995)* ("Singing for Pleasure") † Liebeslieder Waltzes, Op. 52; Motets (2), Op. 74; Neue Liebeslieder Waltzes, Op. 65; Qts (3) SATB, Op. 64 DLS ▲ 3193 [DDD] (14.97)

M. Groop (mez), A. Lubimov (pno)—He, Zigeuner; Hochgetürmte Rimaflut; Wisst ihr, wann mein Kindchen; Leiber Gott, du weisst; Brauner Bursche; Röslein dreie; Kommt dir manchmal in den Sinn; Rote Abendwolken ziehn [arr Brahms voc & pno] *(rec Järvenpää Hall, Germany, Feb 1997)* † Songs; Songs (2), Op. 91; Songs (5), Op. 49; Songs (6), Op. 86 ODE ▲ 896 [DDD] (17.97)

M. Lipovšek (mez), A. Spiri (pno)—He, Zigeuner; Hochgetürmte Rimaflut; Wisst ihr, wann mein Kindchen; Leiber Gott, du weisst; Brauner Bursche; Röslein dreie; Kommt dir manchmal in den Sinn; Rote Abendwolken ziehn † Deutsche Volkslieder (26); Deutsche Volkslieder (49), WoO 33; Marienlieder (7), Op. 22; Romances & Songs (5), Op. 84; Songs; Songs (5), Op. 49; Songs & Romances (6); Songs & Romances (8), Op. 14 *(E,F,G texts)* ORF ▲ 441971 [DDD] (18.97)

M. Müller (sop), M. Raucheisen (pno) *(rec 1944)* † Songs (6), Op. 86; G. Puccini:Bohème (sels); M. Reger:Schlichte Weisen, Op. 76; F. Schubert:Songs (misc colls); R. Wagner:Fliegende Holländer (sels); Lohengrin (sels); Tannhäuser (sels); Walküre (sels); Wesendonck Songs; C. M. von Weber:Freischütz (sels) PRE 2-▲ 89235 (m) (31.97)

A. Planès (pno), M. Creed (cnd), Berlin RIAS Chamber Choir † Qts SATB (misc) HAM ▲ 901593 (18.97)

D. Soffel (mez), C. Spencer (pno) ("Brahms Lieder, Vol. 1") † Songs ARSM ▲ 1190 (17.97)

BRAHMS, JOHANNES (cont.)
Zu Rauch (canon) for 4 Voices
G. Jena (cnd), North German Radio Chorus ("The Complete Brahms Edition, Vol. 7:Choral Works") † Ave Maria, Op. 12; Begräbnisgesang, Op. 13; Canons (13), Op. 113; Dem dunkeln Schoss der heil'gen Erde; Deutsche Volkslieder (26); Fest- und Gedenksprüche, Op. 109; Geistliches Lied, Op. 30; Grausam erweiset sich Amor an mir, Op. 113/2; Kleine Hochzeitskantate; Marienlieder (7), Op. 22; Mir lächelt kein Frühling; Motets (2), Op. 29; Motets (2), Op. 74; Motets (3), Op. 110; O wie sanft; Psalm 13, Op. 27; Sacred Choruses (3), Op. 37; Songs (3), Op. 42; Songs (4), Op. 17; Songs (5), Op. 104; Songs (5), Op. 41; Songs (7), Op. 62; Songs & Romances (12), Op. 44; Songs & Romances (6), Op. 93a; Spruch; Tafellied, Op. 93b; Töne, lindernder Klang; Wann? DGRM 4-▲ 449646
BRAHMS, JOHANNES (1833-1897), **ALBERT DIETRICH** (1829-1908)**& ROBERT SCHUMANN** (1810-1858)
F.A.E. Sonata for Violin & Piano [1 movt each by Brahms, Dietrich, Schumann]
F. Paul (vn), B. Wollenweber (pno) ("Hommage à Joachim") † J. Joachim:Romance Vn; Stücke Vn, Op. 2; Stücke Vn, Op. 5 TACE (Frei aber Einsam, Vol. 4) ▲ 56 (16.97)
J. Rubenstein (vn), D. Ouziel (pno) *(rec Brussels, Belgium, 1997)* † Sons Cl; Sons Vn (comp) PAVA 2-▲ 7398 [DDD] (21.97)
F. Terpitz (vn), B. Witter (pno) † R. Fuchs:Son 1 Vn, Op. 20; Son 6 Vn, Op. 103 AMAT ▲ 9705 (17.97)
BRANCA, GLENN (1948-
Symphony No. 9 for Orchestra & Chorus, "L'eve future"
C. V. Borries (cnd), Polish National RSO Katowice, Camerata Silesia Singers Ensemble *(rec Katowice Poland, Oct 1994)* POIN ▲ 46505 (16.97)
BRANDON, SY (20th cent)
Celebration Overture for Orchestra (1995)
P. Freeman (cnd), Czech National SO *(rec Prague, Austria)* ("Paul Freeman Introduces...Brandon, Griffes, Osbon, Muczynski, Klessig, Lamb & Felciano-Vol. 2") † Griffes:Poems of Fiona McLeod, Op. 11; Klessig:Meditation from Don Juan; M. Lamb:J. B. II; Muczynski:Sym Dialogues, Op. 20; Osbon:Liberty ALBA ▲ 322 [DDD] (16.97)
BRANDT, VASSILY (1869-1923)
Concertpiece No. 2 in E# for Trumpet & Orchestra, Op. 12
K. Christensen (tpt), J. M. Jensen (cnd), Danish Concert Band *(rec 1998-99)* ("Visions from the North") † Akerwall:Ergesia; Almila:Visions from the North; M. Andresen:Con Tpt; J. Gade:Funeral Music; D. W. Jenkins:Con A Sax; Ticheli:Blue Shades ROND ▲ 8368 (18.97)
BRANT, HENRY (1913-
Angels & Devils for Flute & Flute Orchestra (1932; rev 1947)
B. Boyd (fl), D. Hunsberger (cnd) † W. Benson:Leaves Are Falling; H. Hanson:Dies Natalis for Band CENT ▲ 2014 [AAD] (16.97)
F. Morel (cnd) ("Music from Laval University, Vol. 1a") † F. Morel:Aux Marges; Figures, Segments, Ellipses; Oiseau-Demain; I. Stravinsky:Syms of Wind Instrs SNE ▲ 545 (16.97)
Concerto for Trumpet & 9 Instruments (1941; rev. 1970)
G. Schwarz (tpt), H. Brandt (cnd) † E. Carter:Canon for 3; Moryl:Salvos; Whittenberg:Polyphony; S. Wolpe:Solo Piece Tpt PHOE ▲ 115 [AAD] (15.97)
Ghost Nets (Spatial Narratives) for Double Bass Solo & 2 separated Instrumental Groups (1988)
L. Paer (db), J. Stephens (cnd), American Camerata † Cyr:Qt 2 Strs AMCA ▲ 10303 (18.97)
Hieroglyphics III for Soprano, Viola, Piano, Harpsichord, Organ & Percussion
various artists † Orbits; Western Springs CRI ▲ 827 (16.97)
Kingdom Come for Orchestras, Circus Band & Organ (1970)
H. Brant (org), G. Samuel (cnd), Oakland SO, G. Samuel (cnd), Oakland Youth Orch † Macinations PHOE ▲ 127 (15.97)
Machinations for 10 Instruments (1970)
H. Brant (fl/glock/org/perc/ti) † Kingdom Come PHOE ▲ 127 (15.97)
Orbits:A Spatial Symphonic Ritual for Sopranino, 80 Trombones & Organ (1979)
various artists † Hieroglyphics III; Western Springs CRI ▲ 827 (16.97)
Quombex for Viola & Distant Music Boxes (1960)
P. Zukofsky (vn) *(rec Paul Hall Julliard School of Music, June 3, 1972)* † J. Cage:Nocturne; M. Feldman:Vertical Thoughts II; P. Glass:Strung Out; Scelsi:Anahit; S. Wolpe:2nd Piece Vn; Xenakis:Mikka; Mikka S CP2 ▲ 108 [AAD] (19.97)
Verticals Ascending for 2 Wind Bands, "After Rodia Towers"
J. P. Paynter (cnd) ("Winds of Change") † R. R. Bennett:Sym Songs; Finney:Con A Sax; Persichetti:Pageant, Op. 59; H. Smith:Expansions NWW ▲ 80211 [AAD] (16.97)
Western Springs for 2 Orchestras, 2 Choruses & 2 Jazz Ensembles (1984)
various artists † Hieroglyphics III; Orbits CRI ▲ 827 (16.97)
BRASSART, JOHANNES (fl 1420-1445)
Ave Maria for 4 Voices, Op. 19
A. Teichert-Hailperin (sop), K. Smith (ct), W. Jochesn (ten), M. Nitz (ten), Helga Weber Instrumental Circle † Dufay:Magnificat; Dunstable:Sacred Music; Hildegard of Bingen:Sacred Songs ENTE ▲ 41 [ADD] (10.97)
BRASSIN, LOUIS (1840-1884)
Transcriptions for Piano
C. Okashiro (pno)—Wagner:Magic Fire Music [from Die Walküre]; Wagner:Ride of the Valkyries [from Die Walküre]; Wagner:Siegmunds Liebgesang [from Die Walküre] *(rec Academy of Arts & Letters, NY, June 1998)* † G. Fauré:Souvenirs de Bayreuth, Op. posth; Moszkowski:Trans Pno; R. Wagner:Tristan und Isolde (orch sels) PPR ▲ 224521 [DDD] (16.97)
M. Ponti (pno) *(rec ca 1973)* † Liszt:Réminiscences de Don Juan Pno, S.418; Trans, Arrs & Paraphrases; Moszkowski:Operatic Paraphrases & Trans Pno; P. Pabst:Concert Paraphrase on Tchaikovsky's Eugen On; Tausig:Fant on Themes of Moniuszko; Trans & Arrs Pno; Thalberg:Fants & Vars on Opera Themes Pno VB2 2-▲ 5047 [ADD] (9.97)
BRAUN, JEAN DANIEL (fl 1740)
Sonata Terza for Flute & Continuo [from *Oeuvre Premier*]
M. Rasmussen (vl), D. Laurin (rcr) *(rec Furuby Church Sweden, May 8-11, 1995)* ("The French King's Flautists") † Blavet:Sonatas for Transverse Flute & Continuo; Dornel:Sons Vn & Suites Fl, Op. 2; Hotteterre:Première livre de pièce, Op. 5; J.-M. Leclair:Sons Vn (books 1-4) BIS ▲ 745 [DDD] (17.97)
BRAUN, PETER MICHAEL (1936-
Chörale (3) for 4 Trombones (1979)
Triton Trombone Quartet *(rec Furuby Church, Sweden, July 6-10, 1994)* ("Trombone Angels") † G. Jansson:Missa for 4 Trbns; J. Kretz:alles Ding währt seine Zeit; Maklakiewicz:Chrysea Phorminx; F. Peeters:Suite for 4 Trbns, Op. 82; Serocki:Suite for 4 Trbns BIS ▲ 694 [DDD] (17.97)
BRAUNFELS, WALTER (1841-1904)
Die Vögel (opera) [lib Braunfels after Aristophanes], Op. 30 (1913-19)
H. Kwon (sop—Nightingale), E. Wottrich (ten—Good Hope), W. Holzmair (bar—Hoopoe), M. Gorne (b-bar—Prometheus), M. Krause (sgr—Loyal Friend), L. Zagrosek (cnd), Berlin German SO, Berlin Radio Chorus PLON (Entartete Musik) ▲ 448679 (32.97)
BRAXTON, ANTHONY (1945-
Composition No. 107 for Saxophones, Piano, Percussion & Computer Music (1982) (selections)
(rec United States of America) ("The Virtuoso in the Computer Age - I") † L. Austin:Montage; P. Lansky:As If; J. Melby:Con 1 Fl & Computer; D. Rosenboom:Precipice in Time CENT (CDCM Computer Music Series, Vol 10) ▲ 2110 [DDD] (16.97)
Composition No. 136
J. Fonda (db), R. Dahinden (trbn), A. Fuller (dr) *(rec NJ, May & Dec 1995)* ("Naima") † R. Dahinden:Free Lines MODE ▲ 62 [DDD] (17.97)
BRAY, JOHN (1782-1822)
The Indian Princess (opera in 2 acts) (1808)
J. Baldoon (cnd), Federal Music Society Opera Company [ed & arr Victor Fell Yellin] † R. Taylor:Ethiop NWW ▲ 80232 (16.97)
BRAZELTON, KITTY (1951-
Down n Harp n All a Rond o for Harp (1997)
E. Panzer (hp) ("Dancing in Place") † Beglarian:Play Nice; W. M. Chambers:Moments Hp; Einhorn:New Pages Pnos; Hovda:Dancing in Place; Matamoros:Re: Elizabeth; Panzer:Green Tea with Oranges; Invocation Hp; Syncophony Hp OOD ▲ 56 [DDD] (16.97)
BREDEMEYER, REINER (1929-
DiAs (+-) (1973)
L. Güttler (tpt), B. Glaetzner (ob) *(rec Dresden, Germany, Feb 1981)* † B. Franke:Chagall-Impressions; P. Hindemith:Con Tpt; Matthus:Con Tpt; Sauguet:Non morietur in aeternum; S. Thiele:Music Org & Tpt BER ▲ 9057 [DDD] (10.97)
BREHME, HANS (1904-1957)
Paganiniana - Concert Etudes in the Form of Variations on a Theme of Paganini, Op. 52 (1951)
H. C. Jacobs (acc) *(rec Germany, 1988)* ("Paganiniana") † J. Baur:Toccatas (3); J. Haydn:Fl-Clock Pieces, H.XIX; Karg-Elert:Scènes pittoresques, Op. 31; W. A. Mozart:Andante Mechanical Org, K.616; M. Reger:Romance in a Harm *(E, G text)* CPO ▲ 999057 [DDD] (14.97)
BRÉHY, HERCULE PETRUS (1673-1737)
Isti sunt triumphatores for Voices, Strings & Organ
E. van Nevel (cnd), Concerto Currende, Capella Currende *(rec Netherlands, 1996)* † Iubilate Deo; Resurrexit amor meus; Scapulis suis; P. A. Fiocco:Fuge demon, fuge lepra; Helmont:Missa Solemnis Sanctae Gudilae EUFO ▲ 1259 [DDD] (18.97)
Iubilate Deo for Voices
E. van Nevel (cnd), Concerto Currende, Capella Currende *(rec Netherlands, 1996)* † Isti sunt triumphatores; Resurrexit amor meus; Scapulis suis; P. A. Fiocco:Fuge demon, fuge lepra; Helmont:Missa Solemnis Sanctae Gudilae EUFO ▲ 1259 [DDD] (18.97)
Resurrexit amor meus for Voices & String Orchestra
E. van Nevel (cnd), Concerto Currende, Capella Currende *(rec Netherlands, 1996)* † Isti sunt triumphatores; Iubilate Deo; Scapulis suis; P. A. Fiocco:Fuge demon, fuge lepra; Helmont:Missa Solemnis Sanctae Gudilae EUFO ▲ 1259 [DDD] (18.97)
Scapulis suis for Voices & Continuo
E. van Nevel (cnd), Concerto Currende, Capella Currende *(rec Netherlands, 1996)* † Isti sunt triumphatores; Iubilate Deo; Resurrexit amor meus; P. A. Fiocco:Fuge demon, fuge lepra; Helmont:Missa Solemnis Sanctae Gudilae EUFO ▲ 1259 [DDD] (18.97)
BREMER, CAROLYN (1957-
Early Light for Orchestra [trans Bremer for Wind Symphony] (1995)
E. Corporon (cnd), North Texas Wind Sym *(rec Univ of Georgia, Nov 1996)* ("Dialogues & Entertainments") † Corigliano:Gazebo Dances for Band; W. Kraft:Dialogues; Mailman:For Precious Friends; J. Stamp:Maryland Songs; Toch:Miniature Ov KLAV (Wind Recording Project) ▲ 11083 [DDD] (18.97)
Sonata for Clarinet
J. Russo (cl), L. W. Ignacio (pno) *(rec PA, United States of America)* ("Masterworks for Clarinet & Piano") † Son Cl; J. Beck:Son Cl; S. Chandler:Tune & Chase with Quickstep Dirge; H. Cowell:Six Casual Developments; Rochberg:Dialogues; J. Russo:Preludes (3); Studies (2); R. Snyder:Polemics *(E text)* CRSR ▲ 9561
BREMNER, ANTHONY (1939-
In the Shrubbery for Narrator, 2 Pianos, Percussion & Chorus (1989)
J. Glen (nar), D. Miller (pno), G. Willems (pno), P. South (perc), R. Peelman (cnd), Song Company *(rec ABC Ultimo Centre, Apr 1993)* ("The Green CD: Environmentally Friendly Australian Choral Music") † R. Edwards:Flower Songs; S. Greenbaum:Upon the Dark Water; M. Wesley-Smith:Who Killed Cock Robin?; Who Stopped the Rain?; Whiticker:Man, Skin Cancer of the Earth TALP ▲ 64 [DDD] (18.97)
BRENDLER, EDUARD (1800-1831)
Divertissement for Bassoon & Orchestra, Op. 6
A. Engström (bn), T. Svedlund (cnd), Gothenburg SO ("Swedish Bassoon Concertos") † Berwald:Konsertstycke Bn; Crusell:Concertino Bn; Fernström:Concertino Bn, Op.80 ITIM ▲ 15 [DDD] (16.97)
BRENET, THÉRÈSE (1935-
Aeterno certamine for Viola, Cello & String Orchestra with Percussion
D. Fanal (cnd), Sudecka PO † Poem Vn; Return of Quetzalcoatl; Suite concertante Vn DPV ▲ 9894 (15.97)
Poem for Violin & Orchestra
D. Fanal (cnd), Sudecka PO † Aeterno certamine; Return of Quetzalcoatl; Suite concertante Vn DPV ▲ 9894 (15.97)
The Return of Quetzalcoatl (symphonic poem) for Cello & Orchestra
D. Fanal (cnd), Sudecka PO † Aeterno certamine; Poem Vn; Suite concertante Vn DPV ▲ 9894 (15.97)
Suite concertante for Violin & Orchestra
D. Fanal (cnd), Sudecka PO † Aeterno certamine; Poem Vn; Return of Quetzalcoatl DPV ▲ 9894 (15.97)
BRESNICK, MARTIN (1946-
B.'s Garlands for 8 Cellos (1973)
M. Bresnick (cnd) *(rec Sprague Hall Yale Univ., Jan 16, 1994)* ("Music for Strings") † Qt 2 Strs; Qt 3 Strs; Wir weben, wir weben CRI ▲ 682 [DDD] (16.97)
Bag O' Tells (An Archeology of the Mandolin) for Mandolin (1984)
S. Josel (mand) *(rec Yale University New Haven, CT, Mar 21, 1994)* ("Long Distance") † S. Corbett:Arien IV; Kernis:Ciacona Gtr; E. Lyon:Greaseball; Tenney:Water on the Mountain CRI ▲ 697 [DDD] (17.97)
Just Time for Woodwind Quintet (1985)
New York Woodwind Quintet † M. Powell:Qnt Ww; R. Roseman:Double Qnt; R. Shapey:Movts Ww NWW ▲ 80413 [DDD] (16.97)
Lady Neil's Dumpe (all-electronic composition) (1987)
N. B. Rolnick (cmpt) *(rec West Hurley, NJ)* † R. Baitz:Kaleidocycles; S. Lindroth:Syntax; N. B. Rolnick:What Is The Use?; R. Teitelbaum:Golem I CENT (CDCM Computer Music Series, Vol. 2) ▲ 2039 [DDD] (16.97)
Quartet No. 2 for Strings, "Bucephalus" (1983-84)
Alexander String Quartet *(rec Sprague Hall Yale Univ., July 25, 1985)* ("Music for Strings") † B.'s Garlands; Qt 3 Strs; Wir weben, wir weben CRI ▲ 682 [DDD] (16.97)
Quartet No. 3 for Strings (1992)
Harrington String Quartet *(rec Canyon, TX, May 21, 1994)* ("Music for Strings") † B.'s Garlands; Qt 2 Strs; Wir weben, wir weben CRI ▲ 682 [DDD] (16.97)
Trio for Piano, Violin & Cello (1987-88)
Monticello Trio † C. Ives:Trio; Shatin:Ignoto numine CRI ▲ 583 [DDD] (16.97)
Wir weben, wir weben for String Orchestra (1976-78)
D. Asia (cnd) [trans for str sxt] *(rec Sprague Hall Yale Univ., TX, Oct 7, 1985)* ("Music for Strings") † B.'s Garlands; Qt 2 Strs; Qt 3 Strs CRI ▲ 682 [DDD] (16.97)
BRETAN, NICOLAE (1887-1968)
Arald (opera in 1 act) [lib Bretan after M. Eminescu] (1982)
C. Mandeal (cnd), Moldova PO † Golem NIMB ▲ 5424 (16.97)
Choral Music
P. Bryn-Julson (sop), L. Konya (bar), F. Weiss (pno), M. Berkovsky (pno), D. Sutherland (org), R. Stalford (org)—Requiem; Născătoare De Dumnezeu; Tatăl Nostru; Kis, Karácsonyi Enek; Közel A Temetőhz; Isten Drága Pénze; Krisztus-Kereszt Az Erdőn; Az Ur Erkezése; Imdság Háború Után; A Halál Rokona; A Sion-Hegy Alatt; Amen; Futurum Imperfectum; Mors Imperator; Por {ACUEs Virág; Ti Ébe Hulló Órák; Vándorutam; A Csucsai Kert; Siriratok *(rec Bradley Hills Presbyterian Church, MD, Sept 8, 1974)* ("Sacred Songs") NIMB ▲ 5584 [ADD] (16.97)
The Evening Star (opera in 1 act with prologue & epilogue) [lib. Bretan after Eminescu] (1921)
A. Croitoru (sop—King's Daughter), E. Casian (mez—Lady-in-Waiting), M. Budoiu (ten—Mariner), I. Pojar (ten—Page), I. Voineag (ten—Evening Star), B. Szabó (bass—Michael the Archangel), B. Hary (cnd), Transylvania PO Cluj *(rec Cluj, Sept 1994) (Romanian,E,F,G lib texts)* NIMB ▲ 5463 [DDD] (16.97)
Golem (opera in 1 act) [lib Bretan after I. Kaczèv] (1923)
C. Mandeal (cnd), Moldova PO † Arald NIMB ▲ 5424 (16.97)
Horia (opera in 3 acts) [lib Bretan after G. Popp] (1937)
M. Onofrei-Voiculet (sop—Baroness Hunfy), C. Pop (sop—Ileana), I. Buciuceanu (mez—Dochia), C. Iliescu (ten—Nutu), M. Angelescu (ten—Crişan), C. Fănăteanu (ten—Ionel), E. Iuraşcu (bar—Cloşca), L. Martinescu (bar—Baron Nyil), N. Urziceanu (bar—Pavel), G. Crăsnaru (b-bar—Horia), A. Ştefănescu (bass—Costan), D. Zancu (bass—Baron Kemény), C. Trailescu (cnd), Romanian Opera Orch, S. Olariu (cnd), Romanian Opera Chorus *(rec Bucharest, July 1980) (Romanian,E,F,G lib texts)* NIMB 2-▲ 5513 [ADD] (32.97)
BRETÓN, TOMÁS (1850-1923)
La Dolores (selections)
E. F. Arbós (cnd), Madrid SO ("Spanish Orchestral Favorites") † I. Albéniz:Iberia Suite; M. de Falla:Sombrero de tres picos (suite 2); E. Granados:Goyescas:Intermezzo; J. Turina:Danzas fantásticas, Op. 22; Procesión del Rocio, Op. 9 VAIA ▲ 1046 (17.97)
Quartet in D for Strings
New Budapest String Quartet *(rec Budapest, Dec 18-19, 1991)* † Trio Pno MARC ▲ 8223745 [DDD] (13.97)
Trio in E for Piano, Violin & Cello
G. Oravecz (pno), New Budapest String Quartet members *(rec Budapest, Jan 29-30, 1992)* † Qt in D Strs MARC ▲ 8223745 [DDD] (13.97)
La Verbena de la paloma (zarzuela in 1 act) [lib Ricardo de la Vega] (1894)
M. Bayo (sop), S. Tro (sop), R. Pierotti (mez), P. Domingo (ten), E. Baquerizo (sgr), R. Castejon (sgr), M. Martin (sgr), A. Ros-Marbá (cnd), Madrid SO *(lib)* VAL (Zarauela) ▲ 4725 (18.97)

BREUKER, WILLEM (1944-

For Greetje Bijma for Ensemble (1993)
Willem Breuker Ensemble *(rec Bellevue Theater, Amsterdam, Netherlands, Dec 28-30, 1993)* † Hand de Vries; New Pillars in the Field of Art; Overtime; Suzuki Violinenlied; Foresythe:Bereceuse for Unwanted Child; Verdurmen:Pastiche NMCC ▲ 92042 [DDD] (17.97)

Han de Vries for Ensemble (1992)
Willem Breuker Ensemble *(rec Bellevue Theater, Amsterdam, Netherlands, Dec 28-30, 1993)* † For Greetje Bijme; New Pillars in the Field of Art; Overtime; Suzuki Violinenlied; Foresythe:Bereceuse for Unwanted Child; Verdurmen:Pastiche NMCC ▲ 92042 [DDD] (17.97)

New Pillars in the Field of Art for Ensemble (1991)
Willem Breuker Ensemble *(rec Bellevue Theater, Amsterdam, Netherlands, Dec 28-30, 1993)* † For Greetje Bijme; Hand de Vries; Overtime; Suzuki Violinenlied; Foresythe:Bereceuse for Unwanted Child; Verdurmen:Pastiche NMCC ▲ 92042 [DDD] (17.97)

Overtime [Überstunden] for Ensemble (1993)
Willem Breuker Ensemble *(rec Bellevue Theater, Amsterdam, Netherlands, Dec 28-30, 1993)* † For Greetje Bijme; Hand de Vries; New Pillars in the Field of Art; Suzuki Violinenlied; Foresythe:Bereceuse for Unwanted Child; Verdurmen:Pastiche NMCC ▲ 92042 [DDD] (17.97)

Suzuki Violinenlied for Ensemble (1993)
Willem Breuker Ensemble *(rec Bellevue Theater, Amsterdam, Netherlands, Dec 28-30, 1993)* † For Greetje Bijme; Hand de Vries; New Pillars in the Field of Art; Overtime; Foresythe:Bereceuse for Unwanted Child; Verdurmen:Pastiche NMCC ▲ 92042 [DDD] (17.97)

BRÉVAL, JEAN BAPTISTE (1753-1823)

Symphonie concertante for Flute, Bassoon & Orchestra [arr Devienne from Bréval's *Symphonie concertante for Oboe & Horn, Op. 30*], Op. 31
M. Grauwels (fl), A. D. Rijckere (bn), B. Labadie (cnd), Walloon CO † F. Devienne:Con 2 Fl; Con 7 Fl SYRX ▲ 92101 [DDD] (16.97)

Trios (3) for Violin, Cello & Double Bass, Op. 39 (ca 1795)
artists unknown *(rec Eggenburg, Aug 1996)* † F. Devienne:Qts Bn SYM ▲ 96150 [DDD] (18.97)

BREVILLE, PIERRE DE (1861-1949)

Esquisses (7) for Piano (1925)
C. Carnier (pno) † Son Pno; Klingsor:Pno Music LIDI ▲ 103056 (16.97)

Sonata in d for Piano
C. Carnier (pno) † Esquisses Pno; Klingsor:Pno Music LIDI ▲ 103056 (16.97)

BREWAEYS, LUC (1959-**& WERNER VAN CLEEMPUT** (1930-

Namk'cotss for 2 Pianos (1989)
Pianoduo Kolacny ("Muscia a quattro mani") † Buckinx:Four-way Crossroads; Cabus:4 Studies; Celis:Pno Music; Schroyens:Gaia or the 4 Elements of Nature; Westerlinck:Preludio per una danza antica EUFO ▲ 1244 [DDD] (18.97)

BRIAN, HAVERGAL (1876-1972)

Concerto in C for Violin & Orchestra (1934-35)
M. Bisengaliev (vn), L. Friend (cnd), BBC Scottish SO *(rec Jan 12-15, 1993)* † Jolly Miller; Sym 18 MARC ▲ 8223479 [DDD] (13.97)

Festal Dance for Orchestra (1908)
A. Leaper (cnd), Irish National SO *(rec June 15-16, 1992)* † In Memoriam; Sym 17; Sym 32 MARC ▲ 8223481 [DDD] (13.97)

Festival Fanfare for Brass (1967)
T. Rowe (cnd), Moscow SO *(rec Moscow, Russia, May 1996)* † Sym 2 MARC ▲ 8223790 [DDD] (13.97)

In Memoriam (tone poem) for Orchestra (1910)
A. Leaper (cnd), Irish National SO *(rec June 15-16, 1992)* † Festal Dance; Sym 17; Sym 32 MARC ▲ 8223481 [DDD] (13.97)

The Jolly Miller for Orchestra (1962)
L. Friend (cnd), BBC Scottish SO *(rec Jan 12-15, 1993)* † Con Vn; Sym 18 MARC ▲ 8223479 [DDD] (13.97)

Piano Music
R. Clarke (pno)—The Land of Dreams; The Birds; The Defiled Sanctuary [all w. Esther King (mez)]; Prelude, "John Dowland's Fancy"; Double Fugue in E; 4 Miniatures; Prelude & Fugue in c; Prelude & Fugue in d/D; 3 Illuminations Pno; 3 Illuminations Spkr & Pno [w. Tessa Spong (spkr)] *(rec June 1997)* ("Complete Piano Music") ATH ▲ 12 [DDD] (18.97)

Symphony No. 1 for SATB Soloists, Orchestra, Brass Bands & Choruses, "Gothic" (1919-27)
O. Lenárd (cnd), Slovak PO MARC 2-▲ 8223280 (27.97)

Symphony No. 2 in e (1930-31)
T. Rowe (cnd), Moscow SO *(rec Moscow, Russia, May 1996)* † Festival Fanfare MARC ▲ 8223790 [DDD] (13.97)

Symphony No. 17 in c (1961)
A. Leaper (cnd), Irish National SO *(rec June 15-16, 1992)* † Festal Dance; In Memoriam; Sym 32 MARC ▲ 8223481 [DDD] (13.97)

Symphony No. 18 (1961)
L. Friend (cnd), BBC Scottish SO *(rec Jan 12-15, 1993)* † Con Vn; Jolly Miller MARC ▲ 8223479 [DDD] (13.97)

Symphony No. 32 in A♭ (1968)
A. Leaper (cnd), Irish National SO *(rec June 15-16, 1992)* † Festal Dance; In Memoriam; Sym 17 MARC ▲ 8223481 [DDD] (13.97)

The Tigers (selections)
L. Hager (cnd), Luxembourg RSO † Foulds:Mirage; Pasquinade Symphonique 1, Op. 98; St. Joan Suite, Op. 98; H. Parry:Sym 3 FORL 2-▲ 16724 [ADD] (32.97)

Vocal Quartets
M. Piquemal (cnd), Michel Piquemal Vocal Ensemble—Double Fugue in E *(rec Apr 1990)* † J. Brahms:Songs (5), Op. 104; Vocal Qts ARN ▲ 68132 [DDD] (16.97)

BRICCIALDI, GIULIO (1818-1881)

Andantino con variazioni for Flute & Guitar [after Paganini]
A. De Rose (gtr), G. Petrucci (fl) ("Romantic Music for Flute & Guitar") † F. Carulli:Fant on Themes from Bellini's Il pirata, Op. 337; Diabelli:Pot-Pourri on Themes of Beethoven; Trans; M. Giuliani:Trans & Arrs; Reichardt:Trans & Arrs; A. Traeg:Trans & Arrs; Vanhal:Vars (6) on 'Nel cor più non mi sento', Op. 42 BONG ▲ 5555 [DDD] (16.97)

Carnival of Venice for Flute & Piano, Op. 78
S. Bezaly (fl), E. Nagy (pno) *(rec Danderyd Grammar School, Sweden, Feb 1999)* ("Flutissimo") † A. Bazzini:Ronde des lutins, Op. 25; F. Borne:Fant brillante sur Carmen; Chopin:Vars on Rossini; Taffanel:Fant on Freischütz; Mignon Fant BIS ▲ 1039 [DDD] (17.97)

Concerto in A for 2 Flutes & Orchestra, Op. 130
G. Petrucci (fl), J. Bálint (fl), E. Acél (cnd), Szeged SO ("Works for Flute") † Fl Music BONG ▲ 5078 [DDD] (16.97)

Flute Music
G. Petrucci (fl), P. Pisa (pno)—Fant on Themes from Bellini's Norma, Op. 57; Fant on Themes from Donizetti's Lucrezia Borgia, Op. 108; Fant on Themes from Verdi's Aida, Op. 134; Elegia di Ernst, Op. 26; Canzonetta con vars in C on a Theme of Paganini; Le Streghe, Op. 138 ("Works for Flute") † Con Fls BONG ▲ 5078 [DDD] (16.97)

Music of Briccialdi
Arnold Wind Quintet—Qnt in D, Op. 124; Qnts in B series 10/2 & 3; Pot-pourri fantastique on themes from Il barbiere STRV ▲ 33331 (16.97)

Quintets (3) for Winds
Briccialdi Wind Quintet † F. Danzi:Qnts Ww, Op. 56 BONG ▲ 5052 [DDD] (16.97)

Quintet for Winds, Op. 124
Avalon Wind Quintet *(rec Clara-Wieck-Auditorium Sandhausen, Nov 28-Dec 1, 1994)* † Cambini:Qnts Ww NXIN ▲ 553410 [DDD] (5.97)

BRIDGE, FRANK (1879-1941)

Adagio in E for Organ
D. Hill (org) *(rec Trinity Cathedral Portland, OR, May 1994)* ("There Let the Pealing Organ Blow") † J. S. Bach:Toccata & Fugue Org, BWV 565; C. Franck:Chorales Org, M.38-40; Vierne:Org Music HER ▲ 190 [DDD] (19.97)

Elégie for Cello & Piano (1911)
J. L. Webber (vc), J. McCabe (pno) † Scherzetto Vc; J. Ireland:Son Vc; Stanford:Son 2 Vc ASV ▲ 807 (16.97)

Enter Spring (rhapsody) for Orchestra (1927)
B. Britten (cnd), English CO *(rec 1967)* † Sea; B. Britten:Building of the House (ov); G. Holst:Egdon Heath, Op. 47; Fugal Con, Op. 40/2 BBC ▲ 8007 (17.97)
C. Groves (cnd), Royal Liverpool PO *(rec Liverpool Philharmonic Hall, England, July 1975)* † Lament Strs; Old English Songs; Sea; Summer EMIC ▲ 66855 [ADD] (11.97)

BRIDGE, FRANK (cont.)

Idylls (3) for String Quartet (1906)
Coull String Quartet † E. Elgar:Qt Strs, Op. 83; W. Walton:Qt Strs HYP ▲ 66718 (18.97)
Maggini String Quartet *(rec All Saints East Finchley, Dec 16-17, 1994)* † Irish Melody; Novelletten; Old English Songs; Phantasie Qt Strs; Pieces Str Qt; Sir Roger de Coverley NXIN ▲ 553718 [DDD] (5.97)

An Irish Melody [Londonderry Air] for String Quartet (1908)
W. Boughton (cnd), English String Orch † Sir Roger de Coverley; There Is a Willow Grows Aslant; G. Finzi:Ecologue, Op. 10; H. Parry:English Suite NIMB ▲ 5366 (16.97)
Delmé String Quartet † Old English Songs; Qt 2 Strs; Sir Roger de Coverley CHN ▲ 8426 [DDD] (16.97)
Maggini String Quartet *(rec All Saints East Finchley, Dec 16-17, 1994)* † Idylls Str Qt; Novelletten; Old English Songs; Phantasie Qt Strs; Pieces Str Qt; Sir Roger de Coverley NXIN ▲ 553718 [DDD] (5.97)

Lament for Strings (1915)
C. Groves (cnd), Royal Liverpool PO *(rec Liverpool Philharmonic Hall, England, July 1975)* † Enter Spring; Old English Songs; Sea; Summer EMIC ▲ 66855 [ADD] (11.97)
A. Leaper (cnd), Capella Istropolitana *(rec Apr 12-16 & Sept 17-19, 1989)* ("English String Festival") † E. Elgar:Elegy; Intro & Allegro, Op. 47; Serenade Strs, Op. 20; H. Parry:English Suite; Lady Radnor's Suite NXIN ▲ 550331 [DDD] (5.97)

Mélodie for Violin (or Cello) & Piano (1911)
S. Doane (vc), B. Snyder (pno) *(rec Rochester, NY, Jan 14-15 & Apr 10-11, 1994)* ("Bridge & Britten: Music for Cello & Piano") † Scherzetto Vc; Son Vc; Spring Song; B. Britten:Son Vc BRID ▲ 9056 [DDD] (17.97)
R. Rust (vc), D. Apter (pno) *(rec Munich, Feb 21-25, 1994)* † Scherzetto Vc; Son Vc; D. F. Tovey:Elegiac Vars, Op. 25; Son Vc, Op. 4 MARC ▲ 8223637 [DDD] (13.97)

Miniatures (3 sets) for Piano, Violin & Cello (1906-07)
Dussek Piano Trio † Phantasie Trio; Trio 2 Pno MER ▲ 84290 [DDD] (16.97)

Novelletten for String Quartet (1904)
Maggini String Quartet *(rec All Saints East Finchley, Dec 16-17, 1994)* † Idylls Str Qt; Irish Melody; Old English Songs; Phantasie Qt Strs; Pieces Str Qt; Sir Roger de Coverley NXIN ▲ 553718 [DDD] (5.97)

Old English Songs (2) for String Quartet (or Piano Duet) [Sally in Our Alley; Cherry Ripe] (1916)
D. Atherton (cnd), Berlin RIAS Sinfonietta [arr for orch] *(rec 1978)* † Suite Str Orch; Summer; There Is a Willow Grows Aslant; Bantock:Pierrot of the Minute; G. Butterworth:Bredon Hill & Other Songs CHN (Collect) ▲ 6566 (12.97)
Delmé String Quartet † Irish Melody; Qt 2 Strs; Sir Roger de Coverley CHN ▲ 8426 [DDD] (16.97)
C. Groves (cnd), Royal Liverpool PO—Cherry Ripe *(rec Liverpool Philharmonic Hall, England, July 1975)* † Enter Spring; Lament Strs; Sea; Summer EMIC ▲ 66855 [ADD] (11.97)
Maggini String Quartet *(rec All Saints East Finchley, Dec 16-17, 1994)* † Idylls Str Qt; Irish Melody; Novelletten; Phantasie Qt Strs; Pieces Str Qt; Sir Roger de Coverley NXIN ▲ 553718 [DDD] (5.97)

Phantasie Quartet in f# for Piano & Strings (1910)
Amabile Piano Quartet † J. Brahms:Qt 1 Pno, Op. 25; J. Turina:Qt Pno SUMM ▲ 199 (16.97)

Phantasie Quartet in f for Strings (1905)
Maggini String Quartet *(rec All Saints East Finchley, Dec 16-17, 1994)* † Idylls Str Qt; Irish Melody; Novelletten; Old English Songs; Pieces Str Qt; Sir Roger de Coverley NXIN ▲ 553718 [DDD] (5.97)

Phantasie Trio in c for Piano, Violin & Cello (1907)
Dussek Piano Trio † Miniatures; Trio 2 Pno MER ▲ 84290 [DDD] (16.97)
Primavera Trio *(rec Claremont, CA, Nov-Dec 1994)* † F. Campo:Trio Pno; F. Martin:Trio sur les mélodies populaires irlandaises CENT ▲ 2318 [DDD] (16.97)

Pieces (3) for String Quartet
Maggini String Quartet *(rec All Saints East Finchley, Dec 16-17, 1994)* † Idylls Str Qt; Irish Melody; Novelletten; Old English Songs; Phantasie Qt Strs; Sir Roger de Coverley NXIN ▲ 553718 [DDD] (5.97)

A Prayer for Orchestra & Chorus [text after Kempis] (1916)
J. Filsell (org), J. Backhouse (cnd), Vasari Singers ("Songs of Farewell") † H. Parry:Songs of Farewell; Vaughan Williams:Mass GILD ▲ 7132 [DDD] (16.97)

Quartet No. 2 in g for Strings (1915)
Bridge String Quartet *(rec May 20-22, 1996)* † Qt 3 Strs MER ▲ 84311 [DDD] (16.97)
Delmé String Quartet † Irish Melody; Old English Songs; Sir Roger de Coverley CHN ▲ 8426 [DDD] (16.97)

Quartet No. 3 for Strings (1926)
Bochmann String Quartet *(rec 1996-97)* ("British String Quartets") † A. Bush:Dialectic, Op. 15; S. Wesley:Qt Strs RDCL ▲ 13 [DDD] (16.97)
Bridge String Quartet *(rec May 20-22, 1996)* † Qt 2 Strs MER ▲ 84311 [DDD] (16.97)

Quartet No. 4 for Strings (1937)
Bridge String Quartet † Qt Strs MER ▲ 84369 (16.97)

Quartet in e for Strings, "Bologna" (1906)
Bridge String Quartet † Qt 4 Strs MER ▲ 84369 (16.97)

Quintet in d for Piano & Strings (1912)
A. Schiller (pno), Coull String Quartet † E. Elgar:Qnt Pno, Op. 84 ASV ▲ 678 [DDD] (16.97)

Scherzetto for Cello & Piano (1902)
S. Doane (vc), B. Snyder (pno) *(rec Rochester, NY, Jan 14-15 & Apr 10-11, 1994)* ("Bridge & Britten: Music for Cello & Piano") † Mélodie; Son Vc; Spring Song; B. Britten:Son Vc BRID ▲ 9056 [DDD] (17.97)
R. Rust (vc), D. Apter (pno) *(rec Munich, Feb 21-25, 1994)* † Mélodie; Son Vc; D. F. Tovey:Elegiac Vars, Op. 25; Son Vc, Op. 4 MARC ▲ 8223637 [DDD] (13.97)
J. L. Webber (vc), J. McCabe (pno) † Elégie; J. Ireland:Son Vc; Stanford:Son 2 Vc ASV ▲ 807 (16.97)

The Sea (suite) for Orchestra (1911)
B. Britten (cnd), English CO *(rec 1971)* † Enter Spring; B. Britten:Building of the House (ov); G. Holst:Egdon Heath, Op. 47; Fugal Con, Op. 40/2 BBC ▲ 8007 (17.97)
C. Groves (cnd), Royal Liverpool PO *(rec Liverpool Philharmonic Hall, England, July 1975)* † Enter Spring; Lament Strs; Old English Songs; Summer EMIC ▲ 66855 [ADD] (11.97)
V. Handley (cnd), Ulster Orch [sels] † Berlioz:Ovs; B. Britten:Peter Grimes (sea interludes & passacaglia) CHN (Collect) ▲ 6538 [ADD] (12.97)
V. Handley (cnd), Ulster Orch † A. Bax:On the Sea Shore; B. Britten:Peter Grimes (sea interludes & passacaglia) CHN ▲ 8473 [DDD] (16.97)

Sextet for Strings (1906-12)
Academy of St. Martin in the Fields Chamber Ensemble † E. Goossens:Concertino Str Octet, Op. 47; Phantasy Sxt, Op. 37 CHN ▲ 9472 (16.97)

Sir Roger de Coverley, A Christmas Dance for String Quartet (or String Orchestra) (1922)
W. Boughton (cnd), English String Orch † Irish Melody; There Is a Willow Grows Aslant; G. Finzi:Ecologue, Op. 10; H. Parry:English Suite NIMB ▲ 5366 (16.97)
Delmé String Quartet † Irish Melody; Old English Songs; Qt 2 Strs CHN ▲ 8426 [DDD] (16.97)
Maggini String Quartet *(rec All Saints East Finchley, Dec 16-17, 1994)* † Idylls Str Qt; Irish Melody; Novelletten; Old English Songs; Phantasie Qt Strs; Pieces Str Qt NXIN ▲ 553718 [DDD] (5.97)

Sonata in d for Cello & Piano (1913-17)
S. Doane (vc), B. Snyder (pno) *(rec Rochester, NY, Jan 14-15 & Apr 10-11, 1994)* ("Bridge & Britten: Music for Cello & Piano") † Mélodie; Scherzetto Vc; Spring Song; B. Britten:Son Vc BRID ▲ 9056 [DDD] (17.97)
R. Rust (vc), D. Apter (pno) *(rec Munich, Feb 21-25, 1994)* † Mélodie; Scherzetto Vc; D. F. Tovey:Elegiac Vars, Op. 25; Son Vc, Op. 4 MARC ▲ 8223637 [DDD] (13.97)
K. Scholes (vc), E. Blackwood (pno) *(rec Chicago, IL, Sept 1991)* † E. Blackwood:Son Vc CED ▲ 8 [DDD] (16.97)
A. Toth (vc), M. Duchemin (pno) ("Romantic Cello Works from 1901-1950") † Ginastera:Pampeana 2, Op. 21; S. Rachmaninoff:Son Vc SNE ▲ 2030 (16.97)
R. Wallfisch (vc), P. Wallfisch (pno) † A. Bax:Rhapsodic Ballad; Delius:Son Vc; W. Walton:Passacaglia Vc CHN ▲ 8499 [DDD] (16.97)

Songs (complete)
J. Watson (sop), L. Winter (mez), J. MacDougall (ten), G. Finley (bar), R. Vignoles (pno) HYP 2-▲ 67181 (36.97)

Spring Song for Violin (or Cello) & Piano (1912)
S. Doane (vc), B. Snyder (pno) *(rec Rochester, NY, Jan 14-15 & Apr 10-11, 1994)* ("Bridge & Britten: Music for Cello & Piano") † Mélodie; Scherzetto Vc; Son Vc; B. Britten:Son Vc BRID ▲ 9056 [DDD] (17.97)

Suite for String Orchestra (1910)
W. Boughton (cnd), English String Orch † G. Butterworth:Banks of Green Willow Orch; English Idylls; Shropshire Lad; H. Parry:Lady Radnor's Suite NIMB ▲ 5068 [DDD] (16.97)
N. Del Mar (cnd), Bournemouth Sinfonietta † Old English Songs; Summer; There Is a Willow Grows Aslant; Bantock:Pierrot of the Minute; G. Butterworth:Bredon Hill & Other Songs CHN (Collect) ▲ 6566 (12.97)
D. Garforth (cnd), English CO † J. Ireland:Downland Suite; Elegaic Meditation; Holy Boy CHN ▲ 8390 [DDD] (16.97)

BRIDGE, FRANK (cont.)

Summer (symphonic poem) for Orchestra (1914)
N. Del Mar (cnd), Bournemouth Sinfonietta † Old English Songs; Suite Str Orch; There Is a Willow Grows Aslant; Bantock:Pierrot of the Minute; G. Butterworth:Bredon Hill & Other Songs CHN (Collect) ▲ 6566 (12.97)
C. Groves (cnd), Royal Liverpool PO *(rec Liverpool Philharmonic Hall, England, July 1975)* † Enter Spring; Lament Strs; Old English Songs; Sea EMIC ▲ 66855 [ADD] (11.97)

There Is a Willow Grows Aslant a Brook for Small Orchestra (1928)
W. Boughton (cnd), English String Orch † Irish Melody; Sir Roger de Coverley; G. Finzi:Ecologue, Op. 10; H. Parry:English Suite NIMB ▲ 5366 (16.97)
N. Del Mar (cnd), Bournemouth Sinfonietta † Old English Songs; Suite Str Orch; Summer; Bantock:Pierrot of the Minute; G. Butterworth:Bredon Hill & Other Songs CHN (Collect) ▲ 6566 (12.97)

Trio No. 2 for Piano, Violin & Cello (1929)
Dussek Piano Trio † Miniatures; Phantasie Trio MER ▲ 84290 [DDD] (16.97)

BRIEF, TODD (1953-

Nightsong for Piano (1985)
C. O'Riley (pno) † J. Adams:China Gates; Phrygian Gates; R. Helps:Hommages; R. Sessions:Son 1 Pno ALBA ▲ 38 [DDD]

BRIGGS, ROGER (1952-

Tracer for Piano & Orchestra (1993)
J. Jacob (pno), J. Swoboda (cnd), Silesian PO ("MMC New Century, Vol. IV") † P. Farmer:On Mount Pleasant; W. T. McKinley:Con 2 Pno; M. Rossi:Negru Voda; Tomaro:Celestial Navigation MASM ▲ 2028 [DDD] (16.97)

BRIGHT, COLIN (20th cent)

Night for Double Bass & Piano (1976)
austraLYSIS members *(rec ABC Sydney, 1990)* ("austraLYSIS: Windows in Time") † L. Cresswell:Organic Music; Soliloquy on a Lambent Tailpiece; R. T. Dean:TimeStrain; R. Rue:Nocturnal Windows; H. Smith:Simultaneity; Xenakis:Morsima-Amorsima TALP ▲ 39 [DDD] (18.97)

BRINGS, ALLEN (1934-

Bagatelles (5) for Flute, Oboe, Clarinet, Bassoon & Piano (1993)
M. Lifchitz (cnd) ("Music at the Crossroads") † Diemer:Sxt Fl; Rudajev:Petite Suite Parisienne; Toensing:Angels; Ziffrin:Songs of the Trobairitz NSR ▲ 1005 (15.97)

Chimeric Fantasy for Alto Saxophone, Cello & Piano (1993)
L. Grinhauz (vc), C. Sikes (a sax), A. Brings (pno) ("Music da camera") † Fant Fl & Hp; Fant Piece Pno 4-Hands; Son da chiesa; Trio Strs CPS ▲ 8644 [DDD] (16.97)

Concert Piece for 4 Clarinets
P. Gallo (cl), E. Gilmore (cl), B. Hysong (b cl), M. Abt-Greenfield (E♭ cl) *(rec Church of the Holy Trinity, NYC, NY, 1989-90)* † Eclogue Cl; Inventions for 2 Cls; Trio Cl, Vc & Pno; L. Kraft:Episodes; Inventions & Airs; O Primavera CENT ▲ 2079 [ADD] (16.97)

Duo Concertante for Cello & Piano (1968)
P. Rosenfeld (vc), M. Ritt (pno) ("Society of Composers, Inc.: Contrpunctus") † J. Davison:Son Pastorale; C. Folio:Developing Hues; Rokeach:Son Vn CPS ▲ 8615 (16.97)

Eclogue for solo Clarinet
E. Gilmore (cl) *(rec Church of the Holy Trinity, NYC, NY, 1989-90)* † Concert Piece for 4 Cls; Inventions for 2 Cls; Trio Cl, Vc & Pno; L. Kraft:Episodes; Inventions & Airs; O Primavera CENT ▲ 2079 [ADD] (16.97)

Fantaisie for Flute & Harp (1994)
L. Hansen (fl), S. Jolles (hp) ("Music da camera") † Chimeric Fant; Fant Piece Pno 4-Hands; Son da chiesa; Trio Strs CPS ▲ 8644 [DDD] (16.97)

Fantasy Piece for Piano 4-Hands (1986)
M. Ritt (pno), D. Prione (pno) ("Music da camera") † Chimeric Fant; Fant Fl & Hp; Son da chiesa; Trio Strs CPS ▲ 8644 [DDD] (16.97)

Inventions (3) for 2 Clarinets [after J.S. Bach]
M. Abt-Greenfield (cl), E. Gilmore (cl) *(rec Church of the Holy Trinity, NYC, NY, 1989-90)* † Concert Piece for 4 Cls; Eclogue Cl; Trio Cl, Vc & Pno; L. Kraft:Episodes; Inventions & Airs; O Primavera CENT ▲ 2079 [ADD] (16.97)

Sonata for Clarinet & Piano
E. Gilmore (cl), A. Brings (pno) † Son Pno; Son Vn CENT ▲ 2156 (16.97)

Sonata da chiesa for solo Cello (1980)
A. Kouguell (vc) ("Music da camera") † Chimeric Fant; Fant Fl & Hp; Fant Piece Pno 4-Hands; Trio Strs CPS ▲ 8644 [DDD] (16.97)

Sonata for Piano
G. Chinn (pno) † Son Cl; Son Vn CENT ▲ 2156 (16.97)

Sonata for solo Violin
N. Cirillo (vn) † Son Cl; Son Pno CENT ▲ 2156 (16.97)

Trio for Clarinet, Cello & Piano
A. Kouguell (vc), E. Gilmore (cl), G. Chinn (pno) *(rec Church of the Holy Trinity, NYC, NY, 1989-90)* † Concert Piece for 4 Cls; Eclogue Cl; Inventions for 2 Cls; L. Kraft:Episodes; Inventions & Airs; O Primavera CENT ▲ 2079 [ADD] (16.97)

Trio for Strings (1995)
Meridian String Quartet members ("Music da camera") † Chimeric Fant; Fant Fl & Hp; Fant Piece Pno 4-Hands; Son da chiesa CPS ▲ 8644 [DDD] (16.97)

BRIOSCHI, ANTONIO (fl ca 1730-1750)

Overture No. 4 in G for 2 Violins & Continuo (1733)
E. Comparone (hpd), Queen's Chamber Band ("Viva Italia!") † J. Christian Bach:Qnts Fl; J. Dowland:Galliards; Pavanes; Gorzanis:Primo libro di napolitane Ct; G. F. Handel:Giulio Cesare in Egitto (sels); Monteverdi:Scherzi musicali (3) Voices 4TAY ▲ 4011 [DDD] (17.97)

BRIQUET, MARC (1896-1979)

Organ Music
M. Extermann (org)—Prélude pour une fête; Toccata avec interlude; Cantilène; Rhap; Prière pour ceux qui vont mourir; Pastorale; Choral sur la mort de Siddhartha; "Qui al señor habla"; Fant sur l'inscription de la cloche de Schiller *(rec Oct 15-16, 1992)* GALL ▲ 734 [DDD]

BRISMAN, HESKEL (1923-

Concerto for Piano & Strings (1965)
J. Pierce (pno), R. Black (cnd), Slovak RSO Bratislava *(rec Slovak National Republic)* ("Modern American Classics, Vol. 1") † Burwasser:Well Traveled Road; E. Erickson:Shipwrecked Landscape; W. T. McKinley:Fant Variazioni; M. B. Nelson:Medead MASM ▲ 2016 [DDD] (16.97)

BRITTEN, BENJAMIN (LORD BRITTEN OF ALDEBURGH) (1913-1976)

Advance Democracy for Chorus (1938)
P. Spicer (cnd), Finzi Singers ("Choral Edition-Vol. 3") † Boy Was Born, Op. 3; Flower Songs, Op. 47; Sacred & Profane, Op. 91 CHN ▲ 9701 (16.97)

Albert Herring (comic chamber opera in 3 acts) [lib E. Cozier after Maupassant], Op. 39 (1947)
K. Dickerson (sop—Lady Billows), L. Binford (sop—Ms. Wordsworth), B. Kokolus (mez—Mrs. Herring), T. Venditti (cta—Housekeeper), C. Pfund (ten—Albert), S. Bearden (bar—Mr. Gedge), D. Gilbert (cnd), Manhattan School of Music Opera Orch *(rec Manhattan School of Music, Dec 1996)* ("Albert Herring 50th Anniversary") VOXC 2-▲ 7900 (16.97)

Alla Marcia for Bass, Piano & String Quartet (1933)
Maggini String Quartet † Qt 3 Strs, Op. 94; Quartettino Strs; Simple Sym, Op. 4 NXIN ▲ 8554360 (5.97)
Sorrel String Quartet † Divertimenti; Qt 1 Strs, Op. 25; Qt 3 Strs, Op. 94 CHN ▲ 9469 (16.97)

A.M.D.G. (Ad Majorem Dei Gloriam) for Mixed Chorus [text Gerald Manley Hopkins], from, Op. 17 (1939)
P. Spicer (cnd), Finzi Singers ("Choral Edition, Vol. 1") † Gloriana (choral dances); Hymn of St. Columba; Hymn to the Virgin; Hymn to St. Cecilia, Op. 27; Hymn to St. Peter, Op. 56a; Rejoice in the Lamb, Op. 30 CHN ▲ 9511 (16.97)

An American Overture for Orchestra [originally *An Occasional Overture*, renamed by Simon Rattle], Op. 38 (1946)
M. Fredman (cnd), New Zealand SO *(rec Wellington New Zealand, July 1994)* † Peter Grimes (sea interludes & passacaglia); Sinf da requiem, Op. 20 NXIN ▲ 553107 [DDD] (5.97)
R. Hickox (cnd), BBC PO † King Arthur Suite; World of the Spirit CHN ▲ 9487 (16.97)

Antiphon for Soprano, Alto, Tenor, Bass & Organ [text Herbert], Op. 56b (1956)
M. Chance (ct), I. Bostridge (ten) † Canticle II, Op. 51; Ceremony of Carols, Op. 28; Hymn to the Virgin; Rejoice in the Lamb, Op. 30; Wedding Anthem, Op. 46 SNYC ▲ 62615 (16.97)

Ballad of Heroes for Tenor (or Soprano), Chorus & Orchestra [text by Swingler & Auden], Op. 14 (1939)
M. Hill (ten), R. Hickox (cnd), London SO, London Sym Chorus [ENG] † Sinf da requiem, Op. 20; War Requiem, Op. 66 CHN 2-▲ 8983 [DDD] (32.97)

BRITTEN, BENJAMIN (LORD BRITTEN OF ALDEBURGH) (cont.)

Billy Budd (opera in 4 acts) [lib Forster & Cozier after Melville], Op. 50 (1951; rev 1960)
P. Pears (ten), J. Shirley-Quirk (bar), B. Luxon (bar), P. Glossop (bar), M. Langdon (bass), O. Brannigan (bass), B. Britten (cnd), London SO, Ambrosian Singers [ENG] † Holy Sonnets of John Donne, Op. 35; Songs & Proverbs of William Blake, Op. 74 PLON 3-▲ 17428 [ADD] (48.97)
P. Pears (ten), T. Uppman (bar), G. Evans (bar), H. Alan (bass), F. Dalberg (bass), B. Britten (cnd), Royal Opera House Orch Covent Garden, Royal Opera House Covent Garden Chorus *(rec Dec 1, 1951)* VAIA 3-▲ 1034 [ADD] (45.97)
A. Rolfe Johnson (ten), T. Hampson (bar), R. Smythe (bar), E. Halfvarson (b-bar), K. Nagano (cnd), Hallé Orch, Hallé Choir ERAT 3-▲ 21631 (33.97)

The Birds (song) for Mezzo-Soprano (or Baritone) & Piano (1929, rev. 1934)
R. Houghton (pno), H. H. Leck (cnd), Indianapolis Children's Choir *(rec The Lodge, May-June 1995)* † Ceremony of Carols, Op. 28; H. Purcell:Come, ye sons of art, away, Z.323; Now that the sun hath veiled his light (Eve Hymn), Z.193; Odes & Welcome Songs (misc); Pausanias (sels) VAIA ▲ 1130 [DDD]

A Boy Was Born for Mixed Chorus, Op. 3 (1934)
M. Best (cnd), Corydon Singers, M. Best (cnd), Westminster Cathedral Choristers [ENG] † Festival Te Deum, Op. 32; Rejoice in the Lamb, Op. 30; Wedding Anthem, Op. 46 HYP ▲ 66126 (18.97)
P. Spicer (cnd), Finzi Singers ("Choral Edition-Vol. 3") † Advance Democracy; Flower Songs, Op. 47; Sacred & Profane, Op. 91 CHN ▲ 9701 (16.97)
C. Wyn-Rogers (cta), S. Gritton (sgr), D. Goode (org), S. Layton (cnd), Holst Singers ("Christ's Nativity") † Choral Music; Hymn to the Virgin; Te Deum HYP ▲ 66825 (18.97)

Building of the House (overture) for Orchestra (1967)
B. Britten (cnd), English CO † F. Bridge:Enter Spring; Sea; G. Holst:Egdon Heath, Op. 47; Fugal Con, Op. 40/2 BBC ▲ 8007 (17.97)

Cantata misericordium for Tenor, Baritone, Orchestra & Chorus, Op. 69 (1963)
J. M. Ainsley (ten), S. Varcoe (bass), R. Hickox (cnd), City of London Sinfonia, Britten Singers [LAT] † Chorale on an Old French Carol; Deus in adjutorium meum; G. Finzi:Requiem da Camera; G. Holst:Psalms 86 & 148 CHN ▲ 8997 [DDD] (16.97)

Canticles I-V for Voice(s) & Instrument(s) (1947, 1952, 1954, 1971 & 1974)
Aldeburgh Connection ("The Canticles") MARQ ▲ 185 (16.97)
M. Chance (ct), A. Rolfe Johnson (ten), A. Opie (bar), M. Thompson (hn), S. Williams (hp), R. Vignoles (pno) † Purcell Realizations HYP ▲ 66498 (18.97)

Canticle II for Alto, Tenor & Piano, Op. 51, "Abraham & Isaac" (1952)
M. Chance (ct), I. Bostridge (ten) † Antiphon, Op. 56b; Ceremony of Carols, Op. 28; Hymn to the Virgin; Rejoice in the Lamb, Op. 30; Wedding Anthem, Op. 46 SNYC ▲ 62615 (16.97)
C. Russo (cl), D. Hassard (pno), M. Katz (pno) † Sonnets of Michelangelo, Op. 22; D. Argento:To Be Sung Upon The Water PHOE ▲ 129 (15.97)

Canticle V for Tenor & Harp, Op. 89, "The Death of St. Narcissus" (1974)
S. Kim (ten), K. Englichova (hp) ("A Birthday Hansel") † Folksong Arrs BONT ▲ 86

A Ceremony of Carols for Treble Voices, Harp & Chorus, Op. 28 (1942)
All-American Boys Chorus, W. Hall (cnd), William Hall Master Chorale, M. Dickstein (hp) *(rec Santa Ana, CA)* ("Ceremony & Carols") † Anonymous:Angels We Have Heard on High; O Come, All Ye Faithful; There Is No Rose; F. X. Gruber:Silent Night; L. Mason:Joy to the World; Traditional:Good Christian Men; Infant Most Blest; Lo, How a Rose; Nova, Nova, Ave Fit Ex Eva; O Tannenbaum; Tiny Child; Willie Take Your Little Drum KLAV ▲ 11085 [DDD]
M. Brookshaw (sop), C. Wilkinson (alt), R. Marlow (cnd), Trinity College Choir Cambridge *(rec Trinity College Chapel Cambridge, 1996)* ("A Ceremony of Carols") † Hymn to the Virgin; Hymn to St. Cecilia, Op. 27; Missa brevis, Op. 63; Rejoice in the Lamb, Op. 30; Sacred & Profane, Op. 91 CONI ▲ 51287 [DDD] (16.97)
M. Chance (ct), I. Bostridge (ten), A. Brewer (hp), M. Neary (cnd), Westminster Abbey Choir † Antiphon, Op. 56b; Canticle II, Op. 51; Hymn to the Virgin; Rejoice in the Lamb, Op. 30; Wedding Anthem, Op. 46 SNYC ▲ 62615 (16.97)
S. Cleobury (cnd), King's College Choir Cambridge PRGO ▲ 33215 [DDD] (16.97)
K. Goheen (sop), M. D. Kleer (alt), R. Costanzi (hp), Elektra Women's Choir ("A Ceremony of Carols") † P. Csonka:Concierto di Navidad; J. Rutter:Dancing Day SKYL ▲ 9703 [DDD] (15.97)
F. Grier (cnd), Christ Church Cathedral Choir Oxford † Hymn to the Virgin; Hymn to St. Cecilia, Op. 27; Hymn to St. Peter, Op. 56a; Te Deum ASVQ ▲ 6030 [DDD] (10.97)
G. Guest (cnd), St. John's College Choir Cambridge † Jubilate Deo in C; Missa brevis, Op. 63; Rejoice in the Lamb, Op. 30; Te Deum PLON (Jubilee) ▲ 30097 [ADD] (9.97)
D. Hill (cnd), Westminster Cathedral Choir † Deus in adjutorium meum; Hymn to the Virgin; Hymn to St. Peter, Op. 56a; Jubilate Deo in E♭; Missa brevis, Op. 63 HYP ▲ 66220 [DDD] (18.97)
B. Wesner-Hoehn (hp), H. H. Leck (cnd), Indianapolis Children's Choir *(rec The Lodge, May-June 1995)* † Birds; H. Purcell:Come, ye sons of art, away, Z.323; Now that the sun hath veiled his light (Eve Hymn), Z.193; Odes & Welcome Songs (misc); Pausanias (sels) VAIA ▲ 1130 [DDD]
C. Wyn-Rogers (cta), D. Wilson-Johnson (bar), B. Luxon (bar), Finchley Children's Group † Noye's Fludde, Op. 59 SOMM ▲ 212 (17.97)

Choral Music
S. Kanga (hp), A. Wells (pno), R. Corp (cnd) , New London Children's Choir—Friday Afternoons, Op. 7; Sweet was the Song the Virgin Sung; King Herod & the Cock; The Oxen; Fancie; The Birds; Two-part Songs (3); A Wealden Trio [The Song of the Women]; Ceremony of Carols, Op. 28 *(rec Gospel Oak London, England, Sept 17-18, 1994)* NXIN ▲ 553183 [DDD] (5.97)
A. Lumsden (org), P. Spicer (cnd), Finzi Singers *(Jubilate Deo in C; Te Deum; Antiphon, Op. 56b; Missa brevis, Op. 63; Wedding Anthem, Op. 46; Festival Te Deum, Op. 32; Jubilate Deo in E♭)*, S. Drake (hp), P. Spicer (cnd), Finzi Singers *(Ceremony of Carols, Op. 28)*, P. Spicer (cnd), Finzi Singers *(Sweet was the Song the Virgin Sung)* ("Choral Edition, Vol. 2") CHN ▲ 9598 (16.97)
C. Wyn-Rogers (cta), S. Gritton (sgr), D. Goode (org), S. Layton (cnd), Holst Singers—Christ's Nativity; A Shepherd's Carol; Jubilate Deo in C ("Christ's Nativity") † Boy Was Born, Op. 3; Hymn to the Virgin; Te Deum HYP ▲ 66825 (18.97)

Chorale on an Old French Carol for a cappella Choir [text by W.H. Auden] (1944)
R. Hickox (cnd), Britten Singers [ENG] † Cant misericordium, Op. 69; Deus in adjutorium meum; G. Finzi:Requiem da Camera; G. Holst:Psalms 86 & 148 CHN ▲ 8997 [DDD] (16.97)

Concerto in D for Piano & Orchestra, Op. 13 (1938; rev. 1945)
R. Gothóni (pno), O. Kamu (cnd), Helsingborg SO † Matinées musicale, Op. 24; Soirées musicales, Op. 9 ODE ▲ 825 [DDD] (17.97)
G. Lin (pno), J. Hopkins (cnd), Melbourne SO *(rec 1978)* † A. Copland:Con Pno CHN (Collect) ▲ 6580 [ADD] (12.97)

Concerto in d for Violin & Orchestra, Op. 15 (1939)
R. Hirsch (vn), T. Yuasa (cnd), BBC Scottish SO † Sym Vc NXIN ▲ 8553882 (5.97)
R. Ricci (vn), G. Brott (cnd), SWF SO † G. Kubik:Con 2 Vn; B. Lees:Con Vn ONEL (Essential Performance Reference) ▲ 96020 [ADD] (7.97)

Curlew River (church parable in 1 act) [lib. W. Plomer], Op. 71 (1964)
M. Milhofer (ten), M. Evans (bar), G. H. Jones (bar), M. Hargreaves (bass), H. Ticciati (trbn), D. Angus (cnd) KSCH ▲ 313972 (16.97)

Death in Venice (suite) for Orchestra [arr. Bedford]
S. Bedford (cnd), English CO † Sym Vc CHN ▲ 8363 [DDD] (16.97)

Deus in adjutorium meum (motet) for a cappella Choir (1945)
R. Hickox (cnd), Britten Singers [LAT] † Cant misericordium, Op. 69; Chorale on an Old French Carol; G. Finzi:Requiem da Camera; G. Holst:Psalms 86 & 148 CHN ▲ 8997 [DDD] (16.97)
D. Hill (cnd), Westminster Cathedral Choir † Ceremony of Carols, Op. 28; Hymn to the Virgin; Hymn to St. Peter, Op. 56a; Jubilate Deo in E♭; Missa brevis, Op. 63 HYP ▲ 66220 [DDD] (18.97)

Diversions for Piano (left hand) & Orchestra, Op. 21 (1940; rev. 1954)
L. Fleisher (pno), S. Comissiona (cnd), Baltimore SO † E. Laderman:Con Orch PHOE ▲ 122 [ADD] (15.97)
L. Fleisher (pno), S. Ozawa (cnd), Boston SO † S. Prokofiev:Con 4 Pno, Op. 53; M. Ravel:Con Pno (left hand) SNYC ▲ 47188 [DDD] (16.97)

Divertimenti (3) for String Quartet (1935)
Maggini String Quartet *(rec East Woodhay, England, Dec 9-11, 1996)* ("String Quartets, Vol. 1") † Qt 1 Strs, Op. 25; Qt 2 Strs, Op. 36 NXIN ▲ 8553883 [DDD] (5.97)
Sorrel String Quartet † Alla Marcia; Qt 1 Strs, Op. 25; Qt 3 Strs, Op. 94 CHN ▲ 9469 (16.97)

Double Concerto for Violin, Viola & Orchestra [incomplete; compd Colin Matthews] (1938)
G. Kremer (vn), Y. Bashmet (va), K. Nagano (cnd), Hallé Orch † Portraits; Sinfonietta, Op. 1; Young Apollo, Op. 16 ERAT ▲ 25502 (16.97)

CHOPIN, FRÉDERIC (cont.)

Fantaisie in f for Piano, Op. 49 (1841) (cont.)

J. Katchen (pno) *(rec 1949)* ("Julius Katchen") † Ballade 3 Pno, Op. 47; Balakirev:Islamey; J. Brahms:Son 3 Pno, Op. 5; Vars on an Original Theme, Op. 21/1; C. Franck:Prélude, choral et fugue, M.21; Liszt:Hungarian Rhaps, S.244; Mendelssohn (-Bartholdy):Prelude & Fugue Pno; Rondo capriccioso, Op. 14; N. Rorem:Son 2 Pno — PPHI (Great Pianists of the 20th Century) ▲ 456856 (22.97)

W. Kempff (pno) ("Kempff Plays Chopin Vol 2") † Ballade 3 Pno, Op. 47; Polonaises-fant, Op. 61; Son Pno in b, Op. 58 — PLON (The Classic Sound) ▲ 452308 (11.97)

N. Kokinos (pno) † Polonaise 3 Pno, Op. 40/1; Polonaise 6 Pno, Op. 53; Polonaises-fant, Op. 61; Preludes (24) Pno, Op. 28; Scherzos Pno; Waltzes Pno — ANDP ▲ 9592 (15.97)

P. Komen (pno) † Ballades (4) Pno; Barcarolle Pno, Op. 60; Berceuse, Op. 57 — GLOE ▲ 5162 (16.97)

A. Lear (pno) *(rec Brandon Hill Bristol, England, Nov 24, 1993)* ("The Original Chopin") † Andante Spianato & Grand Polonaise, Op. 22; Barcarolle Pno, Op. 60; Fant-Impromptu, Op. 66; Nocturnes (21) Pno; Polonaise 5 Pno, Op. 44 — APR ▲ 5551 [DDD] (19.97)

A. B. Michelangeli (pno) *(rec 1960-73)* ("Michelangeli in Recital") † Waltzes Pno; J. Brahms:Ballades (4), Op. 10; Vars on a Theme by Paganini, Op. 35; Busoni:Chaconne Pno; M. Ravel:Gaspard de la nuit; R. Schumann:Carnaval, Op. 9 — MUA 2-▲ 817 [AAD] (31.97)

A. B. Michelangeli (pno) *(rec Royal Albert Hall London, 1957)* † Ballade 1 Pno, Op. 23; Debussy:Images (6) Pno; Mompou:Cançons i dansas Pno; R. Schumann:Carnaval, Op. 9; Faschingsschwank, Op. 26 — TES 2-▲ 2088 (33.97)

J. Ogdon (pno) † Barcarolle Pno, Op. 60; Berceuse, Op. 57; Polonaise 4 Pno, Op. 40/2; Son Pno in b, Op. 58 — INMP ▲ 2008 (9.97)

M. Perahia (pno) † Barcarolle Pno, Op. 60; Berceuse, Op. 57; Impromptus (4) — SNYC ▲ 39708 [DDD] (16.97)

M. Perahia (pno) † Barcarolle Pno, Op. 60; Berceuse, Op. 57; Con 1 Pno, Op. 11 — SNYC ▲ 42400 [AAD/DDD] (11.97)

M. J. Pires (pno) † Berceuse, Op. 57; Con 1 Pno, Op. 11; Fant-Impromptu, Op. 66 — DEUT ▲ 457585 [DDD] (16.97)

M. Pletnev (pno) *(rec Friedrich Ebert Hall Hamburg-Harburg, Germany, Nov 1996)* † Ecossaises (3) Pno, Op. 72/3; Impromptu in A♭, Op. 29; Son Pno in b, Op. 58; Waltzes Pno — DEUT ▲ 453456 (16.97)

A. Rubinstein (pno) † Son Pno in b, Op. 58; Son Pno in b♭, Op. 35 — RCAV (Red Seal) ▲ 5616 [ADD] (16.97)

F. Ts'ong (pno) † Barcarolle Pno, Op. 60; Berceuse, Op. 57; Polonaises-fant, Op. 61 — SNYC (Essential Classics) ▲ 53515 (7.97) ▮ 53515 (3.98)

T. Ying (pno) *(rec Mar 19-20, 1996)* † W. A. Mozart:Rondo Pno, K.511; S. Rachmaninoff:Vars on a Theme by Corelli, Op. 42; M. Ravel:Gaspard de la nuit; R. Schumann:Toccata Pno, Op. 7 — ARIZ ▲ 96100 [ADD]

K. Zimerman (pno) † Ballades (4) Pno; Barcarolle Pno, Op. 60 — DEUT ▲ 23090 [DDD] (16.97)

Fantasie-Impromptu in c# for Piano, Op. 66 (1835)

W. Backhaus (pno) *(rec 1927; 1933)* † Études Pno; Berceuse, Op. 57 — MTAL ▲ 48032 (6.97)

J. Bolet (pno) *(rec Queens, NY)* ("A Chopin Piano Recital") † Études Pno; Polonaise 3 Pno, Op. 40/1; Polonaise 6 Pno, Op. 53; Preludes (24) Pno, Op. 28; Waltzes Pno — EVC ▲ 9028 [AAD] (13.97)

P. Entremont (pno) *(rec New York City, NY, Mar 30-31, 1966)* † Études Pno; Intro & Polonaise, Op. 3; Mazurkas Pno; Nocturnes Pno; Polonaise 3 Pno, Op. 40/1; Polonaise 6 Pno, Op. 53; Preludes (24) Pno, Op. 28; Son Pno in b♭, Op. 35; Waltzes Pno — SNYC ▲ 51338 [ADD] (7.97)

R. Keller (pno) ("The Kiss: Music for Love and Passion") † Con 2 Pno, Op. 21; Liszt:Hungarian Rhaps, S.244; O. Nicolai:Lustigen Weiber von Windsor (ov); M. Ravel:Boléro; P. Tchaikovsky:Swan Lake (sels); Verdi:Aida (sels); R. Wagner:Tristan und Isolde (orch sels) — INTC ▲ 892923 [AAD] (13.97)

W. Kempff (pno) ("Kempff Plays Chopin Vol 1") † Impromptu in A♭, Op. 29; Son Pno in b♭, Op. 35 — PLON (The Classic Sound) ▲ 452307 (11.97)

A. Lear (pno) *(rec Brandon Hill Bristol, England, Nov 24, 1993)* ("The Original Chopin") † Andante Spianato & Grand Polonaise, Op. 22; Barcarolle Pno, Op. 60; Fantaisie Pno, Op. 49; Nocturnes (21) Pno; Polonaise 5 Pno, Op. 44 — APR ▲ 5551 [DDD] (19.97)

B. Moiseiwitsch (pno) ("In Recital") † Études Pno; Son Pno in b, Op. 58; Beethoven:Andante Pno, WoO 57; Mussorgsky:Pictures at an Exhibition; Palmgren:West Finnish Dance; R. Schumann:Carnaval, Op. 9; Kreisleriana, Op. 16; Symphonic Etudes, Op. 13 — PHS 2-▲ 9192 (33.97)

B. Moiseiwitsch (pno) *(rec 1958)* † Ballade 3 Pno, Op. 47; Ballade 4 Pno, Op. 52; Barcarolle Pno, Op. 60; Nocturnes Pno; Scherzos Pno; Kabalevsky:Son 3 Pno, Op. 46; Liszt:Études de concert (3), S.144; Medtner:Son Pno in g, Op. 22; Mendelssohn (-Bartholdy):Midsummer Night's Dream (sels); S. Prokofiev:Pieces (4) Pno, Op. 4; Toccata Pno, Op. 11; S. Rachmaninoff:Con 2 Pno, Op. 18; Moments musicaux, Op. 16; Preludes Pno — PPHI (Great Pianists of the 20th Century) 2-▲ 456907 (22.97)

G. Montero (pno) † Nocturnes Pno; Polonaise 1 Pno, Op. 26/1; Polonaise 2 Pno, Op. 26/2; Polonaise 6 Pno, Op. 53; Scherzos Pno; Son Pno in b♭, Op. 35; Waltzes Pno — PALE ▲ 510 (17.97)

M. Perahia (pno) *(rec New York City, United States of America, 1983)* ("A Portrait of Murray Perahia") † Preludes (24) Pno, Op. 28; Beethoven:Son 23 Pno, Op. 57; Mendelssohn (-Bartholdy):Rondo capriccioso, Op. 14; W. A. Mozart:Rondo Pno & Orch, K.382; Rondo Pno Orch, K.382; F. Schubert:Impromptus (4) Pno; R. Schumann:Papillons Pno, Op. 2 — SNYC ▲ 42448 [AAD/DDD] (11.97)

M. J. Pires (pno) † Berceuse, Op. 57; Con 1 Pno, Op. 11; Fantaisie Pno, Op. 49 — DEUT ▲ 457585 [DDD] (16.97)

B. Rigutto (pno) *(rec Leiden The Netherlands, Netherlands, Dec 17-19, 1990, Dec 4-8, 1991 & Dec 1-2, 1992)* ("Piano Works, Vol. 3") † Berceuse, Op. 57; Son Pno in b♭, Op. 35 — DNN ▲ 78927 [DDD] (16.97)

Fantasy on Polish Airs in A, Op. 13 (1828)

C. Arrau (pno), E. Inbal (cnd), London SO ("Chopin: Complete Works for Piano & Orchestra") † Andante Spianato & Grand Polonaise, Op. 22; Con 1 Pno, Op. 11; Con 2 Pno, Op. 21; Impromptu in A♭, Op. 29; Impromptu in F#, Op. 36; Impromptu in G♭, Op. 51; Krakowiak, Op. 14; Vars on Mozart, Op. 2 — PPHI 2-▲ 38338 (17.97)

Fugue in a for Piano (1841-2)

I. Biret (pno) *(rec 1991-92)* † Albumleaf (Feuille d'Album); Barcarolle Pno, Op. 60; Bolero; Pno Music (misc colls); Prelude in c#, Op. 45; Prelude in A♭, Op. posth.; Preludes (24) Pno, Op. 28; Wiosna — NXIN ▲ 550366 [DDD] (5.97)

C. Katsaris (pno) † Albumleaf (Feuille d'Album); Allegretto & Mazur; Allegretto in F; Bolero; Bourrées; Cantabile in B♭; Contredanse; Ecossaises (3) Pno, Op. 72/3; Galop Marquis; Largo in E♭; Prelude in c#, Op. 45; Prelude in A♭, Op. posth.; Preludes (24) Pno, Op. 28; Wiosna — SNYC ▲ 53355 [DDD] (16.97)

Funeral March in c for Piano, Op. 72/2

C. Katsaris (pno) *(rec Mar 3-22, 1993)* † Andante Spianato & Grand Polonaise, Op. 22; Mazurkas Pno; Polonaise 1 Pno, Op. 26/1; Polonaise 2 Pno, Op. 26/2; Polonaise 3 Pno, Op. 40/1; Polonaise 4 Pno, Op. 40/2; Polonaise 5 Pno, Op. 44; Polonaise 9 Pno, Op. 71/2; Polonaises Pno; Polonaises-fant, Op. 61 — SNYC 2-▲ 53967 [DDD] (31.97)

Funeral March in b♭ for Piano [from Sonata No. 2, Op. 35] (1837)

I. J. Paderewski (pno) *(rec 1912-30)* ("Ignacy Jan Paderewski") † Études Pno; Berceuse, Op. 57; Mazurkas Pno; Nocturnes Pno; Polonaise 2 Pno, Op. 26/2; Polonaise 3 Pno, Op. 40/1; Preludes (24) Pno, Op. 28; Waltzes Pno; Liszt:Études d'exécution transcendante (6), S.140; Études de concert (3), S.144; Hungarian Rhaps, S.244; Trans, Arrs & Paraphrases; I. J. Paderewski:Minuet; F. Schubert:Impromptus (4) — PPHI (Great Pianists of the 20th Century) 2-▲ 456919 (22.97)

Galop Marquis in A♭ for Piano

C. Katsaris (pno) † Albumleaf (Feuille d'Album); Allegretto & Mazur; Allegretto in F; Bolero; Bourrées; Cantabile in B♭; Contredanse; Ecossaises (3) Pno, Op. 72/3; Fugue in a; Largo in E♭; Prelude in c#, Op. 45; Prelude in A♭, Op. posth.; Preludes (24) Pno, Op. 28; Wiosna — SNYC ▲ 53355 [DDD] (16.97)

Grand Duo in E for Cello & Piano [on themes from Meyerbeer's Robert le diable] (1832)

M. Gendron (vc), K. Toyama (pno) *(rec Iruma-shi Shimin Kaikan, June 1981)* ("Lalo & Chopin: Cello Sonatas") † Intro & Polonaise, Op. 3; Son Vc; Lalo:Son Vc — CAMA ▲ 366 (18.97)

K. Scholes (vc), D. Breitman (pno) *(rec June 1990)* † Intro & Polonaise, Op. 3; Son Vc — TIT ▲ 197 [DDD]

P. Szabó (vc), D. Várjon (pno) ("Chamber Music") † Son Vc; Trio — HUN ▲ 31651 [DDD] (16.97)

Grand Fantasia on Polish Airs in A for Piano & Orchestra, Op. 13 (1828)

E. Ax (pno), C. Mackerras (cnd), Orch of the Age of Enlightenment [original instrs] † Andante Spianato & Grand Polonaise, Op. 22; Con 2 Pno, Op. 21 — SNYC ▲ 63371 [DDD] (16.97)

I. Biret (pno), R. Stankovský (cnd), Czech-Slovak State PO † Andante Spianato & Grand Polonaise, Op. 22; Con 1 Pno, Op. 11 — NXIN ▲ 550368 [DDD] (5.97)

J. Nakamatsu (pno) † Berceuse, Op. 57; Impromptus (4) — HAM ▲ 907244 (18.97)

A. Rubinstein (pno), E. Ormandy (cnd), Philadelphia Orch † Andante Spianato & Grand Polonaise, Op. 22; Con 2 Pno, Op. 21 — RCAV (Gold Seal) ▲ 60404 [ADD] (11.97)

A. Simon (pno), H. Beissel (cnd), Hamburg SO ("Complete Works for Piano & Orchestra") † Andante Spianato & Grand Polonaise, Op. 22; Con 1 Pno, Op. 11; Con 2 Pno, Op. 21; Krakowiak, Op. 14; Vars on Mozart, Op. 2 — VB2 2-▲ 5002 [ADD] (9.97)

Impromptus (4) in A♭, F#, G♭ & c# for Piano, Opp. 29, 36, 51, 66

C. Arrau (pno) † Nocturnes Pno — PPHI (Duo) 2-▲ 456336 (17.97)

A. Cortot (pno) *(rec London, 1933-34)* † Études Pno — 78'S (The 78's) ▲ 78511 [ADD] (13.97)

V. Horowitz (pno) ("Vladimir Horowitz: The Early Studio Recordings, 1932-36") † Mazurkas Pno; Liszt:Son Pno, S.178 — IN ▲ 1303 [ADD] (15.97)

J. Nakamatsu (pno) † Berceuse, Op. 57; Grand Fant on Polish Airs, Op. 13 — HAM ▲ 907244 (18.97)

CHOPIN, FRÉDERIC (cont.)

Impromptus (4) in A♭, F#, G♭ & c# for Piano, Opp. 29, 36, 51, 66 (cont.)

H. Neuhaus (pno) ("Neuhaus Plays Chopin") † Barcarolle Pno, Op. 60; Con 1 Pno, Op. 11; Nocturnes Pno; Polonaises-fant, Op. 61 — RUS ▲ 15007 [AAD] (12.97)

G. Ohlsson (pno) ("The Complete Chopin Piano Works, Vol. 5") † Polonaise 1 Pno, Op. 26/1; Polonaise 2 Pno, Op. 26/2; Polonaise 3 Pno, Op. 40/1; Polonaise 4 Pno, Op. 40/2; Polonaise 9 Pno, Op. 71/2; Polonaises Pno; Polonaises-fant, Op. 61 — ARA 2-▲ 6642 [DDD] (32.97)

M. Perahia (pno) † Barcarolle Pno, Op. 60; Berceuse, Op. 57; Fantaisie Pno, Op. 49 — SNYC ▲ 39708 [DDD] (16.97)

J. Robilette (pno) *(rec 1993)* ("French Piano Album") † C. Franck:Prélude, choral et fugue, M.21; Symphonic Vars, M.46; F. Poulenc:Mouvements perpétuels — PRA ▲ 3491 (14.97)

A. Uninsky (pno) † Berceuse, Op. 57 — PPHI (Duo) 2-▲ 42574 (17.97)

Impromptu in A♭ for Piano, Op. 29

C. Arrau (pno), E. Inbal (cnd), London SO ("Chopin: Complete Works for Piano & Orchestra") † Andante Spianato & Grand Polonaise, Op. 22; Con 1 Pno, Op. 11; Con 2 Pno, Op. 21; Fantasy, Op. 13; Impromptu in F#, Op. 36; Impromptu in G♭, Op. 51; Krakowiak, Op. 14; Vars on Mozart, Op. 2 — PPHI 2-▲ 38338 (17.97)

K. Gekić (pno) *(rec Subotica, Yugoslavia, Apr 27, 1997)* † Impromptu in F#, Op. 36; Polonaise 4 Pno, Op. 40/2; Polonaise 5 Pno, Op. 44; Son Pno in b♭, Op. 35; Liszt:Grand galop chromatique, S.219; Trans, Arrs & Paraphrases — VAIA ▲ 1180 (16.97)

V. Horowitz (pno) ("Vladimir Horowitz: The Early Recordings, 1932-36") † Études (24) Pno, Opp. 10 & 25; Liszt:Harmonies poétiques et religieuses, S.173; Son Pno, S.178 — ENPL (The Piano Library) ▲ 188 (13.97)

V. Horowitz (pno) † Scherzos Pno — MTAL ▲ 48014 (6.97)

W. Kempff (pno) ("Kempff Plays Chopin Vol 1") † Fant-Impromptu, Op. 66; Son Pno in b♭, Op. 35 — PLON (The Classic Sound) ▲ 452307 (11.97)

M. Pletnev (pno) *(rec Friedrich Ebert Hall Hamburg-Harburg, Germany, Nov 1996)* † Ecossaises (3) Pno, Op. 72/3; Fantaisie Pno, Op. 49; Son Pno in b, Op. 58; Waltzes Pno — DEUT ▲ 453456 (16.97)

Impromptu in F# for Piano, Op. 36 (1839)

C. Arrau (pno), E. Inbal (cnd), London SO ("Chopin: Complete Works for Piano & Orchestra") † Andante Spianato & Grand Polonaise, Op. 22; Con 1 Pno, Op. 11; Con 2 Pno, Op. 21; Fantasy, Op. 13; Impromptu in A♭, Op. 29; Impromptu in G♭, Op. 51; Krakowiak, Op. 14; Vars on Mozart, Op. 2 — PPHI 2-▲ 38338 (17.97)

I. Friedman (pno) ("Highlights 1925-36 From His Discography") † Études Pno; Mazurkas Pno; Nocturnes Pno; Polonaise 6 Pno, Op. 53; Son Pno in b♭, Op. 35; Waltzes Pno; Beethoven:Son 14 Pno, Op. 27/2; I. Friedman:Danse; Music Box, Op. 33/3; J. N. Hummel:Rondo Pno, Op. 11; Liszt:Trans, Arrs & Paraphrases; Mendelssohn (-Bartholdy):Fants Pno, Op. 16; Shield:Old English Menuet — APR (Signature Series) ▲ 5508 [ADD] (18.97)

I. Friedman (pno) *(rec Nov 23, 1936)* † Ballade 3 Pno, Op. 47; Mazurkas Pno; Nocturnes Pno; Liszt:Hungarian Rhaps, S.244; Mendelssohn (-Bartholdy):Lieder ohne Worte — BPS ▲ 44 (m) [ADD] (16.97)

K. Gekić (pno) *(rec Subotica, Yugoslavia, Apr 27, 1997)* † Impromptu in A♭, Op. 29; Polonaise 4 Pno, Op. 40/2; Polonaise 5 Pno, Op. 44; Son Pno in b♭, Op. 35; Liszt:Grand galop chromatique, S.219; Trans, Arrs & Paraphrases — VAIA ▲ 1180 (16.97)

J. Gimpel (pno) *(rec Ambassador Auditorium, Los Angeles, CA, May 11, 1978)* ("Jakob Gimpel: All-Chopin Recital") † Ballade 1 Pno, Op. 23; Intro & Vars in B♭, Op. 12; Pno Music (misc colls); Son Pno in b♭, Op. 35; Debussy:Etudes (12) Pno; Liszt:Valses oubliées (4), S.215 — CMB 2-▲ 1070

L. Kraus (pno) *(rec 1938)* † Preludes (24) Pno, Op. 28; B. Bartók:Romanian Folk Dances Pno, Sz.56; Rondos on Folk Tunes, Sz.84; Beethoven:Vars & Fugue Pno, Op. 35; J. Haydn:Andante with Vars Pno, H.XVII/6; F. Schubert:Dances (42), Op. 18; Waltzes, D.969 — PHS (Piano Masters) ▲ 55 (17.97)

G. Novaes (pno) *(rec 1950s)* ("The Romantic Novaes") † Berceuse, Op. 57; Con 1 Pno, Op. 11; Son Pno in b, Op. 58; M. de Falla:Noches en los jardines de España; E. Grieg:Con Pno, Op. 16 — VOXL (Legends) 2-▲ 5513 [ADD] (9.97)

A. Rubinstein (pno) *(rec 1962-65)* ("The Chopin Collection") † Pno Music (misc colls) — RCAV (Gold Seal) 10-▲ 60822 (112.97)

Impromptu in G♭ for Piano, Op. 51 (1842)

C. Arrau (pno), E. Inbal (cnd), London SO ("Chopin: Complete Works for Piano & Orchestra") † Andante Spianato & Grand Polonaise, Op. 22; Con 1 Pno, Op. 11; Con 2 Pno, Op. 21; Fantasy, Op. 13; Impromptu in A♭, Op. 29; Impromptu in F#, Op. 36; Krakowiak, Op. 14; Vars on Mozart, Op. 2 — PPHI 2-▲ 38338 (17.97)

A. Cortot (pno) [Duo-Art pno roll] † Beethoven:Son 30 Pno, Op. 109; Chabrier:Pièces pittoresques; Liszt:Années de pèlerinage 1, S.160; Hungarian Rhaps, S.244; Saint-Saëns:Étude Pno, Op. 52/6 — NIMB (Grand Piano) ▲ 8814 [DDD] (11.97)

A. Cortot (pno) *(rec Royce Hall, University of California, Los Angeles, CA)* † Études Pno; Nocturnes Pno; Preludes (24) Pno, Op. 28; J. S. Bach:Con 5 Hpd, BWV 1056; Beethoven:Son 29 Pno, Op. 106; Son 30 Pno, Op. 109; Chabrier:Feuillet d'album; Pièces pittoresques; Liszt:Au Bord d'une Source; Trans, Arrs & Paraphrases; A. Scriabin:Etudes (12) Pno, Op. 8 — KLAV ▲ 11096 [ADD] (18.97)

S. B. Kovacevich (pno) *(rec 1972)* † Nocturnes Pno; B. Bartók:Con 2 Pno, Sz.95; Out of Doors, Sz.81; Sonatina Pno, Sz.55; Beethoven:Son 5 Pno, Op. 10/1; R. R. Bennett:Con Pno; J. Brahms:Pieces (4) Pno, Op. 119; I. Stravinsky:Con Pno & Ww — PPHI (Great Pianists of the 20th Century, Vol. 61) 2-▲ 456880 (22.97)

Introduction & Polonaise in C for Cello & Piano, Op. 3, "Polonaise brilliante" (1829-30)

H. Brendstrup (vc), C. Edwards (pno) † Son Vc; Liszt:Elegie 1 Vc, S.130; Elegie 2 Vn, S.131; Lugubre gondola Vn or Vc, S.134; Romance oubliée Va, S.132 — KPT ▲ 32026 [DDD]

J. Cox (hn), K. George (pno) *(rec Aug 1991)* † W. Gieseking:Qnt Hn; R. Schumann:Adagio & Allegro Hn, Op. 70 — CENT ▲ 2122 [DDD] (16.97)

M. Gendron (vc), K. Toyama (pno) *(rec Iruma-shi Shimin Kaikan, June 1981)* ("Lalo & Chopin: Cello Sonatas") † Grand Duo; Son Vc; Lalo:Son Vc — CAMA ▲ 366 (18.97)

E. Osinska (pno) *(rec Henry Wood Hall, London, England, Oct 17-19, 1989)* † Son Vc; Trio — SNYC ▲ 53112 [DDD] (16.97)

L. Rose (cel), S. Sanders (pno) *(rec NY, May 2-3, 1966)* † Études Pno; Fant-Impromptu, Op. 66; Mazurkas Pno; Nocturnes Pno; Polonaise 3 Pno, Op. 40/1; Polonaise 6 Pno, Op. 53; Preludes (24) Pno, Op. 28; Son Pno in b♭, Op. 35; Waltzes Pno — SNYC ▲ 51338 [ADD] (7.97)

K. Scholes (vc), D. Breitman (pno) *(rec June 1990)* † Grand Duo; Son Vc — TIT ▲ 197 [DDD]

J. Starker (vc), G. Sebok (pno) † Son Vc; B. Bartók:Rhap Vc, Sz.88; Debussy:Son Vc; Martinů:Vars on a Theme of Rossini, H.290; Mendelssohn (-Bartholdy):Vars concertantes, Op. 17; L. Weiner:Hungarian Wedding Dance — MRCR ▲ 34358 (11.97)

J. Wang (vc), C. Rosenberger (pno) † Son Vc; S. Barber:Son Vc, Op. 6; R. Schumann:Adagio & Allegro Hn, Op. 70 — DLS ▲ 3097 [DDD] (14.97)

Introduction & Variations in B♭ on "Je vends des scalpulaines" [from Hérold's Ludovic] for Piano, Op. 12 (1833)

M. Frager (pno) ("Malcolm Frager Plays Chopin") † Andante Spianato & Grand Polonaise, Op. 22; Pno Music (misc colls); Polonaise 6 Pno, Op. 53; Tarentelle, Op. 43 — TEL ▲ 80280 [DDD] (16.97)

J. Gimpel (pno) *(rec Ambassador Auditorium, Los Angeles, CA, May 11, 1978)* ("Jakob Gimpel: All-Chopin Recital") † Ballade 1 Pno, Op. 23; Impromptu in F#, Op. 36; Pno Music (misc colls); Son Pno in b♭, Op. 35; Debussy:Etudes (12) Pno; Liszt:Valses oubliées (4), S.215 — CMB 2-▲ 1070

K. Skanavi (pno) † Andante Spianato & Grand Polonaise, Op. 22; Berceuse, Op. 57; Nocturnes Pno; Son Pno in b♭, Op. 35 — PPR ▲ 224522

Introduction & Variations in E on a German National Air "Der Schweizerbub" for Piano (1826)

N. Demidenko (pno) † Scherzos Pno; Vars on Mozart, Op. 2 — HYP ▲ 66514 [DDD] (18.97)

Introduction, Theme & Variations in D for Piano 4-Hands (1826)

K. Makowska (pno), A. Wesotowska (pno) *(rec Warsaw, 1987)* † Rondos (4) Pnos; Moniuszko:Pno Music — SELN ▲ 940420 [DDD] (16.97)

Krakowiak (rondo) in F for Piano & Orchestra, Op. 14 (1828)

C. Arrau (pno), E. Inbal (cnd), London SO ("Chopin: Complete Works for Piano & Orchestra") † Andante Spianato & Grand Polonaise, Op. 22; Con 1 Pno, Op. 11; Con 2 Pno, Op. 21; Fantasy, Op. 13; Impromptu in A♭, Op. 29; Impromptu in F#, Op. 36; Impromptu in G♭, Op. 51; Vars on Mozart, Op. 2 — PPHI 2-▲ 38338 (17.97)

I. Biret (pno), R. Stankovský (cnd), Czech-Slovak State PO *(rec 1990-91)* † Con 2 Pno, Op. 21; Vars on Mozart, Op. 2 — NXIN ▲ 550369 [DDD] (5.97)

A. Simon (pno), H. Beissel (cnd), Hamburg SO ("Complete Works for Piano & Orchestra") † Andante Spianato & Grand Polonaise, Op. 22; Con 1 Pno, Op. 11; Con 2 Pno, Op. 21; Grand Fant on Polish Airs, Op. 13; Vars on Mozart, Op. 2 — VB2 2-▲ 5002 [ADD] (9.97)

Largo in E♭ for Piano (?1837)

C. Katsaris (pno) † Albumleaf (Feuille d'Album); Allegretto & Mazur; Allegretto in F; Bolero; Bourrées; Cantabile in B♭; Contredanse; Ecossaises (3) Pno, Op. 72/3; Fugue in a; Galop Marquis; Prelude in c#, Op. 45; Prelude in A♭, Op. posth.; Preludes (24) Pno, Op. 28; Wiosna — SNYC ▲ 53355 [DDD] (16.97)

CHOPIN, FRÉDÉRIC (cont.)

Life & Music of Chopin

I. Haebler (pno) *(Con 1 Pno, Op. 11; Scherzos Pno [No. 2 in b♭/D♭, Op. 31]; Polonaise 3 Pno, Op. 40/1; Polonaise 6 Pno, Op. 53; Mazurkas Pno [No. 23 in D, Op. 33/2; No. 39 in B, Op. 63/1]; Vars on Mozart, Op. 2; Waltzes Pno [No. 1 in E♭, Op. 18, "Grand Valse Brillante"; No. 3 in a, Op. 34/2; No. 4 in F, Op. 34/3; No. 5 in A♭, Op. 42; No. 6 in D♭, Op. 64/1, "Minute"; No. 7 in c#, Op. 64/2; No. 8 in A♭, Op. 64/3; No. 9 in A♭, Op. 69/1, "L'adieu"; No. 10 in b, Op. 69/2; No. 11 in g♭, Op. 70/1; No. 12 in f, Op. 70/2; No. 13 in D♭, Op. 70/3]; Ballade 1 Pno, Op. 23; Preludes (24) Pno, Op. 28 [No. 20 in c]; Études Pno [No. 3 in E, Op. 10/3, "Tristesse"; No. 12 in c, Op. 10/12, "Revolutionary"]; Nocturnes Pno [No. 2 in E♭, Op. 9/2; No. 5 in F#, Op. 15/2]; Fant-Impromptu, Op. 66; Son Pno in b, Op. 58), (Con 2 Pno, Op. 21; Polonaise 5 Pno, Op. 44; Ballade 4 Pno, Op. 52; Son Pno in b♭, Op. 35)* ("The Story of Chopin in Words & Music") MMD (Music Masters) ▲ 8502 [ADD] (3.97) ▮ 8502 [ADD] (2.98)

Mazurkas for Piano

V. Ashkenazy (pno) PLON 2-▲ 48086 (17.97)

A. R. El Bacha (pno)—No. 5 in B♭, Op. 7/1; No. 10 in B♭, Op. 17/1; No. 11 in e, Op. 17/2; No. 12 in A♭, Op. 17/3; No. 13 in a, Op. 17/4 ("El Bacha Plays Chopin, Vol. 4") † Études Pno; Allegro de concert, Op. 46; Ballade 1 Pno, Op. 23; Rondos (4) Pno; Waltzes Pno FORL ▲ 16785 (16.97)

S. Barere (pno)—No. 38 in f#, Op. 59/3 *(rec Oct 15, 1935)* † Waltzes Pno; Balakirev:Islamey; F. Blumenfeld:Etude for the left hand, Op. 36; Glazunov:Etude Pno; Liszt:Pno Music (misc); R. Schumann:Toccata Pno, Op. 7 PHS ▲ 12 [ADD] (17.97)

I. Biret (pno)—No. 30 in G, Op. 50/1; No. 5 in B♭, Op. 7/1; No. 10 in B♭, Op. 17/1; No. 8 in A♭, Op. 7/4; No. 12 in A♭, Op. 17/3; No. 23 in D, Op. 33/2 *(rec 1991)* † Rondos (4) Pno; Rondos (4) Pno, Op. 73; Var 6 Pno; Vars in A, ('Souvenir de Paganini'); Vars on a Theme from La Cenerentola; Vars on Mozart, Op. 2 NXIN ▲ 550367 [DDD] (5.97)

A. Brailowsky (pno) † Polonaises Pno; Songs Sop SNYC (Take Two) 2-▲ 63237 (14.97)

S. Cherkassky (pno)—No. 25 in b, Op. 33/4; No. 41 in c#, Op. 63/3 *(rec Wyastone Leys Monmouth, England, 1984-85)* ("Art of the Encore") † Andante Spianato & Grand Polonaise, Op. 22; Nocturnes (21) Pno; Liszt:Harmonies poétiques et religieuses, S.173; Hungarian Rhaps, S.244; F. Schubert:Impromptus (4) Pno NIMB ▲ 7708 [DDD] (11.97)

J. Coop (pno)—Mazurkas Pno [No. 13 in a, Op. 17/4] *(rec Toronto, Canada)* ("The Romantic Piano") † Etudes (24) Pno, Opp. 10 & 25; Nocturnes Pno; J. Brahms:Pieces (6) Pno, Op. 118; Waltzes (16) Pno, Op. 39; Debussy:Isle joyeuse; Suite bergamasque; Liszt:Etudes de concert (3), S.144; Liebesträume, S.541; Mendelssohn (-Bartholdy):Pno Music (misc); S. Rachmaninoff:Etudes-tableaux Pno, Opp. 33 & 39; Preludes (23) Pno, Opp. 23 & 32; R. Schumann:Kinderszenen Pno, Op. 15 MUVI ▲ 1015 [DDD] (16.97)

S. Cosma (pno)—Mazurkas Pno [No. 41 in c#, Op. 63/3; No. 45 in a, Op. 67/4] † Mazurkas Pno; Beethoven:Vars Pno on Original Theme, WoO 80; J. Brahms:Pieces (8) Pno, Op. 76 TOWN ▲ 29 (17.97)

G. Csalog (pno) † N. Rota:Il capello di paglia di Firenze BMGR 2-▲ 1092 (36.97)

I. Friedman (pno)—Mazurkas Pno [No. 5 in B♭, Op. 7/1; No. 6 in a, Op. 7/2; No. 7 in f, Op. 7/3; No. 17 in b♭, Op. 24/4; No. 23 in D, Op. 33/2; No. 25 in b, Op. 33/4; No. 26 in c#, Op. 41/1; No. 31 in A♭, Op. 50/2; No. 41 in c#, Op. 63/3; No. 44 in C, Op. 67/3; No. 45 in a, Op. 67/4; No. 47 in a, Op. 68/2] *(rec Sept 13, 1930)* † Ballade 3 Pno, Op. 47; Impromptu in F#, Op. 36; Nocturnes Pno; Liszt:Hungarian Rhaps, S.244; Mendelssohn (-Bartholdy):Lieder ohne Worte BPS ▲ 44 (m) [ADD] (16.97)

I. Friedman (pno)—No. 17 in b♭, Op. 24/4; No. 25 in b, Op. 33/4 ("Highlights 1925-36 From His Discography") † Études Pno; Impromptu in F#, Op. 36; Nocturnes Pno; Polonaise 6 Pno, Op. 53; Son Pno in b♭, Op. 35; Waltzes Pno; Beethoven:Son 14 Pno, Op. 27/2; I. Friedman:Danse; Music Box, Op. 33/3; J. N. Hummel:Rondo Pno, Op. 11; Liszt:Trans, Arrs & Paraphrases; Mendelssohn (-Bartholdy):Fants Pno, Op. 16; Shield:Old English Menuet APR (Signature Series) ▲ 5508 [ADD] (18.97)

E. Gabriel (pno)—No. 23 in D, Op. 33/2; No. 25 in b, Op. 33/4; No. 32 in c#, Op. 50/3; No. 19 in b/f#, Op. 30/2 † Nocturnes Pno; Polonaise 2 Pno, Op. 26/2; Polonaise 3 Pno, Op. 40/1; Son Pno in b, Op. 58; Waltzes Pno QUER ▲ 9822 (18.97)

V. Horowitz (pno) ("Vladimir Horowitz: The Early Studio Recordings, 1932-36") † Impromptus (4); Liszt:Son Pno, S.178 IN ▲ 1303 [ADD] (15.97)

J.-M. Luisada—No. 14 in g, Op. 24/1; No. 15 in C, Op. 24/2; No. 16 in A♭, Op. 24/3; No. 17 in b♭, Op. 24/4 ("Masters of Classical Music, Vol. 8: Frederic Chopin") † Études Pno; Nocturnes (21) Pno; Nocturnes Pno; Preludes (24) Pno, Op. 28; Scherzos Pno; Waltzes Pno LALI ▲ 15808 [DDD] (3.97)

W. Kapell (pno)—No. 24 in C, Op. 33/3 † Nocturnes Pno; Polonaises-fant, Op. 61; A. Copland:Son Pno; Mussorgsky:Pictures at an Exhibition; D. Scarlatti:Sons Kbd; R. Schumann:Kinderszenen Pno, Op. 15 RCAV ▲ 68997 [ADD] (16.97)

E. L. Kaplan (pno)—No. 6 in a, Op. 7/2; No. 16 in A♭, Op. 24/3; No. 47 in a, Op. 68/2 *(rec First Congregational Church Los Angeles, CA, Sept 1992)* † Fantaisie Pno, Op. 49; R. Schumann:Carnaval, Op. 9 CMB ▲ 1089 [DDD] (16.97)

E. L. Kaplan (pno)—No. 6 in a, Op. 7/2; No. 16 in A♭, Op. 24/3; No. 47 in a, Op. 68/2 *(rec Los Angeles, CA, Sep 1992)* † Fantaisie Pno, Op. 49; Nocturnes Pno; Waltzes Pno; R. Schumann:Carnaval, Op. 9 CMB ▲ 1098 (16.97)

C. Katsaris (pno) *(rec Mar 3-22, 1993)* † Andante Spianato & Grand Polonaise, Op. 22; Funeral March, Op. 72/2; Polonaise 1 Pno, Op. 26/1; Polonaise 2 Pno, Op. 26/2; Polonaise 3 Pno, Op. 40/1; Polonaise 4 Pno, Op. 40/2; Polonaise 5 Pno, Op. 44; Polonaise 9 Pno, Op. 71/2; Polonaises Pno; Polonaises-fant, Op. 61 SNYC 2-▲ 53967 [DDD] (31.97)

E. Kissin (pno) ("Chopin, Vol. 2") † Son Pno in b, Op. 58 RCAV (Red Seal) ▲ 62542 (16.97)

A. Kitain (pno)—No. 13 in a, Op. 17/4 *(rec 1936-39)* † Études Pno; Ballade 2 Pno, Op. 38; Ballade 3 Pno, Op. 47; Scherzos Pno; J. Brahms:Waltzes Pno, Op. 39; Liszt:Pno Music (misc); R. Schumann:Toccata Pno, Op. 7 ENPL (Piano Library) ▲ 221 (13.97)

Z. Kocsis (pno)—No. 35 in c, Op. 56/3 *(rec 1973-86)* ("Zoltán Kocsis in Concert, 1973-86") † Ballade 1 Pno, Op. 23; Kodály:Pieces (7) Pno, Op. 11; Liszt:Pno Music (misc); S. Rachmaninoff:Etudes-tableaux Pno; Preludes Pno; F. Schubert:Impromptus (4); R. Wagner:Parsifal (sels) HUN ▲ 31679 [AAD] (16.97)

E. Koroliov (pno)—No. 17 in b♭, Op. 24/4 [Moderato]; No. 41 in c#, Op. 63/3 [allegretto]; No. 27 in e, Op. 41/2 [andantino] *(rec 1991)* ("Composers & Their Star Signs: Pisces") † Nocturnes Pno; G. F. Handel:Suites de Pièces (8) Hpd, HWV 426-33; M. Ravel:Pavane pour une infante défunte; Qt Strs; Sonatine Pno; H. Wolf:Gedichte von Goethe TACE ▲ 23

D. Lipatti (pno)—Mazurkas Pno [No. 32 in c#, Op. 50/3] *(rec Switzerland, July 3-12, 1950)* † Barcarolle Pno, Op. 60; Nocturnes Pno; Waltzes Pno EMIC ▲ 66956 [ADD] (11.97)

A. B. Michelangeli (pno)—No. 25 in b, Op. 33/4 † Berceuse, Op. 57; J. S. Bach:Italian Con, BWV 971; Beethoven:Con 5 Pno, Op. 73; E. Grieg:Con Pno, Op. 16; Lyric Pieces; D. Scarlatti:Sons Kbd; Tomeoni:Allegro Pno IMMM (Magic Master series) ▲ 37042 (6.97)

A. B. Michelangeli (pno)—No. 47 in a, Op. 68/2 † Scherzos Pno; Debussy:Images (6) Pno; Galuppi:Presto; Liszt:Con 1 Pno, S.124; Vivaldi:Music of Vivaldi IMMM (Magic Master series) ▲ 37007 (6.97)

G. Montero (pno)—No. 41 in c#, Op. 63/3 *(rec live Montreal Chopin Competition, Canada, 1995)* ("In Concert at Montreal") † Nocturnes Pno; Polonaises-fant, Op. 61; Liszt:Paraphrase on Verdi; S. Rachmaninoff:Preludes Pno; Son 2 Pno, Op. 36 PALE ▲ 501 (17.97)

I. Moravec (pno) *(rec 1969)* ("Ivan Moravec Plays Chopin, Vol. 2") † Ballades (4) Pno VAIA ▲ 1092 (16.97)

L. Mozdzer (pno)—No. 14 in g, Op. 24/1; No. 15 in C, Op. 24/2; No. 23 in D, Op. 33/2; No. 48 in F, Op. 68/3; No. 13 in a, Op. 17/4 ("Tomorrow: Impressions") † Études Pno; Contredanse; Nocturnes Pno; Prelude in A♭, Op. posth.; Preludes (24) Pno, Op. 28 OPUS (Chopin Vol. 9) ▲ 2014 (18.97)

I. J. Paderewski (pno)—No. 13 in a, Op. 17/4; No. 23 in D, Op. 33/2; No. 37 in A, Op. 59/2; No. 38 in f#, Op. 59/3; No. 41 in c#, Op. 63/3 *(rec 1912-30)* ("Ignacy Jan Paderewski") † Études Pno; Berceuse, Op. 57; Funeral March in b♭; Nocturnes Pno; Polonaise 2 Pno, Op. 26/2; Polonaise 3 Pno, Op. 40/1; Preludes (24) Pno, Op. 28; Waltzes Pno; Liszt:Études d'exécution transcendante (6), S.140; Études de concert (3), S.144; Hungarian Rhaps, S.244; Trans, Arrs & Paraphrases; I. J. Paderewski:Minuet; F. Schubert:Impromptus (4) PPHI (Great Pianists of the 20th Century) 2-▲ 456919 (22.97)

M. Perahia (pno) † Études Pno; Ballade 1 Pno, Op. 23; Ballade 2 Pno, Op. 38; Ballade 3 Pno, Op. 47; Ballade 4 Pno, Op. 52; Nocturnes Pno; Waltzes Pno SNYC ▲ 64399 [DDD] (16.97) COL △ 64399 [DDD]

S. Richter (pno)—No. 4 in c, Op. 6/4 *(rec 1992)* † Polonaise 1 Pno, Op. 26/1; Polonaise 3 Pno, Op. 40/1; Polonaises-fant, Op. 61; A. Scriabin:Dances (2) Pno, Op. 73; Fant Pno, Op. 28; Poème-nocturne Pno, Op. 61; Vers la flamme, Op. 72 LV ▲ 441 (17.97)

M. Rosenthal (pno)—No. 41 in c#, Op. 63/3; No. 17 in b♭, Op. 24/4; No. 42 in G, Op. 67/1; No. 41 in c#, Op. 63/3 *(rec May 29, 1929)* † Études Pno; Berceuse, Op. 57; Con 1 Pno, Op. 11; Waltzes Pno; Liszt:Trans, Arrs & Paraphrases; M. Rosenthal:Papillons BPS ▲ 40 (m) [ADD] (16.97)

A. Rubinstein (pno)—No. 26 in c#, Op. 41/1; No. 27 in e, Op. 41/2; No. 28 in B, Op. 41/3; No. 29 in A♭, Op. 41/4; No. 30 in G, Op. 50/1; No. 31 in A♭, Op. 50/2; No. 32 in c#, Op. 50/3; No. 33 in B, Op. 56/1; No. 34 in C, Op. 56/2; No. 35 in c, Op. 56/3; No. 36 in a, Op. 59/1; No. 37 in A, Op. 59/2; No. 38 in f#, Op. 59/3; No. 39 in B, Op. 63/1; No. 40 in f, Op. 63/2; No. 41 in c#, Op. 63/3; No. 42 in G, Op. 67/1; No. 43 in g, Op. 67/2; No. 44 in C, Op. 67/3; No. 45 in a, Op. 67/4; No. 46 in C, Op. 68/1; No. 47 in a, Op. 68/2; No. 48 in F, Op. 68/3; No. 49 in f, Op. 68/4; No. 50 in a, "Notre temps"; No. 51 in a, "A Emile Gaillard" ("Mazurkas, Vol 2") MTAL ▲ 48017 (6.97)

A. Rubinstein (pno)—No. 13 in a, Op. 17/4; No. 23 in D, Op. 33/2; No. 33 in B, Op. 56/1 *(rec Abbey Road, England, Nov 13, 1938)* ("The Legendary Rubinstein") † Barcarolle Pno, Op. 60; Berceuse, Op. 57; Nocturnes Pno; Polonaise 3 Pno, Op. 40/1; Polonaise 6 Pno, Op. 53; Scherzos Pno; Waltzes Pno EMIC ▲ 67007 (m) [ADD] (11.97)

CHOPIN, FRÉDÉRIC (cont.)

Mazurkas for Piano (cont.)

A. Rubinstein (pno) † Con 1 Pno, Op. 11; Con 2 Pno, Op. 21; Nocturnes Pno; Scherzos Pno EMIC 5-▲ 64933 (52.97)

A. Rubinstein (pno) RCAV (Red Seal) 2-▲ 5614 [ADD] (30.97)

G. Sokolov (pno), C. Coin (cnd), Mosaïques Ensemble—No. 11 in e, Op. 17/2; No. 13 in a, Op. 17/4; No. 27 in e, Op. 41/2; No. 15 in C, Op. 24/2 † Études Pno; Con 2 Pno, Op. 21; Nocturnes Pno; Polonaise 5 Pno, Op. 44; Preludes (24) Pno, Op. 28; Son Pno in b♭, Op. 35; Waltzes Pno OPUS (Chopin Vol. 5) ▲ 2010 (18.97)

F. Ts'ong (pno) SNYC ▲ 53246 [DDD] (14.97)

F. Ts'ong (pno)—No. 23 in D, Op. 33/2 † Études Pno; Fant-Impromptu, Op. 66; Intro & Polonaise, Op. 3; Nocturnes Pno; Polonaise 3 Pno, Op. 40/1; Polonaise 6 Pno, Op. 53; Preludes (24) Pno, Op. 28; Son Pno in b♭, Op. 35; Waltzes Pno SNYC ▲ 51338 [ADD] (7.97)

various artists—No. 23 in D, Op. 33/2; No. 5 in B♭, Op. 7/1; No. 14 in g, Op. 24/1 † Études Pno; Con 2 Pno, Op. 21; Polonaise 5 Pno, Op. 44; Preludes (24) Pno, Op. 28; Son Pno in b♭, Op. 35; Son Vc OPUS (Chopin Exploration Vol. 10 (Excerpts from Vols. 1-9)) ▲ 2015 (7.97)

Mazurkas (4) for Piano

A. R. El Bacha (pno)—No. 5 in B♭, Op. 7/1; No. 10 in B♭, Op. 17/1; No. 11 in e, Op. 17/2; No. 12 in A♭, Op. 17/3; No. 13 in a, Op. 17/4 ("El Bacha Plays Chopin, Vol. 4") † Études Pno; Allegro de concert, Op. 46; Ballade 1 Pno, Op. 23; Rondos (4) Pno; Waltzes Pno FORL ▲ 16785 (16.97)

I. Biret (pno)—No. 30 in G, Op. 50/1; No. 5 in B♭, Op. 7/1; No. 10 in B♭, Op. 17/1; No. 8 in A♭, Op. 7/4; No. 12 in A♭, Op. 17/3; No. 23 in D, Op. 33/2 *(rec 1991)* † Rondos (4) Pno; Rondos (4) Pno, Op. 73; Var 6 Pno; Vars in A, ('Souvenir de Paganini'); Vars on a Theme from La Cenerentola; Vars on Mozart, Op. 2 NXIN ▲ 550367 [DDD] (5.97)

Mazurkas for Piano

A. R. El Bacha (pno)—No. 5 in B♭, Op. 7/1; No. 10 in B♭, Op. 17/1; No. 11 in e, Op. 17/2; No. 12 in A♭, Op. 17/3; No. 13 in a, Op. 17/4 ("El Bacha Plays Chopin, Vol. 4") † Études Pno; Allegro de concert, Op. 46; Ballade 1 Pno, Op. 23; Rondos (4) Pno; Waltzes Pno FORL ▲ 16785 (16.97)

I. Biret (pno)—No. 30 in G, Op. 50/1; No. 5 in B♭, Op. 7/1; No. 10 in B♭, Op. 17/1; No. 8 in A♭, Op. 7/4; No. 12 in A♭, Op. 17/3; No. 23 in D, Op. 33/2 *(rec 1991)* † Rondos (4) Pno; Rondos (4) Pno, Op. 73; Var 6 Pno; Vars in A, ('Souvenir de Paganini'); Vars on a Theme from La Cenerentola; Vars on Mozart, Op. 2 NXIN ▲ 550367 [DDD] (5.97)

E. Gabriel (pno)—No. 23 in D, Op. 33/2; No. 25 in b, Op. 33/4; No. 32 in c#, Op. 50/3; No. 19 in b/f#, Op. 30/2 † Nocturnes Pno; Polonaise 2 Pno, Op. 26/2; Polonaise 3 Pno, Op. 40/1; Son Pno in b, Op. 58; Waltzes Pno QUER ▲ 9822 (18.97)

E. Koroliov (pno)—No. 17 in b♭, Op. 24/4 [Moderato]; No. 41 in c#, Op. 63/3 [allegretto]; No. 27 in e, Op. 41/2 [andantino] *(rec 1991)* ("Composers & Their Star Signs: Pisces") † Nocturnes Pno; G. F. Handel:Suites de Pièces (8) Hpd, HWV 426-33; M. Ravel:Pavane pour une infante défunte; Qt Strs; Sonatine Pno; H. Wolf:Gedichte von Goethe TACE ▲ 23

J. Olejniczak (pno), Andrzej Jagodzinski Trio—No. 43 in g, Op. 67/2 ("Jazz: Metamorphoses") † Études Pno; Nocturnes Pno; Polonaise 4 Pno, Op. 40/2; Preludes (24) Pno, Op. 28 OPUS (Chopin Vol. 8) ▲ 2013 (18.97)

M. Rosenthal (pno)—No. 41 in c#, Op. 63/3; No. 17 in b♭, Op. 24/4; No. 42 in G, Op. 67/1; No. 41 in c#, Op. 63/3 *(rec Mar 3, 1931)* † Études Pno; Berceuse, Op. 57; Con 1 Pno, Op. 11; Waltzes Pno; Liszt:Trans, Arrs & Paraphrases; M. Rosenthal:Papillons BPS ▲ 40 (m) [ADD] (16.97)

A. Rubinstein (pno)—No. 26 in c#, Op. 41/1; No. 27 in e, Op. 41/2; No. 28 in B, Op. 41/3; No. 29 in A♭, Op. 41/4; No. 30 in G, Op. 50/1; No. 31 in A♭, Op. 50/2; No. 32 in c#, Op. 50/3; No. 33 in B, Op. 56/1; No. 34 in C, Op. 56/2; No. 35 in c, Op. 56/3; No. 36 in a, Op. 59/1; No. 37 in A, Op. 59/2; No. 38 in f#, Op. 59/3; No. 39 in B, Op. 63/1; No. 40 in f, Op. 63/2; No. 41 in c#, Op. 63/3; No. 42 in G, Op. 67/1; No. 43 in g, Op. 67/2; No. 44 in C, Op. 67/3; No. 45 in a, Op. 67/4; No. 46 in C, Op. 68/1; No. 47 in a, Op. 68/2; No. 48 in F, Op. 68/3; No. 49 in f, Op. 68/4; No. 50 in a, "Notre temps"; No. 51 in a, "A Emile Gaillard" ("Mazurkas, Vol 2") MTAL ▲ 48017 (6.97)

A. Rubinstein (pno)—No. 13 in a, Op. 17/4; No. 23 in D, Op. 33/2; No. 33 in B, Op. 56/1 *(rec Abbey Road, England, May 10, 1939)* ("The Legendary Rubinstein") † Barcarolle Pno, Op. 60; Berceuse, Op. 57; Nocturnes Pno; Polonaise 3 Pno, Op. 40/1; Polonaise 6 Pno, Op. 53; Scherzos Pno; Waltzes Pno EMIC ▲ 67007 (m) [ADD] (11.97)

Music of Chopin

M. Argerich (pno)—Prelude in c#, Op. 45; Prelude in A♭, Op. posth.; Mazurkas Pno [No. 36 in a, Op. 59/1; No. 37 in A, Op. 59/2; No. 38 in f#, Op. 59/3]; Scherzos Pno [No. 3 in c#, Op. 39] ("Chopin Compact Edition, Vol. 5") † Preludes (24) Pno, Op. 28 DEUT ▲ 31584 [ADD] (9.97)

H. Bauer (pno)—Fant-Impromptu, Op. 66; Fantaisie Pno, Op. 49; Nocturnes Pno [No. 2 in E♭, Op. 9/2]; Waltzes Pno [No. 6 in D♭, Op. 64/1, "Minute"; No. 4 in F, Op. 34/3]; Mazurkas Pno [No. 23 in D, Op. 33/2]; Scherzos Pno [No. 3 in c#, Op. 39]; Nouvelles études [No. 1 in f; No. 2 in D♭]; Polonaise 1 Pno, Op. 26/1 † R. Schumann:Kinderszenen Pno, Op. 15; Novelettes, Op. 21 NIMB ▲ 8817 [DDD] (11.97)

J. Hofmann (pno), V. Perlemuter (pno) *(Nocturnes Pno [No. 8 in D♭, Op. 27/2; No. 5 in F#, Op. 15/2])*, J. Hofmann (pno) *(Polonaise 3 Pno, Op. 40/1; Polonaise 6 Pno, Op. 53)*, J. Hofmann (pno), I. Friedman (pno) *(Waltzes Pno [No. 5 in A♭, Op. 42; No. 6 in D♭, Op. 64/1, "Minute"])*, V. Perlemuter (pno) *(Études Pno [No. 5 in G♭, Op. 10/5, "Black Keys"; No. 3 in E, Op. 10/3, "Tristesse"; No. 12 in c, Op. 10/12, "Revolutionary"]; Preludes (24) Pno, Op. 28 [No. 20 in c; No. 4 in e; No. 15 in D♭, "Raindrop"]; Sylphides)*, V. Perlemuter (pno), S. Cherkassky (pno) *(Mazurkas Pno [No. 37 in A, Op. 59/2; No. 15 in C, Op. 24/2; No. 25 in b, Op. 33/4])*, S. Cherkassky (pno) *(Son Pno in b, Op. 58)*, B. D. Ascoli (pno) *(Ballade 1 Pno, Op. 23)*, M. Deyanova (pno) *(Fant-Impromptu, Op. 66)* ("Whad'ya Know About Chopin?") † Vars on Mozart, Op. 2 NIMB ▲ 4003 [ADD] (11.97)

N. Magaloff (pno), C. Arrau (pno), D. Zinman (cnd), London PO, D. Zinman (cnd), Rotterdam PO *(Con 2 Pno, Op. 21 [Larghetto]; Berceuse, Op. 57; Nocturnes Pno [No. 1 in b♭, Op. 9/1; No. 2 in E♭, Op. 9/2; No. 5 in F#, Op. 15/2; No. 8 in D♭, Op. 27/2; No. 20 in c#, Op. posth.; No. 21 in c, Op. posth.]; Preludes (24) Pno, Op. 28 [No. 7 in A; No. 4 in e]; Waltzes Pno [No. 9 in A♭, Op. 69/1, "L'adieu"]; Con 1 Pno, Op. 11 [Rondo (Vivace)])*, N. Magaloff (pno) *(Andante Spianato & Grand Polonaise, Op. 22)* ("Chopin & Champagne") PPHI ▲ 46629 (9.97) ▮ 46629 (5.98)

S. Richter (pno) *(Ballade 3 Pno, Op. 47; Ballade 4 Pno, Op. 52)*, M. Rostropovich (vc), M. Argerich (pno) *(Intro & Polonaise, Op. 3; Son Vc, Op. 65)* ("Chopin Compact Edition, Vol. 4") DEUT ▲ 31583 (9.97)

C. Veen (vc), H. Visser (gtr), P. Vlasman (hp)—Nocturnes Pno [No. 7 in c#, Op. 27/1; No. 8 in D♭, Op. 27/2; No. 2 in E♭, Op. 9/2]; Mazurkas Pno [No. 41 in c#, Op. 63/3]; Preludes (24) Pno, Op. 28 [No. 15 in D♭, "Raindrop"; No. 4 in e; No. 6 in b; No. 23 in F]; Études Pno [No. 3 in E, Op. 10/3, "Tristesse"; No. 7 in C, Op. 10/7]; Marche Funebre in c, Op. 72/2 *(rec Oct & Nov 1995)* ("Stringled: Visser Meets Chopin") OREA ▲ 5283 [DDD] (11.97)

T. Zagorovskaya (pno), V. Vishnevskaya (pno) *(Waltzes Pno [No. 1 in E♭, Op. 18, "Grand Valse Brillante"; No. 6 in D♭, Op. 64/1, "Minute"])*, V. Vishnevskaya (pno) *(Mazurkas Pno [No. 6 in a, Op. 7/2]; Fant-Impromptu, Op. 66)*, T. Zagorovskaya (pno) *(Polonaise 1 Pno, Op. 26/1; Preludes (24) Pno, Op. 28)*, V. Postnikova (pno), USSR SO *(Con 1 Pno, Op. 11)*, A. Orlovetsky (pno) *(Ballade 1 Pno, Op. 23)*, P. Egorov (pno) *(Études Pno [No. 12 in c, Op. 10/12, "Revolutionary"])*, A. Tchernu (pno), St. Petersburg State Academic Cappella SO *(Con 2 Pno, Op. 21)* PUBM (Majestic) ▲ 1027 [DDD] (4.97)

various artists—Con 1 Pno, Op. 11; Con 2 Pno, Op. 21; Son Pno in b♭, Op. 35; Son Pno in b, Op. 58; Mazurkas Pno [No. 36 in a, Op. 59/1; No. 37 in A, Op. 59/2; No. 38 in f#, Op. 59/3; No. 18 in c, Op. 30/1; No. 19 in b/f#, Op. 30/2; No. 20 in D♭, Op. 30/3; No. 21 in c#, Op. 30/4]; Polonaise 6 Pno, Op. 53; Ballade 2 Pno, Op. 38; Scherzos Pno [No. 1 in b, Op. 20; No. 2 in b♭/D♭, Op. 31]; Preludes (24) Pno, Op. 28 [No. 13 in F#; No. 14 in e♭; No. 15 in D♭, "Raindrop"; No. 16 in b♭; No. 17 in A♭; No. 18 in f; No. 21 in B♭; No. 22 in g; No. 23 in F; No. 24 in d]; Ballade 1 Pno, Op. 23 *(rec Warsaw, Poland)* ("Great Chopin Performers") LALI 5-▲ 15961 (20.97)

various artists *(Barcarolle Pno, Op. 60; Berceuse, Op. 57; Études Pno [No. 3 in E, Op. 10/3, "Tristesse"; No. 13 in A♭, Op. 25/1]; Nocturnes Pno [No. 17 in B, Op. 62/1; No. 8 in D♭, Op. 27/2]; Preludes (24) Pno, Op. 28 [No. 7 in A; No. 11 in B; No. 15 in D♭, "Raindrop"; No. 23 in F; No. 13 in F#; No. 3 in G]; Nouvelles études [No. 2 in D♭]; Waltzes Pno [No. 9 in A♭, Op. 69/1, "L'adieu"])*, E. Ormandy (cnd), Philadelphia Orch *(Con 1 Pno, Op. 11; Con 2 Pno, Op. 21)* ("Chopin for Relaxation") RCAV ▲ 63423 (11.97) ▮ 63423 (6.98)

Nocturnes (21) for Piano (Nos. 1-19, Opp. 9, 15, 27, 32, 37, 48, 55, 62, 72; No. 20 in c#, 1830; No. 21 in c, 1837)

C. Arrau (pno) † Impromptus (4) PPHI (Duo) 2-▲ 456336 (17.97)

V. Ashkenazy (pno) PPHI (Double Decker) 2-▲ 452579 (17.97)

D. Barenboim (pno) *(rec 1982)* DEUT (Double) 2-▲ 37464 [DDD] (17.97)

D. Barenboim (pno) *(rec Berlin, Germany, Jan & May 1981)* DEUT (2-Fers) 2-▲ 453022 [DDD] (17.97)

I. Biret (pno)—No. 1 in b♭, Op. 9/1; No. 2 in E♭, Op. 9/2; No. 3 in B, Op. 9/3; No. 4 in F, Op. 15/1; No. 5 in F#, Op. 15/2; No. 6 in g, Op. 15/6; No. 7 in c#, Op. 27/1; No. 8 in D♭, Op. 27/2; No. 9 in B, Op. 32/1; No. 10 in A♭, Op. 32/2; No. 20 in c#, Op. posth.; No. 21 in c, Op. posth. *(rec 1991)* ("Chopin: Nocturnes, Vol. 1") NXIN ▲ 550356 [DDD] (5.97)

J. Browning (pno)—No. 8 in D♭, Op. 27/2 *(rec New York, NY, July 28-31 & Aug 4-6, 20, 1958)* † Études Pno; Waltzes Pno; J. S. Bach:Partitas Hpd; Busoni:Bach Trans Pno; Debussy:Images (6) Pno; Liszt:Mephisto Waltz 3 Pno, S.216; Rimsky-Korsakov:Tale of Tsar Saltan (orch sels); F. Schubert:Impromptus (4) Pno EMIC ▲ 67017 [ADD] (11.97)

L. Bustani (pno)—No. 8 in D♭, Op. 27/2; No. 13 in c, Op. 48/1 *(rec Maria Minor Church, Utrecht, Netherlands, Oct 1998)* † Fantaisie Pno, Op. 49; Scherzos Pno; R. Schumann:Kreisleriana, Op. 16 CSOC ▲ 4230

G. Casalino (pno)—Nocturnes Pno [No. 14 in f#, Op. 48/2; No. 2 in E♭, Op. 9/2; No. 19 in e, Op. 72] *(rec May 1992)* † E. Grieg:Son Pno, Op. 7; S. Rachmaninoff:Prelude in c#, Op. 3/2; F. Schubert:Impromptus (4); Impromptus (4) Pno STRV ▲ 101 [DDD] (16.97)

▲ = CD ♦ = Enhanced CD △ = MD ▮ = Cassette Tape ▯ = DCC

CHOPIN, FRÉDÉRIC (cont.)

Nocturnes (21) for Piano (Nos. 1-19, Opp. 9, 15, 27, 32, 37, 48, 55, 62, 72; No. 20 in c#, 1830; No. 21 in c, 1837) (cont.)

S. Cherkassky (pno)—Nocturnes Pno [No. 8 in D♭, Op. 27/2; No. 19 in e, Op. 72] *(rec Wyastone Leys Monmouth, England, 1984-85)* ("Art of the Encore") † Andante Spianato & Grand Polonaise, Op. 22; Mazurkas Pno; Liszt:Harmonies poétiques et religieuses, S.173; Hungarian Rhaps, S.244; F. Schubert:Impromptus (4) Pno NIMB ▲ 7708 [DDD] (11.97)

J. Coop (pno)—No. 8 in D♭, Op. 27/2 *(rec Toronto, Canada)* ("The Romantic Piano") † Etudes (24) Pno, Opp. 10 & 25; Mazurkas Pno; J. Brahms:Pieces (6) Pno, Op. 118; Waltzes (16) Pno, Op. 39; Debussy:Isle joyeuse; Suite bergamasque; Liszt:Études de concert (3), S.144; Liebesträume, S.541; Mendelssohn (-Bartholdy):Pno Music (misc); S. Rachmaninoff:Etudes-tableaux Pno, Opp. 33 & 39; Preludes (23) Pno, Opp. 23 & 32; R. Schumann:Kinderszenen Pno, Op. 15 MUVI ▲ 1015 [DDD] (16.97)

A. Cortot (pno)—No. 16 in E♭, Op. 55/2 *(rec Royce Hall, University of California, Los Angeles, CA)* † Etudes Pno; Impromptu in G♭, Op. 51; Preludes (24) Pno, Op. 28; J. S. Bach:Con 5 Hpd, BWV 1056; Beethoven:Son 29 Pno, Op. 106; Son 30 Pno, Op. 109; Chabrier:Feuillet d'album; Pièces pittoresques; Liszt:Au Bord d'une Source; Trans, Arrs & Paraphrases; A. Scriabin:Etudes (12) Pno, Op. 8 KLAV ▲ 11096 [ADD] (18.97)

J. R. Crossan (pno)—Nocturnes Pno [No. 16 in E♭, Op. 55/2; No. 19 in e, Op. 72; No. 14 in f#, Op. 48/2; No. 4 in F, Op. 15/1; No. 8 in D♭, Op. 27/2; No. 7 in c#, Op. 27/1; No. 13 in c, Op. 48/1] *(rec Los Angeles, CA, Sept 6 & 13, 1993)* ("Chopin-Liszt") † Liszt:Ballade 2, S.171; Consolations (6), S.172; Légendes, S.175; Pno Music (misc); Valse impromptu, S.213; Valses oubliées (4), S.215 CMB ▲ 1073 [DDD]

J. Darré (pno)—No. 8 in D♭, Op. 27/2 *(rec Konzerthaus Vienna, Germany, June 1966)* ("The Four Scherzi") † Scherzos Pno VC ▲ 95 [AAD] (13.97)

I. Friedman (pno)—No. 16 in E♭, Op. 55/2 ("Highlights 1925-36 From His Discography") † Études Pno; Impromptu in F#, Op. 36; Mazurkas Pno; Polonaise 6 Pno, Op. 53; Son Pno in b♭, Op. 35; Waltzes Pno; Beethoven:Son 14 Pno, Op. 27/2; I. Friedman:Danse; Music Box, Op. 33/3; J. N. Hummel:Rondo Pno, Op. 11; Liszt:Trans, Arrs & Paraphrases; Mendelssohn (-Bartholdy):Fants Pno, Op. 16; Shield:Old English Menuet APR (Signature Series) ▲ 5508 [ADD] (18.97)

I. Friedman (pno)—No. 16 in E♭, Op. 55/2 *(rec Nov 23, 1936)* † Ballade 3 Pno, Op. 47; Impromptu in F#, Op. 36; Mazurkas Pno; Liszt:Hungarian Rhaps, S.244; Mendelssohn (-Bartholdy):Lieder ohne Worte BPS ▲ 44 (m) [ADD] (16.97)

I. Friedman (pno)—No. 11 in g, Op. 37/1; No. 17 in B, Op. 62/1 † Polonaise 6 Pno, Op. 53; Liszt:Grandes études de Paganini, S.141; Hungarian Rhaps, S.244; Réminiscences de Don Juan Pno, S.418 NIMB (Grand Piano) ▲ 8805 [DDD] (11.97)

E. Gabriel (pno)—No. 19 in e, Op. 72 † Mazurkas Pno; Polonaise 2 Pno, Op. 26/2; Polonaise 3 Pno, Op. 40/1; Son Pno in b, Op. 58; Waltzes Pno QUER ▲ 9822 (18.97)

W. Gieseking (pno)—Nocturnes Pno [No. 3 in B, Op. 9/3; No. 5 in F#, Op. 15/2] *(rec 1924-55)* ("Gieseking: A Retrospective, Vol. 3") † Polonaise 6 Pno, Op. 53; J. Brahms:Rhaps (2) Pno, Op. 79; Casella:Son Pno, Op. 28; W. A. Mozart:Con 9 Pno, K.271; M. Ravel:Jeux d'eau PHS ▲ 9038 (17.97)

L. Godowsky (pno)—No. 1 in b♭, Op. 9/1; No. 11 in g, Op. 37/1; No. 12 in G, Op. 37/2; No. 14 in f#, Op. 48/2; No. 15 in f, Op. 55/1; No. 19 in e, Op. 72; No. 2 in E♭, Op. 9/2; No. 4 in F, Op. 15/1; No. 5 in F#, Op. 15/2; No. 7 in c#, Op. 27/1; No. 8 in D♭, Op. 27/2; No. 9 in B, Op. 32/1 *(rec 1926-30)* † Études Pno; Scherzos Pno; Son Pno in b♭, Op. 35; Beethoven:Son 26 Pno, Op. 81a; L. Godowsky:Transcriptions & Paraphrases; E. Grieg:Ballade Pno, Op. 24; Liszt:Paraphrase on Verdi; R. Schumann:Carnaval, Op. 9 PPHI (Great Pianists of the 20th Century, Vol. 37) 2-▲ 456805 (22.97)

L. Godowsky (pno)—No. 2 in E♭, Op. 9/2 [piano roll recording] ("Great Pianists of the Golden Era") † Ballade 1 Pno, Op. 23; Ballade 3 Pno, Op. 47; Polonaise 5 Pno, Op. 44; Debussy:Danse Pno; Henselt:Berceuse; Lanner:Valses Viennoises; W. A. Mozart:Son 16 Pno, K.545; S. Prokofiev:Pieces (4) Pno, Op. 4; Rimsky-Korsakov:Golden Cockerel (sels) FON ▲ 9008 [DDD] (13.97)

A. Harasiewicz (pno) † Prelude in c#, Op. 45; Prelude in A♭, Op. posth.; Preludes (24) Pno, Op. 28 PPHI (Duo) 2-▲ 42266 (17.97)

K. Jablonski (pno), E. Dubourg—No. 3 in B, Op. 9/3; No. 20 in c#, Op. posth. ("Masters of Classical Music, Vol. 8: Frederic Chopin") † Études Pno; Mazurkas Pno; Nocturnes (21) Pno; Preludes (24) Pno, Op. 28; Scherzos Pno; Waltzes Pno LALI ▲ 15808 [DDD] (3.97)

K. H. Kadduri (vc), O. Morzsa (pno)—No. 2 in E♭, Op. 9/2; No. 3 in B, Op. 9/3; No. 4 in F, Op. 15/1; No. 5 in F#, Op. 15/2; No. 7 in c#, Op. 27/1; No. 8 in D♭, Op. 27/2; No. 9 in B, Op. 32/1; No. 10 in A♭, Op. 32/2; No. 11 in g, Op. 37/1; No. 13 in c, Op. 48/1; No. 16 in E♭, Op. 55/2; No. 18 in E, Op. 62/2; No. 20 in c#, Op. posth.; No. 19 in e, Op. 72 [arr Grützmacher] *(rec Hungaraton Studio, Hungary)* HUN ▲ 31814 [DDD] (16.97)

W. Kapell (pno)—No. 16 in E♭, Op. 55/2 † Mazurkas Pno; Polonaises-fant, Op. 61; A. Copland:Son Pno; Mussorgsky:Pictures at an Exhibition; D. Scarlatti:Sons Kbd; R. Schumann:Kinderszenen Pno, Op. 15 RCAV ▲ 68997 [ADD] (16.97)

E. L. Kaplan (pno)—No. 8 in D♭, Op. 27/2 *(rec Los Angeles, CA, Sep 1992)* † Fantaisie Pno, Op. 49; Mazurkas Pno; Waltzes Pno; R. Schumann:Carnaval, Op. 9 CMB ▲ 1098 (16.97)

P. Katin (pno) ICC 2-▲ 6702357 (17.97)

P. Katin (pno)—No. 7 in c#, Op. 27/1 † Polonaise 5 Pno, Op. 44; Son Pno in b, Op. 58 HALM ▲ 35014 (6.97)

N. Kokinos (pno)—No. 8 in D♭, Op. 27/2; No. 17 in B, Op. 62/1; No. 7 in c#, Op. 27/1; No. 1 in b♭, Op. 9/1; No. 9 in B, Op. 32/1; No. 15 in f, Op. 55/1; No. 5 in F#, Op. 15/2; No. 14 in f#, Op. 48/2; No. 10 in A♭, Op. 32/2; No. 19 in e, Op. 72; No. 10 in A♭, Op. 32/2; No. 11 in g, Op. 37/1; No. 4 in F, Op. 15/1; No. 2 in E♭, Op. 9/2 ANDP ▲ 9991 (14.97)

E. Koroliov (pno) *(rec 1991)* ("Composers & Their Star Signs: Pisces") † Mazurkas Pno; G. F. Handel:Suites de Pièces (8) Hpd, HWV 426-33; M. Ravel:Pavane pour une infante défunte; Qt Strs; Sonatine Pno; H. Wolf:Gedichte von Goethe TACE ▲ 23

S. B. Kovacevich (pno)—No. 17 in B, Op. 62/1; No. 18 in E, Op. 62/2 *(rec 1972)* † Impromptu in G♭, Op. 51; B. Bartók:Con 2 Pno, Sz.95; Out of Doors, Sz.81; Sonatina Pno, Sz.55; Beethoven:Son 5 Pno, Op. 10/1; R. R. Bennett:Con Pno; J. Brahms:Pieces (4) Pno, Op. 119; I. Stravinsky:Con Pno & Ww PPHI (Great Pianists of the 20th Century, Vol. 61) 2-▲ 456880 (22.97)

E. Kupiec (pno)—No. 3 in B, Op. 9/3; No. 5 in F#, Op. 15/2; No. 6 in g, Op. 15/6; No. 9 in B, Op. 32/1; No. 13 in c, Op. 48/1; No. 14 in f#, Op. 48/2; No. 16 in E♭, Op. 55/2; No. 17 in B, Op. 62/1; No. 18 in E, Op. 62/2 ("Nocturnes, Vol. 2") KSCH ▲ 365002 (16.97)

E. Kupiec (pno)—No. 1 in b♭, Op. 9/1; No. 2 in E♭, Op. 9/2; No. 4 in F, Op. 15/1; No. 7 in c#, Op. 27/1; No. 20 in c#, Op. posth.; No. 21 in c, Op. posth. ("Nocturnes, Vol. 1") KSCH ▲ 317972 (16.97)

A. Lear (pno)—Nocturnes Pno; Nocturnes Pno *(rec Brandon Hill Bristol, England, Nov 24, 1993)* ("The Original Chopin") † Andante Spianato & Grand Polonaise, Op. 22; Barcarolle Pno, Op. 60; Fant-Impromptu, Op. 66; Fantaisie Pno, Op. 49; Polonaise 5 Pno, Op. 44 APR ▲ 5551 [DDD] (19.97)

E. Leonskaja (pno) TELC 2-▲ 72297 (33.97)

E. Leonskaja (pno) TELC (Ultima) 2-▲ 18949 (16.97)

K. Lifschitz (pno)—Nocturnes Pno [No. 11 in g, Op. 37/1; No. 12 in G, Op. 37/2] ("Live in Milano") † Polonaise 5 Pno, Op. 44; W. A. Mozart:Rondo Pno, K.511; M. Ravel:Gaspard de la nuit DNN ▲ 78908 [DDD] (16.97)

D. Lipatti (pno)—No. 8 in D♭, Op. 27/2 *(rec Abbey Road, London, England, Feb 20, 1947)* † Barcarolle Pno, Op. 60; Mazurkas Pno; Waltzes Pno EMIC ▲ 66956 [ADD] (11.97)

D. Lipatti (pno)—No. 8 in D♭, Op. 27/2 *(rec live, 1950)* † Études Pno; Con 1 Pno, Op. 11; Waltzes Pno; J. S. Bach:Con 2 Hpd, BWV 1053 PALE ▲ 509 (17.97)

D. Lipatti (pno)—No. 8 in D♭, Op. 27/2 † Son Pno in b, Op. 58; Waltzes Pno; J. S. Bach:Jesu, bleibet meine Freude; E. Grieg:Con Pno, Op. 16; Liszt:Sonetti (3) del Petrarca, S.158; D. Scarlatti:Sons Kbd APR ▲ 5509 [ADD] (18.97)

I. Mejoueva (pno)—No. 15 in f, Op. 55/1; No. 16 in E♭, Op. 55/2 † Scherzos Pno; M. Ravel:Miroirs; A. Scriabin:Son 2 Pno, Op. 19 DNN ▲ 18074 (16.97)

B. Moiseiwitsch (pno)—No. 18 in E, Op. 62/2; No. 12 in G, Op. 37/2 *(rec 1958)* † Ballade 3 Pno, Op. 47; Ballade 4 Pno, Op. 52; Barcarolle Pno, Op. 60; Fant-Impromptu, Op. 66; Scherzos Pno; Kabalevsky:Son 3 Pno, Op. 46; Liszt:Études de concert (3), S.144; Medtner:Son Pno in g, Op. 22; Mendelssohn (-Bartholdy):Midsummer Night's Dream (sels); S. Prokofiev:Pieces (4) Pno, Op. 4; Toccata Pno, Op. 11; S. Rachmaninoff:Con 2 Pno, Op. 18; Moments musicaux, Op. 16; Preludes Pno PPHI (Great Pianists of the 20th Century) 2-▲ 456907 (22.97)

G. Montero (pno)—No. 1 in b♭, Op. 9/1; No. 5 in F#, Op. 15/2 *(rec live Montreal Chopin Competition, Canada, 1995)* ("In Concert at Montreal") † Mazurkas Pno; Polonaises-fant, Op. 61; Liszt:Paraphrase on Verdi; S. Rachmaninoff:Preludes Pno; Son 2 Pno, Op. 36 PALE ▲ 501 (17.97)

G. Montero (pno)—No. 13 in c, Op. 48/1; No. 16 in E♭, Op. 55/2 † Fant-Impromptu, Op. 66; Polonaise 1 Pno, Op. 26/1; Polonaise 2 Pno, Op. 26/2; Polonaise 6 Pno, Op. 53; Scherzos Pno; Son Pno in b♭, Op. 35; Waltzes Pno PALE ▲ 510 (17.97)

I. Moravec (pno) NON 2-▲ 79233 (19.97)

L. Mozdzer (pno)—No. 4 in F, Op. 15/1; No. 6 in g, Op. 15/3 ("Tomorrow: Impressions") † Études Pno; Contredanse; Mazurkas Pno; Prelude in A♭, Op. posth.; Preludes (24) Pno, Op. 28 OPUS (Chopin Vol. 9) ▲ 2014 (18.97)

H. Neuhaus (pno) ("Neuhaus Plays Chopin") † Barcarolle Pno, Op. 60; Con 1 Pno, Op. 11; Impromptus (4); Polonaises-fant, Op. 61 RUS ▲ 15007 [AAD] (12.97)

G. Novaes (pno) *(rec 1950s)* ("Guiomar Novaes Plays Chopin") † Études Pno; Son Pno in b♭, Op. 35 VB3 (Legends) 3-▲ 3501 [ADD] (14.97)

CHOPIN, FRÉDÉRIC (cont.)

Nocturnes (21) for Piano (Nos. 1-19, Opp. 9, 15, 27, 32, 37, 48, 55, 62, 72; No. 20 in c#, 1830; No. 21 in c, 1837) (cont.)

G. Ohlsson (pno) *(rec Purchase Performing Arts Center Theatre C, June 13-15 & Oct 3-5, 1994)* ("The Complete Chopin Piano Works, Vol. 6") ARA 2-▲ 6653 [DDD]

J. Olejniczak (pno), Andrzej Jagodzinski Trio—No. 2 in E♭, Op. 9/2; No. 3 in B, Op. 9/3 ("Jazz: Metamorphoses") † Études Pno; Mazurkas Pno; Polonaise 4 Pno, Op. 40/2; Preludes (24) Pno, Op. 28 OPUS (Chopin Vol. 8) ▲ 2013 (18.97)

E. Ormandy (cnd), Philadelphia Orch—No. 2 in E♭, Op. 9/2 [arr A. Harris] † Études Pno; Borodin:Nocturne Str Orch; Liszt:Liebesträume, S.541; Mendelssohn (-Bartholdy):Lieder, Op. 34; S. Rachmaninoff:Sym 2; Vocalise; Rimsky-Korsakov:Sadko (sels); Scheherazade, Op. 35; P. Tchaikovsky:Qt 1 Strs, Op. 11; Snow Maiden (sels); Songs SNYC ▲ 46355 [ADD/DDD] (9.97)

I. J. Paderewski (pno)—No. 4 in F, Op. 15/1; No. 5 in F#, Op. 15/2; No. 2 in E♭, Op. 9/2 *(rec 1912-30)* ("Ignacy Jan Paderewski") † Études Pno; Berceuse, Op. 57; Funeral March in b♭; Mazurkas Pno; Polonaise 2 Pno, Op. 26/2; Polonaise 3 Pno, Op. 40/1; Preludes (24) Pno, Op. 28; Waltzes Pno; Liszt:Études d'exécution transcendante (6), S.140; Études de concert (3), S.144; Hungarian Rhaps, S.244; Trans, Arrs & Paraphrases; I. J. Paderewski:Minuet; F. Schubert:Impromptus (4) PPHI (Great Pianists of the 20th Century) 2-▲ 456919 (22.97)

M. Perahia (pno) † Études Pno; Ballade 1 Pno, Op. 23; Ballade 2 Pno, Op. 38; Ballade 3 Pno, Op. 47; Ballade 4 Pno, Op. 52; Mazurkas Pno; Waltzes Pno SNYC ▲ 64399 [DDD] (16.97) COL △ 64399 [DDD]

E. Petri (pno) *(rec 1936-51)* ("Petri Egon, Vol. 3") † J. Brahms:Vars & Fugue on a Theme by Handel, Op. 24; Busoni:Albumblätter Pno; Elegien Pno PHS ▲ 9078 [AAD] (17.97)

M. J. Pires (pno) *(rec Munich, Germany & London, England, Jan 1995; Jan, Apr & June 1996)* DEUT 2-▲ 47096 [DDD] (32.97)

D. Pollack (pno)—No. 8 in D♭, Op. 27/2; No. 21 in c, Op. posth. ("First Kiss") † Debussy:Arabesques Pno; Fille aux cheveaux de lin (song); Liszt:Études de concert (3), S.144; Consolations (6), S.172; M. Ravel:Pavane pour une infante défunte; R. Schumann:Carnaval, Op. 9; Kinderszenen Pno, Op. 15; P. Tchaikovsky:Saisons FWIN ▲ 3002 (13.97)

L. Rév (pno) HYP (Dyad) 2-▲ 22013 (18.97)

S. Richter (pno) *(rec July, 1988)* † Études Pno; Polonaises-fant, Op. 61; A. Scriabin:Son 2 Pno, Op. 19; Son 5 Pno, Op. 53 PRAG ▲ 254056 (18.97)

M. Rosenthal (pno)—No. 2 in E♭, Op. 9/2; No. 8 in D♭, Op. 27/2 *(rec 1930-37)* † Berceuse, Op. 57; Con 1 Pno, Op. 11; Preludes (24) Pno, Op. 28 ENPL (Piano Library) ▲ 319 (14.97)

A. Rubinstein (pno)—No. 1 in b♭, Op. 9/1; No. 2 in E♭, Op. 9/2; No. 3 in B, Op. 9/3; No. 4 in F, Op. 15/1; No. 5 in F#, Op. 15/2; No. 6 in g, Op. 15/6; No. 7 in c#, Op. 27/1; No. 8 in D♭, Op. 27/2; No. 9 in B, Op. 32/1; No. 10 in A♭, Op. 32/2; No. 11 in g, Op. 37/1; No. 12 in G, Op. 37/2; No. 13 in c, Op. 48/1; No. 14 in f#, Op. 48/2 *(rec 1936-37)* ENPL (Piano Library) ▲ 225 (13.97)

A. Rubinstein (pno) *(rec 1936-37)* † Con 1 Pno, Op. 11; Con 2 Pno, Op. 21 EMIC 2-▲ 64491 (21.97)

A. Rubinstein (pno) † Con 1 Pno, Op. 11; Con 2 Pno, Op. 21; Mazurkas Pno; Scherzos Pno EMIC 5-▲ 64933 (52.97)

A. Rubinstein (pno) RCAV (Red Seal) 2-▲ 5613 [ADD] (30.97)

A. Rubinstein (pno)—No. 1 in b♭, Op. 9/1; No. 2 in E♭, Op. 9/2; No. 3 in B, Op. 9/3; No. 4 in F, Op. 15/1; No. 5 in F#, Op. 15/2; No. 6 in g, Op. 15/6; No. 7 in c#, Op. 27/1; No. 8 in D♭, Op. 27/2; No. 9 in B, Op. 32/1; No. 10 in A♭, Op. 32/2; No. 11 in g, Op. 37/1; No. 12 in G, Op. 37/2; No. 13 in c, Op. 48/1; No. 14 in f#, Op. 48/2 *(rec 1936-37)* MPLY ▲ 2031 (m) (13.97)

A. Rubinstein (pno)—No. 1 in b♭, Op. 9/1; No. 2 in E♭, Op. 9/2; No. 3 in B, Op. 9/3; No. 4 in F, Op. 15/1; No. 5 in F#, Op. 15/2; No. 6 in g, Op. 15/6; No. 7 in c#, Op. 27/1; No. 8 in D♭, Op. 27/2; No. 10 in A♭, Op. 32/2; No. 11 in g, Op. 37/1; No. 12 in G, Op. 37/2; No. 13 in c, Op. 48/1; No. 14 in f#, Op. 48/2; No. 9 in B, Op. 32/1 *(rec 1930s)* GRM2 (The reocrds of the Century) ▲ 78861 (13.97)

A. Rubinstein (pno)—No. 10 in A♭, Op. 32/2; No. 1 in b♭, Op. 9/1; No. 8 in D♭, Op. 27/2; No. 12 in G, Op. 37/2; No. 17 in B, Op. 62/1 *(rec Abbey Road, England, Oct 1936)* ("The Legendary Rubinstein") † Barcarolle Pno, Op. 60; Berceuse, Op. 57; Mazurkas Pno; Polonaise 3 Pno, Op. 40/1; Polonaise 6 Pno, Op. 53; Scherzos Pno; Waltzes Pno EMIC ▲ 67007 (m) [ADD] (11.97)

A. Rubinstein (pno)—No. 15 in f, Op. 55/1; No. 16 in E♭, Op. 55/2 *(rec 1931-37)* ("Rubinstein on Radio in the Golden Thirties") † Con 1 Pno, Op. 11; Con 2 Pno, Op. 21 RY (The Radio Years) ▲ 101 (16.97)

P. Schmalfuss (pno), D. Tomšič (pno)—No. 1 in b♭, Op. 9/1; No. 2 in E♭, Op. 9/2; No. 3 in B, Op. 9/3; No. 4 in F, Op. 15/1; No. 5 in F#, Op. 15/2; No. 6 in g, Op. 15/6; No. 7 in c#, Op. 27/1; No. 8 in D♭, Op. 27/2; No. 9 in B, Op. 32/1; No. 10 in A♭, Op. 32/2; No. 11 in g, Op. 37/1; No. 12 in G, Op. 37/2 PC ▲ 265044 [DDD] (2.97)

A. Simon (pno) *(rec Elite Recordings NYC, 1982)* VB2 2-▲ 5146 (9.97)

K. Skanavi (pno) † Andante Spianato & Grand Polonaise, Op. 22; Berceuse, Op. 57; Intro & Vars in B♭, Op. 12; Son Pno in b♭, Op. 35 PPR ▲ 224522

G. Sokolov (pno), C. Coin (cnd), Mosaïques Ensemble—No. 13 in c, Op. 48/1 † Études Pno; Con 2 Pno, Op. 21; Mazurkas Pno; Polonaise 5 Pno, Op. 44; Preludes (24) Pno, Op. 28; Son Pno in b♭, Op. 35; Waltzes Pno OPUS (Chopin Vol. 5) ▲ 2010 (18.97)

D. T. Son (pno) ("Complete Nocturnes, Vols. I & II") ANAL 2-▲ 27701

I. Tiegerman (pno)—No. 3 in B, Op. 9/3 *(rec Cairo, Egypt, 1950s)* ("The Lost Legend of Cairo: Radio & Private Recordings") † Ballade 4 Pno, Op. 52; Preludes (24) Pno, Op. 28; Scherzos Pno; Son Pno in b, Op. 58; J. Brahms:Con 2 Pno, Op. 83; Intermezzos (3) Pno, Op. 117; Pieces (6) Pno, Op. 118; Pieces (8) Pno, Op. 76; G. Fauré:Nocturnes Pno; J. Field:Nocturnes Pno; C. Franck:Symphonic Vars, M.46; Saint-Saëns:Con 5 Pno, Op. 103; Tiegerman:Meditation Pno ARBT 2-▲ 116 (32.97)

F. Ts'ong (pno) SNYC ▲ 53249 [ADD] (14.97)

F. Ts'ong (pno), P. Entremont (pno)—No. 10 in A♭, Op. 32/2; No. 2 in E♭, Op. 9/2 *(rec New York City, NY, Mar 30-31, 1966)* † Études Pno; Fant-Impromptu, Op. 66; Intro & Polonaise, Op. 3; Mazurkas Pno; Polonaise 3 Pno, Op. 40/1; Polonaise 6 Pno, Op. 53; Preludes (24) Pno, Op. 28; Son Pno in b♭, Op. 35; Waltzes Pno SNYC ▲ 51338 [ADD] (7.97)

A. Wasowski (pno) *(rec Henry Wood Hall London, Sept 30-Oct 1, 1989)* ERTO 2-▲ 42044 [DDD] (22.97)

E. Wild (pno) *(rec Columbus, OH, Mar 3-7, 1996)* IVOR 2-▲ 70701 [DDD] (32.97)

G. Zitterbart (pno)—No. 20 in c#, Op. posth.; No. 1 in b♭, Op. 9/1; No. 7 in c#, Op. 27/1; No. 15 in f, Op. 55/1 † Ballade 1 Pno, Op. 23; Ballade 2 Pno, Op. 38; Ballade 3 Pno, Op. 47; Ballade 4 Pno, Op. 52; Son Pno in b, Op. 58 TACE ▲ 28

various artists—No. 17 in B, Op. 62/1; No. 8 in D♭, Op. 27/2 † Études Pno; Barcarolle Pno, Op. 60; Berceuse, Op. 57; Con 1 Pno, Op. 11; Con 2 Pno, Op. 21; Nouvelles études; Preludes (24) Pno, Op. 28; Waltzes Pno RCAV ▮ 63423 (6.98) ▲ 63423 (11.97)

various artists—Preludes (24) Pno, Op. 28 [No. 15 in D♭, "Raindrop"; No. 20 in c]; Nocturnes Pno [No. 2 in E♭, Op. 9/2; No. 15 in f, Op. 55/1] ("Chopin With Ocean Sounds") † Preludes (24) Pno, Op. 28 CHAC ▲ 944 (14.97)

Nouvelles études (3) for Piano (1839)

C. Arrau (pno) † Études Pno EMIC (Great Recordings of the Century) ▲ 61016 (11.97)

B. Berezovsky (pno) † Études Pno TELC ▲ 73129 [DDD] (16.97)

M. Binns (pno) ("Malcolm Binns Plays Chopin") † Études Pno PHS ▲ 9641 (17.97)

L. Lortie (pno) † Études Pno CHN ▲ 8482 [DDD] (16.97)

Y. Matsuzawa (pno) *(rec London, Mar 1996)* † Études Pno NOVA ▲ 150142 [DDD] (16.97)

G. Ohlsson (pno) *(rec New York, NY, Oct 27-31, 1996)* ("Complete Chopin, Vol. 10") † Études Pno ARA (The Complete Chopin Piano Works) ▲ 6718 [DDD] (16.97)

V. Perlemuter (pno) † Études Pno NIMB ▲ 5095 [DDD] (16.97)

A. Rubinstein (pno) † Pno Music (misc colls) RCAV (Red Seal) ▲ 5617 [ADD] (16.97)

D. Saperton (pno) *(rec 1952 & 1957)* ("Plays Chopin And Godowsky") † Études Pno; L. Godowsky:Studies after Chopin's Etudes; Triakontameron VAIA 2-▲ 1037 (31.97)

E. Wild (pno) † Études Pno CHSK ▲ 77 [DDD] (16.97)

various artists † Études Pno; Barcarolle Pno, Op. 60; Berceuse, Op. 57; Con 1 Pno, Op. 11; Con 2 Pno, Op. 21; Nocturnes Pno; Preludes (24) Pno, Op. 28; Waltzes Pno RCAV ▮ 63423 (6.98) ▲ 63423 (11.97)

Piano Music (complete works for solo piano)

A. R. El Bacha (pno) *(rec 1996)* ("Complete Solo Piano Works, Vol. 1") FORL ▲ 16767 (16.97)

Piano Music (miscellaneous collections)

M. Argerich (pno) *(Mazurkas Pno [No. 13 in a, Op. 17/4]; Études Pno [No. 19 in c#, Op. 25/7]; Berceuse, Op. 57)*, M. Argerich (pno), J. Luisada (pno), M. Pletnev (pno), T. Vásáry (pno), C. Abbado (cnd), London SO *(Preludes (24) Pno, Op. 28 [No. 4 in e; No. 6 in b; No. 7 in A; No. 15 in D♭, "Raindrop"])*, T. Vásáry (pno), J. Kulka (cnd), Berlin PO *(Nocturnes Pno [No. 1 in b♭, Op. 9/1; No. 2 in E♭, Op. 9/2; No. 4 in F, Op. 15/1; No. 5 in F#, Op. 15/2; No. 8 in D♭, Op. 27/2; No. 6 in g, Op. 15/6]; Con 2 Pno, Op. 21; Con 1 Pno, Op. 11)* ("Piano Dreams") PPHI (Night Moods) ▲ 453906 [DDD] (9.97)

M. Argerich (pno)—Preludes (24) Pno, Op. 28; Prelude in c#, Op. 45; Son Pno in b, Op. 58; Scherzos Pno [No. 2 in b♭/D♭, Op. 31; No. 3 in c#, Op. 39]; Mazurkas Pno [No. 36 in a, Op. 59/1; No. 37 in A, Op. 59/2; No. 38 in f#, Op. 59/3]; Polonaises-fant, Op. 61; Polonaises Pno [No. 15 in A♭] *(rec 1960-77)* ("Martha Argerich II") † Liszt:Hungarian Rhaps, S.244; Son Pno, S.178; R. Schumann:Son 2 Pno, Op. 22 PPHI (Great Pianists of the 20th Century) 2-▲ 456703 (22.97)

CHOPIN, FRÉDÉRIC (cont.)

Piano Music (miscellaneous collections) (cont.)

M. Argerich (pno), D. Barenboim (pno), J. Luisada (pno) *(Preludes (24) Pno, Op. 28 [No. 2 in a; No. 4 in e; No. 6 in b; No. 7 in A; No. 21 in B♭; No. 15 in D♭, "Raindrop"])*, M. Argerich (pno) *(Prelude in c#, Op. 45)*, M. Argerich (pno), T. Vásáry (pno) *(Mazurkas Pno [No. 37 in A, Op. 59/2; No. 47 in a, Op. 68/2; No. 5 in B♭, Op. 7/1])*, D. Barenboim (pno), T. Vásáry (pno) *(Nocturnes Pno [No. 2 in E♭, Op. 9/2; No. 1 in b♭, Op. 9/1; No. 3 in B, Op. 9/3; No. 4 in F, Op. 15/1; No. 5 in F#, Op. 15/2; No. 6 in g, Op. 15/6; No. 8 in D♭, Op. 27/2; No. 12 in G, Op. 37/2; No. 21 in c, Op. posth.; No. 20 in c#, Op. posth.; No. 19 in e, Op. 72; No. 9 in B, Op. 32/1])*, J. Luisada (pno) *(Waltzes Pno [No. 1 in E♭, Op. 18, "Grand Valse Brillante"; No. 3 in a, Op. 34/2; No. 4 in F, Op. 34/3; No. 6 in D♭, Op. 64/1, "Minute"; No. 13 in D♭, Op. 70/3; No. 9 in A♭, Op. 69/1, "L'adieu"; No. 10 in b, Op. 69/2; No. 15 in E, Op. posth.])*, A. Ugorski (pno) *(Fant-Impromptu, Op. 66)*, T. Vásáry (pno) *(Ballade 2 Pno, Op. 38; Berceuse, Op. 57)*, T. Vásáry (pno), D. Barenboim (pno), M. Argerich (pno), J. Luisada (pno) *(Études Pno [No. 3 in E, Op. 10/3, "Tristesse"; No. 13 in A♭, Op. 25/1; No. 6 in e♭, Op. 10/6])* ("Music of the Night: The Essential Chopin Collection") DEUT (2-Fers) 2-▲ 457992 [DDD] (17.97)

C. Arrau (pno)—Ballade 3 Pno, Op. 47; Ballade 2 Pno, Op. 38; Études Pno [No. 3 in E, Op. 10/3, "Tristesse"; No. 4 in c#, Op. 10/4; No. 8 in D♭, Op. 10/8; No. 9 in G♭, Op. 10/9]; Waltzes Pno [No. 4 in F, Op. 34/3] † Busoni:Sonatina 6 Pno; Liszt:Années de pèlerinage 3, S.163; R. Schumann:Carnaval, Op. 9 PHS ▲ 9928 [AAD] (17.97)

C. Arrau (pno)—Preludes (24) Pno, Op. 28; Prelude in c#, Op. 45; Prelude in A♭, Op. posth.; Nocturnes Pno [No. 13 in c, Op. 48/1; No. 14 in f#, Op. 48/2] *(rec 1969-90)* ("Claudio Arrau III") † Debussy:Images (6) Pno; E. Granados:Colección de Tonadillas; Liszt:Album d'un voyageur, S.156; Trans, Arrs & Paraphrases; W. A. Mozart:Fant Pno, K.475; F. Schubert:Moments musicaux, D.780 PPHI (Great Pianists of the 20th Century) 2-▲ 456712 (22.97)

V. Ashkenazy (pno)—Berceuse, Op. 57 † Pno Music (misc) PLON 2-▲ 36389 [ADD] (17.97)

V. Ashkenazy (pno)—Waltzes Pno [No. 1 in E♭, Op. 18, "Grand Valse Brillante"; No. 3 in a, Op. 34/2; No. 4 in F, Op. 34/3; No. 5 in A♭, Op. 42; No. 6 in D♭, Op. 64/1, "Minute"; No. 7 in c#, Op. 64/2; No. 8 in A♭, Op. 64/3; No. 9 in A♭, Op. 69/1, "L'adieu"; No. 10 in b, Op. 69/2; No. 11 in g♭, Op. 70/1; No. 12 in f, Op. 70/2; No. 13 in D♭, Op. 70/3]; Fant-Impromptu, Op. 66; Nocturnes Pno [No. 2 in E♭, Op. 9/2; No. 5 in F#, Op. 15/2; No. 9 in B, Op. 32/1; No. 15 in f, Op. 55/1]; Mazurkas Pno [No. 23 in D, Op. 33/2; No. 5 in B♭, Op. 7/1]; Scherzos Pno [No. 2 in b♭/D♭, Op. 31; No. 3 in c#, Op. 39]; Ballade 1 Pno, Op. 23; Ballade 3 Pno, Op. 47; Polonaise 6 Pno, Op. 53; Polonaise 3 Pno, Op. 40/1; Prelude in c#, Op. 45; Preludes (24) Pno, Op. 28 [No. 15 in D♭, "Raindrop"]; Études Pno [No. 3 in E, Op. 10/3, "Tristesse"; No. 5 in G♭, Op. 10/5, "Black Keys"; No. 12 in c, Op. 10/12, "Revolutionary"; No. 23 in a, Op. 25/11, "Winter Wind"]; Barcarolle Pno, Op. 60 *(rec 1972, 1976, 1978-79)* ("Chopin: Favorite Piano Works") PLON 2-▲ 44830 [DDD] (17.97)

E. Auer (pno)—Ballades (4) Pno; Waltzes Pno [No. 17 in e♭, Op. posth.]; Rondos (4) Pno [Intro in c, & Rondo in E♭, Op. 16]; Prelude in A♭, Op. posth.; Vars in A, ('Souvenir de Paganini'); Prelude in c#, Op. 45; Contredanse CAMA ▲ 263

W. Backhaus (pno)—Berceuse, Op. 57; Fant-Impromptu, Op. 66; Waltzes Pno [No. 1 in E♭, Op. 18, "Grand Valse Brillante"; No. 6 in D♭, Op. 64/1, "Minute"] *(rec 1925-33 for HMV)* † Études Pno; Liszt:Etudes de concert (2), S.145 PHS ▲ 9902 [AAD] (18.97)

I. Biret (pno)—Contredanse; Ecossaises (3) Pno, Op. 72/3 *(rec 1991)* † Tarentelle, Op. 43; Waltzes Pno NXIN ▲ 550365 [DDD] (5.97)

I. Biret (pno)—Bourrées *(rec 1991-92)* † Albumleaf (Feuille d'Album); Barcarolle Pno, Op. 60; Bolero; Fugue in a; Prelude in c#, Op. 45; Prelude in A♭, Op. posth.; Preludes (24) Pno, Op. 28; Wiosna NXIN ▲ 550366 [DDD] (5.97)

I. Biret (pno)—Berceuse, Op. 57; Études Pno; Fantaisie Pno, Op. 49; Galop Marquis; Largo in E♭; Funeral March, Op. 72/2; Cantabile in B♭ *(rec 1991)* † Ballades (4) Pno NXIN ▲ 550508 [DDD] (5.97)

I. Biret (pno)—Fant-Impromptu, Op. 66; Nocturnes Pno [No. 2 in E♭, Op. 9/2; No. 8 in D♭, Op. 27/2]; Waltzes Pno [No. 1 in E♭, Op. 18, "Grand Valse Brillante"; No. 6 in D♭, Op. 64/1, "Minute"; No. 7 in c#, Op. 64/2]; Son Pno in b♭, Op. 35; Mazurkas Pno [No. 5 in B♭, Op. 7/1]; Polonaise 3 Pno, Op. 40/1; Polonaise 6 Pno, Op. 53; Preludes (24) Pno, Op. 28 [No. 15 in D♭, "Raindrop"]; Etudes Pno [No. 3 in E, Op. 10/3, "Tristesse"; No. 5 in G♭, Op. 10/5, "Black Keys"; No. 12 in c, Op. 10/12, "Revolutionary"]; Ballade 1 Pno, Op. 23 ("Piano Favourites") NXIN ▲ 553170 [DDD] (5.97)

A. Brailowsky (pno)—Con 1 Pno, Op. 11; Barcarolle Pno, Op. 60; Polonaise 6 Pno, Op. 53; Fant-Impromptu, Op. 66; Impromptu in A♭, Op. 29; Preludes (24) Pno, Op. 28 [No. 6 in b; No. 3 in G; No. 15 in D♭, "Raindrop"]; Mazurkas Pno [No. 5 in B♭, Op. 7/1]; Nocturnes Pno [No. 2 in E♭, Op. 9/2] *(rec 1928-34)* ("A Retrospective, Vol. 2") ENPL (Piano Library) ▲ 248 (13.97)

P. Cavazzini (pno)—Waltzes Pno [No. 1 in E♭, Op. 18, "Grand Valse Brillante"]; Scherzos Pno [No. 1 in b, Op. 20]; Polonaise 3 Pno, Op. 40/1; Etudes Pno [No. 5 in G♭, Op. 10/5, "Black Keys"]; Polonaise 6 Pno, Op. 53 *(rec 1950-60)* ("Un Ritratto") † I. Albéniz:Pno Music (misc); Cavazzini:Pno Music (misc); Debussy:Pno Music (misc colls); Liszt:Études d'exécution transcendante (6), S.140; Hungarian Rhaps, S.244; Liebesträume, S.541; M. Ravel:Jeux d'eau; D. Scarlatti:Sons Kbd STRV 2-▲ 90005 [ADD] (24.97)

S. Cherkassky (pno)—Études Pno [No. 12 in c, Op. 10/12, "Revolutionary"]; Polonaise 6 Pno, Op. 53; Scherzos Pno [No. 4 in E, Op. 54] ("Shura Cherkassky:The Last of the Great Piano Romantics, Vol. 2") † Polonaise 2 Pno, Op. 26/2; Preludes (24) Pno, Op. 28; Liszt:Trans, Arrs & Paraphrases ASVQ ▲ 6109 [DDD] (10.97)

V. Cliburn (pno)—Polonaise 6 Pno, Op. 53; Nocturnes Pno [No. 17 in B, Op. 62/1]; Fantaisie Pno, Op. 49; Études Pno [No. 23 in a, Op. 25/11, "Winter Wind"; No. 3 in E, Op. 10/3, "Tristesse"]; Ballade 3 Pno, Op. 47; Waltzes Pno [No. 6 in D♭, Op. 64/1, "Minute"; No. 7 in c#, Op. 64/2]; Scherzos Pno [No. 3 in c#, Op. 39] *(rec 1961)* ("My Favourite Chopin") RCAV (Living Stereo) ▲ 68813 [ADD] (11.97)

A. Cortot (pno)—Waltzes Pno [No. 1 in E♭, Op. 18, "Grand Valse Brillante"; No. 2 in A♭, Op. 34/1; No. 3 in a, Op. 34/2; No. 4 in F, Op. 34/3; No. 5 in A♭, Op. 42; No. 6 in D♭, Op. 64/1, "Minute"; No. 7 in c#, Op. 64/2; No. 8 in A♭, Op. 64/3; No. 9 in A♭, Op. 69/1, "L'adieu"; No. 10 in b, Op. 69/2; No. 11 in g♭, Op. 70/1; No. 12 in f, Op. 70/2; No. 13 in D♭, Op. 70/3; No. 14 in e, Op. posth.] ("The World of Chopin") † Ballades (4) Pno; Con 2 Pno, Op. 21; Fantaisie Pno, Op. 49; Preludes (24) Pno, Op. 28; Son Pno in b, Op. 58; Son Pno in b♭, Op. 35 ENPL (Piano Library) 3-▲ 206 (39.97)

G. Cziffra (pno)—Polonaises-fant, Op. 61; Fant-Impromptu, Op. 66; Intro & Vars in B♭, Op. 12; Polonaise 6 Pno, Op. 53 *(rec Nov 5, 1978 & Apr 12, 1981)* ("Georges Cziffra Live at Senlis") † Liszt:Études d'exécution transcendante (12), S.139; Études de concert (2), S.145; Années de pèlerinage 3, S.163; Liebesträume, S.541; M. Ravel:Jeux d'eau; Saint-Saëns:Étude Pno, Op. 52/6 APR ▲ 5554 [ADD] (18.97)

R. DeGaetano (pno)—Ballade 1 Pno, Op. 23; Ballade 4 Pno, Op. 52; Nocturnes Pno [No. 18 in E, Op. 62/2; No. 7 in c#, Op. 27/1; No. 5 in F#, Op. 15/2]; Scherzos Pno [No. 3 in c#, Op. 39; No. 1 in b, Op. 20]; Études Pno; Fant-Impromptu, Op. 66; Polonaise 3 Pno, Op. 40/1 ("DeGaetano Plays Chopin") CYST ▲ 1003 (16.97)

M. Frager (pno)—Mazurkas Pno [No. 1 in f#, Op. 6; No. 2 in c#, Op. 6/2; No. 3 in E, Op. 6/3; No. 4 in c, Op. 6/4]; Contredanse; Son Pno in b, Op. 58 ("Malcolm Frager Plays Chopin") † Andante Spianato & Grand Polonaise, Op. 22; Intro & Vars in B♭, Op. 12; Polonaise 6 Pno, Op. 53; Tarentelle, Op. 43 TEL ▲ 80280 [DDD] (16.97)

S. François (pno)—Impromptus (4); Son Pno in b♭, Op. 35; Waltzes Pno [No. 11 in g♭, Op. 70/1; No. 1 in E♭, Op. 18, "Grand Valse Brillante"; No. 13 in D♭, Op. 70/3; No. 7 in c#, Op. 64/2]; Ballades (4) Pno *(rec 1952-61)* † Busoni:Bach Trans Pno; Debussy:Isle joyeuse; Pour le piano; Suite bergamasque; G. Fauré:Impromptus Pno; Nocturnes Pno; W. A. Mozart:Vars "Ah! vous dirai-je, Maman", K.265; M. Ravel:Gaspard de la nuit; R. Schumann:Toccata Pno, Op. 7 PPHI (Great Pianists of the 20th Century, Vol. 28) 2-▲ 456778 (22.97)

I. Friedman (pno)—Mazurkas Pno [No. 5 in B♭, Op. 7/1; No. 6 in a, Op. 7/2; No. 7 in f, Op. 7/3; No. 17 in b♭, Op. 24/4; No. 23 in D, Op. 33/2; No. 25 in b, Op. 33/4; No. 26 in c#, Op. 41/1; No. 31 in A♭, Op. 50/2; No. 41 in c#, Op. 63/3; No. 44 in C, Op. 67/3; No. 45 in a, Op. 67/4; No. 47 in a, Op. 68/2]; Berceuse, Op. 57; Preludes (24) Pno, Op. 28 [No. 15 in D♭, "Raindrop"; No. 19 in E♭]; Études Pno [No. 5 in G♭, Op. 10/5, "Black Keys"; No. 7 in C, Op. 10/7; No. 12 in c, Op. 10/12, "Revolutionary"; No. 18 in g#, Op. 25/6; No. 21 in G♭, Op. 25/9]; Ballade 4 Pno, Op. 52; Waltzes Pno [No. 3 in a, Op. 34/2; No. 6 in D♭, Op. 64/1, "Minute"]; Polonaise 6 Pno, Op. 53; Polonaises Pno [No. 8 in d, Op. 71/1] *(rec Sept 1930)* ENPL (Piano Library) ▲ 262 (13.97)

J. Gimpel (pno)—Barcarolle Pno, Op. 60; Intro & Vars in B♭, Op. 12; Impromptu in F#, Op. 36; Son Pno in b, Op. 58; Mazurkas Pno [No. 20 in D♭, Op. 30/3; No. 32 in c#, Op. 50/3; No. 37 in A, Op. 59/2]; Études Pno [No. 13 in A♭, Op. 25/1; No. 23 in a, Op. 25/11, "Winter Wind"]; Nocturnes Pno [No. 18 in E, Op. 62/2]; Scherzos Pno [No. 1 in b, Op. 20] *(rec Ambassador Auditorium, Los Angeles, CA, May 11, 1978)* ("Jakob Gimpel: All-Chopin Recital") † Ballade 1 Pno, Op. 23; Impromptu in F#, Op. 36; Intro & Vars in B♭, Op. 12; Son Pno in b♭, Op. 35; Debussy:Études (12) Pno; Liszt:Valses oubliées (4), S.215 CMB 2-▲ 1070

L. Godowsky (pno)—Waltzes Pno [No. 1 in E♭, Op. 18, "Grand Valse Brillante"; No. 5 in A♭, Op. 42]; Études Pno [No. 5 in G♭, Op. 10/5, "Black Keys"; No. 14 in f, Op. 25/2; No. 21 in G♭, Op. 25/9]; Nocturnes Pno [No. 1 in b♭, Op. 9/1]; Polonaise 3 Pno, Op. 40/1; Impromptu in A♭, Op. 29; Fant-Impromptu, Op. 66; Berceuse, Op. 57 *(rec 1913-28)* ENPL (Piano Library) ▲ 266 (13.97)

S. Hall (pno)—Ecossaises (3) Pno, Op. 72/3; Polonaises-fant, Op. 61 *(rec Oct 1986)* † Beethoven:Son 16 Pno, Op. 31/1; S. Rachmaninoff:Son 2 Pno, Op. 36 ACAD ▲ 20001 (16.97)

J. Hofmann (pno)—Son Pno in b♭, Op. 35; Nocturnes Pno [No. 8 in D♭, Op. 27/2; No. 15 in f, Op. 55/1]; Polonaise 6 Pno, Op. 53; Scherzos Pno [No. 1 in b, Op. 20; No. 3 in c#, Op. 39]; Waltzes Pno [No. 5 in A♭, Op. 42]; Berceuse, Op. 57; Polonaise 3 Pno, Op. 40/1 NIMB (Grand Piano) ▲ 8803 [DDD] (11.97)

V. Horowitz (pno)—Ballade 1 Pno, Op. 23; Études Pno [No. 3 in E, Op. 10/3, "Tristesse"; No. 4 in c#, Op. 10/4; No. 5 in G♭, Op. 10/5, "Black Keys"; No. 12 in c, Op. 10/12, "Revolutionary"]; Mazurkas Pno [No. 7 in f, Op. 7/3; No. 13 in a, Op. 17/4; No. 20 in D♭, Op. 30/3; No. 23 in D, Op. 33/2; No. 27 in e, Op. 41/2]; Nocturnes Pno [No. 15 in f, Op. 55/1]; Polonaise 3 Pno, Op. 40/1; Polonaise 6 Pno, Op. 53; Preludes (24) Pno, Op. 28 [No. 6 in b]; Scherzos Pno [No. 1 in b, Op. 20]; Waltzes Pno [No. 3 in a, Op. 34/2; No. 7 in c#, Op. 64/2] ("Favorite Chopin") SNYC ▲ 42306 [AAD] (16.97)

CHOPIN, FRÉDÉRIC (cont.)

Piano Music (miscellaneous collections) (cont.)

V. Horowitz (pno)—Etudes Pno [No. 3 in E, Op. 10/3, "Tristesse"; No. 6 in e♭, Op. 10/6; No. 12 in c, Op. 10/12, "Revolutionary"]; Nouvelles études [No. 3 in A♭]; Intro & Rondo, Op. 16; Mazurkas Pno [No. 7 in f, Op. 7/3; No. 13 in a, Op. 17/4; No. 20 in D♭, Op. 30/3; No. 23 in D, Op. 33/2; No. 27 in e, Op. 41/2; No. 32 in c#, Op. 50/3; No. 38 in f#, Op. 59/3]; Polonaise 6 Pno, Op. 53; Polonaise 3 Pno, Op. 40/1; Preludes (24) Pno, Op. 28 [No. 6 in b; No. 15 in D♭, "Raindrop"]; Waltzes Pno [No. 3 in a, Op. 34/2; No. 7 in c#, Op. 64/2] *(rec New York, NY, Apr 14 & May 4, 1971, July 6, 1972 & Feb 8-15, 197)* ("The Complete Masterworks Recordings, Vol. VII: Early Romantics") † R. Schumann:Kreisleriana, Op. 16; Son Pno, Op. 14 SNYC 2-▲ 53468 (31.97)

V. Horowitz (pno)—Andante Spianato & Grand Polonaise, Op. 22; Ballade 1 Pno, Op. 23; Ballade 4 Pno, Op. 52; Barcarolle Pno, Op. 60; Études Pno; Polonaises-fant, Op. 61; Waltzes Pno [No. 9 in A♭, Op. 69/1, "L'adieu"] ("Horowitz Plays Chopin, Vol. 1") RCAV (Gold Seal) ▲ 7752 [ADD] (11.97)

V. Horowitz (pno)—Ballade 1 Pno, Op. 23; Études Pno [No. 3 in E, Op. 10/3, "Tristesse"; No. 4 in c#, Op. 10/4]; Impromptu in A♭, Op. 29; Mazurkas Pno [No. 21 in c#, Op. 30/4]; Nocturnes Pno [No. 2 in E♭, Op. 9/2; No. 15 in f, Op. 55/1]; Scherzos Pno [No. 1 in b, Op. 20] † Son Pno in b♭, Op. 35 RCAV (Gold Seal) ▲ 60376 [ADD] (11.97)

V. Horowitz (pno)—Mazurkas Pno [No. 26 in c#, Op. 41/1; No. 29 in A♭, Op. 41/4; No. 39 in B, Op. 63/1; No. 41 in c#, Op. 63/3; No. 36 in a, Op. 59/1; No. 37 in A, Op. 59/2; No. 38 in f#, Op. 59/3; No. 30 in G, Op. 50/1; No. 31 in A♭, Op. 50/2; No. 32 in c#, Op. 50/3; No. 5 in B♭, Op. 7/1; No. 6 in a, Op. 7/2; No. 7 in f, Op. 7/3; No. 8 in A♭, Op. 7/4; No. 9 in C, Op. 7/5]; Ballade 4 Pno, Op. 52; Nocturnes Pno [No. 19 in e, Op. 72; No. 4 in F, Op. 15/1; No. 5 in F#, Op. 15/2; No. 6 in g, Op. 15/6; No. 3 in B, Op. 9/3]; Polonaises-fant, Op. 61; Scherzos Pno [No. 1 in b, Op. 20; No. 2 in b♭/D♭, Op. 31]; Waltzes Pno [No. 3 in a, Op. 34/2] ("Horowitz Plays Chopin, Vol. 3") RCAV (Gold Seal) ▲ 60987 (11.97)

V. Horowitz (pno) SNYC ▮ 30643 (10.98)

J. Iturbi (pno)—Polonaise 3 Pno, Op. 40/1; Impromptu in A♭, Op. 29; Mazurkas Pno [No. 5 in B♭, Op. 7/1; No. 6 in a, Op. 7/2]; Waltzes Pno [No. 2 in A♭, Op. 34/1; No. 3 in a, Op. 34/2; No. 6 in D♭, Op. 64/1, "Minute"; No. 9 in A♭, Op. 69/1, "L'adieu"] ("Piano Classics") † Debussy:Pno Music (misc colls); M. Ravel:Pno Music RYLC ▲ 70096 (8.97)

B. Janis (pno)—Mazurkas Pno; Nocturnes Pno; Waltzes Pno EMIC ▲ 56196 (16.97)

P. Katin (pno)—Intro & Vars in B♭, Op. 12; Mazurkas Pno [No. 14 in g, Op. 24/1; No. 15 in C, Op. 24/2; No. 16 in A♭, Op. 24/3; No. 17 in b♭, Op. 24/4; No. 49 in f, Op. 68/4]; Rondos (4) Pno; Vars in A, ('Souvenir de Paganini'); Nocturnes Pno [No. 7 in c#, Op. 27/1]; Waltzes Pno [No. 6 in D♭, Op. 64/1, "Minute"; No. 7 in c#, Op. 64/2; No. 8 in A♭, Op. 64/3]; Son Pno in c, Op. 4 [3rd movt]; Polonaises Pno [No. 13 in g; No. 14 in B♭; No. 15 in A♭]; Berceuse, Op. 57; Bolero, Op. 19 ("First & Last") ATH ▲ 11 [DDD] (18.97)

C. Katsaris (pno)—Pno Music (misc) ("Famous Piano Works") TELC 2-▲ 95499 (16.97)

E. Kissin (pno)—Fantaisie Pno, Op. 49; Waltzes Pno [No. 5 in A♭, Op. 42; No. 2 in A♭, Op. 34/1; No. 3 in a, Op. 34/2]; Polonaise 5 Pno, Op. 44; Nocturnes Pno [No. 7 in c#, Op. 27/1; No. 8 in D♭, Op. 27/2; No. 10 in A♭, Op. 32/2]; Scherzos Pno [No. 2 in b♭/D♭, Op. 31] ("Chopin: Recorded Live at Carnegie Hall") RCAV (Red Seal) ▲ 60445 (16.97)

R. Koczalski (pno)—Ballade 4 Pno, Op. 52; Ecossaises (3) Pno, Op. 72/3; Études Pno [No. 5 in G♭, Op. 10/5, "Black Keys"; No. 10 in A♭, Op. 10/10; No. 12 in c, Op. 10/12, "Revolutionary"; No. 13 in A♭, Op. 25/1; No. 14 in f, Op. 25/2; No. 17 in e, Op. 25/5; No. 18 in g#, Op. 25/6]; Nouvelles études; Fant-Impromptu, Op. 66; Waltzes Pno [No. 1 in E♭, Op. 18, "Grand Valse Brillante"; No. 3 in a, Op. 34/2]; Mazurkas Pno [No. 48 in F, Op. 68/3]; Nocturnes Pno [No. 2 in E♭, Op. 9/2]; Polonaise 6 Pno, Op. 53; Preludes (24) Pno, Op. 28 [No. 24 in d]; Prelude in A♭, Op. posth.; Scherzos Pno [No. 2 in b♭/D♭, Op. 31] ("Raoul Koczalski Plays Chopin") PHS ▲ 9472 [AAD] (17.97)

L. Kuzmin (pno)—Nocturnes Pno [No. 16 in E♭, Op. 55/2]; Mazurkas Pno [No. 17 in b♭, Op. 24/4; No. 24 in C, Op. 33/3; No. 25 in b, Op. 33/4; No. 41 in c#, Op. 63/3]; Son Pno in b♭, Op. 35; Barcarolle Pno, Op. 60; Etudes Pno [No. 5 in G♭, Op. 10/5, "Black Keys"; No. 12 in c, Op. 10/12, "Revolutionary"; No. 18 in g#, Op. 25/6]; Scherzos Pno [No. 2 in b♭/D♭, Op. 31] *(rec Dec 1992)* ("For Nina: Chopin—Piano Works") RUS ▲ 10022 [DDD] (12.97)

A. Lear (pno)—Ballade 1 Pno, Op. 23; Ballade 3 Pno, Op. 47; Bolero, Op. 19; Mazurkas Pno [No. 13 in a, Op. 17/4; No. 25 in b, Op. 33/4]; Nocturnes Pno [No. 18 in E, Op. 62/2]; Polonaises-fant, Op. 61; Scherzos Pno [No. 2 in b♭/D♭, Op. 31; No. 3 in c#, Op. 39] *(rec Brandon Hill Bristol, England, July 27, 1994)* ("The Original Chopin Vol. 2") APR ▲ 5555 [DDD] (19.97)

C. Marthé (pno) *(Ballade 4 Pno, Op. 52; Études Pno [No. 6 in e♭, Op. 10/6; No. 12 in c, Op. 10/12, "Revolutionary"]; Impromptu in A♭, Op. 29; Mazurkas Pno [No. 44 in C, Op. 67/3]; Nocturnes Pno [No. 15 in f, Op. 55/1]; Polonaise 6 Pno, Op. 53; Scherzos Pno [No. 2 in b♭/D♭, Op. 31]; Waltzes Pno [No. 7 in c#, Op. 64/2])*, H. Steurer (pno) *(Preludes (24) Pno, Op. 28 [No. 15 in D♭, "Raindrop"])* PC ▲ 267118 [DDD] (2.97)

A. B. Michelangeli (pno)—Andante Spianato & Grand Polonaise, Op. 22; Ballade 1 Pno, Op. 23; Scherzos Pno [No. 1 in b, Op. 20]; Mazurkas Pno [No. 2 in c#, Op. 6/2; No. 3 in E, Op. 6/3; No. 4 in c, Op. 6/4; No. 46 in C, Op. 68/1; No. 47 in a, Op. 68/2; No. 48 in F, Op. 68/3; No. 49 in f, Op. 68/4; No. 18 in c, Op. 30/1; No. 19 in b/f#, Op. 30/2; No. 20 in D♭, Op. 30/3; No. 21 in c#, Op. 30/4; No. 22 in c#, Op. 33/1; No. 23 in D, Op. 33/2; No. 24 in C, Op. 33/3; No. 25 in b, Op. 33/4]; Berceuse, Op. 57; Waltzes Pno [No. 2 in A♭, Op. 34/1; No. 3 in a, Op. 34/2; No. 4 in F, Op. 34/3; No. 9 in A♭, Op. 69/1, "L'adieu"; No. 14 in e, Op. posth.; No. 15 in E, Op. posth.; No. 16 in A♭, Op. posth.; No. 17 in e♭, Op. posth.; No. 18 in E♭, Op. posth.; No. 19 in a, Op. posth.]; Fantaisie Pno, Op. 49 *(rec Turin, Italy, 1962)* MUA ▲ 924

A. B. Michelangeli (pno)—Ballade 1 Pno, Op. 23; Mazurkas Pno; Grande Polonaise brillante in E, Op. 22 *(rec Teatro Grande in Brescia Italy, Italy, June 1967)* † Son Pno in b♭, Op. 35 FON ▲ 9032 [ADD]

E. Mogilevsky (pno)—Scherzos Pno [No. 3 in c#, Op. 39]; Mazurkas Pno [No. 13 in a, Op. 17/4; No. 47 in a, Op. 68/2]; Berceuse, Op. 57 † Pno Music (misc); Preludes (24) Pno, Op. 28 PAVA ▲ 7264 [DDD] (10.97)

G. Novaes (pno)—Études Pno; Fantaisie Pno, Op. 49; Impromptu in F#, Op. 36; Mazurkas Pno; Nocturnes Pno; Preludes (24) Pno, Op. 28; Scherzos Pno [No. 4 in E, Op. 54; No. 3 in c#, Op. 39]; Son Pno in b♭, Op. 35; Son Pno in b, Op. 58 *(rec New York, NY, Nov 26, 1949)* ("The 1949 Town Hall Recital: Unissued Studio Recordings, 1940-1947") † C. W. Gluck:Orfeo ed Euridice (dance); I. Philipp:Feux-Follets MUA 2-▲ 1029 [ADD] (16.97)

G. Ohlsson (pno) *(Polonaise 3 Pno, Op. 40/1)*, D. Adni (pno), J. Ogdon (pno) *(Nocturnes Pno [No. 10 in A♭, Op. 32/2; No. 2 in E♭, Op. 9/2])*, D. Adni (pno), A. Anievas (pno) *(Études Pno [No. 21 in G♭, Op. 25/9; No. 3 in E, Op. 10/3, "Tristesse"; No. 5 in G♭, Op. 10/5, "Black Keys"; No. 12 in c, Op. 10/12, "Revolutionary"])*, W. Malcuzyński (pno) *(Waltzes Pno [No. 1 in E♭, Op. 18, "Grand Valse Brillante"; No. 6 in D♭, Op. 64/1, "Minute"; No. 7 in c#, Op. 64/2])*, R. Orozco (pno) *(Preludes (24) Pno, Op. 28 [No. 7 in A; No. 20 in c])*, J. Ogdon (pno) *(Fant-Impromptu, Op. 66)*, M. Pollini (pno) *(Polonaise 6 Pno, Op. 53)* *(rec 1960-73)* ("Chopin Masterpieces") CFP ▲ 4501 [ADD] (12.97)

J. Olejniczak (pno)—Ballade 1 Pno, Op. 23; Études Pno [No. 12 in c, Op. 10/12, "Revolutionary"]; Mazurkas Pno [No. 13 in a, Op. 17/4]; Nocturnes Pno [No. 20 in c#, Op. posth.]; Polonaise 6 Pno, Op. 53; Scherzos Pno [No. 1 in b, Op. 20]; Waltzes Pno [No. 7 in c#, Op. 64/2] *(rec Warsaw Concert Hall, Poland, Feb-Mar 1978)* ("Chopin Recital") CAMA ▲ 159 [ADD] (18.97)

I. Paderewski (pno)—Ballade 4 Pno, Op. 52; Études Pno [No. 3 in E, Op. 10/3, "Tristesse"; No. 5 in G♭, Op. 10/5, "Black Keys"; No. 7 in C, Op. 10/7; No. 18 in g#, Op. 25/6; No. 21 in G♭, Op. 25/9]; Mazurkas Pno [No. 55 in G, Op. posth.; No. 56 in B♭, Op. posth.]; Nocturnes Pno [No. 2 in E♭, Op. 9/2; No. 17 in B, Op. 62/1]; Polonaise 3 Pno, Op. 40/1; Son Pno in b♭, Op. 35 [Marche funèbre]; Songs Sop [Zyczenie (Maiden's Wish), Op. 74/1; My darling (Moja piesczotka), Op. 74/12]; Waltzes Pno [No. 2 in A♭, Op. 34/1] *(rec 1911-38)* ("Paderewski Plays Chopin, Vol. 2") PHS ▲ 9397 [AAD] (17.97)

I. J. Paderewski (pno)—Études Pno [No. 12 in c, Op. 10/12, "Revolutionary"; No. 13 in A♭, Op. 25/1; No. 14 in f, Op. 25/2; No. 23 in a, Op. 25/11, "Winter Wind"]; Waltzes Pno [No. 7 in c#, Op. 64/2]; Nocturnes Pno [No. 4 in F, Op. 15/1]; Polonaise 6 Pno, Op. 53 *(rec 1911-37)* ("Paderewski Portrait") † J. Brahms:Hungarian Dances Pno; Mendelssohn (-Bartholdy):Lieder ohne Worte; A. Rubinstein:Valse-Caprice Pno; R. Schumann:Pno Music (misc colls) IN ▲ 1366 [ADD] (15.97)

I. J. Paderewski (pno)—Son Pno in b♭, Op. 35 [Marche funèbre]; Études Pno [No. 3 in E, Op. 10/3, "Tristesse"; No. 4 in c#, Op. 10/4; No. 5 in G♭, Op. 10/5, "Black Keys"; No. 18 in g#, Op. 25/6; No. 19 in c#, Op. 25/7; No. 21 in G♭, Op. 25/9]; Waltzes Pno [No. 18 in E♭, Op. posth.; No. 2 in A♭, Op. 34/1; No. 5 in A♭, Op. 42]; Preludes (24) Pno, Op. 28 [No. 15 in D♭, "Raindrop"; No. 17 in A♭]; Mazurkas Pno [No. 13 in a, Op. 17/4; No. 23 in D, Op. 33/2; No. 37 in A, Op. 59/2; No. 38 in f#, Op. 59/3; No. 41 in c#, Op. 63/3]; Berceuse, Op. 57; Nocturnes Pno [No. 2 in E♭, Op. 9/2; No. 4 in F, Op. 15/1; No. 5 in F#, Op. 15/2; No. 17 in B, Op. 62/1] *(rec 1911-38)* ("The Chopin Recordings, 1911-1938") ENPL (Piano Library) ▲ 217 (13.97)

D. Paperno (pno)—Scherzos Pno [No. 2 in b♭/D♭, Op. 31; No. 3 in c#, Op. 39; No. 4 in E, Op. 54]; Ballade 2 Pno, Op. 38; Ballade 4 Pno, Op. 52; Nocturnes Pno; Fantaisie Pno, Op. 49; Prelude in c#, Op. 45; Études Pno [No. 2 in F, Op. 10/2; No. 8 in D♭, Op. 10/8]; Con 2 Pno, Op. 21 [Larghetto]; Mazurkas Pno [No. 38 in f#, Op. 59/3; No. 29 in A♭, Op. 41/4] ("Paperno Plays Chopin") CED ▲ 26 [DDD] (16.97)

V. Perlemuter (pno) *(Nocturnes Pno [No. 1 in b♭, Op. 9/1; No. 3 in B, Op. 9/3; No. 4 in F, Op. 15/1; No. 5 in F#, Op. 15/2; No. 6 in g, Op. 15/6; No. 7 in c#, Op. 27/1; No. 8 in D♭, Op. 27/2; No. 14 in f#, Op. 48/2; No. 17 in B, Op. 62/1; No. 18 in E, Op. 62/2]; Son Pno in b, Op. 58; Barcarolle Pno, Op. 60; Preludes (24) Pno, Op. 28 [No. 1 in C; No. 2 in a; No. 3 in G; No. 4 in e; No. 5 in D; No. 6 in b; No. 7 in A; No. 8 in f#; No. 9 in E; No. 10 in c#; No. 11 in B; No. 12 in g#; No. 13 in F#; No. 14 in e♭; No. 15 in D♭, "Raindrop"; No. 16 in b♭; No. 17 in A♭; No. 18 in f; No. 19 in E♭; No. 20 in c; No. 21 in B♭; No. 22 in g; No. 23 in F; No. 24 in d]; Prelude in c#, Op. 45; Fantaisie Pno, Op. 49; Berceuse, Op. 57; Études Pno; Nouvelles études; Ballades & Polonaises; Scherzos Pno [No. 3 in c#, Op. 39]; Mazurkas Pno; Tarentelle, Op. 43)*, *(Son Pno in b♭, Op. 35)* NIMB 6-▲ 1764 [ADD] (29.97)

CHOPIN, FRÉDÉRIC (cont.)

Piano Music (miscellaneous collections) (cont.)

S. Richter (pno)—Études Pno [No. 1 in C, Op. 10/1; No. 6 in e♭, Op. 10/6; No. 10 in A♭, Op. 10/10; No. 11 in E♭, Op. 10/11; No. 12 in c, Op. 10/12, "Revolutionary"; No. 4 in c#, Op. 10/4; No. 19 in c#, Op. 25/7]; Polonaises-fant, Op. 61; Scherzos Pno [No. 4 in E, Op. 54]; Waltzes Pno [No. 4 in F, Op. 34/3; No. 13 in D♭, Op. 70/3]; Preludes (24) Pno, Op. 28 [No. 8 in f#; No. 9 in E; No. 10 in c#; No. 4 in e; No. 5 in D; No. 6 in b; No. 7 in A; No. 19 in E♭; No. 17 in A♭; No. 11 in B]; Nouvelles études; Impromptu in F#, Op. 36; Impromptu in G♭, Op. 51 *(rec 1954-90)* ("Sviatoslav Richter Archives Vol. 3") DHR (Legendary Treasures) ▲ 7738 (16.97)

M. Rosenthal (pno)—Mazurkas Pno [No. 41 in c#, Op. 63/3; No. 16 in A♭, Op. 24/3; No. 42 in G, Op. 67/1]; Waltzes Pno [No. 5 in A♭, Op. 42]; Nocturnes Pno [No. 2 in E♭, Op. 9/2]; Preludes (24) Pno, Op. 28 [No. 6 in b; No. 7 in A; No. 11 in B; No. 23 in F]; Études Pno [No. 5 in G♭, Op. 10/5, "Black Keys"; No. 1 in C, Op. 10/1]; Nouvelles études [No. 3 in A♭]; Son Pno in b, Op. 58; Tarentelle, Op. 43 *(rec Mar 2, 1929)* † G. F. Handel:Harmonious Blacksmith; Liszt:Trans, Arrs & Paraphrases; Strauss (II):An der schönen blauen Donau, Op. 314 BPS ▲ 39 (m) [ADD] (16.97)

A. Rubinstein (pno)—Mazurkas Pno; Scherzos Pno; Polonaise 1 Pno, Op. 26/1; Polonaise 2 Pno, Op. 26/2; Polonaise 3 Pno, Op. 40/1; Polonaise 4 Pno, Op. 40/2; Polonaise 5 Pno, Op. 44; Polonaise 6 Pno, Op. 53; Polonaises-fant, Op. 61; Barcarolle Pno, Op. 60; Berceuse, Op. 57; Waltzes Pno [No. 2 in A♭, Op. 34/1]; Andante Spianato & Grand Polonaise, Op. 22 *(rec 1928-39)* EMIC 3-▲ 64697 (31.97)

A. Rubinstein (pno)—Andante Spianato & Grand Polonaise, Op. 22; Barcarolle Pno, Op. 60; Impromptus (4); Bolero, Op. 19; Berceuse, Op. 57; Tarentelle, Op. 43 † Nouvelles études RCAV (Red Seal) ▲ 5617 [ADD] (16.97)

A. Rubinstein (pno)—Nocturnes Pno [No. 1 in b♭, Op. 9/1; No. 2 in E♭, Op. 9/2; No. 3 in B, Op. 9/3; No. 4 in F, Op. 15/1; No. 5 in F#, Op. 15/2; No. 6 in g, Op. 15/6; No. 7 in c#, Op. 27/1; No. 8 in D♭, Op. 27/2; No. 9 in B, Op. 32/1; No. 10 in A♭, Op. 32/2; No. 11 in g, Op. 37/1; No. 12 in G, Op. 37/2; No. 13 in c, Op. 48/1; No. 14 in f#, Op. 48/2; No. 15 in f, Op. 55/1; No. 16 in E♭, Op. 55/2; No. 17 in B, Op. 62/1; No. 18 in E, Op. 62/2; No. 19 in e, Op. 72]; Mazurkas Pno [No. 1 in f#, Op. 6; No. 2 in c#, Op. 6/2; No. 3 in E, Op. 6/3; No. 4 in c, Op. 6/4; No. 5 in B♭, Op. 7/1; No. 6 in a, Op. 7/2; No. 7 in f, Op. 7/3; No. 8 in A♭, Op. 7/4; No. 9 in C, Op. 7/5; No. 10 in B♭, Op. 17/1; No. 12 in A♭, Op. 17/3; No. 13 in a, Op. 17/4; No. 14 in g, Op. 24/1; No. 15 in C, Op. 24/2; No. 16 in A♭, Op. 24/3; No. 17 in b♭, Op. 24/4; No. 18 in c, Op. 30/1; No. 19 in b/f#, Op. 30/2; No. 20 in D♭, Op. 30/3; No. 21 in c#, Op. 30/4; No. 22 in c#, Op. 33/1; No. 23 in D, Op. 33/2; No. 24 in C, Op. 33/3; No. 25 in b, Op. 33/4; No. 26 in c#, Op. 41/1; No. 27 in e, Op. 41/2; No. 28 in B, Op. 41/3; No. 29 in A♭, Op. 41/4; No. 30 in G, Op. 50/1; No. 31 in A♭, Op. 50/2; No. 32 in c#, Op. 50/3; No. 33 in B, Op. 56/1; No. 34 in C, Op. 56/2; No. 35 in c, Op. 56/3; No. 36 in a, Op. 59/1; No. 37 in A, Op. 59/2; No. 38 in f#, Op. 59/3; No. 39 in B, Op. 63/1; No. 40 in f, Op. 63/2; No. 41 in c#, Op. 63/3; No. 50 in a, "Notre temps"; No. 51 in a, "A Emile Gaillard"; No. 42 in G, Op. 67/1; No. 43 in g, Op. 67/2; No. 44 in C, Op. 67/3; No. 45 in a, Op. 67/4; No. 46 in C, Op. 68/1; No. 47 in a, Op. 68/2; No. 48 in F, Op. 68/3; No. 49 in f, Op. 68/4]; Ballade 1 Pno, Op. 23; Ballade 2 Pno, Op. 38; Ballade 3 Pno, Op. 47; Ballade 4 Pno, Op. 52; Scherzos Pno [No. 1 in b, Op. 20; No. 2 in b♭/D♭, Op. 31; No. 3 in c#, Op. 39; No. 4 in E, Op. 54]; Polonaise 1 Pno, Op. 26/1; Polonaise 2 Pno, Op. 26/2; Polonaise 3 Pno, Op. 40/1; Polonaise 4 Pno, Op. 40/2; Polonaise 5 Pno, Op. 44; Polonaise 6 Pno, Op. 53; Polonaises-fant, Op. 61; Son Pno in b♭, Op. 35 [Grave; Scherzo; Marche funèbre; Finale (Presto)]; Son Pno in b, Op. 58 [Allegro maestoso; Scherzo; Largo; Presto, non tanto]; Fantaisie Pno, Op. 49; Con 1 Pno, Op. 11 [Allegro maestoso; Larghetto; Rondo (Vivace)]; Con 2 Pno, Op. 21 [Maestoso; Larghetto; Allegro vivace]; Waltzes Pno [No. 1 in E♭, Op. 18, "Grand Valse Brillante"; No. 2 in A♭, Op. 34/1; No. 3 in a, Op. 34/2; No. 4 in F, Op. 34/3; No. 5 in A♭, Op. 42; No. 6 in D♭, Op. 64/1, "Minute"; No. 7 in c#, Op. 64/2; No. 8 in A♭, Op. 64/3; No. 9 in A♭, Op. 69/1, "L'adieu"; No. 10 in b, Op. 69/2; No. 11 in g♭, Op. 70/1; No. 12 in f, Op. 70/2; No. 13 in D♭, Op. 70/3; No. 14 in e, Op. posth.]; Impromptu in A♭, Op. 29; Impromptu in G♭, Op. 51; Fant-Impromptu, Op. 66; Barcarolle Pno, Op. 60; Nouvelles études; Bolero, Op. 19; Berceuse, Op. 57; Tarentelle, Op. 43; Andante Spianato & Grand Polonaise, Op. 22; Preludes (24) Pno, Op. 28 ("The Chopin Collection") † Impromptu in F#, Op. 36 RCAV (Gold Seal) 10-▲ 60822 (112.97)

A. Rubinstein (pno)—Polonaise 3 Pno, Op. 40/1; Nocturnes Pno [No. 2 in E♭, Op. 9/2; No. 11 in g, Op. 37/1; No. 5 in F#, Op. 15/2; No. 8 in D♭, Op. 27/2]; Waltzes Pno [No. 1 in E♭, Op. 18, "Grand Valse Brillante"; No. 7 in c#, Op. 64/2; No. 6 in D♭, Op. 64/1, "Minute"]; Polonaise 6 Pno, Op. 53; Mazurkas Pno [No. 23 in D, Op. 33/2; No. 5 in B♭, Op. 7/1]; Fant-Impromptu, Op. 66; Ballade 1 Pno, Op. 23; Scherzos Pno [No. 2 in b♭/D♭, Op. 31] ("Basic 100, Vol. 20") RCAV ▲ 61717 (10.97) ▮ 61717 (5.98)

A. Rubinstein (pno) *(Nocturnes Pno [No. 1 in b♭, Op. 9/1; No. 2 in E♭, Op. 9/2; No. 3 in B, Op. 9/3; No. 4 in F, Op. 15/1; No. 5 in F#, Op. 15/2; No. 6 in g, Op. 15/6; No. 7 in c#, Op. 27/1; No. 8 in D♭, Op. 27/2; No. 9 in B, Op. 32/1; No. 10 in A♭, Op. 32/2; No. 11 in g, Op. 37/1; No. 12 in G, Op. 37/2; No. 13 in c, Op. 48/1; No. 14 in f#, Op. 48/2; No. 15 in f, Op. 55/1; No. 16 in E♭, Op. 55/2]; Polonaise 1 Pno, Op. 26/1; Polonaise 2 Pno, Op. 26/2; Polonaise 3 Pno, Op. 40/1; Polonaise 4 Pno, Op. 40/2; Polonaise 5 Pno, Op. 44; Polonaises-fant, Op. 61; Andante Spianato & Grand Polonaise, Op. 22; Scherzos Pno; Barcarolle Pno, Op. 60; Berceuse, Op. 57; Waltzes Pno [No. 2 in A♭, Op. 34/1; No. 7 in c#, Op. 64/2])*, A. Rubinstein (pno), J. Barbirolli (cnd), London SO *(Con 1 Pno, Op. 11; Con 2 Pno, Op. 21)* ("The Chopin Experience") GRM2 4-▲ 78654

A. Rubinstein (pno) ("Selections from the Chopin Collection") RCAV (Gold Seal) ▲ 7725 [ADD] (11.97)

V. Shakin (pno)—Barcarolle Pno, Op. 60; Mazurkas Pno [No. 36 in a, Op. 59/1; No. 37 in A, Op. 59/2; No. 38 in f#, Op. 59/3; No. 39 in B, Op. 63/1; No. 40 in f, Op. 63/2; No. 41 in c#, Op. 63/3]; Polonaises-fant, Op. 61; Berceuse, Op. 57 SNYC ▲ 57257 [DDD] (4.97)

Solomon (pno)—Études Pno [No. 8 in D♭, Op. 10/8; No. 13 in A♭, Op. 25/1; No. 15 in F, Op. 25/3]; Fantaisie Pno, Op. 49; Polonaise 3 Pno, Op. 40/1; Polonaise 6 Pno, Op. 53 *(rec 1932 & 1934 for Columbia)* † Liszt:Etudes de concert (3), S.144; Album d'un voyageur, S.156; Rákóczy March Orch, S.117; P. Tchaikovsky:Con 1 Pno, Op. 23 PHS ▲ 9478 [AAD] (17.97)

Solomon (pno)—Études Pno [No. 9 in G♭, Op. 10/9; No. 14 in f, Op. 25/2; No. 15 in F, Op. 25/3]; Nocturnes Pno [No. 8 in D♭, Op. 27/2] ("The First HMV Recordings: 1942-43") † Berceuse, Op. 57; Beethoven:Trio 6 Pno, Op. 97; J. Brahms:Vars & Fugue on a Theme by Handel, Op. 24 APR ▲ 5503 [ADD] (19.97)

S. Tiempo (pno)—Son Pno in b♭, Op. 35; Ballade 1 Pno, Op. 23; Nocturnes Pno [No. 3 in B, Op. 9/3]; Scherzos Pno [No. 1 in b, Op. 20]; Études Pno [No. 18 in g#, Op. 25/6] ("Romantic Recital") † R. Schumann:Fantasiestücke Pno, Op. 12 VRDI ▲ 6806

D. Várjon (pno)—Waltzes Pno [No. 6 in D♭, Op. 64/1, "Minute"; No. 7 in c#, Op. 64/2]; Nocturnes Pno [No. 2 in E♭, Op. 9/2; No. 8 in D♭, Op. 27/2; No. 20 in c#, Op. posth.]; Scherzos Pno [No. 1 in b, Op. 20]; Mazurkas Pno [No. 13 in a, Op. 17/4; No. 23 in D, Op. 33/2] *(rec Budapest, Poland, May-June 1994)* † Son Pno in b, Op. 58 CAPO ▲ 10710 [DDD] (10.97)

D. Wayenberg (pno)—Nocturnes Pno [No. 4 in F, Op. 15/1]; Waltzes Pno [No. 1 in E♭, Op. 18, "Grand Valse Brillante"; No. 6 in D♭, Op. 64/1, "Minute"]; Ballade 1 Pno, Op. 23; Ballade 3 Pno, Op. 47; Études Pno [No. 12 in c, Op. 10/12, "Revolutionary"]; Fant-Impromptu, Op. 66; Mazurkas Pno [No. 13 in a, Op. 17/4; No. 23 in D, Op. 33/2]; Scherzos Pno [No. 2 in b♭/D♭, Op. 31]; Preludes (24) Pno, Op. 28 [No. 15 in D♭, "Raindrop"]; Polonaise 6 Pno, Op. 53 INMP (Classics) ▲ 6700142 (9.97)

Yuval Fichman *(Waltzes Pno [No. 1 in E♭, Op. 18, "Grand Valse Brillante"])*, Kemal Gekic, Jean-Marc Luisada *(Mazurkas Pno [No. 18 in c, Op. 30/1; No. 2 in c#, Op. 6/2; No. 3 in E, Op. 6/3; No. 4 in c, Op. 6/4; No. 14 in g, Op. 24/1; No. 15 in C, Op. 24/2; No. 16 in A♭, Op. 24/3; No. 17 in b♭, Op. 24/4])*, Krzysztof Jablonski, Kemal Gekic *(Études Pno [No. 5 in G♭, Op. 10/5, "Black Keys"; No. 13 in A♭, Op. 25/1])*, Krzysztof Jablonski *(Nocturnes Pno [No. 3 in B, Op. 9/3]; Scherzos Pno [No. 1 in b, Op. 20]) (rec live Warsaw, Poland, 1985)* ("11th International Chopin Competition") LALI ▲ 15604 [DDD] (3.97)

Polonaises (15) for Piano

V. Ashkenazy (pno) † Allegro de concert, Op. 46; Barcarolle Pno, Op. 60; Berceuse, Op. 57 PLON (Double Decker) 2-▲ 452167 (17.97)

I. Biret (pno) ("Vol. 1") NXIN ▲ 550360 [DDD] (5.97)

A. Brailowsky (pno)—No. 16 in g#; No. 8 in d, Op. 71/1; No. 10 in f, Op. 71/3 † Mazurkas Pno; Songs Sop SNYC (Take Two) 2-▲ 63237 (14.97)

F. Clidat (pno)—No. 8 in d, Op. 71/1; No. 10 in f, Op. 71/3 ("The Most Famous Polonaises") † Polonaise 1 Pno, Op. 26/1; Polonaise 2 Pno, Op. 26/2; Polonaise 3 Pno, Op. 40/1; Polonaise 4 Pno, Op. 40/2; Polonaise 5 Pno, Op. 44; Polonaise 6 Pno, Op. 53; Polonaise 9 Pno, Op. 71/2; Polonaises-fant, Op. 61 FORL ▲ 16615 [DDD] (16.97)

A. Harasiewicz (pno) † Waltzes Pno PPHI (Duo) 2-▲ 462874 (17.97)

W. Kapell (pno) *(rec 1940-53)* † Preludes (24) Pno, Op. 28; Beethoven:Con 2 Pno, Op. 19; S. Rachmaninoff:Rhap on a Theme of Paganini, Op. 43; F. Schubert:Songs (misc) PHS ▲ 9194 (17.97)

C. Katsaris (pno)—No. 8 in d, Op. 71/1; No. 10 in f, Op. 71/3; No. 11 in b♭; No. 12 in G♭; No. 13 in g; No. 14 in B♭; No. 15 in A♭; No. 16 in g# *(rec Mar 3-22, 1993)* † Andante Spianato & Grand Polonaise, Op. 22; Funeral March, Op. 72/2; Mazurkas Pno; Polonaise 1 Pno, Op. 26/1; Polonaise 2 Pno, Op. 26/2; Polonaise 3 Pno, Op. 40/1; Polonaise 4 Pno, Op. 40/2; Polonaise 5 Pno, Op. 44; Polonaise 9 Pno, Op. 71/2; Polonaises-fant, Op. 61 SNYC 2-▲ 53967 [DDD] (31.97)

G. Ohlsson (pno), G. Ohlsson (pno)—No. 11 in b♭; No. 12 in G♭; No. 13 in g; No. 14 in B♭; No. 15 in A♭; No. 16 in g#; No. 8 in d, Op. 71/1; No. 10 in f, Op. 71/3 ("The Complete Chopin Piano Works, Vol. 5") † Impromptus (4); Polonaise 1 Pno, Op. 26/1; Polonaise 2 Pno, Op. 26/2; Polonaise 3 Pno, Op. 40/1; Polonaise 4 Pno, Op. 40/2; Polonaise 9 Pno, Op. 71/2; Polonaises-fant, Op. 61 ARA 2-▲ 6642 [DDD] (32.97)

A. Rubinstein (pno) † Andante Spianato & Grand Polonaise, Op. 22 ENPL (The Piano Library) ▲ 187 (13.97)

J. Sterczyński (pno) *(rec Rzeszow, 1992)* SELN 2-▲ 92024 [DDD] (31.97)

CHOPIN, FRÉDÉRIC (cont.)

Polonaise No. 1 in c# for Piano, Op. 26/1 (1834-35)

F. Clidat (pno) ("The Most Famous Polonaises") † Polonaise 2 Pno, Op. 26/2; Polonaise 3 Pno, Op. 40/1; Polonaise 4 Pno, Op. 40/2; Polonaise 5 Pno, Op. 44; Polonaise 6 Pno, Op. 53; Polonaise 9 Pno, Op. 71/2; Polonaises Pno; Polonaises-fant, Op. 61 FORL ▲ 16615 [DDD] (16.97)

C. Katsaris (pno) *(rec Mar 3-22, 1993)* † Andante Spianato & Grand Polonaise, Op. 22; Funeral March, Op. 72/2; Mazurkas Pno; Polonaise 2 Pno, Op. 26/2; Polonaise 3 Pno, Op. 40/1; Polonaise 4 Pno, Op. 40/2; Polonaise 5 Pno, Op. 44; Polonaise 9 Pno, Op. 71/2; Polonaises Pno; Polonaises-fant, Op. 61 SNYC 2-▲ 53967 [DDD] (31.97)

G. Montero (pno) † Fant-Impromptu, Op. 66; Nocturnes Pno; Polonaise 2 Pno, Op. 26/2; Polonaise 6 Pno, Op. 53; Scherzos Pno; Son Pno in b♭, Op. 35; Waltzes Pno PALE ▲ 510 (17.97)

I. Moravec (pno) † Polonaises-fant, Op. 61; Debussy:Estampes; Images (6) Pno; Preludes Pno VB2 2-▲ 5103 [DDD] (9.97)

G. Ohlsson (pno) ("The Complete Chopin Piano Works, Vol. 5") † Impromptus (4); Polonaise 2 Pno, Op. 26/2; Polonaise 3 Pno, Op. 40/1; Polonaise 4 Pno, Op. 40/2; Polonaise 9 Pno, Op. 71/2; Polonaises Pno; Polonaises-fant, Op. 61 ARA 2-▲ 6642 [DDD] (32.97)

M. Pollini (pno) † Études Pno; Polonaise 2 Pno, Op. 26/2; Polonaise 3 Pno, Op. 40/1; Polonaise 4 Pno, Op. 40/2; Polonaise 5 Pno, Op. 44; Polonaise 6 Pno, Op. 53; Polonaises-fant, Op. 61; Preludes (24) Pno, Op. 28 DEUT 3-▲ 31221 [AAD/ADD] (34.97)

M. Pollini (pno) † Polonaise 2 Pno, Op. 26/2; Polonaise 3 Pno, Op. 40/1; Polonaise 4 Pno, Op. 40/2; Polonaise 5 Pno, Op. 44; Polonaise 6 Pno, Op. 53; Polonaises-fant, Op. 61 DEUT (The Originals) ▲ 457711 [ADD] (11.97)

S. Richter (pno) *(rec 1992)* † Mazurkas Pno; Polonaise 3 Pno, Op. 40/1; Polonaises-fant, Op. 61; A. Scriabin:Dances (2) Pno, Op. 73; Fant Pno, Op. 28; Poème-nocturne Pno, Op. 61; Vers la flamme, Op. 72 LV ▲ 441 (17.97)

A. Rubinstein (pno) † Andante Spianato & Grand Polonaise, Op. 22; Polonaise 2 Pno, Op. 26/2; Polonaise 3 Pno, Op. 40/1; Polonaise 4 Pno, Op. 40/2; Polonaise 5 Pno, Op. 44; Polonaise 6 Pno, Op. 53; Polonaises-fant, Op. 61 MTAL ▲ 48003 (6.97)

J. Sterczyński (pno) *(rec Rzeszow, Poland, 1992)* ("Piano Works") † Polonaise 2 Pno, Op. 26/2; Polonaise 3 Pno, Op. 40/1; Polonaise 4 Pno, Op. 40/2; Polonaise 5 Pno, Op. 44; Polonaise 6 Pno, Op. 53; Polonaises-fant, Op. 61; P. Tchaikovsky:Saisons SELN ▲ 930916 [DDD] (16.97)

Polonaise No. 2 in e♭ for Piano, Op. 26/2 (1834-35)

S. Cherkassky (pno) ("Shura Cherkassky:The Last of the Great Piano Romantics, Vol. 2") † Pno Music (misc colls); Preludes (24) Pno, Op. 28; Liszt:Trans, Arrs & Paraphrases ASVQ ▲ 6109 [DDD] (10.97)

F. Clidat (pno) ("The Most Famous Polonaises") † Polonaise 1 Pno, Op. 26/1; Polonaise 3 Pno, Op. 40/1; Polonaise 4 Pno, Op. 40/2; Polonaise 5 Pno, Op. 44; Polonaise 6 Pno, Op. 53; Polonaise 9 Pno, Op. 71/2; Polonaises Pno; Polonaises-fant, Op. 61 FORL ▲ 16615 [DDD] (16.97)

E. Gabriel (pno) † Mazurkas Pno; Nocturnes Pno; Polonaise 3 Pno, Op. 40/1; Son Pno in b, Op. 58; Waltzes Pno QUER ▲ 9822 (18.97)

C. Katsaris (pno) *(rec Mar 3-22, 1993)* † Andante Spianato & Grand Polonaise, Op. 22; Funeral March, Op. 72/2; Mazurkas Pno; Polonaise 1 Pno, Op. 26/1; Polonaise 3 Pno, Op. 40/1; Polonaise 4 Pno, Op. 40/2; Polonaise 5 Pno, Op. 44; Polonaise 9 Pno, Op. 71/2; Polonaises Pno; Polonaises-fant, Op. 61 SNYC 2-▲ 53967 [DDD] (31.97)

G. Montero (pno) † Fant-Impromptu, Op. 66; Nocturnes Pno; Polonaise 1 Pno, Op. 26/1; Polonaise 6 Pno, Op. 53; Scherzos Pno; Son Pno in b♭, Op. 35; Waltzes Pno PALE ▲ 510 (17.97)

G. Ohlsson (pno) ("The Complete Chopin Piano Works, Vol. 5") † Impromptus (4); Polonaise 1 Pno, Op. 26/1; Polonaise 3 Pno, Op. 40/1; Polonaise 4 Pno, Op. 40/2; Polonaise 9 Pno, Op. 71/2; Polonaises Pno; Polonaises-fant, Op. 61 ARA 2-▲ 6642 [DDD] (32.97)

I. J. Paderewski (pno) *(rec 1912-30)* ("Ignacy Jan Paderewski") † Études Pno; Berceuse, Op. 57; Funeral March in b♭; Mazurkas Pno; Nocturnes Pno; Polonaise 3 Pno, Op. 40/1; Preludes (24) Pno, Op. 28; Waltzes Pno; Liszt:Etudes d'exécution transcendante (6), S.140; Études de concert (3), S.144; Hungarian Rhaps, S.244; Trans, Arrs & Paraphrases; I. J. Paderewski:Minuet; F. Schubert:Impromptus (4) PPHI (Great Pianists of the 20th Century) 2-▲ 456919 (22.97)

M. Pollini (pno) † Études Pno; Polonaise 1 Pno, Op. 26/1; Polonaise 3 Pno, Op. 40/1; Polonaise 4 Pno, Op. 40/2; Polonaise 5 Pno, Op. 44; Polonaise 6 Pno, Op. 53; Polonaises-fant, Op. 61; Preludes (24) Pno, Op. 28 DEUT 3-▲ 31221 [AAD/ADD] (34.97)

M. Pollini (pno) † Polonaise 1 Pno, Op. 26/1; Polonaise 3 Pno, Op. 40/1; Polonaise 4 Pno, Op. 40/2; Polonaise 5 Pno, Op. 44; Polonaise 6 Pno, Op. 53; Polonaises-fant, Op. 61 DEUT (The Originals) ▲ 457711 [ADD] (11.97)

A. Rubinstein (pno) † Andante Spianato & Grand Polonaise, Op. 22; Polonaise 1 Pno, Op. 26/1; Polonaise 3 Pno, Op. 40/1; Polonaise 4 Pno, Op. 40/2; Polonaise 5 Pno, Op. 44; Polonaise 6 Pno, Op. 53; Polonaises-fant, Op. 61 MTAL ▲ 48003 (6.97)

J. Sterczyński (pno) *(rec Rzeszow, Poland, 1992)* ("Piano Works") † Polonaise 1 Pno, Op. 26/1; Polonaise 3 Pno, Op. 40/1; Polonaise 4 Pno, Op. 40/2; Polonaise 5 Pno, Op. 44; Polonaise 6 Pno, Op. 53; Polonaises-fant, Op. 61; P. Tchaikovsky:Saisons SELN ▲ 930916 [DDD] (16.97)

Polonaise No. 3 in A for Piano, Op. 40/1, "Military" (1838)

W. Backhaus (pno) *(rec Berlin, Germany, 1916)* † Études Pno; J. Brahms:Vars on a Theme by Paganini, Op. 35; Liszt:Hungarian Rhaps, S.244; A. Rubinstein:Album of Popular Dances, Op. 82; Soirées à Saint-Pétersbourg; F. Schubert:Qnt Pno, D.667 BPS ▲ 38 [ADD] (16.97)

J. Bolet (pno) *(rec Queens, NY)* ("A Chopin Piano Recital") † Études Pno; Fant-Impromptu, Op. 66; Polonaise 6 Pno, Op. 53; Preludes (24) Pno, Op. 28; Waltzes Pno EVC ▲ 9028 [AAD] (13.97)

F. Clidat (pno) ("The Most Famous Polonaises") † Polonaise 1 Pno, Op. 26/1; Polonaise 2 Pno, Op. 26/2; Polonaise 4 Pno, Op. 40/2; Polonaise 5 Pno, Op. 44; Polonaise 6 Pno, Op. 53; Polonaise 9 Pno, Op. 71/2; Polonaises Pno; Polonaises-fant, Op. 61 FORL ▲ 16615 [DDD] (16.97)

P. Entremont (pno) *(rec Winterthur, Switzerland, Nov 18-19, 1968)* † Études Pno; Fant-Impromptu, Op. 66; Intro & Polonaise, Op. 3; Mazurkas Pno; Nocturnes Pno; Polonaise 6 Pno, Op. 53; Preludes (24) Pno, Op. 28; Son Pno in b♭, Op. 35; Waltzes Pno SNYC ▲ 51338 [ADD] (7.97)

E. Gabriel (pno) † Mazurkas Pno; Nocturnes Pno; Polonaise 2 Pno, Op. 26/2; Son Pno in b, Op. 58; Waltzes Pno QUER ▲ 9822 (18.97)

S. Gorodnitzki (pno) *(rec New York City, NY, July 1953)* † J. Brahms:Vars & Fugue on a Theme by Handel, Op. 24; Vars on a Theme by Paganini, Op. 35; Debussy:Preludes Pno; Liszt:Consolations (6), S.172; Trans, Arrs & Paraphrases EMIC ▲ 67018 [ADD] (11.97)

J. Hofmann (pno) [from Duo-Art Pno Rolls] ("Josef Hofmann Plays Chopin") † Con 1 Pno, Op. 11; Polonaise 6 Pno, Op. 53; Waltzes Pno KLAV (Legendary Artists) ▲ 11082 [ADD] (18.97)

C. Katsaris (pno) *(rec Mar 3-22, 1993)* † Andante Spianato & Grand Polonaise, Op. 22; Funeral March, Op. 72/2; Mazurkas Pno; Polonaise 1 Pno, Op. 26/1; Polonaise 2 Pno, Op. 26/2; Polonaise 4 Pno, Op. 40/2; Polonaise 5 Pno, Op. 44; Polonaise 9 Pno, Op. 71/2; Polonaises Pno; Polonaises-fant, Op. 61 SNYC 2-▲ 53967 [DDD] (31.97)

N. Kokinos (pno) † Fantaisie Pno, Op. 49; Polonaise 6 Pno, Op. 53; Polonaises-fant, Op. 61; Preludes (24) Pno, Op. 28; Scherzos Pno; Waltzes Pno ANDP ▲ 9592 (15.97)

G. Ohlsson (pno) ("The Complete Chopin Piano Works, Vol. 5") † Impromptus (4); Polonaise 1 Pno, Op. 26/1; Polonaise 2 Pno, Op. 26/2; Polonaise 4 Pno, Op. 40/2; Polonaise 9 Pno, Op. 71/2; Polonaises Pno; Polonaises-fant, Op. 61 ARA 2-▲ 6642 [DDD] (32.97)

I. J. Paderewski (pno) *(rec 1912-30)* ("Ignacy Jan Paderewski") † Études Pno; Berceuse, Op. 57; Funeral March in b♭; Mazurkas Pno; Nocturnes Pno; Polonaise 2 Pno, Op. 26/2; Preludes (24) Pno, Op. 28; Waltzes Pno; Liszt:Études d'exécution transcendante (6), S.140; Études de concert (3), S.144; Hungarian Rhaps, S.244; Trans, Arrs & Paraphrases; I. J. Paderewski:Minuet; F. Schubert:Impromptus (4) PPHI (Great Pianists of the 20th Century) 2-▲ 456919 (22.97)

M. Pollini (pno) † Études Pno; Polonaise 1 Pno, Op. 26/1; Polonaise 2 Pno, Op. 26/2; Polonaise 4 Pno, Op. 40/2; Polonaise 5 Pno, Op. 44; Polonaise 6 Pno, Op. 53; Polonaises-fant, Op. 61; Preludes (24) Pno, Op. 28 DEUT 3-▲ 31221 [AAD/ADD] (34.97)

M. Pollini (pno) † Polonaise 1 Pno, Op. 26/1; Polonaise 2 Pno, Op. 26/2; Polonaise 4 Pno, Op. 40/2; Polonaise 5 Pno, Op. 44; Polonaise 6 Pno, Op. 53; Polonaises-fant, Op. 61 DEUT (The Originals) ▲ 457711 [ADD] (11.97)

S. Richter (pno) *(rec 1992)* † Mazurkas Pno; Polonaise 1 Pno, Op. 26/1; Polonaises-fant, Op. 61; A. Scriabin:Dances (2) Pno, Op. 73; Fant Pno, Op. 28; Poème-nocturne Pno, Op. 61; Vers la flamme, Op. 72 LV ▲ 441 (17.97)

A. Rubinstein (pno) † Andante Spianato & Grand Polonaise, Op. 22; Polonaise 1 Pno, Op. 26/1; Polonaise 2 Pno, Op. 26/2; Polonaise 4 Pno, Op. 40/2; Polonaise 5 Pno, Op. 44; Polonaise 6 Pno, Op. 53; Polonaises-fant, Op. 61 MTAL ▲ 48003 (6.97)

A. Rubinstein (pno) *(rec Abbey Road, England, Feb 2, 1935)* ("The Legendary Rubinstein") † Barcarolle Pno, Op. 60; Berceuse, Op. 57; Mazurkas Pno; Nocturnes Pno; Polonaise 6 Pno, Op. 53; Scherzos Pno; Waltzes Pno EMIC ▲ 67007 (m) [ADD] (11.97)

J. Sterczyński (pno) *(rec Rzeszow, Poland, 1992)* ("Piano Works") † Polonaise 1 Pno, Op. 26/1; Polonaise 2 Pno, Op. 26/2; Polonaise 4 Pno, Op. 40/2; Polonaise 5 Pno, Op. 44; Polonaise 6 Pno, Op. 53; Polonaises-fant, Op. 61; P. Tchaikovsky:Saisons SELN ▲ 930916 [DDD] (16.97)

Polonaise No. 4 in c for Piano, Op. 40/2 (1839)

F. Clidat (pno) ("The Most Famous Polonaises") † Polonaise 1 Pno, Op. 26/1; Polonaise 2 Pno, Op. 26/2; Polonaise 3 Pno, Op. 40/1; Polonaise 5 Pno, Op. 44; Polonaise 6 Pno, Op. 53; Polonaise 9 Pno, Op. 71/2; Polonaises Pno; Polonaises-fant, Op. 61 FORL ▲ 16615 [DDD] (16.97)

CHOPIN, FRÉDÉRIC (cont.)

Polonaise No. 4 in c for Piano, Op. 40/2 (1839) (cont.)

K. Gekić (pno) *(rec Subotica, Yugoslavia, Apr 27, 1997)* † Impromptu in A♭, Op. 29; Impromptu in F#, Op. 36; Polonaise 5 Pno, Op. 44; Son Pno in b♭, Op. 35; Liszt:Grand galop chromatique, S.219; Trans, Arrs & Paraphrases VAIA ▲ 1180 (16.97)

C. Katsaris (pno) *(rec Mar 3-22, 1993)* † Andante Spianato & Grand Polonaise, Op. 22; Funeral March, Op. 72/2; Mazurkas Pno; Polonaise 1 Pno, Op. 26/1; Polonaise 2 Pno, Op. 26/2; Polonaise 3 Pno, Op. 40/1; Polonaise 5 Pno, Op. 44; Polonaise 9 Pno, Op. 71/2; Polonaises Pno; Polonaises-fant, Op. 61 SNYC 2-▲ 53967 [DDD] (31.97)

J. Ogdon (pno) † Barcarolle Pno, Op. 60; Berceuse, Op. 57; Fantaisie Pno, Op. 49; Son Pno in b, Op. 58 INMP ▲ 2008 (9.97)

G. Ohlsson (pno) ("The Complete Chopin Piano Works, Vol. 5") † Impromptus (4); Polonaise 1 Pno, Op. 26/1; Polonaise 2 Pno, Op. 26/2; Polonaise 3 Pno, Op. 40/1; Polonaise 9 Pno, Op. 71/2; Polonaises Pno; Polonaises-fant, Op. 61 ARA 2-▲ 6642 [DDD] (32.97)

J. Olejniczak (pno), Andrzej Jagodzinski Trio ("Jazz: Metamorphoses") † Études Pno; Mazurkas Pno; Nocturnes Pno; Preludes (24) Pno, Op. 28 OPUS (Chopin Vol. 8) ▲ 2013 (18.97)

M. Pollini (pno) † Études Pno; Polonaise 1 Pno, Op. 26/1; Polonaise 2 Pno, Op. 26/2; Polonaise 3 Pno, Op. 40/1; Polonaise 5 Pno, Op. 44; Polonaise 6 Pno, Op. 53; Polonaises-fant, Op. 61; Preludes (24) Pno, Op. 28 DEUT 3-▲ 31221 [AAD/ADD] (34.97)

M. Pollini (pno) † Polonaise 1 Pno, Op. 26/1; Polonaise 2 Pno, Op. 26/2; Polonaise 3 Pno, Op. 40/1; Polonaise 5 Pno, Op. 44; Polonaise 6 Pno, Op. 53; Polonaises-fant, Op. 61 DEUT (The Originals) ▲ 457711 [ADD] (11.97)

A. Rubinstein (pno) † Andante Spianato & Grand Polonaise, Op. 22; Polonaise 1 Pno, Op. 26/1; Polonaise 2 Pno, Op. 26/2; Polonaise 3 Pno, Op. 40/1; Polonaise 5 Pno, Op. 44; Polonaise 6 Pno, Op. 53; Polonaises-fant, Op. 61 MTAL ▲ 48003 (6.97)

J. Sterczyński (pno) *(rec Rzeszow, Poland, 1992)* ("Piano Works") † Polonaise 1 Pno, Op. 26/1; Polonaise 2 Pno, Op. 26/2; Polonaise 3 Pno, Op. 40/1; Polonaise 5 Pno, Op. 44; Polonaise 6 Pno, Op. 53; Polonaises-fant, Op. 61; P. Tchaikovsky:Saisons SELN ▲ 930916 [DDD] (16.97)

Polonaise No. 5 in f# for Piano, Op. 44 (1840-41)

F. Clidat (pno) ("The Most Famous Polonaises") † Polonaise 1 Pno, Op. 26/1; Polonaise 2 Pno, Op. 26/2; Polonaise 3 Pno, Op. 40/1; Polonaise 4 Pno, Op. 40/2; Polonaise 6 Pno, Op. 53; Polonaise 9 Pno, Op. 71/2; Polonaises Pno; Polonaises-fant, Op. 61 FORL ▲ 16615 [DDD] (16.97)

K. Gekić (pno) *(rec Subotica, Yugoslavia, Apr 27, 1997)* † Impromptu in A♭, Op. 29; Impromptu in F#, Op. 36; Polonaise 4 Pno, Op. 40/2; Son Pno in b♭, Op. 35; Liszt:Grand galop chromatique, S.219; Trans, Arrs & Paraphrases VAIA ▲ 1180 (16.97)

V. Horowitz (pno) *(rec 1968)* † Polonaises-fant, Op. 61; Son Pno in b♭, Op. 35 SNYC ▲ 42412 [AAD] (16.97)

V. Horowitz (pno) *(rec Jan 2-Feb 1, 1968)* ("The Legendary Masterworks Recordings, 1962-1973, Vol. 4") † V. Horowitz:Vars Theme from Bizet's Carmen; D. Scarlatti:Sons Kbd; R. Schumann:Arabeske Pno, Op. 18; Kinderszenen Pno, Op. 15 SNYC ▲ 53465 [ADD] (16.97)

P. Katin (pno) † Nocturnes Pno; Son Pno in b, Op. 58 HALM ▲ 35014 (6.97)

C. Katsaris (pno) *(rec Mar 3-22, 1993)* † Andante Spianato & Grand Polonaise, Op. 22; Funeral March, Op. 72/2; Mazurkas Pno; Polonaise 1 Pno, Op. 26/1; Polonaise 2 Pno, Op. 26/2; Polonaise 3 Pno, Op. 40/1; Polonaise 4 Pno, Op. 40/2; Polonaise 9 Pno, Op. 71/2; Polonaises Pno; Polonaises-fant, Op. 61 SNYC 2-▲ 53967 [DDD] (31.97)

A. Lear (pno) *(rec Brandon Hill Bristol, England, Nov 24, 1993)* ("The Original Chopin") † Andante Spianato & Grand Polonaise, Op. 22; Barcarolle Pno, Op. 60; Fant-Impromptu, Op. 66; Fantaisie Pno, Op. 49; Nocturnes (21) Pno APR ▲ 5551 [DDD] (19.97)

K. Lifschitz (pno) ("Live in Milano") † Nocturnes (21) Pno; W. A. Mozart:Rondo Pno, K.511; M. Ravel:Gaspard de la nuit DNN ▲ 78908 [DDD] (16.97)

Z. Mihailovich (pno) *(rec Pomona College Claremont, CA, May 17-18, 1995)* † Son Pno in b, Op. 58; Son Pno in b♭, Op. 35 CENT ▲ 2270 [DDD] (16.97)

G. Novaes (pno) ("The Art of Guiomar Novaes") † Études Pno; Ballade 3 Pno, Op. 47; Ballade 4 Pno, Op. 52; Berceuse, Op. 57; Ecossaises (3) Pno, Op. 72/3; Polonaise 6 Pno, Op. 53 VC ▲ 8071 (16.97)

V. Perlemuter (pno) † Ballades (4) Pno; Polonaises-fant, Op. 61 NIMB ▲ 5209 [ADD] (16.97)

M. Pollini (pno) † Études Pno; Polonaise 1 Pno, Op. 26/1; Polonaise 2 Pno, Op. 26/2; Polonaise 3 Pno, Op. 40/1; Polonaise 4 Pno, Op. 40/2; Polonaise 6 Pno, Op. 53; Polonaises-fant, Op. 61; Preludes (24) Pno, Op. 28 DEUT 3-▲ 31221 [AAD/ADD] (34.97)

M. Pollini (pno) † Polonaise 1 Pno, Op. 26/1; Polonaise 2 Pno, Op. 26/2; Polonaise 3 Pno, Op. 40/1; Polonaise 4 Pno, Op. 40/2; Polonaise 6 Pno, Op. 53; Polonaises-fant, Op. 61 DEUT (The Originals) ▲ 457711 [ADD] (11.97)

A. Rubinstein (pno) [piano roll recording] ("Great Pianists of the Golden Era") † Ballade 1 Pno, Op. 23; Ballade 3 Pno, Op. 47; Nocturnes Pno; Debussy:Danse Pno; Henselt:Berceuse; Lanner:Valses Viennoises; W. A. Mozart:Son 16 Pno, K.545; S. Prokofiev:Pieces (4) Pno, Op. 4; Rimsky-Korsakov:Golden Cockerel (sels) FON ▲ 9008 [DDD] (13.97)

A. Rubinstein (pno) † Andante Spianato & Grand Polonaise, Op. 22; Polonaise 1 Pno, Op. 26/1; Polonaise 2 Pno, Op. 26/2; Polonaise 3 Pno, Op. 40/1; Polonaise 4 Pno, Op. 40/2; Polonaise 6 Pno, Op. 53; Polonaises-fant, Op. 61 MTAL ▲ 48003 (6.97)

M. Shehori (pno) † Barcarolle Pno, Op. 60; J. S. Bach:Clavier-Büchlein for W. F. Bach; Beethoven:Son 17 Pno, Op. 31/2; G. F. Handel:Suites de Pièces (9) Hpd, HWV 434-42; Liszt:Légendes, S.175; Trans, Arrs & Paraphrases CEMB ▲ 101 [DDD] (15.97)

G. Sokolov (pno), C. Coin (cnd), Mosaïques Ensemble † Études Pno; Con 2 Pno, Op. 21; Mazurkas Pno; Nocturnes Pno; Preludes (24) Pno, Op. 28; Son Pno in b♭, Op. 35; Waltzes Pno OPUS (Chopin Vol. 5) ▲ 2010 (18.97)

J. Sterczyński (pno) *(rec Rzeszow, Poland, 1992)* ("Piano Works") † Polonaise 1 Pno, Op. 26/1; Polonaise 2 Pno, Op. 26/2; Polonaise 3 Pno, Op. 40/1; Polonaise 4 Pno, Op. 40/2; Polonaise 6 Pno, Op. 53; Polonaises-fant, Op. 61; P. Tchaikovsky:Saisons SELN ▲ 930916 [DDD] (16.97)

V. Tropp (pno) † Barcarolle Pno, Op. 60; Prelude in c#, Op. 45; Son Pno in b♭, Op. 35 DNN ▲ 18035 (16.97)

various artists † Études Pno; Con 2 Pno, Op. 21; Mazurkas Pno; Preludes (24) Pno, Op. 28; Son Pno in b♭, Op. 35; Son Vc OPUS (Chopin Exploration Vol. 10 (Excerpts from Vols. 1-9)) ▲ 2015 (7.97)

Polonaise No. 6 in A♭ for Piano, Op. 53, "Heroic" (1842)

J. Bolet (pno) *(rec Queens, NY)* ("A Chopin Piano Recital") † Études Pno; Fant-Impromptu, Op. 66; Polonaise 3 Pno, Op. 40/1; Preludes (24) Pno, Op. 28; Waltzes Pno EVC ▲ 9028 [AAD] (13.97)

F. Clidat (pno) ("The Most Famous Polonaises") † Polonaise 1 Pno, Op. 26/1; Polonaise 2 Pno, Op. 26/2; Polonaise 3 Pno, Op. 40/1; Polonaise 4 Pno, Op. 40/2; Polonaise 5 Pno, Op. 44; Polonaise 9 Pno, Op. 71/2; Polonaises Pno; Polonaises-fant, Op. 61 FORL ▲ 16615 [DDD] (16.97)

G. Cziffra (pno) *(rec 1956-71)* † Études Pno; Liszt:Études d'exécution transcendante (12), S.139; Études de concert (3), S.144; Fant & Fugue on the name B-A-C-H, S.529; Légendes, S.175; Mephisto Waltz 1 Pno, S.514; Polonaises (2) Pno, S.223; Sonetti (3) del Petrarca, S.158; Trans, Arrs & Paraphrases; Venezia e Napoli, S.159 PPHI (Great Pianists of the 20th Century, Vol. 23) 2-▲ 456760 (22.97)

P. Entremont (pno) *(rec Winterthur, Switzerland, Nov 8, 1967)* † Études Pno; Fant-Impromptu, Op. 66; Intro & Polonaise, Op. 3; Mazurkas Pno; Nocturnes Pno; Polonaise 3 Pno, Op. 40/1; Preludes (24) Pno, Op. 28; Son Pno in b♭, Op. 35; Waltzes Pno SNYC ▲ 51338 [ADD] (7.97)

M. Frager (pno) ("Malcolm Frager Plays Chopin") † Andante Spianato & Grand Polonaise, Op. 22; Intro & Vars in B♭, Op. 12; Pno Music (misc colls); Tarentelle, Op. 43 TEL ▲ 80280 [DDD] (16.97)

I. Friedman (pno) † Nocturnes Pno; Liszt:Grandes études de Paganini, S.141; Hungarian Rhaps, S.244; Réminiscences de Don Juan Pno, S.418 NIMB (Grand Piano) ▲ 8805 [DDD] (11.97)

I. Friedman (pno) ("Highlights 1925-36 From His Discography") † Études Pno; Impromptu in F#, Op. 36; Mazurkas Pno; Nocturnes Pno; Son Pno in b♭, Op. 35; Waltzes Pno; Beethoven:Son 14 Pno, Op. 27/2; I. Friedman:Danse; Music Box, Op. 33/3; J. N. Hummel:Rondo Pno, Op. 11; Liszt:Trans, Arrs & Paraphrases; Mendelssohn (-Bartholdy):Fants Pno, Op. 16; Shield:Old English Menuet APR (Signature Series) ▲ 5508 [ADD] (18.97)

W. Gieseking (pno) *(rec 1924-55)* ("Gieseking: A Retrospective, Vol. 3") † Nocturnes (21) Pno; J. Brahms:Rhaps (2) Pno, Op. 79; Casella:Son Pno, Op. 28; W. A. Mozart:Con 9 Pno, K.271; M. Ravel:Jeux d'eau PHS ▲ 9038 (17.97)

W. Gieseking (pno) ("Walter Gieseking: The Homochord Recordings, 1923-25") † J. S. Bach:Partitas Hpd; J. Brahms:Rhaps (2) Pno, Op. 79; Debussy:Images (6) Pno; Liszt:Hungarian Rhaps, S.244; M. Ravel:Jeux d'eau ENPL (Piano Library) ▲ 203 (13.97)

S. D. Groote (pno) *(rec 1977)* ("Van Cliburn International Retrospective Series, Vol. 1") † J. Haydn:Sonatas for Piano; S. Prokofiev:Son 8 Pno, Op. 84; F. Schubert:Son Pno, D.784 VAIA ▲ 1145 [ADD] (16.97)

A. Haraisewicz (pno) † Ballade 3 Pno, Op. 47; Son Pno in b♭, Op. 35 DI ▲ 920180 [DDD] (5.97)

J. Hofmann (pno) [from Duo-Art Pno Rolls] ("Josef Hofmann Plays Chopin") † Con 1 Pno, Op. 11; Polonaise 3 Pno, Op. 40/1; Waltzes Pno KLAV (Legendary Artists) ▲ 11082 [ADD] (18.97)

N. Kokinos (pno) † Fantaisie Pno, Op. 49; Polonaise 3 Pno, Op. 40/1; Polonaises-fant, Op. 61; Preludes (24) Pno, Op. 28; Scherzos Pno; Waltzes Pno ANDP ▲ 9592 (15.97)

N. Magaloff (pno) ("Shine: The Complete Classics") † Preludes (24) Pno, Op. 28; Beethoven:Sym 9; Liszt:Études d'exécution transcendante (6), S.140; Études de concert (3), S.144; Hungarian Rhaps, S.244; S. Rachmaninoff:Con 3 Pno, Op. 30; Prelude in c#, Op. 3/2; Rimsky-Korsakov:Tale of Tsar Saltan (orch sels); R. Schumann:Kinderszenen Pno, Op. 15; Vivaldi:Gloria; Nulla in mundo pax, RV.630 PPHI 2-▲ 456403 (17.97)

CHOPIN, FRÉDÉRIC (cont.)

Polonaise No. 6 in A♭ for Piano, Op. 53, "Heroic" (1842) (cont.)

B. Moiseiwitsch (pno) *(rec 1930-43)* ("A Portrait, Part 2") † Barcarolle Pno, Op. 60; J. Brahms:Vars & Fugue on a Theme by Handel, Op. 24; Liszt:Hungarian Rhaps, S.244; Liebesträume, S.541; Légendes, S.175; C. M. von Weber:Invitation to the Dance Pno, J.260 ENPL (Piano Library) ▲ 265 (13.97)

G. Montero (pno) † Fant-Impromptu, Op. 66; Nocturnes Pno; Polonaise 1 Pno, Op. 26/1; Polonaise 2 Pno, Op. 26/2; Scherzos Pno; Son Pno in b♭, Op. 35; Waltzes Pno PALE ▲ 510 (17.97)

G. Novaes (pno) ("The Art of Guiomar Novaes") † Etudes Pno; Ballade 3 Pno, Op. 47; Ballade 4 Pno, Op. 52; Berceuse, Op. 57; Ecossaises (3) Pno, Op. 72/3; Polonaise 5 Pno, Op. 44 VC ▲ 8071 (16.97)

I. J. Paderewski (pno) *(rec 1911-37)* † Etudes (24) Pno, Opp. 10 & 25; J. Brahms:Hungarian Dances Pno; Mendelssohn (-Bartholdy):Lieder ohne Worte; A. Rubinstein:Valse-Caprice Pno; R. Schumann:Fantasiestücke Pno, Op. 12; Nachtstücke, Op. 23 ENPL (The Piano Library) ▲ 182 (13.97)

M. Pollini (pno) † Études Pno; Polonaise 1 Pno, Op. 26/1; Polonaise 2 Pno, Op. 26/2; Polonaise 3 Pno, Op. 40/1; Polonaise 4 Pno, Op. 40/2; Polonaise 5 Pno, Op. 44; Polonaises-fant, Op. 61; Preludes (24) Pno, Op. 28 DEUT 3-▲ 31221 [AAD/ADD] (34.97)

M. Pollini (pno) *(rec Paris, France, 1968)* † Con 1 Pno, Op. 11 EMIC ▲ 66221 [ADD] (11.97)

M. Pollini (pno) † Polonaise 1 Pno, Op. 26/1; Polonaise 2 Pno, Op. 26/2; Polonaise 3 Pno, Op. 40/1; Polonaise 4 Pno, Op. 40/2; Polonaise 5 Pno, Op. 44; Polonaises-fant, Op. 61 DEUT (The Originals) ▲ 457711 [ADD] (11.97)

S. Richter (pno) ("Sviatoslav Richter Archives Vol. 2") † Barcarolle Pno, Op. 60; Scherzos Pno; Waltzes Pno DHR (Legendary Treasures) ▲ 7724 (16.97)

A. Rubinstein (pno) ("Basic 100, Vol. 20") † Pno Music (misc colls) RCAV ▮ 61717 (5.98) ▲ 61717 (10.97)

A. Rubinstein (pno) † Andante Spianato & Grand Polonaise, Op. 22; Polonaise 1 Pno, Op. 26/1; Polonaise 2 Pno, Op. 26/2; Polonaise 3 Pno, Op. 40/1; Polonaise 4 Pno, Op. 40/2; Polonaise 5 Pno, Op. 44; Polonaises-fant, Op. 61 MTAL ▲ 48003 (6.97)

A. Rubinstein (pno) *(rec Abbey Road, England, Dec 5, 1934)* ("The Legendary Rubinstein") † Barcarolle Pno, Op. 60; Berceuse, Op. 57; Mazurkas Pno; Nocturnes Pno; Polonaise 3 Pno, Op. 40/1; Scherzos Pno; Waltzes Pno EMIC ▲ 67007 (m) [ADD] (11.97)

V. Sofronitzky (pno) *(rec 1948)* † A. Scriabin:Fant Pno, Op. 28; Poèmes (2) Pno, Op. 32 ENPL (Piano Library) ▲ 282 (13.97)

J. Sterczyński (pno) *(rec Rzeszow, Poland, 1992)* ("Piano Works") † Polonaise 1 Pno, Op. 26/1; Polonaise 2 Pno, Op. 26/2; Polonaise 3 Pno, Op. 40/1; Polonaise 4 Pno, Op. 40/2; Polonaise 5 Pno, Op. 44; Polonaises-fant, Op. 61; P. Tchaikovsky:Saisons SELN ▲ 930916 [DDD] (16.97)

Polonaise No. 9 in B♭ for Piano, Op. 71/2 (1828)

F. Clidat (pno) ("The Most Famous Polonaises") † Polonaise 1 Pno, Op. 26/1; Polonaise 2 Pno, Op. 26/2; Polonaise 3 Pno, Op. 40/1; Polonaise 4 Pno, Op. 40/2; Polonaise 5 Pno, Op. 44; Polonaise 6 Pno, Op. 53; Polonaises Pno; Polonaises-fant, Op. 61 FORL ▲ 16615 [DDD] (16.97)

C. Katsaris (pno) *(rec Mar 3-22, 1993)* † Andante Spianato & Grand Polonaise, Op. 22; Funeral March, Op. 72/2; Mazurkas Pno; Polonaise 1 Pno, Op. 26/1; Polonaise 2 Pno, Op. 26/2; Polonaise 3 Pno, Op. 40/1; Polonaise 4 Pno, Op. 40/2; Polonaise 5 Pno, Op. 44; Polonaises Pno; Polonaises-fant, Op. 61 SNYC 2-▲ 53967 [DDD] (31.97)

G. Ohlsson (pno) ("The Complete Chopin Piano Works, Vol. 5") † Impromptus (4); Polonaise 1 Pno, Op. 26/1; Polonaise 2 Pno, Op. 26/2; Polonaise 3 Pno, Op. 40/1; Polonaise 4 Pno, Op. 40/2; Polonaises Pno; Polonaises-fant, Op. 61 ARA 2-▲ 6642 [DDD] (32.97)

Polonaise-fantaisie in A♭ for Piano, Op. 61 (1845-46)

I. Ardašev (pno) † Barcarolle Pno, Op. 60; J. S. Bach:Italian Con, BWV 971; Beethoven:Son 23 Pno, Op. 57 DI ▲ 920242 [DDD] (5.97)

M. Block (pno) [plus others] † A. Scriabin:Son 2 Pno, Op. 19 PPR ▲ 224504 (16.97)

A. Brendel (pno) † Andante Spianato & Grand Polonaise, Op. 22 VC ▲ 4023 [ADD] (13.97)

S. Cherkassky (pno) *(rec San Francisco, CA, Apr 18, 1982)* ("The 1982 San Francisco Recital") † Waltzes Pno; J. Hofmann:Kaleidoskop, Op. 40; Lully:Suite de pièces; Mendelssohn (-Bartholdy):Scherzo a capriccio; P. Tchaikovsky:Son Pno, Op. 37 IVOR ▲ 70904 [DDD] (16.97)

F. Clidat (pno) ("The Most Famous Polonaises") † Polonaise 1 Pno, Op. 26/1; Polonaise 2 Pno, Op. 26/2; Polonaise 3 Pno, Op. 40/1; Polonaise 4 Pno, Op. 40/2; Polonaise 5 Pno, Op. 44; Polonaise 6 Pno, Op. 53; Polonaise 9 Pno, Op. 71/2; Polonaises Pno FORL ▲ 16615 [DDD] (16.97)

A. Di Bonaventura (pno) ("Chopin: Late Works") † Barcarolle Pno, Op. 60; Son Pno in b, Op. 58 TIT ▲ 208 [DDD]

N. Goerner (pno) *(rec London, England, 1996)* ("Piano Works") † Ballade 4 Pno, Op. 52; Barcarolle Pno, Op. 60; Scherzos Pno; Son Pno in b, Op. 58 EMIC (Debut) ▲ 69701 [DDD] (6.97)

R. Goode (pno) † Barcarolle Pno, Op. 60 NON ▲ 79452 (16.97)

V. Horowitz (pno) *(rec 1966)* † Polonaise 5 Pno, Op. 44; Son Pno in b♭, Op. 35 SNYC ▲ 42412 [AAD] (16.97)

V. Horowitz (pno) ("Horowitz In London") † R. Schumann:Kinderszenen Pno, Op. 15 RCAV (Gold Seal) ▲ 61414 (11.97)

V. Horowitz (pno) *(rec 1982)* † Fantaisie Pno, Op. 49; Liszt:Pno Music (misc); Trans, Arrs & Paraphrases; S. Prokofiev:Son 7 Pno, Op. 83; S. Rachmaninoff:Son 2 Pno, Op. 36; A. Scriabin:Son 5 Pno, Op. 53 PPHI (Great Pianists of the 20th Century) ▲ 456844 (22.97)

W. Kapell (pno) † Mazurkas Pno; Nocturnes Pno; A. Copland:Son Pno; Mussorgsky:Pictures at an Exhibition; D. Scarlatti:Sons Kbd; R. Schumann:Kinderszenen Pno, Op. 15 RCAV ▲ 68997 [ADD] (16.97)

C. Katsaris (pno) *(rec Mar 3-22, 1993)* † Andante Spianato & Grand Polonaise, Op. 22; Funeral March, Op. 72/2; Mazurkas Pno; Polonaise 1 Pno, Op. 26/1; Polonaise 2 Pno, Op. 26/2; Polonaise 3 Pno, Op. 40/1; Polonaise 4 Pno, Op. 40/2; Polonaise 5 Pno, Op. 44; Polonaise 9 Pno, Op. 71/2; Polonaises Pno SNYC 2-▲ 53967 [DDD] (31.97)

W. Kempff (pno) ("Kempff Plays Chopin Vol 2") † Ballade 3 Pno, Op. 47; Fantaisie Pno, Op. 49; Son Pno in b, Op. 58 PLON (The Classic Sound) ▲ 452308 (11.97)

N. Kokinos (pno) † Fantaisie Pno, Op. 49; Polonaise 3 Pno, Op. 40/1; Polonaise 6 Pno, Op. 53; Preludes (24) Pno, Op. 28; Scherzos Pno; Waltzes Pno ANDP ▲ 9592 (15.97)

A. Kuerti (pno) ("Last Major Piano Works") † Ballade 4 Pno, Op. 52; Son Pno in b, Op. 58 FL ▲ 23117 [DDD] (12.97)

L. Lortie (pno) † Andante Spianato & Grand Polonaise, Op. 22; Prelude in c#, Op. 45; Preludes (24) Pno, Op. 28 CHN ▲ 9597 (16.97)

G. Montero (pno) *(rec live Montreal Chopin Competition, 1995)* ("In Concert at Montreal") † Mazurkas Pno; Nocturnes Pno; Liszt:Paraphrase on Verdi; S. Rachmaninoff:Preludes Pno; Son 2 Pno, Op. 36 PALE ▲ 501 (17.97)

I. Moravec (pno) † Polonaise 1 Pno, Op. 26/1; Debussy:Estampes; Images (6) Pno; Preludes Pno VB2 2-▲ 5103 [DDD] (9.97)

H. Neuhaus (pno) ("Neuhaus Plays Chopin") † Barcarolle Pno, Op. 60; Con 1 Pno, Op. 11; Impromptus (4); Nocturnes Pno RUS ▲ 15007 [AAD] (12.97)

G. Ohlsson (pno) *(rec SUNY/Purchase Performing Arts Center Theatre C, NY, Mar 24-26 & Aug 23-25, 1993)* ("The Complete Chopin Piano Works, Vol. 5") † Impromptus (4); Polonaise 1 Pno, Op. 26/1; Polonaise 2 Pno, Op. 26/2; Polonaise 3 Pno, Op. 40/1; Polonaise 4 Pno, Op. 40/2; Polonaise 9 Pno, Op. 71/2; Polonaises Pno ARA 2-▲ 6642 [DDD] (32.97)

M. O'Rourke (pno) † Andante Spianato & Grand Polonaise, Op. 22; Ballades (4) Pno CHN ▲ 9353 [DDD] (16.97)

V. Perlemuter (pno) † Ballades (4) Pno; Polonaise 5 Pno, Op. 44 NIMB ▲ 5209 [ADD] (16.97)

M. Pollini (pno) † Études Pno; Polonaise 1 Pno, Op. 26/1; Polonaise 2 Pno, Op. 26/2; Polonaise 3 Pno, Op. 40/1; Polonaise 4 Pno, Op. 40/2; Polonaise 5 Pno, Op. 44; Polonaise 6 Pno, Op. 53; Preludes (24) Pno, Op. 28 DEUT 3-▲ 31221 [AAD/ADD] (34.97)

M. Pollini (pno) † Polonaise 1 Pno, Op. 26/1; Polonaise 2 Pno, Op. 26/2; Polonaise 3 Pno, Op. 40/1; Polonaise 4 Pno, Op. 40/2; Polonaise 5 Pno, Op. 44; Polonaise 6 Pno, Op. 53 DEUT (The Originals) ▲ 457711 [ADD] (11.97)

S. Richter (pno) *(rec Bauerntheater Terofal Schliersee, July 10, 1992)* † Beethoven:Son 22 Pno, Op. 54; Debussy:Isle joyeuse; J. Haydn:Son 31 Kbd, H.XVI/46; A. Scriabin:Mazurkas (2) Pno, Op. 40 LV ▲ 431 (17.97)

S. Richter (pno) *(rec 1992)* † Mazurkas Pno; Polonaise 1 Pno, Op. 26/1; Polonaise 3 Pno, Op. 40/1; A. Scriabin:Dances (2) Pno, Op. 73; Fant Pno, Op. 28; Poème-nocturne Pno, Op. 61; Vers la flamme, Op. 72 LV ▲ 441 (17.97)

S. Richter (pno) *(rec July 1988)* † Études Pno; Nocturnes Pno; A. Scriabin:Son 2 Pno, Op. 19; Son 5 Pno, Op. 53 PRAG ▲ 254056 (18.97)

S. Richter (pno) *(rec Aug 25, 1976)* ("Richter in Helsinki") † Beethoven:Son 7 Pno, Op. 10/3; R. Schumann:Faschingsschwank, Op. 26 MUA ▲ 1020 [ADD] (16.97)

S. Richter (pno) *(rec Munich, May 16, 1992)* ("Richter out of Later Years, Vol. 3: In memoriam Marlene Dietrich") † Beethoven:Son 31 Pno, Op. 110; Debussy:Isle joyeuse; J. Haydn:Andante with Vars Pno, H.XVII/6; M. Ravel:Vallée des cloches; A. Scriabin:Mazurkas (2) Pno, Op. 40; Poème-nocturne Pno, Op. 61 LV ▲ 481 (17.97)

A. Rubinstein (pno) † Andante Spianato & Grand Polonaise, Op. 22; Polonaise 1 Pno, Op. 26/1; Polonaise 2 Pno, Op. 26/2; Polonaise 3 Pno, Op. 40/1; Polonaise 4 Pno, Op. 40/2; Polonaise 5 Pno, Op. 44; Polonaise 6 Pno, Op. 53 MTAL ▲ 48003 (6.97)

J. Sterczyński (pno) *(rec Rzeszow, Poland, 1992)* ("Piano Works") † Polonaise 1 Pno, Op. 26/1; Polonaise 2 Pno, Op. 26/2; Polonaise 3 Pno, Op. 40/1; Polonaise 4 Pno, Op. 40/2; Polonaise 5 Pno, Op. 44; Polonaise 6 Pno, Op. 53; P. Tchaikovsky:Saisons SELN ▲ 930916 [DDD] (16.97)

P. Tengstrand (pno) *(rec Nov 2-4, 1997)* † Liszt:Années de pèlerinage 2, S.161 AZI ▲ 71207 (15.97)

▲ = CD ♦ = Enhanced CD △ = MD ▮ = Cassette Tape ▯ = DCC

CHOPIN, FRÉDÉRIC (cont.)

Polonaise-fantaisie in A♭ for Piano, Op. 61 (1845-46) (cont.)

F. Ts'ong (pno) † Barcarolle Pno, Op. 60; Berceuse, Op. 57; Fantaisie Pno, Op. 49 SNYC (Essential Classics) ▲ 53515 (7.97) ▮ 53515 (3.98)

Preludes (24) for Piano, Op. 28 (1836-39)

M. Argerich (pno) ("Chopin Compact Edition, Vol. 5") † Music of Chopin DEUT ▲ 31584 [ADD] (9.97)

C. Arrau (pno) SNYC ▮ 35934

C. Arrau (pno)—No. 23 in F † Études Pno; Ballade 3 Pno, Op. 47; Tarentelle, Op. 43; R. Schumann:Carnaval, Op. 9; Con Pno in a, Op. 54 ENPL ▲ 287 (13.97)

I. Biret (pno) *(rec 1991-92)* † Albumleaf (Feuille d'Album); Barcarolle Pno, Op. 60; Bolero; Fugue in a; Pno Music (misc colls); Prelude in c#, Op. 45; Prelude in A♭, Op. posth.; Wiosna NXIN ▲ 550366 [DDD] (5.97)

S. Blet (pno)—No. 16 in b♭ ("Favorite Encores") † Blet:Prélude Pno, Op. 5/1; Liszt:Pno Music (misc); Satie:Piccadilly; D. Scarlatti:Sons Kbd; R. Schumann:Kreisleriana, Op. 16; I. Stravinsky:Studies Pno, Op. 7 FORL ▲ 16752 [DDD] (16.97)

J. Bolet (pno)—No. 15 in D♭, "Raindrop" *(rec Queens, NY)* ("A Chopin Piano Recital") † Études Pno; Fant-Impromptu, Op. 66; Polonaise 3 Pno, Op. 40/1; Polonaise 6 Pno, Op. 53; Waltzes Pno EVC ▲ 9028 [AAD] (13.97)

F. Busoni (pno)—No. 1 in C; No. 2 in a; No. 3 in G; No. 4 in e; No. 5 in D; No. 6 in b; No. 7 in A; No. 9 in E; No. 10 in c#; No, 11 in B; No. 14 in e♭; No. 15 in D♭, "Raindrop"; No. 16 in b♭; No. 20 in c; No. 23 in F † J. S. Bach:Suites Vc; Liszt:Etudes d'exécution transcendante (12), S.139; Grandes études de Paganini, S.141; Polonaises (2) Pno, S.223 NIMB (Grand Piano) ▲ 8810 [DDD] (11.97)

S. Cherkassky (pno) ("Shura Cherkassky:The Last of the Great Piano Romantics, Vol. 2") † Pno Music (misc colls); Polonaise 2 Pno, Op. 26/2; Liszt:Trans, Arrs & Paraphrases ASVQ ▲ 6109 [DDD] (10.97)

S. Cherkassky (pno) *(rec Salzburg, Austria, Aug 3, 1968)* † J. S. Bach:Partitas Hpd; R. R. Bennett:Studies Pno; J. Brahms:Son 3 Pno, Op. 5; Liszt:Polonaises (2) Pno, S.223 ORFE (Festspiel Dokumente) 2-▲ 431962 [ADD] (32.97)

A. Cortot (pno) † Ballades (4) Pno ENPL (The Piano Library) ▲ 184 (13.97)

A. Cortot (pno) ("The World of Chopin") † Ballades (4) Pno; Con 2 Pno, Op. 21; Fantaisie Pno, Op. 49; Pno Music (misc colls); Son Pno in b, Op. 58; Son Pno in b♭, Op. 35 ENPL (Piano Library) 3-▲ 206 (39.97)

A. Cortot (pno) *(rec 1933 & 42)* † Ballades (4) Pno GRM2 (The Records of the Century) ▲ 78862 (13.97)

A. Cortot (pno)—No. 15 in D♭, "Raindrop" *(rec Royce Hall, University of California, Los Angeles, CA)* † Études Pno; Impromptu in G♭, Op. 51; Nocturnes Pno; J. S. Bach:Con 5 Hpd, BWV 1056; Beethoven:Son 29 Pno, Op. 106; Son 30 Pno, Op. 109; Chabrier:Feuillet d'album; Pièces pittoresques; Liszt:Au Bord d'une Source; Trans, Arrs & Paraphrases; A. Scriabin:Etudes (12) Pno, Op. 8 KLAV ▲ 11096 [ADD] (18.97)

J. Darré (pno) *(rec Palais Schönburg Vienna, Austria, June 24-25, 1965)* † Berceuse, Op. 57; Fantaisie Pno, Op. 49 VC ▲ 8092 [ADD] (13.97)

P. Entremont (pno) *(rec Switzerland, Feb 2-5, 1970)* † Ballades (4) Pno SNYC (Essential Classics) ▲ 62415 [ADD] (7.97) ▮ 62415 [ADD] (3.98)

N. Freire (pno), G. Graffman (pno)—No. 7 in A; No. 15 in D♭, "Raindrop" *(rec New York City, NY, Dec 28, 1971)* † Études Pno; Fant-Impromptu, Op. 66; Intro & Polonaise, Op. 3; Mazurkas Pno; Nocturnes Pno; Polonaise 3 Pno, Op. 40/1; Polonaise 6 Pno, Op. 53; Son Pno in b♭, Op. 35; Waltzes Pno SNYC ▲ 51338 [ADD] (7.97)

J. Gimpel (pno) *(rec Jan 24, 1976)* ("Jakob Gimpel at Ambassador Auditorium: All-Chopin Recital, Jan 24, 1976") † Fantaisie Pno, Op. 49; Son Pno in b, Op. 58; Waltzes Pno; Debussy:Etudes (12) Pno; Mendelssohn (-Bartholdy):Lieder ohne Worte CMB 2-▲ 1106 (18.97)

A. Harasiewicz (pno) † Nocturnes Pno; Prelude in c#, Op. 45; Prelude in A♭, Op. posth. PPHI (Duo) 2-▲ 42266 (17.97)

L. Jardon (pno) † Prelude in c#, Op. 45; Prelude in A♭, Op. posth. ILD ▲ 642184 (11.97)

W. Kapell (pno) [sels] *(rec 1940-53)* † Polonaises Pno; Beethoven:Con 2 Pno, Op. 19; S. Rachmaninoff:Rhap on a Theme of Paganini, Op. 43; F. Schubert:Songs (misc) PHS ▲ 9194 (17.97)

C. Katsaris (pno) † Albumleaf (Feuille d'Album); Allegretto & Mazur; Allegretto in F; Bolero; Bourrées; Cantabile in B♭; Contredanse; Ecossaises (3) Pno, Op. 72/3; Fugue in a; Galop Marquis; Largo in E♭; Prelude in c#, Op. 45; Prelude in A♭, Op. posth.; Wiosna SNYC ▲ 53355 [DDD] (16.97)

C. Keene (pno) † Mendelssohn (-Bartholdy):Etudes (3) Pno, Op. 104b; Fant "Sonate écossaise", Op. 28; Vars sérieuses, Op. 54 PROT ▲ 1105 [AAD] (18.97)

N. Kokinos (pno)—No. 20 in c; No. 15 in D♭, "Raindrop"; No. 23 in F; No. 24 in d † Fantaisie Pno, Op. 49; Polonaise 3 Pno, Op. 40/1; Polonaise 6 Pno, Op. 53; Polonaises-fant, Op. 61; Scherzos Pno; Waltzes Pno ANDP ▲ 9592 (15.97)

L. Kraus (pno)—No. 4 in e *(rec 1938)* † Impromptu in F#, Op. 36; B. Bartók:Romanian Folk Dances Pno, Sz.56; Rondos on Folk Tunes, Sz.84; Beethoven:Vars & Fugue Pno, Op. 35; J. Haydn:Andante with Vars Pno, H.XVII/6; F. Schubert:Dances (42), Op. 18; Waltzes, D.969 PHS (Piano Masters) ▲ 55 (17.97)

E. Kupiec (pno) † Szymanowski:Preludes (9) Pno, Op. 1 KSCH ▲ 365622 (16.97)

R. Lortat (pno) † Son Pno in b♭, Op. 35 HPC ▲ 37 (17.97)

L. Lortie (pno) † Andante Spianato & Grand Polonaise, Op. 22; Polonaises-fant, Op. 61; Prelude in c#, Op. 45 CHN ▲ 9597 (16.97)

N. Magaloff (pno)—No. 15 in D♭, "Raindrop" ("Shine: The Complete Classics") † Polonaise 6 Pno, Op. 53; Beethoven:Sym 9; Liszt:Études d'exécution transcendante (6), S.140; Études de concert (3), S.144; Hungarian Rhaps, S.244; S. Rachmaninoff:Con 3 Pno, Op. 30; Prelude in c#, Op. 3/2; Rimsky-Korsakov:Tale of Tsar Saltan (orch sels); R. Schumann:Kinderszenen Pno, Op. 15; Vivaldi:Gloria; Nulla in mundo pax, RV.630 PPHI 2-▲ 456403 (17.97)

J. C. Martins (pno), A. Moreira-Lima (pno) ("Bach & Chopin: The Preludes") † J. S. Bach:Wohltemperirte Clavier ERTO 2-▲ 42024 (22.97)

E. Mogilevsky (pno) † Pno Music (misc colls); Pno Music (misc) PAVA ▲ 7264 [DDD] (10.97)

I. Moravec (pno) *(rec 1965)* † Barcarolle Pno, Op. 60 VAIA ▲ 1039 (17.97)

P. Moss (pno) † Son Pno in b, Op. 58 CENT ▲ 2072 [DDD] (16.97)

L. Mozdzer (pno)—No. 3 in G; No. 7 in A ("Tomorrow: Impressions") † Études Pno; Contredanse; Mazurkas Pno; Nocturnes Pno; Prelude in A♭, Op. posth. OPUS (Chopin Vol. 9) ▲ 2014 (18.97)

A. Nikolsky (pno) † Barcarolle Pno, Op. 60; Son Pno in b♭, Op. 35 ARNO ▲ 27774 [DDD] (4.97)

J. Olejniczak (pno), Andrzej Jagodzinski Trio—No. 6 in b ("Jazz: Metamorphoses") † Études Pno; Mazurkas Pno; Nocturnes Pno; Polonaise 4 Pno, Op. 40/2 OPUS (Chopin Vol. 8) ▲ 2013 (18.97)

I. J. Paderewski (pno)—No. 15 in D♭, "Raindrop"; No. 17 in A♭ *(rec 1912-30)* ("Ignacy Jan Paderewski") † Études Pno; Berceuse, Op. 57; Funeral March in b♭; Mazurkas Pno; Nocturnes Pno; Polonaise 2 Pno, Op. 26/2; Polonaise 3 Pno, Op. 40/1; Waltzes Pno; Liszt:Études d'exécution transcendante (6), S.140; Études de concert (3), S.144; Hungarian Rhaps, S.244; Trans, Arrs & Paraphrases; I. J. Paderewski:Minuet; F. Schubert:Impromptus (4) PPHI (Great Pianists of the 20th Century) 2-▲ 456919 (22.97)

M. Perahia (pno)—No. 6 in b; No. 7 in A; No. 15 in D♭, "Raindrop" *(rec New York City, NY, 1975)* ("A Portrait of Murray Perahia") † Fant-Impromptu, Op. 66; Beethoven:Son 23 Pno, Op. 57; Mendelssohn (-Bartholdy):Rondo capriccioso, Op. 14; W. A. Mozart:Rondo Pno & Orch, K.382; Rondo Pno Orch, K.382; F. Schubert:Impromptus (4) Pno; R. Schumann:Papillons Pno, Op. 2 SNYC ▲ 42448 [AAD/DDD] (11.97)

M. J. Pires (pno) † Con 2 Pno, Op. 21 DEUT ▲ 37817 [DDD] (16.97)

I. Pogorelich (pno) DEUT ▲ 29227 [DDD] (16.97)

M. Pollini (pno) DEUT ▲ 13796 [AAD] (16.97)

M. Pollini (pno) † Études Pno; Polonaise 1 Pno, Op. 26/1; Polonaise 2 Pno, Op. 26/2; Polonaise 3 Pno, Op. 40/1; Polonaise 4 Pno, Op. 40/2; Polonaise 5 Pno, Op. 44; Polonaise 6 Pno, Op. 53; Polonaises-fant, Op. 61 DEUT 3-▲ 31221 [AAD/ADD] (34.97)

S. Richter (pno)—No. 4 in e; No. 5 in D; No. 6 in b; No. 7 in A; No. 8 in f#; No. 9 in E; No. 10 in c#; No. 13 in F#; No. 19 in E♭; No. 11 in B; No. 2 in a; No. 23 in F; No. 21 in B♭ *(rec Japan, Feb-Mar 1979)* † R. Schumann:Fantasiestücke Pno, Op. 12; Novelettes, Op. 21 OLY ▲ 287 (16.97)

M. Rosenthal (pno)—No. 3 in G; No. 6 in b; No. 7 in A; No. 13 in F# *(rec 1930-37)* † Berceuse, Op. 57; Con 1 Pno, Op. 11; Nocturnes Pno ENPL (Piano Library) ▲ 319 (14.97)

A. Rubinstein (pno) † Barcarolle Pno, Op. 60; Berceuse, Op. 57; Son Pno in b♭, Op. 35 RCAV (Gold Seal) ▲ 60047 [ADD] (11.97)

S. Bunin—No. 13 in F#; No. 14 in e♭; No. 15 in D♭, "Raindrop"; No. 16 in b♭; No. 17 in A♭; No. 18 in f ("Masters of Classical Music, Vol. 8: Frederic Chopin") † Études Pno; Mazurkas Pno; Nocturnes (21) Pno; Nocturnes Pno; Scherzos Pno; Waltzes Pno LALI ▲ 15808 [DDD] (3.97)

H. Shelley (pno) † Son Pno in b♭, Op. 35 INMP ▲ 6700762 [DDD] (9.97)

H. Shelley (pno) † Ballades (4) Pno ASVQ ▲ 6095 [ADD] (10.97)

Shirim—No. 4 in e [arr McLaughlin] *(rec Carlisle, MA, Oct 31 & Dec 6, 1997)* ("Klezmer Nutcracker") † J. Brahms:Hungarian Dances Pno 4-Hands; Enescu:Romanian Rhap 1, Op. 11/1; G. Mahler:Sym 1; Satie:Gnossiennes; Gymnopédies; P. Tchaikovsky:Nutcracker Suite, Op. 71a; Traditional:Russian Bulgar; Turk in America NPT ▲ 85640 (16.97)

G. Sokolov (pno), C. Coin (cnd), Mosaïques Ensemble—No. 4 in e; No. 7 in A † Études Pno; Con 2 Pno, Op. 21; Mazurkas Pno; Nocturnes Pno; Polonaise 5 Pno, Op. 44; Son Pno in b♭, Op. 35; Waltzes Pno OPUS (Chopin Vol. 5) ▲ 2010 (18.97)

D. Solokov (pno) *(rec St. Petersburg Russia, June 2-4, 1995)* † Mussorgsky:Pictures at an Exhibition ELY ▲ 711 [DDD] (16.97)

CHOPIN, FRÉDÉRIC (cont.)

Preludes (24) for Piano, Op. 28 (1836-39) (cont.)

D. T. Son (pno) † Barcarolle Pno, Op. 60; Prelude in c#, Op. 45 ANAL ▲ 27703

I. Tiegerman (pno)—No. 7 in A; No. 8 in f# *(rec Cairo, Egypt, 1950s)* ("The Lost Legend of Cairo: Radio & Private Recordings") † Ballade 4 Pno, Op. 52; Nocturnes Pno; Scherzos Pno; Son Pno in b, Op. 58; J. Brahms:Con 2 Pno, Op. 83; Intermezzos (3) Pno, Op. 117; Pieces (6) Pno, Op. 118; Pieces (8) Pno, Op. 76; G. Fauré:Nocturnes Pno; J. Field:Nocturnes Pno; C. Franck:Symphonic Vars, M.46; Saint-Saëns:Con 5 Pno, Op. 103; Tiegerman:Meditation Pno ARBT 2-▲ 116 (32.97)

A. Tzerko (pno)—No. 24 in d *(rec 1945-55)* ("In Memoriam Aube Tzerko") † Beethoven:Ecossaises Pno, WoO 83; E. Bloch:Visions & Prophecies; F. Schubert:Fant Pno, D.760 TOWN ▲ 47 (17.97)

various artists—No. 4 in e; No. 15 in D♭, "Raindrop"; No. 20 in c ("Chopin With Ocean Sounds") † Nocturnes (21) Pno CHAC ▲ 944 (14.97)

various artists—No. 3 in G; No. 4 in e; No. 7 in A; No. 14 in e♭ † Études Pno; Con 2 Pno, Op. 21; Mazurkas Pno; Polonaise 5 Pno, Op. 44; Son Pno in b♭, Op. 35; Son Vc OPUS (Chopin Exploration Vol. 10 (Excerpts from Vols. 1-9)) ▲ 2015 (7.97)

various artists—No. 7 in A; No. 11 in B; No. 15 in D♭, "Raindrop"; No. 23 in F; No. 13 in F# † Études Pno; Barcarolle Pno, Op. 60; Berceuse, Op. 57; Con 1 Pno, Op. 11; Con 2 Pno, Op. 21; Nocturnes Pno; Nouvelles études; Waltzes Pno RCAV ▮ 63423 (6.98) ▲ 63423 (11.97)

Prelude in c# for Piano, Op. 45 (1841)

I. Biret (pno) *(rec 1991-92)* † Albumleaf (Feuille d'Album); Barcarolle Pno, Op. 60; Bolero; Fugue in a; Pno Music (misc colls); Prelude in A♭, Op. posth.; Preludes (24) Pno, Op. 28; Wiosna NXIN ▲ 550366 [DDD] (5.97)

A. Harasiewicz (pno) † Nocturnes Pno; Prelude in A♭, Op. posth.; Preludes (24) Pno, Op. 28 PPHI (Duo) 2-▲ 42266 (17.97)

L. Jardon (pno) † Prelude in A♭, Op. posth.; Preludes (24) Pno, Op. 28 ILD ▲ 642184 (11.97)

C. Katsaris (pno) † Albumleaf (Feuille d'Album); Allegretto & Mazur; Allegretto in F; Bolero; Bourrées; Cantabile in B♭; Contredanse; Ecossaises (3) Pno, Op. 72/3; Fugue in a; Galop Marquis; Largo in E♭; Prelude in A♭, Op. posth.; Preludes (24) Pno, Op. 28; Wiosna SNYC ▲ 53355 [DDD] (16.97)

M. Lidsky (pno) † Medtner:Son Pno DNN ▲ 78842 [DDD] (16.97)

L. Lortie (pno) † Andante Spianato & Grand Polonaise, Op. 22; Polonaises-fant, Op. 61; Preludes (24) Pno, Op. 28 CHN ▲ 9597 (16.97)

D. T. Son (pno) † Barcarolle Pno, Op. 60; Preludes (24) Pno, Op. 28 ANAL ▲ 27703

V. Tropp (pno) † Barcarolle Pno, Op. 60; Polonaise 5 Pno, Op. 44; Son Pno in b♭, Op. 35 DNN ▲ 18035 (16.97)

Prelude in A♭ for Piano, Op. posth. (1834)

I. Biret (pno) *(rec 1991-92)* † Albumleaf (Feuille d'Album); Barcarolle Pno, Op. 60; Bolero; Fugue in a; Pno Music (misc colls); Prelude in c#, Op. 45; Preludes (24) Pno, Op. 28; Wiosna NXIN ▲ 550366 [DDD] (5.97)

A. Harasiewicz (pno) † Nocturnes Pno; Prelude in c#, Op. 45; Preludes (24) Pno, Op. 28 PPHI (Duo) 2-▲ 42266 (17.97)

L. Jardon (pno) † Prelude in c#, Op. 45; Preludes (24) Pno, Op. 28 ILD ▲ 642184 (11.97)

C. Katsaris (pno) † Albumleaf (Feuille d'Album); Allegretto & Mazur; Allegretto in F; Bolero; Bourrées; Cantabile in B♭; Contredanse; Ecossaises (3) Pno, Op. 72/3; Fugue in a; Galop Marquis; Largo in E♭; Prelude in c#, Op. 45; Preludes (24) Pno, Op. 28; Wiosna SNYC ▲ 53355 [DDD] (16.97)

L. Mozdzer (pno) ("Tomorrow: Impressions") † Études Pno; Contredanse; Mazurkas Pno; Nocturnes Pno; Preludes (24) Pno, Op. 28 OPUS (Chopin Vol. 9) ▲ 2014 (18.97)

Rondos (4) for solo Piano, Op. 1, 5, 16 & 2 Pianos, Op. 73

A. R. El Bacha (pno) ("El Bacha Plays Chopin, Vol. 4") † Études Pno; Allegro de concert, Op. 46; Ballade 1 Pno, Op. 23; Mazurkas Pno; Waltzes Pno FORL ▲ 16785 (16.97)

I. Biret (pno)—Rondo in c, Op. 1; Rondo in F, Op. 5, "a la Mazur"; Intro in c, & Rondo in E♭, Op. 16 *(rec 1991)* † Mazurkas Pno; Rondos (4) Pno, Op. 73; Var 6 Pno; Vars in A, ('Souvenir de Paganini'); Vars on a Theme from La Cenerentola; Vars on Mozart, Op. 2 NXIN ▲ 550367 [DDD] (5.97)

G. Caillat (pno), D. Duport (pno) † Liszt:Con pathétique Pnos, S.258; D. Shostakovich:Suite Pnos, Op. 6 CASC ▲ 1066 (16.97)

F. Chiu (pno) † Études Pno HAM ▲ 907201 (18.97)

I. Elkina (pno), J. Elkina (pno) ("Cinderella: The Sisters' Version & Other Stories for Duo Piano") † B. Britten:Intro & Rondo alla burlesca; Liszt:Paraphrase on Verdi; S. Prokofiev:Cinderella Suite No. 3, Op. 109; P. Schoenfield:Taschyag; S. Taneyev:Prelude & Fugue, Op. 29 DNC ▲ 1020 (16.97)

K. Makowska (pno), A. Wesotowska (pno) *(rec Warsaw, 1987)* † Intro, Theme & Vars; Moniuszko:Pno Music SELN ▲ 940420 [DDD] (16.97)

J. Rogers (pno), J. Morrison (pno) ("Duo-Piano Favorites") † Debussy:En blanc et noir; D. Milhaud:Scaramouche Pnos, Op. 165b; W. A. Mozart:Son Pnos, K.448; Tailleferre:Jeux de plein air ACAD ▲ 20057 (16.97)

A. Walachowski (pno), I. Walachowski (pno) ("Klavierduo Walachowski") † J. Brahms:Vars on a Theme by Paganini, Op. 35; W. A. Mozart:Andante & Vars, K.501; M. Ravel:Valse; P. Tchaikovsky:Sleeping Beauty, Op. 66 ARS ▲ 368359 [DDD] (15.99)

Scherzos (4) in b, b♭/D♭, c# & E for Piano, Opp. 20, 31, 39 & 54

C. Arrau (pno) *(rec 1928; 1929; 1939)* † Ballade 3 Pno, Op. 47; Bizet:Carmen Fantasie; Debussy:Danse Pno; Estampes; Liszt:Années de pèlerinage 3, S.163; R. Schumann:Carnaval, Op. 9 MTAL ▲ 48044 (6.97)

V. Ashkenazy (pno) † Ballades (4) Pno PLON ▲ 17474 [DDD] (16.97)

E. Ax (pno) SNYC ▲ 44544 [DDD] (16.97)

L. Bustani (pno)—No. 3 in c#, Op. 39 *(rec Maria Minor Church, Utrecht, Netherlands, Oct 1998)* † Fantaisie Pno, Op. 49; Nocturnes Pno; R. Schumann:Kreisleriana, Op. 16 CSOC ▲ 4230

S. Cherkassky (pno) † Barcarolle Pno, Op. 60; Fantaisie Pno, Op. 49 TUD ▲ 720 [ADD] (16.97)

J. Darré (pno) *(rec Konzerthaus Vienna, Germany, June 1966)* ("The Four Scherzi") † Nocturnes Pno VC ▲ 95 [AAD] (13.97)

N. Demidenko (pno) † Intro & Vars in E; Vars on Mozart, Op. 2 HYP ▲ 66514 [DDD] (18.97)

L. Favre-Khan (pno)—No. 1 in b, Op. 20 † Andante Spianato & Grand Polonaise, Op. 22; Ballade 3 Pno, Op. 47; Ballade 4 Pno, Op. 52; Barcarolle Pno, Op. 60; Fantaisie Pno, Op. 49 ARN ▲ 68448 (16.97)

J. Feghali (pno)—No. 1 in b, Op. 20 *(rec Fort Worth, TX, 1985)* ("Van Cliburn Retrospective Series, Vol. 5") † Fantaisie Pno, Op. 49; Beethoven:Son 4 Pno, Op. 7; J. Haydn:Sonatas for Piano; Liszt:Années de pèlerinage 2, S.161; Mephisto Waltz 1 Pno, S.514; S. Prokofiev:Son 3 Pno, Op. 28; M, Ravel:Miroirs VAIA ▲ 1157 [DDD]

L. Godowsky (pno)—No. 4 in E, Op. 54 *(rec 1926-30)* † Études Pno; Nocturnes Pno; Son Pno in b♭, Op. 35; Beethoven:Son 26 Pno, Op. 81a; L. Godowsky:Transcriptions & Paraphrases; E. Grieg:Ballade Pno, Op. 24; Liszt:Paraphrase on Verdi; R. Schumann:Carnaval, Op. 9 PPHI (Great Pianists of the 20th Century, Vol. 37) 2-▲ 456805 (22.97)

N. Goerner (pno)—No. 4 in E, Op. 54 *(rec London, England, 1996)* ("Piano Works") † Ballade 4 Pno, Op. 52; Barcarolle Pno, Op. 60; Polonaises-fant, Op. 61; Son Pno in b, Op. 58 EMIC (Debut) ▲ 69701 [DDD] (6.97)

S. D. Groote (pno)—No. 3 in c#, Op. 39 *(rec Fort Worth, TX, 1977)* ("Van Cliburn Retrospective Series, Vol. 2") † S. Barber:Ballade Pno, Op. 46; B. Bartók:Out of Doors, Sz.81; Liszt:Vars on "Weinen, Klagen, Sorgen, Zagen" Pno, S.180; R. Schumann:Fant Pno, Op. 17; I. Stravinsky:Scenes (3) Pno VAIA ▲ 1146 [ADD] (16.97)

R. Hodgkinson (pno)—No. 4 in E, Op. 54 *(rec Boston, MA)* ("Pétrouchka & Other Prophecies") † Beethoven:Son 32 Pno, Op. 111; R. Schumann:Waldscenen, Op. 82; I. Stravinsky:Scenes (3) Pno ONGA ▲ 24111 [DDD] (16.97)

V. Horowitz (pno)—No. 4 in E, Op. 54 † Impromptu in A♭, Op. 29 MTAL ▲ 48014 (6.97)

K. Jablonski (pno), Y. Fichman—No. 1 in b, Op. 20; No. 2 in b♭/D♭, Op. 31 ("Masters of Classical Music, Vol. 8: Frederic Chopin") † Études Pno; Mazurkas Pno; Nocturnes (21) Pno; Nocturnes Pno; Preludes (24) Pno, Op. 28; Waltzes Pno LALI ▲ 15808 [DDD] (3.97)

E. Kissin (pno)—No. 4 in E, Op. 54 † Ballade 1 Pno, Op. 23; Ballade 2 Pno, Op. 38; Ballade 3 Pno, Op. 47; Ballade 4 Pno, Op. 52; Barcarolle Pno, Op. 60; Berceuse, Op. 57 RCAV ▲ 63259 [DDD] (16.97)

A. Kitain (pno)—No. 1 in b, Op. 20 *(rec 1936-39)* † Études Pno; Ballade 2 Pno, Op. 38; Ballade 3 Pno, Op. 47; Mazurkas Pno; J. Brahms:Waltzes Pno, Op. 39; Liszt:Pno Music (misc); R. Schumann:Toccata Pno, Op. 7 ENPL (Piano Library) ▲ 221 (13.97)

N. Kokinos (pno)—No. 2 in b♭/D♭, Op. 31 † Fantaisie Pno, Op. 49; Polonaise 3 Pno, Op. 40/1; Polonaise 6 Pno, Op. 53; Polonaises-fant, Op. 61; Preludes (24) Pno, Op. 28; Waltzes Pno ANDP ▲ 9592 (15.97)

I. Mejoueva (pno)—No. 2 in b♭/D♭, Op. 31 † Nocturnes Pno; M. Ravel:Miroirs; A. Scriabin:Son 2 Pno, Op. 19 DNN ▲ 18074 (16.97)

A. B. Michelangeli (pno)—No. 2 in b♭/D♭, Op. 31 † Mazurkas Pno; Debussy:Images (6) Pno; Galuppi:Presto; Liszt:Con 1 Pno, S.124; Vivaldi:Music of Vivaldi IMMM (Magic Master series) ▲ 37007 (6.97)

B. Moiseiwitsch (pno)—No. 2 in b♭/D♭, Op. 31; No. 4 in E, Op. 54 *(rec 1958)* † Ballade 3 Pno, Op. 47; Ballade 4 Pno, Op. 52; Barcarolle Pno, Op. 60; Fant-Impromptu, Op. 66; Nocturnes Pno; Kabalevsky:Son 3 Pno, Op. 46; Liszt:Études de concert (3), S.144; Medtner:Son Pno in g, Op. 22; Mendelssohn (-Bartholdy):Midsummer Night's Dream (sels); S. Prokofiev:Pieces (4) Pno, Op. 4; Toccata Pno, Op. 11; S. Rachmaninoff:Con 2 Pno, Op. 18; Moments musicaux, Op. 16; Preludes Pno PPHI (Great Pianists of the 20th Century) 2-▲ 456907 (22.97)

G. Montero (pno)—No. 3 in c#, Op. 39 † Fant-Impromptu, Op. 66; Nocturnes Pno; Polonaise 1 Pno, Op. 26/1; Polonaise 2 Pno, Op. 26/2; Polonaise 6 Pno, Op. 53; Son Pno in b♭, Op. 35; Waltzes Pno PALE ▲ 510 (17.97)

I. Pogorelich (pno) DEUT ▲ 439947 [DDD] (16.97)

CHOPIN, FRÉDERIC (cont.)

Scherzos (4) in b, b♭/D♭, c# & E for Piano, Opp. 20, 31, 39 & 54 (cont.)

M. Pollini (pno)—No. 1 in b, Op. 20 *(rec 1990)* ("Maurizio Pollini") † Debussy:Études (12) Pno; Liszt:Son Pno, S.178; F. Schubert:Pieces Pno, D.946; R. Schumann:Arabeske Pno, Op. 18; Son 1 Pno, Op. 11; I. Stravinsky:Scenes (3) Pno; Webern:Vars Pno, Op. 27 PPHI (Great Pianists of the 20th Century) ▲ 456937 (22.97)

M. Pollini (pno) † Barcarolle Pno, Op. 60; Berceuse, Op. 57 DEUT ▲ 31623 [DDD] (16.97)

S. Rachmaninoff (pno) *(rec 1919-35)* † Ballade 3 Pno, Op. 47; Son Pno in b♭, Op. 35 ENPL (Piano Library) ▲ 264 (13.97)

S. Richter (pno)—No. 4 in E, Op. 54 ("Classic Richter") † Beethoven:Son 27 Pno, Op. 90; S. Rachmaninoff:Preludes Pno; F. Schubert:Son Pno, D.625; R. Schumann:Novelettes, Op. 21; P. Tchaikovsky:Morceaux (6) Pno, Op. 51; Saisons OLY ▲ 580 [ADD] (16.97)

S. Richter (pno)—No. 1 in b, Op. 20; No. 2 in b♭/D♭, Op. 31; No. 3 in c#, Op. 39; No. 4 in E, Op. 54 ("Sviatoslav Richter Archives Vol. 2") † Barcarolle Pno, Op. 60; Polonaise 6 Pno, Op. 53; Waltzes Pno DHR (Legendary Treasures) ▲ 7724 (16.97)

S. Richter (pno)—No. 2 in b♭/D♭, Op. 31 *(rec Aug 26, 1977)* ("Richter in Salzburg") † Barcarolle Pno, Op. 60; Waltzes Pno; Beethoven:Andante Pno, WoO 57; Debussy:Estampes; Preludes Pno; Suite bergamasque; S. Rachmaninoff:Preludes Pno MUA ▲ 1019 [ADD] (16.97)

S. Richter (pno) ("The Richter Collection, Vol. 2") † Beethoven:Son 27 Pno, Op. 90; Son 3 Pno, Op. 2/3; Son 4 Pno, Op. 7; Vars & Fugue Pno, Op. 35; Vars Pno on Original Theme, Op. 34; Vars Pno on Original Theme, Op. 76; J. Brahms:Son 1 Vn, Op. 78; J. Haydn:Son 39 Kbd, H.XVI/24; S. Rachmaninoff:Etudes-tableaux Pno; Preludes Pno; R. Schumann:Bunte Blätter, Op. 99; Symphonic Etudes, Op. 13; D. Shostakovich:Son Vn OLY 5-▲ 5013 [DDD] (64.97)

A. Rubenstein (pno) † Barcarolle Pno, Op. 60; Berceuse, Op. 57 ENPL (The Piano Library) ▲ 201 (13.97)

A. Rubinstein (pno)—No. 2 in b♭/D♭, Op. 31 *(rec Abbey Road, England, Oct 16, 1932)* ("The Legendary Rubinstein") † Barcarolle Pno, Op. 60; Berceuse, Op. 57; Mazurkas Pno; Nocturnes Pno; Polonaise 3 Pno, Op. 40/1; Polonaise 6 Pno, Op. 53; Waltzes Pno EMIC ▲ 67007 (m) [ADD] (11.97)

A. Rubinstein (pno) † Con 1 Pno, Op. 11; Con 2 Pno, Op. 21; Mazurkas Pno; Nocturnes Pno EMIC 5-▲ 64933 (52.97)

A. Rubinstein (pno) † Ballades (4) Pno RCAV (Red Seal) ▲ 7156 (16.97)

A. Schub (pno)—No. 4 in E, Op. 54 *(rec Fort Worth, TX, 1981)* ("The Sixth Cliburn Competition 1981") † Son Pno in b♭, Op. 35; Debussy:Preludes Pno; Liszt:Etudes d'exécution transcendante (6), S.140; Medtner:Fairy Tales (4), Op. 26; Mendelssohn (-Bartholdy):Fant "Sonate écossaise", Op. 28; R. Schumann:Toccata Pno, Op. 7; A. Scriabin:Son 5 Pno, Op. 53 VAIA (Retrospective Series, Vol. 8) ▲ 1176 [ADD] (16.97)

A. Sultanov (pno)—No. 2 in b♭/D♭, Op. 31 *(rec Fort Worth, TX, 1989)* ("Van Cliburn Retrospective Series, Vol. 6") † S. Barber:Son Pno, Op. 26; J. Brahms:Son 3 Pno, Op. 5; J. Haydn:Sonatas for Piano; Liszt:Etudes d'exécution transcendante (12), S.139; W. A. Mozart:Son 10 Pno, K.330; R. Schumann:Son 2 Pno, Op. 22 VAIA ▲ 1158 [DDD]

I. Tiegerman (pno)—No. 1 in b, Op. 20 *(rec Cairo, Egypt, 1950s)* ("The Lost Legend of Cairo: Radio & Private Recordings") † Ballade 4 Pno, Op. 52; Nocturnes Pno; Preludes (24) Pno, Op. 28; Son Pno in b, Op. 58; J. Brahms:Con 2 Pno, Op. 83; Intermezzos (3) Pno, Op. 117; Pieces (6) Pno, Op. 118; Pieces (8) Pno, Op. 76; G. Fauré:Nocturnes Pno; J. Field:Nocturnes Pno; C. Franck:Symphonic Vars, M.46; Saint-Saëns:Con 5 Pno, Op. 103; Tiegerman:Meditation Pno ARBT 2-▲ 116 (32.97)

V. Tryon (pno) *(rec Humbercrest United Church Toronto, Canada)* ("Scherzos & Ballades") † Ballades (4) Pno MUVI (Musica Viva) ▲ 1092 [DDD] (16.97)

E. Wild (pno) † Ballades (4) Pno CHSK ▲ 44 [DDD] (16.97)

Sonata in g for Cello & Piano, Op. 65 (1845-46)

H. Brendstrup (vc), C. Edwards (pno) † Intro & Polonaise, Op. 3; Liszt:Elegie 1 Vc, S.130; Elegie 2 Vn, S.131; Lugubre gondola Vn or Vc, S.134; Romance oubliée Va, S.132 KPT ▲ 32026 [DDD]

D. Finckel (vc), W. Han (pno) *(rec New York, NY, 1996)* † E. Grieg:Son Vc; R. Schumann:Adagio & Allegro Hn, Op. 70 ARLD ▲ 19701

R. Froyen (vc), J. Schmidt (pno) † R. Strauss:Son Vc, Op. 6 DI ▲ 920285 [DDD] (5.97)

M. Gendron (vc), K. Toyama (pno) *(rec Iruma-shi Shimin Kaikan, June 1981)* ("Lalo & Chopin: Cello Sonatas") † Grand Duo; Intro & Polonaise, Op. 3; Lalo:Son Vc CAMA ▲ 366 (18.97)

B. Gregor-Smith (vc), Y. Wrigley (pno) ("Cello Sonatas") † S. Rachmaninoff:Son Vc ASVQ ▲ 6178 (10.97)

Y.-Y. Ma (vc), E. Ax (pno) *(rec New England Conservatory Boston, MA, June 8-10, 1992)* † Intro & Polonaise, Op. 3; Trio SNYC ▲ 53112 [DDD] (16.97)

E. Nyffenegger (vc), G. Wyss (pno) † C. Franck:Son Vn, M.8; E. Grieg:Son Vc DVX ▲ 25204 [ADD] (11.97)

J. D. Pré (vc), D. Barenboim (pno) † C. Franck:Son Vn, M.8 EMIC ▲ 63184 (11.97)

K. Scholes (vc), D. Breitman (pno) *(rec June 1990)* † Grand Duo; Intro & Polonaise, Op. 3 TIT ▲ 197 [DDD]

C. Starck (vc), R. Requejo (pno) † E. Grieg:Son Vc CLAV ▲ 703 [ADD] (16.97)

J. Starker (vc), G. Sebok (pno) † Intro & Polonaise, Op. 3; B. Bartók:Rhap Vc, Sz.88; Debussy:Son Vc; Martinů:Vars on a Theme of Rossini, H.290; Mendelssohn (-Bartholdy):Vars concertantes, Op. 17; L. Weiner:Hungarian Wedding Dance MRCR ▲ 34358 (11.97)

P. Szabó (vc), D. Várjon (pno) ("Chamber Music") † Grand Duo; Trio HUN ▲ 31651 [DDD] (16.97)

J. Wang (vc), C. Rosenberger (pno) † Intro & Polonaise, Op. 3; S. Barber:Son Vc, Op. 6; R. Schumann:Adagio & Allegro Hn, Op. 70 DLS ▲ 3097 [DDD] (14.97)

P. Wispelwey (vc), P. Giacometti (pno) † G. Fauré:Elégie, Op. 24; Papillon, Op. 77; Romance Vc, Op. 69; F. Poulenc:Son Vc CCL ▲ 10797 (18.97)

various artists—Scherzo; Largo † Études Pno; Con 2 Pno, Op. 21; Mazurkas Pno; Polonaise 5 Pno, Op. 44; Preludes (24) Pno, Op. 28; Son Pno in b♭, Op. 35 OPUS (Chopin Exploration Vol. 10 (Excerpts from Vols. 1-9)) ▲ 2015 (7.97)

Sonata in c for Piano, Op. 4 (1828)

L. O. Andsnes (pno) ("Piano Works") † Études Pno; Son Pno in b, Op. 58; Son Pno in b♭, Op. 35 VCL 2-▲ 61317 (21.97)

I. Biret (pno) *(rec Heidelberg, Germany, Sept 3-5, 1990)* † Son Pno in b, Op. 58; Son Pno in b♭, Op. 35 NXIN ▲ 550363 [DDD] (5.97)

I. Biret (pno) *(rec Heidelberg Germany, Sept 3-5, 1990)* † Son Pno in b♭, Op. 35; Liszt:Son Pno, S.178 NXIN ▲ 553237 [DDD] (5.97)

C. Katsaris (pno) † Son Pno in b, Op. 58; Son Pno in b♭, Op. 35 SNYC ▲ 48483 [DDD] (16.97)

G. Ohlsson (pno) † Son Pno in b, Op. 58; Son Pno in b♭, Op. 35 ARA ▲ 6628 [DDD] (16.97)

J. Rose (pno) † Son Pno in b, Op. 58; Son Pno in b♭, Op. 35 SNYC ▲ 62388 [DDD] (4.97)

Sonata in b♭ for Piano, Op. 35 (1839)

L. O. Andsnes (pno) ("Piano Works") † Études Pno; Son Pno in b, Op. 58; Son Pno in c, Op. 4 VCL 2-▲ 61317 (21.97)

I. Biret (pno) *(rec Heidelberg, Germany, Sept 3-5, 1990)* † Son Pno in b, Op. 58; Son Pno in c, Op. 4 NXIN ▲ 550363 [DDD] (5.97)

I. Biret (pno) *(rec Heidelberg, Germany, Sept 3-5, 1990)* † Son Pno in c, Op. 4; Liszt:Son Pno, S.178 NXIN ▲ 553237 [DDD] (5.97)

A. Brailowsky (pno) *(rec 1928-34)* ("A Retrospective, Vol. 1") † Ballade 1 Pno, Op. 23 ENPL (Piano Library) ▲ 245 (13.97)

V. Cliburn (pno) † Son Pno in b, Op. 58; Liszt:Études de concert (3), S.144; Années de pèlerinage 2, S.161; Mephisto Waltz 1 Pno, S.514 RCAV (Gold Seal) ▲ 60417 [ADD] (11.97)

A. Cortot (pno) ("The World of Chopin") † Ballades (4) Pno; Con 2 Pno, Op. 21; Fantaisie Pno, Op. 49; Pno Music (misc colls); Preludes (24) Pno, Op. 28; Son Pno in b, Op. 58 ENPL (Piano Library) 3-▲ 206 (39.97)

A. Cortot (pno) *(rec 1933 & 1935)* ("The World of Chopin, Vol. 1") † Con 2 Pno, Op. 21; Fantaisie Pno, Op. 49 GRM2 ▲ 78516 [ADD] (13.97)

I. Friedman (pno)—Marche funèbre; Finale (Presto) ("Highlights 1925-36 From His Discography") † Études Pno; Impromptu in F#, Op. 36; Mazurkas Pno; Nocturnes Pno; Polonaise 6 Pno, Op. 53; Waltzes Pno; Beethoven:Son 14 Pno, Op. 27/2; I. Friedman:Danse; Music Box, Op. 33/3; J. N. Hummel:Rondo Pno, Op. 11; Liszt:Trans, Arrs & Paraphrases; Mendelssohn (-Bartholdy):Fants Pno, Op. 16; Shield:Old English Menuet APR (Signature Series) ▲ 5508 [ADD] (18.97)

K. Gekić (pno) *(rec Subotica, Yugoslavia, Apr 27, 1997)* † Impromptu in A♭, Op. 29; Impromptu in F#, Op. 36; Polonaise 4 Pno, Op. 40/2; Polonaise 5 Pno, Op. 44; Liszt:Grand galop chromatique, S.219; Trans, Arrs & Paraphrases VAIA ▲ 1180 (16.97)

Em. Gilels (pno) *(rec New York, United States of America, 1955)* † W. A. Mozart:Son 17 Pno, K.570; D. Shostakovich:Preludes & Fugues Pno, Op. 87 TES ▲ 1089 (17.97)

Em. Gilels (pno) *(rec 1959-78)* ("Emil Gilels III") † Études Pno; Son Pno in b, Op. 58; J. Brahms:Con 2 Pno, Op. 83; M. Clementi:Son Pno; E. Grieg:Lyric Pieces; F. Schubert:Fant Pno, D.940; R. Schumann:Arabeske Pno, Op. 18 PPHI (Great Pianists of the 20th Century) 2-▲ 456799 (22.97)

J. Gimpel (pno) *(rec Ambassador Auditorium, Los Angeles, CA, May 11, 1978)* ("Jakob Gimpel: All-Chopin Recital") † Ballade 1 Pno, Op. 23; Impromptu in F#, Op. 36; Intro & Vars in B♭, Op. 12; Pno Music (misc colls); Debussy:Etudes (12) Pno; Liszt:Valses oubliées (4), S.215 CMB 2-▲ 1070

CHOPIN, FRÉDERIC (cont.)

Sonata in b♭ for Piano, Op. 35 (1839) (cont.)

L. Godowsky (pno) *(rec 1926-30)* † Etudes Pno; Nocturnes Pno; Scherzos Pno; Beethoven:Son 26 Pno, Op. 81a; L. Godowsky:Transcriptions & Paraphrases; E. Grieg:Ballade Pno, Op. 24; Liszt:Paraphrase on Verdi; R. Schumann:Carnaval, Op. 9 PPHI (Great Pianists of the 20th Century, Vol. 37) 2-▲ 456805 (22.97)

P. Grainger (pno) *(rec 1908-48)* ("Percy Grainger, Vol. 2") † Son Pno in b, Op. 58; R. Schumann:Romances Pno, Op. 28; Symphonic Etudes, Op. 13; Stanford:Irish Dances Pno, Op. 89 PHS ▲ 9013 [AAD] (18.97)

P. Grainger (pno) *(rec Oct 13 & 15, 1931)* † Son Pno in b, Op. 58 BPS ▲ 10 [ADD]

M.-A. Hamelin (pno) † S. Rachmaninoff:Son 2 Pno, Op. 36; Schulz-Evler:Arabesque Pno; H. Villa-Lobos:Rudepoema PTRY ▲ 2204 (17.97)

A. Haraisewicz (pno) † Ballade 3 Pno, Op. 47; Polonaise 6 Pno, Op. 53 DI ▲ 920180 [DDD] (5.97)

V. Horowitz (pno)—Grave *(rec 1930-36)* ("Solo European Recordings, Vol. 1") † Études (24) Pno, Opp. 10 & 25; Liszt:Harmonies poétiques et religieuses, S.173; Son Pno, S.178 APR ▲ 5516 [ADD] (18.97)

V. Horowitz (pno) *(rec 1962)* † Polonaise 5 Pno, Op. 44; Polonaises-fant, Op. 61 SNYC ▲ 42412 [AAD] (16.97)

V. Horowitz (pno) † Pno Music (misc colls) RCAV (Gold Seal) ▲ 60376 [ADD] (11.97)

C. Katsaris (pno) † Son Pno in b, Op. 58; Son Pno in c, Op. 4 SNYC ▲ 48483 [DDD] (16.97)

W. Kempff (pno) ("Kempff Plays Chopin Vol 1") † Fant-Impromptu, Op. 66; Impromptu in A♭, Op. 29 PLON (The Classic Sound) ▲ 452307 (11.97)

E. Kilenyi (pno) ("Edward Kilenyi: The Pathe Recordings, 1937-39") † Liszt:Pno Music (misc); Trans, Arrs & Paraphrases APR ▲ 7037 [ADD] (38.97)

R. Lortat (pno) † Preludes (24) Pno, Op. 28 HPC ▲ 37 (17.97)

J. Micault (pno) † Son Pno in b, Op. 58 DI ▲ 920286 [DDD] (5.97)

A. B. Michelangeli (pno) *(rec London, England, June 30, 1959)* † M. Ravel:Gaspard de la nuit MUA ▲ 955 (16.97)

A. B. Michelangeli (pno) *(rec Teatro Grande in Brescia Italy, Italy, June 1967)* † Pno Music (misc colls) FON ▲ 9032 [ADD]

A. B. Michelangeli (pno) *(rec 1957, 1960 & 1966)* † Son Pno in b, Op. 58 PRAG ▲ 250042 (18.97)

A. B. Michelangeli (pno) *(rec 1957-60)* † Ballade 1 Pno, Op. 23; Beethoven:Con 5 Pno, Op. 73 PRAG ▲ 256003 (18.97)

A. B. Michelangeli (pno) † Beethoven:Son 11 Pno, Op. 22; Son 12 Pno, Op. 26 MUA ▲ 1036 [AAD] (31.97)

Z. Mihailovich (pno) *(rec Pomona College Claremont, CA, May 17-18, 1995)* † Polonaise 5 Pno, Op. 44; Son Pno in b, Op. 58 CENT ▲ 2270 [DDD] (16.97)

G. Montero (pno) † Fant-Impromptu, Op. 66; Nocturnes Pno; Polonaise 1 Pno, Op. 26/1; Polonaise 2 Pno, Op. 26/2; Polonaise 6 Pno, Op. 53; Scherzos Pno; Waltzes Pno PALE ▲ 510 (17.97)

A. Nikolsky (pno) † Barcarolle Pno, Op. 60; Preludes (24) Pno, Op. 28 ARNO ▲ 27774 [DDD] (4.97)

G. Novaes (pno) *(rec 1950s)* ("Guiomar Novaes Plays Chopin") † Études Pno; Nocturnes Pno VB3 (Legends) 3-▲ 3501 [ADD] (14.97)

G. Ohlsson (pno) † Son Pno in b, Op. 58; Son Pno in c, Op. 4 ARA ▲ 6628 [DDD] (16.97)

D. Paperno (pno) ("Recordings of a Moscow Pianist") † J. Brahms:Rhaps (2) Pno, Op. 79; E. Grieg:Ballade Pno, Op. 24; Liszt:Polonaises (2) Pno, S.223; Rhap espagnole, S.254; Venezia e Napoli, S.159 CED ▲ 37 [ADD] (16.97)

M. Perahia (pno) † Son Pno in b, Op. 58 SNYC ▲ 32780 [ADD] (16.97)

V. Perlemuter (pno) † Barcarolle Pno, Op. 60 NIMB ▲ 5038 [AAD] (16.97)

D. Pollack (pno) † Son Pno in b, Op. 58 SNYC ▲ 64373 [DDD] (4.97)

M. Pollini (pno) † Son Pno in b, Op. 58 DEUT ▲ 15346 [DDD] (16.97)

S. Rachmaninoff (pno) † Waltzes Pno RCAV (Gold Seal) ▲ 62533 (11.97)

S. Rachmaninoff (pno) *(rec 1919-35)* † Ballade 3 Pno, Op. 47; Scherzos Pno ENPL (Piano Library) ▲ 264 (13.97)

S. Rachmaninoff (pno), A. Cortot (pno), A. Brailowsky (pno), E. Kilenyi (pno) *(rec 1930-37)* ("Performers in Comparison 2") ENT (Piano Library) ▲ 294 (13.97)

B. Rigutto (pno) *(rec Leiden, Netherlands, Dec 17-19, 1990, Dec 4-8, 1991 & Dec 1-2, 1992)* ("Piano Works, Vol. 3") † Berceuse, Op. 57; Fant-Impromptu, Op. 66 DNN ▲ 78927 [DDD] (16.97)

S. Rodriguez (pno) *(rec Fort Worth, TX, 1981)* ("The Sixth Cliburn Competition 1981") † Scherzos Pno; Debussy:Preludes Pno; Liszt:Études d'exécution transcendante (6), S.140; Medtner:Fairy Tales (4), Op. 26; Mendelssohn (-Bartholdy):Fant "Sonate écossaise", Op. 28; R. Schumann:Toccata Pno, Op. 7; A. Scriabin:Son 5 Pno, Op. 53 VAIA (Retrospective Series, Vol. 8) ▲ 1176 [ADD] (16.97)

J. Rose (pno) † Son Pno in b, Op. 58; Son Pno in c, Op. 4 SNYC ▲ 62388 [DDD] (4.97)

A. Rubinstein (pno) † Fantaisie Pno, Op. 49; Son Pno in b, Op. 58 RCAV (Red Seal) ▲ 5616 [ADD] (16.97)

A. Rubinstein (pno) † Barcarolle Pno, Op. 60; Berceuse, Op. 57; Preludes (24) Pno, Op. 28 RCAV (Gold Seal) ▲ 60047 [ADD] (11.97)

H. Shelley (pno) † Preludes (24) Pno, Op. 28 INMP ▲ 6700762 [DDD] (9.97)

K. Skanavi (pno) † Andante Spianato & Grand Polonaise, Op. 22; Berceuse, Op. 57; Intro & Vars in B♭, Op. 12; Nocturnes Pno PPR ▲ 224522

G. Sokolov (pno), C. Coin (cnd), Mosaïques Ensemble—Marche funèbre † Études Pno; Con 2 Pno, Op. 21; Mazurkas Pno; Nocturnes Pno; Polonaise 5 Pno, Op. 44; Preludes (24) Pno, Op. 28; Waltzes Pno OPUS (Chopin Vol. 5) ▲ 2010 (18.97)

V. Tropp (pno) † Barcarolle Pno, Op. 60; Polonaise 5 Pno, Op. 44; Prelude in c#, Op. 45 DNN ▲ 18035 (16.97)

A. Watts (pno)—Marche funèbre; Finale (Presto) *(rec NY, Sept 7-8, 1972)* † Études Pno; Fant-Impromptu, Op. 66; Intro & Polonaise, Op. 3; Mazurkas Pno; Nocturnes Pno; Polonaise 3 Pno, Op. 40/1; Polonaise 6 Pno, Op. 53; Preludes (24) Pno, Op. 28; Waltzes Pno SNYC ▲ 51338 [ADD] (7.97)

various artists—Marche funèbre; Finale (Presto) † Études Pno; Con 2 Pno, Op. 21; Mazurkas Pno; Polonaise 5 Pno, Op. 44; Preludes (24) Pno, Op. 28; Son Vc OPUS (Chopin Exploration Vol. 10 (Excerpts from Vols. 1-9)) ▲ 2015 (7.97)

Sonata in b for Piano, Op. 58 (1844)

L. O. Andsnes (pno) ("Piano Works") † Études Pno; Son Pno in b♭, Op. 35; Son Pno in c, Op. 4 VCL 2-▲ 61317 (21.97)

A. Anievas (pno) † Liszt:Son Pno, S.178; S. Rachmaninoff:Liturgy of St. John Chrysostom, Op. 31; Preludes Pno EMIC (Doublefforte) 2-▲ 68664 (16.97)

I. Biret (pno) *(rec Heidelberg, Germany, Sept 3-5, 1990)* † Son Pno in b♭, Op. 35; Son Pno in c, Op. 4 NXIN ▲ 550363 [DDD] (5.97)

A. Brailowsky (pno) SNYC (Essential Classics) ▲ 46346 [ADD] (7.97) ▮ 46346 [ADD] (3.98)

S. Cherkassky (pno) *(rec June 11 & Oct 16-17, 1985)* † Andante Spianato & Grand Polonaise, Op. 22; Liszt:Hungarian Rhaps, S.244; Son Pno, S.178 NIMB ▲ 7701 [DDD] (11.97)

V. Cliburn (pno) † Son Pno in b♭, Op. 35; Liszt:Études de concert (3), S.144; Années de pèlerinage 2, S.161; Mephisto Waltz 1 Pno, S.514 RCAV (Gold Seal) ▲ 60417 [ADD] (11.97)

A. Cortot (pno) *(rec London, May 12, 1931)* ("Alfred Cortot: Chopin Masterworks") IN ▲ 1341 [ADD] (15.97)

A. Cortot (pno) ("The World of Chopin") † Ballades (4) Pno; Con 2 Pno, Op. 21; Fantaisie Pno, Op. 49; Pno Music (misc colls); Preludes (24) Pno, Op. 28; Son Pno in b♭, Op. 35 ENPL (Piano Library) 3-▲ 206 (39.97)

N. Demidenko (pno) HYP ▲ 66577 (18.97)

A. Di Bonaventura (pno) ("Chopin: Late Works") † Barcarolle Pno, Op. 60; Polonaises-fant, Op. 61 TIT ▲ 208 [DDD]

S. Fiorentino (pno) *(rec Berlin, Oct 1994)* ("Fiorentino Edition, Vol. II") † F. Schubert:Son Pno, D.960 APR ▲ 5553 [DDD] (18.97)

E. Gabriel (pno) † Mazurkas Pno; Nocturnes Pno; Polonaise 2 Pno, Op. 26/2; Polonaise 3 Pno, Op. 40/1; Waltzes Pno QUER ▲ 9822 (18.97)

Em. Gilels (pno) *(rec 1959-78)* ("Emil Gilels III") † Études Pno; Son Pno in b♭, Op. 35; J. Brahms:Con 2 Pno, Op. 83; M. Clementi:Son Pno; E. Grieg:Lyric Pieces; F. Schubert:Fant Pno, D.940; R. Schumann:Arabeske Pno, Op. 18 PPHI (Great Pianists of the 20th Century) 2-▲ 456799 (22.97)

J. Gimpel (pno) *(rec Jan 24, 1976)* ("Jakob Gimpel at Ambassador Auditorium: All-Chopin Recital, Jan 24, 1976") † Fantaisie Pno, Op. 49; Preludes (24) Pno, Op. 28; Waltzes Pno; Debussy:Études (12) Pno; Mendelssohn (-Bartholdy):Lieder ohne Worte CMB 2-▲ 1106 (18.97)

N. Goerner (pno) *(rec London, England, 1996)* ("Piano Works") † Ballade 4 Pno, Op. 52; Barcarolle Pno, Op. 60; Polonaises-fant, Op. 61; Scherzos Pno EMIC (Debut) ▲ 69701 [DDD] (6.97)

G. Gould (pno) † Mendelssohn (-Bartholdy):Lieder ohne Worte; S. Prokofiev:Visions fugitives, Op. 22; A. Scriabin:Pno Music (misc colls) SNYC (Glen Gould Edition) 2-▲ 52622 (31.97)

A. Gourari (pno) *(rec Hochschule für Musik Munich, Dec 27-29, 1995)* ARCK ▲ 59001 [DDD]

P. Grainger (pno) *(rec 1908-48)* ("Percy Grainger, Vol. 2") † Son Pno in b♭, Op. 35; R. Schumann:Romances Pno, Op. 28; Symphonic Etudes, Op. 13; Stanford:Irish Dances Pno, Op. 89 PHS ▲ 9013 [AAD] (18.97)

P. Grainger (pno) *(rec Oct 13 & 15, 1931)* † Son Pno in b♭, Op. 35 BPS ▲ 10 [ADD]

P. Katin (pno) † Nocturnes Pno; Polonaise 5 Pno, Op. 44 HALM ▲ 35014 (6.97)

C. Katsaris (pno) † Son Pno in b♭, Op. 35; Son Pno in c, Op. 4 SNYC ▲ 48483 [DDD] (16.97)

W. Kempff (pno) ("Kempff Plays Chopin Vol 2") † Ballade 3 Pno, Op. 47; Fantaisie Pno, Op. 49; Polonaises-fant, Op. 61 PLON (The Classic Sound) ▲ 452308 (11.97)

E. Kissin (pno) ("Chopin, Vol. 2") † Mazurkas Pno RCAV (Red Seal) ▲ 62542 (16.97)

▲ = CD ♦ = Enhanced CD △ = MD ▮ = Cassette Tape ▯ = DCC

CHOPIN, FRÉDÉRIC (cont.)

Sonata in b for Piano, Op. 58 (1844) (cont.)

A. Kuerti (pno) ("Last Major Piano Works") † Ballade 4 Pno, Op. 52; Polonaises-fant, Op. 61 FL ▲ 23117 [DDD] (12.97)

S. Lindgren (pno) † Liszt:Mephisto Waltz 1 Pno, S.514; S. Rachmaninoff:Prelude in c#, Op. 3/2; R. Schumann:Arabeske Pno, Op. 18; A. Scriabin:Fant Pno, Op. 28 OPU ▲ 9202

D. Lipatti (pno) † Nocturnes Pno; Waltzes Pno; J. S. Bach:Jesu, bleibet meine Freude; E. Grieg:Con Pno, Op. 16; Liszt:Sonetti (3) del Petrarca, S.158; D. Scarlatti:Sons Kbd APR ▲ 5509 [ADD] (18.97)

N. Magaloff (pno) *(rec 1957, 1960 & 1966)* † Son Pno in b♭, Op. 35 PRAG ▲ 250042 (18.97)

T. Manshardt (pno) ("Alfred Cortot's Last Pupil") † Liszt:Consolations (6), S.172; Légendes, S.175; T. Manshardt:Hommage à Debussy; Hommage à Liapunov; Hommage à Mendelssohn; W. A. Mozart:Son 5 Pno, K.283 APR ▲ 5550 [DDD] (19.97)

J. Micault (pno) † Son Pno in b♭, Op. 35 DI ▲ 920286 [DDD] (5.97)

Z. Mihailovich (pno) *(rec Pomona College Claremont, CA, May 17-18, 1995)* † Polonaise 5 Pno, Op. 44; Son Pno in b♭, Op. 35 CENT ▲ 2270 [DDD] (16.97)

B. Moiseiwitsch (pno) ("In Recital") † Études Pno; Fant-Impromptu, Op. 66; Beethoven:Andante Pno, WoO 57; Mussorgsky:Pictures at an Exhibition; Palmgren:West Finnish Dance; R. Schumann:Carnaval, Op. 9; Kreisleriana, Op. 16; Symphonic Etudes, Op. 13 PHS 2-▲ 9192 (33.97)

P. Moss (pno) † Preludes (24) Pno, Op. 28 CENT ▲ 2072 [DDD] (16.97)

G. Novaes (pno) *(rec 1950s)* ("The Romantic Novaes") † Berceuse, Op. 57; Con 1 Pno, Op. 11; Impromptu in F#, Op. 36; M. de Falla:Noches en los jardines de España; E. Grieg:Con Pno, Op. 16 VOXL (Legends) 2-▲ 5513 [ADD] (9.97)

J. Ogdon (pno) † Barcarolle Pno, Op. 60; Berceuse, Op. 57; Fantaisie Pno, Op. 49; Polonaise 4 Pno, Op. 40/2 INMP ▲ 2008 (9.97)

G. Ohlsson (pno) † Son Pno in b♭, Op. 35; Son Pno in c, Op. 4 ARA ▲ 6628 [DDD] (16.97)

M. Perahia (pno) † Son Pno in b♭, Op. 35 SNYC ▲ 32780 [ADD] (16.97)

M. Pletnev (pno) *(rec Friedrich Ebert Hall Hamburg-Harburg, Germany, Nov 1996)* † Ecossaises (3) Pno, Op. 72/3; Fantaisie Pno, Op. 49; Impromptu in A♭, Op. 29; Waltzes Pno DEUT ▲ 453456 (16.97)

D. Pollack (pno) † Son Pno in b♭, Op. 35 SNYC ▲ 64373 [DDD] (4.97)

M. Pollini (pno) † Son Pno in b♭, Op. 35 DEUT ▲ 15346 [DDD] (16.97)

J. Rose (pno) † Son Pno in b♭, Op. 35; Son Pno in c, Op. 4 SNYC ▲ 62388 [DDD] (4.97)

A. Rubinstein (pno) † Fantaisie Pno, Op. 49; Son Pno in b♭, Op. 35 RCAV (Red Seal) ▲ 5616 [ADD] (16.97)

R. Slenczynska (pno) *(rec St. Louis, MO, Apr 8, 1994)* ("Slenczynska in Concert") † J. Brahms:Rhaps (2) Pno, Op. 79; A. Copland:Midsummer Nocturne; J. Haydn:Sonatas for Piano; S. Rachmaninoff:Prelude in c#, Op. 3/2; Preludes Pno IVOR ▲ 70902 [DDD] (16.97)

I. Tiegerman (pno) *(rec Cairo, Egypt, ca 1952)* ("The Lost Legend of Cairo: Radio & Private Recordings") † Ballade 4 Pno, Op. 52; Nocturnes Pno; Preludes (24) Pno, Op. 28; Scherzos Pno; J. Brahms:Con 2 Pno, Op. 83; Intermezzos (3) Pno, Op. 117; Pieces (6) Pno, Op. 118; Pieces (8) Pno, Op. 76; G. Fauré:Nocturnes Pno; J. Field:Nocturnes Pno; C. Franck:Symphonic Vars, M.46; Saint-Saëns:Con 5 Pno, Op. 103; Tiegerman:Meditation Pno ARBT 2-▲ 116 (32.97)

D. Várjon (pno) *(rec Budapest, May-June 1994)* † Pno Music (misc colls) CAPO ▲ 10710 [DDD] (10.97)

S. Vladar (pno) *(rec Feb 28, 1989)* ("Stefan Vladar Live at Grosser Musikvereinssaal") † Beethoven:Son 14 Pno, Op. 27/2; Liszt:Consolations (6), S.172; Schmidek:Clock Pieces, Op. 25; F. Schubert:Fant Pno, D.760 CAMA ▲ 104 (18.97)

G. Zitterbart (pno) † Ballade 1 Pno, Op. 23; Ballade 2 Pno, Op. 38; Ballade 3 Pno, Op. 47; Ballade 4 Pno, Op. 52; Nocturnes Pno TACE ▲ 28

Songs for Soprano & Piano [Op. 74/1-17 & the 2 songs without opus numbers]

C. Arrau (pno)—There where she loves (Gdzie lubi), Op. 74/5 † J. Brahms:Vars & Fugue on a Theme by Handel, Op. 24; Liszt:Études de concert (2), S.145; Mephisto Waltz 1 Pno, S.514; M. Ravel:Gaspard de la nuit AURC ▲ 118 (5.97)

A. Brailowsky (pno) [arr for solo piano] † Mazurkas Pno; Polonaises Pno SNYC (Take Two) 2-▲ 63237 (14.97)

C. Verhaeghe (sop), J. Micault (pno) DI ▲ 920272 [DDD] (5.97)

Les Sylphides (ballet) for Orchestra

R. Irving (cnd), Philharmonia Orch [arr Roy Douglas] ("Great Ballet Music I") † A. Adam:Giselle (sels) RYLC ▲ 70112 (8.97)

E. Ormandy (cnd), Philadelphia Orch † J. S. Bach:Passacaglia & Fugue Org, BWV 582; Pastorale Org, BWV 590; Preludes & Fugues, BWV 531-552; Toccata & Fugue Org, BWV 565; Delibes:Coppélia (suite); Sylvia (suite); P. Tchaikovsky:Nutcracker Suite, Op. 71a SNYC (Essential Classics) ▲ 46551 [ADD] (7.97) ▮ 46551 [ADD] (3.98)

D. Zinman (cnd), Rotterdam PO † Delibes:Coppélia; Gounod:Faust (ballet music) PPHI (Duo) 2-▲ 38763 (17.97)

Les Sylphides (selections)

E. Ansermet (cnd), London PO, E. Ansermet (cnd), Straram Concerts Orch, E. Ansermet (cnd), Diaghilev Ballets Russes Orch, E. Ansermet (cnd), London Philharmonic Choir *(rec 1916-47)* ("Ansermet, Vol. 1") † Rimsky-Korsakov:Scheherazade, Op. 35; Snow Maiden (suite); R. Schumann:Carnaval, Op. 9; I. Stravinsky:Capriccio Pno; Firebird Suite 1; Pétrouchka Suite; Sym of Psalms; N. Tcherepnin:Pavillon d'Armide LYS1 2-▲ 451

Tarantelle in A♭ for Piano, Op. 43 (1841)

C. Arrau (pno) † Études Pno; Ballade 3 Pno, Op. 47; Preludes (24) Pno, Op. 28; R. Schumann:Carnaval, Op. 9; Con Pno in a, Op. 54 ENPL ▲ 287 (13.97)

I. Biret (pno) *(rec 1991)* † Pno Music (misc colls); Waltzes Pno NXIN ▲ 550365 [DDD] (5.97)

A. Cortot (pno) *(rec 1933-43)* † Ballades (4) Pno 78'S (The 78's) ▲ 78509 [ADD] (13.97)

M. Frager (pno) ("Malcolm Frager Plays Chopin") † Andante Spianato & Grand Polonaise, Op. 22; Intro & Vars in B♭, Op. 12; Pno Music (misc colls); Polonaise 6 Pno, Op. 53 TEL ▲ 80280 [DDD] (16.97)

N. Mewton-Wood (pno) *(rec 1941)* † C. M. von Weber:Son 1 Pno, Op. 24; Son 2 Pno, J.199 PHS ▲ 31 (17.97)

Trio in g for Piano, Violin & Cello, Op. 8 (1828-29)

P. Frank (vn), Y.-Y. Ma (vc), E. Ax (pno) *(rec New England Conservatory Boston, MA, June 8-10, 1992)* † Intro & Polonaise, Op. 3; Son Vc SNYC ▲ 53112 [DDD] (16.97)

G. T. Nagy (vn), P. Szabó (vc), D. Várjon (pno) ("Chamber Music") † Grand Duo; Son Vc HUN ▲ 31651 [DDD] (16.97)

Variations in E on Rossini's *Non più mesta* for Flute & Piano (1824)

W. Bennett (fl), C. Benson (pno) *(rec Japan, Sept 2-3, 1991)* ("Poulenc: Flute Sonata") † Bizet:Arlésienne (sels); Carmen (sels); W. A. Mozart:Così fan tutte (sels); F. Poulenc:Son Fl; M. Ravel:Vocalise-étude en forme de habanera; Saint-Saëns:Odelette Fl, Op. 162; Widor:Suite Fl, Op. 34 CAMA ▲ 390 [DDD]

S. Bezaly (fl), E. Nagy (pno) *(rec Danderyd Grammar School, Sweden, Feb 1999)* ("Flutissimo") † A. Bazzini:Ronde des lutins, Op. 25; F. Borne:Fant brillante sur Carmen; Bricciaidi:Carnival of Venice, Op. 78; Taffanel:Fant on Freischütz; Mignon Fant BIS ▲ 1039 [DDD] (17.97)

M. Grauwels (fl), C. Michel (hp) † Donizetti:Larghetto & Allegro; L. Drouet:Intro & Vars on an English Theme; G. Rossini:Andante e tema con variazioni Va; L. Spohr:Son 1 Vn & Hp MARC ▲ 8220441 [DDD] (13.97)

Variations on Mozart's *La ci darem la mano* for Piano & Orchestra (or Solo Piano), Op. 2 (1827)

C. Arrau (pno), E. Inbal (cnd), London SO ("Chopin: Complete Works for Piano & Orchestra") † Andante Spianato & Grand Polonaise, Op. 22; Con 1 Pno, Op. 11; Con 2 Pno, Op. 21; Fantasy, Op. 13; Impromptu in A♭, Op. 29; Impromptu in F#, Op. 36; Impromptu in G♭, Op. 51; Krakowiak, Op. 14 PPHI 2-▲ 38338 (17.97)

I. Biret (pno), M. Sauer (pno) *(rec 1991)* † Mazurkas Pno; Rondos (4) Pno; Rondos (4) Pno, Op. 73; Var 6 Pno; Vars in A, ('Souvenir de Paganini'); Vars on a Theme from La Cenerentola NXIN ▲ 550367 [DDD] (5.97)

I. Biret (pno), R. Stanković (cnd), Czech-Slovak State PO *(rec 1990-91)* † Con 2 Pno, Op. 21; Krakowiak, Op. 14 NXIN ▲ 550369 [DDD] (5.97)

S. Cherkassky (pno) ("Whad'ya Know About Chopin?") † Music of Chopin NIMB ▲ 4003 [ADD] (11.97)

N. Demidenko (pno) † Intro & Vars in E; Scherzos Pno HYP ▲ 66514 [DDD] (18.97)

A. Simon (pno), H. Beissel (cnd), Hamburg SO ("Complete Works for Piano & Orchestra") † Andante Spianato & Grand Polonaise, Op. 22; Con 1 Pno, Op. 11; Con 2 Pno, Op. 21; Grand Fant on Polish Airs, Op. 13; Krakowiak, Op. 14 VB2 2-▲ 5002 [ADD] (9.97)

Variation No. 6 in E for Piano [from Hexameron, collab. Liszt, Thalberg, Pixis, Herz & Czerny] (1837)

I. Biret (pno) *(rec 1991)* † Mazurkas Pno; Rondos (4) Pno; Rondos (4) Pno, Op. 73; Vars in A, ('Souvenir de Paganini'); Vars on a Theme from La Cenerentola; Vars on Mozart, Op. 2 NXIN ▲ 550367 [DDD] (5.97)

W. Chen (pno) ("Bolero") † Andante Spianato & Grand Polonaise, Op. 22; Ballades (4) Pno; Barcarolle Pno, Op. 60; Bolero RCMM ▲ 19702 (16.97)

Variations ('Souvenir de Paganini') in A for Piano (1829)

I. Biret (pno) *(rec 1991)* † Mazurkas Pno; Rondos (4) Pno; Rondos (4) Pno, Op. 73; Var 6 Pno; Vars on a Theme from La Cenerentola; Vars on Mozart, Op. 2 NXIN ▲ 550367 [DDD] (5.97)

R. Ricci (vn), B. Smith (pno) [arr Ricci] ("Paganini's Dreams") † F. Kreisler:Vn Pieces; F. Lehár:Paganini (sels); Liszt:Trans, Arrs & Paraphrases; N. Milstein:Paganiniana; Szymanowski:Caprices Vn, Op. 40 JMR ▲ 11 (16.97)

Variations in E on Rossini's La Cenerentola for Flute & Piano, Op. posth

I. Biret (pno) *(rec 1991)* † Mazurkas Pno; Rondos (4) Pno; Rondos (4) Pno, Op. 73; Var 6 Pno; Vars in A, ('Souvenir de Paganini'); Vars on Mozart, Op. 2 NXIN ▲ 550367 [DDD] (5.97)

CHOPIN, FRÉDÉRIC (cont.)

Waltzes (19) for Piano

G. Anda (pno)—No. 1 in E♭, Op. 18, "Grand Valse Brillante"; No. 2 in A♭, Op. 34/1; No. 3 in a, Op. 34/2; No. 4 in F, Op. 34/3; No. 5 in A♭, Op. 42; No. 6 in D♭, Op. 64/1, "Minute"; No. 7 in c#, Op. 64/2; No. 8 in A♭, Op. 64/3; No. 9 in A♭, Op. 69/1, "L'adieu"; No. 10 in b, Op. 69/2; No. 11 in g♭, Op. 70/1; No. 12 in f, Op. 70/2; No. 13 in D♭, Op. 70/3 *(rec 1959-75)* † B. Bartók:Cons Pno (comp); W. A. Mozart:Con 21 Pno, K.467 PPHI (Great Pianists of the 20th Century) 2-▲ 456772 (22.97)

V. Ashkenazy (pno) PLON ▲ 14600 [ADD] (16.97)

A. R. El Bacha (pno)—No. 11 in g♭, Op. 70/1 ("El Bacha Plays Chopin, Vol. 4") † Études Pno; Allegro de concert, Op. 46; Ballade 1 Pno, Op. 23; Mazurkas Pno; Rondos (4) Pno FORL ▲ 16785 (16.97)

S. Barere (pno)—No. 5 in A♭, Op. 42 *(rec Jan 31, 1934)* † Mazurkas Pno; Balakirev:Islamey; F. Blumenfeld:Etude for the left hand, Op. 36; Glazunov:Etude Pno; Liszt:Pno Music (misc); R. Schumann:Toccata Pno, Op. 7 PHS ▲ 12 [ADD] (17.97)

I. Biret (pno) *(rec 1991)* † Pno Music (misc colls); Tarentelle, Op. 43 NXIN ▲ 550365 [DDD] (5.97)

J. Bolet (pno)—No. 6 in D♭, Op. 64/1, "Minute"; No. 7 in c#, Op. 64/2 *(rec Queens, NY)* ("A Chopin Piano Recital") † Études Pno; Fant-Impromptu, Op. 66; Polonaise 3 Pno, Op. 40/1; Polonaise 6 Pno, Op. 53; Preludes (24) Pno, Op. 28 EVC ▲ 9028 [AAD] (13.97)

J. Browning (pno)—No. 1 in E♭, Op. 18, "Grand Valse Brillante" *(rec New York, NY, July 28-31 & Aug 4-6, 20, 1958)* † Études Pno; Nocturnes Pno; J. S. Bach:Partitas Hpd; Busoni:Bach Trans Pno; Debussy:Images (6) Pno; Liszt:Mephisto Waltz 3 Pno, S.216; Rimsky-Korsakov:Tale of Tsar Saltan (orch sels); F. Schubert:Impromptus (4) Pno EMIC ▲ 67017 [ADD] (11.97)

S. Cherkassky (pno)—No. 5 in A♭, Op. 42 *(rec San Francisco, CA, Apr 18, 1982)* ("The 1982 San Francisco Recital") † Polonaises-fant, Op. 61; J. Hofmann:Kaleidoskop, Op. 40; Lully:Suite de pièces; Mendelssohn (-Bartholdy):Scherzo a capriccio; P. Tchaikovsky:Son Pno, Op. 37 IVOR ▲ 70904 [DDD] (16.97)

J. Darré (pno)—Waltzes Pno [No. 3 in a, Op. 34/2] *(rec Konzerthaus Vienna, Austria, June 23-25, 1966)* VC ▲ 91 [AAD] (13.97)

P. Entremont (pno)—No. 6 in D♭, Op. 64/1, "Minute"; No. 7 in c#, Op. 64/2; No. 1 in E♭, Op. 18, "Grand Valse Brillante"; No. 11 in g♭, Op. 70/1 *(rec Winterthur, Switzerland, Nov 6-7, 1967)* † Études Pno; Fant-Impromptu, Op. 66; Intro & Polonaise, Op. 3; Mazurkas Pno; Nocturnes Pno; Polonaise 3 Pno, Op. 40/1; Polonaise 6 Pno, Op. 53; Preludes (24) Pno, Op. 28; Son Pno in b♭, Op. 35 SNYC ▲ 51338 [ADD] (7.97)

I. Friedman (pno)—No. 9 in A♭, Op. 69/1, "L'adieu" ("Highlights 1925-36 From His Discography") † Études Pno; Impromptu in F#, Op. 36; Mazurkas Pno; Nocturnes Pno; Polonaise 6 Pno, Op. 53; Son Pno in b♭, Op. 35; Beethoven:Son 14 Pno, Op. 27/2; I. Friedman:Danse; Music Box, Op. 33/3; J. N. Hummel:Rondo Pno, Op. 11; Liszt:Trans, Arrs & Paraphrases; Mendelssohn (-Bartholdy):Fants Pno, Op. 16; Shield:Old English Menuet APR (Signature Series) ▲ 5508 [ADD] (18.97)

E. Gabriel (pno)—No. 3 in a, Op. 34/2 † Mazurkas Pno; Nocturnes Pno; Polonaise 2 Pno, Op. 26/2; Polonaise 3 Pno, Op. 40/1; Son Pno in b, Op. 58 QUER ▲ 9822 (18.97)

J. Gimpel (pno)—No. 2 in A♭, Op. 34/1 *(rec Jan 24, 1976)* ("Jakob Gimpel at Ambassador Auditorium: All-Chopin Recital, Jan 24, 1976") † Fantaisie Pno, Op. 49; Preludes (24) Pno, Op. 28; Son Pno in b, Op. 58; Debussy:Etudes (12) Pno; Mendelssohn (-Bartholdy):Lieder ohne Worte CMB 2-▲ 1106 (18.97)

A. Harasiewicz (pno) [16 sels] † Polonaises Pno PPHI (Duo) 2-▲ 462874 (17.97)

J. Hofmann (pno)—No. 7 in c#, Op. 64/2; No. 5 in A♭, Op. 42; No. 2 in A♭, Op. 34/1 ("Josef Hofmann Plays Chopin") † Con 1 Pno, Op. 11; Polonaise 3 Pno, Op. 40/1; Polonaise 6 Pno, Op. 53 KLAV (Legendary Artists) ▲ 11082 [ADD] (18.97)

V. Horowitz (pno)—No. 9 in A♭, Op. 69/1, "L'adieu" † Ballade 4 Pno, Op. 52; Liszt:Ballade 2, S.171; S. Rachmaninoff:Preludes Pno; D. Scarlatti:Sons Kbd HP ▲ 63314 (11.97)

J.-M. Luisada—No. 1 in E♭, Op. 18, "Grand Valse Brillante" ("Masters of Classical Music, Vol. 8: Frederic Chopin") † Études Pno; Mazurkas Pno; Nocturnes (21) Pno; Nocturnes Pno; Preludes (24) Pno, Op. 28; Scherzos Pno LALI ▲ 15808 [DDD] (3.97)

E. L. Kaplan (pno)—No. 14 in e, Op. posth. *(rec Los Angeles, CA, Sep 1992)* † Fantaisie Pno, Op. 49; Mazurkas Pno; Nocturnes Pno; R. Schumann:Carnaval, Op. 9 CMB ▲ 1098 (16.97)

N. Kokinos (pno)—No. 2 in A♭, Op. 34/1; No. 13 in D♭, Op. 70/3 † Fantaisie Pno, Op. 49; Polonaise 3 Pno, Op. 40/1; Polonaise 6 Pno, Op. 53; Polonaises-fant, Op. 61; Preludes (24) Pno, Op. 28; Scherzos Pno ANDP ▲ 9592 (15.97)

D. Lipatti (pno) [1 waltz in A♭] † Études Pno; Con 1 Pno, Op. 11; Nocturnes Pno; J. S. Bach:Con 2 Hpd, BWV 1053 PALE ▲ 509 (17.97)

D. Lipatti (pno)—No. 4 in F, Op. 34/3; No. 5 in A♭, Op. 42; No. 6 in D♭, Op. 64/1, "Minute"; No. 9 in A♭, Op. 69/1, "L'adieu"; No. 7 in c#, Op. 64/2; No. 11 in g♭, Op. 70/1; No. 10 in b, Op. 69/2; No. 14 in e, Op. posth.; No. 3 in a, Op. 34/2; No. 8 in A♭, Op. 64/3; No. 12 in f, Op. 70/2; No. 13 in D♭, Op. 70/3; No. 1 in E♭, Op. 18, "Grand Valse Brillante"; No. 2 in A♭, Op. 34/1 *(rec Switzerland, July 3-12, 1950)* † Barcarolle Pno, Op. 60; Mazurkas Pno; Nocturnes Pno EMIC ▲ 66956 [ADD] (11.97)

D. Lipatti (pno)—No. 2 in A♭, Op. 34/1 † Nocturnes Pno; Son Pno in b, Op. 58; J. S. Bach:Jesu, bleibet meine Freude; E. Grieg:Con Pno, Op. 16; Liszt:Sonetti (3) del Petrarca, S.158; D. Scarlatti:Sons Kbd APR ▲ 5509 [ADD] (18.97)

A. B. Michelangeli (pno) *(rec 1960-73)* ("Michelangeli in Recital") † Fantaisie Pno, Op. 49; J. Brahms:Ballades (4), Op. 10; Vars on a Theme by Paganini, Op. 35; Busoni:Chaconne Pno; M. Ravel:Gaspard de la nuit; R. Schumann:Carnaval, Op. 9 MUA 2-▲ 817 [AAD] (31.97)

G. Montero (pno)—No. 6 in D♭, Op. 64/1, "Minute"; No. 2 in A♭, Op. 34/1 † Fant-Impromptu, Op. 66; Nocturnes Pno; Polonaise 1 Pno, Op. 26/1; Polonaise 2 Pno, Op. 26/2; Polonaise 6 Pno, Op. 53; Scherzos Pno; Son Pno in b♭, Op. 35 PALE ▲ 510 (17.97)

I. J. Paderewski (pno)—No. 1 in E♭, Op. 18, "Grand Valse Brillante"; No. 2 in A♭, Op. 34/1; No. 5 in A♭, Op. 42 *(rec 1912-30)* ("Ignacy Jan Paderewski") † Études Pno; Berceuse, Op. 57; Funeral March in b♭; Mazurkas Pno; Nocturnes Pno; Polonaise 2 Pno, Op. 26/2; Polonaise 3 Pno, Op. 40/1; Preludes (24) Pno, Op. 28; Liszt:Études d'exécution transcendante (6), S.140; Études de concert (3), S.144; Hungarian Rhaps, S.244; Trans, Arrs & Paraphrases; I. J. Paderewski:Minuet; F. Schubert:Impromptus (4) PPHI (Great Pianists of the 20th Century) 2-▲ 456919 (22.97)

M. Perahia (pno)—No. 1 in E♭, Op. 18, "Grand Valse Brillante"; No. 5 in A♭, Op. 42 † Études Pno; Ballade 1 Pno, Op. 23; Ballade 2 Pno, Op. 38; Ballade 3 Pno, Op. 47; Ballade 4 Pno, Op. 52; Mazurkas Pno; Nocturnes Pno SNYC ▲ 64399 [DDD] (16.97) COL △ 64399 [DDD]

M. Pletnev (pno)—No. 2 in A♭, Op. 34/1; No. 3 in a, Op. 34/2; No. 14 in e, Op. posth. *(rec Friedrich Ebert Hall Hamburg-Harburg, Germany, Nov 1996)* † Ecossaises (3) Pno, Op. 72/3; Fantaisie Pno, Op. 49; Impromptu in A♭, Op. 29; Son Pno in b, Op. 58 DEUT ▲ 453456 (16.97)

S. Rachmaninoff (pno) † Son Pno in b♭, Op. 35 RCAV (Gold Seal) ▲ 62533 (11.97)

S. Richter (pno)—No. 1 in E♭, Op. 18, "Grand Valse Brillante"; No. 2 in A♭, Op. 34/1; No. 3 in a, Op. 34/2; No. 4 in F, Op. 34/3 ("Sviatoslav Richter Archives Vol. 2") † Barcarolle Pno, Op. 60; Polonaise 6 Pno, Op. 53; Scherzos Pno DHR (Legendary Treasures) ▲ 7724 (16.97)

S. Richter (pno)—No. 4 in F, Op. 34/3; No. 2 in A♭, Op. 34/1; No. 3 in a, Op. 34/2 *(rec Aug 26, 1977)* ("Richter in Salzburg") † Barcarolle Pno, Op. 60; Scherzos Pno; Beethoven:Andante Pno, WoO 57; Debussy:Estampes; Preludes Pno; Suite bergamasque; S. Rachmaninoff:Preludes Pno MUA ▲ 1019 [ADD] (16.97)

M. Rosenthal (pno)—No. 7 in c#, Op. 64/2; No. 14 in e, Op. posth. *(rec Apr 28, 1930)* † Études Pno; Berceuse, Op. 57; Con 1 Pno, Op. 11; Mazurkas Pno; Liszt:Trans, Arrs & Paraphrases; M. Rosenthal:Papillons BPS ▲ 40 (m) [ADD] (16.97)

A. Rubinstein (pno)—No. 7 in c#, Op. 64/2 *(rec Small Queen's Hall, England, Apr 18, 1928)* ("The Legendary Rubinstein") † Barcarolle Pno, Op. 60; Berceuse, Op. 57; Mazurkas Pno; Nocturnes Pno; Polonaise 3 Pno, Op. 40/1; Polonaise 6 Pno, Op. 53; Scherzos Pno EMIC ▲ 67007 (m) [ADD] (11.97)

A. Schiller (pno) ("The Complete Waltzes") † F. Schubert:Minuets & Trios Str Qt, D.89; Qt 12 Strs, D.703; Qt 14 Strs, D.810 ASVQ ▲ 6149 [DDD] (10.97)

A. Simon (pno) *(rec 1974)* † Études Pno VB2 2-▲ 5167 (9.97)

G. Sokolov (pno), C. Coin (cnd), Mosaïques Ensemble—No. 6 in D♭, Op. 64/1, "Minute" † Études Pno; Con 2 Pno, Op. 21; Mazurkas Pno; Nocturnes Pno; Polonaise 5 Pno, Op. 44; Preludes (24) Pno, Op. 28; Son Pno in b♭, Op. 35 OPUS (Chopin Vol. 5) ▲ 2010 (18.97)

D. T. Son (pno) ANAL ▲ 27704 (16.97)

J. Swann (pno) *(rec Milan, Italy, July 14-16, 1995)* AG ▲ 24 [DDD] (18.97)

various artists—No. 9 in A♭, Op. 69/1, "L'adieu" † Études Pno; Barcarolle Pno, Op. 60; Berceuse, Op. 57; Con 1 Pno, Op. 11; Con 2 Pno, Op. 21; Nocturnes Pno; Nouvelles études; Preludes (24) Pno, Op. 28 RCAV ▮ 63423 (6.98) ▲ 63423 (11.97)

Wiosna [Spring] in G for Piano (text Witwicki), Op. 74/2 (1838)

I. Biret (pno) *(rec 1991-92)* † Albumleaf (Feuille d'Album); Barcarolle Pno, Op. 60; Bolero; Fugue in a; Pno Music (misc colls); Prelude in c#, Op. 45; Prelude in A♭, Op. posth.; Preludes (24) Pno, Op. 28 NXIN ▲ 550366 [DDD] (5.97)

C. Katsaris (pno) † Albumleaf (Feuille d'Album); Allegretto & Mazur; Allegretto in F; Bolero; Bourrées; Cantabile in B♭; Contredanse; Ecossaises (3) Pno, Op. 72/3; Fugue in a; Galop Marquis; Largo in E♭; Prelude in c#, Op. 45; Prelude in A♭, Op. posth.; Preludes (24) Pno, Op. 28 SNYC ▲ 53355 [DDD] (16.97)

CHORBAJIAN, JOHN (20th cent)
Bitter for Sweet for Chorus (1971)
P. Rutenberg (cnd), Los Angeles Chamber Singers ("Romancero Gitano") † S. Barber:Songs; Castelnuovo-Tedesco:Romancero gitano, Op. 152; M. Lauridsen:Chansons des roses; H. Stevens:Elizabethan Madrigals; R. Thompson:Odes to Horace RCMM ▲ 19802 (16.97)
CHOU WEN-CHUNG (1923-
Cursive for Flute & Piano (1963)
H. Sollberger (fl), C. Wuorinen (pno) † Landscapes; Pien; Willows Are New; Yü ko CRI ▲ 691 [ADD] (16.97)
Echoes from the Gorge for Percussion Quartet (1989)
New Music Consort † Suite Hp; Windswept Peaks; Yü ko; Yün; Wen-Chung:Music of Wen-Chung ALBA ▲ 155 [DDD] (16.97)
Landscapes for Orchestra (1949)
T. Johnson (cnd), Peninsula Festival Orch † Cursive; Pien; Willows Are New; Yü ko CRI ▲ 691 [ADD] (16.97)
Pien for Piano, Percussion & Winds (1966)
H. Sollberger (cnd), Columbia Univ Group for Contemporary Music † Cursive; Landscapes; Willows Are New; Yü ko CRI ▲ 691 [ADD] (16.97)
Soliloquy of a Bhiksuni for solo Trumpet, Brass Ensemble & Percussion (1958)
T. Stevens (tpt), M. Peters (perc), Los Angeles Brass Society † F. Campo:Times; R. Henderson:Var Movts; W. Kraft:Encounters III; Kupferman:Fires of Prometheus; Revueltas:Little Serious Pieces; V. Reynolds:Signals CRYS ▲ 667 (15.97)
Suite for Harp & Wind Quintet (1950)
Speculum Musicae † Echoes from the Gorge; Windswept Peaks; Yü ko; Yün; Wen-Chung:Music of Wen-Chung ALBA ▲ 155 [DDD] (16.97)
The Willows Are New for Piano (1957)
Y. Chang (pno) † Cursive; Landscapes; Pien; Yü ko CRI ▲ 691 [ADD] (16.97)
Windswept Peaks for Chamber Ensemble (1990)
R. Pittman (cnd) , R. Pittman (cnd), Boston Musica Viva † Echoes from the Gorge; Suite Hp; Yü ko; Yün; Wen-Chung:Music of Wen-Chung ALBA ▲ 155 [DDD] (16.97)
Yü ko for 9 Instruments (1965)
C. Heldrich (cnd) , C. Heldrich (cnd), New Music Consort † Echoes from the Gorge; Suite Hp; Windswept Peaks; Yün; Wen-Chung:Music of Wen-Chung ALBA ▲ 155 [DDD] (16.97)
H. Sollberger (cnd), Columbia Univ Group for Contemporary Music † Cursive; Landscapes; Pien; Willows Are New CRI ▲ 691 [ADD] (16.97)
Yün for Piano, Percussion & Winds (1969)
D. Palma (cnd) , D. Palma (cnd), Speculum Musicae † Echoes from the Gorge; Suite Hp; Windswept Peaks; Yü ko; Wen-Chung:Music of Wen-Chung ALBA ▲ 155 [DDD] (16.97)
CHRISTENSEN, MOGENS (1955-
Birds of a Spring Night for solo Recorder (1993)
H. Kristensen (rcr) *(rec Jetsmark Kirke Denmark, June 1993 & Dec 1994)* ("Play") † Dreamless Fragments; Reflets de cristal; Winter Light; R. Odriozola:Dances; Danish Miniatures; Psalms PONT ▲ 5116
Dreamless Fragments for solo Violin (1994)
R. Odriozola (vn) *(rec Jetsmark Kirke Denmark, June 1993 & Dec 1994)* ("Play") † Birds of a Spring Night; Reflets de cristal; Winter Light; R. Odriozola:Dances; Danish Miniatures; Psalms PONT ▲ 5116
The Lost Poems of Princess Ateh for Ensemble (1991)
Ensemble Nord *(rec Nordjsky Musikkonservatorium, Netherlands, 1992)* † E. Bach:Bagatelles; N. V. Bentzon:Choro Daniensis, Op. 548; E. Bjerno:Star Dust, Op. 182; S. Christiansen:In Reality; RijshøjgArd:Qnt PLAL ▲ 74 [ADD] (18.97)
Music of Christensen
Ensemble Nord—Birds of a Midsummer Night; Snow Light; Esprit Féerique; Dreamtimes; Lost Poems of Princess Ateh; Mellem livets afgrunde; Ange Silencieux ("Vocal & Chamber Music, Vol 3") PLAL ▲ 96 [DDD] (18.97)
C. Meldgaard (sop), Lin Ensemble—Fancyer's Delight; Tale of Adam Ruhani; El Mar, las rosas y el suena perdido; Gura, the growing darkness; Orfiske lldklipper; Pessimisticum PLAL ▲ 86 (18.97)
R. Odriozola (vn), C. Dejour (gtr), K. Thiele (fl), E. Rottingen (pno), F. Stengaard (org)—Eternelle; Solos Vn; Birds of a Spring Night; Dryad's Dream; Khazarian Mirrors PLAL ▲ 110 (18.97)
R. Odriozola (vn), C. Kollavik-Jensen (gtr), H. Kristensen (rcr)—Winter Light; Fancyer's Delight; Bird Nocturnals; Birds of a Spring Night; Birds of a Midsummer Night; Birds of an Autumn Night; Birds of a Winter Night PLAL ▲ 112
L. Øvreb (sop), C. Gottschlack (vn), G. Frenning (perc), R. Odriozola (cnd), Ensemble Nord *(Hyperions Schicksalied)*, E. Lunde (sop), C. Kollavik-Jensen (gtr) *(Morgenhav)*, J. Odriozola (vc) *(El Mar del tiempo perdido)*, R. Odriozola (vn), A. Nitter-Sandvik (pno) *(Elf & Fairy Sprite)*, Ensemble Nord *(Dream within Dream)*, T. A. Olesen (vc), H. Kristensen (rcr), C. Borch (hpd), G. Frenning (perc) *(und helle Musik)*, R. Odriozola (vn) *(Cadenza)*, E. Lunde (sop), A. Dahl (sop), R. Odriozola (vn), C. Gottschlack (vn), K. Steenstrup (tpt), J. O. Nielsen (cnt), G. Frenning (perc), F. Hansen (perc), E. Kullberg (cnd), Ensemble Nord, E. Kullberg (cnd), Da Camera Choir *(Stemmer)* ("Mogens Christensen: Vocal & Chamber Music, Vol. I") PLAL ▲ 66 [DAD] (18.97)
Reflets de cristal for Violin & Cello (1992)
R. Odriozola (vn), J. Odriozola (vc) *(rec Jetsmark Kirke Denmark, June 1993 & Dec 1994)* ("Play") † Birds of a Spring Night; Dreamless Fragments; Winter Light; R. Odriozola:Dances; Danish Miniatures; Psalms PONT ▲ 5116
Winter Light for Recorder & Violin (1990)
R. Odriozola (vn), H. Kristensen (rcr) *(rec Jetsmark Kirke Denmark, June 1993 & Dec 1994)* ("Play") † Birds of a Spring Night; Dreamless Fragments; Reflets de cristal; R. Odriozola:Dances; Danish Miniatures; Psalms PONT ▲ 5116
CHRISTIANSEN, ASGER LUND (1927-
Octet for Winds, Op. 34 (1992)
Danish Wind Octet *(rec Copenhagen, Jan 20, Mar 20 & Apr 10, 1994)* † Graugaard:Summerscapes; H. D. Koppel:Music for Ww Octet, Op. 123; S. S. Schultz:Divert Ww; S. E. Werner:Catch MARC ▲ 8224002 [DDD] (13.97)
CHRISTIANSEN, SVEND (1954-
In Reality [I virkelheden] for Small Ensemble (1992)
Ensemble Nord *(rec Nordjsky Musikkonservatorium, Netherlands, 1992)* † E. Bach:Bagatelles; N. V. Bentzon:Choro Daniensis, Op. 548; E. Bjerno:Star Dust, Op. 182; M. Christensen:Lost Poems of Princess Ateh; RijshøjgArd:Qnt PLAL ▲ 74 [ADD] (18.97)
CHRISTOFF, DIMITER (1933-
Chaconne for Piano (1984)
I. Mantcheva (pno) *(rec Sofia Bulgaria, Jan 1996)* ("The Piano Music, Vol. 1") † Son 1 Pno; Son 2 Pno; Son 3 Pno; Son 4 Pno; Son 5 Pno ERTO ▲ 42037 [DDD] (16.97)
Rain Hoods...After the Storm for Piano (1992)
N. Vlaeva (pno) *(rec Sofia Bulgaria, June 1995)* ("The Piano Music, Vol. 2") † Son 6 Pno; Son 7 Pno; Son 8 Pno; Toccata for All Soul's Day ERTO ▲ 42038 [DDD] (16.97)
Sonata No. 1 for Piano (1962)
I. Mantcheva (pno) *(rec Sofia Bulgaria, Jan 1996)* ("The Piano Music, Vol. 1") † Chaconne; Son 2 Pno; Son 3 Pno; Son 4 Pno; Son 5 Pno ERTO ▲ 42037 [DDD] (16.97)
Sonata No. 2 for Piano (1974)
I. Mantcheva (pno) *(rec Sofia Bulgaria, Jan 1996)* ("The Piano Music, Vol. 1") † Chaconne; Son 1 Pno; Son 3 Pno; Son 4 Pno; Son 5 Pno ERTO ▲ 42037 [DDD] (16.97)
Sonata No. 3 for Piano (1974)
I. Mantcheva (pno) *(rec Sofia Bulgaria, Jan 1996)* ("The Piano Music, Vol. 1") † Chaconne; Son 1 Pno; Son 2 Pno; Son 4 Pno; Son 5 Pno ERTO ▲ 42037 [DDD] (16.97)
Sonata No. 4 for Piano (1974)
I. Mantcheva (pno) *(rec Sofia Bulgaria, Jan 1996)* ("The Piano Music, Vol. 1") † Chaconne; Son 1 Pno; Son 2 Pno; Son 3 Pno; Son 5 Pno ERTO ▲ 42037 [DDD] (16.97)
Sonata No. 5 for Piano (1992)
I. Mantcheva (pno) *(rec Sofia Bulgaria, Jan 1996)* ("The Piano Music, Vol. 1") † Chaconne; Son 1 Pno; Son 2 Pno; Son 3 Pno; Son 4 Pno ERTO ▲ 42037 [DDD] (16.97)
Sonata No. 6 for Piano (1992)
N. Vlaeva (pno) *(rec Sofia Bulgaria, June 1995)* ("The Piano Music, Vol. 2") † Rain Hoods; Son 7 Pno; Son 8 Pno; Toccata for All Soul's Day ERTO ▲ 42038 [DDD] (16.97)
Sonata No. 7 for Piano (1994)
N. Vlaeva (pno) *(rec Sofia Bulgaria, June 1995)* ("The Piano Music, Vol. 2") † Rain Hoods; Son 6 Pno; Son 8 Pno; Toccata for All Soul's Day ERTO ▲ 42038 [DDD] (16.97)
Sonata No. 8 for Piano (1994)
N. Vlaeva (pno) *(rec Sofia Bulgaria, June 1995)* ("The Piano Music, Vol. 2") † Rain Hoods; Son 6 Pno; Son 7 Pno; Toccata for All Soul's Day ERTO ▲ 42038 [DDD] (16.97)
CHRISTOFF, DIMITER (cont.)
Toccata for All Soul's Day for Piano (1992)
N. Vlaeva (pno) *(rec Sofia Bulgaria, June 1995)* ("The Piano Music, Vol. 2") † Rain Hoods; Son 6 Pno; Son 7 Pno; Son 8 Pno ERTO ▲ 42038 [DDD] (16.97)
CHRISTOSKOV, PETER (1917-
Suite No. 1 for Solo Violin, Op. 7
E. Dekov (vn) *(rec 1971 & 1974)* ("Virtuoso Violin Works from the Twentieth Century") † Goleminov:Little Suite; B. Linde:Son Vn; Pergament:Chaconne Vn BIS ▲ 9 [AAD] (17.97)
CHRISTOV, DOBRI (1875-1941)
Choral Music
Philippopolis Chamber Ensemble—Vo Tzarstvij Tvoem Blajenstva; Ize Cheruwimi; Blagoslovi Douche Moia Gospodi *(rec Resurrection Church, Plovdiv, Bulgaria, 1994)* ("Liturgical Songs of Praise of the Orthodox Church") † Arkhangelsky:Gospodji Usliži Molitwu; Bortnyansky:Mnogaja leta; Chesnokov:Djertva Večernaja; Ljubimov:Blažen Muž; Lomakin:Tebe Poem; Traditional:Dnes Vsjaka Twar; Edin svjat; Lord, have mercy [Prositelna Ektenia]; Nine Otpužtaešti; Our Father [Otče Naš] NOVA ▲ 150149 [DDD] (16.97)
CHU, WEI (1917-
Harvest Scenes (symphonic suite) for Orchestra
L. Kektjiang (cnd), Gunma SO *(rec Gumma Prefecture Japan, May 24-25, 1981)* † Du:Mermaid (ballet suite) MARC (Chinese Music) ▲ 8223920 [DDD] (13.97)
CHUECA, FEDERICO (1846-1908)
Operetta Arias
A. Arteta (sop), E. G. Asensio (cnd), RTVE SO—Chotis del Iseo Madrilleno (sels); Tango de La Meneglida (sels); Coro de Nineras (sels) † Chapí:Operetta Arias; Guridi:Operetta Arias; Sorozábal:Operetta Arias; Torroba:Operetta Arias; Vives:Operetta Arias RTVE ▲ 65095 (16.97)
CHUMBLEY, ROBERT (1954-
Self Studies (3) for Piano & Strings (1994)
S. Irek (pno), Broyhill Chamber Ensemble *(rec Appalachian State Univ, July 1995)* ("3 American Piano Quartets") † A. Copland:Qt Pno; W. T. McKinley:Qt 1 Pno MASM ▲ 2041 [DDD] (16.97)
CHURCHILL, FRANK E. (1901-1942)
Songs
J. Ottley (cnd), Columbia SO, J. Ottley (cnd), Mormon Tabernacle Choir—Who's Afraid of the Big Bad Wolf *(rec Salt Lake City, UT)* ("When You Wish Upon a Star") † M. David:Songs; R. Gilbert:Songs; Morey:Songs; R. Sherman:Songs; N. Washington:Songs SNYC ▲ 37200 [DDD] (9.97)
CIAIA, AZZOLINO DELLA BERNARDINO (1671-1755)
Sonatas (6) for Harpsichord & Counterpoints (6) for Keyboard, Op. 4 (?1727)
Y. Rechsteiner (hpd) *(rec Nov 1995)* GALL ▲ 868 [ADD] (18.97)
CIANI, SUZANNE (1946-
History of My Heart for Piano
S. Ciani (pno) PRI ▲ 2058 (11.97)
Hotel Luna for Piano
S. Ciani (pno) PRI ▲ 82090 (11.97)
Neverland for Piano
S. Ciani (pno) PRI ▲ 2036 (11.97)
Pianissimo for Piano
S. Ciani (pno) PRI ▲ 2073 (11.97)
The Private Music of Suzanne Ciani for Piano
S. Ciani (pno) PRI ▲ 82103 (11.97)
CIARDI, CESARE (1818-1877)
Il Pifferaro for Flute & Harp, Op. 122
H. Wegner (fl), E. Wegner (hp) *(rec June 1994)* ("All' Italiana") † Boccherini:Son Fl & Hp; Donizetti:Son Fl & Hp; G. Rossini:Allegretto Hp; Andante e tema con variazioni Va; Son Hp; N. Rota:Sarabande & Toccata; Son Fl & Hp THOR ▲ 2243 [DDD] (16.97)
CICOGNINI, ALESSANDRO (1907-
The Bicycle Thief (selections) (1947)
E. M. Tisi (voc), N. Samale (cnd), Sinfonia Orch delle Marche, St. Cecilia di Fabriano ("Music of Alessandro Cicognini") † Gold of Naples (sels); Last Judgement (sels); Miracle in Milan (sels); Roof (sels); Shoeshine (sels); Umberto D (sels) IMEZ ▲ 23 [DDD] (22.97)
Gold of Naples (selections) (1954)
E. M. Tisi (voc), N. Samale (cnd), Sinfonia Orch delle Marche, St. Cecilia di Fabriano ("Music of Alessandro Cicognini") † Bicycle Thief (sels); Last Judgement (sels); Miracle in Milan (sels); Roof (sels); Shoeshine (sels); Umberto D (sels) IMEZ ▲ 23 [DDD] (22.97)
The Last Judgement (selections) (1961)
E. M. Tisi (voc), N. Samale (cnd), Sinfonia Orch delle Marche, St. Cecilia di Fabriano ("Music of Alessandro Cicognini") † Bicycle Thief (sels); Gold of Naples (sels); Miracle in Milan (sels); Roof (sels); Shoeshine (sels); Umberto D (sels) IMEZ ▲ 23 [DDD] (22.97)
Miracle in Milan (selections) (1951)
E. M. Tisi (voc), N. Samale (cnd), Sinfonia Orch delle Marche, St. Cecilia di Fabriano ("Music of Alessandro Cicognini") † Bicycle Thief (sels); Gold of Naples (sels); Last Judgement (sels); Roof (sels); Shoeshine (sels); Umberto D (sels) IMEZ ▲ 23 [DDD] (22.97)
The Roof (selections) (1956)
E. M. Tisi (voc), N. Samale (cnd), Sinfonia Orch delle Marche, St. Cecilia di Fabriano ("Music of Alessandro Cicognini") † Bicycle Thief (sels); Gold of Naples (sels); Last Judgement (sels); Miracle in Milan (sels); Shoeshine (sels); Umberto D (sels) IMEZ ▲ 23 [DDD] (22.97)
Shoeshine (selections) (1946)
E. M. Tisi (voc), N. Samale (cnd), Sinfonia Orch delle Marche, St. Cecilia di Fabriano ("Music of Alessandro Cicognini") † Bicycle Thief (sels); Gold of Naples (sels); Last Judgement (sels); Miracle in Milan (sels); Roof (sels); Umberto D (sels) IMEZ ▲ 23 [DDD] (22.97)
Umberto D (selections)
E. M. Tisi (voc), N. Samale (cnd), Sinfonia Orch delle Marche, St. Cecilia di Fabriano ("Music of Alessandro Cicognini") † Bicycle Thief (sels); Gold of Naples (sels); Last Judgement (sels); Miracle in Milan (sels); Roof (sels); Shoeshine (sels) IMEZ ▲ 23 [DDD] (22.97)
CICONIA, JOHANNES (ca 1335-1411)
O Padua sidus praeclarum (motets) for 2 Voices & Chorus, C.164
P. Memelsdorff (cnd), Mala Punica ERAT ▲ 21661 (16.97)
Vocal & Instrumental Consort Music
Alla Francesca, Alta—Merçé o morte; Una panthera; Gli alti col dançor; O Padua, sidus preclarum; Ben che da vui; Sus une fontayne; Caçando un giorno; Quod jactatur; Poy che morir; Venecle, mundi splendor; O rosa bella; Chi, vole amar; O felix temptum jubila; Chi nel servir antico; Deduto sey; Aler m'en veus; O virum omaimoda; Gloria; Regina gloriosa ("Motets, Virelais, Ballate, Madrigals") OPUS ▲ 30101 [DDD] (18.97)
L. Meeuwsen (mez), Little Consort *(Panthera; Per quella strada; Chi nel servir anticho; Sus une Fontayne)* [ITA], Little Consort *(Benche da voi Donna; Gli atti col danzar; Quod lactatur)* *(rec Sovana, Italy, June 1988)* ("Johannes Ciconia & His Time") † Anonymous:Lamento di Tristano; Caserta:En remirant vo douce pourtaiture; Casia:Lucida pecorella son; Solage:Hélas, je voy mon cuer CCL ▲ 290 [DDD]
P. van Nevel (cnd) —Italian & French Secular Works; Motets; Masses ("Complete Works") PAVA 3-▲ 7345 (30.97)
CILEA, FRANCESCO (1866-1950)
Adriana Lecouvreur (opera in 4 acts) [lib Colautti after Scribe & Legouvé] (1902)
G. Masini (cnd) , M. Caballé (sop), F. Cossotto (mez), J. Carreras (ten), A. D. Orazi (bar) *(rec Tokyo, Japan, 1976)* MYTO 2-▲ 991199 (34.97)
G. Masini (cnd), French National RSO, M. Caballé (sop), J. Coster (mez), P. Domingo (ten) *(rec live Paris, France, 1975)* ODRO ▲ 1194 (9.97)
M. Olivero (sop), G. Simionato (mez), F. Corelli (ten), E. Bastianini (bar), M. Rossi (cnd), Naples Teatro San Carlo Orch, Naples Teatro San Carlo Chorus *(rec Naples, Nov 28, 1959)* PHO (Phoenix) 2-▲ 502
R. Scotto (sop), E. Obraztsova (mez), P. Domingo (ten), S. Milnes (bar), J. Levine (cnd), Philharmonia Orch *(rec 1977)* SNYC 2-▲ 34588 [ADD] (32.97)
Adriana Lecouvreur (selections)
D. Barioni (ten), F. Guarnieri (cnd), Turin RAI Orch *(rec Turin, Italy, Jan 23, 1968)* ("Daniele Barioni") † Arlesiana (sels); U. Giordano:Andrea Chénier (sels); Fedora (sels); G. Puccini:Bohème (sels); Fanciulla del West (sels); Madama Butterfly (sels); Manon Lescaut (sels); Rondine (sels); Tosca (sels); Turandot (sels); Verdi:Don Carlos (sels); Macbeth (sels); Simon Boccanegra (sels) BONG (Il Mito dell'Opera) ▲ 1077 [ADD] (16.97)

▲ = CD ♦ = Enhanced CD △ = MD ▮ = Cassette Tape ▯ = DCC

CILEA, FRANCESCO (cont.)

Adriana Lecouvreur (selections) (cont.)
M. Caniglia (sop) † A. Catalani:Wally (sels); U. Giordano:Andrea Chénier (sels); P. Mascagni:Cavalleria rusticana (sels); G. Puccini:Tosca (sels); Verdi:Aida (sels); Ballo in maschera (sels); Forza del destino (sels); Otello (sels); Trovatore (sels) WALC ▲ 8033 [ADD]

P. Domingo (ten), J. Carreras (ten), L. Pavarotti (ten)—L'anima ho stanca [plus others] ("The 3 Tenors, Vol. 1") † E. Elgar:Dream of Gerontius (sels); G. Puccini:Bohème (sels); Madama Butterfly (sels); Turandot (sels); G. Rossini:Stabat Mater; Verdi:Ernani (sels); Luisa Miller (sels); Rigoletto (sels); Traviata (sels) OPIT ▲ 54570

L. Gasteen (sop), R. Brydon (cnd), Queensland SO ("Singer of the World") † A. Catalani:Wally (sels); U. Giordano:Andrea Chénier (sels); Ponchielli:Gioconda (sels); G. Puccini:Manon Lescaut (sels); Verdi:Arias PEG ▲ 186 (5.97)

J. Hammond (sop)—Poveri fiori (rec 1942-55) † G. Charpentier:Louise (sels); Korngold:Tote Stadt (sels); Massenet:Cid (sels); Hérodiade (sels); Ponchielli:Gioconda (sels); G. Puccini:Manon Lescaut (sels); Suor Angelica (sels); Verdi:Arias WALC ▲ 8033 [DDD] (16.97)

G. Masini (ten) ("Galliano Masini") † Arlesiana (sels); Donizetti:Lucia di Lammermoor (sels); U. Giordano:Andrea Chénier (sels); Fedora (sels); Leoncavallo:Pagliacci (sels); P. Mascagni:Cavalleria rusticana (sels); G. Puccini:Bohème (sels); Madama Butterfly (sels); Manon Lescaut (sels); Tosca (sels); Verdi:Aida (sels); Forza del destino (sels) BONG (Il Mito dell'Opera) ▲ 1067 [ADD] (16.97)

M. Olivero (sop—Adriana), M. Frusoni (ten—Maurizio), H. Smit (bass—Michonnet), A. Kerjens (cnd) (rec live, May 5, 1973) † Boito:Mefistofele (sels); A. Catalani:Wally (sels); P. Mascagni:Iris (sels) VAIA 2-▲ 1062 [ADD] (31.97)

M. Olivero (sop), B. Gigli (ten) ("Beniamino Gigli in Opera, 1934-40") † U. Giordano:Andrea Chénier (sels); Gounod:Roméo et Juliette (sels); G. Puccini:Manon Lescaut (sels); Tosca (sels); Verdi:Forza del destino (sels); Trovatore (sels) EKLR ▲ 30

M. Olivero (sop—Adriana), M. Moretto (mez—Princess de Bouillon), A. Cupido (ten—Maurizio), O. Mori (bass—Michonnet), C. Gandolfo (pno) (rec Apr 1993) ("Magda Olivero 1993") BONG ▲ 2515 [DDD] (16.97)

N. Stokes (sop) (rec live, 1968-71) † Bizet:Carmen (sels); Leoncavallo:Pagliacci (sels); W. A. Mozart:Nozze di Figaro (sels); G. Puccini:Bohème (sels); Edgar (sels); Tosca (sels); Turandot (sels); Verdi:Traviata (sels) ASOP ▲ 8718 (16.97)

R. Tebaldi (sop), J. E. Martini (cnd), Buenos Aires SO—Io son l'umile ancella (rec Aug 8, 1953) ("Renata Tebaldi a Buenos Aires") † A. Catalani:Wally (sels); W. A. Mozart:Nozze di Figaro (sels); G. Puccini:Bohème (sels); Madama Butterfly (sels); Tosca (sels); Verdi:Otello (sels) MYTO ▲ 972157 (live) (16.97)

L'Arlesiana (opera in 3 acts) [lib Marenco after Daudet] (1897; rev 1898)
artists unknown, artist unknown (rec Budapest, Hungary, Sept 1991) ([ENG,ITA] lib texts) EMIC 2-▲ 66762 [DDD] (23.97)

L'Arlesiana (selections)
D. Barioni (ten), P. Argento (cnd), Turin RAI Orch (rec Turin, Italy, Jan 23, 1968) ("Daniele Barioni") † Adriana Lecouvreur (sels); U. Giordano:Andrea Chénier (sels); Fedora (sels); G. Puccini:Bohème (sels); Fanciulla del West (sels); Madama Butterfly (sels); Manon Lescaut (sels); Rondine (sels); Tosca (sels); Turandot (sels); Verdi:Don Carlos (sels); Macbeth (sels); Simon Boccanegra (sels) BONG (Il Mito dell'Opera) ▲ 1077 [ADD] (16.97)

M. Bolton (sop), S. Mercurio (cnd), Philharmonia Orch ("My Secret Passion") † Donizetti:Elisir d'amore (sels); Flotow:Martha (sels); Leoncavallo:Pagliacci (sels); Massenet:Werther (sels); G. Puccini:Arias; Verdi:Aida (sels) SNYC ▲ 63077 [DDD] (16.97) ■ 63077 [DDD] (10.98) ○ ▲ 63077 [DDD] (15.97)

M. Caniglia (sop) (rec 1939-47) ("Maria Caniglia on Radio") † Verdi:Aida (sels); Traviata (sels); Trovatore (sels) RY (Radio Years) ▲ 86 (16.97)

G. Masini (ten) ("Galliano Masini") † Adriana Lecouvreur (sels); Donizetti:Lucia di Lammermoor (sels); U. Giordano:Andrea Chénier (sels); Fedora (sels); Leoncavallo:Pagliacci (sels); P. Mascagni:Cavalleria rusticana (sels); G. Puccini:Bohème (sels); Madama Butterfly (sels); Manon Lescaut (sels); Tosca (sels); Verdi:Aida (sels); Forza del destino (sels) BONG (Il Mito dell'Opera) ▲ 1067 [ADD] (16.97)

G. D. Stefano (ten)—È la solita storia (rec 1947) † C. A. Bixio:Songs; G. Puccini:Tosca (sels); A. Thomas:Mignon (sels); Traditional:A la Barcillunisa; Cantu a timuni; Verdi:Rigoletto (sels); Traviata (sels) BONG (Il Mito dell'Opera) ▲ 1154 (live) (16.97)

Gloria (opera in 3 acts) [lib Colautti, rev Moschino] (1907; rev 1932)
M. Pace (cnd), San Gimignano Festival Orch, San Gimignano Festival Chorus, F. Cedolins (sop), V. Mosca (mez), A. Cupido (ten), D. D. Monte (sgr) P. Ruggiero (sgr) KICC 2-▲ 13 (34.97)

Sonata in D for Cello & Piano, Op. 38 (1888)
S. Heled (vc), J. Zak (pno) ("20th Century Romantic Cello Music") † Castelnuovo-Tedesco:Notturno sull'acqua & Scherzino Vc, Op. 82; D. Milhaud:Elégie, Op. 251; S. Prokofiev:Son Vc; Saint-Saëns:Cygne CLSO (Simca Heled Collection) ▲ 163 (15.97)

Trio in D for Piano, Violin & Cello
Scaligero Trio † Borodin:Trio Pno; Lalo:Trio 1 Pno, Op. 7 STRV ▲ 26 (16.97)

CIMA, GIOVANNI PAOLO (1570-ca 1622)

Concerti Ecclesiastici for solo Voices & Instruments (1610)
Musica Figurata (rec Dec 1997) DYNC ▲ 212 [DDD] (17.97)

Music of Cima
Convivium ("Early Italian Violin Sonatas") † Castello:Sonate concertate in stil moderno; B. Marini:Sons, Syms & Retornelli, Op. 8; Stradella:Music of; Uccellini:Music of HYP ▲ 66985 (18.97)

Sonatas (2) for Recorder, Viol & Harpsichord
P. Hannan (rcr), C. Thielmann (va da gamba), C. Tilney (hpd) (rec Toronto, Canada) † G. Bassano:Anchor che col partire; Dag bergier; Frescobaldi:Canzonas, Capricci & Ricercari; A. Gabrieli:Anchor che col partire; G. F. Handel:Son Rcr; Telemann:Essercizii Musici SMS ▲ 5049 [DDD] (16.97)

F. Hansen (rcr), V. Boeckman (rcr), L. U. Mortensen (hpd) (rec Sept 1990) † Castello:Sons Rcr; G. B. Fontana:Sons 2, 3 & 4 Rcr; Frescobaldi:Canzona detta la Bernadinia; Canzona quatra; Merula:Music Rcr Vl Hpd KPT ▲ 32059 [DDD]

Sonata for Trumpet & Trombone
R. Wilson (tpt) (rec Mandelsloh Germany, June 11-15, 1994) ("The Feast of San Rocco, Venice 1608") † Son Vn & Tpt; Son Vn & Vle; G. Gabrieli:Music of Gabrieli; A. Grandi:Sacred Music; Monteverdi:Salve regina (1) Voice, M.xvi/502 SNYC (Vivarte) 2-▲ 66254 [DDD] (31.97)

Sonata for Violin, Trumpet & Violone
R. Wilson (tpt) (rec Mandelsloh Germany, June 11-15, 1994) ("The Feast of San Rocco, Venice 1608") † Son Tpt; Son Vn & Vle; G. Gabrieli:Music of Gabrieli; A. Grandi:Sacred Music; Monteverdi:Salve regina (1) Voice, M.xvi/502 SNYC (Vivarte) 2-▲ 66254 [DDD] (31.97)

Sonata for Violin & Violone
R. Wilson (tpt) (rec Mandelsloh Germany, June 11-15, 1994) ("The Feast of San Rocco, Venice 1608") † Son Tpt; Son Vn & Tpt; G. Gabrieli:Music of Gabrieli; A. Grandi:Sacred Music; Monteverdi:Salve regina (1) Voice, M.xvi/502 SNYC (Vivarte) 2-▲ 66254 [DDD] (31.97)

CIMAROSA, DOMENICO (1749-1801)

Amor rende sagace (opera in 1 act) [lib Bertati] (1793)
G. Bertagnolli (sop), D. Bruera (sop), C. Mantese (sop), M. Dalena (ten), E. Dara (bar), M. Nicolini (bar), F. Neri (cnd), Bolzano Claudio Monteverdi Conservatory Youth Orch [ITA] (rec live Bolzano, July 25-27, 1991) BONG 2-▲ 2126 [DDD] (32.97)

L'Armida immaginaria (opera in 3 acts) [lib Giuseppe Palomba] (1777)
G. Donadini (sop), S. Edwards (ten), P. Guarnera (bar), D. Colaianni (bar), A. R. Peraino (sgr), A. Simonischivili (sgr), M. Chiarolla (sgr), E. Hull (cnd), Catania Teatro Massimo Bellini Orch, Petruzelli Artistic Theater Chorus (rec Aug 1997) ([E,I] lib texts) DYNC 3-▲ 205 [DDD] (51.97)

Concerto in c for Clarinet & Strings [1942 arr Arthur Benjamin from various Cimarosa piano sonata movements]
E. Brunner (cl), H. Stadlmair (cnd), Munich CO † A. Benjamin:Con Ob Strs; Donizetti:Concertino Cl; Giampieri:Carnevale di Venezia; Mercadante:Con in B Cl, Op. 101; G. Rossini:Vars Cl TUD ▲ 728 [DDD] (16.97)

Concerto in G for 2 Flutes & Orchestra (1793)
M. Gatti (fl), F. M. Sardelli (fl), R. Cirri (cnd), Ars Cantus (rec Sept 7-10, 1995) † Con Hpd; Maestro di cappella BONG ▲ 2184 [DDD] (16.97)

M. Larrieu (fl), G. Nova (fl), G. Rimonda (cnd), Ducale CO † Con Fls; Boccherini:Sym in D, G.490; G. B. Viotti:Sym Concertante Fls, G.25 BONG ▲ 5077 [DDD] (16.97)

J. Rampal (fl), S. Kudo (fl), J. Rampal (cnd), Salzburg Mozarteum Orch † W. A. Mozart:Concertone Vns, K.190; A. Stamitz:Con Fls; Vivaldi:Con Fls, RV.533 SNYC ▲ 45930 [DDD] (16.97)

S. S. Syrinx (pan fl), J. Rampal (fl), J. Berlingen (cnd), Normandy Orchestral Ensemble [arr Syrinx] (rec Oct 1994) † Con Ob; Albinoni:Cons Ob, Op. 9; B. Bartók:Romanian Folk Dances Vn & Pno; C. Stamitz:Con Fl in G, Op. 29; Vivaldi:Con Fls, RV.533 CASC ▲ 65127

Concerto in B for Harpsichord & Chamber Orchestra
S. Lorenzetti (hpd), R. Cirri (cnd), Ars Cantus (rec Sept 7-10, 1995) † Con Fls; Maestro di cappella BONG ▲ 2184 [DDD] (16.97)

CIMAROSA, DOMENICO (cont.)

Concerto in C for Oboe & Orchestra
J. Anderson (ob), S. Wright (cnd), Philharmonia Orch † A. Benjamin:Con Ob Strs; A. Marcello:Con Ob Strs in d; Vivaldi:Con Ob NIMB ▲ 7027 [DDD] (11.97)

A. Camden (cnd), City of London Sinfonia ("The Art of the Oboe") † Albinoni:Cons Ob, Op. 9; V. Bellini:Con Ob; A. Corelli:Con Ob; G. F. Handel:Cons Ob, HWV 301, 302a & 287; Rondo in G; Suites de Pièces (8) Hpd, HWV 426-33; V. Righini:Con Ob NXIN ▲ 8553991 (5.97)

A. Camden (ob), N. Ward (cnd), City of London Sinfonia (rec East Finchley, England, Apr 1995) ("Italian Oboe Concertos") † J. Barbirolli:Con on Themes of Peroglisi; V. Bellini:Con Ob; A. Corelli:Con in A Ob; Fiorillo:Sinf concertante; V. Righini:Con Ob NXIN ▲ 8553433 [DDD] (5.97)

D'Amore Duo ("Simplicity") † N. Coste:Montegnard, Op. 34; F. Couperin:Music of Couperin; Pièces de clavecin (sels); Ibert:Entracte Fl; M. Moriarty:Simplicity; Pils:Sonatine Ob SO ▲ 22573 [DDD] (16.97)

S. Dent (ob), V. Czarnecki (cnd), Southwest German CO Pforzheim ("The Greatest Oboe Concertos") † J. S. Bach:Con Ob d'amore & Strs; Crusell:Divert Ob, Op. 9; W. A. Mozart:Con Ob AMAT ▲ 9103 [DDD] (17.97)

P. Oostenrijk (ob), Sonora Hungarica (rec Amsterdam, Netherlands, Feb 1993) † Armando:Con Ob; Castelnuovo-Tedesco:Con da Camera, Op. 146; Gibilaro:Fant on British Airs VRDI (Masters) ▲ 32251 [DDD] (13.97)

S. S. Syrinx (pan fl), J. Berlingen (cnd), Normandy Orchestral Ensemble [arr Syrinx] (rec Oct 1994) † Con Fls; Albinoni:Cons Ob, Op. 9; B. Bartók:Romanian Folk Dances Vn & Pno; C. Stamitz:Con Fl in G, Op. 29; Vivaldi:Con Fls, RV.533 CASC ▲ 65127

Le donne rivali (intermezzo in musica in 2 acts) (1780)
A. R. Taliento (sop—Emilia), A. Ruffini (sop—Laurina), B. Lazzaretti (ten—Fernando), B. Praticò (bar—Sempronio), E. Giannino (sgr—Annibale), A. Zedda (cnd), Padova e Veneto Orch (rec Teatro degli Illuminati Castello, Sept 1994) BONG 2-▲ 2186 (32.97)

Il fanatico burlato (comedia per musica in 2 acts) [lib S. Zini] (ca 1787)
G. Morigi (sop), D. Uccello (sop), M. Bolognesi (ten), E. Cossutta (bar), G. Ceccarini (bar), A. Marani (bass), C. F. Cillario (cnd), San Remo SO, Reggio Calabria Francisco Cilea Chorus (rec Savona, 1988) AG 2-▲ 64 (36.97)

L'italiana in Londra (intermezzo in 2 acts) [lib ?Giuseppe Petrosellini] (1779)
C. Rizzi (sop), Piacenza SO, P. Orciani (sop—Livia), M. A. Peters (sop—Mme. Brillante), A. Ariostini (bar—Milord), B. Praticò (bar—Don Polidoro) (rec Teatro Chiabrera di Savona, Italy, Oct 14, 1986) ([E,I] text) BONG 2-▲ 2040 [DDD] (32.97)

Il Maestro di cappella (intermezzo for Baritone & Orchestra (ca 1786-93)
G. Gatti (bar), R. Cirri (cnd), Ars Cantus (rec Sept 7-10, 1995) † Con Fls; Con Hpd BONG ▲ 2184 [DDD] (16.97)
J. Gregor (bass), T. Pál (cnd), Corelli CO [ITA] † Telemann:Schulmeister HUN ▲ 12573 [DDD]

Il Matrimonio segreto (opera in 2 acts) [lib Giovanni Bertati after Colman & Garrick] (1792)
D. Mazzucato (sop), E. Dara (bar), B. D. Simone (bar), A. Cavallaro (cnd), Marchigiano PO NUO ▲ 7014 [DDD] (32.97)

S. Patterson (sop—Carolina), J. Williams (sop—Elisseta), G. Banditelli (cta—Fidalma), W. Matteuzzi (ten—Paolino), P. Salomaa (bass—Count Robinson), A. Antoniozzi (bass—Geronimo), H. L. Hirsch (cnd), G. Bellini (cnd), Eastern Netherlands Orch (rec Muziekcentrum Enschede Holland, Aug 26-Sept 8, 1991) AART 3-▲ 47117 [DDD] (28.97)

E. Szmytka (sop), J. Fischer (sop), A. Owens (mez), A. Romero (bar), F. Le Roux (bar), T. Welborn (sgr), J. López-Cobos (cnd), Lausanne CO (1992) CASC 2-▲ 1022 (32.97)

Music of Cimarosa
H. Tims (gtr), H. Visser (gtr), A. Visser (fl), B. Brouwer (hpd)—Son 5 (rec 1996) ("Buon Giorno: Visser Meets Italian Masters") † Albinoni:Music of Albinoni; D. Scarlatti:Sons Kbd; Vivaldi:Music of Vivaldi OREA ▲ 5284 [DDD] (11.97)

Gli Orazii e i Curiazzi (opera in 3 acts) [lib Sografi] (1797)
G. Simionato (mez), A. Vercelli (mez), G. Del Signore (ten), T. Spataro (ten), C. M. Giulini (cnd), Milan RAI SO, Milan RAI Chorus [ITA] (rec live, Apr 13, 1952) MELO 2-▲ 29500 [AAD]

Overtures
A. Toscanini (cnd), NBC SO—Il matrimonio per ragguir; Il matrimonio segreto ("The Toscanini Collection, Vol. 27") † Cherubini:Ovs; Sinf in D RCAV (Gold Seal) ▲ 60278 [DDD] (11.97)

Requiem pro defunctis (1787)
K. Rymarczyk (sop), B. Krahel (mez), I. Jakubowski (ten), A. Niemierowicz (bar), S. Frontalini (cnd), Warmia National Orch, Olsztyn Academy Chorus [LAT] BONG ▲ 2088 [DDD] (16.97)

Serenade for Flute & Guitar
K. Yamashita (gtr), J. Galway (fl) (rec London, June 23-25, 1986) ("Italian Serenade") † M. Giuliani:Grand Son, Op. 85; Paganini:Son concertata, M.S. 2; G. Rossini:Andante e tema con variazioni Va RCAV (Gold Seal) ▲ 61448 [DDD] (11.97)

Sonatas (50) for Keyboard
D. Kara (pno) ("The Piano Sonatas") AG 2-▲ 118 (36.97)

Sonatas (31) for Keyboard [edition by Vincenzo Vitale, 1972]
D. Failoni (pno) (rec 1981/84) CLDI ▲ 4037 [AAD] (10.97)

Sonatas (50) for Keyboard
R. Bluestone (gtr)—Sonata in b minor; Sonata in A major [trans J. Bream for gtr] † J. S. Bach:Prelude, Fugue & Allegro Lt, BWV 998; Carlevaro:American Preludes; Gomez-Crespo:Norteño, 1940; Mompou:Suite compostelana LINA ▲ 1894 [AAD]

CIRIGLIANO, JUAN CARLOS (1936-)

El sonido de la ciudad for Piano, Violin & Cello (1992)
Montreal Musica Camerata members (rec Laprairie Québec, May 1994) ("Le Grand Tango") † A. Piazzolla:Adiós Nonino; Cuatro estaciones porteñas; Grand Tango; Prelude, Fugue & Divertimento CBC (Musica Viva) ▲ 1079 [DDD] (16.97)

CIRONE, ANTHONY (20th cent)

Sonata No. 2 for Percussion & Trumpet (1973)
E. Sandor (tpt), T. McCutchen (perc) ("The Art of Trumpet & Percussion") † Beney:Flashes; D. Erb:Diversion; W. Kraft:Encounters III; S. Leonard:Fanfare & Allegro; R. Vogel:Temporal Landscape 6; Voyages ACAD ▲ 20042 [DDD] (16.97)

CIRRI, GIACOMO MATTEO IGNAZIO (1711-1787)

Organ Music
A. Macinanti (org) (Sons 3-6, 11 & 12), Francesco Tasini (Sons 1, 2 & 7-10) (rec Forli Cathedral Italy, June 10-11, 1997) LBD ▲ 26 [DDD] (16.97)

CIRRI, GIOVANNI BATTISTA (1724-1808)

Sonatas (6) for 2 Flutes (or Violins) & Continuo, Op. 9
Il Fuggiloto STRV ▲ 33358 [DDD] (16.97)

Sonata Prima for 2 Cellos & Continuo
Concerto Ensemble (rec Nov 1990) † Son Terza; Berteau:Trio (Son Sesta); Cervetto:Sons Vc; G. B. Martini:Son Vc & Hpd TACT ▲ 680001 (16.97)

Sonata Terza for 2 Cellos & Continuo
Concerto Ensemble (rec Nov 1990) † Son Prima; Berteau:Trio (Son Sesta); Cervetto:Sons Vc; G. B. Martini:Son Vc & Hpd TACT ▲ 680001 (16.97)

ČIURLIONIS, MIKOLAJUS KONSTANTINUS (1875-1911)

Canons in c & B♭ for String Quartet
Vilnius String Quartet (rec Vilnius, Lithuania, May 1996) ("Complete Music for String Quartet") † Fugues Str Qt; Qt Strs; Theme, Vars & Fugue Str Qt RUS (Viae Intactae) ▲ 10008 [DDD] (16.97)

Chorale Fugue in a on 'Aus tiefer Not schrei ich zu dir'
H. Ericsson (org) (1987 Grönlund Organ) (rec Sweden, Mar 1992) ("Baltic Organ Music") † Pno Music; Kutavičius:Org Music; Pärt:Annum per annum Org; Süda:Kbd Music; Vasks:Org Music; Zemzaris:Org Music BIS ▲ 561 [DDD] (17.97)

Fugues (2) in G & f# for String Quartet
Vilnius String Quartet (rec Vilnius, Lithuania, May 1996) ("Complete Music for String Quartet") † Canons Str Qt; Qt Strs; Theme, Vars & Fugue Str Qt RUS (Viae Intactae) ▲ 10008 [DDD] (16.97)

In the Forest [Miške] (symphonic poem) for Orchestra (1900)
J. Domarkas (cnd), Slovak PO † Preludes; Sea MARC ▲ 8223323 (13.97)

Piano Music
H. Ericsson (org)—Fugue in c# [Andante con moto] (rec Sweden, Mar 1992) ("Baltic Organ Music") † Chorale Fugue on 'Aus tiefer Not schrei ich zu...'; Kutavičius:Org Music; Pärt:Annum per annum Org; Süda:Kbd Music; Vasks:Org Music; Zemzaris:Org Music BIS ▲ 561 [DDD] (17.97)

M. Rubackyté (pno)—Humoresque, VL 162; Preludes, VL 164, 169, 182a, 184, 185-188, 197 & 2; Nocturnes, VL 178, 183; Impromptu, VL 181; Chansonette, VL 199; Mazurkas, VL 222 & 234; Son, VL 155 ("Mikolajus Konstantinus Čiurlionis: Piano Works, Volume 1") MARC ▲ 8223549 [DDD] (13.97)

ČIURLIONIS, MIKOLAJUS KONSTANTINUS (cont.)

Piano Music (cont.)

M. Rubackytė (pno)—Preludes, VL 239, 241, 256, 259, 295, 298, 304, 32; Pater Noster, VL 260; Autumn, VL 264; Pieces (3) on a Theme, VL 269-71; Fugue, VL 345; Qt Strs ("Mikolajus Konstantinus Ciurlionis: Piano Works, Volume 2") MARC ▲ 8223550 [DDD] (13.97)

Preludes (5) for String Orchestra

J. Domarkas (cnd), Slovak PO † In the Forest; Sea MARC ▲ 8223323 (13.97)

Quartet in c for Strings [4th movement lost] (1903)

Vilnius String Quartet *(rec Vilnius, Lithuania, May 1996)* ("Complete Music for String Quartet") † Canons Str Qt; Fugues Str Qt; Theme, Vars & Fugue Str Qt RUS (Viae Intactae) ▲ 10008 [DDD] (16.97)

Sea [Jura] (symphonic poem) for Orchestra (1903-07)

J. Domarkas (cnd), Slovak PO † In the Forest; Preludes MARC ▲ 8223323 (13.97)

Theme, Variations & Fugue in b for String Quartet (1899)

Vilnius String Quartet *(rec Vilnius, Lithuania, May 1996)* ("Complete Music for String Quartet") † Canons Str Qt; Fugues Str Qt; Qt Strs RUS (Viae Intactae) ▲ 10008 [DDD] (16.97)

CIVITAREALE, WALTER (1954-

Suite estival for 2 Guitars

S. Tordini (gtr), J. Prats (gtr) † M. de Falla:Pièces espagnoles; Gangi:Suite italiana; Santórsola:Suite all'antica Gtrs OTR ▲ 1016 [DDD] (18.97)

CLARK, THOMAS (1949-

LIGHTFORMS 2: Star Spectra for Computer Music on Tape (1993)

T. Clark (tape) *(rec CEMI, Denton, TX, 1993)* † L. Austin:Quadrants: Event/Complex No. 1; J. Klein:Dog; J. C. Nelson:rain has a slap and a curve; M. Thompson:Klank; Y. Tseng:Little Ying Yang; Winsor:Passaggio Spaziale CENT ▲ 2407 [DDD] (16.97)

Peninsula for Piano & Computer Music on Tape (1988)

A. Wodnicki (pno), T. Clark (tape) *(rec Univ. of North Texas, Denton, TX, Apr 1987-Jan 1988)* ("Compositions by Larry Austin, Thomas Clark, Jerry Hunt & Phil Winsor") † L. Austin:Sinf Concertante; Son Concertante; J. Hunt:Fluud; Winsor:Dulcimer Dream CENT (CDCM Computer Series, Volume 1) ▲ 2029 (16.97)

CLARKE, JEREMIAH (ca 1674-1707)

The Prince of Denmark's March for solo Harpsichord

R. Kapp (cnd), Philharmonia Virtuosi, New York *(rec NY, United States of America)* ("Greatest Hits of 1721") † J. S. Bach:Cant 147; Cant 208; Suite 2 Fl, BWV 1067; A. Corelli:Con Grosso in g 2 Vns, Vla & Vc, Op. 6/8; G. F. Handel:Water Music, HWV 348-50; A. Marcello:Con Ob Strs in c; J. P. A. Martini:Plaisir d'Amour; Vivaldi:Con Mand, RV.425; Con Tpts, RV.537; Cons Vn Strs, Op. 8/1-4 SNYC ▲ 35821 (9.97)

W. O'Meara (org) ("Baroque Banquet") † J. S. Bach:Music of Bach; Preludes & Fugues, BWV 531-552; P. Franceschini:Son à 7; G. F. Handel:Samson (sels); Suite Tpt & Org; A. Scarlatti:Endimione e Cintia; Telemann:Marches (12), TWV50: 31-42 (comp) OPDR ▲ 9303 [DDD] (16.97)

Trumpet Voluntary for Trumpet & Organ [formerly attrib Purcell]

Canadian Brass *(rec Toronto, OT, Jan 30-Feb 3, 1995)* ("Fireworks!: Baroque Brass Favorites") † G. F. Handel:Concerti grossi, Op. 3; Royal Fireworks Music, HWV 351; Samson (sels); Serse (sels); Solomon (arrival of the queen of Sheba); Water Music, HWV 348-50; H. Purcell:Abdelazer (sels); Fairy Queen (sels); Fant upon one note, Z.745; Tpt Tune Hpd, Z.678 RCAV (Red Seal) ▲ 68257 [DDD] (16.97)

B. Haley (tpt), D. Foster (org) † J. S. Bach:Cant 51; G. F. Handel:Amadigi di Gaula (sels); Olinto pastore, Tebro fiume, Gloria, HWV 143; A. Scarlatti:Arias Sop; Arias Sop, Tpt & Strs CRYS ▲ 952 [DDD] (15.97) ▮ 952 [DDD] (9.98)

R. Kelley (tpt), M. J. Newman (org) *(rec Mt. Kisco, NY, Aug 1995)* ("The Splendor of the Baroque") † J. S. Bach:Air on the G String; Arioso Ob; Cant 147; Fant Org, BWV 572; G. F. Handel:Cons (16) Org; Messiah (sels); Royal Fireworks Music, HWV 351; Semele (sels); Serse (sels); H. Purcell:Tpt Tune Hpd, Z.678; Telemann:Qnt Tpt HEL ▲ 1006 [DDD] (10.97)

CLARKE, REBECCA (1886-1979)

Epilogue for Cello (1921)

P. Frame (vc) † Son Vc; Beach:Compositions Vn, Op. 40/1-3; Son Vn KOCH ▲ 7281 [DDD] (10.97)

Sonata for Cello & Piano

P. Frame (vc), B. Snyder (pno) † Epilogue; Beach:Compositions Vn, Op. 40/1-3; Son Vn KOCH ▲ 7281 [DDD] (10.97)

Sonata for Viola & Piano (1919)

C. Masson-Bourque (va), M. Sato (pno) † Gougeon:Thèmes-solaires; J. Landry:Poèmes Va; A. Rubinstein:Son Va SNE ▲ 627 (16.97)

T. Riebl (va), C. Höfer (pno) ("Sonatas-1919") † E. Bloch:Suite Va & Pno; P. Hindemith:Son Va PANC ▲ 510098 [DDD] (17.97)

M. Roscoe (pno) † Trio Pno; Beach:Qnt Pno, Op. 67 ASV ▲ 932 [DDD] (16.97)

Y. Schotten (va), K. Collier (pno) ("Viola 1919: Works by E. Bloch, R. Clarke, and Paul Hindemith") † E. Bloch:Suite Va & Pno; P. Hindemith:Son Va CRYS ▲ 637 (15.97)

Trio for Piano, Violin & Cello (1921)

Clementi Trio Cologne † Mendelssohn (-Hensel):Trio Pno, Op. 11 LARG ▲ 5103 (16.97)

M. Roscoe (pno), Endellion String Quartet members † Son Va; Beach:Qnt Pno, Op. 67 ASV ▲ 932 [DDD] (16.97)

CLAUSEN, THOMAS (1949-

Songs (3) for Chorus

M. Viding (db), T. Clausen (pno), J. G. Jørgensen (cnd), Lille MUKO University Choir ("Lille MUKO: Nordisk Suite") † Holten:Nordisk Suite; Langgaard:Rose Garden Songs; Maegaard:Södergran Songs; Nørgård:Evening Country, Op. 10; Sundstrøom:Falcon & the Little Birds PONT ▲ 5125 (19.97)

CLEARFIELD, ANDREA (1960-

Songs of the Wolf for Horn & Piano (1994)

F. R. Werke (hn), A. Clearfield (pno) † S. Berge:Hornlokk; S. Friedman:Topanga Vars; T. Madsen:Dream of the Rhinoceros, Op. 92; Son Hn; W. Plagge:Son 3 Hn, Op. 88 CRYS ▲ 678 (15.97)

CLEARY, DAVID (1954-

Character Studies (5) for String Quartet (1979)

Artaria String Quartet *(rec Viterbo College La Crosse, Wisconsin, July 18-20, 1994)* ("Music for String Quartet by David Cleary") † Qt 1 Strs; Qt 2 Strs CENT ▲ 2251 [DDD] (16.97)

Lake George Overture for Orchestra (1988)

M. Machek (cnd), Bohuslav Martinů PO † Lieuwen:Light Spirit; Loeb:Cant Ob; J. Peel:Diptych; Perron:Double éclat; R. Rooman:Passage VMM (Music from 6 Continents 1993) ▲ 3021 [DDD]

Quartet No. 1 for Strings, "Inventing Situations" (1988)

Artaria String Quartet *(rec Viterbo College La Crosse, Wisconsin, July 18-20, 1994)* ("Music for String Quartet by David Cleary") † Character Studies; Qt 2 Strs CENT ▲ 2251 [DDD] (16.97)

Quartet No. 2 for Strings, "Artaria" (1991)

Artaria String Quartet *(rec Viterbo College La Crosse, Wisconsin, July 18-20, 1994)* ("Music for String Quartet by David Cleary") † Character Studies; Qt 1 Strs CENT ▲ 2251 [DDD] (16.97)

CLEMENCIC, RENÉ (1928-

Moliére (film music) for Orchestra

R. Clemencic (cnd) HMA ▲ 1901020 (9.97)

CLEMENS, AURELIUS PRUDENTIS (348-413)

Salvette Flores Martyrum

J. O'Donnell (cnd), Pro Cantione Antiqua *(rec Holborn, England, Jan 1990)* ("A Gregorian Advent & Christmas") † Anonymous:Adorna Thalamum Tuum; Agnus Dei VIII; Ave Maria; Christe Redemptor Omnium; Conditor alme siderum; Gloria VIII; Hodie Christus natus est; Hodie Nobis Caelorum Rex; Ite Missa Est; Kyrie VIII; Lumen ad Revelationem Gentium; Puer natus est nobis; Reges Tharsis; Sanctus VIII; Sapientia; Tribus Miraculis; Tui sunt caeli; Verbum caro factum est (mode VI); Video Caelos Apertos; Viderunt omnes; Viderunt Omnes & Alleluia dies Sanctificatus; Bourget:Rorate Caeli Desuper; Contractus:Alma Redemptoris Mater; Sedulius:Hostis Herodes *(E,L texts)* CAL ▲ 88007 [DDD]

CLEMENS NON PAPA, JACOBUS (ca 1510-ca 1556)

Choral Music

Henry's Eight—Ego flos campi; Pater peccavi *(rec Royal Masonic School for Girls, Rickmansworth, England, July 1997)* † J. Desprez:Choral Music; Ockeghem:Chansons & Motets; Willaert:Sacred Music ETC ▲ 1214 [DDD] (17.97)

Motets

P. Phillips (cnd), Tallis Scholars—Ego flos campi; Pastores quidnam vidistis; Pater peccavi; Tribulationes civitatum [L] † Pastores quidnam vidistis GIME ▲ 54913 [DDD] (16.97)

Pastores quidnam vidistis (missa & motet) for Vocal Ensemble

P. Phillips (cnd), Tallis Scholars [LAT] † Motets GIME ▲ 54913 [DDD] (16.97)

CLEMENS NON PAPA, JACOBUS (cont.)

Sacred Music

E. van Nevel (cnd), Currende—Vide, Domine quoniam tribulor ("Polyphony for Passion-Tide") † Arcadelt:Lamentationes; Crecquillon:Lamentationes; O. de Lassus:Sacred Music; Rogier:Sacred Music; Wert:Sacred Music EUFO ▲ 1248 [DDD] (18.97)

CLEMENT, SHEREE (1955-

Chamber Concerto (1982)

D. Palma (cnd) *(rec Mar 18, 1986)* † A. Anderson:Charrette; Blaustein:Commedia; D. Rakowski:Imaginary Dances CRI ▲ 617 [DDD] (17.97)

CLEMENTI, MUZIO (1752-1832)

Capriccio in e for Piano, Op. 47/1

I. Hobson (pno) ("The London Piano School, Vol. 2") † J. B. Cramer:Son Pno; J. Field:Sons Pno, Op. 1; G. F. Pinto:Son Pno; C. M. von Weber:Adagio patetico ARA ▲ 6595 (16.97)

Concerto in C for Piano & Orchestra (1796)

F. Blumental (pno), A. Zedda (cnd), Prague New CO † J. B. Cramer:Con 5 Pno, Op. 48; Czerny:Chamber Music; J. Field:Con 2 Pno, H.31; J. N. Hummel:Concertino Pno, Op. 73; F. Ries:Con in c#, Op. 55 VB2 2-▲ 5111 (9.97)

Duet in B♭ for 2 Pianos, Op. 12/5

P. Spada (pno), G. Cozzolino (pno) ("Complete Piano Music, Vo. 5") † Sons (4) Pno, Op. 12/1-4 AART ▲ 47227 (10.97)

Monferrinas (12) for Piano, Op. 49

R. Burnett (pno) [1822 grand fortepiano] † Sons (3) Pno, Op. 50 AMON ▲ 8 [AAD] (16.97)

Orchestral Music (complete)

F. D. Avalos (cnd), Philharmonia Orch—Con Pno Orch; Minuetto Pastorale; 2 Syms, Op. 18 ("Vol. 1") ASV ▲ 802 (16.97)

F. D. Avalos (cnd), Philharmonia Orch—Ov in C; Syms 1 & 3 ("Vol. 2") ASV ▲ 803 (16.97)

F. D. Avalos (cnd), Philharmonia Orch—Ov in D; Syms 2 & 4 ("Vol. 3") ASV ▲ 804 (16.97)

Piano Music (complete)

S. Irmer (pno)—Sons in A, Op. 25/5; in f#, Op. 25/5; in D, Op. 25/6; in A, Op. 33/1; in F, Op. 33/2 *(rec May 12-14, 1996)* ("Piano Works, Vol. 3") MDG (Scene) ▲ 6180653 [DDD] (17.97)

P. Spada (pno)—Sons in c & g, Op. 34/1 & 2; Capricci in A & F, Op. 34/3 & 4 ("Complete Piano Music, Vol. 11") AART ▲ 47233 (10.97)

Sonatas (3) for Flute (or Violin) & Keyboard, Op. 3/4-6

M. Vassilev (vn), M. Anfossi (pno) † Sons (6) Pno, Op. 13 RIVO ▲ 9812 (16.97)

Sonatas (3) in E♭, C & g for Harpsichord (or Piano), Op. 7

M. Leuschner (pno)—No. 3 ("1001") † Sons (3) Pno, Op. 40; Sons (3) Pno, Op. 50 BRIO ▲ 102 (16.97)

P. Spada (pno) ("Complete Edition, Vol. 3") † Sons (3) Pno, Op. 8 AART ▲ 47225 (10.97)

Sonatas for Piano

N. Demidenko (pno)—in f#, Op. 25/5 [Op. 26/2]; in b, Op. 40/2; in D, Op. 40/3; in b, Op. 41/2 [Op. 47/2] ("Demidenko Plays Clementi") HYP ▲ 66808 (18.97)

C. Grante (pno)—Op. 2/ 2, 4 & 6; Op. 7/1; Op. 24/2 ("Complete Piano Sonatas, Vol. 1") ALTA ▲ 9101 (19.97)

G. Hecher (pno)—in B, Op. 12/1; in f#, Op. 25/5; in b, Op. 40/2 *(rec Marble Hall of the Neue Burg Vienna, Mar 1994)* ("Music for Fortepiano") DORD ▲ 80134 [DDD] (13.97)

V. Horowitz (pno)—in E, Op. 12/2; in B, Op. 25/3; in A, Op. 50/1 *(rec New York, June 4 & Sept 16-23, 1964)* ("The Complete Masterworks Recordings, Vol. V: A Baroque & Classical Recital") † Beethoven:Son 28 Pno, Op. 101; J. Haydn:Son 58 Kbd, H.XVI/48; D. Scarlatti:Sons Kbd SNYC ▲ 53466 [ADD] (16.97)

P. Katin (pno)—in f#, Op. 25/5; in B, Op. 24/2; in g, Op. 7/3; in D, Op. 25/6; in f, Op. 13/6 [Clementi Square Pno] ("Clementi on Clementi") ATH ▲ 4 (19.97)

L. Simon (pno)—Son in F, Op. 36/2; Son in f#, Op. 26/2 *(rec Feb 11, 1979)* † G. Fauré:Trio Pno, Op. 120; C. Franck:Son Vn, M.8; J. Haydn:Son 12 Kbd, H.XVI/12; W. A. Mozart:Fant Pno, K.396; S. Prokofiev:Son Vc; Sinding:Son Pno, Op. 91 BIS ▲ 35 [AAD/DDD] (17.97)

P. Spada (pno)—Op. 1/1-4; Op. 2/2; Son in a *(rec Rome Italy, Jan 1981 & Mar 1983)* ("Sonate, Duetti & Capricci: Complete Edition, Vol. 1") AART ▲ 47223 [DDD] (10.97)

P. Spada (pno)—Sons (6) Pno, Op. 13 [No. 4 in B♭]; Chasse, Op. 16; Son Pno in C, Op. 20; Capriccio, Op. 17 *(rec Rome, Italy, Jan 1983)* ("Sonate, Duetti & Capricci: Complete Edition, Vol. 6") AART ▲ 47228 [DDD] (10.97)

P. Spada (pno)—3 Sons, Op. 23; 2 Sons, Op. 24 ("Sonate, Duetti & Capricci: Complete Edition, Vol. 8") AART ▲ 47230 [DDD] (10.97)

P. Spada (pno)—Sons Pno ("Sonate, Duetti & Capricci: Complete Edition, Vol. 9") AART ▲ 47231 (10.97)

P. Spada (pno)—Sons 1-3, Opp. 26 & 33; Son in F ("Sonate, Duetti & Capricci: Complete Edition, Vol. 10") AART ▲ 47232 (10.97)

B. Szokolay (pno)—in G, Op. 25/2; in f#, Op. 25/5; in D, Op. 37/2; in B, Op. 24/2; 6 Progressive Sonatinas, Op. 36/1-6 *(rec Italian Cultural Institute Budapest, June 28-July 4, 1990)* ("Piano Music") NXIN ▲ 550452 [DDD] (5.97)

Sonatas (Duets) for Piano 4-Hands

A. Brings (pno), G. Chinn (pno)—Duets Pno, Op. 3/1-3 [No. 2 in E♭]; 6/1; 14/1 & 3 CENT ▲ 2046 [AAD] (16.97)

P. Spada (pno), G. Cozzolino (pno)—Duets, Op. 14/1-3; Op. 21/1 & 3 *(rec Rome, 1983)* ("Sonate, Duetti & Capricci: Complete Edition, Vol. 7") AART ▲ 47229 [DDD] (10.97)

Sonatas (3) for Piano (or Harpsichord), Op. 8

P. Spada (pno) ("Complete Edition, Vol. 3") † Sons (3) Hpd, Op. 7 AART ▲ 47225 (10.97)

Sonatas (4) in B♭, E♭, F & E♭ for Piano, Op. 12/1-4

P. Spada (pno) ("Complete Piano Music, Vo. 5") † Duet Pnos, Op. 12/5 AART ▲ 47227 (10.97)

Sonatas (6) for Piano [Nos. 1-3 with Flute (or Violin)], Op. 13

I. Hobson (pno)—No. 6 in f *(rec Concordia College, London, England, June 1988)* ("The London Piano School, Vol. 1: Georgian Classicists") † Anonymous:Rondo Pno; J. Christian Bach:Sons Kbd; J. Burton:Son 1 Pno; Busby:Son Pno; J. L. Dussek:Son Pno in E♭, Op. 44 ARA ▲ 6594 (16.97)

A. Marion (fl), D. Roi (hpd) † Cambini:Son 2 Fl & Hpd; Locatelli:Son 10 Fl & Hpd; Nardini:Son Fl; Platti:Sons Fl, Op. 3 FON ▲ 8901 [DDD]

M. Vassilev (vn), M. Anfossi (pno)—No. 1 in G; No. 2 in C; No. 3 in E♭ † Sons (3) Fl, Op. 3/4-6 RIVO ▲ 9812 (16.97)

Sonata in C for Piano, Op. 34/1

Em. Gilels (pno) *(rec 1959-78)* ("Emil Gilels III") † J. Brahms:Con 2 Pno, Op. 83; Chopin:Études Pno; Son Pno in b, Op. 58; Son Pno in b♭, Op. 35; E. Grieg:Lyric Pieces; F. Schubert:Fant Pno, D.940; R. Schumann:Arabeske Pno, Op. 18 PPHI (Great Pianists of the 20th Century) 2-▲ 456799 (22.97)

Sonatas (3) in G, b & d-D for Piano, Op. 40

M. Leuschner (pno)—No. 3 ("1001") † Sons (3) Hpd, Op. 7; Sons (3) Pno, Op. 50 BRIO ▲ 102 (16.97)

P. Spada (pno) † Son E♭ Pno, Op. 41 AART ▲ 47235 (10.97)

Sonata in E♭ for Piano, Op. 41

P. Spada (pno) † Sons (3) Pno, Op. 40 AART ▲ 47235 (10.97)

Sonatas (3) in A, d & g for Piano, Op. 50

R. Burnett (pno)—No. 3 in g, "Didone abbandonata" † Monferrinas, Op. 49 AMON ▲ 8 [AAD] (16.97)

M. Leuschner (pno)—No. 2 ("1001") † Sons (3) Hpd, Op. 7; Sons (3) Pno, Op. 40 BRIO ▲ 102 (16.97)

P. Spada (pno) ("Complete Piano Music, Vol. 15") AART ▲ 47237 (10.97)

Sonatas (3) for Piano (or Harpsichord), Flute & Cello, Op. 21

Nuovo Trio Fauré † Sons Pno, Fl & Vc, Op. 22 DYNC ▲ 93 (17.97)

Sonatas (3) for Piano (or Harpsichord), Flute & Cello, Op. 22

Nuovo Trio Fauré † Sons Pno, Fl & Vc, Op. 21 DYNC ▲ 93 (17.97)

Sonatas (3) in F, D & C for Piano, Flute & Cello, Op. 32 (1793)

Fauré Trio [trans for pno, vn & vc] *(rec Genoa, Dec 1992)* ("Piano Trios, Opp. 28 & 32") † Sons Pno Vn Vc, Op. 28 DYNC ▲ 161 [DDD] (17.97)

Sonata in C for Piano, Flute & Cello, WoO 6 (1794)

Fauré Trio *(rec Genova Italy, 1980)* † Sons Pno, Vn & Vc, Op. 27 DYNC ▲ 19 [ADD] (17.97)

Sonatas in G & D for Piano, Flute & Cello, Op. 29/2 & 3 (1793)

Fauré Trio *(rec Genova Italy, 1980)* † Sons Pno, Vn & Vc, Op. 29/1; Sons Pno, Vn & Vc, Op. 35 DYNC ▲ 32 [ADD] (17.97)

Sonatas (3) in F, D & G for Piano (or Harpsichord), Violin & Cello, Op. 27 (1791)

Fauré Trio *(rec Genova Italy, 1980)* † Son Pno, Fl & Vc, WoO 6 DYNC ▲ 19 [ADD] (17.97)

Sonatas (3) in C, E♭ & G for Piano, Violin & Cello, Op. 28 (1792)

Fauré Trio *(rec Genoa, Dec 1992)* ("Piano Trios, Opp. 28 & 32") † Sons Pno, Fl & Vc, Op. 32 DYNC ▲ 161 [DDD] (17.97)

Sonata in C for Piano, Violin & Cello, Op. 29/1 (1793)

Fauré Trio *(rec Genova Italy, 1980)* † Sons Pno, Fl & Vc; Sons Pno, Vn & Vc, Op. 35 DYNC ▲ 32 [ADD] (17.97)

Sonatas (3) in C, G & D [La chasse] for Piano, Violin & Cello, Op. 35 (1796)

Fauré Trio *(rec Genova Italy, 1980)* † Sons Pno, Fl & Vc; Sons Pno, Vn & Vc, Op. 29/1 DYNC ▲ 32 [ADD] (17.97)

CLEMENTI, MUZIO (cont.)
Symphony No. 1 in C, Wo. 32 [completed & ed. Alfredo Casella, 1938]
("Contemporaries of Mozart: Muzio Clementi") † Syms CHN ▲ 9234 [DDD] (16.97)
Symphonies (2) in B♭ & D, Op. 18 (1787)
artists unknown ("Contemporaries of Mozart: Muzio Clementi") † Sym 1 CHN ▲ 9234 [DDD] (16.97)
CLÉRAMBAULT, LOUIS NICOLAS (1676-1749)
Cantatas
L. Coadou (bass), Concert Spirituel Soloists—Polyphemus *(rec Mar 21-23, 1996)* † Cants Françoises; Instrumental Music NXIN ▲ 8553743 [DDD] (5.97)
Cantates Françoises (5 livres) for Voices & Orchestra (1716)
L. Coadou (bass), Concert Spirituel Soloists—Livre 3, "La mort D'Hercule" *(rec Mar 21-23, 1996)* † Cants; Instrumental Music NXIN ▲ 8553743 [DDD] (5.97)
Instrumental Music
Concert Spirituel Soloists—Son Vn; Son 1 Vns; Son 1 Fl; Son 2 Vns; Son 2 Fl *(rec Mar 21-23, 1996)* † Cants; Cants Françoises NXIN ▲ 8553743 [DDD] (5.97)
Motets
S. Moquet (b vl), E. Mandrin (org), E. Mandrin (cnd), Les Demoiselles de Saint-Cyr *(Justificeris Domine; Miserere mei Deus; Hodie Christus natus est; Domine ante te; Immolabit haedum; Ad caenam Agni providi; Hodie Maria virgo caelos ascendit; Exultate Deo; De profundis clamavi)*, D. Collot (sop), S. Moquet (b vl), E. Mandrin (org) *(Gloria in excelsis Deo)*, D. Michel-Dansac (sop), S. Moquet (b vl), E. Mandrin (org) *(Regina caeli laetare)*, C. Greuillet (sop), S. Moquet (b vl), E. Mandrin (org) *(Factum est silentium) (rec Abbey of Saint-Michel, Thiérache, France, June 20-24, 1993)* ("Clérambault: Chants et Motets pour la Royale Maison de Saint-Louis") VCL (Musique à Versailles) ▲ 61529 [DDD] (11.97)
La Musette (cantata) for Soprano & Instrumental Ensemble
A. Monoyios (sop), J. Richman (cnd), Concert Royal [FRE] † Rameau:Impatience NON ▲ 71371 (9.97)
Premier livre d'orgue contenant deux suites (ca 1710)
P. Bardon (org) ("Organists at the Court of the Sun King") † J. F. Dandrieu:Offertoire sur les Grands Jeux pour la Fête; L. Marchand:Pieces Org; Raison:Vive-le-Roy des Parisiens PVY ▲ 784011 [ADD] (16.97)
H. Spillman (org) ("French Suites for Organ") † Duruflé:Suite Org, Op. 5; Messiaen:Ascension Org TIT ▲ 204 [DDD]
Sonata for Violin & Continuo, "La Magnifique"
Music's Re-Creation MER ▲ 84182 (16.97)
CLERK, JOHN (OF PENICUIK) (1676-1755)
Cantatas
C. Bott (sop), Concerto Caledonia ("The Lion of Scotland") HYP ▲ 67007 (18.97)
CLINGAN, ALTON HOWE (20th cent)
Circle of Faith: The Words of Chief Seattle for Voice, Drum & Orchestra
J. Belindo (nar), T. Russell (cnd), Pro Musica CO, T. Russell (cnd), Young Nation Singers † J. Tate:Iyaaknasha' DNC ▲ 1029 (16.97)
CLOKEY, JOSEPH (1890-1960)
Symphonic Piece for Organ & Piano (1927)
A. Gordon (pno), B. Jones (org) † Demarest:Fant Org; M. Dupré:Vars à deux thèmes, Op. 35; Grasse:Festival Ov, Op. 5; R. Wagner:Walküre (ride of the Valkyries) AFK ▲ 506
COATES, ERIC (1886-1957)
Calling All Workers (march) for Orchestra (1940)
F. Fennell (cnd), London Pops Orch *(rec July 19, 1965)* † Three Elizabeths; P. Grainger:Folk Song Settings; Orchestral Music MRCR ▲ 34330 (11.97)
First Meeting (souvenir) for Viola & Piano
M. Ponder (va), E. Asti (pno) *(rec St. Silas London, Jan 25-27, 1994)* † Songs MARC ▲ 8223806 [DDD] (13.97)
Four Centuries (suite) for Orchestra (1942)
M. Nabarro (cnd), East of England Orch † Jester at the Wedding; Snow White & the 7 Dwarfs ASV (White Line) ▲ 2075 [DDD] (12.97)
Four Ways (suite) for Orchestra (1927)
F. Fennell (cnd) † London; L. Anderson:Music of Anderson MRCR ▲ 34376 (11.97)
From the Countryside (suite) for Orchestra (1915)
M. Nabarro (cnd), East of England Orch *(rec May 1992)* ("Robin Hood Country") † Men of Trent; F. Curzon:Robin Hood; R. Goodwin:City of Lincoln March; Korngold:Adventures of Robin Hood (suite); M. Nabarro:Lincoln Green ASV (White Line) ▲ 2069 [DDD] (12.97)
The Jester at the Wedding (ballet suite) for Orchestra (1932)
M. Nabarro (cnd), East of England Orch † Four Centuries; Snow White & the 7 Dwarfs ASV (White Line) ▲ 2075 [DDD] (12.97)
Knightsbridge March for Orchestra
B. Tovey (cnd), Winnipeg SO † E. Elgar:Cockaigne, Op. 40; G. Holst:Egdon Heath, Op. 47; Vaughan Williams:Lark Ascending; W. Walton:Façade Orch CBC ▲ 5176 (16.97)
London (suite) for Orchestra (1933)
F. Fennell (cnd) † Four Ways Suite; L. Anderson:Music of Anderson MRCR ▲ 34376 (11.97)
Men of Trent (march) for Orchestra (1952)
M. Nabarro (cnd), East of England Orch *(rec May 1992)* ("Robin Hood Country") † From the Countryside; F. Curzon:Robin Hood; R. Goodwin:City of Lincoln March; Korngold:Adventures of Robin Hood (suite); M. Nabarro:Lincoln Green ASV (White Line) ▲ 2069 [DDD] (12.97)
Music of Eric Coates
E. Coates (cnd) —Summer Days; Miniature Suite; 4 Ways; London; London Again; Three Men Suite; Springtime; The Merrymakers; By the Sleepy Lagoon; Wood Nymphs; London Bridge; Three Bears Phantasy; With a Song in My Heart Rhap; Saxo-Rhap; Calling All Workers; plus others ("The Music of Eric Coates") HADA 2-▲ 211 (20.97)
C. Groves (cnd), Royal Liverpool PO—London [London Every Day] (1933); London Again; Three Bears Phantasy (1926); Cinderella Phantasy (1929) ARA ▲ 8036 (16.97)
Inns of Court City Yeomanry Band of Royal Yeomanry—Dam Busters; Youth of Britain; Calling All Workers; By the Sleepy Lagoon; London Again; Music Everywhere † Three Bears Phantasy; Three Men Suite HALM ▲ 30263 (6.97)
A. Penny (cnd), Slovak RSO *(By the Sleepy Lagoon; Springtime Suite; Footlights Waltz; Four Ways Suite; 8th Army (march); Lazy Night; Last Love; High Flight)*, K. Edge (sax), A. Penny (cnd), Slovak RSO *(Saxophone Rhapsody) (rec Bratislava, Czech Republic, April 23-30, 1993)* MARC (British Light Music) ▲ 8223521 [DDD] (13.97)
Royal Liverpool PO, C. Groves *(London [London Every Day] [1933]; London Again [1936]; From Meadow to Mayfair (orch suite) [1932]; Cinderella Phantasy [1929]; Saxo-Rhap for Sax & Orch (1936); Wood Nymphs [valsette] [1918]; Music Everywhere (Rediffusion March) [1949]; The Dam Busters (march) [1955])*, London SO, C. Mackerras *(The Merrymakers (miniature ov) [1922]; Three Bears Phantasy [1926]; At the Dance (from Summer Days suite) [1919]; By the Sleepy Lagoon; Three Men Suite [Man from the Sea])*, City of Birmingham SO, R. Kilbey *(Theree Elizabeths [1944])* CFP 2-▲ 4456 [ADD] (24.97)
J. Wilson (cnd), BBC CO—The Enchanted Garden; Springtime Suite; London Calling, 1942; High Flight ("The Enchanted Garden") ASV ▲ 2112 (12.97)
Snow White & the 7 Dwarfs (ballet suite) for Orchestra (1930; rev. as The Enchanted Garden, 1938)
M. Nabarro (cnd), East of England Orch † Four Centuries; Jester at the Wedding ASV (White Line) ▲ 2075 [DDD] (12.97)
Songs
R. Edgar-Wilson (ten), E. Asti (pno)—4 Old English Songs; The Mill o' Dreams; Rise up & Reach the Stars; At Vesper Bell; The Young Lover; The Grenadier; Because I Miss You So; Sigh No More, Ladies; Tell Me Where Is Fancy Bred; The Fairy Tales of Ireland; Music of the Night; Betty & Johnny; When I Am Dead; The Little Green Balcony; Ship of Dream; The Outlaw's Song; Your Name; Beautiful Lady Moon; Princess of the Dawn *(rec St. Silas London, Jan 25-27, 1994)* † First Meeting MARC ▲ 8223806 [DDD] (13.97)
D. Knox (cnd), Regimental Band of the Gordon Highlanders—Elizabeth of Glamis *(rec Berlin, Germany)* ("Cock O'The North") † D. Knox:Bonnie Black Isle; Rose of Kelvingrove; J. MacGregor:Medley; S. D. Samson:Jock's Favourites; Traditional:Aberdeen Sel; Castlegate to Holborn; Company Marches; Cornkisters; Drummer's Fanfare; Grampian Welcome; Highland Gathering; Highland Troop; Jacobite Prince; Lights Out; Loch Maree; Long Reveille; March Off Colours/Tattoo Last Post; Mess Pipers; Pipe Medley; Regimental Quick March Cock O'the North; Regimental Slow March; Ye Banks and Braes BND ▲ 5077 [DDD] (16.97)
M. Lanza (ten)—With a Song in My Heart † Bizet:Carmen (sels); Leoncavallo:Pagliacci (sels); P. Mascagni:Cavalleria rusticana (sels); S. Romberg:Student Prince (sels); Verdi:Aida (sels); Rigoletto (sels) RCAV ▲ 68134 (10.97) ▮ 68134 (5.98)
B. Rayner (bar), R. Terroni (pno)—I Heard You Singing; Bird Songs of Eventide; Homeward to You; Today Ours ("The Green Hills O' Somerset: The Songs of Eric Coates") ASV (White Line) ▲ 2081 (13.97)

COATES, ERIC (cont.)
The Three Bears (phantasy) for Orchestra (1926)
Inns of Court City Yeomanry Band of Royal Yeomanry † Music of E. Coates; Three Men Suite HALM ▲ 30263 (6.97)
The Three Elizabeths (suite) for Orchestra (1940-44)
F. Fennell (cnd), London Pops Orch *(rec July 19, 1965)* † Calling All Workers; P. Grainger:Folk Song Settings; Orchestral Music MRCR ▲ 34330 (11.97)
The Three Men (suite) for Orchestra (1935)
Inns of Court City Yeomanry Band of Royal Yeomanry—Man from the Sea † Music of E. Coates; Three Bears Phantasy HALM ▲ 30263 (6.97)
COATES, GLORIA (1938-
Quartet No. 1 for Strings, "Protestation Quartet" (1965-66)
Kronos Quartet † Qt 2 Strs; Qt 4 Strs; Bargielski:Qt 2 Strs; Pascher:Qt 1 Strs, Op. 27; Pernes:Qt 1 Strs; Przbylski:ArnolD SCHöNBErG in Memoriam PROV ▲ 173 [ADD] (18.97)
Quartet No. 2 for Strings, "Mobile" (1972)
Kronos Quartet † Qt 1 Strs; Qt 4 Strs; Bargielski:Qt 2 Strs; Pascher:Qt 1 Strs, Op. 27; Pernes:Qt 1 Strs; Przbylski:ArnolD SCHöNBErG in Memoriam PROV ▲ 173 [ADD] (18.97)
Quartet No. 4 for Strings (1977)
Kronos Quartet † Qt 1 Strs; Qt 2 Strs; Bargielski:Qt 2 Strs; Pascher:Qt 1 Strs, Op. 27; Pernes:Qt 1 Strs; Przbylski:ArnolD SCHöNBErG in Memoriam PROV ▲ 173 [ADD] (18.97)
Symphony No. 1, "Music on Open Strings" (1973-74)
E. Howarth (cnd), Bavarian RSO *(rec Munich, Nov 1980)* † Sym 4; Sym 7 CPO ▲ 999392 [DDD] (13.97)
Symphony No. 4, "Chiaroscuro" (1984/90)
W. Hauschild (cnd), Stuttgart PO *(rec Stuttgart, June 1990)* † Sym 1; Sym 7 CPO ▲ 999392 [DDD] (13.97)
Symphony No. 7 [Dedicated to Those Who Brought down the Wall in Peace] (1990-91)
G. Schmöhe (cnd), Stuttgart PO *(rec Stuttgart, Jan 1991)* † Sym 1; Sym 4 CPO ▲ 999392 [DDD] (13.97)
Time Frozen for Chamber Orchestra (1995)
D. Cichewiecz (cnd), Hamburg das neue werk Ensemble *(rec Germany, Aug 14-25, 1995)* ("25 Jahre Ensemble 'das neue werk' Hamburg") † D. Glanert:Son 2; Kelterborn:Ensemble-Buch II; P. Ruzicka:Satyagraha: Approach & Departure MPH ▲ 55706 [DDD] (15.97)
COCCIA, CARLO (1782-1873)
Caterina di Guisa (opera in 2 acts) (1833)
C. Apollonio (sop), N. Ciliento (mez), M. Leonardi (ten), S. Antonucci (bar), M. D. Bernart (cnd), Italian PO, Calabria Francesca Cilea Chorus *(rec Oct 30 & Nov 3, 1990)* BONG 2-▲ 2117 [DDD] (32.97)
Rosmonda (selections)
Y. Kenny (sop), D. Parry (cnd), Philharmonia Orch ("19th Century Heroines") † Carafa (De colobrano):Gabriella di Vergy (sels); Donizetti:Alahor in Granata (sels); Meyerbeer:Crociato in Egitto (sels); G. Nicolini:I Baccanali di Roma (sels); Portugal:Morte di Semiramide (sels) OPR ▲ 201 (18.97)
COCHEREAU, PIERRE (1924-1984)
Boléro on a Theme of Charles Racquet for Organ
D. Briggs (org) ("Popular Organ Music, Vol. 2") † J. Alain:Jardin suspendu, AWV 63; J. S. Bach:Preludes & Fugues (22) Org, BWV 531-552; Preludes & Fugues, BWV 531-552; Dukas:L'Apprenti sorcier; C. Franck:Pièces (3) Org, M.37; P. Tchaikovsky:Nutcracker Suite, Op. 71a PRIO ▲ 568 [DDD] (16.97)
Improvisations (25) sur l'Evangelie selon saint Matthieu for Organ (1984)
P. Cochereau (org) *(rec Feb-Mar 1984)* ("Un testament musical") SOC 2-▲ 150 (31.97)
Organ Music
P. Cochereau (org)—Improvs sur l'evangelie † J. S. Bach:Org Music (misc colls); F. Couperin:Pièces d'orgue consistantes en deux Messes; Messiaen:Banquet céleste; Vierne:Sym 2 Org, Op. 20 AURC ▲ 180 (5.97)
F. Lombard (org) *(Symphonie) (rec Org of Saint-Vincent de Roquevaire, France, Dec 18-19, 1998)*, P. Pincemaille (org), F. Lombard (org), J. Cochereau (cnd), Marseille PO Brass Ensemble, Provence-Alpes-Côte d'Azur Regional Choir *(Paraphrase de la Dédicace) (rec Org of Saint-Vincent de Roquevaire, France, Dec 20, 1998)*, P. Pincemaille (org) *(Vars sur un theme chromatique; Micro Son; Theme & Vars on "Ma jeunesse a une fin") (rec Org of Saint-Vincent de Roquevaire, France, Jan 23-24, 1999)* SOC ▲ 163 (16.97)
Prélude, adagio & choral varié (improvisation) for Organ (1970)
P. Cochereau (org) *(rec Notre-Dame Paris, 1970)* ("Deux Improvisations") † Suite des danses SOC ▲ 118 [ADD] (16.97)
Suite des danses for Organ & Percussion
P. Cochereau (org), M. Cals (perc), M. Gastaud (perc) *(rec Notre-Dame Paris, 1974)* ("Deux Improvisations") † Prélude, adagio & choral varié SOC ▲ 118 [ADD] (16.97)
Symphonie for Organ (1955)
J. S. Whiteley (org) *(rec Cavaillé-Coll org, St. Ouen, Rouen, France)* † M. Dupré:Préludes & Fugues, Op. 36; Vars on Adeste Fidèles; Ibert:Choral sur Justorum animae; Paponaud:Toccata; Vierne:Méditation Org PRIO ▲ 619 [DDD] (16.97)
Variations (3) sur un theme chromatique for Organ (1962)
C. Cramer (org) *(rec St Pierre Cathedral Angoulême, France)* ("Pieces de Concours from the Paris Conservatory") † J.-J. Grunenwald:Pièce en mosaïque; J.-C. Henry:Chaconne Org; J. Langlais:Essai; Sonate en trio; Messiaen:Verset pour la fête ARK ▲ 6146 (16.97)
COCKER, NORMAN (1880-1953)
Tuba Tune
L. Kurpershoek (org) *(rec St. Mary's Anglican Cathedral Org Johannesburg)* ("Popular Organ Music, Vol. 4") † J. Brahms:Chorale Preludes Org, Op. 122; Duruflé:Prélude et fugue, Op. 7; C. Franck:Chorales Org, M.38-40; Grové:Afrika Hymnus; Hollins:Intermezzo PRIO ▲ 610 (16.97)
COELHO, MANUEL RODRIGUES (ca 1555-1635)
Segunda Susana grosada a 4 sobre a de 5 for Harpsichord
S. Yates (hpd) *(rec Somerset, England, Dec 1993)* ("Spanish & Portuguese Harpsichord") † Segunda tento do primeiro tom; Anonymous:Españoleta; Cabanilles:Pasacalles I; Tiento de batalla del octavo tono; H. Cabezón:Dulce memoria glosada; A. de Cabezón:Obras de música (sels); Carreira:Canção a quatro glosada; Ximénez:Obra del primer tono de lleno CHN ▲ 560 [DDD] (16.97)
Segunda tento do primeiro tom for Harpsichord
S. Yates (hpd) *(rec Somerset, England, Dec 1993)* ("Spanish & Portuguese Harpsichord") † Segunda Susana grosada a 4 sobre a de 5; Anonymous:Españoleta; Cabanilles:Pasacalles I; Tiento de batalla del octavo tono; H. Cabezón:Dulce memoria glosada; A. de Cabezón:Obras de música (sels); Carreira:Canção a quatro glosada; Ximénez:Obra del primer tono de lleno CHN ▲ 560 [DDD] (16.97)
COENEN, PAUL (1908-
Variations for 4 French Horns, Op. 69
Berlin PO Horns † Genzmer:Con for 4 Hns; R. Schumann:Konzertstück Hns, Op. 86 KSCH ▲ 311021 [DDD] (16.97)
COGAN, ROBERT (1930-
Polyutterances for Voice & Piano
J. Heller (sop), T. Stumpf (pno) ("To the Verge") † Babbitt:Phonemena Sop & Tape; L. Berio:Sequenza III; T. Stumpf:Lear's Daughters NEU ▲ 45089 (16.97)
COHEN, ALLEN (20th cent)
Song of Myself for Trumpet & Piano
R. Lee (tpt), A. Cohen (pno) *(rec Brooklyn College, Apr 1993 & May 1994)* † Wings of Desire; Baksa:Earth Elegy; Son Tpt; P. Kirby:Son Tpt CPS ▲ 8620 [DDD] (16.97)
Wings of Desire for Trumpet & Piano
R. Lee (tpt), A. Cohen (pno) *(rec Brooklyn College, Apr 1993 & May 1994)* † Song of Myself; Baksa:Earth Elegy; Son Tpt; P. Kirby:Son Tpt CPS ▲ 8620 [DDD] (16.97)
COHEN, DAVID (1927-1991)
Sonata for Piano (1961)
W. Cosand (pno) *(rec June 1993)* ("20th Century American Piano Music") † Aschaffenburg:Conversations, Op. 19; H. Matthews:Preludes; N. Rorem:Etudes Pno SUMM ▲ 154 [DDD] (16.97)
COHEN, FRED (20th cent)
Three for Emily (1990)
Currents New Music Ensemble *(rec Richmond, VA, Sept 1993)* ("Currents") † Trio Ww; A. Blank:Polymorphics; Davidovsky:Biblical Songs; J. Feigin:Poems of Linda Pastan CENT ▲ 2248 [DDD] (16.97)
Trio for Woodwinds (1992)
Currents New Music Ensemble *(rec Richmond, VA, Sept 1993)* ("Currents") † 3 for Emily; A. Blank:Polymorphics; Davidovsky:Biblical Songs; J. Feigin:Poems of Linda Pastan CENT ▲ 2248 [DDD] (16.97)

DONIZETTI, GAETANO (cont.)

Arias (cont.)

L. Tetrazzini (sop), A. Rosza (sop), T. D. Monte (sop), A. Pertile (ten), B. Gigli (ten), M. Stabile (bar), M. Journet (bass), E. Pinza (bass) *(Lucia di Lammermoor (sels) [Cruda, funesta smania; Regnava nel silenzio; Quando rapito in estasi; Dalle stanze; Sulla tomba; Ah! Verranno a te; Spargi d'amaro pianto (Mad Scene); Tomb Scene])*, R. Storchico (sop) *(Linda di Chamounix (sels) [O luce di quest'anima])*, C. Butt (cta), F. Navarrini (bass), C. Albani (sgr) *(Lucrezia Borgia (sels) [Di pescatore ignobile; Vieni: la mia vendetta; Il segreto per esser felici (Brindisi)])*, O. Boronat (sop), L. Bori (sop), G. Anselmi (ten), G. Martinelli (ten), G. De Luca (bar), M. Stabile (bar), M. Lawrence (sgr) *(Don Pasquale (sels) [Sogno soave e casto; So anch'io la virtù magica; Pronta io son; Vado, corro; Com'è gentil; Cheti! cheti immantinente])*, M. Galvany (sop), A. Giorgini (ten), F. De Lucia (ten), T. Schipa (ten), E. Badini (bar), S. Baccaloni (bass) *(Elisir d'amore (sels) [Chiedi all'aura lusinghiera; Obbligato; Udite, o rustici; Una furtiva lagrima])*, M. Battistini (bar) *(Maria di Rudenz (sels) [Ah! Non avea piu lagrime])*, S. Onegin (cta), R. Zanelli (ten), G. Lauri-Volpi (ten), A. Pertile (ten), R. Stracciari (bar), M. Journet (bass), E. Pinza (bass) *(Favorita (sels) [Vieni, amor/ Leonara! A'piedi tuo; Anathème de Balthazar; A tanto amor, Leonora; Spirto gentil; Una vergine, un'angel di Dio; O mio Fernando; Spendon più belle])*, A. Piccaver (ten) *(Dom Sébastien (sels) [Deserto in terra])*, T. D. Monte (sop) *(Fille du régiment (sels) [Convien partir]) (rec 1906-47)* ("Great Singers in Donizetti") NIMB (Prima Voce) 2-▲ 7892 [ADD] (23.97)

R. Vargas (ten), M. Viotti (cnd), Munich Radio Orch—Duca d'Alba (sels) [Inosservata, penetrava; Angelo casto e bel]; Lucia di Lammermoor (sels) [Tombe degl'avi miei; Fra poco a me ricovero]; Favorita (sels) [Spirto gentil]; Elisir d'amore (sels) [Una furtiva lagrima]; Roberto Devereux (sels) [Ed ancor la tremenda porta] ("L'amour L'amour") † Gounod:Roméo et Juliette (sels); Massenet:Manon (sels); Werther (sels); G. Puccini:Bohème (sels); P. Tchaikovsky:Eugene Onegin (sels); Verdi:Ballo in maschera (sels); Rigoletto (sels) RCAV ▲ 61464 (16.97)

L'assedio di Calais (opera in 3 acts) [lib Cammarano after Du Belloy] (1836)

E. Harrhy (sop), D. Jones (mez), R. Serbo (ten), J. Treleaven (ten), R. Smythe (bar), D. Parry (cnd), Philharmonia Orch, Geoffrey Mitchell Choir OPR 2-▲ 9 [DDD] (36.97)

Ballet Music

A. De Almeida (cnd), Philharmonia Orch, A. De Almeida (cnd), Monte Carlo Opera Orch † G. Rossini:Ballet Music PPHI (Duo) 2-▲ 42553 (17.97)

Belisario (opera in 3 acts) [lib Cammarano after J. F. Marmontel] (1836)

G. Gavazzeni (cnd), Venice Theater Orch, C. Mirandola (cnd), Venice Theater Chorus, L. Gencer (sop—Antonina), R. Pallini (mez—Eudora), M. Pecile (cta—Irene), U. Grilli (ten—Alamiro), B. Sebastian (ten—Eutropio), G. Taddei (bar—Belisario), N. Zaccaria (bass—Giustiniano), G. Antonini (bass—Eusebio), A. Veronese (sgr—Ottario), A. Carusi (sgr—Centurion) *(rec live, Venice, Italy, May 1969)* MONM 2-▲ 10301 (36.97)

La bella prigioniera (incomplete farce in 1 act) [rev. by Fabio Maestri]

S. Rigacci (sop), P. Pellegrini (ten), R. Franceschetto (bass), F. Maestri (cnd), In Canto CO *(rec Apr 1992)* † Olimpiade; Pigmalione; Rita, or Le mari battu BONG 2-▲ 2109 [DDD] (32.97)

Betly (or La Capanna Svizzera) (opera buffa in 1 act) [after Scribe] (1836)

S. Rigacci (sop), M. Comencini (ten), R. Scaltriti (bar), B. Rigacci (cnd), Emilia Romagna Toscanini SO, Lugo Teatro Comunale Rossini Chorus *(rec live, June 1990)* † Convenienze ed inconvenienze BONG 2-▲ 2091 [DDD] (32.97)

Il borgomastro di Saardam (opera in 2 acts) [lib Gilardoni after Mélesville, Merle & Cantiran de Boirie] (1827; score re-discovered 1973)

J. Schaap (cnd), P. Langridge (ten), R. Capecchi (bar), P. V. Berg (bass) *(rec Amsterdam, Netherlands, 1973)* MYTO 2-▲ 991202 (34.97)

Il campanello di notte [The Night Bell] (opera farsa in 1 act) [lib Donizetti after Brunswick, Troin & Lhérie] (1836)

M. Bender (sop—Serafina), J. Powell (ten—Spiridone), S. Sims (bar—Enrico), S. Helper (bass—Don Annibale), B. Kokolus (sgr—Madame Rose), C. Larkin (cnd), Manhattan School of Music Opera Orch, Manhattan School of Music Opera Chorus *(rec Apr 1996)* NPT ▲ 85608 [DDD] (16.97)

M. Gentile (sop), P. Guarnera (bar), Gatti (sgr), Rinaldi (sgr), G. Proietti (cnd), Palestrina Conservatory Orch, Palestrina Conservatory Chorus BONG ▲ 2207 (16.97)

A. R. Taliento (sop), C. D. Mola (ten), L. Casalin (ten), L. Nucci (bar), E. Dara (bar), F. M. Carminati (cnd), I Pomeriggi Musicali Orch, Bergamo Teatro Donizetti Chorus BMGR ▲ 5872 (18.97)

Caterina Cornaro (selections)

N. Miricioiu (sop), R. Blake (ten), G. Magee (bar), D. Parry (cnd), Philharmonia Orch † Ajo nell'imbrazzo (sels); Anna Bolena (sels); Gianni di Calais (sels); Maria di Rohan (sels); Maria Stuarda (sels); Marino Faliero (sels); Pia de' Tolomei (sels); Ugo (sels) OPR ▲ 207 (18.97)

Caterina Cornaro (opera in 2 acts) [lib Sacchero after Saint-George] (1844)

L. Gencer (sop), G. Aragall (ten), R. Bruson (bar), L. Risani (sgr), C. F. Cillario (cnd), Naples Teatro San Carlo Orch, Naples Teatro San Carlo Chorus *(rec live, May 28, 1972)* † Lucrezia Borgia (sels) MYTO 2-▲ 92153 [ADD] (34.97)

G. Masini (cnd), ORTF Orch, M. Caballé (sop), G. Aragall (ten), R. Edwards (bar), G. Howell (bass) *(rec Nov 25, 1973)* PHO (Phoenix) 2-▲ 505

Chamber Music

R. Bonucci (vn), V. Bolognese (vn), A. Bonucci (vc), A. Persichilli (fl), A. Loppi (ob), P. Spada (org), A. Vlad (cnd), St. Cecilia CO—Intro Strs; Qnt Gtr; Qnt Strs; Amusement pathétique; Nocturnes; Untitled Ww ("Chamber Music, Vol. 3") AART ▲ 47219 (10.97)

R. Bonucci (vn), A. Bonucci (vc), A. Persichilli (fl), A. Loppi (ob), C. Antonelli (hp), P. Spada (pno) ("Chamber Music, Vol. 2") AART ▲ 47218 (10.97)

R. Bonucci (vn), P. Spada (pno) ("Chamber Music, Vol. 1") AART ▲ 47217 (10.97)

Concertinos (miscellaneous)

L. Kovács (cnd), Budapest Camerata—Con E Hn & Orch; Con Ob & CO; Con Vn, Vc & Orch; Untitled Cl & Orch *(rec Festetich Castle Budapest, Hungary, June 5-11, 1994)* ("Instrumental Concerti") † Sinfonias (misc) MARC ▲ 8223701 [DDD] (13.97)

Concertino in B♭ for Clarinet & Chamber Orchestra

E. Brunner (cl), H. Stadlmair (cnd), Munich CO † A. Benjamin:Con Ob Strs; Cimarosa:Con Cl; Giampieri:Carnevale di Venezia; Mercadante:Con in B Cl, Op. 101; G. Rossini:Vars Cl TUD ▲ 728 [DDD] (16.97)

J. Russo (cl), D. Amos (cnd), Polish National RSO *(rec Alaska, United States of America)* ("Virtuoso Works for Clarinet & Orchestra") † Debussy:Première rapsodie Cl; Joio:Concertante Cl & Orch; I. Stravinsky:Pieces Cl; Swack:Sym 2 Strs; Wolking:Pangaea Orch *(E text)* CRSR ▲ 9459

Le convenienze ed inconvenienze teatrali (opera farsa in 1 act) [lib Donizetti after Sografi] (1827; rev 1831)

M. Peters (sop), A. Cicogna (mez), S. Tedesco (ten), R. Scaltriti (bar), B. Rigacci (cnd), Emilia Romagna Toscanini SO, Lugo Teatro Comunale Rossini Chorus [ITA] *(rec live, June 1990)* † Betly BONG 2-▲ 2091 [DDD] (32.97)

Dom Sébastien, roi de Portugal (opera in 5 acts) [lib Eugène Scribe] (1843)

M. Minarelli (mez—Zayda), Woroniecki (sgr), Jacobsh (sgr), Kim (sgr), Tagadossi (sgr), Joost (sgr), Biebuyck (sgr), Seiz (sgr), Schell (sgr), artists unknown, E. Boncompagni (cnd), Aachen SO, Opera Chorus & Additional Chorus of the Aachen Theater *(rec 1998)* KICC 2-▲ 18 (34.97)

Don Pasquale (opera in 3 acts) [lib Giovanni Ruffini & Donizetti after Anelli] (1843)

M. Freni (sop), G. Winbergh (ten), L. Nucci (bar), S. Bruscantini (b-bar), R. Muti (cnd), Philharmonia Orch, Ambrosian Opera Chorus EMIC 2-▲ 47068 (32.97)

B. Hendricks (sop), L. Canonici (ten), L. Quilico (bar), R. Schirrer (bar), G. Bacquier (bar), G. Ferro (cnd), Lyon Opera Orch, Lyon Opera Chorus [ITA] ERAT 2-▲ 45487 [DDD] (33.97)

M. Kalmár (sop—Norina), J. Bándi (ten—Ernesto), I. Gáti (bar—Dr. Malatesta), J. Gregor (bass—Don Pasquale), T. Szüle (bass—Notary), I. Fischer (cnd), Hungarian State Orch *(rec 1982)* † Vivaldi:Cons Vn Strs, Op. 8/1-12 HUN 2-▲ 12465 [DDD] (32.97)

E. Mei (sop), T. Allen (bar), R. Abbado (cnd), Munich RSO, Bavarian Radio Chorus RCAV (Red Seal) 2-▲ 61924 (30.97)

R. Panerai (bar), F. Corena (bass), R. Muti (cnd) ODRO 2-▲ 1166 (9.97)

D. Parry (cnd), London PO, G. Mitchell (cnd), Geoffrey Mitchell Choir, L. Dawson (sop), B. Bank (ten), A. Shore (bar), J. Howard (bar), C. Bayley (bass) CHN ▲ 3011 (26.97)

C. Sabajno (cnd), La Scala Orch, La Scala Chorus, A. Saraceni (sop), T. Schipa (ten), G. Callegari (ten), E. Badini (bar), A. Poli (bar) *(rec Milan, Italy, 1932)* ("Schipa, Vol. 3") VOCA (Vocal Archives) 2-▲ 1207 (28.97)

H. Steiner (cnd), Berlin Reichssender Orchestra, Berlin Reichssender Chorus, E. Berger (sop), G. Sinimberghi (ten), K. Schmitt-Walter (bar), E. Kandl (bass) *(rec 1939)* KSCH ▲ 316472 (16.97)

Don Pasquale (selections)

L. Aliberti (sop), R. Paternostro (cnd), Berlin RSO—La morale in tutto questo *(rec Jesus Christ Church, Berlin, Germany, Aug 2-10, 1988)* † Anna Bolena (sels); Fille du régiment (sels); Torquato Tasso (sels); V. Bellini:Capuleti e i Montecchi (sels); Puritani (sels) CAPO ▲ 10246 [DDD] (11.97)

L. Bori (sop), G. De Luca (bar) *(rec 1921)* ("Giuseppe De Luca in Opera 1918-1930") † Bizet:Pêcheurs de perles (sels); Ponchielli:Gioconda (sels); G. Puccini:Bohème (sels); Verdi:Aida (sels); Ernani (sels); Forza del destino (sels); Rigoletto (sels); Traviata (sels) MNER ▲ 23 [ADD] (15.97)

DONIZETTI, GAETANO (cont.)

Don Pasquale (selections) (cont.)

J. Gregor (bass), M. Kalmár (sop), I. Gati (bar), I. Fischer (cnd), Hungarian State Orch, T. Pál (cnd), Szombathely SO—Signora, in tanta fretta; Cheti! cheti immantinente; Ah, un foco insolito mi sento addosso *(rec 1975-82)* ("József Gregor, Bass") † Elisir d'amore (sels); J. Haydn:Infedeltà delusa (sels); W. A. Mozart:Arias; Paisiello:Barbiere di Siviglia (sels); G. Rossini:Barbiere di Siviglia (sels); Cenerentola (sels) *([ENG,HUN] texts)* HUN (Great Hungarian Voices) ▲ 31737 [AAD] (16.97)

E. Kohn (cnd), Miami Symphony Orch, A. Panagulias (sop)—Quel guardo il cavaliere † Elisir d'amore (sels); Lucia di Lammermoor (sels); J. Giménez:Boda de Luis Alonso (sels); Meyerbeer:Africaine (sels); Moreno Torroba:Luisa Fernanda (sels); Penella:Gato montés; G. Puccini:Gianni Schicchi (sels); Manon Lescaut (sels); Tosca (sels) HALM ▲ 30833 (6.97)

G. De Luca (bar), A. Gonzaga (sop), F. Corradetti (bar)—Pronta io son; Convien far la semplicità; Cheti! cheti immantinente; Aspetta, aspetta cara sposina *(rec Milan, Italy, 1905-07)* ("The Harold Wayne Collection, Vol 27: Giuseppe De Luca, Part 1") † Favorita (sels); Linda di Chamounix (sels); Berlioz:Damnation de Faust (sels); Meyerbeer:Dinorah (sels); W. A. Mozart:Don Giovanni (sels); Nozze di Figaro (sels); G. Rossini:Barbiere di Siviglia (sels); Guillaume Tell (sels); A. Thomas:Hamlet (sels); Verdi:Arias SYMP ▲ 1197 (18.97)

T. D. Monte (sop) *(rec 1924-41)* ("Arias & Duets") † Fille du régiment (sels); Linda di Chamounix (sels); Lucia di Lammermoor (sels); V. Bellini:Norma (sels); Sonnambula (sels); W. A. Mozart:Don Giovanni (sels); Nozze di Figaro (sels); G. Rossini:Barbiere di Siviglia (sels); Guillaume Tell (sels); Verdi:Falstaff (sels); Rigoletto (sels); Traviata (sels) ENT (Vocal Archives) ▲ 1191 (13.97)

M. Stabile (bar), G. Nessi (ten), A. Poli (bar), L. Donaggio (bass), M. Lawrence (sgr), A. Erede (cnd) —Cheti! cheti immantinente *(rec 1948)* † Boito:Nerone (sels); U. Giordano:Andrea Chénier (sels); W. A. Mozart:Don Giovanni (sels); Nozze di Figaro (sels); G. Puccini:Tosca (sels); Verdi:Aida (sels); Falstaff (sels); Otello (sels); Zandonai:Francesca da Rimini (sels) PRE (Lebendige Vergangenheit) ▲ 89180 (m) (16.97)

L'elisir d'amore (opera in 2 acts) [lib Felice Romani after Scribe] (1832)

I. Cotrubas (sop), L. Watson (sop), P. Domingo (ten), G. Evans (bar), I. Wixell (bar), J. Pritchard (cnd), Royal Opera House Orch Covent Garden, Royal Opera House Covent Garden Chorus *(rec 1977)* SNYC 2-▲ 34585 [ADD] (32.97)

G. Gavazzeni (cnd), Florence Teatro Comunale Orch, Florence Teatro Comunale Chorus, R. Scotto (sop—Adina), C. Bergonzi (ten—Nemorino), G. Taddei (bar—Belcore), C. Cava (bass—Dulcamara) *(rec Florence, Italy, 1967)* MYTO 2-▲ 984194 (34.97)

A. Gheorghiu (sop), E. Dan (sop), R. Alagna (ten), S. Alaimo (bar), R. Scaltriti (bar), E. Pidò (cnd), Lyon Opera Orch, Lyon Opera Chorus PLON ▲ 455691 (32.97)

La Scala Orch, La Scala Chorus, M. Freni (sop), L. Pavarotti (ten), L. Nucci (bar) ODRO 2-▲ 1184 (9.97)

J. Levine (cnd), Metropolitan Opera Orch, Metropolitan Opera Chorus, K. Battle (sop), D. Upshaw (sop), L. Pavarotti (ten), L. Nucci (bar), E. Dara (bar) DEUT 2-▲ 29744 [DDD] (32.97)

A. Ruffini (sop—Adina), M. Spotorno (sop—Gianetta), V. La Scola (ten—Nemorino), S. Alaimo (bar—Dulcamara), R. Frontali (bar—Belcore), P. G. Morandi (cnd), Hungarian State Opera Orch, A. Katona (cnd), Hungarian State Opera Chorus *(rec Budapest, July 1995)* NXIN 2-▲ 660045 [DDD] (14.97)

R. Scotto (sop—Adina), C. Bergonzi (ten—Nemorino), G. Taddei (bar—Belcore), C. Cava (bass—Dulcamara), G. Gavazzeni (cnd), Florence Teatro Comunale Orch, Florence Teatro Comunale Chorus ODRO 2-▲ 1138 (9.97)

H. Soudant (cnd), Emilia Romagna Toscanini SO, Parma Teatro Regio Chorus, A. Scarabelli (sop), B. Briscik (sop), C. Merritt (ten), A. Romero (bar), S. Bruscantini (b-bar) NUO 2-▲ 7292 (32.97)

J. Sutherland (sop), L. Pavarotti (ten), D. Cossa (bar), S. Malas (bass), R. Bonynge (cnd), English CO [ITA] PLON 2-▲ 14461 [ADD] (32.97)

L'elisir d'amore (selections)

M. Álvarez (ten), C. Rizzi (cnd), Welsh National Opera Orch, G. Jones (cnd), Welsh National Opera—Una furtiva lagrima; Inosservato penetrava...Angelo casto e bel *(rec Swansea, Wales, Apr 20-22, 28 & May 2, 1998)* † Favorita (sels); Linda di Chamounix (sels); Lucia di Lammermoor (sels); V. Bellini:Puritani (sels); Verdi:Rigoletto (sels); Traviata (sels) *([ENG] lib text)* SNYC ▲ 60721 [DDD] (16.97)

J. Björling (ten) ("Jussi Björling 1930-45: From Europe to the USA") † P. Mascagni:Cavalleria rusticana (sels); Ponchielli:Gioconda (sels); G. Rossini:Stabat Mater VOCA (Vocal Archives) ▲ 1115 (13.97)

M. Bolton (ten), S. Mercurio (cnd), Philharmonia Orch ("My Secret Passion") † Cilea:Arlesiana (sels); Flotow:Martha (sels); Leoncavallo:Pagliacci (sels); Massenet:Werther (sels); G. Puccini:Arias; Verdi:Aida (sels) SNYC ▲ 63077 [DDD] (16.97) ▮ 63077 [DDD] (10.98) CDL △ 63077 [DDD] (15.97)

A. Bonci (ten)—Una furtiva lagrima ("The 4-Minute Cylinder, Part 1") † Leoncavallo:Pagliacci (sels); P. Mascagni:Cavalleria rusticana (sels); Mendelssohn (-Bartholdy):Songs; G. Puccini:Tosca (sels); G. Rossini:Barbiere di Siviglia (sels); Verdi:Arias SYMP ▲ 1242 (18.97)

E. Caruso (ten), G. Anselmi (ten), M. Chamlee (ten), H. Lazaro (ten), J. McCormack (ten), A. Bonci (ten), A. Pertile (ten), T. Schipa (ten), B. Gigli (ten), J. Schmidt (ten), A. D. Arkor (ten), F. Tagliavini (ten), G. D. Stefano (ten), J. Björling (ten), D. Borgioli (ten) *(rec 1902-45)* ("Una Furtiva Lagrima Sung by Tenors 1902-45") MPLY ▲ 1001 (13.97)

P. Domingo (ten)—Una furtiva lagrima ("A Tenors Valentine") † Lucia di Lammermoor (sels); Bizet:Carmen (sels); U. Giordano:Fedora (sels); Leoncavallo:Pagliacci (sels); G. Puccini:Bohème (sels); Fanciulla del West (sels); Gianni Schicchi (sels); Madama Butterfly (sels); Tosca (sels); Turandot (sels); Verdi:Luisa Miller (sels); Rigoletto (sels) SNYC ▲ 60974 (9.97) ▮ 60974 (5.98)

S. Frontalini (cnd), Moldavian SO—Una furtiva lagrima *(rec Dec 1992)* ("Arias Without Voice: Tenor") † Favorita (sels); Bizet:Pêcheurs de perles (sels); Gounod:Faust (sels); Ponchielli:Gioconda (sels); G. Puccini:Bohème (sels); Manon Lescaut (sels); Tosca (sels); Turandot (sels); Verdi:Ballo in maschera (sels); Forza del destino (sels); Luisa Miller (sels); Macbeth (sels); Rigoletto (sels) BONG ▲ 8001 [DDD] (16.97)

B. Gigli (ten) *(rec 1925-27)* ("Beniamino Gigli Edition 3") † Lucia di Lammermoor (sels); Bizet:Pêcheurs de perles (sels); Boito:Mefistofele (sels); R. Drigo:Arlekinada (sels); Ponchielli:Gioconda (sels); G. Puccini:Bohème (sels); Manon Lescaut (sels); Tosca (sels); Verdi:Forza del destino (sels) VOCA ▲ 1177 (13.97)

J. Gregor (bass), T. Pál (cnd), Szombathely SO—Udite, o rustici *(rec 1975-82)* ("József Gregor, Bass") † Don Pasquale (sels); J. Haydn:Infedeltà delusa (sels); W. A. Mozart:Arias; Paisiello:Barbiere di Siviglia (sels); G. Rossini:Barbiere di Siviglia (sels); Cenerentola (sels) *([ENG,HUN] texts)* HUN (Great Hungarian Voices) ▲ 31737 [AAD] (16.97)

E. Kohn (cnd), Miami Symphony Orch, P. Domingo (ten)—Esulti pur la barbara † Don Pasquale (sels); Lucia di Lammermoor (sels); J. Giménez:Boda de Luis Alonso (sels); Meyerbeer:Africaine (sels); Moreno Torroba:Luisa Fernanda (sels); Penella:Gato montés; G. Puccini:Gianni Schicchi (sels); Manon Lescaut (sels); Tosca (sels) HALM ▲ 30833 (6.97)

M. Lanza (ten)—Una furtiva lagrima † Leoncavallo:Pagliacci (sels); Meyerbeer:Africaine (sels); Ponchielli:Gioconda (sels); G. Puccini:Tosca (sels); Verdi:Aida (sels); Rigoletto (sels) RCAV 2-▲ 63467 (16.97)

P. G. Morandi (cnd), Hungarian State Opera Orch, Hungarian State Opera Chorus ("Italian Opera Choruses") † Leoncavallo:Pagliacci (sels); P. Mascagni:Cavalleria rusticana (sels); G. Puccini:Madama Butterfly (sels); G. Rossini:Tancredi (sels); Verdi:Choruses NXIN ▲ 8553963 [DDD] (5.97)

L. Pavarotti (ten)—Una furtiva lagrima; Quanto è bella † Lucia di Lammermoor (sels); V. Bellini:Capuleti e i Montecchi (sels); Puritani (sels); G. Rossini:Stabat Mater; Verdi:Luisa Miller (sels) LALI ▲ 14308 (3.97)

L. Pavarotti (ten)—Adir forse il cielo † Lucia di Lammermoor (sels); V. Bellini:Capuleti e i Montecchi (sels); Puritani (sels); W. A. Mozart:Idomeneo (sels); G. Puccini:Bohème (sels); Turandot (sels); Verdi:Ballo in maschera (sels); Luisa Miller (sels); Rigoletto (sels) HALM ▲ 30421 (6.97)

L. Pavarotti (ten), R. Bonynge (cnd), Adelaide Opera Orch—Quanto è bella *(rec 1965)* ("The Great Luciano Pavarotti") † Lucia di Lammermoor (sels); V. Bellini:Puritani (sels); G. Puccini:Bohème (sels); Turandot (sels); G. Rossini:Stabat Mater; Verdi:Luisa Miller (sels); Rigoletto (sels) GDIS ▲ 63202 [ADD] (10.97)

B. R. Stees (bn), S. Norris (hp), R. Fusco (pno) [trans for bn, hp & pno] † Lucia di Lammermoor (sels); Hérold:Zampa (ov); W. A. Mozart:Entführung aus dem Serail (sels); G. Rossini:Gazza ladra (sels); P. Tchaikovsky:Eugene Onegin (sels); Verdi:Trovatore (sels); R. Wagner:Tannhäuser (sels) CLAV ▲ 509815 (16.97)

S. Verrett (mez), A. Kraus (ten), L. Pavarotti (ten) *(rec 1975)* † Favorita (sels); G. Rossini:Barbiere di Siviglia (sels); Verdi:Luisa Miller (sels) BELV ▲ 7009 (15.97)

V. Zeani (sop), N. R. Lemeni (bass), F. Vernizzi (cnd), Turin RAI Orch—Come sen va contento; Quanto amore *(rec Italy, 1958)* ("Virginia Zeani") † Anna Bolena (sels); Lucia di Lammermoor (sels); V. Bellini:Puritani (sels); F. Lehár:Lustige Witwe (sels); Verdi:Aida (sels); Don Carlos (sels); Forza del destino (sels) *([ITA]text)* BONG (Il Mito Dell'Opera) ▲ 1060 [ADD] (16.97)

various artists—Una furtiva lagrima † Lucia di Lammermoor (sels); P. Mascagni:Cavalleria rusticana (sels); G. Puccini:Fanciulla del West (sels); Madama Butterfly (sels); Tosca (sels); Verdi:Rigoletto (sels); Traviata (sels); Trovatore (sels) PEG ▲ 196 (5.97)

Emilia di Liverpool (opera in 2 acts) [lib after Scatizzi] (1824)

Y. Kenny (sop), A. Mason (sop), B. Mills (sop), C. Merritt (ten), G. Dolton (bar), C. Thornton-Holmes (bar), S. Bruscantini (b-bar), D. Parry (cnd), Philharmonia Orch, Geoffrey Mitchell Choir † Eremitaggio di Liverpool OPR 3-▲ 8 (54.97)

DONIZETTI, GAETANO (cont.)

Emilia di Liverpool (selections)
J. Sutherland (sop), A. Cantelo (sop), W. McAlpine (ten), D. Dowling (bar), H. Alan (bass), J. Pritchard (cnd), Royal Liverpool PO, Liverpool Music Group Singers *(rec live Liverpool, Sept 1957)* † Lucia di Lammermoor (sels) MYTO ▲ 91545 [ADD] (17.97)

L'Eremitaggio di Liverpool [composer's revised version of his 1824 opera *Emilia in Liverpool*]
Y. Kenny (sop), A. Mason (sop), B. Mills (sop), C. Merritt (ten), G. Dolton (bar), C. Thornton-Holmes (bar), S. Bruscantini (b-bar), D. Parry (cnd), Philharmonia Orch, Geoffrey Mitchell Choir † Emilia di Liverpool OPR 3-▲ 8 (54.97)

L'Esule di Roma (opera in 2 acts) [lib Gilardoni] (1827)
C. Gasdia (sop), E. Palacio (ten), S. Alaimo (bar), A. Ariostini (bar), M. D. Bernart (cnd), Piacenza SO, Paris Opéra-Comique Chorus *(rec live, Oct 14, 1986)* BONG 2-▲ 2045 [DDD]

La favorita (opera in 4 acts) [lib Royer & Vaëz after Baculard D'Arnaud] (1840)
V. Cortez (mez), A. Kraus (ten), R. Bruson (bar), C. Siepi (bass), F. Molinari-Pradelli (cnd) *(rec 1976)* MYTO 2-▲ 983190 (34.97)
K. Lapeyrette (mez), H. Albers (bar) [original version in F] *(rec 1912)* MRSN (Pathe Opera) ▲ 52010 (36.97)
F. Luisi (cnd), Italian International Orch, Slovak Philharmonic Chorus, A. Ruffini (sop), A. Tabiadon (mez), G. Morino (ten), M. Farruggia (ten), P. Coni (bar), A. Verducci (bass) NUO 2-▲ 6823 (32.97)
N. Verchi (cnd), La Scala Orch, La Scala Chorus, F. Cossotto (mez), L. Pavarotti (ten), P. Cappuccilli (bar) *(rec live Milan, Italy, Jan 28, 1974)* ODRO 2-▲ 1196 (9.97)

La favorita (selections)
M. Alvarez (ten), C. Rizzi (cnd), Welsh National Opera Orch, G. Jones (cnd), Welsh National Opera—Spirto gentil *(rec Swansea, Wales, Apr 20-22, 28 & May 2, 1998)* † Elisir d'amore (sels); Linda di Chamounix (sels); Lucia di Lammermoor (sels); V. Bellini:Puritani (sels); Verdi:Rigoletto (sels); Traviata (sels) *([ENG] lib text)* SNYC ▲ 60721 [DDD] (16.97)
O. Borodina (mez), D. Hvorostovsky (bar), P. Summers (cnd), English CO ("Olga & Dmitri") † Rimsky-Korsakov:Tsar's Bride (sels); G. Rossini:Barbiere di Siviglia (sels); Saint-Saëns:Samson et Dalila (sels) PPHI ▲ 454439 (16.97)
R. Bruson (bar), P. Carignani (cnd), Italian PO—Vieni, amor/Leonara! A'piedi tuo; De' nemici tuoi *(rec Teatro civico Vercelli, Italy, Sept 1996)* ("35 Years of Bel Canto") † A. Catalani:Wally (sels); U. Giordano:Andrea Chénier (sels); Verdi:Arias BONG ▲ 2522 (16.97)
S. Frontalini (cnd), Moldavian SO—Favorita del re!; Spirto gentil *(rec Dec 1992)* ("Arias Without Voice: Tenor") † Elisir d'amore (sels); Bizet:Pêcheurs de perles (sels); Gounod:Faust (sels); Ponchielli:Gioconda (sels); G. Puccini:Bohème (sels); Manon Lescaut (sels); Tosca (sels); Turandot (sels); Verdi:Ballo in maschera (sels); Forza del destino (sels); Luisa Miller (sels); Macbeth (sels); Rigoletto (sels) BONG ▲ 8001 [DDD] (16.97)
M. Horne (mez), L. Foster (cnd), Monte Carlo PO † D.-F. Auber:Zerline (sels); B. Godard:Vivandiere (sels); Gounod:Sappho (sels); Saint-Saëns:Samson et Dalila (sels) ERAT (Recital) ▲ 98501 (9.97)
G. De Luca (bar)—Giardini dell'Alcazar; Vieni, amor/Leonara! A'piedi tuo *(rec Milan, Italy, 1905-07)* ("The Harold Wayne Collection, Vol 27: Giuseppe De Luca, Part 1") † Don Pasquale (sels); Linda di Chamounix (sels); Berlioz:Damnation de Faust (sels); Meyerbeer:Dinorah (sels); W. A. Mozart:Don Giovanni (sels); Nozze di Figaro (sels); G. Rossini:Barbiere di Siviglia (sels); Guillaume Tell (sels); A. Thomas:Hamlet (sels); Verdi:Arias SYMP ▲ 1197 (18.97)
E. Pinza (bass) ("Ezio Pinza: The Early Legendary Recordings") † Lucia di Lammermoor (sels); V. Bellini:Norma (sels); Puritani (sels); Boito:Mefistofele (sels); G. Puccini:Bohème (sels); G. Rossini:Mosè in Egitto (sels); Verdi:Arias VOCA (Vocal Archives) ▲ 1132 (13.97)
S. Verrett (mez), A. Kraus (ten), L. Pavarotti (ten) *(rec 1975)* † Elisir d'amore (sels); G. Rossini:Barbiere di Siviglia (sels); Verdi:Luisa Miller (sels) BELV ▲ 7009 (15.97)
M. Zotti (sop), F. Cossotto (mez), A. Kraus (ten), R. Raimondi (bass), O. De Fabritiis (cnd), NHK SO *(rec Sept 13, 1971)* † Fille du régiment MYTO 2-▲ 93276 (34.97)

La fille du régiment (opera in 2 acts) [lib Saint-George & Bayard] (1840)
M. Freni (sop), A. Di Stasio (mez), A. Kraus (ten), W. Ganzarolli (bar), A. Nosotti (bass), A. Bazzini (sgr), N. Sanzogno (cnd), Venice Theater Orch *(rec live, Dec 1975)* MONM (Gran Teatro La Fenice) 2-▲ 10011 (34.97)
M. Freni (sop), L. Pavarotti (ten) ODRO 2-▲ 1147 (9.97)
E. Gruberová (sop), R. Laghezza (mez), D. Walt (ten), P. Fourcade (bass), F. Castel (sgr), M. Panni (cnd), Munich RSO, Bavarian Radio Chorus NIGC 2-▲ 70566 (34.97)
J. Sutherland (sop), R. Resnik (mez), A. Kraus (ten), S. Maias (bass), R. Bonynge (cnd), Chicago Lyric Opera Orch, Chicago Lyric Opera Chorus [FRE] *(rec Nov 20, 1973)* † Favorita (sels) MYTO 2-▲ 93276 (34.97)
J. Sutherland (sop), M. Sinclair (cta), L. Pavarotti (ten), S. Maias (bass), R. Bonynge (cnd), Royal Opera House Orch Covent Garden [FRE] PLON 2-▲ 14520 [ADD] (32.97)

La fille du régiment (selections)
L. Aliberti (sop), R. Paternostro (cnd), Berlin RSO—Convien partir; C'en est donc fait *(rec Jesus Christ Church, Berlin, Germany, Aug 2-10, 1988)* † Anna Bolena (sels); Don Pasquale (sels); Torquato Tasso (sels); V. Bellini:Capuleti e i Montecchi (sels); Puritani (sels) CAPO ▲ 10246 [DDD] (11.97)
K. Battle (sop), M. Chung (cnd), Bastille Opera Orch—C'en est donc fait; Salut à la France *(rec Bastille Opera Paris, France, Nov 1993 & June 1994)* ("Kathleen Battle Sings French Opera Arias") † Berlioz:Béatrice et Benédict (sels); G. Charpentier:Louise (sels); Gounod:Roméo et Juliette (sels); Massenet:Manon (sels); J. Offenbach:Belle Lurette (sels); A. Thomas:Hamlet (sels); Mignon (sels) DEUT ▲ 47114 [DDD] (16.97)
T. D. Monte (sop) *(rec 1924-41)* ("Arias & Duets") † Don Pasquale (sels); Linda di Chamounix (sels); Lucia di Lammermoor (sels); V. Bellini:Norma (sels); Sonnambula (sels); W. A. Mozart:Don Giovanni (sels); Nozze di Figaro (sels); G. Rossini:Barbiere di Siviglia (sels); Guillaume Tell (sels); Verdi:Falstaff (sels); Rigoletto (sels); Traviata (sels) ENT (Vocal Archives) ▲ 1191 (13.97)
L. Pavarotti (ten)—Ah! mes amis; Che voi m'amate † Massenet:Manon (sels); W. A. Mozart:Idomeneo (sels); Verdi:Ballo in maschera (sels); Lombardi (sels) LALI ▲ 14309 (3.97)

Il Fortunato Inganno (opera in 2 acts) [lib Andrea Leone Tottola] (1823)
A. Bosman (cnd), Italian International Opera Orch, Bratislava Chamber Choir, S. Donzelli (sop—Aurelia), E. Lee (sop—Eugenia), M. Todisco (sop—Fiordelisa), M. Damonte (mez—Donna Fulgenzia), S. Fiore (ten—Il tenente Eduardo), N. Rivenq (bar—Colonello Ortenzio), D. Colaianni (bar—Lattanzio Lattughell), M. Chiarolla (bar—Vulcano), L. Miotto (bar—Il signor Bequadro), L. Grassi (bar—B Spizzoletti), M. Nisticò (bar—Ascanio) [score rev Anders Wiklund] *(rec Martina Franca, Palazzo Ducale, Italy, July 27-29, 1998) ([GER,ENG] lib text)* DYNC 2-▲ 228 (live) [DDD] (34.97)

Il furioso all'isola di Santo Domingo (opera in 3 acts) (1833)
L. Serra (sop), P. Antonucci (sop), E. Tandura (mez), L. Canonici (ten), R. Coviello (bar), M. Picconi (bar), C. Rizzi (cnd), Piacenza SO, Piacenza Chorus [ITA] *(rec live, Nov 10, 1987)* BONG 3-▲ 2056 [DDD] (47.97)

Gemma di Vergy (opera in 2 acts) [lib Giovanni Emanuele Biedera after Dumas] (1834)
M. Caballé (sop—Gemma di Vergy), B. Casoni (mez—Ida di Greville), G. Lamberti (ten—Tamas), R. Bruson (bar—Conte di Vergy), M. Rinaudo (bass—Guido), M. Machì (bass—Rolando), A. Gatto (cnd), Naples Teatro San Carlo Orch, Naples Teatro San Carlo Chorus [ITA] *(rec Naples, Dec 12, 1975)* MYTO 2-▲ 952124 (34.97)
M. Caballé (sop—Gemma), A. Ringart (mez—Ida), L. Lima (ten—Tamas), V. Sardinero (bar—Il Conte), J. Pons (bar—Guido), A. Gatto (cnd), Nouvel PO, J. Kreder (cnd), French Radio Chorus *(rec Salle Pleyet Paris, Apr 20, 1976)* PHO (Phoenix) 2-▲ 501 [ADD] (34.97)

Gianni di Calais (selections) (1828)
N. Miricioiu (sop), R. Blake (ten), G. Magee (bar), D. Parry (cnd), Philharmonia Orch—Tu in Grembo all'innocenza † Ajo nell'imbrazzo (sels); Anna Bolena (sels); Caterina Cornaro (sels); Maria di Rohan (sels); Maria Stuarda (sels); Marino Faliero (sels); Pia de' Tolomei (sels); Ugo (sels) OPR ▲ 207 (18.97)

Gianni di Parigi (comic opera in 2 acts) [lib Romani after Saint-Just] (1839)
L. Serra (sop), E. Zilio (mez), G. Morino (ten), A. Romero (bar), E. Fissore (bass), S. Manga (sgr), C. F. Cillario (cnd), Milan RAI Orch, Milan RAI Chorus [ITA] *(rec live)* NUO 2-▲ 6752 [DDD] (32.97)

Il giovedi grasso (opera in 1 act) [lib Gilardoni] (1828)
E. Loehrer (cnd), Swiss-Italian Radio-TV Orch, B. Rizzoli (sop), M. Minetto (cta), R. Malacarne (ten), J. Oncina (ten), T. Rovetta (bar), N. Catalani (bar), J. Loomis (bass), I. Bassi-Ferrari (sgr) *(rec 1961)* NUO ▲ 1131 (16.97)

Imelda de' Lambertazzi (opera in 2 acts) [lib Tottola] (1830)
F. Sovilla (sop), D. D. Auria (ten), F. Tenzi (ten), G. Sarti (bar), A. Martin (bar), M. Andreae (cnd), Swiss-Italian Radio-TV Orch, Swiss-Italian Radio-TV Chorus [ITA] *(rec live)* NUO 2-▲ 6778 [DDD] (32.97)

Instrumental Music
J. Polmear (hn/ob), D. Ambache (pno)—Con E Hn & Orch; Son Ob & Pno; Waltz Pno † Songs; Liszt:Trans, Arrs & Paraphrases; Pasculli:Con on La Favorita; Fant on Poliuto MER ▲ 84147 (16.97)

L'Ajo nell'imbrazzo (selections)
N. Miricioiu (sop), R. Blake (ten), G. Magee (bar), D. Parry (cnd), Philharmonia Orch—Ov † Anna Bolena (sels); Caterina Cornaro (sels); Gianni di Calais (sels); Maria di Rohan (sels); Maria Stuarda (sels); Marino Faliero (sels); Pia de' Tolomei (sels); Ugo (sels) OPR ▲ 207 (18.97)

DONIZETTI, GAETANO (cont.)

Larghetto & Allegro in g for Violin & Harp
Grauwels (fl), B. Michel (hp) † Chopin:Vars on Rossini; L. Drouet:Intro & Vars on an English Theme; G. Rossini:Andante e tema con variazioni Va; L. Spohr:Son 1 Vn & Hp MARC ▲ 8220441 [DDD] (13.97)

Linda di Chamounix (opera in 3 acts) [lib Gaetano Rossi after D'Ennery & Lemoine] (1842)
M. Devia (sop—Linda), S. Ganassi (mez—Pierotto), F. Provvisionato (mez—Maddalena), L. Canonici (ten—Carlo), P. Salomaa (bass—Antonio), A. Antoniozzi (bass—Il Marchese di Boisf), D. Di Stefano (bass—Il Prefetto), B. Fiksinski (sgr—L'intendente), G. Bellini (cnd), Eastern Netherlands Orch, A. Wise (cnd), National Reisopera Choir *(rec Muziekcentrum Enschede Holland, June 24-July 2, 1992) (lib)* AART 3-▲ 47151 [DDD] (28.97)
E. Gruberová (sop), M. Groop (mez), D. Bernardini (ten), E. Kim (sgr), F. Haider (cnd), Swedish RSO, Mikaeli Chamber Choir NIGC 3-▲ 70561

Linda di Chamounix (selections)
M. Alvarez (ten), C. Rizzi (cnd), Welsh National Opera Orch, G. Jones (cnd), Welsh National Opera—Se tanto in ira agli uomini *(rec Swansea, Wales, Apr 20-22, 28 & May 2, 1998)* † Elisir d'amore (sels); Favorita (sels); Lucia di Lammermoor (sels); V. Bellini:Puritani (sels); Verdi:Rigoletto (sels); Traviata (sels) *([ENG] lib text)* SNYC ▲ 60721 [DDD] (16.97)
G. De Luca (bar) *(rec Milan, Italy, 1905-07)* ("The Harold Wayne Collection, Vol 27: Giuseppe De Luca, Part 1") † Don Pasquale (sels); Favorita (sels); Berlioz:Damnation de Faust (sels); Meyerbeer:Dinorah (sels); W. A. Mozart:Don Giovanni (sels); Nozze di Figaro (sels); G. Rossini:Barbiere di Siviglia (sels); Guillaume Tell (sels); A. Thomas:Hamlet (sels); Verdi:Arias SYMP ▲ 1197 (18.97)
T. D. Monte (sop) *(rec 1924-41)* ("Arias & Duets") † Don Pasquale (sels); Fille du régiment (sels); Lucia di Lammermoor (sels); V. Bellini:Norma (sels); Sonnambula (sels); W. A. Mozart:Don Giovanni (sels); Nozze di Figaro (sels); G. Rossini:Barbiere di Siviglia (sels); Guillaume Tell (sels); Verdi:Falstaff (sels); Rigoletto (sels); Traviata (sels) ENT (Vocal Archives) ▲ 1191 (13.97)
R. A. Swenson (sop), N. Rescigno (cnd), London PO—Ah! tardi troppo; O luce di quest'anima *(rec Nov 11-19, 1993)* ("Positively Golden") † Lucia di Lammermoor (sels); V. Bellini:Puritani (sels); Sonnambula (sels); Gounod:Roméo et Juliette (sels); Meyerbeer:Africaine (sels); Dinorah (sels); Huguenots (sels) EMIC ▲ 54827 [DDD] (16.97)
L. Tetrazzini (sop)—O luce di quest'anima ("Luisa Tetrazzini: The London Recordings, Vol. 1 1907-14") † Lucia di Lammermoor (sels); V. Bellini:Puritani (sels); Sonnambula (sels); G. Rossini:Barbiere di Siviglia (sels); Semiramide (sels); Verdi:Arias VOCA (Vocal Archives) ▲ 1122 (13.97)

Lucia di Lammermoor (opera in 3 acts) [lib Salvadore Cammarano after Scott] (1835)
M. Callas (sop—Lucia), A. M. Canali (mez—Alisa), G. Sarri (ten—Normanno), G. Di Stefano (ten—Edgardo), V. Natali (ten—Arturo), T. Gobbi (bar—Enrico), R. Arié (bass—Raimondo), T. Serafin (cnd), Florence Maggio Musicale Orch, Florence Maggio Musicale Chorus *(rec Jan-Feb 1953) (E,I lib texts)* EMIC (Callas Complete Operas) 2-▲ 66438 [ADD] (23.97)
M. Callas (sop), G. Di Stefano (ten), Campolonghi (sgr), G. Picco (cnd), Palacio Bellas Artes Orch, Palacio Bellas Artes Chorus [ITA] *(rec live Mexico City, June 10, 1952)* † V. Bellini:Norma (sels) MYTO 2-▲ 91340 (live) [ADD] (34.97)
M. Callas (sop), E. Fernandi (ten), R. Panerai (bar), G. Modesti (bass), T. Serafin (cnd), Rome RAI SO, Rome RAI Chorus *(rec live Rome, 1957)* ENT (Documents) 2-▲ 973 [ADD] (26.97)
M. Callas (sop), G. Raimondi (ten), R. Panerai (bar), A. Zerbini (bass), F. Molinari-Pradelli (cnd), Naples Teatro San Carlo Orch, Naples Teatro San Carlo Chorus [ITA] *(rec live, Mar 22, 1956)* † Lucia di Lammermoor (sels) MYTO ▲ 90319 [ADD] (34.97)
M. Callas (sop), F. Tagliavini (ten), P. Cappuccilli (bar), B. Ladysz (bass), T. Serafin (cnd), Philharmonia Orch, Philharmonia Chorus EMIC (Callas Edition) 2-▲ 56284 (32.97)
M. Callas (sop—Lucia), L. Villa (mez—Alisa), G. Zampieri (ten—Arturo), G. Di Stefano (ten—Edgardo), M. Carlin (ten—Normanno), R. Panerai (bar—Enrico), N. Zaccaria (bass—Raimondo), H. von Karajan (cnd), Berlin RIAS SO, La Scala Chorus *(rec live Berlin State Opera, Sept 29, 1955) (E,I lib texts)* EMIC (Callas Complete Operas) 2-▲ 66441 [ADD] (23.97)
M. Capsir (sop), E. D. Muro Lomanto (ten), E. Molinari (bar), S. Baccaloni (bass), L. Molajoli (cnd), La Scala Orch, La Scala Chorus *(rec 1933)* GRM2 2-▲ 78762 (26.97)
P. Ciofi (sop), A. Badea (ten), G. Bonfatti (ten), R. Bota (ten), N. Rivenq (bar), J. Lee (bass), M. Benini (cnd), Italian International Orch, Bratislava Chamber Choir [FRE] *(rec Palazzo Ducale Italy, July 1997) (E,F lib texts)* DYNC 2-▲ 204 [DDD] (34.97)
M. Devia (sop—Lucia), E. Scano (mez—Alisa), J. Bros (ten—Edgardo), M. Berti (ten—Arturo), P. Lefebvre (ten—Normanno), R. Fronteli (bar—Enrico), C. Colombara (bass—Raimondo), Z. Mehta (cnd), Florence Maggio Musicale Orch, Florence Maggio Musicale Chorus *(rec live Florence, 1996)* FON (Grand Master) 2-▲ 9606 [DDD] (20.97)
I. Marin (cnd), London SO, C. Studer (sop), P. Domingo (ten), J. Pons (bar), S. Ramey (bass) DEUT 2-▲ 35309 [DDD] (32.97)
D. Mazzola (sop), G. Morino (ten), S. Carroli (bar), M. D. Bernart (cnd), Naples Teatro San Carlo Orch, Naples Teatro San Carlo Chorus *(rec live, 1989)* NUO 3-▲ 6794 (47.97)
L. Pagliughi (sop—Lucia), M. Vinciguerra (mez—Alisa), G. Malipiero (ten—Edgardo), M. Giovagnoli (ten—Arturo), A. Giannotti (ten—Normanno), G. Manacchini (bar—Enrico), L. Neroni (bass—Raimondo), U. Tansini (cnd), Turin EIAR Orch, Turin EIAR Chorus *(rec 1942)* ARKA (The 78's) 2-▲ 78021 [ADD] (26.97)
R. Peters (sop—Lucia), M. T. Pace (mez—Alisa), J. Peerce (ten—Edgardo), P. D. Palma (ten—Lord Arturo Bucklaw), M. Carlin (ten—Normanno), P. Maero (bar—Lord Enrico Ashton), G. Tozzi (bass—Raimondo), E. Leinsdorf (cnd), Rome Opera Orch, Rome Opera Chorus *(rec Rome Opera House, Aug 5-14, 1957)* RCAV (Living Stereo) 2-▲ 68537 [ADD] (22.97)
C. Petrovici (cnd), Romanian Opera Orch, Romanian Opera Chorus, S. Voinea (sop—Lucia), L. Cicoara (mez), F. Georgescu (ten—Sir Edgar Ravenswood), G. Nastase (ten—Lord Arthur Bucklaw), N. Herlea (bar—Lord Henry Ashton), P. Harasteanu (bass), N. Bratu (sgr) GZCL 2-▲ 384 (10.97)
A. Rost (sop—Miss Lucia), L. Winter (mez—Alisa), B. Ford (ten—Sir Edgardo di Raven), P. C. Clarke (ten—Lord Arturo Bucklaw), R. Davies (ten—Normando), A. Michaels-Moore (bar—Lord Enrico Ashton), A. Miles (bass—Raimondo Bidebent), M. Root (fl), A. Moore (hp), C. Mackerras (cnd), Hanover Band, London Voices *(rec London England, Aug 2-13, 1997)* SNYC 2-▲ 63174 [DDD] (32.97)
R. Scotto (sop—Miss Lucia), L. Pavarotti (ten—Sir Edgardo), P. Cappuccilli (bar—Lord Enrico), F. Molinari-Pradelli (cnd), Turin RAI SO, Turin RAI Chorus ODRO 2-▲ 1137 (9.97)
T. Serafin (cnd), Royal Opera House Orch Covent Garden, J. Sutherland (sop—Lucia), M. Elkins (mez—Alisa), J. Gibin (ten—Edgardo), R. Bowman (ten—Normanno), K. McDonald (ten—Arturo), J. Shaw (bar—Enrico), J. Rouleau (bass—Raimondo) *(rec live, London, England, Feb 26, 1959)* MELO (Opera Live) 2-▲ 50024 (m) [ADD] (31.97)
J. Sutherland (sop), L. Pavarotti (ten), S. Milnes (bar), N. Ghiaurov (bass), R. Bonynge (cnd), Royal Opera House Orch Covent Garden [ITA] PLON 3-▲ 10193 [ADD] (48.97)

Lucia di Lammermoor (selections)
M. Alvarez (ten), C. Rizzi (cnd), Welsh National Opera Orch, G. Jones (cnd), Welsh National Opera—Fra poco a me ricovero *(rec Swansea, Wales, Apr 20-22, 28 & May 2, 1998)* † Elisir d'amore (sels); Favorita (sels); Linda di Chamounix (sels); V. Bellini:Puritani (sels); Verdi:Rigoletto (sels); Traviata (sels) *([ENG] lib text)* SNYC ▲ 60721 [DDD] (16.97)
J. Anderson (sop), D. Malvisi (sop), M. A. Martinez (cnd), Emilia Romagna SO—Ancor non giunse?; Regnava nel silenzio; Quando rapito in estasi *(rec Parma, Italy, Nov 24, 1984)* ("June Anderson dal Vivo in Concerto") † V. Bellini:Sonnambula (sels); G. Rossini:Semiramide (sels); Verdi:Battaglia di Legnano (sels); Traviata (sels) BONG ▲ 2504 (16.97)
M. Callas (sop) ("Callas & Company") † V. Bellini:Norma (sels); Pirata (sels); Sonnambula (sels); G. Puccini:Bohème (sels); Tosca (sels); Verdi:Aida (sels); Traviata (sels) EMIC ▲ 56341 (16.97)
M. Callas (sop), G. Raimondi (ten) [ITA] *(rec live, Mar 24, 1956)* † Lucia di Lammermoor MYTO ▲ 90319 [ADD] (34.97)
M. Capsir (sop), E. D. Lomanto (ten), E. Molinari (bar), S. Baccaloni (bass), L. Molajoli (cnd), La Scala Orch, La Scala Chorus OPIT ▲ 54546 (6.97)
C. Deutekom (sop), J. Carreras (ten), R. Benzi (cnd), Rotterdam PO, C. Franci (cnd), Amsterdam PO, C. Franci (cnd), Netherlands Opera Chorus—Lucia perdona; Ah! Verranno a te; Il dolce suono; Ardon gl'incensi; Spargi d'amaro pianto (Mad Scene) *(rec Netherlands, Aug 30, 1975)* ("Cristina Deutekom & José Carreras") † V. Bellini:Norma (sels); Mercadante:Giuramento (sels); Verdi:Attila (sels); Ernani (sels); Luisa Miller (sels) *(E text)* BELV ▲ 7012 [ADD] (15.97)
M. Devia (sop), M. Rota (cnd), Swiss-Italian Orch *(rec June 4, 1992)* † V. Bellini:Capuleti e i Montecchi (sels); Puritani (sels); Sonnambula (sels); G. Charpentier:Louise (sels); Delibes:Lakmé (sels); Gounod:Roméo et Juliette (sels) BONG ▲ 2513 [DDD] (16.97)
G. Di Stefano (ten) † Bizet:Pêcheurs de perles (sels); Leoncavallo:Arias; Pagliacci (sels); P. Mascagni:Cavalleria rusticana (sels); G. Puccini:Bohème (sels); Fanciulla del West (sels); Gianni Schicchi (sels); Madama Butterfly (sels); Manon Lescaut (sels); Tosca (sels); Turandot (sels); Tosti:Songs; Verdi:Ballo in maschera (sels); Forza del destino (sels); Rigoletto (sels); Traviata (sels); Trovatore (sels) GTEN 2-▲ 70482 (13.97)
L. Gencer (sop), L. Hussu (mez), O. D. Fabritiis (cnd), Trieste Teatro Comunale Giuseppe Verdi Orch *(rec 1957)* ("Leyla Gencer, Vol. 2: 1957-58") † Anna Bolena (sels); Pizzetti:Assassinio nella cattedrale (sels); G. Puccini:Suor Angelica (sels); Tabarro (sels); Verdi:Due Foscari (sels); Forza del destino (sels); Trovatore (sels) MYTO ▲ 973160 (17.97)

▲ = CD ♦ = Enhanced CD △ = MD ▮ = Cassette Tape ▯ = DCC

DONIZETTI, GAETANO (cont.)

Lucia di Lammermoor (selections) (cont.)

L. Gencer (sop), G. Prandelli (ten), N. Carta (bar), O. D. Fabritiis (cnd), Trieste Teatro Comunale Giuseppe Verdi Orch, Trieste Teatro Comunale Giuseppe Verdi Chorus *(rec 1957)* † Martyrs MYTO 3-▲ 972154 (51.97)

B. Gigli (ten) *(rec 1925-27)* ("Beniamino Gigli Edition 3") † Elisir d'amore (sels); Bizet:Pêcheurs de perles (sels); Boito:Mefistofele (sels); R. Drigo:Arlekinada (sels); Ponchielli:Gioconda (sels); G. Puccini:Bohème (sels); Manon Lescaut (sels); Tosca (sels); Verdi:Forza del destino (sels) VOCA ▲ 1177 (13.97)

B. Gigli (ten), E. Pinza (bass) ("Opera Masters") † Bizet:Carmen (sels); Gounod:Faust (sels); G. Puccini:Bohème (sels); Tosca (sels); Verdi:Aida (sels); Forza del destino (sels); Traviata (sels) FORL ▲ 16718 [ADD] (16.97)

T. Gobbi (bar), G. Sarri (ten), R. Arié (bass), T. Serafin (cnd), Florence Maggio Musicale Orch—Cruda, funesta smania; La pietade in suo favore ("Opera Heroes: Tito Gobbi") † Leoncavallo:Pagliacci (sels); G. Puccini:Tosca (sels); G. Rossini:Arias; Verdi:Arias EMIC ▲ 66810 (m/s) [ADD] (11.97)

E. Gruberová (sop), A. Agache (bar), A. Miles (bass), R. Bonynge (cnd), London SO, Ambrosian Singers—Giusto ciel, respondete; Il dolce suono; Spargi d'amaro pianto (Mad Scene) † W. A. Mozart:Arias; Strauss (II):Fledermaus (sels); Verdi:Traviata (sels) TELC ▲ 93691 [DDD] (9.97)

E. Kohn (cnd), Miami Symphony Orch, P. Domingo (ten)—Fra poco a me ricovero † Don Pasquale (sels); Elisir d'amore (sels); J. Giménez:Boda de Luis Alonso (sels); Meyerbeer:Africaine (sels); Moreno Torroba:Luisa Fernanda (sels); Penella:Gato montés; G. Puccini:Gianni Schicchi (sels); Manon Lescaut (sels); Tosca (sels) HALM ▲ 30833 (6.97)

J. Lortič (ten), I. Morozov (bar), J. Wildner (cnd), Slovak RSO Bratislava *(rec Slovak Radio Concert Hall Bratislava, Slovak Republic, Feb 15-24, 1994)* ("Operatic Duets for Tenor and Baritone") † Bizet:Pêcheurs de perles (sels); G. Rossini:Guillaume Tell (sels); Verdi:Forza del destino (sels); Otello (sels); Vespri siciliani (sels) NXIN ▲ 553030 [DDD] (5.97)

G. Masini (ten) ("Galliano Masini") † Cilea:Adriana Lecouvreur (sels); Arlesiana (sels); U. Giordano:Andrea Chénier (sels); Fedora (sels); Leoncavallo:Pagliacci (sels); P. Mascagni:Cavalleria rusticana (sels); G. Puccini:Bohème (sels); Madama Butterfly (sels); Manon Lescaut (sels); Tosca (sels); Verdi:Aida (sels); Forza del destino (sels) BONG (Il Mito dell'Opera) ▲ 1067 [ADD] (16.97)

T. D. Monte (sop) *(rec 1924-41)* ("Arias & Duets") † Don Pasquale (sels); Fille du régiment (sels); Linda di Chamounix (sels); V. Bellini:Norma (sels); Sonnambula (sels); W. A. Mozart:Don Giovanni (sels); Nozze di Figaro (sels); G. Rossini:Barbiere di Siviglia (sels); Guillaume Tell (sels); Verdi:Falstaff (sels); Rigoletto (sels); Traviata (sels) ENT (Vocal Archives) ▲ 1191 (13.97)

C. Parmentier (cnd) [arr for mands] ("Opera on Mandolins") † V. Bellini:Puritani (sels); Verdi:Rigoletto (sels); Traviata (sels); Trovatore (sels) PVY ▲ 795042 (16.97)

L. Pavarotti (ten)—Lucia perdona † Elisir d'amore (sels); V. Bellini:Capuleti e i Montecchi (sels); Puritani (sels); W. A. Mozart:Idomeneo (sels); G. Puccini:Bohème (sels); Turandot (sels); Verdi:Ballo in maschera (sels); Luisa Miller (sels); Rigoletto (sels) HALM ▲ 30421 (6.97)

L. Pavarotti (ten)—Tombe degl'avi miei; Fra poco a me ricovero; Tu che a Dio † Elisir d'amore (sels); V. Bellini:Capuleti e i Montecchi (sels); Puritani (sels); G. Rossini:Stabat Mater; Verdi:Luisa Miller (sels) LALI ▲ 14308 (3.97)

L. Pavarotti (ten)—Fra poco a me ricovero ("A Tenors Valentine") † Elisir d'amore (sels); Bizet:Carmen (sels); U. Giordano:Fedora (sels); Leoncavallo:Pagliacci (sels); G. Puccini:Bohème (sels); Fanciulla del West (sels); Gianni Schicchi (sels); Madama Butterfly (sels); Tosca (sels); Turandot (sels); Verdi:Luisa Miller (sels); Rigoletto (sels) SNYC ▲ 60974 (9.97) ▮ 60974 (5.98)

L. Pavarotti (ten), F. Molinari-Pradelli (cnd), Turin SO, Turin Sym Chorus *(rec live, June 30, 1967)* ("Pavarotti: The Early Years, Vol. 2") † V. Bellini:Capuleti e i Montecchi (sels); Puritani (sels); G. Puccini:Turandot (sels); Verdi:Lombardi (sels); Luisa Miller (sels); Rigoletto (sels); Traviata (sels) RCAV (Gold Seal) ▲ 68014 (live) [ADD] (11.97)

E. Pinza (bass) ("Ezio Pinza: The Early Legendary Recordings") † Favorita (sels); V. Bellini:Norma (sels); Puritani (sels); Boito:Mefistofele (sels); G. Puccini:Bohème (sels); G. Rossini:Mosè in Egitto (sels); Verdi:Arias VOCA (Vocal Archives) ▲ 1132 (13.97)

R. Scotto (sop), A. Di Stazio (mez), L. Pavarotti (ten), P. Cappuccilli (bar), F. M. Prandelli (cnd), RAI Orch, RAI Chorus OPIT ▲ 54562 (6.97)

R. Scotto (sop), A. Di Stazio (mez), L. Pavarotti (ten), F. Molinari-Pradelli (cnd), Turin RAI SO *(rec Torino, Oct 10, 1967)* ("The Great Luciano Pavarotti") † Elisir d'amore (sels); V. Bellini:Puritani (sels); G. Puccini:Bohème (sels); Turandot (sels); G. Rossini:Stabat Mater; Verdi:Luisa Miller (sels); Rigoletto (sels) GDIS ▲ 63202 [ADD] (10.97)

B. R. Stees (bn), S. Norris (hp), R. Fusco (pno) [trans for bn, hp & pno] † Elisir d'amore (sels); Hérold:Zampa (ov); W. A. Mozart:Entführung aus dem Serail (sels); G. Rossini:Gazza ladra (sels); P. Tchaikovsky:Eugene Onegin (sels); Verdi:Trovatore (sels); R. Wagner:Tannhäuser (sels) CLAV ▲ 509815 (16.97)

G. D. Stefano (ten), R. Arié (bass), T. Serafin (cnd), Florence Maggio Musicale Orch—Fra poco a me ricovero; Tu che a Dio ("Opera Heroes: Giuseppe di Stefano") † Leoncavallo:Pagliacci (sels); P. Mascagni:Cavalleria rusticana (sels); G. Puccini:Arias; Verdi:Arias EMIC ▲ 66808 (m) [ADD/DDD] (11.97)

C. Studer (sop—Lucia), P. Domingo (ten—Edgardo), I. Marin (cnd), London SO—Ah! Verranno a te ("Domingo Duets") † Bizet:Carmen (sels); P. Mascagni:Cavalleria rusticana (sels); J. Offenbach:Contes d'Hoffmann (sels); G. Puccini:Manon Lescaut (sels); Tosca (sels); Verdi:Duets DEUT ▲ 47270 [ADD/DDD] (16.97)

J. Sutherland (sop) *(rec 1956-60)* ("Recitals") † V. Bellini:Norma (sels); G. F. Handel:Alcina (sels); J. Haydn:Arias; W. A. Mozart:Entführung aus dem Serail (sels); Exsultate, jubilate, K.165 BELV ▲ 7001 [ADD] (15.97)

J. Sutherland (sop), J. McDonald (sop), M. Elkins (mez), J. Bowman (ct), J. Gibin (ten), J. Rouleau (bass), Shaw (sgr), T. Serafin (cnd), Royal Opera House Orch Covent Garden, Royal Opera House Covent Garden Chorus † Emilia di Liverpool (sels) MYTO ▲ 91545 [ADD] (17.97)

R. A. Swenson (sop), N. Rescigno (cnd), London PO—Regnava nel silenzio; Quando rapito in estasi *(rec Nov 11-19, 1993)* ("Positively Golden") † Linda di Chamounix (sels); V. Bellini:Puritani (sels); Sonnambula (sels); Gounod:Roméo et Juliette (sels); Meyerbeer:Africaine (sels); Dinorah (sels); Huguenots (sels) EMIC ▲ 54827 [DDD] (16.97)

D. Takova (sop), M. Matakiev (cnd), Sofia SO—Regnava nel silenzio ("Opera Recital") † Anna Bolena (sels); V. Bellini:Puritani (sels); Sonnambula (sels); Delibes:Lakmé (sels); W. A. Mozart:Zauberflöte (sels); Rimsky-Korsakov:Golden Cockerel (sels); Verdi:Traviata (sels) GEGA ▲ 105 [DDD] (16.97)

L. Tetrazzini (sop)—Regnava nel silenzio; Quando rapito in estasi ("Luisa Tetrazzini: The London Recordings, Vol. 1 1907-14") † Linda di Chamounix (sels); V. Bellini:Puritani (sels); Sonnambula (sels); G. Rossini:Barbiere di Siviglia (sels); Semiramide (sels); Verdi:Arias VOCA (Vocal Archives) ▲ 1122 (13.97)

V. Zeani (sop), A. Kraus (ten), A. Zedda (cnd), Piacenza Theatre Orch—Lucia perdona; Ah! Verranno a te *(rec Italy, 1964)* ("Virginia Zeani") † Anna Bolena (sels); Elisir d'amore (sels); V. Bellini:Puritani (sels); F. Lehár:Lustige Witwe (sels); Verdi:Aida (sels); Don Carlos (sels); Forza del destino (sels) *(I text)* BONG (Il Mito Dell'Opera) ▲ 1060 [ADD] (16.97)

A. Vilumanis (cnd), Latvian National Opera Orch & Chorus, various artists † Bizet:Carmen (sels); Leoncavallo:Pagliacci (sels); P. Mascagni:Cavalleria rusticana (sels); Verdi:Ballo in maschera (sels); Nabucco (sels); Trovatore (sels); R. Wagner:Lohengrin (sels); Tannhäuser (sels) RIGA ▲ 7 (16.97)

various artists—Fra poco a me ricovero † Elisir d'amore (sels); P. Mascagni:Cavalleria rusticana (sels); G. Puccini:Fanciulla del West (sels); Madama Butterfly (sels); Tosca (sels); Verdi:Rigoletto (sels); Traviata (sels); Trovatore (sels) PEG ▲ 196 (5.97)

Lucrezia Borgia (opera in 3 acts) [lib Felice Romani after Hugo] (1833)

M. Caballé (sop), A. M. Rota (cta), G. Raimondi (ten), E. Flagello (bass), E. Gracis (cnd), La Scala Orch, La Scala Chorus [ITA] *(rec live, Mar 2, 1970)* † Lucrezia Borgia (sels) MYTO 2-▲ 90423 [ADD] (34.97)

Lucrezia Borgia (selections)

M. Caballé (sop) ("The Art of Montserrat Caballé") † V. Bellini:Norma (sels); Pirata (sels); G. Rossini:Donna del lago (sels); Verdi:Arias REPL (Butterfly) ▲ 31 [AAD]

L. Gencer (sop—Lucrezia), U. Grilli (ten—Gennaro), A. Camozzo (cnd), Bergamo Teatro Donizetti Orch *(rec live, Oct 4, 1971)* † Caterina Cornaro MYTO 2-▲ 92153 [ADD] (34.97)

L. Gencer (sop), G. Raimondi (ten), L. Roni (bass), E. Gracis (cnd), La Scala Orch, La Scala Chorus *(rec Mar 12, 1970 live)* † Lucrezia Borgia MYTO 2-▲ 90423 [ADD] (34.97)

S. Onegin (cta)—Il segreto per esser felici (Brindisi) [GER] *(rec 1911-24)* ("Vol. 1: 1911-1914") † Bizet:Carmen (sels); Kienzl:Evangelimann (sels); Saint-Saëns:Samson et Dalila (sels); Verdi:Aida (sels); Ballo in maschera (sels); Trovatore (sels); R. Wagner:Götterdämmerung (sels); Rheingold (sels) NIMB (Prima Voce) ▲ 7898 [ADD] (11.97)

D. Soffel (mez), G. Winbergh (ten), R. Bonynge (cnd), Swedish RSO ("Doris Soffel Sings Bel Canto") † V. Bellini:Norma (sels) CAPA ▲ 21601 (16.97)

Maria Padilla (opera in 3 acts) [lib Rossi after Ancelot] (1841)

L. McDonall (sop—Maria Padilla), D. Jones (mez—Ines Padilla), G. Clark (ten—Don Ruiz), C. D. Plessis (bar—Don Pedro), A. Francis (cnd), London SO, Geoffrey Mitchell Choir [ITA] *(rec at Henry Wood Hall London, June 1980)* OPR 3-▲ 6 (54.97)

Maria di Rohan (selections)

N. Miricioiu (sop), R. Blake (ten), G. Magee (bar), D. Parry (cnd), Philharmonia Orch † Ajo nell'imbrazzo (sels); Anna Bolena (sels); Caterina Cornaro (sels); Gianni di Calais (sels); Maria Stuarda (sels); Marino Faliero (sels); Pia de' Tolomei (sels); Ugo (sels) OPR ▲ 207 (18.97)

DONIZETTI, GAETANO (cont.)

Maria di Rohan (selections) (cont.)

K. Ricciarelli (sop), A. Cupido (ten), L. Nucci (bar), E. Inbal (cnd), Orch of Teatro La Fenice, Chorus of Teatro La Fenice OPIT ▲ 54558 (6.97)

Maria di Rohan (opera in 3 acts) [lib Salvadore Cammarano after Lockroy] (1843)

G. Gavazzeni (cnd), Venice Theater Orch, Venice Theater Chorus, R. Scotto (sop—Maria), E. Zilio (sop—Armando), U. Grilli (ten—Riccardo), R. Bruson (bar—Enrico), A. Cassis (bar—Visconte di Suze) *(rec Venice, Italy, Mar 1974)* MONM 2-▲ 10401 [ADD] (36.97)

E. Gruberová (sop), U. Precht (mez), O. Arévalo (ten), E. Kim (bar), E. Boncompagni (cnd), Vienna RSO, Vienna Concert Choir *(rec Vienna, Dec 1996)* NIGC 2-▲ 70567 (34.97)

Maria di Rudenz (opera in 3 acts) [lib Salvadore Cammarano] (1838)

N. Miricoiu (sop—Maria), R. Nathan (sop), B. Ford (ten—Enrico), R. McFarland (bar—Corrado), M. Hargreaves (bass), D. Parry (cnd), Philharmonia Orch OPR ▲ 16 (36.97)

Maria Stuarda (selections)

J. Carreras (ten), M. Mazzieri (bass), N. Santi (cnd), ORTF Lyric Orch *(rec Paris, Mar 26, 1972)* ("The Great José Carreras") † Tosti:Songs; Verdi:Ballo in maschera (sels); Lombardi (sels); Rigoletto (sels); Traviata (sels) GDIS ▲ 63203 [ADD] (10.97)

S. Ehrling (cnd), Royal Swedish Opera Orchestra, Royal Swedish Opera Chorus *(rec Ytterjärna, Sweden, Oct 1995)* ("The Most Beloved Opera Choruses") † Borodin:Prince Igor (Polovtsian Dances); Gounod:Faust (sels); P. Mascagni:Cavalleria rusticana (sels); Verdi:Aida (sels); Nabucco (sels); Traviata (sels); Trovatore (sels); R. Wagner:Fliegende Holländer (sels); Lohengrin (sels); Tannhäuser (sels) CAPA ▲ 21520 (16.97)

L. Gencer (sop), S. Verrett (mez), F. Tagliavini (ten), F. Molinari-Pradelli (cnd), Florence Maggio Musicale Orch, Florence Maggio Musicale Chorus *(rec May 2, 1967)* † Maria Stuarda MYTO 2-▲ 91137 [ADD] (34.97)

E. Gruberová (sop) ("Donizetti's Tudor Queens") † Anna Bolena (sels); Roberto Devereux (sels) NIGC ▲ 180560 (17.97)

N. Miricioiu (sop), R. Blake (ten), G. Magee (bar), D. Parry (cnd), Philharmonia Orch—Overture † Ajo nell'imbrazzo (sels); Anna Bolena (sels); Caterina Cornaro (sels); Gianni di Calais (sels); Maria di Rohan (sels); Marino Faliero (sels); Pia de' Tolomei (sels); Ugo (sels) OPR ▲ 207 (18.97)

Maria Stuarda (opera in 3 acts) [lib Bardari after Schiller] (1835)

M. Caballé (sop), S. Verrett (mez) ODRO 2-▲ 1163 (9.97)

M. Caballé (sop), S. Verrett (mez), O. Garaventa (ten), C. F. Cillario (cnd), La Scala Orch, La Scala Chorus [ITA] *(rec live Milan, Apr 20, 1971)* † Maria Stuarda (sels) MYTO 2-▲ 91137 [ADD] (34.97)

C. Mackerras (cnd), English National Opera Orch, C. Mackerras (cnd), English National Opera Chorus, R. Plowright (sop), J. Baker (mez), A. Opie (bar), J. Tomlinson (bass) [ENG] CHN 2-▲ 3017 (26.97)

Marino Faliero (selections)

N. Miricioiu (sop), R. Blake (ten), G. Magee (bar), D. Parry (cnd), Philharmonia Orch † Ajo nell'imbrazzo (sels); Anna Bolena (sels); Caterina Cornaro (sels); Gianni di Calais (sels); Maria di Rohan (sels); Maria Stuarda (sels); Pia de' Tolomei (sels); Ugo (sels) OPR ▲ 207 (18.97)

Les Martyrs (opera in 4 acts) [2nd version of Poliuto] (1840)

L. Gencer (sop), R. Cazzaniga (ten), O. D. Credico (ten), R. Bruson (bar), L. Roni (bass), A. Riva (bass), V. Sagona (bass), M. Di Felici (sgr), A. Camozzo (cnd), Bergamo Teatro Donizetti Orch, Bergamo Teatro Donizetti Chorus *(rec Bergamo, Sept 22, 1975)* † Lucia di Lammermoor (sels) MYTO 3-▲ 972154 (51.97)

Messa di Gloria e Credo for Voices, Orchestra & Chorus (1837)

H. Mané (sop), G. Vighi (mez), P. Maus (ten), M. Machì (bass), R. Bader (cnd), Berlin RSO, St. Hedwig's Cathedral Choir [LAT] KSCH ▲ 313031 [ADD] (16.97)

Music of Donizetti

E. Corsi (sop), S. Onegin (cta), F. Constantino (ten), C. Albani (ten), M. Renaud (sgr)—Lucrezia Borgia (sels); Dom Sébastien (sels); Poliuto (sels); Favorita (sels); Linda di Chamounix (sels) *(rec 1905-30)* ("Souvenirs of Donizetti Operas") IRCC ▲ 817

S. Frontalini (cnd), Moldava SO—Sinf in C; Sinf concertanta; Preludio funebre; Marino Faliero (sels) [Ov]; Enrico di Borbogna (sels) [Ov]; Gemma di Vergy (sels) [Ov] ("Sinfonias & Overtures from Operas") BONG ▲ 2139 (16.97)

Music for Piano 4-Hands

L. Kondratyeva (pno), R. Schmiedel (pno) ("The Complet Piano Duets") CPO 2-▲ 999163 [DDD] (14.97)

M. E. Sadun (pno), D. Manto (pno)—Pno Music 4-Hands ("Complete Works for Piano 4-Hands") AG ▲ 199 (36.97)

Olimpiade (incomplete opera) [rev Fabio Maestri]

S. Rigacci (sop), D. Broganelli (cta), F. Maestri (cnd), In Canto CO *(rec May 1991)* † Bella prigioniera; Pigmalione; Rita, or Le mari battu BONG 2-▲ 2109 [DDD] (32.97)

Olivo e Pasquale (opera buffa in 2 acts) [lib Ferretti after A. S. Sografi] (ca 1827)

Opera di Barga Chorus, B. Rigacci (cnd), Lucchese Polifonia, G. Sarti (bar), R. Gibbs (bar), J. Del Carlo (bass), Bizzo (sgr), Mastino (sgr) BONG 2-▲ 2005 (32.97)

B. Rigacci (cnd), Swiss-Italian Radio Orch, B. Rigacci (cnd), Swiss-Italian Radio Chorus, E. Czapó (sop), T. Rocchino (mez), B. Pecchioli (cta), M. Bolognese (ten), C. Gaifa (ten), G. Sarti (bass), G. Orlandini (bass), M. Chiappi (bass) *(rec 1980)* NUO ▲ 1112 (32.97)

Overtures

K. Arp (cnd), Southwest German RSO Baden-Baden—Don Pasquale (sels) [Overture]; Roberto Devereux (sels) [Ov] ("Overtures") † V. Bellini:Norma (ov); G. Rossini:Ovs; Verdi:Ovs & Preludes PVY ▲ 730050 (12.97)

S. Frontalini (cnd), Belgian RSO—Roberto Devereux (sels) [Ov]; Diluvio universale (sels) [Ov]; Betly (sels) [Ov]; Zoraida di Granata (sels) [Ov]; Gemma di Vergy (sels) [Ov]; Alina (sels) [Ov]; Follia (sels) [Ov]; Falegname di Livonia (sels) [Ov] BONG ▲ 2049 [DDD] (16.97)

Parafrasi del Christus for Soprano, Alto & String Orchestra [text S. Gatti] (1829; rev 1844)

M. Spindler (sop), G. Prochaska-Stolze (mez), L. Svárovský (cnd), Suk CO † Pergolesi:Stabat mater LT ▲ 13 [DDD] (16.97)

Parisina (opera in 3 acts) [lib Felice Romani after Byron] (1833)

S. Dorigo (sop), E. Belfiore (mez), A. Moretti (ten), C. Caruso (bar), D. Rocca (bass), P. Carignani (cnd), Lugo Teatro Rossini Orch, MASTER Choral Association *(rec live Lugo Teatro Rossini, Nov 1997) (E,I lib texts)* BONG 2-▲ 2212 [DDD] (32.97)

E. Queler (cnd), New York City Opera Orch, New York Opera Chorus, M. Caballé (sop), J. Pruett (ten), L. Quilico (bar), J. Morris (bass) *(rec New York, NY, 1974)* MYTO 2-▲ 984193 (34.97)

I pazzi per progetto (farce in 1 act) [lib Gilardoni] (1830)

S. Rigacci (sop), A. Cicogna (mez), G. Sarti (bar), G. Polidori (bar), E. Fissore (bass), V. M. Brunetti (bass), L. Monreale (bass), G. Micheli (cnd), Emilia Romagna Toscanini SO [ITA] *(rec live, Dec 1988)* BONG ▲ 2070 [DDD] (16.97)

Pia de' Tolomei (selections)

N. Miricioiu (sop), R. Blake (ten), G. Magee (bar), D. Parry (cnd), Philharmonia Orch † Ajo nell'imbrazzo (sels); Anna Bolena (sels); Caterina Cornaro (sels); Gianni di Calais (sels); Maria di Rohan (sels); Maria Stuarda (sels); Marino Faliero (sels); Ugo (sels) OPR ▲ 207 (18.97)

B. Rigacci (cnd), Orch of Swiss-Italian Radio & Television, Chorus of Swiss-Italian Radio & Television † E. de Cavalieri:Rappresentatione di Anima et di Corpo; Rappresentatione di Anima et di Corpo (sels) NUO ▲ 1001 (16.97)

Piano Music (complete)

P. Spada (pno)—Allegro Pno; La ricordanza; Larghetto in a; Motives (2) of the Celebrated Maestro Päer ("Complete Piano Music, Vol. 1") AART ▲ 47381 (10.97)

P. Spada (pno)—Fugue Pno; Pastorale Pno; Grande Offertorio; Vars Pno ("Complete Piano Music, Vol. 3") AART ▲ 47383 (10.97)

Il Pigmalione (opera in 1 act) (1816)

S. Rigacci (sop), P. Pellegrini (ten), F. Maestri (cnd), In Canto CO *(rec Sept 1990)* † Bella prigioniera; Olimpiade; Rita, or Le mari battu BONG 2-▲ 2109 [DDD] (32.97)

Il pirata (selections)

M. Callas (sop), A. Tonini (cnd), Philharmonia Orch—Tranquillo ei posa; Com'è bello *(rec 1953-69)* ("The EMI Rarities") † V. Bellini:Pirata (sels); W. A. Mozart:Don Giovanni (sels); G. Rossini:Arias; Verdi:Arias; C. M. von Weber:Oberon (sels) *([ENG,ITA]lib texts)* EMIC (Callas Edition) 2-▲ 66468 [ADD] (21.97)

Poliuto (opera in 3 acts) [lib Salvadore Cammarano after Corneille] (1848)

M. Callas (sop), F. Corelli (ten), E. Bastianini (bar), A. Votto (cnd), La Scala Orch, La Scala Chorus *(rec live Milan, 1960)* ENT (Documents) 2-▲ 977 (26.97)

M. Callas (sop—Paolina), F. Corelli (ten—Poliuto), P. D. Palma (ten—Nearco), E. Bastianini (bar—Severo), N. Zaccaria (bass—Callistene), A. Votto (cnd), La Scala Orch, La Scala Chorus *(rec Teatro alla Scala Milan, Dec 7, 1960)* EMIC (Callas Edition) 2-▲ 65448 [ADD] (23.97)

M. Gavazzeni (ten), J. Sempere (ten), E. D. Cesare (ten), S. Consolini (ten), I. D. Arcangelo (bass), G. Gavazzeni (cnd), Emilia Romagna Toscanini SO, Bergamo Teatro Donizetti Chorus BMGR (Ricordi) 2-▲ 2023

K. Ricciarelli (sop), J. Carreras (ten), J. Pons (bar), O. Caetani (cnd), Vienna SO, Vienna Chorus SNYC 2-▲ 44821 (32.97)

DONIZETTI, GAETANO (cont.)
Poliuto (selections)
A. Scampini (ten) *(rec 1908-13)* ("Augusto Scampini") † G. Pacini:Saffo (sels); G. Rossini:Guillaume Tell (sels); Verdi:Arias MNER ▲ 61 [ADD] (15.97)
Quartets for Strings
Revolutionary Drawing Room String Quartet—Introduzione; Qt 10 St; Qt 11 Strs; Qt 12 Strs *(rec Heathfield Church East Sussex, July 19-21, 1994)* CPO ▲ 999279 [DDD] (14.97)
Revolutionary Drawing Room String Quartet—Qt 13 Strs; Qt 14 Strs; Qt 15 Strs *(rec Heathfield Church East Sussex, Nov 18-24, 1994)* CPO ▲ 999280 [DDD] (13.97)
Requiem Mass for solo Voices, Orchestra & Chorus
G. Gavazzeni (cnd), Venice Theater Orch, E. Michalopoulos (cnd), Venice Theater Chorus, L. Gencer (sop), M. Pecile (mez), A. Moretti (ten), A. Cassis (bass) *(rec 1970)* † Pizzetti:Agamemnnone MONM 2-▲ 10201 (live) (36.97)
T. Sojat (sop), J. Horska-Maxova (mez), V. Giammarrusco (ten), Z. Hlavka (bar), M. Rosca (bass), A. Rahbari (cnd), Prague Virtuosi, Prague Chamber Choir DI ▲ 920519 [DDD] (5.97)
C. Studer (sop), H. Müller-Molinari (mez), A. Baldin (ten), J. P. Bogart (bass), J. Rootering (bass), M. A. Gómez-Martínez (cnd), Bamberg SO, Bamberg Sym Chorus [LAT] ORF ▲ 172881 [DDD] (18.97)
Rita, or Le mari battu (comic opera in 1 act) [lib Vaëz] (1841)
U. Benelli (ten), R. Franceschetto (bass), S. Figacci (sgr), G. Manini (sgr), F. Maestri (cnd), In Canto CO *(rec Sept 1990)* † Bella prigioniera; Olimpiade; Pigmalione BONG 2-▲ 2109 [DDD] (32.97)
Roberto Devereux (opera in 3 acts) [lib Salvadore Cammarano after Ancelot] (1837)
M. Caballé (sop), L. Londi (sop), M. D. Anna (bar), Raimondi (sgr), Badoer (cnd), Venice Theater Orch *(rec Feb 1972)* MONM 2-▲ 10161 (36.97)
L. Gencer (sop), P. Cappuccilli (bar) ODRO 2-▲ 1159 (9.97)
E. Gruberová (sop), D. Ziegler (mez), D. Bernardini (ten), E. Kim (sgr), F. Haider (cnd), Strasbourg PO, Rhine Opera Chorus NIGC 2-▲ 70563
Roberto Devereux (selections)
E. Gruberová (sop) ("Donizetti's Tudor Queens") † Anna Bolena (sels); Maria Stuarda (sels) NIGC ▲ 180560 (17.97)
Rosmonda d'Inghilterra (opera in 2 acts) [lib Romani] (1834)
R. Fleming (sop), N. Miricioiu (sop), D. Montague (mez), B. Ford (ten), A. Miles (bass), D. Parry (cnd), Philharmonia Orch, Geoffrey Mitchell Choir OPR ▲ 13 (36.97)
Rosmonda d'Inghilterra (selections)
B. Ford (ten), D. Parry (cnd), Philharmonia Orch ("Romantic Heroes") † Alfredo il grande (sels); Mercadante:Virginia (sels); Meyerbeer:Etoile du nord (sels); G. Pacini:Carlo di Borgogna (sels); F. Ricci:Il Marito e l'amante (sels); G. Rossini:Ricciardo e Zoraide (sels) OPR ▲ 202 (18.97)
Sinfonias (miscellaneous)
L. Kovács (cnd), Budapest Camerata—Sinf Ww; Sinf on the Death of A. Capuzzi *(rec Festetich Castle Budapest, June 5-11, 1994)* ("Instrumental Concerti") † Concertinos (misc) MARC ▲ 8223701 [DDD] (13.97)
Sonata for Flute & Harp
R. Aitken (fl), E. Goodman (hp) *(rec Castle Wik Sweden, June 2-4, 1979)* ("Flute & Harp") † A. Hovhaness:Garden of Adonis, Op. 245; Krumpholtz:Son Fl & Hp; L. Spohr:Son 3 Vn & Hp, Op. 113; Son 4 Vn & Hp, Op. 114; Son 5 Vn & Hp, Op. 115 BIS ▲ 143 [AAD] (17.97)
A. Korsakov (vn), V. Dulova (hp) *(rec 1979)* ("Vera Dulova: Russian Performing School") † C. R. G. Pascal:Con Hp; M. Ravel:Pavane pour une infante défunte; Saint-Saëns:Fant Vn RD (Talents of Russia) ▲ 16206 [AAD] (16.97)
H. Wegner (fl), E. Wegner (hp) *(rec June 1994)* ("All' Italiana") † Boccherini:Son Fl & Hp; Ciardi:Pifferaro, Op. 122; G. Rossini:Allegretto Hp; Andante e tema con variazioni Va; Son Hp; N. Rota:Sarabande & Toccata; Son Fl & Hp THOR ▲ 2243 [DDD] (16.97)
Sonata in C for Flute & Piano (1819)
Academic Chamber Ensemble † J. Haydn:Trio 8 Vns & Bc, H.V/G3; Martinů:Madrigal Son; A. Schnittke:Suite in the Old Style; C. M. von Weber:Trio Fl, Op. 63; Yordanov:Bonbonnière Fant GEGA ▲ 103 [DDD] (16.97)
Sonata for Oboe & Piano
T. Indermühle (ob), W. Genuit (pno) *(rec Vienna, Jan 31-Feb 1, 1994)* ("Italian Opera Fantasy") † Daelli:Fant on Verdi's Rigoletto; Lovreglio:Fant on themes from Verdi's Un ballo in masc; Pasculli:Con on La Favorita; Fant on Poliuto; Grand Con Ob; Ponchielli:Capriccio Ob & Pno CAMA ▲ 403 [DDD]
Sonata in G for Violin & Harp
Aurora Duo † Boren:Movts from Liturgical Dance; A. Hovhaness:Son Vn Hp, Op. 406; Lasala:Poema del Pastor Coya; Saint-Saëns:Fant Vn; Shaposhnikov:Son in d Vn 4TAY ▲ 4010 [DDD] (17.97)
Songs
C. Bartoli (mez), J. Levine (pno)—Il barcajuolo; Ah, rammenta, o bella Irene; Amore e morte; La conocchia; Me voglio fa' na' casa ("An Italian Songbook") † V. Bellini:Songs; G. Rossini:Songs PLON ▲ 455513 (17.97) ▮ 455513 (11.98)
I. Caddy (b-bar), S. Comberti (vc), A. Halstead (hn), M. Tan (pno)—Canto d'Ugolino; L'amor funesto; Trovatore in caricatura; Spirito di Dio; Viva il matrimonio; Le renégat; Noé, Scène du Déluge; Le départ pour la chasse; Un coeur pour abri; La hart *(rec Aug 1984 & Dec 1985)* MER ▲ 84183 (16.97)
I. Kertesi (sop), A. Ulbrich (mez), I. Prunyi (pno)—L'aurora; Il sospiro; E morta!; Il giuramento; La zingara; Il fiore; Le crépuscule; La lontananza; Ave Maria; Il pescatore; Il barcajuolo; L'inconstanza di Irene; L'alito di Bice; I bevitori; La ninna-nanna; Lu trademientu; Amor, voce del cielo; Uno sguardo ed una voce ("Songs & Duets") † G. Rossini:Soirées musicales HUN ▲ 31544 [DDD] (16.97)
O. Linsi (ten), C. Walton (pno)—Me voglio fa' na' casa; Il barcajuolo ("Vola, O Serenata") † Arias; G. Puccini:Arias; A. Rotoli:Songs; Tosti:Songs; Verdi:Arias GALL ▲ 886 [ADD] (19.97)
J. Polmear (hn/ob), D. Ambache (pno)—Il barcajuolo † Instrumental Music; Liszt:Trans, Arrs & Paraphrases; Pasculli:Con on La Favorita; Fant on Poliuto MER ▲ 84147 (16.97)
Study for Clarinet (1821)
J. Russo (cl) † Ewazen:Ballade; D. E. Jones:Still Voices; F. Martin:Ballade Fl; Piston:Con Cl; Con Fl; Presser:Partita Cl; G. Rossini:Vars Cl CRSR ▲ 8840
Torquato Tasso (opera in 3 acts) [lib Ferretti after Rosini] (1833)
L. Serra (sop), A. D. Auria (sop), N. Ciliento (mez), E. Palacio (ten), S. Alaimo (bar), R. Coviello (bar), A. Riva (bass), M. D. Bernart (cnd), Genoa Teatro Comunale Orch, Genoa Teatro Comunale Chorus [ITA] *(rec live, Oct 16, 1985)* BONG 3-▲ 2028 [DDD] (47.97)
Torquato Tasso (selections) (1833)
L. Aliberti (sop), R. Paternostro (cnd), Berlin RSO—Fatal! Goffredo *(rec Jesus Christ Church, Berlin, Germany, Aug 2-10, 1988)* † Anna Bolena (sels); Don Pasquale (sels); Fille du régiment (sels); V. Bellini:Capuleti e i Montecchi (sels); Puritani (sels) CAPO ▲ 10246 [DDD] (11.97)
Ugo, conte di Parigi (selections)
N. Miricioiu (sop), R. Blake (ten), G. Magee (bar), D. Parry (cnd), Philharmonia Orch—Ov † Ajo nell'imbrazzo (sels); Anna Bolena (sels); Caterina Cornaro (sels); Gianni di Calais (sels); Maria di Rohan (sels); Maria Stuarda (sels); Marino Faliero (sels); Pia de' Tolomei (sels) OPR ▲ 207 (18.97)
Ugo, conte di Parigi (opera in 2 acts) [lib Romani] (1832)
E. Harrhy (sop), Y. Kenny (sop), J. Price (sop), D. Jones (mez), M. Arthur (ten), C. D. Plessis (bar), A. Francis (cnd), New Philharmonia Orch, Geoffrey Mitchell Choir OPR 3-▲ 1 (54.97)

DOPPER, CORNELIS (1870-1939)
Ciaconna gotica for Orchestra (1920)
K. Bakels (cnd), Netherlands RSO *(rec 1994-95)* † Sym 7; Anrooy:Piet Hein Rhapsody NMCC ▲ 92060 [DDD] (17.97)
Symphony No. 7, "Zuiderzee" (1917)
K. Bakels (cnd), Netherlands RSO *(rec 1994-95)* † Ciaconna gotica; Anrooy:Piet Hein Rhapsody NMCC ▲ 92060 [DDD] (17.97)

DOPPLER, ALBERT FRANZ (1821-1883)
Andante & Rondo for 2 Flutes & Piano, Op. 25
J. Rampal (fl), C. Arimany (fl), J. S. Ritter (pno) *(rec Los Angeles, July 1996)* ("Romantic Music for 2 Flutes & Piano") † Duetto américain, Op. 37; Sonambula, Op. 42; T. Böhm:Duos de Mendelssohn & Lachner; L. Hughes:Grand Con Fant; Kuhlau:Grand Trio, Op. 119; W. A. Mozart:Son Pnos, K.448 DLS ▲ 3212 [DDD] (14.97)
Duetto américain for 2 Flutes & Piano, Op. 37 (1841)
J. Rampal (fl), C. Arimany (fl), J. S. Ritter (pno) *(rec Los Angeles, July 1996)* ("Romantic Music for 2 Flutes & Piano") † Andante & Rondo, Op. 25; Sonambula, Op. 42; T. Böhm:Duos de Mendelssohn & Lachner; L. Hughes:Grand Con Fant; Kuhlau:Grand Trio, Op. 119; W. A. Mozart:Son Pnos, K.448 DLS ▲ 3212 [DDD] (14.97)
Fantasie pastorale hongroise for Flute & Piano, Op. 26
R. Aitken (fl), P. Øien (fl), G. H. Braaten (pno), E. Westenholz (pno) ("The Virtuoso Flute") † T. Böhm:Grande polonaise, Op. 16; Kuhlau:Intro & Rondo on 'Ah! quand il gèle', Op. 98a; Paganini:Caprices Vn, M.S. 25; Saint-Saëns:Airs de ballet d'Ascanio; Taffanel:Fant on Freischütz BIS ▲ 166 (17.97)

DOPPLER, ALBERT FRANZ (cont.)
Fantasie pastorale hongroise for Flute & Piano, Op. 26 (cont.)
Ş. Kutluer (fl), N. Sultanov (pno) ("The Romantic Flute") † Debussy:Syrinx Fl; P. A. Genin:Carnival in Venice, Op. 14; Melikov:Fants of Komde; Morlacchi:Pastore Svizzero; F. Poulenc:Son Fl; Un:At the Tomb of Yunus GALL ▲ 810 [DDD] (19.97)
W. Tast (fl), S. Stöckigt (pno)—Andantino. Moderato; Allegro *(rec Dresden, Germany, Jan 1986)* ("Flute Music in the Salon") † T. Böhm:Fant on a Theme by Schubert Fl, Op. 21; F. Borne:Fant brillante sur Carmen; B. Godard:Suite de trois morceaux, Op. 116; Molique:Musical Sketches Vn, Op. 70; Suppé:Primo Amore BER ▲ 9298 [DDD] (10.97)
Music of Doppler
A. Adorján (fl), W. Bennett (fl), M. Larrieu (fl), A. Nicolet (fl), M. Adorján (fl), M. Bennett (fl), K. Debost (fl), M. Debost (fl), H. Hari (fl), V. Larrieu (fl), V. Haas (hp), S. Soltész (pno)—Andante & Rondo, Op. 25; Nocturne, Op. 19; Mazurka de Salon, Op. 16; La Sonnambula, Op. 42; Souvenir de Rigi, Op. 34; Fant Pastorale Hongroise, Op. 26 *(rec Apr 1984)* ("Doppleriade") † Fl Music (misc); K. Doppler:Csárdás ORF ▲ 154971 [DDD] (18.97)
La Sonambula, paraphrase en souvenir de Adelina Patti for 2 Flutes & Piano [after Bellini], Op. 42
J. Rampal (fl), C. Arimany (fl), J. S. Ritter (pno) *(rec Los Angeles, July 1996)* ("Romantic Music for 2 Flutes & Piano") † Andante & Rondo, Op. 25; Duetto américain, Op. 37; T. Böhm:Duos de Mendelssohn & Lachner; L. Hughes:Grand Con Fant; Kuhlau:Grand Trio, Op. 119; W. A. Mozart:Son Pnos, K.448 DLS ▲ 3212 [DDD] (14.97)
Wallachian Airs for Flute & Piano, Op. 10
C. Régimbald (fl), C. Webster (pno) ("The Virtuoso Flute") † F. Borne:Fant brillante sur Carmen; Demersseman:Homage to Tulou, Op. 43; M. A. Reichert:Melancholy Fant, Op. 1; Tulou:Great Solo 13 Fl SNE ▲ 604 (16.97)

DOPPLER, ALBERT FRANZ (1821-1883)**& KARL DOPPLER** (1825-1900)
Flute Music (miscellaneous)
A. Adorján (fl), W. Bennett (fl), M. Larrieu (fl), A. Nicolet (fl), M. Adorján (fl), M. Bennett (fl), K. Debost (fl), M. Debost (fl), H. Hari (fl), V. Larrieu (fl), V. Haas (hp), S. Soltész (pno)—Fant sur les Motifs Hongrois, Op. 35; Rigoletto-Fant, Op. 38; Valse di Bravura, Op. 33 *(rec Apr 1984)* ("Doppleriade") † Music of Doppler; K. Doppler:Csárdás ORF ▲ 154971 [DDD] (18.97)
Music for Flute (or 2 Flutes) & Piano
R. Aitken (fl), P. Øien (fl), G. H. Braaten (pno) BIS 2-▲ 145 (69.97)
Souvenir de Prague for 2 Flutes & Piano, Op. 24
W. Schulz (fl), F. Bognár (pno) CAMA ▲ 519 [DDD] (18.97)

DOPPLER, KARL (1825-1900)
Csárdás for Flute Ensemble
A. Adorján (fl), W. Bennett (fl), M. Larrieu (fl), A. Nicolet (fl), M. Adorján (fl), M. Bennett (fl), K. Debost (fl), M. Debost (fl), H. Hari (fl), V. Larrieu (fl), V. Haas (hp), S. Soltész (pno) *(rec Apr 1984)* ("Doppleriade") † A. F. Doppler:Fl Music (misc); Music of Doppler ORF ▲ 154971 [DDD] (18.97)

DORAN, MATT (1921-
Movements (4) for Double Bassoon & Piano
S. Nigro (ctbn), M. Lindeblad (pno) *(rec Chicago)* ("Susan Nigro & the Big Bassoon") † Draganski:Heart's Desire; Muradian:Con Ctbn, Op. 86; R. Nicholson:Miniature Suite Ctbn; Palider:Narwhal, Op. 11; F. Warren:Music for Ctbn, Op. 28 CRYS ▲ 346 (15.97)
Poem for Flute & Piano
Aguilar-Delgado Duo † P. Juon:Son Fl; Kuhlau:Sons Fl, Op. 83; A. Molina:Gigue; Sarabande; H. Smith:Faces of Jazz PROT ▲ 2201 [DDD] (19.97)
Sonatina for Oboe & Piano (1982)
E. McCarty (ob), I. Delgado (pno) *(rec Boston, United States of America, Feb 26-27, 1994)* ("Gems for Oboe & Piano") † J. Madden:Songs of Sadness; Rubbra:Son C Ob, Op. 100; Son Ob; E. Schelling:Impressions from an Artist's Life; Nocturne (Ragusa); L. Sinigaglia:Var(s) on Schubert Ob & Pno, Op. 19; Widerkehr:Duo Ob; Duo Pno Orch BOST ▲ 1012 [DDD] (15.97)

DORÁTI, ANTAL (1906-1988)
Duo Concertante for Oboe & Piano (1983)
N. A. King (ob), A. Kuznetsov (pno) ("The Winning Program") † Daelli:Fant on Verdi's Rigoletto; Dring:3 Piece Suite; L. Singer:Memories; Telemann:Kleine Kammermusik BOST ▲ 1019 (15.97)
Jesus oder Barabbas? (melodrama) for Speaker, Orchestra & Choir [after a story by Frigyes Karinthy] (1987)
W. Quadflieg (nar), M. Fischer-Dieskau (cnd), New Berlin CO, Berlin HDK Chamber Choir [GER] *(rec live, 1992)* † Pater Noster; B. Bartók:Divert Strs, Sz.113; Martinů:Concertino Pno BIS ▲ 578 [DDD] (17.97)
Night Music for Flute & Orchestra (1968)
A. Young (fl), C. A. Johnson (cnd), Bohuslav Martinů PO *(rec Zlín, Czech Republic, Jan 1998)* ("Music for All Time") † D. Diamond:Con Fl; Krenek:Suite Fl, Op. 147; B. Rogers:Soliloquy 1 ALBA ▲ 308 [DDD] (16.97)
Pater Noster (prayer) for Mixed Choir (1988)
C. Grube (cnd), Berlin HDK Chamber Choir *(rec live, 1992)* † Jesus oder Barabbas?; B. Bartók:Divert Strs, Sz.113; Martinů:Concertino Pno BIS ▲ 578 [DDD] (17.97)
Symphony No. 1
A. Dorati (cnd), Stockholm PO *(rec 1972)* † Sym 2 BIS ▲ 408 [ADD] (17.97)
Symphony No. 2, "Querela Pacis"
A. Dorati (cnd), Stockholm PO *(rec 1988)* † Sym 1 BIS ▲ 408 [ADD] (17.97)

DORFF, DANIEL (1956-
Sonatina d'Amore for Contrabassoons
S. Nigro (bn), B. Lane (bn) † M. Curtis:Impish Imp; W. A. Mozart:Duo Bn Vc, K.292; Ozi:Son Bns; Vanhal:Con Bns; A. Weisberg:From the Deep CRYS ▲ 349 (15.97)

DØRGE, PIERRE (1946-
Struthio Camelus (3 free pieces) for 2 Guitars
Danish Guitar Duo ("Night Birds: Contemporary Guitar Music") † J. Frandsen:Twilight; S. Nielsen:Barcarole Gtr; W. Siegel:Canons Gtrs PONT ▲ 5120 [DDD]

DORNEL, LOUIS-ANTOINE (ca 1680-after 1756)
Concerts en trio (6) for Flutes, Violins, Oboes & Continuo (ca 1723)
Tripla Concordia *(rec Feb 1998)* ("Concertos & Sonatas") † Suites en trio & Son, Op. 1; Boismortier:Sons, Op. 34; Trio Sons, Op. 37 DYNC ▲ 198 [DDD] (17.97)
Sonatas (8) for Violin & Suites (4) for Flute & Continuo, Op. 2
Le Salon de Mars—Suite No. 1 in G; Suite No. 2 in b; Suite No. 3 in e; Suite No. 4 in D *(rec Oct 1997)* † Suites en trio & Son, Op. 1 BONG ▲ 5084 [DDD] (16.97)
M. Rasmussen (vl), D. Laurin (rcr), L. Meyer (hpd) *(rec Furuby Church Sweden, May 8-11, 1995)* ("The French King's Flautists") † Blavet:Sonatas for Transverse Flute & Continuo; J. D. Braun:Son Terza; Hotteterre:Première livre de pièce, Op. 5; J.-M. Leclair:Sons Vn (books 1-4) BIS ▲ 745 [DDD] (17.97)
Suites en trio (6) & Sonate à 4 for Flutes, Violins, Oboes & Continuo, Op. 1 (ca 1709)
Le Salon de Mars—Suite No. 1 in g *(rec Oct 1997)* † Sons Vn & Suites Fl, Op. 2 BONG ▲ 5084 [DDD] (16.97)
Tripla Concordia *(rec Feb 1998)* ("Concertos & Sonatas") † Concerts en trio; Boismortier:Sons, Op. 34; Trio Sons, Op. 37 DYNC ▲ 198 [DDD] (17.97)

DOSTAL, NICO (1895-1981)
Clivia (selections)
S. Barabas (sop), H. Hoppe (ten), W. Schubert (cnd), Graunke SO, Bavarian Radio Chorus † Ungarische Hochzeit (sels); Fall:Liebe Augustin (sels) EMPE ▲ 86352 (11.97)
Die ungarische Hochzeit (selections)
S. Barabas (sop), H. Hoppe (ten), W. Schubert (cnd), Graunke SO, Bavarian Radio Chorus † Clivia (sels); Fall:Liebe Augustin (sels) EMPE ▲ 86352 (11.97)

DOTZAUER, FRIEDRICH (1783-1860)
Canon in G for 2 Violins
V. Beths (vn), L. Rautenberg (vn) *(rec New York City, Jan 19-22, 1994)* † Etudes Vc; Pieces Vc, Op. 104; Qnt Strs, Op. 134 SNYC (Vivarte) ▲ 64307 [DDD] (16.97)
Etudes (3) for solo Cello
A. Bylsma (vc) *(rec New York City, Jan 19-22, 1994)* † Canon for 2 Vns; Pieces Vc, Op. 104; Qnt Strs, Op. 134 SNYC (Vivarte) ▲ 64307 [DDD] (16.97)
Pieces (6) for 3 Cellos, Op. 104
K. Slowik (vc), A. Bylsma (vc), S. Doane (vc) *(rec New York City, Jan 19-22, 1994)* † Canon for 2 Vns; Etudes Vc; Qnt Strs, Op. 134 SNYC (Vivarte) ▲ 64307 [DDD] (16.97)
Potpourri for Cello & Guitar, Op. 21
M. K. Jones (vc), A. Maruri (gtr) ("Original Romantic Music for Cello & Guitar") † L. von Call:Serenade Vc Gtr, Op. 99; Serenade Vn Gtr, Op. 84; Matiegka:Potpourri on a Form of Serenade, Op. 30 EMEC ▲ 21 (14.97)
Quartet for Strings, Op. 64
V. Beths (vn), J. Gatwood (vn), L. Rautenberg (va), A. Bylsma (vc) *(rec New York City, NY, Jan 19-22, 1994)* † W. A. Mozart:Qnt Strs, K.515; Qnt Strs, K.516 SNYC ▲ 66259 [DDD] (16.97)

▲ = CD ♦ = Enhanced CD △ = MD ▮ = Cassette Tape ▯ = DCC

DOTZAUER, FRIEDRICH (cont.)

Quintet in d for Strings, Op. 134

V. Beths (vn), J. Gatwood (vn), L. Rautenberg (va), K. Slowik (vc), A. Bylsma (vc) *(rec New York City, Jan 19-22, 1994)* † Canon for 2 Vns; Etudes Vc; Pieces Vc, Op. 104 SNYC (Vivarte) ▲ 64307 [DDD] (16.97)

DOUNO, BEINSA (1864-1944)

Music of Douno

B. Brown (fl), D. Bell (hp) *(Izgryava Slunteseto)*, O. Nicolor (ten), D. Bell (hp) *(Vehadi; Kiamen Zenu)*, D. Bell (hp) *(Gospodi, Kolko Te Obicham) (rec England)* † D. Bell:Music of Bell ATH ▲ 14 [DDD] (18.97)

DOW, DANIEL (1732-1783)

Violin & Piano Music

L. Risk (fid), J. Schwab (pno)—Lady Jean Lindsay's Minuet *(rec Troy, NY, Apr 1998)* † W. Forbes:Vn & Pno Music; MacCrimmon:Vn & Pno Music; McGibbon:Vn & Pno Music; H. Purcell:Vn & Pno Music; Traditional:Vn & Pno Music DOR ▲ 90264 [DDD] (16.97)

DOWLAND, JOHN (1563-1626)

Consort Music

J. Feldman (sop), R. Lislevand (gtr/lt/gtr/lt), S. Marq (rcr) *(Lachrimae, or Seaven Teares [The Earl of Essex his Galiard])*, J. Feldman (sop), R. Lislevand (gtr/lt), S. Marq (rcr) *(Can she excuse my wrongs, P42; Second Booke of Songs or Ayres)* † Eyck:Fluyten Lust-Hof ASTR ▲ 8588 (18.97)

G. Weigand (cnd) —Lachrimae, or Seaven Teares [Mr. John Lanton's Pavan; The King of Denmark's Galiard; The Earl of Essex his Galiard] ("Consort Music of the English Renaissance") † Holborne:Instrumental Consort Music MER ▲ 84256

Dances for Lute

R. Spencer (lt) HMA ▲ 1901076 (9.97)

The First Booke of Songs or Ayres for Voice (or Voices) & Lute (1597)

P. Agnew (ten), C. Wilson (lt) ("Flow My Teares: John Dowland") † 2nd Booke of Songs or Ayres MENO ▲ 1010 [DDD] (20.97)

Deller Consort, A. Deller (ct)—Wilt thou unkind thus reave me of my hart; Awake Sweet Love, Thou Art Returnd; If my complaints could passions move; Sleepe wayward thoughts; Come Againe Sweet Love Doth Now Envite; Can she excuse my wrongs *(rec Vienna, Austria, 1966)* ("Awake Sweet Love: Airs & Partsongs") † Galliards; Pilgrimes Solace; Second Booke of Songs or Ayres; Songs; Third & Last Booke of Songs or Ayres VC ▲ 8112 [ADD] (13.97)

C. Högman (voc), J. Lindberg (lt)—Can she excuse my wrongs; Deare if you change Ile never chuse againe; His golden locks time hath to silver turnd *(rec Wik's Castle, Sweden, Dec 1983)* ("Faire, Sweet & Cruell") † In Darknesse Let Me Dwell; Third & Last Booke of Songs or Ayres; T. Campion:First Book of Ayres; Fourth Book of Ayres; Second Book of Ayres; Danyel:Like as the Lute; T. Ford:Faire Sweet Cruell; Pilkington:Rest Sweet Nimphs; Traditional:Greensleeves BIS ▲ 257 [DDD] (17.97)

R. Müller (ten), C. Wilson (lt) ASV (Gaudeamus) ▲ 135 [DDD] (16.97)

Robert DeCormier Singers, J. Baird (sop), D. Tayler (lt/orpharion/lt/orph)—Awake Sweet Love, Thou Art Returnd; Away with these selfe loving lads; His golden locks time hath to silver turnd; If my complaints could passions move; All ye whom love or fortune hath betraide; Come Againe Sweet Love Doth Now Envite; Now, O now I needs must part; Thinkst thou then by thy fayning *(rec Jan 1991)* † In Darknesse Let Me Dwell; Lachrimae, P15; Lt Music; Pilgrimes Solace; Second Booke of Songs or Ayres; Third & Last Booke of Songs or Ayres ARA ▲ 6622 [DDD] (16.97)

Galliards

E. Comparone (hpd), Queen's Chamber Band—Lachrimae, or Seaven Teares [The King of Denmark's Galiard; The Earl of Essex his Galiard] ("Viva Italia!") † Pavanes; J. Christian Bach:Qnts Fl; Brioschi:Ov 4; Gorzanis:Primo libro di napolitane Ct; G. F. Handel:Giulio Cesare in Egitto (sels); Monteverdi:Scherzi musicali (3) Voices 4TAY ▲ 4011 [DDD] (17.97)

D. Dupré (lt)—Queene Elizabeth her Galliard, P41 *(rec Vienna, Austria, 1966)* ("Awake Sweet Love: Airs & Partsongs") † First Booke of Songs or Ayres; Pilgrimes Solace; Second Booke of Songs or Ayres; Songs; Third & Last Booke of Songs or Ayres VC ▲ 8112 [ADD] (13.97)

A. Lawrence-King (hp)—Frog Galliard; Susanna Galliard † Lt Music; Music of Dowland; Second Booke of Songs or Ayres; Songs; Anonymous:Scott's Lament; W. Byrd:Music of Byrd; Le Flelle:Music of Le Flelle; MacDermott:King's Musicon DEHA ▲ 77504 (16.97)

K. Scheit (gtr), H. Tachezi (bc)—King of Denmark his Galliard, P40; Lachrimae, or Seaven Teares [Captain Digorie Piper His Galliard] *(rec Baumgartner Kasino Vienna, Germany, Jan 12-13 & 18, June 23, 1961)* ("The Virtuoso Guitar, Vol. 2") † F. Carulli:Con Gtr; Torelli:Con Vn Gtr; Vivaldi:Con Lt Vns, RV.93; Con Va Lt, RV.540 VC ▲ 1020 [ADD] (13.97)

In Darknesse Let Me Dwell for solo Voice & Lute

C. Högman (voc), J. Lindberg (lt) *(rec Wik's Castle, Sweden, Dec 1983)* ("Faire, Sweet & Cruell") † First Booke of Songs or Ayres; Third & Last Booke of Songs or Ayres; T. Campion:First Book of Ayres; Fourth Book of Ayres; Second Book of Ayres; Danyel:Like as the Lute; T. Ford:Faire Sweet Cruell; Pilkington:Rest Sweet Nimphs; Traditional:Greensleeves BIS ▲ 257 [DDD] (17.97)

Robert DeCormier Singers, J. Baird (sop), D. Tayler (lt/orpharion) *(rec Jan 1991)* † First Booke of Songs or Ayres; Lachrimae, P15; Lt Music; Pilgrimes Solace; Second Booke of Songs or Ayres; Third & Last Booke of Songs or Ayres ARA ▲ 6622 [DDD] (16.97)

Keyboard Music

J. Payne (hpd)—Lachrimae, P15 *(rec Forde Estate, Boston, MA, May & Aug, 1991)* ("The Queenes Command") † J. Bull:Kbd Music; W. Byrd:Kbd Music; Masks (5) Kbd; G. Farnaby:Kbd Music; C. Gibbons:Kbd Music; O. Gibbons:Kbd Music; Masks (5) Kbd; Tisdale:Kbd Music BIS ▲ 539 [DDD] (17.97)

Lachrimae (pavan) for Lute, P15

D. Tayler (lt) *(rec Jan 1991)* † First Booke of Songs or Ayres; In Darknesse Let Me Dwell; Lt Music; Pilgrimes Solace; Second Booke of Songs or Ayres; Third & Last Booke of Songs or Ayres ARA ▲ 6622 [DDD] (16.97)

Lachrimae, or Seaven Teares for 5 Viols (or Violins) & Lute (1604)

R. Festa (cnd), Daedalus Ensemble *(rec France, April 1998)* ("The Anatomy of Melancholy") † Cazzati:Varri, e diversi capricci per camera e per chiesa, Op. 50; Frescobaldi:Capricci Kbd; F. S. Romano:Soprano scherza col cromatico; G. Salvatore:Durezze e ligarure; Trabaci:Music of Trabaci ACCE ▲ 98128 [DDD] (17.97)

J. Lindberg (cnd) BIS ▲ 315 [DDD] (17.97)

P. O'Dette (lt), P. Holman (cnd), Parley of Instruments [period instrs] HYP ▲ 66637 (18.97)

J. Savall (cnd) ASTR ▲ 8701 [DDD] (18.97)

C. Trevor (alt), J. Heringman (lt), Rose Consort of Viols AMON ▲ 55 [DDD] (16.97)

Lute Music

M. A. Girollet (gtr)—Fant Lt; Earl of Essex, His Galliard, P42a; Lachrimae, or Seaven Teares; Sir John Smith his Almain, P47; Melancholy Gaillard, P25 ("Baroque Music for Guitar") † J. S. Bach:Suite Lt, BWV 995; Frescobaldi:Aria detta "La Frescobalda" OTR ▲ 1006 [DDD] (18.97)

K. Heindel (lt) ("Mr. John Langston's Pavan") GAS ▲ 275 (16.97)

A. Lawrence-King (hp)—Fancy Lt, P73; My Lady Hunsdon's Almain, P54 † Galliards; Music of Dowland; Second Booke of Songs or Ayres; Songs; Anonymous:Scott's Lament; W. Byrd:Music of Byrd; Le Flelle:Music of Le Flelle; MacDermott:King's Musicon DEHA ▲ 77504 (16.97)

A. Leonard (gtr)—Shomaker's Wife, a Toy, P58; George Aloe; Fant Lt *(rec Cambridge, MA, May 1996)* ("Music of the Ages") † J. S. Bach:Sons & Partitas Vn; Suites Vc; A. Piazzolla:Milonga del angel; Muerte del angel; Sor:Intro & Vars on "Gentil Housard", Op. 27; Intro & Vars on "Malborough", Op. 28; A. York:Sunburst ACTR ▲ 60101 [DDD] (16.97)

J. Lindberg (lt)—Frog Galliard; Lachrimae, P15; Sir John Smith his Almain, P47; Resolution, P13; King of Denmark his Galliard, P40; Fant Lt, P6; Right Honourable the Lord Viscount Lisle his Gaill, P38; Shomaker's Wife, a Toy, P58; My Lady Hunsdon's Almain, P54; Mrs. Vaux's Jig, P57; Mrs. Brigide Fleetwood's Pavan als Solus Sine Sola, P11; Mignarda, P34; Orlando sleepeth, P61; Can she excuse, P42; Winter Jomps, P55; My Lord Willoughby's Welcome Home, P66; Melancholy Gaillard, P25; Fancy Lt, P73; Dream; Wallsingham, P67; Semper Dowland semper dolens, P9; Mr. Knight's Galliard, P36; Farewell; Tarletones riserrectione, P59 *(rec 1994)* ("Selected Lute Music") BIS ▲ 824 [DDD] (17.97)

M. Lonardi (lt) [31 sels] AG ▲ 124 (18.97)

R. McFarlane (lt)—Sir John Smith his Almain, P47; Lachrimae, or Seaven Teares; My Lord Willoughby's Welcome Home, P66; Melancholy Gaillard, P25; My Lady Hunsdon's Almain, P54; Piper's Pavan, P8; Earl of Essex, His Galliard, P42a; Fant Lt, P1; Fortune my foe, P62; Lady Laiton's Almain, P48a; Lachrimae, P15; Queene Elizabeth her Galliard, P41; Tarletones riserrectione, P59; Winter Jomps, P55; Preludium Lt; Dowland's Galliard, P20; Go from my window, P64; Douland's Rounde Battele Galliard, P39; What is a day, P79; Shomaker's Wife, a Toy, P58; Fant Lt, P5; Mr. Dowland's Midnight; Dr. Case's Pavan, P12; Orlando sleepeth, P61; Lady Clifton's Spirit, P45; Semper Dowland semper dolens, P9; Frog Galliard; Mrs. Whitte's Nothing, P56 DOR ▲ 90148 [DDD] (16.97)

P. O'Dette (lt/orpharion) ("Complete Lute Works, Vol. 1") HAM ▲ 907160 (18.97)

P. O'Dette (lt) ("Complete Lute Works, Vol. 2") HAM ▲ 907161 (18.97)

P. O'Dette (lt) ("Complete Lute Works, Vol. 3") HAM ▲ 907162 (18.97)

DOWLAND, JOHN (cont.)

Lute Music (cont.)

P. O'Dette (lt) ("Complete Lute Works, Vol. 4") HAM ▲ 907163 (18.97)

P. O'Dette (lt) ("Complete Lute Works, Vol. 5") HAM ▲ 907164 (18.97)

P. O'Dette (lt/orpharion) ("Complete Lute Works, Vols. 1-5") HAM 5-▲ 2907160 (69.97)

R. Spencer (lt) ("Come Again, Sweet Love") † Songs HAM ▲ 790245 (12.97)

D. Tayler (lt)—Tarletones riserrectione, P59 *(rec Jan 1991)* † First Booke of Songs or Ayres; In Darknesse Let Me Dwell; Lachrimae, P15; Pilgrimes Solace; Second Booke of Songs or Ayres; Third & Last Booke of Songs or Ayres ARA ▲ 6622 [DDD] (16.97)

Virelai—La Mia Barbara, P95; Lachrimae, or Seaven Teares; Frog Galliard; Lord Strangs March, P65; Second Booke of Songs or Ayres [Fine knacks for ladies, cheap, choice, braue and new]; Mrs Nichols Almand, P52; Fant Lt *(rec Toddington, Gloucestershire, England, June 1996 & Jan-Feb 1997)* † Songs VCL ▲ 45288 (16.97)

Music of Dowland

A. Lawrence-King (hp)—Tarleton's Jigg; Mrs. Winter's Jump; Tarletones riserrectione, P59 † Galliards; Lt Music; Second Booke of Songs or Ayres; Songs; Anonymous:Scott's Lament; W. Byrd:Music of Byrd; Le Flelle:Music of Le Flelle; MacDermott:King's Musicon DEHA ▲ 77504 (16.97)

A. Rooley (cnd), Consort of Musicke PLOI 12-▲ 452563 (80.97)

Pavanes

E. Comparone (hpd), Queen's Chamber Band—Pavan Ob ("Viva Italia!") † Galliards; J. Christian Bach:Qnts Fl; Brioschi:Ov 4; Gorzanis:Primo libro di napolitane Ct; G. F. Handel:Giulio Cesare in Egitto (sels); Monteverdi:Scherzi musicali (3) Voices 4TAY ▲ 4011 [DDD] (17.97)

A Pilgrimes Solace (songs) for Voices & Lute (1612)

Robert DeCormier Singers, J. Baird (sop), D. Tayler (lt/orpharion)—Tell me, true Love *(rec Jan 1991)* † First Booke of Songs or Ayres; In Darknesse Let Me Dwell; Lachrimae, P15; Lt Music; Second Booke of Songs or Ayres; Third & Last Booke of Songs or Ayres ARA ▲ 6622 [DDD] (16.97)

H. Sheppard (sop), A. Deller (ct), V. Redtenbacher (vn), B. Reichert (va da gamba)—Go nightly cares, the enemy to rest; If that a sinner sighes *(rec Vienna, Austria, 1966)* ("Awake Sweet Love: Airs & Partsongs") † First Booke of Songs or Ayres; Galliards; Second Booke of Songs or Ayres; Songs; Third & Last Booke of Songs or Ayres VC ▲ 8112 [ADD] (13.97)

The Second Booke of Songs or Ayres for Voice & Lute (1600)

P. Agnew (ten), C. Wilson (lt)—Second Booke of Songs or Ayres [Flow my teares fall from your springs; If fluds of teares could clense my follies past; Fine knacks for ladies, cheap, choice, braue and new; I saw my lade weepe; Tymes eldest sonne, old age the heire of ease; Then sit thee down and say thy Nunc demittis; When others sing Venite exultemus; Come ye heavy states of night; Shall I sue, shall I seeke for grace?; Sorrow sorrow stay, lend true repentant teares] ("Flow My Teares: John Dowland") † First Booke of Songs or Ayres MENO ▲ 1010 [DDD] (20.97)

Deller Consort, A. Deller (ct)—Sorrow sorrow stay, lend true repentant teares; Fine knacks for ladies, cheap, choice, braue and new; Flow my teares fall from your springs *(rec Vienna, Austria, 1966)* ("Awake Sweet Love: Airs & Partsongs") † First Booke of Songs or Ayres; Galliards; Pilgrimes Solace; Songs; Third & Last Booke of Songs or Ayres VC ▲ 8112 [ADD] (13.97)

A. Lawrence-King (hp)—Fine knacks for ladies, cheap, choice, braue and new † Galliards; Lt Music; Music of Dowland; Songs; Anonymous:Scott's Lament; W. Byrd:Music of Byrd; Le Flelle:Music of Le Flelle; MacDermott:King's Musicon DEHA ▲ 77504 (16.97)

Robert DeCormier Singers, J. Baird (sop), D. Tayler (lt/orpharion/lt/orph)—I saw my lade weepe; Mourne, mourne, day is with darknesse fled; Fine knacks for ladies, cheap, choice, braue and new; O sweet woods, the delight of solitarinesse; Tosse not my soule *(rec Jan 1991)* † First Booke of Songs or Ayres; In Darknesse Let Me Dwell; Lachrimae, P15; Lt Music; Pilgrimes Solace; Third & Last Booke of Songs or Ayres ARA ▲ 6622 [DDD] (16.97)

Songs

P. Agnew (ten), C. Wilson (lt)—Third & Last Booke of Songs or Ayres; Pilgrimes Solace ("In Darknesse Let Me Dwell") † R. Dowland:Songs MENO ▲ 1011 [DDD] (20.97)

B. Asawa (ct), D. Tayler (lt)—First Booke of Songs or Ayres [Come Againe Sweet Love Doth Now Envite; His golden locks time hath to silver turnd; Can she excuse my wrongs; Go christall teares; Away with these selfe loving lads]; Second Booke of Songs or Ayres [Flow my teares fall from your springs; Sorrow sorrow stay, lend true repentant teares; A shepherd in a shade his plaining made; I saw my lade weepe]; Third & Last Booke of Songs or Ayres [It was a time when silly bees could speake; Time stands still] *(rec Jan 1997)* ("The Dark Is My Delight") † T. Campion:Discription of a Maske; First Book of Ayres; Songs (21); Third Book of Ayres RCAV (Red Seal) ▲ 68818 [DDD] (16.97)

J. Bream (lt)—Wallsingham, P67; Go from my window, P64; Robin, P70; Loth to departe, P69; Fant Lt; Farewell † W. Byrd:Lt Music; Cutting:Lt Music; Francesco Canova da Milano:Lt Music; Holborne:Lt Music RCAV ▲ 61587 (11.97)

C. Daniels (ten), D. Miller (lt)—Pilgrimes Solace [Sweet stay a while, why will you rise?; Thou mighty God; When David's life by Saul was often sought; When the poore Criple]; Second Booke of Songs or Ayres [Cleare or cloudie sweet as Aprill showring; I saw my lade weepe; Flow my teares fall from your springs; Shall I sue, shall I seeke for grace?; Now cease my wandring eyes]; First Booke of Songs or Ayres [Come away, come sweet love; All ye whom love or fortune hath betraide; Come heavy sleepe]; Semper Dowland semper dolens, P9; Third & Last Booke of Songs or Ayres [I must complaine, yet do enjoy; What poore astronomers are they; Flow not so fast yee fountaines; Me, me and none but me]; Earl of Essex, His Galliard, P42a; Fant Lt *(rec Jan 1997)* ("Sweet Stay Awhile") EMIC (Debut) ▲ 72266 [DDD] (6.97)

A. Deller (ct)—In Darknesse Let Me Dwell *(rec Vienna, Austria, 1966)* ("Awake Sweet Love: Airs & Partsongs") † First Booke of Songs or Ayres; Galliards; Pilgrimes Solace; Second Booke of Songs or Ayres; Third & Last Booke of Songs or Ayres VC ▲ 8112 [ADD] (13.97)

A. Deller (ct), R. Spencer (lt) ("Come Again, Sweet Love") † Lt Music HAM ▲ 790245 (12.97)

D. Dupré (lt), Saltire Singers ("Music of Love & Friendship") LYR (Early Music) 2-▲ 8031 [ADD] (16.97)

A. Lawrence-King (hp)—Lachrimae, P15; Can she excuse, P42; Robin, P70; Awake, Sweet Love Thou Art Returned; Go Christal Teares; My thoughts are winged; Semper Dowland semper dolens, P9; Farewell; My dear adieu † Galliards; Lt Music; Music of Dowland; Second Booke of Songs or Ayres; Anonymous:Scott's Lament; W. Byrd:Music of Byrd; Le Flelle:Music of Le Flelle; MacDermott:King's Musicon DEHA ▲ 77504 (16.97)

W. Lyons (cnd), Dufay Collective—My Lord Wilobies Welcom Home, P66a *(rec Forde Abbey, England, Sep 1995)* ("Johnny, Cock Thy Beaver") † Anonymous:Songs; G. Farnaby:Music of Farnaby; Playford:Songs; T. Ravenscroft:Songs; C. Simpson:Songs CHN ▲ 9446 [DDD] (16.97)

R. Oberlin (ct), J. Iadone (lt)—First Booke of Songs or Ayres [Come Againe Sweet Love Doth Now Envite; Can she excuse my wrongs]; Pilgrimes Solace [Thou mighty God]; Semper Dowland semper dolens, P9; Third & Last Booke of Songs or Ayres [Flow not so fast yee fountaines; Weepe you no more, sad fountaines]; Second Booke of Songs or Ayres [I saw my lade weepe; Shall I sue, shall I seeke for grace?; Flow my teares fall from your springs]; Lachrimae, or Seaven Teares [Lachrimae antiquae pavan]; Farre from triumphing court; Lady if you so spite me; In Darknesse Let Me Dwell LYR ▲ 8011 (16.97)

S. Rickards (ct), D. Linell (lt)—First Booke of Songs or Ayres [Come Againe Sweet Love Doth Now Envite; His golden locks time hath to silver turnd; If my complaints could passions move; Can she excuse my wrongs; Wilt thou unkind thus reave me of my hart; Thinkst thou then by thy fayning; Now, O now I needs must part; Come heavy sleepe]; Second Booke of Songs or Ayres [Flow my teares fall from your springs; I saw my lade weepe; Sorrow sorrow stay, lend true repentant teares; Fine knacks for ladies, cheap, choice, braue and new]; Lady if you so spite me; In Darknesse Let Me Dwell; Melancholy Gaillard, P25; Third & Last Booke of Songs or Ayres [Say love if ever thou didst find; Time stands still; Me, me and none but me; When Phoebus first did Daphne love]; Greensleeves Divisions; Fortune my foe, P62; Pilgrimes Solace [Stay time a while thy flying]; Robin, P70; Kemp's Jig; Callino; Gaillards by Mary Queen of Scots *(rec Mar & Oct 1995)* ("Lute Songs") NXIN ▲ 8553381 [DDD] (5.97)

D. Taylor (ct), A. Martin (lt), Les Voix Humaines—Third & Last Booke of Songs or Ayres [Time stands still]; Second Booke of Songs or Ayres [Flow my teares fall from your springs; I saw my lade weepe; Sorrow stay, lend true repentant teares]; First Booke of Songs or Ayres [Can she excuse my wrongs; Come Againe Sweet Love Doth Now Envite]; Lachrimae, or Seaven Teares [Lachrimae amantis] *(rec Church of St. Augustin de Mirabel, Québec, Canada, Oct 1997)* † Coprario:Songs of Mourning (sels); Cutting:Mrs. Anne Markham's Pavane; A. I. Ferrabosco:Ayres; T. Hume:Captain Humes Poeticall Musicke; My Hope Is Revived; 1st Part of Ayres (sels); J. Jenkins:Suite for 2 Vls; C. Simpson:VI Music ATMM ▲ 22136 (15.97)

Virelai—First Booke of Songs or Ayres [Come Againe Sweet Love Doth Now Envite; If my complaints could passions move; Awake Sweet Love, Thou Art Returnd; Come away, come sweet love]; Pilgrimes Solace [Go nightly cares, the enemy to rest; From silent night, true register of moanes; Lasso vita mia, mi fa morire]; In Darknesse Let Me Dwell; Second Booke of Songs or Ayres [Flow my teares fall from your springs; Sorrow sorrow stay, lend true repentant teares]; Third & Last Booke of Songs or Ayres [Time stands still] *(rec Toddington, Gloucestershire, England, June 1996 & Jan-Feb 1997)* † Lt Music VCL ▲ 45288 (16.97)

The Third & Last Booke of Songs or Ayres for Voices & Lute (1603)

A. Deller (ct), Deller Consort—Me, me and none but me; Flow not so fast yee fountaines *(rec Vienna, Austria, 1966)* ("Awake Sweet Love: Airs & Partsongs") † First Booke of Songs or Ayres; Galliards; Pilgrimes Solace; Second Booke of Songs or Ayres; Songs VC ▲ 8112 [ADD] (13.97)

DOWLAND, JOHN (cont.)
The Third & Last Booke of Songs or Ayres for Voices & Lute (1603) (cont.)
C. Högman (voc), J. Lindberg (lt)—The lowest trees have tops; Farewell unkind farewell *(rec Wik's Castle, Sweden, Dec 1983)* ("Faire, Sweet & Cruell") † First Booke of Songs or Ayres; In Darknesse Let Me Dwell; T. Campion:First Book of Ayres; Fourth Book of Ayres; Second Book of Ayres; Danyel:Like as the Lute; T. Ford:Faire Sweet Cruell; Pilkington:Rest Sweet Nimphs; Traditional:Greensleeves BIS ▲ 257 [DDD] (17.97)
Robert DeCormier Singers, J. Baird (sop), D. Tayler (lt/orpharion/lt/orph)—Time stands still; The lowest trees have tops; Weepe you no more, sad fountaines; What if I never speede *(rec Jan 1991)* † First Booke of Songs or Ayres; In Darknesse Let Me Dwell; Lachrimae, P15; Lt Music; Pilgrimes Solace; Second Booke of Songs or Ayres ARA ▲ 6622 [DDD] (16.97)

DOWLAND, ROBERT (1591-1641)
Songs
P. Agnew (ten), C. Wilson (lt)—Musicall Banquet ("In Darknesse Let Me Dwell") † J. Dowland:Songs MENO ▲ 1011 [DDD] (20.97)

DOWNEY, JOHN (1927-
Adagio Lyrico for 2 Pianos (1953)
A. Paratore (pno), J. Paratore (pno) † Agort; Dolphin; Lydian Suite; Octet; Pno Music; Tabu; What If?; Duphly:Pièces de clavecin (book 1) GAS ▲ 276 (16.97)
Agort for Woodwind Quintet (1967)
Woodwind Arts Quintet † Adagio Lyrico; Dolphin; Lydian Suite; Octet; Pno Music; Tabu; What If?; Duphly:Pièces de clavecin (book 1) GAS ▲ 276 (16.97)
Chant to Michelangelo for Orchestra (1959)
J. Downey (cnd), Czech RSO † Con Hp; For Those Who Suffered MASM ▲ 2054 [DDD] (16.97)
Concerto for Harp & Orchestra
J. Downey (cnd), Warsaw National PO † Chant to Michelangelo; For Those Who Suffered MASM ▲ 2054 [DDD] (16.97)
A Dolphin for Tenor, Flute, Viola, Percussion & Piano
D. Nelson (ten), B. Zaslav (va), I. Bourachoff (fl), J. Downey (pno), B. Burda (perc) † Adagio Lyrico; Agort; Lydian Suite; Octet; Pno Music; Tabu; What If?; Duphly:Pièces de clavecin (book 1) GAS ▲ 276 (16.97)
The Edge of Space (fantasy) for Bassoon & Orchestra
R. Thompson (bn), G. Simon (cnd), London SO ("The Edge of Space") † J. Andriessen:Concertino Bn; G. Jacob:Con Bn CHN ▲ 9278 [DDD] (16.97)
For Those Who Suffered [Yad Vashem] (impression) for Orchestra (1994)
J. Downey (cnd), Czech RSO † Chant to Michelangelo; Con Hp MASM ▲ 2054 [DDD] (16.97)
Lydian Suite for Cello Solo (1976)
Laufer (pno) † Adagio Lyrico; Agort; Dolphin; Octet; Pno Music; Tabu; What If?; Duphly:Pièces de clavecin (book 1) GAS ▲ 276 (16.97)
Octet for Winds (1954)
Univ of Wisconsin-Milwaukee Wind Ensemble † Adagio Lyrico; Agort; Dolphin; Lydian Suite; Pno Music; Tabu; What If?; Duphly:Pièces de clavecin (book 1) GAS ▲ 276 (16.97)
Piano Music
J. Downey (pno)—Eastlake Terrace (1959); Edges (1960); Portrait No. 1 (1982) † Adagio Lyrico; Agort; Dolphin; Lydian Suite; Octet; Tabu; What If?; Duphly:Pièces de clavecin (book 1) GAS ▲ 276 (16.97)
Tabu for Tuba (1966)
Phillips (tuba), J. Downey (pno) † Adagio Lyrico; Agort; Dolphin; Lydian Suite; Octet; Pno Music; What If?; Duphly:Pièces de clavecin (book 1) GAS ▲ 276 (16.97)
What If? for Instrumental Ensemble & Chorus
Univ of Wisconsin-Milwaukee Chorus † Adagio Lyrico; Agort; Dolphin; Lydian Suite; Octet; Pno Music; Tabu; Duphly:Pièces de clavecin (book 1) GAS ▲ 276 (16.97)

DOWNIE, KENNETH (20th cent)
Capriccio for Brass Ensemble
M. Evans (cnd), Aston-Under-Lyne Band † M. Ball:Midsummer Music; Fernie:Caledonian Journey; Finnegan:Volga Boatman; N. Hefti:L'il Darlin'; Prima:Music of Prima; P. Sparke:Between the Moon & Mexico; Miniatures Brass Band DOY 2-▲ 87 (24.97)

DOYLE, PATRICK (1953-
The Face in the Lake for Narrator & Orchestra
K. Winslet (nar), S. Mercurio (cnd), St. Luke's Orch *(rec Masonic Grand Lodge, New York City, NY, Aug 28, 1997)* ("Listen to the Storyteller") † W. Marsalis:Fiddler and the Dancin' Witch; E. Meyer:Lesson of the Land SNYC ▲ 60283 [DDD] (16.97) ▮ 60283 [DDD] (10.98)
Hamlet (film music) for Orchestra
artists unknown [w. Plácido Domingo (ten) performing Hamlet's] SNYC ▲ 62857 (16.97)
Henry V (film music) for Orchestra
P. Doyle (ten), S. Rattle (cnd), City of Birmingham SO, Stephen Hill Singers EMIC ▲ 49919 (16.97)
Much Ado About Nothing (film music) for Orchestra
artists unknown COL ▲ 54009 (16.97) ▮ 54009 (10.98)
Sense & Sensibility (film music) for Orchestra
J. Eaglen (sop), J. Snowdon (fl), R. Morgan (ob), R. Hill (cl), T. Hymas (pno), R. Ziegler (cnd) *(rec Lyndhurst Hall)* SNYC ▲ 62258 [DDD] (16.97) ▮ 62258 [DDD] (10.98)

DRAESEKE, FELIX (1835-1913)
Grosse Messe in a for Chorus, Op. 85 (1908-09)
U. Gronostay (cnd), Netherlands Chamber Choir *(rec Arts Music Recording, Amsterdam, Netherlands, Nov 1995)* † R. Schumann:Gesänge Double Chorus, Op. 141 GLOE ▲ 5147 [DDD] (16.97)
Mysterium:Christus (prelude & 3 oratorios) for solo Voices, Orchestra & Large Choir [text Draeseke] (1895-99)
A. Vogel (sop), C. Bischoff (sop), E. Dersen (alt), K. Markus (ten), H. J. Ritzerfeld (ten), B. Kämpff (bar), P. Langshaw (bass), J. Sonnenschmidt (org), U. Follert (cnd), Breslau State PO, Evangelical Boys' Choir Palatine, Heilbronn Vocal Ensemble, Palatine Kurrende BAYE 5-▲ 100175 (69.97)
Quintet in B♭ for Piano, Violin, Viola, Cello & Horn, Op. 48 (1888)
G. Langenstein (hn), Mozart Piano Quartet † R. Schumann:Qt Pno in E♭, Op. 47 MDG ▲ 6150673 (17.97)
Sonata for Piano
C. Tanski (pno) † Liszt:Son Pno, S.178 ALTA ▲ 9030

DRAGANSKI, DONALD (1936-
Heart's Desire (fantasy) for Contrabassoon & Piano [after Scheidt]
S. Nigro (ctbn), M. Lindeblad (pno) *(rec Chicago)* ("Susan Nigro & the Big Bassoon") † Doran:Movts Db; Muradian:Con Ctbn, Op. 86; R. Nicholson:Miniature Suite Ctbn; Palider:Narwhal, Op. 11; F. Warren:Music for Ctbn, Op. 28 CRYS ▲ 346 (15.97)

DRAGHI, ANTONIO (?1634/35-1700)
La vita nella morte (oratorio du sepolcro) (ca 1688)
C. Coin (cnd) ASTR ▲ 8616 (18.97)

DRAGHI, GIOVANNI BATTISTA (ca 1640-1708)
Harpsichord Music
R. Egarr (hpd)—Suite in G; Curtain Tune *(rec Utrecht, Aug 1995)* ("A Choice Collection of Restoration Harpsichord Music") † M. Locke:Suite Hpd; H. Purcell:Hpd Music; Suites Hpd GLOE ▲ 5145 [DDD] (16.97)

DRAGONETTI, DOMENICO (1763-1846)
Concerto in G for Double Bass & Orchestra, D.290
U. Fioravanti (db), C. Martignon (cnd), Padova e Veneto CO *(rec Padova Italy, Jan 17-19, 1995)* ("Works for Double Bass") † Duo Vc & Db; Qnt Strs, D.180; Qt 4 Strs, D.350; Waltzes, D.370 DYNC ▲ 133 [DDD] (17.97)
Duo in B♭ for Cello & Double Bass
T. Campagnaro (vc), U. Fioravanti (db) *(rec Padova Italy, Jan 17-19, 1995)* ("Works for Double Bass") † Con Db, D.290; Qnt Strs, D.180; Qt 4 Strs, D.350; Waltzes, D.370 DYNC ▲ 133 [DDD] (17.97)
Quartet No. 4 in e for Strings, D.350
S. Furini (vn), P. Juvarra (vn), G. Di Vacri (va), T. Campagnaro (vc) *(rec Padova Italy, Jan 17-19, 1995)* ("Works for Double Bass") † Con Db, D.290; Duo Vc & Db; Qnt Strs, D.180; Waltzes, D.370 DYNC ▲ 133 [DDD] (17.97)
Quintet in G for Strings, D.180
P. Toso (vn), G. Di Vacri (va), M. Tosi (va), M. Finotti (vc), U. Fioravanti (db) *(rec Padova Italy, Jan 17-19, 1995)* ("Works for Double Bass") † Con Db, D.290; Duo Vc & Db; Qt 4 Strs, D.350; Waltzes, D.370 DYNC ▲ 133 [DDD] (17.97)
Waltzes (3) for Double Bass, D.370
U. Fioravanti (db) *(rec Padova Italy, Jan 17-19, 1995)* ("Works for Double Bass") † Con Db, D.290; Duo Vc & Db; Qnt Strs, D.180; Qt 4 Strs, D.350 DYNC ▲ 133 [DDD] (17.97)

DRATTELL, DEBORAH (20th cent)
Concerto for Clarinet & Orchestra, "Fire Dances" (1986)
D. Shifrin (cl), G. Schwarz (cnd), Seattle SO *(rec Seattle Opera House, June 17, 1994)* ("Sorrow Is Not Melancholy: The Very Intense Music of Deborah Drattell") † Fire Within; Lilith; Sorrow Is Not Melancholy; Syzygy DLS ▲ 3159 [DDD] (14.97)
The Fire Within for Flute & Orchestra (1986-89)
S. Goff (fl), G. Schwarz (cnd), Seattle SO *(rec Seattle Opera House, June 17, 1994)* ("Sorrow Is Not Melancholy: The Very Intense Music of Deborah Drattell") † Con Cl; Lilith; Sorrow Is Not Melancholy; Syzygy DLS ▲ 3159 [DDD] (14.97)
Lilith for Orchestra (1988)
G. Schwarz (cnd), Seattle SO *(rec Seattle Opera House, June 17, 1994)* ("Sorrow Is Not Melancholy: The Very Intense Music of Deborah Drattell") † Con Cl; Fire Within; Sorrow Is Not Melancholy; Syzygy DLS ▲ 3159 [DDD] (14.97)
Sorrow Is Not Melancholy for String Quartet (or String Orchestra) (1993)
G. Schwarz (cnd), Seattle SO *(rec Seattle Opera House, Nov 15-16, 1993)* ("Sorrow Is Not Melancholy: The Very Intense Music of Deborah Drattell") † Con Cl; Fire Within; Lilith; Syzygy DLS ▲ 3159 [DDD] (14.97)
Syzygy for Orchestra (1987)
G. Schwarz (cnd), Seattle SO *(rec Seattle Opera House, Nov 15-16, 1993)* ("Sorrow Is Not Melancholy: The Very Intense Music of Deborah Drattell") † Con Cl; Fire Within; Lilith; Sorrow Is Not Melancholy DLS ▲ 3159 [DDD] (14.97)

DRESDEN, SEM (1881-1957)
Dansflitsen for Orchestra (1951)
W. V. Otterloo (cnd), The Hague PO † H. Badings:Con Vns; Flothuis:Symfonische muziek; Orthel:Sym 2 CV ▲ 26 (19.97)

DRESHER, PAUL (1951-
Casa Vecchia for String Quartet (1982)
Y. Morimoto (cnd) *(rec Vienna, 1994)* ("Casa Vecchia") † Mirrors; Other Fire; Underground STKL ▲ 204 (16.97)
Destiny for Electric Guitar, Percussion & Electronics (1983)
G. Reffkin (perc), P. Dresher (elec gtr/elec) ("This Same Temple") † Liquid & Stellar Music; This Same Temple; Water Dreams LOV ▲ 2011 [ADD] (16.97)
Liquid & Stellar Music for Electric Guitar & Electronics (1981)
P. Dresher (elec gtr/elec) ("This Same Temple") † Destiny; This Same Temple; Water Dreams LOV ▲ 2011 [ADD] (16.97)
Mirrors for Electric Bass & Electronics (1988-89; rev. 1991)
R. Black (elec bass/elec) ("Casa Vecchia") † Casa Vecchia; Other Fire; Underground STKL ▲ 204 (16.97)
Other Fire for Electronics (1984)
P. Dresher (elec) ("Casa Vecchia") † Casa Vecchia; Mirrors; Underground STKL ▲ 204 (16.97)
This Same Temple for 2 Pianos (1976-77)
N. Tiles (pno), E. Neimann (pno) ("This Same Temple") † Destiny; Liquid & Stellar Music; Water Dreams LOV ▲ 2011 [ADD] (16.97)
Underground for Multi-Track Tape Loop System (1982)
P. Dresher (elec) ("Casa Vecchia") † Casa Vecchia; Mirrors; Other Fire STKL ▲ 204 (16.97)
Water Dreams for Electronics (1985)
P. Dresher (elec) ("This Same Temple") † Destiny; Liquid & Stellar Music; This Same Temple LOV ▲ 2011 [ADD] (16.97)

DRESSER, MARK (20th cent)
Armadillo for String Trio
Arcado String Trio *(rec European Community, live, 1994)* ("Arcado String Trio") † Ediface; Harkening; Lanette; M. Feldman:Xanax; Reijseger:Behind the Myth; Biruta AVAK ▲ 58 [DDD] (21.97)
Banquet for Flute, Bass Guitar & String Quartet
M. Feldman (vn), S. Parkins (vn), R. Lawrence (va), E. Friedlander (vc), M. Ziegler (fl) ("Banquet") † Loss of the Innocents TZA (Composer) ▲ 7027 [DDD] (16.97)
Ediface for String Trio
Arcado String Trio *(rec European Community, live, 1994)* ("Arcado String Trio") † Armadillo; Harkening; Lanette; M. Feldman:Xanax; Reijseger:Behind the Myth; Biruta AVAK ▲ 58 [DDD] (21.97)
Harkening for String Trio
Arcado String Trio *(rec European Community, live, 1994)* ("Arcado String Trio") † Armadillo; Ediface; Lanette; M. Feldman:Xanax; Reijseger:Behind the Myth; Biruta AVAK ▲ 58 [DDD] (21.97)
Lanette for String Trio
Arcado String Trio *(rec European Community, live, 1994)* ("Arcado String Trio") † Armadillo; Ediface; Harkening; M. Feldman:Xanax; Reijseger:Behind the Myth; Biruta AVAK ▲ 58 [DDD] (21.97)
Loss of the Innocents for Clarinet, Tuba & Cello
E. Friedlander (vc), C. Speed (cl), M. Rojas (tuba) ("Banquet") † Banquet TZA (Composer) ▲ 7027 [DDD] (16.97)

DREYBLATT, ARNOLD (20th cent)
Music of Dreyblatt
D. Lebahn (b vn), J. Schade (elec bass/tuba/vc), S. Ocougne (elec gtr), P. Brody (tpt), U. Langer (trbn), C. Mello (dlc), P. Berthet (perc)—Point Rotation; Next Slide; Animal Magnetism; Group Velocity; Side Band; Flashbulb History; Epilogue ("Animal Magnetism") TZA (Composer) ▲ 7004 [DDD] (16.97)

DREYSCHOCK, ALEXANDER (1818-1869)
Concerto in d for Piano & Orchestra, Op. 137
P. Lane (pno), N. Willén (cnd), BBC Scottish SO † Kullak:Con Pno, Op. 55 HYP (The Romantic Piano Concerto 21) ▲ 67086 (18.97)

DRIGO, RICCARDO (1846-1930)
Arlekinada (Harlequin's Millions) (selections)
B. Gigli (ten) *(rec 1925-27)* ("Beniamino Gigli Edition 3") † Bizet:Pêcheurs de perles (sels); Boito:Mefistofele (sels); Donizetti:Elisir d'amore (sels); Lucia di Lammermoor (sels); Ponchielli:Gioconda (sels); G. Puccini:Bohème (sels); Manon Lescaut (sels); Tosca (sels); Verdi:Forza del destino (sels) VOCA ▲ 1177 (13.97)
Serenata (song) [from *Arlekinada (Harlequin's Millions)* (ballet)] (1900)
J. Clough (eup), M. Antrobus (cnd), Black Dyke Mills Band *(rec England, Mar 11, 1979)* ("Kings of Brass") † Borodin:Sym 2; D. Bourgeois:Serenade; Lalo:Roi d'Ys (sels); Liszt:Hungarian Rhaps, S.244; Staigers:Carnival of Venice; R. Strauss:Con 1 Hn, Op. 11 *([ENG] text)* CHN ▲ 4517 [ADD] (16.97)

DRING, MADELEINE (1923-1977)
Dances for Flute & Piano
L. Di Tullio (fl), L. Kaplan (pno)—WIB Waltz; Sarabande; Tango ("Leigh Kaplan plays Madeline Dring") † Pastel Panche; Pno Duo Tour; Pno Music; Shades of Dring CMB ▲ 1084 [ADD] (16.97)
Pastel Panche for Small Ensemble
R. Brown (bass), B. Shank (fl), B. Perkins (fl/sax/fl/sax/fl/sax), L. Kaplan (pno), S. Manne (perc) ("Leigh Kaplan plays Madeline Dring") † Dances Fl; Pno Duo Tour; Pno Music; Shades of Dring CMB ▲ 1084 [ADD] (16.97)
Piano Duo Tour
L. Kaplan (pno)—Carribean Dance; Danza Gaya [w Susan Pits (pno)]; Tarantelle; Italian Dance [w Robin Paterson (pno)] ("Leigh Kaplan plays Madeline Dring") † Dances Fl; Pastel Panche; Pno Music; Shades of Dring CMB ▲ 1084 [ADD] (16.97)
Piano Music
L. Kaplan (pno)—Moto Perpetuo; Colour Suite; Valse Française; Waltz Finale; American Dance; Jig ("Leigh Kaplan plays Madeline Dring") † Dances Fl; Pastel Panche; Pno Duo Tour; Shades of Dring CMB ▲ 1084 [ADD] (16.97)
Shades of Dring for Small Ensemble
R. Brown (bass), B. Shank (fl), B. Perkins (fl/sax/fl/sax/fl/sax), L. Kaplan (pno), S. Manne (perc) ("Leigh Kaplan plays Madeline Dring") † Dances Fl; Pastel Panche; Pno Duo Tour; Pno Music CMB ▲ 1084 [ADD] (16.97)
Songs
R. Tear (ten), P. Ledger (pno)—Shakespeare Songs; Mélisande; My proper Bess; Dedications; Betjeman Songs; Night Songs MER ▲ 84386 (16.97)
Three Piece Suite for Oboe & Piano
N. A. King (ob), E. Dalheim (pno) ("The Winning Program") † Daelli:Fant on Verdi's Rigoletto; Doráti:Duo Concertante; L. Singer:Memories; Telemann:Kleine Kammermusik BOST ▲ 1019 (15.97)

DROUET, LOUIS (1792-1873)
Introduction & Variations on an English Theme for Flute & Harp
M. Grauwels (fl), C. Michel (hp) † Chopin:Vars on Rossini; Donizetti:Larghetto & Allegro; G. Rossini:Andante e tema con variazioni Va; L. Spohr:Son 1 Vn & Hp MARC ▲ 8220441 [DDD] (13.97)

DRUCKMAN, JACOB (1928-1996)

Animus II for Soprano (or Mezzo-Soprano), 2 Percussion & Tape (1968)

J. DeGaetani (mez), R. Fitz (perc), G. Gottlieb (perc) † Dark Upon the Harp; Windows CRI (American Masters) ▲ 781 [ADD] (16.97)

Aureole for Orchestra (1979)

L. Slatkin (cnd), St. Louis SO † Colgrass:Déjà Vu Perc; Light Spirit NWW ▲ 318 [ADD] (16.97)

Chiaroscuro for Orchestra (1976-77)

L. Foss (cnd), Juilliard Orch † S. Albert:Into Eclipse; Schwantner:Aftertones of Infinity NWW ▲ 381 [DDD] (16.97)

Come Round for Chamber Ensemble (1992)

New York New Music Ensemble *(rec Vassar College Poughkeepsie, NY, Sept 20, 1992)* ("Music of Carter, Davies & Druckman") † E. Carter:Triple Duo; P. M. Davies:Ave Maris Stella GMR ▲ 2047 (16.97)

Corinna's Going A-Maying (1958)

P. Schubert (cnd), New Calliope Singers *(rec NYC, NY, June 1990)* † Death Be Not Proud; Faery Beam upon You; Madrigals; Shake off Your Heavy Trance; Babbitt:Cultivated Choruses; S. Gerber:Saison en enfer; Gideon:Habitable Earth; Monod:Cantus Contra Cantum IV; M. Wright:Choral Music CRI ▲ 638 [DDD] (16.97)

Dance with Shadows for Brass Quintet

Brass Ring ("New American Classics Written for Brass Ring") † N. Rorem:Diversions; D. Tredici:Heavy Metal Alice CRYS ▲ 564 (15.97)

Dark Upon the Harp (psalms) for Mezzo-Soprano, Brass Quintet & Percussion (1961-62)

J. DeGaetani (mez), R. Ayers (perc), G. Carlyss (perc), New York Brass Quintet † Animus II; Windows CRI (American Masters) ▲ 781 [ADD] (16.97)

J. DeGaetani (mez), B. Herman (perc), J. Haas (perc), J. Druckman (cnd), American Brass Quintet, American Brass Quintet [ENG] *(rec Aspen Music Festival, Aug 6, 1988)* † G. Fauré:Chanson d'Eve, Op. 95 BRID ▲ 9023 [ADD] (17.97)

Death, Be Not Proud (1958)

P. Schubert (cnd), New Calliope Singers *(rec NYC, NY, June 1990)* † Corinna's Going A-Maying; Faery Beam upon You; Madrigals; Shake off Your Heavy Trance; Babbitt:Cultivated Choruses; S. Gerber:Saison en enfer; Gideon:Habitable Earth; Monod:Cantus Contra Cantum IV; M. Wright:Choral Music CRI ▲ 638 [DDD] (16.97)

Duo for Violin & Piano (1950)

Z. Zeitlin (vn), B. Snyder (pno) † S. Adler:Canto III; A. Copland:Son Vn; L. Foss:Early Song; V. Reynolds:Son Vn GAS ▲ 279 (16.97)

The Faery Beam upon You (1958)

New Calliope Singers, K. Krueger (mez) *(rec NYC, NY, June 1990)* † Corinna's Going A-Maying; Death Be Not Proud; Madrigals; Shake off Your Heavy Trance; Babbitt:Cultivated Choruses; S. Gerber:Saison en enfer; Gideon:Habitable Earth; Monod:Cantus Contra Cantum IV; M. Wright:Choral Music CRI ▲ 638 [DDD] (16.97)

In Memoriam Vincent Persichetti for Winds, Brass & Percussion (1987)

E. Corporon (cnd), Cincinnati College Conservatory of Music Wind Sym † Paean; D. Diamond:Tantivy; Kurka:Good Soldier Schweik (suite); D. Wilson:Piece of Mind KLAV ▲ 11051 (18.97)

Madrigals (4) for Vocal Ensemble (1958)

P. Schubert (cnd), New Calliope Singers *(rec NYC, NY, 1990)* † Corinna's Going A-Maying; Death Be Not Proud; Faery Beam upon You; Shake off Your Heavy Trance; Babbitt:Cultivated Choruses; S. Gerber:Saison en enfer; Gideon:Habitable Earth; Monod:Cantus Contra Cantum IV; M. Wright:Choral Music CRI ▲ 638 [DDD] (16.97)

Music of Druckman

C. Macomber (vn), C. Zeavin (vn), L. Martin (va), F. Sherry (vc), D. Druckman (mar)—Dark Wind; Qts 2 & 3 Strs; Reflections on the Nature of Water KOCH ▲ 7409 (16.97)

Other Voices for Brass Quintet (1976)

American Brass Quintet † Bolcom:Qnt; R. Shapey:Qnt Brass; M. Wright:Qnt Brass NWW ▲ 377 [DDD] (16.97)

Paean for Winds (1986)

E. Corporon (cnd), Cincinnati College Conservatory of Music Wind Sym † In Memoriam Vincent Persichetti; D. Diamond:Tantivy; Kurka:Good Soldier Schweik (suite); D. Wilson:Piece of Mind KLAV ▲ 11051 (18.97)

Prism (3 pieces) for Large Orchestra [after Charpentier, Cavalli & Cherubini] (1980)

Z. Mehta (cnd), New York PO † Rochberg:Con Ob NWW ▲ 335 [DDD] (16.97)

Shake off Your Heavy Trance (1958)

P. Schubert (cnd), New Calliope Singers *(rec NYC, NY, June 1990)* † Corinna's Going A-Maying; Death Be Not Proud; Faery Beam upon You; Madrigals; Babbitt:Cultivated Choruses; S. Gerber:Saison en enfer; Gideon:Habitable Earth; Monod:Cantus Contra Cantum IV; M. Wright:Choral Music CRI ▲ 638 [DDD] (16.97)

Windows for Orchestra (1972)

A. Weisberg (cnd), Orch of the 20th Century *(rec Whitman Auditorium Brooklyn College, Apr 22-23, 1981)* † Animus II; Dark Upon the Harp CRI (American Masters) ▲ 781 [ADD] (16.97)

DRUMMOND, DEAN (1949-

Columbus for Flute & Zoomoozophone (1980)

D. Drummond (cnd), Newband ("Newband Play Microtonal Works") † Incredible Time (to live & die); Then or Never; J. La Barbara:Silent Scroll; J. Cage:Haikai; H. Partch:Studies on Ancient Greek Scales MODE ▲ 18

Incredible Time (to live and die) for Flute, Zoomoozophone, Synthesizer & Percussion (1988)

D. Drummond (cnd), Newband ("Newband Play Microtonal Works") † Columbus; Then or Never; J. La Barbara:Silent Scroll; J. Cage:Haikai; H. Partch:Studies on Ancient Greek Scales MODE ▲ 18

Then or Never for Flute, Zoomoozophone, Viola & Double Bass (1984)

D. Drummond (cnd), Newband ("Newband Play Microtonal Works") † Columbus; Incredible Time (to live & die); J. La Barbara:Silent Scroll; J. Cage:Haikai; H. Partch:Studies on Ancient Greek Scales MODE ▲ 18

DRUSCHETZKY, GEORG (1745-1819)

Concerto for Oboe, 8 Timpani & Orchestra

G. Hunt (ob), J. Haas (timp), H. Farberman (cnd), Bournemouth Sinfonietta † Partita; J. C. C. Fischer:Sym for 8 Timp CRD ▲ 3449 [ADD] (17.97)

Missa solemnis in C major for solo Voices, Organ, Orchestra & Chorus (1804)

I. Kertesi (sop), K. Gémes (mez), G. Kállay (ten), A. Ambrus (bar), Z. Kovács (vc), V. Buza (db), B. Arnóth (bn), I. Ella (org), J. Dobra (cnd), Vienna-Szász CO, Tomkins Vocal Ensemble † Bengraf:Sacred Music HUN ▲ 31609 [DDD] (16.97)

Music of Druschetzky

K. Berkes (cnd) —Music for Wind Instrs; Partitas in B, E & C; Vars, Rondos & Marches ("Harmoniemusik") HUN ▲ 31618 (16.97)

Partita in C for 6 Timpani & Orchestra

J. Haas (timp), H. Farberman (cnd), Bournemouth Sinfonietta † Con Ob & Timp; J. C. C. Fischer:Sym for 8 Timp CRD ▲ 3449 [ADD] (17.97)

DU, MINGXIN (1923-

Concerto for Piano, "Spirit of Spring" (1988)

J. Jandó (pno), C. Zuo-huang (cnd), Hungarian State SO *(rec Italian Institute Budapest, July 19-20, 1988)* † Con Vn MARC ▲ 8223269 [DDD] (13.97)

Concerto for Violin (1988)

T. Nishizaki (vn), K. Jean (cnd), Hong Kong PO *(rec Italian Institute Budapest, July 19-20, 1988)* † Con Pno MARC ▲ 8223269 [DDD] (13.97)

Festival Overture for Orchestra

K. Jean (cnd), Hong Kong PO *(rec Tsuen Wan Town Hall, 1988)* † Great Wall Sym MARC (Chinese Composers) ▲ 8223939 [DDD] (13.97)

The Great Wall Symphony

K. Jean (cnd), Hong Kong PO *(rec Tsuen Wan Town Hall, 1988)* † Festival Ov MARC (Chinese Composers) ▲ 8223939 [DDD] (13.97)

Xinjiang Dances (10) for Violin & Orchestra

T. Nishizaki (vn), C. Hoey (cnd), Singapore SO *(rec Victoria Memorial Hall Singapore, June 3-7, 1985)* MARC (Chinese Composers) ▲ 8223903 [DDD] (13.97)

DU, MINGXIN (1923-**& WU ZUJIANG** (20th cent)

The Mermaid:Ballet Suite

L. Kektjiang (cnd), Gunma SO *(rec Gumma Prefecture Japan, May 24-25, 1981)* † Chu:Harvest Scenes MARC (Chinese Music) ▲ 8223920 [DDD] (13.97)

DUARTE, JOHN (1919-

Quintet No. 1 for Guitar & String Quartet, Op. 85 (1992)

M. Tröster (gtr), Das Sächsische String Quartet *(rec Dresden, Germany, Feb 1994)* ("Guitarrenquintette I") † E. Angulo:Vögel, Op. 21; B. Hummel:Konzertante Musik, Op. 39 THOR ▲ 2212 [DDD] (17.97)

DUBOIS, PIERRE-MAX (1930-

Concerto for Alto Saxophone & Chamber Orchestra

G. Banaszak (sax), B. Jarmolowicz (cnd), Polish National CO of Slupsk *(rec Slupsk State Theatre, Poland, Apr 1998)* † Glazunov:Con A Sax, Op. 109; Ibert:Con Vc; S. Rachmaninoff:Vocalise; H. Villa-Lobos:Fant Sax CENT ▲ 2400 [DDD] (16.97)

V. David (a sax), G. Octors (cnd), Walloon CO *(rec Nov 1994)* ("Adolphe Sax International Music Competition") † Glazunov:Con A Sax, Op. 109; H. Pousseur:Caprices de Saxicare RENE ▲ 87518 [DDD]

Petite Suite for Flute & Bassoon

C. Churchfield (fl), C. Millard (bn) † Busser:Portuguesa Bn Pno; Morawetz:Son Bn Pno; W. A. Mozart:Duo Bn Vc, K.292; Sluka:Son Bn; H. Tomasi:Tombeau de Mireille SUMM ▲ 224 (16.97)

Piano Music

E. Katahn (pno)—Son; Toccata; Pour les belles ecouteuses; Hommage a Poulenc; Etudes de Concert (10) GAS ▲ 230 (16.97)

Quartet for Saxophones (1955)

Fairer Sax † J. Gardner:Qt Sax; P. Harvey:Robert Burns Suite; P. Patterson:Diversions SAY ▲ 365 [DDD] (16.97)

Jean-Yves Formeau Saxophone Quartet ("French Masterpieces for Sax Quartet") † Bozza:Andante & Scherzo; A. Desenclos:Quatuor; J. Françaix:Petit Quatuor; G. Pierné:Intro et Vars sur une ronde populaire; Rivier:Grave et presto RENE ▲ 87134 [DDD] (16.97)

Prism Saxophone Quartet † M. Levy:Sax Qt Music; R. Peck:Drastic Measures; Singelée:Qt 1 Saxes, Op. 53; P. Woods:Improvs Sax Qt KOCH ▲ 7024 [DDD] (16.97)

Quartet for Trombones

Triton Trombone Quartet *(rec Bielefeld-Ummeln, Germany, July 1992)* ("French Music For Trombones-Triton Trombone Quartet") † Anonymous:Gallicae (4); Bozza:Pieces (3) Trb Qt; Debussy:Chansons de Charles d'Orléans; F. Desprez:Triptyque pour 3 Trbn; Dukas:La Péri (sels); M. Praetorius:Terpsichore BIS ▲ 604 [DDD] (17.97)

DUBOIS, THÉODORE (1837-1924)

Terzettino for Flute, Viola & Harp

Sabeth Trio Basel ("French Music for Flute, Viola & Harp") † Bondon:Soleil Multicolore; Debussy:Son Fl; Salzedo:Sonatine en Trio; Vellones:Trio Fl PANC ▲ 510096 [DDD] (17.97)

DUBROVAY, LÁSZLÓ (1943-

Buzzing - Polka for Tuba, Harsona, Bassoon & Band (1992)

G. Hóna (bn), J. Bazsinka (tuba), L. Marosi (cnd), Budapest Symphonic Band *(rec July 3-7, 1995)* ("Contemporary Hungarian Wind Music") † I. Bogár:Con Tuba; F. Hidas:Folksongs of the Balaton; Folksongs of Békés County; Lendvay:Last Message from Maestro Tchaikovsky; G. Ránki:Magic Potion; Tales of Father Goose HUN ▲ 31612 [DDD] (16.97)

Concerto for Cimbalom & Strings (1994)

A. Szakály (cimbalom), T. Gál (cnd) ("Works for Cimbalom by Contemporary Hungarian Composers") † Csemiczky:Fant Concertante; Lendvay:Concertno Semplice; G. Ránki:Con Cimbalom; A. Reményi:At the Dawn; At the Twilight HUN ▲ 31669 [DDD] (16.97)

Concerto No. 2 for Piano & Orchestra, "Concerto romantico" (1984)

L. Baranyay (pno), M. Antal (cnd), Budapest SO † Con Vn; Faust, the Damned (suite 1); Faust, the Damned (suite 2); Faust, the Damned (suite 3); Faust, the Damned (suite 4) HUN 2-▲ 31831 [AAD] (32.97)

Concerto for Violin & Orchestra (1992)

A. Falvay (vn), B. Kocsár (cnd), Budapest Sinfonietta † Con 2 Pno; Faust, the Damned (suite 1); Faust, the Damned (suite 2); Faust, the Damned (suite 3); Faust, the Damned (suite 4) HUN 2-▲ 31831 [AAD] (32.97)

Faust, the Damned: Suite No. 1 for Orchestra

L. Kovács (cnd), Budapest SO † Con Vn; Con 2 Pno; Faust, the Damned (suite 2); Faust, the Damned (suite 3); Faust, the Damned (suite 4) HUN 2-▲ 31831 [AAD] (32.97)

Faust, the Damned: Suite No. 2 for Orchestra

L. Kovács (cnd), Budapest SO † Con Vn; Con 2 Pno; Faust, the Damned (suite 1); Faust, the Damned (suite 3); Faust, the Damned (suite 4) HUN 2-▲ 31831 [AAD] (32.97)

Faust, the Damned: Suite No. 3 for Orchestra

L. Kovács (cnd), Budapest SO † Con Vn; Con 2 Pno; Faust, the Damned (suite 1); Faust, the Damned (suite 2); Faust, the Damned (suite 4) HUN 2-▲ 31831 [AAD] (32.97)

Faust, the Damned: Suite No. 4 for Orchestra

L. Kovács (cnd), Budapest SO † Con Vn; Con 2 Pno; Faust, the Damned (suite 1); Faust, the Damned (suite 2); Faust, the Damned (suite 3) HUN 2-▲ 31831 [AAD] (32.97)

DU BUISSON, MONSIEUR (d. before 1688)

Suite in a for 2 Viols & Theorbo

P. Pierlot (vl), S. Watillon (vl), R. Lislevand (thb) † Machy:Suite Vls; Marais:Tombeau pour Monsieur de Ste Colombe; Sainte-Colombe:Fant en rondeau; Tombeau RICE ▲ 118100 [DDD] (17.97)

DU CAURROY, EUSTACHE (1549-1609)

Fantasias (23) for 3-6 Instruments

J. Savall (cnd) ASTR ▲ 7749 (18.97)

DUCHOW, MARVIN (dates unknown)

Chant intime for Piano

L. Altman (pno) *(rec June 17-19, 1996)* † Songs; A. Berg:Early Songs; Son Pno, Op. 1; R. Burns:Songs; Schoenberg:Songs (4), Op. 2; Traditional:Songs; Webern:Poems SNE ▲ 621 (16.97)

Songs (2) for Voice & Piano

V. Kinslow (sop), L. Altman (pno) *(rec June 17-19, 1996)* † Chant intime; A. Berg:Early Songs; Son Pno, Op. 1; R. Burns:Songs; Schoenberg:Songs (4), Op. 2; Traditional:Songs; Webern:Poems SNE ▲ 621 (16.97)

DUCKWORTH, WILLIAM (1943-

Mysterious Numbers for Orchestra (1995-96)

E. London (cnd), Cleveland Chamber SO ("The New American Scene III") † D. Erb:Solstice; S. Martirano:Isabela; Perle:Lyric Intermezzo ALBA ▲ 342 [DDD] (16.97)

Slow Dancing in Yugoslavia for solo Accordian (1990)

G. Klucevsek (acc) *(rec Church of the Holy Trinity, New York, NY, Mar 1993)* † F. Frith:Disinformation Polka; Klucevsek:Music of Klucevsek; J. Zorn:Road Runner STKL ▲ 207 [DDD] (16.97)

Southern Harmony, Books 1-4 for Solo Voice & Chorus (text from William Walker) (1981)

W. Payn (cnd), Rooke Chapel Choir, D. Fortunato (mez), G. Lee (pno) *(rec Bucknell U., Lewisburg, PA, United States of America)* ("An American Collage") † A. Copland:In the Beginning; J. Duke:Songs; J. Hill:Medieval Lyrics; Sweet & Triune Harmony; Hoiby:I Was There; Lady of the Harbor; Let this Mind Be in You; Shepherd; Hundley:Astronomers; Isaac Greentree; Sea is Swimming; R. Palmer:O Magnum Mysterium ALBA ▲ 98 [ADD] (16.97)

Their Song for Baritone & Piano (1991)

T. Buckner (bar), J. Kubera (pno) † Bekaert:Distant Harmony; T. Buckner:Inner Journey; S. Satoh:Burning Meditation; D. Wessel:Situations for Bar & Synth *([ENG] text)* LOV ▲ 3023 [DDD] (16.97)

DUDLEY, ANNE (20th cent)

American History X (film music) for Orchestra (1998)

A. Dudley (cnd) ANGL ▲ 56781 [DDD] (17.97)

The Full Monty (film music) for Orchestra (1997)

A. Dudley (cnd) RCAV ▲ 68904 [DDD] (17.97) ■ 68904 [DDD] (10.98)

Music of Dudley

various artists, A. Dudley (cnd) *(Canticles of the Sun and Moon; Veni Emmanuel; Tallis' Canon; Coventry Carol; Chorales)*, various artists *(Veni Sancte Spiritus)*, A. Dudley (cnd) *(From Darkness To Light; Holly and the Ivy; Canzonetta)*, C. Bott (sop), A. Dudley (cnd) *(Testimony of John) (rec Great Britain & N Ireland)* ("Ancient & Modern") † J. S. Bach:Wohltemperirte Clavier ANGL ▲ 56868 (16.97)

DUESENBERRY, JOHN (1950-

Agitato (Ergo Sum) (1990)

artists unknown ("Electro Acoustic Music II") † J. Berger:Island of Tears; P. Child:Ensemblance; Dashow:Disclosures; G. Shapiro:Phoenix NEU ▲ 45075 [DDD] (16.97)

DUFAY, GUILLAUME (ca 1400-1474)

Agnus Dei 'Custos et pastor' for 3 Voices

K. Boeke (cnd), Cantica Symphonia ("Fragmenta Missarum") † Agnus Dei; Ave regina caelorum; Credo; Gloria; Kyrie 'Fons Bonitatis'; Kyrie di Cambrai; Sanctus; Sanctus 'Ave verum corpus' STRV ▲ 33440 [DDD] (16.97)

Agnus Dei for 3 Voices

K. Boeke (cnd), Cantica Symphonia ("Fragmenta Missarum") † Agnus Dei 'Custos et pastor'; Ave regina caelorum; Credo; Gloria; Kyrie 'Fons Bonitatis'; Kyrie di Cambrai; Sanctus; Sanctus 'Ave verum corpus' STRV ▲ 33440 [DDD] (16.97)

Alma redemptoris Mater

A. Blachly (cnd), Pomerium † Ecclesie militantis; Letabundus; Nuper rosarum flores; Recollectio Festorum Beate Virginis PARC ▲ 447773 [DDD] (16.97)

DUFAY, GUILLAUME (cont.)

Ave regina caelorum (antiphon) for 4 Voices

K. Boeke (cnd), Cantica Symphonia ("Fragmenta Missarum") † Agnus Dei; Agnus Dei 'Custos et pastor'; Credo; Gloria; Kyrie 'Fons Bonitatis'; Kyrie di Cambrai; Sanctus; Sanctus 'Ave verum corpus' STRV ▲ 33440 [DDD] (16.97)

J. Wood (cnd), New London Chamber Choir *(rec Kentish Town, London, England, Nov 1991)* ("The Brightest Heaven of Invention") † Brumel:Nato canunt omnia; Busnois:Music of Busnois; Josquin Desprez:Preter rerum seriem; Obrecht:Factor orbis; Salve crux; Regis:O admirabile commercium AMON ▲ 56 [DDD] (16.97)

Credo for 3 Voices

K. Boeke (cnd), Cantica Symphonia ("Fragmenta Missarum") † Agnus Dei; Agnus Dei 'Custos et pastor'; Ave regina caelorum; Gloria; Kyrie 'Fons Bonitatis'; Kyrie di Cambrai; Sanctus; Sanctus 'Ave verum corpus' STRV ▲ 33440 [DDD] (16.97)

Credo for 4 Voices

K. Boeke (cnd), Cantica Symphonia ("Fragmenta Missarum") † Agnus Dei; Agnus Dei 'Custos et pastor'; Ave regina caelorum; Gloria; Kyrie 'Fons Bonitatis'; Kyrie di Cambrai; Sanctus; Sanctus 'Ave verum corpus' STRV ▲ 33440 [DDD] (16.97)

Ecclesie militantis (motet) for 5 Voices

A. Blachly (cnd), Pomerium † Alma redemptoris Mater; Letabundus; Nuper rosarum flores; Recollectio Festorum Beate Virginis PARC ▲ 447773 [DDD] (16.97)

Gloria for 3 Voices

K. Boeke (cnd), Cantica Symphonia ("Fragmenta Missarum") † Agnus Dei; Agnus Dei 'Custos et pastor'; Ave regina caelorum; Credo; Kyrie 'Fons Bonitatis'; Kyrie di Cambrai; Sanctus; Sanctus 'Ave verum corpus' STRV ▲ 33440 [DDD] (16.97)

Gloria for 4 Voices

K. Boeke (cnd), Cantica Symphonia ("Fragmenta Missarum") † Agnus Dei; Agnus Dei 'Custos et pastor'; Ave regina caelorum; Credo; Kyrie 'Fons Bonitatis'; Kyrie di Cambrai; Sanctus; Sanctus 'Ave verum corpus' STRV ▲ 33440 [DDD] (16.97)

Kyrie di Cambrai for 3 Voices

K. Boeke (cnd), Cantica Symphonia ("Fragmenta Missarum") † Agnus Dei; Agnus Dei 'Custos et pastor'; Ave regina caelorum; Credo; Gloria; Kyrie 'Fons Bonitatis'; Sanctus; Sanctus 'Ave verum corpus' STRV ▲ 33440 [DDD] (16.97)

Kyrie 'Fons Bonitatis' for 3 Voices

K. Boeke (cnd), Cantica Symphonia ("Fragmenta Missarum") † Agnus Dei; Agnus Dei 'Custos et pastor'; Ave regina caelorum; Credo; Gloria; Kyrie di Cambrai; Sanctus; Sanctus 'Ave verum corpus' STRV ▲ 33440 [DDD] (16.97)

Letabundus for 15 Voices

A. Blachly (cnd), Pomerium † Alma redemptoris Mater; Ecclesie militantis; Nuper rosarum flores; Recollectio Festorum Beate Virginis PARC ▲ 447773 [DDD] (16.97)

Magnificat

A. Teichert-Hailperin (sop), K. Smith (ct), W. Jochesn (ten), Helga Weber Instrumental Circle † Brassart:Ave Maria, Op. 19; Dunstable:Sacred Music; Hildegard of Bingen:Sacred Songs ENTE ▲ 41 [ADD] (10.97)

Missa de St. Anthonii de Padua

Binchois Consort ("Music for St. Anthony of Padua") HYP ▲ 66854 (18.97)

Pomerium † Veni Creator Spiritus PARC ▲ 47772 [DDD] (16.97)

Missa Ecce ancilla Domini for 4 Voices

R. Clemencic (cnd) HMA ▲ 190939 (9.97)

C. Gottwald (cnd), Stuttgart Schola Cantorum ("Musica mensurabilis I") † Ockeghem:Requiem BAYE ▲ 100271 [ADD] (17.97)

Missa "L'Homme armé" for 4 Voices

R. Zafir (cnd), Les Jeunes Solistes † Pecou:L'Homme armé MDA7 ▲ 6 (18.97)

Missa Sancti Jacobi for Chorus

A. Planchart (cnd) *(rec Sprague Hall Yale Univ., May 11-12, 1974)* † Se la face ay pale LYR 2-▲ 8013 (16.97)

Music of Dufay

Alla Francesca ("Beauté Parfaite: The Autumn of the Middle Ages") † Binchois:Music of OPUS ▲ 30173 (18.97)

Ensemble Diferencias—Ave maris stella; Bon jour, bon mois; Hélas, ma dame; Je me complains piteusement; Sanctus; Lamentatio sancte matris ecclesiae; Je vous prie; O sancte Sebastiane; Vergene bella; Inclita stella maris *(rec Waldenburg, Switzerland, Jan 17-18, 1996)* ("Cantio Triplex") † Anonymous:Gospodi Wozzwach; Heilige Dreifaltigkeit; Polielej, utrenja; Kreta:Kanon; Sophronios:Oútos ho theós DVX ▲ 79610 [DDD] (16.97)

Nuper rosarum flores

A. Blachly (cnd), Pomerium † Alma redemptoris Mater; Ecclesie militantis; Letabundus; Recollectio Festorum Beate Virginis PARC ▲ 447773 [DDD] (16.97)

Recollectio Festorum Beate Marie Virginis (vespers) for Chorus (ca 1458)

A. Blachly (cnd), Pomerium † Alma redemptoris Mater; Ecclesie militantis; Letabundus; Nuper rosarum flores PARC ▲ 447773 [DDD] (16.97)

Sacred Music

Orlando Consort—Victimae paschali; Vexilla regis *(rec Suffolk, May 1995)* ("Passion") † H. Isaac:Easter Mass; Tinctoris:Lamentationes Jeremie MENO ▲ 1015 [DDD] (20.97)

J. Summerly (cnd), Oxford Camerata—Kyrie; Gloria; Credo; Sanctus; Agnus Dei [all from Missa L'homme armé]; Veni Sancte Spiritus; Jubilate Deo; Illumina faciem tuam; Supremum est mortalibus bonum; L'homme armé [anon song] *(rec Chapel of Hertford College Oxford, Apr 4-5, 1994)* NXIN (Early Music) ▲ 553087 [DDD] (5.97)

Sanctus 'Ave verum corpus' for 4 Voices

K. Boeke (cnd), Cantica Symphonia ("Fragmenta Missarum") † Agnus Dei; Agnus Dei 'Custos et pastor'; Ave regina caelorum; Credo; Gloria; Kyrie 'Fons Bonitatis'; Kyrie di Cambrai; Sanctus STRV ▲ 33440 [DDD] (16.97)

Sanctus for 3 Voices

K. Boeke (cnd), Cantica Symphonia ("Fragmenta Missarum") † Agnus Dei; Agnus Dei 'Custos et pastor'; Ave regina caelorum; Credo; Gloria; Kyrie 'Fons Bonitatis'; Kyrie di Cambrai; Sanctus 'Ave verum corpus' STRV ▲ 33440 [DDD] (16.97)

Se la face ay pale (ballade) for 3 Voices

A. Planchart (cnd) *(rec Sprague Hall Yale Univ., May 11-12, 1974)* † Missa Sancti Jacobi LYR 2-▲ 8013 (16.97)

Secular Music

London Medieval Ensemble PLOI 5-▲ 452557 (33.97)

Songs

B. Landauer (ct), M. Posch (cnd) —J'ay mis mon cuer; Par droit je puis bien complaindre; Quel fronte signorille la dolce vista; Puisque vous estez campieur; Belle, que vous ay je mesfait; Vergene bella; Se la face ay pale; Donnes l'assault à la fortresse; Par le regard de vos beaux yeux; Resvelons nous; Ce jour de l'an; Mon chier amy; Pour l'amour de ma doulce amye; Helas mon dueil; Bon jour, bon mois; Resvelliés vous et faites chiere lye; Adieu ces bons vins de Lannoys *(rec Vienna, Austria, Apr 15-18, 1995)* NXIN ▲ 553458 [DDD] (5.97)

Veni Creator Spiritus (hymn) for 3 Voices

Pomerium † Missa de St. Anthonii de Padua PARC ▲ 47772 [DDD] (16.97)

DUFF, ARTHUR (1899-1956)

Echoes of Georgian Dublin for Orchestra (1955)

P. O. Duinn (cnd), RTE Sinfonietta *(rec UCD Dublin)* ("Romantic Ireland") † Larchet:By the Waters of Moyle; P. O'Connor:Introspect; O Riada:Banks of Sullane; A. J. Potter:Rhap under a High Sky; Victory:Irish Pictures MARC (Irish Composer) ▲ 8223804 [DDD] (13.97)

Irish Suite for Strings

F. Hunt (cnd), Irish Chamber Orch *(rec Limerick, Ireland, July, 1997)* † Meath Pastoral; A. Fleischmann:Elizabeth MacDermott; T. C. Kelly:O'Carolan Suite; Pieces Strs; Larchet:Dirge of Ossian; Mac Ananty's Reel; J. Trimble:Suite Strs BBCL ▲ 1003 [DDD] (16.97)

Meath Pastoral for Orchestra

F. Hunt (cnd), Irish Chamber Orch *(rec Limerick, Ireland, July, 1997)* † Irish Suite; A. Fleischmann:Elizabeth MacDermott; T. C. Kelly:O'Carolan Suite; Pieces Strs; Larchet:Dirge of Ossian; Mac Ananty's Reel; J. Trimble:Suite Strs BBCL ▲ 1003 [DDD] (16.97)

DUFFY, JOHN (1928-

Freedom Overture for Orchestra

Z. Macal (cnd), Milwaukee SO *(rec Milwaukee, WI, Nov 22, 1993)* ("Freedom Works") † Jewish Portraits; Sym 1; Time for Remembrance: A Peace Cant KOSS ▲ 1022 [DDD] (17.97)

Heritage Fanfare & Chorale for Orchestra

R. Williams (cnd), Royal PO † Heritage Suite; Heritage Sym Dances; Sym 1 ALBA ▲ 304 [DDD] (16.97)

Heritage Suite for Orchestra

R. Williams (cnd), Royal PO † Heritage Fanfare & Chorale; Heritage Sym Dances; Sym 1 ALBA ▲ 304 [DDD] (16.97)

Heritage Symphonic Dances for Orchestra

R. Williams (cnd), Royal PO † Heritage Fanfare & Chorale; Heritage Suite; Sym 1 ALBA ▲ 304 [DDD] (16.97)

DUFFY, JOHN (cont.)

Jewish Portraits (3) for Orchestra

Z. Macal (cnd), Milwaukee SO *(rec Milwaukee, WI, Nov 22, 1993)* ("Freedom Works") † Freedom Ov; Sym 1; Time for Remembrance: A Peace Cant KOSS ▲ 1022 [DDD] (17.97)

Symphony No. 1, "Utah" (1988-89)

Z. Macal (cnd), Milwaukee SO *(rec Milwaukee, WI, Nov 22, 1993)* ("Freedom Works") † Freedom Ov; Jewish Portraits; Time for Remembrance: A Peace Cant KOSS ▲ 1022 [DDD] (17.97)

J. Silverstein (cnd), Utah SO † Heritage Fanfare & Chorale; Heritage Suite; Heritage Sym Dances ALBA ▲ 304 [DDD] (16.97)

A Time for Remembrance: A Peace Cantata for Soprano (or Mezzo-Soprano), Narrator & Orchestra (rev 1993)

C. Clarey (sop), J. E. Jones (nar), Z. Macal (cnd), Milwaukee SO *(rec Milwaukee, WI, Nov 22, 1993)* ("Freedom Works") † Freedom Ov; Jewish Portraits; Sym 1 KOSS ▲ 1022 [DDD] (17.97)

DUGGER, EDWIN (1940-

Music for Synthesizer & 6 Instruments (1966)

C. Kiefer (tape), M. Winder (vn), B. Kadinoff (va), S. Geber (vc), R. Domenica (fl), P. Bowman (ob), W. Wrzesien (cl), D. Epstein (cnd) † R. Erickson:Ricercar à 5 Trbns; P. Rhodes:Duo Vn & Vc; H. Sollberger:Grand Qt Fls; Westergaard:Vars for 6 Players NWW ▲ 80563 [ADD] (16.97)

DUHAMEL, ANTOINE (1925-

Contrebasse oblige for Double Bass

P. Feyler (db) *(rec 1994)* ("Trio Sonata Concert") † E. Chausson:Poème Vn, Op. 25; M. Ravel:Tzigane GALL ▲ 801 [DDD]

DUKAS, PAUL (1865-1935)

Ariane et Barbe-Bleue (suite) for Orchestra & Chorus (1907)

A. Toscanini (cnd), NBC SO *(rec 1938-46)* † Debussy:Prélude à l'après-midi d'un faune; C. Franck:Éolides, M.43; Psyché (sels); Roger-Ducasse:Sarabande; A. Roussel:Festin de l'araignée (suite 2) URAN ▲ 107 (m) [DDD] (15.97)

A. Toscanini (cnd), NBC SO, NBC Sym Chorus *(rec 1947)* ("Rare Performances") † Mussorgsky:Pictures at an Exhibition IN ▲ 1389 [AAD] (15.97)

L'Apprenti sorcier [The Sorcerer's Apprentice] (symphonic scherzo) for Orchestra [after Goethe] (1897)

E. Ansermet (cnd), Swiss Romande Orch † Debussy:Mer Orch; Honegger:Pacific 231; M. Ravel:Boléro; Valse PLON (The Classic Sound) ▲ 448576 (11.97)

L. Bernstein (cnd), New York PO *(rec New York, NY, Feb 16, 1965)* † Debussy:Rapsodie Sax; Honegger:Pacific 231; Pastorale d'été; Rugby; D. Milhaud:Création du monde, Op. 81; M. Ravel:Shéhérazade Mez SNYC (Bernstein Century) ▲ 60695 [ADD] (10.97)

D. Briggs (org) [tran for org] ("Popular Organ Music, Vol. 2") † J. Alain:Jardin suspendu, AWV 63; J. S. Bach:Preludes & Fugues (22) Org, BWV 531-552; Preludes & Fugues, BWV 531-552; P. Cochereau:Boléro on a Theme of Charles Racquet; C. Franck:Pièces (3) Org, M.37; P. Tchaikovsky:Nutcracker Suite, Op. 71a PRIO ▲ 568 [DDD] (16.97)

A. Chorosinski (org) [Andrej Chorosinski] *(rec n, Wuppertal Stadhalle, Germany, Sept 1-4, 1997)* ("Virtuoso Organ Music") † Mussorgsky:Pictures at an Exhibition; Saint-Saëns:Danse macabre, Op. 40; Smetana:Moldau MDG ▲ 3200818 [DDD] (17.97)

J. Fournet (cnd), Netherlands Radio PO *(rec Mar 26-27, 1992)* † La Péri; Sym in D DNN ▲ 75284 [DDD] (16.97)

E. Kunzel (cnd), Cincinnati Pops Orch † Liszt:Préludes, S.97; Rimsky-Korsakov:Mlada (procession); Snow Maiden (dance); Saint-Saëns:Samson et Dalila (Bacchanale); J. Weinberger:Schwanda der Dudelsackpfeifer (polka & fugue) TEL ▮ 30115 [DDD] (8.98) ▲ 80115 [DDD] (16.97)

G. Lehel (cnd), Budapest SO, R. Raichev (cnd), Plovdiv PO ("Rhapsodie Espagnole") † Chabrier:España; Debussy:Prélude à l'après-midi d'un faune; M. Ravel:Rapsodie espagnole; Rimsky-Korsakov:Capriccio espagnol, Op. 34 LALI ▲ 15528 [DDD] (3.97)

J. Levine (cnd), Berlin PO † Saint-Saëns:Sym 3 DEUT ▲ 19617 [DDD] (16.97)

J. Loughran (cnd), Hallé Orch ("Children's Classics") † S. Prokofiev:Peter & the Wolf, Op. 67; Saint-Saëns:Carnival of the Animals CFP (Unforgettable Classics) ▲ 69605 (11.97)

D. Mitropoulos (cnd), Minneapolis SO ("Dmitri Mitropoulos: From Minneapolis to New York, Vol. 3") † Beethoven:Coriolan Ov, Op. 62; Leonore (ov 3); P. Tchaikovsky:Sym 4 GRM2 ▲ 78608 (13.97)

D. Mitropoulos (cnd), Minneapolis SO ("Dmitri Mitropoulos: The Minneapolis Years, 1940-45") † Beethoven:Coriolan Ov, Op. 62; Leonore (ov 3); Sym 6; Borodin:Sym 2; G. Mahler:Sym 1; R. Schumann:Sym 2; P. Tchaikovsky:Sym 4 GRM2 4-▲ 78646 (52.97)

C. Munch (cnd), Boston SO ("The French Touch") † C. Franck:Chasseur maudit, M.44; M. Ravel:Ma mère l'oye; Saint-Saëns:Rouet d'Omphale, Op. 31 RCAV (Living Stereo) ▲ 68978 (11.97)

E. Ormandy (cnd), Philadelphia Orch † Berlioz:Sym fantastique, Op. 14; Mussorgsky:Night on Bare Mountain SNYC (Essential Classics) ▲ 46329 [ADD] (7.97) ▮ 46329 [ADD] (3.98)

L. Slatkin (cnd), Orch National de France † La Péri; La Péri (sels); Sym in C RCAV ▲ 68802 [DDD] (16.97)

L. Stokowski (cnd), Philadelphia Orch † J. S. Bach:Toccata & Fugue Org, BWV 565; Mussorgsky:Night on Bare Mountain; Saint-Saëns:Danse macabre, Op. 40; Samson et Dalila (Bacchanale); I. Stravinsky:Sacre du printemps MTAL (Leopold Stokowski Conducts) ▲ 48002 (6.97)

Y. P. Tortelier (cnd), Ulster Orch † La Péri; Chabrier:España; Suite pastorale CHN ▲ 8852 [DDD] (16.97)

A. Toscanini (cnd), NBC SO ("The Toscanini Collection, Vol. 39: All-French Program") † Berlioz:Damnation de Faust (sels); Roméo et Juliette (sels); C. Franck:Psyché (sels); M. Ravel:Daphnis et Chloé (suite 2); Saint-Saëns:Danse macabre, Op. 40; A. Thomas:Mignon (ov) RCAV (Gold Seal) ▲ 60322 (11.97)

A. Toscanini (cnd), New York PO ("The Toscanini Collection, Vol. 65") † J. Brahms:Vars on a Theme by Haydn; Mendelssohn (-Bartholdy):Midsummer Night's Dream (sels); W. A. Mozart:Sym 35, K.385; R. Wagner:Siegfried Idyll RCAV (Gold Seal) ▲ 60317 (11.97)

A. Toscanini (cnd), New York PO *(rec 1928-36)* ("Toscanini Edition, Vol. 4") † J. Brahms:Vars on a Theme by Haydn; C. W. Gluck:Orfeo ed Euridice (dance); Mendelssohn (-Bartholdy):Midsummer Night's Dream (sels); G. Rossini:Barbiere di Siviglia (ov); Italiana in Algeri (ov); Semiramide (ov); Verdi:Traviata (sels) GRM2 ▲ 78817 (13.97)

La Péri (fanfare & poème danse) for Orchestra (1912)

P. Boulez (cnd), New York PO † M. de Falla:Con Hpd; Sombrero de tres picos SNYC (Pierre Boulez Edition) ▲ 68333 (10.97)

J. Fournet (cnd), Netherlands Radio PO *(rec Sept 7, 1990)* † L'Apprenti sorcier; Sym in D DNN ▲ 75284 [DDD] (16.97)

L. Slatkin (cnd), Orch National de France † L'Apprenti sorcier; La Péri (sels); Sym in C RCAV ▲ 68802 [DDD] (16.97)

Y. P. Tortelier (cnd), Ulster Orch † L'Apprenti sorcier; Chabrier:España; Suite pastorale CHN ▲ 8852 [DDD] (16.97)

La Péri (selections) (1907)

L. Slatkin (cnd), Orch National de France—Fanfare † L'Apprenti sorcier; La Péri; Sym in C RCAV ▲ 68802 [DDD] (16.97)

Triton Trombone Quartet [arr Hermann Bäumer] *(rec Bielefeld-Ummeln, Germany, July 1992)* ("French Music For Trombones-Triton Trombone Quartet") † Anonymous:Gallicae (4); Bozza:Pieces (3) Trb Qt; Debussy:Chansons de Charles d'Orléans; F. Desprez:Triptyque pour 3 Trbn; P.-M. Dubois:Qt for Trombones; M. Praetorius:Terpsichore BIS ▲ 604 [DDD] (17.97)

La plainte, au loin, du faune for Piano (1920)

M. Fingerhut (pno) † Prélude élégiaque; Son Pno; Vars, Interlude et Finale sur en thème de Ram CHN ▲ 8765 [DDD] (16.97)

A. Marion (fl), L. Baril (pno) [trans for fl & pno] *(rec July 1997)* ("Autour de Debussy") † Caplet:Improvs Fl; Rêverie & petite valse; Debussy:Prélude à l'après-midi d'un faune; Syrinx Fl; Inghelbrecht:Sonatina en trois parties; Koechlin:Son Fl; G. Pierné:Canzonetta Cl, Op. 19 FL ▲ 23119 [DDD] (16.97)

Polyeucte (overture) for Orchestra [after Corneille] (1891)

Y. P. Tortelier (cnd), BBC PO † Sym in C CHN ▲ 9225 [DDD] (16.97)

Prélude élégiaque for Piano (1908)

M. Fingerhut (pno) † Plainte, au loin, du faune; Son Pno; Vars, Interlude et Finale sur en thème de Ram CHN ▲ 8765 [DDD] (16.97)

Sonata in e♭ for Piano (1901)

M. Fingerhut (pno) † Plainte, au loin, du faune; Prélude élégiaque; Vars, Interlude et Finale sur en thème de Ram CHN ▲ 8765 [DDD] (16.97)

Symphony in C (1895-96)

L. Foster (cnd), Monte Carlo PO *(rec L'Opéra de Monte Carlo, Monaco, Sept 1990)* † G. Fauré:Pelléas et Mélisande, Op. 80 CLAV ▲ 9102 [DDD] (16.97)

L. Slatkin (cnd), Orch National de France † L'Apprenti sorcier; La Péri; La Péri (sels) RCAV ▲ 68802 [DDD] (16.97)

Y. P. Tortelier (cnd), BBC PO † Polyeucte CHN ▲ 9225 [DDD] (16.97)

DUKAS, PAUL (cont.)

Symphony in D (1896)

J. Fournet (cnd), Netherlands Radio PO *(rec Aug 30, 1991)* † L'Apprenti sorcier; La Péri — DNN ▲ 75284 [DDD] (16.97)

Variations, Interlude et Finale sur en thème de Rameau for Piano (ca 1899-1902)

M. Fingerhut (pno) † Plainte, au loin, du faune; Prélude élégiaque; Son Pno — CHN ▲ 8765 [DDD] (16.97)

Villanelle for Horn & Piano (or Orchestra) (1906)

R. Baborák (hn), J. Belohlávek (cnd), Prague Chamber PO *(rec Prague, Aug 28-29 & Oct 31-Nov 1, 1997)* † Busoni:Concertino Cl, Op. 48; A. Copland:Con Cl; D. Milhaud:Scaramouche Cl; O. Schoeck:Con Hn — SUR ▲ 3348 [DDD]

P. Del Vescovo (hn), J. Hubeau (pno) ("The Magic of the French Horn") † N. C. Bochsa:Andante sostenuto; Dauprat:Son Hn & Hp; W. A. Mozart:Con 4 Hn, K.495; Rondo Hn, K.371; R. Schumann:Konzertstück Hns, Op. 86 — ERAT ▲ 94801 (9.97)

W. Slocum (hn), R. Fusco (pno) ("The Expressive Horn") † Beethoven:Son Hn; P. Hindemith:Son Hn — ARUN ▲ 3058 (16.97)

DUKE, GEORGE (20th cent)

Muir Woods Suite for Piano, Bass, Drums, Percussion & Orchestra

S. Clarke (bass), G. Duke (pno), C. Thompson (dr), P. Dacosta (perc), E. Stratta (cnd), Lille National Orch *(rec Montreaux Music Festival Montreaux, Switzerland, July 12, 1993)* — WAR ▲ 46132 [DDD] (11.97)

DUKE, JOHN (1899-1984)

Songs

D. Boothman (bar), J. Duke (pno)—Songs — AFK ▲ 505

D. Fortunato (mez), G. Lee (pno), W. Payn (cnd), Rooke Chapel Choir—Survivor; In the Fields; Acquainted with the Night; To the Thawing Wind *(rec Bucknell U., Lewisburg, PA, United States of America)* ("An American Collage") † A. Copland:In the Beginning; Duckworth:Southern Harmony; J. Hill:Medieval Lyrics; Sweet & Triune Harmony; Hoiby:I Was There; Lady of the Harbor; Let this Mind Be in You; Shepherd; Hundley:Astronomers; Isaac Greentree; Sea is Swimming; R. Palmer:O Magnum Mysterium — ALBA ▲ 98 [ADD] (16.97)

DUKE, VERNON (1903-1969)

Songs

D. Upshaw (sop), E. Stern (cnd) —Round About; Born Too Late; The Love I Long For; Autumn in New York; The Sea-Gull & the Ea-Gull; Remember to Forget; Not a Care in the World; Words without Music; Swattin' the Fly; April in Paris; I Like the Likes of You; Low & Lazy; Water under the Bridge; Ages Ago — NON ▲ 79531 (16.97)

Souvenir de Venise (sonata in 1 movt) for Piano (1955)

A. Mandel (pno) ("American Piano, Vol. 1") † M. Gould:Prelude & Toccata; A. North:Streetcar Named Desire (suite); E. Siegmeister:Sunday in Brooklyn — PREM ▲ 1013 [DDD] (16.97)

DU MONT, HENRY (1610-1684)

Allemanda in g for 2 Violins & Continuo

F. Malgoire (vn), A. Petit (vn), K. Uemura (b vl), C. Rousset (hpd) *(rec Eglise de Cucuron, France, May 27-29, 1992)* † Allemande grave; Allemande in a; Allemande sur les Anches; Motets; Oratorios; Pavane in d; Pavane Hpd; Sarabande; Symphonia — VCL ▲ 61531 [DDD] (11.97)

Allemande grave in d for Organ

C. Rousset (org) *(rec Eglise de Cucuron, France, May 27-29, 1992)* † Allemanda in g Vns; Allemande in a; Allemande sur les Anches; Motets; Oratorios; Pavane in d; Pavane Hpd; Sarabande; Symphonia — VCL ▲ 61531 [DDD] (11.97)

Allemande in a for Keyboard

C. Rousset (org) *(rec Eglise de Cucuron, France, May 27-29, 1992)* † Allemanda in g Vns; Allemande grave; Allemande sur les Anches; Motets; Oratorios; Pavane in d; Pavane Hpd; Sarabande; Symphonia — VCL ▲ 61531 [DDD] (11.97)

Allemande sur les Anches for Organ

C. Rousset (org) *(rec Eglise de Cucuron, France, May 27-29, 1992)* † Allemanda in g Vns; Allemande grave; Allemande in a; Motets; Oratorios; Pavane in d; Pavane Hpd; Sarabande; Symphonia — VCL ▲ 61531 [DDD] (11.97)

Litanies de la vierge for 5 Voices & Continuo

P. Bennett (cnd), Ensemble Dumont † Music of Du Mont; Anonymous:Egredimini Filiae Sion; O veneranda Trinitas; Pater Noster; Veni sponsa mea — LINN ▲ 67 [DDD] (16.97)

Motets

C. Rousset (org), C. Rousset (cnd), Les Talens Lyriques *(Litanies de la vierge)*, K. Uemura (b vl), C. Rousset (hpd), Les Talens Lyriques *(Dialogus angeli)*, M. Boyer (mez), C. Rousset (org) *(In lectulo meo)*, M. Padmore (ct), F. Piolino (ten), S. Van Dyck (ten), P. Gerimon (bass), K. Uemura (b vl), C. Rousset (org) *(In te Domine)* *(rec Eglise de Cucuron, France, May 27-29, 1992)* † Allemanda in g Vns; Allemande grave; Allemande in a; Allemande sur les Anches; Oratorios; Pavane in d; Pavane Hpd; Sarabande; Symphonia — VCL ▲ 61531 [DDD] (11.97)

Motets pour la chapelle du roy (1686)

P. Herreweghe (cnd), La Chapelle Royale Orch, Chapelle Royale Choir *(rec July 1981)* — HMA ▲ 1901077 (9.97)

Music of Du Mont

P. Bennett (cnd), Ensemble Dumont—Pavane Hpd; Prelude; Allemande grave; Antienne de Ste. Cecile; O Sponse mi; Symphonia; Domine salvum fac Regem † Litanies de la vierge; Anonymous:Egredimini Filiae Sion; O veneranda Trinitas; Pater Noster; Veni sponsa mea — LINN ▲ 67 [DDD] (16.97)

Oratorios

F. Malgoire (vn), A. Petit (vn), K. Uemura (b vl), C. Rousset (hpd)—Dialogus de Anima *(rec Eglise de Cucuron, France, May 27-29, 1992)* † Allemanda in g Vns; Allemande grave; Allemande in a; Allemande sur les Anches; Motets; Pavane in d; Pavane Hpd; Sarabande; Symphonia — VCL ▲ 61531 [DDD] (11.97)

Pavane in d for Harpsichord

C. Rousset (hpd) *(rec Eglise de Cucuron, France, May 27-29, 1992)* † Allemanda in g Vns; Allemande grave; Allemande in a; Allemande sur les Anches; Motets; Oratorios; Pavane in d; Sarabande; Symphonia — VCL ▲ 61531 [DDD] (11.97)

B. Schenkman (hpd), B. Schenkman (hpd) *(rec Mar 1996)* ("The Bauyn Manuscript: Music at the Court of Louis XIV") † L. Couperin:Hpd Music; Froberger:Hpd Music — WILD ▲ 9603 [DDD] (16.97)

Pavane in d for 2 Mezzo-Sopranos & Continuo

F. Malgoire (vn), A. Petit (vn), K. Uemura (b vl), C. Rousset (hpd) *(rec Eglise de Cucuron, France, May 27-29, 1992)* † Allemanda in g Vns; Allemande grave; Allemande in a; Allemande sur les Anches; Motets; Oratorios; Pavane Hpd; Sarabande; Symphonia — VCL ▲ 61531 [DDD] (11.97)

Sarabande in d for 2 Mezzo-Sopranos & Continuo

F. Malgoire (vn), A. Petit (vn), K. Uemura (b vl), C. Rousset (hpd) *(rec Eglise de Cucuron, France, May 27-29, 1992)* † Allemanda in g Vns; Allemande grave; Allemande in a; Allemande sur les Anches; Motets; Oratorios; Pavane in d; Pavane Hpd; Symphonia — VCL ▲ 61531 [DDD] (11.97)

Symphonia in g for 2 Violins & Continuo

F. Malgoire (vn), A. Petit (vn), K. Uemura (b vl), C. Rousset (hpd) *(rec Eglise de Cucuron, France, May 27-29, 1992)* † Allemanda in g Vns; Allemande grave; Allemande in a; Allemande sur les Anches; Motets; Oratorios; Pavane in d; Pavane Hpd; Sarabande — VCL ▲ 61531 [DDD] (11.97)

DUNAWAY, JUDY (20th cent)

Balloon Music

J. Dunaway (balalaika), D. E. Farkas (elec) — CRI (Emergency Music) ▲ 778 [DDD] (16.97)

DUNAYEVKY, ISAAC IOSIFOSICH (1900-1955)

Film Music

Moscow Film Orch, Moscow Film Orch Chorus *(rec 1960)* † Muradeli:Songs — ESTO ■ 1006

DUNHILL, THOMAS (1877-1946)

Fantasy Suite for Clarinet and Piano, Op. 91

E. Jóhannesson (cl), P. Jenkins (pno) *(rec Cambridge, England, Sept 1991)* ("British Music for Clarinet and Piano") † M. Arnold:Son Cl; A. Bliss:Pastoral Cl, Op.posth.; H. Ferguson:Short Pieces Cl, Op. 6; Hurlstone:Characteristic Pieces Cl; Stanford:Son Cl; Stoker:Sonatina Cl, Op. 5 — CHN ▲ 9079 (16.97)

C. West (cl), S. Grace (pno) ("Sonatas for Clarinet and Piano") † A. Bax:Son Cl; L. Bernstein:Son Cl; F. Poulenc:Son Cl & Pno; R. Schumann:Romances Ob, Op. 94; Verdi:Rigoletto (sels) — KLAV ▲ 11076 [DDD] (18.97)

Lyric Suite for Bassoon & Piano, Op. 96 (1941)

M. Karr (bn), J. Jamner (pno) *(rec Louisville, 1996)* ("A Bassoonist's Voice") † J. S. Bach:Partita Fl, BWV 1013; Cervetto:Sicilienne Bn; J. Françaix:Divert Bn; R. Schumann:Fantasiestücke Cl, Op. 73; H. Villa-Lobos:Bachiana brasileira 6 — CENT ▲ 2330 [DDD] (16.97)

D. Smith (bn), R. Vignoles (pno) *(rec London, England)* † T. Arne:Son 5 Hpd; Avison:Son Vn; E. Elgar:Romance Vn, Op. 1; Hurlstone:Son Vn; G. Jacob:Four Sketches Bn; Vaughan Williams:Studies in English Folk-Song — ASV ▲ 535 [DDD] (17.97)

DUNLAP, BRUCE

Lute Music

R. Bluestone (gtr)—Just one feather *(rec Loretto Chapel, Santa Fe, NM)* † Holborne:Lt Music; Lauro:Lt Music; D. Milne:Lt Music; M. Ponce:Son 3 Gtr; Tansman:Lt Music; S. L. Weiss:Lt Music — LINA ▲ 1896 [DDD]

DUNN, DAVID (20th cent)

Chaos & the Emergent Mind of the Pond for Electronics

D. Dunn (elec) ("Angels & Insects") † Tabula Angelorum Bonorum 49 — OOWN ▲ 9 [DDD] (16.97)

Entrainments I for Narrator, Electronics & Tape

L. Rymland (nar) *(rec 1973-85)* ("Music, Language & Environment") † (espial); Entrainments II; Mimus; Nexus I; Skydrift — INNO 2-▲ 508 (14.97)

Entrainments II for Narrators, Electronics & Tape

L. Rymland (nar), R. Robby (nar), S. Storer (nar), D. Dunn (elec/tape), L. Rymland (elec), S. Storer (elec), D. Schwartz (elec), P. Seibel (elec) *(rec 1973-85)* ("Music, Language & Environment") † (espial); Entrainments I; Mimus; Nexus I; Skydrift — INNO 2-▲ 508 (14.97)

(espial) for Violin & Tape

D. Dunn (elec/vn) *(rec 1973-85)* ("Music, Language & Environment") † Entrainments I; Entrainments II; Mimus; Nexus I; Skydrift — INNO 2-▲ 508 (14.97)

Mimus Polyglottos for Mockingbird & Tape (1976)

D. Dunn (elec), R. Cupples (elec) *(rec 1973-85)* ("Music, Language & Environment") † (espial); Entrainments I; Entrainments II; Nexus I; Skydrift — INNO 2-▲ 508 (14.97)

Nexus I for 3 Trumpets (1973)

R. Dudgeon (tpt), E. Harkins (tpt), J. Logan (tpt) *(rec 1973-85)* ("Music, Language & Environment") † (espial); Entrainments I; Entrainments II; Mimus; Skydrift — INNO 2-▲ 508 (14.97)

Skydrift for 10 Voices, 4 Flutes, 4 Clarinets, 4 Trumpets, 4 Trombones & Electronics (1977)

R. Robby (voc), P. Seibel (voc), R. Cupples (voc), E. Band (voc), D. Dunn (voc), P. Hamlin (voc), G. Johnson (voc), P. Keeney (voc), C. Robbins (voc), P. W. Simons (voc), N. Bach (fl), D. Caruso (fl), D. Savage (fl), J. Webb (fl), R. Paredes (cl), D. Lakin-Thomas (cl), D. Marlowe (cl), L. Rhodes (cl), J. Logan (tpt), A. Brewer (tpt), D. Dickey (tpt), L. Fant (tpt), B. Burns (trbn), R. Estes (trbn), M. Mayer (trbn), J. Peterson (trbn), E. Wahl (elec) *(rec 1973-85)* ("Music, Language & Environment") † (espial); Entrainments I; Entrainments II; Mimus; Nexus I — INNO 2-▲ 508 (14.97)

Tabula Angelorum Bonorum 49 (7) for Electronics

D. Dunn (elec) ("Angels & Insects") † Chaos & the Emergent Mind — OOWN ▲ 9 [DDD] (16.97)

DUNSTABLE, JOHN (ca 1390-1453)

Alma redemptoris mater

H. Cluett (sop), J. Lambie (ten), B. Martin (bar) *(rec Littleton-on-Severn, Great Britain & N Ireland, July 1995)* ("A Golden Treasury of Mediaeval Music") † Anonymous:Ad regnum epulentum; Conditor alme siderum; Cormacus scripsit; Corps feminin; Estampie; Ex ejus tumba; Gesegnet sey die frucht; Ich bins erfreut; Io son un pellegrin; My Heartly Service; Nu bitt wir den heiligen geist; Peperit virgo; Petrusllied Unsar trohtin hat farsalt; Quen quer que ten en desden (Cantiga 153); Saltarello; Sire cuens j'ai vielé; Tituerl fragment; Hildegard of Bingen:Symphonia virginum; Traditional:Der notter schwantcz; Rosa delectabilis/Regalis exoritur — AMON ▲ 63 (16.97)

Sacred Music

D. Greig (cnd), Orlando Consort—Missa Rex Seculorum; Ave Maris Stella; Gloria in Canon; O Crux Gloriosa; Descendi in Ortum Meum; Speciosa Facta Es; Sub Tuam Portectionem; Veni Sancte Spiritus; Albanus Roseo Rutilat; Specialis Virgo; Preco Preheminencie; Salve Regina — MENO ▲ 1009 (20.97)

A. Teichert-Hailperin (sop), K. Smith (ct), M. Nitz (ten), W. Jochens (ten), H. Deutsch (bar), Helga Weber Instrumental Circle—Sancta Maria; Beata dei genetrix; Beata mater et innupta virgo; Speciosa facta es; Alma redemmptoris mater † Brassart:Ave Maria, Op. 19; Dufay:Magnificat; Hildegard of Bingen:Sacred Songs — ENTE ▲ 41 [ADD] (10.97)

Sancta Maria for Chorus

H. Chaney (cnd), St. Ignatius of Antioch Choir *(rec New York, NY, Nov 17 & Dec 10, 1989)* † Certon:Missa 'Sus le pont d'Avignon'; Duruflé:Mass, "Cum jubilo", Op. 11; Tallis:Motets; Victoria:Cum beatus Ignatius; C. Wuorinen:Missa Brevis *([ENG,LAT,FRE]text)* — MUA ▲ 4798 [DDD]

DUPARC, HENRI (1848-1933)

Chanson triste in E♭ for Voice & Piano [text H. Cazalis] (1868-69; rev 1902; orchd 1912)

W. Holzmair (bar), G. Wyss (pno) ("Mélodies Françaises") † Extase; Manoir de Rosemonde; Songs; Soupir; Sérénade; G. Fauré:Bonne chanson, Op. 61; Mirages; Mélodies 'de Venise', Op. 58; Poèmes d'un jour, Op. 21; M. Ravel:Mélodies populaires grecques — PPHI ▲ 46686 (16.97)

Extase in D for Voice & Piano [text J. Lahor] (1874; rev ?1884)

W. Holzmair (bar), G. Wyss (pno) ("Mélodies Françaises") † Chanson triste; Manoir de Rosemonde; Songs; Soupir; Sérénade; G. Fauré:Bonne chanson, Op. 61; Mirages; Mélodies 'de Venise', Op. 58; Poèmes d'un jour, Op. 21; M. Ravel:Mélodies populaires grecques — PPHI ▲ 46686 (16.97)

Le Manoir de Rosemonde in d for Voice & Piano [text R. de Bonnières] (1879-?82; orchd 1912)

W. Holzmair (bar), G. Wyss (pno) ("Mélodies Françaises") † Chanson triste; Extase; Songs; Soupir; Sérénade; G. Fauré:Bonne chanson, Op. 61; Mirages; Mélodies 'de Venise', Op. 58; Poèmes d'un jour, Op. 21; M. Ravel:Mélodies populaires grecques — PPHI ▲ 46686 (16.97)

Sérénade in G for Voice & Piano [text G. Marc] (1869)

W. Holzmair (bar), G. Wyss (pno) ("Mélodies Françaises") † Chanson triste; Extase; Manoir de Rosemonde; Songs; Soupir; G. Fauré:Bonne chanson, Op. 61; Mirages; Mélodies 'de Venise', Op. 58; Poèmes d'un jour, Op. 21; M. Ravel:Mélodies populaires grecques — PPHI ▲ 46686 (16.97)

Songs

J. Baker (mez), M. Isepp (pno)—Le Manoir de Rosemonde; Phidylé † D. Argento:From the Diary of Virginia Woolf; Debussy:Songs; G. Fauré:Songs; H. Wolf:Spanisches Liederbuch (Geistliche Lieder) — DNC ▲ 1019 [ADD] (16.97)

W. Holzmair (bar), G. Wyss (pno)—L'invitation au voyage ("Mélodies Françaises") † Chanson triste; Extase; Manoir de Rosemonde; Soupir; Sérénade; G. Fauré:Bonne chanson, Op. 61; Mirages; Mélodies 'de Venise', Op. 58; Poèmes d'un jour, Op. 21; M. Ravel:Mélodies populaires grecques — PPHI ▲ 46686 (16.97)

R. Illing (sop), D. McSkimming (pno)—Chanson triste; Extase; Sérénade Florentine; Le manoir de Rosemonde; La vague et la cloche; Testament; Soupir; Elégie; Lamento; Au pays où se fait la guerre; Phidylé; L'invitation au voyage; La vie antérieure ("Songs") † F. Poulenc:Songs — CHN ▲ 9427 (16.97)

K. T. Kanawa (sop), J. Pritchard (cnd), Royal Opera House Orch Covent Garden—Phidylé; L'invitation au voyage; La Vie antérieure; Le Manoir de Rosemonde; Testament; Au Pays où se fait la guerre; Chanson triste ("French Songs & Arias") † Berlioz:Damnation de Faust (sels); G. Charpentier:Louise (sels); Debussy:Enfant prodigue; M. Ravel:Shéhérazade Mez — EMCD (Red Line) ▲ 69802 [DDD] (6.97)

C. Panzéra (ten) *(rec 1926-32)* † Debussy:Pelléas et Mélisande (sels); Songs; D. Milhaud:Chants populaires hébraïques, Op. 86/3 — PHS ▲ 9300 (17.97)

M. Pedrotti (bar), S. Ralls (pno)—Chanson triste; L'invitation au voyage; Le manoir de Rosamonde; Phidylé [F] † J. Brahms:Songs; Songs (6), Op. 86; Morawetz:Songs; R. Strauss:Songs; P. Tchaikovsky:Songs — MUVI (Musica Viva) ▲ 1051 [DDD] (16.97)

M. Price (sop)—3 songs — ORF ▲ 38831 [DDD] (18.97)

L. Simoneau (ten), E. Werba (pno)—Suopir; Chanson triste; Extase; Le Manoir de Rosemonde *(rec live Salzburg, Aug 1959)* † G. Fauré:Songs; G. F. Handel:Arias; J. Haydn:Canzonettas (12); Rameau:Impatience — ORFE ▲ 460971 (16.97)

C. Zay (sop), O. Sörensen (pno)—Chanson triste; Phidylé; La vie antérieure ("Song Recital") † Debussy:Poèmes de Mallarmé; F. Poulenc:Courte paille; R. Strauss:Songs; R. Wagner:Wesendonck Songs — DORO ▲ 5009 [DDD] (16.97)

Soupir in d for Voice & Piano [text S. Prudhomme] (1869-?8; rev 1902)

W. Holzmair (bar), G. Wyss (pno) ("Mélodies Françaises") † Chanson triste; Extase; Manoir de Rosemonde; Songs; Sérénade; G. Fauré:Bonne chanson, Op. 61; Mirages; Mélodies 'de Venise', Op. 58; Poèmes d'un jour, Op. 21; M. Ravel:Mélodies populaires grecques — PPHI ▲ 46686 (16.97)

DUPHLY, JACQUES (1715-1789)

Pièces de clavecin [Book 1] (1744)

K. Heindel (lt)—La Damanzy † J. Downey:Adagio Lyrico; Agort; Dolphin; Lydian Suite; Octet; Pno Music; Tabu; What If? — GAS ▲ 276 (16.97)

Pièces de clavecin [Book 2] (1748)

L. U. Mortensen (hpd)—La de Redemond † Pièces de clavecin (book 4); J.-B. Forqueray:Morangis ou la plissay; Guillemain:Son Vn; J.-M. Leclair:Quatrième livre, Op. 9; Troisième livre, Op. 5; Mondonville:Pièces de clavecin, Op. 3 — CHN (Chaconne) ▲ 531 [DDD] (16.97)

Pièces de clavecin [Book 4] (1768)

L. U. Mortensen (hpd)—La du Buq † Pièces de clavecin (book 2); J.-B. Forqueray:Morangis ou la plissay; Guillemain:Son Vn; J.-M. Leclair:Quatrième livre, Op. 9; Troisième livre, Op. 5; Mondonville:Pièces de clavecin, Op. 3 — CHN (Chaconne) ▲ 531 [DDD] (16.97)

S. Yates (hpd)—La Porthoüin ("La Sophie") † J. S. Bach:Italian Con, BWV 971; F. Couperin:Pièces de clavecin (sels); G. F. Handel:Harmonious Blacksmith; Rameau:Nouvelles suites; Pièces de clavecin; D. Scarlatti:Sons Kbd — CHN (Chaconne) ▲ 598 (16.97)

DUPONT, GABRIEL EDOUARD XAVIER (1878-1914)

La cabrera (selections)

artists unknown *(rec 1903-07)* ("Souvenirs from Verismo Operas, Vol. 3") † Leoncavallo:Roland von Berlin (sels); Mascherone:Lorenza (sels); Samaras:Mademoiselle de Belle-Isle IRCC ▲ 815 (16.97)

Méditation for Organ

S. Armstrong-Ouellette (org) *(rec Mission Church, Boston, MA)* ("Musique de la Basilique") † Gigout:Pièces Org (sels); Guilmant:Son 7 Org, Op. 89; G. Pierné:Pièces Org, Op. 29; Saint-Martin:Toccata de la Libération; Saint-Saëns:Fant 1 Org; Vierne:Pièces de fantaisie AFK ▲ 538 (16.97)

DUPORT, JEAN-LOUIS (1749-1819)

Nocturne concertant No. 3 in g for Cello & Harp

A. Stein (vc), F. Stein (hp) *(rec Neumünster Church, Zurich, Switzerland, May 12-14, 1982)* ("Court Music for Cello & Harp") † Boccherini:Son 7 Vc & Hp; L. Spohr:Son 5 Vn & Hp, Op. 115 DORO ▲ 3025 [ADD] (16.97)

21 exercicesfaisants suite à l'essai sur le doigté (ca 1813)

A. Bylsma (vc), K. Slowick (vc) ("The Cello & the King of Prussia") † Beethoven:Vars Vc on "Bei Männern", WoO 46; Vars Vc, WoO 45; J.-P. Duport:Sons Vc, Op. 2; B. Romberg:Son 1 in E♭ Vc SNYC ▲ 63360 (16.97)

DUPORT, JEAN-PIERRE (1741-1818)

Sonatas (6) for Cello & Continuo, Op. 2 (ca 1770)

A. Bylsma (vc), K. Slowick (vc), S. Hoogland (pno) ("The Cello & the King of Prussia") † Beethoven:Vars Vc on "Bei Männern", WoO 46; Vars Vc, WoO 45; J.-L. Duport:21 exercicesfaisants suite à l'essai sur l; B. Romberg:Son 1 in E♭ Vc SNYC ▲ 63360 (16.97)

DUPRÉ, MARCEL (1886-1971)

Ballade for Organ & Piano, Op. 30 (1932)

S. Engels (org), A. Bax (pno) † Preludes Org, Op. 45; Sinf Pno, Op. 42; Vars à deux thèmes, Op. 35 NXIN ▲ 8554210 (5.97)

M. Jansson (pno), H. Fagius (org) *(rec July 2-5, 1992)* † Sinf Pno, Op. 42; Vars à deux thèmes, Op. 35; C. Franck:Prélude, fugue et var, Op. 18; Karg-Elert:Poesien, Op. 35; Silhouetten, Op. 29; F. Peeters:Con Org Pno, Op. 74 BIS ▲ 551 [DDD] (17.97)

Le Chemin de la croix for Organ, Op. 29 (1931)

H. Feller (org) *(rec Jann-Org in the Waldsassen Basillica, Sept 1996)* † Vision CALG ▲ 50959 [DDD] (18.97)

Concerto in e for Organ & Orchestra, Op. 31 (1934)

U. Meldau (org), D. Schweizer (cnd), Zurich SO † Préludes & Fugues, Op. 36; Tombeau de Titelouze, Op. 38; Demessieux:Poeme MOTE ▲ 40201 (17.97)

Cortège et Litanie, Op. 19/2 (1921)

J. Filsell (org) *(rec St. Boniface Episcopal Church, Sarasota, FL, Sept 1998)* ("Complete Organ Works-Volume 2") † In Memoriam, Op. 61; Lamento, Op. 24; Miserere mei, Op. 46; Vars sur un vieux Noël, Op. 20 GILD ▲ 7157 [DDD] (16.97)

J. Filsell (org), B. Wordsworth (cnd), BBC Concert Orch [org & orch version] ("Masterworks II for Organ & Orchestra") † Sym; Demessieux:Poeme; J. Gilles:Sym Org GILD ▲ 7136 [DDD] (16.97)

J. Longhurst (org) *(rec Great Org of the Mormon Tabernacle Salt Lake City, United States of America)* ("Romantic French Fantasies") † J. Alain:Org Music (misc); Boëllmann:Ronde Française, Op. 37; Suite 2 Org, Op. 27; C. Franck:Pièces (3) Org, M.35; Vierne:Maestoso; Pièces de fant Org (sels); Widor:Sym 1 Org, Op. 13/1; Sym 4 Org, Op. 13/4; Sym 5 Org, Op. 42/1 KLAV ▲ 11069 [DDD] (18.97)

Elévations (3) for Organ, Op. 32 (1935)

M. Preston (org) † Entrée, Méditation, Sortie, Op. 62; Evocation, Op. 37; Org Music; Psalm 18 Org, Op. 47 NXIN ▲ 8554211 (5.97)

Entrée, Méditation, Sortie for Organ, Op. 62 (1962)

M. Preston (org) † Elévations, Op. 32; Evocation, Op. 37; Org Music; Psalm 18 Org, Op. 47 NXIN ▲ 8554211 (5.97)

Esquisses (2) for Organ, Op. 41 (1945)

J. Vaucher (org) *(rec Org of Saint-François Lausanne)* † Evocation, Op. 37; Lamento, Op. 24; Vêpres de la Vierge, Op. 18; Duruflé:Suite Org, Op. 5; M. Reger:Chorale Fants, Op. 52 GALL ▲ 743 [AAD] (19.97)

Evocation for Organ, Op. 37 (1941)

M. Preston (org) † Elévations, Op. 32; Entrée, Méditation, Sortie, Op. 62; Org Music; Psalm 18 Org, Op. 47 NXIN ▲ 8554211 (5.97)

T. Torén (org) † Préludes & Fugues, Op. 36; Sym-Passion, Op. 23 PRPI ▲ 9003

J. Vaucher (org) *(rec Org of Saint-François Lausanne)* † Esquisses, Op. 41; Lamento, Op. 24; Vêpres de la Vierge, Op. 18; Duruflé:Suite Org, Op. 5; M. Reger:Chorale Fants, Op. 52 GALL ▲ 743 [AAD] (19.97)

Fugues modales (4) for Organ, Op. 63 (1963)

J. Filsell (org) *(rec St. Boniface Episcopal Church, Sarasota, FL, Sept 1998)* ("Complete Organ Works-Volume 1") † Inventions, Op. 50; Préludes & Fugues, Op. 7; Triptyque, Op. 51 GILD ▲ 7156 [DDD] (16.97)

Hymnes (3) for Organ, Op. 58 (1958)

J. Filsell (org) *(rec St. Boniface Episcopal Church, Sarasota, FL, Sept. 1998)* ("Complete Organ Works-Volume 3") † Inventions, Op. 50; Préludes & Fugues, Op. 36 GILD ▲ 7159 [DDD] (16.97)

In Memoriam for Organ, Op. 61 (1961)

J. Filsell (org) *(rec St. Boniface Episcopal Church, Sarasota, FL, Sept 1998)* ("Complete Organ Works-Volume 2") † Cortège et Litanie, Op. 19/2; Lamento, Op. 24; Miserere mei, Op. 46; Vars sur un vieux Noël, Op. 20 GILD ▲ 7157 [DDD] (16.97)

Inventions (24) for Organ, Op. 50 (1954-6)

J. Filsell (org)—Book 1 *(rec St. Boniface Episcopal Church, Sarasota, FL, Sept 1998)* ("Complete Organ Works-Volume 1") † Fugues modales, Op. 63; Préludes & Fugues, Op. 7; Triptyque, Op. 51 GILD ▲ 7156 [DDD] (16.97)

J. Filsell (org)—Book 2 *(rec St. Boniface Episcopal Church, Sarasota, FL, Sept. 1998)* ("Complete Organ Works-Volume 3") † Hymnes; Préludes & Fugues, Op. 36 GILD ▲ 7159 [DDD] (16.97)

Lamento for Organ, Op. 24 (1926)

J. Filsell (org) *(rec St. Boniface Episcopal Church, Sarasota, FL, Sept 1998)* ("Complete Organ Works-Volume 2") † Cortège et Litanie, Op. 19/2; In Memoriam, Op. 61; Miserere mei, Op. 46; Vars sur un vieux Noël, Op. 20 GILD ▲ 7157 [DDD] (16.97)

J. Vaucher (org) *(rec Org of Saint-François Lausanne)* † Esquisses, Op. 41; Evocation, Op. 37; Vêpres de la Vierge, Op. 18; Duruflé:Suite Org, Op. 5; M. Reger:Chorale Fants, Op. 52 GALL ▲ 743 [AAD] (19.97)

Miserere mei for Organ, Op. 46 (1948)

J. Filsell (org) *(rec St. Boniface Episcopal Church, Sarasota, FL, Sept 1998)* ("Complete Organ Works-Volume 2") † Cortège et Litanie, Op. 19/2; In Memoriam, Op. 61; Lamento, Op. 24; Vars sur un vieux Noël, Op. 20 GILD ▲ 7157 [DDD] (16.97)

Organ Music

R. Delcamp (org)—Miserere mei, Op. 46; Angélus, Op. 34; Choral Preludes *(rec Augusta, GA)* † Pièces, Op. 27 NXIN (The Organ Encyclopedia) ▲ 8554026 [DDD] (5.97)

M. Dupré (org)—Sym in d; Passacaglia & Fugue in f; Tombeau de Titelouze, Op. 38 [No. 8, Veni creator spiritus]; Spiritus Hymn MOTE ▲ 60011

J. Filsell (org)—De profundis, Op. 17; Chorales, Op. 28 [Christ gisait dans les liens de la mort; Christ qui nous rend heureux; Christ était sur la croix; Aie pitié moi, O Seigneur Dieu; Seigneur Dieu, maintenant ouvre-moi le ciel; Ardemment j'aspire à une fin heureuse; Je t'apelle, Seigneur Jésus; En toi j'ai espéré, Seigneur; Jésus, ma joie; Mon âme exalte le Seigneur; O innocent agneau de Dieu; O homme, pleure la multitude; Pare-toi ô Chèrée amê; Je veux te dire adieu; Notre Père au Royaumme des Cieux]; Des tres Péchés; Miserere mei, Op. 46; Tombeau de Titelouze, Op. 38 [No. 4, Audi benigne conditor; No. 9, Vexilla Regis; No. 10, Pange lingua; No. 12, Iste confessor] ("Passiontide") † J. S. Bach:Chorales (miscellaneous); Ich dank dir, Gott, für all Wohltat, BWV 346; W. Byrd:Cantiones sacrae (1589) GILD ▲ 7131 [DDD] (16.97)

J.-P. Lecaudey (org)—Préludes & Fugues, Op. 7; Vêpres de la Vierge, Op. 18; Cortège et Litanie, Op. 19/2; Vars sur un vieux Noël, Op. 20 *(rec Nov 1996)* ("Organ Works, Vol. 1") PAVA ▲ 7382 [DDD] (10.97)

Murray (org)—Cortège et Litanie, Op. 42/2; Pièces, Op. 27 [No. 7, Final] † J. S. Bach:Preludes & Fugues, BWV 531-552; C. Franck:Chorales Org, M.38-40; Org Music; Vierne:Meditation & Prelude, Op. 31; Widor:Sym 6 Org, Op. 42/2 TEL ▲ 80169 [DDD] (16.97)

M. Preston (org)—Chorales (6), Op. 28 † Elévations, Op. 32; Entrée, Méditation, Sortie, Op. 62; Evocation, Op. 37; Psalm 18 Org, Op. 47 NXIN ▲ 8554211 (5.97)

J. Scott (org) *(rec St. Paul's Cathedral org London)* ("Organ Music 2") † Sym-Passion, Op. 23 HYP ▲ 67047 (18.97)

C. Watters (org)—Vêpres de la Vierge, Op. 18 [Ave Maris Stella]; Cortège et Litanie, Op. 19/2; Chemin de la croix, Op. 29 † Préludes & Fugues, Op. 7; Vars sur un vieux Noël, Op. 20; Widor:Sym 9 Org, Op. 70 AFK ▲ 508 [ADD]

Pièces (7) for Organ, Op. 27 (1931)

S. Chaisemartin (org) † Vêpres de la Vierge, Op. 18 MOTE ▲ 50251 (17.97)

R. Delcamp (org) *(rec Augusta, GA)* † Org Music NXIN (The Organ Encyclopedia) ▲ 8554026 [DDD] (5.97)

Prélude, fugue et variation in b for Organ [from 6 Pièces], Op. 18 (1860-62)

A. Morrison (org) *(rec Morrow, GA, Nov 19, 1995)* ("Festive Duo") † Sinf Pno, Op. 42; Grasse:Festival Ov, Op. 5; S. Rachmaninoff:Con 2 Pno, Op. 18; Preludes Pno; H. Stover:Neumark Vars ACAD ▲ 20050 (16.97)

DUPRÉ, MARCEL (cont.)

Préludes & Fugues (3) for Organ, Op. 36 (1938)

J. S. Whiteley (org)—No. 3 in C *(rec Cavaillé-Coll org, St. Ouen, Rouen, France)* † Vars on Adeste Fidèles; P. Cochereau:Symphonie; Ibert:Choral sur Justorum animae; Paponaud:Toccata; Vierne:Méditation Org PRIO ▲ 619 [DDD] (16.97)

Préludes & Fugues (3) for Organ, Op. 7 (1912)

J. Filsell (org) *(rec St. Boniface Episcopal Church, Sarasota, FL, Sept 1998)* ("Complete Organ Works-Volume 1") † Fugues modales, Op. 63; Inventions, Op. 50; Triptyque, Op. 51 GILD ▲ 7156 [DDD] (16.97)

A. Morrison (org) *(rec Atlanta GA, Aeolian-Skinner Org)* ("St. Philip's Cathedral") † Vars sur un vieux Noël, Op. 20; Demessieux:Te Deum, Op. 11; Duruflé:Suite Org, Op. 5; C. Franck:Chorales Org, M.38-40 GOT ▲ 49083 [DDD] (17.97)

M. Murray (org) † C. Franck:Final B♭, Op. 21; Messiaen:Nativité du Seigneur; Widor:Sym 6 Org, Op. 42/2 TEL ▲ 80097 [DDD] (16.97)

C. Watters (org) † Org Music; Vars sur un vieux Noël, Op. 20; Widor:Sym 9 Org, Op. 70 AFK ▲ 508 [ADD]

Préludes & Fugues (3) for Organ, Op. 36 (1938)

S. Engels (org) *(rec Karl Göckel Org-Catholic Church, Mannheim, France)* † Sym-Passion, Op. 23; Vars sur un vieux Noël, Op. 20 NXIN ▲ 8553920 (5.97)

J. Filsell (org) *(rec St. Boniface Episcopal Church, Sarasota, FL, Sept. 1998)* ("Complete Organ Works-Volume 3") † Hymnes; Inventions, Op. 50 GILD ▲ 7159 [DDD] (16.97)

U. Meldau (org) † Con Org, Op. 31; Tombeau de Titelouze, Op. 38; Demessieux:Poeme MOTE ▲ 40201 (17.97)

T. Torén (org) † Evocation, Op. 37; Sym-Passion, Op. 23 PRPI ▲ 9003

Preludes (8) on Gregorian Themes for Organ, Op. 45 (1948)

S. Engels (org), A. Bax (pno) † Ballade, Op. 30; Sinf Pno, Op. 42; Vars à deux thèmes, Op. 35 NXIN ▲ 8554210 (5.97)

Psalm 18 (Poème symphonique) for Organ, Op. 47 (1950)

M. Preston (org) † Elévations, Op. 32; Entrée, Méditation, Sortie, Op. 62; Evocation, Op. 37; Org Music NXIN ▲ 8554211 (5.97)

Sinfonia for Piano & Organ, Op. 42 (1946)

S. Engels (org), A. Bax (pno) † Ballade, Op. 30; Preludes Org, Op. 45; Vars à deux thèmes, Op. 35 NXIN ▲ 8554210 (5.97)

M. Jansson (pno), H. Fagius (org) *(rec July 2-5, 1992)* † Ballade, Op. 30; Vars à deux thèmes, Op. 35; C. Franck:Prélude, fugue et var, Op. 18; Karg-Elert:Poesien, Op. 35; Silhouetten, Op. 29; F. Peeters:Con Org Pno, Op. 74 BIS ▲ 551 [DDD] (17.97)

J. Morrison (pno), A. Morrison (org) *(rec Morrow, GA, Nov 19, 1995)* ("Festive Duo") † Prélude, fugue et var, Op. 18; Grasse:Festival Ov, Op. 5; S. Rachmaninoff:Con 2 Pno, Op. 18; Preludes Pno; H. Stover:Neumark Vars ACAD ▲ 20050 (16.97)

Symphonie-Passion for Organ, Op. 23 (1924)

J. Biery (org) *(rec CT Org of the Cathedral of St. J, May 17-18, 1994)* † Vêpres de la Vierge, Op. 18 AFK ▲ 537 (16.97)

S. Engels (org) *(rec Karl Göckel Org-Catholic Church, Mannheim, France)* † Préludes & Fugues, Op. 36; Vars sur un vieux Noël, Op. 20 NXIN ▲ 8553920 (5.97)

G. Kime (org) *(rec Dec 30-Jan 1, 1997-98)* ("Paris by the Bay") † Vicrne:Sym 3 Org, Op. 28 RAVN ▲ 450 [DDD] (17.97)

M. Long (org) † Vars sur un vieux Noël, Op. 20; J. Jongen:Toccata Org, Op. 104; Karg-Elert:Impressions, Op. 72; M. Reger:Pieces (12) Org, Op. 59; Vierne:Carillon de Westminster, Op. 54/6; Méditation Org; Naiades, Op. 55; Stèle pour un enfant, Op. 58 KOCH ▲ 7008 [DDD] (16.97)

J. Scott (org) *(rec St. Paul's Cathedral org London)* ("Organ Music 2") † Org Music HYP ▲ 67047 (18.97)

T. Torén (org) † Evocation, Op. 37; Préludes & Fugues, Op. 36 PRPI ▲ 9003

Symphony in g for Organ & Orchestra, Op. 25 (1928)

J. Filsell (org), B. Wordsworth (cnd), BBC Concert Orch ("Masterworks II for Organ & Orchestra") † Cortège et Litanie, Op. 19/2; Demessieux:Poeme; J. Gilles:Sym Org GILD ▲ 7136 [DDD] (16.97)

Murray (org), J. Ling (cnd), Royal PO *(rec 1986)* † Rheinberger:Con 1 Org, Op. 137 TEL ▲ 80136 [DDD] (16.97)

Le tombeau de Titelouze for Organ, Op. 38 (1943)

U. Meldau (org) † Con Org, Op. 31; Préludes & Fugues, Op. 36; Demessieux:Poeme MOTE ▲ 40201 (17.97)

P. Wright (org) *(rec Lewis Org Southwark Cathedral)* † Barié:Pièces Org, Op. 7; Sym Org, Op. 5 PRIO ▲ 406 [DDD]

Triptyque for Organ, Op. 51 (1951)

J. Filsell (org) *(rec St. Boniface Episcopal Church, Sarasota, FL, Sept 1998)* ("Complete Organ Works-Volume 1") † Fugues modales, Op. 63; Inventions, Op. 50; Préludes & Fugues, Op. 7 GILD ▲ 7156 [DDD] (16.97)

Variations on Adeste Fidèles for Organ [trans Rollin Smith from recording of Dupré's improv, 1929]

J. S. Whiteley (org) *(rec Cavaillé-Coll org, St. Ouen, Rouen, France)* † Préludes & Fugues, Op. 36; P. Cochereau:Symphonie; Ibert:Choral sur Justorum animae; Paponaud:Toccata; Vierne:Méditation Org PRIO ▲ 619 [DDD] (16.97)

Variations à deux thèmes for Organ & Piano, Op. 35 (1935)

S. Engels (org), A. Bax (pno) † Ballade, Op. 30; Preludes Org, Op. 45; Sinf Pno, Op. 42 NXIN ▲ 8554210 (5.97)

A. Gordon (pno), B. Jones (org) † Clokey:Symphonic Piece; Demarest:Fant Org; Grasse:Festival Ov, Op. 5; R. Wagner:Walküre (ride of the Valkyries) AFK ▲ 506

M. Jansson (pno), H. Fagius (org) *(rec July 2-5, 1992)* † Ballade, Op. 30; Sinf Pno, Op. 42; C. Franck:Prélude, fugue et var, Op. 18; Karg-Elert:Poesien, Op. 35; Silhouetten, Op. 29; F. Peeters:Con Org Pno, Op. 74 BIS ▲ 551 [DDD] (17.97)

Variations sur un vieux Noël for Organ, Op. 20 (1922)

S. Engels (org) *(rec Karl Göckel Org-Catholic Church, Mannheim, France)* † Préludes & Fugues, Op. 36; Sym-Passion, Op. 23 NXIN ▲ 8553920 (5.97)

H. Fagius (org) *(rec Härnösand Cathedral, Sweden, Jan 15, 1979)* † J. Alain:Vars sur un thème de Clément Janequin; Boëllmann:Suite gothique Org, Op. 25; F. Couperin:Pièces d'orgue consistantes en deux Messes; Daquin:Nouveau livre de noëls, Op. 2; Duruflé:Prélude et fugue, Op. 7; Saint-Saëns:Fant 1 Org BIS ▲ 7 [AAD] (17.97)

J. Farris (org) † J. Alain:Deuxième fant, AWV 91; Duruflé:Prélude et fugue, Op. 7; C. Franck:Pièces (3) Org, M.35; Vierne:Sym 6 Org, Op. 59; Widor:Sym 6 Org, Op. 42/2 DLS ▲ 3049 [DDD] (14.97)

J. Filsell (org) *(rec St. Boniface Episcopal Church, Sarasota, FL, Sept 1998)* ("Complete Organ Works-Volume 2") † Cortège et Litanie, Op. 19/2; In Memoriam, Op. 61; Lamento, Op. 24; Miserere mei, Op. 46 GILD ▲ 7157 [DDD] (16.97)

M. Long (org) † Sym-Passion, Op. 23; J. Jongen:Toccata Org, Op. 104; Karg-Elert:Impressions, Op. 72; M. Reger:Pieces (12) Org, Op. 59; Vierne:Carillon de Westminster, Op. 54/6; Méditation Org; Naiades, Op. 55; Stèle pour un enfant, Op. 58 KOCH ▲ 7008 [DDD] (16.97)

D. Macomber (org) ("Works of the French Masters") † J. Alain:Litanies, Op. 79; Duruflé:Org Music (misc); Prélude et fugue, Op. 7; Roger-Ducasse:Pastoral Org; Vierne:Carillon de Westminster, Op. 54/6; Widor:Andante sostenuto Org ARK ▲ 6152 [DDD] (16.97)

A. Morrison (org) *(rec Atlanta GA, Aeolian-Skinner Org)* ("St. Philip's Cathedral") † Préludes & Fugues, Op. 7; Demessieux:Te Deum, Op. 11; Duruflé:Suite Org, Op. 5; C. Franck:Chorales Org, M.38-40 GOT ▲ 49083 [DDD] (17.97)

D. Schrader (org) *(rec Duluth, MN, Mar 10-11, 1993)* † C. Franck:Final B♭, Op. 21; Pastorale, Op. 19; Pièces (3) Org, M.35; Pièces (3) Org, M.36; Pièces (3) Org, M.37; Prélude, fugue et var, Op. 18 CED ▲ 15 [DDD] (16.97)

C. Watters (org) † Org Music; Préludes & Fugues, Op. 7; Widor:Sym 9 Org, Op. 70 AFK ▲ 508 [ADD]

Les vêpres de la Vierge (15) for Organ, Op. 18 (1919)

J. Biery (org) *(rec CT Org of the Cathedral of St. J, May 17-18, 1994)* † Sym-Passion, Op. 23 AFK ▲ 537 (16.97)

S. Chaisemartin (org) † Pièces, Op. 27 MOTE ▲ 50251 (17.97)

D. Hill (org), P. Lefebvre (org), M. Berry (cnd), Schola Gregoriana ("Gregorian Chant & Grand-Orgue") HER ▲ 170 (19.97)

J. Vaucher (org) *(rec Org of Saint-François Lausanne)* † Esquisses, Op. 41; Evocation, Op. 37; Lamento, Op. 24; Duruflé:Suite Org, Op. 5; M. Reger:Chorale Fants, Op. 52 GALL ▲ 743 [AAD] (19.97)

Versets (15) sur let Vêpres de la Vierge [15 Pieces Founded on Antiphons] for Organ, Op. 18 (1919)

J. Hancock (org) *(rec St. Thomas Church, NYC, NY)* † P. Eben:Sunday Music GOT ▲ 49110 [DDD] (17.97)

Vision for Organ, Op. 44 (1947)

H. Feller (org) *(rec Jann-Org in the Waldsassen Basillica, Sept 1996)* † Chemin de la croix, Op. 29 CALG ▲ 50959 [DDD] (18.97)

DUPUY, JEAN BAPTISTE EDOUARD (ca 1770-1822)

Concerto No. 1 in d for Flute & Orchestra (1814)

T. L. Christiansen (fl), M. Schønwandt (cnd), Copenhagen Collegium Musicum *(rec Odd Fellow Concert Hall, Dec 1996-Jan 1997)* † Youth & Folly MARC 2-▲ 8224066 [DDD] (27.97)

DUPUY, JEAN BAPTISTE EDOUARD (cont.)

Youth & Folly, or Trick for Trick [Ungdom og galskap, eller List over list] (singspiel in 2 acts) [lib N. T. Brunn after J. N. Bouilly] (1806)

D. Mai-Mai (sop—Vilhelmine), P. Elming (ten—Poul), P. Grønlund (ten—Rose), E. Harbo (ten—Mikkel), G. Paevatalu (bar—Johan), U. Cold (bass—Grøndal), M. Schønwandt (cnd), Copenhagen Collegium Musicum *(rec Odd Fellow Concert Hall, Dec 1996-Jan 1997)* † Con 1 Fl MARC 2-▲ 8224066 [DDD] (27.97)

Youth & Folly:Overture

J. Hye-Knudsen (cnd), Royal Danish Orch ("Romantic Danish Overtures") † J. P. E. Hartmann:Little Kristen (ov); Heise:King & Marshal (ov); Horneman:Aladdin (ov); Kuhlau:William Shakespeare (ov); Weyse:Sleeping-draught (ov) STRL ▲ 1018 [AAD] (15.97)

DURAN, GERARDO (dates unknown)

Nepantla for Orchestra

E. Diazmuñoz (cnd), Mexico City PO † Kuri-Aldana:Canto Latinamericano; Lavalle-García:Obertura Colonial; Mabarak:Sym in One Mvt; Moncayo Garcia:Bosques; Sandi:Theme & Vars CLME ▲ 21231 (13.97)

H. de la Fuente (cnd), Mexican State PO † M. K. Aldana:Canto Latinoamericano; R. Halffter:Madrugada del panadero, Op. 12a; Jiménez-Mabarak:Sym in 1 Movt; Lavalle-García:Obertura Colonial; Sandi:Theme & Vars CLME ▲ 21006 (13.97)

DURAND, JOËL FRANÇOIS (20th cent)

Concerto for Piano and Orchestra

S. Litwin (pno), Lubman (cnd), Berlin SO † Innere Grenze; Trio Strs DISQ ▲ 782093 (18.97)

Die innere Grenze for Sextet

Sextour Schoenberg † Con Pno; Trio Strs DISQ ▲ 782093 (18.97)

Trio for Strings

Ensemble Intercontemporain † Con Pno; Innere Grenze DISQ ▲ 782093 (18.97)

DURANTE, FRANCESCO (1684-1755)

Concerti (8) per quartetto

E. Aadland (cnd), European Union CO—Con No. 1 ("Concertos for the Kingdom of the 2 Sicilies") † Pergolesi:Con Fl; Porpora:Con Vc HYP ▲ 55005 (9.97)

Concerto Cologne [period instrs] CAPO ▲ 10371 (11.97)

G. D. Lorenzo (cnd) ("Sinfonie per archi, Vol. 1") AG ▲ 67 [DDD] (18.97)

Vox Aurae Ensemble ("Sinfonias for Strings, Vol. 2") † Con Pno; Hpd Music AG ▲ 125 (18.97)

Concerto in B♭ for Piano & Strings

F. Braga (hpd), Vox Aurae Ensemble ("Sinfonias for Strings, Vol. 2") † Con per quartetto; Hpd Music AG ▲ 125 (18.97)

A. Cristiano (pno), I. Caiazza (cnd) *(rec Mar 1996)* ("Neapolitan Instrumental Music of the 1700's") † A. Prati:Con Pno; Ragazzi:Con Grosso; Con Vn in a; Con Vn in B♭ KICC ▲ 396 [DDD] (17.97)

Duetti da camera (12) for Soprano, Contralto & Continuo

R. Gini (cnd), Concerto Ensemble TACT ▲ 680401 (16.97)

Harpsichord Music

F. Braga (hpd) ("Sinfonias for Strings, Vol. 2") † Con per quartetto; Con Pno AG ▲ 125 (18.97)

Lamentationes Jeremiae Prophetae for solo Voices, Ensemble & Chorus

D. Fasolis (cnd), Sonatori de la Gioiosa Marca, Swiss Radio Chorus Lugano, R. Invernizzi (sop), E. Galli (sop), R. Dominguez (cta), D. Labusch (cta), A. Cantor (cta), M. Beasley (ten), A. Abete (bass), F. Zanasi (bass) † Vespro breve AART ▲ 47522 (10.97)

M. Frimmer (sop), M. Bach (sop), M. Joswig (sgr), P. Neumann (cnd), Collegium Cartusianum, Cologne Chamber Choir CPO ▲ 999325 (14.97)

S. Frontalini (cnd), Moldava Academic National SO, Moldava Academic National Chorus † Requiem in c BONG ▲ 2152 (16.97)

Music of Durante

G. G. Boymann (cnd), Capella Durante—Beatus vir in C; Magnificat in a; Laudate Pueri in C; Magnificat in c; Miserere in c ("Choral Works") THOR ▲ 2266 [DDD] (17.97)

Requiem in c for Chorus (1746)

S. Frontalini (cnd), Moldava Academic National Chorus † Lamentationes Jeremiae Prophetae BONG ▲ 2152 (16.97)

Sonatas (12) Divided into Etudes & Divertimentos for Harpsichord (ca 1732)

L. Alvini (hpd) ("Studii e divertimenti per cembalo") † A. Scarlatti:Variations on La Follia TACT ▲ 680402 [DDD] (16.97)

E. Catemario (gtr) *(rec Lucca Italy, Sept 1994)* ("Barocco Napoletano") † D. Scarlatti:Sons Kbd AART ▲ 47356 [DDD] (10.97)

Vespro breve (Dixit Dominus) in C for 4 Voices

D. Fasolis (cnd), Sonatori de la Gioiosa Marca, Swiss Radio Chorus Lugano † Lamentationes Jeremiae Prophetae AART ▲ 47522 (10.97)

DUREY, LOUIS (EDMOND) (1888-1979)

Le Bestiaire for Voice & Piano [text Apollinaire] (1919; arr for Voice & 13 Instruments, 1958)

C. Lemelin (mez), M. Tabachnik (cnd), Québec Youth Orch ("Bestiaire") † Absil:Poèmes, Op. 45; Caplet:Fables; Daunais:Chansons; J. Kosma:Ménagerie de Tristan SNE ▲ 565 (16.97)

Carillons for Piano 4-Hands

G. Picavet (pno), B. Picavet (pno) † Neige; G. Auric:Waltz Pno 4-Hands; Honegger:Partita Pno 4-Hands; D. Milhaud:Création du monde, Op. 81; Scaramouche Pnos, Op. 165b; F. Poulenc:Capriccio; Elégie Pnos; Embarquement pour Cythère; Tailleferre:Jeux de plein air ILD ▲ 642129 (11.97)

Neige for Piano 4-Hands (1918; orchd 1919)

G. Picavet (pno), B. Picavet (pno) † Carillons; G. Auric:Waltz Pno 4-Hands; Honegger:Partita Pno 4-Hands; D. Milhaud:Création du monde, Op. 81; Scaramouche Pnos, Op. 165b; F. Poulenc:Capriccio; Elégie Pnos; Embarquement pour Cythère; Tailleferre:Jeux de plein air ILD ▲ 642129 (11.97)

Préludes (3) à la mémoire de Juliette Méerowitch for Piano, Op. 26 (1920)

M. Bratke (pno) ("Le Groupe des Six") † G. Auric:Adieu New York; Honegger:Pièces brèves; D. Milhaud:Printemps Pno, Op. 25; F. Poulenc:Mouvements perpétuels; Pièces Pno; Tailleferre:Romance Pno OLY ▲ 487 [DDD] (12.97)

DURKÓ, ZSOLT (1934-1997)

Altamira for Orchestra & Chorus (1967-68)

G. Lehel (cnd), Budapest SO, Hungarian Radio-TV Chamber Chorus *(rec 1972)* † Burial Prayer; History of the Spheres; Iconography 2 HUN ▲ 31654 [AAD/DDD] (16.97)

Burial Prayer (oratorio) for Tenor, Baritone, Orchestra & Chorus (1967-72)

A. Fülöp (ten), E. Ütö (bass), G. Lehel (cnd), Budapest SO, F. Sapszon (cnd), Hungarian Radio-TV Chorus *(rec 1975)* † Altamira; History of the Spheres; Iconography 2 HUN ▲ 31654 [AAD/DDD] (16.97)

Concerto for Piano & Orchestra (1980-81)

K. Körmendi (pno), L. Friend (cnd), Hungarian National PO *(rec live, 1994-97)* † Ludus stellaris; Revelation to John HUN ▲ 31818 [DDD] (16.97)

The History of the Spheres (cycle of 60 pieces in 5 series) for Piano (1989-91)

Z. Durkó (pno) *(rec 1995)* † Altamira; Burial Prayer; Iconography 2 HUN ▲ 31654 [AAD/DDD] (16.97)

Iconography No. 2 for Horn & 7 Instruments (1971)

F. Tarjáni (hn), A. Mihály (cnd) *(rec 1972)* † Altamira; Burial Prayer; History of the Spheres HUN ▲ 31654 [AAD/DDD] (16.97)

Ludus stellaris for Orchestra (1984)

J. Petró (cnd), Hungarian National Phil CO *(rec live, 1994-97)* † Con Pno; Revelation to John HUN ▲ 31818 [DDD] (16.97)

The Revelation to John (oratorio) for Alto, Tenor, Baritone, Orchestra & Chorus (1994-96)

A. Ligeti (cnd), Budapest SO, M. Antal (cnd), Hungarian National Chorus, L. Medgyesi-Schwartz (mez), J. Mukk (ten), L. Szvétek (bar) *(rec live, 1994-97)* † Con Pno; Ludus stellaris *([ENG,HUN] texts)* HUN ▲ 31818 [DDD] (16.97)

Sinfonietta for Brass Ensemble

L. Friend (cnd), Philip Jones Brass Ensemble *(rec Hampstead, London, England, June 1986)* ("Philip Jones Brass Ensemble Finale") † M. Berkeley:Music from Chaucer; W. Lutoslawski:Mini Ov; A. Previn:Triolet; Rautavaara:Playgrounds for Angels CHN ▲ 8490 [DDD] (16.97)

DURÓN, SEBASTIÁN (1660-1716)

El Impossible mayor en amor le venze Amor for Ensemble (1710)

Al Ayre Español † Anonymous:Cancion Franzesa; Discourso de ecos; Ruede la Vola; Literes:Accis y Galatea; Elementos; Estrago en la finesa DEHA ▲ 77696 (16.97)

Sosieguen Descansen for Soprano, Harpsichord & Strings

J. Savall (cnd), Hespèrion XX *(rec Séon, Switzerland, Sep 1976)* ("El Barroco Espanol") † Cabanilles:Music of Cabanilles; J. Hidalgo:Songs; Marín:Songs; Martín y Coll:Songs; Milanes:Songs; Vado:Songs VCL ▲ 61346 [ADD] (11.97)

DURUFLÉ, MAURICE (1902-1986)

Danses (3) for Orchestra, Op. 6 (1932)

A. Goldina (pno), R. Loumbrozo (pno) [trans Duruflé for 2 pnos] *(rec 1992-96)* † R. Casadesus:Danses Mediterranéenes, Op. 36; M. Ravel:Entre cloches; Pièce en forme de Habanera; Rapsodie espagnole; Sites auriculaires; Valse PHOE ▲ 135 [DDD] (15.97)

Fugue sur le Theme du Carillon des Heures de la Cathédrale de Soissons for Organ, Op. 12

F. Ledroit (org) *(rec Angoulême, France)* † Prelude sur l'Introit de l'Epiphany, Op. 13; Prélude et fugue, Op. 7; Prélude, Adagio et Choral varié, Op. 4; Scherzo, Op. 2; Suite Org, Op. 5 SKAR ▲ 1974 [DDD] (18.97)

Mass for Baritone, Male Chorus & Orchestra, Op. 11, "Cum jubilo" (1966)

H. Chaney (cnd), St. Ignatius of Antioch Choir, D. L. Echlard (ten), B. Hurst (bar), H. Chaney (org) [arr for bar, male chorus & org] *(rec Casavant Frères org, New York, NY, Feb 23, 1992)* † Certon:Missa 'Sus le pont d'Avignon'; Dunstable:Sancta Maria; Tallis:Motets; Victoria:Cum beatus Ignatius; C. Wuorinen:Missa Brevis *([ENG,LAT,FRE]text)* MUA ▲ 4798 [DDD]

T. Gödde (bar), T. Götting (org), H. Hennig (cnd), Hanover Boys' Choir *(rec Mar-Apr 1997)* † A. Dvořák:Mass THOR ▲ 2367 [DDD] (16.97)

D. Henry (bar), M. Piquemal (cnd) , Michel Piquemal Vocal Ensemble *(rec Eglise Saint Antoine des Quinze-Vingts Paris, June & Oct 1994)* ("Sacred Choral Works & Organ Works, Vol. 2") † Prélude, Adagio et Choral varié, Op. 4; Suite Org, Op. 5 NXIN ▲ 553197 [DDD] (5.97)

S. Keenlyside (bar), N. Clein (vc), A. Webber (trbn), I. Simcock (org), J. O'Donnell (cnd), Westminster Cathedral Choir † Motets on Gregorian Chants, Op. 10; Notre Père, Op. 14; Requiem, Op. 9 HYP ▲ 66757 (18.97)

F. Le Roux (bar), D. Keene (cnd), Voices of Ascension Orch, Voices of Ascension *(rec Church of the Ascension New York City, May 13, 17-18, 1995)* ("The Duruflé Album") † Requiem, Op. 9 DLS ▲ 3169 [DDD] (14.97)

R. Marlow (cnd), London Musici, Trinity College Choir Cambridge † Motets on Gregorian Chants, Op. 10; G. Fauré:Requiem, Op. 48; Messiaen:O sacrum convivium! CONI ▲ 15351 (16.97)

P. Mattei (bar), M. Wager (org), St. Jacob's Chamber Choir *(rec Nov 9-12, 1992)* † Motets on Gregorian Chants, Op. 10; Requiem, Op. 9 BIS ▲ 602 [DDD] (17.97)

Motets on Gregorian Chants (4) for Chorus, Op. 10 (1960)

G. Guest (org), G. Guest (cnd) , St. John's College Choir Cambridge † Requiem, Op. 9; G. Fauré:Cantique de Jean Racine, Op. 11; Messe basse PLON (Double Decca) 2-▲ 36486 (17.97)

W. Hall (cnd) , Master Chorale of Orange County † Motets on Gregorian Chants, Op. 10; Requiem, Op. 9 SUMM ▲ 134 [DDD] (16.97)

J. Hancock (org), G. Hancock (cnd), St. Thomas Church Men & Boys' Choir New York ("Most Sacret Banquet") † C. Franck:Psalm 150; J. Langlais:Messe solenelle; Messiaen:O sacrum convivium!; F. Poulenc:Exultate Deo KOCH ▲ 7228 (16.97)

S. Keenlyside (bar), N. Clein (vc), A. Webber (trbn), I. Simcock (org), J. O'Donnell (cnd) , Westminster Cathedral Choir † Mass, "Cum jubilo", Op. 11; Notre Père, Op. 14; Requiem, Op. 9 HYP ▲ 66757 (18.97)

R. Marlow (cnd), London Musici, Trinity College Choir Cambridge † Mass, "Cum jubilo", Op. 11; G. Fauré:Requiem, Op. 48; Messiaen:O sacrum convivium! CONI ▲ 15351 (16.97)

St. Jacob's Chamber Choir *(rec Dec 2, 1992)* † Mass, "Cum jubilo", Op. 11; Requiem, Op. 9 BIS ▲ 602 [DDD] (17.97)

Notre Père for Chorus, Op. 14

S. Keenlyside (bar), N. Clein (vc), A. Webber (trbn), I. Simcock (org), J. O'Donnell (cnd) , Westminster Cathedral Choir † Mass, "Cum jubilo", Op. 11; Motets on Gregorian Chants, Op. 10; Requiem, Op. 9 HYP ▲ 66757 (18.97)

Organ Music (miscellaneous)

D. Macomber (org)—Sicilienne; Toccata ("Works of the French Masters") † Prélude et fugue, Op. 7; J. Alain:Litanies, Op. 79; M. Dupré:Vars sur un vieux Noël, Op. 20; Roger-Ducasse:Pastoral Org; Vierne:Carillon de Westminster, Op. 54/6; Widor:Andante sostenuto Org ARK ▲ 6152 [DDD] (16.97)

Organ Music (complete)

D. M. Patrick (org)—Org Music (comp) *(rec Coventry Cathedral Org, United States of America)* † Vierne:Improvs Org ASV ▲ 993 (16.97)

J. Scott (org)—Scherzo, Op. 2; Prélude, adagio et choral varié sur le, Op. 4; Suite, Op. 5; Prélude et fugue, Op. 7; Prelude sur l'Introit de l'Epiphany, Op. 13; Fugue sur le Theme du Carillon des Heures, Op. 12 *(rec St. Paul's Cathedral Org, London, England)* HYP ▲ 66368 (18.97)

T. Torén (org)—Scherzo, Op. 2; Suite, Op. 5; Prélude et fugue, Op. 7 ("Duruflé: L'Oeuvre d'Orgue") PRPI ▲ 9059 (17.97)

T. Wilson (org)—Scherzo, Op. 2; Prélude, adagio et choral varié sur le, Op. 4; Suite, Op. 5; Prélude et fugue, Op. 7; Prelude sur l'Introit de l'Epiphany, Op. 13; Fugue sur le Theme du Carillon des Heures, Op. 12 *(rec St. Thomas Aquinas Dallas, Texas)* DLS ▲ 3047 (14.97)

Prélude, Adagio et Choral varié sur le thème du *Veni Creator* for Organ, Op. 4 (1930)

H. Feller (org) † Messiaen:Messe de la Pentecôte; Tournemire:Orgue mystique, Opp. 55-57 CALG ▲ 50939 (19.97)

E. Lebrun (org) *(rec Eglise Saint Antoine des Quinze-Vingts Paris, June & Oct 1994)* ("Sacred Choral Works & Organ Works, Vol. 2") † Mass, "Cum jubilo", Op. 11; Suite Org, Op. 5 NXIN ▲ 553197 [DDD] (5.97)

F. Ledroit (org) *(rec Angoulême, France)* † Fugue sur le Theme du Carillon des Heures, Op. 12; Prelude sur l'Introit de l'Epiphany, Op. 13; Prélude et fugue, Op. 7; Scherzo, Op. 2; Suite Org, Op. 5 SKAR ▲ 1974 [DDD] (18.97)

J. Lippincott (org) *(rec Princeton Univ Chapel's Mander Org)* † H. Howells:Rhap in c# Org, Op. 17/3; Widor:Sym 6 Org, Op. 42/2 GOT ▲ 49061 [DDD] (17.97)

M. Preston (org) *(rec Dallas, TX)* ("Mary Preston Plays Duruflé & Widor") † Suite Org, Op. 5; Widor:Sym 3 Org, Op. 13/3 GOT ▲ 49079 [DDD] (17.97)

Prélude et fugue sur le nom d'Alain for Organ, Op. 7 (1942)

M. Duruflé (org), D. MacDonald (org)—Prélude; Fugue *(rec Casavant Org, Basilique Notre Dame du Cap, Quebec, Canada, Mar 1993)* † J. Alain:Jardin suspendu, AWV 63; Cardy:Eclat Org; Daveluy:Choral Prelude Org; Son 3 Org; C. Franck:Chorales Org, M.38-40; Messiaen:Nativité du Seigneur; Widor:Sym 5 Org, Op. 42/1 CBC ▲ 1104 [DDD] (16.97)

M. Duruflé-Chevalier (org) *(rec Great Organ of the National Shrine, Wahington, DC, 1967)* † J. S. Bach:Orgelbüchlein; Buxtehude:Fugue; G. F. Handel:Cons (16) Org; R. Schumann:Studies Canon Form, Op. 56; Tournemire:Improvs (5) GOT ▲ 49107 (17.97)

H. Fagius (org) *(rec Nederluleå Church, Gammelstad, Sweden, June 1974)* † J. Alain:Vars sur un thème de Clément Janequin; Boëllmann:Suite gothique Org, Op. 25; F. Couperin:Pièces d'orgue consistantes en deux Messes; Daquin:Nouveau livre de noëls, Op. 2; M. Dupré:Vars sur un vieux Noël, Op. 20; Saint-Saëns:Fant 1 Org BIS ▲ 7 [AAD] (17.97)

J. Farris (org) † J. Alain:Deuxième fant, AWV 91; M. Dupré:Vars sur un vieux Noël, Op. 20; C. Franck:Pièces (3) Org, M.35; Vierne:Sym 6 Org, Op. 59; Widor:Sym 6 Org, Op. 42/2 DLS ▲ 3049 [DDD] (14.97)

L. Kurpershoek (org) *(rec St. Mary's Anglican Cathedral Org Johannesburg)* ("Popular Organ Music, Vol. 4") † J. Brahms:Chorale Preludes Org, Op. 122; N. Cocker:Tuba Tune; C. Franck:Chorales Org, M.38-40; Grové:Afrika Hymnus; Hollins:Intermezzo PRIO ▲ 610 (16.97)

F. Ledroit (org) *(rec Angoulême, France)* † Fugue sur le Theme du Carillon des Heures, Op. 12; Prelude sur l'Introit de l'Epiphany, Op. 13; Prélude, Adagio et Choral varié, Op. 4; Scherzo, Op. 2; Suite Org, Op. 5 SKAR ▲ 1974 [DDD] (18.97)

D. Macomber (org) ("Works of the French Masters") † Org Music (misc); J. Alain:Litanies, Op. 79; M. Dupré:Vars sur un vieux Noël, Op. 20; Roger-Ducasse:Pastoral Org; Vierne:Carillon de Westminster, Op. 54/6; Widor:Andante sostenuto Org ARK ▲ 6152 [DDD] (16.97)

A. Morrison (org)—Prélude *(rec St. Luke's Presbytar. Atlanta, GA)* ("Alan Morrison") † Krape:Choral Triptych Org; J. Langlais:Hommage à Frescobaldi; Org Music; J. Weaver:Passacaglia on a Theme by Dunstable; Widor:Sym 6 Org, Op. 42/2 ACAD ▲ 20015 (16.97)

Prélude, récitatif et variations for Flute, Viola & Piano, Op. 3 (1928)

L. Grunth (va), B. Larsen (fl), S. Larsen (pno) *(rec Copenhagen, Mar 1996)* ("The French Flute") † Gallon:Improv Fl; Suite Fl; R. Hahn:Romanesque; Rhené-Baton:Bourée, Op. 42; Passacaille Fl & Pno, Op. 35; Ropartz:Sonatine Fl CLSO ▲ 160 (15.97)

New Jersey Chamber Music Society † Indy:Suite Fl, Str Trio & Hp, Op. 91; F. Martin:Qnt Pno PREM ▲ 1032 [DDD] (16.97)

South African Chamber Music Society † Bolcom:Afternoon Cakewalk; A. Khachaturian:Trio Cl; Kodály:Intermezzo DI ▲ 920462 [DDD] (5.97)

Prelude sur l'Introit de l'Epiphany for Organ, Op. 13 (1961)

F. Ledroit (org) *(rec Angoulême, France)* † Fugue sur le Theme du Carillon des Heures, Op. 12; Prélude et fugue, Op. 7; Prélude, Adagio et Choral varié, Op. 4; Scherzo, Op. 2; Suite Org, Op. 5 SKAR ▲ 1974 [DDD] (18.97)

Requiem for solo Voices, Organ, Orchestra & Chorus, Op. 9 (1947)

J. Blegen (sop), J. Morris (bass), R. Shaw (cnd), Atlanta SO, Atlanta Sym Chorus [LAT] † G. Fauré:Requiem, Op. 48 TEL ▲ 80135 [DDD] (16.97)

B. Bonney (sop), J. Larmore (mez), T. Hampson (bar), M. Legrand (cnd), Philharmonia Orch, Ambrosian Singers † G. Fauré:Requiem, Op. 48 TELC ▲ 90879 (16.97)

DURUFLÉ, MAURICE (cont.)

Requiem for solo Voices, Organ, Orchestra & Chorus, Op. 9 (1947) (cont.)

R. F. Bragadóttir (mez), M. J. Clarke (bar), I. R. Ingólfsdóttir (vc), H. Lucke (org), H. Áskelsson (cnd), Hallgrímskirkja Motet Choir *(rec Rejkiavik, Oct 1996)* † Suite Org, Op. 5 THOR ▲ 2339 [DDD] (16.97)

M. Chung (cnd), St. Cecilia Academy Orch Rome, St. Cecilia Academy Chorus Rome, C. Bartoli (sop), B. Terfel (b-bar) ("In Paradisum") † G. Fauré:Requiem, Op. 48 DEUT ▲ 459365 [DDD] (16.97)

G. Guest (org), G. Guest (cnd), St. John's College Choir Cambridge † Motets on Gregorian Chants, Op. 10; G. Fauré:Cantique de Jean Racine, Op. 11; Messe basse PLON (Double Decca) 2-▲ 36486 (17.97)

W. Hall (cnd) , Master Chorale of Orange County † Motets; Motets on Gregorian Chants, Op. 10 SUMM ▲ 134 [DDD] (16.97)

E. Higginbottom (cnd), New College Choir Oxford [LAT] † G. Fauré:Requiem, Op. 48 CRD ▲ 3466 [DDD] (17.97)

P. Hofman (ten), P. Mattei (bar), E. Lavotha (vc), M. Wager (org), St. Jacob's Chamber Choir *(rec Nov 9-12, 1992)* † Mass, "Cum jubilo", Op. 11; Motets on Gregorian Chants, Op. 10 BIS ▲ 602 [DDD] (17.97)

S. Keenlyside (bar), N. Clein (vc), A. Webber (trbn), I. Simcock (org), J. O'Donnell (cnd) , Westminster Cathedral Choir † Mass, "Cum jubilo", Op. 11; Motets on Gregorian Chants, Op. 10; Notre Père, Op. 14 HYP ▲ 66757 (18.97)

J. Mayeur (mez), M. Piquemal (bar), F. Dupuis (vc), N. Pien (org), D. Bargier (cnd), Rouen Chamber Choir [2nd version for soloists, org & chorus] † Villette:Motets SOC ▲ 140 [ADD] (16.97)

A. Murray (mez), T. Allen (bar), M. Best (cnd), English CO, Corydon Singers [LAT] HYP ▲ 66191 [DDD] (18.97)

A. Murray (mez), T. Allen (bar), M. Best (cnd), English CO, Corydon Singers † G. Fauré:Requiem, Op. 48 HYP ▲ 67070 (18.97)

P. Spence (mez), F. Le Roux (bar), D. Keene (cnd), Voices of Ascension Orch, Voices of Ascension *(rec Church of the Ascension New York City, June 5-6, 1994)* ("The Duruflé Album") † Mass, "Cum jubilo", Op. 11 DLS ▲ 3169 [DDD] (14.97)

Sacred Choral Music

N. Hutchinson (org), A. Noble (cnd), Farnborough Abbey Choir—Offertory [Veritas mea]; Communion [Beatus servus] *(rec St. Michael's Abbey Farnborough, May 1994)* ("Laetabunda: Gregorian Chant & Chant-Inspired Choral & Organ Music by Langlais & Duruflé") † Suite Org, Op. 5; J. Langlais:Org Music; Sacred Choral Music HER ▲ 179 [DDD]

Scherzo for Organ, Op. 2 (1924)

F. Ledroit (org) *(rec Angoulême, France)* † Fugue sur le Theme du Carillon des Heures, Op. 12; Prelude sur l'Introit de l'Epiphany, Op. 13; Prélude et fugue, Op. 7; Prélude, Adagio et Choral varié, Op. 4; Suite Org, Op. 5 SKAR ▲ 1974 [DDD] (18.97)

Suite for Organ, Op. 5 (1933)

N. Hutchinson (org) *(rec St. Michael's Abbey Farnborough, May 1994)* ("Laetabunda: Gregorian Chant & Chant-Inspired Choral & Organ Music by Langlais & Duruflé") † Sacred Choral Music; J. Langlais:Org Music; Sacred Choral Music HER ▲ 179 [DDD]

E. Lebrun (org) *(rec Eglise Saint Antoine des Quinze-Vingts Paris, June & Oct 1994)* ("Sacred Choral Works & Organ Works, Vol. 2") † Mass, "Cum jubilo", Op. 11; Prélude, Adagio et Choral varié, Op. 4 NXIN ▲ 553197 [DDD] (5.97)

F. Ledroit (org) *(rec Angoulême, France)* † Fugue sur le Theme du Carillon des Heures, Op. 12; Prelude sur l'Introit de l'Epiphany, Op. 13; Prélude et fugue, Op. 7; Prélude, Adagio et Choral varié, Op. 4; Scherzo, Op. 2 SKAR ▲ 1974 [DDD] (18.97)

H. Lucke (org) *(rec Rejkiavik, Oct 1996)* † Requiem, Op. 9 THOR ▲ 2339 [DDD] (16.97)

A. Morrison (org) *(rec Atlanta GA, Aeolian-Skinner Org)* ("St. Philip's Cathedral") † Demessieux:Te Deum, Op. 11; M. Dupré:Préludes & Fugues, Op. 7; Vars sur un vieux Noël, Op. 20; C. Franck:Chorales Org, M.38-40 GOT ▲ 49083 [DDD] (17.97)

M. Preston (org) *(rec Dallas, TX)* ("Mary Preston Plays Duruflé & Widor") † Prélude, Adagio et Choral varié, Op. 4; Widor:Sym 3 Org, Op. 13/3 GOT ▲ 49079 [DDD] (17.97)

H. Spillman (org) ("French Suites for Organ") † Clérambault:Premier livre d'orgue; Messiaen:Ascension Org TIT ▲ 204 [DDD]

J. Vaucher (org) *(rec Org of Saint-François Lausanne)* † M. Dupré:Esquisses, Op. 41; Evocation, Op. 37; Lamento, Op. 24; Vêpres de la Vierge, Op. 18; M. Reger:Chorale Fants, Op. 52 GALL ▲ 743 [AAD] (19.97)

DUSAPIN, PASCAL (1955-

Loop for 8 Cellos

Cello Octet † P. Boulez:Messagesquisse; Capon:A tempo; Pärt:Fratres for 8 Vcs; E. Vásquez:Migrations; H. Villa-Lobos:Bachiana brasileira 1 BUD ▲ 13 [DDD] (16.97)

Medeamaterial (opera) [text Heiner Müller]

Z. Kilanowicz (sop), H. Leidland (sop—Medea), M. D. Callataÿ (sop), R. Popken (alt), F. Beukelaers (sgr), M. Patzakis (sgr), C. Petrick (sgr), P. Herreweghe (cnd), Chapelle Royale Orch, Collegium Vocale *(rec Théâtre Royal de la Monnaie Brussels, Mar 13, 1992)* HAM (Suite) ▲ 7905215 [DDD] (12.97)

Music of Dusapin

E. Krivine (cnd), Lyon National Orch—Apex; Extenso; La Melancholia DISQ ▲ 782073 (18.97)

Quartet for Strings

Arditti String Quartet † Time Zones; Dutilleux:Ainsi la nuit DISQ ▲ 782016 (18.97)

Time Zones for String Quartet

Arditti String Quartet † Qt Str; Dutilleux:Ainsi la nuit DISQ ▲ 782016 (18.97)

DUSATKO, TOMAS (1952-

Traces of Becoming for Orchestra (1986)

A. Pauk (cnd), Esprit Orch *(rec Toronto, Canada)* † Chan Ka Nin:Ecstasy; B. Cherney:Into the Distant Stillness; C. K. Nin:Ecstasy; A. Pauk:Echo Spirit Isle; R. M. Schafer:Dream Rainbow SMS ▲ 5101 [DDD] (16.97)

DUŠECK, FRANTIŠEK XAVER (1731-1799)

Sonata in F

J. Becker (pno) *(rec Sept 1991)* ("Sonate Facile") † W. F. Bach:Son in C Hpd; C.P.E. Bach:Sonatas for Viol & Continuo; J. Christian Bach:Sons Kbd; G. A. Benda:Sonatina 1 Pno; Sonatina 2 Pno; W. A. Mozart:Son 16 Pno, K.545 CAPO ▲ 10415 [DDD] (11.97)

DUSSEK, JAN LADISLAV (1760-1812)

Concerto in E for Harp (or Piano) & Orchestra, Op. 15 (1789)

R. Alessandrini (hp), V. Parisi (cnd), Mantova Orch *(rec Jan 1995)* ("Harp Concertos") † Sons Hp, Op. 34; Krumpholtz:Con 6 Hp, Op. 9; Wagenseil:Con Hp NXIN ▲ 8553622 [DDD] (5.97)

Concerto in F for Piano (or Harp) & Orchestra, Op. 17 (ca 1792)

M. Garzón (pno), J. Corazolla (cnd), New Rhine CO † Con in Pno, Op. 27; Con in Pno, Op. 40 KSCH ▲ 364312 (16.97)

Concerto in F for Piano & Orchestra, Op. 27 (1794)

M. Garzón (pno), J. Corazolla (cnd), New Rhine CO † Con in Pno, Op. 40; Con Pno, Op. 17 KSCH ▲ 364312 (16.97)

Concerto in B♭ for Piano & Orchestra, Op. 40, "Military" (1798)

M. Garzón (pno), J. Corazolla (cnd), New Rhine CO † Con in Pno, Op. 27; Con Pno, Op. 17 KSCH ▲ 364312 (16.97)

Concerto in B♭ for Piano & Strings, Op. 22 (1793)

A. Staier (pno) *(rec German Radio Cologne, Nov 24-28, 1992)* ("Klavierkonzerte") † Con in Pno, Op. 49; Sufferings of the Queen of France, Op. 23 CAPO ▲ 10444 [DDD] (11.97)

Concerto in g for Piano & Strings, Op. 49 (1801)

A. Staier (pno) *(rec German Radio Cologne, Nov 24-28, 1992)* ("Klavierkonzerte") † Con Pno, Op. 22; Sufferings of the Queen of France, Op. 23 CAPO ▲ 10444 [DDD] (11.97)

Harp Music

J. Ellis (vn), H. Verney (vc), D. Perrett (hp), W. Cole (pno)—A Favorite Duet for Hp & Pno, Op. 11; Son in E for Hp, Op. 34/1; Favorite Son for Hp, Vn & Vc, Op. 37; Son in B for Hp, Op. 34/2; Duet Hp, Op. 38 ("Music for Winds") MER ▲ 84244 [DDD] (16.97)

K. Kim (hp) ("Harp Sonatas") MAND ▲ 4909 (18.97)

Quartet in E♭ for Piano & Strings, Op. 56

H. Barton (pno), Apollo String Quartet members ("Chamber Music for Piano") † Qnt Pno, Op. 41; Son Pno, Op. 77 STMA ▲ 20 [DDD] (18.97)

Quintet in f for Piano & Strings, Op. 41 (1799)

H. Barton (pno), Apollo String Quartet ("Chamber Music for Piano") † Qt Pno; Son Pno, Op. 77 STMA ▲ 20 [DDD] (18.97)

Sonatas (3) in B♭, E♭ & F for Harp & Piano, Op. 69 (1810-11)

D. Bell (hp), J. Leach (pno) † Son Pno, Op. 61 ATH ▲ 10 [DDD] (18.97)

Sonata No. 3 in c for Harp, Op. 2

E. Goodman (hp)—Allegro; Andantino; Rondo. Allegro *(rec Peterborough, Ontario, Canada, Nov 1985)* ("The Virtuoso Harp") † Sons Vn, Op. 2; G. Fauré:Impromptu Hp, Op. 86; N. Flagello:Son Hp; S. Prokofiev:Pieces (10) Pno, Op. 12; Salzedo:Scintillation; Tournier:Sonatine Hp, Op. 30 BIS ▲ 319 [DDD] (17.97)

Sonatas (2) in E♭ & B♭ for Harp, Violin & Cello, Op. 34

R. Alessandrini (hp), V. Parisi (cnd) *(rec Jan 1995)* ("Harp Concertos") † Con Hp; Krumpholtz:Con 6 Hp, Op. 9; Wagenseil:Con Hp NXIN ▲ 8553622 [DDD] (5.97)

DUSSEK, JAN LADISLAV (cont.)

Sonatas for Piano

G. Govier (pno)—in C, Op. 9/2; in g, Op. 10/2; in B, G & c, Op. 35/1-3 OLY ▲ 430 [DDD]

F. Marvin (pno)—in C, Op. 4/3; in g, Op. 10/2; in c, Op. 35/3 *(rec Syracuse Univ., 1975-79)* ("Piano Works of Jan Ladislav Dussek, Vol. 2") † Son Pno, Op. 61 DOR ▲ 80125 [ADD] (13.97)

Sonata in a for Piano, Op. 18/2 (1792)

F. Marvin (pno) † Son Pno; Son Pno, Op. 77 DOR (Discovery) ▲ 80110 [ADD] (13.97)

Sonata in E♭ for Piano, Op. 44, "The Farewell" (1800)

I. Hobson (pno)—Grave-Allegro moderato con espressione; Molto adagio e sostenuto; Tempo di minuetto più tosto allegro; Rondo-Allegro moderato ed espressivo *(rec Concordia College, London, England, June 1988)* ("The London Piano School, Vol. 1: Georgian Classicists") † Anonymous:Rondo Pno; J. Christian Bach:Sons Kbd; J. Burton:Son 1 Pno; Busby:Son Pno; M. Clementi:Sons (6) Pno, Op. 13 ARA ▲ 6594 (16.97)

Sonata in f♯ for Piano, Op. 61, "Elégie harmonique sur la mort du Prince Louis" (1806-07)

H. Barton (pno) † Son Pno 4-Hands, Op. 48; Trio Son Pno, Op. 65 STMA ▲ 46 (18.97)

C. Keene (pno) † Beethoven:Son 25 Pno, Op. 79; Griffes:Son Pno; J. Haydn:Son 62 Kbd, H.XVI/52; J. N. Hummel:Son 9 Pno PROT ▲ 1106 [ADD] (18.97)

J. Leach (pno) † Sons Hp, Op. 69 ATH ▲ 10 [DDD] (18.97)

F. Marvin (pno) *(rec Syracuse Univ., 1975-79)* ("Piano Works of Jan Ladislav Dussek, Vol. 2") † Sonatas for Piano DOR ▲ 80125 [ADD] (13.97)

Sonata in D for Piano, Op. 69/3

F. Marvin (pno) † Son Pno; Son Pno, Op. 77 DOR (Discovery) ▲ 80110 [ADD] (13.97)

Sonata in f for Piano, Op. 77, "L'invocation"

H. Barton (pno) ("Chamber Music for Piano") † Qnt Pno, Op. 41; Qt Pno STMA ▲ 20 [DDD] (18.97)

R. Firkušný (pno) *(rec 1972-74)* † G. A. Benda:Son 9 Pno; A. Dvořák:Humoresques, Op. 101; Mazurkas, Op. 56; Poetic Tone Pictures, Op. 85; Theme with Vars, Op. 36; Smetana:Czech Dances Pno; Tomášek:Eclogues (42) Pno; Voříšek:Impromptus Pno, Op. 7 VB2 2-▲ 5058 [ADD] (9.97)

F. Marvin (pno) † Son Pno DOR (Discovery) ▲ 80110 [ADD] (13.97)

Sonata in C for Piano 4-Hands, Op. 48

H. Barton (pno) † Son Pno, Op. 61; Trio Son Pno, Op. 65 STMA ▲ 46 (18.97)

Sonatas (3) for Violin & Piano, Op. 2

E. Goodman (hp) ("The Virtuoso Harp") † Son 3 Hp, Op. 2; G. Fauré:Impromptu Hp, Op. 86; N. Flagello:Son Hp; S. Prokofiev:Pieces (10) Pno, Op. 12; Salzedo:Scintillation; Tournier:Sonatine Hp, Op. 30 BIS ▲ 319 [DDD] (17.97)

J. Suk (vn), K. Englichová (hp) ("Golden Strings") † Massenet:Méditation from Thaïs; O. Respighi:Siciliana; G. Rossini:Andante e tema con variazioni Va; Saint-Saëns:Cygne; Fant Vn; L. Spohr:Son 2 Vn & Hp, Op. 16 LT ▲ 38 [DDD] (16.97)

The Sufferings of the Queen of France for solo Piano, Op. 23 (1793)

J. Forest (spkr—Marie-Antoinette), A. Staier (pno) *(rec German Radio Cologne, Nov 24-28, 1992)* ("Klavierkonzerte") † Con in Pno, Op. 49; Con Pno, Op. 22 CAPO ▲ 10444 [DDD] (11.97)

Trio Sonata in F for Piano, Flute & Violin, Op. 65 (1807)

Apollon Quartet † Son Pno 4-Hands, Op. 48; Son Pno, Op. 61 STMA ▲ 46 (18.97)

M. Valli (vc), F. Pagnini (fl), P. Bidoli (pno) ("Chamber Music in the Biedermeier Period") † Kalkbrenner:Son Fl; C. Kreutzer:Son Fl, Vc & Pno, Op. 23/1 ENT (Tiziano) ▲ 96002 [DDD] (16.97)

DUTILLEUX, HENRI (1916-

Ainsi la nuit for String Quartet (1975-76)

Arditti String Quartet † Dusapin:Qt Str; Time Zones DISQ ▲ 782016 (18.97)

Juilliard String Quartet *(rec May 13-15, 1992)* † Debussy:Qt Strs, Op. 10; M. Ravel:Qt Strs SNYC ▲ 52554 [DDD] (16.97)

Orpheus String Quartet *(rec Jan 1992)* † Debussy:Qt Strs, Op. 10; M. Ravel:Qt Strs CCL ▲ 3892 [DDD] (18.97)

Schoenberg String Quartet † E. Chausson:Concert Vn, Op. 21; Debussy:Son Vn KSCH ▲ 312312 [DDD]

L'Arbe de songes for Violin & Orchestra (1985)

O. Charlier (vn), J. P. Tortelier (cnd), BBC PO † Prière pour nous autres charnels; Sonnets de Jean Cassou; Timbres, espace, mouvement avec interlude CHN ▲ 9504 (16.97)

I. V. Keulen (vn), I. van Keulen (vn), M. Würsch (perc), M. Soustrot (cnd), Bamberg SO *(rec Apr 1997)* † Mystère de l'instant; Timbres, espace, mouvement; Timbres, espace, mouvement avec interlude KSCH ▲ 364912 [DDD] (16.97)

I. Stern (vn), L. Maazel (cnd), French National Orch † P. M. Davies:Con Vn SNYC ▲ 42449 [DDD] (16.97)

Concerto for Cello & Orchestra, "Tout un Monde Lointain" (1970)

B. Pergamenschikow (vc), J. P. Tortelier (cnd), BBC PO † Mystère de l'instant; Métaboles CHN ▲ 9565 (16.97)

Métaboles (5) for Orchestra (1965)

M. Chung (cnd), Bastille Opera Orch † Berlioz:Sym fantastique, Op. 14 DGRM ▲ 445878 [DDD]

J. P. Tortelier (cnd), BBC PO † Con Vc; Mystère de l'instant CHN ▲ 9565 (16.97)

Mystère de l'instant for 24 Strings, Cymbals & Percussion (1989)

I. V. Keulen (vn), I. van Keulen (vn), M. Würsch (perc/cym), M. Soustrot (cnd), Bamberg SO *(rec Apr 1997)* † Arbe de songes; Timbres, espace, mouvement; Timbres, espace, mouvement avec interlude KSCH ▲ 364912 [DDD] (16.97)

J. P. Tortelier (cnd), BBC PO † Con Vc; Métaboles CHN ▲ 9565 (16.97)

Prière pour nous autres charnels for Orchestra [arr from piece by Jehan Alain] (1944)

M. Hill (ten), N. Davies (bar), J. P. Tortelier (cnd), BBC PO † Arbe de songes; Sonnets de Jean Cassou; Timbres, espace, mouvement avec interlude CHN ▲ 9504 (16.97)

Sarabande et Cortège for Bassoon & Piano (1942)

S. Canuti (bn), M. Somenzi (pno) ("Bassoon Images") † M. de Falla:Canciones populares españolas; P. Hindemith:Son Bn; Mompou:Aureana do sil; Combat del somni; A. Piazzolla:Grand Tango; Saint-Saëns:Son Bn STRV ▲ 80013 (16.97)

L. Magnanini (bn), M. Levin (pno) ("Twentieth Century Music for Bassoon & Piano") † Bozza:Récit, Sicilienne & Rondò; Castelnuovo-Tedesco:Sonatina Bn; A. Longo:Suite Bn; Procaccini:Pieces Bn; N. Rota:Toccata Bn ALTA ▲ 9031 (18.97)

M. Monguzzi (bn), G. Brollo (pno) *(rec May 1995)* ("20th Century Bassoon") † U. Bertoni:Con Bn; Bozza:Fant Bn; Récit, Sicilienne & Rondò; P. Hindemith:Son Bn; Saint-Saëns:Son Bn; Tansman:Sonatine Bn; Suite Bn BONG ▲ 5565 [DDD] (16.97)

Sonata for Oboe & Piano (1947)

T. Indermühle (ob), W. Genuit (pno) *(rec Vienna, Feb 10-12, 1993)* † Jolivet:Sérénade Ob; D. Milhaud:Sonatina Ob, Op. 337; M. Ravel:Tombeau; Skalkottas:Concertino Ob, A/K.28 CAMA ▲ 282 [DDD] (18.97)

F. Meyer (ob), E. Le Sage (pno) † B. Britten:Metamorphoses, Op. 49; P. Hindemith:Son Ob; F. Poulenc:Son Ob; Saint-Saëns:Son Ob SONP ▲ 94011 [DDD] (16.97)

Sonata for Piano (1947)

D. Amato (pno) † Balakirev:Son in b♭ for Pno OLY ▲ 354 [DDD] (16.97)

M. Jude (pno) HAM (Les Nouveaux Interprètes) ▲ 911569 (12.97)

Sonatine for Flute & Piano (1942)

E. Pahud (fl), E. Le Sage (pno) *(rec Highgate London, England, Feb 1997)* ("Paris") † Ibert:Aria Cl & Pno; Jeux; Jolivet:Chant de Linos Fl & Pno; Messiaen:Merle noir; D. Milhaud:Sonatina Fl & Pno, Op. 76; F. Poulenc:Son Fl; Sancan:Sonatine Fl EMIC ▲ 56488 [DDD] (16.97)

P. Robison (fl), S. Sanders (pno) † F. Borne:Fant brillante sur Carmen; Delibes:Morceau de concours; G. Fauré:Morceau de concours Fl; Sicilienne, Op. 78; P. Gaubert:Son 1 Fl; Massenet:Morceaux de concours; Taffanel:Andante Pastorale et Scherzettino Fl & Pno VC ▲ 4058 (13.97)

Songs (4) for Baritone (or Mezzo-Soprano) & Piano (or Orchestra) (1942)

P. Mason (bar), R. Spillman (pno) ("Mélodies") † G. Fauré:Bonne chanson, Op. 61; F. Poulenc:Fraîcheur et le feu; M. Ravel:Histoires naturelles BRID ▲ 9058 [DDD] (17.97)

Sonnets de Jean Cassou (2) for Baritone & Piano

N. Davies (bar), J. P. Tortelier (cnd), BBC PO [arr bar & orch] † Arbe de songes; Prière pour nous autres charnels; Timbres, espace, mouvement avec interlude CHN ▲ 9504 (16.97)

Symphony No. 1 (1950)

S. Baudo (cnd), Lyon National Orch † Timbres, espace, mouvement avec interlude HAM (Suite) ▲ 7905159 (12.97)

Y. P. Tortelier (cnd), BBC PO † Sym 2 CHN ▲ 9194 [DDD] (16.97)

Symphony No. 2, "Le Double" (1958-59)

C. Munch (cnd), French National Orch *(rec Jun 1962)* ("Charles Munch Edition, vol. 6") † Honegger:Sym 1 VAL ▲ 4830 [ADD] (12.97)

Y. P. Tortelier (cnd), BBC PO † Sym 1 CHN ▲ 9194 [DDD] (16.97)

Timbres, espace, mouvement avec interlude for Orchestra (1978-91)

S. Baudo (cnd), Lyon National Orch † Sym 1 HAM (Suite) ▲ 7905159 (12.97)

I. V. Keulen (vn), M. Würsch (perc), M. Soustrot (cnd), Bamberg SO *(rec Apr 1997)* † Arbe de songes; Mystère de l'instant; Timbres, espace, mouvement avec interlude KSCH ▲ 364912 [DDD] (16.97)

▲ = CD ♦ = Enhanced CD △ = MD ▮ = Cassette Tape ▯ = DCC

DUTILLEUX, HENRI (cont.)
Timbres, espace, mouvement avec interlude for Orchestra (1978-91) (cont.)
J. P. Tortelier (cnd), BBC PO † Arbe de songes; Prière pour nous autres charnels; Sonnets de Jean Cassou
CHN ▲ 9504 (16.97)
DUTKIEWICZ, ANDRZEJ (20th cent)
A-la for Piano
A. Dutkiewicz (pno) ("Dutkiewicz Plays Dutkiewicz") † Music for Two; Sketches; Sophie's Music; Suite Pno; Tango GAS ▲ 240 [DDD] (16.97)
Music for Two for 2 Pianos (1976)
C. Lewis (pno), A. Dutkiewicz (pno) ("Dutkiewicz Plays Dutkiewicz") † A-la; Sketches; Sophie's Music; Suite Pno; Tango GAS ▲ 240 [DDD] (16.97)
Sketches in Retrospect (3) for Piano (1985)
A. Dutkiewicz (pno) ("Dutkiewicz Plays Dutkiewicz") † A-la; Music for Two; Sophie's Music; Suite Pno; Tango
GAS ▲ 240 [DDD] (16.97)
Sophie's Music for Four for Piano Trio & Electronic Tape (1986)
A. Dutkiewicz (elec), Lanier Trio ("Dutkiewicz Plays Dutkiewicz") † A-la; Music for Two; Sketches; Suite Pno; Tango GAS ▲ 240 [DDD] (16.97)
Suite for Piano (1970)
A. Dutkiewicz (pno) ("Dutkiewicz Plays Dutkiewicz") † A-la; Music for Two; Sketches; Sophie's Music; Tango
GAS ▲ 240 [DDD] (16.97)
Tango for Cello & Piano (1995)
D. Lewis (vc), C. Lewis (pno) ("Dutkiewicz Plays Dutkiewicz") † A-la; Music for Two; Sketches; Sophie's Music; Suite Pno GAS ▲ 240 [DDD] (16.97)
DUTTON, BRENT (1950-
Carnival of Venice (fantasie & variations) for Brass Quintet
1-5 Brass Quintet † Horovitz:Music Hall Suite; A. Hovhaness:Dances Brass Qnt, Op. 79; F. Leclerc:Par Monts et par vaux CRYS ▲ 200 [ADD] (15.97)
DUVERNOY, FRÉDÉRIC (1765-1838)
Nocturne No. 2 for Horn & Harp
S. Hermansson (hn), E. Goodman (hp) *(rec Ontario, Canada, Sept 20-23, 1993)* ("Horn & Harp Soirée - 19th Century French & Italian Duos") † N. C. Bochsa:L'écho (Nocturne 2) Hn & Hp; Boieldieu:Solo Hn & Hp; Chaussier:Elegy Hn & Hp; Dauprat:Air Ecossais Var Hn & Hp, Op. 22; Son Hn & Hp; Paisiello:Andante Hn & Hp; Spontini:Divert Hn & Hp BIS ▲ 648 [DDD] (17.97)
DUVERNOY, J. B. (1802-1880)
Feu roulant for Pianos, Op. 256
J. Rogers (pno), J. Morrison (pno) *(rec Morrow, GA, United States of America, June 8-9, 1993)* ("A Virtuoso Duo-Piano Showcase") † J. Brahms:Vars on a Theme by Haydn; J. Costa:Flying Fingers 2 Pnos; E. von Dohnányi:Suite en valse 2 Pnos, Op. 39a; W. Lutoslawski:Vars Theme Paganini 2 Pnos; H. Stover:Rag Pastorale & Carillon
ACAD ▲ 20023 (16.97)
DVARIONAS, BALYS (1904-1972)
Elegie for Violin & Strings (1947)
G. Kremer (vn) ("From My Home") † Barkauskas:Partita Vn; Pärt:Fratres I Str Qt; Pelécis:Con Vn Pno; Plakidis:2 Grasshopper Dances; Tüür:Conversio; Vasks:Musica Dolorosa TELC ▲ 14654 (16.97)
DVOŘÁK, ANTONÍN (1841-1904)
The American Flag (cantata) for Alto, Tenor, Bass, Orchestra & Chorus, Op. 102, (B.177), (S.116) (1892-93)
J. Evans (ten), B. McDaniel (bar), M. T. Thomas (cnd), Berlin RSO, RIAS Chamber Choir, St. Hedwig's Cathedral Choir † Carnival, Op. 92; Sym 5 SNYC (Essential Classics) ▲ 60297 (7.97) ▮ 60297 (3.98)
Armida (opera in 4 acts) [lib Jaroslav Vrchlický], Op. 115, (B.206), (S.138) (1902-03)
J. Borowska (sop—Armida), W. Ochman (ten—Rinald), R. Sporka (ten—Dudo), V. Nacházel (bar—Roger), J. Markvart (bar—Sven), P. Daniluk (bass—King), G. Fortune (bass—Ismen), Z. Harvánek (bass—Ubald), M. Podskalský (bass—Peter), M. Brychtová (sgr—Siren), M. Bürger (sgr—Gernand), R. Janál (sgr—Hlasatel/Muezzin), V. Kříž (sgr—Gottfried), G. Albrecht (cnd), Czech PO, Prague Chamber Choir *(rec 1995)*
ORF 2-▲ 404962 [DDD] (36.97)
Bagatelles [Maličkosti] (5) for 2 Violins, Cello & Harmonium, Op. 47, (B.79), (S.56) (1878)
V. Black (harm), Alberni String Quartet members *(rec Oct-Nov 1988)* † Gavotte, B.164; Miniatures, Op. 75a; Terzetto, Op. 74; Waltzes Strs, Op. 54 CRD ▲ 3457 [DDD] (17.97)
C. Castleman (vn) † S. Adler:Son 2 Vn; Martinů:Promenades; D. Milhaud:Son Vn & Hpd, Op. 257; Piston:Sonatina Vn; Rubbra:Cant Pastorale, Op. 92; Fant on a Theme of Machaut, Op. 86 ALBA ▲ 41 (16.97)
R. Firkušný (pno), Juilliard String Quartet members † Qnt Pno, Op. 81; Qts Pno, Opp. 23 & 87
SNYC 2-▲ 45672 (14.97)
Lindsay String Quartet [arr for str qt] ("The Bohemians, Vol. 5") † Qnt Strs, Op. 97; Terzetto, Op. 74
ASV ▲ 806 [DDD] (16.97)
J. Panocha (vn), P. Zejfart (vn), J. Kulhan (vc), J. Tůma (harm) *(rec Prague, Nov 3 & Dec 4, 1996)* ("Chamber Works, Vol. 2") † Intermezzos, B.15; Qt 2 Strs, B.17 SUR ▲ 111452 [DDD]
Pražák String Quartet † Qt 12 Strs, Op. 96; Terzetto, Op. 74 PRAG ▲ 250110 (7.97)
J. Suk (vn), I. Ženatý (vn), J. Barta (vc), J. Hála (harm) † Miniatures, Op. 75a; Terzetto, Op. 74
LT ▲ 48 [DDD] (16.97)
J. Tůma (harm), Panocha String Quartet members *(rec Prague, Czech Republic, 1992-1997)* † Cypresses, B.152; Miniatures, Op. 75a; Nocturne Strs, Op. 40; Qt Movt Strs, B.120; Waltzes Strs, Op. 54 SUR ▲ 3391 [DDD] (16.97)
Ballad in d for Violin & Piano, Op. 15/1, (B.139), (S.95) (?1884)
K. Fife (vn), D. Da Silva (pno) *(rec Calabasas, CA)* ("Czech Mate: Music for Violin & Piano") † Nocturne Strs, Op. 40; Janáček:Dumka; Romance Vn; Son Vn; Smetana:From the Homeland RACA ▲ 1006 (16.97)
A. Marwood (vn), S. Tomes (pno) † Nocturne Strs, Op. 40; Romantic Pieces, Op. 75; Son Vn; Sonatina Vn, Op. 100 HYP ▲ 66934 (18.97)
S. Stanzeleit (vn), J. Jacobson (pno) ("Music for Violin & Piano, Vol. 1") † Mazurek, Op. 49; Nocturne Strs, Op. 40; Romance Vn, Op. 11; Son Vn MER ▲ 84274 [DDD] (16.97)
J. Suk (vn), J. Hála (pno) † Nocturne Strs, Op. 40; Romantic Pieces, Op. 75; Son Vn; Sonatina Vn, Op. 100
SUR ▲ 111466
I. Ženatý (vn), A. Kubalek (pno) ("Complete Music for Violin & Piano") † Mazurek, Op. 49; Romantic Pieces, Op. 75; Son Vn; Sonatina Vn, Op. 100 DOR ▲ 90171 [DDD] (16.97)
Biblical Songs [Biblické písně] (10) for solo Voice & Piano, Op. 99, (B.185), (S.122) (1894)
B. R. Cook (bar), N. Järvi (cnd), Royal Scottish National Orch † Sym 4 CHN ▲ 8608 [DDD] (16.97)
B. R. Cook (bar), N. Järvi (cnd), Royal Scottish National Orch [CZE] † Carnival, Op. 92; Slavonic Rhaps, Op. 45; Symphonic Vars, Op. 78(28) CHN ▲ 9002 [DDD] (16.97)
D. Fischer-Dieskau (bar), J. Demus (pno) † Requiem Mass, Op. 89 DEUT (Double) 2-▲ 37377 (17.97)
M. Hemm (bar), Z. Macal (cnd), New Jersey SO *(rec Apr 9, 1994)* † Stabat Mater, Op. 58
DLS 2-▲ 3161 [DDD] (20.97)
I. Kusnjer (bar), M. Lapšanský (pno) *(rec Prague, Czech Republic, Jan 12 & June 16-17, 1998)* † Modern Greek Poems, Op. 50; Zigeunermelodien, Op. 55 *([CZE,ENG,FRE,GER] text)* SUR ▲ 3247 [DDD] (16.97)
I. Siebert (sop), J. Krause (org) † M. Lehmann:Prayer; T. Nilsson:Consolamini popule meus, Op. 16
ENTE ▲ 79 [ADD] (10.97)
V. Smetáček (cnd), Czech PO † Mass; Te Deum SUR ▲ 111821 [AAD]
E. Urbanová (sop), J. Pokorný (pno) † Songs; Zigeunermelodien, Op. 55 GZCL ▲ 326 (6.97)
S. Zambalis (sop), G. Morton (pno) ("Song Cycles") † Love Songs, Op. 83; Zigeunermelodien, Op. 55
OPP ▲ 2578 (10.97)
Carnival [Karneval] (concert overture) for Orchestra, Op. 92, (B.169), (S.113) (1891)
G. Albrecht (cnd), Czech PO † In Nature's Realm, Op. 91; Othello, Op. 93; J. Brahms:Sym 1
SUR (Czech PO Centennial) ▲ 111995
K. Ančerl (cnd), Czech PO † Hussite Ov, Op. 67; In Nature's Realm, Op. 91; My Home, Op. 62; Othello, Op. 93
SUR ▲ 110605 [ADD]
K. Ančerl (cnd), Czech PO *(rec 1966)* † Hussite Ov, Op. 67; My Home, Op. 62; Sym 6 SUR ▲ 111926 [AAD]
J. Bělohlávek (cnd), Czech PO † Sym 9; Symphonic Vars, Op. 78(28) SUR (Czech Philharmonic) ▲ 111987 [DDD]
L. Bernstein (cnd), New York PO *(rec New York, NY, Feb 1, 1965)* † Slavonic Dances (sels); Sym 9
SNYC (Bernstein Century) ▲ 60563 [ADD] (11.97)
S. Comissiona (cnd), Houston SO *(rec May 1987)* PRA ▲ 3432 [DDD] (14.97)
A. Davis (cnd), Philharmonia Orch † Sym 7; Sym 8; Sym 9 SNYC 2-▲ 45618
J. Farrer (cnd), Royal PO † In Nature's Realm, Op. 91; Othello, Op. 93; Scherzo Capriccioso, Op. 66; Symphonic Vars, Op. 78(28) ASV ▲ 794 (16.97)
C. M. Giulini (cnd) † Scherzo Capriccioso, Op. 66; Sym 7; Sym 8; Sym 9 EMIC (Doublefforte) 2-▲ 68628 (16.97)
S. Gunzenhauser (cnd), BBC PO *(rec Mar 23-24, 1992)* † In Nature's Realm, Op. 91; My Home, Op. 62; Othello, Op. 93; Vanda (ov) NXIN ▲ 550600 [DDD] (5.97)

DVOŘÁK, ANTONÍN (cont.)
Carnival [Karneval] (concert overture) for Orchestra, Op. 92, (B.169), (S.113) (1891) (cont.)
V. Handley (cnd), London PO, V. Handley (cnd), Ulster Orch † In Nature's Realm, Op. 91; Nocturne Strs, Op. 40; Sym 8 CHN ▲ 7123 (13.97)
V. Handley (cnd), Ulster Orch † In Nature's Realm, Op. 91; Othello, Op. 93; Scherzo Capriccioso, Op. 66
CHN ▲ 8453 [DDD] (16.97)
N. Järvi (cnd), Royal Scottish National Orch † Sym 3; Symphonic Vars, Op. 78(28) CHN ▲ 8575 [DDD] (16.97)
N. Järvi (cnd), Royal Scottish National Orch † Biblical Songs, Op. 99; Slavonic Rhaps, Op. 45; Symphonic Vars, Op. 78(28) CHN ▲ 9002 [DDD] (16.97)
I. Kertész (cnd), London SO *(rec Kingsway Hall London, Dec 1965)* † Othello, Op. 93; Sym 9
PENG (Penguin Music Classics) ▲ 460604 (11.97)
N. Marriner (cnd), Academy of St. Martin in the Fields † Othello, Op. 93; Sym 9 CAPO ▲ 10386 [DDD] (11.97)
Z. Mehta (cnd), New York PO † Con Vn; Romance Vn, Op. 11 SNYC ▲ 44923 [DDD] (16.97) COL △ 44923 [DDD]
Z. Mehta (cnd), New York PO † American Flag, Op. 102; Sym 5
SNYC (Essential Classics) ▲ 60297 (7.97) ▮ 60297 (3.98)
T. Pál (cnd), Hungarian State Orch † Romance Vn, Op. 11; Sym 9 LALI ▲ 15517 [DDD] (3.97)
T. Pál (cnd), Hungarian State Orch † Romance Vn, Op. 11; Sym 9 LALI ▲ 15824 [DDD] (3.97)
A. Previn (cnd), Los Angeles PO † Sym 9 TEL ▲ 80238 [DDD] (16.97)
F. Reiner (cnd), Chicago SO ("New World Symphony & Other Orchestral Masterpieces") † Sym 9; Smetana:Bartered Bride (ov); J. Weinberger:Schwanda der Dudelsackpfeifer (polka & fugue) RCAV (Living Stereo) ▲ 62587 (11.97)
F. Stupka (cnd), Czech PO † V. Novák:In the Tatras, Op. 26; P. Tchaikovsky:Sym 6
SUR (Czech Philharmonic) ▲ 111909 [AAD]
G. Szell (cnd), Cleveland Orch *(rec Cleveland, OH, Jan 4-5, 1963)* † Sym 7; Sym 8; Sym 9; Smetana:Bartered Bride (ov); Qt 1 Strs SNYC (Masterworks Heritage) 2-▲ 63151 [ADD] (25.97)
V. Talich (cnd), Czech PO † In Nature's Realm, Op. 91; Othello, Op. 93; Sym 8 SUR ▲ 111898 [AAD]
V. Talich (cnd), Czech PO *(rec London, England, Nov, 1935)* † Slavonic Dances (comp) MUA ▲ 4658 (10.97)
B. Tuckwell (cnd), London SO † Sym 9 LSO (LSO) ▲ 6900062 [DDD] (9.97)
Choral Music
L. Mátl (org), L. Mátl (cnd), Czech Phil Chorus—Ave Maria, Op. 19b, (B.68), (S.69); Ave maris stella, Op. 19b, (B.95), (S.69); Hymnus ad laudes, B.82, (S.59); O sanctissima, Op. 19a, (B.95a), (S.69) † Mass SUR ▲ 111430 [DDD]
Concerto in b for Cello & Orchestra, Op. 104, (B.191), (S.125) (1894-95)
O. Ackermann (cnd), Zurich Tonhalle Orch † Sym 9; Beethoven:Sym 5; Sym 7 STRV 2-▲ 12324 [ADD] (25.97)
E. Baeyens (vc), F. Terby (cnd), Brussels BRTN PO *(rec Belgian Radio-TV Concerthall, Jan 1978)* ("Homage to Edmond Baeyens") † Boeck:Cantilena; R. Schumann:Con Vc PHA ▲ 492002 [ADD] (13.97)
P. Casals (vc), G. Szell (cnd), Czech PO *(rec 1937)* † Boccherini:Con Vc, G.482; Bruch:Kol Nidrei, Op. 47
PHS ▲ 9349 [AAD] (17.97)
P. Casals (vc), G. Szell (cnd), Czech PO *(rec 1937)* † Bruch:Kol Nidrei, Op. 47; E. Elgar:Con Vc
EMIC (Great Recordings of the Century) ▲ 63498 [ADD] (11.97)
P. Casals (vc), G. Szell (cnd), Czech PO *(rec 1937)* † J. Brahms:Con Vn & Vc, Op. 102
ENT (Strings) ▲ 99317 (16.97)
P. Casals (vc), G. Szell (cnd), Czech PO *(rec 1937)* † Beethoven:Con Vn MTAL ▲ 48023 (6.97)
P. Casals (vc), G. Szell (cnd), Czech PO *(rec 1937)* † J. Brahms:Con Vn & Vc, Op. 102 GRM2 ▲ 78810 (13.97)
P. Casals (vc), G. Szell (cnd), Czech PO ("The Great Concerto Recordings") † J. Brahms:Con Vn & Vc, Op. 102; Son 2 Vc, Op. 99; Bruch:Kol Nidrei, Op. 47; E. Elgar:Con Vc MPLY 2-▲ 2006 (16.97)
G. Cassado (vc), H. Schmidt-Isserstedt (cnd), Berlin PO *(rec 1931-35)* † G. F. Handel:Serse (sels); Saint-Saëns:Cygne ENT (Strings) ▲ 99314 (16.97)
A. Catell (vc), S. Wislocki (cnd), Polish National PO *(rec Warsaw Philharmonic Hall, 1972)* ("Albert Catell performs Dvořák") † Serenade Orch, Op. 44 APS ▲ 991008 [ADD] (12.97)
J. Chuchro (vc), V. Neumann (cnd), Czech PO † Stabat Mater, Op. 58; Martinů:Con 1 Vc SUR 2-▲ 3093
R. Cohen (vc), Z. Macal (cnd), London PO ("Cello Concertos") † Beethoven:Con Vn, Vc, Pno, Op. 56; E. Elgar:Con Vc; P. Tchaikovsky:Vars on a Rococo Theme, Op. 33 CFP (Silver Doubles) 2-▲ 4775 [ADD] (22.97)
E. Feuermann (vc), M. Taube (cnd), Berlin State Opera Orch *(rec 1928-29)* † J. Brahms:Son 1 Vc, Op. 38; F. Schubert:Son Arpeggione, D.821 ENT (Strings) ▲ 99328 (16.97)
P. Fournier (vc), S. Celibidache (cnd) *(rec 1945)* † F. Schubert:Son Arpeggione, D.821; P. Tchaikovsky:Vars on a Rococo Theme, Op. 33 PHS ▲ 9198 (17.97)
P. Fournier (vc), S. Celibidache (cnd), London PO ("The Legendary 1945 London Broadcast")
GRM2 ▲ 78730 (13.97)
P. Fournier (vc), S. Celibidache (cnd), London PO *(rec London, England, 1945)* † P. Tchaikovsky:Sym 2
URAN ▲ 108 [ADD] (15.97)
P. Fournier (vc), G. Szell (cnd), Berlin PO † E. Bloch:Schelomo; Bruch:Kol Nidrei, Op. 47
DEUT (Resonance) ▲ 29155 [ADD] (7.97)
M. Fujiwara (vc), J. Hirokami (cnd), Norrköping SO † E. Bloch:Schelomo DNN ▲ 78830 (16.97)
F. Helmerson (vc), N. Järvi (cnd), Gothenburg SO † Silent Woods Vc & Orch, Op. 68/5 BIS ▲ 245 [DDD] (17.97)
L. Hoelscher (vc), H. Abendroth (cnd), Leipzig Radio SO BER ▲ 9242 (10.97)
M. Kliegel (vc), M. Halász (cnd), Royal PO *(rec Nov 8-10, 1991)* † E. Elgar:Con Vc NXIN ▲ 550503 [DDD] (5.97)
E. Kurtz (vc), A. Toscanini (cnd), NBC SO ("The Unknown Toscanini") † Beethoven:Con Vn, Vc, Pno, Op. 56
GRM2 ▲ 78636 (13.97)
Y.-Y. Ma (vc), L. Maazel (cnd), Berlin PO † Rondo; Silent Woods Vc & Orch, Op. 68/5
SNYC ▲ 42206 [DDD] (11.97) COL △ 42206 [DDD]
Y.-Y. Ma (vc), L. Maazel (cnd), Berlin PO † E. Elgar:Con Vc; J. Haydn:Con 2 Vc; Saint-Saëns:Con 1 Vc, Op. 33; R. Schumann:Con Vc SNYC 2-▲ 44562 [ADD] (31.97)
Y.-Y. Ma (vc), K. Masur (cnd), New York PO *(rec Avery Fisher Hall Lincoln Center for the Perfor, Jan 27 & 30, 1995)* † V. Herbert:Con 2 Vc, Op. 30 SNYC ▲ 67173 [DDD] (16.97) COL △ 67173 [DDD]
A. May (vc), V. Neumann (cnd), Czech PO † Rondo; Silent Woods Vc & Orch, Op. 68/5 SUR ▲ 111544 [DDD]
J. Metzger (vc), O. Mága (cnd), Nuremberg SO † Con Pno, Op. 33 PC ▲ 267162 [DDD] (2.97)
A. Navarra (vc), F. Stupka (cnd), Prague RSO *(rec ca 1951)* † Con Vn
MUL (Prague Spring Collection) ▲ 310039 [ADD] (13.97)
A. Noras (vc), S. Oramo (cnd), Finnish RSO † Serenade Orch, Op. 44; Serenade Strs, Op. 22; Sym 9
ERAT (Ultima) 2-▲ 18950 (16.97)
G. Piatigorsky (vc), C. Munch (cnd), Boston SO *(rec 1957 & 1960)* † W. Walton:Con Vc
RCAV (Gold Seal) ▲ 61498 (11.97)
J. D. Pré (vc), D. Barenboim (cnd), Chicago SO † J. Haydn:Con 1 Vc EMIC ▲ 47614 (16.97)
L. Rose (vc), E. Ormandy (cnd), Philadelphia Orch † Con Vn
SNYC (Essential Classics) ▲ 46337 [ADD] (7.97) ▮ 46337 [ADD] (3.98)
L. Rose (vc), A. Rodzinski (cnd), New York PO *(rec New York, NY, Jan 7, 1945)* † C. Franck:Sym in d, M.48
IN ▲ 1338 (m) [ADD] (15.97)
M. Rostropovich (vc), K. Ančerl (cnd), Toronto SO † Con Pno, Op. 33; Sym 7 TAHA 2-▲ 136 (34.97)
M. Rostropovich (vc), C. M. Giulini (cnd), London PO † Saint-Saëns:Con 1 Vc, Op. 33 EMIC ▲ 49306 [ADD] (16.97)
M. Rostropovich (vc), H. von Karajan (cnd), Berlin PO † P. Tchaikovsky:Vars on a Rococo Theme, Op. 33
DEUT (The Originals) ▲ 47413 [ADD] (11.97)
M. Rostropovich (vc), V. Talich (cnd), Czech PO ("Prague Spring Inspiring") † Beethoven:Sym 9; Smetana:Má Vlast; P. Tchaikovsky:Con 1 Pno, Op. 23 SUR 3-▲ 546 [AAD]
M. Rostropovich (vc), V. Talich (cnd), Czech PO † Con Pno, Op. 33 SUR ▲ 111901 [AAD]
H. Scherchen (cnd), Swiss-Italian RSO ("Hermann Scherchen in Lugano Vol 1") † J. Brahms:Sym 3
TAHA ▲ 116 (17.97)
J. Starker (vc), A. Dorati (cnd), London SO † Bruch:Kol Nidrei, Op. 47 MRCR ▲ 32001 [ADD] (11.97)
A. Toscanini (cnd), NBC SO *(rec 1940-48)* ("Toscanini, Vol. 6") † Scherzo Capriccioso, Op. 66; Symphonic Vars, Op. 78(28) LYS1 ▲ 449 (17.97)
R. Wallfisch (vc), C. Mackerras (cnd), London SO † E. von Dohnányi:Konzertstück, Op. 12
CHN ▲ 8662 [DDD] (16.97)
Concerto in g for Piano & Orchestra, Op. 33, (B.63), (S.42) (1876)
I. Ardašev (pno), L. Svárovský (cnd), Brno State PO *(rec Brno, Dec 21-23, 1996)* † Ježek:Con Pno
SUR ▲ 3325 [DDD]
R. Firkušný (pno), V. Neumann (cnd), Czech PO † Janáček:Capriccio; Concertino Pno
RCAV (Red Seal) ▲ 60781 (16.97)
J. Jandó (pno), A. Wit (cnd), Polish National RSO Katowice *(rec Nov 9-13, 1993)* † Water Goblin, Op. 107
NXIN ▲ 550896 [DDD] (5.97)
R. Kvapil (pno), F. Jilek (cnd), Brno State PO ("Piano Concerto") SUR ▲ 3067
F. Maxián (pno), K. Ančerl (cnd), Hessian RSO † Con Vc; Sym 7 TAHA 2-▲ 136 (34.97)
R. Molzer (pno), A. von Pitamic (cnd), Munich SO † Con Vc PC ▲ 267162 [DDD] (2.97)

FLURY, URS JOSEPH (cont.)

Concerto in D for Violin & Orchestra (1971-72)

U. J. Flury (vn), T. Hug (cnd) *(rec Phonag Tonstudio, Switzerland, Mar 4, 1977)* † Concertino veneziano; Son Vn; Suite nostalgique GALL ▲ 802 [ADD] (19.97)

Sonata for solo Violin (1976)

R. Ricci (vn) *(rec Bern, Switzerland, Nov 1973)* † Con Vn; Concertino veneziano; Suite nostalgique GALL ▲ 802 [ADD] (19.97)

Suite nostalgique for Violin & Piano (1975)

U. J. Flury (vn), G. Wyss (pno) *(rec Bern, Switzerland, Apr 29, 1977)* † Con Vn; Concertino veneziano; Son Vn GALL ▲ 802 [ADD] (19.97)

FLYNN, GEORGE (1937-

Fantasy Etudes (3) for solo Violin

E. Gratovich (vn) † V. Baley:Figments; A. Blank:Toccatina & Mixtures; R. Shapey:Etudes Vn TIT ▲ 199 [DDD]

FOCCROULLE, BERNARD (1953-

Movements (2) for 2 Viols da Gamba (1981-94)

Nouvelle Musiques de Chambre *(rec Liège Conservatory, 1996)* ("Liàge") † E. Denisov:Son alt Sax; Fourgon:Nuit; Haene:Pessoa Revisited; H. Pousseur:Vue sur les jardins interdits; Scelsi:Anahit CYPR ▲ 4601 (17.97)

FODOR, CAREL ANTON (1768-1846)

Symphony No. 4, Op. 19 (1801)

A. Dorati (cnd), Residentie Orch The Hague *(rec 1978)* † Graaf:Sym; Hellendaal:Concerti grossi, Op. 3; J. N. Lentz:Con 2 Hpd; J. G. Meder:Sym OLY ▲ 501 [AAD] (16.97)

FOERSTER, ADOLPH MARTIN (1854-1927)

On the Sea for Piano

M. Frager (pno) ("Edward MacDowell & Company") † H. F. Gilbert:Mazurka Pno; H. H. Huss:Preludes Pno, Op. 17; MacDowell:Virtuoso Etudes, Op. 46; E. Nevin:Études Pno, Op. 18; Paine:Pieces Pno, Op. 41; Romance Pno, Op. 12; H. Parker:Morceaux caractéristiques, Op. 49 NWW ▲ 80206 [DDD] (16.97)

FOERSTER, JOSEF BOHUSLAV (1859-1951)

Ballad for Violin & Orchestra (1914)

J. Suk (vn), J. Hála (pno) [arr Foester Vn & Pno] *(rec Prague, Czech Republic, Oct 1998)* † Elegy Vn; Fantasy Vn & Pno, Op. 128; Impromptus Vn, Op. 154; Son fant Vn & Pno, Op. 177; Son Vn & Pno, Op. 10; Suite Vn & Pno, Op. 35; Zbiroh Suite, Op. 167 SUR 2-▲ 3401 [DDD] (32.97)

Concerto No. 1 in c for Violin & Orchestra, Op. 88 (1910-11)

A. D. Löwenstein (vn), G. Albrecht (cnd), Vienna RSO † Cyrano de Bergerac, Op. 55 ORF ▲ 403971 [DDD] (18.97)

Cyrano de Bergerac (symphonic suite) for Orchestra, Op. 55 (1903)

G. Albrecht (cnd), Czech PO † Con 1 Vn, Op. 88 ORF ▲ 403971 [DDD] (18.97)

V. Smetáček (cnd), Czech PO † From Shakespeare, Op. 76 SUR ▲ 3041

Dreaming [Snění] for Piano, Op. 47 (1898)

M. Lapšanský (pno) ("Songs of Winter Nights") † Fibich:Scherzos Pno, Op. 4; Janáček:Intimate Sketches; Moravian Dances Pno; V. Novák:Songs of a Winter Night, Op. 30 SUR ▲ 3016 (16.97)

Elegy for solo Violin (1945)

J. Suk (vn) *(rec Prague, Czech Republic, Oct 1998)* † Ballad Vn & Orc; Fantasy Vn & Pno, Op. 128; Impromptus Vn, Op. 154; Son fant Vn & Pno, Op. 177; Son Vn & Pno, Op. 10; Suite Vn & Pno, Op. 35; Zbiroh Suite, Op. 167 SUR 2-▲ 3401 [DDD] (32.97)

Eva (opera in 3 acts) [lib Foerster, after G. Pressová], Op. 50 (1895-97)

E. Děpoltová (sop), A. Barová (cta), L. M. Vodička (ten), J. Souček (bar), F. Vajnar (cnd), Prague RSO, Prague Radio Chorus *(rec 1982)* SUR 2-▲ 3001 (32.97)

Fantasy for Violin & Piano, Op. 128 (1925)

J. Suk (vn), J. Hála (pno) *(rec Prague, Czech Republic, Oct 1998)* † Ballad Vn & Orc; Elegy Vn; Impromptus Vn, Op. 154; Son fant Vn & Pno, Op. 177; Son Vn & Pno, Op. 10; Suite Vn & Pno, Op. 35; Zbiroh Suite, Op. 167 SUR 2-▲ 3401 [DDD] (32.97)

From Shakespeare (symphonic suite) for Orchestra, Op. 76 (1908-09)

V. Smetáček (cnd), Prague SO † Cyrano de Bergerac, Op. 55 SUR ▲ 3041

Impromptus (2) for Violin & Piano, Op. 154 (1934)

J. Suk (vn), J. Hála (pno) *(rec Prague, Czech Republic, Oct 1998)* † Ballad Vn & Orc; Elegy Vn; Fantasy Vn & Pno, Op. 128; Son fant Vn & Pno, Op. 177; Son Vn & Pno, Op. 10; Suite Vn & Pno, Op. 35; Zbiroh Suite, Op. 167 SUR 2-▲ 3401 [DDD] (32.97)

Melody for Cello & Piano

Duo Moravia † Nocturnes, Op. 163; Son 1 Vc, Op. 45; Son 2 Vc, Op. 130 TUD ▲ 7071 (16.97)

Nocturnes (3) for Contralto, Cello & Piano, Op. 163

E. Sporerová (cta), Duo Moravia † Melody Vc; Son 1 Vc, Op. 45; Son 2 Vc, Op. 130 TUD ▲ 7071 (16.97)

Organ Music

J. Hora (org)—Fant in C, Op. 14; Impromptu, Op. 135 ("Complete Organ Music") † A. Dvořák:Preludes & Fugues Org, B.302; Janáček:Org Music; Martinů:Vigilia, H.382 RD (Vixen) ▲ 7 [DDD] (16.97)

Quintet in F for Wind Instruments, Op. 95 (1909)

Berlin Philharmonic Wind Quintet *(rec Nov 1992)* † Pilss:Serenade Ww; C. Reinecke:Sxt Ww; Zemlinsky:Humoresque BIS ▲ 612 [DDD] (17.97)

Sonata No. 1 for Cello & Piano, Op. 45 (1898)

Duo Moravia † Melody Vc; Nocturnes, Op. 163; Son 2 Vc, Op. 130 TUD ▲ 7071 (16.97)

Sonata No. 2 for Cello & Piano, Op. 130 (1926)

Duo Moravia † Melody Vc; Nocturnes, Op. 163; Son 1 Vc, Op. 45 TUD ▲ 7071 (16.97)

Sonata quasi fantasia for Violin & Piano, Op. 177 (1943)

J. Suk (vn), J. Hála (pno) *(rec Prague, Czech Republic, Oct 1998)* † Ballad Vn & Orc; Elegy Vn; Fantasy Vn & Pno, Op. 128; Impromptus Vn, Op. 154; Son Vn & Pno, Op. 10; Suite Vn & Pno, Op. 35; Zbiroh Suite, Op. 167 SUR 2-▲ 3401 [DDD] (32.97)

Sonata in b for Violin & Piano, Op. 10 (1889)

J. Suk (vn), J. Hála (pno) *(rec Prague, Czech Republic, Oct 1998)* † Ballad Vn & Orc; Elegy Vn; Fantasy Vn & Pno, Op. 128; Impromptus Vn, Op. 154; Son fant Vn & Pno, Op. 177; Suite Vn & Pno, Op. 35; Zbiroh Suite, Op. 167 SUR 2-▲ 3401 [DDD] (32.97)

Spring & Longing (symphonic poem) for Orchestra, Op. 93 (1912)

V. Smetáček (cnd), Prague SO † Sym 4 SUR ▲ 111822 [AAD]

Suite for Violin & Piano [from incidental music to *Princess Dandelion*], Op. 35 (1897)

J. Suk (vn), J. Hála (pno) *(rec Prague, Czech Republic, Oct 1998)* † Ballad Vn & Orc; Elegy Vn; Fantasy Vn & Pno, Op. 128; Impromptus Vn, Op. 154; Son fant Vn & Pno, Op. 177; Son Vn & Pno, Op. 10; Zbiroh Suite, Op. 167 SUR 2-▲ 3401 [DDD] (32.97)

Symphony No. 4 in c, Op. 54 (1905)

R. Kubelík (cnd), Czech PO SUR ▲ 111912

V. Smetáček (cnd), Prague SO † Spring & Longing, Op. 93 SUR ▲ 111822 [AAD]

Zbiroh Suite for Viola & Piano, Op. 167 (1940)

J. Suk (va), J. Hála (pno) *(rec Prague, Czech Republic, Oct 1998)* † Ballad Vn & Orc; Elegy Vn; Fantasy Vn & Pno, Op. 128; Impromptus Vn, Op. 154; Son fant Vn & Pno, Op. 177; Son Vn & Pno, Op. 10; Suite Vn & Pno, Op. 35 SUR 2-▲ 3401 [DDD] (32.97)

FOLEY, KEITH (20th cent)

Einstein's Dreams for Wind Quintet

Cumberland Quintet *(rec Tennessee Tech Univ, May 1996)* ("Shadows & Dreams") † H. Baumann:Rondo mit Mozart; Dollarhide:Shadows; K. Hoover:Homage to Bartók; Jager:Mumblety Peg; A. Tcherepnin:Qnt Ww CENT ▲ 2335 [DDD] (16.97)

FOLIO, CYNTHIA (20th cent)

Developing Hues for Flute & Bass Clarinet (1989)

C. Folio (fl), L. R. Thompson (b cl) ("Society of Composers, Inc.: Contrpunctus") † A. Brings:Duo Concertante Vc; J. Davison:Son Pastorale; Rokeach:Son Vn CPS ▲ 8615 (16.97)

FOLQUET DE MARSEILLE (ca 1150/60-1231)

Tant m'abellis l'amoros pessamens for Ensemble

Sequentia *(rec Abbaye de Fontevraud, France, Dec 1993)* ("Dante & the Troubadours") † Aimeric de Peghuilhan:Music of Aimeric de Peghuilhan; Bertran De Born:Rassa, tan creis e monta e poia; A. Daniel:Chanson do'ill mot son plan e prim; Lo ferm voler qu'el cor m'intra; Guiraut de Bornelh:No posc sifrir c'a la dolor; Peire d'Alvernhe:Dejosta'ls breus jorns DEHA ▲ 77227 [DDD] (16.97)

FONSECA BARBOSA, LOURENÇO DA (1904-

Song & Challenge [Toada e desafio] for String Quintet

Paraíba Quintet ("Música Armorial") † Maciel:Kingdom's Stone; Madureira:Aralume; Baque de Luanda; Sloth; The Warrior; Toada e Dobrado da Cavlhada; Toré; Nóbrega de Almeida:Rasgo do Nordeste; C. Pereira:Northeastern Pieces; Variations on a Theme from Guerra Peixe NIMB ▲ 5483 [DDD] (16.97)

FONTANA, GIOVANNI BATTISTA (1571-ca 1630)

Sonatas

J. Feves (bn), G. Schwarz (tpt), H. Katz (hpd) ("The Age of Splendor") † Albinoni:Con Tpt, Ob & Bn; Frescobaldi:Canzonas, Caprici & Ricercari; Hertel:Con à cinque VB2 2-▲ 5124 [ADD] (9.97)

Sonata No. 10 for Flute, Viol & Basso Continuo

Little Consort *(rec Feb 1991)* † Quagliati:Music Voice CCL ▲ 2791 [DDD]

Sonatas Nos. 2, 3 & 4 for Recorder, Viol & Harpsichord

F. Hansen (vl), V. Boeckman (rcr), L. U. Mortensen (hpd) *(rec Sept 1990)* † Castello:Sons Rcr; Cima:Sons Rcr; Frescobaldi:Canzona detta la Bernadinia; Canzona quatra; Merula:Music Rcr Vl Hpd KPT ▲ 32059 [DDD]

Sonata No. 1 for Recorder, Cello & Harpsichord

B. Ericson (vc), C. Pehrsson (rcr), A. Öhrwall (hpd) *(rec Sweden, Feb 29, 1976)* ("Clas Pehrsson Performs Recorder Music") † Barsanti:Sons Rcr, Op. 1; Castello:Sonate concertate in stil moderno; Eyck:Fluyten Lust-Hof; Frescobaldi:Canzonas, Caprici & Ricercari; Toccatas Hpd; Telemann:Essercizii Musici; Sonate (12) metodiche BIS ▲ 48 [AAD] (17.97)

FOOTE, ARTHUR (1853-1937)

Ballad for Violin & Piano, Op. 69

S. Johnson (vn), P. Kairoff (pno) ("American Romantics") † Melody; Pieces Vn & Pno, Op. 9; Beach:Son Vn ALBA ▲ 150 [DDD] (16.97)

K. Lawrence (vn), E. Larsen (pno) *(rec NCSA, NC, Sept 1994)* ("The Violin Music of Arthur Foote") † Legend; Melody; Pieces Vn & Pno, Op. 74; Pieces Vn & Pno, Op. 9; Son Vn NWW ▲ 80464 (16.97)

Flying Cloud & Oriental Dance for Flute, Oboe & Cello [from 5 Silhouettes], Op. 73/4 & 5

Huntingdon Trio † Poem 1 Pno, Op. 41; Czerny:Fant concertante, Op. 256; E. Goossens:Impressions of a Holiday, Op. 7; G. Holst:Terzetto Fl; K. Hoover:Lyric Trio; Musgrave:Impromptu 1 Fl LEON ▲ 325 [DDD] (16.97)

Francesca da Rimini for Orchestra, Op. 90 (1824)

J. Mester (cnd), Louisville Orch † A. Bird:Carneval Scene, Op. 5; G. W. Chadwick:Euterpe; Converse:Endymion's Narrative, Op. 10; Flivver Ten Million ALBA ▲ 30 [ADD]

Legend for Violin & Piano, Op. 76

K. Lawrence (vn), E. Larsen (pno) *(rec NCSA, NC, Sept 1994)* ("The Violin Music of Arthur Foote") † Ballad; Melody; Pieces Vn & Pno, Op. 74; Pieces Vn & Pno, Op. 9; Son Vn NWW ▲ 80464 (16.97)

Melody for Violin & Piano (or Viola & Continuo), Op. 44

S. Johnson (vn), P. Kairoff (pno) ("American Romantics") † Ballad; Pieces Vn & Pno, Op. 9; Beach:Son Vn ALBA ▲ 150 [DDD] (16.97)

K. Lawrence (vn), E. Larsen (pno) *(rec NCSA, NC, Sept 1994)* ("The Violin Music of Arthur Foote") † Ballad; Legend; Pieces Vn & Pno, Op. 74; Pieces Vn & Pno, Op. 9; Son Vn NWW ▲ 80464 (16.97)

Nocturne & Scherzo for Flute & String Quartet (1918)

J. M. Foster (fl), Da Vinci Quartet † Qt Pno; Qt 1 Str, Op. 4 NXIN (American Classics) ▲ 8559014 (5.97)

Pieces (3) for Violin & Piano, Op. 9 (1885)

S. Johnson (vn), P. Kairoff (pno) ("American Romantics") † Ballad; Melody; Beach:Son Vn ALBA ▲ 150 [DDD] (16.97)

K. Lawrence (vn), E. Larsen (pno) *(rec NCSA, NC, Sept 1994)* ("The Violin Music of Arthur Foote") † Ballad; Legend; Melody; Pieces Vn & Pno, Op. 74; Son Vn NWW ▲ 80464 (16.97)

Pieces (2) for Violin & Piano, Op. 74

K. Lawrence (vn), E. Larsen (pno) *(rec NCSA, NC, Sept 1994)* ("The Violin Music of Arthur Foote") † Ballad; Legend; Melody; Pieces Vn & Pno, Op. 9; Son Vn NWW ▲ 80464 (16.97)

Poem No. 1 for Piano, Op. 41

Huntingdon Trio † Flying Cloud & Oriental Dance; Czerny:Fant concertante, Op. 256; E. Goossens:Impressions of a Holiday, Op. 7; G. Holst:Terzetto Fl; K. Hoover:Lyric Trio; Musgrave:Impromptu 1 Fl LEON ▲ 325 [DDD] (16.97)

Quartet in C for Piano, Op. 23 (1890)

J. Barbagallo (pno), Da Vinci Quartet † Nocturne; Qt 1 Str, Op. 4 NXIN (American Classics) ▲ 8559014 (5.97)

Quartet No. 1 in g for Strings, Op. 4 (1883)

J. Barbagallo (pno), Da Vinci Quartet † Nocturne; Qt Pno NXIN (American Classics) ▲ 8559014 (5.97)

Quartet No. 2 in E for Strings, Op. 32 (1894)

J. Barbagallo (pno), Da Vinci Quartet *(rec Lamont School of Music, CO, 1995)* † Qnt Pno, Op. 38; Qt 3 Str, Op. 70 MARC ▲ 8223875 [DDD] (13.97)

Da Vinci Quartet *(rec Lamont School of Music, CO, 1995)* ("Chamber Music, Vol. 1") † Qnt Pno, Op. 38; Qt 3 Str, Op. 70 NXIN (American Classics) ▲ 8559009 [DDD] (5.97)

Quartet No. 3 in D for Strings, Op. 70 (1910)

J. Barbagallo (pno), Da Vinci Quartet *(rec Lamont School of Music, CO, 1995)* † Qnt Pno, Op. 38; Qt 2 Str, Op. 32 MARC ▲ 8223875 [DDD] (13.97)

Da Vinci Quartet *(rec Lamont School of Music, CO, 1995)* ("Chamber Music, Vol. 1") † Qnt Pno, Op. 38; Qt 2 Str, Op. 32 NXIN (American Classics) ▲ 8559009 [DDD] (5.97)

Kohon String Quartet *(rec 1969)* ("The Early String Quartet in the U.S.A.") † G. W. Chadwick:Qt 4 Strs; B. Franklin:Qt Strs; C. M. Loeffler:Music for 4 Str Instrs; D. G. Mason:Qt on Negro Themes, Op. 19 VB2 2-▲ 5057 [ADD] (9.97)

Quintet in a for Piano & Strings, Op. 38 (1897)

J. Barbagallo (pno), Da Vinci Quartet *(rec Lamont School of Music, CO, 1995)* † Qt 2 Str, Op. 32; Qt 3 Str, Op. 70 MARC ▲ 8223875 [DDD] (13.97)

J. Barbagallo (pno), Da Vinci Quartet *(rec Lamont School of Music, CO, 1995)* ("Chamber Music, Vol. 1") † Qt 2 Str, Op. 32; Qt 3 Str, Op. 70 NXIN (American Classics) ▲ 8559009 [DDD] (5.97)

Scherzo for Flute & String Quartet (1918; orchd 1922)

E. Zukerman (fl), Shanghai String Quartet *(rec Church of the Ascension, NYC, NY, Oct 1994)* ("Music for a Sunday Morning") † Beach:Theme & Vars, Op. 80; Ginastera:Impresiones de la Puna; W. A. Mozart:Kleine Nachtmusik, K.525 DLS ▲ 3173 [DDD] (14.97)

Sonata for Cello (or Viola) & Piano, Op. 78 (ca 1913)

A. Diaz (vc), S. Sanders (pno) *(rec Troy, NY, Mar 1996)* ("American Visions") † S. Barber:Son Vc, Op. 6; L. Bernstein:Meditations Vc & Pno DOR ▲ 90241 [DDD] (16.97)

Sonata in g for Violin & Piano, Op. 20 (1889)

K. Lawrence (vn), E. Larsen (pno) *(rec NCSA, NC, Sept 1994)* ("The Violin Music of Arthur Foote") † Ballad; Legend; Melody; Pieces Vn & Pno, Op. 74; Pieces Vn & Pno, Op. 9 NWW ▲ 80464 (16.97)

J. Silverstein (vn), G. Kalish (pno) † Beach:Son Vn; Farwell:From Mesa & Plain, Op. 20; Indian Songs, Op. 102; Orem:American Indian Rhap NWW ▲ 80542 [ADD] (16.97)

Suite in D for Organ, Op. 54 (1904)

H. Mardirosian (org) *(rec Champaign, IL, Apr 1997)* ("Organ Suites") † J. Langlais:Suite médévale; P. Malengreau:Suite Org, Op. 14; Saint-Saëns:Rapsodies sur des cantiques bretons, Op. 7 CENT ▲ 2368 [DDD] (16.97)

Suite in E for String Orchestra, Op. 63 (1907)

K. Klein (cnd), London SO † D. Buck:Festival Ov; J. A. Carpenter:Skyscrapers; MacDowell:Lamia; Paine:Oedipus tyrannus (prelude) ALBA ▲ 235 [DDD] (16.97)

S. Koussevitzky (cnd), Boston SO *(rec 1940 for Victor)* † A. Copland:Salón México; R. Harris:Sym 1; Sym 3; H. McDonald:San Juan Capistrano PHS ▲ 9492 [AAD]

R. Leppard (cnd), Indianapolis SO—Adagietto; Pizzicato ("American Dreams") † S. Barber:Adagio Strs; Canning:Fant on Hymn Tune by Justin Morgan; H. Carmichael:Johnny Appleseed Suite; J. A. Carpenter:Sea Drift; G. W. Chadwick:Noël; G. Gershwin:Lullaby Str Qt DECC ▲ 458157 (16.97)

FORBES, WILLIAM (1662-1740)

Violin & Piano Music

L. Risk (fid), J. Schwab (pno)—Up Tails A'; My Nanny O *(rec Troy, NY, Apr 1998)* † D. Dow:Vn & Pno Music; MacCrimmon:Vn & Pno Music; McGibbon:Vn & Pno Music; H. Purcell:Vn & Pno Music; Traditional:Vn & Pno Music DOR ▲ 90264 [DDD] (16.97)

FORD, ANDREW (1957-

The Art of Puffing (17 elegies for Thomas Chatterton) for Bass Clarinet/Alto Sax & Percussion (1989)

Contemporain Duo *(rec Sydney, Australia, Sept 1993)* ("Whispers") † Pastoral; Sacred Places; Whispers TALP ▲ 53 [DDD] (18.97)

Getting Blue for Alto Saxophone & Vibraphone (1993)

Duo Contemporain ("Tube Makers: Music by Australian Composers") † G. Brophy:we bOp; S. Cronin:Even Love Can Wield a Stealthy Blade; R. Edwards:Enyato IV; A. Schultz:Collide; Sculthorpe:Simori; Smetanin:Tube Makers GLOE ▲ 5176 [DDD] (16.97)

The Laughter of Mermaids for solo Voices

R. Peelman (cnd), Song Company ("The Laughter of Mermaids") † S. Cronin:Carmina Pu!; A. Schultz:Song of Songs (sels); G. Whitehead:Virgin & the Nightingale; Whiticker:As Water Bears Salt VOXA ▲ 16 (18.97)

FORD, ANDREW (cont.)

Music of Ford

G. English (ten), H. McDonald (hn), S. McCallum (pno) *(Martian Sends a Postcard Home)*, J. Nightingale (sax) *(Clarion)*, G. English (ten), A. Evans (vn), A. Ford (bells) *(Epithalamium)*, G. English (ten), D. Stanhope (cnd), Australian CO *(Harbour)*, D. Pratt (conga) *(Composition in Blue, Grey & Pink)*, G. English (ten), M. McGuire (hp) *(Dancing with Smoke)*, G. English (ten), I. Munro (pno) *(Salt Girl; And Now)*, K. Gallagher (fl) *(Female Nude)*, G. English (ten), Tall Poppies Ensemble *(Carbaret Songs) (rec Sydney, Australia)* TALP ▲ 128 [DDD] (18.97)

Pastoral for 3 Violins, 2 Violas, 2 Cellos & Double Bass (1991)

Tasmanian Sym Chamber Players *(rec ABC's Odeon Theater, Hobart, Australia, Nov 1991)* ("Whispers") † Art of Puffing; Sacred Places; Whispers TALP ▲ 53 [DDD] (18.97)

Sacred Places for Tenor & Instrumental Ensemble (1985)

G. English (ten), S. Savage (cnd) *(rec Basil Jones Theater, Queensland Conserv. of Music, Australia, live, Sept 1993)* ("Whispers") † Art of Puffing; Pastoral; Whispers TALP ▲ 53 [DDD] (18.97)

Spinning for solo Alto Flute (1988)

G. Collins (fl) *(rec ABC Ultimo Centre, Jan-Feb 1995)* ("Spinning: New Australian Flute Music") † N. Butterly:Wind Stirs Gently; R. Edwards:Ecstatic Dances Fls; Humble:Son Fl; Smalley:Ceremony III; C. Vine:Son Fl; M. Wesley-Smith:Balibo TALP ▲ 69 [DDD]

Whispers for Tenor & Instrumental Ensemble (1990)

G. English (ten), S. Savage (cnd) *(rec Basil Jones Theater, Queensland Conserv. of Music, Australia, live, Sept 1993)* ("Whispers") † Art of Puffing; Pastoral; Sacred Places TALP ▲ 53 [DDD] (18.97)

FORD, RON (1959-

Cross for Flute, Clarinet, Violin, Viola, Cello, Piano & Vibraphone (1992)

Ives Ensemble members † R. Ayres:Untitled Tpt; G. Carl:Claremont Con; Emmerik:Valise; M. Hamel:There Was Nothing Nobody Could Say; Rijnvos:Gigue et Double CV (Muziepraktijk) ▲ 63 [DDD] (18.97)

Star for 4 Percussionists (1992)

Percussion Group The Hague † J. Cage:First Construction; Donatoni:Omar; N. A. Huber:Clash Music; J. Kondo:Under the Umbrella; S. Reich:Drumming GLOE ▲ 5086 [DDD] (16.97)

Trarre for 5 Percussionists (1987)

Percussion Group The Hague—see Collections, "Percussion: Percussion Group The Hague" † M. Ishii:13 Drums; Xenakis:Okho GLOE ▲ 5066 [DDD] (16.97)

Wanne mine eyhnen misten for Mezzo-Soprano & 4 Percussionists (1991)

Percussion Group The Hague—see Collections, "Percussion: Percussion Group The Hague" † J. Cage:Qt for 4 Perc; P. Smith:Mare a'440; Tsubonoh:Fantom Fire GLOE ▲ 5072 [DDD] (16.97)

FORD, THOMAS (ca 1580-1648)

Faire, Sweet, Cruell

C. Högman (voc), J. Lindberg (lt) *(rec Wik's Castle, Sweden, Dec 1983)* ("Faire, Sweet & Cruell") † T. Campion:First Book of Ayres; Fourth Book of Ayres; Second Book of Ayres; Danyel:Like as the Lute; J. Dowland:First Booke of Songs or Ayres; In Darknesse Let Me Dwell; Third & Last Booke of Songs or Ayres; Pilkington:Rest Sweet Nimphs; Traditional:Greensleeves BIS ▲ 257 [DDD] (17.97)

Musicke of Sundrie Kindes (selections)

W. Kuijken (va da gamba), S. Kuijken (va da gamba) *(rec Melsen, Belgium, May 1980)* ("Music for a Viol") † J. Jenkins:Fant in d Va & Vn; Fant in g Va & Vn; M. Locke:Duos in c for B Vls; Duos in C for B Vls; C. Simpson:Vl Music ACCE ▲ 68014 [DDD] (17.97)

Since First I Saw Your Face (madrigal) for Voice & Chamber Ensemble

J. Bowman (ct), R. King (cnd), King's Consort ("The James Bowman Collection") † Anonymous:Come tread the paths; J. S. Bach:Arias; St. Matthew Passion (sels); G. Gabrieli:O magnum mysterium; G. F. Handel:Music of Handel; H. Purcell:Sacred Music; Songs; Symphonic Poems (misc) HYP ▲ 3 (7.97)

FORESYTHE, REGINALD (1907-1958)

Bereceuse for an Unwanted Child for Ensemble (1929)

Willem Breuker Ensemble *(rec Bellevue Theater, Amsterdam, Netherlands, Dec 28-30, 1993)* † Breuker:For Greetje Bijme; Hand de Vries; New Pillars in the Field of Art; Overtime; Suzuki Violinenlied; Verdurmen:Pastiche NMCC ▲ 92042 [DDD] (17.97)

FORMOSA, RICCARDO (1954-

Dedica for Oboe & Orchestra

J. Crellin (ob), P. Thomas (cnd), Melbourne SO *(rec studio)* † G. Brophy:Forbidden Colours; B. Kos:Con Vn; Smalley:Diptych VOXA ▲ 15 [AAD/DDD] (18.97)

FORONI, JACOPO (1825-1858)

Overture No. 3 in A for Orchestra

M. Liljefors (cnd), St. Petersburg Hermitage Orch *(rec 1985 & 1995)* ("Overtures at the King's Theater") † Berwald:Dressmaker; I Enter a Monastery; J. M. Kraus:Prosperin; L. Norman:Festive Ov, Op 60; Randel:People from Värmland; Söderman:Devil's First Tentative Efforts STRL ▲ 1009 [AAD] (15.97)

FORQUERAY, ANTOINE (1671-1745)

Pièces de viole

Charivari Agréable—La Couperin *(rec St. Andrew's Church, Toddington, Gloucestershire, England, Sept 1995)* ("Chamber Music for the King") † Caix d'Hervelois:Pièces for Fl & Continuo; F. Couperin:Dans le goût; Nouveaux Concerts; Pièces de clavecin (sels); Pièces de violes; Siret:Pièces dediées à Couperin ASV ▲ 159 [DDD] (16.97)

Suites in D & in g for Harpsichord

G. Leonhardt (hpd) SNYC (Vivarte) ▲ 48080 (16.97)

Suites (5) for Viol & Continuo

P. Pandolfo (vl), G. Balestracci (vl), R. Lislevand (thb), E. Eguez (thb), G. Morini (clvd) ("Pièces de Viole avec la Basse Continuë") GLSS 2-▲ 920401 (36.97)

Suite No. 3 in D for Viole da Gambas & Harpsichord

S. Kuijken (vn), R. Köhnen (hpd) ("Late French Viol Music") † Dollé:Suite 2 ACCE ▲ 67808 (17.97)

FORQUERAY, JEAN-BAPTISTE (1699-1782)

La Morangis ou la plissay for Harpsichord

L. U. Mortensen (hpd) † Duphly:Pièces de clavecin (book 2); Pièces de clavecin (book 4); Guillemain:Son Vn; J.-M. Leclair:Quatrième livre, Op. 9; Troisième livre, Op. 5; Mondonville:Pièces de clavecin, Op. 3 CHN (Chaconne) ▲ 531 [DDD] (16.97)

Pièces de clavecin for Harpsichord [trans from Pièces de viole by Antoine Forqueray]

A. Haas (hpd) WILD ▲ 9201 (16.97)

S. Lorenzetti (hpd) *(rec 1997)* ("Pièces de clavecin") DYNC (2000) ▲ 2009 [DDD] (13.97)

FORREST, GEORGE (1915-

Kismet (selections)

B. Ogston (voc), E. Bernstein (cnd), Royal PO, J. McCarthy (cnd), Ambrosian Singers—Night of My Nights [arr Conrad Salinger] *(rec Goldsmiths' College, London, England, Aug 1989)* ("Original Scores from the MGM Classics") † N. H. Brown:Singin' in the Rain (sels); F. Loewe:Brigadoon (sels); Gigi (sels); H. Martin:Meet Me in St. Louis (sels); C. Porter:Pirate (sels); A. Schwartz:Band Wagon (sels); H. Warren:Ziegfeld Follies (selections) CHN ▲ 7053 [DDD] (13.97)

FORSMAN, JOHN VÄINÖ (1924-

Improvisations (5) for Piano, Op. 6/3 (1948)

F. Gräsbeck (pno) † Son 1 Pno, Op. 3; Son 2 Pno, Op. 8; Son 3 Pno, Op. 11; Son 4 Pno, Op. 12; Son 5 Pno, Op. 13 BIS ▲ 902 [DDD] (17.97)

Sonata No. 1 for Piano, Op. 3 (1946)

F. Gräsbeck (pno) † Improvs Pno, Op. 6/3; Son 2 Pno, Op. 8; Son 3 Pno, Op. 11; Son 4 Pno, Op. 12; Son 5 Pno, Op. 13 BIS ▲ 902 [DDD] (17.97)

Sonata No. 2 for Piano, Op. 8 (1950)

F. Gräsbeck (pno) † Improvs Pno, Op. 6/3; Son 1 Pno, Op. 3; Son 3 Pno, Op. 11; Son 4 Pno, Op. 12; Son 5 Pno, Op. 13 BIS ▲ 902 [DDD] (17.97)

Sonata No. 3 for Piano, Op. 11, "Sonata Variata" (1953)

F. Gräsbeck (pno) † Improvs Pno, Op. 6/3; Son 1 Pno, Op. 3; Son 2 Pno, Op. 8; Son 4 Pno, Op. 12; Son 5 Pno, Op. 13 BIS ▲ 902 [DDD] (17.97)

Sonata No. 4 for Piano, Op. 12 (1954)

F. Gräsbeck (pno) † Improvs Pno, Op. 6/3; Son 1 Pno, Op. 3; Son 2 Pno, Op. 8; Son 3 Pno, Op. 11; Son 5 Pno, Op. 13 BIS ▲ 902 [DDD] (17.97)

Sonata No. 5 for Piano, Op. 13 (1957)

F. Gräsbeck (pno) † Improvs Pno, Op. 6/3; Son 1 Pno, Op. 3; Son 2 Pno, Op. 8; Son 3 Pno, Op. 11; Son 4 Pno, Op. 12 BIS ▲ 902 [DDD] (17.97)

FÖRSTER, CHRISTOPH (1693-1745)

Concerto in E♭ for Horn & Orchestra

M. Fank (vc), A. Friedrich (hn), Z. Pertis (hpd) ("Music for Horn") † Cherubini:Sons Hn; J. Haydn:Divert Hn, H.IV/5; Mendelssohn (-Bartholdy):Midsummer Night's Dream (sels); W. A. Mozart:Sinf concertante Ob, K.Anh.9 CLDI ▲ 4033 [AAD] (10.97)

P. Francomb (hn), H. Griffiths (cnd), Northern Sinfonia of England † Stich [or stich-Punto]:Con 5 Hn PANC ▲ 510095 [DDD] (20.97)

H. McDonald (hn), B. Kelly (cnd), Melbourne Academy Orch † J. Haydn:Con 1 Hn; Telemann:Con Hn; Teyber:Con Hn TALP ▲ 42 [DDD] (18.97)

FÖRSTER, KASPAR (1616-1673)

Congregantes Philistei:dialogi Davidis cum Philisteo (oratorio)

R. Wilson (cnd), Musica Fiata, La Capella Ducale *(rec St. Amandus, Cologne, Germany, Feb 1998)* † Domine Dominus noster; Repleta est malis; Son Vns; Trio Son Vns; Trio Son Vns & Bn; Vanitas vanitatum; Viri Israelite *([ENG,LAT] text)* CPO ▲ 999584 [DDD] (14.97)

Domine Dominus noster for 3 Voices & Continuo

R. Wilson (cnd), Musica Fiata, La Capella Ducale *(rec St. Amandus, Cologne, Germany, Feb 1998)* † Congregantes Philistei; Repleta est malis; Son Vns; Trio Son Vns; Trio Son Vns & Bn; Vanitas vanitatum; Viri Israelite *([ENG,LAT] text)* CPO ▲ 999584 [DDD] (14.97)

Repleta est malis for Alto, Tenor, Bass, 2 Violins & Viola

R. Wilson (cnd), Musica Fiata, R. Wilson (cnd), La Capella Ducale *(rec St. Amandus, Cologne, Germany, Feb 1998)* † Congregantes Philistei; Domine Dominus noster; Son Vns; Trio Son Vns; Trio Son Vns & Bn; Vanitas vanitatum; Viri Israelite *([ENG,LAT] text)* CPO ▲ 999584 [DDD] (14.97)

Sonata for 2 Violins, 2 Cornets, Bassoon, Viola & Violone

R. Wilson (cnd), Musica Fiata *(rec St. Amandus, Cologne, Germany, Feb 1998)* † Congregantes Philistei; Domine Dominus noster; Repleta est malis; Trio Son Vns; Trio Son Vns & Bn; Vanitas vanitatum; Viri Israelite CPO ▲ 999584 [DDD] (14.97)

Trio Sonata for 2 Violins & Bassoon

R. Wilson (cnd), Musica Fiata *(rec St. Amandus, Cologne, Germany, Feb 1998)* † Congregantes Philistei; Domine Dominus noster; Repleta est malis; Son Vns; Trio Son Vns; Vanitas vanitatum; Viri Israelite CPO ▲ 999584 [DDD] (14.97)

Trio Sonata for 2 Violins & Violone, "La Pazza"

R. Wilson (cnd), Musica Fiata *(rec St. Amandus, Cologne, Germany, Feb 1998)* † Congregantes Philistei; Domine Dominus noster; Repleta est malis; Son Vns; Trio Son Vns & Bn; Vanitas vanitatum; Viri Israelite CPO ▲ 999584 [DDD] (14.97)

Vanitas vanitatum:dialogo de divite et paupere (oratorio)

R. Wilson (cnd), Musica Fiata, La Capella Ducale *(rec St. Amandus, Cologne, Germany, Feb 1998)* † Congregantes Philistei; Domine Dominus noster; Repleta est malis; Son Vns; Trio Son Vns; Trio Son Vns & Bn; Viri Israelite *([ENG,LAT] text)* CPO ▲ 999584 [DDD] (14.97)

Viri Israelite:dialogus de Juditha et Holoferne (oratorio)

R. Wilson (cnd), Musica Fiata, R. Wilson (cnd), La Capella Ducale *(rec St. Amandus, Cologne, Germany, Feb 1998)* † Congregantes Philistei; Domine Dominus noster; Repleta est malis; Son Vns; Trio Son Vns; Trio Son Vns & Bn; Vanitas vanitatum *([ENG,LAT] text)* CPO ▲ 999584 [DDD] (14.97)

FORSYTH, MALCOLM (1936-

Andante for Sagattarius for Cello & Piano

M. Forsyth (vc), P. Longworth (pno) ("Soaring with Agamemnon") † Burlesque; Duets for Young Cellists; Eclogue; Pop's Cycle; Rondo in Stride; Swan Sees His Reflection; G. Bryars:South Downs; Pärt:Spiegel im Spiegel MARQ ▲ 231 (16.97)

Burlesque for Cello & Piano

M. Forsyth (vc), P. Longworth (pno) ("Soaring with Agamemnon") † Andante for Sagattarius; Duets for Young Cellists; Eclogue; Pop's Cycle; Rondo in Stride; Swan Sees His Reflection; G. Bryars:South Downs; Pärt:Spiegel im Spiegel MARQ ▲ 231 (16.97)

Duets (8) for Young Cellists for Cello & Piano

M. Forsyth (vc), P. Longworth (pno) ("Soaring with Agamemnon") † Andante for Sagattarius; Burlesque; Eclogue; Pop's Cycle; Rondo in Stride; Swan Sees His Reflection; G. Bryars:South Downs; Pärt:Spiegel im Spiegel MARQ ▲ 231 (16.97)

Eclogue for Cello & Piano

M. Forsyth (vc), P. Longworth (pno) ("Soaring with Agamemnon") † Andante for Sagattarius; Burlesque; Duets for Young Cellists; Pop's Cycle; Rondo in Stride; Swan Sees His Reflection; G. Bryars:South Downs; Pärt:Spiegel im Spiegel MARQ ▲ 231 (16.97)

Electra Rising for Cello & Orchestra (1995)

A. Forsyth (vc), G. Nowak (cnd), Edmonton SO *(rec Edmonton, Alberta, Canada, May 1997)* ("Electra Rising: Music of Malcolm Forsyth") † Tre Vie; Valley CBC ▲ 5180 [DDD] (16.97)

Pop's Cycle (Eclectic Suite) for Cello & Piano

M. Forsyth (vc), P. Longworth (pno) ("Soaring with Agamemnon") † Andante for Sagattarius; Burlesque; Duets for Young Cellists; Eclogue; Rondo in Stride; Swan Sees His Reflection; G. Bryars:South Downs; Pärt:Spiegel im Spiegel MARQ ▲ 231 (16.97)

Quintet for Winds (1986)

Essex Winds Woodwind Quintet *(rec Alberta & L.A. East Studios Salt Lake City, 1992-93)* ("Quintette: The Essex Winds") † H. Freedman:Qnt Ww; Hétu:Qnt Ww; Kenins:Vars on a Theme of Schubert CTR ▲ 5595 [DDD] (16.97)

Rondo in Stride for Cello & Piano

M. Forsyth (vc), P. Longworth (pno) ("Soaring with Agamemnon") † Andante for Sagattarius; Burlesque; Duets for Young Cellists; Eclogue; Pop's Cycle; Rondo in Stride; Swan Sees His Reflection; G. Bryars:South Downs; Pärt:Spiegel im Spiegel MARQ ▲ 231 (16.97)

Sketches from Natal for Orchestra (1970)

M. Bernardi (cnd), CBC Vancouver SO † P. Maurice:Tableaux de Provence; D. Milhaud:Globe-trotter, Op. 358; Sowande:African Suite CBC (SM 5000) ▲ 5135 [DDD] (16.97)

Songs from the Q'Appelle Valley for Brass Band

S. Chenette (cnd), Hannaford Street Silver Band *(rec Toronto, Canada, March 19-20, 1992)* ("Canadian Impressions") † H. Cable:Banks of Newfoundland; Irvine:Concertino Eup; Kulesha:Serenade Strs; Luedeke:Circus Music; Weinzweig:Round Dance CBC ▲ 5136 [DDD] (16.97)

L. Comtois (mez), M. Bourdeau (pno) [ion only] ("Songs of the Americas") † S. Barber:Songs (4), Op. 13; L. Bernstein:I Hate Music; Peter Pan (sels); Piccola Serenata; Ginastera:Canciones (2), Op. 3; Canciones populares argentinas, Op. 10; C. Ives:Songs; Mercure:Dissidence; H. Villa-Lobos:Songs BRIO ▲ 112 [DDD] (16.97)

W. Humphreys (sop), S. Laughton (tpt), P. Tiefenbach (org/pno) *(rec Toronto, Canada, 1992-93)* ("Opening Day") † Irvine:Aubade; R. M. Schafer:Aubade; Tiefenbach:Nativity; Opening Day; Poems (3); Traditional:Blooming Bright Star of Belle Isle; She's Like the Swallow *([ENG] text)* OPDR ▲ 9301 [DDD] (16.97)

The Swan Sees His Reflection for Cello & Piano

M. Forsyth (vc), P. Longworth (pno) ("Soaring with Agamemnon") † Andante for Sagattarius; Burlesque; Duets for Young Cellists; Eclogue; Pop's Cycle; Rondo in Stride; G. Bryars:South Downs; Pärt:Spiegel im Spiegel MARQ ▲ 231 (16.97)

Tre Vie for Alto Saxophone & Orchestra (1992)

W. H. Street (a sax), G. Nowak (cnd), Edmonton SO *(rec Edmonton, Alberta, Canada, May 1997)* ("Electra Rising: Music of Malcolm Forsyth") † Electra Rising; Valley CBC ▲ 5180 [DDD] (16.97)

ukuZALWA for Orchestra (1983)

P. Freeman (cnd), Orch of the Americas *(rec Feb & June 1991)* ("An American Composers Salute") † L. Bernstein:Candide (ov); A. Copland:Fanfare for the Common Man; Lieuwen:Angelfire; Locklair:Creation's Seeing Order PRA ▲ 3413 [DDD] (14.97)

Valley of a Thousand Hills for Orchestra (1989)

G. Nowak (cnd), Edmonton SO *(rec Edmonton, Alberta, Canada, May 1997)* ("Electra Rising: Music of Malcolm Forsyth") † Electra Rising; Tre Vie CBC ▲ 5180 [DDD] (16.97)

FORTNER, JACK (1935-

Concertpiece for Cello & Orchestra

M. Flaksman (vc), S. Kawalla (cnd), Koszalin State PO † B. Hobson:Con Orch; D. A. Jaffe:Whoop for Your Life!; Jazwinski:Sequenze Concertanti; P. Moss:Valses VMM ▲ 3024 [DDD]

Quadri for Orchestra & Chorus

S. Kawalla (cnd), Koszalin State PO, Silesian Univ Choir † H. Nakamura:Litaniae; D. Scott:Arras; Van de Vate:Voices; J. J. Yu:Wu-Yu VMM ▲ 3022 [DDD]

Symphonies for Orchestra

J. Fortner (cnd), Transylvania PO Cluj ("Society of Composers, Inc.-Transcendencies") † Z. Browning:Breakpoint Screamer; Cotel:Quatrains; Hankinson:Light/Shadow; F. W.-H. Ho:Bon; Sanchez-Gutierrez:M.E. in Memoriam; Sheffer:Con Sax CPS ▲ 8656 (16.97)

FORTUIN, HAROLD (1964-

Untitled #3: A Transcendental Etude for Computer-controlled Keyboard

H. Fortuin (elec) † Loeb:Yuukuu; Polishook:Tribute VMM ▲ 2008 [DDD]

FORWARD, FAST (1954-

Simultaneous Music for 6 Musicians (1992)

T. Kosugi (voc), D. Moss (voc), T. Kosugi (vn), M. Kinney (vc), A. Tobias (hmc), F. Forward (gtr/instr/perc), D. Moss (elec/perc), D. Shea (elec) *(rec Merkin Hall, NY, NY, Nov 12, 1992)* ("Same Same") † Feeding Frenzy; Yin-Yang Merger XIRE ▲ 108 [DDD]

The Yin-Yang Merger for Voice, Trumpet, Percussion & Electronics (1990)

D. Moss (voc), F. Forward (perc/whistle), B. Neill (elec/müttertrom), D. Moss (perc), Y. Gabay (perc), J. Lo (perc) ("Same Same") † Feeding Frenzy; Simultaneous Music XIRE ▲ 108 [DDD]

FORWARD, FAST (1954-, **GUY KLUCEVSEK** (1947-**& IKUE MORI** (20th cent)

Feeding Frenzy for Cook, Waiter & Instruments (1994)

G. Klucevsek (acc), I. Mori (dr/elec) ("Same Same") † Simultaneous Music; Yin-Yang Merger XIRE ▲ 108 [DDD]

FOSS, LUKAS (1922-

Airs (3) for Frank O'Hara's Angel for Soprano, Flute, Piano, 2 Percussion & Women's Chorus (1972)

J. Kellock (sop), L. Foss (pno) ("The Complete Vocal Chamber Works") † Songs; Thirteen Ways of Looking at a Blackbird; Time Cycle KOCH ▲ 7209 [DDD] (10.97)

American Landscapes for Guitar & Orchestra

S. Isbin (gtr), H. Wolff (cnd), St. Paul CO ("American Landscapes") † Corigliano:Troubadours; Schwantner:From Afar VCL ▲ 55083 (16.97)

American Pieces (3) for Violin & Orchestra

I. Perlman (vn), S. Ozawa (cnd), Boston SO ("The American Album") † S. Barber:Con Vn; L. Bernstein:Serenade EMIC ▲ 55360 (16.97)

Capriccio for Cello & Piano (1946)

S. Honigberg (vc), K. Brake (pno) ("American Music for Cello") † S. Barber:Son Vc, Op. 6; L. Bernstein:Meditations Vc & Pno; D. Diamond:Kaddish; G. Schuller:Fant Vc, Op. 19 ALBA ▲ 82 [DDD] (16.97)

Concerto for Oboe, Winds & String Orchestra (or String Quintet) (1948)

B. Gassman (ob), A. Endo (cnd), Crystal CO [str qnt version] † Heussenstamm:Set for Double Reeds, Op. 39; Pillin:Pieces for Double-Reed Septet CRYS ▲ 871 (15.97)

Curriculum Vitae with Time Bomb for Accordian & Percussion (1977)

B. Schimmel (acc), J. Williams (perc) *(rec 1989-90)* † Paradigm; Thirteen Ways of Looking at a Blackbird; Vn & Pno Music KOSS ▲ 1006 [DDD] (17.97)

Early Song for Violin & Piano (1944)

Z. Zeitlin (vn), L. Foss (pno) † S. Adler:Canto III; A. Copland:Son Vn; J. Druckman:Duo Vn & Pno; V. Reynolds:Son Vn GAS ▲ 279 (16.97)

Fantasy Rondo for Piano (1946)

S. Thompson (pno) ("Music on & off the Keys") † Frankel:Son 1 Vn, Op. 13; Hofmann-Engel:Son 1 Pno; Kershner:Son Bn; Loevendie:Strides; Toccata; Walk; Togawa:Kaze No Ha VMM (Distinguished Performers III) ▲ 2016 [DDD]

The Jumping Frog of Calaveras County (opera in 1 act) [lib Jean Karsavina after Mark Twain] (1950)

J. Baird (sop—Miss Lulu), F. Urrey (ten—Smiley), C. Arneson (bar—Gtr Player), P. Castaldi (bar—Uncle Henry), M. Moliterno (bar—Crapshooter), K. Deas (b-bar—Stranger), G. Friedley (sgr—Crapshooter), R. A. Clark (cnd), Manhattan CO *(rec Church of the Epiphany NYC, Oct 1996)* NPT ▲ 85609 [DDD] (16.97)

Ode for Orchestra (1944, rev 1958)

L. Foss (cnd), Milwaukee SO *(rec Apr 1989)* † Song of Songs; With Music Strong KOSS ▲ 1004 [DDD] (17.97)

Orpheus & Euridice for 2 Violins & Orchestra (1972; rev 1983)

Y. Menuhin (vn), E. Michell (vn), L. Foss (cnd), Brooklyn PO † Renaissance Con; Salomon Rossi Suite NWW ▲ 375 [DDD] (16.97)

Paradigm for Percussion, Electric Guitar (or Sitar), & 3 Instruments (1968)

L. Anderson (vn), J. Grassel (elec gtr), R. Dagon (cl), S. Basson (bn), J. Williams (perc) *(rec 1989-90)* † Curriculum Vitae with Time Bomb; Thirteen Ways of Looking at a Blackbird; Vn & Pno Music KOSS ▲ 1006 [DDD] (17.97)

Phorion (Baroque Variations III) for Harp or Electric Guitar, Electric Organ, Electric Harpsichord & Strings (1967)

L. Bernstein (cnd), New York PO † Song of Songs; Time Cycle SNYC (Bernstein Century) ▲ 63164 (10.97)

Pieces (3) for Flute & Piano (1944)

B. D. Wetter-Smith (fl), S. Seebass (pno) ("The 20th Century Romantic Spirit") † P. Gaubert:Son 1 Fl; G. Pierné:Son Vn; V. Reynolds:Son Fl CRYS ▲ 318 (15.97)

Quartet for Percussion (1983)

New Music Consort † J. Cage:Double Music; Second Construction; Third Construction; H. Cowell:Pulse; H. Sollberger:The 2 & the 1 NWW ▲ 80405 [AAD] (16.97)

Renaissance Concerto for Flute & Orchestra (1986)

C. Wincenc (fl), L. Foss (cnd), Brooklyn PO † Orpheus & Euridice; Salomon Rossi Suite NWW ▲ 375 [DDD] (16.97)

Salomon Rossi Suite for Orchestra (1975)

L. Foss (cnd), Brooklyn PO † Orpheus & Euridice; Renaissance Con NWW ▲ 375 [DDD] (16.97)

Solo for Piano (1981)

K. Supové (pno) *(rec Nov 14-17, 1992)* ("Figure 88") † M. Epstein:Waterbowls; D. Lang:While Nailing at Random; Rzewski:North American Ballads; R. Woolf:Dancétudes CRI (Emergency Music) ▲ 653 [DDD] (17.97)

Song of Songs for Soprano & Orchestra [Biblical text] (1946)

A. Addison (sop), L. Bernstein (cnd), New York PO † Phorion; Time Cycle SNYC (Bernstein Century) ▲ 63164 (10.97)

C. Page (sop), L. Foss (cnd), Milwaukee SO [ENG] *(rec Apr 1989)* † Ode; With Music Strong KOSS ▲ 1004 [DDD] (17.97)

J. Tourel (mez), L. Bernstein (cnd), New York PO [ENG] ("Bernstein: The Royal Edition") † Ben-Haim (Frankenburger):Sweet Psalmist of Israel; E. Bloch:Avodath Hakodesh SNYC ▲ 47533 [ADD] (23.97)

Songs (4) for Voice & Piano

J. Kellock (sop), L. Foss (pno) ("The Complete Vocal Chamber Works") † Airs for Frank O'Hara's Angel; Thirteen Ways of Looking at a Blackbird; Time Cycle KOCH ▲ 7209 [DDD] (10.97)

Thirteen Ways of Looking at a Blackbird for Mezzo-Soprano, Flute, Piano & Percussion [text Wallace Stevens] (1978)

E. L. Bruce (mez), C. Meves (fl), A. Brovan (pno), M. Shadd (perc) [ENG] *(rec 1989-90)* † Curriculum Vitae with Time Bomb; Paradigm; Vn & Pno Music KOSS ▲ 1006 [DDD] (17.97)

J. Kellock (sop), L. Foss (pno) ("The Complete Vocal Chamber Works") † Airs for Frank O'Hara's Angel; Songs; Time Cycle KOCH ▲ 7209 [DDD] (10.97)

Time Cycle for Soprano & Orchestra (1959-60)

A. Addison (sop), L. Bernstein (cnd), New York PO † Phorion; Song of Songs SNYC (Bernstein Century) ▲ 63164 (10.97)

J. Kellock (sop), L. Foss (cnd) ("The Complete Vocal Chamber Works") † Airs for Frank O'Hara's Angel; Songs; Thirteen Ways of Looking at a Blackbird KOCH ▲ 7209 [DDD] (10.97)

Violin & Piano Music

R. Evans (vn), L. Foss (pno)—Composer's Holiday; Dedication; Early Song *(rec 1989-90)* † Curriculum Vitae with Time Bomb; Paradigm; Thirteen Ways of Looking at a Blackbird KOSS ▲ 1006 [DDD] (17.97)

With Music Strong for Orchestra & Chorus (1988)

L. Foss (cnd), Milwaukee SO, Milwaukee Sym Chorus *(rec Apr 1989)* † Ode; Song of Songs KOSS ▲ 1004 [DDD] (17.97)

FOSSA, FRANÇOIS DE (1775-1849)

Trios (3) in A, G & F for Guitar, Violin & Cello, Op. 18

M. Beaver (vn), B. Epperson (vc), S. Wynberg (gtr) *(rec Elora Ontario, Mar 23-25, 1993)* NXIN ▲ 550760 [DDD] (5.97)

FOSTER, STEPHEN COLLINS (1826-1864)

Life & Music of Foster

A. Robinson (nar), M. Diesenroth (cnd), Musikkorps des Wachtbataillons—narration & selected excerpts from Old Folks at Ho; Oh! Susanna; Old Black Joe; Jeanie with the Light Brown Hair; My Old Kentucky Home; Camptown Races; Massa's in De Cold, Cold Ground; Come Where My Love Lies Dreaming; Beautiful Dreamer ("The Stories of Foster & Sousa in Words & Music") MMD (Music Masters) ▮ 8515 [ADD] (2.98) ▲ 8515 [ADD] (3.97)

Music of Foster

K. B. Feeney (vn), C. Wiersma (vn), J. Feeney (db), P. Robison (fl), S. Sanders (pno)—Quadrilles Nos. 1-4; Jig [all from Village Festival]; Andolia; Byerly's Waltz; Rainbow Schottisch; Jennie's Own Schottisch; I Dream of Jeanie with the Light Brown Hair; Oh! Susanna; The Old Pine Tree; Beautiful Dreamer; Maggie by My Side; Gentle Annie; Where Are the Friends of My Youth; Old Folk's Quadrilles [Nos. 1-5]; My Old Kentucky Home, Good Night *(rec Purchase Theater C, Jan 31-Feb 1, 1996)* ("By the Old Pine Tree: Flute Music by Stephen Foster & Sidney Lanier") † S. Lanier:Music of Lanier ARA ▲ 6679 [DDD] (16.97)

FOSTER, STEPHEN COLLINS (cont.)

Music of Foster (cont.)

A. Robinson (nar), M. Diesenroth (cnd), Musikkorps des Wachtbataillons—Old Folks at Home (excerpts); Oh! Susanna; Old Black Joe; Jeanie with the Light Brown Hair; My Old Kentucky Home; Camptown Races; Massa's in De Cold, Cold Ground; Come Where My Love Lies Dreaming; Beautiful Dreamer ("The Stories of Foster & Sousa in Words & Music") † J. P. Sousa:Life & Music of Sousa MMD (Music Masters) ▲ 8515 [ADD] (3.97) ▮ 8515 [ADD] (2.98)

Piano Music

J. Smith (pno)—Old Folks at Home [Swanee River]; Santa Anna's retreat; Village bells polka † Arlen:Pno Music; Ellington:Music of Ellington; G. Gershwin:Pno Music; O. Levant:Sonatina PREM ▲ 1028 [DDD] (16.97)

Songs

J. Baird (sop), L. Russell (alt), F. Urrey (ten), R. Enslow (fid), L. Russell (dlc), J. Buskirk (pno)—The Glendy Burke; Nelly Was a Lady; Melinda May; The Soirée Polka; The Moustache Song; O Willie, Is It You, Dear?; Mr. & Mrs. Brown; Gems from Lucia; Wilt Thou Be Gone Love; Voices That Are Gone; Old Black Joe; Maggie by my Side; Camptown Races; Hard Time Come Again No More; Don't Bet Your Money on de Shanghai; Beautiful Dreamer; Ah! May the Red Rose; Nelly Bly; Jeanie; Oh Susanna ALBA ▲ 119 (16.97)

J. DeGaetani (mez), L. Guinn (bar), G. Kalish (pno) ("Vol. 1") NON ▲ 79158 [AAD] (16.97)

J. Dooley (ct), K. Cok (hpd), L. Nelson (vn), C. Gummere (vc), P. A. Neely (db), J. DeLucia (rcr), D. Dixon (rcr), P. Rand (bn), R. Crafton (cym/dr)—Beautiful Dreamer; The Soirée Polka; Ah! May the Red Rose Live Always; We are coming, Father Abraham; Linger in Blissful Repose; Santa Anna's retreat; Farewell! Mother; Jeanie with the Light Brown Hair; That's What's the Matter; Hard Times Come Again No More; Summer Longings; Nothing but a Plain Old Soldier; My Old Kentucky Home, Good Night LYR ▲ 8036 [DDD] (16.97)

M. Findlay (vn), B. Hutton (bandora), H. Bass (gtr), F. Conlon (pno), Vocal Arts Quartet ("Gentle Annie: Art Songs") † C. Ives:Songs KOCH ▲ 7392 (16.97)

T. Hampson (bar), J. Ungar (vn), M. Mason (gtr), M. Parloff (fl), D. Alpher (pno) *(Jeanie with the Light Brown Hair),* T. Hampson (bar), M. Mason (sgr), G. Keillor (sgr), M. Rust (sgr), J. Ungar (vn), T. Trischka (banjo), D. Alpher (pno) *(Hard Times Come Again No More),* T. Hampson (bar), D. Alpher (pno) *(Voice of Bygone Days; Sweetly She Sleeps, My Alice Fair; My Wife is a Most Knowing Woman; Linger in Blissful Repose),* J. Ungar (vn), M. Glaser (vn), E. Stover (vn), T. Trischka (banjo), P. Ecklund (cnt), D. Bargeron (tuba), M. Mason (gtr/pno), A. Kinsella (perc) *(Ring, Ring the Banjo; Oh! Susanna; Camptown Races),* T. Hampson (bar), J. Ungar (vn), M. Mason (b gtr), D. Alpher (mand) *(Open Thy Lattice, Love),* T. Hampson (bar), M. Mason (gtr), J. Ungar (mand), D. Alpher (pno) *(Beautiful Dreamer),* T. Hampson (bar), J. Kirk (sgr), M. Rust (sgr), J. Ungar (vn), T. Trischka (banjo), M. Mason (gtr), P. Ecklund (cnt), D. Bargeron (tuba), D. Alpher (pno), A. Kinsella (perc) *(That's What's the Matter),* J. Ungar (vn), M. Glaser (vn), E. Stover (vn), T. Trischka (banjo), M. Mason (db/gtr) *(Old Folks at Home; My Old Kentucky Home, Good Night),* T. Hampson (bar), J. Ungar (vn), M. Mason (gtr) *(Molly! Do You Love Me?),* T. Hampson (bar), J. Ungar (vn), E. Stover (vn), M. Mason (db), D. Alpher (pno) *(Comrades, Fill No Glass For Me),* J. Ungar (vn), M. Glaser (vn), E. Stover (db/vn), T. Trischka (banjo), P. Ecklund (cnt), D. Bargeron (tuba), M. Mason (db/pno), A. Kinsella (perc) *(Nelly Bly; Glendy Burk; Angelina Baker),* T. Hampson (bar), J. Ungar (vn), M. Mason (db), D. Alpher (pno) *(Gentle Annie),* T. Hampson (bar), J. Ungar (vn), M. Mason (db/gtr), D. Alpher (pno) *(Ah! May the Red Rose Live Always) (rec New York, NY, Apr-July, 1992)* ("American Dreamer: Songs of Stephen Foster") † Anonymous:Opening Solo Violin ANGL ▲ 54621 [DDD] (16.97)

K. Kuenzi (pno), P. Lambert (pno), D. Kuenzi (cnd), Gloriana—Gentle Annie; Jeanie with the Light Brown Hair ("Songs of America") † H. T. Burleigh:Deep River; A. Copland:Songs (misc); Emmett:Dixie; Traditional:Black Is the Color of My True Love's Hair; Choral Music GLOI ▲ 57114 (16.97)

Robert Shaw Chorale—Beautiful Dreamer; My Old Kentucky Home; Oh! Susanna; Nelly Bly; Steal Away; Camptown Races *(rec 1958 & 1961)* ("Stephen Foster Song Book") RCAV (Living Stereo) ▲ 61253 (11.97) ▮ 61253 (6.98)

L. Russell (voc), L. Russell (dlc/gtr), R. Palmer (pno), W. Payn (cnd), Rooke Chapel Choir *(Why Have My Loved Ones Gone?),* L. Russell (voc), L. Russell (dlc/gtr), R. Palmer (pno), W. Payn (cnd) *(Willie Has Gone to the War; The Voices That Are Gone; For the Dear Old Flag I Die),* M. Cohen (sop), L. Russell (voc), A. Newton (vc), L. Russell (dlc/gtr), C. Patton (dr/fl) *(That's What's the Matter),* L. Russell (voc), L. Russell (dlc/gtr) *(Beautiful Dreamer; Larry's Goodbye; Slumber Song),* S. Epstein (gtr), R. Palmer (pno), W. Payn (cnd), Rooke Chapel Choir Men *(I'll Be a Soldier),* L. Russell (voc), A. Newton (vc), L. Russell (dlc/gtr), S. Epstein (gtr) *(Give This to Mother),* L. Russell (voc), L. Russell (dlc/gtr), S. Epstein (gtr), R. Palmer (pno), W. Payn (cnd), Rooke Chapel Chorus *(Nothing but a Plain Old Soldier),* M. Cohen (sop), L. Russell (voc), A. Newton (vc), L. Russell (dlc/gtr) *(Bring My Brother Back to Me; The Moustache Song),* W. Payn (cnd), Rooke Chapel Choir *(The Merry Month of May),* M. Cohen (sop), L. Russell (voc), A. Newton (vc), L. Russell (dlc/gtr), S. Epstein (gtr), C. Patton (dr/fl) *(While the Bowl Goes Round),* M. Cohen (sop), L. Russell (voc), L. Russell (dlc/gtr), C. Patton (dr/fl) *(Bury Me in the Morning),* R. Palmer (pno), W. Payn (cnd), Rooke Chapel Choir *(We've a Million in the Field) (rec Bucknell Univ.; St. Paul Lutheran Church NYC, May 1995)* ("Civil War Songs") HEL ▲ 1002 (10.97)

D. Warland (cnd), Dale Warland Singers *(Nelly Bly; Hard Times Come Again No More),* T. Tierney (sop), J. Elsbernd (ten), D. Warland (cnd), Dale Warland Singers *(Jeanie with the Light Brown Hair) (rec Univ. of St. Thomas, St. Paul, MN, Aug & Nov 1995)* ("Blue Wheat: A Harvest of American Folk Songs") † H. T. Burleigh:Songs; J. Hodges:Buffalo Gals; Traditional:Black Is the Color; Black Sheep; He's Goin' Away; Johnny Has Gone for a Soldier; My Lord, What a Mornin'; Oh, Shenandoah; Poor Wayfaring Stranger; Pretty Saro; Red River Valley; Single Girl; Skip to My Lou; Soldier, Soldier Won't You Marry Me?; Steal Away; Water Is Wide AME ▲ 122 [DDD] (13.97)

FOUGSTEDT, NILS-ERIC (1910-1961)

Songs

A. Riska (cnd), Jubilate Choir—Björkarnas valv; songs to texts by Nils Ferlin (3), Arvid Mörn; Hjärtats sommar; Smultronbacken; Sommarvişa; Skyn, blomman och en lärka; songs to texts by Jarl Hemmer (3); Sanctus; Mot löftets strand; I jorden går dolda Ådror; Djäknevisa; trad songs (2); Följ oss sång; Silmien laulu *(rec Tapiola Concert Hall, Finland, Nov 11-12, 1995)* ("The Complete Songs for Mixed Choir a cappella") BIS ▲ 721 [DDD] (17.97)

FOULDS, JOHN (1880-1939)

Mirage for Orchestra, Op. 20

L. Hager (cnd), Luxembourg RSO † Pasquinade Symphonique 1, Op. 98; St. Joan Suite, Op. 98; Brian:Tigers (sels); H. Parry:Sym 3 FORL 2-▲ 16724 [ADD] (32.97)

Pasquinade Symphonique No. 1 for Orchestra, Op. 98

L. Hager (cnd), Luxembourg RSO † Mirage; St. Joan Suite, Op. 98; Brian:Tigers (sels); H. Parry:Sym 3 FORL 2-▲ 16724 [ADD] (32.97)

Piano Music

P. Jacobs (pno)—Essays in the Modes (6), Op. 78; Variazioni ed Improvvisati su una Thema Originale, Op. 4; English Tune with Burden, Op. 89; Gandharva-Music; April-England, Op. 48/1 ALTA ▲ 9001

St. Joan Suite for Orchestra, Op. 98

L. Hager (cnd), Luxembourg RSO † Mirage; Pasquinade Symphonique 1, Op. 98; Brian:Tigers (sels); H. Parry:Sym 3 FORL 2-▲ 16724 [ADD] (32.97)

FOURGON, MICHEL (1968-

La Nuit for Chamber Ensemble [after A. Adamov] (1992)

Nouvelle Musiques de Chambre *(rec Liège Conservatory, 1996)* ("Liàge") † E. Denisov:Son alt Sax; B. Foccroulle:Movts; Haene:Pessoa Revisited; H. Pousseur:Vue sur les jardins interdits; Scelsi:Anahit CYPR ▲ 4601 (17.97)

FOWLER, JENNIFER (1939-

Echos from an Antique Land for Percussion Ensemble (1983)

Nova Ensemble ("Mizu to Kori") † Benfall:Rough Cut; Buddle:Just an Inkling for an Angklung; Hille:Mizu to Kori; Smalley:Ceremony I; Travers:Cold Air Rising VOXA ▲ 21 [AAD/ADD] (18.97)

Threaded Stars for solo Harp

M. McGuire (hp) *(rec ABC Ultimo Centre Sydney, 1994)* ("Awakening") † Conyngham:Awakening; Streams; H. Gifford:Fable; Glanville-Hicks:Son Hp; Koehne:To His Servant Bach God Grants a Final Glimpse: Th; Sculthorpe:From Kakadu; Into the Dreaming; Night Pieces Pno TALP ▲ 71 [DDD] (18.97)

FOX, DONAL (1952-

Music of Fox

Fox/Troupe Duo *(River Town Packin' House Blues; The Old People Speak of Death; Following the North Star Boogaloo),* D. Fox (pno) *(T-Cell Countdown; Gone City (ballet); Ballade Cl & Pno [w. Eric Thomas (cl)]; Jazz Sets with T. T. [w. Oliver Lake (a sax)]) (rec 1991-94)* ("Gone City") NWW ▲ 80515 [DDD] (16.97)

Videmus—Dialectics for 2 Grand Pnos (1988); Duetto for Cl & Pno (1991); 4 Chords from T.J.'s Intermezzi for Pno (1991); Jazz Sets & Tone Rows for A Sax & Pno (1991) † T. J. Anderson:Intermezzos Cl; D. Baker:Through This Vale of Tears; O. Wilson:Sometimes NWW ▲ 80423 (16.97)

FOX, FREDERICK (1931-

Auras for Chamber Ensemble (1988)

C. Russell (cnd) *(rec Bloomington, IN, Nov 29, 1990)* † Januaries; Sonaspheres 5; Time Messages IUSM ▲ 3 (16.97)

FOX, FREDERICK (cont.)
Januaries for Orchestra (1984)
H. Sollberger (cnd), Indiana Univ SO *(rec Bloomington, IN, May 1, 1986)* † Auras; Sonaspheres 5; Time Messages IUSM ▲ 3 (16.97)
Sonaspheres 5 for Chamber Ensemble (1983)
H. Sollberger (cnd) *(rec Bloomington, IN, Apr 11, 1985)* † Auras; Januaries; Time Messages IUSM ▲ 3 (16.97)
Time Messages for Brass Quintet (1988)
D. Dzubay (tpt), D. McChesney (tpt), M. Galbraith (hn), A. Glendenning (trbn), A. Oppenheim (tuba) *(rec Bloomington, IN, Nov 30, 1989)* † Auras; Januaries; Sonaspheres 5 IUSM ▲ 3 (16.97)
Time Weaving for Clarinet Trio (1993)
Indiana Trio † J. Defaye:Audition Pieces; M. Kibbe:Ebony Suite; Kulesha:Political Implications; P. Schickele:Dances for 3 CRYS ▲ 734 (15.97)

FRANÇAIX, JEAN (1912-1997)
L'Apocalypse de St. Jean (oratorio) for solo Voices, 2 Orchestras & Chorus (1939)
E. Lind (sop), W. Hoffmann-Mucher (alt), K. Azesberger (ten), R. Holzer (bass), H. Bolterauer (org), C. Simonis (cnd), Göttinger SO, St. Jacobi-Kantorei Göttingen, Jeunesse Chorus Linz *(rec Linz Austria, Dec 7, 1997)* WER ▲ 6632 [DDD] (19.97)
Chamber Music
Y. Naganuma (vn), J. Sajet (cl), J. Françaix (pno), J. Françaix (cnd) —Divert Strs & Pno; Dixtuor Ww & Strs; Qt Strs; Sonatine Vn; Theme & Vars Cl EROL 2-▲ 96004 (36.97)
Concertino for Piano & Orchestra (1934)
S. Cápová (pno), T. Frešo (cnd), Slovak PO † A. Roussel:Con Pno, Op. 36; Saint-Saëns:Con 2 Pno, Op. 22 PC ▲ 267194 [DDD] (2.97)
J. Françaix (pno), A. Doráti (cnd), London SO *(rec London, England, Aug 1965)* † G. Auric:Ov; P. Fetler:Contrasts; D. Milhaud:Boeuf sur le toit, Op. 58; Satie:Parade Orch MRCR ▲ 34335 (11.97)
I. Hobson (pno), Sinfonia da Camera † Saint-Saëns:Con 2 Pno, Op. 22 ARA ▲ 6541 (16.97)
J. Thibaudet (pno), C. Dutoit (cnd), Montreal SO † Honegger:Concertino Pno & Orch; M. Ravel:Con Pno; Con Pno (left hand) PLON ▲ 452448 (16.97)
Concerto for Clarinet & Orchestra (1968)
D. Ashkenazy (cl), C. Mueller (cnd), Cincinnati PO † R. Moser:Con Cl; Rimsky-Korsakov:Concertstück Cl; S. Taneyev:Canzona Cl PANC ▲ 510082 [DDD] (17.97)
Concerto for Flute & Orchestra (1967)
M. Wiesler (fl), P. Auguin (cnd), Helsingborg SO *(rec June 1991)* † Chaminade:Concertino Fl, Op. 107; Ibert:Con Fl; Mouquet:Flûte de Pan, Op. 15 BIS ▲ 529 [DDD] (17.97)
Concerto for 2 Harps & String Orchestra
C. Michel (hp), S. Mildonian (hp), A. Moglia (cnd), Toulouse National CO *(rec Apr 1995)* ("Concertos for 2 Harps") † Debussy:Danses sacrée et profane; Gossec:Sym concertante for 2 Hps; Malecki:Concertino dans un style ancien; M. Ravel:Intro & Allegro Hp PAVA ▲ 7337 [DDD] (10.97)
Concerto for Harpsichord & Instrumental Ensemble (1959)
E. Braito (hpd), P. Kantschieder (cnd) ("Harpsichord Concertos of the 20th Century") † F. Farkas:Concertino Hpd; H. Jelinek:2 Blue O's; Martinů:Con Hpd KSCH ▲ 314222 (16.97)
Danses exotiques (8) for 2 Pianos (1957)
C. Andranian (pno), G. Andranian (pno) ("Distant Ports & Shores") † Ibert:Escales; Jolivet:Hopi Snake Dance; D. Milhaud:Boeuf sur le toit, Op. 58 DI ▲ 920313 [DDD] (5.97)
J. Françaix (pno), C. Françaix (pno) † Scuola di ballo; Chabrier:Bourée fantasque; Valses romantiques; F. Schubert:Divert sur des motifs originaux français, D.823 EROL ▲ 96006 (18.97)
Danses exotiques (5) for Saxophone & Piano (1962)
B. Perconti (a sax), J. March (pno) *(rec University of Iowa, United States of America, May-Aug, 1996)* † Derr:I Never Saw Another Butterfly; Heiden:Son Sax; B. Kolb:Related Characters; W. G. Still:Romance; F. Tull:Concerto da Camera; Threnody CENT ▲ 2345 [DDD] (16.97)
P. Savijoki (sax), M. Rahkonen (pno) ("The French Saxophone") † R. Boutry:Divert Sax & Pno; P. Maurice:Tableaux de Provence; D. Milhaud:Scaramouche BIS ▲ 209 [AAD] (17.97)
Divertissement for Bassoon & Strings (1942)
M. Davis (vn), C. L. Kelly (vn), B. Burge (va), I. Fischer-Bellman (vc), S. King (db), M. Karr (bn) *(rec Louisville, 1996)* ("A Bassoonist's Voice") † J. S. Bach:Partita Fl, BWV 1013; Cervetto:Sicilienne Bn; Dunhill:Lyric Suite Bn & Pno, Op. 96; R. Schumann:Fantasiestücke Cl, Op. 73; H. Villa-Lobos:Bachiana brasileira 6 CENT ▲ 2330 [DDD] (16.97)
Gaudier Ensemble † Heure du berger for Orch; Octet; Qnt Cl HYP ▲ 67036 (18.97)
D. Jensen (bn), W. A. Albert (cnd), Cologne RSO ("Bassoon Concertos") † J. N. Hummel:Con Bn; Jolivet:Con Bn; W. A. Mozart:Con Bn, K.191 CAPO ▲ 10579 [DDD] (11.97)
M. Turkovič (bn), M. Sieghart (cnd), Stuttgart CO † G. Gershwin:Porgy & Bess (sels); M. Haydn:Concertino Bn & Orch; W. A. Mozart:Con Bn, K.191; H. Villa-Lobos:Ciranda das sete notas ORF ▲ 223911 [DDD] (18.97)
A. Wallez (bn), Carl Stamitz Ensemble † Octet; Qnt Cl PVY ▲ 792102 [DDD] (16.97)
Divertissement for Oboe, Clarinet & Bassoon (1947)
Chicago Chamber Musicians *(rec Chicago, IL, 1997)* ("20th Century French Wind Trios") † G. Auric:Trio Ob; Canteloube:Rustiques; Ibert:Pièces (5) en trio; D. Milhaud:Pastorale Ob, Op. 147; Suite d'après Corrette, Op. 161; P. Pierné:Bucolique variée; Tansman:Suite Reed Trio CED ▲ 40 [DDD] (16.97)
Le Gay Paris for Flute, 2 Oboes, 2 Clarinets, Bassoon, Double Bassoon, Trumpet & 2 Horns (1974)
Prague Wind Quintet † Heure du berger for Orch; Qnt 1; Qnt 2 PRAG ▲ 250126 (18.97)
Habanera de Chabrier/Françaix for Cello & Piano
P. Bary (vc), H. Calef (pno) [trans for vc & pno, 1985] † Promenade d'un musicologue eclectique; Rhap Ob; Theme & Vars Cl; Trio Cl; G. F. Handel:Sosarme, HWV 30 NPT 2-▲ 85575 [DDD] (32.97)
L'Heure du berger for Orchestra (1947)
Gaudier Ensemble † Divert Bn; Octet; Qnt Cl HYP ▲ 67036 (18.97)
G. Koukl (pno), Prague National Theater Wind Quintet † Ibert:Pièces brèves Ww; Indy:Sarabande et menuet; D. Milhaud:Son Fl, Cl, Ob & Pno, Op. 47; A. Roussel:Divert Ww, Op. 6; Saint-Saëns:Caprice sur des airs danoises et russes, Op. 79 NUO ▲ 7268 (16.97)
Prague Wind Quintet † Gay Paris; Qnt 1; Qnt 2 PRAG ▲ 250126 (18.97)
J. P. Schulze (pno), Arcis Wind Quintet [trans for pno & wind qnt] *(rec Oct 1996)* ("French Piano Sextets") † Martinů:Sxt Fl, Ob, Cl, 2 Bns & Pno; F. Poulenc:Sxt Pno CALG ▲ 50984 [DDD] (18.97)
L'Heure du berger for Piano & Strings (1947)
Berlin Chamber Ensemble † Qnt 1; Qnt 2 MDG (Scene) ▲ 6030557 [DDD] (17.97)
Hommage à l'ami Papageno for Piano & 10 Wind Instruments (1986)
A. De Groote (pno), Bellerophon Wind Orchestra ("Concertos with Wind Orchestra") † Pièces caractéristiques Ww; Ibert:Con Vc; F. Poulenc:Aubade TLNT ▲ 48 [DDD] (15.97)
L'Horloge de Flore for Oboe & Orchestra (1959)
J. De Lancie (ob), A. Previn (cnd), London SO † Ibert:Symphonie concertante; Satie:Gymnopédies; R. Strauss:Con Ob, AV144 RCAV (Gold Seal) ▲ 7989 [ADD] (11.97)
L. Lencsés (ob), U. Segal (cnd), Stuttgart RSO † Honegger:Con da camera; Ibert:Symphonie concertante CPO ▲ 999193 [ADD] (14.97)
Impromptus (7) for Flute & Bassoon
A. Fröhlich (fl), E. Froelich (bn) † Piccoli duetti; Son Fl Gtr; Suite Fl ORF ▲ 388961 [DDD] (18.97)
Jeu poétique in 6 Mouvements for Harp & Orchestra
J. Zoff (hp), H. Rögner (cnd), Dresden Staatskapelle *(rec Germany)* ("Harfenkonzerte") † Dittersdorf:Con Hp; G. F. Handel:Cons (16) Org *(E, F, G text)* BER ▲ 9313 [ADD] (10.97)
Octet for Clarinet, Bassoon, Horn & String Quintet (1972)
Gaudier Ensemble † Divert Bn; Heure du berger for Orch; Qnt Cl HYP ▲ 67036 (18.97)
J. Sajot (cl), A. Wallez (bn), Carl Stamitz Ensemble † Divert Bn; Qnt Cl PVY ▲ 792102 [DDD] (16.97)
Organ Music
C. Boettcher (sop), B. Kratzer (tpt), M. Maier (tpt), J. Essl (org)—Suite carmelite; Suite profane; Messe de mariage; Apocalypse de St. Jean; Marche solennelle ("Das Orgelwerk") FERM ▲ 20018 (16.97)
Petit Quatuor for Saxophone Quartet (1935)
Jean-Yves Formeau Saxophone Quartet ("French Masterpieces for Sax Quartet") † Bozza:Andante & Scherzo; A. Desenclos:Quatuor; P.-M. Dubois:Qt Sax; G. Pierné:Intro et Vars sur une ronde populaire; Rivier:Grave et presto RENE ▲ 87134 [DDD] (16.97)
Rollin' Phones † Bozza:Andante & Scherzo; Glazunov:Qt Saxes, Op. 109; Singelée:Qt 1 Saxes, Op. 53 BIS ▲ 466 [DDD] (17.97)
Les petits nerveux for Piano & Winds
Hexagon *(rec Aaron Copland School of Music Queens College, NYC, Jan 26 & 29-30, 1996)* ("Les Petits Nerveux") † F. Poulenc:Sxt Pno; Trio Ob; A. Roussel:Divert Ww, Op. 6; Saint-Saëns:Caprice sur des airs danoises et russes, Op. 79; Tarantelle, Op. 6 BRID ▲ 9079 [DDD] (17.97)

FRANÇAIX, JEAN (cont.)
Piccoli duetti (5) for Flute & Harp
A. Fröhlich (fl), U. Mattanovich (hp) † Impromptus Fl Bn; Son Fl Gtr; Suite Fl ORF ▲ 388961 [DDD] (18.97)
S. Kudo (fl), R. Talitman (hp) ("French Music for Flute & Harp") † Bizet:Carmen (sels); Boieldieu:Son Fl & Hp; Damase:Son Fl & Hp; M. Ravel:Pavane pour une infante défunte DI ▲ 920141 [DDD] (5.97)
Pièces caractéristiques (9) for 10 Wind Instruments (1973)
Bellerophon Wind Orchestra ("Concertos with Wind Orchestra") † Hommage à l'ami Papageno; Ibert:Con Vc; F. Poulenc:Aubade TLNT ▲ 48 [DDD] (15.97)
La Promenade d'un musicologue eclectique for Piano (1987)
H. Calef (pno) † Habanera de Chabrier/Françaix; Rhap Ob; Theme & Vars Cl; Trio Cl; G. F. Handel:Sosarme, HWV 30 NPT 2-▲ 85575 [DDD] (32.97)
Quartet for Flute, Oboe, Clarinet & Bassoon
Selandia Wind Ensemble † J. Bentzon:Racconto 3, Op. 31; Bozza:Pièces pour une musique de nuit; G. Pierné:Pastorale Ww; K. Riisager:Divert Fl, Op. 42 KPT ▲ 32032 [DDD]
Quintet for Clarinet & Strings (1977)
Gaudier Ensemble † Divert Bn; Heure du berger for Orch; Octet HYP ▲ 67036 (18.97)
J. Sajot (cl), Carl Stamitz Ensemble † Divert Bn; Octet PVY ▲ 792102 [DDD] (16.97)
Quintet No. 1 for Winds (1948)
Berlin Chamber Ensemble † Heure du berger for Pno; Qnt 2 MDG (Scene) ▲ 6030557 [DDD] (17.97)
Berlin Philharmonic Wind Quintet † Bozza:Scherzo, Op. 48; D. Milhaud:Cheminée du Roi René, Op. 205; H. Tomasi:Printemps BIS ▲ 536 [DDD] (17.97)
New York Woodwind Quintet ("An American and Paris") † F. Poulenc:Sxt Pno BOSK ▲ 141 [AAD] (15.97)
Prague Wind Quintet † Gay Paris; Heure du berger for Orch; Qnt 2 PRAG ▲ 250126 (18.97)
Taffanel Wind Quintet † F. Danzi:Qnt Fl; P. Hindemith:Kleine Kammermusik, Op. 24/2; A. Reicha:Qnts Ww, Op. 88; G. Rossini:Andante e tema con variazioni Fl DNN ▲ 8004 [DDD] (10.97)
Quintet No. 2 for Winds (1987)
Berlin Chamber Ensemble † Heure du berger for Pno; Qnt 1 MDG (Scene) ▲ 6030557 [DDD] (17.97)
Prague Wind Quintet † Gay Paris; Heure du berger for Orch; Qnt 1 PRAG ▲ 250126 (18.97)
Rhapsody for Oboe & Piano (1993)
J. F. Bénatar (ob), H. Calef (pno) † Habanera de Chabrier/Françaix; Promenade d'un musicologue eclectique; Theme & Vars Cl; Trio Cl; G. F. Handel:Sosarme, HWV 30 NPT 2-▲ 85575 [DDD] (32.97)
Scuola di ballo (ballet) for Orchestra [after Boccherini] (1933)
J. Françaix (pno), C. Françaix (pno) [2 pno version] † Danses exotiques Pnos; Chabrier:Bourée fantasque; Valses romantiques; F. Schubert:Divert sur des motifs originaux français, D.823 EROL ▲ 96006 (18.97)
Sextet for Bass Clarinet & Wind Quintet
H. Schuldt (b cl), Berlin Kammervereinigung † F. Poulenc:Sxt Pno; Thuille:Sxt Pno, Op. 6 ARSM ▲ 1163 [DDD] (17.97)
Sonata for Flute & Guitar (1984)
A. Swete (gtr), A. Fröhlich (fl) † Impromptus Fl Bn; Piccoli duetti; Suite Fl ORF ▲ 388961 [DDD] (18.97)
Sonata for Flute & Piano
R. Sherman (fl), R. Votapek (pno) † J. Feld:Son Fl; F. Poulenc:Vocalise; Tailleferre:Forlane Fl; Son 2 Vn; Tansman:Sonatine Fl SUMM ▲ 232 (16.97)
Sonatine for Trumpet & Piano (1952)
H. Hardenberger (tpt), R. Pöntinen (pno) † Arban:Vars on a Theme from Bellini's Norma; P. M. Davies:Son Tpt; J. Hartmann:Vars on Rule Britannia; Honegger:Intrada Tpt & Pno; Rabe:Shazam; Tisné:Héraldiques BIS ▲ 287 [DDD] (17.97)
Suite for solo Flute (1962)
A. Fröhlich (fl) † Impromptus Fl Bn; Piccoli duetti; Son Fl Gtr ORF ▲ 388961 [DDD] (18.97)
M. Wiesler (fl), M. Wiesler (fl) *(rec Sweden, Sep 29-30, 1989)* ("Manuela plays French Solo Flute Music") † Debussy:Fl Music; Ibert:Pièce Fl; Jolivet:Incantation Fl; Pieces (12) from 21 Sounding Minutes Fl; Marais:Vars on "Les Folies d'Espagne"; H. Tomasi:Sonatine Fl *(E, F, G text)* BIS ▲ 459 [DDD] (17.97)
Symphonie d'archets for Orchestra (1948)
A. Lascae (cnd) *(rec Oct 1994)* † Vars de concert; F. Martin:Etudes Str Orch; Passacaglia Org OTT ▲ 109459 [DDD] (16.97)
Theme & Variations for Clarinet & Piano (1974)
P. Beltramini (cl), R. Arosio (pno) † L. Bernstein:Son Cl; Debussy:Première rapsodie Cl; Filas:Little Slovak Melody; W. Lutoslawski:Dance Preludes Cl & Pno PHEX ▲ 98198 (16.97)
E. Brunner (cl), R. Werthen (cnd), I Fiamminghi ("Clarinet Concertos") † Mihalovici:Nocturne Cl; Rivier:Con Cl; H. Tomasi:Con Cl KSCH ▲ 310262 (16.97)
S. Kam (cl), I. Golan (pno) † Debussy:Première rapsodie Cl; F. Poulenc:Son Cl & Pno; R. Schumann:Fantasiestücke Cl, Op. 73 TELC ▲ 11022 (16.97)
K. Leister (cl), F. Bognár (pno) *(rec Vienna, June & Dec 1995)* ("Par exellence: French Music for Clarinet") † Debussy:Première rapsodie Cl; D. Milhaud:Son Cl; F. Poulenc:Son Cl & Pno; Saint-Saëns:Son Cl; Widor:Intro & Rondo Cl, Op. 72 CAMA ▲ 415 [DDD] (18.97)
C. Vergnory-Mion (cl), H. Calef (pno) † Habanera de Chabrier/Françaix; Promenade d'un musicologue eclectique; Rhap Ob; Trio Cl; G. F. Handel:Sosarme, HWV 30 NPT 2-▲ 85575 [DDD] (32.97)
Trio for Clarinet, Oboe & Piano (1990)
J. Bénatar (ob), C. Vergnory-Mion (cl), H. Calef (pno) † Habanera de Chabrier/Françaix; Promenade d'un musicologue eclectique; Rhap Ob; Theme & Vars Cl; G. F. Handel:Sosarme, HWV 30 NPT 2-▲ 85575 [DDD] (32.97)
Trio for Oboe, Bassoon & Piano (1994)
J. Mack (ob), D. McGill (bn), E. DeMio (pno) ("25th Anniversary—International Double Reed Society") † A. Previn:Trio Ob; G. Rossini:Barbiere di Siviglia (wind ensemble); H. Villa-Lobos:Duo Ob & Bn CRYS ▲ 870 (15.97)
Variations de concert for Cello & String Orchestra (1950)
G. Hoogeveen (vc), A. Lascae (cnd) *(rec Oct 1994)* † Sym d'archets; F. Martin:Etudes Str Orch; Passacaglia Org OTT ▲ 109459 [DDD] (16.97)

FRANCESCHINI, GAETANO (18th cent)
Sonatas (6) for 2 Violins & Continuo, Op. 1
E. Casazza (vn), I. Longo (vn), E. Casazza (cnd), Accademia della Magnifica Comunità TACT ▲ 730601 (16.97)

FRANCESCHINI, PETRONIO (ca 1650-1680)
Sonata à 7 for 2 Trumpets, Strings, Trombone, Organ & Theorbo
S. Laughton (tpt), W. O'Meara (org), D. Campion (perc/timp) ("Baroque Banquet") † J. S. Bach:Music of Bach; Preludes & Fugues, BWV 531-552; J. Clarke:Prince of Denmark's March; G. F. Handel:Samson (sels); Suite Tpt & Org; A. Scarlatti:Endimione e Cintia; Telemann:Marches (12), TWV50: 31-42 (comp) OPDR ▲ 9303 [DDD] (16.97)

FRANCESCO CANOVA DA MILANO (1497-1543)
Fantasies for Lute
P. O'Dette (lt)—Fant (Castelfranco MS); Fants 8, 26, 39, 56 & 83; Pourquoy allez-vous seullette; Fant dolcissima et amorosa *(rec Sept 28-29, 1990 & Feb 22, 1992)* ("Dolcissima et Amorosa: Early Italian Renaissance Lute Music") † Borrono:Lt Music; Marco Da l'aquila:Lt Music; Ripa (da Mantova):Lt Music HAM ▲ 907043 (18.97)
Lute Music
J. Bream (lt)—Fantasias † W. Byrd:Lt Music; Cutting:Lt Music; J. Dowland:Songs; Holborne:Lt Music RCAV ▲ 61587 (11.97)
C. Wilson (lt)—Ricercars; Fants; plus others ("Fantasia de mon triste: Renaissance Lute Virtuosi") † Capriola:Lt Music; Spinacino:Lt Music MENO ▲ 1025 (20.97)
Tochata for Lute (1536)
M. Lonardi (lt) † Borrono:Lt Music STRV ▲ 33314 [DDD] (16.97)

FRANCESCONI, LUCA (1956-
Music of Francesconi
Webb (cnd), Bucharest RSO—Les barricades mysterieuses; Passacaglia; Memoria; Trama ("Orchestral Works") BMGR ▲ 1023 (18.97)

FRANCHETTI, ALBERTO (1860-1942)
Cristoforo Colombo (opera in 3 acts) [lib L. Illica] (1892)
R. Ragatzu (sop—Isabella), G. Pasino (mez—Annacoana), M. Berti (ten—Ferdinand), R. Bruson (bar—Cristoforo Colombo), R. Scandiuzzi (bass—Don Roldano Ximenes), M. Viotti (cnd), Frankfurt RSO, Frankfurt Radio Chorus [ITA] *(rec live Alte Oper Frankfurt, Aug 30 & Sept 2, 1991)* KSCH 3-▲ 310302 [DDD] (47.97)

FRANCHOMME, AUGUSTE (JOSEPH) (1808-1884)
Caprices (12) for Cello, Op. 7
O. Bourin (vc), B. Cazauran (db) ("Duo") † Bouknik:Fant Vc; Genzmer:Bagatelles; A. Lindner:Diverts for Young Cellists, Op. 32; G. Rossini:Duet Vc & Db GALL ▲ 795 [ADD]

▲ = CD ♦ = Enhanced CD △ = MD ▮ = Cassette Tape ▯ = DCC

FRANCI, CARLO (1927-

African Oratorio for Soprano, Narrator, Flute, Orchestra, Chorus & Tape (1994)
M. Arroyo (sop), C. Dhlamini (nar), P. Bagshaw (fl), C. Franci (cnd), Transvaal PO, Boisusumu Adult Choir, Kwathema Youth Choir *(rec Johannesburg City Hall South Africa, Nov 1994)* MUIM ▲ 10038 [DDD] (18.97)

Music of Carlo Franci
F. Franci (mez), C. Franci (cnd) ("Dreamtime") MUIM ▲ 10043 (18.97)

FRANCK, CÉSAR (1822-1890)

Andantino quietoso in E♭ for Violin & Piano, Op. 6, (M.5) (1843)
M. Sirbu (vn), M. Sarbu (pno) † Duo based on motifs from Dalayrac's Gulistan, M.6; Quatrième trio concertant, Op. 2; Son Vn, M.8; Trios concertants 1-3, M.1-3 DYNC 2-▲ 21 [DDD] (17.97)

Les Béatitudes (oratorio) for solo Voices, Orchestra & Chorus, M.53 (1869-79)
D. Montague (mez), K. Lewis (ten), G. Cachemaille (bar), J. Cheek (bass), H. Rilling (cnd), Stuttgart RSO, Gächinger Kantorei [FRE] HANS 2-▲ 98964 [DDD] (25.97)

Ce qu'on entend sur la montagne (symphonic poem) for Orchestra [after V. Hugo], Op. 13 (c1845-47)
B. Priestman (cnd), RTBF SO KSCH ▲ 311105

Le Chasseur maudit (symphonic poem) for Orchestra [after G. Bürger], M.44 (1882)
E. Ansermet (cnd), Swiss Romande Orch † Éolides, M.43; Chabrier:España; Joyeuse marche; Roi malgré lui (sels); Suite pastorale PLON (Classic Sound) ▲ 452890 (11.97)
R. Benzi (cnd), Arnhem PO *(rec Arnhem Netherlands, June 14-16, 1995)* † Éolides, M.43; Sym in d, M.48 NXIN ▲ 553631 [DDD] (5.97)
J. Fournet (cnd), Czech PO † Djinns, M.45; Sym in d, M.48 SUR (Collection) ▲ 110613 [ADD]
M. Freccia (cnd), RCA Victor SO *(rec 1968)* † Psyché (sels); Sym in d, M.48; Symphonic Vars, M.46 CHSK ▲ 87 [ADD] (16.97)
J. López-Cobos (cnd), Cincinnati SO † Sym in d, M.48 TEL ▲ 80247 [DDD] (16.97)
C. Munch (cnd), Boston SO ("The French Touch") † Dukas:L'Apprenti sorcier; M. Ravel:Ma mère l'oye; Saint-Saëns:Rouet d'Omphale, Op. 31 RCAV (Living Stereo) ▲ 68978 (11.97)
T. Otaka (cnd), BBC National Orch Wales † Psyché, M.47 CHN ▲ 9342 [DDD] (16.97)

Choral Music
M. Bódi (sop), A. Wendler (ten), I. Rácz (bass), S. Kamp (cnd), Debrecen Kodály Choir—Offertoires (3), M.63-5 [No. 1 Quae est ista; No. 3 Dextera Domini] † Messe à 3 voix, Op. 12 HUN ▲ 31579 [DDD] (16.97)

Chorales (3) for Organ, M.38-40 (1890)
G. Brand (cnd) [arr P. Grainger] † G. Holst:Fugal Con, Op. 40/2; Hammersmith, Op. 52; J. Ireland:Downland Suite; G. Jacob:Sym AD 78 ALBA ▲ 120 [DDD]
M. Dupré (org) † Pièces (3) Org, M.37; Widor:Salve regina; Sym 6 Org, Op. 42/2 MRCR ▲ 34311 [ADD] (11.97)
F. Houbart (org) *(rec Oct 1984)* † Pièces (3) Org, M.37 PVY ▲ 785031 [DDD] (16.97)
M. Murray (org), Murray (org) † J. S. Bach:Preludes & Fugues, BWV 531-552; M. Dupré:Org Music; Vierne:Meditation & Prelude, Op. 31; Widor:Sym 6 Org, Op. 42/2 TEL ▲ 80169 [DDD] (16.97)
G. Robert (org) † Final B♭, Op. 21; Org Music; Pastorale, Op. 19; Pièces (3) Org, M.35; Pièces (3) Org, M.37; Prélude, fugue et var, Op. 18 ILD 2-▲ 642142 (20.97)
F. Swann (org) *(rec Riverside Church, NYC, NY)* ("The Riverside Years") † Pièces (3) Org, M.37; Farnam:Toccata on "O Filii et Filiae"; Gigout:Grand-Choeur Dialogue; Karg-Elert:Symphonic Chorale 1, Op. 87/1; J. Langlais:Hymne d'Actions de grâces "Te Deum" GOT ▲ 49082 (17.97)
B. Turley (org) *(rec Phillips Memorial Baptist Church Cranston, RI)* AFK ▲ 511

Chorales (3) in E, b & a for Organ, M.38-40 (1890)
N. Hakim (org) *(rec Église de Sainte-Trinité Paris, Mar 1997)* ("Canticum: French Organ Music") † Pièces (3) Org, M.36; N. Hakim:Org Music; J. Langlais:Ave Maria, Ave maris stella; Te Deum; Messiaen:Livre du Saint-Sacrement; Nativité du Seigneur; Vierne:Pièces de fant Org (sels) EMIC (Debut) ▲ 72272 [DDD] (6.97)
D. Hill (org) *(rec Trinity Cathedral Portland, OR, May 1994)* ("There Let the Pealing Organ Blow") † J. S. Bach:Toccata & Fugue Org, BWV 565; F. Bridge:Adagio Org; Vierne:Org Music HER ▲ 190 [DDD] (19.97)
S. Hough (pno) [[trans Stephen Hough]] † Danse lente, M.22; Grand caprice, M.13; Plaintes, M.20; Prélude, aria et final, M.23; Prélude, choral et fugue, M.21 HYP ▲ 66918 (18.97)
L. Kurpershoek (org) *(rec St. Mary's Anglican Cathedral Org Johannesburg, England)* ("Popular Organ Music, Vol. 4") † J. Brahms:Chorale Preludes Org, Op. 122; N. Cocker:Tuba Tune; Duruflé:Prélude et fugue, Op. 7; Grové:Afrika Hymnus; Hollins:Intermezzo PRIO ▲ 610 (16.97)
D. MacDonald (org)—No. 3 in a *(rec Casavant Org, Basilique Notre-Dame du Cap, Quebec, Canada, Mar 1993)* † J. Alain:Jardin suspendu, AWV 63; Cardy:Eclat Org; Daveluy:Choral Prelude Org; Son 3 Org; Duruflé:Prélude et fugue, Op. 7; Messiaen:Nativité du Seigneur; Widor:Sym 5 Org, Op. 42/1 CBC ▲ 1104 [DDD] (11.97)
A. Morrison (org) *(rec Atlanta GA, Aeolian-Skinner Org)* ("St. Philip's Cathedral") † Demessieux:Te Deum, Op. 11; M. Dupré:Préludes & Fugues, Op. 7; Vars sur un vieux Noël, Op. 20; Duruflé:Suite Org, Op. 5 GOT ▲ 49083 [DDD] (17.97)
I. Quinn (org) *(rec Methuen Memorial Music Hall Org, Mar 5-7, 1995)* ("Iain Quinn Plays the Great Organ at Methuen") † L. Howard:Moto di Gioia, Op. 27; Josephs:Son Org; Liszt:Org Music; Masson:Meditation RAVN ▲ 360 [DDD]
L. Rogg (org) *(rec Victoria Hall Geneva, Switzerland, Switzerland)* † J. Brahms:Vars on a Theme by Haydn; Vierne:Sym 1 Org, Op. 14; Widor:Sym 5 Org, Op. 42/1 CASC ▲ 1028 (16.97)
F. Swann (org) † J. S. Bach:Passacaglia & Fugue Org, BWV 582; M. S. Wright:Intro, Passacaglia & Fugue GOT ▲ 49049 [DDD] (17.97)

Danse lente for Piano, M.22 (1885)
S. Hough (pno) † Chorales Org, M.38-40; Grand caprice, M.13; Plaintes, M.20; Prélude, aria et final, M.23; Prélude, choral et fugue, M.21 HYP ▲ 66918 (18.97)

Deuxieme grand concerto in g for Piano & Orchestra, Op. 11 (c1835)
J. V. Eynden (pno), E. Doneux (cnd), Belgian RSO † Vars brillantes sur la ronde, Op. 8 KSCH ▲ 311111 [DDD] (16.97)

Les Djinns (symphonic poem) for Piano & Orchestra [after Hugo], M.45 (1884)
K. Åberg (pno), O. Kamu (cnd), Gothenburg SO *(rec May 31, 1979)* † Prélude, choral et fugue, M.21; Symphonic Vars, M.46 BIS ▲ 137 [AAD] (17.97)
F. Maxián (pno), J. Fournet (cnd), Czech PO † Chasseur maudit, M.44; Sym in d, M.48 SUR (Collection) ▲ 110613 [ADD]

Domine non secundum for Solo Voices & Organ [Offertory for Lent], M.66 (1871)
J. Salanne (cnd), Domaine Musical Orch, Henri Duparc Chorus † Sept paroles du Christ sur la croix CYPR ▲ 2610 (17.97)

Duo No. 1 for Piano & Violin based on motifs from Dalayrac's Gulistan, M.6, (Op. 14) (1844)
M. Sirbu (vn), M. Sarbu (pno) † Andantino quietoso, Op. 6; Quatrième trio concertant, Op. 2; Son Vn, M.8; Trios concertants 1-3, M.1-3 DYNC 2-▲ 21 [DDD] (17.97)

Les Éolides (symphonic poem) for Orchestra [after Leconte de Lisle], M.43 (1875-76)
E. Ansermet (cnd), Swiss Romande Orch † Chasseur maudit, M.44; Chabrier:España; Joyeuse marche; Roi malgré lui (sels); Suite pastorale PLON (Classic Sound) ▲ 452890 (11.97)
R. Benzi (cnd), Arnhem PO *(rec Arnhem Netherlands, June 14-16, 1995)* † Chasseur maudit, M.44; Sym in d, M.48 NXIN ▲ 553631 [DDD] (5.97)
A. Toscanini (cnd), NBC SO *(rec 1938-46)* † Psyché (sels); Debussy:Prélude à l'après-midi d'un faune; Dukas:Ariane et Barbe-Bleue (suite); Roger-Ducasse:Sarabande; A. Roussel:Festin de l'araignée (suite 2) URAN ▲ 107 (m) [DDD] (15.97)

Final in B♭ for Organ, Op. 21, (M.33) (1860-62)
M. Murray (org) † M. Dupré:Préludes & Fugues, Op. 7; Messiaen:Nativité du Seigneur; Widor:Sym 6 Org, Op. 42/2 TEL ▲ 80097 [DDD] (16.97)
G. Robert (org) † Chorales Org, M.38-40; Org Music; Pastorale, Op. 19; Pièces (3) Org, M.35; Pièces (3) Org, M.37; Prélude, fugue et var, Op. 18 ILD 2-▲ 642142 (20.97)
D. Schrader (org) *(rec Duluth, MN, Mar 10-11, 1993)* † Pastorale, Op. 19; Pièces (3) Org, M.35; Pièces (3) Org, M.36; Pièces (3) Org, M.37; Prélude, fugue et var, Op. 18; M. Dupré:Vars sur un vieux Noël, Op. 20 CED ▲ 15 [DDD] (16.97)

Grand caprice No. 1 for Piano, M.13, (Op. 5) (1843)
S. Hough (pno) † Chorales Org, M.38-40; Danse lente, M.22; Plaintes, M.20; Prélude, aria et final, M.23; Prélude, choral et fugue, M.21 HYP ▲ 66918 (18.97)

Grande pièce symphonique in f♯ for Organ, Op. 17, (M.29) (1873)
J. E. Eschbach (org) † Guilmant:Son 5 Org, Op. 80 CENT ▲ 2053 [DDD] (16.97)
D. Major (org) *(rec Great Organ, Washington National Cathedral, United States of America)* ("French Masterpieces") † Pièces (3) Org, M.37; Widor:Sym 5 Org, Op. 42/1 GOT ▲ 49108 (17.97)

Messe à 3 voix for Cello, Double Bass, Harp & Choir, Op. 12, (M.61) (1860)
L. Devos (ten), P. Bartholomée (cnd), Brussels Radio-TV Chorus [LAT] *(rec 1976)* † Prélude, fugue et var, Op. 18 KSCH ▲ 310442 [ADD] (17.97)

FRANCK, CÉSAR (cont.)

Messe à 3 voix for Cello, Double Bass, Harp & Choir, Op. 12, (M.61) (1860) (cont.)
S. Kamp (cnd), Debrecen Kodály Choir, A. Wendler (ten), Z. Molnár (vc), F. Nagy (db), A. Kocsis (hp), D. Karasszon (org) † Choral Music HUN ▲ 31579 [DDD] (16.97)

Organ Music (complete)
D. Sanger (org) BIS 2-▲ 214 (69.97)

Organ Music
M. Murray (org), Murray (org)—Chorales Org, M.38-40 † Chorales Org, M.38-40; J. S. Bach:Preludes & Fugues, BWV 531-552; M. Dupré:Org Music; Vierne:Meditation & Prelude, Op. 31; Widor:Sym 6 Org, Op. 42/2 TEL ▲ 80169 [DDD] (16.97)
G. Robert (org)—Fant in C, Op. 16, (M.28); Cantabile; Grande fantasie 1, Op. 11, (M.16); Prière, Op. 20, (M.32) † Chorales Org, M.38-40; Final B♭, Op. 21; Pastorale, Op. 19; Pièces (3) Org, M.35; Pièces (3) Org, M.37; Prélude, fugue et var, Op. 18 ILD 2-▲ 642142 (20.97)

Organ Music (complete)
J. Langlais (org)—Fant in C, Op. 16, (M.28); Grande pièce symphonique, Op. 17, (M.29); Prélude, fugue et var, Op. 18; Prière, Op. 20, (M.32); Final B♭, Op. 21, (M.33); Pastorale, Op. 19, (M.31); Pièces (3) Org, M.35-7; Chorales Org, M.38-40 ("Complete Organ Works") GA 2-▲ 272 (32.97)
D. Roth (org)—Fant in C, Op. 16, (M.28) ("Vol. 1") MOTE ▲ 11381 [DDD]
D. Roth (org)—Pastorale, Op. 19, (M.31); Pièces (3) Org, M.35; Final B♭, Op. 21, (M.33); Prière, Op. 20, (M.32); Prélude, fugue et var, Op. 18 ("Vol. 2") MOTE ▲ 11391 [DDD]
D. Roth (org)—Chorales Org, M.38-40; Pièces (3) Org, M.37; Pièces (3) Org, M.36 [No. 2 Cantabile in B]; Organiste Vol I, M.41 [No.28 Offertoire in E♭; No.35 Offertoire or Communion in e] ("Vol. 3") MOTE ▲ 11401 [DDD]

L'Organiste Volume I (set of 55 pieces) for Organ (or Harmonium), M.41 (1889-90)
D. Bostock (cnd), Bohemian Chamber PO [[orchd Henri Büsser]] ("French Orchestral Miniatures, Vol. 1") † Bizet:Docteur Miracle (ov); Chabrier:Habanera; Delibes:Roi s'amuse; Lalo:Divert Orch; Saint-Saëns:Suite Orch, Op. 49 CLSO ▲ 158 [DDD] (15.97)
P. Delacour (org)—Suite No. 1; Suite No. 2; Suite No. 3; Suite No. 4; Suite No. 5 ("L'Organiste Vol 1: Suites No. 1 to 5") FUGA ▲ 6 (18.97)
P. Gueit (org) ("Noëls Romantiques") † Organiste Vol II, M.24; Boëllmann:Offertoire sur des noëls; Gigout:Rhapsodie sur des Noëls SONP ▲ 92005
R. Silverman (pno) † Prélude, aria et final, M.23; Prélude, choral et fugue, M.21; Prélude, fugue et var, Op. 18 MUVI (Musica Viva) ▲ 1061 [DDD] (16.97)

L'Organiste Volume II (set of 30 pieces) for Organ (or Harmonium), M.24 (1858-63)
P. Gueit (org) ("Noëls Romantiques") † Organiste Vol I, M.41; Boëllmann:Offertoire sur des noëls; Gigout:Rhapsodie sur des Noëls SONP ▲ 92005

Panis angelicus for Tenor, Harp, Cello, Double Bass & Organ [interpolated in Messe solennelle, Op. 12] (1872)
H. Britton (org) [arr for org] ("The 3 Organ Chorales") † Pièces (3) Org, M.36; Prélude, fugue et var, Op. 18 ASVQ ▲ 6175 (10.97)
M. Calvert (ten), D. Di Fiore (org), S. Kershaw (cnd), Auburn SO ("Les Amoureux de l'Orgue") † Gounod:Divine Redeemer; Guilmant:Sym 1; F. Poulenc:Con Org; Vierne:March triomphale, Op. 46 AMBA ▲ 1019 [DDD] (16.97)

Pastorale in E for Organ [from 6 Pièces], Op. 19, (M.31) (1860-62)
M. Murray (org) † Pièces (3) Org, M.35; J. Jongen:Symphonie Concertante, Op. 81 TEL ▲ 80096 [DDD] (16.97)
G. Robert (org) † Chorales Org, M.38-40; Final B♭, Op. 21; Org Music; Pièces (3) Org, M.35; Pièces (3) Org, M.37; Prélude, fugue et var, Op. 18 ILD 2-▲ 642142 (20.97)
D. Schrader (org) *(rec Duluth, MN, Mar 10-11, 1993)* † Final B♭, Op. 21; Pièces (3) Org, M.35; Pièces (3) Org, M.36; Pièces (3) Org, M.37; Prélude, fugue et var, Op. 18; M. Dupré:Vars sur un vieux Noël, Op. 20 CED ▲ 15 [DDD] (16.97)
C. Walsh (org) *(rec Lincoln Cathedral, England, 1994)* ("The Organs of Salisbury & Lincoln Cathedrals") † Boëly:Allegretto; Fant & Fugue in B♭; J. Langlais:Adeste Fidelis; Org Music; Triptyque; Tournemire:Improvs (5); Vierne:Carillon de Westminster, Op. 54/6; Sur le Rhin PRIO ▲ 648 [DDD] (16.97)

Pièces (3) for Organ, M.35 (1878)
J. Farris (org) † J. Alain:Deuxième fant, AWV 91; M. Dupré:Vars sur un vieux Noël, Op. 20; Duruflé:Prélude et fugue, Op. 7; Vierne:Sym 6 Org, Op. 59; Widor:Sym 6 Org, Op. 42/2 DLS ▲ 3049 [DDD] (14.97)
J. Longhurst (org) *(rec Great Org of the Mormon Tabernacle Salt Lake City, United States of America)* ("Romantic French Fantasies") † J. Alain:Org Music (misc); Boëllmann:Ronde Française, Op. 37; Suite 2 Org, Op. 27; M. Dupré:Cortège et Litanie, Op. 19/2; Vierne:Maestoso; Pièces de fant Org (sels); Widor:Sym 1 Org, Op. 13/1; Sym 4 Org, Op. 13/4; Sym 5 Org, Op. 42/1 KLAV ▲ 11069 [DDD] (18.97)
M. Murray (org) † Pastorale, Op. 19; J. Jongen:Symphonie Concertante, Op. 81 TEL ▲ 80096 [DDD] (16.97)
G. Robert (org)—No. 1 Fantasie in A † Chorales Org, M.38-40; Final B♭, Op. 21; Org Music; Pastorale, Op. 19; Pièces (3) Org, M.37; Prélude, fugue et var, Op. 18 ILD 2-▲ 642142 (20.97)
D. Schrader (org) *(rec Duluth, MN, Mar 10-11, 1993)* † Final B♭, Op. 21; Pastorale, Op. 19; Pièces (3) Org, M.36; Pièces (3) Org, M.37; Prélude, fugue et var, Op. 18; M. Dupré:Vars sur un vieux Noël, Op. 20 CED ▲ 15 [DDD] (16.97)

Pièces (3) for Organ, M.36 (1878)
N. Hakim (org) *(rec Eglise de Sainte-Trinité Paris, Mar 1997)* ("Canticum: French Organ Music") † Chorales Org, M.38-40; N. Hakim:Org Music; J. Langlais:Ave Maria, Ave maris stella; Te Deum; Messiaen:Livre du Saint-Sacrement; Nativité du Seigneur; Vierne:Pièces de fant Org (sels) EMIC (Debut) ▲ 72272 [DDD] (6.97)
J. Lancelot (org) *(rec Winchester Cathedral Org)* ("The 3 Organ Chorales") † Panis angelicus; Prélude, fugue et var, Op. 18 ASVQ ▲ 6175 (10.97)
D. Schrader (org) *(rec Duluth, MN, Mar 10-11, 1993)* † Final B♭, Op. 21; Pastorale, Op. 19; Pièces (3) Org, M.35; Pièces (3) Org, M.37; Prélude, fugue et var, Op. 18; M. Dupré:Vars sur un vieux Noël, Op. 20 CED ▲ 15 [DDD] (16.97)

Pièces (3) for Organ, M.37 (1878)
E. P. Biggs (org) † Sym in d, M.48; Symphonic Vars, M.46 SNYC (Essential Classics) ▲ 60287 (7.97) ▮ 60287 (3.98)
D. Briggs (org) ("Popular Organ Music, Vol. 2") † J. Alain:Jardin suspendu, AWV 63; J. S. Bach:Preludes & Fugues (22) Org, BWV 531-552; Preludes & Fugues, BWV 531-552; P. Cochereau:Boléro on a Theme of Charles Racquet; Dukas:L'Apprenti sorcier; P. Tchaikovsky:Nutcracker Suite, Op. 71a PRIO ▲ 568 [DDD] (16.97)
M. Dupré (org)—No. 3 Pièce Héroïque in b † Chorales Org, M.38-40; Widor:Salve regina; Sym 6 Org, Op. 42/2 MRCR ▲ 34311 [ADD] (11.97)
F. Houbart (org) *(rec Oct 1984)* † Chorales Org, M.38-40 PVY ▲ 785031 [DDD] (16.97)
D. Major (org)—No. 3 Pièce Héroïque in b *(rec Great Organ, Washington National Cathedral, United States of America)* ("French Masterpieces") † Grande pièce symphonique, Op. 17; Widor:Sym 5 Org, Op. 42/1 GOT ▲ 49108 (17.97)
P. Monteux (cnd), Chicago SO [orchd] ("Pierre Monteux Edition, Vol. 8") † Sym in d, M.48; Indy:Istar RCAV (Gold Seal) ▲ 61900 (11.97)
G. Robert (org)—No. 3 Pièce Héroïque in b † Chorales Org, M.38-40; Final B♭, Op. 21; Org Music; Pastorale, Op. 19; Pièces (3) Org, M.35; Prélude, fugue et var, Op. 18 ILD 2-▲ 642142 (20.97)
D. Schrader (org) *(rec Duluth, MN, Mar 10-11, 1993)* † Final B♭, Op. 21; Pastorale, Op. 19; Pièces (3) Org, M.35; Pièces (3) Org, M.36; Prélude, fugue et var, Op. 18; M. Dupré:Vars sur un vieux Noël, Op. 20 CED ▲ 15 [DDD] (16.97)
F. Swann (org)—No. 3 Pièce Héroïque in b *(rec Riverside Church, NYC, NY)* ("The Riverside Years") † Chorales Org, M.38-40; Farnam:Toccata on "O Filii et Filiae"; Gigout:Grand-Choeur Dialogue; Karg-Elert:Symphonic Chorale 1, Op. 87/1; J. Langlais:Hymne d'Actions de grâces "Te Deum" GOT ▲ 49082 (17.97)

Les Plaintes d'une poupée for Piano, M.20 (1865)
S. Hough (pno) † Chorales Org, M.38-40; Danse lente, M.22; Grand caprice, M.13; Prélude, aria et final, M.23; Prélude, choral et fugue, M.21 HYP ▲ 66918 (18.97)

Prélude, aria et final for Piano, M.23 (1886-87)
A. Cortot (pno) *(rec 1929-32)* † Prélude, choral et fugue, M.21; Debussy:Preludes Pno ENPL (Piano Library) ▲ 269 (13.97)
S. Hough (pno) † Chorales Org, M.38-40; Danse lente, M.22; Grand caprice, M.13; Plaintes, M.20; Prélude, choral et fugue, M.21 HYP ▲ 66918 (18.97)
R. Silverman (pno) † Organiste Vol I, M.41; Prélude, choral et fugue, M.21; Prélude, fugue et var, Op. 18 MUVI (Musica Viva) ▲ 1061 [DDD] (16.97)

Prélude, choral et fugue for Piano, M.21 (1884)
K. Åberg (pno) *(rec Oct 15, 1979)* † Djinns, M.45; Symphonic Vars, M.46 BIS ▲ 137 [AAD] (17.97)
S. Cherkassky (pno) *(rec Apr 14-16, 1987)* † R. Schumann:Kreisleriana, Op. 16; Symphonic Etudes, Op. 13 NIMB ▲ 7705 [DDD] (11.97)
A. Cortot (pno) *(rec 1929-32)* † Prélude, aria et final, M.23; Debussy:Preludes Pno ENPL (Piano Library) ▲ 269 (13.97)
S. Hough (pno) † Chorales Org, M.38-40; Danse lente, M.22; Grand caprice, M.13; Plaintes, M.20; Prélude, aria et final, M.23 HYP ▲ 66918 (18.97)

FRANCK, CÉSAR (cont.)
Prélude, choral et fugue for Piano, M.21 (1884) (cont.)

J. Katchen (pno) *(rec 1953)* ("Julius Katchen") † Balakirev:Islamey; J. Brahms:Son 3 Pno, Op. 5; Vars on an Original Theme, Op. 21/1; Chopin:Ballade 3 Pno, Op. 47; Fantaisie Pno, Op. 49; Liszt:Hungarian Rhaps, S.244; Mendelssohn (-Bartholdy):Prelude & Fugue Pno; Rondo capriccioso, Op. 14; N. Rorem:Son 2 Pno PPHI (Great Pianists of the 20th Century) ▲ 456856 (22.97)

E. Kissin (pno) † Beethoven:Son 14 Pno, Op. 27/2; J. Brahms:Vars on a Theme by Paganini, Op. 35 RCAV (Red Seal) ▲ 68910 [DDD] (16.97)

I. Moravec (pno) *(rec 1963-69)* ("French Keyboard Masterpieces") † M. Ravel:Sonatine Pno VAIA 2-▲ 1043 [ADD] (31.97)

G. Neuhold (cnd), Royal Flanders PO [orchd Paul Pierné] *(rec July 1988)* † Sym in d, M.48 NXIN ▲ 550155 [DDD] (5.97)

C. Pagano (pno) † Debussy:Images (6) Pno; Preludes Pno; Suite bergamasque SUMM ▲ 110 [DDD] (16.97)

M. Perahia (pno) † Liszt:Pno Music (misc) SNYC ▲ 47180 (16.97)

A. Pratt (pno) † J. Brahms:Ballades (4), Op. 10; Busoni:Chaconne Pno; Liszt:Harmonies poétiques et religieuses, S.173 EMIC ▲ 55025 (16.97)

S. Richter (pno) † R. Schumann:Fantasiestücke Pno, Op. 12; Humoreske Pno, Op. 20 MON ▲ 72022 (11.97)

J. Robilette (pno) *(rec 1993)* ("French Piano Album") † Symphonic Vars, M.46; Chopin:Impromptus (4); F. Poulenc:Mouvements perpétuels PRA ▲ 3491 (14.97)

R. Silverman (pno) † Organiste Vol I, M.41; Prélude, aria et final, M.23; Prélude, fugue et var, Op. 18 MUVI (Musica Viva) ▲ 1061 [DDD] (16.97)

Prélude, fugue et variation in b for Organ [from 6 Pièces], Op. 18 (1860-62)

E. Breidenbach (pno), J. M. Michel (harm) [trans Franck for pno & harm] ("Duos for Harmonium & Piano") † Saint-Saëns:Duos Pno & Harm, Op. 8; Widor:Duos Pno & Harm SIGM ▲ 8700 (17.97)

G. Chevallier (hp), C. Fleischmann (hp) [arr for 2 hps] ("Duo de Harpes") † Andrés:Music of; Dalvimare:Hp Music; L. Rogg:Irisations; J. Thomas:Grand Duo CASC ▲ 1035 (16.97)

A. Davis (org) *(rec Org at Roy Thompson Hall Toronto)* † J. S. Bach:Toccata & Fugue Org, BWV 565; C. Ives:Vars on 'America'; H. Purcell:Cortege Academique; Tpt Tune INMP (IMP Classics) ▲ 6700942 (9.97)

H. Fagius (org) *(rec July 2-5, 1992)* † M. Dupré:Ballade, Op. 30; Sinf Pno, Op. 42; Vars à deux thèmes, Op. 35; Karg-Elert:Poesien, Op. 35; Silhouetten, Op. 29; F. Peeters:Con Org Pno, Op. 74 BIS ▲ 551 [DDD] (17.97)

F. Grier (org) *(rec Christ Church Cathedral Oxford Org)* ("The 3 Organ Chorales") † Panis angelicus; Pièces (3) Org, M.36 ASVQ ▲ 6175 (10.97)

J. Johnson (org) † Son Vn, M.8; J. S. Bach:Org Music (misc colls); Passacaglia & Fugue Org, BWV 582; Pastorale Org, BWV 590; Preludes & Fugues, BWV 531-552 TIT ▲ 164 [DDD]

G. Litaize (org) *(rec 1963)* † Messe à 3 voix, Op. 12 KSCH ▲ 310442 [ADD] (17.97)

A. Pratt (pno) *(rec live, Dec 1995)* ("Live from South Africa") † J. S. Bach:Chromatic Fant & Fugue, BWV 903; J. Brahms:Intermezzos (3) Pno, Op. 117; Busoni:Bach Transcriptions Pno; S. Rachmaninoff:Moments musicaux, Op. 16; Preludes Pno EMIC ▲ 55293 (16.97)

G. Robert (org) † Chorales Org, M.38-40; Final B♭, Op. 21; Org Music; Pastorale, Op. 19; Pièces (3) Org, M.35; Pièces (3) Org, M.37 ILD 2-▲ 642142 (20.97)

D. Schrader (org) *(rec Duluth, MN, Mar 10-11, 1993)* † Final B♭, Op. 21; Pastorale, Op. 19; Pièces (3) Org, M.35; Pièces (3) Org, M.36; Pièces (3) Org, M.37; M. Dupré:Vars sur un vieux Noël, Op. 20 CED ▲ 15 [DDD] (16.97)

R. Seal (org) † J. S. Bach:Fant Org, BWV 572; Liszt:Prelude & Fugue on the name B-A-C-H, S.260; Stanford:For Lo, I Raise Up, Op. 145; Song of Peace; T. A. Walmisley:Remember, O Lord; S. S. Wesley:Thou Wilt Keep Him in Perfect Peace MER ▲ 84140 (16.97)

R. Silverman (pno) † Organiste Vol I, M.41; Prélude, aria et final, M.23; Prélude, choral et fugue, M.21 MUVI (Musica Viva) ▲ 1061 [DDD] (16.97)

Psalm 150 for Organ, Orchestra & Chorus (1884)

J. Hancock (org), G. Hancock (cnd), St. Thomas Church Men & Boys' Choir New York ("Most Sacret Banquet") † Duruflé:Motets on Gregorian Chants, Op. 10; J. Langlais:Messe solenelle; Messiaen:O sacrum convivium!; F. Poulenc:Exultate Deo KOCH ▲ 7228 (16.97)

Psyché (symphonic poem) for Orchestra & Chorus [text Sicard & de Foucard], M.47 (1887-88)

A. Cluytens (cnd), Paris Conservatory Société des Concerts Orch † M. Ravel:Daphnis et Chloé TES ▲ 1128 (17.97)

G. Jochum (cnd), Linz Bruckner Orch *(rec 1944)* † A. Bruckner:Sym 2; Sym 6 LYS 2-▲ 476 (33.97)

T. Otaka (cnd), BBC National Orch Wales, BBC Welsh Chorus † Chasseur maudit, M.44 CHN ▲ 9342 [DDD] (16.97)

Psyché (selections)

C. M. Giulini (cnd), Philharmonia Orch † Sym in d, M.48; B. Britten:Peter Grimes (sea interludes & passacaglia); Young Person's Guide to the Orch, Op. 34 EMIC (Artist Profile) 2-▲ 67723

G. Prêtre (cnd), Royal PO *(rec 1963)* † Chasseur maudit, M.44; Sym in d, M.48; Symphonic Vars, M.46 CHSK ▲ 87 [ADD] (16.97)

A. Toscanini (cnd), NBC SO ("The Toscanini Collection, Vol. 39: All-French Program") † Berlioz:Damnation de Faust (sels); Roméo et Juliette (sels); Dukas:L'Apprenti sorcier; M. Ravel:Daphnis et Chloé (suite 2); Saint-Saëns:Danse macabre, Op. 40; A. Thomas:Mignon (ov) RCAV (Gold Seal) ▲ 60322 (11.97)

A. Toscanini (cnd), NBC SO, NBC Sym Chorus—No. 4, "Psyché et Eros" *(rec 1938-46)* † Eolides, M.43; Debussy:Prélude à l'après-midi d'un faune; Dukas:Ariane et Barbe-Bleue (suite); Roger-Ducasse:Sarabande; A. Roussel:Festin de l'araignée (suite 2) URAN ▲ 107 (m) [DDD] (15.97)

Quartet in D for Strings, M.9 (1889)

Bartholdy Piano Quartet ENTE ▲ 37 (10.97)

Gewandhaus String Quartet † Son Vn, M.8 BER ▲ 9165 (10.97)

Juilliard String Quartet † Smetana:Qt 1 Strs SNYC ▲ 63302 (16.97)

Prague String Quartet † Son Vn, M.8 PRAG ▲ 250024 (18.97)

Pro Arte String Quartet † J. Haydn:Qts (2) Strs, H.III/81-82 ENT ▲ 99370 (16.97)

Quatrième trio concertant in b for Violin, Cello & Piano, Op. 2, (M.4) (1842)

M. Sarbu (pno), Academica Quartet members † Andantino quietoso, Op. 6; Duo based on motifs from Dalayrac's Gulistan, M.6; Son Vn, M.8; Trios concertants 1-3, M.1-3 DYNC 2-▲ 21 [DDD] (17.97)

Quintet in f for Piano & Strings, M.7 (1878-79)

V. Aller (pno), Hollywood String Quartet *(rec 1953)* † D. Shostakovich:Qnt Pno, Op. 57 TES ▲ 1077 (17.97)

W. Bärtschi (pno), Amati String Quartet *(rec 1990)* † G. Fauré:Qt Strs DVX ▲ 29001 [DDD] (16.97)

M. Ciampi (pno), Capet String Quartet *(rec 1927-28)* ("The Capet Quartet in Romantic Works") † Debussy:Qt Strs, Op. 10; M. Ravel:Qt Strs; F. Schubert:Qt 14 Strs, D.810; R. Schumann:Qts Strs, Op. 41 BID 2-▲ 133 [ADD] (31.97)

A. Cortot (pno), International String Quartet *(rec 1927)* † E. Chausson:Concert Vn, Op. 21; G. Fauré:Berceuse, Op. 16 BID ▲ 29 [ADD]

M. Levinas (pno), Quatuor Ludwig † E. Chausson:Qt Strs, Op. 35 NXIN ▲ 8553645 [DDD] (5.97)

P. Rogé (pno), London Festival Orch members † Son Vn, M.8; Symphonic Vars, M.46 ASV ▲ 769 [DDD] (16.97)

G. Tacchino (pno), Athenaeum Enesco String Quartet † E. Chausson:Qt Strs, Op. 35 PVY ▲ 792032 [DDD] (16.97)

Rédemption (poème-symphonie) for Soprano, Speaker, Orchestra & Chorus, M.52 (1875; rev w. new chorus & interlude)

J. Gendille (cnd), Mans SO † Sym in d, M.48 SKAR ▲ 3931 [DDD]

G. Kaunzinger (org)—Symphonic Interlude [arr M. Dupré] † Mussorgsky:Pictures at an Exhibition; M. Ravel:Ma mère l'oye NOVA ▲ 150152 [DDD] (16.97)

Les Sept paroles du Christ sur la croix [Christ's Seven Last Words] (oratorio) for solo Voices, Orchestra & Chorus (1859)

J. Salanne (cnd), Domaine Musical Orch, Henri Duparc Chorus † Domine non Secundum, M.66 CYPR ▲ 2610 (17.97)

Sonata in A for Violin & Piano, M.8 (1886)

E. Baldini (vn), L. Baldini (pno) *(rec Milan, Oct 1996)* † Magnard:Son Vn AG ▲ 97 [DDD] (18.97)

Bekova Sisters CHN ▲ 9680 (16.97)

W. Bennett (fl), C. Benson (pno) *(rec Oct 14, 1987)* ("Concert Live at Nova Hall") † C. Reinecke:Son Fl; F. Schubert:Intro & Vars on "Tröckne Blumen", D.802; Taffanel:Mignon Fant CAMA ▲ 204 [DDD] (18.97)

L. Bobesco (vn), J. Genty (pno) *(rec 1980)* † G. Fauré:Andante Vn, Op. 75; Berceuse, Op. 16; Son 1 Vn, Op. 13; Son 2 Vn, Op. 108; Lekeu:Son Vn PAVA 2-▲ 7292 (10.97)

C. Bruneel (fl), L. Kende (pno) [[arr for Fl]] ("In Flanders' Fields, Vol. 10") † Hoedt:Dialogue; Romance; J. Jongen:Son Fl PHA ▲ 92010 [DDD] (13.97)

K. W. Chung (vn), R. Lupu (pno) † Debussy:Son Vn; M. Ravel:Intro & Allegro Hp PLON ▲ 21154 [ADD] (9.97)

A. Delmoni (vn), M. B. Vas (pno) ("Arturo Delmoni: Sonatas of Fauré & Franck") † G. Fauré:Après un rêve, Op. 7/1; Son 1 Vn, Op. 13 JMR ▲ 8 (16.97)

A. Dumay (vn), M. J. Pires (pno) † Debussy:Son Vn; M. Ravel:Berceuse sur le nom de Fauré; Pièce en forme de Habanera; Tzigane DGRM ▲ 445880 [DDD] (18.97)

M. Faust (fl), R. Hodgkinson (pno) [adapted Faust for fl & pno] *(rec Regis College, MA, Jan 28-29, 1995)* † S. Prokofiev:Son Fl; R. Schumann:Romances Ob, Op. 94 GMR ▲ 2055 (16.97)

FRANCK, CÉSAR (cont.)
Sonata in A for Violin & Piano, M.8 (1886) (cont.)

D. Finckel (vc), W. Han (pno) [trans D. Finckel] *(rec Montclair, NJ, 1995)* † E. Finckel:Vars on "Willow Weep for Me"; R. Strauss:Son Vc, Op. 6 ARLD ▲ 19602

A. Flammer (vn), J. Pennetier (pno) † Debussy:Son Vn; Szymanowski:Myths MDA7 ▲ 82 (18.97)

M. Frasca-Colombier (vn), M. Langot (pno) ("Romantic Sonatas") † Magnard:Son Vn PVY ▲ 730068 [DDD] (12.97)

M. Fukačová (vc), I. Klánský (pno) † A. Dvořák:Rondo; E. Grieg:Son Vc; P. Tchaikovsky:Pezzo capriccioso, Op. 62 KPT ▲ 32013 [DDD]

C. Funke (vn), P. Rösel (pno) ("Virtuoso Violin Sonatas") † Tartini:Son Vn & Pno BER ▲ 9149 (10.97)

J. Galway (fl), M. Argerich (pno) [trans Galway for fl & pno] *(rec May 1975)* ("Flute Sonatas") † S. Prokofiev:Son Fl; C. Reinecke:Son Fl RCAV (Gold Seal) ▲ 61615 [ADD/DDD] (11.97)

A. P. Gerlach (vc), F. Bidini (pno) [trans Delsart] *(rec Mesquite Arts Center, Mesquite, TX, Mar 1997)* † S. Rachmaninoff:Son Vc ENRE ▲ 9714 [DDD] (16.97)

J. Heifetz (vn), A. Rubenstein (pno) *(rec 1937)* † P. Tchaikovsky:Con Vn ENT (Strings) ▲ 99325 (16.97)

N. Imai (va), R. Vignoles (pno) [trans for va & pno] † H. Vieuxtemps:Va & Pno Music CHN ▲ 8873 [DDD] (16.97)

Y. Kamei (vn), C. Okashiro (pno) † W. Walton:Son Vn & Pno PPR ▲ 224505

G. Kremer (vn), O. Maisenberg (pno) *(rec 1978?)* † Qt Strs, M.9 PRAG ▲ 250024 (18.97)

L. Marianiello (fl), R. Morrison (pno) [trans for fl & pno] † P. Gaubert:Son 1 Fl; Liszt:Consolations (6), S.172; Widor:Suite Fl, Op. 34 HEL ▲ 1031 (10.97)

Midori (vn), R. McDonald (pno) † E. Elgar:Son Vn SNYC ▲ 63331 (16.97)

G. Mönch (vn), M. Damerini (pno) *(rec Rome Italy, May 21-25, 1989)* ("French Violin Sonatas") AART ▲ 47106 [DDD] (10.97)

A.-S. Mutter (vn), L. Orkis (pno) ("The Berlin Recital") † J. Brahms:Hungarian Dances Pno 4-Hands; Scherzo Vn; Debussy:Beau soir; Son Vn; W. A. Mozart:Son 21 Vn & Pno, K.304 DEUT ▲ 45826 [DDD] (16.97)

A. Nicolet (fl), B. Berman (pno) † Prélude, fugue et var, Op. 18; J. S. Bach:Org Music (misc colls); Passacaglia & Fugue Org, BWV 582; Pastorale Org, BWV 590; Preludes & Fugues, BWV 531-552 TIT ▲ 164 [DDD]

T. Nishizaki (vn), J. Jandó (pno) *(rec Feb 1990)* NXIN ▲ 550417 [DDD] (5.97)

E. Nyffenegger (vc), G. Wyss (pno) † Chopin:Son Vc; E. Grieg:Son Vc DVX ▲ 25204 [ADD] (11.97)

T. Oxford (b sax), C. McElhaney (pno) [arr Oxford] *(rec U of Texas, Austin, TX, Jul 1996)* ("Finesse") † J. S. Bach:Suites Vc; P. Bonneau:Caprice in forme de valse; Bozza:Caprice-Improvisation EQLB ▲ 22 (16.97)

E. Pahud (fl), E. Le Sage (pno) [trans for fl & pno] † G. Fauré:Fant Fl, Op. 79; Sicilienne, Op. 78; Son 1 Vn, Op. 13 SKAR ▲ 4965 [DDD] (19.97)

D. Peck (fl), M. Lord (pno) [arr for fl & pno] *(rec DePaul Concert Hall, Chicago, IL, June 30, 1996)* ("Live Recital No. 2") † Debussy:Chansons de Bilitis (recitation); Syrinx Fl; W. Ferris:Son Fl BOST ▲ 1014 [DDD] (15.97)

I. Perlman (vn), V. Ashkenazy (pno) † J. Brahms:Trio Hn, Op. 40 PLON (Classic Sound) ▲ 452887 (11.97)

R. Pople (vc), P. Rogé (pno) [vc & pno trans] † Qnt Pno, M.7; Symphonic Vars, M.46 ASV ▲ 769 [DDD] (16.97)

J. D. Pré (vc), D. Barenboim (pno) † Chopin:Son Vc EMIC ▲ 63184 (11.97)

P. Racine (fl), B. Meyer (pno) [trans for fl & pno] † C. Reinecke:Con Fl; Son Fl NOVA ▲ 150139 (16.97)

S. Rolston (vc), M. Pressler (pno) [arr vc & pno] † G. Fauré:Son 1 Vn, Op. 13 SUMM ▲ 109 [DDD] (16.97)

H. Schunk (vn), A. Schmidt (pno) † Qt Strs, M.9 BER ▲ 9165 (10.97)

G. Shaham (vn), G. Oppitz (pno) † M. Ravel:Tzigane; Saint-Saëns:Son 1 Vn, Op. 75 DEUT ▲ 29729 [DDD] (16.97)

M. Sirbu (vn), M. Sarbu (pno) † Andantino quietoso, Op. 6; Duo based on motifs from Dalayrac's Gulistan, M.6; Quatrième trio concertant, Op. 2; Trios concertants 1-3, M.1-3 DYNC 2-▲ 21 [DDD] (17.97)

A. Spalding (vn), A. Benoist (pno) ("The Art of the Violin, Vol. 3") † J. Brahms:Son 2 Vn, Op. 100; G. F. Handel:Son Vn; R. Schumann:Klavierstücke, Op. 85; Tartini:Son Vn & Pno ACLR ▲ 42 (17.97)

I. Stern (vn), A. Zakin (pno) ("Isaac Stern: A Life In Music: Vol. 27") † Debussy:Son Vn; Enescu:Son 3 Vn, Op. 25 SNYC ▲ 64532 [ADD] (10.97)

J. Suk (vn), J. Hála (pno) *(rec Prague, Czech Republic, Sept 1994)* † G. Fauré:Son 2 Vn, Op. 108; M. Ravel:Sonate posthume DI ▲ 920306 [DDD] (5.97)

S. Suzuki (vn), M. Gurlitt (pno) *(rec ca 1928)* ("The Great Violinists: Vol. VII") † E. Chausson:Poème Vn, Op. 25; G. Fauré:Son 1 Vn, Op. 13; M. Ravel:Tzigane SYMP ▲ 1156 (18.97)

H. Szeryng (vn), M. Katz (pno) *(rec June 1973)* ("A Legendary Collaboration") † J. Brahms:Son 3 Vn, Op. 108 CEMB (Historic Series) ▲ 105 [ADD] (15.97)

A. Tellefsen (vn), H. Pålsson (pno) *(rec Oct 24, 1975)* † M. Clementi:Sonatas for Piano; G. Fauré:Trio Pno, Op. 120; J. Haydn:Son 12 Kbd, H.XVI/12; W. A. Mozart:Fant Pno, K.396; S. Prokofiev:Son Vc; Sinding:Son Pno, Op. 91 BIS ▲ 35 [AAD/DDD] (17.97)

J. Thibaud (vn), A. Cortot (pno) *(rec May-June 1929)* † Beethoven:Son 9 Vn, Op. 47; Debussy:Preludes Pno; Son Vn ENT (Strings) ▲ 99353 (16.97)

E. Volckaert (vn), J. V. Eynden (pno) † A. Huybrechts:Son Vn RENE ▲ 99004 [ADD] (16.97)

D. Zsigmondy (vn), A. Nisse (pno) *(rec 1968-74)* † Beethoven:Son 9 Vn, Op. 47 CLDI ▲ 4034 [AAD] (10.97)

P. Zukerman (vn), M. Neikrug (pno) † Debussy:Son Vn; G. Fauré:Son 1 Vn, Op. 13 RCAV (Red Seal) ▲ 62697 (16.97)

Symphonic Variations for Piano & Orchestra, M.46 (1885)

K. Aberg (pno), O. Kamu (cnd), Gothenburg SO *(rec May 31, 1979)* † Djinns, M.45; Prélude, choral et fugue, M.21 BIS ▲ 137 [AAD] (17.97)

R. Casadesus (pno), E. Ormandy (cnd), Philadelphia Orch † Pièces (3) Org, M.37; Sym in d, M.48 SNYC (Essential Classics) ▲ 60287 (7.97) ▮ 60287 (3.98)

F. Clidat (pno), Z. Macal (cnd), Philharmonia Orch † E. Grieg:Con Pno, Op. 16 FORL ▲ 16673 [ADD] (16.97)

P. Crossley (pno), C. M. Giulini (cnd), Vienna PO *(rec Grosser Saal Vienna, Austria, June 12-13, 1993)* † Sym in d, M.48 SNYC ▲ 58958 [DDD] (16.97)

L. Fleisher (pno), G. Szell (cnd), Cleveland Orch *(rec 1956)* † S. Rachmaninoff:Rhap on a Theme of Paganini, Op. 43; M. Ravel:Alborada del gracioso SNYC ▲ 37812 [ADD] (9.97)

W. Gieseking (pno), H. Wood (cnd), London PO *(rec London, Oct 31, 1932)* ("Walter Gieseking: His First Concerto Recordings, Vol. 3") † E. Grieg:Con Pno, Op. 16; Lyric Pieces; Liszt:Con 1 Pno, S.124 APR ▲ 5513 [ADD] (19.97)

D. Goldmann (pno), R. Tschupp (cnd), Nuremberg SO † Sym in d, M.48 PC ▲ 267154 [DDD]

M. Hess (pno), B. Cameron (cnd), City of Birmingham SO † E. Grieg:Con Pno, Op. 16; R. Schumann:Con Pno in a, Op. 54 AVID ▲ 593 (16.97)

E. Joyce (pno) † Mendelssohn (-Bartholdy):Con 1 Pno, Op. 25; S. Rachmaninoff:Con 2 Pno, Op. 18; J. Turina:Rapsodia sinfónica, Op. 66 DLAB (Essential Archives) ▲ 5505 (15.97)

E. Joyce (pno), C. Munch (cnd), Paris Conservatory Société des Concerts Orch ("Munch, Vol. 7") † Indy:Fervaal (sels); Saint-Saëns:Rouet d'Omphale, Op. 31 LYS ▲ 409 (17.97)

P. Katin (pno), E. Goossens (cnd), London SO *(rec Walthamstow Assembly Hall London, 1959-60)* † A. Khachaturian:Con Pno EVC ▲ 9060 [ADD] (13.97)

J. F. Osorio (pno), E. Bátiz (cnd), Royal PO † M. Ravel:Con Pno (left hand); Saint-Saëns:Wedding Cake, Op. 76; R. Schumann:Con Pno in a, Op. 54 ASVQ ▲ 6092 [DDD] (11.97)

D. Protopescu (pno), A. Rahbari (cnd), Brussels BRTN PO † Sym in d, M.48 DI ▲ 920434 [DDD] (5.97)

J. Robilette (pno), P. Freeman (cnd), St. Petersburg PO *(rec 1993)* ("French Piano Album") † Prélude, choral et fugue, M.21; Chopin:Impromptus (4); F. Poulenc:Mouvements perpétuels PRA ▲ 3491 (14.97)

P. Rogé (pno), R. Pople (cnd), London Festival Orch † Qnt Pno, M.7; Son Vn, M.8 ASV ▲ 769 [DDD] (16.97)

A. Rubinstein (pno) † M. de Falla:Amor brujo (Ritual Fire Dance); Noches en los jardines de España; S. Prokofiev:March Pno; Saint-Saëns:Con 2 Pno, Op. 22 RCAV (Gold Seal) ▲ 61863 (11.97)

A. Rubinstein (pno), A. Wallenstein (cnd), Sym of the Air *(rec 1956 & 1958)* † Liszt:Con 1 Pno, S.124; Saint-Saëns:Con 2 Pno, Op. 22 RCAV (Gold Seal) ▲ 61496 (11.97)

F. Thiollier (pno), A. D. Almeida (cnd), Irish National SO *(rec May 1993)* ("French Music for Piano & Orchestra") † G. Fauré:Ballade Pno, Op. 19; Indy:Sym on a French Mountain Air, Op. 25 NXIN ▲ 550754 [DDD] (5.97)

I. Tiegerman (pno), J. Ferriz (cnd), Cairo SO *(rec Cairo, Egypt, June 1, 1963)* ("The Lost Legend of Cairo: Radio & Private Recordings") † J. Brahms:Con 2 Pno, Op. 83; Intermezzos (3) Pno, Op. 117; Pieces (6) Pno, Op. 118; Pieces (8) Pno, Op. 76; Chopin:Ballade 4 Pno, Op. 52; Nocturnes Pno; Preludes (24) Pno, Op. 28; Scherzos Pno; Son Pno in b, Op. 58; G. Fauré:Nocturnes Pno; J. Field:Nocturnes Pno; Saint-Saëns:Con 5 Pno, Op. 103; Tiegerman:Meditation Pno ARBT 2-▲ 116 (32.97)

E. Van Beinum (cnd), Concertgebouw Orch *(rec 1946)* ("Van Beinum, Vol. 3") † Berlioz:Sym fantastique, Op. 14; M. Ravel:Rapsodie espagnole LYS ▲ 473 (17.97)

E. Wild (pno), M. Freccia (cnd), RCA Victor SO *(rec 1968)* † Chasseur maudit, M.44; Psyché (sels); Sym in d, M.48 CHSK ▲ 87 [ADD] (16.97)

Symphony in d, M.48 (1886-88)

K. Akiyama (cnd), Vancouver SO SMS (SM 5000) ▲ 5033 [DDD] (16.97)

K. Ančerl (cnd), (Royal) Concertgebouw Orch † A. Dvořák:Sym 8; J. Haydn:Sym 92; S. Prokofiev:Sym 1 TAHA 2-▲ 124 (34.97)

D. Avalos (cnd), Philharmonia Orch † E. Chausson:Sym in B♭, Op. 20 ASV ▲ 708 (17.97)

J. Barbirolli (cnd), Czech PO *(rec 1962)* † Chasseur maudit, M.44; Djinns, M.45 SUR (Collection) ▲ 110613 [ADD]

T. Beecham (cnd), London PO *(rec 1940)* † F. Schubert:Sym 5 IN ▲ 1394 (15.97)

▲ = CD ♦ = Enhanced CD △ = MD ▮ = Cassette Tape ▯ = DCC

FRANCK, CÉSAR (cont.)
Symphony in d, M.48 (1886-88) (cont.)
R. Benzi (cnd), Arnhem PO *(rec Arnhem Netherlands, June 14-16, 1995)* † Éolides, M.43; Chasseur maudit, M.44
NXIN ▲ 553631 [DDD] (5.97)
L. Bernstein (cnd), New York PO *(rec 1959)* ("Bernstein: The Royal Edition") † E. Chausson:Poème Vn, Op. 25; G. Fauré:Ballade Pno, Op. 19; M. Ravel:Tzigane SNYC ▲ 47548 [ADD] (10.97)
A. Boult (cnd), London Orch Society *(rec 1960)* † Chasseur maudit, M.44; Psyché (sels); Symphonic Vars, M.46
CHSK ▲ 87 [ADD] (16.97)
S. Comissiona (cnd), Houston SO *(rec Apr 1982)* † Saint-Saëns:Sym 3 VC ▲ 4014 [DDD] (13.97)
J. Fournet (cnd), Tokyo Metropolitan SO ("Fournet Conducts French Symphonies") † Berlioz:Sym fantastique, Op. 14; Saint-Saëns:Sym 3 DNN (Classics Exposed) 2-▲ 17009 (16.97)
J. Gendille (cnd), Mans SO † Rédemption, M.52 SKAR ▲ 3931 [DDD]
C. M. Giulini (cnd), Philharmonia Orch † Psyché (sels); B. Britten:Peter Grimes (sea interludes & passacaglia); Young Person's Guide to the Orch, Op. 34 EMIC (Artist Profile) 2-▲ 67723
C. M. Giulini (cnd), Vienna PO *(rec Grosser Saal Vienna, Austria, June 12-13, 1993)* † Symphonic Vars, M.46
SNYC ▲ 58958 [DDD] (16.97)
V. Golschmann (cnd), St. Louis SO † D. Shostakovich:Sym 5 EMIC (Legacy) ▲ 66557 (11.97)
O. Klemperer (cnd), New Philharmonia Orch *(rec London, England, 1966)* † R. Schumann:Sym 1
EMIC (Klemperer Legacy) ▲ 66824 [ADD] (11.97)
J. López-Cobos (cnd), Cincinnati SO † Chasseur maudit, M.44 TEL ▲ 80247 [DDD] (16.97)
L. Maazel (cnd), Berlin PO *(rec ca 1961)* † Mendelssohn (-Bartholdy):Sym 5
DEUT (The Originals) ▲ 449720 [ADD] (11.97)
K. Masur (cnd), New York PO TELC ▲ 74863 (16.97)
W. Mengelberg (cnd), Concertgebouw Orch *(rec 1940)* ("Art of Mengelberg, Vol. 1") † J. Brahms:Sym 3
GRM2 ▲ 78866 (11.97)
D. Mitropoulos (cnd), Minneapolis SO *(rec Jan 8, 1940)* † R. Schumann:Sym 3 GRM2 ▲ 78750 (13.97)
P. Monteaux (cnd), Chicago SO † I. Stravinsky:Pétrouchka (pno reduction) RCAV ▲ 63303 (11.97)
P. Monteux (cnd), Chicago SO ("Pierre Monteux Edition, Vol. 8") † Pièces (3) Org, M.37; Indy:Istar
RCAV (Gold Seal) ▲ 61900 (11.97)
C. Munch (cnd), French National Orch *(rec Montréal, Canada, Sep 1967)* ("Charles Munch Edition, vol. 5") † G. Fauré:Pelléas et Mélisande, Op. 80 VAL ▲ 4829 [ADD] (12.97)
G. Neuhold (cnd), Royal Flanders PO *(rec July 1988)* † Prélude, choral et fugue, M.21
NXIN ▲ 550155 [DDD] (5.97)
E. Ormandy (cnd), Philadelphia Orch *(rec 1961)* † Pièces (3) Org, M.37; Symphonic Vars, M.46
SNYC (Essential Classics) ▲ 60287 (7.97) ■ 60287 (3.98)
A. Rahbari (cnd), Brussels BRTN PO † Symphonic Vars, M.46 DI ▲ 920434 [DDD] (5.97)
A. Rodzinski (cnd), New York PO *(rec New York, NY, Dec 30, 1945)* † A. Dvořák:Con Vc
IN ▲ 1338 (m) [ADD] (15.97)
H. Swarowsky (cnd), South German PO † Symphonic Vars, M.46 PC ▲ 267154 [DDD]
A. Toscanini (cnd), NBC SO *(rec 1940)* ("Toscanini Edition, Vol. 7") † Berlioz:Roméo et Juliette, Op. 17
GRM2 (Record of the Century) ▲ 78843 (13.97)
Trios concertants Nos. 1-3 for Piano, Violin & Cello, M.1-3, (Op. 1) (1839-42)
E. Bekova (vn), A. Bekova (vc), E. Bekova (pno)—No. 2 in B♭, "Trio de Salon"; No. 3 in b † Trio concertant 4, M.4 CHN ▲ 9742 (16.97)
M. Sarbu (pno), Academica Quartet members † Andantino quietoso, Op. 6; Duo based on motifs from Dalayrac's Gulistan, M.6; Quatrième trio concertant, Op. 2; Son Vn, M.8 DYNC 2-▲ 21 [DDD] (17.97)
Trio concertant No. 4 in b for Piano, Violin & Cello, M.4, (Op. 2) (ca 1842)
E. Bekova (vn), A. Bekova (vc), E. Bekova (pno) † Trios concertants 1-3, M.1-3 CHN ▲ 9742 (16.97)
Variations brillantes sur la ronde favorite de Gustave III for Piano & Orchestra, Op. 8 (1834-35)
J. V. Eynden (pno), E. Doneux (cnd), Belgian RSO † Grand Con 2 Pno, Op. 11 KSCH ▲ 311111 [DDD] (16.97)

FRANCK, EDUARD (1817-1893)
Concerto in e for Violin & Orchestra, Op. 30 (ca 1855)
C. Edinger (vn), H. Frank (cnd), Saarbrücken RSO † Sym in A, Op. 47 FERM ▲ 20025 [DDD] (16.97)
Sonata in D for Cello & Piano, Op. 6
T. Blees (vc), M. Bergmann (pno) † R. Franck:Son 2 Vc, Op. 36; C. Reinecke:Pieces Vc, Op. 146
FERM ▲ 20021 (16.97)
Symphony in A, Op. 47
C. Edinger (vn), H. Frank (cnd), Saarbrücken RSO † Con Vn FERM ▲ 20025 [DDD] (16.97)

FRANCK, MAURICE (1897-
Suite for Harp
A. Ravnopolska (hp) ("Légende: French Music for Harp") † G. Fauré:Impromptu Hp, Op. 86; G. Pierné:Impromptu-Caprice Hp, Op. 9; Renié:Légende Hp; Salzedo:Vars Hp, Op. 30; Tailleferre:Son Hp; Tournier:Images Hp
GEGA ▲ 152 [DDD] (16.97)

FRANCK, MELCHIOR (ca 1579-1639)
Music of Franck
D. Bratschke (cnd) —Cant Domino à 8; Domine Deus meus à 6; Exaulte Deo adjutori nostro à 6; Tristis est anima mea à 7; O dolor, o lacrymae à 6; Fahet uns die Füchse à 6; Die Schmach bricht mir mein Hertz à 5; Heulet, denn des Herren Tag à 2; Unser Leben weret siebzig Jahr à 6; Ich danke dir Gott à 3; Lobet den Herrn in seynem Heiligthumb à 7; Ach höchster Schatz à 8; Wie wohl ich arm und elend bin à 4; Ach wie empfind mein hertze à 8; Ach weh à 6; Ein Tochter hat à 4; Wolaudd ihr edlen Jäger gut à 8; Il illo tempore à 4 *(rec Jan 1997)* ("Motetten, Geistliche Konzerte & Deutsche Lieder") THOR ▲ 2343 [DDD] (16.97)

FRANCK, RICHARD (1858-1938)
Sonata No. 2 in e for Cello & Piano, Op. 36
T. Blees (vc), M. Bergmann (pno) † E. Franck:Son Vc, Op. 6; C. Reinecke:Pieces Vc, Op. 146
FERM ▲ 20021 (16.97)

FRANCO, HERNANDO (1532-1585)
Salve Regina for Chorus
Westminster Cathedral Choir [LAT] ("Mexican Polyphony") † López Capillas:Alleluia; Magnificat; J. G. de Padilla:Sacred Music; A. de Salazar:O sacrum convivium HYP ▲ 66330 [DDD] (18.97)

FRANCOEUR, FRANCOIS (1698-1787)
Sonatas (22) for Violin & Continuo [Books 1 & 2; II/12 also w. cello or viol]
J. Baumann (vc), K. Stoll (db), W. Döling (hpd) ("Amazing Duo, Vol. 2") † Boccherini:Adagio & Allegro, G.6; Fesch:Sons Vn & Vc, Op. 8a; Pergolesi:Sinf Vc; J. R. Zumsteeg:Son Vc CAMA ▲ 2044 [DDD] (18.97)
E. Nyffenegger (vc), G. Wyss (pno) † J. S. Bach:Sons Vl; Locatelli:Son Vc; Lully:Passacaglia Vc & Pno
DVX ▲ 25206 [ADD] (11.97)

FRANDSEN, JOHN (1956-
Motets (2) for Chorus [texts Kirkegaard]
M. Bojesen (cnd), Camerata Chamber Choir ("Kirkegaard Set to Music") † Songs; S. Barber:Prayers of Kierkegaard, Op. 30; N. V. Bentzon:Johannes the Seducer; H. Boatwright:Prayers of Kirkegaard; Bojesen:Choral Music; Høffding:Diapsalmata *(Da,E texts)* DANI ▲ 8184 [DDD] (18.97)
Songs
B. Øland (sop), J. Frandsen (org) *(The Lilie & the Bird)*, Wärmekvartetten *(When the Waves Rock)* ("Kirkegaard Set to Music") † Motets (2); S. Barber:Prayers of Kierkegaard, Op. 30; N. V. Bentzon:Johannes the Seducer; H. Boatwright:Prayers of Kirkegaard; Bojesen:Choral Music; Høffding:Diapsalmata DANI ▲ 8184 [DDD] (18.97)
Twilight for 2 Guitars (1992)
Danish Guitar Duo ("Night Birds: Contemporary Guitar Music") † P. Dørge:Struthio Camelus; S. Nielsen:Barcarole Gtr; W. Siegel:Canons Gtrs PONT ▲ 5120 [DDD]

FRANK, ANDREW (1946-
Autumn Rhythm for Piano & String Trio, "Piano Quartet No. 2" (1996)
R. Bauer (cnd) † Range of Light; R. Bauer:Octet; P. Ortiz:Trazos en el Polvo; Vida Furtiva
CENT ▲ 2386 [DDD] (16.97)
Points of Departure for Flute, Clarinet, Violin & Cello (1986)
G. Thomson (cnd), Earplay members, Earplay members *(rec Knuth Hall, SFSU, CA, Nov 25, 1994)* † E. Carter:Esprit rude/esprit doux; Festinger:Spt; Mamlok:Rhap Cl, Va & Pno; G. Moretto:Silenciosamente; W. Peterson:Labyrinth; Vayo:Poem CENT ▲ 2274 [DDD] (16.97)
Range of Light for Chamber Ensemble (1995)
R. Bauer (cnd) † Autumn Rhythm; R. Bauer:Octet; P. Ortiz:Trazos en el Polvo; Vida Furtiva
CENT ▲ 2386 [DDD] (16.97)

FRANKE, BERND (1959-
Chagall-Impressions for Brass Ensemble
L. Güttler (tpt), L. Güttler (cnd), Ludwig Gütler Brass Ensemble *(rec Dresden, Germany, Feb-Mar 1993)* † Bredemeyer:DiAs (+-); P. Hindemith:Con Tpt; Matthus:Con Tpt; Sauguet:Non morietur in aeternum; S. Thiele:Music Org & Tpt BER ▲ 9057 [DDD] (10.97)

FRANKEL, BENJAMIN (1906-1973)
The Aftermath for Tenor, Trumpet, Timpani & Strings [text R. Nichols], Op. 17 (1947)
A. Francis (cnd), Northwest CO Seattle ("Music for Strings") † Concertante lirico, Op. 27; Sketches, Op. 2; Solemn Speech & Discussion, Op. 11; Youth Music, Op. 12 CPO ▲ 999221 [DDD] (14.97)
Concertante lirico for Strings, Op. 27 (1952)
A. Francis (cnd), Northwest CO Seattle ("Music for Strings") † Aftermath, Op. 17; Sketches, Op. 2; Solemn Speech & Discussion, Op. 11; Youth Music, Op. 12 CPO ▲ 999221 [DDD] (14.97)
May Day: A Panorama (symphonic overture) for Orchestra, Op. 22 (1948)
W. A. Albert (cnd), Queensland SO † Sym 1; Sym 5; D. Milhaud:Sym 5; Sym 6 CPO ▲ 999240 [DDD] (14.97)
Mephistopheles' Serenade for Orchestra, Op. 25 (1952)
W. A. Albert (cnd), Queensland SO *(rec ABC Ferry Road Brisbane, 1994-95)* † Sym 4; Sym 6
CPO ▲ 999242 [DDD] (14.97)
Quartets (5) for Strings (complete)
Nomos String Quartet *(rec Bamberg, Feb 1996)* ("Complete String Quartets") CPO 2-▲ 999420 [DDD] (27.97)
Sketches (3) for Strings, Op. 2
A. Francis (cnd), Northwest CO Seattle ("Music for Strings") † Aftermath, Op. 17; Concertante lirico, Op. 27; Solemn Speech & Discussion, Op. 11; Youth Music, Op. 12 CPO ▲ 999221 [DDD] (14.97)
Solemn Speech & Discussion for Strings, Op. 11 (1941)
A. Francis (cnd), Northwest CO Seattle ("Music for Strings") † Aftermath, Op. 17; Concertante lirico, Op. 27; Sketches, Op. 2; Youth Music, Op. 12 CPO ▲ 999221 [DDD] (14.97)
Sonata No. 1 for solo Violin, Op. 13 (1946)
M. Davis (vn) ("Music on & off the Keys") † L. Foss:Fant Rondo; Hofmann-Engel:Son 1 Pno; Kershner:Son Bn; Loevendie:Strides; Toccata; Walk; Togawa:Kaze No Ha VMM (Distinguished Performers III) ▲ 2016 [DDD]
Symphony No. 1, Op. 33 (1958)
W. A. Albert (cnd), Queensland SO † May Day Ov, Op. 22; Sym 5; D. Milhaud:Sym 5; Sym 6
CPO ▲ 999240 [DDD] (14.97)
Symphony No. 4, Op. 44 (1966)
W. A. Albert (cnd), Queensland SO *(rec ABC Ferry Road Brisbane, 1994-95)* † Mephistopheles' Serenade, Op. 25; Sym 6 CPO ▲ 999242 [DDD] (14.97)
Symphony No. 5, Op. 46 (1967)
W. A. Albert (cnd), Queensland SO † May Day Ov, Op. 22; Sym 1; D. Milhaud:Sym 5; Sym 6
CPO ▲ 999240 [DDD] (14.97)
Symphony No. 6, Op. 49 (1969)
W. A. Albert (cnd), Queensland SO *(rec ABC Ferry Road Brisbane, 1994-95)* † Mephistopheles' Serenade, Op. 25; Sym 4 CPO ▲ 999242 [DDD] (14.97)
Youth Music for Strings, Op. 12 (1942)
A. Francis (cnd), Northwest CO Seattle ("Music for Strings") † Aftermath, Op. 17; Concertante lirico, Op. 27; Sketches, Op. 2; Solemn Speech & Discussion, Op. 11 CPO ▲ 999221 [DDD] (14.97)

FRANKLIN, BENJAMIN (1706-1790)
Quartet for Strings (dance suite) for 3 Violins & Cello [attrib to Franklin]
Kohon String Quartet *(rec 1969)* ("The Early String Quartet in the U.S.A.") † G. W. Chadwick:Qt 4 Strs; Foote:Qt 3 Str, Op. 70; C. M. Loeffler:Music for 4 Str Instrs; D. G. Mason:Qt on Negro Themes, Op. 19
VB2 2-▲ 5057 [ADD] (9.97)

FRANSSENS, JOEP (20th cent)
Echos for Orchestra (1983; rev 1984)
T. Fischer (cnd), Netherlands Ballet Orch *(rec Sept 6-11, 1996)* ("Orchestral Music") † Phasing; Sanctus
CV (Jubilee) ▲ 65 [DDD] (18.97)
Phasing for Orchestra & Women's Choir (1985; rev 1991)
T. Fischer (cnd), Netherlands Ballet Orch, H. J. Lindhout (cnd), Netherlands Theater Choir *(rec Sept 6-11, 1996)* ("Orchestral Music") † Echos; Sanctus CV (Jubilee) ▲ 65 [DDD] (18.97)
Sanctus for Orchestra (1996)
T. Fischer (cnd), Netherlands Ballet Orch *(rec Sept 6-11, 1996)* ("Orchestral Music") † Echos; Phasing
CV (Jubilee) ▲ 65 [DDD] (18.97)

FRANZ, ROBERT (1815-1892)
Gesänge (6) for Voice & Piano, Op. 20 (ca 1865)
K. Flagstad (sop)—No. 6, Im Herbst [text Geibel] † Beethoven:Fidelio (sels); F. Schubert:Songs (misc colls); R. Wagner:Lohengrin (sels); Tannhäuser (sels); Tristan und Isolde (sels); C. M. von Weber:Oberon (sels)
PHS ▲ 34 (17.97)

FRANZETTI, CARLOS (1948-
Aubade for Orchestra & Chorus (1985)
C. Franzetti (cnd), Buenos Aires Orch, Buenos Aires Teatro Colón Chorus *(rec Buenos Aires Argentina, 1985)* ("Images Before Dawn") † Con Ob; Concertino Bass Trbn; Images Before Dawn; Suite Fl; Vars Brass
PREM ▲ 1044 [DDD] (16.97)
Concertino for Bass Trombone & Orchestra (1979)
D. Taylor (b trbn), L. Colin (hp), C. Franzetti (pno), C. Franzetti (cnd) *(rec New York)* ("Images Before Dawn") † Aubade; Con Ob; Images Before Dawn; Suite Fl; Vars Brass PREM ▲ 1044 [DDD] (16.97)
Concerto for Oboe & Orchestra (1991)
B. Tindall (ob), A. B. Franzetti (pno), C. Franzetti (cnd) *(rec New York)* ("Images Before Dawn") † Aubade; Concertino Bass Trbn; Images Before Dawn; Suite Fl; Vars Brass PREM ▲ 1044 [DDD] (16.97)
Concierto Del Plata for Guitar & Orchestra
S. Puccini (gtr), A. Koregelos (fl), R. Schwartz (pno), J. L. Moscovich (cnd), San Francisco Camerata Americana ("Camerata Americana") † L. Brouwer:Con 3 Gtr; Ginastera:Impresiones de la Puna; Guastavino:Jeromita Linares; M. Romero:Spirals KLAV ▲ 11093 [DDD] (18.97)
Images Before Dawn for Bass Guitar & String Orchestra
A. Jackson (b gtr), C. Franzetti (cnd) *(rec New York)* ("Images Before Dawn") † Aubade; Con Ob; Concertino Bass Trbn; Suite Fl; Vars Brass PREM ▲ 1044 [DDD] (16.97)
Suite for Flute & Chamber Orchestra (1987)
J. D. Vega (fl), C. Franzetti (pno), C. Franzetti (cnd) *(rec New York)* ("Images Before Dawn") † Aubade; Con Ob; Concertino Bass Trbn; Images Before Dawn; Vars Brass PREM ▲ 1044 [DDD] (16.97)
Variations (5) for Brass
B. Briney (cnd) *(rec Evanston, IL, 1992)* ("Images Before Dawn") † Aubade; Con Ob; Concertino Bass Trbn; Images Before Dawn; Suite Fl PREM ▲ 1044 [DDD] (16.97)

FRÉDÉRIC, CLAUDY (1950-
Peut-être qu'une Valse? for Guitar
D. Azabagic (gtr) *(rec Oct 1996)* ("Printemps de la Guitare 1996") † L. Brouwer:Decameron Negro; J. Rodrigo:Con de Aranjuez CYPR ▲ 5650 [DDD] (17.97)
Regards (2) sur un passé present for Guitar
C. Pérez (gtr) ("Printemps de la Guitar 1998: Carlos Pérez, 1st Prize") † A. Barrios:Gtr Music; Dyens:Hommage à Villa-Lobos; M. Ponce:Concierto del sur; Thème, varié et finale; Pujol Vilarrubí:Gtr Music CYPR ▲ 5651 [DDD] (17.97)

FREDERICK II ("FREDERICK THE GREAT") OF PRUSSIA (1712-1786)
Concerto No. 4 in D for Flute & Orchestra
R. Waage (fl), H. Frank (cnd), Berlin Sym Chamber Orch ("Berlin Composers of the 18th Century") † C.P.E. Bach:Sinfs (6), H.657-62; Eichner:Con Hp BER ▲ 9390 (10.97)
Symphony No. 1 in G
R. A. Clark (cnd), Manhattan CO *(rec St. Jean Baptiste Church, NYC, NY, Jan 1996)* † Sym 2; C.P.E. Bach:Sinfs (6), H.657-62 HEL ▲ 1003 (10.97)
Symphony No. 2 in G
R. A. Clark (cnd), Manhattan CO *(rec St. Jean Baptiste Church, NYC, NY, Jan 1996)* † Sym 1; C.P.E. Bach:Sinfs (6), H.657-62 HEL ▲ 1003 (10.97)

FREEDMAN, HARRY (1922-
Graphic IV for Orchestra, "Town"
A. Pauk (cnd), Esprit Orch *(rec Mar 1992)* ("Iridescence") † Anhalt:Sparkskraps; C. P. Harman:Iridescence; A. Pauk:Cosmos; R. M. Schafer:Scorpius CBC (SM 5000) ▲ 5132 [DDD]
Quintet for Winds (1962)
Essex Winds Woodwind Quintet *(rec Alberta & L.A. East Studios Salt Lake City, 1992-93)* ("Quintette: The Essex Winds") † M. Forsyth:Qnt Ww; Hétu:Qnt Ww; Kenins:Vars on a Theme of Schubert CTR ▲ 5595 [DDD] (16.97)

FREEDMAN, HARRY (cont.)
Touchings for Percussion & Orchestra (1989; rev 1994)
A. Pauk (cnd), Esprit Orch, A. Pauk (cnd), Nexus *(rec Toronto, Canada, Apr 1995)* ("Music for Heaven & Earth") † R. Aitken:Berceuse (For Those Who Sleep Before Us); A. Louie:Music for Heaven & Earth; C. McPhee:Nocturne CBC (SM 5000) ▲ 5154 [DDD] (16.97)
Touchpoints for Flute, Viola & Harp (1994)
Trio Lyra ("Harbord Street") † M. Barnes:Harbord Street; S. I. Glick:Trio Fl; A. MacDonald:Pleiades Vars OPDR ▲ 9315 (16.97)

FREEMAN, JOHN (1928-
Suite for Organ, Percussion & Wind Orchestra
A. Bird (org), J. Somary (cnd) ("Three is Company") † A. Bird:Suite Ww, Op. 29; J. Somary:Songs of Innocence; 3 Is Company PREM ▲ 1042 [DDD] (16.97)

FREIRE, OSMAN PEREZ (1878-1930)
Songs
H. Roswaenge (ten)—Ay, Ay, Ay ("Helge Rosvaenge erzählt sein Leben") † Emborg:Agnes; F. Lehár:Giuditta (sels); Narrative:Helge Roswaenge reminisces; Opa zu sein PRE ▲ 90334 (m)

FRENCH, PERCY (1854-1920)
Songs
M. J. Henderson (cnd), Irish Guards Band—Come Back Paddy Reilly; Phil the Fluter's Ball *(rec Chelsea Barracks, England, Feb 3-5, 1997)* ("Emerald Isle") † Anonymous:Black Velvet Band; Wild Colonial Boy; P. Green:March Hare (sels); M. J. Henderson:Emerald Isle; Micks' March; Traditional:Carrickfergus; Harp That Once through Tara's Halls; Minstrel Boy BND ▲ 5134 (16.97)

FRENCH, TANIA GABRIELLE (1963-
Ancient Echoes for Flute, Violin, Viola & Cello
C. Haslop (vn), R. Kato (va), B. George (vc), S. Greenburg (fl) *(rec June 1997)* ("Chamber Music") † Equinox; Fant Vn; Illuminations; Silhouettes at Sunrise CENT ▲ 2395 [DDD] (16.97)
Equinox for String Quartet
C. Haslop (vn), J. Brand (vn), R. Kato (va), T. Landaeur (vc) *(rec June 1997)* ("Chamber Music") † Ancient Echoes; Fant Vn; Illuminations; Silhouettes at Sunrise CENT ▲ 2395 [DDD] (16.97)
Fantasia for Violin & Piano
C. Haslop (vn), J. P. Martin (pno) *(rec June 1997)* ("Chamber Music") † Ancient Echoes; Equinox; Illuminations; Silhouettes at Sunrise CENT ▲ 2395 [DDD] (16.97)
Illuminations (4) for Oboe, Violin, Cello & Piano
A. Vogel (ob), Los Angeles Piano Trio *(rec June 1997)* ("Chamber Music") † Ancient Echoes; Equinox; Fant Vn; Silhouettes at Sunrise CENT ▲ 2395 [DDD] (16.97)
Silhouettes at Sunrise for Piano Trio
Los Angeles Piano Trio *(rec June 1997)* ("Chamber Music") † Ancient Echoes; Equinox; Fant Vn; Illuminations CENT ▲ 2395 [DDD] (16.97)

FRENGEL, MICHAEL (1972)
Three Short Stories (computer music) for Tape (1995-96)
M. Frengel (tape) *(rec SJSU, San Jose, CA, 1995-96)* ("Music for Players & Digital Media") † Belet:[Mute]ation; P. Furman:Synergy; M. Helms:Whispering Modulations; D. Michael:Extensions #1; A. Strange:Shaman: Sisters of Dreamtime; Wyman:Through the Reed CENT ▲ 2404 (live) [DDD] (16.97)

FRESCOBALDI, GIROLAMO (1583-1643)
Aria detta "La Frescobalda" (variation set) for Keyboard
L. Ghielmi (hpd) † Toccatas Hpd NUO (Ancient Music) ▲ 6799 [DDD] (16.97)
M. A. Girollet (gtr) [trans M. A. Girollet] ("Baroque Music for Guitar") † J. S. Bach:Suite Lt, BWV 995; J. Dowland:Lt Music OTR ▲ 1006 [DDD] (18.97)
Stockholm Guitar Quartet [arr for gtr qt] † J. S. Bach:Brandenburg Con 6, BWV 1051 OPU ▲ 7915
Aria di Follia for Harpsichord
S. Yates (hpd) *(rec Somerset, England, Aug 22-24, 1996)* ("Romanesca: Italian Music for Harpsichord") † Aria di Romanesca; Cento partie sopra Passacagli; Toccatas Hpd; Gesualdo:Canzon francese del Principe; Macque:Seconde stravaganze; Merulo:Susanne un jour; G. Picchi:Ballo alla Polacha; Ballo ditto il Pichi; Ballo hongaro; Toccata; Todescha; M. Rossi:Toccata 7; A. Valente:Tenore del passo e mezo *([ENG,FRE,GER] text)* CHN ▲ 601 [DDD] (16.97)
Aria di Romanesca for Harpsichord
S. Yates (hpd) *(rec Somerset, England, Aug 22-24, 1996)* ("Romanesca: Italian Music for Harpsichord") † Aria di Follia; Cento partie sopra Passacagli; Toccatas Hpd; Gesualdo:Canzon francese del Principe; Macque:Seconde stravaganze; Merulo:Susanne un jour; G. Picchi:Ballo alla Polacha; Ballo ditto il Pichi; Ballo hongaro; Toccata; Todescha; M. Rossi:Toccata 7; A. Valente:Tenore del passo e mezo *([ENG,FRE,GER] text)* CHN ▲ 601 [DDD] (16.97)
Canzonas, Caprici & Ricercari
P. Hannan (rcr), C. Thielmann (va da gamba), C. Tilney (hpd) *(rec Toronto, Canada)* † G. Bassano:Anchor che col partire; Gai bergier; Cima:Sons (2); A. Gabrieli:Anchor che col partire; G. F. Handel:Son Rcr; Telemann:Essercizii Musici SMS ▲ 5049 [DDD] (16.97)
Canzonas, Caprici & Ricercari for Organ
C. Pehrsson (rcr), T. Schuback (org) *(rec Sweden, Feb 29, 1976)* ("Clas Pehrsson Performs Recorder Music") † Toccatas Hpd; Barsanti:Sons Rcr, Op. 1; Castello:Sonate concertate in stil moderno; Eyck:Fluyten Lust-Hof; G. B. Fontana:Son 1 Rcr, Vc & Hpd; Telemann:Essercizii Musici; Sonate (12) metodiche BIS ▲ 48 [AAD] (17.97)
Canzonas, Caprici & Ricercari
J. Feves (bn), G. Schwarz (tpt), H. Katz (hpd) ("The Age of Splendor") † Albinoni:Con Tpt, Ob & Bn; G. B. Fontana:Sons; Hertel:Con a cinque VB2 2-▲ 5124 [ADD] (9.97)
P. Hannan (rcr), C. Thielmann (va da gamba), C. Tilney (hpd) *(rec Toronto, Canada)* † G. Bassano:Anchor che col partire; Gai bergier; Cima:Sons (2); A. Gabrieli:Anchor che col partire; G. F. Handel:Son Rcr; Telemann:Essercizii Musici SMS ▲ 5049 [DDD] (16.97)
Canzoni alla francese in partita [Vol. 4] for Organ, A.13
S. Innocenti (org) *(rec Serassi Org in Church of St. Luborio in Colorno)* † Toccata VI; J. S. Bach:Partite diverse sopra, BWV 767; Pastorale Org, BWV 590; G. Böhm:Capriccio; Prelude, Fugue & Postlude Org; Daquin:Nouveau livre de noëls, Op. 2; Merula:Capricio; Son cromatica LBD ▲ 14 (16.97)
Canzoni (35) for 1-4 Instruments & Continuo [Book 1] (1628)
P. Černý (org) *(rec 1997)* ("Masses for 4 Voices") † W. Byrd:Mass 4 Voc; Monteverdi:Messa et salmi; Paisiello:Re Teodoro in Venezia; C. Simpson:Division on a Ground MONM 3-▲ 20121 [DDD] (54.97)
L. R. Svendsen (rcr), P. van Duren (org) ("Barockmusik für Zwei") † J. S. Bach:Sons Fl; Trio Sons Org; Boismortier:Sons Fl, Op. 91; Buxtehude:Magnificat primi toni, BuxWV 204; Montalbano:Sinfs; Noordt:Tabulature Book PLAL ▲ 99 [DDD] (18.97)
Canzona detta la Bernadinia for Recorder, Viol & Harpsichord
F. Hansen (db), V. Boeckman (rcr), L. U. Mortensen (hpd) *(rec Sept 1990)* † Canzona quatra; Castello:Sons Rcr; Cima:Sons Rcr; G. B. Fontana:Sons 2, 3 & 4 Rcr; Merula:Music Rcr VI Hpd KPT ▲ 32059 [DDD]
Canzona quatra for Recorder, Viol & Harpsichord
F. Hansen (db), V. Boeckman (rcr), L. U. Mortensen (hpd) *(rec Sept 1990)* † Canzona detta la Bernadinia; Castello:Sons Rcr; Cima:Sons Rcr; G. B. Fontana:Sons 2, 3 & 4 Rcr; Merula:Music Rcr VI Hpd KPT ▲ 32059 [DDD]
V.I.F Flute Quartet [arr Blarr] † Org Music; J. S. Bach:Art of the Fugue (sels); Fant & Fugue, BWV 542; Suite 2 Fl, BWV 1067; J. P. Sweelinck:Org Music; Telemann:Musique de Table NCC ▲ 8008 [DDD] (15.99)
Canzona Vigesimaottava for Chamber Ensemble
Icarus Ensemble † Canzona Vigesimasettima; Toccata Quarta; Castello:Music of Castello; Cazzati:Music of Cazzati; Falconieri:Music of Falconieri; Kapsberger:Toccata arpeggiata; B. Marini:Music of Marini; F. Turini:Sons Vns CLAV ▲ 509817 (16.97)
Canzona Vigesimasettima for Chamber Ensemble
Icarus Ensemble † Canzona Vigesimaottava; Toccata Quarta; Castello:Music of Castello; Cazzati:Music of Cazzati; Falconieri:Music of Falconieri; Kapsberger:Toccata arpeggiata; B. Marini:Music of Marini; F. Turini:Sons Vns CLAV ▲ 509817 (16.97)
Capricci (set of 12 capriccios) for Keyboard (1624)
J. Butt (org) ("Il primo libro di capricci") HAM (Suite) ▲ 7907178 (12.97)
R. Festa (cnd), Daedalus Ensemble—Di durezze *(rec France, April 1998)* ("The Anatomy of Melancholy") † Cazzati:Varri, e diversi capricci per camera e per chiesa, Op. 50; J. Dowland:Lachrimae, or Seaven Teares; F. S. Romano:Soprano scherza col cromatico; G. Salvatore:Durezze e ligarure; Trabaci:Music of Trabaci ACCE ▲ 98128 [DDD] (17.97)
S. Vartolo (hpd) TACT 2-▲ 580691 (32.97)

FRESCOBALDI, GIROLAMO (cont.)
Cento partite sopra Passacagli
S. Yates (hpd) *(rec Somerset, England, Aug 22-24, 1996)* ("Romanesca: Italian Music for Harpsichord") † Aria di Follia; Aria di Romanesca; Toccatas Hpd; Gesualdo:Canzon francese del Principe; Macque:Seconde stravaganze; Merulo:Susanne un jour; G. Picchi:Ballo alla Polacha; Ballo ditto il Pichi; Ballo hongaro; Toccata; Todescha; M. Rossi:Toccata 7; A. Valente:Tenore del passo e mezo *([ENG,FRE,GER] text)* CHN ▲ 601 [DDD] (16.97)
Fiori musicali [diverse instrumental compositions, incl 3 Organ Masses] (1635)
L. Ghielmi (org), C. Erkens (cnd), Canticum *(rec Milan, Oct 1994)* ("Fiori musicali, Vol. 2") DEHA ▲ 77345 [DDD] (16.97)
Gagliarda for Orchestra [Book 2, No. 2; trans Stokowski, 1934]
L. Stokowski (cnd), Sym of the Air *(rec Carnegie Hall, 1958)* † G. Gabrieli:Son pian' e forte; Palestrina:Adoramus te Christe; O. Respighi:Pini di Roma; D. Shostakovich:Sym 1 EMIC ▲ 66864 [ADD] (11.97)
Harpsichord Music
J. Chapman (hpd)—Capriccio in G; Fant in e ("Divers styles dans l'eloquence: Pieces de clavecin from The Bauyn Manuscript, Vol. 2") † L. Couperin:Hpd Music; Froberger:Hpd Music COC ▲ 1421 [DDD] (16.97)
S. Henstra (hpd)—Toccata seconda in g; Partita sopra l'Aria di Follia; Canzona sesta detta La presenti; Cento Partite sopra Passacagli ("Toccate, partite et passacagli") † A. Gabrieli:Kbd Music; Merula:Kbd Music; G. Picchi:Kbd Music; B. Storace:Kbd Music RICE ▲ 167136 (17.97)
S. Matthews (hpd) ("Harpsichord Music from 1637") † Toccate e partite d'intavolatura GAS ▲ 241 [ADD] (16.97)
P. Wolfe (hpd) ("When They Had Pedals, Vol. 1, The Pleyel") LYR 2-▲ 8033 (16.97)
Liber secundus diversarum modulationum for 1-4 Voices
D. Cantalupi (cnd), L'aura Soave [18 sels] TACT ▲ 580602 (16.97)
Madrigali (19) for 5 Voices [Book 1]
R. Alessandrini (cnd), Concerto Italiano OPUS ▲ 30133 (18.97)
Music of Frescobaldi
E. P. Biggs (org), R. Burgin (cnd) —Toccatas in d & G; Canzoni Nos 1-5 in G, C, a, g & g *(rec Cambridge, MA, Mar 26-27 & 30-31, 1959)* ("Antiphonal Music of Gabrieli") † G. Gabrieli:Canzoni for Brass Choirs; Fant VI toni; Intonationi; Sacrae symphoniae SNYC (Masterworks Heritage) ▲ 62353 [ADD] (12.97)
K. Coker (cnd) —Balletto; Begli Occhi Io non Provo; Canzona XXXV Detta l'Alessandrina; Oscure Selve; Canzona XIV Detta la Marina; Canzona Ultima Detta la Vittoria; Capriccio Cromatico con Ligature Contrario; Se l'Aura Spira; Canzona VIII Detta l'Ambitsiosa; Vanne, O Carte Amorosa; Capriccio XI; Toccata per Spinettina Sola, Over Liuto; Occhi Che Sete; Canzona Secunda; Passacaglia ("Begli Occhi Io non Provo") RCMM ▲ 19401 [DDD] (16.97)
Ensemble Fitzwilliam ("Canzoni & Partite") AUV ▲ 8514 (12.97)
E.A.B. Nagy (sop), D. Karasszon (org), Schola Calviniana—Ricercari 1-10; Lucis creator optime; Exultet coelum laudibus; Iste confessor; Ave maris stella [L] *(rec Budapest, Hungary, 1994-95)* ("Ricercars & Hymns") HUN ▲ 31645 [DDD] (16.97)
Organ Music
G. Athanasiadès (org)—Aria detta "La Frescobalda"; Toccata per l'Elevatione *(rec Klosterneuburg Vienna)* † W. A. Mozart:Andante Mechanical Org, K.616 TUD ▲ 7053 (16.97)
L. Tamminga (org)—Toccatas "sopra i pedali, e senza" 5 & 7; Toccata ottava "di durreza e leguture"; Canzonas 2, 4, 5 & 7; Capricci et arie [No. 4, Cappricio Quatre la, sol, fa, re mi; No. 9, Capriccio Nono di durezze]; Toccatas per l'Elevazione 1, 3-4; Ricercar 3; Fant 2; Canzon francese "La Pesenti"; Capriccio sopra ut re mi fa lo saO *(rec rgs at Basilica di San Petronio Bologna, Dec 1996)* ("Works for Organ") ACCE ▲ 96120 [DDD] (17.97)
V.I.F Flute Quartet—Toccata per l'Elevatione † Canzona quatra; J. S. Bach:Art of the Fugue (sels); Fant & Fugue, BWV 542; Suite 2 Fl, BWV 1067; J. P. Sweelinck:Org Music; Telemann:Musique de Table NCC ▲ 8008 [DDD] (15.99)
Il primo libro d'intavolatura di toccate di cembalo et organo (1615)
Affetti Musicali—Toccata nona *(rec Micahaelis-Kirche, Ronnenberg Hannover, Germany, May 1995)* ("Marini und seine Zeitgenossen") † Buonamente:Quarto libro de varie Sonate, Sinfonie, Gagliarde; Castello:Sonate concertate in stil moderno; B. Marini:Affetti musicali, Op. 1; Sons, Syms & Retornelli, Op. 8; G. Picchi:Pieces Hpd; S. Rossi:Terzo libro, Op. 12 THOR ▲ 2279 [DDD] (16.97)
Sonetto spirituale:Maddalena all Croce for Solo Voice & Harpsichord (1630)
C. Calvi (cta), R. Gini (vc) [ITA] *(rec May 1991)* † Jommelli:Agonia di Cristo; Sances:Stabat mater dolorosa NUO (Ancient Music) ▲ 7030 [DDD] (16.97)
Toccata Quarta for Chamber Ensemble
Icarus Ensemble † Canzona Vigesimaottava; Canzona Vigesimasettima; Castello:Music of Castello; Cazzati:Music of Cazzati; Falconieri:Music of Falconieri; Kapsberger:Toccata arpeggiata; B. Marini:Music of Marini; F. Turini:Sons Vns CLAV ▲ 509817 (16.97)
Toccatas for Harpsichord
C. Pehrsson (rcr), T. Schuback (hpd), M. Wieslander (org)—Toccata *(rec Stocksund, Sweden, Apr 5-7, 1982)* ("Clas Pehrsson Performs Recorder Music") † Canzonas, Caprici & Ricercari; Barsanti:Sons Rcr, Op. 1; Castello:Sonate concertate in stil moderno; Eyck:Fluyten Lust-Hof; G. B. Fontana:Son 1 Rcr, Vc & Hpd; Telemann:Essercizii Musici; Sonate (12) metodiche BIS ▲ 48 [AAD] (17.97)
S. Yates (hpd)—Toccata in a *(rec Somerset, England, Aug 22-24, 1996)* ("Romanesca: Italian Music for Harpsichord") † Aria di Follia; Aria di Romanesca; Cento partie sopra Passacagli; Gesualdo:Canzon francese del Principe; Macque:Seconde stravaganze; Merulo:Susanne un jour; G. Picchi:Ballo alla Polacha; Ballo ditto il Pichi; Ballo hongaro; Toccata; Todescha; M. Rossi:Toccata 7; A. Valente:Tenore del passo e mezo CHN ▲ 601 [DDD] (16.97)
Toccatas (11) for Harpsichord [from Instrumental Works, Book 2] (1627)
L. Ghielmi (hpd) † Aria detta "La Frescobalda" NUO (Ancient Music) ▲ 6799 [DDD] (16.97)
Toccata VI for Organ
S. Innocenti (org) *(rec Serassi Org in Church of St. Luborio in Colorno)* † Canzoni alla francese; J. S. Bach:Partite diverse sopra, BWV 767; Pastorale Org, BWV 590; G. Böhm:Capriccio; Prelude, Fugue & Postlude Org; Daquin:Nouveau livre de noëls, Op. 2; Merula:Capricio; Son cromatica LBD ▲ 14 (16.97)
Toccate e partite d'intavolatura for Harpsichord & Organ [Books 1 & 2] (1637)
P. Hantaï (hpd) ASTR ▲ 8585 (18.97)
S. Mathews (hpd) ("Harpsichord Music from 1637") † Hpd Music GAS ▲ 241 [ADD] (16.97)
S. Vartolo (hpd/org) TACT 3-▲ 580780 (47.97)

FREUND, DONALD WAYNE (1947-
Backyard Songs for Soprano, Flute & Harp [based on settings of poems by Gwendolyn Brooks] (1990)
Jubal Trio *(rec Music Division SUNY, Purchase, NY, May 29-30, June 14 & Nov 13, 1995)* ("Jubal Songs") † G. Crumb:Federico's Little Songs; T. León:Journey; H. Sollberger:Life Study; E. Stokes:Song Circle CRI ▲ 738 [DDD] (16.97)
Hard Cells for 14 Instruments (1989)
D. Wiley (cnd) *(rec Indiana Univ Bloomington, Oct 1992)* ("New Music from Indiana University, Vol. 1") † C. Baker:Awaking the Winds; Dzubay:Trio; J. Haas:Sussurrando; E. O'Brien:Mysteries of the Horizon IUSM ▲ 5 (16.97)
Jug Blues & Fat Pickin' for Orchestra
E. Corporon (cnd), Cincinnati Wind SO ("Paradigm") † Gregson:Sword & the Crown; J. Harbison:3 City Blocks; P. Hindemith:Sym Concert Band; B. Rands:Ceremonial; I. Stravinsky:Circus Polka KLAV ▲ 11059 (18.97)
Poem Symphonies (7) for Orchestra (1990)
E. F. Brown (cnd), Bowling Green Philharmonia—Radical Light [comments by Freund] ("The Composer's Voice-New Music from Bowling Green") † S. Adler:Requiescat in Pace; K. Husa:Sym 2; J. Ryan:Ophélie; M. Shrude:Into Light; Theofanidis:On the Edge of the Infinte ALBA ▲ 321 [DDD] (16.97)
Triomusic for Violin, Clarinet & Piano (1980)
Verdehr Trio ("The Making of a Medium, Vol. 4") † P. Dickinson:Hymns, Rags & Blues; K. Husa:Son a tre; J. Niblock:Trio Vn CRYS ▲ 744 (15.97)
Viklarbo Chamber Ensemble *(rec 1990)* † I. Dahl:Concerto à tre; M. Rózsa:Intro & Allegro, Op. 44; P. Schickele:Qt Vn RACA ▲ 1005

FRIDERICI, DANIEL (1584-1638)
Aetus carmen melodiae
Retrover Ensemble *(rec Switzerland, Feb 4-6, 1997)* ("Piae Cantiones-Latin Songs in Medieval Finland") † Anonymous:Aetus carmen melodiae; Angelus emittitur; Dies est laetitiae; Dies est laetitiae (Adam von Fulda); Dies est laetitiae (Glogauer Liederbuch); Dies est leticie (Buxheimer Orgelbuch); Jesu dulcis memoria; Jesus Christus nostra salus; Jucundare jugitar; Mars praecurrit in planetis; Mirum si laeteris; Omnis mundus iucundetur; Omnis nunc microcosmus/Omnis mundus; Parvulus nobis nascitur; Personent hodie; Praeambulum; Puer natus in Bethlehem; Ramus virens olivarum; Sum in aliena provincia; Verbum caro factum est; Verbum caro factum est (Canionero de Uppsala); J. H. Schein:Surrexit Christus hodie NXIN ▲ 8554180 [DDD] (5.97)

FRIEDHOFER, HUGO (1901-1981)
Private Parts (film music) for Orchestra
K. Graunke (cnd), Graunke SO † Richthofen & Brown FA ▲ 8105 [AAD] (8.97)

▲ = CD ♦ = Enhanced CD △ = MD ▮ = Cassette Tape ▯ = DCC

FRIEDHOFER, HUGO (cont.)

Richthofen & Brown (film music) for Orchestra
K. Graunke (cnd), Graunke SO † Private Parts FA ▲ 8105 [AAD] (8.97)

FRIEDMAN, IGNAZ (1882-1948)

Elle Danse for Piano, Op. 10/5
I. Friedman (pno) ("Highlights 1925-36 From His Discography") † Music Box, Op. 33/3; Beethoven:Son 14 Pno, Op. 27/2; Chopin:Etudes Pno; Impromptu in F#, Op. 36; Mazurkas Pno; Nocturnes Pno; Polonaise 6 Pno, Op. 53; Son Pno in b♭, Op. 35; Waltzes Pno; J. N. Hummel:Rondo Pno, Op. 11; Liszt:Trans, Arrs & Paraphrases; Mendelssohn (-Bartholdy):Fants Pno, Op. 16; Shield:Old English Menuet APR (Signature Series) ▲ 5508 [ADD] (18.97)

Music Box for Piano, Op. 33/3
I. Friedman (pno) ("Highlights 1925-36 From His Discography") † Danse; Beethoven:Son 14 Pno, Op. 27/2; Chopin:Etudes Pno; Impromptu in F#, Op. 36; Mazurkas Pno; Nocturnes Pno; Polonaise 6 Pno, Op. 53; Son Pno in b♭, Op. 35; Waltzes Pno; J. N. Hummel:Rondo Pno, Op. 11; Liszt:Trans, Arrs & Paraphrases; Mendelssohn (-Bartholdy):Fants Pno, Op. 16; Shield:Old English Menuet APR (Signature Series) ▲ 5508 [ADD] (18.97)

Piano Music
I. Friedman (pno) *(rec 1919-32)* ("The Polish Virtuoso") † J. Hofmann:Pno Music; I. J. Paderewski:Pno Music (misc) NIMB (Grand Piano) ▲ 8802 (11.97)

Studies on a Theme by Paganini for Piano, Op. 47b
M. Raekallio (pno) † J. Brahms:Vars on a Theme by Paganini, Op. 35; Liszt:Études d'exécution transcendante (6), S.140 ODE ▲ 777 [DDD] (17.97)

Transcriptions for solo Piano
L. B. Jensen (pno)—J. S. Bach:Gavotte; Bourée [both from Partita Vn]; Sicilienne [from Son Fl & Hpd]; Sheep May Safely Graze; Toccata & Fugue in d; other sels ("Piano Transcriptions of J. S. Bach") CLSO ▲ 190 (15.97)

FRIEDMAN, STANLEY (1951-

Topanga Variations for Horn (1981-82)
F. R. Werke (hn) † S. Berge:Hornlokk; Clearfield:Songs of the Wolf; T. Madsen:Dream of the Rhinoceros, Op. 92; Son Hn; W. Plagge:Son 3 Hn, Op. 88 CRYS ▲ 678 (15.97)

FRIIS, FLEMMING (1961-

November for Woodwind Trio (1992)
Trio Divertimento ("New Danish Woodwind Music") † B. Andersen:Invocation; Serenade; J. Bentzon:Sonatina, Op. 7; G. Lund:Talks; Tarp:Taffelmusik; F. Weis:Music Fl, Cl & Bn PLAL ▲ 94 [DAD] (18.97)

FRIML, RUDOLF (1879-1972)

Songs
J. Carreras (ten)—Indian Love Call; Rose Marie [both from Rose Marie] ("My Romance") † F. Lehár:Land des Lächelns (sels); Lustige Witwe (sels); Zarewitsch (sels); R. Rodgers:Songs; S. Romberg:Music of Romberg (operetta sels) ERAT ▲ 17789 (16.97)
T. Ringholz (sop), D. Hunsberger (cnd), Eastman-Dryden Orch ("Chansonette") ARA ▲ 6562 (16.97)

FRITH, FRED (20th cent)

The Disinformation Polka for Accordian (1994)
G. Klucevsek (acc) *(rec Church of the Holy Trinity, New York, NY, Mar 1993)* † Duckworth:Slow Dancing in Yugoslavia; Klucevsek:Music of Klucevsek; J. Zorn:Road Runner STKL ▲ 207 [DDD] (16.97)

Pacifica for Voices, Winds, Strings & Percussion
various artists TZA (Composer) ▲ 7034 [DDD] (16.97)

FRITZ, GASPARD (1716-1783)

Concerto in E for Violin & Orchestra
J. Lohmann (vn), H. Griffiths (cnd), English CO † Sym 1; Scherrer:Sym 5 NOVA ▲ 150099 [DDD] (16.97)

Symphony No. 1
H. Griffiths (cnd), English CO † Con Vn; Scherrer:Sym 5 NOVA ▲ 150099 [DDD] (16.97)

FROBERGER, JOHANN JAKOB (1616-1667)

Harpsichord Music
E. Baiano (hpd)—Diverse curiose partite; Suites 16-19 Hpd; Toccata; Fant; Ricercar; Lamentation SYM ▲ 96152 (18.97)
D. Cates (hpd)—Plainte pour passer la Mélancholie; Toccata III in C; Lamentation faite sur la mort très douloureus; Toccata in F; Tombeau sur le mort de Monsieur Blancheroche; Toccata VI in A; Lamentation sur ce que j'ay été vol; Toccata III in G ("Pieces de Clavessin") WILD ▲ 9701 [DDD] (16.97)
J. Chapman (hpd)—Suites in a & G; Toccata in a; Ricercar in C ("Divers styles dans l'eloquence: Pieces de clavecin from The Bauyn Manuscript, Vol. 2") † L. Couperin:Hpd Music; Frescobaldi:Hpd Music COC ▲ 1421 [DDD] (16.97)
J. Johnstone (hpd)—Ricercar in e; Suite in d; Toccatas 1, 4, 6 & 8 ("John Blow's Anthology") † Org Music; Blow:Pieces Hpd; J. C. F. Fischer:Hpd Music MER ▲ 84328 [DDD] (16.97)
G. Leonhardt (hpd)—Tombeau sur la Mort de Monsieur Blancrocher; Suites 7-8; Capriccio 6; Ricercar 11 † M. Weckmann:Hpd Music SNYC (Vivarte) ▲ 62732 (16.97)
S. Mathews (hpd)—Suite VI in C; Toccata II in d; Suite II in d; Lamentation in F; Suite XVII in F; Tombeau fait à Paris; Suite XIX in c; Suite XXIX in E; Toccata XIX in d; Suite XIII in d GAS ▲ 299 [DDD] (16.97)
L. Mortensen (hpd)—6 Suites—Nos. 6 in D, 11 in D, 12 in C, 18 in g; Toccatas I & II (1649); Tombeau KPT ▲ 32040 [DDD]
M. Nabeshima (hpd)—Suite in g; Toccata in F *(rec Brussels, 1991)* ("Bach & His Predecessors") † J. S. Bach:Prelude, Fugue & Allegro Lt, BWV 998; Kuhnau:Musicalische Vorstellung einiger biblischer Histor DI ▲ 920283 [DDD] (5.97)
M. Ohm (hpd) MELI ▲ 7108 (17.97)
E. Parmentier (hpd)—Toccata IV; Canzon VI; Suite in c; Tombeau de Monsieur de Blanrocher ("17th Century French Harpsichord Music") † Anglebert:Pièces de clavecin Hpd WILD ▲ 8502 [DDD] (16.97)
B. Schenkman (hpd)—Suite in g; Tocade ("The Bauyn Manuscript: Music at the Court of Louis XIV") † L. Couperin:Hpd Music; Du Mont:Pavane Hpd WILD ▲ 9603 [DDD] (16.97)
S. Yates (hpd)—Toccata II; Meditation; Suite XVIII; Toccata V; Suite XXX; Suite XIX; Tombeau de Monsier Blancheroche ("Tombeau: German Harpsichord Music of the 17th Century") CHOC ▲ 596 (16.97)

Organ Music
P. Crivellaro (org)—Canzon FbWV 305; Capriccio FbWV 503; Fant FbWV 206; Toccatas FbWV 101, 102 & 107 *(rec Baceno Italy, July & Aug 1997)* † Kerll:Org Music; G. Muffat:Org Music LBD ▲ 25 [DDD] (16.97)
J. Johnstone (org)—Capriccios in G & D; Fant on "Sol La Re"; Ricercar in d; Toccatas 2, 3, 5, 7 *(rec Goetze & Gwynn Org of St. Matthew's Church Sheffie)* ("John Blow's Anthology") † Hpd Music; Blow:Pieces Hpd; J. C. F. Fischer:Hpd Music MER ▲ 84328 [DDD] (16.97)
D. Moroney (org) *(rec Robert-Dallam org Lanvellec)* ("Pièces pour le clavier") TEMR ▲ 316007 (18.97)

FROELICHER, ANDRE (1959-

Muleta for 2 Guitars
J. Moser (gtr), F. Rahm (gtr) ("Musique espagnole pour deux guitares") † I. Albéniz:Suite española 1, Op. 47; Tango Español; A. de Cabezón:Obras de música (sels); E. Granados:Goyescas:Intermezzo; Sor:Waltzes Gtrs, Op. 44bis GALL ▲ 881 [DDD] (19.97)

FRØHLICH, JOHANNES FREDERIK (1806-1860)

Sonata in a for Flute
H. W. Andreasen (fl) *(rec Malmö Sweden, Aug 8-9, 1994)* ("Flute Music of the Danish Golden Age") † J. P. E. Hartmann:Prelude Fl; Son Fl, Op. 1; Kuhlau:Duos brillants, Op. 110; Weyse:Rondeau Fl NXIN ▲ 553333 [DDD] (5.97)

Symphony in E♭, Op. 33 (1830)
C. Hogwood (cnd), Danish National RSO † N. W. Gade:Sym 4 CHN ▲ 9609 (16.97)

FRÖHLICH, JOSEPH (1780-1862)

Concerto in D for Piano 4-Hands & Orchestra
E. Kalvelage (pno), M. Krücker (pno), F. Merz (cnd), Cologne Radio Orch † L. Koželuch:Con Pno 4-Hands KSCH ▲ 365042 (16.97)

FROLOV, IGOR (1937-

Concert Fantasy on Themes from Porgy & Bess for Violin & Orchestra
A. Korsakov (vn) † Conus:Con Vn; K. Khachaturian:Kontsert-rapsodiya RUS ▲ 10010 [DDD]

FROMMEL, GERHARD (1906-1984)

Lieder der Stille [Songs of Silence] for Baritone & Piano, Op. 4 (1924)
R. Lutz (bar), G. Sudau (pno) ("Portrait") † Pia caritatevole amorosissima; Son 2 Vn, Op. 32; Son 3 Pno, Op. 15; Son 4 Pno, Op. 21; Songs (4) after Baudelaire, Op. 16 MPH ▲ 55708 [DDD] (15.97)

Pia caritatevole amorosissima (song) for Soprano & Piano (1924)
A. Vogel (sop), E. Wangler (pno) ("Portrait") † Lieder der Stille, Op. 4; Son 2 Vn, Op. 32; Son 3 Pno, Op. 15; Son 4 Pno, Op. 21; Songs (4) after Baudelaire, Op. 16 MPH ▲ 55708 [DDD] (15.97)

Sonata No. 3 in E for Piano, Op. 15 (1941)
L. Jonsson (pno) ("Portrait") † Lieder der Stille, Op. 4; Pia caritatevole amorosissima; Son 2 Vn, Op. 32; Son 4 Pno, Op. 21; Songs (4) after Baudelaire, Op. 16 MPH ▲ 55708 [DDD] (15.97)

FROMMEL, GERHARD (cont.)

Sonata No. 4 in F for Piano, Op. 21 (1943)
K. Lautner (pno) ("Portrait") † Lieder der Stille, Op. 4; Pia caritatevole amorosissima; Son 2 Vn, Op. 32; Son 3 Pno, Op. 15; Songs (4) after Baudelaire, Op. 16 MPH ▲ 55708 [DDD] (15.97)

Sonata No. 2 in a for Violin & Piano, Op. 32 (1950)
D. Sepec (vn), R. Hoffmann (pno) ("Portrait") † Lieder der Stille, Op. 4; Pia caritatevole amorosissima; Son 3 Pno, Op. 15; Son 4 Pno, Op. 21; Songs (4) after Baudelaire, Op. 16 MPH ▲ 55708 [DDD] (15.97)

Songs (4) after Baudelaire for Soprano & Piano, Op. 16 (1941)
A. Vogel (sop), E. Wangler (pno)—Was erzählst du heut, allein geblieben ("Portrait") † Lieder der Stille, Op. 4; Pia caritatevole amorosissima; Son 2 Vn, Op. 32; Son 3 Pno, Op. 15; Son 4 Pno, Op. 21 MPH ▲ 55708 [DDD] (15.97)

FROOM, DAVID (1951-

Chamber Concerto for Chamber Ensemble (1991)
R. Black (cnd) *(rec Vassar College Poughkeepskie, NY, Sept 20, 1992)* ("To Dance to the Whistling Wind") † Qnt Ob; Qt Strs; Suite Pno; To Dance ARA ▲ 6710 [DDD] (16.97)

Down To A Sunless Sea (rhapsody) for String Quintet (1988)
E. Garth (pno) † Qt Piano; Son Pno; M. Rosenzweig:Diptych CENT ▲ 2103 [DDD] (16.97)

Quartet for Piano & Strings (1985)
E. Garth (pno) † Down To A Sunless Sea; Son Pno; M. Rosenzweig:Diptych CENT ▲ 2103 [DDD] (16.97)

Quartet for Strings (1990)
Ciompi String Quartet *(rec St. Mary's College, MD, Mar 2, 1996)* ("To Dance to the Whistling Wind") † Chamber Con; Qnt Ob; Suite Pno; To Dance ARA ▲ 6710 [DDD] (16.97)

Quintet for Oboe, Strings & Piano (1994)
C. Kendall (cnd) , Twentieth Century Consort *(rec Bethesda, MD, June 30, 1996)* ("To Dance to the Whistling Wind") † Chamber Con; Qt Strs; Suite Pno; To Dance ARA ▲ 6710 [DDD] (16.97)

Sonata for Piano (1980)
E. Garth (pno) † Down To A Sunless Sea; Qt Piano; M. Rosenzweig:Diptych CENT ▲ 2103 [DDD] (16.97)

Suite for Piano (1996)
E. Garth (pno) *(rec St. Mary's College, MD, Sept 21, 1996)* ("To Dance to the Whistling Wind") † Chamber Con; Qnt Ob; Qt Strs; To Dance ARA ▲ 6710 [DDD] (16.97)

To Dance to the Whistling Wind for Flute (1993)
J. Rosenfeld (fl) *(rec St. Mary's College, MD, Sept 21, 1996)* ("To Dance to the Whistling Wind") † Chamber Con; Qnt Ob; Qt Strs; Suite Pno ARA ▲ 6710 [DDD] (16.97)

FROUNBERG, IVAR (1950-

A Dirge: Other Echos Inhabit the Garden for Accordian (1988-94)
G. Draugsvoll (acc) *(rec 1995-96)* ("Works for Classical Accordian") † M. W. Holm:Troglodyt; K. I. Jørgensen:Cadenza; Kanding:Winter Darkness; L. Kayser:Confetti; A. Pape:I've Never Seen A Butterfly MARC ▲ 8224028 [DDD] (13.97)

Worlds Apart for Harp (1993)
S. A. Claro (hp) *(rec Denmark, Nov 1994-Jan 1995)* † Graugaard:Incrustations; Lippe:Music Hp Tape; Parmerud:Strings & Shadows; Saariaho:Fall CENT ▲ 2284 [DDD] (16.97)
S. A. Claro (hp) † Fuzzy:B-Movies; Graugaard:Incrustations; Kanding:Entbergen DCAP ▲ 8224113 (13.97)

FRUMERIE, GUNNAR DE (1908-1987)

Concerto for Clarinet & Orchestra, Op. 51 (1958)
K. Fagéus (cl), E. Klas (cnd), Stockholm Royal Orch ("Clarinet Concertos") † Crusell:Den Lilla Slavinnan (sels); L.-E. Larsson:Hommage à Mozart; W. A. Mozart:Con Cl, K.622 OPU ▲ 19801 (16.97)

Concerto for Horn & Orchestra (1971-72)
I. Lanzky-Otto (hn), S. Westerberg (cnd), Stockholm PO † Musica per novae; Vars & Fugue Pno CAPA ▲ 21400 [AAD] (16.97)

Concerto for Trombone & Orchestra, Op. 81 (1987)
C. Lindberg (trbn), L. Segerstam (cnd), Bamberg SO † F. David:Concertino Trbn, Op. 4; Grondahl:Con Trbn; Guilmant:Morceau symphonique, Op. 88 BIS ▲ 378 [DDD] (17.97)

Music of Frumerie
S. Grippe (cta), F. Wedar (bar), L. Andreasson (vn), G. Roehr (va), C. D. Frumerie-Luthander (vc), G. Gröndahl (vc), G. de Frumerie (pno), S. Frykberg (cnd), Gothenberg SO ("Frumerie Plays Frumerie") CAPA 3-▲ 21535 (31.97)

Musica per novae for Chamber Ensemble
various artists † Con Hn; Vars & Fugue Pno CAPA ▲ 21400 [AAD] (16.97)

Pastoral Suite for Flute, Harp & Strings, Op. 13b (1933)
K. Rudolph (fl), M. Bernardi (cnd), CBC Vancouver SO *(rec Vancouver British Columbia, Mar 1-2, 1992)* ("Northern Landscapes") † L.-E. Larsson:Pastoralsvit, Op. 19; Winter's Tale, Op. 18; K. Riisager:Little Ov; Sibelius:The Lover; D. Wirén:Serenade Strs, Op. 11 SMS ▲ 5157 [DDD] (16.97)

Singoalla (opera) [lib E. Byström-Baeckström after Rydberg], Op. 22 (1937-40)
Y. Ahronovitch (cnd), Stockholm PO, Hägersten Motet Choir CAPA 2-▲ 22023 [DDD] (32.97)

Variations & Fugue for Piano & Orchestra
L. Simon (pno), S. Westerberg (cnd), Stockholm PO † Con Hn; Musica per novae CAPA ▲ 21400 [AAD] (16.97)

Variations on a Swedish Folk Tune for Guitar, Op. 69a
P. Skareng (gtr) ("El Colibri") † J. S. Bach:Sons & Partitas Vn; Carlstedt:Swedish Dances; M. Giuliani:Rossiniana; Lauro:Gtr Music; Sagreras:El Colibri; Tárrega:Recuerdos de la Alhambra CAPA ▲ 21392 [AAD] (16.97)

FRY, JAMES (1949-

Concerto for Clarinet & Wind Ensemble (1994)
E. Rheude (cl), J. Whitwell (cnd), Michigan State Univ Wind Sym ("Kaleidoscope: Music of James Fry") † Drift of the Eastern Gray; Gloria; Impressions Gtr; Kaleidoscope; Studies Pno CPS ▲ 8653 [DDD] (16.97)

Drift of the Eastern Gray for 2 Pianos (1995)
J. Solose (pno), K. Solose (pno) ("Kaleidoscope: Music of James Fry") † Con Cl; Gloria; Impressions Gtr; Kaleidoscope; Studies Pno CPS ▲ 8653 [DDD] (16.97)

Gloria for 2 Pianos & Chorus (1988)
J. Solose (pno), K. Solose (pno), J. Rodde (cnd), Univ of North Dakota Concert Choir ("Kaleidoscope: Music of James Fry") † Con Cl; Drift of the Eastern Gray; Impressions Gtr; Kaleidoscope; Studies Pno CPS ▲ 8653 [DDD] (16.97)

Impressions (3) for Guitar (1997)
V. Mityakov (gtr) ("Kaleidoscope: Music of James Fry") † Con Cl; Drift of the Eastern Gray; Gloria; Kaleidoscope; Studies Pno CPS ▲ 8653 [DDD] (16.97)

Kaleidoscope for Clarinet & Piano (1993)
E. Rheude (cl), J. Hershberger (pno) ("Kaleidoscope: Music of James Fry") † Con Cl; Drift of the Eastern Gray; Gloria; Impressions Gtr; Studies Pno CPS ▲ 8653 [DDD] (16.97)

Metamorphoses on a Theme by Paul Hindemith
J. C. Carmichael (cnd), Furman Civic Wind Ensemble *(rec United States of America)* ("Contemporary Music Festival") † A. Blank:Intro & Rondo Fant; J. Kowalski:Three Koans Str Qt; Lieuwen:Anachronisms; J. Russo:Elegy Ob; Fort Washington Ov Orch; Van Appledorn:Concerto Brevis; Missa Brevis *(E text)* CRSR ▲ 9052

Pierrot's Fancy for Piano (1987)
A. Houle (pno) † W. Alexander:Cambridge Trio; O. Aubert:Solo de Concours 1; L. Bernstein:Son Cl; Diemer:Vars Pno 4-Hands; E. Pellegrini:Divert a tre Bn CRSR ▲ 8949

Studies (12) for Piano (1991)
J. Solose (pno) ("Kaleidoscope: Music of James Fry") † Con Cl; Drift of the Eastern Gray; Gloria; Impressions Gtr; Kaleidoscope CPS ▲ 8653 [DDD] (16.97)

FRYDMAN, ARMAND (20th cent)

Music of Frydman
J. Suk (vn), C. Larde (fl), J. Suk (cnd), Suk CO, A. Zaboronok (cnd), Bolshoi Theater Children's Choir MED7 ▲ 112 (18.97)

FRYKLÖF, HARALD (1882-1919)

Symphonic Piece for Organ
H. Fagius (org) *(rec Katarina Church Org, Stockholm, Sweden, Oct 4, 1981)* ("Hans Fagius Plays the Romantic Swedish Organ") † Symphonic Piece; O. Lindberg:Son Org, Op. 23; O. Olsson:Prelude & Fugue Org, Op. 52; E. Sjögren:Org Music BIS ▲ 191 [AAD] (17.97)

FU, GENG CHEN (20th cent)

Celebration Dance for Orchestra
C. Hoey (cnd), Singapore SO *(rec Victoria Memorial Hall Singapore, Jan 1981)* † A:Con Vn; G. Chen:Fant on a Xinjiang Folk Song; Ge:Horse Cart; K. Ma:Shanbei Suite; Qin:Happy Grassland MARC (Chinese Music) ▲ 8223902 [ADD] (13.97)

FUCHS, ROBERT (1847-1927)

Andante grazioso & Capriccio for Strings, Op. 63
M. Müssauer (cnd), Moravian PO *(rec Philharmonie Olomouc, Oct 1994)* ("Orchesterwerke") † Meeres und der Liebe Wellen, Op. 59; Sym 3 THOR ▲ 2260 [DDD] (17.97)

FUCHS, ROBERT (cont.)

Fantasiestücke (7) for Cello & Piano, Op. 78 (1905)
M. Drobinsky (vc), D. Blumenthal (pno) † Son 1 Pno, Op. 19; Son 2 Pno, Op. 88 MARC ▲ 8223423 [DDD] (13.97)
N. Green (vc), C. Palmer (pno) † Son 1 Vc, Op. 29; Son 2 Vc, Op. 83 BDR ▲ 5 [DDD]

Jugendklänge for Piano
D. Blumenthal (pno) ("Piano Sonatas, Vol. 2") † Son 3 Pno, Op. 109; Waltzes Pno, Op. 110 MARC ▲ 8223474 (13.97)

Des Meeres und der Liebe Wellen (overture) for Orchestra, Op. 59
M. Müssauer (cnd), Moravian PO *(rec Philharmonie Olomouc, Oct 1994)* ("Orchesterwerke") † Andante grazioso & Capriccio, Op. 63; Sym 3 THOR ▲ 2260 [DDD] (17.97)

Quintet in E♭ for Clarinet & Strings, Op. 102 (1914)
P. Meyer (cl), Carmina String Quartet *(rec Landgasthof Riehen Switzerland, Apr 2-3 & 18-19, 1995)* † C. M. von Weber:Qnt Cl DNN ▲ 78801 [DDD] (16.97)
Scarponi Quintet † Kornauth:Qnt Cl NUO ▲ 7252 (16.97)

Serenade No. 3 in e for Strings, Op. 21
R. Padoin (cnd), Accademia Veneta CO ("Late Romantic Serenades") † E. Elgar:Serenade Strs, Op. 20; E. Wolf-Ferrari:Serenade Strs PHEX ▲ 98207 (16.97)

Sonata No. 1 in d for Cello & Piano, Op. 29 (1881)
N. Green (vc), C. Palmer (pno) † Fantasiestücke Vc, Op. 78; Son 2 Vc, Op. 83 BDR ▲ 5 [DDD]

Sonata No. 2 in e♭ for Cello & Piano, Op. 83 (1908)
N. Green (vc), C. Palmer (pno) † Fantasiestücke Vc, Op. 78; Son 1 Vc, Op. 29 BDR ▲ 5 [DDD]

Sonata No. 1 in G♭ for Piano, Op. 19 (?1877)
D. Blumenthal (pno) † Son 2 Pno, Op. 88 MARC ▲ 8223377 [DDD] (13.97)
D. Blumenthal (pno) † Fantasiestücke Vc, Op. 78; Son 2 Pno, Op. 88 MARC ▲ 8223423 [DDD] (13.97)

Sonata No. 2 in g for Piano, Op. 88 (?1910)
D. Blumenthal (pno) † Son 1 Pno, Op. 19 MARC ▲ 8223377 [DDD] (13.97)
D. Blumenthal (pno) † Fantasiestücke Vc, Op. 78; Son 1 Pno, Op. 19 MARC ▲ 8223423 [DDD] (13.97)

Sonata No. 3 in D♭ for Piano, Op. 109 (?1923)
D. Blumenthal (pno) ("Piano Sonatas, Vol. 2") † Jugendklänge; Waltzes Pno, Op. 110 MARC ▲ 8223474 (13.97)

Sonata No. 1 in f# for Violin & Piano, Op. 20
F. Terpitz (vn), B. Witter (pno) † Son 6 Vn, Op. 103; J. Brahms:FAE Son Vn AMAT ▲ 9705 (17.97)

Sonata No. 6 in g for Violin & Piano, Op. 103
F. Terpitz (vn), B. Witter (pno) † Son 1 Vn, Op. 20; J. Brahms:FAE Son Vn AMAT ▲ 9705 (17.97)

Symphony No. 1 in C, Op. 37 (1884)
M. Müssauer (cnd), Moravian PO *(rec Mar 1995)* ("Symphonic Works, Vol. 2") † Sym 2 THOR ▲ 2268 [DDD] (16.97)

Symphony No. 2 in E♭, Op. 45 (1887)
M. Müssauer (cnd), Moravian PO *(rec Mar 1995)* ("Symphonic Works, Vol. 2") † Sym 1 THOR ▲ 2268 [DDD] (16.97)

Symphony No. 3 in E, Op. 79
M. Müssauer (cnd), Moravian PO *(rec Philharmonie Olomouc, Oct 1994)* ("Orchesterwerke") † Andante grazioso & Capriccio, Op. 63; Meeres und der Liebe Wellen, Op. 59 THOR ▲ 2260 [DDD] (17.97)

Trio in A for Strings, Op. 94
Belcanto Strings † C. Reinecke:Trio Strs, Op. 249 MDG ▲ 6340841 (17.97)

Waltzes (12) for Piano, Op. 110
D. Blumenthal (pno) ("Piano Sonatas, Vol. 2") † Jugendklänge; Son 3 Pno, Op. 109 MARC ▲ 8223474 (13.97)

FUCIK, JULIUS (1872-1916)

Der alte Brummbär [The Old Grumbler] (comic polka) for Bassoon & Orchestra, Op. 210
Barbaroque Ensemble [arr for bn, cl, vc, db & barrel org] † G. F. Handel:Cons (16) Org; P. Lavergne:Invariants; C. M. von Weber:Con Ob & Ww GALL ▲ 858 [DDD] (19.97)
M. Rothbauer (bn), D. Bostock (cnd), Carlsbad SO *(rec Karlovy Vary, Czech Republic, Jan 1996)* † Marinarella, Op. 215; A. Dvořák:Romance Vn, Op. 11; Fibich:Idyll; J. Labitzky:Carlsbad Waltz; A. Labitzky:Ouverture characteristique; Nedbal:Valse triste CLSO ▲ 150 (15.97)

Florentine March for Orchestra, Op. 214
K. Jeitler (cnd), Vienna Young Brass-Philharmonic *(rec Vienna, Austria, Dec 1989)* ("Radetzky-Marsch: Favorite Showpieces for Brass") † Mühlberger:Mir sein die Kaiserjäger; E. Strauss:Bahn frei, Op. 45; Joh. Strauss:Radetzky March, Op. 228; Strauss (II):Polkas; Waltzes; Jos. Strauss:Mein Lebenslauf ist Lieb und Lust, Op. 263; Moulinet, Op. 57; Ziehrer:Fesche Geister (ov) CAMA ▲ 140 [DDD] (18.97)

Marches & Waltzes
V. Neumann (cnd), Czech PO—Entrance of the gladiators; Mississippi River; Attila; Triglav (marches); Winterstürme; Donausagen; Traumideale (waltzes) † Marinarella, Op. 215; J. S. Bach:Suites Vc ORF ▲ 146852 [DDD] (36.97)

Marinarella (concert overture) for Orchestra, Op. 215
D. Bostock (cnd), Carlsbad SO *(rec Karlovy Vary, Czech Republic, Jan 1996)* † Alte Brummbär, Op. 210; A. Dvořák:Romance Vn, Op. 11; Fibich:Idyll; J. Labitzky:Carlsbad Waltz; A. Labitzky:Ouverture characteristique; Nedbal:Valse triste CLSO ▲ 150 (15.97)
V. Neumann (cnd), Czech PO † Marches & Waltzes; J. S. Bach:Suites Vc ORF ▲ 146852 [DDD] (36.97)

Music of Fučik
R. Jindra (ten), J. Moravec (bar), V. Mullerova (pno)—Serenade, Op. 19; Invresse Amoureusse, Op. 225; Scherzo, Op. 25; Devotion, Op. 291; Rondo, Op. 26; Ticha Laska, Op. 4; Noc, Op. 16; Symphonia Scandaleuse, Op. 29; Starnem, brachu, Op. 192; Die Gardinenpredikt, Op. 268 STMA ▲ 802 (18.97)

FUENLLANA, MIGUEL DE (ca 1525-1585/1605)

Orphénica lyra (collection of misc music) for Vihuela (or Guitar) (1554)
J. C. Rivera (vih) ("De los alamos se Sevilla: 16th Century Spanish Vihuela Music") † Mudarra:Libros de musica (sels) AL (Musical Heritage of Andalucía) ▲ 106 [DDD] (18.97)

FUGARINO, JOHN (JR.) (1961-

Riding on a Cloud for Orchestra
R. Stankovský (cnd), Slovak RSO Bratislava ("MMC New Century, Vol. II") † Crowell:Black Holes & Anti-Matters; Elkana:Color in Time; Giusto:Peace Cow (it's not a habit, I'm used to it); A. Hoose:Gestures & Intimations; Nytch:Novas MASM ▲ 2017 [DDD] (16.97)

FUHLER, COR (20th cent)

Cinéma for Chamber Ensemble [after Satie's *Entr'acte Symphonique* for Piano 4-Hands] (1924)
Altena Ensemble *(rec May 1996)* † M. Altena:ABCDE; Cantus; Trappel; A. Cameron:Leisure; Isadora:En/Of II; Padding:Ballad CV ▲ 69 [DDD] (18.97)

FUJIEDA, MAMORU (20th cent)

Music of Fujieda
M. Noguchi (vl), E. Ozawa (vl), K. Ishikawa (sho), M. Maruta (koto), Y. Nishi (koto), L. Teycheney (hpd)—Patterns of Plants: 1st Collection [patterns I-IV]; 2nd Collection [hitsu-koto suite: patterns V-VIII]; 3rd Collection [koto-gamelan set: patterns IX-XII]; 4th Collection; 5th Collection [hpd suite: patterns XVII-XX]; 6th Collection [patterns XXI-XXIV] ("Patterns of Plants") TZA (Composer) ▲ 7025 [DDD] (16.97)
M. Sakurai (sho), K. Ebihara (jumon), M. Fujueda (cmpt)—The Night Chant III; Wind Chant; Cocoon Chant; Duct Chant; Falling Chant ("The Night Chant") TZA (The Composers) ▲ 7003 [DDD] (16.97)

FUJITA, MASANORI (1946-

Ichingotoshi I for Percussion (1976)
S. Yoshihara (perc) *(rec 1976-81)* † Ichingotoshi II; Fukushi:Ground; Hachimura:Dolcissima Mia Vita, Op. 16 CAMA ▲ 314 [AAD] (18.97)

Ichingotoshi II for Percussion (1978)
S. Yoshihara (perc) *(rec 1976-81)* † Ichingotoshi I; Fukushi:Ground; Hachimura:Dolcissima Mia Vita, Op. 16 CAMA ▲ 314 [AAD] (18.97)

FUKUSHI, NORIO (1945-

Anima of a Tree for solo Percussion (1995)
A. Sugahara (perc) *(rec Chichibu Myuzu Park Ongaku-do, Oct 5-6, 1995)* ("13 Drums: Music for Percussion Solo") † T. Ichiyanagi:Portrait of Forest; Rhythm Gradation; Ikebe:Monovalence IV; M. Ishii:13 Drums; Kitazume:Shadows III-A; Y. Takahashi:Wolf CAMA ▲ 414 [DDD] (18.97)

Chromosphere for Percussion & Orchestra
J. Arase (perc), M. Okada (perc), S. Sato (perc), H. Yamazaki (perc), S. Yoshihara (perc), T. Otaka (cnd), Tokyo PO *(rec live Tokyo Bunka-Kaikan Large Hall, May 30, 1981)* † A. Otaka:Image Orch; J. Yuasa:Scenes from Basho CAMA ▲ 293 [AAD] (18.97)

Ground for Percussion
M. Leoson (perc) † B. T. Andersson:Apollo Con; Donatoni:Omar; D. Milhaud:Con Mar; T. Tanaka:Movts Perc; Xenakis:Rebonds Perc CAPA ▲ 21466 (16.97)

FUKUSHI, NORIO (cont.)

Ground for Percussion (cont.)
S. Yoshihara (perc) *(rec 1976-81)* † M. Fujita:Ichingotoshi I; Ichingotoshi II; Hachimura:Dolcissima Mia Vita, Op. 16 CAMA ▲ 314 [AAD] (18.97)

FULLMAN, ELLEN (1957-

Music for Long Strings
E. Fullman (strs), S. Lehman (strs), D. Massie (strs) ("Body Music") XIRE ▲ 109 [DDD]

FUMAROLA, MARTIN ALEJANDRO (1966-

Callejuelas for Computer (1996)
M. A. Fumarola (elec) ("Travels of the Spider") † Peregrinar de la Araña; Cromberg:Marimbágenes; Dal Ferra:Ashram; Due Giorni Dopo; Iglesias-Rossi:Ascencíon; Schachter:Tiempo Quebrado POGU ▲ 21015 (16.97)

El Peregrinar de la Araña for Computer (1995)
M. A. Fumarola (elec) ("Travels of the Spider") † Callejuelas; Cromberg:Marimbágenes; Dal Ferra:Ashram; Due Giorni Dopo; Iglesias-Rossi:Ascencíon; Schachter:Tiempo Quebrado POGU ▲ 21015 (16.97)

FUMET, RAPHAËL (1898-1979)

Flute Music
M. Poulet (vc), P. Pierlot (fl), G. Fumet (fl), B. Fromanger (fl), H. D. Villèle (fl) *(Cant Biblique)*, P. Pierlot (fl), G. Fumet (fl), B. Fromanger (fl) *(Trio for Fls)*, G. Caussé (va), G. Fumet (fl) *(Diptyque Baroque)*, G. Fumet (fl) *(Interpolaire)*, P. Pierlot (fl), G. Fumet (fl), B. Fromanger (fl), H. D. Villèle (fl) *(Quatuor [Scherzando])*, G. Fumet (fl), D. N'Kaoua (pno) *(Lacrymosa)*, G. Fumet (fl), G. Jarry (cnd), Jean-François Paillard CO *(Ode concertante) (rec Temple Saint-Marcel Paris, May & June 1995)* MARC ▲ 8223890 [DDD] (13.97)

FUNCK, DAVID (ca 1629-ca 1690)

Stricturae Viola di gambicea, ex sonatis, arris, intradis, allemandis for 4 Viola da gambas
Berlin PO Double Bass Quartet—Adagio; Allemande *(rec Berlin, Germany, Dec 1978)* † Alt:Suite; Chihara:Logs; Findeisen:Prelude; E. Hartmann:Quartet; Jorns:Mobile Perpetuum; W. A. Mozart:Ave verum corpus, K.618 CAMA ▲ 2562 [AAD] (18.97)

FUNDAL, KARSTEN (1966-

The Land of Mists (Anelsernes land) for Piano & Wind Ensemble
Jutland Ensemble † H. D. Koppel:Sxt Ww; F. Poulenc:Sxt Pno; M. Ravel:Tombeau PLAL ▲ 77 (18.97)

FUNK, ERIC (1949-

Concerto for Cello & Orchestra, Op. 55, "Homage to Jaqueline DuPré" (1991)
O. Ogranovitch (vc), V. Válek (cnd), Czech RSO *(rec 1994)* † Con Ob; Lidice; Sym 1 MASM ▲ 2033 [DDD] (16.97)

Concerto for Oboe & Orchestra, Op. 57 (1992)
M. Schuring (ob), V. Válek (cnd), Czech RSO *(rec 1994)* † Con Vc; Lidice; Sym 1 MASM ▲ 2033 [DDD] (16.97)

Lidice (symphonic poem) for Orchestra (1973)
V. Válek (cnd), Czech RSO *(rec 1994)* † Con Ob; Con Vc; Sym 1 MASM ▲ 2033 [DDD] (16.97)

Quartet No. 2 for Strings, "In Memoriam Shostakovich" (1993)
Moyzes String Quartet ("MMC Chamber Music Series, Vol. II") † P. Diehl:On Course; A. Hoose:Allegro Vn; Koplow:Vars on a Hymn Tune; Pond:Modal Vars; Son Pno; B. R. Wishart:Experience MASM ▲ 2030 [DDD] (16.97)

Symphony No. 1 for Orchestra, "Emily" (1978)
V. Válek (cnd), Czech RSO *(rec 1994)* † Con Ob; Con Vc; Lidice MASM ▲ 2033 [DDD] (16.97)

Symphony No. 3 for Clarinet & Orchestra, "Hradcany"
A. M. Baeza (cl), V. Válek (cnd), Czech RSO † Sym 4 MASM ▲ 2076 [DDD] (16.97)

Symphony No. 4 for Contralto & Orchestra [text A. Aizpuriete], Op. 75, "This Eventide Seems Spilt"
J. Swoboda (cnd), Warsaw National PO, J. Stabler (cta) † Sym 3 *([ENG] text)* MASM ▲ 2076 [DDD] (16.97)

FUNK PEARSON, STEPHEN (1950-

Elassomorph for 4 Guitars
JAM Quartet *(rec Helsinki, Finland, Aug 1998)* ("Jamerica") † Mummychogs; Chobanian:Sonics; C. Machado:Danças populares Brasileiras; A. Piazzolla:Music of Piazzolla; W. Siegel:East L.A. Phase BIS ▲ 977 [DDD] (17.97)
Minneapolis Guitar Quartet † S. Assad:Uarekena; Crittenden:Scottish Fantasy; Kalaniemi:Finnish Pieces; I. Stravinsky:Easy Pieces (5); Torroba:Estampas ALBA ▲ 339 [DDD] (16.97)

Mummychogs (Le Monde) for 4 Guitars
Buffalo Guitar Quartet ("New Music For Four Guitars") † Chobanian:Sonics; W. S. Hartley:Qt Gtrs; Ortiz-Alvarado:Abrazo; Piorkowski:Struggle of Jacob NWW ▲ 384 [DDD] (16.97)
JAM Quartet *(rec Helsinki, Finland, Aug 1998)* ("Jamerica") † Elassomorph; Chobanian:Sonics; C. Machado:Danças populares Brasileiras; A. Piazzolla:Music of Piazzolla; W. Siegel:East L.A. Phase BIS ▲ 977 [DDD] (17.97)

FURMAN, PABLO (1955-

Synergy for Flutes & Electronics (1989)
D. Lozano (fl), P. Furman (elec) *(rec Pasadena, CA, Nov 1997)* ("Music for Players & Digital Media") † Belet:[Mute]ation; Frengel:Three Short Stories; M. Helms:Whispering Modulations; D. Michael:Extensions #1; A. Strange:Shaman: Sisters of Dreamtime; Wyman:Through the Reed CENT ▲ 2404 (live) [DDD] (16.97)

FURRER, BEAT (1954-

Narcissus (opera in 6 scenes) [after Ovid's Metamorphoses] (1992-94)
R. Hofmann (sop), M. Oberholzer (bar), B. Furrer (cnd) , Stuttgart South Radio Chorus *(rec Solothur, Sept 1996)* MUSS ▲ 6143 [DDD] (17.97)

FÜRSTENAU, ANTON BERNHARD (1792-1852)

Music of Anton Fürstenau
J. Sommer (gtr), B. Larsen (fl), S. Cavalet (fl) ("The Fürstenaus") † C. Fürstenau:Music of CLSO ▲ 209 (15.97)

FÜRSTENAU, CASPAR (1772-1819)

Music of Caspar Fürstenau
J. Sommer (gtr), B. Larsen (fl), S. Cavalet (fl) ("The Fürstenaus") † A. B. Fürstenau:Music of CLSO ▲ 209 (15.97)

FURTWÄNGLER, WILHELM (1886-1954)

Concerto in b for Piano & Orchestra (1924-36)
D. Lively (pno), A. Walter (cnd), Czech-Slovak State SO MARC ▲ 8223333 (13.97)

Geisterchor [Chorus of Spirits] for Orchestra & Chorus [after Goethe] (1902)
A. Walter (cnd), Frankfurt on the Oder PO, Frankfurt on the Oder Phil Chorus *(rec Konzarthalle C.P.E. Bach Frankfurt on the Oder, June 22-25 1993)* † Religiöser Hymnus; Songs; Te Deum MARC ▲ 8223546 [DDD] (13.97)

Largo in b for Orchestra [1st movt of Symphony in b; rev as 1st movt of Symphony No. 1] (1908)
A. Walter (cnd), Slovak State PO Košice *(rec House of Arts Košice, Feb 12, 1993)* † Ov; Sym in D MARC ▲ 8223645 [DDD] (13.97)

Overture in E♭ for Orchestra, Op. 3 (1899)
A. Walter (cnd), Slovak State PO Košice *(rec House of Arts Košice, June 30, 1993)* † Largo; Sym in D MARC ▲ 8223645 [DDD] (13.97)

Quintet for Piano & Strings (1915-34)
D. Bellik (pno), Elyséen String Quartet BAYE ▲ 100269 [ADD] (17.97)
F. Kerdoncuff (pno), Sine Nomine String Quartet TIMP ▲ 1018 [DDD] (18.97)

Religiöser Hymnus for Soprano, Tenor, Orchestra & Chorus [after Goethe] (1903)
G. Pikal (ten), A. Walter (cnd), Frankfurt on the Oder PO, Frankfurt on the Oder Phil Chorus *(rec Konzarthalle C.P.E. Bach Frankfurt on the Oder, June 22-25 1993)* † Geisterchor; Songs; Te Deum MARC ▲ 8223546 [DDD] (13.97)

Sonata No. 2 in D for Violin & Piano (1938)
A. Galpérine (vn), F. Kerdoncuff (pno) *(rec 1989)* TIMP ▲ 1001 [DDD] (18.97)
W. Müller-Nishio (vn), R. Dennemarck (pno) BAYE ▲ 100268 [ADD] (17.97)

Songs
G. Pikal (ten), A. Walter (pno), A. Walter (cnd), Frankfurt on the Oder PO, Frankfurt on the Oder Phil Chorus—Der traurige Jäger; Der Schatzgräber; Geduld; Auf dem See; Du sendest, Freund, mir Lieder; Erinnerung; Das Vaterland; Möwenflug; Der Soldat *(rec Maison de la Radio Bruxelles, Oct 7-8, 1993)* † Geisterchor; Religiöser Hymnus; Te Deum MARC ▲ 8223546 [DDD] (13.97)

Symphony No. 1 in b (1938-41)
A. Walter (cnd), Czech-Slovak State PO MARC ▲ 8223295 (13.97)

Symphony No. 2 in e (1944-45)
W. Furtwängler (cnd), Berlin PO *(rec Jesus-Christus Church Berlin, Germany, Nov-Dec 1951)* † R. Schumann:Sym 4 DEUT (The Originals) 2-▲ 457722 [ADD] (22.97)
W. Furtwängler (cnd), Vienna PO *(rec live, Feb 22, 1953)* ORFE ▲ 375941 (16.97)
A. Walter (cnd), BBC SO MARC ▲ 8223436 (13.97)

Symphony No. 3 in c# [complete 4-movt version] (1947-54)
W. Sawallisch (cnd), Bavarian State Orch *(rec Bavarian Radio National Theater Munich, Jan 7, 1980)* ORFE ▲ 406961 (16.97)
A. Walter (cnd), RTBF SO MARC ▲ 8223105 (13.97)

FURTWÄNGLER, WILHELM (cont.)

Symphony in D (1903)

A. Walter (cnd), Slovak State PO Košice *(rec House of Arts Košice, Feb 12, 1993)* † Largo; Ov MARC ▲ 8223645 [DDD] (13.97)

Te Deum for Soloists, Orchestra & Chorus (1902-10; rev 1915)

A. Walter (cnd), Frankfurt on the Oder PO, Frankfurt on the Oder Phil Chorus *(rec Konzarthalle C.P.E. Bach Frankfurt on the Oder, June 22-25 1993)* † Geisterchor; Religiöser Hymnus; Songs MARC ▲ 8223546 [DDD] (13.97)

FUSSELL, CHARLES C. (1938-

Being Music for solo Voice, String Quartet & Chorus [text W. Whitman]

S. Sylvan (bar), Lydian String Quartet, D. Hoose (cnd), Cantata Singers † Specimen Days KOCH ▲ 7338 (10.97)

Specimen Days for solo Voice, String Quartet & Chorus [text W. Whitman]

S. Sylvan (bar), Lydian String Quartet, D. Hoose (cnd), Cantata Singers † Being Music KOCH ▲ 7338 (10.97)

FÜSSL, KARL HEINZ (1924-

Duo for Cello & Piano

A. Chitta (vc), S. Chitta (pno) *(rec Vienna, Jan 1989)* ("Music for Cello & Piano") † Fünf Töne—Fünf Finger; Hueber:Capriccio Vc; Son Pno; Son Vc & Pno; Son 2 Vc VMM ▲ 2010 [DDD]

Fünf Töne—Fünf Finger [5 Tones—5 Fingers] (6 small pieces) for Piano

S. Chitta (pno) *(rec Vienna, Jan 1989)* ("Music for Cello & Piano") † Duo Vc & Pno; Hueber:Capriccio Vc; Son Pno; Son Vc & Pno; Son 2 Vc VMM ▲ 2010 [DDD]

FUX, JOHANN JOSEF (1660-1741)

Concentus Musico-Instrumentalis for Orchestra (1701)

L. Duftschmid (cnd), Armonico Tributo Austria ACN ▲ 58 (18.97)

Dafne in Lauro (opera in 1 act) [lib P. Pariati] (1714)

R. Clemencic (cnd) , La Cappella, M. Sluis (sop), L. Akerlund (sop), S. Piccollo (sop), G. Lesne (ct), M. Klietmann (ten) [ITA] NUO (Ancient Music) 2-▲ 6930 [DDD] (32.97)

Keyboard Music

R. Köhnen (hpd)—Harpeggio & Fuga in G; Ciaconna in D; Suite in a [period instr] ("Works for Keyboard") † J. Haydn:Pno Music ACCE ▲ 8222 [DDD] (17.97)

Missa Corporis Christi for SATB Soloists, Orchestra & Chorus (1713)

D. Minter (alt), D. Cordier (male sop), J. Chum (ten), K. Mertens (bass), M. Haselböck (cnd), Vienna Academy Orch, Vienna Academy Choir *(rec Hofburg Vienna, May 19-22, 1997)* † Paries quidem filium; Plaudite, sonat tuba; Victimae paschali laudes *(L,E texts)* CPO ▲ 999528 [DDD] (13.97)

Paries quidem filium (motet) for SATB Soloists, Orchestra & Chorus

D. Minter (alt), D. Cordier (male sop), J. Chum (ten), K. Mertens (bass), M. Haselböck (cnd), Vienna Academy Orch, Vienna Academy Choir *(rec Hofburg Vienna, May 19-22, 1997)* † Missa Corporis; Plaudite, sonat tuba; Victimae paschali laudes *(L,E texts)* CPO ▲ 999528 [DDD] (13.97)

Plaudite, sonat tuba (cantata) for Tenor, Trumpet, Orchestra & Chorus, FWV 165

J. Chum (ten), A. Lackner (tpt), M. Haselböck (cnd), Vienna Academy Orch, Vienna Academy Choir *(rec Hofburg Vienna, May 19-22, 1997)* † Missa Corporis; Paries quidem filium; Victimae paschali laudes *(L,E texts)* CPO ▲ 999528 [DDD] (13.97)

Victimae Paschali Laudes for SATB Soloists, Orchestra & Chorus

D. Minter (alt), D. Cordier (male sop), J. Chum (ten), K. Mertens (bass), M. Haselböck (cnd), Vienna Academy Orch, Vienna Academy Choir *(rec Hofburg Vienna, May 19-22, 1997)* † Missa Corporis; Paries quidem filium; Plaudite, sonat tuba *(L,E texts)* CPO ▲ 999528 [DDD] (13.97)

FUZZY (1939-

B-Movies for Harp & Computer (1997)

S. A. Claro (hp) † Frounberg:Worlds Apart; Graugaard:Incrustations; Kanding:Entbergen DCAP ▲ 8224113 (13.97)

Fireplay for 2 Percussion

Safri Duo ("Works for Percussion") † A. Koppel:Toccata; M. Miki:Mar Spiritual; Nørgård:Echo Zone I-III; A. Pape:CaDance CHN (New Direction) ▲ 9330 [DDD] (16.97)

GAATHAUG, MORTEN (1955-

Chamber Music

artists unknown—Son Vn, Op. 30; Qt 1 Strs, Op. 7; Son Cl, Op. 34 NORW ▲ 2925 (17.97)

Sonata Concertante for Tuba & Brass Quintet

O. Baadsvik (tuba), Swedish Brass Quintet † P. Hindemith:Son Bass Tuba; W. Kraft:Encounters II; T. Madsen:Son Tuba, Op. 34; Sivelöv:Son Tuba, Op. 5 SIMX ▲ 1101 (18.97)

GABRIEL, JUAN (20th cent)

Music of Gabriel

J. Ferrer (cnd) ("Clasicos Mexico, Vol. 6") GLMU ▲ 8546

GABRIELI, ANDREA (1533-1585)

Anchor che col partire for Recorder, Viol & Harpsichord

P. Hannan (rcr), C. Thielmann (va da gamba), C. Tilney (hpd) *(rec Toronto, Canada)* † G. Bassano:Anchor che col partire; Gai bergier; Cima:Sons (2); Frescobaldi:Canzonas, Caprici & Ricercari; G. F. Handel:Son Rcr; Telemann:Essercizii Musici SMS ▲ 5049 [DDD] (16.97)

Keyboard Music

S. Henstra (hpd)—Canzon francese detta Petit Jacquet; Canzon francese detta Le bergier; Canzon francese detta Je ne diray moy bergièr ("Toccate, partite et passacagli") † Frescobaldi:Hpd Music; Merula:Kbd Music; G. Picchi:Kbd Music; B. Storace:Kbd Music RICE ▲ 167136 (17.97)

R. Villani (org)—Toccata per organo del IX tono; Intonazioni per organo del I, II, IV, VI & VII ton *(rec Nov 7-9, 1993)* ("The Complete Works of Adrian Willaert, Vol. 2") STRV ▲ 33326 [DDD] (16.97)

GABRIELI, GIOVANNI (ca 1554/57-1612)

Canticle Jubilate Deo à 18 for Chorus [from Sinfonie Sacrae]

J. E. Gardiner (cnd), Monteverdi Choir London ("Jubilate Deo!") † Monteverdi:Madrigals Book 8; F. Poulenc:Figure humaine; H. Purcell:Anthems & Services; J. Tavener:World Is Burning PPHI ▲ 46116 (16.97)

Canzoni for Brass Choirs

Chicago Brass Ensemble, Philadelphia Brass Ensemble, Cleveland Brass Ensemble *(Canzon per Sonare Nos 2, 27 & 28; Canzon a 12)*, E. P. Biggs (org) *(Canzon per Sonare No 1, "Las Spiritata"; Canzona per Sonare Nos 3 & 4) (rec Cambridge, MA, 1959 & 1968)* ("Antiphonal Music of Gabrieli") † Fant VI toni; Intonationi; Sacrae symphoniae; Frescobaldi:Music of Frescobaldi SNYC (Masterworks Heritage) ▲ 62353 [ADD] (12.97)

Empire Brass Quintet TEL ▲ 80204 [DDD] (16.97)

Summit Brass—3 sels from Symphoniae Sacrae (1597) & 4 sels from; plus 3 Canzoni by contemporaries Orindio Bartolino † J. S. Bach:Cant 147; Fugue Org, BWV 578; Music of Bach; Toccata & Fugue Org, BWV 565 SUMM ▲ 101 [DDD] (16.97)

Canzoni et sonate (21) for Various Instruments & Organ (1615)

R. Clemencic (cnd) , R. Clemencic (cnd), Consort Fontegara *(rec July 1995)* TACT ▲ 550701 [DDD] (16.97)

Choral Music

H. Stinders (org), E. van Nevel (cnd), Concerto Palatino, E. van Nevel (cnd), Currende Consort—In te Domine speravi; Beata es virgo [2 versions]; Sancta et immaculata Virginitas; Angelus Domini; O Jesu mi dulcissime; Canzon III [from Canzoni e Sonate]; Exultavit cor meum; Benedictus es Dominus; Hodie completi sunt ("Venetian Music for Double Choir") † Willaert:Ricercars ACCE ▲ 93101 [DDD] (17.97)

Wilbraham Brass Soloists, D. Willcocks (cnd), Bach Choir, D. Willcocks (cnd), King's College Choir Cambridge † Monteverdi:Vespro della Beata Vergine; Scheidt:Music of Scheidt; H. Schütz:Choral Music EMIC (Doublefforte) 2-▲ 68631 (16.97)

Exaudi me Domine for 16 Voices (1615)

P. van Nevel (cnd), Huelgas Ensemble † Josquin Desprez:Qui habitat in adjutorio Altissimi; Manchicourt:Laudate Dominum; Ockeghem:Deo gratias; C. Porta:Masses; Striggio:Ecce beatam lucem; Tallis:Spem in alium SNYC (Vivarte) ▲ 66261 (16.97)

Fantasia VI toni for Chamber Ensemble

E. P. Biggs (org), Boston Brass Ensemble *(rec Cambridge, MA, 1959)* ("Antiphonal Music of Gabrieli") † Canzoni for Brass Choirs; Intonationi; Sacrae symphoniae; Frescobaldi:Music of Frescobaldi SNYC (Masterworks Heritage) ▲ 62353 [ADD] (12.97)

Guitar Transcriptions

Los Angeles Guitar Quartet—trans of Canzons VI & XI; Canon per sonar primi toni; Son XIII *(rec Apr-May 1992)* † T. Morley:Dances; P. Tchaikovsky:Nutcracker Suite, Op. 71a; Warlock:Capriol Suite DLS ▲ 3132 [DDD] (14.97) ▮ 3132 [DDD] (7.98)

Intonationi d'organo [Book I; formerly attrib A. Gabrieli]

E. P. Biggs (org), Boston Brass Ensemble *(rec Cambridge, MA, 1959)* ("Antiphonal Music of Gabrieli") † Canzoni for Brass Choirs; Fant VI toni; Sacrae symphoniae; Frescobaldi:Music of Frescobaldi SNYC (Masterworks Heritage) ▲ 62353 [ADD] (12.97)

GABRIELI, GIOVANNI (cont.)

Music of Gabrieli

R. Clemencic (rcr), A. Heiller (hpd), H. Tachezi (pno), E. Appia (cnd), Gabrieli Festival Orch, Gabrieli Festival Chorus—Processional & Ceremonial Music; originally released as Bach Guild BGS 5004; O magnum mysterium; Nunc dimittis; Angelus ad pastores; O Jesu mi dulcissime; Exaudi Deus; Hodie completi sunt; O Domine Jesu Christe; Canzona Quarti Toni a 15 (ricercar); Inclina Domine *(rec Vienna, Feb 1958)* VC (The Bach Guild) ▲ 2007 [ADD] (13.97)

D. Cordier (ct), R. Müller (ten), W. Jochens (ten), G. Türk (ten), H. V. Kamp (bass), R. Wilson (cnd) , La Capella Ducale—Toccata [arr Wilson]; Buccinate in neomenia tuba; Canzon XVII à 12; Dulcis Jesu patris imago [Son con voce à 20]; Timor et remor à 6; Son con 3 Vns; Son XIX à 15; In ecclesiis à 14; Canzon V à 7; Jubilate Deo à 10; Son XVIII à 14; Cant Domino à 8; Canzon primi toni à 10; Misericordia tua Domine à 12; Canzon X à 8; Toccata primi toni; Magnificat à 33 [reconstructed by Wilson]; Benedictus es Dominus à 8 *(rec Mandelsloh Germany, June 11-15, 1994)* ("The Feast of San Rocco, Venice 1608") † Cima:Son Tpt; Son Vn & Tpt; Son Vn & Vle; A. Grandi:Sacred Music; Monteverdi:Salve regina (1) Voice, M.xvi/502 SNYC (Vivarte) 2-▲ 66254 [DDD] (31.97)

P. Goodwin (cnd), Academy of Ancient Music, Academy of Ancient Music Chorus ("A Christmas Collection") † H. Schütz:Music of HAM ▲ 907202 (18.97)

P. McCreesh (cnd) , Gabrieli Consort—Toccata; In ecclesiis; Son 19; Suscipe, clementissime Deus; Canzona 14; Buccinate in neomenia tuba; Intonazione del nono tono; Domine Deus meus; Son 21 con tre violini; Timor et tremor; Intonazione duodecimo tono; Jubilate Deo; Son 18; Misericordia tua, Domine; Son 20; Magnificat *(rec Suola Grande di San Rocco Venice, Italy, Aug 1995)* ("Music for San Rocco") † Barbarino:Music of Barbarino PARC ▲ 49180 [DDD] (16.97)

E. Tarr (cnd) —Raveri-Sammlung; Symphoniae Sacrae I & II *(rec Ilbenstadt Basilika, Nov 1992)* † H. Eisler:Kammersinfonie, Op. 69; Kleine Sinf, Op. 29; Orchesterstücke; Pieces (3) Orch; Sturm-Suite; G. Guami:Canzonas; Schelle:Actus Musicus auf Weyh-Nachten; H. Schütz:Weihnachtshistorie CAPO ▲ 10500 [DDD] (10.97)

O magnum mysterium for Chorus (1587)

J. Bowman (ct), R. King (cnd), King's Consort ("The James Bowman Collection") † Anonymous:Come tread the paths; J. S. Bach:Arias; St. Matthew Passion (sels); T. Ford:Since First I Saw Your Face; G. F. Handel:Music of Handel; H. Purcell:Sacred Music; Songs; Symphonic Poems (misc) HYP ▲ 3 (7.97)

Sacrae symphoniae for Instruments & Chorus

Chicago Brass Ensemble, Philadelphia Brass Ensemble, Cleveland Brass Ensemble *(rec Philadelphia, MA, 1968)* ("Antiphonal Music of Gabrieli") † Canzoni for Brass Choirs; Fant VI toni; Intonationi; Frescobaldi:Music of Frescobaldi SNYC (Masterworks Heritage) ▲ 62353 [ADD] (12.97)

T. Roberts (cnd) HYP ▲ 66908 (18.97)

Sacred Music

E. P. Biggs (org), La Fenice Ensemble, Edward Tarr Brass Ensemble, Gregg Smith Singers, Texas Boys' Choir—Deus, in nomine tuo; Beata es, virgo Maria; Juilemus singuli; Deus, Deus meus, ad te de luce vigilo; O quam suavis est; Kyrie; Sanctus; Benedictus; Cant Domino; Domine, exuadi orationem meam; Hodie completi sunt; Magnificat; Surrexit Christus; Nunc dimittis; Jubilate Deo; Intonatio *(rec San Marco Venice, Sept 14-22, 1967)* ("Gabrieli in San Marco") SNYC (Essential Classics) ▲ 62426 [ADD] (7.97) ▮ 62426 [ADD] (3.98)

Sonata pian' e forte for Brass [from Symphoniae Sacrae, 1597]

L. Stokowski (cnd), Sym of the Air [orchd Fritz Stein] *(rec Carnegie Hall, 1958)* † Frescobaldi:Gagliarda; Palestrina:Adoramus te Christe; O. Respighi:Pini di Roma; D. Shostakovich:Sym 1 EMIC ▲ 66864 [ADD] (11.97)

GABRIELLI, DOMENICO (1651-1690)

Canon for 2 Cellos

R. Dieltiens (vc), R. V. Meer (vc) *(rec Haarlem, Germany, Sep 1990)* ("Italian Cello Music") † Ricercares for solo Cello; Vc Music; G. Bononcini:Son in a 2 Vc; Fesch:Son Vc; B. Marcello:Son Vc Bc in g, Op. 2/4; A. Scarlatti:Son Vc ACCE ▲ 9070 [DDD] (17.97)

Cello Music

R. Dieltiens (vc), R. V. Meer (vc) *(Son Vc & Bc in G; Son Vc & Bc in A) (rec Haarlem, Germany, Sep 1990)*, R. Dieltiens (vc), R. V. Meer (vc), K. Junghänel (thb), R. Köhnen (hpd) *(Music by Bononcini (Son in a for 2 Vcs); Ricercare I-VII; Canon for 2 Vcs)* ("Italian Cello Music") † Canon for 2 Vc; Ricercares for solo Cello; G. Bononcini:Son in a 2 Vc; Fesch:Son Vc; B. Marcello:Son Vc Bc in g, Op. 2/4; A. Scarlatti:Son Vc ACCE ▲ 9070 [DDD] (17.97)

Ricercares for solo Cello

R. Dieltiens (vc), R. V. Meer (vc) *(rec Haarlem, Germany, Sep 1990)* ("Italian Cello Music") † Canon for 2 Vc; Vc Music; G. Bononcini:Son in a 2 Vc; Fesch:Son Vc; B. Marcello:Son Vc Bc in g, Op. 2/4; A. Scarlatti:Son Vc ACCE ▲ 9070 [DDD] (17.97)

Sonatas for Trumpet & Strings

G. Cassone (tpt), Pian e Forte Ensemble—Son 2 Tpt, D.11; Son 5 Tpt, D.11 *(rec Feb 17-20, 1992)* ("The Trumpet in San Petronio") † Cazzati:Sons 5 Instr, Op. 35; Grossi:Sons; Jacchini:Sons Tpt; Torelli:Concertino per camera, Op. 4; Sinf Tpt, G.9; Son Tpt, G.1 NUO (Ancient Music) ▲ 7128 [DDD] (16.97)

Sonata No. 4 in D for Trumpet & Strings

J. Schäfer (tpt), A. Popović (cnd) *(rec Dresden, Nov 1997)* ("Concertos for Piccolo Trumpet") † Romanino:Con Tpt; Schwartzkopff:Suite Tpt CHR ▲ 77210 [DDD] (17.97)

GABUNIJA, NODAR (1933-

Sinfonia Gioconda for Chamber Orchestra (1988)

L. Issakadze (cnd), Georgian CO † Nasidze:Con Vn; Taktakishvili:Con 2 Vn; Zinzadse:Phantasie Vn ORF ▲ 304921 [DDD] (18.97)

GABURO, KENNETH (1926-1993)

Antiphony X for Organ & Tape, "Winded" (1991)

G. Verkade (org) ("Winded: Works for Organ & Tape by, of & for Kenneth Gaburo") † P. Blackburn:P.P.S.; W. Burt:Recitative/Tracing Org INNO ▲ 524 [DDD]

GACE BRULE (ca 1160-1213)

Quant voi la flor botoner, R.838

Alla Francesca ("Richard Coeur De Lion:Troubadours et Trouvères") † Chastelain de Couci:Li nouviaus tans; Conon de Béthune:Bien me deüsse targier; Faidit:Fortz causa es; Richard I, Coeur-de-Lion:Ja nuns hons pris; Ventadorn:Can vei la lauzeta OPUS ▲ 30170 (18.97)

GADE, JACOB (1879-1963)

Funeral Music at the Bier of Gustav Esmann for Band

J. M. Jensen (cnd), Danish Concert Band *(rec 1998-99)* ("Visions from the North") † Åkerwall:Ergesia; Almila:Visions from the North; M. Andresen:Con Tpt; V. Brandt:Concertpiece 2 Tpt, Op. 12; D. W. Jenkins:Con A Sax; Ticheli:Blue Shades ROND ▲ 8368 (18.97)

GADE, NIELS WILHELM (1817-1890)

Akvareller for Piano, Op. 19 (1850)

D. Joeres (pno) *(rec Nov 1991)* ("Schumann & His Friends") † Idyller, Op.34; J. Brahms:Ballades (4), Op. 10; S. Heller:Traumbilder, Op. 79; T. Kirchner:Nachtbilder, Op. 25; R. Schumann:Kinderszenen Pno, Op. 15 INMP ▲ 1044 [DDD] (11.97)

Allegro in a for String Quartet

Kontra String Quartet *(rec Humlebaek, Denmark, May 5-8, 1992)* † Andante & Allegro molto; Octet; Qt in F Strs BIS ▲ 545 [DDD] (17.97)

Andante & Allegro molto in f for 2 Violins, Viola & 2 Cellos (1837)

H. Nygaard (vc), Kontra String Quartet *(rec Humlebaek, Denmark, May 5-8, 1992)* † Allegro Str Qt; Octet; Qt in F Strs BIS ▲ 545 [DDD] (17.97)

M. Rachlevsky (cnd), Kremlin CO [arr Rachelevsky] † Novelletter, Op. 53; Novelletter, Op. 58 CLAV ▲ 9607 (16.97)

Comala (cantata) for solo Voices, Orchestra & Chorus (1846)

F. Rasmussen (cnd), South Jutland SO, Canzone Choir KPT ▲ 32180 [DDD]

Concerto in d for Violin & Orchestra, Op. 56

A. Kontra (vn), P. Järvi (cnd), Malmö SO *(rec Malmö Concert Hall Sweden, Aug 23-25, 1994)* † O. Schmidt:Öresund Sym BIS ▲ 672 [DDD] (17.97)

Echoes of Ossian (concert overture) for Orchestra, Op. 1 (1840)

D. Joeres (cnd), Royal PO † Mendelssohn (-Bartholdy):Hebriden, Op. 26; R. Schumann:Ov, Scherzo & Finale, Op. 52; Sterndale-Bennett:Naiads INMP (Classics) ▲ 6700152 (9.97)

D. Kitaienko (cnd), Danish National RSO † Elverskud, Op. 30; Songs CHN ▲ 9075 [DDD] (16.97)

D. Kitaienko (cnd), Danish National RSO † Hamlet (ov); Sym 1 CHN ▲ 9422 (16.97)

O. Schmidt (cnd), Rhineland-Palatinate State PO *(rec Oct 17-20, 1995)* † Hamlet (ov); Holbergiana, Op. 61; Summer's Day in the Country, Op. 55 CPO ▲ 999362 [DDD] (14.97)

Elverskud [The Earl King's Daughter] (cantata) for Vocal Soloists, Orchestra & Chorus [text C. K. F. Molbech], Op. 30 (1853)

L. Balslev (sop), E. Guillaume (mez), M. Melbye (bar), F. Rasmussen (cnd), Collegium Musicum, Canzone Choir [DAN] KPT ▲ 32070 [DDD]

GADE, NIELS WILHELM (cont.)
Elverskud [The Earl King's Daughter] (cantata) for Vocal Soloists, Orchestra & Chorus [text C. K. F. Molbech], Op. 30 (1853) (cont.)
S. Elmark (sop—Elf-King's Daughter), K. Dolberg (mez—Mother), G. Paëvatalu (bar—Oluf), M. Schønwandt (cnd), Tivoli SO, Tivoli Concert Choir *(rec Tivoli Concert Hall, Apr 29-30 & May 4, 1996)* † Frühlings Fant, Op. 23 MARC ▲ 8224051 [DDD] (13.97)
E. Johansson (sop), A. Gjevang (mez), P. Elming (ten), D. Kitaienko (cnd), Danish National RSO, Danish National Radio Chamber Choir [DAN] † Echoes of Ossian, Op. 1; Songs CHN ▲ 9075 [DDD] (16.97)
Et folkesagn (ballet in 3 acts) for Orchestra [after A. Bournonville; act 2 by J. P. E. Hartmann] (1853-4; arr for pno 4-hands)
H. Damgaard (cnd), Danish Radio Sinfonietta *(rec Danish Radio Concert Hall, Aug 1995)* CPO 2-▲ 999426 [DDD] (27.97)

Fantasistykker for Clarinet & Piano, Op. 43 (1864)
K. Leister (cl), F. Bognár (pno) † Beethoven:Duos Cl, WoO 27; E. Elgar:Romance Bn, Op. 62; M. Glinka:Trio pathétique; F. Poulenc:Son Cl & Bn CAMA ▲ 370 [DDD] (18.97)
N. Thomsen (cl), E. Westenholz (pno) † J. Brahms:Sons Cl KPT ▲ 32078 [DDD]
Frühlings Fantasie for solo Voices, Piano & Orchestra, Op. 23 (1852)
A. M. Dahl (sop), K. Dolberg (mez), G. Hennig-Jensen (ten), S. Byriel (b-bar), E. Westenholz (pno), M. Schønwandt (cnd), Tivoli SO *(rec Tivoli Concert Hall, Apr 29-30 & May 4, 1996)* † Elverskud, Op. 30 MARC ▲ 8224051 [DDD] (13.97)

Gefion (cantata) for Baritone, Orchestra & Chorus, Op. 54 (1869)
P. Høyer (bar), F. Rasmussen (cnd), Aalborg SO † Heilige Nacht, Op. 40; Zion KPT ▲ 32149 [DDD]
Hamlet:Overture
D. Kitaienko (cnd), Danish National RSO † Echoes of Ossian, Op. 1; Sym 1 CHN ▲ 9422 (16.97)
O. Schmidt (cnd), Rhineland-Palatinate State PO *(rec Oct 17-20, 1995)* † Echoes of Ossian, Op. 1; Holbergiana, Op. 61; Summer's Day in the Country, Op. 55 CPO ▲ 999362 [DDD] (14.97)
Die heilige Nacht (cantata) in A for Orchestra & Chorus, Op. 40 (1862)
F. Rasmussen (cnd), Aalborg SO † Gefion; Zion KPT ▲ 32149 [DDD]
Holbergiana (suite) for Orchestra, Op. 61
O. Schmidt (cnd), Rhineland-Palatinate State PO *(rec Oct 17-20, 1995)* † Echoes of Ossian, Op. 1; Hamlet (ov); Summer's Day in the Country, Op. 55 CPO ▲ 999362 [DDD] (14.97)
Idyller for Piano, Op.34 (1857)
D. Joeres (pno) *(rec Nov 1991)* ("Schumann & His Friends") † Akvareller, Op. 19; J. Brahms:Ballades (4), Op. 10; S. Heller:Traumbilder, Op. 79; T. Kirchner:Nachtbilder, Op. 25; R. Schumann:Kinderszenen Pno, Op. 15 INMP ▲ 1044 [DDD] (11.97)
Kalanus (cantata) for solo Voices, Orchestra & Chorus [text by C. Andersen], Op. 48
M. Rørholm (mez), N. Gedda (ten), L. Mróz (bass), F. Rasmussen (cnd), Collegium Musicum, Canzone Choir KPT ▲ 32072 [DDD]
Korsfarerne [The Crusader] (cantata) for solo Voices, Orchestra & Chorus [text by C. Andersen], Op. 50 (1865-66)
M. Rørholm (mez), K. Westi (ten), U. Cold (bass), F. Rasmussen (cnd), Aarhus SO, Aarhus Sym Chorus [DAN] BIS ▲ 465 [DDD] (17.97)

Music of Gade
S. Elbæk (vn), E. Westenholz (pno)—Volkstanze, Op. 62; Elegie, Op. 19/1; Scherzo, 19/1; Canzonette, Op. 19/3; Abenddämmerung, Op. 34/4; Allegro Vivace in A; Fantasiestücke, Op. 43; Capriccio in a ("Works for Violin & Piano") KPT ▲ 32164 [DDD]
Novelettes (5) for Violin, Cello & Piano, Op. 29 (1863)
Copenhagen Trio † Trio Movt; Trio Pno, Op. 42 KPT ▲ 32077 [DDD]
Novelletter in F for String Orchestra, Op. 53
O. V. Larsen (cnd), Aarhus CO *(rec Aarhus, Denmark, 1981)* † Novelletter, Op. 58 PLAL ▲ 12 [AAD] (18.97)
Louisiana Museum Art Ensemble † Novelletter, Op. 58 CLSO ▲ 1001 (15.97)
M. Rachlevsky (cnd), Kremlin CO † Andante & Allegro molto; Novelletter, Op. 58 CLAV ▲ 9607 (16.97)
Novelletter in E for String Orchestra, Op. 58 (1883; rev 1886)
O. V. Larsen (cnd), Aarhus CO *(rec Aarhus Denmark, 1981)* † Novelletter, Op. 53 PLAL ▲ 12 [AAD] (18.97)
Louisiana Museum Art Ensemble † Novelletter, Op. 53 CLSO ▲ 1001 (15.97)
M. Rachlevsky (cnd), Kremlin CO † Andante & Allegro molto; Novelletter, Op. 53 CLAV ▲ 9607 (16.97)
Octet in F for 4 Violins, 2 Violas & 2 Cellos, Op. 17
A. Egendal (vn), P. L. Madsen (vn), S. Ranmo (va), H. Nygaard (vc), Kontra String Quartet *(rec Humlebaek, Denmark, May 5-8, 1992)* † Allegro Str Qt; Andante & Allegro molto; Qt in F Strs BIS ▲ 545 [DDD] (17.97)
Smithsonian Chamber Players, L'Archibudelli † Mendelssohn (-Bartholdy):Octet Strs, Op. 20 SNYC (Vivarte) ▲ 48307 (16.97)
South German String Octet † D. Shostakovich:Pieces Str Octet, Op. 11; J. S. Svendsen:Octet Strs, Op. 3 PKST ▲ 10294 [DDD] (15.99)

Piano Music (complete)
A. Blyme (pno)—3 Pno Pieces; Scherzo in f#/F#; Little Pno Story; Dithyrambe; Impromptu in f#; Allegretto grazioso; 30 Scandanavian Folksongs; Saltarella in D; 10 Watercolor Sketches, Op. 19; 3 Album Leaves *(rec May-Nov 1990)* ("Vol. 1") DCAP ▲ 9115 [DDD] (13.97)
A. Blyme (pno)—Calendar; Scherzino & Barcarolle; Arabesque, Op. 27; Son in e, Op. 28; 4 Fant Pieces, Op. 31; Folk Dance & Romance; 8 Pno Pieces (from the Sketch-Book); 4 Idylls, Op. 34 *(rec May-Nov 1990)* ("Vol. 2") DCAP ▲ 9116 [DDD] (13.97)

Psyche (cantata) for solo Voices, Orchestra & Chorus, Op. 60 (1881-82)
A. M. Dahl (sop), H. C. Pedersen (sop), K. Hamnøy (sop), S. Andersen (ten), M. Kristensen (ten), F. Rasmussen (cnd), Canzone Choir *(rec Apr 27-28, 1996)* KPT 2-▲ 32244
Quartets (3) for Strings (complete)
Kontra String Quartet BIS ▲ 516 [DDD] (17.97)
Quartet in D for Strings, Op. 63 (1889)
Copenhagen String Quartet *(rec Copenhagen, 1963 & 1968)* † Qt in e Strs; Qt in F Strs MARC ▲ 8224015 [ADD] (13.97)

Quartet in F for Strings (1830s)
Copenhagen String Quartet *(rec Copenhagen, 1963 & 1968)* † Qt in e Strs; Qt Strs, Op. 63 MARC ▲ 8224015 [ADD] (13.97)
Kontra String Quartet *(rec Humlebaek, Denmark, May 5-8, 1992)* † Allegro Str Qt; Andante & Allegro molto; Octet BIS ▲ 545 [DDD] (17.97)
Quartet in e for Strings (1877)
Copenhagen String Quartet *(rec Copenhagen, 1963 & 1968)* † Qt in F Strs; Qt Strs, Op. 63 MARC ▲ 8224015 [ADD] (13.97)
Songs (5) for a cappella Chorus, Op. 13
S. Parkman (cnd), Danish National Radio Chamber Choir [GER] † Echoes of Ossian, Op. 1; Elverskud, Op. 30 CHN ▲ 9075 [DDD] (16.97)

A Summer's Day in the Country for 5 Piece Orchestra, Op. 55 (1879)
O. Schmidt (cnd), Rhineland-Palatinate State PO *(rec Oct 17-20, 1995)* † Echoes of Ossian, Op. 1; Hamlet (ov); Holbergiana, Op. 61 CPO ▲ 999362 [DDD] (14.97)
Symphony No. 1 in c, Op. 5
N. Järvi (cnd), Stockholm Sinfonietta † Sym 8 BIS ▲ 339 (17.97)
D. Kitaienko (cnd), Danish National RSO † Echoes of Ossian, Op. 1; Hamlet (ov) CHN ▲ 9422 (16.97)
M. Schønwandt (cnd), Copenhagen Collegium Musicum † Sym 2 DCAP ▲ 9201 (13.97)
Symphony No. 2 in E, Op. 10
N. Järvi (cnd), Stockholm Sinfonietta † Sym 7 BIS ▲ 355 (17.97)
M. Schønwandt (cnd), Copenhagen Collegium Musicum † Sym 1 DCAP ▲ 9201 (13.97)
Symphony No. 3 in a, Op. 15
N. Järvi (cnd), Stockholm Sinfonietta † Sym 4 BIS ▲ 338 (17.97)
M. Schønwandt (cnd), Collegium Musicum *(rec Mar 18-20, 1988)* † Sym 5 DCAP ▲ 9004 (13.97)
Symphony No. 4 in B♭, Op. 20
C. Hogwood (cnd), Danish National RSO † Frøhlich:Sym CHN ▲ 9609 (16.97)
N. Järvi (cnd), Stockholm Sinfonietta † Sym 3 BIS ▲ 338 (17.97)
M. Schønwandt (cnd), Copenhagen Collegium Musicum † Sym 6 DCAP ▲ 9202 (13.97)
Symphony No. 5 in d, Op. 25
N. Järvi (cnd), Stockholm Sinfonietta † Sym 6 BIS ▲ 356 (17.97)
A. Malling (pno), M. Schønwandt (cnd), Collegium Musicum *(rec Mar 18-20, 1988)* † Sym 3 DCAP ▲ 9004 (13.97)
Symphony No. 6 in g, Op. 32
N. Järvi (cnd), Stockholm Sinfonietta † Sym 5 BIS ▲ 356 (17.97)
M. Schønwandt (cnd), Copenhagen Collegium Musicum † Sym 4 DCAP ▲ 9202 (13.97)

GADE, NIELS WILHELM (cont.)
Symphony No. 7 in F, Op. 45
N. Järvi (cnd), Stockholm Sinfonietta † Sym 2 BIS ▲ 355 (17.97)
M. Schønwandt (cnd), Copenhagen Collegium Musicum † Sym 8 DCAP ▲ 9301 (13.97)
Symphony No. 8 in b, Op. 47
N. Järvi (cnd), Stockholm Sinfonietta † Sym 1 BIS ▲ 339 (17.97)
M. Schønwandt (cnd), Copenhagen Collegium Musicum † Sym 7 DCAP ▲ 9301 (13.97)
Tone Pieces (3) for Organ, Op. 22
J. Dimmock (org) † J. Brahms:Chorale Preludes Org, Op. 122; Merkel:Son Org 4-Hands, Op. 30; M. Reger:Intro & Passacaglia, Op. 56 ARK ▲ 6113 (16.97)
T. Murray (org) ("1863 E. & G.G. Hook Organ, Op. 322: An American Masterpiece") † E. Elgar:Son Org, Op. 28 AFK ▲ 507

Trio Movement in B♭ for Piano, Violin & Cello (1839)
Copenhagen Trio † Novelettes, Op. 29; Trio Pno, Op. 42 KPT ▲ 32077 [DDD]
Tre Musici *(rec Copenhagen, Oct 1992)* ("Danish Golden Age Piano Trios") † J. P. E. Hartmann:Andantino & 8 Vars; F. Henriques:Børnetrio, Op. 31; Lange-Müller:Trio Pno, Op. 53; Langgaard:Mountain Flowers DCAP ▲ 9310 [DDD] (13.97)
Trio in F for Piano, Violin & Cello, Op. 42
Copenhagen Trio † Novelettes, Op. 29; Trio Movt KPT ▲ 32077 [DDD]
Tre Musici † Mendelssohn (-Bartholdy):Trio 1 Pno, Op. 49 CLSO ▲ 132 (15.97)
Zion (cantata) for Baritone, Orchestra & Chorus, Op. 49 (1874)
P. Høyer (bar), F. Rasmussen (cnd), Aalborg SO † Gefion; Heilige Nacht, Op. 40 KPT ▲ 32149 [DDD]
GÄFVERT, BJORN (dates unknown)
Fantasy for Clarinet & Piano
C. Stjernström (cl), M. Kanarva (pno) *(rec Academy of Music of Malmö, Rosenbergssalen, Sweden, July 1996)* † Bozza:Aria Cl; Debussy:Petite pièce Cl; Première rapsodie Cl; L.-E. Larsson:Pieces Cl, Op. 61; Saint-Saëns:Son Cl; Söderlundh:Petite Suite Cl ITIM ▲ 53 (16.97)
GAGLIANO, MARCO DA (1582-1643)
Dafne (opera in prologue & 6 scenes) [lib Rinuccini after Ovid] (1608)
M. Kiehr (sop), R. Invernizzi (sop), F. Zanasi (bass), J. Ricart (sgr), A. S. Anderson (sgr), A. Fernandez (sgr), G. Garrido (cnd), Musica Antica Studio K617 ▲ 7058 (18.97)
GÁL, HANS (1890-1987)
Serenade for Strings, Op. 46 (1937)
G. Tintner (cnd), Nova Scotia SO *(rec Halifax Nova Scotia, May 5-7, 1993)* ("Late Romantics") † Humperdinck:Hänsel und Gretel (sels); Morawetz:Divert Strs; H. Pfitzner:Sym in C, Op. 46; Rezniček:Donna Diana (ov); Schreker:Valse Lente SMS ▲ 5167 [DDD] (16.97)
Sonata for Clarinet & Piano, Op. 84 (1965)
H. D. Klaus (cl), N. Barrett (pno) *(rec England, May 1997)* † J. Brahms:Son 1 Cl; Son 2 Cl CAMM ▲ 130052 [DDD] (16.97)
GALAN, CARLOS (1963-
Music of Galan
P. M. Martinez (sop), C. Cuellar (gtr), A. Moreno (pno), I. Yepes (cnd) —Como una Ola; Ote fir Therese; Oceanos del Ser; Emanaciones, Op. 26; Commedia Divert I, Op. 36 ("Cántico de Amor del Suicida") EMEC ▲ 11 (16.97)
GALÁN, NATALIO (1919-1985)
Guitar Music
R. Brazzel (gtr)—Son Breve; Son Fácile; Suite Cubana ("Twentieth Century Cuban Music") † L. Brouwer:Gtr Music CENT ▲ 2155 (16.97)
GALANTE, STEVEN (1953-
Saxounds 111 for Saxophone Ensemble
Empire Saxophone Quartet ("Classic Saxophone Vol 2") † D. Baker:Faces of the Blues; G. Fauré:Pelléas et Mélisande, Op. 80; Kechley:In the Dragon's Garden; W. A. Mozart:Qt in F Ob & Strs, K.370/368b LISC ▲ 9193 (16.97)
Shu Gath Manna for Alto Saxophone & Synthesizer (1987)
Duo Vivo † Bolcom:Lilith; P. Cooper:Impromptus; A. Gottschalk:Jeu de chat; R. Rogers:Nature of This Whirling Wheel CRYS ▲ 651 [DDD] (15.97) ▮ 651 [DDD] (9.98)
GALBRAITH, NANCY (1951-
Aeolian Muses for Clarinet, Bassoon & Piano (1993)
T. Thompson (cl), W. Genz (bn), R. Zitterbart (pno) ("4 Chamber Works") † Incantation & Allegro; Qt 1 Strs; Rhythms & Rituals ELAN ▲ 82414 [DDD] (17.97)
Concerto No. 1 for Piano & Orchestra
R. Zitterbart (pno), K. Lockhart (cnd), Cincinnati CO ("New Energy from the Americas") † Alonso-Crespo:Ovs & Dances ORC ▲ 101 (16.97)
Danza de los Duendes for Wind Orchestra (1996)
E. Corporon (cnd), North Texas Wind Sym ("Dream Catchers") † Bassett:Lullaby for Kirsten; Gillingham:Waking Angels; W. Mays:Dreamcatcher; R. Rudin:Dream of Oenghus, Op. 37; Schwantner:From a Dark Millennium; W. L. Thompson:Softly & Tenderly Jesus Is Calling KLAV ▲ 11089 [DDD] (18.97)
Incantation & Allegro for Oboe, Bassoon & Piano (1995)
C. K. DeAlmeida (ob), N. Goeres (bn), L. Manriquez (pno) ("4 Chamber Works") † Aeolian Muses; Qt 1 Strs; Rhythms & Rituals ELAN ▲ 82414 [DDD] (17.97)
Quartet No. 1 for Strings (1996)
Latin American String Quartet ("4 Chamber Works") † Aeolian Muses; Incantation & Allegro; Rhythms & Rituals ELAN ▲ 82414 [DDD] (17.97)

Rhythms & Rituals for Woodwind Quintet & Piano (1995)
P. P. Jennings (pno), Renaissance City Winds ("4 Chamber Works") † Aeolian Muses; Incantation & Allegro; Qt 1 Strs ELAN ▲ 82414 [DDD] (17.97)
GALINDO, BLAS (1910-1993)
La Manda (ballet) for Orchestra
F. Lozano (cnd), Mexico City PO, F. Lozano (cnd), Carlos Chávez SO ("Clásicos Mexicanos") † M. B. Jiménez:Chueco CLME ▲ 21021 (13.97)
Poema de Neruda for Orchestra
B. J. Echenique (cnd), Orch of the Americas ("México Sinfonico") † Carrasco:Preludio Sinfónico; R. Castro:Minueto; J. M. Chávez:Huerfanita; Márquez:Danzón 4; Moncayo Garcia:Huapango; Sinfonieta; Zyman:Encuentros URT ▲ 20 (16.97)

GALIOT, JOHANNES (fl 1380-1395)
Vocal Music
Subtilior Trio—Se vos ne volés; En attendant souffrir; En attendant d'avoir *(rec May 1997)* ("French Ars Subtilior") † B. Cordier:Vocal Music; Cuvelier:Vocal Music; Jacob De senleches:Vocal Music; Vaillant:Vocal Music LAMA (Ars Harmonica) ▲ 25 [DDD] (17.97)

GALLAGHER, JACK (1947-
Berceuse for Orchestra (1985)
S. Kawalla (cnd), Polish Radio-TV SO Cracow † R. Carl:Wide Open Field; I. Heifetz:Raga; Kiraly:Pinocchio (suite 1); T. Myers:Elegy; Wolking:Methenyology VMM (Music from 6 Continents 1994) ▲ 3030 [DDD]
Persistence of Memory for Cello & Orchestra (1995)
B. Peneva (vc), T. Delibozov (cnd), Ruse PO ("New Music for Orchestra") † Beath:Lagu Lagu Manis II; Mageau:Furies; Nuorvala:Notturno urbano; Pelinka:Diagonal, Op. 27 VMM ▲ 3036 [DDD]
GALLAY, JACQUES-FRANÇOIS (1795-1864)
Quartet for Horns, Op. 26, "Grand Quattuor"
NFB Horn Quartet † P. Hindemith:Son Hns; Wadenpfuhl:Tectonica CRYS ▲ 241 (15.97) ▮ 241 (9.98)
GALLIARD, JOHANN ERNST (1687-1749)
Sonata No. 5 in d for Tuba & Piano
R. Bobo (tuba), R. Grierson (pno) *(rec 1969)* † P. Hindemith:Son Bass Tuba; A. Wilder:Children's Suite:Effie the Elephant CRYS ▲ 125 (15.97) ▮ 125 (9.98)
GALLON, NOËL (1891-1966)
Improvisation & Rondo for Flute & Piano
B. Larsen (fl), S. Larsen (pno) *(rec Copenhagen, Mar 1996)* ("The French Flute") † Suite Fl; Duruflé:Prélude, récitatif et vars, Op. 3; R. Hahn:Romanesque; Rhené-Baton:Bourée, Op. 42; Passacaille Fl & Pno, Op. 35; Ropartz:Sonatine Fl CLSO ▲ 160 (15.97)
Suite for Flute & Piano (1921)
B. Larsen (fl), S. Larsen (pno) *(rec Copenhagen, Mar 1996)* ("The French Flute") † Improv Fl; Duruflé:Prélude, récitatif et vars, Op. 3; R. Hahn:Romanesque; Rhené-Baton:Bourée, Op. 42; Passacaille Fl & Pno, Op. 35; Ropartz:Sonatine Fl CLSO ▲ 160 (15.97)

▲ = CD ♦ = Enhanced CD △ = MD ▮ = Cassette Tape ▯ = DCC

GALLOT, JACQUES (ca 1600-ca 1690)
Folies d'Espagne
T. Satoh (lt) *(rec Amsterdam, Netherlands, Feb 1990)* ("Chaconne; Baroque Lute Recital") † J. S. Bach:Sons & Partitas Vn; T. Satoh:Music of Satoh; Tombeau de Mr. D. Philips; Taxin:Qnt Brass; S. L. Weiss:Lt Music CCL ▲ 490 [DDD]
Lute Music
H. Smith (lt) ASTR (Trésors du Baroque) ▲ 128528 (12.97)
Pieces in a for Lute
J. Lindberg (lt) *(rec Sweden, Dec 21 & 23, 1983)* ("Lute Music from Scotland and France") † Anonymous:Balcarres Lute Book (sels); Jane Pickering Lute Book (sels); Lady Margaret Wemyss Book (sels); Panmure 5; Rowallen Lute Book (sels); Straloch Lute Book (sels); F. Couperin:Pièces de violes; E. Gaultier:Pieces in d Lt BIS ▲ 201 [AAD] (17.97)

GALLUS, JACOBUS [JACOB HANDL] (1550-1591)
Choral Music
P. Fiala (cnd), Brno Czech Phil Chorus—Lamentations I, II, V & VI; Oratorio Jermiae Prophetae; Miserere mei Deus; Pater noster, qui es in coelis SUR ▲ 3280 (16.97)
Missa super "Sancta Maria" for Chorus
P. van Nevel (cnd), Huelgas Ensemble † Opus Musicum SNYC (Vivarte) ▲ 64305 (16.97)
Opus Musicum (4 books of motets) for Chorus
P. van Nevel (cnd), Huelgas Ensemble † Missa super "Sancta Maria" SNYC (Vivarte) ▲ 64305 (16.97)

GALUPPI, BALDASSARE (1706-1785)
Il caffè di campagna (drama giocoso) [lib Pierto Chiari] (1761)
M. González (sop—Dorina), A. Szántó (sop—Scaffetta), B. Wiedemann (mez—Lisetta), A. Laczó (ten—Bellagamba), V. Martino (ten—Cicala), M. Kálmándi (bar—Conte Fumana), F. Lufi (bass—Caligo), F. Pirona (cnd), Capella Savaria [period instrs] HUN 2-▲ 31658 [DDD] (32.97)
Concerti a quattro for Strings
Agláia Ensemble STRV ▲ 33316 [DDD] (16.97)
Concerto in D for Flute & Orchestra
J. Galway (fl), C. Scimone (cnd) † Pergolesi:Con Fl; Piacentino:Con Fl; Tartini:Con Fl RCAV (Red Seal) ▲ 61164 (16.97)
Concertos for Harpsichord & Strings
R. Peiretti (hpd), R. Peiretti (cnd), Accademia dei Solinghi [complete] DYNC 2-▲ 215 [DDD] (34.97)
Il Mondo alla roversa (opera in 3 acts) [lib Carlo Goldoni]
F. Piva (cnd), Intermusica Ensemble, P. Saudelli (ten—Rinaldino), G. Sarti (bar—Giacinto), B. Di Castri (sgr—Cintia), C. Ottino (sgr—Graziosino), L. S. Yun (sgr—Tullia), E. Lombardi (sgr—Aurora), C. Olivieri (sgr—Rinaldino) *(rec Teatro "La Concordia" di San Costanzo, Pesaro, Italy, Oct-Nov 1997) (rev Piva, Bongiovanni)* BONG 3-▲ 2230 (live) [DDD] (47.97)
Il mondo della luna [The World on the Moon] (opera in 3 acts) [lib C. Goldoni] (1750)
F. Piva (cnd), Intermusica Ensemble, P. Antonucci (sop—Flaminia), P. Cigna (sop—Lisetta), B. Di Castri (mez—Clarice), E. Facini (ten—Ernesto), G. Sarti (bar—Buonafede), G. Gatti (bar—Ecclittico), C. Ottino (bar—Cecco) *(rec Pesaro, Italy, Oct-Nov, 1997) ([ENG,ITA] lib text)* BONG 3-▲ 2217 [DDD] (47.97)
Music of Galuppi
Quartetto Italiano † Boccherini:Qts Strs; Cambini:Qts Strs; G. B. Vitali:Music of; Vivaldi:Sinf Strs in b, RV.169 TES ▲ 1124 (17.97)
Presto in B♭ for Piano
A. B. Michelangeli (pno) † Chopin:Mazurkas Pno; Scherzos Pno; Debussy:Images (6) Pno; Liszt:Con 1 Pno, S.124; Vivaldi:Music of Vivaldi IMMM (Magic Master series) ▲ 37007 (6.97)
Sonatas for Harpsichord (miscellaneous)
L. Koutalari-Ioannou (pno), B. Papazian (cnd), Orchestral Ensemble—Son in D † Cambini:Cons Hpd, Op.15/3; G. B. Grazioli:Sonata in G; L. D. Rossi:Andantino in G; Zipoli:Suite in b GEGA ▲ 53 (16.97)
Sonatas for Keyboard
W. Glemser (pno) *(Son 8 Pno; Son 7 Pno; Son 3 Pno; Son 10 Pno; Son 9 Pno), (Son 12 Pno) (rec Emmendingen, Germany, July 1-2, 1993)* ARS ▲ 368329 [DDD] (15.99)
Sonata No. 5 in C for Keyboard
A. B. Michelangeli (pno) ("Arturo Benedetti Michelangeli") † Debussy:Images (6) Pno; Preludes Pno; M. Ravel:Con Pno; Gaspard de la nuit; D. Scarlatti:Sons Kbd PPHI (Great Pianists of the 20th Century) ▲ 456901 (22.97)
A. Serdar (pno) *(rec Highgate, London, England, Mar 1997)* † J. Brahms:Waltzes Pno, Op. 39; Busoni:Bach Transcriptions Pno; Chopin:Andante Spianato & Grand Polonaise, Op. 22; Mendelssohn (-Bartholdy):Vars sérieuses, Op. 54 EMIC (Debut) ▲ 72821 [DDD] (6.97)

GAMBARINI, ELISABETTA DE (1731-1765)
Pieces for Harpsichord, Op. 2 (1748)
B. Harbach (hpd) ("18th Century Women Composers: Music for Solo Harpsichord, Vol. 1") † M. V. Auenbrugg:Son in E♭ Hpd; Barthélémon:Son Hpd; M. Martinez:Son in A Hpd; Son in E Hpd; M. H. Park:Son Hpd, Op. 4 GAS ▲ 272 [DDD] (16.97)
P. van Parys (hpd) *(rec Oct 1997)* † Sets of Lessons, Op. 1 PAVA ▲ 7395 [DDD] (10.97)
Sets of Lessons (6) for Harpsichord, Op. 1 (ca 1748)
P. van Parys (hpd) *(rec Oct 1997)* † Pieces Hpd, Op. 2 PAVA ▲ 7395 [DDD] (10.97)

GAMBARO, VINCENZO (1785-1824)
Quartets (3) for Winds
Rossini Wind Quartet *(rec Genoa, June 1993)* † Mercadante:Qts Ww DYNC ▲ 107 [DDD] (17.97)

GAMER, CARLTON (1929-
Sonata for Violin & Piano (1960)
S. Harth (vn), W. Devenny (pno) † E. Bloch:Son 2 Vn; Janáček:Son Vn CRYS ▲ 634 (15.97) ▮ 634 (9.98)

GANDOLFI, MICHAEL (1956-
Caution to the Wind for Flute & String Ensemble (1992)
J. McPhee (cnd), Griffin Music Ensemble, Griffin Music Ensemble *(rec 1993)* ("Academy of Arts & Letters:Composers Award Recording") † Ventaglio di Josephine; T. E. Barker:Pieces F Hn; Trikhyálo; E. Kurtz:From Time to Time CRI ▲ 661 [DDD] (17.97)
Il Ventaglio di Josephine for Piano (1983)
J. Gandolfi (pno) *(rec 1992)* ("Academy of Arts & Letters:Composers Award Recording") † Caution to the Wind; T. E. Barker:Pieces F Hn; Trikhyálo; E. Kurtz:From Time to Time CRI ▲ 661 [DDD] (17.97)

GANGI, MARIO (1923-
Suite italiana for 2 Guitars
S. Tordini (gtr), J. Prats (gtr) † Civitareale:Suite estival; M. de Falla:Pièces espagnoles; Santórsola:Suite all'antica Gtrs OTR ▲ 1016 [DDD] (18.97)

GANN, KYLE (1955-
Desert Sonata for Piano (1994)
L. Svard (pno) *(rec Lewisburg, PA, Oct 11-13, 1996 & Jan 12-13, 1997)* † J. Hunt:Trapani; Lauten:Vars Orange Cycle LOV ▲ 3052 [DDD] (16.97)

GANTSHER, ALEXEI (1895-1937)
Sonatina in e for Viola & Piano, Op. 5
S. Stepchenko (va), Z. Abolitz (pno) *(rec Glinka State Museum Moscow, July 1996)* ("3 Centuries of the Russian Viola, Vol. 2") † P. Juon:Son 1 Va, Op. 15; Son 2 Va; S. Prokofiev:Mélodies Vn, Op. 35bis RUS ▲ 10060 [DDD] (16.97)

GANZ, RUDOLPH (1877-1972)
Concerto in E♭ for Piano & Orchestra, Op. 32 (1940)
R. Salvatore (pno), P. Freeman (cnd), Chicago Sinfonietta *(rec River Forest, IL, Feb 27, 1996)* ("Chicago Concertos") † La Montaine:Con 4 Pno, Op. 59 CED ▲ 28 [DDD] (16.97)

GAOS, ANDRÉS (1874-1959)
Impressión nocturna for Strings (1937)
T. Briccetti (cnd) *(rec Prague, Oct 31-Nov 3, 1994)* ("Mostly French") † Debussy:Danses sacrée et profane; Syrinx Fl; G. Fauré:Fant Fl, Op. 79; Impromptu Hp, Op. 86; Griffes:Poem Fl; M. Ravel:Intro & Allegro Hp; Saint-Saëns:Fant Vn DI ▲ 920281 [DDD] (5.97)

GARANT, SERGE (1929-1986)
Amuya for Winds, Brass, String Quartet, Piano, Harp, Celeste & Percussion (1968)
W. Boudreau (cnd) ("Chamber Music of Serge Garant") † chants d'amours; Offrande I; Qnt ANAL ▲ 29804 [DDD] (16.97)
chants d'amours for solo Cello, Soprano, Mezzo-Soprano, Baritone, Brass, 2 Harps, Percussion & Tape (1975)
W. Boudreau (cnd) ("Chamber Music of Serge Garant") † Amuya; Offrande I; Qnt ANAL ▲ 29804 [DDD] (16.97)
Offrande I for Soprano, Winds, Brass, 2 String Quartets, 2 Harps, Piano & Percussion (1969)
W. Boudreau (cnd) ("Chamber Music of Serge Garant") † chants d'amours; Amuya; Qnt ANAL ▲ 29804 [DDD] (16.97)

GARANT, SERGE (cont.)
Quintet for Flute, Oboe, Cello, Piano & Percussion (1978)
W. Boudreau (cnd) ("Chamber Music of Serge Garant") † chants d'amours; Amuya; Offrande I ANAL ▲ 29804 [DDD] (16.97)

GARCIA, GERALD (1949-
Celtic Airs (6) for Guitar (1994)
J. Holmquist (gtr) *(rec Newmarket Canada, Apr 3-9, 1995)* † Études Esquisses NXIN ▲ 8553419 [DDD] (5.97)
Études Esquisses (25) for Guitar (1992)
J. Holmquist (gtr) *(rec Newmarket Canada, Apr 3-9, 1995)* † Celtic Airs NXIN ▲ 8553419 [DDD] (5.97)

GARCIA, MANUEL (1775-1832)
Songs
E. Palacio (ten), J. C. Rivera (gtr), J. J. Chuquisengo (pno)—Yo que soy contrabandista; Y otras canciones; I Who Am a Bandit; others AL ▲ 114 (18.97)

GARCIA, ORLANDO JACINTO (1954-
Canciones Fragmentadas [Fragmented Songs] for Double Bass (1996)
C. Canonici (db) † Music for Berlin; Pieces Db & Tape; Retratos I; Voces Celestiales OOD ▲ 42 [DDD] (16.97)
Colores Ultraviolados
P. W. Smith (mez), M. Rowell (vn), J. Storck (db), E. Brown (fl) *(rec NYC, NY, 1993)* ("Bang on a Can - Live, Vol. 3") † L. Bouchard:Lung Ta; Didkovsky:I Kick My Hand; B. Marcus:Adam and Eve; P. Reller:Carcass; M. Wright:Lizard Belly Moon CRI ▲ 672 [DDD] (16.97)
Improvisation with Metallic Materials for WX-7 & Stereo Tape (1990)
J. Celli (elec) ("La Belleza del Silencio") † Metallic Images; On the Eve of the 2nd Year Anniversary of Morton's; Sitio sin Nombre OOD ▲ 6 [DDD] (16.97)
Metallic Images for Percussion & Stereo Tape (1991)
J. Williams (perc) ("La Belleza del Silencio") † Improvisation with Metallic Materials; On the Eve of the 2nd Year Anniversary of Morton's; Sitio sin Nombre OOD ▲ 6 [DDD] (16.97)
Music for Berlin for Flute, Piccolo, Alto Flute, Bass Flute & Piano (1990)
R. Dick (fl), A. D. Mare (pno) † Canciones Fragmentadas; Pieces Db & Tape; Retratos I; Voces Celestiales OOD ▲ 42 [DDD] (16.97)
On the Eve of the Second Year Anniversary of Morton's Death for Chorus (1989)
G. Smith (cnd), Gregg Smith Singers ("La Belleza del Silencio") † Improvisation with Metallic Materials; Metallic Images; Sitio sin Nombre OOD ▲ 6 [DDD] (16.97)
Pieces (3) for Double Bass & Tape (1990)
R. Black (db), O. J. Garcia (tape)—No. 2 † Canciones Fragmentadas; Music for Berlin; Retratos I; Voces Celestiales OOD ▲ 42 [DDD] (16.97)
Retratos I for Piano & Tape (1989)
P. Hoffman (pno), O. J. Garcia (tape) † Canciones Fragmentadas; Music for Berlin; Pieces Db & Tape; Voces Celestiales OOD ▲ 42 [DDD] (16.97)
Sitio sin Nombre for Soprano & Stereo Tape (1990)
J. L. Barbara (sop) ("La Belleza del Silencio") † Improvisation with Metallic Materials; Metallic Images; On the Eve of the 2nd Year Anniversary of Morton's OOD ▲ 6 [DDD] (16.97)
Voces Celestiales for 2 Double Basses & Orchestra (1993)
B. Turetzky (db), L. G. Imbert (db), C. Riazuelo (cnd), Caracas Municipal SO † Canciones Fragmentadas; Music for Berlin; Pieces Db & Tape; Retratos I OOD ▲ 42 [DDD] (16.97)

GARCÍA LORCA, FEDERICO (1898-1936)
Songs
G. Montero (sgr)—Canción de Belisa; Las tres hojas; Las morillas de Jaén; Despierte la novia; Zapatera; La guitarra; El grito; El silencio; Prendimiento de Antoñito el Camborio...; Muerte de Antoñito el Camborio; La casada infiel; Romance de la Guardia civil española † Dessau:Mutter Courage (sels) VC ▲ 8095 [ADD] (13.97)
G. Ortega (cant), J. Pons (cnd), Barcelona Teatro Lliure CO † M. de Falla:Corregidor y la molinera HAM ▲ 901520 (18.97)

GARDNER, JOHN (1917-
Quartet for Saxophones, Op. 168 (1985)
Fairer Sax † P.-M. Dubois:Qt Sax; P. Harvey:Robert Burns Suite; P. Patterson:Diversions SAY ▲ 365 [DDD] (16.97)

GARDNER, KAY (1941-
Rainforest for Orchestra (1977)
C. Martin (cnd), Bournemouth Sinfonietta † J. Brockman:Perihelion II; K. Hoover:Summer Night; L. Larsen:Parachute Dancing; Mamlok:Elegy; M. Richter:Lament; Van de Vate:Journeys LEON ▲ 327 [DDD] (16.97)

GARFIELD, BERNARD (1924-
Poème for Bassoon & Piano
D. DeBolt (bn), J. Davidson (pno) ("Bassoon Music of 20th-Century America") † Etler:Son Bn; Farago:Vars on a folia theme of Corelli, Op. 51; Heiden:Serenade; W. Osborne:Rhap Bn CRYS ▲ 347 (15.97)

GARLAND, PETER (1952-
Apple Blossom for Percussion (1972)
Univ of New Mexico Percussion Ensemble † Cantares de la Frontera; Obstacles of Sleep; Old Men of the Fiesta; Songs of Mad Coyote; Three Strange Angels OOWN ▲ 8 [DDD] (16.97)
Cantares de la Frontera for Harp (1986)
R. Simpson (hp) † Apple Blossom; Obstacles of Sleep; Old Men of the Fiesta; Songs of Mad Coyote; Three Strange Angels OOWN ▲ 8 [DDD] (16.97)
Nana & Victorio for Percussion
W. Winant (perc) † Peñasco Blanco AVAK ▲ 12 (21.97)
Obstacles of Sleep for Percussion (1973)
Univ of New Mexico Percussion Ensemble † Apple Blossom; Cantares de la Frontera; Old Men of the Fiesta; Songs of Mad Coyote; Three Strange Angels OOWN ▲ 8 [DDD] (16.97)
Old Men of the Fiesta for Ensemble (1989-90)
Peter Garland Ensemble † Apple Blossom; Cantares de la Frontera; Obstacles of Sleep; Songs of Mad Coyote; Three Strange Angels OOWN ▲ 8 [DDD] (16.97)
Peñasco Blanco for Piano & Vibraphone
J. Steinberg (pno), W. Winant (vib) † Nana & Victorio AVAK ▲ 12 (21.97)
Songs of Mad Coyote (3) for Percussion (1973)
Univ of New Mexico Percussion Ensemble † Apple Blossom; Cantares de la Frontera; Obstacles of Sleep; Old Men of the Fiesta; Three Strange Angels OOWN ▲ 8 [DDD] (16.97)
The Three Strange Angels for Percussion (1972-73)
Univ of New Mexico Percussion Ensemble † Apple Blossom; Cantares de la Frontera; Obstacles of Sleep; Old Men of the Fiesta; Songs of Mad Coyote OOWN ▲ 8 [DDD] (16.97)

GAROFALO, CARLO GIORGIO (dates unknown)
Romantic Symphony of St. Louis
J. Spiegelman (cnd), Moscow Radio Orch RMAN ▲ 1001

GARRIDO, M. (dates unknown)
Guitar Music
H. Salinas (cnd), Inti-Illimani—Libertad ("Fragments of a Dream") † P. Peña:Gtr Music; H. Salinas:Gtr Music COL ▲ 44574 [ADD] (9.97)

GARRIDO-LECCA, CELSO (1926-
Quartet No. 2 for Strings (1988)
Latin American String Quartet † J. Alvarez:Metro Chabacano; Sierra:Memorias Tropicales; Tello:Dansaq II NALB ▲ 51 (16.97)

GARUTA, LUCIJA (dates unknown)
Lord, thy land is burning (cantata) for Voices
L. Vigners (cnd), Latvian National Opera Orch, I. Kokars (cnd), Latvian Radio Choir, L. Greidane (sop), L. Andersone-Silare (mez), J. Sprogis (ten), K. Zarins (ten), A. Krancmanis (bar) † Jurjāns:Sing, Rejoice! [Līgojiet, līksmojiet!]; To my Fatherland [Tēvijai] RIGA ▲ 20 (16.97)

GASLINI, GIORGIO (1929-
Battiti for Violin & Chamber Chorus (1994)
E. Porta (vn), Eurydice Chamber Chorus † Chants-Songs; Chorus Fl; Logar; Myanmar; Open Music LBD ▲ 10 (16.97)
Chants-Songs for Flute & Piano (1995)
R. Fabbriciani (fl), G. Gaslini (pno) † Battiti; Chorus Fl; Logar; Myanmar; Open Music LBD ▲ 10 (16.97)
Chorus for Flute (1965)
R. Fabbriciani (fl) † Battiti; Chants-Songs; Logar; Myanmar; Open Music LBD ▲ 10 (16.97)

GREEN, PHILIP (cont.)
The Man from Galilee:Interpretations for Piano
D. Budway (pno) ("The Man from Galilee") † Ave Maria; Man from Galilee ALAN ▲ 5554 [DDD] (16.97)
The March Hare (selections)
M. J. Henderson (cnd), Irish Guards Band *(rec Chelsea Barracks, England, Feb 3-5, 1997)* ("Emerald Isle") † Anonymous:Black Velvet Band; Wild Colonial Boy; P. French:Songs; M. J. Henderson:Emerald Isle; Micks' March; Traditional:Carrickfergus; Harp That Once through Tara's Halls; Minstrel Boy BND ▲ 5134 (16.97)
St. Patrick's Mass for Chorus
G. Mitchell (cnd), Trinity Chorale † A. Dvořák:Qt 12 Strs, Op. 96; I. Kauffman:D.S. al Fine ALAN ▲ 5552 (16.97)
GREEN, SCOTT (1956-
Onata-say Too (Son of Onata-say) for Piano (1991)
J. Miltenberger (pno) † Aguila:Son Pno; Ginastera:Son 1 Pno, Op. 22; Morillo:Son 4 Pno ACAD ▲ 20021 (16.97)
GREENBAUM, MATTHEW (1950-
Amulet for Piano (1988)
D. Holzman (pno) *(rec Harvard Univ, Jan 1995)* ("Explorations: New American Piano Music") † Boros:Mnem; Cornicello:Son 2 Pno; Pleskow:Son 2 Pno; Yttrehus:Explorations CENT ▲ 2291 [DDD] (16.97)
GREENBAUM, STUART (1966-
But I Want the Harmonica... for Piano (1996)
J. Carrigan (pno) *(rec Univ of Queensland, Australia)* ("But I Want the Harmonica: Australian Contemporary Piano Music") † Broadstock:Aureole 4; Conyngham:ppp; Hiscocks:Piper at the Gates of Dawn; Kats-Chernin:Purple Prelude; Sabin:Another Look at Autumn; Spiers:Elegy & Toccata Pno VOXA ▲ 23 [DDD] (18.97)
Upon the Dark Water for Chorus (1991)
R. Peelman (cnd), Song Company *(rec ABC Ultimo Centre, Apr 1993)* ("The Green CD: Environmentally Friendly Australian Choral Music") † A. Bremner:In the Shrubbery; R. Edwards:Flower Songs; M. Wesley-Smith:Who Killed Cock Robin?; Who Stopped the Rain?; Whiticker:Man, Skin Cancer of the Earth TALP ▲ 64 [DDD] (18.97)
GREENBERG, LAURA (1942-
Child's Play for String Quartet
Alexander String Quartet † Dzubay:Threnody after Josquin's Mille regretz; M. Hess:About the Night; W. Peterson:Qt 2 Strs INNO ▲ 111
This Man Was Your Brother for 2 Sopranos & Orchestra
R. Rosales (sop), L. Vardaman (sop), M. Lifchitz (cnd) ("Of Bondage and Freedom") † Vida Es Sueño; Dvorak:Amandla Mandela!; M. Lifchitz:Of Bondage & Freedom; Pleskow:Arabesques NSR ▲ 1004 [DDD] (15.97)
La Vida Es Sueño for 2 Sopranos & Orchestra
R. Rosales (sop), L. Vardaman (sop), M. Lifchitz (cnd) ("Of Bondage and Freedom") † This Man Was Your Brother; Dvorak:Amandla Mandela!; M. Lifchitz:Of Bondage & Freedom; Pleskow:Arabesques NSR ▲ 1004 [DDD] (15.97)
GREENE, MAURICE (1696-1755)
Anthems
K. Ferrier (cta), G. Moore (pno)—O praise the Lord; I will lay me down in peace *(rec London, England, Sep 21, 1945)* † C. W. Gluck:Orfeo ed Euridice (sels); G. F. Handel:Ottone (sels); G. Mahler:Kindertotenlieder; Mendelssohn (-Bartholdy):Songs; H. Purcell:Come, ye sons of art, away, Z.323; Indian Queen (sels); King Arthur (sels) EMIC (Great Recordings of the Century) ▲ 66963 [ADD] (11.97)
E. Higginbottom (cnd), New College Choir Oxford—10 anthems: How long wilt thou forget me, O Lord?; The King shall rejoice; Let God arise; Lord let me know mine end; O clap your hands; Thou visitest the earth; Voluntary I [E] *(rec Apr 1991)* † W. Boyce:Anthems & Voluntaries CRD ▲ 3483 [DDD] (17.97)
GREER, JOHN (1954-
All Around the Circle for Vocal Quartet & 2 Pianos (1988)
K. Brett (sop), C. Robbin (mez), B. Butterfield (ten), R. Braun (bar), S. Ralls (pno), B. Ubukata (pno) *(rec CBC Toronto, Dec 7-9, 1993)* ("The Aldeburgh Connection") † J. Brahms:Liebeslieder Waltzes Pno 4-Hands, Op. 52a; R. Schumann:Spanische Liebeslieder, Op. 138 CBC (Musica Viva) ▲ 1077 [DDD] (16.97)
GREGORA, FRANTIŠEK (1819-1887)
Music of Gregora
Vienna Waltz Ensemble—Mazurka; Polka *(rec Chicago, IL, July & Oct, 1998)* † Anonymous:Brat-Lenerl; Schellerl-Tanz; Tanz; J. Haydn:Jahreszeiten (sels); J. N. Hummel:German Dances for the Redoutensaal; Pamer:Ländler; Walzer; Pössinger:Minuets Strs; Joh. Strauss:Wiener Carneval-Walzer, Op. 3 DENW ▲ 102 (16.97)
GREGSON, EDWARD (1945-
Concerto for Horn & Brass Band (or Orchestra) (1971)
R. Newsome (cnd), Besses o' th' Barn Band † Con Tuba; Langford:Rhaps Cnt CHN ▲ 4526 [DDD] (16.97)
Concerto for Tuba & Brass Band (1976)
R. Newsome (cnd), Besses o' th' Barn Band † Con Hn; Langford:Rhaps Cnt CHN ▲ 4526 [DDD] (16.97)
Stockholm Symphonic Wind Orch † I. Dahl:Con A Sax; Keuris:Catena: Refrains & Vars; Morthenson:Paraphonia CAPA ▲ 21414 [DDD] (16.97)
Connotations for Brass Band
P. Parkes (cnd), Black Dyke Mills Band *(rec England)* ("Champions of Brass") † G. Bailey:Diadem of Gold (Ov); Bantock:Prometheus Unbound; Langford:Harmonious Vars on a Theme of Handel; W. Mathias:Vivat Regina Bra, Op. 75; Vivat Regina, Op. 75; Vaughan Williams:Vars Brass *([ENG] text)* CHN ▲ 4510 [ADD] (16.97)
Music of Gregson
E. Gregson (cnd), Black Dyke Mills Band—Con Grosso; Essay (in 3 movts); Prelude & Capriccio; Plantagenets; Partita (in 3 movts); Vars on "Laudate Dominum" ("Gregson, Vol. 2") DOY ▲ 44 (16.97)
E. Gregson (cnd), Desford Colliery Caterpillar Band—Con Hn Brass Band [w. Frank Lloyd (hn)]; Dances & Airs; Connotations; Of Men & Mountains ("Gregson, Vol. 1") DOY ▲ 17 (16.97)
The Sword & the Crown for Orchestra (1991)
E. Corporon (cnd), Cincinnati Wind SO ("Paradigm") † D. W. Freund:Jug Blues & Fat Pickin'; J. Harbison:3 City Blocks; P. Hindemith:Sym Concert Band; B. Rands:Ceremonial; I. Stravinsky:Circus Polka KLAV ▲ 11059 (16.97)
GRESSEL, JOEL (1943-
Cold Fusion I for Computer (1994)
J. Gressel (cmpt) ("Points In Time") † Cold Fusion II; Cold Fusion III; Joint Resolution; Meteor Showers; Points in Time CRI ▲ 797 [DDD] (16.97)
Cold Fusion II for Computer (1995)
J. Gressel (cmpt) ("Points In Time") † Cold Fusion I; Cold Fusion III; Joint Resolution; Meteor Showers; Points in Time CRI ▲ 797 [DDD] (16.97)
Cold Fusion III for Computer (1996)
J. Gressel (cmpt) ("Points In Time") † Cold Fusion I; Cold Fusion II; Joint Resolution; Meteor Showers; Points in Time CRI ▲ 797 [DDD] (16.97)
Joint Resolution for Piano & Computer (1976)
J. Gressel (pno) *(rec NYC, NY, 1984)* ("Points In Time") † Cold Fusion I; Cold Fusion II; Cold Fusion III; Meteor Showers; Points in Time CRI ▲ 797 [DDD] (16.97)
Meteor Showers for Computer (1997)
J. Gressel (cmpt) ("Points In Time") † Cold Fusion I; Cold Fusion II; Cold Fusion III; Joint Resolution; Points in Time CRI ▲ 797 [DDD] (16.97)
Points in Time for Computer (1974)
J. Gressel (cmpt) ("Points In Time") † Cold Fusion I; Cold Fusion II; Cold Fusion III; Joint Resolution; Meteor Showers CRI ▲ 797 [DDD] (16.97)
GRETCHANINOFF, ALEXANDER (1864-1956)
Concerto for Cello & Orchestra, Op. 8 (1897)
A. Ivashkin (vc), V. Polianski (cnd), Russian State SO † Missa festiva, Op. 154; Sym 4 CHN ▲ 9559 (16.97)
Histoirettes (12) for Piano, Op. 118 (1929)
C. Favre (pno) *(rec Gland Switzerland, July 1995)* ("Russian Piano Music & the World of Childhood") † A. Khachaturian:Album; S. Prokofiev:Music for Children, Op. 65 DORO ▲ 3016 [DDD] (16.97)
In thy Kingdom (song) for Countertenor & Chorus, Op. 58/3
S. Layton (cnd), Holst Singers, J. Bowman (ct) *(rec Temple Church, London, England, Nov 8-15, 1998)* † Lord, now lettest Thou Thy Servant, Op. 34/1; Now the Powers of Heaven, Op. 58/6; Vespers Liturgy, Op. 59 HYP ▲ 67080 [DDD] (18.97)
Liturgica Domestica for St. John Chrysostom for Chorus, Op. 79 (1917)
Cantus Sacred Music Ensemble OLY ▲ 480 [DDD] (16.97)
V. Polianski (cnd), Russian State SO, Russian State Symphonic Cappella CHN ▲ 9365 [DDD] (16.97)
G. Robev (cnd), Bulgarian National Chorus CAPO ▲ 10537 [DDD] (10.97)
Lord, now lettest Thou Thy Servant (song) for Chorus, Op. 34/1
S. Layton (cnd), Holst Singers *(rec Temple Church, London, England, Nov 8-15, 1998)* † In thy Kingdom, Op. 58/3; Now the Powers of Heaven, Op. 58/6; Vespers Liturgy, Op. 59 HYP ▲ 67080 [DDD] (18.97)

GRETCHANINOFF, ALEXANDER (cont.)
Mass "Et in terra pax" for Organ & Chorus, Op. 166 (1942)
A. Obraztsov (bass), L. Golub (org), V. Polianski (cnd), Russian State Symphonic Cappella † Sym 2 CHN ▲ 9486 (16.97)
Missa festiva for Organ & Chorus, Op. 154 (1937)
L. Golub (org), Russian State Symphonic Cappella † Con Vc, Op. 8; Sym 4 CHN ▲ 9559 (16.97)
Missa Sancti Spiritus for Organ & Chorus, Op. 169 (1943)
T. Jeranje (cta), V. Polianski (cnd), Russian State SO, Russian State Symphonic Cappella † Snowflakes, Op. 47; Sym 1 CHN ▲ 9397 [DDD] (16.97)
Now the Powers of Heaven (song) for Chorus, Op. 58/6
S. Layton (cnd), Holst Singers *(rec Temple Church, London, England, Nov 8-15, 1998)* † In thy Kingdom, Op. 58/3; Lord, now lettest Thou Thy Servant, Op. 34/1; Vespers Liturgy, Op. 59 HYP ▲ 67080 [DDD] (18.97)
Praise the Lord [Kvalite Boga] (cantata) for solo Voice & Chorus, Op. 65 (1914)
V. Polyansky (cnd), Russian State Symphonic Cappella, L. Kuznetsova (mez) † Sym 3 CHN ▲ 9698 (16.97)
Sacred Choral Music
B. Houdy (cnd), Vocal Ensemble of Saint Petersburg—Simcom's Cantide † Bortnyansky:Sacred Choral Music; Glazunov:Easter Hymn; Ippolitov-Ivanov:Psalm 133; Kedrov:Sacred Choral Music; Strokine:Sacred Choral Music; Tchesnokov:Hallelujah; Prayer to the Holy Virgin PMF ▲ 91201 (6.97)
The Seven Days of Passion for a cappella Chorus
V. Polianski (cnd), Russian State Symphonic Cappella CHN (New Direction) ▲ 9303 [DDD] (16.97)
Snowflakes (song cycle) for solo Voice & Piano [after Gorodetsky], Op. 47 (1909)
L. Kuznetsova (mez), V. Polianski (cnd), Russian State SO [arr voice & orch] † Missa Sancti Spiritus, Op. 169; Sym 1 CHN ▲ 9397 [DDD] (16.97)
Symphony No. 1 in b (1894)
R. Edlinger (cnd), Romanian State PO † Sym 2 MARC ▲ 8223163 (13.97)
V. Polianski (cnd), Russian State SO † Missa Sancti Spiritus, Op. 169; Snowflakes, Op. 47 CHN ▲ 9397 [DDD] (16.97)
Symphony No. 2 in A, Op. 27, "Pastoral" (1909)
E. Chivzhel (cnd), USSR RSO † Sym 4 OLY ▲ 586 [ADD] (16.97)
V. Polianski (cnd), Russian State SO † Mass "Et in terra pax", Op. 166 CHN ▲ 9486 (16.97)
J. Wildner (cnd), Czech-Slovak State Radio PO † Sym 1 MARC ▲ 8223163 (13.97)
Symphony No. 4 in C, Op. 102 (1924)
V. Polianski (cnd), Russian State SO † Con Vc, Op. 8; Missa festiva, Op. 154 CHN ▲ 9559 (16.97)
A. Zhuraitis (cnd), USSR RSO † Sym 2 OLY ▲ 586 [ADD] (16.97)
Symphony No. 3 in E, Op. 100 (1923)
V. Polyansky (cnd), Russian State SO † Praise the Lord, Op. 65 CHN ▲ 9698 (16.97)
Trio No. 1 in c for Piano, Violin & Cello, Op. 38 (1906)
Bekova Sisters † Trio 2 Pno, Op. 128 CHN ▲ 9461 (16.97)
Trio No. 2 in G for Piano, Violin & Cello, Op. 128 (1930)
Bekova Sisters † Trio 1 Pno, Op. 38 CHN ▲ 9461 (16.97)
Vespers Liturgy for Chorus, Op. 59
S. Layton (cnd), Holst Singers *(rec Temple Church, London, England, Nov 8-15, 1998)* † In thy Kingdom, Op. 58/3; Lord, now lettest Thou Thy Servant, Op. 34/1; Now the Powers of Heaven, Op. 58/6 HYP ▲ 67080 [DDD] (18.97)
Vokliknite Gospodevi vsya zemlya for Chorus, Op. 19/2
N. Korniev (cnd), St. Petersburg Chamber Choir *(rec St. Petersburg, Russia, Apr 1996)* ("Russian Christmas") † Anonymous:Deva dnes'; Dobr'ii vechir Tobi; Nebo i zemlya; Noch' tikha, noch svyata; Nova radist' stala; Pavochka khodit; Rozhdestvo Christovo angel priletel; Rozhdestvo Khristovo ves' mir prazdnuet; Vzglyani syuda; Chesnokov:Sacred Works, Op. 43; Cui:Presvyatïya bogoroditsï, Op. 93; Liadov:Perelozheniya iz obikhoda; Shvedov:Tebe Poem; A. Yegorov:Bogoroditse Devo PPHI ▲ 454616 [DDD] (16.97)
GRÉTRY, ANDRÉ-ERNEST-MODESTE (1741-1813)
Céphale et Procuris (selections)
F. Mahler (cnd), Hartford SO—Tambourin; Menuetto (Les Nymphes de Diane); Gigue *(rec Hartford, CT, Mar 1961)* † C. W. Gluck:Music of Gluck; H. Purcell:Abdelazer, Z.570; Rameau:Music of Rameau VC ▲ 108 [AAD] (13.97)
Concerto in C for Flute & Orchestra [doubtful]
A. Daboncourt (fl), B. Dawidow (cnd), Russian Philharmonic CO Tomsk *(rec Oct 1995)* ("Concertos pour flûte favoris") † F. Devienne:Con 4 Fl; Gianella:Con 1 Fl; F. X. Pokorny:Con Fl DPV ▲ 9680 [DDD] (15.97)
Quartets (6) for Strings, Op. 3 (1773)
Via Nova String Quartet PVY ▲ 98102 (16.97)
GRIBOYEDOV, ALEXANDER (1795-1829)
Waltz in A♭ for Piano
V. Leyetchkiss (pno) *(rec De Paul University, Chicago, IL, May 1997)* † Waltz in e; Balakirev:Islamey; Polka; Borodin:Petite Suite Pno; M. Glinka:Farewell to St Petersburg; Kalinnikov:Elegy; Nocturne; Rebikov:Christmas Tree (sels); Mazurka; A. Scriabin:Mazurkas (9) Pno, Op. 25; Pieces (2) Pno, Op. 57 CENT ▲ 2398 (live) [DDD] (16.97)
Waltz in e for Piano
V. Leyetchkiss (pno) *(rec De Paul University, Chicago, IL, May 1997)* † Waltz in A♭; Balakirev:Islamey; Polka; Borodin:Petite Suite Pno; M. Glinka:Farewell to St Petersburg; Kalinnikov:Elegy; Nocturne; Rebikov:Christmas Tree (sels); Mazurka; A. Scriabin:Mazurkas (9) Pno, Op. 25; Pieces (2) Pno, Op. 57 CENT ▲ 2398 (live) [DDD] (16.97)
GRIEBLING, STEPHEN (1932-
Queensmere: December 1964 for Orchestra [3rd movement of Symphony in F♯] (1971; rev. 1980 & 1987)
J. Swoboda (cnd), Silesian PO ("Modern American Classics, Vol 2") † Bokhour:Angel Butcher; E. George:Intro & Allegro; J. D. Goodman:Sym 2 MASM ▲ 2027 [DDD] (16.97)
GRIEG, EDVARD (1843-1907)
Album Leaves (4) for Piano, Op. 28 (1864-78)
H. Bauer (pno)—No. 1 in A♭; No. 3 in A † Lyric Pieces; Pictures from Life in the Country, Op. 19; Liszt:Études de concert (2), S.145; Études de concert (3), S.144; R. Schumann:Fantasiestücke Pno, Op. 12; Pno Music (misc colls) BPS ▲ 11 (16.97)
Ballade in g for Piano, Op. 24 (1875-6)
L. Godowsky (pno) *(rec 1926-30)* † Beethoven:Son 26 Pno, Op. 81a; Chopin:Études Pno; Nocturnes Pno; Scherzos Pno; Son Pno in b♭, Op. 35; L. Godowsky:Transcriptions & Paraphrases; Liszt:Paraphrase on Verdi; R. Schumann:Carnaval, Op. 9 PPHI (Great Pianists of the 20th Century, Vol. 37) 2-▲ 456805 (22.97)
L. Godowsky (pno), L. Godowsky (pno) † Con Pno, Op. 16; Lyric Pieces; Piano Music (selections) PHS ▲ 9933 (live) [AAD] (17.97)
D. Paperno (pno) ("Recordings of a Moscow Pianist") † J. Brahms:Rhaps (2) Pno, Op. 79; Chopin:Son Pno in b♭, Op. 35; Liszt:Polonaises (2) Pno, S.223; Rhap espagnole, S.254; Venezia e Napoli, S.159 CED ▲ 37 [ADD] (16.97)
A. Rubinstein (pno) † Con Pno, Op. 16 RCAV (Gold Seal) ▲ 60897 (11.97)
A. Rubinstein (pno) † Con Pno, Op. 16 RCAV (Gold Seal) ▲ 61883 (11.97)
Concerto in a for Piano & Orchestra, Op. 16 (1868; rev 1906-07)
L. O. Andsnes (pno), D. Kitaienko (cnd), Bergen PO † Liszt:Con 2 Pno, S.125 EMIA ▲ 59613 [DDD]
W. Backhaus (pno), J. Barbirolli (cnd), New SO *(rec Oct 1933)* † W. A. Mozart:Con 26 Pno, K.537 MPLY ▲ 2027 (m) (13.97)
E. Ciccarelli (pno), A. Vedernikov (cnd), Milan SO † S. Rachmaninoff:Sym Dances, Op. 45 AG ▲ 114 (18.97)
V. Cliburn (pno), E. Ormandy (cnd), Philadelphia Orch † Liszt:Cons (2) Pno RCAV (Gold Seal) ▲ 7834 [ADD] (11.97)
F. Clidat (pno), Z. Macal (cnd), Philharmonia Orch † C. Franck:Symphonic Vars, M.46 FORL ▲ 16673 [ADD] (16.97)
C. Curzon (pno), ØL. Fjeldstad (cnd), London SO † Peer Gynt, Op. 23 PLON (The Classic Sound) ▲ 448599 (11.97)
B. Davidovich (pno), G. Schwarz (cnd), Seattle SO † Holberg Suite Pno, Op. 40; Lyric Suite, Op. 54/1-4 DLS ▲ 3091 [DDD] (14.97)
L. Derwinger (pno), J. Hirokami (cnd), Norrköping SO [original version] *(rec Mar 28, 1993)* † Piano Music (selections) BIS ▲ 619 (17.97)
L. Derwinger (pno), J. Hirokami (cnd), Norrköping SO † In Autumn, Op. 11; Piano Music (selections); Sym BIS (BIS Twins) 2-▲ 200619 (17.97)
S. Eisenberger (pno), A. D. Greef (pno), A. V. Kreisler (cnd), Cincinnati SO [previously unpublished] *(rec live, Apr 4, 1938)* † Ballade Pno, Op. 24; Lyric Pieces; Piano Music (selections) PHS ▲ 9933 (live) [AAD] (17.97)
P. Entremont (pno), E. Ormandy (cnd), Philadelphia Orch † R. Schumann:Con Pno in a, Op. 54; Intro & Allegro appassionato, Op. 92 SNYC (Essential Classics) ▲ 46543 [ADD] (7.97) ▮ 46543 [ADD] (3.98)
M. Fingerhut (pno), V. Handley (cnd), Ulster Orch † Lyric Suite, Op. 54/1-4; Peer Gynt Suites CHN ▲ 7040 (13.97)
N. Freire (pno), R. Kempe (cnd), Munich PO *(rec 1968)* † R. Schumann:Con Pno in a, Op. 54 SNYC ▲ 46269 [AAD] (7.97)
I. Friedman (pno), P. Gaubert (cnd), Symphony Orch *(rec 1928)* † Mendelssohn (-Bartholdy):Lieder ohne Worte ENPL (Piano Library) ▲ 271 (13.97)
W. Gieseking (pno), W. Furtwängler (cnd), Berlin PO *(rec July 30, 1944)* ("Furtwängler Conducts during the War Years") † Beethoven:Coriolan Ov, Op. 62; Sym 3; Sym 4; Sym 5; Sym 9 IN 3-▲ 1348 [ADD] (43.97)

GRIEG, EDVARD (cont.)

Concerto in a for Piano & Orchestra, Op. 16 (1868; rev 1906-07) (cont.)

W. Gieseking (pno), W. Furtwängler (cnd), Vienna PO *(rec live, Munich, Germany, July 30, 1944)* ("Wilhelm Furtwängler") † Beethoven:Con 4 Pno, Op. 58 RD ▲ 25002 (m) [ADD] (16.97)

W. Gieseking (pno), R. Heger (cnd), Berlin PO *(rec July 1944)* ("Art of Walter Gieseking") † R. Schumann:Con Pno in a, Op. 54 TAHA ▲ 195 (17.97)

W. Gieseking (pno), H. von Karajan (cnd), Philharmonia Orch *(rec 1951)* ("Walter Gieseking Plays") ENT (Palladio) ▲ 4178 [ADD] (13.97)

W. Gieseking (pno), H. Rosbaud (cnd), Berlin State Opera Orch *(rec Berlin, Apr 28-Oct 13, 1937)* ("Walter Gieseking: His First Concerto Recordings, Vol. 3") † Lyric Pieces; C. Franck:Symphonic Vars, M.46; Liszt:Con 1 Pno, S.124 APR ▲ 5513 [ADD] (19.97)

E. Graf (pno), K. Won (cnd), Moscow PO *(rec Great Hall of Moscow Radio Union, Dec 1994)* † Liszt:Son Pno, S.178 INSD ▲ 3539 (14.97)

P. Grainger (pno) [arr Grainger for solo pno] *(rec 1929)* ("Percy Grainger Plays Grieg & Liszt") † Lyric Pieces; Piano Music (selections); Liszt:Hungarian Rhaps, S.244; Polonaises (2) Pno, S.223 KLAV ▲ 11075 [ADD] (18.97)

P. Grainger (pno) [arr Grainger for solo pno] *(rec July 15, 1945)* † P. Grainger:In a Nutshell; S. Rachmaninoff:Con 2 Pno, Op. 18 BPS ▲ 41 [ADD] (16.97)

P. Grainger (pno), P. Dreier (cnd), Aarhus Municipal Orch *(rec Aarhus, Denmark, Feb 25, 1957)* † P. Grainger:Folk Song Settings; Rosenkavalier-Ramble VC ▲ 8205 [AAD] (13.97)

P. Grainger (pno), L. Stokowski (cnd), Hollywood Bowl SO *(rec July 15, 1945)* ("A Grainger/Stokowski Collaboration") † P. Grainger:Folk Song Settings; In a Nutshell ARDO ▲ 2003

J. Jaimes (pno), E. Mata (cnd), London SO † Elegiac Melodies, Op. 34; Holberg Suite Pno, Op. 40; Lyric Suite, Op. 54/1-4 ASVQ ▲ 6176 (10.97)

J. Jandó (pno), A. Ligeti (cnd), Budapest SO † R. Schumann:Con Pno in a, Op. 54 NXIN ▲ 550118 [DDD] (5.97)

J. Jandó (pno), A. Ligeti (cnd), Budapest SO *(rec Italian Institute Budapest, Mar 1-6, 1988)* ("Piano Concertos") † Liszt:Con 1 Pno, S.124; Mendelssohn (-Bartholdy):Con 2 Pno, Op. 40 NXIN ▲ 553267 [DDD] (5.97)

J. Jandó (pno), J. Sándor (cnd), Budapest PO † Peer Gynt Suite 1, Op. 46; Peer Gynt Suite 2, Op. 55 LALI ▲ 15617 [DDD] (3.97)

E. Knardahl (pno), K. Ingebretsen (cnd), Royal PO † Pno Music (comp) BIS ▲ 113 (17.97)

L. Kuzmin (pno), A. Vedernikov (cnd), Moscow PO ("19th Century Live") † Beethoven:Con 5 Pno, Op. 73 RUS ▲ 10023 [DDD] (12.97)

M. Lapansky (pno), B. Rezucha (cnd), Slovak PO † R. Schumann:Con Pno in a, Op. 54 OPP ▲ 1279 (12.97)

D. Lipatti (pno) *(rec 1947)* † W. A. Mozart:Son 8 Pno, K.310; D. Scarlatti:Sons Kbd ENPL (Piano Library) ▲ 300 (14.97)

D. Lipatti (pno), A. Galliera (cnd), Philharmonia Orch † J. S. Bach:Jesu, bleibet meine Freude; Chopin:Nocturnes Pno; Son Pno in b, Op. 58; Waltzes Pno; Liszt:Sonetti (3) del Petrarca, S.158; D. Scarlatti:Sons Kbd APR ▲ 5509 [ADD] (18.97)

R. Lupu (pno), A. Previn (cnd), London SO *(rec 1973)* ("Radu Lupu") † Beethoven:Son 14 Pno, Op. 27/2; Vars Pno on Original Theme, WoO 80; J. Brahms:Intermezzos (3) Pno, Op. 117; Theme & Vars Pno; F. Schubert:Moments musicaux, D.780; Son Pno, D.784; R. Schumann:Kinderszenen Pno, Op. 15 PPHI (Great Pianists of the 20th Century) ▲ 456895 (22.97)

A. Malling (pno), M. Schønwandt (cnd), Danish National Radio SO † Kuhlau:Con Pno, Op. 7 CHN ▲ 9699 (16.97)

A. B. Michelangeli (pno), E. Ansermet (cnd), Swiss Romande Orch † Lyric Pieces; J. S. Bach:Italian Con, BWV 971; Beethoven:Con 5 Pno, Op. 73; Chopin:Berceuse, Op. 57; Mazurkas Pno; D. Scarlatti:Sons Kbd; Tomeoni;Allegro Pno IMMM (Magic Master series) ▲ 37042 (6.97)

A. B. Michelangeli (pno), A. Galliera (cnd), La Scala Orch *(rec 1941)* † Chopin:Berceuse, Op. 57; D. Scarlatti:Sons Kbd ENPL (The Piano Library) ▲ 183 (13.97)

A. B. Michelangeli (pno), A. Galliera (cnd), La Scala Orch † J. S. Bach:Italian Con, BWV 971; Chopin:Berceuse, Op. 57; D. Scarlatti:Sons Kbd ENT (Sirio) ▲ 53003 (13.97)

A. B. Michelangeli (pno), A. Galliera (cnd), La Scala Orch † R. Schumann:Con Pno in a, Op. 54 IMMM (Magic Master series) ▲ 37050 (6.97)

A. B. Michelangeli (pno), A. Pedrotti (cnd), La Scala Orch *(rec 1942)* † R. Schumann:Con Pno in a, Op. 54 MTAL ▲ 48058 (6.97)

B. Moiseiwitsch (pno), L. Heward (cnd), Hallé Orch *(rec Manchester, England, Oct 22-23, 1941)* † Liszt:Fant on Hungarian Folk Tunes, S.123; Saint-Saëns:Con 2 Pno, Op. 22 APR ▲ 5529 (m) [ADD] (18.97)

B. Moseiwitsch (pno), L. Heward (cnd), Hallé Orch † C. Franck:Symphonic Vars, M.46; R. Schumann:Con Pno in a, Op. 54 AVID ▲ 593 (16.97)

Y. Mouravlev (pno), K. Eliasberg (cnd), USSR State SO *(rec 1950)* ("Russian Piano School: Yuri Mouravlev") † Poetic Tone-Pictures, Op. 3 RD (Talents of Russia) ▲ 16328 [ADD] (16.97)

G. Novaes (pno), H. Swarowsky (cnd), Vienna SO *(rec 1950s)* ("The Romantic Novaes") † Chopin:Berceuse, Op. 57; Con 1 Pno, Op. 11; Impromptu in F#, Op. 36; Son Pno in b, Op. 58; M. de Falla:Noches en los jardines de España VOXL (Legends) 2-▲ 5513 [ADD] (9.97)

G. Ohlsson (pno), N. Marriner (cnd), Academy of St. Martin in the Fields *(rec Henry Wood Hall London, Dec 4-6, 1996)* † Symphonic Dances, Op. 64 HANS (Academy) ▲ 98128 [DDD] (15.97)

M. Perahia (pno), C. Davis (cnd), Bavarian RSO † R. Schumann:Con Pno in a, Op. 54 SNYC ▲ 44899 [DDD] (16.97)

J. Perlea (cnd), Bamberg SO ("The Stories of Schumann & Grieg in Words and Music") † Life & Music of Grieg; Lyric Pieces; Lyric Suite, Op. 54/1-4; Norwegian Dances, Op. 35; R. Schumann:Life & Music of Schumann MMD (Music Masters) ▲ 8505 [ADD] (3.97) ▮ 8505 [ADD] (2.98)

E. Poblocka (pno), T. Wojciechowski (cnd), Polish National RSO Katowice † Elegiac Melodies, Op. 34; Holberg Suite Pno, Op. 40; Peer Gynt (sels); Peer Gynt Suites; Symphonic Dances, Op. 64 CONI 2-▲ 51750 [DDD] (16.97)

R. Pöntinen (pno), L. Segerstam (cnd), Bamberg SO † P. Tchaikovsky:Con 1 Pno, Op. 23 BIS ▲ 375 (17.97)

R. Pöntinen (pno), L. Segerstam (cnd), Bamberg SO † G. Pierné:Con Pno, Op. 12; Ramuntcho (suites); P. Tchaikovsky:Con 1 Pno, Op. 23 BIS (BIS Twins) 2-▲ 375381 (17.97)

J. L. Prats (pno), E. Bátiz (cnd), Royal PO † E. von Dohnányi:Vars on a Nursery Song, Op. 25; Litolff:Con Symphonique 4, Op. 102 INMP ▲ 2048 (9.97)

S. Richter (pno), K. Kondrashin (cnd), Moscow Philharmonic SO † Psalms PRAG ▲ 250048 (18.97)

S. Richter (pno), V. Smetáček (cnd), Prague SO *(rec Czech Radio broadcast, 1954-77)* † A. Dvořák:Con Pno, Op. 33 PRAG (Richter in Prague) ▲ 256001 (18.97)

S. Rodriguez (pno), E. Tabakov (cnd), Sofia PO † Liszt:Con 1 Pno, S.124; P. Tchaikovsky:Con 1 Pno, Op. 23 ELAN ▲ 2228 [DDD] (10.97)

A. Rubinstein (pno), A. Dorati (cnd), Dallas SO *(rec 1947)* ("Rubinstein, Vol. 5") † Liszt:Con 1 Pno, S.124; R. Schumann:Con Pno in a, Op. 54 HPC ▲ 148 (17.97)

A. Rubinstein (pno), E. Ormandy (cnd), Philadelphia Orch † Ballade Pno, Op. 24 RCAV (Gold Seal) ▲ 60897 (11.97)

A. Rubinstein (pno), E. Ormandy (cnd), Philadelphia Orch *(rec 1942)* † Ballade Pno, Op. 24 RCAV (Gold Seal) ▲ 61883 (11.97)

A. Rubinstein (pno), A. Wallenstein (cnd), RCA Victor SO *(rec 1961)* † Chopin:Con 2 Pno, Op. 21; Saint-Saëns:Con 2 Pno, Op. 22; R. Schumann:Con Pno in a, Op. 54; P. Tchaikovsky:Con 1 Pno, Op. 23 PPHI (Great Pianists of the 20th Century, Vol. 86) 2-▲ 456958 (22.97)

A. Schmidt (pno), K. Masur (cnd), Dresden PO † P. Tchaikovsky:Sym 2 BER ▲ 9152 (10.97)

D. Tomšič (pno), A. Nanut (cnd), Ljubljana SO † Norwegian Peasant Dances, Op. 72; Sons Vn PC ▲ 265047 [DDD] (2.97)

I. Uryash (pno), A. Titov (cnd), New Philharmonia Orch † R. Schumann:Con Pno in a, Op. 54 SNYC ▲ 57227 [DDD] (4.97)

A. Wallenstein (cnd), Philadelphia Orch ("Basic 100, Vol. 48") † R. Schumann:Con Pno in a, Op. 54 RCAV ▲ 62677 (10.97)

E. Wild (pno), R. Leibowitz (cnd), Royal PO *(rec 1962)* † Liszt:Fant on Hungarian Folk Tunes, S.123; Saint-Saëns:Con 2 Pno, Op. 22 CHSK ▲ 50 [ADD] (16.97)

K. Zimerman (pno), H. von Karajan (cnd), Berlin SO *(rec Sept 1981)* † R. Schumann:Con Pno in a, Op. 54 DEUT (Karajan Gold) ▲ 39015 [DDD] (16.97)

Elegiac Melodies (2) for String Orchestra, Op. 34 (1881)

M. Abravanel (cnd), Utah SO *(rec 1975)* † Holberg Suite Pno, Op. 40; In Autumn, Op. 11; Norwegian Dances, Op. 35; Peer Gynt Suites; Pictures from Life in the Country, Op. 19; Sigurd Jorsalfar (suite), Op. 56; Symphonic Dances, Op. 64 VB2 2-▲ 5048 [ADD] (9.97)

P. Archibald (cnd) [arr for brass ensemble] ("Lyric Brass") † Norwegian Dances, Op. 35; Peer Gynt (sels); Poetic Tone-Pictures, Op. 3 ASVQ ▲ 6181 (10.97)

J. Barbirolli (cnd), Hallé Orch ("Hallé Favorites, Vol. 2") † Peer Gynt (sels); Chabrier:España; F. Lehár:Gold & Silver, Op. 79; Sibelius:Valse triste; Suppé:Schöne Galatea (ov); J. Turina:Danzas fantásticas, Op. 22; E. Waldteufel:Waltzes, Polkas & Galops DLAB (The Barbirolli Society) ▲ 1013 (17.97)

M. Bernardi (cnd), CBC Vancouver SO † Holberg Suite Pno, Op. 40; C. Nielsen:Little Suite, Op. 1; Sibelius:Valse triste SMS (SM 5000) ▲ 5064 [DDD] (16.97)

T. Dausgaard (cnd) † Fugue; Holberg Suite Pno, Op. 40; Lyric Suite, Op. 54/1-4; Melodies, Op. 53; Norwegian Melodies, Op. 63 ROND ▲ 8342 (19.97)

GRIEG, EDVARD (cont.)

Elegiac Melodies (2) for String Orchestra, Op. 34 (1881) (cont.)

A. Duczmal (cnd), Swiss CO † Holberg Suite Pno, Op. 40; J. Suk:Serenade Strs, Op. 6; P. Tchaikovsky:Serenade Strs, Op. 48 ASVQ ▲ 6094 [ADD] (10.97)

V. Handley (cnd), Ulster Orch † Peer Gynt Suite 1, Op. 46; Sigurd Jorsalfar (suite), Op. 56; Symphonic Dances, Op. 64 CHN ▲ 8524 [DDD] (16.97)

H. Hanson (cnd), Eastman-Rochester Orch—No. 2, Last Spring ("Music for Quiet Listening, Vol. 2") † H. Hanson:Fant Vars on a Theme of Youth, Op. 40; La Montaine:Birds of Paradise, Op. 34; Liadov:Enchanted Lake, Op. 62; Kikimora, Op. 63; C. M. Loeffler:Rhaps PPHI ▲ 434390 (11.97)

A. Leaper (cnd), Capella Istropolitana *(rec Apr 1989)* † Melodies, Op. 53; Norwegian Melodies, Op. 63; Sibelius:Andante festivo; Canzonetta, Op. 62a; Romance Strs, Op. 42; The Lover NXIN ▲ 550330 [DDD] (5.97)

E. Mata (cnd), Swiss CO † Con Pno, Op. 16; Holberg Suite Pno, Op. 40; Lyric Suite, Op. 54/1-4 ASVQ ▲ 6176 (10.97)

E. Ormandy (cnd), Philadelphia Orch *(rec Oct 18, 1967)* † Lyric Pieces; Norwegian Dances, Op. 35; Peer Gynt Suites; Sigurd Jorsalfar (suite), Op. 56 SNYC ▲ 53257 (7.97) ▮ 53257 (3.98)

Orpheus CO † Holberg Suite Pno, Op. 40; P. Tchaikovsky:Serenade Strs, Op. 48 DEUT ▲ 23060 [DDD] (16.97)

W. Rajski (cnd), Musica Vitae—No. 1, The wounded heart; No. 2, Last Spring *(rec Furuby Church, Sweden, 1989)* ("Musica Vitae Plays Nordic Music, Vol. 2") † Fernström:Intimate Miniatures, Op. 2; E. von Koch:Concertino pastorale, Op. 35; C. Nielsen:Little Suite, Op. 1; Sallinen:Some Aspects; T. Sigurbjörnsson:Siciliano BIS ▲ 461 [DDD] (17.97)

J. Somary (cnd), English CO—No. 2, Last Spring *(rec Conway Hall London, England, 1973)* † Holberg Suite Pno, Op. 40; B. Britten:Simple Sym, Op. 4; D. Wirén:Serenade Strs, Op. 11 VC ▲ 45 [AAD] (13.97)

M. R. Sørensen (cnd), Copenhagen Young Strings † Holberg Suite Pno, Op. 40; C. Nielsen:Orchestral Music CLSO ▲ 113 (15.97)

T. Wojciechowski (cnd), Polish National RSO Katowice † Con Pno, Op. 16; Holberg Suite Pno, Op. 40; Peer Gynt (sels); Peer Gynt Suites; Symphonic Dances, Op. 64 CONI 2-▲ 51750 [DDD] (16.97)

Fugue in f for String Quartet (1861)

T. Dausgaard (cnd) † Elegiac Melodies, Op. 34; Holberg Suite Pno, Op. 40; Lyric Suite, Op. 54/1-4; Melodies, Op. 53; Norwegian Melodies, Op. 63 ROND ▲ 8342 (19.97)

Kontra String Quartet *(rec May 13, 1993)* † Qt Strs (unfinished); Qt Strs, Op. 27 BIS ▲ 543 [DDD] (17.97)

Funeral March in Memory of Rikard Nordraak [Sörgemarsch over Rikard Nordraak] in a for Piano (1866; rev 1878; orchd in g for military band)

F. Fennell (cnd), Dallas Wind Sym *(rec June 1992)* ("Trittico") † I. Albéniz:Iberia Suite; V. Giannini:Sym 3; Joio:Variants on a Medieval Tune; Nelhybel:Trittico REF ▲ 52 [DDD] (16.97)

E. Knardahl (pno) *(rec Nacka Sweden, 1977-80)* ("The Grieg Collection") † Humoresques, Op. 6; Lyric Pieces; Nordic Folksongs & Dances, Op. 17; Norwegian Peasant Dances, Op. 72; Pictures from Life in the Country, Op. 19; Poetic Tone-Pictures, Op. 3 BIS ▲ 51 [AAD/DDD] (17.97)

J. Panula (cnd), Scandinavian Brass Ensemble [arr Emerson] *(rec 1984)* † Almila:Te Pa Te Pa, Op. 26; Danielsson:Suite 3 Brass; Hallberg:Blacksmith's Tune; Holmboe:Con Brass, Op. 157; T. Madsen:Divert Brass & Perc, Op. 47; Per the Fiddler, Norwegian Folk Song BIS ▲ 265 [DDD] (17.97)

Haugtussa (song cycle) for Soprano & Piano, Op. 67 (1895)

A. S. von Otter (sop), B. Forsberg (pno) † Songs; Songs (6), Op. 48 DEUT ▲ 37521 [DDD] (16.97)

Holberg Suite for Piano, Op. 40 (1884; orchd 1885)

M. Abravanel (cnd), Utah SO *(rec 1975)* † Elegiac Melodies, Op. 34; In Autumn, Op. 11; Norwegian Dances, Op. 35; Peer Gynt Suites; Pictures from Life in the Country, Op. 19; Sigurd Jorsalfar (suite), Op. 56; Symphonic Dances, Op. 64 VB2 2-▲ 5048 [ADD] (9.97)

M. Bernardi (cnd), CBC Vancouver SO † Elegiac Melodies, Op. 34; C. Nielsen:Little Suite, Op. 1; Sibelius:Valse triste SMS (SM 5000) ▲ 5064 [DDD] (16.97)

G. Botnen (pno) *(rec Eidsvoll Church, Jan 15-16, 1996)* ("Edward Grieg in Hardanger") † Improvisations on 2 Norwegian Folksongs, Op. 29; Norwegian folksongs, Op. 66; Norwegian Dances, Op. 35 SIMX ▲ 1133 [DDD] (18.97)

W. Boughton (cnd), English String Orch *(rec Great Hall, Univ of Birmingham, England, 1995)* ("Orchestral Favorites, Vol. 1") † Albinoni:Adagio; G. Holst:St. Paul's Suite, Op. 29/2; J. Pachelbel:Canon & Gigue; Warlock:Capriol Suite NIMB ▲ 7019 [DDD] (11.97)

T. Dausgaard (cnd) † Elegiac Melodies, Op. 34; Fugue; Lyric Suite, Op. 54/1-4; Melodies, Op. 53; Norwegian Melodies, Op. 63 ROND ▲ 8342 (19.97)

A. Duczmal (cnd), Swiss CO † Elegiac Melodies, Op. 34; J. Suk:Serenade Strs, Op. 6; P. Tchaikovsky:Serenade Strs, Op. 48 ASVQ ▲ 6094 [ADD] (10.97)

J. Faukstad (acc) [trans Faukstad] ("Classic Accordion") † Bibalo:Son quasi una fant; Kvandal:Son Acc, Op. 71; W. Plagge:Facsimiles Acc, Op. 66 NORW ▲ 7028 (17.97)

H. Griffiths (cnd), Zurich CO † C. Nielsen:Little Suite, Op. 1; Sibelius:Romance Strs, Op. 42; D. Wirén:Serenade Strs, Op. 11 NOVA ▲ 150140 (16.97)

H. von Karajan (cnd), Berlin PO † Peer Gynt Suites; Sigurd Jorsalfar (suite), Op. 56 DEUT (Galleria) ▲ 19474 [ADD] (9.97)

H. von Karajan (cnd), Berlin PO † Peer Gynt Suite 1, Op. 46; Peer Gynt Suite 2, Op. 55; Sibelius:Finlandia, Op. 26; Swan of Tuonela; Valse triste DEUT (Karajan Gold) ▲ 39010 [DDD] (16.97)

E. Mata (cnd), Swiss CO † Con Pno, Op. 16; Elegiac Melodies, Op. 34; Lyric Suite, Op. 54/1-4 ASVQ ▲ 6176 (10.97)

Orpheus CO † Elegiac Melodies, Op. 34; P. Tchaikovsky:Serenade Strs, Op. 48 DEUT ▲ 23060 [DDD] (16.97)

G. Schwarz (cnd), Seattle SO † Con Pno, Op. 16; Lyric Suite, Op. 54/1-4 DLS ▲ 3091 [DDD] (14.97)

J. Somary (cnd), English CO *(rec Conway Hall London, 1973)* † Elegiac Melodies, Op. 34; B. Britten:Simple Sym, Op. 4; D. Wirén:Serenade Strs, Op. 11 VC ▲ 45 [AAD] (13.97)

M. R. Sørensen (cnd), Copenhagen Young Strings † Elegiac Melodies, Op. 34; C. Nielsen:Orchestral Music CLSO ▲ 113 (15.97)

R. Studt (cnd), Bournemouth Sinfonietta *(rec Bournemouth, UK, May 31-June 1, 1994)* ("Scandinavian String Music") † C. Nielsen:Little Suite, Op. 1; J. S. Svendsen:Icelandic Melodies; Norwegian Folk Melody; Swedish Folk Melodies, Op. 27; D. Wirén:Serenade Strs, Op. 11 NXIN ▲ 553106 [DDD] (5.97)

O. Suitner (cnd), Berlin Staatskapelle † Lyric Suite, Op. 54/1-4; Norwegian Dances, Op. 35; Sigurd Jorsalfar (sels) BER ▲ 9393 (10.97)

Y. Talmi (cnd), Israel CO † S. Barber:Adagio Strs; E. Bloch:Con grosso 1; G. Puccini:Crisantemi CHN ▲ 8593 [DDD] (16.97)

O. Vlček (cnd) *(rec Prague, Nov 22-25, 1993)* † E. Elgar:Serenade Strs, Op. 20; O. Respighi:Ancient Airs & Dances; A. Roussel:Sinfonietta Strs, Op. 52 DI ▲ 920236 [DDD] (5.97)

T. Wojciechowski (cnd), Polish National RSO Katowice † Con Pno, Op. 16; Elegiac Melodies, Op. 34; Peer Gynt (sels); Peer Gynt Suites; Symphonic Dances, Op. 64 CONI 2-▲ 51750 [DDD] (16.97)

S. Yoo (cnd), Metamorphosen CO *(rec Wellesley, MA, Mar 30-Apr 1, 1997)* † A. Dvořák:Serenade Strs, Op. 22; P. Tchaikovsky:Serenade Strs, Op. 48 ACTR ▲ 60105 [DDD] (17.97)

Humoresques (4) for Piano, Op. 6 (1865)

E. Knardahl (pno) *(rec Nacka, Sweden, 1977-80)* ("The Grieg Collection") † Funeral March in Memory of Rikard Nordraak; Lyric Pieces; Nordic Folksongs & Dances, Op. 17; Norwegian Peasant Dances, Op. 72; Pictures from Life in the Country, Op. 19; Poetic Tone-Pictures, Op. 3 BIS ▲ 51 [AAD/DDD] (17.97)

Improvisations on 2 Norwegian Folksongs for Piano, Op. 29 (1878)

G. Botnen (pno) *(rec Eidsvoll Church, Jan 15-16, 1996)* ("Edward Grieg in Hardanger") † Holberg Suite Pno, Op. 40; Norwegian folksongs, Op. 66; Norwegian Dances, Op. 35 SIMX ▲ 1133 [DDD] (18.97)

In Autumn (concert overture) for Orchestra (or Piano 4-Hands), Op. 11 (1866)

M. Abravanel (cnd), Utah SO *(rec 1975)* † Elegiac Melodies, Op. 34; Holberg Suite Pno, Op. 40; Norwegian Dances, Op. 35; Peer Gynt Suites; Pictures from Life in the Country, Op. 19; Sigurd Jorsalfar (suite), Op. 56; Symphonic Dances, Op. 64 VB2 2-▲ 5048 [ADD] (9.97)

T. Beecham (cnd), Royal PO *(rec Abbey Road, London, England, 1955)* † Old Norwegian Romance, Op. 51; Peer Gynt, Op. 23; Symphonic Dances, Op. 64 EMIC (Great Recordings of the Century) ▲ 66966 [ADD] (11.97)

Giarmanà-Lucchetti Duo *(rec May 14-18, 1996)* ("Complete Works for Piano Duet") † Norwegian Dances, Op. 35; Old Norwegian Romance, Op. 51; Sons Pnos; Waltz Caprices Pnos, Op. 37 STRV 2-▲ 33410 (32.97)

O. Kamu (cnd), Gothenburg SO † Sym BIS ▲ 200 [DDD] (17.97)

O. Kamu (cnd), Gothenburg SO † Con Pno, Op. 16; Piano Music (selections); Sym BIS (BIS Twins) 2-▲ 200619 (17.97)

P. Sakari (cnd), Iceland SO † Lyric Pieces; Norwegian Dances, Op. 35; Old Norwegian Romance, Op. 51; Glière:Sym 2; Zaporozhy Cossacks, Op. 64; J. S. Svendsen:Icelandic Melodies CHN ▲ 9071 [DDD] (16.97)

In Heaven for Orchestra

H. Haukas (cnd), Bergen Military Band [plus music by Hansen; Hurum; Forde] † Halvorsen:Bergensiana; Hovland:Fanfare & Chorale; J. S. Svendsen:Norwegian Artists' Carnival, Op. 14 DOY ▲ 70 (16.97)

GRIEG, EDVARD (cont.)

Intermezzo in a for Cello & Piano (1867)

Ø.. Birkeland (vc), H. Gimse (pno) *(rec May & Aug 1993)* † Son Pno, Op. 7; Son Vc NXIN ▲ 550878 [DDD] (5.97)

J. L. Webber (vc), B. Forsberg (pno) ("Complete Music for Cello & Piano") † Son Vc; Delius:Pieces Vc; Romance Vc; Serenade Vc; Son Vc PPHI ▲ 454458 (16.97)

Life & Music of Grieg

J. Perlea (cnd), Bamberg SO—Peer Gynt Suites; Elegiac Melodies, Op. 34; Symphonic Dances, Op. 64 [No. 4]; Melodies of the Heart [Hjertets melodier], Op. 5 [I love thee [Jeg elsker dig]]; Holberg Suite Pno, Op. 40; Moods Pno, Op. 73 [No. 5, Study: Homage to Chopin]; Sigurd Jorsalfar (suite), Op. 56 [No. 3, Homage March] ("The Stories of Schumann & Grieg in Words and Music") † Con Pno, Op. 16; Lyric Pieces; Lyric Suite, Op. 54/1-4; Norwegian Dances, Op. 35; R. Schumann:Life & Music of Schumann MMD (Music Masters) ▲ 8505 [ADD] (3.97) ▮ 8505 [ADD] (2.98)

Lyric Pieces (10 sets) for Piano, Opp. 12, 38, 43, 47, 54, 57, 62, 65, 68, 71

L. O. Andsnes (pno) † Son Pno, Op. 7 VCL ▲ 59300 (16.97)

H. Bauer (pno)—Op. 38/1, "Berecuse"; Op. 43/1, "Schmetterling"; Op. 43/6, "An den Frühlin"; Op. 47/1, "Waltz-Improptu"; Op. 54/4, "Nocturne" † Album Leaves (4) Pno, Op. 28; Pictures from Life in the Country, Op. 19; Liszt:Etudes de concert (2), S.145; Études de concert (3), S.144; R. Schumann:Fantasiestücke Pno, Op. 12; Pno Music (misc colls) BPS ▲ 11 (16.97)

L. Bernstein (cnd), New York PO—Op. 54/3. "March of the Trolls" [Troldtog] *(rec Lincoln Center New York, NY, Jan 3, 10 & 31, 1967)* † Norwegian Dances, Op. 35; Peer Gynt Suite 1, Op. 46; Peer Gynt Suite 2, Op. 55; Sibelius:Finlandia, Op. 26; Swan of Tuonela; Valse triste SNYC (Bernstein Century) ▲ 63156 [ADD] (11.97)

W. Gieseking (pno)—Op. 12/2, "Waltz"; Op. 12/7, "Albumleaf" [Stambogsblad]; Op. 38/1, "Berecuse"; Op. 38/3, "Melodie"; Op. 43/1, "Schmetterling"; Op. 43/2," Einsamer Wanderer"; Op. 43/3, "In der Heimat"; Op. 43/4, "Vöglein"; Op. 43/5, "Erotik"; Op. 43/6, "An den Frühlin"; Op. 47/2, "Albumleaf"; Op. 47/3, "Melody"; Op. 47/4, "Halling" (Norwegian Dance); Op. 54/1, "Shepherd boy" [Gjaetergut]; Op. 54/3. "March of the Trolls" [Troldtog]; Op. 54/4, "Nocturne"; Op. 54/6, "Bell ringing" [Klokkeklang]; Op. 57/6, "Heimweh"; Op. 62/3, "French Serenade"; Op. 62/5, "Phantom" [Drömmesyn]; Op. 62/6, "Homeward" [Hjemad]; Op. 65/1, "From days of youth" [Fra ungdomsdagene]; Op. 65/2, "Peasant's song" [Bondens sang]; Op. 65/6, "Wedding Day at Troldhaugen" [Bryllupsdag på Trolkhaugen]; Op. 68/2, "Grandmother's minuet" [Bedstemors menuet]; Op. 68/3, "At your feet" [For dine födder]; Op. 68/5, "Cradle song" [Bådnlåt]; Op. 71/2, "Summer evening" [Sommeraften]; Op. 71/3, "Puck" [Småtrold]; Op. 71/4, "The woods' peace" [Skovstilhed]; Op. 71/7, "Remembrances" [Efterklang] *(rec London, England, 1948-56)* † Pictures from Life in the Country, Op. 19; Mendelssohn (-Bartholdy):Lieder ohne Worte EMIC (References) 2-▲ 66775 [ADD] (21.97)

W. Gieseking (pno)—Op. 68/5, "Cradle song" [Bådnlåt]; Op. 62/3, "French Serenade" *(rec Berlin, Germany, Apr 29, 1937)* ("Walter Gieseking: His First Concerto Recordings, Vol. 3") † Con Pno, Op. 16; C. Franck:Symphonic Vars, M.46; Liszt:Con 1 Pno, S.124 APR ▲ 5513 [ADD] (19.97)

Em. Gilels (pno)—Op. 12/1, "Arietta"; Op. 38/1, "Berecuse"; Op. 43/1, "Schmetterling"; Op. 43/2," Einsamer Wanderer"; Op. 47/2, "Albumleaf"; Op. 47/3, "Melody"; Op. 47/4, "Halling" (Norwegian Dance); Op. 54/4, "Nocturne"; Op. 54/5, "Scherzo"; Op. 57/6, "Heimweh"; Op. 62/4, "Little brook" [Baekken]; Op. 62/6, "Homeward" [Hjemad]; Op. 65/5, "In ballad style" [I balladetone]; Op. 68/2, "Grandmother's minuet" [Bedstemors menuet]; Op. 68/3, "At your feet" [For dine fööder]; Op. 68/5, "Cradle song" [Bådnlåt]; Op. 71/1, "Once upon a time" [Der var engang]; Op. 71/3, "Puck" [Småtrold]; Op. 71/6, "Gone" [Forbi]; Op. 71/7, "Remembrances" [Efterklang] *(rec 1974)* DEUT (The Originals) ▲ 449721 [ADD] (11.97)

Em. Gilels (pno) [sels] *(rec 1959-78)* ("Emil Gilels III") † J. Brahms:Con 2 Pno, Op. 83; Chopin:Études Pno; Son Pno in b, Op. 58; Son Pno in b♭, Op. 35; M. Clementi:Son Pno; F. Schubert:Fant Pno, D.940; R. Schumann:Arabeske Pno, Op. 18 PPHI (Great Pianists of the 20th Century) 2-▲ 456799 (22.97)

P. Grainger (pno)—Op. 65/6, "Wedding Day at Troldhaugen" [Bryllupsdag på Trolkhaugen]; Op. 43/5, "Erotik"; Op. 43/6, "An den Frühlin" *(rec 1929)* ("Percy Grainger Plays Grieg & Liszt") † Con Pno, Op. 16; Piano Music (selections); Liszt:Hungarian Rhaps, S.244; Polonaises (2) Pno, S.223 KLAV ▲ 11075 [ADD] (18.97)

J. Stockmarr, E. Grieg (pno), A. D. Greef (pno), W. Gieseking (pno), P. Grainger (pno)—Op. 43/6, "An den Frühlin"; Op. 12/1, "Arietta"; Op. 43/1, "Schmetterling"; Op. 62/3, "French Serenade"; Op. 68/5, "Cradle song" [Bådnlåt]; Op. 65/6, "Wedding Day at Troldhaugen" [Bryllupsdag på Trolkhaugen] *(rec 1903-38)* † Ballade Pno, Op. 24; Con Pno, Op. 16; Piano Music (selections) PHS ▲ 9933 (live) [AAD] (17.97)

E. Knardahl (pno) *(rec Nacka Sweden, 1977-80)* ("The Grieg Collection") † Funeral March in Memory of Rikard Nordraak; Humoresques, Op. 6; Nordic Folksongs & Dances, Op. 17; Norwegian Peasant Dances, Op. 72; Pictures from Life in the Country, Op. 19; Poetic Tone-Pictures, Op. 3 BIS ▲ 51 [AAD/DDD] (17.97)

A. B. Michelangeli (pno)—Op. 43/5, "Erotik" † R. Schumann:Con Pno in a, Op. 54; Tomeoni:Allegro Pno ENPL (Piano Library) ▲ 211 (13.97)

A. B. Michelangeli (pno)—Op. 43/5, "Erotik" † Con Pno, Op. 16; J. S. Bach:Italian Con, BWV 971; Beethoven:Con 5 Pno, Op. 73; Chopin:Berceuse, Op. 57; Mazurkas Pno; D. Scarlatti:Sons Kbd; Tomeoni:Allegro Pno IMMM (Magic Master series) ▲ 37042 (6.97)

A. B. Michelangeli (pno)—Op. 47/5, "Melancholy"; Op. 68/5, "Cradle song" [Bådnlåt] † I. Albéniz:Recuerdos de Viaje, Op. 71; Beethoven:Son 3 Pno, Op. 2/3; E. Granados:Andaluza Pno, Op. 37/5; Mompou:Cançons i dansas Pno; D. Scarlatti:Sons Kbd MTAL ▲ 48010 (6.97)

A. B. Michelangeli (pno)—Op. 47/5, "Melancholy"; Op. 68/5, "Cradle song" [Bådnlåt] † I. Albéniz:España, Op. 165; Beethoven:Son 3 Pno, Op. 2/3; E. Granados:Andaluza Pno, Op. 37/5; D. Scarlatti:Sons Kbd IMMM (Magic Master series) ▲ 37025 (6.97)

E. Ormandy (cnd), Philadelphia Orch—Op. 54/3. "March of the Trolls" [Troldtog]; Op. 54/4, "Nocturne" *(rec May 15, 1968)* † Elegiac Melodies, Op. 34; Norwegian Dances, Op. 35; Peer Gynt Suites; Sigurd Jorsalfar (suite), Op. 56 SNYC ▲ 53257 (7.97) ▮ 53257 (3.98)

J. Perlea (cnd), Bamberg SO—Op. 12/4, "Elves' dance" [Elverdans]; Op. 43/1, "Schmetterling"; Op. 65/6, "Wedding Day at Troldhaugen" [Bryllupsdag på Trolkhaugen] ("The Stories of Schumann & Grieg in Words and Music") † Con Pno, Op. 16; Life & Music of Grieg; Lyric Suite, Op. 54/1-4; Norwegian Dances, Op. 35; R. Schumann:Life & Music of Schumann MMD (Music Masters) ▲ 8505 [ADD] (3.97) ▮ 8505 [ADD] (2.98)

S. Richter (pno) ("Sviatoslav Richter, Vol. 8") † Debussy:Preludes Pno STRV 2-▲ 33353 [DDD] (16.97)

S. Richter (pno) *(rec Schliersee, Germany, July 7, 1993)* LV ▲ 442 [DDD] (17.97)

P. Sakari (cnd), Iceland SO—Op. 43/5, "Erotik" [arr Max Spicker] † In Autumn, Op. 11; Norwegian Dances, Op. 35; Old Norwegian Romance, Op. 51; Glière:Sym 2; Zaporozhy Cossacks, Op. 64; J. S. Svendsen:Icelandic Melodies CHN ▲ 9071 [DDD] (16.97)

B. Szokolay (pno)—Op. 12/1, "Arietta"; Op. 12/2, "Waltz"; Op. 12/5, "Folksong" [Folkevise]; Op. 12/7, "Albumleaf" [Stambogsblad]; Op. 43/2," Einsamer Wanderer"; Op. 47/1, "Waltz-Improptu"; Op. 47/2, "Albumleaf"; Op. 47/3, "Melody"; Op. 47/4, "Halling" (Norwegian Dance); Op. 54/2. "Norwegian rustic march" [Gangar]; Op. 57/5, "Sie tanzt"; Op. 65/1, "From days of youth" [Fra ungdomsdagene]; Op. 68/1, "Sailor's song" [Matrosernes opsang]; Op. 68/3, "At your feet" [For dine födder]; Op. 68/6, "Melancholy waltz" *(rec Nov & Dec, 1989)* NXIN ▲ 550450 [DDD] (5.97)

B. Szokolay (pno)—Op. 12/1, "Arietta"; Op. 12/6, "Norwegian melody" [Norsk]; Op. 38/5, "Springtanz"; Op. 54/1, "Shepherd boy" [Gjaetergut]; Op. 54/4, "Nocturne"; Op. 54/5, "Scherzo"; Op. 57/4, "Geheimnis"; Op. 57/6, "Heimweh"; Op. 62/3, "French Serenade"; Op. 62/4, "Little brook" [Baekken]; Op. 62/6, "Homeward" [Hjemad]; Op. 65/1, "From days of youth" [Fra ungdomsdagene]; Op. 65/2, "Peasant's song" [Bondens sang]; Op. 65/3, "Melancholy" [Tungsind]; Op. 65/4, "Salon"; Op. 68/2, "Grandmother's minuet" [Bedstemors menuet]; Op. 68/4, "Evening in the mountains" [Aften på höjfjeldet]; Op. 68/5, "Cradle song" [Bådnlåt]; Op. 71/1, "Once upon a time" [Der var engang] *(rec Feb 1990)* ("Lyric Pieces, Vol. 3") NXIN ▲ 550650 [DDD] (5.97)

B. Szokolay (pno) *(rec Dec 13 & 16-19, 1991)* ("Lyric Pieces, Vol. 2") NXIN ▲ 550577 [DDD] (5.97)

J. Vaabensted (pno) [sels unknown] ("Pearls for Solo Piano in the Nordic Tone") † Palmgren:Majnat; H. Saeverud:Rondo amoroso; Sibelius:Pno Music DANR 2-▲ 493

P. Vairo (pno)—Op. 43/1, "Schmetterling" *(rec May 1992)* † Piano Music (selections); Beethoven:Son 12 Pno, Op. 26; A. Khachaturian:Toccata; Liszt:Liebesträume, S.541; S. Rachmaninoff:Morceaux de salon, Op. 10; R. Schumann:Fantasiestücke Pno, Op. 12 STRV ▲ 102 [DDD] (16.97)

artists unknown—Op. 54/4, "Nocturne"; Op. 54/1, "Shepherd boy" [Gjaetergut]; Op. 68/5, "Cradle song" [Bådnlåt] ("Winter Dreams") † Music of Grieg; Sibelius:Swan of Tuonela; Valse triste; P. Tchaikovsky:Andante cantabile; Con 1 Pno, Op. 23; Serenade Strs, Op. 48 PPHI (Night Moods) ▲ 453908 [DDD] (9.97)

Lyric Suite for Piano, Op. 54/1-4 (1891; orchd 1904)

J. Barbirolli (cnd) *(rec 1957-70)* † Norwegian Melodies, Op. 63; Sigurd Jorsalfar (sels); Symphonic Dances, Op. 64 DLAB ▲ 1012 (17.97)

Y. Butt (cnd), Royal PO † Con Pno, Op. 16; Elegiac Melodies, Op. 34; Holberg Suite Pno, Op. 40 ASVQ ▲ 6176 (10.97)

T. Dausgaard (cnd) † Elegiac Melodies, Op. 34; Fugue; Holberg Suite Pno, Op. 40; Melodies, Op. 53; Norwegian Melodies, Op. 63 ROND ▲ 8342 (19.97)

R. Edlinger (cnd), CSSR State PO Košice *(rec Oct 1988)* † Norwegian Dances, Op. 35; Symphonic Dances, Op. 64; Alfvén:Swedish Rhap 1, Op. 19; Sibelius:Karelia Ov, Op. 10; J. S. Svendsen:Norwegian Artists' Carnival, Op. 14 NXIN ▲ 550090 [DDD] (5.97)

V. Handley (cnd), Ulster Orch † Con Pno, Op. 16; Peer Gynt Suites CHN ▲ 7040 (13.97)

N. Järvi (cnd), Gothenburg SO † Peer Gynt Suites; Sigurd Jorsalfar (suite), Op. 56 DEUT (3D Classics) ▲ 27807 [DDD] (9.97)

GRIEG, EDVARD (cont.)

Lyric Suite for Piano, Op. 54/1-4 (1891; orchd 1904) (cont.)

J. Perlea (cnd), Bamberg SO—Norwegian Rustic March [Gangar]; Nocturne ("The Stories of Schumann & Grieg in Words and Music") † Con Pno, Op. 16; Life & Music of Grieg; Lyric Pieces; Norwegian Dances, Op. 35; R. Schumann:Life & Music of Schumann MMD (Music Masters) ▲ 8505 [ADD] (3.97) ▮ 8505 [ADD] (2.98)

G. Schwarz (cnd), Seattle SO † Con Pno, Op. 16; Holberg Suite Pno, Op. 40 DLS ▲ 3091 [DDD] (14.97)

O. Suitner (cnd), Berlin Staatskapelle [2 movements] † Holberg Suite Pno, Op. 40; Norwegian Dances, Op. 35; Sigurd Jorsalfar (sels) BER ▲ 9393 (10.97)

Melodies of the Heart [Hjertets melodier] (songs) for Voice & Piano, Op. 5 (1863-4)

K. Lövaas (sop), E. Marturet (cnd), Berlin SO—I love thee [Jeg elsker dig] *(rec Netherlands, May 4-5, 1992)* ("Kari Lövaas Sings Songs By Grieg, Sibelius & Strauss") † Peer Gynt (sels); Romances (4), Op. 15; Romances & Songs, Op. 18; Romances, old & new, Op. 39; Songs (12), Op. 33; Songs (6), Op. 25; Sibelius:Songs; R. Strauss:Das Rosenband, Op. 36/1; Heimliche Aufforderung, Op. 27/3; Morgen; Songs; Zueignung, Op. 10/1 VRDI ▲ 32116 [DDD] (13.97)

Melodies (2) for String Orchestra, Op. 53 (1891)

T. Dausgaard (cnd) † Elegiac Melodies, Op. 34; Fugue; Holberg Suite Pno, Op. 40; Lyric Suite, Op. 54/1-4; Norwegian Melodies, Op. 63 ROND ▲ 8342 (19.97)

A. Leaper (cnd), Capella Istropolitana *(rec Apr 1989)* † Elegiac Melodies, Op. 34; Norwegian Melodies, Op. 63; Sibelius:Andante festivo; Canzonetta, Op. 62a; Romance Strs, Op. 42; The Lover NXIN ▲ 550330 [DDD] (5.97)

The Mountain Thrall [Den Bergtekne] for Baritone, 2 Horns & Strings, Op. 32 (1877-78)

K. Skram (b-bar), T. Schuback (cnd), Gothenburg CO *(rec Gothenburg Concert Hall, Sweden, Mar 21-23, 1976)* ("Nordic Vocal Music") † Songs; Kilpinen:Lieder der Liebe I-II, Op. 59; Lieder um den Tod, Op. 62; Rangström:Ur kung Eriks visor; Sibelius:Songs BIS ▲ 43 [AAD] (17.97)

Music of Grieg

J. Silverstein (vn), R. Sherman (pno), A. Gerhardt (cnd), Utah SO, A. Gerhardt (cnd), London Promenade Orch—Peer Gynt Suites; Holberg Suite Pno, Op. 40; Con Pno, Op. 16 [Allegro molto moderato] ("Grieg's Greatest Hits") PRMX ▲ 811

artists unknown—Holberg Suite Pno, Op. 40; Elegiac Melodies, Op. 34; Peer Gynt Suite 1, Op. 46 [Anitra's Dance]; Peer Gynt Suite 2, Op. 55 [Solveig's Song]; Con Pno, Op. 16 [Adagio] ("Winter Dreams") † Lyric Pieces; Sibelius:Swan of Tuonela; Valse triste; P. Tchaikovsky:Andante cantabile; Con 1 Pno, Op. 23; Serenade Strs, Op. 48 PPHI (Night Moods) ▲ 453908 [DDD] (9.97)

Nordic Folksongs & Dances (25) for Piano, Op. 17 (1869)

E. Knardahl (pno) *(rec Nacka Sweden, 1977-80)* ("The Grieg Collection") † Funeral March in Memory of Rikard Nordraak; Humoresques, Op. 6; Lyric Pieces; Norwegian Peasant Dances, Op. 72; Pictures from Life in the Country, Op. 19; Poetic Tone-Pictures, Op. 3 BIS ▲ 51 [AAD/DDD] (17.97)

Norwegian Dances (4) for Piano 4-Hands (or Piano), Op. 35 (1881)

M. Abravanel (cnd), Utah SO *(rec 1975)* † Elegiac Melodies, Op. 34; Holberg Suite Pno, Op. 40; In Autumn, Op. 11; Peer Gynt Suites; Pictures from Life in the Country, Op. 19; Sigurd Jorsalfar (suite), Op. 56; Symphonic Dances, Op. 64 VB2 2-▲ 5048 [ADD] (9.97)

P. Archibald (cnd) [arr for brass ensemble] ("Lyric Brass") † Elegiac Melodies, Op. 34; Peer Gynt (sels); Poetic Tone-Pictures, Op. 3 ASVQ ▲ 6181 (10.97)

L. Bernstein (cnd), New York PO *(rec Lincoln Center New York, NY, NY, Jan 3, 10 & 31, 1967)* † Lyric Pieces; Peer Gynt Suite 1, Op. 46; Peer Gynt Suite 2, Op. 55; Sibelius:Finlandia, Op. 26; Swan of Tuonela; Valse triste SNYC (Bernstein Century) ▲ 63156 [ADD] (11.97)

G. Botnen (pno), J. H. Bratlie (pno) *(rec Eidsvoll Church, Jan 15-16, 1996)* ("Edward Grieg in Hardanger") † Holberg Suite Pno, Op. 40; Improvisations on 2 Norwegian Folksongs, Op. 29; Norwegian folksongs, Op. 66 SIMX ▲ 1133 [DDD] (18.97)

R. Edlinger (cnd), CSSR State PO Košice *(rec Oct 1988)* † Lyric Suite, Op. 54/1-4; Symphonic Dances, Op. 64; Alfvén:Swedish Rhap 1, Op. 19; Sibelius:Karelia Ov, Op. 10; J. S. Svendsen:Norwegian Artists' Carnival, Op. 14 NXIN ▲ 550090 [DDD] (5.97)

Giarmanà-Lucchetti Duo *(rec May 14-18, 1996)* ("Complete Works for Piano Duet") † In Autumn, Op. 11; Old Norwegian Romance, Op. 51; Sons Pnos; Waltz Caprices Pnos, Op. 37 STRV 2-▲ 33410 (32.97)

J. J. Gutiérrez (pno), M. R. Brià (pno) *(rec 1996)* ("Danses romantiques") † A. Dvořák:Slavonic Dances (sels); Moszkowski:Spanische Tänze, Op. 12; R. Schumann:Kinderball, Op. 130 LAMA (Ars Harmonica) ▲ 20 [DDD] (17.97)

E. Ormandy (cnd), Philadelphia Orch—No. 2 in A *(rec Feb 27, 1968)* † Elegiac Melodies, Op. 34; Lyric Pieces; Peer Gynt Suites; Sigurd Jorsalfar (suite), Op. 56 SNYC ▲ 53257 (7.97) ▮ 53257 (3.98)

J. Perlea (cnd), Bamberg SO—No. 1 in d; No. 2 in A ("The Stories of Schumann & Grieg in Words and Music") † Con Pno, Op. 16; Life & Music of Grieg; Lyric Pieces; Lyric Suite, Op. 54/1-4; R. Schumann:Life & Music of Schumann MMD (Music Masters) ▲ 8505 [ADD] (3.97) ▮ 8505 [ADD] (2.98)

P. Sakari (cnd), Iceland SO † In Autumn, Op. 11; Lyric Pieces; Old Norwegian Romance, Op. 51; Glière:Sym 2; Zaporozhy Cossacks, Op. 64; J. S. Svendsen:Icelandic Melodies CHN ▲ 9071 [DDD] (16.97)

E. Steen-Nøkleberg (pno) *(rec Norwegian State Academy of Music Oslo, Norway, Feb 12-14, 1994)* ("Piano Music Vol 12") † Peer Gynt, Op. 23; Pno Music (comp) NXIN ▲ 553398 [DDD] (5.97)

O. Suitner (cnd), Berlin Staatskapelle † Holberg Suite Pno, Op. 40; Lyric Suite, Op. 54/1-4; Sigurd Jorsalfar (sels) BER ▲ 9393 (10.97)

Norwegian folksongs (19) for Piano, Op. 66 (1897)

L. O. Andsnes (pno)—Calling the cows [Kulok]; Tomorrow you shall marry [Morgo ska du få gifte deg]; Cradle song [Bådnlåt]; I wander deep in thought [Jeg gaar i tusind tanker] *(rec Jan 1997)* ("The Long, Long Winter Night") † Norwegian Peasant Dances, Op. 72; D. M. Johansen:Suite 1 Pno, Op. 5; H. Saeverud:Peer Gynt Suites, Op. 28; Tunes & Dances from Siljustøl; Tveitt:Folk Tunes from Hardanger, Op. 150; Valen:Vars Pno, Op. 23 EMIC ▲ 56541 [DDD] (16.97)

G. Botnen (pno) *(rec Eidsvoll Church, Jan 15-16, 1996)* ("Edward Grieg in Hardanger") † Holberg Suite Pno, Op. 40; Improvisations on 2 Norwegian Folksongs, Op. 29; Norwegian Dances, Op. 35 SIMX ▲ 1133 [DDD] (18.97)

Norwegian Melodies (2) for Piano, Op. 63 (1869; orchd 1895)

J. Barbirolli (cnd) *(rec 1957-70)* † Lyric Suite, Op. 54/1-4; Sigurd Jorsalfar (sels); Symphonic Dances, Op. 64 DLAB ▲ 1012 (17.97)

T. Dausgaard (cnd) † Elegiac Melodies, Op. 34; Fugue; Holberg Suite Pno, Op. 40; Lyric Suite, Op. 54/1-4; Melodies, Op. 53 ROND ▲ 8342 (19.97)

A. Leaper (cnd), Capella Istropolitana *(rec Apr 1989)* † Elegiac Melodies, Op. 34; Melodies, Op. 53; Sibelius:Andante festivo; Canzonetta, Op. 62a; Romance Strs, Op. 42; The Lover NXIN ▲ 550330 [DDD] (5.97)

Norwegian Peasant Dances (17) for Piano, Op. 72 (1902-03)

L. O. Andsnes (pno)—Halling from the hills [Haugelåt: halling]; Prillar from the churchplay Os [Prillaren fra Os Praestegjeld]; Gangar; Knut Luråsens halling I; Goblin's bridal procession [Tussebrurefaera på vossevangen] *(rec Jan 1997)* ("The Long, Long Winter Night") † Norwegian folksongs, Op. 66; D. M. Johansen:Suite 1 Pno, Op. 5; H. Saeverud:Peer Gynt Suites, Op. 28; Tunes & Dances from Siljustøl; Tveitt:Folk Tunes from Hardanger, Op. 150; Valen:Vars Pno, Op. 23 EMIC ▲ 56541 [DDD] (16.97)

S. Jeschko (pno) † Con Pno, Op. 16; Sons Vn PC ▲ 265047 [DDD] (2.97)

E. Knardahl (pno)—Rötnamsknut; Bridal March [Bruremarsch] *(rec Nacka Sweden, Sweden, 1977-80)* ("The Grieg Collection") † Funeral March in Memory of Rikard Nordraak; Humoresques, Op. 6; Lyric Pieces; Nordic Folksongs & Dances, Op. 17; Pictures from Life in the Country, Op. 19; Poetic Tone-Pictures, Op. 3 BIS ▲ 51 [AAD/DDD] (17.97)

Old Norwegian Romance with Variations for 2 Pianos (or Orchestra), Op. 51 (1891)

T. Beecham (cnd), Royal PO *(rec Abbey Road, London, England, 1955)* † In Autumn, Op. 11; Peer Gynt, Op. 23; Symphonic Dances, Op. 64 EMIC (Great Recordings of the Century) ▲ 66966 [ADD] (11.97)

Giarmanà-Lucchetti Duo *(rec May 14-18, 1996)* ("Complete Works for Piano Duet") † In Autumn, Op. 11; Norwegian Dances, Op. 35; Sons Pnos; Waltz Caprices Pnos, Op. 37 STRV 2-▲ 33410 (32.97)

P. Sakari (cnd), Iceland SO † In Autumn, Op. 11; Lyric Pieces; Norwegian Dances, Op. 35; Glière:Sym 2; Zaporozhy Cossacks, Op. 64; J. S. Svendsen:Icelandic Melodies CHN ▲ 9071 [DDD] (16.97)

Peer Gynt (incidental music) for solo Voices, Orchestra & Chorus, Op. 23 (1874-75)

T. Beecham (cnd), London PO ("Beecham Favourites") † Bizet:Arlésienne; Chabrier:España; P. Tchaikovsky:Francesca da Rimini, Op. 32 DLAB (Essential Archives) ▲ 5017 (15.97)

T. Beecham (cnd), Royal PO, D. Vaughan (cnd), Beecham Choral Society, I. Hollweg (sop—Solveig) *(rec Abbey Road, London, England, 1956-57)* † In Autumn, Op. 11; Old Norwegian Romance, Op. 51; Symphonic Dances, Op. 64 *([ENG,GER]text)* EMIC (Great Recordings of the Century) ▲ 66966 [ADD] (11.97)

B. Bonney (sop), M. Eklöf (mez), K. M. Sandve (ten), U. Malmberg (bar), N. Järvi (cnd), Gothenburg SO, Gothenburg Sym Chorus [NOR] † Sigurd Jorsalfar, Op. 22 DEUT 2-▲ 23079 [DDD] (32.97)

L. Derwinger (pno) *(rec May 5-6, 1993)* † Piano Music (selections) BIS ▲ 620 [DDD] (17.97)

ØL. Fjeldstad (cnd), London SO † Con Pno, Op. 16 PLON (The Classic Sound) ▲ 448599 (11.97)

V. Hanssen (mez), C. Carlson (mez), K. Bjørkøy (ten), A. Hansli (bar), P. Dreier (cnd), London SO, Oslo Phil Chorus [NOR] UNIC 2-▲ 2003 [AAD] (33.97)

GRIEG, EDVARD (cont.)

Peer Gynt (incidental music) for solo Voices, Orchestra & Chorus, Op. 23 (1874-75) (cont.)

B. Hendricks (sop), E. Salonen (cnd), Oslo PO, Oslo Phil Chorus SNYC ▲ 44528 [DDD] (16.97) COL △ 44528 [DDD]

L. Popp (sop), N. Marriner (cnd), Academy of St. Martin in the Fields, Ambrosian Singers EMIC ▲ 47003 [DDD] (16.97)

E. Steen-Nøkleberg (pno), S. Schioll (cnd), Norwegian State Institute of Music Chamber Choir *(rec Norwegian State Academy of Music Oslo, Feb 12-14, 1994)* ("Piano Music Vol 12") † Norwegian Dances, Op. 35; Pno Music (comp) NXIN ▲ 553398 [DDD] (5.97)

Peer Gynt (selections)

P. Archibald (cnd) —Solvejg's Song ("Lyric Brass") † Elegiac Melodies, Op. 34; Norwegian Dances, Op. 35; Poetic Tone-Pictures, Op. 3 ASVQ ▲ 6181 (10.97)

J. Barbirolli (cnd), Hallé Orch ("Hallé Favorites, Vol. 2") † Elegiac Melodies, Op. 34; Chabrier:España; F. Lehár:Gold & Silver, Op. 79; Sibelius:Valse triste; Suppé:Schöne Galatea (ov); J. Turina:Danzas fantásticas, Op. 22; E. Waldteufel:Waltzes, Polkas & Galops DLAB (The Barbirolli Society) ▲ 1013 (17.97)

E. Grümmer (sop), G. Moore (pno) † J. Brahms:Songs; Songs (5), Op. 49; F. Schubert:Songs (misc colls); Verdi:Arias; Otello (sels) TES ▲ 1086 (17.97)

K. Lövaas (sop), E. Marturet (cnd), Berlin SO—Solvejg's Song; Solvejg's Cradle Song *(rec Netherlands, May 4-5, 1992)* ("Kari Lövaas Sings Songs By Grieg, Sibelius & Strauss") † Melodies of the Heart [Hjertets melodier], Op. 5; Romances (4), Op. 15; Romances & Songs, Op. 18; Romances, old & new, Op. 39; Songs (12), Op. 33; Songs (6), Op. 25; Sibelius:Songs; R. Strauss:Das Rosenband, Op. 36/1; Heimliche Aufforderung, Op. 27/3; Morgen; Songs; Zueignung, Op. 10/1 VRDI ▲ 32116 [DDD] (13.97)

S. McNair (sop), P. Salomaa (bass), S. Borg (spkr), E. Schott (sgr), B. Hoos (sgr), C. Denningham (sgr), J. Tate (cnd), Berlin PO, Ernst Senff Chorus—At the Wedding; Ingrid's Lament; Peer Gynt & the Dairymaids; In the Hall of the Mountain King; Dance of the Mountain King's Daughter; The Death of Åse; Morning Mood (Prelude); Arabian Dance; Anitra's Dance; Peer Gynt's Serenade; Solvejg's Song; Peer Gynt at the Statue of Memnon; Peer Gynt's Homecoming; Solvejg's Song in the Hut; Night Scene; Whitsun hymn, "Oh Blessed Morning" (Churchgoers' Song); Solvejg's Cradle Song CSER ▲ 73287 [DDD] (6.97)

T. Wojciechowski (cnd), Polish National RSO Katowice † Con Pno, Op. 16; Elegiac Melodies, Op. 34; Holberg Suite Pno, Op. 40; Peer Gynt Suites; Symphonic Dances, Op. 64 CONI 2-▲ 51750 [DDD] (16.97)

Peer Gynt Suites (2) for Orchestra, Opp. 46 & 55

M. Abravanel (cnd), Utah SO *(rec 1975)* † Elegiac Melodies, Op. 34; Holberg Suite Pno, Op. 40; In Autumn, Op. 11; Norwegian Dances, Op. 35; Pictures from Life in the Country, Op. 19; Sigurd Jorsalfar (suite), Op. 56; Symphonic Dances, Op. 64 VB2 2-▲ 5048 [ADD] (9.97)

B. Bonney (sop), M. Eklöf (mez), N. Järvi (cnd), Gothenburg SO † Lyric Suite, Op. 54/1-4; Sigurd Jorsalfar (suite), Op. 56 DEUT (3D Classics) ▲ 27807 [DDD] (9.97)

A. Fiedler (cnd), Boston Pops Orch *(rec Symphony Hall Boston, May 20-21, 1957)* ("Classics for Children") † B. Britten:Young Person's Guide to the Orch, Op. 34; Gounod:Funeral March of a Marionette; R. Hayman:Kid Stuff; F. Loesser:Hans Christian Andersen (sels); Saint-Saëns:Carnival of the Animals RCAV (Living Stereo) ▲ 68131 [ADD] (11.97) ▮ 68131 [ADD] (6.98)

V. Handley (cnd), Ulster Orch † Con Pno, Op. 16; Lyric Suite, Op. 54/1-4 CHN ▲ 7040 (13.97)

H. von Karajan (cnd), Berlin PO *(rec 1971)* † Holberg Suite Pno, Op. 40; Sigurd Jorsalfar (suite), Op. 56 DEUT (Galleria) ▲ 19474 [ADD] (9.97)

J. Maksymiuk (cnd), BBC Scottish SO *(rec June 24-25, 1993)* † Sigurd Jorsalfar (suite), Op. 56 NXIN ▲ 550864 [DDD] (5.97)

L. Slatkin (cnd), St. Louis SO † Bizet:Carmen (suites) TEL ▲ 80048 [DDD] (16.97)

E. Söderström (sop), A. Davis (cnd), New Philharmonia Orch *(rec Apr 9-10, 1976)* † Elegiac Melodies, Op. 34; Lyric Pieces; Norwegian Dances, Op. 35; Sigurd Jorsalfar (suite), Op. 56 SNYC ▲ 53257 (7.97) ▮ 53257 (3.98)

T. Wojciechowski (cnd), Polish National RSO Katowice † Con Pno, Op. 16; Elegiac Melodies, Op. 34; Holberg Suite Pno, Op. 40; Peer Gynt (sels); Symphonic Dances, Op. 64 CONI 2-▲ 51750 [DDD] (16.97)

Peer Gynt Suite No. 1 for Orchestra, Op. 46 (1874-75; rev 1888)

J. Barbirolli (cnd), Halle PO *(rec Houldsworth Hall, Manchester, England, Dec 4, 1948)* † Delibes:Sylvia (suite); P. Grainger:Folk Song Settings; Mendelssohn (-Bartholdy):Hebriden, Op. 26; Midsummer Night's Dream (sels); Sym 4 MECL ▲ 446 (17.97)

L. Bernstein (cnd), New York PO *(rec Lincoln Center New York, NY, Oct 20, 1970)* † Lyric Pieces; Norwegian Dances, Op. 35; Peer Gynt Suite 2, Op. 55; Sibelius:Finlandia, Op. 26; Swan of Tuonela; Valse triste SNYC (Bernstein Century) ▲ 63156 [ADD] (11.97)

V. Handley (cnd), Ulster Orch † Elegiac Melodies, Op. 34; Sigurd Jorsalfar (suite), Op. 56; Symphonic Dances, Op. 64 CHN ▲ 8524 [DDD] (16.97)

H. von Karajan (cnd), Berlin PO † Holberg Suite Pno, Op. 40; Peer Gynt Suite 2, Op. 55; Sibelius:Finlandia, Op. 26; Swan of Tuonela; Valse triste DEUT (Karajan Gold) ▲ 39010 [DDD] (16.97)

Progetto Avanti [trans for 2 gtrs] ("Orchestral Classics for 2 Guitars") † W. A. Mozart:Kleine Nachtmusik, K.525; J. Rodrigo:Con de Aranjuez FNL ▲ 18915 (16.97)

J. Sándor (cnd), Budapest PO † Con Pno, Op. 16; Peer Gynt Suite 2, Op. 55 LALI ▲ 15617 [DDD] (3.97)

Peer Gynt Suite No. 2 for Orchestra, Op. 55 (1874-75; rev. 1891 & 1892)

Y. Ahronovitch (cnd), Vienna SO † Con Pno, Op. 16; Peer Gynt Suite 1, Op. 46 LALI ▲ 15617 [DDD] (3.97)

L. Bernstein (cnd), New York PO *(rec New York, NY, Oct 12, 1965)* † Lyric Pieces; Norwegian Dances, Op. 35; Peer Gynt Suite 1, Op. 46; Sibelius:Finlandia, Op. 26; Swan of Tuonela; Valse triste SNYC (Bernstein Century) ▲ 63156 [ADD] (11.97)

H. von Karajan (cnd), Berlin PO † Holberg Suite Pno, Op. 40; Peer Gynt Suite 1, Op. 46; Sibelius:Finlandia, Op. 26; Swan of Tuonela; Valse triste DEUT (Karajan Gold) ▲ 39010 [DDD] (16.97)

Piano Music (complete)

E. Knardahl (pno)—Poetic Tone-Pictures, Op. 3; Funeral March in Memory of Rikard Nordraak; Humoresques, Op. 6; Son Pno, Op. 7 ("Vol. 4") BIS ▲ 107 (17.97)

E. Knardahl (pno)—Norwegian Folksongs & Dances, Op. 17; Album Leaves (4) Pno, Op. 28; Improvisations on 2 Norwegian Folksongs, Op. 29 ("Vol. 5") BIS ▲ 108 (17.97)

E. Knardahl (pno)—Peer Gynt Suites; Sigurd Jorsalfar (suite), Op. 56; Ballade Pno, Op. 24 ("Vol. 6") BIS ▲ 109 (17.97)

E. Knardahl (pno)—Holberg Suite Pno, Op. 40; Elegiac Melodies, Op. 34; Waltz Caprices Pnos, Op. 37; Norwegian Melodies, Op. 63 ("Vol. 7") BIS ▲ 110 (17.97)

E. Knardahl (pno)—Norwegian folksongs, Op. 66; Song Transcriptions Pno, Op. 41; Norwegian Mountain Tunes ("Vol. 8") BIS ▲ 111 (17.97)

E. Knardahl (pno)—Norwegian Peasant Dances, Op. 72; Moods Pno, Op. 73; Drei Klavierstück Pno ("Vol. 9") BIS ▲ 112 (17.97)

E. Knardahl (pno)—Norwegian Dances, Op. 35; Melodies, Op. 53 † Con Pno, Op. 16 BIS ▲ 113 (17.97)

I. Mourao (pno)—Lyric Pieces; Humoresques, Op. 6; Pictures from Life in the Country, Op. 19 ("Solo Piano Music, Vol. 1") VB3 3-▲ 3023 [ADD]

E. Steen-Nøkleberg (pno)—Son Pno, Op. 7; Funeral March in Memory of Rikard Nordraak; Pieces (4) Pno, Op. 1; Melodies of Norway [The sirens' enticement]; Moods Pno, Op. 73; Song Transcriptions Pno, Op. 41 [I love thee (from Op.5/3)]; Humoresques, Op. 6 *(rec Norwegian State Academy of Music Oslo, Norway, July 31-Aug 2, 1993)* ("Piano Music, Vol. 1") NXIN ▲ 550881 [DDD] (5.97)

E. Steen-Nøkleberg (pno)—Improvisations on 2 Norwegian Folksongs, Op. 29; Melodies of Norway [Ballad to Saint Olaf]; Norwegian Folksongs & Dances, Op. 17; Song Transcriptions Pno, Op. 52 [First Meeting (from Op. 21/1)]; Norwegian folksongs, Op. 66 *(rec Norwegian State Academy of Music Oslo, Norway, Aug 3-5, 1993)* ("Piano Music, Vol. 2") NXIN ▲ 550882 [DDD] (5.97)

E. Steen-Nøkleberg (pno)—Album Leaves (4) Pno, Op. 28; Poetic Tone-Pictures, Op. 3; Melodies of Norway [Iceland]; Pictures from Life in the Country, Op. 19; Sigurd Jorsalfar (suite), Op. 56 [No. 1, Prelude: In the King's Hall]; Ballade Pno, Op. 24 *(rec Norwegian State Academy of Music Oslo, Aug 6-9, 1993)* ("Piano Music, Vol. 3") NXIN ▲ 550883 [DDD] (5.97)

E. Steen-Nøkleberg (pno)—Holberg Suite Pno, Op. 40; Melodies of Norway [I went to bed so late]; Norwegian Mountain Tunes; Peer Gynt Suite 1, Op. 46 [Morning mood]; Norwegian Peasant Dances, Op. 72 *(rec Norwegian State Academy of Music Oslo, Norway, Aug 10-12, 1993)* ("Piano Music, Vol. 4") NXIN ▲ 550884 [DDD] (5.97)

E. Steen-Nøkleberg (pno)—Agitato Pno; Album Leaves (4) Pno, Op. 28; The Entry of the Boyars [from Johan Halvorsen]; Peer Gynt (sels) [Dance of the Mountain King's Daughter]; Sigurd Jorsalfar (suite), Op. 56; Waltz Caprices Pnos, Op. 37 *(rec Norwegian State Academy of Music Oslo, Feb 12-14, 1994)* ("Piano Music Vol 12") † Norwegian Dances, Op. 35; Peer Gynt, Op. 23 NXIN ▲ 553398 [DDD] (5.97)

E. Steen-Nøkleberg (pno)—Pno Pieces, EG 105; Elegiac Melodies, Op. 34; Norwegian Melodies Nos. 6 & 22; Melodies, Op. 53; Song Transcriptions Pno, Op. 41; Norwegian Melodies, Op. 63; Pno Pieces, EG 110-12 *(rec Norwegian State Academy of Music Oslo, Mar 7-9, 1994)* ("Piano Music Vol. 13") NXIN ▲ 553399 [DDD] (5.97)

E. Steen-Nøkleberg (pno)—Canon; At Kjeruff's monument; Larvik's Polka Pno; Norweigan Melodies Nos. 87 & 146; Song Transcriptions Pno, Op. 52; Short Pieces Pno; Con in b [frag] *(rec Norwegian State Academy of Music Oslo, Apr 12-14, 1994)* ("Piano Music Vol. 14") † Son Pno, Op. 7 NXIN ▲ 553400 [DDD] (5.97)

GRIEG, EDVARD (cont.)

Piano Music (miscellaneous)

E. Kissin (pno), C. M. Giulini (cnd), Vienna PO ("Ich liebe dich, Op. 41/3") † Pictures from Life in the Country, Op. 19; G. F. Malipiero:I fantisimi; F. Schubert:Qnt Pno, D.667; R. Schumann:Arabeske Pno, Op. 18 SNYC ▲ 52567 (16.97)

A. B. Michelangeli (pno), M. Rossi (cnd), Turin RAI SO *(rec live La Scala, Nov 24, 1947)* † Beethoven:Con 5 Pno, Op. 73; Vivaldi:Music of RY (Radio Years) ▲ 91 (16.97)

Pictures from Life in the Country for Piano, Op. 19 (1870-71)

M. Abravanel (cnd), Utah SO [orchd Johan Halvorsen] *(rec 1975)* † Elegiac Melodies, Op. 34; Holberg Suite Pno, Op. 40; In Autumn, Op. 11; Norwegian Dances, Op. 35; Peer Gynt Suites; Sigurd Jorsalfar (suite), Op. 56; Symphonic Dances, Op. 64 VB2 2-▲ 5048 [ADD] (9.97)

H. Bauer (pno)—The bridal procession passes by [Brudefølget drager forbi] † Album Leaves (4) Pno, Op. 28; Lyric Pieces; Liszt:Études de concert (2), S.145; Etudes de concert (3), S.144; R. Schumann:Fantasiestücke Pno, Op. 12; Pno Music (misc colls) BPS ▲ 11 (16.97)

E. Kissin (pno), C. M. Giulini (cnd), Vienna PO ("Ich liebe dich, Op. 41/3") † Pno Music (misc); G. F. Malipiero:I fantisimi; F. Schubert:Qnt Pno, D.667; R. Schumann:Arabeske Pno, Op. 18 SNYC ▲ 52567 (16.97)

E. Knardahl (pno)—The bridal procession passes by [Brudefølget drager forbi] *(rec Sweden, 1977-80)* ("The Grieg Collection") † Funeral March in Memory of Rikard Nordraak; Humoresques, Op. 6; Lyric Pieces; Nordic Folksongs & Dances, Op. 17; Norwegian Peasant Dances, Op. 72; Poetic Tone-Pictures, Op. 3 BIS ▲ 51 [AAD/DDD] (17.97)

Pièces symphoniques (2) for Piano 4-Hands [2 movts. from Symphony in c], Op. 14 (1863-64)

T. Lenti (pno), M. A. Lenti (pno) *(rec Dec 17, 1990)* ("Forgotten Piano Duets, Vol. 2") † A. Bird:Introduction & Fugue, Op. 16; Liszt:Grande valse di bravura, S.209; Onslow:Grand Duo Pno, Op. 7 ACAD ▲ 20017 (16.97)

Poetic Tone-Pictures (6) for Piano, Op. 3 (1863)

P. Archibald (cnd) [arr for brass ensemble] ("Lyric Brass") † Elegiac Melodies, Op. 34; Norwegian Dances, Op. 35; Peer Gynt (sels) ASVQ ▲ 6181 (10.97)

E. Knardahl (pno) *(rec Nacka Sweden, 1977-80)* ("The Grieg Collection") † Funeral March in Memory of Rikard Nordraak; Humoresques, Op. 6; Lyric Pieces; Nordic Folksongs & Dances, Op. 17; Norwegian Peasant Dances, Op. 72; Pictures from Life in the Country, Op. 19 BIS ▲ 51 [AAD/DDD] (17.97)

Y. Mouravlev (pno) *(rec 1974)* ("Russian Piano School: Yuri Mouravlev") † Con Pno, Op. 16 RD (Talents of Russia) ▲ 16328 [ADD] (16.97)

Psalms (4) [Fire Salmer] for Baritone & Mixed Chorus, Op. 74 (1906)

C. Hogset (cnd), Grex Vocalis ("Crux") † Kverno:Choral Music; Nordheim:Lamentations; Nystedt:O Crux NORW ▲ 9308 (17.97)

P. Kühn (cnd), Kühn Choir † Con Pno, Op. 16 PRAG ▲ 250048 (18.97)

Quartet in g for Strings, Op. 27 (1877-78)

Joachim Koeckert String Quartet *(rec Apr 25-26, 1990)* † Saint-Saëns:Qt 1 Strs, Op. 112 CALG ▲ 50916 [DDD] (19.97)

Kontra String Quartet *(rec Nov 18-21, 1991)* † Fugue; Qt Strs (unfinished) BIS ▲ 543 [DDD] (17.97)

Petersen String Quartet ("Portrait") † Beethoven:Quartets for Strings (miscellaneous collections); W. A. Mozart:Qt 22 Strs, K.589; F. Schubert:Qnt Strs, D.956; Schulhoff:Pieces Str Qt; Qt Strs, Op. 25; R. Schumann:Qts Strs, Op. 41 CAPO ▲ 14862 [DDD] (10.97)

Shanghai String Quartet † Mendelssohn (-Bartholdy):Qt 2 Strs, Op. 13 DLS ▲ 3153 [DDD] (14.97)

Quartet in F for Strings [2 movts; unfinished] (1891)

Kontra String Quartet *(rec Dec 16, 1991)* † Fugue; Qt Strs, Op. 27 BIS ▲ 543 [DDD] (17.97)

Romances & Songs for Voice & Piano, Op. 18 (1869)

K. Lövaas (sop), E. Marturet (cnd), Berlin SO—"Autumn Storms" *(rec Netherlands, May 4-5, 1992)* ("Kari Lövaas Sings Songs By Grieg, Sibelius & Strauss") † Melodies of the Heart [Hjertets melodier], Op. 5; Peer Gynt (sels); Romances (4), Op. 15; Romances, old & new, Op. 39; Songs (12), Op. 33; Songs (6), Op. 25; Sibelius:Songs; R. Strauss:Das Rosenband, Op. 36/1; Heimliche Aufforderung, Op. 27/3; Morgen; Songs; Zueignung, Op. 10/1 VRDI ▲ 32116 [DDD] (13.97)

Romances (4) for Voice & Piano, Op. 15 (1864-68)

K. Lövaas (sop), E. Marturet (cnd), Berlin SO—Margaret's lullaby [Margetes vuggesang] *(rec Netherlands, May 4-5, 1992)* ("Kari Lövaas Sings Songs By Grieg, Sibelius & Strauss") † Melodies of the Heart [Hjertets melodier], Op. 5; Peer Gynt (sels); Romances & Songs, Op. 18; Romances, old & new, Op. 39; Songs (12), Op. 33; Songs (6), Op. 25; Sibelius:Songs; R. Strauss:Das Rosenband, Op. 36/1; Heimliche Aufforderung, Op. 27/3; Morgen; Songs; Zueignung, Op. 10/1 VRDI ▲ 32116 [DDD] (13.97)

Romances, old & new (songs) for Voice & Piano, Op. 39 (1884)

K. Lövaas (sop), E. Marturet (cnd), Berlin SO—"From Monte Pincio" [Fra Monte Pincio] *(rec Netherlands, May 4-5, 1992)* ("Kari Lövaas Sings Songs By Grieg, Sibelius & Strauss") † Melodies of the Heart [Hjertets melodier], Op. 5; Peer Gynt (sels); Romances (4), Op. 15; Romances & Songs, Op. 18; Songs (12), Op. 33; Songs (6), Op. 25; Sibelius:Songs; R. Strauss:Das Rosenband, Op. 36/1; Heimliche Aufforderung, Op. 27/3; Morgen; Songs; Zueignung, Op. 10/1 VRDI ▲ 32116 [DDD] (13.97)

Sigurd Jorsalfar (incidental music) for Voice, Orchestra & Men's Chorus, Op. 22 (1872)

N. Järvi (cnd), Gothenburg SO, Gothenburg Sym Chorus, B. Bonney (sop), M. Eklöf (mez), K. M. Sandve (ten), U. Malmberg (bar) [NOR] † Peer Gynt, Op. 23 DEUT 2-▲ 23079 [DDD] (32.97)

Sigurd Jorsalfar (selections)

J. Barbirolli (cnd) *(rec 1957-70)* † Lyric Suite, Op. 54/1-4; Norwegian Melodies, Op. 63; Symphonic Dances, Op. 64 DLAB ▲ 1012 (17.97)

O. Suitner (cnd), Berlin Staatskapelle † Holberg Suite Pno, Op. 40; Lyric Suite, Op. 54/1-4; Norwegian Dances, Op. 35 BER ▲ 9393 (10.97)

Sigurd Jorsalfar (symphonic suite) for Orchestra, Op. 56 (1872; rev 1892)

M. Abravanel (cnd), Utah SO *(rec 1975)* † Elegiac Melodies, Op. 34; Holberg Suite Pno, Op. 40; In Autumn, Op. 11; Norwegian Dances, Op. 35; Peer Gynt Suites; Pictures from Life in the Country, Op. 19; Symphonic Dances, Op. 64 VB2 2-▲ 5048 [ADD] (9.97)

F. Fennell (cnd), Eastman-Rochester Pops Orch—No. 3, Homage March ("Fabulous Marches") † Borodin:Prince Igor (sels); F. Schubert:Marches militaires, D.733; Sibelius:Karelia Suite, Op. 11; R. Wagner:Ovs, Preludes & Orchestral Sels; W. Walton:Orb & Sceptre MRCR ▲ 434394 (11.97)

V. Handley (cnd), Ulster Orch † Elegiac Melodies, Op. 34; Peer Gynt Suite 1, Op. 46; Symphonic Dances, Op. 64 CHN ▲ 8524 [DDD] (16.97)

N. Järvi (cnd), Gothenburg SO † Lyric Suite, Op. 54/1-4; Peer Gynt Suites DEUT (3D Classics) ▲ 27807 [DDD] (9.97)

H. von Karajan (cnd), Berlin PO † Holberg Suite Pno, Op. 40; Peer Gynt Suites DEUT (Galleria) ▲ 19474 [ADD] (9.97)

J. Maksymiuk (cnd), BBC Scottish SO *(rec June 24-25, 1993)* † Peer Gynt Suites NXIN ▲ 550864 [DDD] (5.97)

E. Ormandy (cnd), Philadelphia Orch *(rec May 15, 1968)* † Elegiac Melodies, Op. 34; Lyric Pieces; Norwegian Dances, Op. 35; Peer Gynt Suites SNYC ▲ 53257 (7.97) ▮ 53257 (3.98)

G. Rozhdestvensky (cnd), Royal Stockholm PO † Songs; Symphonic Dances, Op. 64 CHN ▲ 9113 [DDD] (16.97)

Sonata in a for Cello & Piano, Op. 36 (1883)

Ø. Birkeland (vc), H. Gimse (pno) *(rec May & Aug 1993)* † Intermezzo Vc & Pno; Son Pno, Op. 7 NXIN ▲ 550878 [DDD] (5.97)

R. Cohen (vc), R. Vignoles (pno) CRD ▲ 3391 [ADD] (17.97)

M. Ericsson (vc), F. Malý (pno) † S. Rachmaninoff:Son Vc BONT ▲ 78 (10.97)

D. Finckel (vc), W. Han (pno) *(rec New York, NY, 1996)* † Chopin:Son Vc; R. Schumann:Adagio & Allegro Hn, Op. 70 ARLD ▲ 19701

P. Fournier (vc), J. Fonda (pno) † J. Brahms:Sons Vc (comp) STRV ▲ 33320 [ADD] (16.97)

M. Fukačová (vc), I. Klánský (pno) † A. Dvořák:Rondo; C. Franck:Son Vn, M.8; P. Tchaikovsky:Pezzo capriccioso, Op. 62 KPT ▲ 32013 [DDD]

T. Gill (vc), F. Pavri (pno) † S. Rachmaninoff:Pieces Vc, Op. 2; Son Vc; Vocalise GILD ▲ 7127 [DDD] (16.97)

Hayashi Duo † Martinů:Vars on a Slovak folksong; Vars on a Theme of Rossini, H.290 FON ▲ 8701 [DDD] (13.97)

S. Isserlis (vc), S. Hough (pno) *(rec Abbey Road London, Dec 12-13, 1994)* ("Forgotten Romance") † Liszt:Elegie 1 Vc, S.130; Elegie 2 Vn, S.131; Lugubre gondola Vn or Vc, S.134; Romance oubliée Va, S.132; Zelle in Nonnenwerth Vn, S.382; A. Rubinstein:Son 1 Vc, Op. 18 RCAV (Red Seal) ▲ 68290 [DDD] (16.97)

E. Nyffenegger (vc), G. Wyss (pno) † Chopin:Son Vc; C. Franck:Son Vn, M.8 DVX ▲ 25204 [ADD] (11.97)

C. Starck (vc), R. Requejo (pno) *(rec Gstaad, Dec 1976)* † Chopin:Son Vc CLAV ▲ 703 [ADD] (16.97)

P. Svensson (vc), B. Lundin (pno) ("Scandinavian Cello") † Kokkonen:Son Vc; Lidholm:Fant sopra Laudi; E. Sjögren:Son Vc CAPA ▲ 21590 (16.97)

J. L. Webber (vc), B. Forsberg (pno) ("Complete Music for Cello & Piano") † Intermezzo Vc & Pno; Delius:Pieces Vc; Romance Vc; Serenade Vc; Son Vc PPHI ▲ 454458 (16.97)

Sonata in e for Piano, Op. 7 (1865)

L. O. Andsnes (pno) † Lyric Pieces VCL ▲ 59300 (16.97)

G. Casalino (pno) *(rec May 1992)* † Chopin:Nocturnes (21) Pno; S. Rachmaninoff:Prelude in c#, Op. 3/2; F. Schubert:Impromptus (4); Impromptus (4) Pno STRV ▲ 101 [DDD] (16.97)

▲ = CD ♦ = Enhanced CD △ = MD ▮ = Cassette Tape ▯ = DCC

GRIEG, EDVARD (cont.)

Sonata in e for Piano, Op. 7 (1865) (cont.)

H. Gimse (pno) *(rec May & Aug 1993)* † Intermezzo Vc & Pno; Son Vc NXIN ▲ 550878 [DDD] (5.97)

G. Gould (pno) *(rec 1971)* † Bizet:Nocturne in F; Vars chromatiques de concert; Sibelius:Kyllikki, Op. 41; Sonatinas (3) Pno, Op. 67 SNYC (Glenn Gould Edition) 2-▲ 52654 [ADD] (31.97)

E. Steen-Nøkleberg (org/pno) *(rec Norwegian State Academy of Music Oslo, Apr 12-14, 1994)* ("Piano Music Vol. 14") † Pno Music (comp) NXIN ▲ 553400 [DDD] (5.97)

Sonatas (5) for 2 Pianos [Mozart's Sonatas for Piano, K.283, 457, 533, 545 & Fantasia for Piano, K.475 w. 2nd piano accompaniment added by Grieg] (1877)

Giarmanà-Lucchetti Duo *(rec May 14-18, 1996)* ("Complete Works for Piano Duet") † In Autumn, Op. 11; Norwegian Dances, Op. 35; Old Norwegian Romance, Op. 51; Waltz Caprices Pnos, Op. 37 STRV 2-▲ 33410 (32.97)

Sonatas (3) for Violin & Piano, Opp. 8, 13 & 45

A. Belnick (vn), A. Ruiz (pno) *(rec May 1993)* ("Grieg: Music for Violin & Piano") CMB ▲ 1076 [DDD] (16.97)

J. C. Gehringer (vn), J. Petrov (pno) † Con Pno, Op. 16; Norwegian Peasant Dances, Op. 72 PC ▲ 265047 [DDD] (2.97)

D. Kang (vn), R. Pöntinen (pno) *(rec Sept 14-16, 1993)* ("The Three Sonatas for Violin & Piano") BIS ▲ 647 [DDD] (17.97)

H. Kraggerud (vn), H. Kjekshus (pno) *(rec Hampshire England, Nov 4-6, 1996)* NXIN ▲ 553904 [DDD] (5.97)

G. I. Lotsberg (vn), E. Steen-Nøkleberg (pno) SIMX ▲ 9035 (18.97)

E. Morbitzer (vn), M. Stöckigt (pno) BER ▲ 2103 (10.97)

L. Mordkovitch (vn), E. Mordkovitch (pno) CHN ▲ 9184 [DDD] (16.97)

A. Perpich (vn), F. Bidini (pno) *(rec Mesquite Performing Arts Center, TX, Apr 1996)* ENRE ▲ 9613 [DDD] (16.97)

D. Sitkovetsky (vn), B. Davidovich (pno) ORF ▲ 47831 [DDD] (18.97)

J. Suk (vn), S. Kagan (pno) KOCH ▲ 7419 (16.97)

G. Tarack (vn), D. Hancock (pno) BRID ▲ 9026 [ADD] (17.97)

Sonata No. 1 in F for Violin & Piano, Op. 8 (1865)

M. Marsden (vn), R. Chamberlain (pno) *(rec ABC Melbourne, Sept 1994)* ("Marina Marsden: Violin Recital") † C. Heim:Transformation; F. Kreisler:Caprice viennois; C. Nielsen:Son 1 Vn, Op. 9; Sculthorpe:Irkanda I TALP ▲ 67 [DDD]

J. Palomares (vn), M. Wagemans (pno) *(rec Elder Forest, CA)* ("Sonatas for Violin & Piano") † Son 2 Vn, Op. 13; Son 3 Vn, Op. 45 PROD ▲ 1314 [DDD] (17.97)

I. Ženatý (vn), A. Kubalek (pno) *(rec Troy New York, Oct 1995)* ("The Three Violin Sonatas") † Son 2 Vn, Op. 13; Son 3 Vn, Op. 45 DOR ▲ 90234 [DDD] (16.97)

Sonata No. 2 in G for Violin & Piano, Op. 13 (1867)

J. Heifetz (vn), B. Smith (pno) *(rec Radio Recorders Hollywood, Dec 15, 1955)* ("The Heifetz Chamber Music Collection I") † G. F. Handel:Son Vn; Suites de Pièces (8) Hpd, HWV 426-33; W. A. Mozart:Duo Vn, K.424; Sonatas for Violin & Piano (miscellaneous); Trio Vn, K.563; Sinding:Suite im alten Stil, Op. 10 RCAV (Gold Seal) 2-▲ 61740 [ADD] (21.97)

J. Palomares (vn), M. Wagemans (pno) *(rec Elder Forest, CA)* ("Sonatas for Violin & Piano") † Son 1 Vn, Op. 8; Son 3 Vn, Op. 45 PROD ▲ 1314 [DDD] (17.97)

K. Parlow (vn), E. MacMillan (pno) *(rec Oct 13, 1941)* † G. Holst:Planets, Op. 32; E. MacMillan:Bergerettes du Bas-Canada; England ANAL ▲ 27804 (16.97)

Weiss Duo ("The Weiss Duo in Recital") † W. A. Mozart:Sons Vn & Pno (misc) SUMM ▲ 107 (16.97)

I. Ženatý (vn), A. Kubalek (pno) *(rec Troy New York, Oct 1995)* ("The Three Violin Sonatas") † Son 1 Vn, Op. 8; Son 3 Vn, Op. 45 DOR ▲ 90234 [DDD] (16.97)

Sonata No. 3 in c for Violin & Piano, Op. 45 (1886-87)

L. Josefowicz (vn), J. Novacek (pno) ("For the End of Time") † B. Bartók:Son 1 Vn & Pno, Sz.75; M. de Falla:Suite populaire espagnole; Messiaen:Quatuor PPHI ▲ 456571 (16.97)

F. Kreisler (vn), S. Rachmaninoff (pno) *(rec 1928-29)* † F. Schubert:Son Vn, D.574; R. Schumann:Carnaval, Op. 9 ENPL (Piano Library) ▲ 280 (13.97)

F. Kreisler (vn), S. Rachmaninoff (pno) † Beethoven:Son 8 Vn; F. Kreisler:Vn Pieces; F. Schubert:Son Vn, D.574 MTAL ▲ 48077 (6.97)

F. Kreisler (vn), S. Rachmaninoff (pno) *(rec 1928)* † Beethoven:Son 8 Vn; F. Schubert:Son Vn, D.574 ENT ▲ 99382 (16.97)

F. Kreisler (vn), S. Rachmaninoff (pno) *(rec 1928)* † Beethoven:Son 8 Pno, Op. 13; F. Schubert:Son Vn, D.574 ENT ▲ 99394 (17.97)

G. Kulenkampff (vn) † T. Aulin:Con 3 Vn, Op. 14; Glazunov:Con Vn BLUB ▲ 3003 [ADD] (18.97)

E. León (vn), D. Muñiz (pno) *(rec Estudis Albert Moraleda de Barcelona, Mar 1995)* † Sarasate:Aires bohemios; Toldrá:Sonnets Vn; Turull:Divert Vn EAM ▲ 49523 [DDD] (17.97)

J. Palomares (vn), M. Wagemans (pno) *(rec Elder Forest, CA)* ("Sonatas for Violin & Piano") † Son 1 Vn, Op. 8; Son 2 Vn, Op. 13 PROD ▲ 1314 [DDD] (17.97)

A. Steinhardt (vn), L. Mayorga (pno) ("Steinhardt & Mayorga: Violin & Piano") † Beach:Compositions Vn, Op. 40/1-3; V. Herbert:A la Valse; F. Kreisler:Apple Blossoms (sels) SHLA ▲ 10063 (17.97)

I. Ženatý (vn), A. Kubalek (pno) *(rec Troy New York, Oct 1995)* ("The Three Violin Sonatas") † Son 1 Vn, Op. 8; Son 2 Vn, Op. 13 DOR ▲ 90234 [DDD] (16.97)

Songs

A. Ackté (sop), O. Brønnum (sop), M. Lykseth-Schjerven (sop), C. Monrad (sop), E. Rethberg (sop), G. Stückgold (sop), G. Anselmi (ten) *(Melodies of the Heart [Hjertets melodier], Op. 5 [I love thee [Jeg elsker dig]])* [FRE], M. Barrientos (sop), B. Bryhn (sop), E. Elizza (sop), K. Flagstad (sop), A. Galli-Curci (sop), L. Gates (sop), S. Kruszelnicka (sop), C. Monrad (sop) *(Peer Gynt (sels) [Solvejg's Song; Solvejg's Cradle Song])* [SPA], B. Bryhn (sop) *(Reminiscences from Mountain & Fjord, Op. 44 [Ragnhild])*, B. Bryhn (sop), C. Hultgren (sop) *(Songs (5), Op. 26 ["I wandered one lovely summer evening" [Jeg reiste en deilig sommkvaeld]])*, B. Bryhn (sop), R. Tauber (ten) *(Romances, old & new, Op. 39 ["From Monte Pincio" [Fra Monte Pincio; "Hidden love" [Dulgt kjaerlighed]]])*, B. Bryhn (sop), C. Monrad (sop), E. Clément (ten), P. Cornelius (ten) *(Songs (12), Op. 33; Songs (12), Op. 33)*, E. Burzio (sop), K. Eide (sop), N. H. Grieg (sop), E. Gulbranson (sop), C. Monrad (sop), F. Chaliapin (bass), R. Burg *(Songs (6), Op. 25 ["The Swan" [En Svane; "A birdsong" [En fuglevise; "The Swan" [En Svane; "Album verse" [Stamborsrim]]]]])*, E. Destinn (sop), E. Gulbranson (sop), L. Tetrazzini (sop), E. Gerhardt (mez), R. Olitzka (alt), E. Schumann-Heink (alt), V. Herold (ten), L. Slezak (ten), C. M. Öhman (ten), J. Schwarz (bar), K. Scheidemantel *(Poems by Vilhelm Krag, Op. 60; Poems by Vilhelm Krag, Op. 60)*, G. Farrar (sop), G. Elwes (ten), G. Graarud (ten), R. Tauber (ten) *(Songs (6), Op. 48 ["Ein Traum"])* [ENG], E. Gulbranson (sop) *(Poems (6), Op. 49 ["Greetings, ladies" [Vaer hilset, i damer]])*, M. Heim (sop), F. Hempel (sop), C. Hultgren (sop) *(Haugtussa, Op. 67 ["Kid's dance" [Killingsdans]])*, B. Kernic (sop), O. Kline (sop), L. Lehmann (sop), A. Lütken (sop), C. Monrad (sop) *(Songs (4), Op. 21 ["Good morning" [God morgen; "Thanks for your advice" [Tak for dit råd]]])* [ENG], C. Monrad (sop) *(Romances (4), Op. 15 [Margaret's lullaby [Margetes vuggesang]])*, H. Hedemark (ten), E. Bye *(Norønnafolket; Norønnafolket)*, H. Jadlowker (ten) *(Poems (5), Op. 70 [Eros])* [GER], R. Tauber (ten) *(The Princess [Prinsessen])* [GER], E. Bye *(Kongekvadet [N])*, J. Forsell *(Album, Op. 30 [The great, white flock [Den store, hvide flok]]; Romances & Ballads (4), Op. 9 ["Departure" [Udfarten]])*, J. Schwarz (bar), F. Chaliapin (bass) *(Songs (6), Op. 4 [The Old Song])* SIMX 3-▲ 1810 (54.97)

P. Agnew (ten), D. Wilson-Johnson (bar), S. Layton (cnd), Polyphony—Ave Maris Stella; Psalms, Op. 74 *(rec Oct 10 & 11, 1994)* ("Choral Music by Grainger & Grieg") † P. Grainger:Choral Music; Folk Song Settings; E. Nazareth:Songs HYP ▲ 66793 [DDD] (18.97)

B. Arnesen (sop), E. R. Erikson (pno)—Songs (5), Op. 26 ["Hope" [Et håb; "I wandered one lovely summer evening" [Jeg reiste en deilig sommkvaeld]]]; Lyric Pieces [Op. 47/1, "Waltz-Improptu"; Op. 47/2, "Albumleaf"; Op. 47/3, "Melody"; Op. 47/4, "Halling" (Norwegian Dance)]; Melodies of the Heart [Hjertets melodier], Op. 5; Songs (4), Op. 21; The Princess [Prinsessen]; Romances, old & new, Op. 39 ["From Monte Pincio" [Fra Monte Pincio; Up on the grassy slope [I liden høojt deroppe]]]; Peer Gynt (sels) [Solvejg's Song; Solvejg's Cradle Song]; Songs (6), Op. 48; Romances (4), Op. 15 [Margaret's lullaby [Margetes vuggesang]]; Songs (12), Op. 33 ["Spring" [Våren; "At Rundarne" [Ved Rundarne]]]; Elegiac Poems, Op. 59 ["To the one, II" [Til en II]]; On the Water, Op. 60/3; Songs (6), Op. 25 ["The Swan" [En Svane; "A birdsong" [En fuglevise]]]; Poems (6), Op. 49 ["Spring rain" [Forårsregn]] *(rec Hampshire England, Jan 1996)* ("Songs") NXIN ▲ 8553781 [DDD] (5.97)

T. Beecham (cnd), Royal Philharmonic Society Orch—Songs (6), Op. 48 ["Die verschwiegene Nachtigall"]; Norway, Op. 58 ["The emigrant" [Udvandreren]] † Atterberg:Sym 6; Delius:Walk to the Paradise Garden; W. A. Mozart:Sym 34, K.338; Zauberflöte (ov) DLAB ▲ 7026 (17.97)

M. Groop (mez), L. Derwinger (pno)—Songs (6), Op. 4; Melodies of the Heart [Hjertets melodier], Op. 5; Songs (6), Op. 25; Children's Songs, Op. 61; Haugtussa, Op. 67 ("The Complete Songs, Vol. 1") BIS ▲ 637 [DDD] (17.97)

M. Groop (mez), I. Ranta (pno)—Romances (4), Op. 15; Romances, old & new, Op. 39; Romances & Ballads (4), Op. 9; Poems by Vilhelm Krag, Op. 60; Songs *(rec Danderyd Grammar School, Sweden, Jan 11-14, 1996)* ("The Complete Songs, Vol. 2") BIS ▲ 787 [DDD] (17.97)

M. Groop (mez), I. Ranta (pno)—Songs (4), Op. 2; Haugtussa, Op. 67; Songs (6), Op. 48 ("The Complete Songs, Vol. 3") BIS ▲ 957 [DDD] (17.97)

GRIEG, EDVARD (cont.)

Songs (cont.)

S. Kringelborn (sop), G. Rozhdestvensky (cnd), Royal Stockholm PO—Peer Gynt (sels) [Solvejg's Song; Solvejg's Cradle Song]; Romances, old & new, Op. 39 ["From Monte Pincio" [Fra Monte Pincio]]; Songs (6), Op. 25 ["The Swan" [En Svane]]; Songs (12), Op. 33; Norway, Op. 58 † Sigurd Jorsalfar (suite), Op. 56; Symphonic Dances, Op. 64 CHN ▲ 9113 [DDD] (16.97)

A. S. von Otter (sop), B. Forsberg (pno)—Songs (6), Op. 25 ["The Swan" [En Svane; "With a waterlily" [Med en vanlilje]]]; Songs (12), Op. 33 ["Spring" [Våren; "Beside the river" [Langs ei A]]]; Songs (5), Op. 60 [While I Wait [Mens jeg venter]]; Romances, old & new, Op. 39 [Up on the grassy slope [I liden høojt deroppe]]; Melodies of the Heart [Hjertets melodier; I love thee [Jeg elsker dig]], Op. 5 [Two brown eyes [To brune Øojne]]; Songs (6), Op. 49 [Spring Rain [Forårsregen]] † Haugtussa, Op. 67; Songs (6), Op. 48 DEUT ▲ 37521 [DDD] (16.97)

P. Robison (fl), S. Sanders (pno)—Lyric Pieces [Op. 65/6, "Wedding Day at Troldhaugen" [Bryllupsdag på Trolkhaugen]]; Haugtussa, Op. 67 ["Love" [Elsk]]; Melodies of the Heart [Hjertets melodier; I love thee [Jeg elsker dig]], Op. 5 [Two brown eyes [To brune Øojne]]; Peer Gynt (sels) [Solvejg's Song]; Songs (6), Op. 25 ["The Swan" [En Svane]]; Songs (12), Op. 33; Songs (4), Op. 21 ["Thanks for your advice" [Tak for dit råd]] *(rec SUNY, Purchase, NY, Feb 1995)* † J. Andersen:Fl & Pno Music ARA ▲ 6668 [DDD] (16.97)

K. Skram (b-bar), E. Knardahl (pno)—Reminiscences from Mountain & Fjord, Op. 44; Reminiscences from Mountain & Fjord, Op. 44; Songs (12), Op. 33; Songs (6), Op. 25 ["The Swan" [En Svane]]; Melodies of the Heart [Hjertets melodier], Op. 5 *(rec Gothenburg Concert Hall, Norway, Mar 21-23, 1976)* ("Nordic Vocal Music") † Mountain Thrall, Op. 32; Kilpinen:Lieder der Liebe I-II, Op. 59; Lieder um den Tod, Op. 62; Rangström:Ur kung Eriks visor; Sibelius:Songs BIS ▲ 43 [AAD] (17.97)

Songs (6) for Voice & Piano, Op. 25 (1876)

K. Lövaas (sop), E. Marturet (cnd), Berlin SO—"The Swan" [En Svane]; "Departed"; "A birdsong" [En fuglevise] *(rec Netherlands, May 4-5, 1992)* ("Kari Lövaas Sings Songs By Grieg, Sibelius & Strauss") † Melodies of the Heart [Hjertets melodier], Op. 5; Peer Gynt (sels); Romances (4), Op. 15; Romances & Songs, Op. 18; Romances, old & new, Op. 39; Songs (12), Op. 33; Sibelius:Songs; R. Strauss:Das Rosenband, Op. 36/1; Heimliche Aufforderung, Op. 27/3; Morgen; Songs; Zueignung, Op. 10/1 VRDI ▲ 32116 [DDD] (13.97)

Songs (12) for Voice & Piano [text A. O. Vinje], Op. 33 (1873-80)

K. Lövaas (sop), E. Marturet (cnd), Berlin SO—"Spring" [Våren] *(rec Netherlands, May 4-5, 1992)* ("Kari Lövaas Sings Songs By Grieg, Sibelius & Strauss") † Melodies of the Heart [Hjertets melodier], Op. 5; Peer Gynt (sels); Romances (4), Op. 15; Romances & Songs, Op. 18; Romances, old & new, Op. 39; Songs (6), Op. 25; Sibelius:Songs; R. Strauss:Das Rosenband, Op. 36/1; Heimliche Aufforderung, Op. 27/3; Morgen; Songs; Zueignung, Op. 10/1 VRDI ▲ 32116 [DDD] (13.97)

Songs (6) for Voice & Piano, Op. 48 (1889)

A. S. von Otter (sop), B. Forsberg (pno) † Haugtussa, Op. 67; Songs DEUT ▲ 37521 [DDD] (16.97)

Songs (5) for Voice & Piano [text Krag], Op. 60 (1893-94)

H. Martinpelto (sop), M. Hirvonen (pno) ("Songs from the North") † Kuula:Songs (3); Rangström:Songs (3); Sibelius:Songs (5), Op. 37; E. Sjögren:Songs (5) PHA ▲ 292004 [DDD] (13.97)

Symphonic Dances for Orchestra, Op. 64 (1896-97)

M. Abravanel (cnd), Utah SO *(rec 1975)* † Elegiac Melodies, Op. 34; Holberg Suite Pno, Op. 40; In Autumn, Op. 11; Norwegian Dances, Op. 35; Peer Gynt Suites; Pictures from Life in the Country, Op. 19; Sigurd Jorsalfar (suite), Op. 56 VB2 2-▲ 5048 [ADD] (9.97)

J. Barbirolli (cnd) *(rec 1957-70)* † Lyric Suite, Op. 54/1-4; Norwegian Melodies, Op. 63; Sigurd Jorsalfar (sels) DLAB ▲ 1012 (17.97)

T. Beecham (cnd), Royal PO—No. 2 *(rec Abbey Road, London, England, 1959)* † In Autumn, Op. 11; Old Norwegian Romance, Op. 51; Peer Gynt, Op. 23 EMIC (Great Recordings of the Century) ▲ 66966 [ADD] (11.97)

R. Edlinger (cnd), CSSR State PO Košice *(rec Oct 1988)* † Lyric Suite, Op. 54/1-4; Norwegian Dances, Op. 35; Alfvén:Swedish Rhap 1, Op. 19; Sibelius:Karelia Ov, Op. 10; J. S. Svendsen:Norwegian Artists' Carnival, Op. 14 NXIN ▲ 550090 [DDD] (5.97)

V. Handley (cnd), Ulster Orch † Elegiac Melodies, Op. 34; Peer Gynt Suite 1, Op. 46; Sigurd Jorsalfar (suite), Op. 56 CHN ▲ 8524 [DDD] (16.97)

N. Marriner (cnd), Academy of St. Martin in the Fields *(rec Henry Wood Hall London, Dec 4-6, 1996)* † Con Pno, Op. 16 HANS (Academy) ▲ 98128 [DDD] (15.97)

A. von Pitamic (cnd), South German PO ("Classical Romance") † S. Prokofiev:Love for 3 Oranges (march), Op. 33ter; Pieces (10) Pno, Op. 12; S. Rachmaninoff:Con 2 Pno, Op. 18; M. Reger:Kleine Vortragsstüke, Op. 44 PC ▲ 267121 [DDD] (2.97)

G. Rozhdestvensky (cnd), Royal Stockholm PO † Sigurd Jorsalfar (suite), Op. 56; Songs CHN ▲ 9113 [DDD] (16.97)

T. Wojciechowski (cnd), Polish National RSO Katowice † Con Pno, Op. 16; Elegiac Melodies, Op. 34; Holberg Suite Pno, Op. 40; Peer Gynt (sels); Peer Gynt Suites CONI 2-▲ 51750 [DDD] (16.97)

Symphony in c (1864)

O. Kamu (cnd), Gothenburg SO † In Autumn, Op. 11 BIS ▲ 200 [DDD] (17.97)

O. Kamu (cnd), Gothenburg SO † Con Pno, Op. 16; In Autumn, Op. 11; Piano Music (selections) BIS (BIS Twins) 2-▲ 200619 (17.97)

Waltz Caprices for 2 Pianos, Op. 37 (1883)

Giarmanà-Lucchetti Duo *(rec May 14-18, 1996)* ("Complete Works for Piano Duet") † In Autumn, Op. 11; Norwegian Dances, Op. 35; Old Norwegian Romance, Op. 51; Sons Pnos STRV 2-▲ 33410 (32.97)

T. Lenti (pno), M. Lenti (pno) [arr H. Levine for pno 4-hands, 1925] † G. Gershwin:Rhap in Blue; Liszt:Hungarian Rhaps, S.244; N. Rubinstein:Tarentella, Op. 14; F. Schubert:Fant Pno, D.940 ACAD ▲ 20037 [DDD] (16.97)

GRIER, FRANCIS (1956-

Anthems

J. Bowman (ct), C. Hughes (org), R. Allwood (cnd), Rodolfus Choir—Let us invoke Christ; Great is the Power of Thy Cross; God, Who Made the Earth & Sky; Proclaim His Triumph; Day after Day; Salve Regina; Corpus Christi Carol; O King of the Friday; Christ's Love-Song; The Voice of My Beloved; Dilectus Meus Mihi; Thou, O God, Art Praised in Sion *(rec Eton College Chapel, Dec 1994)* ("12 Anthems") HER ▲ 177 [DDD] (19.97)

GRIER, LITA

Renascence for Flute & Orchestra (1996)

M. Stolper (fl), P. Freeman (cnd), Czech National SO *(rec Prague, Czech Republic, June 21-24, 1998)* † Griffes:Poem Fl; Kennan:Night Soliloquy; E. Siegmeister:Con Fl; V. Thomson:Con Fl CED ▲ 46 [DDD] (16.97)

GRIERSON, RALPH (20th cent)

SometimesNot Always for Piano

R. Grierson (pno) † W. Kraft:Requiescat; Lesemann:Nataraja; Subotnick:Liquid Strata TOWN ▲ 24 (17.97)

GRIFFES, CHARLES TOMLINSON (1884-1920)

Bacchanale for Orchestra (1919)

G. Schwarz (cnd), Seattle SO † Pleasure Dome of Kubla Khan, Op. 8; Poem Fl; Tone-Pictures, Op. 5; White Peacock; D. Taylor:Through the Looking Glass, Op. 12 DLS ▲ 3099 [DDD] (14.97)

Fantasy Pieces (3) for Piano, Op. 6 (1912-15)

G. Landes (pno) † Son Pno; Tone-Pictures, Op. 5; MacDowell:Son 4 Pno, Op. 59 KOCH ▲ 7045 [DDD] (17.97)

P. Rosenbaum (pno) ("Complete Piano Works") † Preludes Pno; Roman Sketches, Op. 7; Son Pno; Tone-Pictures, Op. 5 KPT ▲ 32215 [DDD]

J. Tocco (pno) † Rhap Pno; MacDowell:Son 3 Pno, Op. 57 GAS ▲ 232 (16.97)

J. Tocco (pno) † Legend Pno; Pleasure Dome of Kubla Khan, Op. 8; Pno Music; Rhap Pno; MacDowell:Sons Pno (comp) GAS 4-▲ 1007 (46.97)

Impressions (4 songs) for Mezzo-Soprano & Piano (1912-16)

O. Stapp (mez), D. Richardson (pno) [FRE] † Pleasure Dome of Kubla Khan, Op. 8; Poems of Fiona McLeod, Op. 11; Songs; Tone-Pictures, Op. 5 NWW ▲ 273 [ADD] (16.97)

The Kairn of Koridwen (dance drama in 2 scenes) for Flute, 2 Clarinets, 2 Horns, Harp, Celesta & Piano [after E. Schure] (1916)

E. Decou (cnd) KOCH ▲ 7216 [DDD] (10.97)

Perspectives Ensemble members *(rec St. Paul's Chapel Columbia Univ, NYC, Apr 11, 1995)* ("Goddess of the Moon") † Music of Griffes; Sketches; Son Pno NPT ▲ 85634 [DDD] (16.97)

Legend for Piano (1915)

J. Tocco (pno) † Pleasure Dome of Kubla Khan, Op. 8; Tone-Pictures, Op. 5; MacDowell:Sea Pieces Pno, Op. 55 GAS ▲ 234 (16.97)

J. Tocco (pno) † Fant Pieces, Op. 6; Pleasure Dome of Kubla Khan, Op. 8; Pno Music; Rhap Pno; MacDowell:Sons Pno (comp) GAS 4-▲ 1007 (46.97)

Music of Griffes

Perspectives Ensemble members—3 Japanese melodies; Komori uta; Noge no yama *(rec St. Paul's Chapel Columbia Univ, NYC, NY, Apr 11, 1995)* ("Goddess of the Moon") † Kairn of Koridwen; Sketches; Son Pno NPT ▲ 85634 [DDD] (16.97)

GRIFFES, CHARLES TOMLINSON (cont.)
Notturno for Piano (1915)
C. Rosenberger (pno) † E. Granados:Goyescas (sels); Liszt:Études d'exécution transcendante (12), S.139; Liebesträume, S.541 DLS ▲ 3030 [DDD] (14.97)
Piano Music
I. Klatchev (pno) GEGA ▲ 123 (16.97)
D. Oldham (pno)—The White Peacock; Nightfall; Clouds; The Fountain of the Acqua Paola, Op. 7; Tone-Pictures (3), Op. 5; Piece in B; Piece in d; Legend; De profundis; Dance in a; Piece in E; Preludes (3); Son Pno *(rec New York, 1977-81)* ("Collected Works for Piano") NWW ▲ 80310 [ADD] (16.97)
J. Tocco (pno)—Roman Sketches, Op. 7; Preludes (1919); De profundis; Son Pno; 3 Tone-Pictures, Op. 5 † Fant Pieces, Op. 6; Legend Pno; Pleasure Dome of Kubla Khan, Op. 8; Rhap Pno; MacDowell:Sons Pno (comp) GAS 4-▲ 1007 (46.97)

The Pleasure Dome of Kubla Khan for Piano, Op. 8 (1912; orchd 1917)
L. Botstein (cnd), American Russian Youth Orch *(rec Tanglewood, MA, June 1997)* ("10th Anniversary: American Russian Youth Orchestra in Concert") † C. Ives:Washington's Birthday; Paine:As You Like It, Op. 28; P. Tchaikovsky:Festival Coronation March TOWN ▲ 53 (17.97)
C. Gerhardt (cnd), RCA SO *(rec London, Mar 1968)* ("Great American Composers") † White Peacock; A. Copland:Billy the Kid (sels); Rodeo (sels); M. Gould:Tropical; H. Hanson:Sym 2 CHSK ▲ 112 [ADD] (16.97)
S. Ozawa (cnd), Boston SO † Impressions; Poems of Fiona McLeod, Op. 11; Songs; Tone-Pictures, Op. 5 NWW ▲ 273 [ADD] (16.97)
G. Schwarz (cnd), Seattle SO † Bacchanale; Poem Fl; Tone-Pictures, Op. 5; White Peacock; D. Taylor:Through the Looking Glass, Op. 12 DLS ▲ 3099 [DDD] (14.97)
J. Tocco (pno) † Legend Pno; Tone-Pictures, Op. 5; MacDowell:Sea Pieces Pno, Op. 55 GAS ▲ 234 (16.97)
J. Tocco (pno) † Fant Pieces, Op. 6; Legend Pno; Pno Music; Rhap Pno; MacDowell:Sons Pno (comp) GAS 4-▲ 1007 (46.97)

Poem for Flute & Orchestra (1918)
K. Bryan (fl), Z. Chen (cnd), Czech RSO ("Twentieth Century Flute") † Ibert:Con Fl; C. Nielsen:Con Fl; W. Perry:Summer Nocturne PREM ▲ 1026 [DDD] (16.97)
S. Goff (fl), G. Schwarz (cnd), Seattle SO † Bacchanale; Pleasure Dome of Kubla Khan, Op. 8; Tone-Pictures, Op. 5; White Peacock; D. Taylor:Through the Looking Glass, Op. 12 DLS ▲ 3099 [DDD] (14.97)
A. Jones (fl), T. Briccetti (cnd) *(rec Prague, Oct 31-Nov 3, 1994)* ("Mostly French") † Debussy:Danses sacrée et profane; Syrinx Fl; G. Fauré:Fant Fl, Op. 79; Impromptu Hp, Op. 86; Gaos:Impressión nocturna; M. Ravel:Intro & Allegro Hp; Saint-Saëns:Fant Vn DI ▲ 920281 [DDD] (5.97)
S. Jutt (fl), R. Hodgkinson (pno) [arr G. Barrère] † Jolivet:Chant de Linos Fl & Pno; W. T. McKinley:Romances Fl; A. Piazzolla:Études tanguistiques GMR ▲ 2026 (16.97)
J. Mariano (fl), H. Hanson (cnd), Eastman-Rochester Orch † S. Barber:Capricorn Con, Op. 21; Bergsma:Gold & the Señor Commandante; Piston:Incredible Flutist MRCR ▲ 34307 [ADD] (11.97)
M. Stolper (fl), P. Freeman (cnd), Czech National SO *(rec Prague, Czech Republic, June 21-24, 1998)* † L. Grier:Renascence; Kennan:Night Soliloquy; E. Siegmeister:Con Fl; V. Thomson:Con Fl CED ▲ 46 [DDD] (16.97)
Poems (3) of Fiona McLeod for Soprano & Orchestra, Op. 11 (1918)
P. Bryn-Julson (sop), S. Ozawa (cnd), Boston SO [ENG] † Impressions; Pleasure Dome of Kubla Khan, Op. 8; Songs; Tone-Pictures, Op. 5 NWW ▲ 273 [ADD] (16.97)
L. Toppin (sop), J. Bertelli (cl), P. Freeman (cnd), Czech National SO *(rec Prague, Austria)* ("Paul Freeman Introduces...Brandon, Griffes, Osbon, Muczynski, Klessig, Lamb & Felciano-Vol. 2") † Brandon:Celebration Ov; Klessig:Meditation from Don Juan; M. Lamb:J. B. II; Muczynski:Sym Dialogues, Op. 20; Osbon:Liberty ALBA ▲ 322 [DDD] (16.97)

Preludes (3) for Piano (1919)
P. Rosenbaum (pno) ("Complete Piano Works") † Fant Pieces, Op. 6; Roman Sketches, Op. 7; Son Pno; Tone-Pictures, Op. 5 KPT ▲ 32215 [DDD]
J. Tocco (pno) † Roman Sketches, Op. 7; MacDowell:Son 4 Pno, Op. 59 GAS ▲ 231 (16.97)
De profundis for Piano (1915)
J. Tocco (pno) † Son Pno; MacDowell:Son 2 Pno, Op. 50 GAS ▲ 233 (16.97)
Rhapsody in b for Piano (1914)
J. Tocco (pno) † Fant Pieces, Op. 6; MacDowell:Son 3 Pno, Op. 57 GAS ▲ 232 (16.97)
J. Tocco (pno) † Fant Pieces, Op. 6; Legend Pno; Pleasure Dome of Kubla Khan, Op. 8; Pno Music; MacDowell:Sons Pno (comp) GAS 4-▲ 1007 (46.97)
Roman Sketches (4) for Piano, Op. 7 (1915-16)
P. Rosenbaum (pno) ("Complete Piano Works") † Fant Pieces, Op. 6; Preludes Pno; Son Pno; Tone-Pictures, Op. 5 KPT ▲ 32215 [DDD]
C. Rosenberger (pno) † Debussy:Pno Music (misc colls); Liszt:Années de pèlerinage 3, S.163; M. Ravel:Jeux d'eau DLS ▲ 3006 [DDD] (14.97)
J. Tocco (pno) † Preludes Pno; MacDowell:Son 4 Pno, Op. 59 GAS ▲ 231 (16.97)
Sketches based on Indian Themes (2) for String Quartet (1918-?19)
Budapest String Quartet *(rec May 6, 1943)* ("Souvenir") † Debussy:Danses sacrée et profane; A. Dvořák:Qt 12 Strs, Op. 96; G. F. Handel:Cons (16) Org; D. G. Mason:Qt on Negro Themes, Op. 19 BRID ▲ 9077 (17.97)
Perspectives Ensemble members *(rec St. Paul's Chapel Columbia Univ, NYC, Apr 11, 1995)* ("Goddess of the Moon") † Kairn of Koridwen; Music of Griffes; Son Pno NPT ▲ 85634 [DDD] (16.97)
Sonata in F for Piano (1917-18)
J. Fennimore (pno) ("Joseph Fennimore in Concert") † White Peacock; Liadov:Pieces Pno, Op. 11; R. Schumann:Carnaval, Op. 9; A. Scriabin:Etudes (8) Pno, Op. 42; Sgambati:Melodie ALBA ▲ 102 [ADD] (16.97)
C. Keene (pno) † Beethoven:Son 25 Pno, Op. 79; J. L. Dussek:Son Pno, Op. 61; J. Haydn:Son 62 Kbd, H.XVI/52; J. N. Hummel:Son 9 Pno PROT ▲ 1106 [ADD] (18.97)
G. Landes (pno) † Fant Pieces, Op. 6; Tone-Pictures, Op. 5; MacDowell:Son 4 Pno, Op. 59 KOCH ▲ 7045 [DDD] (17.97)
P. Rosenbaum (pno) ("Complete Piano Works") † Fant Pieces, Op. 6; Preludes Pno; Roman Sketches, Op. 7; Tone-Pictures, Op. 5 KPT ▲ 32215 [DDD]
J. Tocco (pno) † De profundis; MacDowell:Son 2 Pno, Op. 50 GAS ▲ 233 (16.97)
D. Walsh (pno) *(rec St. Paul's Chapel Columbia Univ, NYC, Apr 11, 1995)* ("Goddess of the Moon") † Kairn of Koridwen; Music of Griffes; Sketches NPT ▲ 85634 [DDD] (16.97)
Songs
Milnes (bar), J. Spong (pno)—An den Wind; Am Kreuzweg wird begraben; Meeres Stille; Auf geheimem Waldespfade; Song of the Dagger † Impressions; Pleasure Dome of Kubla Khan, Op. 8; Poems of Fiona McLeod, Op. 11; Tone-Pictures, Op. 5 NWW ▲ 273 [ADD] (16.97)
W. Parker (bar), W. Huckaby (pno)—Das ist ein Brausen und Heulen; Wo ich bin, mich rings umdunkelt; Des Müden Abendlied; Zwei Könige sassen auf Orkadel; The 1st Snowfall; An Old Song Re-sung *(rec New York City, NY)* ("An Old Song Resung") † Cadman:American Indian Songs, Op. 45; Farwell:Indian Songs, Op. 32; C. Ives:Songs NWW ▲ 80463 (16.97)

Tone-Pictures (3) for Piano, Op. 5 (1911-12; orchd 1915)
G. Landes (pno) † Fant Pieces, Op. 6; Son Pno; MacDowell:Son 4 Pno, Op. 59 KOCH ▲ 7045 [DDD] (17.97)
New World Chamber Ensemble † Impressions; Pleasure Dome of Kubla Khan, Op. 8; Poems of Fiona McLeod, Op. 11; Songs NWW ▲ 273 [ADD] (16.97)
S. R. Radcliffe (cnd) ("American Profiles") † A. Copland:Sxt Cl; Piston:Divert Fl; N. Rorem:Studies for 11 ALBA ▲ 175 [DDD] (16.97)
P. Rosenbaum (pno) ("Complete Piano Works") † Fant Pieces, Op. 6; Preludes Pno; Roman Sketches, Op. 7; Son Pno KPT ▲ 32215 [DDD]
G. Schwarz (cnd), Seattle SO † Bacchanale; Pleasure Dome of Kubla Khan, Op. 8; Poem Fl; White Peacock; D. Taylor:Through the Looking Glass, Op. 12 DLS ▲ 3099 [DDD] (14.97)
J. Tocco (pno) † Legend Pno; Pleasure Dome of Kubla Khan, Op. 8; MacDowell:Sea Pieces Pno, Op. 55 GAS ▲ 234 (16.97)

The White Peacock for Piano (1915; orchd 1919)
J. Fennimore (pno) ("Joseph Fennimore in Concert") † Son Pno; Liadov:Pieces Pno, Op. 11; R. Schumann:Carnaval, Op. 9; A. Scriabin:Etudes (8) Pno, Op. 42; Sgambati:Melodie ALBA ▲ 102 [ADD] (16.97)
C. Gerhardt (cnd), Philharmonic Pops Orch *(rec London, Apr 1965)* ("Great American Composers") † Pleasure Dome of Kubla Khan, Op. 8; A. Copland:Billy the Kid (sels); Rodeo (sels); M. Gould:Tropical; H. Hanson:Sym 2 CHSK ▲ 112 [ADD] (16.97)
D. Kitaienko (cnd), Moscow PO *(rec Moscow, Aug 9-18, 1986)* ("The Moscow Sessions") † A. Copland:Appalachian Spring (suite); G. Gershwin:Lullaby Str Qt; Glazunov:Concert Waltz 1, Op. 47; C. Ives:Unanswered Question; D. Shostakovich:Festive Ov, Op. 96 SHLA ▲ 27 (17.97)
A. Litton (cnd), Dallas SO *(rec Morton H. Meyerson Symphony Center Dallas, TX, May 1995)* ("An American Tapestry") † A. Hovhaness:Sym 2; C. Ives:Three Places in New England; Piston:Incredible Flutist; W. Schuman:New England Triptych DOR ▲ 90224 [DDD] (16.97)

GRIFFES, CHARLES TOMLINSON (cont.)
The White Peacock for Piano (1915; orchd 1919) (cont.)
G. Schwarz (cnd), Seattle SO † Bacchanale; Pleasure Dome of Kubla Khan, Op. 8; Poem Fl; Tone-Pictures, Op. 5; D. Taylor:Through the Looking Glass, Op. 12 DLS ▲ 3099 [DDD] (14.97)
GRIGNY, NICOLAS DE (1672-1703)
Organ Music
F. Desenclos (org) *(rec Caen Cathedral org)* † Brossard:Motets ASTR ▲ 8636 (18.97)
J. Payne (org)—Ave maris stella (hymn); A solis ortus [Crudelis Herodes] (hymn); Fugue à 5 *(rec Univ. of Vermont Burlington, Mar 1994)* ("Early French Organ Music, Vol. 1") † L. Compère:Org Music; G. Corrette:Messe du huitième ton à l'usage des dame; Japart:Fortuna d'un gran tempo; L. Marchand:Pieces Org NXIN ▲ 553214 [DDD] (5.97)
M. Touyère (org)—Veni Creator en taille à 5; Récit de tierce en taille *(rec Sain-François-de-Sales Genève)* † Boyvin:Premier livre Org; Guilain:Pièces d'orgue pour le Magnificat; L. Marchand:Pieces Org GALL ▲ 952 [ADD] (18.97)

Premier livre d'orgue (mass & 5 hymns) for Organ & Chorus (1699)
P. Bardon (org) *(rec Oct 1991)* PVY ▲ 792041 [DDD] (16.97)
GRIMSSON, LARUS HALLDOR (1954-
Tales from a Forlorn Fortress for Bassoon, Viola & Cello (1993)
G. O. Gunnarsson (cnd) *(rec Feb 1994)* ("Animato: Icelandic Chamber Works") † Birgisson:Qt Strs, Op. 2; A. Ingólfsson:Vink II; Leifs:Icelandic Dances; Másson:Elja; H. Ragnarsson:Romanza; H. Tómasson:Trio Animato MFIC ▲ 808 [DDD]

GRIPPE, RAGNAR (1951-
Requiem for Soprano & Electronics (1994-95)
M. Kristoffersson (sop), R. Grippe (elec/syn) † Shifting Spirits BIS ▲ 820 [DDD] (17.97)
Shifting Spirits for Electronics (1996)
R. Grippe (elec/syn) † Requiem BIS ▲ 820 [DDD] (17.97)
Situation I for Electronics
R. Grippe (elec) *(rec 1976)* † Ten Temperaments; Ur Undrens Tid BIS ▲ 241 [AAD] (17.97)
Ten Temperaments for Electronics
R. Grippe (elec) *(rec Nov 1981)* † Situation I; Ur Undrens Tid BIS ▲ 241 [AAD] (17.97)
Ur Undrens Tid for Electronics
R. Grippe (elec) *(rec 1975)* † Situation I; Ten Temperaments BIS ▲ 241 [AAD] (17.97)
GROFÉ, FERDE (1892-1972)
Concerto for Piano & Orchestra (1932-59)
J. M. Sanromá (pno), F. Grofé (cnd), Rochester PO *(rec Univ of Rochester, NY, 1960)* † Grand Canyon Suite; G. Gershwin:Rhap in Blue EVC ▲ 9038 [ADD] (13.97)
Death Valley Suite for Orchestra
F. Grofé (cnd), Capitol SO ("Great American Grofé") † Grand Canyon Suite; Grand Canyon:Cloudburst; Mississippi Suite ANGL (Great American) ▲ 66387 (11.97)
Grand Canyon Suite for Orchestra (1931)
L. Bernstein (cnd), New York PO † Mississippi Suite SNYC ▲ 37759 [ADD] (9.97) ▮ 37759 [ADD] (3.98)
L. Bernstein (cnd), New York PO † G. Gershwin:American in Paris; Rhap in Blue SNYC ▲ 42264 [ADD] (16.97)
L. Bernstein (cnd), New York PO † G. Gershwin:American in Paris; Rhap in Blue SNYC (Bernstein Century) ▲ 63086 (11.97)
S. Black (cnd), London Festival Orch † C. Ives:Orch Set 2 PLON (Phase 4 Stereo) ▲ 48956 (9.97)
A. Dorati (cnd), Detroit SO † G. Gershwin:Porgy & Bess (symphonic picture) PLON (Jubilee) ▲ 30712 [DDD] (9.97)
R. Farnon (cnd), London Festival Orch † G. Gershwin:Porgy & Bess (symphonic picture) PLON (Weekend Classics) ▲ 25508 [AAD] (7.97)
A. Fiedler (cnd), Boston Pops Orch † L. Bernstein:Fancy Free (sels); A. Copland:Salón México; G. Gershwin:Cuban Ov; M. Gould:American Salute; R. Rodgers:Slaughter on Tenth Avenue Orch RCAV (Gold Seal) ▲ 6806 [ADD] (11.97)
G. Gershwin (pno), P. Whiteman (cnd), Paul Whiteman Orch † Mississippi Suite; Mississippi Suite Orch; G. Gershwin:Con Pno; Rhap in Blue PHS ▲ 22 [ADD] (17.97)
M. Gould (cnd), Morton Gould Orch *(rec 1960)* † A. Copland:Billy the Kid (suite); Rodeo RCAV (Living Stereo) ▲ 61667 (11.97)
F. Grofé (cnd), Rochester PO *(rec Univ of Rochester, NY, 1960)* † Con Pno; G. Gershwin:Rhap in Blue EVC ▲ 9038 [ADD] (13.97)
H. Hanson (cnd), Eastman-Rochester Orch † Mississippi Suite; V. Herbert:Con 2 Vc, Op. 30 MRCR ▲ 34355 (11.97)
E. Kunzel (cnd), Cincinnati Pops Orch † G. Gershwin:Porgy & Bess (suite) [arr Gershwin] TEL ▮ 30086 [DDD] (8.98) ▲ 80086 [DDD] (16.97)
L. Maazel (cnd), Pittsburgh SO *(rec Oct 13, 1991)* † V. Herbert:Hero & Leander, Op. 33 SNYC ▲ 52491 [DDD] (16.97)
E. Ormandy (cnd), Philadelphia Orch *(rec Philadelphia, Dec 12 & 20, 1967)* † G. Gershwin:American in Paris; Porgy & Bess (symphonic picture) SNYC (Essential Classics) ▲ 62402 [ADD] (7.97) ▮ 62402 [ADD] (3.98)
G. Schwarz (cnd), Seattle SO ("Out West: Tone Poems of the American West") † A. Copland:Billy the Kid (suite); Rodeo DLS ▲ 3104 [DDD] (14.97)
G. Schwarz (cnd), Seattle SO ("The Only American Album You'll Ever Need") † A. Copland:Appalachian Spring (suite); Fanfare for the Common Man; Rodeo (sels); G. Gershwin:American in Paris; Rhap in Blue; J. P. Sousa:Stars & Stripes Forever DLS ▲ 1606 [DDD] (10.97)
F. Slatkin (cnd), Hollywood Bowl SO ("Great American Grofé") † Death Valley; Grand Canyon:Cloudburst; Mississippi Suite ANGL (Great American) ▲ 66387 (11.97)
W. T. Stromberg (cnd), Bournemouth SO † Mississippi Suite; Niagara Falls Suite NXIN ▲ 8559007 (5.97)
A. Toscanini (cnd), NBC SO ("The Toscanini Collection, Vol. 38: All-American Program") † S. Barber:Adagio Strs; G. Gershwin:American in Paris; J. S. Smith:Star-Spangled Banner; J. P. Sousa:Marches & Dances RCAV (Gold Seal) ▲ 60307 (11.97)

Grand Canyon Suite:Cloudburst
F. Grofé (cnd), Capitol SO ("Great American Grofé") † Death Valley; Grand Canyon Suite; Mississippi Suite ANGL (Great American) ▲ 66387 (11.97)

Mississippi Suite for Orchestra (1925)
H. Hanson (cnd), Eastman-Rochester Orch † Grand Canyon Suite; V. Herbert:Con 2 Vc, Op. 30 MRCR ▲ 34355 (11.97)
A. Kostelanetz (cnd), New York PO † Grand Canyon Suite SNYC ▲ 37759 [ADD] (9.97) ▮ 37759 [ADD] (3.98)
F. Slatkin (cnd), Hollywood Bowl SO ("Great American Grofé") † Death Valley; Grand Canyon Suite; Grand Canyon:Cloudburst ANGL (Great American) ▲ 66387 (11.97)
W. T. Stromberg (cnd), Bournemouth SO † Grand Canyon Suite; Niagara Falls Suite NXIN ▲ 8559007 (5.97)
P. Whiteman (cnd), Paul Whiteman Orch † Grand Canyon Suite; Mississippi Suite; G. Gershwin:Con Pno; Rhap in Blue PHS ▲ 22 [ADD] (17.97)
Niagara Falls Suite for Orchestra (1961)
W. T. Stromberg (cnd), Bournemouth SO † Grand Canyon Suite; Mississippi Suite NXIN ▲ 8559007 (5.97)
GRØNDAHL, AGATHE (BACKER-) (1847-1907)
Piano Music
J. M. Bratlie (pno) † Songs NORW ▲ 9802 (17.97)
Songs
E. Tandberg (sop), J. M. Bratlie (pno) † Pno Music NORW ▲ 9802 (17.97)
GRONDAHL, LAUNY (1886-1960)
Concerto for Trombone & Orchestra (1924)
H. Björkman (trbn), J. Hirokami (cnd), Stockholm Symphonic Wind Orch † M. Maros:Aurora; Mayuzumi:Ritual Ov; Mendelssohn (-Bartholdy):Ov Wind, Op. 24; Sallinen:Chorali; Schoenberg:Theme & Vars Band, Op. 43a CAPA ▲ 21516 (16.97)
C. Lindberg (trbn), L. Segerstam (cnd), Bamberg SO † F. David:Concertino Trbn, Op. 4; Frumerie:Con Trbn, Op. 81; Guilmant:Morceau symphonique, Op. 88 BIS ▲ 378 [DDD] (17.97)
GROSSI, ANDREA (17th cent)
Sonatas for 2-5 Instruments, Op. 3
G. Cassone (tpt), G. Cassone (cnd) *(rec Feb 17-20, 1992)* ("The Trumpet in San Petronio") † Cazzati:Sons 5 Instr, Op. 35; Gabrielli:Sonatas for Trumpet & Strings; Jacchini:Sons Tpt; Torelli:Concertino per camera, Op. 4; Sinf Tpt, G.9; Son Tpt, G.1 NUO (Ancient Music) ▲ 7128 [DDD] (16.97)
GROSZ, WILHELM (1894-1939)
Africa Songs for Voice & Chamber Ensemble, Op. 29 (1930)
C. Clarey (sop), R. Ziegler (cnd) † Bankel und Balladen, Op. 31; Rondels, Op. 11; Songs PPHI (Entartete Musik) ▲ 455116 (16.97)
Bankel und Balladen for Voice & Chamber Ensemble [text Sokol & Ringelnatz], Op. 31 (1931)
A. Shore (bass), R. Ziegler (cnd) † Africa Songs, Op. 29; Rondels, Op. 11; Songs PPHI (Entartete Musik) ▲ 455116 (16.97)

▲ = CD ♦ = Enhanced CD △ = MD ▮ = Cassette Tape ▯ = DCC

GROSZ, WILHELM (cont.)
Rondels for Voice & Chamber Ensemble, Op. 11 (1921)
C. Clarey (sop), R. Ziegler (cnd) † Africa Songs, Op. 29; Bankel und Balladen, Op. 31; Songs
PPHI (Entartete Musik) ▲ 455116 (16.97)
Songs
K. Hunter (sgr), R. Ziegler (cnd) —Isle of Capri; Red Sails in the Sunset; Harbour Lights; Along the Santa Fe Trail; When Budapest Was Young † Africa Songs, Op. 29; Bankel und Balladen, Op. 31; Rondels, Op. 11
PPHI (Entartete Musik) ▲ 455116 (16.97)
GROVÉ, STEFANS (1922-
Afrika Hymnus for Organ (1991)
G. Jordaan (org) † Nonyana, the Ceremonial Dancer; Son Va; Songs & Dances from Africa
GSE ▲ 1546 [DDD] (16.97)
L. Kurpershoek (org) *(rec St. Mary's Anglican Cathedral Org Johannesburg)* ("Popular Organ Music, Vol. 4") † J. Brahms:Chorale Preludes Org, Op. 122; N. Cocker:Tuba Tune; Duruflé:Prélude et fugue, Op. 7; C. Franck:Chorales Org, M.38-40; Hollins:Intermezzo PRIO ▲ 610 (16.97)
Nonyana, the Ceremonial Dancer for Piano (1995)
A. Cruickshank (pno) † Afrika Hymnus; Son Va; Songs & Dances from Africa GSE ▲ 1546 [DDD] (16.97)
Sonata for Viola & Piano (1994)
J. Moolman (va), P. Moolman (pno) † Afrika Hymnus; Nonyana, the Ceremonial Dancer; Songs & Dances from Africa GSE ▲ 1546 [DDD] (16.97)
Songs & Dances from Africa for Piano (1990)
A. Cruickshank (pno) † Afrika Hymnus; Nonyana, the Ceremonial Dancer; Son Va GSE ▲ 1546 [DDD] (16.97)
GROVEN, EIVIND (1901-1977)
Concerto for Piano (1950)
W. Plagge (pno), O. K. Ruud (cnd), Trondheim SO † Sym 2 SIMX ▲ 3111 (18.97)
Sunlight Mood [Solstemning] for Flute & Piano (1956)
P. Øien (fl), G. H. Braaten (pno) *(rec Nacka, Sweden, June 13-14, 1980)* ("The Norwegian Flute") † S. Bergh:Pan; F. Mortensen:Son Fl, Op. 6; S. Olsen:Poem Fl; Serenade Fl, Op. 45; Ørbeck:Pastorale & Allegro Fl; Sommerfeldt:Spring Tunes Fl, Op. 44 BIS ▲ 103 [AAD] (17.97)
Symphony No. 2 (1946)
W. Plagge (pno), O. K. Ruud (cnd), Trondheim SO † Con Pno SIMX ▲ 3111 (18.97)
GROVLEZ, GABRIEL (1879-1944)
Sarabande et Allegro for Oboe & Piano (1929)
K. Meier (ob), K. Kolly (pno) ("French Music for Oboe & Piano") † Bozza:Divertissement Sax, Op. 39; Fant pastoral, Op. 37; Maugüé:Pastorale; F. Poulenc:Son Ob; M. Ravel:Pavane pour une infante défunte; Pièce en forme de Habanera; Saint-Saëns:Son Ob PANC ▲ 510092 [DDD] (17.97)
GRUBER, FRANZ XAVER (1787-1863)
Choral Music
E. Hinreiner (cnd), Salzburg Mozart Players—Hornmesse in D; Hochzeitsmesse in D; Stille Nacht, Heilige Nacht! (3 versions); Heiligste Nacht [G,L] KSCH ▲ 313014 [ADD] (16.97)
Silent Night for Voices, Chorus & Organ (1818)
All-American Boys Chorus, W. Hall (cnd), William Hall Master Chorale, M. Dickstein (hp) *(rec Santa Ana, CA)* ("Ceremony & Carols") † Anonymous:Angels We Have Heard on High; O Come, All Ye Faithful; There Is No Rose; B. Britten:Ceremony of Carols, Op. 28; L. Mason:Joy to the World; Traditional:Good Christian Men; Infant Most Blest; Lo, How a Rose; Nova, Nova, Ave Fit Ex Eva; O Tannenbaum; Tiny Child; Willie Take Your Little Drum
KLAV ▲ 11085 [DDD]
C. Byrd (gtr) *(rec San Francisco, CA, June 1982)* ("The Charlie Byrd Christmas Album") † Anonymous:Angels We Have Heard on High; Deck the Halls; Have Yourself a Merry Little Christmas; O Come, All Ye Faithful; I. Berlin:Holiday Inn (sels); G. Holst:In the Bleak Mid-Winter; Mendelssohn (-Bartholdy):Music of Mendelssohn; Tormé:Christmas Song; Traditional:Coventry Carol; First Noel; God Rest Ye Merry, Gentlemen; Good King Wenceslas; Holly & the Ivy; Lully, Lullay; Mistletoe and Holly; O Tannenbaum; What Child Is This? ERTO ▲ 42004 [AAD] (14.97)
GRUBER, H(EINZ) K(ARL) "NALI" (1943-
Frankenstein!! (pan-demonium) for Baritone Chansonnier & Orchestra (1976-77)
H. K. Gruber (bar), F. Welser-Möst (cnd), Salzburg Camerata Academica † Gomorra (sels); MOB Pieces; Nebelsteinmusik EMIC ▲ 56441 [DDD] (16.97)
Gomorra (selections)
H. K. Gruber (bar), H. K. Gruber (cnd) † Frankenstein!!; MOB Pieces; Nebelsteinmusik
EMIC ▲ 56441 [DDD] (16.97)
MOB Pieces (3) for 7 interchangeable Instruments & Percussion (1968; rev 1977)
H. K. Gruber (cnd) † Frankenstein!!; Gomorra (sels); Nebelsteinmusik EMIC ▲ 56441 [DDD] (16.97)
Nebelsteinmusik for Violin & Orchestra, "Violin Concerto No. 2"
E. Kovacic (vn), F. Welser-Möst (cnd), Salzburg Camerata Academica † Frankenstein!!; Gomorra (sels); MOB Pieces EMIC ▲ 56441 [DDD] (16.97)
GRUENBERG, LOUIS (1884-1964)
Animals and Insects for Voice & Piano, Op. 22 (1924)
P. Sperry (ten), I. Vallecillo (pno) *(rec Bedford, NY, 1990)* ("Paul Sperry Sings American Cycles & Sets") † R. Beaser:7 Deadly Sins; C. Berg:Six Poems of Frank O'Hara; L. A. Smith:Songs of the Silence; Talma:Terre de France; R. Wilson:Three Painters *(E text)* ALBA ▲ 58 [DDD] (16.97)
Jazz Epigrams (6) for Piano, Op. 30b (1928)
C. Oldfather (pno) † Rhap Vn, Op. 49; White Lilacs GMR ▲ 2015 (16.97)
Rhapsody for Violin & Piano, Op. 49 (1945)
J. Smirnoff (vn), C. Oldfather (pno) † Jazz Epigrams, Op. 30b; White Lilacs GMR ▲ 2015 (16.97)
White Lilacs for Violin & Piano (1943)
J. Smirnoff (vn), C. Oldfather (pno) † Jazz Epigrams, Op. 30b; Rhap Vn, Op. 49 GMR ▲ 2015 (16.97)
GRUNENWALD, JEAN-JACQUES (1911-1982)
Pièce en mosaïque for Organ (1966)
C. Cramer (org) *(rec St Pierre Cathedral Angoulême, France)* ("Pieces de Concours from the Paris Conservatory") † P. Cochereau:Vars sur un theme chromatique; J.-C. Henry:Chaconne Org; J. Langlais:Essai; Sonate en trio; Messiaen:Verset pour la fête ARK ▲ 6146 (16.97)
GRUSIN, DAVE (1934-
Three Days of the Condor (film music) for Orchestra (1976)
D. Grusin (cnd) IMEZ ▲ 27 [AAD]
GRYC, STEPHEN (1949-
American Portraits (5) for Wind Quintet (1986-87)
A. di Donato (fl), B. Schallhammer (ob), D. Dunn (cl), S. Black (bn), P. Smith (hn) ("Spectra: Connecticut Composers") † R. Dix:Lyric Qt; W. Penn:Chamber Music II; K. Steen:While Conscience Slept; Welwood:Breath inside the Breath CPS ▲ 8650 [ADD] (16.97)
Music of Gryc
T. Pusztai (cnd) —The Moon's Mirror; 5 Preludes for Fl Alone; 6 Mechanicals from A Midsummer Night's Dream; Delicate Balances; 3 Excursions for Ob; Fant Vars On a Theme of Bela Bartók OPS1 ▲ 166 (12.97)
GU, GUANREN (20th cent)
Concerto for Erhu & Orchestra, "Gazing at the Moon" (1988)
M. Xiaohui (erhu), G. Guanren (cnd), Shanghai Chinese Folk Orch *(rec Shanghai, Jan 1994)* † Singapore Glimpses; Spring Suite; Torrent Qnt; Vars Pipa MARC (Chinese Composers) ▲ 8223951 [DDD] (13.97)
Singapore Glimpses (suite) for Orchestra (1989)
G. Guanren (cnd), Shanghai Chinese Folk Orch *(rec Shanghai, Jan 1994)* † Con Erhu; Spring Suite; Torrent Qnt; Vars Pipa MARC (Chinese Composers) ▲ 8223951 [DDD] (13.97)
Spring Suite for Orchestra (1979)
G. Guanren (cnd), Shanghai Chinese Folk Orch *(rec Shanghai, Jan 1994)* † Con Erhu; Singapore Glimpses; Torrent Qnt; Vars Pipa MARC (Chinese Composers) ▲ 8223951 [DDD] (13.97)
Torrent Quintet for Erhu, Pipa, Dulcimer, Konghou & Cello (1982)
G. Guanren (cnd), Shanghai Chinese Folk Orch *(rec Shanghai, Jan 1994)* † Con Erhu; Singapore Glimpses; Spring Suite; Vars Pipa MARC (Chinese Composers) ▲ 8223951 [DDD] (13.97)
Variations for the Pipa (1979)
Y. Wei (pipa) *(rec Shanghai, Jan 1994)* † Con Erhu; Singapore Glimpses; Spring Suite; Torrent Qnt
MARC (Chinese Composers) ▲ 8223951 [DDD] (13.97)
GUAMI, FRANCESCO (ca 1544-1602)
Ricercari (4) for Brass Ensemble
U. Orlandi (cnd) ("I Guami da Lucci") † G. Guami:Canzoni e Toccata; Padovano:Aria della battaglia
FON ▲ 9101 (13.97)
GUAMI, GIOSEFFO (ca 1540-1611)
Canzonas for Instrumental Ensemble
E. Tarr (cnd) —No. 25; "L'Accorta" *(rec Ilbenstadt Basilika, Nov 1992)* † H. Eisler:Kammersinfonie, Op. 69; Kleine Sinf, Op. 29; Orchesterstücke; Pieces (3) Orch; Sturm-Suite; G. Gabrieli:Music of Gabrieli; Schelle:Actus Musicus auf Weyh-Nachten; H. Schütz:Weihnachtshistorie CAPO ▲ 10500 [DDD] (10.97)
Canzoni (11) e Toccata del secondo tuono for Brass
U. Orlandi (cnd) ("I Guami da Lucci") † F. Guami:Ricercari; Padovano:Aria della battaglia FON ▲ 9101 (13.97)
Organ Music
F. Bohme (org), F. Werner (org)—Pieces for 2 Orgs; Taminga † J. Alain:Org Music (misc); Mieg:Org Music; M. Reger:Org Music (misc colls); P. A. Soler:Cons Kbds QUER ▲ 9811 (18.97)
GUARNIERI, CAMARGO MOZART (1907-1993)
Canção sertaneja for Piano (1928)
Brazilian Guitar Quartet [arr Ed. Gloeden for gtr qt] *(rec São Paulo, Brazil, Dec 27-30, 1998)* † Dança brasiliera; Dança negra; Ponteios Pno; Gomes:Son Str Qt; F. Mignone:Lundu; H. Villa-Lobos:Bachiana brasileira 1
DLS ▲ 3245 [DDD] (14.97)
Cantiga de Ninar for Violin & Piano
Upper Valley Duo ("An American Affair") † A. Copland:Rodeo (sels); Corigliano:Son Vn; C. Ives:Son 2 Vn
MARQ ▲ 179 (16.97)
Choro for Piano & Orchestra (1956)
C. Pagano (pno), P. Freeman (cnd), Czech National SO † Dança negra; Homage to Mina; Ponteios Pno; Sonatinas (4) Pno HALM ▲ 35071 (6.97)
Coletanea for Violin & Piano
M. Foster (vn), E. Plawutsky (pno) † Miguez:Son Vn; M. Nobre:Desafio III; H. Villa-Lobos:Son 2 Vn
SNE ▲ 593 (16.97)
Dança brasileira for Piano (1928; orchd 1931)
L. Bernstein (cnd), New York PO *(rec 1962)* † C. Chávez:Sym 2; A. Copland:Danzón Cubano; Salón México; O. L. Fernandez:Batuque; Revueltas:Sensemayá; H. Villa-Lobos:Bachiana brasileira 2; Bachiana brasileira 5
SNYC (Bernstein Century) ▲ 60571 [ADD] (10.97)
Brazilian Guitar Quartet [arr Ed. Gloeden for gtr qt] *(rec São Paulo, Brazil, Dec 27-30, 1998)* † Canção sertaneja; Dança negra; Ponteios Pno; Gomes:Son Str Qt; F. Mignone:Lundu; H. Villa-Lobos:Bachiana brasileira 1
DLS ▲ 3245 [DDD] (14.97)
M. Valdes (cnd), Bolívar SO *(rec Aula Magna of the Universidad Central de Venezuela, July 1995)* ("Caramelos Latinos: Latin American Lollipops") † Dansa selvagem; Dança negra; Encantamento; I. Carreño:Suite margariteña; Ginastera:Creole "Faust" Ov, Op. 9; Moncayo Garcia:Huapango; J. B. Plaza:Fuga romántica venezolana; Revueltas:Renacuajo Paseador DOR ▲ 90227 [DDD] (16.97)
Dança negra for Piano (1946; orchd 1947)
Brazilian Guitar Quartet [arr Ed. Gloeden for gtr qt] *(rec São Paulo, Brazil, Dec 27-30, 1998)* † Canção sertaneja; Dança brasiliera; Ponteios Pno; Gomes:Son Str Qt; F. Mignone:Lundu; H. Villa-Lobos:Bachiana brasileira 1
DLS ▲ 3245 [DDD] (14.97)
C. Pagano (pno), P. Freeman (cnd), Czech National SO † Choro Pno; Homage to Mina; Ponteios Pno; Sonatinas (4) Pno HALM ▲ 35071 (6.97)
M. Valdes (cnd), Bolívar SO *(rec Aula Magna of the Universidad Central de Venezuela, July 1995)* ("Caramelos Latinos: Latin American Lollipops") † Dansa selvagem; Dança brasiliera; Encantamento; I. Carreño:Suite margariteña; Ginastera:Creole "Faust" Ov, Op. 9; Moncayo Garcia:Huapango; J. B. Plaza:Fuga romántica venezolana; Revueltas:Renacuajo Paseador DOR ▲ 90227 [DDD] (16.97)
Dansa selvagem for Piano (1931; orchd 1931)
M. Valdes (cnd), Bolívar SO *(rec Aula Magna of the Universidad Central de Venezuela, July 1995)* ("Caramelos Latinos: Latin American Lollipops") † Dança brasiliera; Dança negra; Encantamento; I. Carreño:Suite margariteña; Ginastera:Creole "Faust" Ov, Op. 9; Moncayo Garcia:Huapango; J. B. Plaza:Fuga romántica venezolana; Revueltas:Renacuajo Paseador DOR ▲ 90227 [DDD] (16.97)
Encantamento for Orchestra (or Violin & Piano) (1941)
M. Valdes (cnd), Bolívar SO *(rec Aula Magna of the Universidad Central de Venezuela, July 1995)* ("Caramelos Latinos: Latin American Lollipops") † Dansa selvagem; Dança brasiliera; Dança negra; I. Carreño:Suite margariteña; Ginastera:Creole "Faust" Ov, Op. 9; Moncayo Garcia:Huapango; J. B. Plaza:Fuga romántica venezolana; Revueltas:Renacuajo Paseador DOR ▲ 90227 [DDD] (16.97)
Homage to Mina for Piano & Orchestra
C. Pagano (pno), P. Freeman (cnd), Czech National SO † Choro Pno; Dança negra; Ponteios Pno; Sonatinas (4) Pno HALM ▲ 35071 (6.97)
Homage to Villa-Lobos for Orchestra (1966)
D. Deroche (cnd), DePaul Univ Wind Ensemble *(rec Depaul Univerity Concert Hall, IL, 1995-98)* † J. Beal:Con Cl; Bozza:Children's Ov; Lopatnikoff:Con Ww; Martinů:Comedy on the Bridge (suite); D. Milhaud:Sym 5
ALBA ▲ 334 [DDD] (16.97)
Ponteios [Preludes] (50) for Piano (1931-1959)
Brazilian Guitar Quartet [arr Ed. Gloeden for gtr qt] *(rec São Paulo, Brazil, Dec 27-30, 1998)* † Canção sertaneja; Dança brasiliera; Dança negra; Gomes:Son Str Qt; F. Mignone:Lundu; H. Villa-Lobos:Bachiana brasileira 1
DLS ▲ 3245 [DDD] (14.97)
C. Pagano (pno), P. Freeman (cnd), Czech National SO—No. 22; No. 24; No. 30; No. 45; No. 46; No. 49 † Choro Pno; Dança negra; Homage to Mina; Sonatinas (4) Pno HALM ▲ 35071 (6.97)
Sonata No. 2 for Violin & Piano (1933)
T. C. Guarnieri (vn), L. D. Souza Brasil (pno) † Son 3 Vn; Son 4 Vn MXHS ▲ 3 (18.97)
L. Kaufman (vn), A. Balsam (pno) ("Pan-Americana: The Violin Artistry of Louis Kaufman") † R. R. Bennett:Con Vn; Song Son; E. Helm:Comment on 2 Spirituals; Mcbride:Aria & Toccata in Swing; D. Milhaud:Saudades do Brasil, Op. 67; W. G. Still:Lenox Ave; Triggs:Danza Braziliana Pnos CMB (Historical) ▲ 1078 [ADD]
Sonata No. 3 for Violin & Piano (1950)
T. C. Guarnieri (vn), L. D. Souza Brasil (pno) † Son 2 Vn; Son 4 Vn MXHS ▲ 3 (18.97)
Sonata No. 4 for Violin & Piano (1956)
T. C. Guarnieri (vn), L. D. Souza Brasil (pno) † Son 2 Vn; Son 3 Vn MXHS ▲ 3 (18.97)
Sonatinas (4) for Piano & Orchestra (1928-58)
C. Pagano (pno), P. Freeman (cnd), Czech National SO—No. 4 (1958) † Choro Pno; Dança negra; Homage to Mina; Ponteios Pno HALM ▲ 35071 (6.97)
GUASTAVINO, CARLOS (1912-
Balicento for solo Guitar
M. I. Siewers (gtr) ("Guitar & Chamber Music") † Cantilena; Cantos Populares; Jeromita Linares; Santa Fé Antiguo ASV ▲ 933 [DDD] (16.97)
Cantilena for solo Guitar
M. I. Siewers (gtr) ("Guitar & Chamber Music") † Balicento; Cantos Populares; Jeromita Linares; Santa Fé Antiguo ASV ▲ 933 [DDD] (16.97)
Cantilenas Argentinas (10) for Piano (1958)
M. Goimard (pno) *(rec Aug 22-24, 1995)* ("Argentine Piano Music") † J. J. Castro:Tangos Pno; Ginastera:Danzas argentinas, Op. 2; Lopez Buchardo:Bailecito Pno; Sonatina Pno; A. Piazzolla:Preludes Pno; Pignoni:Dances Pno
PAVA ▲ 7353 [DDD] (10.97)
Cantilenas Argentinas (3) y Final for Chamber Orchestra
artists unknown *(rec Troy, NY, Feb 1994)* ("Impresiones") † Jeromita Linares; L. Gianneo:Piezas criollas; Ginastera:Impresiones de la Puna; Zorzi:Adagio elegiaco DOR ▲ 90202 [DDD] (16.97)
Cantos Populares (3) for Guitar & Violin
M. I. Siewers (gtr), Stamitz String Quartet members ("Guitar & Chamber Music") † Balicento; Cantilena; Jeromita Linares; Santa Fé Antiguo ASV ▲ 933 [DDD] (16.97)
Jeromita Linares for Guitar & Strings [from Las Presencias]
P. Cohen (gtr) *(rec Troy, NY, Feb 1994)* ("Impresiones") † Cantilenas Argentinas y Final; L. Gianneo:Piezas criollas; Ginastera:Impresiones de la Puna; Zorzi:Adagio elegiaco DOR ▲ 90202 [DDD] (16.97)
S. Puccini (gtr), A. Koregelos (fl), R. Schwartz (pno), J. L. Moscovich (cnd), San Francisco Camerata Americana ("Camerata Americana") † L. Brouwer:Con 3 Gtr; C. Franzetti:Con Del Plata; Ginastera:Impresiones de la Puna; M. Romero:Spirals KLAV ▲ 11093 [DDD] (18.97)
M. I. Siewers (gtr), Stamitz String Quartet ("Guitar & Chamber Music") † Balicento; Cantilena; Cantos Populares; Santa Fé Antiguo ASV ▲ 933 [DDD] (16.97)
Piano Music
N. Lester (pno), N. Roldán (pno)—Romances (3); Bailecito; Gato *(rec Rosenstock Auditorium, Hood College, Frederick, MD, Oct 1992)* ("Music of the Americas") † Aguirre:Huella; A. Benjamin:Jamaican Rhumba; Jamaican Street Songs; A. Copland:Danzón Cubano; R. Cordero:Duo 1954; Joio:Aria & Toccata for 2 Pnos
CENT ▲ 2171 [DDD] (16.97)

GUASTAVINO, CARLOS (cont.)
Piano Music (cont.)
Moreno-Capelli Duo—Romance del plata; 3 Romances; Bailecito; Gato; Llanura; Se equivoco la paloma; La siesta; Las presencias *(rec Feb 25-27, 1992)* MARC ▲ 8223462 [DDD] (13.97)
Preludes on Argentinian Nursery Rhymes for Piano
C. Pillado (pno) ("Cuántas Estrellas") † Ginastera:Son 1 Pno, Op. 22; Pillado:Amazon Vars BER ▲ 1185 (16.97)
Santa Fé Antiguo for solo Guitar
M. I. Siewers (gtr) ("Guitar & Chamber Music") † Balicento; Cantilena; Cantos Populares; Jeromita Linares ASV ▲ 933 [DDD] (16.97)
Sonata for Clarinet & Piano (1969)
D. Pacitti (cl), C. Balzaretti (pno) † A. Copland:Con Cl; A. Piazzolla:Contemplación y danza, Op. 15; I. Stravinsky:Pieces Cl AG ▲ 26 [DDD] (18.97)
Songs
U. Espaillat (ten), P. Zinger (pno)—Desde que te conocí; Viniendo de Chilecito; En los surcos del amor; Mi garganta; Cuando acaba de llover; Préstame tu pañuelito; Ya me voy a retirar; Las puertas de la mañana; Piececitos; Cita; Se equivocó la paloma; Jardin de amores; A volar!; Nana del niño malo; La novia; Geografia Fisica; Alpuente de la golodrina!; Elegía; La rosa y el sauce; Pueblito, mi pueblo *(rec May 1992)* ("Las puertas de la mañana") NALB ▲ 58 (16.97)
M. Fink (bar), L. Ascot (pno)—Quatro canciones argentinas; Flores argentinas; 8 songs CASC ▲ 1059 (16.97)
M. J. Montiel (sop), M. Zanetti (pno)—La rosa y el sauce; El Sampedrino † Ginastera:Songs; E. Granados:Colección de Tonadillas; E. Halffter:Songs; Montsalvage:Canciónes negras; J. Rodrigo:Songs RTVE ▲ 65115 (16.97)
M. Pares-Reyna (sop), G. Rabol (pno)—Alegria de la soledad; Apegado a mi; Cantilena; Corderito; Cuando acaba de llover; Desde que te conoci; Dones sencillos; Deseo; Donde habite el olvido; En los surcos del armor; Encantamiento; Esta iglesia no tiene; Hallazgo; Jardin antiguo; Meciendo; Mi garganta; Pájaro muerto; La palomita; Piececitos; Prestame tu pañuelito; La primera pregunta; La puertas de la mañana; Riqueza; Rocio; Romance de José Cubas; La rosa y el sauce; El Sampedrino; Se equivocó la paloma; Severa Villafañe; Siesta; Violetas; Viniendo de Chilecito; Ya me voy a retirar [Sp] *(rec May 1990)* ("Classics of the Americas, Vol. 2") OPUS ▲ 309002 [DDD] (18.97)

GUBAIDULINA, SOFIA (1931-
Allegro rustico for Flute & Piano (1963)
L. Mironovich (fl), E. Mironovich (pno) *(rec Boston, MA)* ("Magic of the Russian Flute") † E. Denisov:Son Fl; Nagovitzin:Son Fl; Sinisalo:Miniatures Fl; Taktakishvili:Son Fl; Vasilenko:Spring Suite, Op. 138 SO ▲ 22567 [DDD] (16.97)
Alleluia for Boy Soprano, Orchestra & Chorus
D. Kitaienko (cnd), Danish National RSO, Danish National Radio Choir † Górecki:Miserere, Op. 44 CHN ▲ 9523 (16.97)
And: The Feast Is in Full Progress for Cello & Orchestra, "Cello Concerto No. 2"
D. Geringas (vc), J. Saraste (cnd), Finnish RSO † Preludes Vc COLG (Deluxe) ▲ 31881 [DDD] (22.97)
Chaconne for Piano (1962)
M. J. Gothmann (pno) ("180° from Ordinary") † Gleck:2 Tpts; L. Larsen:Black Roller; A. Piazzolla:4, for Tango; Siskind:Rituale; Trenka:WatchWait; F. Zappa:Black Page INNO ▲ 513 [ADD] (14.97)
Concerto for Bassoon & Low Strings (1975)
H. Ahmas (bn), O. Vänskä (cnd) *(rec Aug 16-19, 1993)* † Concordanza; Detto 2 Vc BIS ▲ 636 [DDD] (17.97)
V. Popov (bn), R. Meshchaninov (cnd) † Detto 2 Vc; Mistrioso; Rubayat MELD (Musica non grata) ▲ 49957 (6.97)
Concordanza for Chamber Orchestra (1971)
German Chamber PO † Meditation on a Bach Chorale; 7 Last Words BER ▲ 1113 [DDD] (17.97)
O. Vänskä (cnd) *(rec Aug 16-19, 1993)* † Con Bn; Detto 2 Vc BIS ▲ 636 [DDD] (17.97)
Dancer on a Tightrope for Violin & Piano (1993)
G. Kremer (vn), V. Sakharov (pno) *(rec Lockenhaus Festival Austria, 1995)* † Meditation on a Bach Chorale; Silenzio; Suslin:Capriccio über die Abreise; Choruses on Poems by D. Kharms BIS ▲ 810 [DDD] (17.97)
Detto No. 2 for Cello & Chamber Orchestra (1973)
H. Brendstrup (vc), F. Widekind (cnd) † In Croce; Preludes Vc KPT ▲ 32176 [DDD]
I. Monighetti (vc), Y. Nikolavevsky (cnd) † Con Bn; Mistrioso; Rubayat MELD (Musica non grata) ▲ 49957 (6.97)
I. Pälli (vc), O. Vänskä (cnd) *(rec Aug 16-19, 1993)* † Con Bn; Concordanza BIS ▲ 636 [DDD] (17.97)
Duo-Sonata for 2 Baritone Saxophones (1977)
C. Delangle (bar sax), D. Royannais (bar sax) *(rec Paris, France, July 1995)* ("The Russian Saxophone") † E. Denisov:Son alt Sax; Son alt Sax & Vc; Karasikov:Casus in terminus; Raskatov:Pas de deux; Wustin:Musique pour l'ange BIS ▲ 765 [DDD] (17.97)
V. Popov (bn) † Quasi hoquetus CHN ▲ 9717 (16.97)
The Garden of Joy & Sorrow for Flute, Viola & Harp (1980)
Auréole † Debussy:Épigraphes antiques (6) Pno; Genzmer:Trio Fl, Va & Hp; C. Nielsen:Suite for fl, va, hp KOCH ▲ 7055 [DDD] (16.97)
Hommage à T. S. Eliot for Octet & Soprano (1987)
C. Whittlesey (sop), I. V. Keulen (vn), G. Kremer (vn), T. Zimmermann (va), D. Geringas (vc), A. Posch (db), E. Brunner (cl), K. Thunemann (bn), R. Vlatkovic (hn) *(rec 1987 tour of "Music from Lockenhaus")* † Offertorium DEUT ▲ 27336 [DDD] (16.97)
In Croce for Cello & Organ
M. Beiser (vc), D. Papadakos (org) † Preludes Vc; Ustvolskaya:Grand Duet Vc KOCH ▲ 7258 [DDD] (10.97)
H. Brendstrup (vc), J. E. Christensen (org) † Detto 2 Vc; Preludes Vc KPT ▲ 32176 [DDD]
D. Geringas (vc), E. Krapp (org) ("Russian Chamber Music") † Pärt:Spiegel im Spiegel; A. Schnittke:Son 1 Vc; Suslin:Son Vc & Perc KSCH ▲ 310091 [DDD]
Meditation on a Bach Chorale for Harpsichord & String Quintet (1993)
E. Bekova (vn), H. Weinmeister (vn), M. Stravinsky (va), A. Bekova (vc), A. Posch (db), E. Chojnacka (hpd) *(rec Lockenhaus Festival Austria, 1995)* † Dancer on a Tightrope; Silenzio; Suslin:Capriccio über die Abreise; Choruses on Poems by D. Kharms BIS ▲ 810 [DDD] (17.97)
German Chamber PO † Concordanza; 7 Last Words BER ▲ 1113 [DDD] (17.97)
Mistrioso for 7 Percussionists (1977)
V. Grishin (cnd) † Con Bn; Detto 2 Vc; Rubayat MELD (Musica non grata) ▲ 49957 (6.97)
Offertorium (concerto) for Violin & Orchestra (1980)
G. Kremer (vn), C. Dutoit (cnd), Boston SO † Hommage à T. S. Eliot DEUT ▲ 27336 [DDD] (16.97)
O. Krysa (vn), J. DePreist (cnd), Royal Stockholm PO † Rejoice BIS ▲ 566 [DDD] (17.97)
Piano Music (complete)
D. Baker (pno)—Chaconne; Invention; Toccata-Troncata; Son; Musical Toys ("Complete Works for Solo Piano") STRV ▲ 33393 [DDD] (16.97)
B. Rauchs (pno)—Chaconne; Son Pno; Musical Toys; Toccata-Troncata; Invention; Introitus (con) *(rec Apr & July 1995)* ("The Complete Piano Music") BIS ▲ 853 [DDD] (17.97)
Preludes (10) for Cello (1974)
M. Beiser (vc) † In Croce; Ustvolskaya:Grand Duet Vc KOCH ▲ 7258 [DDD] (10.97)
J. Berger (vc) † J. Cage:One8 WER ▲ 6288 (19.97)
H. Brendstrup (vc) † Detto 2 Vc; In Croce KPT ▲ 32176 [DDD]
D. Geringas (vc) † And the Feast Is in Full Progress, "Con 2 Vc" COLG (Deluxe) ▲ 31881 [DDD] (22.97)
Pro et Contra for Large Orchestra (1989)
T. Otaka (cnd), BBC National Orch Wales *(rec Jan 31, 1994)* † E. Firsova:Cassandra, Op. 60 BIS ▲ 668 [DDD] (17.97)
Punkte, Linien & Zickzack for String Trio
LINensemble [arr for pno trio] † Gorecki:Lerchenmusik, Op. 53 KPT ▲ 32175 [DDD]
Quartet No. 1 for Strings (1971)
Danish String Quartet † Qt 2 Strs; Qt 3 Strs; Trio Strs CPO ▲ 999064 [DDD] (14.97)
Quartet No. 2 for Strings (1987)
Danish String Quartet † Qt 1 Strs; Qt 3 Strs; Trio Strs CPO ▲ 999064 [DDD] (14.97)
Quartet No. 3 for Strings (1987)
Danish String Quartet † Qt 1 Strs; Qt 2 Strs; Trio Strs CPO ▲ 999064 [DDD] (14.97)
Quartet No. 4 for Strings (1993)
Kronos Quartet ("Night Prayers") † Ali-Zade:Mugam Sayagi; Golijov:K'Vakarat; Kancheli:Night Prayers for Str Qt; Tahmizyan:Cool Wind is Blowing; Yanov-Yanovsky:Lacrymosa NON ▲ 79346 (16.97)
Quasi hoquetus for Viola, Bassoon & Piano (1984)
N. Gigashvili (va), V. Popov (bn), A. Bakchiyev (pno) † Duo-Son CHN ▲ 9717 (16.97)
Rejoice (sonata) for Violin & Cello
G. Kremer (vn), Y.-Y. Ma (vc) † D. Shostakovich:Qt 15 Strs, Op. 144 SNYC ▲ 44924 [DDD] (16.97)
O. Krysa (vn), T. Thedéen (vc) † Offertorium BIS ▲ 566 [DDD] (17.97)

GUBAIDULINA, SOFIA (cont.)
Rubayat (cantata) for Baritone & Chamber Ensemble [texts Khakani, Akhmatova & Potapova] (1969)
S. Yanovenko (bar), G. Rozhdestvensky (cnd) † Con Bn; Detto 2 Vc; Mistrioso MELD (Musica non grata) ▲ 49957 (6.97)
The Seven Last Words (partita in 7 movts) for Cello, Bayan & String Orchestra (1982)
German Chamber PO † Concordanza; Meditation on a Bach Chorale BER ▲ 1113 [DDD] (17.97)
Silenzio (5 pieces) for Bayan, Violin & Cello (1991)
G. Kremer (vn), V. Tonkha (vc), F. Lips (bayan) *(rec Lockenhaus Festival Austria, 1995)* † Dancer on a Tightrope; Meditation on a Bach Chorale; Suslin:Capriccio über die Abreise; Choruses on Poems by D. Kharms BIS ▲ 810 [DDD] (17.97)
Stufen for Orchestra
G. Rozhdestvensky (cnd), Royal Stockholm PO † Sym in 12 Movements CHN ▲ 9183 [DDD] (17.97)
Symphony in 12 Movements for Orchestra, "Stimmen...Verstummen"
G. Rozhdestvensky (cnd), Royal Stockholm PO † Stufen CHN ▲ 9183 [DDD] (17.97)
Trio for Strings
Danish String Quartet members † Qt 1 Strs; Qt 2 Strs; Qt 3 Strs CPO ▲ 999064 [DDD] (14.97)

GUDMUNSEN-HOLMGREEN, PELLE (1932-
Concerto grosso for String Quartet & Orchestra (1990; rev 1995)
M. Schønwandt (cnd), Danish National RSO, M. Schønwandt (cnd), Kontra String Quartet † For Vc & Orch; Mester Jakob MARC ▲ 8224060 (13.97)
For Cello & Orchestra (1994-96)
M. Zeuthen (vc), M. Schønwandt (cnd), Danish National RSO † Con grosso Str Qt; Mester Jakob MARC ▲ 8224060 (13.97)
Mester Jakob [Frère Jaques] for Chamber Orchestra (1964)
M. Schønwandt (cnd), Danish National RSO † Con grosso Str Qt; For Vc & Orch MARC ▲ 8224060 (13.97)
Mirror Pieces [Spejlstykker] for Clarinet, Cello & Piano (1980)
Danish Trio *(rec Dec 1987)* † Højsgaard:Fantasistykker; Lorentzen:Mambo; Ruders:Tattoo for 3 PLAL ▲ 57 [AAD] (18.97)
Solo for Electric Guitar (1971-72)
E. Møldrup (gtr) *(rec Århus Denmark, 1988-93)* ("The Frosty Silence: Music for Guitar by Danish Composers") † Gefors:Boîte chinoise, Op. 12/1; T. Nielsen:Frosty Silence in the Gardens; Nørgård:Tales from a Hand; Nørholm:Son Gtr, Op. 69; P. R. Olsen:Nostalgie, Op. 78 MARC (dacapo) ▲ 8224006 [DDD] (13.97)
Symphony No. 3, "Antiphony" (1974-77)
L. Segerstam (cnd), Danish National RSO † K. A. Rasmussen:Sym in Time DCAP ▲ 9010 [DDD] (13.97)
Triptykon for Percussion & Orchestra
G. Mortensen (perc), J. Panula (cnd), Danish National RSO † Nørgård:I Ching; Xenakis:Psappha BIS ▲ 256 [AAD] (17.97)

GUÉDRON, PIERRE (?1570/75-1619/20)
Airs de cour for Voices [or Voice & Lute or Instruments]
C. Ansermet (sop), P. Cherici (lt) ("Soupirs meslés d'amour") SYM ▲ 96153 (18.97)

GUERANDI, MAURIZIO (20th cent)
Towards for Saxophone & Piano (1996)
Duo Dilemme [2 versions] *(rec Jan 1998)* ("Nouvelle musique pour saxophone et piano") † M. Angulo:Bisonante Sax; Charrière:Voix meurtrie; J. A. Lennon:Distances Within Me; M. Nyman:Shaping the Curve; Visvikis:Mondes irisés DORO ▲ 5011 [DDD] (16.97)

GUERAU, FRANCISCO (17th cent)
Poema harmónico for Guitar (1694)
T. Schmitt (gtr) *(rec Apr & Sept 1993)* ("Guitar Music of the Baroque: Spain") † S. De Murcia:Gtr Music; Santa Cruz:Libro donde se verán Pasacalles; G. Sanz:Instrucción de Música MPH ▲ 56819 [DDD] (15.97)

GUERRERO, FRANCISCO (1528-1599)
Choral Music
A. Dixon (cnd), Chapelle du Roi—Missa pro defunctis [Gradual; Tract] *(rec St. Jude's Hampstead, England, May 11-13, 1998)* † N. Gombert:Motets; Infantas:Domine ostende; Josquin Desprez:Secular Songs; A. Lobo:Liber primus missarum; Sacred Music; Richafort:Motets SIUK ▲ 5 (16.97)
His Majesty's Sagbutts & Cornetts, J. O'Donnell (cnd), Westminster Cathedral Choir—Pange lingua; Missa de la batalla escoutez; In exitu Israel; Duo Seraphim; Regina caeli latare; Magnificat Octavi toni; Conditor alme siderum HYP ▲ 67075 (18.97)
J. O'Donnell (cnd), Westminster Cathedral Choir—Missa sancta et immaculata; Magnificat; 2 motets; 3 Vesper hymns ("Missa Sancta et Immaculata") HYP ▲ 66910 (18.97)
Missa del la batalla escoutez for Chorus
M. Dwyer (cnd), Choir of the Church of the Advent *(rec Boston, MA, June 1998)* † Missa Simile est regnum coelorum; Motets ASI ▲ 113 [DDD] (16.97)
Missa Simile est regnum coelorum for Chorus
E. Ho (cnd), Choir of the Church of the Advent *(rec Boston, MA, June 1998)* † Missa del la batalla escoutez; Motets ASI ▲ 113 [DDD] (16.97)
Motets for Chorus
E. Ho (cnd), Choir of the Church of the Advent—Simile est regnum coelorum; Alma Redemptoris Mater; Ave Regina Coelorum; Regina Coeli *(rec Boston, MA, June 1998)* † Missa del la batalla escoutez; Missa Simile est regnum coelorum ASI ▲ 113 [DDD] (16.97)
Sacred Motets for 4, 5, 6, 8 & 12 Voices & Instrumental Ensemble
R. Mallavibarrena (cnd) ("Motecta") CNTS ▲ 9619 (18.97)
P. Phillips (cnd), Tallis Scholars *(rec Salle Norfolk, England)* † A. Lobo:Liber primus missarum PPHI ▲ 454931 [DDD] (16.97)
J. Savall (cnd), Capella Reial de Catalunya [period instrs] *(rec Dec 1991-Jan 1992)* ASTR ▲ 8766 (18.97)
Sacred Music
Sacred Motets *(rec Catalogne, Spain, 1991-92)* ("Musica Sacra") † C. de Morales:Sacred Music; Victoria:Motets; Sacred Choral Music FONT 3-▲ 9916 [DDD] (36.97)
Songs
M. Figueras (sop), E. Tiso (sop), M. Arrubarrena (sop), C. Mena (ct), L. Climent (ten), F. Garrigosa (ten), J. Ricart (bar), D. Carnovich (bass), J. Savall (cnd), Capella Reial de Catalunya—Si la noche haze escura *(rec Catalogne, Spain, Sept 1995)* ("El Cançoner del Duc de Calabria (1526-1554)") † Almodar:Songs; Anonymous:Instrumental Music; Songs; Carceres:Songs; Flexta:Songs; C. de Morales:Songs ASTR ▲ 8582 [DDD] (18.97)
Vocal Music
J. Savall (cnd), Hespèrion XX—Prado verde y florido; Dexó la venda, el arco; Ojos claros y serenos *(rec Catalogne, Spain, Nov 1991-Jan 1992)* ("El Cancionero de Medinaceli") † Anonymous:Aquella voz de Cristo; Instrumental Music; Songs; A. de Cabezón:Obras de música (sels); Cebrián:Songs; P. Guerrero:Instrumental Music; G. de Morata:Songs; Mudarra:Songs ASTR ▲ 8764 [DDD] (18.97)

GUERRERO, PEDRO (ca 1520-?)
Instrumental Music
J. Savall (cnd), Hespèrion XX—Di, perra mora *(rec Catalogne, Spain, Nov 1991-Jan 1992)* ("El Cancionero de Medinaceli") † Anonymous:Aquella voz de Cristo; Instrumental Music; Songs; A. de Cabezón:Obras de música (sels); Cebrián:Songs; F. Guerrero:Vocal Music; G. de Morata:Songs; Mudarra:Songs ASTR ▲ 8764 [DDD] (18.97)

GUGLIELMI, PIETRO ALESSANDRO (1728-1804)
Quartets (6) for Harpsichord, 2 Violins & Cello, Op. 1 (?1768)
F. Costa (pno), F. Pierami (cnd), Esterházy Cappella Musicale [arr for pno & str orch] *(rec live Fivizzano, Nov 1996)* ("6 Concerti da camera, Op. 1") BONG ▲ 5059 [DDD] (16.97)

GUILAIN, JEAN-ADAM (fl 1702-1739)
Pièces d'orgue pour le Magnificat for Organ
R. Hobson (org) *(rec Mayfair England)* † Mendelssohn (-Bartholdy):Sons Org, Op. 65; J. Stanley:Voluntaries Org HER ▲ 156
M. Touyère (org) *(rec Sain-François-de-Sales Genève)* † Boyvin:Premier livre Org; Grigny:Org Music; L. Marchand:Pieces Org GALL ▲ 952 [ADD] (18.97)
Suite du quatrième ton for Organ (1706) [unverified]
T. Muster (org) *(rec Souvigny, Dec 26-28, 1994)* ("Suites Pour Souvigny") † Beauvarlet-Charpentier:Magnificats, Op. 7; G. Bovet:Suite pour Souvigny; Marais:Pièces de viole [Book 2] (sels); Tombeau pour Lully; Rameau:Abaris (sels); Rebel:Eléments GALL 2-▲ 863 [ADD]

GUILLAUME D'AMIENS, PAIGNOUR (fl late 13th cent)

C'est la fins

V. Ellis (voc) *(rec England, Oct 1996)* ("On the Banks of the Seine") † Prendés i garde; Ses tres dous regars; Adam de la Halle:Vocal Music; Anonymous:Amor potest; Chanter voel par grant amour; Doucours; Doucours del tens novel; En ung vergier; Estampie real; L'autre jour par un matin; On parole/A Paris/Frese nouvele; Pucelete—Je languis—Domino; Quant voi la flor novele; Volez vous que je vous chant; Bodel:Music of Bodel; Moniot de Paris:Je chevauchoie l'autrier; Thibaut IV, King:J'aloie l'autrier CHN ▲ 9544 [DDD] (16.97)

Prendés i garde

V. Ellis (voc) *(rec England, Oct 1996)* ("On the Banks of the Seine") † C'est la fins; Ses tres dous regars; Adam de la Halle:Vocal Music; Anonymous:Amor potest; Chanter voel par grant amour; Doucours; Doucours del tens novel; En ung vergier; Estampie real; L'autre jour par un matin; On parole/A Paris/Frese nouvele; Pucelete—Je languis—Domino; Quant voi la flor novele; Volez vous que je vous chant; Bodel:Music of Bodel; Moniot de Paris:Je chevauchoie l'autrier; Thibaut IV, King:J'aloie l'autrier CHN ▲ 9544 [DDD] (16.97)

Ses tres dous regars

V. Ellis (voc) *(rec England, Oct 1996)* ("On the Banks of the Seine") † C'est la fins; Prendés i garde; Adam de la Halle:Vocal Music; Anonymous:Amor potest; Chanter voel par grant amour; Doucours; Doucours del tens novel; En ung vergier; Estampie real; L'autre jour par un matin; On parole/A Paris/Frese nouvele; Pucelete—Je languis—Domino; Quant voi la flor novele; Volez vous que je vous chant; Bodel:Music of Bodel; Moniot de Paris:Je chevauchoie l'autrier; Thibaut IV, King:J'aloie l'autrier CHN ▲ 9544 [DDD] (16.97)

GUILLEMAIN, LOUIS-GABRIEL (1705-1770)

Sonata in A for Violin & Harpsichord, Op. 1/4

S. Standage (vn), L. U. Mortensen (hpd) † Duphly:Pièces de clavecin (book 2); Pièces de clavecin (book 4); J.-B. Forqueray:Morangis ou la plissay; J.-M. Leclair:Quatrième livre, Op. 9; Troisième livre, Op. 5; Mondonville:Pièces de clavecin, Op. 3 CHN (Chaconne) ▲ 531 [DDD] (16.97)

GUILLOU, JEAN (1930-

Hyperion, or The Rhetoric of Fire (suite in 4 movements) for Organ

J. Guillou (org) ("The Great Organ of St. Eustache, Paris: Inaugural Recording") DOR ▲ 90134 [DDD] (16.97)

GUILMANT, ALEXANDRE (1837-1911)

Choral for Organ, Op. 93

D. Roth (org) ("Organ Works, Vol. 3") † Grand Choeur Org, Op. 84; Son 5 Org, Op. 80; Son 6 Org, Op. 86 MOTE ▲ 11531 (17.97)

Grand Choeur for Organ, Op. 84

D. Roth (org) ("Organ Works, Vol. 3") † Choral; Son 5 Org, Op. 80; Son 6 Org, Op. 86 MOTE ▲ 11531 (17.97)

Harmonium Music

J. Verdin (harm)—Canzonetta; Mazurka de salon; Recueillment; Villageoise; Son Harm; Fugue grave; Fughetta; Aspiration; Waltz ("Pièces pour harmonium") † N. J. Lemmens:Harm Music RICE ▲ 206252 (17.97)

March upon Handel's "Lift up Your Hands" for Organ

J. Scott (org) *(rec St. Paul's Cathedral London)* † Gigout:Grand-Choeur Dialogue; J. Langlais:Méditations sur l'apocalypse; Liszt:Fant & Fugue on "Ad nos" Org, S.259 GILD ▲ 7128 [DDD] (16.97)

Marche funèbre et chant séraphique for Organ, Op. 17/3 (1868)

W. Headlee (org) *(rec live Crouse College, Syracuse, NY, 1989)* † J. S. Bach:Org Music (misc colls); D. Johnson:Tpt Tune; D. Milhaud:Preludes Org, Op. 231b; Reubke:Son on 94th Psalm Org; Verrees:O for a Closer Walk with God RAVN ▲ 440 [DDD] (17.97)

Morceau symphonique for Trombone & Orchestra, Op. 88

C. Lindberg (trbn), L. Segerstam (cnd), Bamberg SO † F. David:Concertino Trbn, Op. 4; Frumerie:Con Trbn, Op. 81; Grondahl:Con Trbn BIS ▲ 378 [DDD] (17.97)

Organ Music

J. Hammann (org)—Marche funèbre et chant séraphique; Invocation in B; Final in E *(rec St Martin of Tours Roman Catholic Church Louisvill, KY)* ("Alexandre Guilmant in America") † R. Schumann:Studies Canon Form, Op. 56 RAVN ▲ 330 [DDD]

F. Hauk (org), O. Koch (cnd), Leipzig SO—Allegro for Org & Orch, Op. 81; Marche fant sur deux chantes d'eglise for Org, Hp, Op. 44; Meditation sur le stabat mater for Org & Orch, Op., Op. 63; Final all Schumann sur un Noël languedocien, Op. 83; Sym No. 1 for Org & Orch, Op. 42 † Boëllmann:Fant dialoguée, Op. 35; Fêtis:Fant symphonique INMP (Classics) ▲ 6701092 (9.97)

U. Hauser (org)—Son 1 Org, Op. 42; Prière, Op. 16; Morceau de concert; Allegretto, Op. 19; Final, Op. 40; Marche Nupitale, Op. 25; Son 6 Org, Op. 68; Marche Nupitale 2; Pastorale, Op. 26; Marche de la Sym-Cant, Op. 53; Prière & Berceuse, Op. 27; Allegro, Op. 18; Prière, Op. 56/2; Fant, Op. 19; Postlude Nupitale, Op. 69 ("Organ Works") PANC 2-▲ 510049 [ADD] (17.97)

J. Hermans (org), Capella Sancti-Quintini—L'organiste litugiste, Op. 65; 18 pieces nouvelles, Op. 90 ("Organ Works, Vol. 8") MOTE ▲ 11581 (17.97)

C. Herrick (org)—Deuxième Offertoire sur des Noëls; Introduction et variations sur un ancien noël; Noël Brabançon; Son 1: see Collections, "Organ: Herrick" ("Popular Organ Music from Westminster Abbey") MER ▲ 84148 (16.97)

F. Lombard (org)—Morceau de concert; Marche nuptiale; Fugue in D; Canzone in a; Lamentatio in d; Tempo di minuetto in C; Légende et Final Symphonique in d; Prière et Berceuse in A; Pastorale in A; Morceau Symphonique in a ("Pieces in Various Styles") MOTE ▲ 11561 [DDD]

H. G. van Putten (org)—March on a Theme of Handel, Op. 15/2; Allegretto, Op. 19; Lamentation, Op. 45; Son 7 Org, Op. 89; Choral, "Was Gott tut das ist wohlgetan", Op. 93; Verset Org, Op. 19/5; Scherzo symphonique, Op. 55/2 ("Orgelwerken") LDBG ▲ 60 [DDD] (17.97)

Sonata No. 1 in d for Organ, Op. 42 (1874)

C. Hamberger (org) *(rec Abteikirche Münsterschwarzach, 1979)* ("Organ Recital in the Münsterschwarzach Abbey Church") † Vierne:Sym 3 Org, Op. 28 CALG ▲ 50494 [ADD] (19.97)

Sonata No. 2 in d for Organ, Op. 50

S. Chaisemartin (org) ("Organ Works, Vol. 2") † Son 4 Org, Op. 61 MOTE ▲ 11521 (17.97)

Sonata No. 4 in d for Organ, Op. 61

S. Chaisemartin (org) ("Organ Works, Vol. 2") † Son 2 Org, Op. 50 MOTE ▲ 11521 (17.97)

M. Rost (org) *(rec St. Jakobus zu Ilmenau, Germany, June 1994)* ("Romantische Orgeln IV") † Liszt:Prelude & Fugue on the name B-A-C-H, S.260; M. Reger:Pieces (12) Org, Op. 59; Widor:Sym 4 Org, Op. 13/4 THOR ▲ 2247 [DDD] (16.97)

Sonata No. 5 in c for Organ, Op. 80 (1894)

J. E. Eschbach (org) † C. Franck:Grande pièce symphonique, Op. 17 CENT ▲ 2053 [DDD] (16.97)

J. Parker-Smith (org) *(rec London, England)* ("Popular French Romantics, Vol. 1") † J. Bonnet:Pièces nouvelles, Op. 7; Gigout:Toccata Org; Lefébure-Wély:Org Music; Vierne:Carillon de Westminster, Op. 54/6; Pièces de fantaisie; Widor:Sym 1 Org, Op. 13/1; Sym 9 Org, Op. 70 ASV ▲ 539 [DDD] (16.97)

D. Roth (org) ("Organ Works, Vol. 3") † Choral; Grand Choeur Org, Op. 84; Son 6 Org, Op. 86 MOTE ▲ 11531 (17.97)

Sonata No. 6 for Organ, Op. 86

D. Roth (org) ("Organ Works, Vol. 3") † Choral; Grand Choeur Org, Op. 84; Son 5 Org, Op. 80 MOTE ▲ 11531 (17.97)

Sonata No. 7 in F for Organ, Op. 89 (1902)

S. Armstrong-Ouellette (org) *(rec Mission Church, Boston, MA)* ("Musique de la Basilique") † Dupont:Méditation; Gigout:Pièces Org (sels); G. Pierné:Pièces Org, Op. 29; Saint-Martin:Toccata de la Libération; Saint-Saëns:Fant 1 Org; Vierne:Pièces de fantaisie AFK ▲ 538 (16.97)

Sonata No. 8 in A for Organ, Op. 91 (1906)

S. Armstrong-Ouellette (org) † J. Bonnet:Vars de concert, Op. 1; Hannahs:Tpt Tune AFK ▲ 518

Symphony No. 1 in d for Organ & Orchestra, Op. 42

D. Di Fiore (org), S. Kershaw (cnd), Auburn SO ("Les Amoureux de l'Orgue") † C. Franck:Panis angelicus; Gounod:Divine Redeemer; F. Poulenc:Con Org; Vierne:March triomphale, Op. 46 AMBA ▲ 1019 [DDD] (16.97)

I. Tracey (org), Y. P. Tortelier (cnd), BBC PO † F. Poulenc:Con Org; Widor:Sym 5 Org, Op. 42/1 CHN ▲ 9271 [DDD] (16.97)

GUIMARÃES, JOÃO (1883-1947)

Guitar Music

R. Guthrie (gtr)—Sounds of Bells; Pó de Mico; Graúna *(rec Holy Nativity Episcopal Church, Plano, TX, 1995)* † L. Almeida:Gtr Music; Lauro:Gtr Music; M. Ponce:Gtr Music; J. Silva:Gtr Music; H. Villa-Lobos:Preludes Gtr ENRE ▲ 9509 [DDD] (16.97)

Sons de Carrilhões for Guitar

Y. Storms (gtr) ("A Touch of Latin") † A. Barrios:Gtr Music; L. Brouwer:Gtr Music; J. Cardoso:Gtr Music; Lauro:Gtr Music; Sojo:Pieces from Venezuela; H. Villa-Lobos:Chôro 1 SYRX ▲ 94106 [DDD] (16.97)

GUINJOAN, JOAN (1931-

Flamenco for 2 Pianos (1994-95)

K. Mrongovius (pno), B. Uriarte (pno) *(rec Madrid, Spain, Apr 1, 1998)* † Barce:Nuevas Polifonias; T. Marco:Fandangos; Glasperlenspiel; J. Soler:Coronación WER ▲ 6634 [DDD]

GUIOT DE DIJON (fl 1215-1225)

Chanterai pour mon coraige (song) for Chorus

(rec Columbia, MD, Sept 1993) ("Chanterai-Music of Medieval France") † Anonymous:De bonté, de valour; Estampie real; Gaite de la tor; Je puis trop bien; Ma fin est ma commencement; Non es meravelha s'eu chan; Penser ne doit vilenie; Quan je voy le duc; Quant je suis; Souvent souspire; Girault de Bornelh:Reis glorios *([ENG,FRE] text)* DOR ▲ 80123 [DDD] (13.97)

C. Page (cnd), Gothic Voices ("Jerusalem: Vision of Peace") † Anonymous:Alleluia Pascha nostrum; Congaudet hodie celestis curia; Gospel; Gradual Hec dies quam fecit Dominus; Hac in die Gedeonis; In salvatoris; Invocantes Dominum; Jerusalem accipitur; Jerusalem! grant damage ma fais; Luget Rachel iterum; Luto carens et latere; O levis aurula!; Te Deum; Veri vitis germine; Hildegard of Bingen:O Jerusalem aurea civitatis; St. Quentin:Jerusalem se plainte et li pais HYP ▲ 67039 (18.97)

GUIRAUT DE BORNELH (ca 1140-ca 1200)

No posc sifrir c'a la dolor for Chamber Ensemble

Sequentia *(rec Abbaye de Fontevraud, France, Dec 1993)* ("Dante & the Troubadours") † Aimeric de Peghuilhan:Music of Aimeric de Peghuilhan; Bertran De Born:Rassa, tan creis e monta e poia; A. Daniel:Chanson do'ill mot son plan e prim; Lo ferm voler qu'el cor m'intra; Folquet de Marseille:Tant m'abellis l'amoros pessamens; Peire d'Alvernhe:Dejosta'ls breus jorns DEHA ▲ 77227 [DDD] (16.97)

GULDA, FRIEDRICH (1930-

Gegenwart [3 Duos for Electric Clavichord & Percussion; 1 Solo for Electric Clavichord; 1 Solo for Percussion; 1 Solo for Alto Recorder]

U. Anders (perc) *(rec Jan 1976)* CEHA ▲ 19003 (16.97) ▮ 19003

GULYÁS, LÁSZLÓ (20th cent)

Bottle Dance for Orchestra & Chorus

L. Berki (cnd), Hungarian State Folk Ensemble Orch, Hungarian State Folk Ensemble Chorus *(rec 1969)* ("Wedding at Ecser") † Evening in the Spinning Room; Music from Szék; Triple Jumping Dance; Anonymous:Csárdás; Csámpai:In Memory of Bihari; Csenki:Gypsy Dances of Hungary; Kodály:Kálló Double Dance; R. Maros:Wedding at Ecser HUN ▲ 18008 [AAD] (16.97)

An Evening in the Spinning Room for Orchestra & Chorus

M. Pászti (cnd), Hungarian State Folk Ensemble Orch, Hungarian State Folk Ensemble Chorus *(rec 1969)* ("Wedding at Ecser") † Bottle Dance; Music from Szék; Triple Jumping Dance; Anonymous:Csárdás; Csámpai:In Memory of Bihari; Csenki:Gypsy Dances of Hungary; Kodály:Kálló Double Dance; R. Maros:Wedding at Ecser HUN ▲ 18008 [AAD] (16.97)

Music from Szék for Orchestra & Chorus

L. Berki (cnd), Hungarian State Folk Ensemble Orch, Hungarian State Folk Ensemble Chorus *(rec 1969)* ("Wedding at Ecser") † Bottle Dance; Evening in the Spinning Room; Triple Jumping Dance; Anonymous:Csárdás; Csámpai:In Memory of Bihari; Csenki:Gypsy Dances of Hungary; Kodály:Kálló Double Dance; R. Maros:Wedding at Ecser HUN ▲ 18008 [AAD] (16.97)

Triple Jumping Dance for Orchestra & Chorus

E. Varga (sgr), R. Lantos (cnd), Hungarian State Folk Ensemble Orch, Hungarian State Folk Ensemble Chorus *(rec 1969)* ("Wedding at Ecser") † Bottle Dance; Evening in the Spinning Room; Music from Szék; Anonymous:Csárdás; Csámpai:In Memory of Bihari; Csenki:Gypsy Dances of Hungary; Kodály:Kálló Double Dance; R. Maros:Wedding at Ecser HUN ▲ 18008 [AAD] (16.97)

GUNGE, BO (1964-

Moon Wedding Songs for Piccolo, Trombone, Male Chorus & Female Chorus (1993)

various artists ("Moon Wedding Songs") † Strophes PLAL ▲ 98 [DDD] (18.97)

Strophes (3) from the Middle Ages for Chorus

artists unknown ("Moon Wedding Songs") † Moon Wedding Songs PLAL ▲ 98 [DDD] (18.97)

GURALNICK, TOM (20th cent)

Broken Dances for muted Saxophones & Electronics (1994)

T. Guralnick (elec/sax/elec/sax/el) *(rec Albuquerque, NM, Jan 25-27, 1994)* OOWN ▲ 17 (16.97)

GURDJIEFF, GEORGES (1872-1949)

Piano Music

C. Ketcham (pno), L. Rosenthal (pno) ("Complete Works for Piano, Vol. 1: Asian Songs & Rhythms") WER ▲ 6284 (38.97)

C. Ketcham (pno), L. Rosenthal (pno) ("Complete Works for Piano, Vol. 2: Music of the Sayyids & the Dervishes") WER ▲ 6292 (38.97)

GURIDI, JESÚS (1886-1961)

Una Aventura de Don Quijote (symphonic poem) for Orchestra

M. G. Martinez (cnd), Euskadiko SO † Euzko Irudiak; Homenaje a Walt Disney; Melodias vascas CLAV ▲ 9709 (16.97)

Euzko Irudiak for Orchestra & Chorus (1922)

M. G. Martinez (cnd), Euskadiko SO, Orfeon Donostiarra Choir † Aventura de Don Quijote; Homenaje a Walt Disney; Melodias vascas CLAV ▲ 9709 (16.97)

Homenaje a Walt Disney for Piano & Orchestra (1956)

R. Requejo (pno), M. G. Martinez (cnd), Euskadiko SO † Aventura de Don Quijote; Euzko Irudiak; Melodias vascas CLAV ▲ 9709 (16.97)

Melodias vascas (10) for Orchestra

M. G. Martinez (cnd), Euskadiko SO † Aventura de Don Quijote; Euzko Irudiak; Homenaje a Walt Disney CLAV ▲ 9709 (16.97)

Operetta Arias

A. Arteta (sop), E. G. Asensio (cnd), RTVE SO—Caserío (sels); Mirentxu (sels) † Chapí:Operetta Arias; Chueca:Operetta Arias; Sorozábal:Operetta Arias; Torroba:Operetta Arias; Vives:Operetta Arias RTVE ▲ 65095 (16.97)

GURLITT, MANFRED (1890-1973)

Wozzeck (selections)

C. Lindsley (sop—Marie/Marie/Marie), R. Hermann (bar—Wozzeck/Wozzeck/Wozzeck), G. Albrecht (cnd), Berlin RSO, RIAS Chamber Choir ("German Opera of the 20th Century") † F. Schmidt:Notre Dame (sels); Schreker:Ferne Klang (sels); Schatzgräber (sels); Zemlinsky:Es War Einmal (sels); Kreidekreis (sels); König Kandaules (sels); Traumgörge (sels) CAPO ▲ 10724 [DDD] (10.97)

GURNEY, IVOR (1890-1937)

Songs

B. Luxon (bar), D. Willison (pno)—20 songs: Carol of the Skiddaw Yowes; The apple orchard; The fields are full; The twa corbies; Severn Meadows; Desire in spring; Ha'nacker Mill; Down by the Salley Gardens; The scribe; Hawk & Buckle; On the Downs; The fiddler of Dooney; In Flanders; The folly of being comforted; I praise the tender flower; Black Stichel; An epitaph; By a bierside; Cranham Woods; Sleep † G. Butterworth:Bredon Hill & Other Songs; Songs from A Shropshire Lad CHN ▲ 8831 [DDD] (16.97)

A. Rolfe Johnson (ten), D. Williamson (pno)—Down by the Salley Gardens; An Epitaph; Desire in Spring; Black Stitchel † G. Butterworth:Songs from A Shropshire Lad; J. Ireland:Land of Lost Content; Vaughan Williams:Songs of Travel; Warlock:Songs INMP ▲ 6702032 (9.97)

GUTHRIE, JAMES MARTIN (1953-

Variations (7) on "Herzlich tut mich Verlangen" for Organ

H. Spillman (org) † Berlinski:Burning Bush; Fax:Pieces Org; C. Hampton:Dances Org; T. Kerr:Anguished American Easter, 1968; Persichetti:Chorale Prelude Org, Op. 104 TIT ▲ 205 [DDD]

GWIAZDA, HENRY (20th cent)

Music of Gwiazda

H. Gwiazda (voc), H. Gwiazda (cmpt/elec gtr/elec)—MANEATINGCHIIPSLISTENINGTOAVIOLIN; whErEyoulivE; wM; afterglow; themythofAcceptAnce [w. Jeffery Krieger (elec vc)]; theflLuteintheworLdtheflLuteistheworLd; buzzingreynold'sdreamland ("noTnoTesnoTryhThms") INNO ▲ 505 [DDD] (14.97)

themythofAcceptAnce for Electronic Cello (1991)

J. Krieger (vc) *(rec Glastonbury, CT)* † J. Berger:Lead Plates of the Rom Press; J. Cage:Ryoanji Fl; Knehans:Night Chains; K. Steen:Shadows & Light CRI ▲ 680 [DDD] (16.97)

GYROWETZ, ADALBERT (1763-1850)

Quartets (3) for Flute & Strings, Op. 11 (1795)

M. Mayer (fl), Agora Ensemble FERM ▲ 20013 (16.97)

HAAN, SIMONE DE (20th cent)

Autumn Collage for Trombone, Percussion & Tape (1991)

S. Haan (trbn), D. Pratt (perc), P. Treloar (perc) *(rec South Melbourne, Australia, Dec 1991)* ("In the Pipeline") † Blues Part I; Blues Part II; Response; Shifting Energies; Song Trb; D. Pratt:Reflections; Sock Bop a Dop; Sometimes, Mirrors...; Treloar:Integrations I; Resounds TALP ▲ 95 [DDD] (18.97)

HAAN, SIMONE DE (cont.)
Song for Trombone (1991)
S. Haan (trbn) *(rec South Melbourne, Australia, Dec 1991)* ("In the Pipeline") † Autumn Collage; Blues Part I; Blues Part II; Response; Shifting Energies; D. Pratt:Reflections; Sock Bop a Dop; Sometimes, Mirrors...; Treloar:Integrations I; Resounds TALP ▲ 95 [DDD] (18.97)
HAAN, SIMONE DE (20th cent), **DARYL PRATT** (20th cent)**& PHIL TRELOAR** (1946-
Blues Part I
S. Haan (trbn), D. Pratt (perc), P. Treloar (perc) *(rec South Melbourne, Australia, Dec 1991)* ("In the Pipeline") † Autumn Collage; Blues Part II; Response; Shifting Energies; Song Trb; D. Pratt:Reflections; Sock Bop a Dop; Sometimes, Mirrors...; Treloar:Integrations I; Resounds TALP ▲ 95 [DDD] (18.97)
Blues Part II for Trombone & Percussion (1991)
S. Haan (trbn), D. Pratt (perc), P. Treloar (perc) *(rec South Melbourne, Australia, Dec 1991)* ("In the Pipeline") † Autumn Collage; Blues Part I; Response; Shifting Energies; Song Trb; D. Pratt:Reflections; Sock Bop a Dop; Sometimes, Mirrors...; Treloar:Integrations I; Resounds TALP ▲ 95 [DDD] (18.97)
Response for Trombone & Percussion (1991)
S. Haan (trbn), D. Pratt (perc), P. Treloar (perc) *(rec South Melbourne, Australia, Dec 1991)* ("In the Pipeline") † Autumn Collage; Blues Part I; Blues Part II; Shifting Energies; Song Trb; D. Pratt:Reflections; Sock Bop a Dop; Sometimes, Mirrors...; Treloar:Integrations I; Resounds TALP ▲ 95 [DDD] (18.97)
Shifting Energies for Trombone & Percussion (1991)
S. Haan (trbn), D. Pratt (perc), P. Treloar (perc) *(rec South Melbourne, Australia, Dec 1991)* ("In the Pipeline") † Autumn Collage; Blues Part I; Blues Part II; Response; Song Trb; D. Pratt:Reflections; Sock Bop a Dop; Sometimes, Mirrors...; Treloar:Integrations I; Resounds TALP ▲ 95 [DDD] (18.97)
HAAPALA, TUOMO (dates unknown)
Music of Haapala
artists unknown—The World From Inside-The World From Outside; Midnight Music on the Water; En Doft, Ett Stråk Av Kåda; Tule Petter; Lektion Om Svalor; The Continents Move in the Night ("Movements in Rapid Waters") CAPA ▲ 21524 (16.97)
HAARKLOU, JOHANNES (1847-1925)
Fantasie triomphale for Organ, Op. 61 (1900)
K. Nordstoga (org) ("Organ Works") † Prelude & Fugue on BACH, Op. 121; Sym 1 Org, Op. 106; Sym 2 Org, Op. 116 NKF ▲ 50036 (16.97)
Prelude & Fugue on B-A-C-H for Organ, Op. 121
K. Nordstoga (org) ("Organ Works") † Fant triomphale, Op. 61; Sym 1 Org, Op. 106; Sym 2 Org, Op. 116 NKF ▲ 50036 (16.97)
Symphony No. 1 for Organ, Op. 106 (1916)
K. Nordstoga (org) ("Organ Works") † Fant triomphale, Op. 61; Prelude & Fugue on BACH, Op. 121; Sym 2 Org, Op. 116 NKF ▲ 50036 (16.97)
Symphony No. 2 for Organ, Op. 116 (1924)
K. Nordstoga (org) ("Organ Works") † Fant triomphale, Op. 61; Prelude & Fugue on BACH, Op. 121; Sym 1 Org, Op. 106 NKF ▲ 50036 (16.97)
HAAS, JEFFREY (1953-
Sussurrando for Oboe & Tape (1993)
N. A. Haas (ob) *(rec International Double Reed Society National Convent, Aug 1994)* ("New Music from Indiana University, Vol. 1") † C. Baker:Awaking the Winds; Dzubay:Trio; D. W. Freund:Hard Cells; E. O'Brien:Mysteries of the Horizon IUSM ▲ 5 (16.97)
HAAS, PAVEL (1899-1944)
Broadcasting Overture for 4 Male Voices & Orchestra, Op. 11 (1931)
J. Bělohlávek (cnd) † Psalm 29, Op. 12; Study; Schoenberg:Verklärte Nacht, Op. 4 SUR ▲ 10 [DDD] (16.97)
The Charlatan [Šarlatán] (opera) [lib Haas] (1934-37)
I. Yinon (cnd), Prague Opera Orchestra, Prague Phil Chorus, L. M. Vodička (ten), M. Švejda (ten), V. Chmelo (bar), A. Bogza (sgr) DECC (Entartete Musik) 2-▲ 460042 (32.97)
The Charlatan:Suite
I. Yinon (cnd), Brno State PO † Saddened scherzo, Op. 5; Sym (unfinished) KSCH ▲ 315212 (16.97)
The Chosen One for Tenor, Flute, Horn, Violin & Piano [text Wolker], Op. 8 (1927)
J. Dürmüller (ten), M. Hölszky-Wiedemann (vn), W. Freivogel (fl), F. Pütz (hn), D. R. Davies (pno) † Qnt Ww; Suite Ob, Op. 17; Suite Pno, Op. 13 ORF (Musica Rediviva) ▲ 386961 [DDD] (18.97)
Psalm 29 for Baritone, Female Chorus, Orchestra & Organ, Op. 12 (1932)
J. Bělohlávek (cnd) † Broadcasting Ov, Op. 11; Study; Schoenberg:Verklärte Nacht, Op. 4 SUR ▲ 10 [DDD] (16.97)
Quartet No. 1 for Strings, Op. 3 (1920)
Kocian String Quartet † Qt 2 Strs, Op. 7; Qt 3 Strs, Op. 15 PRAG ▲ 250118 (18.97)
Quartet No. 2 for Strings (w. Jazz Band ad lib), Op. 7 (1925)
Kocian String Quartet † Qt 1 Strs, Op. 3; Qt 3 Strs, Op. 15 PRAG ▲ 250118 (18.97)
Petersen String Quartet *(rec Berlin, Germany, Nov. 1996)* † Janáček:Qt 2 Strs EDA ▲ 11 [DDD]
Quartet No. 3 for Strings, Op. 15 (1938)
Kocian String Quartet † Qt 1 Strs, Op. 3; Qt 2 Strs, Op. 7 PRAG ▲ 250118 (18.97)
Quintet for Wind Instruments, Op. 10 (1929)
Academia Wind Quintet *(rec Prague, Mar 22-May 6, 1997)* † R. Karel:Nonet; G. Klein:Divert; Lucký:Divert SUR ▲ 3339 [DDD]
Stuttgart Wind Quintet [rev Lubomír Peduzzi] † Chosen One, Op. 8; Suite Ob, Op. 17; Suite Pno, Op. 13 ORF (Musica Rediviva) ▲ 386961 [DDD] (18.97)
Saddened scherzo for Orchestra, Op. 5 (1921)
I. Yinon (cnd), Brno State PO † Charlatan (suite); Sym (unfinished) KSCH ▲ 315212 (16.97)
Songs
P. Matuszek (bar) † Krása:Songs; Schulhoff:Songs SUR ▲ 3334
Study for String Orchestra (1943)
G. Albrecht (cnd), Czech PO [compd & rev Lubomír Peduzzi] *(rec May 3-4 & June 2-3, 1993)* ("Musica Rediviva") † G. Klein:Partita Strs; Schulhoff:Sym 2; V. Ullmann:Sym 2 ORF ▲ 337941 [DDD] (18.97)
J. Bělohlávek (cnd) † Broadcasting Ov, Op. 11; Psalm 29, Op. 12; Schoenberg:Verklärte Nacht, Op. 4 SUR ▲ 10 [DDD] (16.97)
F. Obstfeld (cnd), Westphalia PO † Krása:Ov Small Orch; Martinů:Sextet Strs; Schreker:Intermezzo Strs, Op. 8; Scherzo Strs; Wind EDA ▲ 9 [DDD] (19.97)
Suite for Oboe & Piano, Op. 17
S. Michael (ob), D. R. Davies (pno) [rev František Suchý] † Chosen One, Op. 8; Qnt Ww; Suite Pno, Op. 13 ORF (Musica Rediviva) ▲ 386961 [DDD] (18.97)
Suite for Piano, Op. 13 (1935)
D. R. Davies (pno) [rev Bernard Kaff] † Chosen One, Op. 8; Qnt Ww; Suite Ob, Op. 17 ORF (Musica Rediviva) ▲ 386961 [DDD] (18.97)
C. Hacke (pno) *(rec Sandhausen, Germany, 1995-96)* ("The Lost Generation") † J. Alain:Movts Fl; Laparra:Suite Fl; Schulhoff:Son Fl; L. Smit:Son Fl BAYE ▲ 100259 [DDD] (17.97)
F. Lotoro (pno) ("Martyred Musicians of the Holocaust") † R. Karel:Theme & Vars Pno, Op. 13; G. Klein:Son Pno ARN ▲ 68339 (16.97)
Symphony [unfinished]
I. Yinon (cnd), Brno State PO † Charlatan (suite); Saddened scherzo, Op. 5 KSCH ▲ 315212 (16.97)
HÁBA, ALOIS (1893-1973)
Dances (4) for Piano, Op. 39 (1927)
T. Víšek (pno) ("Piano Works") † Morceaux, Op. 2; Pieces, Op. 6; Pno Music SUR ▲ 3146 [DDD] (16.97)
Morceaux (2) for Piano, Op. 2 (1917-18)
T. Víšek (pno) ("Piano Works") † Dances; Pieces, Op. 6; Pno Music SUR ▲ 3146 [DDD] (16.97)
Music of Hába
various artists—Symphonic Fant for Pno & Orch; The Way of Life; New Land Ov; Qts 11, 12 & 16 for Strs; 12-tone Cl & Quarter-tone Pno; other works for various solo instrs SUR 3-▲ 111865 [AAD]
Nonets for Strings
Czech Nonet—No. 1 in 12-note system, Op. 40; No. 2 in 7-note system, Op. 41; No. 3, Op. 82; No. 4, Op. 97 ("Complete Nonets") SUR ▲ 18 [DDD]
Piano Music
T. Víšek (pno)—Scherzo, Op. 2/1; Intermezzo, Op. 2/2; 6 Pieces, Op. 6; 4 Dances, Op. 39; Shimmy-Fox; Romance; Waltz; Toccata quasi una Fant, Op. 38; 6 Moods, Op. 102 *(rec Domovina Studio, June 24-26 & Nov 26, 1996)* ("Piano Works") † Dances; Morceaux, Op. 2; Pieces, Op. 6 SUR ▲ 3146 [DDD] (16.97)
Pieces (6) for Piano, Op. 6 (1920)
T. Víšek (pno) ("Piano Works") † Dances; Morceaux, Op. 2; Pno Music SUR ▲ 3146 [DDD] (16.97)

HÁBA, ALOIS (cont.)
Quarter-Tone (opera in 10 scenes) (1927-29)
J. Jirouš (cnd), Prague National Theater Orch, Prague National Theater Chorus *(lib)* SUR ▲ 108258 [ADD]
HABBESTAD, KJELL (1955-
One Night on Earth (oratorio) for Baritone, String Quartet, Orchestra & Chorus [text Paal-Helge Haugen]
N. Sparbo (bar), T. Mikkelsen (cnd), Lithuanian National SO NORW 2-▲ 2911 (34.97)
HACHIMURA, YOSHIO (1938-1985)
Dolcissima Mia Vita for Percussion, Op. 16 (1981)
S. Yoshihara (perc) *(rec 1976-81)* † M. Fujita:Ichingotoshi I; Ichingotoshi II; Fukushi:Ground CAMA ▲ 314 [AAD] (18.97)
The Logic of Distraction for Piano & Orchestra
Y. Watanabe (pno), T. Otaka (cnd), Tokyo Metropolitan SO *(rec Tokyo Bunka-Kaikan Large Hall, May 24, 1980)* ("The Min-On Contemporary Music Festival, 1980") † K. Mori:Groom; T. Noda:Mutation CAMA ▲ 292 [AAD] (18.97)
Maniera for Flute, Op. 14
M. Nakagawa (fl) *(rec Hadano City Auditorium, July 16, 1982)* ("Flute Music Today") † H. Hayashi:Pieces Sop & Fl; I. Nakagawa:Lied; M. Sato:Bleusy Fragments CAMA ▲ 118 [DDD] (18.97)
Vision of Higanbana for Piano (1969)
M. Matsuya (pno) *(rec Japan, Sept 1993)* ("Light Colored Album for Piano - Midori Matsuya plays Japanese Contemporary Pieces") † Matsumura:Berceuses; A. Miyoshi:Hommage; Ogura:Sonatina; T. Sato:August Laying to Rest; Carpet of Bamboo Leaves Falling onto Northern Sea; Scenery with Tea Gardens; Season of Yellow and Black; Takemitsu:Pno Distance; Yoshimatsu:Pleiades Dances CAMA ▲ 318 [DDD] (18.97)
HADJIDAKIS, MANOS (1925-
Film Music
H. Alexiou (sgr)—Topkapi; Zorba the Greek; Missing; Never on Sunday; Phaedra ("Classic Greek Film Music") † Vangelis [Papathanassiou, Odyssey]:Film Music SIAM ▲ 1052 (16.97)
For a Little White Seashell for Piano, Op. 1 (1947-48)
D. Kara (pno) *(rec Athens Concert Hall, Aug 24, 1995)* ("The Piano Works") † Ionian Suite, Op. 8; Popular Paintings, Op. 4; Rhythmologia, Op. 30 AG ▲ 22 [DDD] (18.97)
Ionian Suite for Piano, Op. 8 (1953)
D. Kara (pno) *(rec Athens Concert Hall, Aug 24, 1995)* ("The Piano Works") † For a Little White Seashell, Op. 1; Popular Paintings, Op. 4; Rhythmologia, Op. 30 AG ▲ 22 [DDD] (18.97)
Popular Paintings (6) for Piano, Op. 4 (1950)
D. Kara (pno) *(rec Athens Concert Hall, Aug 24, 1995)* ("The Piano Works") † For a Little White Seashell, Op. 1; Ionian Suite, Op. 8; Rhythmologia, Op. 30 AG ▲ 22 [DDD] (18.97)
Rhythmologia for Piano, Op. 30 (1971)
D. Kara (pno) *(rec Athens Concert Hall, Aug 24, 1995)* ("The Piano Works") † For a Little White Seashell, Op. 1; Ionian Suite, Op. 8; Popular Paintings, Op. 4 AG ▲ 22 [DDD] (18.97)
HADLEY, HENRY (1871-1937)
Scherzo diabolique for Violin (1934)
I. Hegyi (vn) † J. A. Carpenter:Sea Drift; D. G. Mason:Chanticleer; Q. Porter:Dance in 3-Time NWW ▲ 321 [DDD] (16.97)
Trio for Piano, Violin, Cello, Op. 132 (1932)
Rawlins Piano Trio *(rec June 1996)* ("A World Premier Recording: No. 4") † E. Bloch:Nocturnes; Cadman:Trio Pno, Op. 56; D. G. Mason:Sentimental Sketches, Op. 34 ALBA ▲ 305 [DDD] (16.97)
HADLEY, PATRICK (1899-1973)
La belle dame sans merci (cantata) for Tenor, Orchestra & Chorus [text Keats] (1935)
N. Archer (ten), M. Bamert (cnd), Philharmonia Orch, Philharmonia Chorus † Lenten Meditations; One Morning in Spring; Sainton:Dream of the Marionette; Nadir CHN ▲ 9539 (16.97)
A Cantata for Lent for Tenor, Bass, Orchestra & Chorus (1962)
Gonville & Caius College Choir Cambridge ("English Church Music, Vol. 3") † Songs; Rubbra:Choral Music; Missa in honorem Sancti Dominici, Op. 66 ASV ▲ 881 [DDD] (16.97)
Lenten Meditations for Tenor, Bass, Orchestra & Chorus
N. Archer (ten), S. Richardson (bass), M. Bamert (cnd), Philharmonia Orch, Philharmonia Chorus † Belle dame; One Morning in Spring; Sainton:Dream of the Marionette; Nadir CHN ▲ 9539 (16.97)
One Morning in Spring for Small Orchestra (1942)
M. Bamert (cnd), Philharmonia Orch † Belle dame; Lenten Meditations; Sainton:Dream of the Marionette; Nadir CHN ▲ 9539 (16.97)
A. Boult (cnd) † A. Bax:Mediterranean; A. Bliss:Intro & Allegro, T.40; E. Elgar:Grania & Diarmid (sels); Intro & Allegro, Op. 47; G. Holst:Hammersmith, Op. 52; J. Ireland:Forgotten Rite INMP (BBC Radio Classics) ▲ 9127 (13.97)
Songs
Gonville & Caius College Choir Cambridge—I Sing of a Maiden; A Song for Easter; The Cup of Blessing; My Beloved Spake ("English Church Music, Vol. 3") † Cant for Lent; Rubbra:Choral Music; Missa in honorem Sancti Dominici, Op. 66 ASV ▲ 881 [DDD] (16.97)
The Trees So High for Orchestra (1931)
M. Bamert (cnd), Philharmonia Orch, Philharmonia Chorus † Sainton:Island CHN ▲ 9181 [DDD] (16.97)
HAEFFNER, JOHANN CHRISTIAN FRIEDRICH (1759-1833)
Electra (opera) [lib Guillard & Ristell] (1787)
H. Martinpelto (sop), H. Hinz (sop), P. Mattei (bar), M. Samuelson (bar), T. Schuback (cnd) , Swedish Radio Chorus CAPA 2-▲ 22030 (32.97)
HAENE, FRÉDERIC D' (1961-
Pessoa Revisited for Chamber Ensemble (1991)
Nouvelle Musiques de Chambre *(rec Liège Conservatory, 1996)* ("Liàge") † E. Denisov:Son alt Sax; B. Foccroulle:Movts; Fourgon:Nuit; H. Pousseur:Vue sur les jardins interdits; Scelsi:Anahit CYPR ▲ 4601 (17.97)
HAENTJES, WERNER (1923-
Easter Motets (3) for Chorus
H. Nickoll (cnd), Carmina Chamber Choir ("Choir Music of the 20th Century") † F. Martin:Mass for Double Chorus; Nickoll:Salve regina; Pärt:Magnificat for Chorus; R. Thompson:Alleluia EBS ▲ 6039 [DDD] (17.97)
Music of Haentjes
R. Trexler (sop), et al., Berlin Saxophone Quartet BER ▲ 9240 (10.97)
HAFSTEINSSON, GUETHMUNDUR (1953-
Music of Hafsteinsson
B. Vilhjálmsson (sax), S. Guethmundsson (sax), P. Tompkins (t sax), Ó. Einarsson (bar sax), S. Thorbergsson (bn), Á. Steingŕimsson (tpt), E. Ö. Pálsson (tpt), E. Jónsson (tpt), L. Sveinsson (tpt), E. Friethfinnsson (hn), O. Björnsson (hn), T. Halldórsson (tuba), G. Hafsteinsson (cnd) *(Blastula)*, M. G. Halldórsdóttir (sop), S. Thorbergsson (bn), Á. Steingŕimsson (tpt), E. Ö. Pálsson (tpt), E. Friethfinnsson (hn), L. Mátéova (org) *(He Giveth Power)*, S. Ethvaldsdóttir (va) *(Spinning II)*, E. Waage (hp), G. Hafsteinsson (cimbalom), A. G. Guethmundsdóttir (pno), P. Grétarsson (vib) *(Valediction)*, M. G. Halldórsdóttir (sop), G. Hafsteinsson (pno) *(My Mind Drifts)*, B. H. Gylfadóttir (vc), A. Helgason (cl), G. Hafsteinsson (pno) *(Burned Bright Lights in Both Eyes)* ("Instumental & Vocal Works") ICEM ▲ 198 [DDD] (18.97)
HAGEN, DARON (1961-
Concerto for Cello & Wind Ensemble (1997)
R. L. Rue (vc), M. Haithcock (cnd), Baylor Univ Wind Ensemble ("Night, Again") † Con Flg; Night, Again; Sennets, Cortege & Tuckets ASI ▲ 112 [DDD] (16.97)
Concerto for Flugelhorn & Wind Ensemble (1994)
R. L. Rue (vc), V. Sielert (flgl), M. Haithcock (cnd), Baylor Univ Wind Ensemble ("Night, Again") † Con Vc; Night, Again; Sennets, Cortege & Tuckets ASI ▲ 112 [DDD] (16.97)
Dear Youth (song cycle) for Voice, Flute & Piano (1990)
S. Crowder (sop), S. Stern (fl), B. Moore (pno) *(rec Church of the Epiphany, Washington, DC, Aug 1996)* † Echo's Songs; Love Songs; Merrill Songs ASI ▲ 106 [DDD] (16.97)
Duo for Violin & Cello (1997)
M. P. Neftel (vn), R. L. Rue (vc) *(rec Town Hall, New York City, NY, 1997)* ("Strings Attached") † Higher, Louder, Faster!; Suite Va; Suite Vc; Suite Vn ASI ▲ 111 [DDD] (16.97)
Echo's Songs (song cycle) for Voice & Piano (1983)
S. Crowder (sop), B. Moore (pno) *(rec Church of the Epiphany, Washington, DC, Aug 1996)* † Dear Youth; Love Songs; Merrill Songs ASI ▲ 106 [DDD] (16.97)
Higher, Louder, Faster! for Solo Cello (1987)
R. L. Rue (vc) *(rec Town Hall, New York City, NY, 1997)* ("Strings Attached") † Duo Vn Vc; Suite Va; Suite Vc; Suite Vn ASI ▲ 111 [DDD] (16.97)

HAGEN, DARON (cont.)
Love Songs (song cycle) for Voice & Piano (1988)
S. Crowder (sop), B. Moore (pno) *(rec Church of the Epiphany, Washington, DC, Aug 1996)* † Dear Youth; Echo's Songs; Merrill Songs ASI ▲ 106 [DDD] (16.97)
Merrill Songs (song cycle) for Voice & Piano (1995)
S. Crowder (sop), B. Moore (pno) *(rec Church of the Epiphany, Washington, DC, Aug 1996)* † Dear Youth; Echo's Songs; Love Songs ASI ▲ 106 [DDD] (16.97)
Night, Again for Wind Ensemble (1997)
R. L. Rue (vc), V. Sielert (flgl), M. Haithcock (cnd), Baylor Univ Wind Ensemble ("Night, Again") † Con Flg; Con Vc; Sennets, Cortege & Tuckets ASI ▲ 112 [DDD] (16.97)
Qualities of Light for Piano
J. Golan (pno) *(rec Massachusetts, United States of America, July 1998)* ("American Tonal") † S. Barber:Ballade Pno, Op. 46; Nocturne Pno, Op. 33; Son Pno, Op. 26 ALBA ▲ 324 [DDD] (16.97)
Sennets, Cortege & Tuckets for Wind Ensemble (1989)
R. L. Rue (vc), V. Sielert (flgl), M. Haithcock (cnd), Baylor Univ Wind Ensemble ("Night, Again") † Con Flg; Con Vc; Night, Again ASI ▲ 112 [DDD] (16.97)
Suite for Viola (1986)
C. Noble (va) *(rec Town Hall, New York City, NY, 1997)* ("Strings Attached") † Duo Vn Vc; Higher, Louder, Faster!; Suite Vc; Suite Vn ASI ▲ 111 [DDD] (16.97)
Suite for Violin (1984)
M. P. Neftel (vn) *(rec Town Hall, New York City, NY, 1997)* ("Strings Attached") † Duo Vn Vc; Higher, Louder, Faster!; Suite Va; Suite Vc ASI ▲ 111 [DDD] (16.97)
Suite for Cello (1985)
R. L. Rue (vc) *(rec Town Hall, New York City, NY, 1997)* ("Strings Attached") † Duo Vn Vc; Higher, Louder, Faster!; Suite Va; Suite Vn ASI ▲ 111 [DDD] (16.97)
HAGERUP BULL, EDVARD (1922-
Ad usum amicorum for Flute, Violin, Cello & Piano, Op. 20 (1957)
I. Bergby (cnd) ("Répliques") † Épigrammes, Op. 36; Posthumes, Op. 47 NORW ▲ 4993 (17.97)
Épigrammes (6) for Chamber Ensemble, Op. 36 (1969)
I. Bergby (cnd) ("Répliques") † Ad usum amicorum, Op. 20; Posthumes, Op. 47 NORW ▲ 4993 (17.97)
Posthumes (2) for Chamber Ensemble [in memoriam Jan Østhus & Edvard Fliflet Bræin], Op. 47 (1977)
I. Bergby (cnd) ("Répliques") † Ad usum amicorum, Op. 20 NORW ▲ 4993 (17.97)
Profils for Chamber Ensemble, Op. 45, "Pour un Dame Rustique" (1978)
I. Bergby (cnd) ("Profils") † Sinf a cinq, Op. 54B; Son cantabile, Op. 35; Stèle, Op. 58A; Sxt NORW ▲ 4999 (17.97)
Sextet for Saxophone & Wind Quintet, Op. 31 (1965)
I. Bergby (cnd) ("Profils") † Profils, Op. 45; Sinf a cinq, Op. 54B; Son cantabile, Op. 35; Stèle, Op. 58A NORW ▲ 4999 (17.97)
Sinfonia a cinq for Chamber Ensemble, Op. 54B (1983)
I. Bergby (cnd) ("Profils") † Profils, Op. 45; Son cantabile, Op. 35; Stèle, Op. 58A; Sxt NORW ▲ 4999 (17.97)
Sonata cantabile for Flute, Violin, Cello & Piano, Op. 35 (1966)
I. Bergby (cnd) ("Profils") † Profils, Op. 45; Sinf a cinq, Op. 54B; Stèle, Op. 58A; Sxt NORW ▲ 4999 (17.97)
Stèle pour l'epilogue d'un monde for Chamber Ensemble, Op. 58A (1985)
I. Bergby (cnd) ("Profils") † Profils, Op. 45; Sinf a cinq, Op. 54B; Son cantabile, Op. 35; Sxt NORW ▲ 4999 (17.97)
HÄGG, JACOB ADOLF (1850-1928)
Amerikanische Festklänge (American Festival Music) for Orchestra
M. Liljefors (cnd), Gävelborg SO *(rec Sweden, Jan 11-12, 1996)* † Concert Ov 1, Op. 28; Concert Ov 2, Op. 26; Nordische Sym, Op. 2 STRL ▲ 1007 [ADD/DDD] (15.97)
Concert Overture No. 1 in D, Op. 28 (1870)
M. Liljefors (cnd), Gävelborg SO *(rec Sweden, Jan 11-12, 1996)* † Amerikanische Festklänge; Concert Ov 2, Op. 26; Nordische Sym, Op. 2 STRL ▲ 1007 [ADD/DDD] (15.97)
Concert Overture No. 2 in c, Op. 26 (1871)
M. Liljefors (cnd), Gävelborg SO *(rec Sweden, Jan 11-12, 1996)* † Amerikanische Festklänge; Concert Ov 1, Op. 28; Nordische Sym, Op. 2 STRL ▲ 1007 [ADD/DDD] (15.97)
Nordische Symphonie in E♭, Op. 2 (1871/1899)
G. W. Nilson (cnd), Gävelborg SO *(rec Sweden, Oct 13, 1981)* † Amerikanische Festklänge; Concert Ov 1, Op. 28; Concert Ov 2, Op. 26 STRL ▲ 1007 [ADD/DDD] (15.97)
HAGHIGHI, MOHAMMAD (20th cent)
Rokhsat-e-tabidan for Tar & Orchestra
M. Haghighi (lt), M. Haghighi (cnd) ALSE ▲ 2012 (16.97)
HAHN, REYNALDO (1875-1947)
Concerto in E for Piano & Orchestra (1931)
S. Coombs (pno), J. Ossonce (cnd), BBC Scottish SO ("The Romantic Piano Concerto, Vol. 15") † Massenet:Con Pno HYP ▲ 66897 (18.97)
Music of Hahn
various artists *(rec 1908-35)* ("Reynaldo Hahn: Composer, Conductor, Singer & Accompanist") PEAD ▲ 3 (17.97)
Romanesque for Flute, Viola & Piano
L. Grunth (va), B. Larsen (fl), S. Larsen (pno) *(rec Copenhagen, Mar 1996)* ("The French Flute") † Duruflé:Prélude, récitatif et vars, Op. 3; Gallon:Improv Fl; Suite Fl; Rhené-Baton:Bourée, Op. 42; Passacaille Fl & Pno, Op. 35; Ropartz:Sonatine Fl CLSO ▲ 160 (15.97)
Songs
V. Cole (ten), P. Stephens (pno)—Le rossignol des lilas; A Chloris; Si mes vers avaient des ailes; L'Heure exquise; Cantique; D'Une prison; Infidelité; Paysage; Le souvenir d'avoir chanté *(rec Apr 8-10, 1993)* ("In Love with Love") † Bizet:Songs; Massenet:Songs DLS ▲ 3131 [DDD] (14.97)
S. Graham (mez), R. Vignoles (pno)—À Chloris; Rossignol des lilas; Énamourée; Trois Jours de vendange; Lydé; Tyndaris; Phyllis; Fontaines; Automne; Infidélité; Dans la nuit; D'une Prison; Quand la nuit n'est pas étoilée; Fumée; Printemps; Je me souviens; Quand je fus pris au pavillon; Paysage; Fêtes galantes; Nocturne; Mai; Heure exquise; Offrande; Si mes vers avaient des ailes *(rec New York, NY, Jan 16-19, 1998)* ("La Belle Époque") SNYC ▲ 60168 [DDD] (16.97)
F. Lott (sop), S. Bickley (mez), I. Bostridge (ten), S. Varcoe (bass), G. Johnson (pno), S. Layton (cnd), London Choral Society—[CD 1] Si mes vers avaient des ailes; Paysage; Rêverie; Offrande; Mai; Infidelité; Seule; Les Cygnes; Nocturne; 3 jours de vendange; D'une prison; Séraphine; L'Heure exquise; Fêtes galantes; 12 Rondels; [CD 2] Quand la nuit n'est pas étoilée; Le Plus beau présent; Sur l'eau; Le Rossignol des lilas; A Chloris; Ma jeunesse; Puisque j'ai mis ma lèvre; Etudes Latines; La Nymphe de la Source; Au Rossignol; Je me souviens; Air de la lettre; C'est très vilain d'être infidèle; C'est sa banlieue; Nous avons fait un beau voyage; La Dernière Valse ("Songs") HYP (The Hyperion French Song Edition) 2-▲ 67141 (36.97)
HAILSTORK, ADOLPHUS (1941-
An American Port of Call for Orchestra (1984)
P. Freeman (cnd), Chicago Sinfonietta *(rec Rosary College River Forest, IL, IL, May 10, 1995)* ("Epitaph") † Epitaph: In Memoriam, Martin Luther King, Jr.; R. Cordero:Miniatures; J. Williams:Sym for the Sons of Nam INSD ▲ 3534 (14.97)
Choral Music
D. McCullough (cnd), McCullough Chorale—The Lamb; 7 Songs of the Rubaiyat; A Carol for All Children *(rec live, 1991 & 1994)* † Settings from the Song of Soloman; Songs of Life & Love; Spiritual Songs Chorus ALBA ▲ 156 [DDD] (16.97)
Epitaph: In Memoriam, Martin Luther King, Jr. for Orchestra (1979)
P. Freeman (cnd), Chicago Sinfonietta *(rec Rosary College River Forest, IL, IL, May 10, 1995)* ("Epitaph") † American Port of Call; R. Cordero:Miniatures; J. Williams:Sym for the Sons of Nam INSD ▲ 3534 (14.97)
Settings from the Song of Soloman for Chorus
D. McCullough (cnd), McCullough Chorale *(rec live, 1991 & 1994)* † Choral Music; Songs of Life & Love; Spiritual Songs Chorus ALBA ▲ 156 [DDD] (16.97)
Songs of Life & Love for Chorus
D. McCullough (cnd), McCullough Chorale *(rec live, 1991 & 1994)* † Choral Music; Settings from the Song of Soloman; Spiritual Songs Chorus ALBA ▲ 156 [DDD] (16.97)
Spiritual Songs for Chorus
D. McCullough (cnd), McCullough Chorale—O Praise the Lord; My Lord What a Moanin'; Crucifixion *(rec live, 1991 & 1994)* † Choral Music; Settings from the Song of Soloman; Songs of Life & Love ALBA ▲ 156 [DDD] (16.97)
Symphony No. 1 (1988)
J. P. Williams (cnd), Bohuslav Martinů PO ("Symphonic Brotherhood: The Music of African-American Composers") † D. Baker:Kosbro; H. T. Burleigh:Young Warrior; G. P. Nash:In Memoriam: Sojourner Truth; J. P. Williams:Is It True?; Meditation from the Easter Celebration ALBA ▲ 104 [DDD] (16.97)
HAIMO, ETHAN (1950-
Contrasts for Cello & Piano
K. Buranskas (vc), W. Cerny (pno) *(rec Snite Museum of Art Univ. of Notre Dame, May-June 1994 & Jan 1995)* † Etudes; Rhap Vn; Son Pno; Swenson Songs; Trio Strs CENT ▲ 2253 [DDD] (16.97)
Etudes (3) for Piano
B. D. Salwen (pno) *(rec Snite Museum of Art Univ. of Notre Dame, May-June 1994 & Jan 1995)* † Contrasts; Rhap Vn; Son Pno; Swenson Songs; Trio Strs CENT ▲ 2253 [DDD] (16.97)
Rhapsody for Violin & Piano
C. Plummer (vn), B. D. Salwen (pno) *(rec Snite Museum of Art Univ. of Notre Dame, May-June 1994 & Jan 1995)* † Contrasts; Etudes; Son Pno; Swenson Songs; Trio Strs CENT ▲ 2253 [DDD] (16.97)
Sonata for Piano
B. D. Salwen (pno) *(rec Snite Museum of Art Univ. of Notre Dame, May-June 1994 & Jan 1995)* † Contrasts; Etudes; Rhap Vn; Swenson Songs; Trio Strs CENT ▲ 2253 [DDD] (16.97)
Swenson Songs
G. Resick (sop), B. D. Salwen (pno) *(rec Snite Museum of Art Univ. of Notre Dame, May-June 1994 & Jan 1995)* † Contrasts; Etudes; Rhap Vn; Son Pno; Trio Strs CENT ▲ 2253 [DDD] (16.97)
Trio for Strings
Notre Dame String Trio *(rec Snite Museum of Art Univ. of Notre Dame, May-June 1994 & Jan 1995)* † Contrasts; Etudes; Rhap Vn; Son Pno; Swenson Songs CENT ▲ 2253 [DDD] (16.97)
HAIRSTON, JESTER (1901-
Spirituals (20)
S. H. Kelly (cnd), Belmont Chorale GAS ▲ 269 (16.97)
HAKIM, NAJI (1955-
Organ Music
N. Hakim (org)—Canticum; Pange Lingua *(rec Église de Sainte-Trinité Paris, Mar 1997)* ("Canticum: French Organ Music") † C. Franck:Chorales Org, M.38-40; Pièces (3) Org, M.36; J. Langlais:Ave Maria, Ave maris stella; Te Deum; Messiaen:Livre du Saint-Sacrement; Nativité du Seigneur; Vierne:Pièces de fant Org (sels) EMIC (Debut) ▲ 72272 [DDD] (6.97)
HAKIM, TALIB RASUL (1940-1988)
Sound Gone for Piano (1967)
N. Hinderas (pno) ("Piano Music by African-American Composers") † Dett:In the Bottoms; W. G. Still:Sahdji; G. Walker:Son 1 Pno; O. Wilson:Pno Piece; J. W. Work:Scuppernong CRI 2-▲ 629 [ADD] (31.97)
HALAC, JOSE (1962-
Computer Music
Brooklyn College Center for Computer Music—India vieja, sincretismo #1; Ball, sincretismo #4; Illegal Edge; Uitotos, sincretismo #2; Cueca; Maturity, sincretismo #3 ("Illegal Edge") CENT ▲ 2189 [DDD] (16.97)
HALADYNA, JEREMY (1955-
En la estera del Chilam Balam [On the Mat of the Jaguar Priest] for amplified Flute
J. Felber (fl) ("Premieres") † Bosker:In a State; B. Feldman:Onirica; W. Kraft:Cadeau; Kuchera-Morin:Speira; M. Phillips:Rain Dance NEU ▲ 45094 [DDD] (16.97)
HALÉVY, (JACQUES) FROMENTAL (1799-1862)
La Juive (selections)
G. Grob-Prandl (sop), M. V. Zallinger (cnd) *(rec 1948-63)* ("Recital") † Meyerbeer:Robert le diable (sels); R. Strauss:Elektra (sels); R. Wagner:Arias & Scenes; C. M. von Weber:Oberon (sels) MYTO ▲ 975173 (17.97)
E. Pinza (b-bar) † Meyerbeer:Prophète (sels); W. A. Mozart:Don Giovanni (sels); Entführung aus dem Serail (sels); Mentre ti lascio, o figlia, K.513; Nozze di Figaro (sels); Zauberflöte (sels); G. Rossini:Barbiere di Siviglia (sels); Mosè in Egitto (sels); A. Thomas:Le caïd (sels); Mignon (sels) OPIT ▲ 54519 (6.97)
R. Tucker (ten), E. Cooper (cnd), Metropolitan Opera Orch—Rachel, quand du Seigneur la grâce tutélaire *(rec 1947)* ("Four Famous Met-Tenors of the Past") † Bizet:Carmen (sels); Pêcheurs de perles (sels); Gounod:Faust (sels); Meyerbeer:Africaine (sels); Ponchielli:Gioconda (sels); G. Puccini:Bohème (sels); Tosca (sels); Verdi:Ballo in maschera (sels); Rigoletto (sels); Traviata (sels); Trovatore (sels) PRE ▲ 89952 (m) (16.97)
HALFFTER, CRISTOBAL (1930-
Codex 1 for Guitar (1963)
G. Estarellas (gtr) ("Modern Italian & Spanish Guitar Music") † B. Bettinelli:Quattro pezzi; Ghedini:Studio da concerto; Pablo:Fabula; Petrassi:Suoni Notturni; J. L. Turina:Monologos STRV ▲ 33401 (16.97)
M. Kämmerling (gtr) *(rec Fruering Kirke, 1987)* † Borup-Jørgensen:Für Gitarre, Op. 86; Preludes Gtr, Op. 76; B. Maderna:Serenata per un satellite; Y después PLAL ▲ 60 [AAD] (18.97)
Concerto for Violin & Orchestra (1979)
H. Szeryng (vn), E. Bátiz (cnd), Mexico City PO ("Musica Mexicana 3") † Moncayo Garcia:Huapango; M. Ponce:Concierto del sur; Revueltas:Cuauhnahuac ASV ▲ 871 [DDD] (16.97)
Daliniana (3 pieces) for Orchestra (1994)
P. Halffter-Caro (cnd), Madrid SO *(rec National Music Auditorium Madrid, Dec 15, 1995)* † Fantasía sobre una sonoridad de G. F. Handel; Preludio para Madrid '92; Veni Creator Spiritus MARC ▲ 8225032 [DDD] (13.97)
Elegías a la muerte de tres poetas españoles for Orchestra (1974-75)
C. Halffter (cnd), Frankfurt RSO ("Cristóbal Halffter 3") † No queda más que el silencio DISQ ▲ 78211 [DDD] (18.97)
Fantasía sobre una sonoridad de G. F. Handel for Chorus & Orchestra (1981)
P. Halffter-Caro (cnd), Madrid SO, O. Donostiarra (cnd), St. Thomás de Aquino Chorus *(rec National Music Auditorium Madrid, Dec 15, 1995)* † Daliniana; Preludio para Madrid '92; Veni Creator Spiritus MARC ▲ 8225032 [DDD] (13.97)
No queda más que el silencio (Concerto No. 2) for Cello & Orchestra (1984)
B. Pergamenschikow (vc), C. Halffter (cnd), Frankfurt RSO ("Cristóbal Halffter 3") † Elegías a la muerte DISQ ▲ 78211 [DDD] (18.97)
Preludio para Madrid '92 for Chorus & Orchestra (1991)
P. Halffter-Caro (cnd), Madrid SO, O. Donostiarra (cnd), St. Thomás de Aquino Chorus *(rec National Music Auditorium Madrid, Jan 26, 1993)* † Daliniana; Fantasía sobre una sonoridad de G. F. Handel; Veni Creator Spiritus MARC ▲ 8225032 [DDD] (13.97)
Veni Creator Spiritus for 4 Trumpets, 4 Trombones, Percussion & Chorus (1992)
P. Halffter-Caro (cnd), Madrid SO, O. Donostiarra (cnd), St. Thomás de Aquino Chorus *(rec National Music Auditorium Madrid, Jan 26, 1993)* † Daliniana; Fantasía sobre una sonoridad de G. F. Handel; Preludio para Madrid '92 MARC ▲ 8225032 [DDD] (13.97)
HALFFTER, ERNESTO (1905-1989)
Bocetos sinfónicos (2) for Orchestras (1925)
M. Tang (cnd), Frankfurt RSO *(rec Oct 7-14, 1996)* † Rapsodia portuguesa; Sinfonietta in D CPO ▲ 999493 [DDD] (14.97)
Danzas (2) for Piano (1931)
A. D. Larrocha (pno)—La Pastora *(rec 1970)* † I. Albéniz:Iberia Suite; Navarra; M. P. de Albéniz:Son Pno; E. Granados:Danzas españolas (10) Pno; Goyescas (sels); Mompou:Cançons i dansas Pno; P. A. Soler:Sons Kbd PPHI (Great Pianists of the 20th Century) ▲ 456883 (22.97)
Hommages (petite suite) for String Trio (1922)
Mompou Trio Madrid † F. E. Blanco:Trio Pno; R. Gerhard:Trio Pno; Homs:Impromptu Pno RTVE ▲ 65012 (16.97)
Piano Music
P. Huybregts (pno)—Habanera *(rec Ghent, Belgium, Dec 1986)* ("Spanish Piano Music") † I. Albéniz:Pno Music; E. Granados:Andaluza Pno, Op. 37/5; Danzas españolas (10) Pno; Goyescas (sels); Mompou:Pno Music; J. Turina:Pno Music CENT ▲ 2026 [ADD] (16.97)
Rapsodia portuguesa for Piano & Orchestra (1940; rev 1951)
J. H. Suh (pno), M. Tang (cnd), Frankfurt RSO *(rec Oct 7-14, 1996)* † Bocetos sinfónicos; Sinfonietta in D CPO ▲ 999493 [DDD] (14.97)
Sinfonietta in D for Orchestra (1925)
M. Tang (cnd), Frankfurt RSO *(rec Oct 7-14, 1996)* † Bocetos sinfónicos; Rapsodia portuguesa CPO ▲ 999493 [DDD] (14.97)
Songs
M. J. Montiel (sop), M. Zanetti (pno)—Cancao de berco; Ai, que linda moca † Ginastera:Songs; E. Granados:Colección de Tonadillas; Guastavino:Songs; Montsalvage:Canciónes negras; J. Rodrigo:Songs RTVE ▲ 65115 (16.97)
HALFFTER, RODOLFO (1900-1987)
Don Lindo de Almeria (ballet), Op. 7 (1935)
A. Ros-Marbá (cnd), Seville Real SO *(rec Central Theater, Seville, Spain, July 1995)* ("The Musical Generation of 1927: Spanish Symphonic Music") † Bacarisse:Fant andaluza; Pittaluga:Romeria de los Cornudos AL (Musical Heritage of Andalusia) ▲ 118 [DDD] (18.97)

HALFFTER, RODOLFO (cont.)

La Madrugada del panadero (suite) for Orchestra, Op. 12a (1940)
H. de la Fuente (cnd), Mexican State PO † M. K. Aldana:Canto Latinoamericano; G. Duran:Nepantla; Jiménez-Mabarak:Sym in 1 Movt; Lavalle-García:Obertura Colonial; Sandi:Theme & Vars CLME ▲ 21006 (13.97)

Obertura Festiva for Orchestra, Op. 21 (1952)
E. Bátiz (cnd), Mexico City PO ("Música Mexicana: Volume 5") † Tripartita, Op. 25; Buxtehude:Org Music (misc colls); M. Ponce:Estrellita; Revueltas:Janitzio; Ocho; Sensemayá; P. A. Soler:Sons Kbd; F. Villanueva:Vals Poético ASV (Música Mexicana) ▲ 894 (16.97)

Piano Music
E. Quintana (pno)—Apuntes; Son 1 Pno, Op. 16; Escollo; Danza de Ávila; Homage to Rubenstein; Tres hojas de álbum; Bagatelas (11) for Piano, Op. 19; For Lenin's Tomb; Laberinto; Sons de El Escorial, Op. 2; Homage to Antonio Machado; Dos ensayos; Secuencia; Preludes & Fugue; Minué de La Traviesa Molinera; Facetas; Son 2 Pno, Op. 20; Son 3 Pno, Op. 30 *(rec Aug 1996)* ("Musica de las Americas, Vol. 5") URT 3-▲ 10 (31.97)

Tripartita for Orchestra, Op. 25 (1959)
E. Bátiz (cnd), Mexico City PO ("Música Mexicana: Volume 5") † Obertura Festiva, Op. 21; Buxtehude:Org Music (misc colls); M. Ponce:Estrellita; Revueltas:Janitzio; Ocho; Sensemayá; P. A. Soler:Sons Kbd; F. Villanueva:Vals Poético ASV (Música Mexicana) ▲ 894 (16.97)

HALIER, RONALD (20th cent)

UITT (Particolare) for Cello (1980)
J. Krieger (vc), A. Quadraverb (elec) † S. Hopkins:Cello Chi; A. Lucier:Indian Summer; Saariaho:Petals for Vc; William:Come Windows Gold Coming OOWN ▲ 22 (16.97)

HALL, ROBERT BROWNE (1858-1907)

Tenth Regiment (march) for Band, "Death or Glory"
M. Antrobus (cnd), Black Dyke Mills Band ("World Famous Marches") † Dunlap Commandery; Minstrel Jokes; Richmond Light Infantry Blues; H. L. Blankenburg:Marches; Rimmer:Marches CHN ▲ 6565 [ADD] (12.97)

Dunlap Commandery
M. Antrobus (cnd), Black Dyke Mills Band ("World Famous Marches") † Minstrel Jokes; Richmond Light Infantry Blues; Tenth Regiment; H. L. Blankenburg:Marches; Rimmer:Marches CHN ▲ 6565 [ADD] (12.97)

Minstrel Jokes
M. Antrobus (cnd), Black Dyke Mills Band ("World Famous Marches") † Dunlap Commandery; Richmond Light Infantry Blues; Tenth Regiment; H. L. Blankenburg:Marches; Rimmer:Marches CHN ▲ 6565 [ADD] (12.97)

Richmond Light Infantry Blues
M. Antrobus (cnd), Black Dyke Mills Band ("World Famous Marches") † Dunlap Commandery; Minstrel Jokes; Tenth Regiment; H. L. Blankenburg:Marches; Rimmer:Marches CHN ▲ 6565 [ADD] (12.97)

HALLBERG, BENGT (1932-

Blacksmith's Tune (1984)
J. Panula (cnd), Scandinavian Brass Ensemble *(rec 1984)* † Almila:Te Pa Te Pa, Op. 26; Danielsson:Suite 3 Brass; E. Grieg:Funeral March in Memory of Rikard Nordraak; Holmboe:Con Brass, Op. 157; T. Madsen:Divert Brass & Perc, Op. 47; Per the Fiddler, Norwegian Folk Song BIS ▲ 265 [DDD] (17.97)

HALLEN, ANDREAS (1846-1925)

Harald der Wiking:Act III, Final Scene (1881)
M. Meyerson (sgr—Berta), S. Lindström (sgr—Sigrun), A. Ljungholm (sgr—Harald), S. Sjöstedt (sgr—Sigleif), K. Jacobsson (sgr—Gudmund/Torgrim), S. Rybrant (cnd), Malmö SO, Malmö Radio Chorus [GER] *(rec June 6, 1974)* † Rhap 2; Toteninsel MSV ▲ 621 [AAD/DDD] (16.97)

Rhapsody No. 2 for Orchestra, Op. 23, "Swedish Rhapsody" (1883)
H. Frank (cnd), Helsingborg SO *(rec May 1987)* † Harald der Wiking (act III, final scene); Toteninsel MSV ▲ 621 [AAD/DDD] (16.97)

Toteninsel (symphonic poem) (1898)
H. Frank (cnd), Helsingborg SO *(rec June 1987)* † Harald der Wiking (act III, final scene); Rhap 2 MSV ▲ 621 [AAD/DDD] (16.97)

HALLNÄS, (JOHAN) HILDING (1903-1984)

Partita Amabile for Guitar
G. Söllscher (gtr) † Börtz:Ballad; E. von Koch:Con Gtr; U. Neumann:Con Gtr; D. Wirén:Little Serenade, Op. 39 CAPA ▲ 21514 (16.97)

HALLSTRÖM, IVAR CHRISTIAN (1826-1901)

Den bergtagna [The Bewitched One] (opera) [lib Hedberg] (ca 1874)
A. Hacker (cnd), Umeå SO STRL 2-▲ 1001 (29.97)

HALVORSEN, JOHAN (1864-1935)

Air Norvegien for Orchestra
A. Leaper (cnd), Czech-Slovak RSO Bratislava † Norwegian Dances; Sibelius:Con Vn; Sinding:Légende, Op.46; J. S. Svendsen:Romance Vn, Op. 26 NXIN ▲ 550329 [DDD] (5.97)

Bergensiana for Brass Ensemble
H. Haukas (cnd), Bergen Military Band † E. Grieg:In Heaven; Hovland:Fanfare & Chorale; J. S. Svendsen:Norwegian Artists' Carnival, Op. 14 DOY ▲ 70 (16.97)

Norwegian Dances for Violin & Orchestra (1915)
D. Kang (vn), A. Leaper (cnd), Czech-Slovak RSO Bratislava † Air Norvegien; Sibelius:Con Vn; Sinding:Légende, Op.46; J. S. Svendsen:Romance Vn, Op. 26 NXIN ▲ 550329 [DDD] (5.97)

Norwegian Rhapsodies (2) for Orchestra (1921)
O. K. Ruud (cnd), Trondheim SO † J. S. Svendsen:Norwegian Rhaps SIMX ▲ 1085 [DDD] (18.97)

Orchestral Music
P. Dreier (cnd), Royal PO—Danse Vionaire (1889); Entry of the Boyars (1893); see Collections:Orchestral, Royal PO [dir:Dreier] † J. S. Svendsen:Norwegian Artists' Carnival, Op. 14; Polonaise Orch; Vars on a Norwegian Folk Tune RPO ▲ 5003 [DDD] (11.97)

Passacaglia & Sarabande con variazioni for Violin & Viola [after Handel]
C. Askin (vn), T. Lisboa (vc) ("Octachord: Virtuoso Duos") † Aguiar:Duo; Glière:Duets Vn & Va, Op. 39; Honegger:Sonatina Vns & Vc; Kodály:Duo Vn & Vc, Op. 7 MER ▲ 84321 [DDD] (16.97)
I. Perlman (vn), P. Zukerman (va) *(rec live Tel-Aviv, Dec 26, 1996)* ("Israel Philharmonic 60th Anniversary Gala Concert") † J. S. Bach:Con Vns; J. Brahms:Sym 2; W. A. Mozart:Serenade 6 Orch, K.239; C. M. von Weber:Oberon (ov) RCAV (Red Seal) 2-▲ 68768 [DDD] (16.97)
H. Raudales (vn), F. van Goethem (va) *(rec Mar 1993)* † Glière:Duets Vn & Va, Op. 39; A. Rolla:Duettos Vn & Va, Op. 15 PAVA ▲ 7308 [DDD] (10.97)

HAMBREUS, BENGT (1928-

Music of Hambraeus
various artists—Rota II (1963); Ricordanza per orch (1975-76); Symphonia sacra in tempore passionis (1985-86); I Traditio; II Inquisitio; Ad mortem; III Lux aeterna ("Caprice Composer Series No. 20") CAPA ▲ 21421 (16.97)

HAMBURG, JEFF (1956-

Concertino for Saxophone & Small Orchestra
R. Hekkema (sax), D. Porcelijn (cnd), North-Holland PO † Schuylkill; Sym; Zey CV ▲ 67 [DDD] (18.97)

Schuylkill for String Orchestra
D. Porcelijn (cnd), North-Holland PO † Con Sax; Sym; Zey CV ▲ 67 [DDD] (18.97)

Symphony in E# for Chamber Orchestra
D. Porcelijn (cnd), North-Holland PO † Con Sax; Schuylkill; Zey CV ▲ 67 [DDD] (18.97)

Zey (poems) for Soprano & Orchestra (1994)
J. Mok (sop), L. Markiz (cnd), Amsterdam New Sinfonietta † G. Janssen:Zoek; Jeths:Glenz NMCL ▲ 92041 (16.97)
D. Porcelijn (cnd), North-Holland PO, N. Oostenrijk (sop) † Con Sax; Schuylkill; Sym CV ▲ 67 [DDD] (18.97)

HAMEL, MICHA (1970-

There Was Nothing Nobody Could Say for 5 Instruments (1991)
Ives Ensemble members † R. Ayres:Untitled Tpt; G. Carl:Claremont Con; Emmerik:Valise; R. Ford:Cross; Rijnvos:Gigue et Double CV (Muziepraktijk) ▲ 63 [DDD] (18.97)

HAMELIN, PETER (1951-

Sonata ben melodico for Trumpet & Organ
K. Benjamin (tpt), M. Turnquist (org) ("Clarion: New Music for Trumpet & Organ") † W. Albright:Jericho; P. Eben:Okna; Nelhybel:Metamorphosis; Starer:Preludes Tpt GOT ▲ 49067 [DDD] (18.97)

HAMER, JANICE (20th cent)

Morning Asanas (2) for Piano (1975)
D. Burge (pno) ("Eastman American Music Series, Vol. 3") † W. Albright:Fancies Hpd; N. Dinerstein:Love Songs; Silsbee:Doors ALBA ▲ 251 [ADD] (16.97)

HAMERIK, ASGER (1843-1923)

Concert-Romanze for Cello & Orchestra, Op. 27 (1878)
M. Zeuthen (vc), A. Malling (pno) [arr for vc & pno] *(rec Copenhagen, Mar & June 1996)* ("Cello & Piano") † L. Glass:Romance Vc, Op. 75; Son Vc, Op. 5; P. Grainger:Folk Song Settings; Sehested:Fant Pieces Vc MARC ▲ 8224052 [DDD] (13.97)

Symphony No. 1 in F, Op. 29, "Poétique" (1879-80)
T. Dausgaard (cnd), Helsingborg SO † Sym 2 MARC ▲ 8224076 [DDD] (13.97)
T. Dausgaard (cnd), Helsingborg SO † Sym 2 DCAP ▲ 8224088 (13.97)

Symphony No. 2 in c, Op. 32, "Tragique" (1882-83)
T. Dausgaard (cnd), Helsingborg SO † Sym 1 MARC ▲ 8224076 [DDD] (13.97)
T. Dausgaard (cnd), Helsingborg SO † Sym 1 DCAP ▲ 8224088 (13.97)

HAMES, RICHARD DAVID (20th cent)

Djurunga for Bass Clarinet & Marimba (1985)
C. Rosman (b cl), P. Neville (mar) ("Elision Ensemble: After the Fire") † Zurna; C. Dench:Severance; L. Lim:Amulet; Melchoirre:Halos; T. O'Dwyer:Bar-do'i-thos-grol; Whiticker:After the Fire VOXA ▲ 19 (18.97)

Zurna for Clarinet (1982)
C. Rosman (cl) ("Elision Ensemble: After the Fire") † Djurunga; C. Dench:Severance; L. Lim:Amulet; Melchoirre:Halos; T. O'Dwyer:Bar-do'i-thos-grol; Whiticker:After the Fire VOXA ▲ 19 (18.97)

HAMILTON, DAVID (1955-

Passacaglia for Flute & Orchestra
A. Still (fl), J. Sedares (cnd), New Zealand SO ("Kiwi Flute") † C. Moon:Concertino Fl; A. Ritchie:Con Fl; J. Ritchie:Snow Goose KOCH ▲ 7345 (16.97)

HAMILTON, TOM (1946-

Off-Hour Wait State for Voice, Alto Saxophone, Shakuhachi, Trombone, Synthesizer & Percussion
T. Buckner (bar), R. Samuelson (shak), R. Mitchell (a sax), P. Zummo (trbn), T. Hamilton (elec/syn), J. Haas (perc) OOD ▲ 26 [DDD] (16.97)

HAMLISCH, MARVIN (20th cent)

A Chorus Line (selections)
P. R. Evans (cnd), Royal Engineers Orch *(rec Bedworth, England)* ("Showtime") † A. Lloyd Webber:Aspects of Love (sels); Cats (sels); Phantom of the Opera (sels); F. Loewe:My Fair Lady (sels); R. Rodgers:Flower Drum Song (sels); Sound of Music (sels); Schönberg:Misérables (sels) BND ▲ 5084 [DDD] (16.97)

HAMMERSCHMIDT, ANDREAS (1611 or 1612-1675)

Instrumental Dances, Book I for 5 Viols & Continuo, "Erster Fleiss allerhand..." (pubd 1636)
Ecco la musica, Spirit of Gambo—Suite in a; Suite in g *(rec June 1996)* † Sacred Vocal Music ARSM ▲ 1225 [DDD] (17.97)

Music of Hammerschmidt
J. Baird (sop), S. Duvol (ob), B. Fix-Keller (hpd), V. Radu (cnd), Ama Deus Ensemble—O ihr lieben Hirten † J. S. Bach:Lobet den Herrn, alle Heiden, BWV 230; Magnificat, BWV 243; G. F. Handel:Messiah (sels); A. Scarlatti:Music of A. Scarlatti; Vivaldi:Con in C Ob, RV.554 VOXC ▲ 7548 (5.97)

Sacred Vocal Music
Ecco la musica, Spirit of Gambo, H. Hennig (cnd), Hanover Boys' Choir—Jauchzet, ihr Himmel; Schaffe in mir, Gott, ein reines Herz; Singet dem Herrn ein neues Lied; Herr, mein Gott, wie gross sind deine Wunder; O Vater aller Frommen; Deutsches Magnificat; Ehre sei Gott in der Höhe; Freude, Freude, grosse Freude; Das ist je gewisslich wahr; Alleluja! Freuet euch, ihr Christen alle; Das Wort ward Fleisch *(rec June 1996)* † Instr Dances Book I ARSM ▲ 1225 [DDD] (17.97)

HAMMERTH, JOHAN (1953-

Stockholm Cantata for Soprano, Baritone, Narrator, Orchestra & Chorus
L. Segerstam (cnd), Swedish RSO, Eric Ericson Chamber Choir, Swedish Radio Chorus, K. Dalayman (sop), L. Falkman (bar), R. Wolff (nar) PHNS ▲ 121 (16.97)

HAMPTON, CALVIN (1938-1984)

Alexander Variations for 2 Organs (1984)
T. Wilson (org), D. Higgs (org) *(rec National City Christian Church Orgs, Washington, DC, Jan 1995)* † J. Christian Bach:Sons & Duets Kbd 4-Hands, T.343/3; W. A. Mozart:Adagio & Allegro, K.594; Adagio & Fugue Strs, K.546; Saint-Saëns:Danse macabre, Op. 40; R. Wagner:Walküre (ride of the Valkyries) DLS ▲ 3175 [DDD] (14.97)

Dances (5) for Organ (1982)
H. Spillman (org) † Berlinski:Burning Bush; Fax:Pieces Org; J. M. Guthrie:Vars on "Herzlich tut mich Verlangen"; T. Kerr:Anguished American Easter, 1968; Persichetti:Chorale Prelude Org, Op. 104 TIT ▲ 205 [DDD]

HAMPTON, MITCH (20th cent)

Concerto for Jazz Piano & Orchestra (1994)
M. Hampton (pno), V. Válek (cnd), Czech RSO ("American Legacy") † W. T. McKinley:Patriotic Vars; C. Pizer:Manhattan Impressions; I.-P. Schwarz:Rosa's Rhap; Sladek:Chroma MASM ▲ 2032 [DDD] (16.97)

3 Minute Waltz for Orchestra
R. Black (cnd) † R. Black:Underground; Gideon:Symphonia brevis; Koykkar:Composite; W. T. McKinley:Boston Ov; P. Renz:Symphonic Poem; Warshauer:Revelation MASM ▲ 2008 (16.97)

HAND, FREDERIC (1947-

Late One Night for Guitar (ca 1970)
E. Isaac (gtr) *(rec Jan 1996)* ("The Four Seasons") † Dyens:Libra Sonatine; A. Piazzolla:Cuatro estaciones porteñas; M. Ponce:Son 3 Gtr GHA ▲ 126038 (17.97)

Music of Hand
B. Verdery (gtr), R. Schmidt (fl)—Psalm 100 *(rec NY, Mar 1995)* ("Enchanted Dawn") † Biberian:Armenian Dance Gtr; Armenian Song Gtr; Janáček:On an Overgrown Path; Miyagi:Haru no Umi; A. Piazzolla:Histoire du tango; R. Shankar:Aube enchantée DHR ▲ 5 [DDD] (16.97)

Trilogy for Guitar (1976)
E. Isaac (gtr) † Asencio:Suite valenciana; Bogdanović:Son Gtr; W. Heinze:Gtr Music; A. Piazzolla:Acentuado & Romantico GHA ▲ 126008 (17.97)
S. Robinson (gtr) *(rec DeLand, FL, 1993)* ("The American Record") † S. Adler:Son Gtr; H. Blanchard:Innocent Meandering; N. Rorem:Suite Gtr; D. Schiff:Rhap Gtr CENT ▲ 2204 [DDD] (16.97)

HANDEL, DARRELL (1933-

Barge Music for Alto Flute, Guitar, Double Bass & 2 Percussionists (1994)
J. Pascolini (db), R. Studky (gtr), B. Garner (a fl), R. Burge (perc), A. Otte (perc) ("The Poems of Our Climate") † Fl City; Poems of Our Climate; Recitative Gtr; Scherzo Pno; Trio Ob; Tyger VMM ▲ 2019 [DDD]

Flute City for Flute & Piano (1988)
B. Garner (fl), F. Weinstock (pno) ("The Poems of Our Climate") † Barge Music; Poems of Our Climate; Recitative Gtr; Scherzo Pno; Trio Ob; Tyger VMM ▲ 2019 [DDD]

The Poems of Our Climate for Soprano, Flute, Guitar, Cello, Piano & 3 Percussionists (1977; rev. 1982)
S. Woods (sop), V. Griffen (vc), B. Delay (gtr), P. Watson (fl), A. Nel (pno), A. Otte (perc), J. Brennan (perc), J. Culley (perc), G. Samuel (cnd) ("The Poems of Our Climate") † Barge Music; Fl City; Recitative Gtr; Scherzo Pno; Trio Ob; Tyger VMM ▲ 2019 [DDD]

A Recitative for Guitar (1976)
R. Stucky (gtr) ("The Poems of Our Climate") † Barge Music; Fl City; Poems of Our Climate; Scherzo Pno; Trio Ob; Tyger VMM ▲ 2019 [DDD]

Scherzo for Piano (1965)
E. Pridonoff (pno) ("The Poems of Our Climate") † Barge Music; Fl City; Poems of Our Climate; Recitative Gtr; Trio Ob; Tyger VMM ▲ 2019 [DDD]

Trio for Oboe, English Horn & Piano (1990)
S. L. Bloom (ob), B. Jew (E hn), F. Weinstock (pno) ("The Poems of Our Climate") † Barge Music; Fl City; Poems of Our Climate; Recitative Gtr; Scherzo Pno; Tyger VMM ▲ 2019 [DDD]

The Tyger for Mezzo-Soprano, Oboe, Piano & String Quartet (1984)
M. Henderson (sop), G. Robinson (vn), J. Lee (vn), R. Boughton (va), D. Netanel (vc), S. L. Bloom (ob), M. Butler (pno), C. Zimmerman (cnd) ("The Poems of Our Climate") † Barge Music; Fl City; Poems of Our Climate; Recitative Gtr; Scherzo Pno; Trio Ob VMM ▲ 2019 [DDD]

HANDEL, GEORGE FRIDERIC (1685-1759)

A mirarvi io son intento (duet) for Soprano, Alto & Continuo, HWV 178
R. Bertini (sop), C. Cavina (ct), La Venexiana † Beato in ver chi può, HWV 181; Conservate, raddoppiate, HWV 185; Fronda leggiera e mobile, HWV 186; Langue, geme, sospira, HWV 188; No, di voi non vuo' fidarmi, HWV 190; Se tu non lasci amore, HWV 193; Sono liete, fortunate, HWV 194; Tanti strali al sen mi scocchi, HWV 197; Troppo curda, troppo fiera, HWV 198 CNTS ▲ 9620 [DDD] (18.97)

Aci, Galatea e Polifemo (dramatic cantata) for solo Voices & Orchestra, HWV 72, "Sorge il dì" (1708)
E. Kirkby (sop), C. Watkinson (cta), D. Thomas (bass), C. Medlam (cnd), London Baroque HMA 2-▲ 1901253 (17.97)

▲ = CD ♦ = Enhanced CD △ = MD ▮ = Cassette Tape ▯ = DCC

HANDEL, GEORGE FRIDERIC (cont.)

Acis & Galatea (oratorio) for Vocal Soloists, Orchestra & Chorus [lib J. Gay & others after Ovid], HWV 49

Scholars Baroque Ensemble, K. Amps (sop—Galatea), A. Davidson (ct—Damon), R. Doveton (ten—Acis), D. V. Asch (bass—Polyphemus) *(rec East Finchley, England, Sep 12-14, 1993) ([ENG,FRE] lib texts)* NXIN ▲ 8553188 [DDD] (5.97)

G. Schwarz (cnd), Seattle SO, Seattle Chorale, D. Kotoski (sop—Galatea), D. Gordon (ten—Acis), G. Siebert (ten—Damon), J. Opalach (bass—Polyphemus) [ENG] DLS 2-▲ 3107 [DDD] (20.97)

Acis & Galatea (selections)

J. Baird (sop), E. Brewer (hpd), R. Palmer (cnd), Brewer CO—Stay, shepherd, stay ("Glorious Handel") † Alexander Balus (sels); Berenice (sels); Faramondo (sels); Joshua (sels); Messiah (sels); Mi palpita il cor (sels); Semele (sels); Siroe (sels) NPT ▲ 85646 [DDD] (16.97)

L. Marshall (sop), E. Pedrazzoli (cnd), London SO *(rec Canada, 1959)* ("Arias - Lois Marshall") † Solomon (sels); J. Haydn:Jahreszeiten (sels); Schöpfung (sels); W. A. Mozart:Clemenza di Tito (sels); Don Giovanni (sels); Entführung aus dem Serail (sels) *(E, F text)* CBC ▲ 2001 [ADD] (16.97)

H. Nash (ten), P. Dawson (ten), M. Miles (cnd), Philharmonia CO, G. W. Byng (cnd) —Lo! Here my love; O ruddier than the cherry *(rec London, England, Aug 10, 1945)* ("Stars of English Oratorio, Vol. 2") † Allegro, il Penseroso ed il Moderato (sels); Arias; J. S. Bach:Anna Magdalena Bach Notebook (sels); Arias; A. Dvořák:Spectre's Bride (sels); J. Haydn:Schöpfung (sels); Verdi:Requiem Mass DLAB ▲ 7029 [ADD] (17.97)

Acis & Galatea:Suite

Les Boréades de Montréal *(rec Church of St. Augustin de Mirabel Quebec, May 5-7, 1997)* ("Théâtre Musical") † Rebel:Caractères de la danse (suite); J. H. Schmelzer:Fechtschule; Vivaldi:Griselda (sels) ATMM ▲ 22152 [ADD] (15.97)

Acis & Galatea [arr Mozart, K.566]

T. Pinnock (cnd), English Concert, English Concert Choir, B. Bonney (sop—Galatea), M. Schäfer (ten—Damon), J. MacDougall (ten—Acis), J. Tomlinson (bass—Polyphem) ARCV 2-▲ 447700 [DDD] (26.97)

P. Schreier (cnd), Austrian RSO, George F. Handel Ensemble, E. Mathis (sop), A. Rolfe Johnson (ten), R. Gambill (ten), R. Lloyd (bass) [ENG] ORF 2-▲ 133852 [DDD] (36.97)

Acis & Galatea:Overture

C. Högman (sop), I Quattro Temperamenti ("Nine German Arias") † German Arias, HWV 202-10 BIS ▲ 403 [DDD] (17.97)

Admento (selections)

J. Charvet (ct), S. Intrieri (cnd), La Réjouissance † Amadigi di Gaula (sels); Con a quattro in D; Giulio Cesare in Egitto (sels); Rinaldo (sels); Tamerlano (ov); Tamerlano (sels) MAND ▲ 4944 (18.97)

Admeto, Rè di Tessaglia (opera in 3 acts) [lib ?Haym or Rolli after A. Aureli], HWV 22 (1727)

R. Yakar (sop—Alceste), J. Gomez (sop—Antigone), R. Dams (alt—Orindo), R. Jacobs (ct—Admeto), J. Bowman (ct—Trasimede), M. von Egmond (bar—Meraspe), U. Cold (bass—Apollo/Ercole), A. Curtis (cnd) *(rec Haarlem Netherlands, May 1977)* ("ADMETO") *(E,I lib texts)* VCL (Veritas) 3-▲ 61369 [ADD] (34.97)

Agrippina (opera in 3 acts) [lib V. Grimani], HWV 6

J. E. Gardiner (cnd), English Baroque Soloists, D. Brown (sop—Poppea), D. Jones (mez—Agrippina), A. S. von Otter (mez—Guinone), J. Clarkson (alt—Lesbo), J. P. Kenny (alt—Narciso), D. L. Ragin (ct—Nerone), M. Chance (ct—Ottone), A. Miles (bass—Claudio), G. Mosley (bass—Pallante) PPHI 3-▲ 438009 (48.97)

N. McGegan (cnd), Capella Savaria, S. Bradshaw (sop), W. Hill (sop), L. Saffer (sop), R. Popken (alt), G. Banditelli (cta), D. Minter (ct), B. Szilágyi (bar), M. Dean (b-bar), N. Isherwood (bass) [period instrs] HAM 3-▲ 907063 (36.97)

Agrippina (selections)

D. Brown (sop), D. Jones (mez), D. L. Ragin (ct), M. Chance (ct), A. Miles (bass), J. E. Gardiner (cnd), English Baroque Soloists PPHI ▲ 456025 (16.97)

K. Gauvin (sop), J. Lamon (vn), Tafelmusik—Non hó cor che per amarti; Ogni vento; ; Vaghe perle; Se giunge un dispetto *(rec Grace Church-on-the-Hill, Toronto, Canada, Jan 25-27, 1999)* † Agrippina (ov); Alcina (ov); Alcina (sels) FL ▲ 23137 [DDD] (16.97)

Agrippina:Overture

K. Gauvin (sop), J. Lamon (vn), Tafelmusik *(rec Grace Church-on-the-Hill, Toronto, Canada, Jan 25-27, 1999)* † Agrippina (sels); Alcina (ov); Alcina (sels) FL ▲ 23137 [DDD] (16.97)

Ah! che pur troppo è vero (cantata) for Soprano & Continuo, HWV 77

E. Hargis (sop), Seattle Baroque Orch *(rec Apr-May 1996)* ("Tra le fiamme") † Armida abbandonata, HWV 105; Chamber Music; Serse (sels); Son (Con) Vn, HWV 288; Tra le fiamme, HWV 170 *([I,E] texts)* WILD ▲ 9604 [DDD] (16.97)

Ah! che troppo ineguali/O del ciel! Maria Regina (recitative & aria) for Soprano & Continuo, HWV 230

A. S. von Otter (mez), R. Goebel (cnd), Cologne Musica Antiqua † Donna, che in ciel di tanta luce splendi, HWV 233; Haec est Regina virginum, HWV 235; Pianto di Maria, HWV 234 PARC ▲ 39866 [DDD] (16.97)

Alceste (masque or semi-opera) [based on a play by Tobias Smollet, after Euripides], HWV 45

R. Comiotto (sop), S. Revidat (sop), J. Delescluse (ten), F. Bazola (bass), F. Comte (cnd) *(rec Aug 6-8, 1997) (E,F lib texts)* MED7 ▲ 897 [DDD] (18.97)

The Alchymist (incidental music) for Soprano & Orchestra [for Ben Jonson's play], HWV 43

M. Huggett (cnd), CBC Vancouver SO, N. Argenta (sop) [ITA] † Alcina (sels); H. Purcell:Fairy Queen (sels); King Arthur (sels); Married Beau (sels) SMS (SM 5000) ▲ 5091 [DDD] (16.97)

Alcina (opera in 3 acts) [lib anon after Ariosto], HWV 34 (1735)

F. Leitner (cnd), Cappella Coloniensis, Cologne Radio Chorus, J. Sutherland (sop—Alcina), J. V. Dijck (sop—Morgana), N. Procter (cta—Bradamante), F. Wunderlich (ten—Ruggiero), N. Monti (ten—Oronte), T. Hemsley (bar—Melisso) *(rec live, Cologne, Germany, 1959)* MELO (Opera Live) 2-▲ 50023 (m) [ADD] (31.97)

N. Recsigno (cnd), Venice Theater Orch, Venice Theater Chorus, J. Sutherland (sop), E. Fusco (sop), O. Dominguez (mez), M. Sinclair (cta), N. Monti (ten), P. Clabassi (bass) *(rec 1960)* BELV 2-▲ 7220 (29.97)

Alcina (selections)

N. Argenta (sop), M. Huggett (cnd), CBC Vancouver Orch—Tornami a vagheggiar; Dream Music (Ballet); Mi restano le lagrime † Alchymist, HWV 43; H. Purcell:Fairy Queen (sels); King Arthur (sels); Married Beau (sels) SMS (SM 5000) ▲ 5091 [DDD] (16.97)

K. Gauvin (sop), J. Lamon (vn), Tafelmusik—Musette; Minuett; Di, cor mio, quanto t'amai; Tornami a vagheggiar; Entree; Gavotte; Barbara! Lo ben lo so; Ombre pallide; Mi restano le lagrime *(rec Grace Church-on-the-Hill, Toronto, Canada, Jan 25-27, 1999)* † Agrippina (ov); Agrippina (sels); Alcina (ov) FL ▲ 23137 [DDD] (16.97)

E. Kirkby (sop), C. Hogwood (cnd), Academy of Ancient Music Orch—Credete al mio dolore; Tornami a vagheggiar † Alessandro Severo (sels); Alexander's Feast (ode), HWV 75; Allegro, il Penseroso ed il Moderato (sels); Ariodante (sels); Hornpipe in D, HWV 356; March; Saul (sels); T. Arne:Comus (sels); Rosamond (sels); Tempest (sels); J. Haydn:Schöpfung (sels); J. F. Lampe:Brittania (sels); Dione (sels); W. A. Mozart:Ah, lo previdi & Ah, t'involva agl'occhi miei, K.272; Ch'io mi scordi di te? & Non temer, amato bene, K.505; Nehmt meinen Dank, ihr holden Gönner!, K.383; Rè pastore (sels); Voi avete un cor fedele, K.217; Zaide (sels) PLON (Double Decker) 2-▲ 458084 [DDD] (17.97)

A. Murray (mez), C. Mackerras (cnd), Orch of the Age of Enlightenment—Mi lusinga il dolce affetto; Verdi prati, selve amene; Sta nell'Ircana ("Great Handel Arias") † Ariodante (sels); Giulio Cesare in Egitto (sels); Serse (sels) FORL ▲ 16738 [DDD] (16.97)

J. Sutherland (sop)—Di, cor mio, quanto t'amai; Tornami a vagheggiar *(rec 1956-60)* ("Recitals") † V. Bellini:Norma (sels); Donizetti:Lucia di Lammermoor (sels); J. Haydn:Arias; W. A. Mozart:Entführung aus dem Serail (sels); Exsultate, jubilate, K.165 BELV ▲ 7001 [ADD] (15.97)

J. Sutherland (sop), F. Leitner (cnd), Cappella Coloniensis—Di, cor mio, quanto t'amai; Ah! mio cor! schernito sei! *(rec live May 15, 1959)* † V. Bellini:Sonnambula (sels); J. Haydn:Anima del filosofo, H.XXVIII/13 MYTO 2-▲ 90529 [ADD] (34.97)

F. V. Weingartner (cnd) —Dream Music (Ballet) *(rec 1931-40)* ("The Art of Felix Weingartner") † Beethoven:Geschöpfe des Prometheus (ov); Leonore (ov 2); Ruinen von Athen (ov); J. Brahms:Academic Festival Ov, Op. 80; Liszt:Mephisto Waltz 2 Orch, S.111; Préludes, S.97; Strauss (II):Frühlingsstimmen, Op. 410; Wein, Weib und Gesang, Op. 333; R. Wagner:Rienzi (ov); Siegfried Idyll; Tannhäuser (orch sels); Tristan und Isolde (orch sels) GRM2 2-▲ 78856 (26.97)

Alcina:Overture

K. Gauvin (sop), J. Lamon (vn), Tafelmusik *(rec Grace Church-on-the-Hill, Toronto, Canada, Jan 25-27, 1999)* † Agrippina (ov); Agrippina (sels); Alcina (sels) FL ▲ 23137 [DDD] (16.97)

Alessandro (opera in 3 acts) [lib Rolli adapted from O. Mauro], HWV 21 (1726)

M. Nowakowski (cnd), Sinfonia Varsovia, Watson (sop), A. Terzian (mez), B. J. Rieders (cta), T. Poole (ten), A. Andersson (ten), P. Price (ten), L. Atkinson (trbn) *(rec live)* KSCH 3-▲ 100303 [DDD] (47.97)

Alessandro (selections)

J. Blegen (sop), G. Schwarz (cnd), Mostly Mozart Festival Orch—Lusinghe più care † Ode for the Birthday of Queen Anne; Samson (sels); W. A. Mozart:Exsultate, jubilate, K.165; Idomeneo (sels); Rè pastore (sels); Vorrei spiegarvi, oh Dio, K.418; A. Scarlatti:Su le sponde del Tebro SNYC (Essential Classics) ▲ 62646 (7.97) ▮ 62646 (3.98)

HANDEL, GEORGE FRIDERIC (cont.)

Alessandro Severo (selections)

C. Hogwood (cnd), Academy of Ancient Music—Ov † Alcina (sels); Alexander's Feast (ode), HWV 75; Allegro, il Penseroso ed il Moderato (sels); Ariodante (sels); Hornpipe in D, HWV 356; March; Saul (sels); T. Arne:Comus (sels); Rosamond (sels); Tempest (sels); J. Haydn:Schöpfung (sels); J. F. Lampe:Brittania (sels); Dione (sels); W. A. Mozart:Ah, lo previdi & Ah, t'involva agl'occhi miei, K.272; Ch'io mi scordi di te? & Non temer, amato bene, K.505; Nehmt meinen Dank, ihr holden Gönner!, K.383; Rè pastore (sels); Voi avete un cor fedele, K.217; Zaide (sels) PLON (Double Decker) 2-▲ 458084 [DDD] (17.97)

Alexander Balus (oratorio in 3 acts) for solo Voices, Orchestra & Chorus [lib Morell after I Maccabees], HWV 65 (1748; rev 1754)

R. King (cnd) HYP 2-▲ 67241 (36.97)

R. Palmer (cnd), Brewer CO, Palmer Singers, J. Baird (sop—Cleopatra), D. Fortunato (mez—Aspasia), L. Gratis (mez—Messenger), J. Lane (mez—Alexander), F. Urrey (ten—Jonathan), P. Castaldi (bar—Messenger/Ptolomee/Sycophant Courier) *(rec SUNY Purchase, NY, Summer 1997) (E lib text)* NPT 2-▲ 85625 [DDD] (32.97)

Alexander Balus (selections)

J. Baird (sop), E. Brewer (hpd), R. Palmer (cnd), Brewer CO—O take me from this hateful light; Calm thou my soul; Convey me to some peaceful shore ("Glorious Handel") † Acis & Galatea (sels); Berenice (sels); Faramondo (sels); Joshua (sels); Messiah (sels); Mi palpita il cor (sels); Semele (sels); Siroe (sels) NPT ▲ 85646 [DDD] (16.97)

Alexander's Feast (ode) for solo Voices, Orchestra & Chorus [lib J. Dryden], HWV 75

A. Deller (cnd), Oriana Concert Orch, Oriana Concert Choir, H. Sheppard (sop), A. Deller (ct), M. Worthley (ten), M. Bevan (bar) *(rec Vienna, Austria, 1964)* † Ode for the Birthday of Queen Anne VC 2-▲ 8113 [ADD] (26.97)

E. Kirkby (sop), C. Hogwood (cnd), Academy of Ancient Music Orch—War, he sung, is toil & trouble † Alcina (sels); Alessandro Severo (sels); Allegro, il Penseroso ed il Moderato (sels); Ariodante (sels); Hornpipe in D, HWV 356; March; Saul (sels); T. Arne:Comus (sels); Rosamond (sels); Tempest (sels); J. Haydn:Schöpfung (sels); J. F. Lampe:Brittania (sels); Dione (sels); W. A. Mozart:Ah, lo previdi & Ah, t'involva agl'occhi miei, K.272; Ch'io mi scordi di te? & Non temer, amato bene, K.505; Nehmt meinen Dank, ihr holden Gönner!, K.383; Rè pastore (sels); Voi avete un cor fedele, K.217; Zaide (sels) PLON (Double Decker) 2-▲ 458084 [DDD] (17.97)

Allegro in c for Violin & Continuo, HWV 408

R. Barton (vn), J. M. Rozendaal (vc), D. Schrader (hpd) *(rec Chicago, IL, Dec 1996)* ("The Sonatas for Violin & Continuo") † Aria (Andante), HWV 412; Son Vn CED ▲ 32 [DDD] (16.97)

Berlin Baroque Company *(rec Berlin-Wannsee, Germany, Oct 13-16, 1995)* ("Deutsche Arien") † German Arias, HWV 202-10; German Arias, HWV 202-210, HWV 202-10; Son Fl; Trio Sons, HWV 386-391 CAPO ▲ 10767 [DDD] (10.97)

Cambridge Musick *(rec Utrecht, Netherlands, Aug 1995)* † Aria (Andante), HWV 412; Son Va da Gamba, HWV 364b; Son Vn GLOE 2-▲ 6032 [DDD] (32.97)

L'Ecole d'Orphée ("Chamber Music, Vol. 2") † Aria (Andante), HWV 412; Son Ob; Son Vn CRD ▲ 3374 [ADD] (17.97)

L'Allegro, il Penseroso ed il Moderato (oratorio in 3 parts) for solo Voices, Instrumental Ensemble & Chorus [text by Jennens after Milton], HWV 55 (1740-41)

V. Hruba-Freiberger (sop), D. Schellenberger-Ernst (sop), J. Kowalski (alt), F. Kapellmann (bass), Rabsilber (sgr), R. Reuter (cnd), Berlin Comic Opera Orch, Berlin Radio Chorus BER 2-▲ 1147 [DDD] (32.97)

M. McLaughlin (sop), P. Kwella (sop), M. Ginn (trbn), J. E. Gardiner (cnd) , Monteverdi Choir London ERAT 2-▲ 45377 (33.97)

L'Allegro, il Penseroso ed il Moderato (selections)

E. Kirkby (sop), C. Hogwood (cnd), Academy of Ancient Music Orch—Sweet bird † Alcina (sels); Alessandro Severo (sels); Alexander's Feast (ode), HWV 75; Ariodante (sels); Hornpipe in D, HWV 356; March; Saul (sels); T. Arne:Comus (sels); Rosamond (sels); Tempest (sels); J. Haydn:Schöpfung (sels); J. F. Lampe:Brittania (sels); Dione (sels); W. A. Mozart:Ah, lo previdi & Ah, t'involva agl'occhi miei, K.272; Ch'io mi scordi di te? & Non temer, amato bene, K.505; Nehmt meinen Dank, ihr holden Gönner!, K.383; Rè pastore (sels); Voi avete un cor fedele, K.217; Zaide (sels) PLON (Double Decker) 2-▲ 458084 [DDD] (17.97)

J. Kowalski (alt), R. Reuter (cnd), Berlin Comic Opera Orch—Komm, edle Gottin, hehr und weise; Lasst auch die Trauermuse nun; Birg mich vor dem hellen Schein *(rec Christuskirche, Berlin, Germany, July 1989)* † J. F. Agricola:Achille in Sciro (sels); J. S. Bach:Cant 169; Cant 35; K. H. Graun:Artaserse (sels); J. A. Hasse:Clemenza di Tito (sels); Pergolesi:Salve Regina (sels); Stabat mater (sels); Telemann:Flavius Bertaridus (sels) BER ▲ 9382 [DDD] (10.97)

E. Schwarzkopf (sop), J. Krips (cnd), Vienna PO—Sweet bird *(rec Vienna, Austria, Nov 2, 1946)* ("Stars of English Oratorio, Vol. 2") † Acis & Galatea (sels); Arias; J. S. Bach:Anna Magdalena Bach Notebook (sels); Arias; A. Dvořák:Spectre's Bride (sels); J. Haydn:Schöpfung (sels); Verdi:Requiem Mass DLAB ▲ 7029 [ADD] (17.97)

Alleluja & Amen for solo Voice & Continuo

R. Leanderson (bar), H. Fagius (org) *(rec Stockholm Sweden, May 16-17 & Oct 20, 1978)* ("Baroque & Romantic Vocal Music") † Dolce pur d'amor l'affanno, HWV 109a; E. Elgar:Sea Pictures, Op. 37; H. Purcell:Hail, bright Cecilia, Z.328; Sacred Music; Songs; Telemann:Ew'ge Quelle, milder Strom, TWV1: 546; Kleine Kantate von Wald und Au BIS ▲ 127 [AAD] (17.97)

Almira (selections)

P. Holman (cnd), Parley of Instruments [suite; reconstructed P. Holman] ("Handel in Hamburg") † Cons Ob, HWV 301, 302a & 287; Ov; Rodrigo (ov); Suite Kbd, HWV 453; Suite Orch, HWV 352; Suite Orch, HWV 353; Suite Orch, HWV 354 HYP ▲ 67053 [DDD] (18.97)

Almira:Overture

R. Goodman (cnd), Brandenburg Consort ("Handel Opera Arias") † Arias; Giulio Cesare in Egitto (sels); Scipione (ov); Scipione (sels); Silla (ov); Tamerlano (ov) HYP ▲ 66860 (18.97)

Alpestre monte (cantata) for Soprano & Continuo, HWV 81

J. Baird (sop) † Pensieri notturni di Filli:Nel dolce dell'oblio, HWV 134; Tra le fiamme, HWV 170; Telemann:Essercizii Musici DOR ▲ 90147 [DDD] (16.97)

Amadigi di Gaula (selections)

J. Charvet (ct), S. Intrieri (cnd), La Réjouissance—D'un sventurato amante; Pena tiranna † Admento sel; Con a quattro in D; Giulio Cesare in Egitto (sels); Rinaldo (sels); Tamerlano (ov); Tamerlano (sels) MAND ▲ 4944 (18.97)

B. Norden (sop), B. Haley (tpt), D. Foster (hpd), Alexander String Quartet—Destero dall'empia dite † Olinto pastore, Tebro fiume, Gloria, HWV 143; J. S. Bach:Cant 51; J. Clarke:Trumpet Voluntary; A. Scarlatti:Arias Sop; Arias Sop, Tpt & Strs CRYS ▲ 952 [DDD] (15.97) ▮ 952 [DDD] (9.98)

Andante in d for Recorder & Continuo, HWV 409

A. Bylsma (vc), F. Brüggen (rcr), B. Haynes (ob), H. Lange (bn), B. V. Asperen (hpd) ("The Complete Wind Sonatas") † Son Vn; Sonatas for Recorder (miscellaneous); Sonatas for Recorder & Continuo; Sons Fl; Sons Ob SNYC (Seon) 2-▲ 60100 [ADD] (14.97)

Apollo e Dafne (cantata) for Soprano, Bass & Orchestra, HWV 122 (ca 1709)

R. Alexander (sop), T. Hampson (bar), N. Harnoncourt (cnd), Vienna Concentus Musicus † Giulio Cesare in Egitto (sels) TELC (Das alte Werk) ▲ 98645 (9.97)

N. Argenta (sop), M. George (bass), S. Standage (cnd), Collegium Musicum 90 † Crudel tiranno amor, HWV 97 CHN (Early Music) ▲ 583 [DDD] (16.97)

J. Nelson (sop), D. Thomas (bass), N. McGegan (cnd), Philharmonia Baroque Orch † Cons Ob, HWV 301, 302a & 287 HAM ▲ 1905157 (9.97)

Arias

A. Augér (sop), G. Schwarz (cnd), Mostly Mozart Festival Orch—Atalanta (sels) [Care selve, ombre beate]; Alexander's Feast (ode), HWV 75 [The Prince, unable to conceal his pain; Softly sweet, in Lydian measures]; Giulio Cesare in Egitto (sels) [Piangerò, la sorte mia]; Messiah (sels) [Rejoice greatly, o daughter of Zion; He shall feed His flock; Come unto Him]; Rinaldo (sels) [Lascia ch'io pianga]; Samson (sels) [Let the bright Seraphim] † J. S. Bach:Anna Magdalena Bach Notebook (sels); Cant 202; Cant 209; St. Matthew Passion (sels) DLS ▲ 3026 [DDD] (14.97)

J. Baird (sop), D. Fortunato (mez), J. Aler (ten), W. Watson (ten), P. Castaldi (bar), J. Ostendorf (bass), E. Brewer (hpd), R. Palmer (cnd), Brewer CO, Palmer Singers—Semele (sels) [Where'er you walk; O Sleep! Why dost thou leave me]; Joshua (sels) [See, the raging flames arise; Haste, Israel, haste; While Kedron's brook; Shall I in Mamre's fertile plain; Oh! had I Jubal's lyre]; Messiah (sels) [How beautiful are the feet; Thou shalt break them]; Judas Maccabaeus (sels) [Arm, arm ye brave]; Joseph & His Brethren (sels) [Come, Divine Inspirer]; Acis & Galatea (sels) [Stay, shepherd, stay; Love sounds th'alarm] ("Where'er You Walk") NPT ▲ 85610 [DDD] (16.97)

W. Booth (ten), W. Braithwaite (cnd) *(Acis & Galatea (sels) [Love sounds th'alarm; Love in her eyes sits playing]) (rec Mar 8, 1948)*, W. Booth (ten), W. Braithwaite (cnd), London PO, G. Weldon (cnd), City of Birmingham Orch *(Messiah (sels) [Comfort ye, my people; Every valley shall be exalted; Thy rebuke hath broken His heart; Behold, and see if there be any sorrow; He was cut off out of the land]) (rec Feb 28, 1939)*, W. Booth (ten), M. Sargent (cnd), Liverpool PO *(Jephtha (sels) [Deeper & deeper; Waft her, angels, through the skies]) (rec July 4, 1944)*, W. Booth (ten), S. Robinson (cnd), Symphony Orch *(Samson (sels) [Total eclipse]) (rec Feb 7, 1947)*, W. Booth (ten), W. Reeves (cnd), London PO *(Serse (sels) [Ombra mai fu (Largo)]) (rec Oct 28, 1939)* ("Handel & Operatic Arias") † Coleridge-Taylor:Scenes from the Song of Hiawatha, Op. 30; Leoncavallo:Pagliacci (sels); W. A. Mozart:Arias; G. Puccini:Bohème (sels); Verdi:Aida (sels); R. Wagner:Meistersinger (preludes) DLAB ▲ 7032 [ADD] (17.97)

HANDEL, GEORGE FRIDERIC (cont.)

Arias (cont.)

J. Bowman (ct), R. King (cnd), King's Consort—Alcina (sels) [Verdi prati, selve amene]; Amadigi di Gaula (sels) [Pena tiranna]; Rinaldo (sels) [Cara sposa; Venti, turbini, prestate; Or la tromba in suon festante; Maganimi campioni]; Giulio Cesare in Egitto (sels) [Va tacito e nascosto; Al lampo del armi]; Giustino (sels) [Se parla nel mio cor; Zeffiretto, che scorre nel prato]; Ariodante (sels) [Scherza, infida, in grembo al drudo]; Ottone (sels) [Tanti affanni] ("Heroic Arias") † Serse (ov) HYP ▲ 66483 (18.97)

D. Daniels (ct), R. Norrington (cnd), Orch of the Age of Enlightenment—Serse (sels) [Fronde tenere e belle...Ombra mai fu]; Giulio Cesare in Egitto (sels) [Va tacito e nascosto; Al lampo del armi; Dall' ondoso periglio...Aure, deh, per pietà; Cara speme, questo core; L'angue offeso mai riposa]; Tamerlano (sels) [A dispetto d'un volto ingrato]; Ariodante (sels) [E vivo ancora?; Scherza, infida, in grembo al drudo]; Rodelinda (sels) [Pompe vane di morte!; Dove sei? amato bene!; Vivi tiranno, vivi tiranno]; Rinaldo (sels) [Cara sposa; Venti, turbini, prestate] *(rec Abbey Road, London, England, Feb, 1998)* VCL ▲ 45326 (16.97)

G. Fisher (sop), J. Bowman (ct), J. M. Ainsley (ten), M. George (bass), R. Goodman (vn), L. Besnosiuk (fl), C. Steele-Perkins (tpt), R. King (hpd/org), R. King (cnd) *(Ode for St. Cecilia's Day, HWV 76 [The trumpets loud clangour]; Serse (sels) [Ombra mai fu (Largo)]; Acis & Galatea (sels) [O ruddier than the cherry]; Joshua (sels) [Heroes when with glory burning]; Jephtha (sels) [Waft her, angels, through the skies]; Alexander's Feast (ode), HWV 75 [Revenge, revenge Timotheus cries]; Samson (sels) [How willing my paternal love])*, G. Fisher (sop), J. Bowman (ct), J. M. Ainsley (ten), M. George (bass), R. Goodman (vn), L. Besnosiuk (fl), C. Steele-Perkins (tpt), R. King (hpd/org/hpd/org), R. King (cnd) *(Semele (sels) [Where'er you walk])* ("Great Baroque Arias") ICC ▲ 6600422 (16.97)

S. Gritton (sop), J. Bowman (ct), R. King (cnd), King's Consort—Choice of Hercules (sels) [Yet can I hear that dulcet lay]; Esther (sels) [How can I stay; Tune your harps]; Saul (sels) [O fairest of 10,000 fair; O Lord, whose mercies]; Belshazzar (sels) [Great God! who yest but darkly known; Martial Sym; Destructive war]; Theodora (sels) [Thy raptur'd soul defies the sword; Kind Heav'n, if Virtue be thy care]; Judas Maccabaeus (sels) [Father of Heaven]; Solomon (sels) [What tho' I trace each herb & flower; Welcome as the dawn; Almighty pow'r] ("English Arias") † Esther (sels) HYP ▲ 66797 (18.97)

L. Hunt (sop), N. McGegan (cnd), Philharmonia Baroque Orch—Susanna (sels) [Bending to the throne of glory; Guilt trembling spoke my doom]; Theodora (sels) [Angels ever bright & fair; With darkness, deep as my woe; Oh that I on wings could rise]; Messiah (sels) [He was despised]; Agrippina (sels) [Ogni vento]; Arianna in Creta (sels) [Miriami]; Ottone (sels) [Vieni, o figlio]; Radamisto (sels) [Qual nave]; Clori, Tirsi e Fileno, HWV 96 [Amo Tirsi; Barbaro; Va col canto] HAM ▲ 907149 (18.97)

E. Kirkby (sop), R. Goodman (cnd), Brandenburg Consort—Almira (sels) [Vedrai s'a tuo dispetto]; Rodrigo (sels) [Perché viva il caro sposo]; Rinaldo (sels) [Vo'far guerra]; Amadigi di Gaula (sels) [Ah! spietato; Destero dall'empia dite]; Rodelinda (sels) [Ombre, piante]; Giulio Cesare in Egitto (sels) [V'adoro, pupille, saette d'amore]; Tamerlano (sels) [Cor di padre]; Scipione (sels) [Scoglio d'immota fronte] ("Handel Opera Arias") † Almira (ov); Giulio Cesare in Egitto (sels); Scipione (ov); Scipione (sels); Silla (ov); Tamerlano (ov) HYP ▲ 66860 (18.97)

J. Kowalski (alt), N. Marriner (cnd), Academy of St. Martin in the Fields—Israel in Egypt (sels) [Their land brought forth frogs]; Belshazzar (sels) [Oh sacred oracles of truth]; Allegro, il Penseroso ed il Moderato (sels) [May at last] ("Jochen Kowalski: Händel & Bach Sacred Arias") † Messiah (sels); J. S. Bach:Mass in b, BWV 232; St. Matthew Passion (sels) CAPO ▲ 10532 [DDD] (11.97)

J. Lane (mez), E. Brewer (hpd), R. Palmer (cnd), Brewer CO—Rinaldo (sels) [Lascia ch'io pianga]; Alexander Balus (sels) [Fury with red sparkling eyes; O Mithra]; Muzio Scevola (sels) [Con lui volate; Ah, dolce nome]; Faramondo (sels) [Se ben mi lusinga; Voglio che sia]; Berenice (sels) [Su, Megera, Tisifone, Aletto!; Sì, tra i ceppi]; Semele (sels) [Where'er you walk] ("Fury, with Red Sparkling Eyes") † Joshua (sels) NPT ▲ 85628 [DDD] (16.97)

R. Lewis (ten), M. Sargent (cnd), London SO—Acis & Galatea (sels) [Would you gain the tender creature]; Judas Maccabaeus (sels) [Sound an alarm!; How vain is man; My arms, against this Gorgias will I go; Thanks to my brethren]; Samson (sels) [Total eclipse]; Alexander's Feast (ode), HWV 75 [War, he sung, is toil & trouble]; Joshua (sels) [So long the memory shall last; While Kedron's brook]; Jephtha (sels) [Deeper & deeper; Waft her, angels, through the skies; For ever blessed be Thy holy name]; Semele (sels) [Where'er you walk] † Traditional:British folksongs DLAB ▲ 4003 [ADD] (17.97)

E. Mallas-Godlewska (sop), D. L. Ragin (ct), C. Rousset (cnd) —Rinaldo (sels) [Lascia ch'io pianga; Cara sposa] *(rec Metz, France, July 1993)* ("Farinelli: Il Castrato") † Rinaldo (ov); Broschi:Arias; J. A. Hasse:Artaserse (ov); Pergolesi:Salve regina Sop in a; Porpora:Arias TRAV ▲ 1005 (16.97)

A. Manzotti (male sop), M. Mercelli (fl), P. Pollastri (ob), Anxanum Camerata—Rinaldo (sels) [Venti, turbini, prestate; Cara sposa]; Rodelinda (sels) [Vivi tiranno, vivi tiranno]; Partenope (sels) [Dimmi, pietoso ciel]; Ariodante (sels) [Scherza, infida, in grembo al drudo; Dopo notte atra e funesta]; Aci, Galatea e Polifemo (sels) [Qui l'augel di pianta in pianta]; Arianna in Creta (sels) [Nel pugnar col mostro infido; Sol ristoro de' mortali; Salda querrcia in erta balza] *(rec Aug 1996)* ("Arie per castrato") BONG ▲ 5566 [DDD] (16.97)

H. Nash (sop), C. Raybould (cnd) *(Jephtha (sels) [Waft her, angels, through the skies]) (rec London, England, July 15, 1931)*, E. Suddaby (sop), G. Ripley (sop), A. Alsop (sop), J. Barbirolli (cnd) , M. Miles (cnd), London SO *(Messiah (sels) [Rejoice greatly, o daughter of Zion; He shall feed His flock; I know that my Redeemer liveth]) (rec London, England, May 13, 1929)*, N. Allin (bass), W. Best (pno) *(Samson (sels) [Honour & arms]) (rec London, England, Mar 7, 1930)* ("Stars of English Oratorio, Vol. 2") † Acis & Galatea (sels); Allegro, il Penseroso ed il Moderato (sels); J. S. Bach:Anna Magdalena Bach Notebook (sels); Arias; A. Dvořák:Spectre's Bride (sels); J. Haydn:Schöpfung (sels); Verdi:Requiem Mass DLAB ▲ 7029 [ADD] (17.97)

B. Norden (sop), B. Haley (tpt), D. Foster (hpd), Alexander String Quartet—Amadigi di Gaula (sels) [Destero dall'empia dite]; Olinto pastore, Tebro fiume, Gloria, HWV 143 [Alle voci del bronzo guerriero] † J. S. Bach:Cant 51; J. Clarke:Trumpet Voluntary; A. Scarlatti:Arias Sop; Arias Sop, Tpt & Strs CRYS ▮ 952 [DDD] (9.98) ▲ 952 [DDD] (15.97)

J. Opalach (bass), R. Palmer (cnd), Brewer CO *(Acis & Galatea (sels) [O ruddier than the cherry]; Samson (sels) [Honour & arms]) (rec NYC & St. Jean Baptiste Church NYC, NY)*, F. Urrey (ten), J. Opalach (bass), R. Palmer (cnd), Brewer CO *(Messiah (sels) [Why do the nations?; Thou shalt break them]) (rec NYC & St. Jean Baptiste Church NYC, NY)*, J. Lane (mez), R. Palmer (cnd), Brewer CO *(Serse (sels) [Ombra mai fu (Largo)]; Ariodante (sels) [Dopo notte atra e funesta]) (rec New York City, NY)*, F. Urrey (ten), R. Palmer (cnd), Brewer CO *(Semele (sels) [Where'er you walk]) (rec New York City, NY)*, J. Baird (sop), R. Palmer (cnd), Brewer CO *(Theodora (sels) [Angels ever bright & fair]) (rec NYC & St. Jean Baptiste Church NYC, NY)*, J. Baird (sop), D. Fortunato (mez), J. Ostendorf (bar), R. Palmer (cnd), Brewer CO *(Imeneo (sels) [Deh, m'aiutate; Esser mia; Sorge nell'alma mia; Se potessero]) (rec NYC & St. Jean Baptiste Church NYC, NY)*, M. Tsingopoulos (mez), R. Palmer (cnd), Brewer CO *(Rinaldo (sels) [Lascia ch'io pianga]) (rec NYC & St. Jean Baptiste Church NYC, NY)* ("Handel: Greatest Arias") VOXC ▲ 7527 (5.97)

S. Piau (sop), G. Banditelli (cta), F. Biondi (cnd), Europa Galante—Tolomeo (sels) [Stille amare; Se il cor ti perde]; Muzio Scevola (sels) [Ma come amar?]; Rinaldo (sels) [Lascia ch'io pianga; Cara sposa]; Berenice (sels) [Su, Megera, Tisifone, Aletto!]; Imeneo (sels) [Per le porte del tormento]; Rodelinda (sels) [Ritorna, oh caro]; Con a quattro in D; Arminio (sels) [Il fuggir, cara mia vita]; Parnasso in festa (sels) [Ho perso il caro bien] ("Arie e duetti d'amore") † Trio Sons, HWV 386-391 OPUS ▲ 30174 (18.97)

M. Rigaud (sop), C. Ramona (vc), G. Touvron (tpt), I. Ramona (hpd)—Quel fior che all'alba ride, HWV 154; Samson (sels) [Let the bright Seraphim]; Amadigi di Gaula (sels) [Destero dall'empia dite] *(rec May 1996)* ("Capricci armonici") † A. Scarlatti:Arias Sop; B. Viviani:Capricci armonici, Op. 4 LIDI ▲ 105045 [DDD] (16.97)

L. Saffer (sop—Cuzzoni), L. Hunt (mez—Durastanti), D. Minter (ct—Senesino), D. Thomas (bass—Montagnana), N. McGegan (cnd), Philharmonia Baroque Orch—Acis & Galatea (sels); Agrippina (sels); Alessandro (sels); Arianna in Creta (sels); Athalia (sels); Deborah (sels); Esther (sels); Ezio (sels); Flavio (sels); Giulio Cesare in Egitto (sels); Muzio Scevola (sels); Orlando (sels); Ottone (sels); Radamisto (sels); Riccardo Primo (sels); Rodelinda (sels); Scipione (sels); Sosarme (sels); Tamerlano (sels); Tolomeo (sels) ("Arias for...") HAM 4-▲ 2907171 [ADD] (36.97)

L. Saffer (sop), N. McGegan (cnd), Philharmonia Baroque Orch—Flavio (sels) [Chi mai l'intende...Amante stravagante]; Rodelinda (sels) [Ombre, piante; Spietati, io vi giurai]; Riccardo Primo (sels) [Il volo cosi fido]; Giulio Cesare in Egitto (sels) [Che sento? oh Dio!; Se pietà di me non senti; Piangerò, la sorte mia; Da tempeste il legno infranto]; Scipione (sels) [Scoglio d'immota fronte]; Ottone (sels) [E tale Otton?; Falsa immagine; Giunge Otton?; Affanni del pensier]; Tamerlano (sels) [Serav Asteria...Se non mi vuol amar]; Alessandro (sels) [L'amar, che per te sento] ("Arias for Cuzzoni") HAM ▲ 907036 (18.97)

A. Scholl (ct), R. Norrington (cnd), Orch of the Age of Enlightenment *(Serse (sels) [Frondi tenere e belle; Ombra mai fu (Largo)]; Semele (sels) [Where'er you walk]; Giulio Cesare in Egitto (sels) [Dall' ondoso periglio...Aure, deh, per pietà])*, A. Scholl (ct), F. Kelly (hp), R. Norrington (cnd), Orch of the Age of Enlightenment *(Saul (sels) [Such haughty beauties; O Lord, whose mercies])*, A. Scholl (ct), S. Fulgoni (sop), R. Norrington (cnd), Orch of the Age of Enlightenment *(Rodelinda (sels) [Vivi tiranno, vivi tiranno; Con rauco mormorio])* ("Heroes") † C. W. Gluck:Orfeo ed Euridice (sels); Telemaco (sels); J. A. Hasse:Artaserse (sels); W. A. Mozart:Ascanio in Alba (sels), K.111; Mitridate (sels) DECC ▲ 166196 [DDD] (16.97)

L. Simoneau (ten), E. Werba (pno)—Dettingen Te Deum, HWV 283 [Vouchsafe, oh Lord]; Acis & Galatea (sels) [Would you gain the tender creature; Love sounds th'alarm] *(rec live Salzburg, Austria, Aug 1959)* † Duparc:Songs; G. Fauré:Songs; J. Haydn:Canzonettas (12); Rameau:Impatience ORFE ▲ 460971 (16.97)

HANDEL, GEORGE FRIDERIC (cont.)

Arias (cont.)

B. Terfel (b-bar), J. Fisher (hpd), C. Mackerras (cnd), Scottish CO—Acis & Galatea (sels) [I rage, I melt, I burn; O ruddier than the cherry]; Alcina (sels) [Verdi prati, selve amene]; Alexander's Feast (ode), HWV 75 [Revenge, revenge Timotheus cries; Behold, a ghastly band]; Berenice (sels) [Sì, tra i ceppi]; Dettingen Te Deum, HWV 283 [Vouchsafe, oh Lord]; Giulio Cesare in Egitto (sels) [Va tacito e nascosto]; Judas Maccabaeus (sels) [I feel the Deity within; Arm, arm ye brave]; Messiah (sels) [Thus saith the Lord; But who may abide the day of His coming; Behold, I tell you a mystery; The trumpet shall sound; Why do the nations?]; Orlando (sels) [O voi, del mio poter; Sorge infausta una procella]; Semele (sels) [Where'er you walk]; Serse (sels) [Frondi tenere e belle; Ombra mai fu (Largo)]; Samson (sels) [Honour & arms] *(rec Usher Hall Edinburgh, Scotland, July 1997)* DEUT ▲ 453480 [DDD] (16.97)

F. Wunderlich (ten), F. Leitner (cnd), Capella Coloniensis *(Alcina (sels)) (rec live Vienna, Austria, 1959)*, F. Wunderlich (ten), R. Kubelík (cnd), Bavarian RSO *(Serse (sels)) (rec live Vienna, Austria, 1962)* † G. Rossini:Barbiere di Siviglia MYTO 2-▲ 91752 [ADD] (34.97)

Aria (Andante) in a for Violin & Continuo, HWV 412

R. Barton (vn), J. M. Rozendaal (vc), D. Schrader (hpd) *(rec Chicago, IL, Dec 1996)* ("The Sonatas for Violin & Continuo") † Allegro Vn, HWV 408; Son Vn CED ▲ 32 [DDD] (16.97)

Cambridge Musick *(rec Utrecht, Netherlands, Aug 1995)* † Allegro Vn, HWV 408; Son Va da Gamba, HWV 364b; Son Vn GLOE 2-▲ 6032 [DDD] (32.97)

L'École d'Orphée ("Chamber Music, Vol. 2") † Allegro Vn, HWV 408; Son Ob; Son Vn CRD ▲ 3374 [ADD] (17.97)

Ariodante (opera) [lib after Salvi], HWV 33 (1735)

M. Minkowski (cnd), Musiciens du Louvres, L. Dawson (sop—Ginevra), V. Cangemi (sop—Dalinda), A. S. von Otter (mez—Ariodante), E. Podles (cta), R. Croft (ten—Lurcanio), D. Sedov (bass—King of Scotland) PARC 3-▲ 457271 (48.97)

L. Saffer (sop), J. Gondek (sop), J. Lane (mez), L. Hunt (mez), R. Müller (ten), J. Lindemann (ten), N. Cavallier (bass), N. McGegan (cnd), Freiburg Baroque Orch, R. Popken (cnd), Wilhelmshaven Vocal Ensemble [172-page lib w. production photos] ("Ariodante") HAM 3-▲ 907146 (36.97)

Ariodante (selections)

J. Baird (sop), R. Palmer (cnd), Brewer CO—Dopo notte atra e funesta † Joshua (sels); Ottone (sels); Rinaldo (sels); Semele (sels) NPT ▲ 85568 (16.97)

E. Kirkby (sop), C. Hogwood (cnd), Academy of Ancient Music Orch—Ingrato Polinesso...Neghittosi, or voi che fate? † Alcina (sels); Alessandro Severo (sels); Alexander's Feast (ode), HWV 75; Allegro, il Penseroso ed il Moderato (sels); Hornpipe in D, HWV 356; March; Saul (sels); T. Arne:Comus (sels); Rosamond (sels); Tempest (sels); J. Haydn:Schöpfung (sels); J. F. Lampe:Brittania (sels); Dione (sels); W. A. Mozart:Ah, lo previdi & Ah, t'invola agl'occhi miei, K.272; Ch'io mi scordi di te? & Non temer, amato bene, K.505; Nehmt meinen Dank, ihr holden Gönner!, K.383; Rè pastore (sels); Voi avete un cor fedele, K.217; Zaide (sels) PLON (Double Decker) 2-▲ 458084 [DDD] (17.97)

A. Murray (mez), C. Mackerras (cnd), Orch of the Age of Enlightenment—Scherza, infida, in grembo al drudo; Dopo notte atra e funesta ("Great Handel Arias") † Alcina (sels); Giulio Cesare in Egitto (sels); Serse (sels) FORL ▲ 16738 [DDD] (16.97)

Armida abbandonata (cantata) for Soprano & Strings, HWV 105 (1707)

E. Hargis (sop), Seattle Baroque Orch *(rec Apr-May 1996)* ("Tra le fiamme") † Ah! che pur troppo è vero, HWV 77; Chamber Music; Serse (sels); Son (Con) Vn, HWV 288; Tra le fiamme, HWV 170 *([ENG,ITA] texts)* WILD ▲ 9604 [DDD] (16.97)

Atalanta (selections)

Y. Menuhin (cnd), Menuhin Festival Orch—March *(rec London, England, Dec 1968)* ("Organ Concertos II") † Cons (16) Org; Cons à due Cori, HWV 332-34; Joshua (sels); Occasional Oratorio (sels); Royal Fireworks Music, HWV 351; Son (Con) Vn, HWV 288 EMIC (Doubleforte) 2-▲ 72637 [ADD] (16.97)

Athalia (oratorio in 3 acts) for solo Voices, Orchestra & Chorus [text Humphreys after Racine], HWV 52 (1733)

J. C. Martini (cnd), Frankfurt Baroque Orch, Junge Kantorei, E. Scholl (sop—Athalia), B. Schlick (sop—Josabeth), F. Holzhausen (sop—Joas), A. Reinhold (cta—Joad), M. Brutscher (ten—Mathan), S. MacLeod (bass—Abner) *(rec Eltville am Rhein, Germany, May 1996) ([ENG] lib text)* NXIN 2-▲ 8554364 [DDD] (10.97)

Aure soavi, e lieti (cantata) for Soprano & Continuo, HWV 84 (ca 1707)

I. Troupova-Wilke (sop) † Dolce pur d'amor l'affanno, HWV 109b; German Arias, HWV 202-10 STMA ▲ 13 [DDD] (18.97)

Beato in ver chi può (duet) for Soprano, Alto & Continuo, HWV 181

R. Bertini (sop), C. Cavina (ct), La Venexiana † A mirarvi io son intento, HWV 178; Conservate, raddoppiate, HWV 185; Fronda leggiera e mobile, HWV 186; Langue, geme, sospira, HWV 188; No, di voi non vuo' fidarmi, HWV 190; Se tu non lasci amore, HWV 193; Sono liete, fortunate, HWV 194; Tanti strali al sen mi scocchi, HWV 197; Troppo curda, troppo fiera, HWV 198 CNTS ▲ 9620 [DDD] (18.97)

Concerto Vocale † Langue, geme, sospira, HWV 188; Tanti strali al sen mi scocchi, HWV 197 HMA ▲ 1901004 [DDD] (9.97)

Belshazzar (oratorio in 3 acts) for solo Voices, Orchestra & Chorus [text Jennens], HWV 61 (1745)

R. Frank-Reinecke (sop), U. Trekel-Burckhardt (alt), G. Pohl (cta), P. Schreier (ten), H. C. Polster (bass), R. Münch (hpd), D. Knothe (cnd), Berlin CO, Berlin Singakademie BER 3-▲ 9003 (31.97)

Belshazzar (selections)

J. Elwes (ten), St. Luke's Chamber Ensemble—Let festal joy triumphant reign *(rec New York, NY, Nov 24-26, 1997)* ("With Valour Abounding") † Jephtha (sels); Joseph & His Brethren (ov); Joshua (sels); Solomon (sels) ARA ▲ 6720 [DDD] (16.97)

Berenice [Berenice, Queen of Egypt] (opera in 3 acts) [lib anon after Antonio Salvi], HWV 38 (1736-37)

R. Palmer (cnd), Brewer CO, J. Baird (sop—Berenice), A. Matthews (sop—Alessandro), D. Fortunato (mez—Selene), J. Lane (mez—Demetrio), D. Minter (ct—Arsace), J. McMaster (ten—Fabio), J. Opalach (bass—Aristobolo) *(rec St. Jean Baptiste Church, NYC, NY, Nov 1994) ([ITA,ENG] lib text)* NPT 3-▲ 85620 [DDD] (47.97)

Berenice (selections)

J. Baird (sop), E. Brewer (hpd), R. Palmer (cnd), Brewer CO—Nò, che servire altrui; Traditore ("Glorious Handel") † Acis & Galatea (sels); Alexander Balus (sels); Faramondo (sels); Joshua (sels); Messiah (sels); Mi palpita il cor (sels); Semele (sels); Siroe (sels) NPT ▲ 85646 [DDD] (16.97)

Brockes-Passion [St. John Passion] (oratorio) for solo Voices, Orchestra & Chorus, HWV 48, "Der für die Sünde der Welt gemarterte und sterbende Jesus"

M. Zádori (sop), K. Farkas (sop), D. Minter (ct), G. D. Mey (ten), J. Bándi (ten), M. Klietmann (ten), I. Gáti (bar), N. McGegan (cnd), Capella Savaria, Hallé State Chorus [period instrs] HUN 3-▲ 12734 [DDD] (47.97)

Cantatas for various Voices & Instruments

C. Baumann (sop), J. Corazolla (cnd), Rhenish CO—Silete Venti, HWV 242; Coelestis dum spirat aura, HWV 231; Salve Regina, HWV 241 *(rec June 1984)* ("Sacred Cantatas") ENTE ▲ 86 [DDD] (10.97)

V. Gens (sop), F. Fernandez (vn), M. Glodeanu (vn), Les Basses Réunies—Lucrezia, HWV 145; Armida abbandonata, HWV 105; Agrippina condotta a morire, HWV 110 *(rec Eglise de Bon-Secours, France, Nov 5-8, 1996)* VCL (Musique à Versailles) ▲ 45283 (16.97)

J. Ostendorf (b-bar), R. Palmer (cnd), Brewer CO *(Spande ancor a mio dispetto, HWV 165) (rec Merkin Concert Hall NYC, NY)*, J. Ostendorf (b-bar), R. Palmer (cnd) *(Son como quel nocchiero) (rec Merkin Concert Hall NYC, NY)*, F. Robinson (sop), E. Brewer (hpd) *(Se pari è la tua fè, HWV 158b) (rec Merkin Concert Hall NYC, NY)*, F. Robinson (sop), J. Ostendorf (b-bar), R. Palmer (cnd), Brewer CO *(Scherzano sul tuo volto) (rec Merkin Concert Hall NYC)*, F. Robinson (sop), J. Ostendorf (b-bar), R. Palmer (cnd) *(Senza occhi e senza accenti) (rec Merkin Concert Hall NYC)*, F. Robinson (sop), B. Verdery (gtr), E. Brewer (hpd) *(Nò se emenderá jamás, HWV 140) (rec Merkin Concert Hall NYC, NY)*, F. Robinson (sop), J. Ostendorf (b-bar) *(O Fleeting Joys of Paradise) (rec Merkin Concert Hall NYC, NY)* ("The Romantic Handel") † Suites de Pièces (8) Hpd, HWV 426-33 HEL ▲ 1007 [DDD] (10.97)

Carco sempre di gloria (cantata) for Alto & Continuo, HWV 87

D. L. Ragin (ct), Cologne Divitia Ensemble † Lungi da me pensier tiranno, HWV 125b; Siete rose ruggiadose, HWV 162; Udite il mio consiglio, HWV 172 CCL ▲ 890 [DDD] (18.97)

Chamber Music

Seattle Baroque Orch—Ov in D; Prelude in d; Chaconne in B *(rec Apr-May 1996)* ("Tra le fiamme") † Ah! che pur troppo è vero, HWV 77; Armida abbandonata, HWV 105; Serse (sels); Son (Con) Vn, HWV 288; Tra le fiamme, HWV 170 WILD ▲ 9604 [DDD] (16.97)

Chandos Anthems (11) for solo Voices, Orchestra & Chorus, HWV 246-56

H. Boatwright (sop), C. Bressler (ten), D. Miller (bass), J. Held (bass), M. Raimondi (vn), S. Barab (vc), A. Krilov (ob), H. Shulman (ob), M. Newman (bn), A. Mann (cnd) —No. 1, HWV 246, O be joyful in the Lord; No. 2, HWV 247, In the Lord put I; No. 3, HWV 248, Have mercy upon me; No. 4, HWV 249b, O sing unto the Lord a new song; No. 5a, HWV 250a, I will magnify thee; No. 6a, HWV 251b, As pants the hart *(rec NYC & Vorhees Chapel Rutgers Univ, New Brunswick, NY, 1966-68)* VC 2-▲ 8203 [AAD] (26.97)

H. Christophers (cnd), The Sixteen Orch, The Sixteen Chorus, P. Kwella (sop), L. Dawson (sop), J. Bowman (ct), I. Partridge (ten), M. George (bass) CHN (Chaconne) 4-▲ 554 [DDD] (48.97)

HINDEMITH, PAUL (cont.)

Sonata in B♭ for Bassoon & Piano (1938) (cont.)

R. Bernizzi (bn), M. Damerini (pno) ("Sonatas for Winds & Piano, Vol. 1") † Son Cl; Son Fl; Son Hn; Son Ob AART ▲ 47122 (10.97)

S. Canuti (bn), M. Somenzi (pno) ("Bassoon Images") † Dutilleux:Sarabande et Cortège; M. de Falla:Canciones populares españolas; Mompou:Aureana do sil; Combat del somni; A. Piazzolla:Grand Tango; Saint-Saëns:Son Bn STRV ▲ 80013 (16.97)

B. Grainger (bn), G. Niwa (pno) *(rec DePaul Univ. Concert Hall Chicago, Sept 1992)* † R. Boutry:Interferences; Cascarino:Son Bn; E. Elgar:Romance Bn, Op. 62; Etler:Son Bn; W. A. Mozart:Duo Bn Vc, K.292; Saint-Saëns:Son Bn CENT ▲ 2244 [DDD] (16.97)

D. Jensen (bn), M. Kitagawa (pno) *(rec 1997)* † O. Berg:Sonatine Bn; Vertigo; Nussio:Vars; O. Schoeck:Son Bn; M. Schoof:Impromptus Bn; I. Yun:Monolog Bn MDG ▲ 6030831 [DDD] (17.97)

M. Monguzzi (bn), G. Brollo (pno) *(rec May 1995)* ("20th Century Bassoon") † U. Bertoni:Con Bn; Bozza:Fant Bn; Récit, Sicilienne & Rondò; Dutilleux:Sarabande et Cortège; Saint-Saëns:Son Bn; Tansman:Sonatine Bn; Suite Bn BONG ▲ 5565 [DDD] (16.97)

K. Sønstevold (bn), E. Knardahl (pno) [arr bn & pno] *(rec Nacka, Sweden, April 15, 1978)* ("P. Hindemith: Chamber Music") † Morgenmusik; Son Bass Tuba; Son Hn; Son Tpt; Son Trbn; Trio for 3 Rcrs BIS ▲ 159 [AAD/DDD] (17.97)

K. Thunemann (bn), K. Randalu (pno) *(rec Dec 10, 1996)* ("Complete Sonatas, Vol. 4") † Son Hn; Son Hp; Son Pno 4-Hands; Son Pnos MDG ▲ 3040694 [DDD] (17.97)

M. Turkovič (bn), F. Bognár (pno) † Kleine Kammermusik, Op. 24/2; Son E Hn; Son Fl; Son Hn SNYC ▲ 64400 (16.97)

Sonata for solo Cello, Op. 25/3 (1922)

S. Bagratuni (vc) *(rec Methuen, MA, May 22-23, 1995)* † G. Crumb:Son Vc; Khudoyan:Nostalgia; Son for 2 Vcs; Son 1 Vc; Son 2 Vc; Son 3 Vc ONGA ▲ 104 [DDD] (16.97)

R. Christensen (vc) † Stücke (4) Bn & Vc; Trio 1; Trio 2 GAS ▲ 1009 (11.97)

F. Helmerson (vc) *(rec 1975-77)* ("The Solitary Cello") † G. Crumb:Son Vc; Kodály:Son Vc, Op. 8; Sallinen:Elegy for S. Knight, Op. 10 BIS ▲ 25 [AAD] (17.97)

W. Warner (vc) † Frog He Went a-Courting; Pieces Vc, Op. 8; Son Vc & Pno; Son Vc & Pno, Op. 11/3 BRID ▲ 9088 (17.97)

Sonata for Cello & Piano, Op. 11/3 (1919)

A. Elliot (vc), A. Nel (pno) † Son Db; Son Va; Son Vl; Son Vn & Pno, Op. 11/1 EQLB ▲ 11 [DDD] (16.97)

C. Henkel (vc), G. Pludermacher (pno) ("Cello Sonatas") † H. Pfitzner:Son Vc, Op. 1; R. Strauss:Son Vc, Op. 6 SIGM ▲ 6400 [DDD] (17.97)

J. Krosnick (vc), G. Kalish (pno) *(rec Performing Arts Center SUNY Purchase, May 27-28, 1996)* ("In the Shadow of World War I") † H. Cowell:Son Vc; Debussy:Son Vc; Janáček:Fairy Tale ARA ▲ 6709 [DDD] (16.97)

M. Ostertag (vc), K. Randalu (pno) ("Complete Sonatas, Vol. 1") † Son Va; Son Vn & Pno, Op. 11/1; Son Vn & Pno, Op. 11/2 MDG ▲ 3040691 (17.97)

T. Thedéen (vc), R. Pöntinen (pno) *(rec 1996-97)* ("Cello Music") † Kammermusik 3, Op. 36/2; Son Vc & Pno; Trauermusik BIS ▲ 816 [DDD] (17.97)

W. Warner (vc), E. Buck (pno) † Frog He Went a-Courting; Pieces Vc, Op. 8; Son Vc; Son Vc & Pno BRID ▲ 9088 (17.97)

Sonata for Cello & Piano (1948)

A. Meunier (vc), C. Ivaldi (pno) ("Oeuvres de musique de chambre") † Son Fl; Son Pnos; Son Vn in E ARN ▲ 68319 (16.97)

M. Ostertag (vc), K. Randalu (pno) *(rec Mar 28-29, Dec 5, 1996 & Jan 20, 1997)* ("Complete Sonatas, Vol. 7") † Frog He Went a-Courting; Kleine Son Vc; Son Bass Tuba; Son Db; Son Trbn MDG (Gold) ▲ 3040697 [DDD] (17.97)

T. Thedéen (vc), R. Pöntinen (pno) *(rec 1996-97)* ("Cello Music") † Kammermusik 3, Op. 36/2; Son Vc & Pno, Op. 11/3; Trauermusik BIS ▲ 816 [DDD] (17.97)

W. Warner (vc), E. Buck (pno) † Frog He Went a-Courting; Pieces Vc, Op. 8; Son Vc; Son Vc & Pno, Op. 11/3 BRID ▲ 9088 (17.97)

Sonata for Clarinet & Piano (1939)

D. Altmann (cl), J. Ernst (pno) ("Leÿptziger Allerleÿ") † Musikalisches Blumengärtlein; Son Db; Tanzstücke, Op. 19 TACE ▲ 59

G. Amann (cl), R. Hoffmann (pno) *(rec July 1996)* ("German Works for Clarinet & Piano") † J. Brahms:Son 2 Cl; N. Burgmüller:Duo Cl & Pno, Op. 15; C. M. von Weber:Grand Duo Concertant, J.204 LAVE ▲ 100245 [DDD] (17.97)

M. Carulli (cl), M. Damerini (pno) ("Sonatas for Winds & Piano, Vol. 1") † Son Bn; Son Fl; Son Hn; Son Ob AART ▲ 47122 (10.97)

D. Howard (cl), Z. Carno (pno) *(rec Aug 6-7 & 9, 1991)* ("Capriccio: Mid-Century Music for Clarinet") † L. Bernstein:Son Cl; W. Lutoslawski:Dance Preludes Cl, Hp, Pno, Perc & Strs; F. Poulenc:Son Cl & Pno; Sutermeister:Capriccio Cl CENT ▲ 2201 [DDD] (16.97)

K. Leister (cl), F. Bognár (pno) ("Sonatas for Woodwind") † Son E Hn; Son Fl; Son Ob CAMA ▲ 358 [DDD] (18.97)

K. Leister (cl), F. Bognár (pno) *(rec Berlin, Sept 1992)* † W. Lutoslawski:Dance Preludes Cl & Pno; R. Schumann:Fantasiestücke Cl, Op. 73; Romances Ob, Op. 94 CAMA ▲ 30320 [DDD] (18.97)

R. Manno (cl) ("Clarinet Chamber Music") † Duets Cl & Vn; Qt Cl CPO ▲ 999302 (14.97)

F. Ormand (cl), A. Nel (pno) † Son Bn; Son E Hn; Son Fl; Son Ob EQLB ▲ 9 [DDD] (16.97)

U. Rodenhäuser (cl), K. Randalu (pno) *(rec 1995-96)* ("Complete Sonatas, Vol. 5") † Son E Hn; Son Fl; Son Ob MDG ▲ 3040695 (17.97)

J. Russo (cl), L. W. Ignacio (pno) ("Donaueschingen, Hindemith & Music for Winds") † Kleine Kammermusik, Op. 24/2; Krenek:Marsche, Op. 44; Pepping:Little Serenade; Suite Tpt; Toch:Spiel CRSR ▲ 9051

O. Tantzov (cl), V. Yampolsky (pno) *(rec Mosfilm Studio, Dec 1994)* † Qnt Cl; Qt Cl TRIT ▲ 17005 [DDD] (16.97)

Sonata for Double Bass & Piano (1949)

E. Barker (db), D. D. Emery (pno) † F. Schubert:Son Arpeggione, D.821; Vivaldi:Sons Vc BOST ▲ 1018 [DDD] (15.97)

F. Csontos (db), B. Szokolay (pno) *(rec Jun-July 1997)* ("Original Double Bass Sonatas") † H. Eccles:Son Db; Jentzsch:Son Db; Mišek:Son 1 Db, Op. 5; Montag:Son Db HUN ▲ 31758 [DDD] (16.97)

M. Dobner (db), J. Ernst (pno) ("Leÿptziger Allerleÿ") † Musikalisches Blumengärtlein; Son Cl; Tanzstücke, Op. 19 TACE ▲ 59

W. Güttler (db), K. Randalu (pno) *(rec Mar 28-29, Dec 5, 1996 & Jan 20, 1997)* ("Complete Sonatas, Vol. 7") † Frog He Went a-Courting; Kleine Son Vc; Son Bass Tuba; Son Trbn; Son Vc & Pno MDG (Gold) ▲ 3040697 [DDD] (17.97)

E. Levinson (db), G. Levinson (pno) † Beethoven:Son 3 Vc, Op. 69; Bruch:Kol Nidrei, Op. 47; Koussevitzky:Valse miniature Db, Op. 1/2; S. Rachmaninoff:Trio élégiaque 1; Ranjbaran:Dance of Life; P. Tchaikovsky:Souvenir d'un lieu cher, Op. 42 CAL ▲ 507 [DDD] (15.97)

Q. van Regteren Altena (db), P. B. van Henegouwen (pno) ("Characters: 20th-Century Music for Double Bass & Piano") † L. Andriessen:Elegie; A. Desenclos:Aria & Rondo; Ginastera:Pampeana 2, Op. 21; Thilman:Charaktere; A. Wilder:Small Suite OLY ▲ 467 [DDD] (16.97)

D. Weller (db), S. Bruhn (pno) † Son Va; Son Vc & Pno, Op. 11/3; Son Vl; Son Vn & Pno, Op. 11/1 EQLB ▲ 11 [DDD] (16.97)

Sonata for English Horn & Piano (1941)

P. Borgonovo (E hn), M. Damerini (pno) ("Sonatas for Winds & Piano, Vol. 2") † Son Bass Tuba; Son Hn; Son Tpt; Son Trbn AART ▲ 47123 (10.97)

I. Goritzki (E hn), K. Randalu (pno) *(rec 1995-96)* ("Complete Sonatas, Vol. 5") † Son Cl; Son Fl; Son Ob MDG ▲ 3040695 (17.97)

C. Hove (E hn), G. Cheng (pno) *(rec Little Bridges Auditorium Pomona College, Dec 1994 & Jan 1996)* † E. Carter:Pastorale E Hn; J. Marvin:Pieces E hn & Pno; Persichetti:Parable XV, Op. 128; E.-P. Salonen:2nd Meeting; T. Stevens:Triangles IV CRYS ▲ 328 [DDD] (15.97)

T. Indermühle (E hn), K. Randalu (pno) ("Sonatas for Woodwind") † Son Cl; Son Fl; Son Ob CAMA ▲ 358 [DDD] (18.97)

L. Lencsés (E hn), S. Rudiakov (pno) ("Hindemith's Works for Oboe") † Serenaden, Op. 35; Son Ob; Trio Pno, Op. 47 CPO ▲ 999332 (14.97)

H. Sargous (E hn), A. Nel (pno) † Son Bn; Son Cl; Son Fl; Son Ob EQLB ▲ 9 [DDD] (16.97)

H. Schellenberger (E hn), F. Bognár (pno) † Kleine Kammermusik, Op. 24/2; Son Bn; Son Fl; Son Hn SNYC ▲ 64400 (16.97)

Sonata for Flute & Piano (1936)

M. Beaucoudray (fl), Y. Henry (pno) *(rec 1993)* ("Flûte sans frontière") † B. Bartók:Hungarian Peasant Songs, Sz.71; Martinů:Son Fl & Pno; S. Prokofiev:Son Fl SKAR ▲ 4971 [DDD] (18.97)

K. Bryan (fl), K. Keys (pno) *(rec Bratislava Slovak Republic, July 1989)* ("Twentieth Century Flute, Volume Two") † Martinů:Son Fl & Pno; F. Poulenc:Son Fl; S. Prokofiev:Son Fl PREM ▲ 1053 [DDD] (16.97)

L. Buyse (fl), S. Bruhn (pno) † Son Bn; Son Cl; Son E Hn; Son Ob EQLB ▲ 9 [DDD] (16.97)

M. Debost (fl), C. Ivaldi (pno) ("Oeuvres de musique de chambre") † Son Pnos; Son Vc & Pno; Son Vn in E ARN ▲ 68319 (16.97)

HINDEMITH, PAUL (cont.)

Sonata for Flute & Piano (1936) (cont.)

A. Duchemin (fl), M. Duchemin (pno) ("20th Century Sonatas for Flute & Piano") † E. Burton:Sonatina Fl; F. Poulenc:Son Fl; S. Prokofiev:Son Fl SNE ▲ 2037 (16.97)

A. Garzuly (fl), D. Keilhack (pno) *(rec July 9-11, 1995 & Feb 12-14, 1996)* ("Flute Visions for the 20th Century") † B. Bartók:Hungarian Peasant Songs, Sz.71; L. Berio:Sequenza I; Geszler:Vision; G. Kurtág:Hommage à J. S. B.; Muczynski:Son Fl & Pno, Op. 14 HUN ▲ 31655 [DDD] (16.97)

J. Gérard (fl), K. Randalu (pno) *(rec 1995-96)* ("Complete Sonatas, Vol. 5") † Son Cl; Son E Hn; Son Ob MDG ▲ 3040695 (17.97)

B. Gisler-Haase (fl), M. Mori (pno) ("Sonatas for Woodwind") † Son Cl; Son E Hn; Son Ob CAMA ▲ 358 [DDD] (18.97)

B. Gisler-Haase (fl), M. Mori (pno) *(rec Vienna, Feb 2-3, 1994)* ("Flute Sonatas") † A. Dvořák:Sonatina Vn, Op. 100; J. N. Hummel:Son Vn & Pno, Op. 50; Martinů:Son Fl & Pno CAMA ▲ 393 [DDD] (18.97)

M. Grauwels (fl), D. Blumenthal (pno) ("Paul Hindemith: Music for Flute") † Echo Fl & Pno; Junge Magd, Op. 23/2; Kanonische Sonatine; Kleine Kammermusik, Op. 24/2; Pieces Fl BAT ▲ 26 (20.97)

A. Persichilli (fl), M. Damerini (pno) ("Sonatas for Winds & Piano, Vol. 1") † Son Bn; Son Cl; Son Hn; Son Ob AART ▲ 47122 (10.97)

W. Schulz (fl), F. Bognár (pno) † Kleine Kammermusik, Op. 24/2; Son Bn; Son E Hn; Son Hn SNYC ▲ 64400 (16.97)

J. Válek (fl), J. Hála (pno) ("20th Century Flute Sonatas") † Martinů:Son Fl & Pno; F. Poulenc:Son Fl; S. Prokofiev:Son Fl SUR ▲ 96 [DDD] (10.97)

Sonata for Harp (1939)

C. Antonelli (hp) ("20th Century Harp") † L. Berio:Sequenza II; B. Britten:Suite Hp, Op. 83; S. Bussotti:Labirinto; Nuovi Labirinti; Krenek:Son Hp; Petrassi:Flou; Tailleferre:Son Hp AART ▲ 47532 (10.97)

J. Loman (hp) ("20th Century Masterworks for Harp") † B. Britten:Suite Hp, Op. 83; Buhr:Tanzmusik; Salzedo:Vars Hp, Op. 30; Tailleferre:Son Hp; Tournier:Sonatine Hp, Op. 30 MARQ ▲ 165 (16.97)

H. Storck (hp) *(rec Nov 30, 1995)* ("Complete Sonatas, Vol. 4") † Son Bn; Son Hn; Son Pno 4-Hands; Son Pnos MDG ▲ 3040694 [DDD] (17.97)

Sonata in F for Horn & Piano (1939)

H. Dullaert (hn), M. Bon (pno) *(rec Oct & Dec 1992)* ("Horn Chamber Music") † Kleine Kammermusik, Op. 24/2; Son Hns CPO ▲ 999229 [DDD] (14.97)

D. Geeraert (hn/a hn), G. Callaert (pno) *(rec 1992-96)* ("Complete Brass Sonatas") † Son Bass Tuba; Son Tpt; Son Trbn RENE ▲ 92024 [DDD] (16.97)

L. Giuliani (hn), M. Damerini (pno) ("Sonatas for Winds & Piano, Vol. 1") † Son Bn; Son Cl; Son Fl; Son Ob AART ▲ 47122 (10.97)

G. Högner (hn), F. Bognár (pno) † Kleine Kammermusik, Op. 24/2; Son Bn; Son E Hn; Son Fl SNYC ▲ 64400 (16.97)

M. Jones (hn), G. Gould (pno) *(rec 1975)* † Son Bass Tuba; Son Tpt; Son Trbn SNYC (Glenn Gould Edition) 2-▲ 52671 [ADD] (31.97)

B. Kennedy (hn), C. Daval (a hn), S. Bruhn (pno), R. Conway (pno) † Son Bass Tuba; Son Tpt; Son Trbn EQLB ▲ 10 [DDD] (16.97)

W. Slocum (hn), R. Fusco (pno) ("The Expressive Horn") † Beethoven:Son Hn; Dukas:Villanelle ARUN ▲ 3058 (16.97)

R. Vlatkovic (hn), K. Randalu (pno) *(rec Mar 14, 1996)* ("Complete Sonatas, Vol. 4") † Son Bn; Son Hp; Son Pno 4-Hands; Son Pnos MDG ▲ 3040694 [DDD] (17.97)

G. Williams (hn), L. Strieby (hn), T. Lichtmann (pno) † Concert Music Pno, Brass & Hps, Op. 49; Morgenmusik; Son Bass Tuba; Son Hns; Son Tpt; Son Trbn SUMM 2-▲ 115 [DDD] (32.97)

Z. Zuk (hn), Z. Raubo (pno) † Beethoven:Son Hn; Kilar:Son Hn; Rheinberger:Son Hn; A. Wilder:Son 3 Hn ZUK ▲ 250332 (10.97)

Sonata in E♭ for Horn (or Alto Horn or Alto Saxophone) & Piano (1943)

H. Dullaert (hn), M. Bon (pno) *(rec Oct & Dec 1992)* ("Horn Chamber Music") † Kleine Kammermusik, Op. 24/2; Son Hns CPO ▲ 999229 [DDD] (14.97)

D. Geeraert (hn/a hn), G. Callaert (pno) *(rec 1992-96)* ("Complete Brass Sonatas") † Son Bass Tuba; Son Tpt; Son Trbn RENE ▲ 92024 [DDD] (16.97)

M. Jones (hn), G. Gould (pno) *(rec 1976)* † Son Bass Tuba; Son Tpt; Son Trbn SNYC (Glenn Gould Edition) 2-▲ 52671 [ADD] (31.97)

B. Kennedy (hn), C. Daval (a hn), S. Bruhn (pno), R. Conway (pno) † Son Bass Tuba; Son Tpt; Son Trbn EQLB ▲ 10 [DDD] (16.97)

F. Mondelici (a sax), M. Damerini (pno) ("Sonatas for Winds & Piano, Vol. 2") † Son Bass Tuba; Son E Hn; Son Tpt; Son Trbn AART ▲ 47123 (10.97)

D. Pyatt (hn), M. Jones (pno) ("Recital") † Abbot:Alla caccia; Beethoven:Son Hn; Damase:Berceuse, Op. 19; Koechlin:Son Hn; R. Schumann:Adagio & Allegro Hn, Op. 70; F. Strauss:Nocturne Hn, Op. 7 ERAT ▲ 21632 (16.97)

P. Savijoki (a sax), J. Siirala (pno) *(rec Nacka, Sweden, May 3, 1980)* ("P. Hindemith: Chamber Music") † Morgenmusik; Son Bass Tuba; Son Bn; Son Tpt; Son Trbn; Trio for 3 Rcrs BIS ▲ 159 [AAD/DDD] (17.97)

R. Vlatkovic (hn), K. Randalu (pno) ("Complete Sonatas, Vol. 6") † Son Tpt; Sons Org MDG ▲ 3040696 (17.97)

G. Williams (hn), L. Strieby (hn), T. Lichtmann (pno) † Concert Music Pno, Brass & Hps, Op. 49; Morgenmusik; Son Bass Tuba; Son Hns; Son Tpt; Son Trbn SUMM 2-▲ 115 [DDD] (32.97)

Sonata for 4 Horns (1952)

American Horn Quartet † L. Bernstein:West Side Story (sels); W. Perkins:Con for 4 Hns; K. Turner:Qt 3 Hns EBS ▲ 6038 [DDD] (17.97)

T. Bacon (hn), G. Williams (hn), L. Strieby (hn), A. D. Krehbiel (hn) † Concert Music Pno, Brass & Hps, Op. 49; Morgenmusik; Son Bass Tuba; Son Hn; Son Tpt; Son Trbn SUMM 2-▲ 115 [DDD] (32.97)

NFB Horn Quartet † J.-F. Gallay:Qt Hns; Wadenpfuhl:Tectonica CRYS ▲ 241 (15.97) ■ 241 (9.98)

Pavillon Quartet *(rec Oct & Dec 1992)* ("Horn Chamber Music") † Kleine Kammermusik, Op. 24/2; Son Hn CPO ▲ 999229 [DDD] (14.97)

Villa Musica Ensemble † Qt Cl; Trio Pno, Op. 47 MDG ▲ 3040537 [DDD] (17.97)

Sonata for Oboe & Piano (1938)

P. Borgonovo (ob), M. Damerini (pno) ("Sonatas for Winds & Piano, Vol. 1") † Son Bn; Son Cl; Son Fl; Son Hn AART ▲ 47122 (10.97)

I. Goritzki (ob), K. Randalu (pno) *(rec 1995-96)* ("Complete Sonatas, Vol. 5") † Son Cl; Son E Hn; Son Fl MDG ▲ 3040695 (17.97)

T. Indermühle (ob), K. Randalu (pno) ("Sonatas for Woodwind") † Son Cl; Son E Hn; Son Fl CAMA ▲ 358 [DDD] (18.97)

L. Lencsés (ob), S. Rudiakov (pno) ("Hindemith's Works for Oboe") † Serenaden, Op. 35; Son E Hn; Trio Pno, Op. 47 CPO ▲ 999332 (14.97)

F. Meyer (ob), E. Le Sage (pno) † B. Britten:Metamorphoses, Op. 49; Dutilleux:Son Ob; F. Poulenc:Son Ob; Saint-Saëns:Son Ob SONP ▲ 94011 [DDD] (16.97)

H. Sargous (ob), S. Bruhn (pno) † Son Bn; Son Cl; Son E Hn; Son Fl EQLB ▲ 9 [DDD] (16.97)

Sonatas (3) for Organ (1937-40)

R. Haas (org) ("Complete Sonatas, Vol. 6") † Son Hn; Son Tpt MDG ▲ 3040696 (17.97)

H. Kaiser (org)—No. 2 † J. S. Bach:Chorale Preludes Org; Preludes & Fugues, BWV 531-552; F. Couperin:Pièces d'orgue consistantes en deux Messes; M. Reger:Org Music (misc colls); Widor:Org Music QUER ▲ 9817 (18.97)

P. Kee (org) † M. Reger:Intro & Passacaglia, Op. 56; Org Music (misc colls) CHN ▲ 9097 [DDD]

L. Mazzanti (org) ("Organo Kleuker de l'Alpe d'Huez") † Messiaen:Ascension Org; Scelsi:In nomine lucis V; Schoenberg:Vars on a Recitative Org, Op. 40 FON ▲ 9203 [DDD] (13.97)

Sonatas (3) in A, G & B♭ for Piano (1936)

K. Randalu (pno) *(rec Sept 7 & Oct 21, 1997)* ("Complete Sonatas, Vol. 3") † Vars Pno MDG ▲ 3040693 [DDD] (17.97)

B. Roberts (pno) *(rec Nimbus Foundation Concert Hall, May 17-19 & July 17-18, 1995)* ("Music for 1 & 2 Pianos") † Ludus Tonalis; Son Pno 4-Hands; Son Pnos NIMB 2-▲ 5459 [DDD] (23.97)

Sonata for Piano 4-Hands (1938)

K. Randalu (pno), P. Randalu (pno) *(rec Sept 5-6, 1997)* ("Complete Sonatas, Vol. 4") † Son Bn; Son Hn; Son Hp; Son Pnos MDG ▲ 3040694 [DDD] (17.97)

B. Roberts (pno), D. Strong (pno) *(rec Nimbus Foundation Concert Hall, May 17-19)* ("Music for 1 & 2 Pianos") † Ludus Tonalis; Son Pnos; Sons Pno NIMB 2-▲ 5459 [DDD] (23.97)

Sonata for 2 Pianos (1942)

R. Grunschlag (pno), T. Grunschlag (pno) *(rec NY, United States of America, Jan 23-24, 1991)* ("Piano Duo") † Ballou:Son 2 Pnos; D. Milhaud:Songes (ballet), Op. 124 *(E text)* CRI ▲ 606 [ADD] (16.97)

N. Lee (pno), C. Ivaldi (pno) ("Oeuvres de musique de chambre") † Son Fl; Son Vc & Pno; Son Vn in E ARN ▲ 68319 (16.97)

K. Randalu (pno), P. Randalu (pno) *(rec Sept 5-6, 1997)* ("Complete Sonatas, Vol. 4") † Son Bn; Son Hn; Son Hp; Son Pno 4-Hands MDG ▲ 3040694 [DDD] (17.97)

HINDEMITH, PAUL (cont.)

Sonata for 2 Pianos (1942) (cont.)

B. Roberts (pno), D. Strong (pno) *(rec Nimbus Foundation Concert Hall, May 17-19)* ("Music for 1 & 2 Pianos") † Ludus Tonalis; Son Pno 4-Hands; Sons Pno NIMB 2-▲ 5459 [DDD] (23.97)

Sonatas for solo Viola

N. Imai (va), R. Pöntinen (pno)—Op. 11/5 (1919); Op. 25/1 (1922); Op. 31/4 (1924); Son (1937) *(rec Oct 7-9, 1993)* † Meditation BIS ▲ 651 [DDD] (17.97)

Sonata for solo Violin, Op. 31/1 (1924)

I. Kaler (vn) *(rec Methuen, MA, May 1995)* † Son Vn; J. Martinon:Sonatina 5 Vn, Op. 32/1; S. Prokofiev:Son Vc; Ysaÿe:Sons Vn, Op. 27 ONGA ▲ 103 [DDD] (16.97)

Sonata for solo Violin, Op. 31/2 (1924)

I. Kaler (vn) *(rec Methuen, MA, May 1995)* † Son Vn; J. Martinon:Sonatina 5 Vn, Op. 32/1; S. Prokofiev:Son Vc; Ysaÿe:Sons Vn, Op. 27 ONGA ▲ 103 [DDD] (16.97)

G. R. Schubert (vn) ("Distinguished Performers Series, Vol. 1") † Acker:Cantus Gemellus; L. Berkeley:Intro & Allegro Vn, Op. 24; Sonatina Vn, Op. 17; Jolivet:Chant de Linos Fl & Pno; Kalimullin:Son 2 Pno VMM ▲ 2013 [DDD]

S. Staryk (vn) *(rec Montreal, Aug 1964)* ("Sonatas for Solo Violin") † Papineau-Couture:Aria Vn; Pisendel:Son solo Vn; S. Prokofiev:Son Vc; J. W. A. Stamitz:Diverts solo Vn ORIO ▲ 7809 (13.97)

Sonata for Trombone & Piano (1941)

B. Haemhouts (trbn), G. Callaert (pno) *(rec 1992-96)* ("Complete Brass Sonatas") † Son Bass Tuba; Son Hn; Son Tpt RENE ▲ 92024 [DDD] (16.97)

J. Kitzman (trbn), J. K. Hodges (pno) † Creston:Fant Trbn, Op. 42; J. Defaye:Danses Trbn; A. Pryor:Air varié CRYS ▮ 386 (9.98) ▲ 386 (15.97)

J. Kitzman (trbn), J. K. Hodges (pno) *(rec Southern Methodist Univ Dallas, TX, May 1980)* † S. Baudo:Petite Suite; Creston:Fant Trbn, Op. 42; J. Defaye:Danses Trbn; A. Pryor:Air varié CRYS ▲ 386 (15.97) ▮ 386 (9.98)

M. Lawrence (trbn), T. Lichtmann (pno) † Concert Music Pno, Brass & Hps, Op. 49; Morgenmusik; Son Bass Tuba; Son Hn; Son Hns; Son Tpt SUMM 2-▲ 115 [DDD] (32.97)

C. Lindberg (trbn), R. Pöntinen (pno) *(rec Nacka, Sweden, Nov 12, 1983)* ("P. Hindemith: Chamber Music") † Morgenmusik; Son Bass Tuba; Son Bn; Son Hn; Son Tpt; Trio for 3 Rcrs BIS ▲ 159 [AAD/DDD] (17.97)

C. Lindberg (trbn), R. Pöntinen (pno) † L. Berio:Sequenza V; F. Martin:Ballade Pno BIS ▲ 258 [DDD] (17.97)

M. L. Muto (trbn), M. Damerini (pno) ("Sonatas for Winds & Piano, Vol. 2") † Son Bass Tuba; Son E Hn; Son Hn; Son Tpt AART ▲ 47123 (10.97)

B. Slokar (trbn), K. Randalu (pno) *(rec Mar 28-29, Dec 5, 1996 & Jan 20, 1997)* ("Complete Sonatas, Vol. 7") † Frog He Went a-Courting; Kleine Son Vc; Son Bass Tuba; Son Db; Son Vc & Pno MDG (Gold) ▲ 3040697 [DDD] (17.97)

H. C. Smith (trbn), G. Gould (pno) *(rec 1976)* † Son Bass Tuba; Son Hn; Son Tpt SNYC (Glenn Gould Edition) 2-▲ 52671 [ADD] (31.97)

H. D. Smith (trbn), A. Nel (pno) † Son Bass Tuba; Son Hn; Son Tpt EQLB ▲ 10 [DDD] (16.97)

Sonata for Trumpet & Piano (1939)

V. Camaglia (tpt), M. Damerini (pno) ("Sonatas for Winds & Piano, Vol. 2") † Son Bass Tuba; Son E Hn; Son Hn; Son Trbn AART ▲ 47123 (10.97)

C. Daval (tpt), S. Bruhn (pno) † Son Bass Tuba; Son Hn; Son Trbn EQLB ▲ 10 [DDD] (16.97)

G. Johnson (tpt), G. Gould (pno) *(rec 1975)* † Son Bass Tuba; Son Hn; Son Trbn SNYC (Glenn Gould Edition) 2-▲ 52671 [ADD] (31.97)

H. Läubin (tpt), K. Randalu (pno) ("Complete Sonatas, Vol. 6") † Son Hn; Sons Org MDG ▲ 3040696 [DDD] (17.97)

R. Mase (tpt), T. Lichtmann (pno) † Concert Music Pno, Brass & Hps, Op. 49; Morgenmusik; Son Bass Tuba; Son Hn; Son Hns; Son Trbn SUMM 2-▲ 115 [DDD] (32.97)

A. Plog (tpt), Davis (pno) † F. Campo:Studies Tpt; R. Erickson:Kryl; Petrassi:Fanfare for 3 Tpts; A. Plog:Animal Ditties 2; H. Stevens:Son Tpt; F. Tull:Profiles Tpt CRYS ▲ 663 [DDD] (15.97)

A. D. Rudder (tpt), G. Callaert (pno) *(rec 1992-96)* ("Complete Brass Sonatas") † Son Bass Tuba; Son Hn; Son Trbn RENE ▲ 92024 [DDD] (16.97)

E. H. Tarr (tpt), E. Westenholz (pno) † Alexius:Sonatina Tpt; Cellier:Thème et variations; G. Gershwin:Rhap in Blue; Martinů:Sonatina Tpt; S. Weiner:Phantasy 1 Tpt, Op. 57; F. Werner:Duo Tpt & Org, Op. 53 BIS ▲ 152 [AAD] (17.97)

E. H. Tarr (tpt), E. Westenholz (pno) *(rec Holte, Denmark, Sept 20, 1979)* ("P. Hindemith: Chamber Music") † Morgenmusik; Son Bass Tuba; Son Bn; Son Hn; Son Trbn; Trio for 3 Rcrs BIS ▲ 159 [AAD/DDD] (17.97)

Sonata for Bass Tuba & Piano (1955)

G. Audenaert (tuba), G. Callaert (pno) *(rec 1992-96)* ("Complete Brass Sonatas") † Son Hn; Son Tpt; Son Trbn RENE ▲ 92024 [DDD] (16.97)

O. Baadsvik (tuba), Swedish Brass Quintet † Gaathaug:Son Concertante; W. Kraft:Encounters II; T. Madsen:Son Tuba, Op. 34; Sivelöv:Son Tuba, Op. 5 SIMX ▲ 1101 (18.97)

M. Barsotti (tuba), M. Damerini (pno) ("Sonatas for Winds & Piano, Vol. 2") † Son E Hn; Son Hn; Son Tpt; Son Trbn AART ▲ 47123 (10.97)

W. Hilgers (tuba), K. Randalu (pno) *(rec Mar 28-29, Dec 5, 1996 & Jan 20, 1997)* ("Complete Sonatas, Vol. 7") † Frog He Went a-Courting; Kleine Son Vc; Son Db; Son Trbn; Son Vc & Pno MDG (Gold) ▲ 3040697 [DDD] (17.97)

F. Kaenzig (tuba), S. Bruhn (pno) † Son Hn; Son Tpt; Son Trbn EQLB ▲ 10 [DDD] (16.97)

M. Lind (tuba), S. Harlos (pno) *(rec Nacka, Sweden, Aug 12, 1977)* ("P. Hindemith: Chamber Music") † Morgenmusik; Son Bn; Son Hn; Son Tpt; Son Trbn; Trio for 3 Rcrs BIS ▲ 159 [AAD/DDD] (17.97)

G. Pokorny (tuba), T. Lichtmann (pno) † Concert Music Pno, Brass & Hps, Op. 49; Morgenmusik; Son Hn; Son Hns; Son Tpt; Son Trbn SUMM 2-▲ 115 [DDD] (32.97)

A. Torchinsky (tuba), G. Gould (pno) *(rec 1975)* † Son Hn; Son Tpt; Son Trbn SNYC (Glenn Gould Edition) 2-▲ 52671 [ADD] (31.97)

Sonata for Viol & Piano, Op. 25/2 (1922)

B. Smith (va d'amore), S. Bruhn (pno) † Son Db; Son Va; Son Vc & Pno, Op. 11/3; Son Vn & Pno, Op. 11/1 EQLB ▲ 11 [DDD] (16.97)

Sonatas for solo Viola

P. Cortese (va) ("The Complete Works for Viola, Vol. 2,") ASV ▲ 947 (16.97)

Sonata in F for Viola & Piano, Op. 11/4 (1919)

K. Dreyfus (va), R. McDonald (pno) † Bruch:Romanze Va, Op. 85; Debussy:Beau soir; M. de Falla:Suite populaire espagnole; R. Schumann:Märchenbilder, Op. 113 BRID ▲ 9016 [DDD] (17.97)

W. Primrose (va), J. M. Sanromá (pno) *(rec Apr 1938)* ("20th Century Viola") † A. Bax:Son Va; E. Bloch:Suite Va BID ▲ 148 (mono) [ADD] (16.97)

T. Riebl (va), C. Höfer (pno) ("Sonatas-1919") † E. Bloch:Suite Va & Pno; R. Clarke:Son Va PANC ▲ 510098 [DDD] (17.97)

E. Santiago (va), K. Randalu (pno) ("Complete Sonatas, Vol. 1") † Son Vc & Pno, Op. 11/3; Son Vn & Pno, Op. 11/1; Son Vn & Pno, Op. 11/2 MDG ▲ 3040691 (17.97)

Y. Schotten (va), K. Collier (pno) ("Viola 1919: Works by E. Bloch, R. Clarke, and Paul Hindemith") † E. Bloch:Suite Va & Pno; R. Clarke:Son Va CRYS ▲ 637 (15.97)

Y. Schotten (va), K. Collier (pno) † Son Db; Son Vc & Pno, Op. 11/3; Son Vl; Son Vn & Pno, Op. 11/1 EQLB ▲ 11 [DDD] (16.97)

E. Shumsky (va), S. L. Shames (pno) † Trauermusik; J. Beale:Ballade, Op. 47; E. Bloch:Suite hébraïque; F. Kreisler:Praeludium & Allegro Va AMBA ▲ 1011 [DDD] (16.97)

W. Strehle (va), K. Wisniewska (pno) † Duet Va & Vc; Trauermusik; J. Brahms:Son 1 Cl; A. Dvořák:Sonatina Vn, Op. 100 NIMB ▲ 5473 [DDD] (16.97)

R. Verebes (va), D. Bartlett (pno) ("The Complete Sonatas for Viola") † Son Va; Son Va & Pno in C; Son Va & Pno, Op. 25/4 SNE 2-▲ 546 (32.97)

Sonata for Viola & Piano, Op. 25/4 (1922)

H. Fukai (va) † M. Reger:Suites Va, Op. 131d SIGM ▲ 3800 [ADD] (17.97)

N. Imai (va) BIS ▲ 571 [DDD] (17.97)

E. Santiago (va), K. Randalu (pno) *(rec Oct 2 & Dec 8-9, 1996 & June 29, 1997)* ("Complete Sonatas, Vol. 2") † Kleine Son Va, Op. 25/2; Son Va & Pno in C; Son Vn in C; Son Vn in E MDG ▲ 3040692 [DDD] (17.97)

Z. Tchavdarov (va) *(rec Feb 14, 1977)* † M. Reger:Suites Va, Op. 131d; D. Shostakovich:Son Va BIS ▲ 81 [AAD] (17.97)

R. Verebes (va), D. Bartlett (pno) ("The Complete Sonatas for Viola") † Son Va; Son Va & Pno in C SNE 2-▲ 546 (32.97)

Sonata in C for Viola & Piano (1939)

E. Santiago (va), K. Randalu (pno) *(rec Oct 2 & Dec 8-9, 1996 & June 29, 1997)* ("Complete Sonatas, Vol. 2") † Kleine Son Va, Op. 25/2; Son Va & Pno, Op. 25/4; Son Vn in C; Son Vn in E MDG ▲ 3040692 [DDD] (17.97)

R. Verebes (va), D. Bartlett (pno) ("The Complete Sonatas for Viola") † Son Va; Son Va & Pno, Op. 25/4 SNE 2-▲ 546 (32.97)

Sonata for solo Viola, Op. 11/5 (1919)

R. Verebes (va) ("The Complete Sonatas for Viola") † Son Va; Son Va & Pno in C; Son Va & Pno, Op. 25/4 SNE 2-▲ 546 (32.97)

HINDEMITH, PAUL (cont.)

Sonata for solo Viola, Op. 25/1 (1922)

K. Doležal (va) *(rec Covenant of St. Agnes of Bohemia Prague, Mar 1995)* ("Viola") † E. Bloch:Suite hébraïque; L. Matoušek:Intimate Music; A. Rubinstein:Son Va ARTA ▲ 62 [DDD] (16.97)

P. Hindemith (va) *(rec Jan 1934)* † Scherzo Va & Vc; Trio 2; Beethoven:Serenade Str Trio, Op. 8 MTAL ▲ 48024 (6.97)

R. Verebes (va) ("The Solo Viola") † M. Barnes:Ballade; K. Penderecki:Cadenza Va; M. Reger:Suites Va, Op. 131d; I. Stravinsky:Elégie Va; H. Vieuxtemps:Capriccio Va, Op. 55/9 SNE ▲ 562 (16.97)

R. Verebes (va) ("The Complete Sonatas for Viola") † Son Va; Son Va & Pno in C; Son Va & Pno, Op. 25/4 SNE 2-▲ 546 (32.97)

Sonata in C for Violin & Piano (1939)

T. Brandis (vn), K. Randalu (pno) *(rec Oct 2 & Dec 8-9, 1996 & June 29, 1997)* ("Complete Sonatas, Vol. 2") † Kleine Son Va, Op. 25/2; Son Va & Pno in C; Son Va & Pno, Op. 25/4; Son Vn in E MDG ▲ 3040692 [DDD] (17.97)

O. Kagan (vn), S. Richter (pno) *(rec Moscow, May 7, 1978)* ("Oleg Kagan Edition, Vol. X") † Son Vn & Pno, Op. 11/1; Son Vn & Pno, Op. 11/2; Son Vn in E LV ▲ 161 [ADD] (17.97)

I. Stern (vn), A. Zakin (pno) ("Isaac Stern: A Life In Music: Vol. 28") † E. Bloch:Baal Shem; Son 1 Vn; A. Copland:Son Vn SNYC ▲ 64533 [ADD] (10.97)

U. Wallin (vn), R. Pöntinen (pno) *(rec Stockholm Sweden, Aug 22-25, 1995)* ("The Complete Violin Sonatas") † Son Vn & Pno, Op. 11/1; Son Vn & Pno, Op. 11/2; Son Vn in E BIS ▲ 761 [DDD] (17.97)

Sonata in E for Violin & Piano (1935)

I. Bieler (vn), K. Randalu (pno) *(rec Oct 2 & Dec 8-9, 1996 & June 29, 1997)* ("Complete Sonatas, Vol. 2") † Kleine Son Va, Op. 25/2; Son Va & Pno in C; Son Va & Pno, Op. 25/4; Son Vn in C MDG ▲ 3040692 [DDD] (17.97)

V. Gluzman (vn), A. Yoffe (pno) *(rec Astoria, NY, Mar 27-28, 1995)* † Beethoven:Son 1 Vn; J. Brahms:Son 3 Vn, Op. 108 KOCH ▲ 7323 [DDD] (16.97)

O. Kagan (vn), S. Richter (pno) *(rec Moscow, May 7, 1978)* ("Oleg Kagan Edition, Vol. X") † Son Vn & Pno, Op. 11/1; Son Vn & Pno, Op. 11/2; Son Vn in C LV ▲ 161 [ADD] (17.97)

G. Poulet (vn), C. Ivaldi (pno) ("Oeuvres de musique de chambre") † Son Fl; Son Pnos; Son Vc & Pno ARN ▲ 68319 (16.97)

U. Wallin (vn), R. Pöntinen (pno) *(rec Stockholm Sweden, Aug 22-25, 1995)* ("The Complete Violin Sonatas") † Son Vn & Pno, Op. 11/1; Son Vn & Pno, Op. 11/2; Son Vn in C BIS ▲ 761 [DDD] (17.97)

Sonata in E♭ for Violin & Piano, Op. 11/1 (1918)

I. Bieler (vn), K. Randalu (pno) ("Complete Sonatas, Vol. 1") † Son Va; Son Vc & Pno, Op. 11/3; Son Vn & Pno, Op. 11/2 MDG ▲ 3040691 (17.97)

P. Hirschhorn (vn), L. Petcherskaya (pno) *(rec live, Palais des Beaux-Arts, Brussels, Belgium, June 7, 1967)* † J. S. Bach:Sons & Partitas Vn; B. Bartók:Son Vn; Geminiani:Sons Vn, Op. 4; D. Milhaud:Boeuf sur le toit, Op. 58; M. Ravel:Tzigane; Saint-Saëns:Étude Pno, Op. 52/6 CYPR ▲ 9606 (17.97)

A. Jennings (vn), S. Bruhn (pno) † Son Db; Son Va; Son Vc & Pno, Op. 11/3; Son Vl EQLB ▲ 11 [DDD] (16.97)

O. Kagan (vn), S. Richter (pno) *(rec Moscow, May 7, 1978)* ("Oleg Kagan Edition, Vol. X") † Son Vn & Pno, Op. 11/2; Son Vn in C; Son Vn in E LV ▲ 161 [ADD] (17.97)

G. Kremer (vn), A. Gavrilov (pno) ("Gidon Kramer Plays Great Violin Concertos") † J. Brahms:Con Vn; A. Schnittke:Son 2 Vn; R. Schumann:Con Vn; Sibelius:Con Vn; C. M. von Weber:Grand Duo Concertant, J.204 EMIC 2-▲ 69334 (16.97)

U. Wallin (vn), R. Pöntinen (pno) *(rec Stockholm Sweden, Aug 22-25, 1995)* ("The Complete Violin Sonatas") † Son Vn & Pno, Op. 11/2; Son Vn in C; Son Vn in E BIS ▲ 761 [DDD] (17.97)

Sonata in D for Violin & Piano, Op. 11/2 (1918)

I. Bieler (vn), K. Randalu (pno) ("Complete Sonatas, Vol. 1") † Son Va; Son Vc & Pno, Op. 11/3; Son Vn & Pno, Op. 11/1 MDG ▲ 3040691 (17.97)

O. Kagan (vn), S. Richter (pno) *(rec Moscow, May 7, 1978)* ("Oleg Kagan Edition, Vol. X") † Son Vn & Pno, Op. 11/1; Son Vn in C; Son Vn in E LV ▲ 161 [ADD] (17.97)

U. Wallin (vn), R. Pöntinen (pno) *(rec Stockholm Sweden, Aug 22-25, 1995)* ("The Complete Violin Sonatas") † Son Vn & Pno, Op. 11/1; Son Vn in C; Son Vn in E BIS ▲ 761 [DDD] (17.97)

Songs

J. Banse (sop), A. Bauni (pno)—34 sels including Lieder mit Klavier, Op. 18; Gesang; Vier Lieder nach Texten des Angelus Silesius; Abendständchen; Singet leise; Wer wusste je das Leben; Der Einsiedler; Du bist mein; Zum Abscheid meiner Tochter; Ich will Trauern lassen stehn; Abendwolke ORF ▲ 413961 [DDD] (18.97)

D. Fischer-Dieskau (bar), A. Reimann (pno)—19 songs: Sonnenuntergang; The wild flower's song; The moon; Sing on there in the swamp; On hearing "The Last rose of Summer"; Ehemals und jetzt; Brautgesang; Singet leise; Das ganze, nicht das Einzelne; Des Morgens; Fragment; Der Tod; Ich will nicht klagen mehr; Hymne; Abendphantasie; O, nun heb du an, dort in deinem Moor (1919); Vor dir schein' ich aufgewacht (1920); Die Sonne sinkt; An die Parzen [E,G] ORF ▲ 156861 [DDD] (18.97)

R. Ziesak (sop)—Lieder mit Klavier, Op. 18; Lustige Lieder in Aargauer Mundart, Op. 5; English Songs (2); Songs (2) after Oscar Cox; Das Marienleben (6 orchestral songs), Op. 27 *(rec Jan-Aug 1995)* ("Orchestral Songs & Lieder") CPO ▲ 999331 [DDD] (13.97)

Songs on Old Texts (5) for Chorus (1936)

U. Gronostay (cnd), Danish National Radio Choir † Lieder nach alten Texten, Op. 33; Madrigals; Mass CHN ▲ 9413 [DDD] (16.97)

S. Parkman (cnd), Berlin Radio Chorus † Canons; Chansons; Madrigals WER (Edition Paul Hindemith) ▲ 6629 (19.97)

Stücke (4) for Bassoon & Cello (1941)

R. Christensen (vc), O. Eifert (bn) † Son Vc; Trio 1; Trio 2 GAS ▲ 1009 (11.97)

Stücke (5) for String Orchestra, Op. 44/4

E. Aadland (cnd), European Community CO *(rec July 1991)* † S. Barber:Adagio Strs; B. Bartók:Romanian Folk Dances Pno, Sz.56; B. Britten:Simple Sym, Op. 4; G. Puccini:Crisantemi INMP ▲ 1001 [DDD] (11.97)

E. Aadland (cnd), European Community CO † S. Barber:Adagio Strs; B. Bartók:Romanian Folk Dances Pno, Sz.56; B. Britten:Simple Sym, Op. 4; G. Puccini:Crisantemi; Warlock:Capriol Suite IMPA ▲ 2044 (9.97)

W. A. Albert (cnd), Tasmanian SO *(rec Government House Ballroom Hobart/Tasmanien, Apr & Sept 1994)* ("Orchestral Music") † Kammermusik 1, Op. 24/1; Music of Hindemith; Suite of French Dances CPO ▲ 999301 [DDD] (13.97)

K. Mannberg (cnd), Dalecarlian CO † G. Holst:St. Paul's Suite, Op. 29/2; M. Reger:Lyrisches Andante; J. S. Svendsen:Romance Vn, Op. 26; Warlock:Capriol Suite BLUB ▲ 3007 (18.97)

Stücke (8) for String Quintet, Op. 44/3

Vienna String Quintet *(rec Fuchu-no-Mori Art Theater Wien Hall, Jan 12, 1992)* † A. Dvořák:Qnt Strs, Op. 77; Waltzes Strs, Op. 54 CAMA ▲ 242 [DDD] (18.97)

Suite of French Dances for Orchestra

W. A. Albert (cnd), Tasmanian SO *(rec Government House Ballroom Hobart/Tasmanien, Apr & Sept 1994)* ("Orchestral Music") † Kammermusik 1, Op. 24/1; Music of Hindemith; Stücke (5) Str Orch, Op. 44/4 CPO ▲ 999301 [DDD] (13.97)

Suite "1922" for Piano, Op. 26 (1922)

J. McCabe (pno) † Ludus Tonalis HYP ▲ 66824 (18.97)

Symphonia serena for Orchestra (1946)

W. A. Albert (cnd), Sydney SO *(rec Apr & Aug 1992)* ("Paul Hindemith: Orchestral Works, Vol. 5") † Mathis der Maler (sym); When Lilacs Last in the Dooryard Bloom'd CPO ▲ 999008 [DDD] (14.97)

H. Kegel (cnd), Dresden PO † Con Tpt, Bn & Strs; Mathis der Maler (sym); Nobilissima visione; Sym Orch BER 2-▲ 9054 (21.97)

J. P. Tortelier (cnd), BBC PO † Harmonie der Welt CHN ▲ 9217 [DDD] (16.97)

B. Walter (cnd), Philharmonic SO *(rec New York, United States of America, Feb 15, 1948)* † A. Dvořák:Sym 8; Mendelssohn (-Bartholdy):Hebriden, Op. 26 MUA ▲ 4714 (live) [AAD] (10.97)

Symphonic Metamorphosis on Themes of Carl Maria von Weber for Orchestra (1943)

C. Abbado (cnd), Berlin PO † Mathis der Maler (sym); Nobilissima visione DGRM ▲ 447389 [DDD] (18.97)

W. A. Albert (cnd), Queensland SO ("Orchestral Works, Vol. 1") † Cupid & Psyche; Nobilissima visione; Philharmonisches Konzert CPO ▲ 999004 [DDD] (14.97)

L. Bernstein (cnd), New York PO *(rec 1968)* † Concert Music Brass & Strs, Op. 50; Sym Orch SNYC (Bernstein: The Royal Edition) ▲ 47566 [ADD] (10.97)

E. Corporon (cnd), North Texas College of Music Wind Sym [arr Keith Wilson for winds] ("Luminaries") † Y. Ito:Gloriosa; D. Shostakovich:Folk Dances; Preludes Pno, Op. 34; Whitacre:Ghost Train Triptych KLAV ▲ 11077 [DDD] (18.97)

F. Decker (cnd), New Zealand SO *(rec Wellington New Zealand, Apr 1994)* † Mathis der Maler (sym); Nobilissima visione NXIN ▲ 553078 [DDD] (5.97)

N. Järvi (cnd), Philharmonia Orch † C. M. von Weber:Ovs; Turandot, Prinzessin von China (sels) CHN ▲ 8766 [DDD] (16.97)

R. Kubelík (cnd), Chicago SO † B. Bartók:Miraculous Mandarin (suite), Op. 19; Kodály:Vars on a Hungarian Folk Song; Schoenberg:Pieces Orch, Op. 16 MRCR ▲ 434397 (11.97)

HINDEMITH, PAUL (cont.)

Symphonic Metamorphosis on Themes of Carl Maria von Weber for Orchestra (1943) (cont.)

Y. Levi (cnd), Atlanta SO † Mathis der Maler (sym); Nobilissima visione TEL ▲ 80195 [DDD] (16.97)
W. Sawallisch (cnd), Philadelphia Orch † Mathis der Maler (sym); Nobilissima visione EMIC ▲ 55230 (16.97)
G. Szell (cnd), Cleveland Orch *(rec Oct 10, 1964)* † Mathis der Maler (sym); W. Walton:Vars on a Theme by Hindemith SNYC ▲ 53258 (7.97)

Symphonische Tänze [Symphonic Dances] for Orchestra (1937)

W. A. Albert (cnd), Queensland SO ("Orchestral Works, Vol. 2") † Lustige Sinfonietta, Op. 4; Rag Time CPO ▲ 999005 [DDD] (14.97)
J. Serebrier (cnd), Philharmonia Orch † Con Orch, Op. 38; Con Vn; Kammermusik 4, Op. 36/3; Rag Time ASV ▲ 945 [DDD] (16.97)
J. P. Tortelier (cnd), BBC PO † Pittsburgh Sym; Rag Time CHN ▲ 9530 (16.97)

Symphony in B♭ for Concert Band (1951)

W. A. Albert (cnd), Melbourne SO *(rec Oct-Nov 1989)* † Neues vom Tage (concert ov); Sym Orch CPO ▲ 999007 (14.97)
E. Corporon (cnd), Cincinnati Wind SO ("Paradigm") † D. W. Freund:Jug Blues & Fat Pickin'; Gregson:Sword & the Crown; J. Harbison:3 City Blocks; B. Rands:Ceremonial; I. Stravinsky:Circus Polka KLAV ▲ 11059 (18.97)

Symphony in E♭ for Orchestra (1940)

W. A. Albert (cnd), Melbourne SO *(rec Oct-Nov 1989)* † Neues vom Tage (concert ov); Sym Concert Band CPO ▲ 999007 (14.97)
L. Bernstein (cnd), New York PO *(rec 1967)* † Concert Music Brass & Strs, Op. 50; Symphonic Metamorphosis on Themes of Carl Maria vo SNYC (Bernstein: The Royal Edition) ▲ 47566 [ADD] (10.97)
A. Boult (cnd), London PO † Con Vn EVC ▲ 9009 [AAD] (13.97)
W. Furtwängler (cnd), Berlin PO *(rec Berlin, Germany, Dec 8, 1952)* † Con Orch, Op. 38; I. Stravinsky:Baiser de la fée MUA ▲ 4713 (10.97)
H. Kegel (cnd), Dresden PO † Con Tpt, Bn & Strs; Mathis der Maler (sym); Nobilissima visione; Symphonia serena BER 2-▲ 9054 (21.97)
Y. P. Tortelier (cnd), BBC PO † Neues vom Tage (concert ov); Nobilissima visione CHN ▲ 9060 [DDD] (16.97)

Tanzstücke for Piano, Op. 19 (1920)

J. Ernst (pno) ("Leÿptziger Allerleÿ") † Musikalisches Blumengärtlein; Son Cl; Son Db TACE ▲ 59
S. Mauser (pno) ("Das Klavierwerk, Vol. V") † Klaviermusik Book 1, Op. 37 WER ▲ 6271 (19.97)

Des Todes Tod for Female Voice, 2 Violas & 2 Cellos [text Reinacher], Op. 23a (1922)

C. Oelze (sop), Villa Musica Ensemble ("Vocal Chamber Music") † Junge Magd, Op. 23/2; Melancholie, Op. 13; Serenaden, Op. 35; Wie es wär', wenn's anders wär MDG ▲ 3040535 [DDD] (17.97)

Trauermusik for Viola (or Violin, or Cello) & String Orchestra (1936)

M. Brunello (vc), M. Brunello (cnd), Italian String Orch † A. Piazzolla:Adiós Nonino; G. Rossini:Péchés de vieillesse (sels); Sollima:Violincelles Vibrez!; Takemitsu:Scene Vc; P. Tchaikovsky:Andante cantabile; Nocturne Vc AG ▲ 155 (18.97)
P. Cortese (va), M. Brabbins (cnd), Philharmonia Orch ("Complete Works for Viola, Vol. 3") † Meditation ASV ▲ 978 (16.97)
R. Golani (va), A. Davis (cnd), Toronto SO † E. Bloch:Suite hébraïque; B. Britten:Lachrymae, Op. 48; Colgrass:Chaconne Va SMS (SM 5000) ▲ 5087 [DDD] (16.97)
E. Shumsky (va), J. Shames (pno) † Son Va; J. Beale:Ballade, Op. 47; E. Bloch:Suite hébraïque; F. Kreisler:Praeludium & Allegro Va AMBA ▲ 1011 [DDD] (16.97)
W. Strehle (va), K. Wisniewska (pno) [arr for va & pno] † Duet Va & Vc; Son Va; J. Brahms:Son 1 Cl; A. Dvořák:Sonatina Vn, Op. 100 NIMB ▲ 5473 [DDD] (16.97)
T. Thedéen (vc), L. Markiz (cnd), Amsterdam New Sinfonietta *(rec 1996-97)* ("Cello Music") † Kammermusik 3, Op. 36/2; Son Vc & Pno; Son Vc & Pno, Op. 11/3 BIS ▲ 816 [DDD] (17.97)

Trio for Piano, Viola & Heckelphone (or Tenor Saxophone), Op. 47 (1928)

Arnold Wind Quintet, Stauffer String Quartet members † Octet Winds & Strs; Spt Ww & Tpt STRV ▲ 33435 [DDD] (16.97)
G. Teuffel (va), L. Lencsés (heckelphone), S. Rudiakov (pno) ("Hindemith's Works for Oboe") † Serenaden, Op. 35; Son E Hn; Son Ob CPO ▲ 999332 (14.97)
Villa Musica Ensemble † Qt Cl; Son Hns MDG ▲ 3040537 [DDD] (17.97)

Trio for 3 Recorders [from Plöner Musiktag] (1932)

Musica Dolce members *(rec Wik Castle, Sweden, Dec 18, 1976)* ("P. Hindemith: Chamber Music") † Morgenmusik; Son Bass Tuba; Son Bn; Son Hn; Son Tpt; Son Trbn BIS ▲ 159 [AAD/DDD] (17.97)

Trio No. 1 for Violin, Viola & Cello, Op. 34 (1924)

L'Atelier String Trio † Son Vc; Stücke (4) Bn & Vc; Trio 2 GAS ▲ 1009 (11.97)
Notre Dame String Trio *(rec South Bend, IN, Oct 1995)* † Scherzo Va & Vc; Trio 2 CENT ▲ 2314 [DDD] (16.97)

Trio No. 2 for Violin, Viola & Cello (1933)

S. Goldberg (vn), P. Hindemith (va), E. Feuermann (vc) *(rec 1927-34)* † Mathis der Maler (sym); Qt 3 Strs, Op. 22 KSCH ▲ 311342 [DDD] (16.97)
S. Goldberg (vn), P. Hindemith (va), E. Feuermann (vc) *(rec Jan 1934)* † Scherzo Va & Vc; Son Va; Beethoven:Serenade Str Trio, Op. 8 MTAL ▲ 48024 (6.97)
L'Atelier String Trio † Son Vc; Stücke (4) Bn & Vc; Trio 1 GAS ▲ 1009 (11.97)
Notre Dame String Trio *(rec South Bend, IN, Oct 1995)* † Scherzo Va & Vc; Trio 1 CENT ▲ 2314 [DDD] (16.97)

Tuttifäntchen (Christmas fairy tale in 3 scenes) [text H. Michel & F. Becker] (1922)

A. Myrat (cnd), La Camerata Friends of Music Orch, Kontogeorghiou (cnd), Greek Radio-TV Choir † Saint-Saëns:Oratorio de Noël, Op. 12 AG ▲ 129 (18.97)

Tuttifäntchen:Suite

J. P. Tortelier (cnd), BBC PO † Nusch-Nuschi Dances, Op. 20; Sancta Susanna, Op. 21 CHN ▲ 9620 (16.97)

Das Unaufhörliche (oratorio) for Soprano, Tenor, Baritone, Bass, Orchestra & Chorus [after Gottfried Benn] (1931)

U. Sonntag (sop), R. Wörle (ten), S. Lorenz (bar), A. Korn (bass), L. Zagrosek (cnd), Berlin RSO, Berlin Radio Chorus WER 2-▲ 6603 (38.97)

Variations for Piano (1936)

K. Randalu (pno) *(rec Sept 7 & Oct 21, 1997)* ("Complete Sonatas, Vol. 3") † Sons Pno MDG ▲ 3040693 [DDD] (17.97)

When Lilacs Last in the Dooryard Bloom'd: A Requiem for Those We Love for Mezzo-Soprano, Baritone, Orchestra & Chorus [text Whitman] (1946)

W. A. Albert (cnd), Sydney SO *(rec Apr & Aug 1992)* ("Paul Hindemith: Orchestral Works, Vol. 5") † Mathis der Maler (sym); Symphonia serena CPO ▲ 999008 [DDD] (14.97)
A. Burmeister (mez), G. Leib (bass), H. Koch (cnd), Berlin RSO, Berlin Radio Chorus BER ▲ 9170 (10.97)
J. DeGaetani (mez), W. Stone (bar), R. Shaw (cnd), Atlanta SO, Atlanta Sym Chorus [ENG] TEL ▲ 80132 [DDD] (16.97)
B. Fassbaender (mez), D. Fischer-Dieskau (bar), W. Sawallisch (cnd), Vienna SO, Vienna State Opera Chorus [ENG] *(rec live, Nov 1, 1983)* ORF ▲ 112851 [DDD] (18.97)
P. Hindemith (cnd), Vienna SO, Vienna State Opera Chorus, E. Höngen (cta), H. Braun (bar) *(rec 1956)* TUXE ▲ 1061 [ADD] (10.97)
C. Kallisch (cta), K. St. Hill (bar), L. Zagrosek (cnd), Berlin RSO, Berlin Radio Sym Chorus WER ▲ 6286 (19.97)

Wie es wär', wenn's anders wär for solo Voice & Ensemble (ca 1918)

C. Oelze (sop), Villa Musica Ensemble ("Vocal Chamber Music") † Des Todes Tod, Op. 23a; Junge Magd, Op. 23/2; Melancholie, Op. 13; Serenaden, Op. 35 MDG ▲ 3040535 [DDD] (17.97)

HINTON, ALISTAIR (20th cent)

Pansophiae for John Ogdon for Organ

K. Bowyer (org) *(rec Org of St. Mary Redcliffe Bristol)* † Busoni:Elegien Pno; Fant contrappuntistica Pno; Fant nach J. S. Bach; J. Ogdon:Dance Suite; R. Stevenson:Prelude & Fugue on Liszt; Sonatina 1 Pno ALTA 2-▲ 9063 (38.97)

Variations & Fugue on a Theme of Grieg for Piano

D. Amato (pno) † Sorabji:Variazione maliziosa e perversa; R. Stevenson:Pno Music ALTA ▲ 9021

HIRAI (dates unknown)

Nara-Yama for Chamber Ensemble

H. Naka (db), M. Nakagawa (fl), P. Zander (hpd), S. Yoshiwara (perc), M. Mamiya (cnd), Pro Musica Nipponia [arr Mamiya] *(rec Japan)* ("Japanese Melodies") † Anonymous:Chiran-Bushi; Matsushime-Ondo; Oroku-Musume; Zui-Zui-Zukkorobashi; Konoe:Chin-Chin Chidori; Sugiyama:Defune; Taki:Kojo-No-Tsuki; Traditional:Sakura, Sakura; K. Yamada:Chugoku-Chiho-No-Komoriuta SNYC ▲ 39703 (16.97)

HIRAI, KOZABURO (1910-

Sonata for Koto & Flute (1949-56)

K. Asawa (fl), K. Kudo (koto) † Miyagi:Haru no Umi; Izumi; T. Sawai:Flower; H. Yamamoto:Ichikotsu CRYS ▲ 316 [DDD] (15.97) ▮ 316 [DDD] (9.98)

HIRAO, KISHIO (1907-

Sonata for Violin & Piano (1947)

S. Numata (vn), A. Tadenuma (pno) *(rec July 1997)* ("Japanese Music for Violin & Piano") † K. Kishi:Pieces Vn; H. Otaka:Son Vn; K. Yamada:Chanson triste japonaise; Karatchi no hana CAMA ▲ 30477 [DDD] (18.97)

HIROSE, RYOHEI (1930-

Asura for Violin (1975)

H. Umehara (vn) *(rec 1989-96)* ("Works of Ryohei Hirose") † Élégia Hp; Clima II; Con Shak; Con Vn; Kalavinka; Meditation; Potalaka; Pundarika; Son Fl; Ten Night's Dreams CAMA 2-▲ 25516 [DDD] (34.97)

Clima II for Orchestra (1988)

K. Yamashita (cnd), Tokyo PO *(rec 1989-96)* ("Works of Ryohei Hirose") † Élégia Hp; Asura; Con Shak; Con Vn; Kalavinka; Meditation; Potalaka; Pundarika; Son Fl; Ten Night's Dreams CAMA 2-▲ 25516 [DDD] (34.97)

Concerto for Shakuhachi & Orchestra (1976)

K. Mitsuhashi (shak), S. Araya (cnd), Tokyo PO *(rec 1989-96)* ("Works of Ryohei Hirose") † Élégia Hp; Asura; Clima II; Con Vn; Kalavinka; Meditation; Potalaka; Pundarika; Son Fl; Ten Night's Dreams CAMA 2-▲ 25516 [DDD] (34.97)

Concerto for Violin & Orchestra (1979)

Y. Kuronuma (vn), S. Araya (cnd), Tokyo PO *(rec 1989-96)* ("Works of Ryohei Hirose") † Élégia Hp; Asura; Clima II; Con Shak; Kalavinka; Meditation; Potalaka; Pundarika; Son Fl; Ten Night's Dreams CAMA 2-▲ 25516 [DDD] (34.97)

Élégia for Harp (1994)

Y. Miura (hp) *(rec 1989-96)* ("Works of Ryohei Hirose") † Asura; Clima II; Con Shak; Con Vn; Kalavinka; Meditation; Potalaka; Pundarika; Son Fl; Ten Night's Dreams CAMA 2-▲ 25516 [DDD] (34.97)

Hymn for Recorder (1979-82)

D. Laurin (rcr) *(rec Nov 27-29, 1993)* † Meditation; M. Ishii:east*green*spring; Black Intention; Matsumoto:Pastorale; M. Shinohara:Fragmente Rcr BIS ▲ 655 [DDD] (17.97)

Kalavinka for Recorder, Oboe, Strings & Percussion (1973)

M. Kugota (vn), Y. Yamamoto (va), T. Saito (vc), S. Yamaoka (rcr), H. Kureyama (ob), M. Taneya (perc), T. Yamamoto (perc), H. Takeda (cnd) *(rec 1989-96)* ("Works of Ryohei Hirose") † Élégia Hp; Asura; Clima II; Con Shak; Con Vn; Meditation; Potalaka; Pundarika; Son Fl; Ten Night's Dreams CAMA 2-▲ 25516 [DDD] (34.97)

Meditation for Recorder

D. Laurin (rcr) *(rec Nov 27-29, 1993)* † Hymn; M. Ishii:east*green*spring; Black Intention; Matsumoto:Pastorale; M. Shinohara:Fragmente Rcr BIS ▲ 655 [DDD] (17.97)
S. Yamaoka (rcr) *(rec 1989-96)* ("Works of Ryohei Hirose") † Élégia Hp; Asura; Clima II; Con Shak; Con Vn; Kalavinka; Potalaka; Pundarika; Son Fl; Ten Night's Dreams CAMA 2-▲ 25516 [DDD] (34.97)

Potalaka for Recorder, Cello & Harp (1972)

T. Saito (vc), S. Yamaoka (rcr), E. Nishigaki (hp) *(rec 1989-96)* ("Works of Ryohei Hirose") † Élégia Hp; Asura; Clima II; Con Shak; Con Vn; Kalavinka; Meditation; Pundarika; Son Fl; Ten Night's Dreams CAMA 2-▲ 25516 [DDD] (34.97)

Pundarika for Clarinet & Piano (1972)

T. Morita (cl), A. Jinzai (pno) *(rec 1989-96)* ("Works of Ryohei Hirose") † Élégia Hp; Asura; Clima II; Con Shak; Con Vn; Kalavinka; Meditation; Potalaka; Son Fl; Ten Night's Dreams CAMA 2-▲ 25516 [DDD] (34.97)

Sonata for Flute & Piano (1964)

N. Shimizu (fl), A. Jinzai (pno) *(rec 1989-96)* ("Works of Ryohei Hirose") † Élégia Hp; Asura; Clima II; Con Shak; Con Vn; Kalavinka; Meditation; Potalaka; Pundarika; Ten Night's Dreams CAMA 2-▲ 25516 [DDD] (34.97)

Ten Night's Dreams for Chamber Ensemble (1973)

Pro Musica Nipponia *(rec 1989-96)* ("Works of Ryohei Hirose") † Élégia Hp; Asura; Clima II; Con Shak; Con Vn; Kalavinka; Meditation; Potalaka; Pundarika; Son Fl CAMA 2-▲ 25516 [DDD] (34.97)

HIRSCHFELDER, DAVID (20th cent)

Shine (film music) for Orchestra (1996)

artists unknown PPHI ▲ 54710 (17.97) ▮ 54710 (11.98)

HISCOCKS, WENDY (20th cent)

The Piper at the Gates of Dawn (suite) for Piano (1995)

J. Carrigan (pno) *(rec Univ of Queensland, Australia)* ("But I Want the Harmonica: Australian Contemporary Piano Music") † Broadstock:Aureole 4; Conyngham:ppp; S. Greenbaum:But I Want the Harmonica; Kats-Chernin:Purple Prelude; Sabin:Another Look at Autumn; Spiers:Elegy & Toccata Pno VOXA ▲ 23 [DDD] (18.97)

HISCOTT, JIM (1948-

Romantic Nights for Viola & 2 Percussionists (1993)

R. Golani (va), R. Scott (perc), C. Huang (perc) † Colgrass:Vars Drs & Va; C. P. Harman:Son Va; D. McIntosh:Nanuk CTR ▲ 5798 [DDD] (16.97)

HJÁLMAR, HELGI RAGNARSSON (1952-

Two Etudes (in Black & White) for Solo Flute

M. Wiesler (fl) *(rec Furuby Church, Sweden, June 1989)* ("To Manuela") † Atli:Pieces (12) from 21 Sounding Minutes Fl; Leifur:Fl Music; Magnús:Fl Music; T. Sigurbjörnsson:Fl Music BIS ▲ 456 [DDD] (17.97)

HO, FRED WEI-HAN (20th cent)

Act Up! Before It's Too Late! for Ensemble (1991)

F. Ho (cnd) , F. Ho (cnd), Afro-Asian Music Ensemble ("Turn Pain into Power") † Earth Is Rockin' in Revolution/Drowning in the Yel; Turn Pain into Power!; What's A Girl to Do? OOD ▲ 30 [DDD] (16.97)

Bon for Chamber Ensemble

C. Sun (vn), W. Sung (cl), C. Lee (bn), C. Chen (trbn), C. Lee (hp), B. Yeh (perc), L. Wu (perc), H. Two (cnd) ("Society of Composers, Inc.-Transcendencies") † Z. Browning:Breakpoint Screamer; Cotel:Quatrains; J. Fortner:Symphonies; Hankinson:Light/Shadow; Sanchez-Gutierrez:M.E. in Memoriam; Sheffer:Con Sax CPS ▲ 8656 (16.97)

Contradiction, Please! The Revenge of Charlie Chan for Chamber Ensemble (1992)

Relâche Ensemble ("Outcome Inevitable") † R. Ashley:Outcome Inevitable; Hovda:Borealis Music; Vierk:Timberline OOD ▲ 17 [DDD] (16.97)

The Earth Is Rockin' in Revolution/Drowning in the Yellow River for Vocals & Ensemble [text Janice Mirikitani]

F. Ho (cnd) , F. Ho (cnd), Afro-Asian Music Ensemble ("Turn Pain into Power") † Act Up! Before It's Too Late!; Turn Pain into Power!; What's A Girl to Do? OOD ▲ 30 [DDD] (16.97)

Turn Pain into Power! (suite) for 2 Narrators & Ensemble (1992)

A. Villegas (nar), E. Iverem (nar), F. Ho (cnd) , F. Ho (cnd), Afro-Asian Music Ensemble ("Turn Pain into Power") † Act Up! Before It's Too Late!; Earth Is Rockin' in Revolution/Drowning in the Yel; What's A Girl to Do? OOD ▲ 30 [DDD] (16.97)

What's a Girl to Do? for Vocals & Ensemble [text Janice Mirikitani]

F. Ho (cnd) , F. Ho (cnd), Afro-Asian Music Ensemble ("Turn Pain into Power") † Act Up! Before It's Too Late!; Earth Is Rockin' in Revolution/Drowning in the Yel; Turn Pain into Power! OOD ▲ 30 [DDD] (16.97)

HO ZHAN HAO (20th cent)**& CHEN KANG** (20th cent)

Butterfly Lovers' Concerto for Violin & Orchestra

Vanessa-Mae (vn), V. Fedotov (cnd), London PO ("China Girl: Classical Album 2") † Vanessa-Mae:Fant Vn on Puccini; Happy Valley ANGL ▲ 56483 [DDD] (16.97) ▮ 56483 [DDD] (9.98)

HOAG, CHARLES (1931-

Inventions on the Summer Solstice for Clarinet, Violin & Piano (1979)

Verdehr Trio † Bassett:Trio Cl; Bruch:Pieces Cl, Op. 83; K. Hoover:Images LEON ▲ 326 (16.97)

HOBSON, BRUCE (1943-

Concerto for Orchestra

S. Kawalla (cnd), Slovak RSO Bratislava † J. Fortner:Concertpiece; D. A. Jaffe:Whoop for Your Life!; Jazwinski:Sequenze Concertanti; P. Moss:Valses VMM ▲ 3024 [DDD]

Three for 2 Trumpets & Orchestra (1976)

L. Strešnák (tpt), P. La Garde (tpt), S. Kawalla (cnd), Slovak RSO Bratislava † Konowalski:Brewerie; Loeb:Suite Concertante; T. Myers:Concertino Orch; R. Snyder:Shamanic Dances; K. Steen:Metastasis; G. W. Yasinitsky:Into a Star VMM (Music from 6 Continents 1993) ▲ 3017 [DDD]

HODDINOTT, ALUN (1929-

Chorales, Variants & Fanfares for Organ & Brass Ensemble (1992)

K. Bowyer (org), Fine Arts Brass Ensemble ("Summer Dances") † Quodlibet; Ritornelli for Brass, Op. 100/2; W. Mathias:Soundings; Summer Dances NIMB ▲ 5466 (16.97)

Orchestral Music

H. Kun (vn), D. Cowley (ob), R. Armstrong (hpd), T. Otaka (cnd), BBC Welsh SO—Passaggio, Op. 94 (1977); The Heaventree of Stars (poem) for Vn & Orch, Op. 102; Doubles (concertante) for Ob, Str Orch & Hpd, Op. 106; Star Children, Op. 135 (1989) *(rec 1992)* NIMB ▲ 5357 [DDD] (16.97)

Quodlibet on Welsh Nursery Tunes for Brass Ensemble (1983)

Fine Arts Brass Ensemble ("Summer Dances") † Chorales, Variants & Fanfares; Ritornelli for Brass, Op. 100/2; W. Mathias:Soundings; Summer Dances NIMB ▲ 5466 (16.97)

Ritornelli for Brass Ensemble, Op. 100/2 (1979)

Fine Arts Brass Ensemble ("Summer Dances") † Chorales, Variants & Fanfares; Quodlibet; W. Mathias:Soundings; Summer Dances NIMB ▲ 5466 (16.97)

HODGES, JOHN (COOL WHITE) (dates unknown)
Buffalo Gals (1844)
D. Warland (cnd), Dale Warland Singers, S. Staruch (ten) [arr. Parker] *(rec Univ. of St. Thomas, St. Paul, MN, Aug & Nov 1995)* ("Blue Wheat: A Harvest of American Folk Songs") † H. T. Burleigh:Songs; S. C. Foster:Songs; Traditional:Black Is the Color; Black Sheep; He's Goin' Away; Johnny Has Gone for a Soldier; My Lord, What a Mornin'; Oh, Shenandoah; Poor Wayfaring Stranger; Pretty Saro; Red River Valley; Single Girl; Skip to My Lou; Soldier, Soldier Won't You Marry Me?; Steal Away; Water Is Wide *(E text)* AME ▲ 122 [DDD] (13.97)

HODKINSON, SYDNEY (1934-
Alte Liebeslieder (song cycle) for Voice, Oboe, Cello, Piano & Percussion (1981)
J. DeGaetani (mez), P. West (ob), R. Spillman (pno), R. Sylvester (pno), J. Beck (perc), S. Hodkinson (cnd) ("Eastman American Music Series, Vol. 5") † Maccombie:Leaden Echo, Golden Echo; S. Walden:Some Changes ALBA ▲ 261 [ADD] (16.97)
Chansons de Jadis (6) [Songs of Loneliness] for Voice & Chamber Orchestra (1978-79)
R. Fleming (sop), P. Phillips (cnd), Eastern Connecticut SO [ENG] † Missa brevis CENT ▲ 2073 [DDD] (16.97)
The Edge of the Olde One (chamber concerto) for Electric English Horn, Strings & Percussion (1977)
T. Stacy (E hn), P. Phillips (cnd), Eastman Musica Nova ("Three Concerti") † Persichetti:Con E Hn; N. Rorem:Con E Hn NWW ▲ 80489 (16.97)
Missa brevis for Orchestra & Chorus (1978)
P. Phillips (cnd), Eastern Connecticut SO, Univ of Connecticut Concert Choir [LAT] † Chansons de Jadis CENT ▲ 2073 [DDD] (16.97)

HOEDT, HENRY GEORGES D' (1885-1936)
Chroniques breves de la vie bourgeoise (rhapsody) for Orchestra
A. Rahbari (cnd), Brussels BRTN PO *(rec Magdalena Hall, Brussels, Belgium, Mar 1995)* † Alpaerts:James Ensor Suite; A. Meulemans:Plinius Fontein DI ▲ 920321 [DDD] (5.97)
Dialogue (De L'Improvisateur et du Ménétrier) for Flute & Piano
C. Bruneel (fl), L. Kende (pno) ("In Flanders' Fields, Vol. 10") † Romance; C. Franck:Son Vn, M.8; J. Jongen:Son Fl PHA ▲ 92010 [DDD] (13.97)
Romance for Flute & Piano
C. Bruneel (fl), L. Kende (pno) ("In Flanders' Fields, Vol. 10") † Dialogue; C. Franck:Son Vn, M.8; J. Jongen:Son Fl PHA ▲ 92010 [DDD] (13.97)

HOEKMAN, TIMOTHY (1954-
Margarets for 2 Voices & Piano (1994)
T. Rhodes (sop), E. Williams (mez), T. Hoekman (pno) ("To Sun, to Feast & to Converse: American Vocal Duet Music") † Hoiby:Bermudas; S. Jaffe:Fort Juniper Songs; Kouneva:Aeon; R. Ward:Lady Kate (sels); Roman Fever (sels) ALBA ▲ 172 [DDD] (16.97)

HØFFDING, (NIELS) FINN (1899-1997)
Diapsalmata (4) for Chorus [texts from Kirkegaard's Either/Or]
M. Bojesen (cnd), Camerata Chamber Choir ("Kirkegaard Set to Music") † S. Barber:Prayers of Kierkegaard, Op. 30; N. V. Bentzon:Johannes the Seducer; H. Boatwright:Prayers of Kirkegaard; Bojesen:Choral Music; J. Frandsen:Motets (2); Songs *(Da,E texts)* DANI ▲ 8184 [DDD] (18.97)

HOFFMAN, JOEL (1953-
Duo for Viola & Piano (1983)
T. Hoffman (va), J. Hoffman (pno) † S. Silver:Son Vc; H. Smith:Innerflexions CRI ▲ 590 [DDD] (17.97)

HOFFMANN, E.T.A. [ERNST THEODOR AMADEUS] (1776-1822)
Miserere in b♭ for 2 Sopranos, Alto, Tenor, Bass, Orchestra & Chorus, AV.42 (1809)
C. Nylund (sop), A. Armetia (mez), L. Braun (alt), R. Orrego (ten), J. Schmidt (bass), R. Beck (cnd), Concerto Bamberg, South German Vocal Ensemble † Sym KSCH ▲ 311482 (16.97)
Quintet in c for Harp & String Quartet, AV.24 (1807)
E. Goodman (hp), Amadeus Ensemble members † M. Barnes:Divert Hp; M. Ravel:Intro & Allegro Hp; Samuel-Rousseau:Vars Pastorales; Tournier:Images Hp MUVI (Musica Viva) ▲ 1054 [DDD] (16.97)
Symphony in E♭, AV.23 (1805-06)
R. Beck (cnd), Concerto Bamberg † Miserere, AV.42 KSCH ▲ 311482 (16.97)
Undine (opera in 3 acts) [lib F. Fouqué], AV.70 (1816)
B. Baier (sop—Berthalda), H. Plesch (sop—Undine), C. Tippe (sop—Die Herzogin), M. Hiefinger (mez—Fisherman's Wife), A. Schamberger (ten—Der Herzog), J. Beck (bar—Ritter Huldbrand von), M. Albert (bass—Fisherman), U. Bosch (bass—Heilmann), B. Hofmann (bass—Kühleborn), H. Dechant (cnd), Bamberg Youth Orch BAYE 3-▲ 100256 [DDD] (51.97)
K. Láki (sop), K. Ridderbusch (bass), R. Henry (sgr), R. Bader (cnd), Berlin RSO, St. Hedwig's Cathedral Choir *(rec Feb 1982)* KSCH 3-▲ 310922 [DDD] (47.97)

HOFFMANN, GIOVANNI (b ca 1800)
Chromaticon for Piano & Orchestra
J. Hofmann (pno), F. Reiner (cnd), Curtis Institute Student Orch † Moszkowski:Caprice Espagnole, Op. 37; A. Rubinstein:Con 4 Pno, Op. 70 VAIA 2-▲ 1020 [ADD] (31.97)
Quartets (2) in D & F for Violin, Viola, Mandolin & Lute
Quatuor Plectr'Archi † G. F. Giuliani:Qts Vn PAVA ▲ 7224 [DDD] (10.97)

HOFFMANN, RICHARD (1925-
Orchestra Piece 1961
R. Baustian (cnd), Oberlin College Conservatory Orch *(rec Oberlin Conservatory, OH, Jan 27, 1970)* ("Portraits of 3 Ladies") † E. London:Portraits of 3 Ladies; Whittenberg:Vars 9 Players NWW ▲ 80562 (16.97)

HOFFMEISTER, FRANZ ANTON (1754-1812)
Concerto No. 2 in B♭ for Clarinet & Orchestra
E. Brunner (cl), H. Stadlmair (cnd), Munich CO † F. X. Pokorny:Cons Cl; J. W. A. Stamitz:Con Cl TUD ▲ 7008 [DDD] (16.97)
Concerto in E♭ for 2 Clarinets & Orchestra
W. Boeykens (cl), A. Boeykens (cl), J. Caeyers (cnd), Belgium New CO † F. Krommer:Cons for 2 Cls HAM ▲ 1901433 (9.97)
D. Klöcker (cl), W. Wandel (cl), H. Stadlmair (cnd), Munich CO ("Clarinet Concertos of the Imperial & Royal Court Orchestras") † J. Beer:Con Cl; L. A. Lebrun:Con Cl KSCH ▲ 364222 (16.97)
Concerto (No. 15) in B♭ for Flute & Orchestra
A. Daboncourt (fl), L. Gorelik (cnd), Kharkov PO † J. Haydn:Con Fl & Orch, H.VIIf/1; C. Stamitz:Con Fl in G, Op. 29 DPV ▲ 9127 (15.97)
Concerto in D for Viola & Orchestra
S. Nakariakov (tpt), J. Faerber (cnd), Württemberg CO [trans tpt] † J. Haydn:Con 1 Vc; Mendelssohn (-Bartholdy):Con Vn & Strs TELC ▲ 24276 (16.97)
Grand Sinfonie for Orchestra, Op. 14, "La chasse"
C. Campestrini (cnd), Vienna Volksoper CO ("La chasse") † J. Haydn:Sym 73; F. A. Rosetti:Sinf de chasse ORF ▲ 466971 (18.97)
Quartet in A for Flute & Strings [after Mozart's Sonata in A for Piano, K.331]
Israel Flute Ensemble ("Flute Serenade") † Beethoven:Serenade Fl, Vn & Va, Op. 25; W. A. Mozart:Qt Fl in D, K.285; F. Schubert:Trio Strs, D.471 CACI ▲ 210018 (5.97)
Quintet in E♭ for Horn & Strings
L. Bergé (hn), Arriaga String Quartet ("Kamermuziek voor hoorn") † Amon:Qt Hn; W. A. Mozart:Qnt Hn; Stich [or stich-Punto]:Qt Hn EUFO ▲ 1207 [DDD] (19.97)
L. van Marcke (hn), Apos String Quartet *(rec Berlin, Feb 1996)* ("Chamber Music with Hn") † Hauff:Qnt Hn; Küffner:Qnt Hn; W. A. Mozart:Qnt Hn; A. Reicha:Qnt Hn; C. Stamitz:Qts Strs PAVA ▲ 7363 [DDD] (10.97)
Serenades (6) for Wind Instruments
Consortium Classicum CPO ▲ 999107 [DDD] (14.97)
Serenade in E♭ for Winds
La Gran Partita † Beethoven:Octet Ww, Op. 103; Qnt Ob; Rondino Ww, WoO 25 TUD ▲ 780 (12.97)

HOFMANN, JOSEF (1876-1957)
Kaleidoskop for Piano, Op. 40
S. Cherkassky (pno) *(rec San Francisco, CA, Apr 18, 1982)* ("The 1982 San Francisco Recital") † Chopin:Polonaises-fant, Op. 61; Waltzes Pno; Lully:Suite de pièces; Mendelssohn (-Bartholdy):Scherzo a capriccio; P. Tchaikovsky:Son Pno, Op. 37 IVOR ▲ 70904 [DDD] (16.97)
Piano Music
J. Hofmann (pno) *(rec 1919-32)* ("The Polish Virtuoso") † I. Friedman:Pno Music; I. J. Paderewski:Pno Music (misc) NIMB (Grand Piano) ▲ 8802 (11.97)

HOFMANN, LEOPOLD (1738-1793)
Sonatas (6) for Violin (or Viola), Cello & Double Bass, Op. 1 (1775)
ABC Trio † G. Bassano:Fants; Blendinger:Tonale Skizzen, Op. 56; M. Haydn:Divert for Va, Vc & Db; B. Romberg:Trios Va, Op. 38 BAYE ▲ 100296 [DDD] (17.97)

HOFMANN-ENGEL, LUDGER (1964-
Sonata No. 1 for Piano in 2 Parts (1982)
L. Hofmann-Engel (pno) ("Music on & off the Keys") † L. Foss:Fant Rondo; Frankel:Son 1 Vn, Op. 13; Kershner:Son Bn; Loevendie:Strides; Toccata; Walk; Togawa:Kaze No Ha VMM (Distinguished Performers III) ▲ 2016 [DDD]

HÖGBERG, FREDRIK (1971-
PlastMusikk for Clarinet, Percussion & Tape
M. Fröst (cl), N. Brommare (perc) *(rec Sweden, Mar 1996)* ("Close Ups: Music for Clarinet & Percussion") † E. Denisov:Son Cl; Hillborg:Close Ups; Nursery Rhymes; Kuchera-Morin:Yugen; P. Lindgren:Beep-Ooh; Woodpecker's Chant; Sivelöv:Twist & Shout BIS ▲ 744 [DDD] (17.97)
Su Ba Do Be for Trombone (1993)
C. Lindberg (trbn) ("Unaccompanied") † J. S. Bach:Suites Vc; C. Lindberg:Vars on Gregorian Chants; J. Sandström:Don Quixote; Telemann:Fants (12) Fl, TWV40:2-13 BIS ▲ 858 [DDD] (17.97)

HOIBY, LEE (1926-
Bermudas for 2 Voices, Violin, Viola, Cello & Piano (1984)
T. Rhodes (sop), E. Williams (mez), H. Ku (vn), J. Bagg (va), F. Raimi (vc), T. Warburton (pno) ("To Sun, to Feast & to Converse: American Vocal Duet Music") † T. Hoekman:Margarets; S. Jaffe:Fort Juniper Songs; Kouneva:Aeon; R. Ward:Lady Kate (sels); Roman Fever (sels) ALBA ▲ 172 [DDD] (16.97)
Choral Music
R. Osborne (b-bar), L. King (org), J. A. Simms (cnd), Trinity Church Choir—Ascension (Holy Sonnet No. 7); At the Round Earth's Imagined Corners; Hear Us, O Hear Us Lord; Hymn to the New Age; Inherit the Kingdom; Let this Mind Be in You; Magnificat & Nunc Dimittis; The Offering ("Music from Trinity Church Wall Street, New York City, Vol. 4") GOT ▲ 49035 [DDD] (17.97)
Concerto No. 2 for Piano & Orchestra (1979)
S. Babin (pno), R. Stankovský (cnd), Slovak RSO Bratislava † Narrative; Schubert Vars; Son Vn, Op. 5 MASM ▲ 2038 [DDD] (16.97)
Concerto for Piano & Orchestra, Op. 17 (1957)
J. Atkins (pno), J. Krenz (cnd), Polish National RSO Katowice *(rec 1966)* † J. A. Carpenter:Concertino Pno Orch; La Montaine:Con Pno, Op. 9 CIT ▲ 88118 [ADD] (15.97)
I Was There [text by Walt Whitman] (1988)
W. Payn (cnd), Rooke Chapel Choir, D. Fortunato (mez), G. Lee (pno) *(rec Bucknell U., Lewisburg, PA, United States of America)* ("An American Collage") † Lady of the Harbor; Let this Mind Be in You; Shepherd; A. Copland:In the Beginning; Duckworth:Southern Harmony; J. Duke:Songs; J. Hill:Medieval Lyrics; Sweet & Triune Harmony; Hundley:Astronomers; Isaac Greentree; Sea is Swimming; R. Palmer:O Magnum Mysterium ALBA ▲ 98 [ADD] (16.97)
Lady of the Harbor [text by Emma Lazarus] (1985)
W. Payn (cnd), Rooke Chapel Choir, D. Fortunato (mez), G. Lee (pno) *(rec Bucknell U., Lewisburg, PA, United States of America)* ("An American Collage") † I Was There; Let this Mind Be in You; Shepherd; A. Copland:In the Beginning; Duckworth:Southern Harmony; J. Duke:Songs; J. Hill:Medieval Lyrics; Sweet & Triune Harmony; Hundley:Astronomers; Isaac Greentree; Sea is Swimming; R. Palmer:O Magnum Mysterium ALBA ▲ 98 [ADD] (16.97)
Let this Mind Be in You [text from *Phillipians 2:5*] (1987)
W. Payn (cnd), Rooke Chapel Choir, D. Fortunato (mez), D. Cover (org) *(rec Bucknell U., Lewisburg, PA, United States of America)* ("An American Collage") † I Was There; Lady of the Harbor; Shepherd; A. Copland:In the Beginning; Duckworth:Southern Harmony; J. Duke:Songs; J. Hill:Medieval Lyrics; Sweet & Triune Harmony; Hundley:Astronomers; Isaac Greentree; Sea is Swimming; R. Palmer:O Magnum Mysterium ALBA ▲ 98 [ADD] (16.97)
Narrative for Piano (1983)
L. Hoiby (pno) † Con 2 Pno; Schubert Vars; Son Vn, Op. 5 MASM ▲ 2038 [DDD] (16.97)
Schubert Variations for Piano (1981)
L. Hoiby (pno) † Con 2 Pno; Narrative; Son Vn, Op. 5 MASM ▲ 2038 [DDD] (16.97)
Sextet for Wind Quintet & Piano (ca 1975)
Dorian Wind Quintet † Adolphe:Night Journey; Dejong:Vars on the Spanish La Folia; L. Schifrin:Nouvelle Orléans; Tower:Island Prelude SUMM ▲ 117 [DDD] (16.97)
The Shepherd [text by William Blake] (1987)
W. Payn (cnd), Rooke Chapel Choir, D. Fortunato (mez), G. Lee (pno) *(rec Bucknell U., Lewisburg, PA, United States of America)* ("An American Collage") † I Was There; Lady of the Harbor; Let this Mind Be in You; A. Copland:In the Beginning; Duckworth:Southern Harmony; J. Duke:Songs; J. Hill:Medieval Lyrics; Sweet & Triune Harmony; Hundley:Astronomers; Isaac Greentree; Sea is Swimming; R. Palmer:O Magnum Mysterium ALBA ▲ 98 [ADD] (16.97)
Sonata for Violin & Piano, Op. 5 (1952; rev 1979)
D. Heifetz (vn), L. Hoiby (pno) † Con 2 Pno; Narrative; Schubert Vars MASM ▲ 2038 [DDD] (16.97)
Z. Schiff (vn), C. Grant (pno) *(rec Purchase, NY, Mar 1994)* ("Here's One") † A. Copland:Pieces Vn; Rodeo (sels); H. Cowell:Son 1 Vn; F. Price:Deserted Garden; W. G. Still:Music of Still 4TAY ▲ 4005 [DDD] (17.97)
Songs
P. Stewart (bar), L. Hoiby (pno)—I Was There; poems by Whitman; 2 Songs of Innocence [The Lamb]; poems by Blake; An Immorality [by Pound]; O Florida; poems by Stevens; Why Don't You? [by Beers]; Night [anon]; What if [by Coleridge]; Investiture at Cecconi's [by James Merrill]; Where the Music Comes From [by Lee Hoiby] *(rec Rutgers Church NYC, Sept 13-14, 1993)* ("Songs of Lee Hoiby") CRI ▲ 685 [DDD] (17.97)

HØJSGAARD, ERIK (1954-
Fantasistykker for Clarinet, Cello & Piano (1982-84)
Danish Trio *(rec Dec 1987)* † Gudmunsen-Holmgreen:Mirror Pieces; Lorentzen:Mambo; Ruders:Tattoo for 3 PLAL ▲ 57 [AAD] (18.97)
Pale Landscape for Chamber Ensemble (1991)
Capricorn *(rec London, Jan 17-18, 1993)* † Nordentoft:Nervous Saurian; K. A. Rasmussen:Italian Con; M. Ravel:Pno Music; Rosing-Schow:Inner Voices NXIN ▲ 553008 [DDD] (5.97)

HOLBORNE, ANTHONY (ca 1547-1602)
Instrumental Consort Music
K. Boeke (vl), Amsterdam Loeki Stardust Quartet—Amoretta; Bona Speranza; Ecce quam bonum; Funerals; Galliard; Image of Melancolly; Infernum; Muy Linda; Nec invideo; Paradizo; Pavana Ploravit; Sic semper soleo; The Sighes; Teares of the Muses *(rec Jan 1991)* † K. Boeke:Lacrime CCL ▲ 2891 [DDD] (18.97)
P. O'Dette (lt), D. Douglass (cnd), King's Noyse—Night-Watch; Almayne; Widowes Myte; Muy Linda; Wanton; Passion; Playfellow No. 1; Honie-suckle; Fairie-round; Fruit of Love; Cradle; New-Yeeres Gift; Lullable; Pavan; Galliard; Heigh ho holiday; Il Nodo di Gordio; Sicke, Sicke, and Very Sicke; Funerals; As It Fell on a Holy Eve; Last Will & Testament; Farewell; Fants Nos. 1-3; Paradizo; The Sighes; Posthuma; My selfe; Spero *(rec MA, May 1998)* ("My Selfe-16th Cent Pavans, Galliards & Almains") HAM ▲ 907238 (18.97)
G. Weigand (cnd) —Holborne's Almain; The Countess of Pembroke's Paradise; Nowell's Galliard; The Honie Suckle & the Faerie Round; Pavan & Galliard; The Quadro Pavan & Galliard; Muy Linda; Heres Patemus; Heigh Ho Holiday; The Wanton ("Consort Music of the English Renaissance") † J. Dowland:Consort Music MER ▲ 84256
Lute Music
R. Bluestone (gtr)—Pavane 19; Fants Nos. 1-3 *(rec Loretto Chapel, Santa Fe, NM)* † Dunlap:Lt Music; Lauro:Lt Music; D. Milne:Lt Music; M. Ponce:Son 3 Gtr; Tansman:Lt Music; S. L. Weiss:Lt Music LINA ▲ 1896 [DDD]
J. Bream (lt)—Fairie-round; Heigh Ho Holiday; Heart's Ease † W. Byrd:Lt Music; Cutting:Lt Music; J. Dowland:Songs; Francesco Canova da Milano:Lt Music RCAV ▲ 61587 (11.97)
F. Marincola (lt)—Almaine No. 3 [The Night Watch]; Almaine No. 4; As It Fell on a Holy Eve; Fants Nos. 1-3; Galliard No. 2; Galliard No. 3 [The Fairy Round]; Galliard No. 5 [The New Year's Gift]; Galliard No. 11 [Passion]; Galliard No. 14 [Muy Linda]; Lt Galliard No. 1; Pavan 1 [Last Will & Testament]; Pavan 2; Pavan 3 [Sedet Sola]; Pavan 15 [Countess of Pembrook's Paradise]; Pavan 17 [Patienca]; Piece without Title; Playfellow No. 1; Playfellow No. 2 [Wanton]; Vars ("Pieces for Lute") PVY ▲ 795112 (16.97)
Music of Holborne
S. Pell (va), J. Heringman (bandora/cittern/lt) ("Holburns Passion: Music for Lute, Cittern & Bandora") ASV (Gaudeamus) ▲ 173 (16.97)
Songs
A. Jonsson (rcr), E. Hagberg (rcr), K. Ivarson (rcr), A. Mjönes (rcr), Y. Pehrsson (rcr), L. Karlsson (perc), C. Pehrsson (cnd), Musica Dolce—Funerals; Fairie-round; Choise; Almayne *(rec Uppsala, Sweden, June 18-20, 1985)* ("English Consort Music") † Brade:Paduanen; Songs; W. Byrd:Songs; M. East:Songs; R. Philips:Songs; T. Simpson:Songs BIS ▲ 305 [DDD] (17.97)

HOLBROOKE, JOSEF (1878-1958)
The Birds of Rhiannon (symphonic poem) for Orchestra, Op. 87 (1925)
A. Penny (cnd), Ukrainian National SO *(rec Concert Hall of Ukrainian Radio Kiev, Oct 28-30, 1994)* † Children of Don (ov); Dylan (sels) MARC ▲ 8223721 [DDD] (13.97)

▲ = CD ♦ = Enhanced CD △ = MD ▮ = Cassette Tape ▯ = DCC

HOLST, GUSTAV (cont.)

A Moorside Suite for Brass Band (1928) (cont.)
P. Parkes (cnd), Grimethorpe Colliery Band, G. Cutt (cnd) ("Brass for the Masters-Vol. 2") † M. Arnold:Fant Brass, Op. 114; E. Ball:Kensington Con; Bantock:Frogs; Goffin:Rhaps Brass; G. Lloyd:Diversions on a Bass Theme; Vaughan Williams:Henry V CHN ▲ 4553 (16.97)
J. Watson (cnd), Black Dyke Mills Band *(rec Peel Hall Salford, July 1996)* † Planets, Op. 32 DOY (Master) ▲ 50 [DDD] (16.97)

The Morning of the Year (choral ballet) [lib S. Wilson], Op. 45/2 (1926-27)
H. D. Wetton (cnd), Philharmonia Orch, Guildford Choral Society † Golden Goose, Op. 45/1; King Estmere HYP ▲ 66784 (18.97)

Music of Holst
R. Hickox (cnd), City of London Sinfonia—Double Con, Op. 49; Fugal Con, Op. 40/2; Lyric Movt; Brook Green Suite; St. Paul's Suite, Op. 29/2; Songs without Words, Op. 22 CHN ▲ 9270 [DDD] (16.97)

Orchestral Works
R. Hickox (cnd), London SO—Capriccio; Scherzo † Egdon Heath, Op. 47; Fugal Ov; Hammersmith, Op. 52; Somerset Rhap, Op. 21/2 CHN ▲ 9420 (16.97)

Partsongs (5) for Chorus, Op. 12 (1902-03)
R. Hickox (cnd), London SO, R. Hickox (cnd), City of London Sinfonia, R. Hickox (cnd), London Sym Chorus, R. Hickox (cnd), Finzi Singers, R. Hickox (cnd), Joyful Company of Singers † Choral Fant, Op. 51; Cloud Messenger, Op. 30; Partsongs, Op. 44 CHN ▲ 2406 (16.97)

Partsongs (7) for Soprano, Strings & Female Chorus [text Bridges], Op. 44 (1925-26)
R. Hickox (cnd), London SO, R. Hickox (cnd), City of London Sinfonia, R. Hickox (cnd), London Sym Chorus, R. Hickox (cnd), Finzi Singers, R. Hickox (cnd), Joyful Company of Singers † Choral Fant, Op. 51; Cloud Messenger, Op. 30; Partsongs, Op. 12 CHN ▲ 2406 (16.97)

The Perfect Fool (ballet music) for Orchestra, Op. 39, (H150) (1918-22)
C. Mackerras (cnd), Royal Liverpool PO † Planets, Op. 32; C. Orff:Carmina burana VCL 2-▲ 61510 [DDD] (11.97)
A. Previn (cnd), London SO *(rec Abbey Road, London, England, Aug 3 & 4, 1974)* † Egdon Heath, Op. 47; Planets, Op. 32 EMIC (British Composers) ▲ 66934 [ADD] (11.97)
G. Weldon (cnd) *(rec 1953-55)* † Somerset Rhap, Op. 21/2; Songs without Words, Op. 22; St. Paul's Suite, Op. 29/2; A. Bax:Tintagel; Vaughan Williams:Wasps DLAB ▲ 4002 (17.97)

Piano Music
A. Goldstone (pno)—Arpeggio Study; 2 pièces; Toccata; A Piece for Yvonne; Chrissemas Day in the Morning; 2 Folk Song fragments; Nocturne; Jig; Dances for Pno Duet [w. Caroline Clemmow (pno)] † C. Lambert:Elegiac Blues; Elegy Pno; Son Pno CHN ▲ 9382 [DDD] (17.97)

The Planets (suite) for Orchestra, Op. 32, (H125) (1914-16)
L. Bernstein (cnd), New York PO † W. Walton:Façade SNYC (Essential Classics) ▲ 62400 (7.97) ▮ 62400 (3.98)
L. Bernstein (cnd), New York PO † E. Elgar:Pomp & Circumstance, Op. 39 SNYC (Bernstein Century) ▲ 63087 (11.97)
A. Boult (cnd), London PO † E. Elgar:Enigma Vars, Op. 36 EMIC ▲ 64748 (11.97)
A. Boult (cnd), London PO CFP (Unforgettable Classics) ▲ 68819 (11.97)
A. Boult (cnd), New Philharmonia Orch, Ambrosian Singers *(rec London, England, July 21 & 22, 1966)* † Egdon Heath, Op. 47; Perfect Fool, Op. 39 EMIC (British Composers) ▲ 66934 [ADD] (11.97)
A. Davis (org), A. David (cnd), BBC SO, BBC Sym Women's Chorus *(rec London, Dec 1993)* † Egdon Heath, Op. 47 TELC ▲ 94541 [DDD] (16.97)
C. Dutoit (cnd), Montreal SO, I. Edwards (cnd), Montréal Sym Female Chorus *(rec Montréal, Canada, June 1986)* PENG (Penguin Music Classics) ▲ 460606 [DDD] (11.97)
J. E. Gardiner (cnd), Philharmonia Orch, Monteverdi Choir London members † P. Grainger:Warriors DEUT ▲ 45860 [DDD] (16.97)
A. Gibson (cnd), Royal Scottish National Orch, Royal Scottish National Chorus *(rec Glasgow, Scotland, July 2-3, 1979)* ("The Planets for Orchestra") CHN ▲ 7082 [DDD] (13.97)
A. Goldstone (pno), C. Clemmow (pno) [arr Holst for 2 pnos] *(rec 1996)* † Sym in F, Op. 8; Bainton:Miniature Suite; Bury:Prelude & Fugue; E. Elgar:Serenade Strs, Op. 20 ALBA ▲ 198 [DDD]
R. Goodman (cnd), New Queen's Hall Orch † St. Paul's Suite, Op. 29/2 INMP ▲ 6600432 (16.97)
R. Hickox (cnd), London SO, London Sym Chorus INMP (LSO Classic Masterpieces) ▲ 890 [DDD] (9.97)
G. Holst (cnd), London SO, London Sym Chorus *(rec 1922-24 for Columbia)* ("Holst Conducts Holst: The Acoustic Recordings") † Beni Mora, Op. 29/1; Songs without Words, Op. 22; St. Paul's Suite, Op. 29/2 PHS ▲ 9417 [AAD]
J. Judd (cnd), Royal PO, King's College Choir Cambridge *(rec Dec 1-2, 1991)* DNN ▲ 75076 [DDD] (16.97)
H. von Karajan (cnd), Berlin PO—Venus, the Bringer of Peace ("Summer Adagio") † Beethoven:Sym 6; Debussy:Prélude à l'après-midi d'un faune; J. Haydn:Sym 87; W. A. Mozart:Divert 17 Hns Strs, K.334; Sym 38, K.504; M. Ravel:Rapsodie espagnole; O. Respighi:Fontane di Roma DEUT ▲ 457127 [ADD] (16.97)
H. von Karajan (cnd), Berlin PO, RIAS Chamber Choir DEUT (Karajan Gold) ▲ 39011 [DDD] (16.97)
H. von Karajan (cnd), Vienna PO † E. Elgar:Enigma Vars, Op. 36 PLON (The Classic Sound) ▲ 452303 (11.97)
A. Leaper (cnd), Czech-Slovak RSO Bratislava † Suite de Ballet, Op. 10 NXIN ▲ 550193 [DDD] (5.97)
Y. Levi (cnd), Atlanta SO, A. H. Jones (cnd), Atlanta Sym Chorus TEL ▲ 80466 (16.97)
J. Levine (cnd), Chicago SO, Chicago Sym Chorus DEUT ▲ 29730 [DDD] (16.97)
A. Litton (cnd), Dallas SO, D. R. Davidson (cnd), Dallas Sym Chorus Women *(rec Myerson Center Dallas, TX, Jan 23-26 & Sept 18-21, 1997)* ("Dallas Space Spectacular") † R. Strauss:Also sprach Zarathustra, Op. 30 DLS 2-▲ 3225 [DDD] (20.97)
J. Loughran (cnd), Hallé Orch CFP ▲ 4243 [ADD] (12.97)
L. Maazel (cnd), French National Orch † M. Ravel:Boléro SNYC ▲ 44781 [DDD] (10.97)
C. Mackerras (cnd), Royal Liverpool PO, Royal Liverpool Philharmonic Women's Chorus † Perfect Fool, Op. 39; C. Orff:Carmina burana VCL 2-▲ 61510 [DDD] (11.97)
E. MacMillan (cnd), Toronto SO *(rec 1942)* † E. Grieg:Son 2 Vn, Op. 13; E. MacMillan:Bergerettes du Bas-Canada; England ANAL ▲ 27804 (16.97)
J. Mardjani (cnd), Georgian Festival Orch SNYC ▲ 57258 [DDD] (4.97)
Z. Mehta (cnd), Los Angeles PO † R. Strauss:Also sprach Zarathustra, Op. 30; J. Williams:Close Encounters of the Third Kind (sels); Star Wars (sels) PLON (Double Decker) 2-▲ 452910 (17.97)
E. Ormandy (cnd), Philadelphia Orch ("Basic 100, Vol. 27") † J. Rodrigo:Con de Aranjuez; Fant para un gentilhombre; Vaughan Williams:Fant on a Theme of Tallis; Fant on Greensleeves; H. Villa-Lobos:Bachiana brasileira 5; Preludes Gtr RCAV ▲ 61724 (10.97)
R. Pople (cnd), London Festival Orch † Fugal Ov; St. Paul's Suite, Op. 29/2 ASV ▲ 782 (16.97)
A. Previn (cnd), Royal PO, Brighton Festival Women's Chorus *(rec Apr 14-15, 1986)* TEL ▮ 30133 [DDD] (8.98) ▲ 80133 [DDD] (16.97)
S. Rattle (cnd), Philharmonia Orch, Ambrosian Singers CFP (Eminence) ▲ 9513 [DDD] (16.97)
J. Serebrier (cnd), Melbourne SO † M. Ravel:Boléro; P. Tchaikovsky:Ov 1812, Op. 49 ASVQ ▲ 6078 [DDD] (10.97)
G. Simon (cnd), London SO, London Sym Chorus † Paganini:Intro & Vars on "Dal tuo stellato soglio", M.S. 23 LALI ▲ 14010 [DDD] (3.97)
L. Slatkin (cnd), Philharmonia Orch † Varèse:Arcana RCAV (Red Seal) ▲ 68819 (16.97)
G. Solti (cnd), London PO ("The Solti Collection, Vol. 11") † E. Elgar:Pomp & Circumstance, Op. 39 PLON (Jubilee) ▲ 30447 [ADD] (11.97)
L. Stokowski (cnd), Los Angeles PO, Roger Wagner Chorale † M. Ravel:Alborada del gracioso; I. Stravinsky:Pétrouchka Suite; Verdi:Aida EMIC (Full Dimensional Sound) 3-▲ 65423 [ADD] (11.97)
W. Susskind (cnd), St. Louis SO, Missouri Singers, Ronald Arnatt Chorale † Smetana:Má Vlast VB2 2-▲ 5105 [ADD] (9.97)
P. Sykes (org) [trans Sykes] *(rec Girard College Philadelphia)* RAVN ▲ 380 [DDD] (17.97)
J. Watson (cnd), Black Dyke Mills Band, Hallé Choir [arr Stephen Roberts] *(rec Peel Hall Salford, July 1996)* † Moorside Suite DOY (Master) ▲ 50 [DDD] (16.97)
various artists [excerpt] † B. Bartók:Con Orch, Sz.116; J. Brahms:Vars on a Theme by Haydn; W. A. Mozart:Con 3 Vn, K.216; R. Strauss:Also sprach Zarathustra, Op. 30; Salome (dance of the 7 veils) MTAL ▲ 48095 (6.97)
artists unknown—Mars, the Bringer of War; Venus, the Bringer of Peace ("Mars & Venus") † Berlioz:Béatrice et Bénédict (ov); Roméo et Juliette (sels); Debussy:Nocturnes Orch; Prélude à l'après-midi d'un faune; S. Prokofiev:Romeo & Juliet (sels); R. Strauss:Don Juan, Op. 20; Salome (dance of the 7 veils) RCAV (Red Seal) ▲ 68999 (16.97)
artists unknown—Jupiter, the Bringer of Jollity ("Great British Music II") † B. Britten:Young Person's Guide to the Orch, Op. 34; E. Elgar:Con Vc; Enigma Vars, Op. 36; Vaughan Williams:Fant on Greensleeves CFP (Unforgettable Classics) ▲ 73420 (11.97)

Psalms 86 & 148 for Tenor, Organ, String Orchestra & Chorus (1912)
J. Alley (org), R. Hickox (cnd), City of London Sinfonia, Britten Singers [ENG] † B. Britten:Cant misericordium, Op. 69; Chorale on an Old French Carol; Deus in adjutorium meum; G. Finzi:Requiem da Camera CHN ▲ 8997 [DDD] (16.97)

HOLST, GUSTAV (cont.)

Quintet in a for Piano, Oboe, Clarinet, Horn & Bassoon, Op. 3 (1896)
A. Goldstone (pno), Elysian Wind Quintet members † Qnt Ww; G. Jacob:Sxt Pno & Ww Qnt, Op. 6 CHN ▲ 9077 [DDD] (16.97)

Quintet in A♭ for Winds, Op. 14 (1903)
Aulos Wind Quintet † Jolivet:Sérénade Ob; C. Nielsen:Qnt Ww; P. Pierné:Suite pittoresque; Zemlinsky:Humoresque KSCH ▲ 310100 [DDD] (16.97)
Belgian Wind Quintet *(rec Belgian Radio & Television Concert Hall, Belgium, 1988-89)* ("Summer Music") † Arrieu:Qnt Ww; S. Barber:Summer Music, Op. 31; Beethoven:Qnt Pno, Op. 16 DI ▲ 920322 [DDD] (5.97)
Elysian Wind Quintet † Qnt Pno, Ob, Cl, Hn & Bn, Op. 3; G. Jacob:Sxt Pno & Ww Qnt, Op. 6 CHN ▲ 9077 [DDD] (16.97)

Saint Paul's Suite for String Orchestra, Op. 29/2 (1912-13)
A. Barlow (cnd), Royal PO ("This England") † Brook Green Suite; Delius:Irmelin (prelude); On Hearing the 1st Cuckoo; Summer Night on the River; E. Elgar:Serenade Strs, Op. 20; Warlock:Capriol Suite ASVQ ▲ 6070 [DDD] (10.97)
W. Boughton (cnd), English String Orch *(rec Great Hall, Univ of Birmingham, England, 1995)* ("Orchestral Favorites, Vol. 1") † Albinoni:Adagio; E. Grieg:Holberg Suite Pno, Op. 40; J. Pachelbel:Canon & Gigue; Warlock:Capriol Suite NIMB ▲ 7019 [DDD] (11.97)
R. Goodman (cnd), New Queen's Hall Orch † Planets, Op. 32 INMP ▲ 6600432 (16.97)
G. Holst (cnd) *(rec 1924 for Columbia)* ("Holst Conducts Holst: The Acoustic Recordings") † Beni Mora, Op. 29/1; Planets, Op. 32; Songs without Words, Op. 22 PHS ▲ 9417 [AAD]
G. Hurst (cnd), Bournemouth Sinfonietta † E. Elgar:Serenade Strs, Op. 20; J. Ireland:Concertino pastorale; Warlock:Capriol Suite CHN ▲ 8375 [ADD] (16.97)
K. Mannberg (cnd), Dalecarlian CO † P. Hindemith:Stücke (5) Str Orch, Op. 44/4; M. Reger:Lyrisches Andante; J. S. Svendsen:Romance Vn, Op. 26; Warlock:Capriol Suite BLUB ▲ 3007 (18.97)
R. Pople (cnd), London Festival Orch † Fugal Ov; Planets, Op. 32 ASV ▲ 782 (16.97)
R. Studt (cnd), Bournemouth Sinfonietta *(rec Mar 18-19, 1993)* ("English String Music") † B. Britten:Vars on a Theme of Frank Bridge, Op. 10; Delius:Aquarelles; Vaughan Williams:Variants of Dives & Lazarus; Warlock:Capriol Suite NXIN ▲ 550823 [DDD] (5.97)
G. Weldon (cnd) *(rec 1953-55)* † Perfect Fool, Op. 39; Somerset Rhap, Op. 21/2; Songs without Words, Op. 22; A. Bax:Tintagel; Vaughan Williams:Wasps DLAB ▲ 4002 (17.97)

A Somerset Rhapsody for Orchestra, Op. 21/2 (1906-07)
R. Hickox (cnd), London SO † Egdon Heath, Op. 47; Fugal Ov; Hammersmith, Op. 52; Orchestral Works CHN ▲ 9420 (16.97)
G. Weldon (cnd) *(rec 1953-55)* † Perfect Fool, Op. 39; Songs without Words, Op. 22; St. Paul's Suite, Op. 29/2; A. Bax:Tintagel; Vaughan Williams:Wasps DLAB ▲ 4002 (17.97)

Songs without Words (2) for Chamber Orchestra [Country Song & Marching Song], Op. 22 (1906)
G. Holst (cnd) [in Country Song] *(rec 1924 for Columbia)* ("Holst Conducts Holst: The Acoustic Recordings") † Beni Mora, Op. 29/1; Planets, Op. 32; St. Paul's Suite, Op. 29/2 PHS ▲ 9417 [AAD]
G. Weldon (cnd) *(rec 1953-55)* † Perfect Fool, Op. 39; Somerset Rhap, Op. 21/2; St. Paul's Suite, Op. 29/2; A. Bax:Tintagel; Vaughan Williams:Wasps DLAB ▲ 4002 (17.97)

Suites (2) in E♭ & F for Band, Op. 28 (1909 & 1911)
H. Dunn (cnd), Dallas Wind Sym † Hammersmith, Op. 52; Moorside Suite REF ▲ 39 [DDD] (16.97)
F. Fennell (cnd) † J. S. Bach:Fant Org, BWV 572; G. F. Handel:Royal Fireworks Music, HWV 351 TEL ▲ 80038 [DDD] (16.97)
F. Fennell (cnd), Eastman Wind Ensemble † Mennin:Canzona; Persichetti:Music of Persichetti; H. O. Reed:Fiesta Mexicana; Vaughan Williams:English Folk Song Suite; Toccata marziale MRCR (Living Presence) ▲ 462960 (m) (11.97)
D. Wick (cnd) † Hammersmith, Op. 52; Vaughan Williams:English Folk Song Suite; Toccata marziale ASVQ ▲ 6021 [ADD] (10.97)
artists unknown † Vaughan Williams:English Folk Song Suite; Toccata marziale BND ▲ 5002 [DDD]

Suite de Ballet in E♭ for Orchestra, Op. 10 (1899; rev 1912)
A. Leaper (cnd), Czech-Slovak RSO Bratislava † Planets, Op. 32 NXIN ▲ 550193 [DDD] (5.97)

Suite No. 1 in E♭ for Military Band, Op. 28/1 (1909)
T. Reynish (cnd), Royal College of Music Orch † Hammersmith, Op. 52; Suite 2 Band, Op. 28/2; Vaughan Williams:English Folk Song Suite; Toccata marziale CHN ▲ 9697 (16.97)

Suite No. 2 in F for Military Band, Op. 28/2 (1911)
T. Reynish (cnd), Royal College of Music Orch † Hammersmith, Op. 52; Suite 1 Band, Op. 28/1; Vaughan Williams:English Folk Song Suite; Toccata marziale CHN ▲ 9697 (16.97)

Symphony in F, Op. 8, "The Cotswolds" (1899-1900)
A. Goldstone (pno), C. Clemmow (pno) *(rec 1996)* † Planets, Op. 32; Bainton:Miniature Suite; Bury:Prelude & Fugue; E. Elgar:Serenade Strs, Op. 20 ALBA ▲ 198 [DDD]

Terzetto for Flute, Oboe & Viola (1925)
J. Dunham (va), Barcellona (fl), P. Christ (ob) † Pleyel:Miniatures Va; Sapieyevski:Arioso CRYS ▮ 647 (9.98)
Huntingdon Trio † Czerny:Fant concertante, Op. 256; Foote:Flying Cloud & Oriental Dance; Poem 1 Pno, Op. 41; E. Goossens:Impressions of a Holiday, Op. 7; K. Hoover:Lyric Trio; Musgrave:Impromptu 1 Fl LEON ▲ 325 [DDD] (16.97)

HÖLSZKY, ADRIANA (1953-

Music of Hölszky
Nomos String Quartet, Pelligrini String Quartet—Hängebrücken (Suspension Bridges); Qts I & II; Double Qt; Hunt the Wolves Back for Perc; Audiowindow or Franz Liszt for Pno CPO ▲ 999112 [DDD] (14.97)

HOLT, SIMEON TEN (1923-

Canto ostinato for various Instruments (1979)
G. Bouwhuis (pno), G. Carl (pno), A. Vernède (pno), C. Van Zeeland (pno) *(rec live, Jan 10, 1988)* CV 3-▲ 2 (55.97)

Horizon for Keyboard Instruments (1983-85)
Y. Abe (pno), P. D. Haas (pno), M. Krill (pno), F. Oldenburg (pno) CV 2-▲ 5 (37.97)

HOLT, SIMON (1958-

Banshee for Oboe & Percussion (1994)
M. Maxwell (ob), J. Gruithuyzen (pno), R. Benjafield (perc) *(rec Chapel Studio, Netherlands, May 1996)* † Birtwistle:Pulse Sampler; M. Maxwell:Elegy NMCC ▲ 42 [DDD] (10.97)

HOLTEN, BO (1948-

Grundtvig Motets (5) for Ensemble [texts N.F.S. Grundtvig] (1983)
Ars Nova † Nørgård:Wie ein Kind KPT ▲ 32016 [DDD]

Nordisk Suite for Chorus
J. G. Jørgensen (cnd), Lille MUKO University Choir ("Lille MUKO: Nordisk Suite") † Clausen:Songs; Langgaard:Rose Garden Songs; Maegaard:Södergran Songs; Nørgård:Evening Country, Op. 10; Sundstrøm:Falcon & the Little Birds PONT ▲ 5125 (19.97)

HOLZBAUER, IGNAZ (JAKOB) (1711-1783)

Concerto in d for Oboe
K. Meier (ob), H. Griffiths (cnd), Northern Sinfonia of England ("Oboe Concertos in Premier Recordings") † Eichner:Con 3 Ob; L. A. Lebrun:Con Ob, Op. 7; P. Von Winter:Con 2 Ob PANC ▲ 510088 [DDD] (17.97)

Divertimento in D a 3 parties
Camerata Köln † Qnt 1; Qnt 2; Sinf in G CPO ▲ 999580 (13.97)

Günther von Schwarzburg (singspiel in 3 acts) [lib A. Klein] (1777)
C. McFadden (sop), C. Prégardien (ten), R. Wörle (ten), M. Schopper (bass), M. Schneider (cnd), La Stagione CPO 3-▲ 999265 (41.97)

Quintet No. 1 in G for Flute, Violin, Viola, Bassoon & Concert Harpsichord
Camerata Köln † Divert in D; Qnt 2; Sinf in G CPO ▲ 999580 (13.97)
D. Maiben (va), Zephyrus *(rec Faith Lutheran Church Bloomington, England, July 5-7, 1994)* ("Mozart in Mannheim") † F. Danzi:Petits Duos, Op. 64; F. Lebrun:Sons Vn, Op. 1; W. A. Mozart:Qt Fl in C; C. Stamitz:Duos Vn & Va, Op.1/2; Toeschi:Quartetto FOCU ▲ 945 [DDD] (16.97)

Quintet No. 2 in B♭ for Flute, Violin, Viola, Bassoon & Concert Harpsichord
Camerata Köln † Divert in D; Qnt 1; Sinf in G CPO ▲ 999580 (13.97)

Sinfonia in G à 3 parties for Chamber Ensemble
Camerata Köln † Divert in D; Qnt 1; Qnt 2 CPO ▲ 999580 (13.97)

HOMILIUS, GOTTFRIED AUGUST (1714-1785)

Organ Music
G. Guillard (org)—Trio in G; Straf mich nicht in deinem Zorn; Wer nur den Lieben Gott lässt walten; Schmücke dich, o liebe Seele; Meine Gott, das Herz bring' ich dir; Dies sind die Heilgen Zehn Gebote; Mache dich mein Geist bereit; Christ lag in Todesbanden; Hilft, Herr Jesu, lass gelingen; Wir Christenleut; Sei Lob und Ehr dem höchsten Gut & others *(rec Orgs of Notre-Dame-des-Blancs-Manteaux & Saint-Aug, 1979 & 1996)* ("Organ Works") ARN ▲ 68328 [AAD] (16.97)

HOMILIUS, GOTTFRIED AUGUST (cont.)

Organ Music (cont.)

U. T. Wegele (org)—Mache dich mein Geist bereit; Meinen Jesum lass ich nicht; Meine Gott, das Herz bring' ich dir; Dies sind die Heilgen Zehn Gebote *(rec Basilika Weingarten, Germany, 1993)* † W. F. Bach:Org Music; C.P.E. Bach:Org Music; J. C. Kittel:Org Music; J. L. Krebs:Org Music TACE ▲ 30

HOMS, JOAQUIN (1906-

Impromptu for Piano, Violin & Cello (1996)

Mompou Trio Madrid † F. E. Blanco:Trio Pno; R. Gerhard:Trio Pno; E. Halffter:Hommages RTVE ▲ 65012 (16.97)

Ocells perduts (song cycle) for Voice & Piano [text Tagore] (1940)

I. Aragon (sop), A. Soler (pno) LAMA ▲ 2022 (18.97)

Sonata No. 2 for Piano (1955)

J. Masó (pno) *(rec Waldenburg Switzerland, Sept 18-22, 1993)* † R. Gerhard:Pno Music (comp) MARC ▲ 8223867 [DDD] (13.97)

HONEGGER, ARTHUR (1892-1955)

Les adventures du roi Pausole (operetta in 3 acts) [lib A. Willemetz after Louÿs] (1930)

R. Yakar (sop), B. Antoine (sop), B. Fournier (sop), C. Barbaux (sop), M. Barscha (sop), R. Macias (ten), G. Bacquier (bar), C. Ossola (bass), M. Venzago (cnd), Atelier PO MUSS 2-▲ 6115 [DDD] (36.97)

Allegretto for Orchestra

L. Hager (cnd), RTL SO *(rec Nov 16-20, 1992)* † Blues; Fantasio, Largo, Mort de Sainte Alméenne (interlude); Rédemption de François Villon; Sémiramis; Tempête (suite); Vivace TIMP ▲ 1016 [DDD] (18.97)

Amphion (ballet-melodrama) [text by Paul Valéry] (1929)

I. Bentoiu (sop—muse), O. Lallouette (bass—Apollon), T. Ciucur (sgr—muse), L. Kriska (sgr—muse), A. Mestes (sgr—muse), J. Antonioli (cnd), Timişoara PO, Timişoara Banatul Phil Chorus, Timişoara Children's Chorus *(rec Timisoara Romania, Oct 28 & Nov 1, 1995)* † Impératrice aux rochers TIMP ▲ 1035 [DDD] (18.97)

Blues for Orchestra [from Roses de Métal] (1928)

L. Hager (cnd), RTL SO *(rec Nov 16-20, 1992)* † Allegretto; Fantasio; Largo; Mort de Sainte Alméenne (interlude); Rédemption de François Villon; Sémiramis; Tempête (suite); Vivace TIMP ▲ 1016 [DDD] (18.97)

Cantique de Pâques for solo Voices, Orchestra & Chorus (1918)

N. Okada (sop), M. Brodard (bar), M. Corboz (cnd), Gulbenkian Foundation Orch, Gulbenkian Foundation Chorus † Judith CASC ▲ 1013 (16.97)

Chamber Music (complete)

D. Kang (vn), J. Audoli (vn), P. Xuereb (va), R. Wallfisch (vc), J. Rossi (db), P. Devoyon (pno)—Sonatine for 2 Vns (1920); Sonatine for Vn & Vc (1932); Son for Vc & Pno (1920); Son for Va & Pno (1920); Trio in f for Vn, Vc & Pno (1914); Paduana for Solo Vc (1945); Prelude for Db & Pno (1932) ("Vol. 2") TIMP ▲ 1009 [DDD]

D. Kang (vn), P. Devoyon (pno)—Son in d for Vn & Pno (1912); Sons 1 & 2 for Vn & Pno; 1919; Arioso for Vn & Pno (ca 1927/29); Son for Solo Vn (1940); Morceau de concours for Vn & Pno (1945) ("Honegger: The Chamber Music, Vol. 1") TIMP ▲ 1008 [DDD] (18.97)

F. Kondo (mez), D. Kang (vn), P. Xuereb (va), R. Wallfisch (vc), A. Marion (fl), A. Haraldsdóttir (fl), C. Moreaux (ob), M. Arrignon (cl), T. Caens (tpt), M. Becquet (trbn), P. Zanlonghi (hp), P. Devoyon (pno), Ludwig String Quartet—Sonatine for Cl & Pno (1921-22); Rapsodie for 2 Fls, Cl & Pno (1917); Danse de la Chèvre for Solo Fl (1921); Romance for Fl & Pno (1953); Petite Suite for 2 Fls & Pno (1934); Trois Contrepoints for Pic, Ob, Vn & Vc (1922); Intrada for Tpt & Pno (1947); Hommage du trbn exprimant la tristesse de l'auteur; J'avais un fidèle amant for Str Qt (1929); Chanson de Ronsard & 3 Chansons; Intro et Danse for Fl, Hp & Str Trio [undated]; Colloque for Fl, Cel, Vn & Va [undated] † Rapsodie for 2 Fl; Sonatina Cl TIMP ▲ 1010 [DDD]

F. Kondo (mez), Ludwig String Quartet—Str Qts Nos. 1-3; 1934-36; 1936-37; Pâques à New York (Easter in New York) f † Pâques à New York TIMP ▲ 1011 [DDD] (18.97)

Le Chant de Nigamon for Orchestra [after G. Aymard] (1917)

C. Munch (cnd), French National Orch *(rec Paris, France, June 1962)* ("Charles Munch Edition, Vol. 7") † Pastorale d'été; Sym 2; Sym 2 Tpt & Strs; Sym 5 VAL ▲ 4831 [ADD] (12.97)

Christophe Colomb (radio play) for Soloists, Orchestra & Chorus [text W. Aguet] (1940)

D. McCabe (bar), E. Knecht (spkr—Queen Isabella), S. Rawson (spkr—The Magician), N. Garvey (spkr—Christopher Columbus), A. Furnival (spkr—King Ferdinand), C. Peltz (cnd), Buffalo Opera Sacra Orch, Buffalo Opera Sacra Chorus [ENG] *(rec Buffalo New York, Oct 30-31, 1992)* MODE ▲ 35 [DDD] (17.97)

Concertino for Piano & Orchestra (1925)

F. J. Hirt (pno), O. Nussio (cnd), Swiss-Italian Radio-TV Orch *(rec 1953)* † Idée; Skating Rink GALL ▲ 880 [DDD] (18.97)

J. Thibaudet (pno), C. Dutoit (cnd), Montreal SO † J. Françaix:Concertino; M. Ravel:Con Pno; Con Pno (left hand) PLON ▲ 452448 (16.97)

T. Vásáry (pno), T. Vásáry (cnd), Bournemouth Sinfonietta † Pastorale d'été; Prélude, arioso et fughette sur le nom de BAC; Sym 4 CHN ▲ 8993 [DDD] (16.97)

Concerto for Cello & Orchestra (1934)

M. Maréchal (vc) *(rec 1929-43)* ("Maurice Maréchal, Book 2") † Debussy:Son Vc; Lalo:Con Vc ENT (Strings) ▲ 99316 (16.97)

U. Schmid (vc), D. Roggen (cnd), Northwest German PO † E. Bloch:Schelomo MDG ▲ 3210215 (17.97)

Concerto da camera for Flute, English Horn & Strings (1949)

E. Biessen (fl), M. Hannecart-Jakes (E hn), J. Fournet (cnd), Netherlands Radio PO *(rec Hilversum Music Center Netherlands, May & Dec 1993)* † Pacific 231; Pastorale d'été; Rugby; Sym 3 DNN ▲ 78831 [DDD] (16.97)

G. van Riet (fl), L. Lencsés (E hn), V. Czarnecki (cnd), Southwest German CO Pforzheim † J. Françaix:Horloge de Flore; Ibert:Symphonie concertante CPO ▲ 999193 [ADD] (14.97)

Fantasio (ballet pantomime) for Orchestra (1922)

L. Hager (cnd), RTL SO *(rec Nov 16-20, 1992)* † Allegretto; Blues; Largo; Mort de Sainte Alméenne (interlude); Rédemption de François Villon; Sémiramis; Tempête (suite); Vivace TIMP ▲ 1016 [DDD] (18.97)

Film Music

M. Adriano (cnd), Czech-Slovak RSO Bratislava—Napoléon [orchestral suite, original version]; Misérables; Mermoz [2 suites] (1934); Roue (ov) MARC ▲ 8223134 [DDD] (13.97)

M. Adriano (cnd), Slovak RSO Bratislava—Mayerling:Suite (1936); Regain:Suites 1 & 2 (1937); Démon de l'Himalaya; 1935 *(rec June 22, 1992 & Feb 6-9, 1993)* MARC ▲ 8223467 [DDD] (13.97)

H. Vachey (cnd), Douai Youth SO—Un revenant; Tete d'or; Regain; Redemption de François Villon; Napoléon ("Musiques de films et de scene") SOC ▲ 141 [ADD] (16.97)

L'idée (film music) for Orchestra (1934)

G. Bernasconi (cnd) *(rec 1992)* † Concertino Pno & Orch; Skating Rink GALL ▲ 880 [DDD] (18.97)

L'Impératrice aux rochers [The Emperess of the Rocks] (incidental music) for Orchestra (1925)

J. Antonioli (cnd), Timişoara PO *(rec Timisoara Romania, Oct 28 & Nov 1, 1995)* † Amphion TIMP ▲ 1035 [DDD] (18.97)

Intrada for Trumpet & Piano (1947)

H. Hardenberger (tpt), R. Pöntinen (pno) † Arban:Vars on a Theme from Bellini's Norma; P. M. Davies:Son Tpt; J. Françaix:Sonatine Tpt & Pno; J. Hartmann:Vars on Rule Britannia; Rabe:Shazam; Tisné:Héraldiques BIS ▲ 287 [DDD] (17.97)

Jeanne d'Arc au bûcher (dramatic oratorio) for Vocal Soloists, Orchestra & Chorus [after Paul Claudel] (1934-35)

S. Heinrich (cnd), Cracow RSO, Hersfelder Festival Choir, Frankfurt Children's Choir KSCH ▲ 312922 [DDD] (16.97)

Judith (biblical opera in 3 acts) [lib Morax] (1926)

B. Balleys (mez), L. Bizineche (mez), O. Kisfaludy (nar), M. Corboz (cnd), Gulbenkian Foundation Orch, Gulbenkian Foundation Chorus † Cantique de Pâques CASC ▲ 1013 (16.97)

N. Davrath (sop), B. Christensen (sop), M. Milhaud (nar), M. Abravanel (cnd), Utah SO, Salt Lake City Symphonic Choir [FRE] *(rec Dec 1964)* † D. Milhaud:Création du monde, Op. 81 VC ▲ 8088 [ADD] (13.97)

Largo for String Orchestra

L. Hager (cnd), RTL SO *(rec Nov 16-20, 1992)* † Allegretto; Blues; Fantasio; Mort de Sainte Alméenne (interlude); Rédemption de François Villon; Sémiramis; Tempête (suite); Vivace TIMP ▲ 1016 [DDD] (18.97)

Les Misérables (film music) for Orchestra (1934)

M. Adriano (cnd), Czech-Slovak RSO Bratislava [comp score] MARC ▲ 8223181 (13.97)

Monopartita for Orchestra

D. Zinman (cnd), Zurich Tonhalle Orch † Mouvement symphonique 3; Pacific 231; Pastorale d'été; Rugby; Sym 2 DECC ▲ 455352 (16.97)

La Mort de Sainte Alméenne:Interlude

L. Hager (cnd), RTL SO *(rec Nov 16-20, 1992)* † Allegretto; Blues; Fantasio; Largo; Rédemption de François Villon; Sémiramis; Tempête (suite); Vivace TIMP ▲ 1016 [DDD] (18.97)

Mouvement symphonique No. 3 for Orchestra (1932-33)

S. Baudo (cnd), Czech PO † Pacific 231; Sym 1; Sym 2; Sym 3; Sym 4; Sym 5; Tempête (prelude) SUR 2-▲ 111566 [DDD]

W. Furtwängler (cnd), Berlin PO *(rec Berlin, Germany, Feb 10, 1952)* † Debussy:Nocturnes Orch; M. Ravel:Rapsodie espagnole; R. Strauss:Metamorphosen MUA ▲ 4719 (live) [AAD] (10.97)

HONEGGER, ARTHUR (cont.)

Mouvement symphonique No. 3 for Orchestra (1932-33) (cont.)

D. Zinman (cnd), Zurich Tonhalle Orch † Monopartita; Pacific 231; Pastorale d'été; Rugby; Sym 2 DECC ▲ 455352 (16.97)

Nicolas de Flue (dramatic legend in 3 acts) [lib D. de Rougemont] (1939)

A. Koch (cnd), Central Swiss Youth PO, Lucerne Academy Choir, Lucerne Collegium Musicum Choir MUSS ▲ 6154 (17.97)

Swiss Romande Horn Section, A. Charlet (cnd) , A. Charlet (cnd), Lausanne Pro Arte Chorus, A. Charlet (cnd), Les Copains D'Abord Children's Chorus, A. Charlet (cnd), Fribourg University Chamber Chorus, A. Charlet (cnd), Romand Chamber Chorus, O. Kisfaludy (sgr—Nicolas), J. Bruno (nar) CASC ▲ 1021 (16.97)

Pacific 231 (mouvement symphonique) for Orchestra (1923)

M. Abravanel (cnd), Utah SO *(rec Salt Lake City, UT, 1968)* † Varèse:Amériques; Ecuatorial; Nocturnal VC ▲ 40 [AAD] (13.97)

E. Ansermet (cnd), Swiss Romande Orch † Debussy:Mer Orch; Dukas:L'Apprenti sorcier; M. Ravel:Boléro; Valse PLON (The Classic Sound) ▲ 448576 (11.97)

S. Baudo (cnd), Czech PO † Mouvement symphonique 3; Sym 1; Sym 2; Sym 3; Sym 4; Sym 5; Tempête (prelude) SUR 2-▲ 111566 [DDD]

L. Bernstein (cnd), New York PO † Rugby; D. Milhaud:Choëphores, Op. 24; A. Roussel:Sym 3 SNYC (Masterworks Heritage) ▲ 62352 (12.97)

L. Bernstein (cnd), New York PO *(rec New York, NY, Oct 31, 1962)* † Pastorale d'été; Rugby; Debussy:Rapsodie Sax; Dukas:L'Apprenti sorcier; D. Milhaud:Création du monde, Op. 81; M. Ravel:Shéhérazade Mez SNYC (Bernstein Century) ▲ 60695 [ADD] (10.97)

J. Fournet (cnd), Netherlands Radio PO *(rec Hilversum Music Center Netherlands, May & Dec 1993)* † Con da camera; Pastorale d'été; Rugby; Sym 3 DNN ▲ 78831 [DDD] (16.97)

N. Järvi (cnd), Danish National RSO † Sym 3; Sym 5 CHN ▲ 9176 [DDD] (16.97)

D. Zinman (cnd), Zurich Tonhalle Orch † Monopartita; Mouvement symphonique 3; Pastorale d'été; Rugby; Sym 2 DECC ▲ 455352 (16.97)

Pâques à New York for Mezzo-Soprano & String Quartet (1920)

F. Kondo (mez), Ludwig String Quartet † Chamber Music (comp) TIMP ▲ 1011 [DDD] (18.97)

Partita for Piano 4-Hands (1930)

G. Picavet (pno), B. Picavet (pno) † G. Auric:Waltz Pno 4-Hands; Durey:Carillons; Neige; D. Milhaud:Création du monde, Op. 81; Scaramouche Pnos, Op. 165b; F. Poulenc:Capriccio; Elégie Pnos; Embarquement pour Cythère; Tailleferre:Jeux de plein air ILD ▲ 642129 (11.97)

Pastorale d'été for Orchestra (1920)

E. Ansermet (cnd), Paris Conservatory Société des Concerts Orch, E. Ansermet (cnd), Swiss Romande Orch *(rec 1929-47)* ("Ansermet, Vol. 6") † Roi David; Debussy:Mer Orch; Petite suite Pno; M. de Falla:Noches en los jardines de España LYS1 ▲ 457

L. Bernstein (cnd), New York PO *(rec Lincoln Center New York, NY, NY, Oct 31, 1962)* † Pacific 231; Rugby; Debussy:Rapsodie Sax; Dukas:L'Apprenti sorcier; D. Milhaud:Création du monde, Op. 81; M. Ravel:Shéhérazade Mez SNYC (Bernstein Century) ▲ 60695 [ADD] (10.97)

J. Fournet (cnd), Netherlands Radio PO *(rec Hilversum Music Center Netherlands, May & Dec 1993)* † Con da camera; Pacific 231; Rugby; Sym 3 DNN ▲ 78831 [DDD] (16.97)

C. Munch (cnd), French National Orch *(rec Festival Honegger, Switzerland, June 1962)* ("Charles Munch Edition, Vol. 7") † Chant de Nigamon; Sym 2; Sym 2 Tpt & Strs; Sym 5 VAL ▲ 4831 [ADD] (12.97)

T. Vásáry (cnd), Bournemouth Sinfonietta † Concertino Pno & Orch; Prélude, arioso et fughette sur le nom de BAC; Sym 4 CHN ▲ 8993 [DDD] (16.97)

D. Zinman (cnd), Zurich Tonhalle Orch † Monopartita; Mouvement symphonique 3; Pacific 231; Rugby; Sym 2 DECC ▲ 455352 (16.97)

Pièces brèves (7) for Piano (1919-20)

M. Bratke (pno) ("Le Groupe des Six") † G. Auric:Adieu New York; Durey:Préludes, Op. 26; D. Milhaud:Printemps Pno, Op. 25; F. Poulenc:Mouvements perpétuels; Pièces Pno; Tailleferre:Romance Pno OLY ▲ 487 [DDD] (12.97)

Pieces (3) for Piano (1910)

L. Weiss (pno) *(rec Nacka, Sweden, Apr 30-May 1, 1975)* † A. Berg:Son Pno, Op. 1; H. Eisler:Son 1 Pno, Op. 1; E. Granados:Allegro di concierto; M. Ravel:Sonatine Pno; Schoenberg:Little Pieces Pno, Op. 19 BIS ▲ 23 [AAD] (17.97)

Poésies (6) for solo Voice & Piano [after Cocteau] (1920-23)

F. Katz (mez), B. Desgraupes (cnd) *(rec L'Opéra Comique Paris, France, Dec 1989 & May 1990)* ("Les Mariés de la Tour Eiffel") † D. Milhaud:Machines agricoles, Op. 56; Mariés de la Tour Eiffel MARC ▲ 8223788 [DDD] (13.97)

Prélude, arioso et fughette sur le nom de BACH for Piano (1932)

T. Vásáry (cnd), Bournemouth Sinfonietta † Concertino Pno & Orch; Pastorale d'été; Sym 4 CHN ▲ 8993 [DDD] (16.97)

Rapsodie for 2 Flutes, Clarinet & Piano (1917)

A. Marion (fl) † Chamber Music (comp); Sonatina Cl TIMP ▲ 1010 [DDD]

La Rédemption de François Villon (radio music) for Orchestra (1951)

L. Hager (cnd), RTL SO *(rec Nov 16-20, 1992)* † Allegretto; Blues; Fantasio; Largo; Mort de Sainte Alméenne (interlude); Sémiramis; Tempête (suite); Vivace TIMP ▲ 1016 [DDD] (18.97)

Regain (film score suite) for Orchestra (1937)

E. Theis (cnd), Austrian Chamber Sym *(rec Vienna, May 1996)* † Suite archaique; Sérénade à Angélique; Rot:Con Vn MPH ▲ 56823 [DDD] (15.97)

Le Roi David (dramatic psalm) for Soprano, Contralto, Tenor, 2 Speakers, Orchestra & Chorus [text Morax] (1921)

E. Ansermet (cnd), Paris Conservatory Société des Concerts Orch, E. Ansermet (cnd), Swiss Romande Orch *(rec 1929-47)* ("Ansermet, Vol. 6") † Pastorale d'été; Debussy:Mer Orch; Petite suite Pno; M. de Falla:Noches en los jardines de España LYS1 ▲ 457

N. Davrath (sop), J. Preston (mez), M. Sorensen (ten), M. Singher (nar), M. Milhaud (nar), M. Abravanel (cnd), Utah SO [FRE] VC ▲ 4038 [ADD] (13.97)

D. Pearson (cnd), St. John's Cathedral Orch, St. John's Cathedral Chorus, M. Sorensson (sop), M. Ragonetti (mez), T. Poole (mez—Witch of Endor), J. Matisse (mez) [ENG] *([ENG]lib text)* GOT ▲ 49105 [DDD] (17.97)

Rugby (mouvement symphonique) for Orchestra (1928)

L. Bernstein (cnd), New York PO † Pacific 231; D. Milhaud:Choëphores, Op. 24; A. Roussel:Sym 3 SNYC (Masterworks Heritage) ▲ 62352 (12.97)

L. Bernstein (cnd), New York PO *(rec Lincoln Center New York, NY, NY, Oct 31, 1962)* † Pacific 231; Pastorale d'été; Debussy:Rapsodie Sax; Dukas:L'Apprenti sorcier; D. Milhaud:Création du monde, Op. 81; M. Ravel:Shéhérazade Mez SNYC (Bernstein Century) ▲ 60695 [ADD] (10.97)

J. Fournet (cnd), Netherlands Radio PO *(rec Hilversum Music Center Netherlands, May & Dec 1993)* † Con da camera; Pacific 231; Pastorale d'été; Sym 3 DNN ▲ 78831 [DDD] (16.97)

D. Zinman (cnd), Zurich Tonhalle Orch † Monopartita; Mouvement symphonique 3; Pacific 231; Pastorale d'été; Sym 2 DECC ▲ 455352 (16.97)

Sémiramis (ballet) for Soloists, Orchestra & Chorus (1931)

M. Kemmer (sgr), V. Ivanov (vn), L. Hager (cnd), RTL SO, Brussels Polyphonia Choir, Namur Belgium French Community Symphonic Choir *(rec Nov 16-20, 1992)* † Allegretto; Blues; Fantasio; Largo; Mort de Sainte Alméenne (interlude); Rédemption de François Villon; Tempête (suite); Vivace TIMP ▲ 1016 [DDD] (18.97)

Sérénade à Angélique (radio score) for Orchestra (1946)

E. Theis (cnd), Austrian Chamber Sym *(rec Vienna, May 1996)* † Regain (suite); Suite archaique; Rot:Con Vn MPH ▲ 56823 [DDD] (15.97)

Skating Rink (symphonie chorégraphique) for Orchestra (1921)

M. Andreae (cnd), Swiss-Italian Radio-TV Orch *(rec 1988)* † Concertino Pno & Orch; Idée GALL ▲ 880 [DDD] (18.97)

Sonatina for Clarinet (or Cello) & Piano (1921-22)

M. Arrignon (cl), P. Devoyon (pno) † Chamber Music (comp); Rapsodie for 2 Fl TIMP ▲ 1010 [DDD]

Sonatina for Violins & Cello (1932)

C. Askin (vn), T. Lisboa (vc) ("Octachord: Virtuoso Duos") † Aguiar:Duo; Glière:Duets Vn & Va, Op. 39; Halvorsen:Passacaglia & Sarabande con variazioni; Kodály:Duo Vn & Vc, Op. 7 MER ▲ 84321 [DDD] (16.97)

O. Krysa (vn), T. Thedéen (vc) *(rec 1994-97)* ("Duos for Violin & Cello") † Martinů:Duo 1 Vn & Vc, H.157; M. Ravel:Son Vn & Vc; Schulhoff:Duo Vn & Vc BIS ▲ 916 [DDD] (17.97)

Suite archaique for Orchestra (1952)

E. Theis (cnd), Austrian Chamber Sym *(rec Vienna, May 1996)* † Regain (suite); Sérénade à Angélique; Rot:Con Vn MPH ▲ 56823 [DDD] (15.97)

Symphony No. 1 (1930)

S. Baudo (cnd), Czech PO † Mouvement symphonique 3; Pacific 231; Sym 2; Sym 3; Sym 4; Sym 5; Tempête (prelude) SUR 2-▲ 111566 [DDD]

HONEGGER, ARTHUR (cont.)

Symphony No. 1 (1930) (cont.)

C. Munch (cnd), French National Orch *(rec 1962)* ("Charles Munch Edition, vol. 6") † Dutilleux:Sym 2 VAL ▲ 4830 [ADD] (12.97)

Symphony No. 2 for Trumpet & String Orchestra (1941)

S. Baudo (cnd), Czech PO † Mouvement symphonique 3; Pacific 231; Sym 1; Sym 3; Sym 4; Sym 5; Tempête (prelude) SUR 2-▲ 111566 [DDD]

C. Munch (cnd), Czech PO *(rec ca 1957)* † D. Milhaud:Music for Prague, Op. 415; Sym 10 MUL (Prague Spring Collection) ▲ 310022 [ADD] (13.97)

C. Munch (cnd), French National Orch *(rec San Sebastian, Spain, Sept 1964)* ("Charles Munch Edition, Vol. 7") † Chant de Nigamon; Pastorale d'été; Sym 2; Sym 5 VAL ▲ 4831 [ADD] (12.97)

A. Myrat (cnd) † Martinů:Concertino Pno; Double Con AG ▲ 128 (18.97)

G. Schwarz (cnd), Seattle SO *(rec Apr 17, 1992 & Feb 8-9, 1993)* ("Transformation for Strings") † R. Strauss:Metamorphosen; Webern:Slow Movt Str Qt DLS ▲ 3121 [DDD] (14.97)

D. Schweizer (cnd), Zurich SO *(rec Sept 1993)* † Sym 4 CYPR ▲ 1602 [DDD] (17.97)

F. Wesenigk (tpt), H. von Karajan (cnd), Berlin PO *(rec Aug 1969)* † Sym 3; I. Stravinsky:Con Str Orch DEUT (The Originals) ▲ 47435 [ADD] (11.97)

D. Zinman (cnd), Zurich Tonhalle Orch † Monopartita; Mouvement symphonique 3; Pacific 231; Pastorale d'été; Rugby DECC ▲ 455352 (16.97)

Symphony No. 3, "Liturgique" (1945-46)

S. Baudo (cnd), Czech PO ("The Last World War") † Martinů:Memorial to Lidice; Schoenberg:Survivor from Warsaw, Op. 46 SUR ▲ 177 [AAD] (10.97)

S. Baudo (cnd), Czech PO † Mouvement symphonique 3; Pacific 231; Sym 1; Sym 2; Sym 4; Sym 5; Tempête (prelude) SUR 2-▲ 111566 [DDD]

J. Fournet (cnd), Netherlands Radio PO *(rec Hilversum Music Center Netherlands, May & Dec 1993)* † Con da camera; Pacific 231; Pastorale d'été; Rugby DNN ▲ 78831 [DDD] (16.97)

N. Järvi (cnd), Danish National RSO † Pacific 231; Sym 5 CHN ▲ 9176 [DDD] (16.97)

H. von Karajan (cnd), Berlin PO *(rec Jesus-Christus Church Berlin, Germany, Sept 1969)* † Sym 2; I. Stravinsky:Con Str Orch DEUT (The Originals) ▲ 47435 [ADD] (11.97)

Symphony No. 4, "Deliciae basilienses" (1946)

S. Baudo (cnd), Czech PO † Mouvement symphonique 3; Pacific 231; Sym 1; Sym 2; Sym 3; Sym 5; Tempête (prelude) SUR 2-▲ 111566 [DDD]

D. Schweizer (cnd), Zurich SO *(rec Sept 1993)* † Sym 2 CYPR ▲ 1602 [DDD] (17.97)

T. Vásáry (cnd), Bournemouth Sinfonietta † Concertino Pno & Orch; Pastorale d'été; Prélude, arioso et fughette sur le nom de BAC CHN ▲ 8993 [DDD] (16.97)

Symphony No. 5, "Di tre re" (1951)

S. Baudo (cnd), Czech PO † Mouvement symphonique 3; Pacific 231; Sym 1; Sym 2; Sym 3; Sym 4; Tempête (prelude) SUR 2-▲ 111566 [DDD]

N. Järvi (cnd), Danish National RSO † Pacific 231; Sym 3 CHN ▲ 9176 [DDD] (16.97)

I. Markevitch (cnd), Lamoureux Orch † D. Milhaud:Choëphores, Op. 24; A. Roussel:Bacchus et Ariane, Op. 43 DEUT (The Originals) ▲ 449748 (m) [ADD] (11.97)

C. Munch (cnd), French National Orch *(rec Helsinki, Finland)* ("Charles Munch Edition, Vol. 7") † Chant de Nigamon; Pastorale d'été; Sym 2; Sym 2 Tpt & Strs VAL ▲ 4831 [ADD] (12.97)

La Tempête (prelude) for Orchestra [after Shakespeare] (1923)

S. Baudo (cnd), Czech PO † Mouvement symphonique 3; Pacific 231; Sym 1; Sym 2; Sym 3; Sym 4; Sym 5 SUR 2-▲ 111566 [DDD]

La Tempête:Suite

L. Hager (hpd), M. Kemmer (cnd), RTL SO *(rec Nov 16-20, 1992)* † Allegretto; Blues; Fantasio; Largo; Mort de Sainte Alméenne (interlude); Rédemption de François Villon; Sémiramis; Vivace TIMP ▲ 1016 [DDD] (18.97)

Vivace (danse) for Orchestra

L. Hager (cnd), RTL SO *(rec Nov 16-20, 1992)* † Allegretto; Blues; Fantasio; Largo; Mort de Sainte Alméenne (interlude); Rédemption de François Villon; Sémiramis; Tempête (suite) TIMP ▲ 1016 [DDD] (18.97)

HONOROFF, RICHARD (20th cent)

Symphony No. 1, "Shoah" (1994)

A. Mikhailov (cnd), Moscow RSO *(rec Sept 1994)* † Sym 2; Testament CENT ▲ 2333 [DDD] (16.97)

Symphony No. 2 for Orchestra & Chorus, "From Ashes Reborn" (1994-95)

A. Mikhailov (cnd), Moscow RSO, V. Minin (cnd), Moscow Chamber Chorus *(rec Nov 1995)* † Sym 1; Testament CENT ▲ 2333 [DDD] (16.97)

Testament for Orchestra (1994)

A. Mikhailov (cnd), Moscow RSO *(rec Sept 1994)* † Sym 1; Sym 2 CENT ▲ 2333 [DDD] (16.97)

HOOF, JEF VAN (1886-1959)

Klein Quartet in C for Strings (1919)

R. Morgan (mez), R. Morgan (hp), Gaggini String Quartet † Nietigheden Qt Strs; P. Benoit:My Mother Tongue; Qt Strs in D PHA ▲ 92001 (13.97)

Nietigheden Quartet for Strings (1922)

R. Morgan (mez), R. Morgan (hp), Gaggini String Quartet † Klein Qt Strs; P. Benoit:My Mother Tongue; Qt Strs in D PHA ▲ 92001 (13.97)

Symphony No. 1 in A (1938)

F. Terby (cnd), Brussels BRTN PO † Sym 4; Willem de Zwijger Ov PHA ▲ 92013 (13.97)

Symphony No. 4 in B (1951)

F. Terby (cnd), Brussels BRTN PO † Sym 1; Willem de Zwijger Ov PHA ▲ 92013 (13.97)

Willem de Zwijger Overture for Orchestra (1910)

F. Terby (cnd), Brussels BRTN PO † Sym 1; Sym 4 PHA ▲ 92013 (13.97)

HOOK, JAMES (1746-1827)

Concerto in E♭ for Clarinet & Orchestra (1812)

C. Lawson (cl), P. Holman (cnd), Parley of Instruments † J. Christian Bach:Sinf concertante, T.290/9; Mahon:Con 2 Cl; Duet 1 for Cls; Duet 4 for Cls HYP ▲ 66896 (18.97)

HOORN, MAARTJE TEN (20th cent)

Music of Hoorn

Altena Ensemble—Brokken; Admiraliteit *(rec Theater Frascati, Amsterdam, Netherlands, Dec 1988)* † M. Altena:Music of Altena; Bergeijk:Scène Rurale; G. Carl:Roscoe Blvd HATH ▲ 6029 [DDD] (15.97)

HOOSE, ALFRED (1918-

Allegro for Violin & Piano (1951)

A. Jablokov (vn), D. Buranovsky (pno) ("MMC Chamber Music Series, Vol. II") † P. Diehl:On Course; E. Funk:Qt 2 Strs; Koplow:Vars on a Hymn Tune; Pond:Modal Vars; Son Pno; B. R. Wishart:Experience MASM ▲ 2030 [DDD] (16.97)

Gestures & Intimations for Orchestra

R. Black (cnd), Silesian PO ("MMC New Century, Vol. II") † Crowell:Black Holes & Anti-Matters; Elkana:Color in Time; Fugarino:Riding on a Cloud; Giusto:Peace Cow (it's not a habit, I'm used to it); Nytch:Novas MASM ▲ 2017 [DDD] (16.97)

HOOVER, KATHERINE (1937-

Canyon Echoes for Flute & Guitar (1991)

Duologue *(rec St. Paul, MN, Spring 1996)* ("Canyon Echoes") † Bolcom:Piezas Lindas; L. Larsen:Blue Third Pieces; Paulus:Fant in 3 Parts; Sierra:Segunda Cronica; Tercera Cronica GAS ▲ 336 (16.97)

Double Concerto for 2 Violins & Orchestra

D. Perry (vn), S. Beia (vn), J. E. Suben (cnd), Slovak RSO ("Night Skies: Orchestral Music of Hoover") † Orchestral Music PACD ▲ 96019 (15.97)

Homage to Bartók for Wind Quintet

Cumberland Quintet *(rec Tennessee Tech Univ, May 1996)* ("Shadows & Dreams") † H. Baumann:Rondo mit Mozart; Dollarhide:Shadows; K. Foley:Einstein's Dreams; Jager:Mumblety Peg; A. Tcherepnin:Qnt Ww CENT ▲ 2335 [DDD] (16.97)

Images for Clarinet, Violin & Piano (1981)

Verdehr Trio † Bassett:Trio Cl; Bruch:Pieces Cl, Op. 83; Hoag:Inventions LEON ▲ 326 (16.97)

Lyric Trio for Flute, Oboe & Cello

Huntingdon Trio † Czerny:Fant concertante, Op. 256; Foote:Flying Cloud & Oriental Dance; Poem 1 Pno, Op. 41; E. Goossens:Impressions of a Holiday, Op. 7; G. Holst:Terzetto Fl; Musgrave:Impromptu 1 Fl LEON ▲ 325 [DDD] (16.97)

Orchestral Music

J. E. Suben (cnd), Slovak RSO, V. Manoogian (cnd), Wisconsin Philomusica—Eleni; Night Skies; Sketches Orch ("Night Skies: Orchestral Music of Hoover") † Double Con Vns PACD ▲ 96019 (15.97)

HOOVER, KATHERINE (cont.)

Summer Night for Orchestra

C. Martin (cnd) † J. Brockman:Perihelion II; K. Gardner:Rainforest; L. Larsen:Parachute Dancing; Mamlok:Elegy; M. Richter:Lament; Van de Vate:Journeys LEON ▲ 327 [DDD] (16.97)

HOPKINS, BILL (1943-1981)

Music of Hopkins

A. Wells (sop), A. Balanescu (vn), R. Bernas (cnd) —En attendant for Fl, Ob, Vc & Hpd; 2 Pomes for Sop, Bass Cittern; Tpt, Hp & Va; Penandt for Vn; Sensation for Sop, Sax, Tpt, Hp & Va † A. Gilbert:9 or 10 Osannas NMC ▲ 14 [DDD]

HOPKINS, JAMES (1939-

Quintet No. 1 for Brass

Chicago Brass Quintet † Mattern:Son Breve CRYS ▮ 211 (9.98)

Songs of Eternity for Orchestra & Chorus (1992)

J. Alexander (cnd), Pacific SO, Pacific Chorale † Paulus:Voices ALBA ▲ 182 (16.97)

HOPKINS, SARAH (20th cent)

Cello Chi for a Singing Cellist (1986)

J. Krieger (vc), A. Quadraverb (elec) † Halier:UITT; A. Lucier:Indian Summer; Saariaho:Petals for Vc; William:Come Windows Gold Coming OOWN ▲ 22 (16.97)

HORNEMAN, CHRISTIAN FREDERIK EMIL (1840-1906)

Aladdin (selections)

O. A. Hughes (cnd), Aalborg SO ("Theatre Music") † Esther (sels); Gurre (suite); Kalanus (sels); Kampen med Muserne (suite) BIS ▲ 749 [DDD] (17.97)

Aladdin:Overture

J. Hye-Knudsen (cnd), Royal Danish Orch ("Romantic Danish Overtures") † J. B. E. Dupuy:Youth & Folly (ov); J. P. E. Hartmann:Little Kristen (ov); Heise:King & Marshal (ov); Kuhlau:William Shakespeare (ov); Weyse:Sleeping-draught (ov) STRL ▲ 1018 [AAD] (15.97)

Esther (selections)

O. A. Hughes (cnd), Aalborg SO ("Theatre Music") † Aladdin (sels); Gurre (suite); Kalanus (sels); Kampen med Muserne (suite) BIS ▲ 749 [DDD] (17.97)

Gurre (suite) for Orchestra (1901)

O. A. Hughes (cnd), Aalborg SO ("Theatre Music") † Aladdin (sels); Esther (sels); Kalanus (sels); Kampen med Muserne (suite) BIS ▲ 749 [DDD] (17.97)

Kalanus (selections)

O. A. Hughes (cnd), Aalborg SO ("Theatre Music") † Aladdin (sels); Esther (sels); Gurre (suite); Kampen med Muserne (suite) BIS ▲ 749 [DDD] (17.97)

Kampen med Muserne (suite) for Orchestra (1908)

O. A. Hughes (cnd), Aalborg SO, Danish National Opera Choir Women's Voices ("Theatre Music") † Aladdin (sels); Esther (sels); Gurre (suite); Kalanus (sels) BIS ▲ 749 [DDD] (17.97)

Music of Horneman

G. Paëvatalu (bar), M. Schønwandt (cnd), Danish National RSO, Danish National Choir—Gurre; Helteliv; Alladin Ov CHN ▲ 9373 [DDD] (16.97)

Quartet No. 2 in d for Strings (1861)

Copenhagen String Quartet *(rec Copenhagen, 1969)* † Kuhlau:Qt Strs MARC ▲ 8224016 [AAD] (13.97)

HORNER, JAMES (1953-

Aliens (selections)

C. Eidelman (cnd), Royal Scottish National Orch—Futile Escape ("Titanic and Other Film Scores of James Horner") † Apollo 13 (sels); Brainstorm (sels); Braveheart (sels); Casper (sels); Cocoon:The Return (sels); Courage Under Fire (sels); Film Music; Once Around (sels); Star Trek II:The Wrath of Khan (sels); Titanic (sels); G. F. Handel:Pastor fido (terpsichore) VRS ▲ 5943 (16.97)

Apollo 13 (selections)

J. McNeely (cnd), Royal Scottish National Orch, J. McNeely (cnd), Royal Scottish National Chorus—The Launch ("Titanic and Other Film Scores of James Horner") † Aliens (sels); Brainstorm (sels); Braveheart (sels); Casper (sels); Cocoon:The Return (sels); Courage Under Fire (sels); Film Music; Once Around (sels); Star Trek II:The Wrath of Khan (sels); Titanic (sels); G. F. Handel:Pastor fido (terpsichore) VRS ▲ 5943 (16.97)

Brainstorm (selections)

J. Horner (cnd), London SO, J. Horner (cnd), Ambrosian Singers—Michael's Gift to Karen ("Titanic and Other Film Scores of James Horner") † Aliens (sels); Apollo 13 (sels); Braveheart (sels); Casper (sels); Cocoon:The Return (sels); Courage Under Fire (sels); Film Music; Once Around (sels); Star Trek II:The Wrath of Khan (sels); Titanic (sels); G. F. Handel:Pastor fido (terpsichore) VRS ▲ 5943 (16.97)

Braveheart (selections)

J. McNeely (cnd), Royal Scottish National Orch, J. McNeely (cnd), Royal Scottish National Chorus—End Title ("Titanic and Other Film Scores of James Horner") † Aliens (sels); Apollo 13 (sels); Brainstorm (sels); Casper (sels); Cocoon:The Return (sels); Courage Under Fire (sels); Film Music; Once Around (sels); Star Trek II:The Wrath of Khan (sels); Titanic (sels); G. F. Handel:Pastor fido (terpsichore) VRS ▲ 5943 (16.97)

Casper (selections)

J. McNeely (cnd), Royal Scottish National Orch, J. McNeely (cnd), Royal Scottish National Chorus—Casper's Lullaby; Casper's Lullaby ("Titanic and Other Film Scores of James Horner") † Aliens (sels); Apollo 13 (sels); Brainstorm (sels); Braveheart (sels); Cocoon:The Return (sels); Courage Under Fire (sels); Film Music; Once Around (sels); Star Trek II:The Wrath of Khan (sels); Titanic (sels); G. F. Handel:Pastor fido (terpsichore) VRS ▲ 5943 (16.97)

Cocoon:The Return (selections)

J. Horner (pno), J. Horner (cnd) —Returning Home ("Titanic and Other Film Scores of James Horner") † Aliens (sels); Apollo 13 (sels); Brainstorm (sels); Braveheart (sels); Casper (sels); Courage Under Fire (sels); Film Music; Once Around (sels); Star Trek II:The Wrath of Khan (sels); Titanic (sels); G. F. Handel:Pastor fido (terpsichore) VRS ▲ 5943 (16.97)

Courage Under Fire (selections)

J. McNeely (cnd), Royal Scottish National Orch, J. McNeely (cnd), Royal Scottish National Chorus—Theme ("Titanic and Other Film Scores of James Horner") † Aliens (sels); Apollo 13 (sels); Brainstorm (sels); Braveheart (sels); Casper (sels); Cocoon:The Return (sels); Film Music; Once Around (sels); Star Trek II:The Wrath of Khan (sels); Titanic (sels); G. F. Handel:Pastor fido (terpsichore) VRS ▲ 5943 (16.97)

Deep Impact (film music) for Orchestra

J. Horner (cnd) *(rec CA)* COL ▲ 60690 (17.97) ▮ 60690 (11.98)

Film Music

C. Bell (cnd), Royal Scottish National Orch, C. Bell (cnd), Royal Scottish National Chorus *(Distant Memories [from Titanic])*, J. McNeely (cnd), Royal Scottish National Orch, J. McNeely (cnd), Royal Scottish National Chorus *(Apollo 13 (sels) [The Launch]; Casper (sels) [Casper's Lullaby]; Braveheart (sels) [End Title]; Courage Under Fire (sels) [Theme])*, J. Horner (pno), J. Horner (cnd) *(Once Around (sels) [A Passage of Time]; Cocoon:The Return (sels) [Returning Home])*, C. Eidelman (cnd), Seattle SO *(Star Trek II:The Wrath of Khan (sels) [End Credits])*, C. Eidelman (cnd), Royal Scottish National Orch *(Aliens (sels) [Futile Escape])*, J. Horner (cnd), London SO, J. Horner (cnd), Ambrosian Singers *(Brainstorm (sels) [Michael's Gift to Karen])* ("Titanic and Other Film Scores of James Horner") † Aliens (sels); Apollo 13 (sels); Brainstorm (sels); Braveheart (sels); Casper (sels); Cocoon:The Return (sels); Courage Under Fire (sels); Once Around (sels); Star Trek II:The Wrath of Khan (sels); Titanic (sels); G. F. Handel:Pastor fido (terpsichore) VRS ▲ 5943 (16.97)

The Mask of Zorro (film music) for Orchestra

J. Horner (cnd) *(rec London)* COL ▲ 60627 (17.97) ▮ 60627 (11.98) △ 60627 (15.97)

Once Around (selections)

J. Horner (pno), J. Horner (cnd) —A Passage of Time ("Titanic and Other Film Scores of James Horner") † Aliens (sels); Apollo 13 (sels); Brainstorm (sels); Braveheart (sels); Casper (sels); Cocoon:The Return (sels); Courage Under Fire (sels); Film Music; Star Trek II:The Wrath of Khan (sels); Titanic (sels); G. F. Handel:Pastor fido (terpsichore) VRS ▲ 5943 (16.97)

The Spitfire Grill (film music) for Orchestra (1996)

J. Horner (cnd) ("The Spitfire Grill: Original Motion Picture Soundtrack") SNYC ▲ 62776 (16.97)

Star Trek II:The Wrath of Khan (selections)

C. Eidelman (cnd), Seattle SO—End Credits ("Titanic and Other Film Scores of James Horner") † Aliens (sels); Apollo 13 (sels); Brainstorm (sels); Braveheart (sels); Casper (sels); Cocoon:The Return (sels); Courage Under Fire (sels); Film Music; Once Around (sels); Titanic (sels); G. F. Handel:Pastor fido (terpsichore) VRS ▲ 5943 (16.97)

Titanic (selections)

J. Debney (cnd), Royal Scottish National Orch, C. Bell (cnd), Royal Scottish National Chorus—Distant Memories; Southampton; Take Her to Sea, Mr. Murdoch ("Titanic and Other Film Scores of James Horner") † Aliens (sels); Apollo 13 (sels); Brainstorm (sels); Braveheart (sels); Casper (sels); Cocoon:The Return (sels); Courage Under Fire (sels); Film Music; Once Around (sels); Star Trek II:The Wrath of Khan (sels); G. F. Handel:Pastor fido (terpsichore) VRS ▲ 5943 (16.97)

HORNER, JAMES (cont.)

Titanic (film music) for Orchestra (1997)

artists unknown ("Back to Titanic") COL ▲ 60691 (17.97) ▮ 60691 (11.98) △ 60691 (15.97)

HOROVITZ, JOSEPH (1926-

Canzonet & Rondino for Chamber Orchestra

J. Horovitz (cnd), Royal Ballet Sinfonia † Con Ob; Con Tpt; Jubilee Serenade; Sinfonietta ASV ▲ 2114 (12.97)

Concerto for Oboe & Chamber Orchestra (1993)

N. Daniel (ob), J. Horovitz (cnd), Royal Ballet Sinfonia † Canzonet & Rondino; Con Tpt; Jubilee Serenade; Sinfonietta ASV ▲ 2114 (12.97)

Concerto for Trumpet & Chamber Orchestra

J. Watson (tpt), J. Horovitz (cnd), Royal Ballet Sinfonia † Canzonet & Rondino; Con Ob; Jubilee Serenade; Sinfonietta ASV ▲ 2114 (12.97)

Jubilee Serenade for Chamber Orchestra

J. Horovitz (cnd), Royal Ballet Sinfonia † Canzonet & Rondino; Con Ob; Con Tpt; Sinfonietta ASV ▲ 2114 (12.97)

Music Hall Suite for Brass Quintet (1964)

St. Louis Brass Quintet † B. Dutton:Carnival of Venice; A. Hovhaness:Dances Brass Qnt, Op. 79; F. Leclerc:Par Monts et par vaux CRYS ▲ 200 [ADD] (15.97)

U. Zaiser (tpt), P. Leiner (tpt), S. Scott (hn), R. Rudolph (tuba) † M. Arnold:Qnt Brass, Op. 73; E. Crespo:Suite Americana 1; V. Ewald:Qnt 1 Brass, Op. 5, J. Koetsier:Qnt Brass, Op. 65 BAYF ▲ 100251 [DDD] (17.97)

Sinfonietta for Chamber Orchestra

J. Horovitz (cnd), Royal Ballet Sinfonia † Canzonet & Rondino; Con Ob; Con Tpt; Jubilee Serenade ASV ▲ 2114 (12.97)

Sonatina for Clarinet & Piano (1981)

G. Peyer (cl), G. Pryor (pno) *(rec Rosslyn Hill Chapel, Hempstead, England, 1982-83)* ("English Music for Clarinet & Piano") † M. Arnold:Son Cl; G. Finzi:Bagatelles Cl, Op. 23; P. Harvey:Suite on Themes of Gershwin Clt & Pno; J. Ireland:Fant-Son Cl; A. Richardson:Roundelay CHN ▲ 8549 [DDD] (17.97)

B. Röthlisberger (cl), S. Andres (pno) ("Who Nose") † J. Agrell:Aviary Divert; Blues for D.D.; L. Bernstein:Son Cl; Bolli:Rülpsodie, schön blau; G. Gershwin:Preludes Pno; Schnyder:Son S Sax; Who Nose GALL ▲ 951 [DDD] (18.97)

Variations on a Theme by Paganini for 2 Trumpets, French Horn & Tenor Tuba

London Brass Quintet † D. Bourgeois:Con Trbn; G. Holst:Moorside Suite; J. Ireland:Comedy Ov ALBA ▲ 93 [DDD]

HOROWITZ, VLADIMIR (1903-1989)

Moment exotique for Piano

V. Horowitz (pno) *(rec 1926)* † J. S. Bach:Toccata, Adagio & Fugue Org, BWV 564; Liszt:Trans, Arrs & Paraphrases; S. Rachmaninoff:Preludes Pno INTC ▲ 860864 (13.97)

Variations on a Theme from Bizet's *Carmen* for Piano

V. Horowitz (pno) *(rec Jan 2-Feb 1, 1968)* ("The Legendary Masterworks Recordings, 1962-1973, Vol. 4") † Chopin:Polonaise 5 Pno, Op. 44; D. Scarlatti:Sons Kbd; R. Schumann:Arabeske Pno, Op. 18; Kinderszenen Pno, Op. 15 SNYC ▲ 53465 [ADD] (16.97)

V. Kuleshov (pno) *(rec Fort Worth, TX, 1993)* ("The Ninth Cliburn Competition 1993") † J. S. Bach:Goldberg Vars, BWV 988; Busoni:Bach Trans Pno; J. Haydn:Son 60 Kbd, H.XVI/50; Liszt:Trans, Arrs & Paraphrases; A. Scriabin:Son 9 Pno, Op. 68 VAIA (Retrospective Series, Vol. 9) ▲ 1177 [DDD] (16.97)

HORUSITZKY, ZOLTÁN (1903-1985)

Chinese Songs (6) for Voice & Piano, Op. 13 (1941)

M. László (sop), Z. Horusitzky (pno) *(rec 1964-83)* † French Songs, Op. 58; Pieces Pno, Op. 12; Shakespeare Sonnets, Op. 19; Son for 2 Pnos, Op. 51; Son Pno, "Mountain", Op. 45 HUN ▲ 31670 [ADD] (16.97)

French Songs (5) for Voice & Piano [texts Verlaine & Cros], Op. 58 (1970's)

B. Keönch (ten), I. Rohmann (pno) *(rec 1964-83)* † Chinese Songs, Op. 13; Pieces Pno, Op. 12; Shakespeare Sonnets, Op. 19; Son for 2 Pnos, Op. 51; Son Pno, "Mountain", Op. 45 HUN ▲ 31670 [ADD] (16.97)

Pieces (3) for Piano, Op. 12 (ca 1940)

Sr. (pno) *(rec 1964-83)* † Chinese Songs, Op. 13; French Songs, Op. 58; Shakespeare Sonnets, Op. 19; Son for 2 Pnos, Op. 51; Son Pno, "Mountain", Op. 45 HUN ▲ 31670 [ADD] (16.97)

Shakespeare Sonnets (3) for Voice & Piano, Op. 19

M. László (sop), Z. Horusitzky (pno) *(rec 1964-83)* † Chinese Songs, Op. 13; French Songs, Op. 58; Pieces Pno, Op. 12; Son for 2 Pnos, Op. 51; Son Pno, "Mountain", Op. 45 HUN ▲ 31670 [ADD] (16.97)

Sonata for Piano, Op. 45, "The Mountain" (1968)

Z. Horusitzky (pno) *(rec 1964-83)* † Chinese Songs, Op. 13; French Songs, Op. 58; Pieces Pno, Op. 12; Shakespeare Sonnets, Op. 19; Son for 2 Pnos, Op. 51 HUN ▲ 31670 [ADD] (16.97)

Sonata for 2 Pianos, Op. 51 (1973)

Jr. (pno), Sr. (pno) *(rec 1964-83)* † Chinese Songs, Op. 13; French Songs, Op. 58; Pieces Pno, Op. 12; Shakespeare Sonnets, Op. 19; Son Pno, "Mountain", Op. 45 HUN ▲ 31670 [ADD] (16.97)

HORVIT, MICHAEL (1932-

Aleinu [Adoration] for Baritone, Violin, Organ & Chorus (1985)

S. Smith (bar), F. Lack (vn), R. Jones (org), C. Hausmann (cnd), Moores School Concert Chorale ("Orchestral Music") † Cullen Ov; Even When God is Silent; Fant Vn; Invocation ALBA ▲ 265 [DDD] (16.97)

The Cullen Overture for Orchestra (1988)

A. Gnam (cnd), Texas Festival Orch ("Orchestral Music") † Aleinu; Even When God is Silent; Fant Vn; Invocation ALBA ▲ 265 [DDD] (16.97)

Even When God is Silent for Voices, Cello & Piano

F. A. Krager (cnd), Moores School of Music SO, F. A. Krager (cnd), Ambient Brass Quintet ("Orchestral Music") † Aleinu; Cullen Ov; Fant Vn; Invocation ALBA ▲ 265 [DDD] (16.97)

Fantasy for Violin & Orchestra, "Daughters of Jerusalem" (1996)

F. Lack (vn), F. A. Krager (cnd), Moores School of Music SO ("Orchestral Music") † Aleinu; Cullen Ov; Even When God is Silent; Invocation ALBA ▲ 265 [DDD] (16.97)

Invocation & Exultation for Chamber Orchestra (1990)

L. Spierer (cnd), Norrbotten CO ("Orchestral Music") † Aleinu; Cullen Ov; Even When God is Silent; Fant Vn ALBA ▲ 265 [DDD] (16.97)

Music of Horvit

C. Hausmann (cnd), Texas Music Festival Orch *(The Cullen Ov)*, T. Hester (pno) *(Duo Fant)*, Univ of Houston Chorus *(God Is with Us; You Shall Love the Lord Your God)*, P. Spain (sop), A. Gnam (vc), D. Garrett (vc), R. Jones (org) *(The Prophecy of Amos)*, D. Hayes (sop), T. Franklin (bar), R. Hough (ob), J. Lerner (cl), I. Benevich (tpt), B. Guess (trbn), T. Hester (pno), R. Jones (org) *(3 Shakespeare Sonnets)*, D. Hayes (sop), T. Hester (pno) *(3 Faces of Love)* ALBA ▲ 134 [DDD] (16.97)

HOSOKAWA, TOSHIO (1955-

Fragmente II for Alto Flute & String Quartet

P. Artaud (fl), Arditti String Quartet † Landscape I; Landscape II; Landscape V; Vertical Time Study III DISQ ▲ 782078 (18.97)

Into the Depths of Time for Cello & Accordion

J. Berger (vc), S. Hussong (acc) † J. Cage:Two^4 WER ▲ 6617 (19.97)

J. Berger (vc), S. Hussong (acc) † Melodia Acc; Sen V; Vertical Time Study I; Vertical Time Study III COLG ▲ 20016 (18.97)

N. Imai (va), M. Miki (acc) [trans for va & acc] *(rec Apr 1998)* ("Into the Depth of Time") † Irino:Suite Va; Y. Takahashi:Ins Tal; Like a Water Buffalo; Like Swans Leaving the Lake; I. Yun:Duo Va BIS ▲ 929 [DDD] (17.97)

Landscape I for String Quartet

Arditti String Quartet † Fragmente II; Landscape II; Landscape V; Vertical Time Study III DISQ ▲ 782078 (18.97)

Landscape II for Harp and String Quartet

K. Nakayama (hp), Arditti String Quartet † Fragmente II; Landscape I; Landscape V; Vertical Time Study III DISQ ▲ 782078 (18.97)

Landscape V for Shô and String Quartet

M. Miyata (sho), Arditti String Quartet † Fragmente II; Landscape I; Landscape II; Vertical Time Study III DISQ ▲ 782078 (18.97)

Melodia for Accordian (1979)

S. Hussong (acc) † Into the Depths of Time; Sen V; Vertical Time Study I; Vertical Time Study III COLG ▲ 20016 (18.97)

Sen V for Accordian (1991-92)

S. Hussong (acc) † Into the Depths of Time; Melodia Acc; Vertical Time Study I; Vertical Time Study III COLG ▲ 20016 (18.97)

Vertical Time Study I for Clarinet, Cello & Accordian (1992)

W. Taube (vc), M. Riessler (cl), S. Hussong (acc) † Into the Depths of Time; Melodia Acc; Sen V; Vertical Time Study III COLG ▲ 20016 (18.97)

HOSOKAWA, TOSHIO (cont.)

Vertical Time Study III for Violin & Piano

I. Arditti (vn), I. Nodaira (pno) † Fragmente II; Landscape I; Landscape II; Landscape V DISQ ▲ 782078 (18.97)

A. Urushihara (vn), Y. Sugawara-Lachenmann (pno) † Into the Depths of Time; Melodia Acc; Sen V; Vertical Time Study I COLG ▲ 20016 (18.97)

HOSSEIN, ANDRÉ (1907-1983)

Concerto No. 3 for Piano & Orchestra, "Una Fantasia"

D. Laval (pno), P. Verrot (cnd), Monte Carlo PO *(rec Monte Carlo, July 1995)* ("Musique et cinema") † B. Herrmann:Con Macabre; M. Legrand:Concertino Pno; J. Wiener:Con 1 Pno TRAV (Music & Movies) ▲ 1019 [DDD]

HOTMAN, NICHOLAS (ca 1610-1663)

Music of Hotman

L. Grunth (va), B. Larsen (fl), S. Larsen (pno)—Pièces Thb (5); Suites B VI (4), Pièce B VI; Aris à boire ("The French Flute") CYPR ▲ 3607 [DDD] (17.97)

HOTTETERRE, JACQUES (-MARTIN) (1674-1763)

Deuxième suitte de Pièces à 2 dessus for 2 Flutes (or Recorders, Viols, or other Instruments) and Continuo ad lib, Op. 6 (1717)

L. Dean (trns fl), C. Ahrens (trns fl) ("Le rossignol en amour: French Baroque Music for Transverse Flute without Bass") † Première suitte de Pièces à 2 dessu, Op. 4; Boismortier:Suites Fl, Op. 35; F. Couperin:Nouveaux Concerts; Pièces de clavecin (sels); P. D. Philidor:Suites Trns Fls CHR ▲ 77202 [DDD] (17.97)

Music of Hotteterre

J. T. Linden (vl), K. Junghänel (thb), W. Hazelzet (trns fl), J. Ogg (hpd)—Prélude in D; Suite III in G [from Livre I]; Prélude in b; Passacaille; Suite II in c; Suite 1 Tr Fl; Rochers, je ne veux point que votre Eco fidelle; J'ay passé dexu jours sans vous voir; Dans ces deserts paisibles; Pourquoy, doux rossingol; Le beau berger Tircis; 5 Airs; 8 Preludes in b, c, C, D, g, g, G, G; 3 Suites in c, g, G ("Pièces pour la Flûte Traversiere") GLSS ▲ 920801 [DDD] (18.97)

Pièces for Flute, Other Instruments & Continuo, Op. 2, ""Le Romain"" (1708; rev 1715)

M. Hirao (vl), Y. Imamura (gtr/thb), M. Arita (fl d'amore/trns fl), K. Suga (trns fl), C. Arita (hpd) *(rec Akigawa Kirara Hall, Nov 22-27, 1993)* ("Flute Music of the Grand Siècle") † Première livre de pièce, Op. 5; Blavet:Fl Music; Sons Fl, Op. 3; Boismortier:Sons Fl, Op. 91; J.-M. Leclair:Quatrième livre, Op. 9 DNN 2-▲ 75957 [DDD] (33.97)

Première livre de pièce for Flute & Other Instruments, Op. 5 (1715)

M. Hirao (vl), Y. Imamura (gtr/thb), M. Arita (fl d'amore/trns fl), K. Suga (trns fl), C. Arita (hpd) *(rec Akigawa Kirara Hall, Nov 22-27, 1993)* ("Flute Music of the Grand Siècle") † Pièces, Op. 2; Blavet:Fl Music; Sons Fl, Op. 3; Boismortier:Sons Fl, Op. 91; J.-M. Leclair:Quatrième livre, Op. 9 DNN 2-▲ 75957 [DDD] (33.97)

M. Rasmussen (vl), D. Laurin (rcr), L. Meyer (hpd) *(rec Furuby Church Sweden, May 8-11, 1995)* ("The French King's Flautists") † Blavet:Sonatas for Transverse Flute & Continuo; J. D. Braun:Son Terza; Dornel:Sons Vn & Suites Fl, Op. 2; J.-M. Leclair:Sons Vn (books 1-4) BIS ▲ 745 [DDD] (17.97)

Première suitte de Pièces à 2 dessus for 2 Flutes (or Recorders, Viols or other Instruments), Op. 4 (1712)

L. Dean (trns fl), C. Ahrens (trns fl) ("Le rossignol en amour: French Baroque Music for Transverse Flute without Bass") † Deuxième suitte Fls, Op. 6; Boismortier:Suites Fl, Op. 35; F. Couperin:Nouveaux Concerts; Pièces de clavecin (sels); P. D. Philidor:Suites Trns Fls CHR ▲ 77202 [DDD] (17.97)

HOUGHTON, PHILLIP (1954-

Stélé for Guitar

J. Williams (gtr) *(rec Hampstead, London, England, Mar 17-21, 1998)* ("The Guitarist") † Anonymous:Ductia; Lamento di Tristan; Saltarello; Domeniconi:Koyunbaba, Op. 19; Satie:Gnossiennes; Gymnopédies; Theodorakis:Songs; J. Williams:Aeolian Suite SNYC ▲ 60586 [DDD] (16.97) ▮ 60586 [DDD] (10.98) △ 60586 [DDD] (15.97)

HOUNG, CH'IEN-HUI (1962-

Le récit de cinq marimbas for Percussion Ensemble (1993)

Kroumata Percussion Ensemble *(rec Dec 1997)* ("Kroumata") † J. Cage:Third Construction; Katzer:Schlagmusik 2; S.-D. Sandström:Kroumata Pieces; H. Strindberg:Ursprung/Gläntor BIS ▲ 932 [DDD] (17.97)

HOVDA, ELEANOR (1940-

Ariadne Music for Flute, Clarinet, Violin, Cello, Double Bass, Piano & Percussion (1984)

J. Wagar (cnd), Prism Players ("Ariadne Music") † Leaning into & Away; Onyx; Snapdragon; Song in High Grasses OOD ▲ 46 [DDD] (16.97)

Armonia for Guitar Quartet (1992)

Minneapolis Guitar Quartet ("New Works for Guitar Quartet") † Bassett:Narratives; L. Brouwer:Cuban Landscape with Rumba; Kechley:Voices from the Garden; Sekiya:Tobila; Vandervelde:Genesis V ALBA ▲ 207 [DDD] (16.97)

Borealis Music for Chamber Ensemble (1987)

Relâche Ensemble ("Outcome Inevitable") † R. Ashley:Outcome Inevitable; F. W.-H. Ho:Contradiction, Please! The Revenge of Charlie Chan; Vierk:Timberline OOD ▲ 17 [DDD] (16.97)

Dancing in Place for Harp (1997)

E. Panzer (hp) ("Dancing in Place") † Beglarian:Play Nice; Brazelton:Down n Harp n All a Rond o; W. M. Chambers:Moments Hp; Einhorn:New Pages Pnos; Matamoros:Re: Elizabeth; Panzer:Green Tea with Oranges; Invocation Hp; Syncophony Hp OOD ▲ 56 [DDD] (16.97)

Leaning into & Away for Winds, Strings & Percussion (1994)

J. Wagar (cnd), Prism Players ("Ariadne Music") † Ariadne Music; Onyx; Snapdragon; Song in High Grasses OOD ▲ 46 [DDD] (16.97)

Lemniscates for String Quartet (1988)

Cassatt String Quartet *(rec Jan 1993)* ("Cassatt") † T. Davidson:Cassandra Sings; D. Godfrey:Intermedio; Waggoner:Song:Strophic Vars; J. Wolfe:4 Marys Str Qt CRI ▲ 671 [DDD] (16.97)

Music of Hovda

J. Vees (elec bass/elec gtr/g), L. van Cleve (E hn/ob), E. Hovda (pno)—Coastal Traces Tidepools 1; Shenai Sky; Record of an Ocean Cliff; Crossings in a Mountain Dream; Glacier Track; Glosses/Glacier; Beginnings; Coastal Traces Tidepools 2 ("Coastal Traces") OOD ▲ 29 [DDD] (16.97)

Onyx for Flute, Oboe, Clarinet, Trumpet, Horn, & Strings (1991)

J. Wagar (cnd), Prism Players ("Ariadne Music") † Ariadne Music; Leaning into & Away; Snapdragon; Song in High Grasses OOD ▲ 46 [DDD] (16.97)

Snapdragon for Flute, 2 Oboes, 2 Clarinets, 2 Bassoons & 2 Horns (1993)

J. Wagar (cnd), Prism Players ("Ariadne Music") † Ariadne Music; Leaning into & Away; Onyx; Song in High Grasses OOD ▲ 46 [DDD] (16.97)

Song in High Grasses for Voice, Flute, Cello & Piano (1986)

J. Wagar (cnd), Prism Players ("Ariadne Music") † Ariadne Music; Leaning into & Away; Onyx; Snapdragon OOD ▲ 46 [DDD] (16.97)

HOVHANESS, ALAN (1911-

Alleluia & Fugue for String Orchestra, Op. 40b (1941)

D. Amos (cnd), Philharmonia Orch † Anahid; And God Created Whales, Op. 229; Con 8 Orch, Op. 117; Elibris, Op. 50 CRYS ▲ 810 [DDD] (15.97) ▮ 810 [DDD] (9.98)

G. Schwarz (cnd), Seattle SO *(rec Sept 1993)* ("Mysterious Mountain") † And God Created Whales, Op. 229; Celestial Fant, Op. 44; Prayer of St. Gregory, Op. 62b; Prelude & Quadruple Fugue, Op. 128 DLS ▲ 3157 [DDD] (14.97) ▮ 3157 [DDD] (7.98)

K. Stratton (cnd), Slovak RSO *(rec Slovak Radio Concert Hall Bratislava, Oct 1997)* ("Celestial Fantasy") † Armenian Rhap 2, Op. 51; Armenian Rhap 3, Op. 189; Celestial Fant, Op. 44; Holy City, Op. 218; In Memory of an Artist, Op. 163; Processional & Fugue, Op. 76/5; Psalm & Fugue, Op. 40a DOR ▲ 93166 [DDD] (16.97)

R. Werthen (cnd), I Fiamminghi *(rec Vellereille-les-Brayeux Belgium, Aug 18-20, 1994)* ("Celestial Gate") † Con 7 Orch, Op. 116; Prayer of St. Gregory, Op. 62b; Prelude & Quadruple Fugue, Op. 128; Sym 6; Tzaikerk, Op. 53 TEL ▲ 80392 [DDD] (16.97)

R. Werthen (cnd), I Fiamminghi *(rec Vellereille-les-Brayeux, Belgium, Aug 18-20, 1994)* ("American Adagios") † S. Barber:Adagio Strs; Agnus Dei; Con Vn; Canning:Fant on Hymn Tune by Justin Morgan; A. Copland:Appalachian Spring (suite); Corigliano:Voyage Fl; G. Gershwin:Lullaby Str Qt; C. Rouse:Con Fl TEL ▲ 80503 [DDD] (16.97)

Anahid for Chamber Orchestra, Op. 57 (1945)

D. Amos (cnd), Philharmonia Orch † Alleluia & Fugue, Op. 40b; And God Created Whales, Op. 229; Con 8 Orch, Op. 117; Elibris, Op. 50 CRYS ▲ 810 [DDD] (15.97) ▮ 810 [DDD] (9.98)

And God Created Whales for Orchestra [incorporating taped whale songs], Op. 229 (1970)

D. Amos (cnd), Philharmonia Orch † Alleluia & Fugue, Op. 40b; Anahid; Con 8 Orch, Op. 117; Elibris, Op. 50 CRYS ▲ 810 [DDD] (15.97) ▮ 810 [DDD] (9.98)

G. Schwarz (cnd), Seattle SO *(rec Sept 1993)* ("Mysterious Mountain") † Alleluia & Fugue, Op. 40b; Celestial Fant, Op. 44; Prayer of St. Gregory, Op. 62b; Prelude & Quadruple Fugue, Op. 128 DLS ▲ 3157 [DDD] (14.97) ▮ 3157 [DDD] (7.98)

Armenian Rhapsody No. 1 for String Orchestra, Op. 45 (1944)

Seattle SO † Armenian Rhap 2, Op. 51; Armenian Rhap 3, Op. 189; Con 11 Pno; Sym 38 KSCH ▲ 374222 (16.97)

HOVHANESS, ALAN (cont.)
Armenian Rhapsody No. 2 for String Orchestra, Op. 51 (1944)
D. Amos (cnd), Israel PO † Celestial Fant, Op. 44; Chajes:Israeli Melodies; Creston:Chant of 1942, Op. 33; Suite Str Orch, Op. 109; Joio:Air; Persichetti:Introit Strs, Op. 96 CRYS ▲ 508 (15.97)
Seattle SO † Armenian Rhap 1, Op. 45; Armenian Rhap 3, Op. 189; Con 11 Pno; Sym 38 KSCH ▲ 374222 (16.97)
K. Stratton (cnd), Slovak RSO *(rec Slovak Radio Concert Hall Bratislava, Oct 1997)* ("Celestial Fantasy") † Alleluia & Fugue, Op. 40b; Armenian Rhap 3, Op. 189; Celestial Fant, Op. 44; Holy City, Op. 218; In Memory of an Artist, Op. 163; Processional & Fugue, Op. 76/5; Psalm & Fugue, Op. 40a DOR ▲ 93166 [DDD] (16.97)
Armenian Rhapsody No. 3 for String Orchestra, Op. 189 (1944)
A. Hovhaness (cnd), Royal PO † Fra Angelico, Op. 220; Mountains & Rivers Without End, Op. 225; Sym 21 CRYS ▲ 804 [ADD] (15.97)
Seattle SO † Armenian Rhap 1, Op. 45; Armenian Rhap 2, Op. 51; Con 11 Pno; Sym 38 KSCH ▲ 374222 (16.97)
K. Stratton (cnd), Slovak RSO *(rec Slovak Radio Concert Hall Bratislava, Oct 1997)* ("Celestial Fantasy") † Alleluia & Fugue, Op. 40b; Armenian Rhap 2, Op. 51; Celestial Fant, Op. 44; Holy City, Op. 218; In Memory of an Artist, Op. 163; Processional & Fugue, Op. 76/5; Psalm & Fugue, Op. 40a DOR ▲ 93166 [DDD] (16.97)
artists unknown † Prayer of St. Gregory, Op. 62b; Sym 11; Tzaikerk, Op. 53 CRYS ▲ 801 (15.97)
Artik (concerto) for Horn & String Orchestra, Op. 78 (1949)
M. Rimon (hn), D. Amos (cnd), Israel PO † Sym 9 CRYS ▲ 802 (15.97)
Avak, the Healer (cantata) for Soprano, Trumpet & Strings, Op. 64 (1945; rev 1946)
M. Nixon (sop), T. Stevens (tpt), E. Gold (cnd), Crystal CO † Lady of Light, Op. 227 CRYS ▲ 806 (15.97) ▮ 806 (9.98)
Bagatelles (4) for String Quartet, Op. 30 (1964)
Shanghai String Quartet *(rec May 9-11, 1994)* ("Spirit Murmur") † Qt 1 Strs, Op. 8; Qt 2 Strs, Op. 147; Qt 3 Strs; Qt 4 Strs; Z. Long:Song of the Ch'in DLS ▲ 3162 [DDD] (14.97)
Celestial Canticle for Coloratura Soprano & Piano, Op. 305/2 (1977; orchd 1993; reorchd 1994)
H. Fujihara (sop), S. Goff (fl), A. Hovhaness (cnd), Northwest Sinfonia *(rec Bothell, WA, Jan 1995)* ("Hovhaness Treasures") † Starry Night; Sym 31; Sym 49; Tale of the Sun Goddess Going into the Stone House CRYS ▲ 811 [DDD] (15.97)
Celestial Fantasy, Op. 44 (1935; orchd 1944)
D. Amos (cnd), Israel PO † Armenian Rhap 2, Op. 51; Chajes:Israeli Melodies; Creston:Chant of 1942, Op. 33; Suite Str Orch, Op. 109; Joio:Air; Persichetti:Introit Strs, Op. 96 CRYS ▲ 508 (15.97)
G. Schwarz (cnd), Seattle SO *(rec Sept 1993)* ("Mysterious Mountain") † Alleluia & Fugue, Op. 40b; And God Created Whales, Op. 229; Prayer of St. Gregory, Op. 62b; Prelude & Quadruple Fugue, Op. 128 DLS ▲ 3157 [DDD] (14.97) ▮ 3157 [DDD] (7.98)
K. Stratton (cnd), Slovak RSO *(rec Slovak Radio Concert Hall Bratislava, Oct 1997)* ("Celestial Fantasy") † Alleluia & Fugue, Op. 40b; Armenian Rhap 2, Op. 51; Armenian Rhap 3, Op. 189; Holy City, Op. 218; In Memory of an Artist, Op. 163; Processional & Fugue, Op. 76/5; Psalm & Fugue, Op. 40a DOR ▲ 93166 [DDD] (16.97)
Chahagir for solo Viola, Op. 56/1 (1945)
P. Cortese (va) *(rec June 1991)* † Bergsma:Fantastic Vars on a Theme from Tristan; E. Carter:Elegy Va; Persichetti:Infanta marina; Parable XVI, Op. 130 CRYS ▲ 636 (15.97)
Concerto No. 7 for Orchestra, Op. 116 (1953)
R. Werthen (cnd), I Fiamminghi *(rec Vellereille-les-Brayeux Belgium, Aug 18-20, 1994)* ("Celestial Gate") † Alleluia & Fugue, Op. 40b; Prayer of St. Gregory, Op. 62b; Prelude & Quadruple Fugue, Op. 128; Sym 6; Tzaikerk, Op. 53 TEL ▲ 80392 [DDD] (16.97)
Concerto No. 8 for Orchestra, Op. 117 (1957)
D. Amos (cnd), Philharmonia Orch † Alleluia & Fugue, Op. 40b; Anahid; And God Created Whales, Op. 229; Elibris, Op. 50 CRYS ▲ 810 [DDD] (15.97) ▮ 810 [DDD] (9.98)
Concerto No. 11 for Piano, Trumpet & Strings
M. Berkofsky (pno), Seattle SO † Armenian Rhap 1, Op. 45; Armenian Rhap 2, Op. 51; Armenian Rhap 3, Op. 189; Sym 38 KSCH ▲ 374222 (16.97)
Dances (6) for Brass Quintet, Op. 79 (1967)
Dallas Brass Quintet † B. Dutton:Carnival of Venice; Horovitz:Music Hall Suite; F. Leclerc:Par Monts et par vaux CRYS ▲ 200 [ADD] (15.97)
Elibris (Dawn God of Urardu) for Flute & String Orchestra, Op. 50 (1944)
C. Messiter (fl), D. Amos (cnd), Philharmonia Orch † Alleluia & Fugue, Op. 40b; Anahid; And God Created Whales, Op. 229; Con 8 Orch, Op. 117 CRYS ▲ 810 [DDD] (15.97) ▮ 810 [DDD] (9.98)
Fantasy on Japanese Woodprints for Xylophone & Chamber Orchestra, Op. 211 (1965)
R. Johnson (mar), G. Schwarz (cnd), Seattle SO *(rec Seattle Opera House, June 6-7, 1994)* ("The Rubaiyat") † Meditations on Orpheus, Op. 155; Rubaiyat; Sym 1 DLS ▲ 3168 [DDD] (14.97)
The Flowering Peach (suite) for Orchestra [incidental music for Odets' play]
K. Brion (cnd), Ohio State Univ Concert Band *(rec Ohio State Univ., Nov 21-23, 1993 & Jan 17-18, 1994)* ("Star Dawn") † Sym 20; Sym 29; Sym 53 DLS ▲ 3158 [DDD] (14.97)
Fra Angelico (fantasy) for Orchestra, Op. 220 (1967)
A. Hovhaness (cnd), Royal PO † Armenian Rhap 3, Op. 189; Mountains & Rivers Without End, Op. 225; Sym 21 CRYS ▲ 804 [ADD] (15.97)
The Garden of Adonis (suite) for Flute & Harp, Op. 245 (1971)
R. Aitken (fl), E. Goodman (hp) *(rec Castle Wik Sweden, June 2-4, 1979)* ("Flute & Harp") † Donizetti:Son Fl & Hp; Krumpholtz:Son Fl & Hp; L. Spohr:Son 3 Vn & Hp, Op. 113; Son 4 Vn & Hp, Op. 114; Son 5 Vn & Hp, Op. 115 BIS ▲ 143 [AAD] (17.97)
Haroutiun for Trumpet & String Orchestra, Op. 71 (1948)
C. Gekker (tpt), R. A. Clark (cnd), Manhattan CO † Mountains & Rivers Without End, Op. 225; Prayer of St. Gregory, Op. 62b; Return & Rebuild the Desolate Places, Op. 213; Sym 6 KOCH ▲ 7221 [DDD] (16.97)
The Holy City for Orchestra, Op. 218 (1965)
R. A. Clark (cnd), Manhattan CO † Khirmian Hairig, Op. 49; Kohar; Psalm & Fugue, Op. 40a; Sym 17 KOCH ▲ 7289 [DDD] (16.97)
A. B. Lipkin (cnd), Royal PO *(rec 1970)* † Meditations on Orpheus, Op. 155; Triptych; H. Cowell:Music 1957; Synchrony CIT ▲ 88122 [ADD] (15.97)
K. Stratton (cnd), Slovak RSO *(rec Slovak Radio Concert Hall Bratislava, Oct 1997)* ("Celestial Fantasy") † Alleluia & Fugue, Op. 40b; Armenian Rhap 2, Op. 51; Armenian Rhap 3, Op. 189; Celestial Fant, Op. 44; In Memory of an Artist, Op. 163; Processional & Fugue, Op. 76/5; Psalm & Fugue, Op. 40a DOR ▲ 93166 [DDD] (16.97)
In Memory of an Artist for String Orchestra, Op. 163 (1958)
K. Stratton (cnd), Slovak RSO *(rec Slovak Radio Concert Hall Bratislava, Oct 1997)* ("Celestial Fantasy") † Alleluia & Fugue, Op. 40b; Armenian Rhap 2, Op. 51; Armenian Rhap 3, Op. 189; Celestial Fant, Op. 44; Holy City, Op. 218; Processional & Fugue, Op. 76/5; Psalm & Fugue, Op. 40a DOR ▲ 93166 [DDD] (16.97)
Invocations to Vahakn for Piano & Percussion, Op. 54 (1945)
J. Steinberg (pno), W. Winant (perc) † J. Cage:Nocturne; H. Cowell:Set of Five; L. Harrison:Varied Trio; S. Satoh:Toki No Mon NALB ▲ 36 [DDD] (16.97)
Jhala for Piano, Op. 103 (1952)
M. L. Tan (pno) † Orbit 2; J. Cage:In the Name of the Holocaust; Primitive; G. Crumb:Pieces Pno; Ge Gan-Ru:Gu Yue; S. Satoh:Cosmic Womb MODE ▲ 15 (17.97)
Khirmian Hairig for Trumpet & String Orchestra, Op. 49 (1944)
R. A. Clark (cnd), Manhattan CO † Holy City, Op. 218; Kohar; Psalm & Fugue, Op. 40a; Sym 17 KOCH ▲ 7289 [DDD] (16.97)
Kohar for Chamber Orchestra, Op. 66 (1946)
R. A. Clark (cnd), Manhattan CO † Holy City, Op. 218; Khirmian Hairig, Op. 49; Psalm & Fugue, Op. 40a; Sym 17 KOCH ▲ 7289 [DDD] (16.97)
Komachi (7 miniature tone poems) for Piano, Op. 240 (1971)
A. Hovhaness (pno) *(rec 1987)* † Pno Music; Shalimar, Op. 177; Son Pno FOR ▲ 17062 (16.97) ▮ 17062 (9.98)
Lady of Light (opera-oratorio) for Vocal Soloists, Orchestra & Chorus, Op. 227 (1969)
P. Clark (sop), L. Fyson (bar), A. Hovhaness (cnd), Royal PO, Ambrosian Chorus † Avak, the Healer, Op. 64 CRYS ▲ 806 (15.97) ▮ 806 (9.98)
Lake Samish for Clarinet, Violin & Piano (1989)
Verdehr Trio † B. Bartók:Contrasts, Sz.111; W. A. Mozart:Son Pno 4-Hands, K.381; Pasatieri:Theatrepieces CRYS ▲ 741 (15.97)
Magnificat for solo Voices, Orchestra & Chorus, Op. 157 (1958)
A. Nossaman (sop), E. Johnson (cta), T. East (ten), R. Dales (bar), R. Whitney (cnd), Louisville Orch, Univ of Louisville Choir † Saturn CRYS ▲ 808 (15.97)
Meditations on Orpheus for Orchestra, Op. 155 (1957)
G. Schwarz (cnd), Seattle SO *(rec Seattle Opera House, June 6-7, 1994)* ("The Rubaiyat") † Fant on Japanese Woodprints, Op. 211; Rubaiyat; Sym 1 DLS ▲ 3168 [DDD] (14.97)

HOVHANESS, ALAN (cont.)
Meditations on Orpheus for Orchestra, Op. 155 (1957) (cont.)
W. Strickland (cnd), Japan PO *(rec 1960)* † Holy City, Op. 218; Triptych; H. Cowell:Music 1957; Synchrony CIT ▲ 88122 [ADD] (15.97)
Mountains & Rivers Without End for Chamber Ensemble, Op. 225 (1968)
R. A. Clark (cnd), Manhattan CO † Haroutiun, Op. 71; Prayer of St. Gregory, Op. 62b; Return & Rebuild the Desolate Places, Op. 213; Sym 6 KOCH ▲ 7221 [DDD] (16.97)
A. Hovhaness (cnd), Royal PO † Armenian Rhap 3, Op. 189; Fra Angelico, Op. 220; Sym 21 CRYS ▲ 804 [ADD] (15.97)
Music of Hovhaness
A. Jodry (vn), H. Surmélian (pno), J. Werner (cnd), Léon Barzin Orch—Lousadzak [Coming of Light] for Pno & Str Orch; Saris for Vn & Pno; Oror for Vn & Pno; Shatakh for Vn & Pno; Shatakh II; Khirgiz Suite for Vn & Pno; A Khirgiz Tala; Khirgiz III; Con 2 for Vn & Str Orch *(rec Paris, May 1995)* MED7 ▲ 1001 [DDD] (18.97)
A. Still (fl), M. Rosen (pno), R. A. Clark (cnd), Manhattan CO, R. A. Clark (cnd), New Zealand CO, R. A. Clark (cnd), KBS SO—The Prayer of St. Gregory; Elibris; Mystic Fl; Aria, Hymn & Fugue; Mountain Idylls; Gtr Sym; Adagio; Son; Fred the Cat; Aria [from Harotiun] ("Visions: The Alan Hovhaness Sampler") KOCH ▲ 7311 [DDD] (7.97)
Mystery of the Holy Martyrs [Khorhoort Nahadagats] (17 prayers) for Oud (or Guitar or Lute) & String Quartet (or String Orchestra), Op. 251 (1976)
M. Long (gtr), V. Jordania (cnd), Korean Broadcasting System SO *(rec Seoul, 1996)* † Sym 3 SSET ▲ 1004 [DDD] (16.97)
Nocturne for Harp, Op. 20 (1938)
Y. Kondonassis (hp) *(rec Worcester, MA, Oct 2-5, 1995)* ("Sky Music") † Suite Hp, Op. 270; Debussy:Suite bergamasque; G. Fauré:Impromptu Hp, Op. 86; N. Rorem:Sky Music; Salzedo:Chansons dans la nuit TEL ▲ 80418 [DDD] (16.97)
Orbit No. 2 for Piano, Op. 102 (1952)
M. L. Tan (pno) † Jhala; J. Cage:In the Name of the Holocaust; Primitive; G. Crumb:Pieces Pno; Ge Gan-Ru:Gu Yue; S. Satoh:Cosmic Womb MODE ▲ 15 (17.97)
Piano Music
A. Hovhaness (pno)—Ghazal No. 1, Op. 36/1; Love Song Vanishing into Sounds of Crickets, Op. 3, Op. 327; To Hiroshige's Cat (1st movt), Op. 366 *(rec 1987)* † Komachi; Shalimar, Op. 177; Son Pno FOR ▲ 17062 (16.97) ▮ 17062 (9.98)
W. Johnson (pno)—Macedonian Mountain Dance, Op. 144a; Mountain Dance No. 2, Op. 144b; Blue Job Mountain Son, Op. 340; Mystic Fl, Op. 22; Dance Ghazal, Op. 37a; Love Song Vanishing into Sounds of Crickets, Op. 3, Op. 327; Son Ananda, Op. 303; Fant, Op. 16 *(rec Sept 1991)* CRYS ▲ 813 [DDD] (15.97)
M. Rosen (pno)—Achtamar, Op. 64/1 (1948); Dance Ghazal, Op. 37a (1931); rev 1938; Fant on an Ossetin Tune, Op. 85/6 (1951); Macedonian Mountain Dance, Op. 144 (1938); Mountain Dance No. 2, Op. 144b (1941); rev 1962; Orbit No. 2, Op. 102/2 (1952); Slumber Song, Op. 52/2 (1938); Sons: "Mt. Ossipee," Op. 299/2 (1977); "Fred the Cat," Op. 301 (1977); "Prospect Hill," Op. 346 (1980); "Mt. Chocorua," Op. 335 (1980); rev 1982 ("Fred The Cat: Half A Century of Piano Music") KOCH ▲ 7195 [DDD]
M. Rosen (pno)—Toccata & Fugue No. 1, Op. 6; Prelude & Fugue, Op. 10/1; Do You Remember the Last Silence; Lousang Kisher; Fire Dance; Hymn IV [from Bare November Day]; Madras Son; Son, Op. 145 ("Vision of a Starry Night") KOCH ▲ 7288 [DDD] (10.97)
Prayer of St. Gregory for Trumpet & String Orchestra, Op. 62b (1946)
C. Gekker (tpt), R. A. Clark (cnd), Manhattan CO † Haroutiun, Op. 71; Mountains & Rivers Without End, Op. 225; Return & Rebuild the Desolate Places, Op. 213; Sym 6 KOCH ▲ 7221 [DDD] (16.97)
A. Plog (tpt), H. Ericsson (org) [1987 Grönlund organ] *(rec Sweden, Mar 1992)* ("Twentieth Century Music for Trumpet & Organ") † P. Eben:Okna; Jolivet:Arioso barocco Tpt & Org; D. Lowry:Suburban Measures; Persichetti:Hollow Men Tpt & Strs; A. Plog:Themes (4) on Paintings of Edvard Munch *(E, F, G text)* BIS ▲ 565 [DDD] (17.97)
G. Schwarz (cnd), Seattle SO *(rec Sept 1993)* ("Mysterious Mountain") † Alleluia & Fugue, Op. 40b; And God Created Whales, Op. 229; Celestial Fant, Op. 44; Prelude & Quadruple Fugue, Op. 128 DLS ▲ 3157 [DDD] (14.97) ▮ 3157 [DDD] (7.98)
B. Wiame (tpt), R. Werthen (cnd), I Fiamminghi *(rec Vellereille-les-Brayeux Belgium, Aug 18-20, 1994)* ("Celestial Gate") † Alleluia & Fugue, Op. 40b; Con 7 Orch, Op. 116; Prelude & Quadruple Fugue, Op. 128; Sym 6; Tzaikerk, Op. 53 TEL ▲ 80392 [DDD] (16.97)
B. Wiame (tpt), R. Werthen (cnd), I Fiamminghi ("An I Fiamminghi Collection") † Corigliano:Elegy; Górecki:Stücke im alten Stil; Kancheli:Vom Winde beweint; Pärt:Fratres I Str Qt; Vasks:Musica Dolorosa TEL ▲ 89111 [DDD] (5.97)
J. Wilbraham (tpt), A. Hovhaness (cnd), Polyphonia Orch † Sym 25; Sym 6 CRYS ▲ 807 (15.97)
artists unknown † Armenian Rhap 3, Op. 189; Sym 11; Tzaikerk, Op. 53 CRYS ▲ 801 (15.97)
Prelude & Quadruple Fugue for Orchestra, Op. 128 (1936; orchd 1954)
G. Schwarz (cnd), Seattle SO *(rec Sept 1993)* ("Mysterious Mountain") † Alleluia & Fugue, Op. 40b; And God Created Whales, Op. 229; Celestial Fant, Op. 44; Prayer of St. Gregory, Op. 62b DLS ▲ 3157 [DDD] (14.97) ▮ 3157 [DDD] (7.98)
R. Werthen (cnd), I Fiamminghi *(rec Vellereille-les-Brayeux Belgium, Aug 18-20, 1994)* ("Celestial Gate") † Alleluia & Fugue, Op. 40b; Con 7 Orch, Op. 116; Prayer of St. Gregory, Op. 62b; Sym 6; Tzaikerk, Op. 53 TEL ▲ 80392 [DDD] (16.97)
Processional & Fugue for Orchestra, Op. 76/5 (1967)
K. Stratton (cnd), Slovak RSO *(rec Slovak Radio Concert Hall Bratislava, Oct 1997)* ("Celestial Fantasy") † Alleluia & Fugue, Op. 40b; Armenian Rhap 2, Op. 51; Armenian Rhap 3, Op. 189; Celestial Fant, Op. 44; Holy City, Op. 218; In Memory of an Artist, Op. 163; Psalm & Fugue, Op. 40a DOR ▲ 93166 [DDD] (16.97)
Psalm & Fugue for String Orchestra, Op. 40a (1941)
R. A. Clark (cnd), Manhattan CO † Holy City, Op. 218; Khirmian Hairig, Op. 49; Kohar; Sym 17 KOCH ▲ 7289 [DDD] (16.97)
K. Stratton (cnd), Slovak RSO *(rec Slovak Radio Concert Hall Bratislava, Oct 1997)* ("Celestial Fantasy") † Alleluia & Fugue, Op. 40b; Armenian Rhap 2, Op. 51; Armenian Rhap 3, Op. 189; Celestial Fant, Op. 44; Holy City, Op. 218; In Memory of an Artist, Op. 163; Processional & Fugue, Op. 76/5 DOR ▲ 93166 [DDD] (16.97)
Quartet No. 1 for Strings, Op. 8 (1936)
Shanghai String Quartet *(rec May 9-11, 1994)* ("Spirit Murmur") † Bagatelles, Op. 30; Qt 2 Strs, Op. 147; Qt 3 Strs; Qt 4 Strs; Z. Long:Song of the Ch'in DLS ▲ 3162 [DDD] (14.97)
Quartet No. 2 for Strings, Op. 147 (1951)
Shanghai String Quartet *(rec May 9-11, 1994)* ("Spirit Murmur") † Bagatelles, Op. 30; Qt 1 Strs, Op. 8; Qt 3 Strs; Qt 4 Strs; Z. Long:Song of the Ch'in DLS ▲ 3162 [DDD] (14.97)
Quartet No. 3 for Strings, Op. 208/1 (1964)
Shanghai String Quartet *(rec May 9-11, 1994)* ("Spirit Murmur") † Bagatelles, Op. 30; Qt 1 Strs, Op. 8; Qt 2 Strs, Op. 147; Qt 4 Strs; Z. Long:Song of the Ch'in DLS ▲ 3162 [DDD] (14.97)
Quartet No. 4 for Strings, Op. 208/2 (1970)
Shanghai String Quartet *(rec May 9-11, 1994)* ("Spirit Murmur") † Bagatelles, Op. 30; Qt 1 Strs, Op. 8; Qt 2 Strs, Op. 147; Qt 3 Strs; Z. Long:Song of the Ch'in DLS ▲ 3162 [DDD] (14.97)
Requiem & Resurrection for Brass Choir & Percussion, Op. 224 (1968)
A. Hovhaness (cnd), New Jersey Wind Sym † Sym 19 CRYS ▲ 805 (15.97) ▮ 805 (9.98)
Return & Rebuild the Desolate Places for Trumpet & Wind Ensemble, Op. 213 (1944; rev 1965)
C. Gekker (tpt), R. A. Clark (cnd), Manhattan CO † Haroutiun, Op. 71; Mountains & Rivers Without End, Op. 225; Prayer of St. Gregory, Op. 62b; Sym 6 KOCH ▲ 7221 [DDD] (16.97)
Rubaiyat for Narrator, Accordion & Orchestra, Op. 282 (1975)
M. York (nar), D. Schmidt (acc), G. Schwarz (cnd), Seattle SO *(rec Seattle Opera House, June 6-7, 1994)* ("The Rubaiyat") † Fant on Japanese Woodprints, Op. 211; Meditations on Orpheus, Op. 155; Sym 1 DLS ▲ 3168 [DDD] (14.97)
Sacred Music
E. Plutz (org), D. Pearson (cnd), St. John's Episcopal Cathedral Festival Orch, St. John's Episcopal Cathedral Boy & Girls' Choir, St. John's Episcopal Cathedral Choir—Magnificat, Op. 157; Psalm 23 [Cant from Sym 12, Op. 188]; A Rose Tree Blossoms, Op. 246/4; Jesus, Lover of My Soul, Op. 53b; Jesus Christ Is Risen Today, Op. 100/3b; The Lord's Prayer, Op. 35; Peace be Multiplied, Op. 259/1; O For a Shout of Sacred Joy, Op. 161; Out of the Depths, Op. 142/3; O God, Our Help in Ages Past, Op. 137 *(rec St. John's Episcopal Cathedral Denver, Mar 6-8, 1995)* ("Magnificat") DLS ▲ 3176 [DDD] (14.97)
Saturn (12 pieces) for Soprano, Clarinet & Piano, Op. 243 (1971)
K. Hurney (sop), L. Sobol (cl), M. Berkofsky (pno) † Magnificat, Op. 157 CRYS ▲ 808 (15.97)
Sextet for Recorder, String Quartet & Harpsichord (1958)
J. Starkman (vn), K. Shaw (vn), J. Cosart (va), A. Robbins (vc), J. Tyson (rcr), F. C. Fitch (hpd) † Boismortier:Con Rec & Strs; A. Cooke:Con Rcr; Lovenstein:Fant Rcr TIT ▲ 169 [DDD]
Shalimar (suite) for Piano [musical tribute to the Kashmir region], Op. 177 (1949; rev 1960)
A. Hovhaness (pno) *(rec 1987)* † Komachi; Pno Music; Son Pno FOR ▲ 17062 (16.97) ▮ 17062 (9.98)

HOVHANESS, ALAN (cont.)

Sonatas (2) for Guitar (1979)
D. Tanenbaum (gtr) † Kernis:Partita Gtr; S. Reich:Nagoya Gtrs; Richmond:Preludes Gtr; T. Riley:Barabas; F. Zappa:Waltz Gtr NALB ▲ 95 (16.97)

Sonata for Piano, Op. 346, "Prospect Hill"
A. Hovhaness (pno) *(rec 1987)* † Komachi; Pno Music; Shalimar, Op. 177 FOR ▲ 17062 (16.97) ▮ 17062 (9.98)

Sonata for Violin & Harp, Op. 406
Aurora Duo † Boren:Movts from Liturgical Dance; Donizetti:Son Vn; Lasala:Poema del Pastor Coya; Saint-Saëns:Fant Vn; Shaposhnikov:Son in d Vn 4TAY ▲ 4010 [DDD] (17.97)

Starry Night for Flute, Xylophone & Harp (1984)
S. Goff (fl), J. Carrington (hp), R. Johnson (xyl) *(rec Bothell, WA, Jan 1995)* ("Hovhaness Treasures") † Celestial Canticle, Op. 305/2; Sym 31; Sym 49; Tale of the Sun Goddess Going into the Stone House CRYS ▲ 811 [DDD] (15.97)

Suite for Harp, Op. 270 (1973)
Y. Kondonassis (hp) *(rec Worcester, MA, Oct 2-5, 1995)* ("Sky Music") † Nocturne Hp, Op. 20; Debussy:Suite bergamasque; G. Fauré:Impromptu Hp, Op. 86; N. Rorem:Sky Music; Salzedo:Chansons dans la nuit TEL ▲ 80418 [DDD] (16.97)

Symphony No. 1, Op. 17, "Exile Symphony" (1937)
G. Schwarz (cnd), Seattle SO *(rec Seattle Opera House, June 6-7, 1994)* ("The Rubaiyat") † Fant on Japanese Woodprints, Op. 211; Meditations on Orpheus, Op. 155; Rubaiyat DLS ▲ 3168 [DDD] (14.97)

Symphony No. 2, Op. 132, "Mysterious Mountain" (1955)
A. Litton (cnd), Dallas SO *(rec Morton H. Meyerson Symphony Center Dallas, TX, May 1995)* ("An American Tapestry") † Griffes:White Peacock; C. Ives:Three Places in New England; Piston:Incredible Flutist; W. Schuman:New England Triptych DOR ▲ 90224 [DDD] (16.97)
J. López-Cobos (cnd), Cincinnati SO *(rec Music Hall Cincinnati, Jan 21 & 26, 1997)* ("Into the Light") † D. Brubeck:Joy in the Morning (Suite); Canning:Fant on Hymn Tune by Justin Morgan; S. Rouse:Into the Light; R. Strauss:Tod und Verklärung, Op. 24 TEL ▲ 80462 [DDD] (16.97)
F. Reiner (cnd), Chicago SO † S. Prokofiev:Lt Kijé Suite, Op. 60; I. Stravinsky:Divert Orch RCAV (Living Stereo) ▲ 61957 (11.97)

Symphony No. 3, Op. 148 (1956)
V. Jordania (cnd), Korean Broadcasting System SO *(rec Seoul, 1996)* † Mystery of the Holy Martyrs, Op. 251 SSET ▲ 1004 [DDD] (16.97)

Symphony No. 4 for Winds, Op. 165 (1958)
A. C. Roller (cnd) † V. Giannini:Sym 3; M. Gould:West Point Sym MRCR ▲ 34320 [ADD] (11.97)

Symphony No. 6 for Chamber Orchestra, Op. 173, "Celestial Gate" (1959; rev 1960)
R. A. Clark (cnd), Manhattan CO † Haroutiun, Op. 71; Mountains & Rivers Without End, Op. 225; Prayer of St. Gregory, Op. 62b; Return & Rebuild the Desolate Places, Op. 213 KOCH ▲ 7221 [DDD] (16.97)
A. Hovhaness (cnd), Polyphonia Orch † Prayer of St. Gregory, Op. 62b; Sym 25 CRYS ▲ 807 (15.97)
R. Werthen (cnd), I Fiamminghi *(rec Vellereille-les-Brayeux Belgium, Aug 18-20, 1994)* ("Celestial Gate") † Alleluia & Fugue, Op. 40b; Con 7 Orch, Op. 116; Prayer of St. Gregory, Op. 62b; Prelude & Quadruple Fugue, Op. 128; Tzaikerk, Op. 53 TEL ▲ 80392 [DDD] (16.97)

Symphony No. 9 for Chamber Orchestra, Op. 80 (180), "Saint Vartan" (1950)
A. Hovhaness (cnd), National PO London † Artik CRYS ▲ 802 (15.97)

Symphony No. 11, Op. 186, "All Men Are Brothers" (1960; rev 1969)
A. Hovhaness (cnd), Royal PO † Armenian Rhap 3, Op. 189; Prayer of St. Gregory, Op. 62b; Tzaikerk, Op. 53 CRYS ▲ 801 (15.97)

Symphony No. 17 for 6 Flutes, 3 Trombones & Percussion, Op. 203, "Symphony for Metal Orchestra" (1963)
R. A. Clark (cnd), Manhattan CO † Holy City, Op. 218; Khirmian Hairig, Op. 49; Kohar; Psalm & Fugue, Op. 40a KOCH ▲ 7289 [DDD] (16.97)

Symphony No. 19, Op. 217, "Vishnu" (1966)
A. Hovhaness (cnd), Sevan PO † Requiem & Resurrection, Op. 224 CRYS ▲ 805 (15.97) ▮ 805 (9.98)

Symphony No. 20 for Band, Op. 223, "Three Journeys to a Holy Mountain" (1968)
K. Brion (cnd), Ohio State Univ Concert Band *(rec Ohio State Univ., Nov 21-23, 1993 & Jan 17-18, 1994)* ("Star Dawn") † Flowering Peach; Sym 29; Sym 53 DLS ▲ 3158 [DDD] (14.97)

Symphony No. 21 for 2 Trumpets, Timpani, Percussion & Strings, Op. 234, "Etchmiadzin" (1970)
A. Hovhaness (cnd), Royal PO † Armenian Rhap 3, Op. 189; Fra Angelico, Op. 220; Mountains & Rivers Without End, Op. 225 CRYS ▲ 804 [ADD] (15.97)

Symphony No. 22, Op. 236, "City of Light" (1971)
A. Hovhaness (cnd), Seattle SO *(rec May 17 & 19, 1992)* † Sym 50 DLS ▲ 3137 [DDD] (14.97) ▮ 3137 [DDD] (7.98)

Symphony No. 24 for Tenor, Trumpet, Violin, String Orchestra & Chorus, Op. 273, "Manjun" (1973)
M. Hill (ten), Sax (vn), J. Wilbraham (tpt), A. Hovhaness (cnd), National PO London, John Alldis Choir [ENG] *(rec 1974)* CRYS ▲ 803 [ADD] (15.97)

Symphony No. 25 for Small Orchestra, Op. 275, "Odysseus" (1975)
A. Hovhaness (cnd), Polyphonia Orch † Prayer of St. Gregory, Op. 62b; Sym 6 CRYS ▲ 807 (15.97)

Symphony No. 29 for Horn & Orchestra (1977)
C. Lindberg (trbn), K. Brion (cnd), Ohio State Univ Concert Band *(rec Ohio State Univ., Nov 21-23, 1993 & Jan 17-18, 1994)* ("Star Dawn") † Flowering Peach; Sym 20; Sym 53 DLS ▲ 3158 [DDD] (14.97)

Symphony No. 31 for Strings (1977)
G. Schwarz (cnd), Northwest Sinfonia *(rec Bothell, WA, Jan 1995)* ("Hovhaness Treasures") † Celestial Canticle, Op. 305/2; Starry Night; Sym 49; Tale of the Sun Goddess Going into the Stone House CRYS ▲ 811 [DDD] (15.97)

Symphony No. 38 for Soprano & Orchestra (1978)
H. Fujihara (sop), Seattle SO—My Soul Is a Bird; Lullaby † Armenian Rhap 1, Op. 45; Armenian Rhap 2, Op. 51; Armenian Rhap 3, Op. 189; Con 11 Pno KSCH ▲ 374222 (16.97)

Symphony No. 39 for Guitar & Orchestra (1978)
M. Long (gtr), V. Jordania (cnd), KBS SO † Sym 46 KOCH ▲ 7208 [DDD] (16.97)

Symphony No. 46, "To the Green Mountains" (1980)
V. Jordania (cnd), KBS SO † Sym 39 KOCH ▲ 7208 [DDD] (16.97)

Symphony No. 49 for Strings, "Christmas" (1981)
G. Schwarz (cnd), Northwest Sinfonia *(rec Bothell, WA, Jan 1995)* ("Hovhaness Treasures") † Celestial Canticle, Op. 305/2; Starry Night; Sym 31; Tale of the Sun Goddess Going into the Stone House CRYS ▲ 811 [DDD] (15.97)

Symphony No. 50, Op. 360, "Mount St. Helens"
G. Schwarz (cnd), Seattle SO *(rec May 17 & 19, 1992)* † Sym 22 DLS ▲ 3137 [DDD] (14.97) ▮ 3137 [DDD] (7.98)

Symphony No. 53 for Band, "Star Dawn" (1983)
K. Brion (cnd), Ohio State Univ Concert Band *(rec Ohio State Univ., Nov 21-23, 1993 & Jan 17-18, 1994)* ("Star Dawn") † Flowering Peach; Sym 20; Sym 29 DLS ▲ 3158 [DDD] (14.97)

Tale of the Sun Goddess Going into the Stone House (selections)
H. Fujihara (sop), S. Goff (fl), A. Hovhaness (cnd), Northwest Sinfonia *(rec Bothell, WA, Jan 1995)* ("Hovhaness Treasures") † Celestial Canticle, Op. 305/2; Starry Night; Sym 31; Sym 49 CRYS ▲ 811 [DDD] (15.97)

Triptych for Soprano, Orchestra & Women's Chorus [Ave Maria; Christmas Ode; Easter Cantata] (1952-56)
B. Valente (sop), A. Antonini (cnd), Bamberg SO, Bay Rund Singers *(rec 1967)* † Holy City, Op. 218; Meditations on Orpheus, Op. 155; H. Cowell:Music 1957; Synchrony CIT ▲ 88122 [ADD] (15.97)

Tzaikerk for Chamber Orchestra, Op. 53 (1945)
A. Kobyliansky (vn), P. Edmund-Davies (fl), R. Max (timp), R. Werthen (cnd), I Fiamminghi *(rec Vellereille-les-Brayeux Belgium, Aug 18-20, 1994)* ("Celestial Gate") † Alleluia & Fugue, Op. 40b; Con 7 Orch, Op. 116; Prayer of St. Gregory, Op. 62b; Prelude & Quadruple Fugue, Op. 128; Sym 6 TEL ▲ 80392 [DDD] (16.97)
artists unknown † Armenian Rhap 3, Op. 189; Prayer of St. Gregory, Op. 62b; Sym 11 CRYS ▲ 801 (15.97)

HOVHANNESSIAN, EDGAR SERGEI (1930-

Marmar Suite for Orchestra
L. Tjeknavorian (cnd), Armenian PO *(rec Aram Khachaturian Hall, Yerevan, Armenia, Sept 3-8, 1997)* † Sym 3 ASV ▲ 1033 [DDD] (16.97)

Symphony No. 3 for Orchestra
L. Tjeknavorian (cnd), Armenian PO *(rec Aram Khachaturian Hall, Yerevan, Armenia, Sept 3-8, 1997)* † Marmar ASV ▲ 1033 [DDD] (16.97)

HOVLAND, EGIL (1924-

Cantus II for Descant Recorder & Piano (1974-75)
C. Pehrsson (rcr), T. Schuback (pno) *(rec Sweden, May 11-13, 1981)* † Burkhart:Adventslieder; Kukuck:Brücke; H.-M. Linde:Amarilli, mia bella; L. Lundén:Little Toe & Nine More; M. Shinohara:Fragmente Rcr; Staeps:Son Trb Rcr BIS ▲ 202 [AAD] (17.97)

Choral Music
S. Skold (cnd), Oslo Philharmonic Chamber Choir ("Works for Choir") NORW ▲ 5003 (17.97)

HOVLAND, EGIL (cont.)

Concerto for Piccolo, Flute & Orchestra, Op. 117 (1986)
A. Cunningham (fl/pic), I. Golovchin (cnd), Moscow SO † Con Trbn, Op. 76; Con Vn NORW ▲ 5004 (17.97)

Concerto for Trombone & Orchestra, Op. 76 (1972)
P. Brevig (trbn), A. Dmitriev (cnd), Stavanger SO † Con Pic & Fl, Op. 117; Con Vn NORW ▲ 5004 (17.97)

Concerto for Violin & Orchestra, Op. 81 (1974)
I. Schuldman (vn), A. Dmitriev (cnd), Stavanger SO † Con Pic & Fl, Op. 117; Con Trbn, Op. 76 NORW ▲ 5004 (17.97)

Fanfare & Chorale
H. Haukas (cnd), Bergen Military Band † E. Grieg:In Heaven; Halvorsen:Bergensiana; J. S. Svendsen:Norwegian Artists' Carnival, Op. 14 DOY ▲ 70 (16.97)

HOWARD, JAMES NEWTON (20th cent)

Primal Fear (film music) for Orchestra (1996)
B. Northcutt (E hn), T. Blanchard (hn), A. Kane (cnd) *(rec Scoring Stage M Los Angeles, CA)* ("Primal Fear") † W. Byrd:Mass 4 Voc; W. A. Mozart:Requiem, K.626 MILA ▲ 35716 [DDD] (16.97)

Restoration (film music) for Chamber Ensemble (1996)
A. Kane (cnd) [some period instrs] *(rec Lyndhurst Hall, 1995)* MILA ▲ 35707 [DDD] (16.97)

HOWARD, LESLIE (1948-

Moto di Gioia for Organ, Op. 27 (1993)
I. Quinn (org) *(rec Methuen Memorial Music Hall Org, Mar 5-7, 1995)* ("Iain Quinn Plays the Great Organ at Methuen") † C. Franck:Chorales Org, M.38-40; Josephs:Son Org; Liszt:Org Music; Masson:Meditation RAVN ▲ 360 [DDD]

HOWARTH, ALAN (20th cent)

Film Music
A. Howarth (cnd) —The Dentist; The Dentist 2 CIT ▲ 77120 [DDD] (15.97)

HOWARTH, ELGAR (1935-

Ascendit in Coeli for Brass
E. Howarth (cnd), Eikanger-Bjørsvik Musikklag *(rec Nordhordland Folkehøgskule Assembly Hall Norwa, Dec 1996)* † Cantabile for John Fletcher; Con Trbn; Mosaic; Pieces for Spielberg; Songs for B.L. DOY (Contemporary) ▲ 66 [DDD] (16.97)

Cantabile for John Fletcher for 2 Euphoniums & Brass Band
N. Childs (eup), R. Childs (eup), E. Howarth (cnd), Eikanger-Bjørsvik Musikklag *(rec Nordhordland Folkehøgskule Assembly Hall Norwa, Dec 1996)* † Ascendit in Coeli; Con Trbn; Mosaic; Pieces for Spielberg; Songs for B.L. DOY (Contemporary) ▲ 66 [DDD] (16.97)

Concerto for Trombone & Orchestra, "Concerto Allegorical" (1958)
I. Bousfield (trbn), E. Howarth (cnd), Eikanger-Bjørsvik Musikklag *(rec Nordhordland Folkehøgskule Assembly Hall Norwa, Dec 1996)* † Ascendit in Coeli; Cantabile for John Fletcher; Mosaic; Pieces for Spielberg; Songs for B.L. DOY (Contemporary) ▲ 66 [DDD] (16.97)
C. Lindberg (trbn), G. Llewellyn (cnd), BBC National Orch Wales ("British Trombone Concertos") † D. Bourgeois:Con Trbn; G. Jacob:Con Trbn BIS ▲ 658 [DDD] (17.97)

Mosaic for Brass Band (1957)
E. Howarth (cnd), Eikanger-Bjørsvik Musikklag *(rec Nordhordland Folkehøgskule Assembly Hall Norwa, Dec 1996)* † Ascendit in Coeli; Cantabile for John Fletcher; Con Trbn; Pieces for Spielberg; Songs for B.L. DOY (Contemporary) ▲ 66 [DDD] (16.97)

Pieces for Spielberg (5) for Brass Band (early 1980s)
E. Howarth (cnd), Eikanger-Bjørsvik Musikklag *(rec Nordhordland Folkehøgskule Assembly Hall Norwa, Dec 1996)* † Ascendit in Coeli; Cantabile for John Fletcher; Con Trbn; Mosaic; Songs for B.L. DOY (Contemporary) ▲ 66 [DDD] (16.97)

Songs for B.L. for Brass Band
E. Howarth (cnd), Eikanger-Bjørsvik Musikklag *(rec Nordhordland Folkehøgskule Assembly Hall Norwa, Dec 1996)* † Ascendit in Coeli; Cantabile for John Fletcher; Con Trbn; Mosaic; Pieces for Spielberg DOY (Contemporary) ▲ 66 [DDD] (16.97)

HOWE, MARY (1882-1964)

Castellana for 2 Pianos & Orchestra (1930; rev 1934)
V. Dougherty (pno), V. Ruzicka (pno), W. Strickland (cnd), Vienna Orch † Interlude between 2 Pieces; Pieces after Emily Dickinson; Sand; Spring Pastoral; Stars; Suite Str Qt CRI (American Masters) ▲ 785 [ADD] (16.97)

Interlude between 2 Pieces for Flute & Piano (1942)
W. Mann (fl), E. Meyers (pno) *(rec Washington D.C., July 21-22, 1951)* † Castellana; Pieces after Emily Dickinson; Sand; Spring Pastoral; Stars; Suite Str Qt CRI (American Masters) ▲ 785 [ADD] (16.97)

Pieces after Emily Dickinson (3) for String Quartet (1941)
W. Lywen (vn), G. Steiner (vn), N. Lamb (va), J. Martin (vc) *(rec Washington D.C., July 21-22, 1951)* † Castellana; Interlude between 2 Pieces; Sand; Spring Pastoral; Stars; Suite Str Qt CRI (American Masters) ▲ 785 [ADD] (16.97)

Sand for Orchestra (1928)
W. Strickland (cnd), Vienna Orch *(rec Washington D.C.)* † Castellana; Interlude between 2 Pieces; Pieces after Emily Dickinson; Spring Pastoral; Stars; Suite Str Qt CRI (American Masters) ▲ 785 [ADD] (16.97)

Spring Pastoral for Chorus (1936; orchd)
W. Strickland (cnd), Tokyo Imperial PO *(rec Washington D.C.)* † Castellana; Interlude between 2 Pieces; Pieces after Emily Dickinson; Sand; Stars; Suite Str Qt CRI (American Masters) ▲ 785 [ADD] (16.97)

Stars for Orchestra (1927)
W. Strickland (cnd), Vienna Orch *(rec Washington D.C.)* † Castellana; Interlude between 2 Pieces; Pieces after Emily Dickinson; Sand; Spring Pastoral; Suite Str Qt CRI (American Masters) ▲ 785 [ADD] (16.97)

Suite for String Quartet & Piano (1928)
W. Lywen (vn), G. Steiner (vn), N. Lamb (va), J. Martin (vc), E. Meyers (pno) *(rec Washington D.C., July 21-22, 1951)* † Castellana; Interlude between 2 Pieces; Pieces after Emily Dickinson; Sand; Spring Pastoral; Stars CRI (American Masters) ▲ 785 [ADD] (16.97)

HOWELLS, HERBERT (1892-1983)

Choral Music
H. Bicket (org), P. Spicer (cnd), Finzi Singers—Sequence for St. Michael; House of the Mind (motet—1949) [E] † Requiem; Vaughan Williams:Choral Music CHN ▲ 9019 [DDD] (16.97)
C. Dearnley (org), J. Scott (cnd), St. Paul's Cathedral Choir—Te Deum; Collegium regale; Behold O God Our Defender; Anthems; Take Him, Earth, for Cherishing; Magnificat in G; Nunc Dimittis *(rec June 1987)* ("The St. Paul's Service") † Pieces Org; Psalm-Preludes, Set I; Psalm-Preludes, Set II; Rhaps (3) Org, Op. 17 HYP 2-▲ 22038 [DDD] (18.97)
Finzi Singers—2 Madrigals; Long, Long Ago; The Summer Is Coming *(rec Dec 4-5, 1991)* † A. Bax:Choral Music; H. Mancini:Choral Music CHN ▲ 9139 [DDD] (16.97)
E. Higginbottom (cnd), New College Choir Oxford—Sequence for St. Michael; Hymn for St. Cecilia; House of the Mind (motet—1949); Magnificat & Nunc Dimittis; O Pray for the Peace of Jersalem; King of Glory (1951) ("Howells: Choral & Organ Music, Vol. 1") † Org Music CRD ▲ 3454 [DDD] (17.97)
E. Higginbottom (cnd), New College Choir Oxford—Behold O God Our Defender; Missa Aedis Christi (1958); 3 Carol-Anthems; Here Is the Little Door; Spotless Rose; Where wast thou? (1948) ("Howells: Choral & Organ Music, Vol. 2") † Org Music CRD ▲ 3455 [DDD] (17.97)
L. King (cnd), Trinity Church Choir Broadway & Wall Street—Requiem (1936); Te Deum & Benedictus (1952); Coventry Antiphon (1962); Thee Will I Love (1970); Come, My Soul and Antiphon (1978) GOT ▲ 49033 [DDD] (17.97)
A. Lumsden (org), P. Spicer (cnd), Finzi Singers—Te Deum; Thee Will I Love (1970); Haec dies; Blessed Are the Dead; Behold O God Our Defender; Inheritance; Here Is the Little Door; Spotless Rose; Sing Lullaby; Even Such Is Time; God Is Gone Up; The Scribe ("Choral Works") CHN ▲ 9458 (16.97)
A. Sackett (org), M. Lee (cnd), St. Cecilia Singers *(Hymn for St. Cecilia)*, M. Lee (cnd), St. Cecilia Singers *(Spotless Rose; Here Is the Little Door) (rec Gloucester Cathedral, England, June 1997)* ("Over Hill, Over Dale") † K. Amos:Salisbury Cathedral; Anonymous:Scarborough Fair; She Moved through the Fair; H. Parry:Seven Part Songs; Six Modern Lyrics; Songs of Farewell; J. Sanders:Anthem of the Incarnation; Traditional:Bobby Shaftoe; Dance to Thy Daddy; Frog & the Crow; Vaughan Williams:Shakespeare Songs PRIO ▲ 620 [DDD] (16.97)
P. Spicer (cnd), Finzi Singers—O salutaris Hostia; Salve Regina; Sweetest of sweets; Come, mysoul; Antiphon; Nunc dimittis; Regina caeli [all composed ca 1913-19] † Mass in the Dorian Mode; B. Stevens:Mass CHN ▲ 9021 [DDD] (16.97)

Concerto for Strings (1939)
R. Hickox (cnd), City of London Sinfonia † Elegy Va & Str Qt; Serenade Strs; Suite Strs CHN ▲ 9161 [DDD] (16.97)

HOWELLS, HERBERT (cont.)

Dalby's Fancy for Organ
A. Partington (org) *(rec Organ of Winchester Cathedral, England, Feb 22-23, 1998)* † Dalby's Tocatta; Flourish for a Bidding; Hovingham Sketches; Intrata; Partita; Prelude: De Profundis; Siciliano; Slow Dance; St. Louis comes to Clifton PRIO ▲ 547 [DDD] (16.97)

Dalby's Tocatta for Organ
A. Partington (org) *(rec Organ of Winchester Cathedral, England, Feb 22-23, 1998)* † Dalby's Fancy; Flourish for a Bidding; Hovingham Sketches; Intrata; Partita; Prelude: De Profundis; Siciliano; Slow Dance; St. Louis comes to Clifton PRIO ▲ 547 [DDD] (16.97)

Dances (3) for Violin & Orchestra (1915)
L. Mordkovitch (vn), R. Hickox (cnd), London SO ("Orchestral Works, Vol. 2") † In Green Ways; Suite CHN ▲ 9557 (16.97)

Elegy for Viola & String Quartet (1917)
R. Hickox (cnd), City of London Sinfonia † Con Strs; Serenade Strs; Suite Strs CHN ▲ 9161 [DDD] (16.97)

An English Mass for Mixed Choir (1956)
V. Handley (cnd), Royal Liverpool Phil Choir † Hymnus Paradisi HYP ▲ 66488 (18.97)

Fantasia for Cello & Orchestra (1937)
M. Welsh (vc), R. Hickox (cnd), London SO ("Orchestral Works, Vol. 1") † King's Herald; Paradise Rondel; Pastoral Rhap; Procession; Threnody CHN ▲ 9410 [DDD] (16.97)

Flourish for a Bidding
A. Partington (org) *(rec Organ of Winchester Cathedral, England, Feb 22-23, 1998)* † Dalby's Fancy; Dalby's Tocatta; Hovingham Sketches; Intrata; Partita; Prelude: De Profundis; Siciliano; Slow Dance; St. Louis comes to Clifton PRIO ▲ 547 [DDD] (16.97)

Gadabout for Piano (1928)
J. Filsell (pno) † Pieces Pno; Sonatina Pno; B. Stevens:Aria Pno; Fant on Giles Farnaby; Son Pno in 1 Movt, Op. 25 GILD ▲ 7119 [DDD] (16.97)

Hovingham Sketches for Organ
A. Partington (org)—Epilogue *(rec Organ of Winchester Cathedral, England, Feb 22-23, 1998)* † Dalby's Fancy; Dalby's Tocatta; Flourish for a Bidding; Intrata; Partita; Prelude: De Profundis; Siciliano; Slow Dance; St. Louis comes to Clifton PRIO ▲ 547 [DDD] (16.97)

Hymnus Paradisi for Soprano, Tenor, Orchestra & Chorus (1950)
J. Kennard (sop), J. M. Ainsley (ten), V. Handley (cnd), Royal Liverpool PO, Royal Liverpool Phil Choir † English Mass HYP ▲ 66488 (18.97)

In Green Ways (5 songs) for Voice & Piano (1928)
Y. Kenny (sop), R. Hickox (cnd), London SO ("Orchestral Works, Vol. 2") † Dances; Suite CHN ▲ 9557 (16.97)

Intrata for Organ
A. Partington (org) *(rec Organ of Winchester Cathedral, England, Feb 22-23, 1998)* † Dalby's Fancy; Dalby's Tocatta; Flourish for a Bidding; Hovingham Sketches; Partita; Prelude: De Profundis; Siciliano; Slow Dance; St. Louis comes to Clifton PRIO ▲ 547 [DDD] (16.97)

King's Herald for Organ & Orchestra [arr from Pageantry]
R. Hickox (cnd), London SO ("Orchestral Works, Vol. 1") † Fant Vc & Orch; Paradise Rondel; Pastoral Rhap; Procession; Threnody CHN ▲ 9410 [DDD] (16.97)

Mass in the Dorian Mode (1912)
P. Spicer (cnd), Finzi Singers [LAT] † Choral Music; B. Stevens:Mass CHN ▲ 9021 [DDD] (16.97)

Minuet: Grace for a Fresh Egg for Bassoon & Piano (1945)
L. Perkins (bn), J. Flinders (pno) ("The English Romantics") † Near Minuet Cl; Hurlstone:Characteristic Pieces Cl; Trio Cl; C. H. Lloyd:Trio Cl CLCL ▲ 23 [DDD] (17.97)

Missa sabrinensis for Soprano, Alto, Tenor, Baritone, Orchestra & Chorus (1954)
J. Watson (sop), D. Jones (mez), M. Hill (ten), D. Maxwell (bar), G. Rozhdestvensky (cnd), London SO, London Sym Chorus CHN ▲ 9348 [DDD] (16.97)

A Near Minuet for Clarinet & Piano (1946)
V. Soames (cl), J. Flinders (pno) ("The English Romantics") † Minuet: Grace for a Fresh Egg; Hurlstone:Characteristic Pieces Cl; Trio Cl; C. H. Lloyd:Trio Cl CLCL ▲ 23 [DDD] (17.97)

Organ Music
E. Higginbottom (org)—De La Mare's Pavane; Walton's Toye; Flourish for a Bidding; St. Louis comes to Clifton; Jacob's Brawl ("Howells: Choral & Organ Music, Vol. 1") † Choral Music CRD ▲ 3454 [DDD] (17.97)
E. Higginbottom (org)—Psalm Prelude, Set 1 No. 1, Op. 32; Preludio 'Sine nomine' & Paean ("Howells: Choral & Organ Music, Vol. 2") † Choral Music CRD ▲ 3455 [DDD] (17.97)

Paradise Rondel for Orchestra (1925)
R. Hickox (cnd), London SO ("Orchestral Works, Vol. 1") † Fant Vc & Orch; King's Herald; Pastoral Rhap; Procession; Threnody CHN ▲ 9410 [DDD] (16.97)

Partita for Organ
A. Partington (org) *(rec Organ of Winchester Cathedral, England, Feb 22-23, 1998)* † Dalby's Fancy; Dalby's Tocatta; Flourish for a Bidding; Hovingham Sketches; Intrata; Prelude: De Profundis; Siciliano; Slow Dance; St. Louis comes to Clifton PRIO ▲ 547 [DDD] (16.97)

Pastoral Rhapsody for Orchestra (1923)
R. Hickox (cnd), London SO ("Orchestral Works, Vol. 1") † Fant Vc & Orch; King's Herald; Paradise Rondel; Procession; Threnody CHN ▲ 9410 [DDD] (16.97)

Pieces (6) for Organ (1940-45)
G. Barber (org) *(rec Hereford Cathedral Org, Oct 11, 1995)* ("Organ Music. Vol. 2") † Son Org PRIO ▲ 524 [DDD] (16.97)
C. Dearnley (org)—No. 3, Master Tallis's Testament *(rec June 1987)* ("The St. Paul's Service") † Choral Music; Psalm-Preludes, Set I; Psalm-Preludes, Set II; Rhaps (3) Org, Op. 17 HYP 2-▲ 22038 [DDD] (18.97)

Pieces (3) for Piano (ca 1919)
J. Filsell (pno) † Gadabout; Sonatina Pno; B. Stevens:Aria Pno; Fant on Giles Farnaby; Son Pno in 1 Movt, Op. 25 GILD ▲ 7119 [DDD] (16.97)

Prelude for Harp
D. Perrett (hp) † L. Berkeley:Nocturne Hp; Rubbra:Chamber Music Hp (comp); Songs ASV ▲ 1036 (16.97)

Prelude: De Profundis for Organ
A. Partington (org) *(rec Organ of Winchester Cathedral, England, Feb 22-23, 1998)* † Dalby's Fancy; Dalby's Tocatta; Flourish for a Bidding; Hovingham Sketches; Intrata; Partita; Siciliano; Slow Dance; St. Louis comes to Clifton PRIO ▲ 547 [DDD] (16.97)

Procession for Orchestra (1922)
R. Hickox (cnd), London SO ("Orchestral Works, Vol. 1") † Fant Vc & Orch; King's Herald; Paradise Rondel; Pastoral Rhap; Threnody CHN ▲ 9410 [DDD] (16.97)

Psalm-Preludes (3), Set I for Organ (1915-16)
C. Dearnley (org) *(rec Nov 1989)* ("The St. Paul's Service") † Choral Music; Pieces Org; Psalm-Preludes, Set II; Rhaps (3) Org, Op. 17 HYP 2-▲ 22038 [DDD] (18.97)

Psalm-Preludes (3), Set II for Organ (1938-39)
C. Dearnley (org) *(rec June 1987)* ("The St. Paul's Service") † Choral Music; Pieces Org; Psalm-Preludes, Set I; Rhaps (3) Org, Op. 17 HYP 2-▲ 22038 [DDD] (18.97)

Requiem for solo Voices & Chorus (1936)
J. Alldis (cnd), Netherlands Chamber Choir ("English Choral Music") † D. Bedford:Golden Wine; B. Britten:Flower Songs, Op. 47; G. Holst:Choral Hymns from the Rig-Veda, Op. 26; Vaughan Williams:Shakespeare Songs GLOE ▲ 5170 (16.97)
M. Best (cnd), Corydon Singers [L,E] † Take Him, Earth, for Cherishing; Vaughan Williams:Mass; Te Deum HYP ▲ 66076 [AAD] (18.97)
H. Bicket (org), P. Spicer (cnd), Finzi Singers † Choral Music; Vaughan Williams:Choral Music CHN ▲ 9019 [DDD] (16.97)
P. Flight (ct), D. Honoré (ten), T. Woody (bar), J. Barton (trbn), F. Burgemeister (cnd), Indianapolis Festival Orch, Christ Church Cathedral Men & Boys' Choir Oxford † G. Fauré:Requiem, Op. 48 GOT ▲ 49062 [DDD] (17.97)
D. Warland (cnd), Dale Warland Singers *(rec St. Paul, MN, Aug 1994)* † G. Allegri:Miserere; S. Barber:Agnus Dei; F. Martin:Mass for Double Chorus AME ▲ 120 [DDD] (16.97) ▮ 120 [DDD] (10.98)

Rhapsodies (3) for Organ, Op. 17
C. Dearnley (org) *(rec Nov 1989)* ("The St. Paul's Service") † Choral Music; Pieces Org; Psalm-Preludes, Set I; Psalm-Preludes, Set II HYP 2-▲ 22038 [DDD] (18.97)

Rhapsody in c# for Organ, Op. 17/3
J. Lippincott (org) *(rec Princeton Univ Chapel's Mander Org)* † Duruflé:Prélude, Adagio et Choral varié, Op. 4; Widor:Sym 6 Org, Op. 42/2 GOT ▲ 49061 [DDD] (17.97)

HOWELLS, HERBERT (cont.)

St. Louis comes to Clifton
A. Partington (org) *(rec Organ of Winchester Cathedral, England, Feb 22-23, 1998)* † Dalby's Fancy; Dalby's Tocatta; Flourish for a Bidding; Hovingham Sketches; Intrata; Partita; Prelude: De Profundis; Siciliano; Slow Dance PRIO ▲ 547 [DDD] (16.97)

Serenade for Strings
R. Hickox (cnd), City of London Sinfonia † Con Strs; Elegy Va & Str Qt; Suite Strs CHN ▲ 9161 [DDD] (16.97)

Siciliano for a High Ceremony (1953)
A. Partington (org) *(rec Organ of Winchester Cathedral, England, Feb 22-23, 1998)* † Dalby's Fancy; Dalby's Tocatta; Flourish for a Bidding; Hovingham Sketches; Intrata; Partita; Prelude: De Profundis; Slow Dance; St. Louis comes to Clifton PRIO ▲ 547 [DDD] (16.97)
B. K. Tidwell (org) *(rec 100 Rank Schantz Organ, Cleveland Heights, OH)* † G. Bales:Petite Suite; Hollins:Trumpet Minuet; Paine:Concert Vars Austrian Hymn; Roger-Ducasse:Pastoral Org; Sowerby:Sonatina for Org; Sym 4; Vierne:Pièces de fantaisie ARK ▲ 6157 [DDD] (16.97)

Slow Dance
A. Partington (org) *(rec Organ of Winchester Cathedral, England, Feb 22-23, 1998)* † Dalby's Fancy; Dalby's Tocatta; Flourish for a Bidding; Hovingham Sketches; Intrata; Partita; Prelude: De Profundis; Siciliano; St. Louis comes to Clifton PRIO ▲ 547 [DDD] (16.97)

Sonata for Oboe & Piano (1943)
S. Francis (ob), P. Dickinson (pno) † R. Boughton:Qt 1 Ob; H. Harty:Pieces Ob; Rubbra:Son Ob HYP ▲ 55008 (9.97)

Sonata for Organ (1933)
G. Barber (org) *(rec Hereford Cathedral Org, Oct 11, 1995)* ("Organ Music. Vol. 2") † Pieces Org PRIO ▲ 524 [DDD] (16.97)

Sonatina for Piano (1971)
J. Filsell (pno) † Gadabout; Pieces Pno; B. Stevens:Aria Pno; Fant on Giles Farnaby; Son Pno in 1 Movt, Op. 25 GILD ▲ 7119 [DDD] (16.97)

Songs
J. Bowman (ct), P. Ash (cnd) —2 songs—Full Moon; O my deir hert [E] *(rec 1988)* † A. Ridout:Songs Ct; Steptoe:Elegy on the Death of Cock Robin; Vaughan Williams:Songs; Warlock:Songs MER ▲ 84158 (16.97)

Stabat mater for Tenor, Orchestra & Chorus (1963)
N. Archer (ten), G. Rozhdestvensky (cnd), London SO, London Sym Chorus CHN ▲ 9314 [DDD] (16.97)

Suite for Strings (1944)
R. Hickox (cnd), City of London Sinfonia † Con Strs; Elegy Va & Str Qt; Serenade Strs CHN ▲ 9161 [DDD] (16.97)

Suite "The B's" for Orchestra (ca 1916)
R. Hickox (cnd), London SO ("Orchestral Works, Vol. 2") † Dances; In Green Ways CHN ▲ 9557 (16.97)

Take Him, Earth, for Cherishing (motet on the death of President Kennedy) for Voices [text Prudentius] (1964)
M. Best (cnd), Corydon Singers [L,E] † Requiem; Vaughan Williams:Mass; Te Deum HYP ▲ 66076 [AAD] (18.97)

Threnody for Cello & Orchestra
M. Welsh (vc), R. Hickox (cnd), London SO ("Orchestral Works, Vol. 1") † Fant Vc & Orch; King's Herald; Paradise Rondel; Pastoral Rhap; Procession CHN ▲ 9410 [DDD] (16.97)

HOYLAND, VIC (1945-

The Other Side of the Air for Piano (1992)
R. Hind (pno) *(rec June 1993)* † Sawer:Melancholy of Departure NMCC ▲ 20 [DDD] (8.97)

HUANG, ANLUN (1949-

Chinese Rhapsody No. 3 for Saxophone & Piano, Op. 46 (1989)
J. Demmler (sax), P. Grabinger (pno) ("Cosmopolitan") † Dessau:Suite Sax; Holcombe:Blues Con; Jolivet:Fantaisie-Impromptu; W. Mayer:Inner Voices; M. Rosenthal:Sax-Marmalade BAYE ▲ 100100 [DDD] (17.97)

Concerto in g for Piano & Orchestra (1982)
J. Banowetz (pno), K. Schermerhorn (cnd), Hong Kong PO *(rec Lyric Theatre of the Hong Kong Academy for Perform, June 28, 1986)* ("First Contemporary Chinese Composers Festival 1986") † W. W. Chan:Sym 3; Qu:Mong Dong; Tan Dun:Intermezzo; J. Tang:Sym 3; Ye:Moon over the West River MARC (Chinese Contemporary) ▲ 8223915 [DDD] (13.97)

HUANG, ZI (20th cent)

In Memoriam for Orchestra (1929)
C. Peng (cnd), Shanghai PO *(rec Shanghai China, Apr 1993)* ("Chinese Orchestral Works") † Metropolitan Scene Fant; S. Ding:Music of Ding; Vars on a Chinese Folk Theme; Vars on a Xinjiang Tune; Xinjiang Dances; He:Music of He; Orchestral Works MARC (Chinese Music) ▲ 8223956 [DDD] (13.97)

Metropolitan Scene Fantasia for Orchestra (1935)
C. Peng (cnd), Shanghai PO *(rec Shanghai China, Apr 1993)* ("Chinese Orchestral Works") † In Memoriam; S. Ding:Music of Ding; Vars on a Chinese Folk Theme; Vars on a Xinjiang Tune; Xinjiang Dances; He:Music of He; Orchestral Works MARC (Chinese Music) ▲ 8223956 [DDD] (13.97)

HUBAY, JENŐ (1858-1937)

Concertstück for Cello & Orchestra, Op. 20 (1893)
P. Xuereb (va), L. Devos (pno) [arr va & pno] ("Viola Pieces by Violin Virtuosi") † J. Joachim:Vars on a Theme Va, Op. 10; H. Vieuxtemps:Allegro & Scherzo Va, Op. 60; Wieniawski:Rêverie Va & Pno TLNT ▲ 291012 [DDD] (15.97)

The Flower's Tale for Violin & Orchestra, Op. 30
F. Szecsódi (vn), I. Kassai (pno) ("Works for Violin & Piano, Vol. 2") † Romance Vn, Op. 25; Solo from Vn Maker of Cremona, Op. 40a; Suite Vn, Op. 5; Vars on a Hungarian Song, Op. 72 HUN ▲ 31812 [DDD] (16.97)

Hejre Kati for Violin & Orchestra [from Scènes de la Csárda], Op. 32/4
F. Balogh (vn), M. Antál (cnd), Hungarian State Orch *(rec Apr 1988)* † Kodály:Háry János (suite); Liszt:Hungarian Rhaps, S.244 NXIN ▲ 550142 [DDD] (5.97)
M. Elman (vn), L. Mittman (pno) *(rec Apr 1946)* † Balakirev:Songs; J. Brahms:Son 3 Vn, Op. 108; A. Dvořák:Slavonic Fant; Mendelssohn (-Bartholdy):Con Vn & Orch, Op. 64; Lieder ohne Worte; Smetana:From the Homeland BID ▲ 160 [ADD] (16.97)

Impressions de la Puszta (3 morceaux caractéristiques hongrois) for Violin & Piano, Op. 44 (1893)
F. Szecsódi (vn), I. Kassai (pno) ("Works for Violin & Piano, Vol. 1") † Son Vn; Stücke Vn, Op. 121 HUN ▲ 31733 [DDD] (16.97)

Romance in F for Violin & Piano, Op. 25
F. Szecsódi (vn), I. Kassai (pno) ("Works for Violin & Piano, Vol. 2") † Flower's Tale, Op. 30; Solo from Vn Maker of Cremona, Op. 40a; Suite Vn, Op. 5; Vars on a Hungarian Song, Op. 72 HUN ▲ 31812 [DDD] (16.97)

Solo from *The Violin Maker of Cremona* for Violin, Op. 40a
F. Szecsódi (vn) ("Works for Violin & Piano, Vol. 2") † Flower's Tale, Op. 30; Romance Vn, Op. 25; Suite Vn, Op. 5; Vars on a Hungarian Song, Op. 72 HUN ▲ 31812 [DDD] (16.97)

Sonata in D for Violin & Piano,, Op. 22, "Romantic"
F. Szecsódi (vn), I. Kassai (pno) ("Works for Violin & Piano, Vol. 1") † Impressions de la puszta, Op. 44; Stücke Vn, Op. 121 HUN ▲ 31733 [DDD] (16.97)

Stücke (6) for Violin & Piano, Op. 121 (1925)
F. Szecsódi (vn), I. Kassai (pno) ("Works for Violin & Piano, Vol. 1") † Impressions de la puszta, Op. 44; Son Vn HUN ▲ 31733 [DDD] (16.97)

Suite for Violin & Orchestra, Op. 5
F. Szecsódi (vn), I. Kassai (pno) ("Works for Violin & Piano, Vol. 2") † Flower's Tale, Op. 30; Romance Vn, Op. 25; Solo from Vn Maker of Cremona, Op. 40a; Vars on a Hungarian Song, Op. 72 HUN ▲ 31812 [DDD] (16.97)

Variations on a Hungarian Song for Violin & Orchestra, Op. 72
F. Szecsódi (vn), I. Kassai (pno) ("Works for Violin & Piano, Vol. 2") † Flower's Tale, Op. 30; Romance Vn, Op. 25; Solo from Vn Maker of Cremona, Op. 40a; Suite Vn, Op. 5 HUN ▲ 31812 [DDD] (16.97)

HUBER, HANS (1852-1921)

Eine Lustspiel Overture for Orchestra, Op. 50 (1879)
J. Weigle (cnd), Stuttgart PO *(rec Germany, Dec 1996)* † Sym 2; Symphonic Sel STRL ▲ 1022 [DDD] (15.97)

Serenade No. 1 in E for Orchestra, Op. 86, "Sommernächte" (1885)
J. Weigle (cnd), Stuttgart PO *(rec Stuttgart, Germany, July 1998)* † Sym 5 STRL (World Première) ▲ 1027 [DDD] (15.97)

Sextet in B for Piano & Winds
Swiss Wind Quintet † P. Juon:Arabeske, Op. 73; Qnt Ww DI ▲ 920481 [DDD] (5.97)

Symphonic Selection from the Opera Der Simplicius for Orchestra (1898)
J. Weigle (cnd), Stuttgart PO *(rec Germany, Dec 1996)* † Lustspiel Ov, Op. 50; Sym 2 STRL ▲ 1022 [DDD] (15.97)

Symphony No. 2 in e for Violin, Organ & Orchestra, Op. 115, "Böcklin Symphony" (1900)
M. Wächter (vn), G. Maysenholder (org), J. Weigle (cnd), Stuttgart PO *(rec Germany, Dec 1996)* † Lustspiel Ov, Op. 50; Symphonic Sel STRL ▲ 1022 [DDD] (15.97)

HUBER, HANS (cont.)
Symphony No. 5 in F for Violin & Orchestra, "Romantische, Der Geiger von Gmünd" (1906)
H. Schneeberger (vn), J. Weigle (cnd), Stuttgart PO *(rec Stuttgart, Germany, July 1998)* † Serenade 1 Orch, Op. 86 STRL (World Première) ▲ 1027 [DDD] (15.97)
HUBER, KLAUS (1924-
Ein Hauch von Unzeit VII for Double Bass (1972; 1988)
B. Ianke (db) ("The Contemporary Double Bass") † L. Berio:PSY; Bibalo:Invenzione Evolutiva; Reise med bå uten båt; Feidje:Contrabacchus; Scelsi:C'est bien la nuit SIMX ▲ 1136 [DDD] (18.97)
HUBER, NICOLAUS A. (1939-
An Hölderlins Umnachtung for Chamber Ensemble
Musikfabrik NRW † Bruttger:Monolith; Kalitzke:Salto. Trapez. Ikarus; Stäbler:Traum 1/9/92 CPO ▲ 999259 [DDD] (14.97)
Clash Music for Percussion Ensemble [extracted from Herbstfestival] (1988)
Percussion Group The Hague † J. Cage:First Construction; Donatoni:Omar; R. Ford:Star; J. Kondo:Under the Umbrella; S. Reich:Drumming GLOE ▲ 5086 [DDD] (16.97)
Don't Fence Me In (trio) for Flute, Oboe & Clarinet (1994)
Aventure Ensemble *(rec Apr 1997)* ("Chamber Music") † La Force du Vertige; Mit Erinnerung; Offenes Fragment; Vor und zurück ARSM ▲ 1224 [DDD] (17.97)
La Force du Vertige for Flute, Clarinet, Violin, Cello & Piano (1985)
Aventure Ensemble *(rec Apr 1997)* ("Chamber Music") † Don't Fence Me In; Mit Erinnerung; Offenes Fragment; Vor und zurück ARSM ▲ 1224 [DDD] (17.97)
Mit Erinnerung for Bassoon (1996)
W. Rüdiger (bn) *(rec Apr 1997)* ("Chamber Music") † Don't Fence Me In; La Force du Vertige; Offenes Fragment; Vor und zurück ARSM ▲ 1224 [DDD] (17.97)
Offenes Fragment for Soprano, Flute, Guitar & Percussion [texts Hölderlin's Der Winter & Kitty Kelly's biography of Sinatra, My Way] (1991)
Aventure Ensemble *(rec Apr 1997)* ("Chamber Music") † Don't Fence Me In; La Force du Vertige; Mit Erinnerung; Vor und zurück ARSM ▲ 1224 [DDD] (17.97)
Vor und zurück for Oboe (1981)
C. Hommel (ob) *(rec Apr 1997)* ("Chamber Music") † Don't Fence Me In; La Force du Vertige; Mit Erinnerung; Offenes Fragment ARSM ▲ 1224 [DDD] (17.97)
HUEBER, KURT ANTON (1928-
Capriccio for Cello
A. Chitta (vc) *(rec Vienna, Jan 1989)* ("Music for Cello & Piano") † Son Pno; Son Vc & Pno; Son 2 Vc; Füssl:Duo Vc & Pno; Fünf Töne—Fünf Finger VMM ▲ 2010 [DDD]
Sonata for Cello & Piano
A. Chitta (vc), S. Chitta (pno) *(rec Vienna, Jan 1989)* ("Music for Cello & Piano") † Capriccio Vc; Son Pno; Son 2 Vc; Füssl:Duo Vc & Pno; Fünf Töne—Fünf Finger VMM ▲ 2010 [DDD]
Sonata for Piano
S. Chitta (pno) *(rec Vienna, Jan 1989)* ("Music for Cello & Piano") † Capriccio Vc; Son Vc & Pno; Son 2 Vc; Füssl:Duo Vc & Pno; Fünf Töne—Fünf Finger VMM ▲ 2010 [DDD]
Sonata No. 2 for solo Cello
A. Chitta (vc) *(rec Vienna, Jan 1989)* ("Music for Cello & Piano") † Capriccio Vc; Son Pno; Son Vc & Pno; Füssl:Duo Vc & Pno; Fünf Töne—Fünf Finger VMM ▲ 2010 [DDD]
HUGHES, LUIGI (1836-1913)
Grand Concerto Fantasy on Themes from Verdi's Un ballo en maschera
J. Rampal (fl), C. Arimany (fl), J. S. Ritter (pno) *(rec Los Angeles, July 1996)* ("Romantic Music for 2 Flutes & Piano") † T. Böhm:Duos de Mendelssohn & Lachner; A. F. Doppler:Andante & Rondo, Op. 25; Duetto américain, Op. 37; Sonambula, Op. 42; Kuhlau:Grand Trio, Op. 119; W. A. Mozart:Son Pnos, K.448 DLS ▲ 3212 [DDD] (14.97)
HUGOT, ANTOINE (1761-1803)
Quartet in G for Flute & Strings [arr from Mozart's Sonata in F for Piano 4-Hand] (1799)
Schönbrunn Ensemble Amsterdam *(rec Aug 1990)* † W. A. Mozart:Qts Fl CCL ▲ 1290 [DDD] (18.97)
HUI, MELISSA (1966-
San Rocco for Oboe, Chamber Choir & Percussion (1991)
L. Cherney (ob), R. Hartenberger (perc), N. Edison (cnd), Elora Festival Singers *(rec St Martin-in-the-Fields Church Toronto, July 1995)* ("The Charmer") † Chan Ka Nin:Charmer; B. Cherney:River of Fire; C. P. Harman:Poem; Mather:Vouvray; H. Somers:Miniatures Ob CTR ▲ 5395 [DDD] (16.97)
HULTGREN, CRAIG (1955-
The Chained Cello Improvisation for live amplified Cello (1992)
C. Hultgren (vc) ("Music of the Next Moment - Craig Hultgren") † Double Bow Improvisation; Burrier:II; Marth:They're Still Running; C. N. Mason:Artist & His Model; L. Nielson:Valentine Mechanique; R. Paredes:Small Writing; J. C. Ross:Encore Vc INNO ▲ 502 (14.97)
The Double Bow Improvisation for live amplified Cello (1992)
C. Hultgren (vc) ("Music of the Next Moment - Craig Hultgren") † Chained Vc Improvisation; Burrier:II; Marth:They're Still Running; C. N. Mason:Artist & His Model; L. Nielson:Valentine Mechanique; R. Paredes:Small Writing; J. C. Ross:Encore Vc INNO ▲ 502 (14.97)
HULTQVIST, ANDERS (20th cent)
The Winter Garden for Chamber Orchestra (1993)
P. Csaba (cnd) † Börtz:Vars & Intermezzi; Hillborg:Celestial Mechanics; Liljeholm:Tetrachordon CAPA ▲ 21519 (16.97)
HUMBLE, KEITH (1927-1995)
Short Pieces (5) in 2 Parts for Cello & Piano (1982)
G. Pedersen (vc), D. Bollard (pno) *(rec ABC Sydney, Australia, Dec 1993-Jul 1997)* ("Austrailian Cello") † D. Banks:Sequence; Studies Vc; B. Kos:Evocations; G. Whitehead:Journey of Matuku Moana TALP ▲ 129 [DDD] (18.97)
Sonata for Flute & Piano (1990)
G. Collins (fl), D. Miller (pno) *(rec ABC Ultimo Centre, Jan-Feb 1995)* ("Spinning: New Australian Flute Music") † N. Butterly:Wind Stirs Gently; R. Edwards:Ecstatic Dances Fls; A. Ford:Spinning; Smalley:Ceremony III; C. Vine:Son Fl; M. Wesley-Smith:Balibo TALP ▲ 69 [DDD]
HUME, TOBIAS (ca 1569-1645)
Captain Hume's Poeticall Musicke for Various Instruments
E. Kirkby (sop), Labyrinto *(rec Dec 1995)* ("The Spirit of Gambo") † First Part of Ayres (sels) GLSS ▲ 920402 [DDD] (18.97)
Les Voix Humaines—Cease leaden slumber; What greater griefe [both w. Suzie Le Blanc (sop)]; Sweet Ayre (The Earle of Arundels favoret) *(rec Church of St. Augustin de Mirabel, Québec, Canada, Apr 1997)* † My Hope Is Revived; 1st Part of Ayres (sels); Coprario:Songs of Mourning (sels); Cutting:Mrs. Anne Markham's Pavane; J. Dowland:Songs; A. I. Ferrabosco:Ayres; J. Jenkins:Suite for 2 Vls; C. Simpson:VI Music ATMM ▲ 22136 (15.97)
The First Part of Ayres (selections)
E. Kirkby (sop), Labyrinto *(rec Dec 1995)* ("The Spirit of Gambo") † Captain Humes Poeticall Musicke GLSS ▲ 920402 [DDD] (18.97)
Les Voix Humaines—Touch me sweetly; The Spirite of Musicke *(rec Church of St. Augustin de Mirabel, Québec, Canada, Apr 1997)* † Captain Humes Poeticall Musicke; My Hope Is Revived; Coprario:Songs of Mourning (sels); Cutting:Mrs. Anne Markham's Pavane; J. Dowland:Songs; A. I. Ferrabosco:Ayres; J. Jenkins:Suite for 2 Vls; C. Simpson:VI Music ATMM ▲ 22136 (15.97)
J. Savall (vl) ASTR ▲ 7723 [AAD] (18.97)
My Hope Is Revived (The Lady Suffolkes Delight) for 2 Violas da Gamba
Les Voix Humaines *(rec Church of St. Augustin de Mirabel, Québec, Canada, Oct 1997)* † Captain Humes Poeticall Musicke; 1st Part of Ayres (sels); Coprario:Songs of Mourning (sels); Cutting:Mrs. Anne Markham's Pavane; J. Dowland:Songs; A. I. Ferrabosco:Ayres; J. Jenkins:Suite for 2 Vls; C. Simpson:VI Music ATMM ▲ 22136 (15.97)
HUMMEL, BERTOLD (1925-
Concerto for Percussion & Orchestra, Op. 70
P. Sadlo (perc), W. Rögner (cnd), Bamberg SO ("Percussion in Concert") † Creston:Concertino Mar, Op. 21; D. Milhaud:Con Mar KSCH ▲ 364152 (16.97)
Frescoes '70 for Percussion Ensemble (1970)
Cabaza Percussion Quartet † Brodmann:Greetings to Hermann; W. Heider:Gallery; Ohana:Etudes Chorégraphiques; S. Reich:Music for Pieces of Wood CPO ▲ 999088 [AAD] (14.97)
Konzertante Musik for Guitar & String Quartet, Op. 39 (1989)
M. Tröster (gtr), Das Sächsische String Quartet *(rec Dresden, Germany, Feb 1994)* ("Guitarrenquintette I") † E. Angulo:Vögel, Op. 21; J. Duarte:Qnt 1 Gtr, Op. 85 THOR ▲ 2212 [DDD] (17.97)

HUMMEL, JOHANN NEPOMUK (1778-1837)
Adagio, Variations & Rondo in A on "Schöne Minka" for Piano, Flute & Cello, Op. 78 (1818)
B. Pergamenschikow (vc), A. Adorján (fl), P. Gililov (pno) *(rec Apr 23-25, 1991)* † Son Vc; Son 5 Pno, Op. 81 ORF ▲ 252931 [DDD] (18.97)
Trio Cantabile *(rec Hanover, Germany, July 1997)* ("Trio Cantabile") † Kuhlau:Trio Fls, Op. 119; C. M. von Weber:Trio Fl, Op. 63 THOR ▲ 2383 [DDD] (16.97)
Alma virgo (offertory) for solo Voices, Orchestra & Chorus, Op. 89a (1805)
A. Halgrimson (sop), S. McAdoo (mez), H. Wildhaber (ten), P. Mikuláš (bass), J. Engel (bass), M. Haselböck (cnd), Vienna Academy, Brünn Czech Phil Chorus ("Sacred Music") † Mass in E♭, Op. 80; Quod quod in orbe, Op. 88 KSCH ▲ 317792 (16.97)
Amusement in F for Violin & Piano, Op. 108 (1825)
L. A. Bianchi (vn), A. Orvieto (pno) *(rec May 1998)* ("Works for Violin/Viola & Piano") † Rondo brillant Vn, Op. 126; Son Va; Vars Vn in F, Op.posth.2 DYNC ▲ 192 [DDD] (16.97)
Concertino in G for Piano & Small Orchestra, Op. 73 (1816)
M. Galling (pno), C. Bünte (cnd), Berlin SO † M. Clementi:Con Pno Orch; J. B. Cramer:Con 5 Pno, Op. 48; Czerny:Chamber Music; J. Field:Con 2 Pno, H.31; F. Ries:Con in c#, Op. 55 VB2 2-▲ 5111 (9.97)
H. Shelley (pno) † Con Pno; Gesellschafts Rondo, Op. 117 CHN ▲ 9558 (16.97)
Concerto in F for Bassoon & Orchestra (ca 1805)
C. Davidsson (bn), N. Willén (cnd), Sundsvall CO *(rec Sundsvall Sweden, Dec 5-10, 1994)* ("The Romantic Bassoon") † F. Danzi:Con Bn; Puteanus:Quintetto Bn; C. M. von Weber:Andante & Rondo ungarese Bn BIS ▲ 705 [DDD] (17.97)
D. Jensen (bn), W. A. Albert (cnd), Cologne RSO ("Bassoon Concertos") † J. Françaix:Divert Bn; Jolivet:Con Bn; W. A. Mozart:Con Bn, K.191 CAPO ▲ 10579 [DDD] (11.97)
F. Machats (bn), B. Rezucha (cnd), Cappella Istropolitana ("Instrumental Concertos") † Con Mand & Strs, S.28; Con Tpt in E♭, S.49 OPP ▲ 2632
Y. Nakanishi (bn), N. Cleobury (cnd), London Mozart Players ("Bassoon Concertos") † C. Stamitz:Con Bn; C. M. von Weber:Andante & Rondo ungarese Bn; Con Bn ASVQ ▲ 6159 (10.97)
V. Popov (bn), V. Polyansky (cnd), Russian State SO † W. A. Mozart:Con Bn, K.191; C. M. von Weber:Con Bn CHN ▲ 9656 (16.97)
Concerto in G for Mandolin & Strings, S.28 (1799)
E. Bauer-Slais (mand), V. Hladky (cnd), Vienna Pro Musica Orch *(rec 1973)* † Parthia, S.48; Son Vn & Pno, Op. 5/1 TUXE ▲ 1026 [ADD] (10.97)
K. Harris (mand), J. Valta (cnd), Zilina State CO ("Instrumental Concertos") † Con Bn; Con Tpt in E♭, S.49 OPP ▲ 2632
V. Kruglov (mand), Northern Crown Soloists Ensemble *(rec 1992)* ("Mandolin Concertos") † Vivaldi:Con Lt Vns, RV.93; Con Mands, RV.425; Con Mands, RV.532 OLY ▲ 582 [DDD] (16.97)
Concerto in G for Piano, Violin & Orchestra, Op. 17 (ca 1805)
H. Shaham (vn), H. Shelley (pno), H. Shelley (cnd), London Mozart Players † Con Pno in E, Op. 110 CHN ▲ 9687 (16.97)
Concerto in C for Piano & Orchestra, Op. 34a
P. Kováč (pno), V. Horák (cnd) † Con Pno, Op. 85 KSCH ▲ 311120 (16.97)
P. Kováč (pno), V. Horák (cnd) † Fant Pno, Op. 18 OPP ▲ 2633 (10.97)
Concerto in a for Piano & Orchestra, Op. 85 (ca 1816)
H. Chang (pno), T. Pál (cnd), Budapest CO *(rec Budapest, May 28-30, 1987)* † Con Pno, Op. 89 NXIN ▲ 550837 [DDD] (5.97)
S. Hough (pno), B. Thomson (cnd), English CO † Con Pno, Op. 89 CHN ▲ 8507 [DDD] (16.97)
I. Palovič (pno), L. Slovák (cnd), Slovak PO † Con Pno KSCH ▲ 311120 (16.97)
D. Protopopescu (pno), A. Rahbari (cnd), Slovak Radio New PO † Con Pno, Op. 89 DI ▲ 920117 [DDD] (5.97)
Concerto in b for Piano & Orchestra, Op. 89 (1819)
H. Chang (pno), T. Pál (cnd), Budapest CO *(rec Budapest, May 28-30, 1987)* † Con Pno, Op. 85 NXIN ▲ 550837 [DDD] (5.97)
S. Hough (pno), B. Thomson (cnd), English CO † Con Pno, Op. 85 CHN ▲ 8507 [DDD] (16.97)
D. Protopopescu (pno), A. Rahbari (cnd), Slovak Radio New PO † Con Pno, Op. 85 DI ▲ 920117 [DDD] (5.97)
Concerto in E for Piano & Orchestra, Op. 110, "Les Adieux" (1814)
H. Kann (pno), H. Beissel (cnd), Hamburg SO *(rec 1973)* ("The Romantic Piano Concerto, Vol. 1") † Chopin:Allegro de concert, Op. 46; Henselt:Con Pno, Op. 16; A. Hill:Konzertstück Pno, Op. 113; Kalkbrenner:Con 1 Pno, Op. 61 VB2 2-▲ 5064 [ADD] (9.97)
H. Shelley (pno) † Con Pno & Vn, Op. 17 CHN ▲ 9687 (16.97)
Concerto in A♭ for Piano & Orchestra, Op. 113 (1827)
N. Lahusen (pno), H. Kodama (cnd), South Westphalian PO † Con Pno in F, Op. posth. KSCH ▲ 315672 (16.97)
H. Shelley (pno) † Concertino Pno, Op. 73; Gesellschafts Rondo, Op. 117 CHN ▲ 9558 (16.97)
Concerto in F for Piano & Orchestra, Op. posth.
N. Lahusen (pno), H. Kodama (cnd), South Westphalian PO † Con Pno KSCH ▲ 315672 (16.97)
Concerto in E♭ for Trumpet & Orchestra, S.49 (1803)
M. André (tpt), H. von Karajan (cnd), Berlin PO *(rec Berlin, Germany, May 28-29, 1974)* † L. Mozart:Con Tpt; Telemann:Qnt Tpt; Vivaldi:Cons Tpt EMIC (Great Recordings of the Century) ▲ 66961 [ADD] (11.97)
T. Dokshitzer (tpt), R. Barshaï (cnd), Moscow CO *(rec 1968)* ("Trumpet Rhapsody") † A. Arutiunian:Con Tpt; H. I. Biber:Son à 6 Tpt; G. Gershwin:Rhap in Blue; Glazunov:Album Leaf; Glière:Con Coloratura Sop; P. Tchaikovsky:Swan Lake (sels) RCAV (Gold Seal) ▲ 32045 [ADD] (11.97)
R. Friedrich (tpt), M. Haselböck (cnd) *(rec Sofiensäle Vienna, Oct 17-20, 1994)* ("Konzerte für Klappentrompete") † J. Haydn:Con Tpt; M. Puccini:Concertone Fl CAPO ▲ 10598 [DDD] (11.97)
W. Marsalis (tpt), R. Leppard (cnd), English CO *(rec St. Giles Church, Cripplegate,London, England, Feb 1993)* ("Wynton Marsalis: The London Concert") † Fasch:Con Tpt Obs; J. Haydn:Con Tpt; L. Mozart:Con Tpt SNYC ▲ 57497 [DDD] (16.97) ▮ 57497 [DDD] (10.98)
W. Marsalis (tpt), R. Leppard (cnd), National PO London † J. Haydn:Con Tpt; L. Mozart:Con Tpt SNYC ▲ 37846 [DDD] (11.97)
A. Sandoval (tpt), L. Haza (cnd), London SO *(rec 1993)* † A. Arutiunian:Con Tpt; L. Mozart:Con Tpt; A. Sandoval:Con Tpt RCAV (Red Seal) ▲ 62661 [DDD] (16.97)
G. Schwarz (tpt), G. Schwarz (cnd), New York Chamber SO † J. Haydn:Con Tpt DLS ▲ 3001 [DDD] (14.97)
R. Smedvig (tpt), J. Ling (cnd), Scottish CO † V. Bellini:Con Ob; J. Haydn:Con Tpt; Tartini:Con Tpt; Torelli:Con Tpt TEL ▲ 80232 [DDD] (16.97)
B. Soustrot (tpt), M. Soustrot (cnd), Loire PO † Jolivet:Con 2 Tpt PVY ▲ 788011 [DDD] (16.97)
L. Stresnak (tpt), O. Lenárd (cnd), Bratislava SO ("Instrumental Concertos") † Con Bn; Con Mand & Strs, S.28 OPP ▲ 2632
Concerto in E for Trumpet & Orchestra [2nd version of Concerto in E♭ for Trumpet, S.49, prob revised by either Hummel or Viennese court trumpeter Anton Weidinger, or both]
A. Ghitalla (tpt), P. Monteux (cnd) *(rec 1963-64)* † Albrechtsberger:Con Tpt; M. Haydn:Con in C Tpt; Molter:Con 3 Tpt CRYS ▲ 760 (15.97)
J. Wallace (tpt), C. Warren-Green (cnd), Philharmonia Orch *(rec June 23-25, 1986)* † Fasch:Con Tpt & Ob d'amore; J. Haydn:Con Tpt; Neruda:Con Tpt; F. D. Weber:Vars Tpt NIMB ▲ 7016 [DDD] (11.97)
Fantasie in E♭ for Piano, Op. 18 (ca 1805)
L. Marcinger (pno) † Con Pno OPP ▲ 2633 (10.97)
German Dances for the Redoutensaal for 2 Violins & Bass
Vienna Waltz Ensemble *(rec Chicago, IL, July & Oct, 1998)* † Anonymous:Brat-Lenerl; Schellerl-Tanz; Tanz; Gregora:Music of Gregora; J. Haydn:Jahreszeiten (sels); Pamer:Ländler; Walzer; Pössinger:Minuets Strs; Joh. Strauss:Wiener Carneval-Walzer, Op. 3 DENW ▲ 102 (16.97)
Gesellschafts Rondo in D for Piano & Orchestra, Op. 117 (1829)
H. Shelley (pno) † Con Pno; Concertino Pno, Op. 73 CHN ▲ 9558 (16.97)
Grand Serenades Nos. 1 & 2 for Guitar, Piano, Violin, Clarinet & Bassoon, Opp. 65 & 66
Consortium Classicum † Gragnani:Qt for 2 Gtrs, Op. 8 KSCH ▲ 310006 [DDD]
Introduction, Theme & Variations in F for Oboe & Orchestra, Op. 102
A. Klein (ob), P. Freeman (cnd), Czech National SO *(rec Prague, Czech Republic, June 17-19, 1998)* † F. Krommer:Con Ob CED ▲ 45 [DDD] (16.97)
H. Lee (ob), V. Jordania (cnd), Russian Federal Orch *(rec Moscow Radio Palace Hall, Russia, Oct 1995)* ("Hee-Sun Lee—Oboe") † J. S. Bach:Con 1 for 2 Hpds, BWV 1060; A. Marcello:Con Ob Strs in d; W. A. Mozart:Qt Ob SSET ▲ 1002 [DDD] (16.97)
H. Stadlmair (cnd), Bamberg SO † F. Devienne:Cons Fl (comp); Eybler:Con Cl; F. Krommer:Con Cl TUD ▲ 782 [DDD] (16.97)
Mass in B♭, Op. 77 (ca 1804-10)
J. E. Floreen (cnd), New Brunswick CO, Westminster Oratorio Choir [LAT] † Tantum ergo KOCH ▲ 7117 [DDD] (16.97)

HUMMEL, JOHANN NEPOMUK (cont.)

Mass in E♭ for solo Voices, Orchestra & Chorus, Op. 80 (1804)
A. Halgrimson (sop), S. McAdoo (mez), H. Wildhaber (ten), P. Mikuláš (bass), J. Engel (bass), M. Haselböck (cnd), Vienna Academy, Brünn Czech Phil Chorus ("Sacred Music") † Alma virgo, Op. 89a; Quod quod in orbe, Op. 88 KSCH ▲ 317792 (16.97)

Nocturne in F for Piano 4-Hands, Op. 99 (1822)
R. Holmes (vn), R. Burnett (pno) † Son Va; Son Vn & Pno, Op. 50 AMON ▲ 12 (16.97)
S. Zamborsky (pno), P. Kováč (pno) ("Compositions for 4-Hand Piano") † Sons Pno 4-Hands OPP ▲ 2604

Parthia in E♭ for Wind Octet, S.48 (1803)
Collegium Misicum Prag *(rec 1973)* † Con Mand & Strs, S.28; Son Vn & Pno, Op. 5/1 TUXE ▲ 1026 [ADD] (10.97)
J. Pavlik (cnd) ("Chamber Compositions") † Septet militaire, Op. 114 OPP ▲ 2634 (10.97)

Piano Music
J. Trzeciak (pno)—Caprice, Op. 49; Vars sur un thème d'Armide de Gluck, Op. 57; Bagatelles, Op. 107/1, 3 & 5; Amusements, Op. 105/2; Rondo Pno, Op. 11; Bella Capricciosa, Op. 55 ("La bella Capricciosa & Other Piano Pieces") PAVA ▲ 7359 [DDD] (10.97)

Piano Piece in G, S.39 (1799)
Vienna String Trio *(rec Apr 13-14 & July 20, 1988)* † Dittersdorf:Divert Vn; Pleyel:Trio 3 Strs, Op. 11; Pössinger:Trio Strs CALG ▲ 50876 [DDD]

Quartet in E♭ for Clarinet & Strings, S.98 (1808)
M. Lethiec (cl), Nouveau Trio Pasquier † C. Kreutzer:Qt Cl; Vanhal:Qt Cl TLNT ▲ 291037 (15.97)
C. Neidich (cl), L'Archibudelli *(rec Reitschule Austria, Sept 19-22, 1993)* ("Clarinet Quintets & Quartet") † A. Reicha:Qnt Cl; C. M. von Weber:Qnt Cl SNYC ▲ 57968 [DDD] (16.97)

Quartets (3) in C, G & E♭ for Strings, Op. 30
Delmé String Quartet HYP ▲ 66568 (18.97)

Quartet No. 2 in G for Strings, Op. 30/2 (before 1804)
Hollywood String Quartet *(rec Melrose Studio, Apr 22-23, 1955)* † J. Haydn:Qts (6) Strs, H.III/75-80, Op. 76; W. A. Mozart:Qt 17 Strs, K.458 TES ▲ 1085 (17.97)

Quintet in E♭/e♭ for Piano & Strings, Op. 87 (1802)
Atalanta Fugiens *(rec Accademia del Fortepiano Florence, Jan 13-15, 1997)* † Septet Pno, Op. 74 ARCK ▲ 59003 [DDD]
Minneapolis Artists Ensemble † W. A. Mozart:Grande Sestetto Concertante GMR ▲ 2025 (16.97)
Schubert Ensemble of London † F. Schubert:Qnt Pno, D.667; R. Schumann:Qnt Pno, Op. 44; Qt Pno in c HYP 2-▲ 22008 (18.97)
Sestetto Classico † H.-J. Bertini:Sextet Pno, Op. 90 MDG ▲ 3080067 (17.97)
M. Sirbu (vn), M. Paris (va), M. Dancila (vc), F. Petracchi (db), M. Campanella (pno) † F. Schubert:Qnt Pno, D.667 DYNC ▲ 8 [DDD] (17.97)

Quod quod in orbe (gradual) for solo Voices, Orchestra & Chorus, Op. 88 (ca 1808-11)
A. Halgrimson (sop), S. McAdoo (mez), H. Wildhaber (ten), P. Mikuláš (bass), J. Engel (bass), M. Haselböck (cnd), Vienna Academy, Brünn Czech Phil Chorus ("Sacred Music") † Alma virgo, Op. 89a; Mass in E♭, Op. 80 KSCH ▲ 317792 (16.97)

Rondo brillant in G for Violin & Piano, Op. 126 (1834)
L. A. Bianchi (vn), A. Orvieto (pno) *(rec May 1998)* ("Works for Violin/Viola & Piano") † Amusement Vn, Op. 108; Son Va; Vars Vn in F, Op.posth.2 DYNC ▲ 192 [DDD] (16.97)

Rondo in E♭ for Piano, Op. 11
I. Friedman (pno) ("Highlights 1925-36 From His Discography") † Beethoven:Son 14 Pno, Op. 27/2; Chopin:Études Pno; Impromptu in F#, Op. 36; Mazurkas Pno; Nocturnes Pno; Polonaise 6 Pno, Op. 53; Son Pno in b♭, Op. 35; Waltzes Pno; I. Friedman:Danse; Music Box, Op. 33/3; Liszt:Trans, Arrs & Paraphrases; Mendelssohn (-Bartholdy):Fants Pno, Op. 16; Shield:Old English Menuet APR (Signature Series) ▲ 5508 [ADD] (18.97)

Septet militaire in C for Piano, Flute, Violin, Clarinet, Trumpet & Double Bass, Op. 114 (1829)
R. Macduzinski (pno), J. Pavlik (cnd) ("Chamber Compositions") † Parthia, S.48 OPP ▲ 2634 (10.97)
Nash Ensemble † Septet Pno, Op. 74 CRD ▲ 3418 (17.97)

Septet in d for Piano, Flute, Oboe, Horn, Viola, Cello & Double Bass (or for Piano & String Quartet), Op. 74
Atalanta Fugiens *(rec Accademia del Fortepiano Florence, Jan 13-15, 1997)* † Qnt Pno, Op. 87 ARCK ▲ 59003 [DDD]
Nash Ensemble † Berwald:Septet Vn CRD ▲ 3344 [ADD] (17.97)
Nash Ensemble † Septet militaire, Op. 114 CRD ▲ 3418 (17.97)

Sonata in A for Cello & Piano, Op. 104 (1824)
B. Pergamenschikow (vc), P. Gililov (pno) *(rec Apr 23-25, 1991)* † Adagio, Vars & Rondo, Op. 78; Son 5 Pno, Op. 81 ORF ▲ 252931 [DDD] (18.97)

Sonata in c for Harpsichord, Piano, Mandolin & Violin (c1810)
A. Stephens (mand), R. Burnett (pno) *(rec Finchcocks, Goudhurst, Kent, England, March 1991)* ("Music for Mandolin") † Barbella:Duos (6) Vns; Beethoven:Adagio Mand, WoO 43b; Sonatina Mand in c, WoO 43a; Sonatina Mand in C, WoO 44a; Vars Pno on Original Theme, Op. 76; Calace:Suite 3 mand; W. A. Mozart:Die Zufriedenheit, K.349; Komm, liebe Zither, komm, K.351 AMON ▲ 53 [DDD] (16.97)

Sonata in C for Mandolin (or Violin) & Harpsichord (or Piano), Op. 37a (ca 1810)
R. Walz (mand), V. Sofronitzki (pno) *(rec Apr 1998)* ("Works for Mandolin & Fortepiano") † Beethoven:Adagio Mand, WoO 43b; Sonatina Mand in c, WoO 43a; Sonatina Mand in C, WoO 44a; Neuling:Son Mand, Op. 3 GLOE ▲ 5187 [DDD] (16.97)

Sonata No. 1 in C for Piano, Op. 2a/3
I. Hobson (pno) † Son 6 Pno, Op. 106 ARA ▲ 6564 (16.97)
D. Protopopescu (pno) † Son 2 Pno, Op. 13; Son 3 Pno, Op. 20 DI ▲ 920237 [DDD] (5.97)

Sonata No. 2 in E♭ for Piano, Op. 13
H. Chang (pno) *(rec Santa Rosa, CA, Jan 30-31, 1995)* † Son 3 Pno, Op. 20; Son 5 Pno, Op. 81 NXIN ▲ 8553296 [DDD] (5.97)
I. Hobson (pno) † Son 5 Pno, Op. 81 ARA ▲ 6565 (16.97)
D. Protopopescu (pno) † Son 1 Pno, Op. 2a/3; Son 3 Pno, Op. 20 DI ▲ 920237 [DDD] (5.97)

Sonata No. 3 in f for Piano, Op. 20 (1807)
H. Chang (pno) *(rec Santa Rosa, CA, Jan 30-31, 1995)* † Son 2 Pno, Op. 13; Son 5 Pno, Op. 81 NXIN ▲ 8553296 [DDD] (5.97)
I. Hobson (pno) † Son 4 Pno, Op. 38 ARA ▲ 6566 (16.97)
D. Protopopescu (pno) † Son 1 Pno, Op. 2a/3; Son 2 Pno, Op. 13 DI ▲ 920237 [DDD] (5.97)

Sonata No. 4 in C for Piano, Op. 38
I. Hobson (pno) † Son 3 Pno, Op. 20 ARA ▲ 6566 (16.97)

Sonata No. 5 in f# for Piano, Op. 81
H. Chang (pno) *(rec Santa Rosa, CA, Jan 30-31, 1995)* † Son 2 Pno, Op. 13; Son 3 Pno, Op. 20 NXIN ▲ 8553296 [DDD] (5.97)
P. Gililov (pno) *(rec Apr 23-25, 1991)* † Adagio, Vars & Rondo, Op. 78; Son Vc ORF ▲ 252931 [DDD] (18.97)
I. Hobson (pno) † Son 2 Pno, Op. 13 ARA ▲ 6565 (16.97)

Sonata No. 6 in D for Piano, Op. 106 (1824)
I. Hobson (pno) † Son 1 Pno, Op. 2a/3 ARA ▲ 6564 (16.97)

Sonata No. 9 in C for Piano
C. Keene (pno) † Beethoven:Son 25 Pno, Op. 79; J. L. Dussek:Son Pno, Op. 61; Griffes:Son Pno; J. Haydn:Son 62 Kbd, H.XVI/52 PROT ▲ 1106 [ADD] (18.97)

Sonata in E♭ for Viola & Piano, Op. 5/3
L. A. Bianchi (va), A. Orvieto (pno) *(rec May 1998)* ("Works for Violin/Viola & Piano") † Amusement Vn, Op. 108; Rondo brillant Vn, Op. 126; Vars Vn in F, Op.posth.2 DYNC ▲ 192 [DDD] (16.97)
R. Holmes (vn), Burnett (pno) † Nocturne, Op. 99; Son Vn & Pno, Op. 50 AMON ▲ 12 (16.97)
H. Lindemann (va), B. Martin (pno) † J. S. Bach:Sons & Partitas Vn; A. Bax:Son Va; J. Brahms:Son 2 Cl TACE ▲ 35
R. Verebes (va), M. Lagacé (pno) *(rec Montreal)* ("Classical Sonatas") † Dittersdorf:Son Va; C. Stamitz:Son Va, Op. 6; Vanhal:Son Va SNE ▲ 569 (16.97)

Sonata in B♭ for Violin & Piano, Op. 5/1
Z. Topolski (vn), H. Kann (pno) *(rec 1973)* † Con Mand & Strs, S.28; Parthia, S.48 TUXE ▲ 1026 [ADD] (10.97)

Sonata in D for Violin (or Flute) & Piano, Op. 50
L. Devos (pno) ("Trockneblumen") † Mendelssohn (-Bartholdy):Son Vn, Op. 4; F. X. W. Mozart:Rondo Fl; F. Schubert:Intro & Vars on "Tröckne Blumen", D.802 ACCE ▲ 97125 [DDD] (17.97)
B. Gisler-Haase (fl), M. Mori (pno) *(rec Vienna, Feb 2-3, 1994)* ("Flute Sonatas") † A. Dvořák:Sonatina Vn, Op. 100; P. Hindemith:Son Fl; Martinů:Son Fl & Pno CAMA ▲ 393 [DDD] (18.97)
R. Holmes (vn), R. Burnett (pno) † Nocturne, Op. 99; Son Va AMON ▲ 12 (16.97)

HUMMEL, JOHANN NEPOMUK (cont.)

Sonata in D for Violin (or Flute) & Piano, Op. 50 (cont.)
P. Robison (fl), S. Sanders (pno) *(rec New York City, 1974)* ("The Romantic Flute") † P. Gaubert:Nocturne et Allegro scherzando; P. A. Genin:Carnival in Venice, Op. 14; B. Godard:Suite de trois morceaux, Op. 116 VC ▲ 8089 [ADD] (13.97)

Sonatas for Piano 4-Hands, Opp. 51 & 92
S. Zamborsky (pno), P. Kováč (pno) ("Compositions for 4-Hand Piano") † Nocturne, Op. 99 OPP ▲ 2604

Tantum ergo for Orchestra & Chorus [after Gluck] (1806)
J. E. Floreen (cnd), New Brunswick CO, Westminster Oratorio Choir [LAT] † Mass in B♭, Op. 77 KOCH ▲ 7117 [DDD] (16.97)

Trios for Piano, Violin & Cello (complete)
Trio Parnassus MDG ▲ 3030307 (32.97)

Trio in E♭ for Piano, Violin & Cello, Op. 12
Beaux Arts Trio † Trio Pno, Op. 35; Trio Pno, Op. 65; Trio Pno, Op. 96 PPHI ▲ 446077 (16.97)
Borodin Trio † Trio Pno, Op. 83; Trio Pno, Op. 96 CHN ▲ 9529 (16.97)
Triangulus † Trio Pno, Op. 22; Trio Pno, Op. 35; Trio Pno, Op. 96 MER ▲ 84350 (16.97)

Trio in F for Piano, Violin & Cello, Op. 22 (1799)
Triangulus † Trio Pno, Op. 12; Trio Pno, Op. 35; Trio Pno, Op. 96 MER ▲ 84350 (16.97)

Trio in G for Piano, Violin & Cello, Op. 35
Beaux Arts Trio † Trio Pno, Op. 12; Trio Pno, Op. 65; Trio Pno, Op. 96 PPHI ▲ 446077 (16.97)
Triangulus † Trio Pno, Op. 12; Trio Pno, Op. 22; Trio Pno, Op. 96 MER ▲ 84350 (16.97)

Trio in G for Piano, Violin & Cello, Op. 65
Beaux Arts Trio † Trio Pno, Op. 12; Trio Pno, Op. 35; Trio Pno, Op. 96 PPHI ▲ 446077 (16.97)

Trio in E for Piano, Violin & Cello, Op. 83
Borodin Trio † Trio Pno, Op. 12; Trio Pno, Op. 96 CHN ▲ 9529 (16.97)

Trio in E♭ for Piano, Violin & Cello, Op. 96
Beaux Arts Trio † Trio Pno, Op. 12; Trio Pno, Op. 35; Trio Pno, Op. 65 PPHI ▲ 446077 (16.97)
Borodin Trio † Trio Pno, Op. 12; Trio Pno, Op. 83 CHN ▲ 9529 (16.97)
Triangulus † Trio Pno, Op. 12; Trio Pno, Op. 22; Trio Pno, Op. 35 MER ▲ 84350 (16.97)

Variations on a theme from Gluck's Armide in F for Piano, Op. 57
R. Burnett (pno) † Chopin:Andante Spianato & Grand Polonaise, Op. 22; Czerny:Vars on "La Ricordanza", Op. 33; F. Schubert:Dances (42), Op. 18; Ecossaises (6), D.421; Waltzes (20) Pno, D.146; R. Schumann:Kinderszenen Pno, Op. 15 AMON ▲ 7 (16.97)

Variations in F for Violin & Piano, Op.posth.2
L. A. Bianchi (vn), A. Orvieto (pno) *(rec May 1998)* ("Works for Violin/Viola & Piano") † Amusement Vn, Op. 108; Rondo brillant Vn, Op. 126; Son Va DYNC ▲ 192 [DDD] (16.97)

HUMPERDINCK, ENGELBERT (1854-1921)

Hänsel und Gretel (märchenspiel in 3 acts) [lib Adelheid Wette after Brothers Grimm] (1890-93)
B. Bonney (sop), E. Gruberová (sop), C. Oelze (sop), G. Jones (sop), A. Murray (mez), C. Ludwig (mez), F. Grundheber (bar), C. Davis (cnd), Dresden Staatskapelle PPHI 2-▲ 38013 (32.97)
K. Eichorn (cnd), Munich Radio Orch, L. Popp (sop—The Dew Fairy), H. Donath (sop—Gretel), A. Augér (sop—The Sand Man), A. Moffo (sop—Hänsel), C. Ludwig (mez—The Witch), C. Berthold (mez—Mother), D. Fischer-Dieskau (bar—Father) RCAV ▲ 25281 (22.97)
L. Popp (sop), B. Fassbaender (mez), J. Hamari (mez), A. Schlemm (mez), W. Berry (b-bar), G. Solti (cnd), Vienna PO PLON (Grand Opera) 2-▲ 455063 (22.97)
C. Schäfer (sop—Dew Fairy), R. Ziesak (sop—Gretel), R. Joshua (sop—Sandman), H. Schwarz (mez—Nibblewitch), J. Larmore (mez—Hänsel), D. Runnicles (cnd), Bavarian RSO, Tölz Boys' Choir *(rec Munich, Feb 1994)* TELC 2-▲ 94549 [DDD] (33.97)
G. Schöter (sop), I. Springer (mez), P. Schreier (ten), T. Adam (bar), O. Suitner (cnd), Dresden Staatskapelle, Dresden Kreuz Choir BER (Eterna) 2-▲ 2007 [ADD] (21.97)
E. Schwarzkopf (sop), S. Jurinac (sop), R. Streich (sop), V. Palombini (mez), R. Panerai (bar), B. Ronshini (sgr), H. von Karajan (cnd), Milan Italian Radio-TV Orch, Milan RAI Chorus STRV 2-▲ 12314 (25.97)
E. Söderström (sop), I. Cotrubas (sop), C. Ludwig (mez), F. von Stade (mez), S. Nimsgern (b-bar), J. Pritchard (cnd), Cologne Gürzenich PO [GER] SNYC 2-▲ 35898 [ADD] (32.97)

Hänsel und Gretel (selections)
L. Bernstein (cnd), New York PO † A. Dvořák:Slavonic Dances (sels); K. Goldmark:Ländliche Hochzeit, Op. 26; Smetana:Bartered Bride (dances) SNYC (Bernstein Century) ▲ 61836 (11.97)
R. Hoff (sop), G. Schröter (mez), I. Springer (mez), P. Schreier (ten), T. Adam (b-bar), O. Suitner (cnd), Dresden Staatskapelle *(rec 1969)* BER ▲ 9293 (10.97)
F. Reiner (cnd), Chicago SO † R. Wagner:Ovs, Preludes & Orchestral Sels RCAV (Gold Seal) ▲ 61792 (11.97)
G. Tintner (cnd), Nova Scotia SO *(rec Halifax Nova Scotia, May 5-7, 1993)* ("Late Romantics") † H. Gál:Serenade, Op. 46; Morawetz:Divert Strs; H. Pfitzner:Sym in C, Op. 46; Rezniček:Donna Diana (ov); Schreker:Valse Lente SMS ▲ 5167 [DDD] (16.97)
Vienna Boys' Choir—Abendsegen † A. Bruckner:Choral Music; Locus iste; G. F. Handel:Messiah (choruses); J. Haydn:Schöpfung (sels); Herbeck:Pueri Concinite; W. A. Mozart:Mass 16, K.317; Requiem, K.626; F. Schubert:Ave Maria, Op. 52/6 LALI ▲ 14311 (3.97)

Hänsel und Gretel:Overture
C. Cantieri (cnd), London Festival Orch ("Famous Overtures") † D.-F. Auber:Muette de Portici (ov); M. Glinka:Russlan & Ludmilla (ov); W. A. Mozart:Entführung aus dem Serail (ov); J. Offenbach:Orphée aux enfers (ov); Suppé:Ovs PC ▲ 265013 [DDD] (2.97)

Die Heirat wider Willen (selections)
artists unknown [cnd:Christian Kluttig] *(rec Görrehaus Koblenz, Nov 17-19, 1994)* DSB ▲ 1052 [DDD] (16.97)

Die Heirat wider Willen:Overture
K. A. Rickenbacher (cnd), Bamberg SO † Humoreske; Shakespeare Suites 1 & 2 KSCH ▲ 311972 [DDD] (16.97)

Humoreske for Orchestra (1879)
K. A. Rickenbacher (cnd), Bamberg SO † Heirat wider Willen (ov); Shakespeare Suites 1 & 2 KSCH ▲ 311972 [DDD] (16.97)

Incidental Music
M. Fischer-Dieskau (cnd), Czech-Slovak RSO Bratislava—Die Marketenderin—Prelude; Merchant of Venice—Love Scene; Sleeping Beauty—Tone Pictures *(rec May 1991)* † Moorish Rhap MARC ▲ 8223369 [DDD] (13.97)

Königskinder [The King's Children] (opera in 3 acts) [lib E. Rosmer] (1910)
D. Schellenberger-Ernst (sop—Goose girl), M. Schmiege (mez—Witch), T. Moser (ten—King's Son), H. Weber (ten—Broommaker), D. Henschel (bar—Fiddler), A. Kohn (bass—Woodcutter), F. Luisi (cnd), Munich RSO, M. Gläser (cnd), Bavarian Radio Chorus *(rec live Munich Herkulessaal, Mar 22-24, 1996)* CALG 3-▲ 50968 [DDD] (54.97)

Königskinder (selections)
H. Swarowsky (cnd), Vienna State Opera Orch—Hellafest, Kinderreigen *(rec 1958)* † Orchestral Suites TUXE ▲ 1054 [ADD] (10.97)

Moorish Rhapsody for Orchestra (1898)
M. Fischer-Dieskau (cnd), Czech-Slovak RSO Bratislava *(rec May 1991)* † Incidental Music MARC ▲ 8223369 [DDD] (13.97)

Orchestral Suites
H. Swarowsky (cnd), Vienna State Opera Orch—Tone Pictures from Sleeping Beauty; Fant on theme from Hänsel und Gretel *(rec 1958)* † Königskinder (sels) TUXE ▲ 1054 [ADD] (10.97)

Shakespeare Suites Nos. 1 & 2 for Orchestra
K. A. Rickenbacher (cnd), Bamberg SO † Heirat wider Willen (ov); Humoreske KSCH ▲ 311972 [DDD] (16.97)

HUMPHRIES, JOHN (ca 1707-ca 1740)

Concerto in D for Trumpet & Strings
C. Steele-Perkins (tpt), A. Halstead (cnd), English CO ("Trumpet Concertos") † J. Haydn:Con Tpt; M. Haydn:Con 2 Tpt; Neruda:Con Tpt; Telemann:Con Tpt; Torelli:Con Tpt INMP ▲ 6600662 (16.97)

HUNDLEY, RICHARD (1931-

The Astronomers [An Epitaph from Allegheny, PA] (1960)
W. Payn (cnd), Rooke Chapel Choir, D. Fortunato (mez), G. Lee (pno) *(rec Bucknell U., Lewisburg, PA, United States of America)* ("An American Collage") † Isaac Greentree; Sea is Swimming; A. Copland:In the Beginning; Duckworth:Southern Harmony; J. Duke:Songs; J. Hill:Medieval Lyrics; Sweet & Triune Harmony; Hoiby:I Was There; Lady of the Harbor; Let this Mind Be in You; Shepherd; R. Palmer:O Magnum Mysterium ALBA ▲ 98 [ADD] (16.97)

HUNDLEY, RICHARD (cont.)
Isaac Greentree [An Epitaph from Palmer, *Epitaphs & Epigrams*, London, 1896] (1960)
W. Payn (cnd), Rooke Chapel Choir, D. Fortunato (mez), G. Lee (pno) *(rec Bucknell U., Lewisburg, PA, United States of America)* ("An American Collage") † Astronomers; Sea is Swimming; A. Copland:In the Beginning; Duckworth:Southern Harmony; J. Duke:Songs; J. Hill:Medieval Lyrics; Sweet & Triune Harmony; Hoiby:I Was There; Lady of the Harbor; Let this Mind Be in You; Shepherd; R. Palmer:O Magnum Mysterium ALBA ▲ 98 [ADD] (16.97)
The Sea is Swimming Tonight for Voice & Chorus (1981) *(Text by James Purdy)*
W. Payn (cnd), Rooke Chapel Choir, D. Fortunato (mez), G. Lee (pno) *(rec Bucknell U., Lewisburg, PA, United States of America)* ("An American Collage") † Astronomers; Isaac Greentree; A. Copland:In the Beginning; Duckworth:Southern Harmony; J. Duke:Songs; J. Hill:Medieval Lyrics; Sweet & Triune Harmony; Hoiby:I Was There; Lady of the Harbor; Let this Mind Be in You; Shepherd; R. Palmer:O Magnum Mysterium ALBA ▲ 98 [ADD] (16.97)

HUNT, JERRY (1943-1993)
Bitom (stream): link for Cow Horns, Pianos & Device Arrays
J. Hunt (elec/pno/perc) ("Ground: Five Mechanic Convention Streams") † Chimanzzi; Lattice; Talk; Transform OOD ▲ 9 [DDD] (16.97)
Cantegral Segments for Various Instruments (1973-78)
J. Hunt (elec) ("Lattice") † Kernel; Lattice; Transform; Transphalba CRI ▲ 713 [ADD] (16.97)
Chimanzzi (Olun): core for Violins, Keyed Violin & Device Arrays
J. Henry (elec/vn), J. Hunt (elec) ("Ground: Five Mechanic Convention Streams") † Bitom; Lattice; Talk; Transform OOD ▲ 9 [DDD] (16.97)
Fluud for dual Synclaviers (1988)
J. Hunt (synclavier) *(rec Univ. of North Texas, Denton, TX, Apr 1987-Jan 1988)* ("Compositions by Larry Austin, Thomas Clark, Jerry Hunt & Phil Winsor") † L. Austin:Sinf Concertante; Son Concertante; T. Clark:Peninsula; Winsor:Dulcimer Dream CENT (CDCM Computer Series, Volume 1) ▲ 2029 (16.97)
Haramand Plane: 3 Translation Links for Electronics (1993)
J. Hunt (elec) *(rec Dallas, TX)* OOWN ▲ 15 (16.97)
Kernel for Electronics (1980)
J. Hunt (elec) ("Lattice") † Cantegral Segments; Lattice; Transform; Transphalba CRI ▲ 713 [ADD] (16.97)
Lattice (stream): ordinal for Piano & Auxiliary Device Arrays
J. Hunt (elec/pno) ("Ground: Five Mechanic Convention Streams") † Bitom; Chimanzzi; Talk; Transform OOD ▲ 9 [DDD] (16.97)
J. Hunt (elec) ("Lattice") † Cantegral Segments; Kernel; Transform; Transphalba CRI ▲ 713 [ADD] (16.97)
Song Drapes (20) for Voices & Piano
S. Hirsch (voc), M. Patton (voc), K. Kinley (pno) TZA ▲ 7045 [DDD] (16.97)
Talk (slice): double for Voices & Transient Device Arrays
J. Hunt (elec), R. Stasick (elec) ("Ground: Five Mechanic Convention Streams") † Bitom; Chimanzzi; Lattice; Transform OOD ▲ 9 [DDD] (16.97)
Transform (stream): monopole for Voice & Device Arrays
J. Hunt (elec) ("Ground: Five Mechanic Convention Streams") † Bitom; Chimanzzi; Lattice; Talk OOD ▲ 9 [DDD] (16.97)
J. Hunt (elec) ("Lattice") † Cantegral Segments; Kernel; Lattice; Transphalba CRI ▲ 713 [ADD] (16.97)
Transphalba for Electronics
J. Hunt (elec) ("Lattice") † Cantegral Segments; Kernel; Lattice; Transform CRI ▲ 713 [ADD] (16.97)
Trapani (stream) <<a>> for Piano (1991)
L. Svard (pno) *(rec Lewisburg, PA, Oct 11-13, 1996 & Jan 12-13, 1997)* † Gann:Desert Sonata; Lauten:Vars Orange Cycle LOV ▲ 3052 [DDD] (16.97)

HUNT, OLIVER (1934-
Garuda Ballade for Guitar
L. Young (gtr) ("Solo") † Domeniconi:Vars on an Anatolian Folksong; H. W. Henze:Tentos; Koshkin:Fall of Birds; V. Kučera:Diario Omaggio à Che Guevara; J. Turina:Sevillana, Op. 29 ALSE ▲ 2017 (16.97)

HURÉ, JEAN (1877-1930)
Sonatas (3) for Cello & Piano (1907; 1913; 1920)
R. Chretien (vc), M. Pikulski (pno) MED7 ▲ 9812 (18.97)

HURLEY, SUSAN (1946-
Wind River Songs for solo Voice, Cello & Piano (1988)
N. Philibosian (sop), C. Campbell (vc), M. Coonrod (pno) *(rec Interlochen Center for the Arts)* ("Society of Composers, Inc.: Songfest") † R. Newell:New London; W. Penn:Cornfield in July; Scheidel-Austin:Sonnets from the Portuguese; A. Schmitz:Songs from Green Lotus Man; Van Appledorn:Freedom of Youth CPS ▲ 8618 (16.97)

HURLSTONE, WILLIAM YEATES (1876-1906)
Characteristic Pieces (4) for Clarinet & Piano
E. Johannesson (cl), P. Jenkins (pno) *(rec Cambridge, England, Sept 1991)* ("British Music for Clarinet and Piano") † M. Arnold:Son Cl; A. Bliss:Pastoral Cl, Op.posth.; Dunhill:Fant Suite Cl & Pno, Op. 91; H. Ferguson:Short Pieces Cl, Op. 6; Stanford:Son Cl; Stoker:Sonatina Cl, Op. 5 CHN ▲ 9079 (16.97)
V. Soames (cl), J. Flinders (pno) ("The English Romantics") † Trio Cl; H. Howells:Minuet: Grace for a Fresh Egg; Near Minuet Cl; C. H. Lloyd:Trio Cl CLCL ▲ 23 [DDD] (17.97)
Sonata in F for Violin & Piano
D. Smith (bn), R. Vignoles (pno) *(rec London, England)* † T. Arne:Son 5 Hpd; Avison:Son Vn; Dunhill:Lyric Suite Bn & Pno, Op. 96; E. Elgar:Romance Vn, Op. 1; G. Jacob:Four Sketches Bn; Vaughan Williams:Studies in English Folk-Song ASV ▲ 535 [DDD] (17.97)
Trio in g for Clarinet, Bassoon & Piano (1894)
V. Soames (cl), L. Perkins (bn), J. Flinders (pno) ("The English Romantics") † Characteristic Pieces Cl; H. Howells:Minuet: Grace for a Fresh Egg; Near Minuet Cl; C. H. Lloyd:Trio Cl CLCL ▲ 23 [DDD] (17.97)

HURNÍK, ILJA (1922-
Sonata da camera for Flute, Oboe, Cello & Harpsichord (1953)
Rembrandt Chamber Players ("20th Century Baroque: Modern Reflections On Old Instruments") † D. Argento:Elizabethan Songs Sop & Chamber Ensemble; E. Carter:Son Fl, Ob, Vc & Hpd; M. de Falla:Con Hpd CED ▲ 11 [DDD] (16.97)

HURUM, ALF (THORVALD) (1882-1972)
Benedic og Aarolilja (symphonic poem) for Orchestra, Op. 20 (1923)
A. Dmitriev (cnd), Stavanger SO † Qt Strs, Op. 6; Sym SIMX ▲ 3110 (18.97)
Quartet in a for Strings, Op. 6 (1916)
Vertavo String Quartet † Benedic og Aarolilja, Op. 20; Sym SIMX ▲ 3110 (18.97)
Symphony in d (1927)
A. Dmitriev (cnd), Stavanger SO † Benedic og Aarolilja, Op. 20; Qt Strs, Op. 6 SIMX ▲ 3110 (18.97)

HUSA, KAREL (1921-
Concerto for Wind Ensemble (1982)
M. Thompson (cnd), Cincinnati Wind SO ("Prevailing Winds") † Smetana Fanfare; Maslanka:In Memoriam; J. Rodrigo:Con de Aranjuez SUMM ▲ 192 (16.97)
Les Couleurs Fauves for Wind Ensemble (1995)
F. Battisti (cnd), New England Conservatory Wind Ensemble *(rec Jordan Hall, Boston, MA, Feb 1997)* † J. Harbison:Olympic Dances; W. Kraft:Con Perc; B. Rands:Ceremonial ALBA ▲ 340 [DDD] (16.97)
Divertimento for Brass & Percussion (1959)
L. Sobol (cnd) † Fants Orch; Trojan Women (sels) PHOE ▲ 128 (15.97)
Elegie et Rondeau for Saxophone & Orchestra (1960)
L. Gwozdz (sax), S. Hass (sax), K. Trevor (cnd), Bohuslav Martinů PO *(rec Zlín, Czech Republic, June 12-14, 1998)* † W. Benson:Aeolian Song; W. G. Still:Romance; Wirth:Inglewood Concerto; Jephthah; J. C. Worley:Claremont Concerto ALBA ▲ 331 [DDD] (16.97)
Evocations of Slovakia for Clarinet, Viola & Cello (1951)
Long Island Chamber Ensemble † Qt 2 Strs; Qt 3 Strs PHOE ▲ 113 [AAD] (15.97)
Fantasies (3) for Orchestra (1956)
K. Husa (cnd) † Divert Brass; Trojan Women (sels) PHOE ▲ 128 (15.97)
Landscapes for Brass Quintet (1977)
Western Brass Quintet *(rec 1977)* † Mosaïques; Serenade; Sym 1 CRI ▲ 592 [ADD] (16.97)
Moravian Songs (12) for Soprano & Piano (1955)
B. A. Martin (sop), E. Rodgers (pno) *(rec Sorcerer Sounds NYC)* † Son Vn; Son 2 Pno NWW ▲ 80493 (16.97)
Mosaïques for Orchestra (1961)
K. Husa (cnd), Stockholm RSO *(rec 1967)* † Landscapes; Serenade; Sym 1 CRI ▲ 592 [ADD] (16.97)

HUSA, KAREL (cont.)
Music for Prague 1968 for Band (1969; orchd 1970)
D. Hunsberger (cnd) † A. Copland:Quiet City; P. Hindemith:Concert Music Band, Op. 41; Vaughan Williams:Toccata marziale; Vars Brass SNYC ▲ 44916 [DDD] (16.97)
K. Husa (cnd), Temple Univ Wind Sym *(rec Apr-May 1995)* † S. Prokofiev:Marches, Op. 69; Rimsky-Korsakov:Con Trbn; Concertstück Cl; Vars on a Theme of Glinka ALBA ▲ 271 [DDD] (16.97)
M. A. Machek (cnd), Bohuslav Martinů PO † K. Penderecki:Sinfonietta Strs; Perron:Séquences violées; Van de Vate:Con Va; F. Weiss:Relazioni variabili VMM ▲ 3023 [DDD]
Quartet No. 2 for Strings (1953)
Fine Arts String Quartet † Evocations of Slovakia; Qt 3 Strs PHOE ▲ 113 [AAD] (15.97)
Quartet No. 3 for Strings (1968)
Fine Arts String Quartet † Evocations of Slovakia; Qt 2 Strs PHOE ▲ 113 [AAD] (15.97)
Quartet No. 4 for Strings, "Poems" (1990)
Colorado String Quartet † E. Laderman:Qt 7 Strs; M. Powell:Qt Strs ALBA ▲ 259 [DDD] (16.97)
Serenade for Woodwind Quintet, Strings, Harp & Xylophone (1963)
L. Bergman (pno), Westwood Wind Quintet † I. Dahl:Allegro & Arioso; L. Moyse:Qnt Ww; Sapieyevski:Arioso CRYS ▲ 751 [DDD] (15.97)
K. Husa (cnd), Prague SO *(rec 1970)* † Landscapes; Mosaïques; Sym 1 CRI ▲ 592 [ADD] (16.97)
Smetana Fanfare for Wind Ensemble (1984)
M. Thompson (cnd), Cincinnati Wind SO ("Prevailing Winds") † Con Ww; Maslanka:In Memoriam; J. Rodrigo:Con de Aranjuez SUMM ▲ 192 (16.97)
Sonata a tre for Violin, Clarinet & Piano (1982)
Verdehr Trio ("The Making of a Medium, Vol. 4") † P. Dickinson:Hymns, Rags & Blues; D. W. Freund:Triomusic; J. Niblock:Trio Vn CRYS ▲ 744 (15.97)
Sonata No. 2 for Piano (1975)
P. Basquin (pno) *(rec Rutgers Presbyterian Church NYC)* † Moravian Songs; Son Vn NWW ▲ 80493 (16.97)
Sonata for Violin & Piano (1972-73)
E. Oliveira (vn), D. Oei (pno) *(rec Right Track Recordings NYC)* † Moravian Songs; Son 2 Pno NWW ▲ 80493 (16.97)
Symphony No. 1 (1953)
K. Husa (cnd), Prague SO *(rec 1970)* † Landscapes; Mosaïques; Serenade CRI ▲ 592 [ADD] (16.97)
Symphony No. 2 for Orchestra, "Reflections" (1983)
E. F. Brown (cnd), Bowling Green Philharmonia [comments by Husa] ("The Composer's Voice-New Music from Bowling Green") † S. Adler:Requiescat in Pace; D. W. Freund:Poem Sym; J. Ryan:Ophélie; M. Shrude:Into Light; Theofanidis:On the Edge of the Infinte ALBA ▲ 321 [DDD] (16.97)
The Trojan Women (selections)
K. Husa (cnd), Brno State PO † Divert Brass; Fants Orch PHOE ▲ 128 (15.97)

HUSH, DAVID (20th cent)
Partita No. 1 for solo Cello (1989)
M. Ingolfsson (pno) † E. Carter:Pastorale E Hn; F. Devienne:Son 1 Cl; C. Harrison:Songs from a Child's Garden; J. Russo:Largetto; Son 4 Cl CRSR ▲ 9255
Quartet No. 1 for Strings (1991)
G. Schenk (vn), J. Ingolfsson (vn), C. Chang (va), M. Ingolfsson (vc) ("Excursions") † Son Vc; Bozza:Caprice-Improvisation; J. Russo:Pieces Cl; Son 1 Fl; Van Appledorn:Ayre; E. A. Zappa:Hydra Son CRSR ▲ 9257
Shir Eres for Violin & Piano
Z. Schiff (vn), C. Eisenberg (pno) † Son Vn; J. Achron:Hebrew Melody, Op. 33; Castelnuovo-Tedesco:Sea Murmurs, Op. 24a; Haym:Sephardic Melody; Krein:Caprice Hebraique; M. Lavry:Jewish Dances; Zimbalist:Slavonic Dances (3) 4TAY ▲ 4002 (18.97)
Sonata for Cello & Piano (1990)
M. Ingolfsson (vc), U. Ingolfsson (pno) ("Excursions") † Qt 1 Strs; Bozza:Caprice-Improvisation; J. Russo:Pieces Cl; Son 1 Fl; Van Appledorn:Ayre; E. A. Zappa:Hydra Son CRSR ▲ 9257
Sonata for Violin & Piano
Z. Schiff (vn), C. Eisenberg (pno) † Shir Eres; J. Achron:Hebrew Melody, Op. 33; Castelnuovo-Tedesco:Sea Murmurs, Op. 24a; Haym:Sephardic Melody; Krein:Caprice Hebraique; M. Lavry:Jewish Dances; Zimbalist:Slavonic Dances (3) 4TAY ▲ 4002 (18.97)

HUSS, HENRY HOLDEN (1862-1963)
Concerto in B for Piano & Orchestra, Op. 10
I. Hobson (pno), M. Brabbins (cnd), BBC Scottish SO ("The Romantic Piano Concerto, Vol. 16") † E. Schelling:Suite fantastique, Op. 7 HYP ▲ 66949 (18.97)
Piano Music
B. Kovach (pno)—Menuet, Op. 18/1; Pieces Pno, Op. 20/1, "Valse"; Pieces Pno, Op. 23/1-4 & 6; Sans Souci, Op. 25/2; Pieces (3) Pno, Op. 26; Pieces (2) Pno, Op. 27; Sketches Pno, Op. 32/1, "Optimist Prelude"; Bagatelles Pno, G.199/1-2, Pieces Pno, G.200/2, "The Rivulet"; Intermezzi (3) Pno, G.203; Happy Days, G.246/9, "Lake Como by Moonlight"; Valse petite, G.288 ("Piano Music") ALBA ▲ 287 [DDD] (16.97)
Preludes for Piano, Op. 17
M. Frager (pno) ("Edward MacDowell & Company") † A. M. Foerster:On the Sea; H. F. Gilbert:Mazurka Pno; MacDowell:Virtuoso Etudes, Op. 46; E. Nevin:Etudes Pno, Op. 18; Paine:Pieces Pno, Op. 41; Romance Pno, Op. 12; H. Parker:Morceaux caractéristiques, Op. 49 NWW ▲ 80206 [DDD] (16.97)

HUTCHESON, JERE (1938-
Caricatures (9 impressions) for Wind Orchestra (1997)
E. Corporon (cnd), North Texas Wind Sym ("Deja View") † Bassett:Colors & Contours; Colgrass:Déja Vu Orch; Gorb:Awayday; R. Peck:Cave; Ticheli:Blue Shades KLAV (Wind Recording Project) ▲ 11091 [DDD] (18.97)

HUTCHISON, WARNER (1930-
Poe Songs (2) for Soprano, Horn & Vibraphone (1966)
M. Rowe (sop), N. Joy (hn), F. Bugbee (vib) ("Illuminations") † Bestor:Of Times; H. Bielawa:Stone Settings; Boyadjian:Googleegoo; L. C. Chen:Echo; Richey:Vars Pno 4-Hands CPS (Society of Composers, Inc.) ▲ 8643 (16.97)

HUTCHISON, WILLIAM MARSHALL (1854-?)
Songs
P. Gale (sop), A. Mentschukoff (gtr)—Dream Faces *(rec Cleveland, OH, Sep 1997)* † Anonymous:Songs; H. Birch:Songs; G. Marks:Songs; F. Pascal:Songs; C. A. White:Songs CENT ▲ 2389 [DDD] (16.97)

HUYBRECHTS, ALBERT (1899-1938)
Sicilienne for Piano (1934)
A. Crepin (cnd), Belgian Air Force Royal Symphonic Band [arr Crepin] ("Alain Crepin: Conductor, Composer, Arranger") † Borodin:In the Steppes of Central Asia; Ceuninck:Health Service March; A. Crepin:Music of Crepin; V. Monti:Csárdás RENE ▲ 87151 [DDD] (16.97)
Sonata for Violin & Piano (1925)
V. Bogaerts (vn), D. Corni (pno) † Sonatine Fl; Trio Fl SYRX ▲ 98101 (16.97)
E. Volckaert (vn), J. V. Eynden (pno) † C. Franck:Son Vn, M.8 RENE ▲ 99004 [ADD] (16.97)
Sonatine for Flute & Viola (1934)
J. Dupriez (va), M. Grauwels (fl) † Son Vn; Trio Fl SYRX ▲ 98101 (16.97)
Trio for Flute, Viola & Piano (1926)
J. Dupriez (va), M. Grauwels (fl), D. Corni (pno) † Son Vn; Sonatine Fl SYRX ▲ 98101 (16.97)

HVOSLEF (SAEVERUD), KETIL (1939-
Double Concerto for Flute, Guitar & String Orchestra (1977)
D. Blanco (gtr), G. von Bahr (fl), K. Hvoslef (cnd) † Kvartoni; Mi-Fi-Li; Sxt Fl & Perc BIS ▲ 129 [DDD] (17.97)
Kvartoni for Soprano, Recorder, Guitar & Piano (1974)
S. Faringer (sop), C. Peijel (gtr), C. Pehrsson (rcr), C. Dominique (pno) † Double Con; Mi-Fi-Li; Sxt Fl & Perc BIS ▲ 129 [DDD] (17.97)
Mi-Fi-Li (symphonic poem) for Orchestra (1971)
P. Dreier (cnd), Royal PO † Double Con; Kvartoni; Sxt Fl & Perc BIS ▲ 129 [DDD] (17.97)
Sextet for Flute & Percussion (1986)
M. Wiesler (fl), Kroumata Percussion Ensemble † Double Con; Kvartoni; Mi-Fi-Li BIS ▲ 129 [DDD] (17.97)
M. Wiesler (fl), Kroumata Percussion Ensemble *(rec Mar 19, 1989)* † Nørgård:Square and Round; S.-D. Sandström:Free Music; R. Wallin:Stonewave BIS ▲ 512 [DDD] (17.97)
Solo for Violin (1980)
T. Sæverud (vn) *(rec National Museum for Contemporary Art Oslo, Nov 11, 1995)* ("Ghosts") † G. E. Haugland:Ghosts; TV-Spill 1; Nordheim:Partita for Paul NORW ▲ 2916 (17.97)

HWANG, JASON KAO (1957-

Caverns for Chamber Ensemble
Far East Side Band *(rec New York, Feb 28, 1993)* † Early Hour Vision; Memories & Ice; Palmistry; Still Water NWW ▲ 80458 (16.97)

Early Hour Vision for Chamber Ensemble
Far East Side Band *(rec New York, Feb 28, 1993)* † Caverns; Memories & Ice; Palmistry; Still Water NWW ▲ 80458 (16.97)

Memories & Ice for Chamber Ensemble
Far East Side Band *(rec New York, Feb 28, 1993)* † Caverns; Early Hour Vision; Palmistry; Still Water NWW ▲ 80458 (16.97)

Palmistry for Chamber Ensemble
Far East Side Band *(rec New York, Feb 28, 1993)* † Caverns; Early Hour Vision; Memories & Ice; Still Water NWW ▲ 80458 (16.97)

Still Water for Chamber Ensemble
Far East Side Band *(rec New York, Feb 28, 1993)* † Caverns; Early Hour Vision; Memories & Ice; Palmistry NWW ▲ 80458 (16.97)

HYLA, LEE (1952-

Amnesia Breaks for Wind Quintet (1996)
Quintet of the Americas *(rec Vasser College, June 25-29, 1995)* ("Self Portrait") † Culpo:Qnt Ww; P. Oliveros:Portrait of the Qnt of the Americas; A. Rubin:Loba; E. Sharp:JAG CRI ▲ 722 [DDD] (16.97)

Concerto No. 2 for Piano & Chamber Orchestra (1991)
A. Karis (pno), W. Purvis (cnd) *(rec Purchase, NY, Oct 25, 1995)* ("We Speak Etruscan") † Pre-Pulse Suspended; Qt 2 Strs; Qt 3 Strs; We Speak Etruscan NWW ▲ 80491 (16.97)

The Dream of Innocent III for Cello, Piano & Percussion (1987)
R. Rider (va), L. Hyla (pno), J. Pugliese (perc) † S. Mackey:Rhondo Vars; D. Martino:Parisonatina Al'dodecafonia; Suite of Vars; Webern:Little Pieces, Op. 11; Pieces Vc; Son Vc CRI ▲ 564 [DDD] (16.97)

Howl for Voice & String Quartet [text Allen Ginsberg] (1993)
A. Ginsberg (spkr), Kronos Quartet ("Howl U.S.A.") † M. Daugherty:Sing Sing; S. Johnson:Cold War Suite; H. Partch:Barstow Voice Str Qt NON ▲ 79372 (16.97)

Music of Hyla
various artists—In Double Light; Mythic Birds of Saugerties; Ciao Manhattan *(rec 1986-92)* ("In Double Light") † Qt 2 Strs AVAK ▲ 15 (21.97)

Pre-Pulse Suspended for Chamber Orchestra (1984)
D. Palma (cnd) *(rec Purchase, NY, Oct 24, 1995)* ("We Speak Etruscan") † Con 2 Pno; Qt 2 Strs; Qt 3 Strs; We Speak Etruscan NWW ▲ 80491 (16.97)

Quartet No. 2 for Strings (1985)
Lydian String Quartet *(rec Brandeis Univ, NY, Sept 26, 1995)* ("We Speak Etruscan") † Con 2 Pno; Pre-Pulse Suspended; Qt 3 Strs; We Speak Etruscan NWW ▲ 80491 (16.97)
Lydian String Quartet *(rec 1986-92)* ("In Double Light") † Music of Hyla AVAK ▲ 15 (21.97)

Quartet No. 3 for Strings (1989)
Lydian String Quartet *(rec Brandeis Univ, NY, Dec 18, 1994)* ("We Speak Etruscan") † Con 2 Pno; Pre-Pulse Suspended; Qt 2 Strs; We Speak Etruscan NWW ▲ 80491 (16.97)

We Speak Etruscan for Baritone Saxophone & Bass Clarinet (1992)
T. Smith (b cl), T. Berne (bar sax) *(rec Dec 18, 1994)* ("We Speak Etruscan") † Con 2 Pno; Pre-Pulse Suspended; Qt 2 Strs; Qt 3 Strs NWW ▲ 80491 (16.97)

HYMAN, RICHARD (1927-

Clarinata for Clarinet & Piano
R. Stoltzman (cl), I. Vallecillo-Gray (pno) *(rec Worcester, MA, Jan 1994)* ("Amber Waves: American Clarinet Music") † L. Bernstein:Son Cl; C. Fisher:Sonatine Cl; G. Gershwin:Preludes Pno; W. T. McKinley:Son Cl; Rowles:Peacocks RCAV (Red Seal) ▲ 62685 [DDD] (16.97)

Sextet for Clarinet, Piano & Strings
C. Russo (cl), B. Degoian (pno) ("Clarinet alla Cinema") † R. R. Bennett:Qnt Cl; N. Rota:Trio Cl PREM ▲ 1062 (16.97)

IANNACCONE, ANTHONY (1943-

After a Gentle Rain (2 pieces) for Wind Band (1979)
M. Plank (cnd), Clarion Wind Sym ("Wind Music of Iannaccone") † Antiphonies; Apparitions; Images of Song & Dance; Sea Drift; Toccata Fanfares ALBA ▲ 280 [DDD] (16.97)

Antiphonies for Wind Band (1972)
M. Plank (cnd), Clarion Wind Sym ("Wind Music of Iannaccone") † After a Gentle Rain; Apparitions; Images of Song & Dance; Sea Drift; Toccata Fanfares ALBA ▲ 280 [DDD] (16.97)

Apparitions for Wind Band (1986)
M. Plank (cnd), Clarion Wind Sym ("Wind Music of Iannaccone") † After a Gentle Rain; Antiphonies; Images of Song & Dance; Sea Drift; Toccata Fanfares ALBA ▲ 280 [DDD] (16.97)

Images of Song & Dance (2) for Wind Band (1980)
M. Plank (cnd), Clarion Wind Sym ("Wind Music of Iannaccone") † After a Gentle Rain; Antiphonies; Apparitions; Sea Drift; Toccata Fanfares ALBA ▲ 280 [DDD] (16.97)

Sea Drift (suite) for Wind Band (1992)
M. Plank (cnd), Clarion Wind Sym ("Wind Music of Iannaccone") † After a Gentle Rain; Antiphonies; Apparitions; Images of Song & Dance; Toccata Fanfares ALBA ▲ 280 [DDD] (16.97)

Toccata Fanfares (8 in 2 volumes) for 3 Trumpets & 3 Trombones (or Brass Choir) (1984)
M. Plank (cnd), Clarion Wind Sym ("Wind Music of Iannaccone") † After a Gentle Rain; Antiphonies; Apparitions; Images of Song & Dance; Sea Drift ALBA ▲ 280 [DDD] (16.97)

IBARRA, FREDERICO (1946-

Symphony No. 1
E. Diazmuñoz (cnd), Mexico City PO † Catán:Tu Son, Tu Risa, Tu Sonrisa; S. Contreras:Danza Negra; Márquez:Son; Moncada:Sym 1 CLMX ▲ 21009 (13.97)

IBARRA, MANUEL (20th cent)

Juegos nocturnos for Wind Quintet
Mexico City Woodwind Quintet † C. Chávez:Soli 2; Enriquez:Pentamúsica; A. Lara:Aulós; Lavista:Danzas breves CLME ▲ 21018 (13.97)

IBERT, JACQUES (1890-1962)

Aria for Clarinet (or other instrument) & Piano (1930)
Collegium Musicum Soloists ("Jacques Ibert: Complete Chamber Music with Flute") † Entracte Fl; Interludes (2) Fl Vn & Hpd; Jardinier de Samos (suite); Jeux; Movts (2) Flts; Pièce Fl; Pièces brèves Ww KPT ▲ 32202
E. Pahud (fl), E. Le Sage (pno) [trans for fl & pno] *(rec Highgate London, England, Feb 1997)* ("Paris") † Jeux; Dutilleux:Sonatine Fl; Jolivet:Chant de Linos Fl & Pno; Messiaen:Merle noir; D. Milhaud:Sonatina Fl & Pno, Op. 76; F. Poulenc:Son Fl; Sancan:Sonatine Fl EMIC ▲ 56488 [DDD] (16.97)

La ballade de la geôle de Reading for Orchestra (1920)
M. Adriano (cnd), Slovak RSO Bratislava *(rec Feb 8-13, 1993)* † Féerique; Recontres; Suite élisabéthaine MARC ▲ 8223508 [DDD] (13.97)

Capriccio for 10 Instruments (1937)
R. A. Clark (cnd), Manhattan CO † Con Fl; Suite symphonique; Suite élisabéthaine NPT ▲ 85531 [DDD] (16.97)

Carignane for Bassoon & Piano (1953)
M. Turkovič (bn), K. Engel (pno) † J. Brahms:Son for 2 Pnos, Op. 34b; Saint-Saëns:Son Bn; R. Schumann:Romances Ob, Op. 94 CAMA ▲ 66 (18.97)

Chamber Music
O. Franssen (gtr), H. D. Rijke (gtr), E. Pameijer (fl), A. Bornkamp (sax), P. Gaasterland (bn), P. Masseurs (tpt), E. Stoop (hp), M. van Delft (hpd), S. Grotenhuis (pno), New Netherlands String Quartet—Entracte Fl; Ariette Gtr; L'âge d'or; Pièce Fl; Qt Strs; Trio Vn, Vc & Hp; Interludes (2) Fl Vn & Hpd; Étude-caprice; Ghirlarzana Vc; Caprilena Vn; Impromptu Tpt & Pno; Carignane Bn & Pno *(rec Begijnhof Amsterdam, Holland, Jan & Mar 1996)* ("Complete Chamber Music, Vol. 2") OLY ▲ 469 [DDD] (16.97)
K. Hulsmann (vn), M. van Staalen (vc), O. Franssen (gtr), H. D. Rijke (gtr), E. Pameijer (fl), P. Oostenrijk (ob), H. Colbers (cl), P. Gaasterland (bn), P. Masseurs (tpt), H. Jeurissen (hn), E. Stoop (hp), S. Grotenhuis (pno), A. Marinissen (pipa/perc)—Pièces (6) Hp; Movts (2) Flts; Jeux; Jardinier de Samos (suite); Française Gtr; Aria Pno Trio; Pièces brèves Ww; Pastorale 4 Pipes; Paraboles Gtrs; Pièces (5) en trio ("Complete Chamber Music, Vol. 1") OLY ▲ 468 [DDD]

IBERT, JACQUES (cont.)

Chamber Music (cont.)
C. Macomber (vn), F. Hand (gtr), R. Schmidt (fl), S. A. Kahn (fl), E. Lawrence (fl), P. Schechter (fl), D. Krakauer (cl), L. Goldstein (bn), S. Jolles (hp), A. Willis (pno) *(Movts (2) Flts; Aria Pno Trio; Histoires),* C. Schadeberg (sop), C. Macomber (vn), F. Hand (gtr), R. Schmidt (fl), S. A. Kahn (fl), E. Lawrence (fl), P. Schechter (fl), E. Lawrence (fl), R. Schmidt (fl), P. Schechter (fl), D. Krakauer (cl), L. Goldstein (bn), L. Goldstein (bn), S. Jolles (hp), A. Willis (pno), A. Willis (pno) *(Pastorale 4 Pipes)* ("Around the Clock: Chamber Music for Flute") † Entracte Fl; Interludes (2) Fl Vn & Hpd; Jeux; Pièce Fl; Stèles orientées ALBA ▲ 145 [DDD]

Choral sur *Justorum animae in manu Dei sunt*
J. S. Whiteley (org) *(rec Cavaillé-Coll org, St. Ouen, Rouen, France)* † P. Cochereau:Symphonie; M. Dupré:Préludes & Fugues, Op. 36; Vars on Adeste Fidèles; Paponaud:Toccata; Vierne:Méditation Org PRIO ▲ 619 [DDD] (16.97)

Concertino da camera for Alto Saxophone & 11 Instruments (1935)
J. Harle (sax), N. Marriner (cnd), Academy of St. Martin in the Fields ("Saxophone Concertos") † R. R. Bennett:Con A Sax; Debussy:Rapsodie Sax; Glazunov:Con A Sax, Op. 109; T. Heath:Out of the Cool; H. Villa-Lobos:Fant Sax EMIC ▲ 72109 [DDD] (6.97)
G. Louie (sax), R. A. Clark (cnd), Manhattan CO ("Oeuvres Variées") † Con Vc; Divert Orch; Symphonie concertante NPT (Manhattan CO) ▲ 85598 [DDD] (16.97)
H. Pittel (sax), J. Helmer (pno) [arr Pittel] ("Moving Along with Harvey Pittel") † Albinoni:Con in B Tpt; Creston:Son Sax, Op. 19; I. Dahl:Con A Sax; P. Maurice:Tableaux de Provence; S. Rachmaninoff:Vocalise CRYS ▲ 655 (15.97)
M. Whitcombe (sax), D. Barra (cnd), San Diego CO † Divert Orch; F. Poulenc:Sinfonietta KOCH ▲ 7094 [DDD] (10.97)

Concerto for Cello & Wind Orchestra (1925)
G. Banaszak (sax), B. Jarmolowicz (cnd), Polish National CO of Slupsk *(rec Slupsk State Theatre, Poland, Apr 1998)* † P.-M. Dubois:Con A Sax; Glazunov:Con A Sax, Op. 109; S. Rachmaninoff:Vocalise; H. Villa-Lobos:Fant Sax CENT ▲ 2400 [DDD] (16.97)
N. Rosen (vc), R. A. Clark (cnd), Manhattan CO ("Oeuvres Variées") † Concertino da camera; Divert Orch; Symphonie concertante NPT (Manhattan CO) ▲ 85598 [DDD] (16.97)
V. Spanoghe (vc), Bellerophon Wind Orchestra ("Concertos with Wind Orchestra") † J. Françaix:Hommage à l'ami Papageno; Pièces caractéristiques Ww; F. Poulenc:Aubade TLNT ▲ 48 [DDD] (15.97)

Concerto for Flute & Orchestra (1934)
P. Alanko (fl), J. Saraste (cnd), Finnish RSO † Jolivet:Con Fl; C. Nielsen:Con Fl ODE ▲ 802 [DDD] (17.97)
K. Bryan (fl), Z. Chen (cnd), Czech RSO ("Twentieth Century Flute") † Griffes:Poem Fl; C. Nielsen:Con Fl; W. Perry:Summer Nocturne PREM ▲ 1026 [DDD] (16.97)
N. Buchman (fl), E. Acél (cnd), Oradea PO *(rec Apr 1991)* † C. Nielsen:Con Fl; Partos:Visions OLY ▲ 420 [DDD] (12.97)
R. A. Clark (cnd), Manhattan CO † Capriccio; Suite symphonique; Suite élisabéthaine NPT ▲ 85531 [DDD] (16.97)
P. Graf (fl), R. Leppard (cnd), English CO *(rec EMI Studio London, 1975)* † F. Devienne:Con 2 Fl; Saint-Saëns:Con 1 Vc, Op. 33 CLAV ▲ 105 [ADD]
A. Marion (fl), M. Valdes (cnd), Nice PO † F. Devienne:Con 7 Fl; Molique:Con Fl DNN ▲ 7923 [DDD]
J. Walter (fl), S. Kurz (cnd), Dresden Staatskapelle *(rec Dresden, Germany)* ("Virtuose Flötenmusik") † Debussy:Son Fl; Syrinx Fl; Jolivet:Suite en concert; F. Martin:Ballade Fl BER ▲ 9161 [ADD] (10.97)
M. Wiesler (fl), P. Auguin (cnd), Helsingborg SO *(rec June 1991)* † Chaminade:Concertino Fl, Op. 107; J. Françaix:Con Fl; Mouquet:Flûte de Pan, Op. 15 BIS ▲ 529 [DDD] (17.97)

Diane de Poitiers (ballet) [lib E. de Gramont] (1933-34)
M. Adriano (cnd), Moscow SO *(rec Mosfilm Studio, Aug 1995)* † The Triumph of Chastity MARC ▲ 8223854 [DDD] (13.97)

Divertissement for Chamber Orchestra [from incidental music to *Un chapeau de paille d'Italie*] (1930)
D. Barra (cnd), San Diego CO † Concertino da camera; F. Poulenc:Sinfonietta KOCH ▲ 7094 [DDD] (10.97)
R. A. Clark (cnd), Manhattan CO ("Oeuvres Variées") † Con Vc; Concertino da camera; Symphonie concertante NPT (Manhattan CO) ▲ 85598 [DDD] (16.97)
A. Fiedler (cnd), Boston Pops Orch *(rec 1956)* † J. Offenbach:Contes d'Hoffmann RCAV (Living Stereo) ▲ 61429 (11.97)
P. Järvi (cnd), Tapiola Sinfonietta *(rec June 4 & 9, 1993)* † Jolivet:Con Fl; A. Roussel:Sinfonietta Strs, Op. 52 BIS ▲ 630 [DDD] (17.97)
E. Kunzel (cnd), Cincinnati Pops Orch † J. Offenbach:Dance Music Orch; Gaîté Parisienne TEL ▲ 80294 [DDD] (16.97)
N. Marriner (cnd), Academy of St. Martin in the Fields *(rec London, England)* † Debussy:Danses sacrée et profane; G. Fauré:Dolly; M. Ravel:Tombeau ASV ▲ 517 [DDD] (16.97)
J. Martinon (cnd), Paris Conservatory Société des Concerts Orch † Bizet:Jeux d'enfants; Saint-Saëns:Danse macabre, Op. 40 PLON (The Classic Sound) ▲ 448571 (11.97)
E. Mata (cnd), Dallas SO *(rec Jan 1993)* † Escales; E. Chausson:Sym in B♭, Op. 20 DOR ▲ 90181 [DDD] (16.97)
E. Ormandy (cnd), Philadelphia Orch † Escales; G. Fauré:Pavane; Pelléas et Mélisande, Op. 80; A. Roussel:Bacchus et Ariane (suite 2) SNYC (Essential Classics) ▲ 62644 (7.97) ▮ 62644 (3.98)
Y. P. Tortelier (cnd), Ulster Orch *(rec May 1991)* † D. Milhaud:Boeuf sur le toit, Op. 58; Création du monde, Op. 81; F. Poulenc:Biches CHN ▲ 9023 [DDD] (16.97)

Entracte for Flute (or Violin) & Harp (or Guitar) (1937)
Collegium Musicum Soloists ("Jacques Ibert: Complete Chamber Music with Flute") † Aria Cl & Pno; Interludes (2) Fl Vn & Hpd; Jardinier de Samos (suite); Jeux; Movts (2) Flts; Pièce Fl; Pièces brèves Ww KPT ▲ 32202
D'Amore Duo ("Simplicity") † Cimarosa:Con Ob; N. Coste:Montegnard, Op. 34; F. Couperin:Music of Couperin; Pièces de clavecin (sels); M. Moriarty:Simplicity; Pilss:Sonatine Ob SO ▲ 22573 [DDD] (16.97)
F. Hand (gtr), S. A. Kahn (fl) ("Around the Clock: Chamber Music for Flute") † Chamber Music; Interludes (2) Fl Vn & Hpd; Jeux; Pièce Fl; Stèles orientées ALBA ▲ 145 [DDD]
D. Peck (fl), M. Lord (pno) ("The Flute Heard Round the World") † Caplet:Improvs Fl; Casella:Barcarola et scherzo, Op. 4; P. Gaubert:Son 1 Fl; Rieti:Sonatina Fl; L. Stein:Intro & Rondo Fl; A. Wilder:Air Fl BOST ▲ 1027 [DDD] (15.97)
K. Ragossnig (gtr), P. Graf (fl) † W. Burkhard:Serenade Fl, Op. 71/3; F. Carulli:Serenade Fl & Gtr, Op. 109; M. Giuliani:Grand Duo Concertant, Op. 25; M. Ravel:Pavane pour une infante défunte; Pièce en forme de Habanera CLAV ▲ 408 [ADD]

Escales [Ports of Call] for Orchestra (or Piano) (1922)
C. Andranian (pno), G. Andranian (pno) ("Distant Ports & Shores") † J. Françaix:Danses exotiques Pnos; Jolivet:Hopi Snake Dance; D. Milhaud:Boeuf sur le toit, Op. 58 DI ▲ 920313 [DDD] (5.97)
E. Mata (cnd), Dallas SO *(rec Jan 1993)* † Divert Orch; E. Chausson:Sym in B♭, Op. 20 DOR ▲ 90181 [DDD] (16.97)
P. Monteux (cnd), San Francisco SO † Lalo:Roi d'Ys (sels); M. Ravel:Alborada del gracioso; Daphnis et Chloé (suite 1); Valse; Valses nobles RCAV (Gold Seal) ▲ 61895 (11.97)
C. Munch (cnd), Boston SO *(rec 1956 & 1959)* † Debussy:Mer Orch; Saint-Saëns:Sym 3 RCAV (Living Stereo) ▲ 61500 (11.97)
E. Ormandy (cnd), Philadelphia Orch † Divert Orch; G. Fauré:Pavane; Pelléas et Mélisande, Op. 80; A. Roussel:Bacchus et Ariane (suite 2) SNYC (Essential Classics) ▲ 62644 (7.97) ▮ 62644 (3.98)
E. Oue (cnd), Minnesota Orch *(rec Minneapolis, MN, Oct 1-3, 1996)* ("Ports of Call") † Alfvén:Swedish Rhap 1, Op. 19; Borodin:In the Steppes of Central Asia; Chabrier:España; Sibelius:Finlandia, Op. 26; Smetana:Moldau; P. Tchaikovsky:Capriccio italien, Op. 45 REF ▲ 80 (16.97)
P. Paray (cnd), Detroit SO † M. Ravel:Alborada del gracioso; Pavane pour une infante défunte; Rapsodie espagnole; Tombeau; Valse MRCR ▲ 32003 [ADD] (11.97)
P. Serkin (pno)—Tunis † C. M. Loeffler:Rhaps; W. A. Mozart:Qnt Pno, K.452; F. Poulenc:Son Ob; R. Schumann:Romances Ob, Op. 94 BOST ▲ 1004 (15.97)
W. Straram (cnd), Straram Concerts Orch *(rec 1928-30)* † Debussy:Prélude à l'après-midi d'un faune; M. Ravel:Alborada del gracioso; Daphnis et Chloé (suite 2); A. Roussel:Festin de l'araignée, Op. 17 VAIA ▲ 1074 (17.97)

Féerique for Orchestra (1924)
M. Adriano (cnd), Slovak RSO Bratislava *(rec Feb 8-13, 1993)* † Ballade de la geôle de Reading; Recontres; Suite élisabéthaine MARC ▲ 8223508 [DDD] (13.97)

Film Music
M. Adriano (cnd), Czech-Slovak RSO Bratislava—Don Quichotte [Chanson de Sancho]; Golgotha (suite); Macbeth MARC ▲ 8223287 (13.97)

Ghirlarzana for Cello (1950)
H. Penny (vc) *(rec Dec 1995)* ("Cello") † G. Cassadó:Suite Vc; G. Glynn:Changes Vc; H. W. Henze:Serenade Vc; M. Kelemen:Grand Jeu Classic; Splintery; Varia Melodia; A. Khachaturian:Son-Fant Vc TALP ▲ 103 [DDD] (18.97)

Histoires (10) for Piano [arr Ibert for various instruments] (1922)
W. Feybli (gtr), D. Erni (gtr) [arr Feybli & Erni for 2 gtrs] *(rec June 1995)* ("The Guitar Artistry of W. Feybli & D. Erni") † Gnattali:Suite retratos; Infante:Ritmo; Mersson:Danse Andalouse; T. Wegmann:Rhap Gtrs DORO ▲ 5008 [DDD] (16.97)

IBERT, JACQUES (cont.)
Histoires (10) for Piano [arr Ibert for various instruments] (1922) (cont.)
B. Pergamenschikov (vc), P. Gililov (pno)—No. 1 La meneuse de tortues d'or; No. 08 La cage de cristal; No. 03 Le vieux mendiant; No. 02 Le petit âne blanc *(rec Studio Kraus, Germany, Mar 1994)* ("Beau Soir") † Debussy:Beau soir; Music of Debussy; Preludes Pno; G. Fauré:Après un rêve, Op. 7/1; Berceuse, Op. 16; Elégie, Op. 24; Papillon, Op. 77; Romance Vc, Op. 69; Sicilienne, Op. 78; Sérénade, Op. 98; M. Ravel:Pièce en forme de Habanera; Saint-Saëns:Allegro appassionato, Op. 43; Cygne ORF ▲ 349951 [DDD] (18.97)
Impromptu for Trumpet & Piano (1950)
T. Stevens (tpt), Z. Carno (pno) † Bozza:Badinage; Caprice; Lied Tpt & Pno; F. Poulenc:Son Tpt; Ropartz:Andante & Allegro; H. Tomasi:Triptyque Tpt CRYS ▮ 367 (9.98)
Interludes (2) for Flute, Violin & Harpsichord (or Harp) [from *Le Burlador*] (1946)
Auréole [arr for fl, va & hp] † Debussy:Son Fl; F. Devienne:Duos Fl (sels), Op. 5; G. Fauré:Morceau de concours Fl; Salzedo:Sonatine en Trio KOCH ▲ 7102 [DDD] (16.97)
Collegium Musicum Soloists ("Jacques Ibert: Complete Chamber Music with Flute") † Aria Cl & Pno; Entracte Fl; Jardinier de Samos (suite); Jeux; Movts (2) Flts; Pièce Fl; Pièces brèves Ww KPT ▲ 32202
C. Macomber (vn), S. A. Kahn (fl), S. Jolles (hp) ("Around the Clock: Chamber Music for Flute") † Chamber Music; Entracte Fl; Jeux; Pièce Fl; Stèles orientées ALBA ▲ 145 [DDD]
Le Jardinier de Samos (suite) for Flute, Clarinet, Trumpet, Percussion, Violin & Cello (1924)
Collegium Musicum Soloists ("Jacques Ibert: Complete Chamber Music with Flute") † Aria Cl & Pno; Entracte Fl; Interludes (2) Fl Vn & Hpd; Jeux; Movts (2) Flts; Pièce Fl; Pièces brèves Ww KPT ▲ 32202
Jeux for Flute (or Violin) & Piano (1923)
Collegium Musicum Soloists ("Jacques Ibert: Complete Chamber Music with Flute") † Aria Cl & Pno; Entracte Fl; Interludes (2) Fl Vn & Hpd; Jardinier de Samos (suite); Movts (2) Flts; Pièce Fl; Pièces brèves Ww KPT ▲ 32202
S. A. Kahn (fl), A. Willis (pno) ("Around the Clock: Chamber Music for Flute") † Chamber Music; Entracte Fl; Interludes (2) Fl Vn & Hpd; Pièce Fl; Stèles orientées ALBA ▲ 145 [DDD]
E. Pahud (fl), E. Le Sage (pno) *(rec Highgate London, England, Feb 1997)* ("Paris") † Aria Cl & Pno; Dutilleux:Sonatine Fl; Jolivet:Chant de Linos Fl & Pno; Messiaen:Merle noir; D. Milhaud:Sonatina Fl & Pno, Op. 76; F. Poulenc:Son Fl; Sancan:Sonatine Fl EMIC ▲ 56488 [DDD] (16.97)
K. Redel (fl), N. Lee (pno)—No. 01 Animée; No. 02 Tendre [Ed. Leduc] *(rec France, Nov 1982)* ("French Music for Flute & Piano") † Debussy:Syrinx Fl; D. Milhaud:Sonatina Fl & Pno, Op. 76; F. Poulenc:Son Fl; M. Ravel:Pièce en forme de Habanera; A. Roussel:Andante & Scherzo Fl, Op. 51; Aria Fl; Joueurs de flûte, Op. 27 ARN ▲ 68238 [AAD] (16.97)
Movements (2) for 2 Flutes, Clarinet & Bassoon or (Flute, Oboe, Clarinet & Bassoon) (1922)
Collegium Musicum Soloists ("Jacques Ibert: Complete Chamber Music with Flute") † Aria Cl & Pno; Entracte Fl; Interludes (2) Fl Vn & Hpd; Jardinier de Samos (suite); Jeux; Pièce Fl; Pièces brèves Ww KPT ▲ 32202
Music of Ibert
D. Ascione (gtr), R. Balzani (fl) † B. Bartók:Romanian Folk Dances Vn & Pno; B. Bettinelli:Music of; Castelnuovo-Tedesco:Sonatina Fl & Gtr, Op. 205; E. Cordero:Music of; A. Piazzolla:Histoire du tango; Sauguet:Easy Pieces Fl LBD ▲ 5 (16.97)
Pièce for Flute (1936)
T. L. Christiansen (fl) ("Jacques Ibert: Complete Chamber Music with Flute") † Aria Cl & Pno; Entracte Fl; Interludes (2) Fl Vn & Hpd; Jardinier de Samos (suite); Jeux; Movts (2) Flts; Pièces brèves Ww KPT ▲ 32202
A. Duchemin (fl) † Kabalevsky:Con Vn; Kennan:Night Soliloquy; H. Lipsky:Images; F. Martin:Ballade Fl PAVA ▲ 7197 (10.97)
A. Duchemin (fl) † Kabalevsky:Con Vn; Kennan:Night Soliloquy; H. Lipsky:Trois Images; F. Martin:Ballade Fl SNE ▲ 2033 (16.97)
S. A. Kahn (fl) ("Around the Clock: Chamber Music for Flute") † Chamber Music; Entracte Fl; Interludes (2) Fl Vn & Hpd; Jeux; Stèles orientées ALBA ▲ 145 [DDD]
M. Wiesler (fl) *(rec Sweden, Sep 29-30, 1989)* ("Manuela plays French Solo Flute Music") † Debussy:Fl Music; J. Françaix:Suite Fl; Jolivet:Incantation Fl; Pieces (12) from 21 Sounding Minutes Fl; Marais:Vars on "Les Folies d'Espagne"; H. Tomasi:Sonatine Fl *(E, F, G text)* BIS ▲ 459 [DDD] (17.97)
Pièces brèves (3) for Wind Quintet (1930)
Athena Ensemble *(rec 1978)* † Gounod:Petite Sym; F. Poulenc:Sxt Pno CHN (Collect) ▲ 6543 [ADD] (12.97)
Collegium Musicum Soloists ("Jacques Ibert: Complete Chamber Music with Flute") † Aria Cl & Pno; Entracte Fl; Interludes (2) Fl Vn & Hpd; Jardinier de Samos (suite); Jeux; Movts (2) Flts; Pièce Fl KPT ▲ 32202
Frösunda Wind Quintet *(rec Mar 1979)* ("Favorite Music for Wind Quintet") † M. Arnold:Shanties, Op. 4; F. Farkas:Antique Hungarian Dances; C. Nielsen:Qnt Ww BIS ▲ 136 [AAD] (17.97)
New York Woodwind Quintet ("The Best of the New York Woodwind Quintet, Vol. 2") † I. Fine:Partita; P. Hindemith:Kleine Kammermusik, Op. 24/2; D. Milhaud:Cheminée du Roi René, Op. 205; Van Vactor:Scherzo Ww Qnt; H. Villa-Lobos:Bachiana brasileira 6; Duo Ob & Bn; Qnt forme de chôros; A. Wilder:Up Tempo BOSK ▲ 139 [AAD] (15.97)
Prague National Theater Wind Quintet † J. Françaix:Heure du berger for Orch; Indy:Sarabande et menuet; D. Milhaud:Son Fl, Cl, Ob & Pno, Op. 47; A. Roussel:Divert Ww, Op. 6; Saint-Saëns:Caprice sur des airs danoises et russes, Op. 79 NUO ▲ 7268 (16.97)
Scandinavian Wind Quintet † Bozza:Scherzo, Op. 48; D. Milhaud:Cheminée du Roi René, Op. 205; M. Ravel:Tombeau; Taffanel:Music of Taffanel; H. Villa-Lobos:Qnt forme de chôros PLAL ▲ 58 (18.97)
Sundsvall Wind Quartet † G. Jacob:Sxt Pno & Ww Qnt, Op. 6; Thuille:Sxt Pno, Op. 6; G. Vinter:Miniatures Ww Qnt CAPA ▲ 21497 (16.97)
Pièces (5) en trio for Oboe, Clarinet & Bassoon (1935)
Chicago Chamber Musicians *(rec Chicago, IL, Oct-Dec 1997)* ("20th Century French Wind Trios") † G. Auric:Trio Ob; Canteloube:Rustiques; J. Françaix:Divert Ob, Cl, Bn; D. Milhaud:Pastorale Ob, Op. 147; Suite d'après Corrette, Op. 161; P. Pierné:Bucolique variée; Tansman:Suite Reed Trio CED ▲ 40 [DDD] (16.97)
Les Recontres for Orchestra (1924-25)
M. Adriano (cnd), Slovak RSO Bratislava *(rec Feb 8-13, 1993)* † Ballade de la geôle de Reading; Féerique; Suite élisabéthaine MARC ▲ 8223508 [DDD] (13.97)
Songs
M. Dolorian (sop), C. Cebro (pno)—Berceuse de Galiane; Chanson du Rien; Chansons de Melpomène; Chants (4); Complainte de Florinde; Le jardin du ciel; La verdure dorée; 3 sels from Livre d'Amour; Le roi d'Yvetot sels MED7 ▲ 7 [DDD] (18.97)
Stèles orientées (2) for Voice & Flute [text Segalen] (1925)
C. Schadeberg (sop), S. A. Kahn (fl) ("Around the Clock: Chamber Music for Flute") † Chamber Music; Entracte Fl; Interludes (2) Fl Vn & Hpd; Jeux; Pièce Fl ALBA ▲ 145 [DDD]
Suite élisabéthaine for Voice & Orchestra [from *Le Songe d'une nuit d'été*] (1942)
R. A. Clark (cnd), Manhattan CO † Capriccio; Con Fl; Suite symphonique NPT ▲ 85531 [DDD] (16.97)
D. Kubričká (sop), M. Adriano (cnd), Slovak RSO Bratislava, Slovak Phil Chorus *(rec Feb 8-13, 1993)* † Ballade de la geôle de Reading; Féerique; Recontres MARC ▲ 8223508 [DDD] (13.97)
Suite symphonique for Orchestra, "Paris" (1930)
R. A. Clark (cnd), Manhattan CO † Capriccio; Con Fl; Suite élisabéthaine NPT ▲ 85531 [DDD] (16.97)
Symphonie concertante for Oboe & Strings (1948-49)
J. De Lancie (ob), A. Previn (cnd), London SO † J. Françaix:Horloge de Flore; Satie:Gymnopédies; R. Strauss:Con Ob, AV144 RCAV (Gold Seal) ▲ 7989 [ADD] (11.97)
L. Lencsés (ob), V. Czarnecki (cnd), Southwest German CO Pforzheim † J. Françaix:Horloge de Flore; Honegger:Con da camera CPO ▲ 999193 [ADD] (14.97)
H. Lucarelli (ob), R. A. Clark (cnd), Manhattan CO ("Oeuvres Variées") † Con Vc; Concertino da camera; Divert Orch NPT (Manhattan CO) ▲ 85598 [DDD] (16.97)
H. Schellenberger (ob), Z. Peskó (cnd), Franz Liszt CO *(rec Budapest, Hungary, Apr 1996)* † W. Lutoslawski:Con Ob; F. Martin:Danses CAMM ▲ 130045 [DDD] (16.97)
The Triumph of Chastity (ballet) [lib R. Page] (1950)
M. Adriano (cnd), Moscow SO *(rec Mosfilm Studio, Aug 1995)* † Diane de Poitiers MARC ▲ 8223854 [DDD] (13.97)

IBRAHIMOVA, SEVDA (1940-
Transcriptions de chants populaires azerbaïdjans for Piano
A. Alieva (pno) † Balakirev:Paraphrase Pno; Mustafa-Zade:Con Pno; S. Rachmaninoff:Pno Music (misc colls); Songs (6), Op. 38; Radjabov:Tableaux de la vie hébraïque GALL ▲ 832 [DDD]

ICHIYANAGI, TOSHI (1933-
Cloud Atlas (cycle of 6 pieces) for Piano (1985-87)
K. Kimura (pno) † Flowers Blooming in Summer; Paganini Personal; Scenes II; Two Existence CAMA ▲ 52 (18.97)
Y. Nagai (pno) *(rec Sweden, Dec 1995)* ("Poésie: Yukie Nagai Plays Japanese Piano Music") † Kako:Poésie; A. Miyoshi:Diary of the Sea; Y. Takahashi:Kwanju, May 1980; Takemitsu:For Away; Rain Tree Sketch; Yashiro:Son Pno BIS ▲ 766 [DDD] (17.97)

ICHIYANAGI, TOSHI (cont.)
Cloud Atlas (cycle of 6 pieces) for Piano (1985-87) (cont.)
M. Yuguchi (pno) *(rec Jan 1996)* ("Contemporary Japanese Piano Music") † H. Otaka:Sonatine Pno; Takemitsu:Litany Pno; Uninterrupted Rests; Terauchi:Phoenix Hall and 8 Putto-Figures; Yashiro:Son Pno THOR ▲ 2324 [DDD] (16.97)
Concerto for Violin & Orchestra
P. Zukofsky (vn), T. Otaka (cnd), Tokyo PO ("The Min-On Contemporary Music Festival 1983") † Kawanami:Ondine CAMA ▲ 295 (18.97)
Flowers Blooming in Summer for Harp & Piano
M. Kimura (hp), K. Kimura (pno) † Cloud Atlas; Paganini Personal; Scenes II; Two Existence CAMA ▲ 52 (18.97)
Paganini Personal for Marimba & Piano
K. Kimura (pno), H. Iwaki (mar) † Cloud Atlas; Flowers Blooming in Summer; Scenes II; Two Existence CAMA ▲ 52 (18.97)
Portrait of Forest for solo Marimba (1983)
A. Sugahara (mar) *(rec Chichibu Myuzu Park Ongaku-do, Oct 5-6, 1995)* ("13 Drums: Music for Percussion Solo") † Rhythm Gradation; Fukushi:Anima of a Tree; Ikebe:Monovalence IV; M. Ishii:13 Drums; Kitazume:Shadows III-A; Y. Takahashi:Wolf CAMA ▲ 414 [DDD] (18.97)
Rhythm Gradation for solo Timpani (1993)
A. Sugahara (timp) *(rec Chichibu Myuzu Park Ongaku-do, Oct 5-6, 1995)* ("13 Drums: Music for Percussion Solo") † Portrait of Forest; Fukushi:Anima of a Tree; Ikebe:Monovalence IV; M. Ishii:13 Drums; Kitazume:Shadows III-A; Y. Takahashi:Wolf CAMA ▲ 414 [DDD] (18.97)
Scenes II for Violin & Piano
K. Suzumi (vn), K. Kimura (pno) † Cloud Atlas; Flowers Blooming in Summer; Paganini Personal; Two Existence CAMA ▲ 52 (18.97)
Two Existence for 2 Pianos
K. Kimura (pno), T. Ichiyanagi (pno) † Cloud Atlas; Flowers Blooming in Summer; Paganini Personal; Scenes II CAMA ▲ 52 (18.97)

IFUKUBE, AKIRA (1914-
Ballata Sinfonica for Oboe & Orchestra (1943)
J. Hirokami (cnd), Malmö SO *(rec (Konserthus), Sweden, June 1990)* ("Japanese Orchestral Music") † A. Otaka:Image Orch; K. Tanaka:Prismes Orch; Y. Toyama:Matsura Orch; Wada:Folkloric Dance Suite; Folkloric Dance Suite Orch *(E, F, G text)* BIS ▲ 490 [DDD] (17.97)
Bintatara for Orchestra
T. Tamura (cnd), Pro Musica Nipponia † Lullabies Among the Native Tribes on the Island of; Mono Yu Mai; Son Vn CAMA ▲ 290
Lullabies Among the Native Tribes on the Island of Sakhalin (3) for Soprano & Piano
K. Hirata (sop), Y. Umemura (pno) † Bintatara; Mono Yu Mai; Son Vn CAMA ▲ 290
Mono Yu Mai for Koto
K. Nosaka (koto) † Bintatara; Lullabies Among the Native Tribes on the Island of; Son Vn CAMA ▲ 290
Sonata for Violin & Piano
T. Kobyayashi (vn), Y. Umemura (pno) † Bintatara; Lullabies Among the Native Tribes on the Island of; Mono Yu Mai CAMA ▲ 290

IGLESIAS-ROSSI, ALEJANDRO (1960-
Ascencion for Tape
A. Iglesias-Rossi (elec) ("Travels of the Spider") † Cromberg:Marimbágenes; Dal Ferra:Ashram; Due Giorni Dopo; Fumarola:Callejuelas; Peregrinar de la Araña; Schachter:Tiempo Quebrado POGU ▲ 21015 (16.97)

IKEBE, SHIN-ICHIRO (1943-
Ascension for Piano (1974)
C. Fukunaga (koto) † Kohru; Lion; On the Other Side of Rain; Quinquivalence; Strata I; Strata II; Terre est Bleue Comme Une Orange CAMA ▲ 270 [DDD] (18.97)
Crepa (chamber concerto in 7 movements) for solo Violin, 3 Violas, Cello & Double Bass (1966)
K. Matsubara (vn), K. Kido (va), K. Ona (va), N. Kawango (va), T. Kikuchi (vc), K. Mizoiri (db), S.-I. Ikebe (cnd) *(rec Tsutsuji Hall Tokyo, Oct 21, 1996)* ("Strata: Chamber Music of Ikebe") † Quatrevalence; Son solo Vn; Strata IV; Strata V; Tu sens la terre et la rivière CAMA ▲ 463 [DDD] (18.97)
Dimorphism for Organ & Orchestra (1974)
N. Matsui (org), K. Sato (cnd), Tokyo Metropolitan SO † Sym 3; Sym 5 CAMA ▲ 374 [DDD] (18.97)
Energeia for Soprano, Alto & Tenor Saxophones & Orchestra (1970)
K. Tomioka (a sax/s sax), S. Iwamoto (t sax), H. Iwaki (cnd), New Japan PO † Sym 1; Sym 6 CAMA ▲ 351 [DDD] (18.97)
Fairy Tales Written on the Sky (12) for Chorus
Japan Children's Chorus ("Choral Works for Children") † Lullabies; Poems Engraved on Clay Tablets CAMA ▲ 378 (18.97)
Kageru for 17-String Koto (1979; rev. 1994)
T. Kikuchi (koto) *(rec Saitama Arts Theater Concert Hall, Japan, Apr 1995)* ("Kamunagi") † Matsumura:Air of Prayer; Nishimura:Kamunagi; S. Satoh:Tamaogi-Koto; Yoshimatsu:Nabari CAMA ▲ 267 [DDD] (18.97)
Kohru for Koto (1977)
C. Fukunaga (koto) † Ascension; Lion; On the Other Side of Rain; Quinquivalence; Strata I; Strata II; Terre est Bleue Comme Une Orange CAMA ▲ 270 [DDD] (18.97)
Lion for Brass Intruments (1969)
J. Orita (tpt), A. Nozaki (tpt), N. Maehara (tpt), T. Yoshida (tpt), S. Agata (hn), O. Iwasa (hn), M. Nakamuta (hn), K. Yukawa (hn), K. Shuto (trbn), T. Yamazaki (trbn), A. Odawara (trbn), T. Numata (trbn), M. Ofusa (eup), K. Aoshima (eup), M. Kohiyama (tuba), T. Minagawa (tuba), S.-I. Ikebe (cnd) † Ascension; Kohru; On the Other Side of Rain; Quinquivalence; Strata I; Strata II; Terre est Bleue Comme Une Orange CAMA ▲ 270 [DDD] (18.97)
Lullabies (6) for Chorus
Japan Children's Chorus ("Choral Works for Children") † Fairy Tales Written on the Sky; Poems Engraved on Clay Tablets CAMA ▲ 378 (18.97)
Monovalence IV for Marimba, etc. (1975)
A. Sugahara (perc) *(rec Chichibu Myuzu Park Ongaku-do, Oct 5-6, 1995)* ("13 Drums: Music for Percussion Solo") † Fukushi:Anima of a Tree; T. Ichiyanagi:Portrait of Forest; Rhythm Gradation, M. Ishii:13 Drums; Kitazume:Shadows III-A; Y. Takahashi:Wolf CAMA ▲ 414 [DDD] (18.97)
On a Treetop for Koto (1995)
N. Yoshimura (koto) *(rec Kusatsu Concert Hall, Japan, Nov 17, 1995)* ("On a Treetop") † M. Ishii:Entflohene zeit so-gu, Op. 99; Kitazume:In Resonance; T. Niimi:Altyerre-Dream Time; Nishimura:Kamunagi *([ENG,JAP] text)* CAMA ▲ 30426 [DDD] (18.97)
On the Other Side of Rain for 4 Percussionists (1978)
Percussion Group 72 † Ascension; Kohru; Lion; Quinquivalence; Strata I; Strata II; Terre est Bleue Comme Une Orange CAMA ▲ 270 [DDD] (18.97)
Poems Engraved on Clay Tablets for Chorus
Japan Children's Chorus ("Choral Works for Children") † Fairy Tales Written on the Sky; Lullabies CAMA ▲ 378 (18.97)
Quatrevalence for Violin, Viola, Cello & Piano (1996)
M. Ishii (vn), K. Ono (va), M. Kanda (vc), A. Takahashi (pno) *(rec Tsutsuji Hall Tokyo, Oct 21, 1996)* ("Strata: Chamber Music of Ikebe") † Crepa; Son solo Vn; Strata IV; Strata V; Tu sens la terre et la rivière CAMA ▲ 463 [DDD] (18.97)
Quinquivalence for Violin, Viola, Cello, Doublebass & Piano (1991)
S. Collot (va), T. Kubota (va), M. Kanda (vc), Y. Nagashima (db), T. Mukaiyama (pno), S.-I. Ikebe (cnd) † Ascension; Kohru; Lion; On the Other Side of Rain; Strata I; Strata II; Terre est Bleue Comme Une Orange CAMA ▲ 270 [DDD] (18.97)
Sonata for solo Violin (1965)
M. Ishii (vn) *(rec Tsutsuji Hall Tokyo, Oct 21, 1996)* ("Strata: Chamber Music of Ikebe") † Crepa; Quatrevalence; Strata IV; Strata V; Tu sens la terre et la rivière CAMA ▲ 463 [DDD] (18.97)
Strata I for String Quartet (1988)
H. Ozeki (vn), M. Ishii (vn), S. Collot (va), M. Kanda (vc) † Ascension; Kohru; Lion; On the Other Side of Rain; Quinquivalence; Strata II; Terre est Bleue Comme Une Orange CAMA ▲ 270 [DDD] (18.97)
Strata II for Flute (1988)
H. Koizumi (fl) † Ascension; Kohru; Lion; On the Other Side of Rain; Quinquivalence; Strata I; Terre est Bleue Comme Une Orange CAMA ▲ 270 [DDD] (18.97)
Strata IV for Oboe & Double Bass (1994)
K. Mizoiri (db), Y. Mizoiri (ob) *(rec Tsutsuji Hall Tokyo, Oct 21, 1996)* ("Strata: Chamber Music of Ikebe") † Crepa; Quatrevalence; Son solo Vn; Strata V; Tu sens la terre et la rivière CAMA ▲ 463 [DDD] (18.97)

KREISLER, FRITZ (cont.)

Violin Pieces (original works & arrangements) (cont.)

G. Shaham (vn), Orpheus CO—Con in C for Vn in the style of Vivaldi † Vivaldi:Cons Vn Strs, Op. 8/1-4 DEUT ▲ 39933 [DDD] (17.97) ▮ 39933 [DDD] (10.98)

D. Sitkovetsky (vn), B. Canino (pno) ORF ▲ 48831 [DDD] (18.97)

V. Vaidman (vn), E. Krasovsky (pno)—Schön Rosmarin; Liebesleid; Liebesfreud ("Romantic Strings") † A. Dvořák:Sonatina Vn, Op. 100; F. Schubert:Sonatinas (3) Vn; P. Tchaikovsky:Souvenir d'un lieu cher, Op. 42; Valse-Scherzo Vn, Op. 34 CACI ▲ 210004 (5.97)

O. Volkov (pno)—Liebesleid; Liebesfreud *(rec Moscow, Russia, May 22, 1994)* ("Live From Moscow") † Liszt:Etudes de concert (2), S.145; S. Prokofiev:Sarcasms Pno, Op. 17; F. Schubert:Impromptus (4) Pno; Moments musicaux, D.780; Son Pno, D.537; R. Schumann:Kinderszenen Pno, Op. 15; A. Scriabin:Preludes (24) Pno, Op. 11; Preludes (5) Pno, Op. 16 BRIO ▲ 106 (16.97)

artists unknown *(Hymn to the Sun)*, Tchaikovsky *(Andante cantabile)*, *(Londonderry Air)* † J. Achron:Stimmung; Diciedue:Con Vn; G. Fauré:Con Vn; A. Khachaturian:Con Vn; Martinů:Con 2 Vn; Sibelius:Con Vn CMB ▲ 1063 [ADD/DDD] (16.97)

KRENEK, ERNST (1900-1991)

Capriccio for Cello & Orchestra (1955)

E. Elsing (vc), J. Stephens (cnd), American Camerata † L. Moss:Clouds; Syms Brass; Persichetti:King Lear; Sapieyevski:Mercury Con; H. Villa-Lobos:Chôro 7 AMCA ▲ 10305 (18.97)

Chansons (3) for Voice & Piano, Op. 30a (1924)

N. Pilgrim (sop), W. Nichols (cl), Madison Quartet † Rochberg:In Praise of Krishna; R. Wernick:Haiku of Bashô CRI ▲ 817 (16.97)

Concerto No. 3 for Piano & Orchestra (1946)

D. Mitropoulos (pno), D. Mitropoulos (cnd), NBC SO *(rec 1945-48)* † J. S. Bach:Brandenburg Con 5, BWV 1050; S. Prokofiev:Con 3 Pno, Op. 26 ENPL (Piano Library) ▲ 314 (14.97)

Concerto No. 1 for Violin & Orchestra, Op. 29 (1924)

C. Juillet (vn), J. Mauceri (cnd), Berlin RSO † Korngold:Con Vn; K. Weill:Con Vn PLON (Entartete Musik) ▲ 452481 (16.97)

Jonny spielt auf (opera in 2 acts) [lib Krenek], Op. 45 (1925-26)

H. Hollreiser (cnd), Vienna State Opera Orch, L. Popp (sop—Yvonne), E. Lear (sop—Anita), K. Equiluz (ten—Station Announcer), W. Blankenship (ten—Max), L. Heppe (ten—Manager), T. Stewart (bar—Daniello), G. Feldhoff (bass—Jonny) [GER] VC ▲ 8048 [ADD] (13.97)

Lamentatio Jeremiae Prophatae for a cappella Mixed Chorus, Op. 93 (1941-42)

U. Gronostay (cnd), Netherlands Chamber Choir [LAT] GLOE ▲ 5085 [DDD] (16.97)

Marsche (3) for Winds, Op. 44 (1926)

J. C. Carmichael (cnd) ("Donaueschingen, Hindemith & Music for Winds") † P. Hindemith:Kleine Kammermusik, Op. 24/2; Son Cl; Pepping:Little Serenade; Suite Tpt; Toch:Spiel CRSR ▲ 9051

Miniatures (20) for Piano, Op. 139 (1954)

R. Blumenthal (pno) *(rec Atlanta, GA)* ("Twelve-Tone Miniatures") † Pieces Pno, Op. 110; Short Pieces, Op. 83 GAS ▲ 1016 (11.97)

Music of Krenek

Southwest Chamber Music Society—Zeitlieder (2), Op. 215; Lieder (3), Op. 216; Op. 231 for Vn & Org; Trio Strs, Op. 237; Op. 239 for Hn & Org; Son 7 Pno, Op. 240; Dyophonie, Op. 241 ORF (Musica Rediviva) ▲ 452971 (18.97)

Piano Music

G. D. Madge (pno)—Toccata & Chaconne, Op. 13 (1922); A Little Suite, Op. 13a (1922); 12 Vars in 3 Movts, Op. 79; rev 1940 & 1957; George Washington Vars, Op. 120 (1950); Echoes from Austria, Op. 166 (1958) CPO ▲ 999099 [DDD] (14.97)

Pieces (8) for Piano, Op. 110 (1946)

R. Blumenthal (pno) *(rec Atlanta, GA)* ("Twelve-Tone Miniatures") † Miniatures, Op. 139; Short Pieces, Op. 83 GAS ▲ 1016 (11.97)

Quartet No. 5 for Strings, Op. 65 (1930)

Thouvenel String Quartet *(rec Burbank, CA, July 1983)* † Qt 8 Strs, Op. 233 CRI ▲ 678 [DDD] (16.97)

Quartet No. 8 for Strings, Op. 233 (1980)

Thouvenel String Quartet *(rec Burbank, CA, July 1983)* † Qt 5 Strs, Op. 65 CRI ▲ 678 [DDD] (16.97)

Reisebuch aus den österreichischen Alpen (song cycle) for Tenor & Piano [text Krenek], Op. 62 (1929)

M. Köhler (bar), R. Schmiedel (pno) CPO ▲ 999203 [DDD] (14.97)

Short Pieces (12) for Piano, Op. 83 (1938)

R. Blumenthal (pno) *(rec Atlanta, GA)* ("Twelve-Tone Miniatures") † Miniatures, Op. 139; Pieces Pno, Op. 110 GAS ▲ 1016 (11.97)

Sonata for Harp (1955)

C. Antonelli (hp) ("20th Century Harp") † L. Berio:Sequenza II; B. Britten:Suite Hp, Op. 83; S. Bussotti:Labirinto; Nuovi Labirinti; P. Hindemith:Son Hp; Petrassi:Flou; Tailleferre:Son Hp AART ▲ 47532 (10.97)

Sonata for Organ, Op. 91/1 (1941)

A. Sachetti (org) ("Germany 1920/1940") † H. Distler:Nun komm, der Heiden Heiland, Op. 8/1; Kaminski:Wie schön leucht' uns der Morgenstern; Schoenberg:Vars on a Recitative Org, Op. 40 AART ▲ 47392 (10.97)

Sonatina for solo Oboe (1956)

L. Lencsés (ob) ("Monodien") † B. Britten:Metamorphoses, Op. 49; Koechlin:Suite E Hn, Op. 185; B. Maderna:Solo Ob BAYE ▲ 800915 (17.97)

Songs

C. Schäfer (sop), A. Bauni (pno)—O lacrymosa, Op. 48; Monolog der Stella, Op. 57; Die nachtigall, Op. 68; 5 Lieder, Op. 82; 4 Songs, Op. 112; The Flea, Op. 175; Wechselrahmen, Op. 189 *(rec Bavarian Radio, Germany, Aug 1994)* ("Musica Rediviva") ORF ▲ 373951 [DDD] (18.97)

Der Sprüng über den Schatten (comic opera in 3 acts) [lib Krenek], Op. 17 (1924)

D. Amos (sop), L. Kemeny (sop), S. MacLean (mez), J. Dürmüller (ten), U. Neuweiler (ten), J. Pflieger (bar), T. Brüning (sgr), D. D. Villiers (cnd), Bielefeld PO, Bielefeld Phil Chorus [GER] *(rec live, May 1989)* CPO 2-▲ 999082 [DDD] (27.97)

Suite for Flute & Piano, Op. 147 (1954; orchd)

A. Young (fl), C. A. Johnson (cnd), Bohuslav Martinů PO *(rec Ziln, Czech Republic, Jan 1998)* ("Music for All Time") † D. Diamond:Con Fl; Doráti:Night Music; B. Rogers:Soliloquy 1 ALBA ▲ 308 [DDD] (16.97)

Suite for Guitar (1957)

S. Grondona (gtr) ("'Novecento") † José Martinez Palacios:Son Gtr; F. Martin:Pièces brèves Gtr; E. Morricone:Pieces Gtr; Tansman:Cavatina Gtr PHEX ▲ 98419 (16.97)

Symphonic Elegy on the Death of Anton Webern for String Orchestra (1946)

D. Mitropoulos (cnd), New York PO *(rec Carnegie Hall, 1951)* † A. Berg:Wozzeck; Schoenberg:Erwartung, Op. 17 SNYC (Masterworks Heritage) 2-▲ 62759 (32.97)

Symphony No. 1, Op. 7 (1921)

T. Ukigaya (cnd), Hanover Radio PO † Sym 5 CPO ▲ 999359 (14.97)

Symphony No. 2, Op. 12 (1922)

T. Ukigaya (cnd), North German Radio PO CPO ▲ 999255 (14.97)

L. Zagrosek (cnd), Leipzig Gewandhaus Orch PLON (Entartete Musik) ▲ 452479 (16.97)

Symphony No. 5 (1950)

T. Ukigaya (cnd), Hanover Radio PO † Sym 1 CPO ▲ 999359 (14.97)

KRETA, ANDREAS VON (660-732)

Kanon

Ensemble Diferencias *(rec Waldenburg, Switzerland, Jan 17-18, 1996)* ("Cantio Triplex") † Anonymous:Gospodi Wozzwach; Heilige Dreifaltigkeit; Polielej, utrenja; Dufay:Music of Dufay; Sophronios:Oútos ho theós DVX ▲ 79610 [DDD] (16.97)

KRETZ, JOHANNES (1968-

alles Ding währt seine Zeit for 4 Trombones & Computer-generated Sounds (1993-94)

Triton Trombone Quartet *(rec Furuby Church, Sweden, July 6-10, 1994)* ("Trombone Angels") † P. M. Braun:Chörale; G. Jansson:Missa for 4 Trbns; Maklakiewicz:Chrysea Phorminx; F. Peeters:Suite for 4 Trbns, Op. 82; Serocki:Suite for 4 Trbns BIS ▲ 694 [DDD] (17.97)

KREUTZER, CONRADIN (1780-1849)

Fantasia in B♭ for Bassoon & Orchestra

A. Holder (bn), N. Pasquet (cnd), Stuttgart PO *(rec Stuttgart Phil Hall, June 1995)* ("Bassoon Concertos") † Kalliwoda:Vars et Rondo Bn, Op. 57; Lindpaintner:Con Bn; Molter:Con Bn NXIN ▲ 553456 [DDD] (5.97)

Grand Septet in E♭ for Clarinet, Horn, Bassoon & Strings, Op. 62

Charis Ensemble *(rec Oranienburg, Schloss Nordkirchen, Germany, 1986)* † F. Witt:Septet Cl MDG ▲ 3080232 [DDD] (17.97)

Consortium Classicum † Bruch:Spt ORF ▲ 167881 [DDD] (18.97)

Nash Ensemble CRD ▲ 3390 (17.97)

KREUTZER, CONRADIN (cont.)

Grand Septet in E♭ for Clarinet, Horn, Bassoon & Strings, Op. 62 (cont.)

P. Rivinus (pno), Mithras Octet † Trio Pno, Cl & Bn, Op. 43 ARNO ▲ 54462 (4.97)

Das Nachtlager in Granada (romantic opera in 2 acts) (1834)

R. Klepper (sop), M. Pabst (ten), H. Prey (bar), H. Froschauer (cnd), Cologne RSO, Cologne Radio Chorus CAPO ▲ 60029 [DDD] (17.97)

Quartet for Clarinet & Strings

M. Lethiec (cl), Nouveau Trio Pasquier † J. N. Hummel:Qt Cl, S.98; Vanhal:Qt Cl TLNT ▲ 291037 (15.97)

Sonata for Flute, Cello & Piano, Op. 23/1

M. Valli (vc), F. Pagnini (fl), P. Bidoli (pno) ("Chamber Music in the Biedermeier Period") † J. L. Dussek:Trio Son Pno, Op. 65; Kalkbrenner:Son Fl ENT (Tiziano) ▲ 96002 [DDD] (16.97)

Trio for Piano, Clarinet & Bassoon (or Cello), KWV.5105, Op. 43

P. Rivinus (pno), Mithras Octet † Grand Spt, Op. 62 ARNO ▲ 54462 (4.97)

KREUTZER, JOSEPH (1778-1832)

Grand Trio for Flute, Viola & Guitar, Op. 16

P. Neubauer (va), J. Falletta (gtr), A. Still (fl) ("The Viennese Guitar") † Beethoven:Serenade Str Trio, Op. 8; F. Schubert:Qt Fl KOCH ▲ 7404 (16.97)

P. Silverthorne (va), G. Garcia (gtr), C. Conway (fl) † Beethoven:Serenade Str Trio, Op. 8; F. Molino:Trio Fl, Op. 45 MER ▲ 84199 (16.97)

KRIDEL, JOHANN CHRISTOPH (1672-1733)

Cantatas

A. Hlavenková (sop), M. Štryncl (cnd) —Von dir Gott O!; Mein Jesus mich vergnügt; Dies ist das Brod; Erlaube mir; Wie mein Gott will; Mit ganz zerknirschtem Hertzen *(rec Aug 1996)* ("Concert-Arien") STMA ▲ 35 (18.97)

KRIEGER, JOHANN PHILIPP (1649-1725)

Magnificat for 4 Voices, 2 Trumpets, Timpani, 2 Violins, 2 Violas & Continuo (1685)

K. Strocka (sop), A. Reinhold (alt), A. Sack (ten), D. Schmidt (bass), M. Schönheit (org), M. Schönheit (cnd), Leipzig Chursächsische Capelle *(rec 1995)* ("Konzert in Weissenfels") † J. S. Bach:Cant 11; G. F. Handel:Cons (16) Org; H. Schütz:Danket dem Herren, SWV 45 ARSM ▲ 1169 [DDD] (17.97)

KROEPSCH, FRITZ (dates unknown)

Fantasy on Themes from Weber's Der Freischutz for Clarinet & Piano

K. Leister (cl) ("Pieces for Clarinet & Piano") † Klosé:Little Fant; Küffner:Intro, Theme & Vars; R. Schumann:Fantasiestücke Cl, Op. 73; Romances Ob, Op. 94; C. M. von Weber:Grand Duo Concertant, J.204; Vars on a Theme from *Silvana*, Op. 33 CAMA 2-▲ 329 [DDD] (31.97)

KROL, BERNHARD (1920-

Von Werden und Vergehen (cantata) for 4 Trombones & Chorus [after poems by Theodor Fontane]

Datura Trombone Quartet, R. Gritton (cnd), North German Radio Chorus † Beethoven:Equale Trbns, WoO 30; Candotto:Missa brevis; H. Purcell:Music for the Funeral of Queen Mary; I. Stravinsky:In memoriam Dylan Thomas ARSM ▲ 1154 [DDD] (17.97)

KROMMER, FRANZ (1759-1831)

Concertino for Flute, Clarinet, Violin & Strings, Op. 70 (?1808)

T. Wicky-Borner (vn), W. Schober (fl), H. Stalder (cl), T. Wicky-Borner (cnd) *(rec Dec 1995)* † Concertino, Op. 39 TUD ▲ 7006 (16.97)

Concertino for Flute, Oboe, Violin & Strings, Op. 39 (1803)

T. Wicky-Borner (vn), W. Schober (fl), K. Meier (ob), T. Wicky-Borner (cnd) *(rec Dec 1995)* † Concertino, Op. 70 TUD ▲ 7006 (16.97)

Concerto in E♭ for Clarinet & Orchestra, Op. 36

K. Berkes (cl), K. Berkes (cnd), Nicolaus Esterházy Sinfonia *(rec Scottish Church Budapest, July 14-17, 1994)* † Cons (2) for 2 Cls, Opp. 35 & 91 NXIN ▲ 553178 [DDD] (5.97)

E. Brunner (cl), H. Stadlmair (cnd), Bamberg SO † F. Devienne:Cons Fl (comp); Eybler:Con Cl; J. N. Hummel:Intro, Theme & Vars, Op. 102 TUD ▲ 782 [DDD] (16.97)

E. Johnson (cl), G. Herbig (cnd), Royal PO † Crusell:Con 1 Cl, Op. 1; L. Koželuch:Con Cl ASV ▲ 763 (16.97)

S. Kam (cl) † W. A. Mozart:Con Cl, K.622 TELC ▲ 21462 (16.97)

V. Mareš (cl), L. Pešek (cnd), Prague CO † Cons for 2 Cls SUR ▲ 111596 [DDD]

P. Meyer (cl), J. Rampal (cnd), Franz Liszt CO *(rec Italian Institute Budapest, Jan 4-7, 1993)* † Con Fl; Sinf Concertante, Op. 70 DNN ▲ 75635 [DDD] (16.97)

Concerto for 2 Clarinets & Orchestra, Op. 35 (1802)

S. Drucker (cl), N. Drucker (cl), P. Tiboris (cnd), Bohuslav Martinů PO ("Music for Doubles") † Martinů:Double Con; Saint-Saëns:Muse et la poète, Op. 132 ELY ▲ 714 [DDD] (16.97)

Concertos (2) for 2 Clarinets & Orchestra, Opp. 35 & 91

K. Berkes (cl), K. Berkes (cnd), Nicolaus Esterházy Sinfonia—Op. 35 [w. Kaori Tsutsui (cl)]; Op. 91 [w. Tomoko Takashima (cl)] *(rec Scottish Church Budapest, July 14-17, 1994)* † Con Cl NXIN ▲ 553178 [DDD] (5.97)

W. Boeykens (cl), A. Boeykens (cl), J. Caeyers (cnd), Belgium New CO † F. A. Hoffmeister:Con for 2 Cls HAM ▲ 1901433 (9.97)

L. Legemza (cl), D. Mihely (cl), V. Neumann (cnd), Prague Virtuosi † W. A. Mozart:Sym 40, K.550 DI ▲ 920280 [DDD] (5.97)

V. Mareš (cl), L. Pešek (cnd), Prague CO † Con Cl SUR ▲ 111596 [DDD]

Concerto in e for Flute & Orchestra [arr Joseph Küffner for Clarinet & Orchestra ca 1809], Op. 86

P. Meyer (cl), J. Rampal (cnd), Franz Liszt CO *(rec Italian Institute Budapest, Jan 4-7, 1993)* † Con Cl; Sinf Concertante, Op. 70 DNN ▲ 75635 [DDD] (16.97)

Concerto in F for Oboe & Orchestra, Op. 37

A. Klein (ob), P. Freeman (cnd), Czech National SO *(rec Prague, Czech Republic, June 17-19, 1998)* † Con Ob; J. N. Hummel:Intro, Theme & Vars, Op. 102 CED ▲ 45 [DDD] (16.97)

Concerto in F for Oboe & Orchestra, Op. 52 (1805)

A. Klein (ob), P. Freeman (cnd), Czech National SO *(rec Prague, Czech Republic, June 17-19, 1998)* † Con Ob; J. N. Hummel:Intro, Theme & Vars, Op. 102 CED ▲ 45 [DDD] (16.97)

Octet-Partitas (4) for Winds, Opp. 57, 67, 69 & 79

Nash Ensemble † A. Dvořák:Serenade Orch, Op. 44 CRD ▲ 3410 (17.97)

Zurich Wind Octet ("La Gran Partita") TUD ▲ 7001 [DDD] (16.97)

Partita in E♭ for 2 solo Horns & Wind Ensemble, (FVK 2d)

Michael Thompson Wind Ensemble *(rec Rusthall, Kent, England, July 19, 22 & 23, 1996)* † Partitas Ww, Op. 45 NXIN ▲ 8553868 [DDD] (5.97)

Partitas (3) for Wind Ensemble, Op. 45

Michael Thompson Wind Ensemble—No. 1 in E♭; No. 2 in B♭ *(rec Rusthall, Kent, England, July 19, 22 & 23, 1996)* † Partita in E♭ NXIN ▲ 8553868 [DDD] (5.97)

Partita in E♭ for Wind Octet, Op. 71

Zurich Wind Octet ("La Gran Partita") † Partita, Op. 73; Partita, Op. 77; Partita, Op. 78 TUD ▲ 7027 (16.97)

Partita in F for Wind Octet, Op. 73

Zurich Wind Octet ("La Gran Partita") † Partita, Op. 71; Partita, Op. 77; Partita, Op. 78 TUD ▲ 7027 (16.97)

Partita in F for Wind Octet, Op. 77

Zurich Wind Octet ("La Gran Partita") † Partita, Op. 71; Partita, Op. 73; Partita, Op. 78 TUD ▲ 7027 (16.97)

Partita in B♭ for Wind Octet, Op. 78

Zurich Wind Octet ("La Gran Partita") † Partita, Op. 71; Partita, Op. 73; Partita, Op. 77 TUD ▲ 7027 (16.97)

Quartet in B♭ for Bassoon & String Trio, Op. 46/1

S. Eaton (va), J. Lüthy (va), R. Latzko (vc), E. Hübner (bn) *(rec Hans-Rosbaud Studio, Oct 10-11, 1994)* † Qt Bn; W. A. Mozart:Duo Bn Vc, K.292 CPO ▲ 999297 [DDD] (14.97)

G. Maestri (vn), A. Anjos (va), A. Riccardi (vc), M. Monguzzi (cl) † F. Danzi:Qts Bn BONG ▲ 5520 [DDD] (16.97)

Quartet in E♭ for Bassoon & String Trio, Op. 46/2

S. Eaton (va), J. Lüthy (va), R. Latzko (vc), E. Hübner (bn) *(rec Hans-Rosbaud Studio, Oct 10-11, 1994)* † Qt Bn; W. A. Mozart:Duo Bn Vc, K.292 CPO ▲ 999297 [DDD] (14.97)

Quartets (6) for Clarinet & Strings

D. Klöcker (cl), Consortium Classicum CPO 2-▲ 999141 [DDD] (27.97)

Quartets for Oboe & Strings

S. Fuchs (ob), Novsak Trio † J. Fiala:Qts Ob TUD ▲ 7022 [DDD] (16.97)

Quintet for Clarinet & Strings, Op. 95

V. Mareš (cl), Stamitz String Quartet † W. A. Mozart:Qnt Cl, K.581 SUR ▲ 17 [DDD] (16.97)

Sinfonia Concertante in E♭ for Flute, Clarinet, Violin & Orchestra, Op. 70

J. Rolla (vn), J. Rampal (fl), P. Meyer (cl), J. Rampal (cnd), Franz Liszt CO *(rec Italian Institute Budapest, Jan 4-7, 1993)* † Con Cl; Con Fl DNN ▲ 75635 [DDD] (16.97)

Sinfonia Concertante in D for Flute, Clarinet, Violin & Orchestra, Op. 80

T. Wicky-Borner (vn), P. Graf (fl), H. Stalder (cl), Capriccio Ensemble † Schnyder von Wartensee:Con for 2 Cls TUD ▲ 757 [DDD] (16.97)

KROMMER, FRANZ (cont.)
Symphony No. 2 in D, Op. 40
M. Bamert (cnd), London Mozart Players ("Contemporaries of Mozart: Franz Krommer") † Sym 4
CHN ▲ 9275 [DDD] (16.97)
Symphony No. 4 in c, Op. 102
M. Bamert (cnd), London Mozart Players ("Contemporaries of Mozart: Franz Krommer") † Sym 2
CHN ▲ 9275 [DDD] (16.97)
Trio in F for Oboe, Clarinet & Bassoon
T. Indermühle (ob), D. Carmel (ob), S. Rancourt (E hn) *(rec Vienna, Austria, Feb 24-26, 1996)* † Beethoven:Trio Obs & E Hn, Op. 87; Vars Ww on La ci darem la mano, WoO 28; A. Vranicky:Trio Ob CAMA ▲ 481 [DDD] (18.97)
KROPFFGANSS, JOHANN II (1708-ca 1770)
Sonata in D for Lute, Violin & Cello
Trio Galanterie *(rec Apr 1-3, 1991)* † E. G. Baron:Con Lute; Son Lute; J. Haydn:Qts (6) Strs, H.III/1-6, Op. 1; Kohaut:Trio Lt, Vn & Vc ADQU ▲ 1005 (15.97)
KROUSE, IAN (1956-
Folias for Guitar Quartet (1992)
Los Angeles Guitar Quartet *(rec Dec 1992)* ("Evening in Granada") † Boccherini:Fandango; Debussy:Estampes; M. de Falla:Amor brujo; Rimsky-Korsakov:Capriccio espagnol, Op. 34 DLS ▲ 3144 [DDD] (14.97) ▮ 3144 [DDD] (7.98)
KRUFFT, NIKOLAUS VON (1779-1818)
Sonata in E for Horn & Piano
K. P. Thelander (hn), C. L. Post (pno) *(rec Sept 28-30, 1991)* ("Music of the Early 19th Century") † Beethoven:Son Hn; Dauprat:Son Hn & Pno, Op. 2; Kuhlau:Andante & Polacca; Oestreich:Andante Hn CRYS ▲ 677 (15.97)
Sonata in F for Horn & Piano (ca 1812)
L. Greer (hn), S. Lubin (pno) † Beethoven:Son Hn; J. Brahms:Trio Hn, Op. 40 HAM ▲ 907037 (18.97)
P. V. Zelm (hn), L. V. Doeselaar (pno) *(rec Hilversum, Netherlands, Jan 1997)* ("From Fanfare to Cantilena: 19th Century Horn Music") † Beethoven:Son Hn; Rheinberger:Son Hn; R. Schumann:Adagio & Allegro Hn, Op. 70
ETC ▲ 1210 [DDD] (17.97)
KRUMM, PHILIP (1949-
Concerto for Bass Clarinet & Chamber Ensemble (1964)
S. Vance (b cl), B. Childs (cnd) ("The Orchestra According to the Seven") † F. D. Angeli:Pieces Orch; Dellaira:Three Rivers; Kenessey:Wintersong, Op. 44; Sichel:3 Places in New Jersey; N. Strandberg:Legend of Emmeline Labiche; Van Appledorn:Cycles of Moons & Tides OPS1 ▲ 170 [DDD]
KRUMPHOLTZ, JEAN-BAPTISTE (1742-1790)
Concerto No. 6 for Harp & Orchestra, Op. 9 (ca 1785)
R. Alessandrini (hp), V. Parisi (cnd), Mantova Orch *(rec Jan 1995)* ("Harp Concertos") † J. L. Dussek:Con Hp; Sons Hp, Op. 34; Wagenseil:Con Hp NXIN ▲ 8553622 [DDD] (5.97)
Sonata in F for Flute & Harp
R. Aitken (fl), E. Goodman (hp) *(rec Castle Wik Sweden, June 2-4, 1979)* ("Flute & Harp") † Donizetti:Son Fl & Hp; A. Hovhaness:Garden of Adonis, Op. 245; L. Spohr:Son 3 Vn & Hp, Op. 113; Son 4 Vn & Hp, Op. 114; Son 5 Vn & Hp, Op. 115 BIS ▲ 143 [AAD] (17.97)
Sonatas (6) for solo Harp, Opp. 13/1-4 & 14/1-2
H. Müllerová (hp) SUR ▲ 111573 [DDD]
KRYGELL, JOHAN ADAM (1835-1915)
Organ Music
G. Svensson (org) DANR ▲ 431
KRZYWICKI, JAN (1948-
Deploration for Brass Quintet (1988)
Chestnut Brass Company *(rec Mar & May 1996)* ("Brazen Cartographies") † Bassett:Qnt Brass; Greatbatch:Scenes from the Brothers Grimm; E. Stokes:Brazen Cartographies; R. Wernick:Musica Ptolemica
ALBA ▲ 233 [DDD] (16.97)
Nocturne II for Soprano, Harp, Vibraphone & Piano (1987)
artists unknown ("Postcards: Vocal & Instrumental Music by American Composers") † Deussen:One of Nature's Majesties; San Andreas Suite; I.-P. Schwarz:Chromatic Essay Cl; Sappho; Van Appledorn:Postcards to John; Trio Italiano NSR ▲ 1012 [DDD] (15.97)
Quartet for Strings (1993-94)
Colorado String Quartet *(rec St. Peter's Episcopal Church, New York, NY, Apr 1998)* † Son Tpt; Songs after Rexroth (4); Starscape ALBA ▲ 337 [DDD] (16.97)
Snow Night for Marimba & Piano (1977)
S. Nowicki (pno), A. Orlando (mar) ("Society of Composers, Inc.: Evocations") † Bulow:Contours; Fairlie-Kennedy:Windrider/Final Ascent; B. Fennelly:Scintilla Prisca; J. Hill:Rhap Fl & Pno; D. Kam:Fant Vars; Lubet:Shabbat Shalom CPS ▲ 8631 (16.97)
Sonata for Trumpet & Piano (1994)
T. Everson (tpt), S. Nowicki (pno) *(rec Settlement Music School, Germantown, Philadelphia, PA, Mar 1998)* † Qrt Strs; Songs after Rexroth (4); Starscape ALBA ▲ 337 [DDD] (16.97)
Songs after Rexroth (4) for Mezzosoprano, Harp, Piano & Percussion (1995)
E. Golden (mez), E. Hainen (hp), S. Nowicki (pno), A. Orlando (perc), J. Krzywicki (cnd) *(rec Settlement Music School, Germantown, Philadelphia, PA, Dec 1998)* † Qrt Strs; Son Tpt; Starscape ALBA ▲ 337 [DDD] (16.97)
Starscape for Harp (1983)
M. Coppa (hp) *(rec Settlement Music School, Germantown, Philadelphia, PA, Mar 1998)* † Qrt Strs; Son Tpt; Songs after Rexroth (4) ALBA ▲ 337 [DDD] (16.97)
KUBELÍK, RAFAEL (1914-1996)
Kantate ohne Worte for Orchestra & Chorus
R. Kubelík (cnd), Bavarian RSO, Bavarian Radio Chorus † Orphikon MELI ▲ 7124 [DDD] (17.97)
Orphikon (symphony in 3 movements) for Orchestra
R. Kubelík (cnd), Bavarian RSO, R. Kubelík (cnd), Bavarian Radio Sym Chorus † Kantate ohne Worte
MELI ▲ 7124 [DDD] (17.97)
KUBIK, GAIL (1914-1984)
Concerto No. 2 for Violin & Orchestra (1940; rev 1941)
R. Ricci (vn), G. Kubik (cnd), Rome SO † B. Britten:Con Vn; B. Lees:Con Vn
ONEL (Essential Performance Reference) ▲ 96020 [ADD] (7.97)
Gerald McBoing Boing for Narrator, 9 Instruments & Percussion [text Dr. Seuss]
W. Klemperer (nar), A. Stern (cnd) † B. Rogers:Musicians of Bremen; A. Stern:Fairy's Gift
DLS ▲ 6001 [DDD] (14.97)
KUČERA, VÁCLAV (1929-
Diario Omaggio à Che Guevara for Guitar (1972)
L. Young (gtr) ("Solo") † Domeniconi:Vars on an Anatolian Folksong; H. W. Henze:Tentos; O. Hunt:Garuda Ballade; Koshkin:Fall of Birds; J. Turina:Sevillana, Op. 29 ALSE ▲ 2017 (16.97)
KUCHAR, JAN KŘTITEL (1751-1829)
Organ Music
J. Hora (org)—Fants in e & d; Andante in a; Largo in g; Pastoral in C [2 versions]; Pastoral in G [completed Hora]; Pastorella in D; Adagio in A; Fugue in a *(rec Miličín, Czech Republic, 1997)* ("Complete Organ Works") † Kopřiva:Org Music; Zach:Org Music RD (Vixen) ▲ 10004 [DDD] (16.97)
KUCHARZYK, HENRY (1953-
Impulse for Guitar (1984)
W. Beauvais (gtr) *(rec Toronto, 1989-97)* ("A Bridge Beyond") † Komorous:Amaryllis; Mozetich:Pieces Gtr; Siddall:Skook's Curiosity; S. Wingfield:Teyata; W. R. D. Wraggett:Maya CTR ▲ 6198 [DDD] (16.97)
KUCHERA-MORIN, JOANN (1953-
Speira for Flute
J. Felber (fl) ("Premieres") † Bosker:In a State; B. Feldman:Onirica; Haladyna:En la estera del Chilam Balam; W. Kraft:Cadeau; M. Phillips:Rain Dance NEU ▲ 45094 [DDD] (16.97)
Yugen for Clarinet
M. Fröst (cl) *(rec Sweden, Mar 1996)* ("Close Ups: Music for Clarinet & Percussion") † E. Denisov:Son Cl; Hillborg:Close Ups; Nursery Rhymes; Högberg:PlastMusikk; P. Lindgren:Beep-Ooh; Woodpecker's Chant; Sivelöv:Twist & Shout BIS ▲ 744 [DDD] (17.97)
KÜFFNER, JOSEPH (1776-1856)
Introduction, Theme & Variations in B♭ for Clarinet & Strings [formerly attrib to C. M. von Weber]
K. Leister (cl) ("Pieces for Clarinet & Piano") † Klosé:Little Fant; Kroepsch:Fant on Themes of Weber; R. Schumann:Fantasiestücke Cl, Op. 73; Romances Ob, Op. 94; C. M. von Weber:Grand Duo Concertant, J.204; Vars on a Theme from *Silvana*, Op. 33 CAMA 2-▲ 329 [DDD] (31.97)
S. Meyer (cl), Berlin Philharmonic String Quartet † W. A. Mozart:Qnt Cl, K.581 DNN ▲ 8098 [DDD] (10.97)

KÜFFNER, JOSEPH (cont.)
Quintet in E♭ for Horn & Strings
L. van Marcke (hn), Apos String Quartet *(rec Berlin, Feb 1996)* ("Chamber Music with Hn") † Hauff:Qnt Hn; F. A. Hoffmeister:Qnt Hn; W. A. Mozart:Qnt Hn; A. Reicha:Qnt Hn; C. Stamitz:Qts Strs PAVA ▲ 7363 [DDD] (10.97)
KUHLAU, FRIEDRICH (1786-1832)
Andante & Polacca for Horn & Piano
K. Thelander (hn), C. L. Post (pno) *(rec Sept 28-30, 1991)* ("Music of the Early 19th Century") † Beethoven:Son Hn; Dauprat:Son Hn & Pno, Op. 2; Krufft:Son Hn in E; Oestreich:Andante Hn CRYS ▲ 677 (15.97)
Les Charmes de Copenhagen (introduction & rondo brillant) for Piano, Op. 92 (1828)
T. Trondhjem (pno) *(rec Denmark, 1995-96)* ("Kuhlau-Les Charmes des Copenhague") † Divert en forme de valses, Op. 61; Rondo on a Theme of Rode, Op. 45b; Vars on the Danish Folksong 'Kong Christian stod, Op. 16; Vars on the Danish National Anthem, Op. 35; Vars on the Old Swedish Air Och liten Karin tjente, Op. 91
ROND ▲ 8353 (18.97)
Concerto in C for Piano, Op. 7
A. Malling (pno), M. Schønwandt (cnd), Danish National Radio SO † E. Grieg:Con Pno, Op. 16 CHN ▲ 9699 (16.97)
Divertimentos (6) 'en forme de valses' for Piano, Op. 61
T. Trondhjem (pno) *(rec Denmark, 1995-96)* ("Kuhlau-Les Charmes des Copenhague") † Charmes de Copenhage, Op. 92; Rondo on a Theme of Rode, Op. 45b; Vars on the Danish Folksong 'Kong Christian stod, Op. 16; Vars on the Danish National Anthem, Op. 35; Vars on the Old Swedish Air Och liten Karin tjente, Op. 91
ROND ▲ 8353 (18.97)
Divertimentos (6) for Flute & Piano, Op. 68 (1825)
T. L. Christiansen (fl), E. Westenholz (pno) *(rec Feb 1996)* ("Variations & Divertimenti, Vol. 1") † Vars Irish Folksong, Op. 105; Vars Onslow, Op. 94; Vars Scottish Folksong, Op. 104; Vars Weber, Op. 63 KPT ▲ 32237
Duos brillants (3) in B♭, e & D for Flute & Piano, Op. 110
H. W. Andreasen (fl), A. Øland (pno) *(rec Malmö Sweden, Aug 8-9, 1994)* ("Flute Music of the Danish Golden Age") † Frøhlich:Son Fl; J. P. E. Hartmann:Prelude Fl; Son Fl, Op. 1; Weyse:Rondeau Fl NXIN ▲ 553333 [DDD] (5.97)
K. Redel (fl), N. Lee (pno) † Intro & Rondo on 'Ah! quand il gèle', Op. 98a ETC ▲ 1189 (17.97)
M. Root (fl), R. Egarr (pno)—No. 3 † Intro & Rondo on 'Ah! quand il gèle', Op. 98a; Son Fl GLOE ▲ 5180 (16.97)
Duos concertants (3) for 2 Flutes, Op. 10b (1813)
T. L. Christiansen (fl), M. Beier (fl), U. Miilmann (fl) *(rec 1996-97)* ("Early Works for 1, 2 & 3 Flutes") † Grand Trios Fls, Op. 13; Vars & Solos, Op. 10a KPT 2-▲ 32252
Elverhøj [The Elf's Hill] (incidental music in 5 acts) [lib J. L. Heiberg], Op. 100 (1828)
B. Gøbel (sop), G. Plesner (cta), M. S. Johansen (bar), J. Frandsen (cnd), Danish National RSO, Danish National Radio Choir *(rec Danish Radio Concert Hall, Aug 1974)* MARC ▲ 8224053 [AAD] (13.97)
Flute Music
Kuhlau Flute Quartet—Grand Trio, Op. 90; Grosse Kvartett, Op. 71; Qt for 4 Fls, Op. 103 KPT ▲ 32050 [DDD]
Grand Trio in G for 2 Flutes & Piano, Op. 119
A. L. Christiansen (vc), T. L. Christiansen (fl), E. Westenholz (pno) [arr fl, vc & pno] † Martinů:Trio Fl
KPT ▲ 32064 [DDD]
J. Rampal (fl), C. Arimany (fl), J. S. Ritter (pno) *(rec Los Angeles, July 1996)* ("Romantic Music for 2 Flutes & Piano") † T. Böhm:Duos de Mendelssohn & Lachner; A. F. Doppler:Andante & Rondo, Op. 25; Duetto américain, Op. 37; Sonambula, Op. 42; L. Hughes:Grand Con Fant; W. A. Mozart:Son Pnos, K.448 DLS ▲ 3212 [DDD] (14.97)
Grand Trios (3) in D, g & F for 3 Flutes, Op. 13 (1813)
T. L. Christiansen (fl), M. Beier (fl), U. Miilmann (fl) *(rec 1996-97)* ("Early Works for 1, 2 & 3 Flutes") † Duos concertants, Op. 10b; Vars & Solos, Op. 10a KPT 2-▲ 32252
Introduction & Rondo on 'Ah! quand il gèle' from Le Colporteur for Flute & Piano, Op. 98a
K. Redel (fl), N. Lee (pno) † Duos brillants, Op. 110 ETC ▲ 1189 (17.97)
M. Root (fl), R. Egarr (pno) † Duos brillants, Op. 110; Son Fl GLOE ▲ 5180 (16.97)
artists unknown ("The Virtuoso Flute") † T. Böhm:Grande polonaise, Op. 16; A. F. Doppler:Fant pastorale hongroise, Op. 26; Paganini:Caprices Vn, M.S. 25; Saint-Saëns:Airs de ballet d'Ascanio; Taffanel:Fant on Freischütz
BIS ▲ 166 (17.97)
Lulu (romantic fairy opera in 3 acts) [lib C. F. Güntelberg based on Lulu oder die Zauberflöte from the fairy tale collection of the German poet C. M. Wieland], Op. 65 (1824)
T. Kiberg (sop), K. von Binzer (ten), R. Saarman (ten), U. Cold (bass), A. Frellesvig (sgr), E. Harbo (sgr), M. Schønwandt (cnd), Danish National RSO, Danish National Radio Choir [DAN] KPT 3-▲ 32009 [DDD]
Quartet No. 1 in c for Piano & Strings, Op. 32 (1820)
T. Givskov (vn), L. Grunth (va), A. L. Christiansen (vc), E. Westenholz (pno) *(rec Feb 10-12, May 12, July 16, 1996)* † Qt 2 Pno, Op. 50; Qt 3 Pno, Op. 108; Son Vn MARC 2-▲ 8224044 [DDD] (27.97)
I. Prunyi (pno), New Budapest String Quartet *(rec Dec 20-22, 1991)* † Qt 2 Pno, Op. 50
MARC ▲ 8223482 [DDD] (13.97)
Quartet No. 2 in A for Piano & Strings, Op. 50 (1822)
T. Givskov (vn), L. Grunth (va), A. L. Christiansen (vc), E. Westenholz (pno) *(rec Feb 10-12, May 12, July 16, 1996)* † Qt 1 Pno, Op. 32; Qt 3 Pno, Op. 108; Son Vn MARC 2-▲ 8224044 [DDD] (27.97)
I. Prunyi (pno), New Budapest String Quartet *(rec Dec 20-22, 1991)* † Qt 1 Pno, Op. 32
MARC ▲ 8223482 [DDD] (13.97)
Quartet No. 3 in g for Piano & Strings, Op. 108 (1883)
T. Givskov (vn), L. Grunth (va), A. L. Christiansen (vc), E. Westenholz (pno) *(rec Feb 10-12, May 12, July 16, 1996)* † Qt 1 Pno, Op. 32; Qt 2 Pno, Op. 50; Son Vn MARC 2-▲ 8224044 [DDD] (27.97)
Quartet in a for Strings, Op. 122 (1841)
Copenhagen String Quartet *(rec Copenhagen, 1969)* † Horneman:Qt 2 Strs MARC ▲ 8224016 [AAD] (13.97)
Quintets (3) in D, E & A for Flute, Violin, 2 Violas & Cello, Op. 51
J. S. Hansen (vn), H. Olsen (va), M. Dolgin (va), T. Hermansen (vc), T. Christiansen (fl) † Beethoven:Qnt Fl
KPT 2-▲ 32160 [DDD]
J. Rampal (fl), Juilliard String Quartet SNYC ▲ 44517 [DDD] (16.97)
K. Sjøgren (vn), G. S. Andersen (va), B. B. Rasmussen (va), L. H. Johansen (vc), E. Rafn (fl) *(rec Humlebaek Nordsjaelland, Denmark, Aug 1985)* NXIN ▲ 553303 [DDD] (5.97)
J. Stinton (fl), Prospero Ensemble ASV ▲ 979 (16.97)
Rondo on a Theme of Rode in a for Piano, Op. 45b
T. Trondhjem (pno) *(rec Denmark, 1995-96)* ("Kuhlau-Les Charmes des Copenhague") † Charmes de Copenhage, Op. 92; Divert en forme de valses, Op. 61; Vars on the Danish Folksong 'Kong Christian stod, Op. 16; Vars on the Danish National Anthem, Op. 35; Vars on the Old Swedish Air Och liten Karin tjente, Op. 91
ROND ▲ 8353 (18.97)
Sonatas (3) in G, C & g for Flute & Piano, Op. 83
Aguilar-Delgado Duo † Doran:Poem Fl; P. Juon:Son Fl; A. Molina:Gigue; Sarabande; H. Smith:Faces of Jazz
PROT ▲ 2201 [DDD] (19.97)
Sonata in a for Flute & Piano, Op. 85, "Grande sonate concertante" (1827)
M. Root (fl), R. Egarr (pno) † Duos brillants, Op. 110; Intro & Rondo on 'Ah! quand il gèle', Op. 98a
GLOE ▲ 5180 (16.97)
Sonatas (5) for Violin & Piano (complete)
D. Bratchkova (vn), A. Meyer-Hermann (pno)—in f, Op. 33; in E, Op. 64; in F, a & C, Op. 79/1-3 *(rec May 1995)* ("Complete Violin Sonatas") CPO ▲ 999363 [DDD] (13.97)
Sonata for Violin & Piano in f, Op. 33 (1821)
T. Givskov (vn), L. Grunth (va), A. L. Christiansen (vc), E. Westenholz (pno) *(rec Feb 10-12, May 12, July 16, 1996)* † Qt 1 Pno, Op. 32; Qt 2 Pno, Op. 50; Qt 3 Pno, Op. 108 MARC 2-▲ 8224044 [DDD] (27.97)
Trio in G for 2 Flutes & Piano, Op. 119 (ca 1831)
Trio Cantabile [trans for fl, vc & pno] *(rec Hanover, Germany, July 1997)* ("Trio Cantabile") † J. N. Hummel:Adagio, Vars & Rondo, Op. 78; C. M. von Weber:Trio Fl, Op. 63 THOR ▲ 2383 [DDD] (16.97)
Variations & Solos (12) for Flute, Op. 10a (1806)
T. L. Christiansen (fl), M. Beier (fl), U. Miilmann (fl) *(rec 1996-97)* ("Early Works for 1, 2 & 3 Flutes") † Duos concertants, Op. 10b; Grand Trios Fls, Op. 13 KPT 2-▲ 32252
Variations on a Scottish Folksong for Flute & Piano, Op. 104 (1829)
T. L. Christiansen (fl), E. Westenholz (pno) *(rec Feb 1996)* ("Variations & Divertimenti, Vol. 1") † Diverts, Op. 68; Vars Irish Folksong, Op. 105; Vars Onslow, Op. 94; Vars Weber, Op. 63 KPT ▲ 32237
Variations on a theme from Onslow's Le colporteur for Flute & Piano, Op. 94 (1828)
T. L. Christiansen (fl), E. Westenholz (pno) *(rec Feb 1996)* ("Variations & Divertimenti, Vol. 1") † Diverts, Op. 68; Vars Irish Folksong, Op. 105; Vars Scottish Folksong, Op. 104; Vars Weber, Op. 63 KPT ▲ 32237
Variations on a theme from Weber's Euryanthe for Flute & Piano, Op. 63 (1824)
T. L. Christiansen (fl), E. Westenholz (pno) *(rec Feb 1996)* ("Variations & Divertimenti, Vol. 1") † Diverts, Op. 68; Vars Irish Folksong, Op. 105; Vars Onslow, Op. 94; Vars Scottish Folksong, Op. 104 KPT ▲ 32237

KUHLAU, FRIEDRICH (cont.)

Variations on an Irish Folksong for Flute & Piano, Op. 105 (1829)
T. L. Christiansen (fl), E. Westenholz (pno) *(rec Feb 1996)* ("Variations & Divertimenti, Vol. 1") † Diverts, Op. 68; Vars Onslow, Op. 94; Vars Scottish Folksong, Op. 104; Vars Weber, Op. 63 KPT ▲ 32237

Variations (8) on the Danish Folksong 'Kong Christian stod ved Hojen mast' for Piano, Op. 16 (1818)
T. Trondhjem (pno) *(rec Denmark, 1995-96)* ("Kuhlau-Les Charmes des Copenhague") † Charmes de Copenhage, Op. 92; Divert en forme de valses, Op. 61; Rondo on a Theme of Rode, Op. 45b; Vars on the Danish National Anthem, Op. 35; Vars on the Old Swedish Air Och liten Karin tjente, Op. 91 ROND ▲ 8353 (18.97)

Variations (9) on the Danish National Anthem in F for Piano, Op. 35 (1820)
T. Trondhjem (pno) *(rec Denmark, 1995-96)* ("Kuhlau-Les Charmes des Copenhague") † Charmes de Copenhage, Op. 92; Divert en forme de valses, Op. 61; Rondo on a Theme of Rode, Op. 45b; Vars on the Danish Folksong 'Kong Christian stod, Op. 16; Vars on the Old Swedish Air Och liten Karin tjente, Op. 91 ROND ▲ 8353 (18.97)

Variations (11) on the Old Swedish Air 'Och liten Karin tjente' for Piano, Op. 91 (1828)
T. Trondhjem (pno) *(rec Denmark, 1995-96)* ("Kuhlau-Les Charmes des Copenhague") † Charmes de Copenhage, Op. 92; Divert en forme de valses, Op. 61; Rondo on a Theme of Rode, Op. 45b; Vars on the Danish Folksong 'Kong Christian stod, Op. 16; Vars on the Danish National Anthem, Op. 35 ROND ▲ 8353 (18.97)

William Shakespeare:Overture
J. Hye-Knudsen (cnd), Royal Danish Orch ("Romantic Danish Overtures") † J. B. E. Dupuy:Youth & Folly (ov); J. P. E. Hartmann:Little Kristen (ov); Heise:King & Marshal (ov); Horneman:Aladdin (ov); Weyse:Sleeping-draught (ov) STRL ▲ 1018 [AAD] (15.97)

KUHN, MAX (1896-1994)

Elegie for Basset Horn & Piano (1965)
A. Hacker (bas hn), B. Dolenc (pno) † Mensch lebt und bestehet nur eine kleine Zeit; Missa Brevis; Pieces (5) Pno; Serenata Notturno; Vars on a Melody from Canary Islands GILD ▲ 7153 [DDD] (16.97)

Der Mensch lebt und bestehet nur eine kleine Zeit (motet) for Chorus
Vasari Singers † Elegie Bas Hn; Missa Brevis; Pieces (5) Pno; Serenata Notturno; Vars on a Melody from Canary Islands GILD ▲ 7153 [DDD] (16.97)

Missa Brevis for solo Voices & Double Chorus (1951-59)
Vasari Singers † Elegie Bas Hn; Mensch lebt und bestehet nur eine kleine Zeit; Pieces (5) Pno; Serenata Notturno; Vars on a Melody from Canary Islands GILD ▲ 7153 [DDD] (16.97)

Pieces (5) for Piano (1954)
W. Fong (pno) † Elegie Bas Hn; Mensch lebt und bestehet nur eine kleine Zeit; Missa Brevis; Serenata Notturno; Vars on a Melody from Canary Islands GILD ▲ 7153 [DDD] (16.97)

Serenata Notturno for Wind Quintet (1956)
Haffner Wind Ensemble † Elegie Bas Hn; Mensch lebt und bestehet nur eine kleine Zeit; Missa Brevis; Pieces (5) Pno; Vars on a Melody from Canary Islands GILD ▲ 7153 [DDD] (16.97)

Variations on a Melody from the Canary Islands for Piano (1967)
W. Fong (pno) † Elegie Bas Hn; Mensch lebt und bestehet nur eine kleine Zeit; Missa Brevis; Pieces (5) Pno; Serenata Notturno GILD ▲ 7153 [DDD] (16.97)

KUHNAU, JOHANN (1660-1722)

Biblical Sonata No. 1 for Harpsichord
J. Gagelmann (bc), Datura Trombone Quartet † Ahle:Sacred Vocal Music; W. Byrd:Kbd Music; A. Corelli:Son da chiesa, Op. 3; Mainerio:Il primo libro (sels); H. Schütz:Attendite, popule meus, SWV 270; Fili mi, Absalom, SWV 269 ARSM ▲ 1094 [DDD] (17.97)

Frische Clavier Früchte (7 sonatas) for Harpsichord, 1696
J. Butt (hpd) *(rec Oct 1991)* HAM ▲ 907097 (18.97)

Magnificat in C for Orchestra & Chorus
M. Suzuki (cnd), Japan Bach Collegium ("Magnificat") † J. S. Bach:Magnificat, BWV 243; J. D. Zelenka:Magnificat in C, ZWV 107; Magnificat in D, ZWV 108 BIS ▲ 1011 [DDD] (17.97)

Musicalische Vorstellung einiger biblischer Historien (6 sonatas) for Harpsichord
L. Beauséjour (hpd/org) *(rec McGill Univ Montréal, Québec, Mar 1994)* CBC (Musica Viva) ▲ 1086 [DDD] (16.97)
C. Brembeck (hpd/org) CAPO ▲ 10300 [DDD] (11.97)
M. Nabeshima (hpd) *(rec Brussels, 1991)* ("Bach & His Predecessors") † J. S. Bach:Prelude, Fugue & Allegro Lt, BWV 998; Froberger:Hpd Music DI ▲ 920283 [DDD] (5.97)

Sacred Music
R. King (cnd) —Ihr Himmel jubilirt von oben; Weicht ihr Sorgen aus dem Hertzen; Wie schön leuchtet der Morgenstern; Gott, sei mir gnädig nach deiner Güte; Tristis est anima mea; O heilige Zeit HYP ▲ 67059 (18.97)

Tristis est anima mea (motet) for Chorus
H. Thamm (cnd), Windsbach Boys' Choir *(rec Germany)* ("Kantors and Organists at St. Thomas, Leipzig") † J. S. Bach:Passacaglia & Fugue Org, BWV 582; Preludes & Fugues, BWV 531-552; Calvisius:Unser Leben währet siebnzig Jahr; J. H. Schein:Israels Brünnlein CATA ▲ 57619 [AAD] (15.97)

KUKUCK, FELICITAS (1914-

Die Brücke for Soprano, Recorder & Guitar [text Hans Bethge]
S. Faringer (sop), J. Rörby (gtr), C. Pehrsson (rcr) *(rec Castle Wik, Sweden, Jan 19-20 & 26, 1974)* † Burkhart:Adventslieder; Hovland:Cantus II; H.-M. Linde:Amarilli, mia bella; L. Lundén:Little Toe & Nine More; M. Shinohara:Fragmente Rcr; Staeps:Son Trb Rcr BIS ▲ 202 [AAD] (17.97)

KULESHA, GARY (1954-

Political Implications for Clarinet Quartet (1988)
D. Shea (cl), Indiana Trio † J. Defaye:Audition Pieces; F. Cox:Time Weaving; M. Kibbe:Ebony Suite; P. Schickele:Dances for 3 CRYS ▲ 734 (15.97)

Serenade for Strings
S. Chenette (cnd), Hannaford Street Silver Band—Romance for Brass Band [Romance arr J. Scott Irvine] *(rec Toronto, Canada, March 1992)* ("Canadian Impressions") † H. Cable:Banks of Newfoundland; M. Forsyth:Songs from the Q'Appelle Valley; Irvine:Concertino Eup; Luedeke:Circus Music; Weinzweig:Round Dance CBC ▲ 5136 [DDD] (16.97)

Sinfonia for Piano, Harp & Brass Band
B. Tovey (cnd), Hannaford Street Silver Band ("Brass Links") † J. Curnow:Blenheim Flourishes; J. Ireland:Downland Suite; B. Tovey:Bardfield Ayre; Vaughan Williams:Vars Brass SMS ▲ 5188 (16.97)

KULLAK, THEODOR (1818-1882)

Concerto in c for Piano & Orchestra, Op. 55
P. Lane (pno), N. Willén (cnd), BBC Scottish SO † Dreyschock:Con Pno HYP (The Romantic Piano Concerto 21) ▲ 67086 (18.97)

KÜNNEKE, EDUARD (1885-1953)

The Alluring Flame (romantic singspiel in 8 scenes) [lib P. Knepler & J.M. Welleminsky]
J. Sacher (ten—Master), Z. Todorovic (ten—Jacinto), R. Lukas (bar—Hoffman), B. Fandrey (sgr—Dolores), C. Hossfeld (sgr—Lisbeth), M. Mallé (sgr), G. Grochowski (sgr—1st Neighbor), G. Peters (sgr—Friedrich), T. Weimer (sgr—2nd Neighbor), P. Falk (cnd), Cologne RSO, Cologne Radio Chorus *(rec Cologne, Nov 7-26, 1994)* CAPO ▲ 10753 [DDD] (10.97)

Concerto No. 1 in A♭ for Piano & Orchestra, Op. 36
T. Wirtz (pno), W. Kamirski (cnd), Southwest German RSO † Mendelssohn (-Bartholdy):Capriccio brillante, Op. 22; Serenade & Allegro giocoso, Op. 43 KSCH ▲ 313722 [ADD] (16.97)

Glückliche Reise (selections)
C. Gorner (sop), W. Hoffmann (ten), H. Kudritzki (cnd), Grand Operetta Orch † Vetter aus Dingsda (sels); Benatzky:Im weissen Rössl (sels); Berté:Dreimäderlhaus (sels) EMPE ▲ 86350

Der Vetter aus Dingsda (selections)
E. Köth (sop), H. Hildebrand (sop), R. Schock (ten), M. Schmidt (ten), W. Schmidt-Boelke (cnd), FFB Orch † Glückliche Reise (sels); Benatzky:Im weissen Rössl (sels); Berté:Dreimäderlhaus (sels) EMPE ▲ 86350

KUNZEN, FRIEDRICH LUDWIG AEMILIUS (1761-1817)

The Hallelujah of Creation for solo Voices, Orchestra & Chorus (1797)
S. Elmark (sop), S. Lillesøe (sop), A. Larsson (cta), C. Voight (ten), L. Arvidson (b-bar), P. Marschik (cnd), Danish RSO, S. Birch (cnd), Danish National Radio Chorus *(rec Radio House Copenhagen, Sept 1997)* † Ov on a Theme by Mozart; Sym in g MARC ▲ 8224070 [DDD] (13.97)

Overture on a Theme by Mozart for Orchestra (1807)
P. Marschik (cnd), Danish RSO *(rec Radio House Copenhagen, Sept 1997)* † Hallelujah of Creation; Sym in g MARC ▲ 8224070 [DDD] (13.97)

Symphony in g (ca 1790)
P. Marschik (cnd), Danish RSO *(rec Radio House Copenhagen, Sept 1997)* † Hallelujah of Creation; Ov on a Theme by Mozart MARC ▲ 8224070 [DDD] (13.97)

KUPFERMAN, MEYER (1926-

Abstractions (4) for Flute (1992)
J. Solum (fl) *(rec Vassar College Poughkeepsie, NY, Mar 24-26, 1994)* ("Autumn Rhythms") † J. Beeson:Fant, Ditty & Fughettas; L. Kraft:Cloud Studies; E. Laderman:Epigrams & Canons; Luening:Fantasias Baroque Fl; L. Nowak:Suite Fl CRI ▲ 712 [DDD] (16.97)

Arcana I for Flute
L. A. Maurer (fl) ("Angel Shadows") † T. R. George:American Folk Songs Fl, CN 341; L. Liebermann:Son Fl; Perna:Fant-Son Fl; Piston:Son Fl; A. R. Thomas:Angel Shadows 4TAY ▲ 4006 (17.97)

Atto for Orchestra (1977)
P. Freeman (cnd), Royal PO ("The Orchestral Music of Meyer Kupferman, Vol. 2") † Divert Orch; Libretto; Mask of Electra; Sym 2 SNDS ▲ 112 [ADD] (16.97)

Banners for Orchestra (1994)
E. G. Barrios (cnd), Baja California Orch ("The Orchestral Music of Meyer Kupferman, Vol. 3") † Con Gtr SNDS ▲ 113 [DDD] (16.97)

The Canticles of Ulysses for Piano
C. Vassiliades (pno) ("The Piano Music of Meyer Kupferman, Vol. 1") † Cirrus; Distances; Imprints; Infinities Fant; Partita; Pico (among the smallest particles); Pno Music; Tiananmen Suite SNDS ▲ 115 [DDD] (16.97)

Chaconne Sonata for Flute & Piano (1993)
L. A. Maurer (fl), J. M. Pearce (pno) ("American Flute Works") † S. Barber:Canzone Fl & Pno, Op. 38a; A. Copland:Duo Fl; L. Kraft:Fant Fl & Pno; Muczynski:Son Fl & Pno, Op. 14; Tower:Hexachords Fl ALBA ▲ 167 [DDD] (16.97)

Cirrus for Piano
C. Vassiliades (pno) ("The Piano Music of Meyer Kupferman, Vol. 1") † Canticles of Ulysses; Distances; Imprints; Infinities Fant; Partita; Pico (among the smallest particles); Pno Music; Tiananmen Suite SNDS ▲ 115 [DDD] (16.97)

Concerto brevis for Flute & Orchestra (1998)
L. A. Maurer (fl), M. Kupferman (cnd), Monte Carlo PO ("Orchestral Music, Vol. 11") † Winter Sym SNDS ▲ 125 [DDD] (16.97)

Concerto for Cello & Jazz Band, "Infinities No. 5" (1962; rev 1982)
D. Wells (vc), D. Mattran (cnd) ("The Orchestral Music of Meyer Kupferman, Vol. 1") † Lyric Sym; Ostinato Burlesco; Vars Orch SNDS ▲ 111 [ADD] (16.97)

Concerto for Cello, Tape & Orchestra (1974)
L. Varga (vc), S. Landau (cnd), Westchester SO *(rec 1975)* ("American Concertos") † Bergsma:Con Vn; Colgrass:Concert Masters; L. Harrison:Con Vn; B. Lees:Con Vn; Piston:Concertino Pno; Starer:Con Va VB2 (The American Composers) 2-▲ 5158 (9.97)

Concerto for Clarinet & Orchestra (1984)
P. Alexander (cl), L. Botstein (cnd), Boston Pro Arte CO † R. Wilson:Con Bn; Suite Small Orch CRI ▲ 575 [DDD] (17.97)

Concerto for Guitar & Orchestra (1993)
R. Limón (gtr), E. G. Barrios (cnd), Baja California Orch ("The Orchestral Music of Meyer Kupferman, Vol. 3") † Banners SNDS ▲ 113 [DDD] (16.97)

Concerto for 4 Guitars & Orchestra (1998)
D. Leisner (gtr), D. Starobin (gtr), O. Fader (gtr), M. Delprioria (gtr), G. B. Cortese (cnd), Manhattan School of Music Chamber Sinfonia ("Orchestral Music-Vol. 10") † Poetics 9; Sym for 6 SNDS ▲ 124 [DDD] (16.97)

Distances for Piano
C. Vassiliades (pno) ("The Piano Music of Meyer Kupferman, Vol. 1") † Canticles of Ulysses; Cirrus; Imprints; Infinities Fant; Partita; Pico (among the smallest particles); Pno Music; Tiananmen Suite SNDS ▲ 115 [DDD] (16.97)

Divertimento for Orchestra (1948)
H. Farberman (cnd), Stuttgart Philharmonia ("The Orchestral Music of Meyer Kupferman, Vol. 2") † Atto; Libretto; Mask of Electra; Sym 2 SNDS ▲ 112 [ADD] (16.97)

Echoes from Barcelona for Guitar (1975-77)
W. Anderson (gtr) ("Guitar Music of Kupferman, Vol. 1") † Exordium; Poetics 3; Strumming; Through a Glass Darkly SNDS ▲ 123 [DDD] (16.97)

Exordium for Guitar & Piano (1988)
W. Anderson (gtr), J. Forsyth (pno) ("Guitar Music of Kupferman, Vol. 1") † Echoes from Barcelona; Poetics 3; Strumming; Through a Glass Darkly SNDS ▲ 123 [DDD] (16.97)

Fantasy Concerto for Violin & Orchestra (1995)
R. Katilius (vn), G. Rinkevičius (cnd), Lithuanian State SO ("Orchestral Music of Meyer Kupferman, Vol. 6") SNDS ▲ 119 [DDD] (16.97)

The Fires of Prometheus for Trumpet & 2 Pianos in echo (1986)
T. Stevens (tpt) † F. Campo:Times; Chou Wen-Chung:Soliloquy of a Bhiksuni; R. Henderson:Var Movts; W. Kraft:Encounters III; Revueltas:Little Serious Pieces; V. Reynolds:Signals CRYS ▲ 667 (15.97)

The Flames of Abracadabra for Piano & String Trio (1976)
Cantilena Chamber Players ("Chamber Music, Vol. 1") † Son Guernica; Tunnels of Love SNDS ▲ 118 [ADD] (16.97)

Flavors of the Stars for Chamber Ensemble
Atril5 † Ice Cream Con SNDS ▲ 109 (16.97)

Hexagon Skies for Guitar & Orchestra (1994)
R. Limón (gtr), E. G. Barrios (cnd), Baja California Orch ("Orchestral Music, Vol. 4") † Infinities Projections SNDS ▲ 114 [DDD] (16.97)

Ice Cream Concerto for Chamber Ensemble
Atril5 † Flavors of the Stars SNDS ▲ 109 (16.97)

Imprints (2) for Piano
C. Vassiliades (pno) ("The Piano Music of Meyer Kupferman, Vol. 1") † Canticles of Ulysses; Cirrus; Distances; Infinities Fant; Partita; Pico (among the smallest particles); Pno Music; Tiananmen Suite SNDS ▲ 115 [DDD] (16.97)

Infinities (34) for Chamber Groupings
L. Ranger (tpt), B. Vogt (pno) *(rec Univ of Victoria, May 1994)* ("The Trumpet Comes of Age: 1940-1980") † Coulthard:Fanfare Son; F. Peeters:Son Tpt, Op. 51; H. Shapero:Son Tpt; E. T. Zwilich:Clarino Qt CRYS ▲ 669 (15.97)

Infinities Fantasy for Piano
C. Vassiliades (pno) ("The Piano Music of Meyer Kupferman, Vol. 1") † Canticles of Ulysses; Cirrus; Distances; Imprints; Partita; Pico (among the smallest particles); Pno Music; Tiananmen Suite SNDS ▲ 115 [DDD] (16.97)

Infinities Projections for Chamber Orchestra (1964)
E. G. Barrios (cnd), Baja California Orch ("Orchestral Music, Vol. 4") † Hexagon Skies SNDS ▲ 114 [DDD] (16.97)

Libretto for Orchestra (1948-49)
H. Farberman (cnd) ("The Orchestral Music of Meyer Kupferman, Vol. 2") † Atto; Divert Orch; Mask of Electra; Sym 2 SNDS ▲ 112 [ADD] (16.97)

Little Symphony (1952)
F. Litschauer (cnd), Vienna State Opera Orch ("Orchestral Music of Meyer Kupferman, Vol. 8") † Sym 4 SNDS ▲ 121 [AAD] (16.97)

Lyric Symphony (1956)
A. Watanabe (cnd), Japan PO ("The Orchestral Music of Meyer Kupferman, Vol. 1") † Con Vc & Jazz Band; Ostinato Burlesco; Vars Orch SNDS ▲ 111 [ADD] (16.97)

Masada (A Holocaust Tribute) for Chamber Ensemble (1977)
E. G. Barrios (cnd), Baja California Orch ("Orchestral Music, Vol. 5") † Twilight Sym SNDS ▲ 117 [DDD] (16.97)

Mask of Electra for Mezzo-Soprano, Oboe & Harpsichord
J. De Gaetani (mez), R. Roseman (ob), J. Spiegelman (elec hpd) ("The Orchestral Music of Meyer Kupferman, Vol. 2") † Atto; Divert Orch; Libretto; Sym 2 SNDS ▲ 112 [ADD] (16.97)

The Moor's Concerto for Piano & Orchestra
K. Hayami (pno), K. Krimets (cnd), Moscow SO † Wings of the Highest Tower SNDS ▲ 110 [DDD] (16.97)

O Harlequin for solo Flute (1988)
M. Gates (fl) ("Quintets of Meyer Kupferman") † Qnt Bn; Qnt Cl SNDS ▲ 108 [DDD] (16.97)

Ostinato Burlesco for Orchestra [after piano piece] (1954)
A. Watanabe (cnd), Japan PO ("The Orchestral Music of Meyer Kupferman, Vol. 1") † Con Vc & Jazz Band; Lyric Sym; Vars Orch SNDS ▲ 111 [ADD] (16.97)

Partita for Piano
C. Vassiliades (pno) ("The Piano Music of Meyer Kupferman, Vol. 1") † Canticles of Ulysses; Cirrus; Distances; Imprints; Infinities Fant; Pico (among the smallest particles); Pno Music; Tiananmen Suite SNDS ▲ 115 [DDD] (16.97)

KUPFERMAN, MEYER (cont.)
Piano Music
C. Vassiliades (pno)—2 Imprints; Infinities Fant; Partita; Tiananmen Suite; Cirrus; Distances; Pico [among the smallest particles]; The Canticles of Ulysses ("The Piano Music of Meyer Kupferman, Vol. 1") † Canticles of Ulysses; Cirrus; Distances; Imprints; Infinities Fant; Partita; Pico (among the smallest particles); Tiananmen Suite SNDS ▲ 115 [DDD] (16.97)
Pico (among the smallest particles) for Piano
C. Vassiliades (pno) ("The Piano Music of Meyer Kupferman, Vol. 1") † Canticles of Ulysses; Cirrus; Distances; Imprints; Infinities Fant; Partita; Pno Music; Tiananmen Suite SNDS ▲ 115 [DDD] (16.97)
Poetics No. 3 for 2 Guitars (1982)
W. Anderson (gtr), O. Fader (gtr) ("Guitar Music of Kupferman, Vol. 1") † Echoes from Barcelona; Exordium; Strumming; Through a Glass Darkly SNDS ▲ 123 [DDD] (16.97)
Poetics No. 9 for Chamber Ensemble (1983)
E. G. Barrios (cnd), Baja California Orch ("Orchestral Music-Vol. 10") † Con Gtrs; Sym for 6 SNDS ▲ 124 [DDD] (16.97)
The Proscenium: On the Demise of Gertrude (chamber opera in 1 act)
B. Hardgrave (sop), M. Kupferman (cnd) SNDS ▲ 107
Quasar Symphony for Orchestra (1996)
M. Piečaitis (cnd), Lithuanian State SO ("Orchestral Music, Vol. 9") † Sound Phantoms 8; Sym Odyssey SNDS ▲ 122 [DDD] (16.97)
Quintet for Bassoon & Strings (1947)
W. Scribner (bn), Bronx Arts Ensemble ("Quintets of Meyer Kupferman") † O Harlequin; Qnt Cl SNDS ▲ 108 [DDD] (16.97)
Quintet for Clarinet & Strings (1988)
P. Alexander (cl), Bronx Arts Ensemble ("Quintets of Meyer Kupferman") † O Harlequin; Qnt Bn SNDS ▲ 108 [DDD] (16.97)
Rhapsody for Guitar & Orchestra (1980)
R. Limón (gtr), G. Rinkevičius (cnd), Lithuanian State SO ("Orchestral Music of Meyer Kupferman, Vol. 7") † 3 Faces of Electra SNDS ▲ 120 [DDD] (17.97)
Sonata Guernica for Violin & Piano (1974)
M. Findley (vn), K. Hayami (pno) ("Chamber Music, Vol. 1") † Flames of Abracadabra; Tunnels of Love SNDS ▲ 118 [ADD] (16.97)
Sound Phantoms No. 8 for Orchestra, "Sinfonia brevis No. 2" (1980)
M. Piečaitis (cnd), Lithuanian State SO ("Orchestral Music, Vol. 9") † Quasar Sym; Sym Odyssey SNDS ▲ 122 [DDD] (16.97)
Strumming for Guitar (1988)
W. Anderson (gtr) ("Guitar Music of Kupferman, Vol. 1") † Echoes from Barcelona; Exordium; Poetics 3; Through a Glass Darkly SNDS ▲ 123 [DDD] (16.97)
Symphonic Odyssey for Orchestra (1990)
M. Piečaitis (cnd), Lithuanian State SO ("Orchestral Music, Vol. 9") † Quasar Sym; Sound Phantoms 8 SNDS ▲ 122 [DDD] (16.97)
Symphony for 6 for Chamber Ensemble (1984)
E. G. Barrios (cnd), Baja California Orch ("Orchestral Music-Vol. 10") † Con Gtrs; Poetics 9 SNDS ▲ 124 [DDD] (16.97)
Symphony No. 2, "Chamber Symphony" (1950)
H. Farberman (cnd) ("The Orchestral Music of Meyer Kupferman, Vol. 2") † Atto; Divert Orch; Libretto; Mask of Electra SNDS ▲ 112 [ADD] (16.97)
Symphony No. 4 (1955)
R. Whitney (cnd), Louisville Orch ("Orchestral Music of Meyer Kupferman, Vol. 8") † Little Sym SNDS ▲ 121 [AAD] (16.97)
The 3 Faces of Electra (music for an imaginary ballet) for Orchestra (1995)
G. Rinkevičius (cnd), Lithuanian State SO ("Orchestral Music of Meyer Kupferman, Vol. 7") † Rhap Gtr SNDS ▲ 120 [DDD] (17.97)
Through a Glass Darkly for Guitar (1988)
W. Anderson (gtr) ("Guitar Music of Kupferman, Vol. 1") † Echoes from Barcelona; Exordium; Poetics 3; Strumming SNDS ▲ 123 [DDD] (16.97)
Tiananmen Suite for Piano
C. Vassiliades (pno) ("The Piano Music of Meyer Kupferman, Vol. 1") † Canticles of Ulysses; Cirrus; Distances; Imprints; Infinities Fant; Partita; Pico (among the smallest particles); Pno Music SNDS ▲ 115 [DDD] (16.97)
Tunnels of Love (jazz concerto) for Clarinet, Double Bass & Drums (1969)
M. Foley (db), J. Jones (cl), J. C. Combs (dr) ("Chamber Music, Vol. 1") † Flames of Abracadabra; Son Guernica SNDS ▲ 118 [ADD] (16.97)
Twilight Symphony (For My Father) for Orchestra (1974)
E. G. Barrios (cnd), Baja California Orch ("Orchestral Music, Vol. 5") † Masada SNDS ▲ 117 [DDD] (16.97)
Variations for Orchestra (1959)
A. Watanabe (cnd), Japan PO ("The Orchestral Music of Meyer Kupferman, Vol. 1") † Con Vc & Jazz Band; Lyric Sym; Ostinato Burlesco SNDS ▲ 111 [ADD] (16.97)
Wings of the Highest Tower for Orchestra (1988)
K. Krimets (cnd), Moscow SO † Moor's Con SNDS ▲ 110 [DDD] (16.97)
Winter Symphony (1997)
M. Kupferman (cnd), Monte Carlo PO ("Orchestral Music, Vol. 11") † Con brevis Fl SNDS ▲ 125 [DDD] (16.97)

KUPPER, LEO (1935-
Electro-Acoustic Santur for 2 Santurs, Computers & Electronics (1989)
L. Kupper (elec/santur), K. Peergalou (elec/santur) ("Electro-Acoustic") † Guitarra Cubana; Inflexions Vocales; Rêveur au sourire pasasger POGU ▲ 21009 [DDD] (16.97)
Guitarra Cubana for Guitar (1988)
M. Bonachea (gtr) ("Electro-Acoustic") † Electro-Acoustic Santur; Inflexions Vocales; Rêveur au sourire pasasger POGU ▲ 21009 [DDD] (16.97)
Inflexions Vocales for Soprano & Tape (1982)
F. Vanhecke (sop) ("Electro-Acoustic") † Electro-Acoustic Santur; Guitarra Cubana; Rêveur au sourire pasasger POGU ▲ 21009 [DDD] (16.97)
Le Rêveur au sourire pasasger for Narrator on Tape [text Kupper] (1977)
J. Frison (nar) ("Electro-Acoustic") † Electro-Acoustic Santur; Guitarra Cubana; Inflexions Vocales POGU ▲ 21009 [DDD] (16.97)

KUREK, MICHAEL (1955-
Concerto for Harp & Orchestra (or Chamber Ensemble) (1993-94)
M. Falcao (hp), K. Schermerhorn (cnd) *(rec Nashville, 1996)* † Matisse Impressions; Qt 2 Strs; Son Va & Hp NWW ▲ 80497 (16.97)
Matisse Impressions for Piano & Woodwind Quintet (1991)
J. Helton (pno), Blair Woodwind Quintet *(rec Blair School of Music Recital Hall, 1995)* † Con Hp; Qt 2 Strs; Son Va & Hp NWW ▲ 80497 (16.97)
Quartet No. 2 for Strings (1994-95)
Blair String Quartet *(rec Blair School of Music Recital Hall, 1995)* † Con Hp; Matisse Impressions; Son Va & Hp NWW ▲ 80497 (16.97)
Sonata for Viola & Harp (1989)
J. Kochanowski (va), M. Falcao (hp) *(rec Blair School of Music Recital Hall, 1995)* † Con Hp; Matisse Impressions; Qt 2 Strs NWW ▲ 80497 (16.97)

KURI-ALDANA, MARIO (1931-
Canto Latinamericano for Orchestra
E. Diazmuñoz (cnd), Mexico City PO † G. Duran:Nepantla; Lavalle-García:Obertura Colonial; Mabarak:Sym in One Mvt; Moncayo García:Bosques; Sandi:Theme & Vars CLME ▲ 21231 (13.97)

KURKA, ROBERT (1921-1957)
The Good Soldier Schweik (suite) for Orchestra (1956-57)
E. Corporon (cnd), Cincinnati College Conservatory of Music Wind Sym † D. Diamond:Tantivy; J. Druckman:In Memoriam Vincent Persichetti; Paean; D. Wilson:Piece of Mind KLAV ▲ 11051 (18.97)
R. Whitney (cnd), Louisville Orch *(rec 1965)* † Mennin:Con Vc; Piston:Sym 1 ALBA (First Edition Encores) ▲ 44 [AAD] (16.97)

KURTÁG, GYÖRGY (1926-
Doloroso for Flute (1992)
R. Fabbriciani (fl) *(rec July 1995)* ("Music for the Third Millennium") † Ferneyhough:Mnemosyne; Haubenstock-Ramati:Interpolation mobile; M. Kelemen:Fabliau; B. Maderna:Musica su due dimensioni; L. Nono:atmende Klarsein; Sciarrino:Hermes AG ▲ 113 [DDD] (18.97)
Games [Játékok] (8 Volumes) for Piano (or Piano 4-Hands) (1973-96)
P. Frankl (pno)—Stubbunny *(rec London, England)* ("The Hungarian Anthology") † B. Bartók:Dance Suite, Sz.77; E. von Dohnányi:Gavotte & Musette Pno; Kodály:Pieces (7) Pno, Op. 11; Liszt:Csárdás macabre, S.224; Szöllösy:Paessaggio con morti; L. Weiner:Divert 1 Str Orch, Op. 20 ASV ▲ 860 [DDD] (16.97)
Hommage à J. S. B. for Flute & Lyre (or solo Flute)
A. Garzuly (fl) *(rec July 9-11, 1995 & Feb 12-14, 1996)* ("Flute Visions for the 20th Century") † B. Bartók:Hungarian Peasant Songs, Sz.71; L. Berio:Sequenza I; Geszler:Vision; P. Hindemith:Son Fl; Muczynski:Son Fl & Pno, Op. 14 HUN ▲ 31655 [DDD] (16.97)
Hommage à R. Schumann for Clarinet, Viola & Piano, Op. 15d (1990)
V. Mendelssohn (va), M. Lethiec (cl), C. Ivaldi (pno) † Florentz:Ange du Tamaris, Op. 12; G. Ligeti:Trio Hn, Vn & Pno; Pesson:Récréations françaises ARN ▲ 68414 (16.97)
Plane-Dukes-Rahman Trio ASVQ ▲ 6221 (10.97)
Kafka Fragments (40) for Soprano & Violin
A. Komsi (sop), S. Oramo (vn) ODE ▲ 868 (17.97)
Music of Kurtág
various artists—Quasi una fant; Jatekok Pno; Szalkak; Grabstein for Stephan RIOG ▲ 5816 (18.97)
various artists—Einfuhrung zu, Op. 27; Praeludium & Choral Pno; Tamas Blum in Memorian Va; Antifone in fis Pno; Mikroludien, Op. 13/4-6 & 10; Il pleut sur la ville Sop; Lebehohl, Op. 26/4; Les adieux; Double Con; Requiem po drugu, Op. 26; plus other works ("Portrait Concert: Works from 1961-1992") COLG 2-▲ 31870 (36.97)
Quintet for Winds, Op. 2 (1959)
Arnold Quintet † E. Carter:Etudes & Fant; Qnt Ww; Donatoni:Blow; G. Ligeti:Pieces Ww Qnt STRV ▲ 33304 (16.97)
Berlin Philharmonic Wind Quintet *(rec Jan 19-22, 1994)* † G. Ligeti:Bagatelles; Pieces Ww Qnt; Orbán:Qnt Ww; Szervánszky:Qnt 1 Ww BIS ▲ 662 [DDD] (17.97)
Scenes from a Novel (15 songs) for Soprano, Violin, Double Bass & Cimbalom (1981-82)
J. De Gaetani (mez), Speculum Musicae *(rec live New York City, 1987)* ("Jan De Gaetani in Concert") † D. Shostakovich:From Jewish Folk Poetry, Op. 79; Welcher:Abeja Blanca BRID ▲ 9048 [ADD] (17.97)

KURTLEWICZ, ANDRZEJ (1932-
Blow the Wind for Wind Quintet (1987)
Warsaw Wind Quintet ("Da camera") † Bargielski:Butterfly Cage; Malecki:Suite Ww Qnt; P. Moss:Retours; Palester:Trio d'anches; Stachowski:Pezzo grazioso PROV ▲ 182 [DDD] (18.97)

KURTZ, EUGENE (1923-
From Time to Time for Violin & Piano (1986-87)
A. Auviol (vn), B. Fauchet (pno) *(rec Nov 1992)* ("Academy of Arts & Letters:Composers Award Recording") † T. E. Barker:Pieces F Hn; Trikhyálo; M. Gandolfi:Caution to the Wind; Ventaglio di Josephine CRI ▲ 661 [DDD] (17.97)
Logo I for Clarinet, Piano & Percussion Quartet (1979)
R. Nunemaker (cl), D. Nale (pno), Continuum Percussion Quartet † I. Bazelon:Fourscore; J. Cage:Third Construction; L. Harrison:Con Vn; C. Rouse:Ku-Ka-Ilimoku; Verplanck:Petite Suite NWW ▲ 382 [AAD] (16.97)

KUSS, MARGARITA (1921-
Lyric Poem in D for Orchestra [after Tyutchev] (1988)
V. Fedoseyev (cnd), Moscow RSO † Alfvén:Bergakungen (sels); Berwald:Estrella de Soria (ov); J. M. Kraus:Tragedy of Olympus; Lidholm:Kontakion; Sibelius:Finlandia, Op. 26 CSN ▲ 810011 [DDD] (16.97)

KUSSER, JOHANN SIGISMUND (1660-1727)
Overtures for Theater (6) for Orchestra
P. Zajíček (cnd), Musica Aeterna Ensemble *(rec Mar 1993)* K617 ▲ 7032 [DDD] (18.97)

KUTAVICIUS, BRONISLOVAS (1932-
Organ Music
H. Ericsson (org)—Son Ad Patres *(rec Sweden, Mar 1992)* ("Baltic Organ Music") † Čiurlionis:Chorale Fugue on 'Aus tiefer Not schrei ich zu...; Pno Music; Pärt:Annum per annum Org; Süda:Kbd Music; Vasks:Org Music; Zemzaris:Org Music BIS ▲ 561 [DDD] (17.97)

KUULA, TOIVO (1883-1918)
Piano Music
E. Heinonen (pno)—Kolme Satukuvaa (3 Fairy Tale Pictures), Op. 19; Kolme kappaletta (3 Pieces), Op. 3b *(rec Jan 25-26, 1982)* ("Romantic Finnish Piano Music") † O. Merikanto:From the World of Children, Op. 31 BIS ▲ 198 [AAD] (17.97)
Songs (3) for Soprano & Piano
H. Martinpelto (sop), M. Hirvonen (pno) ("Songs from the North") † E. Grieg:Songs (5), Op. 60; Rangström:Songs (3); Sibelius:Songs (5), Op. 37; E. Sjögren:Songs (5) PHA ▲ 292004 [DDD] (13.97)
Trio in A for Piano, Violin & Cello (1908)
Pohjola Trio † A. Merikanto:Preludio Vn; Meriläinen:Opusculum; L. Segerstam:Poem Vn BIS ▲ 56 [AAD] (17.97)

KVANDAL, JOHAN (1919-
Concerto for Violin & Orchestra, Op. 52 (1979)
Ragin (vn), D. Burkh (cnd), Janáček PO *(rec Czech Republic, Dec 1995)* † Söderlind:Con Vn CENT ▲ 2336 [DDD] (16.97)
I. Schuldman (vn), A. Kantorov (cnd), St. Petersburg State SO ("Orchestral Works") † Sinf concertante, Op. 29; Triptychon, Op. 53; Vars & Fugue Orch, Op. 14 NORW ▲ 2929 (17.97)
Hymn Tunes (3) for Woodwind Quintet
Oslo Wind Ensemble *(rec Oslo, Sept 1993)* ("Scandinavian Wind Quintets") † Qnt Ww; Fernström:Qnt Ww; C. Nielsen:Qnt Ww NXIN ▲ 553050 [DDD] (5.97)
Introduction & Allegro for Horn & Piano, Op. 30 (1969)
I. Ølen (hn), G. H. Braaten (pno) *(rec Sweden, 1980-82)* ("The Scandinavian Horn") † Alfvén:Notturno elegiaco, Op. 5; N. V. Bentzon:Son Hn; Heise:Fant Piece 2; K. Jeppesen:Little Trio Fl, Hn & Pno; C. Nielsen:Canto serioso, FS.132; S. Olsen:Aubade BIS ▲ 171 [AAD] (17.97)
Légende for Bassoon & Piano, Op. 61b (1983)
R. Rønnes (bn), E. Knardahl (pno) ("The Contemporary Norwegian Bassoon") † Bibalo:Son Bn; Lerstad:Son 2 Bn, Op. 192; W. Plagge:Son Bn; H. Saeverud:Autumn; Sonstevold:Sonatina Bn SIMX ▲ 1077 [DDD] (18.97)
Music of Kvandal
A. Berntsen (sop), H. Blomstedt (cnd), Oslo PO—Symphonic Epos, Op. 21; Con for Fl & Strs, Op. 22; Qt No. 2 for Strs, Op. 27; Qt for Fl, Vn, Va & Vc, Op. 42; Duo for Vn & Vc, Op. 19; Son for Vn, Op. 45; Da Lontano for A Fl & Pno, Op. 32; Intro & Allegro for Hn & Pno, Op. 30; Aria Cadenza e Finale, Op. 24; Stevtoner, Op. 40 NORW 2-▲ 4986 (34.97)
Quintet for Winds
Oslo Wind Ensemble *(rec Oslo, Sept 1993)* ("Scandinavian Wind Quintets") † Hymn Tunes; Fernström:Qnt Ww; C. Nielsen:Qnt Ww NXIN ▲ 553050 [DDD] (5.97)
Sinfonia concertante for Orchestra, Op. 29 (1968)
A. Kantorov (cnd), St. Petersburg State SO ("Orchestral Works") † Con Vn; Triptychon, Op. 53; Vars & Fugue Orch, Op. 14 NORW ▲ 2929 (17.97)
Sonata for solo Accordion, Op. 71
J. Faukstad (acc) ("Classic Accordion") † Bibalo:Son quasi una fant; E. Grieg:Holberg Suite Pno, Op. 40; W. Plagge:Facsimiles Acc, Op. 66 NORW ▲ 7028 (17.97)
Triptychon for Orchestra, Op. 53 (1979)
A. Kantorov (cnd), St. Petersburg State SO ("Orchestral Works") † Con Vn; Sinf concertante, Op. 29; Vars & Fugue Orch, Op. 14 NORW ▲ 2929 (17.97)
Variations & Fugue for Orchestra, Op. 14 (1954)
A. Kantorov (cnd), St. Petersburg State SO ("Orchestral Works") † Con Vn; Sinf concertante, Op. 29; Triptychon, Op. 53 NORW ▲ 2929 (17.97)

KVERNO, TROND (1945-
Choral Music
C. Hogset (cnd), Grex Vocalis—Corpus Christi Carol; Ave Maris Stella; Missa in Sono Tubae; Stabat Mater Dolorose ("Crux") † E. Grieg:Psalms; Nordheim:Lamentations; Nystedt:O Crux NORW ▲ 9308 (17.97)

KYBURZ, HANSPETER (20th cent)
Cells for Instrumental Ensemble (1993-94)
J. Ernst (sax), Hirsch (cnd) ("New Saxophone Chamber Music") † Mundry:Komposition Sax; Staude:Obduktion; W. Zimmermann:Fragmente der Liebe COLG ▲ 31890 (18.97)

KYMLICKA, MILAN (1936-
Valses (4) for Piano (1984)
A. Kubalek (pno) † P. Tchaikovsky:Saisons DOR ▲ 90102 [DDD] (16.97)

▲ = CD ♦ = Enhanced CD △ = MD ▮ = Cassette Tape ▯ = DCC

KYR, ROBERT (1952-
From the Circling Wheel (3 motets) for 4 Voices [texts Hildegard trans Kyr] (1997)
L. Monahan (cnd) , Tapestry, (mez) *(rec MA, United States of America, May 28-31, 1997)* ("Celestial Light") † Hildegard of Bingen:Sacred Songs TEL ▲ 80456 [DDD] (16.97)
The Passion According to Four Evangelists for 4 Voices, Orchestra & Chorus [text Kyr] (1995)
C. Haber (sop), G. Raymond (mez), W. Hite (ten), D. Murray (bar), B. Taylor (cnd), Back Bay Chorale NALB ▲ 98 (16.97)
Songs of the Shining Wind (6 motets/madrigals & instrumental intermezzo) for Soprano, Countertenor, Lute & Vielle [to translations by Merwin]
Project Ars Nova Ensemble *(rec Newton, MA, Feb 1993)* ("Unseen Rain") † Threefold Vision; Unseen Rain NALB ▲ 75 (16.97)
Threefold Vision (3 motets) for 3 Voices [texts Machaut, Joubert, Rimbaud & Bingen]
Project Ars Nova Ensemble *(rec South Hadley, MA, Aug 1993)* ("Unseen Rain") † Songs of the Shining Wind; Unseen Rain NALB ▲ 75 (16.97)
Unseen Rain for Soprano, Countertenor, Tenor, Chorus & Instruments [text Rumi]
B. Taylor (cnd), Project Ars Nova Ensemble, Project Ars Nova Ensemble, Back Bay Chorale *(rec Boston, MA, Feb 1993)* ("Unseen Rain") † Songs of the Shining Wind; Threefold Vision NALB ▲ 75 (16.97)
White Tigers for Piano
P. Goodson (pno) ("Strange Attractors: New American Music for Piano") † J. Harbison:Occasional Pieces; M. Herman:Arena; S. Jaffe:Impromptu; A. R. Thomas:Whites; R. Woolf:Nobody Move ALBA ▲ 231 [DDD] (16.97)

LA BARRE, MICHEL DE (ca1743 or 1744)
Sonata in B♭ for 2 Flutes
N. Hadden (fl), E. Walker (fl), E. Headley (va da gamba), L. Carolan (hpd) † Suite 13 Flute; Suite 2 Flute; Suite 4 Flute; Suite 6 Flute ASV ▲ 181 (16.97)
Suite No. 2 for Flute
N. Hadden (fl), E. Headley (va da gamba), L. Carolan (hpd) † Son Fls; Suite 13 Flute; Suite 4 Flute; Suite 6 Flute ASV ▲ 181 (16.97)
Suite No. 4 for Flute
N. Hadden (fl), E. Headley (va da gamba), L. Carolan (hpd) † Son Fls; Suite 13 Flute; Suite 2 Flute; Suite 6 Flute ASV ▲ 181 (16.97)
Suite No. 6 for Flute
N. Hadden (fl), E. Headley (va da gamba), L. Carolan (hpd) † Son Fls; Suite 13 Flute; Suite 2 Flute; Suite 4 Flute ASV ▲ 181 (16.97)
Suite No. 13 for Flute
N. Hadden (fl), E. Headley (va da gamba), L. Carolan (hpd) † Son Fls; Suite 2 Flute; Suite 4 Flute; Suite 6 Flute ASV ▲ 181 (16.97)

LABANCHI, GAETANO (1829-1874)
Fantasia on Verdi's Aida for Clarinet & Piano
B. Röthlisberger (cl), S. Andres (pno) ("Il Clarinetto all'Opera") † L. Bassi:Divertimento on themes from Donizetti's La F; Cavallini:Adagio sentimentale; Fant on Motifs; Lovreglio:Fant da concerto on Motifs of Verdi's La tra; G. Panizza:Ballabile; Spadina:Duetto GALL ▲ 916 [DDD] (18.97)

LABARRE, THEODORE (-FRANÇOIS-JOSEPH) (1805-1870)
Duo No. 1 for Bassoon & Harp
L. Loubry (bn), R. Talitman (hp) ("The Golden Age of Harp & French Bassoon") † Boieldieu:Solo Bn & Hp; Dauprat:Son Hn & Pno, Op. 2; Debussy:Romance Bn & Hp; Naderman:Nocturne I; Nocturne II; Saint-Saëns:Romance Vc, Op. 51 DI ▲ 920193 [DDD] (5.97)

LABITZKY, AUGUST (1832-1903)
Ouverture characteristique [The Hunt of Emperor Charles IV] for Orchestra
D. Bostock (cnd), Carlsbad SO *(rec Karlovy Vary, Czech Republic, Jan 1996)* † A. Dvořák:Romance Vn, Op. 11; Fibich:Idyll; Fučík:Alte Brummbär, Op. 210; Marinarella, Op. 215; J. Labitzky:Carlsbad Waltz; Nedbal:Valse triste CLSO ▲ 150 (15.97)

LABITZKY, JOSEF (1802-1881)
Carlsbad Waltz for Orchestra
D. Bostock (cnd), Carlsbad SO *(rec Karlovy Vary, Czech Republic, Jan 1996)* † A. Dvořák:Romance Vn, Op. 11; Fibich:Idyll; Fučík:Alte Brummbär, Op. 210; Marinarella, Op. 215; A. Labitzky:Ouverture characteristique; Nedbal:Valse triste CLSO ▲ 150 (15.97)

LACHENMANN, HELMUT (1935-
Allegro sostenuto for Piano, Clarinet & Cello (1986-88)
M. Bach (vc), D. Smeyers (cl), B. Wambach (pno) † Dal niente; Kinderspiel; Pression CPO ▲ 999102 [DDD] (14.97)
Dal niente [Interieur III] for Clarinet (1970)
D. Smeyers (cl) † Allegro sostenuto; Kinderspiel; Pression CPO ▲ 999102 [DDD] (14.97)
Harmonica for Tuba & Orch (1981-1983)
R. Nahatzki (tuba), H. Zender (cnd), Saarbrücken RSO ("Hans Zender Edition, Vol. 12") † P. Boulez:Rituel; Riehm:Gewidmet CPO ▲ 999484 (6.97)
Ein Kinderspiel (7 short pieces) for Piano (1981)
B. Wambach (pno) † Allegro sostenuto; Dal niente; Pression CPO ▲ 999102 [DDD] (14.97)
Pression for solo Cello (1969)
M. Bach (vc) † Allegro sostenuto; Dal niente; Kinderspiel CPO ▲ 999102 [DDD] (14.97)
Reigen seliger Geister for String Quartet
Arditti String Quartet † Tanzsuite mit Deutschlandlied DISQ ▲ 782019 (18.97)
Tanzsuite mit Deutschlandlied for String Quartet & Orchestra (1979-80)
O. Henzold (cnd), Berlin RSO † Reigen seliger Geister DISQ ▲ 782019 (18.97)

LACHNER, FRANZ PAUL (1803-1890)
Ball-Suite in D for Orchestra, Op. 170
A. Walter (cnd), Slovak State PO Košice *(rec House of Arts Košice, Sept 3-4, 1993)* † Sym 8 MARC ▲ 8223594 [DDD] (13.97)
Nonet in F for Flute, Oboe, Clarinet, Horn, Bassoon, Violin, Viola, Cello & Double Bass (1875)
Consortium Classicum † Spt Winds & Strs ORF ▲ 382951 (18.97)
I. Grünkorn (vn), M. Gieler (va), T. Ruge (vc), F. Heidenreich (db), A. Duisberg (fl), D. Wollenweber (ob), P. Prieditis (cl), M. Postinghel (bn), P. Douglas (hn) *(rec June 10, 1991)* † Qnt 2 Pno, Op. 145 THOR ▲ 2132 [DDD] (17.97)
Quartet No. 5 in G for Strings, Op. 169 (1849)
Rodin String Quartet ("String Quartets, Vol. 1") † Qt 6 Strs, Op. 173 AMAT ▲ 9601 [DDD] (17.97)
Quartet No. 6 in e for Strings, Op. 173 (1850)
Rodin String Quartet ("String Quartets, Vol. 1") † Qt 5 Strs, Op. 169 AMAT ▲ 9601 [DDD] (17.97)
Quintet No. 2 in c for Piano & Strings, Op. 145 (1869)
O. Duliba (vn), T. Jahnel (vn), S. Clark (va), S. Dörfler (vc), H. Göbel (pno) *(rec June 10, 1991)* † Nonet THOR ▲ 2132 [DDD] (17.97)
Septet in E♭ for Winds & Strings (1824; completed by Franz Beyer)
Consortium Classicum † Nonet ORF ▲ 382951 (18.97)
Symphony No. 1 in E♭, Op. 32 (1828)
C. Hoey (cnd), Singapore SO † L. Spohr:Sym 2 MARC ▲ 8220360 [DDD] (13.97)
Symphony No. 5 in c, Op. 52, "Preis Symphonie" (1835)
P. Robinson (cnd), Slovak State PO Košice *(rec Oct 16-18, 1992)* MARC ▲ 8223502 [DDD] (13.97)
Symphony No. 8 in g, Op. 100
P. Robinson (cnd), Slovak State PO Košice *(rec House of Arts Košice, Oct 18-20, 1992)* † Ball-Suite, Op. 170 MARC ▲ 8223594 [DDD] (13.97)

LACHNER, IGNAZ (1807-1895)
Quartets (7) for Strings [2 for 3 Violins & Viola; 1 for 4 Violins]
Rodin String Quartet ("String Quartets, Vol. 1") AMAT ▲ 9503 [DDD] (17.97)
Rodin String Quartet ("String Quartets, Vol. 2") AMAT ▲ 9504 (17.97)
Rodin String Quartet—in C, Op. 54; in G, Op. 104 ("String Quartets, Vol. 3") AMAT ▲ 9704 (17.97)
Trios (6) for Violin, Viola and Piano
S. Muhmenthaler (vn), A. B. Dutschler (va), M. Pantillon (pno) CLAV ▲ 509802 (27.97)

LACOUR, GUY (1932-
Quartet for Saxophones (1969)
Alexandre Saxophone Quartet ("Réminiscence") † A. Desenclos:Quatuor; Glazunov:Qt Saxes, Op. 109; Pilon:Transparences SNE ▲ 566 (16.97)

LADERMAN, EZRA (1924-
Concerto for Double Orchestra (1989)
H. Wolff (cnd), New Jersey SO *(rec Aug 1990)* † J. Harbison:Con Va NWW ▲ 80404 [DDD] (16.97)

LADERMAN, EZRA (cont.)
Concerto for Orchestra (1968)
S. Comissiona (cnd), Baltimore SO † B. Britten:Diversions, Op. 21 PHOE ▲ 122 [ADD] (15.97)
Epigrams & Canons for 2 Baroque Flutes (1989)
(rec Vassar College Poughkeepsie, NY, Mar 24-26, 1994) ("Autumn Rhythms") † J. Beeson:Fant, Ditty & Fughettas; L. Kraft:Cloud Studies; Kupferman:Abstractions; Luening:Fantasias Baroque Fl; L. Nowak:Suite Fl CRI ▲ 712 [DDD] (16.97)
June 29th for Flute (1983)
Members of the New York Flute Club ("A Tribute to Otto Luening") † Goeb:Divertimenti; Heiss:Etudes Fl; U. Kay:Suite Fl & Ob; Luening:Canons; Canons 2 Fls; Suite 2 Fl; Trio Fls; Trio 3 Fls; H. Sollberger:Killapata/Chaskapata Fl & Fl Ch CRI ▲ 561 [DDD] (16.97)
Pentimento for Orchestra (1985)
J. Hegyi (cnd), Albany SO † L. Trimble:Sym 3 CRI ▲ 555 [DDD] (17.97)
Quartet No. 7 for Strings (1983)
Colorado String Quartet † K. Husa:Qt 4 Strs; M. Powell:Qt Strs ALBA ▲ 259 [DDD] (16.97)

LADMIRAULT, PAUL (1877-1944)
Piano Music
L. Thirion (pno)—4 Pièces Pno; Mémories d'un Ane; 2 Danses Bretonnes; Hommage à Fauré; Carillon; 4 Esquisses *(rec Sept 1995)* ("Complete Works for Piano") SKAR ▲ 1962 [DDD] (18.97)
Sonata for Cello & Piano (1939)
Y. Chiffoleau (vc), R. Plantard (pno) *(rec Radio-France Paris, 1980)* ("Intégrale des Sonates") † Son Cl; Son Vn SKAR ▲ 4952 [ADD] (19.97)
Sonata for Clarinet & Piano (1942)
M. Edwards (cl), T. Bach (pno) *(rec Pomona College Claremont, CA, 1997)* † Bjelinski:Son Cl; Martinů:Sonatina Cl; Rabaud:Solo de Concours, Op. 10; Saint-Saëns:Son Cl CRYS ▲ 735 (15.97)
J. Lancelot (cl), R. Plantard (pno) *(rec Nantes National Conservatory Auditorium, 1980)* ("Intégrale des Sonates") † Son Vc; Son Vn SKAR ▲ 4952 [ADD] (19.97)
Sonata for Violin & Piano (1931)
R. Daugareil (vn), R. Plantard (pno) *(rec Nantes National Conservatory Auditorium, 1980)* ("Intégrale des Sonates") † Son Cl; Son Vc SKAR ▲ 4952 [ADD] (19.97)

LAHUSEN, CHRISTIAN (1886-1975)
Heimkehr im Abend (4-part cycle) for Chorus (1932-39)
K. Reiners (cnd), Birnauer Kantorei *(rec 1989)* DVX ▲ 19003 (16.97)
Music of Lahusen
F. Burgert (pno), U. Kern (org) ("Portrait of a Composer") DVX ▲ 25225 (16.97)

LAJTHA, LASZLO (1892-1963)
Berceuses (3) for Piano (1955-7)
K. Körmendi (pno) *(rec Feb 2-6, 1992)* † Écrits d'un musicien, Op. 1; Contes, Op. 2; Prélude Pno; Scherzo et toccata, Op. 14 MARC ▲ 8223473 (13.97)
Capriccio (ballet in 1 act) for Orchestra, Op. 39 (1944)
N. Pasquet (cnd), Pécs SO *(rec Pécs Hungary, May 1994)* ("Orchestral Works, Vol. 2") MARC ▲ 8223668 [DDD] (13.97)
Contes for Piano, Op. 2 (1915)
K. Körmendi (pno) *(rec Feb 2-6, 1992)* † Écrits d'un musicien, Op. 1; Berceuses; Prélude Pno; Scherzo et toccata, Op. 14 MARC ▲ 8223473 (13.97)
Des Écrits d'un musicien for Piano, Op. 1 (1913)
K. Körmendi (pno) *(rec Feb 2-6, 1992)* † Berceuses; Contes, Op. 2; Prélude Pno; Scherzo et toccata, Op. 14 MARC ▲ 8223473 (13.97)
Hymns for the Holy Virgin (3) for Female Voices & Organ, Op. 65 (1958)
M. Szabó (cnd) , Liszt Academy Chamber Chorus, Györ Girls' Choir [L,F] † Madrigals; Magnificat, Op. 60; Qt 10 Strs, Op. 58 HUN ▲ 31453 [ADD] (16.97)
Madrigals (4) for Chorus
M. Szabó (cnd) , Liszt Academy Chamber Chorus, Györ Girls' Choir [L,F] † Hymns for the Holy Virgin, Op. 65; Magnificat, Op. 60; Qt 10 Strs, Op. 58 HUN ▲ 31453 [ADD] (16.97)
Magnificat for Female Voices & Organ, Op. 60 (1954)
M. Szabó (cnd) , Liszt Academy Chamber Chorus, Györ Girls' Choir [L,F] † Hymns for the Holy Virgin, Op. 65; Madrigals; Qt 10 Strs, Op. 58 HUN ▲ 31453 [ADD] (16.97)
Missa in tono phrygio for Chorus & Orchestra, Op. 50 (1950)
K. Záborszky (cnd), Szent István Király SO, Szent István Király Oratorio Chorus *(rec Matthias Church, Budapest, Hungary)* † G. Ránki:Lament of Jesus; L. Weiner:Romance, Op. 29 HUN ▲ 31833 [ADD] (16.97)
Marionettes for Harp, Flute & String Trio, Op. 26 (1937)
I. Matuz (fl), J. Szilvásy (hp), T. Rónaszegi (vn), E. Ludmány (va), K. Vas (vc) *(rec Hungary, 1997-98)* † Nocturnes (3), Op. 34; Qnt 2 Hp, Op. 46 HUN ▲ 31776 [DDD] (16.97)
Nocturnes (3) for Soprano, Harp, Flute & String Quartet [texts Maupassant & Hugo], Op. 34 (1941)
I. Iván (sop), P. Sárosi (vn), T. Rónaszegi (vn), E. Ludmány (va), K. Vas (vc), I. Matuz (fl), J. Szilvásy (hp), G. Matuz (cnd) *(rec Hungary, 1997-98)* † Marionettes, Op. 26; Qnt 2 Hp, Op. 46 HUN ▲ 31776 [DDD] (16.97)
Pièces (2) for solo Flute, Op. 69 (1958)
I. Matuz (fl) *(rec Jan 1996)* ("Chamber Music with Flute, Vol. 1") † Son en Concert Fl, Op. 64; Trio 1 Fl, Op. 22; Trio 2 Fl, Op. 47 HUN ▲ 31647 [DDD] (16.97)
Prélude for Piano (1918)
K. Körmendi (pno) *(rec Feb 2-6, 1992)* † Écrits d'un musicien, Op. 1; Berceuses; Contes, Op. 2; Scherzo et toccata, Op. 14 MARC ▲ 8223473 (13.97)
Quartet No. 10 for Strings, Op. 58, "Suite transylvaine" (1953)
Tátrai String Quartet [L,F] † Hymns for the Holy Virgin, Op. 65; Madrigals; Magnificat, Op. 60 HUN ▲ 31453 [ADD] (16.97)
Quintet No. 2 for Harp, Flute & String Trio, Op. 46 (1947-48)
I. Matuz (fl), J. Szilvásy (hp), T. Rónaszegi (vn), E. Ludmány (va), K. Vas (vc) *(rec Hungary, 1997-98)* † Marionettes, Op. 26; Nocturnes (3), Op. 34 HUN ▲ 31776 [DDD] (16.97)
Scherzo et toccata for Piano, Op. 14 (1930)
K. Körmendi (pno) *(rec Feb 2-6, 1992)* † Écrits d'un musicien, Op. 1; Berceuses; Contes, Op. 2; Prélude Pno MARC ▲ 8223473 (13.97)
Sinfonietta for String Orchestra, Op. 43 (1946)
V. Tátrai (cnd), Hungarian CO † Sym 4; Sym 9 HUN ▲ 31452 [ADD] (16.97)
Sonate en Concert for Flute & Piano, Op. 64 (1958)
I. Matuz (fl), J. Jandó (pno) *(rec Jan 1996)* ("Chamber Music with Flute, Vol. 1") † Pièces Fl, Op. 69; Trio 1 Fl, Op. 22; Trio 2 Fl, Op. 47 HUN ▲ 31647 [DDD] (16.97)
Sonatina for Violin & Piano, Op. 13 (1930)
G. Takács-Nagy (vn), D. Várjon (pno) ("Original Works & Historical Trio Arrangements") † Trio Pno, Op. 10; Liszt:Hungarian Rhaps, S.244; Orpheus, S.98; Tristia, S.723 HUN ▲ 31815 [DDD] (16.97)
Suite du ballet No. 2 for Orchestra [from the Ballet *Le bosquet des quatre dieux*], Op. 38a (1943)
N. Pasquet (cnd), Pécs SO *(rec Liszt Concert Hall Pécs, Sept 1995)* ("Orchestral Works, Vol. 5") † Sym 3; Sym 4 MARC ▲ 8223671 [DDD] (13.97)
Symphony No. 3, Op. 45 (1948)
N. Pasquet (cnd), Pécs SO *(rec Liszt Concert Hall Pécs, Sept 1995)* ("Orchestral Works, Vol. 5") † Suite 2; Sym 4 MARC ▲ 8223671 [DDD] (13.97)
Symphony No. 4, Op. 52, "Springtime" (1951)
J. Ferencsik (cnd), Hungarian State Orch † Sinfonietta, Op. 43; Sym 9 HUN ▲ 31452 [ADD] (16.97)
N. Pasquet (cnd), Pécs SO *(rec Liszt Concert Hall Pécs, Sept 1995)* ("Orchestral Works, Vol. 5") † Suite 2; Sym 3 MARC ▲ 8223671 [DDD] (13.97)
Symphony No. 9, Op. 67 (1963)
J. Ferencsik (cnd), Hungarian State Orch † Sinfonietta, Op. 43; Sym 4 HUN ▲ 31452 [ADD] (16.97)
Trio No. 1 for Flute, Cello & Harp, Op. 22 (1935)
K. Vas (vc), I. Matuz (fl), J. Szilvásy (hp) *(rec Jan 1996)* ("Chamber Music with Flute, Vol. 1") † Pièces Fl, Op. 69; Son en Concert Fl, Op. 64; Trio 2 Fl, Op. 47 HUN ▲ 31647 [DDD] (16.97)
Trio No. 2 for Flute, Cello & Harp, Op. 47 (1949)
K. Vas (vc), I. Matuz (fl), J. Szilvásy (hp) *(rec Jan 1996)* ("Chamber Music with Flute, Vol. 1") † Pièces Fl, Op. 69; Son en Concert Fl, Op. 64; Trio 1 Fl, Op. 22 HUN ▲ 31647 [DDD] (16.97)
Trio for Piano, Violin & Cello, Op. 10 (1928)
Takács Piano Trio ("Original Works & Historical Trio Arrangements") † Sonatina Vn, Op. 13; Liszt:Hungarian Rhaps, S.244; Orpheus, S.98; Tristia, S.723 HUN ▲ 31815 [DDD] (16.97)

LAKS, SZYMON (1901-1983)
Passacaille for Cello & Piano (1946)
S. Honigberg (vc), C. Honigberg (pno) ("Darkness & Light, Vol. 2") † Ben-Haim (Frankenburger):Pieces Vc; Castelnuovo-Tedesco:Trio 2 Pno, Op. 70; D. Diamond:Qt 1 Strs; Koffler:Son Pno, Op. 12; Messiaen:Quatuor ALBA ▲ 229 [DDD] (16.97)

LALANDE, MICHEL-RICHARD DE (1657-1726)
L'amour, fléchy par la constance (selections)
H. Crook (ten), S. Kuijken (cnd), La Petite Bande ("Concert de danse") † M.-A. Charpentier:Médée (sels); Lully:Acis et Galatée (sels); Armide (sels); Rameau:Music of Rameau; Rebel:Fantaisie; Plaisirs champêtres ACCE ▲ 96122 [DDD] (17.97)
Cantate Dominoquia mirabilia for Orchestra & Chorus (1707)
Ex Cathedra Choir † De profundis; Regina coeli ASV (Gaudeamus) ▲ 141 [DDD] (16.97)
De profundis (motet) for solo Voices, Orchestra & Chorus (1689)
A. Deller (ct), A. Deller (cnd), Vienna State Opera CO, Deller Consort, Vienna Chamber Choir *(rec Baumgartner Hall Vienna, June 1962)* † Blow:Ode on the Death of Mr. Henry Purcell VC (Alfred Deller Edition) ▲ 8108 [ADD] (13.97)
Ex Cathedra Choir † Cant Dominoquia mirabilia; Regina coeli ASV (Gaudeamus) ▲ 141 [DDD] (16.97)
Miserere for solo Voices, Orchestra & Chorus, S.120
W. Christie (cnd), Les Arts Florissants † Motets HAM (Suite) ▲ 7901416 (12.97)
Motets
W. Christie (cnd), Les Arts Florissants † Miserere, S.120 HAM (Suite) ▲ 7901416 (12.97)
Regina coeli for Orchestra & Chorus (1698)
Ex Cathedra Choir † Cant Dominoquia mirabilia; De profundis ASV (Gaudeamus) ▲ 141 [DDD] (16.97)
Symphonies pour les soupers du roi (complete)
H. Reyne (cnd), Marais SO HAM 4-▲ 901337 (69.97)
Symphonies pour les soupers du roi (selections)
H. Reyne (cnd), Marais SO HAM ▲ 901303 (18.97)

LALO, ÉDOUARD (1823-1892)
Arlequin (esquisse-caractéristique) for Violin (or Cello) & Piano (or Orchestra) (ca 1848)
L. Graham (cnd), American Promenade Orch ("Premiere Evening") † Busoni:Lustspiel Ov, K. 245; O. Nicolai:Lustigen Weiber von Windsor (ov); G. B. Viotti:Con 22 Vn, G.97; C. M. von Weber:Drei Pintos (sels) KLAV ▲ 11053 [DDD] (18.97)
Aubades (2) for 10 Instruments (or small Orchestra) [from Fiesque] (1872)
D. Swift (cnd), CBC Vancouver SO ("Parisian Ballets") † D. Milhaud:Rag-Caprices, Op. 78; Ropartz:Serenade Strs; Sauguet:Cigale et la fourmi; Forains; Nuit SMS ▲ 5152 [DDD] (16.97)
Concerto in d for Cello & Orchestra (1877)
E. Bertrand (vc), S. Denève (cnd), Monte Carlo PO † Namouna (suites 1 & 2); R. Schumann:Con Vc ARN ▲ 68458 (16.97)
P. Fournier (vc), J. Martinon (cnd), Lamoureux Orch ("Bizet-Lalo") † Namouna; Rapsodie norvégienne; Bizet:Jeux d'enfants; Jolie fille de Perth (suite); Sym DEUT (Double) 2-▲ 37371 (17.97)
O. Harnoy (vc), A. De Almeida (cnd), Bournemouth SO *(rec Dorset England, May 11-12, 1995)* † J. Offenbach:Andante Vc; Con militaire Vc RCAV (Red Seal) ▲ 68420 [DDD] (16.97)
Y.-Y. Ma (vc), L. Maazel (cnd), French National Orch † Saint-Saëns:Con 1 Vc, Op. 33 SNYC ▲ 35848 [DDD] (16.97)
M. Maréchal (vc) *(rec 1929-43)* ("Maurice Maréchal, Book 2") † Debussy:Son Vc; Honegger:Con Vc ENT (Strings) ▲ 99316 (16.97)
A. Navarra (vc), A. Balsam (pno) ("Navarra, Vol. 3") † Beethoven:Son 3 Vc, Op. 69; Mainguenea:Pieces Vc & Pno; F. Schubert:Son Arpeggione, D.821 LYS ▲ 448
S. Rolland (vc), G. Varga (cnd), BBC PO † Massenet:Fant Vc & Orc; Saint-Saëns:Con 1 Vc, Op. 33 ASV ▲ 867 [DDD] (16.97)
L. Rose (vc), E. Ormandy (cnd), Philadelphia Orch *(rec 1967)* † E. Bloch:Schelomo; G. Fauré:Élégie, Op. 24; P. Tchaikovsky:Vars on a Rococo Theme, Op. 33 SNYC (Essential Classics) ▲ 48278 [ADD] (7.97) ▮ 48278 [ADD] (3.98)
J. Starker (vc), S. Skrowaczewski (cnd), London SO † Saint-Saëns:Con 1 Vc, Op. 33; R. Schumann:Con Vc MRCR ▲ 32010 [ADD] (11.97)
Concerto in f for Piano & Orchestra (1888-89)
D. Gross (pno), N. Athinäos (cnd), Frankfurt on the Oder State Orch † Romance-sérénade; Scherzo; Sym in g SIGM ▲ 6600 [DDD] (17.97)
Concerto russe for Violin & Orchestra, Op. 29 (1879)
H. Merckel (vn), P. Coppola (cnd), Pasdeloup Concerts Association Orch *(rec 1930-35)* ("Coppola, Vol. 7") † Divert Orch; Namouna (suites 1 & 2); Roi d'Ys (sels); Sym espagnole, Op. 21; G. Fauré:Berceuse, Op. 16 LYS1 ▲ 458 (17.97)
R. Ricci (vn), J. Singer (cnd), Orch of the Americas † Con Vn; Fant norvégienne; Guitare, Op. 28 ONEL ▲ 95040 [DDD]
Concerto in F for Violin & Orchestra, Op. 20 (1873)
R. Ricci (vn), J. Singer (cnd), Orch of the Americas † Con russe, Op. 29; Fant norvégienne; Guitare, Op. 28 ONEL ▲ 95040 [DDD]
Divertissement for Orchestra (1872)
G. Andretta (cnd), Basel SO † Rapsodie norvégienne; Scherzo; Sym in g CPO ▲ 999296 [DDD] (14.97)
D. Bostock (cnd), Bohemian Chamber PO ("French Orchestral Miniatures, Vol. 1") † Bizet:Docteur Miracle (ov); Chabrier:Habanera; Delibes:Roi s'amuse; C. Franck:Organiste Vol I, M.41; Saint-Saëns:Suite Orch, Op. 49 CLSO ▲ 158 [DDD] (15.97)
P. Coppola (cnd), Pasdeloup Concerts Association Orch *(rec 1930-35)* ("Coppola, Vol. 7") † Con russe, Op. 29; Namouna (suites 1 & 2); Roi d'Ys (sels); Sym espagnole, Op. 21; G. Fauré:Berceuse, Op. 16 LYS1 ▲ 458 (17.97)
Fantaisie norvégienne for Violin & Orchestra (1878)
R. Ricci (vn), J. Singer (cnd), Orch of the Americas † Con russe, Op. 29; Con Vn; Guitare, Op. 28 ONEL ▲ 95040 [DDD]
Guitare for Violin & Piano, Op. 28 (1882)
R. Ricci (vn), T. Woytowicz (cnd), Zagreb PO † Con russe, Op. 29; Con Vn; Fant norvégienne ONEL ▲ 95040 [DDD]
Namouna (ballet in 2 acts) for Orchestra (1881-82)
J. Martinon (cnd), ORTF Orch ("Bizet-Lalo") † Con Vc; Rapsodie norvégienne; Bizet:Jeux d'enfants; Jolie fille de Perth (suite); Sym DEUT (Double) 2-▲ 37371 (17.97)
D. Robertson (cnd), Monte Carlo PO VAL ▲ 4677 (18.97)
Namouna:Suites 1 & 2
E. Bertrand (vc), S. Denève (cnd), Monte Carlo PO—Suite 1 [sel] † Con Vc; R. Schumann:Con Vc ARN ▲ 68458 (16.97)
Y. Butt (cnd), Royal PO † Gounod:Mors et vita ASV ▲ 878 [DDD] (16.97)
P. Coppola (cnd), Pasdeloup Concerts Association Orch *(rec 1930-35)* ("Coppola, Vol. 7") † Con russe, Op. 29; Divert Orch; Roi d'Ys (sels); Sym espagnole, Op. 21; G. Fauré:Berceuse, Op. 16 LYS1 ▲ 458 (17.97)
P. Paray (cnd), Detroit SO † Roi d'Ys (sels); H. Barraud:Offrande à une ombre; E. Chausson:Sym in B♭, Op. 20 PPHI ▲ 434389 (11.97)
Quartet in E♭ for Strings, Op. 45 [revision of Op. 19] (1880)
Daniel String Quartet † Gounod:Qt 3 Strs; A. Thomas:Qt Strs, Op. 1 DI ▲ 920159 [DDD] (5.97)
Rapsodie norvégienne for Orchestra (1879)
G. Andretta (cnd), Basel SO † Divert Orch; Scherzo; Sym in g CPO ▲ 999296 [DDD] (14.97)
R. Benzi (cnd), Bordeaux-Aquitaine National Orch *(rec Feb 1987)* † Roi d'Ys (sels); Bizet:Roma FORL ▲ 16564 [DDD] (16.97)
H. Gmür (cnd), Nürnberg SO ("Music for Meditation, Vol. 3") † J. Brahms:Sym 2; Debussy:Syrinx Fl; Valse romantique Pno; M. Reger:Con Vn; Rimsky-Korsakov:Scheherazade, Op. 35; I. Stravinsky:Firebird (sels) ECL ▲ 507 (2.97)
J. Martinon (cnd), ORTF Orch ("Bizet-Lalo") † Con Vc; Namouna; Bizet:Jeux d'enfants; Jolie fille de Perth (suite); Sym DEUT (Double) 2-▲ 37371 (17.97)
Le Roi d'Ys (selections)
R. Benzi (cnd), Bordeaux-Aquitaine National Orch *(rec Feb 1987)* † Rapsodie norvégienne; Bizet:Roma FORL ▲ 16564 [DDD] (16.97)
P. Coppola (cnd), Pasdeloup Concerts Association Orch *(rec 1930-35)* ("Coppola, Vol. 7") † Con russe, Op. 29; Divert Orch; Namouna (suites 1 & 2); Sym espagnole, Op. 21; G. Fauré:Berceuse, Op. 16 LYS1 ▲ 458 (17.97)
P. Monteux (cnd), San Francisco SO † Ibert:Escales; M. Ravel:Alborada del gracioso; Daphnis et Chloé (suite 1); Valse; Valses nobles RCAV (Gold Seal) ▲ 61895 (11.97)

LALO, ÉDOUARD (cont.)
Le Roi d'Ys (selections) (cont.)
N. Nozy (cnd), Belgian Guides Symphonic Band *(rec Steurbaut Sound Recording Ctr)* ("Festive Overtures") † Berlioz:Carnaval romain, Op. 9; Mendelssohn (-Bartholdy):Ruy Blas, Op. 95; G. Rossini:Gazza ladra (ov); D. Shostakovich:Festive Ov, Op. 96; Verdi:Vespri siciliani (ov); R. Wagner:Tannhäuser (ov) RENE ▲ 87105 [DDD] (16.97)
P. Paray (cnd), Detroit SO † Namouna (suites 1 & 2); H. Barraud:Offrande à une ombre; E. Chausson:Sym in B♭, Op. 20 PPHI ▲ 434389 (11.97)
P. Parkes (cnd), Black Dyke Mills Band [arr F. Wright] *(rec England, Mar 11, 1979)* ("Kings of Brass") † Borodin:Sym 2; D. Bourgeois:Serenade; R. Drigo:Serenata; Liszt:Hungarian Rhaps, S.244; Staigers:Carnival of Venice; R. Strauss:Con 1 Hn, Op. 11 *([ENG] text)* CHN ▲ 4517 [ADD] (16.97)
Romance-sérénade for Violin & Orchestra (1879)
J. Toschmakow (vn), N. Athinäos (cnd), Frankfurt on the Oder State Orch † Con Pno; Scherzo; Sym in g SIGM ▲ 6600 [DDD] (17.97)
Scherzo for Orchestra [from Trio No. 3 in a for Piano, Op. 26, 1880] (orchd 1884)
G. Andretta (cnd), Basel SO † Divert Orch; Rapsodie norvégienne; Sym in g CPO ▲ 999296 [DDD] (14.97)
N. Athinäos (cnd), Frankfurt on the Oder State Orch † Con Pno; Romance-sérénade; Sym in g SIGM ▲ 6600 [DDD] (17.97)
Sonata in a for Cello & Piano (1856)
M. Gendron (vc), K. Toyama (pno) *(rec Honjo Bunka-kaikan, Sept 1985)* ("Lalo & Chopin: Cello Sonatas") † Chopin:Grand Duo; Intro & Polonaise, Op. 3; Son Vc CAMA ▲ 366 (18.97)
Songs
T. Zylis-Gara (sop), C. Ivaldi (pno)—5 Lieder (1879); 6 mélodies [after V. Hugo], Op. 17 (1856); 3 mélodies [after A. de Musset] (?ca 1870); 3 mélodies (1887); Si j'étais petit oiseau; La pauvre femme [both from 6 romances populaires]; Chant breton; Aubade; Humoresque; Marine; Ballade à la lune; Le rouge-gorge *(rec Paris, Mar 18-19, 1987)* ("Mélodies") PHO ▲ 904 [DDD] (17.97)
Symphonie espagnole for Violin & Orchestra, Op. 21 (1874)
M. Bisengaliev (vn), J. Wildner (cnd), Polish National RSO Katowice *(rec Jan 31-Feb 3, 1992)* † M. Ravel:Tzigane; Saint-Saëns:Havanaise, Op. 83; Sarasate:Zigeunerweisen, Op. 20 NXIN ▲ 550494 [DDD] (5.97)
S. Chang (vn), C. Dutoit (cnd), (Royal) Concertgebouw Orch *(rec Concertgebouw Amsterdam, Jan 4-8, 1995)* † H. Vieuxtemps:Con 5 Vn, Op. 37 EMIC ▲ 55292 [DDD] (16.97)
Chee-Yun (vn), J. López-Cobos (cnd), London PO *(rec London, May 1996)* † Saint-Saëns:Con 3 Vn, Op. 61 DNN ▲ 18017 [DDD] (16.97)
P. Coppola (cnd), Pasdeloup Concerts Association Orch *(rec 1930-35)* ("Coppola, Vol. 7") † Con russe, Op. 29; Divert Orch; Namouna (suites 1 & 2); Roi d'Ys (sels); G. Fauré:Berceuse, Op. 16 LYS1 ▲ 458 (17.97)
R. Daugareil (vn), A. Lombard (cnd), Bordeaux-Aquitaine National Orch † E. Chausson:Poème Vn, Op. 25 FORL ▲ 16723 [DDD] (16.97)
M. Elman (vn), V. Golschmann (cnd), Vienna State Opera Orch *(rec 1959)* † Mendelssohn (-Bartholdy):Con Vn & Orch, Op. 64 VC ▲ 8034 [ADD] (13.97)
I. Haendel (vn), K. Ančerl (cnd), Czech PO † W. A. Mozart:Con 3 Vn, K.216; M. Ravel:Tzigane SUR (Czech Philharmonic) ▲ 111936 [AAD]
J. Heifetz (vn), D. Vorhees (cnd), Bell Telephone Hour Orch [movts 1 & 2] *(rec June 21, 1948)* ("Jascha Heifetz Collection, Vol. 3") † J. Brahms:Con Vn; Hungarian Dances Orch; Saint-Saëns:Havanaise, Op. 83 DHR (Legendary Treasures) ▲ 7717 (16.97)
B. Hubermann (vn) † J. S. Bach:Con 2 Vn; P. Tchaikovsky:Con Vn ENT (Strings) ▲ 99369 (16.97)
B. Huberman (vn), G. Szell (cnd), Vienna PO *(rec June 20 & 22, 1934)* ("Bronislaw Huberman: The 1934 Szell/Vienna Philharmonic Recordings") † Beethoven:Con Vn APR (Signature) ▲ 5506 [ADD] (19.97)
T. Little (vn), V. Handley (cnd), Royal Scottish National Orch † Bruch:Scottish Fant, Op. 46 CFP ▲ 73118 (11.97)
Y. Menuhin (vn), P. Monteux (cnd), San Francisco SO † W. A. Mozart:Con Vn ENT (Strings) ▲ 99384 (16.97)
N. Milstein (vn), V. Golschmann (cnd), St. Louis SO † K. Goldmark:Con 1 Vn, Op. 28 TES ▲ 1047 (17.97)
N. Milstein (vn), V. Golschmann (cnd), St. Louis SO † Bizet:Carmen (sels); M. de Falla:Sombrero de tres picos (dances); Gounod:Faust (ballet music) EMIC (Legacy) ▲ 66552 (11.97)
N. Milstein (vn), E. Ormandy (cnd), Philadelphia Orch † Bruch:Con 1 Vn, Op. 26; Mendelssohn (-Bartholdy):Con Vn & Orch, Op. 64 PHS ▲ 9259 (17.97)
D. Oistrakh (vn), J. Martinon (cnd), Philharmonia Orch † S. Prokofiev:Con 1 Vn, Op. 19 TES ▲ 1116 (17.97)
I. Perlman (vn), D. Barenboim (cnd), Orch de Paris † Saint-Saëns:Con 3 Vn, Op. 61 DEUT (3D Classics) ▲ 29977 [DDD] (9.97)
I. Perlman (vn), D. Barenboim (cnd), Orch de Paris † Berlioz:Rêverie et caprice, Op. 8; Saint-Saëns:Con 3 Vn, Op. 61 DEUT (Masters) ▲ 45549 [DDD] (9.97)
R. Ricci (vn), E. Ansermet (cnd), Swiss Romande Orch † Saint-Saëns:Havanaise, Op. 83; Intro & Rondo capriccioso, Op. 28; Sarasate:Fant on Carmen, Op. 25; Zigeunerweisen, Op. 20 PLON (The Classic Sound) ▲ 452309 (11.97)
P. Zukerman (vn), Z. Mehta (cnd), Los Angeles PO *(rec 1977)* † Bruch:Con 1 Vn, Op. 26; H. Vieuxtemps:Con 5 Vn, Op. 37 SNYC (Essential Classics) ▲ 48274 [ADD] (7.97) ▮ 48274 [ADD] (3.98)
Symphony in g (1886)
G. Andretta (cnd), Basel SO † Divert Orch; Rapsodie norvégienne; Scherzo CPO ▲ 999296 [DDD] (14.97)
N. Athinäos (cnd), Frankfurt on the Oder State Orch † Con Pno; Romance-sérénade; Scherzo SIGM ▲ 6600 [DDD] (17.97)
Trio No. 1 in c for Piano, Violin & Cello, Op. 7 (1850)
Barbican Trio † Trio 2 Pno; Trio 3 Pno, Op. 26 ASV ▲ 899 [DDD] (16.97)
Scaligero Trio † Borodin:Trio Pno; Cilea:Trio Pno STRV ▲ 26 (16.97)
Trio No. 2 in b for Piano, Violin & Cello (?1852)
Barbican Trio † Trio 1 Pno, Op. 7; Trio 3 Pno, Op. 26 ASV ▲ 899 [DDD] (16.97)
Trio No. 3 in a for Piano, Violin & Cello, Op. 26 (1880)
Barbican Trio † Trio 1 Pno, Op. 7; Trio 2 Pno ASV ▲ 899 [DDD] (16.97)

LAM, BUN-CHING (1954-
After Spring for 2 Pianos (1983)
B.-C. Lam (pno), T. Eckert (pno) ("Mountain Clear Water Remote") † Another Spring; Bittersweet Music I; Last Spring; Lü CRI ▲ 726 [DDD] (16.97)
Another Spring for Flute, Cello & Piano (1988)
W. Gray (vc), P. Taub (fl), B.-C. Lam (pno) ("Mountain Clear Water Remote") † After Spring; Bittersweet Music I; Last Spring; Lü CRI ▲ 726 [DDD] (16.97)
Bittersweet Music I for Piccolo (1981)
P. Taub (pic) ("Mountain Clear Water Remote") † After Spring; Another Spring; Last Spring; Lü CRI ▲ 726 [DDD] (16.97)
Last Spring for Piano & String Quartet (1992)
E. M. Gray (vn), J. Weller (vn), M. Hamilton (va), W. Gray (vc), B.-C. Lam (pno) ("Mountain Clear Water Remote") † After Spring; Another Spring; Bittersweet Music I; Lü CRI ▲ 726 [DDD] (16.97)
Like Water for Violin, Viola, Piano & Percussion
Abel-Steinberg-Winant Trio TZA (Composer) ▲ 7021 [DDD] (16.97)
Lü for solo Percussion (1983)
M. Kocmieroski (perc) ("Mountain Clear Water Remote") † After Spring; Another Spring; Bittersweet Music I; Last Spring CRI ▲ 726 [DDD] (16.97)
Music of Lam
B.-C. Lam (cnd) —The Child God; Autumn Sound; The Great River Flows East TZA (Composer) ▲ 7031 [DDD] (16.97)

LAMAN, WIM (1946-
Fleurs du Mal for Mezzo-Soprano, Violin & Orchestra (1981-82)
J. V. Nes (cta), H. Vonk (cnd), Residentie Orch The Hague [FRE] *(rec 1978-82)* ("400 Years of Dutch Music, Vol. 7") † R. Escher:Univers de Rimbaud; G. Janssen:Dans van de Malic Matrijzen; Loevendie:Turkish Folk Poems OLY ▲ 506 [AAD] (16.97)

LAMB, JOSEPH (1887-1960)
Piano Music
J. Novacek (pno)—Top Liner Rag *(rec Univ of Washington, Seattle, WA, Dec 1990)* ("NovaRags") † E. Blake:Eubie Blake Medley Pno; J. W. Johnson:Daintiness Rag Pno; S. Joplin:Gladiolus Rag; Paragon Rag; Solace; Stoptime Rag; J. Novacek:Back Country Rag Pno; Cockles Pno & Gtr; Fourth St. Drag Pno & Gtr; Full Stride Ahead Pno; Hog Wild; Intoxication Pno; Melancholy Drag Pno; Novissong; Rag Brillante Pno & Gtr; Ragamuffin Pno & Gtr; Recuperation for Piano; Schenectady Pno; Waltzee Pno & Gtr; L. Roberts:Pork & Beans Pno; J. Scott:Efficiency Rag Pno; Kansas City Rag Pno AMBA ▲ 1008 [ADD/DDD] (16.97)

▲ = CD ♦ = Enhanced CD △ = MD ▮ = Cassette Tape ▯ = DCC

LAMB, MARVIN (20th cent)
J. B. II for Orchestra (1985)
P. Freeman (cnd), Czech National SO *(rec Prague, Austria)* ("Paul Freeman Introduces...Brandon, Griffes, Osbon, Muczynski, Klessig, Lamb & Felciano-Vol. 2") † Brandon:Celebration Ov; Griffes:Poems of Fiona McLeod, Op. 11; Klessig:Meditation from Don Juan; Muczynski:Sym Dialogues, Op. 20; Osbon:Liberty ALBA ▲ 322 [DDD] (16.97)
LAMBERT, CONSTANT (1905-1951)
Aubade héroïque for Small Orchestra (1942)
D. Lloyd-Jones (cnd), English Northern Philharmonia † Rio Grande; Summer's Last Will & Testament HYP ▲ 66565 [DDD] (18.97)
Concerto for Piano & 9 Instruments (1931)
I. Brown (pno), L. Friend (cnd) † Mr. Bear Squash-you-all-flat; Poems by Li-Po; Son Pno HYP ▲ 66754 (18.97)
A. D. Curtis (pno), G. Grazioli (cnd) † A. Bax:Nonet; Rieti:Serenata Vn AART ▲ 47328 (10.97)
Elegiac Blues for Piano (1927)
A. Goldstone (pno) † Elegy Pno; Son Pno; G. Holst:Pno Music CHN ▲ 9382 [DDD] (17.97)
Elegy for Piano (1938)
A. Goldstone (pno) † Elegiac Blues; Son Pno; G. Holst:Pno Music CHN ▲ 9382 [DDD] (17.97)
Mr. Bear Squash-you-all-flat (ballet) for Orchestra (1924)
I. Brown (pno), L. Friend (cnd) † Con Pno; Poems by Li-Po; Son Pno HYP ▲ 66754 (18.97)
Overture for Piano 4-Hands
P. Lawson (pno), A. MacLean (pno) ("English Music for Piano Duet") † Pièces nègres pour les touches blanches; Berners:Fant espagnole; Morceaux; Valses bourgeoises; P. Lane:Badinages; A. Rawsthorne:Creel; W. Walton:Duets for Children ALBA ▲ 142 [DDD] (16.97)
Pièces nègres (3) pour les touches blanches for Piano 4-Hands (1949)
P. Lawson (pno), A. MacLean (pno) ("English Music for Piano Duet") † Ov Pno 4-Hands; Berners:Fant espagnole; Morceaux; Valses bourgeoises; P. Lane:Badinages; A. Rawsthorne:Creel; W. Walton:Duets for Children ALBA ▲ 142 [DDD] (16.97)
Poems by Li-Po (8) for Soprano & Piano
P. Langridge (ten), N. Hawthorne (nar), I. Brown (pno), L. Friend (cnd) † Con Pno; Mr. Bear Squash-you-all-flat; Son Pno HYP ▲ 66754 (18.97)
The Rio Grande for Contralto, Piano, Orchestra & Chorus [text by Sacheverell Sitwell] (1927)
S. Burgess (mez), J. Gibbons (pno), D. Lloyd-Jones (cnd), English Northern Philharmonia [ENG] † Aubade héroïque; Summer's Last Will & Testament HYP ▲ 66565 [DDD] (18.97)
A. Whitehead (alt), H. Harty (pno), C. Lambert (cnd), Hallé Orch, St. Michael's Singers ("Classics & All That Jazz: The Music of the 20's & 30's Recreated from Recordings of the Time") † Ellington:Music of Ellington; G. Gershwin:Rhap in Blue; R. Rodgers:Slaughter on Tenth Avenue Orch; W. Walton:Façade GSE ▲ 785065 (16.97)
A. Whitehead (alt), C. Lambert (cnd), Hallé Orch, St. Michael's Singers *(rec Jan 11, 1930)* † Berners:Fugue; A. Bliss:Things to Come (sels); W. Walton:Façade; Warlock:Corpus Christi; Curlew SYMP ▲ 1203 [AAD] (16.97)
Sonata for Piano (1928-29)
I. Brown (pno) † Con Pno; Mr. Bear Squash-you-all-flat; Poems by Li-Po HYP ▲ 66754 (18.97)
A. Goldstone (pno) † Elegiac Blues; Elegy Pno; G. Holst:Pno Music CHN ▲ 9382 [DDD] (17.97)
Summer's Last Will & Testament for Baritone, Orchestra & Chorus [text by T. Nashe] (1935)
W. Shimell (bar), D. Lloyd-Jones (cnd), English Northern Philharmonia [ENG] † Aubade héroïque; Rio Grande HYP ▲ 66565 [DDD] (18.97)

LAMBERT, JOHN (1926-1995)
Chamber Music
C. Ramirez (gtr), A. Aarons (tpt), D. Sutton-Anderson (cnd) —Tread Softly; Slide; Meditations; Toccata; Qt 2 Strs; Family Affairs (sels) ("Solos & Ensembles") NMCC ▲ 26 [DDD] (17.97)
LAMBERT, MICHEL (1610-1696)
Airs de Cour for Chamber Ensemble (1689)
W. Christie (cnd), Les Arts Florissants [FRE] HMA ▲ 1901123 (9.97)
U. Imamura (cnd) ETC ▲ 1195 (17.97)
LA MONTAINE, JOHN (1920-
Birds of Paradise for Piano & Orchestra, Op. 34
H. Hanson (cnd), Eastman-Rochester Orch ("Music for Quiet Listening, Vol. 2") † E. Grieg:Elegiac Melodies, Op. 34; H. Hanson:Fant Vars on a Theme of Youth, Op. 40; Liadov:Enchanted Lake, Op. 62; Kikimora, Op. 63; C. M. Loeffler:Rhaps PPHI ▲ 434390 (11.97)
Concerto for Flute & Orchestra (1981)
K. Bryan (fl), Z. Chen (cnd), Slovak RSO Bratislava *(rec Concert Hall of Slovak Radio Bratislava, June 20-24, 1994)* † M. Gould:Con Fl PREM ▲ 1045 [DDD] (16.97)
Concerto for Piano & Orchestra, Op. 9 (1958)
K. Keys (pno), G. F. Harrison (cnd), Oklahoma City SO *(rec 1962)* † J. A. Carpenter:Concertino Pno Orch; Hoiby:Con Pno, Op. 17 CIT ▲ 88118 [ADD] (15.97)
Concerto No. 4 for Piano & Orchestra, Op. 59 (1989)
R. Salvatore (pno), P. Freeman (cnd), Slovak RSO Bratislava *(rec Bratislava, Feb 26-27, 1995)* ("Chicago Concertos") † R. Ganz:Con Pno, Op. 32 CED ▲ 28 [DDD] (16.97)
Sonata for Piano, Op. 3 (1942)
R. Salvatore (pno) ("Music in the American Grain") † P. Bowles:Carretera de Estepona; Latin American Pieces; H. Johnson:Son Pno; R. Palmer:Son 3 Pno CED ▲ 10 [DDD] (16.97)
LAMOTE DE GRIGNON, RICARDO (1899-1962)
Lent expressiu for Chamber Orchestra
G. Comellas (cnd), Gonçal Comellas CO *(rec May 1995)* † Monocromies; Morera:Music of Morera; Toldrá:Vistes al mar LAMA ▲ 2011 [DDD] (18.97)
Monocromies for Chamber Orchestra
G. Claret (cnd), Andorra National CO *(rec Monmouth, England)* ("La Oración del Torero: Spanish Works for String Orchestra") † Manén:Miniatures; J. Rodrigo:Cançoneta; J. Turina:Musas de Andalucía, Op. 93; Oración del torero, Op. 34; Serenata Str Qt, Op. 87 NIMB ▲ 5570 [DDD] (16.97)
G. Comellas (cnd), Gonçal Comellas CO *(rec May 1995)* † Lent expressiu; Morera:Music of Morera; Toldrá:Vistes al mar LAMA ▲ 2011 [DDD] (18.97)
Scherzino for Viola & Piano
P. Cortese (va), A. Soler (pno) † Benejam:Moments musicals Va; Bonet:Sonatina Va; Brotons:Son Va EAM ▲ 7373 [DDD] (17.97)

LAMPE, JOHN FREDERICK (ca 1703-1751)
Britannia (selections)
E. Kirkby (sop), C. Hogwood (cnd), Academy of Ancient Music—Welcome Mars † Dione (sels); T. Arne:Comus (sels); Rosamond (sels); Tempest (sels); G. F. Handel:Alcina (sels); Alessandro Severo (sels); Alexander's Feast (ode), HWV 75; Allegro, il Penseroso ed il Moderato (sels); Ariodante (sels); Hornpipe in D, HWV 356; March; Saul (sels); J. Haydn:Schöpfung (sels); W. A. Mozart:Ah, lo previdi & Ah, t'invola agl'occhi miei, K.272; Ch'io mi scordi di te? & Non temer, amato bene, K.505; Nehmt meinen Dank, ihr holden Gönner!, K.383; Rè pastore (sels); Voi avete un cor fedele, K.217; Zaide (sels) PLON (Double Decker) 2-▲ 458084 [DDD] (17.97)
Dione (selections)
E. Kirkby (sop), C. Hogwood (cnd), Academy of Ancient Music—Prety warblers † Brittania (sels); T. Arne:Comus (sels); Rosamond (sels); Tempest (sels); G. F. Handel:Alcina (sels); Alessandro Severo (sels); Alexander's Feast (ode), HWV 75; Allegro, il Penseroso ed il Moderato (sels); Ariodante (sels); Hornpipe in D, HWV 356; March; Saul (sels); J. Haydn:Schöpfung (sels); W. A. Mozart:Ah, lo previdi & Ah, t'invola agl'occhi miei, K.272; Ch'io mi scordi di te? & Non temer, amato bene, K.505; Nehmt meinen Dank, ihr holden Gönner!, K.383; Rè pastore (sels); Voi avete un cor fedele, K.217; Zaide (sels) PLON (Double Decker) 2-▲ 458084 [DDD] (17.97)
LANCHBERY, JOHN (1923-
The Tales of Beatrix Potter (film music) for Orchestra (1971)
J. Lanchbery (cnd), Royal Opera House Orch Covent Garden CFP ▲ 72813 (11.97)
LANDEGHEM, JAN VAN (1954-
Jobustu for Recorder (1995)
G. Van Gele (rcr) *(rec Belgium, Apr 1995)* ("Flemish Contemporary Recorder Music, Vol. 2") † Biesemans:Slovak Pieces Rcr; Buckinx:Pieces for Pear; F. Geysen:Geproesterol RENE ▲ 92031 [DDD] (16.97)
LANDINI, FRANCESCO (ca 1325-1397)
Vocal Music
Alba Musica Kyo—Gram piant' agli occhi; Conveniens' a fede; Donna, la mente mia; De! dinmi tu; S'i' ti son stato *(rec Renswoude, Netherlands, Sept 7-9, 1992)* ("Landini and His Time") † Anonymous:Estampie; Lamento di Tristano; Saltarello; Jacopo da Bologna:I'me sun un che; Vestisse la cornachia; Lorenzo da Firenze:A poste messe; Come in sul fonte; Non so qual'i' mi volgia; Povero çappator; Matteo da Perugia:Sera quel zorno may CCL ▲ 5793 [DDD]

LANDINI, FRANCESCO (cont.)
Vocal Music (cont.)
J. Sothcott (cnd), St. George's Canzona—Questa fanciulla; Gram piant' agli occhi *(rec London, England)* ("A Medieval Banquet") † Anonymous:Anni novi novitas; Bryd one brere; Danse royale 1; Danse royale 2; Douce dame jolie; Flos florum/Ach Getruys Blut; Fontenella; Gabriel fram evene King sent; Ghaetta; Ježíš, Náš spasitel; Lidové Tance; Pilgrim Song; Saltarello 1; Saltarello 2; Se je souspir; Sexte estampie real; St Thomas Honor We; Sumer is icumen in; Neidhart von Reuental:Winder wie ist nû dń kraft; Traditional:Dance Tune (trad); Drmeš; Folk Song; Janoshka; Robin Hood & Tanner ASVQ ▲ 6131 [ADD] (10.97)
LANDOWSKI, MARCEL (1915-
Cantata No. 1 for Orchestra & Chorus, "Jésus es-tu là?" [text A. Marc] (1948)
J. Prosper (cnd), La Maîtrise des Bouches du Rhône † Chants d'innocence; Rois mages DPV ▲ 9685 (15.97)
Chants d'innocence (5) for female Choir (1952)
J. Prosper (cnd), La Maîtrise des Bouches du Rhône † Cant 1; Rois mages DPV ▲ 9685 (15.97)
Préludes (4) pour l'opéra des Bastilles for Orchestra
A. Moglia (cnd), Toulouse CO ("20th Century French Strings") † Chaynes:Onze Visages ou l'antifugue; Pour faire le portrait d'un oiseau; Daniel-Lesur:Serenade PVY ▲ 798042 (16.97)
Les rois mages [The Wise Men] for Chorus
J. Prosper (cnd), La Maîtrise des Bouches du Rhône † Cant 1; Chants d'innocence DPV ▲ 9685 (15.97)
LANDRY, JEANNE (20th cent)
Poèmes (3) for Viola & Piano
C. Masson-Bourque (va), M. Sato (pno) † R. Clarke:Son Va; Gougeon:Thèmes-solaires; A. Rubinstein:Son Va SNE ▲ 627 (16.97)
LANE, BURTON (1912-
On A Clear Day You Can See Forever (selections)
B. Terfel (b-bar), P. Daniel (cnd), English Northern PO—On A Clear Day; Come Back to Me; She Wasn't You; Hurry, it's Lovely up Here ("If Ever I Would Leave You") † F. Loewe:Brigadoon (sels); Little Prince (sels); My Fair Lady (sels); Paint Your Wagon (sels); Strouse:Dance A Little Closer (sels); K. Weill:Love Life (sels) DEUT ▲ 457628 (16.97)
LANE, EASTWOOD (1879-1951)
Adirondack Sketches for Piano (1922)
M. Polad (pno) ("Piano Deco, Vol. 1: M. Polad Plays American Music of the 1920's") † American Dances; Pno Music; Beiderbecke:Pno Music; R. Bloom:Pno Music PREM ▲ 101 (16.97)
American Dances (5) for Piano (1919)
M. Polad (pno) ("Piano Deco, Vol. 1: M. Polad Plays American Music of the 1920's") † Adirondack Sketches; Pno Music; Beiderbecke:Pno Music; R. Bloom:Pno Music PREM ▲ 101 (16.97)
Piano Music
M. Polad (pno)—Persimmon Pucker; Sea Burial; Girl on Tiptoe ("Piano Deco, Vol. 1: M. Polad Plays American Music of the 1920's") † Adirondack Sketches; American Dances; Beiderbecke:Pno Music; R. Bloom:Pno Music PREM ▲ 101 (16.97)
LANE, PHILIP (1950-
Badinages for Piano 4-Hands
P. Lawson (pno), A. MacLean (pno) ("English Music for Piano Duet") † Berners:Fant espagnole; Morceaux; Valses bourgeoises; C. Lambert:Ov Pno 4-Hands; Pièces nègres pour les touches blanches; A. Rawsthorne:Creel; W. Walton:Duets for Children ALBA ▲ 142 [DDD] (16.97)
LANES, MATHIEU (1660-1725)
Pièces d'orgue
J. Brosse (org) [also includes anon 18th century mass, "Messe Agata] ("Messe Agatange") † Mondonville:Trio Sons, Op. 2 PVY ▲ 798032 (16.97)
LANG, CRAIG SELLAR (1891-1971)
Tuba Tune in D for Organ, Op. 15 (1929)
artist unknown ("Organ Music from the Island of Ireland") † J. S. Bach:Toccata & Fugue Org, BWV 565; J. Dexter:Londonderry Air; Kitson:Communion on an Irish Air; Stanford:Org Music; Widor:Sym 5 Org, Op. 42/1; C. Wood:Preludes Org GILD ▲ 7122 [ADD] (16.97)
LANG, DAVID (1957-
Are You Experienced? for Chamber Orchestra (1988)
D. Lang (nar), H. J. Renes (tuba), S. Mosko (cnd) † Orpheus Over & Under; J. Adams:Grand Pianola Music; Short Ride in a Fast Machine CHN ▲ 9363 [DDD] (16.97)
By Fire (1984)
H. Rosenbaum (cnd), New York Virtuoso Singers, C. Hewes (sop), T. Mount (bar) *(rec United States of America)* ("To Orpheus") † Dallapiccola:Prima serie; Prima serie dei cori di Michelangelo Buonarroti il; Dellaira:Art & Isadora; Art & Isadora Cho; H. W. Henze:Orpheus Behind the Wire; Perle:Sonnets to Orpheus; Sonnets to Orpheus Cho; W. Schuman:Carols of Death; Carols of Death Cho *(E text)* CRI ▲ 615 [DDD] (16.97)
Cheating, Lying, Stealing for Chamber Ensemble (1995)
Bang on a Can members *(rec The Hit Factory New York, Oct 4-8, 1995)* ("Cheating, Lying, Stealing") † Didkovsky:Amalia's Secret; Gosfield:Manufacture of Tangles Ivory; Pascoal:Arapua; Rzewski:Piece 4 Pno; Vierk:Red Shift; Ziporyn:Tsmindao Ghmerto SNYC ▲ 62254 [DDD] (16.97)
Music of Lang
D. Lang (nar), R. Schulte (vn), J. Rozen (elec tuba), U. Oppens (pno), E. Niemann (pno), N. Tilles (pno), L. Vaillancourt (cnd) —Are You Experienced?; Orpheus Over & Under; Spud; Illumination Rounds CRI ▲ 625 [DDD] (16.97)
Orpheus Over & Under for 2 Pianos (1989)
E. Corver (pno), S. Grotenhuis (pno) † Are You Experienced?; J. Adams:Grand Pianola Music; Short Ride in a Fast Machine CHN ▲ 9363 [DDD] (16.97)
While Nailing at Random for Piano (1982)
K. Supové (pno) *(rec Nov 1992)* ("Figure 88") † M. Epstein:Waterbowls; L. Foss:Solo Pno; Rzewski:North American Ballads; R. Woolf:Dancétudes CRI (Emergency Music) ▲ 653 [DDD] (17.97)
LÁNG, GYÖRGY (1908-1976)
Concerto ebraico for Violin & Orchestra (ca 1942)
L. Rásonyi (vn), U. Mayer (cnd), Budapest SO † Vn & Pno Music HUN ▲ 31767 [DDD] (16.97)
Violin & Piano Music
L. Rásonyi (vn), E. Mayer (pno)—Death of the Faun; Chanson d'automne; Love Song of the Cricket; Fleur de délice † Con ebraico HUN ▲ 31767 [DDD] (16.97)
LÁNG, ISTVÁN (1933-
Canto for solo Flute (1994)
Z. Gyöngyössy (fl) † Chagall Flies away over His Sleeping Vitebsk; Son Vc & Pno; Son Vn; Viviofa HUN ▲ 31641 [AAD] (16.97)
Chagall Flies away over His Sleeping Vitebsk for Percussion Ensemble
Amadinda Percussion Group † Canto Fl; Son Vc & Pno; Son Vn; Viviofa HUN ▲ 31641 [AAD] (16.97)
Sonata for Cello & Piano (1992-93)
L. Fenyő (vc), I. Prunyi (pno) † Canto Fl; Chagall Flies away over His Sleeping Vitebsk; Son Vn; Viviofa HUN ▲ 31641 [AAD] (16.97)
Sonata for Violin & Piano (1990)
E. Pérényi (vn), I. Prunyi (pno) † Canto Fl; Chagall Flies away over His Sleeping Vitebsk; Son Vc & Pno; Viviofa HUN ▲ 31641 [AAD] (16.97)
Viviofa for Vibraphone, Viola & Bassoon (1995)
G. Gulyás-Nagy (va), G. Lakatos (bn), Z. Láng (vib) † Canto Fl; Chagall Flies away over His Sleeping Vitebsk; Son Vc & Pno; Son Vn HUN ▲ 31641 [AAD] (16.97)
LANG, JOSEPHINE (1815-1880)
Songs
C. Taha (sop), H. Kommerell (pno)—14 sels including Erinnerung; Den Abschied schnell genommen, Op. 15/1; An de See, Op. 14/4; Am Flusse, Op. 14/2; Frühzeitiger Frühling, Op. 6/3; In weite Ferne, Op. 15/3; Auf dem See in tausend Sterne, Op. 14/6 † Kinkel:Songs BAYE ▲ 100248 [DDD] (17.97)
LANGE-MÜLLER, PETER ERASMUS (1850-1926)
Albumsblade for String Quartet
Carl Nielsen String Quartet † Fant Pieces, Op. 39; Romance, Op. 63; Trio Pno, Op. 53 KPT ▲ 32208
An Autumn Fantasia for Piano, Op. 66
M. Mogensen (pno) ("Piano Music, Vol. 1") † Forest Pieces, Op. 56; In Memoriam; Soft Melodies, Op. 68 KPT ▲ 32228
Danse & Intermezzi for Piano, Op. 49 (1894)
M. Mogensen (pno) *(rec 1996)* ("Complete Piano Works, Vol. 2") † Lamentation; Little Pieces KPT ▲ 32248
Fantasy Pieces (3) for Violin & Piano, Op. 39
S. Elbæk (vn), M. Mogensen (pno) *(rec 1991)* † Albumsblade; Romance, Op. 63; Trio Pno, Op. 53 KPT ▲ 32208

LANGE-MÜLLER, PETER ERASMUS (cont.)

Forest Pieces for Piano, Op. 56

M. Mogensen (pno) ("Piano Music, Vol. 1") † Autumn Fantasia, Op. 66; In Memoriam; Soft Melodies, Op. 68 KPT ▲ 32228

In Memoriam for Piano

M. Mogensen (pno) ("Piano Music, Vol. 1") † Autumn Fantasia, Op. 66; Forest Pieces, Op. 56; Soft Melodies, Op. 68 KPT ▲ 32228

Lamentation in c for Piano

M. Mogensen (pno) *(rec 1996)* ("Complete Piano Works, Vol. 2") † Danse & Intermezzi, Op. 49; Little Pieces KPT ▲ 32248

Little Pieces for Children for Piano (1911)

M. Mogensen (pno) *(rec 1996)* ("Complete Piano Works, Vol. 2") † Danse & Intermezzi, Op. 49; Lamentation KPT ▲ 32248

Romance for Violin & Piano, Op. 63

S. Elbæk (vn), M. Mogensen (pno) † Albumsblade; Fant Pieces, Op. 39; Trio Pno, Op. 53 KPT ▲ 32208

Soft Melodies for Piano, Op. 68

M. Mogensen (pno) ("Piano Music, Vol. 1") † Autumn Fantasia, Op. 66; Forest Pieces, Op. 56; In Memoriam KPT ▲ 32228

Songs

S. Byriel (b-bar), U. Stærk (pno)—Verzogen, verflogen; Die du bist so schön und rein; Nim mich auf, uralte Nacht; Der Zimmermann; Die heil'gen drei Könige; Kæmpens sang; Himlen ulmer svagt i flammerødt; Se blygrå sky'r mod blygrå; Ved solnedgang; Bjørnen; Der stå to roser; Alt dækker nattens vide slægkappe land og; I brændingen liger in kippeblok; En rand af diset hede; I skoven II; Yderst i slæbert, det lette *(rec Danish Radio Concert Hall, May 21-24, 1996)* † Heise:Songs MARC ▲ 8224033 [DDD] (13.97)

I. Dam-Jensen (sop), C. S. Teglbjærg (pno)—Lind; Åkande; Viol; Sulamith sang i Dronninghaven; Skin ud, du clare solskin; Piletæet bøjer sig; Junas første sang; Junas anden sang; Hyrden drager sin kappe på; Solen springer ud som en rose; Jeg synger om en kongesøn; Ak, fagre ejer jeg fingre små; Tal sagte, unge nattergal; I solen kvidre spurve små *(rec Danish Radio Concert Hall, Nov 14-18, 1996)* † Heise:Songs MARC ▲ 8224065 [DDD] (13.97)

Trio in f for Piano, Violin & Cello, Op. 53 (1898)

Copenhagen Trio † Albumsblade; Fant Pieces, Op. 39; Romance, Op. 63 KPT ▲ 32208

Tre Musici *(rec Copenhagen, Oct 1992)* ("Danish Golden Age Piano Trios") † N. W. Gade:Trio Movt; J. P. E. Hartmann:Andantino & 8 Vars; F. Henriques:Børnetrio, Op. 31; Langgaard:Mountain Flowers DCAP ▲ 9310 [DDD] (13.97)

LANGEVIN, PIERRE (dates unknown)

Chansons

Strada—Tresche du jaloux; Carole de Renart; Estampie Aiguebelle et nota; Marche croche ("Strada: A Minstrel's Journey") † Anonymous:Chansons; En mai au douz tens nouvel; Quant voi la flor novele; Volez vous que je vous chant; Erars:Chansons; Gaver:Chansons; Moniot de Paris:Chansons; G. Ross:Chansons; Traditional:Ma mie tant blanche ANAL ▲ 28811 (16.97)

LANGFORD, GORDON (1930-

Carnival Day (march)

R. Bernat (cnd), River City Brass Band † H. Fillmore:Marches (misc); E. F. Goldman:On the Mall; J. P. Sousa:Invictus; Nobles of the Mystic Shrine; Thunderer; E. Tomlinson:Best Foot Forward; M. Wilson:British Grenadiers; Men of Harlech; Seventy-Six Trombones; H. C. Work:Colonel Bogey March; Marching through Georgia RCBB ▲ 191

Harmonious Variations on a Theme of Handel

R. Newsome (cnd), Black Dyke Mills Band *(rec England)* ("Champions of Brass") † G. Bailey:Diadem of Gold (Ov); Bantock:Prometheus Unbound; Gregson:Connotations; W. Mathias:Vivat Regina Bra, Op. 75; Vivat Regina, Op. 75; Vaughan Williams:Vars Brass *([ENG] text)* CHN ▲ 4510 [ADD] (16.97)

Rhapsody for Cornet

R. Newsome (cnd), Besses o' th' Barn Band † Gregson:Con Hn; Con Tuba CHN ▲ 4526 [DDD] (16.97)

LANGGAARD, RUED (1893-1952)

Death of a Hero [Heltedod] for Orchestra (1907-08)

I. Stupel (cnd), Artur Rubinstein PO *(rec Nov 1991)* ("The Complete Symphonies, Vol. 3") † Interdikt; Sym 4; Sym 6 DANR ▲ 406 [DDD] (17.97)

From the Deep [Fra Dybet] for Orchestra

L. Segerstam (cnd), Danish National RSO † Sym 1 CHN ▲ 9249 [DDD] (16.97)

Interdikt for Orchestra, "At the Grave of Christopher I in Ribe" (1947-48)

I. Stupel (cnd), Artur Rubinstein PO *(rec Nov 1991)* ("The Complete Symphonies, Vol. 3") † Death of a Hero; Sym 4; Sym 6 DANR ▲ 406 [DDD] (17.97)

Mountain Flowers [Fjeldblomster] for Violin & Piano (1908)

Tre Musici members *(rec Copenhagen, Oct 1992)* ("Danish Golden Age Piano Trios") † N. W. Gade:Trio Movt; J. P. E. Hartmann:Andantino & 8 Vars; F. Henriques:Børnetrio, Op. 31; Lange-Müller:Trio Pno, Op. 53 DCAP ▲ 9310 [DDD] (13.97)

The Music of the Spheres for Soprano, Orchestra & Chorus (1918)

G. Sjöberg (sop), G. Rozhdestvensky (cnd), Danish National RSO, Danish National Radio Choir † Tone Pictures CHN ▲ 9517 (16.97)

Piano Music

R. Bevan (pno)—Flower Vignettes I & II; Insectarium; Mad Fant Pno; Music of the Abyss; Son Pno CLSO ▲ 240 (15.97)

P. Froundjian (pno) DANR ▲ 430 (17.97)

T. Teirup (pno)—Benguinage; In the Autumn Lamp's Flickering Rays; Insectarium; Son 2 Pno PLAL ▲ 31 (18.97)

Prélude to "Antichrist" for Orchestra (1921-30)

I. Stupel (cnd), Artur Rubinstein PO *(rec Sept 1991)* ("The Complete Symphonies, Vol. 7") † Sym 13; Sym 16 DANR ▲ 410 [DDD]

Quartet No. 2 for Strings (1918; rev 1931)

Kontra String Quartet *(rec Copenhagen, Denmark, 1984)* ("Rued Langgaard: String Quartets") † Qt 3 Strs; Qt 4 Strs; Qt 5 Strs; Qt 6 Strs; Vars Str Qt DCAP (dacapo) 2-▲ 9302 [DDD] (27.97)

Quartet No. 3 for Strings (1924)

Kontra String Quartet *(rec Copenhagen, Denmark, 1984)* ("Rued Langgaard: String Quartets") † Qt 2 Strs; Qt 4 Strs; Qt 5 Strs; Qt 6 Strs; Vars Str Qt DCAP (dacapo) 2-▲ 9302 [DDD] (27.97)

Quartet No. 4 for Strings, "Summer Days" (1918; rev 1931)

Kontra String Quartet *(rec Copenhagen, Denmark, 1984)* ("Rued Langgaard: String Quartets") † Qt 2 Strs; Qt 3 Strs; Qt 5 Strs; Qt 6 Strs; Vars Str Qt DCAP (dacapo) 2-▲ 9302 [DDD] (27.97)

Quartet No. 5 for Strings (1925; rev 1936-38)

Kontra String Quartet *(rec Copenhagen, Denmark, 1984)* ("Rued Langgaard: String Quartets") † Qt 2 Strs; Qt 3 Strs; Qt 4 Strs; Qt 6 Strs; Vars Str Qt DCAP (dacapo) 2-▲ 9302 [DDD] (27.97)

Quartet No. 6 for Strings (1918-19)

Kontra String Quartet *(rec Copenhagen, Denmark, 1984)* ("Rued Langgaard: String Quartets") † Qt 2 Strs; Qt 3 Strs; Qt 4 Strs; Qt 5 Strs; Vars Str Qt DCAP (dacapo) 2-▲ 9302 [DDD] (27.97)

Ribe Early Morning [Ribe tidlig Morgen] for Chamber Ensemble (1949)

K. Christensen (tpt), B. Nielsen (tpt), K. Jørgensen (trbn), M. Andresen (eup) *(rec Anneberg Mansion Denmark, 1986)* ("Trumpet Concertos Vol. 4: Original Danish Romantic Brass Music") † T. Hansen:Con Waltz; Qnt Brass; Romance Tpt; Scherzo Tpt; Son Tpt; A. Jørgensen:Caprice orientale; Qnt Brass; Sehested:Suite Cnt ROND ▲ 8350

The Rose Garden Songs (3) for Chorus (1919)

J. G. Jørgensen (cnd), Lille MUKO University Choir ("Lille MUKO: Nordisk Suite") † Clausen:Songs; Holten:Nordisk Suite; Maegaard:Södergran Songs; Nørgård:Evening Country, Op. 10; Sundstrøom:Falcon & the Little Birds PONT ▲ 5125 (19.97)

Symphony No. 1, "Klippepastoral" (1908-09; rev 1911)

L. Segerstam (cnd), Danish National RSO † From the Deep CHN ▲ 9249 [DDD] (16.97)

Symphony No. 4, "Leaf-fall" (1916)

N. Järvi (cnd), Danish National RSO † Sym 5; Sym 6 CHN ▲ 9064 [DDD] (16.97)

I. Stupel (cnd), Artur Rubinstein PO *(rec Nov 1991)* ("The Complete Symphonies, Vol. 3") † Death of a Hero; Interdikt; Sym 6 DANR ▲ 406 [DDD] (17.97)

Symphony No. 5, "Nature of the Steppe" (1931)

N. Järvi (cnd), Danish National RSO † Sym 4; Sym 6 CHN ▲ 9064 [DDD] (16.97)

I. Stupel (cnd), Artur Rubinstein PO *(rec June 1991)* ("The Complete Symphonies, Vol. 5") † Sym 7; Sym 9 DANR ▲ 407 [DDD] (17.97)

Symphony No. 6, "The Heaven-storming" (1919-20; rev 1926-30)

N. Järvi (cnd), Danish National RSO † Sym 4; Sym 5 CHN ▲ 9064 [DDD] (16.97)

I. Stupel (cnd), Artur Rubinstein PO *(rec Nov 1991)* ("The Complete Symphonies, Vol. 3") † Death of a Hero; Interdikt; Sym 4 DANR ▲ 406 [DDD] (17.97)

LANGGAARD, RUED (cont.)

Symphony No. 7, "By Tordenskjold in Holmen's Church" (1925-26; rev 1932-33)

I. Stupel (cnd), Artur Rubinstein PO *(rec June 1991)* ("The Complete Symphonies, Vol. 5") † Sym 5; Sym 9 DANR ▲ 407 [DDD] (17.97)

Symphony No. 8, "Memories at Amelienborg" (1926-28; rev 1929-34)

I. Stupel (cnd), Artur Rubinstein PO *(rec June & Aug 1992)* ("The Complete Symphonies, Vol. 6") † Sym 14; Sym 15 DANR ▲ 409 [DDD]

Symphony No. 9, "From the Town of Queen Dagmar" (1942)

I. Stupel (cnd), Artur Rubinstein PO *(rec June 1991)* ("The Complete Symphonies, Vol. 5") † Sym 5; Sym 7 DANR ▲ 407 [DDD] (17.97)

Symphony No. 13, "Faithlessness" (1946; rev 1947)

I. Stupel (cnd), Artur Rubinstein PO *(rec Sept 1991)* ("The Complete Symphonies, Vol. 7") † Prélude to "Antichrist"; Sym 16 DANR ▲ 410 [DDD]

Symphony No. 14, "The Morning" (1947-48; rev 1951)

I. Stupel (cnd), Artur Rubinstein PO *(rec June & Aug 1992)* ("The Complete Symphonies, Vol. 6") † Sym 15; Sym 8 DANR ▲ 409 [DDD]

Symphony No. 15, "Sea Storm" (1937; rev 1949)

I. Stupel (cnd), Artur Rubinstein PO *(rec June & Aug 1992)* ("The Complete Symphonies, Vol. 6") † Sym 14; Sym 8 DANR ▲ 409 [DDD]

Symphony No. 16, "Deluge of Sun" (1951)

I. Stupel (cnd), Artur Rubinstein PO *(rec Sept 1991)* ("The Complete Symphonies, Vol. 7") † Prélude to "Antichrist"; Sym 13 DANR ▲ 410 [DDD]

Tone Pictures (4) for Orchestra

G. Rozhdestvensky (cnd), Danish National RSO † Music of the Spheres CHN ▲ 9517 (16.97)

Variations for String Quartet, "O Sacred Head! Now Wounded" (1914; intro 1931)

Kontra String Quartet *(rec Copenhagen, Denmark, 1984)* ("Rued Langgaard: String Quartets") † Qt 2 Strs; Qt 3 Strs; Qt 4 Strs; Qt 5 Strs; Qt 6 Strs DCAP (dacapo) 2-▲ 9302 [DDD] (27.97)

LANGLAIS, JEAN (1907-1991)

Adeste Fidelis for Organ

C. Walsh (org) *(rec Salisbury Cathedral, England, 1984-5)* ("The Organs of Salisbury & Lincoln Cathedrals") † Org Music; Triptyque; Boëly:Allegretto; Fant & Fugue in B♭; C. Franck:Pastorale, Op. 19; Tournemire:Improvs (5); Vierne:Carillon de Westminster, Op. 54/6; Sur le Rhin PRIO ▲ 648 [DDD] (16.97)

Ave Maria, Ave maris stella for Organ

N. Hakim (org) *(rec Église de Sainte-Trinité Paris, Mar 1997)* ("Canticum: French Organ Music") † Te Deum; C. Franck:Chorales Org, M.38-40; Pièces (3) Org, M.36; N. Hakim:Org Music; Messiaen:Livre du Saint-Sacrement; Nativité du Seigneur; Vierne:Pièces de fant Org (sels) EMIC (Debut) ▲ 72272 [DDD] (6.97)

Characteristic Pieces (3) for Organ (1957)

H. Mardirosian (org) † Suite brève CENT ▲ 2042 [DDD] (16.97)

Chorales (7) for Trumpet & Organ (1972)

B. Kratzer (tpt), M. Sander (org) † Deutschmann:Intro & Allegro Tpt; P. Eben:Okna; Karg-Elert:Sinfonische Kanzone, Op. 85/1; H. L. Schilling:Canzona über "Christ ist Erstanden"; H. Tomasi:Semaine Sainte à Cuzco FERM ▲ 20008 [DDD] (16.97)

Essai for Organ (1962)

C. Cramer (org) *(rec St Pierre Cathedral Angoulème, France)* ("Pieces de Concours from the Paris Conservatory") † Sonate en trio; P. Cochereau:Vars sur un theme chromatique; J.-J. Grunenwald:Pièce en mosaïque; J.-C. Henry:Chaconne Org; Messiaen:Verset pour la fête ARK ▲ 6146 (16.97)

Hommage à Frescobaldi for Organ (1951)

A. Morrison (org) *(rec St. Luke's Presbytar. Atlanta, GA)* ("Alan Morrison") † Org Music; Duruflé:Prélude et fugue, Op. 7; Krape:Choral Triptych Org; J. Weaver:Passacaglia on a Theme by Dunstable; Widor:Sym 6 Org, Op. 42/2 ACAD ▲ 20015 (16.97)

Hymne d'Actions de grâces "Te Deum" for Organ

F. Swann (org) *(rec Riverside Church, NYC, NY)* ("The Riverside Years") † Farnam:Toccata on "O Filii et Filiae"; C. Franck:Chorales Org, M.38-40; Pièces (3) Org, M.37; Gigout:Grand-Choeur Dialogue; Karg-Elert:Symphonic Chorale 1, Op. 87/1 GOT ▲ 49082 (17.97)

Méditations (3) for Organ (1962)

S. Farrell (org) *(rec Org of St. Edmundsbury Cathedral)* ("French Connections") † J. Jongen:Son heroïca, Op. 94; Vierne:Sym 2 Org, Op. 20 HER ▲ 208 [DDD] (18.97)

S. Lindley (org) † Boëllmann:Suite gothique, Op. 25; Widor:Sym 5 Org, Op. 42/1 NXIN ▲ 550581 [DDD] (5.97)

Méditations sur l'apocalypse (5) for Organ (1974)

J. Scott (org) *(rec St. Paul's Cathederal London)* † Gigout:Grand-Choeur Dialogue; Guilmant:March upon Handel's; Liszt:Fant & Fugue on "Ad nos" Org, S.259 GILD ▲ 7128 [DDD] (16.97)

Messe solenelle for Chorus (1951)

K. Ek (cnd), Täby Church Choir [LAT] † O. Olsson:Te Deum, Op. 25 BIS ▲ 289 [DDD] (17.97)

J. Hancock (org), G. Hancock (cnd), St. Thomas Church Men & Boys' Choir New York ("Most Sacret Banquet") † Duruflé:Motets on Gregorian Chants, Op. 10; C. Franck:Psalm 150; Messiaen:O sacrum convivium!; F. Poulenc:Exultate Deo KOCH ▲ 7228 (16.97)

C. Robinson (cnd), St. John's College Choir Cambridge ("Set Me as a Seal upon Thine Heart") † A. Copland:In the Beginning; W. Walton:Choral Music LDBG ▲ 55 (17.97)

Music of Langlais

J. Hassler (sop), V. Warner (org)—Messe solennelle, Op. 67; Motets (5), Op. 8; Missa in simplicate, Op. 75; Prières (3), Op. 65; Ventie et audite, Op. 104; Missa miserucordiae Domini, Op. 105 MED7 ▲ 141327 (18.97)

Organ Music

M. Langlais (org)—Con 2 Org; plus others KSCH ▲ 315292 (16.97)

A. Morrison (org) *(rec St. Luke's Presbytar. Atlanta, GA)* ("Alan Morrison") † Hommage à Frescobaldi; Duruflé:Prélude et fugue, Op. 7; Krape:Choral Triptych Org; J. Weaver:Passacaglia on a Theme by Dunstable; Widor:Sym 6 Org, Op. 42/2 ACAD ▲ 20015 (16.97)

A. Noble (org) *(Org acclamation [Improv on Laetabunda]; Offertory [Veritas mea])*, N. Hutchinson (org) *(Communion [Beatus servus]) (rec St. Michael's Abbey Farnborough, May 1994)* ("Laetabunda: Gregorian Chant & Chant-Inspired Choral & Organ Music by Langlais & Duruflé") † Sacred Choral Music; Duruflé:Sacred Choral Music; Suite Org, Op. 5 HER ▲ 179 [DDD]

P. Stubbings (org)—L'Annonciation Org, Op. 2 *(rec Walker Org (1990), St.Martin-in-the-Fields, London, England, Feb 1995)* ("Paul Stubbings Plays the Organ of St Martin-In-the-Fields") † Anonymous:Org Music; J. S. Bach:Chorale Settings, BWV 651-668; Cons Org; C. Gibbons:Org Music; Matter:Org Music; Mendelssohn (-Bartholdy):Sons (6) Org, Op. 65 ARK ▲ 6154 [DDD] (16.97)

C. Walsh (org)—Fête *(rec Salisbury Cathedral, England, 1984-85)* ("The Organs of Salisbury & Lincoln Cathedrals") † Adeste Fidelis; Triptyque; Boëly:Allegretto; Fant & Fugue in B♭; C. Franck:Pastorale, Op. 19; Tournemire:Improvs (5); Vierne:Carillon de Westminster, Op. 54/6; Sur le Rhin PRIO ▲ 648 [DDD] (16.97)

Paraphrases grégoriennes (3) for Organ (1934)

C. Crozier (org) *(rec Rosales Org, Trinity Episcopal, Portland, OR, May 1993)* ("Things Visible & Invisible") † J. Alain:Danses (3) Org, AWV 119; Messiaen:Messe de la Pentecôte DLS ▲ 3147 [DDD] (14.97)

A. Gunning (org) *(rec St John the Evangelist Org Islington)* † Suite médévale; Demessieux:Chorale Preludes on Gregorian Themes, Op. 8; Tournemire:Orgue mystique, Opp. 55-57 HER ▲ 1572 (19.97)

Pièces (73) for Trumpet (or Oboe or Flute) & Organ (or Piano) (1973)

Duo Danica *(rec 1996-97)* ("Works for Oboe & Organ") † Telemann:Marches (12), TWV50: 31-42 (comp) KPT ▲ 32257

Sacred Choral Music

N. Hutchinson (org), A. Noble (cnd), Farnborough Abbey Choir—Kyrie [Missa in simplicitate; Benedictus]; Gloria [Missa in simplicitate]; Gradual [Iustus ut palma]; Alleluia [Beatus vir]; Sequence [Laetabunda]; Gospel [plainsong]; Credo [Plainsong III]; Sanctus [Missa in simplicitate]; Pater Noster [Plainsong]; Agnus Dei [Missa in simplicitate] *(rec St. Michael's Abbey Farnborough, May 1994)* ("Laetabunda: Gregorian Chant & Chant-Inspired Choral & Organ Music by Langlais & Duruflé") † Org Music; Duruflé:Sacred Choral Music; Suite Org, Op. 5 HER ▲ 179 [DDD]

M. Stewart (cnd), London Pro Arte Orch, East London Chorus, Finchley Children's Music Group—Psaumes solennels; Tu es petrus; Cortëge & Ceremony; plus others ("Vol. 2") KSCH ▲ 315302 (16.97)

Sonate en trio for Organ

C. Cramer (org) *(rec St Pierre Cathedral Angoulème, France)* ("Pieces de Concours from the Paris Conservatory") † Essai; P. Cochereau:Vars sur un theme chromatique; J.-J. Grunenwald:Pièce en mosaïque; J.-C. Henry:Chaconne Org; Messiaen:Verset pour la fête ARK ▲ 6146 (16.97)

Suite brève for Organ (1947)

H. Mardirosian (org) † Characteristic Pieces CENT ▲ 2042 [DDD] (16.97)

LANGLAIS, JEAN (cont.)
Suite médévale for Organ (1947)
A. Gunning (org) *(rec St John the Evangelist Org Islington)* † Paraphrases grégoriennes; Demessieux:Chorale Preludes on Gregorian Themes, Op. 8; Tournemire:Orgue mystique, Opp. 55-57 HER ▲ 1572 (19.97)
H. Mardirosian (org) *(rec Champaign, IL, Apr 1997)* ("Organ Suites") † Foote:Suite Org, Op. 54; P. Malengreau:Suite Org, Op. 14; Saint-Saëns:Rapsodies sur des cantiques bretons, Op. 7 CENT ▲ 2368 [DDD] (16.97)
Te Deum for Organ [from Trois Paraphrases Grégoriennes] (1934)
N. Hakim (org) *(rec Eglise de Sainte-Trinité Paris, Mar 1997)* ("Canticum: French Organ Music") † Ave Maria, Ave maris stella; C. Franck:Chorales Org, M.38-40; Pièces (3) Org, M.36; N. Hakim:Org Music; Messiaen:Livre du Saint-Sacrement; Nativité du Seigneur; Vierne:Pièces de fant Org (sels) EMIC (Debut) ▲ 72272 [DDD] (6.97)
Triptyque for Organ
C. Walsh (org)—Finale *(rec Lincoln Cathedral, England, 1994)* ("The Organs of Salisbury & Lincoln Cathedrals") † Adeste Fidelis; Org Music; Boëly:Allegretto; Fant & Fugue in B♭; C. Franck:Pastorale, Op. 19; Tournemire:Improvs (5); Vierne:Carillon de Westminster, Op. 54/6; Sur le Rhin PRIO ▲ 648 [DDD] (16.97)
LANGLEY, JAMES W. (1927-
Quartet for 4 Horns
American Horn Quartet *(rec Dec 1990)* † L. E. Shaw:Fripperies; K. Turner:Fanfare for Barcs; Qt 1 Hns; Qt 2 Hns EBS ▲ 6008 [DDD] (18.97)
LANGTON, STEPHAN (ca 1150-1228)
Vocal Music
K. Ruhland (cnd), Munich Capella Antiqua—Veni sancte spiritus ("Gregorian Chants") † Ambrose [Saint Ambrose]:Vocal Music; Anonymous:Ad coenam agni providi; Antiphony & Canticum Simeonis; Conditor alme siderum; Cum natus esset Jesus; Kyrie fons bonitatis; Lumen ad Revelationem & Nunc Dimittis; Mittit ad virginem; Nato canunt omnia; O Redemptor sume carmen; Surrexit dominus vere; Te deum laudamus CEHA ▲ 13094 (16.97)
LANIER, JARON (20th cent)
Music of Lanier
J. Lanier (pno)—Come Along; Khaen Vn Duo No. 6; The Story of Water Dancing in the Night Sky; Angklung; Suite for Sax Ensemble; Tremolo Silence; Circular Saw; Breaking Song; The Breath of the Earth; Sentiment & Strut; Cream Soda PPHI ▲ 42132 [DDD] (16.97)
LANIER, SIDNEY (1842-1881)
Music of Lanier
K. B. Feeney (vn), C. Wiersma (vn), J. Feeney (db), P. Robison (fl), S. Sanders (pno)—Blackbirds; Waldeinsamkeit 1 & 2; A Melody from Lanier's Fl; Cradle Song; Wind Song *(rec Purchase Theater C, NY, Jan 31-Feb 1, 1996)* ("By the Old Pine Tree: Flute Music by Stephen Foster & Sidney Lanier") † S. C. Foster:Music of Foster ARA ▲ 6679 [DDD] (16.97)
LANNER, JOSEPH (1801-1843)
Hans-Jörgel Polka for Orchestra, Op. 194
Strauss-Lanner Ensemble, Schrammel Ensemble, Montréal Trio Kaffeehaus ("Viennese Telegram") † J. Schrammel:Antoineten Polka; Weana Gmüath Waltz; E. Strauss:Unter der Enns; Joh. Strauss:Jugendfeuer, Op. 90; Wiener Carneval-Walzer, Op. 3; Strauss (II):Lob der Frauen, Op. 315; Telegramme, Op. 318; Ziehrer:Echt Wienerisch; Hoch und Nieder SNE ▲ 644 (16.97)
Die Mozartisten [The Mozartist] for Chamber Ensemble, Op. 196
Vienna Ensemble † W. A. Mozart:Diverts Str Qt, K.136-138; German Dances (6), K.600 SNYC ▲ 47672 (11.97)
Music of Lanner
F. Galimir (vn), I. Cohen (vn), M. Tree (va), J. Levine (db)—Dornbacher ländler, Op. 9; Ländler (Homesickness), Op. 202; Tyroler ländler; Steyerische tänze, Op. 165 *(rec Elisabeth Irwin H.S., NYC, NY, 1988)* ("The Beautiful Blue Danube") † Waltzes; Joh. Strauss:Radetzky March, Op. 228; Strauss (II):An der schönen blauen Donau, Op. 314 SNYC ▲ 44522 [DDD] (9.97)
Vienna Lanner Ensemble—Die Werber, Op. 103; Malapou-Galoppe, Op. 148; Dornbacher Länler, Op. 9; Cerrito Polka, Op. 189; Hofballtänze, Op. 161; Ungarischer Galoppe, Op. 97/3; Ber Herbst; Aufforderung zum Tanze, Op. 7; Marien Waltz, Op. 143; Schönbrunner, Op. 200 *(rec Vienna, July 5-8, 1994)* ("Invitation to the Dance") CAMA ▲ 396 [DDD] (18.97)
Die Romantiker for Orchestra, Op. 167
Vienna Strauss Orch *(rec Stuttgart, Germany)* † E. Strauss:Bahn frei, Op. 45; Telephon Polka, Op. 165; Joh. Strauss:Kettenbrücken-Walzer, Op. 19; Strauss (II):Accellerationen, Op. 234; Music of Joh. Strauss, Jr.; Wiener Blut (waltz), Op. 354; Jos. Strauss:Schwätzerin, Op. 144 TACE ▲ 8
Die Schönbrunner (waltz) for Orchestra, Op. 200
L. Maazel (cnd), Vienna PO ("New Year's Concert 1994") † E. Strauss:Mit Chic, Op. 221; Joh. Strauss:Radetzky March, Op. 228; Strauss (II):An der schönen blauen Donau, Op. 314; Fledermaus (sels); Geschichten aus dem Wienerwald, Op. 325; Music of Joh. Strauss, Jr.; Jos. Strauss:Music of Jos. Strauss SNYC ▲ 46694 [DDD] (16.97)
C. Schulz (vc), M. Mori (pno), G. Jelinek (harm), Biedermeier Ensemble Vienna members [arr Thiemer] *(rec Vienna, Austria, Apr 1993)* † Joh. Strauss:Krapfen-Walden-Walzer, Op. 12; Strauss (II):Kaiser-Walzer, Op. 437; Rosen aus dem Süden, Op. 388; Wein, Weib und Gesang, Op. 333; Zigeunerbaron (sels); Jos. Strauss:Sphären-Klänge, Op. 235 CAMA ▲ 541 [DDD] (18.97)
Valses Viennoises for Piano
W. Landowska (pno) [piano roll recording] ("Great Pianists of the Golden Era") † Chopin:Ballade 1 Pno, Op. 23; Ballade 3 Pno, Op. 47; Nocturnes Pno; Polonaise 5 Pno, Op. 44; Debussy:Danse Pno; Henselt:Berceuse; W. A. Mozart:Son 16 Pno, K.545; S. Prokofiev:Pieces (4) Pno, Op. 4; Rimsky-Korsakov:Golden Cockerel (sels) FON ▲ 9008 [DDD] (13.97)
Waltzes
F. Galimir (vn), I. Cohen (vn), M. Tree (va), J. Levine (db)—Schönbrunner, Op. 200; Romantiker, Op. 167; Mozartisten, Op. 196 *(rec Elisabeth Irwin H.S., NYC, NY, 1988)* ("The Beautiful Blue Danube") † Music of Lanner; Joh. Strauss:Radetzky March, Op. 228; Strauss (II):An der schönen blauen Donau, Op. 314 SNYC ▲ 44522 [DDD] (9.97)
O. Suitner (cnd), Dresden Staatskapelle—Hofballtänze, Op. 161; Steyerische tänze, Op. 165; Schönbrunner, Op. 200 † Strauss (II):Pizzicato-Polka; Jos. Strauss:Auf Ferienreisen, Op. 133; Feuerfest, Op. 269; Frauenherz, Op. 166; Libelle; Moulinet, Op. 57; Plappermäuchen, Op. 245 BER ▲ 9145 (10.97)
LANSKY, PAUL (1944-
As If for String Trio & Computer-Synthesized Sound (1981-82)
P. Lansky (cmpt) *(rec Princeton Univ., NJ)* ("The Virtuoso in the Computer Age - I") † L. Austin:Montage; A. Braxton:Composition 107 (sels); J. Melby:Con 1 Fl & Computer; D. Rosenboom:Precipice in Time CENT (CDCM Computer Music Series, Vol 10) ▲ 2110 [DDD] (16.97)
Computer Music
P. Lansky (cmpt)—Idle Chatter; Word Color; just_more_idle_chatter; The Lesson; Notjustmoreidlechatter; Memory Pages ("More Than Idle Chatter") BRID ▲ 9050 [DDD] (17.97)
Guy's Harp for Computer-Processed Harmonica
G. DeRosa (hmc) † Not So Heavy Metal; Smalltalk & August NALB ▲ 30 [DDD] (16.97)
Music for Computer-Processed Natural Sounds
H. MacKay (nar), J. Lansky (perc), C. Lansky (perc)—Table's Clear (percussive kitchen paraphernalia); Night Traffic (traffic sounds); Now & Then (speech-music); Quakerbridge (people in a suburban shopping mall); The Sound of 2 Hands ("Homebrew") BRID ▲ 9035 [DDD] (17.97)
Music of Lansky
P. Lansky (cmpt/gtr/vn)—Strut; Tender Ladies; Delta; Ash Grove; Hammer; Barbara Allen; Howl; Pine Ridge; Wayfaring Stranger; Pretty Polly; Blue Wine; Motherless Child ("Folk Images") BRID ▲ 9060 [DDD] (17.97)
P. Lansky (cmpt/pno) ("Conversation Pieces") BRID ▲ 9083 (17.97)
Not So Heavy Metal for Computer-Processed Guitar
S. Mackey (gtr) † Guy's Harp; Smalltalk & August NALB ▲ 30 [DDD] (16.97)
Notjustmoreidlechatter for Electronics (1988)
artists unknown ("Electro Acoustic Music I") † N. Boulanger:From Temporal Silence; C. Dodge:Profile; Risset:Autre face; Saariaho:Petals for Vc; D. Warner:Delay in Glass NEU ▲ 45073 [DDD]
Smalltalk & August for Computer-Processed Voices
P. Lansky (sgr), H. McKay (sgr), P. Lansky (elec) † Guy's Harp; Not So Heavy Metal NALB ▲ 30 [DDD] (16.97)
Things She Carried for Computer-Processed Voices & Sounds [text Lansky & Hannah MacKay] (1995-96)
P. Lansky (voc), H. MacKay (voc), P. Lansky (cmpt) BRID ▲ 9076 [DDD] (17.97)
Wayfaring Stranger
S. Mentzer (mez), S. Isbin (gtr) † E. Granados:Spanish Dance 5; J. P. A. Martini:Plaisir d'Amour; J. J. Niles:Black is the color; Go 'way from my window; J. Rodrigo:Aranjuez ma penses; F. Schubert:Songs (misc colls); Tárrega:Capricho árabe ERAT ▲ 23419 (16.97)
LANZETTI, SALVATORE (ca 1780)
Sonatas (12) for Cello & Continuo, Op. 1 (1736)
C. Ronco (vc), S. Veggetti (vc), D. Petech (hpd), J. Held (bc) *(rec May 1991)* NUO (Ancient Music) ▲ 7048 [DDD] (16.97)
LAPARRA, RAOUL (1876-1943)
Suite for Flute & Piano (1926)
C. Thorspecken (fl), C. Hacke (pno) *(rec Sandhausen, Germany, 1995-96)* ("The Lost Generation") † J. Alain:Movts Fl; P. Haas:Suite Pno, Op. 13; Schulhoff:Son Fl; L. Smit:Son Fl BAYE ▲ 100259 [DDD] (17.97)
LAPORTE, ANDRÉ (1931-
Das Schloss [The Castle] (opera in 3 acts) [lib Laporte after M. Brod's adaptation of Kafka] (1986)
A. Rahbari (cnd), Brussels BRTN PO DI 2-▲ 920375 [DDD] (11.97)
LARA, AGUSTIN (1900-1969)
Granada (1932)
A. D. Forno (gtr) *(rec live)* ("In Concert Part I") † Sor:Vars Mozart, Op. 9; H. Villa-Lobos:Chôro 1 JST ▲ 1078 (10.97)
Music of Lara
E. Toussaint (cnd) ("Clasicos Mexico, Vol. 7") GLMU ▲ 8584
Suite Español for solo Voice
P. Domingo (ten) ("Bajo El Cielo Español") SNYC ▲ 62625 (16.97) ▮ 62625 (10.98) COL △ 62625
LARA, ANA (1959-
Aulós for Wind Quintet
Mexico City Woodwind Quintet † C. Chávez:Soli 2; Enriquez:Pentamúsica; M. Ibarra:Juegos nocturnos; Lavista:Danzas breves CLME ▲ 21018 (13.97)
LARCHET, JOHN FRANCIS (1884-1967)
By the Waters of Moyle for Orchestra (1957)
P. O. Duinn (cnd), RTE Sinfonietta *(rec UCD Dublin, Sept 28-29, 1994 & Jan 12, 1995)* ("Romantic Ireland") † Duff:Echoes of Georgian Dublin; P. O'Connor:Introspect; O Riada:Banks of Sullane; A. J. Potter:Rhap under a High Sky; Victory:Irish Pictures MARC (Irish Composer) ▲ 8223804 [DDD] (13.97)
The Dirge of Ossian for Orchestra
F. Hunt (cnd), Irish Chamber Orch *(rec Limerick, Ireland, July, 1997)* † Mac Ananty's Reel; Duff:Irish Suite; Meath Pastoral; A. Fleischmann:Elizabeth MacDermott; T. C. Kelly:O'Carolan Suite; Pieces Strs; J. Trimble:Suite Strs BBCL ▲ 1003 [DDD] (16.97)
Mac Ananty's Reel for Orchestra (1940)
F. Hunt (cnd), Irish Chamber Orch *(rec Limerick, Ireland, July, 1997)* † Dirge of Ossian; Duff:Irish Suite; Meath Pastoral; A. Fleischmann:Elizabeth MacDermott; T. C. Kelly:O'Carolan Suite; Pieces Strs; J. Trimble:Suite Strs BBCL ▲ 1003 [DDD] (16.97)
LARRAÑAGA, JOSÉ (?-1806)
Sonata in d for Piano
S. Yates (hpd) *(rec Sommerset, England, Aug 1997)* ("Fandango-Scarlatti in Iberia") † Son Pno in D; D. Scarlatti:Sons Kbd; Seixas:Sons Kbd; P. A. Soler:Fandango, M.1A CHN ▲ 635 [DDD] (16.97)
Sonata in D for Piano
S. Yates (hpd) *(rec Sommerset, England, Aug 1997)* ("Fandango-Scarlatti in Iberia") † Son Pno in d; D. Scarlatti:Sons Kbd; Seixas:Sons Kbd; P. A. Soler:Fandango, M.1A CHN ▲ 635 [DDD] (16.97)
LARSEN, LIBBY (1950-
Black Birds, Red Hills for Clarinet, Viola & Piano (1987-96)
D. Harding (va), C. Hartig (cl), K. Purrone (pno) ("Dancing Solo: Music of Libby Larsen") † Blue Third Pieces; Corker; Dancing Solo; Pieces Treb Ww; Song without Words INNO ▲ 512 [DDD] (14.97)
Black Roller for Winds, Strings & Piano (1981)
A. Platt (cnd) ("180° from Ordinary") † Gleck:2 Tpts; Gubaidulina:Chaconne Pno; A. Piazzolla:4, for Tango; Siskind:Rituale; Trenka:WatchWait; F. Zappa:Black Page INNO ▲ 513 [ADD] (14.97)
Blue Third Pieces (2) for Clarinet & Guitar (1996)
Duologue *(rec St. Paul, MN, Spring 1996)* ("Canyon Echoes") † Bolcom:Piezas Lindas; K. Hoover:Canyon Echoes; Paulus:Fant in 3 Parts; Sierra:Segunda Cronica; Tercera Cronica GAS ▲ 336 (16.97)
C. Kachian (gtr), C. Hartig (cl) ("Dancing Solo: Music of Libby Larsen") † Black Birds, Red Hills; Corker; Dancing Solo; Pieces Treb Ww; Song without Words INNO ▲ 512 [DDD] (14.97)
Corker for Clarinet & Percussion (1989)
C. Hartig (cl), R. Adney (perc) ("Dancing Solo: Music of Libby Larsen") † Black Birds, Red Hills; Blue Third Pieces; Dancing Solo; Pieces Treb Ww; Song without Words INNO ▲ 512 [DDD] (14.97)
Dancing Solo for Clarinet (1994)
C. Hartig (cl) ("Dancing Solo: Music of Libby Larsen") † Black Birds, Red Hills; Blue Third Pieces; Corker; Pieces Treb Ww; Song without Words INNO ▲ 512 [DDD] (14.97)
How It Thrills Us for Chorus
S. Cleobury (cnd), King's College Choir Cambridge *(rec Cambridge, England, June 23-27, 1990)* † L. Bernstein:Chichester Psalms; A. Copland:In the Beginning; C. Ives:Psalm 90; W. Schuman:Carols of Death EMIC ▲ 66787 [DDD] (11.97)
Missa gaia [Mass for the Earth] for Chorus
G. Seeley (cnd), Oregon Repertory Singers † S. Barber:Songs; Paulus:Echoes KOCH ▲ 7279 [DDD] (10.97)
Parachute Dancing (overture) for Orchestra (1984)
C. Martin (cnd), Bournemouth Sinfonietta † J. Brockman:Perihelion II; K. Gardner:Rainforest; K. Hoover:Summer Night; Mamlok:Elegy; M. Richter:Lament; Van de Vate:Journeys LEON ▲ 327 [DDD] (16.97)
J. Revzen (cnd), London SO † Ring of Fire; Sym; Sym 3 KOCH ▲ 7370 (16.97)
Pieces (3) for Treble Wind & Guitar (1973-74)
C. Kachian (gtr), C. Hartig (cl) ("Dancing Solo: Music of Libby Larsen") † Black Birds, Red Hills; Blue Third Pieces; Corker; Dancing Solo; Song without Words INNO ▲ 512 [DDD] (14.97)
Ring of Fire for Orchestra
J. Revzen (cnd), London SO † Parachute Dancing; Sym; Sym 3 KOCH ▲ 7370 (16.97)
Schoenberg, Schenker & Schillinger for Flute, Oboe, Violin, Viola, Cello & EMAX II Sampler (1991)
D. Crockett (cnd), Los Angeles CO *(rec Simi Valley, CA, Sept 29-30, 1993)* ("Für Wolfgang Amadeus") † Crockett:Celestial Mechanics; Hartke:Wir küssen ihnen tausendmal die Hände; R. Steiger:Woven Serenade CRI ▲ 669 [DDD] (16.97)
Song without Words for Clarinet & Piano (1986)
C. Hartig (cl), K. Purrone (pno) ("Dancing Solo: Music of Libby Larsen") † Black Birds, Red Hills; Blue Third Pieces; Corker; Dancing Solo; Pieces Treb Ww INNO ▲ 512 [DDD] (14.97)
Symphony for Orchestra, "Water Music"
N. Marriner (cnd), Minnesota Orch † Paulus:Sym in 3 Movts NON ▲ 79147 (9.97)
J. Revzen (cnd), London SO † Parachute Dancing; Ring of Fire; Sym 3 KOCH ▲ 7370 (16.97)
Symphony No. 3, "Lyric"
J. Revzen (cnd), London SO † Parachute Dancing; Ring of Fire; Sym KOCH ▲ 7370 (16.97)
What the Monster Saw for Orchestra (1987)
E. London (cnd), Cleveland Chamber SO ("Sound Encounters") † S. Martirano:LON/dons; B. Rands:London Serenade; R. Reynolds:Dream of the Infinite Rooms GMR ▲ 2039 (16.97)
LARSSON, LARS-ERIK (1908-1986)
Concertino for Horn & Strings, Op. 45/5 (1955)
S. Hermansson (hn), E. Chivzhel (cnd), Umeå Sinfonietta † Atterberg:Con Hn; G. Jacob:Con Hn; M. Reger:Scherzino; Seiber:Notturno Hn BIS ▲ 376 [DDD] (17.97)
I. Lanzky-Otto (hn), Stockholm Chamber Ensemble † Con Sax, Op. 14; Divert 2, Op. 15; Qt 3 Strs, Op. 65; Quattro tempi CAPA ▲ 21492 (16.97)
Concertino for Trombone & Strings, Op. 45/7 (1955)
C. Lindberg (trbn), O. Kamu (cnd), New Stockholm CO *(rec Sweden, Sep 23-26 & Nov 27, 1987)* ("The Winter Trombone") † D. Milhaud:Concertino d'hiver, Op. 327; R. Pöntinen:Blue Winter; Telemann:Con Trb; Vivaldi:Cons Vn Strs, Op. 8/1-4 *([ENG,FRE,GER] text)* BIS ▲ 348 [DDD] (17.97)
Concertinos (12) for Various solo Instruments & String Orchestra, Op. 45 (1954-57)
L. Berlin (vn), S. Westerberg (cnd), Stockholm PO † Con Vn; Winter's Tale, Op. 18 SWES ▲ 1156 (17.97)
T. Fredin (db), J. Wedin (cnd) ("Concertos for Double Bass & Orchestra") † G. Bottesini:Con 2 Db; Elegy & Tarantella; E. von Koch:Serenade Db OPU ▲ 8502 (16.97)
artists unknown BIS 2-▲ 473 [AAD] (34.97)
Concerto for Saxophone & Strings, Op. 14 (1934)
C. Johnsson (a sax), L. Segerstam (cnd), Swedish RSO † Concertino Hn, Op. 45/5; Divert 2, Op. 15; Qt 3 Strs, Op. 65; Quattro tempi CAPA ▲ 21492 (16.97)
P. Savijoki (a sax), J. Panula (cnd), Stockholm New CO † Glazunov:Con A Sax, Op. 109; J. Panula:Adagio & Allegro BIS ▲ 218 [DDD] (16.97)

LARSSON, LARS-ERIK (cont.)

Concerto for Violin & Orchestra, Op. 42 (1952)
L. Berlin (vn), S. Westerberg (cnd), Stockholm PO † Concertinos, Op. 45; Winter's Tale, Op. 18 SWES ▲ 1156 (17.97)

Divertimento No. 2 for Small Orchestra, Op. 15 (1935)
J. Wedin (cnd), Stockholm Sinfonietta † Con Sax, Op. 14; Concertino Hn, Op. 45/5; Qt 3 Strs, Op. 65; Quattro tempi CAPA ▲ 21492 (16.97)

God in Disguise [Förklädd Gud] (lyric suite) for Soprano, Baritone, Speaker & Orchestra [set to a poem cycle by Hjalmar Gullberg], Op. 24 (1940)
B. Nordin (sop), H. Hagegård (bar), P. Jonsson (nar), S. Frykberg (cnd), Helsingborg SO, Helsingborg Sym Chorus [SWE] † Sym 3 BIS ▲ 96 [AAD] (17.97)
E. Söderström (sop), E. Sandaen (bar), L. Ekborg (nar), S. Westerberg (cnd), Swedish SO † Orch Vars, Op. 50; Pastoralsvit, Op. 19 SWES ▲ 1020 (17.97)
E. Söderström (sop), S. Westerberg (cnd) † Missa Brevis; Songs SWES ▲ 1096 (17.97)

Hommage à Mozart for Clarinet & Orchestra
K. Fagéus (cl), E. Klas (cnd), Stockholm Royal Orch ("Clarinet Concertos") † Crusell:Den Lilla Slavinnan (sels); Frumerie:Con Cl; W. A. Mozart:Con Cl, K.622 OPU ▲ 19801 (16.97)

Little Serenade for String Orchestra, Op. 12 (1934)
W. Rajski (cnd), Musica Vitae *(rec Sweden, Apr 21/24, 1988)* ("Music Vitae plays Nordic Music Vol. 1") † Carlstedt:Metamorphosi Strs, Op. 42; Rautavaara:Fiddlers; J. H. Roman:Con Ob & Strs, BeRI 46; Sibelius:Romance Strs, Op. 42 *(E, F, G text)* BIS ▲ 460 [DDD] (17.97)
E. Salonen (cnd), Stockholm Sinfonietta † Lidholm:Musik; Söderlundh:Concertino Ob; D. Wirén:Serenade Strs, Op. 11 BIS ▲ 285 [DDD] (17.97)

Missa Brevis for 3 Voices (1954)
E. Söderström (sop), S. Westerberg (cnd) † God in Disguise, Op. 24; Songs SWES ▲ 1096 (17.97)

Orchestral Variations for Orchestra, Op. 50 (1962-63)
S. Westerberg (cnd), Swedish SO † God in Disguise, Op. 24; Pastoralsvit, Op. 19 SWES ▲ 1020 (17.97)

Pastoralsvit [Pastoral Suite] for Orchestra, Op. 19 (1938)
M. Bernardi (cnd), CBC Vancouver SO *(rec Vancouver British Columbia, Mar 1-2, 1992)* ("Northern Landscapes") † Winter's Tale, Op. 18; Frumerie:Pastoral Suite, Op. 13b; K. Riisager:Little Ov; Sibelius:The Lover; D. Wirén:Serenade Strs, Op. 11 SMS ▲ 5157 [DDD] (16.97)
S. Westerberg (cnd), Swedish RSO—Romance *(rec Berwald Hall, Stockholm, Sweden, May 7, 1986)* ("Swedish Highlights") † Alfvén:Bergakungen (sels); Festspel, Op. 25; Gustav II Adolph, Op. 49; Prodigal Son, Op. 217; Swedish Flag; Swedish Rhap 1, Op. 19; O. J. Lindblad:Royal Anthem; Söderman:Swedish Festival; Stenhammar:Ett folk, Op. 22; Sången, Op. 44; Traditional:Du Gamla, Du Fria; D. Wirén:Serenade Strs, Op. 11 CAPA ▲ 21340 [DDD] (16.97)
S. Westerberg (cnd), Swedish SO † God in Disguise, Op. 24; Orch Vars, Op. 50 SWES ▲ 1020 (17.97)

Piano Music
H. Pålsson (pno)—Sju små fugor med preludier i gammal stil, Op., Op. 58; Croquisier, Op. 38; Sons 1-3 Pno ("Piano Music") BIS ▲ 758 [DDD] (17.97)

Pieces (3) for Clarinet & Piano, Op. 61 (1970)
C. Stjernström (cl), M. Kanarva (pno) *(rec Academy of Music of Malmö, Rosenbergssalen, Sweden, July 1996)* † Bozza:Aria Cl; Debussy:Petite pièce Cl; Première rapsodie Cl; Gäfvert:Fant Cl; Saint-Saëns:Son Cl; Söderlundh:Petite Suite Cl ITIM ▲ 53 (16.97)

Quartet No. 3 for Strings, Op. 65 (1975)
Stockholm String Quartet † Con Sax, Op. 14; Concertino Hn, Op. 45/5; Divert 2, Op. 15; Quattro tempi CAPA ▲ 21492 (16.97)

Quattro tempi (divertimento) for Wind Quintet (1968)
Stockholm Wind Quintet † Con Sax, Op. 14; Concertino Hn, Op. 45/5; Divert 2, Op. 15; Qt 3 Strs, Op. 65 CAPA ▲ 21492 (16.97)

Songs
E. Söderström (sop), S. Westerberg (cnd) —Songs of the Naked Trees † God in Disguise, Op. 24; Missa Brevis SWES ▲ 1096 (17.97)

Symphony No. 1 in D, Op. 2 (1927-8)
H. Frank (cnd), Helsingborg SO † Sym 2 BIS ▲ 426 [DDD] (17.97)

Symphony No. 2, Op. 17 (1937)
H. Frank (cnd), Helsingborg SO † Sym 1 BIS ▲ 426 [DDD] (17.97)

Symphony No. 3 in c, Op. 34 (1944-5)
S. Frykberg (cnd), Helsingborg SO † God in Disguise, Op. 24 BIS ▲ 96 [AAD] (17.97)

A Winter's Tale [En Vintersaga] for Violin & Orchestra, Op. 18 (1937-38)
L. Berlin (vn), S. Westerberg (cnd), Stockholm PO † Con Vn; Concertinos, Op. 45 SWES ▲ 1156 (17.97)
M. Bernardi (cnd), CBC Vancouver SO *(rec Vancouver British Columbia, Mar 1-2, 1992)* ("Northern Landscapes") † Pastoralsvit, Op. 19; Frumerie:Pastoral Suite, Op. 13b; K. Riisager:Little Ov; Sibelius:The Lover; D. Wirén:Serenade Strs, Op. 11 SMS ▲ 5157 [DDD] (16.97)

LARSSON, MATS (1965-

Clockworks for Brass Quintet & Wind Band (1992; arr 2 Pianos, Timpani & Brass Quintet, 1994)
L. Derwinger (pno), R. Pöntinen (pno), J. Silvmark (perc), Stockholm Chamber Brass *(rec Swedish Radio, Sweden, Nov 1994)* ("Clockworks") † J. Bach:Rounds & Dances; L. Bernstein:Dance Suite Brass; A. Previn:4 Outings; I. Stravinsky:Histoire du soldat (sels); Ragtime BIS ▲ 699 [DDD] (17.97)

Concerto for Trombone & Winds (1995)
C. Lindberg (trbn), A. V. Beek (cnd) ("Hekas!") † P. Bengtson:Hekas!; Crusell:Intro, Theme & Vars on a Swedish Air, Op. 12; Tykesson:Arabesques BIS ▲ 818 [DDD] (17.97)

LASALA, ANGEL (1914-

Poema del Pastor Coya for Violin & Harp (1942)
Aurora Duo † Boren:Movts from Liturgical Dance; Donizetti:Son Vn; A. Hovhaness:Son Vn Hp, Op. 406; Saint-Saëns:Fant Vn; Shaposhnikov:Son in d Vn 4TAY ▲ 4010 [DDD] (17.97)

LASSUS, FERDINAND DE (ca 1560-1609)

Sacred Music
E. Wickham (cnd), Renaissance Singers ("O Socii Durate") † Manchicourt:Sacred Music; Rore:Sacred Music; Willaert:Sacred Music ASVQ ▲ 6228 (10.97)

LASSUS, ORLANDE (ROLAND) DE (ORLANDO DI LASSO) (1532-1594)

Aurora lucis rutilat (magnificat setting) for 10 Voices (1619)
P. Cao (cnd) , Namur Chamber Choir *(rec St. Lambert à Mozet, Nov 1994)* † Motets; Vinum bonum; Lohet:Org Music RICE ▲ 155141 (17.97)
E. van Nevel (cnd), Concerto Palatino, Currende Consort, Capella Currende, H. Stinders (org) *(rec Hoeven, Netherlands, Nov 11, 1995)* † Motets; Musica Dei donum optimi *((DUT,ENG,FRE,GER)text)* EUFO ▲ 1239 [DDD] (18.97)

Bell'Amfitrit'altera (mass) for 8 Voices (1610)
G. Guest (cnd), St. John's College Choir Cambridge ("Allegri-Miserere") † G. Allegri:Salmo Miserere mei Deus; Palestrina:Veni sponsa Christi CFP (Eminence) ▲ 2180 [DDD] (16.97)
J. O'Donnell (cnd) , J. West (cnd), Westminster Cathedral Choir † C. Erbach:Sacred Music; H. L. Hassler:Sacred Music HYP ▲ 66688 (18.97)
J. Summerly (cnd), Oxford Schola Cantorum *(rec Mar 1993)* ("Early Music: Palestrina and Lassus") † Palestrina:Sacred Music; Stabat mater NXIN ▲ 550836 [DDD] (5.97)

Chansons & Moresche [French Songs & Moreschas]
D. Collot (sop), Ricercar Consort † P. Philips:Kbd Music RICE ▲ 154149 (17.97)

Choral Music
R. Alessandrini (cnd), Concerto Italiano—Allala, pia calia; Saccio 'na cosa; Lucia, celu, ahi, ahi, biscania; S'io ve dico ca sete la chiù bella; Ecco la nimph 'Ebrayca chiamata; Parch'hai lasciato; Io ti vorria contar la pena mia; Hai, Lucia, bona cosa io dic'a tia; Chichilichi? Cucurucu !; Oh Lucia, miau, miau; Ad altrc le voi dare ste passate; Tutto lo di mi dici: canta, canta!; Cathalina, apra finestra; Turro 'l di piango; Matona, mia cara; S'io fusse ciaul'; Ogni giorno m'han ditt'a chi favlli; O belle fusa!; Madonna mia, pietà ("Villanelle, moresche e altre canzoni") OPUS ▲ 3094 (18.97)

Lagrime di San Pietro [The Tears of St. Peter] (madrigal cycle w. closing motet) for 7 Voices (1595)
P. Herreweghe (cnd), Ensemble Vocal Européen HAM ▲ 901483 (18.97)
Huelgas Ensemble *(rec Mar 5-8, 1993)* SNYC ▲ 53373 [DDD] (16.97)

The Lamentations of Jeremiah for Chorus
P. Herreweghe (cnd), Chapelle Royale Vocal Enemble [LAT] HAM ▲ 901299 (18.97)

LASSUS, ORLANDE (ROLAND) DE (ORLANDO DI LASSO) (cont.)

Madrigals
Orlando di Lasso Ensemble—Hor vi riconfortate in vostre fole; O Tempo, o ciel; Pon fren' al gran dolor; Quel rossignuol che si soaue piagne; Viuo sol di speranza; Che fai, alma? che pensi?; Che è fermato di menar sua vita; Come lume di notte; S'io esca viuo de dubbiosi scogli; Perch'io veggio, e mi spiace; In dubbio di mio stato; Occhi, piangete; Di pensier in persier; Amor, che ved'ogni persier; Io son si stanco sotto'l fascio antico; Canzon se l'esser meco; Vedi; Aurora de l'aurato letto; Hor vi riconfoarte in vostre fole; In dubio verno, un instabil sereno; Passan vostri triomphi e vostre pompe *(rec Apr 1995)* ("Madrigals after Petrarch") THOR ▲ 2282 [DDD] (16.97)
M. Zöbeley (cnd) —Il grave dell'età; Vedi l'aurora; Più volte un bel desio; Come pianta; Ben sono i prema tuoi; Canzon, la doglia; Che giova posseder; Così cor mio; Veggio se al vero; Arse la fiamma; Chi è fermato; Chi non sa; Per aspro mar; Ecco che pur vi lasso; Deh lascia anima; Tanto è quel bene; Hor ch'a l'albergo; Prendi l'aurata lira; O fugace dolcezza; Signor, le colpe mie ARSM ▲ 1099 [DDD] (17.97)

Missa "Osculetur me" for 8 Voices (after 1582)
P. Phillips (cnd), Tallis Scholars † Motets GIME ▲ 54918 [DDD] (16.97)

Motets
P. Cao (cnd) , Namur Chamber Choir—Omnes de saba; Da pacem Domine; Timor et tremor; Tui sunt coeli; Surge propera amica mea; Aurora lucis rutilat *(rec St. Lambert à Mozet, Nov 1994)* † Aurora lucis rutilat; Vinum bonum; Lohet:Org Music RICE ▲ 155141 (17.97)
F. Fauché (bass), La Fenice Ensemble—Haec quae ter triplici; Suzanne un jour; Susana un jour; Suzanne un giur; Bonjour mon coeur; Mr Buctons galiard; Et d'où venez vous, Madame Lucette ("Motetti, Madrigali e Canzoni Francesi") † Palestrina:Motets RICE ▲ 152137 (17.97)
P. Phillips (cnd), Tallis Scholars—Alma Redemptoris mater; Ave Regina caelorum; Hodie completi sunt; Osculetur me; Regina caeli; Salve Regina; Timor et tremor † Missa "Osculetur me" GIME ▲ 54918 [DDD] (16.97)
H. Stinders (org), E. van Nevel (cnd), Concerto Palatino, Currende Consort, Capella Currende—Quo properas facunde; Gratia soli Dei pie; Anni nostri sicut; Certa fortier; Dulci sub umbra; Jam lucis orto sidere; In hora ultima; In religione homo vivit; Luxuriosa res vinum; Dulces exuviae; S.U.su.P.E.R.per; Omnia tempus habent; Quid vulgo memorant; Pacis amans; Quid trepidas; Nunc gaudere licet *(rec Hoeven, Netherlands, Nov 11, 1995)* † Aurora lucis rutilat; Musica Dei donum optimi EUFO ▲ 1239 [DDD] (18.97)

Music of Lassus
K. Coker (cnd) —La Cortesia Voi Donne; Occhi Piangete; Audi Dulcis Amica Mea; Per Pianto Mia Carne; O Lucia; Expectatio Iustorum; Fant 25; Trop Endurer; Fant 13; Las voulez vous; Fant 27; Madonna Mia Pietà; Fant Quarta; Oculus Non Vidit; Vatene Lieta Homai ("La Cortesia") RCMM ▲ 19502 [DDD] (16.97)
D. Fallis (cnd) —U jour l'amant; Gallans qui par terre; Ardant amour à 4; Ardant amour à 5; J'ay de vous voir; Toutes les nuis; Puisque vivre; Susana [arr Antonio de Cabezón]; Susanne ung jour [arr Giovanni Bassano]; Susane un jour; Bonjour mon coeur; La nuict froide et sombre; Que dis-tu; Ove sei, vita mia; No giorno; Tu traditora; Come pianta; Poi che'l mio largo pianto; Madonna mia, pietà; Appariran per me; Chi chilichi *(rec Humbercrest United Church Toronto, Jan 1994)* ("Chansons & Madrigals") DOR ▲ 80149 [DDD] (13.97)

Musica Dei donum optimi (motet) for 6 Voices (1594)
E. van Nevel (cnd), Concerto Palatino, Currende Consort, Capella Currende, H. Stinders (org) *(rec Hoeven, Netherlands, Nov 11, 1995)* † Aurora lucis rutilat; Motets *((DUT,ENG,FRE,GER)text)* EUFO ▲ 1239 [DDD] (18.97)

Paschalis for 5 Voices (1576)
P. Elliott (ten), P. Hillier (cnd), Theater of Voices † Passio Domini nostri Jesu Christi secundum Mathheu; Sacred Music HAM ▲ 907076 (18.97)

Passio Domini nostri Jesu Christi secundum Mattheum [St. Matthew Passion] for 5 Voices (1575)
P. Elliott (ten), P. Hillier (cnd), Theater of Voices † Paschalis; Sacred Music HAM ▲ 907076 (18.97)
K. Ruhland (cnd), Capella Antiqua München *(rec Aicha vorm Wald, Bavaria, Germany, Jan 7-9, 1976)* ("Paschale Mysterium") † Anonymous:Alleluia; Ave Rex noster; Christus Dominus resurrexit; Crucem tuam; Cum angelis; Ecce lignum crucis; Hac die, quam fecit Dominus; Hoc corpus; Incipit lamentatio; Nos autem gloriari; Oratio Jeremiae Prophetae; Popule meus; Recessit pastor noster; Ubi est caritas et dilestio SNYC ▲ 60360 [ADD] (7.97)

Patrocinium musicus cantionum [Book 1] for 4-6 Voices (1573)
E. van Nevel (cnd), Concerto Palatino, Currende Vocal Ensemble ACCE ▲ 8855 (17.97)

Psalmi Davidis poenitentiales (7 motets) for 5 Voices (1584)
Henry's Eight HYP 2-▲ 67271 (36.97)
R. Kammler (cnd), Josquin des Préz Chamber Choir RAUM ▲ 9606 (17.97)

Requiem for Chorus
B. Turner (cnd), Pro Cantione Antiqua HYP (Dyad) ▲ 22012 (18.97)

Sacred Music
S. Darlington (cnd), Christ Church Cathedral Choir, Oxford—Missa 'Qual donna'; Tristis est anima mea; Exaltabo te Domine; Psalmi Davidis poenitentiales [De profundis]; Missa 'Jäger' [LAT] *(rec Oxfordshire, England, Nov 16-17, 1987)* ("European Choral Music 1525-1751") † J. R. Esteves:Sacred Music; C. de Morales:O sacrum convivium; Palestrina:Sacred Music; Rore:Qual donn'attende; Victoria:Sacred Choral Music NIMB 5-▲ 1758 [DDD] (29.97)
P. Elliott (ten), P. Hillier (cnd), Theatre of Voices—Visitation † Paschalis; Passio Domini nostri Jesu Christi secundum Mathheu HAM ▲ 907076 (18.97)
E. van Nevel (cnd), Currende—Stabat Mater Dolorosa ("Polyphony for Passion-Tide") † Arcadelt:Lamentationes; Clemens Non Papa:Sacred Music; Crecquillon:Lamentationes; Rogier:Sacred Music; Wert:Sacred Music EUFO ▲ 1248 [DDD] (18.97)
K. Niles (cnd), Munich Cathedral Choir, K. Niles (cnd), Munich Cathedral Boys' Choir, K. Niles (cnd), Munich Cathedral Vocal Ensemble—Gloria Patri à 6; Missa super Entre vous filles à 5; Te Deum à 6; Magnificat à 5; Ave Regina caelorum à 6; Salve Regina à 5 ("Munich Cathedral Music of the Renaissance") † Senfl:Vocal Music CHR ▲ 77196 [DDD] (17.97)
J. Skidmore (cnd) , Ex Cathedra Choir—Sgimus tibi a3; Ave verum corpus a6; Bicinia 3, 9 & 14; Bone Jesu a8; Christus resurgens a5; Justorum animae a5; Laudent Deum a4; Musica De donum a6; Quam pulchra es a6; Salve regina a6; Tristis est anima mea a5; Tui Sunt coeli a8; Vide homo a7; Vinum bonum a8 ("Missa ad Imitationem Vinum Bonum") ASV (Gaudeamus) ▲ 150 (16.97)
J. Summerly (cnd), Oxford Camerata—Missa entre vous filles; Infelix ego; Missa Susanne un jour *(rec Apr 1993)* NXIN ▲ 550842 [DDD] (5.97)
D. Tabbia (cnd), Ricercar Academy Orch, Insieme Vocale Datrocanto—Missa Super Je Suis Deshéritée; Lectiones Matutinae de Nativitate Christi; Lectiones Sacrae ex Libri Hiob; Stabat Mater Dolorosa STRV ▲ 33345 [DDD] (16.97)

Vinum bonum (mass) for 8 Voices
P. Cao (cnd) , Namur Chamber Choir *(rec St. Lambert à Mozet, Nov 1994)* † Aurora lucis rutilat; Motets; Lohet:Org Music RICE ▲ 155141 (17.97)

LAUBER, JOSEPH (1864-1952)

Caprices (6) for Piano, Op. 44 (1923)
H. Sakagami (pno) ("Music in Lucerne, Vol. 1: Solo Piano Music") † P. Benary:Son 2 Pno; Diethelm:Klangfiguren, Op. 244; Eisenmann:Vars Pno, Op. 71; Schnyder von Wartensee:Scherzi Pno; A. Scriabin:Preludes (24) Pno, Op. 11; Willisegger:Sakura GALL 2-▲ 966 [DDD] (36.97)

Concerto for Double Bass & Orchestra (1935)
K. Thalmann (db), O. Henzold (cnd), AML Lucerne SO ("Music in Lucerne") † F. Brun:Sym 2; R. Wagner:Siegfried Idyll GALL ▲ 838 (19.97)

Medieval Dances (4) for Flute & Harp, Op. 45
R. Aitken (fl), E. Goodman (hp) *(rec Ontario Canada, Sept-Oct 1993)* ("Toward the Sea: Music for Flute & Harp") † Damase:Son Fl & Hp; Inghelbrecht:Sonatina en trois parties; Petra-Basacopol:Son Fl Hp; Takemitsu:Toward the Sea III BIS ▲ 650 [DDD] (17.97)

LAUER, ELIZABETH (1932-

Songs on Poems of James Joyce (7) for Mezzo-Soprano & Piano (1955)
A. M. Nelson (mez), E. Lauer (pno) ("Intimate Thoughts") † Cacioppo:Wolf; Constantinides:Intimations; D. K. Eastman:Just Us; Marez Oyens:Hymns CPS ▲ 8632 (16.97)

LAURIDSEN, LAURIDS (1882-1946)

Music of Lauridsen
I. Beck (org) *(Prelude Org in c, Op. 19; Fugue, Op. 19/3; Preludes Org (7), Op. 25; Pastorale Org, Op. 19/2; Org Chorales (6))*, L. T. Bertelsen (bar), I. Beck (org) *(Psalms 62 & 102; "Laer mig at kende dine veje"; "Sung om freden"; Spiritual Songs (4), Op. 25)* ("Organ Music & Spiritual Songs") PLAL ▲ 85 [DDD] (17.97)

LAURIDSEN, MORTEN (1943-

Ave Maria for Chorus
P. Salamunovich (cnd), Los Angeles Master Chorale *(rec Sacred Heart Chapel, Loyola Marymount University, United States of America, June 9 & Aug. 29, 1997/Jan. 9 & 20, 1998)* ("Lux Aeterna") † Chansons des roses; Lux aeterna; Mid-Winter Songs; O magnum mysterium RCMM ▲ 19705 [DDD] (16.97)

LAURIDSEN, MORTEN (cont.)
Les Chansons des roses for Chorus [after Rilke] (1993)
P. Rutenberg (cnd), Los Angeles Chamber Singers ("Romancero Gitano") † S. Barber:Songs; Castelnuovo-Tedesco:Romancero gitano, Op. 152; Chorbajian:Bitter for Sweet; H. Stevens:Elizabethan Madrigals; R. Thompson:Odes to Horace RCMM ▲ 19802 (16.97)
P. Salamunovich (cnd), Los Angeles Master Chorale *(rec Sacred Heart Chapel, Loyola Marymount University, United States of America, June 9 & Aug. 29, 1997/Jan. 9 & 20, 1998)* ("Lux Aeterna") † Ave Maria; Lux aeterna; Mid-Winter Songs; O magnum mysterium RCMM ▲ 19705 [DDD] (16.97)
Lux aeterna for Chorus
P. Salamunovich (cnd), Los Angeles Master Chorale *(rec Sacred Heart Chapel. Loyola Marymount University, United States of America, June 9 & Aug. 29, 1997/Jan. 9 & 20, 1998)* ("Lux Aeterna") † Ave Maria; Chansons des roses; Mid-Winter Songs; O magnum mysterium RCMM ▲ 19705 [DDD] (16.97)
Mid-Winter Songs for Chorus [after poems by Robert Graves]
P. Salamunovich (cnd), Los Angeles Master Chorale [orchd] *(rec Sacred Heart Chapel, Loyola Marymount University, United States of America, June 9 & Aug. 29, 1997/Jan. 9 & 20, 1998)* ("Lux Aeterna") † Ave Maria; Chansons des roses; Lux aeterna; O magnum mysterium RCMM ▲ 19705 [DDD] (16.97)
O magnum mysterium for Chorus (1994)
P. Salamunovich (cnd), Los Angeles Master Chorale *(rec Sacred Heart Chapel, Loyola Marymount University, United States of America, June 9 & Aug. 29, 1997/Jan. 9 & 20, 1998)* ("Lux Aeterna") † Ave Maria; Chansons des roses; Lux aeterna; Mid-Winter Songs RCMM ▲ 19705 [DDD] (16.97)

LAURO, ANTONIO (1909-1986)
Guitar Music
R. Guthrie (gtr)—Adiós a Ocumare; Triptico; Vals Venezolano; El Marabino *(rec Holy Nativity Episcopal Church, Plano, TX, 1995)* † L. Almeida:Gtr Music; J. Guimarães:Gtr Music; M. Ponce:Gtr Music; J. Silva:Gtr Music; H. Villa-Lobos:Preludes Gtr ENRE ▲ 9509 [DDD] (16.97)
P. Skareng (gtr)—2 waltzes Carora & Angostura; Suite Venezolana ("El Colibri") † J. S. Bach:Sons & Partitas Vn; Carlstedt:Swedish Dances; Frumerie:Vars on a Swedish Folk Tune, Op. 69a; M. Giuliani:Rossiniana; Sagreras:El Colibri; Tárrega:Recuerdos de la Alhambra CAPA ▲ 21392 [AAD] (16.97)
Y. Storms (gtr)—Vals; El Marabino; Vals Criollo; Aire de Joropo ("A Touch of Latin") † A. Barrios:Gtr Music; L. Brouwer:Gtr Music; J. Cardoso:Gtr Music; J. Guimarães:Sons de Carrilhões; Sojo:Pieces from Venezuela; H. Villa-Lobos:Chôro 1 SYRX ▲ 94106 [DDD] (16.97)
Lute Music
R. Bluestone (gtr)—Valses Venezolanos (6) Gtr [Maria Luisa] *(rec Loretto Chapel, Santa Fe, NM)* † Dunlap:Lt Music; Holborne:Lt Music; D. Milne:Lt Music; M. Ponce:Son 3 Gtr; Tansman:Lt Music; S. L. Weiss:Lt Music LINA ▲ 1896 [DDD]
Suite Venezolano for Guitar
R. Gauk (gtr) ("Panorama") † L. Brouwer:Paisaje cubano con campanas; Sencillos; O. Daniel:After the Panorama; Moreno Torroba:Pieces caractéristiques; M. Ponce:Piezas Gtr MARQ ▲ 191 (16.97)
Y. Kamata (gtr) ("Serie Americana: Guitar Works of Latin America") † Ayala:Serie Americana; A. Piazzolla:Pieces (5) Gtr; H. Villa-Lobos:Preludes Gtr CAMA ▲ 453 [DDD] (18.97)
Valses Venezolanos (4) for Guitar (1963)
D. Blanco (gtr) *(rec Castle Wik, Sweden, May 25, 1979)* ("Popular Guitar Music") † A. Barrios:Gtr Music; Sojo:Pieces Venezuela (5) Gtr; Sor:Fants Gtr; Grand Solo Gtr, Op. 14; Gtr Music; Son Gtr; Vars Mozart, Op. 9 *(E, F, G text)* BIS ▲ 133 [AAD] (17.97)
G. Kreplin (gtr) *(rec Broad Creek, MD, Spring 1995)* ("Bach in Brazil") † J. S. Bach:Suite Lt, BWV 995; H. Villa-Lobos:Preludes Gtr ASCE ▲ 103 [DDD] (15.97)
Venezuelan Waltz No. 3, ""Natalia"" (1939)
C. Barbosa-Lima (gtr) *(rec Hayward, CA, 1992)* ("Ginastera's Sonata") † L. Almeida:Crepusculo em Copacabana; A. Barrios:Abejas; Fabiniana Gtr; Ginastera:Son Gtr, Op. 47; Gnattali:Sonatina 1 Gtr; A. Harris:Concertino de California; T. D. Mello:Amor Sem Fim ERTO ▲ 42015 (14.97)

LAUTEN, ELODIE (20th cent)
Tronik Involutions (electronic music from the Gaia Cycle Matrix)
E. Lauten (elec/kbd) ("Tronik Involutions") OOD ▲ 27 [DDD] (16.97)
Variations on the Orange Cycle for Piano (1991)
L. Svard (pno) *(rec Lewisburg, PA, Oct 11-13, 1996 & Jan 12-13, 1997)* † Gann:Desert Sonata; J. Hunt:Trapani LOV ▲ 3052 [DDD] (16.97)

LAVALLE-GARCÍA, ARMANDO (1924-
Obertura Colonial for Orchestra
E. Diazmuñoz (cnd), Mexico City PO † G. Duran:Nepantla; Kuri-Aldana:Canto Latinamericano; Mabarak:Sym in One Mvt; Moncayo García:Bosques; Sandi:Theme & Vars CLME ▲ 21231 (13.97)
H. de la Fuente (cnd), Mexican State PO † M. K. Aldana:Canto Latinoamericano; G. Duran:Nepantla; R. Halffter:Madrugada del panadero, Op. 12a; Jiménez-Mabarak:Sym in 1 Movt; Sandi:Theme & Vars CLME ▲ 21006 (13.97)

LAVALLÉE, CALIXA (1842-1891)
The Widow (selections)
J. Kolomyjec (sop), M. DuBois (ten), R. Armenian (cnd), Kitchener-Waterloo SO † Heuberger:Opernball (sels); I. Kálmán:Csárdásfürstin (sels); Gräfin Mariza (sels); F. Lehár:Land des Lächelns (sels); Strauss (II):Nacht in Venedig (sels) CBC (SM 5000) ▲ 5126 [DDD] (16.97)

LAVERGNE, PHILIPPE (20th cent)
Invariants for Clarinet, Bassoon, Cello & Barrel Organ (1990)
Barbaroque Ensemble † Fučík:Alte Brummbär, Op. 210; G. F. Handel:Cons (16) Org; C. M. von Weber:Con Ob & Ww GALL ▲ 858 [DDD] (19.97)

LAVISTA, MARIO (1943-
Danzas breves (5) for Wind Quintet
Mexico City Woodwind Quintet † C. Chávez:Soli 2; Enriquez:Pentamúsica; M. Ibarra:Juegos nocturnos; A. Lara:Aulós CLME ▲ 21018 (13.97)
Fiction for Orchestra
E. Diazmuñoz (cnd), Mexico City PO † Catán:En un doblez tiempo; Espinosa:Ifegenia Cruel (ov); A. L. Ponce:Elegy; Zyman:Soliloquy CLME ▲ 21232 (13.97)
Madrigal for Clarinet (1985)
(rec Jan 13-15, 1996) † Quotations; Davidovsky:Romancero; T. León:Pueblo Mulato; R. X. Rodriguez:Niais Amoureux; Sierra:Trio Tropical CRI ▲ 773 [DDD] (16.97)
Quotations for Cello & Piano (1979)
Voices of Change members *(rec Jan 13-15, 1996)* † Madrigal; Davidovsky:Romancero; T. León:Pueblo Mulato; R. X. Rodriguez:Niais Amoureux; Sierra:Trio Tropical CRI ▲ 773 [DDD] (16.97)

LAVRY, MARC (1903-1967)
Jewish Dances (3) for Violin & Piano
Z. Schiff (vn), C. Eisenberg (pno) † J. Achron:Hebrew Melody, Op. 33; Castelnuovo-Tedesco:Sea Murmurs, Op. 24a; Haym:Sephardic Melody; Hush:Shir Eres; Son Vn; Krein:Caprice Hebraique; Zimbalist:Slavonic Dances (3) 4TAY ▲ 4002 (18.97)

LAWES, HENRY (1596-1662)
Fantasia-Suites (8) for Violin, Bass Viol & Organ
Music's Re-Creation *(rec Jan 1997)* ("Fantazia-Suites") CENT ▲ 2385 (16.97)

LAWES, WILLIAM (1602-1645)
Fantasia-Suites for 2 Violins, Bass Viol & Organ
London Baroque *(rec William Drake org Buckfastleigh, June 1992)* HMA ▲ 1901423 [DDD] (9.97)
Royall Consort Suites (10) for 2 Violins, 2 Bass Viols & Continuo
C. Balding (vn), U. Wild (hpd)—No. 7 *(rec Netherlands)* ("Henry Purcell & His Time") † J. Jenkins:Fant in d Va & Vn; M. Locke:Suite III 2 Vns, Vol & Org; Suite IV 2 Vns, Vol & Hpd; H. Purcell:Fant upon a Ground, Z.731; Pavan à 3; Pavan à 4; C. Simpson:Prelude & Divisions on a Ground; Traditional:John Come Kiss *([ENG,GER] text)* CCL ▲ 4792 [DDD] (18.97)
M. Huggett (vn), Greate Consort ("Vol. 1") ASV (Gaudeamus) ▲ 146 [DDD] (16.97)
M. Huggett (vn), Greate Consort ("Vol. 2") ASV (Gaudeamus) ▲ 147 (16.97)
S. Kuijken (vn), L. van Dael (va), W. Kuijken (vl), B. Kuijken (fl), G. Leonhardt (cnd) † Songs SNYC (Seon) ▲ 63179 (7.97)
N. North (thb), P. O'Dette (thb), Purcell Quartet CHN (Early Music) 2-▲ 584 [DDD] (32.97)
Songs
R. Jacobs (alt) † Royall Consort Suites SNYC (Seon) ▲ 63179 (7.97)

LAY, RAOUL (1964-
Avec amour for Mezzo-Soprano & Chamber Ensemble
F. Bergmann (mez), R. Lay (cnd) ("Jeune ecole de Marseille") † Ombre autour du temps; J. P. Alagna:Palimpseste; Aue:Monologue; Boeuf:Risées; R. Campo:Anima SONP ▲ 96019 [DDD] (16.97)
L'ombre autour du temps for Piano, Winds & Strings
R. Lay (cnd) ("Jeune ecole de Marseille") † Avec amour; J. P. Alagna:Palimpseste; Aue:Monologue; Boeuf:Risées; R. Campo:Anima SONP ▲ 96019 [DDD] (16.97)

LAZAR, SIMON LEON (1948-
Holocaust: A Requiem for the Fate of the Jews for solo Voices, Chorus & Electronics
S. L. Lazar (elec), V. Levy (cnd), Jewish Synagogal Choir GEGA ▲ 104 (16.97)

LAZAREV, EDUARD (1935-
Master & Margarita (ballet) for Orchestra [after Bulgakov]
D. Goya (cnd), Moldavian PO RUS ▲ 10016 [AAD] (12.97)

LAZAROF, HENRI (1932-
Cadence II for Viola & Tape (1969)
M. Thomas (va) *(rec 1970)* † Cadence V; Con 1 Vc; Continuum CRI ▲ 631 (17.97)
Cadence V for Flute & Tape (1972)
J. Galway (fl) *(rec 1973)* † Cadence II; Con 1 Vc; Continuum CRI ▲ 631 (17.97)
Canti (8 songs) for a cappella Chorus [original texts by Lazarof] (1971)
Roger Wagner Chorale [ENG] † Con Fl; Con Orch; Spectrum CRI ▲ 588 [ADD] (17.97)
Chamber Symphony (1977)
G. Schwarz (cnd), Los Angeles CO *(rec Univ of CA Los Angeles)* ("Music for Chamber Orchestra, Viola & Organ") † Intonazione e Variazioni; Serenade Str Sxt; Sinfonietta; Volo LARL ▲ 844 [DDD] (14.97)
Concertante II for Flute, Oboe, Clarinet, Percussion, Piano & String Trio (1988)
C. Kendall (cnd) † Divert Cl; Prayers; Suite Perc DLS ▲ 3124 [DDD] (14.97)
Concerto No. 1 for Cello & Orchestra (1968)
L. Lesser (vc), G. Samuel (cnd), Oakland SO † Cadence II; Cadence V; Continuum CRI ▲ 631 (17.97)
Concerto for Flute & Orchestra (1973)
J. Galway (fl), H. Lazarof (cnd), New Philharmonia Orch † Canti; Con Orch; Spectrum CRI ▲ 588 [ADD] (17.97)
Concerto for Orchestra (1978)
S. Comissiona (cnd), Baltimore SO † Canti; Con Fl; Spectrum CRI ▲ 588 [ADD] (17.97)
Continuum for String Trio (1970)
S. Plummer (vn), M. Thomas (va), L. Lesser (vc) *(rec 1970)* † Cadence II; Cadence V; Con 1 Vc CRI ▲ 631 (17.97)
Divertimento for Clarinet, Vibraphone, Violin & Cello (1989)
F. Epstein (perc), Collage New Music Ensemble † Concertante II; Prayers; Suite Perc DLS ▲ 3124 [DDD] (14.97)
Divertimento No. 3 for Violin & Strings
A. Kavafian (vn), Windham String Quartet *(rec Purchase State Univ New York, NY, Nov 1993)* † Duo Solitaire; Necompe LARL ▲ 856
Duo for Cello & Piano (1973)
J. Solow (vc), J. Lowenthal (pno) † Momenti; Trio Pno, Vn & Vc; Trio Ww Instrs LARL ▲ 845 [AAD] (14.97)
Duo Solitaire for Violin & Cello
Y. Kamei (vn), J. Solow (vc) *(rec NY)* † Divert 3 Vn; Necompe LARL ▲ 856
Icarus for Orchestra, "Concerto No. 2" (1984)
G. Schwarz (cnd), Seattle SO † Poema; Tableaux DLS ▲ 3069 [DDD] (14.97)
Intonazione e Variazioni for Organ (1980)
P. Schwarz (org) ("Music for Chamber Orchestra, Viola & Organ") † Chamber Sym; Serenade Str Sxt; Sinfonietta; Volo LARL ▲ 844 [DDD] (14.97)
Intrada for Horn (1994)
J. Cerminaro (hn) ("Screamers: Difficult Works for the Horn") † J. Haydn:Divert Hn, H.IV/5; W. Kraft:Evening Voluntaries; R. Schumann:Adagio & Allegro Hn, Op. 70; R. Steiger:Hexadecathlon CRYS ▲ 679 (15.97)
Lyric Suite for Violin (1983)
Y. Kamei (vn) ("Music for Strings") † Oct Strs; Qt Strs LARL ▲ 843 [DDD] (14.97)
Momenti for Cello (1987)
J. Solow (vc) † Duo Vc & Pno; Trio Pno, Vn & Vc; Trio Ww Instrs LARL ▲ 845 [AAD] (14.97)
Necompe (8 Soundscapes) for 8 Percussionists (1992)
F. Epstein (cnd), Collage New Music Ensemble *(rec Seiji Ozawa Hall, Tanglewood, Lenox, MA, July 10, 1994)* † Divert 3 Vn; Duo Solitaire LARL ▲ 856
Octet for Strings (1987)
Y. Matsuda (vn), M. Watanabe (vn), Y. Kamei (vn), P. Marsh (vn), P. Silverthorne (va), M. Thomas (va), G. Hoogeveen (vc), D. Speltz (vc), H. Lazarof (cnd) ("Music for Strings") † Lyric Suite; Qt Strs LARL ▲ 843 [DDD] (14.97)
Poema for Orchestra (1985)
G. Schwarz (cnd), Seattle SO † Icarus; Tableaux DLS ▲ 3069 [DDD] (14.97)
Prayers for 10 Players (1990)
S. Mosko (cnd) † Concertante II; Divert Cl; Suite Perc DLS ▲ 3124 [DDD] (14.97)
Quartet for Strings (1980)
artists unknown ("Music for Strings") † Lyric Suite; Oct Strs LARL ▲ 843 [DDD] (14.97)
Serenade for String Sextet (1985)
H. Lazarof (cnd) ("Music for Chamber Orchestra, Viola & Organ") † Chamber Sym; Intonazione e Variazioni; Sinfonietta; Volo LARL ▲ 844 [DDD] (14.97)
Sinfonietta for Chamber Orchestra (1981)
G. Schwarz (cnd), Los Angeles CO *(rec Univ of CA Los Angeles)* ("Music for Chamber Orchestra, Viola & Organ") † Chamber Sym; Intonazione e Variazioni; Serenade Str Sxt; Volo LARL ▲ 844 [DDD] (14.97)
Spectrum for Trumpet, Orchestra & Tape (1972-73)
T. Stevens (tpt), H. Lazarof (cnd), Utah SO † Canti; Con Fl; Con Orch CRI ▲ 588 [ADD] (17.97)
Suite for Percussion & 5 Instrumentalists (1990)
C. Kendall (cnd) † Concertante II; Divert Cl; Prayers DLS ▲ 3124 [DDD] (14.97)
Tableaux for Piano & Orchestra [after Kandinsky] (1987)
G. Schwarz (cnd), Seattle SO † Icarus; Poema DLS ▲ 3069 [DDD] (14.97)
Trio for Piano, Violin & Cello (1988)
Y. Matsuda (vn), J. Solow (vc), J. Lowenthal (pno) † Duo Vc & Pno; Momenti; Trio Ww Instrs LARL ▲ 845 [AAD] (14.97)
Trio for Wind Instruments (1981)
S. Stokes (fl), J. Winter (ob), G. Gray (cl) † Duo Vc & Pno; Momenti; Trio Pno, Vn & Vc LARL ▲ 845 [AAD] (14.97)
Volo (3 canti da requiem) for Viola & 2 String Ensembles
M. Thomas (va), H. Lazarof (cnd) *(rec Los Angeles, CA)* ("Music for Chamber Orchestra, Viola & Organ") † Chamber Sym; Intonazione e Variazioni; Serenade Str Sxt; Sinfonietta LARL ▲ 844 [DDD] (14.97)

LAZKANO, RAMON (20th cent)
Su-Itzalak (Sombras de fuego) for Cello Octet
E. Arizcuren (cnd) † A. Charles:Diverts; J. L. Greco:Invisible; C. Prieto:Caminando CCL ▲ 10597 (18.97)

LAZZARI, SYLVIO (1857-1944)
Sonata in E for Violin & Piano, Op. 24
J. Duhem (vn), M. Virlogeux (pno) *(rec May 1996)* † Trio ARN ▲ 68360 [DDD] (16.97)
Symphony in E♭ for Orchestra
M. Adriano (cnd), Moscow SO *(rec Mosfilm Studio, Aug 1995)* † Tableaux Maritimes MARC ▲ 8223853 [DDD] (13.97)
Tableaux Maritimes for Orchestra (1919-20)
M. Adriano (cnd), Moscow SO *(rec Mosfilm Studio, Aug 1995)* † Sym in E♭ MARC ▲ 8223853 [DDD] (13.97)
Trio in g for Piano, Violin & Cello, Op. 13
Trio de France *(rec May 1996)* † Son Vn ARN ▲ 68360 [DDD] (16.97)

LEACH, MARY JANE (1949-
Ariadne's Lament for Chorus (1993)
V. Davidson (cnd), New York Treble Singers ("Ariadne's Lament") † Call of the Dance; O Magna Vasti Creta; Song of Sorrows; Tricky Pan; Windjammer NWW ▲ 80525 [DDD] (16.97)
Ariel's Song for 8 Sopranos
New York Treble Singers ("Celestial Fires") † Bruckstück; Feu de Joie; Green Mountain Madrigal; Mountain Echoes; Trio for Duo XIRE ▲ 107 [ADD]
Bruckstück for 8 Sopranos [after Bruckner's *Symphony No. 8*]
New York Treble Singers ("Celestial Fires") † Ariel's Song; Feu de Joie; Green Mountain Madrigal; Mountain Echoes; Trio for Duo XIRE ▲ 107 [ADD]

LEACH, MARY JANE (cont.)

Call of the Dance for Soprano & Chorus (1997)
A. Travis (sop), V. Davidson (cnd), New York Treble Singers ("Ariadne's Lament") † Ariadne's Lament; O Magna Vasti Creta; Song of Sorrows; Tricky Pan; Windjammer NWW ▲ 80525 [DDD] (16.97)

Feu de Joie for Bassoon
S. Peet (bn) ("Celestial Fires") † Ariel's Song; Bruckstück; Green Mountain Madrigal; Mountain Echoes; Trio for Duo XIRE ▲ 107 [ADD]

Green Mountain Madrigal for Women's Chorus
New York Treble Singers ("Celestial Fires") † Ariel's Song; Bruckstück; Feu de Joie; Mountain Echoes; Trio for Duo XIRE ▲ 107 [ADD]

Mountain Echoes for Women's Chorus
New York Treble Singers ("Celestial Fires") † Ariel's Song; Bruckstück; Feu de Joie; Green Mountain Madrigal; Trio for Duo XIRE ▲ 107 [ADD]

O Magna Vasti Creta for String Quartet & Chorus (1997)
V. Davidson (cnd), Cassatt String Quartet, V. Davidson (cnd), New York Treble Singers ("Ariadne's Lament") † Ariadne's Lament; Call of the Dance; Song of Sorrows; Tricky Pan; Windjammer NWW ▲ 80525 [DDD] (16.97)

Song of Sorrows for Chorus (1995)
W. Payn (cnd), Rooke Chapel Choir ("Ariadne's Lament") † Ariadne's Lament; Call of the Dance; O Magna Vasti Creta; Tricky Pan; Windjammer NWW ▲ 80525 [DDD] (16.97)

Tricky Pan for Tenor (1995)
D. L. Echlard (ten) ("Ariadne's Lament") † Ariadne's Lament; Call of the Dance; O Magna Vasti Creta; Song of Sorrows; Windjammer NWW ▲ 80525 [DDD] (16.97)

Trio for Duo for Voice, Alto Flute & Tape
M. J. Leach (voc), B. Held (a fl) ("Celestial Fires") † Ariel's Song; Bruckstück; Feu de Joie; Green Mountain Madrigal; Mountain Echoes XIRE ▲ 107 [ADD]

Windjammer for Oboe, Clarinet & Bassoon (1995)
L. van Cleve (ob), P. Burton (cl), K. Johnson (bn) ("Ariadne's Lament") † Ariadne's Lament; Call of the Dance; O Magna Vasti Creta; Song of Sorrows; Tricky Pan NWW ▲ 80525 [DDD] (16.97)

LÉANDRE, JOËLLE (20th cent)

Hommage à J for Double-Bass
J. Léandre (db) † J. Cage:A Flower for Db; Ryoanji Db; The Wonderful Widow of 18 Springs; 59½ DISQ ▲ 782076 (18.97)

LEBARON, ANNE (1953-

Concerto for Active Frogs for Soloists & Chamber Ensemble (1975)
G. Cartwright (voc), D. Shea (voc), J. Staley (voc), W. Trigg (perc), A. LeBaron (cnd) [ENG] ("Rana, Ritual & Revelations") † Lamentation/Invocation; Noh Reflections; Planxty Bowerbird; Rite of the Black Sun MODE ▲ 30 (17.97)

Dish for Soprano, Violin, Keyboards, Electric Bass, Percussion & Tape (1990)
D. Ohrenstein (sop), M. Rowell (vn), J. Thompson (elec bass), P. Bush (pno/syn), J. Cirker (perc), B. Ruyle (perc) *(rec Feb & Apr 1993)* ("Urban Diva") † L. Bouchard:Black Burned Wood; A. Davis:Lost Moon Sisters; S. Johnson:Confetti on Flesh; B. Johnston:Calamity Jane to Her Daughter CRI (Emergency Music) ▲ 654 [DDD] (17.97)

Dog-Gone Cat Act for Prepared Harp (1982)
A. Lebaron (hp) *(rec 1990)* ("The Musical Railism of Anne LeBaron") † E. & O. Line (sels); I Am an American...My Government Will Reward You; Sea & the Honeycomb; Waltz for Qnt MODE ▲ 42 (17.97)

The E. & O. Line (selections)
L. Cloutier (mez—), H. Panero (ten—Hermes), L. Hamilton (bar—Men/Orpheus), D. Williams (gtr), F. Hopkins (elec bass), F. London (tpt), M. Rojas (tuba), M. Melford (kbd/pno), T. Barker (dr), A. Lebaron (cnd) —Juke Joint Jam Session; Eurydice Meets Hermes; Eurydice's Death [Funeral Band]; Eurydice's River Journey; Orpheus Laments [Looked Away] *(rec Coolidge Auditorium Library of Congress, DC, 1987)* ("The Musical Railism of Anne LeBaron") † Dog-Gone Cat Act; I Am an American...My Government Will Reward You; Sea & the Honeycomb; Waltz for Qnt MODE ▲ 42 (17.97)

I Am an American...My Government Will Reward You for Electric Harp & Live Electronics (1988; rev 1994)
A. Lebaron (elec/hp) *(rec 1994)* ("The Musical Railism of Anne LeBaron") † Dog-Gone Cat Act; E. & O. Line (sels); Sea & the Honeycomb; Waltz for Qnt MODE ▲ 42 (17.97)

Lamentation/Invocation for Soloists & Chamber Ensemble (1984)
A. Shearer (sgr), R. Yamins (sgr), M. Shapiro (vc), L. Bouchard (tpt), N. Kellman (perc), New Music Consort [ENG] ("Rana, Ritual & Revelations") † Con for Active Frogs; Noh Reflections; Planxty Bowerbird; Rite of the Black Sun MODE ▲ 30 (17.97)

Noh Reflections for Soloists & Chamber Ensemble (1986)
H. Fujiwara (vn), M. Kawasaki (va), E. Elsing (vc) ("Rana, Ritual & Revelations") † Con for Active Frogs; Lamentation/Invocation; Planxty Bowerbird; Rite of the Black Sun MODE ▲ 30 (17.97)

Planxty Bowerbird for Harp & Tape (1982)
A. LeBaron (elec/hp) ("Rana, Ritual & Revelations") † Con for Active Frogs; Lamentation/Invocation; Noh Reflections; Rite of the Black Sun MODE ▲ 30 (17.97)

Rite of the Black Sun for Soloists & Chamber Ensemble (1980)
F. Cassara (zmz), M. Pugliese (perc), W. Trigg (perc), P. Guerguerian (perc), C. Heldrich (cnd) ("Rana, Ritual & Revelations") † Con for Active Frogs; Lamentation/Invocation; Noh Reflections; Planxty Bowerbird MODE ▲ 30 (17.97)

The Sea & the Honeycomb for Soprano, Flute, Piccolo, Clarinet, Bass Clarinet, 2 Percussionists & Piano (1979)
L. Fleisher (cnd) , L. Fleisher (cnd), Kennedy Center Theater Chamber Players *(rec Hubbard Hall Manhattan School of Music, NY, 1993)* ("The Musical Railism of Anne LeBaron") † Dog-Gone Cat Act; E. & O. Line (sels); I Am an American...My Government Will Reward You; Waltz for Qnt MODE ▲ 42 (17.97)

Waltz for Quintet for Flute, Violin, Viola, Cello & Piano [2nd movt of Telluris Theoria Sacra] (1989)
C. Heldrich (cnd) , C. Heldrich (cnd), New Music Consort *(rec Honrath Germany, Germany, 1982)* ("The Musical Railism of Anne LeBaron") † Dog-Gone Cat Act; E. & O. Line (sels); I Am an American...My Government Will Reward You; Sea & the Honeycomb MODE ▲ 42 (17.97)

LEBEDEV, NICOLAI (1947-

The Liturgy of St. John Chrysotom for solo Voices & Chorus (1990)
V. Matorin (bass), L. Ustinova (sgr), O. Rezaeva (sgr), V. Maximov (cnd), Moscow Chamber Choir *(rec Moscow, 1992)* ("Russian Composing School: Nikolai Lebedev") † Sacred Choral Music RD (Talents of Russia) ▲ 16601 [ADD] (16.97)

Sacred Choral Music
E. Bobrov (cnd), Sheremetev Center Chamber Choir—O Thou Who, with Wisdom Profound; Thee Have We as a Wall & Refuge; Praise Ye the Lord from Heaven [from The Liturgy]; O Come, Let Us Worship; Bless the Lord, O My Soul; Praise Ye the Name of the Lord; In That We Have Beheld the Resurection of Christ *(rec Moscow, 1992)* ("Russian Composing School: Nikolai Lebedev") † Liturgy of St. John RD (Talents of Russia) ▲ 16601 [ADD] (16.97)

LEBÈGUE, NICOLAS-ANTOINE (ca 1631-1702)

Les cloches
P. Kee (org) *(rec Gabler org, Weingarten, Benedictine Abbey Basilika, Germany, Oct 1990)* † J. M. Bach:Org Music; J. S. Bach:Preludes & Fugues, BWV 531-552; Murschhauser:Vars on 'Labt uns das Kindelein wiegen'; J. Pachelbel:Ciaccona in d; Ciaccona, POP 16; Fant in g; Prelude in d, POP 256; J. G. Walther:Vars on Jesu meine Freude Org CHN ▲ 520 [DDD] (16.97)

Les pièces de clavessin [Book 1] (1677)
B. Lapointe (hpd) ("Harpsichord Works") † Pièces de clavessin (book 2) PVY ▲ 796101 [DDD] (16.97)

Les pièces de clavessin [Book 2] (1687)
B. Lapointe (hpd) ("Harpsichord Works") † Pièces de clavessin (book 1) PVY ▲ 796101 [DDD] (16.97)

Les pièces d'orgue [Book 1] (1676)
T. Maeder (org) *(rec Notre-Dame-de-Guibray Falaise)* ("Organ Works") † Pièces d'orgue (book 3) PVY ▲ 796102 [DDD] (16.97)

Les pièces d'orgue [Book 3] (?1685)
T. Maeder (org) *(rec Notre-Dame-de-Guibray Falaise)* ("Organ Works") † Pièces d'orgue (book 1) PVY ▲ 796102 [DDD] (16.97)

LEBRUN, FRANCESCA (1756-1791)

Sonatas (6) for Violin & Piano, Op. 1
D. Maiben (vn), M. Jakuc (pno) *(rec Sage Hall Smith College, Northampton, M, June 1996)* DOR ▲ 80162 [DDD] (13.97)
Zephyrus members *(rec Faith Lutheran Church Bloomington, England, July 5-7, 1994)* ("Mozart in Mannheim") † F. Danzi:Petits Duos, Op. 64; Holzbauer:Qnt 1; W. A. Mozart:Qt Fl in C; C. Stamitz:Duos Vn & Va, Op.1/2; Toeschi:Quartetto FOCU ▲ 945 [DDD] (16.97)

LEBRUN, LUDWIG AUGUST (1752-1790)

Concerto in B♭ for Clarinet & Orchestra [arr from Concerto in C for Oboe & Orchestra]
D. Klöcker (cl), H. Stadlmair (cnd), Munich CO ("Clarinet Concertos of the Imperial & Royal Court Orchestras") † J. Beer:Con Cl; F. A. Hoffmeister:Con for 2 Cls KSCH ▲ 364222 (16.97)

Concerto in F for Oboe, Op. 7 (1787)
K. Meier (ob), H. Griffiths (cnd), Northern Sinfonia of England ("Oboe Concertos in Premier Recordings") † Eichner:Con 3 Ob; Holzbauer:Con Ob; P. Von Winter:Con 2 Ob PANC ▲ 510088 [DDD] (17.97)

LECHNER, LEONHARD (ca1606)

Choral Music
O. Kongsted (cnd), Capella Hafniensis—Dieweil Gott ist mein Zuversicht; Kronborg Motets [spurious]; Nach Gottes Willen heb ich an: see Collections:Cho KPT ▲ 32106 [DDD]

LECLAIR, JEAN-MARIE (1697-1764)

Deuxième Récréation de musique d'une exécution facile for 2 Violins (or Recorders) & Continuo, Op. 8 (1737)
Collegium Musicum 90 † Sons Vns, Op. 3; Trio Vns, Op. 14 CHOC (Early Music) ▲ 582 (16.97)
Music's Re-Creation † Telemann:Qts (6) Fl, "Nouveaux quators" MER ▲ 84114 (16.97)

Music of Leclair
M. Huggett (vn), C. Guimond (fl), Arion Ensemble—Cons (4) ATMM ▲ 22143 (16.97)
I. Stern (vn)—Tambourin ("Caprice Viennois") † C. W. Gluck:Melodie; F. Kreisler:Music of Kreisler SNYC ▲ 62692 (16.97)

Ouvertures et sonates en trio (6) for 2 Violins & Continuo, Op. 13 (1753)
C. Medlam (cnd) HAM ▲ 901646 (18.97)
Palladian Ensemble [arr Palladian Ens] *(rec Highgate & The Warehouse Waterloo, United States of America)* ("Trios for 4") LINN ▲ 5050 (16.97)
Purcell Quartet CHN (Chaconne) ▲ 542 [DDD] (16.97)

Premier livre de sonates (12) for Violin & Continuo, Op. 1 (1723)
Badinage ("Le Premier des François") † Second livre, Op. 2; Sons Vns, Op. 12 MER ▲ 84381 (16.97)
A. Dubeau (vn), A. Tunis (pno) [arr for vn & pno] *(rec 1988)* ("French Sonatas") † Quatrième livre, Op. 9; Second livre, Op. 2; Troisième livre, Op. 5; Debussy:Son Vn; G. Fauré:Son 1 Vn, Op. 13 FL ▲ 23021 [DDD] (16.97)
F. Fernandez (vn), P. Pierlot (vl), P. Hantaï (hpd) ASTR ▲ 8662 (18.97)
Flora Danica [trans fl, vl & hpd] † Quatrième livre, Op. 9; Second livre, Op. 2; Troisième livre, Op. 5 KPT ▲ 32006 [DDD]

Quatrième livre de sonates (12) for Violin & Continuo, Op. 9 (1743)
Convivium—No. 3 in D; No. 2 in e; No. 7 in G; No. 6 in D HYP ▲ 67068 (18.97)
H. Perl (vl), C. Huntgeburth (fl), M. Meyerson (hpd) ("5 Flute Sonatas") † Second livre, Op. 2 ASV (Gaudeamus) ▲ 158 (16.97)
Sonnerie Trio † Troisième livre, Op. 5 ASV (Gaudeamus) ▲ 106 [DDD] (16.97)
R. Stallman (fl), K. Bennion (vc), E. Swanborn (hpd)—No. 7 in G; No. 2 in e *(rec Church of the Good Shepherd, NYC, NY, Mar 1993)* † Second livre, Op. 2 VAIA ▲ 1068 [DDD] (17.97)

Quatrième livre de sonates (12) for Violin & Continuo, Op. 9 (1743)
A. Dubeau (vn), A. Tunis (pno) *(rec 1988)* ("French Sonatas") † Premier livre, Op. 1; Second livre, Op. 2; Troisième livre, Op. 5; Debussy:Son Vn; G. Fauré:Son 1 Vn, Op. 13 FL ▲ 23021 [DDD] (16.97)
F. Fernandez (vn), P. Pierlot (vl), P. Hantaï (hpd) ("Sonates pour violon & basse continue, Livre IV") ASTR ▲ 8586 [DDD] (18.97)
Flora Danica [trans fl, vl & hpd] † Premier livre, Op. 1; Second livre, Op. 2; Troisième livre, Op. 5 KPT ▲ 32006 [DDD]
S. Standage (vn), L. U. Mortensen (hpd) † Troisième livre, Op. 5; Duphly:Pièces de clavecin (book 2); Pièces de clavecin (book 4); J.-B. Forqueray:Morangis ou la plissay; Guillemain:Son Vn; Mondonville:Pièces de clavecin, Op. 3 CHN (Chaconne) ▲ 531 [DDD] (16.97)

Quatrième livre de sonates (12) for Violin & Continuo, Op. 9 (1743)
Convivium—No. 3 in D; No. 2 in e; No. 7 in G; No. 6 in D HYP ▲ 67068 (18.97)

Quatrième livre de sonates (12) for Violin & Continuo, Op. 9 (1743)
Convivium—No. 3 in D; No. 2 in e; No. 7 in G; No. 6 in D HYP ▲ 67068 (18.97)
M. Hirao (vl), Y. Imamura (gtr/thb), M. Arita (fl d'amore/trns fl), K. Suga (trns fl), C. Arita (hpd) *(rec Akigawa Kirara Hall, Japan, Nov 22-27, 1993)* ("Flute Music of the Grand Siècle") † Blavet:Fl Music; Sons Fl, Op. 3; Boismortier:Sons Fl, Op. 91; Hotteterre:Pièces, Op. 2; Première livre de pièce, Op. 5 DNN 2-▲ 75957 [DDD] (33.97)
H. Perl (vl), C. Huntgeburth (fl), M. Meyerson (hpd) ("5 Flute Sonatas") † Second livre, Op. 2 ASV (Gaudeamus) ▲ 158 (16.97)
Sonnerie Trio † Troisième livre, Op. 5 ASV (Gaudeamus) ▲ 106 [DDD] (16.97)
R. Stallman (fl), K. Bennion (vc), E. Swanborn (hpd)—No. 7 in G; No. 2 in e *(rec Church of the Good Shepherd, NYC, NY, Mar 1993)* † Second livre, Op. 2 VAIA ▲ 1068 [DDD] (17.97)

Second livre de sonates (12) for Violin & Continuo, Op. 2 (ca 1728)
Badinage ("Le Premier des François") † Premier livre, Op. 1; Sons Vns, Op. 12 MER ▲ 84381 (16.97)
A. Dubeau (vn), A. Tunis (pno) *(rec 1988)* ("French Sonatas") † Premier livre, Op. 1; Quatrième livre, Op. 9; Troisième livre, Op. 5; Debussy:Son Vn; G. Fauré:Son 1 Vn, Op. 13 FL ▲ 23021 [DDD] (16.97)
Flora Danica [trans fl, vl & hpd] † Premier livre, Op. 1; Quatrième livre, Op. 9; Troisième livre, Op. 5 KPT ▲ 32006 [DDD]
H. Perl (vl), C. Huntgeburth (fl), M. Meyerson (hpd) ("5 Flute Sonatas") † Quatrième livre, Op. 9 ASV (Gaudeamus) ▲ 158 (16.97)
R. Stallman (fl), K. Bennion (vc), E. Swanborn (hpd)—No. 1 in e; No. 11 in b; No. 3 in C *(rec Church of the Good Shepherd, NYC, NY, Mar 1993)* † Quatrième livre, Op. 9 VAIA ▲ 1068 [DDD] (17.97)

Sonatas for Violin (or Flute) & Continuo [Books 1-4, Opp. 1, 2, 5 & 9]
M. Rasmussen (vl), D. Laurin (rcr), L. Meyer (hpd) *(rec Furuby Church Sweden, May 8-11, 1995)* ("The French King's Flautists") † Blavet:Sonatas for Transverse Flute & Continuo; J. D. Braun:Son Terza; Dornel:Sons Vn & Suites Fl, Op. 2; Hotteterre:Première livre de pièce, Op. 5 BIS ▲ 745 [DDD] (17.97)

Sonatas (6) for 2 Violins (or Viols), Op. 12 (ca 1747-49)
Badinage ("Le Premier des François") † Premier livre, Op. 1; Second livre, Op. 2 MER ▲ 84381 (16.97)

Sonatas (6) for 2 Violins, Op. 3
Collegium Musicum 90 † Deuxième Récréation de musique, Op. 8; Trio Vns, Op. 14 CHOC (Early Music) ▲ 582 (16.97)
P. Zukerman (vn), I. Perlman (vn) † W. A. Mozart:Duos Vn RCAV (Red Seal) ▲ 60735 [DDD] (16.97)

Sonates en trio for 2 Violins & Continuo, Op. 4 (1730)
Philharmonia Virtuosi *(rec Purchase, NY, Aug 13-14, 1995)* ("Musical Evenings with the Captain: Music from the Aubrey-Maturin Novels of Patrick O'Brian") † Boccherini:Son Vn Vc; G. F. Handel:Pieces Vn; J. Haydn:Duet Vn & Vc, H.VI/D1; Locatelli:Son Vn, Op. 6; Sons for 2 Vns, Op. 5 ESSY ▲ 1047 [DDD] (16.97)

Trio Sonatas for 2 Violins & Continuo, Op. 4 (1731-33)
C. Medlam (cnd) HAM ▲ 901617 (18.97)
Purcell Quartet [period instrs] *(rec Sept 3-5, 1992)* ("Sonatas for Strings, Op. 4") CHN (Chaconne) ▲ 536 [DDD] (16.97)

Trio in A for 2 Violins & Continuo, Op. 14 (1766, posth.)
Collegium Musicum 90 † Deuxième Récréation de musique, Op. 8; Sons Vns, Op. 3 CHOC (Early Music) ▲ 582 (16.97)

Troisième livre de sonates (12) for Violin & Continuo, Op. 5 (1734)
A. Dubeau (vn), A. Tunis (pno) *(rec 1988)* ("French Sonatas") † Premier livre, Op. 1; Quatrième livre, Op. 9; Second livre, Op. 2; Debussy:Son Vn; G. Fauré:Son 1 Vn, Op. 13 FL ▲ 23021 [DDD] (16.97)
Flora Danica [trans fl, vl & hpd] † Premier livre, Op. 1; Quatrième livre, Op. 9; Second livre, Op. 2 KPT ▲ 32006 [DDD]
Sonnerie Trio † Quatrième livre, Op. 9 ASV (Gaudeamus) ▲ 106 [DDD] (16.97)
S. Standage (vn), L. U. Mortensen (hpd) † Quatrième livre, Op. 9; Duphly:Pièces de clavecin (book 2); Pièces de clavecin (book 4); J.-B. Forqueray:Morangis ou la plissay; Guillemain:Son Vn; Mondonville:Pièces de clavecin, Op. 3 CHN (Chaconne) ▲ 531 [DDD] (16.97)
H. Suzuki (vc), K. Uemura (vl), C. Rousset (hpd) *(rec Feb 26-Mar 9, 1993)* DNN ▲ 75720 [DDD] (16.97)

LECLAIRE, DENNIS (1950-

Episode No. 1 for Clarinet
S. Friedland (cl) ("Music from Concordia: New Music for Clarinet") † Bavicchi:Son Cl; Bottenberg:Son Modalis; Crossman:Desiderata; McGah:Durrell Reflections SNE ▲ 538 (16.97)

Haiku (4) for Orchestra (1990)
R. Black (cnd), Slovak RSO Bratislava—Nos. 1 & 4 † Althans:Valse Excentrique; M. Kessler:Con Pno; W. T. McKinley:Andante & Scherzo; Rahbee:Tapestry 1; Rendelman:Chorale & Toccata; Stango:Sol' per Dirti Addio MASM ▲ 2009 [DDD] (16.97)

▲ = CD ♦ = Enhanced CD △ = MD ▮ = Cassette Tape ▯ = DCC

LECLAIRE, DENNIS (cont.)
Quartet for Horns (1989)
G. Hustis (hn), T. Bacon (hn), W. Caballero (hn), E. Ralske (hn) † A. Gottschalk:Section for 4 Hns; Pinkston:Qt for 4 Hns; A. Schultz:Dragons in the Sky; T-Rex SUMM ▲ 135 [DDD] (16.97)
LECLERC, FÉLIX (1914-
Par Monts et par vaux for Brass Quintet
New York Brass Quintet † B. Dutton:Carnival of Venice; Horovitz:Music Hall Suite; A. Hovhaness:Dances Brass Qnt, Op. 79 CRYS ▲ 200 [ADD] (15.97)
LECUONA, ERNESTO (1896-1963)
A la Antigua
M. Barrueco (gtr) *(rec London, England, Apr 1998)* ("Cuba!") † Comparsa; Danza Lucumi; H. Angulo:Cantos Yoruba; Ardévol:Son Gtr; L. Brouwer:Preludio; Rito de los Orishas; Fariñas:Canción Triste; Preludio; Ubieta:New York Rush EMIC ▲ 56757 [DDD] (16.97)
La Comparsa
M. Barrueco (gtr) *(rec London, England, Apr 1998)* ("Cuba!") † A la Antigua; Danza Lucumi; H. Angulo:Cantos Yoruba; Ardévol:Son Gtr; L. Brouwer:Preludio; Rito de los Orishas; Fariñas:Canción Triste; Preludio; Ubieta:New York Rush EMIC ▲ 56757 [DDD] (16.97)
Danza Lucumi
M. Barrueco (gtr) *(rec London, England, Apr 1998)* ("Cuba!") † A la Antigua; Comparsa; H. Angulo:Cantos Yoruba; Ardévol:Son Gtr; L. Brouwer:Preludio; Rito de los Orishas; Fariñas:Canción Triste; Preludio; Ubieta:New York Rush EMIC ▲ 56757 [DDD] (16.97)
Danzas (10) Cubanas for Piano
C. Pegoraro (pno)—No Hables Mas!; No Puedo Contigo; Ahi Viene el Chino; ¿Por Qué Te Vas?; Lola Está de Fiesta; En Tres por Quatro *(rec Sept 1998)* ("Piano Works, Vol. 2") † Pno Music DYNC (2000) ▲ 2019 [DDD] (13.97)
Gitanerias for 2 Pianos
Y. Mack (pno), T. Mack (pno) *(rec Ann Arbor, MI)* ("Rhapsody") † Malagueña; B. Britten:Intro & Rondo alla burlesca; G. Gershwin:Rhap in Blue; Joio:Aria & Toccata; F. Poulenc:Son for 2 Pnos; D. Shostakovich:Tarantella ARUN ▲ 3076 (16.97)
Malagueña
Y. Mack (pno), T. Mack (pno) *(rec Ann Arbor, MI)* ("Rhapsody") † Gitanerias; B. Britten:Intro & Rondo alla burlesca; G. Gershwin:Rhap in Blue; Joio:Aria & Toccata; F. Poulenc:Son for 2 Pnos; D. Shostakovich:Tarantella ARUN ▲ 3076 (16.97)
Music of Lecuona
M. Gould (cnd), Morton Gould Orch—Malagueña; Sinoney; Guadalquivir; In tres pour quatro; La conga de media noche; Danza negra; Y la negra bailaba; Danza de los ñañigos [all orchd Gould]; La comparsa; Zambra Gitana; Andalucia; Danza lucumi; Córdoba; Rapsodia negra *(rec New York, 1955 & 1964)* ("Lecuona Sinfonica") RCAV (Gold Seal) ▲ 68922 [ADD] (11.97)
S. Henderson (cnd), New York Pops—Andalucia *(rec New York, NY, June 21, 1990)* ("From Berlin to Bernstein") † I. Berlin:Music of Berlin; L. Bernstein:Candide (ov); Music of Bernstein; On the Town (sels); West Side Story (sels); H. Carmichael:Music of Carmichael; Roullier:Music of Roullier; Van Heusen:Here's That Rainy Day CENT ▲ 2427 [DDD] (16.97)
Piano Music
P. Ferman (pno)—Danzas Cubanas; Danzas Afro-Cubanas; Andalucia TLNT ▲ 44 (15.97)
E. Lecuona (pno)—Malagueña; Andalucia; Ante El Escorial; San Francisco El Grande; Siempre en mi corazón; María la O; Siboney; Noche Azul; La comparsa; Danza negra; Danza lucumi; A la Antigua; En tres por cuatro; Canto del Guajiro; La habanera; Damisela encantadora; Crisantemo; Romántico; Rosa la china; Como el Arrullo de Palmas; Palomitas blancas; Poético; Estudiantina; Córdoba; Music Box; Mazurka en Glissando; Polichinela; Zambra Gitana; Aragón; Valencia mora; La brisa y yo; Devuélveme el corazón; Preludio en la noche; Yo te quiero siempre; Pavo real; Vals de las sombras; Bell Flower; Por eso te quiero; Vals Azul; Vals en si mayor; Muñeca de cristal; Mi amor fué una flor; Vals en re bemol; Apasionado Amarosa; Ahí viene el chino; Al fin te ví; ¿Por qué te vas?; Mientras yo comía maullaba un gato; Amorosa; Los minstrels; No hables más; Dame tu amor; La 32; Mis tristezas; Muñequita; Burlesca; La paloma *(rec 1927-54)* ("The Ultimate Collection") RCAV (Gold Seal) 2-▲ 68671 [ADD] (21.97)
C. Pegoraro (pno)—Danzas Afro-Cubanas; Estampas Infantiles; Miniatures Pno; Ante El Escorial; San Francisco El Grande; Andalucia *(rec Sept 1997)* ("Piano Works") DYNC (2000) ▲ 2007 [DDD] (13.97)
C. Pegoraro (pno)—Polka de los Enanos; Crisantemo; Vals del Nilo; Vals del Sena; Zambra Gitana; Aragonesa; Aragón; Granada *(rec Sept 1998)* ("Piano Works, Vol. 2") † Danzas Cubanas DYNC (2000) ▲ 2019 [DDD] (13.97)
F. Spengler (pno)—La comparsa; Mo hables más; Y la negra bailaba; Ahí viene el chino; Danza negra; En tres por cuatro; La Malagueña ("Two Spheres: Memories from Cuba") † Cervantes (Kawanag):Pno Music; Saumell Robredo:Pno Music PIUM ▲ 1
T. Tirino (pno)—Andalucia; Ante El Escorial; Zambra Gitana; Aragonesa; Granada; San Francisco El Grande; Aragón [Vals España]; Preludio en la noche; La Habanera; Mazurka en Glissando; Canto del Guajiro; Miniatures Pno; Canto Siboney; Noche Azul *(rec New York City, 1994-95)* ("The Complete Piano Music, Vol. 1") † Rapsodia negra BIS ▲ 754 [DDD] (17.97)
T. Tirino (pno)—Danzas Afro-Cubanas; Danzas Cubanas; Échate pa'allá María!; Valses Fantásticos; Vals del Nilo; Gardenia; Porcelana China; Polka de los Enanos; Noches de Estrellas; Yo te quiero siempre ("The Complete Piano Music, Vol 3") † Rapsodia Cubana BIS ▲ 794 [DDD] (17.97)
T. Tirino (pno) *(Danzas Cubanas; Amorosa; Futurista; Vals Gitano; A Media Noche; Parisiana; Musetta; Vals de Danubio; Broken Blossoms; Noches de Primavera; Vals de Mariposa)*, E. Henreckson-Farnum (sop), K. Geissinger (mez), A. Montano (alt), T. Tirino (pno), M. Bartos (cnd), Polish National RSO, Silesian PO Chorus *(Rhumba-Rhap)*, T. Tirino (pno), J. Valiente (fl) *(Vals Azul)*, T. Tirino (pno), B. Engel (tpt) *(Paso Doble de los Mantones [w. Bruce Engel (tpt)])* ("Complete Piano Music, Vol. 4") BIS ▲ 874 [DDD] (17.97)
T. Tirino (pno), M. Bartos (cnd), Polish National RSO *(Rapsodia Argentina)*, T. Tirino (pno) *(Diary of a Child; Adiós a las Trincheras; Cuba & America; Black Cat; Cuba at Arms; El Somrero de Yarey:Suite; Quasi Bolero (song trans); Dame de tus Rosas (trans); Waltzes: Crisantemo, Vals del Sena, Locura, Barba) (rec Culture Center, Katowice, Poland)* ("The Complete Piano Music, Vol 2") BIS ▲ 774 [DDD] (17.97)
Rapsodia Cubana (on Cuban Airs) for Piano & Orchestra [arr T. Tirino] (1955)
T. Tirino (pno), M. Bartos (cnd), Polish National RSO Katowice ("The Complete Piano Music, Vol 3") † Pno Music BIS ▲ 794 [DDD] (17.97)
Rapsodia negra for Piano & Orchestra (1943)
T. Tirino (pno), M. Bartos (cnd), Polish National RSO Katowice *(rec Katowice Poland, Feb 27, 1993)* ("The Complete Piano Music, Vol. 1") † Pno Music BIS ▲ 754 [DDD] (17.97)
Songs
P. Domingo (ten), L. Holdridge (cnd), Royal PO—Siboney; Noche Azul; Andalucia; Por eso te quiero; Siempre en mi corazón; María la O; Canto Karabali; Juventud; Malagueña; Damisela encantadora; La comparsa *(rec 1983)* ("Always in My Heart: Songs of Lecuona") SNYC ▲ 63199 (9.97)
LEDESMA, NICOLÁS (1791-1883)
Sonata No. 6 in d for Organ
E. Elizondo (org) *(rec Basilica Org, Apr 1991)* ("The Organs of Guanajuato, Mexico") † De Gamarra:Son in Tone 8; Versos; Oxinaga:Fugues Org; P. A. Soler:Versos para Te Deum TIT ▲ 201 [DDD]
LEDUC, JACQUES (1932-
Ouverture d'été for Orchestra, Op. 28 (1968)
P. Bartholomée (cnd), Liège PO *(rec Liège Conservatory, Oct 1996)* ("Symphonic Works") † Prinetemps, Op. 25; Sym CYPR ▲ 7601 [DDD] (17.97)
Le Printemps (esquisse symphonique) for Orchestra, Op. 25 (1967)
P. Bartholomée (cnd), Liège PO *(rec Liège Conservatory, Oct 1996)* ("Symphonic Works") † Ouverture d'été, Op. 28; Sym CYPR ▲ 7601 [DDD] (17.97)
Symphony, Op. 29 (1969)
P. Bartholomée (cnd), Liège PO *(rec Liège Conservatory, Oct 1996)* ("Symphonic Works") † Ouverture d'été, Op. 28; Prinetemps, Op. 25 CYPR ▲ 7601 [DDD] (17.97)
LEDUC, SIMON (?1777)
Symphonies (3) (1776-77)
B. Wahl (cnd), Versailles CO ARN ▲ 55408 (13.97)
LEE, BRENT (1964-
Maquette V for Violin, Cello & Piano (1987)
Iscles Trio ("Among Friends") † B. M. Feldman:Trio Pno; A. MacDonald:In the Eagle's Eye; C. K. Nin:Among Friends; O. Underhill:Dompe CTR ▲ 6098 [DDD] (16.97)
LEE, NOËL (1924-
Caprices on the name Schönberg for Piano & Orchestra (1973-75)
N. Lee (pno), J. Marty (cnd), Nouvel PO *(rec Paris, France, Nov 23, 1976)* † Convergences; Dialogues; Preludes Prolonged CRI ▲ 798 [ADD/DDD] (16.97)

LEE, NOËL (cont.)
Convergences for Flute & Harpsichord (1972)
A. Adorján (fl), N. Lee (hpd) † Caprices on the name Schönberg; Dialogues; Preludes Prolonged CRI ▲ 798 [ADD/DDD] (16.97)
Dialogues for Violin & Piano (1958)
O. Böhn (vn), N. Lee (pno) † Caprices on the name Schönberg; Convergences; Preludes Prolonged CRI ▲ 798 [ADD/DDD] (16.97)
Double Mosaics for 2 Pianos & Percussion (1994)
C. Ivaldi (pno), N. Lee (pno) *(rec Rueil-Malmaison, France, 1997)* ("American Music for Two Pianos") † S. Barber:Souvenirs, Op. 28; A. Copland:Danzón Cubano; Grohg (sels); Salón México; G. Gershwin:George Gershwin Songbook; Rhap 2 Pno ARN ▲ 68375 [DDD] (16.97)
Preludes Prolonged (5) for Piano (1992)
N. Lee (pno) *(rec Paris, France, May 1994)* † Caprices on the name Schönberg; Convergences; Dialogues CRI ▲ 798 [ADD/DDD] (16.97)
LEE, THOMAS OBOE (1945-
The Mad Frog! for Oboe, Bass Clarinet & Harp (1974)
Collage New Music Ensemble members *(rec Boston, MA, Dec 5, 1983)* † Qt 3 Strs; G. Schuller:Symbiosis GMR ▲ 2007 (16.97)
Marimolin for Violin & Marimba (1986)
artists unknown † Aldridge:threedance; L. Mays:Somewhere in Maine; A. Rogers:Shadow-Play; L. Thimmig:Bluefire Crown III; S. Wheeler:Lyric Vars Vn & Mar GMR ▲ 2023 [DDD] (16.97)
Quartet No. 3 for Strings, "...child of Uranus, father of Zeus" (1982)
Kronos Quartet *(rec San Francisco, CA, June 9, 1983)* † Mad Frog!; G. Schuller:Symbiosis GMR ▲ 2007 (16.97)
LEES, BENJAMIN (1924-
Concerto for Horn & Orchestra (1991)
W. Caballero (hn), L. Maazel (cnd), Pittsburgh SO *(rec Pittsburgh, PN, May 1996)* † Balada:Lament; E. T. Zwilich:Con Bn NWW ▲ 80503 [DDD] (16.97)
Concerto for Violin & Orchestra (1958)
R. Ricci (vn), K. Akiyama (cnd), American SO *(rec 1976)* ("American Concertos") † Bergsma:Con Vn; Colgrass:Concert Masters; L. Harrison:Con Vn; Kupferman:Con Vc, Tape & Orch; Piston:Concertino Pno; Starer:Con Va VB2 (The American Composers) 2-▲ 5158 (9.97)
R. Ricci (vn), G. Brott (cnd), SWF SO † B. Britten:Con Vn; G. Kubik:Con 2 Vn ONEL (Essential Performance Reference) ▲ 96020 [ADD] (7.97)
Fantasy Variations for Piano (1983)
I. Hobson (pno) ("Works for Piano") † Mirrors; Son 4 Pno ALBA ▲ 227 [DDD] (16.97)
Invenzione for Violin (1965)
E. Orner (vn) † Son 1 Vn; Son 2 Vn; Son 3 Vn ALBA ▲ 138 [DDD] (16.97)
Mirrors for Piano (1992-)
I. Hobson (pno) ("Works for Piano") † Fant Vars; Son 4 Pno ALBA ▲ 227 [DDD] (16.97)
Prologue, Capriccio & Epilogue for Orchestra (1959)
J. Avshalomov (cnd), Portland Youth PO *(rec ca 1961)* † Bergsma:Chameleon Vars; E. Bloch:Suite symphonique; Sym Trb; D. Diamond:World of Paul Klee CRI ▲ 634 [ADD] (16.97)
Sonata No. 4 for Piano (1963)
I. Hobson (pno) ("Works for Piano") † Fant Vars; Mirrors ALBA ▲ 227 [DDD] (16.97)
Sonata No. 1 for Violin & Piano (1953)
E. Orner (vn), J. Wizansky (pno) † Invenzione; Son 2 Vn; Son 3 Vn ALBA ▲ 138 [DDD] (16.97)
Sonata No. 2 for Violin & Piano (1973)
R. Druian (vn), J. Laredo (vn), J. Laredo (vn), A. Schein (pno), R. Laredo (pno), I. von Alpenheim (pno), I. V. Alpenheim (pno) ("Music for Violin & Piano") † A. Copland:Son Vn; C. Ives:Son 4 Vn, Op. 22; L. Kirchner:Son concertante PHOE ▲ 136 [ADD] (15.97)
E. Orner (vn), J. Wizansky (pno) † Invenzione; Son 1 Vn; Son 3 Vn ALBA ▲ 138 [DDD] (16.97)
Sonata No. 3 for Violin & Piano (1989)
E. Orner (vn), J. Wizansky (pno) † Invenzione; Son 1 Vn; Son 2 Vn ALBA ▲ 138 [DDD] (16.97)
Symphony No. 4 for Mezzo-Soprano, Violin & Orchestra [text Nelly Sachs], "Memorial Candles" (1985)
K. Wheeler (mez), J. Buswell (vn), T. Kuchar (cnd), Ukraine National SO *(rec Kiev, Ukraine, May 15, 19 & 31, 1998)* NXIN (American Classics) ▲ 8559002 [DDD] (5.97)
LEEUW, TON DE (1926-1996)
Danses sacrees for Piano & Orchestra (1989-90)
D. Kuyken (pno), E. Spanjaard (cnd), Netherlands Radio CO ("Piano Concertos in the Netherlands") † Baaren:Concertino Pno; Bosmans:Concertino Pno; L. Smit:Con Pno NMCL ▲ 92044 (16.97)
Gending for Gamelan (1975-96)
J. Sligter (cnd) *(rec Waalse Church, Amsterdam, Netherlands, July 17, 1984)* † A. Alberts:Haké; Eisma:Mawar Jiwa; Termos:Kendang; Woof:Soundings EMEC ▲ 92062 [DDD]
Haiku II for Soprano & Orchestra (1968)
E. Vink (sop), E. Spanjaard (cnd), The Hague PO † Résonances; Syms of Winds CV ▲ 23 (19.97)
Music of De Leeuw
Quink—Missa Brevis; Prière; En begheeft my niet; Egidius, waer bestu bleven?; Het visschertje *(rec Masonic Temple Cleveland, OH, OH, May 15-17, 1995)* ("Invisible Cities: Contemporary A Capella Music") † Heppener:Canti carnascialeschi; H. Kerstens:Music of Kerstens; Manneke:Choral Music TEL ▲ 80384 [DDD] (16.97)
Résonances for Orchestra
E. Spanjaard (cnd), The Hague PO † Haiku II; Syms of Winds CV ▲ 23 (19.97)
Songs
J. Vindevogel (sop), L. Kende (pno)—Trouvaille; Tu m'as [both text Mistral] *(rec Ghent, Feb 1993)* ("The Nursery") † L. Bernstein:I Hate Music; Debussy:Noël des enfants qui n'ont plus de maison; Mussorgsky:The Nursery; M. Reger:Schlichte Weisen, Op. 76 RENE ▲ 92011 [DDD] (16.97)
Sweelinck-variaties for Organ (1972-73)
L. van der Vliet (org) ("Contemporary Dutch Organ Music") † Brons:Litany Org; Raxach:Looking Glass; Ruiter:Parten Org; Schat:Passacaglia & Fugue; Welmers:Sequens Org CV ▲ 16 (19.97)
Symphonies of Winds for Orchestra (1963)
E. De Waart (cnd), Rotterdam PO † Haiku II; Résonances CV ▲ 23 (19.97)
LEFANU, NICOLA (1947-
A Penny for a Song (cycle of 13 songs) for Soprano & Piano (1981)
P. P. Jones (sop), P. Martin (pno) † S. Barber:Hermit Songs, Op. 29; J. Buckley:Abendlied; J. Kinsella:Last Songs; J. Wilson:Upon Silence ALTA ▲ 9010 (18.97)
Trio 1 for Flute, Cello & Percussion (1980)
Concord Ensemble Ireland ("Celtic Connections") † J. O'Leary:Duo Vn; Silenzio della Terra; Tann:Cresset Stone; Of Erthe & Air CPS ▲ 8640 [DDD] (16.97)
LEFÉBURE-WÉLY, LOUIS JAMES ALFRED (1817-1869)
Duo symphonique No. 1 for 2 Pianos, Op. 163 (1865)
P. Corre (pno), E. Exerjean (pno) ("French Music for 2 Pianos") † A. Blanc:Sonatine concertante, Op. 64; Gouvy:Scherzo, Op. 60; G. Pierné:Tarantella Pnos; Saint-Saëns:Vars on a Theme of Beethoven, Op. 35 PVY ▲ 790041 [DDD] (16.97)
Music of Lefébure-Wély
S. Fournier (sop), S. D. May (sop), C. Ravenne (alt), A. Espagno (db), V. Genvrin (org), La Lyre Seraphique, Pythagore Vocal Ensemble—Sainte cité, demeure permanente; Récit de Hautbois ou de Trompette harmonique; L'Encens divin; Offertoire [grand choeur]; Seigneur dès ma première enfance; Verset; Pleins de ferveur; Marche; Jour heureux, sainte allégresse; Esprit divin, Dieu de lumière; Andante, choeur de voix humaines; Afin d'être docile et sage; Mon fils, pour apprendre; Motet à la Sainte-Vierge; Du Roi des cieux tout célèbre la gloire; Scène pastorale; Andantino ("Cantiques & Organ Pieces") MED7 ▲ 4 [DDD] (18.97)
Organ Music
I. Krüger (org)—Bolero de concert, Op. 166; Scène pastorale; Offertoires; Sorties *(rec Poligny, France)* PANC ▲ 510050 (17.97)
J. Parker-Smith (org) *(rec London, England)* ("Popular French Romantics, Vol. 1") † J. Bonnet:Pièces nouvelles, Op. 7; Gigout:Toccata Org; Guilmant:Son 5 Org, Op. 80; Vierne:Carillon de Westminster, Op. 54/6; Pièces de fantaisie; Widor:Sym 1 Org, Op. 13/1; Sym 9 Org, Op. 70 ASV ▲ 539 [DDD] (16.97)
Suites (3) for Harmonicorde
J. Verdin (harmonicord) *(rec Chapelle de Monty-Charneux, France, May 1995)* RICE ▲ 163147 (17.97)
Symphonic Duo No. 1 for 2 Piano, Op. 163 (1865)
G. Picavet (pno), B. Picavet (pno) † Symphonic Duo 2, Op. 181; L. M. Gottschalk:Pno Music ILD ▲ 642169 (11.97)
Symphonic Duo No. 2 for 2 Pianos, Op. 181 (1868)
G. Picavet (pno), B. Picavet (pno) † Symphonic Duo 1, Op. 163; L. M. Gottschalk:Pno Music ILD ▲ 642169 (11.97)

LE FLELLE, JEAN (fl 1629-1642)
Music of Le Flelle
A. Lawrence-King (hp)—The Queen's Maske † Anonymous:Scott's Lament; W. Byrd:Music of Byrd; J. Dowland:Galliards; Lt Music; Music of Dowland; Second Booke of Songs or Ayres; Songs; MacDermott:King's Musicon DEHA ▲ 77504 (16.97)
LE FLEM, PAUL (1881-1984)
Fantaisie for Piano & Orchestra (1911)
M. Girod (pno), C. Schnitzler (cnd), Bretagne Orch *(rec Oct 22 & 25, 1993)* † Magicienne de la Mer (sels); Sym 1 TIMP ▲ 1021 [DDD] (18.97)
La Magicienne de la Mer (selections)
C. Schnitzler (cnd), Bretagne Orch *(rec Oct 22 & 25, 1993)* † Fantaisie Pno; Sym 1 TIMP ▲ 1021 [DDD] (18.97)
Pièces enfantines [Children's Pieces] (7) for Piano (1912; orchd)
J. Lockhart (cnd), Rhenish PO *(rec Koblenz, June 12-13, 1987)* † Pour les morts; Sym 4 MARC ▲ 8223655 [DDD] (13.97)
Pour les morts [For the Dead] for Orchestra (1913)
J. Lockhart (cnd), Rhenish PO *(rec Koblenz, June 12-13, 1987)* † Pièces enfantines; Sym 4 MARC ▲ 8223655 [DDD] (13.97)
Symphony No. 1 in A (1907)
C. Schnitzler (cnd), Bretagne Orch *(rec Oct 22 & 25, 1993)* † Fantaisie Pno; Magicienne de la Mer (sels) TIMP ▲ 1021 [DDD] (18.97)
Symphony No. 4 (1977-78)
J. Lockhart (cnd), Rhenish PO *(rec Koblenz, June 12-13, 1987)* † Pièces enfantines; Pour les morts MARC ▲ 8223655 [DDD] (13.97)
LE FLEMING, ANTHONY (20th cent)
Choral Music
St. Cecilia Players, M. Smedley (cnd), Oxford Pro Musica Singers—Cant Domino; Nunc Dimittis; Magnificat; Nocturnes; Holy Innocents; Save Me O God ("Some Shadows of Eternity") MER ▲ 84360 (16.97)
LEGLEY, VICTOR (1915-1994)
Le Bal des Halles for Band
N. Nozy (cnd), Belgian Guides Royal Sym Band ("Works for Symphonic Band") † Before Endeavors Fade; Hommage à Jean Absil; Movts; Paradise Regained; Sym 7 RENE ▲ 87123 [DDD] (16.97)
Before Endeavors Fade for Band
N. Nozy (cnd), Belgian Guides Royal Sym Band ("Works for Symphonic Band") † Bal des Halles; Hommage à Jean Absil; Movts; Paradise Regained; Sym 7 RENE ▲ 87123 [DDD] (16.97)
Burlesque for Violin & Piano, Op. 48 (1956)
J. Spanoghe (vn), D. Blumenthal (pno) *(rec Studio 4 Brussels)* † Drie Meisjes, Op. 122; Romance; Son Vn; Son Vn & Pno, Op. 12 RENE ▲ 87114 [DDD] (16.97)
Drie Meisjes (sonata) for Violin & Piano, Op. 122 (1993)
J. Spanoghe (vn), D. Blumenthal (pno) *(rec Studio 4 Brussels)* † Burlesque, Op. 48; Romance; Son Vn; Son Vn & Pno, Op. 12 RENE ▲ 87114 [DDD] (16.97)
Hommage à Jean Absil for Band
N. Nozy (cnd), Belgian Guides Royal Sym Band ("Works for Symphonic Band") † Bal des Halles; Before Endeavors Fade; Movts; Paradise Regained; Sym 7 RENE ▲ 87123 [DDD] (16.97)
Movements (3) pour Cuivres
N. Nozy (cnd), Belgian Guides Royal Sym Band ("Works for Symphonic Band") † Bal des Halles; Before Endeavors Fade; Hommage à Jean Absil; Paradise Regained; Sym 7 RENE ▲ 87123 [DDD] (16.97)
Paradise Regained for Band (1967)
N. Nozy (cnd), Belgian Guides Royal Sym Band ("Works for Symphonic Band") † Bal des Halles; Before Endeavors Fade; Hommage à Jean Absil; Movts; Sym 7 RENE ▲ 87123 [DDD] (16.97)
Romance for Violin & Piano, Op. 120 (1992)
J. Spanoghe (vn), D. Blumenthal (pno) *(rec Studio 4 Brussels)* † Burlesque, Op. 48; Drie Meisjes, Op. 122; Son Vn; Son Vn & Pno, Op. 12 RENE ▲ 87114 [DDD] (16.97)
Sonata No. 2 for Piano, Op. 84
J. D. Beenhouwer (pno) ("In Flanders' Fields, Vol 15") † Son 4 Pno, Op. 107; P. Benoit:Fants (4) Pno, Op. 20; Fants Pno, Op. 18; M. De Jong:Nocturne, Op. 53; Pictures, Op. 58; Scherzo-Idyll, Op. 68; J. Jongen:Pieces Pno, Op. 33; Mortelmans:Minuet Varié; Wielewaalt PHA ▲ 92015 (13.97)
Sonata No. 4 for Piano, Op. 107 (1985)
J. D. Beenhouwer (pno) ("In Flanders' Fields, Vol 15") † Son 2 Pno, Op. 84; P. Benoit:Fants (4) Pno, Op. 20; Fants Pno, Op. 18; M. De Jong:Nocturne, Op. 53; Pictures, Op. 58; Scherzo-Idyll, Op. 68; J. Jongen:Pieces Pno, Op. 33; Mortelmans:Minuet Varié; Wielewaalt PHA ▲ 92015 (13.97)
Sonata for solo Violin, Op. 123 (1994)
J. Spanoghe (vn) *(rec Studio 4 Brussels)* † Burlesque, Op. 48; Drie Meisjes, Op. 122; Romance; Son Vn & Pno, Op. 12 RENE ▲ 87114 [DDD] (16.97)
Sonata for Violin & Piano, Op. 12 (1943)
J. Spanoghe (vn), D. Blumenthal (pno) *(rec Studio 4 Brussels)* † Burlesque, Op. 48; Drie Meisjes, Op. 122; Romance; Son Vn RENE ▲ 87114 [DDD] (16.97)
Symphony No. 7, Op. 112 (1989)
N. Nozy (cnd), Belgian Guides Royal Sym Band ("Works for Symphonic Band") † Bal des Halles; Before Endeavors Fade; Hommage à Jean Absil; Movts; Paradise Regained RENE ▲ 87123 [DDD] (16.97)
LEGNANI, LUIGI (1790-1877)
Capriccios (36) for Guitar, Op. 20 (1922)
L. Matarazzo (gtr) *(rec Sept 1996)* AG ▲ 58 (18.97)
P. Steidl (gtr) *(rec Newmarket, Ontario, Canada, May 16-20, 1997)* † Fantasia Gtr, Op. 19 NXIN ▲ 8554198 [DDD] (5.97)
Duetto concertante for Flute (or Violin) & Guitar, Op. 23
C. Piastra (gtr), C. Ferrarini (fl) † Gran duetto, Op. 87; Battioli:Grandi vars, Op. 5; Grandi vars, Op. 8 MONM (La grande musica Italiana) ▲ 96001 (17.97)
P. Polidori (gtr), P. Depetris (fl) *(rec July 1993)* † G. F. Giuliani:Grand Son, Op. 85; Gragnani:Son Fl; Paganini:Son concertata, M.S. 2 PAVA ▲ 7298 [DDD] (10.97)
Fantasia for Guitar, Op. 19 (1822)
P. Steidl (gtr) *(rec Newmarket, Ontario, Canada, May 16-20, 1997)* † Capriccios (36) Gtr, Op. 20 NXIN ▲ 8554198 [DDD] (5.97)
Gran duetto for Flute & Guitar, Op. 87
C. Piastra (gtr), C. Ferrarini (fl) † Duetto concertante, Op. 23; Battioli:Grandi vars, Op. 5; Grandi vars, Op. 8 MONM (La grande musica Italiana) ▲ 96001 (17.97)
LEGRAND, MICHEL (1932-
Concertino for Piano & Orchestra, "Summer of '42"
D. Laval (pno), P. Verrot (cnd), Monte Carlo PO [from the film Summer of '42] *(rec Monte Carlo, July 1995)* ("Musique et cinema") † B. Herrmann:Con Macabre; Hossein:Con 3 Pno; J. Wiener:Con 1 Pno TRAV (Music & Movies) ▲ 1019 [DDD]
Film Music
C. Michel (hp), M. Legrand (hpd), M. Legrand (cnd), Large SO—Suite for Hp & Orch; Concertino for Hp & Orch [from The Summer of '42]; Suite for Hp, Hpd & Orch [from Le Messager]; Suite for Hp, Hpd & Orch [from Yentl] TRAV (Movies & Music) ▲ 1020 (18.97)
LEGRENZI, GIOVANNI (1626-1690)
La morte del cor penitente (oratorio) (1705)
R. Invernizzi (sop), E. D. Mircovich (sop), P. Costa (alt), M. Cecchetti (ten), M. Bisley (ten), S. Foresti (bass), Sonatori de la Gioiosa Marca DVX ▲ 79504 [DDD] (16.97)
Music of Legrenzi
El Mundo—O mirandum mysterium; O dilectissime Jesu † Sonate; Sonate (16), Op. 8; Sonate da chiesa (30), Op. 4 KOCH ▲ 7446 (16.97)
P. Klikar (cnd) —La squarzona; O dilectissime Jesu; La cremona; Hodie colletantur; O vos qui inter; La marinona; Non susurate; La rosetta; Humili voce; Son prima a 5; Omnes gentes ("Sonate e Motetti") SUR ▲ 3185 [DDD] (16.97)
Sonate (16) for 2, 3, 5, & 6 Instruments, Op. 8
El Mundo † Music of Legrenzi; Sonate; Sonate da chiesa (30), Op. 4 KOCH ▲ 7446 (16.97)
Sonate da chiesa e da camera (30) for 3 Instruments, Op. 4
El Mundo † Music of Legrenzi; Sonate; Sonate (16), Op. 8 KOCH ▲ 7446 (16.97)
Sonate "La cetra" for 2-4 Instruments, Op. 10
El Mundo † Music of Legrenzi; Sonate (16), Op. 8; Sonate da chiesa (30), Op. 4 KOCH ▲ 7446 (16.97)

LEHÁR, FRANZ SR. (1838-1898)
Marches
L. Marosi (cnd), Budapest Symphonic Band—Oliosi Attack March; March of the Prince of Baden; Delegation March ("The Lehár Dynasty: Marches") † F. Lehár:Marches HUN ▲ 16849 [DDD] (16.97)
LEHÁR, FRANZ (1870-1948)
An der grauen Donau (On the Gray Danube) for Orchestra
K. Seibel (cnd), Hanover North German Radio PO *(rec Mar 1996 & Jan 1997)* ("Symphonic Works") † Eine Vision; Fieber; Guado; Tatjana (ovs) CPO ▲ 999423 [DDD] (13.97)
Arias
E. Lind (sop), A. Rost (sop), P. Domingo (ten), J. Carreras (ten), T. Hampson (bar), M. Viotti (cnd), Budapest PO—Lustige Witwe (sels); Zarewitsch (sels); Giuditta (sels); Zigeunerliebe (sels); Paganini (sels); Land des Lächelns (sels) *(rec live Bad Ischl, Austria)* ("A Tribute to Operetta") † I. Kálmán:Csárdásfürstin (sels); Gräfin Mariza (sels); C. Zeller:Vogelhändler (sels) DEUT ▲ 459658 (16.97)
E. Schwarzkopf (sop), O. Ackermann (cnd), Philharmonia Orch—Zarewitsch (sels) [Einer wird kommen]; Graf von Luxemburg (sels) [Hoch, Evoë, Angèle Didier; Heut' noch werd'ich Ehefrau]; Giuditta (sels) [Meine Lippen, sie küssen so heiss] *(rec Kingsway Hall, London, England, July 1957)* † Heuberger:Opernball (sels); Millöcker:Dubarry (sels); Sieczynski:Wien, du Stadt meiner Träume; Strauss (II):Casanova (sels); Suppé:Boccaccio (sels); C. Zeller:Obersteiger (sels); Vogelhändler (sels) EMIC (Great Recordings of the Century) ▲ 67004 [ADD] (11.97)
Eine Vision: Meine Jugend (symphonic fantasy) for Orchestra (1907)
K. Seibel (cnd), Hanover North German Radio PO *(rec Mar 1996 & Jan 1997)* ("Symphonic Works") † An der grauen Donau; Fieber; Guado; Tatjana (ovs) CPO ▲ 999423 [DDD] (13.97)
Eva (selections)
G. Fontana (sop), P. Guth (cnd), Strauss Festival Orch Vienna—Zwanzinette *(rec Ludwigshafen am Rhein, Germany, Oct 1997)* ("Wine, Women & Song") † Giuditta (sels); Waltzes; I. Kálmán:Gräfin Mariza (sels); R. Stolz:Favorit (sels); Venus in Seide (sels); Strauss (II):Fledermaus (sels); Nacht in Venedig (ov); Nacht in Venedig (sels); Prinz Methusalem (sels); Waltzes; Jos. Strauss:Ohne Sorgen, Op. 271; Ziehrer:Waltzes & Other Dances DI ▲ 920532 [DDD] (5.97)
F. Lehár (cnd), Zurich Tonhalle Orch *(rec Radio Zurich Studios, June 1947)* ("Lehár Conducts Lehár") † Graf von Luxemburg (sels); Ovs BEUL ▲ 116 [ADD] (16.97)
Fieber (tone poem) for Tenor & Orchestra
R. Gambill (ten), K. Seibel (cnd), Hanover North German Radio PO *(rec Mar 1996 & Jan 1997)* ("Symphonic Works") † An der grauen Donau; Eine Vision; Guado; Tatjana (ovs) *(E text)* CPO ▲ 999423 [DDD] (13.97)
Frasquita (selections)
N. Gedda (ten), W. Mattes (cnd), Graunke SO † Friederike (sels); Giuditta (sels); Graf von Luxemburg (sels); Land des Lächelns (sels); Lustige Witwe (sels); Schön ist die Welt (sels); Zarewitsch (sels) EMPE ▲ 86354
Friederike (selections)
H. Donath (sop), G. Fuchs (sop), A. Dallapozza (ten), H. Wallberg (cnd), Munich RSO, Bavarian Radio Chorus † Schön ist die Welt (sels) EMPE ▲ 86344 (11.97)
N. Gedda (ten), W. Mattes (cnd), Graunke SO † Frasquita (sels); Giuditta (sels); Graf von Luxemburg (sels); Land des Lächelns (sels); Lustige Witwe (sels); Schön ist die Welt (sels); Zarewitsch (sels) EMPE ▲ 86354
I. Kirtesi (sop), Z. Csonka (sop), J. Berkes (ten), L. Kovács (cnd), Hungarian Operetta Orch—O Mädchen, mein Mädchen *(rec Budapest, Hungary, Oct 1995)* ("Best of Operetta, Vol. 1") † Giuditta (sels); Land des Lächelns (sels); Lustige Witwe (sels); I. Kálmán:Gräfin Mariza (sels); Strauss (II):Arias; Frühlingsstimmen, Op. 410; Zigeunerbaron (ov) NXIN ▲ 8550941 [DDD] (5.97)
E. Réthy (sop), M. Reining (sop), J. Novotná (sop), R. Tauber (ten), F. Lehár (cnd), Vienna PO, F. Lehár (cnd), Vienna SO *(rec 1934-42 for Odeon & HMV)* ("Lehár Conducts Lehár") † Giuditta (sels); Lustige Witwe (ov); Music of Lehár; Paganini (sels); Schön ist die Welt (sels); Zarewitsch (sels); Zigeunerliebe (sels) PRE ▲ 90150 [AAD] (16.97)
Das Füstenkind (selections)
R. Tauber (ten), F. Lehár (cnd), Zurich RSO [plus others] *(rec June 5, 1946)* ("Richard Tauber: The Farewell Recital") † Giuditta (sels); Graf von Luxemburg (sels); Land des Lächelns (sels) KSCH ▲ 310982 [AAD] (16.97)
Giuditta (operetta in 5 acts) [lib Knepler & Löhner] (1933)
D. Riedel (sop—Giuditta), N. Itami (sop—Anita), J. Hadley (ten—Octavio), L. Atkinson (ten—Perrino), W. Dieghan (ten—Innkeeper), J. Carl (bar—Antonio/Manuele), R. Bonynge (cnd), English CO [ENG] *(rec London, Apr 1996)* TEL ▲ 80436 [DDD] (16.97)
Giuditta (selections)
G. Fontana (sop), P. Guth (cnd), Strauss Festival Orch Vienna—Meine Lippen, sie küssen so heiss *(rec Ludwigshafen am Rhein, Germany, Oct 1997)* ("Wine, Women & Song") † Eva (sels); Waltzes; I. Kálmán:Gräfin Mariza (sels); R. Stolz:Favorit (sels); Venus in Seide (sels); Strauss (II):Fledermaus (sels); Nacht in Venedig (ov); Nacht in Venedig (sels); Prinz Methusalem (sels); Waltzes; Jos. Strauss:Ohne Sorgen, Op. 271; Ziehrer:Waltzes & Other Dances DI ▲ 920532 [DDD] (5.97)
N. Gedda (ten), W. Mattes (cnd), Graunke SO † Frasquita (sels); Friederike (sels); Graf von Luxemburg (sels); Land des Lächelns (sels); Lustige Witwe (sels); Schön ist die Welt (sels); Zarewitsch (sels) EMPE ▲ 86354
I. Kirtesi (sop), Z. Csonka (sop), J. Berkes (ten), L. Kovács (cnd), Hungarian Operetta Orch—Freunde, das Leben ist lebenswert; Meine Lippen, sie küssen so heiss *(rec Budapest, Hungary, Oct 1995)* ("Best of Operetta, Vol. 1") † Friederike (sels); Land des Lächelns (sels); Lustige Witwe (sels); I. Kálmán:Gräfin Mariza (sels); Strauss (II):Arias; Frühlingsstimmen, Op. 410; Zigeunerbaron (ov) NXIN ▲ 8550941 [DDD] (5.97)
F. Lehár (cnd), Vienna RSO, Vienna Opera Chorus † Schön ist die Welt (sels); Wo die Lerche singt (sels) BLAG 2-▲ 103352 (29.97)
K. Pitti (sop), G. Leblanc (sgr), G. Oberfrank (cnd), Budapest SO, Hungarian Radio-TV Chorus [HUN] † Land des Lächelns (sels) HUN ▲ 16809 [ADD]
E. Réthy (sop), M. Reining (sop), J. Novotná (sop), R. Tauber (ten), F. Lehár (cnd), Vienna PO, F. Lehár (cnd), Vienna SO—Freunde, das Leben ist lebenswert; Schön, Wie die blaue Sommernacht; Schönste der Frau'n' behann das Lied; Meine Lippen, sie küssen so heiss *(rec 1934-42 for Odeon & HMV)* ("Lehár Conducts Lehár") † Friederike (sels); Lustige Witwe (ov); Music of Lehár; Paganini (sels); Schön ist die Welt (sels); Zarewitsch (sels); Zigeunerliebe (sels) PRE ▲ 90150 [AAD] (16.97)
H. Roswaenge (ten), B. Seidler-Winkler (cnd), Berlin German Opera Orch—Freunde, das Leben ist lebenswert *(rec 1943)* ("Helge Rosvaenge erzählt sein Leben") † Emborg:Agnes; O. P. Freire:Songs; Narrative:Helge Roswaenge reminisces; Opa zu sein PRE ▲ 90334 (m)
A. Rothenberger (sop), N. Gedda (ten), W. Mattes (cnd), Graunke SO, Munich Theater Gartnerplatz Chorus † Graf von Luxemburg (sels); Zigeunerliebe (sels) EMPE ▲ 86342
J. Scharkowskaja (sop), T. Dewald (ten), H. Froschauer (cnd), Cologne Radio Orch, Cologne Radio Chorus—Meine Lippen, sie küssen so heiss ("Gold & Silber") † Land des Lächelns (sels); Lustige Witwe (sels); Paganini (sels); Zarewitsch (sels) CAPO ▲ 10819 [DDD] (10.97)
R. Tauber (ten), F. Lehár (cnd), Zurich RSO *(rec June 5, 1946)* ("Richard Tauber: The Farewell Recital") † Füstenkind (sels); Graf von Luxemburg (sels); Land des Lächelns (sels) KSCH ▲ 310982 [AAD] (16.97)
various artists † Graf von Luxemburg (sels); Land des Lächelns (sels); Lustige Witwe (sels); Paganini (sels); Zarewitsch (sels); Zigeunerliebe (sels) EMPE 3-▲ 70004
Gold and Silver Waltz for Orchestra, Op. 79
J. Barbirolli (cnd), Hallé Orch ("Hallé Favorites, Vol. 2") † Chabrier:España; E. Grieg:Elegiac Melodies, Op. 34; Peer Gynt (sels); Sibelius:Valse triste; Suppé:Schöne Galatea (ov); J. Turina:Danzas fantásticas, Op. 22; E. Waldteufel:Waltzes, Polkas & Galops DLAB (The Barbirolli Society) ▲ 1013 (17.97)
R. Stolz (cnd), Vienna SO *(rec 1969)* ("The Genius of Robert Stolz") † Komzák:Badener Madeln; R. Stolz:Music of Stolz; Strauss (II):Annen-Polka, Op. 117; Fledermaus (ov); Zigeunerbaron (ov) TUXE ▲ 1023 (10.97)
Der Graf von Luxemburg (selections)
N. Gedda (ten), W. Mattes (cnd), Graunke SO † Frasquita (sels); Friederike (sels); Giuditta (sels); Land des Lächelns (sels); Lustige Witwe (sels); Schön ist die Welt (sels); Zarewitsch (sels) EMPE ▲ 86354
M. Hill Smith (sop), E. Harrhy (sop), J. Davies (mez), R. Remedios (ten), N. Jenkins (ten), B. Wordsworth (cnd), New Sadler's Wells Opera Orch, New Sadler's Wells Opera Chorus [ENG] JAYR ▲ 1271 (16.97)
I. Kertesi (sop), Z. Csonka (sop), J. Berkes (ten), L. Kovács (cnd), Hungarian Operetta Orch—Mein Anherr war der Luxemburg *(rec Budapest, Hungary, Jan 1995)* ("Best of Operetta, Vol. II") † Lustige Witwe (sels); Paganini (sels); Zarewitsch (sels); Zigeunerliebe (sels); I. Kálmán:Operetta Arias; R. Stolz:Music of Stolz; Strauss (II):Nacht in Venedig (ov) NXIN ▲ 8550942 [DDD] (5.97)
E. Köth (sop), H. Hildebrand (sop), R. Schock (ten), M. Schmidt (ten), G. Niedlinger (b-bar) † Giuditta (sels); Zigeunerliebe (sels) EMPE ▲ 86342
F. Lehár (cnd), Zurich Tonhalle Orch *(rec Radio Zurich Studios, June 1947)* ("Lehár Conducts Lehár") † Eva (sels); Ovs BEUL ▲ 116 [ADD] (16.97)
E. Liebesberg (sop), R. Holm (sop), D. Hermann (mez), H. Brauner (cta), R. Christ (ten), H. Prikopa (bar), F. Bauer-Theussl (cnd), Vienna Volksoper Orch, Vienna Volksoper Chorus [GER] ("Golden Operetta, Vol. 1") † Straus:Walzertraum (sels) KOCP ▲ 399223 [AAD] (8.97)
R. Tauber (ten), F. Lehár (cnd), Zurich RSO *(rec June 5, 1946)* ("Richard Tauber: The Farewell Recital") † Füstenkind (sels); Giuditta (sels); Land des Lächelns (sels) KSCH ▲ 310982 [AAD] (16.97)

MACY, CARLETON (cont.)
Maria Music for Piano (1976)
J. Jensen (pno) *(rec Macalester College, Mar 11-12, 1994)* ("Music of Carelton Macy") † Ostinato Studies; Reflections; Solstice & Equinox INNO ▲ 503 (14.97)
Ostinato Studies (3) for 2 Pianos (1985)
J. Jensen (pno), C. Dahl (pno) *(rec Macalester College, Mar 11-12, 1994)* ("Music of Carelton Macy") † Maria Music; Reflections; Solstice & Equinox INNO ▲ 503 (14.97)
Reflections for Piano (1988-92)
J. Jensen (pno) *(rec Macalester College, Mar 11-12, 1994)* ("Music of Carelton Macy") † Maria Music; Ostinato Studies; Solstice & Equinox INNO ▲ 503 (14.97)
Solstice & Equinox for 2 Flutes & Piano (1992)
J. Bogorad (fl), A. Keunzel (fl), J. Jensen (pno) *(rec Macalester College, Mar 11-12, 1994)* ("Music of Carelton Macy") † Maria Music; Ostinato Studies; Reflections INNO ▲ 503 (14.97)
Twigs (serenade) for Woodwind Quintet (1980)
Georgia Woodwind Quintet *(rec 1994-95)* ("Twigs: Winning Compositions from the Univ of Georgia Symposia for New Woodwind Quintet Music") † T. L. McKinley:Bagatelles; Sieg:Suite Ww Qnt; Vayo:Qnt Winds ACAD ▲ 20032 (16.97)

MADARÁSZ, IVÁN (1949-
Chapters of a Story for Orchestra & Chorus (1989)
L. Kovács (cnd), Miskolc SO, Hungarian State Chorus † Con F(L)A; Echo; Embroidered; Speeds HUN ▲ 31671 [DDD] (16.97)
Concerto F(L)A for Flute & Orchestra (1993)
J. Bálint (fl), T. Szabó (cnd), Bartók Youth SO † Chapters; Echo; Embroidered; Speeds HUN ▲ 31671 [DDD] (16.97)
Echo for Orchestra (1982)
T. Szabó (cnd), Bartók Youth SO † Chapters; Con F(L)A; Embroidered; Speeds HUN ▲ 31671 [DDD] (16.97)
Embroidered Sounds for Voice, Violin, Flute, Synthesizer & Percussion (1989)
M. Kosztolányi (sgr), E. Pérényi (vn), Z. Gyöngyössy (fl), G. Eckhardt (syn), A. Holló (perc), L. Tihanyi (cnd) † Chapters; Con F(L)A; Echo; Speeds HUN ▲ 31671 [DDD] (16.97)
Lót (opera in 1 act) [lib A. Romhányi] (1985)
T. Koncz (cnd), Hungarian State Opera Orch, F. Sapszon (cnd), Hungarian Radio-TV Chorus, V. Botka (cnd), Hungarian State Opera Children's Chorus, J. Pászthy (sop—Lót's daughter), M. Takács (sop—Lót's daughter), K. Mészöly (mez—Lót's wife), M. Kuthy (mez—Prostitute), A. Fülöp (ten—Gentle angel), P. Korcsmáros (ten—Pickpocket), F. Gerdesits (ten—Irate angel), L. Kokas (ten—Homosexual), L. Miller (bar—Lót), J. Tóth (bar—Beggar), J. Schwimmer (bass—Vendor) *(rec Hungarian Television, Hungary, 1985)* † Refrain *([ENG,HUN] lib text)* HUN ▲ 31819 [AAD] (16.97)
Refrain (solo cantatas) [text Buddha] (1991)
A. Csengery (sop), K. Balázs (vc), E. Olsvai (syn), B. Faragó (syn), M. Sugár (cnd) *(rec Hungary, 1985)* † Lót *([ENG,HUN] text)* HUN ▲ 31819 [AAD] (16.97)
Speeds for 2 Flutes (1984)
G. Csetényi (fl), I. Matuz (fl) † Chapters; Con F(L)A; Echo; Embroidered HUN ▲ 31671 [DDD] (16.97)

MADDEN, JOHN (1956-
Songs of Sadness & Pitie for Oboe & Piano (1973)
E. McCarty (ob), I. Delgado (pno) *(rec Boston, United States of America, Feb 26-27, 1994)* ("Gems for Oboe & Piano") † Doran:Sonatina Ob; Rubbra:Son C Ob, Op. 100; Son Ob; E. Schelling:Impressions from an Artist's Life; Nocturne (Ragusa); L. Sinigaglia:Var(s) on Schubert Ob & Pno, Op. 19; Widerkehr:Duo Ob; Duo Pno Orch BOST ▲ 1012 [DDD] (15.97)

MADENSKY, EDUARD (1877-1923)
Tarantella for Double Bass
Y. Goilav (db) *(rec 1972)* ("The Virtuoso Romantic Double Bass") † G. Bottesini:Music Db; Dimitrescu:Danse Taranesc, Op. 15; H. Eccles:Son Va; M. Glinka:Music Db; Koussevitzky:Con Db, Op. 3; Valse miniature Db, Op. 1/2; M. Ravel:Pièce en forme de Habanera TUXE ▲ 1090 [ADD] (10.97)

MADERNA, BRUNO (1920-1973)
Chamber Music
Ex Novo Ensemble—Divert in due tempi; Qt Strs; Honeyrêves; Aulodia per Lothar; Widmung; Serenata per unsatellite; Viola; Dialodia *(rec Dec 1993)* STRV ▲ 33330 (16.97)
Concerto No. 2 for Oboe & Orchestra (1967)
P. Borgonovo (ob), A. Plotino (cnd), New Music Studium Production *(rec 1993-96)* ("Maderna & Berio") † Giardino Religioso; Serenata per un satellite; L. Berio:Chamber Music; Linea; Sequenza VIII DYNC ▲ 174 [DDD] (17.97)
Concerto for 2 Pianos & Instruments (1948)
A. Orvieto (pno), R. Maioli (pno), G. Facchin (cnd) *(rec July 1992)* ("Piano & Percussion in the 20th Century") † Serenata per un satellite; Donatoni:Cloches III; Tailleferre:Hommage à Rameau; Premières prouesses; Suite burlesque for Pno 4-Hands DYNC (2000) ▲ 2010 [DDD] (13.97)
Dimensioni No. 2 for Voice & Tape, "Invenzione su una voce" (1960)
C. Berberian (mez), B. Maderna (elec), M. Zuccheri (elec) † Electronic Music; Musica su due dimensioni STRV ▲ 33349 (16.97)
Don Perlimpin (radio opera) [lib Maderna after Lorca] (1962)
A. Caiello (sop), L. Missaglia (fl), A. Calò (a sax), M. Marzi (t sax), M. Longoni (bar sax), S. Gorli (cnd) *(rec Apr-May 1996)* STRV ▲ 33436 (16.97)
Electronic Music
C. Berberian (mez), R. Rivolta (fl), B. Maderna (syn), M. Zuccheri (syn) *(Notturno; Syntaxis; Continuo; Dimensioni II [Invenzione su una voce]; Serenata III; Le Rire) (rec 1956-62)*, C. Berberian (mez), R. Rivolta (fl), B. Maderna (syn), M. Zuccheri (syn), B. Maderna (elec), M. Zuccheri (elec) *(Musica su due dimensioni) (rec 1956-62)*, B. Maderna (elec), M. Zuccheri (elec) *(Le rire (1964))* † Dimensioni 2; Musica su due dimensioni STRV ▲ 33349 (16.97)
Giardino Religioso for Chamber Ensemble (1972)
A. Plotino (cnd), New Music Studium Production *(rec 1993-96)* ("Maderna & Berio") † Con 2 Ob; Serenata per un satellite; L. Berio:Chamber Music; Linea; Sequenza VIII DYNC ▲ 174 [DDD] (17.97)
Grande aulodia for Flute, Oboe & Orchestra (1970)
S. Gazzelloni (fl), L. Faber (ob), B. Maderna (cnd), Rome RAI SO † Julliard Serenade; Music of Gaity RIOG ▲ 5818 [AAD/ADD] (18.97)
Julliard Serenade for Small Orchestra & Tape (1971)
B. Maderna (cnd), Rome RAI SO † Grande aulodia; Music of Gaity RIOG ▲ 5818 [AAD/ADD] (18.97)
Music of Gaity [arr of 5 pieces from the Fitzwilliam Virginal Book] for Chamber Orchestra (1969)
B. Maderna (cnd), Rome RAI SO † Grande aulodia; Julliard Serenade RIOG ▲ 5818 [AAD/ADD] (18.97)
Musica su due dimensioni for Flute, Cymbals & Tape, "Dimensioni No. 1" (1952; rev for Flute & Tape, 1963)
C. Berberian (mez), R. Rivolta (fl), B. Maderna (syn), M. Zuccheri (syn), B. Maderna (elec), M. Zuccheri (elec) † Dimensioni 2; Electronic Music STRV ▲ 33349 (16.97)
R. Fabbriciani (fl) *(rec July 1995)* ("Music for the Third Millennium") † Ferneyhough:Mnemosyne; Haubenstock-Ramati:Interpolation mobile; M. Kelemen:Fabliau; G. Kurtág:Doloroso; L. Nono:atmende Klarsein; Sciarrino:Hermes AG ▲ 113 [DDD] (18.97)
Quartet for Strings (1955)
Fonè String Quartet † B. Bartók:Qt 2 Strs, Op. 17; D. Shostakovich:Qt 8 Strs, Op. 110 ARCK ▲ 59004 (16.97)
Serenata per un satellite for Ensemble (1969)
S. Antonello (vn), G. Carrer (gtr), A. Tamiozzo (mand), D. Ruggieri (fl/pic), A. Vignato (ob d'amore/ob), R. Rosetti (cl), G. Facchin (cnd) *(rec July 1992)* ("Piano & Percussion in the 20th Century") † Con for 2 Pnos; Donatoni:Cloches III; Tailleferre:Hommage à Rameau; Premières prouesses; Suite burlesque for Pno 4-Hands DYNC (2000) ▲ 2010 [DDD] (13.97)
M. Kämmerling (gtr) *(rec Fruering Kirke, 1987)* † Y después; Borup-Jørgensen:Für Gitarre, Op. 86; Preludes Gtr, Op. 76; C. Halffter:Codex 1 PLAL ▲ 60 [AAD] (18.97)
A. Plotino (cnd), New Music Studium Production *(rec 1993-96)* ("Maderna & Berio") † Con 2 Ob; Giardino Religioso; L. Berio:Chamber Music; Linea; Sequenza VIII DYNC ▲ 174 [DDD] (17.97)
Solo for Oboe + Oboe d'amore + English Horn + Musette (1971)
L. Lencsés (E hn/musette/ob d'am) ("Monodien") † B. Britten:Metamorphoses, Op. 49; Koechlin:Suite E Hn, Op. 185; Krenek:Sonatina Ob BAYE ▲ 800915 (17.97)
Y después for Guitar (1972)
M. Kämmerling (gtr) *(rec Fruering Kirke, 1987)* † Serenata per un satellite; Borup-Jørgensen:Für Gitarre, Op. 86; Preludes Gtr, Op. 76; C. Halffter:Codex 1 PLAL ▲ 60 [AAD] (18.97)

MADETOJA, LEEVI (1887-1947)
Huvinäytelmäalku (comedy overture) for Orchestra, Op. 53 (1923)
P. Sakari (cnd), Iceland SO *(rec Reykjavik, Iceland, 1991-1992)* † Okun Fuoko Suite 1; Ostrobothnians; Sym 1; Sym 2; Sym 3 CHN 2-▲ 7097 [DDD] (26.97)

MADETOJA, LEEVI (cont.)
Okon Fuoko:Suite No. 1 for Orchestra
P. Sakari (cnd), Iceland SO *(rec Reykjavik, Iceland, 1991-1992)* † Huvinäytelmäalku, Op. 53; Ostrobothnians; Sym 1; Sym 2; Sym 3 CHN 2-▲ 7097 [DDD] (26.97)
J. Saraste (cnd), Finnish RSO *(rec Cultural Hall Helsinki, June 1994)* † Ostrobothnians (sels); Sym 3 FNL ▲ 96867 [DDD] (16.97)
The Ostrobothnians (selections)
J. Saraste (cnd), Finnish RSO *(rec Cultural Hall Helsinki, Aug 1993)* † Okun Fuoko (suite 1); Sym 3 FNL ▲ 96867 [DDD] (16.97)
The Ostrobothnians (opera), Op. 45 (1923)
J. Saraste (cnd), Finnish RSO FNL ▲ 21440 (33.97)
The Ostrobothnians:Suite
P. Sakari (cnd), Iceland SO *(rec Reykjavik, Iceland, 1991-1992)* † Huvinäytelmäalku, Op. 53; Okon Fuoko Suite 1; Sym 1; Sym 2; Sym 3 CHN 2-▲ 7097 [DDD] (26.97)
Symphony No. 1 in F, Op. 29 (1915-16)
P. Sakari (cnd), Iceland SO *(rec Reykjavik, Iceland, 1991-1992)* † Huvinäytelmäalku, Op. 53; Okon Fuoko Suite 1; Ostrobothnians; Sym 2; Sym 3 CHN 2-▲ 7097 [DDD] (26.97)
Symphony No. 2 in E♭, Op. 35 (1917-18)
D. Kolbeinsson (ob), J. Ognibene (hn), P. Sakari (cnd), Iceland SO *(rec Reykjavik, Iceland, 1991-1992)* † Huvinäytelmäalku, Op. 53; Okon Fuoko Suite 1; Ostrobothnians; Sym 1; Sym 3 CHN 2-▲ 7097 [DDD] (26.97)
Symphony No. 3 in A, Op. 55 (1926)
P. Sakari (cnd), Iceland SO *(rec Reykjavik, Iceland, 1991-1992)* † Huvinäytelmäalku, Op. 53; Okon Fuoko Suite 1; Ostrobothnians; Sym 1; Sym 2 CHN 2-▲ 7097 [DDD] (26.97)
J. Saraste (cnd), Finnish RSO *(rec Cultural Hall Helsinki, Mar 1993)* † Okun Fuoko (suite 1); Ostrobothnians (sels) FNL ▲ 96867 [DDD] (16.97)

MADIN, HENRI (1698-1748)
Missa "Dico opera mea regi" for Voices (1743)
J. Pappas (cnd), Ensemble Almasis † Missa "Velociter currit sermo ejus"; Motets ARN ▲ 68432 (13.97)
Missa "Velociter currit sermo ejus" for Voices (1746)
J. Pappas (cnd), Ensemble Almasis † Missa "Dico opera mea regi"; Motets ARN ▲ 68432 (13.97)
Motets for Voices
J. Pappas (cnd), Ensemble Almasis [6 sels] † Missa "Dico opera mea regi"; Missa "Velociter currit sermo ejus" ARN ▲ 68432 (13.97)

MADSEN, TRYGVE (1940-
Clarinet Marmalade for Clarinet Quartet, Op. 79
Francilien Clarinet Quartet ("Sonatas, Marmalades & Faxes") † Sax Marmalade, Op. 96; Son A Sax, Op. 95; Son Cl; 3 Faxes, Op. 75 NORW ▲ 2921 (17.97)
Concerto for Horn & Orchestra, Op. 45
F. R. Werke (hn), O. K. Ruud (cnd), Trondheim SO ("Corno di Norvegia") † Nystedt:Con Hn; W. Plagge:Con Hn SIMX ▲ 1100 (18.97)
Divertimento for Brass & Percussion, Op. 47 (1984)
J. Panula (cnd), Scandinavian Brass Ensemble *(rec 1984)* † Per the Fiddler, Norwegian Folk Song; Almila:Te Pa Te Pa, Op. 26; Danielsson:Suite 3 Brass; E. Grieg:Funeral March in Memory of Rikard Nordraak; Hallberg:Blacksmith's Tune; Holmboe:Con Brass, Op. 157 BIS ▲ 265 [DDD] (17.97)
The Dream of the Rhinoceros for Horn, Op. 92 (1994)
F. R. Werke (hn) † Son Hn; S. Berge:Hornlokk; Clearfield:Songs of the Wolf; S. Friedman:Topanga Vars; W. Plagge:Son 3 Hn, Op. 88 CRYS ▲ 678 (15.97)
Hommage à Ravel for Piano, Op. 10
J. H. Bratlie (pno) ("Piano Works") † Prelude & Fugue, Op. 51; Preludes Pno, Op. 20; Vars & Fugue, Op. 28 NORW ▲ 2913 (17.97)
Per the Fiddler, Norwegian Folk Song
J. Panula (cnd), Scandinavian Brass Ensemble *(rec 1984)* † Divert Brass & Perc, Op. 47; Almila:Te Pa Te Pa, Op. 26; Danielsson:Suite 3 Brass; E. Grieg:Funeral March in Memory of Rikard Nordraak; Hallberg:Blacksmith's Tune; Holmboe:Con Brass, Op. 157 BIS ▲ 265 [DDD] (17.97)
Prelude & Fugue on the Name of Bach for Piano, Op. 51
J. H. Bratlie (pno) ("Piano Works") † Hommage à Ravel, Op. 10; Preludes Pno, Op. 20; Vars & Fugue, Op. 28 NORW ▲ 2913 (17.97)
Preludes (24) for Piano, Op. 20
J. H. Bratlie (pno) ("Piano Works") † Hommage à Ravel, Op. 10; Prelude & Fugue, Op. 51; Vars & Fugue, Op. 28 NORW ▲ 2913 (17.97)
Saxophone Marmalade for Saxophone Quartet, Op. 96
Jean Ledieu Sax Quartet ("Sonatas, Marmalades & Faxes") † Cl Marmalade, Op. 79; Son A Sax, Op. 95; Son Cl; 3 Faxes, Op. 75 NORW ▲ 2921 (17.97)
Sonata for Alto Saxophone & Piano, Op. 95
P. Portejoie (a sax), F. Lagarde (pno) ("Sonatas, Marmalades & Faxes") † Cl Marmalade, Op. 79; Sax Marmalade, Op. 96; Son Cl; 3 Faxes, Op. 75 NORW ▲ 2921 (17.97)
Sonata for Clarinet & Piano, Op. 23
S. Hue (cl), R. Boutry (pno) ("Sonatas, Marmalades & Faxes") † Cl Marmalade, Op. 79; Sax Marmalade, Op. 96; Son A Sax, Op. 95; 3 Faxes, Op. 75 NORW ▲ 2921 (17.97)
Sonata for Horn & Piano, Op. 24 (1978)
F. R. Werke (hn), J. H. Bratlie (pno) † Dream of the Rhinoceros, Op. 92; S. Berge:Hornlokk; Clearfield:Songs of the Wolf; S. Friedman:Topanga Vars; W. Plagge:Son 3 Hn, Op. 88 CRYS ▲ 678 (15.97)
Sonata for Oboe & Piano, Op. 22
B. Hoff (ob), K. Ørnung (pno) ("The Contemporary Oboe") † Karlsen:Sonatina Ob, Op. 44; F. Mortensen:Son Ob; S. Olsen:Poems; Sommerfeldt:Divert Ob, Op. 41; Strømholm:Con minimo Ob NORW ▲ 1005 (17.97)
Sonata for Tuba & Piano, Op. 34
O. Baadsvik (tuba), Swedish Brass Quintet † Gaathaug:Son Concertante; P. Hindemith:Son Bass Tuba; W. Kraft:Encounters II; Sivelöv:Son Tuba, Op. 5 SIMX ▲ 1101 (18.97)
Variations & Fugue over a Theme by Beethoven for Piano, Op. 28
J. H. Bratlie (pno) ("Piano Works") † Hommage à Ravel, Op. 10; Prelude & Fugue, Op. 51; Preludes Pno, Op. 20 NORW ▲ 2913 (17.97)
3 Faxes for 6 Saxes, Op. 75
A. Jousset (t sax), P. Duchesne (b sax), Jean Ledieu Sax Quartet ("Sonatas, Marmalades & Faxes") † Cl Marmalade, Op. 79; Sax Marmalade, Op. 96; Son A Sax, Op. 95; Son Cl NORW ▲ 2921 (17.97)

MADUREIRA, ANTÔNIO JOSÉ (1949-
Aralume for String Quintet
Paraíba Quintet ("Música Armorial") † Baque de Luanda; Sloth; The Warrior; Toada e Dobrado da Cavlhada; Toré; Fonseca Barbosa:Song & Challenge; Maciel:Kingdom's Stone; Nóbrega de Almeida:Rasgo do Nordeste; C. Pereira:Northeastern Pieces; Variations on a Theme from Guerra Peixe NIMB ▲ 5483 [DDD] (16.97)
Baque de Luanda for String Quintet
Paraíba Quintet ("Música Armorial") † Aralume; Sloth; The Warrior; Toada e Dobrado da Cavlhada; Toré; Fonseca Barbosa:Song & Challenge; Maciel:Kingdom's Stone; Nóbrega de Almeida:Rasgo do Nordeste; C. Pereira:Northeastern Pieces; Variations on a Theme from Guerra Peixe NIMB ▲ 5483 [DDD] (16.97)
Sloth [Preguiça] for String Quintet [from Suassuna's O Homen da Vaca e o Poder da Fortuna]
Paraíba Quintet ("Música Armorial") † Aralume; Baque de Luanda; The Warrior; Toada e Dobrado da Cavlhada; Toré; Fonseca Barbosa:Song & Challenge; Maciel:Kingdom's Stone; Nóbrega de Almeida:Rasgo do Nordeste; C. Pereira:Northeastern Pieces; Variations on a Theme from Guerra Peixe NIMB ▲ 5483 [DDD] (16.97)
Toada e Dobrado da Cavlhada for String Quintet
Paraíba Quintet ("Música Armorial") † Aralume; Baque de Luanda; Sloth; The Warrior; Toré; Fonseca Barbosa:Song & Challenge; Maciel:Kingdom's Stone; Nóbrega de Almeida:Rasgo do Nordeste; C. Pereira:Northeastern Pieces; Variations on a Theme from Guerra Peixe NIMB ▲ 5483 [DDD] (16.97)
Toré for String Quintet
Paraíba Quintet ("Música Armorial") † Aralume; Baque de Luanda; Sloth; The Warrior; Toada e Dobrado da Cavlhada; Fonseca Barbosa:Song & Challenge; Maciel:Kingdom's Stone; Nóbrega de Almeida:Rasgo do Nordeste; C. Pereira:Northeastern Pieces; Variations on a Theme from Guerra Peixe NIMB ▲ 5483 [DDD] (16.97)
The Warrior [O Guerreiro] for String Quintet
Paraíba Quintet ("Música Armorial") † Aralume; Baque de Luanda; Sloth; Toada e Dobrado da Cavlhada; Toré; Fonseca Barbosa:Song & Challenge; Maciel:Kingdom's Stone; Nóbrega de Almeida:Rasgo do Nordeste; C. Pereira:Northeastern Pieces; Variations on a Theme from Guerra Peixe NIMB ▲ 5483 [DDD] (16.97)

MAEGAARD, JAN (1926-

Canon for 3 Flutes, Op. 68 (1981)

T. L. Christiansen (fl), H. Svitzer (fl), U. M. Jørgensen (fl) *(rec Copenhagen, 1995-96)* ("Chamber Music") † Elegy; Labirinto I, Op. 77; Musica Riservata II, Op. 61 MARC ▲ 8224050 [DDD] (13.97)

Elegy of Equinox for Soprano, Cello & Organ, Op. 28 (1955)

A. Simonsen (mez), H. Brendstrup (vc), E. Feldbæk (org) *(rec Copenhagen, 1995-96)* ("Chamber Music") † Canon Fls, Op. 68; Labirinto I, Op. 77; Musica Riservata II, Op. 61 MARC ▲ 8224050 [DDD] (13.97)

Labirinto I for Viola, Op. 77 (1986)

T. Frederiksen (va) *(rec Copenhagen, 1995-96)* ("Chamber Music") † Canon Fls, Op. 68; Elegy; Musica Riservata II, Op. 61 MARC ▲ 8224050 [DDD] (13.97)

Musica Riservata II for Wind Quartet, Op. 61 (1976)

K. Sjöblom (E hn/ob), J. H. Madsen (cl), J. Bove (sax), P. Andersen (bn) *(rec Copenhagen, 1995-96)* ("Chamber Music") † Canon Fls, Op. 68; Elegy; Labirinto I, Op. 77 MARC ▲ 8224050 [DDD] (13.97)

Södergran Songs (3) for Chorus

J. G. Jørgensen (cnd), Lille MUKO University Choir ("Lille MUKO: Nordisk Suite") † Clausen:Songs; Holten:Nordisk Suite; Langgaard:Rose Garden Songs; Nørgård:Evening Country, Op. 10; Sundstrøm:Falcon & the Little Birds PONT ▲ 5125 (19.97)

MAES, JEF (1905-

Arabesque & Scherzo for Flute & Orchestra

F. Vanhove (fl), G. Oskamp (cnd), Royal Flanders PO *(rec Elisabeth Hall Antwerp, July 1994)* † Con Va; Ov concertante; Sym 2 MARC (Anthology of Flemish Music) ▲ 8223741 [DDD] (13.97)

Concerto for Viola & Orchestra (1946)

L. D. Neve (va), G. Oskamp (cnd), Royal Flanders PO *(rec Elisabeth Hall Antwerp, July 1994)* † Arabesque & Scherzo; Ov concertante; Sym 2 MARC (Anthology of Flemish Music) ▲ 8223741 [DDD] (13.97)

Ouverture concertante for Orchestra (1961)

G. Oskamp (cnd), Royal Flanders PO *(rec Elisabeth Hall Antwerp, July 1994)* † Arabesque & Scherzo; Con Va; Sym 2 MARC (Anthology of Flemish Music) ▲ 8223741 [DDD] (13.97)

Symphony No. 2 in A (1965)

G. Oskamp (cnd), Royal Flanders PO *(rec Elisabeth Hall Antwerp, July 1994)* † Arabesque & Scherzo; Con Va; Ov concertante MARC (Anthology of Flemish Music) ▲ 8223741 [DDD] (13.97)

MAGEAU, MARY JANE (1934-

An Early Autumn's Dreaming for Orchestra

S. Kawalla (cnd), Polish Radio-TV SO Cracow ("I Am An American Woman") † E. Bell:Andromeda; S. Hershey:Arrival; A. Pierce:Sym 2 VMM (Music from 6 Continents 1994) ▲ 3029 [DDD]

The Furies for Piano & Orchestra (1995)

W. Lorenz (pno), L. Williams (cnd), Queensland SO ("New Music for Orchestra") † Beath:Lagu Lagu Manis II; J. Gallagher:Persistence of Memory; Nuorvala:Notturno urbano; Pelinka:Diagonal, Op. 27 VMM ▲ 3036 [DDD]

MAGGIO, ROBERT (1964-

Fantasy: Spontaneous Lines for Clarinet & Piano (1989)

N. Williams (cl), A. Andrist (pno) *(rec Jan 1998)* ("Spontaneous Lines") † Bassett:Arias Cl; S. Currier:Intimations Cl; Muczynski:Time Pieces, Op. 43; Rokeach:North Beach Rhap Cl ALBA ▲ 311 [DDD] (16.97)

MAGILL, RONAN (1954-

Titanic: 10th-15th April, 1912 (atmospheric poem in 5 pictures) for Piano (1988)

R. Magill (pno) ATH ▲ 13 [DDD] (18.97)

MAGNARD, ALBERIC (1865-1914)

Promenades (7) for Piano, Op. 7 (1893)

S. McCallum (pno) *(rec Sydney, Australia, June 1995)* † Alkan:Etudes in minor keys, Op. 39; Preludes Pno, Op. 31 TALP ▲ 81 [DDD] (18.97)

Quintet in d for Flute, Oboe, Clarinet, Bassoon & Piano, Op. 8 (1894)

Aura Ensemble *(rec July 1997)* † Caplet:Qnt Fl THOR ▲ 2375 [DDD] (16.97)

Montreal Société des Vents *(rec Radio-Canada Building Montreal)* † Caplet:Qnt Fl CBC ▲ 1097 [DDD] (16.97)

Quintet for Piano & Winds, Op. 8

B. Fromanger (fl), L. Martin (pno), Trio OZI † Caplet:Qnt Fl KSCH ▲ 367162 (6.97)

Sonata in A for Cello & Piano, Op. 20 (1910)

S. Heled (vc), J. Zak (pno) † J. Brahms:Son Vc in D CLSO (Simca Heled Collection) ▲ 243 (15.97)

X. Phillips (vc), H. Sermet (pno) † Trio Pno, Op. 18 VAL ▲ 4807 (18.97)

Sonata in G for Violin & Piano, Op. 13 (1901)

E. Baldini (vn), L. Baldini (pno) *(rec Milan, Oct 1996)* † C. Franck:Son Vn, M.8 AG ▲ 97 [DDD] (18.97)

M. Frasca-Colombier (vn), M. Langot (pno) ("Romantic Sonatas") † C. Franck:Son Vn, M.8 PVY ▲ 730068 [DDD] (12.97)

Symphony No. 1 in c, Op. 4 (1890)

J. Ossance (cnd), BBC Scottish SO † Sym 2 HYP ▲ 67030 (18.97)

T. Sanderling (cnd), Malmö SO *(rec Sept 1998)* † Sym 3 BIS ▲ 927 [DDD] (17.97)

Symphony No. 2 in E, Op. 6 (1893)

J. Ossance (cnd), BBC Scottish SO † Sym 1 HYP ▲ 67030 (18.97)

Symphony No. 3 in b♭, Op. 11 (1896)

J. Ossance (cnd), BBC Scottish SO † Sym 4 HYP ▲ 67040 (18.97)

T. Sanderling (cnd), Malmö SO *(rec Sept 1998)* † Sym 1 BIS ▲ 927 [DDD] (17.97)

Symphony No. 4 in c#, Op. 21 (1913)

J. Ossance (cnd), BBC Scottish SO † Sym 3 HYP ▲ 67040 (18.97)

Trio in f for Piano, Violin & Cello, Op. 18 (1904)

R. Pasquier (vn), X. Phillips (vc), H. Sermet (pno) † Son Vc VAL ▲ 4807 (18.97)

MAGNUS, BLONDAL JOHANNSSON (1925-

Flute Music

M. Wiesler (fl)—Solitude *(rec Furuby Church, Sweden, June 1989)* ("To Manuela") † Atli:Pieces (12) from 21 Sounding Minutes Fl; Hjálmar:Two Etudes Fl; Leifur:Fl Music; T. Sigurbjörnsson:Fl Music BIS ▲ 456 [DDD] (17.97)

MAHIN, BRUCE (20th cent)

Flautus Aeterna for Flute & Computer (1991)

B. Mahin (elec) [includes 2 music videos; plays on any stereo or Ma] *(rec Presbyterian Church of Radford, Oct 1994)* † For Every Season; Synapse; Time Chants I. Los Angeles; Time Chants II. Monhegan Island CPS ▲ 8624 [DDD]

For Every Season for solo Instrument (1994)

B. Mahin (elec) [includes 2 music videos; plays on any stereo or Ma] *(rec Presbyterian Church of Radford, Oct 1994)* † Flautus Aeterna; Synapse; Time Chants I. Los Angeles; Time Chants II. Monhegan Island CPS ▲ 8624 [DDD]

Synapse for Soloist & Computer (1993)

B. Mahin (elec) [includes 2 music videos; plays on any stereo or Ma] *(rec Presbyterian Church of Radford, Oct 1994)* † Flautus Aeterna; For Every Season; Time Chants I. Los Angeles; Time Chants II. Monhegan Island CPS ▲ 8624 [DDD]

Time Chants I. Los Angeles, April-May 1992 for Soloist & Computer

B. Mahin (elec) [includes 2 music videos; plays on any stereo or Ma] *(rec Presbyterian Church of Radford, Oct 1994)* † Flautus Aeterna; For Every Season; Synapse; Time Chants II. Monhegan Island CPS ▲ 8624 [DDD]

Time Chants II. Monhegan Island, August 1992 for Piano & Digital Delay

C. Conger (pno) [includes 2 music videos; plays on any stereo or Ma] *(rec Radford University's Preston Hall, May 8-9, 1994)* † Flautus Aeterna; For Every Season; Synapse; Time Chants I. Los Angeles CPS ▲ 8624 [DDD]

MAHLER, GUSTAV (1860-1911)

Arrangements

L. A. Myers (sop), I. Sameth (mez), J. Clark (ten), R. Conant (bass), P. Tiboris (cnd), Brno State PO, Janáček Opera Chorus—Beethoven:Sym 9 † Beethoven:Sym 9 BRID ▲ 9033 [DDD] (17.97)

M. Senn (fl), P. Schwarz (hpd), P. Siegele (org), P. Ruzicka (cnd), Berlin RSO—Bach, J.S.:Suite aus den Orchesterwerken [arr from SuitesNos. 2 & 3, BWV 1067/68] † Totenfeier KSCH ▲ 312042 [ADD] (16.97)

P. Tiboris (cnd), Warsaw PO—Beethoven:Sym 5 † H. Distler:Neues Chorliederbuch, Op. 16 EBS 2-▲ 6076 [DDD] (17.97)

Blumine (andante) for Orchestra [discarded 5th movt of Symphony No. 1 in D] (1884)

N. Järvi (cnd), Royal Scottish National Orch † Sym 1 CHN ▲ 9308 [DDD] (16.97)

J. Judd (cnd), Florida PO † Sym 1 HAM ▲ 907118 [DDD] (18.97)

Im Lenz for Tenor & Piano [text Mahler] (1880)

J. Baker (mez), G. Parsons (pno) [GER] † Lieder eines fahrenden Gesellen; Lieder und Gesänge aus der Jugendzeit; Winterlied HYP ▲ 66100 (18.97)

Kindertotenlieder (cycle of 5 songs) for Voice & Orchestra [text Rückert] (1901-04)

M. Anderson (cta), P. Monteux (cnd), San Francisco SO ("Vol 3") † J. Brahms:Schicksalslied, Op. 54; Sym 2 RCAV (Gold Seal) ▲ 61891 (11.97)

MAHLER, GUSTAV (cont.)

Kindertotenlieder (cycle of 5 songs) for Voice & Orchestra [text Rückert] (1901-04) (cont.)

J. Baker (mez), J. Barbirolli (cnd), Hallé Orch † Knaben Wunderhorn; Lied von der Erde; Lieder eines fahrenden Gesellen; Songs from Rückert EMIC ▲ 62707 (13.97)

J. Baker (mez), J. Barbirolli (cnd), Hallé Orch *(rec Abbey Road, London, England, 1967)* † Lieder eines fahrenden Gesellen; Songs from Rückert *([ENG,GER] text)* EMIC (Great Recordings of the Century) ▲ 66996 [ADD] (11.97)

J. Baker (cta), L. Bernstein (cnd), Israel PO *(rec Mann Auditorium, Tel Aviv, Israel, Nov 1974)* † Sym 8 SNYC (Bernstein Century) ▲ 61837 (11.97)

K. Ferrier (cta), B. Walter (cnd), Vienna PO *(rec London, England, Sep 21, 1945)* † C. W. Gluck:Orfeo ed Euridice (sels); M. Greene:Anthems; G. F. Handel:Ottone (sels); Mendelssohn (-Bartholdy):Songs; H. Purcell:Come, ye sons of art, away, Z.323; Indian Queen (sels); King Arthur (sels) EMIC (Great Recordings of the Century) ▲ 66963 [ADD] (11.97)

L. Finnie (mez), N. Järvi (cnd), Royal Scottish National Orch [GER] † Sym 3 CHN 2-▲ 9117 [DDD] (32.97)

L. Finnie (mez), N. Järvi (cnd), Royal Scottish National Orch † Lieder eines fahrenden Gesellen; R. Strauss:Songs CHN ▲ 9545 (16.97)

N. Foster (bass), J. Horenstein (cnd), Bamberg SO *(rec 1955)* † Sym 9 VOXL (Legends) 2-▲ 5509 [ADD] (9.97)

T. Hampson (bar), L. Bernstein (cnd), Vienna PO [GER] † Sym 6 DEUT 2-▲ 27697 [DDD] (32.97)

T. Hampson (bar), L. Bernstein (cnd), Vienna PO † Songs from Rückert DEUT ▲ 31682 [DDD] (16.97)

T. Hampson (bar), W. Reger (pno) *(rec Abbey Road Studio 1, Mar 1996)* † Lied von der Erde; Songs from Rückert EMIC ▲ 56443 [DDD] (16.97)

H. Komatsu (bar), C. Garben (cnd), Hannover Radio PO † Lieder eines fahrenden Gesellen; Songs from Rückert NXIN ▲ 8554164 (5.97)

G. London (b-bar), O. Klemperer (cnd) *(rec Cologne, 1955)* † P. Tchaikovsky:Eugene Onegin, Op. 24 MYTO 2-▲ 971153 (34.97)

S. Lorenz (bar) † Knaben Wunderhorn; Lieder eines fahrenden Gesellen; Songs from Rückert BER ▲ 9397 (10.97)

C. Ludwig (mez), H. von Karajan (cnd), Berlin PO *(rec Philharmonie Berlin, Germany, May 1974)* † Songs from Rückert; Sym 6 DEUT (The Originals) 2-▲ 457716 [ADD] (22.97)

W. Meier (mez), L. Maazel (cnd), Bavarian Radio SO † Knaben Wunderhorn; Songs from Rückert RCAV ▲ 57129 (16.97)

J. Norman (sop), S. Ozawa (cnd), Boston SO † Sym 7 PPHI 2-▲ 26249 [DDD] (32.97)

D. Pecková (mez), J. Bělohlávek (cnd), Prague Chamber PO † Lieder eines fahrenden Gesellen; Songs from Rückert; Sym 5 SUR ▲ 3030 (16.97)

H. Rehkemper (bar), J. Horenstein (cnd), Munich National Theater Orch [GER] *(rec 1928 for Polydor)* ("Mahler: The First Three Orchestral Recordings") † Sym 2 PHS 2-▲ 9929 [AAD] (34.97)

C. Robbin (mez), R. Armenian (cnd), Kitchener-Waterloo SO [GER] † Lieder eines fahrenden Gesellen; Songs from Rückert SMS (SM 5000) ▲ 5098 [DDD] (16.97)

A. Schmidt (bar), J. López-Cobos (cnd), Cincinnati SO [GER] † Lieder eines fahrenden Gesellen; Songs from Rückert TEL ▲ 80269 [DDD] (16.97)

B. Svendén (mez), J. Carewe (cnd), Nice PO [GER] *(rec July & Nov 1990)* † Zemlinsky:Songs to Poems by Maeterlinck, Op. 13 FORL ▲ 16642 [DDD] (16.97)

J. Tourel (mez), L. Bernstein (cnd), New York PO *(rec 1960)* † Knaben Wunderhorn; Songs from Rückert; Sym 3 SNYC (Bernstein: The Royal Edition) 2-▲ 47576 [ADD] (23.97)

J. Tourel (mez), L. Bernstein (cnd), New York PO *(rec St. George Hotel, Brooklyn, NY, February 16, 1960)* † Knaben Wunderhorn; Songs from Rückert; Sym 3 SNYC (Bernstein Century) 2-▲ 61831 [ADD] (23.97)

various artists ("Complete Symphonies & Orchestral Songs") † Knaben Wunderhorn; Lied von der Erde; Lieder eines fahrenden Gesellen; Songs from Rückert; Syms (comp) DEUT 16-▲ 459080 (182.97)

Das klagende Lied (cantata) for Soprano, Alto, Tenor, Orchestra & Chorus (1880; rev 1892-93 & 1898-99)

T. Cahill (sop), J. Baker (mez), R. Tear (ten), G. Howell (bass), G. Rozhdestvensky (cnd), BBC SO, BBC Sym Chorus INMP (BBC Radio) ▲ 5691412 (13.97)

P. Coburn (sop), J. Rappe (alt), H. P. Blochwitz (ten), H. Hagegaard (bar), K. Nagano (cnd), Hallé Orch ERAT ▲ 21664 (16.97)

H. Döse (sop), A. Hodgson (cta), R. Tear (ten), S. Rattle (cnd), City of Birmingham SO, City of Birmingham Sym Chorus EMIA ▲ 47089

E. Lear (sop), E. Söderström (sop), G. Hoffman (mez), E. Haefliger (ten), S. Burrows (ten), G. Nienstedt (bass), P. Boulez (cnd), London SO, London Sym Chorus SNYC (Pierre Boulez Edition) ▲ 45841 (10.97)

J. Rodgers (sop), L. Finnie (cta), H. Blochwitz (ten), R. Hickox (cnd), Bournemouth SO, Waynflete Singers, Bath Festival Chorus CHN ▲ 9247 [DDD] (16.97)

M. Shaguch (sop), M. DeYoung (mez), T. Moser (ten), S. Leiferkus (bar), M. T. Thomas (cnd), San Francisco SO, San Francisco Sym Chorus *(rec San Francisco, May-June 1996)* RCAV (Red Seal) ▲ 68599 [DDD] (16.97)

K. Szendrényi (sop), K. Takács (cta), D. Gulyás (ten), A. Ligeti (cnd), Budapest SO, P. Erdei (cnd), Hungarian Radio-TV Chorus † Sym 10 CLDI ▲ 4010 [DDD] (10.97)

Des Knaben Wunderhorn (cycle of 12 songs) for Voice & Piano (or Orchestra) [text Brentano & Arnim] (1892-98)

E. Ameling (sop), B. Britten (cnd), London SO *(rec Aldeburgh, England, 1969)* † Lieder eines fahrenden Gesellen; Sym 4 BBC (Britten the Performer) ▲ 8004 (17.97)

J. Baker (mez), R. Hermann (bar), G. Evans (bar), W. Morris (cnd), London PO, W. Morris (cnd), Symphonica of London † Lieder eines fahrenden Gesellen INMP ▲ 2020 (9.97)

L. Bernstein (cnd), New York PO—Das irdische Leben *(rec St. George Hotel, Brooklyn, NY, February 8, 1960)* † Kindertotenlieder; Songs from Rückert; Sym 3 SNYC (Bernstein Century) 2-▲ 61831 [ADD] (23.97)

S. L. Comtois (sop), M. Bourdeau (pno) [5 sels] ("Songs of Folk Inspriation") † Canteloube:Chants de France; M. de Falla:Canciones populares españolas; M. Ravel:Chants populaires; Melodies hébraïques SNE ▲ 626 (16.97)

J. DeGaetani (mez), D. Effron (cnd) [GER] † Songs from Rückert; Berlioz:Nuits d'été, Op. 7 BRID ▲ 9017 [DDD] (17.97)

C. Elsner (ten), C. Spencer (pno)—Lob des hohen Verstandes; Des Antonius von Padua Fischpredigt; Rheinlegendchen ("Gesellen- und Lumpenlieder") † Lieder aus letzter Zeit; Lieder eines fahrenden Gesellen; Lieder und Gesänge aus der Jugendzeit; Hessenberg:Lieder eines lumpen, Op. 51 ARSM ▲ 1172 [DDD] (17.97)

B. Fassbaender (mez), D. Fischer-Dieskau (bar), H. Zender (cnd), Saarbrücken RSO [11 sels] ("Hans Zender Edition, Vol. 7") † Sym 9 CPO 2-▲ 999479 (6.97)

A. Felbermayer (sop), A. Poell (bar), V. Gräf (pno), F. Prohaska (cnd), Vienna State Opera Orch—Rheinlegendchen; Lob des hohen Verstandes *(rec Vienna, Austria, 1952)* † Lieder und Gesänge aus der Jugendzeit; Songs from Rückert VC ▲ 8202 [ADD] (13.97)

M. Forrester (cta), H. Rehfuss (bar), F. Prohaska (cnd), Vienna Festival Orch *(rec May-June 1963)* VC ▲ 4045 [ADD] (13.97)

T. Hampson (bar), G. Parsons (pno) TELC ▲ 74726 (16.97)

C. Kallisch (sop), G. Dobner (pno)—Rheinlegendchen; Lob des hohen Verstandes *(rec Germany, Sep 11-12, 1997)* † Lieder und Gesänge aus der Jugendzeit; A. Dvořák:Zigeunermelodien, Op. 55; Liszt:Songs *([ENG,FRE,GER]text)* MDG ▲ 6390840 [DDD] (17.97)

S. Keenlyside (bar), S. Rattle (cnd), City of Birmingham SO—Der Schildwache Nachtlied; Verlor'ne Müh; Wer hat dies Liedlein erdacht?; Wo die schönen Trompeten blasen; Des Antonius von Padua Fischpredigt *(rec Birmingham, United States of America, Sept 1997)* † Lieder aus letzter Zeit; Lieder und Gesänge aus der Jugendzeit; Sym 3 *([ENG,GER]text)* EMIC 2-▲ 56657 [DDD] (32.97)

E. Lear (sop), T. Stewart (bar), R. Kraus (cnd), Berlin PO *(rec 1962 & 1983)* † Sym 2; Sym 3 VAIA ▲ 1061 [ADD] (16.97)

S. Lorenz (bar) [4 songs] † Kindertotenlieder; Lieder eines fahrenden Gesellen; Songs from Rückert BER ▲ 9397 (10.97)

W. Meier (mez), L. Maazel (cnd), Bavarian Radio SO † Kindertotenlieder; Songs from Rückert RCAV ▲ 57129 (16.97)

A. Murray (mez), T. Allen (bar), C. Mackerras (cnd), London PO *(rec London, England, Oct 1990)* † Lieder eines fahrenden Gesellen; Sym 5 VCL 2-▲ 61507 [DDD] (11.97)

A. S. von Otter (mez), T. Quasthoff (bar), C. Abbado (cnd), Berlin PO † Sym 2 DEUT ▲ 459646 (16.97)

D. Pecková (mez), J. Bělohlávek (cnd), Prague Chamber PO—Das irdische Leben; Rheinlegendchen; Wer hat dies Liedlein erdacht?; Wo die schönen Trompeten blasen *(rec Prague, Czech Republic, July 1-2 & Sept 11-13, 1996)* † Lieder und Gesänge aus der Jugendzeit; Sym 2; L. Berio:Folk Songs Sop SUR ▲ 3264 [DDD]

L. Popp (sop), J. Baker (mez), M. Dickie (ten), D. Fischer-Dieskau (bar), B. Weikl (bar), K. Tennstedt (cnd), London PO † Kindertotenlieder; Lied von der Erde; Lieder eines fahrenden Gesellen; Songs from Rückert EMIC ▲ 62707 (13.97)

L. Popp (sop), A. Schmidt (bar), L. Bernstein (cnd), (Royal) Concertgebouw Orch [GER] DGRM ▲ 27302 [DDD] (17.97)

M. Price (sop), T. Dewey (pno)—Des Antonius von Padua Fischpredigt; Rheinlegendchen; Wo die schönen Trompeten blasen; Lob des hohen Verstandes; Das irdische Leben † Lieder eines fahrenden Gesellen; Songs from Rückert FORL ▲ 16744 [DDD] (16.97)

▲ = CD ♦ = Enhanced CD △ = MD ▮ = Cassette Tape ▯ = DCC

MAHLER, GUSTAV (cont.)

Des Knaben Wunderhorn (cycle of 12 songs) for Voice & Piano (or Orchestra) [text Brentano & Arnim] (1892-98) (cont.)

J. Raskin (sop), G. Schick (pno)—Wer hat dies Liedlein erdacht?; Wo die schönen Trompeten blasen ("Songs & Duets") † Lieder und Gesänge aus der Jugendzeit; Songs from Rückert; J. Brahms:Ballads & Romances, Op. 75; Duets (3), Op. 20; Duets (4), Op. 61; Duets (5), Op. 66; Mendelssohn (-Bartholdy):Songs; R. Schumann:Spanisches Liederspiel, Op. 74 SNYC (Essential Classics) ▲ 60269 (7.97) ▮ 60269 (3.98)

M. Shirai (mez), H. Höll (pno)—Das irdische Leben; Des Antonius von Padua Fischpredigt; Rheinlegendchen; Wo die schönen Trompeten blasen ("Mahler:Leider") † Lieder und Gesänge aus der Jugendzeit; Songs from Rückert CAPO ▲ 10712 [DDD] (11.97)

J. Tourel (mez), L. Bernstein (cnd), New York PO—Das irdische Leben *(rec 1960)* † Kindertotenlieder; Songs from Rückert; Sym 3 SNYC (Bernstein: The Royal Edition) 2-▲ 47576 [ADD] (23.97)

J. Van Dam (b-bar) [FRE] ("Le chant d'un maître") † Songs from Rückert; W. A. Mozart:Don Giovanni (sels); Nozze di Figaro (sels); Zauberflöte (sels); G. Puccini:Bohème (sels); G. Rossini:Barbiere di Siviglia (sels); Verdi:Don Carlos (sels); Rigoletto (sels); R. Wagner:Tannhäuser (sels); Walküre (sels) FORL ▲ 302270 [ADD]

I. Vermillion (mez), B. Weikl (bar), E. Inbal (cnd), Vienna SO † Lieder eines fahrenden Gesellen DNN ▲ 18018 (16.97)

various artists ("Complete Symphonies & Orchestral Songs") † Kindertotenlieder; Lied von der Erde; Lieder eines fahrenden Gesellen; Songs from Rückert; Syms (comp) DEUT 16-▲ 459080 (182.97)

Das Lied von der Erde (symphony) for solo Voices & Orchestra [text after H. Bethge] (1908-09)

E. Cavelti (alt), A. Dermota (ten), O. Klemperer (cnd), Vienna SO *(rec 1957)* TUXE ▲ 1036 [ADD] (10.97)

L. Chookasian (mez), R. Lewis (ten), E. Ormandy (cnd), Philadelphia Orch *(rec Feb 9, 1966)* † Songs from Rückert SNYC (Essential Classics) ▲ 53518 [ADD] (7.97) ▮ 53518 [ADD] (3.98)

M. DeYoung (mez), J. Villars (ten), E. Oue (cnd), Minnesota Orch REF ▲ 88 (16.97)

R. Donose (mez), T. Harper (ten), M. Halász (cnd), Irish National SO *(rec National Concert Hall Dublin, Apr 11-12, 1994)* NXIN ▲ 550933 [DDD] (5.97)

H. Fassbender (mez), J. Wagner (ten), A. Jordan (cnd) CASC ▲ 1034 (16.97)

M. Groop (mez), J. Silvasti (ten), O. Vänskä (cnd) [trans A. Schoenberg for chamber ensemble & compd R] BIS ▲ 681 [DDD] (17.97)

T. Hampson (bar), W. Reger (pno) *(rec Abbey Road Studio 1, Mar 1996)* † Kindertotenlieder; Songs from Rückert EMIC ▲ 56443 [DDD] (16.97)

G. Hoffmann (alt), H. Melchert (ten), H. Rosbaud (cnd), Southwest German RSO Baden-Baden *(rec 1957)* ("Hans Rosbaud Conducts Mahler & Bruckner") † A. Bruckner:Sym 7 VOXL 2-▲ 5518 (9.97)

J. King (ten), D. Fischer-Dieskau (bar), L. Bernstein (cnd), Vienna PO *(rec 1966)* DECC ▲ 466381 (11.97)

G. Linos (mez), Z. Vandersteene (ten) PC ▲ 265043 [DDD] (2.97)

C. Ludwig (mez), R. Kollo (ten), L. Bernstein (cnd), Israel PO SNYC ▲ 47589 (10.97)

C. Ludwig (mez), F. Wunderlich (ten), O. Klemperer (cnd), Philharmonia Orch, O. Klemperer (cnd), New Philharmonia Orch *(rec London, England, 1964 & 1966) ([ENG,GER])* EMIC (Great Recordings of the Century) ▲ 66944 [ADD] (11.97)

N. Merriman (mez), F. Wunderlich (ten), H. Schmidt-Isserstedt (cnd), North German SO *(rec Hamburg, Apr 1965)* BELV ▲ 7011 (15.97)

J. V. Nes (cta), P. Schreier (ten), E. Inbal (cnd), Frankfurt RSO [GER] DNN ▲ 72605 [DDD] (16.97)

E. Nikolaidi (cta), S. Svanholm (ten), B. Walter (cnd), Philharmonic SO *(rec 1953)* MUA ▲ 950 (16.97)

J. Norman (sop), S. Jerusalem (ten), J. Levine (cnd), Berlin PO *(rec live)* DEUT ▲ 439948 [DDD] (16.97)

J. Norman (sop), J. Vickers (ten), C. Davis (cnd), London SO [GER] PPHI ▲ 11474 [DDD] (16.97)

L. Popp (sop), J. Baker (mez), M. Dickie (ten), D. Fischer-Dieskau (bar), B. Weikl (bar), P. Kletzki (cnd), Philharmonia Orch † Kindertotenlieder; Knaben Wunderhorn; Lieder eines fahrenden Gesellen; Songs from Rückert EMIC ▲ 62707 (13.97)

B. Remmert (cta), H. Blochwitz (ten), P. Herreweghe (cnd) [arr Schoenberg & Riehn for CO] HAM ▲ 901477 (18.97)

I. Schmithusen (sop), A. Baldin (ten), R. Platz (cnd) [arr Schoenberg for chamber ens] CANT ▲ 1031 (17.97)

K. Thorborg (alt), C. Kullman (ten), A. Rodzinski (cnd), New York PO *(rec 1944)* GRM2 ▲ 78623 (13.97)

K. Thorborg (mez), C. Kullman (ten), B. Walter (cnd), Vienna PO [GER] *(rec live, Musikvereinsaal, Vienna, Austria, May 24, 1936)* † Songs from Rückert; Sym 5 PHS ▲ 9413 [AAD] (17.97)

K. Thorborg (mez), C. Kullman (ten), B. Walter (cnd), Vienna PO *(rec Vienna, May 1936)* ("Bruno Walter in Vienna, Vol. 3") GRM2 ▲ 78553 (13.97)

K. Thorborg (mez), C. Kullman (ten), B. Walter (cnd), Vienna PO ("Bruno Walter in Vienna") † Sym 9 ENT (Palladio) ▲ 4172 [ADD] (26.97)

K. Thorborg (mez), C. Kullman (ten), B. Walter (cnd), Vienna PO *(rec 1936)* † Songs from Rückert; Sym 5 DLAB (Essential Archive) ▲ 5014 (15.97)

K. Thorborg (mez), C. M. Öhmann (ten), C. Schuricht (cnd), (Royal) Concertgebouw Orch *(rec Amsterdam, Oct 5, 1939)* ("Schuricht Conducts Mahler") GRM2 ▲ 78978 (13.97)

K. Thorborg (mez), C. M. Öhmann (ten), C. Schuricht (cnd), (Royal) Concertgebouw Orch *(rec live Amsterdam, Netherlands, Oct 5, 1939)* MNER ▲ 30 [ADD] (15.97)

F. Wunderlich (ten), D. Fischer-Dieskau (bar), J. Keilberth (cnd), Bamberg SO *(rec Bamberg, 1964)* † H. Wolf:Songs (misc) *(G texts)* MYTO ▲ 975171 (17.97)

various artists ("Complete Symphonies & Orchestral Songs") † Kindertotenlieder; Knaben Wunderhorn; Lieder eines fahrenden Gesellen; Songs from Rückert; Syms (comp) DEUT 16-▲ 459080 (182.97)

Lieder aus letzter Zeit (7) for Voice & Orchestra (or Piano) (1899-1901)

C. Elsner (ten), C. Spencer (pno)—Der Tamboursg'sell ("Gesellen- und Lumpenlieder") † Knaben Wunderhorn; Lieder eines fahrenden Gesellen; Lieder und Gesänge aus der Jugendzeit; Hessenberg:Lieder eines lumpen, Op. 51 ARSM ▲ 1172 [DDD] (17.97)

S. Keenlyside (bar), S. Rattle (cnd), City of Birmingham SO—Revelge; Der Tamboursg'sell *(rec Birmingham, United States of America, Sept 1997)* † Knaben Wunderhorn; Lieder und Gesänge aus der Jugendzeit; Sym 3 *([ENG,GER]text)* EMIC 2-▲ 56657 [DDD] (32.97)

J. Van Dam (b-bar), J. Casadesus (cnd), Lille National Orch—Revelge; Der Tamboursg'sell *(rec Nov 1986)* † Sym 2 FORL 2-▲ 16654 [DDD] (32.97)

Lieder eines fahrenden Gesellen [Songs of a Wayfarer] (song cycle) for Voice & Orchestra (or Piano) (1883-85; rev 1891-96; orchd 1896)

J. Baker (mez), J. Barbirolli (cnd), Hallé Orch † Kindertotenlieder; Knaben Wunderhorn; Lied von der Erde; Songs from Rückert EMIC ▲ 62707 (13.97)

J. Baker (mez), J. Barbirolli (cnd), Hallé Orch *(rec Abbey Road, London, England, 1967)* † Kindertotenlieder; Songs from Rückert *([ENG,GER] text)* EMIC (Great Recordings of the Century) ▲ 66996 [ADD] (11.97)

J. Baker (mez), R. Hermann (bar), G. Evans (bar), W. Morris (cnd), London PO, W. Morris (cnd), Symphonica of London † Knaben Wunderhorn INMP ▲ 2020 (9.97)

J. Baker (mez), G. Parsons (pno) [GER] † Im Lenz; Lieder und Gesänge aus der Jugendzeit; Winterlied HYP ▲ 66100 (18.97)

J. Benton (bar), G. Kirkland (pno) [ENG] † Beethoven:An die ferne Geliebte, Op. 98; R. Schumann:Dichterliebe, Op. 48 SYMP ▲ 1221 [DDD] (18.97)

C. Elsner (ten), C. Spencer (pno)—Wenn mein Schatz Hochzeit macht; Ging heut' morgens übers Feld; Ich hab' ein glühend Messer; Die zwei blauen Augen ("Gesellen- und Lumpenlieder") † Knaben Wunderhorn; Lieder aus letzter Zeit; Lieder und Gesänge aus der Jugendzeit; Hessenberg:Lieder eines lumpen, Op. 51 ARSM ▲ 1172 [DDD] (17.97)

L. Finnie (mez), N. Järvi (cnd), Royal Scottish National Orch † Kindertotenlieder; R. Strauss:Songs CHN ▲ 9545 (16.97)

D. Fischer-Dieskau (bar), L. Bernstein (pno) [GER] *(rec live, Lincoln Center, New York City, NY, Nov 8, 1968)* † Lieder und Gesänge aus der Jugendzeit; Songs from Rückert MYTO ▲ 89008 [ADD] (17.97)

D. Fischer-Dieskau (bar), R. Kubelík (cnd), Bavarian RSO *(rec Residenz Munich, Germany, Dec 1968)* † Sym 1 DEUT (The Originals) ▲ 449735 [ADD] (11.97)

N. Foster (b-bar), J. Horenstein (cnd), Bamberg SO *(rec Bamberg, 1954)* † Schoenberg:Chamber Sym 1, Op. 9; Verklärte Nacht, Op. 4; R. Strauss:Don Juan, Op. 20; Till Eulenspiegels lustige Streiche, Op. 28; Tod und Verklärung, Op. 24; R. Wagner:Lohengrin (preludes); Tristan und Isolde (prelude & liebestod) VB2 2-▲ 5529 (9.97)

J. Hynninen (bar), E. Inbal (cnd), Vienna SO † Knaben Wunderhorn DNN ▲ 18018 (16.97)

H. Komatsu (bar), C. Garben (cnd), Hannover Radio PO † Kindertotenlieder; Songs from Rückert NXIN ▲ 8554164 (5.97)

Y. Levi (cnd), Atlanta SO, F. von Stade (mez) *(rec Atlanta, GA, July 1998)* † Sym 4 TEL ▲ 80499 [DDD] (16.97)

S. Lorenz (bar) † Kindertotenlieder; Knaben Wunderhorn; Songs from Rückert BER ▲ 9397 (10.97)

A. Murray (mez), A. Litton (cnd), Royal PO *(rec London, England, July-Aug 1987)* † Knaben Wunderhorn; Sym 5 VCL 2-▲ 61507 [DDD] (11.97)

J. Norman (sop), B. Haitink (cnd), Berlin PO † Sym 6 PPHI 2-▲ 26257 [DDD] (32.97)

A. S. von Otter (mez), J. E. Gardiner (cnd), North German SO *(rec Hamburg, Germany, 1993)* ("Mahler & Zemlinsky Lieder") † Songs from Rückert; Zemlinsky:Songs to Poems by Maeterlinck, Op. 13 PPHI ▲ 439928 [DDD] (16.97)

MAHLER, GUSTAV (cont.)

Lieder eines fahrenden Gesellen [Songs of a Wayfarer] (song cycle) for Voice & Orchestra (or Piano) (1883-85; rev 1891-96; orchd 1896) (cont.)

D. Pecková (mez), J. Bělohlávek (cnd), Prague Chamber PO † Kindertotenlieder; Songs from Rückert; Sym 5 SUR ▲ 3030 (16.97)

M. Price (sop), T. Dewey (pno) † Knaben Wunderhorn; Songs from Rückert FORL ▲ 16744 [DDD] (16.97)

A. Reynolds (sop), B. Britten (cnd), London SO *(rec 1969)* † Knaben Wunderhorn; Sym 4 BBC (Britten the Performer) ▲ 8004 (17.97)

C. Robbin (mez), R. Armenian (cnd), Kitchener-Waterloo SO [GER] † Kindertotenlieder; Songs from Rückert SMS (SM 5000) ▲ 5098 [DDD] (16.97)

A. Schmidt (bar), J. López-Cobos (cnd), Cincinnati SO [GER] † Kindertotenlieder; Songs from Rückert TEL ▲ 80269 [DDD] (16.97)

F. von Stade (mez), A. Davis (cnd), London PO † Sym 4 SNYC (Essential Classics) ▲ 46535 [ADD] (7.97) ▮ 46535 [ADD] (3.98)

E. Zareska (mez), C. Schuricht (cnd), French National Orch † Sym 1 STRV ▲ 10010 [ADD] (12.97)

various artists ("Complete Symphonies & Orchestral Songs") † Kindertotenlieder; Knaben Wunderhorn; Lied von der Erde; Songs from Rückert; Syms (comp) DEUT 16-▲ 459080 (182.97)

Lieder und Gesänge aus der Jugendzeit (set of 14 songs) for Voice & Piano (1880-90)

J. Baker (mez), G. Parsons (pno) [GER] † Im Lenz; Lieder eines fahrenden Gesellen; Winterlied HYP ▲ 66100 (18.97)

C. Elsner (ten), C. Spencer (pno)—Frühlingsmorgen; Ablösung im Sommer; Serenade aus Don Juan; Selbstgefühl ("Gesellen- und Lumpenlieder") † Knaben Wunderhorn; Lieder aus letzter Zeit; Lieder eines fahrenden Gesellen; Hessenberg:Lieder eines lumpen, Op. 51 ARSM ▲ 1172 [DDD] (17.97)

A. Felbermayer (sop), A. Poell (bar), V. Gräf (pno), F. Prohaska (cnd), Vienna State Opera Orch *(rec Vienna, Austria, 1952)* † Knaben Wunderhorn; Songs from Rückert VC ▲ 8202 [ADD] (13.97)

D. Fischer-Dieskau (bar), L. Bernstein (pno) [GER;11 sels] *(rec live, Lincoln Center, New York City, Nov 8, 1968)* † Lieder eines fahrenden Gesellen; Songs from Rückert MYTO ▲ 89008 [ADD] (17.97)

D. Halban (sop), B. Walter (cnd), New York PO [sel] ("Bruno Walter: First American Recordings") † Sym 5; Beethoven:Sym 3 GRM2 2-▲ 78838 (26.97)

C. Kallisch (sop), G. Dobner (pno)—Ablösung im Sommer; Um schlimme Kinder artig zu machen; Ich ging mit Lust durch einen grünen Wald; Zu Strassburg auf der Schanz; Nicht wiedersehen! *(rec Germany, Sep 11-12, 1997)* † Knaben Wunderhorn; A. Dvořák:Zigeunermelodien, Op. 55; Liszt:Songs *([ENG,FRE,GER]text)* MDG ▲ 6390840 [DDD] (17.97)

K. Karnéus (mez), R. Vignoles (pno)—Frühlingsmorgen; Ich ging mit Lust durch einen grünen Wald; Ablösung im Sommer; Erinnerung; Hans und Grethe; Scheiden und Meiden *(rec St. Michael's Church, Highgate, London, England, July 1998)* † Songs from Rückert; J. Marx:Italianisches Liederbuch; Lieder und Gesänge; R. Strauss:Die Nacht, Op. 10/3; Morgen; Ruhe, meine Seele, Op. 27/1; Songs EMIC ▲ 73168 [DDD] (6.97)

S. Keenlyside (bar), S. Rattle (cnd), City of Birmingham SO—Ablösung im Sommer [orch Luciano Berio] *(rec Birmingham, AL, Sept 1997)* † Knaben Wunderhorn; Lieder aus letzter Zeit; Sym 3 *([ENG,GER]text)* EMIC 2-▲ 56657 [DDD] (32.97)

D. Pecková (mez), J. Bělohlávek (cnd), Prague Chamber PO—Erinnerung *(rec Prague, July 1-2 & Sept 11-13, 1996)* † Knaben Wunderhorn; Sym 2; L. Berio:Folk Songs Sop SUR ▲ 3264 [DDD]

L. Popp (sop), G. Parsons (pno)—Frühlingsmorgen; Ich ging mit Lust durch einen grünen Wald; Nicht wiedersehen!; Scheiden und Meiden; Um schlimme Kinder artig zu machen; Hans und Grethe; Starke Einbildungskraft; Ablösung im Sommer; Erinnerung *(rec Munich, Germany, 1983)* ("Lieder") † J. Brahms:Songs AART ▲ 47367 [DDD] (10.97)

J. Raskin (sop), G. Schick (pno)—Frühlingsmorgen; Erinnerung; Hans und Grethe; Ich ging mit Lust durch einen grünen Wald; Ablösung im Sommer; Scheiden und Meiden ("Songs & Duets") † Knaben Wunderhorn; Songs from Rückert; J. Brahms:Ballads & Romances, Op. 75; Duets (3), Op. 20; Duets (4), Op. 61; Duets (5), Op. 66; Mendelssohn (-Bartholdy):Songs; R. Schumann:Spanisches Liederspiel, Op. 74 SNYC (Essential Classics) ▲ 60269 (7.97) ▮ 60269 (3.98)

M. Shirai (mez), H. Höll (pno)—Frühlingsmorgen; Erinnerung; Phantasie aus Don Juan; Um schlimme Kinder artig zu machen; Ich ging mit Lust durch einen grünen Wald; Ablösung im Sommer; Scheiden und Meiden; Nicht wiedersehen! ("Mahler:Leider") † Knaben Wunderhorn; Songs from Rückert CAPO ▲ 10712 [DDD] (11.97)

Music of Mahler

D. Bowman (voc), A. Lindsay (voc), M. Feldman (vn), L. Gold (vc), M. Formanek (db), D. Blume (elec/gtr/elec/gtr), D. Byron (cl), D. Binney (s sax), D. Douglas (tpt), J. Roseman (trbn), U. Caine (pno), J. Baron (dr) *(Sym 5 [Trauermarsch; Adagietto]; Kindertotenlieder [Nun will die Sonn' so hell aufgeh'n; Oft denk' ich, sie sind nur ausgegangen]; Lied von der Erde [Der Trunkene im Frühling; Der Abschied])*, D. Bowman (voc), A. Lindsay (voc), M. Feldman (vn), L. Gold (vc), M. Formanek (db), D. Blume (elec/gtr), D. Byron (cl), D. Binney (s sax), D. Douglas (tpt), J. Roseman (trbn), U. Caine (pno), J. Baron (dr) *(Lieder aus letzter Zeit [Der Tamboursg'sell]; Knaben Wunderhorn [Wer hat dies Liedlein erdacht?]; Sym 1 [Feierlich und gemessen]; Lieder eines fahrenden Gesellen [Ging heut' morgens übers Feld])*, D. Bowman (voc), A. Lindsay (voc), M. Feldman (vn), L. Gold (vc), M. Formanek (db), D. Blume (elec/gtr/elec/gtr/el), D. Byron (cl), D. Binney (s sax), D. Douglas (tpt), J. Roseman (trbn), U. Caine (pno), J. Baron (dr) *(Sym 2 [Urlicht; Andante moderato])* ("Urlicht/Primal Light") WNTR ▲ 4 (16.97)

E. Podles (cta), A. Wit (cnd), Polish National RSO Katowice *(Sym 3 [Sehr langsam: 'O Mensch! Gib acht']*), A. Wit (cnd), Polish National RSO Katowice *(Sym 4 [Ruhevoll]; Sym 5 [Adagietto]; Sym 6 [Andante])* ("Adagio Mahler") NXIN ▲ 8552243 [DDD] (5.97)

Songs (5) from Rückert for Voice & Orchestra (or Piano) (1901-02)

J. Baker (mez), J. Barbirolli (cnd), New Philharmonia Orch † Kindertotenlieder; Knaben Wunderhorn; Lied von der Erde; Lieder eines fahrenden Gesellen EMIC ▲ 62707 (13.97)

J. Baker (mez), J. Barbirolli (cnd), New Philharmonia Orch *(rec Watford Town Hall, England, 1969)* † Kindertotenlieder; Lieder eines fahrenden Gesellen *([ENG,GER] text)* EMIC (Great Recordings of the Century) ▲ 66996 [ADD] (11.97)

J. Baker (mez), M. T. Thomas (cnd), London SO, London Sym Chorus [GER] † Sym 3 SNYC 2-▲ 44553 [DDD] (31.97)

K. Berman (bass), V. Neumann (cnd), Czech PO [GER;3 sels] *(rec Oct 10-12, 1977)* SUR 2-▲ 111978

L. Bernstein (cnd), New York PO—Ich atmet' einen linden Duft; Ich bin der Welt abhanden gekommen; Um Mitternacht † Kindertotenlieder; Knaben Wunderhorn; Sym 3 SNYC (Bernstein Century) 2-▲ 61831 [ADD] (23.97)

J. DeGaetani (mez), D. Effron (cnd) [GER] † Knaben Wunderhorn; Berlioz:Nuits d'été, Op. 7 BRID ▲ 9017 [DDD] (17.97)

A. Felbermayer (sop), A. Poell (bar), V. Gräf (pno), F. Prohaska (cnd), Vienna State Opera Orch *(rec Vienna, Austria, 1952)* † Knaben Wunderhorn; Lieder und Gesänge aus der Jugendzeit VC ▲ 8202 [ADD] (13.97)

K. Ferrier (cta), B. Walter (cnd), Vienna PO [3 sels] ("Great Voices of the 50s, Vol 1") † R. Strauss:Four Last Songs, AV150; R. Wagner:Wesendonck Songs PLON ▲ 448150 (11.97)

D. Fischer-Dieskau (bar), L. Bernstein (pno)—Blicke mir nicht in die Lieder; Ich atmet' einen linden Duft; Ich bin der Welt abhanden gekommen; Um Mitternacht [GER] *(rec live, Lincoln Center, New York City, NY, Nov 8, 1968)* † Lieder eines fahrenden Gesellen; Lieder und Gesänge aus der Jugendzeit MYTO ▲ 89008 [ADD] (17.97)

T. Hampson (bar), L. Bernstein (cnd), Vienna PO *(rec live Feb 1990)* † Kindertotenlieder DEUT ▲ 31682 [DDD] (16.97)

T. Hampson (bar), W. Reger (pno) *(rec Abbey Road Studio 1, Mar 1996)* † Kindertotenlieder; Lied von der Erde EMIC ▲ 56443 [DDD] (16.97)

K. Karnéus (mez), R. Vignoles (pno)—Blicke mir nicht in die Lieder; Ich atmet' einen linden Duft; Liebst du um Schönheit; Ich bin der Welt abhanden gekommen *(rec St. Michael's Church, Highgate, London, England, July 1998)* † Lieder und Gesänge aus der Jugendzeit; J. Marx:Italianisches Liederbuch; Lieder und Gesänge; R. Strauss:Die Nacht, Op. 10/3; Morgen; Ruhe, meine Seele, Op. 27/1; Songs EMIC ▲ 73168 [DDD] (6.97)

H. Komatsu (bar), C. Garben (cnd), Hannover Radio PO † Kindertotenlieder; Lieder eines fahrenden Gesellen NXIN ▲ 8554164 (5.97)

M. Lipovšek (mez), E. Werba (pno)—Ich atmet' einen linden Duft; Liebst du um Schönheit; Ich bin der Welt abhanden gekommen; Um Mitternacht [GER] † Schreker:Songs; R. Strauss:Songs ORF ▲ 176891 [DDD] (18.97)

S. Lorenz (bar) † Kindertotenlieder; Knaben Wunderhorn; Lieder eines fahrenden Gesellen BER ▲ 9397 (10.97)

C. Ludwig (mez), H. von Karajan (cnd), Berlin PO *(rec Philharmonie Berlin, Germany, May 1974)* † Kindertotenlieder; Sym 6 DEUT (The Originals) 2-▲ 457716 [ADD] (22.97)

W. Meier (mez), L. Maazel (cnd), Bavarian Radio SO † Kindertotenlieder; Knaben Wunderhorn RCAV ▲ 57129 (16.97)

Y. Minton (mez), P. Boulez (cnd) † R. Wagner:Das Liebesmahl der Apostel; Wesendonck Songs SNYC (Pierre Boulez Edition) ▲ 68330 (10.97)

A. S. von Otter (mez), J. E. Gardiner (cnd), North German SO *(rec Hamburg, Germany, 1993)* ("Mahler & Zemlinsky Lieder") † Lieder eines fahrenden Gesellen; Zemlinsky:Songs to Poems by Maeterlinck, Op. 13 PPHI ▲ 439928 [DDD] (16.97)

D. Pecková (mez), J. Bělohlávek (cnd), Prague Chamber PO † Kindertotenlieder; Lieder eines fahrenden Gesellen; Sym 5 SUR ▲ 3030 (16.97)

MAHLER, GUSTAV (cont.)

Songs (5) from Rückert for Voice & Orchestra (or Piano) (1901-02) (cont.)

M. Price (sop), T. Dewey (pno) † Knaben Wunderhorn; Lieder eines fahrenden Gesellen FORL ▲ 16744 [DDD] (16.97)
J. Raskin (sop), G. Schick (pno)—Ich atmet' einen linden Duft; Liebst du um Schönheit ("Songs & Duets") † Knaben Wunderhorn; Lieder und Gesänge aus der Jugendzeit; J. Brahms:Ballads & Romances, Op. 75; Duets (3), Op. 20; Duets (4), Op. 61; Duets (5), Op. 66; Mendelssohn (-Bartholdy):Songs; R. Schumann:Spanisches Liederspiel, Op. 74 SNYC (Essential Classics) ▲ 60269 (7.97) ▮ 60269 (3.98)
C. Robbin (mez), R. Armenian (cnd), Kitchener-Waterloo SO [GER] † Kindertotenlieder; Lieder eines fahrenden Gesellen SMS (SM 5000) ▲ 5098 [DDD] (16.97)
M. Sargent (cnd), Vienna PO—Ich atmet' einen linden Duft [ENG] † Lied von der Erde; Sym 5 DLAB (Essential Archive) ▲ 5014 (15.97)
A. Schmidt (bar), J. López-Cobos (cnd), Cincinnati SO [GER] † Kindertotenlieder; Lieder eines fahrenden Gesellen TEL ▲ 80269 [DDD] (16.97)
M. Shirai (mez), N. Marriner (cnd), Academy of St. Martin in the Fields ("Mahler:Leider") † Knaben Wunderhorn; Lieder und Gesänge aus der Jugendzeit CAPO ▲ 10712 [DDD] (11.97)
F. von Stade (mez), A. Davis (cnd), London PO *(rec Dec 8-16, 1978)* † Lied von der Erde SNYC (Essential Classics) ▲ 53518 [ADD] (7.97) ▮ 53518 [ADD] (3.98)
K. Thorborg (mez), B. Walter (cnd), Vienna PO—Ich bin der Welt abhanden gekommen [GER] *(rec live, Musikvereinsaal, Vienna, Austria, May 24, 1936)* † Lied von der Erde; Sym 5 PHS ▲ 9413 [AAD] (17.97)
J. Tourel (mez), L. Bernstein (cnd), New York PO—Ich atmet' einen linden Duft; Ich bin der Welt abhanden gekommen; Um Mitternacht *(rec 1960)* † Kindertotenlieder; Knaben Wunderhorn; Sym 3 SNYC (Bernstein: The Royal Edition) 2-▲ 47576 [ADD] (23.97)
J. Van Dam (b-bar) ("Le chant d'un maître") † Knaben Wunderhorn; W. A. Mozart:Don Giovanni (sels); Nozze di Figaro (sels); Zauberflöte (sels); G. Puccini:Bohème (sels); G. Rossini:Barbiere di Siviglia (sels); Verdi:Don Carlos (sels); Rigoletto (sels); R. Wagner:Tannhäuser (sels); Walküre (sels) FORL ▲ 302270 [ADD]
various artists ("Complete Symphonies & Orchestral Songs") † Kindertotenlieder; Knaben Wunderhorn; Lied von der Erde; Lieder eines fahrenden Gesellen; Syms (comp) DEUT 16-▲ 459080 (182.97)

Symphonisches Praeludium for Orchestra (?1876)

N. Järvi (cnd), Royal Scottish National Orch † Sym 6 CHN ▲ 9207 [DDD] (16.97)

Symphonies (complete:Nos. 1-9 & Sym No. 10—Agadio only)

M. Abravanel (cnd), Utah SO VC 11-▲ 2030 (100.97)
M. Abravanel (cnd), Utah SO, R. Kubelík (cnd), Bavarian RSO, L. Segerstam (cnd), Danish National RSO, Bavarian Radio Chorus, Danish National Radio Chorus ("Complete Symphonies & Orchestral Songs") † Kindertotenlieder; Knaben Wunderhorn; Lied von der Erde; Lieder eines fahrenden Gesellen; Songs from Rückert DEUT 16-▲ 459080 (182.97)
R. Kubelík (cnd), Bavarian RSO, Bavarian Radio Chorus DEUT 10-▲ 29042 [ADD] (67.97)
L. Segerstam (cnd), Danish National RSO, Danish National Radio Choir CHN 12-▲ 9572 (111.97)

Symphony No. 1 in D, "Titan" (1888; rev 1893-96)

C. Abbado (cnd), Berlin PO DEUT ▲ 31769 [DDD] (16.97)
M. Abravanel (cnd), Utah SO VC ▲ 20 [AAD] (13.97)
C. F. Adler (cnd), Vienna SO † A. Bruckner:Sym 6 TAHA ▲ 239 (34.97)
K. Ančerl (cnd), Czech PO SUR (Czech Philharmonic Series) ▲ 111953 [ADD]
J. Barbirolli (cnd), Hallé Orch *(rec 1957)* † J. Barbirolli:Purcell Suite DLAB (The Barbirolli Society) ▲ 1015 (17.97)
L. Bernstein (cnd), (Royal) Concertgebouw Orch DEUT ▲ 27303 [DDD] (16.97)
A. Boult (cnd), London PO *(rec Walthamstow Assembly Hall London)* EVC ▲ 9022 [AAD] (13.97)
R. Chailly (cnd), (Royal) Concertgebouw Orch † A. Berg:Son Pno, Op. 1 PLON ▲ 448813 (16.97)
C. Eschenbach (cnd), Houston SO KOCH ▲ 7405 (16.97)
H. Farberman (cnd), London SO *(rec 1979)* † Sym 4 VB2 2-▲ 5123 (9.97)
M. Halász (cnd), Polish National RSO Katowice *(rec Polish Radio Concert Hall Katowice, Dec 11-14, 1993)* NXIN ▲ 550522 [DDD] (5.97)
J. Horenstein (cnd), Vienna SO † A. Bruckner:Sym 9 VOXL (Legends) 2-▲ 5508 (9.97)
J. Horenstein (cnd), Vienna SO *(rec 1958)* TUXE ▲ 1048 [ADD] (10.97)
E. Inbal (cnd), Frankfurt RSO DNN ▲ 7537 [DDD] (16.97)
N. Järvi (cnd), Royal Scottish National Orch † Blumine CHN ▲ 9308 [DDD] (16.97)
A. Joó (cnd), Amsterdam PO *(rec Amsterdam The Netherlands, July 1983)* AART ▲ 47239 [DDD] (10.97)
J. Judd (cnd), Florida PO † Blumine HAM ▲ 907118 [DDD] (18.97)
R. Kubelík (cnd), Bavarian RSO *(rec Residenz Munich, Germany, Oct 1967)* † Lieder eines fahrenden Gesellen DEUT (The Originals) ▲ 449735 [ADD] (11.97)
A. Litton (cnd), Royal PO *(rec 1987)* † Sym 9 VCL 2-▲ 61475 [DDD] (11.97)
L. Maazel (cnd), Vienna PO † Sym 5 SNYC ▲ 44907 [DDD] (10.97)
I. Markevitch (cnd), Leipzig Gewandhaus Orch † F. Schubert:Sym 3; P. Tchaikovsky:Sym 4 TAHA (Markevitch Edition) 2-▲ 282 (34.97)
I. Markevitch (cnd), Turin RAI Orch † Lieder eines fahrenden Gesellen STRV ▲ 10010 [ADD] (12.97)
Z. Mehta (cnd), Israel PO † Sym 3 PLON (Double Decker) 2-▲ 43030 (17.97)
Z. Mehta (cnd), New York PO *(rec Nov 10-25, 1980)* † Sym 10 SNYC ▲ 53259 (7.97)
D. Mitropoulos (cnd), Minneapolis SO † S. Rachmaninoff:Isle of the Dead, Op. 29 SNYC (Masterworks Heritage) ▲ 62342 (12.97)
D. Mitropoulos (cnd), Minneapolis SO *(rec Nov 4, 1940)* ("Dmitri Mitropoulos: From Minneapolis to New York, Vol. 2") GRM2 ▲ 78566 (13.97)
D. Mitropoulos (cnd), Minneapolis SO ("Dmitri Mitropoulos: The Minneapolis Years, 1940-45") † Beethoven:Coriolan Ov, Op. 62; Leonore (ov 3); Sym 6; Borodin:Sym 2; Dukas:L'Apprenti sorcier; R. Schumann:Sym 2; P. Tchaikovsky:Sym 4 GRM2 4-▲ 78646 (52.97)
D. Mitropoulos (cnd), Minneapolis SO *(rec 1940)* ENT (Sirio) ▲ 530030 (13.97)
D. Mitropoulos (cnd), Philharmonic SO † Sym 3; Sym 5; Sym 6; Sym 8; Sym 9 MUA 6-▲ 1021 (63.97)
A. Nanut (cnd), Ljubljana SO PC ▲ 265038 [DDD] (2.97)
V. Neumann (cnd), Czech PO *(rec Oct 3-8, 1979)* † Sym 10 SUR ▲ 111970 [AAD]
H. Rosbaud (cnd), Southwest German RSO Baden-Baden *(rec Sept 13, 1961)* STRV ▲ 10036 (12.97)
H. Schmidt-Isserstedt (cnd), North German RSO † Sym 4 TAHA 2-▲ 9903 (33.97)
Shirim—Feierlich und gemessen [arr Dickson] *(rec Carlisle, MA, Oct 31 & Dec 6, 1997)* ("Klezmer Nutcracker") † J. Brahms:Hungarian Dances Pno 4-Hands; Chopin:Preludes (24) Pno, Op. 28; Enescu:Romanian Rhap 1, Op. 11/1; Satie:Gnossiennes; Gymnopédies; P. Tchaikovsky:Nutcracker Suite, Op. 71a; Traditional:Russian Bulgar; Turk in America NPT ▲ 85640 (16.97)
G. Solti (cnd), Chicago SO PLON ▲ 11731 [DDD] (16.97)
W. Steinberg (cnd), Pittsburgh SO † E. Bloch:Con grosso 1 EMIC (Legacy) ▲ 66555 (11.97)
E. Tabakov (cnd), Sofia PO *(rec Bulgarian Concert Hall Sofia, Mar 1989)* ("Complete Edition: 10 Symphonies") † Sym 10; Sym 2; Sym 3; Sym 4; Sym 5; Sym 6; Sym 7; Sym 8; Sym 9 CAPO 15-▲ 49043 [DDD] (89.97)
P. Urbanek (cnd), Prague Festival Orch LALI ▲ 15529 [DDD] (3.97)
P. Urbanek (cnd), Prague Festival Orch ("The World of Symphony, Vol. 8: Gustav Mahler") LALI ▲ 15828 [DDD] (3.97)
B. Walter (cnd), NBC SO ("Bruno Walter Conducts") GRM2 ▲ 78595 (13.97)
B. Walter (cnd), New York PO *(rec 1954)* † J. Brahms:Vars on a Theme by Haydn SNYC (Masterworks Heritage) ▲ 63328 [ADD] (12.97)

Symphony No. 2 in c-E♭ for Soprano, Mezzo-Soprano, Orchestra & Chorus, "Resurrection" (1888-94; rev 1903)

C. Abbado (cnd), Chicago SO, Chicago Sym Chorus, C. Neblett (sop), M. Horne (mez) *(rec Medinah Temple Chicago, IL, Feb 1976)* † Sym 4 DEUT 2-▲ 453037 [ADD] (17.97)
A. Augér (sop), J. Baker (mez), S. Rattle (cnd), City of Birmingham SO, City of Birmingham Sym Chorus [GER] EMIC 2-▲ 47962 [DDD] (32.97)
K. Battle (sop), M. Forrester (cta), L. Slatkin (cnd), St. Louis SO, St. Louis Sym Chorus TEL 2-▲ 80081 [DDD] (25.97)
G. Benačková (sop), E. Randová (mez), V. Neumann (cnd), Czech PO, Czech Phil Chorus *(rec June 11-16, 1980)* SUR ▲ 111971 [AAD]
L. Bernstein (cnd), New York PO, Westminster Choir, B. Hendricks (sop), C. Ludwig (mez) DEUT 2-▲ 23395 [DDD] (32.97)
G. Bindernagel (sop), E. Leisner (cta), O. Fried (cnd), Berlin State Opera Orch, Berlin Cathedral Choir *(rec 1923 for Polydor)* ("Mahler: The First Three Orchestral Recordings") † Kindertotenlieder PHS 2-▲ 9929 [AAD] (34.97)
I. Buchanan (sop), M. Zakai (cta), G. Solti (cnd), Chicago SO, Chicago Sym Chorus [GER] PLON 2-▲ 10202 [DDD] (32.97)
I. Cotrubas (sop), C. Ludwig (mez), Z. Mehta (cnd), Vienna PO, Vienna State Opera Chorus *(rec 1975)* † F. Schmidt:Sym 4 PLON (Double Decker) 2-▲ 40615 [ADD] (17.97)

MAHLER, GUSTAV (cont.)

Symphony No. 2 in c-E♭ for Soprano, Mezzo-Soprano, Orchestra & Chorus, "Resurrection" (1888-94; rev 1903) (cont.)

T. Genova (sop), V. Zorova (mez), E. Tabakov (cnd), Sofia PO, Bulgarian National Chorus *(rec Bulgarian Concert Hall Sofia, Jan 1987)* ("Complete Edition: 10 Symphonies") † Sym 1; Sym 10; Sym 3; Sym 4; Sym 5; Sym 6; Sym 7; Sym 8; Sym 9 CAPO 15-▲ 49043 [DDD] (89.97)
S. Greenberg (sop), F. Quivar (mez), Z. Mehta (cnd), Israel PO, Tel Aviv Phil Choir, National Choir Rinat, Ihud Choir CACI ▲ 210012 (5.97)
N. Gustafson (sop), F. Quivar (cta), Z. Mehta (cnd), Israel PO, Prague Phil Chorus *(rec Fredric R. Mann Auditorium Tel Aviv, Jan-Feb 1994)* TELC ▲ 94545 [DDD] (16.97)
M. Hajóssyová (sop), U. Priew (alt), O. Suitner (cnd), Berlin Staatskapelle, Berlin German Opera Chorus BER ▲ 9011 (10.97)
E. Lear (sop), R. Weikert (cnd), Venice Theater Orch—Urlicht *(rec 1978)* † Knaben Wunderhorn; Sym 3 VAIA ▲ 1061 [ADD] (16.97)
H. Lisowska (sop), J. Rappé (ten), A. Wit (cnd), Polish National RSO Katowice, Cracow Radio-TV Chorus *(rec Jan 9-17, 1993)* NXIN 2-▲ 8550523 [DDD] (15.97)
A. Litton (cnd), Dallas SO, Dallas Sym Chorus, H. G. Murphy (sop), P. Lang (mez) *(rec Symphony Center, Dallas, TX, Sept 10-13, 1998)* DLS 2-▲ 3237 [DDD] (14.97)
F. Lott (sop), J. Hamari (mez), M. Jansons (cnd), Oslo PO, Oslo Phil Chorus CHN (Collect) 2-▲ 6595 [DDD] (25.97)
A. S. von Otter (mez), C. Abbado (cnd), Berlin PO—Urlicht † Knaben Wunderhorn DEUT ▲ 459646 (16.97)
D. Pecková (mez), J. Bělohlávek (cnd), Prague Chamber PO—Urlicht *(rec Prague, Czech Republic, July 1-2 & Sept 11-13, 1996)* † Knaben Wunderhorn; Lieder und Gesänge aus der Jugendzeit; L. Berio:Folk Songs Sop SUR ▲ 3264 [DDD]
E. Schwarzkopf (sop), H. Rössl-Majdan (mez), O. Klemperer (cnd), Philharmonia Orch, Philharmonia Chorus [GER] EMIC (Studio) ▲ 69662 [ADD] (11.97)
B. Sills (sop), F. Kopleff (cta), M. Abravanel (cnd), Utah SO [GER] *(rec 1967)* VC ▲ 4004 [ADD] (13.97)
B. Sills (sop), F. Kopleff (cta), M. Abravanel (cnd), Utah SO, University of Utah Civic Chorale *(rec Salt Lake City, 1967)* VC ▲ 21 [AAD] (13.97)
G. Sinopoli (cnd), Philharmonia Orch, New London Children's Choir, Philharmonia Chorus, H. Schwarz (mez) DGRM 2-▲ 447051 [DDD] (35.97)
L. Stokowski (cnd), London SO, L. Stokowski (cnd), London Sym Chorus, M. Price (sop), B. Fassbaender (mez) † J. Brahms:Sym 4 RCAV ▲ 62606 (21.97)
B. Valente (sop), M. Forrester (cta), G. Kaplan (cnd), London SO, London Sym Chorus, Alwyn Singers ("10th Anniversary Edition") CONI 2-▲ 51337 [DDD] (16.97)
L. Venora (sop), J. Tourel (mez), L. Bernstein (cnd), New York PO, Collegiate Chorale † Sym 5; Sym 8 SNYC (Bernstein Century) 2-▲ 63159 (23.97)
G. Vishnevskaya (sop), H. Rössl-Majdan (mez), O. Klemperer (cnd), Vienna PO, Vienna Phil Chorus MUA ▲ 881 [ADD] (16.97)
B. Walter (cnd), Vienna PO *(rec 1948)* † Sym 4 GRM2 2-▲ 78787 (26.97)
R. Woodland (sop), J. Baker (mez), L. Stokowski (cnd), London SO, BBC Sym Chorus *(rec 1963)* MUA ▲ 885 [AAD] (16.97)
R. Ziesak (sop), C. Hellekant (mez), H. Blomstedt (cnd), San Francisco SO, San Francisco Sym Chorus PLON ▲ 43350 (17.97)
T. Zylis-Gara (sop), E. Podles (cta), J. Casadesus (cnd), Lille National Orch *(rec Feb 1991)* † Lieder aus letzter Zeit FORL 2-▲ 16654 [DDD] (32.97)

Symphony No. 3 in d-D for Mezzo-Soprano, Orchestra & Chorus (1893-96; rev 1906)

C. Abbado (cnd), Vienna PO, Vienna Boys' Choir, Vienna State Opera Chorus, J. Norman (sop) [GER] DEUT 2-▲ 10715 [DDD] (32.97)
O. Alexandrova (mez), E. Svetlanov (cnd), Russian State SO, Russian Academic Choir, Moscow Boys' Cappella *(rec Large Hall of the Conservatory Moscow, Dec 1994)* RUSS 2-▲ 288111 [DDD]
J. Baker (mez), M. T. Thomas (cnd), London SO, London Sym Chorus [GER] † Songs from Rückert SNYC 2-▲ 44553 [DDD] (31.97)
L. Bernstein (cnd), New York PO, New York Choral Artists, Brooklyn Boys' Chorus, C. Ludwig (mez) [GER] DEUT 2-▲ 27328 [DDD] (32.97)
G. B. Cortese (cnd), Manhattan School of Music SO, T. Smith (cnd), Riverside Women's Choir, H. Cha-Pyo (cnd), Manhattan School of Music Festival Chorus, C. Jordanoff (cnd), Manhattan School of Music Children's Festival Chorus, G. Archer (cnd), Columbia/Barnard Chorus, M. Dunn (mez) *(rec New York City, United States of America, Mar 1998)* TIT 2-▲ 252 [DDD] (31.97)
L. Finnie (mez), N. Järvi (cnd), Royal Scottish National Orch, Royal Scottish National Chorus [GER] † Kindertotenlieder CHN 2-▲ 9117 [DDD] (32.97)
M. Forrester (cta), Z. Mehta (cnd), Los Angeles PO † Sym 1 PLON (Double Decker) 2-▲ 43030 (17.97)
A. Larsson (cta), E.-P. Salonen (cnd), Los Angeles PO SNYC 2-▲ 60250 (31.97)
E. Lear (sop), R. Weikert (cnd), Venice Theater Orch—Lustig im Tempo: 'Es sungen drei Engel' *(rec 1978)* † Knaben Wunderhorn; Sym 2 VAIA ▲ 1061 [ADD] (16.97)
M. Lipton (cta), L. Bernstein (cnd), New York PO, New York Phil Chorus *(rec 1961)* † Kindertotenlieder; Knaben Wunderhorn; Songs from Rückert SNYC (Bernstein: The Royal Edition) 2-▲ 47576 [ADD] (23.97)
M. Lipton (mez), J. Ware (psthn), L. Bernstein (cnd), New York PO, H. Ross (cnd), Schola Cantorum, S. Gardner (cnd), Boy's Choir of the Church of the Transfiguration *(rec Manhattan Center, NY, April 3, 1961)* † Kindertotenlieder; Knaben Wunderhorn; Songs from Rückert SNYC (Bernstein Century) 2-▲ 61831 [ADD] (23.97)
J. López-Cobos (cnd), Cincinnati SO, J. López-Cobos (cnd), Cincinnati Symphony Chorus TEL 2-▲ 80481 (16.97)
C. Ludwig (mez), V. Neumann (cnd), Czech PO, Czech Phil Chorus *(rec Dec 16-19, 1981)* † Sym 8 SUR 3-▲ 111972 [DDD]
K. Meyer (mez), J. Barbirolli (cnd), Hallé Orch, Manchester Grammar School Choir, Hallé Choir (ladies) BBC ▲ 4004 (24.97)
D. Mitropoulos (cnd), Philharmonic SO † Sym 1; Sym 5; Sym 6; Sym 8; Sym 9 MUA 6-▲ 1021 (63.97)
E. Podles (cta), A. Wit (cnd), Polish National RSO Katowice, J. Mentel (cnd), Cracow Phil Chorus, J. Mentel (cnd), Cracow Boys' Choir *(rec Concert Hall of the Polish National Radio Katowice, Nov 12-16, 1994)* † Sym 10 NXIN 2-▲ 550525 [DDD] (15.97)
B. Pretschner (alt), E. Tabakov (cnd), Sofia PO, Bulgarian National Chorus, Bodra-Smyana Children's Choir *(rec Bulgarian Concert Hall Sofia, Apr 1990)* ("Complete Edition: 10 Symphonies") † Sym 1; Sym 10; Sym 2; Sym 4; Sym 5; Sym 6; Sym 7; Sym 8; Sym 9 CAPO 15-▲ 49043 [DDD] (89.97)
N. Procter (cta), J. Horenstein (cnd), London SO, Ambrosian Singers, Wandsworth Boys' School Choir [GER] UNIC (Souvenir) 2-▲ 2006 [ADD] (36.97)
J. Rappé (alt), H. Rögner (cnd), Berlin RSO, Berlin Radio Women's Chorus, Berlin Radio Youth Chorus BER 2-▲ 2121 (21.97)
S. Rattle (cnd), City of Birmingham SO, S. Halsey (cnd), City of Birmingham Sym Youth Chorus, S. Halsey (cnd), Ladies of the City of Birmingham Sym Chorus, B. Remmert (cta) *(rec Birmingham, United States of America, Oct 1997)* † Knaben Wunderhorn; Lieder aus letzter Zeit; Lieder und Gesänge aus der Jugendzeit *([ENG,GER]text)* EMIC 2-▲ 56657 [DDD] (32.97)
R. Siewert (cta), C. Schuricht (cnd), Stuttgart RSO, Eberhard Ludwig Gymnasium Children's Choir, South German Radio Chorus *(rec 1960)* † F. Schubert:Sym 8 STRV 2-▲ 10051 (24.97)
D. Soffel (mez), E. Inbal (cnd), Frankfurt RSO, Frankfurt Radio Chorus [GER] DNN 2-▲ 7828 [DDD] (33.97)

Symphony No. 4 in G-E for Soprano & Orchestra (1892, 1899-1900; rev 1901-02)

C. Abbado (cnd), Vienna PO, F. von Stade (mez), G. Hetzel (vn) *(rec Musikverein Vienna, Austria, May 1977)* † Sym 2 DEUT 2-▲ 453037 [ADD] (17.97)
H. Adolph (cnd), Slovak PO PC ▲ 267140 [DDD] (2.97)
K. Battle (sop), L. Maazel (cnd), Vienna PO SNYC ▲ 44908 [DDD] (10.97)
J. Carlyle (sop), B. Britten (cnd), London SO *(rec Aldeburgh, England, 1961)* † Knaben Wunderhorn; Lieder eines fahrenden Gesellen BBC (Britten the Performer) ▲ 8004 (17.97)
C. Casapietra (sop), H. Kegel (cnd), Leipzig RSO BER ▲ 9303 (10.97)
C. Curry (mez), H. Farberman (cnd), London SO *(rec 1979)* † Sym 1 VB2 2-▲ 5123 (9.97)
I. Dam-Jensen (sop), J. Hirokami (cnd), Royal PO *(rec Abbey Road Studio, Apr 25-26, 1995)* † Webern:Im Sommerwind DNN ▲ 78832 [DDD] (16.97)
N. Davrath (sop), M. Abravanel (cnd), Utah SO VC ▲ 24 (13.97)
H. Donath (sop), E. Inbal (cnd), Frankfurt RSO [GER] DNN ▲ 7952 [DDD] (16.97)
L. Hadzhieva (sop), E. Tabakov (cnd), Sofia PO *(rec Bulgarian Concert Hall Sofia, Jan 1990)* ("Complete Edition: 10 Symphonies") † Sym 1; Sym 10; Sym 2; Sym 3; Sym 5; Sym 6; Sym 7; Sym 8; Sym 9 CAPO 15-▲ 49043 [DDD] (89.97)
M. Hajóssyová (sop), V. Neumann (cnd), Czech PO [GER] *(rec 1980)* SUR ▲ 111975 [AAD]
A. Hargan (sop), S. Skrowaczewski (cnd), Hallé Orch [GER] INMP ▲ 972 [DDD]
H. Harper (sop), J. Barbirolli (cnd), BBC SO *(rec Prague, Czech Republic, 1967)* † Berlioz:Corsaire, Op. 21 BBC ▲ 4014 (17.97)

▲ = CD ♦ = Enhanced CD △ = MD ▮ = Cassette Tape ▯ = DCC

MAHLER, GUSTAV (cont.)
Symphony No. 4 in G-E for Soprano & Orchestra (1892, 1899-1900; rev 1901-02) (cont.)
B. Hendricks (sop), E. Salonen (cnd), Los Angeles PO [GER] SNYC ▲ 48380 [DDD] (16.97)
K. T. Kanawa (sop), G. Solti (cnd), Chicago SO [GER] PLON ▲ 10188 [DDD] (16.97)
Y. Kenny (sop), M. Inoue (cnd), Royal PO RPO ▲ 5007 [DDD] (11.97)
Y. Levi (cnd), Atlanta SO, F. von Stade (mez) *(rec Atlanta, GA, July 1998)* † Lieder eines fahrenden Gesellen TEL ▲ 80499 [DDD] (16.97)
E. Loose (sop), P. Kletzki (cnd), Philharmonia Orch † Sym 5 RYLC ▲ 6468
L. Lootens (sop), A. Ostrowsky (cnd), Brussels BRTN PO DI ▲ 920404 [DDD] (5.97)
S. McNair (sop), B. Haitink (cnd), Berlin PO PPHI ▲ 34123 (16.97)
M. Marshall (sop), S. Stalanowski (vn), C. Danel (hn), J. Casadesus (cnd), Lille National Orch *(rec Sept 1986)* FORL ▲ 16563 (16.97)
J. Raskin (sop), G. Szell (cnd), Cleveland Orch † Lieder eines fahrenden Gesellen SNYC (Essential Classics) ▲ 46535 [ADD] (7.97) ▮ 46535 [ADD] (3.98)
A. Roocroft (sop), S. Rattle (cnd), City of Birmingham SO *(rec May 1997)* EMIC ▲ 56563 [DDD] (16.97)
L. Russell (sop), A. Wit (cnd), Polish National RSO Katowice *(rec June 26-28 & Sept 5, 1992)* NXIN ▲ 550527 [DDD] (5.97)
H. Schmidt-Isserstedt (cnd), North German RSO † Sym 1 TAHA 2-▲ 9903 (33.97)
D. Upshaw (sop), C. von Dohnányi (cnd), Cleveland Orch *(rec May 1992)* PLON ▲ 40315 [DDD] (16.97)
J. Vincent (sop), W. Mengelberg (cnd), (Royal) Concertgebouw Orch *(rec Nov 1939)* IN ▲ 1386 (15.97)
J. Vincent (sop), W. Mengelberg (cnd), Concertgebouw Orch *(rec Amsterdam, Holland, 1939)* GRM2 (Records of the Century) ▲ 78844 (13.97)
B. Walter (cnd), New York PO *(rec 1945)* † Sym 2 GRM2 2-▲ 78787 (26.97)
C. Whittlesey (sop), M. Gielen (cnd), Southwest German SO Baden-Baden INTC (Gielen Edition) ▲ 860900 (13.97)
H. Wittek (trbn), L. Bernstein (cnd), (Royal) Concertgebouw Orch [GER] DEUT ▲ 23607 [DDD] (16.97)
Symphony No. 5 in c#-D (1901-02)
C. Abbado (cnd), Berlin PO DEUT ▲ 37789 [DDD] (16.97)
M. Abravanel (cnd), Utah SO VC ▲ 25 [AAD] (13.97)
J. Barbirolli (cnd), New Philharmonia Orch *(rec London, England, July 16-18, 1969)* EMIC (Great Recordings of the Century) ▲ 66962 [ADD] (11.97)
J. Bělohlávek (cnd), Prague Chamber PO † Kindertotenlieder; Lieder eines fahrenden Gesellen; Songs from Rückert SUR ▲ 3030 (16.97)
L. Bernstein (cnd), New York PO SNYC (Bernstein Century) ▲ 63084 (10.97)
L. Bernstein (cnd), New York PO—Adagietto † S. Barber:Adagio Strs; P. Tchaikovsky:Andante cantabile; Qt 1 Strs, Op. 11; Vaughan Williams:Fant on a Theme of Tallis; Fant on Greensleeves SNYC ▲ 38484 [AAD] (9.97) ▮ 38484 [AAD] (3.98)
L. Bernstein (cnd), New York PO—Adagietto † Sym 2; Sym 8 SNYC (Bernstein Century) 2-▲ 63159 (23.97)
L. Bernstein (cnd), Vienna PO DEUT ▲ 23608 [DDD] (16.97)
P. Boulez (cnd), Vienna PO DEUT ▲ 453416 [DDD] (16.97)
R. Chailly (cnd), (Royal) Concertgebouw Orch PLON ▲ 458860 [DDD] (16.97)
H. Farberman (cnd), London SO VOXC ▲ 97205 (5.97)
D. Gatti (cnd), Royal PO CONI ▲ 51318 [DDD] (16.97)
G. Herbig (cnd), BBC PO INMP (BBC Radio) ▲ 5691432 (13.97)
E. Inbal (cnd), Frankfurt RSO DNN ▲ 1088 [DDD] (16.97)
N. Järvi (cnd), Royal Scottish National Orch CHN ▲ 8829 [DDD] (16.97)
N. Järvi (cnd), Royal Scottish National Orch—Adagietto *(rec Oct 23-24, 1989)* ("Elegy—Music for Strings") † S. Barber:Adagio Strs; Eller:Elegia; Pärt:Cantus in Memory of Benjamin Britten; R. Strauss:Metamorphosen CHN ▲ 7039 (13.97)
H. von Karajan (cnd), Berlin PO *(rec Jesus Christ Church Berlin, Germany, Feb 1973)* DEUT (The Originals) ▲ 47450 [ADD] (11.97)
P. Kletzki (cnd), Philharmonia Orch—Adagietto † Sym 4 RYLC ▲ 6468
K. Kondrashin (cnd), USSR Radio-TV Large SO APC (Legacy Collection) ▲ 101501 [ADD]
E. Leinsdorf (cnd), Boston SO RCAV (Basic 100) ▲ 68365 (10.97) ▮ 68365 (5.98)
Y. Levi (cnd), Atlanta SO *(rec Woodruff Arts Center Atlanta, GA, Feb 13-14, 1995)* TEL ▲ 80394 [DDD] (16.97)
A. Litton (cnd), Dallas SO *(rec live, Sept 1993)* DOR ▲ 90193 (16.97)
A. Lombard (cnd), Bordeaux-Aquitaine National Orch FORL ▲ 16779 (16.97)
L. Maazel (cnd), Vienna PO SNYC ▲ 44782 [DDD] (10.97)
L. Maazel (cnd), Vienna PO † Sym 1 SNYC ▲ 44907 [DDD] (10.97)
C. Mackerras (cnd), Royal Liverpool PO CFP (Eminence) ▲ 2164 [DDD] (16.97)
Z. Mehta (cnd), New York PO TELC ▲ 46152 [DDD] (16.97)
W. Mengelberg (cnd), Concertgebouw Orch—Adagietto *(rec 1926-41)* ("The Art of Willem Mengelberg, Vol. 2") † Beethoven:Coriolan Ov, Op. 62; Leonore (ov 1), Op. 138; Ruinen von Athen (sels); Berlioz:Damnation de Faust (sels); Cherubini:Anacréon (ov); F. Schubert:Rosamunde (sels); Suppé:Poet & Peasant (ov); C. M. von Weber:Euryanthe (ov) GRM2 ▲ 78867 (14.97)
D. Mitropoulos (cnd), Philharmonic SO † Sym 1; Sym 3; Sym 6; Sym 8; Sym 9 MUA 6-▲ 1021 (63.97)
A. Nanut (cnd), Ljubljana RSO—Trauermarsch ("Music for Meditation, Vol. 2") † A. Adam:Giselle (sels); A. Bruckner:Qnt Strs; Chopin:Berceuse, Op. 57; Gounod:Ave Maria; Massenet:Méditation from Thaïs; F. Schubert:Sym 8 ECL ▲ 506 (2.97)
A. Nanut (cnd), Ljubljana RSO PC ▲ 267023 [DDD] (2.97)
V. Neumann (cnd), Czech PO SUR ▲ 111976 [AAD]
A. Ostrowsky (cnd), Brussels BRTN PO *(rec Concert Hall of the Belgian Radio & Television, 1994)* DI ▲ 920220 [DDD] (5.97)
T. Otaka (cnd), Tokyo PO—Adagietto ("Orchestra Plays Adagio") † A. Bruckner:Qt Strs; Sym 2; P. Tchaikovsky:Serenade Strs, Op. 48; Yoshimatsu:Threnody to Toki, Op. 12; Zi:3 Wishes for a Rose CAMA (After Hours Classics) ▲ 423 [DDD] (15.97)
J. Saraste (cnd), Finnish RSO *(rec Helsinki, Finland, May 1990)* † Knaben Wunderhorn; Lieder eines fahrenden Gesellen VCL 2-▲ 61507 [DDD] (11.97)
H. Scherchen (cnd), French National Orch *(rec 1965)* HMA ▲ 1905179 [AAD] (9.97)
R. Schwarz (cnd), London SO *(rec Walthamstow Assembly Hall London)* EVC ▲ 9032 [AAD] (13.97)
L. Segerstam (cnd), Danish National RSO CHN ▲ 9403 [DDD] (16.97)
G. Solti (cnd), Chicago SO ("The Solti Collection, Vol. 7") PLON (Jubilee) ▲ 30443 [ADD] (11.97)
G. Solti (cnd), Chicago SO *(rec 1991)* PLON ▲ 33329 [DDD] (16.97)
E. Tabakov (cnd), Sofia PO *(rec Bulgarian Concert Hall Sofia, Oct 1988)* ("Complete Edition: 10 Symphonies") † Sym 1; Sym 10; Sym 2; Sym 3; Sym 4; Sym 6; Sym 7; Sym 8; Sym 9 CAPO 15-▲ 49043 [DDD] (89.97)
B. Walter (cnd), New York PO ("Bruno Walter: First American Recordings") † Lieder und Gesänge aus der Jugendzeit; Beethoven:Sym 3 GRM2 2-▲ 78838 (26.97)
B. Walter (cnd), Vienna PO—Adagietto *(rec live, Musikvereinsaal, Vienna, Austria, Jan 15, 1938)* † Lied von der Erde; Songs from Rückert PHS ▲ 9413 [AAD] (17.97)
B. Walter (cnd), Vienna PO *(rec 1938)* † Lied von der Erde; Songs from Rückert DLAB (Essential Archive) ▲ 5014 (15.97)
A. Wit (cnd), Polish National RSO Katowice NXIN ▲ 550528 [DDD] (5.97)
B. Zander (cnd), New England Conservatory Youth PO CPRO ▲ 329407 (16.97)
Symphony No. 6 in a (1903-04; rev 1906)
M. Abravanel (cnd), Utah SO VC ▲ 26 (13.97)
J. Barbirolli (cnd), New Philharmonia Orch † R. Strauss:Heldenleben, Op. 40 EMIC (Doublefforte) 2-▲ 69349 (16.97)
L. Bernstein (cnd), New York PO SNYC (Bernstein Century) ▲ 60208 (11.97)
L. Bernstein (cnd), Vienna PO † Kindertotenlieder DEUT 2-▲ 27697 [DDD] (32.97)
L. A. Bianchi (vn)—Allegro energico, ma non troppo *(rec Genoa, Italy, June 22-23, 1995)* ("Centone di sonate for Violin & Guitar, Vol. 1") † Paganini:Cantabile, M.S. 109; Centone di sonate, M.S. 112 DYNC ▲ 148 [DDD] (17.97)
P. Boulez (cnd), Vienna PO DEUT ▲ 45835 [DDD] (16.97)
H. Haenchen (cnd), Netherlands PO LALI 2-▲ 14140 [DDD] (3.97)
B. Haitink (cnd), Berlin PO † Lieder eines fahrenden Gesellen PPHI 2-▲ 26257 [DDD] (32.97)
N. Järvi (cnd), Royal Scottish National Orch † Symphonisches Praeludium CHN ▲ 9207 [DDD] (16.97)
H. von Karajan (cnd), Berlin PO *(rec Philharmonie Berlin, Germany, Jan-Feb 1975 & Feb-Mar 1977)* † Kindertotenlieder; Songs from Rückert DEUT (The Originals) 2-▲ 457716 [ADD] (22.97)
Y. Levi (cnd), Atlanta SO TEL ▲ 80444 (16.97)
D. Mitropoulos (cnd), West German RSO † Sym 1; Sym 3; Sym 5; Sym 8; Sym 9 MUA 6-▲ 1021 (63.97)
V. Neumann (cnd), Czech PO *(rec 1979)* SUR ▲ 111977 [AAD]
G. Szell (cnd), Cleveland Orch SNYC (Essential Classics) ▲ 47654 (7.97) ▮ 47654 (3.98)

MAHLER, GUSTAV (cont.)
Symphony No. 6 in a (1903-04; rev 1906) (cont.)
E. Tabakov (cnd), Sofia PO *(rec Bulgarian Concert Hall Sofia, Oct 1993)* ("Complete Edition: 10 Symphonies") † Sym 1; Sym 10; Sym 2; Sym 3; Sym 4; Sym 5; Sym 7; Sym 8; Sym 9 CAPO 15-▲ 49043 [DDD] (89.97)
A. Wit (cnd), Polish National RSO Katowice *(rec Dec 15-19, 1992)* NXIN 2-▲ 550529 [DDD] (15.97)
H. Zender (cnd), Saarbrücken RSO ("Hans Zender Edition, Vol. 5") CPO ▲ 999477 (6.97)
Symphony No. 7 in e-C (1904-05)
C. Abbado (cnd), Chicago SO DEUT (Masters) ▲ 45513 [DDD] (9.97)
M. Abravanel (cnd), Utah SO VC ▲ 27 (13.97)
L. Bernstein (cnd), New York PO DEUT 2-▲ 19211 [DDD] (32.97)
L. Bernstein (cnd), New York PO *(rec Philharmonia Hall New York, Dec 14-15, 1965)* SNYC (Bernstein Century) ▲ 60564 [ADD] (10.97)
P. Boulez (cnd), Cleveland Orch *(rec Masonic Auditorium Cleveland, OH, Nov 1994)* DEUT ▲ 47756 [DDD] (16.97)
R. Chailly (cnd), (Royal) Concertgebouw Orch † Diepenbrock:Im grossen Schweigen PLON 2-▲ 44446 (32.97)
M. Halász (cnd), Polish National RSO Katowice *(rec Concert Hall of the Polish National Radio Katowice, Nov 28-Dec 2, 1994)* NXIN ▲ 550531 [DDD] (5.97)
K. Kondrashin (cnd), Leningrad PO *(rec Concert Hall of the Leningrad Philharmony, Russia, Mar 3, 1975)* CONE ▲ 9427 [ADD]
K. Masur (cnd), Leipzig Gewandhaus Orch BER (Eterna) ▲ 2058 [AAD] (10.97)
K. Masur (cnd), Leipzig Gewandhaus Orch BER (Masur Edition) ▲ 9159 (10.97)
V. Neumann (cnd), Leipzig Opera Orch BER ▲ 9046 [ADD] (11.97)
S. Ozawa (cnd), Boston SO † Kindertotenlieder PPHI 2-▲ 26249 [DDD] (32.97)
H. Rosbaud (cnd), Berlin RSO *(rec 1952)* † A. Bruckner:Sym 4 VOXL 2-▲ 5520 (9.97)
H. Rosbaud (cnd), Southwest German RSO Baden-Baden, H. Rosbaud (cnd), Southwest German SO *(rec Baden Germany, Feb 20, 1957)* PHO (Phoenix) ▲ 702 [ADD] (17.97)
E. Tabakov (cnd), Sofia PO *(rec Bulgarian Concert Hall Sofia, Oct 1989)* ("Complete Edition: 10 Symphonies") † Sym 1; Sym 10; Sym 2; Sym 3; Sym 4; Sym 5; Sym 6; Sym 8; Sym 9 CAPO 15-▲ 49043 [DDD] (89.97)
M. Tilson Thomas (cnd), London SO RCAV ▲ 63510 (16.97)
H. Zender (cnd), Saarbrücken RSO ("Hans Zender Edition, Vol. 6") CPO ▲ 999478 (6.97)
Symphony No. 8 in E♭ for 3 Sopranos, 2 Altos, Tenor, Bass, Orchestra, Boys' Chorus & Mixed Chorus, "Symphony of a Thousand" (1906)
C. Abbado (cnd), Berlin PO, Berlin Radio Chorus, Tölz Boys' Choir, Prague Phil Chorus, S. McNair (sop), C. Studer (sop), A. Rost (sop), A. S. von Otter (mez), R. Lang (cta), P. Seiffert (ten), B. Terfel (b-bar), J. Rootering (bass) DEUT 2-▲ 45843 [DDD] (32.97)
M. Abravanel (cnd), Utah SO, Utah Sym Chorus VC ▲ 28 (13.97)
A. Augér (sop), L. Popp (sop), H. Harper (sop), Y. Minton (mez), H. Watts (cta), A. Kollo (ten), J. Shirley-Quirk (bar), M. Talvela (bass), G. Solti (cnd), Chicago SO, Vienna Boys' Choir, Vienna State Opera Chorus, Vienna Singverein [G,L] PLON 2-▲ 14493 [ADD] (32.97)
L. Bernstein (cnd), New York PO—Komm! Ich hebe dich zu höhern sphären † Sym 2; Sym 5 SNYC (Bernstein Century) 2-▲ 63159 (23.97)
M. Bjerno (sop), H. Bonde-Hansen (sop), I. Nielsen (sop), A. Gjevang (mez), K. Dolberg (mez), R. Sirkiä (ten), J. Hynninen (bar), C. Stabell (bass), L. Segerstam (cnd), Danish National RSO, Danish National Radio Choir, Berlin Philharmonic Chorus, Copenhagen Boys' Choir † Sym 10 CHN 2-▲ 9305 [DDD] (32.97)
G. Boiko (sop), N. Gerasimova (sop), O. Alexandrova (mez), G. Borisova (mez), A. Martynov (ten), A. Safiulin (bass), D. Trapeznikov (sgr), E. Svetlanov (cnd), Russian State SO, V. Popov (cnd), Moscow Academy Children's Choir, V. Popov (cnd), Moscow Academy Double Mixed Choir RUSS 2-▲ 288151 (36.97)
I. Cotrubas (sop), H. Harper (sop), H. Bork (sop), B. Finnilä (mez), M. Dieleman (cta), W. Cochran (ten), H. Prey (bar), H. Sotin (bass), B. Haitink (cnd), (Royal) Concertgebouw Orch PPHI (Solo) ▲ 46195 (9.97)
M. Gielen (cnd), Frankfurt Opera House & Museum Orch, Frankfurt Opera House & Museum Choruses *(rec 1981)* SNYC (Essential Classics) ▲ 48281 [ADD] (7.97) ▮ 48281 [ADD] (3.98)
L. Hadzhieva (sop), M. Temeshi (sop), D. Takova (sop), T. Takac (alt), B. Tabakova (alt), J. Bándi (ten), P. Kovács (bar), T. Syule (bass), E. Tabakov (cnd), Sofia PO, Bulgarian National Chorus, Bulgarian National Radio Chorus, Bulgarian National Radio Children's Choir *(rec National Palace of Culture Sofia, June 1991)* ("Complete Edition: 10 Symphonies") † Sym 1; Sym 10; Sym 2; Sym 3; Sym 4; Sym 5; Sym 6; Sym 7; Sym 9 CAPO 15-▲ 49043 [DDD] (89.97)
M. A. Häggander (sop), U. Gustafsson (sop), C. Sandgren (sop), A. Gjevang (mez), U. Tenstam (alt), S. Ruohonen (ten), M. Persson (bar), J. Tilli (bass), N. Järvi (cnd), Gothenburg SO, N. Järvi (cnd), Gothenburg Opera Orch, Gothenburg Sym Chorus, Estonian Boys' Choir, Brunnsbo Children's Choir, Gothenburg Opera Chorus, Royal Stockholm Phil Choir *(rec live Gothenburg Opera House, Nov 1994)* BIS ▲ 700 [DDD] (17.97)
E. Inbal (cnd), Frankfurt RSO [G,L] DNN 2-▲ 1564 [DDD] (33.97)
D. Mitropoulos (cnd), Vienna PO, Vienna State Opera Chorus; Vienna Boys Choir † Sym 1; Sym 3; Sym 5; Sym 6; Sym 9 MUA 6-▲ 1021 (63.97)
V. Neumann (cnd), Czech PO, Czech Phil Chorus *(rec Feb 10-14, 1982)* † Sym 3 SUR 3-▲ 111972 [DDD]
E. Norberg-Schulz (sop), A. Marc (sop), S. Sweet (sop), N. Liang (mez), V. Kasarova (mez), B. Heppner (ten), S. Leiferkus (bar), R. Pape (bass), C. Davis (cnd), Bavarian RSO, Bavarian Radio Chorus, Berlin Radio Chorus, Stuttgart Southern Radio Chorus, Tölz Boys' Choir *(rec live Munich, July 7-8, 1996)* RCAV (Red Seal) 2-▲ 68348 [DDD] (16.97)
H. Scherchen (cnd) ("Edition Hermann Abendroth Vol 2") † J. Brahms:Sym 1; Kalinnikov:Sym 1; R. Schumann:Sym 1; Strauss (II):An der schönen blauen Donau, Op. 314; Kaiser-Walzer, Op. 437; Ovs TAHA 2-▲ 120 (17.97)
R. Shaw (cnd), Atlanta SO, Atlanta Sym Chorus [GER] TEL ▲ 80267 [DDD] (16.97)
E. Spoorenberg (sop—Magna Peccatrix), G. Jones (sop—Una poenitentium), N. Procter (alt—Maria Aegyptiaca), A. Reynolds (alt—Mulier Samaritana), G. Annear (alt—Mater Gloriosa), J. Mitchinson (ten—Doctor Marianus), V. Ruzdjak (bar—Pater Ecstaticus), D. McIntyre (bass—Pater Profundus), H. Vollenweider (org), L. Bernstein (cnd), London SO, Leeds Festival Chorus, London Sym Chorus, Finchley Children's Music Group, Highgate School Boys Choir, S. Mossman (cnd), Orpington Junior Singers *(rec Walthamstow assembly Hall, London, England, April 18-20, 1966)* † Kindertotenlieder SNYC (Bernstein Century) ▲ 61837 (11.97)
K. Tennstedt (cnd), London PO, London Phil Chorus, Tiffin Boys' School Choir [G,L] EMIC 2-▲ 47625 [DDD] (32.97)
Symphony No. 9 in D-D♭ (1908-09)
M. Abravanel (cnd), Utah SO VC ▲ 29 (26.97)
K. Ančerl (cnd), Czech PO SUR (Czech Philharmonic Series) ▲ 111954 [ADD]
J. Barbirolli (cnd), Berlin PO EMIC (Studio) ▲ 63115 [ADD] (11.97)
R. Barshaï (cnd), Moscow RSO *(rec Apr 1993)* BIS ▲ 632 [DDD] (17.97)
L. Bernstein (cnd), (Royal) Concertgebouw Orch DEUT 2-▲ 19208 [DDD] (32.97)
L. Bernstein (cnd), Berlin PO *(rec live 1979)* DEUT 2-▲ 35378 [DDD] (32.97)
L. Bernstein (cnd), New York PO *(rec Lincoln Center New York, NY, Dec 16, 1965)* SNYC (Bernstein Century) ▲ 60597 [ADD] (11.97)
P. Boulez (cnd), Chicago SO *(rec Medinah Temple Chicago, IL, Dec 1995)* DEUT ▲ 457581 [DDD] (16.97)
C. von Dohnányi (cnd), Cleveland Orch † K. A. Hartmann:Sym 2 DECC ▲ 458902 (32.97)
C. M. Giulini (cnd), Chicago SO DEUT (Double) 2-▲ 37467 (17.97)
M. Halász (cnd), Polish National RSO *(rec Apr 1993)* NXIN 2-▲ 8550535 [DDD] (5.97)
J. Horenstein (cnd), London SO *(rec live, 1966)* MUA 2-▲ 235
J. Horenstein (cnd), Vienna SO *(rec 1954)* † Kindertotenlieder VOXL (Legends) 2-▲ 5509 [ADD] (9.97)
E. Inbal (cnd), Frankfurt RSO † Sym 10 DNN 2-▲ 1566 [DDD] (33.97)
H. von Karajan (cnd), Berlin PO DEUT (Karajan Gold) 2-▲ 39024 [DDD] (32.97)
J. López-Cobos (cnd), Cincinnati SO *(rec Cincinnati Music Hall, May 1996)* TEL 2-▲ 80426 [DDD] (16.97)
C. Ludwig (mez), H. von Karajan (cnd), Berlin PO DEUT (2-Fer) 2-▲ 453040 [ADD] (17.97)
L. Ludwig (cnd), London SO *(rec Walthamstow Assembly Hall London, 1960)* EVC ▲ 9059 [ADD] (13.97)
K. Masur (cnd), New York PO *(rec Avery Fischer Hall New York, Apr 1994)* TELC ▲ 90882 [DDD] (16.97)
D. Mitropoulos (cnd), Philharmonic SO † Sym 1; Sym 3; Sym 5; Sym 6; Sym 8 MUA 6-▲ 1021 (63.97)
W. Morris (cnd), Symphonica of London † Beethoven:Grosse Fuge Str Qt, Op. 133 INMP 2-▲ 1025 (21.97)
V. Neumann (cnd), Czech PO SUR ▲ 111980 [DDD]
V. Neumann (cnd), Leipzig Gewandhaus Orch BER ▲ 2187 [ADD] (10.97)
L. Pešek (cnd), Royal Liverpool PO *(rec 1990)* † Sym 1 VCL 2-▲ 61475 [DDD] (11.97)
S. Rattle (cnd), Vienna PO *(rec Vienna, Austria, 1993-97)* † R. Strauss:Metamorphosen EMIC 2-▲ 56580 [DDD] (32.97)
E. Tabakov (cnd), Sofia PO *(rec Bulgarian Concert Hall Sofia, Mar 1991)* ("Complete Edition: 10 Symphonies") † Sym 1; Sym 10; Sym 2; Sym 3; Sym 4; Sym 5; Sym 6; Sym 7; Sym 8 CAPO 15-▲ 49043 [DDD] (89.97)
B. Walter (cnd), Vienna PO *(rec 1938)* EMIC (Great Recordings of the Century) ▲ 63029 [ADD] (11.97)
B. Walter (cnd), Vienna PO ("Bruno Walter in Vienna") † Lied von der Erde ENT (Palladio) ▲ 4172 [ADD] (26.97)
B. Walter (cnd), Vienna PO *(rec Jan 16, 1938)* MTAL (Great Conductors) ▲ 48007 (6.97)
B. Walter (cnd), Vienna PO *(rec 1938)* GRM2 ▲ 78818 (13.97)

COMPOSERS 509

MAHLER, GUSTAV (cont.)

Symphony No. 9 in D-D♭ (1908-09) (cont.)
B. Walter (cnd), Vienna PO *(rec Vienna, Austria, 1938)* HCO ▲ 37017 (7.97)
H. Zender (cnd), Saarbrücken RSO ("Hans Zender Edition, Vol. 7") † Knaben Wunderhorn CPO 2-▲ 999479 (6.97)

Symphony No. 10 in f# [only Adagio movt finished by Mahler; completed versions by Cooke & others] (1910)
V. Baley (cnd) —Adagio [arr Hans Stadlmair for 15 solo strs] *(rec Kiev, Ukraine, Jan 5, 1996)* ("Kiev Camerata, Vol. 1") † W. A. Mozart:Sym 29, K.201; Schoenberg:Verklärte Nacht, Op. 4 CMB ▲ 1402 (16.97)
M. Gielen (cnd), Southwest German SO Baden-Baden—Adagio † R. Wagner:Tristan und Isolde (prelude & liebestod) INTC (Gielen Edition) ▲ 860908 (13.97)
E. Inbal (cnd), Frankfurt RSO † Sym 9 DNN 2-▲ 1566 [DDD] (33.97)
E. Inbal (cnd), Frankfurt RSO [Cooke version] DNN ▲ 75129 [DDD] (16.97)
A. Ligeti (cnd), Budapest SO—Adagio † Klagende Lied CLDI ▲ 4010 [DDD] (10.97)
V. Neumann (cnd), Czech PO—Adagio *(rec Feb 27, 1976)* † Sym 1 SUR ▲ 111970 [AAD]
S. Rattle (cnd), Bournemouth SO [Cooke version, w. slight adjustments by Rattle] EMIC ▲ 54406 (16.97)
L. Segerstam (cnd), Danish National RSO—Adagio † Sym 8 CHN 2-▲ 9305 [DDD] (32.97)
L. Slatkin (cnd), St. Louis SO [reconstructed Remo Mazetti Jr.] *(rec St Louis, MS, Mar 10-13, 1995)* RCAV (Red Seal) ▲ 68190 [DDD] (16.97)
G. Szell (cnd), Cleveland Orch—Adagio *(rec Nov 1, 1958)* † Sym 1 SNYC ▲ 53259 (7.97)
E. Tabakov (cnd), Sofia PO—Adagio *(rec Sofia, Bulgaria, Apr 1987)* ("Complete Edition: 10 Symphonies") † Sym 1; Sym 2; Sym 3; Sym 4; Sym 5; Sym 6; Sym 7; Sym 8; Sym 9 CAPO 15-▲ 49043 [DDD] (89.97)
A. Wit (cnd), Polish National RSO Katowice—Adagio *(rec Katowice, Poland, Nov 12-16, 1994)* † Sym 3 NXIN 2-▲ 550525 [DDD] (15.97)

Totenfeier (symphonic poem) for Orchestra [original version of 1st movt of Symphony No. 2] (1888)
J. López-Cobos (cnd), Berlin RSO † Arrangements KSCH ▲ 312042 [ADD] (16.97)
S. Magad (vn), P. Boulez (cnd), Chicago SO † R. Strauss:Also sprach Zarathustra, Op. 30 DEUT ▲ 457649 (16.97)

Winterlied for Tenor & Piano [text Mahler] (1880)
J. Baker (mez), G. Parsons (pno) [GER] † Im Lenz; Lieder eines fahrenden Gesellen; Lieder und Gesänge aus der Jugendzeit HYP ▲ 66100 (18.97)

MAHLER (-WERFEL), ALMA MARIA (1879-1964)

Songs
V. Dupuy (mez), S. Sargon (pno)—Die stille Stadt; In meines Vaters Garten; Laue Sommernacht; Bei dir ist es traut; Ich wandle unter Blumen; Licht in der Nacht; Waldseligkeit; Ansturm; Erntelied; Hymne; Ekstase; Der Erkennende; Lobgesang; Hymne an die Nacht *(rec Dallas, TX)* GAS ▲ 1015 (11.97)
C. Högman (sop), R. Pöntinen (pno)—Licht in der Nacht; Waldseligkeit; Ansturm; Erntelied; Laue Sommernacht; Ich wandle unter Blumen; Der Erkennende; Lobgesang *(rec Stockholm Sweden, May 24-27, 1995)* † Mendelssohn (-Hensel):Songs; C. Schumann:Songs BIS ▲ 738 [DDD] (17.97)
I. Lippitz (sop), B. Heller (pno)—Licht in der Nacht; Waldseligkeit; Ansturm; Erntelied; Hymne; Ekstase; Der Erkennende; Lobgesang; Hymne an die Nacht; Die stille Stadt; In meines Vaters Garten; Laue Sommernacht; Bei dir ist es traut; Ich wandle unter Blumen [G] CPO ▲ 999018 [DDD] (14.97)

MAHON, JOHN (ca 1749-1834)

Concerto No. 2 in F for Clarinet (or Oboe or Flute or Violin) & Orchestra
C. Lawson (cl), P. Holman (cnd), Parley of Instruments † Duet 1 for Cls; Duet 4 for Cls; J. Christian Bach:Sinf concertante, T.290/9; Hook:Con Cl HYP ▲ 66896 (18.97)

Duet No. 1 in F for 2 Clarinets
C. Lawson (cl), M. Harris (cl) † Con 2 Cl; Duet 4 for Cls; J. Christian Bach:Sinf concertante, T.290/9; Hook:Con Cl HYP ▲ 66896 (18.97)

Duet No. 4 in B♭ for 2 Clarinets
C. Lawson (cl), M. Harris (cl) † Con 2 Cl; Duet 1 for Cls; J. Christian Bach:Sinf concertante, T.290/9; Hook:Con Cl HYP ▲ 66896 (18.97)

MAILMAN, MARTIN (1932-

For Precious Friends Hid in Death's Dateless Night (3 songs) for Soprano & Wind Orchestra [after Shakespeare] (1988)
T. M. Gomez (sop), E. Corporon (cnd), North Texas Wind Sym *(rec Texas Women's Univ, Nov 1996)* ("Dialogues & Entertainments") † Bremer:Early Light; Corigliano:Gazebo Dances for Band; W. Kraft:Dialogues; J. Stamp:Maryland Songs; Toch:Miniature Ov KLAV (Wind Recording Project) ▲ 11083 [DDD] (18.97)

MAINERIO, GIORGIO (ca 1535-1582)

Il primo libro de balli (selections)
R. Haeger (bc), Datura Trombone Quartet † Ahle:Sacred Vocal Music; W. Byrd:Kbd Music; A. Corelli:Son da chiesa, Op. 3; Kuhnau:Biblical Son 1 Hpd; H. Schütz:Attendite, popule meus, SWV 270; Fili mi, Absalom, SWV 269 ARSM ▲ 1094 [DDD] (17.97)

Il primo libro de balli (21 4-part dances) for Ensemble
Ensemble Consort Veneto *(rec Oct 1-7, 1992)* TACT ▲ 531301 [DDD] (16.97)

MAINGUENEAU (dates unknown)

Pieces (3) for Cello & Piano
A. Navarra (vc), A. Balsam (pno) ("Navarra, Vol. 3") † Beethoven:Son 3 Vc, Op. 69; Lalo:Con Vc; F. Schubert:Son Arpeggione, D.821 LYS ▲ 448

MAKAROVA, NINA (1908-1976)

Symphony in d (1938)
O. Koch (cnd), USSR SO † Levina:Con 2 Pno RUS ▲ 11382 [DDD] (12.97)

MAKLAKIEWICZ, TADEUSZ (20th cent)

Chrysea Phorminx (ode) for 4 Trombones
Triton Trombone Quartet *(rec Furuby Church, Sweden, July 6-10, 1994)* ("Trombone Angels") † P. M. Braun:Chörale; G. Jansson:Missa for 4 Trbns; J. Kretz:alles Ding währt seine Zeit; F. Peeters:Suite for 4 Trbns, Op. 82; Serocki:Suite for 4 Trbns BIS ▲ 694 [DDD] (17.97)

MALATS, JOAQUÍN (1872-1912)

Impresiones de España for Guitar
A. Segovia (gtr)—Serenata [arr for gtr] *(rec Oct 6, 1930)* ("The Young Segovia, 1927-39") † J. S. Bach:Sons & Partitas Vn; Suites Vc; M. Ponce:Gtr Music IN ▲ 1347 [ADD] (15.97)

Serenata Andaluza for Guitar
N. Ruiz (gtr) *(rec Columbia College, Chicago, IL, 1995)* † Serenata Española; I. Albéniz:Gtr Music; Moreno Torroba:Gtr Music; J. Rodrigo:Por los campos de España CENT ▲ 2279 [DDD] (16.97)

Serenata Española for Guitar
N. Ruiz (gtr) *(rec Columbia College, Chicago, IL, 1995)* † Serenata Andaluza; I. Albéniz:Gtr Music; Moreno Torroba:Gtr Music; J. Rodrigo:Por los campos de España CENT ▲ 2279 [DDD] (16.97)

Trio for Piano, Violin & Cello (1898)
Mompou Trio Madrid † J. Serra:Trio in E; J. Turina:Trio 1 Pno, Op. 35 RTVE ▲ 65011 (16.97)

MALAWSKI, ARTUR (1904-1957)

Overture for Orchestra (1948)
J. Krenz (cnd), Polish National RSO Katowice *(rec 1964)* † Turski:Con 1 Vn; Sym 2 OLY ▲ 327 [AAD] (16.97)

MALDERE, PIETER VAN (1729-1768)

Sinfonias (miscellaneous)
P. Peire (cnd) —Sinf No. 23 in E♯, Op. 4; Sinfs Nos. 18, 38 & 43 in A, D & D EUFO ▲ 1206 [DDD]

MALECKI, MACIEJ (1940-

Concertino dans un style ancien for 2 Harps & String Orchestra
C. Michel (hp), S. Mildonian (hp), A. Moglia (cnd), Toulouse National CO *(rec Apr 1995)* ("Concertos for 2 Harps") † Debussy:Danses sacrée et profane; J. Françaix:Con for 2 Hps; Gossec:Sym concertante for 2 Hps; M. Ravel:Intro & Allegro Hp PAVA ▲ 7337 [DDD] (10.97)

Suite for Wind Quintet (1983)
Warsaw Wind Quintet ("Da camera") † Bargielski:Butterfly Cage; Kurtlewicz:Blow the Wind; P. Moss:Retours; Palester:Trio d'anches; Stachowski:Pezzo grazioso PROV ▲ 182 [DDD] (18.97)

MALENGREAU, PAUL (EUGÈNE) (1887-1959)

Suite for Organ, Op. 14 (1919)
H. Mardirosian (org) *(rec Champaign, IL, Apr 1997)* ("Organ Suites") † Foote:Suite Org, Op. 54; J. Langlais:Suite médévale; Saint-Saëns:Rapsodies sur des cantiques bretons, Op. 7 CENT ▲ 2368 [DDD] (16.97)

MALIPIERO, GIAN FRANCESCO (1882-1973)

Chamber Music
Ex Novo Ensemble—Son à tre; Son à cinque; Dialogo 4; Qt for Elisabeth ("Chamber Music") BMGR ▲ 1024 (18.97)

Commedie goldoniane (3 orchestral fragments) for Orchestra (1925)
M. D. Bernart (cnd), Emilia Romagna SO † Casella:Symphonic Fragments, Op. 19; C. Pedrotti:Tutti en maschera; V. Tommasini:Carnevale di Venezia AURC ▲ 404 (5.97)

MALIPIERO, GIAN FRANCESCO (cont.)

Dialogo No. 2 for 2 Pianos (1955)
Brusca-Solastra Piano Duo ("Italian 4 Hand Piano Music") † Busoni:Duettino concertante; Fugue on the folksong O du lieber Augustin; Casella:Pagine di guerra, Op. 25; Pupazzetti, Op. 27; Petrassi:Siciliana e marcetta; O. Respighi:Pezzi (6) per bambini PHEX ▲ 97309 (16.97)

Dialogo No. 4 for Wind Quintet (1956)
Wind Quintette of the 1900s *(rec Mar 1989)* † Ghedini:Qnt Ww; R. Malipiero:Musica da camera; O. Respighi:Qnt Ww FON ▲ 9001 (13.97)

Dialogo No. 5 for Viola & Orchestra, "Quasi Concerto" (1956)
E. Wallfisch (va), S. Comissiona (cnd), Jerusalem SO † Paganini:Son Va; Vanhal:Con Va; C. M. von Weber:Andante & Rondo ungarese Va, J.79; Vars on A Schüsserl und a Reind'r'l, J.49 BAYE ▲ 200028 [ADD] (17.97)

Dialogo No. 7 for 2 Pianos & Orchestra (1956)
J. Pierce (pno), D. Jonas (pno), D. Amos (cnd), Slovak State PO Košice † Lopatnikoff:Con for 2 Pnos; Tansman:Suite for 2 Pnos CENT ▲ 2269 (16.97)

I fantisimi
E. Kissin (pno), C. M. Giulini (cnd), Vienna PO ("Ich liebe dich, Op. 41/3") † E. Grieg:Pictures from Life in the Country, Op. 19; Pno Music (misc); F. Schubert:Qnt Pno, D.667; R. Schumann:Arabeske Pno, Op. 18 SNYC ▲ 52567 (16.97)

Invenzioni (4) for Orchestra, "La festa degli indolenti" (1933)
P. Maag (cnd), Venice PO *(rec Mar 1-8, 1991)* † Finto Arlecchino (sels); Invenzioni (7) MARC ▲ 8223397 [DDD] (13.97)

Invenzioni (7) for Orchestra (1933)
P. Maag (cnd), Venice PO *(rec Mar 1-8, 1991)* † Finto Arlecchino (sels); Invenzioni (4) MARC ▲ 8223397 [DDD] (13.97)

Il finto Arlecchino (selections)
P. Maag (cnd), Venice PO *(rec Mar 1-8, 1991)* † Invenzioni (4); Invenzioni (7) MARC ▲ 8223397 [DDD] (13.97)

Pause del silenzio I for Orchestra (1917)
Dirani-Ameletti Piano Duo [arr for pno 4-hands] † Casella:Pagine di guerra, Op. 25; Pupazzetti, Op. 27; Martucci:Pensiero sull'opera, Op. 8; O. Respighi:Pezzi (6) per bambini FON ▲ 9030 [DDD] (13.97)

Piano Music
G. Gorino (pno)—La notte dei Monti; Barlumi; 3 Preludes & a Fugue; Risonanze; Hortus Conclusus; 5 Studi per domani ("Piano Works") RIVO ▲ 9810 (16.97)
F. Quarti (pno)—Notturno pastorale; I fantisimi *(rec Italy, June 5-7, 1996)* ("..il regno della Notte..") † Debussy:Nocturnes in D♭ Pno; Martucci:Notturni Pno, Op. 70; O. Respighi:Pezzi (6) Pno PHEX ▲ 96206 (16.97)

Quartets (8) for Strings (complete)
Venice String Quartet *(rec Genova, 1996)* ("I Quartetti d'Archi") DYNC 2-▲ 168 [DDD] (34.97)

Quartet No. 1 for Strings, "Rispetti e strambotti" (1920)
Christopher String Quartet ("Christopher Quartet") † J. Turina:Oración del torero, Op. 34; K. Weigl:Qt 1 Strs, Op. 20 IUSM ▲ 1 [DDD] (16.97)

Sinfonia No. 1, "in quattro tempi, come le quattro stagioni" (1933)
A. D. Almeida (cnd), Moscow SO *(rec May-June 1993)* † Sinf del silenzo; Sinf 2 MARC ▲ 8223603 [DDD] (13.97)

Sinfonia No. 2, "elegiaca" (1936)
A. D. Almeida (cnd), Moscow SO *(rec May-June 1993)* † Sinf del silenzo; Sinf 1 MARC ▲ 8223603 [DDD] (13.97)

Sinfonia No. 3, "delle campane" (1944-45)
A. D. Almeida (cnd), Moscow SO *(rec May-June 1993)* † Sin del mare; Sinf 4 MARC ▲ 8223602 [DDD] (13.97)

Sinfonia No. 4, "in memoriam" (1946)
(rec May-June 1993) † Sin del mare; Sinf 3 MARC ▲ 8223602 [DDD] (13.97)

Sinfonia No. 6 for String Orchestra (1947; arr for String Quintet 1953)
Italian Solisti *(rec Piazzola sul Brenta Italy, June 19-23, 1994)* ("Italian Compositions of the 20th Century") † E. Morricone:Esercizi; Porena:Vivaldi; N. Rota:Con Strs DNN ▲ 78949 [DDD] (16.97)

Sinfonia No. 7, "delle canzoni" (1948)
A. D. Almeida (cnd), Moscow SO *(rec May-June 1993)* † Sinf in un tempo; Sinf per Antigenida MARC ▲ 8223604 [DDD] (13.97)

Sinfonia No. 9, "dell'ahimè" (1966)
A. De Almeida (cnd), Moscow SO *(rec Moscow, Feb 1994)* † Sinf dello zodiaco; Sinf 10 MARC ▲ 8223697 [DDD] (13.97)

Sinfonia No. 10, "atropo" (1967)
A. De Almeida (cnd), Moscow SO *(rec Moscow, Feb 1994)* † Sinf dello zodiaco; Sinf 9 MARC ▲ 8223697 [DDD] (13.97)

Sinfonia del mare for Orchestra (1906)
A. D. Almeida (cnd), Moscow SO *(rec May-June 1993)* † Sinf 3; Sinf 4 MARC ▲ 8223602 [DDD] (13.97)

Sinfonia del silenzo e de la morte for Orchestra (1909-10)
A. D. Almeida (cnd), Moscow SO *(rec May-June 1993)* † Sinf 1; Sinf 2 MARC ▲ 8223603 [DDD] (13.97)

Sinfonia dello zodiaco for Orchestra (1951)
A. De Almeida (cnd), Moscow SO *(rec Moscow, Feb 1994)* † Sinf 10; Sinf 9 MARC ▲ 8223697 [DDD] (13.97)

Sinfonia in un tempo for Orchestra (1950)
A. D. Almeida (cnd), Moscow SO *(rec May-June 1993)* † Sinf per Antigenida; Sinf 7 MARC ▲ 8223604 [DDD] (13.97)

Sinfonia per Antigenida for Orchestra (1962)
A. D. Almeida (cnd), Moscow SO *(rec May-June 1993)* † Sinf in un tempo; Sinf 7 MARC ▲ 8223604 [DDD] (13.97)

MALIPIERO, RICHARD (1914-

Musica da camera for Wind Quintet (1959)
Wind Quintette of the 1900s *(rec Mar 1989)* † Ghedini:Qnt Ww; G. F. Malipiero:Dialogo 4; O. Respighi:Qnt Ww FON ▲ 9001 (13.97)

MALLING, OTTO (1848-1915)

Concerto in c for Piano & Orchestra, Op. 43
A. Malling (pno), P. Sundkvist (cnd), Danish RSO † Trio Pno, Op. 36 DCAP ▲ 8224114 (13.97)

Paulus (tone poem) for Organ, Op. 78 (1903)
H. Gramstrup (org) *(rec St. Markus church Arhus, Oct 1995)* † 7 Last Words, Op. 81 DCAP ▲ 9423 [DDD] (13.97)

The Seven Last Words on the Cross (tone poem) for Organ & Chorus, Op. 81 (1904)
H. Gramstrup (org), M. Dahl (cnd), Jjyske Choir *(rec St. Markus church Arhus, Oct 1995)* † Paulus DCAP ▲ 9423 [DDD] (13.97)

Trio in a for Piano, Violin & Cello, Op. 36
E. Z. Schneider (vn), M. Zeuthen (vc), A. Malling (pno) † Con Pno, Op. 43 DCAP ▲ 8224114 (13.97)

MAMANGAKIS, NIKOS (1929-

Folk Dance Suite
E. Papandreou (gtr)—Hassapiko; Zeimbekiko No. 1; Tsifteteli; Karsilamas *(rec Newmarket, Canada, Oct 27-30, 1996)* ("Elena Papandreou") † Hroes; Boudounis:Cocktail; Summaries; Tsifteteli for Elena; Dyens:Songe capricorne; Tango en Skaï; Koshkin:Usher Gtr, Op. 29; I. Stravinsky:Histoire du soldat (sels); Theodorakis:Lyricotera; Music of Theodorakis NXIN (Laureate Series) ▲ 8554001 [DDD] (5.97)

Hroes *(Dedicated to E Papandreou)*
E. Papandreou (gtr) *(rec Newmarket, Canada, Oct 27-30, 1996)* ("Elena Papandreou") † Folk Dance Suite; Boudounis:Cocktail; Summaries; Tsifteteli for Elena; Dyens:Songe capricorne; Tango en Skaï; Koshkin:Usher Gtr, Op. 29; I. Stravinsky:Histoire du soldat (sels); Theodorakis:Lyricotera; Music of Theodorakis NXIN (Laureate Series) ▲ 8554001 [DDD] (5.97)

MAMIYA, MICHIO (1929-

Concerto III for Piano & Orchestra
I. Tateno (pno), K. Akiyama (cnd), Tokyo SO *(rec live Tokyo Metropolitan Theater Large Hall, June 23, 1993)* † Nishimura:Mantra of the Light; K. Tanaka:Initium CAMA ▲ 319 [DDD] (18.97)

MAMLOK, URSULA (1928-

Der Andreas Garten for Piano Trio (1987)
Jubal Trio † Constellations; Girasol; Polarities; Qrt Strings *([ENG,GER])* CRI ▲ 806 [DDD] (16.97)

Constellations for Orchestra (1993)
G. Schwarz (cnd), Seattle SO *(rec Sept 26, 1997)* † Andreas Garten; Girasol; Polarities; Qrt Strings CRI ▲ 806 [DDD] (16.97)

Designs for Violin & Piano
C. Tait (vn), B. Snyder (pno) ("American Women Composers") † From My Garden; Son Vn; Crawford (Seeger):Son Vn & Pno; Talma:Son Vn; E. T. Zwilich:Son Vn in 3 Movts GAS ▲ 300 (16.97)

Elegy for Orchestra [from Concertino for Woodwind Quintet, String Orchestra & Percussion]
C. Martin (cnd), Bournemouth Sinfonietta † J. Brockman:Perihelion II; K. Gardner:Rainforest; K. Hoover:Summer Night; L. Larsen:Parachute Dancing; M. Richter:Lament; Van de Vate:Journeys LEON ▲ 327 [DDD] (16.97)

▲ = CD ♦ = Enhanced CD △ = MD ▮ = Cassette Tape ▯ = DCC

MAMLOK, URSULA (cont.)
From My Garden for Violin (or Viola) (1983)
C. Tait (vn) ("American Women Composers") † Designs; Son Vn; Crawford (Seeger):Son Vn & Pno; Talma:Son Vn; E. T. Zwilich:Son Vn in 3 Movts GAS ▲ 300 (16.97)
Girasol for Flute, Clarinet, Violin, Viola, Cello & Piano (1990)
C. Stevens (vn), S. Adams (va), C. Finckel (vc), K. Underwood (fl), A. R. Kay (cl), C. Oldfather (pno) *(rec State University of New York, NY, May 1998)* † Andreas Garten; Constellations; Polarities; Qrt Strings CRI ▲ 806 [DDD] (16.97)
Polarities for Flute, Violin, Cello & Piano (1995)
A. Korf (cnd), Parnassus *(rec State University of New York, NY, May 1998)* † Andreas Garten; Constellations; Girasol; Qrt Strings CRI ▲ 806 [DDD] (16.97)
Quartet No. 2 for Strings (1998)
(rec Performing Arts Center, SUNY, NY, Jan 1998) † Andreas Garten; Constellations; Girasol; Polarities CRI ▲ 806 [DDD] (16.97)
Rhapsody for Clarinet, Viola & Piano (1989)
G. Thomson (cnd), Earplay members *(rec Knuth Hall, SFSU, CA, Nov 25, 1994)* † E. Carter:Esprit rude/esprit doux; Festinger:Spt; A. Frank:Points of Departure; G. Moretto:Silenciosamente; W. Peterson:Labyrinth; Vayo:Poem CENT ▲ 2274 [DDD] (16.97)
Sonata for Violin & Piano
C. Tait (vn), B. Snyder (pno) ("American Women Composers") † Designs; From My Garden; Crawford (Seeger):Son Vn & Pno; Talma:Son Vn; E. T. Zwilich:Son Vn in 3 Movts GAS ▲ 300 (16.97)

MANCHICOURT, PIERRE DE (ca 1510-1564)
Laudate Dominum for Chorus
P. van Nevel (cnd), Huelgas Ensemble † G. Gabrieli:Exaudi me Domine; Josquin Desprez:Qui habitat in adjutorio Altissimi; Ockeghem:Deo gratias; C. Porta:Masses; Striggio:Ecce beatam lucem; Tallis:Spem in alium SNYC (Vivarte) ▲ 66261 (16.97)
Music of Manchicourt
P. van Nevel (cnd) —Missa veni sancte; Chansons; Motets SNYC ▲ 62694 (16.97)
Sacred Music
E. Wickham (cnd), Renaissance Singers ("O Socii Durate") † F. De Lassus:Sacred Music; Rore:Sacred Music; Willaert:Sacred Music ASVQ ▲ 6228 (10.97)

MANCINA, MARK (20th cent)
Moll Flanders (film music) for Chamber Ensemble
("Moll Flanders") † J. S. Bach:Brandenburg Con 3, BWV 1048; Suite 3 Orch, BWV 1068; G. F. Handel:Water Music, HWV 348-50; J. Offenbach:Contes d'Hoffmann (sels); Vivaldi:Con Mand, RV.425 PLON ▲ 52485 (16.97)

MANCINI, FRANCESCO (1672-1737)
Solos (12) for Violin (or Flute) & Continuo, "Which Solos Are Proper Lessons for the Harpsichord" (1724; rev Geminiani, 1727)
C. Ferrarini (fl), L. Fontana (hpd) *(rec July 1995)* ("12 Sonatas for Flute") MONM 2-▲ 96003 [DDD] (17.97)

MANCINI, HENRY (1924-1994)
Breakfast at Tiffany's (film music) for Orchestra
artist unknown RCA ▲ 2362 (9.97)
Choral Music
Finzi Singers—Film Music *(rec Dec 4-5, 1991)* † A. Bax:Choral Music; H. Howells:Choral Music CHN ▲ 9139 [DDD] (16.97)
Film Music
W. Kanengiser (gtr), F. J. Castillo (instr) ("Classic Film Scores of Henry Mancini") CMB ▲ 1069 [DDD] (16.97)
H. Mancini (cnd) —Breakfast at Tiffany's (sels); Hatari & others RCA ▲ 53822 (11.97) ▮ 3822 (7.98)
J. Mathis (sop), A. Williams (sgr), L. Albright (sgr), B. Hackett (sgr), B. Greco (sgr), C. Byrd (sgr), P. Page (sgr), H. Mancini (cnd), Costa Orch, H. Mancini (cnd), Conniff Orch, H. Mancini (cnd), Mancini Orch—Breakfast at Tiffany's (sels); Peter Gunn; Mr. Lucky & others COL ▲ 66505 (11.97)
artists unknown ("The Pink Panther, Baby Elephant Walk, Moon River & Other Hits") RCAV ▲ 55938 (16.97)
Peter Gunn (selections)
M. Pugliese (perc), K. Grossman (perc), C. Nappi (perc), W. Trigg (perc)—Peter Gunn Theme [arr Michael Pugliese for perc ensemble] *(rec NYC, NY, live, Apr 4, 1989)* ("Perkin' at Merkin") † J. Cage:Music for...; M. Feldman:King of Denmark; Nørgård:Waves; Vigeland:Progress; Xenakis:Psappha MODE ▲ 25
Songs
M. Mancini (sgr), Patrick Williams Orch *(Moment to Moment; Two for the Road; Crazy World; Anywhere the Heart Goes; Loss of Love; Whistling Away the Dark; Charade; Days of Wine & Roses; Slow Hot Wind; Dear Heart; Moon River; Music on the Way)*, M. Mancini (sgr), J. Mathis (sgr), Patrick Williams Orch *(Dreamsville)* WAR ▲ 47115 (16.97) ▮ 47115 (10.98)
Victor/Victoria (film music) for Orchestra
J. Andrews (sop), R. Preston (sgr), L. A. Warren (sgr) GNP ▲ 8038 (16.97)

MANDONICO, CLAUDIO (1957-
Suite No. 1 for String Orchestra
G. D. Lorenzo (cnd) ("Novecento Barocco") † M. E. Bossi:Pieces Strs; O. Respighi:Ancient Airs & Dances; Toni:Parafrasi settecentesca AG ▲ 104 [DDD] (18.97)

MANÉN, JUAN (1883-1971)
Miniatures for Orchestra
G. Claret (cnd), Andorra National CO *(rec Monmouth, England)* ("La Oración del Torero: Spanish Works for String Orchestra") † Lamote De Grignon:Monocromies; J. Rodrigo:Cançoneta; J. Turina:Musas de Andalucía, Op. 93; Oración del torero, Op. 34; Serenata Str Qt, Op. 87 NIMB ▲ 5570 [DDD] (16.97)

MANFREDINI, FRANCESCO (ca 1680-1748)
Concerti (12) for 2 Violins, Strings & Continuo, Op. 3
T. Füri (cnd), Bern Camerata † Albinoni:Adagio; J. S. Bach:Brandenburg Con 3, BWV 1048; J. Pachelbel:Canon & Gigue; H. Purcell:Pavane & Chaconne NOVA ▲ 150004 (16.97)
J. Maksymiuk (cnd), Polish CO *(rec 1978-82)* † J. S. Bach:Brandenburg Cons; A. Corelli:Con grosso, Op. 6/8; Locatelli:Concerti grossi, Op. 1 EMIC 2-▲ 69749 [ADD] (16.97)
S. Standage (cnd), Collegium Musicum 90—No. 12 in C † A. Corelli:Con grosso, Op. 6/8; A. Scarlatti:Pastorale per nascita di Nostro Signore; Telemann:In dulci jubilo, TWV1: 939; Vivaldi:Con Vn CHN ▲ 634 (16.97)
Concerto in D for 2 Trumpets, Harpsichord & Strings
Z. Nagy-Major (tpt), B. Nemes (tpt), M. Pommer (cnd), Thüringian Weimar CO ("Virtuose Trompetenkonzerte") † Fasch:Con Tpt Obs; Hertel:Con 1 Tpt; Molter:Con 1 Tpt; Telemann:Qnt Tpt DSB ▲ 1062 [DDD] (16.97)
H. Wobisch (tpt), A. Holler (tpt), E. Heiller (hpd), A. Heiller (org), A. Janigro (cnd) *(rec Baumgarten Hall, Vienna, Austria, May 1961)* ("The Virtuoso Trumpet, Vol. 2") † G. M. Alberti:Son Tpts; H. I. Biber:Son for 6 Tpts; J. Haydn:Con Tpt; L. Mozart:Con Tpt; Torelli:Con for 2 Tpts VC ▲ 2535 [ADD] (13.97)
Music of Manfredini
Musica Petropolitana ("Music at the Court of St. Petersburg, Vol VI") † Khandoshkin:Music of OPUS ▲ 30231 (18.97)

MANFROCE, NICOLA ANTONIO (1791-1813)
Ecuba (opera in 3 acts) (1812)
A. C. Antonacci (sop), D. Di Domenico (ten), F. Piccoli (ten), G. D. Bellida (sgr), M. D. Bernart (cnd), Italian PO, Italian Phil Chorus [ITA] *(rec live, 1990)* BONG 2-▲ 2119 [DDD] (32.97)

MANGOLD, CARL AMAND (1813-1889)
Abraham (oratorio) for solo Voices, Orchestra & Chorus (1859)
M. Frimmer (sop), G. Mechthild (mez), G. Türk (ten), B. Gärtner (ten), G. Cachemaille (bar), Darmstadt Concert Choir CHR 2-▲ 77172 (17.97)

MANINO, F. (dates unknown)
Canzoni per Arpa (3) for Harp
V. Dulova (hp) *(rec 1982)* ("Vera Dulova - Russian Performing School") † Damase:Sonatine Hp; Debussy:Suite bergamasque; Jolivet:Con Hp; Salzedo:Preludes Hp; A. Zecchi:Divert Fl RD (Talents of Russia) ▲ 16204 [AAD] (16.97)

MANKELL, HENNING (1868-1930)
Nocturne
M. Lidström (vc), B. Forsberg (pno) *(rec Stockholm, Sweden, Nov 6-9, 1995)* ("Swedish Cello Sonatas") † Berwald:Duo Vn; Lidström:Tango; Melchers:Son Vc & Pno; J. H. Roman:Largo; H. Rosenberg:Son Vc & Pno *([ENG,SWE] text)* CAPA ▲ 21460 (16.97)

MANNEKE, DAAN (1939-
Choral Music
Quink—Madrigal: "Le città sottili" (1986); Psaume 121, "I Lift up Mine Eyes" (1960); Due Canti for Solo Voice & Chorus (1986) *(rec Masonic Temple Cleveland, OH, OH, May 15-17, 1995)* ("Invisible Cities: Contemporary A Capella Music") † Heppener:Canti carnascialeschi; H. Kerstens:Music of Kerstens; T. Leeuw:Music of De Leeuw TEL ▲ 80384 [DDD] (16.97)

MANNIS, JOSÉ AUGUSTO (1958-
Reflexos for Percussion
Duo Dialogos *(rec Sao Paolo, Brazil, 1994)* ("Contemporary Percussion Music from Brazil") † Alvares:Pocema; Cerqueira:Sketches to Frighten Guido d'Arezzo; Csekö:Volume em sombras; Menezes:A dialética da praia; Seincman:A dança do Dibuk GHA ▲ 126033 (17.97)

MANOURY, PHILIPPE (1952-
Pluton for Midi Piano & Electronics
I. Ranta (pno), P. Manoury (elec) [MIDI pno] ODE ▲ 888 (17.97)

MANSHARDT, THOMAS (1927-
Hommage à Debussy for Piano
T. Manshardt (pno) ("Alfred Cortot's Last Pupil") † Hommage à Liapunov; Hommage à Mendelssohn; Chopin:Son Pno in b, Op. 58; Liszt:Consolations (6), S.172; Légendes, S.175; W. A. Mozart:Son 5 Pno, K.283 APR ▲ 5550 [DDD] (19.97)
Hommage à Liapunov for Piano
T. Manshardt (pno) ("Alfred Cortot's Last Pupil") † Hommage à Debussy; Hommage à Mendelssohn; Chopin:Son Pno in b, Op. 58; Liszt:Consolations (6), S.172; Légendes, S.175; W. A. Mozart:Son 5 Pno, K.283 APR ▲ 5550 [DDD] (19.97)
Hommage à Mendelssohn for Piano
T. Manshardt (pno) ("Alfred Cortot's Last Pupil") † Hommage à Debussy; Hommage à Liapunov; Chopin:Son Pno in b, Op. 58; Liszt:Consolations (6), S.172; Légendes, S.175; W. A. Mozart:Son 5 Pno, K.283 APR ▲ 5550 [DDD] (19.97)

MANSURIAN, TIGRAN (1939-
Bagatellen (5) for Piano Trio (1985)
artists unknown *(rec Bolshoi Hall, Moscow, Russia)* † Capriccio; Madrigals (2); Shadow of the Sash MEGD ▲ 7839 [DDD] (18.97)
Capriccio for Cello (1981)
artist unknown *(rec Bolshoi Hall, Moscow, Russia)* † Bagatellen (5); Madrigals (2); Shadow of the Sash MEGD ▲ 7839 [DDD] (18.97)
Concerto No. 2 for Cello & Orchestra (1978)
I. Monighetti (vc), L. Issakadze (cnd), Georgian CO *(rec Dec 1995)* † Con Vn; Con Vn & Vc ORF ▲ 415971 [DDD] (18.97)
Concerto for Violin & String Orchestra (1981)
L. Issakadze (vn), L. Issakadze (cnd), Georgian CO *(rec Dec 1995)* † Con Vn & Vc; Con 2 Vc ORF ▲ 415971 [DDD] (18.97)
Concerto for Violin, Cello & String Orchestra (1978)
L. Issakadze (vn), I. Monighetti (vc), L. Issakadze (cnd), Georgian CO *(rec Dec 1995)* † Con Vn; Con 2 Vc ORF ▲ 415971 [DDD] (18.97)
Madrigals (2) for Soprano & Ensemble (1976/1982)
artists unknown *(rec Bolshoi Hall, Moscow, Russia)* † Bagatellen (5); Capriccio; Shadow of the Sash MEGD ▲ 7839 [DDD] (18.97)
Shadow of the Sash for Ensemble (1995)
artists unknown *(rec Bolshoi Hall, Moscow, Russia)* † Bagatellen (5); Capriccio; Madrigals (2) MEGD ▲ 7839 [DDD] (18.97)

MANZIARLY, MARCELLE DE (1899-1989)
Trio for Flute, Cello & Piano (1952)
Trio Aperto ("Chamber Music by French Female Composers") † N. Boulanger:Pieces Vc; Chaminade:Concertino Fl, Op. 107; Farrenc:Trio Pno, Op. 45 TLNT ▲ 49 (15.97)

MANZONI, GIACOMO (1932-
Chamber Music
E. Pomárico (cnd) —Preludio-Grave-Finale; Hommage à Josquin [both w. Diane Rama (sop)]; Klavieralbum; Incipit; Musica Notturna ("Musica da camera") BMGR ▲ 1008 (18.97)

MARAIS, MARIN (1656-1728)
Alcione (selections)
J. Savall (cnd), Concert des Nations ASTR ▲ 8525 (18.97)
Le Basque for Chamber Ensemble
D. Shostac (fl), R. Kato (va), J. Walz (vc), J. Smith (gtr), G. Levant (hp), A. Perry (pno) *(rec North Hollywood, CA)* ("The Romantic Flute") † J. S. Bach:Air on the G String; Arioso Ob; Sons Fl; Debussy:Prélude à l'après-midi d'un faune; Suite bergamasque; G. Fauré:Pavane; Sicilienne, Op. 78; Gossec:Tambourin Fl; W. A. Mozart:Andante Fl, K.315; Con 21 Pno, K.467; J. Pachelbel:Canon & Gigue XCEL ▲ 30006
Dances [arr for viola & harpsichord]
Y. Schotten (va), E. Parmentier (hpd) † B. Britten:Lachrymae, Op. 48; F. Schubert:Son Arpeggione, D.821; A. Shulman:Theme & Vars Va CRYS ▲ 635 (15.97) ▮ 635 (9.98)
La Gamme et autres morceaux de simphonie for Violin, Viol & Harpsichord (1723)
Boston Museum Trio [period instrs] † Son à la Marésienne; Sonnerie CENT ▲ 2129 (16.97)
Music of Marais
Oberlin Baroque Ensemble—Sonnerie de Ste. Genviève (1723); Suite in D (1711); Feste champètre (1717); Tambourin (1717); Allamande la Singulière & l'Arabesque (1717); Suite for 3 Vls in G (1717) GAS ▲ 1002 [AAD] (11.97)
Pièces de viole (miscellaneous)
Charivari Agréable—Suite in F/f; Suite in e/G; Caprice ou Sonate; Suite in D/d ("Musique pour la viole") ASV (Gaudeamus) ▲ 152 (16.97)
Pièces de viole [Book 1] for 1 & 2 Viols & Continuo (1686-89) (complete)
P. Pierlot (b vl), Ricarcar Consort RICE 3-▲ 205842 (34.97)
Pièces de viole [Book 2] (selections)
Chicago Baroque Ensemble members—Tombeau de Lully *(rec Chicago, IL, March, 1998)* † Lully:Armide (sels); Music of Lully CED ▲ 43 [DDD] (16.97)
L. Dreyfus (vl), K. Haugsand (hpd) † Vars on "Les Folies d'Espagne" SIMX ▲ 1053 [DDD] (18.97)
M. Luolajan-Mikkola (vl), V. Haavisto (vl), E. Palviainen (lt), E. Mustonen (hpd) *(rec Sept 1997)* BIS ▲ 909 [DDD] (17.97)
T. Muster (org) [trans Thilo Muster] *(rec Souvigny, Dec 26-28, 1994)* ("Suites Pour Souvigny") † Tombeau pour Lully; Beauvarlet-Charpentier:Magnificats, Op. 7; G. Bovet:Suite pour Souvigny; Guilain:Suite du quatrième ton; Rameau:Abaris (sels); Rebel:Elémens GALL 2-▲ 863 [ADD]
Pièces de viole [Book 3] (selections)
E. Matiffa (va da gamba), G. Robert (lt/thb), J. C. Veilhan (fl/rcr), E. Maserati (hpd) † Vars on "Les Folies d'Espagne" ARN ▲ 55410 (13.97)
J. Savall (b vl), H. Smith (thb), T. Koopman (hpd) ASTR ▲ 8761 (18.97)
Pièces de viole [Book 4] (selections)
Music's Re-Creation *(rec Sept 1995)* CENT ▲ 2334 [DDD] (16.97)
J. Savall (b vl), H. Smith (gtr), T. Koopman (hpd) ASTR ▲ 7727 [AAD] (18.97)
Pièces de viole [Book 5] (1725)
W. Kuijken (vl), K. Uemura (vl), R. Köhnen (hpd) ACCE ▲ 78744 [DDD] (17.97)
Pièces en trio (dance pieces) for Flutes, Strings & Continuo (1692)
Fitzwilliam Ensemble VAL ▲ 4638 (18.97)
Musica Pacifica VCL (Vertias) 2-▲ 61365 [DDD] (21.97)
P. Pierlot (cnd), Ricercar Consort RICE ▲ 206482 (17.97)
Sonata à la Marésienne for Violin & Continuo (1723)
Boston Museum Trio [period instrs] † Gamme et autres; Sonnerie CENT ▲ 2129 (16.97)
La Sonnerie de Ste. Genevieve du Mont de Paris for Ensemble
Boston Museum Trio [period instrs] † Gamme et autres; Son à la Marésienne CENT ▲ 2129 (16.97)
Suite d'un goût étranger [Suite to Suit Strange Tastes] for Viol & Continuo
C. Coin (b vl), C. Rousset (hpd) DECC ▲ 458144 (16.97)
M. Luolajan-Mikkola (vl), Battalia Continuo Group MARQ ▲ 207 (16.97)
Suite No. 2 in G for 2 Viols
S. Napper (vl), M. Little (vl) *(rec Saint-Joseph-de-Rivière-des-prairies Church M, Nov 29-30, 1993)* ("Violes Esgales") CBC (Musica Viva) ▲ 1082 [DDD] (16.97)

MARAIS, MARIN (cont.)

Tombeau pour Lully for Organ

T. Muster (org) ("Suites Pour Souvigny") † Pièces de viole [Book 2] (sels); Beauvarlet-Charpentier:Magnificats, Op. 7; G. Bovet:Suite pour Souvigny; Guilain:Suite du quatrième ton; Rameau:Abaris (sels); Rebel:Elémens GALL 2-▲ 863 [ADD]

Tombeau pour Monsieur de Ste Colombe for Bass Viol & Continuo

P. Pierlot (vl), S. Watillon (vl), R. Lislevand (thb) † Du Buisson:Suite Vls; Machy:Suite Vls; Sainte-Colombe:Fant en rondeau; Tombeau RICE ▲ 118100 [DDD] (17.97)

Variations (32) on *Les Folies d'Espagne*

R. Aitken (fl) *(rec Nacka, Sweden, Sept 14-16, 1980)* † Bozza:Image; F. X. W. Mozart:Rondo Fl; C. Reinecke:Son Fl; F. Schubert:Intro & Vars on "Tröckne Blumen", D.802 BIS ▲ 183 [AAD] (17.97)

R. Canter (ob), A. Pleeth (bc) [original instruments] *(rec Goudhurst, Kent, England, Feb 1985)* † Anonymous:Quinte estampie real; C.P.E. Bach:Son Ob, H.549; Kalliwoda:Morceau de Salon, Op. 228; Traditional:Alborada; An Dro Nevez; Etenraku; Traditional Turkish; Verdi:Vespri siciliani (sels); T. A. Walmisley:Sonatina 2 in G Ob & Pno AMON ▲ 22 [DDD] (16.97)

L. Dreyfus (vl), K. Haugsand (hpd) † Pièces de viole [Book 2] (sels) SIMX ▲ 1053 [DDD] (18.97)

E. Matiffa (va da gamba), G. Robert (lt/thb), J. C. Veilhan (fl/rcr), E. Maserati (hpd) † Pièces de viole [Book 3] (sels) ARN ▲ 55410 (13.97)

J. Paull (ob), S. Canuti (bn), C. Sartoretti (hpd) *(rec Villars Switzerland, Switzerland, Apr 21-22, 1995)* † Caix d'Hervelois:Music of Caix d'Hervelois DORO ▲ 5006 [DDD] (16.97)

M. Wiesler (fl) *(rec Sweden, 1989)* ("Manuela plays French Solo Flute Music") † Debussy:Fl Music; J. Françaix:Suite Fl; Ibert:Pièce Fl; Jolivet:Incantation Fl; Pieces (12) from 21 Sounding Minutes Fl; H. Tomasi:Sonatine Fl BIS ▲ 459 [DDD] (17.97)

Viol Music

Spectre de la Rose—Sonnerie de Sainte Geneviève du Mont de Paris; Le badinage; Le labyrinth; La rêveuse; L'arabesque; Prelude in G; Tombeau pour Monsieur de Sainte-Colombe *(rec Jan 6-7, 1993)* † Sainte-Colombe:Vl Music NXIN ▲ 550750 [DDD] (5.97)

MARBE, MYRIAM (1931-

Concerto for Daniel Kientzy & Saxophones for Saxophone & Orchestra [including various types of saxophones] (1986)

D. Kientzy (sax), H. Andreescu (cnd), Ploieşti PO ("The Romanian Saxophone") † S. Niculescu:Concertante Sym 3; A. Vieru:Narration II OLY (Explorer) ▲ 410 [AAD] (16.97)

MARCEL, LUC (1962-

Wind (ballet) for Saxophone Quartet (1994)

C. Z. Bornstein (cnd) VAND ▲ 2 (16.97)

MARCELLO, ALESSANDRO (1684-1750)

Concerto in B♭ for 2 Flutes & Orchestra

artists unknown ("Oboe Concertos & Rarities") † Con Ob Strs in d; Con 2 Obs in A; Con 2 Obs in F; Irene sdegnata; Lontananza AART ▲ 47505 (10.97)

Concertos for Oboe & Strings

J. Kiss (ob) *(rec 1991)* † C.P.E. Bach:Con Ob, H.466; Con Ob, H.468; Son Fl, H.562 NXIN ▲ 550556 [DDD] (5.97)

G. Krčková (ob), J. Krček (cnd), Musica Bohemica *(rec 1989)* † Telemann:Essercizii Musici; Qt Rcr SUR ▲ 111290 [DDD]

Concerto in c for Oboe & Strings

R. Kapp (cnd), Philharmonia Virtuosi, New York—Adagio *(rec NYC, NY)* ("Greatest Hits of 1721") † J. S. Bach:Cant 147; Cant 208; Suite 2 Fl, BWV 1067; J. Clarke:Prince of Denmark's March; A. Corelli:Con Grosso in g 2 Vns, Vla & Vc, Op. 6/8; G. F. Handel:Water Music, HWV 348-50; J. P. A. Martini:Plaisir d'Amour; Vivaldi:Con Mand, RV.425; Con Tpts, RV.537; Cons Vn Strs, Op. 8/1-4 SNYC ▲ 35821 (9.97)

Concerto in d for Oboe & Strings

J. Anderson (ob), S. Wright (cnd), Philharmonia Orch † A. Benjamin:Con Ob Strs; Cimarosa:Con Ob; Vivaldi:Con Ob NIMB ▲ 7027 [DDD] (11.97)

S. Dent (ob), W. Rajski (cnd), Polish CO ("Greatest Oboe Concertos, Vol. 2") † J. S. Bach:Con 1 for 2 Hpds, BWV 1060; J. Haydn:Con Ob; E. Wolf-Ferrari:Idillio-Concertino Ob, Op. 15 AMAT ▲ 9502 [DDD] (17.97)

P. Grazzi (ob), A. Marcon (cnd) ("Oboe Concertos & Rarities") † Con 2 Fls in B♭; Con 2 Obs in A; Con 2 Obs in F; Irene sdegnata; Lontananza AART ▲ 47505 (10.97)

H. Lee (ob), V. Jordania (cnd), Russian Federal Orch *(rec Moscow Radio Palace Hall, Russia, Oct 1995)* ("Hee-Sun Lee—Oboe") † J. S. Bach:Con 1 for 2 Hpds, BWV 1060; J. N. Hummel:Intro, Theme & Vars, Op. 102; W. A. Mozart:Qt Ob SSET ▲ 1002 [DDD] (16.97)

Concerto in d for Oboe & Strings, Op. 1

N. Black (ob), R. Leppard (cnd), English CO ("Sunday Brunch. Vol 2") † J. S. Bach:Cant 147; Cant 156; Cant 78; Con 5 Hpd, BWV 1056; Suite 2 Fl, BWV 1067; G. F. Handel:Minuet Vc & Pno; Solomon (arrival of the queen of Sheba); Water Music (sels); Mouret:Suite de symphonies; H. Purcell:Abdelazer (sels); Gordian Knot Unty'd (sels); V. Tommasini:Donne di buon umore (sels); Vivaldi:Con Mand, RV.425; Con Mands, RV.532; Cons Fl, Op. 10/1-6; Cons Vn Strs, Op. 8/1-4 SNYC (Dinner Classics) ▲ 46359 [AAD] (9.97)

G. Mattes (ob) *(rec Apr 1994)* ("Oboenkonzerte") † A. Corelli:Con in F Ob; Vivaldi:Con Ob NOVA ▲ 150141 (16.97)

Concerto in A for 2 Oboes & Orchestra

artists unknown ("Oboe Concertos & Rarities") † Con Ob Strs in d; Con 2 Fls in B♭; Con 2 Obs in F; Irene sdegnata; Lontananza AART ▲ 47505 (10.97)

Concerto in F for 2 Oboes & Orchestra

artists unknown ("Oboe Concertos & Rarities") † Con Ob Strs in d; Con 2 Fls in B♭; Con 2 Obs in A; Irene sdegnata; Lontananza AART ▲ 47505 (10.97)

Concerto for Oboe & Strings [often attrib to Benedetto Marcello]

M. Messiter (ob), Guildhall String Ensemble † Albinoni:Cons Ob, Op. 9; J. S. Bach:Con Ob; G. F. Handel:Cons Ob, HWV 301, 302a & 287 RCAV (Red Seal) ▲ 60224 [DDD] (16.97)

J. Williams (gtr) [arr Williams] † J. S. Bach:Con 2 Vn; Sons & Partitas Vn; G. F. Handel:Cons (16) Org SNYC ▲ 39560 [DDD] (16.97)

Concertos (6) in D, E, b, e, B♭ & G for Violin & Orchestra, "La Cetra"

S. Standage (vn), S. Standage (cnd), Collegium Musicum 90 † Con Vn in B♭ CHN (Chaconne) ▲ 563 [DDD] (16.97)

Concerto in B♭ for Violin & Orchestra

S. Standage (vn), S. Standage (cnd), Collegium Musicum 90 † Cons Vn CHN (Chaconne) ▲ 563 [DDD] (16.97)

Irene sdegnata (cantata) for solo Voices, Orchestra & Chorus

artists unknown ("Oboe Concertos & Rarities") † Con Ob Strs in d; Con 2 Fls in B♭; Con 2 Obs in A; Con 2 Obs in F; Lontananza AART ▲ 47505 (10.97)

La Lontananza (duet) for 2 Voices

S. Pozzer (sop), R. Balconi (ct) ("Oboe Concertos & Rarities") † Con Ob Strs in d; Con 2 Fls in B♭; Con 2 Obs in A; Con 2 Obs in F; Irene sdegnata AART ▲ 47505 (10.97)

MARCELLO, BENEDETTO (1686-1739)

Concertos a cinque (12) for Violin, Cello & Continuo, Op. 1

L. Aretini (vn), S. Frontalini (cnd), Kaunas CO BONG 2-▲ 5550 [DDD] (32.97)

Concerto in c for Trumpet & Orchestra

B. Soustrot (tpt), M. Tardue (cnd) *(rec Oct 1992)* ("6 Italian Concertos for Trumpet & Strings") † Tartini:Con Tpt; Torelli:Con Tpt FORL ▲ 16682 [DDD] (16.97)

Estro poetico-armonico (25 psalms) for Chorus (1724-26)

C. Brua (cta), P. Franco (cta), R. Martinini (vc), R. Martinini (cnd) KICC ▲ 19 (17.97)

Il mio bel foco (song) for Voice & Piano

E. Höngen (cta), artist unknown *(rec Apr 1946)* † J. Brahms:Liebeslieder Waltzes Pno 4-Hands, Op. 52a; F. Schubert:Songs (misc colls); R. Schumann:Gesänge, Op. 31; Liederkreis, Op. 39; Myrthen, Op. 25; R. Wagner:Wesendonck Songs; H. Wolf:Gedichte von Goethe; Gedichte von Mörike PRE ▲ 90356 (m) (16.97)

Music of Benedetto Marcello

A. Zagorinsky (vc), A. Schmitov (org)—Sons Vc; Con Ob [arr J. S. Bach for org] ICC ▲ 6600732 (16.97)

Requiem in the Venetian Manner for Voices & Chamber Ensemble

F. M. Bressan (cnd), Academia de li Musici, Athestis Chorus CHN ▲ 637 (16.97)

Salmo Decimoquinto for Baritone, Bassoon, Cello & Continuo

Maryland Bach Aria Group members ("The Italian Voyage") † Son 2 Vls; J. S. Bach:Cant 110; Cant 20; Stradella:Sinf alla Serenata; Torelli:Son Tpt, G.1 CRYS ▲ 705 [DDD] (15.97)

Sonatas (6) for Cello & Continuo

B. Slawinska (vc), L. Duron (hpd) PROF ▲ 232

Sonata in g for Cello & Continuo, Op. 2/4

R. Dieltiens (vc), R. V. Meer (vc) *(rec Haarlem, Germany, Sep 1990)* ("Italian Cello Music") † G. Bononcini:Son in a 2 Vc; Fesch:Son Vc; Gabrielli:Canon for 2 Vc; Ricercares for solo Cello; Vc Music; A. Scarlatti:Son Vc ACCE ▲ 9070 [DDD] (17.97)

MARCELLO, BENEDETTO (cont.)

Sonatas (12) for Recorder (or Flute) & Continuo, Op. 2

Collegium Pro Musica *(rec Genoa Italy, Oct 9-11, 1995)* DYNC ▲ 155 [DDD] (17.97)

H. L. Hirsch (cnd) *(rec Italy, Italy, Nov 1985)* ("Sonatas, Op. 2, Vol. 1") AART ▲ 47213 [DDD] (10.97)

H. L. Hirsch (cnd) *(rec Italy, Italy, Nov 1985)* ("Sonatas, Op. 2, Vol. 2") AART ▲ 47214 [DDD] (10.97)

A. Mosca (vc), S. Balestracci (rcr), O. Dantone (hpd) *(rec Feb-Mar 1995)* ("Complete Recorder Sonatas, Vol. 1") STRV ▲ 33390 [DDD] (16.97)

A. Mosca (vc), S. Balestracci (rcr), O. Dantone (hpd) *(rec Feb-Mar 1995)* ("Complete Sonatas for Recorder, Vol. 2") STRV ▲ 33391 (16.97)

Sonata for 2 Viols & Continuo

Maryland Bach Aria Group members [played on vc & bn] ("The Italian Voyage") † Salmo Decimoquinto; J. S. Bach:Cant 110; Cant 20; Stradella:Sinf alla Serenata; Torelli:Son Tpt, G.1 CRYS ▲ 705 [DDD] (15.97)

MARCH, ANDREW (1973-

Marine-à travers les arbres for Orchestra

D. Harding (cnd), London SO *(rec London, England, Dec 1997)* † Borisova-Ollas:Wings of the Wind; D. Gasparini:Through the Looking Glass; Hartke:Ascent of the Equestrian in a Balloon; Z. Long:Poems from Tang; C. Vine:Descent EMIC (Debut) ▲ 72826 [DDD] (6.97)

MARCHAND, LOUIS (1669-1732)

Pieces for Organ [4 Books]

P. Bardon (org) ("Organists at the Court of the Sun King") † Clérambault:Premier livre d'orgue; J. F. Dandrieu:Offertoire sur les Grands Jeux pour la Fête; Raison:Vive-le-Roy des Parisiens PVY ▲ 784011 [ADD] (16.97)

P. van Copponolle (org), Ensemble Quintessence RENE ▲ 87141 [DDD] (16.97)

J. Payne (org) *(rec Univ. of Vermont Burlington, Mar 1994)* ("Early French Organ Music, Vol. 1") † L. Compère:Org Music; G. Corrette:Messe du huitième ton à l'usage des dame; Grigny:Org Music; Japart:Fortuna d'un gran tempo NXIN ▲ 553214 [DDD] (5.97)

M. Touyère (org) *(rec Sain-François-de-Sales Genève)* † Boyvin:Premier livre Org; Grigny:Org Music; Guilain:Pièces d'orgue pour le Magnificat GALL ▲ 952 [ADD] (18.97)

MARCHETTI, FILIPO (1831-1902)

Ruy Blas (selections)

N. Margarit (sop), S. Frontalini (cnd), Moldava SO *(rec Sept 1997)* ("Rare Operatic Arias") † Floridia:Maruzza (sels); Gomes:Guarany (sels); Leoncavallo:Arias; G. Puccini:Edgar (sels) BONG ▲ 2528 [DDD] (16.97)

MARCIANO, SERGIO (20th cent)

Organ Music (complete)

S. Marciano (org) BONG 7-▲ 5590 (63.97)

MARCO, TOMÁS (1942-

Árbol de arcángeles (serenata virtual) for String Orchestra (1995)

J. Pons (cnd), Granada City Orch † Con del alma; Ojos verdes de luna BIS ▲ 811 [DDD] (17.97)

Concierto del alma for Violin & String Orchestra (1982)

V. Martín (vn), J. Pons (cnd), Granada City Orch † Árbol de arcángeles; Ojos verdes de luna BIS ▲ 811 [DDD] (17.97)

Fandangos, Fados y Tangos for 2 Pianos (or Piano 4-Hands) (1991)

K. Mrongovius (pno), B. Uriarte (pno) *(rec Madrid, Spain, Apr 1, 1998)* † Glasperlenspiel; Barce:Nuevas Polifonias; Guinjoan:Flamenco; J. Soler:Coronación WER ▲ 6634 [DDD]

Glasperlenspiel [Glass Bead Game] for 2 Pianos (1993-94)

K. Mrongovius (pno), B. Uriarte (pno) *(rec Madrid, Spain, Apr 1, 1998)* † Fandangos; Barce:Nuevas Polifonias; Guinjoan:Flamenco; J. Soler:Coronación WER ▲ 6634 [DDD]

Ojos verdes de luna for Soprano, 2 Percussionists & String Orchestra [after G. A. Bécquer & Ariosto]

M. J. Montiel (sop), J. Pons (cnd), Granada City Orch † Árbol de arcángeles; Con del alma BIS ▲ 811 [DDD] (17.97)

Tarots (22 pieces) for Guitar

J. C. Laguna (gtr) URT ▲ 5 [DDD] (16.97)

Trio concertante No. 1 for Piano, Violin & Cello (1983)

Mompou Trio Madrid † Alvez:Trio; Blanquer:Celista; J. L. Turina:Trio Pno RTVE ▲ 65014 (16.97)

MARCO DA L'AQUILA (16th cent)

Lute Music

P. O'Dette (lt)—Ricercar; Il est bel et bon; Ricercar Lautre jour No. 101; Nous bergiers; La traditora No. 3; Ricercar No. 16; La traditora No. 2; La battaglia; Ricercar No. 33 *(rec Sept 28-29, 1990 & Feb 22, 1992)* ("Dolcissima et Amorosa: Early Italian Renaissance Lute Music") † Borrono:Lt Music; Francesco Canova da Milano:Fants Lt; Ripa (da Mantova):Lt Music HAM ▲ 907043 (18.97)

MARCUS, BUNITA (20th cent)

Adam and Eve for Ensemble

M. Gibson (vn), J. Gordon (vc), S. Stenger (fl), S. Bauer (pno), Y. K. Chung (perc), T. Goldstein (perc), B. Marcus (cnd) *(rec NYC, NY, 1989, 1992)* ("Bang on a Can - Live, Vol. 3") † L. Bouchard:Lung Ta; Didkovsky:I Kick My Hand; O. J. Garcia:Colores Ultraviolados; P. Reller:Carcass; M. Wright:Lizard Belly Moon CRI ▲ 672 [DDD] (16.97)

MAREK, CZESLAW (1891-1985)

Capriccio for Orchestra (1914)

G. Brain (cnd), Philharmonia Orch ("Vol. 2") † Serenade Vn; Sinfonietta KSCH ▲ 364402

Choral Music

Polish Hymn; Death Melody; Greeting; Alps † Rural Scenes, Op. 30; Village Songs, Op. 34 KSCH ▲ 364412 (16.97)

Méditations for Orchestra, Op. 14 (1911-13)

G. Brain (cnd), Philharmonia Orch ("Complete Works, Vol. 1") † Sinfonia; Suita KSCH ▲ 6439 (16.97)

Rural Scenes [Na wsi] for High Voice & Chamber Orchestra, Op. 30 (1929)

J. Fischer (sop), R. Tschupp (cnd), Zurich Camerata *(rec 1993-94)* ("Von der Spätromantik zur Moderne: Schweizer Musik in der Zentralbibliothek Zürich") † Toccata Pno, Op. 27/2; O. Schoeck:Pieces Pno, Op. 29; W. Vogel:Hörformen; Intervalle; Variétude JEC ▲ 306

E. Szmytka (sop), G. Brain (cnd), London Philharmonia † Choral Music; Village Songs, Op. 34 KSCH ▲ 364412 (16.97)

Serenade for Violin & Orchestra (1916-18)

I. Turban (vn), G. Brain (cnd), Philharmonia Orch ("Vol. 2") † Capriccio; Sinfonietta KSCH ▲ 364402

Sinfonia for Orchestra (1927)

G. Brain (cnd), Philharmonia Orch ("Complete Works, Vol. 1") † Méditations, Op. 14; Suita KSCH ▲ 6439 (16.97)

Sinfonietta for Orchestra (1914-16)

G. Brain (cnd), Philharmonia Orch ("Vol. 2") † Capriccio; Serenade Vn KSCH ▲ 364402

Suita for Orchestra, Op. 25 (1925)

G. Brain (cnd), Philharmonia Orch ("Complete Works, Vol. 1") † Méditations, Op. 14; Sinfonia KSCH ▲ 6439 (16.97)

Toccata for Piano, Op. 27/2

W. Bärtschi (pno) *(rec 1993-94)* ("Von der Spätromantik zur Moderne: Schweizer Musik in der Zentralbibliothek Zürich") † Rural Scenes, Op. 30; O. Schoeck:Pieces Pno, Op. 29; W. Vogel:Hörformen; Intervalle; Variétude JEC ▲ 306

Village Songs for Soprano & Orchestra, Op. 34

E. Szmytka (sop), G. Brain (cnd), London Philharmonia † Choral Music; Rural Scenes, Op. 30 KSCH ▲ 364412 (16.97)

MARENCO, ROMUALDO (1841-1907)

Teodora [ballet] for Orchestra (1889)

S. Frontalini (cnd), Volgograd PO *(rec Volgograd Philharmonic, Volgograd, Russia, Dec 11, 1991)* BONG ▲ 2140 (live) [DDD] (16.97)

MARENZIO, LUCA (1553-1599)

Motets

G. Monaco (cnd), Insieme vocale e strumentale di Progretto Musica, G. Monaco (cnd), Ensemble Perfidie Armoniche—Motectorum Pro Festis Totus Anni [(parte seconda) Mottetti 23-42] TACT ▲ 551302 (16.97)

Qual mormorio soave for Chorus (1584)

M. Berry (cnd), Schola Gregoriana of Cambridge *(rec Apr 1998)* ("Angels from the Vatican") † Anonymous:Agnus Dei; Alleluia, assumpta est Maria; Angeli, Archangeli; Angelis suis mandavitde te; Angelus Domini descendit; Ave Maria; Benedicite Dominum; Christe, sanctorum decus Angelorum; Dixit Angelus ad Iacob; Domine Jesu Christe; Exsultet iam Angelica turba caelorum; Facta est cum Angelo; Gloria; Hodie nobis caelorum Rex; In Paradisum; Kyrie; Sanctus; Stetit Angelus; Te laudamus; Te Deum laudamus; Palestrina:Ave Regina coelorum; Venit Michaël Archangelus; Traditional:Angelus ad pastores ait; Victoria:Duo Seraphim HER ▲ 220 [DDD] (18.97)

MAREZ OYENS, TERA DE (1932-

Charon's Gift for Piano & Tape (1982)

T. de Marez Oyens (pno) † Litany; Sinf Testimonial CV ▲ 8702 [AAD]

▲ = CD ♦ = Enhanced CD △ = MD ▮ = Cassette Tape ▯ = DCC

MAREZ OYENS, TERA DE (cont.)
Hymns (3) for Soprano & Piano [text M. Arnoni] (1979)
M. Michael (sop), T. de Marez Oyens (pno) ("Intimate Thoughts") † Cacioppo:Wolf; Constantinides:Intimations; D. K. Eastman:Just Us; E. Lauer:Songs on Poems of James Joyce CPS ▲ 8632 (16.97)
Litany of the Victims of War for Orchestra (1985)
J. Stulen (cnd), Hilversum Radio Orch † Charon's Gift; Sinf Testimonial CV ▲ 8702 [AAD]
Sinfonia Testimonial for Orchestra, Chorus & Tape (1987)
K. Montgomery (cnd), Hilversum Radio Orch, Hilversum Radio Chorus † Charon's Gift; Litany CV ▲ 8702 [AAD]
MARGOLA, FRANCO (1908-1992)
Concertos (2) for Guitar & Strings
C. Piastra (gtr), Accademia Farnese † Castelnuovo-Tedesco:Qnt Gtr Strs, Op. 143 MONM (La nuova musica Italiana) ▲ 96007 (17.97)
Flute Music
G. Petrucci (fl)—Qt 7 Fl & Strs, dC.87; La Longobarda, dC.208; Son 4 Fl & Gtr, dC.191; Impressioni (5) Fl & Gtr, dC.698; Duo Fl & Va, dC.104 [w. Enrico Balboni (va)]; Partita Fl & Ob, dC.115; Duetti (6) Fls, dC.184 [w. Manuela Tiberi (fl)]; Contrasti Fl & Db, dC.324; Notturino, dC.80; Pezzi (3), dC.116; Son Fl, dC.230 [all w. Paola Pisa (pno)]; Eppigrami Greci (3), dC.126 ("Opere per flauto") BONG ▲ 5058 [DDD] (16.97)
Guitar Music
P. Spadetto (gtr)—Sons 1-2 Gtr; 6 Bagatelles; Trittico; Meditativo; Ballata; Caccia; Ultimo Canto; 8 Miniatures; 2 Etudes ("The Essential Music for Guitar") PHEX (Rainbow) ▲ 9701 (16.97)
Music of Margola
F. Lama (vn), S. Bertoletti (pno)—Sons 1 & 4 Vn; Son breve 3; Piccola Son DI ▲ 920444 [DDD] (5.97)
MARGOLIS, AL (20th cent)
Music of Margolis
if, bwana—3 out of 4 ain't bad; PR-DR; Tripping India ("Tripping India") POGU ▲ 21013 [DDD] (16.97)
artists unknown *(Breathing), (R.Ism V.2PF; Barump Poe) (rec 1996)* ("Breathing") POGU ▲ 21010 [DDD] (16.97)
MARGOLIS, JEROME (1941-
Terpsichore for Orchestra
E. Corporon (cnd), Cincinnati Wind SO ("Postcards") † J. Adams:Short Ride in a Fast Machine; D. Milhaud:Suite française, Op. 248; R. Nelson:Passacaglia Orch; Ticheli:Postcard KLAV ▲ 11058 (18.97)
MARIN, JOSE (ca 1618-1699)
Songs
M. Figueras (sop), R. Lislevand (gtr), P. Estevan (perc), A. Gonzales-Campa (perc) ("Tonos Humanos") AVOX ▲ 9802 (18.97)
J. Savall (cnd), Hespèrion XX—Aquella Sierra Nevada *(rec Séon, Switzerland, Sep 1976)* ("El Barroco Espanol") † Cabanilles:Music of Cabanilles; Durón:Sosieguen Descansen; J. Hidalgo:Songs; Martín y Coll:Songs; Milanes:Songs; Vado:Songs VCL ▲ 61346 [ADD] (11.97)
MARINER, FRANCISCO (fl 1742-1771)
Toccata in C for Flute & Continuo
Barcelona Consort *(rec Barcelona, Sept 1994)* ("Affetti Musicali") † Castello:Sonate concertate in stil moderno; Oliver y Astorga:Sons Fls, Op. 3; Pla:Trio Son 12; M. Soler:Son Bn; Telemann:Essercizii Musici; Musique de Table LAMA ▲ 2020 [DDD] (17.97)
MARINI, BIAGIO (ca 1587-1663)
Affetti musicali for 1-3 Violins & Continuo, Op. 1 (1617)
Affetti Musicali—Cornera; Bocca; Zorzi; Martinenga; Albana; Candela *(rec Micahaelis-Kirche, Ronnenberg Hannover, Germany, May 1995)* ("Marini und seine Zeitgenossen") † Sons, Syms & Retornelli, Op. 8; Buonamente:Quarto libro de varie Sonate, Sinfonie, Gagliarde; Castello:Sonate concertate in stil moderno; Frescobaldi:Primo libro d'intavolatura di toccate di cembalo e; G. Picchi:Pieces Hpd; S. Rossi:Terzo libro, Op. 12 THOR ▲ 2279 [DDD] (16.97)
Conserto Vago *(rec Genova, Feb 1994)* AG ▲ 85 [DDD] (16.97)
Lacrime di Davide sparse nel miserere for 2-4 (or More) Voices, 2 Violins & Organ, Op. 21
A. Casari (cnd), Gli Erranti STRV ▲ 33474 (16.97)
Music of Marini
Corde—Son per sonar; Son prima; Son sopra Fuggi; Canzon prima a 4 Cnts; Aria,"la Soranza"; Son ecco; Son senza cadenza; Canzon Ottava a 6; Capriccio for 2 Vns & Strs; Balletto secondo; Son Vn; Son Vns; Sinf:La Zorzi; Canzon 5 a 4; Son La Foscarina; Son seconda; Sons, Syms & Retornelli, Op. 8 [Son a 3 sopra La Monica]; Son variata *(rec 1995)* ("Echos from Venice") DAPH ▲ 1004 [DDD] (16.97)
E. Galli (sop), P. Beier (cnd) ("Allegrezza del Nuovo Maggio") STRV ▲ 33446 [DDD] (16.97)
Icarus Ensemble—La Foscarina; Son terza † Castello:Music of Castello; Cazzati:Music of Cazzati; Falconieri:Music of Falconieri; Frescobaldi:Canzona Vigesimaottava; Canzona Vigesimasettima; Toccata Quarta; Kapsberger:Toccata arpeggiata; F. Turini:Sons Vns CLAV ▲ 509817 (16.97)
La Fenice Ensemble—Intrada:Canzon octava; Son seconda; Madre non mi far monaca; Son sopra la Monica; Aria,"la Soranza"; Capriccio for 2 Vns & Strs; Grotte ombrose; Son Org & Cnt; Son La Foscarina; Ligature e durezze; Canzon prima a 4 Cnts; Sinf:Passacalio a 4; Miserere a 3 voci ("Moderne e Curiose Inventioni") RICE ▲ 205852 (17.97)
Sonatas, Symphonies & Retornelli for 1-6 Instruments, Op. 8 (1629)
Affetti Musicali—Sons prima, seconda & quarta; Son a 3 sopra La Monica *(rec Micahaelis-Kirche, Ronnenberg Hannover, Germany, May 1995)* ("Marini und seine Zeitgenossen") † Affetti musicali, Op. 1; Buonamente:Quarto libro de varie Sonate, Sinfonie, Gagliarde; Castello:Sonate concertate in stil moderno; Frescobaldi:Primo libro d'intavolatura di toccate di cembalo e; G. Picchi:Pieces Hpd; S. Rossi:Terzo libro, Op. 12 THOR ▲ 2279 [DDD] (16.97)
Convivium ("Early Italian Violin Sonatas") † Castello:Sonate concertate in stil moderno; Cima:Music of; Stradella:Music of; Uccellini:Music of HYP ▲ 66985 (18.97)
M. Kiehr (sop), Concerto Soave ("Sacri Musicali Affetti") † Giancelli:Tastegiati; Merula:Music of Merula; B. Strozzi:Sacred Music ED ▲ 13048 (18.97)
La Romanesca ("Curiose & Moderne Inventioni") HAM ▲ 907175 (18.97)
MARKEVITCH, IGOR (1912-1983)
Cantique d'amour for Orchestra (1936)
C. Lyndon-Gee (cnd), Arnhem PO *(rec Arnhem The Netherlands, Dec 7, 1995)* ("Complete Orchestral Music, Vol. 2") † Concerto grosso; Envol d'Icare Orch MARC ▲ 8223666 [DDD] (13.97)
Cinéma-Ouverture for Orchestra (1931)
C. Lyndon-Gee (cnd), Arnhem PO *(rec Arnhem The Netherlands, Dec 6-7, 1995)* ("Complete Orchestral Music, Vol. 1") † Nouvel âge; Sinfonietta MARC ▲ 8223653 [DDD] (13.97)
Concerto grosso for Orchestra (1930)
C. Lyndon-Gee (cnd), Arnhem PO *(rec Arnhem The Netherlands, June 10-11, 1996)* ("Complete Orchestral Music, Vol. 2") † Cantique; Envol d'Icare Orch MARC ▲ 8223666 [DDD] (13.97)
Hymnes for Orchestra (1933)
C. Lyndon-Gee (cnd), Arnhem PO ("Complete Orchestral Music, Vol. 3") † Rébus MARC ▲ 8223724 [DDD] (13.97)
L'Envol d'Icare (ballet) for Orchestra [arr for Piano as La Mort d'Icare] (1932)
C. Lyndon-Gee (cnd), Arnhem PO *(rec Arnhem The Netherlands, Dec 5-6, 1995)* ("Complete Orchestral Music, Vol. 2") † Cantique; Concerto grosso MARC ▲ 8223666 [DDD] (13.97)
Lorenzo il Magnifico for Soprano & Orchestra (1940)
L. Shelton (sop), C. Lyndon-Gee (cnd), Arnhem PO *(rec Arnheim, Netherlands, Sept 3-6, 1996)* † Psaume MARC ▲ 8223882 [DDD] (13.97)
Le Nouvel âge for Orchestra (1938)
C. Lyndon-Gee (cnd), Arnhem PO *(rec Arnhem The Netherlands, Dec 6-7, 1995)* ("Complete Orchestral Music, Vol. 1") † Cinéma-Ouverture; Sinfonietta MARC ▲ 8223653 [DDD] (13.97)
Psaume for Soprano & Orchestra (1933)
S. von Osten (sop), I. Markevitch (cnd), Swiss Romande Orch *(rec live, 1982)* † I. Stravinsky:Sacre du printemps CASC ▲ 2004 (16.97)
L. Shelton (sop), C. Lyndon-Gee (cnd), Arnhem PO *(rec Arnheim, Netherlands, Sept 3-6, 1996)* † Lorenzo il Magnifico MARC ▲ 8223882 [DDD] (13.97)
Rébus (ballet) for Orchestra (1931)
C. Lyndon-Gee (cnd), Arnhem PO ("Complete Orchestral Music, Vol. 3") † Hymnes Orch MARC ▲ 8223724 [DDD] (13.97)
Sinfonietta in F for Orchestra (1928-29)
C. Lyndon-Gee (cnd), Arnhem PO *(rec Arnhem The Netherlands, Dec 6-7, 1995)* ("Complete Orchestral Music, Vol. 1") † Cinéma-Ouverture; Nouvel âge MARC ▲ 8223653 [DDD] (13.97)
MARKS, GODFREY (dates unknown)
Songs
P. Gale (sop), A. Mentschukoff (gtr)—Steering Home *(rec Cleveland, OH, Sep 1997)* † Anonymous:Songs; H. Birch:Songs; W. M. Hutchison:Songs; F. Pascal:Songs; C. A. White:Songs CENT ▲ 2389 [DDD] (16.97)
MAROS, MIKLÓS (1943-
Aurora for Orchestra
J. Hirokami (cnd), Stockholm Symphonic Wind Orch † Grondahl:Con Trbn; Mayuzumi:Ritual Ov; Mendelssohn (-Bartholdy):Ov Wind, Op. 24; Sallinen:Chorali; Schoenberg:Theme & Vars Band, Op. 43a CAPA ▲ 21516 (16.97)
Burattinata for Saxophone & Piano
J. Kelly (sax), B. Versteegh (pno) ("Saxophone & Piano 3") † Denhoff:Unverändert verandert; Keuris:Canzone Sax; Rojko:Godba; D. Terzakis:Holle Nachklang COLG ▲ 31891 (18.97)
Saxazione for 18 Saxophones
L. Bangs-Urban (bar sax), L. Bangs-Urban (cnd), South German Saxophone CO ("Saxazione") † W. W. Glaser:Konzertstück; Pieces Saxes; E. von Koch:Moderato PHNS ▲ 98 (16.97)
MAROS, RUDOLF (1917-1982)
Euphony No. 1 for Orchestra (1963)
G. Lehel (cnd), Budapest SO † Euphony 2; Euphony 3; Gemma; Kaleidoscope; Lament; Musica da camera HUN ▲ 31699 [AAD] (16.97)
Euphony No. 2 for Orchestra (1964)
G. Lehel (cnd), Budapest SO † Euphony 1; Euphony 3; Gemma; Kaleidoscope; Lament; Musica da camera HUN ▲ 31699 [AAD] (16.97)
Euphony No. 3 for Orchestra (1965)
G. Lehel (cnd), Budapest SO † Euphony 1; Euphony 2; Gemma; Kaleidoscope; Lament; Musica da camera HUN ▲ 31699 [AAD] (16.97)
Gemma (in memoriam Zoltán Kodály) for Orchestra (1968)
G. Lehel (cnd), Budapest SO † Euphony 1; Euphony 2; Euphony 3; Kaleidoscope; Lament; Musica da camera HUN ▲ 31699 [AAD] (16.97)
Kaleidoscope for Chamber Ensemble (1976)
A. Mihály (cnd), Budapest Chamber Ensemble † Euphony 1; Euphony 2; Euphony 3; Gemma; Lament; Musica da camera HUN ▲ 31699 [AAD] (16.97)
Lament for Soprano & Chamber Ensemble (1969)
E. Sziklay (sop), A. Mihály (cnd), Budapest Chamber Ensemble † Euphony 1; Euphony 2; Euphony 3; Gemma; Kaleidoscope; Musica da camera HUN ▲ 31699 [AAD] (16.97)
Musica da camera for 11 Instruments (1966)
A. Mihály (cnd), Budapest Chamber Ensemble † Euphony 1; Euphony 2; Euphony 3; Gemma; Kaleidoscope; Lament HUN ▲ 31699 [AAD] (16.97)
The Wedding at Ecser (ballet) for Orchestra & Chorus (1950)
R. Lantos (cnd), Hungarian State Folk Ensemble Orch, Hungarian State Folk Ensemble Chorus *(rec 1969)* ("Wedding at Ecser") † Anonymous:Csárdás; Csámpai:In Memory of Bihari; Csenki:Gypsy Dances of Hungary; L. Gulyás:Bottle Dance; Evening in the Spinning Room; Music from Szék; Triple Jumping Dance; Kodály:Kálló Double Dance HUN ▲ 18008 [AAD] (16.97)
MÁRQUEZ, ARTURO (1950-
Danzón No. 4 for Orchestra
B. J. Echenique (cnd), Orch of the Americas ("México Sinfonico") † Carrasco:Preludio Sinfónico; R. Castro:Minueto; J. M. Chávez:Huerfanita; Galindo:Poema de Neruda; Moncayo Garcia:Huapango; Sinfonieta; Zyman:Encuentros URT ▲ 20 (16.97)
Sonata for Orchestra
E. Diazmuñoz (cnd), Mexico City PO † Catán:Tu Son, Tu Risa, Tu Sonrisa; S. Contreras:Danza Negra; F. Ibarra:Sym 1; Moncada:Sym 1 CLMX ▲ 21009 (13.97)
MARQUINA, PASQUAL (dates unknown)
Espaãna Caãi for Guitar
G. Tinturin (gtr), N. C. Tinturin (pno) [arr Tinturin] *(rec Hollywood, CA)* † I. Albéniz:Suite española 1, Op. 47; Castelnuovo-Tedesco:Fant Gtr & Pno, Op. 145; Romancero gitano, Op. 152; M. de Falla:Vida breve (sels); M. Ravel:Pièce en forme de Habanera; P. Tinturin:Crazy Quilt of Memories; Latin Rhapsody; Syncopated Nocturne CMB ▲ 1099 (16.97)
MARSALIS, WYNTON (20th cent)
The Fiddler and the Dancin' Witch for Narrator, Violin & Orchestra
W. Marsalis (nar), J. Bell (vn), R. Sadin (cnd), St. Luke's Orch *(rec Masonic Grand Lodge, New York City, NY, Jan 8-14, 1998)* ("Listen to the Storyteller") † P. Doyle:Face in the Lake; E. Meyer:Lesson of the Land SNYC ▲ 60283 [DDD] (16.97) ▮ 60283 [DDD] (10.98)
MARSCHNER, HEINRICH AUGUST (1795-1861)
Bagatelles (12) for Guitar, Op. 4
T. Hoppstock (gtr) *(rec Darmstadt, 1995-96)* ("Werke für Gitarre") † Sor:Gtr Music; Werthmüller:Son Pno, Op. 17 SIGM ▲ 7500 [DDD] (17.97)
MARSH, JOHN (1752-1828)
A Conversation Symphony for 2 Orchestras (1784)
I. Graham-Jones (cnd), Chichester Concert [period instrs] † Sym 1; Sym 3; Sym 4; Sym 6 OLY (Explorer) ▲ 400 [DDD] (12.97)
Symphony No. 1 in B♭ (1783)
I. Graham-Jones (cnd), Chichester Concert [period instrs] † Conversation Sym; Sym 3; Sym 4; Sym 6 OLY (Explorer) ▲ 400 [DDD] (12.97)
Symphony No. 3 in D (?1770)
I. Graham-Jones (cnd), Chichester Concert [period instrs] † Conversation Sym; Sym 1; Sym 4; Sym 6 OLY (Explorer) ▲ 400 [DDD] (12.97)
Symphony No. 4 in F (ca 1788)
I. Graham-Jones (cnd), Chichester Concert [period instrs] † Conversation Sym; Sym 1; Sym 3; Sym 6 OLY (Explorer) ▲ 400 [DDD] (12.97)
Symphony No. 6 in D (1784)
I. Graham-Jones (cnd), Chichester Concert [period instrs] † Conversation Sym; Sym 1; Sym 3; Sym 4 OLY (Explorer) ▲ 400 [DDD] (12.97)
MARSHALL, INGRAM (1942-
Alcatraz (sound-scape of Alcatraz prison) [recorded on-site] (1982-84)
I. Marshall (elec) NALB ▲ 40 [DDD] (16.97)
Cortez (electronic music) [after McCaig] (1970)
S. McCaig (voc), I. Marshall (elec) *(rec 1961-73)* ("Columbia-Princeton Electronic Music Center") † B. Arel:Music for a Sacred Service; Out of into; C. Dodge:Earth's Magnetic Field; I. K. Mimaroglu:Prelude 8, "To the Memory of Varèse"; Semegen:Elec Comp 1; A. Shields:Dance Piece 3; Study Voc & Tape NWW ▲ 80521 (16.97)
Entrada (At the River) for String Quartet amplified with processing (1984)
Maia String Quartet † Evensongs; In My Beginning NALB ▲ 92 (16.97)
Evensongs for String Quartet (1991-92; rev 1996)
Maia String Quartet *(rec Purchase New York, Feb 1996)* † Entrada; In My Beginning NALB ▲ 92 (16.97)
Fog Tropes for Brass Sextet, Fog Horns & Tape (1982)
J. Adams (cnd) † Gambuh 1; Gradual Requiem NALB ▲ 2 [ADD] (16.97)
J. Adams (cnd), Orch of St. Luke's ("American Elegies") † J. Adams:Eros Pno; D. Diamond:Elegy in Memory of Ravel; M. Feldman:Madame Press; C. Ives:Songs; Unanswered Question NON ▲ 79249 [DDD] (16.97)
Gambuh 1 for Gambuh [Balinese bamboo flute], Synthesizer & Tape Delay (1972-75)
I. Marshall (elec/gam), F. Reed (tape) † Fog Tropes; Gradual Requiem NALB ▲ 2 [ADD] (16.97)
Gradual Requiem for Voices, Synthesizer, Mandolin, Gambuh, Piano & Tape Delay
I. Marshall (elec/gam), F. Reed (tape) † Fog Tropes; Gambuh 1 NALB ▲ 2 [ADD] (16.97)
Hidden Voices (electronic music) (1989)
artists unknown [electronically manipulated acoustic instrumental &] † 3 Penitential Visions NON ▲ 79227 (16.97)
In My Beginning Is My End for Piano Quartet (1986-87; rev 1995)
Dunsmuir Piano Quartet *(rec Berkeley, CA, May 1996)* † Entrada; Evensongs NALB ▲ 92 (16.97)
Three Penitential Visions (electronic music) (1986)
[electronically manipulated acoustic instrumental &] † Hidden Voices NON ▲ 79227 (16.97)
MARTÁ, ISTVÁN (1952-
Doom. A Sigh for String Quartet
Kronos Quartet † G. Crumb:Black Angels (Images I); C. Ives:They Are There!; D. Shostakovich:Qt 8 Strs, Op. 110; Tallis:Spem in alium NON ▲ 79242 (16.97)
The Wind Rises for Chamber Ensemble (1985)
I. Martá (voc), E. Szkárosi (voc), Ş. Bernáth (voc), M. Sebestyén (voc), F. Nagy (voc), C. Szabó (voc), T. Cseh (voc), K. Nagy (nar), S. Bernáth (gtr), A. Török (fl), T. Szemző (pipes), L. Dés (sax), G. Róbert (shm), P. Füzes (hn), L. Göz (trbn), T. Kiss (hp), K. Balog (cembalo), I. Martá (perc/syn), E. Szkárosi (dr/elec), Mandel Quartet, Amadinda Group, WYXIMPHONIC group RREC ▲ 91 [DDD] (18.97)

MARTH, MATTHEW (1967-
They're Still Running to the West, Rex for Cello, Speaking Cellist & Electronic Tape (1992)
C. Hultgren (vc) ("Music of the Next Moment - Craig Hultgren") † Burrier:II; C. Hultgren:Chained Vc Improvisation; Double Bow Improvisation; C. N. Mason:Artist & His Model; L. Nielson:Valentine Mechanique; R. Paredes:Small Writing; J. C. Ross:Encore Vc INNO ▲ 502 (14.97)

MARTIN, FRANK (1890-1974)
Ballade for Alto Saxophone & Orchestra (1938)
M. Robertson (a sax), M. Bamert (cnd), London PO ("Ballades") † Ballade Fl; Ballade Pno; Ballade Trb; Ballade Va, Www, Hpd & Hp; Ballade Vc CHN ▲ 9380 [DDD] (16.97)
Ballade for Cello & Piano (or Orchestra) (1949)
Britten-Pears Ensemble † Ballade Fl; Qnt Pno; Son Vn; Sonnets à Cassandre ASV ▲ 1010 (16.97)
W. Conway (vc), P. Evans (pno) † Debussy:Son Vc; F. Poulenc:Son Vc HODU ▲ 2 (16.97)
P. Dixon (vc), M. Bamert (cnd), London PO ("Ballades") † Ballade A Sax; Ballade Fl; Ballade Pno; Ballade Trb; Ballade Va, Www, Hpd & Hp CHN ▲ 9380 [DDD] (16.97)
Ballade for Flute & Piano (or Flute, String Orchestra & Piano) (1939)
S. Baron (fl), U. Barnea (cnd), Billings SO [orchestral version] † Donizetti:Study Cl; Ewazen:Ballade; D. E. Jones:Still Voices; Piston:Con Cl; Con Fl; Presser:Partita Cl; G. Rossini:Vars Cl CRSR ▲ 8840
J. Baxtresser (fl), P. Muzijevic (pno) *(rec Bronxville, NY, 1996)* ("New York Legends") † Amirov:Pieces Fl; Debussy:Prélude à l'après-midi d'un faune; P. Gaubert:Three Water Colours; W. Gieseking:Sonatine Fl; Taktakishvili:Son Fl CAL ▲ 512 [DDD] (15.97)
Britten-Pears Ensemble † Ballade Vc; Qnt Pno; Son Vn; Sonnets à Cassandre ASV ▲ 1010 (16.97)
R. Brown (fl), R. Kapp (cnd) [orchestral version] † Con for 7 Winds; Petite sym concertante ESSY ▲ 1014 [DDD] (16.97)
C. Chambers (fl), R. Elms (pno), M. Bamert (cnd), London PO ("Ballades") † Ballade A Sax; Ballade Pno; Ballade Trb; Ballade Va, Www, Hpd & Hp; Ballade Vc CHN ▲ 9380 [DDD] (16.97)
A. Duchemin (fl), M. Duchemin (pno), M. Bélanger (cnd), Montreal Metropolitan Orch † Ibert:Pièce Fl; Kabalevsky:Con Vn; Kennan:Night Soliloquy; H. Lipsky:Trois Images SNE ▲ 2033 (16.97)
A. Duchemin (fl), M. Duchemin (pno), B. Jean (cnd), Montreal Metropolitan Orch [orchestral version] † Ibert:Pièce Fl; Kabalevsky:Con Vn; Kennan:Night Soliloquy; H. Lipsky:Images PAVA ▲ 7197 (10.97)
S. Milan (fl), M. Dussek (pno), R. Hickox (cnd), City of London Sinfonia ("La flûte enchantée") † Chaminade:Concertino Fl, Op. 107; B. Godard:Suite de trois morceaux, Op. 116; Saint-Saëns:Airs de ballet d'Ascanio CHN ▲ 8840 [DDD] (16.97)
A. Pépin (fl), F. Martin (cnd), Swiss Romande Orch *(rec 1951-67)* † Con Vc; Petite sym concertante; Sturm (sels) CASC ▲ 2001 (16.97)
J. Walter (fl), S. Kurz (cnd), Dresden Staatskapelle *(rec Dresden, Germany)* ("Virtuose Flötenmusik") † Debussy:Son Fl; Syrinx Fl; Ibert:Con Fl; Jolivet:Suite en concert *(E, F, G text)* BER ▲ 9161 [ADD] (10.97)
M. Wiesler (fl), J. Jacobson (pno) *(rec Malmö Concert Hall, Sweden, Apr 1990)* ("Vocal & Chamber Music") † Étude de lecture; Ballade Trb; Chants de Noël; Preludes; Son da chiesa BIS ▲ 71 [AAD/DDD] (17.97)
Ballade for Piano & Orchestra (1939)
R. Elms (pno), M. Bamert (cnd), London PO ("Ballades") † Ballade A Sax; Ballade Fl; Ballade Trb; Ballade Va, Www, Hpd & Hp; Ballade Vc CHN ▲ 9380 [DDD] (16.97)
C. Lindberg (trbn), R. Pöntinen (pno) † L. Berio:Sequenza V; P. Hindemith:Son Trbn BIS ▲ 258 [DDD] (17.97)
Ballade for Trombone (or Tenor Saxophone) & Piano (or Orchestra) (1940)
I. Bousfield (trbn), M. Bamert (cnd), London PO ("Ballades") † Ballade A Sax; Ballade Fl; Ballade Pno; Ballade Va, Www, Hpd & Hp; Ballade Vc CHN ▲ 9380 [DDD] (16.97)
C. Lindberg (trbn), R. Pöntinen (pno) *(rec Nacka Aula, Sweden, Nov 11, 1983)* ("Vocal & Chamber Music") † Étude de lecture; Ballade Fl; Chants de Noël; Preludes; Son da chiesa BIS ▲ 71 [AAD/DDD] (17.97)
C. Lindberg (trbn), L. Segerstam (cnd), Swedish RSO ("Trombone Odyssey: 20th Century Landmarks For Trombone & Orchestra") † E. Bloch:Sym Trb; J. Sandström:Con Trbn; Serocki:Con Trbn BIS ▲ 538 [DDD] (17.97)
Ballade for Viola, Winds, Harpsichord & Harp (1972)
P. Dukes (va), M. Bamert (cnd), London PO ("Ballades") † Ballade A Sax; Ballade Fl; Ballade Pno; Ballade Trb; Ballade Vc CHN ▲ 9380 [DDD] (16.97)
Chants de Noël (3) for Soprano, Flute & Piano [text Rudhardt] (1947)
J. Delman (sop), G. von Bahr (fl), L. Negro (pno) *(rec Nacka Aula, Sweden, Aug 23, 1975)* ("Vocal & Chamber Music") † Étude de lecture; Ballade Fl; Ballade Trb; Preludes; Son da chiesa BIS ▲ 71 [AAD/DDD] (17.97)
A. S. von Otter (mez), A. Alin (fl), B. Forsberg (pno) *(rec Stockholm, Nov 1994)* ("La Bonne Chanson: French Chamber Songs") † E. Chausson:Chanson perpétuelle, Op. 37; M. Delage:Poèmes hindous; G. Fauré:Bonne chanson, Op. 61; F. Poulenc:Rapsodie nègre; M. Ravel:Poèmes de Mallarmé; Saint-Saëns:Flûte invisible DEUT ▲ 47752 [DDD] (16.97)
Concerto for Cello & Orchestra (1965-66)
P. Fournier (vc), E. Ansermet (cnd), Swiss Romande Orch *(rec 1951-67)* † Ballade Fl; Petite sym concertante; Sturm (sels) CASC ▲ 2001 (16.97)
Concerto for Violin & Orchestra (1950-51)
S. Canin (vn), K. Nagano (cnd), Berkeley SO *(rec Pittsburgh, CA, Feb 25-26, 1995)* † Etudes Str Orch; Maria-Triptychon NALB ▲ 86 (16.97)
W. Schneiderhan (vn), E. Ansermet (cnd), Swiss Romande Orch † Con for 7 Winds; In terra pax; Passacaglia Org; Petite sym concertante PLON (Double Decker) 2-▲ 448264 (17.97)
Concerto for 7 Winds, Wind Quintet, Trumpet, Trombone, Percussion & Strings (1949)
E. Ansermet (cnd), Swiss Romande Orch † Con Vn; In terra pax; Passacaglia Org; Petite sym concertante PLON (Double Decker) 2-▲ 448264 (17.97)
M. Bamert (cnd), London PO † Erasmi Monumentum; Etudes Str Orch CHN ▲ 9283 [DDD] (16.97)
R. Kapp (cnd) † Ballade Fl; Petite sym concertante ESSY ▲ 1014 [DDD] (16.97)
Danses (3) for Oboe, Harp & Strings (1970)
H. Schellenberger (ob), M. Süss (hp), Z. Peskó (cnd), Franz Liszt CO *(rec Budapest, Hungary, Apr 1996)* † Ibert:Symphonie concertante; W. Lutoslawski:Con Ob CAMM ▲ 130045 [DDD] (16.97)
Erasmi Monumentum for Orchestra (1969)
M. Bamert (cnd), London PO † Con for 7 Winds; Etudes Str Orch CHN ▲ 9283 [DDD] (16.97)
L. Lohmann (org) † In terra pax MOTE ▲ 40141 (17.97)
Étude de lecture for Piano (1966)
L. Negro (pno) *(rec Nacka Aula, Sweden, Oct 10, 1976)* ("Vocal & Chamber Music") † Ballade Fl; Ballade Trb; Chants de Noël; Preludes; Son da chiesa BIS ▲ 71 [AAD/DDD] (17.97)
Etudes for String Orchestra (1955-56)
M. Bamert (cnd), London PO † Con for 7 Winds; Erasmi Monumentum CHN ▲ 9283 [DDD] (16.97)
S. Canin (cnd), New Century CO *(rec Belvedere, CA, May 29, 1995)* † Con Vn; Maria-Triptychon NALB ▲ 86 (16.97)
A. Lascae (cnd) *(rec Oct 1994)* † Passacaglia Org; J. Françaix:Sym d'archets; Vars de concert OTT ▲ 109459 [DDD] (16.97)
Gesänge (5) des Ariel for a capella Choir [from opera Der Sturm] (1950)
J. Straube (cnd), North German Figural Choir, S. Fischer (sgr) *(rec St. Osdag Mandelsloh, Germany, 1994-1995)* † Mass for Double Chorus; Passacaglia Org THOR ▲ 2261 [DDD] (16.97)
In terra pax (oratorio) for Soprano, Alto, Tenor, Baritone, Bass, Orchestra & 2 Choruses [after the Bible] (1944)
E. Ansermet (cnd), Swiss Romande Orch † Con for 7 Winds; Con Vn; Passacaglia Org; Petite sym concertante PLON (Double Decker) 2-▲ 448264 (17.97)
M. Bamert (cnd), London PO, L. Heltay (cnd), Brighton Festival Chorus, J. Howarth (sop), D. Jones (mez), M. Hill (ten), S. Roberts (bar), R. Williams (bar) † Quatre éléments CHN ▲ 9465 (16.97)
L. Lohmann (org), Altenburg Cathedral Choir † Erasmi Monumentum MOTE ▲ 40141 (17.97)
Ludwig (cnd), Weisbaden Bach Orch, Weisbaden Bach Chorus MELI ▲ 27032 (17.97)
Maria-Triptychon for Soprano, Violin & Orchestra (1968-69)
S. Ganz (sop), S. Canin (vn), K. Nagano (cnd), Berkeley SO *(rec Pittsburgh, CA, Feb 25-26, 1995)* † Con Vn; Etudes Str Orch NALB ▲ 86 (16.97)
L. Russell (sop), D. Riddell (vn), M. Bamert (cnd), London PO † Monologe; Sturm CHN ▲ 9411 [DDD] (16.97)
Mass for Double Chorus (1922-26)
M. Corboz (cnd), Lausanne Vocal Ensemble ("Messes A Capella") † Monteverdi:Messa et salmi CASC ▲ 1025 [DDD] (16.97)
S. Darlington (cnd), Christ Church Cathedral Choir Oxford † F. Poulenc:Mass NIMB ▲ 5197 [DDD]
Mikaeli Chamber Choir † Pizzetti:Messa di Requiem PRPI ▲ 9965
H. Nickoll (cnd), Carmina Chamber Choir ("Choir Music of the 20th Century") † Haentjes:Easter Motets; Nickoll:Salve regina; Pärt:Magnificat for Chorus; R. Thompson:Alleluia EBS ▲ 6039 [DDD] (17.97)
J. O'Donnell (cnd), Westminster Cathedral Choir † Passacaglia Org; Pizzetti:De profundis; Messa di Requiem HYP ▲ 67017 (18.97)

MARTIN, FRANK (cont.)
Mass for Double Chorus (1922-26) (cont.)
R. Shaw (cnd), Robert Shaw Festival Singers *(rec Gramat France, July 26-28, 1994)* ("Evocation of the Spirit") † S. Barber:Agnus Dei; Górecki:Totus tuus; Pärt:Magnificat-Antiphones; Schoenberg:Friede auf Erden, Op. 13 TEL ▲ 80406 [DDD] (16.97)
J. Straube (cnd), North German Figural Choir *(rec St. Osdag Mandelsloh, Germany, Sept 1994-Mar 1995)* † Gesänge des Ariel; Passacaglia Org THOR ▲ 2261 [DDD] (16.97)
D. Warland (cnd), Dale Warland Singers *(rec St. Paul, MN, Aug 1994)* † G. Allegri:Miserere; S. Barber:Agnus Dei; H. Howells:Requiem AME ▲ 120 [DDD] (16.97) ▮ 120 [DDD] (10.98)
Monologe (6) aus "Jedermann" for Alto (or Baritone) & Piano [after H. von Hoffmansthal] (1943; orchd 1949)
D. Wilson-Johnson (bar), M. Bamert (cnd), London PO † Maria-Triptychon; Sturm CHN ▲ 9411 [DDD] (16.97)
Passacaglia for Organ [adapted Martin for large orch] (1944)
E. Ansermet (cnd), Swiss Romande Orch † Con for 7 Winds; Con Vn; In terra pax; Petite sym concertante PLON (Double Decker) 2-▲ 448264 (17.97)
M. Bamert (cnd), London PO † Sym; Sym concertante CHN ▲ 9312 [DDD] (16.97)
A. Lascae (cnd) *(rec Oct 1994)* † Etudes Str Orch; J. Françaix:Sym d'archets; Vars de concert OTT ▲ 109459 [DDD] (16.97)
J. O'Donnell (org) † Mass for Double Chorus; Pizzetti:De profundis; Messa di Requiem HYP ▲ 67017 (18.97)
U. Smidt (org) *(rec Wöhl Org of Petrikirche zu Cuxhaven, Germany, Sept 1994-Mar 1995)* † Gesänge des Ariel; Mass for Double Chorus THOR ▲ 2261 [DDD] (16.97)
Petite symphonie concertante for Harp, Harpsichord, Piano & 2 String Orchestras (1944-45)
E. Ansermet (cnd), Swiss Romande Orch *(rec 1951-67)* † Ballade Fl; Con Vc; Sturm (sels) CASC ▲ 2001 (16.97)
E. Ansermet (cnd), Swiss Romande Orch † Con for 7 Winds; Con Vn; In terra pax; Passacaglia Org PLON (Double Decker) 2-▲ 448264 (17.97)
V. Drake (hp), A. Newman (hpd), C. Hoca (pno), R. Kapp (cnd) † Ballade Fl; Con for 7 Winds ESSY ▲ 1014 [DDD] (16.97)
Pièces brèves (4) for Guitar (1933)
S. Grondona (gtr) ("Novecento") † José Martinez Palacios:Son Gtr; Krenek:Suite Gtr; E. Morricone:Pieces Gtr; Tansman:Cavatina Gtr PHEX ▲ 98419 (16.97)
J. Rost (gtr) *(rec Leipzig, Germany, Nov 1979)* † L. Brouwer:Micro piezas Gtr; F. Carulli:Little Duet Gtr, Op. 34/2; Narváez:Diferencias sobre Gtr; Guárdame las vacas Gtr; Seys libros del delphin (sels); J. Rodrigo:Invocación y danza; Sor:Grand Solo Gtr, Op. 14 BER ▲ 9331 [ADD] (10.97)
R. Smits (gtr), R. Smits (gtr) *(rec Boom, Belgium, July 1990)* † A. Barrios:Gtr Music; R. R. Bennett:Impromptus Gtr; Burkhart:Passacaglia Gtr; J. Morel:Sonatina Gtr; J. Turina:Son Gtr, Op. 61 ACCE ▲ 8966 [DDD] (17.97)
Poèmes païens (3) for Baritone & Orchestra [text de Lisle] (1910)
J. Van Dam (b-bar), S. Baudo (cnd), Swiss-Italian Orch † Berlioz:Nuits d'été, Op. 7 FORL ▲ 16768 (16.97)
Preludes (8) for Piano (1947-48)
L. Negro (pno) *(rec Nacka Aula, Sweden, Oct 10, 1976)* ("Vocal & Chamber Music") † Étude de lecture; Ballade Fl; Ballade Trb; Chants de Noël; Son da chiesa BIS ▲ 71 [AAD/DDD] (17.97)
D. Walsh (pno) † S. Barber:Son Pno, Op. 26; B. Bartók:Son Pno, Sz.80; S. Prokofiev:Son 2 Pno, Op. 14 MUA ▲ 4669 (10.97)
Les quatre éléments for Orchestra (1964)
M. Bamert (cnd), London PO † In terra pax CHN ▲ 9465 (16.97)
Quintet for Piano & Strings (1919)
Britten-Pears Ensemble † Ballade Fl; Ballade Vc; Son Vn; Sonnets à Cassandre ASV ▲ 1010 (16.97)
New Jersey Chamber Music Society † Duruflé:Prélude, récitatif et vars, Op. 3; Indy:Suite Fl, Str Trio & Hp, Op. 91 PREM ▲ 1032 [DDD] (16.97)
Sonata da chiesa for Viola d'amore & Organ [arr Flute & Organ, 1938] (1938, orchd 1938)
G. von Bahr (fl), H. Fagius (org) *(rec Härnösand Cathedral, Sweden, Feb 29, 1980)* ("Vocal & Chamber Music") † Étude de lecture; Ballade Fl; Ballade Trb; Chants de Noël; Preludes BIS ▲ 71 [AAD/DDD] (17.97)
Sonata for Violin & Piano (1931-32)
Britten-Pears Ensemble † Ballade Fl; Ballade Vc; Qnt Pno; Sonnets à Cassandre ASV ▲ 1010 (16.97)
Sonnets à Cassandre (4) for Mezzo-Soprano, Flute, Viola & Cello [text Ronsard] (1921)
B. Rearick (mez), Britten-Pears Ensemble † Ballade Fl; Ballade Vc; Qnt Pno; Son Vn ASV ▲ 1010 (16.97)
Der Sturm (opera in 3 acts) (1956)
M. Bamert (cnd), London PO † Maria-Triptychon; Monologe CHN ▲ 9411 [DDD] (16.97)
Der Sturm (selections)
D. Fischer-Dieskau (bar), E. Ansermet (cnd), Swiss Romande Orch *(rec 1951-67)* † Ballade Fl; Con Vc; Petite sym concertante CASC ▲ 2001 (16.97)
Symphonie concertante for Orchestra (1945)
M. Bamert (cnd), London PO † Passacaglia Org; Sym CHN ▲ 9312 [DDD] (16.97)
Symphony for Orchestra (1937)
M. Bamert (cnd), London PO † Passacaglia Org; Sym concertante CHN ▲ 9312 [DDD] (16.97)
Trio sur les mélodies populaires irlandaises for Piano, Violin & Cello (1925)
Osiris Trio ("Folk Music") † Beethoven:Trio 1 Pno, Op. 1/1; A. Dvořák:Trio 4 Pno, Op. 90; C. Ives:Trio; V. Novák:Trio Pno, Op. 27; D. Shostakovich:Trio 2 Pno, Op. 67 CCL 2-▲ 13098 (18.97)
Primavera Trio *(rec Claremont, CA, Nov-Dec 1994)* † F. Bridge:Phantasie Trio; F. Campo:Trio Pno CENT ▲ 2318 [DDD] (16.97)
Die Weise von Liebe und Tod des Cornets Christoph Rilke [The Way of Love & Death of the Cornet Christopher Rilke] for Contralto & Orchestra, "Der Cornet" (1942-43)
B. Balleys (mez), J. López-Cobos (cnd), Lausanne CO CASC ▲ 1020 (16.97)
P. Huttenlocher (bar), R. Dunand (cnd), Geneva Collegium Academicum *(rec Oct 8, 1984)* GALL ▲ 725 [ADD] (19.97)
M. Lipovšek (mez), L. Zagrosek (cnd), Austrian RSO [GER] ORF ▲ 164881 [DDD] (18.97)

MARTIN, HENRY (20th cent)
Preludes & Fugues (6) [Group 1] for Piano (1990)
D. Buechner (pno) *(rec Regis College Weston, MA, Aug 24-26, 1994)* † Preludes & Fugues (Group 2) GMR ▲ 2049 (16.97)
Preludes & Fugues (6) [Group 2] for Piano (1991-92)
D. Buechner (pno) *(rec Regis College Weston, MA, Aug 24-26, 1994)* † Preludes & Fugues (Group 1) GMR ▲ 2049 (16.97)

MARTIN, HUGH (1914-
Meet Me in St. Louis (selections)
M. Carewe (voc), E. Bernstein (cnd), Royal PO, J. McCarthy (cnd), Ambrosian Singers—The Trolley Song [arr Conrad Salinger] *(rec Goldsmiths' College, London, England, Aug 1989)* ("Original Scores from the MGM Classics") † N. H. Brown:Singin' in the Rain (sels); G. Forrest:Kismet (sels); F. Loewe:Brigadoon (sels); Gigi (sels); C. Porter:Pirate (sels); A. Schwartz:Band Wagon (sels); H. Warren:Ziegfeld Follies (selections) CHN ▲ 7053 [DDD] (13.97)

MARTIN, PHILIP (1947-
Beato Angelico for Orchestra (1989-90)
K. D. Roo (cnd), Ireland National SO *(rec 1995)* † Con Hp; Con 2 MARC (Irish Composer) ▲ 8223834 [DDD] (13.97)
Concerto for Harp & Orchestra (1993)
A. Malir (hp), K. D. Roo (cnd), Ireland National SO *(rec 1995)* † Beato Angelico; Con 2 MARC (Irish Composer) ▲ 8223834 [DDD] (13.97)
Concerto No. 2 for Piano & Orchestra (1991)
P. Martin (pno), K. D. Roo (cnd), Ireland National SO *(rec 1995)* † Beato Angelico; Con Hp MARC (Irish Composer) ▲ 8223834 [DDD] (13.97)
Elegies (2) for Violin & Piano (1993-94)
R. Colan (vn), P. Martin (pno) † Light Music; Rainbow Comes & Goes; Songs for the 4 Parts of the Night; Trio 1 Pno ALTA ▲ 9011
Light Music (cycle of 25 songs) for solo Voice & Piano (1992)
P. P. Jones (sop), P. Martin (pno) † Elegies; Rainbow Comes & Goes; Songs for the 4 Parts of the Night; Trio 1 Pno ALTA ▲ 9011
The Rainbow Comes & Goes (4 fragments) for Piano [after Wordsworth's Ode: Intimations of Immortality from Recollections of Early Childhood] (1987)
P. Martin (pno) † Elegies; Light Music; Songs for the 4 Parts of the Night; Trio 1 Pno ALTA ▲ 9011
Songs
P. P. Jones (sop), P. Martin (pno) ALTA ▲ 9009 (19.97)
Songs for the 4 Parts of the Night for solo Voice & Violin (1981)
P. P. Jones (sop), R. Colan (vn) † Elegies; Light Music; Rainbow Comes & Goes; Trio 1 Pno ALTA ▲ 9011
Trio No. 1 for Piano, Violin & Cello, "Serendipity" (1993)
Crawford Trio † Elegies; Light Music; Rainbow Comes & Goes; Songs for the 4 Parts of the Night ALTA ▲ 9011

▲ = CD ♦ = Enhanced CD △ = MD ▮ = Cassette Tape ▯ = DCC

MARTINEZ, MARIANNE (1744-1812)
Sonata in A for Harpsichord
B. Harbach (hpd) ("18th Century Women Composers: Music for Solo Harpsichord, Vol. 1") † Son in E Hpd; M. V. Auenbrugg:Son in E♭ Hpd; Barthélémon:Son Hpd; E. De Gambarini:Pieces Hpd, Op. 2; M. H. Park:Son Hpd, Op. 4 GAS ▲ 272 [DDD] (16.97)
M. Jakuc (pno) † Son in E Hpd; M. V. Auenbrugg:Son in E♭ Hpd; J. Haydn:Son 49 Kbd, H.XVI/36; Son 50 Kbd, H.XVI/37 TIT ▲ 214
Sonata in E for Harpsichord (1765)
B. Harbach (hpd) ("18th Century Women Composers: Music for Solo Harpsichord, Vol. 1") † Son in A Hpd; M. V. Auenbrugg:Son in E♭ Hpd; Barthélémon:Son Hpd; E. De Gambarini:Pieces Hpd, Op. 2; M. H. Park:Son Hpd, Op. 4 GAS ▲ 272 [DDD] (16.97)
M. Jakuc (pno) † Son in A Hpd; M. V. Auenbrugg:Son in E♭ Hpd; J. Haydn:Son 49 Kbd, H.XVI/36; Son 50 Kbd, H.XVI/37 TIT ▲ 214

MARTINEZ-SOBRAL, MANUEL (1879-1946)
Acuarelas Chapinas (4 scenes) for Orchestra (1907)
A. De Almeida (cnd), Moscow SO *(rec Moscow, Feb 1994)* ("Guatemala, Vol. 1") † R. Castillo:Guatemala for Orch; Guatemala for Pno; Sinfonietta; Xibalbá MARC (Latin American Classics) ▲ 8223710 [DDD] (13.97)

MARTINI, GIOVANNI BATTISTA (1706-1784)
Sonata al'Postcommunio for Organ
B. Kratzer (tpt), M. Nuber (org) [arr for tpt & org] *(rec Münster zu Villingen, Germany, Feb 1990)* ("Virtuoso Trumpet Music of the Baroque") † Toccata; Albinoni:Cons Tpt & Org; H. Purcell:Cons Tpt & Org; Stradella:Sinf alla Serenata; Telemann:Qnt Tpt; Torelli:Con Tpt; J. G. Walther:Cons Tpt & Org FERM ▲ 20001 [DDD] (16.97)
Sonata for Cello & Harpsichord Obbligato
Concerto Ensemble † Berteau:Trio (Son Sesta); Cervetto:Sons Vc; G. B. Cirri:Son Prima; Son Terza TACT ▲ 680001 (16.97)
Toccata for Keyboard
B. Kratzer (tpt), M. Nuber (org) [arr for tpt & org] *(rec Münster zu Villingen, Germany, Feb 1990)* ("Virtuoso Trumpet Music of the Baroque") † Son al'Postcommunio; Albinoni:Cons Tpt & Org; H. Purcell:Cons Tpt & Org; Stradella:Sinf alla Serenata; Telemann:Qnt Tpt; Torelli:Con Tpt; J. G. Walther:Cons Tpt & Org FERM ▲ 20001 [DDD] (16.97)

MARTINI, JOHANN PAUL AEGIDIUS (1741-1816)
Plaisir d'Amour (song)
R. Kapp (cnd), Philharmonia Virtuosi, New York *(rec NYC, NY)* ("Greatest Hits of 1721") † J. S. Bach:Cant 147; Cant 208; Suite 2 Fl, BWV 1067; J. Clarke:Prince of Denmark's March; A. Corelli:Con Grosso in g 2 Vns, Vla & Vc, Op. 6/8; G. F. Handel:Water Music, HWV 348-50; A. Marcello:Con Ob Strs in c; Vivaldi:Con Mand, RV.425; Con Tpts, RV.537; Cons Vn Strs, Op. 8/1-4 SNYC ▲ 35821 (9.97)
S. Mentzer (mez), S. Isbin (gtr) † E. Granados:Spanish Dance 5; P. Lansky:Wayfaring Stranger; J. J. Niles:Black is the color; Go 'way from my window; J. Rodrigo:Aranjuez ma penses; F. Schubert:Songs (misc colls); Tárrega:Capricho árabe ERAT ▲ 23419 (16.97)

MARTINO, DONALD (1931-
Canzone e Tarantella sul nome Petrassi for Clarinet & Cello (1984)
A. Mark (vc), I. Greitzer (cl) *(rec New England Conservatory of Music Boston, MA, June 1996)* ("A Jazz Set") † Jazz Set; Parisonatina Al'dodecafonia; Preludes; Set Mar NWW ▲ 80518 (16.97)
Concerto for Alto Saxophone & Orchestra (1987)
K. Radnofsky (a sax), R. Hoenich (cnd), New England Conservatory SO † Paradiso Choruses NWW ▲ 80529 [DDD] (16.97)
Concerto for Wind Quintet (1964)
A. Weisberg (cnd) † Fant-Vars Pno; Quodlibets; Set Cl; Strata; Trio Cl CRI ▲ 693 [ADD] (17.97)
Fantasies & Impromptus for Piano (1981)
E. Garth (pno) † Pianississimo; Suite in the Old Form CENT ▲ 2173 (16.97)
R. Hodgkinson (pno) † R. Sessions:Son 2 Pno; Son 3 Pno NWW ▲ 80546 (16.97)
D. Holzman (pno) *(rec Paine Hall Harvard Univ, 1994)* † Fant Pno; Impromptu for Roger; Preludes ALBA ▲ 169 [DDD] (16.97)
Fantasy for solo Piano (1958)
E. Garth (pno) † Impromptu for Roger; Preludes; Son Cl; Son Vn; Trio Cl CENT ▲ 2321 (16.97)
D. Holzman (pno) *(rec Paine Hall Harvard Univ, 1994)* † Fants & Impromptus; Impromptu for Roger; Preludes ALBA ▲ 169 [DDD] (16.97)
Fantasy-Variations for Violin (1962)
P. Zukofsky (vn) † Con Ww Qnt; Quodlibets; Set Cl; Strata; Trio Cl CRI ▲ 693 [ADD] (17.97)
From the Other Side for Flute & Ensemble
R. Rudich (fl), B. Lubman (cnd), Group for Contemporary Music † Notturno; Quodlibets II KOCH ▲ 7613 (10.97)
Impromptu for Roger for Piano (1977)
E. Garth (pno) † Fant Pno; Preludes; Son Cl; Son Vn; Trio Cl CENT ▲ 2321 (16.97)
D. Holzman (pno) *(rec Paine Hall Harvard Univ, 1994)* † Fant Pno; Fants & Impromptus; Preludes ALBA ▲ 169 [DDD] (16.97)
A Jazz Set for Ensemble (1957; trans Martino 1990)
Core Ensemble *(rec Wellesley College & WGBH Studios Boston, MA, MA, June & Sept 1995)* ("A Jazz Set") † Canzone e Tarantella; Parisonatina Al'dodecafonia; Preludes; Set Mar NWW ▲ 80518 (16.97)
Notturno for Piccolo, Flute, Alto Flute, Clarinet, Bass Clarinet, Violin, Viola, Cello, Piano & Percussion (1973)
R. Rudich (fl), B. Lubman (cnd), Group for Contemporary Music † From the Other Side; Quodlibets II KOCH ▲ 7613 (10.97)
D. Shulman (cnd) *(rec Feb 1974)* † Pianississimo; Triple Con ALBA ▲ 168 [DDD] (16.97)
Paradiso Choruses for Voice, Orchestra, Choruses & Tape [from Dante] (1974)
L. C. DeVaron (cnd), New England Conservatory Repertory Orch, New England Conservatory Chorus, New England Conservatory Opera Department, New England Conservatory Boys' Choir, New England Conservatory Youth Singers † Con A Sax NWW ▲ 80529 [DDD] (16.97)
Parisonatina Al'Dodecafonia for solo Cello (1963)
S. Kluksdahl (vc) *(rec Esther Boyer College of Music Temple Univ)* ("Lines for Solo Cello") † Broadhead:Lament; G. Schuller:Fantasia Vc; R. Shapey:Krosnick Soli; A. R. Thomas:Spring Song; R. Wernick:Cadenzas & Vars 3 CRI ▲ 762 [DDD] (16.97)
A. Mark (vc) *(rec Wellesley College, MA, June 1995)* ("A Jazz Set") † Canzone e Tarantella; Jazz Set; Preludes; Set Mar NWW ▲ 80518 (16.97)
R. Rider (vc) † Suite of Vars; L. Hyla:The Dream of Innocent III; S. Mackey:Rhondo Vars; Webern:Little Pieces, Op. 11; Pieces Vc; Son Vc CRI ▲ 564 [DDD] (16.97)
Pianississimo (sonata) for Piano (1970)
E. Garth (pno) † Fants & Impromptus; Suite in the Old Form CENT ▲ 2173 (16.97)
D. Holzman (pno) *(rec Paine Hall Harvard Univ, 1991)* † Notturno; Triple Con ALBA ▲ 168 [DDD] (16.97)
Pious Pieces (7) for Chorus (& Piano or Organ) [set to poems by R. Herrick] (1972)
John Oliver Chorale † S. Martirano:Mass NWW ▲ 80210 (16.97)
Preludes (12) for Piano (1991)
E. Garth (pno) † Fant Pno; Impromptu for Roger; Son Cl; Son Vn; Trio Cl CENT ▲ 2321 (16.97)
H. Hinton (pno) *(rec Wellesley College, MA, June 1995)* ("A Jazz Set") † Canzone e Tarantella; Jazz Set; Parisonatina Al'dodecafonia; Set Mar NWW ▲ 80518 (16.97)
D. Holzman (pno) *(rec Paine Hall Harvard Univ, 1994)* † Fant Pno; Fants & Impromptus; Impromptu for Roger ALBA ▲ 169 [DDD] (16.97)
Quartet for Strings (1983)
Juilliard String Quartet † F. Lerdahl:Qt 1 Strs CRI ▲ 551 [DDD] (17.97)
Quodlibets for Flute (1954)
S. Baron (fl) † Con Ww Qnt; Fant-Vars Pno; Set Cl; Strata; Trio Cl CRI ▲ 693 [ADD] (17.97)
Quodlibets II for Flute
R. Rudich (fl) † From the Other Side; Notturno KOCH ▲ 7613 (10.97)
A Set for Clarinet (1954)
M. Webster (cl) † Con Ww Qnt; Fant-Vars Pno; Quodlibets; Strata; Trio Cl CRI ▲ 693 [ADD] (17.97)
J. B. Yeh (cl) ("Dialogues With My Shadow") † P. Boulez:Dialogue de l'ombre double; R. Carl:Towards the Crest; R. Levin:New Leaf; Sandroff:Tephillah KOCH ▲ 7088 (10.97)
A Set for Marimba [trans Martino from A Set for Clarinet, 1995]
M. Parola (mar) *(rec Wellesley College, MA, June 1995)* ("A Jazz Set") † Canzone e Tarantella; Jazz Set; Parisonatina Al'dodecafonia; Preludes NWW ▲ 80518 (16.97)
Sonata for Clarinet & Piano (1950-51)
J. Kopperud (cl), E. Garth (pno) † Fant Pno; Impromptu for Roger; Preludes; Son Vn; Trio Cl CENT ▲ 2321 (16.97)
Sonata for Violin & Piano
R. Schulte (vn), E. Garth (pno) † Fant Pno; Impromptu for Roger; Preludes; Son Cl; Trio Cl CENT ▲ 2321 (16.97)

MARTINO, DONALD (cont.)
Strata for Bass Clarinet (1966)
D. Smylie (b cl) † Con Ww Qnt; Fant-Vars Pno; Quodlibets; Set Cl; Trio Cl CRI ▲ 693 [ADD] (17.97)
Suite of Variations on Medieval Melodies for Cello (1952)
R. Rider (vc) † Parisonatina Al'dodecafonia; L. Hyla:The Dream of Innocent III; S. Mackey:Rhondo Vars; Webern:Little Pieces, Op. 11; Pieces Vc; Son Vc CRI ▲ 564 [DDD] (16.97)
Suite in the Old Form for Piano (1982)
E. Garth (pno) † Fants & Impromptus; Pianississimo CENT ▲ 2173 (16.97)
Trio for Clarinet, Violin & Piano (1959)
R. Schulte (vn), J. Kopperud (cl), E. Garth (pno) † Fant Pno; Impromptu for Roger; Preludes; Son Cl; Son Vn CENT ▲ 2321 (16.97)
P. Zukofsky (vn), A. Bloom (cl), G. Kalish (pno) † Con Ww Qnt; Fant-Vars Pno; Quodlibets; Set Cl; Strata CRI ▲ 693 [ADD] (17.97)
Triple Concerto for Clarinet, Bass Clarinet, Contrabass Clarinet & Orchestra (1977)
L. Thimmig (cl), D. Smylie (cl), A. Devendra (cl), H. Sollberger (cnd) *(rec Dec 1978)* † Notturno; Pianississimo ALBA ▲ 168 [DDD] (16.97)

MARTINON, JEAN (1910-1976)
Sonatina No. 5 for Violin, Op. 32/1 (1942)
I. Kaler (vn) *(rec Methuen, MA, May 1995)* † P. Hindemith:Son Vn; S. Prokofiev:Son Vc; Ysaÿe:Sons Vn, Op. 27 ONGA ▲ 103 [DDD] (16.97)

MARTINŮ, BOHUSLAV (1890-1959)
Alexandre bis (opera in 1 act) [lib A. Wurmser] (1937)
J. Krátká (sop), A. Barová (cta), R. Tuček (bar), R. Novák (bass), F. Jílek (cnd), Brno Janáček Opera Orch † Comedy on the Bridge SUR ▲ 112140 [AAD]
Arabesques (7) for Violin (or Cello) & Piano, H. 201A (1931)
B. Matoušek (vn), P. Adamec (pno) *(rec Martinů Hall, Lichtenstein Palace, Prague, Czech Republic, Feb & June 1997)* † Études rythmiques; Ariette; Czech Rhapsody, H. 307; Intermezzos Vn, H. 261; Madrigal Stanzas, H. 297; Son 2 Vn, H. 208; Son 3 Vn, H.303; Sonatina Vn, H. 262 SUR 2-▲ 3412 [DDD] (16.97)
J. Talich (vn), J. Klepác (pno) † Études rythmiques; Czech Rhapsody, H. 307; Intermezzos Vn, H. 261; Madrigal Stanzas, H. 297 GZCL ▲ 305 (6.97)
Ariette for Violin (or Cello) & Piano, H. 188A (1930)
B. Matoušek (vn), P. Adamec (pno) *(rec Martinů Hall, Lichtenstein Palace, Prague, Czech Republic, Feb & June 1997)* † Études rythmiques; Arabesques, H. 201A; Czech Rhapsody, H. 307; Intermezzos Vn, H. 261; Madrigal Stanzas, H. 297; Son 2 Vn, H. 208; Son 3 Vn, H.303; Sonatina Vn, H. 262 SUR 2-▲ 3412 [DDD] (16.97)
Bergerettes for Violin, Cello & Piano (1939)
Iscles Trio ("Complete Piano Trios") † Trio 1 Pno; Trio 2 Pno; Trio 3 Pno MDA7 ▲ 4 (18.97)
Philadelphia Trio *(rec Curtis Institute of Music Philadelphia, PA, May 1994)* † J. Turina:Trio 1 Pno, Op. 35; Trio 2 Pno, Op. 76 CENT ▲ 2259 [DDD] (16.97)
The Butterfly That Stamped [Motýl, který depal] (ballet) for Orchestra [after Kipling] (1926)
J. Bělohlávek (cnd), Prague SO SUR ▲ 110380 [DDD]
Cello Music (complete works for cello & piano)
M. Fukačová (vc), I. Klánský (pno)—7 Arabesques; Ariette; 4 Nocturnes; 6 Pastorales; Rossini Vars; Sons 1-3; Suite Miniature; Vars On a Theme from a Slovak Folk Song *(rec June 1991)* KPT 3-▲ 32084 [DDD]
Chamber Music
Darlington Ensemble—La revue de cuisine; Nonet; 3 Madrigals; plus others HYP (Dyad) 2-▲ 22039 (18.97)
J. Klusoň (va), M. Kaňka (vc), B. Krajný (pno), D. Wiesner (pno), Kocian String Quartet *(2 Dances; Son 2 Vn, H. 208; Ritournelles; 2 Sons Vn)*, J. Klusoň (va), M. Kaňka (vc), B. Krajný (pno), D. Wiesner (pno), et al., Kocian String Quartet *(Deux chansons; Sérénade 2; Sxt Strs)* ("Paris, Spring of 1932") PRAG ▲ 250111 (18.97)
Chamber Music No. 1 for Clarinet, Harp, Piano, Violin, Viola & Cello (1959)
Danish Chamber Players ("Musique de Chambre") † Nonet Ww, Strs & Db; Revue de Cuisine; Rondes KPT ▲ 32227
Philadelphia Orch members *(rec 1996)* † K. Penderecki:Qt Cl; F. Poulenc:Trio Ob BOST ▲ 1026 (15.97)
Choral Music
M. Cejková (sop), H. Pracnová (cta), P. Frýbort (ten), M. Pařízek (bar), P. Messiereur (vn), P. Kühn (cnd), Kühn Choir, P. Kühn (cnd), Prague Radio Chorus Male Voices—Brigand Songs I, II (1957); Czech Nursery Rhymes (1931); 3 Part-Songs (1952); Czech Madrigals (1939); 4 Songs of the Virgin (1934); 5 Czech Madrigals (1948); Madrigals (1959); 3 Sacred Songs (1952) *(rec Prague, Nov 13, 1989-May 13, 1990)* ("Male, Female & Mixed Choruses") SUR 2-▲ 3101 [DDD]
Comedy on the Bridge (radio opera in 1 act) [lib Martinů after V. K. Klispera] (1935)
J. Krátká (sop), A. Barová (cta), R. Tuček (bar), R. Novák (bass), F. Jílek (cnd), Brno Janáček Opera Orch † Alexandre bis SUR ▲ 112140 [AAD]
Comedy on the Bridge:suite
D. Deroche (cnd), DePaul Univ Wind Ensemble *(rec Depaul Univerity Concert Hall, IL, 1995-98)* † J. Beal:Con Cl; Bozza:Children's Ov; C. M. Guarnieri:Homage to Villa-Lobos; Lopatnikoff:Con Ww; D. Milhaud:Sym 5 ALBA ▲ 334 [DDD] (16.97)
Concertino for Cello, Wind Instruments, Piano & Percussion (1924)
M. Fukačová (vc), P. Csaba (cnd), Odense SO *(rec May 1996)* † Con 1 Vc; Con 2 Vc KPT ▲ 32256
M. Rummel (vc), E. Theis (cnd), Austrian Chamber Sym † Con da camera; W. Steinmetz:Solo & Kammermusik MPH ▲ 56821 [DDD] (15.97)
R. Wallfisch (vc), J. Bělohlávek (cnd), Czech PO † Con 1 Vc; Con 2 Vc CHN ▲ 9015 [DDD] (16.97)
Concertino for Piano, Violin, Cello & String Orchestra (1933)
M. Fischer-Dieskau (cnd), New Berlin CO *(rec live, 1992)* † B. Bartók:Divert Strs, Sz.113; Doráti:Jesus oder Barabbas?; Pater Noster BIS ▲ 578 [DDD] (17.97)
A. Myrat (cnd) † Double Con; Honegger:Sym 2 AG ▲ 128 (18.97)
Concerto No. 1 for Cello & Orchestra (1930; rev 1955)
J. Chuchro (vc), Z. Košler (cnd), Czech PO † A. Dvořák:Con Vc; Stabat Mater, Op. 58 SUR 2-▲ 3093
P. Fournier (vc) *(rec live, 1957-78)* † R. Schumann:Con Vc; D. Shostakovich:Con 1 Vc, Op. 107 CASC ▲ 2009 (16.97)
M. Fukačová (vc), P. Csaba (cnd), Odense SO *(rec May 1996)* † Con 2 Vc; Concertino Vc KPT ▲ 32256
R. Wallfisch (vc), J. Bělohlávek (cnd), Czech PO [1955 version] † Con 2 Vc; Concertino Vc CHN ▲ 9015 [DDD] (16.97)
Concerto No. 2 for Cello & Orchestra (1944-45)
M. Fukačová (vc), P. Csaba (cnd), Odense SO *(rec May 1996)* † Con 1 Vc; Concertino Vc KPT ▲ 32256
R. Wallfisch (vc), J. Bělohlávek (cnd), Czech PO † Con 1 Vc; Concertino Vc CHN ▲ 9015 [DDD] (16.97)
Concerto da camera for Violin, Piano, Percussion & Strings (1941)
P. Rybar (vn), M. Rybar (pno), U. Voegelin (cnd), Swiss Romande Orch *(rec May 1960)* ("Peter Rybar Edition, Vol. 2") † Con 1 for 2 Vns; Qt 6 Strs TELO (Violin Legends) ▲ 23 [AAD] (16.97)
S. Windbacher (vn), E. Theis (cnd), Austrian Chamber Sym † Concertino Vc; W. Steinmetz:Solo & Kammermusik MPH ▲ 56821 [DDD] (15.97)
Concerto grosso for 2 Pianos & Chamber Orchestra (1937)
artists unknown ("Czech Philharmonic Centenary Homage") † A. Dvořák:Suite Orch, Op. 98b; Smetana:Bartered Bride (ov); J. Suk:Ripening, Op. 34 SUR ▲ 111996
Concerto for Harpsichord & Chamber Orchestra (1935)
E. Braito (hpd), P. Kantschieder (cnd) ("Harpsichord Concertos of the 20th Century") † F. Farkas:Concertino Hpd; J. Françaix:Con Hpd; H. Jelinek:2 Blue O's KSCH ▲ 314222 (16.97)
Z. Růžičová (hpd), Slovak Radio CO † Con 4 Pno; Con 5 Pno CAPI ▲ 1321 [DDD]
Concerto for Oboe & Orchestra (1955)
D. Doherty (ob), O. Henzold (cnd), Lucerne SO ("Oboe Concertos") † J. Haydn:Con Ob; W. A. Mozart:Con Ob; B. A. Zimmermann:Con Ob PANC ▲ 510090 [DDD] (17.97)
T. Indermühle (ob), C. Schnitzler (cnd), Bretagne Orch † R. Strauss:Con Ob, AV144; Vaughan Williams:Con Ob; B. A. Zimmermann:Con Ob CAMA ▲ 346 (18.97)
L. Pešek (cnd), Czech PO *(rec live, 1992-94)* † W. A. Mozart:Sinf concertante Ob, K.Anh.9; Smetana:Festive Sym SUR ▲ 180 [DDD] (16.97)
Concertos Nos. 1-5 for Piano (complete)
E. Leichner (pno) SUR ▲ 111313 [DDD]
Concerto No. 2 for Piano & Orchestra (1934)
R. Firkušný (pno), J. Bělohlávek (cnd), Czech PO † Estampes; Parables; Ricercari SUR ▲ 111988
Concerto No. 3 for Piano & Orchestra (1948)
J. Paleníček (pno), K. Ančerl (cnd), Czech PO † Janáček:Sinfonietta; Taraš Bulba SUR (Czech Philharmonic) ▲ 111929 [AAD]

MARTINŮ, BOHUSLAV (cont.)

Concerto No. 4 for Piano & Orchestra, "Incantations" (1955-56)

K. Havlikova (pno), O. Lenárd (cnd), Slovak Radio CO † Con Hpd; Con 5 Pno CAPI ▲ 1321 [DDD]

Concerto No. 5 for Piano & Orchestra, "Fantasia Concertante" (1957)

K. Havlikova (pno), T. Koutník (cnd), Slovak Radio CO † Con Hpd; Con 4 Pno CAPI ▲ 1321 [DDD]

Concerto for 2 Pianos & Orchestra (1943)

J. Pierce (pno), D. Jonas (pno), E. Stratta (cnd), Luxembourg RSO, E. Stratta (cnd), Luxembourg Radio Orch † Czech Dances; Fant for 2 Pnos; B. Britten:Scottish Ballad, Op. 26 PHOE ▲ 104 (15.97)

J. Pierce (pno), D. Jonas (pno), E. Stratta (cnd), Luxembourg Radio-TV Orch *(rec 1981)* † Czech Dances; Fant for 2 Pnos; B. Britten:Scottish Ballad, Op. 26 ICC ▲ 6701732 [DDD] (9.97)

Concerto for String Quartet & Orchestra (1931)

R. Hickox (cnd), City of London Sinfonia † Double Con; Sinfonia concertante Ob EMIA ▲ 59575 [DDD] (16.97)

Concerto No. 1 for Violin & Orchestra (1933)

J. Suk (vn), V. Neumann (cnd), Czech PO † Con 2 Vn; Rhap-Con Va SUR ▲ 111969 [AAD]

Concerto No. 2 for Violin & Orchestra (1943)

L. Kaufman (vn), J. Rachmilovich (cnd), Santa Monica Orch *(rec ca 1946)* † J. Achron:Stimmung; Diciedue:Con Vn; G. Fauré:Con Vn; A. Khachaturian:Con Vn; F. Kreisler:Vn Pieces (original works & arrs); Sibelius:Con Vn CMB ▲ 1063 [ADD/DDD] (16.97)

J. Suk (vn), V. Neumann (cnd), Czech PO † Con 1 Vn; Rhap-Con Va SUR ▲ 111969 [AAD]

Concerto for Violin & Piano, H. 13 (1910)

B. Matoušek (vn), P. Adamec (pno) *(rec Martinů Hall, Lichtenstien Palace, Prague, Czech Republic, July & Sept 1996)* † Elegy; Impromptu, H. 166; Short Pieces (5), H. 184; Son Vn & Pno, H. 120; Son Vn & Pno, H. 152; Son 1 Vn SUR 2-▲ 3410 [DDD] (16.97)

Concerto No. 1 for 2 Violins & Orchestra (1937)

P. Rybar (vn), K. Conzelmann (vn), J. Horenstein (cnd), Zurich Tonhalle Orch *(rec May 1960)* ("Peter Rybar Edition, Vol. 2") † Con da camera; Qt 6 Strs TELO (Violin Legends) ▲ 23 [AAD] (16.97)

Concerto No. 2 for 2 Violins & Orchestra (1950)

A. Siwy (vn), Y. Siwy (vn), R. Barshaï (cnd), Belgian Radio-TV French SO *(rec 1989)* † S. Prokofiev:Son 2 Vns, Op. 56; Szymanowski:Con 2 Vn, Op. 61 DI ▲ 920161 [DDD] (5.97)

Czech Dances (3) for 2 Pianos (1949)

J. Pierce (pno), D. Jonas (pno) *(rec 1987)* † Con for 2 Pnos; Fant for 2 Pnos; B. Britten:Scottish Ballad, Op. 26 ICC ▲ 6701732 [DDD] (9.97)

J. Pierce (pno), D. Jonas (pno), E. Stratta (cnd), Luxembourg RSO † Con for 2 Pnos; Fant for 2 Pnos; B. Britten:Scottish Ballad, Op. 26 PHOE ▲ 104 (15.97)

Czech Rhapsody for Violin & Piano, H. 307 (1945)

E. Bekova (vn), E. Bekova (pno) † Nocturnes Vc; Trio 2 Pno; Trio 3 Pno CHN ▲ 9632 (16.97)

H. Kotkova (vn), S. Mulligan (pno) † Son 1 Vn; Son 2 Vn, H. 208; Son 3 Vn, H.303 STMA ▲ 45 (18.97)

B. Matoušek (vn), P. Adamec (pno) *(rec Martinů Hall, Lichtenstein Palace, Prague, Czech Republic, Oct 1997 & Apr 1998)* † Études rythmiques; Arabesques, H. 201A; Ariette; Intermezzos Vn, H. 261; Madrigal Stanzas, H. 297; Son 2 Vn, H. 208; Son 3 Vn, H.303; Sonatina Vn, H. 262 SUR 2-▲ 3412 [DDD] (16.97)

J. Talich (vn), J. Klepác (pno) † Études rythmiques; Arabesques, H. 201A; Intermezzos Vn, H. 261; Madrigal Stanzas, H. 297 GZCL ▲ 305 (6.97)

Dandelion Romance for Soprano & Mixed Chorus [text Bureš] (1957)

M. Cejková (sop), P. Kühn (cnd), Kühn Choir [CZE] † Spaliček; Primrose SUR 2-▲ 110752 [DDD]

Double Concerto for Piano, Timpani & 2 String Orchestras (1938)

J. Bělohlávek (cnd), Czech PO † Sym 1 CHN ▲ 8950 [DDD] (17.97)

J. DePreist (cnd), Malmö SO † Fresques de Piero; Rhap-Con Va BIS ▲ 501 [DDD] (17.97)

R. Hickox (cnd), City of London Sinfonia † Con Str Qt; Sinfonia concertante Ob EMIA ▲ 59575 [DDD] (16.97)

H. Lester (pno), C. Mackerras (cnd), BBC SO † Janáček:Ballad of Blanik; Sinfonietta; Taraš Bulba INMP (BBC Radio Classics) ▲ 9135 (13.97)

A. Myrat (cnd) † Concertino Pno; Honegger:Sym 2 AG ▲ 128 (18.97)

J. Schiller (pno), G. Kruyer (timp), P. Tiboris (cnd), Bohuslav Martinů PO ("Music for Doubles") † F. Krommer:Con for 2 Cls, Op. 35; Saint-Saëns:Muse et la poète, Op. 132 ELY ▲ 714 [DDD] (16.97)

K. Šejna (cnd), Czech PO † Sym 3; A. Dvořák:Suite Orch, Op. 98b SUR ▲ 111924

Duo No. 1 for Violin & Cello, H.157 (1927)

Bekova Sisters † Trio 1 Pno; M. Ravel:Son Vn & Vc; Trio Pno CHN ▲ 9452 (16.97)

O. Krysa (vn), T. Thedéen (vc) *(rec 1994-97)* ("Duos for Violin & Cello") † Honegger:Sonatina Vns & Vc; M. Ravel:Son Vn & Vc; Schulhoff:Duo Vn & Vc BIS ▲ 916 [DDD] (17.97)

Duo No. 2 for Violin & Cello (1958)

Angell Piano Trio † Trio 1 Pno; Trio 2 Pno; Trio 3 Pno ASLE ▲ 6230 (10.97)

R. Barton (vn), W. Warner (vc) *(rec Chicago, IL, Dec 1-10, 1998)* ("Double Play") † Kodály:Duo Vn & Vc, Op. 7; M. Ravel:Son Vn & Vc; Schulhoff:Duo Vn & Vc CED ▲ 47 [DDD] (16.97)

Echec au roi (ballet) for Alto & Orchestra [text Coeuroy] (1930)

J. Bělohlávek (cnd), Prague SO † Revolt SUR ▲ 111415 [DDD]

Elegy for Violin & Piano (1909)

B. Matoušek (vn), P. Adamec (pno) *(rec Martinů Hall, Lichtenstien Palace, Prague, Czech Republic, July & Sept 1996)* † Con Vn & Pno, H. 13; Impromptu, H. 166; Short Pieces (5), H. 184; Son Vn & Pno, H. 120; Son Vn & Pno, H. 152; Son 1 Vn SUR 2-▲ 3410 [DDD] (16.97)

The Epic of Gilgamesh (oratorio) for solo Voices, Orchestra & Chorus (1954-55)

M. Machotková (sop), J. Zaradníček (ten), V. Zítek (bar), K. Průša (bass), J. Bělohlávek (cnd), Prague SO, Czech Phil Chorus SUR ▲ 111824 [ADD]

Slovak PO, Slovak Phil Chorus MARC ▲ 8223316 (13.97)

Estampes for Orchestra (1958)

J. Bělohlávek (cnd), Czech PO † Con 2 Pno; Parables; Ricercari SUR ▲ 111988

Études & Polkas for Piano [Books 1-3] (1945)

R. Kvapil (pno) *(rec Apr 1983)* † Son Fl & Pno; Son Pno BIS ▲ 234 [AAD] (17.97)

Études rythmiques (7) for Violin & Piano (1931)

B. Matoušek (vn), P. Adamec (pno) *(rec Martinů Hall, Lichtenstein Palace, Prague, Czech Republic, Oct 1997 & Apr 1998)* † Arabesques, H. 201A; Ariette; Czech Rhapsody, H. 307; Intermezzos Vn, H. 261; Madrigal Stanzas, H. 297; Son 2 Vn, H. 208; Son 3 Vn, H.303; Sonatina Vn, H. 262 SUR 2-▲ 3412 [DDD] (16.97)

J. Talich (vn), J. Klepác (pno) † Arabesques, H. 201A; Czech Rhapsody, H. 307; Intermezzos Vn, H. 261; Madrigal Stanzas, H. 297 GZCL ▲ 305 (6.97)

Fantasie for 2 Pianos (1929)

J. Pierce (pno), D. Jonas (pno) † Con for 2 Pnos; Czech Dances; B. Britten:Scottish Ballad, Op. 26 PHOE ▲ 104 (15.97)

J. Pierce (pno), D. Jonas (pno) *(rec 1987)* † Con for 2 Pnos; Czech Dances; B. Britten:Scottish Ballad, Op. 26 ICC ▲ 6701732 [DDD] (9.97)

Field Mass for Baritone, Orchestra & Male Chorus (1939)

I. Kusnjer (bar), M. Kejmar (tpt), B. Kotmel (cnd), Czech PO, Czech Phil Chorus [CZE] † Memorial to Lidice; Sym 4 CHN ▲ 9138 [DDD] (16.97)

Les Fresques de Piero della Francesca for Orchestra (1953)

E. Ansermet (cnd), Swiss Romande Orch † Parables; Sym 4 CASC ▲ 2007 [ADD] (16.97)

J. DePreist (cnd), Malmö SO † Double Con; Rhap-Con Va BIS ▲ 501 [DDD] (17.97)

The Greek Passion (opera in 4 acts) [lib Martinů after Kazantzakis's Christ Recrucified] (1959)

H. Field (sop), J. Mitchinson (ten), P. Joll (b-bar), J. Tomlinson (bass), C. Mackerras (cnd), Brno State PO, Czech Phil Chorus [ENG] *(rec 1981)* SUR 2-▲ 103611 [DDD]

C. Mackerras (cnd), Czech PO, C. Mackerras (cnd), Czech Phil Chorus, M. Field (sop), J. Mitchinson (ten), J. Tomlinson (bass) SUR ▲ 3611 (32.97)

Hymn to St. James for Vocal Soloists, Chamber Ensemble & Chorus [text J. Daněk] (1954)

N. Romanová (sop), D. Drobková (cta), R. Novák (ten), P. Haničinec (nar), P. Kühn (cnd) , Prague Radio Chorus [CZE] *(rec Feb-Mar 1988)* † Mount of 3 Lights; Prophecy of Isaiah SUR ▲ 110751 [DDD]

Impromptu for Violin & Piano, H. 166 (1927)

B. Matoušek (vn), P. Adamec (pno) *(rec Martinů Hall, Lichtenstien Palace, Prague, Czech Republic, Sept 1996)* † Con Vn & Pno, H. 13; Elegy; Short Pieces (5), H. 184; Son Vn & Pno, H. 120; Son Vn & Pno, H. 152; Son 1 Vn SUR 2-▲ 3410 [DDD] (16.97)

Intermezzos (4) for Violin & Piano, H. 261 (1937)

B. Matoušek (vn), P. Adamec (pno) *(rec Martinů Hall, Lichtenstein Palace, Prague, Czech Republic, Feb & June 1997)* † Études rythmiques; Arabesques, H. 201A; Ariette; Czech Rhapsody, H. 307; Madrigal Stanzas, H. 297; Son 2 Vn, H. 208; Son 3 Vn, H.303; Sonatina Vn, H. 262 SUR 2-▲ 3412 [DDD] (16.97)

J. Suk (vn), J. Hála (pno) *(rec Prague, Czech Republic, 1996)* ("Sonatas for Violin, Flute & Piano") † Madrigal Son; Promenades; Son Fl & Pno; Son Fl, Vn & Pno LT ▲ 41 [DDD] (16.97)

MARTINŮ, BOHUSLAV (cont.)

Intermezzos (4) for Violin & Piano, H. 261 (1937) (cont.)

J. Talich (vn), J. Klepác (pno) † Études rythmiques; Arabesques, H. 201A; Czech Rhapsody, H. 307; Madrigal Stanzas, H. 297 GZCL ▲ 305 (6.97)

Julietta (opera in 3 acts) [lib Martinů after Neveux] (1936-38)

M. Tauberová (sop), I. Zídek (ten), J. Krombholc (cnd), Prague National Theater Orch, Prague National Theater Chorus [CZE] *(rec 1964)* SUR 3-▲ 108176 [AAD]

Legend of the Smoke from Potato Fires (chamber cantata) for Soprano, Alto, Baritone, Flute, Clarinet, Horn, Accordion, Piano & Chorus [text Bureš] (1956)

P. Kühn (cnd) , Kühn Choir † Mikeš of the Mountains; Opening of the Wells SUR ▲ 110767 [DDD]

Madrigal Sonata for Flute, Violin & Piano (1942)

Academic Chamber Ensemble † Donizetti:Son Fl; J. Haydn:Trio 8 Vns & Bc, H.V/G3; A. Schnittke:Suite in the Old Style; C. M. von Weber:Trio Fl, Op. 63; Yordanov:Bonbonnière Fant GEGA ▲ 103 [DDD] (16.97)

E. Saltzman (vn), Y. Arnheim (fl), I. Rub-Levi (pno) ("Bohuslav Martinů: Chamber Music with Flute") † Promenades; Son Fl & Pno; Son Fl, Vn & Pno; Trio Fl KPT ▲ 32205

J. Suk (vn), J. Válek (fl), J. Hála (pno) *(rec Prague, 1996)* ("Sonatas for Violin, Flute & Piano") † Intermezzos Vn, H. 261; Promenades; Son Fl & Pno; Son Fl, Vn & Pno LT ▲ 41 [DDD] (16.97)

Madrigal Stanzas (5) for Violin & Piano, H. 297 (1943)

Y. Kless (vn), S. Rudiakov (pno) † Son 3 Vn, H.303; Enescu:Impromptu Concertant; Son 2 Vn, Op. 6 TACE ▲ 62

B. Matoušek (vn), P. Adamec (pno) *(rec Martinů Hall, Lichtenstein Palace, Prague, Czech Republic, Oct 1997 & Apr 1998)* † Études rythmiques; Arabesques, H. 201A; Ariette; Czech Rhapsody, H. 307; Intermezzos Vn, H. 261; Son 2 Vn, H. 208; Son 3 Vn, H.303; Sonatina Vn, H. 262 SUR 2-▲ 3412 [DDD] (16.97)

J. Suk (vn), J. Hála (pno) † A. Dvořák:Romantic Pieces, Op. 75; Janáček:Son Vn; Smetana:From the Homeland; J. Suk:Balada Vn & Pno DI ▲ 920317 [DDD] (5.97)

J. Talich (vn), J. Klepác (pno) † Études rythmiques; Arabesques, H. 201A; Czech Rhapsody, H. 307; Intermezzos Vn, H. 261 GZCL ▲ 305 (6.97)

Madrigals (3) for Violin & Viola (1947)

Stamitz String Quartet members † Qts Strs; Trio 2 Vn BAYE 3-▲ 100152 [DDD] (51.97)

Memorial to Lidice [Památnik Lidicim] for Orchestra (1943)

K. Ančerl (cnd), Czech PO ("The Last World War") † Honegger:Sym 3; Schoenberg:Survivor from Warsaw, Op. 46 SUR ▲ 177 [AAD] (10.97)

B. Kotmel (cnd), Czech PO † Field Mass; Sym 4 CHN ▲ 9138 [DDD] (16.97)

Mikeš of the Mountains (chamber cantata) for Soprano, Tenor, Piano, Strings & Chorus [text Bureš] (1959)

P. Kühn (cnd) , Kühn Choir † Legend of the Smoke; Opening of the Wells SUR ▲ 110767 [DDD]

The Miracles of Mary [Hry o Marii] (opera) [lib Martinů after H. Ghéon] (1933-34)

J. Bělohlávek (cnd), Prague SO, Prague Radio Chorus † Smetana:Brandenbergers in Bohemia SUR 2-▲ 111802 [AAD/DDD]

Mount of 3 Lights (cantata) for Vocal Soloists, Speaker, Organ & Male Chorus [text W. E. Morton] (1954)

V. Doležal (ten), R. Novák (bass), P. Haničinec (nar), J. Hora (org), P. Kühn (cnd) , Prague Radio Men's Chorus, Kühn Chorus [CZE] *(rec Feb-Mar 1988)* † Hymn to St. James; Prophecy of Isaiah SUR ▲ 110751 [DDD]

Music of Martinů

(La Revue de Cuisine), artists unknown *(Jazz-Suite; Sxt for Pno & Wind Instrs; Shimmy Foxtrot; Le Jazz; Half-time; La Bagarre; Thunderbolt, P.47)* ("Works Inspired by Jazz & Sport") SUR ▲ 3058

Nocturnes (4) for Cello & Piano (1930)

A. Bekova (vc), E. Bekova (pno) † Czech Rhapsody, H. 307; Trio 2 Pno; Trio 3 Pno CHN ▲ 9632 (16.97)

Nonet for Wind Quintet & Piano Quartet (1924-25)

Lahti SO Chamber Ensemble *(rec Järvenpää Hall Finland, Feb 28-Mar 4, 1994)* † Nonet Ww, Strs & Db; Revue de Cuisine; Trio Fl BIS ▲ 653 [DDD] (17.97)

Nonet for Wind Quintet, String Trio & Double Bass (1959)

Danish Chamber Players ("Musique de Chambre") † Chamber Music 1; Revue de Cuisine; Rondes KPT ▲ 32227

L. Graham (cnd) ("Nonets & Septets") † Indy:Chanson et Danses, Op. 50; Jaroch:Children's Suite; I. Stravinsky:Septet; H. Villa-Lobos:Chôro 7 KLAV ▲ 11080 [DDD] (18.97)

A. Jordan (cnd) *(rec Oct 1992)* ("L'Ecole de Paris") † T. Harsányi:Nonet; Tansman:Septet GALL ▲ 729 [DDD] (19.97)

Lahti SO Chamber Ensemble *(rec Järvenpää Hall Finland, Feb 28-Mar 4, 1994)* † Nonet Ww & Pno; Revue de Cuisine; Trio Fl BIS ▲ 653 [DDD] (17.97)

The Opening of the Wells (chamber cantata) for Soprano, Alto, Baritone, Narrator, Strings, Piano & Female Chorus [text Bureš] (1955)

P. Kühn (cnd) , Kühn Choir † Legend of the Smoke; Mikeš of the Mountains SUR ▲ 110767 [DDD]

Parables for Orchestra (1957-58)

E. Ansermet (cnd), Swiss Romande Orch † Fresques de Piero; Sym 4 CASC ▲ 2007 [ADD] (16.97)

J. Bělohlávek (cnd), Czech PO † Con 2 Pno; Estampes; Ricercari SUR ▲ 111988

Pastorales (6) for Cello & Piano (1930)

M. Zukovsky (cl), Bohemian Ensemble Los Angeles ("Otiose Odalisque") † Qt Cl; Revue de Cuisine; Sonatina Cl SUMM ▲ 214 (16.97)

Piano Music (complete works for solo piano)

E. Leichner (pno)—Les Marionettes [14 miniatures for pno] (1912-14); Études & Polkas [16 pieces in 3 books] (1945); Son 1 (1954); Fant & Toccata, H.281; Les Papillons [Butterflies & Birds of Paradise]; Trois Danses Tchéques; Sept Danses Tchéques (1929); Trois Esquisses (1927); Huit Préludes (1929); Les Ritournelles (1932); Esquisses de Danses (1932); Fenêtre sur le Jardin (1938) SUR 3-▲ 111010 [DDD]

Primrose (5 duets) for Sopranos, Contraltos, Violin & Piano [on texts of Moravian folk poetry] (1954)

P. Messiereur (vn), S. Bogunia (pno), P. Kühn (cnd) , Kühn Women's Chorus † Spaliček; Dandelion Romance SUR 2-▲ 110752 [DDD]

Promenades for Flute, Violin & Harpsichord (1939)

C. Castleman (vn), B. Boyd (fl), B. Harbach (hpd) † S. Adler:Son 2 Vn; A. Dvořák:Bagatelles, Op. 47; D. Milhaud:Son Vn & Hpd, Op. 257; Piston:Sonatina Vn; Rubbra:Cant Pastorale, Op. 92; Fant on a Theme of Machaut, Op. 86 ALBA ▲ 41 (16.97)

E. Saltzman (vn), Y. Arnheim (fl), I. Rub-Levi (pno) ("Bohuslav Martinů: Chamber Music with Flute") † Madrigal Son; Son Fl & Pno; Son Fl, Vn & Pno; Trio Fl KPT ▲ 32205

J. Suk (vn), J. Válek (fl), J. Hála (pno) *(rec Prague, 1996)* ("Sonatas for Violin, Flute & Piano") † Intermezzos Vn, H. 261; Madrigal Son; Son Fl & Pno; Son Fl, Vn & Pno LT ▲ 41 [DDD] (16.97)

The Prophecy of Isaiah for Vocal Soloists, Chamber Ensemble & Male Chorus [Biblical text] (1959)

N. Romanová (sop), R. Novák (bass), J. Pěruška (va), V. Kozderka (tpt), S. Bogunia (pno), I. Kiezlich (timp), P. Kühn (cnd) , Prague Radio Men's Chorus, Kühn Chorus [CZE] *(rec Feb-Mar 1988)* † Hymn to St. James; Mount of 3 Lights SUR ▲ 110751 [DDD]

Quartet for Clarinet, Horn, Cello & Side Drum (1924)

Ensemble Villa Musica † Serenade 1 Strs; Serenade 2 Strs; Serenade 3 Strs; Serenade 4 Strs MDG ▲ 3040774 (17.97)

M. Zukovsky (cl), Bohemian Ensemble Los Angeles ("Otiose Odalisque") † Pastorales; Revue de Cuisine; Sonatina Cl SUMM ▲ 214 (16.97)

Quartet for Oboe & Piano Trio (1947)

P. Enoksson (vn), M. Rondin (vc), H. Jahren (ob), S. Bojsten (pno) † Messiaen:Quatuor; Schoenberg:Stelldichein CAPA ▲ 21481 (16.97)

C. Gadd (vn), A. Ivashkin (vc), J. Marangella (ob), K. Selby (pno) *(rec Australian Festival of Chamber Music, July 1994)* ("Chamber Music") † Qnt Strs; Qt 1 Pno; Son 1 Va NXIN ▲ 553916 [DDD] (5.97)

Quartet No. 1 for Piano & Strings (1942)

I. van Keulen (vn), R. Moog (va), Y. Cho (vc), D. Adni (pno) *(rec Australian Festival of Chamber Music, July 1994)* ("Chamber Music") † Qnt Strs; Qt Ob; Son 1 Va NXIN ▲ 553916 [DDD] (5.97)

Quartets (7) for Strings (1918-47) (complete)

Panocha String Quartet SUR 3-▲ 110994 [AAD]

Stamitz String Quartet † Madrigals Vn; Trio 2 Vn BAYE 3-▲ 100152 [DDD] (51.97)

Quartet No. 6 for Strings (1946)

Winterthur String Quartet *(rec Feb 1957)* ("Peter Rybar Edition, Vol. 2") † Con da camera; Con 1 for 2 Vns TELO (Violin Legends) ▲ 23 [AAD] (16.97)

Quintet No. 2 for Piano & Strings (1944)

P. Frankl (pno), Lindsay String Quartet † A. Dvořák:Qnt Pno, Op. 81 ASV ▲ 889 [DDD] (16.97)

Quintet for Strings (1927)

C. Gadd (vn), S. Soroka (vn), T. Kuchar (va), R. Moog (va), Y. Cho (vc) *(rec Australian Festival of Chamber Music, July 1994)* ("Chamber Music") † Qt Ob; Qt 1 Pno; Son 1 Va NXIN ▲ 553916 [DDD] (5.97)

MARTINŮ, BOHUSLAV (cont.)

Short Pieces (5) for Violin & Piano, H. 184 (1929)

B. Matoušek (vn), P. Adamec (pno) *(rec Martinů Hall, Lichtenstien Palace, Prague, Czech Republic, Sept 1996)* † Con Vn & Pno, H. 13; Elegy; Impromptu, H. 166; Son Vn & Pno, H. 120; Son Vn & Pno, H. 152; Son 1 Vn SUR 2-▲ 3410 [DDD] (16.97)

Revolt [Vzpoura] (ballet) for Orchestra (1925)

J. Bělohlávek (cnd), Prague SO † Echec au roi SUR ▲ 111415 [DDD]

La Revue de Cuisine (ballet) for Orchestra (1927)

Chicago Pro Musica † P. Bowles:Music for a Farce; Varèse:Octandre; K. Weill:Kleine Dreigroschenmusik REF ▲ 29 [DDD] (16.97)

Danish Chamber Players ("Musique de Chambre") † Chamber Music 1; Nonet Ww, Strs & Db; Rondes KPT ▲ 32227

Lahti SO Chamber Ensemble *(rec Järvenpää Hall Finland, Feb 28-Mar 4, 1994)* † Nonet Ww & Pno; Nonet Ww, Strs & Db; Trio Fl BIS ▲ 653 [DDD] (17.97)

M. Zukovsky (cl), Bohemian Ensemble Los Angeles [orig score for cl, bn, tpt, vn, vc, pno] ("Otiose Odalisque") † Pastorales; Qt Cl; Sonatina Cl SUMM ▲ 214 (16.97)

Rhapsody-Concerto for Viola & Orchestra (1952)

N. Imai (va), J. DePreist (cnd), Malmö SO † Double Con; Fresques de Piero BIS ▲ 501 [DDD] (17.97)

J. Suk (va), V. Neumann (cnd), Czech PO † Con 1 Vn; Con 2 Vn SUR ▲ 111969 [AAD]

M. Tolpygo (va), E. Chivzhel (cnd), State SO *(rec 1990)* † Rakhmadiev:Con Vn; Dairabay; Kudasha-Duman CSN ▲ 810003 [DDD] (16.97)

Ricercari (3) for Orchestra (1938)

J. Bělohlávek (cnd), Czech PO † Con 2 Pno; Estampes; Parables SUR ▲ 111988

Les Rondes for Oboe, Clarinet, Bassoon, Trumpet, 2 Violins & Piano (1930)

Danish Chamber Players ("Musique de Chambre") † Chamber Music 1; Nonet Ww, Strs & Db; Revue de Cuisine KPT ▲ 32227

Serenade No. 1 for String Orchestra

Ensemble Villa Musica † Qt Cl; Serenade 2 Strs; Serenade 3 Strs; Serenade 4 Strs MDG ▲ 3040774 (17.97)

Serenade No. 2 for String Orchestra (1931)

Academy of St. Martin in the Fields Chamber Ensemble † Sextet Strs; A. Dvořák:Sxt Strs, Op. 48 CHN ▲ 8771 [DDD] (16.97)

Ensemble Villa Musica † Qt Cl; Serenade 1 Strs; Serenade 3 Strs; Serenade 4 Strs MDG ▲ 3040774 (17.97)

Serenade No. 3 for String Orchestra

Ensemble Villa Musica † Qt Cl; Serenade 1 Strs; Serenade 2 Strs; Serenade 4 Strs MDG ▲ 3040774 (17.97)

Serenade No. 4 for String Orchestra

Ensemble Villa Musica † Qt Cl; Serenade 1 Strs; Serenade 2 Strs; Serenade 3 Strs MDG ▲ 3040774 (17.97)

Sextet for Flute, Oboe, Clarinet, 2 Bassoons & Piano (1929)

Forrás Ensemble ("Chamber Music") † Son Fl & Pno; Sonatina Cl; Trio Fl; Vars on a Theme of Rossini, H.290 HUN ▲ 31674 [DDD] (16.97)

J. P. Schulze (pno), Arcis Wind Quintet *(rec Oct 1996)* ("French Piano Sextets") † J. Françaix:Heure du berger for Orch; F. Poulenc:Sxt Pno CALG ▲ 50984 [DDD] (18.97)

Sextet for Strings (1932)

Academy of St. Martin in the Fields Chamber Ensemble † Serenade 2 Strs; A. Dvořák:Sxt Strs, Op. 48 CHN ▲ 8771 [DDD] (16.97)

F. Obstfeld (cnd), Westphalia PO [arr composer for str orch] † P. Haas:Study; Krása:Ov Small Orch; Schreker:Intermezzo Strs, Op. 8; Scherzo Strs; Wind EDA ▲ 9 [DDD] (19.97)

Sinfonia concertante for Oboe, Bassoon, Violin, Cello & Orchestra (1949)

R. Hickox (cnd), City of London Sinfonia † Con Str Qt; Double Con EMIA ▲ 59575 [DDD] (16.97)

Sinfonietta giocosa for Piano & Small Orchestra (1940)

J. Jacobson (pno), T. Vásáry (cnd), Bournemouth Sinfonietta † Sinfonietta Pno; Toccata e due canzoni CHN ▲ 8859 [DDD] (16.97)

Sinfonietta for Piano & Orchestra, "La Jolla" (1950)

J. Jacobson (pno), T. Vásáry (cnd), Bournemouth Sinfonietta † Sinfonietta giocosa Pno; Toccata e due canzoni CHN ▲ 8859 [DDD] (16.97)

M. Singerova (pno), J. Valta (cnd), Zilina State CO † O. Respighi:Trittico botticelliano OPP ▲ 1844 (10.97)

M. Singerová (pno), J. Valta (cnd), Žilina State CO † O. Respighi:Trittico botticelliano PC ▲ 267185 [DDD] (2.97)

Sonatas (3) for Cello & Piano (complete)

J. Hanousek (vc), P. Kaspar (pno) CENT ▲ 2207 (16.97)

J. Starker (vc), R. Firkušný (pno) RCAV (Red Seal) ▲ 61220 (16.97)

Sonata No. 1 for Cello & Piano (1939)

F. Guye (vc), D. Lively (pno) † Vars on a Slovak folksong; S. Rachmaninoff:Romance Vc; Son Vc CASC ▲ 1019 (16.97)

Sonata No. 2 for Cello & Piano (1941)

G. Epperson (vc), F. Burnett (pno) *(rec Moore College Musical Arts Bowling Green State, OH, Aug 2-3, 1994)* † S. Barber:Son Vc, Op. 6; B. Bartók:Rhap Vc, Sz.88; Bavicchi:Son 2 Vc, Op. 25 CENT ▲ 2275 [DDD] (16.97)

P. Rejto (vc), E. Rowley (pno) *(rec 1991)* † S. Barber:Son Vc, Op. 6; Janáček:Fairy Tale; Kodály:Son Vc & Pno, Op. 4 SUMM ▲ 137 [DDD] (16.97)

Sonata for Flute & Piano (1945)

Y. Arnheim (fl), I. Rub-Levi (pno) ("Bohuslav Martinů: Chamber Music with Flute") † Madrigal Son; Promenades; Son Fl, Vn & Pno; Trio Fl KPT ▲ 32205

G. von Bahr (fl), K. Hindart (pno) *(rec Apr 1973)* † Études & Polkas; Son Pno BIS ▲ 234 [AAD] (17.97)

M. Beaucoudray (fl), Y. Henry (pno) *(rec 1993)* ("Flûte sans frontière") † B. Bartók:Hungarian Peasant Songs, Sz.71; P. Hindemith:Son Fl; S. Prokofiev:Son Fl SKAR ▲ 4971 [DDD] (18.97)

M. Bellavance (fl), M. Bourdeau (pno) † B. Bartók:Hungarian Peasant Songs, Sz.71; S. Prokofiev:Son Fl; Taktakishvili:Son Fl BRIO ▲ 121 (16.97)

K. Bryan (fl), K. Keys (pno) *(rec Bratislava Slovak Republic, July 1989)* ("Twentieth Century Flute, Volume Two") † P. Hindemith:Son Fl; F. Poulenc:Son Fl; S. Prokofiev:Son Fl PREM ▲ 1053 [DDD] (16.97)

B. Gisler-Haase (fl), M. Mori (pno) *(rec Vienna, Feb 2-3, 1994)* ("Flute Sonatas") † A. Dvořák:Sonatina Vn, Op. 100; P. Hindemith:Son Fl; J. N. Hummel:Son Vn & Pno, Op. 50 CAMA ▲ 393 [DDD] (18.97)

E. Horgas (fl), B. Simon (pno) ("Chamber Music") † Sonatina Cl; Sxt Fl, Ob, Cl, 2 Bns & Pno; Trio Fl; Vars on a Theme of Rossini, H.290 HUN ▲ 31674 [DDD] (16.97)

S. Milan (fl), I. Brown (pno) † C. Reinecke:Son Fl; F. Schubert:Intro & Vars on "Tröckne Blumen", D.802 CHN ▲ 8823 [DDD] (16.97)

J. Válek (fl), J. Hála (pno) ("20th Century Flute Sonatas") † P. Hindemith:Son Fl; F. Poulenc:Son Fl; S. Prokofiev:Son Fl SUR ▲ 96 [DDD] (10.97)

J. Válek (fl), J. Hála (pno) *(rec Prague, 1996)* ("Sonatas for Violin, Flute & Piano") † Intermezzos Vn, H. 261; Madrigal Son; Promenades; Son Fl, Vn & Pno LT ▲ 41 [DDD] (16.97)

Sonata for Flute, Violin & Piano (1937)

E. Saltzman (vn), Y. Arnheim (fl), I. Rub-Levi (pno) ("Bohuslav Martinů: Chamber Music with Flute") † Madrigal Son; Promenades; Son Fl & Pno; Trio Fl KPT ▲ 32205

J. Suk (vn), J. Válek (fl), J. Hála (pno) *(rec Prague, 1996)* ("Sonatas for Violin, Flute & Piano") † Intermezzos Vn, H. 261; Madrigal Son; Promenades; Son Fl & Pno LT ▲ 41 [DDD] (16.97)

Sonata for Piano (1954)

R. Kvapil (pno) *(rec Apr 1983)* † Études & Polkas; Son Fl & Pno BIS ▲ 234 [AAD] (17.97)

Sonata No. 1 for Viola & Piano (1955)

R. Moog (va), D. Adni (pno) *(rec Australian Festival of Chamber Music, July 1994)* ("Chamber Music") † Qnt Strs; Qt Ob; Qt 1 Pno NXIN ▲ 553916 [DDD] (5.97)

R. Verebes (va), D. Bartlett (pno) *(rec Boucherville Quebec)* † Coulthard:Son Rhap; Mendelssohn (-Bartholdy):Son Va SNE ▲ 550 (16.97)

Sonata in C for Violin & Piano, H. 120 (1919)

B. Matoušek (vn), P. Adamec (pno) *(rec Martinů Hall, Lichtenstien Palace, Prague, Czech Republic, July & Sept 1996)* † Con Vn & Pno, H. 13; Elegy; Impromptu, H. 166; Short Pieces (5), H. 184; Son Vn & Pno, H. 152; Son 1 Vn SUR 2-▲ 3410 [DDD] (16.97)

Sonata in d for Violin & Piano, H. 152 (1926)

B. Matoušek (vn), P. Adamec (pno) *(rec Martinů Hall, Lichtenstien Palace, Prague, Czech Republic, Sept 1996)* † Con Vn & Pno, H. 13; Elegy; Impromptu, H. 166; Short Pieces (5), H. 184; Son Vn & Pno, H. 120; Son 1 Vn SUR 2-▲ 3410 [DDD] (16.97)

Sonata No. 1 for Violin & Piano (1927)

H. Kotkova (vn), S. Mulligan (pno) † Czech Rhapsody, H. 307; Son 2 Vn, H. 208; Son 3 Vn, H.303 STMA ▲ 45 (18.97)

MARTINŮ, BOHUSLAV (cont.)

Sonata No. 1 for Violin & Piano (1927) (cont.)

F. Lack (vn), T. Hester (pno) *(rec Dudley Recital Hall Univ of Houston School of Mus, TX, Aug 18-20, 1993)* † Son 2 Vn, H. 208; Son 3 Vn, H.303; Sonatina for 2 Vns CENT ▲ 2276 [DDD] (16.97)

B. Matoušek (vn), P. Adamec (pno) *(rec Martinů Hall, Lichtenstien Palace, Prague, Czech Republic, Sept 1996)* † Con Vn & Pno, H. 13; Elegy; Impromptu, H. 166; Short Pieces (5), H. 184; Son Vn & Pno, H. 120; Son Vn & Pno, H. 152 SUR 2-▲ 3410 [DDD] (16.97)

Sonata No. 2 for Violin & Piano, H. 208 (1931)

H. Kotkova (vn), S. Mulligan (pno) † Czech Rhapsody, H. 307; Son 1 Vn; Son 3 Vn, H.303 STMA ▲ 45 (18.97)

F. Lack (vn), T. Hester (pno) *(rec Dudley Recital Hall Univ of Houston School of Mus, Aug 18-20, 1993)* † Son 1 Vn; Son 3 Vn, H.303; Sonatina for 2 Vns CENT ▲ 2276 [DDD] (16.97)

B. Matoušek (vn), P. Adamec (pno) *(rec Martinů Hall, Lichtenstein Palace, Prague, Czech Republic, Feb & June 1997)* † Études rythmiques; Arabesques, H. 201A; Ariette; Czech Rhapsody, H. 307; Intermezzos Vn, H. 261; Madrigal Stanzas, H. 297; Son 3 Vn, H.303; Sonatina Vn, H. 262 SUR 2-▲ 3412 [DDD] (16.97)

P. Rejto (vc), R. Rowley (pno) † S. Barber:Son Vc, Op. 6; Janáček:Fairy Tale; Kodály:Son Vc & Pno, Op. 4 RTOP ▲ 8617 (16.97)

Sonata No. 3 for Violin & Piano, H.303 (1944)

Y. Kless (vn), S. Rudiakov (pno) † Madrigal Stanzas, H. 297; Enescu:Impromptu Concertant; Son 2 Vn, Op. 6 TACE ▲ 62

H. Kotkova (vn), S. Mulligan (pno) † Czech Rhapsody, H. 307; Son 1 Vn; Son 2 Vn, H. 208 STMA ▲ 45 (18.97)

F. Lack (vn), T. Hester (pno) *(rec Dudley Recital Hall Univ of Houston School of Mus, Aug 18-20, 1993)* † Son 1 Vn; Son 2 Vn, H. 208; Sonatina for 2 Vns CENT ▲ 2276 [DDD] (16.97)

B. Matoušek (vn), P. Adamec (pno) *(rec Martinů Hall, Lichtenstein Palace, Prague, Czech Republic, Oct 1997 & Apr 1998)* † Études rythmiques; Arabesques, H. 201A; Ariette; Czech Rhapsody, H. 307; Intermezzos Vn, H. 261; Madrigal Stanzas, H. 297; Son 2 Vn, H. 208; Sonatina Vn, H. 262 SUR 2-▲ 3412 [DDD] (16.97)

Sonatina for Clarinet & Piano (1956)

M. Edwards (cl), T. Bach (pno) *(rec Pomona College Claremont, CA, 1997)* † Bjelinski:Son Cl; Ladmirault:Son Cl; Rabaud:Solo de Concours, Op. 10; Saint-Saëns:Son Cl CRYS ▲ 735 (15.97)

L. Rozmán (cl), B. Simon (pno) ("Chamber Music") † Son Fl & Pno; Sxt Fl, Ob, Cl, 2 Bns & Pno; Trio Fl; Vars on a Theme of Rossini, H.290 HUN ▲ 31674 [DDD] (16.97)

H. Wright (cl), L. Batlle (pno) *(rec Jan 26, 1992)* ("Harold Wright Live Recital No. 1") † Debussy:Arabesques Pno; Petite pièce Cl; Plus que lente; Pno Music (misc colls); W. Lutoslawski:Dance Preludes Cl & Pno; F. Poulenc:Son Cl & Pno; Saint-Saëns:Son Cl BOST ▲ 1023 (15.97)

M. Zukovsky (cl), Bohemian Ensemble Los Angeles ("Otiose Odalisque") † Pastorales; Qt Cl; Revue de Cuisine SUMM ▲ 214 (16.97)

Sonatina for Trumpet & Piano (1956)

E. H. Tarr (tpt), E. Westenholz (pno) † Alexius:Sonatina Tpt; Cellier:Thème et variations; G. Gershwin:Rhap in Blue; P. Hindemith:Son Tpt; S. Weiner:Phantasy 1 Tpt, Op. 57; F. Werner:Duo Tpt & Org, Op. 53 BIS ▲ 152 [AAD] (17.97)

Sonatina in G for Violin & Piano, H. 262 (1937)

B. Matoušek (vn), P. Adamec (pno) *(rec Martinů Hall, Lichtenstein Palace, Prague, Czech Republic, Feb & June 1997)* † Études rythmiques; Arabesques, H. 201A; Ariette; Czech Rhapsody, H. 307; Intermezzos Vn, H. 261; Madrigal Stanzas, H. 297; Son 2 Vn, H. 208; Son 3 Vn, H.303 SUR 2-▲ 3412 [DDD] (16.97)

Sonatina for 2 Violins & Piano (1930)

F. Lack (vn), L. Spierer (vn), T. Hester (pno) *(rec Dudley Recital Hall Univ of Houston School of Mus, Aug 18-20, 1993)* † Son 1 Vn; Son 2 Vn, H. 208; Son 3 Vn, H.303 CENT ▲ 2276 [DDD] (16.97)

Špalíček (ballet in 3 acts) for Soprano, Tenor, Bass, Orchestra & Chorus [text Martinů] (1933; rev 1940)

A. Kratochvílová (sop), M. Kopp (ten), R. Novák (bass), F. Jílek (cnd), Brno State PO, Kantiléna Children's Chorus [CZE] † Dandelion Romance; Primrose SUR 2-▲ 110752 [DDD]

Symphonies (6) for Orchestra (complete)

V. Neumann (cnd), Czech PO *(rec 1976-77)* SUR 3-▲ 110382 [AAD]

V. Neumann (cnd), Czech PO SUR ▲ 111966 [AAD]

V. Neumann (cnd), Czech PO SUR 3-▲ 382 (30.97)

B. Thomson (cnd), Royal Scottish National Orch CHN 3-▲ 9103 [DDD] (48.97)

Symphony No. 1 (1942)

K. Ančerl (cnd), Czech PO *(rec ca 1963)* † Sym 3; Sym 5 MUL (Prague Spring Collection) 2-▲ 310023 [ADD]

J. Bělohlávek (cnd), Czech PO † Double Con CHN ▲ 8950 [DDD] (17.97)

A. Fagen (cnd), Ukrainian National SO *(rec Ukraine National Radio Company Concert Hall Kiev, June 1995)* † Sym 6 NXIN ▲ 8553348 [DDD] (5.97)

N. Järvi (cnd), Bamberg SO † Sym 2 BIS ▲ 362 (17.97)

B. Thomson (cnd), Royal Scottish National Orch † Sym 5 CHN ▲ 8915 [DDD] (17.97)

Symphony No. 2 (1943)

N. Järvi (cnd), Bamberg SO † Sym 1 BIS ▲ 362 (17.97)

B. Thomson (cnd), Royal Scottish National Orch † Sym 6 CHN ▲ 8916 [DDD] (16.97)

Symphony No. 3 (1944)

K. Ančerl (cnd), Czech PO *(rec ca 1966)* † Sym 1; Sym 5 MUL (Prague Spring Collection) 2-▲ 310023 [ADD]

N. Järvi (cnd), Bamberg SO † Sym 4 BIS ▲ 363 (17.97)

K. Sejna (cnd), Czech PO † Double Con; A. Dvořák:Suite Orch, Op. 98b SUR ▲ 111924

B. Thomson (cnd), Royal Scottish National Orch † Sym 4 CHN ▲ 8917 [DDD] (16.97)

Symphony No. 4 (1945)

E. Ansermet (cnd), Swiss Romande Orch † Fresques de Piero; Parables CASC ▲ 2007 [ADD] (16.97)

N. Järvi (cnd), Bamberg SO † Sym 3 BIS ▲ 363 (17.97)

B. Kotmel (cnd), Czech PO † Field Mass; Memorial to Lidice CHN ▲ 9138 [DDD] (16.97)

B. Thomson (cnd), Royal Scottish National Orch † Sym 3 CHN ▲ 8917 [DDD] (16.97)

Symphony No. 5 (1946)

K. Ančerl (cnd), Czech PO *(rec ca 1962)* † Sym 1; Sym 3 MUL (Prague Spring Collection) 2-▲ 310023 [ADD]

N. Järvi (cnd), Bamberg SO † Sym 6 BIS ▲ 402 (17.97)

B. Thomson (cnd), Royal Scottish National Orch † Sym 1 CHN ▲ 8915 [DDD] (17.97)

Symphony No. 6, "Fantaisies symphoniques" (1951-53)

J. Bělohlávek (cnd), Czech PO † Janáček:Sinfonietta; J. Suk:Fantastické scherzo, Op. 25 CHN ▲ 8897 [DDD] (16.97)

A. Fagen (cnd), Ukrainian National SO *(rec Ukraine National Radio Company Concert Hall Kiev, June 1995)* † Sym 1 NXIN ▲ 8553348 [DDD] (5.97)

N. Järvi (cnd), Bamberg SO † Sym 5 BIS ▲ 402 (17.97)

B. Thomson (cnd), Royal Scottish National Orch † Sym 2 CHN ▲ 8916 [DDD] (16.97)

The Three Wishes (film opera in 3 acts) [lib G. Ribemont-Dessaignes] (1929)

M. Kloboučková (sop—Eblouie Barbichette/La mendiante bossue), J. Marková (sop—Indolende/Nina Valencia), Y. Škvárová (mez—La fée Nulle/Lillian Nevermore), A. Barová (cta—Adélaïde), V. Krejčík (ten—Le garçon), J. Skrobánek (ten—Le majordome), Z. Šmukař (ten—Adolphe/Serge Eliacin), J. Souček (bar—Arthur de St. Barbe/Monsieur Juste), V. Chmelo (bar—Le ministre des fina), J. Hladík (bass—Le capitaine), A. Šťáva (bass—Le général), M. Grym (sgr), M. Važanský (sgr), M. Vojta (sgr), V. Nosek (cnd), Brno Janáček Opera Orch, J. Pančík (cnd), Brno Janáček Opera Chorus [Cz, F] *(rec Brno Dukla Studio, Oct 25, 1989-June 25, 1990)* SUR ▲ 3103 [AAD] (16.97)

Toccata e due canzoni for Orchestra (1946)

T. Vásáry (cnd), Bournemouth Sinfonietta † Sinfonietta giocosa Pno; Sinfonietta Pno CHN ▲ 8859 [DDD] (16.97)

Trio in F for Flute, Cello & Piano (1944)

M. Bergman (vc), Y. Arnheim (fl), I. Rub-Levi (pno) ("Bohuslav Martinů: Chamber Music with Flute") † Madrigal Son; Promenades; Son Fl & Pno; Son Fl, Vn & Pno KPT ▲ 32205

A. L. Christiansen (vc), T. Christiansen (fl), E. Westenholz (pno) † Kuhlau:Grand Trio, Op. 119 KPT ▲ 32064 [DDD]

Huntingdon Trio † Loeb:Nocturnes; B. Marx:Divert a Tre; N. Rorem:Trio Fl LEON ▲ 330 [DDD] (16.97)

Lahti SO Chamber Ensemble members *(rec Järvenpää Hall Finland, Feb 28-Mar 4, 1994)* † Nonet Ww & Pno; Nonet Ww, Strs & Db; Revue de Cuisine BIS ▲ 653 [DDD] (17.97)

B. Lasserson (vc), E. Horgas (fl), B. Simon (pno) ("Chamber Music") † Son Fl & Pno; Sonatina Cl; Sxt Fl, Ob, Cl, 2 Bns & Pno; Vars on a Theme of Rossini, H.290 HUN ▲ 31674 [DDD] (16.97)

Trio No. 1 for Piano, Violin & Cello, "5 pièces brèves" (1930)

Angell Piano Trio † Duo 2 Vn & Vc; Trio 2 Pno; Trio 3 Pno ASLE ▲ 6230 (10.97)

Bekova Sisters † Duo 1 Vn & Vc, H.157; M. Ravel:Son Vn & Vc; Trio Pno CHN ▲ 9452 (16.97)

Iscles Trio ("Complete Piano Trios") † Bergerettes; Trio 2 Pno; Trio 3 Pno MDA7 ▲ 4 (18.97)

Trio No. 2 in d for Piano, Violin & Cello (1950)

Angell Piano Trio † Duo 2 Vn & Vc; Trio 1 Pno; Trio 3 Pno ASLE ▲ 6230 (10.97)

E. Bekova (vn), A. Bekova (vc), E. Bekova (pno) † Czech Rhapsody, H. 307; Nocturnes Vc; Trio 3 Pno CHN ▲ 9632 (16.97)

MOZART, WOLFGANG AMADEUS (cont.)

Arias (cont.)

L. Simoneau (ten) *(Per pietà, non ricercate, K.420)*, E. Köth (sop) *(Nehmt meinen Dank, ihr holden Gönner!, K.383)*, E. Mathis (sop) *(Misera, dove son! & Ah, non son'io che parlo, K.369)*, G. Tozzi (bass) *(Così dunque tradisci & Aspri rimorsi atroci, K.432)*, H. Güden (sop) *(Rè pastore (sels) [L'amerò, sarò costante])*, G. Sciutti (sop) *(Voi avete un cor fedele, K.217)*, G. Evans (bass) *(Un bacio di mano, K.541)*, R. Grist (sop) *(Vorrei spiegarvi, oh Dio, K.418)*, I. Hallstein (sop) *(No, che non sei capace, K.419)*, P. Schreier (ten) *(Misero! O sogno! & Aura, che intorno spiri, K.431)*, I. Cotrubas (sop) *(Basta, vincesti & Ah, non lasciarmi, K.486a)*, J. Van Dam (bass) *(Mentre ti lascio, o figlia, K.513)* ("Great Mozart Singers, Vol. 4: Concert Arias, 1956-70") ORFE (Festspiel Dokumente) ▲ 394401 (16.97)

E. Steber (sop) *(Tu virginum corona; Idomeneo (sels) [D'Oreste, d'Ajace]; Nozze di Figaro (sels) [Deh vieni, non tardar, o gioja bella; Voi, che sapete che cosa è amor; Porgi amor qualche ristoro; Dove sono i bei momenti]; Resta, o cara; A questo seno deh vieni, K.374; Nehmt meinen Dank, ihr holden Gönner!, K.383)*, E. Steber (sop), F. Eyle (vn) *(Rè pastore (sels) [L'amerò, sarò costante]) (rec 1946-51)* ("Eleanor Steber Sings Mozart") † Qnts (110) Various Instrs; Sacred Music VAIA ▲ 1031 [ADD] (17.97)

N. Stutzmann (cta), V. Spivakov (cnd), Moscow Virtuosi—Ombra felice & Io ti lascio, K.255; Io ti lascio, oh cara, addio, K.Anh.245 *(rec Neumarkt Germany, Germany, July 27-30, 1994)* ("Rare Mozart Arias") † Ascanio in Alba (sels), K.111; Betulia liberata (sels); Mitridate (sels) RCAV (Red Seal) ▲ 68187 [DDD] (16.97)

J. Van Dam (b-bar), J. Wallez (cnd) *(Così fan tutte (sels); Nozze di Figaro (sels); Zauberflöte (sels); Un bacio di mano, K.541)*, artist unknown, J. Van Dam (b-bar), J. Wallez (cnd) *(Mentre ti lascio, o figlia, K.513; Mentre ti lascio, o figlia, K.513) (rec live, Nov 22, 1986)* † Così fan tutte (ov); Nozze di Figaro (ov) FORL ▲ 16562 [DDD] (16.97)

H. Zadek (sop), B. Paumgartner (cnd), Vienna SO, B. Paumgartner (cnd), Vienna PO—Idomeneo (sels) [Tutte nel cor vi sento]; Nozze di Figaro (sels) [E Susanna non vien!]; Clemenza di Tito (sels) [Deh se piacer mi vuoi; Ecco il punto, oh Vitellia]; Basta, vincesti & Ah, non lasciarmi, K.486a; Alma grande e nobil core, K.578; Bella mia fiamma & Resta, o cara, K.528 ("Hilde Zadek singt") † Alma grande e nobil core, K.578; Basta, vincesti & Ah, non lasciarmi, K.486a; Bella mia fiamma & Resta, o cara, K.528; Clemenza di Tito (sels); Idomeneo (sels); Nozze di Figaro (sels); R. Strauss:Ariadne auf Naxos (sels); Elektra (sels); R. Wagner:Arias & Scenes; Fliegende Holländer (sels); Lohengrin (sels); Tannhäuser (sels) PRE ▲ 90335 (m) [ADD] (16.97)

Ascanio in Alba (selections), K.111

A. Scholl (ct), R. Norrington (cnd), Orch of the Age of Enlightenment—Al mio ben mi veggio avanti ("Heroes") † Mitridate (sels); C. W. Gluck:Orfeo ed Euridice (sels); Telemaco (sels); G. F. Handel:Arias; J. A. Hasse:Artaserse (sels) DECC ▲ 166196 [DDD] (16.97)

N. Stutzmann (cta), V. Spivakov (cnd), Moscow Virtuosi *(rec Neumarkt Germany, Germany, July 27-30, 1994)* ("Rare Mozart Arias") † Arias; Betulia liberata (sels); Mitridate (sels) RCAV (Red Seal) ▲ 68187 [DDD] (16.97)

H. Vonk (cnd), Dresden Staatskapelle—Ov † Clemenza di Tito (ov); Così fan tutte (ov); Don Giovanni (ov); Entführung aus dem Serail (ov); Finta giardiniera (ov); Idomeneo (ov); Lucio Silla (ov); Nozze di Figaro (ov); Schauspieldirektor (sels); Zauberflöte (ov) LALI ▲ 15885 [DDD] (3.97)

various artists, N. McGegan (cnd), Royal Opera House Orch—Si, ma d'un altro amore † Clemenza di Tito (ov); Clemenza di Tito (sels); Così fan tutte (sels); Don Giovanni (sels); Entführung aus dem Serail (sels); Nozze di Figaro (sels); Zaide (sels); Zauberflöte (sels) CONI ▲ 55031 (16.97)

Ave verum corpus (motet) for SATB Voices, Organ & Strings, K.618 (1791)

N. Argenta (sop), C. Robbin (cta), J. M. Ainsley (ten), A. Miles (bass), R. Norrington (cnd), Schütz Consort *(rec Kilburn, London, England, Sept 1991)* † Maurerische Trauermusik, K.477; Requiem, K.626 *([ENG,LAT]text)* VCL (The Norrington Collection) ▲ 61520 (11.97)

M. Atzmon (cnd), BBC Welsh SO, BBC Welsh Choral Society † Maurerische Trauermusik, K.477; Requiem, K.626 INMP (BBC Radio) ▲ 5691452 (13.97)

Berlin PO Double Bass Quartet *(rec Berlin, Germany, Dec 1978)* † Alt:Suite; Chihara:Logs; Findeisen:Prelude; Funck:Stricturae Viola di gambicea; E. Hartmann:Quartet; Jorns:Mobile Perpetuum CAMA ▲ 2562 [AAD] (18.97)

L. Bernstein (cnd), Bavarian RSO, Bavarian Radio Chorus *(rec live Apr 1990)* † Exsultate, jubilate, K.165; Mass 18, K.427 DEUT ▲ 31791 [DDD] (16.97)

S. Cleobury (cnd) , Hilliard Ensemble, King's College Choir Cambridge [LAT] † Vesperae de Dominica, K.321; Vesperae solennes de confessore, K.339 EMIC ▲ 49672 [DDD] (16.97)

C. Davis (cnd), London SO, London Sym Chorus † Exsultate, jubilate, K.165; Kyrie; Vesperae solennes de confessore, K.339 PPHI ▲ 12873 [ADD] (11.97)

M. Devia (sop), D. Callegari (cnd), Marchigiano PO, Chorus Lirico Marchigiana † Exsultate, jubilate, K.165; Kleine Nachtmusik, K.525; Regina coeli in C, K.108/74d; Vesperae solennes de confessore, K.339 FON ▲ 9830 (13.97)

F. Grier (cnd), Christ Church Cathedral Choir, Oxford, C. Daniels (vc), H. Bicket (org) *(rec Christ Church Catheral, Oxford, England)* ("O For the Wings of a Dove") † Anonymous:Church Music; J. S. Bach:Cant 147; Mendelssohn (-Bartholdy):Choral Music; Stanford:Church Music; C. Wood:Hail Gladdening Light ASVQ ▲ 6019 [ADD] (10.97)

K. T. Kanawa (sop), A. S. von Otter (mez), A. Rolfe Johnson (ten), R. Lloyd (bass), N. Marriner (cnd), Academy of St. Martin in the Fields, Academy Chorus *(rec London, Mar 10-12, 1993)* † Mass 18, K.427 PPHI ▲ 38999 (16.97)

B. Klee (cnd), English CO, Tallis Chamber Choir [LAT] † Exsultate, jubilate, K.165; Sacred Music; Schuldigkeit des ersten Gebotes (sels) NOVA ▲ 150064 [DDD] (16.97)

Z. Kloubová (sop), J. Žigmund (va), J. Krejčí (ob), D. Dimitrov (tpt), V. Roubal (org) † Exsultate, jubilate, K.165; Vesperae solennes de confessore, K.339; J. S. Bach:Cant 51; Cant 92; G. F. Handel:German Arias, HWV 202-10; Joshua (sels); Messiah (sels); J. Haydn:Schöpfung (sels); Saint-Saëns:Ave Maria; F. Schubert:Ave Maria, Op. 52/6; Vivaldi:Gloria; Motets GZCL ▲ 276 (6.97)

T. Koopman (cnd) † Requiem, K.626 ERAT ▲ 17909 (9.97)

S. McNair (sop), B. Bonney (sop), C. Margiono (sop), E. von Magnus (cta), C. Prégardien (ten), T. Hampson (bar), N. Harnoncourt (cnd), Vienna Concentus Musicus, Arnold Schoenberg Choir † Grabmusik, K.42; Regina coeli in B♭, K.127 TELC ▲ 98928 (16.97)

A. Michael (sop), B. Fink (cta), M. Tucker (ten), M. Brodard (bar), M. Corboz (cnd) , Lausanne Vocal Ensemble *(rec Switzerland, 1989)* † Mass 18, K.427 CASC ▲ 1011 (16.97)

E. Mirgová (sop), M. Kozená (cta), J. Griffett (ten), J. Klecker (bass), A. Kröper (cnd), Prague Concertino Notturno, R. Válek (cnd), Brnensky Academy Chorus Sbor *(rec Dec 5-7, 1991)* † Requiem, K.626 ICC ▲ 6702112 [DDD] (9.97)

N. Rime (sop), C. Batty (mez), S. Patterson (ten), B. Delétré (bass), G. Vashegyi (cnd), Budapest Orfeo Orch, P. Marco (cnd), Maîtrise de Paris † Mass 16, K.317; Vesperae solennes de confessore, K.339 PVY ▲ 730058 [DDD] (12.97)

G. Schmidt-Gaden (cnd) , Tölz Boys' Choir [LAT] † Inter natos mulierum, K.72; Mass 14, K.262; Regina coeli in C, K.276/371b; Te Deum, K.141; Venite populi, K.260 SNYC (Vivarte) ▲ 46493 (16.97)

A. Titov (cnd), St. Petersburg Conservatory CO, St. Petersburg Conservatory Chorus † J. S. Bach:Cant 122; Cant 191; Christmas Oratorio (sels); Gounod:Ave Maria; G. F. Handel:Messiah (sels); F. Schubert:Ave Maria, Op. 52/6 SNYC ▲ 57254 [DDD] (4.97)

I. Verebics (sop), J. Németh (mez), J. Mukk (ten), J. Moldvay (bar), G. Oláh (bar), I. Ella (org), J. Reményi (cnd), Hungarian Radio-TV Children's Chorus Girls' Voices, J. Reményi (cnd), Hungarian Radio-TV Male Chamber Choir *(rec Hungaroton Studio, June 14-16, 1991)* † Alma Dei creatoris, K.277; Mass 2, K.65; Mass 8, K.194; Miserere, K. 85; Misericordias Domini, K.222; Sancta Maria, K.273 CLDI ▲ 4003 [DDD] (10.97)

F. Wolf (cnd), St. Augustin Orch, St. Augustin Chorus † F. Schubert:Deutsche Messe; Mass 3, D.324 PRE ▲ 93325 (16.97)

Basta, vincesti (recitation) & Ah, non lasciarmi (aria) for Soprano & Orchestra, K.486a (1778)

H. Zadek (sop), B. Paumgartner (cnd), Vienna SO, B. Paumgartner (cnd), Vienna PO ("Hilde Zadek singt") † Alma grande e nobil core, K.578; Arias; Bella mia fiamma & Resta, o cara, K.528; Clemenza di Tito (sels); Idomeneo (sels); Nozze di Figaro (sels); R. Strauss:Ariadne auf Naxos (sels); Elektra (sels); R. Wagner:Arias & Scenes; Fliegende Holländer (sels); Lohengrin (sels); Tannhäuser (sels) PRE ▲ 90335 (m) [ADD] (16.97)

Bastien und Bastienne (selections)

M. Bernardi (cnd), Calgary PO—Ov *(rec Jack Singer Hall Calgary Centre for the Perfor, Canada)* ("Mozart: 12 Overtures") † Clemenza di Tito (ov); Così fan tutte (ov); Don Giovanni (ov); Entführung aus dem Serail (ov); Finta semplice (ov); Idomeneo (ov); Lucio Silla (ov); Mitridate (Ov); Nozze di Figaro (ov); Schauspieldirektor (sels); Zauberflöte (ov) SMS (SM 5000) ▲ 5149 [DDD] (16.97)

C. Davis (cnd), Staatskapelle Dresden—Ov † Così fan tutte (ov); Entführung aus dem Serail (ov); Finta giardiniera (ov); Lucio Silla (ov); Nozze di Figaro (ov); Ovs; Schauspieldirektor (sels) RCAV ▲ 63500 (16.97)

L. Hager (cnd), English CO—Ov † Betulia liberata, K.118; Clemenza di Tito (ov); Così fan tutte (ov); Don Giovanni (ov); Finta semplice (ov); Idomeneo (ov); Lucio Silla (ov); Mitridate (Ov); Nozze di Figaro (ov); Schauspieldirektor (sels); Zauberflöte (ov) NOVA ▲ 150041 [DDD] (16.97)

B. Wordsworth (cnd), Capella Istropolitana—Ov *(rec Czechoslovak Radio Concert Hall Bratislava, Czech Republic, Sept 6-9, 1988)* ("Famous Overtures") † Apollo et Hyacinthus (sels), K.38; Clemenza di Tito (ov); Così fan tutte (ov); Don Giovanni (ov); Entführung aus dem Serail (ov); Finta giardiniera (ov); Idomeneo (ov); Lucio Silla (ov); Mitridate (Ov); Nozze di Figaro (ov); Rè pastore (sels); Schauspieldirektor (sels); Zauberflöte (ov); G. Rossini:Barbiere di Siviglia (ov); Cenerentola (sels); Elisabetta; Guillaume Tell (ov); Italiana in Algeri (ov); Scala di seta (ov); Semiramide (ov); Signor Bruschino (sels); Verdi:Ovs & Preludes NXIN 4-▲ 504013 [DDD] (19.97)

MOZART, WOLFGANG AMADEUS (cont.)

Bastien und Bastienne (selections) (cont.)

B. Wordsworth (cnd), Capella Istropolitana—Ov *(rec Sept 6-9, 1988)* † Clemenza di Tito (ov); Così fan tutte (ov); Don Giovanni (ov); Entführung aus dem Serail (ov); Finta giardiniera (ov); Idomeneo (ov); Lucio Silla (ov); Mitridate (Ov); Nozze di Figaro (ov); Ovs; Rè pastore (sels); Schauspieldirektor (sels); Zauberflöte (ov) NXIN ▲ 550185 [DDD] (5.97)

Bastien und Bastienne (opera in 1 act) [lib Wieskern & Schachtner after Rousseau], K.50 (1768)

R. Clemencic (cnd), Alpe Adria Ensemble, E. Kirchner (sop), M. D. Vries (sgr), D. Chou (sgr) [GER] † Beethoven:Songs; J.-J. Rousseau:Devin du village NUO 2-▲ 7106 [DDD] (32.97)

E. Gruberová (sop), V. Cole (ten), L. Polgár (bass), R. Leppard (cnd), Franz Liszt CO SNYC ▲ 45855 (16.97)

A. Stolte (sop), P. Schreier (ten), T. Adam (bass), H. Koch (cnd), Berlin CO † Arias BER ▲ 9129 (10.97)

Bella mia fiamma & Resta, o cara (aria) for Soprano & Orchestra, K.528 (1787)

H. Zadek (sop), B. Paumgartner (cnd), Vienna SO, B. Paumgartner (cnd), Vienna PO ("Hilde Zadek singt") † Alma grande e nobil core, K.578; Arias; Basta, vincesti & Ah, non lasciarmi, K.486a; Clemenza di Tito (sels); Idomeneo (sels); Nozze di Figaro (sels); R. Strauss:Ariadne auf Naxos (sels); Elektra (sels); R. Wagner:Arias & Scenes; Fliegende Holländer (sels); Lohengrin (sels); Tannhäuser (sels) PRE ▲ 90335 (m) [ADD] (16.97)

Benedictus sit Deus (offertory) in C for Soprano, Orchestra & Chorus, K.117 (1768)

B. Bonney (sop), N. Harnoncourt (cnd), Vienna Concentus Musicus, Arnold Schoenberg Choir *(rec Casino Zögernitz Vienna, Dec 1990)* † Litaniae Lauretanae BVM, K.109; Regina coeli in C, K.108/74d; Sacred Music TELC (Das alte Werke) ▲ 96147 [DDD] (16.97)

La Betulia liberata (selections)

N. Stutzmann (cta), V. Spivakov (cnd), Moscow Virtuosi—Parto inerme, e non pavento *(rec Neumarkt Germany, Germany, July 27-30, 1994)* ("Rare Mozart Arias") † Arias; Ascanio in Alba (sels), K.111; Mitridate (sels) RCAV (Red Seal) ▲ 68187 [DDD] (16.97)

La betulia liberata (selections)

N. Stutzmann (cta), V. Spivakov (cnd), Moscow Virtuosi—Parto inerme, e non pavento *(rec Neumarkt Germany, Germany, July 27-30, 1994)* ("Rare Mozart Arias") † Arias; Ascanio in Alba (sels), K.111; Mitridate (sels) RCAV (Red Seal) ▲ 68187 [DDD] (16.97)

La Betulia liberata (oratorio in 2 parts) for Voice, Orchestra & Chorus, K.118 (1771)

L. Hager (cnd), English CO † Bastien und Bastienne (sels); Clemenza di Tito (ov); Così fan tutte (ov); Don Giovanni (ov); Finta semplice (ov); Idomeneo (ov); Lucio Silla (ov); Mitridate (Ov); Nozze di Figaro (ov); Schauspieldirektor (sels); Zauberflöte (ov) NOVA ▲ 150041 [DDD] (16.97)

Canons

Tölz Boys' Choir—Alleluja, K.553; Ave Maria, K.554; Lacrimoso son' io, K.555; Nascoso è il mio sol, K.557; Caro bell'idol, idol mio, K.562 † Mendelssohn (-Bartholdy):Choral Music KOC ▲ 340172 (16.97)

Cassation in G for 2 Oboes, 2 Horns & Strings, K.63 (1769)

G. Hölscher (ob), S. Winiarczyk (ob), R. Schnepps (hn), H. Nerat (hn) *(rec Mar 28-30, 1992)* † Cassation Obs, K.100; Cassation Obs, K.99 NXIN ▲ 550609 [DDD] (5.97)

L. Maazel (cnd), English CO ("Mozart Violin Concertos") † Cassation Obs, K.100; Cassation Obs, K.99; Con 3 Vn, K.216; Con 5 Vn, K.219 KLAV ▲ 11046 [ADD] (18.97)

Cassation in B♭ for 2 Oboes, 2 Horns & Strings, K.99 (1769)

G. Hölscher (ob), S. Winiarczyk (ob), R. Schnepps (hn), H. Nerat (hn) *(rec Mar 28-30, 1992)* † Cassation Obs, K.100; Cassation Obs, K.63 NXIN ▲ 550609 [DDD] (5.97)

L. Maazel (vn), L. Maazel (cnd), English CO ("Mozart Violin Concertos") † Cassation Obs, K.100; Cassation Obs, K.63; Con 3 Vn, K.216; Con 5 Vn, K.219 KLAV ▲ 11046 [ADD] (18.97)

Cassation in D for 2 Oboes (or Flutes), 2 Horns, 2 Trumpets & Strings, K.100 (1769)

W. Boskovsky (cnd) *(rec Sofiensaal Vienna, Austria)* † Kleine Nachtmusik, K.525; Serenade Vn; Serenade 6 Orch, K.239; Serenade 9 Orch, K.320 PLON 2-▲ 43458 [ADD] (17.97)

C. Hogwood (bc), J. Schröder (cnd), Academy of Ancient Music ("The Symphonies") † Gallimathias musicum, K.32; Music of Mozart; Symphonies (miscellaneous) PLOI 19-▲ 452496 [ADD] (127.97)

G. Hölscher (ob), S. Winiarczyk (ob), R. Schnepps (hn), H. Nerat (hn) *(rec Mar 28-30, 1992)* † Cassation Obs, K.63; Cassation Obs, K.99 NXIN ▲ 550609 [DDD] (5.97)

L. Maazel (cnd), English CO ("Mozart Violin Concertos") † Cassation Obs, K.63; Cassation Obs, K.99; Con 3 Vn, K.216; Con 5 Vn, K.219 KLAV ▲ 11046 [ADD] (18.97)

C. Scimone (cnd) *(rec Vicenza Italy, Italy, 1994)* ("Early Symphonies, Vol 3") † Sym 10, K.74; Sym 12, K.110; Sym 13, K.112; Sym 14, K.114 AART ▲ 47277 [DDD] (10.97)

Ch'io mi scordi di te? & Non temer, amato bene (scene & rondo) for Soprano & Orchestra, K.505 (1786)

S. Ehrling (cnd), Swedish CO *(rec Sweden, Sept 1996)* ("Debra Kitabjian Every") † Montsalvage:Canciónes negras; O. Respighi:Aretusa; Uccelli BLUB ▲ 68 (18.97)

E. Kirkby (sop), C. Hogwood (cnd), Academy of Ancient Music Orch † Ah, lo previdi & Ah, t'invola agl'occhi miei, K.272; Nehmt meinen Dank, ihr holden Gönner!, K.383; Rè pastore (sels); Voi avete un cor fedele, K.217; Zaide (sels); T. Arne:Comus (sels); Rosamond (sels); Tempest (sels); G. F. Handel:Alcina (sels); Alessandro Severo (sels); Alexander's Feast (ode), HWV 75; Allegro, il Penseroso ed il Moderato (sels); Ariodante (sels); Hornpipe in D, HWV 356; March; Saul (sels); J. Haydn:Schöpfung (sels); J. F. Lampe:Brittania (sels); Dione (sels) PLON (Double Decker) 2-▲ 458084 [DDD] (17.97)

C. Ludwig (mez), B. Paumgartner (cnd), Salzburg Mozarteum Orch † Con 16 Pno, K.451; Marches Orch, K.408; Sym 36, K.425 ORFE ▲ 330931 (16.97)

B. Weil (cnd), Tafelmusik † Serenade Vn; Serenade Vn, K.185/167a; Serenade Vn, K.203/189b; Serenade Vn, K.204/213a; Serenade 9 Orch, K.320 SNYC (Vivarte) ▲ 47260 (31.97)

Church Sonatas (17) for 2 Violins (or Trumpets/Oboes), Double Bass & Organ, "Epistle Sonatas" (1772-80)

A. Frigé (org), Pian e Forte Ensemble *(rec St. Francis of Paola Church Milan, Aug 1994)* AG ▲ 2 (18.97)

C. Medlam (cnd) HMA ▲ 1901137 (9.97)

J. Messner (cnd), Salzburg Mozarteum Orch *(rec Aug 24, 1952)* † Grabmusik, K.42; Requiem, K.626 ORFE (Festspiel Dokumente) ▲ 396951 (16.97)

A. Parrott (cnd), Boston Early Music Festival Orch—K.67, Sonata da Chiesa No. 1 in E♭; K.329, Sonata da Chiesa No. 16 in C † Mass 18, K.427 DNN ▲ 79573 [DDD] (16.97)

J. Sebestyén (org) *(rec Feb 15-18, 1991)* NXIN ▲ 550512 [DDD] (5.97)

Y. Turovsky (cnd), Montreal Musici CHN ▲ 8745 [DDD] (16.97)

I. Watson (org), R. King (cnd), King's Consort HYP ▲ 66377 [DDD] (18.97)

La clemenza di Tito (opera in 2 acts) [lib C. Mazzolà after Metastasio], K.621 (1791)

B. Bonney (sop—Servilia), D. Jones (mez—Vitellia), D. Montague (mez—Annio), C. Bartoli (mez—Sesto), U. Heilmann (ten—Tito), G. Cachemaille (bar—Publio), C. Hogwood (cnd), Academy of Ancient Music, Academy of Ancient Music Chorus PLOI 2-▲ 44131 [DDD] (32.97)

J. E. Gardiner (cnd), English Baroque Soloists, Monteverdi Choir London, J. Varady (sop), S. McNair (sop), A. S. von Otter (mez), A. Rolfe Johnson (ten) PARC 2-▲ 31806 [DDD] (32.97)

La clemenza di Tito (selections)

Albert Schweitzer Octet members—Vitellia's Aria; Annio's Aria; Duet Vitellia - Sesto; Duet Servilia - Annio; Terzet: Vitellia, Annio, Publio; Sesto's Aria; Vitellia's Rondo [arr A. Tarkmann] *(rec Germany, Apr 15-17, 1997)* ("Harmoniemusiken") † Clemenza di Tito (ov); Bizet:Carmen (sels); O. Nicolai:Lustigen Weiber von Windsor (sels) CPO ▲ 999519 [DDD] (14.97)

C. Bartoli (mez), L. Schatzberger (b cl), C. Hogwood (cnd), Academy of Ancient Music *(rec 1992)* ("A Portrait") † Così fan tutte (sels); Don Giovanni (sels); Nozze di Figaro (sels); G. Caccini:Amarilli mia bella; Parisotti:Se tu m'ami; G. Rossini:Cenerentola (sels); Maometto II (sels); Semiramide (sels); F. Schubert:Songs (misc colls) PLON ▲ 48300 [DDD] (17.97) ▮ 48300 [DDD] (11.98)

J. Carden (sop), R. Brydon (cnd), Queensland PO *(rec 1996)* ("Great Opera Heroines") † Così fan tutte (sels); B. Britten:Peter Grimes (sels); A. Catalani:Wally (sels); G. Puccini:Arias; P. Tchaikovsky:Eugene Onegin (sels); Verdi:Traviata (sels) WALC ▲ 8026 [DDD] (16.97)

J. Kovács (cnd), Hungarian State Orch, M. Szalay (cnd), Hungarian State Opera Male Chorus—Tardi s'avvede d'un tradimento; Tardi s'avvede d'un tradimento *(rec Budapest, Hungary, 1997)* ("Operatic Recitals") † Arias; Don Giovanni (sels); Entführung aus dem Serail (sels); Mentre ti lascio, o figlia, K.513; Nozze di Figaro (sels); Per questa bella mano, K.612; Zauberflöte (sels) *([ENG,GER,ITA]texts)* HUN ▲ 31660 [DDD] (16.97)

L. Marshall (sop), E. Pedrazzoli (cnd), London SO—Parto, parto, ma tu ben mio *(rec Canada, 1959)* ("Arias - Lois Marshall") † Don Giovanni (sels); Entführung aus dem Serail (sels); G. F. Handel:Acis & Galatea (sels); Solomon (sels); J. Haydn:Jahreszeiten (sels); Schöpfung (sels) *([ENG,FRE] text)* CBC ▲ 2001 [ADD] (16.97)

E. Ritchie (sop), V. Soames (cl), J. Purvis (pno)—Parto, parto, ma tu ben mio † I. Müller:Qt 2 Cl; F. Paer:Una voce; L. Spohr:Faust (sels); Vars on a Theme from Alruna CLCL ▲ 6 [ADD] (17.97)

G. Sabbatini (ten), R. Paternostro (cnd) † Così fan tutte (sels); Don Giovanni (ov); Entführung aus dem Serail (sels) LALI ▲ 15890 [DDD] (3.97)

MOZART, WOLFGANG AMADEUS (cont.)
La clemenza di Tito (selections) (cont.)
H. Zadek (sop), B. Paumgartner (cnd), Vienna SO, B. Paumgartner (cnd), Vienna PO—Ecco il punto, oh Vitellia; Deh se piacer mi vuoi; Ecco il punto, oh Vitellia ("Hilde Zadek singt") † Alma grande e nobil core, K.578; Arias; Basta, vincesti & Ah, non lasciarmi, K.486a; Bella mia fiamma & Resta, o cara, K.528; Idomeneo (sels); Nozze di Figaro (sels); R. Strauss:Ariadne auf Naxos (sels); Elektra (sels); R. Wagner:Arias & Scenes; Fliegende Holländer (sels); Lohengrin (sels); Tannhäuser (sels) PRE ▲ 90335 (m) [ADD] (16.97)
various artists, N. McGegan (cnd), Royal Opera House Orch—Parto, parto, ma tu ben mio † Ascanio in Alba (sels), K.111; Clemenza di Tito (ov); Così fan tutte (sels); Don Giovanni (sels); Entführung aus dem Serail (sels); Nozze di Figaro (sels); Zaide (sels); Zauberflöte (sels) CONI ▲ 55031 (16.97)
La clemenza di Tito:Overture
Albert Schweitzer Octet members [arr A. Tarkmann] *(rec Germany, Apr 15-17, 1997)* ("Harmoniemusiken") † Clemenza di Tito (sels); Bizet:Carmen (sels); O. Nicolai:Lustigen Weiber von Windsor (sels) CPO ▲ 999519 [DDD] (14.97)
T. Beecham (cnd), London PO ("Beecham & London PO, 1944-45, Vol. 1") † Kleine Nachtmusik, K.525; G. F. Handel:Great Elopement; J. Haydn:Sym 97 BCS ▲ 41 (16.97)
M. Bernardi (cnd), Calgary PO *(rec Jack Singer Hall Calgary Centre for the Perfor, Canada)* ("Mozart: 12 Overtures") † Bastien und Bastienne (sels); Così fan tutte (ov); Don Giovanni (ov); Entführung aus dem Serail (ov); Finta semplice (ov); Idomeneo (ov); Lucio Silla (ov); Mitridate (Ov); Nozze di Figaro (ov); Schauspieldirektor (sels); Zauberflöte (ov) SMS (SM 5000) ▲ 5149 [DDD] (16.97)
L. Christensen (gtr), M. Kammerling (gtr) [arr for 2 gtrs] † V. Bellini:Pirata (sels); G. Rossini:Ovs; Spontini:Vestale (sels) PLAL ▲ 54 (18.97)
Duo Sonare [arr Mauro Giuliani for 2 gtrs] *(rec Nov 1996)* † Larghetto & Vars; Rondo Pno, K.485; Son 16 Pno, K.545; F. Carulli:Duos Gtrs, Op. 241; M. Giuliani:Polonaise; Rondo alla Pollacca; Tarantella MDG (Scene) ▲ 6300629 [DDD] (17.97)
L. Hager (cnd), English CO † Bastien und Bastienne (sels); Betulia liberata, K.118; Così fan tutte (ov); Don Giovanni (ov); Finta semplice (ov); Idomeneo (ov); Lucio Silla (ov); Mitridate (Ov); Nozze di Figaro (ov); Schauspieldirektor (sels); Zauberflöte (ov) NOVA ▲ 150041 [DDD] (16.97)
Z. Kosler (cnd), Slovak PO [plus others] † Così fan tutte (ov); Don Giovanni (ov); Entführung aus dem Serail (ov); Idomeneo (ov); Nozze di Figaro (ov); Zauberflöte (ov) GZCL ▲ 74 (6.97)
N. Marriner (cnd), Academy of St. Martin in the Fields † Così fan tutte (ov); Don Giovanni (ov); Entführung aus dem Serail (ov); Idomeneo (ov); Lucio Silla (ov); Nozze di Figaro (ov); Schauspieldirektor (sels); Zauberflöte (ov) EMIC ▲ 47014 [DDD] (16.97)
H. Vonk (cnd), Dresden Staatskapelle † Ascanio in Alba (sels), K.111; Così fan tutte (ov); Don Giovanni (ov); Entführung aus dem Serail (ov); Finta giardiniera (ov); Idomeneo (ov); Lucio Silla (ov); Nozze di Figaro (ov); Schauspieldirektor (sels); Zauberflöte (ov) LALI ▲ 15885 [DDD] (3.97)
B. Wordsworth (cnd), Capella Istropolitana *(rec Czechoslovak Radio Concert Hall Bratislava, Czech Republic, Sept 6-9, 1988)* ("Famous Overtures") † Apollo et Hyacinthus (sels), K.38; Bastien und Bastienne (sels); Così fan tutte (ov); Don Giovanni (ov); Entführung aus dem Serail (ov); Finta giardiniera (ov); Idomeneo (ov); Lucio Silla (ov); Mitridate (Ov); Nozze di Figaro (ov); Rè pastore (sels); Schauspieldirektor (sels); Zauberflöte (ov); G. Rossini:Barbiere di Siviglia (ov); Cenerentola (sels); Elisabetta; Guillaume Tell (ov); Italiana in Algeri (ov); Scala di seta (ov); Semiramide (ov); Signor Bruschino (sels); Verdi:Ovs & Preludes NXIN 4-▲ 504013 [DDD] (19.97)
B. Wordsworth (cnd), Capella Istropolitana *(rec Sept 6-9, 1988)* † Bastien und Bastienne (sels); Così fan tutte (ov); Don Giovanni (ov); Entführung aus dem Serail (ov); Finta giardiniera (ov); Idomeneo (ov); Lucio Silla (ov); Mitridate (Ov); Nozze di Figaro (ov); Ovs; Rè pastore (sels); Schauspieldirektor (sels); Zauberflöte (ov) NXIN ▲ 550185 [DDD] (5.97)
various artists, N. McGegan (cnd), Royal Opera House Orch † Ascanio in Alba (sels), K.111; Clemenza di Tito (sels); Così fan tutte (sels); Don Giovanni (sels); Entführung aus dem Serail (sels); Nozze di Figaro (sels); Zaide (sels); Zauberflöte (sels) CONI ▲ 55031 (16.97)
The "Complete Mozart Edition" (the complete works by Mozart in 45 volumes)
Academy of St. Martin in the Fields Chamber Ensemble ("Vol. 4—Divertimenti for Strings & Winds") PPHI 5-▲ 22504 [ADD] (57.97)
Academy of St. Martin in the Fields Chamber Ensemble, Grumiaux Trio ("Vol. 10—Quartets, Quintets, etc. for Strings & Winds") PPHI 3-▲ 22510 [ADD] (34.97)
E. Ameling (sop), D. Baldwin (pno), Netherlands Wind Ensemble ("Vol. 24—Lieder & Notturni") PPHI 2-▲ 22524 [ADD] (22.97)
M. Arroyo (sop), M. Freni (sop), K. T. Kanawa (sop), S. Burrows (ten), I. Wixell (bar), C. Davis (cnd), Royal Opera House Orch Covent Garden, Royal Opera House Covent Garden Chorus ("Vol. 41—Don Giovanni") PPHI 3-▲ 22541 [ADD] (34.97)
A. Augér (sop), E. Gruberová (sop), I. Cotrubas (sop), A. Baltsa (mez), W. Hollweg (ten), L. Hager (cnd), Salzburg Mozarteum Orch ("Vol. 29—Mitridate") PPHI 3-▲ 22529 [ADD] (34.97)
W. Boskovsky (cnd) ("Vol. 6—Dances & Marches") PPHI 6-▲ 22506 [ADD] (68.97)
A. Brendel (pno), S. B. Kovacevich (pno), B. Hoffmann (g ar), Beaux Arts Trio ("Vol. 14—Piano Trios, Quartets, Quintet, etc.") PPHI 5-▲ 22514 [ADD] (57.97)
A. Brendel (pno), N. Marriner (cnd), Academy of St. Martin in the Fields—Con 5 Pno, K.175; Con 6 Pno, K.238; Con 7 Pnos, K.242; Con 8 Pno, K.246; Con 9 Pno, K.271; Con 10 Pnos, K.365; Con 11 Pno, K.413; Con 12 Pno, K.414; Con 13 Pno, K.415; Con 14 Pno, K.449; Con 15 Pno, K.450; Con 16 Pno, K.451; Con 17 Pno, K.453; Con 18 Pno, K.456; Con 19 Pno, K.459; Con 20 Pno, K.466; Con 21 Pno, K.467; Con 22 Pno, K.482; Con 23 Pno, K.488; Con 24 Pno, K.491; Con 25 Pno, K.503; Con 26 Pno, K.537; Con 27 Pno, K.595 ("Vol. 7—Piano Concertos") PPHI 12-▲ 22507 [ADD] (137.97)
M. Caballé (sop), I. Cotrubas (sop), J. Baker (mez), N. Gedda (ten), C. Davis (cnd), Royal Opera House Orch Covent Garden, Royal Opera House Covent Garden Chorus ("Vol. 42—Così fan tutte") PPHI 3-▲ 22542 [ADD] (34.97)
P. Coburn (sop), I. Nielsen (sop), E. Wiens (sop), P. Schreier (ten), D. Fischer-Dieskau (bar), P. Schreier (cnd), CPE Bach CO *(L'oca del Cairo, K.422)*, F. Palmer (sop), I. Cotrubas (sop), R. Tear (ten), A. Rolfe Johnson (ten), C. Davis (cnd), London SO *(Sposo deluso)* ("Vol. 39— L'oca de Cairo & Lo sposo deluso") PPHI ▲ 22539 [ADD] (11.97)
J. Demus (pno), I. Haebler (pno), P. Badura-Skoda (pno), L. Hoffmann (pno) ("Vol. 16—Music for Two Pianos & Piano Duets") PPHI 2-▲ 22516 [ADD] (22.97)
H. Donath (sop), J. Norman (sop), I. Cotrubas (sop), T. Troyanos (mez), W. Hollweg (ten), H. Prey (bar), H. Schmidt-Isserstedt (cnd), North German RSO ("Vol. 34—Die Gärtnerin aus Liebe") PPHI 3-▲ 22534 [ADD] (34.97)
C. Eda-Pierre (sop), N. Burrowes (sop), R. Tear (ten), S. Burrows (ten), C. Davis (cnd), Academy of St. Martin in the Fields, John Alldis Choir ("Vol. 38—Die Entführung aus dem Serail") PPHI 2-▲ 22538 [ADD] (22.97)
B. Fassbaender (mez), T. Moser (ten), B. McDaniel (bar), L. Hager (cnd), Salzburg Mozarteum Orch ("Vol. 33—La finta giardiniera") PPHI 3-▲ 22533 [ADD] (34.97)
A. Grumiaux (vn) ("Vol. 15—Violin Sonatas") PPHI 7-▲ 22515 [ADD] (80.97)
Grumiaux Ensemble ("Vol. 11—String Quintets") PPHI 3-▲ 22511 [ADD] (34.97)
Grumiaux Piano Trio, Academy of St. Martin in the Fields Chamber Ensemble ("Vol. 13—String Trios & Duos") PPHI 2-▲ 22513 [ADD] (22.97)
U. C. Harrer (cnd) , Vienna Boys' Choir ("Vol. 27—Bastien und Bastienne") PPHI ▲ 22527 [ADD] (11.97)
B. Hendricks (sop), H. Blochwitz (ten), P. Schreier (cnd), C.P.E. Bach CO ("Vol. 28—La finta semplice") PPHI 2-▲ 22528 [ADD] (22.97)
H. Kegel (cnd) ("Vol. 19—Missae; Requiem") PPHI 9-▲ 22519 [ADD] (102.97)
H. Kegel (cnd) ("Vol. 20—Litanies, Vespers, etc.") PPHI 5-▲ 22520 [ADD] (57.97)
T. Koopman (hpd), M. Uchida (pno), I. Haebler (pno) ("Vol. 18—Piano Variations; Rondos; etc.") PPHI 5-▲ 22518 [ADD] (57.97)
S. McNair (sop), A. M. Blasi (sop), I. Vermillion (mez), C. H. Ahnsjö (ten), J. Hadley (ten), N. Marriner (cnd), Academy of St. Martin in the Fields ("Vol. 35—Il re pastore") PPHI 2-▲ 22535 [ADD] (22.97)
N. Marriner (cnd), Academy of St. Martin in the Fields ("Vol. 1—Early Symphonies") PPHI 6-▲ 22501 [ADD] (68.97)
N. Marriner (cnd), Academy of St. Martin in the Fields ("Vol. 2—Symphonies 21-41") PPHI 6-▲ 22502 [ADD] (68.97)
N. Marriner (cnd), Academy of St. Martin in the Fields ("Vol. 3—Serenades for Orchestra") PPHI 7-▲ 22503 [ADD] (80.97)
N. Marriner (cnd), Academy of St. Martin in the Fields ("Vol. 5—Serenades & Divertimenti for Winds") PPHI 6-▲ 22505 [ADD] (68.97)
N. Marriner (cnd), Academy of St. Martin in the Fields ("Vol. 9—Wind Concertos") PPHI 5-▲ 22509 [ADD] (57.97)
E. Mathis (sop), A. Augér (sop), A. Baltsa (mez), P. Schreier (ten), L. Hager (cnd), Salzburg Mozarteum Orch ("Vol. 30—Ascanio in Alba") PPHI 3-▲ 22530 [ADD] (34.97)
E. Mathis (sop), A. Augér (sop), H. Schwarz (mez), A. Rolfe Johnson (ten), L. Hager (cnd), Salzburg Mozarteum Orch, Salzburg Mozarteum Chorus ("Vol. 26—Apollo et Hyacinthus") PPHI 2-▲ 22526 [ADD] (22.97)
E. Mathis (sop), L. Popp (sop), E. Gruberová (sop), P. Schreier (ten), F. Araiza (ten), W. Berry (b-bar) ("Vol. 23—Arias, Vocal Ensembles, Canons") PPHI 8-▲ 22523 [ADD] (91.97)
E. Mathis (sop), L. Popp (sop), E. Moser (sop), E. Gruberová (sop), P. Schreier (ten), L. Hager (cnd), Salzburg Mozarteum Orch ("Vol. 31—Il sogno di Scipione") PPHI 2-▲ 22531 [ADD] (22.97)
E. Mathis (sop), P. Schreier (ten), W. Hollweg (ten), I. Wixell (bar), B. Klee (cnd), Berlin Staatskapelle ("Vol. 36—Zaïde") PPHI 2-▲ 22536 [ADD] (22.97)

MOZART, WOLFGANG AMADEUS (cont.)
The "Complete Mozart Edition" (the complete works by Mozart in 45 volumes) (cont.)
J. Norman (sop), M. Freni (sop), Y. Minton (mez), I. Wixell (bar), C. Davis (cnd), BBC SO, BBC Sym Chorus ("Vol. 40—Le nozze di Figaro") PPHI 3-▲ 22540 [ADD] (34.97)
L. Popp (sop), J. Baker (mez), Y. Minton (mez), F. von Stade (mez), S. Burrows (ten), R. Lloyd (bass), C. Davis (cnd), Royal Opera House Orch Covent Garden, Royal Opera House Covent Garden Chorus ("Vol. 44—La clemenza di Tito") PPHI 2-▲ 22544 [ADD] (22.97)
Quartetto Italiano ("Vol. 12—String Quartets") PPHI 8-▲ 22512 [ADD] (91.97)
P. Schreier (ten), N. Marriner (cnd) ("Vol. 22—Oratorios; Cantatas; Masonic Music") PPHI 6-▲ 22522 [ADD] (68.97)
L. Serra (sop), M. Price (sop), P. Schreier (ten), R. Tear (ten), T. Adam (b-bar), K. Moll (bass), C. Davis (cnd), Dresden Staatskapelle, Dresden State Chorus ("Vol. 43—Die Zauberflöte") PPHI 3-▲ 22543 [ADD] (34.97)
H. Szeryng (vn), N. Imai (va), I. Brown (cnd) ("Vol. 8—Violin Concertos") PPHI 4-▲ 22508 [ADD] (45.97)
M. Uchida (pno) ("Vol. 17—Piano Sonatas") PPHI 5-▲ 22517 [ADD] (57.97)
J. Varady (sop), B. Hendricks (sop), S. Mentzer (mez), F. Araiza (ten), T. Allen (bar), C. Davis (cnd), Bavarian RSO ("Vol. 37—Idomeneo") PPHI 3-▲ 22537 [ADD] (34.97)
J. Varady (sop), E. Mathis (sop), A. Augér (sop), H. Donath (sop), P. Schreier (ten), L. Hager (cnd), Salzburg Mozarteum Orch ("Vol. 32—Lucio Silla") PPHI 3-▲ 22532 [ADD] (34.97)
H. Winschermann (ob), D. Chorzempa (org), German Bach Soloists ("Vol. 21—Organ Sonatas & Solos") PPHI 2-▲ 22521 [ADD] (22.97)
Concerto in B♭ for Bassoon & Orchestra, K.191 (1774)
S. Azzolini (bn), E. Aadland (cnd), European Community CO † Con Cl, K.622; Con Ob IMPA ▲ 2047 (9.97)
K. Bidlo (bn), K. Ančerl (cnd), Czech PO *(rec 1952-66)* † Con 23 Pno, K.488; Con 3 Hn, K.447; Zauberflöte (sels) SUR ▲ 111935 [AAD]
A. Camden (bn), H. Blech (cnd), London Mozart Players *(rec 1952-56)* † Con 17 Pno, K.453; Lucio Silla (ov); Sym 31, K.297 DLAB ▲ 4005 (17.97)
A. Camden (bn), H. Harty (cnd), London SO † Con Cl, K.622; Con 2 Hn, K.417; Con 4 Hn, K.495 AVID (Classical Masters) ▲ 605 (16.97)
J. Chevallier (eup), G. Lloyd (cnd), City of London Sinfonia † F. Danzi:Con Bn; G. F. Handel:Cons Ob, HWV 301, 302a & 287 ALBA ▲ 201 [DDD]
B. Garfield (bn), E. Ormandy (cnd), Philadelphia Orch † Con Ob; R. Strauss:Con Ob, AV144; C. M. von Weber:Andante & Rondo ungarese Bn SNYC (Essential Classics) ▲ 62652 (7.97)
L. Hara (bn), J. Ferencsik (cnd), Hungarian State Orch *(rec 1981-82)* ("Concertos for Horn & Bassoon") † Con 2 Hn, K.417; Con 3 Hn, K.447; Con 4 Hn, K.495 CLDI ▲ 4027 [ADD] (10.97)
K. Hellmann (bn), H. Kraus (cnd) † Andante Fl, K.315; Con Cl, K.622; Con Ob LALI ▲ 15875 [DDD] (3.97)
C. Hogwood (cnd), Academy of Ancient Music Orch † Con Cl, K.622; Con Fl & Hp, K.299; Con Ob; Con 1 Fl, K.313; Cons (4) Hn DECC 3-▲ 460027 (32.97)
D. Jensen (bn), W. A. Albert (cnd), Cologne RSO ("Bassoon Concertos") † J. Françaix:Divert Bn; J. N. Hummel:Con Bn; Jolivet:Con Bn CAPO ▲ 10579 [DDD] (11.97)
B. Karel (bn), V. Smetáček (cnd), Czech PO † Sinf concertante Ob, K.Anh.9 SUR ▲ 3053 (10.97)
D. McGill (bn), C. von Dohnányi (cnd), Cleveland Orch † Con Cl, K.622; Con Ob PLON ▲ 443176 (16.97)
F. Morelli (bn), Orpheus CO † Con Ob; Con 2 Hn, K.417; Con 3 Hn, K.447 DEUT ▲ 23623 [DDD] (16.97)
F. Morelli (bn), Orpheus CO ("The Wind Concerti") † Con Cl, K.622; Con Fl & Hp, K.299; Con Ob; Cons (4) Hn; Cons Fl; Sinf concertante Ob, K.Anh.9 DEUT 3-▲ 31665 [DDD] (34.97)
Y. Nakanishi (bn), J. Glover (cnd), London Mozart Players † Con Cl, K.622 CFP ▲ 4484 [DDD] (12.97)
D. Noyen (bn), D. Vermeulen (cnd), Prima La Musica ("Wind Concertos") † Con Ob; Con 1 Fl, K.313; Con 4 Hn, K.495; Sinf concertante Ob, K.Anh.9 EUFO 2-▲ 1234 [DDD] (36.97)
G. Piesk (bn), H. von Karajan (cnd), Berlin PO † Con Cl, K.622; Con Ob EMIC ▲ 64355 [ADD] (11.97)
V. Popov (bn), V. Polyansky (cnd), Russian State SO † J. N. Hummel:Con Bn; C. M. von Weber:Con Bn CHN ▲ 9656 (16.97)
G. Prêtre (cnd), Paris Opera Orch ("Homage to Georges Prêtre") † Con Cl, K.622; Con Fl & Hp, K.299; Con Ob; Con 1 Fl, K.313; Cons (4) Hn FORL ▲ 16747 [DDD] (47.97)
L. Sharrow (bn), A. Toscanini (cnd), NBC SO ("The Toscanini Collection, Vol. 10") † Divert 15 Hns & Strs, K.287; Sym 35, K.385 RCAV (Gold Seal) ▲ 60286 (11.97)
L. Sharrow (bn), A. Toscanini (cnd), NBC SO *(rec live New York, Nov 8, 1947)* ("Toscanini Conducts Mozart") † Sym 29, K.201; Sym 38, K.504 IN ▲ 1400 [ADD] (15.97)
K. Sønstevold (bn), S. Comissiona (cnd), Swedish RSO † A. Pettersson:Sym 7 CAPA ▲ 21411 [DDD] (16.97)
K. Sreter (bn), A. Lizzio (cnd), Mozart Festival Orch † Rondo Vn; Sym 25, K.183 PC ▲ 265055 [DDD] (2.97)
R. Stoltzman (cl), A. Schneider (cnd), English CO [trans Stoltzman] † Con Cl, K.622 RCAV (Gold Seal) ▲ 60379 [ADD] (11.97)
K. Thunemann (bn), N. Marriner (cnd), Academy of St. Martin in the Fields † Con Cl, K.622; Duo Bn Vc, K.292 PPHI ▲ 22390 [DDD] (16.97)
M. Turkovič (bn), M. Sieghart (cnd), Stuttgart CO † J. Françaix:Divert Bn; G. Gershwin:Porgy & Bess (sels); M. Haydn:Concertino Bn & Orch; H. Villa-Lobos:Ciranda das sete notas ORF ▲ 223911 [DDD] (18.97)
S. Turnovsky (bn), J. Wildner (cnd), Vienna Mozart Academy † Con Cl, K.622; Con 2 Fl, K.314 NXIN ▲ 550345 [DDD] (5.97)
D. Zeman (bn), K. Böhm (cnd), Vienna PO † Con Cl, K.622; Con Ob DEUT ▲ 29816 [ADD] (7.97)
D. Zeman (bn), K. Böhm (cnd), Vienna PO *(rec Great Hall Vienna Musikverein, Austria, May 1973)* † Con Cl, K.622; Con 1 Fl, K.313 DEUT (The Originals) ▲ 457719 [ADD] (11.97)
Concerto in A for Clarinet & Orchestra, K.622 (1791)
J. Campbell (cl), F. Decker (cnd), National Arts Center Canada Orch † A. Copland:Con Cl; C. M. von Weber:Concertino Cl, Op. 26 SMS (SM 5000) ▲ 5096 [DDD] (16.97)
D. Campbell (cl), R. Hickox (cnd), City of London Sinfonia † Con Fl & Hp, K.299 INMP ▲ 2011 (9.97)
A. Carbonare (cl), V. Czarnecki (cnd), Southwest German PO Pforzheim † G. Rossini:Theme & Vars Cl; Vars Cl AG ▲ 111 (18.97)
M. Carulli (cl), E. Aadland (cnd), European Community CO † Con Bn, K.191; Con Ob IMPA ▲ 2047 (9.97)
F. Cohen (cl), C. von Dohnányi (cnd), Cleveland Orch † Con Bn, K.191; Con Ob PLON ▲ 443176 (16.97)
K. Fagéus (cl), E. Klas (cnd), Stockholm Royal Orch ("Clarinet Concertos") † Crusell:Den Lilla Slavinnan (sels); Frumerie:Con Cl; L.-E. Larsson:Hommage á Mozart OPU ▲ 19801 (16.97)
D. Glazer (cl), G. Simon (cnd), English CO † Andante Fl, K.315; Con Bn, K.191; Con Ob LALI ▲ 15875 [DDD] (3.97)
B. Goodman (cl), C. Munch (cnd), Boston SO *(rec Tanglewood Music Festival, 1956)* ("Mozart at Tanglewood") † Qnt Cl, K.581 RCAV (Gold Seal) ▲ 68804 [ADD] (11.97)
C. Hogwood (cnd), Academy of Ancient Music Orch † Con Bn, K.191; Con Fl & Hp, K.299; Con Ob; Con 1 Fl, K.313; Cons (4) Hn DECC 3-▲ 460027 (32.97)
E. Johnson (cl), R. Leppard (cnd), English CO † Con Fl & Hp, K.299 ASV ▲ 532 (16.97)
S. Kam (cl) † F. Krommer:Con Cl TELC ▲ 21462 (16.97)
R. Kell (cl), M. Sargent (cnd), London PO † Con Bn, K.191; Con 2 Hn, K.417; Con 4 Hn, K.495 AVID (Classical Masters) ▲ 605 (16.97)
T. King (cl), A. Francis (cnd), English CO † L. Spohr:Con 4 Cl MER ▲ 84022 (16.97)
D. Klöcker (cl), W. Hauschild (cnd), English CO † Eybler:Con Cl; Süssmayr:Con Cl NOVA ▲ 150061 [DDD] (16.97)
D. Klöcker (cl), M. Lajcik (cnd), Prague CO *(rec Domovina Prague, May 28-31, 1997)* † Con 6 Vn, K.268; Vars Cl Orch MDG ▲ 3010755 [DDD] (17.97)
J. Lancelot (cl), J. Paillard (cnd), Jean-François Paillard CO ("The Magic of the Clarinet") † J. Brahms:Son 1 Cl; Son 2 Cl; Bruch:Pieces Cl, Op. 83; Debussy:Premiere rapsodie Cl; C. M. von Weber:Con 1 Cl, Op. 73; Con 2 Cl, Op. 74; Grand Duo Concertant, J.204 ERAT ▲ 94679 (9.97)
K. Leister (cl), H. von Karajan (cnd), Berlin PO † Con Bn, K.191; Con Ob EMIC ▲ 64355 [ADD] (11.97)
K. Leister (cl), N. Marriner (cnd), Academy of St. Martin in the Fields † Con Bn, K.191; Duo Bn Vc, K.292 PPHI ▲ 22390 [DDD] (16.97)
K. Leister (cl), K. Toyoda (cnd), Gunma SO *(rec Takasaki Japan, Apr 1980)* † J. Haydn:Arianna a Naxos, H.XXVIb/2; Canzonettas (12); Mercadante:Con in B Cl, Op. 101; C. M. von Weber:Con 1 Cl, Op. 73; Con 2 Cl, Op. 74; Concertino Cl, Op. 26; Divert Cl CAMA 2-▲ 323 [DDD] (34.97)
A. Malsbury (cl), J. Glover (cnd), London Mozart Players † Con Ob; Con 1 Fl, K.313 ASV ▲ 795 [DDD] (16.97)
R. Marcellus (cl), G. Szell (cnd), Cleveland Orch *(rec Cleveland, OH, Oct 21, 1961)* † Cons Fl SNYC (Essential Classics) ▲ 62424 [ADD] (7.97) ▮ 62424 [ADD] (3.98)
V. Mareš (cl), L. Pešek (cnd), Prague RSO *(rec 1966-85)* ("Mozart in Prague") † Don Giovanni (ov); Sym 38, K.504 SUR ▲ 3367 [ADD] (7.97)
N. Marriner (cnd), Academy of St. Martin in the Fields ("The Mozart Experience") † Con Fl & Hp, K.299; Con Movt Hn, K.Anh.98a; Con 20 Pno, K.466; Con 21 Pno, K.467; Divert Ww; German Dances (3), K.605; Kleine Nachtmusik, K.525; Musikalischer Spass, K.522; Nozze di Figaro (sels); Serenade 6 Orch, K.239; Sym 40, K.550; Sym 41, K.551 PPHI 5-▲ 26204 (33.97)
A. Marriner (cl), J. Glover (cnd), London Mozart Players † Con Bn, K.191 CFP ▲ 4484 [DDD] (12.97)

▲ = CD ♦ = Enhanced CD △ = MD ▮ = Cassette Tape ▯ = DCC

MOZART, WOLFGANG AMADEUS (cont.)

Concerto in A for Clarinet & Orchestra, K.622 (1791) (cont.)

P. Meyer (cl), D. Zinman (cnd), English CO *(rec Mar 27-29, 1992)* † Busoni:Concertino Cl, Op. 48; A. Copland:Con Cl DNN ▲ 75289 [DDD] (16.97)

S. Meyer (b cl), D. Jonas (ob), S. Azzolini (bn), B. Schneider (hn), H. Vonk (cnd), Dresden Staatskapelle *(rec Dresden, Germany, June 6-8, 1990)* † Sinf concertante Ob, K.Anh.9 EMIC (Great Recordings of the Century) ▲ 66949 [DDD] (11.97)

S. Meyer (cl), H. Vonk (cnd), Dresden Staatskapelle *(rec Lukaskirche Dresden, June 6-8, 1990)* ("Clarinet Connection: Sabine Meyer") † Serenade; C. Stamitz:Cons Cl; C. M. von Weber:Con 1 Cl, Op. 73 EMIC ▲ 55155 [DDD] (16.97)

C. Neidich (cl), Orpheus CO † Con 1 Hn, K.412; Con 4 Hn, K.495 DEUT ▲ 23377 [DDD] (16.97)

C. Neidich (cl), Orpheus CO ("The Wind Concerti") † Con Bn, K.191; Con Fl & Hp, K.299; Con Ob; Cons (4) Hn; Cons Fl; Sinf concertante Ob, K.Anh.9 DEUT 3-▲ 31665 [DDD] (34.97)

E. Ottensamer (cl), J. Wildner (cnd), Vienna Mozart Academy *(rec Oct 1989)* † Con Bn, K.191; Con 2 Fl, K.314 NXIN ▲ 550345 [DDD] (5.97)

A. Pay (cl), C. Hogwood (cnd), Academy of Ancient Music † Con Ob PLOI ▲ 14339 [DDD] (16.97)

M. Portal (cl), P. Entremont (cnd), Vienna CO † Sym 21, K.134; Sym 27, K.199 HMA ▲ 2901304 (7.97)

G. Prêtre (cnd), Paris Opera Orch ("Homage to Georges Prêtre") † Con Bn, K.191; Con Fl & Hp, K.299; Con Ob; Con 1 Fl, K.313; Cons (4) Hn FORL ▲ 16747 [DDD] (47.97)

A. Prinz (cl), K. Böhm (cnd), Vienna PO † Con Bn, K.191; Con Ob DEUT ▲ 29816 [ADD] (7.97)

A. Prinz (cl), K. Böhm (cnd), Vienna PO *(rec Great Hall Vienna Musikverein, Austria, Sept 1972)* † Con Bn, K.191; Con 1 Fl, K.313 DEUT (The Originals) ▲ 457719 [ADD] (11.97)

V. Riha (cl), V. Talich (cnd), Czech PO *(rec 1954)* † Sinf concertante Ob, K.Anh.9 SUR ▲ 111907 [AAD]

J. Rutter (cnd), City of London Sinfonia *(rec London, England, July 29, 1985)* ("The Mozart Collection") † Con Fl & Hp, K.299; Con 12 Pno, K.414; Con 21 Pno, K.467; Diverts Str Qt, K.136-138; Music of Mozart; Nozze di Figaro (ov); Sym 39, K.543 AMG ▲ 586 (15.99)

P. Schmidl (cl), L. Bernstein (cnd), Vienna PO † Sym 25, K.183; Sym 29, K.201 DEUT ▲ 29221 [DDD] (16.97)

D. Shifrin (cl), G. Schwarz (cnd), Mostly Mozart Festival Orch † Qnt Cl, K.581 DLS ▲ 3020 [DDD] (14.97)

R. Stoltzman (cl) † Qnt Cl, K.581 RCAV (Red Seal) ▲ 60723 [DDD] (16.97)

R. Stoltzman (cl) ("Basic 100, Vol. 55") † Andante Fl, K.315; Con Fl & Hp, K.299 RCAV ▲ 68024 (10.97) ■ 68024 (5.98)

R. Stoltzman (cl), A. Schneider (cnd), English CO † Con Bn, K.191 RCAV (Gold Seal) ▲ 60379 [ADD] (11.97)

P. Taillard (b cl) † Adagio E Hn, K.580a; Qnt Ob, K.406; Qt Ob; Qt 22 Strs, K.589 CAPO ▲ 10525 [DDD] (10.97)

G. Touvron (tpt) † Con Fl & Hp, K.299; Con Ob; Zauberflöte (sels); L. Mozart:Con Tpt LIDI ▲ 105057 (16.97)

J. Valdepeñas (cl), J. Garcia (cnd), English CO † Con 3 Hn, K.447; Con 4 Hn, K.495 SUMM ▲ 131 [DDD] (16.97)

M. Van de Wiel (b cl), J. Clayton (cnd), Chetham's CO ("Mozart Reflections") † Birtwistle:Linoi 1; Süssmayr:Con Movt; Woolrich:Si va Facendo Notte OLY ▲ 484 [DDD] (16.97)

various artists—Adagio † Con 20 Pno, K.466; Con 21 Pno, K.467; Con 3 Vn, K.216; Così fan tutte (ov); Kleine Nachtmusik, K.525; Son 11 Pno, K.331; Sym 40, K.550; Sym 41, K.551; Zauberflöte (ov) RCAV ▲ 60829 (10.97) ■ 60829 (5.98)

various artists—Adagio † Andante Fl, K.315; Con Fl & Hp, K.299; Con 21 Pno, K.467; Con 3 Vn, K.216; Così fan tutte (sels); Kleine Nachtmusik, K.525; Qt in A Cl Strs, K.581; Serenade; Son 13 Pno, K.333 RCAV ■ 63329 (5.98) ▲ 63329 (11.97)

artists unknown—Adagio ("Adagios") † Adagio Pno, K.540; Adagio Vn, K.261; Con Fl & Hp, K.299; Con 2 Hn, K.417; Con 20 Pno, K.466; Con 21 Pno, K.467; Con 23 Pno, K.488; Con 26 Pno, K.537; Con 27 Pno, K.595; Con 3 Hn, K.447; Con 3 Vn, K.216; Diverts Str Qt, K.136-138; Kleine Nachtmusik, K.525; Qnt Cl, K.581; Serenade; Serenade Ww, K.388/384a; Sinf concertante Vn, K.364; Son 12 Pno, K.332; Son 16 Pno, K.545; Sym 40, K.550; Sym 41, K.551 DECC (2-Fers) 2-▲ 460191 (17.97)

Concertos (2) in G & D for Flute & Orchestra, K.313-14 (1778)

A. Adorján (fl), H. Stadlmair (cnd), Munich CO † Andante Fl, K.315 DNN ▲ 7803 [DDD] (10.97)

R. Aitken (fl), F. Mannino (cnd), National Arts Center Canada Orch † Andante Fl, K.315; Rondo Fl SMS (SM 5000) ▲ 5076 [DDD] (16.97)

C. Arimany (fl), J. Rampal (cnd), Hungarian Virtuosi CO † Andante Fl, K.315; Rondo Fl PROD ▲ 2419 [DDD] (17.97)

K. Berger (fl), H. Kraus (cnd) † Con 1 Hn, K.412; Con 3 Hn, K.447 LALI ▲ 15624 [DDD] (3.97)

J. Galway (fl), J. Galway (cnd), CO of Europe † Andante Fl, K.315; Con Fl & Hp, K.299; Divert 17 Hns Strs, K.334; Kleine Nachtmusik, K.525; Son 11 Pno, K.331 RCAV (Red Seal) 2-▲ 7861 [DDD] (30.97)

J. Galway (fl), N. Marriner (cnd), Academy of St. Martin in the Fields *(rec Watford England, 1995)* ("Flute Concertos") † Con Fl & Hp, K.299 RCAV (Red Seal) ▲ 68256 [DDD] (16.97)

J. Hall (fl), P. Thomas (cnd), Philharmonia Orch INMP (Classic) ▲ 2036 (9.97)

R. Krimsier (fl), S. Argiris (cnd), English CO *(rec Hampstead London, Sept 20-22, 1995)* † Con Fl & Hp, K.299 CCL ▲ 10297 [DDD] (18.97)

C. Lardé (fl), P. Kuentz (cnd), Paul Kuentz Orch † Con Fl & Hp, K.299 PVY ▲ 730078 (11.97)

S. Milan (fl), R. Leppard (cnd), English CO † Andante Fl, K.315; Rondo Vn, K.373 CHN ▲ 8613 [DDD] (16.97)

M. Moyse (fl), E. Bigot (cnd) *(rec 1930-36)* † Con Fl & Hp, K.299 PHS ▲ 9118 [ADD] (17.97)

E. Pahud (fl), C. Abbado (cnd), Berlin PO † Con Fl & Hp, K.299 EMIC ▲ 56365 (16.97)

S. Palma (fl), Orpheus CO ("The Wind Concerti") † Con Bn, K.191; Con Cl, K.622; Con Fl & Hp, K.299; Con Ob; Cons (4) Hn; Sinf concertante Ob, K.Anh.9 DEUT 3-▲ 31665 [DDD] (34.97)

G. Pretto (fl), E. Aadland (cnd), European Community CO *(rec Rosslyn Hill Chapel London, Apr 16-19, 1992)* † Andante Fl, K.315; Rondo Fl INMP (Classics) ▲ 1107 (11.97)

J. Rampal (fl), Z. Mehta (cnd), Israel PO † Andante Fl, K.315; Rondo Fl SNYC ▲ 44919 [DDD] (16.97)

W. Tast (fl), H. Haenchen (cnd), C.P.E. Bach CO † Mercadante:Con Fl LALI ▲ 14037 [DDD] (3.97)

W. Tast (fl), H. Haenchen (cnd), C.P.E. Bach CO † Con Fl & Hp, K.299 LALI ▲ 15873 [DDD] (3.97)

A. G. Tatu (fl) † Andante Fl, K.315 PC ▲ 265050 [DDD] (2.97)

K. Zöller (fl), B. Klee (cnd), English CO † Con Fl & Hp, K.299 DEUT ▲ 29815 [ADD] (7.97)

E. Zukerman (fl), P. Zukerman (cnd), English CO *(rec London, June 22-24, 1977)* † Con Cl, K.622 SNYC (Essential Classics) ▲ 62424 [ADD] (7.97) ■ 62424 [ADD] (3.98)

Concerto No. 1 in G for Flute & Orchestra, K.313 (1778)

J. Baker (fl), A. Janigro (cnd) *(rec Vienna, 1965)* ("Virtuoso Flute, Vol. 2") † Andante Fl, K.315; Vaughan Williams:Fant on Greensleeves VC ▲ 54 [AAD] (13.97)

C. Bruneel (fl), D. Vermeulen (cnd), Prima La Musica ("Wind Concertos") † Con Bn, K.191; Con Ob; Con 4 Hn, K.495; Sinf concertante Ob, K.Anh.9 EUFO 2-▲ 1234 [DDD] (36.97)

P. Davies (fl), J. Glover (cnd), London Mozart Players † Con Cl, K.622; Con Ob ASV ▲ 795 [DDD] (16.97)

J. Galway (fl), B. Baumgartner (cnd) † Andante Fl, K.315; Con Fl & Hp, K.299 RCAV (Gold Seal) ▲ 6723 [ADD] (11.97)

C. Hogwood (cnd), Academy of Ancient Music Orch † Con Bn, K.191; Con Cl, K.622; Con Fl & Hp, K.299; Con Ob; Cons (4) Hn DECC 3-▲ 460027 (32.97)

S. Palma (fl), Orpheus CO † Andante Fl, K.315; Con Fl & Hp, K.299 DEUT ▲ 27677 [DDD] (16.97)

G. Prêtre (cnd), Paris Opera Orch ("Homage to Georges Prêtre") † Con Bn, K.191; Con Cl, K.622; Con Fl & Hp, K.299; Con Ob; Cons (4) Hn FORL ▲ 16747 [DDD] (47.97)

J. Snowden (fl) *(rec 1987-91)* † Con Fl & Hp, K.299; Con Ob; Sinf concertante Ob, K.Anh.9 CFP 2-▲ 4808 [DDD] (21.97)

W. Tripp (fl), K. Böhm (cnd), Vienna PO *(rec Great Hall Vienna Musikverein, Austria, Apr 1974)* † Con Bn, K.191; Con Cl, K.622 DEUT (The Originals) ▲ 457719 [ADD] (11.97)

F. Vester (trns fl), F. Brüggen (cnd), Mozart-Ensemble Amsterdam *(rec Amsterdam, Holland, May 1971)* ("The Flute Concertos") † Andante Fl, K.315; Con Fl & Hp, K.299; Con 2 Fl, K.314; Rondo Fl SNYC 2-▲ 60381 [ADD] (7.97)

Concerto No. 2 in D for Flute & Orchestra [trans of Oboe Concerto, K.271], K.314 (1778)

J. Baker (fl), F. Prohaska (cnd), Vienna State Opera Orch *(rec Vienna, 1966)* ("Virtuoso Flute, Vol. 3") † C. W. Gluck:Orfeo ed Euridice (dance) VC ▲ 55 [AAD] (13.97)

M. Gabriel (ob), J. Wildner (cnd), Vienna Mozart Academy *(rec Oct 1989)* † Con Bn, K.191; Con Cl, K.622 NXIN ▲ 550345 [DDD] (5.97)

I. Schnöller (fl), A. Apolin (cnd), Pilsen RSO *(rec Sept 1994)* ("Concertos for Flute") † Mercadante:Con Fl; C. Reinecke:Con Fl JEC ▲ 704 [DDD]

F. Vester (trns fl), F. Brüggen (cnd), Mozart-Ensemble Amsterdam *(rec Amsterdam, Holland, Aug 1971)* ("The Flute Concertos") † Andante Fl, K.315; Con Fl & Hp, K.299; Con 1 Fl, K.313; Rondo Fl SNYC 2-▲ 60381 [ADD] (7.97)

Concerto in C for Flute, Harp & Orchestra, K.299 (1778)

J. Baker (fl), H. Jelinek (hp), A. Janigro (cnd) *(rec Baumgarten Hall Vienna, May 5-7, 1962)* ("Julius Baker: The Virtuoso Flute") † Telemann:Cons & Suites Fl; Vivaldi:Con Fl Bn, RV.104 VC ▲ 42 [AAD] (13.97)

W. Bennett (fl), O. Ellis (hp), R. Leppard (cnd), English CO † Con Cl, K.622 ASV ▲ 532 (16.97)

P. Davies (fl), R. Masters (hp), R. Hickox (cnd), City of London Sinfonia † Con Cl, K.622 INMP ▲ 2011 (9.97)

H. Friedrich (fl), A. Berger (hp), H. Kraus (cnd) † Cons Fl LALI ▲ 15873 [DDD] (3.97)

J. Galway (fl), M. Robles (hp), J. Galway (cnd), CO of Europe † Andante Fl, K.315; Cons Fl; Divert 17 Hns Strs, K.334; Kleine Nachtmusik, K.525; Son 11 Pno, K.331 RCAV (Red Seal) 2-▲ 7861 [DDD] (30.97)

MOZART, WOLFGANG AMADEUS (cont.)

Concerto in C for Flute, Harp & Orchestra, K.299 (1778) (cont.)

J. Galway (fl), M. Robles (hp), N. Marriner (cnd), Academy of St. Martin in the Fields *(rec Watford England, 1995)* ("Flute Concertos") † Cons Fl RCAV (Red Seal) ▲ 68256 [DDD] (16.97)

J. Galway (fl), M. Robles (hp), E. Mata (cnd), London SO † Andante Fl, K.315; Con 1 Fl, K.313 RCAV (Gold Seal) ▲ 6723 [ADD] (11.97)

J. Galway (fl), M. Robles (hp), E. Mata (cnd), London SO ("Basic 100, Vol. 55") † Andante Fl, K.315; Con Cl, K.622 RCAV ▲ 68024 (10.97) ■ 68024 (5.98)

J. Galway (fl), M. Robles (hp), E. Mata (cnd), London SO ("Better Thinking through Mozart") † Con 21 Pno, K.467; Kleine Nachtmusik, K.525; Serenade; Son Pnos, K.448; Son 11 Pno, K.331 RCAV (Gold Seal) ▲ 68113 [ADD] (11.97) ■ 68113 [ADD] (6.98)

C. Hogwood (cnd), Academy of Ancient Music Orch † Con Bn, K.191; Con Cl, K.622; Con Ob; Con 1 Fl, K.313; Cons (4) Hn DECC 3-▲ 460027 (32.97)

R. Krimsier (fl), Y. Kondonassis (hp), M. Stefanelli (cnd), English CO *(rec Hampstead London, Mar 25-27, 1996)* † Cons Fl CCL ▲ 10297 [DDD] (18.97)

C. Lardé (fl), M. Jamet (hp), P. Kuentz (cnd), Paul Kuentz Orch † Cons Fl PVY ▲ 730078 (11.97)

N. Marriner (cnd), Academy of St. Martin in the Fields ("The Mozart Experience") † Con Cl, K.622; Con Movt Hn, K.Anh.98a; Con 20 Pno, K.466; Con 21 Pno, K.467; Divert Ww; German Dances (3), K.605; Kleine Nachtmusik, K.525; Musikalischer Spass, K.522; Nozze di Figaro (sels); Serenade 6 Orch, K.239; Sym 40, K.550; Sym 41, K.551 PPHI 5-▲ 26204 (33.97)

S. Milan (fl), S. Kang (hp), R. Hickox (cnd), City of London Sinfonia † Con Ob; A. Salieri:Con Fl CHN ▲ 9051 [DDD] (16.97)

M. Moyse (fl), L. Laskine (hp), E. Bigot (cnd) *(rec 1930-36)* † Cons Fl PHS ▲ 9118 [ADD] (17.97)

A. Nicolet (fl), U. Holliger (hp), H. Holliger (cnd), English CO ("Mozart Masterworks") † Con 3 Vn, K.216; Con 5 Vn, K.219; Kleine Nachtmusik, K.525; Minuets, K.568; Music of Mozart; Sym 32, K.318; Sym 35, K.385; Sym 41, K.551; 11 Contredanses; 13 German Dances NOVA 5-▲ 150060 [DDD] (51.97)

E. Pahud (fl), M. Langlamet (hp), C. Abbado (cnd), Berlin PO † Cons Fl EMIC ▲ 56365 (16.97)

S. Palma (fl), N. Allen (hp), Orpheus CO † Andante Fl, K.315; Con 1 Fl, K.313 DEUT ▲ 27677 [DDD] (16.97)

S. Palma (fl), N. Allen (hp), Orpheus CO ("The Wind Concerti") † Con Bn, K.191; Con Cl, K.622; Con Ob; Cons (4) Hn; Cons Fl; Sinf concertante Ob, K.Anh.9 DEUT 3-▲ 31665 [DDD] (34.97)

G. Prêtre (cnd), Paris Opera Orch ("Homage to Georges Prêtre") † Con Bn, K.191; Con Cl, K.622; Con Ob; Con 1 Fl, K.313; Cons (4) Hn FORL ▲ 16747 [DDD] (47.97)

R. le Roy (fl), L. Laskine (hp), T. Beecham (cnd), Royal PO *(rec 1947-49)* † Divert 2 Fl, K.131; Sym 27, K.199; Zauberflöte (ov) DLAB (RPO Legacy Vol. 4) ▲ 7037 (17.97)

J. Rutter (cnd), City of London Sinfonia *(rec London, England, July 29, 1985)* ("The Mozart Collection") † Con Cl, K.622; Con 12 Pno, K.414; Con 21 Pno, K.467; Diverts Str Qt, K.136-138; Music of Mozart; Nozze di Figaro (ov); Sym 39, K.543 AMG ▲ 586 (15.99)

M. Sandhoff (fl), S. Kwast (hp) † Con Ob CAPO ▲ 10375 (11.97)

H. Scherchen (cnd), Champs Elysées Orch † Sym 40, K.550; Sym 41, K.551 TAHA ▲ 147 (34.97)

W. Schulz (fl), N. Zabaleta (hp), K. Böhm (cnd), Vienna PO † Cons Fl DEUT ▲ 29815 [ADD] (7.97)

J. Snowden (fl), C. Thomas (hp) *(rec 1987-91)* † Con Ob; Con 1 Fl, K.313; Sinf concertante Ob, K.Anh.9 CFP 2-▲ 4808 [DDD] (21.97)

G. Touvron (tpt) † Con Cl, K.622; Con Ob; Zauberflöte (sels); L. Mozart:Con Tpt LIDI ▲ 105057 (16.97)

J. Válek (fl), H. Müllerová (hp), R. Edlinger (cnd), Capella Istropolitana *(rec 1988)* † Sinf concertante Ob, K.Anh.9 NXIN ▲ 550159 [DDD] (5.97)

F. Vester (trns fl), E. Witsenburg (hp), F. Brüggen (cnd), Mozart-Ensemble Amsterdam *(rec Amsterdam, Holland, Aug 1971)* ("The Flute Concertos") † Andante Fl, K.315; Con 1 Fl, K.313; Con 2 Fl, K.314; Rondo Fl SNYC 2-▲ 60381 [ADD] (7.97)

various artists—Andantino † Andante Fl, K.315; Con Cl, K.622; Con 21 Pno, K.467; Con 3 Vn, K.216; Così fan tutte (sels); Kleine Nachtmusik, K.525; Qt in A Cl Strs, K.581; Serenade; Son 13 Pno, K.333 RCAV ■ 63329 (5.98) ▲ 63329 (11.97)

artists unknown—Andantino ("Adagios") † Adagio Pno, K.540; Adagio Vn, K.261; Con Cl, K.622; Con 2 Hn, K.417; Con 20 Pno, K.466; Con 21 Pno, K.467; Con 23 Pno, K.488; Con 26 Pno, K.537; Con 27 Pno, K.595; Con 3 Hn, K.447; Con 3 Vn, K.216; Diverts Str Qt, K.136-138; Kleine Nachtmusik, K.525; Qnt Cl, K.581; Serenade; Serenade Ww, K.388/384a; Sinf concertante Vn, K.364; Son 12 Pno, K.332; Son 16 Pno, K.545; Sym 40, K.550; Sym 41, K.551 DECC (2-Fers) 2-▲ 460191 (17.97)

Concertos (4) for Horn & Orchestra

D. Bourgue (hn), B. Papazian (cnd) † Con 1 Hn, K.412; Rondo Hn, K.371 ARN ▲ 68198 [DDD] (16.97)

J. Cerminaro (hn), G. Schwarz (cnd), Seattle SO *(rec Seattle, WA, Sept 1997)* CRYS ▲ 515 (15.97)

A. Civil (hn), O. Klemperer (cnd), Philharmonia Orch *(rec 1961)* † Mendelssohn (-Bartholdy):Midsummer Night's Dream (sels); G. Rossini:Prelude, Theme & Vars Hn TES ▲ 1102 (17.97)

D. Clevenger (hn) † Rondo Hn, K.371; L. Mozart:Sym in G, G3 SNYC (Essential Classics) ▲ 62639 (7.97) ■ 62639 (3.98)

P. Damm (hn), N. Marriner (cnd), Academy of St. Martin in the Fields PPHI ▲ 22330 [DDD] (16.97)

L. Greer (hn), N. McGegan (cnd), Philharmonia Baroque Orch † Con 1 Hn, K.412; Rondo Hn, K.371 HAM ▲ 907012 [AAD] (18.97)

X. Han (hn), J. Lü (cnd), English CO † Rondo Hn, K.371 ASVQ ▲ 6213 (10.97)

C. Hogwood (cnd), Academy of Ancient Music Orch † Con Bn, K.191; Con Cl, K.622; Con Fl & Hp, K.299; Con Ob; Con 1 Fl, K.313 DECC 3-▲ 460027 (32.97)

H. Jeurissen (hn), R. Goodman (cnd), Netherlands CO *(rec 1996)* ("The Complete Horn Concertos") † Con Movt Hn, K.Anh.98a; Con Movt Hn, K.370b; Con 1 Hn, K.412; Rondo Hn, K.371 OLY ▲ 470 [DDD] (16.97)

D. Jolley (hn), Orpheus CO ("The Wind Concerti") † Con Bn, K.191; Con Cl, K.622; Con Fl & Hp, K.299; Con Ob; Cons Fl; Sinf concertante Ob, K.Anh.9 DEUT 3-▲ 31665 [DDD] (34.97)

A. Koster (hn), B. Weil (cnd), Tafelmusik *(rec 1992-93)* † Rondo Hn, K.371 SNYC ▲ 53369 [DDD] (16.97)

F. Lloyd (hn), R. Hickox (cnd), Northern Sinfonia of England † Rondo Hn, K.371 CHN ▲ 9150 [DDD] (17.97)

W. V. Meulen (hn), C. Eschenbach (cnd), Houston SO ICC ▲ 6600972 (16.97)

G. Prêtre (cnd), Paris Opera Orch ("Homage to Georges Prêtre") † Con Bn, K.191; Con Cl, K.622; Con Fl & Hp, K.299; Con Ob; Con 1 Fl, K.313 FORL ▲ 16747 [DDD] (47.97)

E. Ruske (hn), C. Mackerras (cnd), Scottish CO *(rec Edinburgh, Scotland, Dec 4-5, 1993)* † Con Movt Hn, K.Anh.98a; Rondo Hn, K.371 TEL ▲ 80367 [DDD] (16.97)

M. Števove (hn), J. Kopelman (cnd), Capella Istropolitana *(rec Nov 1988)* † Rondo Hn, K.371 NXIN ▲ 550148 [DDD] (5.97)

M. Thompson (hn), M. Thompson (cnd), Bournemouth Sinfonietta *(rec Dorset, England, Dec 18-20, 1995)* ("Complete Works for Horn & Orchestra") † Con "0" Hn; Con Movt Hn, K.Anh.98a; Rondo Hn, K.371 NXIN ▲ 8553592 [DDD] (5.97)

B. Tuckwell (hn), N. Marriner (cnd), Academy of St. Martin in the Fields † Rondo Hn, K.371 EMIC ▲ 69569 (11.97)

B. Tuckwell (hn), B. Tuckwell (cnd), English CO PLON ▲ 10284 [DDD] (16.97)

R. Vlatkovic (hn), J. Tate (cnd), English CO † Rondo Hn, K.371 RYLC ▲ 6469 (8.97)

S. Weigle (hn), J. Weigle (cnd), Dresden PO—Con 1 Hn, K.412 [Rondo (Allegro)]; Con 2 Hn, K.417; Con 3 Hn, K.447; Con 4 Hn, K.495 † Con Movt Hn, K.Anh.98a; Con Movt Hn, K.370b; Con 1 Hn, K.412; Rondo Hn, K.371 LALI ▲ 15874

Concerto "No. 0" in E♭ for Horn & Orchestra [arr of K.370b & K.371]

J. Sommerville (hn), M. Bernardi (cnd), CBC Vancouver SO [arr Levin] *(rec CBC Vancouver, Canada, Feb 10-12, 1996)* ("Mozart Horn Concertos") † Con 1 Hn, K.412; Con 2 Hn, K.417; Con 3 Hn, K.447; Con 4 Hn, K.495 SMS ▲ 5172 [DDD] (16.97)

M. Thompson (hn), M. Thompson (cnd), Bournemouth Sinfonietta [arr John Humphries] *(rec Dorset, England, Dec 18-20, 1995)* ("Complete Works for Horn & Orchestra") † Con Movt Hn, K.Anh.98a; Cons (4) Hn; Rondo Hn, K.371 NXIN ▲ 8553592 [DDD] (5.97)

Concerto No. 2 in E♭ for Horn & Orchestra, K.417 (1783)

D. Brain (hn) *(rec 1939-46)* ("Dennis Brain: His Early Recordings") † Con 3 Hn, K.447; Divert 17 Hns Strs, K.334 GRM2 ▲ 78729 (13.97)

D. Brain (hn), H. von Karajan (cnd), Philharmonia Orch *(rec London, England, 1953)* † Con 1 Hn, K.412; Con 3 Hn, K.447; Con 4 Hn, K.495; Qnt Pno & Winds, K.452 EMIC (Great Recordings of the Century) ▲ 66950 [ADD] (11.97)

D. Brain (hn), W. Susskind (cnd), Philharmonia Orch *(rec 1939-46)* † Divert 17 Hns Strs, K.334; Beethoven:Son Hn GRM2 (Records of the Century) ▲ 78881 (14.97)

D. Brain (hn), W. Susskind (cnd), Philharmonia Orch † Con Bn, K.191; Con Cl, K.622; Con 4 Hn, K.495 AVID (Classical Masters) ▲ 605 (16.97)

D. Brain (hn), W. Susskind (cnd), Philharmonia Orch † Con 3 Hn, K.447; Qnt Hn; Beethoven:Son Hn; R. Strauss:Con 1 Hn, Op. 11 PHS ▲ 26 (17.97)

J. Dokupil (hn), A. Lizzio (cnd), Mozart Festival Orch † Con Ob; Con 1 Hn, K.412; Con 3 Hn, K.447 PC ▲ 265051 [DDD] (2.97)

COMPOSERS 555

MOZART, WOLFGANG AMADEUS (cont.)

Concerto No. 2 in E♭ for Horn & Orchestra, K.417 (1783) (cont.)

I. Magyari (hn), J. Ferencsik (cnd), Hungarian State Orch *(rec 1981-82)* ("Concertos for Horn & Bassoon") † Con Bn, K.191; Con 3 Hn, K.447; Con 4 Hn, K.495 CLDI ▲ 4027 [ADD] (10.97)
W. Purvis (hn), Orpheus CO † Con Bn, K.191; Con Ob; Con 3 Hn, K.447 DEUT ▲ 23623 [DDD] (16.97)
J. Sommerville (hn), M. Bernardi (cnd), CBC Vancouver SO *(rec CBC Vancouver, Feb 10-12, 1996)* ("Mozart Horn Concertos") † Con "0" Hn; Con 1 Hn, K.412; Con 3 Hn, K.447; Con 4 Hn, K.495 SMS ▲ 5172 [DDD] (16.97)
R. Watkins (hn), R. Hickox (cnd), City of London Sinfonia † Con 1 Hn, K.412; Con 3 Hn, K.447; Con 4 Hn, K.495; Rondo Hn, K.371 INMP ▲ 2013 (9.97)
Z. Zuk (hn), G. Dalinkevičius (cnd), Baltic Virtuosi ("Horn Classics") † J. Haydn:Con 1 Hn; G. Rossini:Prelude, Theme & Vars Hn; Telemann:Con Hn ZUK ▲ 310355 (10.97)
artists unknown—Andante ("Adagios") † Adagio Pno, K.540; Adagio Vn, K.261; Con Cl, K.622; Con Fl & Hp, K.299; Con 20 Pno, K.466; Con 21 Pno, K.467; Con 23 Pno, K.488; Con 26 Pno, K.537; Con 27 Pno, K.595; Con 3 Hn, K.447; Con 3 Vn, K.216; Diverts Str Qt, K.136-138; Kleine Nachtmusik, K.525; Qnt Cl, K.581; Serenade; Serenade Ww, K.388/384a; Sinf concertante Vn, K.364; Son 12 Pno, K.332; Son 16 Pno, K.545; Sym 40, K.550; Sym 41, K.551 DECC (2-Fers) 2-▲ 460191 (17.97)

Concerto No. 3 in E♭ for Horn & Orchestra, K.447 (?1784-87)

D. Brain (hn) *(rec 1939-46)* ("Dennis Brain: His Early Recordings") † Con 2 Hn, K.417; Divert 17 Hns Strs, K.334 GRM2 ▲ 78729 (13.97)
D. Brain (hn), H. von Karajan (cnd), Philharmonia Orch *(rec London, England, 1953)* † Con 1 Hn, K.412; Con 2 Hn, K.417; Con 4 Hn, K.495; Qnt Pno & Winds, K.452 EMIC (Great Recordings of the Century) ▲ 66950 [ADD] (11.97)
D. Brain (hn), L. Turner (cnd), Hallé Orch † Con 2 Hn, K.417; Qnt Hn; Beethoven:Son Hn; R. Strauss:Con 1 Hn, Op. 11 PHS ▲ 26 (17.97)
J. Falout (hn), K. Redel (cnd), Camerata Labacensis † Con Ob; Con 1 Hn, K.412; Con 2 Hn, K.417 PC ▲ 265051 [DDD] (2.97)
Á. Friedrich (hn), J. Ferencsik (cnd), Hungarian State Orch *(rec 1981-82)* ("Concertos for Horn & Bassoon") † Con Bn, K.191; Con 2 Hn, K.417; Con 4 Hn, K.495 CLDI ▲ 4027 [ADD] (10.97)
B. Heiser (hn), H. Kraus (cnd) † Con 1 Hn, K.412; Cons Fl LALI ▲ 15624 [DDD] (3.97)
W. Purvis (hn), Orpheus CO † Con Bn, K.191; Con Ob; Con 2 Hn, K.417 DEUT ▲ 23623 [DDD] (16.97)
F. Rizner (hn), J. Garcia (cnd), English CO † Con Cl, K.622; Con 4 Hn, K.495 SUMM ▲ 131 [DDD] (16.97)
J. Sommerville (hn), M. Bernardi (cnd), CBC Vancouver SO *(rec CBC Vancouver, Feb 10-12, 1996)* ("Mozart Horn Concertos") † Con "0" Hn; Con 1 Hn, K.412; Con 2 Hn, K.417; Con 4 Hn, K.495 SMS ▲ 5172 [DDD] (16.97)
M. Stefek (hn), K. Ančerl (cnd), Czech PO *(rec 1952-66)* † Con Bn, K.191; Con 23 Pno, K.488; Zauberflöte (sels) SUR ▲ 111935 [AAD]
R. Watkins (hn), R. Hickox (cnd), City of London Sinfonia † Con 1 Hn, K.412; Con 2 Hn, K.417; Con 4 Hn, K.495; Rondo Hn, K.371 INMP ▲ 2013 (9.97)
Z. Zuk (hn), J. Stanienda (cnd), Wroclaw CO Leopoldinum ("Eine kleine Hornmusik") † Con 4 Hn, K.495; Rondo Hn, K.371; L. Mozart:Con Hn; Con Hns ZUK ▲ 160114 (10.97)
artists unknown—Romance (Larghetto) ("Adagios") † Adagio Pno, K.540; Adagio Vn, K.261; Con Cl, K.622; Con Fl & Hp, K.299; Con 2 Hn, K.417; Con 20 Pno, K.466; Con 21 Pno, K.467; Con 23 Pno, K.488; Con 26 Pno, K.537; Con 27 Pno, K.595; Con 3 Vn, K.216; Diverts Str Qt, K.136-138; Kleine Nachtmusik, K.525; Qnt Cl, K.581; Serenade; Serenade Ww, K.388/384a; Sinf concertante Vn, K.364; Son 12 Pno, K.332; Son 16 Pno, K.545; Sym 40, K.550; Sym 41, K.551 DECC (2-Fers) 2-▲ 460191 (17.97)

Concerto (No. 4) in E♭ for Horn & Orchestra, K.495 (1786)

P. Del Vescovo (hn), J. Paillard (cnd), Jean-François Paillard CO ("The Magic of the French Horn") † Rondo Hn, K.371; N. C. Bochsa:Andante sostenuto; Dauprat:Son Hn & Hp; Dukas:Villanelle; R. Schumann:Konzertstück Hns, Op. 86 ERAT ▲ 94801 (9.97)
J. Rolla (cnd), Liszt CO—Rondo (Allegro vivace) *(rec Vac Franciscan Church, Vac, Hungary, Aug 1987)* ("The Essential Mozart") † Con 21 Pno, K.467; Don Giovanni (sels); Exsultate, jubilate, K.165; Kleine Nachtmusik, K.525; Nozze di Figaro (ov); Nozze di Figaro (sels); Requiem, K.626; Serenade; Sym 40, K.550; Sym 41, K.551; Vars "Ah! vous dirai-je, Maman", K.265; Zauberflöte (ov) SNYC (Essential Classics) ▲ 64225 [ADD] (7.97)

Concerto No. 4 in E♭ for Horn & Orchestra, K.495 (1786)

L. Bergé (hn), D. Vermeulen (cnd), Prima La Musica ("Wind Concertos") † Con Bn, K.191; Con Ob; Con 1 Fl, K.313; Sinf concertante Ob, K.Anh.9 EUFO 2-▲ 1234 [DDD] (36.97)
D. Brain (hn), H. von Karajan (cnd), Philharmonia Orch *(rec London, England, 1953)* † Con 1 Hn, K.412; Con 2 Hn, K.417; Con 3 Hn, K.447; Qnt Pno & Winds, K.452 EMIC (Great Recordings of the Century) ▲ 66950 [ADD] (11.97)
D. Brain (hn), M. Sargent (cnd), Hallé Orch † Con Bn, K.191; Con Cl, K.622; Con 2 Hn, K.417 AVID (Classical Masters) ▲ 605 (16.97)
D. Jolley (hn), Orpheus CO † Con Cl, K.622; Con 1 Hn, K.412 DEUT ▲ 23377 [DDD] (16.97)
A. Klisans (hn), V. Sinaisky (cnd), Latvian National SO, L. Vigners (cnd) † P. Hindemith:Con Hn; L. Mozart:Con Hn; C. M. von Weber:Con Hn RIGA ▲ 17 (16.97)
I. Magyari (hn), J. Ferencsik (cnd), Hungarian State Orch *(rec 1981-82)* ("Concertos for Horn & Bassoon") † Con Bn, K.191; Con 2 Hn, K.417; Con 3 Hn, K.447 CLDI ▲ 4027 [ADD] (10.97)
F. Rizner (hn), J. Garcia (cnd), English CO † Con Cl, K.622; Con 3 Hn, K.447 SUMM ▲ 131 [DDD] (16.97)
J. Sommerville (hn), M. Bernardi (cnd), CBC Vancouver SO *(rec CBC Vancouver, Feb 10-12, 1996)* ("Mozart Horn Concertos") † Con "0" Hn; Con 1 Hn, K.412; Con 2 Hn, K.417; Con 3 Hn, K.447 SMS ▲ 5172 [DDD] (16.97)
R. Watkins (hn), R. Hickox (cnd), City of London Sinfonia † Con 1 Hn, K.412; Con 2 Hn, K.417; Con 3 Hn, K.447; Rondo Hn, K.371 INMP ▲ 2013 (9.97)
Z. Zuk (hn), J. Stanienda (cnd), Wroclaw CO Leopoldinum ("Eine kleine Hornmusik") † Con 3 Hn, K.447; Rondo Hn, K.371; L. Mozart:Con Hn; Con Hns ZUK ▲ 160114 (10.97)

Concerto (No. 1) in D for Horn & Orchestra [2nd Movt rondo completed by Süssmayr], K.412 (1791)

D. Bourgue (hn), B. Papazian (cnd) [rondo movt by Herman Jeurissen] † Cons (4) Hn; Rondo Hn, K.371 ARN ▲ 68198 [DDD] (16.97)
L. Greer (nat hn), N. McGegan (cnd), Philharmonia Baroque Orch—Rondo (Allegro) [rondo movt by Herman Jeurissen] † Cons (4) Hn; Rondo Hn, K.371 HAM ▲ 907012 [AAD] (18.97)

Concerto No. 1 in D for Horn & Orchestra [2nd movt rondo completed by Süssmayr], K.412 (1791)

D. Brain (hn), H. von Karajan (cnd), Philharmonia Orch *(rec London, England, 1953)* † Con 2 Hn, K.417; Con 3 Hn, K.447; Con 4 Hn, K.495; Qnt Pno & Winds, K.452 EMIC (Great Recordings of the Century) ▲ 66950 [ADD] (11.97)
J. Falout (hn), K. Redel (cnd), Camerata Labacensis † Con Ob; Con 2 Hn, K.417; Con 3 Hn, K.447 PC ▲ 265051 [DDD] (2.97)
B. Heiser (hn), H. Kraus (cnd) † Con 3 Hn, K.447; Cons Fl LALI ▲ 15624 [DDD] (3.97)
H. Jeurissen (hn), R. Goodman (cnd), Netherlands CO [Rondo; w. Mozart's original texts narrated by Gior] *(rec 1996)* ("The Complete Horn Concertos") † Con Movt Hn, K.Anh.98a; Con Movt Hn, K.370b; Cons (4) Hn; Rondo Hn, K.371 OLY ▲ 470 [DDD] (16.97)
D. Jolley (hn), Orpheus CO † Con Cl, K.622; Con 4 Hn, K.495 DEUT ▲ 23377 [DDD] (16.97)
J. Sommerville (hn), M. Bernardi (cnd), CBC Vancouver SO *(rec CBC Vancouver, Canada, Feb 10-12, 1996)* ("Mozart Horn Concertos") † Con "0" Hn; Con 2 Hn, K.417; Con 3 Hn, K.447; Con 4 Hn, K.495 SMS ▲ 5172 [DDD] (16.97)
R. Watkins (hn), R. Hickox (cnd), City of London Sinfonia † Con 2 Hn, K.417; Con 3 Hn, K.447; Con 4 Hn, K.495; Rondo Hn, K.371 INMP ▲ 2013 (9.97)
S. Weigle (hn), J. Weigle (cnd), Dresden PO—Rondo (Allegro) † Con Movt Hn, K.Anh.98a; Con Movt Hn, K.370b; Cons (4) Hn; Rondo Hn, K.371 LALI ▲ 15874

Concerto Movement in E♭ for Horn & Orchestra [fragment; reconstructed Herman Jeurissen], K.370b (?1781)

H. Jeurissen (hn), R. Goodman (cnd), Netherlands CO *(rec 1996)* ("The Complete Horn Concertos") † Con Movt Hn, K.Anh.98a; Con 1 Hn, K.412; Cons (4) Hn; Rondo Hn, K.371 OLY ▲ 470 [DDD] (16.97)
S. Weigle (hn), J. Weigle (cnd), Dresden PO † Con Movt Hn, K.Anh.98a; Con 1 Hn, K.412; Cons (4) Hn; Rondo Hn, K.371 LALI ▲ 15874

Concerto Movement in E for Horn & Orchestra [fragment], K.Anh.98a (1785)

H. Jeurissen (hn), R. Goodman (cnd), Netherlands CO [completed by H. Jeurissen] *(rec 1996)* ("The Complete Horn Concertos") † Con Movt Hn, K.370b; Con 1 Hn, K.412; Cons (4) Hn; Rondo Hn, K.371 OLY ▲ 470 [DDD] (16.97)
N. Marriner (cnd), Academy of St. Martin in the Fields ("The Mozart Experience") † Con Cl, K.622; Con Fl & Hp, K.299; Con 20 Pno, K.466; Con 21 Pno, K.467; Divert Ww; German Dances (3), K.605; Kleine Nachtmusik, K.525; Musikalischer Spass, K.522; Nozze di Figaro (sels); Serenade 6 Orch, K.239; Sym 40, K.550; Sym 41, K.551 PPHI 5-▲ 26204 (33.97)
E. Ruske (hn), C. Mackerras (cnd), Scottish CO *(rec Usher Hall Edinburgh, Scotland, Dec 4-5, 1993)* † Cons (4) Hn; Rondo Hn, K.371 TEL ▲ 80367 [DDD] (16.97)
M. Thompson (hn), M. Thompson (cnd), Bournemouth Sinfonietta *(rec Dorset, England, Dec 18-20, 1995)* ("Complete Works for Horn & Orchestra") † Con "0" Hn; Cons (4) Hn; Rondo Hn, K.371 NXIN ▲ 8553592 [DDD] (5.97)
S. Weigle (hn), J. Weigle (cnd), Dresden PO † Con Movt Hn, K.370b; Con 1 Hn, K.412; Cons (4) Hn; Rondo Hn, K.371 LALI ▲ 15874

Concerto in C for Oboe & Orchestra, K.271k (1777)

A. Baccini (ob), E. Aadland (cnd), European Community CO † Con Bn, K.191; Con Cl, K.622 IMPA ▲ 2047 (9.97)

MOZART, WOLFGANG AMADEUS (cont.)

Concerto in C for Oboe & Orchestra, K.271k (1777) (cont.)

J. DeLancie (ob), E. Ormandy (cnd), Philadelphia Orch † Con Bn, K.191; R. Strauss:Con Ob, AV144; C. M. von Weber:Andante & Rondo ungarese Bn SNYC (Essential Classics) ▲ 62652 (7.97)
S. Dent (ob), V. Czarnecki (cnd), Southwest German CO Pforzheim ("The Greatest Oboe Concertos") † J. S. Bach:Con Ob d'amore & Strs; Cimarosa:Con Ob; Crusell:Divert Ob, Op. 9 AMAT ▲ 9103 [DDD] (17.97)
D. Doherty (ob), O. Henzold (cnd), Lucerne SO ("Oboe Concertos") † J. Haydn:Con Ob; Martinů:Con Ob; B. A. Zimmermann:Con Ob PANC ▲ 510090 [DDD] (17.97)
B. Glaetzner (ob), H. Haenchen (cnd), C.P.E. Bach CO † Andante Fl, K.315; Con Bn, K.191; Con Cl, K.622 LALI ▲ 15875 [DDD] (3.97)
B. Glaetzner (ob), H. Haenchen (cnd), C.P.E. Bach CO † Ferlendis:Con 1 Ob CAPO ▲ 10087 [DDD] (11.97)
J. V. Hauwe (ob), D. Vermeulen (cnd), Prima La Musica ("Wind Concertos") † Con Bn, K.191; Con 1 Fl, K.313; Con 4 Hn, K.495; Sinf concertante Ob, K.Anh.9 EUFO 2-▲ 1234 [DDD] (36.97)
C. Hogwood (cnd), Academy of Ancient Music Orch † Con Bn, K.191; Con Cl, K.622; Con Fl & Hp, K.299; Con 1 Fl, K.313; Cons (4) Hn DECC 3-▲ 460027 (32.97)
B. Horlitz (ob), R. Reuter (cnd), Thüringian CO Weimar *(rec Weimar Johannis Church, Mar 10-13, 1997)* ("Serenade im Park") † Divert 11 Ob, K.251; Divert 7 Hns, K.205 GRH ▲ 1068 [DDD] (16.97)
G. Hunt (ob) *(rec 1987-91)* † Con Fl & Hp, K.299; Con 1 Fl, K.313; Sinf concertante Ob, K.Anh.9 CFP 2-▲ 4808 [DDD] (21.97)
L. Koch (ob), H. von Karajan (cnd), Berlin PO † Con Bn, K.191; Con Cl, K.622 EMIC ▲ 64355 [ADD] (11.97)
J. Mack (ob), C. von Dohnányi (cnd), Cleveland Orch † Con Bn, K.191; Con Cl, K.622 PLON ▲ 443176 (16.97)
C. Nicklin (ob), J. Glover (cnd), London Mozart Players † Con Cl, K.622; Con 1 Fl, K.313 ASV ▲ 795 [DDD] (16.97)
M. Niesemann (ob) † Con Fl & Hp, K.299 CAPO ▲ 10375 (11.97)
Piquet (ob), C. Hogwood (cnd), Academy of Ancient Music † Con Cl, K.622 PLOI ▲ 14339 [DDD] (16.97)
G. Prêtre (cnd), Paris Opera Orch ("Homage to Georges Prêtre") † Con Bn, K.191; Con Cl, K.622; Con Fl & Hp, K.299; Con 1 Fl, K.313; Cons (4) Hn FORL ▲ 16747 [DDD] (47.97)
I. Rogeljic (ob), K. Redel (cnd), Camerata Labacensis † Con 1 Hn, K.412; Con 2 Hn, K.417; Con 3 Hn, K.447 PC ▲ 265051 [DDD] (2.97)
D. Theodore (ob), R. Hickox (cnd), City of London Sinfonia † Con Fl & Hp, K.299; A. Salieri:Con Fl CHN ▲ 9051 [DDD] (16.97)
G. Touvron (tpt) † Con Cl, K.622; Con Fl & Hp, K.299; Zauberflöte (sels); L. Mozart:Con Tpt LIDI ▲ 105057 (16.97)
G. Turetschek (ob), K. Böhm (cnd), Vienna PO † Con Bn, K.191; Con Cl, K.622 DEUT ▲ 29816 [ADD] (7.97)
R. Wolfgang (ob), Orpheus CO † Con Bn, K.191; Con 2 Hn, K.417; Con 3 Hn, K.447 DEUT ▲ 23623 [DDD] (16.97)
R. Wolfgang (ob), Orpheus CO ("The Wind Concerti") † Con Bn, K.191; Con Cl, K.622; Con Fl & Hp, K.299; Cons (4) Hn; Cons Fl; Sinf concertante Ob, K.Anh.9 DEUT 3-▲ 31665 [DDD] (34.97)

Concertos (27) for Piano & Orchestra (complete)

G. Anda (pno), Salzburg Mozarteum Camerata Academica DEUT 10-▲ 29001 [ADD] (67.97)
D. Barenboim (pno), D. Barenboim (cnd), English CO [all except 7 & 10] *(rec London, England, 1967-74)* † Rondo Pno & Orch, K.382 EMIC 10-▲ 72930 [ADD] (66.97)
M. Bilson (pno), R. Levin (pno), M. Tan (pno), J. E. Gardiner (cnd), English Baroque Soloists PARC 9-▲ 31211 [DDD] (80.97)
J. van Immerseel (pno) ("Vols. 1-10, boxed-set") CCL 10-▲ 10 [DDD] (69.97)
M. Uchida (pno), J. Tate (cnd), English CO PPHI 9-▲ 38207 (112.97)

Concertos (3) for Piano & Orchestra [arr from J. C. Bach, Op.5], K.107 (1772)

M. Perahia (pno), M. Perahia (cnd), English CO † J. S. Schroeter:Con Pno SNYC ▲ 39222 [DDD] (16.97)

Concerto No. 1 in F for Piano & Orchestra [arr from works by Raupach & Honauer], K.37 (1767)

H. Francesch (pno), K. Weise (cnd), Nice PO ("Mozart Piano Concertos, Vol. 1") † Con 2 Pno, K.39; Con 3 Pno, K.40; Con 4 Pno, K.41 KPT ▲ 32109 [DDD]
J. Jandó (pno), I. Hegyi (cnd), Concentus Hungaricus † Con 2 Pno, K.39; Con 3 Pno, K.40; Con 4 Pno, K.41 NXIN ▲ 550212 [DDD] (5.97)
M. Perahia (pno), M. Perahia (cnd), English CO † Con 2 Pno, K.39; Con 3 Pno, K.40; Con 4 Pno, K.41 SNYC ▲ 39225 [DDD] (16.97)
S. Richter (pno), R. Barshai (cnd), Japan Shinsei SO *(rec Tokyo, Japan, Mar 3, 1993)* ("The Last Concert") † Con 18 Pno, K.456; Con 5 Pno, K.175 LARL ▲ 902 (15.97)

Concerto No. 2 in B♭ for Piano & Orchestra [arr from works by Raupach & Schobert], K.39 (1767)

H. Francesch (pno), K. Weise (cnd), Nice PO ("Mozart Piano Concertos, Vol. 1") † Con 1 Pno, K.37; Con 3 Pno, K.40; Con 4 Pno, K.41 KPT ▲ 32109 [DDD]
J. Jandó (pno), I. Hegyi (cnd), Concentus Hungaricus † Con 1 Pno, K.37; Con 3 Pno, K.40; Con 4 Pno, K.41 NXIN ▲ 550212 [DDD] (5.97)
M. Perahia (pno), M. Perahia (cnd), English CO † Con 1 Pno, K.37; Con 3 Pno, K.40; Con 4 Pno, K.41 SNYC ▲ 39225 [DDD] (16.97)

Concerto No. 3 in D for Piano & Orchestra [arr from works by Honauer, Eckard & C. P. E. Bach], K.40 (1767)

H. Francesch (pno), K. Weise (cnd), Nice PO ("Mozart Piano Concertos, Vol. 1") † Con 1 Pno, K.37; Con 2 Pno, K.39; Con 4 Pno, K.41 KPT ▲ 32109 [DDD]
J. Jandó (pno), I. Hegyi (cnd), Concentus Hungaricus † Con 1 Pno, K.37; Con 2 Pno, K.39; Con 4 Pno, K.41 NXIN ▲ 550212 [DDD] (5.97)
M. Perahia (pno), M. Perahia (cnd), English CO † Con 1 Pno, K.37; Con 2 Pno, K.39; Con 4 Pno, K.41 SNYC ▲ 39225 [DDD] (16.97)

Concerto No. 4 in G for Piano & Orchestra [arr from works by Honauer & Raupach], K.41 (1767)

H. Francesch (pno), K. Weise (cnd), Nice PO ("Mozart Piano Concertos, Vol. 1") † Con 1 Pno, K.37; Con 2 Pno, K.39; Con 3 Pno, K.40 KPT ▲ 32109 [DDD]
J. Jandó (pno), I. Hegyi (cnd), Concentus Hungaricus † Con 1 Pno, K.37; Con 2 Pno, K.39; Con 3 Pno, K.40 NXIN ▲ 550212 [DDD] (5.97)
M. Perahia (pno), M. Perahia (cnd), English CO † Con 1 Pno, K.37; Con 2 Pno, K.39; Con 3 Pno, K.40 SNYC ▲ 39225 [DDD] (16.97)

Concerto No. 5 in D for Piano & Orchestra, K.175 (1773)

D. Barenboim (pno), D. Barenboim (cnd), Berlin PO † Con 6 Pno, K.238; Con 8 Pno, K.246 TELC ▲ 21483 (16.97)
R. Buchbinder (pno), Vienna SO *(rec Nov 30, 1997)* † Con 6 Pno, K.238; Con 8 Pno, K.246; Rondo Pno & Orch, K.382 CALG ▲ 51009 [DDD]
J. Jandó (pno), M. Antál (cnd), Concentus Hungaricus *(rec Jan 4-10, 1991)* ("Complete Piano Concertos, Vol. 9") † Con 26 Pno, K.537; Rondo Pno Orch, K.382 NXIN ▲ 550209 [DDD] (5.97)
M. Perahia (pno), M. Perahia (cnd), English CO † Con 25 Pno, K.503 SNYC ▲ 37267 [DDD] (16.97)
S. Richter (pno), R. Barshai (cnd), Japan Shinsei SO *(rec Tokyo, Japan, Mar 3, 1993)* ("The Last Concert") † Con 1 Pno, K.37; Con 18 Pno, K.456 LARL ▲ 902 (15.97)
M. Uchida (pno), J. Tate (cnd), English CO † Con 6 Pno, K.238; Rondo Pno Orch, K.382 PPHI ▲ 32082 [DDD] (16.97)

Concerto No. 6 in B♭ for Piano & Orchestra, K.238 (1776)

G. Anda (pno), G. Anda (cnd), Salzburg Mozarteum Camerata Academia *(rec Neues Festspielhaus Salzburg, Austria, Apr 1962)* † Con 17 Pno, K.453; Con 21 Pno, K.467 DEUT (The Originals) ▲ 47436 [ADD] (11.97)
V. Ashkenazy (pno), D. Zinman (cnd), London SO † J. S. Bach:Con 1 Hpd, BWV 1052; Chopin:Con 2 Pno, Op. 21 PLON (The Classic Sound) ▲ 448598 (11.97)
D. Barenboim (pno), D. Barenboim (cnd), Berlin PO † Con 5 Pno, K.175; Con 8 Pno, K.246 TELC ▲ 21483 (16.97)
R. Buchbinder (pno), Vienna SO *(rec May 17, 1998)* † Con 5 Pno, K.175; Con 8 Pno, K.246; Rondo Pno & Orch, K.382 CALG ▲ 51009 [DDD]
M. Erxleben (vn), M. Erxleben (cnd), New Berlin CO † Adagio Vn, K.261; Con 7 Vn, K.271a; Rondo Vn, K.373 LALI ▲ 15881 [DDD] (3.97)
J. Jandó (pno), M. Antál (cnd), Concentus Hungaricus *(rec 1990)* ("Complete Piano Concertos, Vol. 8") † Con 18 Pno, K.456; Con 19 Pno, K.459; Con 8 Pno, K.246 NXIN ▲ 550208 [DDD] (5.97)
M. Perahia (pno), M. Perahia (cnd), English CO † Con 13 Pno, K.415 SNYC ▲ 39223 (16.97)
M. Uchida (pno), J. Tate (cnd), English CO † Con 5 Pno, K.175; Rondo Pno Orch, K.382 PPHI ▲ 32082 [DDD] (16.97)
A. Vardi (pno), A. Vardi (cnd), Israel CO † Con 21 Pno, K.467 CACI ▲ 210015

Concerto No. 8 in C for Piano & Orchestra, K.246 (1776)

V. Ashkenazy (pno), I. Kertész (cnd), London SO † Con 9 Pno, K.271 PPHI (The Classic Sound) ▲ 443576 (11.97)
D. Barenboim (pno), D. Barenboim (cnd), Berlin PO † Con 5 Pno, K.175; Con 6 Pno, K.238 TELC ▲ 21483 (16.97)
P. Bruni (pno), E. Aadland (cnd), European Community CO † J. S. Bach:Con 1 Hpd, BWV 1052; J. Haydn:Con Org & Strs, H.XVIII/2 INMP ▲ 964 [DDD] (11.97)
R. Buchbinder (pno), Vienna SO *(rec June 20, 1998)* † Con 5 Pno, K.175; Con 6 Pno, K.238; Rondo Pno & Orch, K.382 CALG ▲ 51009 [DDD]
J. Jandó (pno), M. Antál (cnd), Concentus Hungaricus *(rec 1990)* ("Complete Piano Concertos, Vol. 8") † Con 18 Pno, K.456; Con 19 Pno, K.459; Con 6 Pno, K.238 NXIN ▲ 550208 [DDD] (5.97)

▲ = CD ♦ = Enhanced CD △ = MD ▮ = Cassette Tape ▯ = DCC

MOZART, WOLFGANG AMADEUS (cont.)

Concerto No. 8 in C for Piano & Orchestra, K.246 (1776) (cont.)

S. Kagan (pno), P. Macecek (cnd), Suk CO † Con 9 Pno, K.271; Rondo Pno Orch, K.386 DI ▲ 920517 [DDD] (5.97)

W. Kempff (pno), F. Leitner (cnd), Berlin PO † Con 23 Pno, K.488; Con 24 Pno, K.491; Con 27 Pno, K.595 DEUT (Double) 2-▲ 39699 (17.97)

W. Kempff (pno), F. Leitner (cnd), Berlin PO ("Wilhelm Kempff III") † Vars on "Unser dummer Pöbel", K.455; Beethoven:Rondos Pno, Op. 51; Son 11 Pno, Op. 22; Son 2 Pno, Op. 2/2; J. Brahms:Rhaps (2) Pno, Op. 79; G. Fauré:Nocturnes Pno; F. Schubert:Son Pno, D.840; R. Schumann:Romances Pno, Op. 28 PPHI (Great Pianists of the 20th Century) 2-▲ 456868 (22.97)

Concerto No. 9 in E♭ for Piano & Orchestra, K.271, "Jeunehomme" (1777)

V. Ashkenazy (pno), I. Kertész (cnd), London SO † Con 8 Pno, K.246 PPHI (The Classic Sound) ▲ 443576 (11.97)

D. Barenboim (pno), D. Barenboim (cnd), Berlin PO † Con 17 Pno, K.453 TELC ▲ 73128 [DDD] (16.97)

A. Brendel (pno), A. Janigro (cnd), Zagreb Solisti *(rec Vienna, Austria, 1965)* † Con 14 Pno, K.449 VC ▲ 116 [AAD] (13.97)

A. Brendel (pno), N. Marriner (cnd), Academy of St. Martin in the Fields ("Complete Piano Concerti, Vol. 2") † Con 15 Pno, K.450; Con 22 Pno, K.482; Con 25 Pno, K.503; Con 27 Pno, K.595 PPHI (Duo) 2-▲ 42571 (17.97)

R. Buchbinder (pno), Vienna SO *(rec Dec 1997)* † Con 19 Pno, K.459 CALG ▲ 51010 [DDD] (11.97)

A. Cheng (pno), M. Bernardi (cnd), CBC Vancouver SO † Con 17 Pno, K.453 SMS (SM 5000) ▲ 5104 [DDD] (16.97)

R. Firkušný (pno), E. Bour (cnd), Southwest German RSO Baden-Baden † Con 24 Pno, K.491 INTC ▲ 820547 (9.97)

R. Firkušný (pno), G. Szell (cnd), (Royal) Concertgebouw Orch † Sym 41, K.551 SNYC (Festspiel Dokumente: Salzburger Festspiele) ▲ 68445 (10.97)

H. Francesch (pno), K. Weise (cnd), Nice PO † Con 25 Pno, K.503 KPT ▲ 32209

N. Frisardi (pno), G. Korsten (cnd), Salzburg Mozarteum Orch † Con 27 Pno, K.595 CHSK ▲ 136 [DDD] (16.97)

D. Gerard (pno), H. Kraus (cnd) † Con 23 Pno, K.488 LALI ▲ 15632 [DDD] (3.97)

W. Gieseking (pno) *(rec 1924-55)* ("Gieseking: A Retrospective, Vol. 3") † J. Brahms:Rhaps (2) Pno, Op. 79; Casella:Son Pno, Op. 28; Chopin:Nocturnes (21) Pno; Polonaise 6 Pno, Op. 53; M. Ravel:Jeux d'eau PHS ▲ 9038 (17.97)

W. Gieseking (pno), H. Rosbaud (cnd), Berlin State Opera Orch *(rec Berlin, Sept 29, 1936)* ("His First Concerto Recordings, Vol. 1") † Son 18 Pno, K.576; Beethoven:Con 1 Pno, Op. 15 APR ▲ 5511 [ADD] (19.97)

R. Goode (pno) † Con 25 Pno, K.503 NON ▲ 79454 (16.97)

C. Haskil (pno), O. Ackermann (cnd), Northwest German RSO *(rec Nov 6, 1954)* † Con 20 Pno, K.466 MUA ▲ 4715 (10.97)

M. Hess (pno) *(rec University of Illinois, IL, Mar 18, 1949)* † Con 21 Pno, K.467 APR ▲ 5539 [ADD] (18.97)

M. Horszowski (pno), F. Waldman (cnd), Musica Aeterna Ensemble *(rec 1962-72)* † Con 12 Pno, K.414; Con 13 Pno, K.415; Con 14 Pno, K.449; Con 19 Pno, K.459; Son 16 Pno, K.545 PHS 2-▲ 9138 [ADD] (33.97)

J. Jandó (pno), A. Ligeti (cnd), Concentus Hungaricus *(rec July 1989)* † Con 27 Pno, K.595 NXIN ▲ 550203 [DDD] (5.97)

K. Jarrett (pno), D. R. Davies (cnd), Stuttgart CO *(rec Mozart-Saal, Stuttgart, Germany, 1996-98)* † Adagio & Fugue Strs, K.546; Con 17 Pno, K.453; Con 20 Pno, K.466 UECM 2-▲ 462651 [DDD] (34.97)

S. Kagan (pno), P. Macecek (cnd), Suk CO † Con 8 Pno, K.246; Rondo Pno Orch, K.386 DI ▲ 920517 [DDD] (5.97)

B. Meyer (pno), I. Brown (cnd), Norwegian CO † Con 23 Pno, K.488 VC ▲ 1003 [DDD] (13.97)

L. Nicholson (pno), N. Kraemer (cnd), Cappella Coloniensis ("Cappella Edition") † Con 21 Pno, K.467 CAPO ▲ 10621 [DDD] (11.97)

G. Novaes (pno), H. Swarowsky (cnd), Vienna SO *(rec 1950s)* ("The Classical Novaes") † Con 20 Pno, K.466; Son 11 Pno, K.331; Son 16 Pno, K.545; Son 5 Pno, K.283; Beethoven:Con 5 Pno, Op. 73 VOXL (Legends) 2-▲ 5512 [ADD] (9.97)

M. Perahia (pno), M. Perahia (cnd), English CO † Con 21 Pno, K.467 SNYC ▲ 34562 [AAD] (16.97)

H. Shelley (pno), H. Shelley (cnd), London Mozart Players † Con 17 Pno, K.453 CHN ▲ 9068 [DDD] (16.97)

K. Tabe (pno), J. López-Cobos (cnd), Lausanne CO *(rec Musica Théâtre La Chaux-de-Fonds, June 10-11, 1995)* † Con 24 Pno, K.491 DNN ▲ 78833 [DDD] (16.97)

M. Uchida (pno), J. Tate (cnd), English CO *(rec 1990)* ("Mitsuko Uchida") † Adagio Pno, K.540; Rondo Pno, K.511; Son 18 Pno, K.576; Vars on "Unser dummer Pöbel", K.455; Debussy:Études (12) Pno; Schoenberg:Pieces (3) Pno, Op. 11 PPHI (Great Pianists of the 20th Century) 2-▲ 456982 (22.97)

Concerto No. 10 in E♭ for 2 Pianos & Orchestra, K.365 (1779)

M. Argerich (pno), A. Rabinovitch (pno) † Con 19 Pno, K.459; Con 20 Pno, K.466 TELC ▲ 98407 (16.97)

R. Fizdale (pno), A. Gold (pno), L. Bernstein (cnd), New York PO *(rec Lincoln Center New York, NY, Feb 17, 1970)* † Con 7 Pnos, K.242; Qt Pno, K.478 SNYC (Bernstein Century) ▲ 60598 [ADD] (10.97)

A. Grau (pno), G. Schumacher (pno), W. Gönnenwein (cnd), Stuttgart CO ("Homage to Karl Münchinger") † Idomeneo (ballet music), K.367 DI ▲ 920275 [DDD] (5.97)

J. Jandó (pno), M. Antál (pno) † Con 22 Pno, K.482 NXIN ▲ 550206 [DDD] (5.97)

J. Jandó (pno), D. Várjon (pno), M. Antál (cnd), Concentus Hungaricus *(rec Jan 7-10, 1991)* † Con 15 Pno, K.450; Con 7 Pnos, K.242 NXIN ▲ 550210 [DDD] (5.97)

A. D. Larrocha (pno), A. Previn (pno), A. Previn (cnd), Orch of St. Luke's *(rec New York City, July 26-27, 1993)* † Son Pnos, K.448 RCAV (Red Seal) ▲ 68044 (16.97)

G. Pekinel (pno), S. Pekinel (pno) † Bruch:Con for 2 Pnos, Op. 88a; Mendelssohn (-Bartholdy):Cons Pnos CHN ▲ 9711 (16.97)

M. Perahia (pno), R. Lupu (pno) † Andante & Vars, K.501; Con 7 Pnos, K.242; Busoni:Fant Org, K.608 SNYC ▲ 44915 (16.97)

M. Perahia (pno), M. Perahia (cnd), English CO † Con 12 Pno, K.414; Con 14 Pno, K.449 SNYC ▲ 42243 [AAD] (16.97)

A. Schnabel (pno), K. U. Schnabel (pno) ("Artur Schnabel Plays Mozart") † Con 19 Pno, K.459; Con 21 Pno, K.467; Con 27 Pno, K.595; Rondo Pno, K.511; Son 8 Pno, K.310 PHS 2-▲ 6 (33.97)

R. Serkin (pno), P. Serkin (pno), A. Schneider (cnd), Marlboro Festival Orch *(rec 1962)* † Con 12 Pno, K.414; Trio Pno, K.502 SNYC ▲ 46255 [ADD] (10.97)

R. Serkin (pno), P. Serkin (pno), A. Schneider (cnd), Marlboro Festival Orch ("Mozart: Legendary Interpretations") † Con 12 Pno, K.414; Con 14 Pno, K.449; Con 17 Pno, K.453; Con 18 Pno, K.456; Con 19 Pno, K.459; Con 20 Pno, K.466; Con 27 Pno, K.595; Rondo Pno Orch, K.382; Rondo Pno, K.511 SNYC 3-▲ 47207 (33.97)

G. Solti (cnd), English CO † Con 20 Pno, K.466; Con 7 Pnos, K.242 PLON ▲ 30232 [DDD] (16.97)

Concerto No. 11 in F for Piano & Orchestra, K.413 (1782-83)

D. Barenboim (pno), D. Barenboim (cnd) † Con 12 Pno, K.414; Con 13 Pno, K.415 TELC ▲ 13162 (15.97)

R. Buchbinder (pno), R. Buchbinder (cnd), Vienna SO † Con 12 Pno, K.414; Con 13 Pno, K.415 CALG ▲ 51011 [DDD] (11.97)

P. Dechorgnat (pno), Henschel String Quartet [Mozart's version for pno & str qt] *(rec July 1997)* † Con 12 Pno, K.414; Con 13 Pno, K.415 EMIC (Debut) ▲ 72525 [DDD] (6.97)

K. Lechner (pno), Franciscan String Quartet ["qnt" version] † Con 12 Pno, K.414; Con 13 Pno, K.415 VRDI (Masters) ▲ 32291 (13.97)

Concerto No. 12 in A for Piano & Orchestra, K.414 (1782)

D. Barenboim (pno), D. Barenboim (cnd) † Con 11 Pno, K.413; Con 13 Pno, K.415 TELC ▲ 13162 (15.97)

R. Buchbinder (pno), R. Buchbinder (cnd), Vienna SO † Con 11 Pno, K.413; Con 13 Pno, K.415 CALG ▲ 51011 [DDD] (11.97)

E. Ciccarelli (pno), G. D. Lorenzo (cnd), Vox Aurae Ensemble † Con 14 Pno, K.449; Sym 25, K.183 AG ▲ 183 (18.97)

P. Dechorgnat (pno), Henschel String Quartet [Mozart's version for pno & str qt] *(rec July 1997)* † Con 11 Pno, K.413; Con 13 Pno, K.415 EMIC (Debut) ▲ 72525 [DDD] (6.97)

M. Hess (pno), R. Scholz (cnd), American CO *(rec Mar 20, 1956)* ("In Concert 1949-1960") † Con 21 Pno, K.467; Con 27 Pno, K.595; Beethoven:Con 4 Pno, Op. 58; Con 5 Pno, Op. 73; Son 10 Vn, Op. 96; J. Brahms:Con 2 Pno, Op. 83; Son 2 Vn, Op. 100; F. Schubert:Sonatinas (3) Vn MUA 3-▲ 779 [AAD] (47.97)

M. Horszowski (pno), F. Waldman (cnd), Musica Aeterna Ensemble *(rec 1962-72)* † Con 13 Pno, K.415; Con 14 Pno, K.449; Con 19 Pno, K.459; Con 9 Pno, K.271; Son 16 Pno, K.545 PHS 2-▲ 9138 [ADD] (33.97)

J. Jandó (pno), A. Ligeti (cnd), Concentus Hungaricus *(rec June 1989)* † Con 14 Pno, K.449; Con 21 Pno, K.467 NXIN ▲ 550202 [DDD] (5.97)

E. Kissin (pno), V. Spivakov (cnd), Moscow Virtuosi † Con 20 Pno, K.466; Rondo Pno Orch, K.382 RCAV (Red Seal) ▲ 60400 (16.97)

E. Kissin (pno), V. Spivakov (cnd), Moscow Virtuosi ("Evgeny Kissin: A Musical Portrait") † S. Prokofiev:Con 3 Pno, Op. 26; S. Rachmaninoff:Con 2 Pno, Op. 18; D. Shostakovich:Con 1 Pno, Op. 35 RCAV (Red Seal) 2-▲ 60567 [DDD] (24.97)

P. Lang (pno), A. Lizzio (cnd), South German PO † Beethoven:Con 4 Pno, Op. 58 PC ▲ 267159 [DDD] (2.97)

K. Lechner (pno), Franciscan String Quartet ["qnt" version] † Con 11 Pno, K.413; Con 13 Pno, K.415 VRDI (Masters) ▲ 32291 (13.97)

S. Lubin (pno), S. Lubin (cnd) † Con 15 Pno, K.450 ARA ▲ 6552 [DDD] (16.97)

M. Migdal (pno), U. Björlin (cnd), Cappella Coloniensis † Con 25 Pno, K.503 LALI ▲ 15870 [DDD] (3.97)

L. Nicholson (pno), N. Kraemer (cnd), Cappella Coloniensis ("Cappella Edition") † Con 18 Pno, K.456 CAPO ▲ 10622 [DDD] (11.97)

MOZART, WOLFGANG AMADEUS (cont.)

Concerto No. 12 in A for Piano & Orchestra, K.414 (1782) (cont.)

M. Perahia (pno), M. Perahia (cnd), English CO † Con 10 Pnos, K.365; Con 14 Pno, K.449 SNYC ▲ 42243 [AAD] (16.97)

J. Rutter (cnd), City of London Sinfonia *(rec London, England, July 29, 1985)* ("The Mozart Collection") † Con Cl, K.622; Con Fl & Hp, K.299; Con 21 Pno, K.467; Diverts Str Qt, K.136-138; Music of Mozart; Nozze di Figaro (ov); Sym 39, K.543 AMG ▲ 586 (15.99)

R. Serkin (pno), C. Abbado (cnd), London SO *(rec 1981-82)* ("Rudolf Serkin") † Con 14 Pno, K.449; Con 16 Pno, K.451; Con 17 Pno, K.453; Con 19 Pno, K.459; Beethoven:Son 23 Pno, Op. 57 PPHI (Great Pianists of the 20th Century) ▲ 456964 (22.97)

R. Serkin (pno), A. Schneider (cnd), Columbia SO ("Mozart: Legendary Interpretations") † Con 10 Pnos, K.365; Con 14 Pno, K.449; Con 17 Pno, K.453; Con 18 Pno, K.456; Con 19 Pno, K.459; Con 20 Pno, K.466; Con 27 Pno, K.595; Rondo Pno Orch, K.382; Rondo Pno, K.511 SNYC 3-▲ 47207 (33.97)

R. Serkin (pno), A. Schneider (cnd), Marlboro Festival Orch *(rec 1962)* † Con 10 Pnos, K.365; Trio Pno, K.502 SNYC ▲ 46255 [ADD] (10.97)

H. Shelley (pno), H. Shelley (cnd), London Mozart Players † Con 19 Pno, K.459 CHN ▲ 9256 [DDD] (16.97)

Concerto No. 13 in C for Piano & Orchestra, K.415 (1782-83)

D. Barenboim (pno), D. Barenboim (cnd) † Con 11 Pno, K.413; Con 12 Pno, K.414 TELC ▲ 13162 (15.97)

R. Buchbinder (pno), R. Buchbinder (cnd), Vienna SO † Con 11 Pno, K.413; Con 12 Pno, K.414 CALG ▲ 51011 [DDD] (11.97)

P. Dechorgnat (pno), Henschel String Quartet [Mozart's version for pno & str qt] *(rec July 1997)* † Con 11 Pno, K.413; Con 12 Pno, K.414 EMIC (Debut) ▲ 72525 [DDD] (6.97)

C. Haskil (pno), B. Paumgartner (cnd), Lucerne Festival Strings *(rec 1960)* ("Clara Haskil") † Con 20 Pno, K.466; Con 23 Pno, K.488; Con 24 Pno, K.491; Con 27 Pno, K.595; Rondo Pno Orch, K.386 PPHI (Great Pianists of the 20th Century) ▲ 456826 (22.97)

M. Horszowski (pno), F. Waldman (cnd), Musica Aeterna Ensemble *(rec 1962-72)* † Con 12 Pno, K.414; Con 14 Pno, K.449; Con 19 Pno, K.459; Con 9 Pno, K.271; Son 16 Pno, K.545 PHS 2-▲ 9138 [ADD] (33.97)

J. Jandó (pno), A. Ligeti (cnd), Concentus Hungaricus *(rec May 1989)* † Con 20 Pno, K.466 NXIN ▲ 550201 [DDD] (5.97)

W. Landowska (pno), A. Rodzinski (cnd), New York PO *(rec New York, NY, 1945)* ("Wanda Landowska Plays Mozart's Piano Concertos") † Con 22 Pno, K.482 IN ▲ 1336 (m) [ADD] (15.97)

W. Landowska (pno), A. Rodzinski (cnd), New York PO *(rec 1945-46)* † Con 22 Pno, K.482 ENT (Sirio) ▲ 530032 (13.97)

W. Landowska (pno), A. Rodzinski (cnd), New York PO *(rec mid 1940s)* † Con 22 Pno, K.482 ENPL (The Piano Library) ▲ 283 (13.97)

K. Lechner (pno), Franciscan String Quartet ["qnt" version] † Con 11 Pno, K.413; Con 12 Pno, K.414 VRDI (Masters) ▲ 32291 (13.97)

H. Menuhin (pno), G. Cleve (cnd), Midsummer Mozart Festival Orch *(rec Berkeley, CA, July 25, 1987)* BAIN ▲ 6273 [DDD] (16.97)

L. Nicholson (pno), N. Kraemer (cnd), Cappella Coloniensis † Con 23 Pno, K.488 LALI ▲ 15871 [DDD] (3.97)

L. Nicholson (pno), N. Kraemer (cnd), Cappella Coloniensis ("Cappella Edition") † Con 23 Pno, K.488 CAPO ▲ 10623 [DDD] (11.97)

M. Perahia (pno), M. Perahia (cnd), English CO † Con 6 Pno, K.238 SNYC ▲ 39223 (16.97)

H. Shelley (pno), H. Shelley (cnd), London Mozart Players † Con 24 Pno, K.491 CHN ▲ 9326 [DDD] (17.97)

Concerto No. 14 in E♭ for Piano & Orchestra, K.449 (1784)

A. Brendel (pno), A. Janigro (cnd), Zagreb Solisti *(rec Vienna, Austria, 1965)* † Con 9 Pno, K.271 VC ▲ 116 [AAD] (13.97)

R. Buchbinder (cnd), Vienna SO *(rec live, Vienna, Austria, Dec 7, 1997)* † Con 15 Pno, K.450; Con 16 Pno, K.451 CALG ▲ 51012 [DDD]

E. Ciccarelli (pno), G. D. Lorenzo (cnd), Vox Aurae Ensemble † Con 12 Pno, K.414; Sym 25, K.183 AG ▲ 183 (18.97)

H. Francesch (pno), K. Weise (cnd), Nice PO *(rec live, 1991)* † Con 15 Pno, K.450; Con 16 Pno, K.451 KPT ▲ 32139 [DDD]

M. Horszowski (pno), F. Waldman (cnd), Musica Aeterna Ensemble *(rec 1962-72)* † Con 12 Pno, K.414; Con 13 Pno, K.415; Con 19 Pno, K.459; Con 9 Pno, K.271; Son 16 Pno, K.545 PHS 2-▲ 9138 [ADD] (33.97)

J. Jandó (pno), A. Ligeti (cnd), Concentus Hungaricus *(rec June 1989)* † Con 12 Pno, K.414; Con 21 Pno, K.467 NXIN ▲ 550202 [DDD] (5.97)

M. Perahia (pno), M. Perahia (cnd), English CO † Con 10 Pnos, K.365; Con 12 Pno, K.414 SNYC ▲ 42243 [AAD] (16.97)

C. Seemann (pno), L. Hager (cnd), North German RSO *(rec Kiel, Feb 1972)* † Con 25 Pno, K.503 ORFE ▲ 447961 (16.97)

R. Serkin (pno), Adolf Busch Chamber Players † Adagio & Fugue Strs, K.546; Con 5 Vn, K.219; Serenade 6 Orch, K.239 PHS ▲ 9278 (17.97)

R. Serkin (pno), A. Busch (cnd), Adolf Busch Chamber Players *(rec 1938)* ("Rudolf Serkin") † Con 12 Pno, K.414; Con 16 Pno, K.451; Con 17 Pno, K.453; Con 19 Pno, K.459; Beethoven:Son 23 Pno, Op. 57 PPHI (Great Pianists of the 20th Century) ▲ 456964 (22.97)

R. Serkin (pno), A. Schneider (cnd), Columbia SO ("Mozart: Legendary Interpretations") † Con 10 Pnos, K.365; Con 12 Pno, K.414; Con 17 Pno, K.453; Con 18 Pno, K.456; Con 19 Pno, K.459; Con 20 Pno, K.466; Con 27 Pno, K.595; Rondo Pno Orch, K.382; Rondo Pno, K.511 SNYC 3-▲ 47207 (33.97)

H. Shelley (pno), H. Shelley (cnd), London Mozart Players † Con 27 Pno, K.595 CHN ▲ 9137 [DDD] (16.97)

Concerto No. 15 in B♭ for Piano & Orchestra, K.450 (1784)

L. Bernstein (pno), L. Bernstein (cnd), Vienna PO † Sym 36, K.425 PLON (The Classic Sound) ▲ 48570 (11.97)

A. Brendel (pno), N. Marriner (cnd), Academy of St. Martin in the Fields ("Complete Piano Concerti, Vol. 2") † Con 22 Pno, K.482; Con 25 Pno, K.503; Con 27 Pno, K.595; Con 9 Pno, K.271 PPHI (Duo) 2-▲ 42571 (17.97)

R. Buchbinder (cnd), Vienna SO *(rec live, Vienna, Austria, Nov 10, 1997)* † Con 14 Pno, K.449; Con 16 Pno, K.451 CALG ▲ 51012 [DDD]

H. Francesch (pno), K. Weise (cnd), Nice PO *(rec live, 1991)* † Con 14 Pno, K.449; Con 16 Pno, K.451 KPT ▲ 32139 [DDD]

J. Jandó (pno), M. Antál (cnd), Concentus Hungaricus *(rec Jan 7-10, 1991)* † Con 10 Pnos, K.365; Con 7 Pnos, K.242 NXIN ▲ 550210 [DDD] (5.97)

S. Lubin (pno), S. Lubin (cnd) † Con 12 Pno, K.414 ARA ▲ 6552 [DDD] (16.97)

M. Perahia (pno), M. Perahia (cnd), English CO † Con 16 Pno, K.451 SNYC ▲ 37824 [DDD] (16.97)

Concerto No. 16 in D for Piano & Orchestra, K.451 (1784)

G. Anda (pno), B. Paumgartner (cnd), Salzburg Mozarteum Orch † Ch'io mi scordi di te? & Non temer, amato bene, K.505; Marches Orch, K.408; Sym 36, K.425 ORFE ▲ 330931 (16.97)

R. Buchbinder (cnd), Vienna SO *(rec live, Vienna, Austria, Nov 10, 1997)* † Con 14 Pno, K.449; Con 15 Pno, K.450 CALG ▲ 51012 [DDD]

R. Firkušný (pno), E. Bour (cnd), Southwest German RSO Baden-Baden † Con 20 Pno, K.466 INTC ▲ 820546 (9.97)

H. Francesch (pno), K. Weise (cnd), Nice PO *(rec live, 1991)* † Con 14 Pno, K.449; Con 15 Pno, K.450 KPT ▲ 32139 [DDD]

J. Jandó (pno), M. Antál (cnd), Concentus Hungaricus *(rec 1990)* ("Complete Piano Concertos, Vol. 7") † Con 25 Pno, K.503; Rondo Pno Orch, K.386 NXIN ▲ 550207 [DDD] (5.97)

M. Perahia (pno), M. Perahia (cnd), English CO † Con 15 Pno, K.450 SNYC ▲ 37824 [DDD] (16.97)

R. Serkin (pno), C. Abbado (cnd), London SO † Con 20 Pno, K.466 DGRM (Masters) ▲ 445597 [DDD]

R. Serkin (pno), C. Abbado (cnd), London SO *(rec 1981-82)* ("Rudolf Serkin") † Con 12 Pno, K.414; Con 14 Pno, K.449; Con 17 Pno, K.453; Con 19 Pno, K.459; Beethoven:Son 23 Pno, Op. 57 PPHI (Great Pianists of the 20th Century) ▲ 456964 (22.97)

Concerto No. 17 in G for Piano & Orchestra, K.453 (1784)

D. Ambache (pno) *(rec Jan 1990)* † Adagio Pno, K.540; Con 19 Pno, K.459; Con 21 Pno, K.467; Con 25 Pno, K.503; Fant Pno, K.397 VCL 2-▲ 61445 [DDD] (11.97)

G. Anda (pno), G. Anda (cnd), Salzburg Mozarteum Camerata Academia *(rec Neues Festspielhaus Salzburg, Austria, May 1961)* † Con 21 Pno, K.467; Con 6 Pno, K.238 DEUT (The Originals) ▲ 47436 [ADD] (11.97)

D. Bardin (pno), J. Lopez-Cobos (cnd), Lausanne CO † Son 4 Pno, K.282; R. Schumann:Waldscenen, Op. 82 CLAV ▲ 509710 (16.97)

D. Barenboim (pno), D. Barenboim (cnd), Berlin PO † Con 9 Pno, K.271 TELC ▲ 73128 [DDD] (16.97)

A. Brendel (pno), P. Angerer (cnd), Vienna State Opera Orch † Con 27 Pno, K.595 TUXE ▲ 1027 (10.97)

R. Buchbinder (pno), R. Buchbinder (cnd), Vienna SO † Con 18 Pno, K.456 CALG ▲ 51013 [DDD] (11.97)

A. Cheng (pno), M. Bernardi (cnd), CBC Vancouver SO † Con 9 Pno, K.271 SMS (SM 5000) ▲ 5104 [DDD] (16.97)

E. von Dohnányi (pno), E. von Dohnányi (cnd), Budapest PO † E. von Dohnányi:Ruralia hungarica Orch, Op. 32b; Vars on a Nursery Song, Op. 25; Strauss (II):Fledermaus (sels); Zigeunerbaron (sels) PHS (Piano Masters) ▲ 18 (17.97)

MOZART, WOLFGANG AMADEUS (cont.)
Concerto No. 17 in G for Piano & Orchestra, K.453 (1784) (cont.)
E. Fischer (pno), E. Fischer (cnd), Edwin Fischer CO *(rec 1933-47)* ("Mozart Piano Recordings, Vol. 2") † Con 24 Pno, K.491; Fant Pno, K.396; Son 11 Pno, K.331 APR ▲ 5524 (m) [ADD] (18.97)
V. Fischer (pno), H. Kraus (cnd) † Con 21 Pno, K.467 LALI ▲ 15618 [DDD] (3.97)
H. Francesch (pno), K. Weise (cnd), Nice PO † Con 18 Pno, K.456 KPT ▲ 32159 [DDD]
R. Goode (pno) † Con 23 Pno, K.488 NON ▲ 79042 [DDD] (9.97)
M.-A. Hamelin (pno), V. Lacroix (cnd), Montreal Ensemble Contemporain † Gonneville:Adonwe PTRY ▲ 2207 (17.97)
M. Horszowski (pno), F. Waldman (cnd), Musica Aeterna Ensemble † Con 18 Pno, K.456; Con 20 Pno, K.466; Con 22 Pno, K.482; Fant Pno, K.475 PHS 2-▲ 9153 [ADD] (33.97)
J. Jandó (pno), M. Antál (cnd), Concentus Hungaricus † Con 18 Pno, K.456 NXIN ▲ 550205 [DDD] (5.97)
K. Jarrett (pno), D. R. Davies (cnd), Stuttgart CO *(rec Mozart-Saal, Stuttgart, Germany, 1996-98)* † Adagio & Fugue Strs, K.546; Con 20 Pno, K.466; Con 9 Pno, K.271 UECM 2-▲ 462651 [DDD] (34.97)
R. Levin (pno), C. Hogwood (cnd), Academy of Ancient Music † Con 20 Pno, K.466 PLON ▲ 455607 (16.97)
D. Matthews (pno), H. Blech (cnd), London Mozart Players *(rec 1952-56)* † Con Bn, K.191; Lucio Silla (ov); Sym 31, K.297 DLAB ▲ 4005 (17.97)
J. O'Conor (pno), C. Mackerras (cnd), Scottish CO † Con 24 Pno, K.491 TEL ▲ 80306 [DDD] (16.97)
M. Perahia (pno), M. Perahia (cnd), English CO † Con 18 Pno, K.456 SNYC ▲ 36686 [DDD] (16.97)
M. J. Pires (pno), C. Abbado (cnd), CO of Europe *(rec Teatro Comunale Ferrara, Italy, June 1993)* † Con 21 Pno, K.467 DEUT ▲ 39941 [DDD] (16.97)
C. Schornsheim (pno), B. Glaetzner (cnd), Leipzig New Bach Collegium Musicum † Con 18 Pno, K.456; Con 19 Pno, K.459 LALI ▲ 15872 [DDD] (3.97)
R. Serkin (pno), C. Abbado (cnd), London SO *(rec 1981-82)* ("Rudolf Serkin") † Con 12 Pno, K.414; Con 14 Pno, K.449; Con 16 Pno, K.451; Con 19 Pno, K.459; Beethoven:Son 23 Pno, Op. 57 PPHI (Great Pianists of the 20th Century) ▲ 456964 (22.97)
R. Serkin (pno), A. Schneider (cnd), Columbia SO ("Mozart: Legendary Interpretations") † Con 10 Pnos, K.365; Con 12 Pno, K.414; Con 14 Pno, K.449; Con 18 Pno, K.456; Con 19 Pno, K.459; Con 20 Pno, K.466; Con 27 Pno, K.595; Rondo Pno Orch, K.382; Rondo Pno, K.511 SNYC 3-▲ 47207 (33.97)
H. Shelley (pno), H. Shelley (cnd), London Mozart Players † Con 9 Pno, K.271 CHN ▲ 9068 [DDD] (16.97)

Concerto No. 18 in B♭ for Piano & Orchestra, K.456 (1784)
D. Barenboim (pno), D. Barenboim (cnd), Berlin PO *(rec Philharmonie Hall Berlin, Apr 1993)* † Con 19 Pno, K.459; Rondo Pno Orch, K.382 TELC ▲ 90674 [DDD] (16.97)
R. Buchbinder (pno), R. Buchbinder (cnd), Vienna SO † Con 17 Pno, K.453 CALG ▲ 51013 [DDD] (11.97)
H. Francesch (pno), K. Weise (cnd), Nice PO † Con 17 Pno, K.453 KPT ▲ 32159 [DDD]
R. Goode (pno) *(rec Manhattan Center New York, June 1996)* † Con 20 Pno, K.466 NON ▲ 79439 (16.97)
M. Horszowski (pno), F. Waldman (cnd), Musica Aeterna Ensemble † Con 17 Pno, K.453; Con 20 Pno, K.466; Con 22 Pno, K.482; Fant Pno, K.475 PHS 2-▲ 9153 [ADD] (33.97)
J. Jandó (pno), M. Antál (cnd), Concentus Hungaricus *(rec 1989)* † Con 17 Pno, K.453 NXIN ▲ 550205 [DDD] (5.97)
J. Jandó (pno), M. Antál (cnd), Concentus Hungaricus *(rec 1990)* ("Complete Piano Concertos, Vol. 8") † Con 19 Pno, K.459; Con 6 Pno, K.238; Con 8 Pno, K.246 NXIN ▲ 550208 [DDD] (5.97)
L. Nicholson (pno), N. Kraemer (cnd), Cappella Coloniensis ("Cappella Edition") † Con 12 Pno, K.414 CAPO ▲ 10622 [DDD] (11.97)
J. O'Conor (pno), C. Mackerras (cnd), Scottish CO † Con 19 Pno, K.459; Con 23 Pno, K.488; Rondo Pno Orch, K.386 TEL ▲ 80285 [DDD] (16.97)
M. Perahia (pno), M. Perahia (cnd), English CO † Con 17 Pno, K.453 SNYC ▲ 36686 [DDD] (16.97)
M. Perahia (pno), M. Perahia (cnd), English CO † Con 19 Pno, K.459; Con 23 Pno, K.488 SNYC ▲ 39064 [DDD] (16.97)
S. Richter (pno) *(rec Tokyo, Japan, Mar 3, 1993)* ("The Last Concert") † Con 1 Pno, K.37; Con 5 Pno, K.175 LARL ▲ 902 (15.97)
A. Schmidt (pno), K. Masur (cnd), Dresden PO ("Famous Piano Concertos") † Con 20 Pno, K.466; Con 21 Pno, K.467; Con 27 Pno, K.595 BER 2-▲ 9251 (21.97)
C. Schornsheim (pno), B. Glaetzner (cnd), Leipzig New Bach Collegium Musicum † Con 17 Pno, K.453; Con 19 Pno, K.459 LALI ▲ 15872 [DDD] (3.97)
B. Schulman (pno), R. Freisitzer (cnd), Moscow Orch † Fant Pno, K.396; Vars "Salve tu, Domine", K.398; M. Ravel:Con Pno RD ▲ 30006 (16.97)
R. Serkin (pno), G. Szell (cnd), Columbia SO † Con 19 Pno, K.459; Con 20 Pno, K.466 SNYC ▲ 37236 [ADD] (9.97) ▮ 37236 [ADD] (3.98)
R. Serkin (pno), G. Szell (cnd), Columbia SO ("Mozart: Legendary Interpretations") † Con 10 Pnos, K.365; Con 12 Pno, K.414; Con 14 Pno, K.449; Con 17 Pno, K.453; Con 19 Pno, K.459; Con 20 Pno, K.466; Con 27 Pno, K.595; Rondo Pno Orch, K.382; Rondo Pno, K.511 SNYC 3-▲ 47207 (33.97)
M. Tan (pno), N. McGegan (cnd), Philharmonia Baroque Orch *(rec Walnut Creek Regional Center for the Arts, CA, 1995)* † Con 19 Pno, K.459 HAM ▲ 907138 (18.97)

Concerto No. 19 in F for Piano & Orchestra, K.459 (1784)
D. Ambache (pno) *(rec Jan 1990)* † Adagio Pno, K.540; Con 17 Pno, K.453; Con 21 Pno, K.467; Con 25 Pno, K.503; Fant Pno, K.397 VCL 2-▲ 61445 [DDD] (11.97)
M. Argerich (pno), A. Rabinovitch (pno) † Con 10 Pnos, K.365; Con 20 Pno, K.466 TELC ▲ 98407 (16.97)
D. Barenboim (pno), D. Barenboim (cnd), Berlin PO *(rec Philharmonie Hall Berlin, Apr 1994)* † Con 18 Pno, K.456; Rondo Pno Orch, K.382 TELC ▲ 90674 [DDD] (16.97)
R. Buchbinder (pno), Vienna SO *(rec Dec 1997)* † Con 9 Pno, K.271 CALG ▲ 51010 [DDD] (11.97)
G. Casadesus (pno), Lamoureux Orch † Con 25 Pno, K.503; Vars on an Allegretto, K.500; Chabrier:Pièces pittoresques; F. Couperin:Pièces de clavecin (sels); G. Fauré:Impromptus Pno; Rameau:Pièces de clavecin HPC ▲ 155 (50.97)
H. Franesch (pno), K. Weise (cnd), Nice PO † Con 20 Pno, K.466 KPT ▲ 32179 [DDD]
C. Haskil (pno), F. Fricsay (cnd), Berlin PO *(rec Jesus-Christus Church Berlin, Germany, Sept 1955)* † Con 27 Pno, K.595; Son 2 Pno, K.280 DEUT (The Originals) ▲ 449722 [ADD] (11.97)
M. Horszowski (pno), F. Waldman (cnd), Musica Aeterna Ensemble *(rec 1962-72)* † Con 12 Pno, K.414; Con 13 Pno, K.415; Con 14 Pno, K.449; Con 9 Pno, K.271; Son 16 Pno, K.545 PHS 2-▲ 9138 [ADD] (33.97)
J. Jandó (pno), M. Antál (cnd), Concentus Hungaricus *(rec 1990)* ("Complete Piano Concertos, Vol. 8") † Con 18 Pno, K.456; Con 6 Pno, K.238; Con 8 Pno, K.246 NXIN ▲ 550208 [DDD] (5.97)
N. Marriner (cnd), Academy of St. Martin in the Fields ("Vol. I") † Con 20 Pno, K.466; Con 21 Pno, K.467; Con 23 Pno, K.488; Con 24 Pno, K.491 PPHI 2-▲ 42269 (17.97)
J. O'Conor (pno), C. Mackerras (cnd), Scottish CO † Con 18 Pno, K.456; Con 23 Pno, K.488; Rondo Pno Orch, K.386 TEL ▲ 80285 [DDD] (16.97)
M. Perahia (pno), M. Perahia (cnd), English CO † Con 18 Pno, K.456; Con 23 Pno, K.488 SNYC ▲ 39064 [DDD] (16.97)
A. Schnabel (pno) ("Artur Schnabel Plays Mozart") † Con 10 Pnos, K.365; Con 21 Pno, K.467; Con 27 Pno, K.595; Rondo Pno, K.511; Son 8 Pno, K.310 PHS 2-▲ 6 (33.97)
C. Schornsheim (pno), B. Glaetzner (cnd), Leipzig New Bach Collegium Musicum † Con 17 Pno, K.453; Con 18 Pno, K.456 LALI ▲ 15872 [DDD] (3.97)
R. Serkin (pno), C. Abbado (cnd), London SO *(rec 1981-82)* ("Rudolf Serkin") † Con 12 Pno, K.414; Con 14 Pno, K.449; Con 16 Pno, K.451; Con 17 Pno, K.453; Beethoven:Son 23 Pno, Op. 57 PPHI (Great Pianists of the 20th Century) ▲ 456964 (22.97)
R. Serkin (pno), G. Szell (cnd), Columbia SO † Con 18 Pno, K.456; Con 20 Pno, K.466 SNYC ▲ 37236 [ADD] (9.97) ▮ 37236 [ADD] (3.98)
R. Serkin (pno), G. Szell (cnd), Columbia SO ("Mozart: Legendary Interpretations") † Con 10 Pnos, K.365; Con 12 Pno, K.414; Con 14 Pno, K.449; Con 17 Pno, K.453; Con 18 Pno, K.456; Con 20 Pno, K.466; Con 27 Pno, K.595; Rondo Pno Orch, K.382; Rondo Pno, K.511 SNYC 3-▲ 47207 (33.97)
H. Shelley (pno), H. Shelley (cnd), London Mozart Players † Con 12 Pno, K.414 CHN ▲ 9256 [DDD] (16.97)
M. Tan (pno), N. McGegan (cnd), Philharmonia Baroque Orch *(rec Walnut Creek Regional Center for the Arts, CA, 1995)* † Con 18 Pno, K.456 HAM ▲ 907138 (18.97)
S. Uryvayev (pno), A. Titov (cnd), St. Petersburg Classical Music Studio Orch SNYC ▲ 64333 [DDD] (4.97)

Concerto No. 20 in d for Piano & Orchestra, K.466 (1785)
L. Alvini (pno), Aglāia String Quartet [trans Lichtenthal for str qt & pno] † Requiem, K.626 STRV ▲ 33470 (16.97)
M. Argerich (pno), A. Rabinovitch (pno) † Con 10 Pnos, K.365; Con 19 Pno, K.459 TELC ▲ 98407 (16.97)
V. Ashkenazy (pno) † Con 21 Pno, K.467; Con 22 Pno, K.482; Con 23 Pno, K.488; Con 24 Pno, K.491; Con 25 Pno, K.503 PPHI (Double Decker) 2-▲ 452958 (17.97)
V. Ashkenazy (pno), V. Ashkenazy (cnd), Philharmonia Orch ("Favourite Mozart") † Con 21 Pno, K.467; Con 23 Pno, K.488; Con 27 Pno, K.595; Rondo Pno, K.511; Son 18 Pno, K.576 PLON 2-▲ 36383 [ADD] (17.97)

MOZART, WOLFGANG AMADEUS (cont.)
Concerto No. 20 in d for Piano & Orchestra, K.466 (1785) (cont.)
D. Barenboim (pno), D. Barenboim (cnd), Berlin PO ("The Late Piano Concertos") † Con 21 Pno, K.467; Con 22 Pno, K.482; Con 23 Pno, K.488; Con 24 Pno, K.491; Con 25 Pno, K.503; Con 26 Pno, K.537; Con 27 Pno, K.595 TELC 4-▲ 72024 [DDD] (50.97)
D. Barenboim (pno), D. Barenboim (cnd), Berlin PO † Con 21 Pno, K.467 TELC ▲ 75710 [DDD] (16.97)
D. Barenboim (pno), D. Barenboim (cnd), Berlin PO † Con 21 Pno, K.467; Con 22 Pno, K.482; Con 23 Pno, K.488 ERAT (Ultima) 2-▲ 18956 (16.97)
A. Brendel (pno), N. Marriner (cnd), Academy of St. Martin in the Fields † Con 24 Pno, K.491; Rondo Pno Orch, K.382 PPHI (Concert Classics) ▲ 20867 [ADD] (9.97)
J. Doyen (pno), C. Munch (cnd), Paris Conservatory Société des Concerts Orch *(rec 1941-42)* ("Munch, Vol. 6") † Fant Pno, K.397; P. Tchaikovsky:Con 1 Pno, Op. 23 LYS ▲ 400 (17.97)
Y. Egorov (pno), W. Sawallisch (cnd), Philharmonia Orch *(rec London, England, Feb 1985)* † Beethoven:Con 5 Pno, Op. 73; Sym 9 EMIC 2-▲ 73329 [DDD] (16.97)
R. Firkušný (pno), E. Bour (cnd), Southwest German RSO Baden-Baden † Con 16 Pno, K.451 INTC ▲ 820546 (9.97)
A. Fischer (pno), E. Lukács (cnd), Budapest SO *(rec 1965)* † Con 21 Pno, K.467; Rondo Pno Orch, K.382 HUN ▲ 31492 (16.97)
E. Fischer (pno), E. Fischer (cnd), London PO *(rec London, Nov 11, 1933)* ("The Mozart Piano Concerto Recordings, Vol. 1") † Con 22 Pno, K.482; Minuet Pno, K.1; Rondo Pno Orch, K.382 APR ▲ 5523 [ADD] (18.97)
H. Franesch (pno), K. Weise (cnd), Nice PO † Con 19 Pno, K.459 KPT ▲ 32179 [DDD]
R. Goode (pno) [movt 1 cadenza by Beethoven; movt 3 cadenza by Goo] *(rec Manhattan Center New York, June 1996)* † Con 18 Pno, K.456 NON ▲ 79439 (16.97)
C. Haskil (pno), O. Ackermann (cnd), Northwest German RSO *(rec Nov 11, 1956)* † Con 9 Pno, K.271 MUA ▲ 4715 (10.97)
C. Haskil (pno), I. Markevitch (cnd), Lamoureux Concerts Orch *(rec 1960)* ("Clara Haskil") † Con 13 Pno, K.415; Con 23 Pno, K.488; Con 24 Pno, K.491; Con 27 Pno, K.595; Rondo Pno Orch, K.386 PPHI (Great Pianists of the 20th Century) ▲ 456826 (22.97)
M. Horszowski (pno), F. Waldman (cnd), Musica Aeterna Ensemble † Con 17 Pno, K.453; Con 18 Pno, K.456; Con 22 Pno, K.482; Fant Pno, K.475 PHS 2-▲ 9153 [ADD] (33.97)
J. Jandó (pno), A. Ligeti (cnd), Concentus Hungaricus *(rec May 1989)* † Con 13 Pno, K.415 NXIN ▲ 550201 [DDD] (5.97)
J. Jandó (pno), A. Ligeti (cnd), Concentus Hungaricus *(rec May 1989)* † Con 21 Pno, K.467 NXIN ▲ 550434 [DDD] (5.97)
K. Jarrett (pno), D. R. Davies (cnd), Stuttgart CO *(rec Mozart-Saal, Stuttgart, Germany, 1996-98)* † Adagio & Fugue Strs, K.546; Con 17 Pno, K.453; Con 9 Pno, K.271 UECM 2-▲ 462651 [DDD] (34.97)
E. Kissin (pno), V. Spivakov (cnd), Moscow Virtuosi † Con 12 Pno, K.414; Rondo Pno Orch, K.382 RCAV (Red Seal) ▲ 60400 (16.97)
Y. Lefébure (pno), P. Casals (cnd), Perpignan Festival Orch *(rec June 17, 1951)* † Con 22 Pno, K.482 SNYC ▲ 66570 [ADD] (10.97)
R. Levin (pno), C. Hogwood (cnd), Academy of Ancient Music † Con 17 Pno, K.453 PLON ▲ 455607 (16.97)
S. Lubin (pno), S. Lubin (cnd) † Con 23 Pno, K.488 ARA ▲ 6530 (16.97)
B. McFerrin (cnd), St. Paul CO, B. McFerrin (sgr), C. Corea (pno)—Allegro [a capella voc & pno improv] *(rec Bethel College St. Paul & Masonic Grand Lodge, United States of America, 1996)* ("The Mozart Sessions") † Con 23 Pno, K.488; Son 2 Pno, K.280 SNYC ▲ 62601 [DDD] (16.97) ▮ 62601 [DDD] (10.98) COL △ 62601 [DDD]
R. Mamou (pno), G. Oskamp (cnd), Berlin SO † Con 24 Pno, K.491 VRDI ▲ 32147 (13.97)
N. Marriner (cnd), Academy of St. Martin in the Fields ("The Mozart Experience") † Con Cl, K.622; Con Fl & Hp, K.299; Con Movt Hn, K.Anh.98a; Con 21 Pno, K.467; Divert Ww; German Dances (3), K.605; Kleine Nachtmusik, K.525; Musikalischer Spass, K.522; Nozze di Figaro (sels); Serenade 6 Orch, K.239; Sym 40, K.550; Sym 41, K.551 PPHI 5-▲ 26204 (33.97)
N. Marriner (cnd), Academy of St. Martin in the Fields ("Vol. I") † Con 19 Pno, K.459; Con 21 Pno, K.467; Con 23 Pno, K.488; Con 24 Pno, K.491 PPHI 2-▲ 42269 (17.97)
I. Moravec (pno), N. Marriner (cnd), Academy of St. Martin in the Fields † Con 23 Pno, K.488 HANS (Academy) ▲ 98142 (15.97)
E. Naoumoff (pno), A. Lombard (cnd), Bordeaux-Aquitaine National Orch † Con 24 Pno, K.491 FORL ▲ 16626 [DDD] (16.97)
G. Novaes (pno), H. Swarowsky (cnd), Vienna SO *(rec 1950s)* ("The Classical Novaes") † Con 9 Pno, K.271; Son 11 Pno, K.331; Son 16 Pno, K.545; Son 5 Pno, K.283; Beethoven:Con 5 Pno, Op. 73 VOXL (Legends) 2-▲ 5512 [ADD] (9.97)
J. O'Conor (pno), C. Mackerras (cnd), Scottish CO *(rec Oct 30-31, 1991)* † Con 22 Pno, K.482 TEL ▲ 80308 [DDD] (16.97)
M. Perahia (pno), M. Perahia (cnd), English CO † Con 27 Pno, K.595 COL ▲ 42241 [AAD] (16.97)
A. Rubinstein (pno), A. Wallenstein (cnd), RCA Victor SO † Con 21 Pno, K.467; J. Haydn:Son Kbd RCAV (Gold Seal) ▲ 7967 [ADD] (11.97)
A. Rubinstein (pno), A. Wallenstein (cnd), RCA Victor SO ("Basic 100, Vol. 69") † Con 23 Pno, K.488 RCAV ▲ 68337 (10.97) ▮ 68337 (5.98)
A. Schmidt (pno), K. Masur (cnd), Dresden PO ("Famous Piano Concertos") † Con 18 Pno, K.456; Con 21 Pno, K.467; Con 27 Pno, K.595 BER 2-▲ 9251 (21.97)
A. Schnabel (pno), W. Susskind (cnd), Philharmonia Orch *(rec 1946-48)* † Con 24 Pno, K.491; Rondo Pno, K.511 ENPL (Piano Library) ▲ 274 (13.97)
R. Serkin (pno), C. Abbado (cnd), London SO † Con 21 Pno, K.467 DEUT (3D Classics) ▲ 31278 [DDD] (9.97)
R. Serkin (pno), C. Abbado (cnd), London SO † Con 16 Pno, K.451 DGRM (Masters) ▲ 445597 [DDD]
R. Serkin (pno), G. Szell (cnd), Columbia SO † Con 18 Pno, K.456; Con 19 Pno, K.459 SNYC ▲ 37236 [ADD] (9.97) ▮ 37236 [ADD] (3.98)
R. Serkin (pno), G. Szell (cnd), Columbia SO ("Mozart: Legendary Interpretations") † Con 10 Pnos, K.365; Con 12 Pno, K.414; Con 14 Pno, K.449; Con 17 Pno, K.453; Con 18 Pno, K.456; Con 19 Pno, K.459; Con 27 Pno, K.595; Rondo Pno Orch, K.382; Rondo Pno, K.511 SNYC 3-▲ 47207 (33.97)
H. Shelley (pno), H. Shelley (cnd), London Mozart Players † Con 23 Pno, K.488 CHN ▲ 8992 [DDD] (16.97)
G. Solti (pno), G. Solti (cnd), English CO † Con 10 Pnos, K.365; Con 7 Pnos, K.242 PLON ▲ 30232 [DDD] (16.97)
S. Stanceva (pno), A. Lizzio (cnd), Mozart Festival Orch † Con 26 Pno, K.537 PC ▲ 267143 [DDD] (2.97)
S. Sugitani (pno), T. Ukigaya (cnd), Polish National RSO Katowice *(rec May 1998)* † Con 23 Pno, K.488 THOR ▲ 2394 [DDD] (16.97)
M. Uchida (pno), J. Tate (cnd), English CO † Con 21 Pno, K.467 PPHI ▲ 16381 [DDD] (16.97)
M. Uchida (pno), J. Tate (cnd), English CO † Con 23 Pno, K.488 PPHI (Insignia) ▲ 34164 [DDD] (9.97)
S. Uryvayev (pno), A. Titov (cnd), St. Petersburg New Philharmony Orch † Con 21 Pno, K.467 SNYC ▲ 57232 [DDD] (4.97)
B. Walter (cnd) † German Dances (3), K.605; Kleine Nachtmusik, K.525; Sym 38, K.504 MTAL ▲ 48028 (6.97)
B. Walter (pno), B. Walter (cnd), NBC SO *(rec live New York, Mar 11, 1939)* ("Bruno Walter Plays & Conducts Mozart") † Divert 15 Hns & Strs, K.287 GRM2 ▲ 78622 (13.97)
E. Westenholz (pno), M. Schønwandt (cnd), Copenhagen Collegium Musicum † Con 23 Pno, K.488 BIS ▲ 283 [DDD] (17.97)
artists unknown—Romance ("Adagios") † Adagio Pno, K.540; Adagio Vn, K.261; Con Cl, K.622; Con Fl & Hp, K.299; Con 2 Hn, K.417; Con 21 Pno, K.467; Con 23 Pno, K.488; Con 26 Pno, K.537; Con 27 Pno, K.595; Con 3 Hn, K.447; Con 3 Vn, K.216; Diverts Str Qt, K.136-138; Kleine Nachtmusik, K.525; Qnt Cl, K.581; Serenade; Serenade Ww, K.388/384a; Sinf concertante Vn, K.364; Son 12 Pno, K.332; Son 16 Pno, K.545; Sym 40, K.550; Sym 41, K.551 DECC (2-Fers) 2-▲ 460191 (17.97)
various artists—Rondo (Allegro assai) † Con Cl, K.622; Con 21 Pno, K.467; Con 3 Vn, K.216; Cosi fan tutte (ov); Kleine Nachtmusik, K.525; Son 11 Pno, K.331; Sym 40, K.550; Sym 41, K.551; Zauberflöte (ov) RCAV ▲ 60829 (10.97) ▮ 60829 (5.98)

Concerto No. 21 in C for Piano & Orchestra, K.467, "Elvira Madigan" (1785)
D. Ambache (pno) *(rec Jan 1990)* † Adagio Pno, K.540; Con 17 Pno, K.453; Con 19 Pno, K.459; Con 25 Pno, K.503; Fant Pno, K.397 VCL 2-▲ 61445 [DDD] (11.97)
G. Anda (pno), G. Anda (cnd), Salzburg Mozarteum Camerata Academia *(rec Neues Festspielhaus Salzburg, Austria, May 1961)* † Con 17 Pno, K.453; Con 6 Pno, K.238 DEUT (The Originals) ▲ 47436 [ADD] (11.97)
G. Anda (pno), G. Anda (cnd), Salzburg Mozarteum Camerata Academica *(rec 1959-75)* † B. Bartók:Cons Pno (comp); Chopin:Waltzes Pno PPHI (Great Pianists of the 20th Century) 2-▲ 456772 (22.97)
G. Anda (pno), G. Anda (cnd), Vienna SO ("Better Thinking through Mozart") † Con Fl & Hp, K.299; Kleine Nachtmusik, K.525; Serenade; Son Pnos, K.448; Son 11 Pno, K.331 RCAV (Gold Seal) ▲ 68113 [ADD] (11.97) ▮ 68113 [ADD] (6.98)
V. Ashkenazy (pno) † Con 20 Pno, K.466; Con 22 Pno, K.482; Con 23 Pno, K.488; Con 24 Pno, K.491; Con 25 Pno, K.503 PPHI (Double Decker) 2-▲ 452958 (17.97)
V. Ashkenazy (pno), V. Ashkenazy (cnd), Philharmonia Orch ("Favourite Mozart") † Con 20 Pno, K.466; Con 23 Pno, K.488; Con 27 Pno, K.595; Rondo Pno, K.511; Son 18 Pno, K.576 PLON 2-▲ 36383 [ADD] (17.97)

▲ = CD ◆ = Enhanced CD △ = MD ▮ = Cassette Tape ▯ = DCC

MOZART, WOLFGANG AMADEUS (cont.)

Concerto No. 21 in C for Piano & Orchestra, K.467, "Elvira Madigan" (1785) (cont.)

S. Askenase (pno), K. Böhm (cnd), Berlin PO † Beethoven:Con 5 Pno, Op. 73; J. Brahms:Con Vn & Vc, Op. 102; R. Schumann:Con Pno in a, Op. 54 STRV 2-▲ 12305 [ADD] (25.97)

D. Barenboim (pno), D. Barenboim (cnd), Berlin PO ("The Late Piano Concertos") † Con 20 Pno, K.466; Con 22 Pno, K.482; Con 23 Pno, K.488; Con 24 Pno, K.491; Con 25 Pno, K.503; Con 26 Pno, K.537; Con 27 Pno, K.595 TELC 4-▲ 72024 [DDD] (50.97)

D. Barenboim (pno), D. Barenboim (cnd), Berlin PO † Con 20 Pno, K.466 TELC ▲ 75710 [DDD] (16.97)

D. Barenboim (pno), D. Barenboim (cnd), Berlin PO † Con 20 Pno, K.466; Con 22 Pno, K.482; Con 23 Pno, K.488 ERAT (Ultima) 2-▲ 18956 (16.97)

R. Casadesus (pno), G. Szell (cnd), Cleveland Orch—Andante *(rec Severance Hall, Cleveland, OH, Nov 5, 1961)* ("The Essential Mozart") † Con 4 Hn, K.495; Don Giovanni (sels); Exsultate, jubilate, K.165; Kleine Nachtmusik, K.525; Nozze di Figaro (ov); Nozze di Figaro (sels); Requiem, K.626; Serenade; Sym 40, K.550; Sym 41, K.551; Vars "Ah! vous dirai-je, Maman", K.265; Zauberflöte (ov) SNYC (Essential Classics) ▲ 64225 [ADD] (7.97)

R. Casadesus (pno), G. Szell (cnd), Cleveland Orch † Con 24 Pno, K.491 SNYC ▲ 38523 [AAD] (9.97)

C. Corea (pno), R. Kapp (cnd), Philharmonia Virtuosi, New York *(rec NY)* ("Greatest Hits of 1790") † Son 11 Pno, K.331; Beethoven:Bagatelle Pno in B♭, WoO 60; Minuets (6) Orch, WoO 10; Ruinen von Athen (sels); Boccherini:Qnt Strs, G.275; C. W. Gluck:Orfeo ed Euridice (sels); Gossec:Gavotte Fl; J. Haydn:Con Tpt; Qts (6) Strs, H.III/13-18, Op. 3 SNYC ▲ 37216 [DDD] (9.97)

A. Fischer (pno), E. Lukács (cnd), Budapest SO *(rec 1965)* † Con 20 Pno, K.466; Rondo Pno Orch, K.382 HUN ▲ 31492 (16.97)

V. Fischer (pno), H. Kraus (cnd) † Con 17 Pno, K.453 LALI ▲ 15618 [DDD] (3.97)

H. Francesch (pno), K. Weise (cnd), Nice PO † Con 22 Pno, K.482 KPT ▲ 32189 [DDD]

W. Gieseking (pno), G. Cantelli (cnd), New York Philharmonic SO *(rec live, 1948-56)* ("Gieseking Plays Mozart") † Con 27 Pno, K.595; Son 18 Pno, K.576 PHS ▲ 9236 (17.97)

M. Hess (pno) *(rec University of Illinois, IL, Mar 17, 1949)* † Con 9 Pno, K.271 APR ▲ 5539 [ADD] (18.97)

M. Hess (pno), L. Heward (cnd), Hallé Orch *(rec 1938)* ("Myra Hess") † R. Schumann:Carnaval, Op. 9 ENPL (Piano Library) ▲ 231 (13.97)

M. Hess (pno), L. Stokowski (cnd), Philharmonic SO *(rec Feb 6, 1949)* ("In Concert 1949-1960") † Con 12 Pno, K.414; Con 27 Pno, K.595; Beethoven:Con 4 Pno, Op. 58; Con 5 Pno, Op. 73; Son 10 Vn, Op. 96; J. Brahms:Con 2 Pno, Op. 83; Son 2 Vn, Op. 100; F. Schubert:Sonatinas (3) Vn MUA 3-▲ 779 [AAD] (47.97)

H. Huang (pno), K. Masur (cnd), New York PO † Mendelssohn (-Bartholdy):Capriccio brillante, Op. 22; Con 1 Pno, Op. 25 TELC ▲ 15869 (16.97)

E. Istomin (pno), G. Schwarz (cnd), Seattle SO *(rec Bothell, WA, Oct 10, 1995)* † Con 24 Pno, K.491 REF ▲ 68 (16.97)

J. Jandó (pno), A. Ligeti (cnd), Concentus Hungaricus *(rec June 1989)* † Con 12 Pno, K.414; Con 14 Pno, K.449 NXIN ▲ 550202 [DDD] (5.97)

J. Jandó (pno), A. Ligeti (cnd), Concentus Hungaricus *(rec June 1989)* † Con 20 Pno, K.466 NXIN ▲ 550434 [DDD] (5.97)

M. Kwok (pno), P. Freeman (cnd), Czech National SO † Con 24 Pno, K.491 HALM ▲ 35063 (6.97)

N. Marriner (cnd), Academy of St. Martin in the Fields ("The Mozart Experience") † Con Cl, K.622; Con Fl & Hp, K.299; Con Movt Hn, K.Anh.98a; Con 20 Pno, K.466; Divert Ww; German Dances (3), K.605; Kleine Nachtmusik, K.525; Musikalischer Spass, K.522; Nozze di Figaro (sels); Serenade 6 Orch, K.239; Sym 40, K.550; Sym 41, K.551 PPHI 5-▲ 26204 (33.97)

N. Marriner (cnd), Academy of St. Martin in the Fields ("Vol. I") † Con 19 Pno, K.459; Con 20 Pno, K.466; Con 23 Pno, K.488; Con 24 Pno, K.491 PPHI 2-▲ 42269 (17.97)

Myra Hess Trio ("Myra Hess: A Vignette") † J. Brahms:Trio 2 Pno, Op. 87; J. Haydn:Son 50 Kbd, H.XVI/37; F. Schubert:Rosamunde (sels); Son Pno, D.664; Trio 1 Pno, D.898 APR 2-▲ 7012 [AAD] (38.97)

L. Nicholson (pno), N. Kraemer (cnd), Cappella Coloniensis ("Cappella Edition") † Con 9 Pno, K.271 CAPO ▲ 10621 [DDD] (11.97)

J. O'Conor (pno), C. Mackerras (cnd), Scottish CO † Con 27 Pno, K.595 TEL ▲ 80219 [DDD] (16.97)

M. Perahia (pno), M. Perahia (cnd), English CO † Con 9 Pno, K.271 SNYC ▲ 34562 [AAD] (16.97)

M. J. Pires (pno), C. Abbado (cnd), CO of Europe *(rec Teatro Comunale Ferrara, Italy, June 1993)* † Con 17 Pno, K.453 DEUT ▲ 39941 [DDD] (16.97)

A. Rubinstein (pno), J. Levine (cnd), Chicago SO ("Basic 100, Vol. 11") † Sym 40, K.550; Sym 41, K.551 RCAV ▲ 61708 (10.97)

A. Rubinstein (pno), A. Wallenstein (cnd), RCA Victor SO † Con 20 Pno, K.466; J. Haydn:Son Kbd RCAV (Gold Seal) ▲ 7967 [ADD] (11.97)

J. Rutter (cnd), City of London Sinfonia—Andante *(rec London, England, July 29, 1985)* ("The Mozart Collection") † Con Cl, K.622; Con Fl & Hp, K.299; Con 12 Pno, K.414; Diverts Str Qt, K.136-138; Music of Mozart; Nozze di Figaro (ov); Sym 39, K.543 AMG ▲ 586 (15.99)

S. Scheja (pno), J. Wedin (cnd), Stockholm Sinfonietta † Sinf concertante Vn, K.364 BIS ▲ 205 (17.97)

A. Schmidt (pno), K. Masur (cnd), Dresden PO ("Famous Piano Concertos") † Con 18 Pno, K.456; Con 20 Pno, K.466; Con 27 Pno, K.595 BER 2-▲ 9251 (21.97)

A. Schnabel (pno) ("Artur Schnabel Plays Mozart") † Con 10 Pnos, K.365; Con 19 Pno, K.459; Con 27 Pno, K.595; Rondo Pno, K.511; Son 8 Pno, K.310 PHS 2-▲ 6 (33.97)

A. Schnabel (pno), M. Sargent (cnd), London SO † Con 27 Pno, K.595 ENPL (Piano Library) ▲ 210 (13.97)

A. Schnabel (pno), M. Sargent (cnd), London SO † Con 27 Pno, K.595 ENT (Sirio) ▲ 53006 (13.97)

P. Serkin (pno), C. Abbado (cnd), London SO † Con 20 Pno, K.466 DEUT (3D Classics) ▲ 31278 [DDD] (9.97)

R. Serkin (pno), C. Abbado (cnd), London SO † Con 27 Pno, K.595 DEUT (Masters) ▲ 45516 [DDD] (9.97)

H. Shelley (pno), H. Shelley (cnd), City of London Sinfonia † Con 24 Pno, K.491 INMP ▲ 2007 (9.97)

H. Shelley (pno), H. Shelley (cnd), London Mozart Players † Con 22 Pno, K.482 CHN ▲ 9404 [DDD] (16.97)

D. Shostac (fl), R. Kato (va), J. Walz (vc), J. Smith (gtr), G. Levant (hp), A. Perry (pno)—Andante *(rec North Hollywood, CA)* ("The Romantic Flute") † Andante Fl, K.315; J. S. Bach:Air on the G String; Arioso Ob; Sons Fl; Debussy:Prélude à l'après-midi d'un faune; Suite bergamasque; G. Fauré:Pavane; Sicilienne, Op. 78; Gossec:Tambourin Fl; Marais:Basque; J. Pachelbel:Canon & Gigue XCEL ▲ 30006

S. Stanceva (pno), A. Lizzio (cnd), Mozart Festival Orch † Con 23 Pno, K.488 PC ▲ 265093 [DDD] (2.97)

J. Thibaud (vn), T. Janopoulo (pno)—Andante [arr Saint-Saëns for vn & pno] *(rec 1930)* † Con 23 Pno, K.488; Con 5 Vn, K.219; Sons Vn & Pno (misc) BID ▲ 114 [ADD] (16.97)

M. Tipo (pno), J. Perlea (cnd), Vienna SO † Con 25 Pno, K.503; D. Scarlatti:Sons Kbd VOXL (Legends) 2-▲ 5515 [ADD] (9.97)

M. Uchida (pno), J. Tate (cnd), English CO † Con 20 Pno, K.466 PPHI ▲ 16381 [DDD] (16.97)

S. Uryvayev (pno), A. Titov (cnd), St. Petersburg New Philharmony Orch † Con 20 Pno, K.466 SNYC ▲ 57232 [DDD] (4.97)

A. Vardi (pno), A. Vardi (cnd), Israel CO † Con 6 Pno, K.238 CACI ▲ 210015

E. Wild (pno), A. Randall (cnd), Royal PO [cadenzas by Wild] *(rec London, England, Apr 3, 1982)* ("Earl Wild Goes to the Movies") † Chopin:Andante Spianato & Grand Polonaise, Op. 22; Liszt:Etudes de concert (3), S.144; R. Rodgers:Slaughter on Tenth Avenue Orch; M. Rózsa:Spellbound; M. Steiner:Four Wives (sels) IVOR ▲ 70801 [ADD] (16.97)

various artists—Andante † Con Cl, K.622; Con 20 Pno, K.466; Con 3 Vn, K.216; Così fan tutte (ov); Kleine Nachtmusik, K.525; Son 11 Pno, K.331; Sym 40, K.550; Sym 41, K.551; Zauberflöte (ov) RCAV ▲ 60829 (10.97) ■ 60829 (5.98)

various artists—Andante † Andante Fl, K.315; Con Cl, K.622; Con Fl & Hp, K.299; Con 3 Vn, K.216; Così fan tutte (sels); Kleine Nachtmusik, K.525; Qt in A Cl Strs, K.581; Serenade; Son 13 Pno, K.333 RCAV ■ 63329 (5.98) ▲ 63329 (11.97)

artists unknown—Andante ("Adagios") † Adagio Pno, K.540; Adagio Vn, K.261; Con Cl, K.622; Con Fl & Hp, K.299; Con 2 Hn, K.417; Con 20 Pno, K.466; Con 23 Pno, K.488; Con 26 Pno, K.537; Con 27 Pno, K.595; Con 3 Hn, K.447; Con 3 Vn, K.216; Diverts Str Qt, K.136-138; Kleine Nachtmusik, K.525; Qnt Cl, K.581; Serenade; Serenade Ww, K.388/384a; Sinf concertante Vn, K.364; Son 12 Pno, K.332; Son 16 Pno, K.545; Sym 40, K.550; Sym 41, K.551 DECC (2-Fers) 2-▲ 460191 (17.97)

Concerto No. 22 in E♭ for Piano & Orchestra, K.482 (1785)

V. Ashkenazy (pno) † Con 20 Pno, K.466; Con 21 Pno, K.467; Con 23 Pno, K.488; Con 24 Pno, K.491; Con 25 Pno, K.503 PPHI (Double Decker) 2-▲ 452958 (17.97)

D. Barenboim (pno), D. Barenboim (cnd), Berlin PO ("The Late Piano Concertos") † Con 20 Pno, K.466; Con 21 Pno, K.467; Con 23 Pno, K.488; Con 24 Pno, K.491; Con 25 Pno, K.503; Con 26 Pno, K.537; Con 27 Pno, K.595 TELC 4-▲ 72024 [DDD] (50.97)

D. Barenboim (pno), D. Barenboim (cnd), Berlin PO † Con 23 Pno, K.488 TELC ▲ 75711 [DDD] (16.97)

D. Barenboim (pno), D. Barenboim (cnd), Berlin PO † Con 20 Pno, K.466; Con 21 Pno, K.467; Con 23 Pno, K.488 ERAT (Ultima) 2-▲ 18956 (16.97)

D. Barenboim (pno), D. Barenboim (cnd), English CO † Con 23 Pno, K.488 EMIC (Red Line) ▲ 69822 [DDD] (6.97)

M. Bilson (pno), J. E. Gardiner (cnd), English Baroque Soloists † Con 26 Pno, K.537 PARC ▲ 47283 [DDD] (9.97)

A. Brendel (pno), P. Angerer (cnd), Vienna CO *(rec 1958)* † Con 25 Pno, K.503 TUXE ▲ 1046 [ADD] (10.97)

MOZART, WOLFGANG AMADEUS (cont.)

Concerto No. 22 in E♭ for Piano & Orchestra, K.482 (1785) (cont.)

A. Brendel (pno), N. Marriner (cnd), Academy of St. Martin in the Fields ("Complete Piano Concerti, Vol. 2") † Con 15 Pno, K.450; Con 25 Pno, K.503; Con 27 Pno, K.595; Con 9 Pno, K.271 PPHI (Duo) 2-▲ 42571 (17.97)

R. Buchbinder (pno), R. Buchbinder (cnd), Vienna SO † Con 23 Pno, K.488 CALG ▲ 51015 [DDD] (11.97)

E. Fischer (pno), J. Barbirolli (cnd) *(rec London, June 6, 1935)* ("The Mozart Piano Concerto Recordings, Vol. 1") † Con 20 Pno, K.466; Minuet Pno, K.1; Rondo Pno Orch, K.382 APR ▲ 5523 [ADD] (18.97)

H. Francesch (pno), K. Weise (cnd), Nice PO † Con 21 Pno, K.467 KPT ▲ 32189 [DDD]

M. Horszowski (pno), F. Waldman (cnd), Musica Aeterna Ensemble † Con 17 Pno, K.453; Con 18 Pno, K.456; Con 20 Pno, K.466; Fant Pno, K.475 PHS 2-▲ 9153 [ADD] (33.97)

J. Jandó (pno), M. Antál (cnd), Concentus Hungaricus † Con 10 Pnos, K.365 NXIN ▲ 550206 [DDD] (5.97)

W. Landowska (pno), A. Rodzinski (cnd), New York PO *(rec New York, NY, Dec 2, 1945)* ("Wanda Landowska Plays Mozart's Piano Concertos") † Con 13 Pno, K.415 IN ▲ 1336 (m) [ADD] (15.97)

W. Landowska (pno), A. Rodzinski (cnd), New York PO *(rec 1945-46)* † Con 13 Pno, K.415 ENT (Sirio) ▲ 530032 (13.97)

W. Landowska (pno), A. Rodzinski (cnd), New York PO *(rec mid 1940s)* † Con 13 Pno, K.415 ENPL (The Piano Library) ▲ 283 (13.97)

A. D. Larrocha (pno), C. Davis (cnd), English CO † Con 26 Pno, K.537 RCAV (Red Seal) ▲ 61698 (16.97)

J. O'Conor (pno), C. Mackerras (cnd), Scottish CO *(rec Oct 30-31, 1991)* † Con 20 Pno, K.466 TEL ▲ 80308 [DDD] (16.97)

M. Perahia (pno), M. Perahia (cnd), English CO † Con 24 Pno, K.491 SNYC ▲ 42242 [AAD] (16.97)

S. Richter (pno), B. Britten (cnd), English CO *(rec June 1967)* † Adagio & Fugue Strs, K.546; Sinf concertante Vn, K.364 BBC ▲ 8010 (17.97)

A. Schnabel (pno), B. Walter (cnd), New York PO ("Artur Schnabel & Bruno Walter on American Radio") † Sinf concertante Vn, K.364 RY (The Radio Years) ▲ 69 (16.97)

R. Serkin (pno), P. Casals (cnd), Perpignan Festival Orch *(rec July 26, 1951)* † Con 20 Pno, K.466 SNYC ▲ 66570 [ADD] (10.97)

H. Shelley (pno), H. Shelley (cnd), London Mozart Players † Con 21 Pno, K.467 CHN ▲ 9404 [DDD] (16.97)

M. Uchida (pno), J. Tate (cnd), English CO † Con 23 Pno, K.488 PPHI ▲ 20187 [DDD] (16.97)

Concerto No. 23 in A for Piano & Orchestra, K.488 (1786)

V. Ashkenazy (pno) † Con 20 Pno, K.466; Con 21 Pno, K.467; Con 22 Pno, K.482; Con 24 Pno, K.491; Con 25 Pno, K.503 PPHI (Double Decker) 2-▲ 452958 (17.97)

V. Ashkenazy (pno), V. Ashkenazy (cnd), Philharmonia Orch ("Favourite Mozart") † Con 20 Pno, K.466; Con 21 Pno, K.467; Con 27 Pno, K.595; Rondo Pno, K.511; Son 18 Pno, K.576 PLON 2-▲ 36383 [ADD] (17.97)

D. Barenboim (pno), D. Barenboim (cnd), Berlin PO ("The Late Piano Concertos") † Con 20 Pno, K.466; Con 21 Pno, K.467; Con 22 Pno, K.482; Con 24 Pno, K.491; Con 25 Pno, K.503; Con 26 Pno, K.537; Con 27 Pno, K.595 TELC 4-▲ 72024 [DDD] (50.97)

D. Barenboim (pno), D. Barenboim (cnd), Berlin PO † Con 22 Pno, K.482 TELC ▲ 75711 [DDD] (16.97)

D. Barenboim (pno), D. Barenboim (cnd), Berlin PO † Con 20 Pno, K.466; Con 21 Pno, K.467; Con 22 Pno, K.482 ERAT (Ultima) 2-▲ 18956 (16.97)

D. Barenboim (pno), D. Barenboim (cnd), English CO † Con 22 Pno, K.482 EMIC (Red Line) ▲ 69822 [DDD] (6.97)

R. Buchbinder (pno), R. Buchbinder (cnd), Vienna SO † Con 22 Pno, K.482 CALG ▲ 51015 [DDD] (11.97)

E. Ciccarelli (pno), T. Pál (cnd), Salieri CO *(rec Szeged Opera House Hungary, June 1996)* † Con 24 Pno, K.491; Diverts Str Qt, K.136-138 AG ▲ 57 [DDD] (18.97)

J. Cullen (pno), P. Freeman (cnd), Moscow PO † Son 12 Pno, K.332 HALM ▲ 35074 (6.97)

C. Curzon (pno), I. Kertész (cnd), London SO † Con 24 Pno, K.491 PLON (Classic Sound) ▲ 452888 (11.97)

C. Curzon (pno), B. Neel (cnd), National SO † Liszt:Mephisto Waltz 1 Pno, S.514; Trans, Arrs & Paraphrases; F. Schubert:Impromptus (4) Pno PHS ▲ 27 (17.97)

C. Curzon (pno), B. Neel (cnd), National SO † J. Brahms:Con 1 Pno, Op. 15 DLAB ▲ 5507 (15.97)

H. Czerny-Stefańska (pno), K. Ančerl (cnd), Czech PO *(rec 1952-66)* † Con Bn, K.191; Con 3 Hn, K.447; Zauberflöte (sels) SUR ▲ 111935 [AAD]

D. Gerard (pno), H. Kraus (cnd) † Con 9 Pno, K.271 LALI ▲ 15632 [DDD] (3.97)

D. Gerard (pno), H. Kraus (cnd) LALI ▲ 15649 [DDD] (3.97)

R. Goode (pno) † Con 17 Pno, K.453 NON ▲ 79042 [DDD] (9.97)

F. Gulda (pno), N. Harnoncourt (cnd), (Royal) Concertgebouw Orch † Con 26 Pno, K.537 TELC ▲ 92150

C. Haskil (pno), P. Sacher (cnd), Vienna SO *(rec 1954)* ("Clara Haskil") † Con 13 Pno, K.415; Con 20 Pno, K.466; Con 24 Pno, K.491; Con 27 Pno, K.595; Rondo Pno Orch, K.386 PPHI (Great Pianists of the 20th Century) ▲ 456826 (22.97)

V. Horowitz (pno), C. M. Giulini (cnd), La Scala Orch † Son 13 Pno, K.333 DEUT ▲ 23287 [DDD] (16.97)

W. Kempff (pno), F. Leitner (cnd), Berlin PO † Con 24 Pno, K.491; Con 27 Pno, K.595; Con 8 Pno, K.246 DEUT (Double) 2-▲ 39699 (17.97)

S. Lubin (pno), S. Lubin (cnd) † Con 20 Pno, K.466 ARA ▲ 6530 (16.97)

B. McFerrin (cnd), St. Paul CO, B. McFerrin (sgr), C. Corea (pno) [a capella voc & pno improv w voc prelude] *(rec Bethel College St. Paul & Masonic Grand Lodge, United States of America, 1996)* ("The Mozart Sessions") † Con 20 Pno, K.466; Son 2 Pno, K.280 SNYC ▲ 62601 [DDD] (16.97) ■ 62601 [DDD] (10.98) COL △ 62601 [DDD]

N. Marriner (cnd), Academy of St. Martin in the Fields ("Vol. I") † Con 19 Pno, K.459; Con 20 Pno, K.466; Con 21 Pno, K.467; Con 24 Pno, K.491 PPHI 2-▲ 42269 (17.97)

B. Meyer (pno), I. Brown (cnd), Norwegian CO † Con 9 Pno, K.271 VC ▲ 1003 [DDD] (13.97)

I. Moravec (pno), N. Marriner (cnd), Academy of St. Martin in the Fields † Con 20 Pno, K.466 HANS (Academy) ▲ 98142 [DDD] (15.97)

L. Nicholson (pno), N. Kraemer (cnd), Cappella Coloniensis † Con 13 Pno, K.415 LALI ▲ 15871 [DDD] (3.97)

L. Nicholson (pno), N. Kraemer (cnd), Cappella Coloniensis ("Cappella Edition") † Con 13 Pno, K.415 CAPO ▲ 10623 [DDD] (11.97)

J. O'Conor (pno), C. Mackerras (cnd), Scottish CO † Con 18 Pno, K.456; Con 19 Pno, K.459; Rondo Pno Orch, K.386 TEL ▲ 80285 [DDD] (16.97)

M. Perahia (pno), M. Perahia (cnd), English CO † Con 18 Pno, K.456; Con 19 Pno, K.459 SNYC ▲ 39064 [DDD] (16.97)

D. Ránki (pno), I. Karabtchevsky (cnd), Venice Theater Orch † Sym 40, K.550 MONM ▲ 10014 (18.97)

V. Reznikovskaya (pno), A. Titov (cnd), St. Petersburg Classical Music Studio Orch † Con 27 Pno, K.595 SNYC ▲ 57259 [DDD] (4.97)

A. Rubinstein (pno), A. Wallenstein (cnd), RCA Victor SO † Con 24 Pno, K.491; Rondo Pno, K.511 RCAV (Gold Seal) ▲ 7968 [ADD] (11.97)

A. Rubinstein (pno), A. Wallenstein (cnd), RCA Victor SO ("Basic 100, Vol. 69") † Con 20 Pno, K.466 RCAV ▲ 68337 (10.97) ■ 68337 (5.98)

A. Schnabel (pno), A. Rodzinski (cnd), New York PO ("Schnabel & Rodzinski") † Kleine Nachtmusik, K.525; Sym 35, K.385 IN ▲ 1363 (15.97)

A. Schnabel (pno), A. Rodzinski (cnd), Philharmonic Society Orch † Con 24 Pno, K.491 MUA ▲ 4632 (10.97)

H. Shelley (pno), H. Shelley (cnd), London Mozart Players † Con 20 Pno, K.466 CHN ▲ 8992 [DDD] (16.97)

S. Stanceva (pno), A. Lizzio (cnd), Mozart Festival Orch † Con 21 Pno, K.467 PC ▲ 265093 [DDD] (2.97)

S. Sugitani (pno), T. Ukigaya (cnd), Polish National RSO Katowice *(rec May 1998)* † Con 20 Pno, K.466 THOR ▲ 2394 [DDD] (16.97)

J. Thibaud (vn), P. Gaubert (cnd), Paris SO *(rec 1935)* † Con 21 Pno, K.467; Con 5 Vn, K.219; Sons Vn & Pno (misc) BID ▲ 114 [ADD] (16.97)

M. Tipo (pno), A. Jordan (cnd) † Con 27 Pno, K.595 EMIA ▲ 54234 (16.97)

M. Uchida (pno), J. Tate (cnd), English CO † Con 22 Pno, K.482 PPHI ▲ 20187 [DDD] (16.97)

M. Uchida (pno), J. Tate (cnd), English CO † Con 20 Pno, K.466 PPHI (Insignia) ▲ 34164 [DDD] (9.97)

E. Westenholz (pno), M. Schønwandt (cnd), Copenhagen Collegium Musicum † Con 20 Pno, K.466 BIS ▲ 283 [DDD] (17.97)

artists unknown—Adagio ("Adagios") † Adagio Pno, K.540; Adagio Vn, K.261; Con Cl, K.622; Con Fl & Hp, K.299; Con 2 Hn, K.417; Con 20 Pno, K.466; Con 21 Pno, K.467; Con 26 Pno, K.537; Con 27 Pno, K.595; Con 3 Hn, K.447; Con 3 Vn, K.216; Diverts Str Qt, K.136-138; Kleine Nachtmusik, K.525; Qnt Cl, K.581; Serenade; Serenade Ww, K.388/384a; Sinf concertante Vn, K.364; Son 12 Pno, K.332; Son 16 Pno, K.545; Sym 40, K.550; Sym 41, K.551 DECC (2-Fers) 2-▲ 460191 (17.97)

Concerto No. 24 in c for Piano & Orchestra, K.491 (1786)

V. Ashkenazy (pno) † Con 20 Pno, K.466; Con 21 Pno, K.467; Con 22 Pno, K.482; Con 23 Pno, K.488; Con 25 Pno, K.503 PPHI (Double Decker) 2-▲ 452958 (17.97)

D. Barenboim (pno), D. Barenboim (cnd), Berlin PO ("The Late Piano Concertos") † Con 20 Pno, K.466; Con 21 Pno, K.467; Con 22 Pno, K.482; Con 23 Pno, K.488; Con 25 Pno, K.503; Con 26 Pno, K.537; Con 27 Pno, K.595 TELC 4-▲ 72024 [DDD] (50.97)

D. Barenboim (pno), D. Barenboim (cnd), Berlin PO † Con 25 Pno, K.503 TELC ▲ 75715 [DDD]

COMPOSERS 559

MOZART, WOLFGANG AMADEUS (cont.)

Concerto No. 24 in c for Piano & Orchestra, K.491 (1786) (cont.)

A. Brendel (pno), N. Marriner (cnd), Academy of St. Martin in the Fields † Con 20 Pno, K.466; Rondo Pno Orch, K.382 PPHI (Concert Classics) ▲ 20867 [ADD] (9.97)
R. Buchbinder (pno), R. Buchbinder (cnd), Vienna SO † Con 25 Pno, K.503 CALG ▲ 51016 [DDD] (11.97)
R. Casadesus (pno), G. Szell (cnd), Cleveland Orch † Con 21 Pno, K.467 SNYC ▲ 38523 [AAD] (9.97)
E. Ciccarelli (pno), T. Pál (cnd), Salieri CO *(rec Szeged Opera House Hungary, June 1996)* † Con 23 Pno, K.488; Diverts Str Qt, K.136-138 AG ▲ 57 [DDD] (18.97)
C. Curzon (pno), I. Kertész (cnd), London SO † Con 23 Pno, K.488 PLON (Classic Sound) ▲ 452888 (11.97)
R. Firkušný (pno), E. Bour (cnd), Southwest German RSO Baden-Baden † Con 9 Pno, K.271 INTC ▲ 820547 (9.97)
E. Fischer (pno), L. Collingwood (cnd), London PO *(rec 1933-47)* ("Mozart Piano Recordings, Vol. 2") † Con 17 Pno, K.453; Fant Pno, K.396; Son 11 Pno, K.331 APR ▲ 5524 (m) [ADD] (18.97)
E. Fischer (pno), L. Collingwood (cnd), London PO *(rec 1937-47)* † Con 25 Pno, K.503; Son 10 Pno, K.330 ENPL (The Piano Libary) ▲ 297 (13.97)
G. Gould (pno), G. L. Jochum (cnd), Swedish RSO † Beethoven:Con 2 Pno, Op. 19; Son 31 Pno, Op. 110; A. Berg:Son Pno, Op. 1; J. Haydn:Son 59 Kbd, H.XVI/49 BIS 2-▲ 323 (34.97)
G. Gould (pno), W. Susskind (cnd), CBC Vancouver SO *(rec 1961)* † Prelude & Fugue Pno, K.394; Son 10 Pno, K.330; J. Haydn:Son 59 Kbd, H.XVI/49 SNYC (Glenn Gould Edition) ▲ 52626 [ADD] (16.97)
C. Haskil (pno), I. Markevitch (cnd), Lamoureaux Concerts Orch *(rec 1960)* ("Clara Haskil") † Con 13 Pno, K.415; Con 20 Pno, K.466; Con 23 Pno, K.488; Con 27 Pno, K.595; Rondo Pno Orch, K.386 PPHI (Great Pianists of the 20th Century) ▲ 456826 (22.97)
E. Istomin (pno), G. Schwarz (cnd), Seattle SO *(rec Bothell, WA, Oct 10, 1995)* † Con 21 Pno, K.467 REF ▲ 68 (16.97)
W. Kempff (pno), F. Leitner (cnd), Berlin PO † Con 23 Pno, K.488; Con 27 Pno, K.595; Con 8 Pno, K.246 DEUT (Double) 2-▲ 39699 (17.97)
M. Kwok (pno), P. Freeman (cnd), Czech National SO † Con 21 Pno, K.467 HALM ▲ 35063 (6.97)
K. Long (pno), London PO, E. Van Beinum (cnd), Concertgebouw Orch *(rec 1946-47)* ("Van Beinum, Vol. 3") † J. Haydn:Sym 100; Sym 96 LYS ▲ 472 (17.97)
R. Mamou (pno), G. Oskamp (cnd), Berlin SO † Con 20 Pno, K.466 VRDI ▲ 32147 (13.97)
N. Marriner (cnd), Academy of St. Martin in the Fields ("Vol. I") † Con 19 Pno, K.459; Con 20 Pno, K.466; Con 21 Pno, K.467; Con 23 Pno, K.488 PPHI 2-▲ 42269 (17.97)
E. Naoumoff (pno), A. Lombard (cnd), Bordeaux-Aquitaine National Orch † Con 20 Pno, K.466 FORL ▲ 16626 [DDD] (16.97)
J. O'Conor (pno), C. Mackerras (cnd), Scottish CO † Con 17 Pno, K.453 TEL ▲ 80306 [DDD] (16.97)
P. Osetinskaya (pno), S. Litkov (cnd), St. Petersburg Festival Orch † Divert 10 Hns, K.247; Diverts Str Qt, K.136-138 SNYC ▲ 64332 [DDD] (4.97)
M. Perahia (pno), M. Perahia (cnd), English CO † Con 22 Pno, K.482 SNYC ▲ 42242 [AAD] (16.97)
A. Rubinstein (pno), J. Krips (cnd), RCA Victor SO † Con 23 Pno, K.488; Rondo Pno, K.511 RCAV (Gold Seal) ▲ 7968 [ADD] (11.97)
A. Schnabel (pno), A. Rodzinski (cnd), Philharmonic Society Orch † Con 23 Pno, K.488 MUA ▲ 4632 (10.97)
A. Schnabel (pno), W. Susskind (cnd), Philharmonia Orch *(rec 1946-48)* † Con 20 Pno, K.466; Rondo Pno, K.511 ENPL (Piano Library) ▲ 274 (13.97)
H. Shelley (pno), H. Shelley (cnd), City of London Sinfonia † Con 21 Pno, K.467 INMP ▲ 2007 (9.97)
H. Shelley (pno), H. Shelley (cnd), London Mozart Players † Con 13 Pno, K.415 CHN ▲ 9326 [DDD] (17.97)
K. Tabe (pno), J. López-Cobos (cnd), Lausanne CO *(rec Musica Théâtre La Chaux-de-Fonds, June 10-11, 1995)* † Con 9 Pno, K.271 DNN ▲ 78833 [DDD] (16.97)
M. Uchida (pno), J. Tate (cnd), English CO † Con 25 Pno, K.503 PPHI ▲ 22331 [DDD] (16.97)

Concerto No. 25 in C for Piano & Orchestra, K.503 (1786)

D. Ambache (pno) *(rec Jan 1990)* † Adagio Pno, K.540; Con 17 Pno, K.453; Con 19 Pno, K.459; Con 21 Pno, K.467; Fant Pno, K.397 VCL 2-▲ 61445 [DDD] (11.97)
V. Ashkenazy (pno) † Con 20 Pno, K.466; Con 21 Pno, K.467; Con 22 Pno, K.482; Con 23 Pno, K.488; Con 24 Pno, K.491 PPHI (Double Decker) 2-▲ 452958 (17.97)
D. Barenboim (pno), D. Barenboim (cnd), Berlin PO ("The Late Piano Concertos") † Con 20 Pno, K.466; Con 21 Pno, K.467; Con 22 Pno, K.482; Con 23 Pno, K.488; Con 24 Pno, K.491; Con 26 Pno, K.537; Con 27 Pno, K.595 TELC 4-▲ 72024 [DDD] (50.97)
D. Barenboim (pno), D. Barenboim (cnd), Berlin PO † Con 24 Pno, K.491 TELC ▲ 75715 [DDD]
L. Bernstein (pno), L. Bernstein (cnd), Israel PO ("Bernstein: The Royal Edition") † Beethoven:Con 1 Pno, Op. 15 SNYC ▲ 47519 [ADD] (10.97)
A. Brendel (pno), P. Angerer (cnd), Vienna State Opera Orch *(rec 1958)* † Con 22 Pno, K.482 TUXE ▲ 1046 [ADD] (10.97)
A. Brendel (pno), N. Marriner (cnd), Academy of St. Martin in the Fields ("Complete Piano Concerti, Vol. 2") † Con 15 Pno, K.450; Con 22 Pno, K.482; Con 27 Pno, K.595; Con 9 Pno, K.271 PPHI (Duo) 2-▲ 42571 (17.97)
R. Buchbinder (pno), R. Buchbinder (cnd), Vienna SO † Con 24 Pno, K.491 CALG ▲ 51016 [DDD] (11.97)
G. Casadesus (pno), Lamoureux Orch † Con 19 Pno, K.459; Vars on an Allegretto, K.500; Chabrier:Pièces pittoresques; F. Couperin:Pièces de clavecin (sels); G. Fauré:Impromptus Pno; Rameau:Pièces de clavecin HPC ▲ 155 (50.97)
D. Ciani (pno), J. Barbirolli (cnd), Naples RAI Orch † Con 5 Vn, K.219 STRV ▲ 10005 [ADD] (13.97)
E. Fischer (pno), J. Krips (cnd), Philharmonia Orch *(rec 1937-47)* † Con 24 Pno, K.491; Son 10 Pno, K.330 ENPL (The Piano Libary) ▲ 297 (13.97)
E. Fischer (pno), J. Krips (cnd), Philharmonia Orch *(rec Oct 1947)* † Fant Pno, K.396; Fant Pno, K.475; Minuet Pno, K.1; Romance Pno, K.Anh.205; Son 11 Pno, K.331 PHS (Edwin Fischer Plays Mozart-Vol. II) ▲ 43 [ADD] (17.97)
L. Fleisher (pno), G. Szell (cnd), Cleveland Orch † Beethoven:Con 4 Pno, Op. 58 SNYC ▲ 37762 [ADD] (9.97)
L. Fleisher (pno), G. Szell (cnd), Cleveland Orch † Beethoven:Cons Pno (comp) SNYC 3-▲ 42445 (47.97)
H. Francesch (pno), K. Weise (cnd), Nice PO † Con 9 Pno, K.271 KPT ▲ 32209
R. Goode (pno) † Con 9 Pno, K.271 NON ▲ 79454 (16.97)
F. Gulda (pno) *(rec 1954)* † Con 26 Pno, K.537 ENT ▲ 2020 (14.97)
J. Jandó (pno), M. Antál (cnd), Concentus Hungaricus *(rec 1990)* ("Complete Piano Concertos, Vol. 7") † Con 16 Pno, K.451; Rondo Pno Orch, K.386 NXIN ▲ 550207 [DDD] (5.97)
M. Migdal (pno), U. Björlin (cnd), Cappella Coloniensis † Con 12 Pno, K.414 LALI ▲ 15870 [DDD] (3.97)
M. Perahia (pno), M. Perahia (cnd), English CO † Con 5 Pno, K.175 SNYC ▲ 37267 [DDD] (16.97)
C. Seemann (pno), W. Boettcher (cnd), North German RSO *(rec Hamburg, Dec 1979)* † Con 14 Pno, K.449 ORFE ▲ 447961 (16.97)
M. Tipo (pno), J. Perlea (cnd), Vienna SO † Con 21 Pno, K.467; D. Scarlatti:Sons Kbd VOXL (Legends) 2-▲ 5515 [ADD] (9.97)
M. Uchida (pno), J. Tate (cnd), English CO † Con 24 Pno, K.491 PPHI ▲ 22331 [DDD] (16.97)

Concerto No. 26 in D for Piano & Orchestra, K.537, "Coronation" (1788)

W. Backhaus (pno), F. Zaun (cnd), Berlin City Orch *(rec 1940)* † E. Grieg:Con Pno, Op. 16 MPLY ▲ 2027 (m) (13.97)
D. Barenboim (pno), D. Barenboim (cnd), Berlin PO ("The Late Piano Concertos") † Con 20 Pno, K.466; Con 21 Pno, K.467; Con 22 Pno, K.482; Con 23 Pno, K.488; Con 24 Pno, K.491; Con 25 Pno, K.503; Con 27 Pno, K.595 TELC 4-▲ 72024 [DDD] (50.97)
D. Barenboim (pno), D. Barenboim (cnd), Berlin PO † Con 27 Pno, K.595 TELC ▲ 75716 [DDD] (16.97)
M. Bilson (pno), J. E. Gardiner (cnd), English Baroque Soloists † Con 22 Pno, K.482 PARC ▲ 47283 [DDD] (9.97)
R. Buchbinder (pno), V. Fedoseyev (cnd), Vienna SO *(rec Konzerthaus Wien, Austria, live May 1998)* † Con 27 Pno, K.595 CALG ▲ 51017 [DDD] (11.97)
R. Casadesus (pno), E. Ansermet (cnd), Swiss Romande Orch [also includes 1970 interview w. Casadesus] *(rec 1950s)* † M. de Falla:Noches en los jardines de España; Liszt:Con 2 Pno, S.125 CASC ▲ 2008 (16.97)
F. Gulda (pno) *(rec 1954)* † Con 25 Pno, K.503 ENT ▲ 2020 (14.97)
F. Gulda (pno), N. Harnoncourt (cnd), (Royal) Concertgebouw Orch † Con 23 Pno, K.488 TELC ▲ 92150
J. Jandó (pno), M. Antál (cnd), Concentus Hungaricus *(rec Jan 4-10, 1991)* ("Complete Piano Concertos, Vol. 9") † Con 5 Pno, K.175; Rondo Pno Orch, K.382 NXIN ▲ 550209 [DDD] (5.97)
W. Landowska (pno), W. Goehr (cnd) *(rec Mar 1937)* ("Wanda Landowska: Piano & Harpsichord") † J. Haydn:Con Hpd ENPL (Piano Library) ▲ 230 (13.97)
A. D. Larrocha (pno), C. Davis (cnd), English CO † Con 22 Pno, K.482 RCAV (Red Seal) ▲ 61698 (16.97)
M. K. Luria (pno), P. Freeman (cnd), London SO † Son 12 Pno, K.332; Son 9 Pno, K.311 CENT ▲ 2093 [DDD] (16.97)
M. Perahia (pno), M. Perahia (cnd), English CO † Rondo Pno Orch, K.382; Rondo Pno Orch, K.386 SNYC ▲ 39224 [DDD] (16.97)
S. Stanceva (pno), A. Lizzio (cnd), Mozart Festival Orch † Con 20 Pno, K.466 PC ▲ 267143 [DDD] (2.97)
M. Uchida (pno), J. Tate (cnd), English CO † Con 27 Pno, K.595 PPHI (Digital Classics) ▲ 20951 [DDD] (16.97)

MOZART, WOLFGANG AMADEUS (cont.)

Concerto No. 26 in D for Piano & Orchestra, K.537, "Coronation" (1788) (cont.)

artists unknown—Larghetto ("Adagios") † Adagio Pno, K.540; Adagio Vn, K.261; Con Cl, K.622; Con Fl & Hp, K.299; Con 2 Hn, K.417; Con 20 Pno, K.466; Con 21 Pno, K.467; Con 23 Pno, K.488; Con 27 Pno, K.595; Con 3 Hn, K.447; Con 3 Vn, K.216; Diverts Str Qt, K.136-138; Kleine Nachtmusik, K.525; Qnt Cl, K.581; Serenade; Serenade Ww, K.388/384a; Sinf concertante Vn, K.364; Son 12 Pno, K.332; Son 16 Pno, K.545; Sym 40, K.550; Sym 41, K.551 DECC (2-Fers) 2-▲ 460191 (17.97)

Concerto No. 27 in B♭ for Piano & Orchestra, K.595 (1788-91)

V. Ashkenazy (pno), V. Ashkenazy (cnd), Philharmonia Orch ("Favourite Mozart") † Con 20 Pno, K.466; Con 21 Pno, K.467; Con 23 Pno, K.488; Rondo Pno, K.511; Son 18 Pno, K.576 PLON 2-▲ 36383 [ADD] (17.97)
W. Backhaus (pno), K. Böhm (cnd), Vienna PO † J. Brahms:Con 2 Pno, Op. 83 PLON (The Classic Sound) ▲ 448600 (11.97)
W. Backhaus (pno), K. Böhm (cnd), Vienna PO *(rec 1967)* † J. Brahms:Con 2 Pno, Op. 83 DECC ▲ 466380 (11.97)
D. Barenboim (pno), D. Barenboim (cnd), Berlin PO ("The Late Piano Concertos") † Con 20 Pno, K.466; Con 21 Pno, K.467; Con 22 Pno, K.482; Con 23 Pno, K.488; Con 24 Pno, K.491; Con 25 Pno, K.503; Con 26 Pno, K.537 TELC 4-▲ 72024 [DDD] (50.97)
D. Barenboim (pno), D. Barenboim (cnd), Berlin PO † Con 26 Pno, K.537 TELC ▲ 75716 [DDD] (16.97)
A. Brendel (pno), P. Angerer (cnd), Vienna State Opera Orch † Con 17 Pno, K.453 TUXE ▲ 1027 (10.97)
A. Brendel (pno), N. Marriner (cnd), Academy of St. Martin in the Fields ("Complete Piano Concerti, Vol. 2") † Con 15 Pno, K.450; Con 22 Pno, K.482; Con 25 Pno, K.503; Con 9 Pno, K.271 PPHI (Duo) 2-▲ 42571 (17.97)
R. Buchbinder (pno), V. Fedoseyev (cnd), Vienna SO *(rec Konzerthaus Wien, Austria, live June 1998)* † Con 26 Pno, K.537 CALG ▲ 51017 [DDD] (11.97)
N. Frisardi (pno), G. Korsten (cnd), Salzburg Mozarteum Orch † Con 9 Pno, K.271 CHSK ▲ 136 [DDD] (16.97)
W. Gieseking (pno), V. Desarzens (cnd), Lausanne CO *(rec live, 1948-56)* ("Gieseking Plays Mozart") † Con 21 Pno, K.467; Son 18 Pno, K.576 PHS ▲ 9236 (17.97)
Em. Gilels (pno), K. Böhm (cnd), Vienna PO [y] *(rec 1973)* † J. S. Bach:French Suites; Preludes & Fugues, BWV 531-552; Beethoven:Con 4 Pno, Op. 58; Debussy:Images (6) Pno; M. Ravel:Alborada del gracioso; Jeux d'eau; Tombeau PPHI (Great Pianists of the 20th Century) ▲ 456793 (22.97)
C. Haskil (pno), F. Fricsay (cnd), Bavarian State Orch *(rec Residenz Munich, Germany, May 1957)* † Con 19 Pno, K.459; Son 2 Pno, K.280 DEUT (The Originals) ▲ 449722 [ADD] (11.97)
C. Haskil (pno), F. Fricsay (cnd), Bavarian State Orch *(rec 1957)* ("Clara Haskil") † Con 13 Pno, K.415; Con 20 Pno, K.466; Con 23 Pno, K.488; Con 24 Pno, K.491; Rondo Pno Orch, K.386 PPHI (Great Pianists of the 20th Century) ▲ 456826 (22.97)
M. Hess (pno), R. Scholz (cnd), American CO *(rec Mar 20, 1956)* ("In Concert 1949-1960") † Con 12 Pno, K.414; Con 21 Pno, K.467; Beethoven:Con 4 Pno, Op. 58; Con 5 Pno, Op. 73; Son 10 Vn, Op. 96; J. Brahms:Con 2 Pno, Op. 83; Son 2 Vn, Op. 100; F. Schubert:Sonatinas (3) Vn MUA 3-▲ 779 [AAD] (47.97)
J. Jandó (pno), A. Ligeti (cnd), Concentus Hungaricus *(rec June 1989)* † Con 9 Pno, K.271 NXIN ▲ 550203 [DDD] (5.97)
W. Kempff (pno), F. Leitner (cnd), Berlin PO † Con 23 Pno, K.488; Con 24 Pno, K.491; Con 8 Pno, K.246 DEUT (Double) 2-▲ 39699 (17.97)
J. O'Conor (pno), C. Mackerras (cnd), Scottish CO † Con 21 Pno, K.467 TEL ▲ 80219 [DDD] (16.97)
M. Perahia (pno), M. Perahia (cnd), English CO † Con 20 Pno, K.466 COL ▲ 42241 [AAD] (16.97)
V. Reznikovskaya (pno), A. Titov (cnd), St. Petersburg Classical Music Studio Orch † Con 23 Pno, K.488 SNYC ▲ 57259 [DDD] (4.97)
S. Richter (pno), B. Britten (cnd), English CO † Exsultate, jubilate, K.165; Qt Pno, K.478 BBC (Britten the Performer) ▲ 8005 (17.97)
A. Schmidt (pno), K. Masur (cnd), Dresden PO ("Famous Piano Concertos") † Con 18 Pno, K.456; Con 20 Pno, K.466; Con 21 Pno, K.467 BER 2-▲ 9251 (21.97)
A. Schnabel (pno), J. Barbirolli (cnd), London SO † Con 21 Pno, K.467 ENPL (Piano Library) ▲ 210 (13.97)
A. Schnabel (pno), J. Barbirolli (cnd), London SO † Con 21 Pno, K.467 ENT (Sirio) ▲ 53006 (13.97)
A. Schnabel (pno), J. Barbirolli (cnd), London SO ("Artur Schnabel Plays Mozart") † Con 10 Pnos, K.365; Con 19 Pno, K.459; Con 21 Pno, K.467; Rondo Pno, K.511; Son 8 Pno, K.310 PHS 2-▲ 6 (33.97)
R. Serkin (pno), C. Abbado (cnd), London SO † Con 21 Pno, K.467 DEUT (Masters) ▲ 45516 [DDD] (9.97)
R. Serkin (pno), E. Ormandy (cnd), Philadelphia Orch ("Mozart: Legendary Interpretations") † Con 10 Pnos, K.365; Con 12 Pno, K.414; Con 14 Pno, K.449; Con 17 Pno, K.453; Con 18 Pno, K.456; Con 19 Pno, K.459; Con 20 Pno, K.466; Rondo Pno Orch, K.382; Rondo Pno, K.511 SNYC 3-▲ 47207 (33.97)
H. Shelley (pno), H. Shelley (cnd), London Mozart Players † Con 14 Pno, K.449 CHN ▲ 9137 [DDD] (16.97)
M. Tipo (pno), A. Jordan (cnd) † Con 23 Pno, K.488 EMIA ▲ 54234 (16.97)
M. Uchida (pno), J. Tate (cnd), English CO † Con 26 Pno, K.537 PPHI (Digital Classics) ▲ 20951 [DDD] (16.97)
artists unknown—Larghetto ("Adagios") † Adagio Pno, K.540; Adagio Vn, K.261; Con Cl, K.622; Con Fl & Hp, K.299; Con 2 Hn, K.417; Con 20 Pno, K.466; Con 21 Pno, K.467; Con 23 Pno, K.488; Con 26 Pno, K.537; Con 3 Hn, K.447; Con 3 Vn, K.216; Diverts Str Qt, K.136-138; Kleine Nachtmusik, K.525; Qnt Cl, K.581; Serenade; Serenade Ww, K.388/384a; Sinf concertante Vn, K.364; Son 12 Pno, K.332; Son 16 Pno, K.545; Sym 40, K.550; Sym 41, K.551 DECC (2-Fers) 2-▲ 460191 (17.97)

Concerto No. 7 in F for 3 (or 2) Pianos & Orchestra, K.242, "Lodron" (1766)

L. Bernstein (pno), R. Fizdale (pno), A. Gold (pno), L. Bernstein (cnd), New York PO *(rec Lincoln Center New York, NY, Mar 21, 1968)* † Con 10 Pnos, K.365; Qt Pno, K.478 SNYC (Bernstein Century) ▲ 60598 [ADD] (10.97)
B. Ganz (pno), F. Braley (pno), S. Prutsman (pno), P. Peire (cnd), Collegium Instrumentale Brugense † J. S. Bach:Cons for 3 Hpds (comp); S. Rachmaninoff:Piano Music (works for 2 pianos & piano 4- & 6-hands); Pieces Pno 6-Hands RENE ▲ 87065 [DDD] (16.97)
J. Jandó (pno), D. Várjon (pno), M. Antál (pno) [arr Mozart for 2 pnos & orch] *(rec Jan 7-10, 1991)* † Con 10 Pnos, K.365; Con 15 Pno, K.450 NXIN ▲ 550210 [DDD] (5.97)
M. Perahia (pno), R. Lupu (pno) [arr Mozart for 2 pnos & orch] † Andante & Vars, K.501; Con 10 Pnos, K.365; Busoni:Fant Org, K.608 SNYC ▲ 44915 (16.97)
A. Schiff (pno), D. Barenboim (pno), G. Solti (pno), G. Solti (cnd), English CO † Con 10 Pnos, K.365; Con 20 Pno, K.466 PLON ▲ 30232 [DDD] (16.97)

Concertos (7) for Violin & Orchestra (complete)

A. Grumiaux (vn), C. Davis (cnd), London SO † Beethoven:Son 27 Pno, Op. 90 PPHI 2-▲ 38323 (17.97)

Concerto No. 1 in B♭ for Violin & Orchestra, K.207 (1775)

S. Accardo (vn), S. Accardo (cnd), Prague Chamber Orch † Con 2 Vn, K.211; Con 4 Vn, K.218; Rondo Vn, K.373 FON ▲ 9803 (13.97)
E. Kovacic (vn), E. Kovacic (cnd), Scottish CO *(rec Aug 1990)* † Con 3 Vn, K.216; Con 7 Vn, K.271a INMP ▲ 6700822 [DDD] (9.97)
G. Kremer (vn), N. Harnoncourt (cnd), Vienna PO † Con 2 Vn, K.211; Con 3 Vn, K.216; Con 4 Vn, K.218; Con 5 Vn, K.219; Sinf concertante Vn, K.364 DEUT (2CD) 2-▲ 453043 [DDD] (17.97)
S. Kuijken (vn), La Petite Bande † Con 2 Vn, K.211; Concertone Vns, K.190 DNN ▲ 18066 (16.97)
C. Lin (vn), R. Leppard (cnd), English CO † Con 4 Vn, K.218; Rondo Vn SNYC ▲ 44503 [DDD] (11.97)
A.-S. Mutter (vn), N. Marriner (cnd), Academy of St. Martin in the Fields † Sinf concertante Vn, K.364 EMIC ▲ 54302 (16.97)
T. Nishizaki (vn), J. Wildner (cnd), Capella Istropolitana † Con 2 Vn, K.211; Rondo Vn; Saint-Saëns:Andante Vn NXIN ▲ 550414 [DDD] (5.97)
I. Perlman (vn), J. Levine (cnd), Vienna PO † Adagio Vn, K.261; Con 2 Vn, K.211; Con 3 Vn, K.216; Con 4 Vn, K.218; Con 5 Vn, K.219; Rondo Vn; Rondo Vn, K.373 DEUT (Masters) 2-▲ 45535 [DDD] (19.97)
V. Spivakov (vn), V. Spivakov (cnd), English CO † Con 2 Vn, K.211; Sinf concertante Vn, K.364 RYLC ▲ 70121
S. Standage (vn), C. Hogwood (cnd), Academy of Ancient Music † Con 2 Vn, K.211; Con 3 Vn, K.216; Con 4 Vn, K.218; Con 5 Vn, K.219 PLON (Double Decker) 2-▲ 455721 (17.97)
I. Stern (vn), G. Szell (cnd), Cleveland Orch ("Isaac Stern: A Life in Music") † Adagio Vn, K.261; Con 2 Vn, K.211; Con 3 Vn, K.216; Con 4 Vn, K.218; Con 5 Vn, K.219; Concertone Vns, K.190; Rondo Vn, K.373; Sinf concertante Vn, K.364 SNYC 3-▲ 66475 (33.97)
I. Stern (vn), G. Szell (cnd), Columbia SO † Adagio Vn, K.261; Con 2 Vn, K.211; Con 3 Vn, K.216; Con 4 Vn, K.218; Con 5 Vn, K.219; Rondo Vn, K.373; Serenade Vn SNYC 2-▲ 42494 [ADD] (31.97)
I. Stern (vn), G. Szell (cnd), Columbia SO † Con 2 Vn, K.211; Con 3 Vn, K.216; Con 4 Vn, K.218; Con 5 Vn, K.219 SNYC 2-▲ 45614 (14.97)
M. Tenenbaum (vn), R. Kapp (cnd), Czech Chamber PO † Con 2 Vn, K.211; Con 4 Vn, K.218 ESSY ▲ 1070 (16.97)
E. Verhey (vn), E. Marturet (cnd), Concertgebouw CO † Adagio Vn, K.261; Con 2 Vn, K.211; Con 3 Vn, K.216; Con 4 Vn, K.218; Con 5 Vn, K.219; Concertone Vns, K.190; Rondo Vn; Rondo Vn, K.373; Sinf concertante Vn, K.364 FIGA 3-▲ 99077 (11.97)
F. P. Zimmermann (vn), J. Faerber (cnd), Württemberg CO † Adagio Vn, K.261; Con 2 Vn, K.211; Con 3 Vn, K.216; Con 4 Vn, K.218; Con 5 Vn, K.219; Rondo Vn; Rondo Vn, K.373 EMIC 2-▲ 69355 (16.97)
P. Zukerman (vn), P. Zukerman (cnd), St. Paul CO † Con 2 Vn, K.211; Con 3 Vn, K.216 SNYC (Essential Classics) ▲ 46539 [ADD] (7.97) ▮ 46539 [ADD] (3.98)

MOZART, WOLFGANG AMADEUS (cont.)

Concerto No. 2 in D for Violin & Orchestra, K.211 (1775)

S. Accardo (vn), S. Accardo (cnd), Prague Chamber Orch † Con 1 Vn, K.207; Con 4 Vn, K.218; Rondo Vn, K.373 FON ▲ 9803 (13.97)

E. Kovacic (vn), E. Kovacic (cnd), Scottish CO † Adagio Vn, K.261; Con 5 Vn, K.219 ICC ▲ 6701112 (9.97)

G. Kremer (vn), N. Harnoncourt (cnd), Vienna PO † Con 1 Vn, K.207; Con 3 Vn, K.216; Con 4 Vn, K.218; Con 5 Vn, K.219; Sinf concertante Vn, K.364 DEUT (2CD) 2-▲ 453043 [DDD] (17.97)

S. Kuijken (vn), La Petite Bande † Con 1 Vn, K.207; Concertone Vns, K.190 DNN ▲ 18066 (16.97)

C. Lin (vn), R. Leppard (cnd), English CO † Con 7 Vn, K.271a; Rondo Vn, K.373 SNYC ▲ 44913 [DDD] (11.97)

T. Nishizaki (vn), J. Wildner (cnd), Capella Istropolitana *(rec Apr 3-9, 1990)* † Con 1 Vn, K.207; Rondo Vn; Saint-Saëns:Andante Vn NXIN ▲ 550414 [DDD] (5.97)

I. Perlman (vn), J. Levine (cnd), Vienna PO † Con 4 Vn, K.218 DEUT ▲ 15975 [DDD] (16.97)

I. Perlman (vn), J. Levine (cnd), Vienna PO † Adagio Vn, K.261; Con 1 Vn, K.207; Con 3 Vn, K.216; Con 4 Vn, K.218; Con 5 Vn, K.219; Rondo Vn; Rondo Vn, K.373 DEUT (Masters) 2-▲ 45535 [DDD] (19.97)

V. Repin (vn), Y. Menuhin (cnd), Vienna CO † Con 3 Vn, K.216; Con 5 Vn, K.219 ERAT ▲ 21660 (16.97)

V. Spivakov (vn), V. Spivakov (cnd), English CO † Con 1 Vn, K.207; Sinf concertante Vn, K.364 RYLC ▲ 70121

S. Standage (vn), C. Hogwood (cnd), Academy of Ancient Music † Con 1 Vn, K.207; Con 3 Vn, K.216; Con 4 Vn, K.218; Con 5 Vn, K.219 PLON (Double Decker) 2-▲ 455721 (17.97)

I. Stern (vn), G. Szell (cnd), Cleveland Orch ("Isaac Stern: A Life in Music") † Adagio Vn, K.261; Con 1 Vn, K.207; Con 3 Vn, K.216; Con 4 Vn, K.218; Con 5 Vn, K.219; Concertone Vns, K.190; Rondo Vn, K.373; Sinf concertante Vn, K.364 SNYC 3-▲ 66475 (33.97)

I. Stern (vn), G. Szell (cnd), Columbia SO † Adagio Vn, K.261; Con 1 Vn, K.207; Con 3 Vn, K.216; Con 4 Vn, K.218; Con 5 Vn, K.219; Rondo Vn, K.373; Serenade Vn SNYC 2-▲ 42494 [ADD] (31.97)

I. Stern (vn), G. Szell (cnd), Columbia SO † Con 1 Vn, K.207; Con 3 Vn, K.216; Con 4 Vn, K.218; Con 5 Vn, K.219 SNYC 2-▲ 45614 (14.97)

J. Suk (vn), J. Suk (cnd), Suk CO ("Josef Suk Plays Mozart") † Con 3 Vn, K.216; Sinf concertante Vn, K.364 VC ▲ 7001 [DDD] (13.97)

M. Tenenbaum (vn), R. Kapp (cnd), Czech Chamber PO † Con 1 Vn, K.207; Con 4 Vn, K.218 ESSY ▲ 1070 (16.97)

E. Verhey (vn), E. Marturet (cnd), Concertgebouw CO † Adagio Vn, K.261; Con 1 Vn, K.207; Con 3 Vn, K.216; Con 4 Vn, K.218; Con 5 Vn, K.219; Concertone Vns, K.190; Rondo Vn; Rondo Vn, K.373; Sinf concertante Vn, K.364 FIGA 3-▲ 99077 (11.97)

R. Wenzel (vn), H. Adolph (cnd), Munich SO † Con 3 Vn, K.216; Con 4 Vn, K.218 PC ▲ 265008 [DDD] (2.97)

F. P. Zimmermann (vn), J. Faerber (cnd), Württemberg CO † Adagio Vn, K.261; Con 1 Vn, K.207; Con 3 Vn, K.216; Con 4 Vn, K.218; Con 5 Vn, K.219; Rondo Vn; Rondo Vn, K.373 EMIC 2-▲ 69355 (16.97)

P. Zukerman (vn), P. Zukerman (cnd), St. Paul CO † Con 1 Vn, K.207; Con 3 Vn, K.216 SNYC (Essential Classics) ▲ 46539 [ADD] (7.97) ▮ 46539 [ADD] (3.98)

Concerto No. 3 in G for Violin & Orchestra, K.216 (1775)

S. Accardo (vn), S. Accardo (cnd), Prague Chamber Orch † Adagio Vn, K.261; Con 5 Vn, K.219; Rondo Vn FON ▲ 9805 (13.97)

C. Altenburger (vn), H. Winschermann (cnd) † Con 4 Vn, K.218; Con 5 Vn, K.219 LALI ▲ 15525 [DDD] (3.97)

C. Altenburger (vn), H. Winschermann (cnd) [selections] ("The Great Violin Concertos") † Con 4 Vn, K.218; Con 5 Vn, K.219; Sinf concertante Vn, K.364 LALI ▲ 15650 [DDD] (3.97)

C. Altenburger (vn), H. Winschermann (cnd) † Con 4 Vn, K.218; Fant Mechanical Org, K.608 LALI ▲ 15879 [DDD] (3.97)

D. Brazda (vn), C. Cantieri (cnd), Mozart Festival Orch † Con 2 Vn, K.211; Con 4 Vn, K.218 PC ▲ 265008 [DDD] (2.97)

A. Dumay (vn), A. Dumay (cnd), Salzburg Camerata Academica † Con 4 Vn, K.218; Con 5 Vn, K.219 DGRM ▲ 457645 [DDD]

Z. Francescatti (vn), B. Walter (cnd), Columbia SO *(rec Hollywood, CA, Dec 10-17, 1958)* ("Volume 2") † Con 4 Vn, K.218; Kleine Nachtmusik, K.525 SNYC (Bruno Walter Edition) ▲ 64468 [ADD] (10.97)

J. Fuchs (vn), E. Goossens (cnd), London SO *(rec Walthamstow Assembly Hall London)* ("Sampler") † Sym 40, K.550; A. Dvořák:Sym 9; F. Schubert:Sym 8; R. Schumann:Con Pno in a, Op. 54 EVC 2-▲ 9045 [AAD] (19.97)

B. Huberman (vn), I. Dobrowen (cnd), Vienna PO *(rec 1934)* † J. S. Bach:Cons Vn (comp) PHS ▲ 9341 [AAD] (18.97)

B. Huberman (vn), I. Dobrowen (cnd), Vienna PO *(rec 1934)* † J. S. Bach:Con 1 Vn; Beethoven:Con Vn ENT (Strings) ▲ 99321 (16.97)

E. Kovacic (vn), E. Kovacic (cnd), Scottish CO *(rec Aug 1990)* † Con 1 Vn, K.207; Con 7 Vn, K.271a INMP ▲ 6700822 [DDD] (9.97)

G. Kremer (vn), N. Harnoncourt (cnd), Vienna PO † Con 1 Vn, K.207; Con 2 Vn, K.211; Con 4 Vn, K.218; Con 5 Vn, K.219; Sinf concertante Vn, K.364 DEUT (2CD) 2-▲ 453043 [DDD] (17.97)

C. Lin (vn), R. Leppard (cnd), English CO † Adagio Vn, K.261; Con 5 Vn, K.219 SNYC ▲ 42364 [DDD] (11.97)

L. Maazel (vn), L. Maazel (cnd), English CO ("Mozart Violin Concertos") † Cassation Obs, K.100; Cassation Obs, K.63; Cassation Obs, K.99; Con 5 Vn, K.219 KLAV ▲ 11046 [ADD] (18.97)

A.-S. Mutter (vn), H. von Karajan (cnd), Berlin PO † Con 5 Vn, K.219; Beethoven:Con Vn; J. Brahms:Con Vn; Bruch:Con 1 Vn, Op. 26; Mendelssohn (-Bartholdy):Con Vn & Orch, Op. 64 DEUT 4-▲ 15565 [ADD/DDD] (38.97)

A.-S. Mutter (vn), H. von Karajan (cnd), Berlin PO † Con 5 Vn, K.219 DEUT ▲ 29814 [ADD] (7.97)

A.-S. Mutter (vn), H. von Karajan (cnd), Berlin PO † Con 5 Vn, K.219 DEUT (Originals) ▲ 457746 (11.97)

T. Nishizaki (vn), S. Gunzenhauser (cnd), Capella Istropolitana † Adagio Vn, K.261; Con 5 Vn, K.219; Rondo Vn, K.373 NXIN ▲ 550418 [DDD] (5.97)

D. Oistrakh (vn), K. Ančerl (cnd), Czech PO † Lalo:Sym espagnole, Op. 21; M. Ravel:Tzigane SUR (Czech Philharmonic) ▲ 111936 [AAD]

D. Oistrakh (vn), M. Sargent (cnd), Philharmonia Orch † Beethoven:Con Vn, Vc, Pno, Op. 56; J. Brahms:Con Vn & Vc, Op. 102; S. Prokofiev:Con 2 Vn, Op. 63 EMIC 2-▲ 69331 (16.97)

I. Perlman (vn), J. Levine (cnd), Vienna PO † Con 4 Vn, K.218; Rondo Vn; Rondo Vn, K.373 DEUT (3D Classics) ▲ 31282 [DDD] (9.97)

I. Perlman (vn), J. Levine (cnd), Vienna PO † Adagio Vn, K.261; Con 1 Vn, K.207; Con 2 Vn, K.211; Con 4 Vn, K.218; Con 5 Vn, K.219; Rondo Vn; Rondo Vn, K.373 DEUT (Masters) 2-▲ 45535 [DDD] (19.97)

V. Příhoda (vn) ("Vasa Prihoda Vol 2") † A. Dvořák:Con Vn PODM ▲ 1002

V. Repin (vn), Y. Menuhin (cnd), Vienna CO † Con 2 Vn, K.211; Con 5 Vn, K.219 ERAT ▲ 21660 (16.97)

D. Sitkovetsky (vn), D. Sitkovetsky (cnd) ("Mozart Masterworks") † Con Fl & Hp, K.299; Con 5 Vn, K.219; Kleine Nachtmusik, K.525; Minuets, K.568; Music of Mozart; Sym 32, K.318; Sym 35, K.385; Sym 41, K.551; 11 Contredanses; 13 German Dances NOVA 5-▲ 150060 [DDD] (51.97)

K. Sjøgren (vn), M. Schønwandt (cnd), Copenhagen Collegium Musicum † Con 5 Vn, K.219 BIS ▲ 282 [DDD] (17.97)

S. Standage (vn), C. Hogwood (cnd), Academy of Ancient Music † Con 1 Vn, K.207; Con 2 Vn, K.211; Con 4 Vn, K.218; Con 5 Vn, K.219 PLON (Double Decker) 2-▲ 455721 (17.97)

A. Stang (vn), L. Korkhin (cnd), Orch del'Arte † Adagio & Fugue Strs, K.546; Con 5 Vn, K.219 SNYC ▲ 64331 [DDD] (4.97)

I. Stern (vn), G. Szell (cnd), Cleveland Orch ("Isaac Stern: A Life in Music") † Adagio Vn, K.261; Con 1 Vn, K.207; Con 2 Vn, K.211; Con 4 Vn, K.218; Con 5 Vn, K.219; Concertone Vns, K.190; Rondo Vn, K.373; Sinf concertante Vn, K.364 SNYC 3-▲ 66475 (33.97)

I. Stern (vn), G. Szell (cnd), Columbia SO † Adagio Vn, K.261; Con 1 Vn, K.207; Con 2 Vn, K.211; Con 4 Vn, K.218; Con 5 Vn, K.219; Rondo Vn, K.373; Serenade Vn SNYC 2-▲ 42494 [ADD] (31.97)

I. Stern (vn), G. Szell (cnd), Columbia SO † Con 1 Vn, K.207; Con 2 Vn, K.211; Con 4 Vn, K.218; Con 5 Vn, K.219 SNYC 2-▲ 45614 (14.97)

J. Suk (vn), J. Suk (cnd), Suk CO ("Josef Suk Plays Mozart") † Con 2 Vn, K.211; Sinf concertante Vn, K.364 VC ▲ 7001 [DDD] (13.97)

R. Terakado (vn), S. Kuijken (cnd), La Petite Bande † Sinf concertante Vn, K.364 DNN ▲ 78837 (16.97)

E. Verhey (vn), E. Marturet (cnd), Concertgebouw CO † Adagio Vn, K.261; Con 1 Vn, K.207; Con 2 Vn, K.211; Con 4 Vn, K.218; Con 5 Vn, K.219; Concertone Vns, K.190; Rondo Vn; Rondo Vn, K.373; Sinf concertante Vn, K.364 FIGA 3-▲ 99077 (11.97)

F. P. Zimmermann (vn), J. Faerber (cnd), Württemberg CO † Adagio Vn, K.261; Con 1 Vn, K.207; Con 2 Vn, K.211; Con 4 Vn, K.218; Con 5 Vn, K.219; Rondo Vn; Rondo Vn, K.373 EMIC 2-▲ 69355 (16.97)

P. Zukerman (vn), P. Zukerman (cnd), St. Paul CO † Con 1 Vn, K.207; Con 2 Vn, K.211 SNYC (Essential Classics) ▲ 46539 [ADD] (7.97) ▮ 46539 [ADD] (3.98)

Concerto No. 4 in D for Violin & Orchestra, K.218 (1775)

S. Accardo (vn), S. Accardo (cnd), Prague Chamber Orch † Con 1 Vn, K.207; Con 2 Vn, K.211; Rondo Vn, K.373 FON ▲ 9803 (13.97)

C. Altenberger (vn), H. Winschermann (cnd) † Con 3 Vn, K.216; Con 5 Vn, K.219 LALI ▲ 15525 [DDD] (3.97)

C. Altenberger (vn), H. Winschermann (cnd) ("The Great Violin Concertos") † Con 3 Vn, K.216; Con 5 Vn, K.219; Sinf concertante Vn, K.364 LALI ▲ 15650 [DDD] (3.97)

MOZART, WOLFGANG AMADEUS (cont.)

Concerto No. 4 in D for Violin & Orchestra, K.218 (1775) (cont.)

C. Altenberger (vn), H. Winschermann (cnd) † Con 3 Vn, K.216; Fant Mechanical Org, K.608 LALI ▲ 15879 [DDD] (3.97)

D. Brazda (vn), C. Cantieri (cnd), Mozart Festival Orch † Con 2 Vn, K.211; Con 3 Vn, K.216 PC ▲ 265008 [DDD] (2.97)

A. Dumay (vn), A. Dumay (cnd), Salzburg Camerata Academica † Con 3 Vn, K.216; Con 5 Vn, K.219 DGRM ▲ 457645 [DDD]

Z. Francescatti (vn), B. Walter (cnd), Columbia SO *(rec Hollywood, CA, Dec 10-17, 1958)* ("Volume 2") † Con 3 Vn, K.216; Kleine Nachtmusik, K.525 SNYC (Bruno Walter Edition) ▲ 64468 [ADD] (10.97)

D. Garrett (vn), C. Abbado (cnd), CO of Europe † Con 7 Vn, K.271a; Son 32 Vn & Pno, K.454 DGRM ▲ 447110 [DDD] (18.97)

B. Huberman (vn), B. Walter (cnd), Philharmonic SO *(rec Dec, 1945)* † P. Tchaikovsky:Con Vn MUA ▲ 4299 (10.97)

F. Kreisler (vn) *(rec 1924-27)* † Beethoven:Con Vn; J. Brahms:Con Vn; Mendelssohn (-Bartholdy):Con Vn & Orch, Op. 64 MUA ▲ 4290 (20.97)

F. Kreisler (vn), L. Ronald (cnd), London SO *(rec 1924)* † J. S. Bach:Con Vns; Beethoven:Con Vn; J. Brahms:Con Vn; Mendelssohn (-Bartholdy):Con Vn & Orch, Op. 64 PHS 2-▲ 9996 [AAD] (33.97)

G. Kremer (vn), N. Harnoncourt (cnd), Vienna PO † Con 1 Vn, K.207; Con 2 Vn, K.211; Con 3 Vn, K.216; Con 5 Vn, K.219; Sinf concertante Vn, K.364 DEUT (2CD) 2-▲ 453043 [DDD] (17.97)

S. Kuijken (vn) [cadenzas by S. Kuijken] *(rec May 10-13, 1996)* † Con 5 Vn, K.219 DNN ▲ 18021 [DDD] (16.97)

C. Lin (vn), R. Leppard (cnd), English CO † Con 1 Vn, K.207; Rondo Vn SNYC ▲ 44503 [DDD] (11.97)

A. Lizzio (cnd), Mozart Festival Orch † Sym 28, K.200; Sym 33, K.319 PC ▲ 265053 [DDD] (2.97)

E. Morini (vn) *(rec 1927)* ("Erica Morini Plays Mozart") † Con 5 Vn, K.219; Divert 17 Hns Strs, K.334 ARBT ▲ 107 (16.97)

T. Nishizaki (vn), S. Gunzenhauser (cnd), Capella Istropolitana *(rec Nov 1989)* † Sinf concertante Vn, K.364 NXIN ▲ 550332 [DDD] (5.97)

J. Novak (vn), V. Talich (cnd), Czech PO *(rec 1954-55)* † J. S. Bach:Con 8 Hpd, BWV 1059; G. F. Handel:Cons Ob, HWV 301, 302a & 287 SUR ▲ 111906 [AAD]

I. Perlman (vn), J. Levine (cnd), Vienna PO † Con 2 Vn, K.211 DEUT ▲ 15975 [DDD] (16.97)

I. Perlman (vn), J. Levine (cnd), Vienna PO † Con 3 Vn, K.216; Rondo Vn; Rondo Vn, K.373 DEUT (3D Classics) ▲ 31282 [DDD] (9.97)

I. Perlman (vn), J. Levine (cnd), Vienna PO † Adagio Vn, K.261; Con 1 Vn, K.207; Con 2 Vn, K.211; Con 3 Vn, K.216; Con 5 Vn, K.219; Rondo Vn; Rondo Vn, K.373 DEUT (Masters) 2-▲ 45535 [DDD] (19.97)

W. Schneiderhan (vn), H. Rosbaud (cnd), Berlin PO *(rec Jesus-Christus Church Berlin, Germany, Mar 1956)* † J. Haydn:Sym 104; Sym 92 DEUT (The Originals) ▲ 457720 [ADD] (11.97)

D. Sitkovetsky (vn), D. Sitkovetsky (cnd), English CO † Con 5 Vn, K.219 NOVA ▲ 150007 [DDD] (16.97)

S. Standage (vn), C. Hogwood (cnd), Academy of Ancient Music † Con 1 Vn, K.207; Con 2 Vn, K.211; Con 3 Vn, K.216; Con 5 Vn, K.219 PLON (Double Decker) 2-▲ 455721 (17.97)

I. Stern (vn), A. Schneider (cnd), English CO † Con 5 Vn, K.219 SNYC ▲ 37808 [ADD] (9.97) ▮ 37808 [ADD] (3.98)

I. Stern (vn), G. Szell (cnd), Cleveland Orch ("Isaac Stern: A Life in Music") † Adagio Vn, K.261; Con 1 Vn, K.207; Con 2 Vn, K.211; Con 3 Vn, K.216; Con 5 Vn, K.219; Concertone Vns, K.190; Rondo Vn, K.373; Sinf concertante Vn, K.364 SNYC 3-▲ 66475 (33.97)

I. Stern (vn), G. Szell (cnd), Columbia SO † Adagio Vn, K.261; Con 1 Vn, K.207; Con 2 Vn, K.211; Con 3 Vn, K.216; Con 5 Vn, K.219; Rondo Vn, K.373; Serenade Vn SNYC 2-▲ 42494 [ADD] (31.97)

I. Stern (vn), G. Szell (cnd), Columbia SO † Con 1 Vn, K.207; Con 2 Vn, K.211; Con 3 Vn, K.216; Con 5 Vn, K.219 SNYC 2-▲ 45614 (14.97)

A. Szigeti (vn), T. Beecham (cnd), London PO *(rec Oct 8, 1934 for Columbia)* † Mendelssohn (-Bartholdy):Con Vn & Orch, Op. 64; S. Prokofiev:Con 1 Vn, Op. 19 PHS ▲ 9377 [AAD] (18.97)

J. Szigeti (vn), T. Beecham (cnd), London PO *(rec 1947)* † Beethoven:Con Vn ENT (Strings) ▲ 99367 (16.97)

M. Tenenbaum (vn), R. Kapp (cnd), Czech Chamber PO † Con 1 Vn, K.207; Con 2 Vn, K.211 ESSY ▲ 1070 (16.97)

E. Verhey (vn), E. Marturet (cnd), Concertgebouw CO † Adagio Vn, K.261; Con 1 Vn, K.207; Con 2 Vn, K.211; Con 3 Vn, K.216; Con 5 Vn, K.219; Concertone Vns, K.190; Rondo Vn; Rondo Vn, K.373; Sinf concertante Vn, K.364 FIGA 3-▲ 99077 (11.97)

F. P. Zimmermann (vn), J. Faerber (cnd), Württemberg CO † Adagio Vn, K.261; Con 1 Vn, K.207; Con 2 Vn, K.211; Con 3 Vn, K.216; Con 5 Vn, K.219; Rondo Vn; Rondo Vn, K.373 EMIC 2-▲ 69355 (16.97)

P. Zukerman (vn), P. Zukerman (cnd), St. Paul CO † Con 5 Vn, K.219 SNYC (Essential Classics) ▲ 46540 [ADD] (7.97) ▮ 46540 [ADD] (3.98)

Concerto No. 5 in A for Violin & Orchestra, K.219 (1775)

S. Accardo (vn), S. Accardo (cnd), Prague Chamber Orch † Adagio Vn, K.261; Con 3 Vn, K.216; Rondo Vn FON ▲ 9805 (13.97)

C. Altenberger (vn), H. Winschermann (cnd) † Con 3 Vn, K.216; Con 4 Vn, K.218 LALI ▲ 15525 [DDD] (3.97)

C. Altenberger (vn), H. Winschermann (cnd) † Sinf concertante Vn, K.364 LALI ▲ 15880 [DDD] (3.97)

C. Altenberger (vn), H. Winschermann (cnd) [selections] ("The Great Violin Concertos") † Con 3 Vn, K.216; Con 4 Vn, K.218; Sinf concertante Vn, K.364 LALI ▲ 15650 [DDD] (3.97)

B. Belkin (vn), Salzburg Chamber Soloists *(rec Mozarteum Grosse Saal Salzburg, Feb 21-23, 1994)* † Divert 7 Hns, K.205; Sinf concertante Vn, K.364 DNN ▲ 78918 [DDD] (16.97)

A. Busch (vn), Adolf Busch Chamber Players † Adagio & Fugue Strs, K.546; Con 14 Pno, K.449; Serenade 6 Orch, K.239 PHS ▲ 9278 (17.97)

A. Dumay (vn), A. Dumay (cnd), Salzburg Camerata Academica † Con 3 Vn, K.216; Con 4 Vn, K.218 DGRM ▲ 457645 [DDD]

J. Heifetz (vn), J. Barbirolli (cnd), London PO *(rec 1934-40)* ("Jascha Heifetz: Concerto Recordings, Vol. 1") † Glazunov:Con Vn; Sibelius:Con Vn; P. Tchaikovsky:Con Vn PHS ▲ 9157 [ADD] (33.97)

J. Heifetz (vn), J. Barbirolli (cnd), London PO *(rec Feb 23, 1934 for HMV)* BID ▲ 12 [AAD]

J. Heifetz (vn), J. Barbirolli (cnd), London PO *(rec 1934-40)* † Beethoven:Con Vn ENT (Strings) ▲ 99366 (16.97)

J. Heifetz (vn), J. Barbirolli (cnd), London PO † P. Tchaikovsky:Con Vn IMMM ▲ 37016 (6.97)

A. Ioffe (vn), A. Titov (cnd), St. Petersburg Classical Music Studio Orch † Adagio & Fugue Strs, K.546; Con 3 Vn, K.216 SNYC ▲ 64331 [DDD] (4.97)

O. Kagan (vn), D. Oistrakh (cnd), Moscow Philharmony CO *(rec Moscow, Russia, Feb 1970)* † Con 7 Vn, K.271a CONE ▲ 9405 [ADD] (16.97)

E. Kovacic (vn), Scottish CO † Adagio Vn, K.261; Con 2 Vn, K.211 ICC ▲ 6701112 (9.97)

G. Kremer (vn), N. Harnoncourt (cnd), Vienna PO † Con 1 Vn, K.207; Con 2 Vn, K.211; Con 3 Vn, K.216; Con 4 Vn, K.218; Sinf concertante Vn, K.364 DEUT (2CD) 2-▲ 453043 [DDD] (17.97)

C. Lin (vn), R. Leppard (cnd), English CO † Adagio Vn, K.261; Con 3 Vn, K.216 SNYC ▲ 42364 [DDD] (11.97)

L. Maazel (vn), L. Maazel (cnd), English CO ("Mozart Violin Concertos") † Cassation Obs, K.100; Cassation Obs, K.63; Cassation Obs, K.99; Con 3 Vn, K.216 KLAV ▲ 11046 [ADD] (18.97)

E. Morini (vn) ("Erica Morini Plays Mozart") † Con 4 Vn, K.218; Divert 17 Hns Strs, K.334 ARBT ▲ 107 (16.97)

E. Morini (vn), P. Casals (cnd), Perpignan Festival Orch *(rec Perpignan France, July 13, 1951)* † Sinf concertante Vn, K.364 SNYC (The Casals Edition) ▲ 58983 [ADD] (10.97)

E. Morini (vn), G. Szell (cnd), RTF National Orch † Sym 35, K.385; J. Haydn:Sym 92 SNYC (Festspiel Dokumente: Salzburger Festspiele) ▲ 68446 (10.97)

A.-S. Mutter (vn), H. von Karajan (cnd), Berlin PO † Con 3 Vn, K.216; Beethoven:Con Vn; J. Brahms:Con Vn; Bruch:Con 1 Vn, Op. 26; Mendelssohn (-Bartholdy):Con Vn & Orch, Op. 64 DEUT 4-▲ 15565 [ADD/DDD] (38.97)

A.-S. Mutter (vn), H. von Karajan (cnd), Berlin PO † Con 3 Vn, K.216 DEUT ▲ 29814 [ADD] (7.97)

A.-S. Mutter (vn), H. von Karajan (cnd), Berlin PO † Con 3 Vn, K.216 DEUT (Originals) ▲ 457746 (11.97)

T. Nishizaki (vn), S. Gunzenhauser (cnd), Capella Istropolitana † Adagio Vn, K.261; Con 3 Vn, K.216; Rondo Vn, K.373 NXIN ▲ 550418 [DDD] (5.97)

D. Oistrakh (vn), K. Kondrashin (cnd), USSR State Orch *(rec 1958-59)* † P. Tchaikovsky:Con Vn TUXE ▲ 1052 [ADD] (10.97)

D. Oistrakh (vn), E. Mravinsky (cnd), Leningrad PO † Con 25 Pno, K.503 STRV ▲ 10005 [ADD] (13.97)

D. Oistrakh (vn), F. Konwitschny (cnd), Leipzig Gewandhaus Orch ("Vol. II") † Wieniawski:Con 2 Vn, Op. 22 BER (Dokumente) ▲ 2131 [ADD]

I. Perlman (vn), J. Levine (cnd), Vienna PO † Adagio Vn, K.261; Con 1 Vn, K.207; Con 2 Vn, K.211; Con 3 Vn, K.216; Con 4 Vn, K.218; Rondo Vn; Rondo Vn, K.373 DEUT (Masters) 2-▲ 45535 [DDD] (19.97)

V. Repin (vn), Y. Menuhin (cnd), Vienna CO † Con 2 Vn, K.211; Con 3 Vn, K.216 ERAT ▲ 21660 (16.97)

W. Schneiderhan (vn), W. Schneiderhan (cnd), Berlin PO *(rec 1962-67)* † Beethoven:Con Vn DEUT (The Originals) ▲ 47403 [ADD] (11.97)

D. Sitkovetsky (vn), D. Sitkovetsky (cnd) ("Mozart Masterworks") † Con Fl & Hp, K.299; Con 3 Vn, K.216; Kleine Nachtmusik, K.525; Minuets, K.568; Music of Mozart; Sym 32, K.318; Sym 35, K.385; Sym 41, K.551; 11 Contredanses; 13 German Dances NOVA 5-▲ 150060 [DDD] (51.97)

D. Sitkovetsky (vn), D. Sitkovetsky (cnd), English CO † Con 4 Vn, K.218 NOVA ▲ 150007 [DDD] (16.97)

MOZART, WOLFGANG AMADEUS (cont.)
Concerto No. 5 in A for Violin & Orchestra, K.219 (1775) (cont.)
K. Sjøgren (vn), M. Schønwandt (cnd), Copenhagen Collegium Musicum † Con 3 Vn, K.216 BIS ▲ 282 [DDD] (17.97)
S. Standage (vn), C. Hogwood (cnd), Academy of Ancient Music † Con 1 Vn, K.207; Con 2 Vn, K.211; Con 3 Vn, K.216; Con 4 Vn, K.218 PLON (Double Decker) 2-▲ 455721 (17.97)
I. Stern (vn), G. Szell (cnd), Cleveland Orch ("Isaac Stern: A Life in Music") † Adagio Vn, K.261; Con 1 Vn, K.207; Con 2 Vn, K.211; Con 3 Vn, K.216; Con 4 Vn, K.218; Concertone Vns, K.190; Rondo Vn, K.373; Sinf concertante Vn, K.364 SNYC 3-▲ 66475 (33.97)
I. Stern (vn), G. Szell (cnd), Columbia SO † Con 4 Vn, K.218 SNYC ▲ 37808 [ADD] (9.97) ▮ 37808 [ADD] (3.98)
I. Stern (vn), G. Szell (cnd), Columbia SO † Adagio Vn, K.261; Con 1 Vn, K.207; Con 2 Vn, K.211; Con 3 Vn, K.216; Con 4 Vn, K.218; Rondo Vn, K.373; Serenade Vn SNYC 2-▲ 42494 [ADD] (31.97)
I. Stern (vn), G. Szell (cnd), Columbia SO † Con 1 Vn, K.207; Con 2 Vn, K.211; Con 3 Vn, K.216; Con 4 Vn, K.218 SNYC 2-▲ 45614 (14.97)
J. Szigeti (vn), D. Mitropoulos (cnd), New York PO *(rec live, 1948)* † J. Brahms:Con Vn IN ▲ 1417 [ADD] (15.97)
R. Terakado (vn) [cadenzas by R. Terakado] *(rec May 10-13, 1996)* † Con 4 Vn, K.218 DNN ▲ 18021 [DDD] (16.97)
J. Thibaud (vn), C. Munch (cnd), Paris Conservatory Société des Concerts Orch *(rec 1941)* † Con 21 Pno, K.467; Con 23 Pno, K.488; Sons Vn & Pno (misc) BID ▲ 114 [ADD] (16.97)
E. Verhey (vn), E. Marturet (cnd), Concertgebouw CO † Adagio Vn, K.261; Con 1 Vn, K.207; Con 2 Vn, K.211; Con 3 Vn, K.216; Con 4 Vn, K.218; Concertone Vns, K.190; Rondo Vn; Rondo Vn, K.373; Sinf concertante Vn, K.364 FIGA 3-▲ 99077 (11.97)
F. P. Zimmermann (vn), J. Faerber (cnd), Württemberg CO † Adagio Vn, K.261; Con 1 Vn, K.207; Con 2 Vn, K.211; Con 3 Vn, K.216; Con 4 Vn, K.218; Rondo Vn; Rondo Vn, K.373 EMIC 2-▲ 69355 (16.97)
P. Zukerman (vn), P. Zukerman (cnd), St. Paul CO † Con 4 Vn, K.218 SNYC (Essential Classics) ▲ 46540 [ADD] (7.97) ▮ 46540 [ADD] (3.98)

Concerto No. 6 in E♭ for Violin & Orchestra [spurious], K.268 (1780)
D. Klöcker (cl), M. Lajcik (cnd), Prague CO *(rec Domovina Prague, Czech Republic, May 28-31, 1997)* † Con Cl, K.622; Vars Cl Orch MDG ▲ 3010755 [DDD] (17.97)

Concerto No. 7 in D for Violin & Orchestra [spurious], K.271a (1777)
M. Erxleben (vn), M. Erxleben (cnd), New Berlin CO † Adagio Vn, K.261; Con 6 Pno, K.238; Rondo Vn, K.373 LALI ▲ 15881 [DDD] (3.97)
M. Fikhtenkholts (vn), D. Oistrakh (cnd), Moscow Philharmony CO *(rec Moscow, Russia, Apr 1971)* † Con 5 Vn, K.219 CONE ▲ 9405 [ADD] (16.97)
D. Garrett (vn), C. Abbado (cnd), CO of Europe † Con 4 Vn, K.218; Son 32 Vn & Pno, K.454 DGRM ▲ 447110 [DDD] (18.97)
E. Kovacic (vn), E. Kovacic (cnd), Scottish CO † Con 1 Vn, K.207; Con 3 Vn, K.216 INMP ▲ 6700822 [DDD] (9.97)
H. Kurosaki (vn), U. Björlin (cnd), Cappella Coloniensis ("Cappella Edition") † Sym 25, K.183; Sym 31, K.297 CAPO ▲ 10620 [DDD] (11.97)
C. Lin (vn), R. Leppard (cnd), English CO † Con 2 Vn, K.211; Rondo Vn, K.373 SNYC ▲ 44913 [DDD] (11.97)

Concerto in D for Violin & Orchestra [spurious], K.Anh.294a, "Adelaide"
Y. Menuhin (vn), P. Monteux (cnd), Paris SO † Lalo:Sym espagnole, Op. 21 ENT (Strings) ▲ 99384 (16.97)
Y. Menuhin (vn), P. Monteux (cnd), Paris SO *(rec 1934)* ("Monteux, Vol. 3") † A. Bazzini:Ronde des lutins, Op. 25; Nováček:Perpetuum mobile; Paganini:Con 1 Vn, M.S. 21; Moto perpetuo Vn, M.S. 66 LYS ▲ 479 (17.97)

Concerto No. 3 in G for Violin & Orchestra, K.216 (1775)
various artists—Adagio † Con Cl, K.622; Con 20 Pno, K.466; Con 21 Pno, K.467; Così fan tutte (ov); Kleine Nachtmusik, K.525; Son 11 Pno, K.331; Sym 40, K.550; Sym 41, K.551; Zauberflöte (ov) RCAV ▲ 60829 (10.97) ▮ 60829 (5.98)
various artists [excerpt; plus others] † B. Bartók:Con Orch, Sz.116; J. Brahms:Vars on a Theme by Haydn; G. Holst:Planets, Op. 32; R. Strauss:Also sprach Zarathustra, Op. 30; Salome (dance of the 7 veils) MTAL ▲ 48095 (6.97)
various artists [excerpt] † J. S. Bach:Sons & Partitas Vn; Beethoven:Son 9 Vn, Op. 47; Mendelssohn (-Bartholdy):Con Vn & Orch, Op. 64; Tartini:Son Vn & Pno; P. Tchaikovsky:Con Vn MTAL ▲ 48099 (6.97)
various artists—Adagio † Andante Fl, K.315; Con Cl, K.622; Con Fl & Hp, K.299; Con 21 Pno, K.467; Così fan tutte (sels); Kleine Nachtmusik, K.525; Qt in A Cl Strs, K.581; Serenade; Son 13 Pno, K.333 RCAV ▮ 63329 (5.98) ▲ 63329 (11.97)
artists unknown—Adagio ("Adagios") † Adagio Pno, K.540; Adagio Vn, K.261; Con Cl, K.622; Con Fl & Hp, K.299; Con 2 Hn, K.417; Con 20 Pno, K.466; Con 21 Pno, K.467; Con 23 Pno, K.488; Con 26 Pno, K.537; Con 27 Pno, K.595; Con 3 Hn, K.447; Diverts Str Qt, K.136-138; Kleine Nachtmusik, K.525; Qnt Cl, K.581; Serenade; Serenade Ww, K.388/384a; Sinf concertante Vn, K.364; Son 12 Pno, K.332; Son 16 Pno, K.545; Sym 40, K.550; Sym 41, K.551 DECC (2-Fers) 2-▲ 460191 (17.97)

Concertone in C for 2 Violins & Orchestra, K.190 (1774)
A. Hobling (vn), G. Hobling (vn), B. Warchal (cnd), Slovak CO † Adagio Vn, K.261; Con 1 Vn, K.207; Con 2 Vn, K.211; Con 3 Vn, K.216; Con 4 Vn, K.218; Con 5 Vn, K.219; Rondo Vn; Rondo Vn, K.373; Sinf concertante Vn, K.364 FIGA 3-▲ 99077 (11.97)
M. Huggett (vn), P. Beznoisuk (vn), M. Huggett (cnd), Portland Baroque Orch *(rec Portland, OR, Apr 1997)* † Rondo Vn, K.373; Sinf concertante Vn, K.364 VCL (Veritas) ▲ 45290 [DDD] (17.97)
I. van Keulen (vn) † Sinf concertante Vn, K.364 KOCC ▲ 6443 (16.97)
S. Kuijken (vn), R. Terakado (vn), La Petite Bande † Con 1 Vn, K.207; Con 2 Vn, K.211 DNN ▲ 18066 (16.97)
R. Kussmaul (vn), V. Beths (vn) *(rec Mar 1991)* † Sinf concertante Vn, K.Anh.104; Sinf concertante Vn, K.364 CCL ▲ 3992 [DDD]
C. Lin (vn), J. Laredo (vn), R. Leppard (cnd), English CO † Sinf concertante Vn, K.364 SNYC ▲ 47693 (16.97)
I. Perlman (vn), P. Zukerman (vn), Z. Mehta (cnd), Israel PO † Sinf concertante Vn, K.364 DEUT ▲ 15486 [DDD] (16.97)
J. Rampal (fl), S. Kudo (fl), J. Rampal (cnd), Salzburg Mozarteum Orch † Cimarosa:Con Fls; A. Stamitz:Con Fls; Vivaldi:Con Fls, RV.533 SNYC ▲ 45930 [DDD] (16.97)
I. Stern (vn), P. Zukerman (vn), G. Szell (cnd), English CO ("Isaac Stern: A Life in Music") † Adagio Vn, K.261; Con 1 Vn, K.207; Con 2 Vn, K.211; Con 3 Vn, K.216; Con 4 Vn, K.218; Con 5 Vn, K.219; Rondo Vn, K.373; Sinf concertante Vn, K.364 SNYC 3-▲ 66475 (33.97)
O. Vlček (cnd), Prague Virtuosi † Don Giovanni (ov); Sym 38, K.504 DI ▲ 920201 [DDD] (5.97)

Contredanse in D for Piano, K.534, "Das Donnerwetter" (1788)
F. Litschauer (cnd), Vienna State Opera CO *(rec Vienna, Austria, 1952)* ("Contradances from Old Vienna") † Contredanses (5), K.609; German Dances (3), K.605; German Dances (4), K.602; German Dances (6), K.600; German Dances (6), K.606; Beethoven:Contredanses Orch, WoO 14; Dances Fls, WoO 17; F. Schubert:German Dances & Trios Str Qt, D.90 VC ▲ 8206 [ADD] (13.97)
G. Tintner (cnd), Nova Scotia SO † Contredanses (2), K.463; Contredanses (5), K.609; German Dances (3), K.605; German Dances (6), K.536; German Dances (6), K.567; Marches Orch, K.408; Minuets Orch, K.585; Minuets, K.601; Petits riens (sels) SMS (SM 5000) ▲ 5095 [DDD] (16.97)

Contredanses (2) in F & B♭ for Orchestra, K.463 (1784)
G. Tintner (cnd), Nova Scotia SO † Contredanse, K.534; Contredanses (5), K.609; German Dances (3), K.605; German Dances (6), K.536; German Dances (6), K.567; Marches Orch, K.408; Minuets Orch, K.585; Minuets, K.601; Petits riens (sels) SMS (SM 5000) ▲ 5095 [DDD] (16.97)

Contredanses (5) in C, E♭, D, C & G for Orchestra, K.609 (1791)
F. Litschauer (cnd), Vienna State Opera CO *(rec Vienna, Austria, 1952)* ("Contradances from Old Vienna") † Contredanse, K.534; German Dances (3), K.605; German Dances (4), K.602; German Dances (6), K.600; German Dances (6), K.606; Beethoven:Contredanses Orch, WoO 14; Dances Fls, WoO 17; F. Schubert:German Dances & Trios Str Qt, D.90 VC ▲ 8206 [ADD] (13.97)
G. Tintner (cnd), Nova Scotia SO † Contredanse, K.534; Contredanses (2), K.463; German Dances (3), K.605; German Dances (6), K.536; German Dances (6), K.567; Marches Orch, K.408; Minuets Orch, K.585; Minuets, K.601; Petits riens (sels) SMS (SM 5000) ▲ 5095 [DDD] (16.97)

Così fan tutte (opera in 2 acts) [lib L. Da Ponte], K.588 (1790)
A. C. Antonacci (sop—Fiordiligi), L. Cherici (sop—Despina), M. Bacelli (mez—Dorabella), R. Decker (ten—Ferrando), A. Dohmen (bar—Gugliemo), S. Bruscantini (b-bar—Don Alfonso), G. Kuhn (cnd), Marchigiano PO, Marchigiano Phil Chorus [ITA] *(rec live Teatro Lauro Rossi at the Fes, Aug 3, 1990)* ORF 3-▲ 243913 [DDD] (54.97)
J. Borowska (sop—Fiordiligi), P. Coles (sop—Despina), R. Yachmi-Caucig (cta—Dorabella), J. Dickie (ten—Ferrando), A. Martin (bar—Guglielmo), P. Mikuláš (bass—Don Alfonso), J. Wildner (cnd), Capella Istropolitana, Slovak Phil Chorus [ITA] *(rec 1990)* NXIN 3-▲ 660008 [DDD] (20.97)
C. Deutekom (sop), T. Troyanos (mez), R. Casellato (ten), P. Montarsolo (bass), P. Maag (cnd), Venice Theater Orch, Venice Theater Chorus *(rec live, 1968)* MONM (Teatro La Fenice) 2-▲ 10171 (36.97)
R. Fleming (sop—Fiordiligi), A. Scarabelli (sop—Despina), A. S. von Otter (mez—Dorabella), F. Lopardo (ten—Ferrando), O. Bar (bar—Guglielmo), M. Pertusi (bass—Don Alfonso), G. Solti (cnd), CO of Europe PLON 3-▲ 44174 (48.97)

MOZART, WOLFGANG AMADEUS (cont.)
Così fan tutte (opera in 2 acts) [lib L. Da Ponte], K.588 (1790) (cont.)
J. E. Gardiner (cnd), English Baroque Soloists, R. Mannion (sop), A. Roocroft (sop), E. James (mez), R. Trost (ten), R. Gilfry (bar), C. Feller (bass) PARC 3-▲ 37829 [DDD] (48.97)
L. Helletsgruber (sop—Dorabella), I. Eisinger (sop—Despina), I. Souez (sop—Fiordiligi), H. Nash (ten—Ferrando), J. Brownlee (bar—Don Alfonso), W. Domgraf-Fassbaender (bass—Guglielmo), F. Busch (cnd), Glyndebourne Festival Orch, Glyndebourne Festival Chorus *(rec June 25-28, 1935)* ARKA (The 78's) 2-▲ 78011 [ADD] (26.97)
R. Jacobs (cnd), Concerto Cologne, Cologne Chamber Choir, V. Gens (sop—Fiordiligi), G. Oddone (sop—Despina), B. Fink (cta—Dorabella), W. Güra (ten—Ferrando), M. Boone (ten—Guglielmo), P. Spagnoli (bar—Don Alfonso) HAM 3-▲ 951663 (52.97)
J. Levine (cnd), Vienna PO, Vienna State Opera Chorus, M. McLaughlin (sop), K. T. Kanawa (sop), A. Murray (mez), H. Blochwitz (ten), T. Hampson (bar), G. Furlanetto (bar) [ITA] DEUT 3-▲ 23897 [DDD] (48.97)
J. Malgoire (cnd), La Grande Écurie et la Chambre du Roy, S. Marin-Degor (sop—Despina), S. Fournier (sop—Fiordiligi), L. Polverelli (mez—Dorabella), S. Edwards (ten—Ferrando), N. Rivenq (bar—Guglielmo), P. Donnelly (bass—Don Alfonso) ASTR (The Da Ponte Trilogy) 3-▲ 8658 (36.97)
L. Price (sop), J. Raskin (sop), T. Troyanos (mez), G. Shirley (ten), S. Milnes (bar), E. Leinsdorf (cnd), New Philharmonia Orch, New Philharmonia Chorus [ITA] RCAV (Gold Seal) 3-▲ 6677 [ADD] (33.97)
E. Schwarzkopf (sop), H. Steffek (sop), C. Ludwig (mez), A. Kraus (ten), G. Taddei (bar), W. Berry (b-bar), K. Böhm (cnd), Philharmonia Orch, Philharmonia Chorus [ITA] EMIC (Studio) 3-▲ 69330 [ADD] (34.97)
F. Stiedry (cnd), Metropolitan Opera Orch, K. Adler (cnd) , E. Steber (sop—Fiordiligi), R. Peters (sop—Despina), B. Thebom (mez—Dorabella), R. Tucker (ten—Ferrando), F. Guarrera (bar—Guglielmo), L. Alvary (bass—Don Alfonso), J. Blatt (kbd) [ENG] *(rec New York City, NY, June 1952)* SNYC (Masterworks Heritage) ▲ 60652 [ADD] (32.97)
C. Vaness (sop), D. Ziegler (mez), C. Watson (cta), J. Aler (ten), D. Duesing (bar), C. Desderi (bar), B. Haitink (cnd), London PO, Glyndebourne Festival Chorus EMIA 3-▲ 47727 (47.97)

Così fan tutte (selections)
C. Bartoli (mez), G. Fischer (cnd), Vienna CO—Temerari; Come scoglio *(rec 1993)* ("A Portrait") † Clemenza di Tito (sels); Don Giovanni (sels); Nozze di Figaro (sels); G. Caccini:Amarilli mia bella; Parisotti:Se tu m'ami; G. Rossini:Cenerentola (sels); Maometto II (sels); Semiramide (sels); F. Schubert:Songs (misc colls) PLON ▲ 48300 [DDD] (17.97) ▮ 48300 [DDD] (11.98)
W. Bennett (fl), C. Benson (pno)—Adagio & Rondo *(rec Japan, Oct 21, 1987)* ("Poulenc: Flute Sonata") † Bizet:Arlésienne (sels); Carmen (sels); Chopin:Vars on Rossini; F. Poulenc:Son Fl; M. Ravel:Vocalise-étude en forme de habanera; Saint-Saëns:Odelette Fl, Op. 162; Widor:Suite Fl, Op. 34 CAMA ▲ 390 [DDD]
K. Böhm (cnd), Vienna PO ("Great Mozart Singers, Vol. 3: Opera Arias, 1961-82") † Don Giovanni (sels); Entführung aus dem Serail (sels); Idomeneo (sels); Nozze di Figaro (sels); Zauberflöte (sels) ORFE (Festspiel Dokumente) ▲ 394301 (16.97)
J. Borowska (sop—Fiordiligi), P. Coles (sop—Despina), R. Yachmi-Caucig (cta—Dorabella), J. Dickie (ten—Ferrando), A. Martin (bar—Gugliemo), P. Mikuláš (bass—Don Alfonso), M. Synkova (hpd), J. Wildner (cnd), Capella Istropolitana, Slovak Phil Chorus—La mia Dorabella capace non è; E la fede delle femine come l'araba fenice; Una bella serenata; Ah guarda, sorella; Vorrei dir, e cor non ho; Sento, o Dio; Bella vita militar; Soave sia il vento; Smanie implacabili; In uomini, in soldati; Alla bella Despinetta; Come scoglio; Non siate ritrosi; Un'aura amorosa; Una donna a quindici anni; Prenderò quel brunettino; La mano a me date; Ei Parte...Per pietà, ben mio, perdona, all'error; Donne mie, la fate a tanti; Fra gli amplessi in pochi istanti; Fortunato l'uom che prende *(rec Slovak Philharmonic Moyzes Hall Bratislava, Slovak Republic, 1990)* † Così fan tutte (ov) NXIN ▲ 553172 [DDD] (5.97)
J. Carden (sop), R. Brydon (cnd), Queensland PO *(rec 1996)* ("Great Opera Heroines") † Clemenza di Tito (sels); B. Britten:Peter Grimes (sels); A. Catalani:Wally (sels); G. Puccini:Arias; P. Tchaikovsky:Eugene Onegin (sels); Verdi:Traviata (sels) WALC ▲ 8026 [DDD] (16.97)
P. Curtin (sop) ("Phyllis Curtin: Opera Arias 1960-1968") † Nozze di Figaro (sels); G. Charpentier:Louise (sels); C. Floyd:Susannah (sels); U. Giordano:Andrea Chénier (sels); G. Puccini:Gianni Schicchi (sels); Rondine; R. Strauss:Salome (sels); Verdi:Traviata (sels) VAIA ▲ 1152 [AAD] (16.97)
I. Kirilova (sop—Dorabella), E. Seniglova (sop—Fiordiligi), I. Tannenbergerova (sop—Despina), O. Dohnányi (cnd), Bratislava Opera Orch—La mia Dorabella capace non è; Una bella serenata; Vorrei dir, e cor non ho; In uomini, in soldati; Smanie implacabili; Rivolgete a lui lo sguardo; E voi ridete?; Come scoglio; Una donna a quindici anni; Un'aura amorosa; Donne mie, la fate a tanti; E Amore un ladroncello † Don Giovanni (sels) PC ▲ 267027 [DDD] (2.97)
F. Lott (sop), M. McLaughlin (sop), N. Focile (sop), J. Hadley (ten), G. Cachemaille (bar), A. Corbelli (bar) *(rec Edinburgh Scotland)* TEL ▲ 80399 [DDD] (16.97)
C. Margiono (sop), V. D. Walt (sop), D. Ziegler (mez), G. Cachemaille (bar), N. Harnoncourt (cnd), (Royal) Concertgebouw Orch TELC ▲ 76455 (9.97)
E. Schwarzkopf (sop), L. Otto (sop), N. Merriman (mez), L. Simoneau (ten), R. Panerai (bar), S. Bruscantini (b-bar), H. von Karajan (cnd), Philharmonia Orch CFP (Eminence) ▲ 2211 [DDD] (16.97)
E. Schwarzkopf (sop), I. Seefried (sop), C. Ludwig (mez), A. Dermota (ten), E. Kunz (bar), P. Schöffler (b-bar), K. Böhm (cnd), Vienna PO—Sento, o Dio; Prenderò quel brunettino ("Great Mozart Singers, Vol. 2: Opera Arias, 1949-60") † Don Giovanni (sels); Entführung aus dem Serail (sels); Nozze di Figaro (sels); Zauberflöte (sels) ORFE (Festspiel Dokumente) ▲ 394201 (16.97)
F. von Stade (mez), R. Leppard (cnd), Scottish CO ("Recital: Frederica von Stade") † P. F. Cavalli:Music of Cavalli; Monteverdi:Music of Monteverdi ERAT ▲ 98504 (9.97)
A. Tomowa-Sintow (sop), V. Stefanov (cnd), Bulgarian RSO—Un'aura amorosa † Clemenza di Tito (sels); Don Giovanni (ov); Entführung aus dem Serail (sels) LALI ▲ 15890 [DDD] (3.97)
various artists, N. McGegan (cnd), Royal Opera House Orch—Soave sia il vento; Ah, scostasi; Un'aura amorosa † Ascanio in Alba (sels), K.111; Clemenza di Tito (ov); Clemenza di Tito (sels); Don Giovanni (sels); Entführung aus dem Serail (sels); Nozze di Figaro (sels); Zaide (sels); Zauberflöte (sels) CONI ▲ 55031 (16.97)
various artists—Soave sia il vento † Andante Fl, K.315; Con Cl, K.622; Con Fl & Hp, K.299; Con 21 Pno, K.467; Con 3 Vn, K.216; Kleine Nachtmusik, K.525; Qt in A Cl Strs, K.581; Serenade; Son 13 Pno, K.333 RCAV ▮ 63329 (5.98) ▲ 63329 (11.97)

Così fan tutte:Overture
M. Bernardi (cnd), Calgary PO *(rec Jack Singer Hall Calgary Centre for the Perfor, Canada)* ("Mozart: 12 Overtures") † Bastien und Bastienne (sels); Clemenza di Tito (ov); Don Giovanni (ov); Entführung aus dem Serail (ov); Finta semplice (ov); Idomeneo (ov); Lucio Silla (ov); Mitridate (Ov); Nozze di Figaro (ov); Schauspieldirektor (sels); Zauberflöte (ov) SMS (SM 5000) ▲ 5149 [DDD] (16.97)
J. Borowska (sop—Fiordiligi), P. Coles (sop—Despina), R. Yachmi-Caucig (cta—Dorabella), J. Dickie (ten—Ferrando), A. Martin (bar—Gugliemo), P. Mikuláš (bass—Don Alfonso), M. Synkova (hpd), J. Wildner (cnd), Capella Istropolitana, Slovak Phil Chorus *(rec Slovak Philharmonic Moyzes Hall Bratislava, Czech Republic, 1990)* † Così fan tutte (sels) NXIN ▲ 553172 [DDD] (5.97)
C. Davis (cnd), Staatskapelle Dresden † Bastien und Bastienne (sels); Entführung aus dem Serail (ov); Finta giardiniera (ov); Lucio Silla (ov); Nozze di Figaro (ov); Ovs; Schauspieldirektor (sels) RCAV ▲ 63500 (16.97)
L. Hager (cnd), English CO † Bastien und Bastienne (sels); Betulia liberata, K.118; Clemenza di Tito (ov); Don Giovanni (ov); Finta semplice (ov); Idomeneo (ov); Lucio Silla (ov); Mitridate (Ov); Nozze di Figaro (ov); Schauspieldirektor (sels); Zauberflöte (ov) NOVA ▲ 150041 [DDD] (16.97)
Z. Kosler (cnd), Slovak PO † Clemenza di Tito (ov); Don Giovanni (ov); Entführung aus dem Serail (ov); Idomeneo (ov); Nozze di Figaro (ov); Zauberflöte (ov) GZCL ▲ 74 (6.97)
N. Marriner (cnd), Academy of St. Martin in the Fields † Clemenza di Tito (ov); Don Giovanni (ov); Entführung aus dem Serail (ov); Idomeneo (ov); Lucio Silla (ov); Nozze di Figaro (ov); Schauspieldirektor (sels); Zauberflöte (ov) EMIC ▲ 47014 [DDD] (16.97)
Omnibus Wind Ensemble [arr Lars-Erik Lidström] *(rec 1996-97)* ("Opera Pearls") † Don Giovanni (ov); Don Giovanni (sels); Zauberflöte (ov); Zauberflöte (sels); Bizet:Carmen (ov); C. Nielsen:Maskarade (orch sels); G. Rossini:Italiana in Algeri (ov); Semiramide (ov); R. Wagner:Tannhäuser (ov); Tannhäuser (sels) OPU ▲ 19602 [AAD] (16.97)
H. Vonk (cnd), Dresden Staatskapelle † Ascanio in Alba (sels), K.111; Clemenza di Tito (ov); Don Giovanni (ov); Entführung aus dem Serail (ov); Finta giardiniera (ov); Idomeneo (ov); Lucio Silla (ov); Nozze di Figaro (ov); Schauspieldirektor (sels); Zauberflöte (ov) LALI ▲ 15885 [DDD] (3.97)
J. Wallez (cnd) *(rec live, Nov 22, 1986)* † Arias; Nozze di Figaro (ov) FORL ▲ 16562 [DDD] (16.97)
B. Wordsworth (cnd), Capella Istropolitana *(rec Czechoslovak Radio Concert Hall Bratislava, Czech Republic, Sept 6-9, 1988)* ("Famous Overtures") † Apollo et Hyacinthus (sels), K.38; Bastien und Bastienne (sels); Clemenza di Tito (ov); Don Giovanni (ov); Entführung aus dem Serail (ov); Finta giardiniera (ov); Idomeneo (ov); Lucio Silla (ov); Mitridate (Ov); Nozze di Figaro (ov); Rè pastore (sels); Schauspieldirektor (sels); Zauberflöte (ov); G. Rossini:Barbiere di Siviglia (ov); Cenerentola (sels); Elisabetta; Guillaume Tell (ov); Italiana in Algeri (ov); Scala di seta (ov); Semiramide (ov); Signor Bruschino (sels); Verdi:Ovs & Preludes NXIN 4-▲ 504013 [DDD] (19.97)
B. Wordsworth (cnd), Capella Istropolitana *(rec Sept 6-9, 1988)* † Bastien und Bastienne (sels); Clemenza di Tito (ov); Don Giovanni (ov); Entführung aus dem Serail (ov); Finta giardiniera (ov); Idomeneo (ov); Lucio Silla (ov); Mitridate (Ov); Nozze di Figaro (ov); Ovs; Rè pastore (sels); Schauspieldirektor (sels); Zauberflöte (ov) NXIN ▲ 550185 [DDD] (5.97)
various artists † Con Cl, K.622; Con 20 Pno, K.466; Con 21 Pno, K.467; Con 3 Vn, K.216; Kleine Nachtmusik, K.525; Son 11 Pno, K.331; Sym 40, K.550; Sym 41, K.551; Zauberflöte (ov) RCAV ▲ 60829 (10.97) ▮ 60829 (5.98)

562 ▲ = CD ♦ = Enhanced CD △ = MD ▮ = Cassette Tape ▯ = DCC

MOZART, WOLFGANG AMADEUS (cont.)

Dances & Marches

H. Graf (cnd), Salzburg Mozarteum Orch—Idomeneo (sels); Nozze di Figaro (sels); March Obs, K.62; March Orch, K.189; March Orch, K.215; March Orch, K.237; March Hns, K.248; March Orch, K.249; Marches Orch, K.335; Marches Orch, K.408; March Hns, K.445 LALI ▲ 15886 [DDD] (3.97)

H. Graf (cnd), Salzburg Mozarteum Orch—Contredanse, K.534; Contredanse, K.535; Contredanse, K.587; Contredanses (2), K.603; Contredanses (6), K.462; German Dances (3), K.605; German Dances (6), K.509; German Dances (6), K.600; Minuets Orch, K.461; Contredanses (2), K.463 LALI ▲ 15887 [DDD] (3.97)

S. Végh (cnd), Salzburg Mozarteum Orch, S. Végh (cnd), Salzburg Camerata Academica—Cassation Obs, K.63; Contredanses (4), K.101; German Dances (3), K.605 [No. 1 in D]; German Dances (6), K.606; March Orch, K.189; March Orch, K.215; March Hns, K.248; Marches Orch, K.408 [No. 1 in C; No. 2 in D]; Entführung aus dem Serail (sels) [March of the Janissaries]; Marches Orch, K.335; Contredanses (5), K.609; Idomeneo (sels) [Marches]; Nozze di Figaro (sels) [March] LALI ▲ 15653 [DDD] (3.97)

Davidde penitente (oratorio) for 3 solo Voices & Orchestra, K.469 (1785)

C. Bartoli (mez), G. Fischer (cnd), Vienna CO ("Mozart Portraits") † Arias; Exsultate, jubilate, K.165 PLON ▲ 43452 (17.97) ■ 43452 (10.98)

M. A. Tapia (cnd), Orch Pro-Musica, Chorus Tapia Colman, T. Maruschak (sop), E. Vasquez (mez), F. Becerra (ten) CLME ▲ 21026 (13.97)

Divertimentos

Berlin PO Winds—Divert 3 Winds, K.166; Divert 4 Winds, K.186 ORF ▲ 163881 [DDD] (18.97)

Selandia Wind Ensemble—Divert 14 Obs, K.270; Diverts Bas Hns, K.Anh.229 ("Wind Chamber Music 2") † Andante Mechanical Org, K.616; Qt 17 Strs, K.458 KPT ▲ 32058 [DDD]

Divertimentos (5) in B♭ for 3 Basset Horns (or 2 Basset Horns/Clarinets & Bassoon), K.Anh.229 (?1783)

Berlin PO Winds—No. 1; No. 3; No. 5 † Duos Hns, K.487 ORF ▲ 217901 [DDD] (18.97)

Berlin PO Winds—No. 2; No. 4 † Adagio Bas Hns & Bn, K.410; Notturnos Sops; Nozze di Figaro (winds); Più non si trovano, K.549 ORF ▲ 218911 [DDD] (18.97)

Classical Winds [period instrs] AMON ▲ 25 [DDD] (16.97)

In Modo Camerale—No. 3 † Qnt in A Cl & Strs, K.581; Qt Ob STMA ▲ 2 (18.97)

New World Basset Horn Trio ("Music for Basset Horns") † Duos Hns, K.487; A. Stadler:Trios Bas Hns HAM ▲ 1907017 (9.97)

Stadler Trio—No. 1; No. 3; No. 5 ("Music for Basset Horns") † Adagio Cl & Bas Hns, Ka.94; Nozze di Figaro (winds) GLSS ▲ 920602 (18.97)

Divertimento No. 1 in E♭ for 2 Clarinets, 2 Horns & Strings, K.113 (1771)

S. Végh (cnd), Salzburg Camerata Academica † Diverts Str Qt, K.136-138; Kleine Nachtmusik, K.525 LALI ▲ 15861 [DDD] (3.97)

Divertimento No. 2 in D for Flute, Oboe, Bassoon, 4 Horns & Strings, K.131 (1772)

D. Brain (hn), T. Beecham (cnd), Royal PO *(rec 1947-49)* † Con Fl & Hp, K.299; Sym 27, K.199; Zauberflöte (ov) DLAB (RPO Legacy Vol. 4) ▲ 7037 (17.97)

S. Végh (cnd), Salzburg Camerata Academica † Divert 7 Hns, K.205; Serenade 6 Orch, K.239 LALI ▲ 15862 [DDD] (3.97)

Divertimento for 2 Horns & Strings [fragment], K.246b (1772-73)

L'Archibudelli † Divert Vn, K.288; Duos Hns, K.487; March Hns, K.248; March Hns, K.290; March Hns, K.445; Musikalischer Spass, K.522; Qnt Hn SNYC (Vivarte) ▲ 46702 (16.97)

Divertimento No. 10 in F for 2 Horns & Strings, K.247 (1776)

L'Archibudelli † Bach Trans, K.404a; Divert 17 Hns Strs, K.334; Trio Vn, K.563 SNYC (Vivarte) ▲ 46497 (16.97)

W. Sobotka (cnd), Capella Istropolitana † Kleine Nachtmusik, K.525; Serenade 6 Orch, K.239 NXIN ▲ 550026 [DDD] (5.97)

A. Titov (cnd), St. Petersburg Classical Music Studio Orch † Con 24 Pno, K.491; Diverts Str Qt, K.136-138 SNYC ▲ 64332 [DDD] (4.97)

S. Végh (cnd), Salzburg Camerata Academica † Divert 11 Ob, K.251 LALI ▲ 15863 [DDD] (3.97)

artists unknown † Kleine Nachtmusik, K.525 NIMB ▲ 7808 [DDD] (11.97)

Divertimento No. 15 in B♭ for 2 Horns & Strings, K.287 (1777)

M. Goberman (cnd) *(rec 1938)* † Busoni:Son 2 Vn, Op. 36a GRM2 (The Records of the Century) ▲ 78873 (13.97)

W. Janezic (hn), R. Janezic (hn), Vienna Ensemble † Kleine Nachtmusik, K.525 KOCC ▲ 6445 (16.97)

H. von Karajan (cnd), Berlin PO † Kleine Nachtmusik, K.525; Serenade 6 Orch, K.239 DEUT (3D Classics) ▲ 31272 [DDD] (9.97)

J. Szigeti (vn), M. Goberman (cnd) *(rec 1938)* † J. S. Bach:Arioso Ob; Con 1 Hpd, BWV 1052; Tartini:Con Vn, D.45 BID ▲ 64 [ADD]

J. Szigeti (vn), M. Goberman (cnd) *(rec 1938)* † Busoni:Son 2 Vn, Op. 36a ENT (Strings) ▲ 99351 (16.97)

A. Toscanini (cnd), NBC SO ("The Toscanini Collection, Vol. 10") † Con Bn, K.191; Sym 35, K.385 RCAV (Gold Seal) ▲ 60286 (11.97)

B. Walter (cnd), NBC SO *(rec live New York, Mar 11, 1939)* ("Bruno Walter Plays & Conducts Mozart") † Con 20 Pno, K.466 GRM2 ▲ 78622 (13.97)

artists unknown † Divert 12 Obs, K.252 SNYC ▲ 64557 (4.97)

Divertimento No. 17 in D for 2 Horns & Strings, K.334 (1779-80)

A. Brain (hn), D. Brain (hn), Liner Quartet † J. Brahms:Trio Hn, Op. 40 MTAL ▲ 48021 (6.97)

A. Brain (hn), D. Brain (hn), Léner String Quartet *(rec 1939-46)* ("Dennis Brain: His Early Recordings") † Con 2 Hn, K.417; Con 3 Hn, K.447 GRM2 ▲ 78729 (13.97)

A. Brain (hn), D. Brain (hn), Léner String Quartet *(rec 1939-46)* † Con 2 Hn, K.417; Beethoven:Son Hn GRM2 (Records of the Century) ▲ 78881 (14.97)

A. Brain (hn), D. Brain (hn), Léner String Quartet *(rec 1924-39)* ("Complete Electrical & Acoustic Recordings, Vol. 2") † J. Haydn:Qts (6) Strs, H.III/13-18, Op. 3; Qts (6) Strs, H.III/63-68, Op. 64 RPTR ▲ 5006 (m) (17.97)

J. Galway (fl), J. Galway (cnd), CO of Europe † Andante Fl, K.315; Con Fl & Hp, K.299; Cons Fl; Kleine Nachtmusik, K.525; Son 11 Pno, K.331 RCAV (Red Seal) 2-▲ 7861 [DDD] (30.97)

H. von Karajan (cnd), Berlin PO ("Summer Adagio") † Sym 38, K.504; Beethoven:Sym 6; Debussy:Prélude à l'après-midi d'un faune; J. Haydn:Sym 87; G. Holst:Planets, Op. 32; M. Ravel:Rapsodie espagnole; O. Respighi:Fontane di Roma DEUT ▲ 457127 [ADD] (16.97)

H. von Karajan (cnd), Vienna PO *(rec 1946-47)* ("The Young Karajan, Vol. 10") † Adagio & Fugue Strs, K.546; F. Schubert:Sym 9 GRM2 ▲ 78770 (13.97)

L'Archibudelli † Bach Trans, K.404a; Divert 10 Hns, K.247; Trio Vn, K.563 SNYC (Vivarte) ▲ 46497 (16.97)

L. Markiz (cnd), Stuttgart CO † Sym 33, K.319 DI ▲ 920302 [DDD] (5.97)

E. Morini (vn), M. Rauchstein (pno)—Menuetto [trans for vn & pno] *(rec 1927)* ("Erica Morini Plays Mozart") † Con 4 Vn, K.218; Con 5 Vn, K.219 ARBT ▲ 107 (16.97)

J. Rampal (fl), Pasquier Trio † Adagio & Rondo, K.617; Andante Mechanical Org, K.616; Qnt Strs SNYC ▲ 47230 (16.97)

S. Végh (cnd), Salzburg Camerata † Diverts Str Qt, K.136-138 CAPO ▲ 10153 [DDD] (11.97)

S. Végh (cnd), Salzburg Mozarteum Camerata Academia *(rec 1986)* † Diverts Str Qt, K.136-138; Kleine Nachtmusik, K.525; Serenade 6 Orch, K.239 CAPO 3-▲ 49176 [DDD] (16.97)

Vienna Flautists † Diverts Str Qt, K.136-138 DI ▲ 920158 [DDD] (5.97)

Divertimento No. 7 in D for 2 Horns, Bassoon & Strings, K.205 (?1773)

R. Edlinger (cnd), Capella Istropolitana *(rec Mar 1988)* † Diverts Str Qt, K.136-138 NXIN ▲ 550108 [DDD] (5.97)

R. Reuter (cnd), Thüringian CO Weimar *(rec Weimar Johannis Church, Mar 10-13, 1997)* ("Serenade im Park") † Con Ob; Divert 11 Ob, K.251 GRH ▲ 1068 [DDD] (16.97)

Salzburg Chamber Soloists *(rec Mozarteum Grosse Saal Salzburg, Feb 21-23, 1994)* † Con 5 Vn, K.219; Sinf concertante Vn, K.364 DNN ▲ 78918 [DDD] (16.97)

C. Straka (cnd), Zeljko Musica † C. Stamitz:Qts concertantes, Op. 15; Vivaldi:Con Strs, RV.151; Cons Vn(s) Strs, Op. 3/1-12 BER ▲ 9349 (10.97)

S. Végh (cnd), Salzburg Camerata Academica † Divert 2 Fl, K.131; Serenade 6 Orch, K.239 LALI ▲ 15862 [DDD] (3.97)

Divertimento No. 11 in D for Oboe, 2 Horns & Strings, K.251 (1776)

C. Abbado (cnd), Berlin PO *(rec Nov 28-29, 1992)* † Marches Orch, K.335; Serenade 9 Orch, K.320 SNYC ▲ 53277 [DDD] (16.97)

R. Canter (ob), London Baroque [period instrs] † Qnt Ob, K.516; Qt Ob AMON ▲ 34 [DDD] (16.97)

T. Cobb (db), J. Robinson (ob), L. W. Kuyper (hn), R. A. Spanjer (hn), Elysium String Quartet *(rec Academy of Arts & Letters, NY, 1998)* † Qnt Cl, K.581; Qnt Hn ELY ▲ 716 [DDD] (16.97)

S. Fuchs (ob) † Adagio E Hn, K.580a; Qt Fl in C; Qt Ob TUD ▲ 7049 (16.97)

N. Harnoncourt (cnd), Vienna Concentus Musicus [period instrs] † Kleine Nachtmusik, K.525; Musikalischer Spass, K.522 TELC ▲ 44809 [DDD] (16.97)

B. Horlitz (ob), R. Reuter (cnd), Thüringian CO Weimar *(rec Weimar Johannis Church, Mar 10-13, 1997)* ("Serenade im Park") † Con Ob; Divert 7 Hns, K.205 GRH ▲ 1068 [DDD] (16.97)

T. Koopman (cnd), Amsterdam Baroque Orch [period instrs] ERAT ▲ 45471 [DDD] (16.97)

MOZART, WOLFGANG AMADEUS (cont.)

Divertimento No. 11 in D for Oboe, 2 Horns & Strings, K.251 (1776) (cont.)

S. Végh (cnd), Salzburg Camerata Academica † Kleine Nachtmusik, K.525; Serenade Ww, K.375; Serenade Ww, K.388/384a; Serenade 6 Orch, K.239 LALI ▲ 15648 [DDD] (3.97)

S. Végh (cnd), Salzburg Camerata Academica † Divert 10 Hns, K.247 LALI ▲ 15863 [DDD] (3.97)

B. Wahl (cnd), Versailles CO † Qt 4 Strs, K.157; Qt 7 Strs; Sym 13, K.112 ARN ▲ 68140 (16.97)

Divertimento No. 8 in F for 2 Oboes, 2 Bassoons & 2 Horns, K.213 (1775)

P. Järvi (cnd) † Serenade CHN (Collect) ▲ 6575 [DDD] (12.97)

Vienna Quintet † Zauberflöte (ww); F. Danzi:Qnts Ww, Op. 56; F. Farkas:Antique Hungarian Dances; J. Haydn:Diverts Obs; J. Takács:Serenade nach Alt-Grazer Kontratänzen NIMB ▲ 5479 [DDD] (16.97)

Divertimento No. 12 in E for 2 Oboes, 2 Bassoons & 2 Horns, K.252 (1776)

artists unknown † Divert 15 Hns & Strs, K.287 SNYC ▲ 64557 (4.97)

Divertimento No. 13 in F for 2 Oboes, 2 Bassoons & 2 Horns, K.253 (1776)

Collegium dell'Arte † Divert 14 Obs, K.270; Kleine Nachtmusik, K.525 SNYC ▲ 57230 (4.97)

Divertimento No. 14 in B♭ for 2 Oboes, 2 Bassoons & 2 Horns, K.270 (1777)

Collegium dell'Arte † Divert 13 Obs, K.253; Kleine Nachtmusik, K.525 SNYC ▲ 57230 (4.97)

Divertimento No. 16 in E♭ for 2 Oboes, 2 Bassoons & 2 Horns [doubtful], K.289 (1777)

Ottetto Italiano *(rec Italy, 1992)* ("Music for Winds, Vol. 3") † Serenade AART ▲ 47281 [DDD] (10.97)

Divertimento in B♭ for Piano Trio, K. 254 (1776)

Vienna Schubert Trio *(rec Doopsgezinde Gemeente Kerk, Haarlem, Netherlands, 1990)* † Trio Pno, K.496; Trio Pno, K.502; Trio Pno, K.542; Trio Pno, K.548; Trio Pno, K.564 EMIC 2-▲ 73350 [DDD] (16.97)

Divertimentos (3) in D, B♭ & F for String Quartet, K.136-138, "Salzburg Symphonies" (1772)

R. Edlinger (cnd), Capella Istropolitana *(rec Mar 1988)* † Divert 7 Hns, K.205 NXIN ▲ 550108 [DDD] (5.97)

H. von Karajan (cnd), Berlin PO † Kleine Nachtmusik, K.525; Serenade 6 Orch, K.239 DEUT ▲ 29805 [ADD] (7.97)

B. Khadem-Missagh (cnd), Vienna Tonkünstler CO † Sinf concertante Vn, K.364 DI ▲ 920355 [DDD] (5.97)

A. Martini (cnd), Accademia I Filarmonici *(rec Palazzo Pizzini Trento, Italy, Dec 1995)* † Adagio & Fugue Strs, K.546; Kleine Nachtmusik, K.525 AART ▲ 47359 [DDD] (10.97)

Mirring String Quartet † Divert 1 Cls, K.113; Kleine Nachtmusik, K.525 LALI ▲ 15861 [DDD] (3.97)

M. Sieghart (cnd), Stuttgart CO *(rec Ludwigsburg Germany, Oct 4-5, 1994)* † Sym 28, K.200 DI ▲ 920288 [DDD] (5.97)

C. Traunfellner (cnd), Vienna Chamber PO *(rec Casino Zögarnitz Vienna, June 1990)* † Kleine Nachtmusik, K.525; Serenade 6 Orch, K.239 CAMA ▲ 119 [DDD] (18.97)

Y. Turovsky (cnd), Montreal Musici † Kleine Nachtmusik, K.525 CHN ▲ 9045 [DDD] (16.97)

S. Végh (cnd), Salzburg Mozarteum Camerata Academia *(rec 1986)* † Divert 17 Hns Strs, K.334; Kleine Nachtmusik, K.525; Serenade 6 Orch, K.239 CAPO 3-▲ 49176 [DDD] (16.97)

Vienna Ensemble † German Dances (6), K.600; Lanner:Mozartisten, Op. 196 SNYC ▲ 47672 (11.97)

G. Wich (cnd), Southwest German CO † Kleine Nachtmusik, K.525 INTC ▲ 820504 (9.97)

Divertimentos (3) for String Quartet, K.136-138, "Salzburg Symphonies" (1772)

I. Brown (cnd), Norwegian CO † Kleine Nachtmusik, K.525; Sym 29, K.201 ORG ▲ 1004 [DDD] (13.97)

N. Marriner (cnd) † Kleine Nachtmusik, K.525; Musikalischer Spass, K.522 PPHI ▲ 12269 [DDD] (16.97)

T. Pál (cnd), Salieri CO *(rec Szeged Opera House Hungary, June 1996)* † Con 23 Pno, K.488; Con 24 Pno, K.491 AG ▲ 57 [DDD] (18.97)

J. Rolla (cnd), Franz Liszt CO † Adagio & Fugue Strs, K.546; Kleine Nachtmusik, K.525; Serenade 6 Orch, K.239 HUN ▲ 12471 [DDD] (16.97)

J. Rolla (cnd), Franz Liszt CO, S. Végh (cnd), Salzburg Camerata, S. Végh (cnd), Mirring String Quartet † Sym 1, K.16; Sym 5, K.22; Sym 6, K.43 LALI ▲ 15647 [DDD] (3.97)

J. Rutter (cnd), City of London Sinfonia—K.136, No. 1 in D [Presto] *(rec London, England, July 29, 1985)* ("The Mozart Collection") † Con Cl, K.622; Con Fl & Hp, K.299; Con 12 Pno, K.414; Con 21 Pno, K.467; Music of Mozart; Nozze di Figaro (ov); Sym 39, K.543 AMG ▲ 586 (15.99)

J. Stanienda (cnd), Polish CO *(rec Mayfest City Halls, Glasgow, 1990)* † J. S. Bach:Con 1 Vn; B. Bartók:Divert Strs, Sz.113; E. Elgar:Intro & Allegro, Op. 47 LINN ▲ 1 (16.97)

A. Titov (cnd), St. Petersburg Classical Music Studio Orch † Con 24 Pno, K.491; Divert 10 Hns, K.247 SNYC ▲ 64332 [DDD] (4.97)

S. Végh (cnd), Salzburg Camerata † Divert 17 Hns Strs, K.334 CAPO ▲ 10153 [DDD] (11.97)

Vienna Flautists † Divert 17 Hns Strs, K.334 DI ▲ 920158 [DDD] (5.97)

Vienna Flautists [arr Mozart for fl ensemble] † Adagio & Allegro, K.594; Andante & Vars, K.501; Andante Mechanical Org, K.616; Fant Mechanical Org, K.608; A. Prinz:Zauberflötiana ORF ▲ 239911 [DDD] (18.97)

artists unknown † J. S. Bach:Brandenburg Con 1, BWV 1046; Bizet:Carmen (suite 1); A. Dvořák:Slavonic Dances (sels) PC ▲ 265088 [DDD] (2.97)

artists unknown—K.137, No. 2 in B♭ [Andante] ("Adagios") † Adagio Pno, K.540; Adagio Vn, K.261; Con Cl, K.622; Con Fl & Hp, K.299; Con 2 Hn, K.417; Con 20 Pno, K.466; Con 21 Pno, K.467; Con 23 Pno, K.488; Con 26 Pno, K.537; Con 27 Pno, K.595; Con 3 Hn, K.447; Con 3 Vn, K.216; Kleine Nachtmusik, K.525; Qnt Cl, K.581; Serenade; Serenade Ww, K.388/384a; Sinf concertante Vn, K.364; Son 12 Pno, K.332; Son 16 Pno, K.545; Sym 40, K.550; Sym 41, K.551 DECC (2-Fers) 2-▲ 460191 (17.97)

Divertimento in E♭ for String Trio, K.563 (1788)

Budapest String Quartet members *(rec Nov 2, 1944)* ("Mozart Recordings (1940-45)") † Qnt in A Cl & Strs, K.581; Qt Pno, K.493; Qt 15 Strs; Qt 18 Strs, K.464 BRID 2-▲ 9085 (32.97)

Dresden String Trio † F. Schubert:Trio Strs, D.581 QUER ▲ 9901 (18.97)

Divertimento in F for Violin, Viola, Cello & 2 Horns [fragment], K.288 (1777)

L'Archibudelli † Divert Hns, K.246b; Duos Hns, K.487; March Hns, K.248; March Hns, K.290; March Hns, K.445; Musikalischer Spass, K.522; Qnt Hn SNYC (Vivarte) ▲ 46702 (16.97)

Divertimento No. 3 in E for Wind Ensemble, K.166 (1773)

Zefiro Ensemble † Serenade ASTR ▲ 8605 (18.97)

Divertimento No. 4 in B♭ for Wind Ensemble, K.186 (1773)

Zefiro Ensemble [period instrs] ("Serenades & Divertimeno") † Serenade Ww, K.375; Serenade Ww, K.388/384a ASTR ▲ 8573 (18.97)

Divertimento in D for Winds

N. Marriner (cnd), Academy of St. Martin in the Fields ("The Mozart Experience") † Con Cl, K.622; Con Fl & Hp, K.299; Con Movt Hn, K.Anh.98a; Con 20 Pno, K.466; Con 21 Pno, K.467; German Dances (3), K.605; Kleine Nachtmusik, K.525; Musikalischer Spass, K.522; Nozze di Figaro (sels); Serenade 6 Orch, K.239; Sym 40, K.550; Sym 41, K.551 PPHI 5-▲ 26204 (33.97)

Don Giovanni (opera in 2 acts) [lib Lorenzo Da Ponte], K.527 (1787)

C. Abbado (cnd), CO of Europe, S. Isokoski (sop), C. Remigio (sop), P. Pace (sop), U. Heilmann (ten), S. Keenlyside (bar), B. Terfel (b-bar), M. Salminen (bass), I. D. Arcangelo (bass) DEUT 3-▲ 457601 [DDD] (48.97)

B. Bonney (sop), E. Gruberová (sop), R. Alexander (sop), T. Hampson (bar), N. Harnoncourt (cnd), (Royal) Concertgebouw Orch [ITA] TELC 3-▲ 44184 [DDD] (50.97)

L. D. Casa (sop—D. Elvira), E. Grümmer (sop—D. Anna), R. Streich (sop—Zerlina), L. Simoneau (ten—Don Ottavio), W. Berry (b-bar—Masetto), C. Siepi (b-bar—Don Giovanni), G. Frick (bass—Il Commendatore), F. Corena (bass—Leporello), D. Mitropoulos (cnd), Vienna PO, Vienna State Opera Chorus *(rec Salzburg, July 24, 1956)* SNYC 3-▲ 64263 [ADD] (33.97)

E. Děpoltová (sop—Anna), M. Hajóssyová (sop—Elvira), J. Jonášová (sop—Zerlina), V. Kocián (ten—Ottavio), V. Zítek (b-bar—Don Giovanni), K. Berman (bass—Leporello), E. Haken (bass—Commendatore), D. Jedlička (bass—Masetto), J. Pokorný (hpd), L. Pešek (cnd), Prague CO, M. Malý (cnd), Prague National Theater Chorus *(rec Rudolfinum Prague, Mar 7-23, 1981)* ("Prague Version") *(I lib text)* SUR 2-▲ 3296

R. Fleming (sop—Donna Anna), A. Murray (mez—Donna Elvira), M. Groop (mez—Zerlina), H. Lippert (ten—Don Ottavio), R. Scaltriti (bar—Masetto), B. Terfel (b-bar—Don Giovanni), M. Pertusi (bass—Leporello), M. Luperi (bass—Commendatore), G. Solti (cnd), London PO PLON ▲ 455500 (48.97)

J. E. Gardiner (cnd), English Baroque Soloists, Monteverdi Choir London, L. Orgonasova (sop—Donna Anna), C. Margiono (sop—Donna Elvira), E. James (mez—Zerlina), J. Clarkson (alt—Masetto), C. Prégardien (ten—Don Ottavio), R. Gilfry (bar—Don Giovanni), I. D. Arcangelo (bass—Leporello), A. Silvestrelli (bass—Il Commendatore) PARC 3-▲ 45870 [DDD] (48.97)

V. Gens (sop), D. Borst (sop), S. Marin-Degor (sop), S. Edwards (ten), N. Revenq (bar), H. Claessens (bass), P. Donnelly (bass), J. Malgoire (cnd) [period instrs] ASTR 2-▲ 8635 (18.97)

L. Helletsgruber (sop), I. Souez (sop), A. Mildmay (sop), K. von Pataky (ten), J. Brownlee (bar), R. Henderson (bar), S. Baccaloni (bass), D. Franklin (bass), F. Busch (cnd), Glyndebourne Festival Orch, Glyndebourne Festival Chorus *(rec 1936)* ("Fritz Busch at Glyndebourne: The Legendary Cycle of the Da Ponte-Mozart Operas, Vol. 3") GRM2 3-▲ 78693 (39.97)

H. von Karajan (cnd), Berlin PO, Berlin German Opera Chorus, K. Battle (sop), A. Tomowa-Sintow (sop), A. Baltsa (mez), G. Winbergh (ten), S. Ramey (bass), F. Furlanetto (bass), P. Burchuladze (bass) [ITA] DEUT 3-▲ 19179 [DDD] (48.97)

MOZART, WOLFGANG AMADEUS (cont.)

Don Giovanni (opera in 2 acts) [lib Lorenzo Da Ponte], K.527 (1787) (cont.)

O. Klemperer (cnd), Cologne Radio SO & Chorus, H. Zadek (sop), R. Streich (sop), M. Cunitz (sop), L. Simoneau (ten), B. Kusche (bar), G. London (b-bar), L. Weber (bass), H. Günter (sgr) *(rec live, Cologne, Germany, 1955)* TES ▲ 2149 (33.97)

A. Kraus (ten), S. Bruscantini (b-bar), N. Ghiaurov (bass) ODRO 3-▲ 1144 (13.97)

F. Lott (sop—Donna Elvira), C. Brewer (sop—Donna Anna), N. Focile (sop—Zerlina), J. Hadley (ten—Don Ottavio), A. Corbelli (bar—Leporello), B. Skovhus (bar—Don Giovanni), U. Chiummo (bass—Il Commendatore/Masetto), C. Mackerras (cnd), Scottish CO, Scottish Chamber Chorus *(rec Edinburgh, Scotland, 1995)* TEL 3-▲ 80420 [DDD] (41.97)

E. Moser (sop), K. T. Kanawa (sop), T. Berganza (mez), K. Riegel (ten), G. Raimondi (ten), J. Van Dam (b-bar), J. Macurdy (bass), L. Maazel (cnd), Paris Opera Orch, Paris Opera Chorus [ITA] SNYC 3-▲ 35192 (51.97)

E. Rethberg (sop), L. Helletsgruber (sop), D. Borgioli (ten), E. Pinza (bass), V. Lazzari (bass), B. Walter (cnd), Vienna PO, Vienna State Opera Chorus *(rec Salzburg Festival, Aug 2, 1937)* RY (Radio Years) 3-▲ 83 (47.97)

E. Schwarzkopf (sop), E. Berger (sop), E. Grümmer (sop), A. Dermota (ten), W. Berry (b-bar), O. Edelmann (bass), C. Siepi (bass), W. Furtwängler (cnd), Vienna PO, Vienna State Opera Chorus *(rec Salzburg, Aug 3, 1953)* EMIC (Great Recordings of the Century) 2-▲ 63860 (34.97)

E. Schwarzkopf (sop—Donna Elvira), J. Sutherland (sop—Donna Anna), G. Sciutti (sop—Zerlina), L. Alva (ten—Don Ottavio), P. Cappuccilli (bar—Masetto), E. Wächter (bar—Don Giovanni), G. Taddei (bar—Leporello), G. Frick (bass—Commendatore), C. M. Giulini (cnd), Philharmonia Orch, Philharmonia Chorus *(rec 1959) (E,F,G,I lib texts)* EMIC 3-▲ 56232 [ADD] (47.97)

G. Sciutti (sop—Zerlina), I. Ligabue (sop—Donna Elvira), C. C. Kegel (sop—Donna Anna), L. Kozma (ten—Ottavio), G. Taddei (bar—Leporello), R. Raimondi (bass—Don Giovanni), A. Zerbini (bass—Commandatore), L. Monreale (bass—Masetto), P. Maag (cnd), Venice Theater Orch, Venice Theater Chorus *(rec live Venice, Dec 3, 1971)* MONM 3-▲ 10211 (54.97)

I. Seefried (sop—Zerline), S. Jurinac (sop—Donna Elvira), L. D. Casa (sop—Donna Anna), G. London (b-bar—Don Giovanni), L. Weber (bass—Commandatore), K. Böhm (cnd), Vienna State Opera Orch, Vienna State Opera Chorus *(rec live Vienna, Nov 6, 1955)* RCAV (Red Seal-Vienna State Opera) 3-▲ 57737 (33.97)

I. Souez (sop), L. Helletsgruber (sop), A. Mildmay (sop), K. von Pataky (ten), J. Brownlee (bar), R. Henderson (bar), T. Franklin (bar), S. Baccaloni (bass), F. Busch (cnd), Glyndebourne Festival Orch, Glyndebourne Festival Chorus [ITA] *(rec 1936; orig. issued by HMV)* PHS 3-▲ 9369 [AAD] (49.97)

T. Stich-Randall (sop—Donn'Anna), L. Gencer (sop—Donn'Elvra), M. Petri (bar—Don Giovanni), S. Bruscantini (b-bar—Leporello), F. Molinari-Pradelli (cnd), Milan RAI SO, Milan RAI Chorus STRV 3-▲ 12321 [ADD] (37.97)

C. Studer (sop), C. Vaness (sop), W. Shimell (bar), S. Ramey (bass), R. Muti (cnd), Vienna PO EMIC 3-▲ 54255 (47.97)

B. Walter (cnd), Metropolitan Opera Orch, Metropolitan Opera Chorus, R. Bampton (sop), J. Novotná (sop), B. Sayão (sop), C. Kullman (ten), M. Harrell (bar), A. Kipnis (bass), N. Cordon (bass), E. Pinza (bass) *(rec live Met, NY, 1942)* PHG 3-▲ 5081 (36.97)

Don Giovanni (selections)

R. Bampton (sop), J. Novotná (sop), B. Sayão (sop), C. Kullman (ten), M. Harrell (bar), A. Kipnis (bass), E. Pinza (bass), B. Walter (cnd), New York Opera Orch, New York Opera Chorus OPIT ▲ 54555 (6.97)

C. Bartoli (mez), G. Fischer (cnd), Vienna CO *(rec 1993)* ("A Portrait") † Clemenza di Tito (sels); Così fan tutte (sels); Nozze di Figaro (sels); G. Caccini:Amarilli mia bella; Parisotti:Se tu m'ami; G. Rossini:Cenerentola (sels); Maometto II (sels); Semiramide (sels); F. Schubert:Songs (misc colls) PLON ▲ 48300 [DDD] (17.97) ▮ 48300 [DDD] (11.98)

K. Battle (sop), A. Tomowa-Sintow (sop), A. Baltsa (mez), G. Winbergh (ten), S. Ramey (bass), F. Furlanetto (bass), P. Burchuladze (bass), H. von Karajan (cnd), Berlin PO, Berlin German Opera Chorus [ITA] DEUT ▲ 19635 [DDD] (16.97)

E. Baude-Delhommais (cnd) [arr Vent] ("Mozart/Vent Transcriptions by Ensemble Philedor") † Entführung aus dem Serail (sels) SUR ▲ 3018 (16.97)

M. Bäumer (sop), W. Schupp (sgr), F. Weissmann (cnd), Berlin State Opera Orch—Du kennst nun den Frevler [GER] *(rec 1932)* ("Four German Sopranos of the Past") † Nozze di Figaro (sels); Zauberflöte (sels); Beethoven:Fidelio (sels); Verdi:Arias; R. Wagner:Fliegende Holländer (sels); Lohengrin (sels); Tannhäuser (sels); Walküre (sels); C. M. von Weber:Freischütz (sels) PRE ▲ 89964 (m) (16.97)

M. Bayo (sop), V. P. Pérez (cnd), Galicia SO—Batti, batti, o bel Masetto † Ah, lo previdi & Ah, t'invola agl'occhi miei, K.272; Exsultate, jubilate, K.165; Idomeneo (sels); Voi avete un cor fedele, K.217; Zaide (sels) VAL ▲ 4790 (18.97)

B. Berkyova (sop—Zerlina), H. Kaupova (sop—Donna Elvira), P. Oswald (ten—Don Ottavio), O. Dohnányi (cnd), Bratislava Opera Orch—Ah! pietà, signori miei!; Il mio tesoro intanto; In quali eccessi, o Numi; Ah, chi mi dice mai; Vedrai, carino, se sei buonino; Metà di voi quà vadano † Così fan tutte (sels) PC ▲ 267027 [DDD] (2.97)

J. Björling (ten)—Il mio tesoro intanto ("O Paradiso") † Bizet:Carmen (sels); P. Mascagni:Cavalleria rusticana (sels); Massenet:Manon (sels); Meyerbeer:Africaine (sels); G. Puccini:Bohème (sels); Manon Lescaut (sels); Tosca (sels); Turandot (sels); Verdi:Aida (sels); Rigoletto (sels); Trovatore (sels) RCAV (Gold Seal) ▲ 68429 (11.97)

K. Böhm (cnd), Vienna PO ("Great Mozart Singers, Vol. 3: Opera Arias, 1961-82") † Così fan tutte (sels); Entführung aus dem Serail (sels); Idomeneo (sels); Nozze di Figaro (sels); Zauberflöte (sels) ORFE (Festspiel Dokumente) ▲ 394301 (16.97)

M. Callas (sop), N. Rescigno (cnd), Paris Conservatory Société des Concerts Orch—Crudele! Ah nò, mio bene; Non mi dir, bell'idol mio; In quali eccessi, o Numi; Mi tradì quell' alma ingrata *(rec Salle Wagram Paris, France, 1963-64)* ("Mozart, Beethoven & Weber") † Nozze di Figaro (sels); Beethoven:Ah, perfido!, Op. 65; C. M. von Weber:Oberon (sels) *([ENG,ITA] lib texts)* EMIC (Callas Edition) ▲ 66465 [ADD] (11.97)

M. Callas (sop), T. Serafin (cnd), Florence Maggio Musicale Orch—Non mi dir, bell'idol mio [2 versions] *(rec 1953-69)* ("The EMI Rarities") † V. Bellini:Pirata (sels); Donizetti:Pirata (sels); G. Rossini:Arias; Verdi:Arias; C. M. von Weber:Oberon (sels) *([ENG,ITA]lib texts)* EMIC (Callas Edition) 2-▲ 66468 [ADD] (21.97)

M. Cebotari (sop), A. Dermota (ten), H. von Karajan (cnd), Vienna PO—Or sai chi l'onore; Dalla sua pace *(rec 1944)* ("Vienna Opera Favorites of the Past (1942-1947)") † Entführung aus dem Serail (sels); Nozze di Figaro (sels); G. Puccini:Turandot (sels); R. Strauss:Rosenkavalier (sels); Verdi:Aida (sels); Don Carlos (sels); R. Wagner:Meistersinger (sels); Walküre (sels) PRE ▲ 90345 [ADD] (16.97)

P. Freeman (cnd), National Opera Orch—Madamina! Il catalogo è questo (Catalog song); Là ci darem la mano, là mi dirai di si; Finch'han dal vino calda la testa (Champagne Aria); Il mio tesoro intanto ("Opera for Orchestra") † Don Giovanni (ov); Nozze di Figaro (ov); Nozze di Figaro (sels); Zauberflöte (ov) INSD ▲ 3675 (11.97)

S. Frontalini (cnd), Moldava SO—Madamina! Il catalogo è questo (Catalog song) *(rec Dec 1992)* ("Arie senza voce: Baritono") † Nozze di Figaro (sels); Verdi:Ernani (sels); Orchestral Sels BONG ▲ 8002 [DDD] (16.97)

W. Furtwängler (cnd) ("Great Mozart Singers, Vol. 2: Opera Arias, 1949-60") † Così fan tutte (sels); Entführung aus dem Serail (sels); Nozze di Figaro (sels); Zauberflöte (sels) ORFE (Festspiel Dokumente) ▲ 394201 (16.97)

H. de Garmo (bass)—Finch'han dal vino calda la testa (Champagne Aria); Horch auf den Klang der Zither [GER] *(rec 1917)* † E. D. Albert:Tiefland (sels); Bizet:Carmen (sels); Leoncavallo:Pagliacci (sels); J. Offenbach:Contes d'Hoffmann (sels); Verdi:Otello (sels); R. Wagner:Fliegende Holländer (sels); Meistersinger (sels); Rheingold (sels); Siegfried (sels); Tannhäuser (sels); Walküre (sels) PRE (Lebendige Vergangenheit) ▲ 89175 (m) (16.97)

A. Gibson (cnd), Scottish CO † R. Strauss:Rosenkavalier (sels) CFP (Silver Doubles) 2-▲ 4739 [ADD] (22.97)

K. T. Kanawa (sop), T. Berganza (mez), J. Van Dam (b-bar), R. Raimondi (bass), L. Maazel (cnd), Paris Opera Orch, Paris Opera Chorus SNYC (Essential Classics) ▲ 62663 (7.97) ▮ 62663 (3.98)

P. Koci (bar) † Beethoven:Fidelio (sels); Janáček:From the House of the Dead (sels); G. Rossini:Barbiere di Siviglia (sels); Smetana:Kiss (sels); Secret (sels); P. Tchaikovsky:Eugene Onegin (sels); R. Wagner:Fliegende Holländer (sels); Tannhäuser (sels) GZCL ▲ 303 (6.97)

J. Kovács (cnd), Hungarian State Orch, M. Szalay (cnd), Hungarian State Opera Male Chorus—Madamina! Il catalogo è questo (Catalog song); Deh! vieni alla finestra (canzonetta); Ah! pietà, signori miei!; Ah! pietà, signori miei!; Madamina! Il catalogo è questo (Catalog song); Hò capito, Signor, sì; Deh! vieni alla finestra (canzonetta); Metà di voi quà vadano; Ah! pietà, signori miei!; Ah! pietà, signori miei! *(rec Budapest, Hungary, 1997)* ("Operatic Recitals") † Arias; Clemenza di Tito (sels); Entführung aus dem Serail (sels); Mentre ti lascio, o figlia, K.513; Nozze di Figaro (sels); Per questa bella mano, K.612; Zauberflöte (sels) *([ENG,GER,ITA]texts)* HUN ▲ 31660 [DDD] (16.97)

W. Landowska (hpd/pno) † Fant Pno, K.397; Son 11 Pno, K.331; Son 12 Pno, K.332; Son 18 Pno, K.576; Son 9 Pno, K.311; J. Haydn:German Dances, H.IX/12; Son 49 Kbd, H.XVI/36 PHS ▲ 9286 (17.97)

E. Lear (sop), T. Stewart (bar), H. Fricke (cnd), Berlin Staatskapelle *(rec Berlin, Germany, June 1975)* ("Reich Mir die Hand, Mein Leben-Opernduette") † G. F. Handel:Giulio Cesare in Egitto (sels); R. Strauss:Arabella (sels); Verdi:Aida (sels); Simon Boccanegra (sels) BER ▲ 9105 [ADD] (10.97)

F. Leider (sop) † Nozze di Figaro (sels); Beethoven:Ah, perfido!, Op. 65; Fidelio (sels); R. Strauss:Ariadne auf Naxos (sels); C. M. von Weber:Oberon (sels) LYS ▲ 399 (17.97)

F. Lott (sop—Donna Elvira), C. Brewer (sop—Donna Anna), N. Focile (sop—Zerlina), J. Hadley (ten—Don Ottavio), A. Corbelli (bar—Leporello), B. Skovhus (bar—Don Giovanni), U. Chiummo (bass—Commendatore/Masetto), C. Mackerras (cnd), Scottish CO, Scottish Chamber Chorus *(rec 1995)* † Don Giovanni (ov) TEL ▲ 80442 [DDD] (16.97)

MOZART, WOLFGANG AMADEUS (cont.)

Don Giovanni (selections) (cont.)

G. De Luca (bar)—Deh! vieni alla finestra (canzonetta) *(rec Milan, Italy, 1905-07)* ("The Harold Wayne Collection, Vol 27: Giuseppe De Luca, Part 1") † Nozze di Figaro (sels); Berlioz:Damnation de Faust (sels); Donizetti:Don Pasquale (sels); Favorita (sels); Linda di Chamounix (sels); Meyerbeer:Dinorah (sels); G. Rossini:Barbiere di Siviglia (sels); Guillaume Tell (sels); A. Thomas:Hamlet (sels); Verdi:Arias SYMP ▲ 1197 (18.97)

L. Maazel (cnd), Paris National Opera Theater Orch—Là ci darem la mano, là mi dirai di si *(rec Église du Liban, Paris, France, 1978)* ("The Essential Mozart") † Con 21 Pno, K.467; Con 4 Hn, K.495; Exsultate, jubilate, K.165; Kleine Nachtmusik, K.525; Nozze di Figaro (ov); Nozze di Figaro (sels); Requiem, K.626; Serenade; Sym 40, K.550; Sym 41, K.551; Vars "Ah! vous dirai-je, Maman", K.265; Zauberflöte (ov) SNYC (Essential Classics) ▲ 64225 [ADD] (7.97)

L. Marshall (sop), E. Pedrazzoli (cnd), London SO *(rec Canada, 1959)* ("Arias - Lois Marshall") † Clemenza di Tito (sels); Entführung aus dem Serail (sels); G. F. Handel:Acis & Galatea (sels); Solomon (sels); J. Haydn:Jahreszeiten (sels); Schöpfung (sels) *(E, F text)* CBC ▲ 2001 [ADD] (16.97)

T. D. Monte (sop) *(rec 1924-41)* ("Arias & Duets") † Nozze di Figaro (sels); V. Bellini:Norma (sels); Sonnambula (sels); Donizetti:Don Pasquale (sels); Fille du régiment (sels); Linda di Chamounix (sels); Lucia di Lammermoor (sels); G. Rossini:Barbiere di Siviglia (sels); Guillaume Tell (sels); Verdi:Falstaff (sels); Rigoletto (sels); Traviata (sels) ENT (Vocal Archives) ▲ 1191 (13.97)

Omnibus Wind Ensemble—Là ci darem la mano, là mi dirai di si; Dalla sua pace; Deh! vieni alla finestra (canzonetta) [arr Lars-Erik Lidstr] *(rec 1996-97)* ("Opera Pearls") † Così fan tutte (ov); Don Giovanni (ov); Zauberflöte (ov); Zauberflöte (sels); Bizet:Carmen (ov); C. Nielsen:Maskarade (orch sels); G. Rossini:Italiana in Algeri (ov); Semiramide (ov); R. Wagner:Tannhäuser (ov); Tannhäuser (sels) OPU ▲ 19602 [AAD] (16.97)

L. Orgonasova (sop), C. Margiono (sop), E. James (mez), J. Clarkson (alt), C. Prégardien (ten), R. Gilfry (ten), I. D. Arcangelo (bass), A. Silvestrelli (bass), J. E. Gardiner (cnd), English Baroque Soloists, Monteverdi Choir ARCV ▲ 449139 [DDD] (18.97)

E. Pinza (b-bar) † Entführung aus dem Serail (sels); Mentre ti lascio, o figlia, K.513; Nozze di Figaro (sels); Zauberflöte (sels); Halévy:Juive (sels); Meyerbeer:Prophète (sels); G. Rossini:Barbiere di Siviglia (sels); Mosè in Egitto (sels); A. Thomas:Le caïd (sels); Mignon (sels) OPIT ▲ 54519 (6.97)

T. Ruffo (bar) *(rec 1912-14)* ("The Golden Years of Titta Ruffo") † Ponchielli:Gioconda (sels); G. Puccini:Tosca (sels); G. Rossini:Barbiere di Siviglia (sels); Verdi:Arias IN ▲ 1356 [ADD] (15.97)

T. Schipa (ten), E. Pinza (bass), Roselle (sgr), L. Halász (cnd) ("Tito Schipa in Opera, 1939-41") † Massenet:Manon (sels) EKLR ▲ 41 (17.97)

E. Schwarzkopf (sop), J. Sutherland (sop), G. Sciutti (sop), L. Alva (ten), E. Wächter (bar), C. M. Giulini (cnd), Philharmonia Orch EMIC ▲ 63078 (11.97)

M. Stabile (bar)—Deh! vieni alla finestra (canzonetta) *(rec 1926)* ("Four Italian Baritones of the Past") † Nozze di Figaro (sels); P. Mascagni:Guglielmo Ratcliff (sels); Meyerbeer:Africaine (sels); G. Rossini:Barbiere di Siviglia (sels); Guillaume Tell (sels); Verdi:Aida (sels); Due Foscari (sels); Falstaff (sels); Otello (sels); Rigoletto (sels); Trovatore (sels); R. Wagner:Tannhäuser (sels) PRE ▲ 89962 (m) (16.97)

M. Stabile (bar)—Deh! vieni alla finestra (canzonetta) *(rec 1926)* † Nozze di Figaro (sels); Boito:Nerone (sels); Donizetti:Don Pasquale (sels); U. Giordano:Andrea Chénier (sels); G. Puccini:Tosca (sels); Verdi:Aida (sels); Falstaff (sels); Otello (sels); Zandonai:Francesca da Rimini (sels) PRE (Lebendige Vergangenheit) ▲ 89180 (m) (16.97)

K. Te Kanawa (sop), L. Maazel (cnd), Paris Opera Orch—Mi tradì quell' alma ingrata † Ponchielli:Gioconda (sels); G. Puccini:Bohème (sels); Edgar (sels); Madama Butterfly (sels); Manon Lescaut (sels); Suor Angelica (sels); G. Rossini:Cenerentola (sels); Verdi:Forza del destino (sels); Otello (sels); Trovatore (sels); R. Wagner:Götterdämmerung (sels); Tristan und Isolde (sels) SNYC ▲ 46288 [ADD] (9.97)

J. Van Dam (b-bar)—Finch'han dal vino calda la testa (Champagne Aria); Deh! vieni alla finestra (canzonetta) ("Le chant d'un mâitre") † Nozze di Figaro (sels); Zauberflöte (sels); G. Mahler:Knaben Wunderhorn; Songs from Rückert; G. Puccini:Bohème (sels); G. Rossini:Barbiere di Siviglia (sels); Verdi:Don Carlos (sels); Rigoletto (sels); R. Wagner:Tannhäuser (sels); Walküre (sels) FORL ▲ 302270 [ADD]

Vienna Volksoper Mozart Ensemble—Madamina! Il catalogo è questo (Catalog song); Là ci darem la mano, là mi dirai di si; Dalla sua pace; Batti, batti, o bel Masetto; Vedrai, carino, se sei buonino; Non mi dir, bell'idol mio *(rec Kittsee, Austria)* ("Mozart Opera for Flute & String Trio") † Entführung aus dem Serail (ov); Entführung aus dem Serail (sels); Zauberflöte (sels) NIMB ▲ 5576 [DDD] (16.97)

B. Walter (cnd), Vienna PO ("Great Mozart Singers, Vol. 1: Opera Arias, 1922-42") † Entführung aus dem Serail (sels); Nozze di Figaro (sels); Zauberflöte (sels) ORFE (Festspiel Dokumente) ▲ 394101 (16.97)

various artists, N. McGegan (cnd), Royal Opera House Orch—Là ci darem la mano, là mi dirai di si; Finch'han dal vino calda la testa (Champagne Aria); Deh! vieni alla finestra (canzonetta) † Ascanio in Alba (sels), K.111; Clemenza di Tito (ov); Clemenza di Tito (sels); Così fan tutte (sels); Entführung aus dem Serail (sels); Nozze di Figaro (sels); Zaide (sels); Zauberflöte (sels) CONI ▲ 55031 (16.97)

artists unknown *(rec Glyndebourne Recordings of 1936)* PHS ▲ 9231 (17.97)

Don Giovanni:Overture

M. Bernardi (cnd), Calgary PO *(rec Jack Singer Hall Calgary Centre for the Perfor, Canada)* ("Mozart: 12 Overtures") † Bastien und Bastienne (sels); Clemenza di Tito (ov); Così fan tutte (ov); Entführung aus dem Serail (ov); Finta semplice (ov); Idomeneo (ov); Lucio Silla (ov); Mitridate (Ov); Nozze di Figaro (ov); Schauspieldirektor (sels); Zauberflöte (ov) SMS (SM 5000) ▲ 5149 [DDD] (16.97)

English Concert Winds [arr Triebensee for winds] † Nozze di Figaro (ov); Serenade Ww, K.375; Serenade Ww, K.388/384a; Zauberflöte (ov) HYP ▲ 66887 (18.97)

P. Freeman (cnd), National Opera Orch ("Opera for Orchestra") † Don Giovanni (sels); Nozze di Figaro (ov); Nozze di Figaro (sels); Zauberflöte (ov) INSD ▲ 3675 (11.97)

L. Hager (cnd), English CO † Bastien und Bastienne (sels); Betulia liberata, K.118; Clemenza di Tito (ov); Così fan tutte (ov); Finta semplice (ov); Idomeneo (ov); Lucio Silla (ov); Mitridate (Ov); Nozze di Figaro (ov); Schauspieldirektor (sels); Zauberflöte (ov) NOVA ▲ 150041 [DDD] (16.97)

Z. Kosler (cnd), Slovak PO † Clemenza di Tito (ov); Così fan tutte (ov); Entführung aus dem Serail (ov); Idomeneo (ov); Nozze di Figaro (ov); Zauberflöte (ov) GZCL ▲ 74 (6.97)

F. Lott (sop—Donna Elvira), C. Brewer (sop—Donna Anna), N. Focile (sop—Zerlina), J. Hadley (ten—Don Ottavio), A. Corbelli (bar—Leporello), B. Skovhus (bar—Don Giovanni), U. Chiummo (bass—Commendatore/Masetto), C. Mackerras (cnd), Scottish CO, Scottish Chamber Chorus *(rec 1995)* † Don Giovanni (sels) TEL ▲ 80442 [DDD] (16.97)

N. Marriner (cnd), Academy of St. Martin in the Fields † Clemenza di Tito (ov); Così fan tutte (ov); Entführung aus dem Serail (ov); Idomeneo (ov); Lucio Silla (ov); Nozze di Figaro (ov); Schauspieldirektor (sels); Zauberflöte (ov) EMIC ▲ 47014 [DDD] (16.97)

Omnibus Wind Ensemble *(rec 1996-97)* ("Opera Pearls") † Così fan tutte (ov); Don Giovanni (sels); Zauberflöte (ov); Zauberflöte (sels); Bizet:Carmen (ov); C. Nielsen:Maskarade (orch sels); G. Rossini:Italiana in Algeri (ov); Semiramide (ov); R. Wagner:Tannhäuser (ov); Tannhäuser (sels) OPU ▲ 19602 [AAD] (16.97)

L. Pešek (cnd), Prague CO *(rec 1966-85)* ("Mozart in Prague") † Con Cl, K.622; Sym 38, K.504 SUR ▲ 3367 [ADD] (7.97)

O. Vlček (cnd), Prague Virtuosi † Concertone Vns, K.190; Sym 38, K.504 DI ▲ 920201 [DDD] (5.97)

H. Vonk (cnd), Dresden Staatskapelle † Ascanio in Alba (sels), K.111; Clemenza di Tito (ov); Così fan tutte (ov); Entführung aus dem Serail (ov); Finta giardiniera (ov); Idomeneo (ov); Lucio Silla (ov); Nozze di Figaro (ov); Schauspieldirektor (sels); Zauberflöte (ov) LALI ▲ 15885 [DDD] (3.97)

B. Wordsworth (cnd), Capella Istropolitana *(rec Czechoslovak Radio Concert Hall Bratislava, Czech Republic, Sept 6-9, 1988)* ("Famous Overtures") † Apollo et Hyacinthus (sels), K.38; Bastien und Bastienne (sels); Clemenza di Tito (ov); Così fan tutte (ov); Entführung aus dem Serail (ov); Finta giardiniera (ov); Idomeneo (ov); Lucio Silla (ov); Mitridate (Ov); Nozze di Figaro (ov); Rè pastore (sels); Schauspieldirektor (sels); Zauberflöte (ov); G. Rossini:Barbiere di Siviglia (ov); Cenerentola (sels); Elisabetta; Guillaume Tell (ov); Italiana in Algeri (ov); Scala di seta (ov); Semiramide (ov); Signor Bruschino (sels); Verdi:Ovs & Preludes NXIN 4-▲ 504013 [DDD] (19.97)

B. Wordsworth (cnd), Capella Istropolitana *(rec Sept 6-9, 1988)* † Bastien und Bastienne (sels); Clemenza di Tito (ov); Così fan tutte (ov); Entführung aus dem Serail (ov); Finta giardiniera (ov); Idomeneo (ov); Lucio Silla (ov); Mitridate (Ov); Nozze di Figaro (ov); Ovs; Rè pastore (sels); Schauspieldirektor (sels); Zauberflöte (ov) NXIN ▲ 550185 [DDD] (5.97)

artists unknown † Clemenza di Tito (sels); Così fan tutte (sels); Entführung aus dem Serail (sels) LALI ▲ 15890 [DDD] (3.97)

Duo in B♭ for Bassoon & Cello, K.292 (1775)

J. Baumann (vc), K. Stoll (db) ("Amazing Duo") † F. Barrière:Son Vc & Db; F. Couperin:Con Vc; G. Rossini:Duet Vc & Db CAMA ▲ 5 (18.97)

J. Baumann (vc), K. Stoll (db) ("Works for Violoncello") † J. S. Bach:Suites Vc; M. Reger:Suites Vc, Op. 131c CAMA ▲ 373

D. Hoebig (vc), C. Millard (bn) † Busser:Portuguesa Bn Pno; P.-M. Dubois:Petite Suite Fl Bn; Morawetz:Son Bn Pno; Sluka:Son Bn; H. Tomasi:Tombeau de Mireille SUMM ▲ 224 (16.97)

L. Jeppeson (vl), J. Hershey (vl) [2 vc arr] ("Music for Viola da Gamba") † C. F. Abel:Suite Vl; Machy:Music of De Machy; Schaffrath:Duet Vdg TIT ▲ 183 [DDD] (16.97)

R. Latzko (vc), E. Hübner (bn) *(rec Hans-Rosbaud Studio, Oct 10-11, 1994)* † F. Krommer:Qt Bn CPO ▲ 999297 [DDD] (14.97)

564 ▲ = CD ♦ = Enhanced CD △ = MD ▮ = Cassette Tape ▯ = DCC

MOZART, WOLFGANG AMADEUS (cont.)

Duo in B♭ for Bassoon & Cello, K.292 (1775) (cont.)

Y.-Y. Ma (vc), A. Heller (bn) † Serenade SNYC ▲ 46248 [ADD] (10.97)

S. Nigro (bn), B. Lane (bn) [arr Andraud for bassoons] † M. Curtis:Impish Imp; D. Dorff:Son d'Armore; Ozi:Son Bns; Vanhal:Con Bns; A. Weisberg:From the Deep CRYS ▲ 349 (15.97)

S. Orton (vc), K. Thunemann (bn) † Con Bn, K.191; Con Cl, K.622 PPHI ▲ 22390 [DDD] (16.97)

F. Pollet (bn), Eugene Ysaÿe String Trio † F. Devienne:Qts Bn; C. Stamitz:Qt Bn; J. C. Vogel:Qts Bn SYRX ▲ 93103 [DDD] (16.97)

G. Stucka (vc), B. Grainger (bn) *(rec DePaul Univ. Concert Hall Chicago, Sept 1992)* † R. Boutry:Interferences; Cascarino:Son Bn; E. Elgar:Romance Bn, Op. 62; Etler:Son Bn; P. Hindemith:Son Bn; Saint-Saëns:Son Bn CENT ▲ 2244 [DDD] (16.97)

Duos (12) for 2 Horns (or Basset Horns), K.487 (1785)

Berlin PO Winds † Diverts Bas Hns, K.Anh.229 ORF ▲ 217901 [DDD] (18.97)

A. Clark (nat hn), Ensemble Galant—No. 1, Allegro; No. 3, Andante *(rec Highgate, London, England, Sept 1997)* † Qnt Hn; Beethoven:Son Hn; Sxt Hns; J. Brahms:Trio Hn, Op. 40 EMIC (Debut) ▲ 72822 [DDD] (6.97)

L'Archibudelli † Divert Hns, K.246b; Divert Vn, K.288; March Hns, K.248; March Hns, K.290; March Hns, K.445; Musikalischer Spass, K.522; Qnt Hn SNYC (Vivarte) ▲ 46702 (16.97)

New World Basset Horn Trio ("Music for Basset Horns") † Diverts Bas Hns, K.Anh.229; A. Stadler:Trios Bas Hns HAM ▲ 1907017 (9.97)

M. Van de Merwe (hn), B. Stoel (hn) ("Chamber Music with Horn") † Musikalischer Spass, K.522; Qnt Hn HEL ▲ 1036 (10.97)

Duo in G for Violin & Viola, K.423 (1783)

S. Goldberg (vn), F. Riddle (va) *(rec 1940)* † Duo Vn, K.424; Sonatas for Violin & Piano (miscellaneous); Beethoven:Son 10 Vn, Op. 96; Son 5 Vn, Op. 24; Son 9 Vn, Op. 47 MUA 3-▲ 4665 (30.97)

Uppsala Chamber Soloists † Grande Sestetto Concertante; Qnt Strs BLUB ▲ 54 [DDD] (18.97)

Duo in B♭ for Violin & Viola, K.424 (1783)

S. Goldberg (vn), P. Hindemith (va) *(rec 1934)* † Duo Vn, K.423; Sonatas for Violin & Piano (miscellaneous); Beethoven:Son 10 Vn, Op. 96; Son 5 Vn, Op. 24; Son 9 Vn, Op. 47 MUA 3-▲ 4665 (30.97)

J. Heifetz (vn), W. Primrose (va) *(rec New York City & RCA Studios Hollywood, NY, 1941)* ("The Heifetz Chamber Music Collection I") † Sonatas for Violin & Piano (miscellaneous); Trio Vn, K.563; E. Grieg:Son 2 Vn, Op. 13; G. F. Handel:Son Vn; Suites de Pièces (8) Hpd, HWV 426-33; Sinding:Suite im alten Stil, Op. 10 RCAV (Gold Seal) 2-▲ 61740 [ADD] (21.97)

Duos (2) in G & B♭ for Violin & Viola, K.423-24 (1783)

L'Archibudelli † Grande Sestetto Concertante SNYC (Vivarte) ▲ 46631 (16.97)

R. Pasquier (vn), B. Pasquier (va) HMA ▲ 1901052 [DDD] (9.97)

I. Perlman (vn), P. Zukerman (va) † J.-M. Leclair:Sons Vns, Op. 3 RCAV (Red Seal) ▲ 60735 [DDD] (16.97)

Die Entführung aus dem Serail [The Abduction from the Seraglio] (opera in 3 acts) [lib J. G. Stephanie, Jr. after C. F. Bretzner], K.384 (1782)

K. Battle (sop), E. Gruberová (sop), H. Zednik (ten), G. Winbergh (ten), M. Talvela (bass), W. Quadflieg (nar), G. Solti (cnd), Vienna PO [GER] PLON 2-▲ 17402 [DDD] (32.97)

J. E. Gardiner (cnd), English Baroque Soloists, Monteverdi Choir London, L. Orgonasova (sop), C. Sieden (sop), U. Peper (ten), S. Olsen (ten), C. Hauptmann (bass), H. Minetti (nar) [GER] PARC 2-▲ 35857 [DDD] (32.97)

S. Greenberg (sop), J. Thames (sop), J. van der Schaaf (ten), W. Gahmlich (ten), K. Rydl (bass), M. Viotti (cnd), Frankfurt RSO, Bamberg Sym Chorus LALI ▲ 14117 [DDD] (3.97)

Y. Kenny (sop), C. Watson (cta), P. Schreier (ten), W. Gamlich (ten), M. Salminen (bass), W. Reichmann (nar), N. Harnoncourt (cnd), Zurich Mozart Opera Orch, Zurich Mozart Opera Chorus [GER] TELC 2-▲ 35673 (33.97)

R. Ronisch (sop), J. Vulpius (sop), R. Apreck (ten), J. Förster (ten), A. van Mill (bass), O. Suitner (cnd), Dresden State Opera Orch, Dresden State Opera Chorus BER 2-▲ 9116 (21.97)

A. Rothenberger (sop—Konstanze), R. Grist (sop—Blondchen), F. Wunderlich (ten—Belmonte), G. Unger (ten—Pedrillo), F. Corena (bass—Osmin), M. Heltau (nar—Selim), Z. Mehta (cnd), Vienna PO, Vienna State Opera Chorus *(rec July 28, 1965)* ORFE (Festspiel Dokumente) 2-▲ 392952 (32.97)

M. Stader (sop—Konstanze), R. Streich (sop—Blondchen), E. Haefliger (ten), M. Vantin (ten), J. Greindl (bass), F. Fricsay (cnd), Berlin RSO, RIAS Chamber Choir *(rec 1954)* † Exsultate, jubilate, K.165 DEUT (The Originals) 2-▲ 457730 (22.97)

C. Studer (sop), E. Szmytka (sop), K. Streit (ten), R. Gambill (ten), G. Missenhardt (bar), M. Heltau (nar), B. Weil (cnd), Vienna SO, Vienna State Opera Chorus SNYC 2-▲ 48053 (32.97)

Die Entführung aus dem Serail (selections)

H. Alsen (bass), R. Moralt (cnd), Vienna PO—Solche hergelauf'ne Laffen *(rec 1944)* ("Vienna Opera Favorites of the Past (1942-1947)") † Don Giovanni (sels); Nozze di Figaro (sels); G. Puccini:Turandot (sels); R. Strauss:Rosenkavalier (sels); Verdi:Aida (sels); Don Carlos (sels); R. Wagner:Meistersinger (sels); Walküre (sels) PRE ▲ 90345 [ADD] (16.97)

E. Baude-Delhommais (cnd) [arr Vent] ("Mozart/Vent Transcriptions by Ensemble Philedor") † Don Giovanni (sels) SUR ▲ 3018 (16.97)

T. Beecham (cnd), London PO ("Beecham & London PO, 1944-45, Vol. 2") † Beethoven:Sym 4; F. Schubert:Sym 6 BCS ▲ 42 (16.97)

E. Berger (sop), M. Perras (sop), A. Kern (sop), M. Ivogün (sop), J. Patzak (ten), P. Anders (ten), H. Jadlowker (ten), H. Roswaenge (ten), K. von Pataky (ten), M. Hirzel (ten), C. Jöken (bar), A. Kipnis (bass), W. Hesch (bass), E. Kandl (sgr) *(rec 1906-37)* ("Great Singers Sing Mozart's Die Entführung aus dem Serail") VOCA (Vocal Archives) ▲ 1151 (13.97)

W. Furtwängler (cnd), Berlin PO *(rec 1929-36)* ("Wilhelm Furtwängler: The Early Recordings, Vol. 1") † Kleine Nachtmusik, K.525; J. S. Bach:Air on the G String; Beethoven:Egmont (ov); Mendelssohn (-Bartholdy):Hebriden, Op. 26; G. Rossini:Gazza ladra (ov); R. Wagner:Lohengrin (preludes); C. M. von Weber:Invitation to the Dance Orch GRM2 ▲ 78574 (13.97)

E. Köth (sop), R. Schock (ten), G. Szell (cnd), Vienna PO—Welch ein Geschick! O Qual der Seele! ("Great Mozart Singers, Vol. 2: Opera Arias, 1949-60") † Così fan tutte (sels); Don Giovanni (sels); Nozze di Figaro (sels); Zauberflöte (sels) ORFE (Festspiel Dokumente) ▲ 394201 (16.97)

J. Kovács (cnd), Hungarian State Orch, M. Szalay (cnd), Hungarian State Opera Male Chorus—Solche hergelauf'ne Laffen; Ha, wie will ich triumphieren; Wer ein Liebchen hat gefunden; Solche hergelauf'ne Laffen; Ha, wie will ich triumphieren *(rec Budapest, Hungary, 1997)* ("Operatic Recitals") † Arias; Clemenza di Tito (sels); Don Giovanni (sels); Mentre ti lascio, o figlia, K.513; Nozze di Figaro (sels); Per questa bella mano, K.612; Zauberflöte (sels) *([ENG,GER,ITA]texts)* HUN ▲ 31660 [DDD] (16.97)

Les Arts Florissants ERAT ▲ 25490 (33.97)

L. Marshall (sop), T. Beecham (cnd), Royal PO *(rec Canada, 1957)* ("Arias - Lois Marshall") † Clemenza di Tito (sels); Don Giovanni (sels); G. F. Handel:Acis & Galatea (sels); Solomon (sels); J. Haydn:Jahreszeiten (sels); Schöpfung (sels) *(E, F text)* CBC ▲ 2001 [ADD] (16.97)

M. Perras (sop), K. Alwin (cnd), Vienna PO—Ach ich liebte, war so glücklich ("Great Mozart Singers, Vol. 1: Opera Arias, 1922-42") † Don Giovanni (sels); Nozze di Figaro (sels); Zauberflöte (sels) ORFE (Festspiel Dokumente) ▲ 394101 (16.97)

E. Pinza (b-bar) † Don Giovanni (sels); Mentre ti lascio, o figlia, K.513; Nozze di Figaro (sels); Zauberflöte (sels); Halévy:Juive (sels); Meyerbeer:Prophète (sels); G. Rossini:Barbiere di Siviglia (sels); Mosè in Egitto (sels); A. Thomas:Le caïd (sels); Mignon (sels) OPIT ▲ 54519 (6.97)

J. Protschka (ten) † Clemenza di Tito (sels); Così fan tutte (sels); Don Giovanni (ov) LALI ▲ 15890 [DDD] (3.97)

H. Roswaenge (ten) *(rec 1928-42)* ("The German Repertoire") † Zauberflöte (sels); Beethoven:Fidelio (sels); P. Cornelius:Barbier von Bagdad (sels); Flotow:Martha (sels); R. Wagner:Lohengrin (sels); Meistersinger (sels); C. M. von Weber:Freischütz (sels); Oberon (sels) VOCA (Vocal Archives) ▲ 1197 (13.97)

H. Roswaenge (ten) *(rec 1937)* ("Helge Rosvaenge: The German Repertoire, 1928-42") † Zauberflöte (sels); Beethoven:Fidelio (sels); P. Cornelius:Barbier von Bagdad (sels); Flotow:Martha (sels); R. Wagner:Lohengrin (sels); Meistersinger (sels); C. M. von Weber:Freischütz (sels); Oberon (sels) MNER ▲ 35 [ADD] (15.97)

B. R. Stees (bn), S. Norris (hp), R. Fusco (pno) [trans for bn, hp & pno] † Donizetti:Elisir d'amore (sels); Lucia di Lammermoor (sels); Hérold:Zampa (ov); G. Rossini:Gazza ladra (sels); P. Tchaikovsky:Eugene Onegin (sels); Verdi:Trovatore (sels); R. Wagner:Tannhäuser (sels) CLAV ▲ 509815 (16.97)

C. Studer (sop), E. Szmytka (sop), K. Streit (ten), R. Gambill (ten), G. Missenhardt (bar), B. Weil (cnd), Vienna SO, Vienna State Opera Chorus *(rec Vienna, Apr 2-10, 1991)* † G. Puccini:Tosca (sels) SNYC (Opera Highlights) ▲ 53500 [DDD] (10.97)

J. Sutherland (sop)—Martern aller Arten *(rec 1956-60)* ("Recitals") † Exsultate, jubilate, K.165; V. Bellini:Norma (sels); Donizetti:Lucia di Lammermoor (sels); G. F. Handel:Alcina (sels); J. Haydn:Arias BELV ▲ 7001 [ADD] (15.97)

R. A. Swenson (sop), C. Mackerras (cnd), Orch of the Age of Enlightenment—Welcher Wechsel herrscht in meiner Seele...Traurigkeit ward mir zum Losse; Martern aller Arten *(rec London, England, Feb 1998)* ("Endless Pleasure") † Lucio Silla (sels); Misera, dove son! & Ah, non son'io che parlo, K.369; G. F. Handel:Giulio Cesare in Egitto (sels); Semele (sels) EMIC ▲ 56672 [DDD] (16.97)

MOZART, WOLFGANG AMADEUS (cont.)

Die Entführung aus dem Serail (selections) (cont.)

Vienna Volksoper Mozart Ensemble—Hier soll ich dich denn sehen, Constanze!; Ich gehe, doch rate ich dir; Frisch zum Kampfe!; Vivat Bacchus!; Ha, wie will ich triumphieren; March of the Janissaries *(rec Kittsee, Austria)* ("Mozart Opera for Flute & String Trio") † Don Giovanni (sels); Entführung aus dem Serail (ov); Zauberflöte (sels) NIMB ▲ 5576 [DDD] (16.97)

F. Wunderlich (ten), I. Kertész (cnd), Vienna PO—Constanze, dich wiederzusehen ("Great Mozart Singers, Vol. 3: Opera Arias, 1961-82") † Così fan tutte (sels); Don Giovanni (sels); Idomeneo (sels); Nozze di Figaro (sels); Zauberflöte (sels) ORFE (Festspiel Dokumente) ▲ 394301 (16.97)

various artists, N. McGegan (cnd), Royal Opera House Orch—Constanze! Constanze! O wie ängstlich, o wie feurig † Ascanio in Alba (sels), K.111; Clemenza di Tito (ov); Clemenza di Tito (sels); Così fan tutte (sels); Don Giovanni (sels); Nozze di Figaro (sels); Zaide (sels); Zauberflöte (sels) CONI ▲ 55031 (16.97)

Die Entführung aus dem Serail:Overture

M. Bernardi (cnd), Calgary PO *(rec Jack Singer Hall Calgary Centre for the Perfor, Canada)* ("Mozart: 12 Overtures") † Bastien und Bastienne (sels); Clemenza di Tito (ov); Così fan tutte (ov); Don Giovanni (ov); Finta semplice (ov); Idomeneo (ov); Lucio Silla (ov); Mitridate (Ov); Nozze di Figaro (ov); Schauspieldirektor (sels); Zauberflöte (ov) SMS (SMS 5000) ▲ 5149 [DDD] (16.97)

K. Böhm (cnd), Saxon State Orch *(rec 1938-39)* † Nozze di Figaro (ov); Leoncavallo:Pagliacci (sels); P. Mascagni:Cavalleria rusticana (sels); Verdi:Aida (sels); R. Wagner:Ovs, Preludes & Orchestral Sels; C. M. von Weber:Freischütz (ov) MTAL ▲ 48061 (6.97)

K. Böhm (cnd), Saxon State Orch *(rec 1930s)* † Nozze di Figaro (ov); Leoncavallo:Pagliacci (sels); Verdi:Aida (sels); R. Wagner:Fliegende Holländer (ov); Meistersinger (ov); Tannhäuser (ov); C. M. von Weber:Freischütz (ov) HCO ▲ 37055 (7.97)

K. Böhm (cnd), Saxon State Orch † Nozze di Figaro (ov); Leoncavallo:Pagliacci (sels); Verdi:Aida (sels); R. Wagner:Fliegende Holländer (ov); Meistersinger (preludes); Tannhäuser (ov); C. M. von Weber:Freischütz (ov) IMMM ▲ 37055 (6.97)

C. Cantieri (cnd), London Festival Orch ("Famous Overtures") † D.-F. Auber:Muette de Portici (ov); M. Glinka:Russlan & Ludmilla (ov); Humperdinck:Hänsel und Gretel (ov); J. Offenbach:Orphée aux enfers (ov); Suppé:Ovs PC ▲ 265013 [DDD] (2.97)

Z. Kosler (cnd), Slovak PO † Clemenza di Tito (ov); Così fan tutte (ov); Don Giovanni (ov); Idomeneo (ov); Nozze di Figaro (ov); Zauberflöte (ov) GZCL ▲ 74 (6.97)

N. Marriner (cnd), Academy of St. Martin in the Fields † Clemenza di Tito (ov); Così fan tutte (ov); Don Giovanni (ov); Idomeneo (ov); Lucio Silla (ov); Nozze di Figaro (ov); Schauspieldirektor (sels); Zauberflöte (ov) EMIC ▲ 47014 [DDD] (16.97)

S. Richman (cnd), Harmonie Ensemble New York [trans for wind ensemble] *(rec Rye, NY, 1992)* † Beethoven:Fidelio (ov); G. Rossini:Barbiere di Siviglia (ov); Guillaume Tell (ov); Semiramide (ov); C. M. von Weber:Freischütz (ov) MUA ▲ 4797 [DDD]

Vienna Volksoper Mozart Ensemble *(rec Kittsee, Austria)* ("Mozart Opera for Flute & String Trio") † Don Giovanni (sels); Entführung aus dem Serail (sels); Zauberflöte (sels) NIMB ▲ 5576 [DDD] (16.97)

H. Vonk (cnd), Dresden Staatskapelle † Ascanio in Alba (sels), K.111; Clemenza di Tito (ov); Così fan tutte (ov); Don Giovanni (ov); Finta giardiniera (ov); Idomeneo (ov); Lucio Silla (ov); Nozze di Figaro (ov); Schauspieldirektor (sels); Zauberflöte (ov) LALI ▲ 15885 [DDD] (3.97)

B. Wordsworth (cnd), Capella Istropolitana *(rec Czechoslovak Radio Concert Hall Bratislava, Czech Republic, Sept 6-9, 1988)* ("Famous Overtures") † Apollo et Hyacinthus (sels), K.38; Bastien und Bastienne (sels); Clemenza di Tito (ov); Così fan tutte (ov); Don Giovanni (ov); Finta giardiniera (ov); Idomeneo (ov); Lucio Silla (ov); Mitridate (Ov); Nozze di Figaro (ov); Rè pastore (sels); Schauspieldirektor (sels); Zauberflöte (ov); G. Rossini:Barbiere di Siviglia (ov); Cenerentola (sels); Elisabetta; Guillaume Tell (ov); Italiana in Algeri (ov); Scala di seta (ov); Semiramide (ov); Signor Bruschino (sels); Verdi:Ovs & Preludes NXIN 4-▲ 504013 [DDD] (19.97)

B. Wordsworth (cnd), Capella Istropolitana *(rec Sept 6-9, 1988)* † Bastien und Bastienne (sels); Clemenza di Tito (ov); Così fan tutte (ov); Don Giovanni (ov); Finta giardiniera (ov); Idomeneo (ov); Lucio Silla (ov); Mitridate (Ov); Nozze di Figaro (ov); Ovs (ov); Rè pastore (sels); Schauspieldirektor (sels); Zauberflöte (ov) NXIN ▲ 550185 [DDD] (5.97)

Die Entführung aus dem Serail [arr for wind ensemble ca late 18th/early 19th cent]

Linos Ensemble † Nozze di Figaro (winds) CAPO ▲ 10493 [DDD] (11.97)

Exsultate, jubilate (motet) in F for Soprano, Orchestra & Organ, K.165 (ca 1773)

E. Ameling (sop), B. Britten (cnd), English CO *(rec 1969)* † Con 27 Pno, K.595; Qt Pno, K.478 BBC (Britten the Performer) ▲ 8005 (17.97)

C. Bartoli (mez), G. Fischer (cnd), Vienna CO ("Mozart Portraits") † Arias; Davidde penitente, K.469 PLON ▲ 43452 (17.97) ▮ 43452 (10.98)

K. Battle (sop), A. Previn (cnd), Royal PO [LAT] EMIC ▲ 47355 [DDD] (16.97)

M. Bayo (sop), V. P. Pérez (cnd), Galicia SO † Ah, lo previdi & Ah, t'invola agl'occhi miei, K.272; Don Giovanni (sels); Idomeneo (sels); Voi avete un cor fedele, K.217; Zaide (sels) VAL ▲ 4790 (18.97)

L. Bernstein (cnd), Bavarian RSO, Bavarian Radio Chorus, A. Augér (sop) *(rec live Apr 1990)* † Ave verum corpus, K.618; Mass 18, K.427 DEUT ▲ 31791 [DDD] (16.97)

J. Blegen (sop), P. Zukerman (cnd), Mostly Mozart Festival Orch † Idomeneo (sels); Rè pastore (sels); Vorrei spiegarvi, oh Dio, K.418; G. F. Handel:Alessandro (sels); Ode for the Birthday of Queen Anne; Samson (sels); A. Scarlatti:Su le sponde del Tebro SNYC (Essential Classics) ▲ 62646 (7.97) ▮ 62646 (3.98)

J. Blegen (sop), P. Zukerman (cnd), Mostly Mozart Festival Orch—Allegro *(rec NYC, NY, July 19, 1978)* ("The Essential Mozart") † Con 21 Pno, K.467; Con 4 Hn, K.495; Don Giovanni (sels); Kleine Nachtmusik, K.525; Nozze di Figaro (ov); Nozze di Figaro (sels); Requiem, K.626; Serenade; Sym 40, K.550; Sym 41, K.551; Vars "Ah! vous dirai-je, Maman", K.265; Zauberflöte (ov) SNYC (Essential Classics) ▲ 64225 [ADD] (7.97)

G. Bohman (sop), J. Wedin (cnd), Kalmar Läns CO [LAT] BIS ▲ 299 [DDD] (17.97)

B. Bonney (sop), N. Harnoncourt (cnd), Vienna Concentus Musicus [LAT] † Mass 4, K.139 TELC ▲ 44180 [DDD] (16.97)

L. Cuberli (sop), M. Lutero (cnd), Il Quartettone CO, Milan City Chorus *(rec live 1998)* † Pergolesi:Miserere 2 in c STRV ▲ 50005 (16.97)

M. Devia (sop), D. Callegari (cnd), Marchigiano PO, Chorus Lirico Marchigiana † Ave verum corpus, K.618; Kleine Nachtmusik, K.525; Regina coeli in C, K.108/74d; Vesperae solennes de confessore, K.339 FON ▲ 9830 (13.97)

G. Fuchs (sop), E. Hinreiner (cnd), Mozarteum Orch, Mozarteum Chorus † Mass 16, K.317; Vesperae de Dominica, K.321 PC ▲ 267142 [DDD] (2.97)

K. T. Kanawa (sop), C. Davis (cnd), London SO [LAT] † Ave verum corpus, K.618; Kyrie; Vesperae solennes de confessore, K.339 PPHI ▲ 12873 [ADD] (11.97)

Z. Kloubová (sop), J. Žigmund (va), J. Krejčí (ob), D. Dimitrov (tpt), V. Roubal (org)—Alleluia † Ave verum corpus, K.618; Vesperae solennes de confessore, K.339; J. S. Bach:Cant 51; Cant 92; G. F. Handel:German Arias, HWV 202-10; Joshua (sels); Messiah (sels); J. Haydn:Schöpfung (sels); Saint-Saëns:Ave Maria; F. Schubert:Ave Maria, Op. 52/6; Vivaldi:Gloria; Motets GZCL ▲ 276 (6.97)

F. Lott (sop), J. Glover (cnd), London Mozart Players [LAT] † Arias ASV ▲ 683 [DDD] (16.97)

S. McNair (sop), J. E. Gardiner (cnd) , Monteverdi Choir London [GER] † G. F. Handel:Laudate pueri Dominum, HWV 236 PPHI ▲ 34920 [DDD] (16.97)

N. Marriner (cnd), Academy of St. Martin in the Fields † Mass 16, K.317; Requiem, K.626 PLON (Double Decker) 2-▲ 43009 (17.97)

E. Mathis (sop), B. Klee (cnd), English CO [LAT] † Ave verum corpus, K.618; Sacred Music; Schuldigkeit des ersten Gebotes (sels) NOVA ▲ 150064 [DDD] (16.97)

J. Micheau (sop), E. Ansermet (cnd), Paris Conservatory Société des Concerts Orch *(rec 1942-47)* ("Ansermet, Vol. 2") † Sym 40, K.550; Sym 41, K.551 LYS1 ▲ 453

A. Muzerelle (cnd), Muzerelle CO, Maîtrise de la Cathédrale *(rec Ardennes, France, Sept 28, 1996)* † J. S. Bach:Mass in b, BWV 232; Moineau:Baptême de Clovis; Messe solennelle de s. Remi; Van Berchem:O Jesu Christe PAVA ▲ 7410 [DDD] (10.97)

T. Pinnock (cnd), English Concert, English Concert Choir, B. Bonney (sop) † Mass 16, K.317; Vesperae solennes de confessore, K.339 PARC ▲ 45353 [DDD] (16.97)

C. Schäfer (sop), C. Abbado (cnd), Berlin PO *(rec Jesus-Christus Church Berlin, Germany, Sept 1997)* † Arias; Idomeneo (sels); Zaide (sels); R. Strauss:Songs DEUT ▲ 457582 [DDD] (16.97)

E. Schumann (sop), H. Wood (cnd), BBC SO ("A Salute to Sir Henry Wood") † Rè pastore (sels); Sinf concertante Vn, K.364; A. Bax:Con Vc; Sym 3 SYMP ▲ 1150 (18.97)

M. Stader (sop), F. Fricsay (cnd), Berlin RIAS SO † Litaniae Lauretanae BVM, K.195; Mass 16, K.317; Mass 18, K.427; Vesperae de Dominica, K.321; Vesperae solennes de confessore, K.339; J. Haydn:Mass 3, "Cäcilienmesse", H.XXII/5 DEUT 2-▲ 37383 [ADD] (17.97)

M. Stader (sop), F. Fricsay (cnd), Berlin RSO † Entführung aus dem Serail, K.384 DEUT (The Originals) 2-▲ 457730 (22.97)

J. Sutherland (sop) *(rec 1956-60)* ("Recitals") † Entführung aus dem Serail (sels); V. Bellini:Norma (sels); Donizetti:Lucia di Lammermoor (sels); G. F. Handel:Alcina (sels); J. Haydn:Arias BELV ▲ 7001 [ADD] (16.97)

MOZART, WOLFGANG AMADEUS (cont.)

Fantasia in f for Mechanical Organ, K.608 (1791)

J. Banowetz (pno), R. Stevenson (pno) [arr Busoni for pno 4-hands] † Busoni:Fant contrappuntistica Pnos; Finnländische Volksweisen, Op. 27; Fugue on the folksong O du lieber Augustin ALTA ▲ 9044 (19.97)

M. M. Faulkner (org), Q. Faulkner (org) [arr for 4-hands] ("Duetto: Early Music for Keyboard-Four Hands") † Adagio & Allegro, K.594; H. L. Hassler:Sacred Music PROO ▲ 7049 [DDD]

T. Vásáry (pno), P. Frankl (pno) [arr for pno duet] † Fugue Pno, K.401; Son Pno 4-Hands, K.19d; Son Pno 4-Hands, K.381; Son Pno 4-Hands, K.497 ASV ▲ 799 [DDD] (16.97)

S. Végh (cnd), Salzburg Camerata Academica † Con 3 Vn, K.216; Con 4 Vn, K.218 LALI ▲ 15879 [DDD] (3.97)

Vienna Flautists [arr performers for fl ensemble] † Adagio & Allegro, K.594; Andante & Vars, K.501; Andante Mechanical Org, K.616; Diverts Str Qt, K.136-138; A. Prinz:Zauberflötiana ORF ▲ 239911 [DDD] (18.97)

Fantasia in d for Piano, K.397 (1782 or 1786-87)

V. Afanassiev (pno) *(rec Musica Théâtre La Chaux-de-Fonds, Apr 6-7, 1993)* † Adagio Pno, K.540; Fant Pno, K.396; Fant Pno, K.475; Son 14 Pno, K.457 DNN ▲ 78945 [DDD] (16.97)

D. Ambache (pno) *(rec Jan 1990)* † Adagio Pno, K.540; Con 17 Pno, K.453; Con 19 Pno, K.459; Con 21 Pno, K.467; Con 25 Pno, K.503 VCL 2-▲ 61445 [DDD] (11.97)

P. Badura-Skoda (pno) † Adagio Pno, K.540; Pno Music (misc colls); Prelude & Fugue Pno, K.394; Rondo Pno, K.511; Vars "Ah! vous dirai-je, Maman", K.265 ASTR ▲ 7710 [AAD] (19.97)

J. Doyen (pno), C. Munch (cnd), Paris Conservatory Société des Concerts Orch *(rec 1941-42)* ("Munch, Vol. 6") † Con 20 Pno, K.466; P. Tchaikovsky:Con 1 Pno, Op. 23 LYS ▲ 400 (17.97)

H. Francesch (pno) † Fant Pno, K.396; Fant Pno, K.475; Son 15 Pno, K.533; Sons Pno KPT 5-▲ 32092 [DDD]

G. Gould (pno) *(rec 1972)* † Son 11 Pno, K.331; Son 12 Pno, K.332; Son 13 Pno, K.333; Son 14 Pno, K.457; Son 15 Pno, K.533; Son 16 Pno, K.545; Son 17 Pno, K.570 SNYC 2-▲ 45613 (14.97)

M. Horszowski (pno) † Beethoven:Son 2 Pno, Op. 2/2; Debussy:Children's Corner NON ▲ 79160 [DDD] (16.97)

M. Horszowski (pno) ("Complete Piano Sonatas, Vol. 2") † Rondo Pno, K.511; Son Pno; Son 10 Pno, K.330; Son 11 Pno, K.331; Son 12 Pno, K.332; Son 13 Pno, K.333; Son 14 Pno, K.457; Son 15 Pno, K.533; Son 16 Pno, K.545; Son 17 Pno, K.570; Son 18 Pno, K.576; Son 9 Pno, K.311 ARBT 3-▲ 104 (16.97)

W. Landowska (hpd/pno) † Don Giovanni (sels); Son 11 Pno, K.331; Son 12 Pno, K.332; Son 18 Pno, K.576; Son 9 Pno, K.311; J. Haydn:German Dances, H.IX/12; Son 49 Kbd, H.XVI/36 PHS ▲ 9286 (17.97)

A. D. Larrocha (pno) ("Vol. 4") † Fant Pno, K.475; Rondo Pno, K.485; Son 1 Pno, K.279; Son 14 Pno, K.457; Son 2 Pno, K.280 RCAV (Red Seal) ▲ 60453 (16.97)

J. Leach (pno) ("4 Square:A Selection of Favourite 18th & 19th Century Piano Pieces") † Son 11 Pno, K.331; J. S. Bach:Partitas Hpd; Mendelssohn (-Bartholdy):Lieder ohne Worte ATH ▲ 3 (19.97)

M. J. Pires (pno) ("W.A. Mozart: The Complete Piano Sonatas, Vol. 5") † Son 15 Pno, K.533; Son 16 Pno, K.545; Son 17 Pno, K.570; Son 18 Pno, K.576 DNN ▲ 8075 (10.97)

I. Pogorelich (pno) † Son 11 Pno, K.331; Son 5 Pno, K.283 DEUT ▲ 37763 [DDD] (16.97)

M. Shehori (pno) † Adagio Pno, K.540; Andante Mechanical Org, K.616; Rondo Pno, K.485; Beethoven:Son 2 Pno, Op. 2/2; Liszt:Rhap espagnole, S.254; Trans, Arrs & Paraphrases CEMB ▲ 100 [DDD] (15.97)

M. Uchida (pno) † Son 11 Pno, K.331; Son 12 Pno, K.332 PPHI ▲ 12123 [DDD] (16.97)

Fantasia in c for Piano, K.396 (1782)

V. Afanassiev (pno) *(rec Musica Théâtre La Chaux-de-Fonds, Apr 6-7, 1993)* † Adagio Pno, K.540; Fant Pno, K.397; Fant Pno, K.475; Son 14 Pno, K.457 DNN ▲ 78945 [DDD] (16.97)

A. Brendel (pno) † Rondo Pno, K.511; Son 8 Pno, K.310; Vars on a Minuet, K.573 VC ▲ 4025 [ADD] (13.97)

E. Fischer (pno) ("Edwin Fischer: The Recordings, 1933-38") † Minuet Pno, K.1; Son 11 Pno, K.331; F. Schubert:Impromptus (8) ENPL (The Piano Library) ▲ 191 (13.97)

E. Fischer (pno) *(rec 1933-38)* † Minuet Pno, K.1; Son 11 Pno, K.331; F. Schubert:Impromptus (8) ENT (Sirio) ▲ 530025 (13.97)

E. Fischer (pno) *(rec 1933-47)* ("Mozart Piano Recordings, Vol. 2") † Con 17 Pno, K.453; Con 24 Pno, K.491; Son 11 Pno, K.331 APR ▲ 5524 (m) [ADD] (18.97)

E. Fischer (pno) *(rec Oct 1947)* † Con 25 Pno, K.503; Fant Pno, K.475; Minuet Pno, K.1; Romance Pno, K.Anh.205; Son 11 Pno, K.331 PHS (Edwin Fischer Plays Mozart-Vol. II) ▲ 43 [ADD] (17.97)

H. Francesch (pno) † Fant Pno, K.397; Fant Pno, K.475; Son 15 Pno, K.533; Sons Pno KPT 5-▲ 32092 [DDD]

L. Nadelmann (pno) ("The Renowned WQXR Recordings of 1956/7") † Son 10 Pno, K.330; Beethoven:Son 10 Pno, Op. 14/2; J. Haydn:Son Kbd; Son 59 Kbd, H.XVI/49; Vars (6) Kbd, H.XVII/5; F. Schubert:Impromptus (4); Son Pno, D.960 APR ▲ 7026 [AAD]

H. Půlsson (pno) *(rec Apr 11, 1976)* † M. Clementi:Sonatas for Piano; G. Fauré:Trio Pno, Op. 120; C. Franck:Son Vn, M.8; J. Haydn:Son 12 Kbd, H.XVI/12; S. Prokofiev:Son Vc; Sinding:Son Pno, Op. 91 BIS ▲ 35 [AAD/DDD] (17.97)

B. Schulman (pno) † Con 18 Pno, K.456; Vars "Salve tu, Domine", K.398; M. Ravel:Con Pno RD ▲ 30006 (16.97)

Fantasia in c for Piano, K.475 (1785)

V. Afanassiev (pno) *(rec Musica Théâtre La Chaux-de-Fonds, Apr 6-7, 1993)* † Adagio Pno, K.540; Fant Pno, K.396; Fant Pno, K.397; Son 14 Pno, K.457 DNN ▲ 78945 [DDD] (16.97)

C. Arrau (pno) *(rec 1969-90)* ("Claudio Arrau III") † Chopin:Pno Music (misc colls); Debussy:Images (6) Pno; E. Granados:Colección de Tonadillas; Liszt:Album d'un voyageur, S.156; Trans, Arrs & Paraphrases; F. Schubert:Moments musicaux, D.780 PPHI (Great Pianists of the 20th Century) 2-▲ 456712 (22.97)

W. Backhaus (pno) *(rec Salzburg Mozart Festival, 1956)* † Rondo Pno, K.511; Son 10 Pno, K.330; Son 11 Pno, K.331; Son 14 Pno, K.457 APS ▲ 991009 (12.97)

M. Bilson (pno) ("Vol. 3") † Son 15 Pno, K.533; Sons Pno HUN 2-▲ 31013 [DDD] (16.97)

R. Brautigam (pno) ("Complete Piano Sonatas, Vol. 5") † Son 13 Pno, K.333; Son 14 Pno, K.457 BIS ▲ 839 [DDD] (17.97)

A. Brendel (pno) *(rec 1991)* ("Alfred Brendel") † J. Haydn:Sonatas for Piano; F. Schubert:Impromptus (4); Impromptus (4) Pno; R. Schumann:Fantasiestücke Pno, Op. 12 PPHI (Great Pianists of the 20th Century) ▲ 456727 (22.97)

A. Ciccolini (pno) ("Piano Sonatas, Vol. 1") † Son 14 Pno, K.457; Son 2 Pno, K.280; Son 4 Pno, K.282 DI ▲ 920144 [DDD] (5.97)

P. Crawford (pno) † Rondo Pno, K.511; Son 14 Pno, K.457; Son 6 Pno, K.284 TIT ▲ 206 [DDD]

Y. Egorov (pno) *(rec Dec 16, 1978)* † J. S. Bach:Chromatic Fant & Fugue, BWV 903; Chopin:Fantaisie Pno, Op. 49; R. Schumann:Fant Pno, Op. 17 GLOE ▲ 6015 [ADD] (16.97)

M. A. Estrella (pno) *(rec Nov 14, 1991)* † Son 14 Pno, K.457; Liszt:Son Pno, S.178 GALL ▲ 719 [DDD]

E. Fischer (pno) *(rec Oct 1947)* † Con 25 Pno, K.503; Fant Pno, K.396; Minuet Pno, K.1; Romance Pno, K.Anh.205; Son 11 Pno, K.331 PHS (Edwin Fischer Plays Mozart-Vol. II) ▲ 43 [ADD] (17.97)

H. Francesch (pno) † Fant Pno, K.396; Fant Pno, K.397; Son 15 Pno, K.533; Sons Pno KPT 5-▲ 32092 [DDD]

A. Haefliger (pno) † Son 12 Pno, K.332; Son 13 Pno, K.333; Son 14 Pno, K.457 SNYC ▲ 46748 (11.97)

M. Horszowski (pno), F. Waldman (cnd), Musica Aeterna Ensemble † Con 17 Pno, K.453; Con 18 Pno, K.456; Con 20 Pno, K.466; Con 22 Pno, K.482 PHS 2-▲ 9153 [ADD] (33.97)

J. Jandó (pno) *(rec 1991)* ("Mozart: Piano Sonatas, Vol. 5") † Son 13 Pno, K.333; Son 14 Pno, K.457; Son 2 Pno, K.280 NXIN ▲ 550449 [DDD] (5.97)

A. Karis (pno) † Adagio Glass Amc, K.356; Gigue Pno, K.574; Minuet Pno, K.355; Rondo Pno, K.485; Son 12 Pno, K.332; Son 18 Pno, K.576; Son 8 Pno, K.310 BRID ▲ 9011 [ADD] (17.97)

P. Katin (pno) † Son 10 Pno, K.330; Son 11 Pno, K.331; Son 14 Pno, K.457 OLY ▲ 230 [DDD] (16.97)

W. Klien (pno) *(rec 1964)* ("Vol. 2") † Son 12 Pno, K.332; Son 13 Pno, K.333; Son 14 Pno, K.457; Son 15 Pno, K.533; Son 16 Pno, K.545; Son 17 Pno, K.570; Son 18 Pno, K.576 VB2 2-▲ 5046 [ADD] (9.97)

Z. Kocsis (pno) ("Piano Sonatas, Vol. 2") † Son 1 Pno, K.279; Son 10 Pno, K.330; Son 11 Pno, K.331; Son 14 Pno, K.457; Son 15 Pno, K.533; Son 17 Pno, K.570; Son 18 Pno, K.576; Son 3 Pno, K.281; Son 7 Pno, K.309 HUN 3-▲ 31804 [AAD] (47.97)

A. D. Larrocha (pno) ("Vol. 4") † Fant Pno, K.397; Rondo Pno, K.485; Son 1 Pno, K.279; Son 14 Pno, K.457; Son 2 Pno, K.280 RCAV (Red Seal) ▲ 60453 (16.97)

I. Moravec (pno) *(rec 1967)* † Son 14 Pno, K.457; Son 17 Pno, K.570; Beethoven:Bagatelle Pno in a, WoO 59; Bagatelles; J. Brahms:Intermezzos (3) Pno, Op. 117 VAIA ▲ 1096 (17.97)

S. Richter (pno) *(rec Oct 2, 1991)* † Son 14 Pno, K.457; J. Haydn:Son Kbd; Son 33 Kbd, H.XVI/20 STRV ▲ 33343 [DDD] (16.97)

S. Richter (pno) *(rec Bochum Germany, Oct 21, 1992)* † Son 14 Pno, K.457; Beethoven:Son 30 Pno, Op. 109; Son 31 Pno, Op. 110 LV ▲ 422 [DDD] (17.97)

M. Uchida (pno) † Son 1 Pno, K.279; Son 14 Pno, K.457; Son 18 Pno, K.576 PPHI ▲ 12617 [DDD] (16.97)

E. Wirssaladze (pno) *(rec Munich, Jan 15, 1995)* † Son 14 Pno, K.457; Vars "Lison dormait", K.264; S. Prokofiev:Son 8 Pno, Op. 84 LV ▲ 351 [DDD] (17.97)

La finta giardiniera (opera buffa in 3 acts) [lib ?Calzabigi, rev Coltellini], K.196 (1775)

D. Upshaw (sop), C. Margiono (sop), E. Gruberová (sop), M. Bacelli (mez), U. Heilmann (ten), A. Scharinger (bass), N. Harnoncourt (cnd), Vienna Concentus Musicus TELC 3-▲ 72309 (50.97)

La finta giardiniera:Overture

C. Davis (cnd), Staatskapelle Dresden † Bastien und Bastienne (sels); Così fan tutte (ov); Entführung aus dem Serail (ov); Lucio Silla (ov); Nozze di Figaro (ov); Ovs; Schauspieldirektor (sels) RCAV ▲ 63500 (16.97)

MOZART, WOLFGANG AMADEUS (cont.)

La finta giardiniera:Overture (cont.)

C. Groves (cnd), English Sinfonia † Nozze di Figaro (ov); Sinf concertante Ob, K.Anh.9; Sym 25, K.183 ICC ▲ 6702502 (9.97)

H. Vonk (cnd), Dresden Staatskapelle † Ascanio in Alba (sels), K.111; Clemenza di Tito (ov); Così fan tutte (ov); Don Giovanni (ov); Entführung aus dem Serail (ov); Idomeneo (ov); Lucio Silla (ov); Nozze di Figaro (ov); Schauspieldirektor (sels); Zauberflöte (ov) LALI ▲ 15885 [DDD] (3.97)

B. Wordsworth (cnd), Capella Istropolitana *(rec Czechoslovak Radio Concert Hall Bratislava, Czech Republic, Sept 6-9, 1988)* ("Famous Overtures") † Apollo et Hyacinthus (sels), K.38; Bastien und Bastienne (sels); Clemenza di Tito (ov); Così fan tutte (ov); Don Giovanni (ov); Entführung aus dem Serail (ov); Idomeneo (ov); Lucio Silla (ov); Mitridate (Ov); Nozze di Figaro (ov); Rè pastore (sels); Schauspieldirektor (sels); Zauberflöte (ov); G. Rossini:Barbiere di Siviglia (ov); Cenerentola (sels); Elisabetta; Guillaume Tell (ov); Italiana in Algeri (ov); Scala di seta (ov); Semiramide (ov); Signor Bruschino (sels); Verdi:Ovs & Preludes NXIN 4-▲ 504013 [DDD] (19.97)

B. Wordsworth (cnd), Capella Istropolitana *(rec Sept 6-9, 1988)* † Bastien und Bastienne (sels); Clemenza di Tito (ov); Così fan tutte (ov); Don Giovanni (ov); Entführung aus dem Serail (ov); Idomeneo (ov); Lucio Silla (ov); Mitridate (Ov); Nozze di Figaro (ov); Ovs; Rè pastore (sels); Schauspieldirektor (sels); Zauberflöte (ov) NXIN ▲ 550185 [DDD] (5.97)

La finta semplice (opera buffa in 3 acts) [lib M. Coltellini after Goldoni], K.51 (1769)

H. Donath (sop), J. Ihloff (sop), T. Berganza (mez), A. Rolfe Johnson (ten), T. Moser (ten), R. Holl (bass), R. Lloyd (bass), L. Hager (cnd), Salzburg Mozarteum Orch [ITA] ORF 3-▲ 85843 [DDD] (54.97)

La finta semplice:Overture

M. Bernardi (cnd), Calgary PO *(rec Jack Singer Hall Calgary Centre for the Perfor, Canada)* ("Mozart: 12 Overtures") † Bastien und Bastienne (sels); Clemenza di Tito (ov); Così fan tutte (ov); Don Giovanni (ov); Entführung aus dem Serail (ov); Idomeneo (ov); Lucio Silla (ov); Mitridate (Ov); Nozze di Figaro (ov); Schauspieldirektor (sels); Zauberflöte (ov) SMS (SM 5000) ▲ 5149 [DDD] (16.97)

L. Hager (cnd), English CO † Bastien und Bastienne (sels); Betulia liberata, K.118; Clemenza di Tito (ov); Così fan tutte (ov); Don Giovanni (ov); Idomeneo (ov); Lucio Silla (ov); Mitridate (Ov); Nozze di Figaro (ov); Schauspieldirektor (sels); Zauberflöte (ov) NOVA ▲ 150041 [DDD] (16.97)

Fugue in g for Piano [completed M. Stadler], K.401 (1782)

Phantasm [arr Phantasm] † Fugues Str Qt, K.405; J. S. Bach:Art of the Fugue, BWV 1080 SIMX ▲ 1135 (18.97)

T. Vásáry (pno), P. Frankl (pno) [duet version] † Fant Mechanical Org, K.608; Son Pno 4-Hands, K.19d; Son Pno 4-Hands, K.381; Son Pno 4-Hands, K.497 ASV ▲ 799 [DDD] (16.97)

Fugue in c for 2 Pianos, K.426 (1783)

N. Palmier (pno), J. Rigal (pno) † Adagio & Fugue Strs, K.546; Pno Music for 2 Pnos; Son Pno 4-Hands, K.19d; Son Pnos, K.448 ARN ▲ 68028 [DDD] (16.97)

P. Serkin (pno), A. Schiff (pno) *(rec Academy of Arts and Letters, NYC, NY, Nov 1997)* † Son Pnos, K.448; Busoni:Fant contrappuntistica Pnos; M. Reger:Vars & Fugue on a Theme of Beethoven, Op. 86 UECM 2-▲ 465062 [DDD] (34.97)

Fugues (5) for String Quartet [arr of 5 J. S. Bach Fugues, BWV 871, 876, 878, 877 & 874], K.405 (1782)

Phantasm [arr Phantasm] † Fugue Pno, K.401; J. S. Bach:Art of the Fugue, BWV 1080 SIMX ▲ 1135 (18.97)

Gallimathias musicum for Harpsichord, 2 Oboes, 2 Horns, 2 Bassoons & Strings, K.32 (1766)

C. Hogwood (bc), J. Schröder (cnd), Academy of Ancient Music ("The Symphonies") † Cassation Obs, K.100; Music of Mozart; Symphonies (miscellaneous) PLOI 19-▲ 452496 [ADD] (127.97)

C. Scimone (cnd) *(rec Vicenza Italy, June 10-14, 1994)* ("Early Symphonies, Vol 1") † Sym in F; Sym 1, K.16; Sym 4, K.19; Sym 5, K.22; Sym 6, K.43 AART ▲ 47100 [DDD] (10.97)

German Dances (6) for Orchestra, K.509 (1787)

E. Leinsdorf (cnd), London SO *(rec 1975)* † Kleine Nachtmusik, K.525; Minuet Orch, K.338; Serenade 9 Orch, K.320 SNYC (Essential Classics) ▲ 48266 [ADD] (7.97) ▮ 48266 [ADD] (3.98)

German Dances (6) for Orchestra, K.536 (1787)

G. Tintner (cnd), Nova Scotia SO † Contredanse, K.534; Contredanses (2), K.463; Contredanses (5), K.609; German Dances (3), K.605; German Dances (6), K.567; Marches Orch, K.408; Minuets Orch, K.585; Minuets, K.601; Petits riens (sels) SMS (SM 5000) ▲ 5095 [DDD] (16.97)

German Dances (6) for Orchestra, K.567 (1788)

G. Tintner (cnd), Nova Scotia SO † Contredanse, K.534; Contredanses (2), K.463; Contredanses (5), K.609; German Dances (3), K.605; German Dances (6), K.536; Marches Orch, K.408; Minuets Orch, K.585; Minuets, K.601; Petits riens (sels) SMS (SM 5000) ▲ 5095 [DDD] (16.97)

German Dances (6) for Orchestra, K.600 (1791)

H. von Karajan (cnd), Vienna PO *(rec 1946)* ("The Young Karajan: The First Recordings, Vol. 7: The Early Recordings with Walter Legge") † German Dances (3), K.605; Sym 33, K.319; Beethoven:Sym 8; P. Tchaikovsky:Romeo & Juliet GRM2 ▲ 78691 (13.97)

F. Litschauer (cnd), Vienna State Opera CO—No. 1 in C; No. 4 in E♭; No. 5 in G; No. 2 in F; No. 3 in B♭ *(rec Vienna, Austria, 1952)* ("Contradances from Old Vienna") † Contredanse, K.534; Contredanses (5), K.609; German Dances (3), K.605; German Dances (4), K.602; German Dances (6), K.606; Beethoven:Contredanses Orch, WoO 14; Dances Fls, WoO 17; F. Schubert:German Dances & Trios Str Qt, D.90 VC ▲ 8206 [ADD] (13.97)

Vienna Ensemble † Diverts Str Qt, K.136-138; Lanner:Mozartisten, Op. 196 SNYC ▲ 47672 (11.97)

German Dances (4) for Orchestra, K.602 (1791)

F. Litschauer (cnd), Vienna State Opera CO—No. 3 in C, "Organ Grinder" *(rec Vienna, Austria, 1952)* ("Contradances from Old Vienna") † Contredanse, K.534; Contredanses (5), K.609; German Dances (3), K.605; German Dances (6), K.600; German Dances (6), K.606; Beethoven:Contredanses Orch, WoO 14; Dances Fls, WoO 17; F. Schubert:German Dances & Trios Str Qt, D.90 VC ▲ 8206 [ADD] (13.97)

German Dances (3) for Orchestra, K.605 (1791)

A. Doráti (cnd), London SO † Kleine Nachtmusik, K.525; March Orch, K.249; Marches Orch, K.335; Minuet Orch, K.338; Sym 51; G. F. Handel:Royal Fireworks Music, HWV 351; Water Music (arr suite) MRCR ▲ 434398 (11.97)

H. von Karajan (cnd), Vienna PO *(rec 1946)* ("The Young Karajan: The First Recordings, Vol. 7: The Early Recordings with Walter Legge") † German Dances (6), K.600; Sym 33, K.319; Beethoven:Sym 8; P. Tchaikovsky:Romeo & Juliet GRM2 ▲ 78691 (13.97)

F. Litschauer (cnd), Vienna State Opera CO *(rec Vienna, Austria, 1952)* ("Contradances from Old Vienna") † Contredanse, K.534; Contredanses (5), K.609; German Dances (4), K.602; German Dances (6), K.600; German Dances (6), K.606; Beethoven:Contredanses Orch, WoO 14; Dances Fls, WoO 17; F. Schubert:German Dances & Trios Str Qt, D.90 VC ▲ 8206 [ADD] (13.97)

J. Lubbock (cnd), St. John's Smith Square Orch † L. Mozart:Cassation ASVQ ▲ 6197 (10.97)

N. Marriner (cnd), Academy of St. Martin in the Fields ("The Mozart Experience") † Con Cl, K.622; Con Fl & Hp, K.299; Con Movt Hn, K.Anh.98a; Con 20 Pno, K.466; Con 21 Pno, K.467; Divert Ww; Kleine Nachtmusik, K.525; Musikalischer Spass, K.522; Nozze di Figaro (sels); Serenade 6 Orch, K.239; Sym 40, K.550; Sym 41, K.551 PPHI 5-▲ 26204 (33.97)

G. Tintner (cnd), Nova Scotia SO † Contredanse, K.534; Contredanses (2), K.463; Contredanses (5), K.609; German Dances (6), K.536; German Dances (6), K.567; Marches Orch, K.408; Minuets Orch, K.585; Minuets, K.601; Petits riens (sels) SMS (SM 5000) ▲ 5095 [DDD] (16.97)

Vienna Ensemble—No. 1 in D; No. 3 in C, "Die Schlittenfahrt" ("Age of Elegance Greatest Hits") † Kleine Nachtmusik, K.525; Beethoven:Bagatelle Pno in a, WoO 59; Contredanses Orch, WoO 14; Boccherini:Minuetto Strs; C. W. Gluck:Iphigénie en Aulide (sels); Orfeo ed Euridice (dance); G. F. Handel:Cons (16) Org; Serse (sels); Water Music (sels); J. Haydn:Qts (6) Strs, H.III/13-18, Op. 3; Sym 82; H. Purcell:King Arthur (sels); Trumpet Tune & Ayre SNYC ▲ 62369 [ADD] (9.97) ▮ 62369 [ADD] (5.98)

B. Walter (cnd) † Con 20 Pno, K.466; Kleine Nachtmusik, K.525; Sym 38, K.504 MTAL ▲ 48028 (6.97)

B. Walter (cnd), Columbia SO *(rec New York, NY, Dec. 1954)* ("Volume 4") † Minuets, K.568; Music of Mozart; Ovs; J. Haydn:Sym 96 SNYC (The Bruno Walter Edition) ▲ 64486 [ADD] (10.97)

B. Walter (cnd), Los Angeles PO *(rec 1949-50)* ("Bruno Walter in Concert, Vol. 1") † Berlioz:Damnation de Faust (sels); C. M. von Weber:Freischütz (ov); Invitation to the Dance Orch; Konzertstück Pno, J.282; Oberon (ov) EKLR ▲ 1402 (17.97)

German Dances (6) in B♭ for Orchestra, K.606 (1791)

F. Litschauer (cnd), Vienna State Opera CO—No. 1; No. 2; No. 3; No. 4; No. 5 *(rec Vienna, Austria, 1952)* ("Contradances from Old Vienna") † Contredanse, K.534; Contredanses (5), K.609; German Dances (3), K.605; German Dances (4), K.602; German Dances (6), K.600; Beethoven:Contredanses Orch, WoO 14; Dances Fls, WoO 17; F. Schubert:German Dances & Trios Str Qt, D.90 VC ▲ 8206 [ADD] (13.97)

Gigue in G for Piano, K.574 (1789)

M. Hess (pno) *(rec 1958)* ("Hess & Fournier in a New York Sonata Recital") † Rondo Pno, K.485; J. S. Bach:Sons Vl; Beethoven:Son 4 Vc; Vars Vc on "Ein Mädchen oder Weibchen", Op. 66; J. Brahms:Son 2 Vc, Op. 99 RELE ▲ 1895 [ADD]

A. Karis (pno) † Adagio Glass Amc, K.356; Fant Pno, K.475; Minuet Pno, K.355; Rondo Pno, K.485; Son 12 Pno, K.332; Son 18 Pno, K.576; Son 8 Pno, K.310 BRID ▲ 9011 [ADD] (17.97)

M. Uchida (pno) † Adagio Pno, K.540; Son 10 Pno, K.330; Son 13 Pno, K.333 PPHI ▲ 12616 [DDD] (16.97)

NYMAN, MICHAEL (cont.)
Zoo Caprices for Violin
A. Balanescu (vn) † And do they do JAYR ▲ 1322 (16.97)
NYORD, MORTEN (20th cent)
Rørdrum for Wind Quartet (1995)
Reed Quartet *(rec June 1996)* ("Scandinavian Contemporary Works") † F. C. Hansen:Prélude, Estampie et Fugue; Roikjer:Little Intermezzi; Sagvik:Roughs from the Wooden Wind; F. Weis:Studies Ww Qnt; Wiernik:Feelings KPT ▲ 32243
NYSTEDT, KNUT (1915-
Concerto for Horn & Orchestra, Op. 114 (1986)
F. R. Werke (hn), O. K. Ruud (cnd), Trondheim SO ("Corno di Norvegia") † T. Madsen:Con Hn; W. Plagge:Con Hn SIMX ▲ 1100 (18.97)
O Crux for Chorus
C. Hogset (cnd), Grex Vocalis ("Crux") † E. Grieg:Psalms; Kverno:Choral Music; Nordheim:Lamentations NORW ▲ 9308 (17.97)
Organ Music
G. Petersen-Øverlier (org)—Fant trionfale, Op. 57; Le verbe éternal, Op. 133; Intro & Passacaglia, Op. 7; Pietà, Op. 50; Toccata, Op. 9; Pastorale, Op. 20/1; Prélude Héroïque, Op. 123; Veni Creator Spiritus, Op. 75; Ressurrexit, Op. 68 ("Organ Works") † M. Ravel:Pno Music SIMX ▲ 1127 [DDD] (18.97)
NYSTROEM, GÖSTA (1890-1966)
The Arctic Sea [Is havet] (symphonic poem) for Orchestra (1924-25)
P. Erös (cnd), Stockholm PO † Sinf breve; Sym 5 CAPA ▲ 21332 [ADD] (16.97)
P. Järvi (cnd), Malmö SO *(rec Malmö Concert Hall Sweden, Aug 8-9, 1994)* † Con Va; Sinf concertante BIS ▲ 682 [DDD] (17.97)
Concerto for Viola & Orchestra, "Hommage à la France" (1941)
N. Imai (va), P. Järvi (cnd), Malmö SO *(rec Malmö Concert Hall Sweden, May 14, 1994)* † Arctic Sea; Sinf concertante BIS ▲ 682 [DDD] (17.97)
Sinfonia breve for Orchestra (1931)
P. Erös (cnd), Stockholm PO † Arctic Sea; Sym 5 CAPA ▲ 21332 [ADD] (16.97)
Sinfonia concertante for Cello & Orchestra (1944; rev. 1951-52)
E. B. Bengtsson (vc), S. Westerberg (cnd), Swedish RSO † Sym 3 SWES ▲ 1015 (17.97)
N. Ullner (vc), P. Järvi (cnd), Malmö SO *(rec Malmö Concert Hall Sweden, Aug 16-18, 1994)* † Arctic Sea; Con Va BIS ▲ 682 [DDD] (17.97)
Songs at the Sea [Sanger vid havet] for Voice & Orchestra (1941)
R. Lang (cta), H. Frank (cnd), Helsingborg SO [SWE] *(rec 1991)* † E. Elgar:Sea Pictures, Op. 37; R. Wagner:Wesendonck Songs BIS ▲ 530 [DDD] (17.97)
M. Schéle (sop), B. Finnila (cta), R. Leanderson (bar), E. Lundén (pno) ("Swedish Vocal Music") † Gefors:Songs of Trusting; H. Rosenberg:Chinese Songs; Werle:Night Hunt BIS ▲ 38 (17.97)
Symphony No. 2, "Sinfonia espressiva" (1935)
P. Järvi (cnd), Malmö SO *(rec Mar-Apr 1996)* † Sym 5 BIS ▲ 782 [DDD] (17.97)
Symphony No. 3 for Soprano & Orchestra, "Sinfonia del Mare" (1947-48)
E. Söderström (sop), S. Westerberg (cnd), Swedish RSO † Sinf concertante SWES ▲ 1015 (17.97)
Symphony No. 5, "Sinfonia seria" (1963)
P. Erös (cnd), Stockholm PO † Arctic Sea; Sinf breve CAPA ▲ 21332 [ADD] (16.97)
P. Järvi (cnd), Malmö SO *(rec Mar-Apr 1996)* † Sym 2 BIS ▲ 782 [DDD] (17.97)
NYTCH, JEFFREY (1964-
Novas for Orchestra (1992)
R. Black (cnd), Slovak RSO Bratislava ("MMC New Century, Vol. II") † Crowell:Black Holes & Anti-Matters; Elkana:Color in Time; Fugarino:Riding on a Cloud; Giusto:Peace Cow (it's not a habit, I'm used to it); A. Hoose:Gestures & Intimations MASM ▲ 2017 [DDD] (16.97)
NYVANG, MICHAEL (1963-
Movements for a Monument to the Lonliness of Our World for Piano (1986-93)
E. Kaltoft (pno) *(rec Royal Danish Academy of Music Århus, June 17-20, 1997)* MARC ▲ 8224074 [DDD] (13.97)
OAKES, RODNEY (1937-
Blues Danube for MIDI Trombone & Synthesizer Tracks (1991)
R. Oakes (trbn) [MIDI trbn] ("Simple Requests: New American Music for Computers & Live Performers") † E. Chambers:Rothko-Tobey Continuum; Kothman:Interrupted Dances; R. Lyons:Electronique; Gigue Vn; Ice Cream Truck from Hell; J. Stolet:Simple Requests; S. Sung:Mobiles; P. Terry:Aria & Accidental Music CMB ▲ 1088 (16.97)
OBERDOERFFER, FRITZ (1895-1979)
Fantasy & Fugue in e for Organ
J. Callahan (org) † M. Reger:Intro & Passacaglia, Op. 56; Org Music (misc colls); F. Schmidt:Chorale Preludes Org CENT ▲ 2081 [DAD] (16.97)
OBRADORS, FERNANDO (1897-1945)
Canciones clásicas españolas for Voice & Piano (1920)
M. D. Campos (sop), K. Durran (pno) *(rec West Road Concert Hall Univ, Cambridge, England, Jan 1995)* ("Classical Spanish Songs") † Esplá:Canciones playeras; M. de Falla:Canciones populares españolas; E. Granados:Colección de Tonadillas; Mompou:Combat del somni; J. Turina:Poema en forma de canciones, Op. 19 HER ▲ 184 [DDD] (19.97)
El Poema de la Jungla for Orchestra
A. Leaper (cnd), Orquestra Filarmonica de Gran Canaria † Rodó:Sym 2 ASV ▲ 1043 (16.97)
OBRECHT, JACOB (ca 1450-1505)
Factor orbis for Chorus
J. Wood (cnd), New London Chamber Choir *(rec Kentish Town, London, England, Nov 1991)* ("The Brightest Heaven of Invention") † Salve crux; Brumel:Nato canunt omnia; Busnois:Music of Busnois; Dufay:Ave regina caelorum; Josquin Desprez:Preter rerum seriem; Regis:O admirabile commercium AMON ▲ 56 [DDD] (16.97)
Laudes Christo Redemptori (motet) for 4 Voices
E. Wickham (cnd), The Clerk's Group † Missa "Malheur me bat" ASV (Gaudeamus) ▲ 171 (16.97)
Missa "Malheur me bat" for 4 Voices
E. Wickham (cnd), The Clerk's Group † Laudes Christo ASV (Gaudeamus) ▲ 171 (16.97)
Missa "Maria zart" for 4 Voices
P. Phillips (cnd), Tallis Scholars GIME ▲ 54932 [DDD] (16.97)
Salve crux for Chorus
J. Wood (cnd), New London Chamber Choir *(rec Kentish Town, London, England, Nov 1991)* ("The Brightest Heaven of Invention") † Factor orbis; Brumel:Nato canunt omnia; Busnois:Music of Busnois; Dufay:Ave regina caelorum; Josquin Desprez:Preter rerum seriem; Regis:O admirabile commercium AMON ▲ 56 [DDD] (16.97)
Salve Regina for Chorus
M. Ghijs (cnd), Capilla Flamenca ("Missa Alleluia") † Josquin Desprez:Sacred Music; Pipelare:Memorare, Mater Christi EUFO ▲ 1232 [DDD] (18.97)
O'BRIEN, EUGENE (1945-
Mysteries of the Horizon for Chamber Ensemble (1987)
H. Sollberger (cnd) *(rec Indiana Univ Bloomington, Mar 1989)* ("New Music from Indiana University, Vol. 1") † C. Baker:Awaking the Winds; Dzubay:Trio; D. W. Freund:Hard Cells; J. Haas:Sussurrando IUSM ▲ 5 (16.97)
OCHSE, ORPHA (1925-
Prelude & Fugue for Flute & Organ
F. Shelly (fl), S. Egler (org) *(rec Wiedemann Recital Hall, Wichita State University, KS)* ("The Dove Descending") † M. Albrecht:Psalms; Berlinski:Adagietto; Roush:Dove Descending; B. W. Sanders:Pieces Fl; J. Weaver:Rhapsody; G. Young:Triptych SUMM ▲ 174 [DDD] (16.97)
OCKEGHEM, JOHANNES (ca 1410-1497)
Celeste Beneficium (motet) for 5 Voices
E. Wickham (cnd), Clerks' Group † Masses for 3 Voc; Missa Cuiusvis toni ASV ▲ 189 (16.97)
Chansons & Motets
Henry's Eight—Ave Maria *(rec Royal Masonic School for Girls, Rickmansworth, England, July 1997)* † Clemens Non Papa:Choral Music; J. Desprez:Choral Music; Willaert:Sacred Music ETC ▲ 1214 [DDD] (17.97)
K. van Laethem (sop), P. Malfeyt (cnd) —Ma bouche rit; Petite camusette; J'en ay deuil; Malheur me bat [2 versions]; Ma maitresse; Prenez sur moi [2 versions]; Aultre Venus; L'autre d'antan; Baisez moy; D'un autre amer; Fors seulment; ¿Ques mi vida? ("Chansons") RICE ▲ 206302 (17.97)
Orlando Consort—Presque transi; Prenez sur moi vostre exemple; O rosa bella; Aultre Venus estés; S'elle m'amera je ne sçay; Tant fuz gentement resjouy; Mort, tu as navré/Miserere *(rec Mandelsloh (Neustadt) St. Osdag Church, Germany, Mar 1996)* † Missa De plus en plus PARC ▲ 453419 [DDD] (16.97)

OCKEGHEM, JOHANNES (cont.)
Deo gratias (canon) for 9 groups of 4 Voices [doubtful]
P. van Nevel (cnd), Huelgas Ensemble † G. Gabrieli:Exaudi me Domine; Josquin Desprez:Qui habitat in adjutorio Altissimi; Manchicourt:Laudate Dominum; C. Porta:Masses; Striggio:Ecce beatam lucem; Tallis:Spem in alium SNYC (Vivarte) ▲ 66261 (16.97)
Gaude Maria (motet) for Chorus
E. Wickham (cnd), Clerks' Group † Missa De plus en plus; Barbireau:Osculetur me; Binchois:De plus en plus se renouvelle; Pipelare:Salve Regina ASV (Gaudeamus) ▲ 153 (16.97)
Masses (2) for 3 Voices
K. Moll (cnd), Schola Discantus LYR ▲ 8010 [DDD] (16.97)
E. Wickham (cnd), Clerks' Group—Missa quinti Tone † Celeste Beneficium; Missa Cuiusvis toni ASV ▲ 189 (16.97)
Missa Caput for Chorus
E. Wickham (cnd), Clerks' Group † Missa ma Maistresse; Motets (3); Venit ad Petrum ASV ▲ 186 (16.97)
Missa "Cuiusvis toni" for 4 Voices
C. Gottwald (cnd), Stuttgart Schola Cantorum *(rec Stiftskirche Stuttgart, June 1984)* ("Musica mensurabilis III") † H. Finck:Missa in summis; Josquin Desprez:Missa, "Malheur me bat" BAYE ▲ 100273 [ADD] (17.97)
P. Urquhart (cnd), Capella Alamire *(rec Portsmouth, NH, May 15-17, 1995 & Feb 19-20, 1996)* ("Music of the Modes") † Missa Fors seulement; Missa Sine nomine DORD ▲ 80152 [DDD] (13.97)
E. Wickham (cnd), Clerks' Group † Celeste Beneficium; Masses for 3 Voc ASV ▲ 189 (16.97)
Missa "Fors seulement" for 5 Voices
K. Moll (cnd), Schola Discantus † Missa De plus en plus LYR (Early Music) ▲ 8029 [DDD] (16.97)
P. Urquhart (cnd), Capella Alamire *(rec Portsmouth, NH, May 15-17, 1995 & Feb 19-20, 1996)* ("Music of the Modes") † Missa Cuiusvis toni; Missa Sine nomine DORD ▲ 80152 [DDD] (13.97)
E. Wickham (cnd), Clerks' Group † Requiem ASV (Gaudeamus) ▲ 168 (16.97)
Missa "L'homme armé" for 4 Voices
Coeli et Terra Vocal Ensemble [LAT] † Requiem ARN ▲ 68149 [DDD] (16.97)
Missa ma Maistresse for Chorus
E. Wickham (cnd), Clerks' Group † Missa Caput; Motets (3); Venit ad Petrum ASV ▲ 186 (16.97)
Missa "Mi-mi" for 4 Voices, "Missa quarti toni"
R. Stewart (cnd), Capella Pratensis RICE ▲ 206402 (17.97)
Missa "De plus en plus" for 4 Voices
K. Moll (cnd), Schola Discantus † Missa Fors seulement LYR (Early Music) ▲ 8029 [DDD] (16.97)
Orlando Consort *(rec Mandelsloh (Neustadt) St. Osdag Church, Germany, Mar 1996)* † Chansons & Motets PARC ▲ 453419 [DDD] (16.97)
P. Phillips (cnd), Tallis Scholars † Missa Au travail suis; Barbingant:Au travail suis; Binchois:De plus en plus se renouvelle GIME ▲ 454935 [DDD] (16.97)
E. Wickham (cnd), Clerks' Group † Gaude Maria; Barbireau:Osculetur me; Binchois:De plus en plus se renouvelle; Pipelare:Salve Regina ASV (Gaudeamus) ▲ 153 (16.97)
Missa prolationum for 4 Voices
C. Gottwald (cnd), Stuttgart Schola Cantorum ("Musica mensurabilis II") † Josquin Desprez:Missa, "Da Pacem" BAYE ▲ 100272 [ADD] (17.97)
E. Wickham (cnd), Clerk's Group ("Ockeghem, Vol. 2") † Busnois:Music of Busnois; J. Pullois:Flos de spina ASV (Gaudeamus) ▲ 143 [DDD] (16.97)
Missa "Sine nomine" for 5 Voices
P. Urquhart (cnd), Capella Alamire *(rec Portsmouth, NH, May 15-17, 1995 & Feb 19-20, 1996)* ("Music of the Modes") † Missa Cuiusvis toni; Missa Fors seulement DORD ▲ 80152 [DDD] (13.97)
Missa "Au travail suis" for 4 Voices
P. Phillips (cnd), Tallis Scholars † Missa De plus en plus; Barbingant:Au travail suis; Binchois:De plus en plus se renouvelle GIME ▲ 454935 [DDD] (16.97)
Motets for Choir & Orchestra
E. Bonnardot (cnd), Obsidienne ("Vox aurea") † Faugues:Missa 'La basse danse' OPUS ▲ 30222 (18.97)
Motets (3) for Chorus
E. Wickham (cnd), Clerks' Group † Missa ma Maistresse; Missa Caput; Venit ad Petrum ASV ▲ 186 (16.97)
Requiem for 4 Voices
C. Gottwald (cnd), Stuttgart Schola Cantorum ("Musica mensurabilis I") † Dufay:Missa Ecce ancilla Domini BAYE ▲ 100271 [ADD] (17.97)
Paris Métamorphoses Ensemble [LAT] † Missa L'homme armé ARN ▲ 68149 [DDD] (16.97)
M. Pérès (cnd) , Les Pages de la Chapelle HAM ▲ 901441 (18.97)
E. Wickham (cnd), Clerks' Group † Missa Fors seulement ASV (Gaudeamus) ▲ 168 (16.97)
Sine nomine (credo) for Chorus
P. Urquhart (cnd), Capella Alamire *(rec Cambridge, MA, May 11, 1993)* ("The Early Josquin") † Josquin Desprez:Missa, "L'ami Baudechon"; Music of Josquin Desprez DOR ▲ 80131 [DDD] (13.97)
Venit ad Petrum for Chorus
E. Wickham (cnd), Clerks' Group † Missa ma Maistresse; Missa Caput; Motets (3) ASV ▲ 186 (16.97)
OCKER, MARSHALL (1926-
Gettysburg: July 1, 1863 for Orchestra (1993)
R. Silva (cnd), Moravian PO ("Music from 6 Continents: 1995 Series") † A. Bertrand:Creatures of Proteus; Loeb:Fantasias on East Asian Modes; M. Matsunaga:Constellations; T. Myers:Cadenza & Lament VMM ▲ 3034 [DDD]
OCÓN, EDUARDO (19th cent)
Bolero for Piano
P. Cohen (pno) *(rec Auditorio de Cuenca, Spain, Apr 1995)* ("El Último Adiós: Romantic Piano Music from Spain") † Adalid y Gurréa:Ultimo adiós; Lamento; Petits riens; Allú:Peregrino; T. Power:Barcarola Pno; Quesada:Allegro de concierto; Grandes estudios GLSS ▲ 920501 [DDD] (18.97)
O'CONNOR, MARK (1962-
Chamber Music
E. Meyer (bass), M. O'Connor (vn), Y.-Y. Ma (vc)—Appalachia Waltz; Butterfly's Day Out; F.C.'s Jig; Old Country Fairytale; Fair Dancer Reel *(rec Sound Emporium Nashville, Aug 17-20, 1995)* ("Appalachia Waltz") † E. Meyer:Chamber Music SNYC ▲ 68460 [DDD] (16.97) ▮ 68460 [DDD] (10.98) COL △ 68460 [DDD]
Fiddle Concerto for Violin & Orchestra (1991-92)
M. O'Connor (vn), M. Alsop (cnd), Concordia Orch *(rec Englewood, NJ, Oct 1994)* † Qt Vn WAR ▲ 45846 (15.97)
Liberty! (film music) for Voice, Trumpet, Violin, Cello & Orchestra (1997)
J. Taylor (ten), M. O'Connor (vn), Y.-Y. Ma (vc), W. Marsalis (tpt) SNYC ▲ 63216 (16.97) COL ▮ 63216 (10.98)
Music of O'Connor
M. O'Connor (vn)—Cricket Dance; Improvisations 1-4; Caprices 1-6; Follow the Scout; Fancy Stops & Goes; River Out Back; Flailing; Midnight on the Water/Bonaparte's Retreat; arr O'Connor *(rec St. Louis, MO, Aug 29-Sept 2, 1996)* ("Midnight on the Water") SNYC ▲ 62862 [DDD] (16.97)
Quartet for Violin, Viola, Cello & Double Bass (1989-90)
M. O'Connor (vn), D. Phillips (va), C. Brey (vc), E. Meyer (db) *(rec Vanderbilt Univ. Nashville, TN, Dec 1990)* † Fid Con WAR ▲ 45846 (15.97)
O'CONNOR, PADRAIG (1942-
Introspect for Orchestra (1978; rev 1992)
P. O. Duinn (cnd), RTE Sinfonietta *(rec UCD Dublin, Sept 28-29, 1994 & Jan 12, 1995)* ("Romantic Ireland") † Duff:Echoes of Georgian Dublin; Larchet:By the Waters of Moyle; O Riada:Banks of Sullane; A. J. Potter:Rhap under a High Sky; Victory:Irish Pictures MARC (Irish Composer) ▲ 8223804 [DDD] (13.97)
ODRIOZOLA, RICARDO (1965-
Dances (4) for Violin & Cello (1987-89)
R. Odriozola (vn), J. Odriozola (vc) *(rec Jetsmark Kirke Denmark, June 1993 & Dec 1994)* ("Play") † Danish Miniatures; Psalms; M. Christensen:Birds of a Spring Night; Dreamless Fragments; Reflets de cristal; Winter Light PONT ▲ 5116
Danish Miniatures (7) for Violin & Cello (1990)
R. Odriozola (vn), J. Odriozola (vc) *(rec Jetsmark Kirke Denmark, June 1993 & Dec 1994)* ("Play") † Dances; Psalms; M. Christensen:Birds of a Spring Night; Dreamless Fragments; Reflets de cristal; Winter Light PONT ▲ 5116
Psalms for Cello (1992-94)
J. Odriozola (vc) *(rec Jetsmark Kirke Denmark, June 1993 & Dec 1994)* ("Play") † Dances; Danish Miniatures; M. Christensen:Birds of a Spring Night; Dreamless Fragments; Reflets de cristal; Winter Light PONT ▲ 5116
O'DWYER, TIMOTHY (20th cent)
Bar-do'i-thos-grol for Saxophone
T. O'Dwyer (sax) ("Elision Ensemble: After the Fire") † C. Dench:Severance; Hames:Djurunga; Zurna; L. Lim:Amulet; Melchoirre:Halos; Whiticker:After the Fire VOXA ▲ 19 (18.97)

OE, HIKARI (1963-

Flute & Piano Music

H. Koizumi (fl), A. Ebi (pno)—A Favourite Waltz; Nocturne; Magic Flute; Sad Waltz; Pied Piper; Graduation (w. vars) *(rec Nippon Columbia Studio 1, June 8-9, 1992)* ("Music of Hikari Oe 1") † Pno Music DNN ▲ 78952 [DDD] (16.97)

H. Koizumi (fl), A. Ebi (pno)—Snow; June Lullaby; Merry Waltz; Siciliano in e; Adagio in d; Nocturne No. 2 *(rec Asahikawa City Hokkaido, June 27 & 29-30, 1994)* ("Music of Hikari Oe 2") † Pno Music; Sonatina Pno; Vn & Pno Music DNN ▲ 78953 [DDD] (16.97)

Piano Music

A. Ebi (pno)—Forest Ballad; Birthday Waltz; Ave Maria; Bluebird March; Star; Mister Prelude; Waltz in a; Rondo; Summer in Kitakaru; Winter; Requiem for M; Lullaby for Keiko; Dance; Siciliano; Ländler; Grief; Stream; Barcarolle; Hiroshima Requiem *(rec Nippon Columbia Studio 1, June 8-9, 1992)* ("Music of Hikari Oe 1") † Fl & Pno Music DNN ▲ 78952 [DDD] (16.97)

A. Ebi (pno)—Grief No. 3; Minuet for Children; Baroque Waltz; Salzburg; Grief No. 2; Wistful Adagio; May the Plane Not Fall; Requiem for Mrs. I *(rec Asahikawa City Hokkaido, June 27 & 29-30, 1994)* ("Music of Hikari Oe 2") † Fl & Pno Music; Sonatina Pno; Vn & Pno Music DNN ▲ 78953 [DDD] (16.97)

Sonatina in C for Piano

A. Ebi (pno) *(rec Asahikawa City Hokkaido, June 27 & 29-30, 1994)* ("Music of Hikari Oe 2") † Fl & Pno Music; Pno Music; Vn & Pno Music DNN ▲ 78953 [DDD] (16.97)

Violin & Piano Music

T. Kato (vn), A. Ebi (pno)—Dream; Summer Holidays; Nocturnal Capriccio; Andante Cantabile; August Capriccio *(rec Asahikawa City Hokkaido, June 27 & 29-30, 1994)* ("Music of Hikari Oe 2") † Fl & Pno Music; Pno Music; Sonatina Pno DNN ▲ 78953 [DDD] (16.97)

OESTREICH, CARL (1800-1840)

Andante for Horn & Piano

K. P. Thelander (nat hn), C. Post (pno) *(rec Sept 28-30, 1991)* ("Music of the Early 19th Century") † Beethoven:Son Hn; Dauprat:Son Hn & Pno, Op. 2; Krufft:Son Hn in E; Kuhlau:Andante & Polacca CRYS ▲ 677 (15.97)

OFFENBACH, JACQUES (1819-1880)

Andante for Cello & Orchestra (1845)

O. Harnoy (vc), A. De Almeida (cnd), Bournemouth SO *(rec Dorset England, May 11-12, 1995)* † Con militaire Vc; Lalo:Con Vc RCAV (Red Seal) ▲ 68420 [DDD] (16.97)

La Belle Hélène (selections)

L. Frémaux (cnd), City of Birmingham SO † Berlioz:Damnation de Faust (sels); B. Britten:War Requiem, Op. 66; Massenet:Cid (ballet suite); Suite 4; Vierge (sels) KLAV ▲ 11007 [ADD] (18.97)

La Belle Hélène:Overture

A. Fiedler (cnd), Boston Pops Orch † Contes d'Hoffmann; Gaîté Parisienne; Orphée aux enfers (sels) RCAV (Basic 100) ▲ 68366 (10.97) ▮ 68366 (5.98)

O. Klemperer (cnd), Berlin State Opera Orch *(rec 1929)* ("Otto Klemperer: The Kroll Opera Years, 1926-29") † D.-F. Auber:Fra Diavolo (ov); Beethoven:Coriolan Ov, Op. 62; Debussy:Nocturnes Orch; M. Ravel:Alborada del gracioso; R. Wagner:Siegfried Idyll IN ▲ 1339 [ADD] (15.97)

A. Walter (cnd), Czech-Slovak State PO † Orphée aux enfers (ov); Strauss (II):Fledermaus (ov); Nacht in Venedig (ov); Zigeunerbaron (ov); Suppé:Ovs NXIN ▲ 550468 [DDD] (5.97)

Belle Lurette (selections)

K. Battle (sop), M. Chung (cnd), Bastille Opera Orch *(rec Bastille Opera Paris, France, Nov 1993 & June 1994)* ("Kathleen Battle Sings French Opera Arias") † Berlioz:Béatrice et Bénédict (sels); G. Charpentier:Louise (sels); Donizetti:Fille du régiment (sels); Gounod:Roméo et Juliette (sels); Massenet:Manon (sels); A. Thomas:Hamlet (sels); Mignon (sels) DEUT ▲ 47114 [DDD] (16.97)

Concerto militaire for Cello & Orchestra (1848)

O. Harnoy (vc), A. De Almeida (cnd), Bournemouth SO *(rec Dorset England, Jan 16-17, 1995)* † Andante Vc; Lalo:Con Vc RCAV (Red Seal) ▲ 68420 [DDD] (16.97)

O. Harnoy (vc), E. Kunzel (cnd), Cincinnati Pops Orch ("Viva la France!") † Gaîté Parisienne; Music of Offenbach VB2 2-▲ 5131 (9.97)

Les Contes d'Hoffmann [Tales of Hoffmann] (opera in 5 acts) [completed Guiraud] (1881)

S. Danco (sop), I. Borkh (sop), P. Alarie (sop), M. Krásová (mez), M. Musilová (cta), T. Altmeyer (ten), L. Simoneau (ten), B. Blachut (ten), I. Zidek (ten), G. London (b-bar), Jelinkova (sgr), West (sgr), Beier (sgr), R. Heger (cnd), Bavarian State Opera Orch, J. Vogel (cnd), Prague National Theater Orch, L. Schaenen (cnd), Vienna State Opera Orch, Bavarian State Opera Chorus, Vienna State Opera Chorus, Prague National Theater Chorus † M. Glinka:Russlan & Ludmilla; J. Offenbach:Contes d'Hoffmann; Schillings:Mona Lisa; F. Schubert:Winterreise, D.911; R. Strauss:Frau ohne Schatten, Op. 65; R. Wagner:Arias & Scenes; Wesendonck Songs VL 3-▲ 2000 (30.97)

A. Fiedler (cnd), Boston Pops Orch *(rec 1956)* † Ibert:Divert Orch RCAV (Living Stereo) ▲ 61429 (11.97)

A. Fiedler (cnd), Boston Pops Orch † Belle Hélène (ov); Gaîté Parisienne; Orphée aux enfers (sels) RCAV (Basic 100) ▲ 68366 (10.97) ▮ 68366 (5.98)

S. Ozawa (cnd), French National Orch, French Radio Chorus, E. Gruberová (sop), C. Eder (mez), P. Domingo (ten), M. Sénéchal (ten), G. Bacquier (bar), J. Diaz (bass), J. Morris (bass), A. Schmidt (sgr) [FRE] DEUT 2-▲ 27682 [DDD] (32.97)

A. Rother (cnd), Berlin Radio Orch, Berlin Radio Chorus, E. Berger (sop—Antonia), R. Streich (sop—Olympia), I. Klein (sop—Giulietta), P. Anders (ten—Hoffmann), G. Witting (ten), J. Prohaska (bar) [GER] *(rec Berlin, Germany, July 29, 1946)* MYTO (Historical Line) 2-▲ 991026 (live) (34.97)

E. Schwarzkopf (sop), V. D. Angeles (sop), G. D. Angelo (sop), N. Gedda (ten), E. Blanc (bar), G. London (b-bar), A. Cluytens (cnd), Paris Conservatory Société des Concerts Orch, René DuClos Chorus [FRE] EMIC (Studio) 2-▲ 63222 [ADD] (23.97)

B. Sills (sop—Antonia/Giulietta/Olympia/Stella), E. Evans (mez—Mother's Voice/Nicklausse), A. Turp (ten—Hoffmann), L. Vellucci (ten—Andrès/Cochenille/Frantz/Pitichinaccio), D. Bernard (bar—Luther/Schlemil), M. Devlin (b-bar—Spalanzani), N. Treigle (bass—Coppélius/Dapertutto/Dr. Miracl/Lindorf), J. West (bass—Crespel), R. Hall (bass—Hermann), A. Brim (sgr—Nathanaël), K. Andersson (cnd), New Orleans Opera Orch, New Orleans Opera Chorus *(rec Feb 27, 1964)* ("New Orleans Opera Archives, Vol. 8") VAIA 2-▲ 1121 [ADD] (30.97)

C. Studer (sop), J. Norman (sop), E. Lind (sop), A. S. von Otter (mez), F. Araiza (ten), S. Ramey (bass), J. Tate (cnd), Dresden Staatskapelle PPHI 3-▲ 22374 [DDD] (48.97)

J. Sutherland (sop), H. Tourangeau (mez), P. Domingo (ten), H. Cuénod (ten), G. Bacquier (bar), R. Bonynge (cnd), Swiss Romande Orch PLON 2-▲ 17363 [ADD] (32.97)

Les Contes d'Hoffmann (selections)

R. Bonynge (cnd), Swiss Romande Orch—Belle nuit, ô nuit d'amour (Barcarolle) ("Moll Flanders") † J. S. Bach:Brandenburg Con 3, BWV 1048; Suite 3 Orch, BWV 1068; G. F. Handel:Water Music, HWV 348-50; Mancina:Moll Flanders; Vivaldi:Con Mand, RV.425 PLON ▲ 52485 [DDD] (16.97)

N. Dessay (sop), S. Jo (sop), L. Vaduva (sop), C. Dubosc (sop), D. Lamprecht (mez), R. Alagna (ten), G. Ragon (ten), G. Bacquier (bar), J. Van Dam (b-bar), K. Nagano (cnd), Lyon Opera Orch, Lyon Opera Chorus ERAT ▲ 17355 (15.97)

G. Farrar (sop), A. Scotti (bar)—Belle nuit, ô nuit d'amour (Barcarolle) *(rec Oct 6, 1909)* ("Geraldine Farrar: In French Opera") † Bizet:Carmen (sels); Gounod:Roméo et Juliette (sels); Massenet:Manon (sels); Thaïs (sels); A. Thomas:Mignon (sels) NIMB ▲ 7872 [ADD] (11.97)

H. de Garmo (bass)—Leuchte, heller Spiegel [GER] *(rec 1917)* † E. D. Albert:Tiefland (sels); Bizet:Carmen (sels); Leoncavallo:Pagliacci (sels); W. A. Mozart:Don Giovanni (sels); Verdi:Otello (sels); R. Wagner:Fliegende Holländer (sels); Meistersinger (sels); Rheingold (sels); Siegfried (sels); Tannhäuser (sels); Walküre (sels) PRE (Lebendige Vergangenheit) ▲ 89175 (m) (16.97)

E. Gruberová (sop—Giulietta), P. Domingo (ten—Hoffmann), S. Ozawa (cnd), French National Orch ("Domingo Duets") † Bizet:Carmen (sels); Donizetti:Lucia di Lammermoor (sels); P. Mascagni:Cavalleria rusticana (sels); G. Puccini:Manon Lescaut (sels); Tosca (sels); Verdi:Duets DEUT ▲ 47270 [ADD/DDD] (16.97)

J. Norman (sop) † Berlioz:Roméo et Juliette (sels); J. Brahms:Deutsches Requiem, Op. 45; F. Poulenc:Songs; M. Ravel:Songs; R. Wagner:Fliegende Holländer (sels); Tannhäuser (sels); Tristan und Isolde (sels); Wesendonck Songs GOD 2-▲ 70395 (13.97)

L. Warren (bar), W. Pelletier (cnd) —Scintille, diamant † Bizet:Carmen (sels); Gounod:Faust (sels); Leoncavallo:Pagliacci (sels); Ponchielli:Gioconda (sels); G. Rossini:Barbiere di Siviglia (sels); Verdi:Arias MYTO (Historical Line) ▲ 991023 (17.97)

L. Warren (bar), Robert Shaw Chorale † Bizet:Carmen (sels); Gounod:Faust (sels); Leoncavallo:Pagliacci (sels); Ponchielli:Gioconda (sels); G. Rossini:Barbiere di Siviglia (sels); Verdi:Ballo in maschera (sels); Falstaff (sels); Otello (sels); Rigoletto (sels); Trovatore (sels) OPIT ▲ 54543 (6.97)

Dance Music for Orchestra

E. Kunzel (cnd), Cincinnati Pops Orch—Belles américaines Pno; Geneviève de Brabant (sels) † Gaîté Parisienne; Ibert:Divert Orch TEL ▲ 80294 [DDD] (16.97)

OFFENBACH, JACQUES (cont.)

Dance Music for Orchestra (cont.)

M. Swierczewski (cnd), Lisbon Gulbenkian Foundation Orch—American Eagle Waltz; Souvenir d'Aix-les-Bains Valse Pno; Ballet des Flocons de Neige; Ballet des Mouches ("Music from the Operettas") † Ovs NIMB ▲ 5303 [DDD] (16.97)

Gaîté Parisienne for Orchestra [arr Manuel Rosenthal, 1938]

L. Bernstein (cnd), New York PO ("Bernstein: The Royal Edition") † Orphée aux enfers (sels); Bizet:Sym SNYC ▲ 47532 [ADD] (10.97)

A. Dorati (cnd), Minneapolis SO † A. Adam:Giselle; Strauss (II):Abschieds-Walzer in F MRCR (Living Presence) 2-▲ 34365 (22.97)

A. Fiedler (cnd), Boston Pops Orch † O. Respighi:Boutique fantasque RCAV (Living Stereo) ▲ 61847 (11.97)

A. Fiedler (cnd), Boston Pops Orch † Belle Hélène (ov); Contes d'Hoffmann; Orphée aux enfers (sels) RCAV (Basic 100) ▲ 68366 (10.97) ▮ 68366 (5.98)

E. Kunzel (cnd), Cincinnati Pops Orch ("Viva la France!") † Con militaire Vc; Music of Offenbach VB2 2-▲ 5131 (9.97)

E. Kunzel (cnd), Cincinnati Pops Orch † Dance Music Orch; Ibert:Divert Orch TEL ▲ 80294 [DDD] (16.97)

E. Ormandy (cnd), Philadelphia Orch *(rec 1963)* † S. Rachmaninoff:Sym Dances, Op. 45; Smetana:Bartered Bride (dances) SNYC (Essential Classics) ▲ 48279 [ADD] (7.97) ▮ 48279 [ADD] (3.98)

A. Previn (cnd), Pittsburgh SO *(rec Oct 1-2, 1982)* † Orphée aux enfers (sels); Voyage dans la lune (sels) PPHI (Solo) ▲ 42403 (9.97)

Grand duos concertants (3) for 2 Cellos, Op. 43

R. Pidoux (vc), E. Péclard (vc) HMA ▲ 1901043 (9.97)

La Grande-Duchesse de Gérolstein (opera in 3 acts) [lib H. Meilhac & L. Halévy] (1867)

C. Di Censo (sop), L. V. Terrani (mez), C. Allemano (ten), E. Ligot (sgr), R. A. Peraino (sgr), R. Marcantoni (sgr), M. G. Pani (sgr), A. L. Iongo (sgr), T. Morris (sgr), R. Plaza (sgr), B. Imbert (sgr), F. Cassard (sgr), E. Villaume (cnd), Italian International Orch, Bratislava Chamber Chorus *(rec Palazzo Ducale Italy, July 1996)* DYNC 2-▲ 173 [DDD] (34.97)

La Grande-Duchesse de Gérolstein (selections)

R. Leibowitz (cnd), Pasdeloup Concerts Association Orch *(rec 1958)* † Massenet:Espada; Meyerbeer:Africaine (sels); Dinorah (ov); Prophète (sels) FORL ▲ 16586 [AAD] (16.97)

F. Von Stade (mez), J. Pritchard (cnd), London PO—Dites-lui qu'on l'a remarqué distigué *(rec London, England, Jan 1976)* ("French Opera Arias") † Périchole (sels); Berlioz:Béatrice et Bénédict (sels); Damnation de Faust (sels); Gounod:Roméo et Juliette (sels); Massenet:Cendrillon (sels); Werther (sels); Meyerbeer:Huguenots (sels); A. Thomas:Mignon (sels) *([ENG,FRE] texts)* SNYC ▲ 60527 [ADD] (10.97)

Harmonie du soir for Cello (1852)

A. Noferini (vc), S. Roach (pno) ("Cello Miniatures") † Chants du soir Vc; Larmes de Jacqueline; Rêveries Vc BONG ▲ 5569 [DDD] (16.97)

Les Larmes de Jacqueline for Cello & Piano

A. Noferini (vc), S. Roach (pno) ("Cello Miniatures") † Chants du soir Vc; Harmonie du soir Vc; Rêveries Vc BONG ▲ 5569 [DDD] (16.97)

Music of Offenbach

E. Kunzel (cnd), Cincinnati Pops Orch—Ov to a Grand Orch; Souvenir d'Aix-les-Bains Valse Pno; Schüler Polka Pno; American Eagle Waltz; Belle Hélène (ov); Ile de Tulipatan (sels) ("Viva la France!") † Con militaire Vc; Gaîté Parisienne VB2 2-▲ 5131 (9.97)

F. von Stade (mez), A. De Almeida (cnd), Scottish CO—Périchole (sels) [Ov; Lettre de la Périchole; Ah! que les hommes sont bêtes!; Ariette de la griserie; Entr'acte]; Fille du tambour-major (sels) [Chanson de la fille du tambour-major]; Belle Hélène (sels) [Amours divins!]; Pomme d'api (sels) [Couplets de pomme, d'api; J'en prendrai un, deux, trois]; Madame l'archiduc (sels) [Couplets de l'alphabet]; Romance de la rose (sels) [Ov]; Vie parisienne (sels) [Rondeau et valse]; Orphée aux enfers (sels) [Couplets du berger joli]; Barbe-bleue (sels) [Couplets de Boulette; Couplets de la rosière]; Grande-Duchesse de Gérolstein (sels) [Dites-lui qu'on l'a remarqué distigué; Ah! que j'aime les militaires!] *(rec Glasgow Scotland, Scotland, Dec 16-18, 1994)* ("Offenbach Arias and Overtures") RCAV (Red Seal) ▲ 68116 [DDD] (16.97)

artists unknown—Orphée aux enfers (sels); Belle Hélène (sels); Chanson de Fortunio (sels); Violoneux (sels); Princesse de Trébizonde (sels); Brésilien (sels); Bavards (sels); Geneviève de Brabant (sels) [Galop]; Mariage aux lanternes (sels); Lischen et Fritzchen (sels); Barbe-bleue (sels) ("Anthology, Vol. 1") FORL ▲ 16766 [ADD] (16.97)

Orphée aux enfers [Orpheus in the Underworld] (opera in 2 acts) [lib Crémieux & Halévy] (1858: revd in 4 acts 1874)

M. Minkowski (cnd), Lyon Opera Orch, M. Minkowski (cnd), Grenoble Chamber Orch, M. Minkowski (cnd), Lyon Opera Chorus, N. Dessay (sop—Eurydice), P. Petibon (sop—Cupidon), V. Gens (sop—Vénus), J. Smith (sop—Diane), E. Podles (cta—L'Opinion publique), J. Fouchécourt (ten—Aristée-Pluton), S. Cole (ten—John Styx), É. Lescroart (ten—Mercure), Y. Beuron (ten—Orpheus), L. Naouri (bar—Jupiter), V. Pochon (voc—Minerve), L. Pruvot (voc—Junon) *(rec Lyon, France, Nov-Dec 1998)* EMIC 2-▲ 56725 (32.97)

Orphée aux enfers [Orpheus in the Underworld] (selections)

A. D. Almeida (cnd), Philharmonia Orch *(rec Aug 7-9, 1987)* † Gaîté Parisienne; Voyage dans la lune (sels) PPHI (Solo) ▲ 42403 (9.97)

L. Bernstein (cnd), New York PO ("Bernstein: The Royal Edition") † Gaîté Parisienne; Bizet:Sym SNYC ▲ 47532 [ADD] (10.97)

A. Fiedler (cnd), Boston Pops Orch † Belle Hélène (ov); Contes d'Hoffmann; Gaîté Parisienne RCAV (Basic 100) ▲ 68366 (10.97) ▮ 68366 (5.98)

Orphée aux enfers:Overture

(rec Jan 1997) ("Centenary of the Vichy Municipal Wind Band") † A. Arutiunian:Con Tpt; J. B. Chance:Vars on a Korean Theme; A. Reed:Hymn Vars; Vivaldi:Con Tpts, RV.537 LIDI ▲ 301049 [DDD] (16.97)

C. Cantieri (cnd), London Festival Orch ("Famous Overtures") † D.-F. Auber:Muette de Portici (ov); M. Glinka:Russlan & Ludmilla (ov); Humperdinck:Hänsel und Gretel (ov); W. A. Mozart:Entführung aus dem Serail (ov); Suppé:Ovs PC ▲ 265013 [DDD] (2.97)

F. Shipway (cnd), Royal PO † O. Nicolai:Lustigen Weiber von Windsor (ov); Smetana:Bartered Bride (ov); Strauss (II):Zigeunerbaron (ov); R. Wagner:Meistersinger (ov); C. M. von Weber:Freischütz (ov) PC ▲ 267147 [DDD] (2.97)

A. Walter (cnd), Czech-Slovak State PO † Belle Hélène (ov); Strauss (II):Fledermaus (ov); Nacht in Venedig (ov); Zigeunerbaron (ov); Suppé:Ovs NXIN ▲ 550468 [DDD] (5.97)

Overtures

L. Frémaux (cnd), City of Birmingham SO—Orphée aux enfers (ov); Grande-Duchesse de Gérolstein (sels); Belle Hélène (ov); Barbe-bleue (sels) [Ov]; Vie parisienne (sels) [Ov] † Berlioz:Ovs KLAV ▲ 11040 (18.97)

H. von Karajan (cnd), Berlin PO—Orphée aux enfers (ov); Barbe-bleue (sels) [Ov]; Grande-Duchesse de Gérolstein (sels) [Ov]; Belle Hélène (ov); Vert-vert (sels) [Ov]; Kakadu (sels) [Ov]; Barcarolle Orch DEUT ▲ 44 [DDD] (16.97)

M. Swierczewski (cnd), Lisbon Gulbenkian Foundation Orch—Orphée aux enfers (ov); Voyage dans la lune (sels) [Ov]; Die Rheinnixen (sels); Grande-Duchesse de Gérolstein (sels) [Ov] ("Music from the Operettas") † Dance Music Orch NIMB ▲ 5303 [DDD] (16.97)

B. Weil (cnd), Vienna SO—Fille du tambour-major (sels) [Ov]; Orphée aux enfers (ov); Belle Hélène (ov); Barbe-bleue (sels) [Ov]; Grande-Duchesse de Gérolstein (sels) [Ov]; Monsieur et Madame Denis (sels) [Ov]; Vie parisienne (sels) [Ov]; Vert-vert (sels) [Ov] *(rec Dec 11-14, 1992)* † A. Dvořák:Qt 14 Strs, Op. 105; Smetana:Qt 1 Strs SNYC ▲ 53288 [DDD] (16.97)

Le Papillon (ballet in 2 acts) for Orchestra (1860)

R. Bonynge (cnd), London SO *(rec Kingsway Hall London, Jan 1972)* † P. Tchaikovsky:Nutcracker, Op. 71 PLON (Double Decker) 2-▲ 44827 [ADD] (17.97)

La Périchole (selections)

F. Von Stade (mez), F. von Stade (mez), J. Pritchard (cnd), London PO—Ah! quel dîner je viens de faire *(rec London, England, Jan 1976)* ("French Opera Arias") † Grande-Duchesse de Gérolstein (sels); Berlioz:Béatrice et Bénédict (sels); Damnation de Faust (sels); Gounod:Roméo et Juliette (sels); Massenet:Cendrillon (sels); Werther (sels); Meyerbeer:Huguenots (sels); A. Thomas:Mignon (sels) *([ENG,FRE] texts)* SNYC ▲ 60527 [ADD] (10.97)

Robinson Crusoe (selections)

S. Jo (sop), G. Carella (cnd), English CO—Conduisez-moi vers celui que l'adore † Bizet:Pêcheurs de perles (sels); G. Charpentier:Louise (sels); Gounod:Arias; Massenet:Manon (sels); Meyerbeer:Étoile du nord (sels); Huguenots (sels); A. Thomas:Hamlet (sels); Mignon (sels) ERAT ▲ 23140 (16.97)

Le Voyage dans la lune (selections)

A. D. Almeida (cnd), Philharmonia Orch *(rec Aug 7-9, 1987)* † Gaîté Parisienne; Orphée aux enfers (sels) PPHI (Solo) ▲ 42403 (9.97)

OFFENBACH, JACQUES (1819-1880)**& FRIEDRICH VON FLOTOW** (1812-1883)

Chants du soir for Cello & Piano [Cello part composed by Offenbach, Piano part by Flotow] (1839)

A. Noferini (vc), S. Roach (pno) ("Cello Miniatures") † Harmonie du soir Vc; Larmes de Jacqueline; Rêveries Vc BONG ▲ 5569 [DDD] (16.97)

Rêveries for Cello & Piano [Cello part composed by Offenbach & Piano part by Flotow] (1839)

A. Noferini (vc), S. Roach (pno) ("Cello Miniatures") † Chants du soir Vc; Harmonie du soir Vc; Larmes de Jacqueline BONG ▲ 5569 [DDD] (16.97)

O'GALLAGHER, EAMMON (1906-
Harp Music
R. Chenut (hp)—Meioreiseac *(rec Médias-Waimes, Belgium)* ("The Art of the Celtic Harp") † Anonymous:Hp Music; Motets; Chenut:Hp Music; Judenkünig:Hp Music; Milán:Hp Music; H. Purcell:Hpd Music; Vogelweide:Hp Music
ARN (The Art of...) ▲ 60357 [AAD] (13.97)

OGDON, JOHN (1937-1989)
Dance Suite for Piano
J. Ogdon (pno) † Busoni:Elegien Pno; Fant contrappuntistica Pno; Fant nach J. S. Bach; A. Hinton:Pansophiae for John Ogdon; R. Stevenson:Prelude & Fugue on Liszt; Sonatina 1 Pno ALTA 2-▲ 9063 (38.97)

OGERMANN, CLAUS (1930-
Concerto Lirico for Violin & Orchestra
A. Rosand (vn), Anonymous (cnd), London National PO, C. Ogermann (cnd), London SO, C. Ogermann (cnd), National PO London † Preludio & Chant; Sarabande-Fant KSCH ▲ 364522 [DDD] (16.97)
Preludio & Chant for Violin & Orchestra (1979)
A. Rosand (vn), Anonymous (cnd), London National PO, C. Ogermann (cnd), London SO † Con Lirico; Sarabande-Fant KSCH ▲ 364522 [DDD] (16.97)
Sarabande-Fantasie for Violin & Orchestra
A. Rosand (vn), Anonymous (cnd), London National PO, C. Ogermann (cnd), London SO † Con Lirico; Preludio & Chant KSCH ▲ 364522 [DDD] (16.97)

OGINSKI, FRANTISEK KSAWERY (1801-1837)
Piano Music
I. Zaluski (pno)—Polonaise in g; Polonaise in E♭; Polonaise in f; Polonaise in d *(rec St. Ives, Cambridge, England, Jan 1998)* ("Music of the Ogiński Dynasty, Vol. 2") † M. K. Ogiński:Pno Music; K. O. Ostaszewski:Funeral March in Honour of Marshal Piludski; W. O. Ostaszewski:Turn of the Wave; K. B. Zaluski:Pno Music; I. Zaluski:Vars on a Theme of Amelia Zaluska OLY ▲ 645 [DDD] (16.97)

OGINSKI, MICHAL KLEOFAS (1765-1833)
Piano Music
I. Zaluski (pno)—Minuet Pno; Polonaise 19; Polonaise 20; Polonaise 23; Polonaise 24 *(rec St. Ives, Cambridge, England, Jan 1998)* ("Music of the Ogiński Dynasty, Vol. 2") † F. K. Ogiński:Pno Music; K. O. Ostaszewski:Funeral March in Honour of Marshal Piludski; W. O. Ostaszewski:Turn of the Wave; K. B. Zaluski:Pno Music; I. Zaluski:Vars on a Theme of Amelia Zaluska OLY ▲ 645 [DDD] (16.97)

OGURA, ROH (1916-1990)
Sonatina for Piano (1937)
M. Matsuya (pno) *(rec Japan, Sept 1993)* ("Light Colored Album for Piano - Midori Matsuya plays Japanese Contemporary Pieces") † Hachimura:Vision of Higanbana; Matsumura:Berceuses; A. Miyoshi:Hommage; T. Sato:August Laying to Rest; Carpet of Bamboo Leaves Falling onto Northern Sea; Scenery with Tea Gardens; Season of Yellow and Black; Takemitsu:Pno Distance; Yoshimatsu:Pleiades Dances CAMA ▲ 318 [DDD] (18.97)

OHANA, MAURICE (1914-1992)
Cantigas for Soprano, Mezzo-Soprano, Winds, Piano, Percussion & Chorus (1953-54)
M. Quercia (sop), F. Atlan (mez), R. Conil (pno), R. Hayrabedian (cnd) , Choeur Contemporain [SPA] † I. Stravinsky:Noces PVY ▲ 787032 [DDD] (16.97)
Caprices (3) for Piano (1944-53)
J. Pennetier (pno) *(rec 1989)* † Préludes Pno ARN ▲ 68091 [AAD/DDD] (16.97)
Chiffres de clavecin for Harpsichord & Chamber Orchestra (1967-68)
A. Tamayo (cnd), Luxembourg PO † Silenciaire; Tombeau de Debussy TIMP ▲ 1044 (18.97)
Concerto for Cello & Orchestra
S. Wieder-Atherton (vc), A. Tamayo (cnd), Luxembourg PO † Con Pno; T'harân-Ngô TIMP ▲ 1039 (18.97)
Concerto for Piano & Orchestra (1980-81)
J. Pennetier (pno), A. Tamayo (cnd), Luxembourg PO † Con Vc; T'harân-Ngô TIMP ▲ 1039 (18.97)
Etudes Chorégraphiques for Percussion Ensemble (1955)
Cabaza Percussion Quartet † Brodmann:Greetings to Hermann; W. Heider:Gallery; B. Hummel:Frescoes '70; S. Reich:Music for Pieces of Wood CPO ▲ 999088 [AAD] (14.97)
Préludes (24) for Piano (1972-73)
J. Pennetier (pno) † Caprices Pno ARN ▲ 68091 [AAD/DDD] (16.97)
Silenciaire for 6 Percussion & Strings (1969)
A. Tamayo (cnd), Luxembourg PO † Chiffres de clavecin; Tombeau de Debussy TIMP ▲ 1044 (18.97)
T'harân-Ngô for Orchestra (1974)
A. Tamayo (cnd), Luxembourg PO † Con Pno; Con Vc TIMP ▲ 1039 (18.97)
Le Tombeau de Claude Debussy for Soprano, Guitar, Piano & Chamber Orchestra (1962)
A. Tamayo (cnd), Luxembourg PO † Chiffres de clavecin; Silenciaire TIMP ▲ 1044 (18.97)

OJEDA, RICARDO (dates unknown)
Rasguido Doble for 2 Guitars
J. Cardoso (gtr), R. Smits (gtr) † Bilhar:Tira poeira; J. Cardoso:Gtr Music; A. Ramirez:Alfonsina; H. Villa-Lobos:Chôro 1; Preludes Gtr; Suite populaire brésilienne ACCE ▲ 96121 [DDD] (17.97)

OJEDA, SANTIAGO (1963-
Zappaloapan for Percussion Ensemble (1994)
Tambuco Percussion Ensemble *(rec Sala Nezahualcóyotl Mexico City, Sept-Oct 1996)* ("Rítmicas") † G. Fitkin:Hook; M. Miki:Mar Spiritual; G. Ortiz:Altar de Neón; A. Roldán:Rítmicas V-VI; Toussaint:Chunga de la Jungla
DOR ▲ 90245 [DDD] (16.97)

OKASHIRO, ICHIZO (1959-
Moon for Piano
C. Okashiro (pno) † Debussy:Images (6) Pno; A. Scriabin:Son 5 Pno, Op. 53 PPR ▲ 224502 (16.97)

OKUNEV, GERMAN (1931-1973)
Adagio & Scherzo for Trombone & Piano
C. Lindberg (trbn), R. Pöntinen (pno) *(rec Eskilstuna, Sweden, Jan 4-6, 1990)* ("The Russian Trombone") † E. Denisov:Choral varié; V. Ewald:Mélodie; Goedicke:Improv; S. Prokofiev:Romeo & Juliet (sels); P. Tchaikovsky:Queen of Spades (sels) BIS ▲ 478 [DDD] (17.97)

ÓLAFSSON, KJARTAN (1958-
Calculus for Solo Flute (1990)
M. Nardeau (fl) ("Music from Calmus") † Útstrok; Mónetta Vn; Nonet; Thorithoraut ICEM ▲ 5 (18.97)
Dark Days [Skammdegi] for Jazz Guitar, Classical Guitar, Percussion & Computer (1996)
H. Jensson (gtr), P. Jónasson (gtr), M. Hemstock (perc), K. Ólafsson (cmpt) ("3 Worlds according to 1") † Diphthong 1; Summary: 3 Worlds according to 1; A. Bush:Pno Music ALTA ▲ 9004 [DDD] (19.97)
Diphthong 1 [Tvíhljóð 1] for Guitar & Computer Orchestra (1993)
P. Jónasson (gtr), K. Ólafsson (cmpt) ("3 Worlds according to 1") † Dark Days; Summary: 3 Worlds according to 1; A. Bush:Pno Music ALTA ▲ 9004 [DDD] (19.97)
Mónetta for Violin & Piano (1997)
S. Ethvaldsdóttir (vn), S. S. Birgisson (pno) ("Music from Calmus") † Útstrok; Calculus; Nonet; Thorithoraut
ICEM ▲ 5 (18.97)
Nonetta for Chamber Orchestra (1995)
Camerartica ("Music from Calmus") † Útstrok; Calculus; Mónetta Vn; Thorithoraut ICEM ▲ 5 (18.97)
Summary: 3 Worlds according to 1 [Samantekt: Þrír heimar í einem] (computer music) [composed from short segments of Olafsson's works] (1994)
K. Ólafsson (cmpt) ("3 Worlds according to 1") † Dark Days; Diphthong 1; A. Bush:Pno Music
ALTA ▲ 9004 [DDD] (19.97)
Thorithoraut for Clarinet Trio (1993)
Chalumeau Trio ("Music from Calmus") † Útstrok; Calculus; Mónetta Vn; Nonet ICEM ▲ 5 (18.97)
Útstrok for Orchestra (1992:rev 1996)
H. Andreescu (cnd), Iceland SO ("Music from Calmus") † Calculus; Mónetta Vn; Nonet; Thorithoraut
ICEM ▲ 5 (18.97)

OLAN, DAVID (1948-
After Great Pain for Soprano & Electronic Sounds (1982)
J. Bettina (sop) † Composition Cl; Prism; C. Biscardi:Mestiere; Son Pno; Trasumanar
CRI ▲ 565 [AAD/DDD] (17.97)
Composition for Clarinet & Tape (1976)
L. Flax (cl) † After Great Pain; Prism; C. Biscardi:Mestiere; Son Pno; Trasumanar CRI ▲ 565 [AAD/DDD] (17.97)
Prism for 6 Percussionists & Tape (1978)
P. Jarvis (cnd) † After Great Pain; Composition Cl; C. Biscardi:Mestiere; Son Pno; Trasumanar
CRI ▲ 565 [AAD/DDD] (17.97)

ÖLANDER, PER AUGUST (1824-1886)
Symphony in E♭ (1868?)
H. Damgaard (cnd), Västerås SO *(rec Västerås Concert Hall, Oct 8, 1977)* † A. F. Lindblad:Sym 2
STRL ▲ 1005 [AAD/ADD] (15.97)

OLDBERG, ARNE (1874-1962)
Sonata in b for Piano, Op. 28 (ca 1910)
M. L. Boehm (pno) *(rec Oct-Nov 1997)* ("3 American Romantics") † Beach:Vars Balkan Theme, Op. 60; Converse:Son 1 Pno ALBA ▲ 293 [DDD] (16.97)

OLDHAM, KEVIN (1960-1993)
Music of Oldham
K. Kushner (pno) *(Ballade, Op. 17; Sarabande & Toccata; Andante Tranquilo [from Con Pno]; 2 Nocturnes, Op. 15)*, C. Johnson (sop), K. Kushner (pno) *(Sleep & Dream)*, S. Rosenbaum (sop), K. Kushner (pno) *(Across the Sea; Gaspard de la Nuit)*, M. Russo (sop), C. Halvorson (ten), A. Schroeder (bar), K. Kushner (pno) *(Row, I Love to Row)*, M. Russo (sop), K. Kushner (pno) *(Paint Me)*, A. Halvorson (ten), K. Kushner (pno) *(Not Even If I Try)*, K. Oldham (pno) *(Vars on a French Noël)* ("Piano & Vocal Music") ALBA ▲ 213 [DDD] (16.97)

O'LEARY, JANE (1946-
Duo for Violin & Cello (1994)
Concord Ensemble Ireland ("Celtic Connections") † Silenzio della Terra; Lefanu:Trio 1 Fl; Tann:Cresset Stone; Of Erthe & Air CPS ▲ 8640 [DDD] (16.97)
Silenzio della Terra for Flute & Percussion (1993)
Concord Ensemble Ireland ("Celtic Connections") † Duo Vn; Lefanu:Trio 1 Fl; Tann:Cresset Stone; Of Erthe & Air
CPS ▲ 8640 [DDD] (16.97)

OLIVER, JOHN (20th cent)
El Reposo del Fuego for Digital Keyboard
S. Barroso (kbd) † Barroso:Canzona; Soledad; Denis:Trajectoires SNE ▲ 556 (16.97)

OLIVERO, BETTY (1954-
Bakashot for Clarinet, Orchestra & Chorus
G. Feidman (cl), L. Shambadal (cnd), North German Radio PO, Hamburg North German Radio Choir † Bat Chaim:Prayer; E. Bloch:Schelomo KSCH ▲ 364702 (16.97)

OLIVEROS, PAULINE (1932-
Electronic Music
artists unknown—Bye Bye Butterfly *(rec San Francisco, CA)* ("Women in Electronic Music - 1977") † R. Anderson:Electronic Music; L. Anderson:Electronic Music; J. M. Beyer:Electronic Music; A. Lockwood:Electronic Music; M. Roberts:Electronic Music; Spiegel:Electronic Music CRI ▲ 728 [ADD] (16.97)
In Memoriam Mr. Whitney for Voice, Accordion & Vocal Ensemble (1991)
P. Oliveros (voc), P. Oliveros (acc), American Voices *(rec CN, Mar 10, 1991)* MODE ▲ 40
Lion's Tale for Digital Sampler (1989)
C. Scholz (elec) ("CDCM Computer Music Series, Vol. 7") † J. Chadabe:Modalities; Kabat:Child & the Moon-Tree; B. McLean:Visions of a Summer Night (sels); N. B. Rolnick:Robert Johnson Sampler; Vocal Chords
CENT ▲ 2047 [DDD] (16.97)
Portrait of Malcom for Violin (1987)
M. Goldstein (vn) *(rec Dartmouth College, United States of America, July, 19991)* † J. Cage:Eight Whiskus; O. Coleman:Trinity; Corner:The Gold Stone; M. Goldstein:Sounding the Fragility of the Line; Tenney:Postal Pieces
OOWN ▲ 5 [DDD] (16.97)
Portrait of the Quintet of the Americas for Wind Quintet (1996)
Quintet of the Americas *(rec Vassar College, June 25-29, 1995)* ("Self Portrait") † Culpo:Qnt Ww; L. Hyla:Amnesia Breaks; A. Rubin:Loba; E. Sharp:JAG CRI ▲ 722 [DDD] (16.97)

OLIVER Y ASTORGA, JUAN (ca 1733-1830)
Sonatas (6) for 2 Flutes (or 2 Violins) & Continuo, Op. 3 (?1769)
Barcelona Consort *(rec Barcelona, Sept 1994)* ("Affetti Musicali") † Castello:Sonate concertate in stil moderno; Mariner:Toccata; Pla:Trio Son 12; M. Soler:Son Bn; Telemann:Essercizii Musici; Musique de Table
LAMA ▲ 2020 [DDD] (17.97)

OLMSTEAD, R. NEIL (1953-
Sinfonia Borealis for Orchestra (1995)
J. Swoboda (cnd), Warsaw PO † J. Caldwell:Elegy; D. Kowalski:Double Helix; Lomon:Terra Incognita; N. Strandberg:Preludes for Orchestra; Womack:Pentacle
MASM (MMC New Century: Volume XI) ▲ 2069 [DDD] (16.97)

OLROG, ULF PEDER (1919-1972)
SÅna Metoder; En död i Skönhet; Glöm inte for Voice, Piano & Recorder
E. Söderström (sop), H. Sund (pno) [arr Håkan Sund] *(rec Djursholm, Sweden, June 15-18, 1981)* ("Örhängen") † Anonymous:Viktoria; R. Davidson:Gudlös bön; Norlén:Visa vid midsommartid; Tauro:Songs; Traditional:Ekovisan; Godmorgon, min docka; Vallåt; Vinden drar; Wennerberg:Man borde inte sofva BIS ▲ 187 [AAD] (17.97)

OLSEN, (CARL GUSTAV) SPARRE (1903-1984)
Aubade for Flute & Horn, Op. 57/3 (1979)
P. Øien (fl), I. Øien (hn) *(rec Sweden, 1980-82)* ("The Scandinavian Horn") † Alfvén:Notturno elegiaco, Op. 5; N. V. Bentzon:Son Hn; Heise:Fant Piece 2; K. Jeppesen:Little Trio Fl, Hn & Pno; Kvandal:Intro & Allegro, Op. 30; C. Nielsen:Canto serioso, FS.132 BIS ▲ 171 [AAD] (17.97)
Poem for Flute & Piano (1933)
P. Øien (fl), G. H. Braaten (pno) *(rec Nacka, Sweden, June 13-14, 1980)* ("The Norwegian Flute") † Serenade Fl, Op. 45; S. Bergh:Pan; Groven:Sunlight Mood; F. Mortensen:Son Fl, Op. 6; Ørbeck:Pastorale & Allegro Fl; Sommerfeldt:Spring Tunes Fl, Op. 44 BIS ▲ 103 [AAD] (17.97)
Poems (3) for Oboe & Piano
B. Hoff (ob), R. Levin (pno) ("The Contemporary Oboe") † Karlsen:Sonatina Ob, Op. 44; T. Madsen:Son Ob; F. Mortensen:Son Ob; Sommerfeldt:Divert Ob, Op. 41; Strømholm:Con minimo Ob NORW ▲ 1005 (17.97)
Serenade for Flute & String Orchestra, Op. 45 (1957)
P. Øien (fl), T. Tønnesen (cnd), Norwegian CO *(rec Oslo, Norway, Feb 1-4, 1978)* ("The Norwegian Flute") † Poem Fl; S. Bergh:Pan; Groven:Sunlight Mood; F. Mortensen:Son Fl, Op. 6; Ørbeck:Pastorale & Allegro Fl; Sommerfeldt:Spring Tunes Fl, Op. 44 BIS ▲ 103 [AAD] (17.97)

OLSEN, POUL ROVSING (1922-1982)
Concertino for Clarinet, Op. 73 (1973)
P. Elbaek (vn), V. Skovlund (va), S. Winsløv (vc), J. Schou (cl), R. Bevan (pno) *(rec PAULA's Recording Hall, 1984)* † Qt 2 Strs, Op. 62; Serenade Vn, Op. 14; Trio II Pno, Op. 77 PLAL ▲ 36 [AAD] (18.97)
Images (4) for Piano, Op. 51 (1965)
R. Bevan (pno) ("Poul Rovsing Olsen: Four Piano Works") † Medardus Pno, Op. 35; Nocturnes Pno, Op. 21; Preludes Pno, Op. 12 PLAL ▲ 76 [DAD] (18.97)
Medardus (4) for Piano, Op. 35 (1956)
R. Bevan (pno) ("Poul Rovsing Olsen: Four Piano Works") † Images; Nocturnes Pno, Op. 21; Preludes Pno, Op. 12
PLAL ▲ 76 [DAD] (18.97)
Nocturnes (3) for Piano, Op. 21 (1951)
R. Bevan (pno) ("Poul Rovsing Olsen: Four Piano Works") † Images; Medardus Pno, Op. 35; Preludes Pno, Op. 12
PLAL ▲ 76 [DAD] (18.97)
Nostalgie for Guitar, Op. 78 (1976)
E. Møldrup (gtr) *(rec Arhus Denmark, 1988-93)* ("The Frosty Silence: Music for Guitar by Danish Composers") † Gefors:Boîte chinoise, Op. 12/1; Gudmunsen-Holmgreen:Solo for Gtr; T. Nielsen:Frosty Silence in the Gardens; Nørgård:Tales from a Hand; Nørholm:Son Gtr, Op. 69 MARC (dacapo) ▲ 8224006 [DDD] (13.97)
Preludes (12) for Piano, Op. 12 (1948)
R. Bevan (pno) ("Poul Rovsing Olsen: Four Piano Works") † Images; Medardus Pno, Op. 35; Nocturnes Pno, Op. 21 PLAL ▲ 76 [DAD] (18.97)
Quartet No. 2 for Strings, Op. 62 (1969)
P. Elbaek (vn), J. Larsen (vn), V. Skovlund (va), S. Winsløv (vc) *(rec PAULA's Recording Hall, 1984)* † Concertino Cl, Op. 73; Serenade Vn, Op. 14; Trio II Pno, Op. 77 PLAL ▲ 36 [AAD] (18.97)
Serenade for Violin & Piano, Op. 14 (1949)
P. Elbaek (vn), R. Bevan (pno) *(rec PAULA's Recording Hall, 1984)* † Concertino Cl, Op. 73; Qt 2 Strs, Op. 62; Trio II Pno, Op. 77 PLAL ▲ 36 [AAD] (18.97)
Trio II for Piano, Violin & Cello, Op. 77 (1976)
P. Elbaek (vn), S. Winsløv (vc), R. Bevan (pno) *(rec PAULA's Recording Hall, 1984)* † Concertino Cl, Op. 73; Qt 2 Strs, Op. 62; Serenade Vn, Op. 14 PLAL ▲ 36 [AAD] (18.97)

OLSSON, OTTO (1879-1964)
Credo symphoniacum for Organ, Op. 50 (1925)
E. Lundkvist (org) *(rec Gustaf Vasa Church Org)* PRPI ▲ 9025 (17.97)

OLSSON, OTTO (cont.)

Etudes (3) for Organ, Op. 45

H. Fagius (org) *(rec May 2-3, 1977)* † Prelude & Fugue Org, Op. 52; Prelude & Fugue, Op. 56; Son Org, Op. 38; Vars on "Ave Maris Stella", Op. 42 BIS ▲ 85 [AAD] (17.97)

Introduction & Scherzo for Piano & Orchestra, Op. 19

I. Mannheimer (pno), G. Staern (cnd), Royal Stockholm PO *(rec 1997)* † Pno Music STRL ▲ 1024 [DDD] (15.97)

Piano Music

I. Mannheimer (pno)—Pieces Pno, Op. 2/1 & 4; Scherzi Pno, Op. 9/1, 2, 4-5; Pieces Pno, Op. 18b/2; Elegaic Dances, Op. 34/1, 2 & 5 *(rec 1997)* † Intro & Scherzo Pno, Op. 19 STRL ▲ 1024 [DDD] (15.97)

Prelude & Fugue in f# for Organ, Op. 52 (1918)

H. Fagius (org) *(rec Katarina Church Org, Stockholm, Sweden, Oct 4, 1981)* † Études Org, Op. 45; Prelude & Fugue, Op. 56; Son Org, Op. 38; Vars on "Ave Maris Stella", Op. 42 BIS ▲ 85 [AAD] (17.97)

H. Fagius (org) *(rec Katarina Church Org, Stockholm, Sweden, Oct 4, 1981)* ("Hans Fagius Plays the Romantic Swedish Organ") † Fryklöf:Symphonic Piece; Symphonic Piece Org; O. Lindberg:Son Org, Op. 23; E. Sjögren:Org Music BIS ▲ 191 [AAD] (17.97)

Prelude & Fugue in d# for Organ, Op. 56

H. Fagius (org) *(rec June 17, 1974)* † Etudes Org, Op. 45; Prelude & Fugue Org, Op. 52; Son Org, Op. 38; Vars on "Ave Maris Stella", Op. 42 BIS ▲ 85 [AAD] (17.97)

Requiem in g for solo Voices, Orchestra & Chorus, Op. 13 (1901-03)

M. A. Häggander (sop), E. Paaske (cta), A. Andersson (ten), L. Wedin (bar), A. Öhrwall (cnd), Stockholm PO, Stockholm Phil Chorus CAPA ▲ 21368 [DDD] (16.97)

Sacred Music

E. Westberg (cnd), Erik Westberg Vocal Ensemble—Jesu dulcis memoria; Ave maris stella ("Musica Sacra") † J. S. Bach:Cons Org; L. Jansson:Sacred Music; A. Paulsson:Lullaby; J. Sandström:Sanctus OPU ▲ 9506 [AAD] (16.97)

Sonata in E for Organ, Op. 38

H. Fagius (org) *(rec May 2-3, 1977)* † Études Org, Op. 45; Prelude & Fugue Org, Op. 52; Prelude & Fugue, Op. 56; Vars on "Ave Maris Stella", Op. 42 BIS ▲ 85 [AAD] (17.97)

Symphony in g, Op. 11 (1901-02)

M. Liljefors (cnd), Gävelborg SO *(rec Gävle, May 22-24, 1996)* STRL ▲ 1020 [DDD] (15.97)

Te Deum for Harp, Organ, Strings & Chorus, Op. 25 (1906)

K. Ek (cnd), Täby Church Choir [LAT] † J. Langlais:Messe solenelle BIS ▲ 289 [DDD] (17.97)

Variations (10) on "Ave Maris Stella" for Organ, Op. 42

H. Fagius (org) *(rec May 2-3, 1977)* † Études Org, Op. 45; Prelude & Fugue Org, Op. 52; Prelude & Fugue, Op. 56; Son Org, Op. 38 BIS ▲ 85 [AAD] (17.97)

O'NEILL, MICHAEL (1955-

Ur Og & Aji for 4 Bagpipes, Bass Clarinet & Tabla

O. Underhill (cnd) *(rec Vancouver B.C., Mar 7-9, 1995)* ("Tree Line: Music from Canada & Japan") † Bushnell:Night's Swift Dragons; C. Butterfield:Jappements; J. Kondo:Still Life; A. Louie:Winter Music; Takemitsu:Tree Line CBC (Musica Viva) ▲ 1109 [DDD] (16.97)

ONSLOW, GEORGES (1784-1853)

Grand Duo in e for Piano 4-Hands, Op. 7

A. Brings (pno), G. Chinn (pno) *(rec Episcopal Church of the Holy Trinity, New York, United States of America)* † Grand Duo Pno, Op. 22 CENT ▲ 2393 [ADD] (16.97)

T. Lenti (pno), M. A. Lenti (pno) *(rec Dec 17, 1990)* ("Forgotten Piano Duets, Vol. 2") † A. Bird:Introduction & Fugue, Op. 16; E. Grieg:Pièces symphoniques, Op. 14; Liszt:Grande valse di bravura, S.209 ACAD ▲ 20017 (16.97)

Grand Duo in f for Piano 4-Hands, Op. 22

A. Brings (pno), G. Chinn (pno) *(rec Episcopal Church of the Holy Trinity, New York, United States of America)* † Grand Duo Pno, Op. 7 CENT ▲ 2393 [ADD] (16.97)

Quartet in B♭ for Strings, Op. 4/1

Mandelring String Quartet *(rec Germany, Dec 10-12, 1997)* † Qt Strs CPO ▲ 999329 [DDD] (13.97)

Quartet in c for Strings, Op. 47

Mandelring String Quartet † Qts Strs, Op. 9 CPO ▲ 999060 [DDD] (14.97)

Quartet in E♭ for Strings, Op. 56

Coull String Quartet † Qt Strs ASV ▲ 808 [DDD] (16.97)

Quartet in f# for Strings, Op. 46/1

Coull String Quartet † Qt Strs, Op. 56 ASV ▲ 808 [DDD] (16.97)

Quartet in G for Strings, Op. 10/1

Mandelring String Quartet *(rec Germany, Dec 10-12, 1997)* † Qt Strs CPO ▲ 999329 [DDD] (13.97)

Quartet in g for Strings, Op. 46/3

Mandelring String Quartet *(rec Germany, Dec 10-12, 1997)* † Qt Strs CPO ▲ 999329 [DDD] (13.97)

Quartets (3) in g, C & f for Strings, Op. 9

Mandelring String Quartet † Qt Strs, Op. 47 CPO ▲ 999060 [DDD] (14.97)

Quintets (34) for Strings

Smithsonian Chamber Players, L'Archibudelli—in c, Op. 38 [The Bullet]; in E, Op. 39; in b, Op. 40 SNYC (Vivarte) ▲ 64308 (16.97)

Sonatas (3) in F, c & A for Cello (or Violin) & Piano, Op. 16

P. Franck (va), F. Thiollier (pno) PVY ▲ 796032 [DDD] (16.97)

Symphony No. 2, Op. 42

J. Leger (cnd), Hradec Kralove PO † Sym 4 LIDI ▲ 301036 (16.97)

Symphony No. 4, Op. 71

J. Leger (cnd), Hradec Kralove PO † Sym 2 LIDI ▲ 301036 (16.97)

Trio (No. 8) in c for Piano, Violin & Cello (or Horn), Op. 26

Göbel Trio Berlin † Czerny:Trio 4 Pno, Op. 289 SIGM ▲ 9400 (17.97)

ORBÁN, GYÖRGY (1947-

Missa Quinta for Clarinet, Double Bass & Chorus (1992)

E. Ludányi (db), J. Maczák (cl), K. Kiss (cnd), Ars Nova Vocal Ensemble ("Contemporary Hungarian Masses") † G. Selmeczi:Missa Secunda; Missa Tertia HUN ▲ 31711 [DDD] (16.97)

Passion to Hungarian Words for solo Voices, Organ, Orchestra & Chorus (1998)

G. Baross (cnd), Loránd Eötvös Univ of Sciences Orch, Bartók Chorus, I. Cserna (sop), X. Rivadeneira (ten), Á. Ambrus (bar), T. Szüle (bass), Z. Elekes (org) *(rec Sept 1998)* HUN ▲ 31824 [DDD] (16.97)

Quintet for Winds (1985)

Berlin Philharmonic Wind Quintet *(rec Jan 19-22, 1994)* † G. Kurtág:Qnt Winds, Op. 2; G. Ligeti:Bagatelles; Pieces Ww Qnt; Szervánszky:Qnt 1 Ww BIS ▲ 662 [DDD] (17.97)

ØRBECK, ANNE-MARIE (1911-

Pastorale & Allegro for Flute & String Orchestra (1959)

P. Øien (fl), T. Tønnesen (cnd), Norwegian CO *(rec Oslo, Norway, Feb 1-4, 1978)* ("The Norwegian Flute") † S. Bergh:Pan; Groven:Sunlight Mood; F. Mortensen:Son Fl, Op. 6; S. Olsen:Poem Fl; Serenade Fl, Op. 45; Sommerfeldt:Spring Tunes Fl, Op. 44 BIS ▲ 103 [AAD] (17.97)

ORBÓN, JULIÁN (1925-1991)

Cantigas del rey (3) for Soprano, Harpsichord, Percussion & String Quartet (1960)

R. Puyana (hpd), E. Mata (cnd) *(rec Nezahualcóyotl Hall, Univ Natl Autónoma, Mexico, Oct 1994)* † Himnus ad galli cantum; M. de Falla:Con Hpd; Retablo de maese Pedro DOR ▲ 90214 [ADD/DDD] (16.97)

Concerto grosso for Orchestra & String Quartet (1958)

E. Mata (cnd), Bolívar SO ("Music of Latin American Masters") † Versiones sinfónicas; C. Chávez:Caballos de vapor (suite); Sym 2; Estévez:Mediodia en el Llano; Ginastera:Estancia (sels); Pampeana 3, Op. 24; Revueltas:Redes; Sensemayá; H. Villa-Lobos:Bachiana brasileira 2; Uirapurú DOR 3-▲ 98102 [DDD] (36.97)

E. Mata (cnd), Bolívar SO, Latin American String Quartet † Ginastera:Pampeana 3, Op. 24; Revueltas:Redes; Sensemayá DOR ▲ 90178 [DDD] (16.97)

Himnus ad galli cantum for Soprano, Flute, Oboe, Clarinet, Harp & String Quartet (1955)

E. Mata (cnd) *(rec Nezahualcóyotl Hall, Univ Natl Autónoma, Mexico, Oct 1994)* † Cantigas del rey; M. de Falla:Con Hpd; Retablo de maese Pedro DOR ▲ 90214 [ADD/DDD] (16.97)

Partita No. 4 (symphonic movement) for Piano & Orchestra

T. Joselson (pno), E. Mata (cnd), Frankfurt RSO † M. de Falla:Noches en los jardines de España OLY ▲ 351 [DDD] (16.97)

Prelude y danza for Guitar

M. Barrueco (gtr) *(rec 1988)* † L. Brouwer:Gtr Music; H. Villa-Lobos:Chôro 1; Preludes Gtr EMIC ▲ 66576 [DDD] (11.97)

Versiones sinfónicas (3) for Orchestra (1953)

E. Mata (cnd), Bolívar SO *(rec Nov 1992 & July 1993)* † C. Chávez:Sym 2; Estévez:Mediodia en el Llano DOR ▲ 90179 [DDD] (16.97)

ORBÓN, JULIÁN (cont.)

Versiones sinfónicas (3) for Orchestra (1953) (cont.)

E. Mata (cnd), Bolívar SO ("Music of Latin American Masters") † Con grosso; C. Chávez:Caballos de vapor (suite); Sym 2; Estévez:Mediodia en el Llano; Ginastera:Estancia (sels); Pampeana 3, Op. 24; Revueltas:Redes; Sensemayá; H. Villa-Lobos:Bachiana brasileira 2; Uirapurú DOR 3-▲ 98102 [DDD] (36.97)

OREFICE, GIACOMO (1865-1922)

Music of Orefice

G. Turconi (vn), M. Sala (pno) ("Giacomo Orefice: The Complete Works for Violin & Piano") DUC ▲ 16 [DDD]

OREJON Y APARICIO, JOSE DE (1705-1765)

Ah del dia for 2 Sopranos, 2 Violins & Basso Continuo, ""Our Lady of Copacabana""

E. Gieco (cnd), Agrupación Música ("Peru-Guatemala: Music of the Latin American Cathedrals") † Anonymous:Hanac Pachap; Juguetico de fuego; Ceruti:A cantar un villancico; Pascual:Tres Villancicos; Ponce de Léon:Venid, venid, deidades AB ▲ 1425 (16.97)

OREM, PRESTON WARE (1865-1938)

American Indian Rhapsody for Piano (ca 1918; orchd)

P. Basquin (pno) † Beach:Son Vn; Farwell:From Mesa & Plain, Op. 20; Indian Songs, Op. 102; Foote:Son Vn NWW ▲ 80542 [ADD] (16.97)

ORFF, CARL (1895-1982)

Antigonae (opera in 5 acts) [text Sophocles translated to German by Friedrich Hölderlin] (1949)

C. Goltz (sop), P. Kuen (ten), K. Ostertag (ten), B. Kusche (bar), H. Uhde (bar), N. Barth (bar), G. Solti (cnd), Bavarian State Opera Orch, Bavarian State Opera Chorus *(rec Prinzregententheater, Jan 12, 1951)* ORFE 2-▲ 407952 (32.97)

Der Bernauerin [A Bavarian Play] for solo Voices, Orchestra & Chorus (1947)

L. Popp (sop), Laubenthal (ten), H. Lippert (ten), Ostermayer (sgr), K. Eichhorn (cnd), Munich RSO, Munich Radio Chorus [GER] ORF 2-▲ 255912 [DDD] (18.97)

Carmina burana (scenic cantata) for Soprano, Tenor, Baritone, Orchestra & Chorus (1935-36)

S. Armstrong (sop), P. Hall (ten), B. R. Cook (bar), M. Handford (cnd), Hallé Orch, Hallé State Chorus CFP ▲ 9005 [ADD] (12.97)

R. Bareva (sop), C. Kamenov (ten), Yanukov (bar), G. Robev (cnd), Sofia PO, Bulgarian choirs [G, L] † G. Fauré:Music Vc Pno FORL ▲ 16556 [DDD] (16.97)

J. Blegen (sop), W. Brown (ten), H. Hagegård (bar), R. Shaw (cnd), Atlanta SO, Atlanta Sym Chorus [G, L] TEL ▲ 80056 [DDD] (16.97)

J. Blegen (sop), K. Riegel (ten), P. Binder (bar), M. T. Thomas (cnd), Cleveland Orch, Cleveland Orch Chorus [G, L] SNYC ▲ 33172 [ADD] (16.97)

H. Blomstedt (cnd), San Francisco SO, San Francisco Sym Chorus [G, L] PLON ▲ 30509 [DDD] (16.97)

A. Carmignani (ct), A. Ariostini (bar), Kollaku (sgr), D. Alberti (pno), A. Malazzi (pno), O. Ben (perc), L. Casiraghi (perc), F. Pinetti (perc), G. Saveri (perc), A. Scotillo (perc), G. Andreoli (cnd), Venice Theater Chorus *(rec live, 1996)* MONM ▲ 10034 (18.97)

A. M. Dahl (sop), B. Grek (ten), J. Wolański (bass), I. Stupel (cnd), Artur Rubinstein PO, Artur Rubinstein Phil Chorus VRDI (Masters) ▲ 8932 (13.97)

N. Dessay (sop), G. Lesne (ct), T. Hampson (bar), M. Plasson (cnd), Toulouse Capitole Orch, Midi-Pyrénées Children's Choir *(rec Halle-aux-Grains Toulouse, Dec 2, 4 & 6, 1994)* EMIC ▲ 55392 [DDD] (16.97)

E. Gruberová (sop), J. Aler (ten), T. Hampson (bar), S. Ozawa (cnd), Berlin PO, Shin-Yuh Kai Chorus, Berlin Cathedral Boys' Choir [G, L] PPHI ▲ 22363 [DDD] (16.97)

J. Harsanyi (sop), R. Petrak (ten), H. Presnell (bar), E. Ormandy (cnd), Philadelphia Orch, Rutgers Univ Choir SNYC (Essential Classics) ▲ 47668 (7.97) ▮ 47668 (3.98)

B. Hendricks (sop), J. Aler (ten), H. Hagegård (bar), E. Mata (cnd), London SO, London Sym Chorus ("Basic 100, Vol. 60") RCAV ▲ 68085 (10.97) ▮ 68085 (5.98)

B. Hendricks (sop), M. Chance (ct), J. Black (bar), F. Welser-Möst (cnd), London PO, London Phil Chorus, St. Alban's Cathedral Choristers [G, L] EMIC ▲ 54054 [DDD] (16.97)

G. Herrera (sop), F. Kelley (ten), B. Holt (bar), H. D. Fuente (cnd), Mineria SO, Mineria Sym Choir INMP (Classic) ▲ 2024 (9.97)

D. Hill (cnd), Bournemouth SO, Waynflete Singers, Bournemouth Sym Chorus, Highcliffe Junior Choir, J. Watson (sop), J. Bowman (ct), D. Maxwell (bar) † G. Holst:Perfect Fool, Op. 39; Planets, Op. 32 VCL 2-▲ 61510 [DDD] (11.97)

B. Hoch (sop), H. Oswald (ten), Olsen (bar), C. Dutoit (cnd), Montreal SO PLON ▲ 455290 (16.97)

E. Jenisová (sop), V. Dolezal (ten), I. Kusnjer (bar), S. Gunzenhauser (cnd), Czech-Slovak RSO Bratislava, Slovak Phil Chorus NXIN ▲ 550196 [DDD] (5.97)

E. Jochum (cnd), Berlin German Opera Orch, Berlin German Opera Chorus, G. Janowitz (sop), G. Stolze (ten), D. Fischer-Dieskau (bar) *(rec Berlin, Germany, Oct 1967)* DEUT (The Originals) ▲ 47437 [ADD] (11.97)

S. Jo (sop), J. Kowalski (alt), B. Skovhus (bar), Z. Mehta (cnd), London PO, London Phil Chorus, Southend Boys' Choir TELC ▲ 74886 (16.97)

H. Kegel (cnd), Leipzig RSO, Dresden Children's Choir, Berlin Radio Chorus, Leipzig Radio Chorus ("Trionfi") † Catulli Carmina; Trionfo di Afrodite BER 2-▲ 2047 [ADD]

Z. Kloubová (sop), V. Dolezal (ten), I. Kusnjer (bar), G. Delogu (cnd), Prague SO, Kühn Choir, Bambini di Praga *(rec live Prague, Dec 12, 1995)* SUR ▲ 3160 (16.97)

J. Levine (cnd), Chicago SO, Chicago Sym Chorus, J. Anderson (sop), P. Creech (ten), B. Weikl (bar) DEUT ▲ 15136 [DDD] (16.97)

S. McNair (sop), J. Aler (ten), H. Hagegård (bar), L. Slatkin (cnd), St. Louis SO RCAV (Red Seal) ▲ 61673 (16.97) ▮ 61673 (9.98)

F. Mahler (cnd), Hartford SO, Hartford Sym Chorale, S. Stahlman (sop), J. Ferrante (ten), M. Meredith (bar) *([LAT,ENG] lib text)* VC ▲ 8208 [ADD] (13.97)

E. Mandac (sop), S. Kolk (ten), S. Milnes (bar), S. Ozawa (cnd), Boston SO, New England Conservatory Chorus [G, L] RCAV (Gold Seal) ▲ 56533 [ADD] (11.97)

L. Nordin (sop), H. Dornbusch (ten), P. Mattei (bar), R. Pöntinen (pno), L. Derwinger (pno), Kroumata Percussion Ensemble, C. R. Alin (cnd), Allmänna Sången, C. R. Alin (cnd), Uppsala Choir School Children's Chorus [chamber version] *(rec Uppsala Sweden, June 9-11, 1995)* BIS ▲ 734 [DDD] (17.97)

R. Pople (cnd), London Festival Orch, P. Simms (cnd), Tallis Chamber Choir, R. Corp (cnd), New London Children's Choir, A. Liebeck (sop), M. Hill (ten), D. Barrell (bar) *(rec King Square, London, England, Jan 20, 1996)* ("Carmina Burana") ARNO ▲ 34048 [DDD] (4.97)

L. Popp (sop), G. Unger (ten), R. Wolansky (bar), J. Noble (bar), R. Frühbeck de Burgos (cnd), New Philharmonia Orch, New Philharmonia Chorus † M. Ravel:Boléro EMIC ▲ 64328 (11.97)

K. Prestel (cnd), Salzburg Mozarteum Orch, K. Prestel (cnd), Salzburg Mozarteum Chorus INTC (Classical Creations) ▲ 820545 (9.97)

A. Previn (cnd), London SO, A. Oldham (cnd), London Sym Chorus, A. Clifford (cnd), St. Clement Danes Grammar School Boys' Choir, S. Armstrong (sop), G. English (ten), T. Allen (bar) *(rec London, England, Nov 25-27, 1974) ([ENG,LAT] text)* EMIC (Great Recordings of the Century) ▲ 66951 [ADD] (11.97)

A. Previn (cnd), Vienna PO, Vienna Boys' Choir, Arnold Schoenberg Choir, B. Bonney (sop), F. Lopardo (ten), A. Michaels-Moore (bar) DEUT ▲ 39950 [DDD] (16.97)

S. Roberts (sop), L. Griffith (sop), Frankfurt Kantorei, Frankfurt Singakademie (" Trionfi trittico teatrale ") † Catulli Carmina; Trionfo di Afrodite WER 2-▲ 6275 (38.97)

L. Stokowski (cnd), Houston SO, Houston Chorale *(rec 1955)* † I. Stravinsky:Firebird Suite 1 EMIC (FDS) ▲ 65207 (11.97)

C. Thielemann (cnd), Berlin German Opera Orch, Berlin German Opera Chorus, C. Oelze (sop), S. Keenlyside (ten), D. Kuebler (bar) DEUT ▲ 453587 (16.97)

P. Urbanek (cnd), Prague Festival Orch, Prague Festival Chorus *(rec live)* LALI ▲ 14020 [DDD] (3.97)

E. Vidal (sop), A. Stevenson (ten), A. Cognet (bass), P. Kuentz (cnd), Paul Kuentz Orch, Paul Kuentz Choir, Mouez Armor Chorale, Lorient Conservatory Chorus, Notre Dame College Chorus PVY ▲ 730044 (12.97)

P. Walmsley-Clark (sop), J. Graham-Hall (ten), D. Maxwell (bar), R. Hickox (cnd), London SO, London Sym Chorus [G, L] INMP ▲ 855 (9.97)

H. R. Zöbeley (cnd), Munich Residenz Orch, Munich Motet Choir † Catulli Carmina; Dithyrambe CALG 2-▲ 50937

Catulli Carmina (scenic cantata) for Soprano, Tenor, 4 Pianos, Percussion Ensemble & Chorus (1943)

L. Griffith (sop), T. Dewald (ten), W. Schäfer (cnd), Royal Flanders PO members, Frankfurt Kantorei INTU ▲ 3169 (16.97)

H. Kegel (cnd), Leipzig RSO, Dresden Children's Choir, Berlin Radio Chorus, Leipzig Radio Chorus ("Trionfi") † Carmina burana; Trionfo di Afrodite BER 2-▲ 2047 [ADD]

S. Roberts (sop), L. Griffith (sop), Frankfurt Kantorei, Frankfurt Singakademie (" Trionfi trittico teatrale ") † Carmina burana; Trionfo di Afrodite WER 2-▲ 6275 (38.97)

E. Stoyanova (sop), K. Kaludov (ten), M. Milkov (cnd), Bulgarian Radio-TV SO, Bulgarian Radio-TV Chorus [LAT] *(rec live in Sofia, 1988)* † B. Britten:Missa brevis, Op. 63 FORL ▲ 16610 [DDD] (16.97)

H. R. Zöbeley (cnd), Munich Residenz Orch, Munich Motet Choir † Carmina burana; Dithyrambe CALG 2-▲ 50937

604 ▲ = CD ♦ = Enhanced CD △ = MD ▮ = Cassette Tape ▯ = DCC

ORFF, CARL (cont.)
Dithyrambe for solo Voices, Orchestra & Chorus
H. R. Zöbeley (cnd), Munich Residenz Orch, Munich Motet Choir † Carmina burana; Catulli Carmina
CALG 2-▲ 50937
Die Kluge for solo Voices, Orchestra & Chorus (1943)
G. Frick (bass)—O hätt' ich meiner Tochter nur geglaubt *(rec 1943)* ("Four German Basses of the Past") † W. A. Mozart:Arias; Zauberflöte (sels); G. Rossini:Barbiere di Siviglia (sels); Verdi:Luisa Miller (sels); R. Wagner:Arias & Scenes; Götterdämmerung (sels); Lohengrin (sels); Tristan und Isolde (sels); H. Wolf:Corregidor (sels)
PRE ▲ 89968 (m) (16.97)
H. Kegel (cnd), Leipzig RSO, Leipzig Radio Chorus † Mond—Ein kleines Weltteater BER 2-▲ 2104 [ADD] (21.97)
Der Mond—Ein kleines Weltteater [The Moon—A Little World Theater] for solo Voices, Orchestra & Chorus [text Orff after Brothers Grimm] (1939)
H. Kegel (cnd), Leipzig RSO, Leipzig Radio Chorus † Kluge BER 2-▲ 2104 [ADD] (21.97)
P. Kuen (ten—Lad 3), B. Kusche (bar—Lad 1), J. Knapp (bar—Lad 2), G. Hann (bass—St. Peter), G. Wieter (bass—Lad 4), R. Wünzer (bass—The Farmer), K. Hanft (sgr—Innkeeper), W. Rösner (sgr—The Major), K. Erb (nar), R. Alberth (cnd), Bavarian RSO, Bavarian Radio Chorus *(rec Bavarian Radio, Jan 19-20, 1950)*
CALG ▲ 50948 [ADD] (19.97)
Schulwerk (complete)
M. Koppelstetter (mez), G. Orff (nar), C. Widmann (vn), S. Lehrmann (vc), M. Zahnhausen (rcr), Karl Peinkofer Percussion Ensemble—Schulwerk (complete) *(rec Munich, Germany, 1994-95)* ("Orff-Schulwerk, Vol. 1: Musica poetica") CEHA ▲ 13104 (16.97)
Trionfo di Afrodite (scenic cantata) for solo Voices, Orchestra & Chorus (1950-51)
H. Kegel (cnd), Leipzig RSO, Dresden Children's Choir, Berlin Radio Chorus, Leipzig Radio Chorus ("Trionfi") † Carmina burana; Catulli Carmina BER 2-▲ 2047 [ADD]
S. Roberts (sop), L. Griffith (sop), Frankfurt Kantorei, Frankfurt Singakademie (" Trionfi trittico teatrale ") † Carmina burana; Trionfo di Afrodite WER 2-▲ 6275 (38.97)
Ó RIADA, SEAN (1931-1971)
The Banks of Sullane (symphonic essay) for Orchestra (1956)
P. O. Duinn (cnd), RTE Sinfonietta *(rec UCD Dublin, Sept 28-29, 1994 & Jan 12, 1995)* ("Romantic Ireland") † Duff:Echoes of Georgian Dublin; Larchet:By the Waters of Moyle; P. O'Connor:Introspect; A. J. Potter:Rhap under a High Sky; Victory:Irish Pictures MARC (Irish Composer) ▲ 8223804 [DDD] (13.97)
ORIOLA, PIETRO (fl ca 1440-1480)
O vos homines
Unknown, Daedalus Ensemble *(rec Switzerland, July 1990)* ("Il Cantar Moderno") † Anonymous:Amor tu non me gabasti; Ben so che la mia mente; Cor mio voluntorioso; Fate d'arera; Giù per la mala via; Hora may che fora son; La gratia de voe; O tempo bono; Per la mya cara; Piangete done; Una vechia sempiternosa; Voca la galiera; J. Cornago:Morte merce/Mort en mercy; H. Isaac:Morte che fay ACCE ▲ 9068 [DDD] (17.97)
ORLANDINI, GIUSEPPE MARIA (1675-1760)
La Griselda (selections)
G. Banditelli (cta), P. Pasquini (hpd) † Marito giocatore BONG ▲ 2198 [DDD] (16.97)
Il marito giocatore e la moglie becchatona (intermezzo) [lib A. Salvi] (1719)
G. Banditelli (cta), A. Abete (ten), A. Bares (cnd), Il Viaggio Musicale † Griselda (sels)
BONG ▲ 2198 [DDD] (16.97)
ORNSTEIN, LEO (1892-
Arabesques (9) for Piano, Op. 42 (1918)
M. Verbit (pno) ("Past Futurists") † Son 4 Pno; C. Scott:Pno Music ALBA ▲ 70 [ADD] (16.97)
Quartet No. 3 for Strings (1976)
Lydian String Quartet † Qnt Pno NWW ▲ 80509 [DDD] (16.97)
Quintet for Piano & Strings (1927)
J. Weber (pno), Lydian String Quartet † Qt 3 Strs NWW ▲ 80509 [DDD] (16.97)
Sonata No. 4 for Piano (1919)
M. Verbit (pno) ("Past Futurists") † Arabesques Pno, Op. 42; C. Scott:Pno Music ALBA ▲ 70 [ADD] (16.97)
Sonata for Violin & Piano, Op. 31
G. Fulkerson (vn), A. Feinberg (pno) *(rec NY)* ("Cadenza & Variations") † A. Copland:Duo Fl; P. Glass:Einstein on the Beach (sels); R. Wernick:Cadenzas & Vars 2 NWW ▲ 80313 (16.97)
O'ROURKE, JIM (1969-
Terminal Pharmacy for Instrumental Ensemble
M. Dockter (vc), H. Franck (vc), R. Keck (vc), M. L. Breque (vc), D. Loch (vc), S. Saderk (vc), J. O'Rourke (gtr), L. Hemmer (fl), S. Oberg (fl), W. Lev (fl), J. Vanden (fl), T. Burr (cl), J. Cortazzo (b trbn), R. Prosser (acc), I. Suftin (acc), J. McEntire (dr), S. Braack (elec) TZA ▲ 7011 [DDD] (16.97)
ORREGO-SALAS, JUAN (1919-
Concerto for Violin & Orchestra, Op. 86 (1983)
F. Gulli (vn), T. Baldner (cnd), Indiana Univ SO *(rec Bloomington, IN, Oct 4, 1984)* † Glosas; Mobili; Serenata, Op. 70; Tangos IUSM ▲ 2 (16.97)
Glosas for Violin & Guitar, Op. 91 (1984)
G. Decuyper (vn), F. G. I Altisent (gtr) *(rec Bloomington, IN, Dec 2, 1988)* † Con Vn; Mobili; Serenata, Op. 70; Tangos IUSM ▲ 2 (16.97)
Mobili for Viola & Piano, Op. 63 (1967)
K. Kashkashian (va), J. Tocco (pno) *(rec Bloomington, IN, Apr 3, 1987)* † Con Vn; Glosas; Serenata, Op. 70; Tangos IUSM ▲ 2 (16.97)
Serenata for Flute & Cello, Op. 70 (1972)
F. Magg (vc), K. Magg (fl) *(rec Bloomington, IN, Mar 12, 1989)* † Con Vn; Glosas; Mobili; Tangos
IUSM ▲ 2 (16.97)
Tangos for 11 Instruments, Op. 82 (1982)
H. Sollberger (cnd) *(rec Bloomington, IN, Feb 3, 1984)* † Con Vn; Glosas; Mobili; Serenata, Op. 70
IUSM ▲ 2 (16.97)
ORTHEL, LÉON (1905-1985)
Scherzo No. 2 for Orchestra (1957)
M. Soustrot (cnd), Het Brabants Chamber Orchestra *(rec Jun 4, 1998)* † H. Andriessen:Con Org; H. Badings:Con Hp; Flothuis:Con Fl CV ▲ 77 (18.97)
Symphony No. 2, Op. 18, "Piccola sinfonia" (1940)
W. V. Otterloo (cnd), The Hague PO † H. Badings:Con Vns; Dresden:Dansflitsen; Flothuis:Symfonische muziek
CV ▲ 26 (19.97)
ORTIZ, DIEGO (ca 1510-ca 1570)
Trattado de Glosas (27 instrumental works or "recercadas") [2 books] for Chamber Ensemble (1553) (complete)
L. Duftschmid (vn), J. Savall (vl), P. Pandolfo (b vl), R. Lislevand (vih), A. Lawrence-King (hp), T. Koopman (hpd/org) ASTR ▲ 8717 [DDD] (18.97)
ORTIZ, GABRIELA (1964-
Altar de Neón for Chamber Orchestra & Percussion Quartet (1995)
E. A. Diemecke (cnd), Camerata de las Américas, Tambuco Percussion Ensemble *(rec Sala Nezahualcóyotl Mexico City, Sept-Oct 1996)* ("Ritmicas") † G. Fitkin:Hook; M. Miki:Mar Spiritual; S. Ojeda:Zappaloapan; A. Roldán:Ritmicas V-VI; Toussaint:Chunga de la Jungla DOR ▲ 90245 [DDD] (16.97)
ORTIZ, PABLO (1956-
Trazos en el Polvo for Chamber Ensemble (1994)
R. Bauer (cnd) † Vida Furtiva; R. Bauer:Octet; A. Frank:Autumn Rhythm; Range of Light
CENT ▲ 2386 [DDD] (16.97)
Vida Furtiva for Chamber Ensemble (1992)
R. Bauer (cnd) † Trazos en el Polvo; R. Bauer:Octet; A. Frank:Autumn Rhythm; Range of Light
CENT ▲ 2386 [DDD] (16.97)
ORTIZ-ALVARADO, WILLIAM (1947-
Abrazo for 4 Guitars
Buffalo Guitar Quartet ("New Music For Four Guitars") † Chobanian:Sonics; Funk Pearson:Mummychogs; W. S. Hartley:Qt Gtrs; Piorkowski:Struggle of Jacob NWW ▲ 384 [DDD] (16.97)
Cantilena for Guitar (1996)
J. Piorkowski (gtr) *(rec Lenna Hall, Chautauqua Institution, Chautauqua, NY, July-Nov 1996)* ("Freedom Flight: Guitar Music of Ortiz & Piorkowski") † Pavana; Piezas Tipicas Puertorriquenas; Rhapsody; Romance; Piorkowski:Freedom Flight; Once was Lost...; Sonnetas; Uraca; 51 CENT ▲ 2413 [DDD] (16.97)
Pavana for Guitar (1977)
J. Piorkowski (gtr) *(rec Lenna Hall, Chautauqua Institution, Chautauqua, NY, July-Nov 1996)* ("Freedom Flight: Guitar Music of Ortiz & Piorkowski") † Cantilena; Piezas Tipicas Puertorriquenas; Rhapsody; Romance; Piorkowski:Freedom Flight; Once was Lost...; Sonnetas; Uraca; 51 CENT ▲ 2413 [DDD] (16.97)

ORTIZ-ALVARADO, WILLIAM (cont.)
Piezas Tipicas Puertorriquenas (5) for 2 Guitars (1981)
J. Piorkowski (gtr) *(rec Lenna Hall, Chautauqua Institution, Chautauqua, NY, July-Nov 1996)* ("Freedom Flight: Guitar Music of Ortiz & Piorkowski") † Cantilena; Pavana; Rhapsody; Romance; Piorkowski:Freedom Flight; Once was Lost...; Sonnetas; Uraca; 51 CENT ▲ 2413 [DDD] (16.97)
Rhapsody for Guitar (1970; rev 1979 & 89)
J. Piorkowski (gtr) *(rec Lenna Hall, Chautauqua Institution, Chautauqua, NY, July-Nov 1996)* ("Freedom Flight: Guitar Music of Ortiz & Piorkowski") † Cantilena; Pavana; Piezas Tipicas Puertorriquenas; Romance; Piorkowski:Freedom Flight; Once was Lost...; Sonnetas; Uraca; 51 CENT ▲ 2413 [DDD] (16.97)
Romance for Soprano & Guitar (1988)
J. Piorkowski (gtr) *(rec Lenna Hall, Chautauqua Institution, Chautauqua, NY, July-Nov 1996)* ("Freedom Flight: Guitar Music of Ortiz & Piorkowski") † Cantilena; Pavana; Piezas Tipicas Puertorriquenas; Rhapsody; Piorkowski:Freedom Flight; Once was Lost...; Sonnetas; Uraca; 51 CENT ▲ 2413 [DDD] (16.97)
OSBON, DAVID (1963-
Liberty for Orchestra
P. Freeman (cnd), Czech National SO *(rec Prague, Austria)* ("Paul Freeman Introduces...Brandon, Griffes, Osbon, Muczynski, Klessig, Lamb & Feliciano-Vol. 2") † Brandon:Celebration Ov; Griffes:Poems of Fiona McLeod, Op. 11; Klessig:Meditation from Don Juan; M. Lamb:J. B. II; Muczynski:Sym Dialogues, Op. 20
ALBA ▲ 322 [DDD] (16.97)
OSBORNE, GEORGE ALEXANDER (1806-1893)
Duo brillant for 2 Pianos, Op. 69
B. Posner (pno), D. Garvelmann (pno) ("Celtic Keyboard: Duets by Irish Composers") KOCH ▲ 7287 [DDD] (10.97)
OSBORNE, WILLSON (1906-1979)
Rhapsody for Bassoon (or Clarinet) (1952)
D. DeBolt (bn) ("Bassoon Music of 20th-Century America") † Etler:Son Bn; Farago:Vars on a folia theme of Corelli, Op. 51; Garfield:Poème; Heiden:Serenade CRYS ▲ 347 (15.97)
OSTASZEWSKI, KAZIMIERZ OSTOIA (1864-1948)
Funeral March in Honour of Marshal Piludski for Piano
I. Zaluski (pno) *(rec St. Ives, Cambridge, England, Jan 1998)* ("Music of the Ogiński Dynasty, Vol. 2") † M. K. Ogiński:Pno Music; F. K. Ogiński:Pno Music; W. O. Ostaszewski:Turn of the Wave; K. B. Zaluski:Pno Music; I. Zaluski:Vars on a Theme of Amelia Zaluska OLY ▲ 645 [DDD] (16.97)
OSTASZEWSKI, WOJCIECH OSTOIA (1902-1975)
The Turn of the Wave [Powrotna Fala] for Piano
I. Zaluski (pno) *(rec St. Ives, Cambridge, England, Jan 1998)* ("Music of the Ogiński Dynasty, Vol. 2") † M. K. Ogiński:Pno Music; F. K. Ogiński:Pno Music; K. O. Ostaszewski:Funeral March in Honour of Marshal Piludski; K. B. Zaluski:Pno Music; I. Zaluski:Vars on a Theme of Amelia Zaluska OLY ▲ 645 [DDD] (16.97)
OSTERTAG, BOB (20th cent)
All the Rage for String Quartet (1992)
Kronos Quartet NON ▲ 79332 (9.97)
OSTRČIL, OTAKAR (1879-1935)
Symfonietta for Orchestra, Op. 20 (1921)
J. Bělohlávek (cnd), Prague SO † Sym in A, Op. 7 SUR ▲ 111826 [AAD]
Symphony in A, Op. 7 (1905)
J. Bělohlávek (cnd), Prague SO † Symfonietta, Op. 20 SUR ▲ 111826 [AAD]
OSTROWSKI, MATTHEW (20th cent.)
Computer Music
M. Ostrowski (cmpt)—Vertebra *(rec Holland)* ("Vertebra") POGU ▲ 21016 (16.97)
OSWALD, HENRIQUE (1852-1931)
Piano Music
M. I. Guimarães (pno)—Feuilles d'Album, Op. 20; Valse Lente; Três Peças, Op. 23; Nocturnes, Op. 6/1 & 2; Il Neige; Seis Peças, Op. 14 *(rec Clara-Wieck-Auditorium Sandhausen, Sept 13-14 & Nov 7-8, 1994)*
MARC (Latin American Classics) ▲ 8223639 [DDD] (13.97)
OSWALD, JAMES (1711-1769)
Airs for the Seasons (selections)
J. Barlow (hpd), J. Barlow (cnd) DOR ▲ 80164 (13.97)
OSWALD, JOHN (1953-
Music of John Oswald
J. Oswald (samples) ("Plexure") AVAK ▲ 16 (21.97)
OSWALD VON WOLKENSTEIN (ca 1377-1445)
Gelück und hail
Freiburg Spielleyt Ensemble *(rec Freiburg, Germany, Feb 1996)* ("O Fortuna: Luck & Misfortune in Songs & Texts of the Middle Ages") † Anonymous:Carmina Burana (sels); Lamento de Tristano/Rotta; Under der linden an der heide; Willekomen si der sumer schoene; Moniot d'Arras:Ce fu en mai; Walther von der Vogelweide:Carmina Burana (sels) *(E,G text)* ARSM ▲ 1181 [DDD] (17.97)
Songs
C. Bott (sop), P. Agnew (ten), M. George (bass), P. Pickett (cnd), New London Consort ("Knightly Passions")
PLOI ▲ 444173 (16.97)
OTAKA, ATSUTADA (1944-
Image for Orchestra
J. Hirokami (cnd), Malmö SO *(rec (Konserthus), Sweden, June 1990)* ("Japanese Orchestral Music") † Ifukube:Ballata Sinfonica; K. Tanaka:Prismes Orch; Y. Toyama:Matsura Orch; Wada:Folkloric Dance Suite; Folkloric Dance Suite Orch *(E, F, G text)* BIS ▲ 490 [DDD] (17.97)
T. Otaka (cnd), Tokyo PO *(rec live Tokyo Bunka-Kaikan Large Hall, May 30, 1981)* † Fukushi:Chromosphere; J. Yuasa:Scenes from Basho CAMA ▲ 293 [AAD] (18.97)
OTAKA, HISATADA (1911-1951)
Sonata for Violin & Piano [unfinished] (1932)
S. Numata (vn), A. Tadenuma (pno) *(rec July 1997)* ("Japanese Music for Violin & Piano") † K. Hirao:Son Vn; K. Kishi:Pieces Vn; K. Yamada:Chanson triste japonaise; Karatchi no hana CAMA ▲ 30477 [DDD] (18.97)
Sonatine for Piano (1940)
M. Yuguchi (pno) *(rec Jan 1996)* ("Contemporary Japanese Piano Music") † T. Ichiyanagi:Cloud Atlas; Takemitsu:Litany Pno; Uninterrupted Rests; Terauchi:Phoenix Hall and 8 Putto-Figures; Yashiro:Son Pno
THOR ▲ 2324 [DDD] (16.97)
OTT, DAVID (1947-
Concerto for 2 Cellos & Orchestra (1988)
D. Laufer (vc), W. Laufer (vc), Z. Macal (cnd), Milwaukee SO *(rec Uihlein Hall Milwaukee, WI, Oct 4, 1992)* † Music of the Canvas; Water Garden KOSS ▲ 1023 [DDD] (17.97)
Music of the Canvas for Orchestra (1990)
Z. Macal (cnd), Milwaukee SO *(rec Uihlein Hall Milwaukee, WI, Jan 23, 1994)* † Con for 2 Vcs; Water Garden
KOSS ▲ 1023 [DDD] (17.97)
Symphony No. 2 (1991)
C. Comet (cnd), Grand Rapids SO † Sym 3 KOSS ▲ 3301 [DDD] (17.97)
Symphony No. 3 (1992)
C. Comet (cnd), Grand Rapids SO † Sym 2 KOSS ▲ 3301 [DDD] (17.97)
Triple Concerto for Violin, Clarinet, Piano & Orchestra (1993)
L. Gregorian (cnd), Solisti di Praga, Verdehr Trio ("Verdehr Trio, Vol. 8") † W. Wallace:Triple Con
CRYS (Making of a Medium) ▲ 748 [DDD] (15.97)
Water Garden for Orchestra (1986)
Z. Macal (cnd), Milwaukee SO *(rec Uihlein Hall Milwaukee, Jan 23, 1994)* † Con for 2 Vcs; Music of the Canvas
KOSS ▲ 1023 [DDD] (17.97)
OTTE, HANS (1926-
Das Buch der Klänge [The Book of Sounds] for Piano (1983)
H. Otte (pno) KUC ▲ 11069 (16.97) ▮ 12069 (15.98)
Wassermannmusik for Chamber Ensemble
A. Ceccomori (fl), G. D. Esposti (rcr), P. Wehage (sax), C. Chailly (hp), F. Ottaviucci (pno) *(rec Italy)* ("New Music Masters") † Einaudi:Quattro Passi; Górecki:For You Ann, Op. 58; Pärt:Pari intervallo; S. Reich:N.Y. Counterpoint; Vermont Counterpoint AMI ▲ 496 [DDD] (15.97)
OTTMAN, JOHN (20th cent)
The Usual Suspects (film music) for Orchestra (1995)
D. Intrabartolo (pno), L. Groupé (cnd) *(rec Rancho Bernardo, CA)* MILA ▲ 35721 (16.97)

OTTO, LUIGI (ca 1750)

Concerto in E♭ for Trumpet, 2 Oboes, 2 Horns, Strings & Continuo

L. Güttler (tpt), C. Schornsheim (hpd), M. Pommer (cnd), Leipzig New Bach Collegium Musicum *(rec Dresden, Germany, May 1986)* ("Classical Trumpet Concertos") † Molter:Con 3 Tpt; F. X. Richter:Con Tpt; Sperger:Con Tpt CAPO ▲ 10051 [DDD] (11.97)

OTTO, VALERIUS (1579-?1612)

Praha Dances (suites) for Chamber Ensemble (1611)

V. Návrat (cnd), Antiquarius Consort Prague ARTA ▲ 88 (16.97)

OUELLETTE, ANTOINE (1960-

Music of Ouellette

D. Habel (hp), P. Wedd (org), A. Ouellette (cnd) —Hymn & Processional "Veni Creator Spiritus"; A Mass for the Wind That Blows; Celtic Suite SNE ▲ 611 (16.97)

OWEN, JERRY (1944-

Encounters for Piano

J. Jensen (pno) *(rec Cedar Rapids, IA, May 5, 1989)* ("Intimate Dances") † Intimate Dances; Songs; Studies Gtr CENT ▲ 2233 [DDD] (16.97)

Intimate Dances for Flute & Guitar

C. Egger (gtr), J. Boland (fl) *(rec Aug 10, 1991)* ("Intimate Dances") † Encounters Pno; Songs; Studies Gtr CENT ▲ 2233 [DDD] (16.97)

Songs (4) for Soprano & Piano [after poems by William Blake]

L. Morgan (sop), J. Jensen (pno) *(rec July 7, 1989)* ("Intimate Dances") † Encounters Pno; Intimate Dances; Studies Gtr CENT ▲ 2233 [DDD] (16.97)

Studies (4) for Guitar

C. Egger (gtr) *(rec Cedar Rapids, IA, Aug 11, 1991)* ("Intimate Dances") † Encounters Pno; Intimate Dances; Songs CENT ▲ 2233 [DDD] (16.97)

OXINAGA, JOAQUIN DE (1719-1789)

Fugues for Organ

E. Elizondo (org)—Fuga airosa; Intento in G *(rec La Valenciana Org, Apr 1991)* ("The Organs of Guanajuato, Mexico") † De Gamarra:Son in Tone 8; Versos; N. Ledesma:Son 6 Org; P. A. Soler:Versos para Te Deum TIT ▲ 201 [DDD]

OZI, ETIENNE (1754-1813)

Sonata No. 1 for Bassoons

S. Nigro (bn), B. Lane (bn) † M. Curtis:Impish Imp; D. Dorff:Son d'Armore; W. A. Mozart:Duo Bn Vc, K.292; Vanhal:Con Bns; A. Weisberg:From the Deep CRYS ▲ 349 (15.97)

PABLO, LUIS DE (1930-

Fabula for Guitar

G. Estarellas (gtr) ("Modern Italian & Spanish Guitar Music") † B. Bettinelli:Quattro pezzi; Ghedini:Studio da concerto; C. Halffter:Codex 1; Petrassi:Suoni Notturni; J. L. Turina:Monologos STRV ▲ 33401 (16.97)

Music of Pablo

P. Méfano (cnd) —Notturnino; Con da camera; Dibujos; Meditatiónes (5); Fragmentos (4) de Kiu 2E2M ▲ 1009 (20.97)

Tarde de Poetas for Voices & Orchestra

L. Castellani (sop), J. Chaminé (bar), J. Pons (cnd), Barcelona Teatro Lliure CO HAM 2-▲ 901568 (18.97)

PABST, PAUL (1854-1897)

Concert Paraphrase on Tchaikovsky's Eugen Onegin for Piano

M. Ponti (pno) *(rec ca 1973)* † Brassin:Trans Pno; Liszt:Réminiscences de Don Juan Pno, S.418; Trans, Arrs & Paraphrases; Moszkowski:Operatic Paraphrases & Trans Pno; Tausig:Fant on Themes of Moniuszko; Trans & Arrs Pno; Thalberg:Fants & Vars on Opera Themes Pno VB2 2-▲ 5047 [ADD] (9.97)

PACCIONE, PAUL (1952-

Like Spring for Prerecorded & Overdubbed Flutes & Electronic Tape Recording (1988)

J. Walker (fl), D. Scheele (fl) ("Society of Composers, Inc.: Extended Resources") † C. A. Cox:Studies of Light & Dark; C. P. First:Tantrum; E. Mattila:Primordius; Veeneman:Wiry Concord CPS ▲ 8626

PACHELBEL, JOHANN (1653-1706)

Alle Menschen müssen sterben (chorale variation) for Organ, POP 102 (1683)

J. Payne (org) *(rec H.G. Trost Organ (1735), Altenburg Castle Church, Germany, June 7, 1997)* † Allein zu dir, Herr Jesu Christ; Allein Gott in der Höh sei Ehr, POP 25; Ciaccona, POP 16; Fugue Org, POP 127; Magnificat fugues in tone 8; Toccata Org, POP 274 CENT (Complete Organ Works Vol. 7) ▲ 2418 [DDD] (16.97)

Allein Gott in der Höh sei Ehr (chorale) for Organ, POP 25

J. Payne (org) *(rec H.G. Trost Organ (1735), Altenburg Castle Church, Germany, June 7, 1997)* † Alle Menschen müssen sterben, POP 102; Allein zu dir, Herr Jesu Christ; Ciaccona, POP 16; Fugue Org, POP 127; Magnificat fugues in tone 8; Toccata Org, POP 274 CENT (Complete Organ Works Vol. 7) ▲ 2418 [DDD] (16.97)

Allein zu dir, Herr Jesu Christ (chorale) for Organ

J. Payne (org) *(rec H.G. Trost Organ (1735), Altenburg Castle Church, Germany, June 7, 1997)* † Alle Menschen müssen sterben, POP 102; Allein Gott in der Höh sei Ehr, POP 25; Ciaccona, POP 16; Fugue Org, POP 127; Magnificat fugues in tone 8; Toccata Org, POP 274 CENT (Complete Organ Works Vol. 7) ▲ 2418 [DDD] (16.97)

Arias & Duets

J. Németh (alt), G. Kállay (ten), J. Malina (cnd), Affetti Musicali, Z. Szabó (cnd), Musica Profana Viola da Gamba Ensemble *(Augen streuet Perlen-Tränen; Widder Abrahams)*, G. Kállay (ten), J. Malina (cnd), Affetti Musicali, Z. Szabó (cnd), Musica Profana Viola da Gamba Ensemble *(Wie nichtig, ach; Guter Walter unsers Rats; Mein Leben, dessen Kreuz; Es muss die Sinne ja erfreuen; O grosses Musenlicht; Gewitter)*, M. Zádori (sop), J. Malina (cnd), Affetti Musicali, Z. Szabó (cnd), Musica Profana Viola da Gamba Ensemble *(Freuderfüllten Abendstunden; Auf, werte Gäst)*, J. Németh (alt), J. Malina (cnd), Affetti Musicali, Z. Szabó (cnd), Musica Profana Viola da Gamba Ensemble *(Mäecenas lebet noch; Hör, grosser Mäcenat)*, I. Kovács (bass), J. Malina (cnd), Affetti Musicali, Z. Szabó (cnd), Musica Profana Viola da Gamba Ensemble *(Geliebtes Vaterherz)* *(rec Budapest, Hungary, Aug 29-Sep 5, 1997)* HUN ▲ 31736 [DDD] (16.97)

Canon & Gigue in D for 3 Violins & Continuo

W. Boughton (cnd), English SO † Vaughan Williams:Fant on a Theme of Tallis; Fant on Greensleeves NIMB ▲ 7007 [DDD] (11.97)

W. Boughton (cnd), English SO *(rec Great Hall, Univ of Birmingham, England, 1995)* ("Orchestral Favorites, Vol. 1") † Albinoni:Adagio; E. Grieg:Holberg Suite Pno, Op. 40; G. Holst:St. Paul's Suite, Op. 29/2; Warlock:Capriol Suite NIMB ▲ 7019 [DDD] (11.97)

Canadian Brass † G. F. Handel:Water Music, HWV 348-50 RCAV (Gold Seal) ▲ 3554 (16.97)

Canadian Brass RCAV (Red Seal) ▲ 4733 (16.97) ▮ 4733 (9.98)

L. Chan (vn), P. Cochand (vn), P. Cochand (cnd) *(rec Oct 19-21, 1992)* † F. X. Richter:Grandes simphonies; Telemann:Don Quichotte (suite); Vivaldi:Cons Vn(s) Strs, Op. 3/1-12 GALL ▲ 723

H. Farberman (cnd) [arr Farberman] *(rec 1982)* † Beethoven:Sym 9; Berlioz:Sym fantastique, Op. 14; Bizet:Carmen (suite 1) ALLO ▲ 8195 (3.97)

T. Füri (cnd), Bern Camerata † Albinoni:Adagio; J. S. Bach:Brandenburg Con 3, BWV 1048; Manfredini:Cons Vns, Op. 3; H. Purcell:Pavane & Chaconne NOVA ▲ 150004 (16.97)

R. Goebel (cnd), Cologne Musica Antiqua † J. S. Bach:Ov Orch; Suite 2 Fl, BWV 1067; G. F. Handel:Trio Sons, HWV 396-402; Vivaldi:Sons Vns Vl, Op. 1/1-12 PARC (Masters) ▲ 47285 [DDD] (9.97)

C. Hogwood (cnd), Academy of Ancient Music † G. F. Handel:Solomon (arrival of the queen of Sheba) PLOI ▲ 10553 [ADD] (16.97)

I Musici † Albinoni:Adagio; W. A. Mozart:Kleine Nachtmusik, K.525 PPHI (Digital Classics) ▲ 10606 [DDD] (16.97)

Italian Solisti † Albinoni:Adagio DNN ▲ 73335 [DDD] (16.97)

R. Kapp (cnd), Philharmonia Virtuosi, New York—Canon *(rec NYC, NY)* ("Greatest Hits of 1720") † Albinoni:Adagio; J. S. Bach:Air on the G String; Anna Magdalena Bach Notebook (sels); Con 1 for 2 Hpds, BWV 1060; Con 5 Hpd, BWV 1056; Campra:Tancrède (sels); A. Corelli:Sonatas (12) for Violin (or Violone) & Continuo Instruments [including No. 12, "La Follia"], Op. 5; G. F. Handel:Suites de Pièces (9) Hpd, HWV 434-42; Mouret:Rondeau SNYC ▲ 34544 [ADD] (9.97)

R. Kapp (cnd), Philharmonia Virtuosi, New York—Canon ("Build Your Baby's Brain") † J. S. Bach:Air on the G String; Cant 147; Cant 208; Beethoven:Bagatelle Pno in a, WoO 59; G. F. Handel:Solomon (sels); W. A. Mozart:Kleine Nachtmusik, K.525; Son 11 Pno, K.331; F. Schubert:Qnt Pno, D.667; Vivaldi:Cons Vn Strs, Op. 8/1-4 SNYC ▲ 60815 [DDD] (9.97) ▮ 60815 [DDD] (5.98)

H. von Karajan (cnd), Berlin PO † Albinoni:Adagio; J. S. Bach:Suite 3 Orch, BWV 1068; C. W. Gluck:Orfeo ed Euridice (dance); W. A. Mozart:Serenade 6 Orch, K.239; Vivaldi:Cons Fl, Op. 10/1-6 DEUT ▲ 13309 [DDD] (16.97)

Y. Kondonassis (hp) *(rec Cleveland, OH, June 1994)* ("A New Baroque") † J. S. Bach:Arioso Ob; Cant 147; Suite Lt, BWV 996; Wohltemperirte Clavier; G. F. Handel:Suites de Pièces (8) Hpd, HWV 426-33; D. Scarlatti:Sons Kbd TEL ▲ 80403 [DDD] (16.97)

J. Lamon (vn), K. Solway (fl), J. Lamon (cnd), Tafelmusik † J. S. Bach:Air on the G String; G. F. Handel:Solomon (sels); H. Purcell:Abdelazer (sels); Telemann:Musique de Table REF ▲ 13 (16.97)

R. Leppard (cnd), English CO † Albinoni:Adagio SNYC ▮ 38482 (3.98) ▲ 38482 (9.97)

PACHELBEL, JOHANN (cont.)

Canon & Gigue in D for 3 Violins & Continuo (cont.)

R. Leppard (cnd), English CO † H. Purcell:Abdelazer (sels); Music of Purcell SNYC ▮ 44650 [DDD] (5.98) ▲ 44650 [DDD] (10.97)

N. Marriner (cnd), Academy of St. Martin in the Fields † W. A. Mozart:Adagio & Fugue Strs, K.546; Kleine Nachtmusik, K.525 PPHI ▲ 16386 [DDD] (16.97)

W. Marsalis (tpt), R. Leppard (cnd), English CO [arr R. Leppard for 3 tpts & strs] † H. I. Biber:Son in A Tpts; M. Haydn:Con Tpt, Hns & Strs; Telemann:Con Tpts; Vivaldi:Con Tpts, RV.537 SNYC ▲ 42478 [DDD] (16.97) ▮ 42478 [DDD] (10.98)

Orpheus CO—Canon † Albinoni:Adagio; J. S. Bach:Jesu, bleibet meine Freude; Suite 3 Orch, BWV 1068; A. Corelli:Con grosso, Op. 6/8; G. F. Handel:Solomon (arrival of the queen of Sheba); H. Purcell:Chacony Strs, Z.730; Vivaldi:Cons Vn(s) Strs, Op. 3/1-12 DEUT ▲ 29390 [DDD] (16.97)

J. Paillard (cnd), Jean-François Paillard CO *(rec 1968)* † Fasch:Con Tpt Obs; Syms ERAT ▲ 98475 [ADD] (9.97)

J. Paillard (cnd), Jean-François Paillard CO † Albinoni:Adagio RCAV (Red Seal) ▲ 65468 [DDD] (16.97) ▮ 65468 [DDD] (9.98)

T. Pinnock (cnd), English Concert † Avison:Concerti grossi; H. Purcell:Chacony Strs, Z.730 PARC ▲ 15518 [DDD] (16.97)

D. Shostac (fl), R. Kato (va), J. Walz (vc), J. Smith (gtr), G. Levant (hp), A. Perry (pno)—Canon *(rec North Hollywood, CA)* ("The Romantic Flute") † J. S. Bach:Air on the G String; Arioso Ob; Sons Fl; Debussy:Prélude à l'après-midi d'un faune; Suite bergamasque; G. Fauré:Pavane; Sicilienne, Op. 78; Gossec:Tambourin Fl; Marais:Basque; W. A. Mozart:Andante Fl, K.315; Con 21 Pno, K.467 XCEL ▲ 30006

L. Slatkin (cnd), St. Louis SO † Borodin:Nocturne Str Orch; P. Tchaikovsky:Serenade Strs, Op. 48; Vaughan Williams:Fant on Greensleeves TEL ▲ 80080 [DDD] (16.97)

J. Williams (cnd), Boston Pops Orch—Canon † Albinoni:Adagio; G. Fauré:Pavane; Satie:Gymnopédies PPHI ▲ 16361 [DDD] (11.97)

artists unknown ("Pachelbel's Greatest Hit") RCAV (Gold Seal) ▲ 60712 [ADD] (11.97) ▮ 60712 [ADD] (6.98)

various artists—Canon † Albinoni:Adagio; J. S. Bach:Brandenburg Con 2, BWV 1047; Brandenburg Con 3, BWV 1048; Brandenburg Con 5, BWV 1050; Jesu, bleibet meine Freude; Suite 2 Fl, BWV 1067; Suite 3 Orch, BWV 1068; G. F. Handel:Messiah (sels); Royal Fireworks Music, HWV 351; Serse (sels); Water Music, HWV 348-50; Mouret:Rondeau; Vivaldi:Con Gtr; Cons Vn Strs, Op. 8/1-4 RCAV ▲ 60840 (10.97) ▮ 60840 (5.98)

various artists—Canon ("Baby Needs Baroque") † J. S. Bach:Brandenburg Con 1, BWV 1046; French Suites; Goldberg Vars, BWV 988; Inventions Hpd; Son Vn; Sons & Partitas Vn; Suite 2 Fl, BWV 1067; G. F. Handel:Water Music, HWV 348-50; Telemann:Qnt Tpt; Son Fl; Torelli:Son 5 No. 1 in D; Vivaldi:Cons Vn Strs, Op. 8/1-4 DLS ▲ 1609 [DDD] (10.97) ▮ 1609 [DDD] (8.98)

various artists—Canon † Albinoni:Adagio; J. S. Bach:Brandenburg Con 2, BWV 1047; Brandenburg Con 3, BWV 1048; Brandenburg Con 5, BWV 1050; Suite 2 Fl, BWV 1067; Suite 3 Orch, BWV 1068; G. F. Handel:Music of Handel; Mouret:Music of Mouret; Vivaldi:Con in D Gtr; Cons Vn Strs, Op. 8/1-4 RCAV ▲ 63501 (11.97)

Ciaccona in d for Organ

P. Kee (org) *(rec Gabler org, Weingarten, Benedictine Abbey Basilika, Germany, Oct 1990)* † Ciaccona, POP 16; Fant in g; Prelude in d, POP 256; J. M. Bach:Org Music; J. S. Bach:Preludes & Fugues, BWV 531-552; Lebègue:Cloches; Murschhauser:Vars on 'Labt uns das Kindelein wiegen'; J. G. Walther:Vars on Jesu meine Freude Org CHN ▲ 520 [DDD] (16.97)

Ciaccona for Organ, POP 16

P. Kee (org) *(rec Gabler org, Weingarten, Benedictine Abbey Basilika, Germany, Oct 1990)* † Ciaccona in d; Fant in g; Prelude in d, POP 256; J. M. Bach:Org Music; J. S. Bach:Preludes & Fugues, BWV 531-552; Lebègue:Cloches; Murschhauser:Vars on 'Labt uns das Kindelein wiegen'; J. G. Walther:Vars on Jesu meine Freude Org CHN ▲ 520 [DDD] (16.97)

J. Payne (org) *(rec H.G. Trost Organ (1735), Altenburg Castle Church, Germany, June 7, 1997)* † Alle Menschen müssen sterben, POP 102; Allein zu dir, Herr Jesu Christ; Allein Gott in der Höh sei Ehr, POP 25; Fugue Org, POP 127; Magnificat fugues in tone 8; Toccata Org, POP 274 CENT (Complete Organ Works Vol. 7) ▲ 2418 [DDD] (16.97)

Fantasia in g for Organ

P. Kee (org) *(rec Gabler org, Weingarten, Benedictine Abbey Basilika, Germany, Oct 1990)* † Ciaccona in d; Ciaccona, POP 16; Prelude in d, POP 256; J. M. Bach:Org Music; J. S. Bach:Preludes & Fugues, BWV 531-552; Lebègue:Cloches; Murschhauser:Vars on 'Labt uns das Kindelein wiegen'; J. G. Walther:Vars on Jesu meine Freude Org CHN ▲ 520 [DDD] (16.97)

Fugues (11) on the Magnificat tertii toni for Organ

M. J. Newman (pno), Parthenia XII members VOXC ▲ 93043

Fugue in C for Organ, POP 127

J. Payne (org) *(rec H.G. Trost Organ (1735), Altenburg Castle Church, Germany, June 7, 1997)* † Alle Menschen müssen sterben, POP 102; Allein zu dir, Herr Jesu Christ; Allein Gott in der Höh sei Ehr, POP 25; Ciaccona, POP 16; Magnificat fugues in tone 8; Toccata Org, POP 274 CENT (Complete Organ Works Vol. 7) ▲ 2418 [DDD] (16.97)

Hexachordum Apollinis (6 arias) for Organ (1699)

J. Butt (org) HAM (Suite) ▲ 7907029 (12.97)

Magnificat fugues (13) in tone 8 for Organ

J. Payne (org) *(rec H.G. Trost Organ (1735), Altenburg Castle Church, Germany, June 7, 1997)* † Alle Menschen müssen sterben, POP 102; Allein zu dir, Herr Jesu Christ; Allein Gott in der Höh sei Ehr, POP 25; Ciaccona, POP 16; Fugue Org, POP 127; Toccata Org, POP 274 CENT (Complete Organ Works Vol. 7) ▲ 2418 [DDD] (16.97)

Magnificat in D for 4 Voices & Continuo

A. Jacob (org), W. Jacob (cnd), Capella Sebaldina Nuremberg † Missa brevis; Motets; Org Music ENTE ▲ 50 [ADD] (10.97)

Missa brevis in D for 4 Voices (1704)

A. Jacob (org), W. Jacob (cnd), Capella Sebaldina Nuremberg † Magnificat; Motets; Org Music ENTE ▲ 50 [ADD] (10.97)

Motets

A. Jacob (org), W. Jacob (cnd), Capella Sebaldina Nuremberg—Singet dem Herrn ein neues Lied; Der Herr ist König; Nun danket alle Gott; Jauchzet dem Herrn; Exsurgat Deus; Tröste uns Gott; Gott ist unsre Zuversicht † Magnificat; Missa brevis; Org Music ENTE ▲ 50 [ADD] (10.97)

Organ Music

M. Aberg (org)—Was Gott tut, das ist wohlgetan, Partita Org; Fantasia in g *(rec 1724 Cahman Organ, Kristine Church, Falun, Sweden, Jan 28, 1983)* † J. S. Bach:Orgelbüchlein; Buxtehude:Passacaglia Org, BuxWV 161; Kauffmann:Org Music; J. P. Kellner:Org Music; J. L. Krebs:Org Music; J. P. Sweelinck:Org Music BIS ▲ 229 [DDD] (17.97)

A. Bouchard (org)—Ciaccona, POP 16; Hexachordum Apollinis; Herr Christ, der einig Gott's Sohn, POP 54; Nun komm der Heiden Heiland, POP 72; Toccata Org, POP 282; Tag der ist so freudenreich, POP 38; Gelobet seist du, Jesu Christ, POP 50; Vom Himmel hoch da komm ich her; Lob sei Gott in des Himmels Thron, POP 67; Christus, der ist mein Leben, POP 101; Magnificat fugues in tone 1 [No. 1, POP 151; No. 2, POP 152; No. 3, POP 153; No. 4, POP 154; No. 5, POP 155; No. 6, POP 156; No. 7, POP 157; No. 8, POP 158; No. 9, POP 159; No. 10, POP 160; No. 11, POP 161; No. 12, POP 162] *(rec Casavant org, 1964, St-Pascal de Kamouraska Church, Canada)* ("Complete Organ Works, Vol. 1") DOR ▲ 93173 [DDD] (16.97)

A. Bouchard (org)—Ciaccona in C, POP 11; Hexachordum Apollinis; Toccata Org, POP 274; Fugue Org, POP 127; Wie schön leuchtet der Morgenstern, POP 88; Christ unser Herr zum Jordan kam, POP 34; Erhalt uns, Herr, bei deinem Wort, POP 45; Durch Adams Fall; Alle Menschen müssen sterben, POP 102; Magnificat fugues in tone 2 *(rec Casavant org, 1964, St-Pascal de Kamouraska Church, Canada)* ("Complete Organ Works, Vol. 2") DOR ▲ 93174 [DDD] (16.97)

B. Harbach (org)—Canon & Gigue [Canon]; Ciaccona, POP 16; Vom Himmel hoch da komm ich her; Allein Gott in der Höh sei Ehr, POP 25; Nun lob, mein Seel', den Herren; Ach Herr, mich armen Sünder; Nun komm der Heiden Heiland, POP 72; Jesus Christus, unser Heiland, der von uns; Wenn wir in höchsten Nöten sein; An Wasserflüssen Babylon, POP 29; Ich ruf zu dir; Feste Burg; Wie schön leuchtet der Morgenstern, POP 88; Nun freut euch, lieben Christen g'mein; Ciaccona in d GAS (Silver) ▲ 2001 [DDD] (7.97)

H. Heintze (org) ("Works for Organ") † J. G. Walther:Org Music BER ▲ 9213 (10.97)

W. Jacob (org)—Ricercare in c; Toccata in c *(rec Org of St. Sebald Nuremberg)* † Magnificat; Missa brevis; Motets ENTE ▲ 50 [ADD] (10.97)

J. Payne (org)—Fugues (11) Org; Toccata Org, POP 273; Allein zu dir, Herr Jesu Christ; Ach Herr, mich armen Sünder; Ricercar in c; Non lob, mein' Seel, den Herren; Toccata, Prelude & Fugue in e; Vom Himmel hoch da komm ich her; Chaconne in D; Partite:Was Gott tut ist wohlgetan; Nun komm der Heiden Heiland, POP 72; Tag der ist so freudenreich, POP 38; Allein Gott in der Höh sei Ehr, POP 25; Gelobet seist du, Jesu Christ, POP 50 *(rec Houston, Dec 1995)* ("Complete Organ Works, Vol. 2") CENT ▲ 2306 [DDD] (16.97)

J. Payne (org)—Toccata & Fugue in d; Fugues Magnificat quinti toni 1-12; Fant in d; Durch Adams Fall; Partita, "Herzlich tut mich verlangen"; Ach wie elend ist unsre Zeit; Gott hat das Evangelium; Fugue in b; Ciaccona in D *(rec Sept 1996)* ("Complete Organ Works, Vol. 4") CENT ▲ 2352 [DDD] (16.97)

▲ = CD ♦ = Enhanced CD △ = MD ▮ = Cassette Tape ▯ = DCC

PACHELBEL, JOHANN (cont.)

Organ Music (cont.)

J. Payne (org)—Toccata Org, POP 276; Fugue Magnificat sexti toni, No. 1; Prelude in d, POP 256; Dies sind die heil'gen zehn Gebot, POP 39; Ciaccona in C, POP 11; Hexachordum Apollinis [Arias 1-5] *(rec Sept 1996)* ("Complete Organ Works, Vol. 5") CENT ▲ 2353 [DDD] (16.97)

J. Payne (org) *(rec Steinwedel, Germany, June 1997)* ("Complete Organ Works, Vol. 6") CENT ▲ 2383 [DDD] (16.97)

J. Tůma (org) *(rec Kladruby Monastery, Czech Republic)* ("Historic Organs of Bohemia, Vol. 4") SUR ▲ 3355 [DDD] (16.97)

G. Wachowski (org) ("Organ Works") MDG ▲ 6060273 (17.97)

J. Zehnder (org)—Nun lob, mein Seel', den Herren; Choralsatz; Fuga super Dies sind die heilgen zehn Gebot; Choralsatz von M. Praetorius *(rec Pere Casulleras CH-Waldenburg, 1992)* ("The Five Organs of the Abbey Church of Muri") † J. S. Bach:Chorales (miscellaneous); Org Music (misc colls); Heron:Voluntary Org; J. L. Krebs:Org Music JEC ▲ 309 [DDD]

Prelude in d for Organ, POP 256

P. Kee (org) *(rec Gabler org, Weingarten, Benedictine Abbey Basilika, Germany, Oct 1990)* † Ciaccona in d; Ciaccona, POP 16; Fant in g; J. M. Bach:Org Music; J. S. Bach:Preludes & Fugues, BWV 531-552; Lebègue:Cloches; Murschhauser:Vars on 'Labt uns das Kindelein wiegen'; J. G. Walther:Vars on Jesu meine Freude Org CHN ▲ 520 [DDD] (16.97)

Toccata & Fugue in B♭ for Organ

D. Hollick (org) ("The Young Bach") † J. S. Bach:Fant & Fugue, BWV 542; Fugue on "Meine Seele"; Org Music (misc colls); G. Böhm:Preludes & Fugues; Buxtehude:Magnificat primi toni, BuxWV 204 SUR ▲ 3015 (16.97)

Toccata in C for Organ, POP 274

J. Payne (org) *(rec H.G. Trost Organ (1735), Altenburg Castle Church, Germany, June 7, 1997)* † Alle Menschen müssen sterben, POP 102; Allein zu dir, Herr Jesu Christ; Allein Gott in der Höh sei Ehr, POP 25; Ciaccona, POP 16; Fugue Org, POP 127; Magnificat fugues in tone 8 CENT (Complete Organ Works Vol. 7) ▲ 2418 [DDD] (16.97)

PACHELBEL, WILHELM HIERONYMUS (1686-1764)

Musicalisches Vergnügen in D for Organ or Harpsichord (?1725)

C. Brembeck (org) *(rec Intzgrund, Germany, Oct 24-26, 1988)* ("Lahm-Itzgrund Herbst-Orgel") † J. S. Bach:Chorale Preludes Org; Chorales Org; Fant & Imitatio Org, BWV 563; Org Music (misc colls); Partite diverse sopra, BWV 770; J. Lorenz Bach:Prelude & Fugue Org; J. S. Bach:Preludes & Fugues, BWV 531-552; Trio Org, BWV 583 CAPO ▲ 10351 [DDD] (11.97)

PACINI, GIOVANNI (1796-1867)

Carlo di Borgogna (selections)

B. Ford (ten), D. Parry (cnd), Philharmonia Orch ("Romantic Heroes") † Donizetti:Alfredo il grande (sels); Rosmonda d'Inghilterra (sels); Mercadante:Virginia (sels); Meyerbeer:Étoile du nord (sels); F. Ricci:Il Marito e l'amante (sels); G. Rossini:Ricciardo e Zoraide (sels) OPR ▲ 202 (18.97)

Medea (opera tragico in 3 acts) [lib B. Castiglia] (1843; rev 1845)

R. Bonynge (cnd), Giocosa Opera Festival, J. Omilian (sop), M. Lippi (bass), M. C. Zanni (sgr), S. Panajia (sgr) AG ▲ 86 (36.97)

Saffo (opera in 3 acts) [lib S. Cammarano] (1840)

G. Bertagnolli (sop—Dirce), F. Pedaci (sop—Saffo), M. Pentcheva (cta—Climene), C. Ventre (ten—Faone), A. Hall (ten—Ippia), R. D. Candia (bar—Alcandro), D. Baronchelli (bass—Lisimaco), M. Benini (cnd), Irish National SO, L. Mátl (cnd), Wexford Festival Opera Chorus *(rec Wexford, Oct-Nov 1995)* MARC 2-▲ 8223883 [DDD] (27.97)

Saffo (selections)

A. Scampini (ten) *(rec 1908-13)* ("Augusto Scampini") † Donizetti:Poliuto (sels); G. Rossini:Guillaume Tell (sels); Verdi:Arias MNER ▲ 61 [ADD] (15.97)

L'Ultimo giorno di Pompei (opera seria in 2 acts) [lib A. L. Tottola] (1825)

I. Tamar (sop), S. Sidorova (sop), R. Giménez (ten), G. Bonfatti (ten), N. Rivenq (bar), S. Lee (sgr), R. Novaro (sgr), E. Alekperov (sgr), G. Carella (cnd), Catania Teatro Massimo Bellini Orch, Bratislava Chamber Chorus *(rec Palazza Ducale Italy, Aug 1996)* DYNC 2-▲ 178 [DDD] (34.97)

PACKALES, JOSEPH (1948-

I Was on the Sea (tone poem) for Orchestra

R. Stankovský (cnd), Slovak RSO Bratislava, Slovak Radio Chorus *(rec Slovak Radio & Television Studios)* ("MMC New Century Volume IV") † F. E. Levy:Sym 4; Vali:Persian Folk Songs MASM ▲ 2021 [DDD] (16.97)

PADDING, MARTIJN VAN (1956-

Ballad for Chamber Ensemble

Altena Ensemble *(rec May 1996)* † M. Altena:ABCDE; Cantus; Trappel; A. Cameron:Leisure; Fuhler:Cinéma; Isadora:En/Of II CV ▲ 69 [DDD] (18.97)

Nicht eilen, nicht schleppen (tribute to Mahler) for Chamber Ensemble (1993)

Altena Ensemble *(rec Doopsgezinde Church, Amsterdam, Netherlands, 1995)* ("Working on Time") † M. Altena:Dowlands; R. Ayres:Short Arrs; Bergeijk:Sym joyeuse; Isadora:America Is Waiting; G. van Keulen:Trompeau; H. van der Meulen:Music for a While NMCL ▲ 92063 [DDD] (16.97)

PADEREWSKI, IGNACE JAN (1860-1941)

Concerto in a for Piano & Orchestra, Op. 17 (1888)

E. Kupiec (pno), H. Wolff (cnd), Frankfurt Radio SO † Fant polonaise, Op. 19 KSCH ▲ 365502 (16.97)

P. Lane (pno), J. Maksymiuk (cnd), BBC Scottish SO ("The Romantic Piano Concerto, Vol. 1") † Moszkowski:Con Pno, Op. 59 HYP ▲ 66452 [DDD] (18.97)

Danses polonaises for Piano, Op. 5 (1883)

E. Kupiec (pno) † Humoresques, Op. 14; Nocturne Pno, Op. 16/4; Tatra Album, Op. 12; Variations et fugue sur un thème original, Op. 11 KSCH ▲ 311762 (16.97)

Fantaisie polonaise for Piano & Orchestra, Op. 19 (1893)

E. Kupiec (pno), H. Wolff (cnd), Frankfurt Radio SO † Con Pno, Op. 17 KSCH ▲ 365502 (16.97)

Humoresques de concert (6) for Piano, Op. 14 (1887-88)

E. Kupiec (pno) † Danses polonaises, Op. 5; Nocturne Pno, Op. 16/4; Tatra Album, Op. 12; Variations et fugue sur un thème original, Op. 11 KSCH ▲ 311762 (16.97)

Minuet in G for Keyboard, Op. 14/1

I. J. Paderewski (pno) *(rec 1912-30)* ("Ignacy Jan Paderewski") † Chopin:Études Pno; Berceuse, Op. 57; Funeral March in b♭; Mazurkas Pno; Nocturnes Pno; Polonaise 2 Pno, Op. 26/2; Polonaise 3 Pno, Op. 40/1; Preludes (24) Pno, Op. 28; Waltzes Pno; Liszt:Études d'exécution transcendante (6), S.140; Études de concert (3), S.144; Hungarian Rhaps, S.244; Trans, Arrs & Paraphrases; F. Schubert:Impromptus (4) PPHI (Great Pianists of the 20th Century) 2-▲ 456919 (22.97)

Nocturne in B for Piano, Op. 16/4 (ca 1888)

E. Kupiec (pno) † Danses polonaises, Op. 5; Humoresques, Op. 14; Tatra Album, Op. 12; Variations et fugue sur un thème original, Op. 11 KSCH ▲ 311762 (16.97)

Piano Music (complete)

A. Wodnicki (pno)—Miscellanea, Op. 16; Son Pno, Op. 21; Tatra Album, Op. 12 ("Piano Works, Vol. 1") ALTA ▲ 9045 (18.97)

Piano Music (miscellaneous collections)

I. J. Paderewski (pno) *(rec 1919-32)* ("The Polish Virtuoso") † I. Friedman:Pno Music; J. Hofmann:Pno Music NIMB (Grand Piano) ▲ 8802 (11.97)

Sonata in a for Violin & Piano, Op. 13 (ca 1882-84)

R. Szreder (vn), B. J. Strobel (pno) † W. Lutoslawski:Partita Vn & Pno; Szymanowski:Son Vn, Op. 9 PAVA ▲ 7283 [DDD] (10.97)

Symphony in b, Op. 24, "Polonia" (1903-09)

J. Maksymiuk (cnd), BBC Scottish SO HYP ▲ 67056 (18.97)

Tatra Album for Piano, Op. 12 (ca 1883)

E. Kupiec (pno) † Danses polonaises, Op. 5; Humoresques, Op. 14; Nocturne Pno, Op. 16/4; Variations et fugue sur un thème original, Op. 11 KSCH ▲ 311762 (16.97)

Variations et fugue sur un thème original in a for Piano, Op. 11 (ca 1883)

E. Kupiec (pno) † Danses polonaises, Op. 5; Humoresques, Op. 14; Nocturne Pno, Op. 16/4; Tatra Album, Op. 12 KSCH ▲ 311762 (16.97)

PADILLA, JUAN GUTIÉRREZ DE (ca 1590-1664)

Maitines de Natividad for Double Chorus

B. J. Echenique (cnd), Angelicum de Puebla, B. J. Echenique (cnd), Mexico Schola Cantorum ("Mexico Barroco, Puebla 1") URT ▲ 2004 [DDD] (16.97)

Missa "Ego flos campi" for 8 Voices

P. Schmidt (cnd), Mixolydian † Stabat mater; Victoria:Alma Redemptoris mater; Surge propera ICC ▲ 6600802 (16.97)

PADILLA, JUAN GUTIÉRREZ DE (cont.)

Sacred Music

P. Rutenberg (cnd), Capella—Missa "Ego flos campi"; Psalm for None, "Mirabilia testimonium"; Mirabilia testimonia; Deus in adiutorium meum intende; Lamentation for Maundy Thursday; Holy Week Motets ("Music of the Mexican Baroque") RCMM ▲ 19901 (16.97)

Westminster Cathedral Choir—Lamentation for Maundy Thursday; Salve Regina; Psalm for None, "Mirabilia testimonium"; Versicle & Response, "Deus in adiutorium"—see Col ("Mexican Polyphony") † H. Franco:Salve Regina; López Capillas:Alleluia; Magnificat; A. de Salazar:O sacrum convivium HYP ▲ 66330 [DDD] (18.97)

Stabat mater for 4 Voices

P. Schmidt (cnd), Mixolydian † Missa "Ego flos campi"; Victoria:Alma Redemptoris mater; Surge propera ICC ▲ 6600802 (16.97)

PADOVANO, ANNIBALE (1527-1575)

Aria della battaglia for Brass

U. Orlandi (cnd) ("I Guami da Lucci") † G. Guami:Canzoni e Toccata; F. Guami:Ricercari FON ▲ 9101 (13.97)

PAER, FERDINANDO (1771-1839)

Sonatas (3) for Piano, Violin & Cello ad lib (?1810)

Brahms Trio ("Tre Grandi Sonate") BONG ▲ 5538 [DDD] (16.97)

A. D. Renzo (pno) [fortepno] STRV ▲ 33535 (16.97)

Una voce al cor mi parla for Voice, Clarinet & Piano [arr Veston & Voxman from Sargino, ossia L'allievo dell'amore]

E. Ritchie (sop), V. Soames (cl), J. Purvis (pno) † W. A. Mozart:Clemenza di Tito (sels); I. Müller:Qt 2 Cl; L. Spohr:Faust (sels); Vars on a Theme from Alruna CLCL ▲ 6 [ADD] (17.97)

PAGANELLI, GIUSEPPE ANTONIO (1710-ca 1763)

Sonatas (6) for Flute & Continuo, Op. 16

C. Ferrarini (cnd), Accademia Farnese MONM ▲ 96020 (18.97)

PAGANINI, NICCOLÒ (1782-1840)

Cantabile in D for Violin & Guitar, M.S. 109, (Op. 17) (1822-24)

S. Accardo (vn), L. Manzini (pno) [arr for vn & pno] ("Violinist Composers") † Sarasate:Fant on Carmen, Op. 25; Tartini:Son Vn & Pno; T. A. Vitali:Chaconne Vn; Wieniawski:Légende Vn, Op. 17; Polonaise 2, Op. 21 FON ▲ 9602 [DDD] (13.97)

L. A. Bianchi (vn), M. Preda (gtr) *(rec Dynamic's Genova, June 22-23, 1995)* ("Centone di sonate for Violin & Guitar, Vol. 1") † Centone di sonate, M.S. 112; G. Mahler:Sym 6 DYNC ▲ 148 [DDD] (17.97)

L. A. Bianchi (vn), M. Preda (gtr) *(rec Genoa Italy, June 22-23, 1995)* ("Centone di Sonate: Complete Edition") † Caprices Vn, M.S. 25; Centone di sonate, M.S. 112 DYNC 3-▲ 157 [DDD] (51.97)

J. Grey (gtr) ("Music for Guitar & Strings") † Qts (15) Gtr & Strs, M.S. 28-42; Son concertata, M.S. 2; Terzetto concertante, M.S. 114 DOR ▲ 90237 (16.97)

I. Gringolts (vn), I. Ryumina (pno) *(rec 1998-99)* † Con 1 Vn, M.S. 21; Con 2 Vn, M.S. 48; Intro & Vars on Nel cor più non mi sento, M.S. 44 BIS ▲ 999 [DDD] (17.97)

V. Hudeček (vn), L. Brabec (gtr) *(rec Prague, Czech Republic, Sept 6 & 8, 1998)* ("Hudeček & Brabec Play Paganini") † Centone di sonate, M.S. 112; Grand Son, M.S. 3; Intro & Vars on Nel cor più non mi sento, M.S. 44; Son concertata, M.S. 2; Sons Vn & Gtr, M.S. 27 SUR ▲ 3395 [DDD] (16.97)

F. Mezzena (vn), A. Sebastiani (gtr) † Cantabile & Waltz, M.S. 45; Duetto amoroso, M.S. 111; Sons Vn & Gtr, M.S. 26; Sons Vn & Gtr, M.S. 27 DYNC ▲ 62 [DDD] (17.97)

S. Milenkovich (vn), M. Paderni (pno) ("Paganini Recital") † Music of Paganini DYNC ▲ 165 [DDD] (17.97)

I. Perlman (vn), J. Williams (gtr) † Son concertata, M.S. 2; Sons Vn & Gtr, M.S. 27; M. Giuliani:Son Vn SNYC ▲ 34508 [AAD] (16.97) ▮ 34508 [AAD] (10.98)

R. Ricci (vn), S. Cardi (gtr) ("Hommage to Paganini") † Music of Paganini ONEL ▲ 93070 [DDD] (7.97)

S. St. John (vn), S. Wynberg (gtr) *(rec Mar 1993)* ("Music for Violin & Guitar I") † Son concertata, M.S. 2; Sons Vn & Gtr, M.S. 27; Vars on "Barucabà", M.S. 71 NXIN ▲ 8550690 [DDD] (5.97)

S. St. John (vn), S. Wynberg (gtr) ("Best of Paganini") † Music of Paganini NXIN ▲ 8556680 [DDD] (5.97)

G. Shaham (vn), G. Söllscher (gtr) † Centone di sonate, M.S. 112; Grand Son, M.S. 3; Moto perpetuo 2, M.S. 72; Son a preghiera; Son concertata, M.S. 2; Sons Vn & Gtr, M.S. 27 DEUT ▲ 37837 [DDD] (16.97)

M. Szenthelyi (vn), D. Benkö (gtr) † Centone di sonate, M.S. 112; Duetto amoroso, M.S. 111 HUN ▲ 31478 [DDD] (16.97)

M. Yashvili (vn), N. Walter (pno) [arr for vn & pno] *(rec 1975)* ("Russian Violin School: Marina Yashvili") † Moto perpetuo Vn, M.S. 66; Babadjanyan:Music of Babadjanyan; J. Brahms:Hungarian Dances Pno 4-Hands; Son 2 Vn, Op. 100; M. de Falla:Canciones populares españolas RD (Talents of Russia) ▲ 16251 [ADD] (16.97)

Cantabile & Waltz in E for Violin & Guitar, M.S. 45, (Op. 19) (1823)

A. Dubeau (vn), A. Pierri (gtr) † Centone di sonate, M.S. 112; Son concertata, M.S. 2; M. de Falla:Canciones populares españolas; A. Piazzolla:Pieces (5) Gtr FL ▲ 23034 (16.97)

F. Mezzena (vn), A. Sebastiani (gtr) † Cantabile, M.S. 109; Duetto amoroso, M.S. 111; Sons Vn & Gtr, M.S. 26; Sons Vn & Gtr, M.S. 27 DYNC ▲ 62 [DDD] (17.97)

S. St. John (vn), S. Wynberg (gtr) *(rec Mar 1993)* ("Music for Violin & Guitar II") † Duetto amoroso, M.S. 111; Son Va; Sons Vn & Gtr, M.S. 26; Variazioni di bravura NXIN ▲ 550759 [DDD] (5.97)

Caprice d'adieux for Violin & Piano (?1831)

R. Ricci (vn) † Caprices Vn, M.S. 25; Con 2 Vn, M.S. 48; J. Brahms:Vars on a Theme by Paganini, Op. 35; Liszt:Grandes études de Paganini, S.141; S. Rachmaninoff:Rhap on a Theme of Paganini, Op. 43; R. Schumann:Studien nach Capricen von Paganini, Op. 3 VB3 3-▲ 3020 [ADD] (14.97)

Caprices (24) for solo Violin, M.S. 25, (Op. 1) (ca 1805)

S. Accardo (vn) DEUT (Galleria) ▲ 29714 [ADD] (9.97)

R. Aitken (fl), E. Westenholz (pno)—No. 24 in a [arr Callimahos fl & pno] ("The Virtuoso Flute") † T. Böhm:Grande polonaise, Op. 16; A. F. Doppler:Fant pastorale hongroise, Op. 26; Kuhlau:Intro & Rondo on 'Ah! quand il gèle', Op. 98a; Saint-Saëns:Airs de ballet d'Ascanio; Taffanel:Fant on Freischütz BIS ▲ 166 (17.97)

L. A. Bianchi (vn) *(rec Genoa Italy, June 22-23, 1995)* ("Centone di Sonate: Complete Edition") † Cantabile, M.S. 109; Centone di sonate, M.S. 112 DYNC 3-▲ 157 [DDD] (51.97)

J. Cawdrey (fl) [arr Cawdrey] *(rec May 1997)* PAVA ▲ 7403 [DDD] (10.97)

R. Dick (fl) [No. 15; arr Dick for solo fl] † R. Dick:Solo Fl Music; Dolphy:Gazzelloni; Varèse:Density 21.5 GMR ▲ 2013 [DDD] (16.97)

J. Ehnes (vn) *(rec Cleveland, OH, Aug 7-10, 1995)* TEL ▲ 80398 [DDD] (16.97)

J. Epstein (vn) AG ▲ 108 [DDD] (18.97)

D. Garrett (vn), B. Canino (pno) DGRM ▲ 453489 [DDD] (18.97)

J. Heifetz (vn)—No. 13 in B♭ † J. S. Bach:Sons & Partitas Vn; J. Brahms:Con Vn & Vc, Op. 102; Saint-Saëns:Havanaise, Op. 83; Wieniawski:Scherzo-tarantelle, Op. 16 IMMM ▲ 37095 (6.97)

T. Hoppstock (gtr) [trans for guitar] ("Werke für Gitarre") † L. Brouwer:Estudios Sencillos; H. Villa-Lobos:Etudes Gtr SIGM ▲ 4100 [DDD] (17.97)

I. Kaler (vn) *(rec Oct 19-22, 1992)* NXIN ▲ 550717 [DDD] (5.97)

L. Kavakos (vn) DYNC ▲ 66 [DDD] (17.97)

H. Lindemann (va)—No. 24 in a [trans Primrose] ("Hommage a Primrose") † J. Brahms:Son 1 Cl; J. Joachim:Vars on a Theme Va, Op. 10; S. Rachmaninoff:Vocalise; T. A. Vitali:Chaconne Vn; Wieniawski:Etude-caprices Vn, Op. 18 TACE ▲ 45

A. Markov (vn) ERAT ▲ 45502 [DDD] (16.97)

Y.-Y. Ma (vc), P. Zander (pno)—No. 9 in E; No. 13 in B♭; No. 14 in E♭; No. 17 in E♭; No. 24 in a † Intro & Vars on "Dal tuo stellato soglio", M.S. 23 SNYC ▲ 37280 [DDD] (16.97)

Midori (vn) SNYC ▲ 44944 [DDD] (16.97)

N. Milstein (vn)—No. 5 in a *(rec Aug 4, 1957)* † J. S. Bach:Sons & Partitas Vn ORFE (Festspiel Dokumente) ▲ 400951 (16.97)

I. Perlman (vn) EMIC ▲ 47171 (16.97)

M. Rabin (vn) EMIC ▲ 64560 (11.97)

R. Ricci (vn) † Caprice d'adieux; Con 2 Vn, M.S. 48; J. Brahms:Vars on a Theme by Paganini, Op. 35; Liszt:Grandes études de Paganini, S.141; S. Rachmaninoff:Rhap on a Theme of Paganini, Op. 43; R. Schumann:Studien nach Capricen von Paganini, Op. 3 VB3 3-▲ 3020 [ADD] (14.97)

R. Ricci (vn) † Moto perpetuo Vn, M.S. 66 ONEL ▲ 94010 (7.97)

R. Ricci (vn) *(rec 1947)* ("First Complete Recording of Op. 1 Caprices") IDI ▲ 309 (m) (13.97)

R. Ricci (vn), R. Weininger (cnd), Weiner CO [orchd from Schumann's vn & pno arr] *(rec Szezed Synagogue, Hungary, May 1998)* DYNC ▲ 244 [DDD] (13.97)

B. Schmid (vn), L. Smirnova (pno) [arr Robert Schumann for vn & pno] MDG ▲ 3330674 (17.97)

J. Williams (gtr)—No. 24 in a *(rec New York City, NY, May 21-22, 1964)* ("John Williams Guitar Recital") † M. Giuliani:Vars on a Theme by Handel; D. Scarlatti:Sons Kbd; H. Villa-Lobos:Preludes Gtr SNYC (Essential Classics) ▲ 62425 [ADD] (7.97) ▮ 62425 [ADD] (3.98)

D. Zsigmondy (vn)—No. 9 in E; No. 13 in B♭; No. 14 in E♭; No. 17 in E♭; No. 19 in E♭; No. 20 in D; No. 23 in E♭; No. 24 in a † Music of Paganini; F. Schubert:Rondo Vn, D.895; Sonatinas (3) Vn TUXE ▲ 1044 [ADD] (10.97)

PAGANINI, NICCOLÒ (cont.)

Centone di sonate (18) for Violin & Guitar, M.S. 112, (Op. 64) (ca 1828)

L. A. Bianchi (vn), M. Preda (gtr) ("Vol. 3") DYNC ▲ 34 [DDD] (17.97)

L. A. Bianchi (vn), M. Preda (gtr) *(rec Genoa Italy, Jan & Oct 1991, June 22-23, 1995)* ("Centone di Sonate: Complete Edition") † Cantabile, M.S. 109; Caprices Vn, M.S. 25 DYNC 3-▲ 157 [DDD] (51.97)

L. A. Bianchi (vn), M. Preda (gtr)—No. 1 in A; No. 2 in D; No. 3 in C; No. 4 in A; No. 5 in E; No. 6 in A *(rec Genoa, Italy, June 22-23, 1995)* ("Centone di sonate for Violin & Guitar, Vol. 1") † Cantabile, M.S. 109; G. Mahler:Sym 6 DYNC ▲ 148 [DDD] (17.97)

L. A. Bianchi (vn), M. Preda (gtr)—No. 7 in F; No. 8 in G; No. 9 in A; No. 10 in C; No. 11 in a; No. 12 in D ("Vol. 2") DYNC ▲ 84 [DDD] (17.97)

A. Dubeau (vn), A. Pierri (gtr) † Cantabile & Waltz, M.S. 45; Son concertata, M.S. 2; M. de Falla:Canciones populares españolas; A. Piazzolla:Pieces (5) Gtr FL ▲ 23034 (16.97)

Duo Nova ("Duo Nova") † L. von Call:Serenade Vn Gtr, Op. 84; A. Corelli:Sons Vn, Op. 5; Sarasate:Serenata andaluza, Op. 28; F. Schubert:Originaltänze, D.365; Smith Brindle:Sketches Vn & Gtr GALL ▲ 936 [DDD] (18.97)

M. Hammer (vn), N. Kraft (gtr)—No. 7 in F; No. 8 in G; No. 9 in A; No. 10 in C; No. 11 in a; No. 12 in D *(rec Newmarket, Canada, Sept 24-26, 1994)* ("Centone di sonate, Vol. 2") NXIN (Guitar Collection) ▲ 553142 [DDD] (5.97)

M. Hammer (vn), N. Kraft (gtr)—No. 13 in E; No. 14 in G; No. 15 in A; No. 16 in E; No. 17 in A; No. 18 in C *(rec Newmarket, Canada, Nov 1995)* ("Centone di sonate, Vol. 3") NXIN ▲ 8553143 [DDD] (5.97)

V. Hudeček (vn), L. Brabec (gtr)—No. 1 in A; No. 2 in D; No. 3 in C; No. 4 in A *(rec Prague, Czech Republic, Sept 6 & 8, 1998)* ("Hudeček & Brabec Play Paganini") † Cantabile, M.S. 109; Grand Son, M.S. 3; Intro & Vars on Nel cor più non mi sento, M.S. 44; Son concertata, M.S. 2; Sons Vn & Gtr, M.S. 27 SUR ▲ 3395 [DDD] (16.97)

G. Shaham (vn), G. Söllscher (gtr)—No. 2 in D; No. 4 in A † Cantabile, M.S. 109; Grand Son, M.S. 3; Moto perpetuo 2, M.S. 72; Son a preghiera; Son concertata, M.S. 2; Sons Vn & Gtr, M.S. 27 DEUT ▲ 37837 [DDD] (16.97)

I. Suzuki (gtr), B. Fromanger (fl)—No. 1 in A; No. 4 in A [arr flt & gtr] *(rec 1990)* † F. Carulli:Fant on Themes from Bellini's Il pirata, Op. 337; Diabelli:Pieces Fl Gtr; M. Giuliani:Grand Son, Op. 85 FORL ▲ 16635 [DDD] (16.97)

M. Szenthelyi (vn), D. Benkö (gtr)—No. 1 in A; No. 2 in D; No. 3 in C; No. 4 in A † Cantabile, M.S. 109; Duetto amoroso, M.S. 111 HUN ▲ 31478 [DDD] (16.97)

Concerto No. 1 in D (or E♭) for Violin & Orchestra, M.S. 21, (Op. 6) (?1817)

S. Accardo (vn), C. Dutoit (cnd), London PO † Con 2 Vn, M.S. 48 DEUT ▲ 15378 [ADD] (16.97)

S. Accardo (vn), C. Dutoit (cnd), London PO † Con 2 Vn, M.S. 48; Con 3 Vn, M.S. 50; Con 4 Vn, M.S. 60; Con 5 Vn, M.S. 78; Con 6 Vn DEUT 3-▲ 37210 [ADD] (34.97)

S. Ashkenasi (vn), H. Esser (cnd), Vienna SO † Con 2 Vn, M.S. 48 DEUT (Resonance) ▲ 29524 [ADD] (7.97)

S. Chang (vn), W. Sawallisch (cnd), Philadelphia Orch † Saint-Saëns:Havanaise, Op. 83; Intro & Rondo capriccioso, Op. 28 EMIC ▲ 55026 (16.97)

O. Colbentson (vn), H. Gmür (cnd), South German PO † Wieniawski:Con 2 Vn, Op. 22 PC ▲ 267150 [DDD] (2.97)

Z. Francescatti (vn), E. Ormandy (cnd), Philadelphia Orch † Con 4 Vn, M.S. 60; G. Bottesini:Gran Duo Concertant SNYC (Essential Classics) ▲ 47661 (7.97) ▮ 47661 (3.98)

I. Gringolts (vn), O. Vänskä (cnd), Lahti SO *(rec 1998-99)* † Cantabile, M.S. 109; Con 2 Vn, M.S. 48; Intro & Vars on Nel cor più non mi sento, M.S. 44 BIS ▲ 999 [DDD] (17.97)

I. Grubert (vn), C. Orbelian (cnd), Moscow CO † Con 2 Vn, M.S. 48 CHN ▲ 9492 (16.97)

P. Hirschhorn (vn), P. Bartholomée (cnd), Liège PO *(rec live, May 1967)* † Beethoven:Con Vn; A. Berg:Con Vn CYPR 2-▲ 9605 (17.97)

I. Kaler (vn), S. Gunzenhauser (cnd), Polish National RSO Katowice *(rec Sept 3-6, 1992)* † Con 2 Vn, M.S. 48 NXIN ▲ 550649 [DDD] (5.97)

F. Kreisler (vn), E. Ormandy (cnd), Philadelphia Orch *(rec 1938 for HMV)* † Beethoven:Con Vn; J. Brahms:Con Vn; Mendelssohn (-Bartholdy):Con Vn & Orch, Op. 64 PHS 2-▲ 9362 [AAD] (33.97)

A. Markov (vn), M. Viotti (cnd), Saarbrücken RSO † Con 2 Vn, M.S. 48 ERAT ▲ 45788 (16.97)

Y. Menuhin (vn), P. Monteux (cnd), Paris SO ("Monteux, Vol. 3") † Moto perpetuo Vn, M.S. 66; A. Bazzini:Ronde des lutins, Op. 25; W. A. Mozart:Con Vn; Nováček:Perpetuum mobile LYS ▲ 479 (17.97)

I. Perlman (vn), L. Foster (cnd), Royal PO † Sarasate:Fant on Carmen, Op. 25 EMIC ▲ 47101 (16.97)

V. Příhoda (vn), C. Cerné (pno) [arr for vn & pno] † I palpiti, M.S. 77; Sons Vn & Gtr, M.S. 27; Streghe; H. Vieuxtemps:Con 4 Vn, Op. 31; Wieniawski:Con 2 Vn, Op. 22 BID ▲ 135 (16.97)

R. Ricci (vn), K. Bakels (cnd), Polish National RSO Katowice *(rec June 1997)* ("Ricci: 70 Years of Performing") † P. Tchaikovsky:Con Vn DYNC ▲ 203 [DDD] (17.97)

R. Ricci (vn), H. D. Fuente (cnd), Orch of the Americas † Ginastera:Con Vn ONEL ▲ 94020 (7.97)

R. Ricci (vn), G. Thiele (cnd), Warsaw PO † S. Barber:Con Vn; Saint-Saëns:Intro & Rondo capriccioso, Op. 28 ONEL ▲ 96030 [ADD] (7.97)

R. Ricci (vn), K. Woss (cnd), Berlin Municipal Orch, P. Mordini (cnd), Virtuosi d'Assisi—Rondo (allegro spiritoso) ("Paganini & Ricci") † Con 2 Vn, M.S. 48; Con 4 Vn, M.S. 60; Con 6 Vn; Music of Paganini ONEL (Essential Performance Reference) 2-▲ 95013 [ADD]

G. Shaham (vn), G. Sinopoli (cnd), New York PO † Saint-Saëns:Con 3 Vn, Op. 61 DEUT ▲ 29786 [DDD] (16.97)

V. Tretyakov (vn), N. Järvi (cnd), Moscow PO *(rec Moscow, 1966)* ("Neeme Järvi: The Early Recordings, Vol. 2") † P. Tchaikovsky:Con Vn MELD ▲ 40720 [ADD] (6.97)

M. Vengerov (vn), Z. Mehta (cnd), Israel PO † Saint-Saëns:Havanaise, Op. 83; Intro & Rondo capriccioso, Op. 28; F. Waxman:Carmen Fant TELC ▲ 73266 (16.97)

Concerto No. 2 in b for Violin & Orchestra, M.S. 48, (Op. 7) (1826)

S. Accardo (vn), C. Dutoit (cnd), London PO † Con 1 Vn, M.S. 21 DEUT ▲ 15378 [ADD] (16.97)

S. Accardo (vn), C. Dutoit (cnd), London PO † Con 1 Vn, M.S. 21; Con 3 Vn, M.S. 50; Con 4 Vn, M.S. 60; Con 5 Vn, M.S. 78; Con 6 Vn DEUT 3-▲ 37210 [ADD] (34.97)

S. Ashkenasi (vn), H. Esser (cnd), Vienna SO † Con 1 Vn, M.S. 21 DEUT (Resonance) ▲ 29524 [ADD] (7.97)

D. Chan (vn), R. Koenig (pno)—Rondo á la clochette ("La campanella") [arr vn & pno] *(rec Aspen, CO, May 1995)* † G. Gershwin:Songs; Saint-Saëns:Son 1 Vn, Op. 75; Tartini:Son Vn & Pno; P. Tchaikovsky:Souvenir d'un lieu cher, Op. 42; Valse-Scherzo Vn, Op. 34; Ysaÿe:Sons Vn, Op. 27 AMBA ▲ 1017 [DDD] (16.97)

I. Gringolts (vn), I. Ryumina (pno)—Rondo á la clochette ("La campanella") *(rec 1998-99)* † Cantabile, M.S. 109; Con 1 Vn, M.S. 21; Intro & Vars on Nel cor più non mi sento, M.S. 44 BIS ▲ 999 [DDD] (17.97)

I. Grubert (vn), C. Orbelian (cnd), Moscow CO † Con 1 Vn, M.S. 21 CHN ▲ 9492 (16.97)

I. Kaler (vn), S. Gunzenhauser (cnd), Polish National RSO Katowice *(rec Sept 3-6, 1992)* † Con 1 Vn, M.S. 21 NXIN ▲ 550649 [DDD] (5.97)

J. Kantorow (vn), J. Kantorow (cnd), Bernard Thomas CO † Caprice d'adieux; Caprices Vn, M.S. 25; J. Brahms:Vars on a Theme by Paganini, Op. 35; Liszt:Grandes études de Paganini, S.141; S. Rachmaninoff:Rhap on a Theme of Paganini, Op. 43; R. Schumann:Studien nach Capricen von Paganini, Op. 3 VB3 3-▲ 3020 [ADD] (14.97)

A. Markov (vn), M. Viotti (cnd), Saarbrücken RSO † Con 1 Vn, M.S. 21 ERAT ▲ 45788 (16.97)

R. Ricci (vn), K. Akiyama (cnd), American SO ("Paganini & Ricci") † Con 1 Vn, M.S. 21; Con 4 Vn, M.S. 60; Con 6 Vn; Music of Paganini ONEL (Essential Performance Reference) 2-▲ 95013 [ADD]

Concerto No. 3 in E for Violin & Orchestra, M.S. 50 (1826)

S. Accardo (vn), C. Dutoit (cnd), London PO † Con 4 Vn, M.S. 60 DEUT ▲ 23370 [ADD] (16.97)

S. Accardo (vn), C. Dutoit (cnd), London PO † Con 1 Vn, M.S. 21; Con 2 Vn, M.S. 48; Con 4 Vn, M.S. 60; Con 5 Vn, M.S. 78; Con 6 Vn DEUT 3-▲ 37210 [ADD] (34.97)

Concerto No. 4 in d for Violin & Orchestra, M.S. 60 (1829-30)

S. Accardo (vn), C. Dutoit (cnd), London PO † Con 3 Vn, M.S. 50 DEUT ▲ 23370 [ADD] (16.97)

S. Accardo (vn), C. Dutoit (cnd), London PO † Con 1 Vn, M.S. 21; Con 2 Vn, M.S. 48; Con 3 Vn, M.S. 50; Con 5 Vn, M.S. 78; Con 6 Vn DEUT 3-▲ 37210 [ADD] (34.97)

Z. Francescatti (vn), E. Ormandy (cnd), Philadelphia Orch † Con 1 Vn, M.S. 21; G. Bottesini:Gran Duo Concertant SNYC (Essential Classics) ▲ 47661 (7.97) ▮ 47661 (3.98)

R. Ricci (vn) ("Paganini & Ricci") † Con 1 Vn, M.S. 21; Con 2 Vn, M.S. 48; Con 6 Vn; Music of Paganini ONEL (Essential Performance Reference) 2-▲ 95013 [ADD]

Concerto No. 5 in a for Violin & Orchestra, M.S. 78 (1830)

S. Accardo (vn), C. Dutoit (cnd), London PO † Con 1 Vn, M.S. 21; Con 2 Vn, M.S. 48; Con 3 Vn, M.S. 50; Con 4 Vn, M.S. 60; Con 6 Vn DEUT 3-▲ 37210 [ADD] (34.97)

Concerto No. 6 in e for Violin & Orchestra, Op. posth (ca 1815)

S. Accardo (vn), C. Dutoit (cnd), London PO † Con 1 Vn, M.S. 21; Con 2 Vn, M.S. 48; Con 3 Vn, M.S. 50; Con 4 Vn, M.S. 60; Con 5 Vn, M.S. 78 DEUT 3-▲ 37210 [ADD] (34.97)

R. Ricci (vn) ("Paganini & Ricci") † Con 1 Vn, M.S. 21; Con 2 Vn, M.S. 48; Con 4 Vn, M.S. 60; Music of Paganini ONEL (Essential Performance Reference) 2-▲ 95013 [ADD]

Divertimenti carnevaleschi for 2 Violins & Cello, M.S. 4

S. Milenkovich (vn), P. D. Sommati (vn), R. Agosti (vc) *(rec Dynamic's Genova, Italy, Feb 22-24, 1995)* † Duets Vn & Vc, M.S. 107; In cuor più non mi sento, M.S. 117 DYNC ▲ 120 [DDD] (17.97)

Duets (3) for Violin & Bassoon [newly discovered manuscript], M.S. 130

S. Accardo (vn), C. Gonella (bn) ("Paganini: A Recent Discovery") DYNC ▲ 184 (17.97)

PAGANINI, NICCOLÒ (cont.)

Duets (3) for Violin & Cello, M.S. 107, (Op. 16) (ca 1802)

S. Milenkovich (vn), R. Agosti (vc) *(rec Dynamic's Genova, Italy, Feb 22-24, 1995)* † Divertimenti carnevaleschi, M.S. 4; In cuor più non mi sento, M.S. 117 DYNC ▲ 120 [DDD] (17.97)

Duetto amoroso for Violin & Guitar, M.S. 111, (Op. 63) (?1807)

F. Mezzena (vn), A. Sebastiani (gtr) † Cantabile & Waltz, M.S. 45; Cantabile, M.S. 109; Sons Vn & Gtr, M.S. 26; Sons Vn & Gtr, M.S. 27 DYNC ▲ 62 [DDD] (17.97)

B. Pignata (vn), P. Briasco (gtr) *(rec Dynamic's Genova, Italy, Dec 10-13, 1995)* † Nocturnes, M.S. 15 DYNC ▲ 152 [DDD] (17.97)

S. St. John (vn), S. Wynberg (gtr) *(rec Mar 1993)* ("Music for Violin & Guitar II") † Cantabile & Waltz, M.S. 45; Son Va; Sons Vn & Gtr, M.S. 26; Variazioni di bravura NXIN ▲ 550759 [DDD] (5.97)

M. Szenthelyi (vn), D. Benkö (gtr) † Cantabile, M.S. 109; Centone di sonate, M.S. 112 HUN ▲ 31478 [DDD] (16.97)

S. Volta (gtr), C. Aonzo (mand) † Son Mand & Gtr, M.S. 14 ARN ▲ 68420 (16.97)

Grand Sonata in A for Violin & Guitar, M.S. 3, (Op. 39) (1803-04)

V. Hudeček (vn), L. Brabec (gtr)—Romance, più tosto largo, amorosamente *(rec Prague, Czech Republic, Sept 6 & 8, 1998)* ("Hudeček & Brabec Play Paganini") † Cantabile, M.S. 109; Centone di sonate, M.S. 112; Intro & Vars on Nel cor più non mi sento, M.S. 44; Son concertata, M.S. 2; Sons Vn & Gtr, M.S. 27 SUR ▲ 3395 [DDD] (16.97)

M. Huggett (vn), R. Savino (gtr) ("Romanza") † Son concertata, M.S. 2; M. Giuliani:Grand Duo Concertant, Op. 25 HAM ▲ 907116 (18.97)

N. Kraft (gtr) ("Romantic Works for Guitar") † Castelnuovo-Tedesco:Capriccio diabolico Gtr, Op. 85; Son Cl; M. Ponce:Son romántica CHN ▲ 9033 [DDD] (16.97)

P. Martelli (gtr) [arr Abreu gtr] *(rec Feb-Mar 1993)* † Castelnuovo-Tedesco:Son Gtr, Op. 77; Diabelli:Sons Gtr, Op. 29; A. Harris:Vars & Fugue DHR ▲ 4 [DDD] (16.97)

G. Shaham (vn), G. Söllscher (gtr) † Cantabile, M.S. 109; Centone di sonate, M.S. 112; Moto perpetuo 2, M.S. 72; Son a preghiera; Son concertata, M.S. 2; Sons Vn & Gtr, M.S. 27 DEUT ▲ 37837 [DDD] (16.97)

Guitar Music

F. Zigante (gtr)—Allegretto Gtr, M.S. 86; Allegretto Gtr, M.S. 90; Allegretto Gtr, M.S. 91; Andantino Gtr, M.S. 88; Andantino Gtr, M.S. 89; Andantino Gtr, M.S. 97; Andantino Gtr, M.S. 99; Andantino Gtr, M.S. 102; Marche, M.S. 103; Marziale, M.S. 105, (Op. 41); Rondoncino, M.S. 94; Sinf Lodovisia, M.S. 98, (Op. 58); Minuetto & Perigourdine, M.S. 104, (Op. 52); Waltz, M.S. 92; Waltz, M.S. 96; Waltz, M.S. 100; Trio, M.S. 101 *(rec Torino, Italy, 1988-89)* ("Guitar Music, Vol. 3") † Sonatas for Violin & Guitar; Sonatines, M.S. 85 AART ▲ 47194 [DDD] (10.97)

In cuor più non mi sento for 2 Violins & Cello, M.S. 117 (1820)

S. Milenkovich (vn), P. D. Sommati (vn), R. Agosti (vc) *(rec Dynamic's Genova, Feb 22-24, 1995)* † Divertimenti carnevaleschi, M.S. 4; Duets Vn & Vc, M.S. 107 DYNC ▲ 120 [DDD] (17.97)

Inno patriottico con variazioni for Violin & Guitar, M.S. 81

F. Mezzena (vn), A. Sebastiani (gtr) † Moto perpetuo Vn, M.S. 66; Theme & Vars Vn, M.S. 82; Vars on "La Carmagnole", M.S. 1; Vars on "O mamma, mamma cara", M.S. 59 DYNC ▲ 3 [AAD] (17.97)

Introduction & Variations on "Dal tuo stellato soglio" for Violin & Orchestra [from Rossini's *Mosè in Egitto*], M.S. 23, (Op. 24) (?1819)

Z. Borowicz (db) [arr db] ("The Paganini of the Double Bass") † G. Bottesini:Con 2 Db; Elegy & Tarantella; Fant on *Lucia di Lammermoor*, Rêverie; Vars on "Nel cor più non mi sento" SNE ▲ 581 (16.97)

R. Fontanarosa (vc), F. Fontanarosa (pno) † Debussy:Son Vc; G. Fauré:Elégie, Op. 24; R. Strauss:Son Vc, Op. 6 ILD ▲ 642119 (11.97)

G. Karr (db), U. Lajovic (cnd), Berlin RSO [arr Karr] † Boismortier:Sons; G. Bottesini:Con 2 Db; Grande con for 2 Dbs KSCH ▲ 313382 [ADD] (16.97)

G. Karr (db), G. Simon (cnd), London SO † G. Holst:Planets, Op. 32 LALI ▲ 14010 [DDD] (3.97)

Y.-Y. Ma (vc), P. Zander (pno) [arr Silva] † Caprices Vn, M.S. 25 SNYC ▲ 37280 [DDD] (16.97)

Introduction & Variations on "Nel cor più non mi sento" for solo Violin [from Paisiello's La Molinara], M.S. 44 (?1820)

M. Fornaciari (vn) † Son Va; Beethoven:Notturno Va; Son 9 Vn, Op. 47 FON ▲ 9320 [DDD]

I. Gringolts (vn), I. Ryumina (pno) *(rec 1998-99)* † Cantabile, M.S. 109; Con 1 Vn, M.S. 21; Con 2 Vn, M.S. 48 BIS ▲ 999 [DDD] (17.97)

V. Hudeček (vn), L. Brabec (gtr) *(rec Prague, Czech Republic, Sept 6 & 8, 1998)* ("Hudeček & Brabec Play Paganini") † Cantabile, M.S. 109; Centone di sonate, M.S. 112; Grand Son, M.S. 3; Son concertata, M.S. 2; Sons Vn & Gtr, M.S. 27 SUR ▲ 3395 [DDD] (16.97)

L. Josefowicz (vn) † B. Bartók:Son Vn; H. W. Ernst:Roi des aulnes, Op. 26; F. Kreisler:Recitativo & Scherzo-caprice, Op. 6; Ysaÿe:Sons Vn, Op. 27 PPHI ▲ 46700 (16.97)

Maestoso sonata sentimentale (variations on the Austrian National Hymn) for Violin & Orchestra, M.S. 51, (Op. 27) (1828)

M. Quarta (vn), S. Redaelli (pno) *(rec Genova, Italy, sept 22/24, 1998)* † I palpiti, M.S. 77; Son & vars on Weigl; Son Napoleone, M.S. 5; Streghe DYNC ▲ 232 [DDD] (17.97)

Moto perpetuo in C for Violin & Orchestra, M.S. 66, (Op. 11) (after 1830)

Y. Menuhin (vn), P. Monteux (cnd), Paris SO ("Monteux, Vol. 3") † Con 1 Vn, M.S. 21; A. Bazzini:Ronde des lutins, Op. 25; W. A. Mozart:Con Vn; Nováček:Perpetuum mobile LYS ▲ 479 (17.97)

F. Mezzena (vn), A. Sebastiani (gtr) [trans for vn & gtr in D] † Inno patriottico, M.S. 81; Theme & Vars Vn, M.S. 82; Vars on "La Carmagnole", M.S. 1; Vars on "O mamma, mamma cara", M.S. 59 DYNC ▲ 3 [AAD] (17.97)

R. Ricci (vn), C. Furstner (pno) [arr for vn & pno] † Caprices Vn, M.S. 25 ONEL ▲ 94010 (7.97)

Sejong Soloists *(rec American Academy of Arts & Letters NYC, June 1995)* † J. Haydn:7 Last Words of Christ on the Cross; G. Puccini:Crisantemi; H. Wolf:Italian Serenade Str Qt SSCL ▲ 81 (16.97)

M. Yashvili (vn), N. Walter (pno) [arr for vn & pno] *(rec 1975)* ("Russian Violin School: Marina Yashvili") † Cantabile, M.S. 109; Babadjanyan:Music of Babadjanyan; J. Brahms:Hungarian Dances Pno 4-Hands; Son 2 Vn, Op. 100; M. de Falla:Canciones populares españolas RD (Talents of Russia) ▲ 16251 [ADD] (16.97)

Moto perpetuo No. 2 in C for Violin & Guitar (allegro vivace), M.S. 72, (Op. 11) (1835)

G. Shaham (vn), G. Söllscher (gtr) † Cantabile, M.S. 109; Centone di sonate, M.S. 112; Grand Son, M.S. 3; Son a preghiera; Son concertata, M.S. 2; Sons Vn & Gtr, M.S. 27 DEUT ▲ 37837 [DDD] (16.97)

Music of Paganini

I. Kaler (vn), S. Gunzenhauser (cnd), Polish National RSO, S. Gunzenhauser (cnd) *(Con 2 Vn, M.S. 48, (Op. 7) [Rondo á la clochette ("La campanella"); Adagio])*, I. Kaler (vn), S. Gunzenhauser (cnd) *(Con 1 Vn, M.S. 21, (Op. 6) [Rondo (allegro spiritoso)])*, M. Hammer (vn), N. Kraft (gtr) *(Centone di sonate, M.S. 112, (Op. 64))*, G. Garcia (gtr) *(Grand Son, M.S. 3, (Op. 39) [Allegro risoluto; Andantino variato, scherzando])*, I. Kaler (vn) *(Caprices Vn, M.S. 25, (Op. 1))*, S. St. John (vn), S. Wynberg (gtr) *(Son concertata, M.S. 2, (Op. 61) [Adagio, assai espressivo; Rondo:allegretto con brio, scherzando])* ("Best of Paganini") † Cantabile, M.S. 109 NXIN ▲ 8556680 [DDD] (5.97)

S. Milenkovich (vn), M. Paderni (pno)—Carnevale di Venezia, M.S. 59, (Op. 10); Polacca, M.S. 18, (Op. 28); Con 2 Vn, M.S. 48, (Op. 7) [Rondo á la clochette ("La campanella")]; Intro & Vars on "Non più mesta", M.S. 22, (Op. 12); I palpiti, M.S. 77, (Op. 13); Streghe, M.S. 19, (Op. 8); Intro & Vars on "Dal tuo stellato soglio", M.S. 23, (Op. 24) [Sonata a preghiera]; Moto perpetuo 2, M.S. 72, (Op. 11) ("Paganini Recital") † Cantabile, M.S. 109 DYNC ▲ 165 [DDD] (17.97)

R. Ricci (vn), S. Cardi (gtr)—Tarantella, M.S. 76, (Op. 33); Intro & Vars on Nel cor più non mi sento, M.S. 44; Cantabile & Waltz, M.S. 45, (Op. 19); Centone di sonate, M.S. 112, (Op. 64) [No. 1 in A]; Sons Vn & Gtr, M.S. 26, (Op. 2) [No. 1 in A; No. 4 in A]; Sons Vn & Gtr, M.S. 27, (Op. 3) [No. 1 in A; No. 2 in G; No. 3 in D; No. 4 in a; No. 6 in e]; Intro & Vars on "Dal tuo stellato soglio", M.S. 23, (Op. 24); Variazioni di bravura; Grand Son, M.S. 3, (Op. 39) ("Hommage to Paganini") † Cantabile, M.S. 109 ONEL ▲ 93070 [DDD] (7.97)

R. Ricci (vn), U.S. Army Air Force SO *(Moto perpetuo Vn, M.S. 66, (Op. 11))*, R. Ricci (vn), H. W. Zimmermann (cnd), Academic SO *(I palpiti, M.S. 77, (Op. 13))*, R. Ricci (vn), P. Bellugi (cnd), Royal PO *(Streghe, M.S. 19, (Op. 8))* ("Paganini & Ricci") † Con 1 Vn, M.S. 21; Con 2 Vn, M.S. 48; Con 4 Vn, M.S. 60; Con 6 Vn ONEL (Essential Performance Reference) 2-▲ 95013 [ADD]

D. Zsigmondy (vn), A. Nissen (pno)—Sons Vn & Gtr, M.S. 27, (Op. 3) [No. 4 in a; No. 6 in e]; Sons Vn & Gtr, M.S. 26, (Op. 2) [No. 2 in C]; Streghe, M.S. 19 [Hexentänze [Witches' Dance]] † Caprices Vn, M.S. 25; F. Schubert:Rondo Vn, D.895; Sonatinas (3) Vn TUXE ▲ 1044 [ADD] (10.97)

Quartets (15) for Guitar & Strings (1818-20)

Paganini String Quartet—No. 4 in D, M.S. 31 (Op. 5/1); No. 5 in C, M.S. 32 (Op. 5/2); No. 6 in d, M.S. 33 (Op. 5/3) ("The 15 Quartets for Strings & Guitar, Vol. 4") DYNC ▲ 98 [DDD] (17.97)

Nocturnes (4) for String Quartet, M.S. 15 (1805-08)

Paganini String Quartet *(rec Dynamic's Genova, Italy, Dec 10-13, 1995)* † Duetto amoroso, M.S. 111 DYNC ▲ 152 [DDD] (17.97)

I palpiti for Violin & Orchestra (introduction & variations on "Di tanti palpiti" from Rossini's *Tancredi*), M.S. 77, (Op. 13) (1819)

V. Příhoda (vn), C. Cerné (pno) † Con 1 Vn, M.S. 21; Sons Vn & Gtr, M.S. 27; Streghe; H. Vieuxtemps:Con 4 Vn, Op. 31; Wieniawski:Con 2 Vn, Op. 22 BID ▲ 135 (16.97)

M. Quarta (vn), S. Redaelli (pno) *(rec Genova, Italy, sept 22/24, 1998)* † Maestoso son sentimentale, M.S. 51; Son & vars on Weigl; Son Napoleone, M.S. 5; Streghe DYNC ▲ 232 [DDD] (17.97)

PAGANINI, NICCOLÒ (cont.)

Quartets (3) for Guitar & Strings, Op. 4 (1806-16)
Paganini String Quartet SYMO ▲ 206 (18.97)

Quartets (3) in d, Eb & a for Strings, M.S. 20, (Op. 78) (ca 1800)
Paganini String Quartet *(rec Genova, Italy, Nov 21-25, 1994)* ("The Complete String Quartets") DYNC ▲ 134 [DDD] (17.97)

Quartets (15) for Guitar & Strings, M.S. 28-42 (1818-20)
J. Grey (gtr), Diaz Trio ("Music for Guitar & Strings") † Cantabile, M.S. 109; Son concertata, M.S. 2; Terzetto concertante, M.S. 114 DOR ▲ 90237 (16.97)

Sonata in e for Mandolin & Guitar, M.S. 14, "Sonata per Rovene" (1805-08)
S. Volta (gtr), C. Aonzo (mand) † Duetto amoroso, M.S. 111 ARN ▲ 68420 (16.97)

Serenata in C for Viola, Cello & Guitar, M.S. 17, (Op. 69) (before 1808)
A. Farulli (va), A. Noferini (vc), A. Sebastiani (gtr) † Serenata Vns, M.S. 115; Terzetto concertante, M.S. 114; Terzetto Vn, M.S. 69; Terzetto Vns, M.S. 116 DYNC ▲ 76 [DDD] (17.97)

Serenata in F for 2 Violins & Guitar, M.S. 115, (Op. 67)
D. Bratchkova (vn), G. Hartmann (vn), A. Sebastiani (gtr) † Serenata Va, Vc & Gtr, M.S. 17; Terzetto concertante, M.S. 114; Terzetto Vn, M.S. 69; Terzetto Vns, M.S. 116 DYNC ▲ 76 [DDD] (17.97)
M. Tenenbaum (vn), A. Tenenbaum (vn), P. Bernard (gtr) *(rec Conservatory of Music Purchase College, Purchase, Oct 28-29, 1996)* ("The Paganinis at Home: An Evening of Casual Virtuosity") † Terzetto concertante, M.S. 114; Terzetto Vn, M.S. 69 ESSY ▲ 1053 [DDD] (16.97)

Sonata Napoleone in Eb for Violin & Orchestra, M.S. 5, (Op. 31) (1807)
M. Quarta (vn), S. Redaelli (pno) *(rec Genova, Italy, sept 22/24, 1998)* † I palpiti, M.S. 77; Maestoso son sentimentale, M.S. 51; Son & vars on Weigl; Streghe DYNC ▲ 232 [DDD] (17.97)

Sonata a preghiera for Violin & Guitar
G. Shaham (vn), G. Söllscher (gtr) † Cantabile, M.S. 109; Centone di sonate, M.S. 112; Grand Son, M.S. 3; Moto perpetuo 2, M.S. 72; Son concertata, M.S. 2; Sons Vn & Gtr, M.S. 27 DEUT ▲ 37837 [DDD] (16.97)

Sonata and Variations on "Pria ch'io l'impegno" from Joseph Weigl's "L'amor marinaro" for Piano and Orchestra (1828)
M. Quarta (vn), S. Redaelli (pno) [arr vln & pno Kinsky/Rothschild] *(rec Genova, Italy, sept 22/24, 1998)* † I palpiti, M.S. 77; Maestoso son sentimentale, M.S. 51; Son Napoleone, M.S. 5; Streghe DYNC ▲ 232 [DDD] (17.97)

Sonata concertata in A for Violin & Guitar, M.S. 2, (Op. 61) (1804)
A. Dubeau (vn), A. Pierri (gtr) † Cantabile & Waltz, M.S. 45; Centone di sonate, M.S. 112; M. de Falla:Canciones populares españolas; A. Piazzolla:Pieces (5) Gtr FL ▲ 23034 (16.97)
J. Grey (gtr) ("Music for Guitar & Strings") † Cantabile, M.S. 109; Qts (15) Gtr & Strs, M.S. 28-42; Terzetto concertante, M.S. 114 DOR ▲ 90237 (16.97)
V. Hudeček (vn), L. Brabec (gtr) *(rec Prague, Czech Republic, Sept 6 & 8, 1998)* ("Hudeček & Brabec Play Paganini") † Cantabile, M.S. 109; Centone di sonate, M.S. 112; Grand Son, M.S. 3; Intro & Vars on Nel cor più non mi sento, M.S. 44; Sons Vn & Gtr, M.S. 27 SUR ▲ 3395 [DDD] (16.97)
M. Huggett (vn), R. Savino (gtr) ("Romanza") † Grand Son, M.S. 3; M. Giuliani:Grand Duo Concertant, Op. 25 HAM ▲ 907116 (18.97)
I. Perlman (vn), J. Williams (gtr) † Cantabile, M.S. 109; Sons Vn & Gtr, M.S. 27; M. Giuliani:Son Vn SNYC ▲ 34508 [AAD] (16.97) ▮ 34508 [AAD] (10.98)
C. Piastra (gtr), C. Ferrarini (fl) [trans for fl & gtr] † F. Carulli:Fant on Themes from Bellini's Il pirata, Op. 337; Nocturne Fl, Op. 115; M. Giuliani:Grand Duo Concertant, Op. 52; Grand Son, Op. 85 MONM (La grande musica Italiana) ▲ 96010 (17.97)
P. Polidori (gtr), P. Depetris (fl) [arr fl & gtr] *(rec July 1993)* † G. F. Giuliani:Grand Son, Op. 85; Gragnani:Son Fl; Legnani:Duetto concertante, Op. 23 PAVA ▲ 7298 [DDD] (10.97)
R. Ricci (vn), S. Cardi (gtr) † Terzetto concertante, M.S. 114; Terzetto Vn, M.S. 69 BONG ▲ 5507 [DDD] (16.97)
S. St. John (vn), S. Wynberg (gtr) *(rec Mar 1993)* ("Music for Violin & Guitar I") † Cantabile, M.S. 109; Sons Vn & Gtr, M.S. 27; Vars on "Barucabà", M.S. 71 NXIN ▲ 8550690 [DDD] (5.97)
G. Shaham (vn), G. Söllscher (gtr) † Cantabile, M.S. 109; Centone di sonate, M.S. 112; Grand Son, M.S. 3; Moto perpetuo 2, M.S. 72; Son a preghiera; Sons Vn & Gtr, M.S. 27 DEUT ▲ 37837 [DDD] (16.97)
K. Yamashita (gtr), J. Galway (fl) *(rec London, June 23-25, 1986)* ("Italian Serenade") † Cimarosa:Serenade Fl & Gtr; M. Giuliani:Grand Son, Op. 85; G. Rossini:Andante e tema con variazioni Va RCAV (Gold Seal) ▲ 61448 (11.97)

Sonata in c for large Viola & Orchestra, M.S. 70, (Op. 35) (1834)
M. Fornaciari (vn) † Intro & Vars on Nel cor più non mi sento, M.S. 44; Beethoven:Notturno Va; Son 9 Vn, Op. 47 FON ▲ 9320 [DDD]
S. St. John (vn), S. Wynberg (gtr) [arr for va & gtr] *(rec Mar 1993)* ("Music for Violin & Guitar II") † Cantabile & Waltz, M.S. 45; Duetto amoroso, M.S. 111; Sons Vn & Gtr, M.S. 26; Variazioni di bravura NXIN ▲ 550759 [DDD] (5.97)
E. Wallfisch (va), F. Allers (cnd), Northwest German PO † G. F. Malipiero:Dialogo 5; Vanhal:Con Va; C. M. von Weber:Andante & Rondo ungarese Va, J.79; Vars on A Schüsserl und a Reind'r'l, J.49 BAYE ▲ 200028 [ADD] (17.97)

Sonatas for Violin & Guitar
S. Ishikawa (vn), J. Hála (pno)—Centone di sonate, M.S. 112, (Op. 64) [No. 2 in D; No. 4 in A]; Son Vn, M.S. 505; Sons Vn & Gtr, M.S. 26, (Op. 2) ("Virtuoso Pieces") † Szymanowski:Caprices Vn, Op. 40 LT ▲ 28 [DDD] (16.97)
F. Zigante (gtr)—Grand Son, M.S. 3, (Op. 39); Son Gtr, M.S. 87 *(rec Torino, Italy, 1988-89)* ("Guitar Music, Vol. 3") † Gtr Music; Sonatines, M.S. 85 AART ▲ 47194 [DDD] (10.97)

Sonatas (6) for Violin & Guitar, M.S. 26, (Op. 2) (ca 1805)
F. Mezzena (vn), A. Sebastiani (gtr) † Cantabile & Waltz, M.S. 45; Cantabile, M.S. 109; Duetto amoroso, M.S. 111; Sons Vn & Gtr, M.S. 27 DYNC ▲ 62 [DDD] (17.97)
S. St. John (vn), S. Wynberg (gtr) *(rec Mar 1993)* ("Music for Violin & Guitar II") † Cantabile & Waltz, M.S. 45; Duetto amoroso, M.S. 111; Son Va; Variazioni di bravura NXIN ▲ 550759 [DDD] (5.97)

Sonatas (6) for Violin & Guitar, M.S. 27, (Op. 3) (ca 1805)
V. Hudeček (vn), L. Brabec (gtr)—No. 6 in e *(rec Prague, Czech Republic, Sept 6 & 8, 1998)* ("Hudeček & Brabec Play Paganini") † Cantabile, M.S. 109; Centone di sonate, M.S. 112; Grand Son, M.S. 3; Intro & Vars on Nel cor più non mi sento, M.S. 44; Son concertata, M.S. 2 SUR ▲ 3395 [DDD] (16.97)
F. Mezzena (vn), A. Sebastiani (gtr) † Cantabile & Waltz, M.S. 45; Cantabile, M.S. 109; Duetto amoroso, M.S. 111; Sons Vn & Gtr, M.S. 26 DYNC ▲ 62 [DDD] (17.97)
I. Perlman (vn), J. Williams (gtr) † Cantabile, M.S. 109; Son concertata, M.S. 2; M. Giuliani:Son Vn SNYC ▲ 34508 [AAD] (16.97) ▮ 34508 [AAD] (10.98)
V. Příhoda (vn), C. Cerné (pno)—No. 6 in e [arr vn & pno] † Con 1 Vn, M.S. 21; I palpiti, M.S. 77; Streghe; H. Vieuxtemps:Con 4 Vn, Op. 31; Wieniawski:Con 2 Vn, Op. 22 BID ▲ 135 (16.97)
S. St. John (vn), S. Wynberg (gtr) *(rec Mar 1993)* ("Music for Violin & Guitar I") † Cantabile, M.S. 109; Son concertata, M.S. 2; Vars on "Barucabà", M.S. 71 NXIN ▲ 8550690 [DDD] (5.97)
G. Shaham (vn), G. Söllscher (gtr)—No. 1 in A; No. 4 in a; No. 6 in e † Cantabile, M.S. 109; Centone di sonate, M.S. 112; Grand Son, M.S. 3; Moto perpetuo 2, M.S. 72; Son a preghiera; Son concertata, M.S. 2 DEUT ▲ 37837 [DDD] (16.97)

Sonatines (5) for solo Guitar, M.S. 85 (1818)
F. Zigante (gtr) *(rec Torino, Italy, 1988-89)* ("Guitar Music, Vol. 3") † Gtr Music; Sonatas for Violin & Guitar AART ▲ 47194 [DDD] (10.97)

Le Streghe for Violin & Orchestra [variations on a theme from Süssmayr's *Il Noce di Benevento*], M.S. 19, (Op. 8) (1813)
V. Příhoda (vn), C. Cerné (pno) [arr vn & pno] † Con 1 Vn, M.S. 21; I palpiti, M.S. 77; Sons Vn & Gtr, M.S. 27; H. Vieuxtemps:Con 4 Vn, Op. 31; Wieniawski:Con 2 Vn, Op. 22 BID ▲ 135 (16.97)
M. Quarta (vn), S. Redaelli (pno) *(rec Genova, Italy, sept 22/24, 1998)* † I palpiti, M.S. 77; Maestoso son sentimentale, M.S. 51; Son & vars on Weigl; Son Napoleone, M.S. 5 DYNC ▲ 232 [DDD] (17.97)

Tarantella in a for Violin & Orchestra, M.S. 76, (Op. 33) (ca 1838)
F. Mezzena (vn), A. Plotino (cnd), Genoa CO DYNC ▲ 27 [ADD] (17.97)

Terzetto concertante in D for Viola, Cello & Guitar, M.S. 114, (Op. 68) (1833)
A. Farulli (va), A. Noferini (vc), A. Sebastiani (gtr) † Serenata Va, Vc & Gtr, M.S. 17; Serenata Vns, M.S. 115; Terzetto Vn, M.S. 69; Terzetto Vns, M.S. 116 DYNC ▲ 76 [DDD] (17.97)
J. Grey (gtr), Diaz Trio members ("Music for Guitar & Strings") † Cantabile, M.S. 109; Qts (15) Gtr & Strs, M.S. 28-42; Son concertata, M.S. 2 DOR ▲ 90237 (16.97)
M. Tenenbaum (va), D. Lawson (vc), P. Bernard (gtr) *(rec Conservatory of Music Purchase College, Purchase, Oct 28-29, 1996)* ("The Paganinis at Home: An Evening of Casual Virtuosity") † Serenata Vns, M.S. 115; Terzetto Vn, M.S. 69 ESSY ▲ 1053 [DDD] (16.97)
A. Vismara (va), L. Signorini (vc), S. Cardi (gtr) † Son concertata, M.S. 2; Terzetto Vn, M.S. 69 BONG ▲ 5507 [DDD] (16.97)

PAGANINI, NICCOLÒ (cont.)

Terzetto in D for Violin, Cello & Guitar, M.S. 69, (Op. 66) (1833)
D. Bratchkova (vn), A. Noferini (vc), A. Sebastiani (gtr) † Serenata Va, Vc & Gtr, M.S. 17; Serenata Vns, M.S. 115; Terzetto concertante, M.S. 114; Terzetto Vns, M.S. 116 DYNC ▲ 76 [DDD] (17.97)
R. Ricci (vn), L. Signorini (vc), S. Cardi (gtr) † Son concertata, M.S. 2; Terzetto concertante, M.S. 114 BONG ▲ 5507 [DDD] (16.97)
M. Tenenbaum (vn), D. Lawson (vc), P. Bernard (gtr) *(rec Conservatory of Music Purchase College, Purchase, Oct 28-29, 1996)* ("The Paganinis at Home: An Evening of Casual Virtuosity") † Serenata Vns, M.S. 115; Terzetto concertante, M.S. 114 ESSY ▲ 1053 [DDD] (16.97)

Terzetto in a for 2 Violins & Guitar, M.S. 116, (Op. 67)
D. Bratchkova (vn), G. Hartmann (vn), A. Sebastiani (gtr) † Serenata Va, Vc & Gtr, M.S. 17; Serenata Vns, M.S. 115; Terzetto concertante, M.S. 114; Terzetto Vn, M.S. 69 DYNC ▲ 76 [DDD] (17.97)

Theme & Variations for Violin & Guitar, M.S. 82
F. Mezzena (vn), A. Sebastiani (gtr) † Inno patriottico, M.S. 81; Moto perpetuo Vn, M.S. 66; Vars on "La Carmagnole", M.S. 1; Vars on "O mamma, mamma cara", M.S. 59 DYNC ▲ 3 [AAD] (17.97)

Variations (60) on "Barucabà" for Violin & Guitar, M.S. 71, (Op. 14) (1835)
S. St. John (vn), S. Wynberg (gtr) *(rec Mar 1993)* ("Music for Violin & Guitar I") † Cantabile, M.S. 109; Son concertata, M.S. 2; Sons Vn & Gtr, M.S. 27 NXIN ▲ 8550690 [DDD] (5.97)

Variations on "God Save the King" for Violin & Orchestra, M.S. 56, (Op. 9) (1829)
R. Ricci (vn), T. Paul (cnd), Paris National Orch † Beethoven:Con Vn; Bruch:Con 1 Vn, Op. 26 ONEL ▲ 95020 [ADD] (7.97)

Variations on "La Carmagnole" for Violin & Orchestra (or Violin & Guitar), M.S. 1 (ca 1794)
F. Mezzena (vn), A. Sebastiani (gtr) † Inno patriottico, M.S. 81; Moto perpetuo Vn, M.S. 66; Theme & Vars Vn, M.S. 82; Vars on "O mamma, mamma cara", M.S. 59 DYNC ▲ 3 [AAD] (17.97)

Variations on "O mamma, mamma cara" for Violin & Orchestra (or Violin & Guitar) [from *Il Carnevale di Venezia*], M.S. 59, (Op. 10) (1829)
F. Mezzena (vn), A. Sebastiani (gtr) † Inno patriottico, M.S. 81; Moto perpetuo Vn, M.S. 66; Theme & Vars Vn, M.S. 82; Vars on "La Carmagnole", M.S. 1 DYNC ▲ 3 [AAD] (17.97)

Variazioni di bravura on Caprice No. 24 for Violin & Guitar
S. St. John (vn), S. Wynberg (gtr) *(rec Mar 1993)* ("Music for Violin & Guitar II") † Cantabile & Waltz, M.S. 45; Duetto amoroso, M.S. 111; Son Va; Sons Vn & Gtr, M.S. 26 NXIN ▲ 550759 [DDD] (5.97)

PAHISSA, JAIME (1880-1969)

Songs
J. Cabero (ten), M. Cabero (pno)—Balades (3); Rosa; Per un bes; L'enyor; El mocador; Un ventall; El record; Cançó del lladre *(rec Sept 1994)* ("Cançons de carrer") † Morera:Songs LAMA ▲ 2015 [DDD] (17.97)

PAIK, SEUNG-WOO (20th cent)

PAN I for Clarinet
I.-S. Lee (cl) ("Presenting Im-Soo Lee") † L. Bassi:Fant di concerto on Verdi's Rigoletto; R. Schumann:Fantasiestücke Cl, Op. 73; Romances Ob, Op. 94; L. Weiner:Pereg Recruiting Dance, Op. 40 SUMM ▲ 235 (16.97)

PAINE, JOHN KNOWLES (1839-1906)

As You Like It (concert overture) for Orchestra, Op. 28 (1876)
L. Botstein (cnd), American Russian Youth Orch *(rec Tanglewood, MA, June 1997)* ("10th Anniversary: American Russian Youth Orchestra in Concert") † Griffes:Pleasure Dome of Kubla Khan, Op. 8; C. Ives:Washington's Birthday; P. Tchaikovsky:Festival Coronation March TOWN ▲ 53 (17.97)
Z. Mehta (cnd), New York PO † Sym 1 NWW ▲ 374 [DDD] (16.97)

Concert Variations on the Austrian Hymn (1860)
B. K. Tidwell (org) *(rec 100 Rank Schantz Organ, Cleveland Heights, OH)* † G. Bales:Petite Suite; Hollins:Trumpet Minuet; H. Howells:Siciliano; Roger-Ducasse:Pastoral Org; Sowerby:Sonatina for Org; Sym 4; Vierne:Pièces de fantaisie ARK ▲ 6157 [DDD] (16.97)

Fantaisie on Ein feste Burg ist unser Gott for Organ, Op. 13
R. Morris (org) ("Fugues, Fantasia, and Variations: 19th Century American Concert Organ Music") † D. Buck:Grand Son, Op. 22; H. Parker:Compositions Org, Op. 36; Thayer:Vars on Russian National Hymn, Op. 12; G. Whiting:Postlude Org, Op. 53 NWW ▲ 80280 [DDD] (16.97)

Mass in D for solo Voices, Organ, Orchestra & Chorus, Op. 10 (1866)
C. Balthrop (sop), J. Blackett (cta), V. Cole (ten), J. Cheek (bass), J. Lange (org), G. Schuller (cnd), St. Louis SO, St. Louis Sym Chorus [LAT] *(rec mid-1970s)* NWW 2-▲ 80262 [AAD] (29.97)

Oedipus tyrannus:Prelude
K. Klein (cnd), London SO † D. Buck:Festival Ov; J. A. Carpenter:Skyscrapers; Foote:Suite Str Orch, Op. 63; MacDowell:Lamia ALBA ▲ 235 [DDD] (16.97)

Piano Music
D. Oldham (pno)—Christmas Gift; Characteristic Pieces (4); Romance, Op. 12; Pno Pieces (3); Valse Caprice; Sketches (10):In the Country; Character Pieces (4); Funeral March in Memory of President Lincoln; Romance, Op. 39; Son Pno, Op. 1; Nocturne *(rec 1992)* ("Selected Piano Works") NWW 2-▲ 80424 (29.97)

Pieces (3) for Piano, Op. 41 (ca 1882-84)
M. Frager (pno) ("Edward MacDowell & Company") † Romance Pno, Op. 12; A. M. Foerster:On the Sea; H. F. Gilbert:Mazurka Pno; H. H. Huss:Preludes Pno, Op. 17; MacDowell:Virtuoso Etudes, Op. 46; E. Nevin:Etudes Pno, Op. 18; H. Parker:Morceaux caractéristiques, Op. 49 NWW ▲ 80206 [DDD] (16.97)

Romance in c for Piano, Op. 12 (ca 1868)
M. Frager (pno) ("Edward MacDowell & Company") † Pieces Pno, Op. 41; A. M. Foerster:On the Sea; H. F. Gilbert:Mazurka Pno; H. H. Huss:Preludes Pno, Op. 17; MacDowell:Virtuoso Etudes, Op. 46; E. Nevin:Etudes Pno, Op. 18; H. Parker:Morceaux caractéristiques, Op. 49 NWW ▲ 80206 [DDD] (16.97)

St. Peter (oratorio) for solo Voices, Orchestra & Chorus, Op. 20 (1870-72)
J. Ommerlé (sop), A. Fortunato (mez), P. Kelly (ten), D. Evitts (bar), G. Schuller (cnd), Boston Pro Arte CO, Back Bay Chorale [ENG] *(rec Cambridge Mass., May 21, 1989)* GMR 2-▲ 2027 (32.97)

Sonata for Violin & Piano, Op. 24 (1875; rev 1905)
R. Druian (vn), B. Pasternack (pno) † G. Schuller:Duologue GMR ▲ 2021 (16.97)

Symphony No. 1 in c, Op. 23 (1875)
Z. Mehta (cnd), New York PO † As You Like It, Op. 28 NWW ▲ 374 [DDD] (16.97)

Symphony No. 2 in A, Op. 34, "Im Frühling" (1879)
Z. Mehta (cnd), New York PO NWW ▲ 350 [DDD] (16.97)

PAISIBLE, JAMES (d. 1721)

Music of Paisible
P. Goodwin (cnd), London Oboe Band—Mr. Paisible's Airs in the Comedy of the Humors of; Mr. Paisible's Airs in the Comedy of She Wou'd & S; The Queen's Farewell ("Playhouse Aires: 18th Century English Theatre Music") † W. Croft:Music of Croft HAM ▲ 907181 [DDD] (18.97)

Recorder Music
Bergen Baroque—Son Rcr in F, Sibley 9 [Vivace]; Son Rcr in D *(rec June 1998)* ("The Lonely Shepherd") † Blow:Music Kbd; Finger:VI Music; Pepusch:English Cants Book I; English Cants Book II; H. Purcell:Fairy Queen (sels) BIS ▲ 965 [DDD] (17.97)

Sonata in F for Recorder & Continuo, Sibley 9
Trio Basiliensis *(rec Freiburg, Germany, Apr 1996)* ("Concerning Babell & Son") † Babell:Son 2 Rcr; A. Corelli:Son 5 Va da Gamba, Op. 5; P. A. Fiocco:Son in C; G. F. Handel:Rinaldo (sels); Rosier:Son in g; Steffani:Son in d ARSM ▲ 1167 [DDD] (17.97)

PAISIELLO, GIOVANNI (1740-1816)

Andante for Horn & Harp
S. Hermansson (nat hn), E. Goodman (hp) *(rec Ontario, Canada, Sept 20-23, 1993)* ("Horn & Harp Soirée - 19th Century French & Italian Duos") † N. C. Bochsa:L'écho (Nocturne 2) Hn & Hp; Boieldieu:Solo Hn & Hp; Chaussier:Elegy Hn & Hp; Dauprat:Air Ecossais Var Hn & Hp, Op. 22; Son Hn & Hp; F. Duvernoy:Nocturne 2 Hn & Hp; Spontini:Divert Hn & Hp BIS ▲ 648 [DDD] (17.97)

Il barbiere di Siviglia (selections)
J. Gregor (bass), A. Fischer (cnd), Hungarian State Orch—Veramente ho torto *(rec 1975-82)* ("József Gregor, Bass") † Donizetti:Don Pasquale (sels); Elisir d'amore (sels); J. Haydn:Infedeltà delusa (sels); W. A. Mozart:Arias; G. Rossini:Barbiere di Siviglia (sels); Cenerentola (sels) *([ENG,HUN] texts)* HUN (Great Hungarian Voices) ▲ 31737 [AAD] (16.97)

Divertimenti (3) for Violin
T. Grindenko (vn) ("Music at the Court of St. Petersburg, Vol. 3") OPUS ▲ 30180 (18.97)

La Molinara (opera in 3 acts) [lib Giuseppe Palomba] (1788)
A. Scarabelli (sop), G. Banditelli (cta), B. Lazzaretti (ten), W. Matteuzzi (ten), B. Praticò (bar), C. Remigio (sgr), I. Bolton (cnd), Bologna Teatro Comunale Orch BMGR ▲ 5862 (18.97)

PAISIELLO, GIOVANNI (cont.)

Il mondo della luna (opera in 2 acts) [lib Carlo Goldoni] (1782)
C. Di Censo (sop—Flaminia), G. Bertagnolli (sop—Clarice), E. Dara (bar—Buonafede), M. Nicolini (bar—Ernesto), D. Gaspari (sgr—Ecclittico), F. Neri (cnd), Bolzano Claudio Monteverdi Conservatory Youth Orch *(rec Aug 4-6, 1993) (E,I lib texts)* BONG 2-▲ 2173 [DDD] (32.97)

Nina, o sia La pazza per amore (opera in 1 act) [lib G. Carpani after B. J. Mersollier w. additions by Lorenzi] (1789)
J. M. Bima (sop—Nina), G. Banditelli (cta—Susanna), W. Matteuzzi (ten—Lindoro), N. D. Carolis (b-bar—Conte), A. Antoniozzi (bass—Giorgio), H. L. Hirsch (cnd), Concentus Hungaricus, Hungarian Chamber Chorus *(rec Budapest, Dec 1992)* AART 2-▲ 47166 [DDD] (19.97)
R. Bonynge (cnd), Teatro Massimo Orchestra, M. Bolgan (sop) NUO ▲ 6872 (32.97)

La passione di Gesù Cristo (oratorio) for solo Voices, Orchestra & Chorus (1783; rev 1815)
H. Górzyńska (sop), J. Knetig (ten), J. Mahler (bass), M. Kacprzak (sgr), W. Czepiel (cnd), Warsaw Sinfonietta, Warsaw Chamber Opera Chorus *(I text)* AART 2-▲ 47191 (19.97)

Quartets (6) for Flute, Violin, Viola & Cello [perhaps arrs], Op. 23
Accademia Farnese *(rec Aug 1997)* MONM (Grande Musica Italiana) ▲ 96021 [DDD] (18.97)
Flautarte Quartet STRV ▲ 24 [DDD] (16.97)

Quartets (9) for Strings in C, A, D, E♭, E♭, C, D, G & A
Quartetto Modi *(rec Jan 20-22, 1993)* BONG ▲ 5526 [DDD] (16.97)

Il re Teodoro in Venezia (opera in 2 acts) [lib Casti] (1784)
E. Barazia (sop), R. Stanisci (sop), M. Comencini (ten), S. Kale (ten), F. Previati (bar), A. Cognet (b-bar), D. Baronchelli (bass), M. Buda (sgr), I. Karabtchevsky (cnd), Venice Theater Orch, Venice Theater Chorus *(rec live Venice, 1998)* ("Masses for 4 Voices") † W. Byrd:Mass 4 Voc; Frescobaldi:Canzoni for 1-4 Instr; Monteverdi:Messa et salmi; C. Simpson:Division on a Ground MONM 3-▲ 20121 [DDD] (54.97)

Sacred Music
St. Petersburg Cappella—Mass; Te Deum *(rec La Chaise-Dieu Abbey, Aug 22-23, 1995)* ("Coronation Music for Napoleon I") † Roze:Vivat in aeternum—Vivat Rex; Sueur:Sacred Music KSCH ▲ 312082 (16.97)

La Serva padrona (intermezzo in 2 acts) [lib G. A. Federico] (1781)
J. M. Bima (sop), P. Salomaa (bass), H. L. Hirsch (pno), H. L. Hirsch (cnd), Munich RSO AART ▲ 47152 (10.97)

PALADILHE, EMILE (1844-1926)

Solo de concert for Oboe
J. Mack (ob) † B. Britten:Metamorphoses, Op. 49; C. M. Loeffler:Rhaps; W. A. Mozart:Qt Ob CRYS ▲ 323 (15.97) ▮ 323 (9.98)
J. Mack (ob) † B. Britten:Metamorphoses, Op. 49; Saint-Saëns:Son Ob; R. Schumann:Romances Ob, Op. 94 CRYS ▮ 325 (9.98)

PALESTER, ROMAN (1907-1989)

Concertino for Alto Saxophone & String Orchestra (1938)
D. Pituch (sax), J. Maksymiuk (cnd), Polish CO *(rec Polish Radio, 1982)* ("David Pituch Plays New Compositions for the E Alto Saxophone") † A. Bloch:Notes; B. Fennelly:Con Sax; Tesserae VIII; J. Yuasa:Not I, But the Wind PROV ▲ 175 [ADD]

Trio d'anches for Oboe, Clarinet & Bassoon (1967)
Warsaw Wind Quintet members ("Da camera") † Bargielski:Butterfly Cage; Kurtlewicz:Blow the Wind; Malecki:Suite Ww Qnt; P. Moss:Retours; Stachowski:Pezzo grazioso PROV ▲ 182 [DDD] (18.97)

PALESTINE, CHARLEMAGNE (1945-

The Lower Depths for Piano
C. Palestine (pno) *(rec Washington Square Church NYC, Jan 1987)* ("Godbear") † Strumming Music; Timbral Assault BARO ▲ 19 [DDD]

Schlingen-Blängen for Organ (1979)
C. Palestine (org) NWW ▲ 80578 (16.97)

Strumming Music for Piano
C. Palestine (pno) *(rec Washington Square Church NYC, Jan 1987)* ("Godbear") † Lower Depths; Timbral Assault BARO ▲ 19 [DDD]

Timbral Assault for Piano
C. Palestine (pno) *(rec Washington Square Church NYC, Jan 1987)* ("Godbear") † Lower Depths; Strumming Music BARO ▲ 19 [DDD]

PALESTRINA, GIOVANNI (ca 1525-1594)

Adoramus te Christe (motet) for Chorus (1581)
L. Stokowski (cnd), Sym of the Air [orchd Stokowski, 1934] *(rec Carnegie Hall, 1958)* † Frescobaldi:Gagliarda; G. Gabrieli:Son pian' e forte; O. Respighi:Pini di Roma; D. Shostakovich:Sym 1 EMIC ▲ 66864 [ADD] (11.97)

Ave Regina coelorum
M. Berry (cnd), Schola Gregoriana of Cambridge *(rec Apr 1998)* ("Angels from the Vatican") † Venit Michaël Archangelus; Anonymous:Agnus Dei; Alleluia, assumpta est Maria; Angeli, Archangeli; Angelis suis mandavitde te; Angelus Domini descendit; Ave Maria; Benedicite Dominum; Christe, sanctorum decus Angelorum; Dixit Angelus ad Iacob; Domine Jesu Christe; Exsultet iam Angelica turba caelorum; Facta est cum Angelo; Gloria; Hodie nobis caelorum Rex; In Paradisum; Kyrie; Sanctus; Stetit Angelus; Te laudamus; Te Deum laudamus; Marenzio:Qual mormorio soave; Traditional:Angelus ad pastores ait; Victoria:Duo Seraphim HER ▲ 220 [DDD] (18.97)

Hodie Beata Virgo
D. Willcocks (cnd), King's College Choir *(rec 1963)* † Litaniae de Beata Virgine Maria; Magnificat octavi toni; Senex puerum portabat; Stabat mater; G. Allegri:Miserere DECC ▲ 466373 (11.97)

Hymns
J. Miller (cnd), Chicago a Cappella—A solis ortus cardine; Christe redemptor omnium; Hostis Herodis impie *(rec Northbrook Illinois, Mar 2-3, 1996)* ("Music for the Christmas Season") CENT ▲ 2303 [DDD] (16.97)

Lamentationum Hieremiae prophetae liber primus (1588)
B. Turner (cnd), Pro Cantione Antiqua ICC ▲ 6600762 (16.97)

Litaniae de Beata Virgine Maria for 8 Voices
D. Willcocks (cnd), King's College Choir *(rec 1963)* † Hodie Beata Virgo; Magnificat octavi toni; Senex puerum portabat; Stabat mater; G. Allegri:Miserere DECC ▲ 466373 (11.97)

Magnificat octavi toni
D. Willcocks (cnd), King's College Choir *(rec 1963)* † Hodie Beata Virgo; Litaniae de Beata Virgine Maria; Senex puerum portabat; Stabat mater; G. Allegri:Miserere DECC ▲ 466373 (11.97)

Missa Aeterna Christi Munera
J. Summerly (cnd), Oxford Camerata *(rec Dorchester Abbey, Oxon, England, Sept 1991)* † Missa "Papae marcelli", R. 12; Stabat mater; G. Allegri:Miserere NXIN ▲ 8553238 [DDD] (5.97)

Missa "Aspice Domine" for 5 Voices, K.10 (1567)
M. Longhini (cnd), Delitiae Musicae † Missa "Salvum me fac", K.11; Jacquet Of mantua:Aspice Domine; Salvum me fac Domine STRV ▲ 33477 (16.97)

Missa "Assumpta est Maria" for 6 Voices, R.82
T. Brown (cnd), Clare College Choir Cambridge *(rec Lady Chapel Ely Cathedral, Jan 1996)* † Motets EMIC (Debut) ▲ 69703 [DDD] (6.97)
P. Phillips (cnd), Tallis Scholars † Missa "Sicut lilium inter spinas", R.34; Motets GIME ▲ 54920 [DDD] (16.97)

Missa "Benedicta es" for 6 Voices [text Josquin], R.91
P. Phillips (cnd), Tallis Scholars GIME ▲ 54901 [AAD] (16.97)

Missa brevis for 4 Voices, R.15 (1570)
M. Brown (cnd), Pro Cantione Antiqua † Missa "Lauda Sion", R.21 ICC ▲ 6600742 (16.97)
F. Monego (cnd), Syntagma ("Sacred Polyphony of the 16th Century") STRV ▲ 35 (16.97)
A. Sanna (cnd), Coro Polifonico Turritano † Missa De feria; Missa Ut re mi fa sol la; Motets FON 2-▲ 9020 [DDD] (20.97)

Missa de Beata Marie II for 5 Voices [text Mantuan], R.99
Gloriae Dei Cantores ("Prince of Music") † Missa "Descendit angelus", R.68; Sacred Music PAR ▲ 13 [DDD]

Missa de Beata Virgine for 6 Voices, R.19 (1570)
J. O'Donnell (cnd), Westminster Cathedral Choir HYP ▲ 66364 (18.97)
I. Segarra (cnd), Montserrat Escolania, I. Segarra (cnd), Montserrat Capella KSCH ▲ 317962 (16.97)
B. Turner (cnd), Pro Cantione Antiqua † Missa "Papae marcelli", R. 12; Stabat mater ASVQ ▲ 6086 [ADD] (10.97)

Missa De feria for 4 Voices (1570)
A. Sanna (cnd), Coro Polifonico Turritano † Missa brevis, R.15; Missa Ut re mi fa sol la; Motets FON 2-▲ 9020 [DDD] (20.97)

Missa "Descendit angelus Domini" for 4 Voices, R.68 (1600)
Gloriae Dei Cantores ("Prince of Music") † Missa de Beata Marie II, R.99; Sacred Music PAR ▲ 13 [DDD]

Missa "L'Homme armé" for 4 Voices, R.24 (1582)
S. Vartolo (cnd), Bologna St. Petronio Cappella Musicale *(rec Church de S. Zeno a Cavalo Verona, Oct 1995)* ("Masses & Motets, Vol. 2") † Missa "Sine nomine", R.36; Motets NXIN (Early Music) ▲ 8553314 [DDD] (5.97)

PALESTRINA, GIOVANNI (cont.)

Missa "In minoribus duplicibus" for 4 Voices, R.84
G. Monaco (cnd), Progetto Musica Vocal Ensemble *(rec Santuario di Graglia, Mar 1995)* ("Sacred Music Connected with St. Philip Neri") † Ancina:Vocal Music; Arascione:Nuove laudi ariose della Beatissima Virgine scelte; G. Razzi:Laude spirituale TACT ▲ 520001 [DDD] (16.97)

Missa "Lauda Sion" for 4 Voices, R.21 (1582)
M. Brown (cnd), Pro Cantione Antiqua † Missa brevis, R.15 ICC ▲ 6600742 (16.97)

Missa "Nigra sum" for 5 Voices, R. 33 (1590)
P. Phillips (cnd), Tallis Scholars [LAT] † Lhéritier:Motet & Plainchant; A. Silva:Nigra sum GIME ▲ 54903 [AAD] (16.97)

Missa "Papae marcelli" for 6 Voices, R. 12 (1567)
Hägersten Motet Choir *(rec 1980-93)* † Sicut cervus; W. Byrd:Laudibus in sanctis; Mass 4-Part Chorus NSAG ▲ 6 [AAD] (16.97)
P. Phillips (cnd), Tallis Scholars *(rec 1980)* † G. Allegri:Miserere; W. Mundy:Vox Patris GIME ▲ 54939 [AAD] (16.97)
P. Phillips (cnd), Tallis Scholars *(rec live, Rome, Italy)* † Sacred Music; Stabat mater; G. Allegri:Miserere GIME ▲ 54994 [DDD] (16.97)
S. Preston (cnd), Westminster Abbey Choir—Kyrie; Gloria; Credo; Sanctus; Benedictus; Angus Dei I/II *(rec All Saints' Church, London, England, Feb 1985)* † Tu es Petrus; G. Allegri:Miserere; Anerio:Vocal Music; Giovannelli:Jubilate Deo; G. B. Nanino:Haec dies PARC ▲ 15517 [DDD] (16.97)
J. Summerly (cnd), Oxford Camerata *(rec Dorchester Abbey, Oxon, England, Sept 1991)* † Missa Aeterna Christi Munera; Stabat mater; G. Allegri:Miserere NXIN ▲ 8553238 [DDD] (5.97)
B. Turner (cnd), Pro Cantione Antiqua [LAT] † Missa de Beata Virgine, R.19; Stabat mater ASVQ ▲ 6086 [ADD] (10.97)

Missa "Pro defunctis" for 5 Voices, R.37, "Requiem" (1591)
Chanticleer *(rec San Rafael, CA, June 1994)* † Motets; Song of Songs TELC ▲ 94561 [DDD] (16.97) ▮ 94561 [DDD] (10.98)
M. Michielsen (cnd), Cappella Palestrina ("Requiem") ERAS ▲ 42 [DDD]

Missa "Qual è il più grand'amore" for 5 Voices [text Rore], R.76 (1550)
P. Bertin (alt), C. Cavina (alt), G. Maletto (ten), R. Abbondanza (bass), M. Vargetto (bass), M. Longhini (cnd) *(rec Sept 1995)* ("Missæ ex Cipriano de Rore") † Missa "Quando lieta sperai", R.70 STRV ▲ 33423 (16.97)

Missa "Quando lieta sperai" for 5 Voices [text Rore], R.70 (1552)
P. Bertin (alt), C. Cavina (alt), G. Maletto (ten), R. Abbondanza (bass), M. Vargetto (bass), M. Longhini (cnd) *(rec Sept 1995)* ("Missæ ex Cipriano de Rore") † Missa "Qual è il più grand'amore", R.76 STRV ▲ 33423 (16.97)

Missa "Salvum me fac" for 5 Voices, K.11 (1567)
M. Longhini (cnd), Delitiae Musicae † Missa "Aspice Domine", K.10; Jacquet Of mantua:Aspice Domine; Salvum me fac Domine STRV ▲ 33477 (16.97)

Missa "Sicut lilium inter spinas" for 5 Voices, R.34 (1590)
P. Phillips (cnd), Tallis Scholars † Missa "Assumpta est Maria", R.82; Motets GIME ▲ 54920 [DDD] (16.97)

Missa "Sine nomine" for 6 Voices, R.36 (1590)
D. Fasolis (cnd), Theatrum Instrumentorum Milano, Chorus of Swiss-Italian Radio & Television † Motets AART ▲ 47521 (10.97)
S. Vartolo (cnd), Bologna St. Petronio Cappella Musicale *(rec Church de S. Zeno a Cavalo Verona, Oct 1995)* ("Masses & Motets, Vol. 2") † Missa "L'Homme armé" 4 Voices, R.24; Motets NXIN (Early Music) ▲ 8553314 [DDD] (5.97)

Missa Ut re mi fa sol la for 6 Voices (1570)
C. Jackson (cnd), Montreal Ancient Music Studio Choir † Sacred Choral Music; Victoria:Sacred Choral Music *(E,F,L texts)* FL ▲ 23120 [DDD] (16.97)
A. Sanna (cnd), Coro Polifonico Turritano † Missa brevis, R.15; Missa De feria; Motets FON 2-▲ 9020 [DDD] (20.97)

Motets
T. Brown (cnd), Clare College Choir Cambridge—Assumpta est Maria; Ave Maria; Beata es, Virgo Maria; Hodie gloriosa semper Virgo Maria; Regina coeli *(rec Lady Chapel Ely Cathedral, Jan 1996)* † Missa "Assumpta est Maria", R.82 EMIC (Debut) ▲ 69703 [DDD] (6.97)
Chanticleer—Gaude gloriosa; Gaude, B. *(rec San Rafael, CA, June 1994)* † Missa "Pro defunctis", R.37; Song of Songs TELC ▲ 94561 [DDD] (16.97) ▮ 94561 [DDD] (10.98)
D. Fasolis (cnd), Theatrum Instrumentorum Milano, Chorus of Swiss-Italian Radio & Television—Motets (4) † Missa "Sine nomine", R.36 AART ▲ 47521 (10.97)
F. Fauché (bass), La Fenice Ensemble—Io son ferito, ahi lasso; Vestiva i colli; Ricercar noni toni; Pulchra es amica mea ("Motetti, Madrigali e Canzoni Francesi") † O. de Lassus:Motets RICE ▲ 152137 (17.97)
P. Phillips (cnd), Tallis Scholars—Assumpta est Maria; Sicut lilium inter spinas I † Missa "Assumpta est Maria", R.82; Missa "Sicut lilium inter spinas", R.34 GIME ▲ 54920 [DDD] (16.97)
A. Sanna (cnd), Coro Polifonico Turritano—Ave Maria; Adoramus te Christe; Pueri Habraeorum; Domine quando pavesco; Hodie Christus natus est; Jubilate Deo; Quam pulchri sunt; Duo ubera tua; Quam pulchra es; Exsultate Deo; Magnificat octavi toni; In festo unius Martyris; Figlio immortal d'immortal Padre; E se mai voci di qua giù son grate; Hor tu sol, che di vivi almi splendori; Dammi, scala del ciel e del ciel porta; E se fur già de le mie mani immonde; Vello di Gedeon, cui Dio sì largo; Novella aurora che nascend'allegri; Stabat Mater † Missa brevis, R.15; Missa De feria; Missa Ut re mi fa sol la FON 2-▲ 9020 [DDD] (20.97)
L. Taglioni (cnd), Camerata Nova—Ave Maria; Alma Redemptoris mater; Tu quæ genuisti; Veni sponsa Christi; Surge propera; Quæ est ista; Magnificat IV toni; Hodie Beata Virgo; Ave Regina coelorum; Gaude Virgo gloriosa; Magnificat VII toni; Ave maris stella *(rec Sept 19-22, 1996)* ("Ave Maris Stella: Motets for the Blessed Virgin") STRV ▲ 33375 [DDD] (16.97)
S. Vartolo (cnd), Bologna St. Petronio Cappella Musicale—Peccantem me quotidie; Sicut cervus; Super flumina Babylonis *(rec Church de S. Zeno a Cavalo Verona, Oct 1995)* ("Masses & Motets, Vol. 2") † Missa "L'Homme armé" 4 Voices, R.24; Missa "Sine nomine", R.36 NXIN (Early Music) ▲ 8553314 [DDD] (5.97)

Organ Music
L. Tamminga (org)—Ricercares 1st-8th tones; Canzon *(rec May 1996)* ("Works for Organ") † Macque:Org Music ACCE ▲ 96115 [DDD] (17.97)

Sacred Choral Music
C. Jackson (cnd), Montreal Ancient Music Studio Choir—Ecce nunc benedicite † Missa Ut re mi fa sol la; Victoria:Sacred Choral Music FL ▲ 23120 [DDD] (16.97)

Sacred Music
S. Darlington (cnd), Christ Church Cathedral Choir Oxford—Mass for Pentecost; 5 Motets [L] NIMB ▲ 5100 [DDD] (16.97)
S. Darlington (cnd), Christ Church Cathedral Choir, Oxford—Missa "Dum complerentur", R.55; Super flumina Babylonis; Exsultate Deo; Sicut cervus; O bone Jesu; Missa "O sacrum convivium", R.86; Coenantibus illis; Magnificat Sexti Toni [LAT] *(rec Oxfordshire, England, May 16-17, 1988)* ("European Choral Music 1525-1751") † J. R. Esteves:Sacred Music; O. de Lassus:Sacred Music; C. de Morales:O sacrum convivium; Rore:Qual donn'attende; Victoria:Sacred Choral Music NIMB 5-▲ 1758 [DDD] (29.97)
Gloriae Dei Cantores—Super flumina Babylonis; Ad Te levavi oculos meos; Miserere nostri, Domine; Sicut cervus; Sitivit anima mea; Jubilate Deo ("Prince of Music") † Missa "Descendit angelus", R.68; Missa de Beata Marie II, R.99 PAR ▲ 13 [DDD]
P. Herreweghe (cnd), Organum Ensemble, P. Herreweghe (cnd), Royal Chapel European Vocal Ensemble—Missa Viri Galilaei; Motet Viri Galilaei; Magnificat Primi Toni [L] HAM ▲ 901388 (18.97)
E. Iseler (cnd), Elmer Iseler Singers—Ascendo ad patrem; Missa Ascendo ad Patrem; Quem vidistis, pastores; Surge illuminare Jerusalem; Stabat Mater; Assumpta est Maria; Magnificat Primi Toni ("The Glory of Palestrina") CBC (Musica Viva) ▲ 1067 [DDD] (16.97)
D. Keene (cnd), Voices of Ascension—Missa "Papae marcelli", R. 12; Secundum multitudinem; Tu es Petrus; Dum complerentur; O Domine Jesu Christe; Super flumina Babylonis; Canite tuba; Peccantem me quotidie; Agnus Dei; Alma Redemptoris mater; Sicut cervus *(rec Church of Ascension, NYC, NY, May 18-24, 1996)* DLS ▲ 3210 [DDD] (14.97)
P. Ledger (cnd), King's College Choir Cambridge—Missa, "Hodie Christus natus est"; Motets EMIC (Classics for Pleasure) ▲ 64045 (11.97)
E. Munk (cnd), Copenhagen Boys' Choir—Missa Papae Marcelli; Motets for the Major Festivals of the Church Year DANI ▲ 8163
Musica Contexta ("Music for Maundy Thursday") CHOC ▲ 617 (16.97)
J. O'Donnell (cnd), Westminster Cathedral Choir—Motet & Mass, "O Rex Gloriae"; Motet & Mass, "Viri Galilaei" [L] HYP ▲ 66316 (18.97)
J. O'Donnell (cnd), Westminster Cathedral Choir—Missa, "Hodie Christus natus est"; Magnificat Primi Toni; 3 Motets; Super flumina Babylonis; Vidi turbam magnum; 4 Motets from Canticum Canticorum; Duo ubera tua; Nigra sum, sed formosa; Surge, amica mea HYP ▲ 66490 [DDD] (18.97)

PALESTRINA, GIOVANNI (cont.)

Sacred Music (cont.)

P. Phillips (cnd), Tallis Scholars—Missa brevis; Missa, "Nasce la gioia mia" [L] GIME ▲ 54908 [DDD] (16.97)

P. Phillips (cnd), Tallis Scholars—Alma redemptoris mater; Magnificat primi toni; Nunc dimittis; Surge, illuminare *(rec live, Rome, Italy)* † Missa "Papae marcelli", R. 12; Stabat mater; G. Allegri:Miserere GIME ▲ 54994 [DDD] (16.97)

P. Phillips (cnd), Tallis Scholars—Assumpta est Maria; Benedicta est; Missa brevis; Nasce la gioia mia; Nigra sum; Papae marcelli; Sicut lilium [all masses]; Sicut lilium I [both motets] ("Palestrina 400 Collection") † Lhéritier:Motet & Plainchant PPHI 4-▲ 454890 (45.97)

J. Summerly (cnd), Oxford Schola Cantorum—Missa Hodie Christus natus est; Motet:Hodie Christus natus est *(rec Mar 1993)* ("Early Music: Palestrina and Lassus") † Stabat mater; O. de Lassus:Bell'Amfitrit'altera NXIN ▲ 550836 [DDD] (5.97)

Senex puerum portabat (motet) for 5 Voices (1569)

D. Willcocks (cnd), King's College Choir *(rec 1963)* † Hodie Beata Virgo; Litaniae de Beata Virgine Maria; Magnificat octavi toni; Stabat mater; G. Allegri:Miserere DECC ▲ 466373 (11.97)

Sicut cervus (motet) for 4 Voices (1581)

Hägersten Motet Choir *(rec 1980-93)* † Missa "Papae marcelli", R. 12; W. Byrd:Laudibus in sanctis; Mass 4-Part Chorus NSAG ▲ 6 [AAD] (16.97)

The Song of Songs [Motettorum liber quartus ex Canticis canticorum] (cycle of 29 motets) for Chorus (1584)

Chanticleer *(rec San Rafael, CA, June 1994)* † Missa "Pro defunctis", R.37; Motets TELC ▲ 94561 [DDD] (16.97) ▮ 94561 [DDD] (10.98)

F. Lasserre (cnd), Champagne-Ardenne Akademia Regional Vocal Ensemble PVY ▲ 795092 (16.97)

J. Rutter (cnd), Cambridge Singers *(rec Nov 1993)* CLL ▲ 122 [DDD] (15.97)

B. Turner (cnd), Pro Cantione Antiqua HYP ▲ 66733 (18.97)

Stabat mater for Chorus

P. Phillips (cnd), Tallis Scholars *(rec live, Rome, Italy)* † Missa "Papae marcelli", R. 12; Sacred Music; G. Allegri:Miserere GIME ▲ 54994 [DDD] (16.97)

J. Summerly (cnd), Oxford Schola Cantorum *(rec Mar 1993)* ("Early Music: Palestrina and Lassus") † Sacred Music; O. de Lassus:Bell'Amfitrit'altera NXIN ▲ 550836 [DDD] (5.97)

J. Summerly (cnd), Schola Cantorum *(rec Hertford College Chapel, Oxford, England, Mar 1993)* † Missa "Papae marcelli", R. 12; Missa Aeterna Christi Munera; G. Allegri:Miserere NXIN ▲ 8553238 [DDD] (5.97)

B. Turner (cnd), Pro Cantione Antiqua [LAT] † Missa "Papae marcelli", R. 12; Missa de Beata Virgine, R.19 ASVO ▲ 6086 [ADD] (10.97)

D. Willcocks (cnd), King's College Choir *(rec 1963)* † Hodie Beata Virgo; Litaniae de Beata Virgine Maria; Magnificat octavi toni; Senex puerum portabat; G. Allegri:Miserere DECC ▲ 466373 (11.97)

D. Willcocks (cnd), King's College Choir Cambridge ("Great Choral Classics from King's") † G. Allegri:Miserere; J. S. Bach:Cant 41; G. F. Handel:Coronation Anthems for George II, HWV 258-61; Tallis:Spem in alium; Vivaldi:Gloria (& Intro), RV.588 PLON 2-▲ 452949 (17.97)

Tu es Petrus for 6 Voices (1572)

S. Preston (cnd), Westminster Abbey Choir *(rec All Saints' Church, London, England, Feb 1985)* † Missa "Papae marcelli", R. 12; G. Allegri:Miserere; Anerio:Vocal Music; Giovannelli:Jubilate Deo; G. B. Nanino:Haec dies PARC ▲ 15517 [DDD] (16.97)

Veni sponsa Christi (motet) for 4 Voices (1563)

G. Guest (cnd), St. John's College Choir Cambridge ("Allegri-Miserere") † G. Allegri:Salmo Miserere mei Deus; O. de Lassus:Bell'Amfitrit'altera CFP (Eminence) ▲ 2180 [DDD] (16.97)

Venit Michaël Archangelus (1569)

M. Berry (cnd), Schola Gregoriana of Cambridge *(rec Apr 1998)* ("Angels from the Vatican") † Ave Regina coelorum; Anonymous:Agnus Dei; Alleluia, assumpta est Maria; Angeli, Archangeli; Angelis suis mandavitde te; Angelus Domini descendit; Ave Maria; Benedicite Dominum; Christe, sanctorum decus Angelorum; Dixit Angelus ad Iacob; Domine Jesu Christe; Exsultet iam Angelica turba caelorum; Facta est cum Angelo; Gloria; Hodie nobis caelorum Rex; In Paradisum; Kyrie; Sanctus; Stetit Angelus; Te laudamus; Te Deum laudamus; Marenzio:Qual mormorio soave; Traditional:Angelus ad pastores ait; Victoria:Duo Seraphim HER ▲ 220 [DDD] (18.97)

PALIDER, ALAN (1959-

The Narwhal for Contrabassoon & Piano, Op. 11 (1993)

S. Nigro (ctbn), M. Lindeblad (pno) *(rec Chicago)* ("Susan Nigro & the Big Bassoon") † Doran:Movts Db; Draganski:Heart's Desire; Muradian:Con Ctbn, Op. 86; R. Nicholson:Miniature Suite Ctbn; F. Warren:Music for Ctbn, Op. 28 CRYS ▲ 346 (15.97)

PALMER, ROBERT (1915-

Quintet for Clarinet, Strings & Piano (1952; rev 1953)

K. Kooper (vn), P. Doktor (va), F. Sherry (vc), A. Bloom (cl), M. L. Boehm (pno) † R. Cordero:Qnt Fl; Rochberg:Trio 1 Pno ALBA ▲ 153 [DDD] (16.97)

Sonata No. 3 for Piano (1979)

R. Salvatore (pno) ("Music in the American Grain") † P. Bowles:Carretera de Estepona; Latin American Pieces; H. Johnson:Son Pno; La Montaine:Son Pno, Op. 3 CED ▲ 10 [DDD] (16.97)

PALMER, RUDOLPH (1952-

O Magnum Mysterium (1993)

W. Payn (cnd), Rooke Chapel Choir, D. Fortunato (mez) *(rec Bucknell U., Lewisburg, PA, United States of America)* ("An American Collage") † A. Copland:In the Beginning; Duckworth:Southern Harmony; J. Duke:Songs; J. Hill:Medieval Lyrics; Sweet & Triune Harmony; Hoiby:I Was There; Lady of the Harbor; Let this Mind Be in You; Shepherd; Hundley:Astronomers; Isaac Greentree; Sea is Swimming ALBA ▲ 98 [ADD] (16.97)

PALMGREN, SELIM (1878-1951)

Majnat for Piano

J. Vaabensted (pno) ("Pearls for Solo Piano in the Nordic Tone") † E. Grieg:Lyric Pieces; H. Saeverud:Rondo amoroso; Sibelius:Pno Music DANR 2-▲ 493

West Finnish Dance for Piano

B. Moiseiwitsch (pno) ("In Recital") † Beethoven:Andante Pno, WoO 57; Chopin:Études Pno; Fant-Impromptu, Op. 66; Son Pno in b, Op. 58; Mussorgsky:Pictures at an Exhibition; R. Schumann:Carnaval, Op. 9; Kreisleriana, Op. 16; Symphonic Etudes, Op. 13 PHS 2-▲ 9192 (33.97)

PÁLSSON, PÁLL PAMPICHLER (1928-

Music of Pálsson

S. Saemundsdóttir (sop), R. F. Bragadóttir (mez)—Gudis-Mana-Hasi; Crystals; Tomorro; August Sonnet; September Sonnet; Lantao; 6 Thoughtful Songs ("Chamber Works") MFIC ▲ 807

PAMER, IGNAZ MICHAEL (1782-1827)

Ländler for Strings

Vienna Waltz Ensemble *(rec Chicago, IL, July & Oct, 1998)* † Walzer; Anonymous:Brat-Lenerl; Schellerl-Tanz; Tanz; Gregora:Music of Gregora; J. Haydn:Jahreszeiten (sels); J. N. Hummel:German Dances for the Redoutensaal; Pössinger:Minuets Strs; Joh. Strauss:Wiener Carneval-Walzer, Op. 3 DENW ▲ 102 (16.97)

Walzer for 2 Violins & Bass

Vienna Waltz Ensemble *(rec Chicago, IL, July & Oct, 1998)* † Ländler; Anonymous:Brat-Lenerl; Schellerl-Tanz; Tanz; Gregora:Music of Gregora; J. Haydn:Jahreszeiten (sels); J. N. Hummel:German Dances for the Redoutensaal; Pössinger:Minuets Strs; Joh. Strauss:Wiener Carneval-Walzer, Op. 3 DENW ▲ 102 (16.97)

PANDOLFI MEALLI, GIOVANNI ANTONIO (fl 1660-69)

Sonatas (6) for Violin & optional Continuo, Op. 3 (1660)

A. Manze (vn), R. Egarr (hpd) † Sons Vn, Op. 4 HAM ▲ 907241 (18.97)

Sonatas (6) for Violin & optional Continuo, Op. 4 (1660)

A. Manze (vn), R. Egarr (hpd) † Sons Vn, Op. 3 HAM ▲ 907241 (18.97)

A. Manze (vn), F. Jacobs (thb), R. Egarr (hpd) CCL ▲ 5894 [DDD] (18.97)

PANHUYSEN, PAUL (20th cent)

Partitas (3) for Long Strings (1997)

P. Panhuysen (strs) *(rec Het Apollohuis, Eindhoven, Netherlands)* XIRE ▲ 122 [DDD]

PANIZZA, GIACOMO (1804-1860)

Ballabile con variazioni from the Ballet Ettore Fieramosca for Clarinet & Piano

B. Röthlisberger (cl), S. Andres (pno) ("Il Clarinetto all'Opera") † L. Bassi:Divertimento on themes from Donizetti's La F; Cavallini:Adagio sentimentale; Fant on Motifs; Labanchi:Fant on Verdi's Aida; Lovreglio:Fant da concerto on Motifs of Verdi's La tra; Spadina:Duetto GALL ▲ 916 [DDD] (18.97)

PANTILLON, FRANÇOIS (1928-

Bethlehem (oratorio) for Soprano, Narrator, Organ, Orchestra & Chorus (1995)

C. Goetze (sop), R. Rosen (nar), P. Laubschet (org), F. Pantillon (cnd), Biel SO, Pro Arte Chorale, Bern Vocal Ensemble † W. A. Mozart:Mass 17, K.337 GALL ▲ 893 [DDD] (18.97)

Missa brevis di San Pedro for Organ & Chorus (1992)

P. Laubschet (org), F. Pantillon (cnd), Bern Vocal Ensemble *(rec La Salle Musica de La Chaux-de-Fonds)* † Noël des Bergers; Poème Org; Trio 1029 GALL ▲ 884 [DDD] (19.97)

PANTILLON, FRANÇOIS (cont.)

Le Noël des Bergers (cantata) for Soprano, Organ & Chorus [after Arnoul Gréban] (1962)

C. Gaetze (sop), P. Laubschet (org), F. Pantillon (cnd), Bern Vocal Ensemble *(rec La Salle Musica de La Chaux-de-Fonds)* † Missa brevis; Poème Org; Trio 1029 GALL ▲ 884 [DDD] (19.97)

Poème for Organ [after Psalm 130] (1991; rev 1994)

P. Laubschet (org) *(rec l'Eglise française de Berne)* † Missa brevis; Noël des Bergers; Trio 1029 GALL ▲ 884 [DDD] (19.97)

Trio 1029 for Piano, Violin & Cello (1992)

Pantillon Trio *(rec La Salle Musica de La Chaux-de-Fonds)* † Missa brevis; Noël des Bergers; Poème Org GALL ▲ 884 [DDD] (19.97)

PANUFNIK, ANDRZEJ (1914-1991)

Arbor Cosmica (12 evocations) for 12 Strings (or String Orchestra) (1983)

A. Panufnik (cnd), (Royal) Concertgebouw Orch † Sinf sacra NON ▲ 79228 (16.97)

Sinfonia sacra (1963)

A. Panufnik (cnd), New York Chamber SO † Arbor Cosmica NON ▲ 79228 (16.97)

Song to the Virgin Mary for Chorus (or 6 solo Voices) (1964; rev 1970)

S. Cleobury (cnd), King's College Choir Cambridge ("Credo") † K. Penderecki:Choral Music; S. Rachmaninoff:All-Night Vigil, Op. 37; Liturgy of St. John Chrysostom, Op. 31; I. Stravinsky:Choral Music EMIC ▲ 56439 (16.97)

Symphony No. 8, "Sinfonia votiva" (1981)

S. Ozawa (cnd), Boston SO † R. Sessions:Con Orch HYP ▲ 66050 [DDD] (18.97)

PANULA, JORMA (1930-

Adagio & Allegro for Saxophone & Strings (1982)

P. Savijoki (sax), J. Panula (cnd), Stockholm New CO † Glazunov:Con A Sax, Op. 109; L.-E. Larsson:Con Sax, Op. 14 BIS ▲ 218 [DDD] (17.97)

PANZER, ELIZABETH (20th cent)

Green Tea with Oranges for Harp (1998)

E. Panzer (hp) ("Dancing in Place") † Invocation Hp; Syncophony Hp; Beglarian:Play Nice; Brazelton:Down n Harp n All a Rond o; W. M. Chambers:Moments Hp; Einhorn:New Pages Pnos; Hovda:Dancing in Place; Matamoros:Re: Elizabeth OOD ▲ 56 [DDD] (16.97)

Invocation for Harp (1998)

E. Panzer (hp) ("Dancing in Place") † Green Tea with Oranges; Syncophony Hp; Beglarian:Play Nice; Brazelton:Down n Harp n All a Rond o; W. M. Chambers:Moments Hp; Einhorn:New Pages Pnos; Hovda:Dancing in Place; Matamoros:Re: Elizabeth OOD ▲ 56 [DDD] (16.97)

Syncophony for Harp (1998)

E. Panzer (hp) ("Dancing in Place") † Green Tea with Oranges; Invocation Hp; Beglarian:Play Nice; Brazelton:Down n Harp n All a Rond o; W. M. Chambers:Moments Hp; Einhorn:New Pages Pnos; Hovda:Dancing in Place; Matamoros:Re: Elizabeth OOD ▲ 56 [DDD] (16.97)

PANZINI, ANGELO (1820-1886)

Divertimento on themes from Verdi's I Lombardi for Piano 6-Hands

L. Bavaj (pno), F. Venanzoni (pno), G. Galterio (pno) *(rec Oct 1996)* ("Fantasie e Divertimenti su Opera di Verdi") † Divert on Luisa Miller; Divert on Nabucco; Divert on Trovatore; Dacci:Fantasia brilliante on themes from Verdi's Vespri; Fantasia on themes from Verdi's La Traviata MUIM ▲ 10037 [DDD] (18.97)

Divertimento on themes from Verdi's Luisa Miller for Piano 6-Hands

L. Bavaj (pno), F. Venanzoni (pno), G. Galterio (pno) *(rec Oct 1996)* ("Fantasie e Divertimenti su Opera di Verdi") † Divert on Lombardi; Divert on Nabucco; Divert on Trovatore; Dacci:Fantasia brilliante on themes from Verdi's Vespri; Fantasia on themes from Verdi's La Traviata MUIM ▲ 10037 [DDD] (18.97)

Divertimento on themes from Verdi's Nabucco for Piano 6-Hands

L. Bavaj (pno), F. Venanzoni (pno), G. Galterio (pno) *(rec Oct 1996)* ("Fantasie e Divertimenti su Opera di Verdi") † Divert on Lombardi; Divert on Luisa Miller; Divert on Trovatore; Dacci:Fantasia brilliante on themes from Verdi's Vespri; Fantasia on themes from Verdi's La Traviata MUIM ▲ 10037 [DDD] (18.97)

Divertimento on themes from Verdi's Il Trovatore for Piano 6-Hands

L. Bavaj (pno), F. Venanzoni (pno), G. Galterio (pno) *(rec Oct 1996)* ("Fantasie e Divertimenti su Opera di Verdi") † Divert on Lombardi; Divert on Luisa Miller; Divert on Nabucco; Dacci:Fantasia brilliante on themes from Verdi's Vespri; Fantasia on themes from Verdi's La Traviata MUIM ▲ 10037 [DDD] (18.97)

PAPA, FRANCESCO (18th cent)

Concerto in G for Flute & Strings

G. Petrucci (fl), C. F. Sedazzari (cnd), Schubert Camerata *(rec live, Rome, Italy, July 27, 1995)* ("5 Concertos for Flute & Strings from the Neapolitan School of the 1700's") † Angrisani:Con Fl; Prota:Con Fl; Sciroli:Con Fl; Servillo:Con 1 Fl BONG ▲ 5553 [ADD] (16.97)

PAPE, ANDY (1955-

CaDance 4 2 for 2 Percussion

Safri Duo ("Works for Percussion") † Fuzzy:Fireplay; A. Koppel:Toccata; M. Miki:Mar Spiritual; Nørgård:Echo Zone I-III CHN (New Direction) ▲ 9330 [DDD] (16.97)

I've Never Seen a Butterfly Here (song cycle) for Soprano, Violin & Accordian (1990-92)

L. Nielsen (sop), S. K. Claesson (vn), G. Draugsvoll (acc) *(rec 1995-96)* ("Works for Classical Accordian") † Frounberg:Dirge: Other Echos Inhabit the Garden; M. W. Holm:Troglodyt; K. I. Jørgensen:Cadenza; Kanding:Winter Darkness; L. Kayser:Confetti MARC ▲ 8224028 [DDD] (13.97)

PAPE, GERARD (1955-

Music of Pape

J. Pape (sop), C. Daroux (fl) *(2 Electro-Acoustic Songs)*, The Arditti String Quartet *(Le Fleuve au Désir)*, N. Isherwood (db) *(Monologue)*, Vox Nova *(Battle)*, P. Kientzy (sax), P. Mefano (cnd), Ensemble 2e2m *(Makebenach)* MODE ▲ 67 [DDD] (17.97)

PAPINEAU-COUTURE, JEAN (1916-

Aria for solo Violin (1946)

S. Staryk (vn) *(rec Montreal, Aug 1964)* ("Sonatas for Solo Violin") † P. Hindemith:Son Vn; Pisendel:Son solo Vn; S. Prokofiev:Son Vc; J. W. A. Stamitz:Diverts solo Vn ORIO ▲ 7809 (13.97)

Départ for Flute (1974-75)

R. Aitken (fl) *(rec Toronto, Canada)* † Dialogues; Idée; Nuit; Slano; Verségéres CTR ▲ 6499 [DDD] (16.97)

Dialogues for Violin & Piano (1967)

D. Lupien (vn), L. Pelletier (pno) *(rec Toronto, Canada)* † Départ; Idée; Nuit; Slano; Verségéres CTR ▲ 6499 [DDD] (16.97)

Idée for Piano (1979-82)

L. Pelletier (pno) *(rec Toronto, Canada)* † Dialogues; Départ; Nuit; Slano; Verségéres CTR ▲ 6499 [DDD] (16.97)

Nuit for Piano

C. Athparia (pno) † Debussy:Estampes; Images (6) Pno; Isle joyeuse; E. Granados:Danzas españolas (10) Pno; F. Morel:Études de sonorité; M. Ravel:Jeux d'eau SNE ▲ 584 (16.97)

L. Pelletier (pno) *(rec Toronto, Canada)* † Dialogues; Départ; Idée; Slano; Verségéres CTR ▲ 6499 [DDD] (16.97)

Slano for Strings (1976)

Accordes String Trio *(rec Toronto, Canada)* † Dialogues; Départ; Idée; Nuit; Verségéres CTR ▲ 6499 [DDD] (16.97)

Verségéres for Flute (1975)

R. Aitken (fl) *(rec Toronto, Canada)* † Dialogues; Départ; Idée; Nuit; Slano CTR ▲ 6499 [DDD] (16.97)

PAPONAUD, MARCEL (1893-1988)

Toccata for Organ

J. S. Whiteley (org) *(rec Cavaillé-Coll org, St. Ouen, Rouen, France)* † P. Cochereau:Symphonie; M. Dupré:Préludes & Fugues, Op. 36; Vars on Adeste Fidèles; Ibert:Choral sur Justorum animae; Vierne:Méditation Org PRIO ▲ 619 [DDD] (16.97)

PARADIES, PIETRO DOMENICO (1707-1791)

Sonatas (12) for Harpsichord (1754)

E. Baiano (hpd) SYM ▲ 95140 (18.97)

O. Dantone (hpd) ("Complete Sonatas for Harpsichord, Vol. 1") STRV ▲ 33420 [DDD] (16.97)

O. Dantone (hpd) ("Complete Sonatas for Harpsichord, Vol. 2") STRV ▲ 33421 (16.97)

E. Smith (hpd) *(rec Aug 27-29, 1996)* † G. B. Grazioli:Sons Hpd; Pescetti:Sons Hpd; Platti:Sons Hpd, Op. 4; D. Scarlatti:Sons Kbd STRV ▲ 80007 [DDD] (12.97)

PARASKEVAÍDIS, GRACIELA (1940-

sendas for 7 Winds & Piano (1992)

Aventure Ensemble † Aharonián:Gente; Bruttger:Monolith; Etkin:Abgesang Mambo; Luzuriaga:Grave Bossa; Riehm:Sarca - il fiume Sarca; Varèse:Octandre ARSM ▲ 1147 [DDD] (17.97)

PARAY, PAUL (1886-1979)

Mass for the 500th Anniversary of the Death of Joan of Arc for solo Voices, Orchestra & Chorus (1931)

L. Haywood (sop), T. Patrick-Harris (mez), J. Harris (ten), J. Koc (b-bar), J. Paul (cnd), Royal Scottish National Orch, Royal Scottish National Chorus † Sym 1 REF ▲ 78 [DDD] (16.97)

PARAY, PAUL (cont.)
Symphony No. 1 in C (1935)
J. Paul (cnd), Royal Scottish National Orch † Mass for the 500th Anniversary of the Death of Joa
REF ▲ 78 [DDD] (16.97)
PAREDES, HILDA (1957-
Permutaciones (2 versions) for Violin (1985)
I. Arditti (vn) *(rec Univ of Mexico City, Apr 1995)* † 7th Seed MODE ▲ 60 [DDD] (17.97)
The Seventh Seed (chamber opera in 3 acts) for Soprano, Baritone, String Quartet, Percussion & Chorus [lib Karen Whiteson] (1990-91)
L. Ambriz (sop), J. Oakley-Tucker (bar), S. Schick (perc), Arditti String Quartet [w. Virginia Sublett (sop), Carol Plantamura (mez),] *(rec Univ of CA San Diego, Mar 2-3, 1995)* † Permutaciones *(E lib text)*
MODE ▲ 60 [DDD] (17.97)
PAREDES, ROBERT (1948-
Small Writing for Cello, Speaking Cellist & Percussion [to the memory of Kenneth Gaburo] (1993-94)
C. Hultgren (vc), K. Collins (perc) ("Music of the Next Moment - Craig Hultgren") † Burrier:II; C. Hultgren:Chained Vc Improvisation; Double Bow Improvisation; Marth:They're Still Running; C. N. Mason:Artist & His Model; L. Nielson:Valentine Mechanique; J. C. Ross:Encore Vc INNO ▲ 502 (14.97)
PARISOTTI, ALESSANDRO (1835-1913)
Se tu m'ami (aria) for Voice & Piano [formerly attrib Pergolesi]
C. Bartoli (mez), G. Fischer (pno) *(rec 1990)* ("A Portrait") † G. Caccini:Amarilli mia bella; W. A. Mozart:Clemenza di Tito (sels); Così fan tutte (sels); Don Giovanni (sels); Nozze di Figaro (sels); G. Rossini:Cenerentola (sels); Maometto II (sels); Semiramide (sels); F. Schubert:Songs (misc colls) PLON ▲ 48300 [DDD] (17.97) ▮ 48300 [DDD] (11.98)
PARK, MARIA HESTER (1775-1822)
Concerto in E♭ for Harpsichord (ca 1795)
B. Harbach (hpd) † Son Hpd, Op. 7; Barthélémon:Son Hpd, Op. 3; E. Turner:Lesson I Hpd; Lesson II Hpd
GAS ▲ 281 (16.97)
Sonata in F for Harpsichord, Op. 4
B. Harbach (hpd) ("18th Century Women Composers: Music for Solo Harpsichord, Vol. 1") † M. V. Auenbrugg:Son in E♭ Hpd; Barthélémon:Son Hpd; E. De Gambarini:Pieces Hpd, Op. 2; M. Martinez:Son in A Hpd; Son in E Hpd
GAS ▲ 272 [DDD] (16.97)
B. A. Miller (pno) *(rec Bethesda, MD, Mar 1996)* † Son Hpd, Op. 7; Mendelssohn (-Hensel):Pno Music
CENT ▲ 2320 [DDD] (16.97)
Sonata in C for Harpsichord, Op. 7 (ca 1796)
B. Harbach (hpd) † Con Hpd; Barthélémon:Son Hpd, Op. 3; E. Turner:Lesson I Hpd; Lesson II Hpd
GAS ▲ 281 (16.97)
B. A. Miller (pno) *(rec Bethesda, MD, Mar 1996)* † Son Hpd, Op. 4; Mendelssohn (-Hensel):Pno Music
CENT ▲ 2320 [DDD] (16.97)
PARKER, HORATIO (1863-1919)
Compositions (4) for Organ, Op. 36 (1893)
R. Morris (org) ("Fugues, Fantasia, and Variations: 19th Century American Concert Organ Music") † D. Buck:Grand Son, Op. 22; Paine:Fantaisie on Ein feste, Op. 13; Thayer:Vars on Russian National Hymn, Op. 12; G. Whiting:Postlude Org, Op. 53 NWW ▲ 80280 (16.97)
Concerto in e♭ for Organ & Orchestra, Op. 55 (1902)
J. Levick (cnd), Nebraska CO † Hora novissima ALBA 2-▲ 124 (25.97)
Hora novissima for solo Voices, Orchestra & Chorus (1893)
A. Soranno (sop), J. Simson (mez), D. Andersen (b-bar), K. Hall (b-bar), J. Levick (cnd), Nebraska CO, Abendmusik Chorus, Nebraska Wesleyan Univ Choir † Con Org, Op. 55 ALBA 2-▲ 124 (25.97)
Lyrics (6) for Piano, Op. 25 (1891)
P. Kairoff (pno) *(rec May 7, 1998)* † Morceaux caractéristiques, Op. 49; Morceaux caractéristiques, Op. 9; Sketches Pno, Op. 19 ALBA ▲ 315 [DDD] (16.97)
Morceaux caractéristiques (5) for Piano, Op. 9 (1886)
P. Kairoff (pno)—Gavotte; Caprice; Elegie *(rec May 7, 1998)* † Lyrics Pno, Op. 25; Morceaux caractéristiques, Op. 49; Sketches Pno, Op. 19 ALBA ▲ 315 [DDD] (16.97)
Morceaux caractéristiques (3) for Piano, Op. 49 (1899)
M. Frager (pno) ("Edward MacDowell & Company") † A. M. Foerster:On the Sea; H. F. Gilbert:Mazurka Pno; H. H. Huss:Preludes Pno, Op. 17; MacDowell:Virtuoso Etudes, Op. 46; E. Nevin:Etudes Pno, Op. 18; Paine:Pieces Pno, Op. 41; Romance Pno, Op. 12 NWW ▲ 80206 [DDD] (16.97)
P. Kairoff (pno)—No. 3, "Valse Gracile" *(rec May 7, 1998)* † Lyrics Pno, Op. 25; Morceaux caractéristiques, Op. 9; Sketches Pno, Op. 19 ALBA ▲ 315 [DDD] (16.97)
A Northern Ballad for Orchestra (1899)
I. Hegyi (cnd), Albany SO † G. W. Chadwick:Sym 2 NWW ▲ 339 [DDD] (16.97)
Sketches (4) for Piano, Op. 19 (1890)
P. Kairoff (pno) *(rec May 7, 1998)* † Lyrics Pno, Op. 25; Morceaux caractéristiques, Op. 49; Morceaux caractéristiques, Op. 9 ALBA ▲ 315 [DDD] (16.97)
Suite for Piano, Violin & Cello, Op. 35 (1893)
Rawlins Piano Trio † Trio Pno, Op. 7; S. Adler:Trio 1 Pno; Heilman:Suite Pno Trio; Trio Pno
ALBA ▲ 107 [DDD] (16.97)
Trio in C for Piano, Violin & Cello, Op. 7
Rawlins Piano Trio † Suite Pno, Op. 35; S. Adler:Trio 1 Pno; Heilman:Suite Pno Trio; Trio Pno
ALBA ▲ 107 [DDD] (16.97)
PARKER, JIM (1934-
Betjeman's London (6 poems) for Speaker & Chamber Orchestra
G. Benson (spkr), C. Herbert (spkr), D. Chernaik (cnd), Apollo CO † Con Cl; Oscar Wilde:Sym in Yellow; G. Gershwin:Damsel in Distress (sels); B. Powell:Songs MER ▲ 84396 (16.97)
Concerto for Clarinet & Strings (1954)
I. Herbert (cl), D. Chernaik (cnd), Apollo CO † Betjeman's London; Oscar Wilde:Sym in Yellow; G. Gershwin:Damsel in Distress (sels); B. Powell:Songs MER ▲ 84396 (16.97)
Oscar Wilde:Symphony in Yellow for Speaker & Chamber Orchestra
G. Benson (spkr), C. Herbert (spkr), D. Chernaik (cnd), Apollo CO † Betjeman's London; Con Cl; G. Gershwin:Damsel in Distress (sels); B. Powell:Songs MER ▲ 84396 (16.97)
PARKER, JON KIMURA (20th cent)
Pan Dreams for Flute & Piano (1989)
J. Walker (fl), K. Fitz-Gerald (pno) *(rec Tuscon, AZ, Mar 1997)* ("The 4th Tuscon Winter Chamber Music Festival") † B. Bartók:Contrasts, Sz.111; I. Dahl:Concerto à tre; J. Harbison:Twilight Music ARIZ ▲ 97101 [DDD] (16.97)
PARKER, PHILIP (20th cent)
Beneath the Canopy for Flute & Percussion
Armstrong Flute & Percussion Duo *(rec Penn State Univ School of Music University Park, PA, May 1995)* ("Exotic Chamber Music") † J. L. Adams:Songbirdsongs; I. Dahl:Duo concertante; Marttinen:Alfa; Mols:Interplay; E. Vercoe:Fantavia CENT ▲ 2273 [DDD] (16.97)
PARKIN, ERIC (1924-
Mayerl Shots (Set 3) for Piano (1995)
E. Parkin (pno) *(rec Dec 11-12, 1995)* ("Scallywag: A Further Tribute to Billy Mayerl") † W. J. Mayerl:Piano Music (ragtime & novelty compositions); Trans Pno PRIO ▲ 565 (16.97)
PARKINS, ZEENA (20th cent)
Music of Zeena Parkins
Gangster Band—Maul:Benya Krik; Zero Hour; Wie Sieben Meilen Miesen Dirach; Betrayer; Torrid Zone; Dough; Weaponistic Charms; Italyid; No Thing; Simcha; Chase; Hod; Blue Mirror:Ice Pick; The Dasher; Red; 2Gun; Abaddabbah; Phrases; Nails ("Mouth=Maul=Betrayer") TZA ▲ 7109 [DDD] (16.97)
S. Parkins (vn), M. Parkins (vc), Z. Parkins (elec/kbd), I. Mori (perc)—Isabelle: outside; The Magician; EL QUED:Romance; Si Mahmoud Essadi:The Convert; La Petite Gironde:Victor Barrucand lends a hand; Fever; Monastery of Kenadsa; AIN SEFRA:In Captivity & Flood; Oblivion Seekers; The Breath of Night; Look out for Gail Garrity-Girl Wonder; Chamber of Eternal Wisdom; the uncanny feeling of being watched; MY GOD! Have I flung myself into an endless void?; Ju-Jitsu Jimmy-Impulse Beam Rising ("Isabelle") AVAK ▲ 18 (21.97)
PARMERUD, AKE (20th cent)
Retur for Saxophone Quartet
Stockholm Saxophone Quartet ("Links") † Enström:Vigil; Feiler:Anvil & Parachutes; Lindwall:Cut Up; Rydberg:Link/Sequence; Samuelsson:Signal Sax Qt CAPA ▲ 21517 (16.97)
Strings & Shadows for Harp (1993)
S. A. Claro (hp) *(rec Denmark, Nov 1994-Jan 1995)* † Frounberg:Worlds Apart; Graugaard:Incrustations; Lippe:Music Hp Tape; Saariaho:Fall CENT ▲ 2284 [DDD] (16.97)

PARRIS, ROBERT (1924-
Book of Imaginary Beings for Orchestra
Polish National RSO † Con Trbn; Con Vn; Fant & Fugue Vc CRI ▲ 792 (16.97)
Concerto for Trombone & Orchestra
R. Siwek (trbn), Polish National RSO † Book of Imaginary Beings; Con Vn; Fant & Fugue Vc CRI ▲ 792 (16.97)
Concerto for Violin, Cello, Piano & Percussion
Polish National RSO † Book of Imaginary Beings; Con Trbn; Fant & Fugue Vc CRI ▲ 792 (16.97)
Fantasy & Fugue for Cello
L. Barnet (vc), Polish National RSO † Book of Imaginary Beings; Con Trbn; Con Vn CRI ▲ 792 (16.97)
Sonata for Violin (1965)
C. Macomber (vn) *(rec Music Division SUNY, Purchase, New York, May 10, 1991, Feb 5, 1993 & Feb 19-22, 1995)* ("Songs of Solitude: American Works for Solo Violin") † E. Carter:Riconoscenza; Davidovsky:Synchronism 9; S. Gerber:Fant Vn; Songs without Words; J. Harbison:Songs of Solitude; Ran:Inscriptions CRI ▲ 706 [DDD] (16.97)
PARRY, (CHARLES) HUBERT (HASTINGS) (1848-1918)
Adagissimo for Piano
A. Goldstone (pno) *(rec 1994)* † Charakterbilder; Son 1 Pno; Son 2 Pno; Theme & Vars; M. Gould:American Symphonette 2; Columbia; Con Va; Flourishes & Galop; Housewarming; Soundings; Sym of Spirituals
ALBA 2-▲ 13 [AAD]
Blest Pair of Sirens (ode) for Orchestra & Chorus [text Milton] (1887)
R. Hickox (cnd), London SO, London Sym Chorus † I Was Glad; E. Elgar:Dream of Gerontius, Op. 38
CHN 2-▲ 8641 [DDD] (33.97)
Charakterbilder for Piano (1872)
A. Goldstone (pno) *(rec 1994)* † Charakterbilder; Son 1 Pno; Son 2 Pno; Theme & Vars; M. Gould:American Symphonette 2; Columbia; Con Va; Flourishes & Galop; Housewarming; Soundings; Sym of Spirituals
ALBA 2-▲ 13 [AAD]
Choral Music
R. Allwood (cnd), Rodolfus Choir—There rolls the deep; If I had but two little wings; Love is a sickness; Tell me, O love; Phillis; How sweet the answer; What voice of gladness; Seven Part Songs; La belle dame sans merci; Sorrow and Pain; Six Modern Lyrics *(rec England)* ("Songs of Farewell") † Shulbrede Tunes HER ▲ 217 [DDD] (18.97)
Concertstück in g for Orchestra [single movt] (1877)
M. Bamert (cnd), London PO † Elegy for Brahms; From Death to Life; Sym Vars CHN ▲ 7006 [DDD] (13.97)
M. Bamert (cnd), London PO † Sym 1 CHN ▲ 9062 [DDD] (16.97)
Elegy for Brahms for Orchestra (1897)
M. Bamert (cnd), London PO † Concertstück; From Death to Life; Sym Vars CHN ▲ 7006 [DDD] (13.97)
M. Bamert (cnd), London PO † From Death to Life; Sym 5 CHN ▲ 8955 [DDD] (16.97)
An English Suite for String Orchestra [Prelude; Sarabande; Minuet]
W. Boughton (cnd), English String Orch † F. Bridge:Irish Melody; Sir Roger de Coverley; There Is a Willow Grows Aslant; G. Finzi:Ecologue, Op. 10 NIMB ▲ 5366 (16.97)
A. Leaper (cnd), Capella Istropolitana *(rec Apr 12-16 & Sept 17-19, 1989)* ("English String Festival") † Lady Radnor's Suite; F. Bridge:Lament Strs; E. Elgar:Elegy; Intro & Allegro, Op. 47; Serenade Strs, Op. 20
NXIN ▲ 550331 [DDD] (5.97)
From Death to Life (symphonic poem) for Orchestra [in 2 connected movts] (1914)
M. Bamert (cnd), London PO † Concertstück; Elegy for Brahms; Sym Vars CHN ▲ 7006 [DDD] (13.97)
M. Bamert (cnd), London PO † Elegy for Brahms; Sym 5 CHN ▲ 8955 [DDD] (16.97)
Hands across the Centuries (suite) for Piano
P. Jacobs (pno) ("Piano Music of Charles Parry") † Shulbrede Tunes; Theme & Vars PRIO ▲ 451 [DDD] (16.97)
I Was Glad (anthem with processional music for the coronation of Edward VII) for Orchestra & Chorus (1902)
P. Daniel (cnd), English Northern Philharmonia, Leeds Festival Chorus *(rec Town Hall, Leeds, England, 1996)* † Jerusalem; M. Arnold:Tam o'Shanter Ov, Op. 51; E. Elgar:Enigma Vars, Op. 36; Pomp & Circumstance, Op. 39; W. Walton:Crown Imperial; Orb & Sceptre; H. J. Wood:Fant on British Seas Songs NXIN ▲ 8553981 [DDD] (5.97)
R. Hickox (cnd), London SO, London Sym Chorus † Blest Pair of Sirens; E. Elgar:Dream of Gerontius, Op. 38
CHN 2-▲ 8641 [DDD] (33.97)
Invocation to Music (ode) for Soprano, Tenor, Bass, Orchestra & Chorus [text R. Bridges in honor of Purcell] (1895)
L. Dawson (sop), A. Davies (ten), B. R. Cook (bar), M. Bamert (cnd), London PO, London Phil Chorus [ENG]
CHN ▲ 9025 [DDD] (16.97)
Jerusalem for Orchestra & Chorus
P. Daniel (cnd), English Northern Philharmonia, Leeds Festival Chorus *(rec Town Hall, Leeds, England, 1996)* † I Was Glad; M. Arnold:Tam o'Shanter Ov, Op. 51; E. Elgar:Enigma Vars, Op. 36; Pomp & Circumstance, Op. 39; W. Walton:Crown Imperial; Orb & Sceptre; H. J. Wood:Fant on British Seas Songs NXIN ▲ 8553981 [DDD] (5.97)
Job (oratorio) for SATB solo Voices, Orchestra & Chorus (1892)
H. D. Wetton (cnd), Royal PO, H. D. Wetton (cnd), Guildford Choral Society, T. Spence (bar), P. Coleman-Wright (bar), N. Davies (bar), J. M. Hitchcock (bar) HYP ▲ 67025 (18.97)
Lady Radnor's Suite for String Orchestra (1894)
W. Boughton (cnd), English String Orch † F. Bridge:Suite Str Orch; G. Butterworth:Banks of Green Willow Orch; English Idylls; Shropshire Lad NIMB ▲ 5068 [DDD] (16.97)
A. Leaper (cnd), Capella Istropolitana *(rec Apr 12-16 & Sept 17-19, 1989)* ("English String Festival") † English Suite; F. Bridge:Lament Strs; E. Elgar:Elegy; Intro & Allegro, Op. 47; Serenade Strs, Op. 20 NXIN ▲ 550331 [DDD] (5.97)
The Lotus Eaters for Soprano, Orchestra & Chorus [text Tennyson] (1892)
D. Jones (mez), M. Bamert (cnd), London PO, London Phil Chorus [ENG] † Soul's Ransom
CHN ▲ 8990 [DDD] (16.97)
Overture to an Unwritten Tragedy in a for Orchestra (1893)
D. Lloyd-Jones (cnd), English Northern Philharmonia ("Victorian Concert Overtures") † E. Elgar:Froissart, Op. 19; Macfarren:Chevy Chace; A. Mackenzie:Brittania, Op. 52; H. Pierson:Romeo & Juliet, Op. 86; A. Sullivan:Macbeth (concert ov) HYP ▲ 66515 [DDD] (18.97)
A. Penny (cnd), Royal Scottish National Orch *(rec Glasgow, Aug 7-8 & Sept 20-21, 1995)* † Sym Vars; Sym 2
NXIN ▲ 553469 [DDD] (5.97)
Part Songs (7) for a capella Mixed Chorus (1909)
M. Lee (cnd), St. Cecilia Singers—My delight and thy delight *(rec Gloucester Cathedral, England, June 1997)* ("Over Hill, Over Dale") † Six Modern Lyrics; Songs of Farewell; K. Amos:Salisbury Cathedral; Anonymous:Scarborough Fair; She Moved through the Fair; H. Howells:Choral Music; J. Sanders:Anthem of the Incarnation; Traditional:Bobby Shaftoe; Dance to Thy Daddy; Frog & the Crow; Vaughan Williams:Shakespeare Songs
PRIO ▲ 620 [DDD] (16.97)
Shulbrede Tunes (10) for Piano
R. Allwood (cnd), Rodolfus Choir *(rec England)* ("Songs of Farewell") † Choral Music HER ▲ 217 [DDD] (18.97)
P. Jacobs (pno) ("Piano Music of Charles Parry") † Hands accross the Centuries; Theme & Vars
PRIO ▲ 451 [DDD] (16.97)
Six Modern Lyrics for a capella Mixed Chorus (1897)
M. Lee (cnd), St. Cecilia Singers—Music, when soft voices die *(rec Gloucester Cathedral, England, June 1997)* ("Over Hill, Over Dale") † Seven Part Songs; Songs of Farewell; K. Amos:Salisbury Cathedral; Anonymous:Scarborough Fair; She Moved through the Fair; H. Howells:Choral Music; J. Sanders:Anthem of the Incarnation; Traditional:Bobby Shaftoe; Dance to Thy Daddy; Frog & the Crow; Vaughan Williams:Shakespeare Songs
PRIO ▲ 620 [DDD] (16.97)
Sonata No. 1 in F for Piano (1877)
A. Goldstone (pno) *(rec 1994)* † Charakterbilder; Son 1 Pno; Son 2 Pno; Theme & Vars; M. Gould:American Symphonette 2; Columbia; Con Va; Flourishes & Galop; Housewarming; Soundings; Sym of Spirituals
ALBA 2-▲ 13 [AAD]
Sonata No. 2 in A for Piano (1878)
A. Goldstone (pno) *(rec 1994)* † Charakterbilder; Son 1 Pno; Son 2 Pno; Theme & Vars; M. Gould:American Symphonette 2; Columbia; Con Va; Flourishes & Galop; Housewarming; Soundings; Sym of Spirituals
ALBA 2-▲ 13 [AAD]
Songs
S. Varcoe (bar), C. Benson (pno)—Poet's Song; More Fond Than Cushat Dove; Music; Take, O Take Those Lips Away; No Longer Mourn for Me; To Lucasta, on Going to the Wars; If Thou Would'st Ease Thine Heart; To Althea, from Prison; Why So Pale & Wan?; Through the Ivory Gate; Thine Eyes Still Shined for Me; Weep You No More, Sad Fountains; Proud Maisie; Lay a Garland on My Hearse; When Comes My Gwen; Love Is a Bable; And Yet I Love Her Till I Die; Under the Greenwood Tree; On a Time the Amorous Silvy; O Never Say That I Was False of Heart; Ye Little Birds That Sit & Sing; Sleep; Julia; Nightfall in Winter; Dirge in Woods; Spirit of the Spring; What Part of Dread Eternity; Blackbird; She Is My Love Beyond All Thought; Faithful Lover HYP ▲ 67044 (18.97)
Songs of Farewell (6 motets) for Chorus [texts Vaughn, Campian, Davies, Lockhart, Donne] (1916-18)
J. Filsell (org), J. Backhouse (cnd), Vasari Singers ("Songs of Farewell") † F. Bridge:Prayer; Vaughan Williams:Mass GILD ▲ 7132 [DDD] (16.97)

▲ = CD ♦ = Enhanced CD △ = MD ▮ = Cassette Tape ▯ = DCC

PARRY, (CHARLES) HUBERT (HASTINGS) (cont.)
Songs of Farewell (6 motets) for Chorus [texts Vaughn, Campian, Davies, Lockhart, Donne] (1916-18) (cont.)
M. Lee (cnd), St. Cecilia Singers—No. 1, "My Soul, There is a Country" *(rec Gloucester Cathedral, England, June 1997)* ("Over Hill, Over Dale") † Seven Part Songs; Six Modern Lyrics; K. Amos:Salisbury Cathedral; Anonymous:Scarborough Fair; She Moved through the Fair; H. Howells:Choral Music; J. Sanders:Anthem of the Incarnation; Traditional:Bobby Shaftoe; Dance to Thy Daddy; Frog & the Crow; Vaughan Williams:Shakespeare Songs PRIO ▲ 620 [DDD] (16.97)
The Soul's Ransom (sinfonia sacra) for Soprano, Bass, Orchestra & Chorus (1906)
D. Jones (mez), D. Wilson-Johnson (bar), M. Bamert (cnd), London PO, London Phil Chorus [ENG] † Lotus Eaters CHN ▲ 8990 [DDD] (16.97)
Symphonic Variations for Orchestra (1897)
M. Bamert (cnd), London PO † Concertstück; Elegy for Brahms; From Death to Life CHN ▲ 7006 [DDD] (13.97)
M. Bamert (cnd), London PO † Sym 2 CHN ▲ 8961 [DDD] (16.97)
M. Bamert (cnd), London PO † Syms (comp) CHN 3-▲ 9120 [DDD] (48.97)
A. Penny (cnd), Royal Scottish National Orch *(rec Glasgow, Aug 7-8 & Sept 20-21, 1995)* † Ov to an Unwritten Tragedy; Sym 2 NXIN ▲ 553469 [DDD] (5.97)
Symphonies (5) (complete)
M. Bamert (cnd), London PO † Sym Vars CHN 3-▲ 9120 [DDD] (48.97)
Symphony No. 1 in G (1882)
M. Bamert (cnd), London PO † Concertstück CHN ▲ 9062 [DDD] (16.97)
Symphony No. 2 in F, "The Cambridge" (1882-83)
M. Bamert (cnd), London PO † Sym Vars CHN ▲ 8961 [DDD] (16.97)
A. Penny (cnd), Royal Scottish National Orch *(rec Glasgow, Aug 7-8 & Sept 20-21, 1995)* † Ov to an Unwritten Tragedy; Sym Vars NXIN ▲ 553469 [DDD] (5.97)
Symphony No. 3 in C, "The English" (1889)
M. Bamert (cnd), London PO † Sym 4 CHN ▲ 8896 [DDD] (16.97)
L. Hager (cnd), Luxembourg RSO † Brian:Tigers (sels); Foulds:Mirage; Pasquinade Symphonique 1, Op. 98; St. Joan Suite, Op. 98 FORL 2-▲ 16724 [ADD] (32.97)
Symphony No. 4 in e (1889)
M. Bamert (cnd), London PO † Sym 3 CHN ▲ 8896 [DDD] (16.97)
Symphony No. 5 in b, "Symphonic Fantasia" (1912)
M. Bamert (cnd), London PO † Elegy for Brahms; From Death to Life CHN ▲ 8955 [DDD] (16.97)
Theme & Variations (19) in d for Piano (1878-85)
A. Goldstone (pno) *(rec 1994)* † Charakterbilder; Son 1 Pno; Son 2 Pno; Theme & Vars; M. Gould:American Symphonette 2; Columbia; Con Va; Flourishes & Galop; Housewarming; Soundings; Sym of Spirituals ALBA 2-▲ 13 [AAD]
P. Jacobs (pno) ("Piano Music of Charles Parry") † Hands accross the Centuries; Shulbrede Tunes PRIO ▲ 451 [DDD] (16.97)
Trio No. 2 in b for Piano, Violin & Cello (1884)
Deakin Piano Trio † Trio 3 Pno MER ▲ 84225 (16.97)
Trio No. 3 in G for Piano, Violin & Cello (1884-?90)
Deakin Piano Trio † Trio 2 Pno MER ▲ 84225 (16.97)

PARSADANIAN, BORIS (1925-
Symphony No. 1, "To the Memory of the 26 Commisars of Baku"
E. Svetlanov (cnd), Moscow RSO † Sym 2 RUS ▲ 11050 [ADD] (12.97)
Symphony No. 2, "Martyros Sarian"
E. Svetlanov (cnd), Moscow RSO † Sym 1 RUS ▲ 11050 [ADD] (12.97)

PÄRT, ARVO (1935-
Adagio for Piano, Violin & Cello (1992)
Kalichstein-Laredo-Robinson Trio ("Legacies") † L. Kirchner:Trio 2 Pno; S. Silverman:In Celebration; E. T. Zwilich:Trio Pno ARA ▲ 6676 (16.97)
And One of the Pharisees for Chorus (1990)
P. Hillier (cnd), Theater of Voices ("De Profundis") † Beatitudes; Cant Domino; Choral Music; Magnificat for Chorus; Magnificat-Antiphones; Missa sillabica; Solfeggio; Summa Chorus HAM ▲ 907182 [DDD] (18.97)
Annum per annum for Organ (1980)
H. Ericsson (org) [1987 Grönlund Organ] *(rec Sweden, Mar 1992)* ("Baltic Organ Music") † Čiurlionis:Chorale Fugue on 'Aus tiefer Not schrei ich zu...'; Pno Music; Kutavičius:Org Music; Süda:Kbd Music; Vasks:Org Music; Zemzaris:Org Music BIS ▲ 561 [DDD] (17.97)
C. M. Moosmann (org) *(rec St. Martin Cathedral Rottenburg, Apr 12-14, 1994)* ("Annum per annum") † Mein Weg hat Gipfel; Pari intervallo; Trivium; J. Cage:Souvenir Org; Scelsi:In nomine lucis V NALB ▲ 74 (16.97)
Arbos for Brass Ensemble & Percussion (1977-86)
Calefax Reed Quintet [arr Eduard Wesly for reed qnt] *(rec Martin Luther Church Gütersloh, Sept 17-18 & 23-24, 1996)* † Magnificat-Antiphones; Pari intervallo; Summa Orch; W. Byrd:Magnificat; Mass 5 Voc; Senex puerum portabatadoravit; Senex puerum portabatregebat MDG (Scene) ▲ 6190745 [DDD] (17.97)
The Beatitudes for Chorus (1990; rev 1991)
S. Cleobury (cnd), King's College Choir Cambridge ("Ikos") † Magnificat for Chorus; Górecki:Amen; Totus tuus; J. Tavener:Funeral Ikos; Magnificat EMIC ▲ 55096 (16.97)
S. Cleobury (cnd), King's College Choir Cambridge ("Sanctuary") † Cantus in Memory of Benjamin Britten; De Profundis; Festina lente; Fratres VI; Magnificat for Chorus; Summa Orch; Tabula rasa VCL ▲ 45314 [DDD] (16.97)
P. Hillier (cnd), Theater of Voices ("De Profundis") † And 1 of the Pharisees; Cant Domino; Choral Music; Magnificat for Chorus; Magnificat-Antiphones; Missa sillabica; Solfeggio; Summa Chorus HAM ▲ 907182 [DDD] (18.97)
S. Layton (cnd), Polyphony † Berliner Messe; De Profundis; Magnificat for Chorus; Magnificat-Antiphones HYP ▲ 66960 (18.97)
Berliner Messe [Berlin Mass] for Organ & Chorus
S. Layton (cnd), Polyphony † Beatitudes; De Profundis; Magnificat for Chorus; Magnificat-Antiphones HYP ▲ 66960 (18.97)
Oregon Repertory Singers *(rec May 1992)* † L. Harrison:Mass to St. Anthony KOCH ▲ 7177 [DDD] (16.97)
Cantate Domino for Chorus (1977)
P. Hillier (cnd), Theater of Voices ("De Profundis") † And 1 of the Pharisees; Beatitudes; Choral Music; Magnificat for Chorus; Magnificat-Antiphones; Missa sillabica; Solfeggio; Summa Chorus HAM ▲ 907182 [DDD] (18.97)
Cantus in Memory of Benjamin Britten for Bell & String Orchestra (1977)
N. Järvi (cnd), Bergen PO † B. Britten:Peter Grimes (sea interludes & passacaglia); Sym Vc; Young Person's Guide to the Orch, Op. 34 BIS ▲ 420 [DDD] (17.97)
N. Järvi (cnd), Royal Scottish National Orch *(rec Henry Wood Hall Glasgow, Aug 23-24, 1987)* ("Elegy—Music for Strings") † S. Barber:Adagio Strs; Eller:Elegia; G. Mahler:Sym 5; R. Strauss:Metamorphosen CHN ▲ 7039 (13.97)
N. Järvi (cnd), Royal Scottish National Orch ("Music from Estonia, Vol. 2") † Eller:Twilight; Lemba:Sym in c♯; R. Tobias:Julius Caesar; Tormis:Ov 2 CHN ▲ 8656 [DDD] (16.97)
R. Studt (cnd), Bournemouth Sinfonietta ("Sanctuary") † Beatitudes; De Profundis; Festina lente; Fratres VI; Magnificat for Chorus; Summa Orch; Tabula rasa VCL ▲ 45314 [DDD] (16.97)
J. Vartianinen (bells), J. Kantorow (cnd), Tapiola Sinfonietta *(rec Tapiola Concert Hall Finland, 1996)* ("Summa") † Collage on the Theme B-A-C-H; Festina lente; Fratres I Str Qt; Summa Orch; Tabula rasa BIS ▲ 834 [DDD] (17.97)
Choral Music
P. Hillier (cnd), Theater of Voices—De Profundis; Missa Sabilica; Solfeggio; And 1 of the Pharisees..; Cant Domino; Summa; Magnificat Antiphons (7); The Beatitudes ("De Profundis") † And 1 of the Pharisees; Beatitudes; Cant Domino; Magnificat for Chorus; Magnificat-Antiphones; Missa sillabica; Solfeggio; Summa Chorus HAM ▲ 907182 [DDD] (18.97)
Collage on the Theme B-A-C-H for Oboe, Harpsichord, Piano & Strings (1964)
B. Berman (pno), N. Järvi (cnd), Philharmonia Orch † Credo; Festina lente; Fratres I Str Qt; Summa Orch; Sym 2; Wenn Bach Bienen CHN ▲ 9134 [DDD] (16.97)
M. Talka (ob), J. Laivuori (hpd/pno), J. Kantorow (cnd), Tapiola Sinfonietta *(rec Tapiola Concert Hall Finland, 1996)* ("Summa") † Cantus in Memory of Benjamin Britten; Festina lente; Fratres I Str Qt; Summa Orch; Tabula rasa BIS ▲ 834 [DDD] (17.97)
Credo for Piano, Orchestra & Mixed Choir (1968)
B. Berman (pno), N. Järvi (cnd), Philharmonia Orch, Philharmonia Chorus † Collage on the Theme B-A-C-H; Festina lente; Fratres I Str Qt; Summa Orch; Sym 2; Wenn Bach Bienen CHN ▲ 9134 [DDD] (16.97)
Festina lente for String Orchestra (1989)
N. Järvi (cnd), Philharmonia Orch † Collage on the Theme B-A-C-H; Credo; Fratres I Str Qt; Summa Orch; Sym 2; Wenn Bach Bienen CHN ▲ 9134 [DDD] (16.97)

PÄRT, ARVO (cont.)
Festina lente for String Orchestra (1989) (cont.)
J. Kantorow (cnd), Tapiola Sinfonietta *(rec Tapiola Concert Hall Finland, 1996)* ("Summa") † Cantus in Memory of Benjamin Britten; Collage on the Theme B-A-C-H; Fratres I Str Qt; Summa Orch; Tabula rasa BIS ▲ 834 [DDD] (17.97)
R. Studt (cnd), Bournemouth Sinfonietta ("Sanctuary") † Beatitudes; Cantus in Memory of Benjamin Britten; De Profundis; Fratres VI; Magnificat for Chorus; Summa Orch; Tabula rasa VCL ▲ 45314 [DDD] (16.97)
Fratres I for String Quartet (or String Orchestra & Percussion)
J. Barta (vc), M. Lapšanský (pno) [arr vc & pno] † S. Rachmaninoff:Son Vc; A. Schnittke:Son 1 Vc SUR ▲ 112156 [DDD]
L. Derwinger (pno), Tallinn String Quartet ("Chamber Music from Estonia") † Tubin:Music of Tubin; Tüür:Qt Strs BIS ▲ 574 [DDD] (17.97)
N. Järvi (cnd), Philharmonia Orch † Collage on the Theme B-A-C-H; Credo; Festina lente; Summa Orch; Sym 2; Wenn Bach Bienen CHN ▲ 9134 [DDD] (16.97)
G. Kremer (vn) ("From My Home") † Barkauskas:Partita Vn; Dvarionas:Elegie; Pelēcis:Con Vn Pno; Plakidis:2 Grasshopper Dances; Tüür:Conversio; Vasks:Musica Dolorosa TELC ▲ 14654 (16.97)
J. Vartianinen (perc), J. Kantorow (cnd), Tapiola Sinfonietta *(rec Tapiola Concert Hall Finland, 1996)* ("Summa") † Cantus in Memory of Benjamin Britten; Collage on the Theme B-A-C-H; Festina lente; Summa Orch; Tabula rasa BIS ▲ 834 [DDD] (17.97)
R. Werthen (cnd), I Fiamminghi ("An I Fiamminghi Collection") † Corigliano:Elegy; Górecki:Stücke im alten Stil; A. Hovhaness:Prayer of St. Gregory, Op. 62b; Kancheli:Vom Winde beweint; Vasks:Musica Dolorosa TEL ▲ 89111 [DDD] (5.97)
Fratres VI for Orchestra
F. Welser-Möst (cnd), London PO ("Sanctuary") † Beatitudes; Cantus in Memory of Benjamin Britten; De Profundis; Festina lente; Magnificat for Chorus; Summa Orch; Tabula rasa VCL ▲ 45314 [DDD] (16.97)
Fratres VII for Cello & Piano
T. Benedek (cnd), Hungarian State Opera Orch *(rec Festetich Castle Budapest, Hungary, Dec 10-16, 1995)* ("Fratres") † Fratres for 8 Vcs; Music of Pärt NXIN ▲ 553750 [DDD] (5.97)
U. Boeckheler (vc), S. Starr (pno) † S. Prokofiev:Son Vc; D. Shostakovich:Son Vc ICC ▲ 6702362 (9.97)
R. Werthen (cnd), I Fiamminghi *(rec Vellereille-les-Brayeux Belgium, Spain, Aug 18-20, 1994)* ("Fratres") † Fratres for 8 Vcs; Music of Pärt TEL ▲ 80387 [DDD] (16.97)
Fratres for 8 Cellos
T. Benedek (cnd), Hungarian State Opera Orch *(rec Festetich Castle Budapest, Hungary, Dec 10-16, 1995)* ("Fratres") † Fratres Vc Pno; Music of Pärt NXIN ▲ 553750 [DDD] (5.97)
Cello Octet † P. Boulez:Messagesquisse; Capon:A tempo; Dusapin:Loop; E. Vásquez:Migrations; H. Villa-Lobos:Bachiana brasileira 1 BUD ▲ 13 [DDD] (16.97)
R. Werthen (cnd), I Fiamminghi *(rec Vellereille-les-Brayeux Belgium, Spain, Aug 18-20, 1994)* ("Fratres") † Fratres Vc Pno; Music of Pärt TEL ▲ 80387 [DDD] (16.97)
Für Alina for Piano (1976)
D. Arden (pno) † Variationen zur Gesundung; Górecki:Preludes Pno; Son 1 Pno; Ustvolskaya:Preludes Pno; Son 6 Pno KOCH ▲ 7301 [DDD] (16.97)
Magnificat for Chorus (1989)
S. Cleobury (cnd), King's College Choir Cambridge ("Ikos") † Beatitudes; Górecki:Amen; Totus tuus; J. Tavener:Funeral Ikos; Magnificat EMIC ▲ 55096 (16.97)
S. Cleobury (cnd), King's College Choir Cambridge ("Sanctuary") † Beatitudes; Cantus in Memory of Benjamin Britten; De Profundis; Festina lente; Fratres VI; Summa Orch; Tabula rasa VCL ▲ 45314 [DDD] (16.97)
P. Hillier (cnd), Theater of Voices ("De Profundis") † And 1 of the Pharisees; Beatitudes; Cant Domino; Choral Music; Magnificat-Antiphones; Missa sillabica; Solfeggio; Summa Chorus HAM ▲ 907182 [DDD] (18.97)
S. Layton (cnd), Polyphony † Beatitudes; Berliner Messe; De Profundis; Magnificat-Antiphones HYP ▲ 66960 (18.97)
H. Nickoll (cnd), Carmina Chamber Choir ("Choir Music of the 20th Century") † Haentjes:Easter Motets; F. Martin:Mass for Double Chorus; Nickoll:Salve regina; R. Thompson:Alleluia EBS ▲ 6039 [DDD] (17.97)
Magnificat-Antiphones (7) for Chorus (1988; rev 1991)
P. Hillier (cnd), Theater of Voices ("De Profundis") † And 1 of the Pharisees; Beatitudes; Cant Domino; Choral Music; Magnificat for Chorus; Missa sillabica; Solfeggio; Summa Chorus HAM ▲ 907182 [DDD] (18.97)
S. Layton (cnd), Polyphony † Beatitudes; Berliner Messe; De Profundis; Magnificat for Chorus HYP ▲ 66960 (18.97)
R. Shaw (cnd), Robert Shaw Festival Singers [original 1988 version] *(rec Gramat France, July 26-28, 1994)* ("Evocation of the Spirit") † S. Barber:Agnus Dei; Górecki:Totus tuus; F. Martin:Mass for Double Chorus; Schoenberg:Friede auf Erden, Op. 13 TEL ▲ 80406 [DDD] (16.97)
K. Wessel (alt), Calefax Reed Quintet [arr Raaf Hekkema for voice & reed qnt] *(rec Martin Luther Church Gütersloh, Sept 17-18 & 23-24, 1996)* † Arbos for Brass; Pari intervallo; Summa Orch; W. Byrd:Magnificat; Mass 5 Voc; Senex puerum portabatadoravit; Senex puerum portabatregebat MDG (Scene) ▲ 6190745 [DDD] (17.97)
Mein Weg hat Gipfel und Wellentäler for Organ (1989)
C. M. Moosmann (org) *(rec St. Martin Cathedral Rottenburg, Apr 12-14, 1994)* ("Annum per annum") † Annum per annum Org; Pari intervallo; Trivium; J. Cage:Souvenir Org; Scelsi:In nomine lucis V NALB ▲ 74 (16.97)
Missa sillabica for 4 Voices & 6 Instruments (or Chamber Choir) (1977; rev 1996)
P. Hillier (cnd), Theater of Voices ("De Profundis") † And 1 of the Pharisees; Beatitudes; Cant Domino; Choral Music; Magnificat for Chorus; Magnificat-Antiphones; Solfeggio; Summa Chorus HAM ▲ 907182 [DDD] (18.97)
Music of Pärt
T. Benedek (cnd), Hungarian State Opera Orch—Fratres for Strs & Perc; Fratres for Vn, Strs & Perc; Fratres for Str Qt; Fratres for Wind Octet & Perc; Festina Lente for Strs & Hp; Summa for Strs; Cantus in Memory of Benjamin Britten *(rec Festetich Castle Budapest, Dec 10-16, 1995)* ("Fratres") † Fratres for 8 Vcs; Fratres Vc Pno NXIN ▲ 553750 [DDD] (5.97)
R. Werthen (cnd), I Fiamminghi—Fratres for Strs & Perc; Fratres for Vn, Strs & Perc; Cantus in Memory of Benjamin Britten; Fratres for Wind Octet & Perc; Summa for Strs; Fratres for Str Qt; Festina Lente for Strs & Hp *(rec Vellereille-les-Brayeux Belgium, Aug 18-20, 1994)* ("Fratres") † Fratres for 8 Vcs; Fratres Vc Pno TEL ▲ 80387 [DDD] (16.97)
Nekrolog for Orchestra, Op. 5
J. Carewe (cnd), Rhineland-Palatinate State PO ("20th Century Russian Orchestral Works") † I. Stravinsky:Faune et bergère, Op. 2; I. Tcherepnin:Va et le vient; A. Volkonsky:Serenade for an Insect MELI ▲ 7115 (17.97)
Pari intervallo for Organ (1976)
Calefax Reed Quintet [arr Eduard Wesly for reed qnt] *(rec Martin Luther Church Gütersloh, Sept 17-18 & 23-24, 1996)* † Arbos for Brass; Magnificat-Antiphones; Summa Orch; W. Byrd:Magnificat; Mass 5 Voc; Senex puerum portabatadoravit; Senex puerum portabatregebat MDG (Scene) ▲ 6190745 [DDD] (17.97)
A. Ceccomori (fl), G. D. Esposti (rcr), P. Wehage (sax), C. Chailly (hp), F. Ottaviucci (pno) *(rec Italy)* ("New Music Masters") † Einaudi:Quattro Passi; Górecki:For You Ann, Op. 58; H. Otte:Wassermannsmusik; S. Reich:N.Y. Counterpoint; Vermont Counterpoint AMI ▲ 496 [DDD] (15.97)
C. M. Moosmann (org) *(rec St. Martin Cathedral Rottenburg, Apr 12-14, 1994)* ("Annum per annum") † Annum per annum Org; Mein Weg hat Gipfel; Trivium; J. Cage:Souvenir Org; Scelsi:In nomine lucis V NALB ▲ 74 (16.97)
Perpetuum mobile for Orchestra, Op. 10 (1963)
N. Järvi (cnd), Bamberg SO † Pro et contra; Syms (comp) BIS ▲ 434 [DDD] (17.97)
Pro et contra for Cello & Orchestra (1964)
F. Helmerson (vc), N. Järvi (cnd), Bamberg SO † Perpetuum mobile, Op. 10; Syms (comp) BIS ▲ 434 [DDD] (17.97)
De Profundis for Chorus, Organ & Percussion [text Psalm 130] (1980)
T. Kaljuste (cnd), Estonian Philharmonic Chamber Choir ("Sanctuary") † Beatitudes; Cantus in Memory of Benjamin Britten; Festina lente; Fratres VI; Magnificat for Chorus; Summa Orch; Tabula rasa VCL ▲ 45314 [DDD] (16.97)
S. Layton (cnd), Polyphony † Beatitudes; Berliner Messe; Magnificat for Chorus; Magnificat-Antiphones HYP ▲ 66960 (18.97)
Solfeggio for Chorus (1964)
P. Hillier (cnd), Theater of Voices ("De Profundis") † And 1 of the Pharisees; Beatitudes; Cant Domino; Choral Music; Magnificat for Chorus; Magnificat-Antiphones; Missa sillabica; Summa Chorus HAM ▲ 907182 [DDD] (18.97)
Spiegel im Spiegel for Cello & Piano (1978)
M. Forsyth (vc), P. Longworth (pno) ("Soaring with Agamemnon") † G. Bryars:South Downs; M. Forsyth:Andante for Sagattarius; Burlesque; Duets for Young Cellists; Eclogue; Pop's Cycle; Rondo in Stride; Swan Sees His Reflection MARQ ▲ 231 (16.97)
D. Geringas (vc), T. Schatz (pno) ("Russian Chamber Music") † Gubaidulina:In Croce; A. Schnittke:Son 1 Vc; Suslin:Son Vc & Perc KSCH ▲ 310091 [DDD]

PÄRT, ARVO (cont.)
Summa for Chorus (1997)
P. Hillier (cnd), Theater of Voices ("De Profundis") † And 1 of the Pharisees; Beatitudes; Cant Domino; Choral Music; Magnificat for Chorus; Magnificat-Antiphones; Missa sillabica; Solfeggio HAM ▲ 907182 [DDD] (18.97)
Summa for Orchestra (1991)
Calefax Reed Quintet [arr Eduard Wesly for reed qnt] *(rec Martin Luther Church Gütersloh, Sept 17-18 & 23-24, 1996)* † Arbos for Brass; Magnificat-Antiphones; Pari intervallo; W. Byrd:Magnificat; Mass 5 Voc; Senex puerum portabatadoravit; Senex puerum portabatregebat MDG (Scene) ▲ 6190745 [DDD] (17.97)
N. Järvi (cnd), Philharmonia Orch † Collage on the Theme B-A-C-H; Credo; Festina lente; Fratres I Str Qt; Sym 2; Wenn Bach Bienen CHN ▲ 9134 [DDD] (16.97)
J. Kantorow (cnd), Tapiola Sinfonietta *(rec Tapiola Concert Hall Finland, 1996)* ("Summa") † Cantus in Memory of Benjamin Britten; Collage on the Theme B-A-C-H; Festina lente; Fratres I Str Qt; Tabula rasa BIS ▲ 834 [DDD] (17.97)
R. Studt (cnd), Bournemouth Sinfonietta ("Sanctuary") † Beatitudes; Cantus in Memory of Benjamin Britten; De Profundis; Festina lente; Fratres VI; Magnificat for Chorus; Tabula rasa VCL ▲ 45314 [DDD] (16.97)
Symphonies (3) (complete)
N. Järvi (cnd), Bamberg SO † Perpetuum mobile, Op. 10; Pro et contra BIS ▲ 434 [DDD] (17.97)
Symphony No. 2 (1966)
N. Järvi (cnd), Philharmonia Orch † Collage on the Theme B-A-C-H; Credo; Festina lente; Fratres I Str Qt; Summa Orch; Wenn Bach Bienen CHN ▲ 9134 [DDD] (16.97)
Tabula rasa (concerto) for Violin, Prepared Piano & String Orchestra (1977)
J. Söderblom (vn), T. Latvala (vn), J. Laivuori (prepared pno), J. Kantorow (cnd), Tapiola Sinfonietta *(rec Tapiola Concert Hall Finland, 1996)* ("Summa") † Cantus in Memory of Benjamin Britten; Collage on the Theme B-A-C-H; Festina lente; Fratres I Str Qt; Summa Orch BIS ▲ 834 [DDD] (17.97)
R. Studt (vn), T. Little (vn), R. Studt (cnd), Bournemouth Sinfonietta ("Sanctuary") † Beatitudes; Cantus in Memory of Benjamin Britten; De Profundis; Festina lente; Fratres VI; Magnificat for Chorus; Summa Orch VCL ▲ 45314 [DDD] (16.97)
E. Turovsky (vn), N. Turovsky (vn), Y. Turovsky (cnd), Montreal Musici † Górecki:Con Hpd; A. Schnittke:Con grosso 1 CHN ▲ 9590 [DDD] (16.97)
Trivium for Organ (1976)
C. M. Moosmann (org) *(rec St. Martin Cathedral Rottenburg, Apr 12-14, 1994)* ("Annum per annum") † Annum per annum Org; Mein Weg hat Gipfel; Pari intervallo; J. Cage:Souvenir Org; Scelsi:In nomine lucis V NALB ▲ 74 (16.97)
Variationen zur Gesundung von Arinuschka [Variations for Arinuschka's Recuperation] for Piano (1977)
D. Arden (pno) † Für Alina; Górecki:Preludes Pno; Son 1 Pno; Ustvolskaya:Preludes Pno; Son 6 Pno KOCH ▲ 7301 [DDD] (16.97)
Wenn Bach Bienen gezüchtet hätte for Piano & Orchestra (1978)
B. Berman (pno), N. Järvi (cnd), Philharmonia Orch † Collage on the Theme B-A-C-H; Credo; Festina lente; Fratres I Str Qt; Summa Orch; Sym 2 CHN ▲ 9134 [DDD] (16.97)

PARTCH, HARRY (1901-1974)
And on the 7th Day, Petals Fell In Petaluma for Large Ensemble of original Instruments (1963-66)
H. Partch (cnd) *(rec Petaluma & Venice, CA, 1964 & 1966)* ("The Harry Partch Collection, Vol. 2") † Barstow; Letter for Voice; San Francisco; US Highball CRI ▲ 752 [ADD] (16.97)
Barstow - 8 Hitchhiker Inscriptions from a Highway Railing at Barstow, California (stage piece) for solo Voices, original Instruments & Chorus (1941)
D. Mitchell (cnd) *(rec Oakland, CA, 1982)* ("The Harry Partch Collection, Vol. 2") † And on the 7th Day; Letter for Voice; San Francisco; US Highball CRI ▲ 752 [ADD] (16.97)
H. Partch (voc), W. Wendlandt (voc), H. Partch (gtr), L. Hoiby (kithara), C. Charnstrom (chromelodeon) [adapted gtr] *(rec 1945)* ("Enclosure Two: Harry Partch") † Bitter Music; Bless This Home; By the Rivers of Babylon; Dark Brother; Lyrics by Li Po; Mock Turtle Song; Music of Partch; Plectra & Percussion Dances (sels); San Francisco; San Francisco II; Settings from "Finnegan's Wake"; US Highball; While My Heart; Yankee Doodle Fant INNO 4-▲ 401 (43.97)
Barstow - 8 Hitchhiker Inscriptions from a Highway Railing at Barstow, California (stage piece) for Voice & Adapted Guitar (1941)
J. Schneider (bar), J. Schneider (gtr) [adapted gtr] *(rec KPFK-FM, CA, 1993)* ("Just West Coast") † Studies on Ancient Greek Scales; J. Cage:Dream Pno; In a Landscape; L. Harrison:Suite 2 Gtr; L. Young:Sarabande BRID ▲ 9041 [DDD] (17.97)
Barstow - 8 Hitchhiker Inscriptions from a Highway Railing at Barstow, California (stage piece) for Voice & String Quartet [arr B. Johnston, 1994]
B. Johnston (cnd), Kronos Quartet ("Howl U.S.A.") † M. Daugherty:Sing Sing; L. Hyla:Howl; S. Johnson:Cold War Suite NON ▲ 79372 (16.97)
The Bewitched (a dance-satire) for solo Voice & Instrumental Ensemble (1952-55)
J. Garvey (cnd) *(rec Univ of Illinois Champaign-Urbana, 1957)* ("The Harry Partch Collection, Vol. 4") CRI ▲ 754 [ADD] (16.97)
Bitter Music for Voice & Piano [abridged] (1935-36)
artists unknown, W. Burt (voc), S. Guymer (pno) [prepared Warren Burt] *(rec Melbourne Australia, Jan 24, 1992)* ("Enclosure Two: Harry Partch") † Barstow; Bless This Home; By the Rivers of Babylon; Dark Brother; Lyrics by Li Po; Mock Turtle Song; Music of Partch; Plectra & Percussion Dances (sels); San Francisco; San Francisco II; Settings from "Finnegan's Wake"; US Highball; While My Heart; Yankee Doodle Fant INNO 4-▲ 401 (43.97)
Bless This Home for Voice, Oboe & original Instruments (1961)
artists unknown, H. Partch (voc), H. Partch (va), V. Prockelo (ob), D. Mitchell (harmonic canon/kitha), J. Garvey (cnd) [adapted va] *(rec Univ of Illinois, 1961)* ("Enclosure Two: Harry Partch") † Barstow; Bitter Music; By the Rivers of Babylon; Dark Brother; Lyrics by Li Po; Mock Turtle Song; Music of Partch; Plectra & Percussion Dances (sels); San Francisco; San Francisco II; Settings from "Finnegan's Wake"; US Highball; While My Heart; Yankee Doodle Fant INNO 4-▲ 401 (43.97)
By the Rivers of Babylon for Voices & original Instruments [from Psalm 137] (1931; rev 1943)
artists unknown, W. Wendlandt (bar), H. Partch (va), L. Hoiby (kithara), C. Charnstrom (chromelodeon) [adapted va] *(rec 1945)* ("Enclosure Two: Harry Partch") † Barstow; Bitter Music; Bless This Home; Dark Brother; Lyrics by Li Po; Mock Turtle Song; Music of Partch; Plectra & Percussion Dances (sels); San Francisco; San Francisco II; Settings from "Finnegan's Wake"; US Highball; While My Heart; Yankee Doodle Fant INNO 4-▲ 401 (43.97)
Dark Brother for Voice & original Instruments [after Thomas Wolfe] (1943)
artists unknown, W. Wendlandt (bar), H. Partch (va), L. Hoiby (kithara), C. Charnstrom (chromelodeon), F. Hancock (perc) [adapted va] *(rec 1945)* ("Enclosure Two: Harry Partch") † Barstow; Bitter Music; Bless This Home; By the Rivers of Babylon; Lyrics by Li Po; Mock Turtle Song; Music of Partch; Plectra & Percussion Dances (sels); San Francisco; San Francisco II; Settings from "Finnegan's Wake"; US Highball; While My Heart; Yankee Doodle Fant INNO 4-▲ 401 (43.97)
The Dreamer that Remains: a Portrait of Harry Partch (film score) for Voices & original Instruments (1972)
J. Logan (cnd) *(rec San Diego, CA, 1972)* ("The Harry Partch Collection, Vol. 3") † Rotate the Body; Water! Water! (sels); Windsong CRI ▲ 753 [ADD] (16.97)
Eleven Intrusions for Voices & original Instruments (1949-50)
H. Partch (voc), H. Partch (instr), B. Johnston (instr), B. Johnston (instr), D. Pippin (instr), B. Snead (instr) *(rec Gualala, CA, 1950-51)* ("The Harry Partch Collection, Vol. 1") † Plectra & Percussion Dances (sels); Ulysses at the Edge of the World CRI ▲ 751 [ADD] (16.97)
The Letter for Voice & original Instruments (1943)
H. Partch (voc), D. Dunn (harmonicord), H. Partch (omicron belly dr), R. Hoffman (omicron belly dr) [w. dubbed-in interludes from 1950 recording] *(rec Encinitas & San Diego, CA, 1972)* ("The Harry Partch Collection, Vol. 2") † And on the 7th Day; Barstow; San Francisco; US Highball CRI ▲ 752 [ADD] (16.97)
Lyrics by Li Po (17) for Voice & Adapted Viola (1931)
S. Kalm (voc), T. Mook (t vn) TZA ▲ 7012 [DDD] (16.97)
W. Wendlandt (voc), H. Partch (va) *(rec 1947)* ("Enclosure Two: Harry Partch") † Barstow; Bitter Music; Bless This Home; By the Rivers of Babylon; Dark Brother; Mock Turtle Song; Music of Partch; Plectra & Percussion Dances (sels); San Francisco; San Francisco II; Settings from "Finnegan's Wake"; US Highball; While My Heart; Yankee Doodle Fant INNO 4-▲ 401 (43.97)
The Mock Turtle Song & Jabberwocky for Voice & original Instruments (1952)
H. Partch (voc), H. Partch (harmonic canon), D. Mitchell (b mar) *(rec Mill Valley Outdoor Club's Young People's Concert, Feb 13, 1954)* ("Enclosure Two: Harry Partch") † Barstow; Bitter Music; Bless This Home; By the Rivers of Babylon; Dark Brother; Lyrics by Li Po; Music of Partch; Plectra & Percussion Dances (sels); San Francisco; San Francisco II; Settings from "Finnegan's Wake"; US Highball; While My Heart; Yankee Doodle Fant INNO 4-▲ 401 (43.97)

PARTCH, HARRY (cont.)
Music of Partch
artists unknown, W. Wendlandt (bar), H. Partch (va), L. Hoiby (kithara), C. Charnstrom (chromelodeon) *(By the Rivers of Babylon)*, artists unknown *(10 Li Po Lyrics; San Francisco [Newsboy Cries]; U.S. Highball; While My Heart Keeps Beating Time; 2 Settings from Joyce's Finnegans Wake; A Quarter-Saw Section of Motivations & Intonations; Y.D. Fant [On the Words of an Early American Tune]; O Frabjous Day!; Ring around the Moon)*, artists unknown, Illinois Performers' Workshop Ensemble *(San Francisco II)*, artists unknown, W. Wendlandt (bar), H. Partch (va), L. Hoiby (kithara), C. Charnstrom (chromelodeon), F. Hancock (perc) *(Dark Brother)*, artists unknown, W. Burt (voc), S. Guymer (pno) *(Bitter Music)*, artists unknown, H. Partch (voc), H. Partch (va), V. Prockelo (ob), D. Mitchell (harmonic canon/kitha), J. Garvey (cnd) *(Bless This Home)* ("Enclosure Two: Harry Partch") † Barstow; Bitter Music; Bless This Home; By the Rivers of Babylon; Dark Brother; Lyrics by Li Po; Mock Turtle Song; Plectra & Percussion Dances (sels); San Francisco; San Francisco II; Settings from "Finnegan's Wake"; US Highball; While My Heart; Yankee Doodle Fant INNO 4-▲ 401 (43.97)
Plectra & Percussion Dances (selections)
L. Ludlow (spkr), Gate 5 Ensemble *(rec International House KPFA-Berkeley, Nov 19, 1953)* ("Enclosure Two: Harry Partch") † Barstow; Bitter Music; Bless This Home; By the Rivers of Babylon; Dark Brother; Lyrics by Li Po; Mock Turtle Song; Music of Partch; San Francisco; San Francisco II; Settings from "Finnegan's Wake"; US Highball; While My Heart; Yankee Doodle Fant INNO 4-▲ 401 (43.97)
H. Schwartz (cnd) *(rec Sausalito, CA, 1953)* ("The Harry Partch Collection, Vol. 1") † Ulysses at the Edge of the World; 11 Intrusions CRI ▲ 751 [ADD] (16.97)
Rotate the Body in all its Planes for Soprano, Instruments & Chorus (1961)
F. Pierce (sop), J. Garvey (cnd) *(rec Univ of Illinois Champaign-Urbana, 1961)* ("The Harry Partch Collection, Vol. 3") † Dreamer that Remains; Water! Water! (sels); Windsong CRI ▲ 753 [ADD] (16.97)
San Francisco for Voices & original Instruments (1943)
H. Partch (va), L. Hoiby (kithara), C. Charnstrom (chromelodeon) [adapted va] *(rec 1945)* ("Enclosure Two: Harry Partch") † Barstow; Bitter Music; Bless This Home; By the Rivers of Babylon; Dark Brother; Lyrics by Li Po; Mock Turtle Song; Music of Partch; Plectra & Percussion Dances (sels); San Francisco II; Settings from "Finnegan's Wake"; US Highball; While My Heart; Yankee Doodle Fant INNO 4-▲ 401 (43.97)
H. Partch (voc), H. Partch (va), D. Mitchell (kithara), E. Gentry (chromelodeon) [adapted va] *(rec Evanston, IL, 1958)* ("The Harry Partch Collection, Vol. 2") † And on the 7th Day; Barstow; Letter for Voice; US Highball CRI ▲ 752 [ADD] (16.97)
San Francisco II for Ensemble (1943; rev 1955)
artists unknown, Illinois Performers' Workshop Ensemble [arr Mark Enslin] *(rec Karlsruhe Germany, Jan 24, 1990)* ("Enclosure Two: Harry Partch") † Barstow; Bitter Music; Bless This Home; By the Rivers of Babylon; Dark Brother; Lyrics by Li Po; Mock Turtle Song; Music of Partch; Plectra & Percussion Dances (sels); San Francisco; Settings from "Finnegan's Wake"; US Highball; While My Heart; Yankee Doodle Fant INNO 4-▲ 401 (43.97)
Settings from "Finnegan's Wake" (2) for Voice, Flute & Kithara (1944)
L. Harding (sop), D. Holden (fl), H. Luckhardt (fl), H. Partch (kithara) *(rec 1945)* ("Enclosure Two: Harry Partch") † Barstow; Bitter Music; Bless This Home; By the Rivers of Babylon; Dark Brother; Lyrics by Li Po; Mock Turtle Song; Music of Partch; Plectra & Percussion Dances (sels); San Francisco; San Francisco II; US Highball; While My Heart; Yankee Doodle Fant INNO 4-▲ 401 (43.97)
Studies on Ancient Greek Scales (2) for Harmonic Canon & Bass Marimba (1946-50)
J. Schneider (gtr), A. Shulman (hp) [arr J. Schneider for gtr & hp] *(rec KPFK-FM, CA, 1993)* ("Just West Coast") † Barstow Gtr; J. Cage:Dream Pno; In a Landscape; L. Harrison:Suite 2 Gtr; L. Young:Sarabande BRID ▲ 9041 [DDD] (17.97)
Studies on Ancient Greek Scales (2) for Plucked Strings & Bass Marimba [newly arr Dean Drummond for Flute & Zoomoozophone] (1946)
Newband ("Newband Play Microtonal Works") † J. La Barbara:Silent Scroll; J. Cage:Haikai; D. Drummond:Columbus; Incredible Time (to live & die); Then or Never MODE ▲ 18
Ulysses at the Edge of the World for Voice, Tenor Saxophone, Trumpet & original Instruments [text Partch] (1955)
D. Reid (voc), D. Schleppe (a sax), D. Reid (bar sax), D. Mitchell (bamboo mar) *(rec Evanston, IL, 1958)* ("The Harry Partch Collection, Vol. 1") † Plectra & Percussion Dances (sels); 11 Intrusions CRI ▲ 751 [ADD] (16.97)
US Highball (dramatic work) for solo Voices, original Instruments & Chorus (1943)
J. McKenzie (cnd) *(rec Evanston, IL, 1958)* ("The Harry Partch Collection, Vol. 2") † And on the 7th Day; Barstow; Letter for Voice; San Francisco CRI ▲ 752 [ADD] (16.97)
W. Wendlandt (bar), H. Partch (voc), F. Hancock (db), H. Partch (gtr), L. Hoiby (kithara), C. Charnstrom (chromelodeon) [adapted gtr] *(rec 1946)* ("Enclosure Two: Harry Partch") † Barstow; Bitter Music; Bless This Home; By the Rivers of Babylon; Dark Brother; Lyrics by Li Po; Mock Turtle Song; Music of Partch; Plectra & Percussion Dances (sels); San Francisco; San Francisco II; Settings from "Finnegan's Wake"; While My Heart; Yankee Doodle Fant INNO 4-▲ 401 (43.97)
Water! Water! (selections)
J. Garvey (cnd) *(rec Univ of Illinois Champaign-Urbana, 1962)* ("The Harry Partch Collection, Vol. 3") † Dreamer that Remains; Rotate the Body; Windsong CRI ▲ 753 [ADD] (16.97)
While My Heart Keeps Beating Time (song) for Voice & Piano (1929)
P. Blackburn (voc), L. Schmidt (pno) [orig published under alias Paul Pirate] *(rec 1995)* ("Enclosure Two: Harry Partch") † Barstow; Bitter Music; Bless This Home; By the Rivers of Babylon; Dark Brother; Lyrics by Li Po; Mock Turtle Song; Music of Partch; Plectra & Percussion Dances (sels); San Francisco; San Francisco II; Settings from "Finnegan's Wake"; US Highball; Yankee Doodle Fant INNO 4-▲ 401 (43.97)
Windsong (film music) for 10 Instruments (1958)
H. Partch (instr) *(rec Chicago, IL, 1958)* ("The Harry Partch Collection, Vol. 3") † Dreamer that Remains; Rotate the Body; Water! Water! (sels) CRI ▲ 753 [ADD] (16.97)
Yankee Doodle Fantasy for Soprano, Flexotone, Synthesizer, Tin Flute & Oboe (1941)
L. Harding (sop), H. Luckhardt (tin whistle), D. Thompson (ob/tin whistle), H. Partch (chromelodeon) *(rec 1945)* ("Enclosure Two: Harry Partch") † Barstow; Bitter Music; Bless This Home; By the Rivers of Babylon; Dark Brother; Lyrics by Li Po; Mock Turtle Song; Music of Partch; Plectra & Percussion Dances (sels); San Francisco; San Francisco II; Settings from "Finnegan's Wake"; US Highball; While My Heart INNO 4-▲ 401 (43.97)

PARTOS, OEDEON (1907-1977)
Visions for Flute, Piano & Strings (1957)
N. Buchman (fl), E. Acél (cnd), Oradea PO *(rec Apr 1991)* † Ibert:Con Fl; C. Nielsen:Con Fl OLY ▲ 420 [DDD] (12.97)

PASATIERI, THOMAS (1945-
Theatrepieces (an opera for 3 instruments) for Violin, Clarinet & Piano (1986)
Verdehr Trio † B. Bartók:Contrasts, Sz.111; A. Hovhaness:Lake Samish; W. A. Mozart:Son Pno 4-Hands, K.381 CRYS ▲ 741 (15.97)
Yizkor [In Memoriam] for Strings (1947)
A. Heatherington (cnd) *(rec June 2-3, 1992)* † E. Bloch:Con grosso 1; From Jewish Life; Suite modale; Chajes:Israeli Melodies; M. Gould:Holocaust Suite CENT ▲ 2140 [DDD] (16.97)

PASCAL, CLAUDE RENÉ GEORGES (1921-
Concerto for Harp & Orchestra (1967)
V. Dulova (hp), A. Korneiev (cnd), Moscow Radio-TV SO *(rec 1970)* ("Vera Dulova: Russian Performing School") † Donizetti:Son Fl & Hp; M. Ravel:Pavane pour une infante défunte; Saint-Saëns:Fant Vn RD (Talents of Russia) ▲ 16206 [AAD] (16.97)

PASCAL, FLORIAN [JOSEPH WILLIAMS] (1842-1923)
Songs
P. Gale (sop), A. Mentschukoff (gtr)—Only a Little While *(rec Cleveland, OH, Sep 1997)* † Anonymous:Songs; H. Birch:Songs; W. M. Hutchison:Songs; G. Marks:Songs; C. A. White:Songs CENT ▲ 2389 [DDD] (16.97)

PASCHA, EDMUND (1714-1772)
Harmonia pastoralis for Chorus
K. Hron (org), J. Krček (cnd), Musica Bohemica, J. Kolář (cnd), Iuventus Paedagogica † Prosae pastorales PC ▲ 267183 [DDD] (2.97)
M. Venhoda (cnd), Prague Madrigal Singers † Prosae pastorales CAPI ▲ 1305 [AAD] (16.97)
Prosae pastorales for Chorus
J. Krček (cnd), Musica Bohemica † Harmonia pastoralis CAPI ▲ 1305 [AAD] (16.97)
J. Krček (cnd), Musica Bohemica † Harmonia pastoralis PC ▲ 267183 [DDD] (2.97)

PASCHER, HARTMUT (1956-
Quartet No. 1 for Strings, Op. 27
Franz Schubert String Quartet † Bargielski:Qt 2 Strs; G. Coates:Qt 1 Strs; Qt 2 Strs; Qt 4 Strs; Pernes:Qt 1 Strs; Przbylski:ArnolD SCHönBErG in Memoriam PROV ▲ 173 [ADD] (18.97)

▲ = CD ♦ = Enhanced CD △ = MD ▮ = Cassette Tape ▯ = DCC

PURCELL, HENRY (cont.)

Anthems & Services (cont.)

R. King (cnd), King's Consort—Awake, put on thy strength, Z.1; Praise the Lord, O my soul, O Lord my God, Z.48; O Lord, thou art my God, Z.41; Hear me, O Lord, Z.13a/b; Turn thou us, O good Lord, Z.62; Close thine eyes & sleep secure, Z.184; Lord, how long wilt thou be angry?, Z.25; Magnificat & Nunc Dimittis, Z.231 ("Complete Anthems & Services, Vol. 11") HYP ▲ 66716 (18.97)

R. King (cnd), King's Consort, King's Consort Choir—In thee, O Lord, do I put my trust, D.16; Blessed is the man that feareth the Lord, Z.9 HYP ▲ 66686 (18.97)

R. King (cnd), King's Consort, King's Consort Choir—I will sing unto the Lord, Z.22; Kyrie in B; Nicene Creed in B; Benedictus in B; I will give thanks unto the Lord, Z.21; Out of the deep have I called, Z.45 ("Complete Anthems & Services, Vol. 10") HYP ▲ 66707 (18.97)

R. King (cnd), King's Consort, New College Choir Oxford—Let mine eyes run down with tears, Z.24; Rejoice in the Lord alway, Z.49; Thou knowest, Lord, the secrets of our hearts, Z.58b ("Essential Purcell") † Dido & Aeneas (sels); King Arthur (sels); Music of Purcell; Odes & Welcome Songs (misc); Sacred Music; Songs HYP ▲ 2 (7.97)

M. Laplénie (cnd), Les Menus Plaisirs, L'Abbaye aux Dames—Man that is born of a woman, Z.27; In the midst of life, Z.17a/b; Thou knowest, Lord, the secrets of our hearts, Z.58b ("Baroque Sacré en Europe") † J. Ludwig Bach:Motets; J. M. Bach:Motets; J. Christoph Bach:Motets & Cants; Monteverdi:Selva morale e spirituale (sels) CYPR ▲ 1614 [DDD] (17.97)

J. Nibbs (sop), G. Mitchell (ct), P. Hall (ten), D. Thomas (bass), M. Phillips (org), M. Howard (cnd), Cantores in Ecclesia—Magnificat & Nunc Dimittis, Z.231; Thy word is a lantern unto my feet, Z.61; Man that is born of a woman, Z.27; Thou knowest, Lord, the secrets of our hearts, Z.58b; O God, thou art my God, Z.41; Turn thou us, O good Lord, Z.62; O give thanks unto the Lord, Z.33 ("Music for Westminster Abbey") † Songs INMP (BBC Radio Classics) ▲ 9126 (13.97)

Arias & Duets

J. Dooley (ct), H. Crook (ten) ("Airs & Duets") LYR (Early Music) ▲ 8024 (16.97)

Awake, ye dead (song) for Chorus [text G. Sandys], Z.182

P. McCreesh (cnd), Gabrieli Players, Gabrieli Consort ("Harmonia Sacra") † Close thine eyes & sleep secure, Z.184; Ground in c, Z. T681; In guilty night, Z.134; In the black dismal dungeon of despair, Z.190; Lord, what is man?, Z.192; Lord, I can suffer thy rebukes, Z.136; O solitude, my sweetest choice, Z.406; O, I'm sick of life, Z.140; Plung'd in the confines of despair, Z.142; The earth trembled, Z.197; Voluntary in C; Voluntary, Z.720; With sick & famish'd eyes, Z.200 PARC ▲ 45829 [DDD] (16.97)

Bonduca, or The British Heroine (selections)

A. Deller (ct), R. Skeaping (vn), W. Kuijken (vl), J. Ryan (vl), W. Christie (hpd), R. Elliott (hpd)—O lead me to some peaceful gloom *(rec Apr 1979)* † Fairy Queen (sels); Indian Queen (sels); King Arthur (sels); Pausanias (sels); Prophetess (sels); Sacred Music; Songs HAM ▲ 90249 (18.97)

A. Deller (ct), R. Skeaping (vn), W. Kuijken (b vl), J. Ryan (b vl), W. Christie (hpd), R. Elliot (org)—O lead me to some peaceful gloom ("Music for a while") † Comical History of Don Quixote (sels); Fairy Queen (sels); Indian Queen (sels); King Arthur (sels); Oedipus (sels); Pausanias (sels); Sacred Music; Songs HAM (40th Anniversary Edition) ▲ 94249 [ADD] (12.97)

S. McNair (sop), L. Dreyfus (vc/vl), P. O'Dette (archlt), C. Hogwood (hpd/org), C. Hogwood (cnd), Academy of Ancient Music—To arms, your ensigns straight display; O lead me to some peaceful gloom *(rec St. John's, London, England, 1994)* ("The Echoing Air") † Chacony Strs, Z.730; Fairy Queen (sels); Indian Queen (sels); King Arthur (sels); Libertine (sels); Music of Purcell; Pausanias (sels); Songs PPHI ▲ 46081 (16.97)

Chaconne for Baroque Ensemble

Minstrelsey! *(rec Minneapolis, MN, Nov 1996)* † Fairy Queen (sels); Adson:Adsonns Maske; Anonymous:Black Nag; Cupararee; King's Mistress; Love's Triumph; Mountebanks Dance; Second of Grey's Inn; Sir Francis Bacon; Sir Francis Bacon II; Standing Masque; Trip to Paris; Wilsons Love; J. Gay:Beggar's Opera (sels); Kapsberger:Kapsberger; Pepusch:Allegro; Traditional:Arran Boat; Morning Dew/Sally Gardens; Swallows Tail Reel LYR ▲ 8032 [AAD/DDD] (16.97)

Chacony in g for 4 Strings, Z.730, "London"

R. Browder (va/vn), Purcell Quartet ("Vol. 2") † Music of Purcell; Pavans; Sons (22) Vns, Z.790-811 CHN ▲ 8663 [DDD] (16.97)

J. Lamon (cnd), Tafelmusik *(rec CBC Toronto, Apr 26-29, 1995)* † Abdelazer (sels); Dido & Aeneas, Z.626; Overture à 5, Z.772 SMS ▲ 5147 [DDD] (16.97)

S. McNair (sop), L. Dreyfus (vc/vl), P. O'Dette (archlt), C. Hogwood (hpd/org), C. Hogwood (cnd), Academy of Ancient Music [all arr Hogwood] *(rec St. John's, London, England, 1994)* ("The Echoing Air") † Bonduca (sels); Fairy Queen (sels); Indian Queen (sels); King Arthur (sels); Libertine (sels); Music of Purcell; Pausanias (sels); Songs PPHI ▲ 46081 (16.97)

Orpheus CO † Albinoni:Adagio; J. S. Bach:Jesu, bleibet meine Freude; Suite 3 Orch, BWV 1068; A. Corelli:Con grosso, Op. 6/8; G. F. Handel:Solomon (arrival of the queen of Sheba); J. Pachelbel:Canon & Gigue; Vivaldi:Cons Vn(s) Strs, Op. 3/1-12 DEUT ▲ 29390 [DDD] (16.97)

T. Pinnock (cnd), English Concert † Avison:Concerti grossi; J. Pachelbel:Canon & Gigue PARC ▲ 15518 [DDD] (16.97)

Close thine eyes & sleep secure for 2 Voices & Continuo [text F. Quarles], Z.184

P. McCreesh (cnd), Gabrieli Players, Gabrieli Consort ("Harmonia Sacra") † Awake, ye dead, Z.182; Ground in c, Z. T681; In guilty night, Z.134; In the black dismal dungeon of despair, Z.190; Lord, what is man?, Z.192; Lord, I can suffer thy rebukes, Z.136; O solitude, my sweetest choice, Z.406; O, I'm sick of life, Z.140; Plung'd in the confines of despair, Z.142; The earth trembled, Z.197; Voluntary in C; Voluntary, Z.720; With sick & famish'd eyes, Z.200 PARC ▲ 45829 [DDD] (16.97)

Come, ye sons of art, away (song) for solo Voices, 2 Oboes, 2 Trumpets, Timpani & Chorus [on the bithday of Queen Mary], Z.323 (1694)

N. Burrowes (sop), J. Bowman (ct), C. Brett (ct), R. Lloyd (bass), D. Munrow (cnd) *(rec 1975)* ("Birthday Odes for Queen Mary") † Love's goddess sure was blind, Z.331 *([ENG,GER] text)* VCL (Veritas) ▲ 61333 [ADD] (11.97)

K. Ferrier (cta), I. Baillie (sop), G. Moore (pno) *(rec London, England, Sep 21, 1945)* † Indian Queen (sels); King Arthur (sels); C. W. Gluck:Orfeo ed Euridice (sels); M. Greene:Anthems; G. F. Handel:Ottone (sels); G. Mahler:Kindertotenlieder; Mendelssohn (-Bartholdy):Songs EMIC (Great Recordings of the Century) ▲ 66963 [ADD] (11.97)

H. H. Leck (cnd), Indianapolis Children's Choir, D. Brooks (vn), L. Brooks (vn), J. Cosart (va), V. Reese (db), M. Burke (vl), L. Goetz (ob), S. Weiner (ob), T. Gerber (hpd) [arr M. Blower] *(rec May-June 1995)* † Now that the sun hath veiled his light (Eve Hymn), Z.193; Odes & Welcome Songs (misc); Pausanias (sels); B. Britten:Birds; Ceremony of Carols, Op. 28 VAIA ▲ 1130 [DDD]

E. Söderström (sop), K. Meyer (mez), J. Eyron (pno) *(rec Nacka, Sweden, Nov 1 & 3, 1974)* ("Elisabeth Söderström & Kerstin Meyer") † Indian Queen (sels); King Arthur (sels); A. Dvořák:Moravian Duets, Opp. 20, 32, 38; Geijer:Songs; Kodály:Songs; G. Rossini:Soirées musicales; Songs; P. Tchaikovsky:Duets; Wennerberg:Songs *(E text)* BIS ▲ 17 [AAD] (17.97)

The Comical History of Don Quixote (selections)

A. Deller (ct), R. Skeaping (vn), W. Kuijken (b vl), J. Ryan (b vl), W. Christie (hpd), R. Elliot (org)—From rosy bow'rs ("Music for a while") † Bonduca (sels); Fairy Queen (sels); Indian Queen (sels); King Arthur (sels); Oedipus (sels); Pausanias (sels); Sacred Music; Songs HAM (40th Anniversary Edition) ▲ 94249 [ADD] (12.97)

S. Sanford (sop), B. Wissick (vl), R. Erickson (hpd/org)—From rosy bow'rs † Fairy Queen (sels); Hail, bright Cecilia, Z.328; Songs; Tyrannic Love (sels) ALBA ▲ 127 (16.97)

Concertos for Trumpet & Organ

B. Kratzer (tpt), M. Nuber (org)—Suite Tpt & Org *(rec Münster zu Villingen, Germany, Feb 1990)* ("Virtuoso Trumpet Music of the Baroque") † Albinoni:Cons Tpt & Org; G. B. Martini:Son al'Postcommunio; Toccata; Stradella:Sinf alla Serenata; Telemann:Qnt Tpt; Torelli:Con Tpt; J. G. Walther:Cons Tpt & Org FERM ▲ 20001 [DDD] (16.97)

Cortege Academique

A. Davis (org) *(rec Org at Roy Thompson Hall Toronto)* † Tpt Tune; J. S. Bach:Toccata & Fugue Org, BWV 565; C. Franck:Prélude, fugue et var, Op. 18; C. Ives:Vars on 'America' INMP (IMP Classics) ▲ 6700942 (9.97)

Dido & Aeneas (opera in 3 acts) [lib Nahum Tate], Z.626 (ca 1689)

S. Baker (sop—2nd Woman), S. Waters (sop—Belinda), M. O'Keefe (sop—1st Witch), N. Maultsby (mez—Dido), L. Tucker (mez—Sorceress), D. Ames (alt—Spirit), R. Clement (ten—Sailor), R. Braun (bar—Aeneas), M. Pearlman (cnd), Boston Baroque Orch † Abdelazer (sels); Fairy Queen (sels); Gordian Knot Unty'd (sels); Married Beau (sels); Timon of Athens (sels) TEL ▲ 80424 [DDD] (16.97)

C. Brandes (sop), D. Deam (sop), L. Hunt (sop), L. Saffer (sop), R. Rainero (sop), E. Rabiner (mez), P. Elliott (ten), M. Dean (b-bar), N. McGegan (cnd), Philharmonia Baroque Orch, Clare College Choir Cambridge † Gordian Knot Unty'd, Z.597 HAM ▲ 907110 (18.97)

B. Britten (cnd), English Opera Group Orch, Purcell Singers, C. Watson (sop), P. Pears (ten) [score by Britten & Imogen Holst] *(rec 1959)* † When night her purple veil had softly spread, Zd201 BBC (Purcell the Performer) ▲ 8003 (17.97)

J. Feldman (sop), G. Laurens (mez), P. Cantor (ten), W. Christie (cnd), Les Arts Florissants [ENG] HAM ▲ 905173 (18.97)

PURCELL, HENRY (cont.)

Dido & Aeneas (opera in 3 acts) [lib Nahum Tate], Z.626 (ca 1689) (cont.)

V. Gens (sop—Dido), C. Brua (sop—Sorceress), S. Daneman (sop—1st witch/2nd woman), G. Mechaly (sop—2nd witch), S. Marin-Degor (sop—Belinda), S. Dugardin (alt—Chorus), J. Fouchécourt (ten—Sailor/Spirit), N. Berg (bass—Aeneas), J. Arnold (bass—Chorus), W. Christie (hpd), W. Christie (cnd), Les Arts Florissants *(rec Massy Opera Theatre, Nov 8-11, 1994)* ERAT ▲ 98477 [DDD] (16.97)

R. Holton (sop—Belinda), E. Priday (sop—2nd Woman), D. Deam (sop—1st Witch), S. Beesley (sop—2nd Witch), T. Shaw (mez—Sorceress), J. P. Kenny (alt—Spirit), C. Watkinson (cta—Dido), P. Tindall (ten—Sailor), G. Mosley (bass—Aeneas), J. E. Gardiner (cnd) , Monteverdi Choir London *(rec Bristol, UK, July 12-14, 1990)* † Welcome to all the pleasures, Z.339 PPHI ▲ 32114 (16.97)

E. Kirkby (sop), J. Nelson (mez), D. Thomas (bass), A. Parrott (cnd) , Taverner Choir [ENG] CHN (Chaconne) ▲ 521 [DDD] (16.97)

A. Monoyios (sop—Belinda), M. Hall (sop—Spirit/2nd Witch), S. Saunders (sop—1st Woman/2nd Woman), J. Lane (mez—Dido/Sorceress), B. Butterfield (ten—Sailor), R. Braun (bar—Aeneas), J. Lamon (cnd), Tafelmusik, Tafelmusik Chamber Choir *(rec CBC Toronto, Apr 26-29, 1995)* † Abdelazer (sels); Chacony Strs, Z.730; Overture à 5, Z.772 SMS ▲ 5147 [DDD] (16.97)

J. Norman (sop), M. McLaughlin (sop), T. Allen (bar), R. Leppard (cnd), English CO, Ambrosian Singers [ENG] PPHI ▲ 16299 [DDD] (16.97)

A. Parrott (cnd), Taverner Players, Taverner Choir, E. V. Evera (sop—Dido), J. Lax (sop—Belinda), H. M. Orbaek (sop—2nd Woman), K. Eckersley (sop—Enchantress I), L. Skeaping (sop—Enchantress II), S. Stowe (sop—Spirit), H. Andrews (ten—Sorceress), D. Wootton (ten—Sailor), B. Parry (bar—Aeneas) SNYC ▲ 62993 (16.97)

T. Pinnock (cnd), English Concert, L. Dawson (sop), A. S. von Otter (mez), N. Rogers (ten), S. Varcoe (bass) [ENG] PARC ▲ 27624 [DDD] (16.97)

M. Plazas (sop—1st witch), R. Evans (sop—Belinda), M. Ewing (sop—Dido), P. Rozario (sop—2nd woman), P. H. Stephens (mez—2nd witch), S. Burgess (mez—Sorceress), J. Bowman (ct—Spirit), J. MacDougall (ten—Sailor), K. Daymond (bar—Aeneas), R. Hickox (cnd), Collegium Musicum 90 CHN (Early Music) ▲ 586 [DDD] (16.97)

A. Travis (sop—2nd Witch), C. Hoffman (sop—Belinda), J. Lane (mez—Dido), D. Halac (mez—Sorceress/Spirit), E. Norman (alt), T. Bogdan (ten—A Sailor), M. Brown (bar—Aeneas), C. Streetman (bar), C. O'Leary (sgr—2nd Woman), S. Pillow (sgr—1st Witch), B. Brookshire (cnd), San Cassiano Musici *(rec St. Ignatius of Antioch Episcopal Church New York, Spring 1995) (lib)* VOXC ▲ 7518 (5.97)

R. Yakar (sop), A. Murray (mez), A. Scharinger (bass), N. Harnoncourt (cnd), Vienna Concentus Musicus, Arnold Schoenberg Choir TELC (Das alte Werke) ▲ 93686 (10.97)

Dido & Aeneas (selections)

G. Fischer (sop), R. King (cnd), King's Consort, New College Choir Oxford—When I am laid in earth ("Essential Purcell") † Anthems & Services; King Arthur (sels); Music of Purcell; Odes & Welcome Songs (misc); Sacred Music; Songs HYP ▲ 2 (7.97)

G. Laurens (mez), P. Cantor (ten), W. Christie (cnd), Les Arts Florissants ("A Purcell Companion") † Anthems & Services; King Arthur (sels); Music of Purcell; Oedipus (sels) HAM 6-▲ 2901528 (52.97)

E. Podles (cta), P. Peire (cnd) ("Ewa Podles: Recital") FORL ▲ 16620 [DDD] (16.97)

L. Stokowski (cnd), Royal PO—Dido's lament [arr Stokowski] *(rec London, England, Aug 1975)* † A. Dvořák:Serenade Strs, Op. 22; Vaughan Williams:Fant on a Theme of Tallis EMIC ▲ 66760 [ADD] (11.97)

The earth trembled for 2 Voices & Continuo, Z.197

P. McCreesh (cnd), Gabrieli Players, Gabrieli Consort ("Harmonia Sacra") † Awake, ye dead, Z.182; Close thine eyes & sleep secure, Z.184; Ground in c, Z. T681; In guilty night, Z.134; In the black dismal dungeon of despair, Z.190; Lord, what is man?, Z.192; Lord, I can suffer thy rebukes, Z.136; O solitude, my sweetest choice, Z.406; O, I'm sick of life, Z.140; Plung'd in the confines of despair, Z.142; Voluntary in C; Voluntary, Z.720; With sick & famish'd eyes, Z.200 PARC ▲ 45829 [DDD] (16.97)

The Fairy Queen (semi-opera in 5 acts) [anon adaption from Shakespeare's A Midsummer Night's Dream], Z.629 (1692)

A. Deller (cnd), Stour Music Orch, Stour Music Chorus, A. Deller (cnd), Deller Consort HAM 2-▲ 190257 (29.97)

J. E. Gardiner (cnd), English Baroque Soloists, Monteverdi Choir London [ENG] PARC 2-▲ 19221 [DDD] (32.97)

The Fairy Queen (selections)

N. Argenta (sop), M. Huggett (cnd), CBC Vancouver Orch—See, even Night herself is here; Hark how all things † King Arthur (sels); Married Beau (sels); G. F. Handel:Alchymist, HWV 43; Alcina (sels) SMS (SM 5000) ▲ 5091 [DDD] (16.97)

Bergen Baroque—If love's a sweet passion *(rec June 1998)* ("The Lonely Shepherd") † Blow:Music Kbd; Finger:Vl Music; Paisible:Rcr Music; Pepusch:English Cants Book I; English Cants Book II *([ENG] texts)* BIS ▲ 965 [DDD] (17.97)

C. Bott (sop), Purcell Quartet—Hark how all things; If love's a sweet passion; See, even Night herself is here; Thus the ever grateful spring ("Purcell Miscellany") † Music of Purcell; Prophetess (suite); Songs; Suites Hpd CHN (Chaconne) ▲ 571 [DDD] (17.97)

Canadian Brass *(rec Toronto, OT, Jan 30-Feb 3, 1995)* ("Fireworks!: Baroque Brass Favorites") † Abdelazer (sels); Fant upon one note, Z.745; Tpt Tune Hpd, Z.678; J. Clarke:Trumpet Voluntary; G. F. Handel:Concerti grossi, Op. 3; Royal Fireworks Music, HWV 351; Samson (sels); Serse (sels); Solomon (arrival of the queen of Sheba); Water Music, HWV 348-50 RCAV (Red Seal) ▲ 68257 [DDD] (16.97)

T. Charlston (hpd)—Ov *(rec Crypt of St. Etheldrea's London, England, June 26-27, 1994)* ("Suites and Transcriptions for Harpsichord") † Hpd Music; Hpd Music (misc); King Arthur (sels) NXIN ▲ 8553982 [DDD] (5.97)

A. Deller (ct), R. Skeaping (vn), W. Kuijken (b vl), J. Ryan (b vl), W. Christie (hpd), R. Elliot (org)—O let me weep; Thrice happy lovers ("Music for a while") † Bonduca (sels); Comical History of Don Quixote (sels); Indian Queen (sels); King Arthur (sels); Oedipus (sels); Pausanias (sels); Sacred Music; Songs HAM (40th Anniversary Edition) ▲ 94249 [ADD] (12.97)

A. Deller (ct), R. Skeaping (vn), W. Kuijken (vl), J. Ryan (vl), W. Christie (hpd), R. Elliott (hpd)—O let me weep; Thrice happy lovers *(rec Apr 1979)* † Bonduca (sels); Indian Queen (sels); King Arthur (sels); Pausanias (sels); Prophetess (sels); Sacred Music; Songs HAM ▲ 90249 (18.97)

L. Habeck (sop), Minstrelsey!—If love's a sweet passion *(rec Minneapolis, MN, Nov 1996)* † Chaconne; Adson:Adsonns Maske; Anonymous:Black Nag; Cupararee; King's Mistress; Love's Triumph; Mountebanks Dance; Second of Grey's Inn; Sir Francis Bacon; Sir Francis Bacon II; Standing Masque; Trip to Paris; Wilsons Love; J. Gay:Beggar's Opera (sels); Kapsberger:Kapsberger; Pepusch:Allegro; Traditional:Arran Boat; Morning Dew/Sally Gardens; Swallows Tail Reel LYR ▲ 8032 [AAD/DDD] (16.97)

J. Lamon (cnd), Tafelmusik—Ov; Prelude *(rec Toronto, Canada, Apr 8-10, 1994)* ("Ayres for the Theatre") † Indian Queen (sels); King Arthur (sels); Prophetess (sels) SNYC ▲ 66169 [DDD] (16.97)

S. McNair (sop), L. Dreyfus (vc/vl/vc/vl), P. O'Dette (archlt), C. Hogwood (hpd/org/org), S. Standage (vn), C. S. Perkins (tpt), C. Hogwood (cnd), Academy of Ancient Music—Hark, the Ech'ing air; O let me weep *(rec St. John's, London, England, 1994)* ("The Echoing Air") † Bonduca (sels); Chacony Strs, Z.730; Indian Queen (sels); King Arthur (sels); Libertine (sels); Music of Purcell; Pausanias (sels); Songs PPHI ▲ 46081 (16.97)

M. Papadopoulos (cnd), City of Oxford Orch—Suite *(rec St. Barnabas Church, Oxford, England, May 1994)* ("Baroque Encores") † Albinoni:Adagio; A. Corelli:Con grosso, Op. 6/8; G. F. Handel:Solomon (arrival of the queen of Sheba); Water Music, HWV 348-50; Torelli:Con for 2 Tpts INMP (Classics) ▲ 1104 (11.97)

M. Pearlman (cnd), Boston Baroque Orch—Hornpipe; Dance for the Fairies; Chaconne † Abdelazer (sels); Dido & Aeneas, Z.626; Gordian Knot Unty'd (sels); Married Beau (sels); Timon of Athens (sels) TEL ▲ 80424 [DDD] (16.97)

Pro Arte Antiqua Prague *(rec Korunní Prague, Czech Republic, Feb 1993)* ("Theatre Music") † Abdelazer, Z.570; Gordian Knot Unty'd, Z.597 ARTA ▲ 43 (16.97)

S. Sanford (sop), B. Wissick (vl), R. Erickson (hpd/org)—Hark, the Ech'ing air † Comical History of Don Quixote (sels); Hail, bright Cecilia, Z.328; Songs; Tyrannic Love (sels) ALBA ▲ 127 (16.97)

T. Svendsen (vn), T. Træholt (vn), W. T. Have (va), K. Englund (hpd)—Prelude; Hornpipe; Dance for the Fairies; Jig; Air; Monkey's Dance *(rec Copenhagen, Denmark)* ("Violon-Bande: The Danish Violon-Bande") † Fants Vls; Hpd Music; Music of Purcell; Telemann:Geographical Suite; Getreue Music-Meister; Sonate (12) metodiche; Sons (6) Corellisantes ROND ▲ 8363 [DDD] (18.97)

The Fairy Queen:Orchestral Suites

J. Savall (cnd), Concert des Nations *(rec Collégiale Romane du Château de Cardona, Sept 1996)* † Prophetess (sels) FONT ▲ 8583 [DDD] (18.97)

Scholars Baroque Ensemble *(rec Nov 1992)* NXIN 2-▲ 550660 [DDD] (15.97)

Fantasia upon a Ground in D/F for 3 Violins (or Recorders) & Continuo, Z.731 (c1680)

C. Balding (vn), U. Wild (hpd) *(rec Netherlands)* ("Henry Purcell & His Time") † Pavan à 3; Pavan à 4; J. Jenkins:Fant in d Va & Vn; W. Lawes:Royall Consort Suites; M. Locke:Suite III 2 Vns, Vol & Org; Suite IV 2 Vns, Vol & Hpd; C. Simpson:Prelude & Divisions on a Ground; Traditional:John Come Kiss CCL ▲ 4792 [DDD] (18.97)

Fantasia upon one note in F for 5 Viols, Z.745 (ca 1680)

Canadian Brass *(rec Toronto, OT, Jan 30- Feb 3, 1995)* ("Fireworks!: Baroque Brass Favorites") † Abdelazer (sels); Fairy Queen (sels); Tpt Tune Hpd, Z.678; J. Clarke:Trumpet Voluntary; G. F. Handel:Concerti grossi, Op. 3; Royal Fireworks Music, HWV 351; Samson (sels); Serse (sels); Solomon (arrival of the queen of Sheba); Water Music, HWV 348-50 RCAV (Red Seal) ▲ 68257 [DDD] (16.97)

PURCELL, HENRY (cont.)

Fantasia upon one note in F for 5 Viols, Z.745 (ca 1680) (cont.)

N. Harnoncourt (cnd), Vienna Concentus Musicus *(rec Vienna, 1965)* ("The Fantasias for Viols") † Fants Vls; In Nomine, Z.746; In Nomine, Z.747 VC ▲ 8091 [ADD] (13.97)

L. Köhler (cnd), HR Brass *(rec Justinukirsche Höchst, Germany, June 1990)* † In Nomine, Z.746; In Nomine, Z.747; J. S. Bach:Brandenburg Con 3, BWV 1048; S. Barber:Mutations from Bach; E. Carter:Fantasy; A. Copland:Fanfare for the Common Man; G. F. Handel:Royal Fireworks Music, HWV 351 CAPO ▲ 10361 [DDD] (11.97)

Fantasias for Viols (complete)

J. Savall (cnd) † In Nomine, Z.746; In Nomine, Z.747 ASTR ▲ 8536 (18.97)

Fantasias (3) in d, F & g for 3 Viols, Z.732-734 (ca 1680)

N. Harnoncourt (cnd), Vienna Concentus Musicus *(rec Vienna, 1965)* ("The Fantasias for Viols") † Fant upon one note, Z.745; In Nomine, Z.746; In Nomine, Z.747 VC ▲ 8091 [ADD] (13.97)

Fantasias (9) in g, B♭, F, c, d, a, e, G & d for 4 Viols, Z.735-743 (1680)

T. Svendsen (vn), T. Træholt (vn), W. T. Have (va), M. Rasmussen (va da gamba) *(rec Copenhagen, Denmark)* ("Violon-Bande: The Danish Violon-Bande") † Fairy Queen (sels); Hpd Music; Music of Purcell; Telemann:Geographical Suite; Getreue Music-Meister; Sonate (12) metodiche; Sons (6) Corellisantes ROND ▲ 8363 [DDD] (18.97)

The Gordian Knot Unty'd (incidental music) for Ensemble, Z.597 (1691)

N. McGegan (cnd), Philharmonia Baroque Orch † Dido & Aeneas, Z.626 HAM ▲ 907110 (18.97)

F. Mahler (cnd), Hartford CO *(rec 1960)* † Abdelazer, Z.570; Married Beau, Z.603; Musick's Hand-maid; Virtuous Wife, Z.611 VC ▲ 4044 [ADD] (13.97)

Pro Arte Antiqua Prague *(rec Korunni Prague, Feb 1993)* ("Theatre Music") † Abdelazer, Z.570; Fairy Queen (sels) ARTA ▲ 43 (16.97)

The Gordian Knot Unty'd (selections)

R. Leppard (cnd), English CO † Old Bachelor (sels); Son Tpt, Z.850; Vivaldi:Cons Vn Strs, Op. 8/1-4 SNYC ▲ 44644 [DDD] (10.97)

R. Leppard (hpd), R. Leppard (cnd), English CO ("Sunday Brunch. Vol 2") † Abdelazer (sels); J. S. Bach:Cant 147; Cant 156; Cant 78; Con 5 Hpd, BWV 1056; Suite 2 Fl, BWV 1067; G. F. Handel:Minuet Vc & Pno; Solomon (arrival of the queen of Sheba); Water Music (sels); A. Marcello:Con Ob Strs in d, Op. 1; Mouret:Suite de symphonies; V. Tommasini:Donne di buon umore (sels); Vivaldi:Con Mand, RV.425; Con Mands, RV.532; Cons Fl, Op. 10/1-6; Cons Vn Strs, Op. 8/1-4 SNYC (Dinner Classics) ▲ 46359 [AAD] (9.97)

M. Pearlman (cnd), Boston Baroque Orch—Air; Rondeau minuet † Abdelazer (sels); Dido & Aeneas, Z.626; Fairy Queen (sels); Married Beau (sels); Timon of Athens (sels) TEL ▲ 80424 [DDD] (16.97)

Ground in c for Harpsichord, Z. T681

P. McCreesh (cnd), Gabrieli Players, Gabrieli Consort ("Harmonia Sacra") † Awake, ye dead, Z.182; Close thine eyes & sleep secure, Z.184; In guilty night, Z.134; In the black dismal dungeon of despair, Z.190; Lord, what is man?, Z.192; Lord, I can suffer thy rebukes, Z.136; O solitude, my sweetest choice, Z.406; O, I'm sick of life, Z.140; Plung'd in the confines of despair, Z.142; The earth trembled, Z.197; Voluntary in C; Voluntary, Z.720; With sick & famish'd eyes, Z.200 PARC ▲ 45829 [DDD] (16.97)

Hail, bright Cecilia (song) for solo Voices, Chamber Ensemble & Chorus [for St. Cecilia's Day], Z.328 (1692)

A. Cantelo (sop), A. Deller (ct), W. Brown (ten), M. Bevan (bar), M. Tippett (cnd), Kalmar CO London, Ambrosian Singers VC ▲ 8020 [ADD] (13.97)

P. Herreweghe (cnd), Collegium Vocale † Welcome to all the pleasures, Z.339 HAM ▲ 901643 (18.97)

R. Leanderson (bar), H. Fagius (org) *(rec Stockholm Sweden, May 16-17 & Oct 20, 1978)* ("Baroque & Romantic Vocal Music") † Sacred Music; Songs; E. Elgar:Sea Pictures, Op. 37; G. F. Handel:Alleluja & Amen; Dolce pur d'amor l'affanno, HWV 109a; Telemann:Ew'ge Quelle, milder Strom, TWV1: 546; Kleine Kantate von Wald und Au BIS ▲ 127 [AAD] (17.97)

S. Sanford (sop), B. Wissick (vl), R. Erickson (hpd/org)—'Tis nature's voice † Comical History of Don Quixote (sels); Fairy Queen (sels); Songs; Tyrannic Love (sels) ALBA ▲ 127 (16.97)

Harpsichord Music

T. Charlston (hpd)—New Ground Hpd, Z.T682 *(rec Crypt of St. Etheldrea's London, England, June 26-27, 1994)* ("Suites and Transcriptions for Harpsichord") † Fairy Queen (sels); Hpd Music (misc); King Arthur (sels) NXIN ▲ 8553982 [DDD] (5.97)

R. Chenut (hp)—Ground in Gamut, Z.645 *(rec Médias-Waimes, Belgium)* ("The Art of the Celtic Harp") † Anonymous:Hp Music; Motets; Chenut:Hp Music; Judenkünig:Hp Music; Milán:Hp Music; O'Gallagher:Hp Music; Vogelweide:Hp Music ARN (The Art of...) ▲ 60357 [AAD] (13.97)

R. Egarr (hpd)—Ground Hpd, Z.D221; Ground Hpd, Z.D222; New Ground Hpd, Z.T682 *(rec Utrecht, Netherlands, Aug 1995)* ("A Choice Collection of Restoration Harpsichord Music") † Suites Hpd; G. B. Draghi:Hpd Music; M. Locke:Suite Hpd GLOE ▲ 5145 [DDD] (16.97)

K. Englund (hpd)—New Scotch Tune Hpd, Z.655; New Irish Tune Hpd, Z.646; Hornpipe Hpd, Z.685 *(rec Copenhagen, Denmark)* ("Violon-Bande: The Danish Violon-Bande") † Fairy Queen (sels); Fants Vls; Music of Purcell; Telemann:Geographical Suite; Getreue Music-Meister; Sonate (12) metodiche; Sons (6) Corellisantes ROND ▲ 8363 [DDD] (18.97)

J. Gibbons (hpd)—Ground in c, Z. T681; Ah! how pleasant 'tis to love, Z.353; March Hpd, Z.647; Minuet Hpd, Z.649; Minuet Hpd, Z.650; New Scotch Tune Hpd, Z.655; New Ground Hpd, Z.T682; New Irish Tune Hpd, Z.646; Rigadoon, Z.653; Sefauchi's farewell, Z.656; Minuet d Hpd, Z.T688; Suite of Lessons, Z.665; Song Tune Hpd, Z.T695; March Hpd, Z.648; New Minuet Hpd, Z.T689 *(rec The Music Room, Cambridge, MA, Nov 3-4, 1995)* † Suites Hpd CENT ▲ 2313 [DDD] (16.97)

S. Yates (hpd)—Ground Hpd, Z.D222; Round O Hpd, Z.684; Ground Hpd, Z.D221 ("Harpsichord") † Music of Purcell; Suites Hpd CHN (Early Music) ▲ 587 [DDD] (16.97)

In guilty night for Voices & Continuo, Z.134

P. McCreesh (cnd), Gabrieli Players, Gabrieli Consort ("Harmonia Sacra") † Awake, ye dead, Z.182; Close thine eyes & sleep secure, Z.184; Ground in c, Z. T681; In the black dismal dungeon of despair, Z.190; Lord, what is man?, Z.192; Lord, I can suffer thy rebukes, Z.136; O solitude, my sweetest choice, Z.406; O, I'm sick of life, Z.140; Plung'd in the confines of despair, Z.142; The earth trembled, Z.197; Voluntary in C; Voluntary, Z.720; With sick & famish'd eyes, Z.200 PARC ▲ 45829 [DDD] (16.97)

In Nomine in g for 6 Viols, Z.746 (ca 1680)

N. Harnoncourt (cnd), Vienna Concentus Musicus *(rec Vienna, Germany, 1965)* ("The Fantasias for Viols") † Fant upon one note, Z.745; Fants Vls; In Nomine, Z.747 VC ▲ 8091 [ADD] (13.97)

L. Köhler (cnd), HR Brass *(rec Justinukirsche Höchst, Germany, 1990)* † Fant upon one note, Z.745; In Nomine, Z.747; J. S. Bach:Brandenburg Con 3, BWV 1048; S. Barber:Mutations from Bach; E. Carter:Fantasy; A. Copland:Fanfare for the Common Man; G. F. Handel:Royal Fireworks Music, HWV 351 CAPO ▲ 10361 [DDD] (11.97)

J. Savall (cnd) † Fants Vls (comp); In Nomine, Z.747 ASTR ▲ 8536 (18.97)

In Nomine in g for 7 Viols, Z.747 (ca 1680)

N. Harnoncourt (cnd), Vienna Concentus Musicus *(rec Vienna, Germany, 1965)* ("The Fantasias for Viols") † Fant upon one note, Z.745; Fants Vls; In Nomine, Z.746 VC ▲ 8091 [ADD] (13.97)

L. Köhler (cnd), HR Brass *(rec Justinukirsche Höchst, Germany, June 1990)* † Fant upon one note, Z.745; In Nomine, Z.746; J. S. Bach:Brandenburg Con 3, BWV 1048; S. Barber:Mutations from Bach; E. Carter:Fantasy; A. Copland:Fanfare for the Common Man; G. F. Handel:Royal Fireworks Music, HWV 351 CAPO ▲ 10361 [DDD] (11.97)

J. Savall (cnd) † Fants Vls (comp); In Nomine, Z.746 ASTR ▲ 8536 (18.97)

In the black dismal dungeon of despair for Voice & Continuo, Z.190

P. McCreesh (cnd), Gabrieli Players, Gabrieli Consort ("Harmonia Sacra") † Awake, ye dead, Z.182; Close thine eyes & sleep secure, Z.184; Ground in c, Z. T681; In guilty night, Z.134; Lord, what is man?, Z.192; Lord, I can suffer thy rebukes, Z.136; O solitude, my sweetest choice, Z.406; O, I'm sick of life, Z.140; Plung'd in the confines of despair, Z.142; The earth trembled, Z.197; Voluntary in C; Voluntary, Z.720; With sick & famish'd eyes, Z.200 PARC ▲ 45829 [DDD] (16.97)

The Indian Queen (semi-opera in prologue & 5 acts) [lib Purcell after Dryden & Howard], Z.630 (1695)

T. Bonner (sop), S. Bruce-Payne (alt), S. Liley (ten), E. Caswell (bass), C. Mackintosh (cnd), Purcell Simfony Voices *(rec Orford Suffolk, Sept 21-23, 1994)* LINN ▲ 5035 (16.97)

A. Deller (cnd), Deller Choir HAM (Suite) ▲ 790243 (12.97)

The Indian Queen (selections)

A. Deller (ct), R. Skeaping (vn), W. Kuijken (vl), J. Ryan (vl), W. Christie (hpd), R. Elliott (hpd)—I attempt from love's sickness to fly *(rec Apr 1979)* † Bonduca (sels); Fairy Queen (sels); King Arthur (sels); Pausanias (sels); Prophetess (sels); Sacred Music; Songs HAM ▲ 90249 (18.97)

A. Deller (ct), R. Skeaping (vn), W. Kuijken (b vl), J. Ryan (b vl), W. Christie (hpd), R. Elliot (org)—I attempt from love's sickness to fly ("Music for a while") † Bonduca (sels); Comical History of Don Quixote (sels); Fairy Queen (sels); King Arthur (sels); Oedipus (sels); Pausanias (sels); Sacred Music; Songs HAM (40th Anniversary Edition) ▲ 94249 [ADD] (12.97)

PURCELL, HENRY (cont.)

The Indian Queen (selections) (cont.)

K. Ferrier (cta), I. Baillie (sop), G. Moore (pno)—Let us wander, not unseen *(rec London, England, Sep 21, 1945)* † Come, ye sons of art, away, Z.323; King Arthur (sels); C. W. Gluck:Orfeo ed Euridice (sels); M. Greene:Anthems; G. F. Handel:Ottone (sels); G. Mahler:Kindertotenlieder; Mendelssohn (-Bartholdy):Songs EMIC (Great Recordings of the Century) ▲ 66963 [ADD] (11.97)

J. Lamon (cnd), Tafelmusik *(rec Toronto Canada, Apr 8-10, 1994)* ("Ayres for the Theatre") † Fairy Queen (sels); King Arthur (sels); Prophetess (sels) SNYC ▲ 66169 [DDD] (16.97)

R. Leppard (cnd), English CO † King Arthur (sels); Songs; Fasch:Con Tpt Obs; G. F. Handel:Ode for the Birthday of Queen Anne; Samson (sels); Molter:Con 2 Tpt; Torelli:Sons à 5 Tpts SNYC ▲ 39061 [DDD] (16.97)

S. McNair (sop), L. Dreyfus (vc/vl), P. O'Dette (archlt), C. Hogwood (hpd/org), C. Hogwood (cnd), Academy of Ancient Music—I attempt from love's sickness to fly *(rec St. John's, London, England, 1994)* ("The Echoing Air") † Bonduca (sels); Chacony Strs, Z.730; Fairy Queen (sels); King Arthur (sels); Libertine (sels); Music of Purcell; Pausanias (sels); Songs PPHI ▲ 46081 (16.97)

E. Söderström (sop), K. Meyer (mez), J. Eyron (pno)—Let us wander, not unseen *(rec Nacka, Sweden, Nov 1 & 3, 1974)* ("Elisabeth Söderström & Kerstin Meyer") † Come, ye sons of art, away, Z.323; King Arthur (sels); A. Dvořák:Moravian Duets, Opp. 20, 32, 38; Geijer:Songs; Kodály:Songs; G. Rossini:Soirées musicales; Songs; P. Tchaikovsky:Duets; Wennerberg:Songs *(E text)* BIS ▲ 17 [AAD] (17.97)

King Arthur, or the British Worthy (semi-opera in 5 acts) [text J. Dryden], Z.628 (1691)

A. Deller (cnd), King's Musick, A. Deller (cnd), Deller Choir, H. Sheppard (sop), R. Hardy (sop), J. Knibbs (cta), A. Deller (ct), M. Deller (ct), P. Elliott (ten), L. Nixon (ten), M. Bevan (bar), N. Beavan (bass) HAM 2-▲ 90252 (36.97)

King Arthur, or the British Worthy (selections)

D. Brooks (vn), L. Brooks (vn), J. Cosart (va), V. Reese (db), M. Burke (vl), L. Goetz (ob), S. Weiner (ob), T. Gerber (hpd), H. H. Leck (cnd), Indianapolis Children's Choir—Fairest isle [arr S. Rickards] *(rec May-June 1995)* VAIA ▲ 1030 [DDD]

T. Charlston (hpd)—Ov *(rec Crypt of St. Etheldrea's London, England, June 26-27, 1994)* ("Suites and Transcriptions for Harpsichord") † Fairy Queen (sels); Hpd Music; Hpd Music (misc) NXIN ▲ 8553982 [DDD] (5.97)

A. Deller (cnd), Deller Consort & Choir, A. Deller (cnd), King's Music ("A Purcell Companion") † Anthems & Services; Dido & Aeneas (sels); Music of Purcell; Oedipus (sels) HAM 6-▲ 2901528 (52.97)

A. Deller (ct), R. Skeaping (vn), W. Kuijken (vl), J. Ryan (vl), W. Christie (hpd), R. Elliott (hpd)—Fairest isle *(rec Apr 1979)* † Bonduca (sels); Fairy Queen (sels); Indian Queen (sels); Pausanias (sels); Prophetess (sels); Sacred Music; Songs HAM ▲ 90249 (18.97)

A. Deller (ct), R. Skeaping (vn), W. Kuijken (b vl), J. Ryan (b vl), W. Christie (hpd), R. Elliot (org)—Fairest isle ("Music for a while") † Bonduca (sels); Comical History of Don Quixote (sels); Fairy Queen (sels); Indian Queen (sels); Oedipus (sels); Pausanias (sels); Sacred Music; Songs HAM (40th Anniversary Edition) ▲ 94249 [ADD] (12.97)

K. Ferrier (cta), I. Baillie (sop), G. Moore (pno)—Shepherd, shepherd, leave decoying *(rec London, England, Sep 21, 1945)* † Come, ye sons of art, away, Z.323; Indian Queen (sels); C. W. Gluck:Orfeo ed Euridice (sels); M. Greene:Anthems; G. F. Handel:Ottone (sels); G. Mahler:Kindertotenlieder; Mendelssohn (-Bartholdy):Songs EMIC (Great Recordings of the Century) ▲ 66963 [ADD] (11.97)

M. Huggett (cnd), CBC Vancouver SO—Ov; Air; Hornpipe; Fairest isle; Air; Chaconne † Fairy Queen (sels); Married Beau (sels); G. F. Handel:Alchymist, HWV 43; Alcina (sels) SMS (SM 5000) ▲ 5091 [DDD] (16.97)

R. King (cnd), King's Consort, New College Choir Oxford—Fairest isle ("Essential Purcell") † Anthems & Services; Dido & Aeneas (sels); Music of Purcell; Odes & Welcome Songs (misc); Sacred Music; Songs HYP ▲ 2 (7.97)

J. Lamon (cnd), Tafelmusik ("Age of Elegance Greatest Hits") † Trumpet Tune & Ayre; Beethoven:Bagatelle Pno in a, WoO 59; Contredanses Orch, WoO 14; Boccherini:Minuetto Strs; C. W. Gluck:Iphigénie en Aulide (sels); Orfeo ed Euridice (dance); G. F. Handel:Cons (16) Org; Serse (sels); Water Music (sels); J. Haydn:Qts (6) Strs, H.III/13-18, Op. 3; Sym 82; W. A. Mozart:German Dances (3), K.605; Kleine Nachtmusik, K.525 SNYC ▲ 62369 [ADD] (9.97) ▮ 62369 [ADD] (5.98)

J. Lamon (cnd), Tafelmusik *(rec Toronto Canada, Apr 8-10, 1994)* ("Ayres for the Theatre") † Fairy Queen (sels); Indian Queen (sels); Prophetess (sels) SNYC ▲ 66169 [DDD] (16.97)

R. Leppard (cnd), English CO † Indian Queen (sels); Songs; Fasch:Con Tpt Obs; G. F. Handel:Ode for the Birthday of Queen Anne; Samson (sels); Molter:Con 2 Tpt; Torelli:Sons à 5 Tpts SNYC ▲ 39061 [DDD] (16.97)

C. McFadden (sop), V. Gens (sop), S. Piau (sop), M. Padmore (ten), I. Paton (ten), P. Salomaa (bass), J. Best (bass), W. Christie (cnd), Les Arts Florissants ERAT ▲ 17351 (16.97)

S. McNair (sop), L. Dreyfus (vc/vl), P. O'Dette (archlt), C. Hogwood (hpd/org), C. Hogwood (cnd), Academy of Ancient Music—Fairest isle *(rec St. John's, London, England, 1994)* ("The Echoing Air") † Bonduca (sels); Chacony Strs, Z.730; Fairy Queen (sels); Indian Queen (sels); Libertine (sels); Music of Purcell; Pausanias (sels); Songs PPHI ▲ 46081 (16.97)

E. Söderström (sop), K. Meyer (mez), J. Eyron (pno)—Two daughters of this aged stream *(rec Nacka, Sweden, Nov 1 & 3, 1974)* ("Elisabeth Söderström & Kerstin Meyer") † Come, ye sons of art, away, Z.323; Indian Queen (sels); A. Dvořák:Moravian Duets, Opp. 20, 32, 38; Geijer:Songs; Kodály:Songs; G. Rossini:Soirées musicales; Songs; P. Tchaikovsky:Duets; Wennerberg:Songs *(E text)* BIS ▲ 17 [AAD] (17.97)

King Richard II, or the History of the Sicillian Usurper (selections)

R. Jacobs (ct), W. Kuijken (vl), K. Junghänel (thb)—Retired from any mortal's sight † Music of Purcell; Oedipus (sels); Pausanias (sels); Prophetess (sels); Songs ACCE ▲ 57802 (17.97)

The Libertine, or the Libertine Destroyed (selections) (1692)

S. McNair (sop), L. Dreyfus (vc/vl), P. O'Dette (archlt), C. Hogwood (hpd/org), C. S. Perkins (tpt), C. Hogwood (cnd), Academy of Ancient Music—To arms, heroic Prince *(rec St. John's, London, England, 1994)* ("The Echoing Air") † Bonduca (sels); Chacony Strs, Z.730; Fairy Queen (sels); Indian Queen (sels); King Arthur (sels); Music of Purcell; Pausanias (sels); Songs PPHI ▲ 46081 (16.97)

Lord, I can suffer thy rebukes for Voices & Continuo, Z.136

P. McCreesh (cnd), Gabrieli Players, Gabrieli Consort ("Harmonia Sacra") † Awake, ye dead, Z.182; Close thine eyes & sleep secure, Z.184; Ground in c, Z. T681; In guilty night, Z.134; In the black dismal dungeon of despair, Z.190; Lord, what is man?, Z.192; O solitude, my sweetest choice, Z.406; O, I'm sick of life, Z.140; Plung'd in the confines of despair, Z.142; The earth trembled, Z.197; Voluntary in C; Voluntary, Z.720; With sick & famish'd eyes, Z.200 PARC ▲ 45829 [DDD] (16.97)

Lord, what is man? for Voices & Continuo, Z.192

P. McCreesh (cnd), Gabrieli Players, Gabrieli Consort ("Harmonia Sacra") † Awake, ye dead, Z.182; Close thine eyes & sleep secure, Z.184; Ground in c, Z. T681; In guilty night, Z.134; In the black dismal dungeon of despair, Z.190; Lord, I can suffer thy rebukes, Z.136; O solitude, my sweetest choice, Z.406; O, I'm sick of life, Z.140; Plung'd in the confines of despair, Z.142; The earth trembled, Z.197; Voluntary in C; Voluntary, Z.720; With sick & famish'd eyes, Z.200 PARC ▲ 45829 [DDD] (16.97)

Love's goddess sure was blind (ode) for Strings, Continuo & Chorus [for Queen Mary's Birthday], Z.331 (1692)

N. Burrowes (sop), J. Bowman (ct), C. Brett (ct), R. Lloyd (bass), D. Munrow (cnd) *(rec 1975)* ("Birthday Odes for Queen Mary") † Come, ye sons of art, away, Z.323 *([ENG,GER] text)* VCL (Veritas) ▲ 61333 [ADD] (11.97)

Deller Consort † Welcome to all the pleasures, Z.339 HMA ▲ 190222 (9.97)

The Married Beau, or The Curious Impertinent (incidental music) for Chamber Ensemble [text Crowne], Z.603 (1694)

F. Mahler (cnd), Hartford CO *(rec 1960)* † Abdelazer, Z.570; Gordian Knot Unty'd, Z.597; Musick's Hand-maid; Virtuous Wife, Z.611 VC ▲ 4044 [ADD] (13.97)

The Married Beau (selections)

N. Argenta (sop), M. Huggett (cnd), CBC Vancouver SO—Ov; Slow Air; Hornpipe; See! Where repenting Celia lyes; Air; Hornpipe; Jig; Tpt Air; March; Hornpipe on a ground † Fairy Queen (sels); King Arthur (sels); G. F. Handel:Alchymist, HWV 43; Alcina (sels) SMS (SM 5000) ▲ 5091 [DDD] (16.97)

M. Pearlman (cnd), Boston Baroque Orch—Hornpipe on a ground † Abdelazer (sels); Dido & Aeneas, Z.626; Fairy Queen (sels); Gordian Knot Unty'd (sels); Timon of Athens (sels) TEL ▲ 80424 [DDD] (16.97)

The Mock Marriage (selections)

J. Shirley-Quirk (bar), N. Liddell (vn), I. McMahon (vn), A. Gauntlett (vl), M. Isepp (hpd/pno)—Man is for the woman made; 'Twas within a furlong of Edinboro' town ("A Recital of English Songs") † Songs; G. Butterworth:Songs from A Shropshire Lad; Moeran:Songs SAGA ▲ 3336 (15.97)

Music of Purcell

B. Borden (sop), R. Shaw (hpd), Academy of the Begynhof Amsterdam *(High on a throne of glitt'ring ore, Z.465)*, R. Shaw (hpd) *(Son 3 in d (from 12 Sons of 3 Parts, 1683), Z.792; Son 6 in g (from 10 Sons of 4 Parts, 1697), Z.807)* † Odes & Welcome Songs (misc); Songs; Tempest (sels); Blow:No, Lesbia, No, You Ask in Vain GLOE ▲ 5029 [DDD] (16.97)

R. Browder (va/vn), Purcell Quartet—Fant upon a Ground, Z.731 ("Vol. 2") † Chacony Strs, Z.730; Pavans; Sons (22) Vns, Z.790-811 CHN ▲ 8663 [DDD] (16.97)

A. Cantelo (sop), A. Deller (ct), M. Bevan (bar), N. Marriner (vn), G. Jones (vn), P. Gibbs (vn), D. Dupré (vl), G. Malcolm (hpd), W. Bergmann (hpd)—Fant upon a Ground, Z.731; Fant upon one note, Z.745; Music Lessons 1-12 from Musick's Hand-Maid, Part I; New Irish Tune Hpd, Z.646; Pavan Vn, Z.752; Son in g for Vn & Bc, Z.780; Son 9 in F, "Golden Son," Z.810 ("Celebrated Songs, Sacred Airs, Concerted Pieces for Strings & Harpsichord") † Old Bachelor (sels); Songs; Suites Hpd BG (The Bach Guild) 2-▲ 2002 [ADD] (26.97)

▲ = CD ♦ = Enhanced CD △ = MD ▮ = Cassette Tape ▯ = DCC

PURCELL, HENRY (cont.)
Music of Purcell (cont.)
L. Cummings (org), J. Summerly (cnd), Oxford Camerata—March Tpts, Z.860a; Canzona Tpts, Z.860b *(rec Chapel of Hertford College Oxford, England, June 9-10, 1994)* † Anthems & Services; Songs; Thou knowest, Lord, the secrets of our hearts, Z.58c NXIN ▲ 553129 [DDD] (5.97)
D. Fasolis (cnd) , Swiss Radio Chorus—Music for the Funeral of Queen Mary † Odes & Welcome Songs (misc); Sacred Music AART ▲ 47375 [DDD] (10.97)
P. Herreweghe (cnd), Collegium Vocale *(Te Deum)*, C. Medlam (cnd), London Baroque *(Trio Sons; Pavans, Z.748-751; Ovs)*, J. Butt (org) *(Org Works)* ("A Purcell Companion") † Anthems & Services; Dido & Aeneas (sels); King Arthur (sels); Oedipus (sels) HAM 6-▲ 2901528 (52.97)
R. Jacobs (ct), W. Kuijken (vl), K. Junghänel (thb)—Pious Celinda goes to prayers, Z.410; Old Bachelor (sels) [As Amoret & Thirsis]; I lov'd fair Celia, Z.381 † King Richard II (sels); Oedipus (sels); Pausanias (sels); Prophetess (sels); Songs ACCE ▲ 57802 (17.97)
R. King (cnd), King's Consort, New College Choir Oxford—O! fair Cedaria, hide those eyes, Z.402; Hear my prayer, O Lord, Z.15; From hardy climes, Z.325 [The sparrow & the gentle dove]; Hosanna to the highest, Z.187; Raise, raise the voice, Z.334 [Mark how readily each pliant string]; She loves & she confesses too, Z.413; O How Blest Is the Isle; Vouchsafe, O Lord, to Keep Us This Day; Hail, bright Cecilia, Z.328 [With rapture of delight] ("Essential Purcell") † Anthems & Services; Dido & Aeneas (sels); King Arthur (sels); Odes & Welcome Songs (misc); Sacred Music; Songs HYP ▲ 2 (7.97)
R. Leppard (cnd), English CO—Abdelazer (sels) [Ov; Rondeau; Minuet; Jig; Hornpipe] † Abdelazer (sels); J. Pachelbel:Canon & Gigue SNYC ▮ 44650 [DDD] (5.98) ▲ 44650 [DDD] (10.97)
S. McNair (sop), L. Dreyfus (vc/vl), P. O'Dette (archlt), C. Hogwood (hpd/org), C. Hogwood (cnd), Academy of Ancient Music *(Cebell; We Come to Sing; Slow Air; Jig; Hear, Mighty Love; Staircase Ov; Tell me, some pitying angel; O solitude, my sweetest choice, Z.406; She that would gain a faithful lover, Z.414; Cupid, the slyest rogue alive, Z.367)*, S. McNair (sop), L. Dreyfus (vc/vl), P. O'Dette (archlt), C. S. Perkins (tpt), C. Hogwood (hpd/org), C. Hogwood (cnd), Academy of Ancient Music *(Tpt Tune Hpd, Z.678)*, S. McNair (sop), L. Dreyfus (vc/vl/vc/vl), P. O'Dette (archlt), C. Hogwood (hpd/org/hpd/org), C. Hogwood (cnd), Academy of Ancient Music *(Bonduca (sels) [O lead me to some peaceful gloom])*, S. McNair (sop), P. O'Dette (archlt), C. Hogwood (cnd), Academy of Ancient Music *(Oedipus (sels) [Music for a while]) (rec St. John's, London, England, 1994)* ("The Echoing Air") † Bonduca (sels); Chacony Strs, Z.730; Fairy Queen (sels); Indian Queen (sels); King Arthur (sels); Libertine (sels); Pausanias (sels); Songs PPHI ▲ 46081 (16.97)
P. Pears (ten), B. Britten (pno)—I Attempt from Love's Sickness to Fly *(rec Aldeburgh Festival, European Community, 1958-59)* † G. Fauré:Bonne chanson, Op. 61; F. Schubert:Die Sterne, D.939; R. Schumann:Liederkreis, Op. 39 BBC ▲ 8006 (17.97)
Purcell Quartet *(Timon of Athens (sels) [Curtain tune on a ground]; Overture à 5, Z.772; New Scotch Tune Hpd, Z.655; Sefauchi's farewell, Z.656; New Irish Tune Hpd, Z.646; Suite in G, Z.770; Suite [from Abdelazer]; Ov & Suite, Z.770 [Ov]; Staircase Ov; Ov Strs, Z.771; Son for Tpt & Strs [w. Bennett])*, M. Bennett (tpt), Purcell Quartet *(Cibell Tpt)* ("Purcell Miscellany") † Fairy Queen (sels); Prophetess (suite); Songs; Suites Hpd CHN (Chaconne) ▲ 571 [DDD] (17.97)
T. Svendsen (vn)—Prelude Vn, ZN.773 *(rec Copenhagen, Denmark)* ("Violon-Bande: The Danish Violon-Bande") † Fairy Queen (sels); Fants Vls; Hpd Music; Telemann:Geographical Suite; Getreue Music-Meister; Sonate (12) metodiche; Sons (6) Corellisantes ROND ▲ 8363 [DDD] (18.97)
S. Yates (hpd)—Ground in Gamut, Z.645; Prelude; Suite of Lessons, Z.665; New Ground Hpd, Z.T682; Saraband, Z.654 ("Harpsichord") † Hpd Music; Suites Hpd CHN (Early Music) ▲ 587 [DDD] (16.97)
Music for the Funeral of Queen Mary
Collegium Vocale † Te Deum & Jubilate, Z.232 HAM ▲ 901462 (18.97)
Datura Trombone Quartet, R. Gritton (cnd), North German Radio Chorus † Beethoven:Equale Trbns, WoO 30; Candotto:Missa brevis; B. Krol:Von Werden und Vergehen; I. Stravinsky:In memoriam Dylan Thomas ARSM ▲ 1154 [DDD] (17.97)
S. Gritton (sop), M. Kennedy (sop), J. Bowman (ct), N. Short (ct), R. Covey-Crump (ten), C. Daniels (ten), M. Milhofer (ten), M. George (bass), R. Evans (bass), E. O'Dwyer (trbn), J. Goodman (trbn), R. King (cnd), King's Consort ("Vol. VII") † Anthems & Services HYP ▲ 66677 [DDD] (18.97)
Music for the Theater
P. Holman (cnd), Parley of Instruments ("Ayres for the Theatre") HYP ▲ 55010 (9.97)
Musick's Hand-maid for Harpsichord [2nd part] (1687)
G. Malcolm (hpd) *(rec 1958)* † Abdelazer, Z.570; Gordian Knot Unty'd, Z.597; Married Beau, Z.603; Virtuous Wife, Z.611 VC ▲ 4044 [ADD] (13.97)
Musick's Hand-maid (consort music) for Voices & Instruments
E. Hargis (sop), R. Del Pozo (ten), I. Honeyman (ten), H. V. Kamp (bass), P. O'Dette (cittern/lt/thb), A. Lawrence-King (hpd/org), A. Lawrence-King (cnd) ("Musick's Hand-Maid") ASTR ▲ 8564 (18.97)
Now that the sun hath veiled his light (An Evening Hymn on a Ground) for Soprano & Continuo [text Fuller], Z.193 (1688)
R. Houghton (pno), H. H. Leck (cnd), Indianapolis Children's Choir [arr W.G. Whitaker] *(rec The Lodge, May-June 1995)* † Come, ye sons of art, away, Z.323; Odes & Welcome Songs (misc); Pausanias (sels); B. Britten:Birds; Ceremony of Carols, Op. 28 VAIA ▲ 1130 [DDD]
O solitude, my sweetest choice (song) for Voice & Continuo [text K. Phillips], Z.406
P. McCreesh (cnd), Gabrieli Players, Gabrieli Consort ("Harmonia Sacra") † Awake, ye dead, Z.182; Close thine eyes & sleep secure, Z.184; Ground in c, Z. T681; In guilty night, Z.134; In the black dismal dungeon of despair, Z.190; Lord, what is man?, Z.192; Lord, I can suffer thy rebukes, Z.136; O, I'm sick of life, Z.140; Plung'd in the confines of despair, Z.142; The earth trembled, Z.197; Voluntary in C; Voluntary, Z.720; With sick & famish'd eyes, Z.200 PARC ▲ 45829 [DDD] (16.97)
O, I'm sick of life for Voices & Continuo, Z.140
P. McCreesh (cnd), Gabrieli Players, Gabrieli Consort ("Harmonia Sacra") † Awake, ye dead, Z.182; Close thine eyes & sleep secure, Z.184; Ground in c, Z. T681; In guilty night, Z.134; In the black dismal dungeon of despair, Z.190; Lord, what is man?, Z.192; Lord, I can suffer thy rebukes, Z.136; O solitude, my sweetest choice, Z.406; Plung'd in the confines of despair, Z.142; The earth trembled, Z.197; Voluntary in C; Voluntary, Z.720; With sick & famish'd eyes, Z.200 PARC ▲ 45829 [DDD] (16.97)
Odes & Welcome Songs (complete)
R. King (cnd), King's Consort—Welcome to all the pleasures, Z.339; Now does the glorious day appear, Z.332; Arise, my Muse, Z.320 ("Complete Odes & Welcome Songs, Vol. 1") HYP ▲ 66314 [DDD] (18.97)
R. King (cnd), King's Consort—Hail, bright Cecilia, Z.328; Who can from joy refrain?, Z.342 ("Complete Odes & Welcome Songs, Vol. 2") HYP ▲ 66349 [DDD] (18.97)
R. King (cnd), King's Consort—Fly, bold rebellion, Z.324; Sound the trumpet, Z.335; Celebrate this festival, Z.321 ("Complete Odes & Welcome Songs, Vol. 3") HYP ▲ 66412 [DDD] (18.97)
Oedipus (selections)
A. Deller (alt), W. Kuijken (va), W. Christie (hpd)—Music for a while ("A Purcell Companion") † Anthems & Services; Dido & Aeneas (sels); King Arthur (sels); Music of Purcell HAM 6-▲ 2901528 (52.97)
A. Deller (ct), R. Skeaping (vn), W. Kuijken (b vl), J. Ryan (b vl), W. Christie (hpd), R. Elliot (org)—Music for a while ("Music for a while") † Bonduca (sels); Comical History of Don Quixote (sels); Fairy Queen (sels); Indian Queen (sels); King Arthur (sels); Pausanias (sels); Sacred Music; Songs HAM (40th Anniversary Edition) ▲ 94249 [ADD] (12.97)
R. Jacobs (ct), W. Kuijken (vl), K. Junghänel (thb)—Music for a while † King Richard II (sels); Music of Purcell; Pausanias (sels); Prophetess (sels); Songs ACCE ▲ 57802 (17.97)
The Old Bachelor (selections)
A. Cantelo (sop), A. Deller (ct), M. Bevan (bar), N. Marriner (vn), G. Jones (vn), P. Gibbs (vn), D. Dupré (vl), G. Malcolm (hpd), W. Bergmann (hpd)—Hornpipe ("Celebrated Songs, Sacred Airs, Concerted Pieces for Strings & Harpsichord") † Music of Purcell; Songs; Suites Hpd BG (The Bach Guild) 2-▲ 2002 [ADD] (26.97)
R. Leppard (cnd), English CO † Gordian Knot Unty'd (sels); Son Tpt, Z.850; Vivaldi:Cons Vn Strs, Op. 8/1-4 SNYC ▲ 44644 [DDD] (10.97)
Overture à 5 in g for 2 Violins, 2 Violas & Continuo, Z.772 (ca 1680)
J. Lamon (cnd), Tafelmusik *(rec CBC Toronto, Canada, Apr 26-29, 1995)* † Abdelazer (sels); Chacony Strs, Z.730; Dido & Aeneas, Z.626 SMS ▲ 5147 [DDD] (16.97)
Pausanias, the Betrayer of His Country (selections)
A. Deller (ct), R. Skeaping (vn), W. Kuijken (vl), J. Ryan (vl), W. Christie (hpd), R. Elliott (hpd)—Sweeter than roses *(rec Apr 1979)* † Bonduca (sels); Fairy Queen (sels); Indian Queen (sels); King Arthur (sels); Prophetess (sels); Sacred Music; Songs HAM ▲ 90249 (18.97)
A. Deller (ct), R. Skeaping (vn), W. Kuijken (b vl), J. Ryan (b vl), W. Christie (hpd), R. Elliot (org)—Sweeter than roses ("Music for a while") † Bonduca (sels); Comical History of Don Quixote (sels); Fairy Queen (sels); Indian Queen (sels); King Arthur (sels); Oedipus (sels); Sacred Music; Songs HAM (40th Anniversary Edition) ▲ 94249 [ADD] (12.97)
R. Jacobs (ct), W. Kuijken (vl), K. Junghänel (thb)—Sweeter than roses † King Richard II (sels); Music of Purcell; Oedipus (sels); Prophetess (sels); Songs ACCE ▲ 57802 (17.97)

PURCELL, HENRY (cont.)
Pausanias, the Betrayer of His Country (selections) (cont.)
S. McNair (sop), L. Dreyfus (vc/vl), P. O'Dette (archlt), C. Hogwood (hpd/org), C. Hogwood (cnd), Academy of Ancient Music—Sweeter than roses *(rec St. John's, London, England, 1994)* ("The Echoing Air") † Bonduca (sels); Chacony Strs, Z.730; Fairy Queen (sels); Indian Queen (sels); King Arthur (sels); Libertine (sels); Music of Purcell; Songs PPHI ▲ 46081 (16.97)
S. Rickards (ct), R. Houghton (pno)—Sweeter than roses [arr B. Britten] *(rec May-June 1995)* † Come, ye sons of art, away, Z.323; Now that the sun hath veiled his light (Eve Hymn), Z.193; Odes & Welcome Songs (misc); B. Britten:Birds; Ceremony of Carols, Op. 28 VAIA ▲ 1130 [DDD]
J. Vickers (ten), R. Woitach (pno) *(rec live New York, United States of America, Apr 30, 1967)* ("Jon Vickers in Concert") † Songs; A. Dvořák:Zigeunermelodien, Op. 55; G. F. Handel:Messiah (sels); A. Scarlatti:Cants & Duets; R. Schumann:Dichterliebe, Op. 48 VAIA ▲ 1032 [ADD]
Pavane & Chaconne for Orchestra
T. Füri (cnd), Bern Camerata † Albinoni:Adagio; J. S. Bach:Brandenburg Con 3, BWV 1048; Manfredini:Cons Vns, Op. 3; J. Pachelbel:Canon & Gigue NOVA ▲ 150004 (16.97)
Pavan à 3
C. Balding (vn), U. Wild (hpd) *(rec Netherlands)* ("Henry Purcell & His Time") † Fant upon a Ground, Z.731; Pavan à 4; J. Jenkins:Fant in d Va & Vn; W. Lawes:Royall Consort Suites; M. Locke:Suite III 2 Vns, Vol & Org; Suite IV 2 Vns, Vol & Hpd; C. Simpson:Prelude & Divisions on a Ground; Traditional:John Come Kiss *([ENG,GER] text)* CCL ▲ 4792 [DDD] (18.97)
Pavan à 4
C. Balding (vn), U. Wild (hpd) *(rec Netherlands)* ("Henry Purcell & His Time") † Fant upon a Ground, Z.731; Pavan à 3; J. Jenkins:Fant in d Va & Vn; W. Lawes:Royall Consort Suites; M. Locke:Suite III 2 Vns, Vol & Org; Suite IV 2 Vns, Vol & Hpd; C. Simpson:Prelude & Divisions on a Ground; Traditional:John Come Kiss *([ENG,GER] text)* CCL ▲ 4792 [DDD] (18.97)
Pavans (4) in A, a, B & g for 2 Violins & Continuo, Z.748-751 (ca 1680)
R. Browder (va/vn/va/vn), Purcell Quartet—No. 1 in A; No. 4 in g ("Vol. 2") † Chacony Strs, Z.730; Music of Purcell; Sons (22) Vns, Z.790-811 CHN ▲ 8663 [DDD] (16.97)
Plung'd in the confines of despair for Chorus, Z.142 (ca 1680)
P. McCreesh (cnd), Gabrieli Players, Gabrieli Consort ("Harmonia Sacra") † Awake, ye dead, Z.182; Close thine eyes & sleep secure, Z.184; Ground in c, Z. T681; In guilty night, Z.134; In the black dismal dungeon of despair, Z.190; Lord, what is man?, Z.192; Lord, I can suffer thy rebukes, Z.136; O solitude, my sweetest choice, Z.406; O, I'm sick of life, Z.140; The earth trembled, Z.197; Voluntary in C; Voluntary, Z.720; With sick & famish'd eyes, Z.200 PARC ▲ 45829 [DDD] (16.97)
The Prophetess, or The History of Dioclesian (semi-opera in 5 acts) [lib Thomas Betterton after Fletcher & Massinger], Z.627 (1690)
A. Deller (cnd), Vienna Concentus Musicus, H. Sheppard (sop), S. Le Sage (sop), A. Deller (ct), P. Todd (ten), M. Worthley (ten), M. Bevan (bar) *(rec June 1965)* † Prophetess (suite) BG (The Bach Guild) ▲ 2517 [ADD] (13.97)
C. Pierard (mez), J. Bowman (ct), J. M. Ainsley (ten), M. George (bass), R. Hickox (cnd), Collegium Musicum 90 CHN ▲ 569 [DDD] (33.97)
The Prophetess, or The History of Dioclesian (selections)
A. Deller (ct), R. Skeaping (vn), W. Kuijken (vl), J. Ryan (vl), W. Christie (hpd), R. Elliott (hpd)—Since from my dear Astrea's sight *(rec Apr 1979)* † Bonduca (sels); Fairy Queen (sels); Indian Queen (sels); King Arthur (sels); Pausanias (sels); Sacred Music; Songs HAM ▲ 90249 (18.97)
R. Jacobs (ct), W. Kuijken (vl), K. Junghänel (thb)—Since from my dear Astrea's sight † King Richard II (sels); Music of Purcell; Oedipus (sels); Pausanias (sels); Songs ACCE ▲ 57802 (17.97)
J. Lamon (cnd), Tafelmusik—Prelude; Tpt tune *(rec Toronto Canada, Apr 8-10, 1994)* ("Ayres for the Theatre") † Fairy Queen (sels); Indian Queen (sels); King Arthur (sels) SNYC ▲ 66169 [DDD] (16.97)
J. Savall (cnd), Concert des Nations—First music; Second music; Dance of the Furies; Chair Dance *(rec Collégiale Romane du Château du Cardona, France, Sept 1996)* † Fairy Queen (orch suites) FONT ▲ 8583 [DDD] (18.97)
The Prophetess, or The History of Dioclesian (suite)
A. Deller (cnd), Vienna Concentus Musicus, Deller Consort—Dances † Prophetess, Z.627 BG (The Bach Guild) ▲ 2517 [ADD] (13.97)
Purcell Quartet—Dances ("Purcell Miscellany") † Fairy Queen (sels); Music of Purcell; Songs; Suites Hpd CHN (Chaconne) ▲ 571 [DDD] (17.97)
Raise, raise the voice (song) for solo Voices, 2 Violins, Continuo & Chorus [for St. Cecilia's Day], Z.334 (ca 1685)
S. Bisatt (sop), J. Bern (sop), C. Robson (ct), W. Purefoy (ct), I. Honeyman (ten), T. Guthrie (bass), R. Glenton (cnd), Orch of the Golden Age, Golden Age Choir *(rec Manchester Grammar School England, May 13-14, 1995)* † Son Tpt, Z.850; Te Deum & Jubilate, Z.232; Welcome to all the pleasures, Z.339 NXIN ▲ 553444 [DDD] (5.97)
Sacred Choral & Vocal Music
A. Deller (cnd), Deller Consort—In guilty night, Z.134; Man that is born of a woman, Z.27 † Te Deum & Jubilate, Z.232 HMA ▲ 190207 [DDD] (9.97)
Sacred Music
J. Bowman (ct), R. King (cnd), King's Consort—Now that the sun hath veiled his light (Eve Hymn), Z.193 ("The James Bowman Collection") † Songs; Symphonic Poems (misc); Anonymous:Come tread the paths; J. S. Bach:Arias; St. Matthew Passion (sels); T. Ford:Since First I Saw Your Face; G. Gabrieli:O magnum mysterium; G. F. Handel:Music of Handel HYP ▲ 3 (7.97)
A. Deller (ct), R. Skeaping (vn), W. Kuijken (vl), J. Ryan (vl), W. Christie (hpd), R. Elliott (hpd)—Now that the sun hath veiled his light (Eve Hymn), Z.193 *(rec Apr 1979)* † Bonduca (sels); Fairy Queen (sels); Indian Queen (sels); King Arthur (sels); Pausanias (sels); Prophetess (sels); Songs HAM ▲ 90249 (18.97)
A. Deller (ct), R. Skeaping (vn), W. Kuijken (b vl), J. Ryan (b vl), W. Christie (hpd), R. Elliot (org)—Now that the sun hath veiled his light (Eve Hymn), Z.193 ("Music for a while") † Bonduca (sels); Comical History of Don Quixote (sels); Fairy Queen (sels); Indian Queen (sels); King Arthur (sels); Oedipus (sels); Pausanias (sels); Songs HAM (40th Anniversary Edition) ▲ 94249 [ADD] (12.97)
D. Fasolis (cnd) , Swiss Radio Chorus *(Motets)*, D. Fasolis (cnd) , Svizzera Radio Chorus *(Jehova, quam multi sunt, Z.135; Beati omnes qui timent Dominum, Z.131)* † Music of Purcell; Odes & Welcome Songs (misc) AART ▲ 47375 [DDD] (10.97)
R. King (cnd), King's Consort, New College Choir Oxford—Now that the sun hath veiled his light (Eve Hymn), Z.193 ("Essential Purcell") † Anthems & Services; Dido & Aeneas (sels); King Arthur (sels); Music of Purcell; Odes & Welcome Songs (misc); Songs HYP ▲ 2 (7.97)
R. Leanderson (bar), H. Fagius (org)—The earth trembled, Z.197 *(rec Stockholm, Sweden, May 16-17 & Oct 20, 1978)* ("Baroque & Romantic Vocal Music") † Hail, bright Cecilia, Z.328; Songs; E. Elgar:Sea Pictures, Op. 37; G. F. Handel:Alleluja & Amen; Dolce pur d'amor l'affanno, HWV 109a; Telemann:Ew'ge Quelle, milder Strom, TWV1: 546; Kleine Kantate von Wald und Au BIS ▲ 127 [AAD] (17.97)
Sonatas (12) of 3 Parts for 2 Violins, Bass Viol & Continuo, Z.790-801 (ca 1680)
J. Williams (gtr), C. Bonell (gtr), K. Marjoram (b chl), B. Gascoigne (mar), M. Pert (vib)—Son 11 in f 2 Vns, Vla & Bc, Z.800 *(rec NYC, NY)* ("John Williams & Friends") † J. S. Bach:Cant 147; Cons Org; Suites Vc; Trio Son for 2 Vns; Daquin:Pièces de clavecin (sels); W. A. Mozart:Adagio Glass Amc, K.356; Son 11 Pno, K.331; Telemann:Bourree alla Polacca; Vivaldi:Con Mands, RV.532 SNYC ▲ 35108 [AAD] (16.97)
Sonata No. 1 in D for Trumpet & Organ
B. Soustrot (tpt), F. Houbart (org) *(rec Sully-sur-Loire Org St. Ythier's Church, May 1992)* ("The European Concert") † Son 2 Tpt Org; Boismortier:Son 2 Tpt Org; Loeillet:Son Tpt; B. Viviani:Capricci armonici, Op. 4 FORL ▲ 16672 [DDD] (16.97)
Sonata No. 2 in D for Trumpet & Organ
B. Soustrot (tpt), F. Houbart (org) *(rec Sully-sur-Loire Org St. Ythier's Church, May 1992)* ("The European Concert") † Son 1 Tpt Org; Boismortier:Son 2 Tpt Org; Loeillet:Son Tpt; B. Viviani:Capricci armonici, Op. 4 FORL ▲ 16672 [DDD] (16.97)
Sonata in D for Trumpet & Strings, Z.850 (?1694)
N. Sparf (cnd) *(rec Petruskyrkan, Stockholm, Sweden, Aug 1995)* ("The Art of the Baroque Trumpet, Vol 1") † Fasch:Con Tpt Obs; G. F. Handel:Ov; Molter:Con 1 Tpt; L. Mozart:Con Tpt; Telemann:Qnt Tpt; Torelli:Son Tpt, G.1 NXIN ▲ 553531 [DDD] (5.97)
D. Staff (tpt), R. Glenton (cnd), Orch of the Golden Age *(rec Manchester Grammar School England, May 13-14, 1995)* † Raise, raise the voice, Z.334; Te Deum & Jubilate, Z.232; Welcome to all the pleasures, Z.339 NXIN ▲ 553444 [DDD] (5.97)
J. Wilbraham (tpt), R. Leppard (cnd), English CO † Gordian Knot Unty'd (sels); Old Bachelor (sels); Vivaldi:Cons Vn Strs, Op. 8/1-4 SNYC ▲ 44644 [DDD] (10.97)
Sonatas (22) for 2 Violins, Bass Viol & Continuo Instruments, Z.790-811 (ca 1680)
C. Ferrarini (cnd) MONM (Baroque) 3-▲ 96027 (54.97)
Les Nièces de Rameau PVY ▲ 795093 (16.97)
Locke Consort *(rec Jan 1993)* ("The World of Purcell") † Baltazar:Suite for 2 Vns; Blow:Ground; Trio Son; J. Jenkins:Lady Katherine Audley's Bells; Suite Strs; M. Locke:Suites for 2 Vns GLOE ▲ 5058 [DDD] (16.97)

PURCELL, HENRY (cont.)

Sonatas (22) for 2 Violins, Bass Viol & Continuo Instruments, Z.790-811 (ca 1680) (cont.)
Purcell Quartet ("Vol. 1") CHN ▲ 8591 [DDD] (16.97)
Purcell Quartet ("Vol. 2") † Chacony Strs, Z.730; Music of Purcell; Pavans CHN ▲ 8663 [DDD] (16.97)
Purcell Quartet ("Vol. 3") CHN ▲ 8763 [DDD] (16.97)

Sonatas (12) of 3 Parts for 2 Violins, Bass Viol & Continuo, Z.790-801 (ca 1680)
London Baroque HAM (Suite) ▲ 7901439 (12.97)

Sonatas (10) in 4 Parts for 2 Violins, Bass Viol & Continuo, Z.802-811 (ca 1680)
London Baroque members HAM (Suite) ▲ 7901438 (12.97)
E. Selig-Plaskurova (vn), V. Simcisko (vn), D. Dockal (vc), M. Dobiášová (hpd) *(rec Bratislava, 1994)* ("Purcell: Sonatas") DI ▲ 920251 [DDD] (5.97)

Songs
B. Bonney (sop), S. Gritton (sop), J. Bowman (ct), R. Covey-Crump (ten), C. Daniels (ten), M. George (bass), M. Caudle (b vl), D. Miller (archlt/thb), R. King (chamber org)—Draw near, you lovers, Z.462; While Thyrsis, wrapt in downy sleep, Z.437; Love, thou can't hear tho' thou art blind, Z.396; I lov'd fair Celia, Z.381; What hope for us remains now he is gone; Pastora's beauties, when unblown, Z.407; A thousand sev'ral ways I tried, Z.359; Urge me no more, Z.426; Farewell all joys, Z.368; If music be the food of love, D.379a; Amidst the shades & cool refreshing streams, Z.355; They say you're angry, Z.422; Let each gallant heart, Z.390; This poet sings the Trojan wars, Z.423; Ah! how pleasant 'tis to love, Z.353; My heart whenever you appear, Z.399; On the brow of Richmond Hill, Z.405; Rashly I swore I would disown, Z.411; Since the pox or the plague, Z.471; Beneath a dark & melancholy grove, Z.461; Musing on cares of human fate, Z.467; Whilst Cynthia sung, all angry winds lay still, Z.438 ("The Secular Songs of Henry Purcell, Vol. 1") HYP ▲ 66710 (18.97)
B. Bonney (sop), S. Gritton (sop), J. Bowman (ct), R. Covey-Crump (ten), C. Daniels (ten), M. George (bass), M. Caudle (b vl), D. Miller (archlt/thb), R. King (hpd/org)—Incassum, Lesbia, rogas, Z.383; Gentle Shepherds, you that know, Z.464; I love & I must, Z.382; Through mournful shades & solitary groves, Z.424; The Knotting Song, Z.371 ("The Secular Solo Songs of Henry Purcell, Vol. 2") HYP ▲ 66720 [DDD] (18.97)
B. Bonney (sop), S. Gritton (sop), J. Bowman (ct), R. Covey-Crump (ten), C. Daniels (ten), M. George (bass), R. King (cnd), King's Consort—When Strephon found his passions in vain, Z.435; Let us, kind Lesbia, give away, Z.466; Corinna is divinely fair, Z.365; Olinda in the shades unseen, Z.404; If music be the food of love, D.379c; Lovely Albina's come ashore, Z.394; I came, I saw, and was undone, Z.375; No, to what purpose should I speak, Z.468; Young Thirsis' fate, Z.473; She loves & she confesses too, Z.413; From silent shades, Z.370; O solitude, my sweetest choice, Z.406; If prayers and tears, D.380; The fatal hour comes on apace, Z.421; Sylvia, 'tis true you're fair, Z.512; Amintor, heedless of his flocks, Z.357; Love is now become a trade, Z.393; Phyllis, I can ne'er forgive it, Z.408; Who can behold Florella's charms?, Z.441; He himself courts his own ruin, Z.372; Let formal lovers still pursue, Z.391; Ask me to love no more, Z.358; In Cloris all soft charms, Z.384; Spite of the godhead, pow'rful love, Z.417 ("Secular Songs, Vol. 3") HYP ▲ 66730 (18.97)
B. Borden (sop), R. Shaw (hpd), Academy of the Begynhof Amsterdam—Incassum, Lesbia, rogas, Z.383; O dive Custos Auriacae domus, Z.504; If music be the food of love, D.379c † Music of Purcell; Odes & Welcome Songs (misc); Tempest (sels); Blow:No, Lesbia, No, You Ask in Vain GLOE ▲ 5029 [DDD] (16.97)
C. Bott (sop), Purcell Quartet—Fairy Queen (sels) [Hark how all things; Thus the ever grateful spring]; If music be the food of love, D.379; Lord, what is man?, Z.192 ("Purcell Miscellany") † Fairy Queen (sels); Music of Purcell; Prophetess (suite); Suites Hpd CHN (Chaconne) ▲ 571 [DDD] (17.97)
J. Bowman (ct), R. King (cnd), King's Consort—Why, why are all the Muses mute?, Z.343 [Britain, thou now art great]; O solitude, my sweetest choice, Z.406; Now does the glorious day appear, Z.332 [By beauteous softness]; On the brow of Richmond Hill, Z.405 ("The James Bowman Collection") † Sacred Music; Symphonic Poems (misc); Anonymous:Come tread the paths; J. S. Bach:Arias; St. Matthew Passion (sels); T. Ford:Since First I Saw Your Face; G. Gabrieli:O magnum mysterium; G. F. Handel:Music of Handel HYP ▲ 3 (7.97)
A. Cantelo (sop), A. Deller (ct), M. Bevan (bar), N. Marriner (vn), G. Jones (vn), P. Gibbs (vn), D. Dupré (vl), G. Malcolm (hpd), W. Bergmann (hpd)—Songs ("Celebrated Songs, Sacred Airs, Concerted Pieces for Strings & Harpsichord") † Music of Purcell; Old Bachelor (sels); Suites Hpd BG (The Bach Guild) 2-▲ 2002 [ADD] (26.97)
A. Deller (ct), R. Skeaping (vn), W. Kuijken (vl), J. Ryan (vl), W. Christie (hpd), R. Elliott (hpd)—Comical History of Don Quixote (sels) [From rosy bow'rs]; If music be the food of love, D.379; Not all my torments can your pity move, Z.400; O solitude, my sweetest choice, Z.406; Fairy Queen (sels) [Thrice happy lovers] *(rec Apr 1979)* † Bonduca (sels); Fairy Queen (sels); Indian Queen (sels); King Arthur (sels); Pausanias (sels); Prophetess (sels); Sacred Music HAM ▲ 90249 (18.97)
A. Deller (ct), R. Skeaping (vn), W. Kuijken (b vl), J. Ryan (b vl), W. Christie (hpd), R. Elliot (org)—If music be the food of love, D.379; Not all my torments can your pity move, Z.400; King Richard II (sels) [Retired from any mortal's sight]; Prophetess (sels) [Since from my dear Astrea's sight]; O solitude, my sweetest choice, Z.406 ("Music for a while") † Bonduca (sels); Comical History of Don Quixote (sels); Fairy Queen (sels); Indian Queen (sels); King Arthur (sels); Oedipus (sels); Pausanias (sels); Sacred Music HAM (40th Anniversary Edition) ▲ 94249 [ADD] (12.97)
R. Jacobs (ct), W. Kuijken (vl), K. Junghänel (thb)—Hail, bright Cecilia, Z.328 ['Tis nature's voice]; Incassum, Lesbia, rogas, Z.383; Ah! cruel nymph, you give despair, Z.352; The fatal hour comes on apace, Z.421; Young Thirsis' fate, Z.473 † King Richard II (sels); Music of Purcell; Oedipus (sels); Pausanias (sels); Prophetess (sels) ACCE ▲ 57802 (17.97)
R. King (cnd), King's Consort, New College Choir Oxford—If music be the food of love, D.379 ("Essential Purcell") † Anthems & Services; Dido & Aeneas (sels); King Arthur (sels); Music of Purcell; Odes & Welcome Songs (misc); Sacred Music HYP ▲ 2 (7.97)
E. Kirkby (sop), M. Chance (ct), M. Neary (cnd), New London Consort, Westminster Abbey Choir—I was glad when they said unto me, Z.19; Praise the Lord, O Jerusalem, Z.46; Stript of their green our groves appear, Z.444; Ode for Queen Mary's Birthday; O dive Custos Auriacae domus, Z.504; Incassum, Lesbia, rogas, Z.383; March; The Burial Service [composed w. Thomas Morley] ("Music for Queen Mary") † Blow:Songs SNYC ▲ 66243 (16.97)
C. Lane (sop), L. Cummings (org), J. Summerly (cnd), Oxford Camerata—Incassum, Lesbia, rogas, Z.383 *(rec Chapel of Hertford College Oxford, England, June 9-10, 1994)* † Anthems & Services; Music of Purcell; Thou knowest, Lord, the secrets of our hearts, Z.58c NXIN ▲ 553129 [DDD] (5.97)
R. Leanderson (bar), H. Fagius (org)—If music be the food of love, D.379; How long, great God, Z.189 *(rec Stockholm, Sweden, May 16-17 & Oct 20, 1978)* ("Baroque & Romantic Vocal Music") † Hail, bright Cecilia, Z.328; Sacred Music; E. Elgar:Sea Pictures, Op. 37; G. F. Handel:Alleluja & Amen; Dolce pur d'amor l'affanno, HWV 109a; Telemann:Ew'ge Quelle, milder Strom, TWV1: 546; Kleine Kantate von Wald und Au BIS ▲ 127 [AAD] (17.97)
R. Leppard (cnd), English CO—Come, ye sons of art, away, Z.323 † Indian Queen (sels); King Arthur (sels); Fasch:Con Tpt Obs; G. F. Handel:Ode for the Birthday of Queen Anne; Samson (sels); Molter:Con 2 Tpt; Torelli:Sons à 5 Tpts SNYC ▲ 39061 [DDD] (16.97)
S. McNair (sop), L. Dreyfus (vc/vl), P. O'Dette (archlt), C. Hogwood (hpd/org), C. Hogwood (cnd), Academy of Ancient Music—If music be the food of love, D.379; The fatal hour comes on apace, Z.421 *(rec St. John's, London, England, 1994)* ("The Echoing Air") † Bonduca (sels); Chacony Strs, Z.730; Fairy Queen (sels); Indian Queen (sels); King Arthur (sels); Libertine (sels); Music of Purcell; Pausanias (sels) PPHI ▲ 46081 (16.97)
D. Minter (ct), M. Springfels (vl), P. O'Dette (archlt), M. Meyerson (hpd/org) ("Sweeter Than Roses") HAM ▲ 7907035 (12.97)
J. Nibbs (sop), G. Mitchell (ct), P. Hall (ten), D. Thomas (bass), M. Phillips (org), M. Howard (cnd), Cantores in Ecclesia—Hear my prayer, O Lord, Z.15; Morning & Evening Service, Z.230; Remember not, Lord, our offences, Z.50; Voluntary for Single Org; In the midst of life, Z.17a/b; Voluntary on the 100th Psalm Tune ("Music for Westminster Abbey") † Anthems & Services INMP (BBC Radio Classics) ▲ 9126 (13.97)
S. Sanford (sop), B. Wissick (vl), R. Erickson (hpd/org)—Come, ye sons of art, away, Z.323 [Strike the viol, touch the lute]; Ye Gentle Spirits; Round O'; Hornpipe; Let Us Dance † Comical History of Don Quixote (sels); Fairy Queen (sels); Hail, bright Cecilia, Z.328; Tyrannic Love (sels) ALBA ▲ 127 (16.97)
J. Shirley-Quirk (bar), N. Liddell (vn), I. McMahon (vn), A. Gauntlett (vl), M. Isepp (hpd/pno)—Mock Marriage (sels) [Man is for the woman made]; Oedipus (sels) [Music for a while]; When night her purple veil had softly spread, Zd201 ("A Recital of English Songs") † Mock Marriage (sels); G. Butterworth:Songs from A Shropshire Lad; Moeran:Songs SAGA ▲ 3336 (15.97)
J. Vickers (ten), R. Woitach (pno)—Rule a Wife & Have a Wife (sels) [There's not a swain on the plain]; Not all my torments can your pity move, Z.400; Mock Marriage (sels) [Man is for the woman made] *(rec live New York, Apr 30, 1967)* ("Jon Vickers in Concert") † Pausanias (sels); A. Dvořák:Zigeunermelodien, Op. 55; G. F. Handel:Messiah (sels); A. Scarlatti:Cants & Duets; R. Schumann:Dichterliebe, Op. 48 VAIA ▲ 1032 [ADD]

Suites (8) in G, g, G, a, C, D, d & F for Harpsichord, Z.660-663 & 666-669
A. Cantelo (sop), A. Deller (ct), M. Bevan (bar), N. Marriner (vn), G. Jones (vn), P. Gibbs (vn), D. Dupré (vl), G. Malcolm (hpd), W. Bergmann (hpd)—No. 6 in D ("Celebrated Songs, Sacred Airs, Concerted Pieces for Strings & Harpsichord") † Music of Purcell; Old Bachelor (sels); Songs BG (The Bach Guild) 2-▲ 2002 [ADD] (26.97)
R. Egarr (hpd)—No. 3 in G; No. 6 in D *(rec Utrecht, Netherlands, Aug 1995)* ("A Choice Collection of Restoration Harpsichord Music") † Hpd Music; G. B. Draghi:Hpd Music; M. Locke:Suite Hpd GLOE ▲ 5145 [DDD] (16.97)
J. Gibbons (hpd)—No. 1 in G; No. 2 in g; No. 3 in G; No. 4 in a; No. 5 in C; No. 6 in D; No. 7 in d [trans Purcell from Hornpipe, Z.603]; No. 8 in F [trans Purcell from Minuet, Z. 592] *(rec The Music Room, Cambridge, MA, Nov 3-4, 1995)* † Hpd Music CENT ▲ 2313 [DDD] (16.97)

PURCELL, HENRY (cont.)

Suites (8) in G, g, G, a, C, D, d & F for Harpsichord, Z.660-663 & 666-669 (cont.)
A. Haas (hpd)—No. 6 in D; No. 2 in g ("The Age of Purcell: English Harpsichord Music of the Restoration") † Hpd Music (misc); W. Croft:Hpd Music MUA ▲ 998 [DDD] (16.97)
M. Proud (hpd) ("8 Suites & Other Pieces") MER ▲ 84280 [DDD] (16.97)
Purcell Quartet—No. 6 in D ("Purcell Miscellany") † Fairy Queen (sels); Music of Purcell; Prophetess (suite); Songs CHN (Chaconne) ▲ 571 [DDD] (17.97)
R. Touyère (hpd) *(rec Collège St-Louis à Genève, May-June 1972)* ("Les Suites pour Clavecin") GALL ▲ 852 [ADD] (19.97)
S. Yates (hpd) ("Harpsichord") † Hpd Music; Music of Purcell CHN (Early Music) ▲ 587 [DDD] (16.97)

Suite for Winds & Strings [arr Barbirolli]
J. Barbirolli (cnd), New York PO *(rec Carnegie Hall New York, Feb 7, 1938)* † Creston:Threnody, Op. 16; G. C. Menotti:Old Maid & the Thief (ov); O. Respighi:Ancient Airs & Dances; Fontane di Roma; F. Schubert:German Dances & Trios Str Qt, D.90 DLAB (Essential Archives) ▲ 5019 [ADD] (15.97)

Symphonic Poems (miscellaneous)
J. Bowman (ct), R. King (cnd), King's Consort—Vouchsafe, O Lord, to Keep Us This Day ("The James Bowman Collection") † Sacred Music; Songs; Anonymous:Come tread the paths; J. S. Bach:Arias; St. Matthew Passion (sels); T. Ford:Since First I Saw Your Face; G. Gabrieli:O magnum mysterium; G. F. Handel:Music of Handel HYP ▲ 3 (7.97)

Te Deum & Jubilate in D for Continuo & Chorus, Z.232 (1694)
S. Bisatt (sop), J. Bern (sop), C. Robson (ct), W. Purefoy (ct), I. Honeyman (ten), T. Guthrie (bass), D. Staff (tpt), R. Glenton (cnd), Orch of the Golden Age, Golden Age Choir *(rec Manchester Grammar School England, May 13-14, 1995)* † Raise, raise the voice, Z.334; Son Tpt, Z.850; Welcome to all the pleasures, Z.339 NXIN ▲ 553444 [DDD] (5.97)
Collegium Vocale † Music for the Funeral of Queen Mary HAM ▲ 901462 (18.97)
A. Deller (cnd), Deller Consort [LAT] † Sacred Choral & Vocal Music HMA ▲ 190207 [ADD] (9.97)

The Tempest, or The Enchanted Island (selections)
B. Borden (sop), R. Shaw (hpd), Academy of the Begynhof Amsterdam—Dry those eyes † Music of Purcell; Odes & Welcome Songs (misc); Songs; Blow:No, Lesbia, No, You Ask in Vain GLOE ▲ 5029 [DDD] (16.97)

Thou knowest, Lord, the secrets of our hearts for Trumpets, Organ & Chorus, Z.58c
L. Cummings (org), J. Summerly (cnd), Oxford Camerata *(rec Chapel of Hertford College Oxford, June 9-10, 1994)* † Anthems & Services; Music of Purcell; Songs NXIN ▲ 553129 [DDD] (5.97)

Timon of Athens (selections)
M. Pearlman (cnd), Boston Baroque Orch—Curtain tune on a ground † Abdelazer (sels); Dido & Aeneas, Z.626; Fairy Queen (sels); Gordian Knot Unty'd (sels); Married Beau (sels) TEL ▲ 80424 [DDD] (16.97)

Trumpet Tune, "Bonducco"
J. Culp (org) *(rec Kilgore, TX)* † H. W. Davies:Solemn Melody; P. Graham:Crimond; C. Ives:Abide with Me; Ketèlbey:In a Monastery Garden; Traditional:Londonderry Air; Rigaudon; Were You There? HALM ▲ 35028 (6.97)

Trumpet Tune & Ayre for Trumpet & Organ
E. Carroll (tpt), W. Nell (org) ("Age of Elegance Greatest Hits") † King Arthur (sels); Beethoven:Bagatelle Pno in a, WoO 59; Contredanses Orch, WoO 14; Boccherini:Minuetto Strs; C. W. Gluck:Iphigénie en Aulide (sels); Orfeo ed Euridice (dance); G. F. Handel:Cons (16) Org; Serse (sels); Water Music (sels); J. Haydn:Qts (6) Strs, H.III/13-18, Op. 3; Sym 82; W. A. Mozart:German Dances (3), K.605; Kleine Nachtmusik, K.525 SNYC ▲ 62369 [ADD] (9.97) ▮ 62369 [ADD] (5.98)

Trumpet Tune in C for Harpsichord
A. Davis (org) *(rec Org at Roy Thompson Hall Toronto)* † Cortege Academique; J. S. Bach:Toccata & Fugue Org, BWV 565; C. Franck:Prélude, fugue et var, Op. 18; C. Ives:Vars on 'America' INMP (IMP Classics) ▲ 6700942 (9.97)

Trumpet Tune in C for Harpsichord, Z.678, "Cibell"
Canadian Brass *(rec Toronto, OT, Jan 30-Feb 3, 1995)* ("Fireworks!: Baroque Brass Favorites") † Abdelazer (sels); Fairy Queen (sels); Fant upon one note, Z.745; J. Clarke:Trumpet Voluntary; G. F. Handel:Concerti grossi, Op. 3; Royal Fireworks Music, HWV 351; Samson (sels); Serse (sels); Solomon (arrival of the queen of Sheba); Water Music, HWV 348-50 RCAV (Red Seal) ▲ 68257 [DDD] (16.97)
R. Kelley (tpt), M. J. Newman (org) *(rec Mt. Kisco, NY, Aug 1995)* ("The Splendor of the Baroque") † J. S. Bach:Air on the G String; Arioso Ob; Cant 147; Fant Org, BWV 572; J. Clarke:Trumpet Voluntary; G. F. Handel:Cons (16) Org; Messiah (sels); Royal Fireworks Music, HWV 351; Semele (sels); Serse (sels); Telemann:Qnt Tpt HEL ▲ 1006 [DDD] (10.97)

Tyrannic Love (selections)
S. Sanford (sop), B. Wissick (vl), R. Erickson (hpd/org)—Ah! how sweet it is to love † Comical History of Don Quixote (sels); Fairy Queen (sels); Hail, bright Cecilia, Z.328; Songs ALBA ▲ 127 (16.97)

Violin & Piano Music
L. Risk (fid), J. Schwab (pno)—Old Sir Symon the King *(rec Troy, NY, Apr 1998)* † D. Dow:Vn & Pno Music; W. Forbes:Vn & Pno Music; MacCrimmon:Vn & Pno Music; McGibbon:Vn & Pno Music; Traditional:Vn & Pno Music DOR ▲ 90264 [DDD] (16.97)

The Virtuous Wife, or Good Luck at Last (incidental music) for Chamber Ensemble [text D'Urfey], Z.611 (?1694)
F. Mahler (cnd), Hartford CO *(rec 1960)* † Abdelazer, Z.570; Gordian Knot Unty'd, Z.597; Married Beau, Z.603; Musick's Hand-maid VC ▲ 4044 [ADD] (13.97)

Voluntaries (4) in C, d, d & G for Organ, Z.717-720
A. Wills (org) *(rec Org of Ely Cathedral)* ("Full Stops") † Albinoni:Adagio; R. Wagner:Walküre (ride of the Valkyries); Widor:Marche pontificale, Op. 13/1; A. Wills:Vars on Amazing Grace MER ▲ 84305 (16.97)

Voluntary in C
P. McCreesh (cnd), Gabrieli Players, Gabrieli Consort ("Harmonia Sacra") † Awake, ye dead, Z.182; Close thine eyes & sleep secure, Z.184; Ground in c, Z. T681; In guilty night, Z.134; In the black dismal dungeon of despair, Z.190; Lord, what is man?, Z.192; Lord, I can suffer thy rebukes, Z.136; O solitude, my sweetest choice, Z.406; O, I'm sick of life, Z.140; Plung'd in the confines of despair, Z.142; The earth trembled, Z.197; Voluntary, Z.720; With sick & famish'd eyes, Z.200 PARC ▲ 45829 [DDD] (16.97)

Voluntary in G for Organ, Z.720
P. McCreesh (cnd), Gabrieli Players, Gabrieli Consort ("Harmonia Sacra") † Awake, ye dead, Z.182; Close thine eyes & sleep secure, Z.184; Ground in c, Z. T681; In guilty night, Z.134; In the black dismal dungeon of despair, Z.190; Lord, what is man?, Z.192; Lord, I can suffer thy rebukes, Z.136; O solitude, my sweetest choice, Z.406; O, I'm sick of life, Z.140; Plung'd in the confines of despair, Z.142; The earth trembled, Z.197; Voluntary in C; With sick & famish'd eyes, Z.200 PARC ▲ 45829 [DDD] (16.97)

Welcome to All the pleasures (song) for solo Voices, 2 Violins, Viola & Chorus [for St. Cecilia's Day], Z.339 (1683)
S. Bisatt (sop), J. Bern (sop), C. Robson (ct), W. Purefoy (ct), I. Honeyman (ten), T. Guthrie (bass), R. Glenton (cnd), Orch of the Golden Age, Golden Age Choir *(rec Manchester Grammar School England, May 13-14, 1995)* † Raise, raise the voice, Z.334; Son Tpt, Z.850; Te Deum & Jubilate, Z.232 NXIN ▲ 553444 [DDD] (5.97)
Deller Consort [ENG] † Love's goddess sure was blind, Z.331 HMA ▲ 190222 (9.97)
P. Herreweghe (cnd), Collegium Vocale † Hail, bright Cecilia, Z.328 HAM ▲ 901643 (18.97)
R. Holton (sop), N. Jenkin (sop), M. Chance (ct), P. Tindall (ten), G. Mosley (bass), J. E. Gardiner (cnd), Monteverdi Choir London *(rec Bristol, UK, July 12-14, 1990)* † Dido & Aeneas, Z.626 PPHI ▲ 32114 (16.97)

When night her purple veil had softly spread (song) for Voice, 2 Violins & Continuo, Zd201
D. Fischer-Dieskau (bar), B. Britten (pno), Alberni String Quartet † Dido & Aeneas, Z.626 BBC (Purcell the Performer) ▲ 8003 (17.97)

With sick & famish'd eyes for Chorus, Z.200 (1688)
P. McCreesh (cnd), Gabrieli Players, Gabrieli Consort ("Harmonia Sacra") † Awake, ye dead, Z.182; Close thine eyes & sleep secure, Z.184; Ground in c, Z. T681; In guilty night, Z.134; In the black dismal dungeon of despair, Z.190; Lord, what is man?, Z.192; Lord, I can suffer thy rebukes, Z.136; O solitude, my sweetest choice, Z.406; O, I'm sick of life, Z.140; Plung'd in the confines of despair, Z.142; The earth trembled, Z.197; Voluntary in C; Voluntary, Z.720 PARC ▲ 45829 [DDD] (16.97)

PUTEANUS, ERYCIUS (1574-1646)

Quintetto in a for Bassoon & Strings
C. Davidsson (bn), N. Willén (cnd), Sundsvall CO *(rec Sundsvall, Sweden, Dec 1994)* ("The Romantic Bassoon") † F. Danzi:Con Bn; J. N. Hummel:Con Bn; C. M. von Weber:Andante & Rondo ungarese Bn BIS ▲ 705 [DDD] (17.97)

PYGOTT, RICHARD (16th cent)

Missa'Veni Sancte Spiritus' for 5 Voices
S. Darlington (cnd), Christ Church Cathedral Choir Oxford *(rec Monmouth, England)* ("Music for Cardinal Wolsey") † J. Mason:O rex gloriose NIMB ▲ 5578 [DDD] (16.97)

QIN, YONG CHENG (20th cent)
Happy Grassland for Orchestra (1957)
C. Hoey (cnd), Singapore SO *(rec Victoria Memorial Hall Singapore, Jan 1981)* † A:Con Vn; G. Chen:Fant on a Xinjiang Folk Song; Fu:Celebration Dance; Ge:Horse Cart; K. Ma:Shanbei Suite
MARC (Chinese Music) ▲ 8223902 [ADD] (13.97)

QU, XIAOSONG (20th cent)
Mong Dong for Voices & Orchestra (1984)
M. Rippon (bass), K. Schermerhorn (cnd), Hong Kong PO *(rec Lyric Theatre of the Hong Kong Academy for Perform, June 28, 1986)* ("First Contemporary Chinese Composers Festival 1986") † W. W. Chan:Sym 3; A. Huang:Con Pno; Tan Dun:Intermezzo; J. Tang:Sym 3; Ye:Moon over the West River
MARC (Chinese Contemporary) ▲ 8223915 [DDD] (13.97)

QUADRENY, JOSEP M. MESTRES (1929-
Branca de Branques for Orchestra (1997)
S. Brotons (cnd), Balaers Ciutat de Palma SO † Doble Concert; Sym in B♭; Vara per dos; Vara per quatre
LAMA ▲ 38 (17.97)
Cançons de bressol for solo Voice & Piano (1959)
A. Ricci (mez), A. Soler (pno) *(rec Albert Moraleda Studio, 1993-95)* ("Compositors del Cercle Manuel de Falla/Joan Comellas") † J. Casanovas:Joan Miró; Cercós:Hinamatsuri; A. Cerdà:Tres letras asturianas; J. Comellas:Music of Comellas; Giró:Chansons françaises; M. Valls:Music of M. Valls
EAM 2-▲ 32 [DDD] (33.97)
Doble Concert for Ondes Martenot, Percussion & Orchestra (1970)
K. Simonovitch (cnd), Barcelona & Cataluna National SO † Branca de Branques; Sym in B♭; Vara per dos; Vara per quatre
LAMA ▲ 38 (17.97)
Symphony in B♭ (1983)
F. Decker (cnd), Barcelona & Cataluna National SO † Branca de Branques; Doble Concert; Vara per dos; Vara per quatre
LAMA ▲ 38 (17.97)
Vara per dos for Piano 4-Hands (1992)
E. Vela (pno), E. V. López (pno) † Branca de Branques; Doble Concert; Sym in B♭; Vara per quatre
LAMA ▲ 38 (17.97)
Vara per quatre for Piano 8-Hands (1982)
E. Vela (pno), E. V. López (pno), E. Gómez (pno), C. Olivella (pno) † Branca de Branques; Doble Concert; Sym in B♭; Vara per dos
LAMA ▲ 38 (17.97)

QUAGLIA, BRUCE (1965-
Quartetto
J. Evans (vn), K. Cardon (vc), C. Vickers (fl), J. Hinckley (cl), M. Rosenzweig (cnd), Canyonlands *(rec Salt Lake City, UT, 1994-95)* ("New Music from Utah") † Cathey:Bardol Saga; M. Johnson:Nocturne; Roens:Delicate Arch; Invocation; Time & Again; Wolking:Reaching; Yao:Drifting About *([ENG] text)*
CENT ▲ 2360 [DDD] (16.97)

QUAGLIATI, PAOLO (?1555-1628)
Music for Voice
Little Consort—E ver che nel partire; Io vo cantar; Felice chi vi mira [I]—see Collections † G. B. Fontana:Son 10 Fl
CCL ▲ 2791 [DDD]

QUANTZ, JOHANN JOACHIM (1697-1773)
Concertos (4) in C, D, G & g for Flute & Orchestra
J. Galway (fl), J. Faerber (cnd), Württemberg CO
RCAV (Red Seal) ▲ 60247 [DDD] (16.97)
Concerto in e for Flute & Strings
N. McLaren (fl), J. H. Jones (cnd), Cambridge Baroque Camerata [period instrs] ("Rare Baroque Flute Concertos") † F. Benda:Cons (4) Fl; Tartini:Con Fl
AMON ▲ 52 [DDD] (16.97)
Concerto in G for Flute & Strings
R. Brown (fl), R. Goodman (cnd), Hanover Band [period instrs] *(rec BBC Studio 1, May 1993)* ("Concert in Sanssouci") † C.P.E. Bach:Con Ob, H.468; K. H. Graun:Arias; Kirnberger:Sym in D
RCAV (Red Seal) ▲ 61903 [DDD] (16.97)
P. Øien (fl), T. Tønnesen (cnd), Norwegian CO *(rec Sept 2-3, 1978)* † Blavet:Con Fl; Tartini:Con Fl; Vivaldi:Con Rcr, RV.441
BIS ▲ 118 [AAD] (17.97)
Sonatas for Flute & Continuo
M. Caudle (vc), R. Brown (fl), J. Johnstone (hpd)—Sons Nos. 231, 273, 275 & 348; Son XIV; 2 Sons Fl Hpd; Minuetto *(rec Orford Church, June 24-26, 1996)*
CHN (Chaconne) ▲ 607 [DDD] (16.97)
Suite for solo Flute
B. Csalog (fl) † J. S. Bach:Partita Fl, BWV 1013; C.P.E. Bach:Son Fl, H.562; J. C. C. Fischer:Menuet w. Vars Fl; Telemann:Fants (12) Fl, TWV40:2-13
HUN ▲ 31677 [DDD] (16.97)

QUESADA, ADOLFO DE (1830-?)
Allegro de concierto for Piano
P. Cohen (pno) *(rec Auditorio de Cuenca, Spain, Apr 1995)* ("El Último Adiós: Romantic Piano Music from Spain") † Grandes estudios; Adalid y Gurréa:Ultimo adiós; Lamento; Petits riens; Allú:Peregrino; Ocón:Bolero; T. Power:Barcarola Pno
GLSS ▲ 920501 [DDD] (18.97)
Grandes estudios (6) for Piano
P. Cohen (pno) *(rec Auditorio de Cuenca, Spain, Apr 1995)* ("El Último Adiós: Romantic Piano Music from Spain") † Allegro de concierto; Adalid y Gurréa:Ultimo adiós; Lamento; Petits riens; Allú:Peregrino; Ocón:Bolero; T. Power:Barcarola Pno
GLSS ▲ 920501 [DDD] (18.97)

QUILLING, HOWARD (1935-
Sonata No. 4 for Piano (1992)
M. Lifchitz (pno) *(rec Recital Hall of the Univ at Albany, May 25-26, 1995)* ("New American Romantics: Music for Solo Piano") † L. Bell:Son Pno; Pleskow:Quatrains Pno; H. Rovics:Son Pno; Toutant:Small Suite Pno; Van Appledorn:Set of 5 Pno
NSR ▲ 1007 [DDD] (15.97)

QUILTER, ROGER (1877-1953)
The Arnold Book of Old Songs for Voice & Piano (1947)
J. Benton (bar), R. Lowe (pno) † Songs; Traditional:Songs
SYMP ▲ 1159 (18.97)
Music of Quilter
A. Leaper (cnd), Czech-Slovak RSO Bratislava—A Children's Ov; Where the Rainbow Ends (suite); As You Like It (suite); Country Pieces; The Rake (suite); 3 English Dances *(rec Jan 1992)*
MARC ▲ 8223444 [DDD] (13.97)
Shakespeare Songs (miscellaneous)
J. Benton (bar), G. Kirkland (pno), R. Lowe (pno)—Orpheus with His Lt, Op. 32/1; When Icicles Hang by the Wall, Op. 32/2; Shakespeare Songs, Op. 6 [Come Away, Death]; Oh Mistress Mine, Op. 6/2; Blow, Blow, Thou Winter Wind, Op. 6/3; Who Is Sylvia?, Op. 30/1; When Daffodils Begin to Peer, Op. 30/2; How Should I Your True Love Know?, Op. 30/3; Sigh No More, Ladies, Op. 30/4; Fear No More the Heat of the Sun, Op. 23/1; Under the Greenwood Tree, Op. 23/2; It Was a Lover & His Lass, Op. 23/3; Take, O Take Those Lips away, Op. 23/4; Hey, Ho, the Wind & the Rain, Op. 23/5 ("Roger Quilter, Vol. 2") † Songs
SYMP ▲ 1184 (18.97)
Shakespeare Songs (3) for Voice & Piano, Op. 6 (1905)
S. Varcoe (bass), R. Hickox (cnd), City of London Sinfonia [ENG] ("English Orchestral Songs") † G. Butterworth:Songs from A Shropshire Lad; Songs Voc & Strs; E. Elgar:Songs; G. Finzi:Let Us Garlands Bring, Op. 18; Vaughan Williams:Songs
CHN ▲ 8743 [DDD] (16.97)
Songs
J. M. Ainsley (ten), M. Martineau (pno)—Now Sleeps the Crimson Petal; Go, Lovely Rose; plus others ("Songs by Roger Quilter")
HYP ▲ 66878 (18.97)
J. Benton (bar), G. Kirkland (pno), R. Lowe (pno)—To Julia; poems by Herrick, Op. 8; Weep You No More; My Life's Delight [Campion]; Damask Roses; The Faithless Shepherdess [Byrd]; Brown Is My Love; By a Fountainside [Ben Johnson]; Fair House of Joy ("Roger Quilter, Vol. 2") † Shakespeare Songs (misc)
SYMP ▲ 1184 (18.97)
J. Benton (bar), R. Lowe (pno)—Fairy Lullaby; Wind from the South, Thomas Moore; Oh, tis sweet to think, Burns; a Manx ballad (The Fuchsia tree) † Arnold Book of Old Songs; Traditional:Songs
SYMP ▲ 1159 (18.97)
B. Luxon (bar), D. Willison (pno)—5 song groups: 3 Shakespeare Songs, Op. 6; To Julia, Op. 8; 7 Elizabethan Lyrics, Op. 12; 4 Songs, Op. 14; 3 Songs of William Blake, Op. 20; 8 individual songs—Love's philosophy, Op. 3/1; Now sleeps the crimson petal, Op. 3/2; At close of day; Go, lovely rose, op. 24/3; Arab love song, Op. 25/4; Music, when soft voices die, Op. 25/5; In the bud of the morning O, Op. 25/6; I arise from dreams of thee, Op. 29
CHN ▲ 8782 [DDD] (16.97)

QUINET, FERNAND (1898-1971)
Chamber Music
J. Petit (cnd), Jean-Louis Petit CO—L'Ecole buissonnière; Mélodies (5) orientales; Suite pour 3 Cls; Charade; Son Va; Moralités non légendaires *(rec Ville d'Avray, June 1995)* ("Musique de chambre")
CYPR ▲ 3604 [DDD] (17.97)

RAAIJMAKERS, DICK (1930-
Tape Music
D. Raaijmakers (tape) *(rec 1959-96)* ("Complete Tape Music")
CV (Composer's Voice) 3-▲ 9 (54.97)

RAASTED, NIELS OTTO (1888-1966)
Prelude & Fugue in C for Organ, Op. 20 (1918)
P. S. Jacobsen (org) ("Organ Works") † Son 2 Org, Op. 23; Son 3 Org, Op. 33; Son 4 Org, Op. 50
PONT ▲ 5131 [DDD] (18.97)
Sonata No. 1 in c for Organ, Op. 16
A. Riber (org) *(rec May-June 1996)* ("Danish Organ Works") † Buxtehude:Te Deum laudamus, BuxWV 218; E. Haumann:Chaconne; S. Møller:Te Deum; C. Nielsen:Commotio, Op. 58
KPT ▲ 32242
Sonata No. 2 in e for Organ, Op. 23 (1919)
P. S. Jacobsen (org) ("Organ Works") † Prelude & Fugue Org, Op. 20; Son 3 Org, Op. 33; Son 4 Org, Op. 50
PONT ▲ 5131 [DDD] (18.97)
Sonata No. 3 in d for Organ, Op. 33 (1922)
P. S. Jacobsen (org) ("Organ Works") † Prelude & Fugue Org, Op. 20; Son 2 Org, Op. 23; Son 4 Org, Op. 50
PONT ▲ 5131 [DDD] (18.97)
Sonata No. 4 in f for Organ, Op. 50 (1926)
P. S. Jacobsen (org) ("Organ Works") † Prelude & Fugue Org, Op. 20; Son 2 Org, Op. 23; Son 3 Org, Op. 33
PONT ▲ 5131 [DDD] (18.97)

RÄÄTS, JAAN (1932-
Concerto for Trumpet, Piano & String Orchestra, Op. 92
R. Friedrich (tpt), T. Duis (pno), L. Köhler (cnd), Berlin SO † E. Denisov:Con sordino; Jolivet:Concertino Tpt; D. Shostakovich:Con 1 Pno, Op. 35
CAPO ▲ 10575 [DDD] (10.97)

RABAUD, HENRI (1873-1949)
Divertissement sur des chansons russes for Orchestra, Op. 2 (1899)
L. Segerstam (cnd), Rhineland-Palatinate State PO *(rec Ludwigshafen, June 21-22, 1990)* † Eclogue, Op. 7; Mârouf, Savetier du Caire (sels); Procession Nocturne, Op. 6; The Merchant of Venice (sels)
MARC ▲ 8223503 [DDD] (13.97)
Eclogue (symphonic poem) for Orchestra [after Virgil], Op. 7
L. Segerstam (cnd), Rhineland-Palatinate State PO *(rec Ludwigshafen, June 21-22, 1990)* † Divertissement sur des chansons russes, Op. 2; Mârouf, Savetier du Caire (sels); Procession Nocturne, Op. 6; The Merchant of Venice (sels)
MARC ▲ 8223503 [DDD] (13.97)
Mârouf, Savetier du Caire (selections)
H. Rabaud (cnd) ("French Composers Conduct") † Procession Nocturne, Op. 6; G. Charpentier:Impressions d'Italie; P. Gaubert:Chants de la mer; Orch Music
VAIA ▲ 1075 (17.97)
L. Segerstam (cnd), Rhineland-Palatinate State PO *(rec Ludwigshafen, June 21-22, 1990)* † Divertissement sur des chansons russes, Op. 2; Eclogue, Op. 7; Procession Nocturne, Op. 6; The Merchant of Venice (sels)
MARC ▲ 8223503 [DDD] (13.97)
The Merchant of Venice (selections)
L. Segerstam (cnd), Rhineland-Palatinate State PO *(rec Ludwigshafen, June 28, 1990 & Nov 11, 1992)* † Divertissement sur des chansons russes, Op. 2; Eclogue, Op. 7; Mârouf, Savetier du Caire (sels); Procession Nocturne, Op. 6
MARC ▲ 8223503 [DDD] (13.97)
Procession Nocturne for Orchestra, Op. 6
H. Rabaud (cnd) ("French Composers Conduct") † Mârouf, Savetier du Caire (sels); G. Charpentier:Impressions d'Italie; P. Gaubert:Chants de la mer; Orch Music
VAIA ▲ 1075 (17.97)
L. Segerstam (cnd), Rhineland-Palatinate State PO *(rec Ludwigshafen, June 21-22, 1990)* † Divertissement sur des chansons russes, Op. 2; Eclogue, Op. 7; Mârouf, Savetier du Caire (sels); The Merchant of Venice (sels)
MARC ▲ 8223503 [DDD] (13.97)
Solo de Concours for Clarinet & Piano, Op. 10
W. Boeykens (cl), R. Groslot (pno) ("French Music for Clarinet & Piano") † E. Chausson:Andante et Allegro; Debussy:Première rapsodie Cl; P. Gaubert:Fant Fl; Messager:Solo de concours Cl; G. Pierné:Canzonetta Cl, Op. 19; Saint-Saëns:Son Cl
TLNT ▲ 51 (15.97)
M. Edwards (cl), T. Bach (pno) *(rec Pomona College Claremont, CA, 1997)* † Bjelinski:Son Cl; Ladmirault:Son Cl; Martinů:Sonatina Cl; Saint-Saëns:Son Cl
CRYS ▲ 735 (15.97)

RABE, FOLKE (1935-
Concerto for Trombone & Orchestra, "All the Lonely People..." (1989)
C. Lindberg (trbn), O. Vänskä (cnd), Tapiola Sinfonietta † Rimsky-Korsakov:Con Trbn; N. Rota:Con Trbn; A. Schnittke:Dialogue Vc; H. Tomasi:Con Trbn
BIS ▲ 568 [DDD] (17.97)
Shazam for Trumpet (1984)
H. Hardenberger (tpt) † Arban:Vars on a Theme from Bellini's Norma; P. M. Davies:Son Tpt; J. Françaix:Sonatine Tpt & Pno; J. Hartmann:Vars on Rule Britannia; Honegger:Intrada Tpt & Pno; Tisné:Héraldiques
BIS ▲ 287 [DDD] (17.97)

RABL, WALTER (1873-1940)
Quartet for Clarinet, Violin, Cello & Piano, Op. 1 (ca 1897)
Ensemble Kontraste † J. Brahms:Trio Cl; Zemlinsky:Trio Cl, Op. 3
THOR ▲ 2368 [DDD] (16.97)

RABUSHKA, AARON (1958-
Canzona e Scherzo Capriccioso for Wind & Percussion Ensemble, Op. 4 (1974)
M. Machek (cnd), Bohuslav Martinů PO ("Music in Mixed Accents") † Etude Fantasque Pno, Op. 7; Suite Va, Op. 23; R. Snyder:Son Ob; Sukegawa:Komoriuta; Trojanowski:Treatment; G. W. Yasinitsky:Music of Wood, Silver & Ivory; On Wings of Angels
VMM ▲ 2012 [DDD]
Concerto for Harp & Chamber Orchestra, Op. 24 (1978)
A. Antalová (hp), M. Machek (cnd), Bohuslav Martinů PO ("Music from 6 Continents 1995") † J. M. Kennedy:Portrait...; D. Patterson:Hermit's Blue; R. Snyder:Namdaemun; Winges:Aural Colors
VMM ▲ 3032 [DDD]
Etude Fantasque for Piano, Op. 7 (1974)
A. Flajšinová (pno) ("Music in Mixed Accents") † Canzona e Scherzo Capriccioso, Op. 4; Suite Va, Op. 23; R. Snyder:Son Ob; Sukegawa:Komoriuta; Trojanowski:Treatment; G. W. Yasinitsky:Music of Wood, Silver & Ivory; On Wings of Angels
VMM ▲ 2012 [DDD]
Suite for Viola & Piano, Op. 23 (1978)
M. Kašný (va), A. Flajšinová (pno) ("Music in Mixed Accents") † Canzona e Scherzo Capriccioso, Op. 4; Etude Fantasque Pno, Op. 7; R. Snyder:Son Ob; Sukegawa:Komoriuta; Trojanowski:Treatment; G. W. Yasinitsky:Music of Wood, Silver & Ivory; On Wings of Angels
VMM ▲ 2012 [DDD]

RACHMANINOFF, SERGEI (1873-1943)
Again You Are Bestirred, My Heart for Piano
H. Shelley (pno) *(rec Highgate, England, July 24-27, 1994, Sept 19-20, 1994 & Jan 23-25)* † All-Night Vigil, Op. 37; Songs (12), Op. 14; Songs (12), Op. 21; Songs (14), Op. 34; Songs (15), Op. 26; Songs (6), Op. 38; Songs (6), Op. 4; Songs (6), Op. 8; Vocalise
CHN ▲ 9644 [DDD] (16.97)
Aleko (opera in 1 act) [lib V. Nemirovich-Danchenko after Pushkin] (1892)
N. Erassova (sop), G. Borissova (mez), V. Taraschenko (ten), V. Matorin (bass), V. Potchapski (bass), A. Tchistiakov (cnd), Bolshoi Theater Orch, Russian State Choir ("The 3 Operas") † Francesca da Rimini, Op. 25; Miserly Knight, Op. 24
RUSS 3-▲ 388053 (36.97)
B. Karnobatlova-Dobreva (sop—Tsemfira), P. Kurshumov (ten—Gypsy), N. Ghiuselev (bass—Aleko), D. Petkov (bass—Father), T. Hirstova (sgr—Gypsy woman), R. Raichev (cnd), Plovdiv PO, Choir Ensemble for Songs
CAPO ▲ 10782 [DDD] (10.97)
M. Lapina (sop), S. Isoumov (sgr), O. Koulko (sgr), L. Tischenko (sgr), R. Kofman (cnd), Donetsk PO *(rec 1995)*
VRDI (Masters) ▲ 6803
A. Tchistiakov (cnd), Bolshoi Theater Orch
RUSS (Midline) ▲ 788079 (12.97)
Aleko (selections)
S. Aleksashkin (bass), G. Rozhdestvensky (cnd), Philharmonia Orch ("Russian Arias, Vol. 2") † Borodin:Prince Igor (sels); Mussorgsky:Boris Godunov (sels); Rimsky-Korsakov:Arias; P. Tchaikovsky:Arias
CHN ▲ 9629 (16.97)
N. Järvi (cnd), Philharmonia Orch † Capriccio bohémien, Op. 12; Sym Dances, Op. 45
CHN ▲ 9081 [DDD] (16.97)
E. Nesterenko (bass), E. Shenderovich (pno)
RUS ▲ 11372 [DDD] (12.97)
Sofia National Opera Chorus ("The Russian Opera Experience") † M. Glinka:Life for the Tsar (sels); Mussorgsky:Khovanshchina (sels); Rimsky-Korsakov:Boyarinya Vera Sheloga (sels); Golden Cockerel (sels); May Night (sels); Snow Maiden (sels)
CAPO ▲ 14864 [DDD] (5.97)
Y. Temirkanov (cnd), St. Petersburg PO † Rhap on a Theme of Paganini, Op. 43; Sym Dances, Op. 45
RCAV (Red Seal) ▲ 62710 (16.97)
All-Night Vigil (vespers) for Contralto, Tenor & a cappella Mixed Chorus, Op. 37 (1915)
O. Borodina (mez), V. Mostowoy (ten), N. Korniev (cnd), St. Petersburg Chamber Choir *(rec St. Petersburg, Oct 3-6, 1993)*
PPHI ▲ 42344 (16.97)
V. Chernushenko (cnd), St. Petersburg Cappella
RUSS (Midline) ▲ 788050 (12.97)
S. Cleobury (cnd), King's College Choir Cambridge ("Credo") † Liturgy of St. John Chrysostom, Op. 31; A. Panufnik:Song to the Virgin Mary Chorus; K. Penderecki:Choral Music; I. Stravinsky:Choral Music
EMIC ▲ 56439 (16.97)

RACHMANINOFF, SERGEI (cont.)

All-Night Vigil (vespers) for Contralto, Tenor & a cappella Mixed Chorus, Op. 37 (1915) (cont.)

K. Linke (cnd), Johannes Damascenus Choir Essen, P. L. Pichler (cnd), Papal Russian College Choir Rome [includes traditional Russian liturgy] ("All Night Vigil 2") ENTE ▲ 89 [DDD] (10.97)

K. Linke (cnd), Johannes Damascenus Choir Essen, P. L. Pichler (cnd), Papal Russian College Choir Rome [includes traditional Russian liturgy] ("All Night Vigil I") ENTE ▲ 90 [DDD] (10.97)

J. Mack (ten), W. Hall (cnd), Master Chorale of Orange County *(rec Santa Ana, CA)* KLAV ▲ 11065 [DDD] (18.97)

Y. Necheporenko (ten), A. Zlobin (ten), R. Sevostyanov (ten), O. Shepel (cnd), Voronezh Chamber Choir GLOE ▲ 5077 [DDD] (16.97)

J. Pančík (cnd), Prague Chamber Choir DI ▲ 920273 [DDD] (5.97)

V. Polianski (cnd), USSR Ministry of Culture Chamber Choir ("Vespers") MELD (Russian Choral Music) ▲ 25188 [DDD] (6.97)

V. Rumantsev (ten), V. Polianski (cnd), USSR Ministry of Culture Choir ("Rachmaninoff in Hollywood") † Con 2 Pno, Op. 18; Con 3 Pno, Op. 30; Rhap on a Theme of Paganini, Op. 43; Sym Dances, Op. 45 RCAV (Greatest Hits) ▲ 68874 (11.97)

R. Shaw (cnd), Robert Shaw Festival Singers [RUS] TEL ▲ 80172 [DDD] (16.97)

H. Shelley (pno)—Glory to God in the Highest *(rec Highgate, England, July 24-27, 1994, Sept 19-20, 1994 & Jan 23-25)* † Again You Are Bestirred, My Heart; Songs (12), Op. 14; Songs (12), Op. 21; Songs (14), Op. 34; Songs (15), Op. 26; Songs (6), Op. 38; Songs (6), Op. 4; Songs (6), Op. 8; Vocalise CHN ▲ 9644 [DDD] (16.97)

The Bells (choral symphony) for Soprano, Tenor, Baritone, Orchestra & Chorus [text Bal'mont after Poe], Op. 35 (1913)

V. Ashkenazy (cnd), (Royal) Concertgebouw Orch † Isle of the Dead, Op. 29; Sym Dances, Op. 45; Syms (comp) PLON (Budget Box) 3-▲ 455798 (20.97)

Christos (sop), W. Planté (ten), A. Voketaitis (b-bar), L. Slatkin (cnd), St. Louis SO, St. Louis Sym Chorus *(rec 1980)* † Capriccio bohémien, Op. 12; Isle of the Dead, Op. 29; Prince Rostislav; Rock; Russian Songs, Op. 41; Scherzo; Spring; Sym in d; Sym Dances, Op. 45; Vocalise VB3 3-▲ 3002 [ADD] (14.97)

M. Kurenko (sop), V. Pastukhoff (pno), L. Rosenthal (pno)—Arion ("Maria Kurenko: Rachmaninoff Recital") † Songs; Songs (12), Op. 21; Songs (14), Op. 34; Songs (15), Op. 26; Songs (6), Op. 38; Songs (6), Op. 4; Songs (6), Op. 8; Vocalise VAIA ▲ 1094 [ADD] (16.97)

S. Murphy (sop), K. Lewis (ten), D. Wilson-Johnson (bar), N. Järvi (cnd), Royal Scottish National Orch, Scottish National Chorus [RUS] † Vocalise; S. Taneyev:Duet for Romeo & Juliet; P. Tchaikovsky:Festival Coronation March CHN ▲ 8476 [DDD] (16.97)

R. Shaw (cnd), Atlanta SO, Atlanta Sym Chorus *(rec Atlanta, Nov 4-5, 1995)* † J. Adams:Harmonium TEL ▲ 80365 [DDD] (16.97)

Y. Shumskaya (sop), M. Dovenman (ten), A. Bolshakov (bar), K. Kondrashin (cnd), Moscow PO, A. Yurlov (cnd), Russian Republican Capella † Sym Dances, Op. 45 RCAV (Gold Seal) ▲ 32046 [ADD] (11.97)

E. Ustinova (sop), K. Westi (ten), J. Hynninen (bar), D. Kitaienko (cnd), Danish National RSO, Danish National Radio Choir † Spring CHN ▲ 8966 [DDD] (16.97)

Boris Godunov (selections) (1890-91)

S. Larin (ten), G. Rozhdestvensky (cnd), Philharmonia Orch, J. McCarthy (cnd), Ambrosian Opera Chorus—One last story (Pimen's monologue) *(rec London, England, Aug 14-17, 1997)* ("Russian Arias, Vol. 1") † Borodin:Prince Igor (sels); Dargomyzhsky:Ruslan and Lyudmila (sels); M. Glinka:Russlan & Ludmilla (sels); Rimsky-Korsakov:May Night (sels); Sadko (sels); P. Tchaikovsky:Eugene Onegin (sels); Mazeppa (sels); Queen of Spades (sels); Slippers (sels) *([FRE,GER,RUS,ENG] lib text)* CHN ▲ 9603 [DDD] (16.97)

Capriccio bohémien [Capriccio on Gypsy Themes] for Orchestra, Op. 12 (1892)

A. Anissimov (cnd), Ireland National SO † Sym 1 NXIN ▲ 8550806 [DDD] (5.97)

S. Comissiona (cnd), Vancouver SO *(rec The Orpheum Vancouver, June 1 & 4, 1993 & June 13, 1994)* † Prelude in c#, Op. 3/2; Preludes Pno; Sym Dances, Op. 45 CBC ▲ 5143 [DDD] (16.97)

N. Järvi (cnd), Philharmonia Orch † Aleko (sels); Sym Dances, Op. 45 CHN ▲ 9081 [DDD] (16.97)

L. Slatkin (cnd), St. Louis SO *(rec 1979)* † Bells; Isle of the Dead, Op. 29; Prince Rostislav; Rock; Russian Songs, Op. 41; Scherzo; Spring; Sym in d; Sym Dances, Op. 45; Vocalise VB3 3-▲ 3002 [ADD] (14.97)

E. Svetlanov (cnd), USSR SO *(rec 1966-90)* ("Symphonic Poems from Russia") † Isle of the Dead, Op. 29; Prince Rostislav; Scherzo; Balakirev:Ov on Czech Themes; Rus; Tamara; Glazunov:Ballade, Op. 78; Stenka Razin, Op. 13; Liapunov:Zhelyazova Volya, Op. 37 MELD (2fer) 2-▲ 34166 [ADD] (13.97)

Choruses (6) for Piano & Female (or Children's) Chorus, Op. 15 (1895-96)

V. Krainev (pno), A. Zaboronok (cnd), Bolshoi Theater Children's Choir † Kastalski:Liturgy of St. John Chrysostom RUSS ▲ 788013 [DDD] (12.97)

Concertos (4) for Piano & Orchestra (complete)

A. Anievas (pno), R. Frühbeck de Burgos (cnd), New Philharmonia Orch † Rhap on a Theme of Paganini, Op. 43 EMIC (Doublefforte) 2-▲ 68619 (16.97)

V. Ashkenazy (pno), B. Haitink (cnd), (Royal) Concertgebouw Orch PLON 2-▲ 21590 [DDD] (32.97)

V. Ashkenazy (pno), A. Previn (cnd), London SO PLON 2-▲ 25576 [ADD] (22.97)

V. Ashkenazy (pno), A. Previn (cnd), London SO *(rec Kingsway Hall London, Apr 1970-Nov 1971)* PLON 2-▲ 44839 [ADD] (17.97)

V. Ashkenazy (pno), A. Previn (cnd), London SO † Études-tableaux Pno; Prelude in c#, Op. 3/2; Preludes Pno; Rhap on a Theme of Paganini, Op. 43; Son 2 Pno, Op. 36; Suite 1 for 2 Pnos, Op. 5; Suite 2 for 2 Pnos, Op. 17 PPHI (Budget Box) 6-▲ 455234 (40.97)

V. Eresko (pno), G. Provatorov (cnd), USSR SO *(rec Leningrad, 1984)* † Rhap on a Theme of Paganini, Op. 43 MELD 2-▲ 40068 [ADD] (13.97)

S. Rachmaninoff (pno), E. Ormandy (cnd), Philadelphia Orch ("Rachmaninoff Plays Rachmaninoff") † Rhap on a Theme of Paganini, Op. 43 RCAV (Gold Seal) 2-▲ 61658 (21.97)

H. Shelley (pno), B. Thomson (cnd), Royal Scottish National Orch † Rhap on a Theme of Paganini, Op. 43 CHN 2-▲ 8882 [DDD] (32.97)

A. Simon (pno), L. Slatkin (cnd), St. Louis SO ("Complete Works for Piano & Orchestra") † Rhap on a Theme of Paganini, Op. 43 VB2 2-▲ 5008 [ADD] (9.97)

T. Vásáry (pno), Y. Ahronovitch (cnd), London SO *(rec 1976-77)* DEUT (2-Fers) 2-▲ 453136 [ADD] (17.97)

E. Wild (pno), J. Horenstein (cnd), Royal PO † Rhap on a Theme of Paganini, Op. 43 CHN 2-▲ 7114 (26.97)

Concerto No. 1 in f# for Piano & Orchestra, Op. 1 (1890-91; rev 1917)

P. Entremont (pno), E. Ormandy (cnd), Philadelphia Orch † Con 4 Pno, Op. 40 SNYC (Essential Classics) ▲ 46541 [ADD] (7.97) ▮ 46541 [ADD] (3.98)

B. Janis (pno), K. Kondrashin (cnd), Moscow PO *(rec Tchaikovsky Conservatory Moscow, June 13, 1962)* † Mendelssohn (-Bartholdy):Lieder ohne Worte; S. Prokofiev:Con 3 Pno, Op. 26; Toccata Pno, Op. 11; R. Schumann:Impromptus on a Theme by Clara Wieck, Op. 5 MRCR ▲ 34333 (11.97)

B. Janis (pno), K. Kondrashin (cnd), Moscow PO *(rec 1960-63)* ("Byron Janis II") † Con 2 Pno, Op. 18; Liszt:Con 1 Pno, S.124; S. Prokofiev:Con 3 Pno, Op. 26; Toccata Pno, Op. 11; R. Schumann:Concert sans orch, Op. 14; Romances Pno, Op. 28; P. Tchaikovsky:Con 1 Pno, Op. 23 PPHI (Great Pianists of the 20th Century) 2-▲ 456850 (22.97)

J. Lill (pno), T. Otaka (cnd), BBC National Orch Wales *(rec Brangwyn Hall Swansea, Nov 3, 1996)* † Con 2 Pno, Op. 18 NIMB ▲ 5511 [DDD] (16.97)

J. Lill (pno), T. Otaka (cnd), BBC Welsh National Orch † Études-tableaux Pno; Con 2 Pno, Op. 18; Con 3 Pno, Op. 30; Con 4 Pno, Op. 40; Music of Rachmaninoff; Rhap on a Theme of Paganini, Op. 43; Sym 1; Sym 2; Sym 3; Vars on a Theme by Corelli, Op. 42; Vocalise NIMB 6-▲ 1761 [DDD] (29.97)

A. Ozolins (pno), M. Bernardi (cnd), Toronto SO † E. von Dohnányi:Vars on a Nursery Song, Op. 25; Litolff:Con Symphonique 3, Op. 45 SMS (SM 5000) ▲ 5052 [DDD] (16.97)

S. Rachmaninoff (pno), E. Ormandy (cnd), Philadelphia Orch *(rec 1939-40)* † Con 3 Pno, Op. 30 ENPL (Piano Library) ▲ 258 (13.97)

S. Rachmaninoff (pno), E. Ormandy (cnd), Philadelphia Orch † Con 2 Pno, Op. 18; Con 3 Pno, Op. 30; Con 4 Pno, Op. 40 MPLY 2-▲ 2030 (26.97)

P. Rösel (pno), K. Sanderling (cnd), Berlin SO † Con 2 Pno, Op. 18 BER ▲ 9307 (10.97)

H. Shelley (pno), B. Thomson (cnd), Royal Scottish National Orch † Con 4 Pno, Op. 40; Rhap on a Theme of Paganini, Op. 43 CHN ▲ 9192 [DDD] (16.97)

J. Thibaudet (pno), V. Ashkenazy (cnd), Cleveland Orch *(rec Cleveland Ohio, Apr 25, 1994)* † Con 2 Pno, Op. 18; Con 3 Pno, Op. 30 PLON ▲ 48219 [DDD] (16.97)

O. Volkov (pno), A. Tchistiakov (cnd), Moscow PO *(rec Moscow, Russia, June 1996)* † Rhap on a Theme of Paganini, Op. 43; Vocalise BRIO ▲ 111 (16.97)

O. Volkov (pno), A. Tchistiakov (cnd), Moscow PO ("Celebrate Rachmaninoff") † Con 2 Pno, Op. 18; Preludes Pno; Rhap on a Theme of Paganini, Op. 43; Son 2 Pno, Op. 36; Songs (14), Op. 34 BRIO 2-▲ 116 [DDD] (18.97)

E. Wild (pno), J. Horenstein (cnd), Royal PO † Con 4 Pno, Op. 40; Rhap on a Theme of Paganini, Op. 43 CHN (Collect) ▲ 6605 [ADD] (12.97)

E. Wild (pno), J. Horenstein (cnd), Royal PO *(rec 1965)* † Con 4 Pno, Op. 40; Rhap on a Theme of Paganini, Op. 43 CHSK ▲ 41 [ADD] (16.97)

RACHMANINOFF, SERGEI (cont.)

Concerto No. 2 in c for Piano & Orchestra, Op. 18 (1900-01)

V. Ashkenazy (pno), B. Haitink (cnd), (Royal) Concertgebouw Orch † Con 4 Pno, Op. 40 PLON ▲ 14475 [DDD] (16.97)

V. Ashkenazy (pno), K. Kondrashin (cnd), Moscow PO † Con 3 Pno, Op. 30 DECC ▲ 466375 (11.97)

V. Ashkenazy (pno), A. Previn (cnd), London SO † Rhap on a Theme of Paganini, Op. 43 PLON ▲ 17702 [ADD] (9.97)

V. Ashkenazy (pno), A. Previn (cnd), London SO ("Favourite Rachmaninoff") † Études-tableaux Pno; Con 3 Pno, Op. 30; Prelude in c#, Op. 3/2; Preludes Pno; Rhap on a Theme of Paganini, Op. 43 PLON 2-▲ 36386 [ADD] (17.97)

B. Berezovsky (pno), F. Duchable (cnd) † Con 3 Pno, Op. 30 ERAT ▲ 18411 (9.97)

F. Blumenthal (pno), M. Gielen (cnd), Vienna State Opera Orch *(rec 1958)* † R. Schumann:Con Pno in a, Op. 54 TUXE ▲ 1045 [ADD] (10.97)

R. Bohnke (pno), N. Kirchmann (cnd), Tübingen Medical Orch ("Classical Romance") † E. Grieg:Symphonic Dances, Op. 64; S. Prokofiev:Love for 3 Oranges (march), Op. 33ter; Pieces (10) Pno, Op. 12; M. Reger:Kleine Vortragsstüke, Op. 44 PC ▲ 267121 [DDD] (2.97)

E. Bolkvadze (pno) † Rhap on a Theme of Paganini, Op. 43 SNYC ▲ 62294 [DDD] (4.97)

A. Brailowsky (pno), E. Jordá (cnd), San Francisco SO ("Rachmaninoff in Hollywood") † All-Night Vigil, Op. 37; Con 3 Pno, Op. 30; Rhap on a Theme of Paganini, Op. 43; Sym Dances, Op. 45 RCAV (Greatest Hits) ▲ 68874 (11.97)

Y. Bronfman (pno), E.-P. Salonen (cnd), Philharmonia Orch † Con 3 Pno, Op. 30 SNYC ▲ 47183 (16.97) COL △ 47183

V. Cliburn (pno), F. Reiner (cnd), Chicago SO † P. Tchaikovsky:Con 1 Pno, Op. 23 RCAV (Red Seal) ▲ 55912 [ADD] (16.97)

V. Cliburn (pno), F. Reiner (cnd), Chicago SO † Beethoven:Con 5 Pno, Op. 73 RCAV (Living Stereo) ▲ 61961 [AAD] (11.97) ▮ 61961 [AAD] (6.98)

S. Costa (pno), C. Seaman (cnd), Royal PO † Con 4 Pno, Op. 40 INMP (IMP Classics) ▲ 6701132 (9.97)

P. Entremont (pno), L. Bernstein (cnd), New York PO † Preludes Pno; Rhap on a Theme of Paganini, Op. 43 SNYC ▲ 46271 [AAD] (7.97) ▮ 46271 [AAD] (3.98)

P. Entremont (pno), L. Bernstein (cnd), New York PO *(rec Feb 3, 1960)* † Con 3 Pno, Op. 30 SNYC (Essential Classics) ▲ 53512 [ADD] (7.97) ▮ 53512 [ADD] (3.98)

P. Fowke (pno), Y. Temirkanov (cnd), Royal PO CFP (Eminence) ▲ 9509 [DDD] (16.97)

B. Glemser (pno), A. Wit (cnd), Polish National RSO *(rec Polish Radio Concert Hall, Katowice, Poland, June 1996)* † Con 3 Pno, Op. 30 NXIN ▲ 8550810 [DDD] (5.97)

D. Golub (pno), W. Morris (cnd), London SO † Rhap on a Theme of Paganini, Op. 43 INMP (LSO Classic Masterpieces) ▲ 903 [DDD] (9.97)

G. Graffman (pno), L. Bernstein (cnd), New York PO † Rhap on a Theme of Paganini, Op. 43 SNYC ▲ 36722 (9.97) ▮ 36722 (3.98)

G. Graffman (pno), L. Bernstein (cnd), New York PO *(rec May 26, 1964)* ("Leonard Bernstein: The Royal Edition") † P. Tchaikovsky:Con 1 Pno, Op. 23 SNYC ▲ 47630 [ADD] (10.97)

G. Graffman (pno), L. Bernstein (cnd), New York PO ("Rachmaninoff Goes to the Movies") † Con 3 Pno, Op. 30; Rhap on a Theme of Paganini, Op. 43 SNYC ▲ 63032 (9.97) ▮ 63032 (5.98)

H. Grimaud (pno), J. López-Cobos (cnd), Royal PO † M. Ravel:Con Pno DNN ▲ 75368 [DDD] (16.97)

H. Grimaud (pno), J. Lopez-Cobos (cnd), Royal PO *(rec London, England, June 1992)* ("Romantic Piano Concertos") † Chopin:Con 1 Pno, Op. 11; R. Schumann:Con Pno in a, Op. 54; P. Tchaikovsky:Con 1 Pno, Op. 23 DNN 2-▲ 17013 (16.97)

S. D. Groote (pno), D. D. Villiers (cnd), Cape Town SO *(rec 1987-88)* ("Romantic Piano Concertos") † Beethoven:Con 4 Pno, Op. 58 GSE ▲ 1554 [ADD] (16.97)

H. Gutiérrez (pno), L. Maazel (cnd), Pittsburgh SO † Con 3 Pno, Op. 30 TEL ▲ 80259 [DDD] (16.97)

D. Han (pno), P. Kogan (cnd), Moscow State SO † Rhap on a Theme of Paganini, Op. 43 VRDI (Masters) ▲ 6809 (13.97)

J. Jandó (pno), G. Lehel (cnd), Budapest SO *(rec Italian Institute Budapest, Hungary, 1988)* ("Famous Piano Concertos") † Rhap on a Theme of Paganini, Op. 43; Beethoven:Con 2 Pno, Op. 19; Con 5 Pno, Op. 73; Chopin:Con 1 Pno, Op. 11; Con 2 Pno, Op. 21; P. Tchaikovsky:Con 1 Pno, Op. 23; Eugene Onegin (sels); Tempest, Op. 18 NXIN 4-▲ 504011 [DDD] (19.97)

J. Jandó (pno), G. Lehel (cnd), Budapest SO † Rhap on a Theme of Paganini, Op. 43 NXIN ▲ 550117 [DDD] (5.97)

B. Janis (pno), A. Dorati (cnd), Minneapolis SO † Con 3 Pno, Op. 30; Prelude in c#, Op. 3/2; Preludes Pno MRCR ▲ 32759 [ADD] (11.97)

B. Janis (pno), A. Dorati (cnd), Minneapolis SO *(rec 1960-63)* ("Byron Janis II") † Con 1 Pno, Op. 1; Liszt:Con 1 Pno, S.124; S. Prokofiev:Con 3 Pno, Op. 26; Toccata Pno, Op. 11; R. Schumann:Concert sans orch, Op. 14; Romances Pno, Op. 28; P. Tchaikovsky:Con 1 Pno, Op. 23 PPHI (Great Pianists of the 20th Century) 2-▲ 456850 (22.97)

E. Joyce (pno), E. Leinsdorf (cnd), London PO † C. Franck:Symphonic Vars, M.46; Mendelssohn (-Bartholdy):Con 1 Pno, Op. 25; J. Turina:Rapsodia sinfónica, Op. 66 DLAB (Essential Archives) ▲ 5505 (15.97)

J. Katchen (pno), G. Solti (cnd), London SO † Rhap on a Theme of Paganini, Op. 43; E. von Dohnányi:Vars on a Nursery Song, Op. 25 PLON (The Classic Sound) ▲ 448604 (11.97)

R. Kerer (pno), K. Kondrashin (cnd), Moscow PO *(rec 1952-63)* ("Famous Russian Pianists") † S. Prokofiev:Con 1 Pno, Op. 10; Rimsky-Korsakov:Con Pno, Op. 30 MUL ▲ 310353 (13.97)

H. Kim (pno), G. Rozhdestvensky (cnd), USSR Ministry of Culture Orch † Con 3 Pno, Op. 30 SSCL ▲ 20 (16.97)

E. Kissin (pno) † Études-tableaux Pno RCAV ▲ 57982 (16.97)

E. Kissin (pno), V. Gergiev (cnd), London SO ("Evgeny Kissin: A Musical Portrait") † W. A. Mozart:Con 12 Pno, K.414; S. Prokofiev:Con 3 Pno, Op. 26; D. Shostakovich:Con 1 Pno, Op. 35 RCAV (Red Seal) 2-▲ 60567 [DDD] (24.97)

J. Lill (pno), T. Otaka (cnd), BBC National Orch Wales *(rec Brangwyn Hall Swansea, Apr 15, 1996)* † Con 1 Pno, Op. 1 NIMB ▲ 5511 [DDD] (16.97)

J. Lill (pno), T. Otaka (cnd), BBC Welsh National Orch † Études-tableaux Pno; Con 1 Pno, Op. 1; Con 3 Pno, Op. 30; Con 4 Pno, Op. 40; Music of Rachmaninoff; Rhap on a Theme of Paganini, Op. 43; Sym 1; Sym 2; Sym 3; Vars on a Theme by Corelli, Op. 42; Vocalise NIMB 6-▲ 1761 [DDD] (29.97)

J. Lill (pno), T. Otaka (cnd), BBC Welsh SO—Allegro scherzando ("Whad' Ya Know About Rachmaninoff") † Con 3 Pno, Op. 30; Liturgy of St. John Chrysostom, Op. 31; Prelude in c#, Op. 3/2; Preludes Pno; Rhap on a Theme of Paganini, Op. 43; Son 2 Pno, Op. 36; Sym 2; Vocalise NIMB ▲ 4007 [DDD] (11.97)

D. Lively (pno), A. Rahbari (cnd), Brussels BRTN PO *(rec Concert Hall of the Belgian Radio & Television Bru, May 19-21, 1994)* † Con 3 Pno, Op. 30 DI ▲ 920221 [DDD] (5.97)

B. Moiseiwitsch (pno), W. Goehr (cnd), London PO *(rec Nov 24 & Dec 13, 1937)* ("The Complete Rachmaniov Recordings, 1937-43") † Moments musicaux, Op. 16; Prelude in c#, Op. 3/2; Preludes Pno; Rhap on a Theme of Paganini, Op. 43; A. Scarlatti:Preludes (23) Pno, Opp. 23 & 32 APR ▲ 5505 [ADD] (19.97)

B. Moiseiwitsch (pno), H. Rignold (cnd), Philharmonia Orch *(rec 1955)* † Moments musicaux, Op. 16; Preludes Pno; Chopin:Ballade 3 Pno, Op. 47; Ballade 4 Pno, Op. 52; Barcarolle Pno, Op. 60; Fant-Impromptu, Op. 66; Nocturnes Pno; Scherzos Pno; Kabalevsky:Son 3 Pno, Op. 46; Liszt:Études de concert (3), S.144; Medtner:Son Pno in g, Op. 22; Mendelssohn (-Bartholdy):Midsummer Night's Dream (sels); S. Prokofiev:Pieces (4) Pno, Op. 4; Toccata Pno, Op. 11 PPHI (Great Pianists of the 20th Century) 2-▲ 456907 (22.97)

J. Morrison (pno), A. Morrison (org)—Adagio sostenuto [trans pno & org] *(rec Morrow, GA, Nov 19, 1995)* ("Festive Duo") † Preludes Pno; M. Dupré:Prélude, fugue et var, Op. 18; Sinf Pno, Op. 42; Grasse:Festival Ov, Op. 5; H. Stover:Neumark Vars ACAD ▲ 20050 (16.97)

B. Moseiwitsch (pno), W. Goehr (cnd), London PO † Mendelssohn (-Bartholdy):Midsummer Night's Dream (sels); P. Tchaikovsky:Con 1 Pno, Op. 23 AVID ▲ 585 (16.97)

N. Ogawa (pno), O. A. Hughes (cnd), Malmö SO *(rec May 1997)* † Con 3 Pno, Op. 30 BIS ▲ 900 [DDD] (17.97)

G. Ohlsson (pno), N. Marriner (cnd), Academy of St. Martin in the Fields † P. Tchaikovsky:Con 1 Pno, Op. 23 HANS ▲ 98932 [DDD] (15.97)

R. Orozco (pno), E. De Waart (cnd), Royal PO † Rhap on a Theme of Paganini, Op. 43; Sym 2; Vocalise PPHI 2-▲ 38383 (17.97)

A. Ozolins (pno), M. Bernardi (cnd), Toronto SO † Vocalise; Willan:Con Pno, Op. 76 SMS (SM 5000) ▲ 5108 [DDD] (16.97)

J. L. Prats (pno), E. Bátiz (cnd), Mexico City PO † Rhap on a Theme of Paganini, Op. 43 ASVQ ▲ 6128 [DDD] (11.97)

S. Rachmaninoff (pno), L. Stokowski (cnd), Philadelphia Orch † Rhap on a Theme of Paganini, Op. 43; Vocalise INMP ▲ 104 [ADD] (14.97)

S. Rachmaninoff (pno), L. Stokowski (cnd), Philadelphia Orch *(rec 1929)* † Con 3 Pno, Op. 30 RCAV (Red Seal) ▲ 5997 [ADD] (16.97)

S. Rachmaninoff (pno), L. Stokowski (cnd), Philadelphia Orch † Rhap on a Theme of Paganini, Op. 43 MTAL ▲ 48075 (6.97)

S. Rachmaninoff (pno), L. Stokowski (cnd), Philadelphia Orch *(rec 1929)* † Con 4 Pno, Op. 40 ENPL (Piano Library) ▲ 276 (13.97)

S. Rachmaninoff (pno), L. Stokowski (cnd), Philadelphia Orch *(rec 1929)* † Con 1 Pno, Op. 1; Con 3 Pno, Op. 30; Con 4 Pno, Op. 40 MPLY 2-▲ 2030 (26.97)

652

▲ = CD ♦ = Enhanced CD △ = MD ▮ = Cassette Tape ▯ = DCC

RACHMANINOFF, SERGEI (cont.)

Concerto No. 2 in c for Piano & Orchestra, Op. 18 (1900-01) (cont.)

S. Richter (pno), S. Wislocki (cnd), Warsaw PO † P. Tchaikovsky:Con 1 Pno, Op. 23 DEUT (The Originals) ▲ 47420 [ADD] (11.97)
S. Richter (pno), S. Wislocki (cnd), Warsaw PO *(rec 1952-59)* ("Sviatoslav Richter III") † Preludes Pno; Trans & Arrs; A. Scriabin:Etudes (12) Pno, Op. 8; Etudes (3) Pno, Op. 65; Etudes (8) Pno, Op. 42; Pieces (3) Pno, Op. 2 PPHI (Great Pianists of the 20th Century) 2-▲ 456952 (22.97)
P. Rösel (pno), K. Sanderling (cnd), Berlin SO † Con 1 Pno, Op. 1 BER ▲ 9307 (10.97)
A. Rubinstein (pno), V. Golschmann (cnd), NBC SO *(rec 1946-47)* ("Rubinstein, Vol. 4") † Rhap on a Theme of Paganini, Op. 43 HPC1 ▲ 132 (17.97)
A. Rubinstein (pno), F. Reiner (cnd), Chicago SO † Rhap on a Theme of Paganini, Op. 43 RCAV (Red Seal) ▲ 4934 (16.97)
A. Rubinstein (pno), L. Stokowski (cnd), Hollywood Bowl SO *(rec Aug 1, 1945)* † P. Grainger:In a Nutshell; E. Grieg:Con Pno, Op. 16 BPS ▲ 41 [ADD] (16.97)
H. Shelley (pno), B. Thomson (cnd), Royal Scottish National Orch † Con 3 Pno, Op. 30 CHN ▲ 9193 [DDD] (17.97)
C. Smith (pno), M. Sargent (cnd), Liverpool PO *(rec 1947-48)* † Rhap on a Theme of Paganini, Op. 43; Suite 2 for 2 Pnos, Op. 17 DLAB ▲ 4004 (17.97)
E. S. Son (pno), M. Ermler (cnd), Moscow PO † Sym 3 RUS ▲ 10011 [DDD] (12.97)
A. Sultanov (pno), A. Lazarev (cnd) † Con 3 Pno, Op. 30; Sym 2; Vocalise TELC (Ultima) 2-▲ 18958 (16.97)
J. Thibaudet (pno)—Adagio sostenuto † Rhap on a Theme of Paganini, Op. 43; Addinsell:Warsaw Con; G. Gershwin:Rhap in Blue; D. Shostakovich:Con 2 Pno, Op. 102 DECC ▲ 460503 (16.97)
J. Thibaudet (pno), V. Ashkenazy (cnd), Cleveland Orch † Rhap on a Theme of Paganini, Op. 43 PLON ▲ 40653 [DDD] (16.97)
J. Thibaudet (pno), V. Ashkenazy (cnd), Cleveland Orch *(rec Cleveland Ohio, Apr 25, 1994)* † Con 1 Pno, Op. 1; Con 3 Pno, Op. 30 PLON ▲ 48219 [DDD] (16.97)
O. Volkov (pno), A. Tchistiakov (cnd), Moscow PO † Saint-Saëns:Con 2 Pno, Op. 22 BRIO ▲ 114 (16.97)
O. Volkov (pno), A. Tchistiakov (cnd), Moscow PO ("Celebrate Rachmaninoff") † Con 1 Pno, Op. 1; Preludes Pno; Rhap on a Theme of Paganini, Op. 43; Son 2 Pno, Op. 36; Songs (14), Op. 34 BRIO 2-▲ 116 [DDD] (18.97)
E. Wild (pno), J. Horenstein (cnd), Royal PO † Con 3 Pno, Op. 30 CHN (Collect) ▲ 6507 [ADD] (12.97)
E. Wild (pno), J. Horenstein (cnd), Royal PO *(rec 1966)* † Isle of the Dead, Op. 29; Tausig:Trans & Arrs Pno CHSK ▲ 2 (16.97)
E. Wild (pno), J. Horenstein (cnd), Royal PO † Isle of the Dead, Op. 29 CHGR ▲ 902 [DDD] (29.97)
various artists [excerpt] † Borodin:Prince Igor (sels); Liszt:Hungarian Rhaps, S.244; W. A. Mozart:Serenade No. 13, K.525, "Eine kleine Nachtmusik"; Sibelius:Finlandia, Op. 26; R. Strauss:Also sprach Zarathustra, Op. 30; P. Tchaikovsky:Sym 6 MTAL ▲ 48097 (6.97)

Concerto No. 3 in d for Piano & Orchestra, Op. 30 (1909)

M. Argerich (pno), R. Chailly (cnd), Berlin RSO *(rec live Berlin)* † P. Tchaikovsky:Con 1 Pno, Op. 23 PPHI ▲ 46673 (16.97)
M. Argerich (pno), R. Chailly (cnd), Berlin RSO *(rec 1982)* ("Martha Argerich") † J. S. Bach:Partitas Hpd; Liszt:Con 1 Pno, S.124; S. Prokofiev:Con 3 Pno, Op. 26; M. Ravel:Con Pno; Gaspard de la nuit; Sonatine Pno PPHI (Great Pianists of the 20th Century) ▲ 456700 (22.97)
V. Ashkenazy (pno), A. Fistoulari (cnd), London SO † Con 2 Pno, Op. 18 DECC ▲ 466375 (11.97)
V. Ashkenazy (pno), B. Haitink (cnd), (Royal) Concertgebouw Orch PLON ▲ 17239 [DDD] (16.97)
V. Ashkenazy (pno), E. Ormandy (cnd), Philadelphia Orch ("Rachmaninoff in Hollywood") † All-Night Vigil, Op. 37; Con 2 Pno, Op. 18; Rhap on a Theme of Paganini, Op. 43; Sym Dances, Op. 45 RCAV (Greatest Hits) ▲ 68874 (11.97)
V. Ashkenazy (pno), A. Previn (cnd), London SO ("Favourite Rachmaninoff") † Études-tableaux Pno; Con 2 Pno, Op. 18; Prelude in c#, Op. 3/2; Preludes Pno; Rhap on a Theme of Paganini, Op. 43 PLON 2-▲ 36386 [ADD] (17.97)
V. Ashkenazy (pno), A. Previn (cnd), London SO † Con 4 Pno, Op. 40 PENG (Penguin Music Classics) ▲ 460608 (11.97)
B. Berezovsky (pno), F. Duchable (cnd) † Con 2 Pno, Op. 18 ERAT ▲ 18411 (9.97)
J. Bolet (pno) ("Live in Concert") † Liszt:Trans, Arrs & Paraphrases PALE ▲ 503 (17.97)
Y. Bronfman (pno), E.-P. Salonen (cnd), Philharmonia Orch † Con 2 Pno, Op. 18 SNYC ▲ 47183 (16.97) COL △ 47183
V. Cliburn (pno), K. Kondrashin (cnd), Sym of the Air † S. Prokofiev:Con 3 Pno, Op. 26 RCAV (Red Seal) ▲ 6209 [ADD] (16.97)
S. Costa (pno), C. Seaman (cnd), Royal PO † Rhap on a Theme of Paganini, Op. 43 INMP (IMP Classics) ▲ 6701142 [DDD] (9.97)
V. Feltsman (pno), Z. Mehta (cnd), Israel PO † Rhap on a Theme of Paganini, Op. 43 SNYC ▲ 44761 [DDD] (16.97)
Em. Gilels (pno), A. Cluytens (cnd), Paris Conservatory Société des Concerts Orch † Saint-Saëns:Con 2 Pno, Op. 22; D. Shostakovich:Preludes & Fugues Pno, Op. 87 TES ▲ 1029 [ADD] (17.97)
B. Glemser (pno), J. Maksymiuk (cnd), Irish National SO *(rec National Concert Hall Dublin, Dec 17-18, 1992)* † Prince Rostislav NXIN ▲ 550666 [DDD] (5.97)
B. Glemser (pno), J. Maksymuik (cnd), Ireland National SO—Allegro ma non tanto ("Best of Rachmaninov") † Music of Rachmaninoff; Prelude in c#, Op. 3/2; Preludes Pno; Rhap on a Theme of Paganini, Op. 43; Sym 2; Vocalise NXIN ▲ 8556682 [DDD] (5.97)
B. Glemser (pno), A. Wit (cnd), Polish National RSO *(rec Polish Radio Concert Hall, Katowice, Poland, June 1996)* † Con 2 Pno, Op. 18 NXIN ▲ 8550810 [DDD] (5.97)
H. Gutiérrez (pno), L. Maazel (cnd), Pittsburgh SO † Con 2 Pno, Op. 18 TEL ▲ 80259 [DDD] (16.97)
D. Helfgott (pno), M. Horvat (cnd), Copenhagen PO *(rec Tivoli Concert Hall Copenhagen, Nov 2, 1995)* ("David Helfgott Plays Rachmaninoff") † Prelude in c#, Op. 3/2; Preludes Pno; Son 2 Pno, Op. 36 RCAV (Red Seal) ▲ 40378 [DDD] (16.97) ▮ 40378 [DDD] (9.98)
V. Horowitz (pno), S. Koussevitzky (cnd), Los Angeles PO *(rec live, Aug 1948)* ("Horowitz Plays Rachmaninoff & Tchaikovsky") † P. Tchaikovsky:Con 1 Pno, Op. 23 IN ▲ 1398 [ADD] (15.97)
V. Horowitz (pno), E. Ormandy (cnd), New York PO RCAV (Red Seal) ▲ 61564 (16.97)
V. Horowitz (pno), F. Reiner (cnd), RCA Victor SO † Pno Music (misc colls); Son 2 Pno, Op. 36 RCAV (Gold Seal) ▲ 7754 [ADD] (11.97)
B. Janis (pno), A. Dorati (cnd), London SO † Con 2 Pno, Op. 18; Prelude in c#, Op. 3/2; Preludes Pno MRCR ▲ 32759 [ADD] (11.97)
B. Janis (pno), C. Munch (cnd), Boston SO RCAV (Silver Seal) ▲ 60540 [ADD] (6.97)
W. Kapell (pno), E. MacMillan (cnd), Toronto SO *(rec live, Apr 13, 1948)* ("W. Kapell, Vol. 1") † A. Khachaturian:Con Pno VAIA ▲ 1027 [ADD]
H. Kim (pno), G. Rozhdestvensky (cnd), USSR Ministry of Culture Orch † Con 2 Pno, Op. 18 SSCL ▲ 20 (16.97)
A. Laplante (pno), A. Lazarev (cnd), Moscow PO *(rec live Tchaikovsky Int'l Music Compe, July 4, 1978)* † Preludes Pno; P. Tchaikovsky:Saisons FL ▲ 23107 [DDD] (16.97)
J. Lill (pno), T. Otaka (cnd), BBC National Orch Wales † Son 2 Pno, Op. 36 NIMB ▲ 5348 [DDD] (16.97)
J. Lill (pno), T. Otaka (cnd), BBC Welsh National Orch † Études-tableaux Pno; Con 1 Pno, Op. 1; Con 2 Pno, Op. 18; Con 4 Pno, Op. 40; Music of Rachmaninoff; Rhap on a Theme of Paganini, Op. 43; Sym 1; Sym 2; Sym 3; Vars on a Theme by Corelli, Op. 42; Vocalise NIMB 6-▲ 1761 [DDD] (29.97)
J. Lill (pno), T. Otaka (cnd), BBC Welsh SO—Finale. Alla breve-Scherzando-Alla breve ("Whad' Ya Know About Rachmaninoff") † Con 2 Pno, Op. 18; Liturgy of St. John Chrysostom, Op. 31; Prelude in c#, Op. 3/2; Preludes Pno; Rhap on a Theme of Paganini, Op. 43; Son 2 Pno, Op. 36; Sym 2; Vocalise NIMB ▲ 4007 [DDD] (11.97)
D. Lively (pno), A. Rahbari (cnd), Brussels BRTN PO *(rec Concert Hall of the Belgian Radio & Television Bru, May 19-21, 1994)* † Con 2 Pno, Op. 18 DI ▲ 920221 [DDD] (5.97)
W. Malcuzyński (pno), P. Kletzki (cnd), Philharmonia Orch *(rec 1946-49)* † Chopin:Con 2 Pno, Op. 21 HPC ▲ 144 (17.97)
N. Ogawa (pno), O. A. Hughes (cnd), Malmö SO *(rec May 1997)* † Con 2 Pno, Op. 18 BIS ▲ 900 [DDD] (17.97)
A. Orlovetsky (pno), A. Titov (cnd), St. Petersburg New Classical Orch † Liszt:Fant on Hungarian Folk Tunes, S.123 SNYC ▲ 57260 [DDD] (4.97)
R. Orozco (pno), E. Waart (cnd), Royal PO ("Shine: The Complete Classics") † Prelude in c#, Op. 3/2; Beethoven:Sym 9; Chopin:Polonaise 6 Pno, Op. 53; Preludes (24) Pno, Op. 28; Liszt:Études d'exécution transcendante (6), S.140; Études de concert (3), S.144; Hungarian Rhaps, S.244; Rimsky-Korsakov:Tale of Tsar Saltan (orch sels); R. Schumann:Kinderszenen Pno, Op. 15; Vivaldi:Gloria; Nulla in mundo pax, RV.630 PPHI 2-▲ 456403 (17.97)
S. Rachmaninoff (pno), E. Ormandy (cnd), Philadelphia Orch *(rec 1940)* † Con 2 Pno, Op. 18 RCAV (Red Seal) ▲ 5997 [ADD] (16.97)
S. Rachmaninoff (pno), E. Ormandy (cnd), Philadelphia Orch *(rec 1939-40)* † Con 1 Pno, Op. 1 ENPL (Piano Library) ▲ 258 (13.97)
S. Rachmaninoff (pno), E. Ormandy (cnd), Philadelphia Orch † Con 1 Pno, Op. 1; Con 2 Pno, Op. 18; Con 4 Pno, Op. 40 MPLY 2-▲ 2030 (26.97)
P. Rösel (pno), K. Sanderling (cnd), Berlin SO † Con 4 Pno, Op. 40 BER ▲ 9302
H. Shelley (pno), B. Thomson (cnd), Royal Scottish National Orch † Con 2 Pno, Op. 18 CHN ▲ 9193 [DDD] (17.97)

RACHMANINOFF, SERGEI (cont.)

Concerto No. 3 in d for Piano & Orchestra, Op. 30 (1909) (cont.)

C. Smith (pno), G. Weldon (cnd), City of Birmingham SO *(rec 1944-46)* ("The Complete Rachmaninoff & Dohnányi Recordings") † Preludes Pno; E. von Dohnányi:Trans Pno; Vars on a Nursery Song, Op. 25 APR (Signature) ▲ 5507 [ADD] (18.97)
A. Sultanov (pno), A. Lazarev (cnd) † Con 2 Pno, Op. 18; Sym 2; Vocalise TELC (Ultima) 2-▲ 18958 (16.97)
J. Thibaudet (pno), V. Ashkenazy (cnd), Cleveland Orch *(rec Cleveland Ohio, Apr 25, 1994)* † Con 1 Pno, Op. 1; Con 2 Pno, Op. 18 PLON ▲ 48219 [DDD] (16.97)
N. Trull (pno), A. Anichanov (cnd), St. Petersburg State SO † Rhap on a Theme of Paganini, Op. 43 APC ▲ 101038
A. Watts (pno), S. Ozawa (cnd), New York PO *(rec Oct 1, 1969)* † Con 2 Pno, Op. 18 SNYC (Essential Classics) ▲ 53512 [ADD] (7.97) ▮ 53512 [ADD] (3.98)
A. Watts (pno), S. Ozawa (cnd), New York PO ("Rachmaninoff Goes to the Movies") † Con 2 Pno, Op. 18; Rhap on a Theme of Paganini, Op. 43 SNYC ▲ 63032 (9.97) ▮ 63032 (5.98)
E. Wild (pno), J. Horenstein (cnd), Royal PO † Con 2 Pno, Op. 18 CHN (Collect) ▲ 6507 [ADD] (12.97)
E. Wild (pno), J. Horenstein (cnd), Royal PO *(rec 1965)* † MacDowell:Con 2 Pno, Op. 23 CHSK ▲ 76 [ADD] (16.97)

Concerto No. 4 in g for Piano & Orchestra, Op. 40 (1926; rev 1941)

V. Ashkenazy (pno), B. Haitink (cnd), (Royal) Concertgebouw Orch † Con 2 Pno, Op. 18 PLON ▲ 14475 [DDD] (16.97)
V. Ashkenazy (pno), A. Previn (cnd), London SO † Con 3 Pno, Op. 30 PENG (Penguin Music Classics) ▲ 460608 (11.97)
W. Black (pno), I. Buketoff (cnd), Iceland SO [original 1927 version] † Monna Vanna CHN ▲ 8987 [DDD] (16.97)
S. Costa (pno), C. Seaman (cnd), Royal PO † Con 2 Pno, Op. 18 INMP (IMP Classics) ▲ 6701132 (9.97)
P. Entremont (pno), E. Ormandy (cnd), Philadelphia Orch † Con 1 Pno, Op. 1 SNYC (Essential Classics) ▲ 46541 [ADD] (7.97) ▮ 46541 [ADD] (3.98)
H. Kim (pno), J. Rudel (cnd), Philharmonia Orch † Rhap on a Theme of Paganini, Op. 43 HEL ▲ 1035 (10.97)
J. Lill (pno), T. Otaka (cnd), BBC National Orch Wales † Liturgy of St. John Chrysostom, Op. 31; Rhap on a Theme of Paganini, Op. 43; Vars on a Theme by Corelli, Op. 42 NIMB 2-▲ 5478 (16.97)
J. Lill (pno), T. Otaka (cnd), BBC Welsh National Orch † Études-tableaux Pno; Con 1 Pno, Op. 1; Con 2 Pno, Op. 18; Con 3 Pno, Op. 30; Music of Rachmaninoff; Rhap on a Theme of Paganini, Op. 43; Sym 1; Sym 2; Sym 3; Vars on a Theme by Corelli, Op. 42; Vocalise NIMB 6-▲ 1761 [DDD] (29.97)
A. Lubimov (pno), J. Saraste (cnd), Toronto SO *(rec Roy Thomson Hall Toronto)* † A. Scriabin:Prométhée, Op. 60; I. Stravinsky:Con Pno & Ww FNL ▲ 17277 (16.97)
S. Rachmaninoff (pno), E. Ormandy (cnd), Philadelphia Orch *(rec 1941)* † Con 2 Pno, Op. 18 ENPL (Piano Library) ▲ 276 (13.97)
S. Rachmaninoff (pno), E. Ormandy (cnd), Philadelphia Orch *(rec 1941)* ("Composer, Pianist, Conductor") † Sym 3; Vocalise GSE ▲ 785077 (m) [ADD] (16.97)
S. Rachmaninoff (pno), E. Ormandy (cnd), Philadelphia Orch *(rec 1941)* † Con 1 Pno, Op. 1; Con 2 Pno, Op. 18; Con 3 Pno, Op. 30 MPLY 2-▲ 2030 (26.97)
P. Rösel (pno), K. Sanderling (cnd), Berlin SO † Con 3 Pno, Op. 30 BER ▲ 9302
H. Shelley (pno), B. Thomson (cnd), Royal Scottish National Orch † Con 1 Pno, Op. 1; Rhap on a Theme of Paganini, Op. 43 CHN ▲ 9192 [DDD] (16.97)
P. Stewart (pno), I. Golovchin (cnd), Moscow RSO ("Rachmaninoff & Mednter") † Medtner:Son Pno PALE ▲ 506 (17.97)
J. Thibaudet (pno), V. Ashkenazy (cnd), Cleveland Orch † Prelude in c#, Op. 3/2; Son 2 Pno, Op. 36; Vars on a Theme by Corelli, Op. 42 PLON ▲ 458930 (16.97)
E. Wild (pno), J. Horenstein (cnd), Royal PO † Con 1 Pno, Op. 1; Rhap on a Theme of Paganini, Op. 43 CHN (Collect) ▲ 6605 [ADD] (12.97)
E. Wild (pno), J. Horenstein (cnd), Royal PO *(rec 1965)* † Con 1 Pno, Op. 1; Rhap on a Theme of Paganini, Op. 43 CHSK ▲ 41 [ADD] (16.97)

Duets (6) for Piano 4-Hands, Op. 11 (1894)

A. Goldenweiser (pno), G. Ginzburg (pno) *(rec 1948-52)* ("Russian Piano School") † Suite 1 for 2 Pnos, Op. 5; Suite 2 for 2 Pnos, Op. 17 RD (Talents of Russia) ▲ 16260 [ADD] (16.97)
T. Hecht (pno), S. Shapiro (pno) *(rec Euclid, OH, Aug 31-Sept 2, 1991)* ("Sentimiento") † Infante:Danzas andaluzas; Liszt:Réminiscences de Don Juan Pno, S.418 AZI ▲ 1201 [DDD] (15.97)
Reine Elisabeth Duo ("Russian Music for 2 Pianos") † A. Scriabin:Fant Pnos; D. Shostakovich:Concertino Pnos, Op. 94; I. Stravinsky:Pétrouchka (pno reduction) DI ▲ 920150 [DDD] (5.97)
I. Thorson (pno), J. Thurber (pno) † Pieces Pno 6-Hands; Polka italienne; Preludes Pno; Romance in G; Russian Rhap; Suite 1 for 2 Pnos, Op. 5; Suite 2 for 2 Pnos, Op. 17; Sym Dances, Op. 45 PLAL 2-▲ 46 (35.97)

Études-tableaux for Piano, Opp. 33 & 39 (1911; 1916-17)

N. Angelich (pno) † Preludes Pno HAM (Les Nouveaux Interprètes) ▲ 911547 (12.97)
V. Ashkenazy (pno) *(rec All Sants' Church Petersham & St George the Mar, 1977 & 1981)* † Russian Rhap; Suite 1 for 2 Pnos, Op. 5; Suite 2 for 2 Pnos, Op. 17; Sym Dances, Op. 45; Vars on a Theme by Corelli, Op. 42 PLON (Double Decker) 2-▲ 44845 [ADD] (17.97)
V. Ashkenazy (pno) † Cons Pno (comp); Prelude in c#, Op. 3/2; Preludes Pno; Rhap on a Theme of Paganini, Op. 43; Son 2 Pno, Op. 36; Suite 1 for 2 Pnos, Op. 5; Suite 2 for 2 Pnos, Op. 17 PPHI (Budget Box) 6-▲ 455234 (40.97)
V. Ashkenazy (pno)—Op. 39/1 in c; Op. 39/2 in a; Op. 39/5 in e♭ ("Favourite Rachmaninoff") † Con 2 Pno, Op. 18; Con 3 Pno, Op. 30; Prelude in c#, Op. 3/2; Preludes Pno; Rhap on a Theme of Paganini, Op. 43 PLON 2-▲ 36386 [ADD] (17.97)
I. Biret (pno) NXIN ▲ 550347 [DDD] (5.97)
J. Browning (pno)—Op. 33/2 in C; Op. 33/3 in c; Op. 39/5 in e♭; Op. 33 † Moments musicaux, Op. 16; Pno Music (misc colls); Preludes Pno; Son 2 Pno, Op. 36 DLS ▲ 3044 [DDD] (14.97)
M. P. Carola (pno) † Vars on a Theme by Corelli, Op. 42 SYMO ▲ 103 (17.97)
V. Cliburn (pno)—Op. 39/5 in e♭ † Preludes Pno; Son 2 Pno, Op. 36; S. Prokofiev:Son 6 Pno, Op. 82 RCAV (Gold Seal) ▲ 7941 [ADD] (11.97)
J. Coop (pno)—Études-tableaux Pno [Op. 39/8 in d] *(rec Toronto, Canada)* ("The Romantic Piano") † Preludes (23) Pno, Opp. 23 & 32; J. Brahms:Pieces (6) Pno, Op. 118; Waltzes (16) Pno, Op. 39; Chopin:Etudes (24) Pno, Opp. 10 & 25; Mazurkas Pno; Nocturnes Pno; Debussy:Isle joyeuse; Suite bergamasque; Liszt:Études de concert (3), S.144; Liebesträume, S.541; Mendelssohn (-Bartholdy):Pno Music (misc); R. Schumann:Kinderszenen Pno, Op. 15 MUVI ▲ 1015 [DDD] (16.97)
J. DePreist (cnd), Oregon SO—Op. 39/2 in a [arr Respighi] † Sym 2; Vocalise DLS ▲ 3071 [DDD] (14.97)
A. Gavrilov (pno)—Op. 39/3 in f#; Op. 39/5 in e♭ † Morceaux de fant, Op. 3; Pno Music (misc colls); Preludes Pno; Balakirev:Islamey; P. Tchaikovsky:Morceaux (6) Pno, Op. 19 RYLC ▲ 6471
P. Gillot (pno) DANT ▲ 9435 (17.97)
N. Goerner (pno) *(rec Switzerland, Dec 19-21, 1993)* † Son 2 Pno, Op. 36; Songs (12), Op. 21; Songs (6), Op. 38; Trans & Arrs CASC ▲ 1037 [DDD] (16.97)
M. Gon (pno)—Op. 39 † Moments musicaux, Op. 16 DI ▲ 920278 [DDD] (5.97)
I. Hobson (pno) ARA ▲ 6609 (16.97)
C. Keene (pno) *(rec Pepperdine Univ)* ("Constance Keene Plays Rachmaninoff") PROT ▲ 2207 (19.97)
E. Kissin (pno) [6 sels] † Con 2 Pno, Op. 18 RCAV ▲ 57982 (16.97)
Z. Kocsis (pno)—Op. 33/7 in E♭ *(rec 1973-86)* ("Zoltán Kocsis in Concert, 1973-86") † Preludes Pno; Chopin:Ballade 1 Pno, Op. 23; Mazurkas Pno; Kodály:Pieces (7) Pno, Op. 11; Liszt:Pno Music (misc); F. Schubert:Impromptus (4); R. Wagner:Parsifal (sels) HUN ▲ 31679 [AAD] (16.97)
J. Lill (pno) *(rec Concert Hall of the Nimbus Foundation, Jan 25-26, 1995)* NIMB ▲ 5439 [DDD] (16.97)
J. Lill (pno), T. Otaka (cnd), BBC Welsh National Orch—Op. 39 † Con 1 Pno, Op. 1; Con 2 Pno, Op. 18; Con 3 Pno, Op. 30; Con 4 Pno, Op. 40; Music of Rachmaninoff; Rhap on a Theme of Paganini, Op. 43; Sym 1; Sym 2; Sym 3; Vars on a Theme by Corelli, Op. 42; Vocalise NIMB 6-▲ 1761 [DDD] (29.97)
J. López-Cobos (cnd), Cincinnati SO—Op. 33/7 in E♭; Op. 39/2 in a; Op. 39/6 in a; Op. 39/7 in c; Op. 39/9 [orchd Respighi] *(rec Cincinatti, OH, 1995)* ("Respighi: Transcriptions for Orchestra") † O. Respighi:Boutique fantasque TEL ▲ 80396 [DDD] (16.97)
F. Moyer (pno)—Op. 33/3 in c; Op. 39/6 in a; Op. 39/9 † Preludes Pno; J. S. Bach:Sons & Partitas Vn JUP ▲ 106 (13.97)
J. Ogdon (pno)—Op. 33 † Prelude in c#, Op. 3/2; Preludes Pno; Balakirev:Islamey; Liszt:Pno Music (misc); Trans, Arrs & Paraphrases PPHI (Great Pianists of the 20th Century, Vol. 73) ▲ 456916 (22.97)
M. Perahia (pno)—Op. 33/2 in C; Op. 39/5 in e♭; Op. 39/6 in a; Op. 39/9 ("The Aldeburgh Recital, 1990") † Beethoven:Vars Pno on Original Theme, WoO 80; Liszt:Consolations (6), S.172; Hungarian Rhaps, S.244; R. Schumann:Faschingsschwank, Op. 26 SNYC ▲ 46437 [DDD] (16.97)
M. Petkova (pno) *(rec Nov 1996)* † Preludes Pno DORO ▲ 3026 [DDD] (16.97)
M. Pletnev (pno)—Op. 33/6; Op. 33/8 in g; Op. 33/9; Op. 39/5 in e♭ *(rec Villa Senar, Switzerland)* ("Hommage à Rachmaninov") † Vars on a Theme by Corelli, Op. 42; Beethoven:Son 26 Pno, Op. 81a; Chopin:Andante Spianato & Grand Polonaise, Op. 22; Mendelssohn (-Bartholdy):Rondo capriccioso, Op. 14 DEUT ▲ 459634 (16.97)

RACHMANINOFF, SERGEI (cont.)

Études-tableaux for Piano, Opp. 33 & 39 (1911; 1916-17) (cont.)

S. Prutsman (pno) *(rec Fairfax, VA, Dec 1996)* † Liadov:Pieces (3) Pno, Op. 11; A. Scriabin:Son 3 Pno, Op. 23 BRIO ▲ 113 (16.97)

S. Richter (pno) ("The Richter Collection, Vol. 2") † Preludes Pno; Beethoven:Son 27 Pno, Op. 90; Son 3 Pno, Op. 2/3; Son 4 Pno, Op. 7; Vars & Fugue Pno, Op. 35; Vars Pno on Original Theme, Op. 34; Vars Pno on Original Theme, Op. 76; J. Brahms:Son 1 Vn, Op. 78; Chopin:Scherzos Pno; J. Haydn:Son 39 Kbd, H.XVI/24; R. Schumann:Bunte Blätter, Op. 99; Symphonic Etudes, Op. 13; D. Shostakovich:Son Vn OLY 5-▲ 5013 [DDD] (64.97)

S. Richter (pno) *(rec 1984)* † Mussorgsky:Pictures at an Exhibition PRAG ▲ 254034 (18.97)

H. Shelley (pno) HYP ▲ 66091 (18.97)

V. Viardo (pno), C. Zacharias (pno)—Op. 39/1 in c; Op. 33/2 in C *(rec Fort Worth, TX, 1973)* ("The Fourth Cliburn Competition 1973") † J. S. Bach:Wohltemperirte Clavier; Beethoven:Son 28 Pno, Op. 101; Son 32 Pno, Op. 111; Debussy:Estampes; Images (6) Pno; Pour le piano; S. Prokofiev:Visions fugitives, Op. 22; Webern:Vars Pno, Op. 27 VAIA (Retrospective Series, Vol. 7) ▲ 1175 (m) [ADD] (16.97)

The Flower Has Faded for Voice & Piano (1893)

J. Rodgers (sop), M. Popescu (mez), A. Naoumenko (ten), S. Leiferkus (bar), H. Shelley (pno) ("Volume 1") † Songs; Songs (12), Op. 14; Songs (6), Op. 4; Songs (6), Op. 8 CHN ▲ 9405 (16.97)

Francesca da Rimini (opera in prologue, 2 scenes & epilogue) [lib M. Tchaikovsky after Dante], Op. 25 (1900, 1904-05)

M. Lapina (sop), V. Taraschenko (ten), N. Vassiliev (ten), N. Mechetniak (bar), V. Matorin (bass), A. Tchistiakov (cnd), Bolshoi Theater Orch, Russian State Choir ("The 3 Operas") † Aleko; Miserly Knight, Op. 24 RUSS 3-▲ 388053 (36.97)

V. Taraschenko (ten), N. Vasiliev (bar), V. Matorin (bass), A. Tchistiakov (cnd), Bolshoi Theater Orch RUSS ▲ 788081 (12.97)

The Isle of the Dead (symphonic poem) for Orchestra [after Böcklin], Op. 29 (1909)

V. Ashkenazy (cnd), (Royal) Concertgebouw Orch † Sym Dances, Op. 45 PLON ▲ 30733 [DDD] (9.97)

V. Ashkenazy (cnd), (Royal) Concertgebouw Orch † Bells; Sym Dances, Op. 45; Syms (comp) PLON (Budget Box) 3-▲ 455798 (20.97)

E. Bátiz (cnd), Royal Liverpool PO † Sym Dances, Op. 45 ALFA ▲ 1011 [DDD]

E. Bátiz (cnd), Royal PO *(rec Nov 1991)* † Sym Dances, Op. 45 NXIN ▲ 550583 [DDD] (5.97)

A. Davis (cnd), Royal Stockholm PO † Rock; Sym Dances, Op. 45 FNL ▲ 19091 (15.97)

J. Horenstein (cnd), Royal PO † Con 2 Pno, Op. 18; Tausig:Trans & Arrs Pno CHSK ▲ 2 (16.97)

J. Horenstein (cnd), Royal PO † Con 2 Pno, Op. 18 CHGR ▲ 902 [DDD] (29.97)

D. Mitropoulos (cnd), Minneapolis SO † G. Mahler:Sym 1 SNYC (Masterworks Heritage) ▲ 62342 (12.97)

S. Rachmaninoff (cnd), Philadelphia Orch *(rec 1929)* † Sym 3; Vocalise PHS ▲ 9414 [AAD] (17.97)

S. Rachmaninoff (cnd), Philadelphia Orch † Rhap on a Theme of Paganini, Op. 43; Sym 3 RCAV (Gold Seal) 10-▲ 61265 (102.97)

S. Rachmaninoff (cnd), Philadelphia Orch *(rec Apr 20, 1929)* ("Rachmaninoff Conducts Rachmaninoff") † Sym 3; Vocalise RCAV (Gold Seal) ▲ 62532 [ADD] (11.97)

S. Rachmaninoff (cnd), Philadelphia Orch † Sym 3; Vocalise MTAL ▲ 48038 (6.97)

F. Reiner (cnd), Chicago SO *(rec 1957)* ("The Reiner Sound") † Liszt:Totentanz Pno & Orch, S.126; M. Ravel:Pavane pour une infante défunte; Rapsodie espagnole; C. M. von Weber:Invitation to the Dance Orch RCAV (Gold Seal) ▲ 61250 (11.97)

F. Reiner (cnd), Chicago SO ("Basic 100, Vol. 53") † Sym 2 RCAV ▲ 68022 (10.97)

L. Slatkin (cnd), St. Louis SO *(rec 1979)* † Bells; Capriccio bohémien, Op. 12; Prince Rostislav; Rock; Russian Songs, Op. 41; Scherzo; Spring; Sym in d; Sym Dances, Op. 45; Vocalise VB3 3-▲ 3002 [ADD] (14.97)

L. Stokowski (cnd), Hollywood Bowl SO *(rec 1945-46)* † P. Tchaikovsky:Marche slave, Op. 31; Sym 6 PHS ▲ 9261 (17.97)

E. Svetlanov (cnd), USSR SO *(rec 1966-90)* ("Symphonic Poems from Russia") † Capriccio bohémien, Op. 12; Prince Rostislav; Scherzo; Balakirev:Ov on Czech Themes; Rus; Tamara; Glazunov:Ballade, Op. 78; Stenka Razin, Op. 13; Liapunov:Zhelyazova Volya, Op. 37 MELD (2fer) 2-▲ 34166 [ADD] (13.97)

H. Williams (cnd), Pécs SO † Rhap on a Theme of Paganini, Op. 43; Sym Dances, Op. 45 HUN ▲ 31551 [DDD] (16.97)

Liturgy of St. John Chrysostom for a cappella Chorus, Op. 31 (1910)

M. Best (cnd), Corydon Singers HYP ▲ 66703 (18.97)

C. Bruffy (cnd), Kansas City Chorale—Glory be to the Father ("Whad' Ya Know About Rachmaninoff") † Con 2 Pno, Op. 18; Con 3 Pno, Op. 30; Prelude in c#, Op. 3/2; Preludes Pno; Rhap on a Theme of Paganini, Op. 43; Son 2 Pno, Op. 36; Sym 2; Vocalise NIMB ▲ 4007 [DDD] (11.97)

C. Bruffy (cnd), Kansas City Chorale † Con 4 Pno, Op. 40; Rhap on a Theme of Paganini, Op. 43; Vars on a Theme by Corelli, Op. 42 NIMB 2-▲ 5478 (16.97)

S. Cleobury (cnd), King's College Choir Cambridge ("Credo") † All-Night Vigil, Op. 37; A. Panufnik:Song to the Virgin Mary Chorus; K. Penderecki:Choral Music; I. Stravinsky:Choral Music EMIC ▲ 56439 (16.97)

S. Leiferkus (bar), H. Shelley (pno) *(rec Highgate, England, Sept 19-20, 1994 & Jan 30-31, 1995)* † Songs; Songs (12), Op. 14; Songs (12), Op. 21; Songs (14), Op. 34; Songs (15), Op. 26; Songs (6), Op. 4; Songs (6), Op. 8 CHN ▲ 9374 [DDD] (16.97)

K. Linke (cnd), Johannes Damascenus Choir Essen *(rec 1979)* ENTE ▲ 88 [DDD] (10.97)

M. Milkov (cnd), Bulgarian Radio Chorus Sofia † Preludes Pno; Chopin:Son Pno in b, Op. 58; Liszt:Son Pno, S.178 EMIC (Doublefforte) 2-▲ 68664 (16.97)

V. Minin (cnd), Moscow Chamber Choir MELD (Russian Choral Music) ▲ 25187 [DDD] (6.97)

V. Popov (cnd), Moscow Academy of Choral Singing RUSS ▲ 288154 (18.97)

J. Rodgers (sop), M. Popescu (mez), A. Naoumenko (ten), S. Leiferkus (bass), H. Shelley (pno) ("Complete Songs, Vol. 3") † Songs; Songs (14), Op. 34; Songs (6), Op. 38; Vocalise CHN ▲ 9477 (16.97)

The Miserly Knight [Skupoy rïtsar'] (opera in 3 acts) [lib Pushkin], Op. 24 (1903-05)

V. Kudriashov (ten), V. Verestnikov (bar), M. Krutikov (bass), A. Arkhipov (sgr), P. Gluboky (sgr), A. Tchistiakov (cnd), Bolshoi Theater Orch, Russian State Choir ("The 3 Operas") † Aleko; Francesca da Rimini, Op. 25 RUSS 3-▲ 388053 (36.97)

A. Tchistiakov (cnd), Bolshoi Theater Orch RUSS ▲ 788080 (12.97)

Moments musicaux (6) for Piano, Op. 16 (1896)

L. Berman (pno) † Liszt:Harmonies poétiques et religieuses, S.173; Trans, Arrs & Paraphrases; A. Scriabin:Fant Pno, Op. 28 AURC ▲ 161 (5.97)

I. Biret (pno) *(rec Oct 1989)* † Son 2 Pno, Op. 36; Vars on a Theme by Corelli, Op. 42 NXIN ▲ 550349 [DDD] (5.97)

V. Bogolubov (pno) ("Unfamiliar Masterpieces") † Preludes Pno; Vars on a Theme by Chopin, Op. 22 SNE ▲ 620 (16.97)

J. Browning (pno) † Études-tableaux Pno; Pno Music (misc colls); Preludes Pno; Son 2 Pno, Op. 36 DLS ▲ 3044 [DDD] (14.97)

M. Gon (pno) † Études-tableaux Pno DI ▲ 920278 [DDD] (5.97)

I. Heifetz (pno)—No. 4 in e (presto); No. 5 in D♭ (adagio sostenuto) † Morceaux de fant, Op. 3; S. Prokofiev:Son 3 Pno, Op. 28; Toccata Pno, Op. 11; P. Tchaikovsky:Dumka; Morceaux (6) Pno, Op. 19 SO ▲ 22562 (16.97)

I. Heifetz (pno)—No. 1 in b♭ (andantino); No. 5 in D♭ (adagio sostenuto) ("The Maiden's Wish") † Liszt:Pno Music (misc); Trans, Arrs & Paraphrases; S. Prokofiev:Pno Music (misc colls); P. Tchaikovsky:Album pour enfants Pno, Op. 39; Morceaux (6) Pno, Op. 19 SO ▲ 22565 [DDD] (16.97)

I. Hobson (pno) *(rec Houston TX & Great Hall of the Kranne, United States of America, Sept 9-10, 1994 & Jan 25, 1995)* ("The Complete Solo Piano Transcriptions & Arrangements of Sergei Rachmaninoff") † Morceaux de fant, Op. 3; Morceaux de salon, Op. 10; Pno Music (misc colls); Pno Trans; Polka WR; Trans & Arrs; Mendelssohn (-Bartholdy):Capriccio brillante, Op. 22 ARA ▲ 6663 (16.97)

I. Hobson (pno) ("Early Piano Works") † Morceaux de fant, Op. 3; Morceaux de salon, Op. 10 ARA ▲ 6685

V. Horowitz (pno)—No. 3 in b (andante cantabile) *(rec Washington D.C. & New York, United States of America, Dec 10, 1967 & Dec 15, 1968)* ("The Complete Masterworks Recordings, Vol. IX") † Pno Music (misc colls); Preludes Pno; Son 2 Pno, Op. 36; Medtner:Fairy Tales, Op. 51; A. Scriabin:Etudes (12) Pno, Op. 8; Pno Music (misc colls) SNYC ▲ 53472 (16.97)

J. Lill (pno) † Prelude in c#, Op. 3/2; Son 1 Pno, Op. 28 NIMB ▲ 5575 [DDD] (16.97)

B. Moiseiwitsch (pno) *(rec Oct 20, 1943)* ("The Complete Rachmaniov Recordings, 1937-43") † Con 2 Pno, Op. 18; Prelude in c#, Op. 3/2; Preludes Pno; Rhap on a Theme of Paganini, Op. 43; A. Scarlatti:Preludes (23) Pno, Opp. 23 & 32 APR ▲ 5505 [ADD] (19.97)

B. Moiseiwitsch (pno)—No. 4 in e (presto) *(rec 1956)* † Con 2 Pno, Op. 18; Preludes Pno; Chopin:Ballade 3 Pno, Op. 47; Ballade 4 Pno, Op. 52; Barcarolle Pno, Op. 60; Fant-Impromptu, Op. 66; Nocturnes Pno; Scherzos Pno; Kabalevsky:Son 3 Pno, Op. 46; Liszt:Études de concert (3), S.144; Medtner:Son Pno in g, Op. 22; Mendelssohn (-Bartholdy):Midsummer Night's Dream (sels); S. Prokofiev:Pieces (4) Pno, Op. 4; Toccata Pno, Op. 11 PPHI (Great Pianists of the 20th Century) 2-▲ 456907 (22.97)

RACHMANINOFF, SERGEI (cont.)

Moments musicaux (6) for Piano, Op. 16 (1896) (cont.)

D. Paperno (pno)—No. 5 in D♭ (adagio sostenuto) *(rec 1980-95)* ("Paperno Live") † J. Brahms:Intermezzos (3) Pno, Op. 117; J. Haydn:Sonatas for Piano; Liszt:Années de pèlerinage 2, S.161; Trans, Arrs & Paraphrases; Medtner:Forgotten Melodies 1, Op. 38; R. Schumann:Bunte Blätter, Op. 99; P. Tchaikovsky:Dumka CED ▲ 44 [DDD] (16.97)

A. Pratt (pno)—No. 3 in b (andante cantabile) *(rec live, South Africa, Dec 1995)* ("Live from South Africa") † Preludes Pno; J. S. Bach:Chromatic Fant & Fugue, BWV 903; J. Brahms:Intermezzos (3) Pno, Op. 117; Busoni:Bach Transcriptions Pno; C. Franck:Prélude, fugue et var, Op. 18 EMIC ▲ 55293 (16.97)

S. Rachmaninoff (pno), E. Ormandy (cnd), Philadelphia Orch *(rec 1920-42)* † Morceaux de fant, Op. 3; Morceaux de salon, Op. 10; Pno Music (misc colls) MTAL ▲ 48074 (6.97)

Monna Vanna for Orchestra [from composer's piano score of opera, Act 1; orchd Igor Buketoff] (1907)

S. McCoy (ten), S. Milnes (bar), I. Buketoff (cnd), Iceland SO, Icelandic Opera Chorus † Con 4 Pno, Op. 40 CHN ▲ 8987 [DDD] (16.97)

Morceaux de fantaisie (5 fantasy pieces) for Piano [including No. 2, Prelude in c#], Op. 3 (1892)

B. Bekhterev (pno) ("Miniatures by Great Russian Composers") † A. Scriabin:Pno Music (misc colls) PHEX ▲ 97322 (16.97)

I. Biret (pno) *(rec Oct 1989 & 1990)* † Preludes Pno NXIN ▲ 550348 [DDD] (5.97)

N. Demidenko (pno) [plus others] † Pno Music (misc colls) HYP ▲ 66713 (18.97)

A. Gavrilov (pno)—Elégie in e♭ † Études-tableaux Pno; Pno Music (misc colls); Preludes Pno; Balakirev:Islamey; P. Tchaikovsky:Morceaux (6) Pno, Op. 19 RYLC ▲ 6471

I. Heifetz (pno)—Polichinelle in f# † Moments musicaux, Op. 16; S. Prokofiev:Son 3 Pno, Op. 28; Toccata Pno, Op. 11; P. Tchaikovsky:Dumka; Morceaux (6) Pno, Op. 19 SO ▲ 22562 (16.97)

I. Hobson (pno)—Sérénade in b♭ *(rec Houston TX & Great Hall of the Kranne, United States of America, Sept 9-10, 1994 & Jan 25, 1995)* ("The Complete Solo Piano Transcriptions & Arrangements of Sergei Rachmaninoff") † Moments musicaux, Op. 16; Morceaux de salon, Op. 10; Pno Music (misc colls); Pno Trans; Polka WR; Trans & Arrs; Mendelssohn (-Bartholdy):Capriccio brillante, Op. 22 ARA ▲ 6663 (16.97)

I. Hobson (pno) ("Early Piano Works") † Moments musicaux, Op. 16; Morceaux de salon, Op. 10 ARA ▲ 6685

F. Lushtak (pno) *(rec Recital Hall Univ of New Orleans, Apr-May 1995)* † Preludes Pno; A. Scriabin:Son 2 Pno, Op. 19; Son 3 Pno, Op. 23 CENT ▲ 2287 [DDD] (16.97)

S. Rachmaninoff (pno)—Elégie in e♭; Prelude in c# [plus others] ("Rachmaninoff Plays Rachmaninoff") † Morceaux de salon, Op. 10 PLON (Historic) ▲ 25964 [ADD] (11.97)

S. Rachmaninoff (pno)—Elégie in e♭; Prelude in c#; Polichinelle in f#; Sérénade in b♭ ("A Window in Time") † Pno Music (misc colls); Pno Trans; Polka WR; Prelude in c#, Op. 3/2; Preludes Pno; Songs (12), Op. 21; Trans & Arrs TEL ▲ 80489 [DDD] (16.97)

S. Rachmaninoff (pno), E. Ormandy (cnd), Philadelphia Orch—Mélodie in E *(rec 1920-42)* † Moments musicaux, Op. 16; Morceaux de salon, Op. 10; Pno Music (misc colls) MTAL ▲ 48074 (6.97)

I. Sztankov (db), E. Tóth (pno) [arr for Db & Pno] *(rec May 1997)* ("Double-Bass Parade") † Koussevitzky:Andante Db, Op. 1/1; Chanson triste Db, Op. 2; Humoresque Db, Op. 4; Valse miniature Db, Op. 1/2; Liszt:Lugubre gondola Vn or Vc, S.134; Rimsky-Korsakov:Tale of Tsar Saltan (orch sels); F. Schubert:Son Arpeggione, D.821; E. Tabakov:Motivs Db HUN ▲ 31732 [DDD] (16.97)

V. Tropp (pno) † P. Tchaikovsky:Saisons DNN ▲ 18003 (16.97)

Morceaux de salon (7) for Piano, Op. 10 (1893-94)

D. Golub (pno)—Humoresque in G *(rec Purchase Conservatory of Music, United States of America, Sept 14-16, 1996)* ("Humoresque") † A. Dvořák:Humoresques, Op. 101; R. Schumann:Humoreske Pno, Op. 20; J. Suk:Humoreska; P. Tchaikovsky:Morceaux (2) Pno, Op. 10 ARA ▲ 6706 [DDD] (16.97)

I. Hobson (pno) ("Early Piano Works") † Moments musicaux, Op. 16; Morceaux de fant, Op. 3 ARA ▲ 6685

I. Hobson (pno)—Humoresque in G *(rec Houston TX & Great Hall of the Kranne, United States of America, Sept 9-10, 1994 & Jan 25, 1995)* ("The Complete Solo Piano Transcriptions & Arrangements of Sergei Rachmaninoff") † Moments musicaux, Op. 16; Morceaux de fant, Op. 3; Pno Music (misc colls); Pno Trans; Polka WR; Trans & Arrs; Mendelssohn (-Bartholdy):Capriccio brillante, Op. 22 ARA ▲ 6663 (16.97)

S. Rachmaninoff (pno)—Barcarolle; Humoresque in G ("Rachmaninoff Plays Rachmaninoff") † Morceaux de fant, Op. 3; Pno Music (misc colls) PLON (Historic) ▲ 25964 [ADD] (11.97)

S. Rachmaninoff (pno), E. Ormandy (cnd), Philadelphia Orch—Humoresque in G *(rec 1920-42)* † Moments musicaux, Op. 16; Morceaux de fant, Op. 3; Pno Music (misc colls) MTAL ▲ 48074 (6.97)

P. Vairo (pno)—Barcarolle *(rec May 1992)* † Beethoven:Son 12 Pno, Op. 26; E. Grieg:Lyric Pieces; Piano Music (selections); A. Khachaturian:Toccata; Liszt:Liebesträume, S.541; R. Schumann:Fantasiestücke Pno, Op. 12 STRV ▲ 102 [DDD] (16.97)

Music of Rachmaninoff

J. Jandó (pno), G. Lehel (cnd), Budapest SO *(Con 2 Pno, Op. 18 [Moderato])*, E. Bátiz (cnd), Royal PO *(Sym Dances, Op. 45 [Andante con moto])* ("Best of Rachmaninov") † Con 3 Pno, Op. 30; Prelude in c#, Op. 3/2; Preludes Pno; Rhap on a Theme of Paganini, Op. 43; Sym 2; Vocalise NXIN ▲ 8556682 [DDD] (5.97)

J. Lill (pno), T. Otaka (cnd), BBC Welsh National Orch—Son 2 Pno, Op. 36; The Isle of the Dead, Op. 29 † Études-tableaux Pno; Con 1 Pno, Op. 1; Con 2 Pno, Op. 18; Con 3 Pno, Op. 30; Con 4 Pno, Op. 40; Rhap on a Theme of Paganini, Op. 43; Sym 1; Sym 2; Sym 3; Vars on a Theme by Corelli, Op. 42; Vocalise NIMB 6-▲ 1761 [DDD] (29.97)

Piano Music (miscellaneous collections)

A. Alieva (pno)—Con 1 Pno, Op. 1 † Songs (6), Op. 38; Balakirev:Paraphrase Pno; S. Ibrahimova:Trans de chants populaires azerbaïdjans; Mustafa-Zade:Con Pno; Radjabov:Tableaux de la vie hébraïque GALL ▲ 832 [DDD]

J. Browning (pno)—Songs (6), Op. 38 [Daisies]; Études-tableaux Pno [Op. 33]; Moments musicaux, Op. 16 † Études-tableaux Pno; Moments musicaux, Op. 16; Preludes Pno; Son 2 Pno, Op. 36 DLS ▲ 3044 [DDD] (14.97)

N. Demidenko (pno)—Études-tableaux Pno [Op. 33/2 in C; Op. 33/8 in g; Op. 39/3 in f#; Op. 39/4 in b; Op. 39/5 in e♭] † Morceaux de fant, Op. 3 HYP ▲ 66713 (18.97)

A. Gavrilov (pno)—Études-tableaux Pno [Op. 39/3 in f#]; Moments musicaux, Op. 16 [No. 3 in b (andante cantabile); No. 4 in e (presto); No. 5 in D♭ (adagio sostenuto); No. 6 in C (maestoso)] † Études-tableaux Pno; Morceaux de fant, Op. 3; Preludes Pno; Balakirev:Islamey; P. Tchaikovsky:Morceaux (6) Pno, Op. 19 RYLC ▲ 6471

I. Hobson (pno)—Trans & Arrs [Smith:The Star-Spangled Banner; Tchaikovsky:Lullaby (Op. 16/1); Kreisler:Liebesfreud]; Songs (12), Op. 21 [Lilacs]; Songs (6), Op. 38 [Daisies] *(rec Houston TX & Great Hall of the Kranne, Sept 9-10, 1994 & Jan 25, 1995)* ("The Complete Solo Piano Transcriptions & Arrangements of Sergei Rachmaninoff") † Moments musicaux, Op. 16; Morceaux de fant, Op. 3; Morceaux de salon, Op. 10; Pno Trans; Polka WR; Trans & Arrs; Mendelssohn (-Bartholdy):Capriccio brillante, Op. 22 ARA ▲ 6663 (16.97)

V. Horowitz (pno)—Études-tableaux Pno [Op. 33/2 in C; Op. 33/5 in d; Op. 39/8 in d] *(rec Washington D.C. & New York, Dec 10, 1967 & Dec 15, 1968)* ("The Complete Masterworks Recordings, Vol. IX") † Moments musicaux, Op. 16; Preludes Pno; Son 2 Pno, Op. 36; Medtner:Fairy Tales, Op. 51; A. Scriabin:Etudes (12) Pno, Op. 8; Pno Music (misc colls) SNYC ▲ 53472 (16.97)

V. Horowitz (pno)—Moments musicaux, Op. 16 [No. 2 in e♭ (allegretto)]; Polka WR; Preludes Pno [Op. 32/5 in G] † Con 3 Pno, Op. 30; Son 2 Pno, Op. 36 RCAV (Gold Seal) ▲ 7754 [ADD] (11.97)

S. Rachmaninoff (pno)—Morceaux de fant, Op. 3 [Elégie in e♭] ("Rachmaninoff Plays Rachmaninoff") † Morceaux de fant, Op. 3; Morceaux de salon, Op. 10 PLON (Historic) ▲ 25964 [ADD] (11.97)

S. Rachmaninoff (pno)—Morceaux de salon, Op. 10 [Barcarolle; Humoresque in G]; Études-tableaux Pno [Op. 39/4 in b; Op. 39/6 in a] ("A Window in Time") † Morceaux de fant, Op. 3; Pno Trans; Polka WR; Prelude in c#, Op. 3/2; Preludes Pno; Songs (12), Op. 21; Trans & Arrs TEL ▲ 80489 [DDD] (16.97)

S. Rachmaninoff (pno), E. Ormandy (cnd), Philadelphia Orch—Con 1 Pno, Op. 1; Oriental Sketch Pno *(rec 1920-42)* † Moments musicaux, Op. 16; Morceaux de fant, Op. 3; Morceaux de salon, Op. 10 MTAL ▲ 48074 (6.97)

Piano Transcriptions

I. Hobson (pno)—Trans & Arrs [Mendelssohn:Scherzo [from A Midsummer Night's Dream]] *(rec Houston TX & Great Hall of the Kranne, United States of America, Sept 9-10, 1994 & Jan 25, 1995)* ("The Complete Solo Piano Transcriptions & Arrangements of Sergei Rachmaninoff") † Moments musicaux, Op. 16; Morceaux de fant, Op. 3; Morceaux de salon, Op. 10; Pno Music (misc colls); Polka WR; Trans & Arrs; Mendelssohn (-Bartholdy):Capriccio brillante, Op. 22 ARA ▲ 6663 (16.97)

S. Rachmaninoff (pno)—Trans & Arrs [Kreisler:Liebeslied; Schubert:Wohin?; Bizet:L'Arlésienne (suite 1); Mussorgsky:Hopak [from Sorochintsy Fair]] ("A Window in Time") † Morceaux de fant, Op. 3; Pno Music (misc colls); Polka WR; Prelude in c#, Op. 3/2; Preludes Pno; Songs (12), Op. 21; Trans & Arrs TEL ▲ 80489 [DDD] (16.97)

J. Weber (pno) *(Aleko (sels) [Men's Dance])*, B. Michel (tpt), J. Weber (pno) *(Polka italienne)* † Polka WR; Preludes Pno; Songs (12), Op. 21; Trans & Arrs INMP ▲ 1051 [DDD] (11.97)

Pieces (2) for Cello & Piano, Op. 2 (1892)

T. Gill (vc), F. Pavri (pno)—Oriental Dance † Son Vc; Vocalise; E. Grieg:Son Vc GILD ▲ 7127 [DDD] (16.97)

J. L. Webber (vc), Y. Seow (pno)—Oriental Dance † Son Vc; Debussy:Son Vc ASVQ ▲ 6072 [ADD] (10.97)

Pieces (2) in A for Piano 6-Hands (1890-91)

S. Prutsman (pno), F. Braley (pno), B. Ganz (pno)—Romance † Piano Music (works for 2 pianos & piano 4- & 6-hands); J. S. Bach:Cons for 3 Hpds (comp); W. A. Mozart:Con 7 Pnos, K.242 RENE ▲ 87065 [DDD] (16.97)

RACHMANINOFF, SERGEI (cont.)

Pieces (2) in A for Piano 6-Hands (1890-91) (cont.)

I. Thorson (pno), J. Thurber (pno) † Duets Pno 4-Hands, Op. 11; Polka italienne; Preludes Pno; Romance in G; Russian Rhap; Suite 1 for 2 Pnos, Op. 5; Suite 2 for 2 Pnos, Op. 17; Sym Dances, Op. 45 PLAL 2-▲ 46 (35.97)

Pieces (2) for Violin & Piano, Op. 6 (1893)

G. Varga (cnd), Stuttgart CO *(rec Stuttgart, Germany, 1994)* † Arensky:Vars on a Theme of Tchaikovsky; M. Glinka:Divert brillante; P. Tchaikovsky:Serenade Strs, Op. 48 DI ▲ 920323 [DDD] (5.97)

Polka italienne for Piano 4-Hands (?1906)

I. Thorson (pno), J. Thurber (pno) † Duets Pno 4-Hands, Op. 11; Pieces Pno 6-Hands; Preludes Pno; Romance in G; Russian Rhap; Suite 1 for 2 Pnos, Op. 5; Suite 2 for 2 Pnos, Op. 17; Sym Dances, Op. 45 PLAL 2-▲ 46 (35.97)

Polka "WR" in A♭ for Piano [Transcription of Behr:Lachtäuben, Op. 303] (ca 1911)

I. Hobson (pno) *(rec Houston TX & Great Hall of the Kranne, United States of America, Sept 9-10, 1994 & Jan 25, 1995)* ("The Complete Solo Piano Transcriptions & Arrangements of Sergei Rachmaninoff") † Moments musicaux, Op. 16; Morceaux de fant, Op. 3; Morceaux de salon, Op. 10; Pno Music (misc colls); Pno Trans; Trans & Arrs; Mendelssohn (-Bartholdy):Capriccio brillante, Op. 22 ARA ▲ 6663 (16.97)

S. Rachmaninoff (pno) ("A Window in Time") † Morceaux de fant, Op. 3; Pno Music (misc colls); Pno Trans; Prelude in c#, Op. 3/2; Preludes Pno; Songs (12), Op. 21; Trans & Arrs TEL ▲ 80489 [DDD] (16.97)

J. Weber (pno) † Pno Trans; Preludes Pno; Songs (12), Op. 21; Trans & Arrs INMP ▲ 1051 [DDD] (11.97)

Prelude in c# for Piano [from *Morceau de fantasie*], Op. 3/2 (1897; arr 2 Pianos, 1938)

V. Ashkenazy (pno) ("Favourite Rachmaninoff") † Études-tableaux Pno; Con 2 Pno, Op. 18; Con 3 Pno, Op. 30; Preludes Pno; Rhap on a Theme of Paganini, Op. 43 PLON 2-▲ 36386 [ADD] (17.97)

V. Ashkenazy (pno) † Preludes Pno; Son 2 Pno, Op. 36 PLON (Double Decca) 2-▲ 43841 (17.97)

V. Ashkenazy (pno) † Études-tableaux Pno; Cons Pno (comp); Preludes Pno; Rhap on a Theme of Paganini, Op. 43; Son 2 Pno, Op. 36; Suite 1 for 2 Pnos, Op. 5; Suite 2 for 2 Pnos, Op. 17 PPHI (Budget Box) 6-▲ 455234 (40.97)

I. Biret (pno) ("Best of Rachmaninov") † Con 3 Pno, Op. 30; Music of Rachmaninoff; Preludes Pno; Rhap on a Theme of Paganini, Op. 43; Sym 2; Vocalise NXIN ▲ 8556682 [DDD] (5.97)

G. Casalino (pno) *(rec May 1992)* † Chopin:Nocturnes (21) Pno; E. Grieg:Son Pno, Op. 7; F. Schubert:Impromptus (4); Impromptus (4) Pno STRV ▲ 101 [DDD] (16.97)

S. Comissiona (cnd), Vancouver SO [orchd Lucien Cailliet] *(rec 1993-94)* † Capriccio bohémien, Op. 12; Preludes Pno; Sym Dances, Op. 45 CBC ▲ 5143 [DDD] (16.97)

M. Deyanova (pno) † Preludes Pno NIMB ▲ 5094 [DDD] (16.97)

M. Deyanova (pno) ("Whad' Ya Know About Rachmaninoff") † Con 2 Pno, Op. 18; Con 3 Pno, Op. 30; Liturgy of St. John Chrysostom, Op. 31; Preludes Pno; Rhap on a Theme of Paganini, Op. 43; Son 2 Pno, Op. 36; Sym 2; Vocalise NIMB ▲ 4007 [DDD] (11.97)

D. Helfgott (pno) ("David Helfgott Plays Rachmaninoff") † Con 3 Pno, Op. 30; Preludes Pno; Son 2 Pno, Op. 36 RCAV (Red Seal) ▲ 40378 [DDD] (16.97) ▮ 40378 [DDD] (9.98)

B. Janis (pno) † Con 2 Pno, Op. 18; Con 3 Pno, Op. 30; Preludes Pno MRCR ▲ 32759 [ADD] (11.97)

W. Kapell (pno) † Beethoven:Con 2 Pno, Op. 19; J. Brahms:Fants Pno, Op. 116; A. Khachaturian:Con Pno; D. Shostakovich:Preludes Pno, Op. 34 PHS ▲ 9277 (17.97)

C. Keene (pno) † Preludes Pno PROT ▲ 1101 (18.97)

J. Lill (pno) † Moments musicaux, Op. 16; Son 1 Pno, Op. 28 NIMB ▲ 5575 [DDD] (16.97)

S. Lindgren (pno) † Chopin:Son Pno in b, Op. 58; Liszt:Mephisto Waltz 1 Pno, S.514; R. Schumann:Arabeske Pno, Op. 18; A. Scriabin:Fant Pno, Op. 28 OPU ▲ 9202

C. F. Miller (pno) *(rec Portsmouth, NH, May 13 & 26, 1995)* † Preludes Pno; J. Haydn:Trio Strs; Paulus:Miniatures; M. Ravel:Alborada del gracioso; Jeux d'eau; D. Scarlatti:Sons Kbd; R. Schumann:Fant Pno, Op. 17; H. Villa-Lobos:Trio Strs TIT ▲ 231 [DDD]

B. Moiseiwitsch (pno) *(rec Aug 2, 1940)* ("The Complete Rachmaniov Recordings, 1937-43") † Con 2 Pno, Op. 18; Moments musicaux, Op. 16; Preludes Pno; Rhap on a Theme of Paganini, Op. 43; A. Scarlatti:Preludes (23) Pno, Opp. 23 & 32 APR ▲ 5505 [ADD] (19.97)

J. Ogdon (pno) † Études-tableaux Pno; Preludes Pno; Balakirev:Islamey; Liszt:Pno Music (misc); Trans, Arrs & Paraphrases PPHI (Great Pianists of the 20th Century, Vol. 73) ▲ 456916 (22.97)

R. Orozco (pno) ("Shine: The Complete Classics") † Con 3 Pno, Op. 30; Beethoven:Sym 9; Chopin:Polonaise 6 Pno, Op. 53; Preludes (24) Pno, Op. 28; Liszt:Études d'exécution transcendante (6), S.140; Études de concert (3), S.144; Hungarian Rhaps, S.244; Rimsky-Korsakov:Tale of Tsar Saltan (orch sels); R. Schumann:Kinderszenen Pno, Op. 15; Vivaldi:Gloria; Nulla in mundo pax, RV.630 PPHI 2-▲ 456403 (17.97)

S. Rachmaninoff (pno) ("A Window in Time") † Morceaux de fant, Op. 3; Pno Music (misc colls); Pno Trans; Polka WR; Preludes Pno; Songs (12), Op. 21; Trans & Arrs TEL ▲ 80489 [DDD] (16.97)

R. Slenczynska (pno) *(rec St. Louis, MO, Apr 8, 1984)* ("Slenczynska in Concert") † Preludes Pno; J. Brahms:Rhaps (2) Pno, Op. 79; Chopin:Son Pno in b, Op. 58; A. Copland:Midsummer Nocturne; J. Haydn:Sonatas for Piano IVOR ▲ 70902 [DDD] (16.97)

J. Thibaudet (pno) † Con 4 Pno, Op. 40; Son 2 Pno, Op. 36; Vars on a Theme by Corelli, Op. 42 PLON ▲ 458930 (16.97)

Preludes (23) for Piano, Op. 23 (1903) & Op. 32 (1910)

N. Angelich (pno) † Études-tableaux Pno HAM (Les Nouveaux Interprètes) ▲ 911547 (12.97)

A. Anievas (pno) † Liturgy of St. John Chrysostom, Op. 31; Chopin:Son Pno in b, Op. 58; Liszt:Son Pno, S.178 EMIC (Doublefforte) 2-▲ 68664 (16.97)

V. Ashkenazy (pno)—Op. 23/2 in B♭; Op. 23/5 in g; Op. 32/10 in b; Op. 32/13 in D♭ ("Favourite Rachmaninoff") † Études-tableaux Pno; Con 2 Pno, Op. 18; Con 3 Pno, Op. 30; Prelude in c#, Op. 3/2; Rhap on a Theme of Paganini, Op. 43 PLON 2-▲ 36386 [ADD] (17.97)

V. Ashkenazy (pno) † Prelude in c#, Op. 3/2; Son 2 Pno, Op. 36 PLON (Double Decca) 2-▲ 43841 (17.97)

V. Ashkenazy (pno) † Études-tableaux Pno; Cons Pno (comp); Prelude in c#, Op. 3/2; Rhap on a Theme of Paganini, Op. 43; Son 2 Pno, Op. 36; Suite 1 for 2 Pnos, Op. 5; Suite 2 for 2 Pnos, Op. 17 PPHI (Budget Box) 6-▲ 455234 (40.97)

I. Biret (pno)—Op. 23/5 in g ("Best of Rachmaninov") † Con 3 Pno, Op. 30; Music of Rachmaninoff; Prelude in c#, Op. 3/2; Rhap on a Theme of Paganini, Op. 43; Sym 2; Vocalise NXIN ▲ 8556682 [DDD] (5.97)

I. Biret (pno)—Op. 32 † Trans & Arrs NXIN ▲ 550466 [DDD] (5.97)

I. Biret (pno)—Op. 23 *(rec 1989-90)* † Morceaux de fant, Op. 3 NXIN ▲ 550348 [DDD] (5.97)

V. Bogolubov (pno)—Op. 32/5 in G; Op. 32/12 in g# ("Unfamiliar Masterpieces") † Moments musicaux, Op. 16; Vars on a Theme by Chopin, Op. 22 SNE ▲ 620 (16.97)

A. D. Bonaventura (pno)—Op. 32 TIT ▲ 195

J. Browning (pno)—Op. 23/4 in D; Op. 23/5 in g; Op. 23/6 in E♭; Op. 32/5 in G; Op. 32/12 in g#; Op. 32/13 in D♭ † Études-tableaux Pno; Moments musicaux, Op. 16; Pno Music (misc colls); Son 2 Pno, Op. 36 DLS ▲ 3044 [DDD] (14.97)

E. Ciccarelli (pno)—Op. 23/5 in g; Op. 32/12 in g# † Mussorgsky:Pictures at an Exhibition; S. Prokofiev:Son 7 Pno, Op. 83 AG ▲ 6 (18.97)

V. Cliburn (pno)—Op. 23/4 in D † Études-tableaux Pno; Son 2 Pno, Op. 36; S. Prokofiev:Son 6 Pno, Op. 82 RCAV (Gold Seal) ▲ 7941 [ADD] (11.97)

S. Comissiona (cnd), Vancouver SO [orchd Lucien Cailliet] *(rec 1993-94)* † Capriccio bohémien, Op. 12; Prelude in c#, Op. 3/2; Sym Dances, Op. 45 CBC ▲ 5143 [DDD] (16.97)

J. Coop (pno)—Preludes Pno [Op. 23/7 in c] *(rec Toronto, Canada)* ("The Romantic Piano") † Études-tableaux Pno, Opp. 33 & 39; J. Brahms:Pieces (6) Pno, Op. 118; Waltzes (16) Pno, Op. 39; Chopin:Etudes (24) Pno, Opp. 10 & 25; Mazurkas Pno; Nocturnes Pno; Debussy:Isle joyeuse; Suite bergamasque; Liszt:Etudes de concert (3), S.144; Liebesträume, S.541; Mendelssohn (-Bartholdy):Pno Music (misc); R. Schumann:Kinderszenen Pno, Op. 15 MUVI ▲ 1015 [DDD] (16.97)

M. Deyanova (pno)—Op. 23/5 in g ("Whad' Ya Know About Rachmaninoff") † Con 2 Pno, Op. 18; Con 3 Pno, Op. 30; Liturgy of St. John Chrysostom, Op. 31; Prelude in c#, Op. 3/2; Rhap on a Theme of Paganini, Op. 43; Son 2 Pno, Op. 36; Sym 2; Vocalise NIMB ▲ 4007 [DDD] (11.97)

M. Deyanova (pno) † Prelude in c#, Op. 3/2 NIMB ▲ 5094 [DDD] (16.97)

P. Entremont (pno) [3 preludes] † Con 2 Pno, Op. 18; Rhap on a Theme of Paganini, Op. 43 SNYC ▲ 46271 [AAD] (7.97) ▮ 46271 [AAD] (3.98)

A. Gavrilov (pno)—Op. 23/1 in f#; Op. 23/3 in d; Op. 23/5 in g; Op. 23/6 in E♭; Op. 32/12 in g# † Études-tableaux Pno; Morceaux de fant, Op. 3; Pno Music (misc colls); Balakirev:Islamey; P. Tchaikovsky:Morceaux (6) Pno, Op. 19 RYLC ▲ 6471

N. Gavrilova (pno)—Op. 23/6 in E♭; Op. 23/7 in c; Op. 32/12 in g# *(rec 1976-90)* ("Russian Piano School: Natalia Gavrilova") † Babadjanyan:Pno Music; D. Shostakovich:Pno Music; Strauss (II):Pno Trans; Tso Chenhuan:Pno Music RD (Talents of Russia) ▲ 16238 [ADD] (16.97)

G. Graffman (pno)—Op. 23/5 in g; Op. 32/12 in g#; Op. 32/8 in a † P. Tchaikovsky:Con 1 Pno, Op. 23 SNYC ▲ 37263 [ADD] (9.97)

D. Helfgott (pno)—Op. 23/5 in g; Op. 32/5 in G; Op. 32/12 in g# ("David Helfgott Plays Rachmaninoff") † Con 3 Pno, Op. 30; Prelude in c#, Op. 3/2; Son 2 Pno, Op. 36 RCAV (Red Seal) ▲ 40378 [DDD] (16.97) ▮ 40378 [DDD] (9.98)

V. Horowitz (pno)—Op. 23/5 in g † J. S. Bach:Toccata, Adagio & Fugue Org, BWV 564; V. Horowitz:Moment exotique; Liszt:Trans, Arrs & Paraphrases INTC ▲ 860864 (13.97)

RACHMANINOFF, SERGEI (cont.)

Preludes (23) for Piano, Op. 23 (1903) & Op. 32 (1910) (cont.)

V. Horowitz (pno)—Op. 23/5 in g † Chopin:Ballade 4 Pno, Op. 52; Waltzes Pno; Liszt:Ballade 2, S.171; D. Scarlatti:Sons Kbd HP ▲ 63314 (11.97)

V. Horowitz (pno)—Op. 32/12 in g# *(rec Washington D.C. & New York, United States of America, Dec 10, 1967 & Dec 15, 1968)* ("The Complete Masterworks Recordings, Vol. IX") † Moments musicaux, Op. 16; Pno Music (misc colls); Son 2 Pno, Op. 36; Medtner:Fairy Tales, Op. 51; A. Scriabin:Etudes (12) Pno, Op. 8; Pno Music (misc colls) SNYC ▲ 53472 (16.97)

B. Janis (pno)—Op. 23/6 in E♭ † Con 2 Pno, Op. 18; Con 3 Pno, Op. 30; Prelude in c#, Op. 3/2 MRCR ▲ 32759 [ADD] (11.97)

K. Jordan (pno) [3 preludes] *(rec Waco, TX, Jan 16-20, 1995)* ("Slavic Masterpieces for Piano") † R. Shchedrin:Pno Music (misc colls); Smetana:Pno Music (misc colls); Szymanowski:Metopes, Op. 29; P. Tchaikovsky:Dumka; P. Vladigerov:Pno Music (misc colls) ALBA ▲ 203 [DDD] (16.97)

C. Keene (pno) † Prelude in c#, Op. 3/2 PROT ▲ 1101 (18.97)

Z. Kocsis (pno)—Op. 32/9 in A; Op. 32/3 in E *(rec 1973-86)* ("Zoltán Kocsis in Concert, 1973-86") † Études-tableaux Pno; Chopin:Ballade 1 Pno, Op. 23; Mazurkas Pno; Kodály:Pieces (7) Pno, Op. 11; Liszt:Pno Music (misc); F. Schubert:Impromptus (4); R. Wagner:Parsifal (sels) HUN ▲ 31679 [AAD] (16.97)

A. Laplante (pno)—Op. 23/1 in f# *(rec Montreal, Canada, June 1992)* † Con 3 Pno, Op. 30; P. Tchaikovsky:Saisons FL ▲ 23107 [DDD] (16.97)

K. Lifschitz (pno)—Op. 32/1 in C; Op. 32/13 in D♭; Op. 32/2; Op. 32/5 in G; Op. 32/7 in F; Op. 32/6 *(rec Wigmore Hall London, England)* ("London Debut Recital Live") † J. Brahms:Vars on a Hungarian Song, Op. 21/2; Vars on an Original Theme, Op. 21/1; F. Couperin:Pièces de clavecin (sels) DNN ▲ 78773 (16.97)

K. Lifschitz (pno) *(rec Nov 13-15, 1995)* ("Constantin Lifschitz Plays Scriabin & Rachmaninoff") † A. Scriabin:Pieces (2) Pno, Op. 59; Pieces (3) Pno, Op. 52; Son 5 Pno, Op. 53 DNN ▲ 18026 (16.97)

J. Lill (pno) *(rec Dec 19-20, 1996)* NIMB ▲ 5555 [DDD] (16.97)

F. Lushtak (pno)—Op. 23/6 in E♭; Op. 32/5 in G; Op. 32/12 in g#; Op. 32/8 in a *(rec Recital Hall Univ of New Orleans, LA, Apr-May 1995)* † Morceaux de fant, Op. 3; A. Scriabin:Son 2 Pno, Op. 19; Son 3 Pno, Op. 23 CENT ▲ 2287 [DDD] (16.97)

C. F. Miller (pno) *(rec Portsmouth, NH, May 13 & 26, 1995)* † Prelude in c#, Op. 3/2; J. Haydn:Trio Strs; Paulus:Miniatures; M. Ravel:Alborada del gracioso; Jeux d'eau; D. Scarlatti:Sons Kbd; R. Schumann:Fant Pno, Op. 17; H. Villa-Lobos:Trio Strs TIT ▲ 231 [DDD]

B. Moiseiwitsch (pno)—Op. 23/5 in g; Op. 32/10 in b; Op. 32/12 in g# *(rec Aug 2 & Oct 3, 1940 & Oct 19, 1943)* ("The Complete Rachmaniov Recordings, 1937-43") † Con 2 Pno, Op. 18; Moments musicaux, Op. 16; Prelude in c#, Op. 3/2; Rhap on a Theme of Paganini, Op. 43; A. Scarlatti:Preludes (23) Pno, Opp. 23 & 32 APR ▲ 5505 [ADD] (19.97)

B. Moiseiwitsch (pno)—Op. 32/5 in G *(rec 1956)* † Con 2 Pno, Op. 18; Moments musicaux, Op. 16; Chopin:Ballade 3 Pno, Op. 47; Ballade 4 Pno, Op. 52; Barcarolle Pno, Op. 60; Fant-Impromptu, Op. 66; Nocturnes Pno; Scherzos Pno; Kabalevsky:Son 3 Pno, Op. 46; Liszt:Etudes de concert (3), S.144; Medtner:Son Pno in g, Op. 22; Mendelssohn (-Bartholdy):Midsummer Night's Dream (sels); S. Prokofiev:Pieces (4) Pno, Op. 4; Toccata Pno, Op. 11 PPHI (Great Pianists of the 20th Century) 2-▲ 456907 (22.97)

G. Montero (pno)—Op. 23/4 in D; Op. 32/5 in G *(rec live Montreal Chopin Competition, Canada, 1995)* ("In Concert at Montreal") † Son 2 Pno, Op. 36; Chopin:Mazurkas Pno; Nocturnes Pno; Polonaises-fant, Op. 61; Liszt:Paraphrase on Verdi PALE ▲ 501 (17.97)

A. Morrison (org) [trans Federlein for org] *(rec Morrow, GA, Nov 19, 1995)* ("Festive Duo") † Con 2 Pno, Op. 18; M. Dupré:Prélude, fugue et var, Op. 18; Sinf Pno, Op. 42; Grasse:Festival Ov, Op. 5; H. Stover:Neumark Vars ACAD ▲ 20050 (16.97)

F. Moyer (pno)—Op. 23 † Études-tableaux Pno; J. S. Bach:Sons & Partitas Vn JUP ▲ 106 (13.97)

J. Ogdon (pno)—Op. 23/5 in g; Op. 32/5 in G; Op. 32/12 in g# † Études-tableaux Pno; Prelude in c#, Op. 3/2; Balakirev:Islamey; Liszt:Pno Music (misc); Trans, Arrs & Paraphrases PPHI (Great Pianists of the 20th Century, Vol. 73) ▲ 456916 (22.97)

D. Paperno (pno)—Op. 23/7 in c; Op. 23/10 in G♭; Op. 32/5 in G; Op. 32/10 in b; Op. 32/11 in B; Op. 32/12 in g# † Liadov:Vars on a Polish Folk Theme, Op. 51; Medtner:Forgotten Melodies 1, Op. 38; A. Scriabin:Son 2 Pno, Op. 19; P. Tchaikovsky:Pno Music CED ▲ 1 [DDD] (16.97)

M. Petkova (pno)—Op. 32/5 in G *(rec Nov 1996)* † Études-tableaux Pno DORO ▲ 3026 [DDD] (16.97)

A. Pratt (pno)—Op. 32 [2 preludes] *(rec live, South Africa, Dec 1995)* ("Live from South Africa") † Moments musicaux, Op. 16; J. S. Bach:Chromatic Fant & Fugue, BWV 903; J. Brahms:Intermezzos (3) Pno, Op. 117; Busoni:Bach Transcriptions Pno; C. Franck:Prélude, fugue et var, Op. 18 EMIC ▲ 55293 (16.97)

S. Rachmaninoff (pno)—Op. 23/5 in g ("A Window in Time") † Morceaux de fant, Op. 3; Pno Music (misc colls); Pno Trans; Polka WR; Prelude in c#, Op. 3/2; Songs (12), Op. 21; Trans & Arrs TEL ▲ 80489 [DDD] (16.97)

S. Richter (pno)—Op. 23/2 in B♭; Op. 23/4 in D; Op. 23/5 in g; Op. 23/7 in c; Op. 32/1 in C; Op. 32/2 *(rec 1952-59)* ("Sviatoslav Richter III") † Con 2 Pno, Op. 18; Trans & Arrs; A. Scriabin:Etudes (12) Pno, Op. 8; Etudes (3) Pno, Op. 65; Etudes (8) Pno, Op. 42; Pieces (3) Pno, Op. 2 PPHI (Great Pianists of the 20th Century) 2-▲ 456952 (22.97)

S. Richter (pno)—Op. 32/12 in g# *(rec 1977)* ("Richter in Salzburg") † Beethoven:Andante Pno, WoO 57; Chopin:Barcarolle Pno, Op. 60; Scherzos Pno; Waltzes Pno; Debussy:Estampes; Preludes Pno; Suite bergamasque MUA ▲ 1019 [ADD] (16.97)

S. Richter (pno) [13 sels from opp. 23 & 32] ("The Richter Collection, Vol. 2") † Études-tableaux Pno; Beethoven:Son 27 Pno, Op. 90; Son 3 Pno, Op. 2/3; Son 4 Pno, Op. 7; Vars & Fugue Pno, Op. 35; Vars Pno on Original Theme, Op. 34; Vars Pno on Original Theme, Op. 76; J. Brahms:Son 1 Vn, Op. 78; Chopin:Scherzos Pno; J. Haydn:Son 39 Kbd, H.XVI/24; R. Schumann:Bunte Blätter, Op. 99; Symphonic Etudes, Op. 13; D. Shostakovich:Son Vn OLY 5-▲ 5013 [DDD] (64.97)

S. Richter (pno)—Op. 23 [3 preludes] ("Classic Richter") † Beethoven:Son 27 Pno, Op. 90; Chopin:Scherzos Pno; F. Schubert:Son Pno, D.625; R. Schumann:Novelettes, Op. 21; P. Tchaikovsky:Morceaux (6) Pno, Op. 51; Saisons OLY ▲ 580 [ADD] (16.97)

R. Rudnytsky (pno)—Op. 32/10 in b; Op. 32/5 in G ("Pianistic Portraits") † Liszt:Légendes, S.175; Rollin:Night Thoughts II; A. Rudnytsky:Vars Pno, Op. 38; Talma:Son 1 Pno ARUN ▲ 3059 (16.97)

R. Slenczynska (pno)—Op. 23/1 in f#; Op. 23/4 in D; Op. 23/6 in E♭; Op. 32/1 in C; Op. 32/10 in b; Op. 32/12 in g#; Op. 32/13 in D♭ *(rec St. Louis, MO, Apr 8, 1984)* ("Slenczynska in Concert") † Prelude in c#, Op. 3/2; J. Brahms:Rhaps (2) Pno, Op. 79; Chopin:Son Pno in b, Op. 58; A. Copland:Midsummer Nocturne; J. Haydn:Sonatas for Piano IVOR ▲ 70902 [DDD] (16.97)

C. Smith (pno)—Op. 23/5 in g; Op. 32/5 in G *(rec 1944-46)* ("The Complete Rachmaninoff & Dohnányi Recordings") † Con 3 Pno, Op. 30; E. von Dohnányi:Trans Pno; Vars on a Nursery Song, Op. 25 APR (Signature) ▲ 5507 [ADD] (18.97)

G. Sokolov (pno)—Op. 23/4 in D † S. Prokofiev:Son 9 Pno, Op. 103; A. Scriabin:Son 3 Pno, Op. 23; Son 9 Pno, Op. 68 OPUS ▲ 409104 (18.97)

I. Thorson (pno), J. Thurber (pno)—Op. 32/1 in C † Duets Pno 4-Hands, Op. 11; Pieces Pno 6-Hands; Polka italienne; Romance in G; Russian Rhap; Suite 1 for 2 Pnos, Op. 5; Suite 2 for 2 Pnos, Op. 17; Sym Dances, Op. 45 PLAL 2-▲ 46 (35.97)

O. Volkov (pno)—Op. 23/2 in B♭; Op. 23/5 in g ("Celebrate Rachmaninoff") † Con 1 Pno, Op. 1; Con 2 Pno, Op. 18; Rhap on a Theme of Paganini, Op. 43; Son 2 Pno, Op. 36; Songs (14), Op. 34 BRIO 2-▲ 116 [DDD] (18.97)

J. Weber (pno)—Op. 32/12 in g# † Pno Trans; Polka WR; Songs (12), Op. 21; Trans & Arrs INMP ▲ 1051 [DDD] (11.97)

E. Wild (pno) † Son 2 Pno, Op. 36 CHSK ▲ 114 (16.97)

Prince Rostislav (symphonic poem) for Orchestra [after Tolstoy] (1891)

B. Glemser (pno), J. Maksymiuk (cnd), Irish National SO *(rec National Concert Hall Dublin, Dec 17-18, 1992)* † Con 3 Pno, Op. 30 NXIN ▲ 550666 [DDD] (5.97)

L. Slatkin (cnd), St. Louis SO *(rec 1980)* † Bells; Capriccio bohémien, Op. 12; Isle of the Dead, Op. 29; Rock; Russian Songs, Op. 41; Scherzo; Spring; Sym in d; Sym Dances, Op. 45; Vocalise VB3 3-▲ 3002 [ADD] (14.97)

E. Svetlanov (cnd), USSR SO *(rec 1966-90)* ("Symphonic Poems from Russia") † Capriccio bohémien, Op. 12; Isle of the Dead, Op. 29; Scherzo; Balakirev:Ov on Czech Themes; Rus; Tamara; Glazunov:Ballade, Op. 78; Stenka Razin, Op. 13; Liapunov:Zhelyazova Volya, Op. 37 MELD (2fer) 2-▲ 34166 [ADD] (13.97)

Quartet for Strings [in 2 movts only] (1889)

Budapest String Quartet *(rec Coolidge Auditorium Library of Congress, Apr 4, 1952)* † Trio élégiaque 2, Op. 9 BRID ▲ 9063 (17.97)

Rhapsody on a Theme of Paganini for Piano & Orchestra, Op. 43 (1934)

A. Alieva (pno), W. Proost (cnd), San Remo SO ("Classical Music around the World, Vol. 1: Russia") † S. Prokofiev:Con 2 Pno, Op. 16; Ov on Hebrew Themes, Op. 34 GALL ▲ 849 [DAD] (18.97)

A. Anievas (pno), R. Frühbeck de Burgos (cnd), New Philharmonia Orch † Cons Pno (comp) EMIC (Doublefforte) 2-▲ 68619 (16.97)

V. Ashkenazy (pno), A. Previn (cnd), London SO † Con 2 Pno, Op. 18 PLON ▲ 17702 [ADD] (9.97)

V. Ashkenazy (pno), A. Previn (cnd), London SO ("Favourite Rachmaninoff") † Études-tableaux Pno; Con 2 Pno, Op. 18; Con 3 Pno, Op. 30; Prelude in c#, Op. 3/2; Preludes Pno PLON 2-▲ 36386 [ADD] (17.97)

RACHMANINOFF, SERGEI (cont.)

Rhapsody on a Theme of Paganini for Piano & Orchestra, Op. 43 (1934) (cont.)

V. Ashkenazy (pno), A. Previn (cnd), London SO † Études-tableaux Pno; Cons Pno (comp); Prelude in c#, Op. 3/2; Preludes Pno; Son 2 Pno, Op. 36; Suite 1 for 2 Pnos, Op. 5; Suite 2 for 2 Pnos, Op. 17 PPHI (Budget Box) 6-▲ 455234 (40.97)

V. Cliburn (pno), K. Kondrashin (cnd), Moscow PO *(rec 1972)* † J. Brahms:Con 2 Pno, Op. 83 RCAV (Red Seal) ▲ 62695 [ADD] (16.97) ▮ 62695 [ADD] (9.98)

V. Cliburn (pno), E. Ormandy (cnd), Philadelphia Orch † Chopin:Con 1 Pno, Op. 11 RCAV (Gold Seal) ▲ 7945 [ADD] (11.97)

S. Costa (pno), C. Seaman (cnd), Royal PO † Con 3 Pno, Op. 30 INMP (IMP Classics) ▲ 6701142 [DDD] (9.97)

P. Entremont (pno), E. Ormandy (cnd), Philadelphia Orch † Con 2 Pno, Op. 18; Preludes Pno SNYC ▲ 46271 [AAD] (7.97) ▮ 46271 [AAD] (3.98)

V. Eresko (pno), V. Ponkin (cnd), Leningrad PO *(rec Leningrad, 1983)* † Cons Pno (comp) MELD 2-▲ 40068 [ADD] (13.97)

V. Feltsman (pno), Z. Mehta (cnd), Israel PO † Con 3 Pno, Op. 30 SNYC ▲ 44761 [DDD] (16.97)

L. Fleisher (pno), G. Szell (cnd), Cleveland Orch *(rec 1956)* † C. Franck:Symphonic Vars, M.46; M. Ravel:Alborada del gracioso SNYC ▲ 37812 [ADD] (9.97)

D. Golub (pno), D. Golub (pno), W. Morris (cnd), London SO † Con 2 Pno, Op. 18 INMP (LSO Classic Masterpieces) ▲ 903 [DDD] (9.97)

G. Graffman (pno), L. Bernstein (cnd), New York PO † Con 2 Pno, Op. 18 SNYC ▲ 36722 (9.97) ▮ 36722 (3.98)

G. Graffman (pno), L. Bernstein (cnd), New York PO *(rec 1964)* † Liszt:Con 1 Pno, S.124; M. Ravel:Con Pno SNYC (Bernstein: The Royal Edition) ▲ 47571 [ADD] (10.97)

G. Graffman (pno), L. Bernstein (cnd), New York PO ("Rachmaninoff Goes to the Movies") † Con 2 Pno, Op. 18; Con 3 Pno, Op. 30 SNYC ▲ 63032 (9.97) ▮ 63032 (5.98)

H. Gutiérrez (pno), D. Zinman (cnd), Baltimore SO † P. Tchaikovsky:Con 1 Pno, Op. 23 TEL ▲ 80193 [DDD] (16.97)

D. Han (pno), P. Kogan (cnd), Moscow State SO † Con 2 Pno, Op. 18 VRDI (Masters) ▲ 6809 (13.97)

J. Jandó (pno), G. Lehel (cnd) ("Best of Rachmaninov") † Con 3 Pno, Op. 30; Music of Rachmaninoff; Prelude in c#, Op. 3/2; Preludes Pno; Sym 2; Vocalise NXIN ▲ 8556682 [DDD] (5.97)

J. Jandó (pno), G. Lehel (cnd), Budapest SO *(rec Italian Institute Budapest, Hungary, 1988)* ("Famous Piano Concertos") † Con 2 Pno, Op. 18; Beethoven:Con 2 Pno, Op. 19; Con 5 Pno, Op. 73; Chopin:Con 1 Pno, Op. 11; Con 2 Pno, Op. 21; P. Tchaikovsky:Con 1 Pno, Op. 23; Eugene Onegin (sels); Tempest, Op. 18 NXIN 4-▲ 504011 [DDD] (19.97)

J. Jandó (pno), G. Lehel (cnd), Budapest SO † Con 2 Pno, Op. 18 NXIN ▲ 550117 [DDD] (5.97)

W. Kapell (pno) *(rec 1940-53)* † Beethoven:Con 2 Pno, Op. 19; Chopin:Polonaises Pno; Preludes (24) Pno, Op. 28; F. Schubert:Songs (misc) PHS ▲ 9194 (17.97)

J. Katchen (pno), G. Solti (cnd), London SO † Con 2 Pno, Op. 18; E. von Dohnányi:Vars on a Nursery Song, Op. 25 PLON (The Classic Sound) ▲ 448604 (11.97)

H. Kim (pno), J. Rudel (cnd), Philharmonia Orch † Con 4 Pno, Op. 40 HEL ▲ 1035 (10.97)

J. Lill (pno), T. Otaka (cnd), BBC National Orch Wales † Con 4 Pno, Op. 40; Liturgy of St. John Chrysostom, Op. 31; Vars on a Theme by Corelli, Op. 42 NIMB 2-▲ 5478 (16.97)

J. Lill (pno), T. Otaka (cnd), BBC Welsh National Orch † Études-tableaux Pno; Con 1 Pno, Op. 1; Con 2 Pno, Op. 18; Con 3 Pno, Op. 30; Con 4 Pno, Op. 40; Music of Rachmaninoff; Sym 1; Sym 2; Sym 3; Vars on a Theme by Corelli, Op. 42; Vocalise NIMB 6-▲ 1761 [DDD] (29.97)

J. Lill (pno), T. Otaka (cnd), BBC Welsh SO—Vars 17 & 18 ("Whad' Ya Know About Rachmaninoff") † Con 2 Pno, Op. 18; Con 3 Pno, Op. 30; Liturgy of St. John Chrysostom, Op. 31; Prelude in c#, Op. 3/2; Preludes Pno; Son 2 Pno, Op. 36; Sym 2; Vocalise NIMB ▲ 4007 [DDD] (11.97)

B. Moiseiwitsch (pno), B. Cameron (cnd), London PO *(rec Dec 5, 1938)* ("The Complete Rachmaniov Recordings, 1937-43") † Con 2 Pno, Op. 18; Moments musicaux, Op. 16; Prelude in c#, Op. 3/2; Preludes Pno; A. Scarlatti:Preludes (23) Pno, Opp. 23 & 32 APR ▲ 5505 [ADD] (19.97)

R. Orozco (pno), E. De Waart (cnd), Royal PO † Con 2 Pno, Op. 18; Sym 2; Vocalise PPHI 2-▲ 38383 (17.97)

L. Pennario (pno), A. Fiedler (cnd), Boston Pops Orch ("Rachmaninoff in Hollywood") † All-Night Vigil, Op. 37; Con 2 Pno, Op. 18; Con 3 Pno, Op. 30; Sym Dances, Op. 45 RCAV (Greatest Hits) ▲ 68874 (11.97)

J. Pierce (pno), A. Nanut (cnd), Slovenian Radio-TV Orch *(rec Apr 10-11, 1991)* † Casella:Partita, Op. 42; O. Respighi:Toccata Pno PHOE ▲ 124 [DDD] (15.97)

M. Pletnev (pno), C. Abbado (cnd), Berlin PO *(rec live Berlin Philharmonie, Dec 31, 1997)* ("The Berlin Gala: A Salute to Carmen") † Bizet:Carmen (sels); J. Brahms:Hungarian Dances Orch; M. Ravel:Rapsodie espagnole; Sarasate:Fant on Carmen, Op. 25 DEUT ▲ 457583 [DDD] (16.97)

J. L. Prats (pno), E. Bátiz (cnd), Mexico City PO † Con 2 Pno, Op. 18 ASVQ ▲ 6128 [DDD] (11.97)

I. Prunyi (pno), H. Williams (cnd), Pécs SO † Isle of the Dead, Op. 29; Sym Dances, Op. 45 HUN ▲ 31551 [DDD] (16.97)

S. Rachmaninoff (pno), L. Stokowski (cnd), Philadelphia Orch † Con 2 Pno, Op. 18; Vocalise INMP ▲ 104 [ADD] (14.97)

S. Rachmaninoff (pno), L. Stokowski (cnd), Philadelphia Orch † Isle of the Dead, Op. 29; Sym 3 RCAV (Gold Seal) 10-▲ 61265 (102.97)

S. Rachmaninoff (pno), L. Stokowski (cnd), Philadelphia Orch ("Rachmaninoff Plays Rachmaninoff") † Cons Pno (comp) RCAV (Gold Seal) 2-▲ 61658 (21.97)

S. Rachmaninoff (pno), L. Stokowski (cnd), Philadelphia Orch † Con 2 Pno, Op. 18 MTAL ▲ 48075 (6.97)

A. Rubinstein (pno), F. Reiner (cnd), Chicago SO † Con 2 Pno, Op. 18 RCAV (Red Seal) ▲ 4934 (16.97)

A. Rubinstein (pno), F. Reiner (cnd), Chicago SO *(rec Chicago Orch Hall, IL, Jan 16, 1956)* † Chopin:Andante Spianato & Grand Polonaise, Op. 22; M. de Falla:Noches en los jardines de España RCAV (Living Stereo) ▲ 68886 [ADD] (11.97)

A. Rubinstein (pno), W. Susskind (cnd), Philharmonia Orch *(rec 1946-47)* ("Rubinstein, Vol. 4") † Con 2 Pno, Op. 18 HPC1 ▲ 132 (17.97)

K. Serovatov (pno), A. Anichanov (cnd), St. Petersburg State SO † Con 3 Pno, Op. 30 APC ▲ 101038

H. Shelley (pno), B. Thomson (cnd), Royal Scottish National Orch † Cons Pno (comp) CHN 2-▲ 8882 [DDD] (32.97)

H. Shelley (pno), B. Thomson (cnd), Royal Scottish National Orch † Con 1 Pno, Op. 1; Con 4 Pno, Op. 40 CHN ▲ 9192 [DDD] (16.97)

A. Simon (pno), L. Slatkin (cnd), St. Louis SO ("Complete Works for Piano & Orchestra") † Cons Pno (comp) VB2 2-▲ 5008 [ADD] (9.97)

C. Smith (pno), M. Sargent (cnd), Philharmonia Orch *(rec 1947-48)* † Con 2 Pno, Op. 18; Suite 2 for 2 Pnos, Op. 17 DLAB ▲ 4004 (17.97)

Y. Temirkanov (cnd), St. Petersburg PO † Aleko (sels); Sym Dances, Op. 45 RCAV (Red Seal) ▲ 62710 (16.97)

J. Thibaudet (pno) † Con 2 Pno, Op. 18; Addinsell:Warsaw Con; G. Gershwin:Rhap in Blue; D. Shostakovich:Con 2 Pno, Op. 102 DECC ▲ 460503 (16.97)

J. Thibaudet (pno), V. Ashkenazy (cnd), Cleveland Orch † Con 2 Pno, Op. 18 PLON ▲ 40653 [DDD] (16.97)

D. Tomšič (pno), A. Nanut (cnd), Ljubljana SO † J. Brahms:Vars on a Theme by Paganini, Op. 35; Liszt:Grandes études de Paganini, S.141; Paganini:Caprice d'adieux; Caprices Vn, M.S. 25; Con 2 Vn, M.S. 48; R. Schumann:Studien nach Capricen von Paganini, Op. 3 VB3 3-▲ 3020 [ADD] (14.97)

O. Volkov (pno), A. Tchistiakov (cnd), Moscow PO *(rec Moscow, Russia, June 1996)* † Con 1 Pno, Op. 1; Vocalise BRIO ▲ 111 (16.97)

O. Volkov (pno), A. Tchistiakov (cnd), Moscow PO ("Celebrate Rachmaninoff") † Con 1 Pno, Op. 1; Con 2 Pno, Op. 18; Preludes Pno; Son 2 Pno, Op. 36; Songs (14), Op. 34 BRIO 2-▲ 116 [DDD] (18.97)

E. Wild (pno), J. Horenstein (cnd), Royal PO † Con 1 Pno, Op. 1; Con 4 Pno, Op. 40 CHN (Collect) ▲ 6605 [ADD] (12.97)

E. Wild (pno), J. Horenstein (cnd), Royal PO *(rec 1965)* † Con 1 Pno, Op. 1; Con 4 Pno, Op. 40 CHSK ▲ 41 [ADD] (16.97)

E. Wild (pno), J. Horenstein (cnd), Royal PO † Cons Pno (comp) CHN 2-▲ 7114 (26.97)

M. Zeltser (pno), R. Barshaï (cnd), Cologne RSO *(rec Cologne Philharmonic, Germany)* † S. Prokofiev:Con 3 Pno, Op. 26 LARL ▲ 904 (14.97)

artists unknown † Con 2 Pno, Op. 18 SNYC ▲ 62294 [DDD] (4.97)

The Rock (symphonic fantasy) for Orchestra [after Chekhov], Op. 7 (1893)

D. Achatz (pno), Y. Nagai (pno) [trans Rachmaninoff for pno duo] *(rec Växjö Concert Hall, Sweden, Aug 6-8, 1995)* † A. Scriabin:Poème de l'extase, Op. 54 BIS ▲ 746 [DDD] (17.97)

A. Davis (cnd), Royal Stockholm PO † Isle of the Dead, Op. 29; Sym Dances, Op. 45 FNL ▲ 19091 (15.97)

E. De Waart (cnd), Rotterdam PO † Syms (comp) PPHI (Duo) 2-▲ 38724 (17.97)

C. Dutoit (cnd), Philadelphia Orch † Sym 2 PLON ▲ 40604 [DDD] (16.97)

L. Maazel (cnd), Berlin PO † Syms (comp) DGRM (Masters) 2-▲ 445590 [DDD]

M. Pletnev (cnd), Russian National Orch † Sym 2 DEUT ▲ 39888 [DDD] (16.97)

L. Slatkin (cnd), St. Louis SO *(rec 1979)* † Bells; Capriccio bohémien, Op. 12; Isle of the Dead, Op. 29; Prince Rostislav; Russian Songs, Op. 41; Scherzo; Spring; Sym in d; Sym Dances, Op. 45; Vocalise VB3 3-▲ 3002 [ADD] (14.97)

RACHMANINOFF, SERGEI (cont.)

The Rock (symphonic fantasy) for Orchestra [after Chekhov], Op. 7 (1893) (cont.)

W. Weller (cnd), Basel SO † Sym 1 ARSM ▲ 1121 [DDD] (17.97)

Romance in f for Cello & Piano (1890)

F. Guye (vc), D. Lively (pno) † Son Vc; Martinů:Son 1 Vc; Vars on a Slovak folksong CASC ▲ 1019 (16.97)

Romance in G for Piano 4-Hands (1893)

I. Thorson (pno), J. Thurber (pno) † Duets Pno 4-Hands, Op. 11; Pieces Pno 6-Hands; Polka italienne; Preludes Pno; Russian Rhap; Suite 1 for 2 Pnos, Op. 5; Suite 2 for 2 Pnos, Op. 17; Sym Dances, Op. 45 PLAL 2-▲ 46 (35.97)

Romance for Violin & Piano, Op. 6/1 (1893)

L. Mordkovitch (vn), M. Gusak-Grin (pno) *(rec Frognal, Hampstead, United States of America, Mar 21/22, 1986)* ("Russian Music for Violin & Piano") † Glazunov:Grand Waltz; Raymonda (sels); S. Prokofiev:Mélodies Vn, Op. 35bis; I. Stravinsky:Mavra (sels); Russian Dance; P. Tchaikovsky:Souvenir d'un lieu cher, Op. 42; Sérénade mélancolique, Op. 26; Valse-Scherzo Vn, Op. 34 *([ENG] text)* CHN ▲ 8500 [DDD] (16.97)

I. Politkovsky (vn), I. Kollegorskaya (pno) *(rec 1957)* ("Igor Politkovsky: Russian Violin School") † Balakirev:Impromptu Vn; A. Dvořák:Zigeunermelodien, Op. 55; A. Rubinstein:Son 1 Vn, Op. 13; S. Taneyev:Son Vn; P. Tchaikovsky:Souvenir d'un lieu cher, Op. 42 RD (Talents of Russia) ▲ 16279 [ADD] (16.97)

Russian Rhapsody in e for 2 Pianos (1891)

V. Ashkenazy (pno), A. Previn (pno) *(rec Kingsway Hall London, 1979)* † Études-tableaux Pno; Suite 1 for 2 Pnos, Op. 5; Suite 2 for 2 Pnos, Op. 17; Sym Dances, Op. 45; Vars on a Theme by Corelli, Op. 42 PLON (Double Decker) 2-▲ 44845 [ADD] (17.97)

N. Demidenko (pno), D. Alexeev (pno) † Suite 2 for 2 Pnos, Op. 17; Sym Dances, Op. 45; Medtner:Knight Errant, Op. 58/2; Russian Round Dance, Op. 58/1 HYP ▲ 66654 [DDD] (18.97)

I. Thorson (pno), J. Thurber (pno) † Duets Pno 4-Hands, Op. 11; Pieces Pno 6-Hands; Polka italienne; Preludes Pno; Romance in G; Suite 1 for 2 Pnos, Op. 5; Suite 2 for 2 Pnos, Op. 17; Sym Dances, Op. 45 PLAL 2-▲ 46 (35.97)

Russian Songs (3) for Orchestra & Chorus, Op. 41 (1926)

V. Polyanski (cnd), Russian State SO, Russian State Symphonic Cappella † Sym 2 CHN ▲ 9665 (16.97)

L. Slatkin (cnd), St. Louis SO, St. Louis Sym Chorus *(rec 1980)* † Bells; Capriccio bohémien, Op. 12; Isle of the Dead, Op. 29; Prince Rostislav; Rock; Scherzo; Spring; Sym in d; Sym Dances, Op. 45; Vocalise VB3 3-▲ 3002 [ADD] (14.97)

Scherzo in d for Orchestra (1887)

L. Slatkin (cnd), St. Louis SO *(rec 1980)* † Bells; Capriccio bohémien, Op. 12; Isle of the Dead, Op. 29; Prince Rostislav; Rock; Russian Songs, Op. 41; Spring; Sym in d; Sym Dances, Op. 45; Vocalise VB3 3-▲ 3002 [ADD] (14.97)

E. Svetlanov (cnd), USSR SO *(rec 1966-90)* ("Symphonic Poems from Russia") † Capriccio bohémien, Op. 12; Isle of the Dead, Op. 29; Prince Rostislav; Balakirev:Ov on Czech Themes; Rus; Tamara; Glazunov:Ballade, Op. 78; Stenka Razin, Op. 13; Liapunov:Zhelyazova Volya, Op. 37 MELD (2fer) 2-▲ 34166 [ADD] (13.97)

Sonata in g for Cello & Piano, Op. 19 (1901)

J. Barta (vc), M. Lapšanský (pno) † Pärt:Fratres I Str Qt; A. Schnittke:Son 1 Vc SUR ▲ 112156 [DDD]

E. Bengtsson (vc), N. Kavtaradze (pno) † D. Shostakovich:Son Vc KPT ▲ 32018 [DDD]

W. Conway (vc), P. Evans (pno) † W. Lutoslawski:Grave; Webern:Little Pieces, Op. 11 LINN ▲ 9 (16.97)

M. Ericsson (vc), F. Malý (pno) † E. Grieg:Son Vc BONT ▲ 78 (10.97)

A. P. Gerlach (vc), F. Bidini (pno) *(rec Mesquite Arts Center, Mesquite, TX, Mar 1997)* † C. Franck:Son Vn, M.8 ENRE ▲ 9714 [DDD] (16.97)

T. Gill (vc), F. Pavri (pno) † Pieces Vc, Op. 2; Vocalise; E. Grieg:Son Vc GILD ▲ 7127 [DDD] (16.97)

B. Gregor-Smith (vc), Y. Wrigley (pno) ("Cello Sonatas") † Chopin:Son Vc ASVQ ▲ 6178 (10.97)

F. Guye (vc), D. Lively (pno) † Romance Vc; Martinů:Son 1 Vc; Vars on a Slovak folksong CASC ▲ 1019 (16.97)

D. Hoebig (vc), A. Tunis (pno) ("Rachmaninoff & Shostakovich") † Vocalise; D. Shostakovich:Son Vc CBC ▲ 1093 [DDD] (16.97)

Y.-Y. Ma (vc), E. Ax (pno) † S. Prokofiev:Son Vc SNYC ▲ 46486 (16.97)

H. Stegenga (vc), J. Bogaart (pno) ("Recital of Russian Music") † D. Shostakovich:Son Vc DI ▲ 920187 [DDD] (5.97)

T. Thedéen (vc), R. Pöntinen (pno) † S. Prokofiev:Son Vc BIS ▲ 386 [DDD] (17.97)

A. Toth (vc), M. Duchemin (pno) ("Romantic Cello Works from 1901-1950") † F. Bridge:Son Vc; Ginastera:Pampeana 2, Op. 21 SNE ▲ 2030 (16.97)

Y. Turovsky (vc), L. Edlina (pno) † Miaskovsky:Son 2 Vc, Op. 81 CHN ▲ 8523 [DDD] (17.97)

J. L. Webber (vc), Y. Seow (pno) † Pieces Vc, Op. 2; Debussy:Son Vc ASVQ ▲ 6072 [ADD] (10.97)

Sonata No. 1 in d for Piano, Op. 28 (1907)

B. Berezovsky (pno) † Vars on a Theme by Chopin, Op. 22 TELC ▲ 90890 (16.97)

I. Biret (pno) *(rec Sandhausen Germany, 1994-95)* † Son 2 Pno, Op. 36 NXIN ▲ 8553003 [DDD] (5.97)

S. Fiorentino (pno) *(rec Berlin, Oct 1995)* ("Fiorentino Edition, Vol. 3") † A. Scriabin:Son 1 Pno, Op. 6; Son 4 Pno, Op. 30 APR ▲ 5556 [DDD] (18.97)

Y. Kasman (pno) † Son 2 Pno, Op. 36 CALL ▲ 9259 (18.97)

J. Lill (pno) † Moments musicaux, Op. 16; Prelude in c#, Op. 3/2 NIMB ▲ 5575 [DDD] (16.97)

Sonata No. 2 in b♭ for Piano, Op. 36 (1913; rev 1931)

V. Ashkenazy (pno) † Prelude in c#, Op. 3/2; Preludes Pno PLON (Double Decca) 2-▲ 43841 (17.97)

V. Ashkenazy (pno) † Études-tableaux Pno; Cons Pno (comp); Prelude in c#, Op. 3/2; Preludes Pno; Rhap on a Theme of Paganini, Op. 43; Suite 1 for 2 Pnos, Op. 5; Suite 2 for 2 Pnos, Op. 17 PPHI (Budget Box) 6-▲ 455234 (40.97)

F. Bidini (pno) [1931 version] *(rec Mesquite Arts Center, TX, Mar 1998)* ("Fabio Bidini in Recital II") † Debussy:Images (6) Pno; M. de Falla:Fant bética; I. Stravinsky:Scenes (3) Pno ENRE ▲ 9816 [DDD] (16.97)

I. Biret (pno) *(rec Oct 1989)* † Moments musicaux, Op. 16; Vars on a Theme by Corelli, Op. 42 NXIN ▲ 550349 [DDD] (5.97)

I. Biret (pno) [original 1913 version] *(rec Sandhausen Germany, 1994-95)* † Son 1 Pno, Op. 28 NXIN ▲ 8553003 [DDD] (5.97)

J. Browning (pno) † Études-tableaux Pno; Moments musicaux, Op. 16; Pno Music (misc colls); Preludes Pno DLS ▲ 3044 [DDD] (14.97)

V. Cliburn (pno) † Études-tableaux Pno; Preludes Pno; S. Prokofiev:Son 6 Pno, Op. 82 RCAV (Gold Seal) ▲ 7941 [ADD] (11.97)

N. Goerner (pno) *(rec Switzerland, Dec 19-21, 1993)* † Études-tableaux Pno; Songs (12), Op. 21; Songs (6), Op. 38; Trans & Arrs CASC ▲ 1037 [DDD] (16.97)

S. Hall (pno) *(rec Oct 1986)* † Beethoven:Son 16 Pno, Op. 31/1; Chopin:Pno Music (misc colls) ACAD ▲ 20001 (16.97)

M.-A. Hamelin (pno) † Chopin:Son Pno in b♭, Op. 35; Schulz-Evler:Arabesque Pno; H. Villa-Lobos:Rudepoema PTRY ▲ 2204 (17.97)

D. Helfgott (pno) ("David Helfgott Plays Rachmaninoff") † Con 3 Pno, Op. 30; Prelude in c#, Op. 3/2; Preludes Pno RCAV (Red Seal) ▲ 40378 [DDD] (16.97) ▮ 40378 [DDD] (9.98)

V. Horowitz (pno) *(rec Washington D.C. & New York, United States of America, Dec 10, 1967 & Dec 15, 1968)* ("The Complete Masterworks Recordings, Vol. IX") † Moments musicaux, Op. 16; Pno Music (misc colls); Preludes Pno; Medtner:Fairy Tales, Op. 51; A. Scriabin:Etudes (12) Pno, Op. 8; Pno Music (misc colls) SNYC ▲ 53472 (16.97)

V. Horowitz (pno) † Con 3 Pno, Op. 30; Pno Music (misc colls) RCAV (Gold Seal) ▲ 7754 [ADD] (11.97)

V. Horowitz (pno) *(rec 1980)* † Chopin:Fantaisie Pno, Op. 49; Polonaises-fant, Op. 61; Liszt:Pno Music (misc); Trans, Arrs & Paraphrases; S. Prokofiev:Son 7 Pno, Op. 83; A. Scriabin:Son 5 Pno, Op. 53 PPHI (Great Pianists of the 20th Century) ▲ 456844 (22.97)

Y. Kasman (pno) † Son 1 Pno, Op. 28 CALL ▲ 9259 (18.97)

J. Lill (pno)—Allegro molto ("Whad' Ya Know About Rachmaninoff") † Con 2 Pno, Op. 18; Con 3 Pno, Op. 30; Liturgy of St. John Chrysostom, Op. 31; Prelude in c#, Op. 3/2; Preludes Pno; Rhap on a Theme of Paganini, Op. 43; Sym 2; Vocalise NIMB ▲ 4007 [DDD] (11.97)

J. Lill (pno) † Con 3 Pno, Op. 30 NIMB ▲ 5348 [DDD] (16.97)

G. Montero (pno) *(rec live Montreal Chopin Competition, 1995)* ("In Concert at Montreal") † Preludes Pno; Chopin:Mazurkas Pno; Nocturnes Pno; Polonaises-fant, Op. 61; Liszt:Paraphrase on Verdi PALE ▲ 501 (17.97)

H. Shelley (pno) [1913 version] HYP ▲ 66198 [DDD] (18.97)

C. Sorel (pno) [plus others] *(rec 1973)* EMSO 2-▲ 5852 (9.97)

J. Thibaudet (pno) † Con 4 Pno, Op. 40; Prelude in c#, Op. 3/2; Vars on a Theme by Corelli, Op. 42 PLON ▲ 458930 (16.97)

O. Volkov (pno) [2nd version] ("Celebrate Rachmaninoff") † Con 1 Pno, Op. 1; Con 2 Pno, Op. 18; Preludes Pno; Rhap on a Theme of Paganini, Op. 43; Songs (14), Op. 34 BRIO 2-▲ 116 [DDD] (18.97)

E. Wild (pno) † Preludes Pno CHSK ▲ 114 (16.97)

Songs

D. Hvorostovsky (bar), M. Arkadiev (pno)—Songs (6), Op. 4 [Morning] ("My Restless Soul") † Songs (12), Op. 14; Songs (12), Op. 21; Songs (6), Op. 8; Rimsky-Korsakov:Songs; P. Tchaikovsky:Songs PPHI ▲ 42536 (16.97)

D. Hvorostovsky (bar), M. Arkadiev (pno)—Choruses, Op. 15 [Night] † Songs (12), Op. 14; Songs (12), Op. 21; Songs (15), Op. 26; Songs (6), Op. 4; Sviridov:Russia Cast Adrift PPHI ▲ 46666 (16.97)

656

▲ = CD ♦ = Enhanced CD △ = MD ▮ = Cassette Tape ▯ = DCC

RACHMANINOFF, SERGEI (cont.)

Songs (cont.)

M. Kurenko (sop), V. Pastukhoff (pno), L. Rosenthal (pno)—I Remember That Day ("Maria Kurenko: Rachmaninoff Recital") † Bells; Songs (12), Op. 21; Songs (14), Op. 34; Songs (15), Op. 26; Songs (6), Op. 38; Songs (6), Op. 4; Songs (6), Op. 8; Vocalise VAIA ▲ 1094 [ADD] (16.97)

S. Leiferkus (bar), H. Shelley (pno)—At the Gates of the Holy Cloister; I Shall Tell You Nothing; Song of the Disillusioned; Do You Remember the Evening?; Were You Hiccoughing, Natasha?; Letter to K.S. Stanislavsky *(rec Highgate London, England, Sept 19-20, 1994 & Jan 30-31, 1995)* † Liturgy of St. John Chrysostom, Op. 31; Songs (12), Op. 14; Songs (12), Op. 21; Songs (14), Op. 34; Songs (15), Op. 26; Songs (6), Op. 4; Songs (6), Op. 8 CHN ▲ 9374 [DDD] (16.97)

M. Popescu (mez)—Choruses, Op. 15 [Night] ("Complete Songs, Vol 2") † Songs (12), Op. 21; Songs (15), Op. 26; Songs (6), Op. 4; Were You Hiccoughing, Natasha? CHN ▲ 9451 (16.97)

A. Pusar-Jeric (sop), T. Hans (pno)—Songs (12), Op. 14 [Do Not Believe Me, Friend] *(rec Nov 12-15, 1992)* ("Lieder und Romanzen") † Songs (12), Op. 14; Songs (12), Op. 21; Songs (14), Op. 34; Songs (15), Op. 26; Songs (6), Op. 38; Songs (6), Op. 4; Songs (6), Op. 8; Schnyder:monde miniscule ORF ▲ 340941 [DDD] (18.97)

J. Rodgers (sop), M. Popescu (mez), A. Naoumenko (ten), S. Leiferkus (bar), H. Shelley (pno)—At the Gates of the Holy Cloister; I Shall Tell You Nothing; Again You Are Bestirred, My Heart; April! A Festive Day in the Spring; Twilight Has Fallen; Song of the Disillusioned; Do You Remember the Evening? ("Volume 1") † Songs (12), Op. 14; Songs (6), Op. 4; Songs (6), Op. 8; The Flower Has Faded CHN ▲ 9405 (16.97)

J. Rodgers (sop), M. Popescu (mez), A. Naoumenko (ten), S. Leiferkus (bass), H. Shelley (pno)—Letter to K.S. Stanislavsky; Songs (14), Op. 34 [In the Soul of Each of Us; The Storm; A Passing Breeze; The Raising of Lazarus; It Cannot Be; Music; You Knew Him; I Remember this Day; The Peasant; What Happiness]; Bells, Op. 35 [Arion]; Songs (6), Op. 38 [At Night in My Garden; A-u]; Songs (6), Op. 8 [A Prayer]; All-Night Vigil, Op. 37 [Glory to God in the Highest] ("Complete Songs, Vol. 3") † Liturgy of St. John Chrysostom, Op. 31; Songs (14), Op. 34; Songs (6), Op. 38; Vocalise CHN ▲ 9477 (16.97)

Songs (6) for Voice & Piano, Op. 4 (1890)

B. Asawa (ct), N. Marriner (cnd), Academy of St. Martin in the Fields—In the Silence of the Secret Night *(rec Henry Wood Hall, England, Nov 1997)* † Songs (12), Op. 14; Songs (6), Op. 38; Vocalise; G. Fauré:Mélodies 'de Venise', Op. 58; Pavane; Songs; Medtner:Songs; H. Villa-Lobos:Bachiana brasileira 5; Canções Típicas Brasileiras; Forest of the Amazon RCAV (Red Seal) ▲ 68903 [DDD] (16.97)

J. DeGaetani (mez), G. Kalish (pno)—Oh Thou, My Field *(rec New York, NY, Apr 1979)* ("Russian Songs") † Songs (12), Op. 14; Songs (12), Op. 21; Songs (14), Op. 34; Songs (15), Op. 26; Mussorgsky:The Nursery; P. Tchaikovsky:Songs ARA ▲ 6674 [ADD] (16.97)

I. Galante (sop), V. Chochlov (pno)—Sing Not, O Lovely One † Songs (12), Op. 21; Songs (15), Op. 26; Goldins:Jewish Folksongs CAPI ▲ 1340 [AAD] (16.97)

D. Hvorostovsky (bar), M. Arkadiev (pno)—Oh Thou, My Field † Songs; Songs (12), Op. 14; Songs (12), Op. 21; Songs (15), Op. 26; Sviridov:Russia Cast Adrift PPHI ▲ 46666 (16.97)

M. Kurenko (sop), V. Pastukhoff (pno), L. Rosenthal (pno)—Oh No, I Beg You, Forsake Me Not ("Maria Kurenko: Rachmaninoff Recital") † Bells; Songs; Songs (12), Op. 21; Songs (14), Op. 34; Songs (15), Op. 26; Songs (6), Op. 38; Songs (6), Op. 8; Vocalise VAIA ▲ 1094 [ADD] (16.97)

S. Leiferkus (bar), H. Shelley (pno)—Oh No, I Beg You, Forsake Me Not; Morning; In the Silence of the Secret Night; Sing Not, O Lovely One *(rec Highgate, England, Sept 19-20, 1994 & Jan 30-31, 1995)* † Liturgy of St. John Chrysostom, Op. 31; Songs; Songs (12), Op. 14; Songs (12), Op. 21; Songs (14), Op. 34; Songs (15), Op. 26; Songs (6), Op. 8 CHN ▲ 9374 [DDD] (16.97)

N. Makarova (sop), M. Agaffonikova (pno)—Sing Not, O Lovely One † Songs (12), Op. 14; Songs (12), Op. 21; Songs (6), Op. 8; P. Tchaikovsky:Songs MED7 ▲ 9149 [DDD] (18.97)

A. Naoumenko (ten)—Oh No, I Beg You, Forsake Me Not ("Complete Songs, Vol 2") † Songs; Songs (12), Op. 21; Songs (15), Op. 26; Were You Hiccoughing, Natasha? CHN ▲ 9451 (16.97)

A. Pusar-Jeric (sop), T. Hans (pno)—Sing Not, O Lovely One; Oh Thou, My Field; How Long, My Friend *(rec Nov 12-15, 1992)* ("Lieder und Romanzen") † Songs; Songs (12), Op. 14; Songs (12), Op. 21; Songs (14), Op. 34; Songs (15), Op. 26; Songs (6), Op. 38; Songs (6), Op. 8; Schnyder:monde miniscule ORF ▲ 340941 [DDD] (18.97)

N. Rautio (sop), S. Skigin (pno)—Sing Not, O Lovely One; In the Silence of the Secret Night; Oh No, I Beg You, Forsake Me Not † Songs (12), Op. 14; Songs (12), Op. 21; Songs (15), Op. 26; Songs (6), Op. 38; Songs (6), Op. 8 CONI ▲ 51276 (16.97)

J. Rodgers (sop), M. Popescu (mez), A. Naoumenko (ten), S. Leiferkus (bar), H. Shelley (pno)—Oh No, I Beg You, Forsake Me Not; Morning; In the Silence of the Secret Night; Sing Not, O Lovely One; Oh Thou, My Field; How Long, My Friend ("Volume 1") † Songs; Songs (12), Op. 14; Songs (6), Op. 8; The Flower Has Faded CHN ▲ 9405 (16.97)

H. Shelley (pno) *(rec Highgate, England, July 24-27, 1994, Sept 19-20, 1994 & Jan 23-25)* † Again You Are Bestirred, My Heart; All-Night Vigil, Op. 37; Songs (12), Op. 14; Songs (12), Op. 21; Songs (14), Op. 34; Songs (15), Op. 26; Songs (6), Op. 38; Songs (6), Op. 8; Vocalise CHN ▲ 9644 [DDD] (16.97)

Songs (6) for Voice & Piano, Op. 8 (1893)

G. Gorchakova (sop), L. Gergieva (pno)—The Dream; A Prayer ("Memories of Love: Russian Romances") † Songs (12), Op. 14; Songs (12), Op. 21; Balakirev:Songs; Dargomyzhsky:Songs; M. Glinka:Songs; P. Tchaikovsky:Songs PPHI ▲ 446720 (16.97)

D. Hvorostovsky (bar), M. Arkadiev (pno)—Child, Thou Art as Beautiful as a Flower ("My Restless Soul") † Songs; Songs (12), Op. 14; Songs (12), Op. 21; Rimsky-Korsakov:Songs; P. Tchaikovsky:Songs PPHI ▲ 42536 (16.97)

M. Kurenko (sop), V. Pastukhoff (pno), L. Rosenthal (pno)—The Dream ("Maria Kurenko: Rachmaninoff Recital") † Bells; Songs; Songs (12), Op. 21; Songs (14), Op. 34; Songs (15), Op. 26; Songs (6), Op. 38; Songs (6), Op. 4; Vocalise VAIA ▲ 1094 [ADD] (16.97)

S. Leiferkus (bar), H. Shelley (pno)—Child, Thou Art as Beautiful as a Flower; Brooding, Reflection *(rec Highgate London, England, Sept 19-20, 1994 & Jan 30-31, 1995)* † Liturgy of St. John Chrysostom, Op. 31; Songs; Songs (12), Op. 14; Songs (12), Op. 21; Songs (14), Op. 34; Songs (15), Op. 26; Songs (6), Op. 4 CHN ▲ 9374 [DDD] (16.97)

N. Makarova (sop), M. Agaffonikova (pno)—I Fell in Love to My Sorrow; The Dream † Songs (12), Op. 14; Songs (12), Op. 21; Songs (6), Op. 4; P. Tchaikovsky:Songs MED7 ▲ 9149 [DDD] (18.97)

A. Pusar-Jeric (sop), T. Hans (pno)—I Fell in Love to My Sorrow; The Dream; A Prayer *(rec Nov 12-15, 1992)* ("Lieder und Romanzen") † Songs; Songs (12), Op. 14; Songs (12), Op. 21; Songs (14), Op. 34; Songs (15), Op. 26; Songs (6), Op. 38; Songs (6), Op. 4; Schnyder:monde miniscule ORF ▲ 340941 [DDD] (18.97)

N. Rautio (sop), S. Skigin (pno)—A Prayer; I Fell in Love to My Sorrow; The Waterlily † Songs (12), Op. 14; Songs (12), Op. 21; Songs (15), Op. 26; Songs (6), Op. 38; Songs (6), Op. 4 CONI ▲ 51276 (16.97)

J. Rodgers (sop), M. Popescu (mez), A. Naoumenko (ten), S. Leiferkus (bar), H. Shelley (pno)—The Waterlily; Child, Thou Art as Beautiful as a Flower; Brooding, Reflection; I Fell in Love to My Sorrow; The Dream; A Prayer ("Volume 1") † Songs; Songs (12), Op. 14; Songs (6), Op. 4; The Flower Has Faded CHN ▲ 9405 (16.97)

H. Shelley (pno)—A Prayer; A Prayer *(rec Highgate, England, July 24-27, 1994, Sept 19-20, 1994 & Jan 23-25)* † Again You Are Bestirred, My Heart; All-Night Vigil, Op. 37; Songs (12), Op. 14; Songs (12), Op. 21; Songs (14), Op. 34; Songs (15), Op. 26; Songs (6), Op. 38; Songs (6), Op. 4; Vocalise CHN ▲ 9644 [DDD] (16.97)

Songs (12) for Voice & Piano, Op. 14 (1896)

B. Asawa (ct), N. Marriner (cnd), Academy of St. Martin in the Fields—I Await You; She Is as Beautiful as the Midday *(rec Henry Wood Hall, England, Nov 1997)* † Songs (6), Op. 38; Songs (6), Op. 4; Vocalise; G. Fauré:Mélodies 'de Venise', Op. 58; Pavane; Songs; Medtner:Songs; H. Villa-Lobos:Bachiana brasileira 5; Canções Típicas Brasileiras; Forest of the Amazon RCAV (Red Seal) ▲ 68903 [DDD] (16.97)

J. DeGaetani (mez), G. Kalish (pno)—Oh, Do Not Grieve; For Long There Has Been Little Consolation in Love *(rec New York, United States of America, Apr 1979)* ("Russian Songs") † Songs (12), Op. 21; Songs (14), Op. 34; Songs (15), Op. 26; Songs (6), Op. 4; Mussorgsky:The Nursery; P. Tchaikovsky:Songs ARA ▲ 6674 [ADD] (16.97)

G. Gorchakova (sop), L. Gergieva (pno)—For Long There Has Been Little Consolation in Love; Do Not Believe Me, Friend ("Memories of Love: Russian Romances") † Songs (12), Op. 21; Songs (6), Op. 8; Balakirev:Songs; Dargomyzhsky:Songs; M. Glinka:Songs; P. Tchaikovsky:Songs PPHI ▲ 446720 (16.97)

D. Hvorostovsky (bar), M. Arkadiev (pno)—Do Not Believe Me, Friend; I Await You † Songs; Songs (12), Op. 21; Songs (15), Op. 26; Songs (6), Op. 4; Sviridov:Russia Cast Adrift PPHI ▲ 46666 (16.97)

D. Hvorostovsky (bar), M. Arkadiev (pno)—Spring Torrents ("My Restless Soul") † Songs; Songs (12), Op. 21; Songs (6), Op. 8; Rimsky-Korsakov:Songs; P. Tchaikovsky:Songs PPHI ▲ 42536 (16.97)

S. Leiferkus (bar), H. Shelley (pno)—I Was with Her; You Are So Loved by All; She Is as Beautiful as the Midday; Spring Torrents; It Is Time *(rec Highgate London, England, Sept 19-20, 1994 & Jan 30-31, 1995)* † Liturgy of St. John Chrysostom, Op. 31; Songs; Songs (12), Op. 21; Songs (14), Op. 34; Songs (15), Op. 26; Songs (6), Op. 4; Songs (6), Op. 8 CHN ▲ 9374 [DDD] (16.97)

N. Makarova (sop), M. Agaffonikova (pno)—I Await You; Spring Torrents [FRE] † Songs (12), Op. 21; Songs (6), Op. 4; Songs (6), Op. 8; P. Tchaikovsky:Songs MED7 ▲ 9149 [DDD] (18.97)

A. Pusar-Jeric (sop), T. Hans (pno)—I Await You; Small island; Do Not Believe Me, Friend *(rec Nov 12-15, 1992)* ("Lieder und Romanzen") † Songs (12), Op. 21; Songs (14), Op. 34; Songs (15), Op. 26; Songs (6), Op. 38; Songs (6), Op. 4; Songs (6), Op. 8; Schnyder:monde miniscule ORF ▲ 340941 [DDD] (18.97)

RACHMANINOFF, SERGEI (cont.)

Songs (12) for Voice & Piano, Op. 14 (1896) (cont.)

N. Rautio (sop), S. Skigin (pno)—Oh, Do Not Grieve; Do Not Believe Me, Friend; I Await You; Spring Torrents † Songs (12), Op. 21; Songs (15), Op. 26; Songs (6), Op. 38; Songs (6), Op. 4; Songs (6), Op. 8 CONI ▲ 51276 (16.97)

J. Rodgers (sop), M. Popescu (mez), A. Naoumenko (ten), S. Leiferkus (bar), H. Shelley (pno)—I Await You; Small island; For Long There Has Been Little Consolation in Love; I Was with Her; These Summer Nights; You Are So Loved by All; Do Not Believe Me, Friend; Oh, Do Not Grieve; She Is as Beautiful as the Midday; In My Soul; Spring Torrents; It Is Time ("Volume 1") † Songs; Songs (6), Op. 4; Songs (6), Op. 8; The Flower Has Faded CHN ▲ 9405 (16.97)

H. Shelley (pno) *(rec Highgate, England, July 24-27, 1994, Sept 19-20, 1994 & Jan 23-25)* † Again You Are Bestirred, My Heart; All-Night Vigil, Op. 37; Songs (12), Op. 21; Songs (14), Op. 34; Songs (15), Op. 26; Songs (6), Op. 38; Songs (6), Op. 4; Songs (6), Op. 8; Vocalise CHN ▲ 9644 [DDD] (16.97)

Songs (12) for Voice & Piano, Op. 21 (1902)

J. DeGaetani (mez), G. Kalish (pno)—Lilacs; They Answered *(rec New York, United States of America, Apr 1979)* ("Russian Songs") † Songs (12), Op. 14; Songs (14), Op. 34; Songs (15), Op. 26; Songs (6), Op. 4; Mussorgsky:The Nursery; P. Tchaikovsky:Songs ARA ▲ 6674 [ADD] (16.97)

I. Galante (sop), V. Chochlov (pno)—They Answered; How Fair This Place † Songs (15), Op. 26; Songs (6), Op. 4; Goldins:Jewish Folksongs CAPI ▲ 1340 [AAD] (16.97)

N. Goerner (pno) *(rec Switzerland, Dec 19-21, 1993)* † Études-tableaux Pno; Son 2 Pno, Op. 36; Songs (6), Op. 38; Trans & Arrs CASC ▲ 1037 [DDD] (16.97)

G. Gorchakova (sop), L. Gergieva (pno)—Lilacs ("Memories of Love: Russian Romances") † Songs (12), Op. 14; Songs (6), Op. 8; Balakirev:Songs; Dargomyzhsky:Songs; M. Glinka:Songs; P. Tchaikovsky:Songs PPHI ▲ 446720 (16.97)

D. Hvorostovsky (bar), M. Arkadiev (pno)—How Painful for Me ("My Restless Soul") † Songs; Songs (12), Op. 14; Songs (6), Op. 8; Rimsky-Korsakov:Songs; P. Tchaikovsky:Songs PPHI ▲ 42536 (16.97)

D. Hvorostovsky (bar), M. Arkadiev (pno)—How Fair This Place; They Answered † Songs; Songs (12), Op. 14; Songs (15), Op. 26; Songs (6), Op. 4; Sviridov:Russia Cast Adrift PPHI ▲ 46666 (16.97)

M. Kurenko (sop), V. Pastukhoff (pno), L. Rosenthal (pno)—Twilight; On the Death of a Siskin; Lilacs; How Fair This Place ("Maria Kurenko: Rachmaninoff Recital") † Bells; Songs; Songs (14), Op. 34; Songs (15), Op. 26; Songs (6), Op. 38; Songs (6), Op. 4; Songs (6), Op. 8; Vocalise VAIA ▲ 1094 [ADD] (16.97)

S. Leiferkus (bar), H. Shelley (pno)—Fate; By a Fresh Grave; Lilacs; Before the Icon; I Am Not a Prophet *(rec Highgate, England, Sept 19-20, 1994 & Jan 30-31, 1995)* † Liturgy of St. John Chrysostom, Op. 31; Songs; Songs (12), Op. 14; Songs (14), Op. 34; Songs (15), Op. 26; Songs (6), Op. 4; Songs (6), Op. 8 CHN ▲ 9374 [DDD] (16.97)

N. Makarova (sop), M. Agaffonikova (pno)—Lilacs; How Painful for Me; Lilacs † Songs (12), Op. 14; Songs (6), Op. 4; Songs (6), Op. 8; P. Tchaikovsky:Songs MED7 ▲ 9149 [DDD] (18.97)

A. Pusar-Jeric (sop), T. Hans (pno)—Twilight; They Answered; Lilacs; Fragment from A. Musset; How Fair This Place; Twilight; I Am Not a Prophet; How Painful for Me; Twilight *(rec Nov 12-15, 1992)* ("Lieder und Romanzen") † Songs; Songs (12), Op. 14; Songs (14), Op. 34; Songs (15), Op. 26; Songs (6), Op. 38; Songs (6), Op. 4; Songs (6), Op. 8; Schnyder:monde miniscule ORF ▲ 340941 [DDD] (18.97)

S. Rachmaninoff (pno)—Lilacs ("A Window in Time") † Morceaux de fant, Op. 3; Pno Music (misc colls); Pno Trans; Polka WR; Prelude in c#, Op. 3/2; Preludes Pno; Trans & Arrs TEL ▲ 80489 [DDD] (16.97)

N. Rautio (sop), S. Skigin (pno)—Fragment from A. Musset; Lilacs; How Fair This Place † Songs (12), Op. 14; Songs (15), Op. 26; Songs (6), Op. 38; Songs (6), Op. 4; Songs (6), Op. 8 CONI ▲ 51276 (16.97)

J. Rodgers (sop), M. Popescu (mez), A. Naoumenko (ten), S. Leiferkus (bass)—Lilacs; Fragment from A. Musset; How Fair This Place; I Am Not a Prophet; How Painful for Me; On the Death of a Siskin; Before the Icon; Twilight; They Answered; Twilight; Fate; By a Fresh Grave ("Complete Songs, Vol 2") † Songs; Songs (15), Op. 26; Songs (6), Op. 4; Were You Hiccoughing, Natasha? CHN ▲ 9451 (16.97)

H. Shelley (pno)—How Fair This Place *(rec Highgate, England, July 24-27, 1994, Sept 19-20, 1994 & Jan 23-25)* † Again You Are Bestirred, My Heart; All-Night Vigil, Op. 37; Songs (12), Op. 14; Songs (14), Op. 34; Songs (15), Op. 26; Songs (6), Op. 38; Songs (6), Op. 4; Songs (6), Op. 8; Vocalise CHN ▲ 9644 [DDD] (16.97)

J. Weber (pno)—Lilacs † Pno Trans; Polka WR; Preludes Pno; Trans & Arrs INMP ▲ 1051 [DDD] (11.97)

Songs (15) for Voice & Piano, Op. 26 (1906)

J. DeGaetani (mez), G. Kalish (pno)—Christ Is Risen; To My Children *(rec New York, NY, Apr 1979)* ("Russian Songs") † Songs (12), Op. 14; Songs (12), Op. 21; Songs (14), Op. 34; Songs (6), Op. 4; Mussorgsky:The Nursery; P. Tchaikovsky:Songs ARA ▲ 6674 [ADD] (16.97)

I. Galante (sop), V. Chochlov (pno)—At My Window † Songs (12), Op. 21; Songs (6), Op. 4; Goldins:Jewish Folksongs CAPI ▲ 1340 [AAD] (16.97)

D. Hvorostovsky (bar), M. Arkadiev (pno)—All Passes; Night Is Sorrowful; I Am Again Alone † Songs; Songs (12), Op. 14; Songs (12), Op. 21; Songs (6), Op. 4; Sviridov:Russia Cast Adrift PPHI ▲ 46666 (16.97)

M. Kurenko (sop), V. Pastukhoff (pno), L. Rosenthal (pno)—Night Is Sorrowful; The Fountain; Yesterday We Met; Two Partings; All Passes; The Ring; I Am Again Alone; Let Us Rest ("Maria Kurenko: Rachmaninoff Recital") † Bells; Songs; Songs (12), Op. 21; Songs (14), Op. 34; Songs (6), Op. 38; Songs (6), Op. 4; Songs (6), Op. 8; Vocalise VAIA ▲ 1094 [ADD] (16.97)

S. Leiferkus (bar), H. Shelley (pno)—He Took All from Me; Let Us Rest; Christ Is Risen; Yesterday We Met; All Passes *(rec Highgate London, England, Sept 19-20, 1994 & Jan 30-31, 1995)* † Liturgy of St. John Chrysostom, Op. 31; Songs; Songs (12), Op. 14; Songs (12), Op. 21; Songs (14), Op. 34; Songs (6), Op. 4; Songs (6), Op. 8 CHN ▲ 9374 [DDD] (16.97)

A. Pusar-Jeric (sop), T. Hans (pno)—At My Window *(rec Nov 12-15, 1992)* ("Lieder und Romanzen") † Songs; Songs (12), Op. 14; Songs (12), Op. 21; Songs (14), Op. 34; Songs (6), Op. 38; Songs (6), Op. 4; Songs (6), Op. 8; Schnyder:monde miniscule ORF ▲ 340941 [DDD] (18.97)

N. Rautio (sop), S. Skigin (pno)—Night Is Sorrowful; Christ Is Risen; Let Us Rest; He Took All from Me; Let Us Leave, My Sweet † Songs (12), Op. 14; Songs (12), Op. 21; Songs (6), Op. 38; Songs (6), Op. 4; Songs (6), Op. 8 CONI ▲ 51276 (16.97)

J. Rodgers (sop), M. Popescu (mez), A. Naoumenko (ten), S. Leiferkus (bass)—Let Us Leave, My Sweet; I Am Again Alone; At My Window; Night Is Sorrowful; There Are Many Sounds; He Took All from Me; Christ Is Risen; To My Children; Yesterday We Met; The Ring; The Fountain; Let Us Rest; Two Partings; All Passes ("Complete Songs, Vol 2") † Songs; Songs (12), Op. 21; Songs (6), Op. 4; Were You Hiccoughing, Natasha? CHN ▲ 9451 (16.97)

H. Shelley (pno) *(rec Highgate, England, July 24-27, 1994, Sept 19-20, 1994 & Jan 23-25)* † Again You Are Bestirred, My Heart; All-Night Vigil, Op. 37; Songs (12), Op. 14; Songs (12), Op. 21; Songs (14), Op. 34; Songs (6), Op. 38; Songs (6), Op. 4; Songs (6), Op. 8; Vocalise CHN ▲ 9644 [DDD] (16.97)

Songs (14) for Voice & Piano, Op. 34 (1912)

J. DeGaetani (mez), G. Kalish (pno)—A Passing Breeze *(rec New York, NY, Apr 1979)* ("Russian Songs") † Songs (12), Op. 14; Songs (12), Op. 21; Songs (15), Op. 26; Songs (6), Op. 4; Mussorgsky:The Nursery; P. Tchaikovsky:Songs ARA ▲ 6674 [ADD] (16.97)

M. Kurenko (sop), V. Pastukhoff (pno), L. Rosenthal (pno)—Music; A Passing Breeze; What Happiness; The Muse; Dissonance ("Maria Kurenko: Rachmaninoff Recital") † Bells; Songs; Songs (12), Op. 21; Songs (15), Op. 26; Songs (6), Op. 38; Songs (6), Op. 4; Songs (6), Op. 8; Vocalise VAIA ▲ 1094 [ADD] (16.97)

S. Leiferkus (bar), H. Shelley (pno)—In the Soul of Each of Us; The Raising of Lazarus; You Knew Him; The Peasant *(rec Highgate London, England, Sept 19-20, 1994 & Jan 30-31, 1995)* † Liturgy of St. John Chrysostom, Op. 31; Songs; Songs (12), Op. 14; Songs (12), Op. 21; Songs (15), Op. 26; Songs (6), Op. 4; Songs (6), Op. 8 CHN ▲ 9374 [DDD] (16.97)

A. Pusar-Jeric (sop), T. Hans (pno)—A Passing Breeze; It Cannot Be; You Knew Him *(rec Nov 12-15, 1992)* ("Lieder und Romanzen") † Songs; Songs (12), Op. 14; Songs (12), Op. 21; Songs (15), Op. 26; Songs (6), Op. 38; Songs (6), Op. 4; Songs (6), Op. 8; Schnyder:monde miniscule ORF ▲ 340941 [DDD] (18.97)

J. Rodgers (sop), M. Popescu (mez), A. Naoumenko (ten), S. Leiferkus (bass), H. Shelley (pno)—The Muse; In the Soul of Each of Us; The Storm; A Passing Breeze; The Raising of Lazarus; It Cannot Be; Music; You Knew Him; I Remember this Day; The Peasant; What Happiness; Dissonance ("Complete Songs, Vol. 3") † Liturgy of St. John Chrysostom, Op. 31; Songs; Songs (6), Op. 38; Vocalise CHN ▲ 9477 (16.97)

H. Shelley (pno)—A Passing Breeze *(rec Highgate, England, July 24-27, 1994, Sept 19-20, 1994 & Jan 23-25)* † Again You Are Bestirred, My Heart; All-Night Vigil, Op. 37; Songs (12), Op. 14; Songs (12), Op. 21; Songs (15), Op. 26; Songs (6), Op. 38; Songs (6), Op. 4; Songs (6), Op. 8; Vocalise CHN ▲ 9644 [DDD] (16.97)

G. Vinogradov (ten), G. Orentlicher (pno) † Rimsky-Korsakov:Songs, Op. 51; A. Rubinstein:Songs; R. Schumann:Dichterliebe, Op. 48; Gedichte, Op. 90; Liederkreis, Op. 24; Myrthen, Op. 25; P. Tchaikovsky:Songs PRE ▲ 89118 (16.97)

O. Volkov (pno)—Vocalise [trans for pno Edward Leiter] ("Celebrate Rachmaninoff") † Con 1 Pno, Op. 1; Con 2 Pno, Op. 18; Preludes Pno; Rhap on a Theme of Paganini, Op. 43; Son 2 Pno, Op. 36 BRIO 2-▲ 116 [DDD] (18.97)

Songs (6) for Voice & Piano, Op. 38 (1916)

A. Alieva (pno)—Daisies † Pno Music (misc colls); Balakirev:Paraphrase Pno; S. Ibrahimova:Trans de chants populaires azerbaïdjans; Mustafa-Zade:Con Pno; Radjabov:Tableaux de la vie hébraïque GALL ▲ 832 [DDD]

RACHMANINOFF, SERGEI (cont.)
Songs (6) for Voice & Piano, Op. 38 (1916) (cont.)
B. Asawa (ct), N. Marriner (cnd), Academy of St. Martin in the Fields—To Her *(rec Henry Wood Hall, England, Nov 1997)* † Songs (12), Op. 14; Songs (6), Op. 4; Vocalise; G. Fauré:Mélodies 'de Venise', Op. 58; Pavane; Songs; Medtner:Songs; H. Villa-Lobos:Bachiana brasileira 5; Canções Típicas Brasileiras; Forest of the Amazon RCAV (Red Seal) ▲ 68903 [DDD] (16.97)
N. Goerner (pno)—Daisies *(rec Switzerland, Dec 19-21, 1993)* † Études-tableaux Pno; Son 2 Pno, Op. 36; Songs (12), Op. 21; Trans & Arrs CASC ▲ 1037 [DDD] (16.97)
M. Kurenko (sop), V. Pastukhoff (pno), L. Rosenthal (pno)—At Night in My Garden; To Her; Daisies; The Rat Catcher; A-u ("Maria Kurenko: Rachmaninoff Recital") † Bells; Songs; Songs (12), Op. 21; Songs (14), Op. 34; Songs (15), Op. 26; Songs (6), Op. 4; Songs (6), Op. 8; Vocalise VAIA ▲ 1094 [ADD] (16.97)
A. Pusar-Jeric (sop), T. Hans (pno)—At Night in My Garden; Daisies *(rec Nov 12-15, 1992)* ("Lieder und Romanzen") † Songs; Songs (12), Op. 14; Songs (12), Op. 21; Songs (14), Op. 34; Songs (15), Op. 26; Songs (6), Op. 4; Songs (6), Op. 8; Schnyder:monde miniscule ORF ▲ 340941 [DDD] (18.97)
N. Rautio (sop), S. Skigin (pno)—At Night in My Garden † Songs (12), Op. 14; Songs (12), Op. 21; Songs (15), Op. 26; Songs (6), Op. 4; Songs (6), Op. 8 CONI ▲ 51276 (16.97)
J. Rodgers (sop), M. Popescu (mez), A. Naoumenko (ten), S. Leiferkus (bass), H. Shelley (pno)—At Night in My Garden; To Her; Daisies; The Rat Catcher; A Dream; A-u ("Complete Songs, Vol. 3") † Liturgy of St. John Chrysostom, Op. 31; Songs; Songs (14), Op. 34; Vocalise CHN ▲ 9477 (16.97)
H. Shelley (pno)—A-u *(rec Highgate, England, July 24-27, 1994, Sept 19-20, 1994 & Jan 23-25)* † Again You Are Bestirred, My Heart; All-Night Vigil, Op. 37; Songs (12), Op. 14; Songs (12), Op. 21; Songs (14), Op. 34; Songs (15), Op. 26; Songs (6), Op. 4; Songs (6), Op. 8; Vocalise CHN ▲ 9644 [DDD] (16.97)
Spring [Vesna] (cantata) for Baritone, Orchestra & Chorus [text Nekrasov], Op. 20 (1902)
J. Hynninen (bar), D. Kitaienko (cnd), Danish National RSO, Danish National Radio Choir † Bells CHN ▲ 8966 [DDD] (16.97)
A. Voketaitis (b-bar), L. Slatkin (cnd), St. Louis SO, St. Louis Sym Chorus *(rec 1980)* † Bells; Capriccio bohémien, Op. 12; Isle of the Dead, Op. 29; Prince Rostislav; Rock; Russian Songs, Op. 41; Scherzo; Sym in d; Sym Dances, Op. 45; Vocalise VB3 3-▲ 3002 [ADD] (14.97)
Suite No. 1 for 2 Pianos, Op. 5, "Fantaisie-tableaux" (1893)
M. Argerich (pno), A. Rabinovitch (pno) † Suite 2 for 2 Pnos, Op. 17; Sym Dances, Op. 45 TELC ▲ 74717 (16.97)
V. Ashkenazy (pno), A. Previn (pno) *(rec All Saints' Church Petersham, 1974)* † Études-tableaux Pno; Russian Rhap; Suite 2 for 2 Pnos, Op. 17; Sym Dances, Op. 45; Vars on a Theme by Corelli, Op. 42 PLON (Double Decker) 2-▲ 44845 [ADD] (17.97)
V. Ashkenazy (pno), A. Previn (pno) † Études-tableaux Pno; Cons Pno (comp); Prelude in c#, Op. 3/2; Preludes Pno; Rhap on a Theme of Paganini, Op. 43; Son 2 Pno, Op. 36; Suite 2 for 2 Pnos, Op. 17 PPHI (Budget Box) 6-▲ 455234 (40.97)
A. Goldenweiser (pno), G. Ginzburg (pno) *(rec 1948-52)* ("Russian Piano School") † Duets Pno 4-Hands, Op. 11; Suite 2 for 2 Pnos, Op. 17 RD (Talents of Russia) ▲ 16260 [ADD] (16.97)
S. Gordon (pno), N. Gordon (pno) † Suite 2 for 2 Pnos, Op. 17 CIT ▲ 88101 [ADD] (15.97)
N. Lugansky (pno), V. Rudenko (pno) *(rec Moscow Conservatory Great Hall, Dec 1995)* † Suite 2 for 2 Pnos, Op. 17; F. Poulenc:Son for 2 Pnos; M. Ravel:Valse TRIT ▲ 17018 [DDD] (16.97)
Reine Elisabeth Duo † Suite 2 for 2 Pnos, Op. 17; Debussy:En blanc et noir; Marche écossaise; M. Ravel:Rapsodie espagnole THOR ▲ 2297 (16.97)
I. Thorson (pno), J. Thurber (pno) † Duets Pno 4-Hands, Op. 11; Pieces Pno 6-Hands; Polka italienne; Preludes Pno; Romance in G; Russian Rhap; Suite 2 for 2 Pnos, Op. 17; Sym Dances, Op. 45 PLAL 2-▲ 46 (35.97)
Suite No. 2 for 2 Pianos, Op. 17 (1900-01)
M. Argerich (pno), A. Rabinovitch (pno) † Suite 1 for 2 Pnos, Op. 5; Sym Dances, Op. 45 TELC ▲ 74717 (16.97)
V. Ashkenazy (pno), A. Previn (pno) *(rec All Saints' Church Petersham, 1974)* † Études-tableaux Pno; Russian Rhap; Suite 1 for 2 Pnos, Op. 5; Sym Dances, Op. 45; Vars on a Theme by Corelli, Op. 42 PLON (Double Decker) 2-▲ 44845 [ADD] (17.97)
V. Ashkenazy (pno), A. Previn (pno) † Études-tableaux Pno; Cons Pno (comp); Prelude in c#, Op. 3/2; Preludes Pno; Rhap on a Theme of Paganini, Op. 43; Son 2 Pno, Op. 36; Suite 1 for 2 Pnos, Op. 5 PPHI (Budget Box) 6-▲ 455234 (40.97)
N. Demidenko (pno), D. Alexeev (pno) † Russian Rhap; Sym Dances, Op. 45; Medtner:Knight Errant, Op. 58/2; Russian Round Dance, Op. 58/1 HYP ▲ 66654 [DDD] (18.97)
A. Goldenweiser (pno), G. Ginzburg (pno) *(rec 1948-52)* ("Russian Piano School") † Duets Pno 4-Hands, Op. 11; Suite 1 for 2 Pnos, Op. 5 RD (Talents of Russia) ▲ 16260 [ADD] (16.97)
R. Laredo (pno), J. Tocco (pno) *(rec St. Hugo of the Hills Catholic Church, MI)* ("Rachmaninoff & Stravinsky Meet Again!") † I. Stravinsky:Sacre du printemps Pno GAS ▲ 313 (16.97)
N. Lugansky (pno), V. Rudenko (pno) *(rec Moscow Conservatory Great Hall, Dec 1995)* † Suite 1 for 2 Pnos, Op. 5; F. Poulenc:Son for 2 Pnos; M. Ravel:Valse TRIT ▲ 17018 [DDD] (16.97)
J. Mester (cnd), London PO [orchd R. Harkness] † Suite 1 for 2 Pnos, Op. 5 CIT ▲ 88101 [ADD] (15.97)
Reine Elisabeth Duo † Suite 1 for 2 Pnos, Op. 5; Debussy:En blanc et noir; Marche écossaise; M. Ravel:Rapsodie espagnole THOR ▲ 2297 (16.97)
C. Smith (pno), P. Sellick (pno) *(rec 1947-48)* † Con 2 Pno, Op. 18; Rhap on a Theme of Paganini, Op. 43 DLAB ▲ 4004 (17.97)
I. Thorson (pno), J. Thurber (pno) † Duets Pno 4-Hands, Op. 11; Pieces Pno 6-Hands; Polka italienne; Preludes Pno; Romance in G; Russian Rhap; Suite 1 for 2 Pnos, Op. 5; Sym Dances, Op. 45 PLAL 2-▲ 46 (35.97)
E. Wild (pno), C. Steiner (pno)—Waltz *(rec London, England, Apr 1968)* ("Dances for 2 Pianos") † Sym Dances, Op. 45; M. Ravel:Valse IVOR ▲ 70803 [ADD] (16.97)
Symphonic Dances for Orchestra (or 2 Pianos), Op. 45 (1940)
M. Argerich (pno), A. Rabinovitch (pno) † Suite 1 for 2 Pnos, Op. 5; Suite 2 for 2 Pnos, Op. 17 TELC ▲ 74717 (16.97)
V. Ashkenazy (cnd), (Royal) Concertgebouw Orch † Isle of the Dead, Op. 29 PLON ▲ 30733 [DDD] (9.97)
V. Ashkenazy (cnd), (Royal) Concertgebouw Orch † Bells; Isle of the Dead, Op. 29; Syms (comp) PLON (Budget Box) 3-▲ 455798 (20.97)
V. Ashkenazy (pno), A. Previn (pno) *(rec Kingsway Hall London, 1979)* † Études-tableaux Pno; Russian Rhap; Suite 1 for 2 Pnos, Op. 5; Suite 2 for 2 Pnos, Op. 17; Vars on a Theme by Corelli, Op. 42 PLON (Double Decker) 2-▲ 44845 [ADD] (17.97)
E. Bátiz (cnd), Royal Liverpool PO † Isle of the Dead, Op. 29 ALFA ▲ 1011 [DDD]
E. Bátiz (cnd), Royal PO *(rec Nov 1991)* † Isle of the Dead, Op. 29 NXIN ▲ 550583 [DDD] (5.97)
S. Comissiona (cnd), Vancouver SO *(rec The Orpheum Vancouver, June 1 & 4, 1993 & June 13, 1994)* † Capriccio bohémien, Op. 12; Prelude in c#, Op. 3/2; Preludes Pno CBC ▲ 5143 [DDD] (16.97)
A. Davis (cnd), Royal Stockholm PO † Isle of the Dead, Op. 29; Rock FNL ▲ 19091 (15.97)
N. Demidenko (pno), D. Alexeev (pno) † Russian Rhap; Suite 2 for 2 Pnos, Op. 17; Medtner:Knight Errant, Op. 58/2; Russian Round Dance, Op. 58/1 HYP ▲ 66654 [DDD] (18.97)
J. E. Gardiner (cnd), North German RSO † Janáček:Taraš Bulba DEUT ▲ 45838 [DDD] (16.97)
E. Goossens (cnd), London SO † I. Stravinsky:Sacre du printemps EVC ▲ 9002 [AAD] (13.97)
N. Järvi (cnd), Philharmonia Orch † Aleko (sels); Capriccio bohémien, Op. 12 CHN ▲ 9081 [DDD] (16.97)
K. Kondrashin (cnd), Moscow PO † Bells RCAV (Gold Seal) ▲ 32046 [ADD] (11.97)
E. Ormandy (cnd), Philadelphia Orch *(rec 1960)* † J. Offenbach:Gaîté Parisienne; Smetana:Bartered Bride (dances) SNYC (Essential Classics) ▲ 48279 [ADD] (7.97) ▮ 48279 [ADD] (3.98)
M. Pletnev (cnd), Russian National Orch *(rec Moscow State Conservatory, Russia, June 1997)* † Sym 3 DEUT ▲ 457598 [DDD] (16.97)
I. Prunyi (pno), H. Williams (cnd), Pécs SO † Isle of the Dead, Op. 29; Rhap on a Theme of Paganini, Op. 43 HUN ▲ 31551 [DDD] (16.97)
L. Slatkin (cnd), St. Louis SO *(rec 1979)* † Bells; Capriccio bohémien, Op. 12; Isle of the Dead, Op. 29; Prince Rostislav; Rock; Russian Songs, Op. 41; Scherzo; Spring; Sym in d; Vocalise VB3 3-▲ 3002 [ADD] (14.97)
Y. Temirkanov (cnd), St. Petersburg PO † Aleko (sels); Rhap on a Theme of Paganini, Op. 43 RCAV (Red Seal) ▲ 62710 (16.97)
Y. Temirkanov (cnd), St. Petersburg State SO ("Rachmaninoff in Hollywood") † All-Night Vigil, Op. 37; Con 2 Pno, Op. 18; Con 3 Pno, Op. 30; Rhap on a Theme of Paganini, Op. 43 RCAV (Greatest Hits) ▲ 68874 (11.97)
I. Thorson (pno), J. Thurber (pno) † Duets Pno 4-Hands, Op. 11; Pieces Pno 6-Hands; Polka italienne; Preludes Pno; Romance in G; Russian Rhap; Suite 1 for 2 Pnos, Op. 5; Suite 2 for 2 Pnos, Op. 17 PLAL 2-▲ 46 (35.97)
A. Vedernikov (cnd), Milan SO † E. Grieg:Con Pno, Op. 16 AG ▲ 114 (18.97)
E. Wild (pno), C. Steiner (pno) *(rec London, England, Apr 1968)* ("Dances for 2 Pianos") † Suite 2 for 2 Pnos, Op. 17; M. Ravel:Valse IVOR ▲ 70803 [ADD] (16.97)
D. Zinman (cnd), Baltimore SO *(rec Baltimore, May 28-29, 1994)* † Sym 3 TEL ▲ 80331 [DDD] (16.97)
Symphonies (3) (complete)
V. Ashkenazy (cnd), (Royal) Concertgebouw Orch PPHI (Double Decker) 2-▲ 448116 (17.97)

RACHMANINOFF, SERGEI (cont.)
Symphonies (3) (complete) (cont.)
V. Ashkenazy (cnd), (Royal) Concertgebouw Orch † Bells; Isle of the Dead, Op. 29; Sym Dances, Op. 45 PLON (Budget Box) 3-▲ 455798 (20.97)
E. De Waart (cnd), Rotterdam PO † Rock PPHI (Duo) 2-▲ 38724 (17.97)
L. Maazel (cnd), Berlin PO † Rock DGRM (Masters) 2-▲ 445590 [DDD]
A. Previn (cnd), London SO EMIC 3-▲ 64530 [DDD] (31.97)
L. Slatkin (cnd), St. Louis SO *(rec 1976-79)* VB2 2-▲ 5034 [ADD] (9.97)
USSR SO, E. Svetlanov (cnd), Bolshoi Theater Orch *(Sym 1, Op. 13)*, Bolshoi Theater Orch *(Sym 2, Op. 27)*, USSR Radio-TV Large SO, E. Svetlanov (cnd), Bolshoi Theater Orch *(Sym 3, Op. 44) (rec Moscow, Russia, 1962-66)* † Vocalise MELD 2-▲ 40064 [ADD] (13.97)
Symphony No. 1 in d, Op. 13 (1895)
A. Anissimov (cnd), Ireland National SO † Capriccio bohémien, Op. 12 NXIN ▲ 8550806 [DDD] (5.97)
J. Lill (pno), T. Otaka (cnd), BBC Welsh National Orch † Études-tableaux Pno; Con 1 Pno, Op. 1; Con 2 Pno, Op. 18; Con 3 Pno, Op. 30; Con 4 Pno, Op. 40; Music of Rachmaninoff; Rhap on a Theme of Paganini, Op. 43; Sym 2; Sym 3; Vars on a Theme by Corelli, Op. 42; Vocalise NIMB 6-▲ 1761 [DDD] (29.97)
P. Przytocki (cnd), Gdansk PO PC ▲ 265098 [DDD] (2.97)
W. Weller (cnd), Basel SO † Rock ARSM ▲ 1121 [DDD] (17.97)
Symphony No. 2 in e, Op. 27 (1906-07)
E. De Waart (cnd), Royal PO † Con 2 Pno, Op. 18; Rhap on a Theme of Paganini, Op. 43; Vocalise PPHI 2-▲ 38383 (17.97)
J. DePreist (cnd), Oregon SO † Études-tableaux Pno; Vocalise DLS ▲ 3071 [DDD] (14.97)
C. Dutoit (cnd), Philadelphia Orch † Rock PLON ▲ 40604 [DDD] (16.97)
V. Gergiev (cnd), Kirov Theater Orch PPHI ▲ 38864 (16.97)
A. Gibson (cnd), Royal Scottish National Orch CHN (Collect) ▲ 6606 [DDD]
I. Golovchin (cnd), Olsztyn National SO PC ▲ 265099 [DDD] (2.97)
S. Gunzenhauser (cnd), Czecho-Slovak Radio SO—Adagio ("Best of Rachmaninov") † Con 3 Pno, Op. 30; Music of Rachmaninoff; Prelude in c#, Op. 3/2; Preludes Pno; Rhap on a Theme of Paganini, Op. 43; Vocalise NXIN ▲ 8556682 [DDD] (5.97)
M. Jansons (cnd), Philharmonia Orch CHN ▲ 8520 [DDD] (16.97)
A. Lazarev (cnd) † Con 2 Pno, Op. 18; Con 3 Pno, Op. 30; Vocalise TELC (Ultima) 2-▲ 18958 (16.97)
J. Lill (pno), T. Otaka (cnd), BBC Welsh National Orch † Études-tableaux Pno; Con 1 Pno, Op. 1; Con 2 Pno, Op. 18; Con 3 Pno, Op. 30; Con 4 Pno, Op. 40; Music of Rachmaninoff; Rhap on a Theme of Paganini, Op. 43; Sym 1; Sym 3; Vars on a Theme by Corelli, Op. 42; Vocalise NIMB 6-▲ 1761 [DDD] (29.97)
E. Ormandy (cnd), Philadelphia Orch † Vocalise; Borodin:Nocturne Str Orch; Chopin:Études Pno; Nocturnes Pno; Liszt:Liebesträume, S.541; Mendelssohn (-Bartholdy):Lieder, Op. 34; Rimsky-Korsakov:Sadko (sels); Scheherazade, Op. 35; P. Tchaikovsky:Qt 1 Strs, Op. 11; Snow Maiden (sels); Songs SNYC ▲ 46355 [ADD/DDD] (9.97)
E. Ormandy (cnd), Philadelphia Orch RCAV (Victrola) ▲ 60132 [ADD] (6.97)
E. Ormandy (cnd), Philadelphia Orch ("Basic 100, Vol. 53") † Isle of the Dead, Op. 29 RCAV ▲ 68022 (10.97)
T. Otaka (cnd), BBC Welsh SO—Adagio ("Whad' Ya Know About Rachmaninoff") † Con 2 Pno, Op. 18; Con 3 Pno, Op. 30; Liturgy of St. John Chrysostom, Op. 31; Prelude in c#, Op. 3/2; Preludes Pno; Rhap on a Theme of Paganini, Op. 43; Son 2 Pno, Op. 36; Vocalise NIMB ▲ 4007 [DDD] (11.97)
M. Pletnev (cnd), Russian National Orch † Rock DEUT ▲ 39888 [DDD] (16.97)
V. Polyanski (cnd), Russian State SO † Russian Songs, Op. 41 CHN ▲ 9665 (16.97)
A. Previn (cnd), Royal PO TEL ▲ 80113 [DDD] (16.97)
S. Rattle (cnd), Los Angeles PO CSER (Seraphim) ▲ 73292 [DDD] (6.97)
G. Rozhdestvensky (cnd), London SO INMP (LSO Classic Masterpieces) ▲ 904 [DDD] (9.97)
K. Sanderling (cnd), Leningrad PO *(rec Jesus-Christus Church Berlin, Germany, May 1956)* DEUT (The Originals) ▲ 449767 [ADD] (11.97)
W. Steinberg (cnd), Pittsburgh SO *(rec 1953-54)* † S. Prokofiev:Sym 1; R. Strauss:Till Eulenspiegels lustige Streiche, Op. 28 EMIC (Legacy) ▲ 66554 [ADD] (11.97)
Y. Temirkanov (cnd), Royal PO *(rec 1977)* † P. Tchaikovsky:Manfred, Op. 58; Marche slave, Op. 31; Romeo & Juliet EMIC (Doubleforte) 2-▲ 69776 [ADD] (16.97)
Y. Temirkanov (cnd), St. Petersburg PO † Vocalise RCAV (Red Seal) ▲ 61281 (16.97)
D. Zinman (cnd), Baltimore SO † Vocalise TEL ▲ 80312 [DDD] (16.97)
artists unknown SNYC ▲ 64559 (4.97)
Symphony No. 3 in a, Op. 44 (1935-36; rev 1938)
M. Abravanel (cnd), Utah SO VC ▲ 8 [ADD] (13.97)
M. Ermler (cnd), Moscow PO † Con 2 Pno, Op. 18 RUS ▲ 10011 [DDD] (12.97)
I. Golovchin (cnd), Moscow SO PC ▲ 265037 [DDD] (2.97)
N. Järvi (cnd), London SO † Kalinnikov:Intermezzi CHN ▲ 8614 [DDD] (16.97)
J. Lill (pno), T. Otaka (cnd), BBC Welsh National Orch † Études-tableaux Pno; Con 1 Pno, Op. 1; Con 2 Pno, Op. 18; Con 3 Pno, Op. 30; Con 4 Pno, Op. 40; Music of Rachmaninoff; Rhap on a Theme of Paganini, Op. 43; Sym 1; Sym 2; Vars on a Theme by Corelli, Op. 42; Vocalise NIMB 6-▲ 1761 [DDD] (29.97)
M. Pletnev (cnd), Russian National Orch *(rec Moscow State Conservatory, Russia, June 1997)* † Sym Dances, Op. 45 DEUT ▲ 457598 [DDD] (16.97)
S. Rachmaninoff (cnd), Philadelphia Orch *(rec 1939)* † Isle of the Dead, Op. 29; Vocalise PHS ▲ 9414 [AAD] (17.97)
S. Rachmaninoff (cnd), Philadelphia Orch † Isle of the Dead, Op. 29; Rhap on a Theme of Paganini, Op. 43 RCAV (Gold Seal) 10-▲ 61265 (102.97)
S. Rachmaninoff (cnd), Philadelphia Orch *(rec Dec 11, 1939)* ("Rachmaninoff Conducts Rachmaninoff") † Isle of the Dead, Op. 29; Vocalise RCAV (Gold Seal) ▲ 62532 [ADD] (11.97)
S. Rachmaninoff (cnd), Philadelphia Orch † Isle of the Dead, Op. 29; Vocalise MTAL ▲ 48038 (6.97)
S. Rachmaninoff (cnd), Philadelphia Orch *(rec 1939)* ("Composer, Pianist, Conductor") † Con 4 Pno, Op. 40; Vocalise GSE ▲ 785077 (m) [ADD] (16.97)
L. Stokowski (cnd), National PO *(rec London, Apr-May 1975)* † Vocalise EMIC ▲ 66759 [ADD] (11.97)
D. Zinman (cnd), Baltimore SO *(rec Baltimore, May 28-29, 1994)* † Sym Dances, Op. 45 TEL ▲ 80331 [DDD] (16.97)
various artists [excerpt; plus others] † Borodin:Prince Igor (Polovtsian Dances); G. Gershwin:Rhap in Blue; C. W. Gluck:Alceste (ov); P. Hindemith:Mathis der Maler; I. Stravinsky:Jeu de cartes MTAL ▲ 48094 (6.97)
Symphony in d, "Youth Symphony" (1891)
L. Slatkin (cnd), St. Louis SO *(rec 1980)* † Bells; Capriccio bohémien, Op. 12; Isle of the Dead, Op. 29; Prince Rostislav; Rock; Russian Songs, Op. 41; Scherzo; Spring; Sym Dances, Op. 45; Vocalise VB3 3-▲ 3002 [ADD] (14.97)

Transcriptions & Arrangements
I. Biret (pno)—Kreisler:Liebesfreud; Kreisler:Liebeslied † Preludes Pno NXIN ▲ 550466 [DDD] (5.97)
J. Browning (pno)—Mussorgsky:Hopak [from Sorochintsy Fair] [[arr Rachmaninoff]] † Mussorgsky:Pictures at an Exhibition; Pno Music DLS ▲ 1008 [AAD] (10.97)
N. Goerner (pno)—Mendelssohn:Scherzo [from A Midsummer Night's Dream] *(rec Switzerland, Dec 19-21, 1993)* † Études-tableaux Pno; Son 2 Pno, Op. 36; Songs (12), Op. 21; Songs (6), Op. 38 CASC ▲ 1037 [DDD] (16.97)
I. Hobson (pno)—Smith:The Star-Spangled Banner; J.S.Bach:Vn Part (prelude, gavotte & gigue); Rimsky-Korsakov:The Flight of the Bumblebee; Mussorgsky:Hopak [from Sorochintsy Fair]; Schubert:Wohin?; Bizet:L'Arlésienne (suite 1); Tchaikovsky:Lullaby (Op. 16/1); Mendelssohn:Scherzo [from A Midsummer Night's Dream]; Kreisler:Liebeslied; Kreisler:Liebesfreud *(rec Houston TX & Great Hall of the Kranne, United States of America, Sept 9-10, 1994 & Jan 25, 1995)* ("The Complete Solo Piano Transcriptions & Arrangements of Sergei Rachmaninoff") † Moments musicaux, Op. 16; Morceaux de fant, Op. 3; Morceaux de salon, Op. 10; Pno Music (misc colls); Polka WR; Mendelssohn (-Bartholdy):Capriccio brillante, Op. 22 ARA ▲ 6663 (16.97)
S. Rachmaninoff (pno)—Rimsky-Korsakov:The Flight of the Bumblebee; Kreisler:Liebeslied; Schubert:Wohin?; Bizet:L'Arlésienne (suite 1); Mussorgsky:Hopak [from Sorochintsy Fair] ("A Window in Time") † Morceaux de fant, Op. 3; Pno Music (misc colls); Polka WR; Prelude in c#, Op. 3/2; Preludes Pno; Songs (12), Op. 21 TEL ▲ 80489 [DDD] (16.97)
S. Richter (pno)—Schumann:Waldszenen *(rec 1952-59)* ("Sviatoslav Richter III") † Con 2 Pno, Op. 18; Preludes Pno; A. Scriabin:Etudes (12) Pno, Op. 8; Etudes (3) Pno, Op. 65; Etudes (8) Pno, Op. 42; Pieces (3) Pno, Op. 2 PPHI (Great Pianists of the 20th Century) 2-▲ 456952 (22.97)
J. Weber (pno)—J.S.Bach:Vn Part (prelude, gavotte & gigue); Liszt:Hungarian Rhap 2 (cadenza); Kreisler:Liebeslied; Kreisler:Liebesfreud; Rimsky-Korsakov:The Flight of the Bumblebee † Pno Trans; Polka WR; Preludes Pno; Songs (12), Op. 21 INMP ▲ 1051 [DDD] (11.97)
Trio élégiaque (No. 1) in g for Piano, Violin & Cello (1892)
V. Abramyan (vn), A. Bourikov (vc), G. Dzubenko (pno) *(rec 1995)* ("Romantic Trio") † M. Glinka:Trio pathétique; D. Shostakovich:Trio 2 Pno, Op. 67 RD ▲ 10401 [DDD] (16.97)
Bekova Sisters ("The Bekova Sisters") † Trio élégiaque 2, Op. 9 CHN (New Direction) ▲ 9329 [DDD] (16.97)
Borodin Trio † Trio élégiaque 2, Op. 9 CHN ▲ 8341 [DDD] (16.97)

▲ = CD ♦ = Enhanced CD △ = MD ▮ = Cassette Tape ▯ = DCC

RACHMANINOFF, SERGEI (cont.)
Trio élégiaque (No. 1) in g for Piano, Violin & Cello (1892) (cont.)
E. Levinson (db), G. Levinson (pno) † Beethoven:Son 3 Vc, Op. 69; Bruch:Kol Nidrei, Op. 47; P. Hindemith:Son Db; Koussevitzky:Valse miniature Db, Op. 1/2; Ranjbaran:Dance of Life; P. Tchaikovsky:Souvenir d'un lieu cher, Op. 42 CAL ▲ 507 [DDD] (15.97)
Moscow Conservatory Piano Trio ("Great Piano Trios: Rachmaninoff & Tchaikovsky") † P. Tchaikovsky:Trio Pno, Op. 50 CMH ▲ 8020 (13.97)
Rachmaninoff Trio † Trio élégiaque 2, Op. 9 CENT ▲ 2059 [DDD] (16.97)
Trio élégiaque (No. 2) in d for Piano, Violin & Cello, Op. 9 (1893; rev 1907, 1917)
Bekova Sisters ("The Bekova Sisters") † Trio élégiaque 1 CHN (New Direction) ▲ 9329 [DDD] (16.97)
Borodin Trio † Trio élégiaque 1 CHN ▲ 8341 [DDD] (16.97)
L. Kogan (vn), F. Luzanov (vc), E. Svetlanov (pno) RUS ▲ 10046 [AAD]
A. Kogosowski (pno), N. Järvi (cnd), Detroit SO [orchd A. Kogosowski] † Vars on a Theme by Corelli, Op. 42; Vocalise CHN ▲ 9261 [DDD] (16.97)
Rachmaninoff Trio † Trio élégiaque 1 CENT ▲ 2059 [DDD] (16.97)
J. Roisman (vn), M. Schneider (vc), A. Balsam (pno), Budapest String Quartet *(rec Coolidge Auditorium Library of Congress, Apr 4, 1952)* † Qt Strs BRID ▲ 9063 (17.97)
P. Serebrekov (pno), M. Vajman (vn), M. Rostropovich (vc) MTRC ▲ 8408
Variations on a Theme by Chopin for Piano, Op. 22 (1902-03)
B. Berezovsky (pno) † Son 1 Pno, Op. 28 TELC ▲ 90890 (16.97)
V. Bogolubov (pno) ("Unfamiliar Masterpieces") † Moments musicaux, Op. 16; Preludes Pno SNE ▲ 620 (16.97)
E. Wild (pno) † Vars on a Theme by Corelli, Op. 42; Vocalise CHSK ▲ 58 [DDD] (16.97)
Variations on a Theme by Corelli for Piano, Op. 42 (1931)
V. Ashkenazy (pno) *(rec Kingsway Hall London, 1972)* † Études-tableaux Pno; Russian Rhap; Suite 1 for 2 Pnos, Op. 5; Suite 2 for 2 Pnos, Op. 17; Sym Dances, Op. 45 PLON (Double Decker) 2-▲ 44845 [ADD] (17.97)
I. Biret (pno) *(rec Oct 1989)* † Moments musicaux, Op. 16; Son 2 Pno, Op. 36 NXIN ▲ 550349 [DDD] (5.97)
M. P. Carola (pno) † Études-tableaux Pno SYMO ▲ 103 (17.97)
S. Cherkassky (pno) † J. Brahms:Vars on a Theme by Paganini, Op. 35; Mussorgsky:Pictures at an Exhibition NIMB ▲ 7706 (11.97)
C. Keene (pno) ("C. Keene Plays Variations") † Beethoven:Vars Pno on Original Theme, WoO 80; G. F. Handel:Harmonious Blacksmith; Mendelssohn (-Bartholdy):Vars sérieuses, Op. 54; R. Schumann:Vars on A-B-E-G-G, Op. 1 PROT ▲ 1112 (18.97)
H. Kim (pno) ("Essential") † Debussy:Preludes Pno; Ginastera:Son 1 Pno, Op. 22; Mendelssohn (-Bartholdy):Vars sérieuses, Op. 54; D. Scarlatti:Sons Kbd SSCL ▲ 5 (16.97)
A. Kogosowski (pno), N. Järvi (cnd), Detroit SO † Trio élégiaque 2, Op. 9; Vocalise CHN ▲ 9261 [DDD] (16.97)
J. Lill (pno), T. Otaka (cnd), BBC National Orch Wales † Con 4 Pno, Op. 40; Liturgy of St. John Chrysostom, Op. 31; Vars on a Theme by Corelli, Op. 42 NIMB 2-▲ 5478 (16.97)
J. Lill (pno), T. Otaka (cnd), BBC Welsh National Orch † Études-tableaux Pno; Con 1 Pno, Op. 1; Con 2 Pno, Op. 18; Con 3 Pno, Op. 30; Con 4 Pno, Op. 40; Music of Rachmaninoff; Rhap on a Theme of Paganini, Op. 43; Sym 1; Sym 2; Sym 3; Vocalise NIMB 6-▲ 1761 [DDD] (29.97)
M. Pletnev (pno) *(rec Villa Senar, Switzerland)* ("Hommage à Rachmaninov") † Études-tableaux Pno; Beethoven:Son 26 Pno, Op. 81a; Chopin:Andante Spianato & Grand Polonaise, Op. 22; Mendelssohn (-Bartholdy):Rondo capriccioso, Op. 14 DEUT ▲ 459634 (16.97)
J. Thibaudet (pno) † Con 4 Pno, Op. 40; Prelude in c#, Op. 3/2; Son 2 Pno, Op. 36 PLON ▲ 458930 (16.97)
V. Viardo (pno) † Medtner:Forgotten Melodies 1, Op. 38; Forgotten Melodies 2, Op. 39; Son in a Pno, Op. 30 NON ▲ 79283 (16.97)
E. Wild (pno) † Vars on a Theme by Chopin, Op. 22; Vocalise CHSK ▲ 58 [DDD] (16.97)
T. Ying (pno) *(rec Mar 19-20, 1996)* † Chopin:Fantaisie Pno, Op. 49; W. A. Mozart:Rondo Pno, K.511; M. Ravel:Gaspard de la nuit; R. Schumann:Toccata Pno, Op. 7 ARIZ ▲ 96100 [ADD]
Vocalise in e for Soprano, Op. 34/14 (1912, rev 1915)
B. Asawa (ct), N. Marriner (cnd), Academy of St. Martin in the Fields *(rec Henry Wood Hall, England, Nov 1997)* † Songs (12), Op. 14; Songs (6), Op. 38; Songs (6), Op. 4; G. Fauré:Mélodies 'de Venise', Op. 58; Pavane; Songs; Medtner:Songs; H. Villa-Lobos:Bachiana brasileira 5; Canções Típicas Brasileiras; Forest of the Amazon RCAV (Red Seal) ▲ 68903 [DDD] (16.97)
G. Banaszak (sax), B. Jarmolowicz (cnd), Polish National CO of Slupsk—Lentemente *(rec Slupsk State Theatre, Poland, Apr 1998)* † P.-M. Dubois:Con A Sax; Glazunov:Con A Sax, Op. 109; Ibert:Con Vc; H. Villa-Lobos:Fant Sax CENT ▲ 2400 [DDD] (16.97)
M. Bernardi (cnd), Toronto SO † Con 2 Pno, Op. 18; Willan:Con Pno, Op. 76 SMS (SM 5000) ▲ 5108 [DDD] (16.97)
C. Delafontaine (fl), M. Mourtazine-Chapochnikova (pno) [trans fl & pno] ("Decouvertes Transcaucasiennes") † Amirov:Pieces Fl; Glière:Pieces various instrs, Op. 35; Liadov:Prelude Fl & Pno; Taktakishvili:Son Fl GALL ▲ 894 [DDD] (19.97)
J. DePreist (cnd), Oregon SO † Études-tableaux Pno; Sym 2 DLS ▲ 3071 [DDD] (14.97)
T. Gill (vc), F. Pavri (pno) [arr vc & pno] † Pieces Vc, Op. 2; Son Vc; E. Grieg:Son Vc GILD ▲ 7127 [DDD] (16.97)
D. Hoebig (vc), A. Tunis (pno) [trans Leonard Rose for vc & pno] ("Rachmaninoff & Shostakovich") † Son Vc; D. Shostakovich:Son Vc CBC ▲ 1093 [DDD] (16.97)
N. Järvi (cnd), Detroit SO † Trio élégiaque 2, Op. 9; Vars on a Theme by Corelli, Op. 42 CHN ▲ 9261 [DDD] (16.97)
M. Kliegel (vc), R. Havenith (pno) ("Best of Rachmaninov") † Con 3 Pno, Op. 30; Music of Rachmaninoff; Prelude in c#, Op. 3/2; Preludes Pno; Rhap on a Theme of Paganini, Op. 43; Sym 2 NXIN ▲ 8556682 [DDD] (5.97)
M. Kurenko (sop), V. Pastukhoff (pno), L. Rosenthal (pno) ("Maria Kurenko: Rachmaninoff Recital") † Bells; Songs; Songs (12), Op. 21; Songs (14), Op. 34; Songs (15), Op. 26; Songs (6), Op. 38; Songs (6), Op. 4; Songs (6), Op. 8 VAIA ▲ 1094 [ADD] (16.97)
A. Lazarev (cnd) † Con 2 Pno, Op. 18; Con 3 Pno, Op. 30; Sym 2 TELC (Ultima) 2-▲ 18958 (16.97)
M. Lidström (vc), V. Ashkenazy (pno) *(rec Gothenburg Concert Hall en, Sweden, 1995)* † Kabalevsky:Con 2 Vc, Op. 77; A. Khachaturian:Con Vc BIS ▲ 719 [DDD] (17.97)
J. Lill (pno), T. Otaka (cnd), BBC Welsh National Orch † Études-tableaux Pno; Con 1 Pno, Op. 1; Con 2 Pno, Op. 18; Con 3 Pno, Op. 30; Con 4 Pno, Op. 40; Music of Rachmaninoff; Rhap on a Theme of Paganini, Op. 43; Sym 1; Sym 2; Sym 3; Vars on a Theme by Corelli, Op. 42 NIMB 6-▲ 1761 [DDD] (29.97)
H. Lindemann (va), B. Martin (pno) ("Hommage a Primrose") † J. Brahms:Son 1 Cl; J. Joachim:Vars on a Theme Va, Op. 10; Paganini:Caprices Vn, M.S. 25; T. A. Vitali:Chaconne Vn; Wieniawski:Etude-caprices Vn, Op. 18 TACE ▲ 45
C. Lin (vn), S. Rivers (pno) [tran Michel Press] *(rec Lehman Center for the Performing Arts, NYC, NY)* ("Bravura") † M. de Falla:Suite populaire espagnole; Vida breve (sels); F. Kreisler:Liebesfreud; Liebesleid; Tambourin Chinois Vc & Pno; Tempo di Minuetto; W. A. Mozart:Serenade Vn, K.250/248b; Sarasate:Intro & Tarantella, Op. 43; R. Schumann:Romances Ob, Op. 94; Wieniawski:Capriccio-valse, Op. 7 SNYC ▲ 39133 [DDD] (11.97)
S. McNair (sop), D. Zinman (cnd), Baltimore SO † Sym 2 TEL ▲ 80312 [DDD] (16.97)
A. Moffo (sop), L. Stokowski (cnd), American SO † Canteloube:Songs of Auvergne (sels); H. Villa-Lobos:Bachiana brasileira 5 RCAV (Gold Seal) ▲ 7831 [ADD] (11.97)
S. Murphy (sop), N. Järvi (cnd), Royal Scottish National Orch † Bells; S. Taneyev:Duet for Romeo & Juliet; P. Tchaikovsky:Festival Coronation March CHN ▲ 8476 [DDD] (16.97)
E. Ormandy (cnd), Philadelphia Orch † Sym 2; Borodin:Nocturne Str Orch; Chopin:Études Pno; Nocturnes Pno; Liszt:Liebesträume, S.541; Mendelssohn (-Bartholdy):Lieder, Op. 34; Rimsky-Korsakov:Sadko (sels); Scheherazade, Op. 35; P. Tchaikovsky:Qt 1 Strs, Op. 11; Snow Maiden (sels); Songs SNYC ▲ 46355 [ADD/DDD] (9.97)
R. Orozco (pno), E. Waart (cnd), Royal PO † Con 2 Pno, Op. 18; Rhap on a Theme of Paganini, Op. 43; Sym 2 PPHI 2-▲ 38383 (17.97)
T. Otaka (cnd), BBC Welsh SO ("Whad' Ya Know About Rachmaninoff") † Con 2 Pno, Op. 18; Con 3 Pno, Op. 30; Liturgy of St. John Chrysostom, Op. 31; Prelude in c#, Op. 3/2; Preludes Pno; Rhap on a Theme of Paganini, Op. 43; Son 2 Pno, Op. 36; Sym 2 NIMB ▲ 4007 [DDD] (11.97)
H. Pittel (sax), J. Helmer (pno) [arr Pittel] ("Moving Along with Harvey Pittel") † Albinoni:Con in B Tpt; Creston:Son Sax, Op. 19; I. Dahl:Con A Sax; Ibert:Concertino da camera; P. Maurice:Tableaux de Provence CRYS ▲ 655 (15.97)
S. Rachmaninoff (cnd), Philadelphia Orch *(rec 1929)* † Isle of the Dead, Op. 29; Sym 3 PHS ▲ 9414 [AAD] (17.97)
S. Rachmaninoff (cnd), Philadelphia Orch [orchd Rachmaninoff] *(rec Apr 20, 1929)* ("Rachmaninoff Conducts Rachmaninoff") † Isle of the Dead, Op. 29; Sym 3 RCAV (Gold Seal) ▲ 62532 [ADD] (11.97)
S. Rachmaninoff (cnd), Philadelphia Orch † Isle of the Dead, Op. 29; Sym 3 MTAL ▲ 48038 (6.97)
S. Rachmaninoff (cnd), Philadelphia Orch [orchd Rachmaninoff] *(rec 1929)* ("Composer, Pianist, Conductor") † Con 4 Pno, Op. 40; Sym 3 GSE ▲ 785077 (m) [ADD] (16.97)
S. Rachmaninoff (pno), L. Stokowski (cnd), Philadelphia Orch † Con 2 Pno, Op. 18; Rhap on a Theme of Paganini, Op. 43 INMP ▲ 104 [ADD] (14.97)
J. Rodgers (sop), M. Popescu (mez), A. Naoumenko (ten), S. Leiferkus (bass), H. Shelley (pno) ("Complete Songs, Vol. 3") † Liturgy of St. John Chrysostom, Op. 31; Songs; Songs (14), Op. 34; Songs (6), Op. 38 CHN ▲ 9477 (16.97)

RACHMANINOFF, SERGEI (cont.)
Vocalise in e for Soprano, Op. 34/14 (1912, rev 1915) (cont.)
H. Shelley (pno) *(rec Highgate, England, July 24-27, 1994, Sept 19-20, 1994 & Jan 23-25)* † Again You Are Bestirred, My Heart; All-Night Vigil, Op. 37; Songs (12), Op. 14; Songs (12), Op. 21; Songs (14), Op. 34; Songs (15), Op. 26; Songs (6), Op. 38; Songs (6), Op. 4; Songs (6), Op. 8 CHN ▲ 9644 [DDD] (16.97)
L. Slatkin (cnd), St. Louis SO *(rec 1979)* † Bells; Capriccio bohémien, Op. 12; Isle of the Dead, Op. 29; Prince Rostislav; Rock; Russian Songs, Op. 41; Scherzo; Spring; Sym in d; Sym Dances, Op. 45 VB3 3-▲ 3002 [ADD] (14.97)
L. Stokowski (cnd), National PO *(rec London, Apr-May 1975)* † Sym 3 EMIC ▲ 66759 [ADD] (11.97)
L. Stokowski (cnd), New SO London, Norman Luboff Choir † J. S. Bach:Mass in b, BWV 232; St. Matthew Passion (sels); S. Barber:Agnus Dei; Carissimi:Vocal Music (misc); G. F. Handel:Messiah (choruses); W. A. Mozart:Requiem, K.626; Verdi:Requiem Mass RCAV ▲ 63450 (11.97)
E. Svetlanov (cnd), USSR SO [trans V. Kin for orch] *(rec Moscow, 1973)* † Syms (3) (comp) MELD 2-▲ 40064 [ADD] (13.97)
Y. Temirkanov (cnd), St. Petersburg PO † Sym 2 RCAV (Red Seal) ▲ 61281 (16.97)
O. Volkov (pno) [trans for pno Edward J. Leitner] *(rec Moscow, Russia)* † Con 1 Pno, Op. 1; Rhap on a Theme of Paganini, Op. 43 BRIO ▲ 111 (16.97)
E. Wild (pno) [solo pno trans Earl Wild] † Vars on a Theme by Chopin, Op. 22; Vars on a Theme by Corelli, Op. 42 CHSK ▲ 58 [DDD] (16.97)
M. Wordtmann (sax), N. Kitano (pno) *(rec Germany, Apr 1995)* † Albinoni:Cons Ob, Op. 9; Debussy:Rapsodie Sax; G. Fauré:Impromptus Pno; Sicilienne, Op. 78; Lully:Music of Lully; R. Noda:Improvisation I; M. Ravel:Pièce en forme de Habanera; Tombeau FSM ▲ 97237 [DDD] (15.99)
Were You Hiccoughing, Natasha? for Voice & Piano (1899)
S. Leiferkus (bass) ("Complete Songs, Vol 2") † Songs; Songs (12), Op. 21; Songs (15), Op. 26; Songs (6), Op. 4 CHN ▲ 9451 (16.97)

RADANOVICS, MICHAEL (1958-
Introversion for Orchestra
E. Theis (cnd), Austrian Chamber Sym *(rec Casino Zögernitz Vienna, Austria, June 6-19, 1995)* † D. Milhaud:Con Mar; Cortège funèbre, Op. 202; Simphoniette, Op. 363 MPH ▲ 56809 [DDD] (15.97)

RADIGUE, ELIANE (1932-
Kyema (6 intermediate states) for Synthesizer & Electronics [after The Tibetan Book of the Dead] (1988)
E. Radigue (elec/syn) XIRE ▲ 103 [ADD]
Songs (5) of Milarepa
R. Ashley (voc), K. Rinpoche (voc), E. Radigue (elec) *(rec 1981-1983)* LOV 2-▲ 2001 [ADD] (31.97)
Trilogie de la Mort (3 pieces) for Synthesizer [Kyema; Kailasha; Koumé] (1988-93)
E. Radigue (syn/elec) XIRE 3-▲ 119 [ADD]

RADJABOV, OCTAI (1943-
Tableaux (6) de la vie hébraïque for Piano
A. Alieva (pno) † Balakirev:Paraphrase Pno; S. Ibrahimova:Trans de chants populaires azerbaïdjans; Mustafa-Zade:Con Pno; S. Rachmaninoff:Pno Music (misc colls); Songs (6), Op. 38 GALL ▲ 832 [DDD]

RADULESCU, HORATIU (1942-
Concerto for Piano & Orchestra, Op. 90, "The Quest"
O. Stürmer (pno), L. Zagrosek (cnd), Frankfurt RSO *(rec live, Germany, June 8, 1996)* CPO ▲ 999589 [DDD] (13.97)

RADZYNSKI, JAN (1950-
Music of Radzynski
Aviv Str Qt *(Qt Strs) (rec 1991)*, A. Erez (pno) *(Canto Pno) (rec 1991)*, M. Beiser (vc), Z. Plesser (vc) *(Duets Vcs) (rec 1992)* † R. Helps:Music of Helps; T. Street:Trio Vn; D. Tredici:Fant Pieces; Trio Vn, Va & Vc CRI ▲ 649 [DDD] (16.97)

RAES, GODFRIED-WILLEM (20th cent)
Fuga Memento for Flute & Piano (1992)
K. De Fleyt (fl), M. Maes (pno) ("Logos Works") † Fuga Otto Nove; Jonas; Shifts; Spring '94; Darge:AlviCeba; Man-Mo; ShSh XIRE ▲ 117 [DDD]
Fuga Otto Nove for 4 Instruments (1991)
K. De Fleyt (fl), M. Maes (pno/syn) ("Logos Works") † Fuga Memento; Jonas; Shifts; Spring '94; Darge:AlviCeba; Man-Mo; ShSh XIRE ▲ 117 [DDD]
Jonas for Organ (1988)
A. De Masi (org) ("Logos Works") † Fuga Memento; Fuga Otto Nove; Shifts; Spring '94; Darge:AlviCeba; Man-Mo; ShSh XIRE ▲ 117 [DDD]
Shifts for Electronic Percussion Sounds (1988)
G. Raes (cmpt/syn) ("Logos Works") † Fuga Memento; Fuga Otto Nove; Jonas; Spring '94; Darge:AlviCeba; Man-Mo; ShSh XIRE ▲ 117 [DDD]
Spring '94 for Sampled Orchestra (1994)
G. Raes (cmpt) ("Logos Works") † Fuga Memento; Fuga Otto Nove; Jonas; Shifts; Darge:AlviCeba; Man-Mo; ShSh XIRE ▲ 117 [DDD]

RAFF, JOACHIM (1822-1882)
Abends Rhapsodie (idyll) for Orchestra
D. Avalos (cnd), Philharmonia Orch † Romeo & Juliet Ov; Sym 3 ASV ▲ 793 (16.97)
Chaconne in a for 2 Pianos, Op. 150 (1868)
T. Hitzlberger (pno), G. Shütz (pno) † C. Reinecke:Pno Music; Rheinberger:Duo Pnos, Op. 15 CPO ▲ 999106 [DDD] (14.97)
Chamber Music
Y. Butt (cnd), Philharmonia Orch—Cavatina [w. Yuko Nishino (vn)]; Canzona; Scherzino; Tarantella [all orchd] † Sym 5 ASV ▲ 1000 (16.97)
Concerto in c for Piano & Orchestra, Op. 185 (1873)
P. Aronsky (pno), M. Bamert (cnd), Basel RSO † Ode au printemps, Op. 76 TUD ▲ 7035 (12.97)
M. Ponti (pno), R. Kapp (cnd), Hamburg SO *(rec 1973)* ("The Romantic Piano Concerto, Vol. 4") † E. D. Albert:Con 2 Pno, Op. 12; Bronsart Von schellendorf:Con Pno, Op. 10; Liszt:Malédiction, S.121; Mosonyi:Con Pno; Stavenhagen:Con 1 Pno, Op. 4 VB2 2-▲ 5067 [ADD] (9.97)
Dame Kobold:Overture
U. Schneider (cnd), Slovak State PO Košice *(rec House of Arts Košice, Jan 14-17, 1994)* † Festmarsch, Op. 159; Jubel-Ov, Op. 103; Sym 6 MARC ▲ 8223638 [DDD] (13.97)
Ein feste Burg ist unser Gott for Orchestra, Op. 127 (1865)
U. Schneider (cnd), Slovak State PO Košice *(rec Mar 5, 1993)* † Sym 5 MARC ▲ 8223455 [DDD] (13.97)
Festmarsch for Orchestra, Op. 159
U. Schneider (cnd), Slovak State PO Košice *(rec House of Arts Košice, Jan 14-17, 1994)* † Dame Kobald (ov); Jubel-Ov, Op. 103; Sym 6 MARC ▲ 8223638 [DDD] (13.97)
Jubel-Overtüre in C for Orchestra, Op. 103 (1864)
U. Schneider (cnd), Slovak State PO Košice *(rec House of Arts Košice, Jan 14-17, 1994)* † Dame Kobald (ov); Festmarsch, Op. 159; Sym 6 MARC ▲ 8223638 [DDD] (13.97)
Konzert-Overtüre in F for Orchestra, Op. 123 (1862)
U. Schneider (cnd), Slovak State PO Košice *(rec Apr 27, 1993)* † Sym 7 MARC ▲ 8223506 [DDD] (13.97)
P. Steinberg (cnd), Basel RSO † Sym 10 TUD ▲ 786 [ADD]
Macbeth Overture for Orchestra (1879)
U. Schneider (cnd), Slovak State PO Košice *(rec House of Arts Košice, Oct 22-26, 1993)* † Romeo & Juliet Ov; Sym 2 MARC ▲ 8223630 [DDD] (13.97)
Octet in C for Strings, Op. 176 (1872)
Academy of St. Martin in the Fields Chamber Ensemble † Mendelssohn (-Bartholdy):Octet Strs, Op. 20 CHN ▲ 8790 [DDD] (16.97)
Ode au printemps in G for Piano & Orchestra, Op. 76 (1857)
P. Aronsky (pno), M. Bamert (cnd), Basel RSO † Con Pno TUD ▲ 7035 (12.97)
P. Aronsky (pno), J. Meier (cnd), Basel RSO † Sym 8 TUD ▲ 784 [ADD] (16.97)
Romeo & Juliet Overture for Orchestra (1879)
D. Avalos (cnd), Philharmonia Orch † Abends Rhap; Sym 3 ASV ▲ 793 (16.97)
U. Schneider (cnd), Slovak State PO Košice *(rec House of Arts Košice, Oct 22-26, 1993)* † Macbeth Ov; Sym 2 MARC ▲ 8223630 [DDD] (13.97)
Symphony No. 1 in D, Op. 96, "An das Vaterland" (1859-61)
S. Friedmann (cnd), Rhenish PO MARC ▲ 8223165 (13.97)
Symphony No. 2 in C, Op. 140 (1866)
U. Schneider (cnd), Slovak State PO Košice *(rec House of Arts Košice, Oct 22-26, 1993)* † Macbeth Ov; Romeo & Juliet Ov MARC ▲ 8223630 [DDD] (13.97)

RAFF, JOACHIM (cont.)
Symphony No. 3 in F, Op. 153, "Im Walde" (1869)
D. Avalos (cnd), Philharmonia Orch † Abends Rhap; Romeo & Juliet Ov — ASV ▲ 793 (16.97)
H. Davan (cnd), Milton Keynes City Orch † Sym 4 — HYP ▲ 55017 (9.97)
U. Schneider (cnd), CSSR State PO Košice † Sym 10 — MARC ▲ 8223321 (13.97)
Symphony No. 4 in G, Op. 167
H. Davan (cnd), Milton Keynes City Orch † Sym 3 — HYP ▲ 55017 (9.97)
Symphony No. 5 in E, Op. 177, "Lenore" (1872)
M. Bamert (cnd), Berlin RSO — KSCH ▲ 311013 [ADD] (16.97)
Y. Butt (cnd), Philharmonia Orch † Chamber Music — ASV ▲ 1000 (16.97)
U. Schneider (cnd), Slovak State PO Košice *(rec Apr 13-15, 1992)* † Ein feste Burg ist unser Gott, Op. 127 — MARC ▲ 8223455 [DDD] (13.97)
Symphony No. 6 in d, Op. 189 (1873)
U. Schneider (cnd), Slovak State PO Košice *(rec House of Arts Košice, Mar 1-3, 1993)* † Dame Kobald (ov); Festmarsch, Op. 159; Jubel-Ov, Op. 103 — MARC ▲ 8223638 [DDD] (13.97)
Symphony No. 7 in B♭, Op. 201, "In den Alpen" (1875)
U. Schneider (cnd), Slovak State PO Košice *(rec Mar 4-6 1993)* † Konzert-Ov, Op. 123 — MARC ▲ 8223506 [DDD] (13.97)
Symphony No. 8 in A, Op. 205, "Frühlingsklänge" (1876)
G. Lehel (cnd), Basel RSO † Ode au printemps, Op. 76 — TUD ▲ 784 [ADD] (16.97)
U. Schneider (cnd), Czech-Slovak State PO † Sym 9 — MARC ▲ 8223362 [DDD] (13.97)
Symphony No. 9 in e, Op. 208, "Im Sommer" (1878)
U. Schneider (cnd), Czech-Slovak State PO † Sym 8 — MARC ▲ 8223362 [DDD] (13.97)
Symphony No. 10 in f, Op. 213, "Zur Herbstzeit" (1879)
U. Schneider (cnd), CSSR State PO Košice † Sym 3 — MARC ▲ 8223321 (13.97)
F. Travis (cnd), Basel RSO † Konzert-Ov, Op. 123 — TUD ▲ 786 [ADD]

RAGAZZI, ANGELO (1680-1750)
Concerto Grosso in C for 2 Violins, Viola, Cello, Strings & Continuo
M. Rogliano (vn), A. Guerrini (vn), E. Pitone (va), A. Bertucci (vc), A. Cristiano (hpd), I. Caiazza (cnd) *(rec Mar 1996)* ("Neapolitan Instrumental Music of the 1700's") † Con Vn in a; Con Vn in B♭; Durante:Con Pno; A. Prati:Con Pno — KICC ▲ 396 [DDD] (17.97)
Concerto in B♭ for Violin, Strings & Continuo (1728)
M. Rogliano (vn), I. Caiazza (cnd) *(rec Mar 1996)* ("Neapolitan Instrumental Music of the 1700's") † Con Grosso; Con Vn in a; Durante:Con Pno; A. Prati:Con Pno — KICC ▲ 396 [DDD] (17.97)
Concerto in a for Violin, Strings & Continuo (1729)
M. Rogliano (vn), I. Caiazza (cnd) *(rec Mar 1996)* ("Neapolitan Instrumental Music of the 1700's") † Con Grosso; Con Vn in B♭; Durante:Con Pno; A. Prati:Con Pno — KICC ▲ 396 [DDD] (17.97)

RAGNARSSON, HJÁLMAR (1952-
Music of Ragnarsson
S. E. Magnúşdóttir (mez), H. Halldórsdóttir (vn), G. Gudnadóttir (vn), G. Kristmundsson (va), S. Halldórsson (vc), R. Korn (db), O. V. Albertsson (pno), S. A. Jónsdóttir (pno), H. Ragnarsson (pno), E. Erlendsdóttir (pno), M. H. Fridriksson (org), P. Sakari (cnd), Iceland SO—Meine kleine Freundin [In the Ballroom]; Lovers Duet; After the Concert; Meine kleine Freundin [Annie listens to the Radio]; Lif's Theme [On the Beach]; Lif's Theme II [Night Prayer]; Composing Ov [Vars I, II & III] ("Tears of Stone: Music from the Motion Picture") † Leifs:Music of Leifs — MFIC ▲ 605 [DDD]
Romanza for Flute, Clarinet & Piano (1981)
G. O. Gunnarsson (cnd) *(rec Feb-July 1995)* ("Animato: Icelandic Chamber Works") † Birgisson:Qt Strs, Op. 2; Grímsson:Tales from a Forlorn Fortress; A. Ingólfsson:Vink II; Leifs:Icelandic Dances; Másson:Elja; H. Tómasson:Trio Animato — MFIC ▲ 808 [DDD]

RAHBARI, ALEXANDER (20th cent)
Beirut for Flute Ensemble
Vienna Flautists ("Discover the Magic of the Flute") † Debussy:Chansons de Charles d'Orléans; Marche écossaise; Petite suite Pno; G. Fauré:Dolly — DI ▲ 920255 [DDD] (5.97)

RAHBEE, DIANNE GOOLKASIAN (1938-
Preludes (3) for Piano (or Piano 4-Hands), Op. 68 (1994)
N. K. Solomon (pno) *(rec Slippery Rock University, PA, Sept 1996)* ("Sunbursts") † Diemer:Fant Pno; Kenessey:Sunburst, Op. 33; Rudow:Rebecca's Suite; Schonthal:In Homage of...; S. Silver:Fant Quasi Theme & Vars; D. Thome:Pianismus — LEON ▲ 345 [DDD] (16.97)
Tapestry No. 1 for Orchestra, "Proclamation" (1991)
R. Black (cnd), Slovak RSO Bratislava † Althans:Valse Excentrique; M. Kessler:Con Pno; Leclaire:Haiku; W. T. McKinley:Andante & Scherzo; Rendelman:Chorale & Toccata; Stango:Sol' per Dirti Addio — MASM ▲ 2009 [DDD] (16.97)

RAHN, JOHN (1944-
Kali for Electronics (1986)
J. Rahn (elec) ("CDCM Computer Music Series, Vol. 12") † Miranda; Karpen:Denouement; Saxonomy; D. Thome:Ruins of the Heart — CENT ▲ 2144 [DDD] (16.97)
Miranda for Electronics (1990)
J. Rahn (elec) ("CDCM Computer Music Series, Vol. 12") † Kali; Karpen:Denouement; Saxonomy; D. Thome:Ruins of the Heart — CENT ▲ 2144 [DDD] (16.97)

RAICKOVICH, MILOŠ (1956-
Dream Quartet for Violin, Viola, Cello & Piano (1986)
Musica da Camera *(rec Yugoslavia, 1987)* ("New Classicism") † Happy Ov; Prelude & Fugue; Romances; Sym 1 — MODE ▲ 45 (17.97)
Happy Overture for Orchestra (1987)
M. Raickovich (cnd), Moscow SO *(rec Moscow, Aug 24-25, 1993)* ("New Classicism") † Dream Qt; Prelude & Fugue; Romances; Sym 1 — MODE ▲ 45 (17.97)
Prelude & Fugue for Keyboard (1987; arr 2 toy pianos, 1993)
M. L. Tan (prepared pno) *(rec Harmonic Ranch New York City, Apr 5, 1994)* ("New Classicism") † Dream Qt; Happy Ov; Romances; Sym 1 — MODE ▲ 45 (17.97)
Romances (3) for Violin & Orchestra (1988)
I. Frolov (vn), M. Raickovich (cnd), Moscow SO *(rec Moscow, Aug 24-25, 1993)* ("New Classicism") † Dream Qt; Happy Ov; Prelude & Fugue; Sym 1 — MODE ▲ 45 (17.97)
Symphony No. 1 (1992)
M. Raickovich (cnd), Moscow SO *(rec Moscow, Aug 24-25, 1993)* ("New Classicism") † Dream Qt; Happy Ov; Prelude & Fugue; Romances — MODE ▲ 45 (17.97)

RAID, KALJO (1922-
Symphony No. 1 in c (1944)
N. Järvi (cnd), Royal Scottish National Orch ("Music from Estonia, Vol. 1") † Eller:Dawn; Elegia; Pieces Str Orch — CHN ▲ 8525 [DDD] (16.97)

RAINIER, PRIAULX (1903-1986)
Ploërmel for Winds & Percussion (1973)
T. Reynish (cnd) *(rec BBC Studio 2, 1991)* ("Music by Rainier") † Qt Strs; Trio Strs — RDCL ▲ 7 (16.97)
Quartet for Strings (1939)
Edinburgh String Quartet *(rec BBC Studio 2, 1991)* ("Music by Rainier") † Ploërmel; Trio Strs — RDCL ▲ 7 (16.97)
Requiem for Chorus (1956)
M. Brewer (cnd), Great Britain National Youth Choir ("British Choral Music") † A. Rawsthorne:Partsongs; Routh:On a Deserted Shore — RDCL ▲ 11 [DDD] (16.97)
Trio for Strings (1966)
Redcliffe Ensemble members *(rec BBC Studio 2, 1991)* ("Music by Rainier") † Ploërmel; Qt Strs — RDCL ▲ 7 (16.97)

RAISON, ANDRÉ (1650-1719)
Le Vive-le-Roy des Parisiens for Organ [from 1st Organ Book]
P. Bardon (org) ("Organists at the Court of the Sun King") † Clérambault:Premier livre d'orgue; J. F. Dandrieu:Offertoire sur les Grands Jeux pour la Fête; L. Marchand:Pieces Org — PVY ▲ 784011 [ADD] (16.97)

RAJNA, THOMAS (1928-
Music for Violin & Piano (1957)
G. Pauk (vn), T. Rajna (pno) *(rec 1982)* ("The Hungarian Connection") † Qt Strs; E. von Dohnányi:Son Vn; Trans Pno — GSE ▲ 785050 [DDD] (16.97)
Quartet for Strings (1948)
Schwietering String Quartet *(rec 1995-96)* ("The Hungarian Connection") † Music Vn & Pno; E. von Dohnányi:Son Vn; Trans Pno — GSE ▲ 785050 [DDD] (16.97)

RAK, ŠTĚPÁN (1945-
Music for Guitar
V. Mikulka (gtr)—Farewell Finland; Romance; Temptation of the Renaissance † Koshkin:Prince's Toys — BIS ▲ 240 [DDD] (17.97)

RAKHMADIEV, ERKEGALY (1932-
Concerto for Violin & Orchestra (1985)
A. Musakodzhaeva (vn), P. Kogan (cnd), Moscow SO *(rec 1990)* † Dairabay; Kudasha-Duman; Martinů:Rhap-Con Va — CSN ▲ 810003 [DDD] (16.97)
Dairabay for Orchestra (1963)
P. Kogan (cnd), Moscow SO *(rec 1990)* † Con Vn; Kudasha-Duman; Martinů:Rhap-Con Va — CSN ▲ 810003 [DDD] (16.97)
Kudasha-Duman for Orchestra (1973)
P. Kogan (cnd), Moscow SO *(rec 1990)* † Con Vn; Dairabay; Martinů:Rhap-Con Va — CSN ▲ 810003 [DDD] (16.97)

RAKOV, NIKOLAI (1908-1990)
Concerto No. 1 for Violin & Orchestra (1944)
A. Hardy (vn), V. Dudarova (cnd), Russian SO ("Russian Violin Concertos") † Kabalevsky:Con Vn; V. Shebalin:Con Vn — OLY ▲ 573 (16.97)

RAKOWSKI, DAVID (1958-
Attitude Problem for Piano Trio (1996-97)
Triple Helix *(rec Recital Hall, Performing Arts Center-Purchse Coll., NY, Sept 18, 1997)* † Études; Hyperblue; Sesso e Violenza; Songs — CRI ▲ 820 [DDD] (16.97)
Études (20) for Piano
M. Nonken (pno)—No. 14, Martler; No. 7, Les Arbres Embués; No. 10, Corrente; No. 1, E-Machines; No. 2, Bam! *(rec Purchase College, NY, Sept 16, 1997)* † Attitude Problem; Hyperblue; Sesso e Violenza; Songs — CRI ▲ 820 [DDD] (16.97)
Hyperblue for Piano Trio (1991-93)
Triple Helix *(rec Purchase College, NY, Sept 17, 1997)* † Études; Attitude Problem; Sesso e Violenza; Songs — CRI ▲ 820 [DDD] (16.97)
Imaginary Dances for Chamber Ensemble (1986)
D. Palma (cnd) *(rec Mar 23, 1989)* † A. Anderson:Charrette; Blaustein:Commedia; S. Clement:Chamber Con — CRI ▲ 617 [DDD] (17.97)
Sesso e Violenza for Flute & Chamber Ensemble (1995-96)
T. H. O'Connor (fl), D. Fedele (a fl), P. Jarvis (cnd), Ensemble 21 *(rec Purchase College, NY, Mar 11, 1997)* † Études; Attitude Problem; Hyperblue; Songs — CRI ▲ 820 [DDD] (16.97)
Songs (3) for Voice & Piano [poems Louise Bogan] (1989)
J. Bettina (sop), J. Goldsworthy (pno) *(rec Purchase College, NY, Mar 11, 1997)* † Études; Attitude Problem; Hyperblue; Sesso e Violenza — CRI ▲ 820 [DDD] (16.97)

RAKSIN, DAVID (1912-
The Bad & the Beautiful (film music) for Orchestra (1952)
D. Raksin (cnd), MGM Studio Orch [full score & outtakes] *(rec Culver City, CA, 1952)* — RHI ▲ 72400 [AAD] (16.97)
Film Music
artists unknown *(suites from Laura)*, *(Forever Amber; The Bad & the Beautiful)* — RCAV ▲ 1490 (11.97)

RAMEAU, JEAN-PHILIPPE (1683-1764)
Abaris (Les Boréades) (selections)
T. Muster (org) [sels trans Thilo Muster] *(rec Souvigny, France, Dec 26-28, 1994)* ("Suites Pour Souvigny") † Beauvarlet-Charpentier:Magnificats, Op. 7; G. Bovet:Suite pour Souvigny; Guilain:Suite du quatrième ton; Marais:Pièces de viole [Book 2] (sels); Tombeau pour Lully; Rebel:Elémens — GALL 2-▲ 863 [ADD]
M. Térey-Smith (cnd), Capella Savaria [period instrs] *(rec Köszeg Castle, Mar 1995)* ("Orchestral Suites") † Naissance d'Osiris — NXIN ▲ 553388 [DDD] (5.97)
Acante et Céphise (selections)
F. Bruggen (cnd), Orch of the 18th Century [arr Wim ten Have as orchestral suite] † Fêtes d'Hébé (sels) — GLSS ▲ 921103 (18.97)
Anacréon (selections)
M. Térey-Smith (cnd) [period instrs] *(rec Koszeg Castle Knight Hall, July 2-12, 1995)* ("Orchestral Suites, Vol. 2") † Daphnis et Eglé (sels) — NXIN ▲ 8553746 [DDD] (5.97)
Anacréon (ballet in 1 act) [lib Cahusac] (1757)
W. Christie (cnd), Les Arts Florissants — HMA ▲ 1901090 (9.97)
Arlequinade (selections)
B. James (kbd) † Nouvelles suites; Nouvelles suites (sels); Pièces (5) de clavecin en concert; Pièces de clavecin; Songs — SNYC ▲ 39540 (9.97)
Le Berger fidèle (cantata) for Tenor, 2 Violins & Continuo (1728)
A. Monoyios (sop), C. Brandes (sop), H. Crook (ten), N. Wilson (b-bar) ("L'Amour règne") † Fêtes d'Hébé (sels) — NPT ▲ 85555 (16.97)
Cantatas (5) for Voice & Chamber Ensemble
New Opera Chamber Ensemble ("Complete Cantatas") — ASV ▲ 234 (31.97)
Castor et Pollux (opera in 5 acts) [lib P.-J. Bernard] (1737)
J.-C. Frisch (cnd) — ASTR 2-▲ 8624 (36.97)
A. Mellon (sop), V. Gens (sop), H. Cook (ten), J. Corréas (bass), W. Christie (cnd), Les Arts Florissants — HAM 3-▲ 901435 (36.97)
Castor et Pollux (selections)
W. Christie (cnd), Les Arts Florissants — HMA ▲ 1901501 (9.97)
Castor et Pollux (overture)
C. Rousset (cnd) † Fêtes de Polymnie (sels); Indes galantes (sels); Zaïs (sels) — PLOI ▲ 455293 (16.97)
Daphnis et Eglé (selections)
M. Térey-Smith (cnd) [period instrs] *(rec Koszeg Castle Knight Hall, July 2-12, 1995)* ("Orchestral Suites, Vol. 2") † Anacréon (sels) — NXIN ▲ 8553746 [DDD] (5.97)
Dardanus (selections)
B. Christoff (bass), E. Gracis (cnd), Bulgarian RSO, Bulgarian National Chorus ("Boris Christoff Recital") † Beethoven:Fidelio (sels); C. W. Gluck:Iphigénie en Aulide (sels); Verdi:Macbeth (sels) — FORL ▲ 16651 [AAD] (16.97)
V. Loriaut (org) *(rec St. Laurent d'Aubenas Church Org)* — GALL ▲ 768 [DDD] (19.97)
N. McGegan (cnd), Philharmonia Baroque Orch † Platée (sels) — CONI ▲ 51313 [DDD] (16.97)
La Dauphine in g for Keyboard [extemporized for the wedding of the Dauphin with Maria-Josepha of Saxony] (1747)
A. Fuller (hpd) † Nouvelles suites; Pièces (5) de clavecin en concert; Pièces de clavecin — REF ▲ 27 [DDD] (16.97)
F. Haas (hpd) † Nouvelles suites; Pièces (5) de clavecin en concert — CALL ▲ 9279 (18.97)
M. Shehori (pno) † Nouvelles suites; Pièces (5) de clavecin en concert; Pièces de clavecin; Premier livre de pièces de clavecin — CEMB ▲ 104 [DDD] (15.97)
Les Fêtes d'Hébé (selections)
F. Bruggen (cnd), Orch of the 18th Century [arr Wim ten Have as orchestral suite] † Acante et Céphise (sels) — GLSS ▲ 921103 (18.97)
A. Monoyios (sop), C. Brandes (sop), H. Crook (ten), N. Wilson (b-bar) ("L'Amour règne") † Berger fidèle — NPT ▲ 85555 (16.97)
Les Fêtes d'Hébé [Les Talents lyriques] (opera-ballet in prologue & 3 acts) [lib A. G. de Montdorge] (1739)
S. Daneman (sop), S. Connolly (cta), P. Agnew (ten), J. Fouchécourt (ten), T. Félix (bar), W. Christie (cnd), Les Arts Florissants — ERAT ▲ 21064 (33.97)
Gavotte for Orchestra
O. Klemperer (cnd), Philharmonia Orch † J. S. Bach:Suites Orch; Cherubini:Anacréon (ov); C. W. Gluck:Iphigénie en Aulide (ov); G. F. Handel:Con grosso, HWV 318 — TES ▲ 2131 (33.97)
Harpsichord Music (miscellaneous collections)
P. Sykes (hpd)—Allemande; Courante; Sarabande; Nouvelles suites; Nouvelles suites (sels); Gavotte; Doubles 1-6 [all from Pièces de clavecin] ("Music of Couperin & Rameau") † Pièces de clavecin; F. Couperin:Art de toucher le clavecin; Pièces de clavecin (sels) — TIT ▲ 229 (16.97)
Hippolyte et Aricie (musical tragedy in prologue & 5 acts) [lib S.-J. Pellegrin] (1733)
M. Minkowski (cnd), Musiciens du Louvres, Sagittarius Vocal Ensemble, V. Gens (sop), B. Fink (cta), J. Fouchécourt (ten), R. Smythe (bar), L. Naouri (b-bar) — PARC 3-▲ 45853 [DDD] (48.97)
L'Impatience (cantata) for Soprano, Cello & Continuo (1715-22)
A. Monoyios (sop), J. Richman (cnd), Concert Royal [FRE] † Clérambault:Musette — NON ▲ 71371 (9.97)
S. Piau (sop), C. Coin (va da gamba), W. Jansen (pno) *(rec Sept 14-16, 1994)* † Pièces (5) de clavecin en concert; Thétis — VCL (Music á Versailles) ▲ 61540 [DDD] (11.97)
L. Simoneau (ten), E. Werba (pno) *(rec live Salzburg, Aug 1959)* † Duparc:Songs; G. Fauré:Songs; G. F. Handel:Arias; J. Haydn:Canzonettas (12) — ORFE ▲ 460971 (16.97)

ROSSINI, GIOACCHINO (cont.)

Piano Music (complete)

S. Irmer (pno)—Péchés de vieillesse (sels) [Book 10, No. 6, "Petit caprice" (in C for Pno); Book 6, No. 3, "Momento homo" (in c); Book 6, No. 4, "Assez de Momento:dansons" (in F); Book 6, No. 7, "Une caresse à ma femme" (in G); Book 12, No. 7, "Un profond sommeil; Un reveil en sursaut" (in b/D for Pno); Book 6, No. 12, "Un enterrement en Carnaval" (in D for Pno); Book 6, No. 1, "Mon prélude hygienique du matin" (in C); Book 5, No. 9, "La lagune de Venise" (in G♭ for Pno); Book 9, No. 7, "Marche et réminiscences pour mon dernier voyage" (in A♭ for Pno)] *(rec Feb 2-4, 1997)* ("Piano Works, Vol. 1") MDG ▲ 6180654 [DDD] (17.97)

Il pianto delle Muse in morte di Lord Byron (cantata) for Voice, Chorus and Orchestra *(Includes music from Maometto II)*

Prague Virtuosi, Czech Chorus, T. Korovina (sop—Argene), A. Manzotti (cta—Alceo), W. Matteuzzi (ten—Fileno), H. Iturralde (bass—Elpino) *(rec 1997)* BONG ▲ 2236 [DDD] (16.97)

La pietra del paragone (comic opera in 2 acts) [lib L. Romanelli] (1812)

T. Carraro (sop—Fulvia), E. Gutierrez (mez—Baronessa Aspasia), S. Mingardo (cta—Clarice), W. Matteuzzi (ten—Giocondo), M. Camastra (bar—Pacuvio), P. Spagnoli (bar—Conte Asdrubale), G. Zarrelli (bar—Fabrizio), J. Fardilha (bass—Macrobio), B. Aprea (cnd), Graz SO, Sluk Chamber Chorus Bratislava *(rec 1993) (E,I lib texts)* BONG 2-▲ 2179 [DDD] (32.97)

A. Elgar (sop), B. Wolff (mez), E. Bonazzi (mez), J. Carreras (ten), J. Reardon (bar), R. Murcell (bar), A. Foldi (b-bar), J. Diaz (bass), N. Jenkins (cnd), Clarion Concerts Orch, Clarion Concerts Chorus [ITA] *(rec ca 1972)* ("La Petra del Paragone") VC 3-▲ 8043 [ADD] (39.97)

M. C. Nocentini (sop), H. Müller-Molinari (mez), A. Trovarelli (mez), P. Barbacini (ten), R. Scaltriti (bar), V. Di Matteo (bar), A. Svab (bar), P. Rumetz (bass), C. Desderi (cnd), Camerata Musicale Orch, Modeno Teatro Comunale Chorus [ITA] *(rec 1992)* NUO 2-▲ 7132 [DDD] (32.97)

Prelude, Theme & Variations for Horn & Piano (1857)

A. Civil (hn), G. Moore (pno) *(rec 1961)* † Mendelssohn (-Bartholdy):Midsummer Night's Dream (sels); W. A. Mozart:Cons (4) Hn TES ▲ 1102 (17.97)

Z. Zuk (hn), G. Dalinkevičius (cnd), Baltic Virtuosi [orchd] ("Horn Classics") † J. Haydn:Con 1 Hn; W. A. Mozart:Con 2 Hn, K.417; Telemann:Con Hn ZUK ▲ 310355 (10.97)

Quartets (6) for Flute, Clarinet, Horn & Bassoon

Paris Quartet † Theme & Vars Fl PVY ▲ 797112 (16.97)

La regatta Veneziana (3 canzonettas) for Voice & Piano

V. Genaux (mez), M. Dubé (pno) † Donna del lago (sels); Italiana in Algeri (sels); Petite messe solennelle; Siège de Corinthe (sels); Verdi:Giovanna d'Arco (sels) EPC ▲ 401 (16.97)

Ricciardo e Zoraide (opera in 2 acts) [lib Berio di Salsa] (1818)

N. Miricioiu (sop), D. Jones (mez), C. Smith (mez), A. Coote (mez), B. Ford (ten), W. Matteuzzi (ten), P. Nilon (ten), T. Spence (bar), A. Miles (bass), D. Parry (cnd), Academy of St. Martin in the Fields, Geoffrey Mitchell Choir OPR ▲ 14 (54.97)

Ricciardo e Zoraide (selections)

B. Ford (ten), D. Parry (cnd), Philharmonia Orch ("Romantic Heroes") † Donizetti:Alfredo il grande (sels); Rosmonda d'Inghilterra (sels); Mercadante:Virginia (sels); Meyerbeer:Étoile du nord (sels); G. Pacini:Carlo di Borgogna (sels); F. Ricci:Il Marito e l'amante (sels) OPR ▲ 202 (18.97)

Sacred Music

M. Callas (sop), M. Mesplé (sop), M. Caballé (sop), J. Anderson (sop), P. Lorengar (sop), E. Gruberová (sop), N. Gedda (ten), T. Gobbi (bar), S. Ramey (bass)—Petite messe solennelle; Stabat Mater *(rec 1958-89)* ("The Best of Rossini") † Arias; Ovs EMIC 2-▲ 67440 [ADD] (13.97)

R. Gandolfi (cnd), Prague Chamber Choir—O salutaris hostia; Ave Maria *(rec Prague, Sept 10-12, 1994)* † Petite messe solennelle; Songs DI 2-▲ 920324 [DDD] (11.97)

J. Lavender (ten), H. Williams (cnd), Bournemouth SO—Stabat Mater † Arias; Donizetti:Arias INMP (Classics) ▲ 6700102 (9.97)

Scala di seta:Overture

M. Halász (cnd), Zagreb Festival Orch *(rec Lisinski Concert Hall Zagreb, Croatia, Jan 9-11, 1989)* ("Famous Overtures") † Barbiere di Siviglia (ov); Cenerentola (sels); Elisabetta; Guillaume Tell (ov); Italiana in Algeri (ov); Semiramide (ov); Signor Bruschino (sels); W. A. Mozart:Apollo et Hyacinthus (sels), K.38; Bastien und Bastienne (sels); Clemenza di Tito (ov); Così fan tutte (ov); Don Giovanni (ov); Entführung aus dem Serail (ov); Finta giardiniera (ov); Idomeneo (ov); Lucio Silla (ov); Mitridate (Ov); Nozze di Figaro (ov); Rè pastore (sels); Schauspieldirektor (sels); Zauberflöte (ov); Verdi:Ovs & Preludes NXIN 4-▲ 504013 [DDD] (19.97)

A. Toscanini (cnd), BBC SO *(rec June 1938)* ("Toscanini in London 1935-39, Vol. 3") † Debussy:Mer Orch; E. Elgar:Enigma Vars, Op. 36; W. A. Mozart:Zauberflöte (ov) GRM2 ▲ 78613 (13.97)

A. Toscanini (cnd), La Scala Orch *(rec La Scala, Milan, Italy, Sept 16, 1948)* † Mussorgsky:Pictures at an Exhibition; P. Tchaikovsky:Romeo & Juliet; Verdi:Otello (sels) RY (The Radio Years) ▲ 99 (16.97)

J. Wedin (cnd), Stockholm Sinfonietta *(rec Stockholm, Sweden, May 1, 1981)* ("Classics for Chamber Orchestra") † S. Barber:Adagio Strs; Grandjany:Aria in Classic Style, Op. 19; H. C. Lumbye:Champagne Galop, Op. 14; W. Lutoslawski:Dance Preludes Cl & Pno; Sibelius:Canzonetta, Op. 62a; Suite mignonne, Op. 98/1; Swan of Tuonela; The Lover BIS ▲ 180 [AAD] (17.97)

Semiramide (opera in 2 acts) [lib Rossi after Voltaire] (1823)

I. Marin (cnd), London SO, Ambrosian Opera Chorus, C. Studer (sop), J. Larmore (mez), F. Lopardo (ten), S. Ramey (bass) DEUT 3-▲ 37797 [DDD] (48.97)

J. Sutherland (sop—Semiramide), M. Sinclair (cta—Arsace), O. Garaventa (ten—Idreno), M. Petri (bar—Assur), R. Bonynge (cnd), Rome RAI SO, Rome RAI Chorus ODRO 2-▲ 1136 (9.97)

Semiramide (selections)

J. Anderson (sop), M. A. Martinez (cnd), Emilia Romagna SO *(rec Parma, Italy, Nov 24, 1984)* ("June Anderson dal Vivo in Concerto") † V. Bellini:Sonnambula (sels); Donizetti:Lucia di Lammermoor (sels); Verdi:Battaglia di Legnano (sels); Traviata (sels) BONG ▲ 2504 (16.97)

C. Bartoli (mez), I. Marin (cnd), Venice Theater Orch, Venice Theater Chorus *(rec 1991)* ("A Portrait") † Cenerentola (sels); Maometto II (sels); G. Caccini:Amarilli mia bella; W. A. Mozart:Clemenza di Tito (sels); Così fan tutte (sels); Don Giovanni (sels); Nozze di Figaro (sels); Parisotti:Se tu m'ami; F. Schubert:Songs (misc colls) PLON ▲ 48300 [DDD] (17.97) ■ 48300 [DDD] (11.98)

H. von Karajan (cnd) ("The Young Karajan: The 1st Polydor Recordings, 1939-43") † Beethoven:Leonore (ov 3); Smetana:Moldau; Strauss (II):Fledermaus (ov); Verdi:Forza del destino (sels); R. Wagner:Meistersinger (preludes); C. M. von Weber:Freischütz (ov) GRM2 ▲ 78523 (13.97)

H. von Karajan (cnd) ("Karajan Orchestral Favorites") † Beethoven:Leonore (ov 3); Smetana:Moldau; Strauss (II):Fledermaus (sels); Verdi:Forza del destino (sels); R. Wagner:Meistersinger (sels); C. M. von Weber:Freischütz (sels) ENT (Sirio) ▲ 53007 (13.97)

V. Kasarova (sop), A. Fagen (cnd), Munich Radio Orch, Bavarian Radio Chorus—Ecco mi alfine in Babilonia; Ah! quel giorno ognor rammento † Armida (sels); Bianca e Falliero (sels); Cenerentola (sels); Donna del lago (sels); Italiana in Algeri (sels); Otello (sels) RCAV ▲ 57131 (16.97)

Mayr Ensemble [arr B. Carulli] *(rec Sept 1996)* † Beethoven:Vars Ww on La ci darem la mano, WoO 28; S. Mayr:Bagatelles Fl PHEX ▲ 9608 (16.97)

G. Merola (cnd), San Francisco Opera Orch—Sinf [incl introduction] *(rec San Francisco, CA, Oct 23, 1949)* † Gounod:Roméo et Juliette (sels); E. Granados:Goyescas (sels); Massenet:Manon (sels); G. Puccini:Bohème (sels); Gianni Schicchi (sels) URAN ▲ 120 (m) [ADD] (15.97)

L. Tetrazzini (sop) ("Luisa Tetrazzini: The London Recordings, Vol. 1 1907-14") † Barbiere di Siviglia (sels); V. Bellini:Puritani (sels); Sonnambula (sels); Donizetti:Linda di Chamounix (sels); Lucia di Lammermoor (sels); Verdi:Arias VOCA (Vocal Archives) ▲ 1122 (13.97)

Semiramide:Overture

M. Halász (cnd), Zagreb Festival Orch *(rec Lisinski Concert Hall Zagreb, Croatia, Jan 9-11, 1989)* ("Famous Overtures") † Barbiere di Siviglia (ov); Cenerentola (sels); Elisabetta; Guillaume Tell (ov); Italiana in Algeri (ov); Scala di seta (ov); Signor Bruschino (sels); W. A. Mozart:Apollo et Hyacinthus (sels), K.38; Bastien und Bastienne (sels); Clemenza di Tito (ov); Così fan tutte (ov); Don Giovanni (ov); Entführung aus dem Serail (ov); Finta giardiniera (ov); Idomeneo (ov); Lucio Silla (ov); Mitridate (Ov); Nozze di Figaro (ov); Rè pastore (sels); Schauspieldirektor (sels); Zauberflöte (ov); Verdi:Ovs & Preludes NXIN 4-▲ 504013 [DDD] (19.97)

Omnibus Wind Ensemble [arr Lars-Erik Lidström] *(rec 1996-97)* ("Opera Pearls") † Italiana in Algeri (ov); Bizet:Carmen (ov); W. A. Mozart:Così fan tutte (ov); Don Giovanni (ov); Don Giovanni (sels); Zauberflöte (ov); Zauberflöte (sels); C. Nielsen:Maskarade (orch sels); R. Wagner:Tannhäuser (ov); Tannhäuser (sels) OPU ▲ 19602 [AAD] (16.97)

S. Richman (cnd), Harmonie Ensemble New York [trans for wind ensemble] *(rec Rye, NY, 1992)* † Barbiere di Siviglia (ov); Guillaume Tell (ov); Beethoven:Fidelio (ov); W. A. Mozart:Entführung aus dem Serail (ov); C. M. von Weber:Freischütz (ov) MUA ▲ 4797 [DDD]

A. Toscanini (cnd), New York Philharmonic SO † Barbiere di Siviglia (ov); Italiana in Algeri (ov); Verdi:Traviata (sels); R. Wagner:Götterdämmerung (sels); Lohengrin (preludes) MTAL ▲ 48041 (6.97)

A. Toscanini (cnd), New York PO *(rec 1928-36)* ("Toscanini Edition, Vol. 4") † Barbiere di Siviglia (ov); Italiana in Algeri (ov); J. Brahms:Vars on a Theme by Haydn; Dukas:L'Apprenti sorcier; C. W. Gluck:Orfeo ed Euridice (dance); Mendelssohn (-Bartholdy):Midsummer Night's Dream (sels); Verdi:Traviata (sels) GRM2 ▲ 78817 (13.97)

ROSSINI, GIOACCHINO (cont.)

Serenade in E♭ for Flute, Oboe, English Horn, 2 Violins, Viola & Cello (1823)

Stanislas Ensemble † Andante e tema con variazioni Fl; Andante e tema con variazioni Va; L. Spohr:Nonet Strs & Ww, Op. 31 GALL ▲ 721 [DDD] (19.97)

Le siège de Corinthe (opera in 3 acts) [lib Balocchi & A Soumet] (1826)

G. Santini (cnd), Naples Teatro San Carlo Orch, Naples Teatro San Carlo Chorus, R. Tebaldi (sop), M. Pirazzini (mez), M. Picchi (ten), M. Petri (bar) *(rec live, Jan 2, 1952)* HDY 2-▲ 6001 (34.97)

Le siège de Corinthe (selections)

V. Genaux (mez), M. Dubé (pno)—L'ora fatal; Giusto ciel! In tal periglio † Donna del lago (sels); Italiana in Algeri (sels); Petite messe solennelle; Regatta Veneziana; Verdi:Giovanna d'Arco (sels) EPC ▲ 401 (16.97)

A. Toscanini (cnd), NBC SO—Ov *(rec 1939-45)* ("Toscanini Edition Vol. 3") † Barbiere di Siviglia (ov); Cenerentola (sels); Gazza ladra (ov); Guillaume Tell (ov); Verdi:Aida (sels); Forza del destino (sels); Traviata (sels); Vespri siciliani (ov) GRM2 ▲ 78809 (13.97)

Sigismondo (drama in 2 acts) [lib G. Foppa] (1814)

S. Ganassi (mez), N. Zanini (mez), B. Lazzaretti (ten), G. Prestia (bass), F. Pina (sgr), R. Bonynge (cnd), Venezze di Rovigo Conservatory of Music Orch, Autunna Trevigiano Chorus *(rec Oct 1992)* BONG 2-▲ 2131 [DDD] (32.97)

Il Signor Bruschino (selections)

M. Halász (cnd), Zagreb Festival Orch—Ov *(rec Lisinski Concert Hall Zagreb, Croatia, Jan 9-11, 1989)* ("Famous Overtures") † Barbiere di Siviglia (ov); Cenerentola (sels); Elisabetta; Guillaume Tell (ov); Italiana in Algeri (ov); Scala di seta (ov); Semiramide (ov); W. A. Mozart:Apollo et Hyacinthus (sels), K.38; Bastien und Bastienne (sels); Clemenza di Tito (ov); Così fan tutte (ov); Don Giovanni (ov); Entführung aus dem Serail (ov); Finta giardiniera (ov); Idomeneo (ov); Lucio Silla (ov); Mitridate (Ov); Nozze di Figaro (ov); Rè pastore (sels); Schauspieldirektor (sels); Zauberflöte (ov); Verdi:Ovs & Preludes NXIN 4-▲ 504013 [DDD] (19.97)

Les Soirées musicales (12 songs) for Voice (or 2 Voices) & Piano (ca 1830-35)

J. Aragall (ten), E. Arnaltes (pno)—La danza; La promessa † V. Bellini:Ariette da camera; Songs; Leoncavallo:Songs; G. Puccini:Songs; Tosti:Songs RTVE ▲ 65026 (16.97)

A. Augér (sop), J. Larmore (mez), M. Kimbrough (bar), D. Baldwin (pno)—La pesca † Péchés de vieillesse (sels); Songs ARA ▲ 6623 [ADD] (16.97)

I. Kertesi (sop), A. Ulbrich (mez), I. Prunyi (pno)—La pesca; La regata veneziana ("Songs & Duets") † Donizetti:Songs HUN ▲ 31544 [DDD] (16.97)

E. Söderström (sop), K. Meyer (mez), J. Eyron (pno)—La pesca; La regata veneziana *(rec Nacka, Sweden, Nov 1 & 3, 1974)* ("Elisabeth Söderström & Kerstin Meyer") † Songs; A. Dvořák:Moravian Duets, Opp. 20, 32, 38; Geijer:Songs; Kodály:Songs; H. Purcell:Come, ye sons of art, away, Z.323; Indian Queen (sels); King Arthur (sels); P. Tchaikovsky:Duets; Wennerberg:Songs *([ENG,ITA]text)* BIS ▲ 17 [AAD] (17.97)

R. Tebaldi (sop), L. Gardelli (cnd) —La regata veneziana ("Renata Tebaldi: The Concert at Lewisohn Stadium, 1966") † Boito:Mefistofele (sels); P. Mascagni:Cavalleria rusticana (sels); W. A. Mozart:Nozze di Figaro (sels); R. Rodgers:Carousel (sels); Verdi:Arias VAIA ▲ 1148 [AAD] (16.97)

Sonata for Harp

E. Wegner (hp) *(rec June 1994)* ("All' Italiana") † Allegretto Hp; Andante e tema con variazioni Va; Boccherini:Son Fl & Hp; Ciardi:Pifferaro, Op. 122; Donizetti:Son Fl & Hp; N. Rota:Sarabande & Toccata; Son Fl & Hp THOR ▲ 2243 [DDD] (16.97)

Sonatas (6) for String Quartet (ca 1804)

T. Benedek (cnd), Hungarian Virtuosi CO—No. 1 in G; No. 2 in A; No. 3 in C ("Vol. 1") NXIN ▲ 8554418 [DDD] (5.97)

T. Benedek (cnd), Hungarian Virtuosi CO ("Vol. 2") † Vars Cl NXIN ▲ 8554419 [DDD] (5.97)

I Musici † G. Bottesini:Gran Duo Concertant; Mendelssohn (-Bartholdy):Octet Strs, Op. 20; H. Wolf:Italian Serenade Str Qt PPHI (Duo) 2-▲ 456330 (17.97)

M. Rachlevsky (cnd), Kremlin CO *(rec July 1992)* CLAV ▲ 9222 [DDD] (16.97)

E. Wallfisch (vn), M. Marcus (vn), R. Tunnicliffe (vc), C. Nwanoku (db) HYP ▲ 66595 (18.97)

Songs

A. Augér (sop), J. Larmore (mez), M. Kimbrough (bar), D. Baldwin (pno)—Il trovatore † Péchés de vieillesse (sels); Soirées musicales ARA ▲ 6623 [ADD] (16.97)

C. Bartoli (mez), J. Levine (pno)—Péchés de vieillesse (sels) [Book 11, No. 6, "Aragonese" (for Voice & Pno); Book 11, No. 4, "A ma belle mère" (in A for Voice & Pno); Book 3, No. 2, "L'esule" (for Voice & Pf)]; La passeggiata; Bolero; Soirées musicales [La danza] ("An Italian Songbook") † V. Bellini:Songs; Donizetti:Songs PLON ▲ 455513 (17.97) ■ 455513 (11.98)

R. Gandolfi (cnd), Prague Chamber Choir—Péchés de vieillesse (sels) [Book 3, No. 10, "Cantemus Domino" (for Voices)] *(rec Prague, Czech Republic, Sept 10-12, 1994)* † Petite messe solennelle; Sacred Music DI 2-▲ 920324 [DDD] (11.97)

E. Söderström (sop), K. Meyer (mez), J. Eyron (pno)—Duetto buffo di due gatti *(rec Nacka, Sweden, Nov 1 & 3, 1974)* ("Elisabeth Söderström & Kerstin Meyer") † Soirées musicales; A. Dvořák:Moravian Duets, Opp. 20, 32, 38; Geijer:Songs; Kodály:Songs; H. Purcell:Come, ye sons of art, away, Z.323; Indian Queen (sels); King Arthur (sels); P. Tchaikovsky:Duets; Wennerberg:Songs BIS ▲ 17 [AAD] (17.97)

L. V. Terrani (mez), M. Carnelli (pno)—Addio di Rossini; Canzonetta spagnola; Ave Maria; Soirées musicales [La danza] ("Pietre Preziose") † Giovanna d'Arco; J. Haydn:Arianna a Naxos, H.XXVIb/2 KICC ▲ 196 [DDD] (17.97)

Songs & Song Cycles

V. Genaux (mez), J. D. Florez (ten), N. Ulivieri (ten), M. Benzi (cnd), Giuseppe Verdi SO Milan—Soirées musicales ("Rossiniana") † Arias AG ▲ 164 (18.97)

T. Ichihara (ten), L. Bavaj (pno)—Soirées musicales [L'orgia; La promessa; La partenza; La gita in gondola] *(rec 1995)* ("Italian Chamber Songs") † Arias; F. Gasparini:Arias; Tosti:Songs BONG ▲ 2519 [DDD] (16.97)

M. Pertusi (bass), C. Ferrarini (cnd) —Soirées musicales [Il rimprovero; La danza; La promessa; L'orgia; La gita in gondola; La partenza] ("Chamber Arias") † Arias MONM 2-▲ 90061 (34.97)

Stabat Mater for solo Voices, Orchestra & Chorus (1832; rev 1842)

M. Arroyo (sop), B. Wolff (mez), T. Del Bianco (ten), J. Diaz (bass), T. Schippers (cnd), New York PO, Camerata Singers † Verdi:Requiem Mass SNYC ▲ 53252 (14.97)

J. Björling (ten) ("Jussi Björling 1930-45: From Europe to the USA") † Donizetti:Elisir d'amore (sels); P. Mascagni:Cavalleria rusticana (sels); Ponchielli:Gioconda (sels) VOCA (Vocal Archives) ▲ 1115 (13.97)

M. Chung (cnd), Vienna PO, Vienna State Opera Chorus, L. Orgonasova (sop), C. Bartoli (mez), R. Giménez (ten), R. Scandiuzzi (bass) DEUT ▲ 49178 [DDD] (16.97)

P. Domingo (ten), J. Carreras (ten), L. Pavarotti (ten)—Cujus animam gementem ("The 3 Tenors, Vol. 1") † Cilea:Adriana Lecouvreur (sels); E. Elgar:Dream of Gerontius (sels); G. Puccini:Bohème (sels); Madama Butterfly (sels); Turandot (sels); Verdi:Ernani (sels); Luisa Miller (sels); Rigoletto (sels); Traviata (sels) PEG ▲ 186 (5.97)

H. Field (sop), D. Jones (mez), A. Davies (ten), R. Earle (bass), R. Hickox (cnd), City of London Sinfonia, London Sym Chorus [LAT] CHN ▲ 8780 [DDD] (16.97)

C. Malfitano (sop), A. Baltsa (mez), R. Gambill (ten), G. Howell (bass), R. Muti (cnd), Florence Maggio Musicale Orch, Florence Maggio Musicale Chorus † Petite messe solennelle EMIC (Doublefforte) 2-▲ 68658 (16.97)

L. Pavarotti (ten)—Cujus animam gementem † V. Bellini:Capuleti e i Montecchi (sels); Puritani (sels); Donizetti:Elisir d'amore (sels); Lucia di Lammermoor (sels); Verdi:Luisa Miller (sels) LALI ▲ 14308 (3.97)

L. Pavarotti (ten) PPHI (Double Decker) 2-▲ 455023 (17.97)

L. Pavarotti (ten), C. M. Giulini (cnd), Rome RAI SO—Cujus animam gementem *(rec Rome, Italy, Dec 22, 1967)* ("The Great Luciano Pavarotti") † V. Bellini:Puritani (sels); Donizetti:Elisir d'amore (sels); Lucia di Lammermoor (sels); G. Puccini:Bohème (sels); Turandot (sels); Verdi:Luisa Miller (sels); Rigoletto (sels) GDIS ▲ 63202 [ADD] (10.97)

C. Remigio (sop), J. D. Florez (ten), I. D. Arcangelo (bass), D. Barcellona (sgr), G. Gelmetti (cnd), Toscana Orch, Prague Chorus AG ▲ 161 (18.97)

C. Scimone (cnd) ERAT ▲ 17917 (9.97)

Tancredi (opera in 2 acts) [lib Gaetano Rossi after Voltaire] (1813)

S. Jo (sop—Amenaide), L. Lendi (mez—Roggiero), A. M. Di Micco (mez—Isaura), E. Podles (cta—Tancredi), S. Olsen (ten—Argirio), P. Spagnoli (bar—Orbazzano), L. Baert (vc), F. Coryn (db), E. Demeyere (hpd), A. Zedda (cnd), Collegium Instrumentale Brugense, Capella Brugensis *(rec Poissy Theatre & Centre Musical-Lyrique-Phonograph, Jan 26-31, 1994) (lib)* NXIN (Opera Classics) 2-▲ 660037 [DDD] (14.97)

E. Mei (sop—Amenaide), V. Cangemi (sop—Roggiero), M. Paulsen (mez—Isaura), V. Kasarova (mez—Tancredi), R. Vargas (ten—Argirio), H. Peeters (bass—Orbazzano), J. Maté (vn), G. Greiner (vc), I. Nawra (db), D. Syrus (hpd), R. Abbado (cnd), Munich RSO, Bavarian Radio Chorus *(rec Munich, July 17-30, 1995)* RCAV (Red Seal) 3-▲ 68349 [DDD] (46.97)

Tancredi (selections)

Italian Solisti ("Operisti") † Barbiere di Siviglia (sels); Italiana in Algeri (sels); A. Catalani:Sera, in Paganini; G. Puccini:Crisantemi DNN ▲ 18070 (16.97)

A. Zedda (cnd), Collegium Instrumentale Brugense, Capella Brugensis ("Italian Opera Choruses") † Donizetti:Elisir d'amore (sels); Leoncavallo:Pagliacci (sels); P. Mascagni:Cavalleria rusticana (sels); G. Puccini:Madama Butterfly (sels); Verdi:Choruses NXIN ▲ 8553963 [DDD] (5.97)

ROTA, NINO (cont.)
Trio for Clarinet, Cello & Piano
L. Paykin (vc), C. Russo (cl), B. Charlap (pno) ("Clarinet alla Cinema") † R. R. Bennett:Qnt Cl; R. Hyman:Sxt Cl PREM ▲ 1062 (16.97)
Trio for Flute, Violin & Piano (1958)
Ex Novo Ensemble † Casella:Serenata, Op. 46; Pizzetti:Trio Pno STRV ▲ 33312 [DDD] (16.97)
C. Parazzoli (vn), M. Carbotta (fl), C. Balzaretti (pno) *(rec Genova, Italy, Jan 1998)* ("Chamber Music for Flute") † Duets Fl & Ob; Pieces Fl; Qnt Fl; Son Fl & Hp DYNC ▲ 172 [DDD] (17.97)
Variations & Fugue on the Name B-A-C-H for Piano (1950)
M. F. Battista (pno) † Preludes Pno; Ginastera:Son 1 Pno, Op. 22 KICC ▲ 294 (17.97)
La visita meravigliosa [The Wonderful Visit] (opera in 3 acts) [lib Rota after H. G. Wells] (1970)
M. C. Nocentini (sop), A. Vespasiani (mez), A. Trevisan (mez), F. P. Castiglioni (ten), M. Frusoni (ten—Angel), G. Sarti (bar), G. L. Ricci (bar), D. Rigosa (bass—Reverend Hilyer), G. Grazioli (cnd), Rovigo Teatro Sociale SO, Rovigo Teatro Sociale Chorus *(rec Rovigo Teatro Sociale, Nov 1993)* LBD 2-▲ 2 (27.97)
ROTA, NINO (1911-1979)**& CARMINE COPPOLA** (20th cent)
The Godfather, Part III (film music) for Orchestra
artists unknown COL ▲ 47078 (11.97) ▮ 47078 (5.98) △ 47078 (15.97)
ROTH, BERTRAND (1855-1938)
Piano Music
F. Ruch (pno)—Capriccioso Pno, Op. 3/1; Degersheimer Weisen, Op. 23; Gavottina Pno, Op. 3/2; Gondoliera Pno, Op. 1; Nocturne Pno, Op. 26/2; Serenade Pno, Op. 4/2; Vars Pno, Op. 20; Waltz Pno PANC ▲ 510380 (17.97)
ROTHMAN, DANIEL (1958-
Cézanne's Doubt (chamber opera) for solo Voice, Clarinet, Trumpet, Cello & Electronics [text Rothman] (1996)
T. Buckner (bar), T. Mook (vc), D. Smeyers (cl), W. L. Smith (tpt), K. Celland (elec) NWW ▲ 80528 [DDD] (16.97)
ROTHROCK, CARSON (1935-
Vertigo (scherzo) for Orchestra
R. Ciorei (cnd), Black Sea PO *(rec Constanța Romania, 1995-96)* ("Black Sea Idyll") † Constantinides:Dedications; T. Flaherty:Intrada; Kessner:Images of Romania; Tomaro:Celestial Navigation; Toutant:Arcanae; Peregrinations II CPS ▲ 8648 [DDD] (16.97)
ROTOLI, AUGUSTO (1847-1904)
Songs
O. Linsi (ten), C. Walton (pno)—Gondola nera; Ho sognato; Il tuo pensiero ("Vola, O Serenata") † Donizetti:Arias; Songs; G. Puccini:Arias; Tosti:Songs; Verdi:Arias GALL ▲ 886 [ADD] (19.97)
ROTT, HANS (1858-1884)
Symphony in E (1878-80)
L. Segerstam (cnd), Norrköping SO BIS ▲ 563 [DDD] (17.97)
ROUGH ASSEMBLAGE (20th cent)
Music of Rough Assemblage
artists unknown—Mit Starken Schlagen Streckt Ich Dich; Construction et Demolition; Year One; Ring 'Em ("Construction & Deconstruction") AVAK ▲ 17 (21.97)
ROULLIER, RON (20th cent)
Music of Roullier
S. Henderson (cnd), New York Pops—Pops Are Marching on *(rec New York, NY, June 21, 1990)* ("From Berlin to Bernstein") † I. Berlin:Music of Berlin; L. Bernstein:Candide (ov); Music of Bernstein; On the Town (sels); West Side Story (sels); H. Carmichael:Music of Carmichael; E. Lecuona:Music of Lecuona; Van Heusen:Here's That Rainy Day CENT ▲ 2427 [DDD] (16.97)
ROUSE, CHRISTOPHER (1949-
Concerto for Cello & Orchestra
Y.-Y. Ma (vc), D. Zinman (cnd), Philadelphia Orch ("Premieres") † Danielpour:Con Vc; L. Kirchner:Con Vc SNYC ▲ 66299 (16.97)
Concerto for Flute & Orchestra (1993)
C. Wincenc (fl), C. Eschenbach (cnd), Houston SO—Ànhran *(rec Houston, TX, Sept & Oct 1996)* ("American Adagios") † S. Barber:Adagio Strs; Agnus Dei; Con Vn; Canning:Fant on Hymn Tune by Justin Morgan; A. Copland:Appalachian Spring (suite); Corigliano:Voyage Fl; G. Gershwin:Lullaby Str Qt; A. Hovhaness:Alleluia & Fugue, Op. 40b TEL ▲ 80503 [DDD] (16.97)
C. Wincenc (fl), C. Eschenbach (cnd), Houston SO *(rec Houston, Sept-Oct 1996)* † Phaethon; Sym 2 TEL ▲ 80452 [DDD] (16.97)
Concerto for Trombone & Orchestra (1991)
J. Alessi (trbn), M. Alsop (cnd), Colorado SO *(rec Denver, Feb 1995)* † Gorgon; Iscariot RCAV (Red Seal) ▲ 68410 [DDD] (16.97)
C. Lindberg (trbn), G. Llewellyn (cnd), BBC National Orch Wales *(rec Brangwyn Hall, Swansea, Wales, England, Dec 14-15, 1995)* ("American Trombone Concertos, Vol. 2") † C. Chávez:Con Trbn; A. R. Thomas:Meditation Trbn BIS ▲ 788 [DDD] (17.97)
Gorgon for Orchestra (1984)
M. Alsop (cnd), Colorado SO *(rec Denver, Nov 1995)* † Con Trbn; Iscariot RCAV (Red Seal) ▲ 68410 [DDD] (16.97)
Iscariot for Orchestra (1989)
M. Alsop (cnd), Colorado SO *(rec Denver, Nov 1995)* † Con Trbn; Gorgon RCAV (Red Seal) ▲ 68410 [DDD] (16.97)
Ku-Ka-Ilimoku for Percussion Quartet (1978)
Continuum Percussion Quartet † I. Bazelon:Fourscore; J. Cage:Third Construction; L. Harrison:Con Vn; E. Kurtz:Logo I; Verplanck:Petite Suite NWW ▲ 382 [AAD] (16.97)
Madrigals (4) for Voices & Chamber Ensemble
D. Neuen (cnd) , Graduate Chamber Singers *(rec Eastman Theater, NY, Feb 22, 1984)* ("Eastman American Music Series, Vol 1") † Mitternachtlieder; S. Albert:Into Eclipse ALBA ▲ 192 [ADD] (16.97)
Mitternachtlieder for Bass-Baritone & Chamber Ensemble (1979)
L. Guinn (b-bar), S. Hodkinson (cnd) *(rec Eastman Theater, NY, Nov 29, 1983)* ("Eastman American Music Series, Vol 1") † Madrigals; S. Albert:Into Eclipse ALBA ▲ 192 [ADD] (16.97)
Ogoun Badagris for Percussion Ensemble (1976)
Univ of Michigan Percussion Ensemble ("Border Crossing") † M. Daugherty:Lex; Hollinden:Whole Toy Laid Down; M. Kowalski:Vapor Trails; G. Shapiro:Sxt Kbd; Udow:Flashback; Vayo:Border Crossing EQLB ▲ 2 (16.97)
Phaethon for Orchestra (1986)
C. Eschenbach (cnd), Houston SO *(rec Houston, Sept-Oct 1996)* † Con Fl; Sym 2 TEL ▲ 80452 [DDD] (16.97)
Phantasmata for Orchestra (1981-85)
D. Zinman (cnd), Baltimore SO † Sym 1 NON ▲ 79230 (16.97)
Symphony No. 1 (1986)
D. Zinman (cnd), Baltimore SO † Phantasmata NON ▲ 79230 (16.97)
Symphony No. 2 (1994)
C. Eschenbach (cnd), Houston SO *(rec Houston, Sept-Oct 1996)* † Con Fl; Phaethon TEL ▲ 80452 [DDD] (16.97)
ROUSE, MIKEL (1957-
Dennis Cleveland (opera) (1996)
M. Rouse (sgr), M. Rouse (elec) NWW ▲ 80506 (16.97)
ROUSE, STEVE (1953-
Into the Light for Orchestra (1991)
J. López-Cobos (cnd), Cincinnati SO *(rec Music Hall Cincinnati, Jan 21 & 26, 1997)* ("Into the Light") † D. Brubeck:Joy in the Morning (Suite); Canning:Fant on Hymn Tune by Justin Morgan; A. Hovhaness:Sym 2; R. Strauss:Tod und Verklärung, Op. 24 TEL ▲ 80462 [DDD] (16.97)
ROUSH, DEAN K. (1952-
The Dove Descending for Flute & Organ
F. Shelly (fl), S. Egler (org) *(rec Wiedemann Recital Hall, Wichita State University, KS)* ("The Dove Descending") † M. Albrecht:Psalms; Berlinski:Adagietto; Ochse:Prelude & Fugue Ft & Org; B. W. Sanders:Pieces Fl; J. Weaver:Rhapsody; G. Young:Triptych SUMM ▲ 174 [DDD] (16.97)
ROUSSAKIS, NICOLAS (1934-1994)
Ephemeris for String Quartet (1979)
Group for Contemporary Music String Quartet *(rec 1981)* † Hymn to Apollo CRI ▲ 624 [ADD] (17.97)
Fire & Earth & Water & Air for Orchestra (1983)
P. Dunkel (cnd), American Composers Orch † E. Carter:Sym 1; F. Thorne:Sym 5 CRI ▲ 552 [DDD] (16.97)
Hymn to Apollo for Chamber Ensemble (1989)
D. Stock (cnd) *(rec 1990)* † Ephemeris CRI ▲ 624 [ADD] (17.97)
MI e FA for Piano (1991)
X. Pan (pno) *(rec American Academy of Arts & Letters Auditorium New, Sept 19, 1994)* ("Chamber & Solo Works") † Night Speech; Pas de deux; Short Pieces Fls; Son Hpd; Trigono CRI ▲ 709 [DDD] (16.97)

ROUSSAKIS, NICOLAS (cont.)
Night Speech for Chorus & Percussion (1968)
D. Warland (cnd), Macalester Concert Choir *(rec St. Paul, MN, Nov 1969)* ("Chamber & Solo Works") † MI e FA; Pas de deux; Short Pieces Fls; Son Hpd; Trigono CRI ▲ 709 [DDD] (16.97)
Pas de deux for Violin & Piano (1985)
R. Mao (vn), X. Pan (pno) *(rec American Academy of Arts & Letters Auditorium New, Sept 19, 1994)* ("Chamber & Solo Works") † MI e FA; Night Speech; Short Pieces Fls; Son Hpd; Trigono CRI ▲ 709 [DDD] (16.97)
Short Pieces (6) for 2 Flutes (1969)
H. Sollberger (fl), S. Sollberger (fl) *(rec 1975)* ("Chamber & Solo Works") † MI e FA; Night Speech; Pas de deux; Son Hpd; Trigono CRI ▲ 709 [DDD] (16.97)
Sonata for Harpsichord (1967)
H. Chaney (hpd) *(rec New York, May 1970)* ("Chamber & Solo Works") † MI e FA; Night Speech; Pas de deux; Short Pieces Fls; Trigono CRI ▲ 709 [DDD] (16.97)
Trigono for Trombone, Vibraphone & Drums (1986)
R. Borror (trbn), S. Paysen (vib), G. Charnon (perc) ("Chamber & Solo Works") † MI e FA; Night Speech; Pas de deux; Short Pieces Fls; Son Hpd CRI ▲ 709 [DDD] (16.97)
ROUSSEAU, JEAN-JACQUES (1712-1778)
Le Devin du village (opera in 1 act) (1752)
E. Kirchner (sop), M. D. Vries (sgr), D. Chou (sgr), R. Clemencic (cnd), Alpe Adria Ensemble [FRE] † Beethoven:Songs; W. A. Mozart:Bastien und Bastienne, K.50 NUO 2-▲ 7106 [DDD] (32.97)
Le printemps di Vivaldi for Flute
C. Ferrarini (fl) ("Musica per Flauto e Clavicembalo") † G. F. Handel:Royal Fireworks Music, HWV 351; Water Music, HWV 348-50; Vivaldi:Cons Vn Strs, Op. 8/1-4 STRV ▲ 33301 [DDD] (16.97)
ROUSSEAU, SAMUEL (1853-1904)
Organ Music
D. Modersohn (org)—Prélude in E; Prière in D; Écho in b; Double Thème Varié in c ("Historic Organ of St. Gertraudkirche in Frankfurt on Oder") † M. Reger:Pieces (12) Org, Op. 59; R. Schumann:Fugues on B-A-C-H Org, Op. 60 THOR ▲ 2285 [DDD] (16.97)
ROUSSEL, ALBERT (1869-1937)
L'Accueil des muses (in memoriam Debussy) for Piano (1920)
E. Katahn (pno) *(rec Vanderbilt University Nashville, TN)* † Heures passent, Op. 1; Pieces Pno, Op. 49; Rustiques, Op. 5; Sonatine Pno, Op. 16; Suite Pno, Op. 14 GAS ▲ 295 (16.97)
Andante & Scherzo for Flute & Piano, Op. 51
K. Redel (fl), N. Lee (pno) [Ed. Durand] *(rec France, Nov 1982)* ("French Music for Flute & Piano") † Aria Fl; Joueurs de flûte, Op. 27; Debussy:Syrinx Fl; Ibert:Jeux; D. Milhaud:Sonatina Fl & Pno, Op. 76; F. Poulenc:Son Fl; M. Ravel:Pièce en forme de Habanera ARN ▲ 68238 [AAD] (16.97)
Aria for Flute (or Oboe or Clarinet or Viola or Cello) & Piano (or Orchestra) [arr A. Hoérée from *Vocalise No. 2*]
J. Hilton (cl), K. Swallow (pno) † Debussy:Première rapsodie Cl; D. Milhaud:Duo concertante Cl & Pno, Op. 351; F. Poulenc:Son Cl & Pno; M. Ravel:Pièce en forme de Habanera; Saint-Saëns:Son Cl CHN (Collect) ▲ 6589 [DDD] (12.97)
K. Redel (fl), N. Lee (pno) [Ed. Leduc] *(rec France, Nov 1982)* ("French Music for Flute & Piano") † Andante & Scherzo Fl, Op. 51; Joueurs de flûte, Op. 27; Debussy:Syrinx Fl; Ibert:Jeux; D. Milhaud:Sonatina Fl & Pno, Op. 76; F. Poulenc:Son Fl; M. Ravel:Pièce en forme de Habanera ARN ▲ 68238 [AAD] (16.97)
Bacchus et Ariane (ballet in 2 acts) for Orchestra, Op. 43 (1930)
I. Markevitch (cnd), Lamoureux Orch † Honegger:Sym 5; D. Milhaud:Choëphores, Op. 24 DEUT (The Originals) ▲ 449748 (m) [ADD] (11.97)
J. P. Tortelier (cnd), BBC PO † Festin de l'araignée, Op. 17 CHN ▲ 9494 (16.97)
Bacchus et Ariane:Suite No. 2
N. Järvi (cnd), Detroit SO † Sinfonietta Strs, Op. 52; Sym 3; Sym 4 CHN ▲ 7007 [DDD] (13.97)
C. Munch (cnd), French National Orch ("Charles Munch Edition, Vol 8.") † Sym 3; Sym 4 VAL ▲ 4832 [ADD] (12.97)
E. Ormandy (cnd), Philadelphia Orch † G. Fauré:Pavane; Pelléas et Mélisande, Op. 80; Ibert:Divert Orch; Escales SNYC (Essential Classics) ▲ 62644 (7.97) ▮ 62644 (3.98)
Chamber Music
M. Bjerno (sop), A. S. Hansen (vn), Z. Carmelli (va), P. Zelazny (va), N. Ullner (vc), M. Dabelsteen (db), T. L. Christiansen (fl), B. C. Nielsen (ob), N. Thomsen (cl), A. Svendsen (bn), K. Christensen (tpt), P. Jacobsen (hn), T. Rehling (hp), P. Salo (pno), M. Mogensen (pno), P. Jensen (perc)—Divert Ww, Op. 6; Trio Fl, Op. 40; Joueurs de flûte, Op. 27; Sérénade, Op. 30; Marchand de sable qui passe, Op. 13; Andante & Scherzo Fl, Op. 51; Poèmes de Ronsard, Op. 26; Aria Fl; Elpénor; Pipe ("Complete Chamber Music with Flute") KPT 2-▲ 32218 [DDD]
Concerto in G for Piano & Orchestra, Op. 36 (1927)
S. Cápová (pno), T. Frešo (cnd), Slovak PO † J. Françaix:Concertino; Saint-Saëns:Con 2 Pno, Op. 22 PC ▲ 267194 [DDD] (2.97)
S. Lemelin (pno), M. Bernardi (cnd), CBC Vancouver Orch † G. Fauré:Ballade Pno, Op. 19; Fant Pno, Op. 111; Saint-Saëns:Con 2 Pno, Op. 22 CBC ▲ 5178 (16.97)
J. Michiels (pno), F. Bollon (cnd), Flanders SO *(rec 1996-97)* † Pour une fête de printemps, Op. 22; Sym 1 CYPR ▲ 2620 (17.97)
Divertissement for Wind Quintet & Piano, Op. 6 (1906)
Hexagon *(rec Aaron Copland School of Music, Queens College, NYC, NY, 1996)* ("Les Petits Nerveux") † J. Françaix:Petits nerveux; F. Poulenc:Sxt Pno; Trio Ob; Saint-Saëns:Caprice sur des airs danoises et russes, Op. 79; Tarantelle, Op. 6 BRID ▲ 9079 [DDD] (17.97)
G. Koukl (pno), Prague National Theater Wind Quintet † J. Françaix:Heure du berger for Orch; Ibert:Pièces brèves Ww; Indy:Sarabande et menuet; D. Milhaud:Son Fl, Cl, Ob & Pno, Op. 47; Saint-Saëns:Caprice sur des airs danoises et russes, Op. 79 NUO ▲ 7268 (16.97)
Orphée Piano & Wind Quintet *(rec Saitama, Japan, July 1992)* † G. Fauré:Pavane; Sicilienne, Op. 78; F. Poulenc:Aubade; Suite française; Sxt Pno ARTA ▲ 61 (16.97)
Evocations for Alto, Tenor, Baritone, Orchestra & Chorus (1910-11)
M. Mrázová (cta), Z. Svehla (ten), J. Jindrák (bar), Z. Košler (cnd), Czech PO, Czech Phil Chorus ("Serenades") † J. Brahms:Serenade 1 Orch, Op. 11; Serenade 2 Orch, Op. 16; Fibich:Fall of Arkona (ov); Komenský, Op. 34; Toman & the Wood Nymph, Op. 49; Záboj, Slavoj & Luděk, Op. 37; J. Suk:Praga; Summer's Tale, Op. 29 SUR ▲ 111823 [AAD]
Le Festin de l'araignée [The Spider's Feast] (ballet in 1 act) for Orchestra, Op. 17 (1912)
C. Munch (cnd), London PO, C. Munch (cnd), Paris Conservatory Société des Concerts Orch *(rec 1946-47)* ("Munch, Vol. 8") † Little Suite, Op. 39; Suite Orch, Op. 33; Debussy:Berceuse héroïque Pno; Images Orch LYS ▲ 438
W. Straram (cnd), Straram Concerts Orch *(rec 1928-30)* † Debussy:Prélude à l'après-midi d'un faune; Ibert:Escales; M. Ravel:Alborada del gracioso; Daphnis et Chloé (suite 2) VAIA ▲ 1074 (17.97)
J. P. Tortelier (cnd), BBC PO † Bacchus et Ariane, Op. 43 CHN ▲ 9494 (16.97)
Le Festin de l'araignée:Suite No. 2
A. Toscanini (cnd), NBC SO *(rec 1938-46)* † Debussy:Prélude à l'après-midi d'un faune; Dukas:Ariane et Barbe-Bleue (suite); C. Franck:Eolides, M.43; Psyché (sels); Roger-Ducasse:Sarabande URAN ▲ 107 (m) [DDD] (15.97)
Des heures passent for Piano, Op. 1 (1898)
E. Katahn (pno) *(rec Vanderbilt University Nashville, TN)* † Accueil des muses; Pieces Pno, Op. 49; Rustiques, Op. 5; Sonatine Pno, Op. 16; Suite Pno, Op. 14 GAS ▲ 295 (16.97)
Impromptu for Harp, Op. 21 (1919)
F. Bartholomée (hp) ("Harp Landscapes") † Debussy:Danses sacrée et profane; Enescu:Allegro de Concert; Koechlin:Nocturne Hp, Op. 33; G. C. Menotti:Cantilena e scherzo Hp; Rohozinski:Suite brève; Vierne:Rhap Hp CYPR ▲ 1615 [DDD] (17.97)
Joueurs de flûte for Flute & Piano, Op. 27 (1924)
K. Redel (fl), N. Lee (pno) [Ed. Durand] *(rec France, Nov 1982)* ("French Music for Flute & Piano") † Andante & Scherzo Fl, Op. 51; Aria Fl; Debussy:Syrinx Fl; Ibert:Jeux; D. Milhaud:Sonatina Fl & Pno, Op. 76; F. Poulenc:Son Fl; M. Ravel:Pièce en forme de Habanera ARN ▲ 68238 [AAD] (16.97)
Little Suite for Orchestra, Op. 39 (1929)
C. Munch (cnd), London PO, C. Munch (cnd), Paris Conservatory Société des Concerts Orch *(rec 1946-47)* ("Munch, Vol. 8") † Festin de l'araignée, Op. 17; Suite Orch, Op. 33; Debussy:Berceuse héroïque Pno; Images Orch LYS ▲ 438
Pieces (3) for Piano, Op. 49 (1933)
E. Katahn (pno) *(rec Vanderbilt University Nashville, TN)* † Accueil des muses; Heures passent, Op. 1; Rustiques, Op. 5; Sonatine Pno, Op. 16; Suite Pno, Op. 14 GAS ▲ 295 (16.97)
Poèmes de Ronsard (2) for Soprano & Flute, Op. 26 (1924)
Scarborough Chamber Players † A. Blank:Poems; R. Schumann:Faschingsschwank, Op. 26; L. Spohr:German Songs, Op. 103; Starer:Songs of Youth & Age; H. Villa-Lobos:Bachiana brasileira 6 CENT ▲ 2106 [DDD] (16.97)

ROUSSEL, ALBERT (cont.)

Pour une fête de printemps (symphonic poem) for Orchestra, Op. 22 (1921)

F. Bollon (cnd), Flanders SO *(rec 1996-97)* † Con Pno, Op. 36; Sym 1 CYPR ▲ 2620 (17.97)

Rustiques (3) for Piano, Op. 5 (1904-06)

E. Katahn (pno) *(rec Vanderbilt University Nashville, TN)* † Accueil des muses; Heures passent, Op. 1; Pieces Pno, Op. 49; Sonatine Pno, Op. 16; Suite Pno, Op. 14 GAS ▲ 295 (16.97)

Sérénade for Flute, Violin, Viola, Cello & Harp, Op. 30 (1925)

O. Ellis (hp), Melos Ensemble † Debussy:Son Fl; M. Ravel:Intro & Allegro Hp; Ropartz:Prélude, Marine et Chanson PLON (Classic Sound) ▲ 452891 (11.97)

S. Kang (hp), Academy of St. Martin in the Fields Chamber Ensemble † Debussy:Danses sacrée et profane; Son Fl; M. Ravel:Intro & Allegro Hp; Saint-Saëns:Fant Vn CHN ▲ 8621 [DDD] (16.97)

Sinfonietta in d for Strings, Op. 52 (1934)

N. Järvi (cnd), Detroit SO † Bacchus et Ariane (suite 2); Sym 3; Sym 4 CHN ▲ 7007 [DDD] (13.97)

P. Järvi (cnd), Tapiola Sinfonietta *(rec June 4 & 9, 1993)* † Ibert:Divert Orch; Jolivet:Con Fl BIS ▲ 630 [DDD] (17.97)

O. Vlček (cnd) *(rec Prague, Nov 22-25, 1993)* † E. Elgar:Serenade Strs, Op. 20; E. Grieg:Holberg Suite Pno, Op. 40; O. Respighi:Ancient Airs & Dances DI ▲ 920236 [DDD] (5.97)

Sonata No. 2 in A for Violin & Piano, Op. 28

P. Schmidt (vn), A. van Den Bossche (pno) † Enescu:Son 3 Vn, Op. 25; Tournemire:Sonate-poème, Op. 65 CYPR ▲ 2617 (17.97)

Sonatine for Piano, Op. 16 (1912)

E. Katahn (pno) *(rec Vanderbilt University Nashville, TN)* † Accueil des muses; Heures passent, Op. 1; Pieces Pno, Op. 49; Rustiques, Op. 5; Suite Pno, Op. 14 GAS ▲ 295 (16.97)

Songs

A. Martel (sop), M. Bourdeau (pno)—Poèmes, Op. 8 [No. 3, Nuit d'automne]; Le jardin mouillé; Mélodies, Op. 20 [Sarabande; Le bachelier de Salamanque]; Light; Flammes, Op. 10 *(rec June 1993)* ("French Songs") † E. Chausson:Songs; Debussy:Songs; Mercure:Dissidence SNE ▲ 588 (16.97)

Suite in F for Orchestra, Op. 33 (1926)

L. D. Froment (cnd), Luxembourg RSO *(rec 1978)* † M. Constant:Turner; Daniel-Lesur:Andrea del Sarto; H. Tomasi:Fanfares Liturgiques CIT ▲ 88106 [ADD] (15.97)

C. Munch (cnd), London PO, C. Munch (cnd), Paris Conservatory Société des Concerts Orch *(rec 1946-47)* ("Munch, Vol. 8") † Festin de l'araignée, Op. 17; Little Suite, Op. 39; Debussy:Berceuse héroïque Pno; Images Orch LYS ▲ 438

P. Paray (cnd), Detroit SO † Chabrier:Bourée fantasque; España; Gwendoline (ov); Joyeuse marche; Roi malgré lui (sels); Suite pastorale MRCR ▲ 34303 [ADD] (11.97)

Suite in f# for Piano, Op. 14 (1909-10)

E. Katahn (pno) *(rec Vanderbilt University Nashville, TN)* † Accueil des muses; Heures passent, Op. 1; Pieces Pno, Op. 49; Rustiques, Op. 5; Sonatine Pno, Op. 16 GAS ▲ 295 (16.97)

Symphony No. 1, Op. 7, "La poème de la forêt" (1904-06)

F. Bollon (cnd), Flanders SO *(rec 1996-97)* † Con Pno, Op. 36; Pour une fête de printemps, Op. 22 CYPR ▲ 2620 (17.97)

Symphony No. 3 in g, Op. 42 (1929-30)

L. Bernstein (cnd), New York PO † Honegger:Pacific 231; Rugby; D. Milhaud:Choëphores, Op. 24 SNYC (Masterworks Heritage) ▲ 62352 (12.97)

N. Järvi (cnd), Detroit SO † Bacchus et Ariane (suite 2); Sinfonietta Strs, Op. 52; Sym 4 CHN ▲ 7007 [DDD] (13.97)

C. Munch (cnd), French National Orch ("Charles Munch Edition, Vol 8.") † Bacchus et Ariane (suite 2); Sym 4 VAL ▲ 4832 [ADD] (12.97)

Symphony No. 4 in A, Op. 53 (1934)

N. Järvi (cnd), Detroit SO † Bacchus et Ariane (suite 2); Sinfonietta Strs, Op. 52; Sym 3 CHN ▲ 7007 [DDD] (13.97)

C. Munch (cnd), French National Orch ("Charles Munch Edition, Vol 8.") † Bacchus et Ariane (suite 2); Sym 3 VAL ▲ 4832 [ADD] (12.97)

P. Verrot (cnd), Quebec SO FL ▲ 23052 (16.97)

Trio for Flute, Viola & Cello, Op. 40 (1929)

K. Plummer (va), C. Meints (vc), R. Willoughby (fl) † G. Pierné:Canzonetta Fl & Vc; Son da camera Fl, Op. 48; M. Reger:Serenade; Suite Vn Pno, Op. 103a GAS ▲ 1003 [AAD] (12.97)

Trio for Strings, Op. 58 (1937)

Jerusalem String Trio ("French Impressions") † Caplet:Conte fantastique; Debussy:Son Fl; M. Ravel:Intro & Allegro Hp CACI ▲ 210019 (5.97)

ROUTH, FRANCIS (1927-

On a Deserted Shore for Soprano, 2 Pianos, Percussion & 2 Choruses (1975)

M. Brewer (cnd), Great Britain National Youth Choir ("British Choral Music") † Rainier:Requiem; A. Rawsthorne:Partsongs RDCL ▲ 11 [DDD] (16.97)

Quartet for Oboe & Strings, Op. 34 (1977)

Redcliffe Ensemble *(rec BBC Studio 2, June 1987)* ("British Chamber Music for Oboe & Strings") † Tragic Interludes, Op. 43; Lutyens:Driving out the Death, Op. 81; A. Rawsthorne:Qt Ob; Theme & Vars Vns RDCL ▲ 6 (16.97)

Quintet for Clarinet & Strings (1994)

Redcliffe Ensemble ("British Chamber Music for Clarinet & Strings") † A. Bliss:Qnt Cl, T.50; A. Rawsthorne:Qnt Cl RDCL ▲ 10 [DDD] (16.97)

A Sacred Tetralogy for Organ [The Manger Throne; Lumen Christi; Aeterne Rex Altissime], Opp. 3, 10 & 15 (1959-70)

C. Bowers-Broadbent (org) *(rec Coventry Cathedral Org)* ("British Organ Music 1") RDCL ▲ 12 [DDD] (16.97)

Tragic Interludes for Oboe, Op. 43 (1983)

R. Canter (ob) *(rec BBC Studio 2, June 1987)* ("British Chamber Music for Oboe & Strings") † Qt Ob; Lutyens:Driving out the Death, Op. 81; A. Rawsthorne:Qt Ob; Theme & Vars Vns RDCL ▲ 6 (16.97)

A Woman Young & Old (cycle of 7 songs) for Soprano & Piano [text W. B. Yeats] (1962)

M. Field (sop), A. Ball (pno) *(rec Bristol, May 1995)* ("British Song") † D. Matthews:Golden Kingdom; Rushby-Smith:Love's Legacy; M. Tippett:Heart's Assurance RDCL ▲ 9 (16.97)

ROVICS, HOWARD (1936-

Cybernetic Study for Alto Flute & Piano (1967)

T. Pagano (fl), H. Rovics (pno) *(rec Danbury, CT, Feb-June 1997)* ("Retrospective") † Do You Not See; Incantation; My Stage Is Tied to Heaven; Serenade Fl; Songs on Chinese Poetry; Songs Med Voc; Tangere *([ENG] text)* NSR ▲ 1016 [DDD] (15.97)

Do You Not See (cycle of 6 songs) for Soprano & Piano [texts Chinese poetry] (1978)

C. Rovics (sop), H. Rovics (pno) *(rec Danbury, CT, Feb-June 1997)* ("Retrospective") † Cybernetic Study; Incantation; My Stage Is Tied to Heaven; Serenade Fl; Songs on Chinese Poetry; Songs Med Voc; Tangere *([ENG] text)* NSR ▲ 1016 [DDD] (15.97)

Incantation for Cello & Piano (1982)

D. Wells (vc), H. Rovics (pno) *(rec Danbury, CT, Feb-June 1997)* ("Retrospective") † Cybernetic Study; Do You Not See; My Stage Is Tied to Heaven; Serenade Fl; Songs on Chinese Poetry; Songs Med Voc; Tangere *([ENG] text)* NSR ▲ 1016 [DDD] (15.97)

My Stage Is Tied to Heaven (song) for Soprano, Flute & Piano [text Rivka Kashtan] (1996)

C. Rovics (sop), L. Hansen (fl), H. Rovics (pno) *(rec Danbury, CT, Feb-June 1997)* ("Retrospective") † Cybernetic Study; Do You Not See; Incantation; Serenade Fl; Songs on Chinese Poetry; Songs Med Voc; Tangere *([ENG] text)* NSR ▲ 1016 [DDD] (15.97)

Serenade for Flute & Piano (1967)

T. Pagano (fl), H. Rovics (pno) *(rec Danbury, CT, Feb-June 1997)* ("Retrospective") † Cybernetic Study; Do You Not See; Incantation; My Stage Is Tied to Heaven; Songs on Chinese Poetry; Songs Med Voc; Tangere *([ENG] text)* NSR ▲ 1016 [DDD] (15.97)

Sonata for Piano (1987)

M. Lifchitz (pno) *(rec Recital Hall of the Univ at Albany, May 25-26, 1995)* ("New American Romantics: Music for Solo Piano") † L. Bell:Son Pno; Pleskow:Quatrains Pno; Quilling:Son 4 Pno; Toutant:Small Suite Pno; Van Appledorn:Set of 5 Pno NSR ▲ 1007 [DDD] (15.97)

Songs (2) for Medium Voice & Piano [texts Duane Niatum] (1984)

C. Rovics (sop), H. Rovics (pno) *(rec Danbury, CT, Feb-June 1997)* ("Retrospective") † Cybernetic Study; Do You Not See; Incantation; My Stage Is Tied to Heaven; Serenade Fl; Songs on Chinese Poetry; Tangere *([ENG] text)* NSR ▲ 1016 [DDD] (15.97)

Songs on Chinese Poetry (6) for Soprano & Ensemble (1982)

C. Rovics (sop), M. Lifchitz (cnd), North/South Consonance Ensemble *(rec Danbury, CT, Feb-June 1997)* ("Retrospective") † Cybernetic Study; Do You Not See; Incantation; My Stage Is Tied to Heaven; Serenade Fl; Songs Med Voc; Tangere *([ENG] text)* NSR ▲ 1016 [DDD] (15.97)

ROVICS, HOWARD (cont.)

Tangere for Soprano, Flute & Piano [text Rivka Kashtan] (1996)

C. Rovics (sop), L. Hansen (fl), H. Rovics (pno) *(rec Danbury, CT, Feb-June 1997)* ("Retrospective") † Cybernetic Study; Do You Not See; Incantation; My Stage Is Tied to Heaven; Serenade Fl; Songs on Chinese Poetry; Songs Med Voc *([ENG] text)* NSR ▲ 1016 [DDD] (15.97)

ROWLES, JIMMY (1918-

The Peacocks for Clarinet & Piano

R. Stoltzman (cl), I. Vallecillo-Gray (pno) *(rec Worcester, MA, Jan 1994)* ("Amber Waves: American Clarinet Music") † L. Bernstein:Son Cl; C. Fisher:Sonatine Cl; G. Gershwin:Preludes Pno; R. Hyman:Clarinata; W. T. McKinley:Son Cl RCAV (Red Seal) ▲ 62685 [DDD] (16.97)

ROXBURY, RONALD (1946-1986)

Songs (2) of Walt Whitman for Baritone, Flute & Guitar (1986)

P. Mason (bar), D. Starobin (gtr), S. Palma (fl) [ENG] ("New Music with Guitar, Vol. 4") † T. Machover:Bug-Mudra; Saxton:Night Dance Gtr; Searle:2 Practical Cats; M. Starobin:Chase BRID ▲ 9022 [DDD] (17.97)

ROY, ADRIAN LE (ca 1520-1598)

Songs

C. LaRue (sop), Baltimore Consort—Has tu point veu ("Ballads") † Akeroyde:Songs; Anonymous:Geordie; My Heartly Service; The Rebel Soldier; A. Campbell:Gloomy Winter's Now Awa'; T. Ravenscroft:Songs; Traditional:Aupres de ma blonde; Barbara Allen; Charlie's Sweet; Edward; Il a tout dit; In a Garden So Green; J'ai vû le loup; Le matin en me levant; Marlbru s'en va t'en guerre; Mignonne, allons voir si la rose; Soldier Boy for Me; The Fox Went out on a Chilly Night; The True Lover's Farewell; The Wren Song DOR ▲ 90014 [DDD] (11.97)

ROY, KLAUS GEORGE (1924-

Miracles Are Not Ceased for Soprano & Oboe [text Izaak Walton], Op. 126 (1985)

Plymouth Trio † S. Adler:Rocking Horse Winner CRYS ▲ 640 (15.97) ▮ 640 (9.98)

ROYER, JOSEPH-NICOLAS-PANCRACE (ca 1705-1755)

Pièces de clavecin (15 pieces) for Harpsichord (1746)

L. G. Crawford (hpd) † Rameau:Pièces de clavecin GAS ▲ 1006 [DDD] (12.97)

ROZE, NICOLAS (1745-1819)

Vivat in aeternum—Vivat Rex (motet) for Vocal Soloists, Orchestra & Chorus (1802)

St. Petersburg Cappella *(rec La Chaise-Dieu Abbey, Aug 22-23, 1995)* ("Coronation Music for Napoleon I") † Paisiello:Sacred Music; Sueur:Sacred Music KSCH ▲ 312082 (16.97)

RÓZSA, MIKLÓS (1907-1995)

Andante for String Orchestra, Op. 22a (1950; rev 1992)

I. Jackson (cnd), Berlin SO † Con Str Orch; B. Herrmann:Sinfonietta Str Orch; F. Waxman:Sinfonietta Timp KOCH ▲ 7152 [DDD] (16.97)

J. Sedares (cnd), New Zealand SO ("Complete Orchestral Music, Vol. IV") † Con Str Orch; Con Vn KOCH ▲ 7379 (16.97)

Bagatellen for Piano, Op. 12 (1932)

S. D. Buechner (pno) † Kaleidoscope, Op. 19; Son Pno; Valse Crepuscalence; Vars Pno, Op. 9; Vintner's Daughter, Op. 23 KOCH ▲ 7435 (16.97)

E. Parkin (pno) † Son Pno; Vars Pno, Op. 9; Vintner's Daughter, Op. 23 CMB ▲ 1081 [ADD] (16.97)

Ben-Hur (film music) for Orchestra (1959)

M. Rózsa (cnd), MGM Studio Orch, MGM Studio Chorus *(rec CA & Rome Italy)* ("Ben-Hur:A Tale of Christ") RHI 2-▲ 72197 (31.97)

Ben-Hur (selections)

J. Williams (cnd), Boston Pops Orch—Parade of the Charioteers *(rec Boston, MA, Jan 6, 10 & 13, 1996)* ("Summon The Heroes: The Official Centennial Olympic Theme") † L. Bernstein:Olympic Hymn; D. Shostakovich:Festive Ov, Op. 96; J. Suk:Towards a New Life, Op. 35c; Theodorakis:Canto olympico; J. Williams:Olympic Spirit; Summon the Heroes SNYC ▲ 62592 [DDD] (16.97) ▮ 62592 [DDD] (10.98) COL △ 62592 [DDD]

El Cid (film music) for Orchestra (1962)

T. S. Fine (org), J. Sedares (cnd), New Zealand SO, New Zealand Youth Choir *(rec Wellington New Zealand, May 1995)* ("El Cid") KOCH ▲ 7340 [DDD] (16.97)

artists unknown ("Hungarian Sketches") † Con Str Orch; Hungarian Sketches, Op. 14; Sinf concertante, Op. 29; Vars on Hungarian Peasant Song, Op. 4; Vintner's Daughter, Op. 23 KOCH ▲ 7601 (10.97)

Concerto for Cello & Orchestra, Op. 32 (1971)

B. Smith (vc), J. Sedares (cnd), New Zealand SO ("Complete Orchestral Music, Vol. 5") † Con Pno, Op. 31 KOCH ▲ 7402 (16.97)

Concerto for Piano & Orchestra, Op. 31 (1966)

E. Chen (pno), J. Sedares (cnd), New Zealand SO ("Complete Orchestral Music, Vol. 5") † Con Vc KOCH ▲ 7402 (16.97)

Concerto for String Orchestra (1943)

P. Csaba (cnd), Virtuosi di Kuhmo † B. Bartók:Divert Strs, Sz.113; Romanian Folk Dances Pno, Sz.56 ODE ▲ 919 (17.97)

I. Jackson (cnd), Berlin SO † Andante; B. Herrmann:Sinfonietta Str Orch; F. Waxman:Sinfonietta Timp KOCH ▲ 7152 [DDD] (16.97)

J. Sedares (cnd), New Zealand SO ("Complete Orchestral Music, Vol. IV") † Andante; Con Vn KOCH ▲ 7379 (16.97)

artists unknown ("Hungarian Sketches") † Cid; Hungarian Sketches, Op. 14; Sinf concertante, Op. 29; Vars on Hungarian Peasant Song, Op. 4; Vintner's Daughter, Op. 23 KOCH ▲ 7601 (10.97)

Concerto for Viola & Orchestra, Op. 37

P. Silverthorne (va), J. Sedares (cnd), New Zealand SO ("The Complete Orchestral Music, Vol. 3") † Sinf concertante, Op. 29 KOCH ▲ 7304 [DDD] (16.97)

Concerto for Violin & Orchestra, Op. 24 (1956)

I. Gruppman (vn), J. Sedares (cnd), New Zealand SO ("Complete Orchestral Music, Vol. IV") † Andante; Con Str Orch KOCH ▲ 7379 (16.97)

Crisis (film suite) for Guitar (1950; arr 1978)

D. Denning (gtr) † Lydia (suite); Private Files of J. Edgar Hoover CIT (Legendary Hollywood) ▲ 77118 [ADD] (15.97)

Double Indemnity (film music) for Orchestra (1944)

J. Sedares (cnd), New Zealand SO † Killers; Lost Weekend KOCH ▲ 7375 (16.97)

Duo for Violin & Piano, Op. 7 (1931)

E. Granat (vn), L. Pennario (pno) † Qnt Pno, Op. 2; Trio-Serenade, Op. 1 CMB ▲ 1034 [ADD] (16.97)

I. Lippi (vn), J. Novacek (pno) ("Complete Music for Solo Violin") † North Hungarian Peasant Songs & Dances, Op. 5; Son Vn; Vars on Hungarian Peasant Song, Op. 4 KOCH ▲ 7256 [DDD] (10.97)

Film Music

K. Alwyn (cnd), Prague PO—Ben-Hur (sels); King of Kings (sels); Sodom & Gomorrah (sels); Golden Voyage of Sinbad (sels); El Cid (sels); Quo Vadis (sels) ("The Epic Film Music of Miklos Rozsa") SIAM ▲ 1056 (16.97)

E. Bernstein (cnd), Utah SO *(World, the Flesh & the Devil (sels) [Ov]; Because of Him (sels) [Ov])*, R. Padberg (cnd), Royal PO *(El Cid (sels) [Palace music]; Young Bess (sels) [Danish dance]; Julius Ceasar (sels) [Ceasar's procession]; Sodom & Gomorrah (sels) [Triumphal march & wedding]; King of Kings (sels) [Via Dolorosa; Jugglers & Tumblers]; Ben-Hur (sels) [Parade of the Charioteers; Victory Parade]; Story of 3 Lovers (sels) [Java de la Seine]; Festive Flourish)*, C. Bowers-Broadbent (org), R. Padberg (cnd), Royal PO *(Fant on Themes from Young Bess) (rec 1984-85)* ("Legendary Hollywood: Miklós Rózsa") CIT ▲ 77111 [DDD] (15.97)

C. Gerhardt (cnd), National PO London, Ambrosian Singers—Spellbound ("Spellbound: The Classic Film Music of Miklos Rózsa") RCAV (Classic Film Scores) ▲ 911 (11.97)

D. Robbins (pno)—Man in Half Moon Street (sels); Other Love (sels); Fedora (sels); Knight without Armor (sels); Macomber Affair (sels); Kiss the Blood Off My Hands (sels); Woman's Vengeance (sels) ("Knight without Armor:Miklos Rozsa Film Music for Piano") INTR ▲ 7057 [DDD] (16.97)

Hungarian Sketches (3) for Orchestra, Op. 14 (1938)

J. Sedares (cnd), New Zealand SO *(rec Nov 1992)* † Notturno ungherese, Op. 28; Ov to Sym Concert, Op. 26a; Theme, Vars & Finale, Op. 13a KOCH ▲ 7191 [DDD] (16.97)

artists unknown ("Hungarian Sketches") † Cid; Con Str Orch; Sinf concertante, Op. 29; Vars on Hungarian Peasant Song, Op. 4; Vintner's Daughter, Op. 23 KOCH ▲ 7601 (10.97)

Introduction & Allegro for Viola, Op. 44 (1988)

M. Newman (va) *(rec 1990)* † I. Dahl:Concerto à tre; D. W. Freund:Triomusic; P. Schickele:Qt Vn RACA ▲ 1005

Ivanhoe (film music) for Orchestra (1952)

B. Broughton (cnd), London Sinfonia INTR ▲ 7055 [DDD] (16.97)

Julius Caesar (film music) for Orchestra

B. Broughton (cnd), London Sinfonia, Sinfonia Chorus INTR ▲ 7056 (16.97)

B. Herrmann (cnd), National PO London † D. Shostakovich:Hamlet (film music), Op. 116; W. Walton:Richard III (film music) PLON (Phase 4 Stereo) ▲ 455156 (9.97)

▲ = CD ♦ = Enhanced CD △ = MD ▮ = Cassette Tape ▯ = DCC

RÓZSA, MIKLÓS (cont.)

Kaleidoscope for Piano, Op. 19 (ca 1948)
S. D. Buechner (pno) † Bagatellen Pno, Op. 12; Son Pno; Valse Crepuscalence; Vars Pno, Op. 9; Vintner's Daughter, Op. 23 KOCH ▲ 7435 (16.97)

The Killers (film music) for Orchestra (1946)
J. Sedares (cnd), New Zealand SO † Double Indemnity; Lost Weekend KOCH ▲ 7375 (16.97)

The King's Thief (film music) for Orchestra (1955)
R. Kaufman (cnd), Brandenburg PO [reconstructed Christopher Palmer] *(rec Jesus Christ Church Berlin, Germany, 1994)* ("Captain Blood") † Korngold:Captain Blood; M. Steiner:Three Musketeers; V. Young:Scaramouche MARC ▲ 8223607 [DDD] (13.97)

The Lost Weekend (film music) for Orchestra (1945)
J. Sedares (cnd), New Zealand SO † Double Indemnity; Killers KOCH ▲ 7375 (16.97)

Lydia (film suite) for Piano (1941; arr 1979)
A. Dominguez (pno) † Crisis (suite); Private Files of J. Edgar Hoover CIT (Legendary Hollywood) ▲ 77118 [ADD] (15.97)

North Hungarian Peasant Songs & Dances for Violin & Orchestra (or Piano), Op. 5 (1929)
I. Lippi (vn), J. Novacek (pno) ("Complete Music for Solo Violin") † Duo Vn, Op. 7; Son Vn; Vars on Hungarian Peasant Song, Op. 4 KOCH ▲ 7256 [DDD] (10.97)

Notturno ungherese for Orchestra, Op. 28 (1964)
J. Sedares (cnd), New Zealand SO *(rec Nov 1992)* † Hungarian Sketches, Op. 14; Ov to Sym Concert, Op. 26a; Theme, Vars & Finale, Op. 13a KOCH ▲ 7191 [DDD] (16.97)

Overture to a Symphony Concert, Op. 26a (1957)
J. Sedares (cnd), New Zealand SO *(rec Nov 1992)* † Hungarian Sketches, Op. 14; Notturno ungherese, Op. 28; Theme, Vars & Finale, Op. 13a KOCH ▲ 7191 [DDD] (16.97)

The Private Files of J. Edgar Hoover (film music) for Orchestra (1978)
M. Rózsa (cnd) † Crisis (suite); Lydia (suite) CIT (Legendary Hollywood) ▲ 77118 [ADD] (15.97)

Quartet No. 1 for Strings, Op. 22 (1950)
Pro Arte String Quartet † Qt 2 Strs, Op. 38; Rhap Vc, Op. 3 LARL ▲ 842 [DDD] (14.97)

Quartet No. 2 for Strings, Op. 38 (1981)
Pro Arte String Quartet † Qt 1 Strs, Op. 22; Rhap Vc, Op. 3 LARL ▲ 842 [DDD] (14.97)

Quintet for Piano & Strings, Op. 2 (1928)
E. Granat (vn), S. Sanov (vn), M. Thomas (va), N. Rosen (vc), L. Pennario (pno) † Duo Vn, Op. 7; Trio-Serenade, Op. 1 CMB ▲ 1034 [ADD] (16.97)

Rhapsody for Cello & Orchestra (or Piano), Op. 3 (1929)
P. Karp (vc), H. Karp (pno) † Qt 1 Strs, Op. 22; Qt 2 Strs, Op. 38 LARL ▲ 842 [DDD] (14.97)

Sinfonia concertante for Violin, Cello & Orchestra, Op. 29 (1968)
I. Gruppman (vn), R. Boch (vc), J. Sedares (cnd), New Zealand SO ("The Complete Orchestral Music, Vol. 3") † Con Va KOCH ▲ 7304 [DDD] (16.97)
artists unknown ("Hungarian Sketches") † Cid; Con Str Orch; Hungarian Sketches, Op. 14; Vars on Hungarian Peasant Song, Op. 4; Vintner's Daughter, Op. 23 KOCH ▲ 7601 (10.97)

Sodom & Gomorrah (film music) for Orchestra
artists unknown CMB ▲ 1050 [ADD] (16.97)

Sonata for Piano (ca 1949)
S. D. Buechner (pno) † Bagatellen Pno, Op. 12; Kaleidoscope, Op. 19; Valse Crepuscalence; Vars Pno, Op. 9; Vintner's Daughter, Op. 23 KOCH ▲ 7435 (16.97)
E. Parkin (pno) † Bagatellen Pno, Op. 12; Vars Pno, Op. 9; Vintner's Daughter, Op. 23 CMB ▲ 1081 [ADD] (16.97)

Sonata for Violin, Op. 40 (1985)
I. Lippi (vn) ("Complete Music for Solo Violin") † Duo Vn, Op. 7; North Hungarian Peasant Songs & Dances, Op. 5; Vars on Hungarian Peasant Song, Op. 4 KOCH ▲ 7256 [DDD] (10.97)

Sonatina for Clarinet (1957)
L. Combs (cl) † Rochberg:Trio Cl; G. Schuller:Romantic Son Cl CRYS ▮ 731 (9.98)

Spellbound (concerto) for Piano & Orchestra
E. Wild (pno), C. Gerhardt (cnd), London Promenade Orch *(rec London, England, Aug 19, 1965)* ("Earl Wild Goes to the Movies") † Chopin:Andante Spianato & Grand Polonaise, Op. 22; Liszt:Etudes de concert (3), S.144; W. A. Mozart:Con 21 Pno, K.467; R. Rodgers:Slaughter on Tenth Avenue Orch; M. Steiner:Four Wives (sels) IVOR ▲ 70801 [ADD] (16.97)

Symphony, Op. 6 (1930; rev 1990)
J. Sedares (cnd), New Zealand SO † Vintner's Daughter, Op. 23 KOCH ▲ 7244 [DDD] (16.97)

Theme, Variations & Finale for Orchestra, Op. 13a (1933, rev 1943)
J. Sedares (cnd), New Zealand SO *(rec Nov 1992)* † Hungarian Sketches, Op. 14; Notturno ungherese, Op. 28; Ov to Sym Concert, Op. 26a KOCH ▲ 7191 [DDD] (16.97)

Trio-Serenade for Violin, Viola & Cello, Op. 1 (1927, rev 1974)
E. Granat (vn), M. Thomas (va), N. Rosen (vc) † Duo Vn, Op. 7; Qnt Pno, Op. 2 CMB ▲ 1034 [ADD] (16.97)

Valse Crepuscalence for Piano
S. D. Buechner (pno) † Bagatellen Pno, Op. 12; Kaleidoscope, Op. 19; Son Pno; Vars Pno, Op. 9; Vintner's Daughter, Op. 23 KOCH ▲ 7435 (16.97)

Variations on a Hungarian Peasant Song for Violin & Orchestra (or Piano), Op. 4 (1929)
I. Lippi (vn), J. Novacek (pno) ("Complete Music for Solo Violin") † Duo Vn, Op. 7; North Hungarian Peasant Songs & Dances, Op. 5; Son Vn KOCH ▲ 7256 [DDD] (10.97)
artists unknown ("Hungarian Sketches") † Cid; Con Str Orch; Hungarian Sketches, Op. 14; Sinf concertante, Op. 29; Vintner's Daughter, Op. 23 KOCH ▲ 7601 (10.97)

Variations for Piano, Op. 9 (1932)
S. D. Buechner (pno) † Bagatellen Pno, Op. 12; Kaleidoscope, Op. 19; Son Pno; Valse Crepuscalence; Vintner's Daughter, Op. 23 KOCH ▲ 7435 (16.97)
E. Parkin (pno) † Bagatellen Pno, Op. 12; Son Pno; Vintner's Daughter, Op. 23 CMB ▲ 1081 [ADD] (16.97)

The Vintner's Daughter (12 variations on a French folksong) for Orchestra (or Piano), Op. 23 (1952)
S. D. Buechner (pno) † Bagatellen Pno, Op. 12; Kaleidoscope, Op. 19; Son Pno; Valse Crepuscalence; Vars Pno, Op. 9 KOCH ▲ 7435 (16.97)
E. Parkin (pno) † Bagatellen Pno, Op. 12; Son Pno; Vars Pno, Op. 9 CMB ▲ 1081 [ADD] (16.97)
J. Sedares (cnd), New Zealand SO † Sym KOCH ▲ 7244 [DDD] (16.97)
artists unknown ("Hungarian Sketches") † Cid; Con Str Orch; Hungarian Sketches, Op. 14; Sinf concertante, Op. 29; Vars on Hungarian Peasant Song, Op. 4 KOCH ▲ 7601 (10.97)

RÓZSAVÖLGYI [ROSENTHAL], MÁRK (1789-1848)

Ballroom Dances for Strings
Festetics String Quartet—Censorship; Circle of Opposition; Diet Dance; Hear! Hear!; Hungarian Round Dance 1; Mazurka; Mazurka of Pétervár; Polonaise in A; Polonaise in C; Polonaise in G; Slogan; Sounds of Hope from the East; Souvenir of Nógrád; Spinning Tune; Spur; The Dream; Uniting [period instrs] HUN ▲ 31781 [DDD] (16.97)

RUBBRA, EDMUND (1901-1986)

Cantata Pastorale for Tenor, Recorder, Cello & Harpsichord, Op. 92 (1956)
B. Boyd (fl), B. Harbach (hpd) † Fant on a Theme of Machaut, Op. 86; S. Adler:Son 2 Vn; A. Dvořák:Bagatelles, Op. 47; Martinů:Promenades; D. Milhaud:Son Vn & Hpd, Op. 257; Piston:Sonatina Vn ALBA ▲ 41 (16.97)

Chamber Music for Harp (complete)
D. Perrett (hp) † Songs; L. Berkeley:Nocturne Hp; H. Howells:Prelude Hp ASV ▲ 1036 (16.97)

Choral Music
Gloriae Dei Cantores—Magnificat; Nunc Dimittis; Tenebrae Motets [Nocturnes 1-3]; Salutation; Missa in honorem Sancti Dominici; Festival Gloria ("The Sacred Muse") GLRI ▲ 24 (15.97)
Gonville & Caius College Choir Cambridge—3 Motets; 3 Hymn Tunes; Magnificat & Nunc Dimittis ("English Church Music, Vol. 3") † Missa in honorem Sancti Dominici, Op. 66; P. Hadley:Cant for Lent; Songs ASV ▲ 881 [DDD] (16.97)

Fantasy on a Theme of Machaut for Flute, Harpsichord & String Quartet, Op. 86
B. Boyd (fl), B. Harbach (hpd) † Cant Pastorale, Op. 92; S. Adler:Son 2 Vn; A. Dvořák:Bagatelles, Op. 47; Martinů:Promenades; D. Milhaud:Son Vn & Hpd, Op. 257; Piston:Sonatina Vn ALBA ▲ 41 (16.97)

Missa in honorem Sancti Dominici for Chorus, Op. 66 (1948)
Gonville & Caius College Choir Cambridge ("English Church Music, Vol. 3") † Choral Music; P. Hadley:Cant for Lent; Songs ASV ▲ 881 [DDD] (16.97)

The Morning Watch for SATB Soloists & Orchestra [after Vaughan] (1941)
R. Hickox (cnd), BBC National Orch Wales, BBC Welsh Chorus † Sym 9 CHN ▲ 9441 (16.97)

Ode to the Queen (song-cycle) for Soprano & Orchestra, Op. 83
S. Bickley (sop), R. Hickox (cnd), BBC National Orch Wales † Sym 5; Sym 8 CHN (Rubbra Symphonies) ▲ 9714 (16.97)

RUBBRA, EDMUND (cont.)

Quartet No. 2 in E♭ for Strings, Op. 73 (1952)
English String Quartet *(rec May 1992)* † P. Tate:Qt Strs; P. Wishart:Qt Strs, Op. 22 RD ▲ 26002 (16.97)

Sinfonia concertante for Piano & Orchestra, Op. 38 (1934)
H. Shelley (pno), R. Hickox (cnd), BBC National Orch Wales † Sym 1; Tribute, Op. 56 CHN ▲ 9538 (16.97)

Sonata in g for Cello, Op. 60 (1946)
T. Gill (vc), F. Pavri (pno) [arr vc & pno] † B. Britten:Son Vc; J. Mayer:Calcutta-Nagar; Prabhanda GILD ▲ 7114 [DDD] (16.97)
R. Wallfisch (vc) *(rec East Woodhay Berkshire, Mar 16-17, 1994)* ("English Cello Sonatas") † J. Ireland:Son Vc; Moeran:Son Vc MARC ▲ 8223718 [DDD] (13.97)

Sonata in C for Oboe & Piano, Op. 100 (1958)
S. Francis (ob), P. Dickinson (pno) † R. Boughton:Qt 1 Ob; H. Harty:Pieces Ob; H. Howells:Son Ob HYP ▲ 55008 (9.97)
E. McCarty (ob), I. Delgado (pno) *(rec Boston, United States of America, Feb 26-27, 1994)* ("Gems for Oboe & Piano") † Son Ob; Doran:Sonatina Ob; J. Madden:Songs of Sadness; E. Schelling:Impressions from an Artist's Life; Nocturne (Ragusa); L. Sinigaglia:Var(s) on Schubert Ob & Pno, Op. 19; Widerkehr:Duo Ob; Duo Pno Orch BOST ▲ 1012 [DDD] (15.97)

Songs
T. Chadwell (sop), T. Gill (vc), D. Perrett (hp)—The Jade Mountain; Transformations; plus others † Chamber Music Hp (comp); L. Berkeley:Nocturne Hp; H. Howells:Prelude Hp ASV ▲ 1036 (16.97)

Symphony No. 1, Op. 44 (1935-37)
R. Hickox (cnd), BBC National Orch Wales † Sinf concertante, Op. 38; Tribute, Op. 56 CHN ▲ 9538 (16.97)

Symphony No. 2, Op. 45 (1937)
R. Hickox (cnd), BBC National Orch Wales † Sym 6 CHN ▲ 9481 (16.97)

Symphony No. 3, Op. 49 (1939)
R. Hickox (cnd), BBC National Orch Wales † Sym 7 CHN ▲ 9634 (16.97)

Symphony No. 4, Op. 53 (1941)
R. Hickox (cnd), BBC National Orch Wales † Sym 10; Sym 11 CHN ▲ 9401 [DDD] (16.97)

Symphony No. 5 in B♭, Op. 63 (1947-48)
R. Hickox (cnd), BBC National Orch Wales † Ode to the Queen, Op. 83; Sym 8 CHN (Rubbra Symphonies) ▲ 9714 (16.97)
H. Schönzeler (cnd), Melbourne SO † A. Bliss:Checkmate, T.57; M. Tippett:Little Music Strs CHN (Collect) ▲ 6576 [ADD] (12.97)

Symphony No. 6, Op. 80 (1954)
R. Hickox (cnd), BBC National Orch Wales † Sym 2 CHN ▲ 9481 (16.97)

Symphony No. 7, Op. 88 (1957)
R. Hickox (cnd), BBC National Orch Wales † Sym 3 CHN ▲ 9634 (16.97)

Symphony No. 8, Op. 132 (1966-68)
R. Hickox (cnd), BBC National Orch Wales † Ode to the Queen, Op. 83; Sym 5 CHN (Rubbra Symphonies) ▲ 9714 (16.97)

Symphony No. 9 for Soprano, Alto, Baritone, Orchestra & Chorus, Op. 140, "Sinfonia Sacra" (1971-72)
L. Dawson (sop), D. Jones (mez), S. Roberts (bar), R. Hickox (cnd), BBC National Orch Wales, BBC Welsh Chorus † Morning Watch CHN ▲ 9441 (16.97)

Symphony No. 10, Op. 145, "Sinfonia da camera" (1974)
R. Hickox (cnd), BBC National Orch Wales † Sym 11; Sym 4 CHN ▲ 9401 [DDD] (16.97)

Symphony No. 11, Op. 153 (1978-79)
R. Hickox (cnd), BBC National Orch Wales † Sym 10; Sym 4 CHN ▲ 9401 [DDD] (16.97)

A Tribute for Orchestra [for Ralph Vaughan Williams on his 70th Birthday], Op. 56 (1942)
R. Hickox (cnd), BBC National Orch Wales † Sinf concertante, Op. 38; Sym 1 CHN ▲ 9538 (16.97)

Variations on "The Shining River" for Band, Op. 101 (1958)
J. Gourlay (cnd), Williams Fairey Band *(rec Dewsbury Town Hall, England, Feb 1997)* ("Brass From the Masters, Vol. 1") † W. Alwyn:Moor of Venice; E. Elgar:Severn Suite Brass, Op. 87; C. Jenkins:Life Divine; R. Simpson:Energy; Vaughan Williams:Vars Brass CHN ▲ 4547 [DDD] (16.97)
artists unknown ("Epic Brass: British Music for Brass Band") † E. Ball:Sinfonietta; E. Elgar:Severn Suite Brass, Op. 87; P. E. Fletcher:Epic Sym; G. Vinter:James Cook CHN ▲ 4508 [ADD] (16.97)

RUBIN, AMY (20th cent)

La Loba for Wind Quintet & Piano (1994; rev 1995)
A. Rubin (pno), Quintet of the Americas *(rec Vassar College, June 25-29, 1995)* ("Self Portrait") † Culpo:Qnt Ww; L. Hyla:Amnesia Breaks; P. Oliveros:Portrait of the Qnt of the Americas; E. Sharp:JAG CRI ▲ 722 [DDD] (16.97)

RUBINSTEIN, ANTON (1829-1894)

Album of Popular Dances (7) of the Different Nations for Piano, Op. 82 (1868)
W. Backhaus (pno)—Polka in G (No. 7) *(rec Berlin, Germany, 1916)* † Soirées à Saint-Pétersbourg; J. Brahms:Vars on a Theme by Paganini, Op. 35; Chopin:Etudes Pno; Polonaise 3 Pno, Op. 40/1; Liszt:Hungarian Rhaps, S.244; F. Schubert:Qnt Pno, D.667 BPS ▲ 38 [ADD] (16.97)

Barcarolle No. 4 in G for Piano (or Orchestra)
A. Rubinstein (pno) † Pieces Pno, Op. 5; Valse-Caprice Pno RCAV (Gold Seal) ▲ 61860 (11.97)

Concertos (2) in a & d for Cello & Orchestra, Opp. 65 & 96
W. Thomas-Mifune (vc), Y. Ahronovitch (cnd), Bamberg SO KSCH ▲ 311103 [DDD] (16.97)

Concerto No. 1 in e for Piano & Orchestra, Op. 25 (1850)
J. Banowetz (pno), A. Walter (cnd), Czech-Slovak State PO *(rec Mar 3-7, 1992)* † Con 2 Pno, Op. 35 MARC ▲ 8223456 [DDD] (13.97)

Concerto No. 2 in F for Piano & Orchestra, Op. 35 (1851)
J. Banowetz (pno), A. Walter (cnd), Czech-Slovak State PO *(rec Mar 3-7, 1992)* † Con 1 Pno, Op. 25 MARC ▲ 8223456 [DDD] (13.97)

Concerto No. 3 in G for Piano & Orchestra, Op. 45 (1853-54)
J. Banowetz (pno), R. Stankovský (cnd), Czech-Slovak State PO † Con 4 Pno, Op. 70 MARC ▲ 8223382 [DDD] (13.97)
V. Traficante (pno), J. Serebrier (cnd), Rheinische Philharmonie VOXC ▲ 7533 (5.97)

Concerto No. 4 in d for Piano & Orchestra, Op. 70 (1864; arr 2 pianos, 1866)
J. Banowetz (pno), R. Stankovský (cnd), Czech-Slovak State PO † Con 3 Pno, Op. 45 MARC ▲ 8223382 [DDD] (13.97)
J. Hofmann (pno), F. Reiner (cnd), Curtis Institute Student Orch *(rec live, Nov 28, 1937)* † G. Hoffmann:Chromaticon; Moszkowski:Caprice Espagnole, Op. 37 VAIA 2-▲ 1020 [ADD] (31.97)
M. Ponti (pno), O. Mága (cnd), Philharmonia Hungarica *(rec 1968)* † Moszkowski:Con Pno, Op. 59; X. Scharwenka:Con 2 Pno, Op. 56; Thalberg:Con Pno, Op. 5 VB2 2-▲ 5066 [ADD] (9.97)

Concerto No. 5 in E♭ for Piano & Orchestra, Op. 94 (1874)
J. Banowetz (pno), R. Stankovský (cnd), Slovak RSO Bratislava *(rec Dec 13-18, 1993)* † Russian Capriccio, Op. 102 MARC ▲ 8223489 [DDD] (13.97)
A. Ruiz (pno), Z. Deáky (cnd), Nuremberg SO GNSI ▲ 103 [ADD] (15.97)

Concerto in G for Violin & Orchestra, Op. 46 (1857)
T. Nishizaki (vn), M. Halász (cnd), Slovak PO † Don Quixote, Op. 87 MARC ▲ 8220359 [DDD] (13.97)

Concertstück in A♭ for Piano & Orchestra, Op. 113 (1889)
J. Banowetz (pno), O. Dohnányi (cnd), Czech-Slovak RSO Bratislava † Fant Pno, Op. 84 MARC ▲ 8223190 (13.97)

The Demon (opera in prologue, 3 acts & apotheosis) [lib P. A. Viskovatov after Lermontov] (1871)
V. Fedoseyev (cnd), Vienna SO, M. Mescheriakova (sop), O. Alexandrova (mez), E. Silins (bass), P. Daniluk (bass) ("The Demon") KSCH 2-▲ 365432
M. Mescheriakova (sop—Tamara), L. Andrew (sop—Nanny), A. Browner (mez—Angel), V. Serkin (ten—Prince Sinodal), W. Weinorowski (ten—Messenger), L. Zimnenko (bass—Prince Gudal), A. Lochak (sgr—Demon), R. Robson (sgr—Old Servant), A. Anissimov (cnd), Irish National SO, G. Rose (cnd), Wexford Festival Opera Chorus *(rec Wexford, Oct-Nov 1994)* MARC 2-▲ 8223781 [DDD] (27.97)

The Demon (orchestral selections)
M. Halász (cnd), Slovak PO † Feramors (orch sels); Nero (orch sels) MARC ▲ 8220451 [DDD] (13.97)

Dmitry Donskoy:Overture
H. Andreescu (cnd), Enescu State PO † Faust; Sym 5 MARC ▲ 8223320 (13.97)

Don Quixote for Orchestra, Op. 87 (1870)
I. Golovchin (cnd), Russian State SO † Ivan the Terrible, Op. 79 RUS ▲ 11397 [DDD] (12.97)
M. Halász (cnd), Slovak PO † Con Vn MARC ▲ 8220359 [DDD] (13.97)

Fantaisie in C for Piano & Orchestra, Op. 84 (1869; arr 2 pianos, 1870)
J. Banowetz (pno), O. Dohnányi (cnd), Czech-Slovak RSO Bratislava † Concertstück Pno, Op. 113 MARC ▲ 8223190 (13.97)

RUBINSTEIN, ANTON (cont.)

Faust (symphonic portrait) for Orchestra [after Goethe], Op. 68 (1864)
H. Andreescu (cnd), Enescu State PO † Dmitry Donskoy (ov); Sym 5 MARC ▲ 8223320 (13.97)

Feramors (orchestral selections)
M. Halász (cnd), Slovak PO † Demon (orch sels); Nero (orch sels) MARC ▲ 8220451 [DDD] (13.97)

Feramors:Ballet Music
I. Golovchin (cnd), Moscow State SO † Sym 2 RUS ▲ 11356 [DDD] (12.97)

Ivan the Terrible (symphonic portrait) for Orchestra [after L. A. Mey], Op. 79 (1869)
I. Golovchin (cnd), Russian State SO † Don Quixote, Op. 87 RUS ▲ 11397 [DDD] (12.97)
R. Stankovský (cnd), Slovak State PO Košice † Sym 1 MARC ▲ 8223277 (13.97)

Nero (orchestral selections)
M. Halász (cnd), Slovak PO † Demon (orch sels); Feramors (orch sels) MARC ▲ 8220451 [DDD] (13.97)

Nocturne for Viola & Piano
N. Imai (va), R. Pöntinen (pno) † M. Glinka:Son Va; D. Shostakovich:Son Va; I. Stravinsky:Elégie Va BIS ▲ 358 (17.97)

Piano Music
L. Howard (pno)—Fant in e, Op. 77; Thème et Vars, Op. 88; plus others ("Solo Piano Music") HYP (Dyad) ▲ 22023 (18.97)
Z. Mihailovich (pno)—Kamennoi-Ostrow, Op. 10/22; Polka-Bohème, Op. 82/7; Melody in F, Op. 3/1; Ruins of Athens (sels) [Turkish March]; Barcarolles, No. 1, Op. 30/1; No. 2, Op. 45; No. 3, Op. 50/5; No. 4; No. 5, Op. 90/4; No. 6, Op. 104/4; Romance, Op. 44; Valse-Caprice Pno *(rec Los Angeles, CA, Oct 1994)* ("Works for Piano") CENT ▲ 2235 [DDD] (16.97)
L. Sirota (pno)—Prés du ruisseau; Serenade; Prelude; Polonaise; Valse-Caprice Pno *(rec 1955)* ("The Sirota Archives, Vol. 1") † Glazunov:Son 1 Pno, Op. 74; P. Tchaikovsky:Son Pno, Op. 37 ARBT ▲ 110 (16.97)

Pieces (3) for Piano, Op. 5 (1852)
A. Rubinstein (pno) † Barcarolle 4 Pno; Valse-Caprice Pno RCAV (Gold Seal) ▲ 61860 (11.97)

Quintet in F for Flute, Clarinet, Horn, Bassoon & Piano, Op. 55 (ca 1855; rev 1860)
V. Zverov (fl), V. Sokolov (cl), S. Krasavin (bn), A. Demim (hn), A. Nasedkin (pno) † Son Va RUS (The A. Rubinstein Edition) ▲ 11061 [ADD] (12.97)

Quintet in g for Piano & Strings, Op. 99 (1876)
Pihtipudas Quintet *(rec Kuopio Finland, May 1996)* † D. Shostakovich:Qnt Pno, Op. 57 EDA ▲ 10 [DDD] (18.97)

Rêve Angelique for Orchestra
H. Adolph (cnd), Slovak PO ("A Night at the Ballet: Great Moments of Ballet Music") † M. Ravel:Boléro; F. Schubert:Rosamunde (sels); Strauss (II):Champagner-Polka, Op. 211; Egyptischer Marsch, Op. 335; P. Tchaikovsky:Swan Lake (suite), Op. 20a; Verdi:Aida (sels) ECL ▲ 511 (2.97)

Russian Capriccio for Piano & Orchestra, Op. 102 (1878)
J. Banowetz (pno), R. Stankovský (cnd), Slovak RSO Bratislava *(rec Dec 13-18, 1993)* † Con 5 Pno, Op. 94 MARC ▲ 8223489 [DDD] (13.97)

Soirées à Saint-Pétersbourg (6 pieces) for Piano (1860)
W. Backhaus (pno)—Romance in E (No. 1) *(rec Berlin, Germany, 1916)* † Album of Popular Dances, Op. 82; J. Brahms:Vars on a Theme by Paganini, Op. 35; Chopin:Études Pno; Polonaise 3 Pno, Op. 40/1; Liszt:Hungarian Rhaps, S.244; F. Schubert:Qnt Pno, D.667 BPS ▲ 38 [ADD] (16.97)

Sonata No. 1 in D for Cello & Piano, Op. 18 (1852)
S. Isserlis (vc) *(rec Abbey Road London, Dec 12-13, 1994)* ("Forgotten Romance") † E. Grieg:Son Vc; Liszt:Elegie 1 Vc, S.130; Elegie 2 Vn, S.131; Lugubre gondola Vn or Vc, S.134; Romance oubliée Va, S.132; Zelle in Nonnenwerth Vn, S.382 RCAV (Red Seal) ▲ 68290 [DDD] (16.97)
A. Vasilieva (vc), M. Muntian (pno) *(rec State House for Radio Broadcasting, May 1994)* † Son 2 Vc, Op. 39 RUS ▲ 10038 [AAD] (16.97)

Sonata No. 2 in G for Cello & Piano, Op. 39 (1857)
A. Vasilieva (vc), A. Shchmitov (pno) *(rec State House for Radio Broadcasting, May 1994)* † Son 1 Vc, Op. 18 RUS ▲ 10038 [AAD] (16.97)

Sonatas for Piano (complete)
L. Howard (pno) ("Anton Rubenstein: Complete Piano Sonatas") HYP 2-▲ 22007 (18.97)

Sonata in f for Viola & Piano, Op. 49 (1855)
K. Doležal (va) *(rec Covenent of St. Agnes of Bohemia Prague, Mar 1995)* ("Viola") † E. Bloch:Suite hébraïque; P. Hindemith:Son Va; L. Matoušek:Intimate Music ARTA ▲ 62 [DDD] (16.97)
F. Druzhinin (va), L. Panteyeva (pno) † Qnt Fl RUS (The A. Rubinstein Edition) ▲ 11061 [ADD] (12.97)
C. Masson-Bourque (va), M. Sato (pno) † R. Clarke:Son Va; Gougeon:Thèmes-solaires; J. Landry:Poèmes Va SNE ▲ 627 (16.97)

Sonata No. 1 in G for Violin & Piano, Op. 13 (1851)
I. Politkovsky (vn), E. Epstein (pno) *(rec 1981)* ("Igor Politkovsky: Russian Violin School") † Balakirev:Impromptu Vn; A. Dvořák:Zigeunermelodien, Op. 55; S. Rachmaninoff:Romance Vn & Pno, Op. 6/1; S. Taneyev:Son Vn; P. Tchaikovsky:Souvenir d'un lieu cher, Op. 42 RD (Talents of Russia) ▲ 16279 [ADD] (16.97)

Songs
B. Fassbaender (mez), H. Komatsu (bar), K. Moll (bass), C. Garben (pno)—Engel; Wanderers Nachtlied; Lied; Waldlied *(rec Nov 1989)* ("Romantic Duets") † J. Brahms:Songs; P. Cornelius:Songs; Liszt:Songs; Mendelssohn (-Bartholdy):Songs; R. Schumann:Songs HMA ▲ 1905210 [DDD] (9.97)

Songs (6) for Voice & Piano [text Heine], Op. 32 (1856)
G. Vinogradov (ten), G. Orentlicher (pno) † S. Rachmaninoff:Songs (14), Op. 34; Rimsky-Korsakov:Songs, Op. 51; R. Schumann:Dichterliebe, Op. 48; Gedichte, Op. 90; Liederkreis, Op. 24; Myrthen, Op. 25; P. Tchaikovsky:Songs PRE ▲ 89118 (16.97)

Symphony No. 1 in F, Op. 40 (1850)
R. Stankovský (cnd), Slovak State PO Košice † Ivan the Terrible, Op. 79 MARC ▲ 8223277 (13.97)

Symphony No. 2 in C [1st version in 4 movts; 2nd version in 6 movts; 3rd version in 7 movts], Op. 42, "Ocean" (1851; 1853; 1880)
I. Golovchin (cnd), Moscow State SO † Feramors (ballet music) RUS ▲ 11356 [DDD] (12.97)
S. Gunzenhauser (cnd), Slovak PO MARC ▲ 8220449 [DDD] (13.97)

Symphony No. 3 in A, Op. 56 (1854-55)
B. H. Kolman (cnd), Slovak State PO Košice *(rec Sept 1993)* † Sym 5 CENT ▲ 2185 [DDD] (16.97)

Symphony No. 4 in d, Op. 95, "Dramatic" (1874)
I. Golovchin (cnd), Russian State SO RUS (The A. Rubinstein Edition) ▲ 11357 [DDD] (12.97)
R. Stankovský (cnd), Czech PO MARC ▲ 8223319 (13.97)

Symphony No. 5 in g, Op. 107 (1880)
H. Andreescu (cnd), Enescu State PO † Dmitry Donskoy (ov); Faust MARC ▲ 8223320 (13.97)
B. H. Kolman (cnd), Slovak State PO Košice *(rec Sept 1993)* † Sym 3 CENT ▲ 2185 [DDD] (16.97)

Trio No. 1 in F for Piano, Violin & Cello, Op. 15/1 (1851)
Romantic Trio † Trio 3 Pno, Op. 52 RUS ▲ 10041 [DDD] (16.97)

Trio No. 3 in B♭ for Piano, Violin & Cello, Op. 52 (1857)
Romantic Trio † Trio 1 Pno, Op. 15/1 RUS ▲ 10041 [DDD] (16.97)

Valse-Caprice in E♭ for Piano (1870)
I. J. Paderewski (pno) *(rec 1911-37)* ("Paderewski Portrait") † J. Brahms:Hungarian Dances Pno; Chopin:Pno Music (misc colls); Mendelssohn (-Bartholdy):Lieder ohne Worte; R. Schumann:Pno Music (misc colls) IN ▲ 1366 [ADD] (15.97)
I. J. Paderewski (pno) *(rec 1911-37)* † J. Brahms:Hungarian Dances Pno; Chopin:Études (24) Pno, Opp. 10 & 25; Polonaise 6 Pno, Op. 53; Mendelssohn (-Bartholdy):Lieder ohne Worte; R. Schumann:Fantasiestücke Pno, Op. 12; Nachtstücke, Op. 23 ENPL (The Piano Library) ▲ 182 (13.97)
A. Rubinstein (pno) † Barcarolle 4 Pno; Pieces Pno, Op. 5 RCAV (Gold Seal) ▲ 61860 (11.97)
A. Toscanini (cnd), NBC SO ("Toscanini Rarities on Radio, 1939-43") † Bizet:Jolie fille de Perth (suite); Enescu:Romanian Rhap 1, Op. 11/1; Liszt:Hungarian Rhaps, S.244; M. Ravel:Boléro RY (The Radio Years) ▲ 42 (16.97)

RUBINSTEIN, ARTUR (1887-1982)

Fake Out (film music) for Orchestra
A. Rubinstein (cnd) LALI (Soundtracks) ▲ 12920 (5.97)

RUBINSTEIN, BERYL (1898-1952)

Concert Transcriptions (3) from Gershwin's *Porgy & Bess* for Piano
R. Glazier (pno) *(rec Christel DeHaan Fine Arts Center University, IN, May 2-4, 1995)* ("Gershwin: Remembrance and Discovery") † G. Gershwin:Bars (16) without a Name; Goldwyn Follies (sels); Impromptu in Two Keys; Melody No. 40; Pno Music; Preludes Pno; Primrose (sels); Promenade; Shall We Dance (sels); Sleepless Night Pno; Strike Up The Band (sels); 3/4 Blues; L. M. Gottschalk:Minuit à Séville, RO 170; E. Wild:Etudes on Gershwin Songs CENT ▲ 2271 [DDD] (16.97)

RUBINSTEIN, NIKOLAI (1835-1881)

Tarentella in g for 2 Pianos, Op. 14
T. Lenti (pno), M. Lenti (pno) † G. Gershwin:Rhap in Blue; E. Grieg:Waltz Caprices Pnos, Op. 37; Liszt:Hungarian Rhaps, S.244; F. Schubert:Fant Pno, D.940 ACAD ▲ 20037 [DDD] (16.97)

RUDAJEV, ALEXANDRE (1935-

Petite Suite Parisienne for Wind Quintet
M. Lifchitz (cnd) ("Music at the Crossroads") † A. Brings:Bagatelles; Diemer:Sxt Fl; Toensing:Angels; Ziffrin:Songs of the Trobairitz NSR ▲ 1005 (15.97)

Sonata for Violin & Piano (1992)
P. Eret (vn), D. Weisner (pno) ("Society of Composers, Inc. "Chamber Works"") † Belet:Proportional Preludes; C. Delgado:Fugaz; D. Epstein:Vars Pno; Juusela:Ilta Pala(a); Rindfleisch:Tears CPS ▲ 8651 [ADD] (16.97)

RUDERS, POUL (1949-

The Bells for Soprano & Chamber Ensemble [text Edgar Allan Poe] (1993)
L. Shelton (sop), D. Starobin (cnd) *(rec American Academy of Arts & Letters, NYC, NY, Apr 1994)* ("Speculum Musicae Plays the New Danes") † Abrahamsen:Winternacht; J. S. Bach:Sons & Partitas Vn; K. A. Rasmussen:Movements on a Moving Line; B. Sørensen:Deserted Churchyards BRID ▲ 9054 [DDD] (17.97)

Compositions (4) for Flute, Clarinet, Horn, Piano, String Quartet & Double Bass (1980)
O. Knussen (cnd), London Sinfonietta *(rec Kiddapore Ave London, England, Dec 1984)* † Abrahamsen:Walden; Winternacht PLAL ▲ 37 [DDD] (18.97)

Concerto No. 2 for Violin & Orchestra (1990-91)
R. Hirsch (vn), M. Schønwandt (cnd), Copenhagen Collegium Musicum *(rec Odd Fellow Palaeet Copenhagen, Feb 2, 1992)* † Dramaphonia DCAP (dacapo) ▲ 9308 [DDD] (13.97)

Corona for Orchestra (1993-95)
M. Schønwandt (cnd), Odense SO *(rec Odense Concert Hall, Nov 6-8, 1996)* ("Solar Trilogy") † Gong; Zenith MARC ▲ 8224054 [DDD] (13.97)

Corpus Cum Figuris for Ensemble (1984)
S. K. Hansen (cnd), Aarhus Sinfonia † Dramaphonia; 4 Dances in 1 Movt BIS ▲ 720 [DDD] (17.97)

The Death of Queen Dagmar for Chorus (1990)
S. Asmussen (alt), M. Bojesen (cnd), Camerata Chamber Choir ("Works for A Cappella Choir") † Motets; Stabat Mater DANI ▲ 8178 [DDD] (18.97)

Dramaphonia for Piano & Chamber Ensemble (1987)
E. Kaltoft (pno), S. K. Hansen (cnd), Aarhus Sinfonia † Corpus Cum Figuris; 4 Dances in 1 Movt BIS ▲ 720 [DDD] (17.97)
P. Rosenbaum (pno), O. D. Martinez (cnd), Lontano *(rec Danish Radio Concert Hall Copenhagen, Feb 10, 1990)* † Con 2 Vn DCAP (dacapo) ▲ 9308 [DDD] (13.97)

Four Dances in One Movement for Chamber Ensemble (1984)
S. K. Hansen (cnd), Aarhus Sinfonia † Corpus Cum Figuris; Dramaphonia BIS ▲ 720 [DDD] (17.97)

Gong for Orchestra (1992)
M. Schønwandt (cnd), Odense SO *(rec Odense Concert Hall, Nov 6-8, 1996)* ("Solar Trilogy") † Corona; Zenith MARC ▲ 8224054 [DDD] (13.97)

Motets
M. Bojesen (cnd), Camerata Chamber Choir—Pregheria semplice; Psalm 86; Caritas nunquam exidit ("Works for A Cappella Choir") † Death of Queen Dagmar; Stabat Mater DANI ▲ 8178 [DDD] (18.97)

Music of Ruders
L. Segerstam (cnd), Danish National RSO—Gong; Sym; Tundra; Saledes Saaes Johannes CHN ▲ 9179 [DDD] (17.97)

Nightshade for 9 Instruments (1986)
O. Knussen (cnd) † Psalmodies; Vox in Rama BRID ▲ 9037 [DDD] (17.97)

Psalmodies for Guitar & 9 Instruments (1989)
D. Starobin (gtr), D. Palma (cnd) † Nightshade; Vox in Rama BRID ▲ 9037 [DDD] (17.97)
D. Starobin (gtr), W. Purvis (cnd) *(rec June 1, 1992)* ("Guitar Concertante") † G. Crumb:Quest; J. A. Lennon:Zingari BRID ▲ 9071 [DDD] (17.97)

Stabat Mater for Boy Treble, Tenor, Out-of-tune Piano, Organ, Percussion & Mixed Chorus (1974)
F. Rasmussen (ten), M. La Cour Rasmussen (trbn), M. Bojesen (pno), H. Palsmar (org), S. Gaston (perc), M. Bojesen (cnd), Camerata Chamber Choir ("Works for A Cappella Choir") † Death of Queen Dagmar; Motets DANI ▲ 8178 [DDD] (18.97)

Tattoo for One for Clarinet (1984)
J. Kruse (cl) *(rec Det Fynske Musikkonservatorium, 1993)* ("Contemporary Danish Works for Clarinet") † Throne; N. V. Bentzon:Qt Cl; Son Cl; H. D. Koppel:Variazioni Libère, Op. 98; Vars Cl & Pno, Op. 72; B. Sørensen:Songs of the Decaying Garden Cl; Troll-Playing PLAL ▲ 78 [DAD] (18.97)

Tattoo for Three for Clarinet, Cello & Piano (1984)
Danish Trio *(rec Dec 1987)* † Gudmunsen-Holmgreen:Mirror Pieces; Højsgaard:Fantasistykker; Lorentzen:Mambo PLAL ▲ 57 [AAD] (18.97)

Throne for Clarinet & Piano (1988)
J. Kruse (cl), P. Salo (pno) *(rec Det Fynske Musikkonservatorium, 1993)* ("Contemporary Danish Works for Clarinet") † Tattoo for 1; N. V. Bentzon:Qt Cl; Son Cl; H. D. Koppel:Variazioni Libère, Op. 98; Vars Cl & Pno, Op. 72; B. Sørensen:Songs of the Decaying Garden Cl; Troll-Playing PLAL ▲ 78 [DAD] (18.97)

Vox in Rama for Amplified Violin, Clarinet & Piano (1983)
Capricorn members † Nightshade; Psalmodies BRID ▲ 9037 [DDD] (17.97)

Zenith for Orchestra (1992-93)
M. Schønwandt (cnd), Odense SO *(rec Odense Concert Hall, Nov 6-8, 1996)* ("Solar Trilogy") † Corona; Gong MARC ▲ 8224054 [DDD] (13.97)

RUDHYAR, DANE (1895-1985)

Advent for String Quartet (1976)
Kronos Quartet *(rec 1979)* † Crisis & Overcoming; Transmutation Pno CRI ▲ 604 [AAD] (16.97)

Crisis & Overcoming for String Quartet (1978)
Kronos Quartet † Advent; Transmutation Pno CRI ▲ 604 [AAD] (16.97)

Piano Music
W. Masselos (pno)—Paeans (1927); Stars (1926); Granites (1929) † W. Mayer:Octagon; Son 1 Pno CRI ▲ 584 [ADD] (17.97)

Transmutation for Piano (1976)
M. Mikulak (pno) † Advent; Crisis & Overcoming CRI ▲ 604 [AAD] (16.97)

RUDIN, ROLF (1961-

The Dream of Oenghus for Wind Orchestra, Op. 37 (1994-96)
E. Corporon (cnd), North Texas Wind Sym ("Dream Catchers") † Bassett:Lullaby for Kirsten; N. Galbraith:Danza de los Duendes; Gillingham:Waking Angels; W. Mays:Dreamcatcher; Schwantner:From a Dark Millennium; W. L. Thompson:Softly & Tenderly Jesus Is Calling KLAV ▲ 11089 [DDD] (18.97)

RUDNYTSKY, ANTIN (1902-1975)

Variations for Piano, Op. 38
R. Rudnytsky (pno) ("Pianistic Portraits") † Liszt:Légendes, S.175; S. Rachmaninoff:Preludes Pno; Rollin:Night Thoughts II; Talma:Son 1 Pno ARUN ▲ 3059 (16.97)

RUDOLPH [ARCHDUKE OF AUSTRIA] (1788-1831)

Septet in e for Clarinet, Bassoon, Horn & Strings
Consortium Classicum † J. M. Weber:Septet Cl ORF ▲ 182891 [DDD] (18.97)

Sonata in A for Clarinet & Piano, Op. 2 (1822)
R. Morales (cl), S. Kagan (pno) *(rec Astoria, NY, Apr 1995)* † Trio Cl KOCH ▲ 7339 [DDD] (10.97)

Sonata in f for Violin & Piano (ca 1812)
J. Suk (vn), S. Kagan (pno) † Vars Vn KOCH ▲ 7082 [DDD] (17.97)

Trio in E♭ for Clarinet, Cello & Piano (1814)
G. Kagan (vc), R. Morales (cl), S. Kagan (pno) *(rec Astoria, NY, Apr 1995)* † Son Cl, Op. 2 KOCH ▲ 7339 [DDD] (10.97)

Variations in F for Vioin & Piano [on a Theme by Prince Louis Ferdinand of Prussia] (ca 1810)
J. Suk (vn), S. Kagan (pno) † Son Vn KOCH ▲ 7082 [DDD] (17.97)

RUDOW, VIVIAN ADELBERG (20th cent)

Rebecca's Suite for Piano (1989-1991)
N. K. Solomon (pno) *(rec Slippery Rock University, PA, Sept 1996)* ("Sunbursts") † Diemer:Fant Pno; Kenessey:Sunburst, Op. 33; Rahbee:Preludes Pno, Op. 68; Schonthal:In Homage of...; S. Silver:Fant Quasi Theme & Vars; D. Thome:Pianismus LEON ▲ 345 [DDD] (16.97)

RUE, PIERRE DE LA (ca 1455-ca 1518)
Lamentationes Hieremiae for 4 Voices
K. Moll (cnd), Schola Discantus *(rec Harvard Univ Cambridge, MA)* † Missa de Sancta Anna
LYR (Early Music) ▲ 8021 (16.97)
Missa de feria for 5 Voices
C. Page (cnd), Gothic Voices † Missa "Sancta Dei genitrix" HYP ▲ 67010 (18.97)
Missa de Sancta Anna [Missa Felix Anna] for 4 Voices
K. Moll (cnd), Schola Discantus *(rec Harvard Univ Cambridge, MA, MA)* † Lamentationes Hieremiae
LYR (Early Music) ▲ 8021 (16.97)
Missa, "L'Homme armé" for 4 Voices
B. Holten (cnd), Ars Nova Vocal Ensemble [LAT] † N. Gombert:Motets KPT ▲ 32008 [DDD]
Missa pro defunctis (requiem) for 4 Voices
B. Holten (cnd), Ars Nova Vocal Ensemble [LAT] † Wert:Sacred Music KPT ▲ 32001 [DDD]
J. Wood (cnd), New London Chamber Choir [LAT] † Josquin Desprez:Déploration de Johannes Ockeghem; Missa, "L'ami Baudechon" AMON ▲ 24 [DDD] (16.97)
Missa "Sancta Dei genitrix" for 4 Voices
C. Page (cnd), Gothic Voices † Missa de feria HYP ▲ 67010 (18.97)

RUE, RIK (20th cent)
Nocturnal Windows (3) for Tape & 2 Instrumentalists (1992)
austraLYSIS members *(rec 2MBS-FM, 1993)* ("austraLYSIS: Windows in Time") † Bright:Night Db; L. Cresswell:Organic Music; Soliloquy on a Lambent Tailpiece; R. T. Dean:TimeStrain; H. Smith:Simultaneity; Xenakis:Morsima-Amorsima TALP ▲ 39 [DDD] (18.97)

RUEHR, ELENA (20th cent)
Shimmer for String Orchestra (1994)
S. Yoo (cnd), Metamorphosen CO *(rec Weston, MA, Apr 1994)* ("Metamorphosen Performs Chamber Orchestral Works") † E. Carter:Elegy Va; D. Coleman:Long Ago, This Radiant Day; Corigliano:Voyage Strs; I. Fine:Serious Song; E. T. Zwilich:Prologue & Vars Strs ALBA ▲ 194 [DDD] (16.97)

RUFFO, VINCENZO (ca 1508-1587)
Capricci in musica for 3 Voices
A. Rasi (cnd) *(rec Oct 27-30, 1993)* STRV ▲ 33337 [DDD] (16.97)

RUGGIERO, CHARLES (1947-
Interplay for Saxophone & Piano (1988)
J. Lulloff (sax), P. Hosford (pno) *(rec Illinois, United States of America, Mar 3-11 & May 23-35, 1994)* ("Interplay") † P. Cooper:Impromptus; A. Desenclos:Prélude, cadence et finale; F. Poulenc:Son Ob; Vaughan Williams:Studies in English Folk-Song *([ENG] text)* CCL ▲ 10497 [DDD] (18.97)

RUGGLES, CARL (1876-1971)
Angels for Brass [from symphonic suite Men & Angels, 1920-22] (1920; rev 1938)
A. Weisberg (cnd) † Messiaen:Et exspecto; Revueltas:Homenaje a Federico García Lorca
SUMM ▲ 122 [DDD] (16.97)
Evocations (4 chants) for Piano (1935-43; rev 1954)
M. Boriskin (pno) † I. Fine:Music for Pno; G. C. Menotti:Ricercare & Toccata; H. Shapero:Sons Pno
NWW ▲ 80402 [DDD] (16.97)
Men & Mountains for Chamber Orchestra (1924-35)
C. von Dohnányi (cnd), Cleveland Orch † Sun-treader; Crawford (Seeger):Andante; C. Ives:Orch Set 2; Three Places in New England PLON ▲ 443776 (16.97)
W. Strickland (cnd), Polish National RSO Katowice † Organum; L. Harrison:Sym on G
CRI (American Masters) ▲ 715 [ADD] (16.97)
Organum for Large Orchestra (1944-47)
A. Watanabe (cnd), Japan PO † Men & Mountains; L. Harrison:Sym on G
CRI (American Masters) ▲ 715 [ADD] (16.97)
Sun-treader for Orchestra (1926-31)
C. von Dohnányi (cnd), Cleveland Orch † Men & Mountains; Crawford (Seeger):Andante; C. Ives:Orch Set 2; Three Places in New England PLON ▲ 443776 (16.97)

RUITER, WIM DE (1943-
Parten for Organ (1969; rev 1983)
L. van der Vliet (org) ("Contemporary Dutch Organ Music") † Brons:Litany Org; T. Leeuw:Sweelinck-variaties; Raxach:Looking Glass; Schat:Passacaglia & Fugue; Welmers:Sequens Org CV ▲ 16 (19.97)

RUIZ DE RIBAYAZ, LUCAS (before 1650-?)
Luz Y norte musical (selections)
A. Lawrence-King (hpd/hp/org/psaltery), A. Lawrence-King (cnd) *(rec Valkkoog, Sept 1994)* ("Spanish Dances")
DEHA ▲ 77340 [DDD] (16.97)

RULON, C. BRYAN (20th cent)
Res Facta for Electro-Acoustic Ensemble
R. Black (cnd), New York New Music Ensemble *(rec 1991-94)* ("New Electro-Acoustic Music") † Primosch:Sacra Conversazione; R. Steiger:13 Loops CENT ▲ 2338 [DDD] (16.97)
Self Requiem for Taped Ensemble (1994-95)
C. Bahn (tape), C. B. Rulon (cnd) , Musicians' Accord ("And Trouble Came") † De Blasio:All the Way through Evening; Kaminsky:And Trouble Came: An African AIDS Diary CRI ▲ 729 [DDD] (16.97)

RUPPE, CHRISTIAN FRIEDRICH (1753-1826)
Christmas Cantata for Vocalists, Ensemble & Chorus
Musica ad Rhenum, Ensemble Bouzignac, F. V. Heidjen (sop), K. V. Poel (mez), O. Bouwknegt (ten), M. Sandler (bass) *(rec Jun 28-30, 1995)* † Easter Cantata NMCC ▲ 92067 [DDD] (17.97)
Easter Cantata for Vocalists, Ensemble & Chorus
Musica ad Rhenum, Ensemble Bouzignac, F. V. Heidjen (sop), K. V. Poel (mez), O. Bouwknegt (ten), M. Sandler (bass) *(rec Jun 28-30, 1995)* † Christmas Cantata NMCC ▲ 92067 [DDD] (17.97)

RUSH, STEPHEN (1958-
Aeneas in Strophades for 4 Harps & Tape, "Attack of the Harpies!" (1990)
L. Aspnes (hp), D. Watkins-Chou (hp), L. Cleaver (hp), K. Allwin (hp) ("Music of Stephen Rush") † Humandiños; Murders in the Rue Morgue; Nature's Course; Save Changes before Quitting MASM ▲ 2056 [DDD] (16.97)
Humandiños for Tape (1986/1996)
S. Rush (tape) ("Music of Stephen Rush") † Aeneas in Strophades; Murders in the Rue Morgue; Nature's Course; Save Changes before Quitting MASM ▲ 2056 [DDD] (16.97)
Murders in the Rue Morgue (opera in 1 act) for Singers, Synthesizer, Mallet Synthesizer & Computer [lib Delanghe & Rush after Poe] (1995)
S. Asplund (sop), D. Rentz (alt), E. Santos (voc), K. March (voc), B. Thomas (syn), S. Rush (tape) ("Music of Stephen Rush") † Aeneas in Strophades; Humandiños; Nature's Course; Save Changes before Quitting
MASM ▲ 2056 [DDD] (16.97)
Nature's Course for Marimba & Tape (1992)
N. Petrella (mar), S. Rush (tape) ("Music of Stephen Rush") † Aeneas in Strophades; Humandiños; Murders in the Rue Morgue; Save Changes before Quitting MASM ▲ 2056 [DDD] (16.97)
Save Changes before Quitting for Tape (1993)
S. Rush (tape) ("Music of Stephen Rush") † Aeneas in Strophades; Humandiños; Murders in the Rue Morgue; Nature's Course MASM ▲ 2056 [DDD] (16.97)

RUSHBY-SMITH, JOHN (1936-
Love's Legacy (cycle of 4 songs) for Soprano & Piano [text P. Shelly & M. Shelly] (1994)
M. Field (sop), A. Ball (pno) *(rec Bristol, May 1995)* ("British Song") † D. Matthews:Golden Kingdom; Routh:Woman Young & Old; M. Tippett:Heart's Assurance RDCL ▲ 9 (16.97)

RUSSELL, ARMAND (1932-
Suite Concertante for Tuba & Woodwind Quintet (1961)
J. Ketchum (fl), E. Dumler (ob), J. Kanter (cl), C. Ullery (bn), A. D. Krehbiel (hn), F. Cooley (tuba) ("The Romantic Tuba") † J. S. Bach:Sons Fl; J. Brahms:Ernste Gesänge, Op. 121; Zindars:Trigon CRYS ▲ 120 (15.97) ▮ 120 (9.98)

RUSSELL, WILLIAM (1905-1992)
Music of Russell
Essential Music—Prelude, Chorale & Fugue (1932); rev 1985; 4 Dance Movts; rev 1990; 3 Cuban Pieces (1935); Tpt Con (1937); Chicago Scketches (1940); March Suite (1936); rev 1984; Obou Badagri [ballet based on voodoo rites] (1933); Made in America (1936) MODE ▲ 34 (17.97)

RUSSO, JOHN (1943-
Elegy for Oboe (1971)
J. DeLancie (ob) *(rec United States of America)* ("Contemporary Music Festival") † Fort Washington Ov Orch; A. Blank:Intro & Rondo Fant; J. Fry:Metamorphoses on a Theme by P. Hindemith; J. Kowalski:Three Koans Str Qt; Lieuwen:Anachronisms; Van Appledorn:Concerto Brevis; Missa Brevis *(E text)* CRSR ▲ 9052

RUSSO, JOHN (cont.)
Fort Washington Overture for Orchestra (1971)
J. Russo (cnd), National Festival Orchestra *(rec United States of America)* ("Contemporary Music Festival") † Elegy Ob; A. Blank:Intro & Rondo Fant; J. Fry:Metamorphoses on a Theme by P. Hindemith; J. Kowalski:Three Koans Str Qt; Lieuwen:Anachronisms; Van Appledorn:Concerto Brevis; Missa Brevis *(E text)* CRSR ▲ 9052
Largetto for Clarinet, Viola & Piano (1964)
S. Curtiss (va), J. Russo (cl), L. W. Ignacio (pno) † Son 4 Cl; E. Carter:Pastorale E Hn; F. Devienne:Son 1 Cl; C. Harrison:Songs from a Child's Garden; Hush:Partita 1 Vc CRSR ▲ 9255
Pieces (4) for Clarinet
J. Russo (cl) ("Excursions") † Son 1 Fl; Bozza:Caprice-Improvisation; Hush:Qt 1 Strs; Son Vc; Van Appledorn:Ayre; E. A. Zappa:Hydra Son CRSR ▲ 9257
Preludes (3) for Clarinet & Piano
J. Russo (cl), L. W. Ignacio (pno) *(rec PA, United States of America)* ("Masterworks for Clarinet & Piano") † Studies (2); J. Beck:Son Cl; Bremer:Son Cl; Son Clt; S. Chandler:Tune & Chase with Quickstep Dirge; H. Cowell:Six Casual Developments; Rochberg:Dialogues; R. Snyder:Polemics *(E text)* CRSR ▲ 9561
Preludes (3)
J. Russo (cl), L. W. Ignacio (pno) *(rec PA, United States of America)* ("Masterworks for Clarinet & Piano") † Studies (2); J. Beck:Son Cl; Bremer:Son Cl; Son Clt; S. Chandler:Tune & Chase with Quickstep Dirge; H. Cowell:Six Casual Developments; Rochberg:Dialogues; R. Snyder:Polemics *(E text)* CRSR ▲ 9561
Sonata No. 4 for Clarinet & Piano (1966)
J. Russo (cl), L. W. Ignacio (pno) † Largetto; E. Carter:Pastorale E Hn; F. Devienne:Son 1 Cl; C. Harrison:Songs from a Child's Garden; Hush:Partita 1 Vc CRSR ▲ 9255
Sonata No. 1 for Flute & Piano (1971)
L. Lind (fl), L. W. Ignacio (pno) ("Excursions") † Pieces Cl; Bozza:Caprice-Improvisation; Hush:Qt 1 Strs; Son Vc; Van Appledorn:Ayre; E. A. Zappa:Hydra Son CRSR ▲ 9257
Studies (2) for Clarinet & Piano
J. Russo (cl), L. W. Ignacio (pno) *(rec PA, United States of America)* ("Masterworks for Clarinet & Piano") † Preludes (3); J. Beck:Son Cl; Bremer:Son Cl; Son Clt; S. Chandler:Tune & Chase with Quickstep Dirge; H. Cowell:Six Casual Developments; Rochberg:Dialogues; R. Snyder:Polemics *(E text)* CRSR ▲ 9561
Toccata No. 1 for Piano (1969)
K. Rasmussen (pno) ("Danish/American Composers") † Toccata 2 Pno; J. Beck:Son 1 Pno; F. Germani:Immotus; Hegaard:Preludes Pno; Lorentzen:Abgrund; Goldranken; G. Lund:Dialogues; Van Appledorn:Contrasts Pno
CRSR ▲ 9664
Toccata No. 2 for Piano
K. Rasmussen (pno) ("Danish/American Composers") † Toccata 1 Pno; J. Beck:Son 1 Pno; F. Germani:Immotus; Hegaard:Preludes Pno; Lorentzen:Abgrund; Goldranken; G. Lund:Dialogues; Van Appledorn:Contrasts Pno
CRSR ▲ 9664

RUTENBERG, PETER (1951-
Ballad of the Buffalo Skinners for Chorus (1990)
J. Reyheim (ten), R. McLeod (bass), P. Rutenberg (cnd), Los Angeles Chamber Singers [trad; ed & expanded Peter Rutenberg] ("Shenandoah: An American Chorister 1890-1990") † S. Barber:Songs; MacDowell:Northern Songs, Op. 43; Mechem:5 Centuries of Spring; H. Stevens:Campion Suite KLAV ▲ 11052 [DDD] (18.97)

RUTTER, JOHN (1945-
Brother Heinrich's Christmas for Voices & Chamber Orchestra
A. Holt (sgr—St. George), S. Carrington (sgr—Master of Ceremonies), B. Ives (sgr—Dragon), J. Jackman (sgr—Boy), R. Hickox (cnd), City of London Sinfonia, King's Singers *(rec London, England, June 1983)* ("Three Musical Fables") † Reluctant Dragon; Wind in the Willows CLL ▲ 115 (15.97)
Church Music
J. Martinson (org), T. Seelig (cnd), Turtle Creek Chorale, T. Seelig (cnd), Dallas Women's Chorus—Praise Ye the Lord; The Lord Is My Light & My Salvation; All Things Bright & Beautiful; Lord, Make Me an Instr of Thy Peace *(rec July 28-29, 1993)* † Requiem REF ▲ 57 [DDD] (16.97)
M. O'Neal (cnd), Michael O'Neal Singers—Te Deum; Be Thou My Vision; All Things Bright & Beautiful; The Lord Bless You & Keep You *(rec Roswell United Methodist Church Atlanta GA, GA, Mar 27, 1995)* ("Sacred Sounds of John Rutter") † Requiem ACAD ▲ 20048 [DDD] (16.97)
J. Rutter (cnd), City of London Sinfonia, Cambridge Singers—Te Deum; Be thou my vision; I believe in springtime; Lord, make me an instr of thy peace; O be joyful in the Lord; All creatures of our God & King; A choral fanfare; As the bridegroom to his chosen; Christ the Lord is risen again; Thy perfect love; The Lord is my light & my salvation; Go forth into the world in peace; Now thank we all our God ("Te Deum & other Church Music")
CLL ▲ 112 [DDD] (15.97) ▮ 112 [DDD] (7.98)
Dancing Day for Harp & Chorus (1974)
K. Goheen (sop), M. Barry (sop), C. Hanney (sop), M. D. Kleer (alt), M. Burr (alt), R. Costanzi (hp), Elektra Women's Choir ("A Ceremony of Carols") † B. Britten:Ceremony of Carols, Op. 28; P. Csonka:Concierto di Navidad
SKYL ▲ 9703 [DDD] (15.97)
Toronto Children's Chorus, J. Loman (hp) MARQ ▲ 135 [DDD] (16.97)
Gloria for Brass Ensemble, Organ, Percussion & Chorus (1974)
J. Rutter (cnd) , Cambridge Singers [LAT] CLL ▲ 100 [DDD] (15.97) ▮ 100 [DDD] (7.98)
Magnificat for Soprano, Orchestra & Chorus (1990)
J. Rutter (cnd), City of London Sinfonia, Cambridge Singers, P. Forbes (sop) † Requiem
CLL ▲ 504 [DDD] (10.97) ▮ 504 [DDD] (6.98)
Music of Rutter
City of London Sinfonia, S. Cleobury (cnd), King's College Choir Cambridge *(Requiem; Hymn to the Creator of Light; Cantate Domino)*, R. Quinney (org), City of London Sinfonia, S. Cleobury (cnd), King's College Choir Cambridge *(Veni sancte spiritus; What Sweeter Music)*, Wallace Collection, S. Cleobury (cnd), King's College Choir Cambridge *(Cantus)*, R. Quinney (org), Wallace Collection, S. Cleobury (cnd), King's College Choir Cambridge *(Te Deum) (rec Cambridge, England, July 15-18, 1997)* EMIC ▲ 56605 [DDD] (16.97)
S. Layton (cnd), Bournemouth Sinfonietta, Polyphony—Requiem; Hymn to the Creator of Light; God Be in My Head; Gaelic Blessing; Cantate Domino; Open Thou Mine Eyes; A Prayer of St. Patrick; A Choral Fanfare; Draw on, Sweet Night; My True Love Hath My Heart; The Lord Bless You & Keep You HYP ▲ 66947 (18.97)
The Reluctant Dragon for Voices & Chamber Orchestra (1978)
B. Kay (nar), J. Rutter (cnd), City of London Sinfonia, Cambridge Singers, King's Singers *(rec London, England, June 1983)* ("Three Musical Fables") † Brother Heinrich's Christmas; Wind in the Willows CLL ▲ 115 (15.97)
Requiem for Voice, Organ, Orchestra & Chorus (1985)
D. Deam (sop), C. Ashton (sop), J. Rutter (cnd), City of London Sinfonia, Cambridge Singers [E,L]
CLL ▲ 103 [DDD] ▮ 103 [DDD] (7.98)
N. Keith (sop), J. Martinson (org), T. Seelig (cnd), Turtle Creek Chorale, T. Seelig (cnd), Dallas Women's Chorus *(rec July 28-29, 1993)* † Church Music REF ▲ 57 [DDD] (16.97)
K. List (sop), M. A. Swope (vc), K. Farmer (fl), B. Cook (ob), J. Albertson (hp), T. Alderman (org), J. Mautz (timp), M. Del Campo (perc), M. O'Neal (cnd), Michael O'Neal Singers *(rec Atlanta, GA, Mar 27, 1995)* ("Sacred Sounds of John Rutter") † Church Music ACAD ▲ 20048 [DDD] (16.97)
J. Rutter (cnd), City of London Sinfonia, Cambridge Singers, C. Ashton (sop), D. Deam (sop) † Magnificat
CLL ▲ 504 [DDD] (10.97) ▮ 504 [DDD] (6.98)
The Wind in the Willows for Voices & Chamber Orchestra (1981)
A. Holt (sgr—Rat/Rat/Saint George), S. Carrington (sgr—Magistrate/Magistrate/Master of Ceremonies), C. Mason (sgr—Badger/Badger), B. Ives (sgr—Toad/Dragon/Toad), J. Jackman (sgr—Gaolers Daughter/Boy/Gaoler's daughter), A. Hume (sgr—Mole), R. Baker (nar), B. Kay (nar), R. Hickox (cnd), City of London Sinfonia, J. Rutter (cnd), King's Singers, Cambridge Singers, King's Singers *(rec London, England, June 1983)* ("Three Musical Fables") † Brother Heinrich's Christmas; Reluctant Dragon CLL ▲ 115 (15.97)

RÜTTI, CARL (1949-
Ave Maria for Organ & Chorus (1993)
I. Moore (cnd), Cambridge Voices, A. Page (org) *(rec England, Oct 1997 & Mar 1998)* ("Veni Creator Spiritus") † Ave maris stella; Tabor; Veni Creator Spiritus; Veni Creator Spiritus Org; T. Rütti:Stiller Kanon *([ENG,GER,LAT] text)*
HER ▲ 210 [DDD] (18.97)
Ave maris stella for 8 A Cappella Voices
I. Moore (cnd), Cambridge Voices *(rec England, Oct 1997 & Mar 1998)* ("Veni Creator Spiritus") † Ave Maria; Tabor; Veni Creator Spiritus; Veni Creator Spiritus Org; T. Rütti:Stiller Kanon *([ENG,GER,LAT] text)*
HER ▲ 210 [DDD] (18.97)
Choral Music
V. Henderson (vc), I. Moore (cnd), Cambridge Voices—O magnum mysterium; Lieder; Der Liebe; Fortis ut mors; Osculetur; Que tu es belle, ma bien-aimée; Ich schlief, doch mein Herz; Behold; Thou Hast Ravished My Heart; In meinem Garten; Vater Unser; Gloria (Missa Angelorum) *(rec St. Cyriac's Church Swaffham Prior, Mar 1995)* ("Songs of Love") HER ▲ 183 [DDD]

RÜTTI, CARL (cont.)
Choral Music (cont.)
S. Jackson (cnd), BBC Sym Chorus—O Magnum Mysterium; Nunc Dumittis; Missa Angelorum; Magnificat; Alpha et Omega ("Sacred Choral Music") ASV ▲ 954 (16.97)
Panta Rhei for Piano (1994)
C. Rütti (pno) *(rec London, England, Aug 1998)* ("Carl Rütti Plays His Own Piano Music") † Parabel; Stundenbuch; Symbole HER ▲ 226 [DDD] (18.97)
Parabel for Piano
C. Rütti (pno) *(rec London, England, Aug 1998)* ("Carl Rütti Plays His Own Piano Music") † Panta Rhei; Stundenbuch; Symbole HER ▲ 226 [DDD] (18.97)
Stundenbuch for Piano
C. Rütti (pno) *(rec London, England, Aug 1998)* ("Carl Rütti Plays His Own Piano Music") † Panta Rhei; Parabel; Symbole HER ▲ 226 [DDD] (18.97)
Symbole (suite) for Piano
C. Rütti (pno) *(rec London, England, Aug 1998)* ("Carl Rütti Plays His Own Piano Music") † Panta Rhei; Parabel; Stundenbuch HER ▲ 226 [DDD] (18.97)
Tabor (suite) for Organ
A. Page (org)—Berg der Verklärung; Die Wolke; Lerche *(rec England, Oct 1997 & Mar 1998)* ("Veni Creator Spiritus") † Ave maris stella; Ave Maria; Veni Creator Spiritus; Veni Creator Spiritus Org; T. Rütti:Stiller Kanon HER ▲ 210 [DDD] (18.97)
Veni Creator Spiritus for 40 A Cappella Voices
I. Moore (cnd), Cambridge Voices, L. Smallwood (voc) *(rec England, Oct 1997 & Mar 1998)* ("Veni Creator Spiritus") † Ave maris stella; Ave Maria; Tabor; Veni Creator Spiritus Org; T. Rütti:Stiller Kanon *([ENG,GER,LAT] text)* HER ▲ 210 [DDD] (18.97)
Veni Creator Spiritus for Organ (1983)
A. Page (org) *(rec England, Oct 1997 & Mar 1998)* ("Veni Creator Spiritus") † Ave maris stella; Ave Maria; Tabor; Veni Creator Spiritus; T. Rütti:Stiller Kanon HER ▲ 210 [DDD] (18.97)
Verena, die Quelle (oratorio) for Narrator, Chamber Ensemble & Chorus
S. Walter (nar), I. Moore (cnd) , Cambridge Voices HER 2-▲ 186 [DDD] (36.97)

RÜTTI, TOBIAS (1979-
Stiller Kanon for Chorus (1995)
I. Moore (cnd), Cambridge Voices *(rec England, Oct 1997 & Mar 1998)* ("Veni Creator Spiritus") † C. Rütti:Ave maris stella; Ave Maria; Tabor; Veni Creator Spiritus; Veni Creator Spiritus Org *([ENG,GER,LAT] text)* HER ▲ 210 [DDD] (18.97)

RUZICKA, PETER (1948-
...Islands, Unbounded... for Violin, Orchestra & Chorus (1995)
V. Ashkenazy (cnd), Berlin SO, RIAS Chamber Choir, C. Tetzlaff (vn) † Gestalt und Abbruch; Presentiments; Sonne skint THOR ▲ 2402 [DDD] (16.97)
Approach & Peace (4 fragments) for Piano & 42 Strings [after Schumann] (1981)
J. Frantz (pno), G. Herbig (cnd), Southwest German RSO Baden-Baden *(rec Nov 1984)* ("Orchesterwerke") † Blessed, the Damned; Etym; Tallis; Torso THOR ▲ 2220 (16.97)
Befragung (5 pieces) for Orchestra (1974)
M. Atzmon (cnd), North German RSO † Feedback; Metamorphoses on a Sound Plane by Haydn; Sinf for 25 CPO ▲ 999053 [DDD] (14.97)
The Blessed, the Damned for Orchestra (1984)
S. Bychkov (cnd), Bavarian RSO *(rec Nov 1992)* ("Orchesterwerke") † Approach & Peace; Etym; Tallis; Torso THOR ▲ 2220 (16.97)
Etym for Orchestra, "Cross-fades for 72 Musicians" (1973)
P. Moll (pno), P. Ruzicka (cnd), Berlin RSO *(rec Mar 1975)* ("Orchesterwerke") † Approach & Peace; Blessed, the Damned; Tallis; Torso THOR ▲ 2220 (16.97)
Feedback for 4 Orchestral Groups (1973)
E. Bour (cnd), Southwest German RSO Baden-Baden, Zurich Sprechchor † Befragung; Metamorphoses on a Sound Plane by Haydn; Sinf for 25 CPO ▲ 999053 [DDD] (14.97)
Das Gesagnete, das Verfluchte for Orchestra
P. Ruzicka (cnd), Berlin German SO † A. Pettersson:Sym 15; Sym 3; Sym 4 CPO ▲ 999223 [DDD] (14.97)
Gestalt und Abbruch for Chorus (1979)
W. Hagen (cnd), NDR Chorus † ...Islands, Unbounded...; Presentiments; Sonne skint THOR ▲ 2402 [DDD] (16.97)
Metamorphoses on a Sound Plane by Joseph Haydn for Orchestra
G. Albrecht (cnd), Cologne RSO † Befragung; Feedback; Sinf for 25 CPO ▲ 999053 [DDD] (14.97)
Presentiments for Orchestra (1998)
P. Ruzicka (cnd), Schleswig-Holstein Festival Orch † ...Islands, Unbounded...; Gestalt und Abbruch; Sonne skint THOR ▲ 2402 [DDD] (16.97)
Satyagraha: Approach & Departure for Chamber Ensemble (1984-95)
D. Cichewiecz (cnd), Hamburg das neue werk Ensemble *(rec Germany, Aug 14-25, 1995)* ("25 Jahre Ensemble 'das neue werk' Hamburg") † G. Coates:Time Frozen; D. Glanert:Son 2; Kelterborn:Ensemble-Buch II MPH ▲ 55706 [DDD] (15.97)
Sinfonia for 25 solo Strings, 16 Vocalists & Percussion (1971)
M. Gielen (cnd), Stuttgart RSO, South German Radio Chorus † Befragung; Feedback; Metamorphoses on a Sound Plane by Haydn CPO ▲ 999053 [DDD] (14.97)
Die sonne sinkt [The Sun Sets] for Baritone & Orchestra (1997)
P. Ruzicka (cnd), Frankfurt RSO, A. Schmidt (bar) † ...Islands, Unbounded...; Gestalt und Abbruch; Presentiments THOR ▲ 2402 [DDD] (16.97)
Tallis for Orchestra
P. Ruzicka (cnd), North German SO *(rec Oct 1994)* ("Orchesterwerke") † Approach & Peace; Blessed, the Damned; Etym; Torso THOR ▲ 2220 (16.97)
Torso [Materials] for Orchestra
L. Vis (cnd), Cologne RSO *(rec Dec 1973)* ("Orchesterwerke") † Approach & Peace; Blessed, the Damned; Etym; Tallis THOR ▲ 2220 (16.97)

RYABCHIKOVA, TATYANA (20th cent)
Barcarolle for Piano
T. Riabchikova (pno) *(rec Tsai Performance Center Boston)* ("The Monogram") † Dedication to J. S. Bach; Pno Music; Scenes from Nature; Son Pno, "Bells" SO ▲ 22570 [DDD] (16.97)
Dedication to J. S. Bach for Piano
T. Riabchikova (pno) *(rec Tsai Performance Center Boston)* ("The Monogram") † Barcarolle; Pno Music; Scenes from Nature; Son Pno, "Bells" SO ▲ 22570 [DDD] (16.97)
Piano Music
T. Riabchikova (pno)—Son in d; The Bells; Barcarolle; Dedication to J.S. Bach; Scenes from Nature [Landscapes] ("The Monogram") † Barcarolle; Dedication to J. S. Bach; Scenes from Nature; Son Pno, "Bells" SO ▲ 22570 [DDD] (16.97)
Scenes from Nature [Landscapes] for Piano
T. Riabchikova (pno) *(rec Tsai Performance Center Boston)* ("The Monogram") † Barcarolle; Dedication to J. S. Bach; Pno Music; Son Pno, "Bells" SO ▲ 22570 [DDD] (16.97)
Sonata in d for Piano, "The Bells"
T. Riabchikova (pno) *(rec Tsai Performance Center Boston)* ("The Monogram") † Barcarolle; Dedication to J. S. Bach; Pno Music; Scenes from Nature SO ▲ 22570 [DDD] (16.97)

RYABOV, VLADIMIR (1950-
Concerto of Waltzes for Orchestra, Op. 36
V. Ziva (cnd), Moscow SO † Sym 4 MARC ▲ 8223749 (13.97)
Symphony No. 4 in e, Op. 22
V. Ziva (cnd), Moscow SO † Con of Waltzes, Op. 36 MARC ▲ 8223749 (13.97)

RYAN, JEFFREY (20th cent)
Ophélie for Voices & Large Orchestra (1994)
E. F. Brown (cnd), Bowling Green Philharmonia [comments by Ryan] ("The Composer's Voice-New Music from Bowling Green") † S. Adler:Requiescat in Pace; D. W. Freund:Poem Sym; K. Husa:Sym 2; M. Shrude:Into Light; Theofanidis:On the Edge of the Infinte ALBA ▲ 321 [DDD] (16.97)

RYDBERG, BO (1960-
LINK/Sequence for Saxophone Quartet
Stockholm Saxophone Quartet ("Links") † Enström:Vigil; Feiler:Anvil & Parachutes; Lindwall:Cut Up; Parmerud:Retur; Samuelsson:Signal Sax Qt CAPA ▲ 21517 (16.97)

RYELANDT, JOSEPH (1870-1965)
Agnus Dei (oratorio in 5 parts) for Vocal Soloists, Orchestra & Chorus, Op. 56 (1913-15)
I. Kapelle (sop), L. van Deyck (mez), J. Cornwell (ten), S. Macleod (bass), H. Claessens (bass), G. Llewellyn (cnd), Royal Flanders PO, Altra Voce, Audite Nova Vocal Ensemble *(rec Elisabeth Hall Antwerp, Holland, Dec 9, 1994)* MARC 2-▲ 8223785 [DDD] (27.97)
Flos Carmeli (cantata) for Soprano, Small Orchestra, Female Chorus & Piano, Op. 106 (1932)
G. D. Reyghere (sop), P. Peire (cnd) , Capella Brugensis *(rec 1997-98)* ("Sacred Works") † Missa 4 vocibus, Op. 84; Motets; Thème & Vars Org, Op. 119 RENE ▲ 92040 [DDD] (16.97)
Idylle Mystique for Soprano & Orchestra, WW 23, Op. 55 (1901)
F. Bollon (cnd), Flanders SO, Koor Novecento, M. Capelle (sop) † Sym 4 CYPR ▲ 1616 [DDD] (17.97)
Missa 4 vocibus for Mixed Choir & Organ, Op. 84 (1925)
I. Michiels (org), P. Peire (cnd), Capella Brugensis *(rec 1997-98)* ("Sacred Works") † Flos Carmelli, Op. 106; Motets; Thème & Vars Org, Op. 119 RENE ▲ 92040 [DDD] (16.97)
Missa 6 vocibus for Voices, Op. 111
Malmö Chamber Choir *(rec Mar 28-29, 1981)* † Peterson-Berger:Album of 8 Songs, Op. 11; Söderman:Spiritual Songs BIS ▲ 181 [AAD] (17.97)
Motets
P. Peire (cnd), Capella Brugensis—Audi Filia à 4; Panem de Coelo, Op. 87/1; Ave Maria, Op. 87/2 *(rec 1997-98)* ("Sacred Works") † Flos Carmelli, Op. 106; Missa 4 vocibus, Op. 84; Thème & Vars Org, Op. 119 RENE ▲ 92040 [DDD] (16.97)
Symphony No. 4 for Orchestra & Choir, WW 111, Op. 55 (1913)
F. Bollon (cnd), Flanders SO, Koor Novecento † Idylle Mystique, WW 23 CYPR ▲ 1616 [DDD] (17.97)
Thème & Variations for Organ, Op. 119 (1937)
I. Michiels (org) *(rec 1997-98)* ("Sacred Works") † Flos Carmelli, Op. 106; Missa 4 vocibus, Op. 84; Motets RENE ▲ 92040 [DDD] (16.97)

RZEWSKI, FREDERIC (1938-
Antigone-Legend for Voice & Piano [text B. Brecht; translated J. Malma] (1982)
C. Plantamura (sop), F. Rzewski (pno) *(rec Univ of CA San Diego, Oct 25-26, 1986)* † Jefferson CRI ▲ 747 [ADD] (16.97)
Coming Together—Attica for Narrator & Instruments (1972)
Group 180 [ENG] † L. Melis:Etude for 3 Mirrors; Szemző:Water-Wonder HUN ▲ 12545 (16.97)
Crusoe for Percussion, Keyboards & Woodwinds (1993)
Zeitgeist *(rec St. Paul, MN, Mar 1994)* ("Zeitgeist Plays Rzewski") † Lost Melody; Spots; Wails OOD ▲ 15 (16.97)
De profundis for Piano (1991)
A. D. Mare (pno) † Piece 4 Pno; Son Pno; Winnsboro Cotton Mill Blues OOD ▲ 16 [DDD] (16.97)
Jefferson [setting of excerpts from Thomas Jefferson's *Declaration of Independence*] for Voice & Piano (1970)
C. Plantamura (sop), F. Rzewski (pno) *(rec Cologne Germany, Oct 1970)* † Antigone-Legend CRI ▲ 747 [ADD] (16.97)
The Lost Melody for Percussion, Keyboards & Woodwinds (1989)
J. Holmquist (perc), Zeitgeist *(rec St. Paul, MN, Mar 1994)* ("Zeitgeist Plays Rzewski") † Crusoe; Spots; Wails OOD ▲ 15 (16.97)
Ludes (12) for Piano [Book 1] (1990)
F. Rzewski (pno) *(rec Univ of Iowa School of Music Iowa City, 1996)* ("Night Crossing: Works for 1 & 2 Pianos") † Ludes (book 2); Night Crossing; Winnsboro Cotton Mill Blues MUA ▲ 988 [DDD] (16.97)
Ludes (12) for Piano [Book 2] (1991)
F. Rzewski (pno) *(rec Univ of Iowa School of Music Iowa City, 1996)* ("Night Crossing: Works for 1 & 2 Pianos") † Ludes (book 1); Night Crossing; Winnsboro Cotton Mill Blues MUA ▲ 988 [DDD] (16.97)
Moonrise with Memories for Bass Trombone & 6 Instruments (1978)
L. Schulman (vn), R. Wolinsky (gtr), W. Blount (cl), A. Dean (tpt), D. Taylor (b trbn), D. Carp (kazoo), B. Moersch (dlc/mar) *(rec NYC, June 4, 1981)* ("David Taylor: Bass Trombone") † Dlugoszewski:Duende Quidditas; Ewazen:Dagon II; Liebman:Remembrance NWW ▲ 80494 (16.97)
Night Crossing with Fisherman for 2 Pianos (1994)
U. Oppens (pno), F. Rzewski (pno) *(rec Univ of Iowa School of Music Iowa City, 1996)* ("Night Crossing: Works for 1 & 2 Pianos") † Ludes (book 1); Ludes (book 2); Winnsboro Cotton Mill Blues MUA ▲ 988 [DDD] (16.97)
North American Ballads (4) for Piano (1978-79)
M.-A. Hamelin (pno)—Down by the Riverside; Winnsboro Cotton Mill Blues † People United Will Never Be Defeated HYP ▲ 67077 (18.97)
K. Supové (pno) *(rec Nov 1992)* ("Figure 88") † M. Epstein:Waterbowls; L. Foss:Solo Pno; D. Lang:While Nailing at Random; R. Woolf:Dancétudes CRI (Emergency Music) ▲ 653 [DDD] (17.97)
The People United Will Never Be Defeated (36 variations on a Chilean song) for Piano (1975)
S. Drury (pno) *(rec June 1992)* NALB ▲ 63 [DDD] (16.97)
M.-A. Hamelin (pno) † North American Ballads HYP ▲ 67077 (18.97)
U. Oppens (pno) *(rec Apr 1978)* VC ▲ 8056 [ADD] (13.97)
Piece No. 4 for Piano (1977)
A. D. Mare (pno) † De Profundis; Son Pno; Winnsboro Cotton Mill Blues OOD ▲ 16 [DDD] (16.97)
L. Moore (pno) *(rec The Hit Factory New York, Oct 4-8, 1995)* ("Cheating, Lying, Stealing") † Didkovsky:Amalia's Secret; Gosfield:Manufacture of Tangles Ivory; D. Lang:Cheating, Lying, Stealing; Pascoal:Arapua; Vierk:Red Shift; Ziporyn:Tsmindao Ghmerto SNYC ▲ 62254 [DDD] (16.97)
The Road for Piano (1996)
F. Rzewski (pno) *(rec Other Minds Festival Yerba Buena Gardens Theater, Nov 22, 1996)* ("New Works") † To the Earth; Whangdoodles MUA ▲ 1000 [DDD] (16.97)
Sonata for Piano (1991)
A. D. Mare (pno) † De Profundis; Piece 4 Pno; Winnsboro Cotton Mill Blues OOD ▲ 16 [DDD] (16.97)
Spots for Percussion, Keyboards & Woodwinds (1986)
J. Holmquist (perc), Zeitgeist *(rec St. Paul, MN, Mar 1994)* ("Zeitgeist Plays Rzewski") † Crusoe; Lost Melody; Wails OOD ▲ 15 (16.97)
To the Earth for Percussion (1985)
W. Winant (perc) *(rec Mills College)* ("New Works") † Road; Whangdoodles MUA ▲ 1000 [DDD] (16.97)
Wails for Percussion, Keyboards & Woodwinds (1984)
J. Holmquist (perc), Zeitgeist *(rec St. Paul, MN, Mar 1994)* ("Zeitgeist Plays Rzewski") † Crusoe; Lost Melody; Spots OOD ▲ 15 (16.97)
Whangdoodles for Violin, Piano & Percussion (1990)
Abel-Steinberg-Winant Trio *(rec Mills College Concert Hall, 1994)* ("New Works") † Road; To the Earth MUA ▲ 1000 [DDD] (16.97)
Winnsboro Cotton Mill Blues for Piano (1979; arr for 2 Pianos, 1980)
A. D. Mare (pno) † De Profundis; Piece 4 Pno; Son Pno OOD ▲ 16 [DDD] (16.97)
U. Oppens (pno), F. Rzewski (pno) *(rec Univ of Iowa School of Music Iowa City, 1996)* ("Night Crossing: Works for 1 & 2 Pianos") † Ludes (book 1); Ludes (book 2); Night Crossing MUA ▲ 988 [DDD] (16.97)

SAARIAHO, KAIJA (1952-
A la fumée for Alto Flute, Cello & Orchestra (1990)
A. Karttunen (vc), P. Alanko (a fl), E. Salonen (cnd), Los Angeles PO † Du cristal; Nymphea ODE ▲ 804 [DDD] (17.97)
Du cristal for Orchestra (1989-90)
E. Salonen (cnd), Los Angeles PO † À la fumée; Nymphea ODE ▲ 804 [DDD] (17.97)
Fall for Harp (1991)
S. A. Claro (hp) *(rec Denmark, Nov 1994-Jan 1995)* † Frounberg:Worlds Apart; Graugaard:Incrustations; Lippe:Music Hp Tape; Parmerud:Strings & Shadows CENT ▲ 2284 [DDD] (16.97)
Jardin secret I (electronic music) (1984-85)
K. Saariaho (elec) ("A Portrait of Kaija Saariaho") † Laconisme de laile; NoaNoa; Sah den Vögeln; Verblendungen BIS ▲ 307 [AAD] (17.97)
Laconisme de l'aile for Flute (1982)
C. Hoitenga (fl) ("A Portrait of Kaija Saariaho") † Jardin secret I; NoaNoa; Sah den Vögeln; Verblendungen BIS ▲ 307 [AAD] (17.97)
Lonh for Soprano & Electronics
D. Upshaw (sop), K. Saariaho (elec) ("Private Gardens") † NoaNoa; Près; Six Japanese Gardens ODE ▲ 906 (17.97)
Maa (ballet in 7 scenes) for Acoustic-Electronic Chamber Ensemble (1991)
T. Tuomela (cnd) ODE ▲ 791 [DDD] (17.97)
NoaNoa for Flute & Electronics (1991)
C. Hoitenga (fl) ("A Portrait of Kaija Saariaho") † Jardin secret I; Laconisme de laile; Sah den Vögeln; Verblendungen BIS ▲ 307 [AAD] (17.97)

SAARIAHO, KAIJA (cont.)
NoaNoa for Flute & Electronics (1991) (cont.)
C. Hoitenga (fl), K. Saariaho (elec) ("Private Gardens") † Lonh; Près; Six Japanese Gardens ODE ▲ 906 (17.97)
Nymphea for String Quartet & Electronics (1987)
Arditti String Quartet ("From Scandanavia") † M. Lindberg:Qnt Cl; B. Sørensen:Adieu; Alman; Angel's Music; Tiensuu:Arsenic & Old Lace DISQ ▲ 782033 (18.97)
Kronos Quartet † À la fumée; Du cristal ODE ▲ 804 [DDD] (17.97)
Petals for Cello (1988)
A. Karttunen (vc) ("Electro Acoustic Music I") † N. Boulanger:From Temporal Silence; C. Dodge:Profile; P. Lansky:Notjustmoreidlechatter; Risset:Autre face; D. Warner:Delay in Glass NEU ▲ 45073 [DDD]
J. Krieger (vc), A. Quadraverb (elec) † Halier:UITT; S. Hopkins:Cello Chi; A. Lucier:Indian Summer; William:Come Windows Gold Coming OOWN ▲ 22 (16.97)
Près for Cello & Electronics
A. Karttunen (vc), K. Saariaho (elec) ("Private Gardens") † Lonh; NoaNoa; Six Japanese Gardens ODE ▲ 906 (17.97)
Sah den Vögeln for Soprano, Flute, Oboe, Cello, Piano & Harmonizer (1981)
T. Tuomela (sop), E. Ojanen (vc), T. Laivaara (fl), J. Teikari (ob), K. Saariaho (harmonizer), M. Rahkonen (pno), A. Almila (cnd) ("A Portrait of Kaija Saariaho") † Jardin secret I; Laconisme de laile; NoaNoa; Verblendungen BIS ▲ 307 [AAD] (17.97)
Six Japanese Gardens for Percussion & Electronics
F. Jodelet (perc), K. Saariaho (elec) ("Private Gardens") † Lonh; NoaNoa; Près ODE ▲ 906 (17.97)
Verblendungen for Orchestra (1982-84)
E.-P. Salonen (cnd), Finnish RSO ("A Portrait of Kaija Saariaho") † Jardin secret I; Laconisme de laile; NoaNoa; Sah den Vögeln BIS ▲ 307 [AAD] (17.97)
SABANEYEV, BORIS (1880-1918)
Inner-City Counterpoints for Chamber Ensemble
Perihelion Ensemble † R. Davidson:Tapestry; A. Schultz:Barren Grounds VOXA ▲ 14 (18.97)
SABANEYEV, LEONID (1881-1968)
Suite for Woodwind Quintet
Viento Ensemble *(rec Portland, OR, Mar 1992)* ("Music of Eastern Europe: Woodwind Works") † F. Hidas:Qnt 3 Ww; Janáček:Moravian Dances Orch; T. Svoboda:Trio Fl; Zeiger:Estonian Suite CENT ▲ 2211 [DDD] (16.97)
SABIN, NIGEL (20th cent)
Another Look at Autumn for Piano (1993)
J. Carrigan (pno) *(rec Univ of Queensland, Australia)* ("But I Want the Harmonica: Australian Contemporary Piano Music") † Broadstock:Aureole 4; Conyngham:ppp; S. Greenbaum:But I Want the Harmonica; Hiscocks:Piper at the Gates of Dawn; Kats-Chernin:Purple Prelude; Spiers:Elegy & Toccata Pno VOXA ▲ 23 [DDD] (18.97)
SACCHINI, ANTONIO (1730-1786)
Quartets (6) for Strings, Op. 2 (1778)
Stauffer String Quartet *(rec Milan, Dec 1993)* AG ▲ 84 [DDD] (18.97)
Trios (6) for 2 Violins & Continuo, Op. 1
Stauffer Trio K617 ▲ 7089 (18.97)
SACCO, P. PETER (1928-
Flying Saucer Overture for Orchestra (1959)
R. Stankovský (cnd), Slovak RSO ("MMC New Century, Vol. VII") † Sketches on Emerson; W. Alexander:Salphynx; E. George:Thanksgiving Ov; Wendelburg:Sinf MASM ▲ 2029 [DDD] (16.97)
Sketches (4) on Emerson Essays for Band (or Orchestra) [Deeds; Circles; Gossip; Self] (ca 1963)
R. Stankovský (cnd), Slovak RSO ("MMC New Century, Vol. VII") † Flying Saucer Ov; W. Alexander:Salphynx; E. George:Thanksgiving Ov; Wendelburg:Sinf MASM ▲ 2029 [DDD] (16.97)
SACKMAN, NICHOLAS (1950-
Hawthorn for Orchestra (1991-93)
A. Davis (cnd), BBC SO NMCC (Singles) ▲ 27 [DDD] (10.97)
SAEVERUD, HARALD (1897-1992)
Autumn [Høst] for Bassoon & Piano (1916)
R. Rønnes (bn), E. Knardahl (pno) ("The Contemporary Norwegian Bassoon") † Bibalo:Son Bn; Kvandal:Légende, Op. 61b; Lerstad:Son 2 Bn, Op. 192; W. Plagge:Son Bn; Sonstevold:Sonatina Bn SIMX ▲ 1077 [DDD] (18.97)
Concerto for Bassoon & Orchestra, Op. 44 (1963; rev 1964)
R. Rønnes (bn), A. Dmitriev (cnd), Stavanger SO *(rec Jan 1997)* ("Orchestral Music, Vol. 2") † Lucretia-suite, Op. 10; Sym 7 BIS ▲ 822 [DDD] (17.97)
Concerto for Piano & Orchestra, Op. 31 (1948-50)
N. Ogawa (pno), A. Dmitriev (cnd), Stavanger SO *(rec Stavanger, Norway)* ("Saeverud, Vol. 4") † Fanfare & Hymn, Op. 48; Sym 9 BIS ▲ 962 [DDD] (17.97)
Concerto for Violin & Orchestra, Op. 37 (1956; rev 1982)
T. Sæverud (vn), O. K. Ruud (cnd), Stavanger SO *(rec June 1997)* † Sym 3 BIS ▲ 872 [DDD] (17.97)
Fanfare & Hymn for Orchestra, Op. 48 (1970)
A. Dmitriev (cnd), Stavanger SO *(rec Stavanger, Norway)* ("Saeverud, Vol. 4") † Con Pno, Op. 31; Sym 9 BIS ▲ 962 [DDD] (17.97)
Galdreslåtten for Orchestra, Op. 20 (1942; rev 1955)
A. Dmitriev (cnd), Stavanger SO *(rec Stavanger Konserthus, Norway, Nov 13-17, 1995)* † Kjempeviseslåtten, Op. 22a/5; Peer Gynt Suites, Op. 28; Sinf dolorosa, Op. 19 BIS ▲ 762 [DDD] (17.97)
Kjempeviseslåtten for Orchestra, [after piano piece], Op. 22a/5 (1943)
A. Dmitriev (cnd), Stavanger SO *(rec Stavanger Konserthus, Norway, Nov 13-17, 1995)* † Galdreslåtten, Op. 20; Peer Gynt Suites, Op. 28; Sinf dolorosa, Op. 19 BIS ▲ 762 [DDD] (17.97)
Lucretia-suite for Orchestra [from incidental music for *The Rape of Lucretia*], Op. 10 (1936)
A. Dmitriev (cnd), Stavanger SO *(rec Jan 1997)* ("Orchestral Music, Vol. 2") † Con Bn; Sym 7 BIS ▲ 822 [DDD] (17.97)
Orchestral Music
K. Andersen (cnd), Bergen PO *(Casto Rivoltoso, Op. 22a/5; Siljuslåtten, Op. 17a; Her Last Cradle Song, Op. 22a/3; Fanfare & Hymn, Op. 48; Vade mors, Op. 38; Peer Gynt Suites 1-2, Op.28/1-2; Syljetone; Vars piccole, Op. 8; Divert Fl, Op. 13; Gjætlevise Vars, Op. 15; Småfugvals, Op. 18/2)*, T. Saeverud (vn), K. Andersen (cnd), Bergen PO *(Romanza Vn, Op. 23)*, E. Rottingen (pno), K. Andersen (cnd), Bergen PO *(Con Pno, Op. 31)* ("Orchestral Music, Vol. 2") RICE 2-▲ 3125 (39.97)
D. Kitaienko (cnd), Bergen PO—Sym 8, Op. 40; Canto ostinato, Op. 9; Galdreslåtten, Op. 20; Sym 6, Op. 19; Rondo amoroso, Op. 14a/7; Sym 5, Op. 16; Sym 4, Op. 11; Sym 7, Op. 27, "Salme sinfoni" ("Orchestral Music, Vol. 1") SIMX 2-▲ 3124 (39.97)
Peer Gynt Suites (Nos. 1 & 2) for Orchestra, Op. 28 (1947)
L. O. Andsnes (pno) *(rec Jan 1997)* ("The Long, Long Winter Night") † Tunes & Dances from Siljustøl; E. Grieg:Norwegian folksongs, Op. 66; Norwegian Peasant Dances, Op. 72; D. M. Johansen:Suite 1 Pno, Op. 5; Tveitt:Folk Tunes from Hardanger, Op. 150; Valen:Vars Pno, Op. 23 EMIC ▲ 56541 [DDD] (16.97)
S. Sand (vn), A. Dolezych (va), K. Dahle (E hn/ob), G. Erlandsen (cl), B. Maliska (hn), A. Dmitriev (cnd), Stavanger SO *(rec Stavanger Konserthus, Norway, Nov 13-17, 1995)* † Galdreslåtten, Op. 20; Kjempeviseslåtten, Op. 22a/5; Sinf dolorosa, Op. 19 BIS ▲ 762 [DDD] (17.97)
Piano Music
J. H. Kayser (pno)—Easy Pieces, Op. 14; Siljuslåtten, Op. 17; Suite 1 & 2, "Tunes & Dances from Siljustol," Opp. *(rec 1976)* ("Piano Music from Norway") † Valen:Pno Music BIS 2-▲ 173 [AAD] (69.97)
J. H. Kayser (pno)—Capricci, Op. 1; Easy Pieces Pno; Symphonic Dances, Op. 17; Birdeall Vars, Op. 13; Tunes & Dances from Siljostol, Op. 22 ("Piano Music") NORW ▲ 2 (17.97)
Quartets (3) for Strings, Opp. 49, 52 & 55
Hansa String Quartet SIMX ▲ 1141 (18.97)
Quartet No. 3 for Strings, Op. 55
Norwegian String Quartet ("Hommage à Saeverud") NORW ▲ 970041 (17.97)
Rondo amoroso for Piano
J. Vaabensted (pno) ("Pearls for Solo Piano in the Nordic Tone") † E. Grieg:Lyric Pieces; Palmgren:Majnat; Sibelius:Pno Music DANR 2-▲ 493
Sinfonia dolorosa for Orchestra, Op. 19 (1942)
A. Dmitriev (cnd), Stavanger SO *(rec Stavanger Konserthus, Norway, Nov 13-17, 1995)* † Galdreslåtten, Op. 20; Kjempeviseslåtten, Op. 22a/5; Peer Gynt Suites, Op. 28 BIS ▲ 762 [DDD] (17.97)
Suite No. 1 for Piano [from Tunes & Dances from Siljustøl], Op. 21a (1942; arr for Wind Quintet, 1980)
Bergen Wind Quintet † S. Barber:Summer Music, Op. 31; P. Hindemith:Kleine Kammermusik, Op. 24/2; Jolivet:Sérénade Ob BIS ▲ 291 [DDD] (17.97)
Symphony No. 3 in B♭, Op. 5 (1925-26)
O. K. Ruud (cnd), Stavanger SO *(rec June 1997)* † Con Vn BIS ▲ 872 [DDD] (17.97)

SAEVERUD, HARALD (cont.)
Symphony No. 7, Op. 27, "Salme" (1944-45)
A. Dmitriev (cnd), Stavanger SO *(rec Jan 1997)* ("Orchestral Music, Vol. 2") † Con Bn; Lucretia-suite, Op. 10 BIS ▲ 822 [DDD] (17.97)
Symphony No. 9, Op. 45 (1966)
A. Dmitriev (cnd), Stavanger SO *(rec Stavanger, Norway)* ("Saeverud, Vol. 4") † Con Pno, Op. 31; Fanfare & Hymn, Op. 48 BIS ▲ 962 [DDD] (17.97)
Tunes & Dances from Siljustøl [Slåtter og stev fra Siljustøl] (5 suites) for Piano, Opp. 21, 22, 24-26 (1942-ca 1946)
L. O. Andsnes (pno) *(rec Jan 1997)* ("The Long, Long Winter Night") † Peer Gynt Suites, Op. 28; E. Grieg:Norwegian folksongs, Op. 66; Norwegian Peasant Dances, Op. 72; D. M. Johansen:Suite 1 Pno, Op. 5; Tveitt:Folk Tunes from Hardanger, Op. 150; Valen:Vars Pno, Op. 23 EMIC ▲ 56541 [DDD] (16.97)
SAGRERAS, JULIO S. (1879-1942)
El Colibri for Guitar
P. Skareng (gtr) ("El Colibri") † J. S. Bach:Sons & Partitas Vn; Carlstedt:Swedish Dances; Frumerie:Vars on a Swedish Folk Tune, Op. 69a; M. Giuliani:Rossiniana; Lauro:Gtr Music; Tárrega:Recuerdos de la Alhambra CAPA ▲ 21392 [AAD] (16.97)
SAGVIK, STELLAN
Roughs from the Wooden Wind for Wind Quartet (1980)
Reed Quartet *(rec June 1996)* ("Scandinavian Contemporary Works") † F. C. Hansen:Prèlude, Estampie et Fugue; Nyord:Rørdrum; Roikjer:Little Intermezzi; F. Weis:Studies Ww Qnt; Wiernik:Feelings KPT ▲ 32243
ST. QUENTIN, HUON DE (ca 1100)
Jerusalem se plainte et li pais for Chorus (ca 1130)
C. Page (cnd), Gothic Voices ("Jerusalem: Vision of Peace") † Anonymous:Alleluia Pascha nostrum; Congaudet hodie celestis curia; Gospel; Gradual Hec dies quam fecit Dominus; Hac in die Gedeonis; In salvatoris; Invocantes Dominum; Jerusalem accipitur; Jerusalem! grant damage ma fais; Luget Rachel iterum; Luto carens et latere; O levis aurula!; Te Deum; Veri vitis germine; Guiot de Dijon:Chanterai pour mon coraige; Hildegard of Bingen:O Jerusalem aurea civitatis HYP ▲ 67039 (18.97)
SAINT-GEORGES, JOSEPH BOULOGNE (ca 1739-1799)
Aria with Variations in G for Violin & Harpsichord
J. Kantorow (vn), B. Haudebourg (hpd) † Sons Hpd ARN ▲ 55445 (14.97)
Concerto No. 11 in G for Violin & Orchestra, Op. 7
A. Villars (vn), B. Wahl (cnd), Versailles CO † Sinfonies (2), Op. 11 ARN (Premières) ▲ 55434 (13.97)
Quartets (6) for Strings, Op. 1 (ca 1772)
Jean Noël Molard String Quartet ARN ▲ 55425 (13.97)
Sinfonies (2) in G & D for Orchestra, Op. 11
B. Wahl (cnd), Versailles CO † Con 11 Vn, Op. 7 ARN (Premières) ▲ 55434 (13.97)
Sonatas (3) for Harpsichord (or Piano) & Violin obbligato
J. Kantorow (vn), B. Haudebourg (hpd) † Aria w. Vars ARN ▲ 55445 (14.97)
SAINT-LUC, LAURENT [JACQUES-ALEXANDRE] DE (1663-after 1700)
Music of Laurent de Saint-Luc
D. Fournier (lt/thb), J. Vandeville (ob)—Suites 1, 9 & 13 for Ob & Bc; La prise de Barcelonne; La Reyne de Prusse-Caprice ARN ▲ 55395 (13.97)
SAINT-MARTIN, LÉONCE DE (1886-1945)
Cantique Spirituel for Organ (1950)
P. Cochereau (org) *(rec Notre-Dame, France)* † In Memoriam; Magnificat; Mass; Paraphase Psalm 136; Passacaille SOC ▲ 161 (16.97)
In Memoriam for Organ (1941)
P. Cochereau (org) *(rec Notre-Dame, France)* † Cantique Spirituel; Magnificat; Mass; Paraphase Psalm 136; Passacaille SOC ▲ 161 (16.97)
Magnificat for Chorus & Organ (1952)
P. Cochereau (org), G. Roussel (org) *(rec Notre-Dame, France)* † Cantique Spirituel; In Memoriam; Mass; Paraphase Psalm 136; Passacaille SOC ▲ 161 (16.97)
Mass in E for 4 Voices & 2 Organs (1932)
P. Cochereau (org), J. Revert (org) *(rec Notre-Dame, France)* † Cantique Spirituel; In Memoriam; Magnificat; Paraphase Psalm 136; Passacaille SOC ▲ 161 (16.97)
Paraphase of Psalm 136 for Organ (1932)
P. Cochereau (org) *(rec Notre-Dame, France)* † Cantique Spirituel; In Memoriam; Magnificat; Mass; Passacaille SOC ▲ 161 (16.97)
Passacaille for Organ (1940)
P. Cochereau (org) *(rec Notre-Dame, France)* † Cantique Spirituel; In Memoriam; Magnificat; Mass; Paraphase Psalm 136 SOC ▲ 161 (16.97)
Toccata de la Libération for Organ (1944)
S. Armstrong-Ouellette (org) *(rec Mission Church, Boston, MA)* ("Musique de la Basilique") † Dupont:Méditation; Gigout:Pièces Org (sels); Guilmant:Son 7 Org, Op. 89; G. Pierné:Pièces Org, Op. 29; Saint-Saëns:Fant 1 Org; Vierne:Pièces de fantaisie AFK ▲ 538 (16.97)
SAINTE CROIX, JUDITH
Music of Sainte Croix
A. Bolotowsky (fl/Native American f), G. Kitzis (vn), M. Levin (vn), C. Ims (va), T. Ulrich (vc), S. Carter (cl), J. Reinhard (bn), M. Helias (ctbn), T. H. Bynum (tpt), J. Van Nostrand (hn), L. Wolf (pno), B. Hayes (perc), J. Sainte Croix (cnd) *(Vision I) (rec NYC, NY, June 1998)*, J. Sainte Croix (pno) *(Preludes [Tukwinong]) (rec NYC, NY, July 1998)*, T. Alioto (ten), J. Sainte Croix (syn) *(Dear One) (rec NYC, NY, Aug 1998)*, D. Barrett (vc), L. Arkis (fl), J. Sainte Croix (pno) *(The Bright Leaf Trios) (rec NYC, NY, 1998)*, R. Bergman (vn), S. Kephart (va), T. Ulrich (vc), M. Sullivan (dr/Native American f) *(Vision II) (rec NYC, NY, June 1998)* SNCM ▲ 3000 [DDD] (17.97)
SAINTE-COLOMBE, MONSIEUR DE (d. 1691-1701)
Concerts for 2 Bass Viols
S. Moquet (b vl), A. Lasla (b vl) *(rec Jan 1993)* ALPE ▲ 9308002 [DDD] (18.97)
J. Savall (vl), W. Kuijken (b vl)—Concerts XXVII, "Bourrasque"; XLVIII, "Le raporté"; XLI, "Le retour"; XLIV, "Tombeau les regrets"; LIV, "[La] Dubois" ASTR ▲ 7729 [AAD] (18.97)
Fantaisie en rondeau for 2 Viols
R. Zipperling (vc), P. Pierlot (vl) † Tombeau; Du Buisson:Suite Vls; Machy:Suite Vls; Marais:Tombeau pour Monsieur de Ste Colombe RICE ▲ 118100 [DDD] (17.97)
Tombeau for 2 Viols
R. Zipperling (vc), P. Pierlot (vl) † Fant en rondeau; Du Buisson:Suite Vls; Machy:Suite Vls; Marais:Tombeau pour Monsieur de Ste Colombe RICE ▲ 118100 [DDD] (17.97)
Viol Music
L. Duftschmid (vl), H. Perl (vl), L. Santana (archlt/lt/thb), A. Lawrence-King (hp/org)—Prélude; Les Couplets; Le Retrouvé; La Conférence; Le Changé; Tombeau Les Regrets; Le Raporté; Le Majestueux; Le Précipité; Le Varié; L'Infidelle *(rec Toddington England, Mar 1996)* ("Retrouvé & Changé: Seven Strings & More") DEHA ▲ 77373 [DDD] (16.97)
Spectre de la Rose—Le retour; Tombeau les Regrets *(rec Jan 6-7, 1993)* † Marais:Vl Music NXIN ▲ 550750 [DDD] (5.97)
SAINTON, PHILIP (1891-1967)
The Dream of the Marionette (ballet) for Orchestra
M. Bamert (cnd), Philharmonia Orch † Nadir; P. Hadley:Belle dame; Lenten Meditations; One Morning in Spring CHN ▲ 9539 (16.97)
The Island for Orchestra & Chorus
M. Bamert (cnd), Philharmonia Orch, Philharmonia Chorus † P. Hadley:Trees So High CHN ▲ 9181 [DDD] (16.97)
Nadir for Orchestra
M. Bamert (cnd), Philharmonia Orch † Dream of the Marionette; P. Hadley:Belle dame; Lenten Meditations; One Morning in Spring CHN ▲ 9539 (16.97)
SAINT-SAËNS, CAMILLE (1835-1921)
Africa in g for Piano & Orchestra, Op. 89 (1891)
J. Collard (pno), A. Previn (cnd), Royal PO † Allegro appassionato, Op. 43; Con 1 Pno, Op. 17; Rapsodie d'Auvergne, Op. 73; Wedding Cake, Op. 76 EMIC ▲ 49757 (16.97)
L. Mikkola (pno), J. Kantorow (cnd), Tapiola Sinfonietta † Sym in F; Sym 2 BIS ▲ 790 [DDD] (17.97)
Airs de ballet d'Ascanio (adagio & variations) for Flute & Orchestra
Collegium Musicum Soloists ("Complete Works for Piano & Winds") † Caprice sur des airs danoises et russes, Op. 79; Cavatina Trb & Pno, Op. 144; Odelette Fl, Op. 162; Romance Fl, Op. 37; Romance Hn Orch, Op. 36; Romance Hn Pno, Op. 67; Son Bn; Son Cl; Son Ob; Spt Tpt, Op. 65; Suite algérienne, Op. 60; Tarantelle, Op. 6 KPT 2-▲ 32062 [DDD]

SAINT-SAËNS, CAMILLE (cont.)

Airs de ballet d'Ascanio (adagio & variations) for Flute & Orchestra (cont.)

S. Milan (fl), R. Hickox (cnd), City of London Sinfonia ("La flûte enchantée") † Chaminade:Concertino Fl, Op. 107; B. Godard:Suite de trois morceaux, Op. 116; F. Martin:Ballade Fl CHN ▲ 8840 [DDD] (16.97)

artists unknown ("The Virtuoso Flute") † T. Böhm:Grande polonaise, Op. 16; A. F. Doppler:Fant pastorale hongroise, Op. 26; Kuhlau:Intro & Rondo on 'Ah! quand il gèle', Op. 98a; Paganini:Caprices Vn, M.S. 25; Taffanel:Fant on Freischütz BIS ▲ 166 (17.97)

Album for Piano, Op. 72 (1884)

M. Lee (pno) † Études (6) Pno, Op. 111; Études (6) Pno, Op. 52 MDG ▲ 6040590 [DDD] (17.97)

Allegro appassionato in b for Cello & Piano (or Orchestra), Op. 43 (1875)

J. Collard (pno), A. Previn (cnd), Royal PO † Africa; Con 1 Pno, Op. 17; Rapsodie d'Auvergne, Op. 73; Wedding Cake, Op. 76 EMIC ▲ 49757 (16.97)

J. Gamard (vc), P. Kuentz (cnd), Paul Kuentz Orch † Con 1 Vc, Op. 33; R. Schumann:Con Vc PVY ▲ 730053 [DDD] (12.97)

I. Hobson (pno) † Bagatelles Pno, Op. 3; Carnival of the Animals; Spt Tpt, Op. 65 ARA ▲ 6570 (16.97)

M. Kliegel (vc), J. Monnard (cnd), Bournemouth Sinfonietta *(rec Poole Arts Ctr England, Jan 1995)* † Con 1 Vc, Op. 33; Con 2 Vc, Op. 119; Cygne; Suite Vc, Op. 16 NXIN ▲ 8553039 [DDD] (5.97)

B. Pergamenschikov (vc), P. Gililov (pno) *(rec Walchstadt, Germany, Mar 1994)* ("Beau Soir") † Cygne; Debussy:Beau soir; Music of Debussy; Preludes Pno; G. Fauré:Après un rêve, Op. 7/1; Berceuse, Op. 16; Elégie, Op. 24; Papillon, Op. 77; Romance Vc, Op. 69; Sicilienne, Op. 78; Sérénade, Op. 98; Ibert:Histoires; M. Ravel:Pièce en forme de Habanera ORF ▲ 349951 [DDD] (18.97)

L. Tooten (vc), B. Rawitz (pno) *(rec Brussels, Belgium, Feb 1998)* ("Works for Cello & Piano") † Cygne; Son 1 Vc, Op. 32; Son 2 Vc, Op. 123 PAVA ▲ 7407 [DDD] (10.97)

L. Varga (vc), L. De Froment (cnd), Luxembourg RSO † Caprice andalous, Op. 122; Con 1 Vc, Op. 33; Con 1 Vn, Op. 20; Con 2 Vc, Op. 119; Con 2 Vn, Op. 58; Con 3 Vn, Op. 61; Havanaise, Op. 83; Intro & Rondo capriccioso, Op. 28; Morceau de concert Vn, Op. 62; Romance Vn, Op. 48 VB2 2-▲ 5084 [ADD] (9.97)

D. D. Williencourt (vc), P. Verrot (cnd), Monte Carlo PO † Con 1 Vc, Op. 33; Con 2 Vc, Op. 119; Cygne; Suite Vc, Op. 16 ARN ▲ 68347 (16.97)

Allegro appassionato in c# for Orchestra, Op. 70 (1874)

C. Mackerras (cnd), Academy of St. Martin in the Fields † Carnival of the Animals; Con 3 Vn, Op. 61 ILOV 2-▲ 531 (9.97)

Andante in F for Violin & Orchestra [trans from Mozart's *Concerto No. 21 for Piano*]

T. Nishizaki (vn), J. Wildner (cnd), Capella Istropolitana † W. A. Mozart:Con 1 Vn, K.207; Con 2 Vn, K.211; Rondo Vn NXIN ▲ 550414 [DDD] (5.97)

Ave Maria in B♭ for Soprano and Organ (1859)

Z. Kloubová (sop), J. Zigmund (va), J. Krejčí (ob), D. Dimitrov (tpt), V. Roubal (org) † J. S. Bach:Cant 51; Cant 92; G. F. Handel:German Arias, HWV 202-10; Joshua (sels); Messiah (sels); J. Haydn:Schöpfung (sels); W. A. Mozart:Ave verum corpus, K.618; Exsultate, jubilate, K.165; Vesperae solennes de confessore, K.339; F. Schubert:Ave Maria, Op. 52/6; Vivaldi:Gloria; Motets GZCL ▲ 276 (6.97)

Bagatelles (6) for Piano, Op. 3 (1855)

I. Hobson (pno) † Allegro appassionato, Op. 43; Carnival of the Animals; Spt Tpt, Op. 65 ARA ▲ 6570 (16.97)

Bénédiction nuptiale for Organ, Op. 9 (1859)

H. Fagius (org) † Fant 1 Org; Fant 2 Org, Op. 101; Fant 3 Org, Op. 157; Preludes & Fugues Org, Op. 109; Preludes & Fugues Org, Op. 99 BIS ▲ 556 [DDD] (17.97)

Berceuse in B♭ for Violin & Piano, Op. 38 (1871)

G. Poulet (vn), N. Lee (pno) *(rec Aug 1996)* ("Complete Works for Violin & Piano") † Elégie, Op. 143; Elégie, Op. 160; Son 1 Vn, Op. 75; Son 2 Vn, Op. 102; Tryptique, Op. 136 ARN ▲ 68362 [DDD] (16.97)

Caprice andalous in G for Violin & Orchestra, Op. 122 (1904)

D. Kang (vn), A. Wit (cnd), Polish National RSO Katowice *(rec May 24-26, 1993)* † Con 3 Vn, Op. 61; Intro & Rondo capriccioso, Op. 28; Morceau de concert Vn, Op. 62; Romance Vn, Op. 48 NXIN ▲ 550752 [DDD] (5.97)

R. Ricci (vn), L. De Froment (cnd), Luxembourg RSO † Allegro appassionato, Op. 43; Con 1 Vc, Op. 33; Con 1 Vn, Op. 20; Con 2 Vc, Op. 119; Con 2 Vn, Op. 58; Con 3 Vn, Op. 61; Havanaise, Op. 83; Intro & Rondo capriccioso, Op. 28; Morceau de concert Vn, Op. 62; Romance Vn, Op. 48 VB2 2-▲ 5084 [ADD] (9.97)

Caprice arabe for 2 Pianos, Op. 96 (1884)

C. Ivaldi (pno), N. Lee (pno) † Caprice héroïque, Op. 106; Polonaise Pnos, Op. 77; Scherzo Pnos, Op. 87; Vars on a Theme of Beethoven, Op. 35 ARN ▲ 68011 [AAD] (16.97)

J. Reynolds (pno), P. Lockwood (pno) *(rec Utrecht, Netherlands, Apr 1996)* † Carnival of the Animals; Danse macabre, Op. 40; Polonaise Pnos, Op. 77; Scherzo Pnos, Op. 87; Vars on a Theme of Beethoven, Op. 35 GLOE ▲ 5152 [DDD] (16.97)

Caprice héroïque for 2 Pianos, Op. 106 (1898)

C. Ivaldi (pno), N. Lee (pno) † Caprice arabe, Op. 96; Polonaise Pnos, Op. 77; Scherzo Pnos, Op. 87; Vars on a Theme of Beethoven, Op. 35 ARN ▲ 68011 [AAD] (16.97)

Caprice sur des airs danoises et russes for Flute, Oboe, Clarinet & Piano, Op. 79 (1887)

Collegium Musicum Soloists ("Complete Works for Piano & Winds") † Airs de ballet d'Ascanio; Cavatina Trb & Pno, Op. 144; Odelette Fl, Op. 162; Romance Fl, Op. 37; Romance Hn Orch, Op. 36; Romance Hn Pno, Op. 67; Son Bn; Son Cl; Son Ob; Spt Tpt, Op. 65; Suite algérienne, Op. 60; Tarantelle, Op. 6 KPT 2-▲ 32062 [DDD]

Hexagon *(rec Aaron Copland School of Music, Queens College, NYC, NY, 1996)* ("Les Petits Nerveux") † Tarantelle, Op. 6; J. Françaix:Petits nerveux; F. Poulenc:Sxt Pno; Trio Ob; A. Roussel:Divert Ww, Op. 6 BRID ▲ 9079 [DDD] (17.97)

G. Koukl (pno), Prague National Theater Wind Quintet † J. Françaix:Heure du berger for Orch; Ibert:Pièces brèves Ww; Indy:Sarabande et menuet; D. Milhaud:Son Fl, Cl, Ob & Pno, Op. 47; A. Roussel:Divert Ww, Op. 6 NUO ▲ 7268 (16.97)

Carnival of the Animals for 2 Pianos & Orchestra [sometimes performed with special verses by Ogden Nash] (1886)

ERAT (Ultima) 2-▲ 18971 (16.97)

K. Beikircher (nar), L. Köhler (cnd), HR Brass † S. Prokofiev:Peter & the Wolf, Op. 67 CAPO ▲ 10836 (10.97)

L. Bernstein (nar), L. Bernstein (cnd), New York PO † S. Prokofiev:Peter & the Wolf, Op. 67 SNYC ▲ 37765 (9.97) ▮ 37765 (3.98)

L. Bernstein (nar), L. Bernstein (cnd), New York PO ("Children's Classics") † B. Britten:Young Person's Guide to the Orch, Op. 34; S. Prokofiev:Peter & the Wolf, Op. 67 SNYC (Bernstein Century) ▲ 60175 (10.97)

I. Brown (pno), A. Goldstone (pno), O. A. Hughes (cnd), Royal PO † S. Prokofiev:Peter & the Wolf, Op. 67 ASVQ ▲ 6017 [ADD] (10.97)

M. Dosse (pno), A. Petit (pno), J. Faerber (cnd), Württemberg CO † B. Britten:Young Person's Guide to the Orch, Op. 34; S. Prokofiev:Peter & the Wolf, Op. 67 ALLO ▲ 8219 (5.97)

H. Downs (nar), M. Hoherman (vc), L. Litwin (pno), S. Lipman (pno), A. Fiedler (cnd), Boston Pops Orch [verses rec June 12, 1963] *(rec Symphony Hall Boston, June 14, 1961)* ("Classics for Children") † B. Britten:Young Person's Guide to the Orch, Op. 34; Gounod:Funeral March of a Marionette; E. Grieg:Peer Gynt Suites; R. Hayman:Kid Stuff; F. Loesser:Hans Christian Andersen (sels) RCAV (Living Stereo) ▲ 68131 [ADD] (11.97) ▮ 68131 [ADD] (6.98)

A. Fiedler (cnd), Boston Pops Orch ("Classics for Children") † S. Prokofiev:Peter & the Wolf, Op. 67; P. Tchaikovsky:Nutcracker Suite, Op. 71a RCAV (Gold Seal) ▲ 6718 [ADD] (11.97) ▮ 6718 [ADD] (6.98)

C. Frank (pno), L. Kallir (pno), E. Ormandy (cnd), Philadelphia Orch † B. Britten:Young Person's Guide to the Orch, Op. 34; S. Prokofiev:Peter & the Wolf, Op. 67 SNYC (Essential Classics) ▲ 62638 (7.97) ▮ 62638 (3.98)

A. Gibson (cnd), Scottish National Orch ("Children's Classics") † Dukas:L'Apprenti sorcier; S. Prokofiev:Peter & the Wolf, Op. 67 CFP (Unforgettable Classics) ▲ 69605 (11.97)

J. Gielgud (nar), R. Stamp (cnd), Academy of London Orch † S. Prokofiev:Peter & the Wolf, Op. 67 VCL (Ultraviolet) ▲ 61137 (9.97)

H. Gmür (cnd), South German PO † Sym 3 PC ▲ 267029 [DDD] (2.97)

S. Gorkovenko (cnd), St. Petersburg TV & Broadcast Company SO † S. Prokofiev:Peter & the Wolf, Op. 67; Tales of an Old Grandmother, Op. 31 SNYC ▲ 57234 [DDD] (4.97)

I. Hobson (cnd), Sinfonia da Camera † Allegro appassionato, Op. 43; Bagatelles Pno, Op. 3; Spt Tpt, Op. 65 ARA ▲ 6570 (16.97)

V. Jennings (pno), P. Jennings (pno), A. Previn (cnd), Pittsburgh SO † M. Ravel:Ma mère l'oye PPHI ▲ 16 [DDD] (16.97)

P. Katin (pno), P. Fowke (pno), A. Gibson (cnd), Royal Scottish National Orch † Bizet:Jeux d'enfants; M. Ravel:Ma mère l'oye CFP ▲ 4086 [ADD] (12.97)

Y. Kim (pno), J. Kim (pno), D. V. Yu (cnd), Philharmonia Orch † Cyprès et Lauriers, Op. 156; Sym 3 ICC ▲ 6600012 (16.97)

M. Lapšanský (pno), P. Toperczer (pno), O. Lenárd (cnd), Czech-Slovak RSO Bratislava † B. Britten:Young Person's Guide to the Orch, Op. 34; S. Prokofiev:Peter & the Wolf, Op. 67 NXIN ▲ 550499 [DDD] (5.97)

C. Mackerras (cnd), Academy of St. Martin in the Fields † Allegro appassionato, Op. 70; Con 3 Vn, Op. 61 ILOV 2-▲ 531 (9.97)

SAINT-SAËNS, CAMILLE (cont.)

Carnival of the Animals for 2 Pianos & Orchestra [sometimes performed with special verses by Ogden Nash] (1886) (cont.)

Nash Ensemble *(rec 1988)* † Spt Tpt, Op. 65; Trio 1 for Pno, Op. 18; A. Dvořák:Qnt Pno, Op. 81; Trio 4 Pno, Op. 90 VCL 2-▲ 61516 [DDD] (11.97)

D. O. Norris (pno), Y. Turovsky (cnd), Montreal Musici † Wedding Cake, Op. 76; W. A. Mozart:Musikalischer Spass, K.522 CHN ▲ 9246 [DDD] (16.97)

F. Onder (pno), F. Onder (pno), H. Griffiths (cnd), Zurich CO † Intro & Rondo capriccioso, Op. 28; Vars on a Theme of Beethoven, Op. 35 PANC ▲ 510106 (17.97)

E. Ormandy (cnd), Philadelphia Orch † Danse macabre, Op. 40; Marche militaire française; Samson et Dalila (Bacchanale); Sym 3 SNYC (Essential Classics) ▲ 47655 (7.97) ▮ 47655 (3.98)

C. Ortiz (pno), P. Rogé (pno), C. Dutoit (cnd), London Sinfonietta † Danse macabre, Op. 40; Phaéton, Op. 39; Rouet d'Omphale, Op. 31 PLON ▲ 14460 [ADD] (16.97)

C. Ortiz (pno), P. Rogé (pno), C. Dutoit (cnd), London Sinfonietta † Sym 3 PLON ▲ 30720 [DDD] (9.97)

G. Pekinel (pno), S. Pekinel (pno), M. Janowski (cnd), ORTF SO † F. Poulenc:Con for 2 Pnos TELC (M Line) ▲ 97445 (9.97)

I. Perlman (nar), Y. Levi (cnd), Atlanta SO [w. new poetry, Bruce Adolphe (nar)] ("Classical Zoo") † O. Respighi:Uccelli; G. Rossini:Gazza ladra (ov); Sibelius:Swan of Tuonela TEL ▲ 80443 (16.97)

J. Reynolds (pno), P. Lockwood (pno), J. Reynolds (cnd) *(rec Utrecht, Netherlands, Apr 1996)* † Caprice arabe, Op. 96; Danse macabre, Op. 40; Polonaise Pnos, Op. 77; Scherzo Pnos, Op. 87; Vars on a Theme of Beethoven, Op. 35 GLOE ▲ 5152 [DDD] (16.97)

G. Salvador, Sr (pno), G. Salvador, Jr. (pno), E. Bátiz (cnd), Mexico City PO † Danse macabre, Op. 40; Sym 3; Wedding Cake, Op. 76 ASV ▲ 665 [DDD] (16.97)

P. Schickele (nar), R. Markham (pno), K. Broadway (pno), Y. Levi (cnd), Atlanta SO [poems by Schickele] *(rec Mar 20 & June 16, 1993)* ("Sneaky Pete & the Wolf") † S. Prokofiev:Peter & the Wolf, Op. 67 TEL ▮ 30350 [DDD] (8.98) ▲ 80350 [DDD] (16.97)

L. Stokowski (cnd), Philadelphia Orch † Bizet:Jeux d'enfants; B. Britten:Young Person's Guide to the Orch, Op. 34; S. Prokofiev:Peter & the Wolf, Op. 67 AVID ▲ 601 (16.97)

B. Wordsworth (cnd), London SO [chamber version] † Bizet:Jeux d'enfants; M. Ravel:Ma mère l'oye Suite Pno LSO (LSO) ▲ 6900082 (9.97)

Cavatina for Trombone & Piano, Op. 144 (1915)

Collegium Musicum Soloists ("Complete Works for Piano & Winds") † Airs de ballet d'Ascanio; Caprice sur des airs danoises et russes, Op. 79; Odelette Fl, Op. 162; Romance Fl, Op. 37; Romance Hn Orch, Op. 36; Romance Hn Pno, Op. 67; Son Bn; Son Cl; Son Ob; Spt Tpt, Op. 65; Suite algérienne, Op. 60; Tarantelle, Op. 6 KPT 2-▲ 32062 [DDD]

Chant saphique in D for Cello & Piano, Op. 91 (1892)

W. Thomas-Mifune (vc), C. Piazzini (pno) *(rec Dec 22-23, 1986)* † Son 1 Vc, Op. 32; Son 2 Vc, Op. 123 CALG ▲ 50862 [DDD] (19.97)

Choeurs (2) for Chorus (with Piano ad lib) [Calme des nuits; Les Fleurs et les arbres], Op. 68 (1882)

J. E. Gardiner (cnd), Monteverdi Choir London † Choeurs; Debussy:Chansons de Charles d'Orléans; G. Fauré:Djinns; Madrigal, Op. 35; Requiem, Op. 48; M. Ravel:Chansons Chorus PPHI ▲ 38149 (16.97)

Choeurs (2) for Chorus [Des pas dans l'allée; Trinquons], Op. 141 (1913)

J. E. Gardiner (cnd), Monteverdi Choir London † Choeurs, Op. 68; Debussy:Chansons de Charles d'Orléans; G. Fauré:Djinns; Madrigal, Op. 35; Requiem, Op. 48; M. Ravel:Chansons Chorus PPHI ▲ 38149 (16.97)

Concerto No. 1 in a for Cello & Orchestra, Op. 33 (1872)

H. Chang (vc), M. Rostropovich (cnd), London SO † Bruch:Kol Nidrei, Op. 47; G. Fauré:Elégie, Op. 24; P. Tchaikovsky:Vars on a Rococo Theme, Op. 33 EMIC ▲ 56126 (16.97)

P. Fournier (vc), W. Susskind (cnd), Philharmonia Orch *(rec 1939-47)* † Cygne; F. Schubert:Son Arpeggione, D.821; P. Tchaikovsky:Vars on a Rococo Theme, Op. 33 ENT (Strings) ▲ 99344 (16.97)

J. Gamard (vc), P. Kuentz (cnd), Paul Kuentz Orch † Allegro appassionato, Op. 43; R. Schumann:Con Vc PVY ▲ 730053 [DDD] (12.97)

M. Kliegel (vc), J. Monnard (cnd), Bournemouth Sinfonietta *(rec Poole Arts Ctr England, Jan 1995)* † Allegro appassionato, Op. 43; Con 2 Vc, Op. 119; Cygne; Suite Vc, Op. 16 NXIN ▲ 8553039 [DDD] (5.97)

Y.-Y. Ma (vc), L. Maazel (cnd), French National Orch † Lalo:Con Vc SNYC ▲ 35848 [DDD] (16.97)

Y.-Y. Ma (vc), L. Maazel (cnd), French National Orch † A. Dvořák:Con Vc; E. Elgar:Con Vc; J. Haydn:Con 2 Vc; R. Schumann:Con Vc SNYC 2-▲ 44562 [ADD] (31.97)

C. Prieto (vc), H. D. Fuente (cnd), Mineria SO † D. Shostakovich:Con 1 Vc, Op. 107; Son Vc INMP ▲ 1084 [DDD] (11.97)

S. Rolland (vc), G. Varga (cnd), BBC PO † Lalo:Con Vc; Massenet:Fant Vc & Orc ASV ▲ 867 [DDD] (16.97)

S. Rolston (vc), M. Bernardi (cnd), Calgary PO *(rec Calgary Centre for the Performing Arts, Mar 15-16, 1994)* † E. Elgar:Con Vc; Glazunov:Chant du ménestrel, Op. 71; Popper:Hungarian Rhap, Op. 68; P. Tchaikovsky:Andante cantabile CBC (SM 5000) ▲ 5153 [DDD] (16.97)

L. Rose (vc), E. Ormandy (cnd), Philadelphia Orch *(rec 1967)* † Con 2 Pno, Op. 22; Con 4 Pno, Op. 44 SNYC (Essential Classics) ▲ 48276 [ADD] (7.97) ▮ 48276 [ADD] (3.98)

M. Rostropovich (vc), C. M. Giulini (cnd), London PO † A. Dvořák:Con Vc EMIC ▲ 49306 [ADD] (16.97)

C. Starck (vc), R. Leppard (cnd), English CO *(rec EMI Studio London, 1975)* † F. Devienne:Con 2 Fl; Ibert:Con Fl CLAV ▲ 105 [ADD]

J. Starker (vc), A. Dorati (cnd), London SO † Lalo:Con Vc; R. Schumann:Con Vc MRCR ▲ 32010 [ADD] (11.97)

T. Thedéen (vc), J. Kantorow (cnd), Tapiola Sinfonietta *(rec Tapiola, Finland, June 1998)* † Con 2 Vc, Op. 119; Romance Hn Orch, Op. 36; Sym in A BIS ▲ 956 [DDD] (17.97)

L. Varga (vc), L. De Froment (cnd), Luxembourg RSO † Allegro appassionato, Op. 43; Caprice andalous, Op. 122; Con 1 Vn, Op. 20; Con 2 Vc, Op. 119; Con 2 Vn, Op. 58; Con 3 Vn, Op. 61; Havanaise, Op. 83; Intro & Rondo capriccioso, Op. 28; Morceau de concert Vn, Op. 62; Romance Vn, Op. 48 VB2 2-▲ 5084 [ADD] (9.97)

D. D. Williencourt (vc), P. Verrot (cnd), Monte Carlo PO † Allegro appassionato, Op. 43; Con 2 Vc, Op. 119; Cygne; Suite Vc, Op. 16 ARN ▲ 68347 (16.97)

Concerto No. 2 in d for Cello & Orchestra, Op. 119 (1902)

M. Kliegel (vc), J. Monnard (cnd), Bournemouth Sinfonietta *(rec Poole Arts Ctr England, Jan 1995)* † Allegro appassionato, Op. 43; Con 1 Vc, Op. 33; Cygne; Suite Vc, Op. 16 NXIN ▲ 8553039 [DDD] (5.97)

T. Thedéen (vc), J. Kantorow (cnd), Tapiola Sinfonietta *(rec Tapiola, Finland, June 1998)* † Con 1 Vc, Op. 33; Romance Hn Orch, Op. 36; Sym in A BIS ▲ 956 [DDD] (17.97)

L. Varga (vc), S. Landau (cnd), Westphalia SO † Allegro appassionato, Op. 43; Caprice andalous, Op. 122; Con 1 Vc, Op. 33; Con 1 Vn, Op. 20; Con 2 Vn, Op. 58; Con 3 Vn, Op. 61; Havanaise, Op. 83; Intro & Rondo capriccioso, Op. 28; Morceau de concert Vn, Op. 62; Romance Vn, Op. 48 VB2 2-▲ 5084 [ADD] (9.97)

D. D. Williencourt (vc), P. Verrot (cnd), Monte Carlo PO † Allegro appassionato, Op. 43; Con 1 Vc, Op. 33; Cygne; Suite Vc, Op. 16 ARN ▲ 68347 (16.97)

Concertos (5) for Piano & Orchestra (complete)

A. Ciccolini (pno), S. Baudo (cnd), Orch de Paris EMIC (Studio) 2-▲ 69443 [ADD] (21.97)

P. Rogé (pno), C. Dutoit (cnd) PLON (Double Decca) 2-▲ 43865 (17.97)

Concerto No. 1 in D for Piano & Orchestra, Op. 17 (1858)

J. Collard (pno), A. Previn (cnd), Royal PO † Africa; Allegro appassionato, Op. 43; Rapsodie d'Auvergne, Op. 73; Wedding Cake, Op. 76 EMIC ▲ 49757 (16.97)

Concerto No. 2 in g for Piano & Orchestra, Op. 22 (1868)

I. Biret (pno), J. Loughran (cnd), Philharmonia Orch † Con 4 Pno, Op. 44 NXIN ▲ 550334 [DDD] (5.97)

J. Collard (pno), A. Previn (cnd), Royal PO † Con 4 Pno, Op. 44 EMIC ▲ 47816 (16.97)

J. Covelli (pno), K. Won (cnd), Moscow PO † Wedding Cake, Op. 76; D. Shostakovich:Con 2 Pno, Op. 102 INMP ▲ 6701842 (9.97)

P. Entremont (pno), E. Ormandy (cnd), Philadelphia Orch *(rec 1964)* † Con 1 Vc, Op. 33; Con 4 Pno, Op. 44 SNYC (Essential Classics) ▲ 48276 [ADD] (7.97) ▮ 48276 [ADD] (3.98)

Em. Gilels (pno), A. Cluytens (cnd), Paris Conservatory Société des Concerts Orch † S. Rachmaninoff:Con 3 Pno, Op. 30; D. Shostakovich:Preludes & Fugues Pno, Op. 87 TES ▲ 1029 [ADD] (17.97)

Em. Gilels (pno), K. Kondrashin (cnd), Russian State SO † Liszt:Con 1 Pno, S.124 VC ▲ 1029 (m) [ADD] (13.97)

I. Hobson (pno), Sinfonia da Camera † J. Françaix:Concertino ARA ▲ 6541 (16.97)

S. Lemelin (pno), M. Bernardi (cnd), CBC Vancouver Orch † G. Fauré:Ballade Pno, Op. 19; Fant Pno, Op. 111; A. Roussel:Con Pno, Op. 36 CBC ▲ 5178 (16.97)

I. Margalit (pno), B. Thomson (cnd), London PO ("Romantic Piano Concertos") † J. Brahms:Con 1 Pno, Op. 15; Mendelssohn (-Bartholdy):Capriccio brillante, Op. 22; R. Schumann:Con Pno in a, Op. 54 CHN 2-▲ 7070 (26.97)

B. Moiseiwitsch (pno), B. Cameron (cnd), Philharmonia Orch *(rec 1944-48)* † P. Tchaikovsky:Con 2 Pno, Op. 44 HPC ▲ 146 (17.97)

B. Moiseiwitsch (pno), B. Cameron (cnd), Philharmonia Orch *(rec Abbey Road, London, England, Apr 25, 1947)* † E. Grieg:Con Pno, Op. 16; Liszt:Fant on Hungarian Folk Tunes, S.123 APR ▲ 5529 (m) [ADD] (18.97)

G. Rozhdestvensky (pno) † Carnival of the Animals; Con 3 Vn, Op. 61; Havanaise, Op. 83; Intro & Rondo capriccioso, Op. 28; Sym 3 ERAT (Ultima) 2-▲ 18971 (16.97)

704 ▲ = CD ♦ = Enhanced CD △ = MD ▮ = Cassette Tape ▯ = DCC

SAINT-SAËNS, CAMILLE (cont.)

Concerto No. 2 in g for Piano & Orchestra, Op. 22 (1868) (cont.)

A. Rubinstein (pno) † M. de Falla:Amor brujo (Ritual Fire Dance); Noches en los jardines de España; C. Franck:Symphonic Vars, M.46; S. Prokofiev:March Pno RCAV (Gold Seal) ▲ 61863 (11.97)

A. Rubinstein (pno), P. Gaubert (cnd), Paris Conservatory Société des Concerts Orch † Beethoven:Con 4 Pno, Op. 58 TES ▲ 1154 (17.97)

A. Rubinstein (pno), A. Wallenstein (cnd), RCA Victor SO *(rec 1958)* † Chopin:Con 2 Pno, Op. 21; E. Grieg:Con Pno, Op. 16; R. Schumann:Con Pno in a, Op. 54; P. Tchaikovsky:Con 1 Pno, Op. 23 PPHI (Great Pianists of the 20th Century, Vol. 86) 2-▲ 456958 (22.97)

A. Rubinstein (pno), A. Wallenstein (cnd), Sym of the Air *(rec 1956 & 1958)* † C. Franck:Symphonic Vars, M.46; Liszt:Con 1 Pno, S.124 RCAV (Gold Seal) ▲ 61496 (11.97)

G. Sokolov (pno), N. Järvi (cnd), USSR SO *(rec Moscow, 1967)* ("Neeme Järvi: The Early Recordings, Vol. 3") † P. Tchaikovsky:Con 1 Pno, Op. 23 MELD ▲ 40721 [ADD] (6.97)

M. Vaiman (vn), B. Režucha (cnd), Slovak PO † J. Françaix:Concertino; A. Roussel:Con Pno, Op. 36 PC ▲ 267194 [DDD] (2.97)

O. Volkov (pno), A. Tchistiakov (cnd), Moscow PO † S. Rachmaninoff:Con 2 Pno, Op. 18 BRIO ▲ 114 (16.97)

A. Watts (pno), Y. Levi (cnd), Atlanta SO *(rec Woodruff Arts Center Atlanta, GA, Nov 21, 1994)* † P. Tchaikovsky:Con 1 Pno, Op. 23 TEL ▲ 80386 [DDD] (16.97)

E. Wild (pno), M. Freccia (cnd), RCA Victor SO *(rec 1967)* † E. Grieg:Con Pno, Op. 16; Liszt:Fant on Hungarian Folk Tunes, S.123 CHSK ▲ 50 [ADD] (16.97)

artists unknown † P. Tchaikovsky:Con 1 Pno, Op. 23 SNYC ▲ 64560 (4.97)

Concerto No. 4 in c for Piano & Orchestra, Op. 44 (1875)

I. Biret (pno), J. Loughran (cnd), Philharmonia Orch † Con 2 Pno, Op. 22 NXIN ▲ 550334 [DDD] (5.97)

R. Casadesus (pno), L. Bernstein (cnd), New York PO † Intro & Rondo capriccioso, Op. 28; Sym 3 SNYC ▲ 47608

J. Collard (pno), A. Previn (cnd), Royal PO † Con 2 Pno, Op. 22 EMIC ▲ 47816 (16.97)

A. Cortot (pno), C. Munch (cnd), Paris Conservatory Société des Concerts Orch *(rec 1935 for Victor)* ("Alfred Cortot Plays French Concertos") † Étude Pno, Op. 52/6; Chopin:Con 2 Pno, Op. 21; M. Ravel:Con Pno (left hand) PHS ▲ 9491 [AAD] (17.97)

P. Entremont (pno), E. Ormandy (cnd), Philadelphia Orch *(rec 1961)* † Con 1 Vc, Op. 33; Con 2 Pno, Op. 22 SNYC (Essential Classics) ▲ 48276 [ADD] (7.97) ▮ 48276 [ADD] (3.98)

Concerto No. 5 in F for Piano & Orchestra, Op. 103, "Egyptian" (1896)

I. Tiegerman (pno), J. Ferriz (cnd), Cairo SO *(rec Cairo, Egypt, June 1, 1963)* ("The Lost Legend of Cairo: Radio & Private Recordings") † J. Brahms:Con 2 Pno, Op. 83; Intermezzos (3) Pno, Op. 117; Pieces (6) Pno, Op. 118; Pieces (8) Pno, Op. 76; Chopin:Ballade 4 Pno, Op. 52; Nocturnes Pno; Preludes (24) Pno, Op. 28; Scherzos Pno; Son Pno in b, Op. 58; G. Fauré:Nocturnes Pno; J. Field:Nocturnes Pno; C. Franck:Symphonic Vars, M.46; Tiegerman:Meditation Pno ARBT 2-▲ 116 (32.97)

Concerto No. 1 in A for Violin & Orchestra, Op. 20 (1859)

P. Graffin (vn), M. Brabbins (cnd), BBC Scottish SO † Con 2 Vn, Op. 58; Con 3 Vn, Op. 61 HYP (Romantic Violin Concerto Vol. 1) ▲ 67074 (18.97)

J. Kantorow (vn), J. Kantorow (cnd), Tapiola Sinfonietta ("Capriccio: Music for Violin & Orchestra") † Havanaise, Op. 83; Intro & Rondo capriccioso, Op. 28; Morceau de concert Vn, Op. 62; Romance Vn, Op. 48; Sarabande & rigaudon, Op. 93 BIS ▲ 860 [DDD] (17.97)

R. Ricci (vn), P. Cao (cnd), Luxembourg RSO † Allegro appassionato, Op. 43; Caprice andalous, Op. 122; Con 1 Vc, Op. 33; Con 2 Vc, Op. 119; Con 2 Vn, Op. 58; Con 3 Vn, Op. 61; Havanaise, Op. 83; Intro & Rondo capriccioso, Op. 28; Morceau de concert Vn, Op. 62; Romance Vn, Op. 48 VB2 2-▲ 5084 [ADD] (9.97)

R. Ricci (vn), T. Koetsier (cnd), Polish National Orch † Con 2 Vn, Op. 58; K. Goldmark:Con 1 Vn, Op. 28 ONEL ▲ 96040 [ADD] (7.97)

Concerto No. 2 in C for Violin & Orchestra, Op. 58 (1858)

P. Graffin (vn), M. Brabbins (cnd), BBC Scottish SO † Con 1 Vn, Op. 20; Con 3 Vn, Op. 61 HYP (Romantic Violin Concerto Vol. 1) ▲ 67074 (18.97)

R. Ricci (vn), P. Cao (cnd), Luxembourg RSO † Allegro appassionato, Op. 43; Caprice andalous, Op. 122; Con 1 Vc, Op. 33; Con 1 Vn, Op. 20; Con 2 Vc, Op. 119; Con 3 Vn, Op. 61; Havanaise, Op. 83; Intro & Rondo capriccioso, Op. 28; Morceau de concert Vn, Op. 62; Romance Vn, Op. 48 VB2 2-▲ 5084 [ADD] (9.97)

R. Ricci (vn), T. Koetsier (cnd), Polish National Orch † Con 1 Vn, Op. 20; K. Goldmark:Con 1 Vn, Op. 28 ONEL ▲ 96040 [ADD] (7.97)

Concerto No. 3 in b for Violin & Orchestra, Op. 61 (1880)

P. Amoyal (vn) † Carnival of the Animals; Con 2 Pno, Op. 22; Havanaise, Op. 83; Intro & Rondo capriccioso, Op. 28; Sym 3 ERAT (Ultima) 2-▲ 18971 (16.97)

Chee-Yun (vn), J. López-Cobos (cnd), London PO *(rec London, May 1996)* † Lalo:Sym espagnole, Op. 21 DNN ▲ 18017 [DDD] (16.97)

Z. Francescatti (vn), D. Mitropoulos (cnd), New York PO *(rec New York, NY, Jan 23, 1950)* ("Great Violin Concertos") † Bruch:Con 1 Vn, Op. 26; E. Chausson:Chanson perpétuelle, Op. 37; Poème Vn, Op. 25; Mendelssohn (-Bartholdy):Con Vn & Orch, Op. 64; S. Prokofiev:Con 2 Vn, Op. 63; P. Tchaikovsky:Con Vn SNYC 2-▲ 62339 (m) [ADD] (25.97)

P. Graffin (vn), M. Brabbins (cnd), BBC Scottish SO † Con 1 Vn, Op. 20; Con 2 Vn, Op. 58 HYP (Romantic Violin Concerto Vol. 1) ▲ 67074 (18.97)

D. Kang (vn), A. Wit (cnd), Polish National RSO Katowice *(rec May 24-26, 1993)* † Caprice andalous, Op. 122; Intro & Rondo capriccioso, Op. 28; Morceau de concert Vn, Op. 62; Romance Vn, Op. 48 NXIN ▲ 550752 [DDD] (5.97)

E. Oliveira (vn), G. Schwarz (cnd), Seattle SO † J. Brahms:Con Vn ARTK ▲ 3 (15.97)

I. Perlman (vn), D. Barenboim (cnd), Orch de Paris † Lalo:Sym espagnole, Op. 21 DEUT (3D Classics) ▲ 29977 [DDD] (9.97)

I. Perlman (vn), D. Barenboim (cnd), Orch de Paris † Berlioz:Rêverie et caprice, Op. 8; Lalo:Sym espagnole, Op. 21 DEUT (Masters) ▲ 45549 [DDD] (9.97)

R. Ricci (vn), P. Cao (cnd), Luxembourg RSO † Allegro appassionato, Op. 43; Caprice andalous, Op. 122; Con 1 Vc, Op. 33; Con 1 Vn, Op. 20; Con 2 Vc, Op. 119; Con 2 Vn, Op. 58; Havanaise, Op. 83; Intro & Rondo capriccioso, Op. 28; Morceau de concert Vn, Op. 62; Romance Vn, Op. 48 VB2 2-▲ 5084 [ADD] (9.97)

M. Schwalbe (vn), F. Prausnitz (cnd), Swiss Romande Orch *(rec Jan 1961)* † Mendelssohn (-Bartholdy):Con Vn & Orch, Op. 64; Wieniawski:Con 2 Vn, Op. 22 BID ▲ 164 (16.97)

G. Shaham (vn), G. Sinopoli (cnd), New York PO † Paganini:Con 1 Vn, M.S. 21 DEUT ▲ 29786 [DDD] (16.97)

S. Tönz (vn), C. Mackerras (cnd), Academy of St. Martin in the Fields † Allegro appassionato, Op. 70; Carnival of the Animals ILOV 2-▲ 531 (9.97)

S. Tönz (vn), N. Marriner (cnd), Academy of St. Martin in the Fields † Son 1 Vn, Op. 75; Son 2 Vn, Op. 102 NOVA ▲ 150147 (16.97)

Xue-Wei (vn), K. Bakels (cnd), Philharmonia Orch † Bruch:Con 1 Vn, Op. 26 ASV ▲ 680 [DDD] (16.97)

Le Cygne [The Swan] for Cello & Piano (or Orchestra) [from *Carnival of the Animals*]

G. Cassado (vc), H. Schmidt-Isserstedt (cnd), Berlin PO *(rec 1931-35)* † A. Dvořák:Con Vc; G. F. Handel:Serse (sels) ENT (Strings) ▲ 99314 (16.97)

P. Fournier (vc), G. Moore (pno) *(rec 1939-47)* † Con 1 Vc, Op. 33; F. Schubert:Son Arpeggione, D.821; P. Tchaikovsky:Vars on a Rococo Theme, Op. 33 ENT (Strings) ▲ 99344 (16.97)

S. Heled (vc), J. Zak (pno) ("20th Century Romantic Cello Music") † Castelnuovo-Tedesco:Notturno sull'acqua & Scherzino Vc, Op. 82; Cilea:Son Vc; D. Milhaud:Elégie, Op. 251; S. Prokofiev:Son Vc CLSO (Simca Heled Collection) ▲ 163 (15.97)

M. Kliegel (vc), J. Monnard (cnd), Bournemouth Sinfonietta *(rec Poole Arts Center, England, Jan 1995)* † Allegro appassionato, Op. 43; Con 1 Vc, Op. 33; Con 2 Vc, Op. 119; Suite Vc, Op. 16 NXIN ▲ 8553039 [DDD] (5.97)

B. Pergamenschikov (vc), P. Gililov (pno) *(rec Walchstadt, Germany, Mar 1994)* ("Beau Soir") † Allegro appassionato, Op. 43; Debussy:Beau soir; Music of Debussy; Preludes Pno; G. Fauré:Après un rêve, Op. 7/1; Berceuse, Op. 16; Elégie, Op. 24; Papillon, Op. 77; Romance Vc, Op. 69; Sicilienne, Op. 78; Sérénade, Op. 98; Ibert:Histoires; M. Ravel:Pièce en forme de Habanera ORF ▲ 349951 [DDD] (18.97)

J. Suk (vn), K. Englichová (hp) [trans for vn & hp] ("Golden Strings") † Fant Vn; J. L. Dussek:Sons Vn, Op. 2; Massenet:Méditation from Thaïs; O. Respighi:Siciliana; G. Rossini:Andante e tema con variazioni Va; L. Spohr:Son 2 Vn & Hp, Op. 16 LT ▲ 38 [DDD] (16.97)

L. Tooten (vc), B. Rawitz (pno) *(rec Brussels, Belgium, Feb 1998)* ("Works for Cello & Piano") † Allegro appassionato, Op. 43; Son 1 Vc, Op. 32; Son 2 Vc, Op. 123 PAVA ▲ 7407 [DDD] (10.97)

D. D. Williencourt (vc), P. Verrot (cnd), Monte Carlo PO † Allegro appassionato, Op. 43; Con 1 Vc, Op. 33; Con 2 Vc, Op. 119; Suite Vc, Op. 16 ARN ▲ 68347 (16.97)

Cyprès et Lauriers in d for Organ & Orchestra, Op. 156 (1919)

N. Kynaston (org), D. V. Yu (cnd), Philharmonia Orch † Carnival of the Animals; Sym 3 ICC ▲ 6600012 (16.97)

Danse macabre in g for Orchestra, Op. 40 (1874)

E. Bátiz (cnd), Mexican State SO † Carnival of the Animals; Sym 3; Wedding Cake, Op. 76 ASV ▲ 665 [DDD] (16.97)

SAINT-SAËNS, CAMILLE (cont.)

Danse macabre in g for Orchestra, Op. 40 (1874) (cont.)

A. Chorosinski (org) [Andrej Chorosinski] *(rec n, Wuppertal Stadhalle, Germany, Sept 1-4, 1997)* ("Virtuoso Organ Music") † Dukas:L'Apprenti sorcier; Mussorgsky:Pictures at an Exhibition; Smetana:Moldau MDG ▲ 3200818 [DDD] (17.97)

J. DePreist (cnd), Royal Stockholm PO † Rapsodies sur des cantiques bretons, Op. 7; Samson et Dalila (Bacchanale); Sym 3 BIS ▲ 555 [DDD] (17.97)

C. Dutoit (cnd), Philharmonia Orch † Carnival of the Animals; Phaéton, Op. 39; Rouet d'Omphale, Op. 31 PLON ▲ 14460 [ADD] (16.97)

C. Dutoit (cnd), Philharmonia Orch † Havanaise, Op. 83; Intro & Rondo capriccioso, Op. 28; Jeunesse d'Hercule, Op. 50; Marche héroïque, Op. 34; Phaéton, Op. 39; Rouet d'Omphale, Op. 31 PLON (Jubilee) ▲ 25021 [ADD] (9.97)

V. Horowitz (pno) *(rec 1945)* † J. S. Bach:Chorales Org; S. Barber:Excursions, Op. 20; Kabalevsky:Preludes Pno, Op. 38; Son 2 Pno, Op. 45; Mussorgsky:By the Water; S. Prokofiev:Toccata Pno, Op. 11 ENPL (Piano Library) ▲ 239 (13.97)

E. Krivine (cnd), Lyon National Orch † Phaéton, Op. 39; Sym 3 DNN ▲ 75024 [DDD] (16.97)

L. Maazel (cnd), Pittsburgh SO † Phaéton, Op. 39; Samson et Dalila (Bacchanale); Sym 3 SNYC ▲ 53979 (16.97)

J. Martinon (cnd), Paris Conservatory Société des Concerts Orch † Bizet:Jeux d'enfants; Jbert:Divert Orch PLON (The Classic Sound) ▲ 448571 (11.97)

T. Murray (org) † Lemare:Org Music; Rameau:Temple de la gloire (sels) AFK ▲ 515

E. Ormandy (cnd), Philadelphia Orch † Carnival of the Animals; Marche militaire française; Samson et Dalila (Bacchanale); Sym 3 SNYC (Essential Classics) ▲ 47655 (7.97) ▮ 47655 (3.98)

P. Paray (cnd), Detroit SO † Liszt:Mephisto Waltz 1 Orch, S.110; F. Schmitt:Tragédie de Salomé (sels); R. Strauss:Salome (dance of the 7 veils); C. M. von Weber:Invitation to the Dance Orch MRCR ▲ 34336 (11.97)

J. Reynolds (pno), P. Lockwood (pno) [trans Saint-Saëns for 2 pnos] *(rec Utrecht, Netherlands, Apr 1996)* † Caprice arabe, Op. 96; Carnival of the Animals; Polonaise Pnos, Op. 77; Scherzo Pnos, Op. 87; Vars on a Theme of Beethoven, Op. 35 GLOE ▲ 5152 [DDD] (16.97)

H. Scherchen (cnd), Vienna State Opera Orch ("Hermann Scherchen Conducts") † Rimsky-Korsakov:Scheherazade, Op. 35 ENT (Palladio) ▲ 4159 [DDD] (13.97)

L. Stokowski (cnd), Philadelphia Orch ("Leopold Stokowski: The Philadelphia Years") † A. Dvořák:Sym 9; Liszt:Hungarian Rhaps, S.244; Mussorgsky:Khovanshchina (orch sels); C. M. von Weber:Invitation to the Dance Orch GRM2 ▲ 78552 (13.97)

L. Stokowski (cnd), Philadelphia Orch † Samson et Dalila (Bacchanale); J. S. Bach:Toccata & Fugue Org, BWV 565; Dukas:L'Apprenti sorcier; Mussorgsky:Night on Bare Mountain; I. Stravinsky:Sacre du printemps MTAL (Leopold Stokowski Conducts) ▲ 48002 (6.97)

A. Toscanini (cnd), NBC SO ("The Toscanini Collection, Vol. 39: All-French Program") † Berlioz:Damnation de Faust (sels); Roméo et Juliette (sels); Dukas:L'Apprenti sorcier; C. Franck:Psyché (sels); M. Ravel:Daphnis et Chloé (suite 2); A. Thomas:Mignon (ov) RCAV (Gold Seal) ▲ 60322 (11.97)

T. Wilson (org), D. Higgs (org) [arr Dikinson & Mathewson] *(rec National City Christian Church Orgs, Washington, DC, Jan 1995)* † J. Christian Bach:Sons & Duets Kbd 4-Hands, T.343/3; C. Hampton:Alexander Vars; W. A. Mozart:Adagio & Allegro, K.594; Adagio & Fugue Strs, K.546; R. Wagner:Walküre (ride of the Valkyries) DLS ▲ 3175 [DDD] (14.97)

Duos (6) for Piano & Harmonium, Op. 8 (1858)

E. Breidenbach (pno), J. M. Michel (harm) ("Duos for Harmonium & Piano") † C. Franck:Prélude, fugue et var, Op. 18; Widor:Duos Pno & Harm SIGM ▲ 8700 (17.97)

Elégie for Piano & Violin, Op. 160 (1920)

G. Poulet (vn), N. Lee (pno) *(rec Aug 1996)* ("Complete Works for Violin & Piano") † Berceuse Vn, Op. 38; Elégie, Op. 143; Son 1 Vn, Op. 75; Son 2 Vn, Op. 102; Tryptique, Op. 136 ARN ▲ 68362 [DDD] (16.97)

Elégie for Violin & Piano, Op. 143 (1915)

G. Poulet (vn), N. Lee (pno) *(rec Aug 1996)* ("Complete Works for Violin & Piano") † Berceuse Vn, Op. 38; Elégie, Op. 160; Son 1 Vn, Op. 75; Son 2 Vn, Op. 102; Tryptique, Op. 136 ARN ▲ 68362 [DDD] (16.97)

Études (6) for Piano, Op. 52 (1877)

P. Lane (pno) ("The Complete Études") † Études (6) Pno, Op. 111; Études (6) Pno, Op. 135; Thème varié, Op. 97 HYP ▲ 67037 (18.97)

M. Lee (pno) † Études (6) Pno, Op. 111; Album Pno, Op. 72 MDG ▲ 6040590 [DDD] (17.97)

Étude in D♭ for Piano, Op. 52/6, "Etude en forme de valse" (1877)

A. Cortot (pno) *(rec 1931 for Victor)* ("Alfred Cortot Plays French Concertos") † Con 4 Pno, Op. 44; Chopin:Con 2 Pno, Op. 21; M. Ravel:Con Pno (left hand) PHS ▲ 9491 [AAD] (17.97)

A. Cortot (pno) [Duo-Art pno roll] † Beethoven:Son 30 Pno, Op. 109; Chabrier:Pièces pittoresques; Chopin:Impromptu in G♭, Op. 51; Liszt:Années de pèlerinage 1, S.160; Hungarian Rhaps, S.244 NIMB (Grand Piano) ▲ 8814 [DDD] (11.97)

G. Cziffra (pno) *(rec Nov 5, 1978 & Apr 12, 1981)* ("Georges Cziffra Live at Senlis") † Chopin:Pno Music (misc colls); Liszt:Etudes d'exécution transcendante (12), S.139; Etudes de concert (2), S.145; Années de pèlerinage 3, S.163; Liebesträume, S.541; M. Ravel:Jeux d'eau APR ▲ 5554 [ADD] (18.97)

P. Hirschhorn (vn), L. Petcherskaya (pno) [arr for vn & pno] *(rec live, Palais des Beaux-Arts, Brussels, Belgium, June 7, 1967)* † J. S. Bach:Sons & Partitas Vn; B. Bartók:Son Vn; Geminiani:Sons Vn, Op. 4; P. Hindemith:Son Vn & Pno, Op. 11/1; D. Milhaud:Boeuf sur le toit, Op. 58; M. Ravel:Tzigane CYPR ▲ 9606 (17.97)

H. Udagawa (vn), K. Klein (cnd), London PO † E. Chausson:Poème Vn, Op. 25; Glazunov:Con Vn; P. Tchaikovsky:Souvenir d'un lieu cher, Op. 42 INMP (Classics) ▲ 6700312 (9.97)

Études (6) for Piano, Op. 111 (1899)

P. Lane (pno) ("The Complete Études") † Études (6) Pno, Op. 135; Études (6) Pno, Op. 52; Thème varié, Op. 97 HYP ▲ 67037 (18.97)

M. Lee (pno) † Études (6) Pno, Op. 52; Album Pno, Op. 72 MDG ▲ 6040590 [DDD] (17.97)

Études (6) for Piano (left hand), Op. 135 (1912)

P. Lane (pno) ("The Complete Études") † Études (6) Pno, Op. 111; Études (6) Pno, Op. 52; Thème varié, Op. 97 HYP ▲ 67037 (18.97)

Fantaisie in a for Harp, Op. 95 (1893)

C. Antonelli (hp) *(rec Rome, Italy, 1987)* ("Harp Festival") † C.P.E. Bach:Son Hp, H.563; B. Britten:Suite Hp, Op. 83; G. Fauré:Impromptu Hp, Op. 86; L. Spohr:Fant 2 Hp, Op. 35; G. B. Viotti:Son Hp AART ▲ 47202 [DDD] (10.97)

Fantaisie No. 1 in E♭ for Organ (1857)

S. Armstrong-Ouellette (org) *(rec Mission Church, Boston, MA)* ("Musique de la Basilique") † Dupont:Méditation; Gigout:Pièces Org (sels); Guilmant:Son 7 Org, Op. 89; G. Pierné:Pièces Org, Op. 29; Saint-Martin:Toccata de la Libération; Vierne:Pièces de fantaisie AFK ▲ 538 (16.97)

H. Fagius (org)—Con moto; Allegro di molto e con fuoco *(rec Härnösand Cathedral, Sweden, July 8, 1977)* † J. S. Bach:Cant 147; Toccata & Fugue Org, BWV 565; Boëllmann:Suite gothique Org, Op. 25; O. Lindberg:Music of Lindberg; Mendelssohn (-Bartholdy):Preludes & Fugues Org, Op. 37; Sons Org, Op. 65; Vierne:Sym 1 Org, Op. 14 BIS 2-▲ 156 [AAD] (34.97)

H. Fagius (org) *(rec Härnösand Cathedral, Sweden, July 8, 1977)* † J. Alain:Vars sur un thème de Clément Janequin; Boëllmann:Suite gothique Org, Op. 25; F. Couperin:Pièces d'orgue consistantes en deux Messes; Daquin:Nouveau livre de noëls, Op. 2; M. Dupré:Vars sur un vieux Noël, Op. 20; Duruflé:Prélude et fugue, Op. 7 BIS ▲ 7 [AAD] (17.97)

H. Fagius (org) † Bénédiction nuptiale, Op. 9; Fant 2 Org, Op. 101; Fant 3 Org, Op. 157; Preludes & Fugues Org, Op. 109; Preludes & Fugues Org, Op. 99 BIS ▲ 556 [DDD] (17.97)

Fantaisie No. 2 in D♭ for Organ, Op. 101 (1895)

H. Fagius (org) † Bénédiction nuptiale, Op. 9; Fant 1 Org; Fant 3 Org, Op. 157; Preludes & Fugues Org, Op. 109; Preludes & Fugues Org, Op. 99 BIS ▲ 556 [DDD] (17.97)

Fantaisie No. 3 in C for Organ, Op. 157 (1919)

H. Fagius (org) † Bénédiction nuptiale, Op. 9; Fant 1 Org; Fant 2 Org, Op. 101; Preludes & Fugues Org, Op. 109; Preludes & Fugues Org, Op. 99 BIS ▲ 556 [DDD] (17.97)

Fantaisie in A for Violin & Harp, Op. 124 (1907)

Aurora Duo † Boren:Movts from Liturgical Dance; Donizetti:Son Vn; A. Hovhaness:Son Vn Hp, Op. 406; Lasala:Poema del Pastor Coya; Shaposhnikov:Son in d Vn 4TAY ▲ 4010 [DDD] (17.97)

C. Henkel (vc), I. Moretti (hp) † Qt Pno; Suite Vc, Op. 16 VAL (Musique Française) ▲ 4657 (18.97)

A. Jones (fl), R. Yamahata (hp) *(rec Prague, Oct 31-Nov 3, 1994)* ("Mostly French") † Debussy:Danses sacrée et profane; Syrinx Fl; G. Fauré:Fant Fl, Op. 79; Impromptu Hp, Op. 86; Gaos:Impressión nocturna; Griffes:Poem Fl; M. Ravel:Intro & Allegro Hp DI ▲ 920281 [DDD] (5.97)

A. Korsakov (vn), V. Dulova (hp) *(rec 1979)* ("Vera Dulova: Russian Performing School") † Donizetti:Son Fl & Hp; C. R. G. Pascal:Con Hp; M. Ravel:Pavane pour une infante défunte RD (Talents of Russia) ▲ 16206 [AAD] (16.97)

K. Sillito (vn), S. Kang (hp) † Debussy:Danses sacrée et profane; Son Fl; M. Ravel:Intro & Allegro Hp; A. Roussel:Sérénade, Op. 30 CHN ▲ 8621 [DDD] (16.97)

SAINT-SAËNS, CAMILLE (cont.)

Fantaisie in A for Violin & Harp, Op. 124 (1907) (cont.)

J. Suk (vn), K. Englichová (hp) ("Meditation") † Massenet:Méditation from Thaïs; G. Pierné:Impromptu-Caprice Hp, Op. 9; O. Respighi:Siciliana; G. Rossini:Andante e tema con variazioni Va; L. Spohr:Son 1 Vn & Hp DI ▲ 920318 [DDD] (5.97)

J. Suk (vn), K. Englichová (hp) ("Golden Strings") † Cygne; J. L. Dussek:Sons Vn, Op. 2; Massenet:Méditation from Thaïs; O. Respighi:Siciliana; G. Rossini:Andante e tema con variazioni Va; L. Spohr:Son 2 Vn & Hp, Op. 16 LT ▲ 38 [DDD] (16.97)

Une Flûte invisible for Voice, Flute & Piano (1885)

A. S. von Otter (mez), A. Alin (fl), B. Forsberg (pno) *(rec Stockhom, Nov 1994)* ("La Bonne Chanson: French Chamber Songs") † E. Chausson:Chanson perpétuelle, Op. 37; M. Delage:Poèmes hindous; G. Fauré:Bonne chanson, Op. 61; F. Martin:Chants de Noël; F. Poulenc:Rapsodie nègre; M. Ravel:Poèmes de Mallarmé DEUT ▲ 47752 [DDD] (16.97)

Havanaise in E for Violin & Orchestra, Op. 83 (1887)

P. Amoyal (vn) † Carnival of the Animals; Con 2 Pno, Op. 22; Con 3 Vn, Op. 61; Intro & Rondo capriccioso, Op. 28; Sym 3 ERAT (Ultima) 2-▲ 18971 (16.97)

M. Bisengaliev (vn), J. Wildner (cnd), Polish National RSO ("The Lark Ascending") † Intro & Rondo capriccioso, Op. 28; Beethoven:Romance 2 Vn, Op. 50; Massenet:Méditation from Thaïs; W. A. Mozart:Adagio Vn, K.261; M. Ravel:Tzigane; Sarasate:Zigeunerweisen, Op. 20; Vaughan Williams:Lark Ascending NXIN ▲ 8553509 [DDD] (5.97)

M. Bisengaliev (vn), J. Wildner (cnd), Polish National RSO Katowice *(rec Jan 31-Feb 3, 1992)* † Lalo:Sym espagnole, Op. 21; M. Ravel:Tzigane; Sarasate:Zigeunerweisen, Op. 20 NXIN ▲ 550494 [DDD] (5.97)

S. Chang (vn), W. Sawallisch (cnd), Philadelphia Orch † Intro & Rondo capriccioso, Op. 28; Paganini:Con 1 Vn, M.S. 21 EMIC ▲ 55026 (16.97)

K. Chung (vn), C. Dutoit (cnd), Royal PO † Danse macabre, Op. 40; Intro & Rondo capriccioso, Op. 28; Jeunesse d'Hercule, Op. 50; Marche héroïque, Op. 34; Phaéton, Op. 39; Rouet d'Omphale, Op. 31 PLON (Jubilee) ▲ 25021 [ADD] (9.97)

J. Heifetz (vn), J. Barbirolli (cnd) † J. S. Bach:Sons & Partitas Vn; J. Brahms:Con Vn & Vc, Op. 102; Paganini:Caprices Vn, M.S. 25; Wieniawski:Scherzo-tarantelle, Op. 16 IMMM ▲ 37095 (6.97)

J. Heifetz (vn), J. Barbirolli (cnd), London SO *(rec Abbey Road London, Apr 9, 1937)* ("The Heifetz Collection, Volume 4, 1935-1939") † Intro & Rondo capriccioso, Op. 28; J. Brahms:Con Vn; Son 2 Vn, Op. 100; G. Fauré:Son 1 Vn, Op. 13; S. Prokofiev:Con 2 Vn, Op. 63; Sarasate:Zigeunerweisen, Op. 20 RCAV (Gold Seal) 2-▲ 61735 [ADD] (21.97)

J. Heifetz (vn), J. Barbirolli (cnd), London SO *(rec London, 1935 & 1937)* ("J. Heifetz in the Golden Thirties, Vol. 1") † Intro & Rondo capriccioso, Op. 28; J. S. Bach:Sons & Partitas Vn; Wieniawski:Con 2 Vn, Op. 22 GRM2 ▲ 78511 [ADD] (13.97)

J. Heifetz (vn), D. Vorhees (cnd), Bell Telephone Hour Orch *(rec Aug 30, 1943)* ("Jascha Heifetz Collection, Vol. 3") † J. Brahms:Con Vn; Hungarian Dances Orch; Lalo:Sym espagnole, Op. 21 DHR (Legendary Treasures) ▲ 7717 (16.97)

J. Kantorow (vn), J. Kantorow (cnd), Tapiola Sinfonietta ("Capriccio: Music for Violin & Orchestra") † Con 1 Vn, Op. 20; Intro & Rondo capriccioso, Op. 28; Morceau de concert Vn, Op. 62; Romance Vn, Op. 48; Sarabande & rigaudon, Op. 93 BIS ▲ 860 [DDD] (17.97)

L. Kogan (vn), V. Vasiligv (cnd), USSR SO ("Leonid Kogan in Concert") † G. Gershwin:Pno Music; Songs; M. Ravel:Tzigane; Sarasate:Zigeunerweisen, Op. 20; M. Vainberg:Con Vn; F. Waxman:Carmen Fant ONEL ▲ 50500 [ADD] (7.97)

P. Monteux (cnd), San Francisco SO ("Vol 6") † Debussy:Mer Orch; Liszt:Préludes, S.97; A. Scriabin:Poème de l'extase, Op. 54 RCAV (Gold Seal; Pierre Monteux Edition) ▲ 61890 (11.97)

I. Perlman (vn), J. Martinon (cnd), Orch de Paris † Intro & Rondo capriccioso, Op. 28; E. Chausson:Poème Vn, Op. 25; M. Ravel:Tzigane EMIC ▲ 47725 (16.97)

I. Perlman (vn), Z. Mehta (cnd), New York PO † Intro & Rondo capriccioso, Op. 28; E. Chausson:Poème Vn, Op. 25; M. Ravel:Tzigane; Sarasate:Fant on Carmen, Op. 25 DEUT ▲ 23063 [DDD] (16.97)

R. Ricci (vn), E. Ansermet (cnd), Swiss Romande Orch † Intro & Rondo capriccioso, Op. 28; Lalo:Sym espagnole, Op. 21; Sarasate:Fant on Carmen, Op. 25; Zigeunerweisen, Op. 20 PLON (The Classic Sound) ▲ 452309 (11.97)

R. Ricci (vn), P. Cao (cnd), Luxembourg RSO † Allegro appassionato, Op. 43; Caprice andalous, Op. 122; Con 1 Vc, Op. 33; Con 1 Vn, Op. 20; Con 2 Vc, Op. 119; Con 2 Vn, Op. 58; Con 3 Vn, Op. 61; Intro & Rondo capriccioso, Op. 28; Morceau de concert Vn, Op. 62; Romance Vn, Op. 48 VB2 2-▲ 5084 [ADD] (9.97)

N. Salerno-Sonnenberg (vn), G. Schwarz (cnd), New York Chamber SO † Intro & Rondo capriccioso, Op. 28; Massenet:Thaïs (sels); Mendelssohn (-Bartholdy):Con Vn & Orch, Op. 64 EMIC ▲ 49276 [DDD] (16.97)

M. Vengerov (vn), Z. Mehta (cnd), Israel PO † Intro & Rondo capriccioso, Op. 28; Paganini:Con 1 Vn, M.S. 21; F. Waxman:Carmen Fant TELC ▲ 73266 (16.97)

Henry VIII (selections)

A. Mogrelia (cnd), Razumovsky Sinfonia *(rec Slovak Radio Concert Hall Bratislava, Mar 27-Apr 4, 1995)* † Delibes:Sylvia NXIN 2-▲ 553338 [DDD] (15.97)

Improvisations (7) for Organ, Op. 150 (1917)

J. Higdon (org) † Preludes & Fugues Org, Op. 109; Preludes & Fugues Org, Op. 99 ARK ▲ 6107 [DDD] (16.97)

Introduction & Rondo capriccioso in a for Violin & Orchestra, Op. 28 (1863)

P. Amoyal (vn) † Carnival of the Animals; Con 2 Pno, Op. 22; Con 3 Vn, Op. 61; Havanaise, Op. 83; Sym 3 ERAT (Ultima) 2-▲ 18971 (16.97)

S. Chang (vn), W. Sawallisch (cnd), Philadelphia Orch † Havanaise, Op. 83; Paganini:Con 1 Vn, M.S. 21 EMIC ▲ 55026 (16.97)

K. Chung (vn), C. Dutoit (cnd), Royal PO † Danse macabre, Op. 40; Havanaise, Op. 83; Jeunesse d'Hercule, Op. 50; Marche héroïque, Op. 34; Phaéton, Op. 39; Rouet d'Omphale, Op. 31 PLON (Jubilee) ▲ 25021 [ADD] (9.97)

M. Elman (vn), V. Golschmann (cnd), Vienna State Opera Orch *(rec 1959)* † A. Khachaturian:Con Vn VC ▲ 8035 [ADD] (13.97)

Z. Francescatti (vn), L. Bernstein (cnd), New York PO † Con 4 Pno, Op. 44; Sym 3 SNYC ▲ 47608

H. Griffiths (cnd), Zurich CO † Carnival of the Animals; Vars on a Theme of Beethoven, Op. 35 PANC ▲ 510106 (17.97)

J. Heifetz (vn) *(rec 1935-39)* † J. S. Bach:Sons & Partitas Vn; J. Brahms:Con Vn & Vc, Op. 102; Glazunov:Con Vn; Wieniawski:Con 2 Vn, Op. 22 ENT (Strings) 2-▲ 99312 (32.97)

J. Heifetz (vn), J. Barbirolli (cnd), London PO *(rec Abbey Road London, Mar 18, 1935)* ("The Heifetz Collection, Volume 4, 1935-1939") † Havanaise, Op. 83; J. Brahms:Con Vn; Son 2 Vn, Op. 100; G. Fauré:Son 1 Vn, Op. 13; S. Prokofiev:Con 2 Vn, Op. 63; Sarasate:Zigeunerweisen, Op. 20 RCAV (Gold Seal) 2-▲ 61735 [ADD] (21.97)

J. Heifetz (vn), J. Barbirolli (cnd), London SO *(rec London, 1935 & 1937)* ("J. Heifetz in the Golden Thirties, Vol. 1") † Havanaise, Op. 83; J. S. Bach:Sons & Partitas Vn; Wieniawski:Con 2 Vn, Op. 22 GRM2 ▲ 78511 [ADD] (13.97)

L. Josefowicz (vn), N. Marriner (cnd), Academy of St. Martin in the Fields ("Bohemian Rhapsodies") † E. Chausson:Poème Vn, Op. 25; Massenet:Méditation from Thaïs; M. Ravel:Tzigane; Sarasate:Fant on Carmen, Op. 25; Zigeunerweisen, Op. 20; Wieniawski:Polonaise 1, Op. 4 PPHI ▲ 454440 (16.97)

O. Kagan (vn), V. Sinaisky (cnd), Moscow State PO *(rec 1980)* ("Oleg Kagan Edition, Vol. XIII") † S. Prokofiev:Con 1 Vn, Op. 19; M. Ravel:Tzigane; R. Schumann:Fant Vn LV ▲ 173 [ADD] (17.97)

D. Kang (vn), A. Wit (cnd), Polish National RSO ("The Lark Ascending") † Havanaise, Op. 83; Beethoven:Romance 2 Vn, Op. 50; Massenet:Méditation from Thaïs; W. A. Mozart:Adagio Vn, K.261; M. Ravel:Tzigane; Sarasate:Zigeunerweisen, Op. 20; Vaughan Williams:Lark Ascending NXIN ▲ 8553509 [DDD] (5.97)

D. Kang (vn), A. Wit (cnd), Polish National RSO Katowice *(rec May 24-26, 1993)* † Caprice andalous, Op. 122; Con 3 Vn, Op. 61; Morceau de concert Vn, Op. 62; Romance Vn, Op. 48 NXIN ▲ 550752 [DDD] (5.97)

J. Kantorow (vn), J. Kantorow (cnd), Tapiola Sinfonietta ("Capriccio: Music for Violin & Orchestra") † Con 1 Vn, Op. 20; Havanaise, Op. 83; Morceau de concert Vn, Op. 62; Romance Vn, Op. 48; Sarabande & rigaudon, Op. 93 BIS ▲ 860 [DDD] (17.97)

D. Oistrakh (vn), C. Munch (cnd), Boston SO † E. Chausson:Sym in B♭, Op. 20 RCAV (Gold Seal) ▲ 60683

I. Perlman (vn), J. Martinon (cnd), Orch de Paris † Havanaise, Op. 83; E. Chausson:Poème Vn, Op. 25; M. Ravel:Tzigane EMIC ▲ 47725 (16.97)

I. Perlman (vn), Z. Mehta (cnd), New York PO † Havanaise, Op. 83; E. Chausson:Poème Vn, Op. 25; M. Ravel:Tzigane; Sarasate:Fant on Carmen, Op. 25 DEUT ▲ 23063 [DDD] (16.97)

R. Ricci (vn), E. Ansermet (cnd), Swiss Romande Orch † Havanaise, Op. 83; Lalo:Sym espagnole, Op. 21; Sarasate:Fant on Carmen, Op. 25; Zigeunerweisen, Op. 20 PLON (The Classic Sound) ▲ 452309 (11.97)

R. Ricci (vn), P. Cao (cnd), Luxembourg RSO † Allegro appassionato, Op. 43; Caprice andalous, Op. 122; Con 1 Vc, Op. 33; Con 1 Vn, Op. 20; Con 2 Vc, Op. 119; Con 2 Vn, Op. 58; Con 3 Vn, Op. 61; Havanaise, Op. 83; Morceau de concert Vn, Op. 62; Romance Vn, Op. 48 VB2 2-▲ 5084 [ADD] (9.97)

R. Ricci (vn), G. Thiele (cnd), Warsaw PO † S. Barber:Con Vn; Paganini:Con 1 Vn, M.S. 21 ONEL ▲ 96030 [ADD] (7.97)

N. Salerno-Sonnenberg (vn), G. Schwarz (cnd), New York Chamber SO † Havanaise, Op. 83; Massenet:Thaïs (sels); Mendelssohn (-Bartholdy):Con Vn & Orch, Op. 64 EMIC ▲ 49276 [DDD] (16.97)

M. Vengerov (vn), Z. Mehta (cnd), Israel PO † Havanaise, Op. 83; Paganini:Con 1 Vn, M.S. 21; F. Waxman:Carmen Fant TELC ▲ 73266 (16.97)

SAINT-SAËNS, CAMILLE (cont.)

La Jeunesse d'Hercule (symphonic poem) in E♭ for Orchestra, Op. 50 (1877)

C. Dutoit (cnd), Philharmonia Orch † Danse macabre, Op. 40; Havanaise, Op. 83; Intro & Rondo capriccioso, Op. 28; Marche héroïque, Op. 34; Phaéton, Op. 39; Rouet d'Omphale, Op. 31 PLON (Jubilee) ▲ 25021 [ADD] (9.97)

La Libellule for Voice & Piano (1894)

C. Hartglass (sop), B. Leroy (pno) *(rec Châteaugay Church France, June 1995)* ("Caryn Hartglass") † Rossignol et la rose; J. Benedict:Gitane et l'oiseau; L. Bernstein:I Hate Music; Mass (sels); Longas:Rossignol et l'Empereur; D. Milhaud:Chansons de Ronsard, Op. 223; R. Strauss:Songs (6), Op. 68 LIDI ▲ 201033 [DDD] (16.97)

Marche héroïque in E♭ for Orchestra, Op. 34 (1871)

C. Dutoit (cnd), Philharmonia Orch † Danse macabre, Op. 40; Havanaise, Op. 83; Intro & Rondo capriccioso, Op. 28; Jeunesse d'Hercule, Op. 50; Phaéton, Op. 39; Rouet d'Omphale, Op. 31 PLON (Jubilee) ▲ 25021 [ADD] (9.97)

Marche militaire française for Orchestra [final section from Suite Algérienne, Op. 60]

E. P. Biggs (org), E. Ormandy (cnd), Philadelphia Orch † Carnival of the Animals; Danse macabre, Op. 40; Samson et Dalila (Bacchanale); Sym 3 SNYC (Essential Classics) ▲ 47655 (7.97) ▮ 47655 (3.98)

Morceau de concert in G for Harp & Orchestra, Op. 154 (1918)

I. Moretti (hp), K. Arp (cnd), Southwest German RSO Baden-Baden ("French Harp Concertos") † Boieldieu:Con Hp; G. Pierné:Concertstück Hp, Op. 39 KSCH ▲ 311422 (16.97)

Morceau de concert in f for Horn & Orchestra, Op. 94 (1887)

P. Damm (hn), S. Kurz (cnd), Dresden Staatskapelle ("Romantic Horn Concerti") † Lortzing:Konzertstück Hn; R. Schumann:Konzertstück Hns, Op. 86; C. M. von Weber:Con Hn BER ▲ 9324 (10.97)

Morceau de concert in G for Violin & Orchestra, Op. 62 (1880)

D. Kang (vn), A. Wit (cnd), Polish National RSO Katowice *(rec May 24-26, 1993)* † Caprice andalous, Op. 122; Con 3 Vn, Op. 61; Intro & Rondo capriccioso, Op. 28; Romance Vn, Op. 48 NXIN ▲ 550752 [DDD] (5.97)

J. Kantorow (vn), J. Kantorow (cnd), Tapiola Sinfonietta ("Capriccio: Music for Violin & Orchestra") † Con 1 Vn, Op. 20; Havanaise, Op. 83; Intro & Rondo capriccioso, Op. 28; Romance Vn, Op. 48; Sarabande & rigaudon, Op. 93 BIS ▲ 860 [DDD] (17.97)

R. Ricci (vn), L. De Froment (cnd), Luxembourg RSO † Allegro appassionato, Op. 43; Caprice andalous, Op. 122; Con 1 Vc, Op. 33; Con 1 Vn, Op. 20; Con 2 Vc, Op. 119; Con 2 Vn, Op. 58; Con 3 Vn, Op. 61; Havanaise, Op. 83; Intro & Rondo capriccioso, Op. 28; Romance Vn, Op. 48 VB2 2-▲ 5084 [ADD] (9.97)

La Muse et la poète for Violin, Cello & Piano (or Orchestra), Op. 132 (1910)

C. Rex (vn), C. Rex (vc), P. Tiboris (cnd), Bohuslav Martinů PO ("Music for Doubles") † F. Krommer:Con for 2 Cls, Op. 35; Martinů:Double Con ELY ▲ 714 [DDD] (16.97)

Music of Saint-Saëns

Banff Camerata—Spt Tpt, Op. 65; Son Ob, Op. 166; Wedding Cake, Op. 76; Fant Vn, Op. 124; Morceau de concert Hn, Op. 94; Duos Pno & Harm, Op. 8; Cloches du soir, Op. 85 ("Chamber Works") SUMM ▲ 157 [DDD] (16.97)

L. De Froment (cnd), Luxembourg Radio Orch *(Con 1 Pno, Op. 17; Con 2 Pno, Op. 22; Con 3 Pno, Op. 29; Con 4 Pno, Op. 44; Con 5 Pno, Op. 103; Africa, Op. 89; Rapsodie d'Auvergne, Op. 73; Wedding Cake, Op. 76; Muse et la poète, Op. 132; Cyprès et Lauriers, Op. 156; Morceau de concert Hn, Op. 94; Romance Hn Orch, Op. 36),* R. Ricci (vn), S. Mildonian (hp) *(Fant Vn, Op. 124)* VB3 3-▲ 3028 [ADD] (14.97)

N. Milstein (vn)—Carnival of the Animals; Danse macabre, Op. 40; Phaéton, Op. 39; Rouet d'Omphale, Op. 31; Samson et Dalila (Bacchanale); Intro & Rondo capriccioso, Op. 28; Havanaise, Op. 83 EMIC (Studio) ▲ 69112 (11.97)

Odelette in D for Flute & Orchestra, Op. 162 (1920)

W. Bennett (fl), C. Benson (pno) *(rec Japan, Oct 21, 1987)* ("Poulenc: Flute Sonata") † Bizet:Arlésienne (sels); Carmen (sels); Chopin:Vars on Rossini; W. A. Mozart:Così fan tutte (sels); F. Poulenc:Son Fl; M. Ravel:Vocalise-étude en forme de habanera; Widor:Suite Fl, Op. 34 CAMA ▲ 390 [DDD]

Collegium Musicum Soloists ("Complete Works for Piano & Winds") † Airs de ballet d'Ascanio; Caprice sur des airs danoises et russes, Op. 79; Cavatina Trb & Pno, Op. 144; Romance Fl, Op. 37; Romance Hn Orch, Op. 36; Romance Hn Pno, Op. 67; Son Bn; Son Cl; Son Ob; Spt Tpt, Op. 65; Suite algérienne, Op. 60; Tarantelle, Op. 6 KPT 2-▲ 32062 [DDD]

Oratorio de Noël [Christmas Oratorio] for solo Voices, Orchestra & Chorus, Op. 12 (1858)

M. Flämig (cnd), Dresden PO, Dresden Kreuz Choir, U. Selbig (sop), E. Wilke (mez), A. Markert (cta), A. Ude (ten), E. Junghans (bar), J. Zoff (hp), M. Winkler (org) *(rec Dresden, Germany, Mar-Apr 1987)* † Mendelssohn (-Bartholdy):Vom Himmel hoch; P. Tchaikovsky:Suite 3 Orch, Op. 55; Suite 4 Orch, Op. 61; Verdi:Traviata CAPO 2-▲ 10200 [DDD] (11.97)

A. Myrat (cnd), La Camerata Friends of Music Orch, Kontogeorghiou (cnd), Greek Radio-TV Choir † P. Hindemith:Tuttifäntchen AG ▲ 129 (18.97)

E. Wiens (sop), V. Schweizer (sop), H. Jung (mez), F. Melzer (ten), K. Widmer (bass), D. Hellmann (cnd), Mainz Bach Orch, Mainz Bach Choir *(rec 1976)* CALG ▲ 50512 [AAD] (19.97)

Phaéton (symphonic poem) in C for Orchestra, Op. 39 (1873)

C. Badea (cnd), Royal PO † Sym 3 TEL ▲ 80274 [DDD] (16.97)

Y. Butt (cnd), London SO † Suite algérienne, Op. 60; Sym 2 ASV ▲ 599 [DDD] (16.97)

C. Dutoit (cnd), Philharmonia Orch † Carnival of the Animals; Danse macabre, Op. 40; Rouet d'Omphale, Op. 31 PLON ▲ 14460 [ADD] (16.97)

C. Dutoit (cnd), Philharmonia Orch † Danse macabre, Op. 40; Havanaise, Op. 83; Intro & Rondo capriccioso, Op. 28; Jeunesse d'Hercule, Op. 50; Marche héroïque, Op. 34; Rouet d'Omphale, Op. 31 PLON (Jubilee) ▲ 25021 [ADD] (9.97)

E. Krivine (cnd), Lyon National Orch † Danse macabre, Op. 40; Sym 3 DNN ▲ 75024 [DDD] (16.97)

L. Maazel (cnd), Pittsburgh SO † Danse macabre, Op. 40; Samson et Dalila (Bacchanale); Sym 3 SNYC ▲ 53979 (16.97)

Polonaise in f for 2 Pianos, Op. 77 (1886)

C. Ivaldi (pno), N. Lee (pno) † Caprice arabe, Op. 96; Caprice héroïque, Op. 106; Scherzo Pnos, Op. 87; Vars on a Theme of Beethoven, Op. 35 ARN ▲ 68011 [AAD] (16.97)

J. Reynolds (pno), P. Lockwood (pno) *(rec Utrecht, Netherlands, Apr 1996)* † Caprice arabe, Op. 96; Carnival of the Animals; Danse macabre, Op. 40; Scherzo Pnos, Op. 87; Vars on a Theme of Beethoven, Op. 35 GLOE ▲ 5152 [DDD] (16.97)

Preludes & Fugues (3) for Organ, Op. 99 (1894)

H. Fagius (org) † Bénédiction nuptiale, Op. 9; Fant 1 Org; Fant 2 Org, Op. 101; Fant 3 Org, Op. 157; Preludes & Fugues Org, Op. 109 BIS ▲ 556 [DDD] (17.97)

J. Higdon (org) † Improvs Org, Op. 150; Preludes & Fugues Org, Op. 109 ARK ▲ 6107 [DDD] (16.97)

A. Partington (org) ("Great European Organs No. 31") † Preludes & Fugues Org, Op. 109 PRIO ▲ 384 [DDD]

Preludes & Fugues (3) for Organ, Op. 109 (1898)

H. Fagius (org) † Bénédiction nuptiale, Op. 9; Fant 1 Org; Fant 2 Org, Op. 101; Fant 3 Org, Op. 157; Preludes & Fugues Org, Op. 99 BIS ▲ 556 [DDD] (17.97)

J. Higdon (org) † Improvs Org, Op. 150; Preludes & Fugues Org, Op. 99 ARK ▲ 6107 [DDD] (16.97)

A. Partington (org) ("Great European Organs No. 31") † Preludes & Fugues Org, Op. 99 PRIO ▲ 384 [DDD]

Quartet in B♭ for Piano & Strings, Op. 41 (1875)

H. Sermet (pno) † Fant Vn; Suite Vc, Op. 16 VAL (Musique Française) ▲ 4657 (18.97)

Quartet No. 1 in e for Strings, Op. 112 (1899)

Joachim Koeckert String Quartet *(rec Apr 25-26, 1990)* † E. Grieg:Qt Strs, Op. 27 CALG ▲ 50916 [DDD] (19.97)

Medici String Quartet † Qt 2 Strs, Op. 153 KSCH ▲ 364842 (16.97)

Miami String Quartet † Qt 2 Strs, Op. 153; G. Fauré:Qt Strs CONI ▲ 51291 (16.97)

Venice String Quartet *(rec Genova, May 1997)* ("The String Quartets") † Qt 2 Strs, Op. 153 DYNC ▲ 179 [DDD] (17.97)

Quartet No. 2 in G for Strings, Op. 153 (1918)

Medici String Quartet † Qt 1 Strs, Op. 112 KSCH ▲ 364842 (16.97)

Miami String Quartet † Qt 1 Strs, Op. 112; G. Fauré:Qt Strs CONI ▲ 51291 (16.97)

Venice String Quartet *(rec Genova, May 1997)* ("The String Quartets") † Qt 1 Strs, Op. 112 DYNC ▲ 179 [DDD] (17.97)

Rapsodie d'Auvergne in C for Piano & Orchestra, Op. 73 (1884)

J. Collard (pno), A. Previn (cnd), Royal PO † Africa; Allegro appassionato, Op. 43; Con 1 Pno, Op. 17; Wedding Cake, Op. 76 EMIC ▲ 49757 (16.97)

Rapsodies sur des cantiques bretons (3) for Organ, Op. 7 (1866)

H. Fagius (org) † Danse macabre, Op. 40; Samson et Dalila (Bacchanale); Sym 3 BIS ▲ 555 [DDD] (17.97)

H. Mardirosian (org) *(rec Champaign, IL, Apr 1997)* ("Organ Suites") † Foote:Suite Org, Op. 54; J. Langlais:Suite médévale; P. Malengreau:Suite Org, Op. 14 CENT ▲ 2368 [DDD] (16.97)

Requiem for solo Voices, Orchestra & Chorus, Op. 54 (1878)

Watson (sgr), Hewes (sgr), Weld (sgr), MacMaster (sgr), J. Somary (cnd), Amor Artis Orch, Amor Artis Chorale *(rec live)* † J. Somary:Ballad of God & His People PREM ▲ 1025 [DDD] (16.97)

706 ▲ = CD ♦ = Enhanced CD △ = MD ▮ = Cassette Tape ▯ = DCC

SAINT-SAËNS, CAMILLE (cont.)

Romance in D for Cello & Piano, Op. 51 (1877)

L. Loubry (bn), R. Talitman (hp) ("The Golden Age of Harp & French Bassoon") † Boieldieu:Solo Bn & Hp; Dauprat:Son Hn & Pno, Op. 2; Debussy:Romance Bn & Hp; Labarre:Duo 1; Naderman:Nocturne I; Nocturne II — DI ▲ 920193 [DDD] (5.97)

Romance in D♭ for Flute (or Violin) & Orchestra, Op. 37 (1871)

Collegium Musicum Soloists ("Complete Works for Piano & Winds") † Airs de ballet d'Ascanio; Caprice sur des airs danoises et russes, Op. 79; Cavatina Trb & Pno, Op. 144; Odelette Fl, Op. 162; Romance Hn Orch, Op. 36; Romance Hn Pno, Op. 67; Son Bn; Son Cl; Son Ob; Spt Tpt, Op. 65; Suite algérienne, Op. 60; Tarantelle, Op. 6 — KPT 2-▲ 32062 [DDD]

T. Hutchins (fl), M. Bernardi (cnd), Vancouver SO † Chaminade:Concertino Fl, Op. 107; Coulthard:Music on a Quiet Song; G. Fauré:Fant Fl, Op. 79; W. McCauley:Miniatures Fl; J. Rodrigo:Con pastorale — CBC ▲ 5171 (16.97)

Romance in F for Horn (or Cello) & Orchestra, Op. 36 (1874)

Collegium Musicum Soloists ("Complete Works for Piano & Winds") † Airs de ballet d'Ascanio; Caprice sur des airs danoises et russes, Op. 79; Cavatina Trb & Pno, Op. 144; Odelette Fl, Op. 162; Romance Fl, Op. 37; Romance Hn Pno, Op. 67; Son Bn; Son Cl; Son Ob; Spt Tpt, Op. 65; Suite algérienne, Op. 60; Tarantelle, Op. 6 — KPT 2-▲ 32062 [DDD]

T. Thedéen (vc), J. Kantorow (cnd), Tapiola Sinfonietta *(rec Tapiola, Finland, June 1998)* † Con 1 Vc, Op. 33; Con 2 Vc, Op. 119; Sym in A — BIS ▲ 956 [DDD] (17.97)

Romance in E for Horn & Piano, Op. 67 (1885)

Collegium Musicum Soloists ("Complete Works for Piano & Winds") † Airs de ballet d'Ascanio; Caprice sur des airs danoises et russes, Op. 79; Cavatina Trb & Pno, Op. 144; Odelette Fl, Op. 162; Romance Fl, Op. 37; Romance Hn Orch, Op. 36; Son Bn; Son Cl; Son Ob; Spt Tpt, Op. 65; Suite algérienne, Op. 60; Tarantelle, Op. 6 — KPT 2-▲ 32062 [DDD]

Romance in C for Violin & Orchestra, Op. 48 (1874)

D. Kang (vn), A. Wit (cnd), Polish National RSO Katowice *(rec May 24-26, 1993)* † Caprice andalous, Op. 122; Con 3 Vn, Op. 61; Intro & Rondo capriccioso, Op. 28; Morceau de concert Vn, Op. 62 — NXIN ▲ 550752 [DDD] (5.97)

J. Kantorow (vn), J. Kantorow (cnd), Tapiola Sinfonietta ("Capriccio: Music for Violin & Orchestra") † Con 1 Vn, Op. 20; Havanaise, Op. 83; Intro & Rondo capriccioso, Op. 28; Morceau de concert Vn, Op. 62; Sarabande & rigaudon, Op. 93 — BIS ▲ 860 [DDD] (17.97)

R. Ricci (vn), L. De Froment (cnd), Luxembourg RSO † Allegro appassionato, Op. 43; Caprice andalous, Op. 122; Con 1 Vc, Op. 33; Con 1 Vn, Op. 20; Con 2 Vc, Op. 119; Con 2 Vn, Op. 58; Con 3 Vn, Op. 61; Havanaise, Op. 83; Intro & Rondo capriccioso, Op. 28; Morceau de concert Vn, Op. 62 — VB2 2-▲ 5084 [ADD] (9.97)

Le Rossignol et la rose (song) for Voice & Piano (1894)

C. Hartglass (sop), B. Leroy (pno) *(rec Châteaugay Church France, June 1995)* ("Caryn Hartglass") † Libellule; J. Benedict:Gitane et l'oiseau; L. Bernstein:I Hate Music; Mass (sels); Longas:Rossignol et l'Empereur; D. Milhaud:Chansons de Ronsard, Op. 223; R. Strauss:Songs (6), Op. 68 — LIDI ▲ 201033 [DDD] (16.97)

Le Rouet d'Omphale in A for Orchestra, Op. 31 (1872)

C. Dutoit (cnd), Philharmonia Orch † Carnival of the Animals; Danse macabre, Op. 40; Phaéton, Op. 39 — PLON ▲ 14460 [ADD] (16.97)

C. Dutoit (cnd), Philharmonia Orch † Danse macabre, Op. 40; Havanaise, Op. 83; Intro & Rondo capriccioso, Op. 28; Jeunesse d'Hercule, Op. 50; Marche héroïque, Op. 34; Phaéton, Op. 39 — PLON (Jubilee) ▲ 25021 [ADD] (9.97)

S. Gunzenhauser (cnd), Czech-Slovak State Radio PO † Samson et Dalila (Bacchanale); Sym 3 — NXIN ▲ 550138 [DDD] (5.97)

C. Munch (cnd), Boston SO † Berlioz:Ovs; Roméo et Juliette (sels); Troyens (sels) — RCAV (Gold Seal) ▲ 61400 (11.97)

C. Munch (cnd), Boston SO ("The French Touch") † Dukas:L'Apprenti sorcier; C. Franck:Chasseur maudit, M.44; M. Ravel:Ma mère l'oye — RCAV (Living Stereo) ▲ 68978 (11.97)

C. Munch (cnd), Paris Conservatory Société des Concerts Orch ("Munch, Vol. 7") † C. Franck:Symphonic Vars, M.46; Indy:Fervaal (sels) — LYS ▲ 409 (17.97)

Samson et Dalila (opera in 3 acts) [lib Ferdinand Lemaire] (1877)

D. Barenboim (cnd), Orch de Paris, E. Obraztsova (mez), P. Domingo (ten), R. Bruson (bar), R. Lloyd (bass) — DEUT 2-▲ 13297 [ADD] (22.97)

S. Cambreling (cnd), Vienna SO, Bregenz Festival Choir, Anonymous (cnd), Sofia Chamber Choir, P. Burian (cnd), Vienna Volksoper Chorus *(rec Vorarlberg, Germany, July 21, 1988)* — KSCH 3-▲ 317742 [DDD] (31.97)

W. Meier (mez), P. Domingo (ten), A. Fondary (bar), S. Ramey (bass), M. Chung (cnd), Bastille Opera Orch, Bastille Opera Chorus — EMIC 2-▲ 54470 (32.97)

F. Molinari-Pradelli (cnd), Naples Teatro San Carlo Orch, Naples Teatro San Carlo Chorus, J. Madeira (mez—Dalila), M. del Monaco (ten—Samson), A. Cesarini (ten—1st Philistine), A. Flauto (ten—Philistine Messanger), L. Puglisi (bar—High Priest), P. Clabassi (bass—Abimelecco), I. Riccò (bass—Old Hebrew), E. Feliciati (bass—2nd Philistine) *(rec Naples, Italy, May 5, 1959)* — HDY 2-▲ 6006 (m) (34.97)

G. Prêtre (cnd), Paris National Opera Theater Orch, F. Cossotto (mez), G. Chauvet (ten), R. Massard (bar), J. Rouleau (bass), J. Bastin (bass) *(rec Paris, France)* † Bizet:Carmen (sels) — BELV 2-▲ 7222 (29.97)

R. Stevens (mez—Dalila), R. Vinay (ten—Samson), T. Carter (ten—1st Philistine), T. Lopez (ten—Philistine Messenger), J. Mordino (bar—High Priest), A. Cosenza (bar—Abimélech), J. Knight (bass—2nd Philistine), A. Berberian (bass—Old Hebrew), R. Cellini (cnd), New Orleans Opera Orch, New Orleans Opera Chorus *(rec live, Apr 2, 1960)* ("New Orleans Opera Archives, Vol. 3") — VAIA 2-▲ 1055 [ADD]

F. Tamagno (ten) *(rec 1903-05)* ("The Mythical Recordings") † U. Giordano:Andrea Chénier (sels); Massenet:Hérodiade (sels); Meyerbeer:Prophète (sels); G. Rossini:Guillaume Tell (sels); Verdi:Otello (sels); Trovatore (sels) — VOCA (Vocal Archives) ▲ 1200 (14.97)

Samson et Dalila (selections)

O. Borodina (mez), D. Hvorostovsky (bar), P. Summers (cnd), English CO ("Olga & Dmitri") † Donizetti:Favorita (sels); Rimsky-Korsakov:Tsar's Bride (sels); G. Rossini:Barbiere di Siviglia (sels) — PPHI ▲ 454439 (16.97)

M. Callas (sop), G. Prêtre (cnd), French National RSO *(rec Salle Wagram Paris, Mar-Apr 1961)* ("Callas à Paris I") † Bizet:Carmen (sels); G. Charpentier:Louise (sels); C. W. Gluck:Alceste (sels); Orfeo ed Euridice (sels); Gounod:Roméo et Juliette (sels); Massenet:Cid (sels); A. Thomas:Mignon (sels) *(E,F lib texts)* — EMIC (Callas Edition) ▲ 66466 [ADD] (11.97)

M. Horne (mez), L. Foster (cnd), Monte Carlo PO † D.-F. Auber:Zerline (sels); Donizetti:Favorita (sels); B. Godard:Vivandiere (sels); Gounod:Sappho (sels) — ERAT (Recital) ▲ 98501 (9.97)

S. Onegin (cta)—Printemps qui commence; Mon coeur s'ouvre à ta voix [GER] *(rec 1911-24)* ("Vol. 1: 1911-1914") † Bizet:Carmen (sels); Donizetti:Lucrezia Borgia (sels); Kienzl:Evangelimann (sels); Verdi:Aida (sels); Ballo in maschera (sels); Trovatore (sels); R. Wagner:Götterdämmerung (sels); Rheingold (sels) — NIMB (Prima Voce) ▲ 7898 [ADD] (11.97)

E. Stignani (mez) † V. Bellini:Norma (sels); C. W. Gluck:Orfeo ed Euridice (sels); A. Thomas:Mignon (sels); Verdi:Aida (sels); Don Carlos (sels); Forza del destino (sels); Trovatore (sels) — PHG (Great Voices) ▲ 5101 (12.97)

G. Taccani (ten), C. Formichi (bar), H. Harty (cnd), orch unknown—Maudite à jamais *(rec 1924)* † Leoncavallo:Pagliacci (sels); Massenet:Jongleur de Nôtre Dame (sels); Thaïs (sels); G. Puccini:Tosca (sels); Verdi:Otello (sels); Rigoletto; Rigoletto (sels) — PRE 2-▲ 89234 (m) (31.97)

J. Tourel (mez) *(rec 1945-46)* ("Jennie Tourel in Opera & Concert, 1944-46") † Bizet:Carmen (sels); G. Rossini:Barbiere di Siviglia (sels) — EKLR ▲ 55 (16.97)

Samson et Dalila:Bacchanale

L. Bernstein (cnd), New York PO *(rec May 15, 1967)* † Borodin:Prince Igor (Polovtsian Dances); Gounod:Faust (ballet music); Ponchielli:Gioconda (sels); Rimsky-Korsakov:Snow Maiden (dance); Verdi:Aida (sels) — SNYC ▲ 47600 [ADD] (10.97)

J. DePreist (cnd), Royal Stockholm PO † Danse macabre, Op. 40; Rapsodies sur des cantiques bretons, Op. 7; Sym 3 — BIS ▲ 555 [DDD] (17.97)

S. Gunzenhauser (cnd), Czech-Slovak State Radio PO † Rouet d'Omphale, Op. 31; Sym 3 — NXIN ▲ 550138 [DDD] (5.97)

E. Kunzel (cnd), Cincinnati Pops Orch † Dukas:L'Apprenti sorcier; Liszt:Préludes, S.97; Rimsky-Korsakov:Mlada (procession); Snow Maiden (dance); J. Weinberger:Schwanda der Dudelsackpfeifer (polka & fugue) — TEL ▮ 30115 [DDD] (8.98) ▲ 80115 [DDD] (16.97)

L. Maazel (cnd), Pittsburgh SO † Danse macabre, Op. 40; Phaéton, Op. 39; Sym 3 — SNYC ▲ 53979 (16.97)

E. Ormandy (cnd), Philadelphia Orch † Carnival of the Animals; Danse macabre, Op. 40; Marche militaire française; Sym 3 — SNYC (Essential Classics) ▲ 47655 (7.97) ▮ 47655 (3.98)

L. Stokowski (cnd), Philadelphia Orch *(rec 1927-30)* ("Leopold Stokowski: The Philadelphia Years, Vol. 3") † Berlioz:Damnation de Faust (sels); Sibelius:Swan of Tuonela; P. Tchaikovsky:Nutcracker Suite, Op. 71a — GRM2 ▲ 78586 (13.97)

L. Stokowski (cnd), Philadelphia Orch † Danse macabre, Op. 40; J. S. Bach:Toccata & Fugue Org, BWV 565; Dukas:L'Apprenti sorcier; Mussorgsky:Night on Bare Mountain; I. Stravinsky:Sacre du printemps — MTAL (Leopold Stokowski Conducts) ▲ 48002 (6.97)

SAINT-SAËNS, CAMILLE (cont.)

Sarabande & rigaudon in E for Orchestra, Op. 93 (1892)

J. Kantorow (vn), J. Kantorow (cnd), Tapiola Sinfonietta ("Capriccio: Music for Violin & Orchestra") † Con 1 Vn, Op. 20; Havanaise, Op. 83; Intro & Rondo capriccioso, Op. 28; Morceau de concert Vn, Op. 62; Romance Vn, Op. 48 — BIS ▲ 860 [DDD] (17.97)

Scherzo for 2 Pianos, Op. 87 (1889)

C. Ivaldi (pno), N. Lee (pno) † Caprice arabe, Op. 96; Caprice héroïque, Op. 106; Polonaise Pnos, Op. 77; Vars on a Theme of Beethoven, Op. 35 — ARN ▲ 68011 [AAD] (16.97)

J. Reynolds (pno), P. Lockwood (pno) *(rec Utrecht, Netherlands, Apr 1996)* † Caprice arabe, Op. 96; Carnival of the Animals; Danse macabre, Op. 40; Polonaise Pnos, Op. 77; Vars on a Theme of Beethoven, Op. 35 — GLOE ▲ 5152 [DDD] (16.97)

Septet in E♭ for Trumpet, Strings & Piano, Op. 65 (1881)

Collegium Musicum Soloists ("Complete Works for Piano & Winds") † Airs de ballet d'Ascanio; Caprice sur des airs danoises et russes, Op. 79; Cavatina Trb & Pno, Op. 144; Odelette Fl, Op. 162; Romance Fl, Op. 37; Romance Hn Orch, Op. 36; Romance Hn Pno, Op. 67; Son Bn; Son Cl; Son Ob; Suite algérienne, Op. 60; Tarantelle, Op. 6 — KPT 2-▲ 32062 [DDD]

I. Hobson (pno), I. Hobson (cnd), Sinfonia da Camera † Allegro appassionato, Op. 43; Bagatelles Pno, Op. 3; Carnival of the Animals — ARA ▲ 6570 (16.97)

Nash Ensemble *(rec 1988)* † Carnival of the Animals; Trio 1 for Pno, Op. 18; A. Dvořák:Qnt Pno, Op. 81; Trio 4 Pno, Op. 90 — VCL 2-▲ 61516 [DDD] (11.97)

J. Rosenfeld (vn), A. Kavafian (vn), T. Hoffman (va), C. Brey (vc), J. Kulowitsch (db), T. Stevens (tpt), A. Previn (pno) *(rec New York City, May 25-26, 1993)* ("French Chamber Music") † D. Milhaud:Création du monde:Suite; F. Poulenc:Sxt Pno — RCAV (Red Seal) ▲ 68181 [DDD] (16.97)

Sérénade d'hiver for Male Vocal Quartet [text H. Cazalis] (1867)

Asbury Brass Quintet [arr G. Flint] ("Asbury Brass Quintet") † O. Böhme:Sxt Brass, Op. 30; Bozza:Sonatine; P. Grainger:Folk Song Settings; Jevtic:Qnt Victoria; W. Lutoslawski:Mini Ov — ALBA ▲ 273 [DDD] (16.97)

Sonata in G for Bassoon & Piano, Op. 168 (1921)

S. Canuti (bn), M. Somenzi (pno) ("Bassoon Images") † Dutilleux:Sarabande et Cortège; M. de Falla:Canciones populares españolas; P. Hindemith:Son Bn; Mompou:Aureana do sil; Combat del somni; A. Piazzolla:Grand Tango — STRV ▲ 80013 (16.97)

Collegium Musicum Soloists ("Complete Works for Piano & Winds") † Airs de ballet d'Ascanio; Caprice sur des airs danoises et russes, Op. 79; Cavatina Trb & Pno, Op. 144; Odelette Fl, Op. 162; Romance Fl, Op. 37; Romance Hn Orch, Op. 36; Romance Hn Pno, Op. 67; Son Cl; Son Ob; Spt Tpt, Op. 65; Suite algérienne, Op. 60; Tarantelle, Op. 6 — KPT 2-▲ 32062 [DDD]

B. Grainger (bn), G. Niwa (pno) *(rec DePaul Univ. Concert Hall Chicago, Sept 1992)* † R. Boutry:Interferences; Cascarino:Son Bn; E. Elgar:Romance Bn, Op. 62; Etler:Son Bn; P. Hindemith:Son Bn; W. A. Mozart:Duo Bn Vc, K.292 — CENT ▲ 2244 [DDD] (16.97)

P. Hannevold (bn), G. H. Braaten (pno) ("L'Esprit") † Son Ob; Bozza:Divertissement Sax, Op. 39; Fant pastoral, Op. 37; Récit, Sicilienne & Rondò; Chagrin:Pieces Bn; Jolivet:Sonatine Ob; F. Poulenc:Trio Ob — NORW ▲ 960038 [DDD] (17.97)

M. Monguzzi (bn), G. Brollo (pno) *(rec May 1995)* ("20th Century Bassoon") † U. Bertoni:Con Bn; Bozza:Fant Bn; Récit, Sicilienne & Rondò; Dutilleux:Sarabande et Cortège; P. Hindemith:Son Bn; Tansman:Sonatine Bn; Suite Bn — BONG ▲ 5565 [DDD] (16.97)

M. Turkovič (bn), K. Engel (pno) † J. Brahms:Son for 2 Pnos, Op. 34b; Ibert:Carignane Bn & Pno; R. Schumann:Romances Ob, Op. 94 — CAMA ▲ 66 (18.97)

Sonata No. 1 in c for Cello & Piano, Op. 32 (1872)

Drinkall-Baker Duo ("Cello Sonatas") † Suite Vc, Op. 16; Beethoven:Son 3 Vc, Op. 69 — KLAV ▲ 11068 [DDD] (18.97)

N. Gutman (vc), S. Richter (pno) *(rec Kur- und Kongresszentrum Rottach-Egern, July 12, 1992)* † B. Britten:Son Vc; S. Prokofiev:Son Vc — LV ▲ 641 [DDD] (17.97)

W. Thomas-Mifune (vc), C. Piazzini (pno) *(rec Dec 22-23, 1986)* † Chant saphique Vc, Op. 91; Son 2 Vc, Op. 123 — CALG ▲ 50862 [DDD] (19.97)

L. Tooten (vc), B. Rawitz (pno) *(rec Brussels, Belgium, Feb 1998)* ("Works for Cello & Piano") † Allegro appassionato, Op. 43; Cygne; Son 2 Vc, Op. 123 — PAVA ▲ 7407 [DDD] (10.97)

Sonata No. 2 in F for Cello & Piano, Op. 123 (1905)

W. Thomas-Mifune (vc), C. Piazzini (pno) *(rec Dec 22-23, 1986)* † Chant saphique Vc, Op. 91; Son 1 Vc, Op. 32 — CALG ▲ 50862 [DDD] (19.97)

L. Tooten (vc), B. Rawitz (pno) *(rec Brussels, Belgium, Feb 1998)* ("Works for Cello & Piano") † Allegro appassionato, Op. 43; Cygne; Son 1 Vc, Op. 32 — PAVA ▲ 7407 [DDD] (10.97)

Sonata in E♭ for Clarinet & Piano, Op. 167 (1921)

W. Boeykens (cl), R. Groslot (pno) ("French Music for Clarinet & Piano") † E. Chausson:Andante et Allegro; Debussy:Première rapsodie Cl; P. Gaubert:Fant Fl; Messager:Solo de concours Cl; G. Pierné:Canzonetta Cl, Op. 19; Rabaud:Solo de Concours, Op. 10 — TLNT ▲ 51 (15.97)

Collegium Musicum Soloists ("Complete Works for Piano & Winds") † Airs de ballet d'Ascanio; Caprice sur des airs danoises et russes, Op. 79; Cavatina Trb & Pno, Op. 144; Odelette Fl, Op. 162; Romance Fl, Op. 37; Romance Hn Orch, Op. 36; Romance Hn Pno, Op. 67; Son Bn; Son Ob; Spt Tpt, Op. 65; Suite algérienne, Op. 60; Tarantelle, Op. 6 — KPT 2-▲ 32062 [DDD]

M. Edwards (cl), T. Bach (pno) *(rec Pomona College Claremont, CA, 1997)* † Bjelinski:Son Cl; Ladmirault:Son Cl; Martinů:Sonatina Cl; Rabaud:Solo de Concours, Op. 10 — CRYS ▲ 735 (15.97)

J. Hilton (cl), K. Swallow (pno) † Debussy:Première rapsodie Cl; D. Milhaud:Duo concertante Cl & Pno, Op. 351; F. Poulenc:Son Cl & Pno; M. Ravel:Pièce en forme de Habanera; A. Roussel:Aria Fl — CHN (Collect) ▲ 6589 [DDD] (12.97)

K. Leister (cl), F. Bognár (pno) *(rec Vienna, Austria, 1995)* ("Par exellence: French Music for Clarinet") † Debussy:Première rapsodie Cl; J. Françaix:Theme & Vars Cl; D. Milhaud:Son Cl; F. Poulenc:Son Cl & Pno; Widor:Intro & Rondo Cl, Op. 72 — CAMA ▲ 415 [DDD] (18.97)

G. Peyer (cl), G. Pryor (pno) *(rec Hampstead, London, England, 1982-83)* ("French Music for Clarinet and Piano") † Debussy:Arabesques Pno; Preludes Pno; Première rapsodie Cl; G. Pierné:Canzonetta Cl, Op. 19; F. Poulenc:Son Cl & Pno; M. Ravel:Pièce en forme de Habanera; F. Schmitt:Andantino, Op. 30/1 — CHN ▲ 8526 [DDD] (16.97)

C. Stjernström (cl), M. Kanarva (pno) *(rec Academy of Music of Malmö, Rosenbergssalen, Sweden, July 1996)* † Bozza:Aria Cl; Debussy:Petite pièce Cl; Première rapsodie Cl; Gäfvert:Fant Cl; L.-E. Larsson:Pieces Cl, Op. 61; Söderlundh:Petite Suite Cl — ITIM ▲ 53 (16.97)

H. Wright (cl), L. Batlle (pno) *(rec Jan 26, 1992)* ("Harold Wright Live Recital No. 1") † Debussy:Arabesques Pno; Petite pièce Cl; Plus que lente; Pno Music (misc colls); W. Lutoslawski:Dance Preludes Cl & Pno; Martinů:Sonatina Cl; F. Poulenc:Son Cl & Pno — BOST ▲ 1023 (15.97)

D. Wright (cl), G. Davis (pno) † D. G. Mason:Son Cl (or Vn), Op. 14; C. M. von Weber:Grand Duo Concertant, J.204 — CENT ▲ 2067 [DDD] (16.97)

Sonata in D for Oboe & Piano, Op. 166 (1921)

Collegium Musicum Soloists ("Complete Works for Piano & Winds") † Airs de ballet d'Ascanio; Caprice sur des airs danoises et russes, Op. 79; Cavatina Trb & Pno, Op. 144; Odelette Fl, Op. 162; Romance Fl, Op. 37; Romance Hn Orch, Op. 36; Romance Hn Pno, Op. 67; Son Bn; Son Cl; Spt Tpt, Op. 65; Suite algérienne, Op. 60; Tarantelle, Op. 6 — KPT 2-▲ 32062 [DDD]

S. Hannevold (ob), G. H. Braaten (pno) ("L'Esprit") † Son Bn; Bozza:Divertissement Sax, Op. 39; Fant pastoral, Op. 37; Récit, Sicilienne & Rondò; Chagrin:Pieces Bn; Jolivet:Sonatine Ob; F. Poulenc:Trio Ob — NORW ▲ 960038 [DDD] (17.97)

J. Mack (ob), E. Podis (pno) † B. Britten:Metamorphoses, Op. 49; Paladilhe:Solo de concert Ob; R. Schumann:Romances Ob, Op. 94 — CRYS ▮ 325 (9.98)

K. Meier (ob), K. Kolly (pno) ("French Music for Oboe & Piano") † Bozza:Divertissement Sax, Op. 39; Fant pastoral, Op. 37; Grovlez:Sarabande et Allegro; Maugüé:Pastorale; F. Poulenc:Son Ob; M. Ravel:Pavane pour une infante défunte; Pièce en forme de Habanera — PANC ▲ 510092 [DDD] (17.97)

F. Meyer (ob), E. Le Sage (pno) † B. Britten:Metamorphoses, Op. 49; Dutilleux:Son Ob; P. Hindemith:Son Ob; F. Poulenc:Son Ob — SONP ▲ 94011 [DDD] (16.97)

W. Rapier (ob), M. Amlin (pno) ("Wayne Rapier Plays Oboe") † J. S. Bach:Cant 187; Partita Fl, BWV 1013; E. Goossens:Con Ob; Hollingsworth:Son Ob; Piston:Suite Ob; Vaughan Williams:Blake Songs — BOST ▲ 1013 (15.97)

Sonata No. 1 in d for Violin & Piano, Op. 75 (1885)

S. Accardo (vn), B. Canino (pno) ("Salvatore Accardo & Friends") † Borodin:Qt 2 Strs; E. Chausson:Concert Vn, Op. 21; A. Dvořák:Qnt Pno, Op. 81; Qnt Strs, Op. 77; Romantic Pieces, Op. 75; Terzetto, Op. 74; Verdi:Qt Strs — DYNC 4-▲ 207 [DDD] (34.97)

D. Chan (vn), R. Koenig (pno) *(rec Aspen, CO, May 1995)* † G. Gershwin:Songs; Paganini:Con 2 Vn, M.S. 48; Tartini:Son Vn & Pno; P. Tchaikovsky:Souvenir d'un lieu cher, Op. 42; Valse-Scherzo Vn, Op. 34; Ysaÿe:Sons Vn, Op. 27 — AMBA ▲ 1017 [DDD] (16.97)

Chee-Yun (vn), A. Eguchi (pno) *(rec May 1990)* † Debussy:Son Vn; G. Fauré:Son 1 Vn, Op. 13 — DNN ▲ 75625 [DDD] (16.97)

SAINT-SAËNS, CAMILLE (cont.)

Sonata No. 1 in d for Violin & Piano, Op. 75 (1885) (cont.)

P. Clarke (vn), S. Holshouser (pno) † E. Chausson:Poème Vn, Op. 25; P. Tchaikovsky:Valse-Scherzo Vn, Op. 34; F. Waxman:Carmen Fant CJL ▲ 101 (15.97)

D. Kang (vn), P. Devoyon (pno) ("French Violin Sonatas") † Debussy:Son Vn; F. Poulenc:Son Vn; M. Ravel:Son Vn Pno NXIN ▲ 550276 [DDD] (5.97)

J. Kantorow (vn), J. Rouvier (pno) *(rec Mar 11-12, 1991)* † Son 2 Vn, Op. 102 DNN ▲ 79552 [DDD] (16.97)

I. van Keulen (vn), R. Brautigam (pno) ("French Violin Sonatas, Vol. 2") † Messiaen:Thème et vars Vn; D. Milhaud:Son 2 Vn, Op. 40; M. Ravel:Son Vn Pno KOCC ▲ 6416 (16.97)

G. Poulet (vn), N. Lee (pno) *(rec Aug 1996)* ("Complete Works for Violin & Piano") † Berceuse Vn, Op. 38; Elégie, Op. 143; Elégie, Op. 160; Son 2 Vn, Op. 102; Tryptique, Op. 136 ARN ▲ 68362 [DDD] (16.97)

G. Shaham (vn), G. Oppitz (pno) † C. Franck:Son Vn, M.8; M. Ravel:Tzigane DEUT ▲ 29729 [DDD] (16.97)

S. Tönz (vn), O. Triendl (pno) † Con 3 Vn, Op. 61; Son 2 Vn, Op. 102 NOVA ▲ 150147 (16.97)

Sonata No. 2 in E♭ for Violin & Piano, Op. 102 (1896)

J. Kantorow (vn), J. Rouvier (pno) *(rec Mar 11-12, 1991)* † Son 1 Vn, Op. 75 DNN ▲ 79552 [DDD] (16.97)

G. Poulet (vn), N. Lee (pno) *(rec Aug 1996)* ("Complete Works for Violin & Piano") † Berceuse Vn, Op. 38; Elégie, Op. 143; Elégie, Op. 160; Son 1 Vn, Op. 75; Tryptique, Op. 136 ARN ▲ 68362 [DDD] (16.97)

S. Tönz (vn), O. Triendl (pno) † Con 3 Vn, Op. 61; Son 1 Vn, Op. 75 NOVA ▲ 150147 (16.97)

Suite algérienne in C for Orchestra, Op. 60 (1880)

Y. Butt (cnd), London SO † Phaéton, Op. 39; Sym 2 ASV ▲ 599 [DDD] (16.97)

Collegium Musicum Soloists [arr for ob, fl & pno] ("Complete Works for Piano & Winds") † Airs de ballet d'Ascanio; Caprice sur des airs danoises et russes, Op. 79; Cavatina Trb & Pno, Op. 144; Odelette Fl, Op. 162; Romance Fl, Op. 37; Romance Hn Orch, Op. 36; Romance Hn Pno, Op. 67; Son Bn; Son Cl; Son Ob; Spt Tpt, Op. 65; Tarantelle, Op. 6 KPT 2-▲ 32062 [DDD]

Suite for Cello & Piano, Op. 16 (1862)

Drinkall-Baker Duo ("Cello Sonatas") † Son 1 Vc, Op. 32; Beethoven:Son 3 Vc, Op. 69 KLAV ▲ 11068 [DDD] (18.97)

M. Kliegel (vc), J. Monnard (cnd), Bournemouth Sinfonietta [trans for vc & orch] *(rec Poole Arts Ctr England, Jan 1995)* † Allegro appassionato, Op. 43; Con 1 Vc, Op. 33; Con 2 Vc, Op. 119; Cygne NXIN ▲ 8553039 [DDD] (5.97)

R. Pidoux (vc), H. Sermet (pno) † Fant Vn; Qt Pno VAL (Musique Française) ▲ 4657 (18.97)

D. D. Williencourt (vc), P. Verrot (cnd), Monte Carlo PO † Allegro appassionato, Op. 43; Con 1 Vc, Op. 33; Con 2 Vc, Op. 119; Cygne ARN ▲ 68347 (16.97)

Suite in D for Orchestra, Op. 49 (1863)

D. Bostock (cnd), Bohemian Chamber PO ("French Orchestral Miniatures, Vol. 1") † Bizet:Docteur Miracle (ov); Chabrier:Habanera; Delibes:Roi s'amuse; C. Franck:Organiste Vol I, M.41; Lalo:Divert Orch CLSO ▲ 158 [DDD] (15.97)

Symphonies (5) (complete)

B. Gavoty (org), J. Martinon (cnd), ORTF National Orch EMIC (Studio) 2-▲ 62643 [ADD] (21.97)

Symphony in A (ca 1850)

D. Joeres (cnd), West German Sinfonia † Bizet:Sym ICC ▲ 6700582 (9.97)

J. Kantorow (cnd), Tapiola Sinfonietta *(rec Tapiola, Finland, June 1998)* † Con 1 Vc, Op. 33; Con 2 Vc, Op. 119; Romance Hn Orch, Op. 36 BIS ▲ 956 [DDD] (17.97)

Symphony in F, "Urbs Roma" (1856)

J. Kantorow (cnd), Tapiola Sinfonietta † Africa; Sym 2 BIS ▲ 790 [DDD] (17.97)

Symphony No. 1 in E♭, Op. 2 (1853)

C. Comet (cnd), Grand Rapids SO † Sym 2 KOSS ▲ 2217 [DDD] (17.97)

Symphony No. 2 in a, Op. 55 (1859)

Y. Butt (cnd), London SO † Phaéton, Op. 39; Suite algérienne, Op. 60 ASV ▲ 599 [DDD] (16.97)

C. Comet (cnd), Grand Rapids SO † Sym 1 KOSS ▲ 2217 [DDD] (17.97)

J. Kantorow (cnd), Tapiola Sinfonietta † Africa; Sym in F BIS ▲ 790 [DDD] (17.97)

Y. P. Tortelier (cnd), Ulster Orch † Sym 3 CHN ▲ 8822 [DDD] (16.97)

Symphony No. 3 in c for Organ & Orchestra, Op. 78, "Organ Symphony" (ca 1886)

E. P. Biggs (org), E. Ormandy (cnd), Philadelphia Orch † Carnival of the Animals; Danse macabre, Op. 40; Marche militaire française; Samson et Dalila (Bacchanale) SNYC (Essential Classics) ▲ 47655 (7.97) ▮ 47655 (3.98)

D. Chjorzempa (org), P. Maag (cnd), Bern SO INMP ▲ 2010 (9.97)

P. Cochereau (org), H. von Karajan (cnd), Berlin PO DEUT (Karajan Gold) ▲ 39014 [DDD] (16.97)

J. Dalitz (org), C. P. Flor (cnd), Berlin SO † F. Poulenc:Con Org BER ▲ 2138 [DDD] (17.97)

F. Eibner (org), H. Swarowsky (cnd), Vienna State Opera Orch † Mendelssohn (-Bartholdy):Sym 5 FORL ▲ 16587 [AAD] (16.97)

H. Fagius (org), J. DePreist (cnd), Royal Stockholm PO † Danse macabre, Op. 40; Rapsodies sur des cantiques bretons, Op. 7; Samson et Dalila (Bacchanale) BIS ▲ 555 [DDD] (17.97)

J. Fournet (cnd), Tokyo Metropolitan SO ("Fournet Conducts French Symphonies") † Berlioz:Sym fantastique, Op. 14; C. Franck:Sym in d, M.48 DNN (Classics Exposed) 2-▲ 17009 (16.97)

J. Guillou (org), E. Mata (cnd), Dallas SO *(rec Jan 1994)* † J. Jongen:Symphonie Concertante, Op. 81 DOR ▲ 90200 [DDD] (16.97)

S. Gunzenhauser (cnd), Czech-Slovak State Radio PO † Rouet d'Omphale, Op. 31; Samson et Dalila (Bacchanale) NXIN ▲ 550138 [DDD] (5.97)

P. Hurford (org), C. Dutoit (cnd), Montreal SO † Carnival of the Animals PLON ▲ 30720 [DDD] (9.97)

Y. Kim (pno), J. Kim (pno), N. Kynaston (org), D. V. Yu (cnd), Philharmonia Orch † Carnival of the Animals; Cyprès et Lauriers, Op. 156 ICC ▲ 6600012 (16.97)

A. Lizzio (cnd), Munich SO † Carnival of the Animals PC ▲ 267029 [DDD] (2.97)

M. Matthes (org), E. Krivine (cnd), Lyon National Orch † Danse macabre, Op. 40; Phaéton, Op. 39 DNN ▲ 75024 [DDD] (16.97)

F. Minger (org), S. Comissiona (cnd), Baltimore SO *(rec 1980)* † C. Franck:Sym in d, M.48 VC ▲ 4014 [DDD] (13.97)

F. Minger (org), S. Comissiona (cnd), Baltimore SO *(rec Washington, DC, Nov 14, 1980)* † Berlioz:Requiem, Op. 5 VC 2-▲ 100 [AAD] (26.97)

M. Murray (org), C. Badea (cnd), Royal PO † Phaéton, Op. 39 TEL ▲ 80274 [DDD] (16.97)

T. Murray (org), E. Ormandy (cnd), Philadelphia Orch TEL ▲ 80051 [DDD] (16.97)

A. Newman (org), L. Maazel (cnd), Pittsburgh SO † Danse macabre, Op. 40; Phaéton, Op. 39; Samson et Dalila (Bacchanale) SNYC ▲ 53979 (16.97)

S. Preston (org), J. Levine (cnd), Berlin PO † Dukas:L'Apprenti sorcier DEUT ▲ 19617 [DDD] (16.97)

L. Raver (org), L. Bernstein (cnd), New York PO † Con 4 Pno, Op. 44; Intro & Rondo capriccioso, Op. 28 SNYC ▲ 47608

N. Rawsthorne (org), E. Bátiz (cnd), London PO † Carnival of the Animals; Danse macabre, Op. 40; Wedding Cake, Op. 76 ASV ▲ 665 [DDD] (16.97)

G. Weir (org), Y. P. Tortelier (cnd), Ulster Orch † Sym 2 CHN ▲ 8822 [DDD] (16.97)

B. Zamkochian (org), C. Munch (cnd), Boston SO *(rec 1956 & 1959)* † Debussy:Mer Orch; Ibert:Escales RCAV (Living Stereo) ▲ 61500 (11.97)

artists unknown † Carnival of the Animals; Con 2 Pno, Op. 22; Con 3 Vn, Op. 61; Havanaise, Op. 83; Intro & Rondo capriccioso, Op. 28 ERAT (Ultima) 2-▲ 18971 (16.97)

Tarantelle in a for Flute, Clarinet & Orchestra, Op. 6 (1857)

L. Buyse (fl), M. Webster (cl), K. Collier (pno) [trans M. Webster] ("Tour de France") † Bizet:Jeux d'enfants; Debussy:Petite pièce Cl; Première rapsodie Cl; Prélude à l'après-midi d'un faune; Syrinx Fl; G. Fauré:Dolly; Morceau de concours Fl CRYS ▲ 356 (15.97)

Collegium Musicum Soloists ("Complete Works for Piano & Winds") † Airs de ballet d'Ascanio; Caprice sur des airs danoises et russes, Op. 79; Cavatina Trb & Pno, Op. 144; Odelette Fl, Op. 162; Romance Fl, Op. 37; Romance Hn Orch, Op. 36; Romance Hn Pno, Op. 67; Son Bn; Son Cl; Son Ob; Spt Tpt, Op. 65; Suite algérienne, Op. 60 KPT 2-▲ 32062 [DDD]

Hexagon *(rec Aaron Copland School of Music, Queens College, NYC, NY, 1996)* ("Les Petits Nerveux") † Caprice sur des airs danoises et russes, Op. 79; J. Françaix:Petits nerveux; F. Poulenc:Sxt Pno; Trio Ob; A. Roussel:Divert Ww, Op. 6 BRID ▲ 9079 [DDD] (17.97)

Thème varié for Piano, Op. 97 (1894)

P. Lane (pno) ("The Complete Etudes") † Études (6) Pno, Op. 111; Études (6) Pno, Op. 135; Études (6) Pno, Op. 52 HYP ▲ 67037 (18.97)

Trio No. 1 in F for Piano, Violin & Cello, Op. 18 (1863)

Golub/Kaplan/Carr Trio ("French Piano Trios") † Debussy:Trio Pno; G. Fauré:Trio Pno, Op. 120 ARA ▲ 6643 [DDD] (16.97)

R. Hirsch (vn), C. Dearnley (vc), J. Lenehan (pno) *(rec Conway Hall London, Oct 11-12, 1993)* † Trio 2 for Pno, Op. 92 NXIN ▲ 550935 [DDD] (5.97)

Nash Ensemble *(rec 1988)* † Carnival of the Animals; Spt Tpt, Op. 65; A. Dvořák:Qnt Pno, Op. 81; Trio 4 Pno, Op. 90 VCL 2-▲ 61516 [DDD] (11.97)

SAINT-SAËNS, CAMILLE (cont.)

Trio No. 1 in F for Piano, Violin & Cello, Op. 18 (1863) (cont.)

Ravel Trio † Trio 2 for Pno, Op. 92 ARN ▲ 68010 [AAD] (16.97)

Rembrandt Trio † Chaminade:Romanza appassionata, Op. 31; Sérénade espagnole; M. Ravel:Trio Pno DOR ▲ 90187 [DDD] (16.97)

Triangulus † C. Schumann:Trio Pno, Op. 17 MER ▲ 84355 (16.97)

Yuval Trio *(rec 1988)* ("Piano Trios 1 & 2") † Trio 2 for Pno, Op. 92 CENT ▲ 2292 [ADD] (16.97)

Trio No. 2 in e for Piano, Violin & Cello, Op. 92 (1892)

Arden Trio † M. Ravel:Trio Pno DLS ▲ 3055 (14.97)

R. Hirsch (vn), C. Dearnley (vc), J. Lenehan (pno) *(rec Conway Hall London, Oct 11-12, 1993)* † Trio 1 for Pno, Op. 18 NXIN ▲ 550935 [DDD] (5.97)

Ravel Trio † Trio 1 for Pno, Op. 18 ARN ▲ 68010 [AAD] (16.97)

Yuval Trio *(rec 1988)* ("Piano Trios 1 & 2") † Trio 1 for Pno, Op. 18 CENT ▲ 2292 [ADD] (16.97)

Tryptique for Piano & Violin, Op. 136 (1912)

G. Poulet (vn), N. Lee (pno) *(rec Aug 1996)* ("Complete Works for Violin & Piano") † Berceuse Vn, Op. 38; Elégie, Op. 143; Elégie, Op. 160; Son 1 Vn, Op. 75; Son 2 Vn, Op. 102 ARN ▲ 68362 [DDD] (16.97)

Variations on a Theme of Beethoven for 2 Pianos, Op. 35 (1874)

P. Corre (pno), E. Exerjean (pno) ("French Music for 2 Pianos") † A. Blanc:Sonatine concertante, Op. 64; Gouvy:Scherzo, Op. 60; Lefébure-Wély:Duo symphonique 1, Op. 163; G. Pierné:Tarantella Pnos PVY ▲ 790041 [DDD] (16.97)

C. Ivaldi (pno), N. Lee (pno) † Caprice arabe, Op. 96; Caprice héroïque, Op. 106; Polonaise Pnos, Op. 77; Scherzo Pnos, Op. 87 ARN ▲ 68011 [AAD] (16.97)

H. Martina (pno), B. Uribe (pno) ("Piano Duos") † Debussy:Nocturnes Orch; Infante:Danzas andaluzas; D. Milhaud:Scaramouche Pnos, Op. 165b; M. Ravel:Valse HEL ▲ 1020 (10.97)

F. Onder (pno), F. Onder (pno) † Carnival of the Animals; Intro & Rondo capriccioso, Op. 28 PANC ▲ 510106 (17.97)

J. Reynolds (pno), P. Lockwood (pno) *(rec Utrecht, Netherlands, Apr 1996)* † Caprice arabe, Op. 96; Carnival of the Animals; Danse macabre, Op. 40; Polonaise Pnos, Op. 77; Scherzo Pnos, Op. 87 GLOE ▲ 5152 [DDD] (16.97)

Wedding Cake in A♭ for Piano & Orchestra, Op. 76 (1885)

J. Collard (pno), A. Previn (cnd), Royal PO † Africa; Allegro appassionato, Op. 43; Con 1 Pno, Op. 17; Rapsodie d'Auvergne, Op. 73 EMIC ▲ 49757 (16.97)

J. Covelli (pno), J. Covelli (cnd), Moscow PO † Con 2 Pno, Op. 22; D. Shostakovich:Con 2 Pno, Op. 102 INMP ▲ 6701842 (9.97)

D. O. Norris (pno), Y. Turovsky (cnd), Montreal Musici † Carnival of the Animals; W. A. Mozart:Musikalischer Spass, K.522 CHN ▲ 9246 [DDD] (16.97)

J. Osorio (pno), E. Bátiz (cnd), Royal PO † C. Franck:Symphonic Vars, M.46; M. Ravel:Con Pno (left hand); R. Schumann:Con Pno in a, Op. 54 ASVO ▲ 6092 [DDD] (11.97)

J. Osorio (pno), E. Bátiz (cnd), Royal PO † Carnival of the Animals; Danse macabre, Op. 40; Sym 3 ASV ▲ 665 [DDD] (16.97)

SAINZ DE LA MAZA, EDUARDO (1903-1982)

Guitar Music

A. Garrobe (gtr)—Platero y Yo; Confidencia; Bolero; Habanera; Camino de Colorado; Sonando caminos; Evocacion criolla; Campanas del alba; Homenaje a Toulouse-Lautrec; Homenaje a la guitarra; Homenaje a Haydn ("Works for Guitar") OTR ▲ 1022 (18.97)

SAKAMOTO, RYUICHI (1952-

The Handmaid's Tale (film music) for Orchestra

artists unknown GNP ▲ 8020 (16.97) ▮ 8020 (11.98)

High Heels (film music) for Orchestra

E. Nelson (vn), J. Morelenbaum (vc), R. Sakamoto (pno)—Main Theme *(rec New York, NY, 1996)* ("1996") † Merry Christmas Mr. Lawrence; Music of Sakamoto; Sheltering Sky MILA ▲ 35759 [DDD] (16.97)

artists unknown VERV ▲ 10855 (16.97)

Little Buddha (film music) for Orchestra

artists unknown MILA ▲ 35676 (16.97)

Merry Christmas Mr. Lawrence (film music) for Orchestra

E. Nelson (vn), J. Morelenbaum (vc), R. Sakamoto (pno) *(rec New York, 1996)* ("1996") † High Heels; Music of Sakamoto; Sheltering Sky MILA ▲ 35759 [DDD] (16.97)

A. Stalteri (pno) ("Flowers") † Sheltering Sky; A. A. Corea:Fiesta; Debussy:Preludes Pno; P. Glass:Metamorphosis 1-5; Stalteri:Pno Music MASO ▲ 90071 [DDD] (16.97)

artists unknown MILA ▲ 35691 (11.97)

Music of Sakamoto

D. Nadien (vn), E. Nelson (vn), J. Morelenbaum (vc), R. Sakamoto (pno)—A Day a Gorilla Gives a Banana; Rain; Bibo no Aozora; 1919; The Last Emperor; M.A.Y. in the Backyard; A Tribute to N.J.P.; Aoneko no Torso; The Wuthering Heights *(rec New York, 1996)* ("1996") † High Heels; Merry Christmas Mr. Lawrence; Sheltering Sky MILA ▲ 35759 [DDD] (16.97)

The Sheltering Sky (film music) for Orchestra

D. Nadien (vn), J. Morelenbaum (vc), R. Sakamoto (pno) *(rec New York, 1996)* ("1996") † High Heels; Merry Christmas Mr. Lawrence; Music of Sakamoto MILA ▲ 35759 [DDD] (16.97)

A. Stalteri (pno) ("Flowers") † Merry Christmas Mr. Lawrence; A. A. Corea:Fiesta; Debussy:Preludes Pno; P. Glass:Metamorphosis 1-5; Stalteri:Pno Music MASO ▲ 90071 [DDD] (16.97)

Untitled 01 for DJ, Guitar, Piano & Orchestra

artists unknown ("Discord") SNYC ▲ 60121 (16.97)

SAKAMOTO, RYUICHI (1952-, **DAVID BYRNE** (1952-& **CONG SU** (20th cent)

The Last Emperor (film music) for Orchestra

artists unknown VRGN ▲ 86029 (15.97)

SALADIN, LOUIS (17th cent)

Canticum hebraicum for Vocal Ensemble (ca 1670)

Boston Camerata [HEB] † S. Rossi:Songs of Solomon HMA ▲ 1901021 [ADD] (9.97)

SALAZAR, ANTONIO DE (ca 1650-1715)

O sacrum convivium for Chorus

Westminster Cathedral Choir [LAT] ("Mexican Polyphony") † H. Franco:Salve Regina; López Capillas:Alleluia; Magnificat; J. G. de Padilla:Sacred Music HYP ▲ 66330 [DDD] (18.97)

SALERNO, MICHAEL (20th cent)

Enter when Ready (rock symphony in 9 movements)

M. Salerno (cnd) ARUN ▲ 3055 (16.97)

SALIERI, ANTONIO (1750-1825)

Arlecchinata (scherzo musicale) for solo Voices & Orchestra [compiled by Cesare Brero using arias & other music by Salieri, ca 1961]

P. Pellegrini (ten), U. Benelli (ten), G. Gatti (bar), G. Catalucci (cnd), In Canto di Terni Youth Orch [ITA] *(rec live, Sept 1990)* † C. W. Gluck:Innocenza giustificata BONG 2-▲ 2111 [DDD] (32.97)

Armonia per un tempio della notte in E♭ for Winds

Zurich Wind Octet † Triebensee:Suite Ww after Don Giovanni TUD ▲ 779 [DDD] (16.97)

Axur, Re d'Ormus (opera in 4 acts) [lib Da Ponte] (1788)

E. Mei (sop), M. Valenti (sop), A. Vespasiani (mez), C. Rayam (ten), A. Martin (bar), E. Nova (bass), R. Clemencic (cnd), Guido d'Arezzo Orch, Guido d'Arezzo Chorus [ITA] *(rec live, 1989)* NUO 3-▲ 6852 [DDD] (47.97)

Concerto in C for Flute, Oboe & Orchestra

S. Milan (fl), D. Theodore (ob), R. Hickox (cnd), City of London Sinfonia † W. A. Mozart:Con Fl & Hp, K.299; Con Ob CHN ▲ 9051 [DDD] (16.97)

Concerto for Organ & Orchestra (1773)

U. C. Harrer (cnd), Leondinger SO † Sacred Music KSCH ▲ 312882 (16.97)

Concertos (2) in B♭ & C for Piano & Orchestra (1773)

P. Spada (pno), P. Spada (cnd), Philharmonia Orch † Horaces (ov); Semiramide (ov); Vars on "La folia di Spagnia" ASV ▲ 955 (16.97)

Falstaff, ossia Le tre burle (opera in 2 acts) [lib C. P. Defranceschi after Shakespeare] (1799)

C. Calli (sop), L. Myeounghee (sop), N. Valli (sop), G. D. Filippo (ten), R. Franceschetto (bar), F. Bettoschi (bass), F. Ciuffo (bass), A. Veronesi (cnd), Guido Cantelli Orch Milan, Milan Madrigalists CHN 2-▲ 9613 (32.97)

Les Horaces:Overture

P. Spada (cnd), Philharmonia Orch † Cons Pno; Semiramide (ov); Vars on "La folia di Spagnia" ASV ▲ 955 (16.97)

La Locandiera (opera buffa in 3 acts) [lib D. Poggi after C. Goldini] (1773)

M. Dittrich (cnd), Czech-Slovak RSO Bratislava MARC ▲ 8223381 (13.97)

A. Ruffini (sop), O. D. Credico (ten), G. Sarti (bar), P. Guarnera (bar), F. Luisi (cnd), Emilia Romagna Toscanini SO [ITA] *(rec live, 1989)* NUO 2-▲ 6888 [DDD] (32.97)

SALIERI, ANTONIO (cont.)
Music of Antonio Salieri
P. Pollastri (ob), Amati String Quartet—Ov prima; Ov seconda; Les Danäides; Concertinos 1T-4T; Diverts 1-4; La fuga *(rec Montepulciano, Apr 1994)* ("Overtures, Scherzi, Divertimenti") TACT ▲ 751901 [DDD]
La passione di Gesù Cristo (oratorio) for Reciter, solo Voices, Orchestra & Chorus [after Metastasio] (1776)
D. Citino (sop), M. T. Toso (alt), N. Yovanovitch (ten), M. Scardoni (bass), G. Scardoni (voc), A. Turco (cnd) , Verona Cathedral Cappella Musicale *(rec Verona Cathedral Italy, Mar 30, 1995)* BONG ▲ 2190 [DDD] (16.97)
Sacred Music
U. C. Harrer (cnd), Leondinger SO, St. Florian Boys' Choir—Emperor's Mass; Magnificat; Dixit Dominus † Con Org KSCH ▲ 312882 (16.97)
A. Turco (cnd) , Verona Cathedral Cappella Musicale—Gesu al Limbo; Il Giudizio Finale; Te Deum BONG ▲ 2167 (16.97)
Semiramide:Overture
P. Spada (cnd), Philharmonia Orch † Cons Pno; Horaces (ov); Vars on "La folia di Spagnia" ASV ▲ 955 (16.97)
Te Deum for Chorus, "Coronation"
A. Grossman (cnd), Vienna CO, Vienna Boys' Choir, Chorus Viennensis ("500th Anniversary") † J. Haydn:Te Deum; W. A. Mozart:Mass 16, K.317; F. Schubert:Gesang der Geister über den Wassern, D.714; Magnificat, D.486 KOCC ▲ 365632 (16.97)
Variations (24) on "La folia di Spagnia" for Orchestra (1815)
P. Spada (cnd), Philharmonia Orch † Cons Pno; Horaces (ov); Semiramide (ov) ASV ▲ 955 (16.97)

SALIERI, GIROLAMO (dates unknown)
Adagio e Tema con variazioni for Clarinet & String Quartet
C. Scarponi (cl), Rome Solisti ("Discoveries") † P. Bottesini:Andante e Tema con variazioni; Cherubini:Sons Hn; Mercadante:Qts Fl MUIM ▲ 10031 (18.97)

SALINAS, HORACIO (dates unknown)
Guitar Music
H. Salinas (cnd), Inti-Illimani *(Danza di cala luna; Corazon a contraluz; Preguntona; Carnaval; Fragmento de un seuño; Ciudad; Mercado testaccio)*, J. Williams (gtr) *(Cristalino)* ("Fragments of a Dream") † M. Garrido:Gtr Music; P. Peña:Gtr Music COL ▲ 44574 [ADD] (9.97)

SALLINEN, AULIS (1935-
Cadenze for Violin (1965)
P. Pohjola (vn) † Chorali; Elegy for S. Knight, Op. 10; Qt 3 Strs, Op. 19; Sym 1; Sym 3 BIS ▲ 41 [AAD] (17.97)
Chamber Music
J. Wedin (cnd), Stockholm Chamber Ensemble *(Chamber Music I, Op. 38 (1975))*, G. von Bahr (a fl), O. Kamu (cnd), Stockholm Chamber Ensemble *(Chamber Music II [w. solo a fl], Op. 41 (1976))*, A. Angervo (vn), V. Höylä (vc), G. von Bahr (a fl), E. Nordwall (hpd) *(Quattro per Quattro for Fl, Vn, Vc & Hpd, Op. 12)*, F. Forsman (org) *(Chaconne for Org)*, E. Pohjola (cnd), Tapiola Children's Choir *(Vintern var hard & Sakura for Children's Choir)*, T. Valjakka (sop), R. Gothóni (pno) *(4 Dream Songs for Sop & Pno)*, J. Hynninen (bar), R. Gothóni (pno) *(Simple Simme & Homeless Hamme for Bar & Pno)* BIS ▲ 64 [AAD] (17.97)
Chamber Music II for Alto Flute & String Orchestra, Op. 41 (1976)
P. Alanko (a fl), O. Vänskä (cnd), Lahti SO *(rec Church of the Cross, Lahti, Finland, Aug 8-11, 1995)* ("Dances with the Winds: Finnish Flute Concertos") † Bashmakov:Impressioni marine; Marttinen:Con espagnole, Op. 144; Rautavaara:Dances with the Winds, Op. 69 BIS ▲ 687 [DDD] (17.97)
Chorali for Winds, Harp, Celesta & Percussion (1970)
P. Berglund (cnd), Helsinki PO † Cadenze Vn; Elegy for S. Knight, Op. 10; Qt 3 Strs, Op. 19; Sym 1; Sym 3 BIS ▲ 41 [AAD] (17.97)
J. Hirokami (cnd), Stockholm Symphonic Wind Orch † Grondahl:Con Trbn; M. Maros:Aurora; Mayuzumi:Ritual Ov; Mendelssohn (-Bartholdy):Ov Wind, Op. 24; Schoenberg:Theme & Vars Band, Op. 43a CAPA ▲ 21516 (16.97)
Concerto for Violin & Orchestra, Op. 18 (1968)
E. Koskinen (vn), O. Vänskä (cnd), Tapiola Sinfonietta † Nocturnal Dances, Op. 58; Some Aspects; Vars Orch, Op. 8 BIS ▲ 560 [DDD] (17.97)
Elegy for Sebastian Knight for Cello, Op. 10 (1964)
F. Helmerson (vc) *(rec 1975-77)* ("The Solitary Cello") † G. Crumb:Son Vc; P. Hindemith:Son Vc; Kodály:Son Vc, Op. 8 BIS ▲ 25 [AAD] (17.97)
F. Helmerson (vc) † Cadenze Vn; Chorali; Qt 3 Strs, Op. 19; Sym 1; Sym 3 BIS ▲ 41 [AAD] (17.97)
The Iron Age (suite) for Soprano, Orchestra, Mixed Chorus & Children's Chorus (1983)
O. Kamu (cnd), Helsinki PO, Helsinki Music Institute Choir † Songs of Life & Death, Op. 69 ODE ▲ 844 [DDD] (17.97)
Kullervo (opera in 2 acts) (1986-88)
J. Silvasti (ten), J. Hynninen (bar), M. Salminen (bass), G. Saarinen (pno), U. Söderblom (cnd), Finnish National Opera Orch, Finnish National Opera Chorus [FIN] *(E,Fin lib texts)* ODE 3-▲ 780 [DDD] (49.97)
The Nocturnal Dances of Don Juanquixote for Cello & Orchestra, Op. 58, "Chamber Music III" (1985-86)
T. Thedéen (vc), O. Vänskä (cnd), Tapiola Sinfonietta † Con Vn; Some Aspects; Vars Orch, Op. 8 BIS ▲ 560 [DDD] (17.97)
Palatsi [The Palace] (opera) [lib Hans Magnus Enzensberger] (1995)
J. Silvasti (ten), V. Varpio (ten), T. Krause (bar), S. Tiilikainen (bar), J. Mäntynen (sgr), O. Kamu (cnd), Savonlinna Opera Festival Orch, Savonlinna Opera Festival Chorus *(rec Savonlinna Festival Finland, 1995)* KOCC 2-▲ 6465 (31.97)
Quartet No. 3 for Strings, Op. 19, "Aspects of Peltoniemi Hintrik's Funeral March" (1969)
Kronos Quartet † P. Glass:Company; Hendrix:Purple Haze; Nancarrow:Qt Strs NON ▲ 79111 [DDD] (16.97)
Voces Intimae String Quartet † Cadenze Vn; Chorali; Elegy for S. Knight, Op. 10; Sym 1; Sym 3 BIS ▲ 41 [AAD] (17.97)
Shadows (prelude) for Orchestra, Op. 52 (1982)
J. DePreist (cnd), Malmö SO *(rec Malmö Concert Hall Sweden, Mar 11-June 17, 1993)* † Sym 4; Sym 5 BIS ▲ 607 [DDD] (17.97)
Some Aspects of Peltoniemi Hintrik's Funeral March (marche funèbre w. 5 variations) for String Orchestra [arr from his *Quartet No. 3 for Strings, Op. 19*]
W. Rajski (cnd), Musica Vitae *(rec Furuby Church, Sweden, 1989)* ("Musica Vitae Plays Nordic Music, Vol. 2") † Fernström:Intimate Miniatures, Op. 2; E. Grieg:Elegiac Melodies, Op. 34; E. von Koch:Concertino pastorale, Op. 35; C. Nielsen:Little Suite, Op. 1; T. Sigurbjörnsson:Siciliano BIS ▲ 461 [DDD] (17.97)
O. Vänskä (cnd), Tapiola Sinfonietta † Con Vn; Nocturnal Dances, Op. 58; Vars Orch, Op. 8 BIS ▲ 560 [DDD] (17.97)
Songs of Life & Death for Baritone, Orchestra & Chorus, Op. 69 (1962-65)
J. Hynninen (bar), O. Kamu (cnd), Helsinki PO, Helsinki Music Institute Choir † Iron Age ODE ▲ 844 [DDD] (17.97)
Suita grammaticale for Strings & Chorus (1972)
Tapiola Choir † Vinten var hard; E. Bergman:Dreams; B. Johansson:Pater Noster; Kortekangas:A for Instrs & Choir; Rautavaara:Children's Mass ODE ▲ 786 [DDD] (17.97)
Sunrise Serenade for Orchestra, Op. 63 (1989)
O. Kamu (cnd), Malmö SO † Sym 2; Sym 6 BIS ▲ 511 [DDD] (17.97)
Symphony No. 1 (1970-71)
O. Kamu (cnd), Finnish RSO † Cadenze Vn; Chorali; Elegy for S. Knight, Op. 10; Qt 3 Strs, Op. 19; Sym 3 BIS ▲ 41 [AAD] (17.97)
Symphony No. 2 for Percussion & Orchestra, Op. 29, "Symphonic Dialogue" (1972)
G. Mortensen (perc), O. Kamu (cnd), Malmö SO † Sunrise Serenade, Op. 63; Sym 6 BIS ▲ 511 [DDD] (17.97)
Symphony No. 3 (1974-75)
O. Kamu (cnd), Finnish RSO † Cadenze Vn; Chorali; Elegy for S. Knight, Op. 10; Qt 3 Strs, Op. 19; Sym 1 BIS ▲ 41 [AAD] (17.97)
Symphony No. 4, Op. 49 (1979)
J. DePreist (cnd), Malmö SO *(rec Malmö Concert Hall Sweden, Mar 11-June 17, 1993)* † Shadows, Op. 52; Sym 5 BIS ▲ 607 [DDD] (17.97)
Symphony No. 5, Op. 57, "Washington Mosaics" (1984-85; rev 1987)
J. DePreist (cnd), Malmö SO *(rec Malmö Concert Hall Sweden, Mar 11-June 17, 1993)* † Shadows, Op. 52; Sym 4 BIS ▲ 607 [DDD] (17.97)
Symphony No. 6, Op. 65, "From a New Zealand Diary" (1989-90)
O. Kamu (cnd), Malmö SO † Sunrise Serenade, Op. 63; Sym 2 BIS ▲ 511 [DDD] (17.97)
Variations for Orchestra, Op. 8 (1963)
O. Vänskä (cnd), Tapiola Sinfonietta † Con Vn; Nocturnal Dances, Op. 58; Some Aspects BIS ▲ 560 [DDD] (17.97)
Vinten var hard for Strings & Chorus
Tapiola Choir † Suita grammaticale; E. Bergman:Dreams; B. Johansson:Pater Noster; Kortekangas:A for Instrs & Choir; Rautavaara:Children's Mass ODE ▲ 786 [DDD] (17.97)

SALMANOV, VADIM (1912-1978)
Symphony No. 2 in G
E. Mravinsky (cnd), Leningrad PO *(rec 1966)* ("Mravinsky Live") † D. Shostakovich:Sym 5 RUS ▲ 11023 [AAD]

SALMENHAARA, ERKKI (1941-
Quintet for Winds (1964)
Gothenburg Wind Quintet *(rec May 5-6, 1975)* † Carlstedt:Qnt Winds; Holmboe:Notturno, Op. 19; F. Mortensen:Qnt Ww, Op. 4; F. Poulenc:Sxt Pno BIS ▲ 24 [AAD] (17.97)

SALMHOFER, FRANZ (1900-1975)
Heiteres Herbarium (song cycle) for Voice & Piano [text K. H. Waggerl]
E. Buchner (ten), N. Shelter (pno) † C. Loewe:Ballads; S. Prokofiev:Ugly Duckling, Op. 18 BER ▲ 9144 (10.97)

SALONEN, ESA-PEKKA (1958-
Mimo II for Oboe & Orchestra (1992)
B. Rosengren (ob), E.-P. Salonen (cnd), Swedish RSO *(rec live Berwald Hall, Stockholm, Sweden, Sept 23, 1994)* † Börtz:Con Ob; Nordheim:Boomerang; O. Schmidt:Con Ob DAPH ▲ 1002 [DDD] (16.97)
Second Meeting for Oboe & Piano (1992)
C. Hove (ob), G. Cheng (pno) *(rec Little Bridges Auditorium Pomona College, Dec 1994 & Jan 1996)* † E. Carter:Pastorale E Hn; P. Hindemith:Son E Hn; J. Marvin:Pieces E hn & Pno; Persichetti:Parable XV, Op. 128; T. Stevens:Triangles IV CRYS ▲ 328 [DDD] (15.97)
Sonata for Cello & Piano (1977)
A. Cooke (vc), A. Watkins (pno) *(rec CA, Oct 1997)* ("Splendors of the 20th Century") † P. Hindemith:Leichte Stücke; Thuille:Son Vc HRM ▲ 3004 [DDD] (14.97)

SALTER, HANS J. (1896-1995)
Horror Rhapsody (suite of selections from Salter's horror film scores) for Orchestra (ca 1940)
H. J. Salter (cnd) *(rec 1966)* ("Legendary Hollywood") † Maya CIT ▲ 77115 [ADD] (15.97)
Maya (TV music) for Orchestra (1966)
K. Graunke (cnd), Graunke SO *(rec 1966)* ("Legendary Hollywood") † Horror Rhap CIT ▲ 77115 [ADD] (15.97)
Wichita Town (TV music) for Orchestra
H. Salter (cnd), Graunke SO *(rec 1959)* ("Adventures in Hollywood: Original Soundtracks & Scores") † B. Broughton:Silverado; R. Farnon:Captain Horatio Hornblower; D. Tiomkin:President's Country CIT ▲ 77108 [ADD] (15.97)

SALTER, HANS J. (1896-1995)**& PAUL DESSAU** (1894-1979)
House of Frankenstein (film music) for Orchestra (1944)
W. T. Stromberg (cnd), Moscow SO *(rec Mosfilm Studios, Moscow, Russia, Dec 1994)* MARC ▲ 8223748 [DDD] (13.97)

SALTZMAN, PETER (20th cent)
Walls for Orchestra (1995-96)
P. Freeman (cnd), Czech National SO *(rec Prague, Czech Republic, 1996)* ("Paul Freeman Introduces American Music") † W. Logan:Runagate, Runagate; Narrative:Paul Freeman Introduces American Music 1; Rendelman:Oct 9, 1943; J. Williams:Fanfare for Life; Yardumian:Veni, Sancte Spiritus ALBA (Exploratory Series, Vol. 1) ▲ 312 [DDD] (16.97)

SALULINI, PAOLO (1709-1780)
Concerto in G for Dulcimer, Strings & Orchestra
K. Schickhaus (dlc), H. Stadlmair (cnd), Munich CO † Jommelli:Sinf Dulcimer; L. Mozart:Bauernhochzeit TUD ▲ 712 [ADD] (16.97)

SALVATORE, GIOVANNI (early 17th cent-?1688)
Durezze e ligarure for Keyboard (1603)
R. Festa (cnd), Daedalus Ensemble *(rec France, April 1998)* ("The Anatomy of Melancholy") † Cazzati:Varri, e diversi capricci per camera e per chiesa, Op. 50; J. Dowland:Lachrimae, or Seaven Teares; Frescobaldi:Capricci Kbd; F. S. Romano:Soprano scherza col cromatico; Trabaci:Music of Trabaci ACCE ▲ 98128 [DDD] (17.97)
Organ Music
A. Marcon (org) ("The Heritage of Frescobaldi, Vol. 1") † B. Pasquini:Org Music; B. Storace:Org Music; G. Strozzi:Org Music APS (Historic Organ) ▲ 79405 [DDD] (16.97)

SALZEDO, CARLOS (1885-1961)
Chanson dans la nuit for Harp
Y. Kondonassis (hp) *(rec Worcester, MA, Oct 2-5, 1995)* ("Sky Music") † Debussy:Suite bergamasque; G. Fauré:Impromptu Hp, Op. 86; A. Hovhaness:Nocturne Hp, Op. 20; Suite Hp, Op. 270; N. Rorem:Sky Music TEL ▲ 80418 [DDD] (16.97)
Harp Music [original works & transcriptions for solo harp]
J. Loman (hp) MARQ ▲ 117 [DDD] (16.97)
Morceaux (3) for Harp, Op. 28 (1913)
A. Giles (hp) † Poetical Studies; Scintillation; Suite Hp; Vars Hp, Op. 30 KSCH ▲ 312232 [DDD] (16.97)
Poetical Studies (5) for Harp
A. Giles (hp) † Morceaux Hp, Op. 28; Scintillation; Suite Hp; Vars Hp, Op. 30 KSCH ▲ 312232 [DDD] (16.97)
Preludes (5) for Harp (1924)
V. Dulova (hp) *(rec 1957)* ("Vera Dulova - Russian Performing School") † Damase:Sonatine Hp; Debussy:Suite bergamasque; Jolivet:Con Hp; Manino:Canzoni per Arpa; A. Zecchi:Divert Fl RD (Talents of Russia) ▲ 16204 [AAD] (16.97)
Scintillation for Harp (1936)
A. Giles (hp) † Morceaux Hp, Op. 28; Poetical Studies; Suite Hp; Vars Hp, Op. 30 KSCH ▲ 312232 [DDD] (16.97)
E. Goodman (hp) *(rec Peterborough, Ontario, Canada, Nov 1985)* ("The Virtuoso Harp") † J. L. Dussek:Son 3 Hp, Op. 2; Sons Vn, Op. 2; G. Fauré:Impromptu Hp, Op. 86; N. Flagello:Son Hp; S. Prokofiev:Pieces (10) Pno, Op. 12; Tournier:Sonatine Hp, Op. 30 BIS ▲ 319 [DDD] (17.97)
Y. Kondonassis (hp) *(rec Nov 23-25, 1992)* ("Scintillation") † Debussy:Arabesques Pno; Danses sacrée et profane; Preludes Pno; G. Gershwin:Preludes Pno; Grandjany:Fant Hp; M. Ravel:Intro & Allegro Hp; Pavane pour une infante défunte TEL ▲ 80361 [DDD] (16.97)
Sonatine en Trio for Flute, Viola & Harp [arr from Ravel's *Sonatine for Piano*]
Auréole † Debussy:Son Fl; F. Devienne:Duos Fl (sels), Op. 5; G. Fauré:Morceau de concours Fl; Ibert:Interludes (2) Fl Vn & Hpd KOCH ▲ 7102 [DDD] (16.97)
Dallas Tryptych Players *(rec Dallas, TX)* ("Tryptych") † Beethoven:Serenade Fl, Vn & Va, Op. 25; W. Mathias:Zodiac Trio KLAV ▲ 11055 [DDD] (18.97)
Sabeth Trio Basel ("French Music for Flute, Viola & Harp") † Bondon:Soleil Multicolore; Debussy:Son Fl; T. Dubois:Terzettino; Vellones:Trio Fl PANC ▲ 510096 [DDD] (17.97)
Suite of 8 Dances for Harp
A. Giles (hp) † Morceaux Hp, Op. 28; Poetical Studies; Scintillation; Vars Hp, Op. 30 KSCH ▲ 312232 [DDD] (16.97)
Variations on a Theme in the Olden Style for Harp, Op. 30
A. Giles (hp) † Morceaux Hp, Op. 28; Poetical Studies; Scintillation; Suite Hp KSCH ▲ 312232 [DDD] (16.97)
J. Loman (hp) ("20th Century Masterworks for Harp") † B. Britten:Suite Hp, Op. 83; Buhr:Tanzmusik; P. Hindemith:Son Hp; Tailleferre:Son Hp; Tournier:Sonatine Hp, Op. 30 MARQ ▲ 165 (16.97)
A. Ravnopolska (hp) ("Légende: French Music for Harp") † G. Fauré:Impromptu Hp, Op. 86; M. Franck:Suite Hp; G. Pierné:Impromptu-Caprice Hp, Op. 9; Renié:Légende Hp; Tailleferre:Son Hp; Tournier:Images Hp GEGA ▲ 152 [DDD] (16.97)

SAMARAS, SPYRIDON (FILISKOS) (?1863-1917)
Mademoiselle de Belle-Isle (selections)
artists unknown *(rec 1903-07)* ("Souvenirs from Verismo Operas, Vol. 3") † Dupont:Cabrera (sels); Leoncavallo:Roland von Berlin (sels); Mascherone:Lorenza (sels) IRCC ▲ 815 (16.97)

SAMETZ, STEVEN (1954-
in time of for Vocal Ensemble
Chanticleer † Z. Long:Words of the Sun; B. Rands:Canti d'Amor; S. Stucky:Cradle Songs; Taverner:Village Wedding; A. R. Thomas:Love Songs; Rub of Love; C. Yi:Tang Poems TELC ▲ 24570 (16.97)

SAMINSKY, LAZARE (1882-1959)
Danse rituelle du Sabbath [Ritual Dance on the Sabbath] for Piano (1919)
J. Nemtsov (pno) † Etude Pno; Hebrew Fairy Tale Pno; J. Achron:Begrüssung Pno; Kindersuite Pno; Symphonic Vars & Son; Traum Pno; Weprik:Folk Dances Pno; Son 2 Pno EDA ▲ 14 (18.97)
Etude for Piano (1919)
J. Nemtsov (pno) † Danse rituelle Pno; Hebrew Fairy Tale Pno; J. Achron:Begrüssung Pno; Kindersuite Pno; Symphonic Vars & Son; Traum Pno; Weprik:Folk Dances Pno; Son 2 Pno EDA ▲ 14 (18.97)
Hebrew Fairy Tale for Piano (1919)
J. Nemtsov (pno) † Danse rituelle Pno; Etude Pno; J. Achron:Begrüssung Pno; Kindersuite Pno; Symphonic Vars & Son; Traum Pno; Weprik:Folk Dances Pno; Son 2 Pno EDA ▲ 14 (18.97)

SAMINSKY, LAZARE (cont.)
Vision for Piano (1919)
J. Nemtsov (pno) *(rec Leipzig, Nov 1996)* ("Discovering Russia, Vol. 1: Visions 1910-1940") † J. Achron:Statuettes; S. Feinberg:Berceuse; Lourié:Pno Music; S. Prokofiev:Visions fugitives, Op. 22; Weprik:Dance Pno, Op. 13a EDA (Across Boundries) ▲ 12 [DDD]

SAMMARTINI, GIOVANNI BATTISTA (1701-1775)
Cantatas (8) for the Fridays in Lent for solo Voices & Ensemble, J.118 (1751-1760)
S. Mapelli (sop), C. Calvi (cta), V. Martino (ten), D. Ferrari (cnd) NUO ▲ 7269 (16.97)
Chamber Music
Aglàia Ensemble—Qnts 2 & 3 in G; Concertinos for 4 in G, E & B *(rec Apr 9-12, 1996)* ("Quintets & Quartets") STRV ▲ 33426 [DDD] (16.97)
Concertos (2) in G & D for Flute, Strings & Harpsichord
M. Mercelli (fl), V. Paternoster (cnd), Benedetto Marcello CO BONG ▲ 5552 [DDD] (16.97)
Magnificat in B♭ for SATB Soloists, Orchestra & Chorus
F. Szekeres (cnd), Budapest Strings, Budapest Madrigal Choir, M. Szücs (sop), K. Takács (alt), D. Gulyás (ten), T. Bátor (bass) † Albinoni:Magnificat; Caldara:Magnificat; Vivaldi:Magnificat, RV.610; Magnificat, RV.611 HUN ▲ 31259 [DDD] (16.97)
Quintet in G for Strings
C. Banchini (cnd) † Sym in D; Sym in G; G. Sammartini:Con grossi, Op. 5 HMA ▲ 1901245 [DDD] (9.97)
Sinfonia in A for Orchestra
J. Corazolla (cnd), Rhenish CO ("Symphonies of the Italian Baroque") † Sym in G; Albinoni:Cons Strs, Op. 10; A. Corelli:Concerti grossi, Op. 6; Geminiani:Concerti grossi (6) for 2 Vns, Op. 3; Locatelli:Concerti grossi, Op. 1; Torelli:Con musicali, Op. 6; Vivaldi:Incoronazione di Dario (sels) ENTE ▲ 92 [DDD] (10.97)
Sonatas (6) for Flute, Violin & Continuo
Accademia Farnese MONM (Il grande barocco italiano) ▲ 96017 (18.97)
Sonatas (6) for Strings, Op. 1 (pubd. 1744)
M. Conti (fl), A. Marion (fl), D. Roi (hpd) † Son terza Fls; Cambini:Trio 1 for 2 Fls & Hpd; Nardini:Sons (6) for 2 Fls; Platti:Trio Fls FON ▲ 8903 [DDD] (13.97)
Sonata terza in C for 2 Flutes & Harpsichord
M. Conti (fl), A. Marion (fl), D. Roi (hpd) † Sons (6) Strs, Op. 1; Cambini:Trio 1 for 2 Fls & Hpd; Nardini:Sons (6) for 2 Fls; Platti:Trio Fls FON ▲ 8903 [DDD] (13.97)
Symphony in D
C. Banchini (cnd), Ensemble 415 *(rec 1986)* † Qnt Strs; Sym in G; G. Sammartini:Con grossi, Op. 5 HMA ▲ 1901245 [DDD] (9.97)
Symphony in G
C. Banchini (cnd), Ensemble 415 *(rec 1986)* † Qnt Strs; Sym in D; G. Sammartini:Con grossi, Op. 5 HMA ▲ 1901245 [DDD] (9.97)
J. Corazolla (cnd), Rhenish CO ("Symphonies of the Italian Baroque") † Sinf in A; Albinoni:Cons Strs, Op. 10; A. Corelli:Concerti grossi, Op. 6; Geminiani:Concerti grossi (6) for 2 Vns, Op. 3; Locatelli:Concerti grossi, Op. 1; Torelli:Con musicali, Op. 6; Vivaldi:Incoronazione di Dario (sels) ENTE ▲ 92 [DDD] (10.97)

SAMMARTINI, GIUSEPPE (ca 1693-ca 1750)
Concerti grossi (6) for 2 Violins, Viola & Cello Concertino (or 2 Violins & Bass), Op. 2 (1728)
S. Frontalini (cnd), Kaunas CO *(rec Kaunas Lithuania, June 1993)* † Giuseppe St. Martini's Cons, Op. 9 BONG ▲ 5559 [DDD] (16.97)
P. Zajíček (cnd), Musica Aeterna Ensemble ("Baroque Christmas") † A. Corelli:Con grosso, Op. 6/8; G. F. Handel:Messiah (sels) SLOV ▲ 4
Concerti grossi (6) in e, B♭, g, a, c & g for 2 Violins, Viola & Cello concertino, Op. 5, "Christmas Concerto" (1747)
C. Banchini (cnd) † G. B. Sammartini:Qnt Strs; Sym in D; Sym in G HMA ▲ 1901245 [DDD] (9.97)
S. M. Lucarelli (cnd), Milan Piccola Sinfonica ("Concerti Grossi") † A. Corelli:Con grosso, Op. 6/8; Pez:Con pastorale FON ▲ 9705 (13.97)
Concerto in D for Flute & Strings
P. Ferrigato (fl), P. Suppa (cnd), I Musici Ambrosiani *(rec Auditorium Marcelline Tommaseo, Milan, Italy, Sep 1998)* † Con 12 Ob; Con 9 Ob; Giuseppe St. Martini's Cons, Op. 9 DYNC ▲ 2020 [DDD] (13.97)
Concerto in A for Flute & Strings
P. Ferrigato (fl), P. Suppa (cnd), I Musici Ambrosiani *(rec Auditorium Marcelline Tommaseo, Milan, Italy, Sep 1998)* † Con 12 Ob; Con 9 Ob; Giuseppe St. Martini's Cons, Op. 9 DYNC ▲ 2020 [DDD] (13.97)
Concerto in G for Harpsichord, 2 Violins & Continuo
Musica Alta Ripa *(rec June 1997)* ("Londoner's Taste") † Babell:Con Rcr; W. Boyce:Son 11 Vns; Geminiani:Vars on a Subject; G. F. Handel:Son Rcr; Porpora:Son Vc; R. Valentine:Con Rcr MDG ▲ 3090779 [DDD] (17.97)
Concerto No. 9 in B♭ for Oboe & Strings
F. Quaranta (ob), P. Suppa (cnd), I Musici Ambrosiani *(rec Auditorium Marcelline Tommaseo, Milan, Italy, Sep 1998)* † Con Fl; Con 12 Ob; Giuseppe St. Martini's Cons, Op. 9 DYNC ▲ 2020 [DDD] (13.97)
Concerto No. 12 in C for Oboe & Strings
F. Quaranta (ob), P. Suppa (cnd), I Musici Ambrosiani *(rec Auditorium Marcelline Tommaseo, Milan, Italy, Sep 1998)* † Con Fl; Con 9 Ob; Giuseppe St. Martini's Cons, Op. 9 DYNC ▲ 2020 [DDD] (13.97)
Concerto in B♭ for Oboe, Strings & Continuo
L. Avanzi (ob), A. Molino (cnd) ("Oboe Concertos in Italy") † Dall'Abaco:Con Ob; J. A. Hasse:Con Ob STRV ▲ 33346 [DDD] (16.97)
Giuseppe St. Martini's Concertos (4) in A, F, G & B♭ for Harpsichord (or Organ) & Strings, Op. 9 (1754)
D. Bianchi (hpd), P. Suppa (cnd), I Musici Ambrosiani—No. 1 in A *(rec Auditorium Marcelline Tommaseo, Milan, Italy, Sep 1998)* † Con Fl; Con 12 Ob; Con 9 Ob DYNC ▲ 2020 [DDD] (13.97)
S. Frontalini (cnd), Kaunas CO *(rec Kaunas Lithuania, June 1993)* † Con grossi, Op. 2 BONG ▲ 5559 [DDD] (16.97)
Solos (6) for Flute (or Violin, or Oboe) & Continuo, Op. 13 (ca 1760)
O. Zoboli (ob), A. Cremonesi (hpd) *(rec Apr 4-6, 1995)* ("The Apotheosis of the Oboe") † J. S. Bach:Sons Fl; Geminiani:Son 3 Ob; Telemann:Kleine Kammermusik STRV ▲ 80005 (12.97)
Sonatas (12) for Flute & Continuo, Op. 2 (ca 1745)
C. Frigeiro (vc), V. Bottazzini (fl), M. Frige (clvd) ("Vol. 2") SYMO ▲ 105 (17.97)
V. Paternoster (vc), M. Mercelli (fl), G. Kiss (clvd) BONG ▲ 5562 [DDD] (16.97)
V. Paternoster (vc), M. Mercelli (fl), G. Kiss (hpd) ("Flute Sonatas, Vol. 1") BONG ▲ 5561 [DDD] (16.97)
Sonatas (4) in C, G, D & A for Flute & Harpsichord [attrib] (ca 1720-28)
R. Gini (vc), M. Henry (ob), D. Petech (hpd) *(rec Bellagio)* ("Italian Musicians in London") † Barsanti:Collection of Old Scots Tunes; Geminiani:Pièces de clavecin AART ▲ 47141 [DDD] (10.97)
Sonatas (12) for 2 Flutes (or Violins) & Continuo
G. Matteoli (fl), T. Rossi (fl) † Sons for 2 Vns AG ▲ 44 (18.97)
G. Matteoli (fl), T. Rossi (fl), Fête Rustique *(rec Milan, June 25-26, 1995)* AG ▲ 20 [DDD] (18.97)
Sonatas (12) for 2 Violins & Continuo (ca 1743)
D. Nuzzoli (vn), P. Cantamessa (vn) † Sons 2 Fls AG ▲ 44 (18.97)

SAMPSON, DAVID (1951-
Distant Voices for Brass Quintet (1990)
American Brass Quintet *(rec SUNY College, Purchase, NY)* ("Premiere!") † J. Bach:Triptych; G. Schuller:Qnt 2 Brass; Welcher:Qnt Brass SUMM ▲ 187 [DDD] (16.97)
Morning Music for Brass Quintet (1986)
American Brass Quintet *(rec Mar 1991)* † Adolphe:Triskelion; R. Dennis:Blackbird Vars; Ewazen:Colchester Fant; D. Snow:Dance Movts SUMM ▲ 133 [DDD] (16.97)
Reflections on a Dance for Brass (1988)
Summit Brass † J. Cheetham:Keystone Celebration; D. Erb:Sonneries; G. Schuller:Sym Brass, Op. 16; J. Stevens:Moondance SUMM ▲ 127 [DDD] (16.97)

SAMSON, S. D. (dates unknown)
Jock's Favourites for Band
T. Cooper (cnd), Drums & Pipes of the Gordon Highlanders—Between the Don & the Dee/Crossing the Spey/ Juggernaut/Clumsy Lover *(rec Berlin, Germany)* ("Cock O'The North") † E. Coates:Songs; D. Knox:Bonnie Black Isle; Rose of Kelvingrove; J. MacGregor:Medley; Traditional:Aberdeen Sel; Castlegate to Holborn; Company Marches; Cornkisters; Drummer's Fanfare; Grampian Welcome; Highland Gathering; Highland Troop; Jacobite Prince; Lights Out; Loch Maree; Long Reveille; March Off Colours/Tattoo Last Post; Mess Pipers; Pipe Medley; Regimental Quick March Cock O'the North; Regimental Slow March; Ye Banks and Braes BND ▲ 5077 [DDD] (16.97)

SAMUEL, GERHARD (1924-
Quartet No. 1 for Strings (1978)
LaSalle String Quartet *(rec College-Conservatory of Music Univ. of Cincinnati, OH, Oct 15, 1978)* † Qt 2 Strs; Transformations Vn CENT ▲ 2238 [DDD] (16.97)

SAMUEL, GERHARD (cont.)
Quartet No. 2 for Strings (1981)
Essex String Quartet *(rec College-Conservatory of Music Univ. of Cincinnati, OH, Feb 21, 1994)* † Qt 1 Strs; Transformations Vn CENT ▲ 2238 [DDD] (16.97)
Transformations for Violin & Chamber Orchestra
P. Yeager (vn), K. Sassmannshaus (cnd), Starling CO *(rec College-Conservatory of Music Univ. of Cincinnati, OH, Sept 25, 1994)* † Qt 1 Strs; Qt 2 Strs CENT ▲ 2238 [DDD] (16.97)

SAMUEL-ROUSSEAU, MARCEL (1882-1955)
Variations Pastorales sur un vieux Noël for Orchestra (1916)
E. Goodman (hp), Amadeus Ensemble members [trans for hp & str qt] † M. Barnes:Divert Hp; E.T.A. Hoffmann:Qnt Hp, AV.24; M. Ravel:Intro & Allegro Hp; Tournier:Images Hp MUVI (Musica Viva) ▲ 1054 [DDD] (16.97)

SAMUELSSON, MARIE (20th cent)
Signal for Saxophone Quartet
Stockholm Saxophone Quartet ("Links") † Enström:Vigil; Feiler:Anvil & Parachutes; Lindwall:Cut Up; Parmerud:Retur; Rydberg:Link/Sequence CAPA ▲ 21517 (16.97)

SANCAN, PIERRE (1916-
Sonatine for Clarinet & Piano (1963)
H. Wright (cl), L. Battle (pno) ("Recital No. 2") † I. Dahl:Son da Camera; Debussy:Arabesques Pno; F. Schubert:Der Hirt auf dem Felsen, D.965; C. M. von Weber:Grand Duo Concertant, J.204 BOST ▲ 1024 (15.97)
Sonatine for Flute & Piano
E. Pahud (fl), E. Le Sage (pno) *(rec Highgate London, England, Feb 1997)* ("Paris") † Dutilleux:Sonatine Fl; Ibert:Aria Cl & Pno; Jeux; Jolivet:Chant de Linos Fl & Pno; Messiaen:Merle noir; D. Milhaud:Sonatina Fl & Pno, Op. 76; F. Poulenc:Son Fl EMIC ▲ 56488 [DDD] (16.97)

SANCES, GIOVANNI FELICE (ca 1600-1679)
Music of Sances
J. Walters (cnd) ("17th Century Music for Sopranos, Harp & Guitar") ASV (Gaudeamus) ▲ 155 (16.97)
Stabat mater dolorosa for solo Voice & Organ (1638)
C. Calvi (cta), R. Gini (vc) [LAT] *(rec May 1991)* † Frescobaldi:Sonetto spirituale:Maddalena all Croce; Jommelli:Agonia di Cristo NUO (Ancient Music) ▲ 7030 [DDD] (16.97)

SANCHEZ-GUTIERREZ, CARLOS (1964-
M.E. in Memoriam for Chamber Ensemble
M. Pratt (cnd), Princeton Composers Ensemble ("Society of Composers, Inc.-Transcendencies") † Z. Browning:Breakpoint Screamer; Cotel:Quatrains; J. Fortner:Symphonies; Hankinson:Light/Shadow; F. W.-H. Ho:Bon; Sheffer:Con Sax CPS ▲ 8656 (16.97)

SANDERS, BERNARD WAYNE (1951-
Pieces (3) for Flute & Organ (1987)
F. Shelly (fl), S. Egler (org) *(rec Wiedemann Recital Hall, Wichita State University, KS)* ("The Dove Descending") † M. Albrecht:Psalms; Berlinski:Adagietto; Ochse:Prelude & Fugue Ft & Org; Roush:Dove Descending; J. Weaver:Rhapsody; G. Young:Triptych SUMM ▲ 174 [DDD] (16.97)

SANDERS, JOHN (20th cent)
Anthem of the Incarnation for Mixed Chorus (1995)
M. Lee (cnd), St. Cecilia Singers, A. Sackett (org) *(rec Gloucester Cathedral, England, June 1997)* ("Over Hill, Over Dale") † K. Amos:Salisbury Cathedral; Anonymous:Scarborough Fair; She Moved through the Fair; H. Howells:Choral Music; H. Parry:Seven Part Songs; Six Modern Lyrics; Songs of Farewell; Traditional:Bobby Shaftoe; Dance to Thy Daddy; Frog & the Crow; Vaughan Williams:Shakespeare Songs PRIO ▲ 620 [DDD] (16.97)

SANDI, LUIS (1905-
Theme & Variations for Orchestra (1944)
E. Diazmuñoz (cnd), Mexico City PO † G. Duran:Nepantla; Kuri-Aldana:Canto Latinamericano; Lavalle-García:Obertura Colonial; Mabarak:Sym in One Mvt; Moncayo Garcia:Bosques CLME ▲ 21231 (13.97)
H. de la Fuente (cnd), Mexican State PO † M. K. Aldana:Canto Latinoamericano; G. Duran:Nepantla; R. Halffter:Madrugada del panadero, Op. 12a; Jiménez-Mabarak:Sym in 1 Movt; Lavalle-García:Obertura Colonial CLME ▲ 21006 (13.97)

SANDKE, RANDY (20th cent)
Music of Sandke
R. Sandke (tpt), L. Denev (pno), L. Denev (cnd), Bulgarian National SO *(Ellington-Strayhorn Boquet)*, R. Sandke (tpt), L. Denev (cnd) *(Cloudy; Orphic Mystery; Remembrance)*, L. Denev (cnd), Bulgarian National SO *(Ov for the Year 2000)*, R. Sandke (elec/tpt) *(Fugue State I)*, Randy Sandke Quintet *(Persistence; Sea Change)*, Randy Sandke Trio *(Fugue State II; Awakening)* *(rec Sofia, Bulgaria, Apr 1997)* ("Awakening") † C. Ives:Unanswered Question ERTO ▲ 42049 [DDD] (16.97)

SANDOVAL, ARTURO (1949-
Concerto for Trumpet & Orchestra [orchd Zito Zelanti]
A. Sandoval (tpt), L. Haza (cnd), London SO *(rec 1993)* † A. Arutiunian:Con Tpt; J. N. Hummel:Con Tpt in E♭, S.49; L. Mozart:Con Tpt RCAV (Red Seal) ▲ 62661 [DDD] (16.97)

SANDROFF, HOWARD (20th cent)
La Joie for 3 Clarinets (1996)
L. Combs (cl), J. DeRoche (cl), J. B. Yeh (b cl) *(rec Chicago, Nov 25, 1996)* ("Chicago Clarinet Trio") † Bouffil:Trio 2 for 3 Cls, Op. 8/2; Mihalovici:Son Cls, Op. 35; A. Prinz:Con a Cinque; Zonn:Ultimate Nimbus HEL ▲ 1028 (10.97)
Tephillah for Clarinet & Electronics
J. B. Yeh (cl), H. Sandroff (elec) ("Dialogues With My Shadow") † P. Boulez:Dialogue de l'ombre double; R. Carl:Towards the Crest; R. Levin:New Leaf; D. Martino:Set Cl KOCH ▲ 7088 (10.97)

SANDSTRÖM, JAN (1954-
BombiBone BrassBitt (suite) for Trombone & Wind Orchestra [from Bombi Bitt] (1996)
C. Lindberg (trbn), C. Imamura (cnd), Kosei Wind Orch *(rec Dec 1996)* ("Wind Power") † Berlioz:Grande Symphonie funèbre et triomphale, Op. 15; D. Bourgeois:Con Trbn; G. Holst:Duet Trbn; Rimsky-Korsakov:Con Trbn BIS ▲ 848 [DDD] (17.97)
Concerto for Trombone & Orchestra (1986-89)
C. Lindberg (trbn), L. Segerstam (cnd), Swedish RSO ("Trombone Odyssey: 20th Century Landmarks For Trombone & Orchestra") † E. Bloch:Sym Trb; F. Martin:Ballade Trb; Serocki:Con Trbn BIS ▲ 538 [DDD] (17.97)
Don Quixote (Concerto No. 2) for Trombone & Orchestra (1994)
C. Lindberg (trbn) ("Unaccompanied") † J. S. Bach:Suites Vc; Högberg:Su Ba Do Be; C. Lindberg:Vars on Gregorian Chants; Telemann:Fants (12) Fl, TWV40:2-13 BIS ▲ 858 [DDD] (17.97)
C. Lindberg (trbn), O. Vänskä (cnd), Lahti SO ("Lindberg Plays Sandström") † Emperor's Chant; Short Ride; Wahlberg Vars BIS ▲ 828 [DDD] (17.97)
Emperor's Chant for Trombone & Orchestra (1994)
C. Lindberg (trbn), O. Vänskä (cnd), Lahti SO ("Lindberg Plays Sandström") † Don Quixote; Short Ride; Wahlberg Vars BIS ▲ 828 [DDD] (17.97)
Sanctus for Chorus (ca 1990)
E. Westberg (cnd), Erik Westberg Vocal Ensemble ("Musica Sacra") † J. S. Bach:Cons Org; L. Jansson:Sacred Music; O. Olsson:Sacred Music; A. Paulsson:Lullaby OPU ▲ 9506 [AAD] (16.97)
A Short Ride on a Motorbike for Trombone & Orchestra (1989)
C. Lindberg (trbn), O. Vänskä (cnd), Lahti SO ("Lindberg Plays Sandström") † Don Quixote; Emperor's Chant; Wahlberg Vars BIS ▲ 828 [DDD] (17.97)
Wahlberg Variations (5) for Trombone & Orchestra (1996)
C. Lindberg (trbn), O. Vänskä (cnd), Lahti SO ("Lindberg Plays Sandström") † Don Quixote; Emperor's Chant; Short Ride BIS ▲ 828 [DDD] (17.97)

SANDSTRÖM, SVEN-DAVID (1942-
Drums for Percussion Ensemble (1980)
Kroumata Percussion Ensemble † J. Cage:Amores; L. Harrison:Con 1 Fl; Jolivet:Suite en concert BIS ▲ 272 [DDD] (17.97)
Free Music for Flute & 6 Percussion Players (1900)
M. Wiesler (fl), Kroumata Percussion Ensemble † Hvoslef (Saeverud):Sxt Fl & Perc; Nørgård:Square and Round; R. Wallin:Stonewave BIS ▲ 512 [DDD] (17.97)
Kroumata Pieces for Percussion Ensemble (1995)
Kroumata Percussion Ensemble *(rec Dec 1997)* ("Kroumata") † J. Cage:Third Construction; Houng:Récit de cinq marimbas; Katzer:Schlagmusik 2; H. Strindberg:Ursprung/Gläntor BIS ▲ 932 [DDD] (17.97)
Mute the Bereaved Memories Speak (requiem) for solo Voices, Orchestra, Mixed Chorus, Children's Chorus & Tape (1979)
L. Segerstam (cnd), Swedish RSO, Stockholm Chamber Choir, Swedish Radio Chorus, Stockholm Children's Choir CAPA 2-▲ 22027 [AAD] (32.97)

▲ = CD ♦ = Enhanced CD △ = MD ▮ = Cassette Tape ▯ = DCC

SANDSTRÖM, SVEN-DAVID (cont.)

Quartet No. 3 for Strings (1987)

Zetterqvist String Quartet *(rec Apr-May 1997)* ("Zetterqvist String Quartet") † M. Edlund:brains & dancin'; Stenhammar:Qt 6 Strs, Op. 35 OPU ▲ 19702 [DDD] (16.97)

SANFORD, DAVID (20th cent)

Concerto No. 3 for Clarinet & Chamber Ensemble (1992)

A. Blustine (cl), W. Purvis (cnd) *(rec Queens College New York, May 14, 1995)* † E. Moe:Kicking & Screaming; M. Rosenzweig:Delta, the Perfect King CRI ▲ 705 [DDD] (16.97)

SAN JUAN, JOSE DE (18th cent)

Missa à 8 con violines, trompas y clarines

I. Terrazas (sop), G. Thierry (mez), F. Becerra (ten), E. Carsi (bass), E. Moreno (vn), A. Baciero (org), B. J. Echenique (cnd), Mexico City CO, Mexico City Chamber Chorus ("México Barroco, Puebla IV") URT ▲ 2007 (16.97)

SANTACREU, JAVIER (1965-

Quartet de Tardor for String Quartet

Floregium String Quartet ("Quattuor at Magistrum") † Botella:Noix; Darias:Miniatura; Relato; Valle:Cants Cordals; Verdu:Sombra de Ailanto EMEC ▲ 12 (16.97)

Sextet de la Naixenca for Ensemble

L. Danceanu (cnd) ("Concert in Bucharest") † Vitae; Botella:Anihila; Darias:Sunday Suite; Verdu:Krameria; Sueño de Neire EMEC ▲ 8 (16.97)

Vitae for Ensemble

L. Danceanu (cnd) ("Concert in Bucharest") † Sxt de la Naixenca; Botella:Anihila; Darias:Sunday Suite; Verdu:Krameria; Sueño de Neire EMEC ▲ 8 (16.97)

SANTA CRUZ, ANTONIO DE (17th cent)

Guitar Music

A. Gonzales-Campa (castanets)—Jacaras; Españoletas; Canarios; Marionas ("Encuentro Sanz & Santa Cruz") † G. Sanz:Gtr Music ASTR ▲ 8575 [DDD] (18.97)

Libro donde se verán Pasacalles for Guitar (ca 1705)

T. Schmitt (gtr) *(rec Apr & Sept 1993)* ("Guitar Music of the Baroque: Spain") † Guerau:Poema harmónico; S. De Murcia:Gtr Music; G. Sanz:Instrucción de Música MPH ▲ 56819 [DDD] (15.97)

SANTANA, ANTONIO (20th cent)

Un Chant pour la planete [A Song for the Planet] (oratorio) for Soprano, Baritone, Piano, Orchestra & Chorus [text Bernard Chotil]

C. Sylvestre (sop), J. Perroni (bar), J. Distel (pno), J. Loré (cnd), French Oratorio Orch, Pléiade de Maurepas Choir, Mesnil Saint-Denis Choir, Cernay la Ville Choir, Paris New Polyphonic Ensemble, Sainte-Marie d'Antony Petits Chanteurs EROL ▲ 96002 [DDD] (18.97)

SANTINI, ALESSANDRO (18th cent)

Sonatas (6) for Flute & Continuo

L'Offerta Musicale BONG ▲ 5577 [DDD] (16.97)

SANTORE, JONATHAN (20th cent)

Divertimento for Chamber Ensemble

Octagon ("Octagon, Vol. 1") † Doe:Solstice Fragments; E. Harrison:Cité du globe captif; Jelliffe:Chinese Teapot Teaches Patience; Kothman:G-R-K; Mateus-Vasquez:Song Cycle ALBA ▲ 130 [DDD] (16.97)

SANTÓRSOLA, GUIDO (1904-

Sonata a duo for 2 Guitars

F. Halász (gtr), D. Halász (pno) *(rec Stockholm Sweden, Jan 22-25, 1995)* † Castelnuovo-Tedesco:Fant Gtr & Pno, Op. 145; H. Haug:Fant Gtr & Pno; D. Shostakovich:Preludes Vn BIS ▲ 717 [DDD] (17.97)

Suite all'antica for 2 Guitars

S. Tordini (gtr), J. Prats (gtr) † Civitareale:Suite estival; M. de Falla:Pièces espagnoles; Gangi:Suite italiana OTR ▲ 1016 [DDD] (18.97)

SANTOS, ENRIQUE (1930-

Sonata No. 2 for Piano

E. M. Zuk (pno) † Son 6 Pno; Suite de los Grindeles; Suite para Ninos Traviosos CLMX ▲ 21035 (16.97)

Sonata No. 6 for Piano

A. Leon (pno) † Son 2 Pno; Suite de los Grindeles; Suite para Ninos Traviosos CLMX ▲ 21035 (16.97)

Suite de los Grindeles for Piano

D. Noli (pno) † Son 2 Pno; Son 6 Pno; Suite para Ninos Traviosos CLMX ▲ 21035 (16.97)

Suite para Ninos Traviosos for Piano

D. Noli (pno) † Son 2 Pno; Son 6 Pno; Suite de los Grindeles CLMX ▲ 21035 (16.97)

SANZ, GASPAR (mid-17th cent-early 18th cent)

Guitar Music

A. Gonzales-Campa (castanets)—Canarios; Españoletas; Rugero; Paradetas; Folias; Chaconne; Hachas; Vacas; Pavana por la D; Maricapalos; Preludio & fant; Zarabanda francesca; Giga Ingles; Passacales por la X; Clarinas y trompetas; Marionas ("Encuentro Sanz & Santa Cruz") † Santa Cruz:Gtr Music ASTR ▲ 8575 [DDD] (18.97)

Instrucción de Música sobre la guitarra española y método de sus primeros rudimentos hasta tañerla con destreza for Guitar (1674)

T. Schmitt (gtr) *(rec Apr & Sept 1993)* ("Guitar Music of the Baroque: Spain") † Guerau:Poema harmónico; S. De Murcia:Gtr Music; Santa Cruz:Libro donde se verán Pasacalles MPH ▲ 56819 [DDD] (15.97)

H. Smith (gtr) ASTR ▲ 8576 (18.97)

Suite Española for Guitar

C. Romero (gtr) † J. S. Bach:Sons & Partitas Vn; Suites Vc DLS ▲ 1005 [AAD] (10.97)

A. Romero (gtr) ("A Touch of Romance") † A. Barrios:Gtr Music; C. Romero:Suite Andaluza TEL ▲ 80213 [DDD] (16.97)

SAPIEYEVSKI, JERZY (1945-

Arioso for Chamber Ensemble

J. Dunham (va), Boatman (perc), Westwood Wind Quintet † G. Holst:Terzetto Fl; Pleyel:Miniatures Va CRYS ▮ 647 (9.98)

Westwood Wind Quintet † I. Dahl:Allegro & Arioso; K. Husa:Serenade; L. Moyse:Qnt Ww CRYS ▲ 751 [DDD] (15.97)

Mercury Concerto for Trumpet & Chamber Ensemble

A. Ghitalla (tpt), J. Stephens (cnd), American Camerata † Krenek:Capriccio Vc; L. Moss:Clouds; Syms Brass; Persichetti:King Lear; H. Villa-Lobos:Chôro 7 AMCA ▲ 10305 (18.97)

SAPP, ALLEN DWIGHT (1922-

And the Bombers Went Home for Violin & Piano, W.53 (1943)

M. Gelland (vn), L. Wallin (pno) *(rec Sweden, 1995)* ("Lyrische Aspekte unseres Jahrhundert") † Acker:Son Vn; W. Burkhard:Son Vn; H. Jelinek:Zahme Xenien, Op. 32; O. Schoeck:Son Vn; R. Strauss:Allegretto Vn, AV149; Wyshnegradsky:Chant douloureux et étude, Op. 6; Chant nocturne, Op. 12 bis VMM ▲ 2017 [DDD]

The Four Reasons (concerto) for Chamber Orchestra (1994)

K. Lockhart (cnd), Cincinnati CO *(rec Nov 4, 1996)* † Imaginary Creatures; Women of Trachis CRI ▲ 765 [DDD] (16.97)

Imaginary Creatures: A Bestiary for the Credulous for Harpsichord & Orchestra (1981)

E. Hashimoto (hpd), K. Lockhart (cnd), Cincinnati CO *(rec Oct 1 & Nov 4, 1996)* † Women of Trachis; 4 Reasons CRI ▲ 765 [DDD] (16.97)

The Women of Trachis (overture) for Orchestra (1960)

K. Lockhart (cnd), Cincinnati CO *(rec Oct 1, 1996)* † Imaginary Creatures; 4 Reasons CRI ▲ 765 [DDD] (16.97)

SARASATE, PABLO DE (1844-1908)

Aires bohemios for Violin & Piano

E. León (vn), D. Muñiz (pno) *(rec Estudis Albert Moraleda de Barcelona, Mar 1995)* † E. Grieg:Son 3 Vn, Op. 45; Toldrá:Sonnets Vn; Turull:Divert Vn EAM ▲ 49523 [DDD] (17.97)

Capriccio Basque for Violin & Piano, Op. 24

L. Csury (vn), B. Simon (pno) † Danzas Españolas; Fant on Carmen, Op. 25; Zigeunerweisen, Op. 20 CLDI ▲ 4007 [DDD] (10.97)

A. Rosand (vn), E. Flissler (pno) ("Aaron Rosand Plays Sarasate") † Danzas Españolas; Fant on Carmen, Op. 25; Navarra, Op. 33; Zigeunerweisen, Op. 20 ALLO ▲ 8160 [ADD] (3.97)

Danzas Españolas (8) for Violin & Piano [Opp. 21-23 & 26]

R. Barton (vn), S. Sanders (pno) ("Homage to Sarasate") † Fant on Carmen, Op. 25; Intro & Tarantella, Op. 43; Vn & Pno Music DOR ▲ 90183 [DDD] (16.97)

L. Csury (vn), B. Simon (pno) † Capriccio Basque, Op. 24; Fant on Carmen, Op. 25; Zigeunerweisen, Op. 20 CLDI ▲ 4007 [DDD] (10.97)

A. Rosand (vn), E. Flissler (pno) ("Aaron Rosand Plays Sarasate") † Capriccio Basque, Op. 24; Fant on Carmen, Op. 25; Navarra, Op. 33; Zigeunerweisen, Op. 20 ALLO ▲ 8160 [ADD] (3.97)

SARASATE, PABLO DE (cont.)

Fantasy on Carmen for Violin & Orchestra [after Bizet], Op. 25

S. Accardo (vn), L. Manzini (pno) [arr for vn & pno] ("Violinist Composers") † Paganini:Cantabile, M.S. 109; Tartini:Son Vn & Pno; T. A. Vitali:Chaconne Vn; Wieniawski:Légende Vn, Op. 17; Polonaise 2, Op. 21 FON ▲ 9602 [DDD] (13.97)

R. Barton (vn), S. Sanders (pno) [arr for vn & pno] ("Homage to Sarasate") † Danzas Españolas; Intro & Tarantella, Op. 43; Vn & Pno Music DOR ▲ 90183 [DDD] (16.97)

S. Chang (vn), S. Rivers (pno) EMIC ▲ 54352 [DDD] (16.97)

L. Csury (vn), B. Simon (pno) [arr for vn & pno] † Capriccio Basque, Op. 24; Danzas Españolas; Zigeunerweisen, Op. 20 CLDI ▲ 4007 [DDD] (10.97)

C. Haslop (vn), J. Sanders (gtr) [vn-gtr arr] † B. Bartók:Romanian Folk Dances Pno, Sz.56; M. Giuliani:Grand Son, Op. 85; K. Kohn:Concords; D. Leisner:Dances in the Madhouse CENT ▲ 2061 [DDD] (16.97)

L. Josefowicz (vn), N. Marriner (cnd), Academy of St. Martin in the Fields ("Bohemian Rhapsodies") † Zigeunerweisen, Op. 20; E. Chausson:Poème Vn, Op. 25; Massenet:Méditation from Thaïs; M. Ravel:Tzigane; Saint-Saëns:Intro & Rondo capriccioso, Op. 28; Wieniawski:Polonaise 1, Op. 4 PPHI ▲ 454440 (16.97)

I. Perlman (vn), L. Foster (cnd), Royal PO † Paganini:Con 1 Vn, M.S. 21 EMIC ▲ 47101 (16.97)

I. Perlman (vn), L. Foster (cnd), Royal PO † Zigeunerweisen, Op. 20; M. de Falla:Suite populaire espagnole EMIC ▲ 63533 (11.97)

I. Perlman (vn), Z. Mehta (cnd), New York PO † E. Chausson:Poème Vn, Op. 25; M. Ravel:Tzigane; Saint-Saëns:Havanaise, Op. 83; Intro & Rondo capriccioso, Op. 28 DEUT ▲ 23063 [DDD] (16.97)

R. Ricci (vn), E. Ansermet (cnd), Swiss Romande Orch † Zigeunerweisen, Op. 20; Lalo:Sym espagnole, Op. 21; Saint-Saëns:Havanaise, Op. 83; Intro & Rondo capriccioso, Op. 28 PLON (The Classic Sound) ▲ 452309 (11.97)

A. Rosand (vn), R. Reinhardt (cnd), Southwest German RSO Baden-Baden ("Aaron Rosand Plays Sarasate") † Capriccio Basque, Op. 24; Danzas Españolas; Navarra, Op. 33; Zigeunerweisen, Op. 20 ALLO ▲ 8160 [ADD] (3.97)

G. Shaham (vn), C. Abbado (cnd), Berlin PO *(rec live Berlin Philharmonie, Dec 31, 1997)* ("The Berlin Gala: A Salute to Carmen") † Bizet:Carmen (sels); J. Brahms:Hungarian Dances Orch; S. Rachmaninoff:Rhap on a Theme of Paganini, Op. 43; M. Ravel:Rapsodie espagnole DEUT ▲ 457583 [DDD] (16.97)

Introduction & Tarantella for Violin & Orchestra, Op. 43 (1899)

R. Barton (vn), S. Sanders (pno) [arr vn & pno] ("Homage to Sarasate") † Danzas Españolas; Fant on Carmen, Op. 25; Vn & Pno Music DOR ▲ 90183 [DDD] (16.97)

C. Lin (vn), S. Rivers (pno) [tran Michel Press] *(rec Lehman Center for the Performing Arts, NYC, NY)* ("Bravura") † M. de Falla:Suite populaire espagnole; Vida breve (sels); F. Kreisler:Liebesfreud; Liebesleid; Tambourin Chinois Vc & Pno; Tempo di Minuetto; W. A. Mozart:Serenade Vn, K.250/248b; S. Rachmaninoff:Vocalise; R. Schumann:Romances Ob, Op. 94; Wieniawski:Capriccio-valse, Op. 7 SNYC ▲ 39133 [DDD] (11.97)

Navarra for 2 Violins & Piano, Op. 33

A. Rosand (vn), E. Flissler (pno) [Rosand plays both vn parts] ("Aaron Rosand Plays Sarasate") † Capriccio Basque, Op. 24; Danzas Españolas; Fant on Carmen, Op. 25; Zigeunerweisen, Op. 20 ALLO ▲ 8160 [ADD] (3.97)

Serenata andaluza for Violin & Piano, Op. 28

Duo Nova [arr for vn & gtr] ("Duo Nova") † L. von Call:Serenade Vn Gtr, Op. 84; A. Corelli:Sons Vn, Op. 5; Paganini:Centone di sonate, M.S. 112; F. Schubert:Originaltänze, D.365; Smith Brindle:Sketches Vn & Gtr GALL ▲ 936 [DDD] (18.97)

Violin & Piano Music

R. Barton (vn), S. Sanders (pno)—Muiñeira, Op. 32; Zortzico Miramar, Op. 42; Zortzico Adiós montañas mías, Op. 37 ("Homage to Sarasate") † Danzas Españolas; Fant on Carmen, Op. 25; Intro & Tarantella, Op. 43 DOR ▲ 90183 [DDD] (16.97)

M. Kaplan (vn), B. Canino (pno)—Navarra, Op. 33; Danzas Españolas; Capriccio Basque, Op. 24; Bolero, Op. 30; Zortzico D'Iparraguirre, Op. 39; Zortzico Miramar, Op. 42; Intro & Tarantella, Op. 43 *(rec Aug 6-8 & Dec 29, 1989)* ARA ▲ 6614

R. Ricci (vn), G. McNaught (pno)—Fant on Faust, Op. 13; Jota de San Fermín, Op. 36; Melodia Rumana, Op. 47; Jota Aragonesa, Op. 27; Serenata andaluza, Op. 28; Canto del ruiseñor, Op. 29; Peteneras, Op. 35; Zortzico Adiós montañas mías, Op. 37; Zortzico D'Iparraguirre, Op. 39; Zortzico Miramar, Op. 42; Canciones rusas, Op. 49; Jota de Pablo, Op. 52 ("Pablo de Sarasate: A Homage by Ruggiero Ricci") DYNC ▲ 94 [DDD] (17.97)

E. Rose (va), K. Collier (pno)—Danzas Españolas [Op. 26/1, Dance in C; Op. 26/2, Dance in C; Op. 21/1, Malagueña; Op. 23/2, Zapateado] *(rec SMU, Dallas, TX, Jan 1995)* ("Spanish Treasures") † I. Albéniz:Pno Music (misc); M. de Falla:Suite populaire espagnole; M. Ravel:Pièce en forme de Habanera; Toldrá:Sonnets Vn CENT ▲ 2315 [DDD] (16.97)

Zigeunerweisen for Violin & Piano, Op. 20

M. Bisengaliev (vn), J. Wildner (cnd), Polish National RSO ("The Lark Ascending") † Beethoven:Romance 2 Vn, Op. 50; Massenet:Méditation from Thaïs; W. A. Mozart:Adagio Vn, K.261; M. Ravel:Tzigane; Saint-Saëns:Havanaise, Op. 83; Intro & Rondo capriccioso, Op. 28; Vaughan Williams:Lark Ascending NXIN ▲ 8553509 [DDD] (5.97)

M. Bisengaliev (vn), J. Wildner (cnd), Polish National RSO Katowice *(rec Jan 31-Feb 3, 1992)* † Lalo:Sym espagnole, Op. 21; M. Ravel:Tzigane; Saint-Saëns:Havanaise, Op. 83 NXIN ▲ 550494 [DDD] (5.97)

L. Csury (vn), B. Simon (pno) † Capriccio Basque, Op. 24; Danzas Españolas; Fant on Carmen, Op. 25 CLDI ▲ 4007 [DDD] (10.97)

J. Heifetz (vn), J. Barbirolli (cnd), London PO † P. Tchaikovsky:Con Vn; H. Vieuxtemps:Con 4 Vn, Op. 31 IMMM ▲ 37063 (6.97)

J. Heifetz (vn), J. Barbirolli (cnd), London SO *(rec Abbey Road London, Apr 9, 1937)* ("The Heifetz Collection, Volume 4, 1935-1939") † J. Brahms:Con Vn; Son 2 Vn, Op. 100; G. Fauré:Son 1 Vn, Op. 13; S. Prokofiev:Con 2 Vn, Op. 63; Saint-Saëns:Havanaise, Op. 83; Intro & Rondo capriccioso, Op. 28 RCAV (Gold Seal) 2-▲ 61735 [ADD] (21.97)

L. Josefowicz (vn), N. Marriner (cnd), Academy of St. Martin in the Fields ("Bohemian Rhapsodies") † Fant on Carmen, Op. 25; E. Chausson:Poème Vn, Op. 25; Massenet:Méditation from Thaïs; M. Ravel:Tzigane; Saint-Saëns:Intro & Rondo capriccioso, Op. 28; Wieniawski:Polonaise 1, Op. 4 PPHI ▲ 454440 (16.97)

L. Kogan (vn), V. Vasiligv (cnd), USSR SO ("Leonid Kogan in Concert") † G. Gershwin:Pno Music; Songs; M. Ravel:Tzigane; Saint-Saëns:Havanaise, Op. 83; M. Vainberg:Con Vn; F. Waxman:Carmen Fant ONEL ▲ 50500 [ADD] (7.97)

I. Perlman (vn), A. Previn (cnd), Pittsburgh SO † Fant on Carmen, Op. 25; M. de Falla:Suite populaire espagnole EMIC ▲ 63533 (11.97)

R. Ricci (vn), E. Ansermet (cnd), Swiss Romande Orch † Fant on Carmen, Op. 25; Lalo:Sym espagnole, Op. 21; Saint-Saëns:Havanaise, Op. 83; Intro & Rondo capriccioso, Op. 28 PLON (The Classic Sound) ▲ 452309 (11.97)

A. Rosand (vn), R. Reinhardt (cnd), Southwest German RSO Baden-Baden ("Aaron Rosand Plays Sarasate") † Capriccio Basque, Op. 24; Danzas Españolas; Fant on Carmen, Op. 25; Navarra, Op. 33 ALLO ▲ 8160 [ADD] (3.97)

G. Shaham (vn), L. Foster (cnd), London SO † Wieniawski:Con 1 Vn, Op. 14; Con 2 Vn, Op. 22; Légende Vn, Op. 17 DEUT ▲ 31815 [DDD] (16.97)

I. Stern (vn) *(rec 1945-46)* † Beethoven:Son 7 Vn; Bizet:Carmen Fantasie; Rimsky-Korsakov:Tale of Tsar Saltan (orch sels); R. Wagner:Fant on *Tristan und Isolde*; Wieniawski:Con 2 Vn, Op. 22 ENT (Strings) ▲ 99387 (14.97)

SARDINHA, ANNIBAL AUGUSTO (GAROTO) (1915-1955)

Chôro triste for Flute & Guitar

P. Rudolph (gtr), H. C. Porto (fl) *(rec Belgium, May-June 1995)* ("Music of Latin America") † Everts:Agua con Gas; Falú:Chôro; C. Machado:Brazilian Folk Themes; A. Piazzolla:Etudes tanguistiques; Histoire du tango; R. Riera:Prélude Créole; Senanes:Don Mondongo RENE ▲ 87128 [DDD] (16.97)

SARGON, SIMON (1938-

Ash un Flamen (5 songs) for High Voice & Piano [text Yiddish poems of the Holocaust]

C. Klein (sop), S. Sargon (pno) *(rec Dallas, TX)* ("A Clear Midnight") † Bitter for Sweet; Clear Midnight; Waves of the Sea GAS ▲ 333 [DDD] (16.97)

Bitter for Sweet for Low Voice & Piano [texts C. Rossetti]

E. Halfvarson (bass), S. Sargon (pno) *(rec Dallas, TX)* ("A Clear Midnight") † Ash un Flamen; Clear Midnight; Waves of the Sea GAS ▲ 333 [DDD] (16.97)

A Clear Midnight for Baritone, Horn & Piano [texts W. Whitman]

D. R. Albert (b-bar), G. Hustis (hn), S. Sargon (pno) *(rec Dallas, TX)* ("A Clear Midnight") † Ash un Flamen; Bitter for Sweet; Waves of the Sea GAS ▲ 333 [DDD] (16.97)

Deep Ellum Nights (3 sketches) for Clarinet & Piano (1991)

J. Cohler (cl), J. Gordon (pno) *(rec May 29-30, 1992)* ("Cohler on Clarinet") † Bärmann:Qnt 3 Cl & Str Qt, Op. 23; J. Brahms:Son 1 Cl; C. M. von Weber:Grand Duo Concertant, J.204 ONGA ▲ 101 [DDD] (16.97)

Music of Sargon

L. Deis (sop), S. Dubov (ten), V. Demirev (vn), C. Adkins (vc), D. Baron (fl), S. Girko (cl), S. Sargon (pno)—Shemà [Hear] for Sop, Fl, Cl, Vc & Pno; Before the Ark for Vn & Pno; Wedding Dance for Vn & Pno; Klezmuzik for Cl & Pno; At Grandmother's Knee [5 Yiddish Folk Songs] for T; Meditation for Vc & Pno; At Grandfather's Knee [5 Judeo-Spanish Folk Songs] *(rec SMU Dallas, TX, Jan 1996)* ("Shemà") GAS ▲ 318 (16.97)

SCHUBERT, FRANZ (cont.)

Songs (miscellaneous collections) (cont.)

L. Gien (bar), A. Kontarsky (pno)—Schwanengesang, D.957 [Liebesbotschaft; Frühlingssehnsucht]; Auf der Donau, D.553; Der Wanderer an den Mond, D.870; Das Zügenglöcklein, D.871; Wie Ulfru fischt, D.525; Fischerweise, D.881b; Der Schiffer, D.536; Am Fenster, D.878; Des Fräuleins, D.698; Die Sterne, D.939; Der Einsame, D.800b; Der Geistertanz III, D.116; Gruppe aus dem Tartarus, D.583; Heliopolis II, D.754; Totengräbers Heimweh, D.842; Des Sängers Habe, D.832 ("Wenn Sie am Ufer in Träume versenkt") OTT ▲ 19861 [DDD] (16.97)

M. Groop (mez), R. Jansen (pno)—Fischerweise, D.881; Seligkeit, D.433; Lied der Mignon; Die Forelle, D.550; Romanz aus Rosamunde; Lachen und Weinen, D.777; Auf dem Wasser zu singen, D.774; Schäfers Klagelied, D.121; Pax Vobiscum; Vier Refrainlieder, D.866 [Die Männer sind méchant]; An die Musik, D.547; An Silvia, D.891; Du bist die Ruh; Ganymed, D.544; Wiegenlied, D.304; Der Musensohn, D.764; Ständchen, D.957/4 † Ave Maria, Op. 52/6; Meeres Stille, D.216 ODE ▲ 886 (17.97)

E. Grümmer (sop), G. Moore (pno)—Suleika II, D.717; Auf dem Wasser zu singen, D.774; Wiegenlied, D.304; Rastlose Liebe; Vor meiner Wiege, D.927; Die Forelle, D.550; Fischerweise, D.881 † J. Brahms:Songs; Songs (5), Op. 49; E. Grieg:Peer Gynt (sels); Verdi:Arias; Otello (sels) TES ▲ 1086 (17.97)

H. Hinz (sop), H. Metz (pno)—An die Musik, D.547; An die Nachtigall, D.196; An Silvia, D.891; Fischerweise, D.881; Die Forelle, D.550; Frühlingsglaube; Ganymed, D.544; Im Frühling, D.882; Heidenröslein, D.257; Lachen und Weinen, D.777; Wiegenlied, D.304 † W. A. Mozart:Songs KPT ▲ 32052 [DDD]

W. Holzmair (bar), I. Cooper (pno)—Widerspruch, D.865a; Der Wanderer an den Mond, D.870; Sehnsucht; Vier Refrainliederck, D.866 [Irdisches Glück]; Lebensmut, D.883; Herbst, D.945 *(rec Vienna Konzerthaus, Austria, Jan 10-12, 1994)* † Schwanengesang, D.957 PPHI ▲ 42460 (16.97)

W. Holzmair (bar), G. Wyss (pno)—Die Forelle, D.550 † Intro & Vars on "Tröckne Blumen", D.802; Qnt Pno, D.667; Schöne Müllerin, D.795 TUD ▲ 778 (12.97)

V. Horowitz (pno)—Geistes-Gruss, D.142a; Geistes-Gruss, D.142b *(rec New York, NY, Jan 10-24, 1973)* ("The Complete Masterworks Recordings, Vol. VIII: The Romantic & Impressionist Era") † Impromptus (8) Pno, D.899 & 935; Debussy:Etudes (12) Pno; Preludes Pno; Liszt:Consolations (6), S.172; Scherzo & March, S.177; Mendelssohn (-Bartholdy):Etudes (3) Pno, Op. 104b SNYC ▲ 53471 (16.97)

H. Hotter (b-bar), M. Raucheisen (pno)—Der Wanderer; Wandrers Nachtlied I, D.224; Gesänge des Hafners; Geheimes, D.719; An die Musik, D.547; Pilgerweise; Atys; Abschied, D.578; Orest auf Turis, D.548; Liedesend; Alinde, D.904; Die Liebe hat gelogen, D.751; Greisengesang, D.778; Das Zügenglöcklein, D.871 *(rec 1944)* ("16 Lieder") † Meeres Stille, D.216 GRM2 ▲ 78690 (13.97)

H. Hotter (b-bar), M. Raucheisen (pno) *(rec 1942-44)* † Winterreise, D.911 VOCA (Vocal Archives) 2-▲ 1166 (26.97)

G. Janowitz (sop), I. Gage (pno)—The Shepherd on the Rock DEUT 2-▲ 453082 (17.97)

H. Jerke (ten), H. Bertram (b-bar), C. Keymer (pno), Detmold Hornists, Berlin Carl Maria von Weber Vocal Ensemble—Das Dörfchen; Unendliche Freude; Die Nachtigall; Mailied; 5 Deutsche Tänze; Trinklied; Dessen Fahne Donnerstürme wallte, D.58; Der Gondelfahrer II, D.809; Nächtliches Ständchen; Geist der Liebe, D.233; Winterreise, D.911, (Op. 89) [Das Wirtshaus; Der Lindenbaum]; Nachthelle, D.892; Nachtgesang im Walde, D.913; Grab und Mond, D.93; Ruhe, schönstes Glück der Erde *(rec Martin Luther Church Gütersloh, Mar 18-21, 1996)* ("Der Lindenbaum") MDG (Scene) ▲ 6160679 [DDD] (17.97)

S. Koch (mez), S. Raynaud (pno)—Ganymed, D.544; Suleika I, D.720; Geheimes, D.719; Suleika II, D.717; Der König in Thule, D.367; Gretchen am Spinnrade, D.118; Rastlose Liebe, D.138; Nur wer die Sehnsucht kennt; Heiss mich nicht reden; So lasst mich scheinen; Kennst du das Land; Heidenröslein, D.257; Der Musensohn, D.764 ("Goethe-Lieder") † H. Wolf:Gedichte von Goethe LCDM ▲ 2781111 (18.97)

E. van Lier (sop), R. Holl (bass), D. Lutz (pno)—Licht und Liebe, D.352; Abendröte, D.690; Die Berge, D.634; Die Vögel; Der Knabe, D.692; Der Fluss, D.693; Die Rose; Der Schmetterling, D.633; Der Wanderer; Das Mädchen; Die Sterne; Die Gebüsche, D.646; Gesäng us Wilhelm Meister, D.877 [Mignon und der Harfner]; Wer sich der Einsamkeit ergibt; Harfenspieler III, D.480; An die Türen will ich schleichen; Kennst du das Land; Nur wer die Sehnsucht kennt; Heiss mich nicht reden; So lasst mich scheinen; Gesänge des Harfners, D.478-480 *(rec Casino Baumgarten, Dec 1996)* PRE ▲ 93406 [DDD] (16.97)

F. Lott (sop), G. Johnson (pno)—Die Forelle, D.550; An Silvia, D.891; Heidenröslein, D.257; Du bist die Ruh, D.776; Der Musensohn, D.764; An die Musik, D.547; Auf dem Wasser zu singen, D.774; Sei mir gegrüsst, D.741; Am Tage aller Seelen, D.343; Die junge Nonne, D.828; Im Frühling, D.882; Gretchen am Spinnrade, D.118; Nacht und Träume, D.827; Ganymed, D.544; Lied der Mignon; Seligkeit, D.433 ("Felicity Lott Sings Schubert") † Ave Maria, Op. 52/6 INMP ▲ 2016 (9.97)

F. Lott (sop), A. Murray (mez), A. Rolfe Johnson (ten), R. Jackson (bar), G. Johnson (pno)—Die junge Nonne, D.828; Der zürnenden Diana, D.707; Vom Mitleiden Mariä, D.632; Lachen und Weinen, D.777; Selige Welt, D.743; Gesäng us Wilhelm Meister, D.877 [Mignon und der Harfner]; Auflösung, D.807; Lebensmut, D.883; Willkommen und Abschied, D.767a; An die Laute, D.905; Wiegenlied, D.867; Ellens Gesang II, D.838; Nacht und Träume, D.827; Licht und Liebe, D.352; Ständchen, D.889; Der Tod und das Mädchen, D.531; Abschied, D.829; Fischerweise, D.881; Das Lied im Grünen, D.917; Der Schiffer, D.694; Nähe des Geliebten, D.162; Frühlingsglaube, D.686; Wandrers Nachtlied I, D.224; Im Frühling, D.882; Wehmuth, D.772; Auf der Bruck, D.853; An mein Klavier, D.342; Zum Punsche, D.492; Geheimnis, D.491; Viola, D.786; Der Hochzeitsbraten, D.930 *(rec London, England, Nov 22-31, 1989)* HYP (Dyad) 2-▲ 22010 [AAD] (18.97)

K. McMillan (bar), P. Stewart (pno)—Schöne Müllerin, D.795, (Op. 25) [Morgengruss; Das Wandern; Wohin?]; Schwanengesang, D.957 [Ständchen]; An die Musik, D.547; Die Forelle, D.550; Erlkönig, D.328 *(rec Église de la Visitation Montreal, Canada, Oct 26-29, 1992)* ("An die Musik") † Music of Schubert CBC (Musica Viva) ▲ 1106 [DDD] (16.97)

M. Maisky (vc), D. Hovora (pno)—Schöne Müllerin, D.795, (Op. 25) [Der Neugierige; Der Müller und der Bach]; Gesäng us Wilhelm Meister, D.877 [Lied der Mignon VI]; Winterreise, D.911, (Op. 89) [Täuschung; Der Leiermann]; Nacht und Träume, D.827; Schwanengesang, D.957 [Am Meer; Ständchen]; An die Musik, D.547; Die Forelle, D.550; Der Einsame, D.800; Heidenröslein, D.257; Am Tage aller Seelen, D.343; Du bist die Ruh, D.776 *(rec Rittersaal Rapperswil Palace, Germany, Jan 1996)* † Son Arpeggione, D.821 DEUT ▲ 49817 [DDD] (16.97)

H. Mammel (ten), L. Holtmeier (pno) [Goethe lieder] ("Goethe Lieder") † Zelter:Songs ARSM 2-▲ 1246 (34.97)

S. Mentzer (mez), S. Isbin (gtr)—Ständchen, D.889; Heidenröslein, D.257; Nachtstück, D.672 † E. Granados:Spanish Dance 5; P. Lansky:Wayfaring Stranger; J. P. A. Martini:Plaisir d'Amour; J. J. Niles:Black is the color; Go 'way from my window; J. Rodrigo:Aranjuez ma penses; Tárrega:Capricho árabe ERAT ▲ 23419 (16.97)

M. Mödl (sop), R. von Zustrow (pno) ("Liederabende, Vol. 1") † R. Wagner:Wesendonck Songs; H. Wolf:Songs (misc) GEBH ▲ 1 (17.97)

K. Moll (bass), C. Garben (cnd), Hanover Radio PO—Gruppe aus dem Tartarus, D.583; Im Abendrot, D.799; Heliopolis I, D.753; Der Tod und das Mädchen, D.531 ("Portrait, Vol. 1") † R. Strauss:Songs; H. Wolf:Gedichte von Michelangelo CANT ▲ 1071 (17.97)

M. Müller-Brachmann (b-bar), M. Martineau (pno) HAM ▲ 911648 (12.97)

M. Müller (sop), M. Raucheisen (pno)—Suleika I, D.720; Lied der Mignon I; Lied der Mignon III *(rec 1943)* † J. Brahms:Songs (6), Op. 86; Zigeunerlieder, Op. 103; G. Puccini:Bohème (sels); M. Reger:Schlichte Weisen, Op. 76; R. Wagner:Fliegende Holländer (sels); Lohengrin (sels); Tannhäuser (sels); Walküre (sels); Wesendonck Songs; C. M. von Weber:Freischütz (sels) PRE 2-▲ 89235 (m) (31.97)

A. S. von Otter (mez), B. Forsberg (pno)—Abendstern, D.806; An Silvia, D.891; Vier Refrainlieder, D.866 [Bei dir allein]; Dass sie hier gewesen, D.775; Ellens Gesang III, D.839; Erntelied, D.434; Geheimes, D.719; Heidenröslein, D.257; Im Abendrot, D.799; Im Frühling, D.882; Der Jüngling an der Quelle, D.300; Ständchen, D.920; Suleika I, D.720; Totengräbers Heimweh, D.842; Viola, D.786; Der Wanderer an den Mond, D.870; Wonne der Wehmut, D.260; Waldesnacht, D.708 *(rec Kungl. Musialiska Akademien Stockholm; Concert Hal, May & June 1996)* DEUT ▲ 453481 (16.97)

I. Partridge (ten), J. Partridge (pno)—An Silvia, D.891; Auflösung, D.807; Fischerweise, D.881; Der Wanderer an den Mond, D.870; Wandrers Nachtlied II, D.768; Die Forelle, D.550; An die Laute, D.905; Der Einsame, D.800; Der Schiffer, D.536; An die Musik, D.547 † Schwanengesang, D.957 ASVQ ▲ 6171 (10.97)

J. Patzak (ten), M. Raucheisen (pno)—Auf der Bruck, D.853; Drang in die Ferne, D.770; Über Wildemann, D.884; Stimme der Liebe, D.412; Als ich sie erröten sah, D.153; An die Apfelbäume, wo ich Julien erblickte, D.197; Im Walde, D.834; Schäfers Klagelied, D.121; Willkommen und Abschied, D.767; Vier Refrainlieder, D.866; Abschied, D.578; Vier Canzonen, D.688 *(rec 1943-44)* † J. Brahms:Songs; W. A. Mozart:Songs; R. Strauss:Songs; H. Wolf:Songs (misc colls) PRE ▲ 90347 (m) (16.97)

R. Porroni (gtr)—Ständchen, D.957/4; Lob der Tränen, D.711 *(rec Feb 1992)* ("The 19th Century Guitar") † Mertz:Gtr Music; Sor:Fant Gtr, Op. 59 STRV ▲ 23 (16.97)

C. Prégardien (ten), T. Hoppstock (gtr) ("Lieder on Love & Death") † J. Brahms:Songs; L. Spohr:Songs SIGM ▲ 9500 (17.97)

M. Price (sop), G. Johnson (pno)—An die Laute, D.905; Im Frühling, D.882; Lachen und Weinen, D.777; Nacht und Träume, D.827; Frühlingsglaube, D.686b; An die Musik, D.547; Seligkeit, D.433; Fischerweise, D.881; An Silvia, D.891; Der Tod und das Mädchen, D.531; Am Tage aller Seelen, D.343; Die Allmacht, D.852; Gesäng us Wilhelm Meister, D.877 [Lied der Mignon VI]; Rastlose Liebe, D.138; Ganymed, D.544; Wandrers Nachtlied II, D.768; Der Musensohn, D.764; Suleika I, D.720; Suleika II, D.717; Erlkönig, D.328 ("21 Famous Lieder") † Meeres Stille, D.216 FORL ▲ 16698 (16.97)

SCHUBERT, FRANZ (cont.)

Songs (miscellaneous collections) (cont.)

H. Rehfuss (bar), F. Martin (pno)—Frühlingsglaube; Winterreise, D.911, (Op. 89); Der Wanderer; Der Wanderer an den Mond, D.870; An die Laute, D.905; Schwanengesang, D.957 [Der Doppelgänger] † Schoenberg:Verklärte Nacht, Op. 4; R. Strauss:Metamorphosen; Webern:Movts (5) Str Qt, Op. 5; Slow Movt Str Qt CLAV ▲ 9412 [ADD/DDD] (16.97)

H. Rehkemper (bar), M. Gurlitt (pno)—Das Rosenband, D.280; Erlkönig, D.328; Am Bach im Frühlinge, D.361; Lied des Orpheus, D.474; Sei mir gegrüsst, D.741; Der Musensohn, D.764; Auf dem Wasser zu singen, D.774 *(rec 1924-28)* † Schwanengesang, D.957; Winterreise, D.911 PRE (Lebendige Vergangenheit) ▲ 89058 [AAD] (16.97)

C. Robbin (mez), M. McMahon (pno)—Der Fischer, D.225; Der König † J. Brahms:Songs MARQ ▲ 113 (16.97)

L. Russell (sop), D. Campbell (cl), P. Hill (pno)—Ganymed, D.544; Liebhaber in allen Gestalten, D.558; Nacht und Träume, D.827; Geheimes, D.719; Abendstern, D.806; Der Hirt auf dem Felsen, D.965; Suleika I, D.720; Seligkeit, D.433; Wiegenlied, D.498; Gretchen am Spinnrade, D.118; An die Entfernte, D.765; Im Frühling, D.882; Suleika II, D.717; Du bist die Ruh, D.776; Gesäng us Wilhelm Meister, D.877 [Lied der Mignon VI]; Nachtviolen, D.752; Der Musensohn, D.764; Die Forelle, D.550 *(rec East Woodhay Hampshire, England, England, Nov 7-9, 1994)* NXIN ▲ 553113 [DDD] (5.97)

C. Schäfer (sop), I. Gage (pno)—Im Frühling, D.882; Die Blumensprache, D.519; An den Mond; Der Knabe, D.692; Im Abendrot, D.799; Glaube; Hoffnung, D.251; Liebe; Das Mädchen; Die Rose; Die junge Nonne, D.828; Der Fluss, D.693; Nacht und Träume, D.827 ORF ▲ 450971 (18.97)

H. Schlusnus (bar), M. Raucheisen (pno) *(Der Musensohn, D.764; Sei mir gegrüsst, D.741)*, H. Schlusnus (bar), F. Rupp (pno) *(Ständchen, Op. 135) (rec 1919-27)* † Beethoven:Adelaide, Op. 46; J. Brahms:Songs (6), Op. 86; Songs (9), Op. 32; R. Schumann:Dichterliebe, Op. 48; R. Strauss:Songs; H. Wolf:Songs (misc) PRE (Lebendige Vergangenheit) ▲ 89188 (m) (16.97)

H. Schlusnus (bar), F. Rupp (pno), S. Peschko (pno)—Erlkönig, D.328; Wandrers Nachtlied I, D.224; Wandrers Nachtlied II, D.768; Im Frühling, D.882; Schöne Müllerin, D.795, (Op. 25) [Der Neugierige]; Winterreise, D.911, (Op. 89) [Der Lindenbaum; Frühlingstraum]; Schwanengesang, D.957 [Liebesbotschaft; Kriegers Ahnung; Ständchen; Der Doppelgänger; Die Taubenpost]; Lied des Harfners II; An die Leier, D.737; Der Jüngling an der Quelle, D.300; Am See, D.746; Der Wanderer, D.489; Nachtstück, D.672; Der Blumenbrief, D.622; Die Forelle, D.550; An die Musik, D.547; Alinde, D.904 *(rec 1927-43)* ("Schlusnus: Schubert Lieder") NIMB (Prima Voce) ▲ 7883 [ADD] (11.97)

E. Schumann (sop)—Die Forelle, D.550; An die Musik, D.547; Gretchen am Spinnrade, D.118; Nacht und Träume, D.827; Schwanengesang, D.957 [Liebesbotschaft]; Seligkeit, D.433; Winterreise, D.911, (Op. 89) [Frühlingstraum]; An die Geliebte, D.303; Der Schmetterling, D.633; Schöne Müllerin, D.795, (Op. 25); Die Jüngling und der Tod *(rec 1933-45)* ("26 Lieder") † Ave Maria, Op. 52/6 GRM2 ▲ 78679 (13.97)

E. Schumann (sop), G. Moore (pno), L. Rosenek (pno), E. Coleman (pno), G. Reeves (pno)—Die Forelle, D.550; An die Musik, D.547; Gretchen am Spinnrade, D.118; Nacht und Träume, D.827; Schwanengesang, D.957 [Liebesbotschaft]; Seligkeit, D.433; An die Geliebte, D.303 *(rec 1933-45)* ("The Most Famous Lieder") † Ave Maria, Op. 52/6 VOCA (Vocal Archives) ▲ 1170 (13.97)

E. Schumann (sop), L. Rosenek (pno), E. Coleman (pno)—An die Nachtigall, D.497; Die Forelle, D.550; An die Musik, D.547; Auf dem Wasser zu singen, D.774; Des Fischers Liebesglück, D.933; Der Musensohn, D.764; Fischerweise, D.881; Gretchen am Spinnrade, D.118; Schwanengesang, D.957 [Liebesbotschaft]; Nacht und Träume, D.827; Seligkeit, D.433; Nähe des Geliebten, D.162; Lachen und Weinen, D.777; Winterreise, D.911, (Op. 89) [Frühlingstraum]; Der Einsame, D.800; Nachtviolen, D.752; An die Geliebte, D.303; Wiegenlied, D.498; Der Schmetterling, D.633; Schöne Müllerin, D.795, (Op. 25) [Des Baches Wiegenlied]; Der Jüngling und der Tod, D.545; Das Heimweh, D.456; Dass sie hier gewesen, D.775; Romanze zum Drama Rosamunde, D.797; Die junge Nonne, D.828 *(rec 1933-45)* † Ave Maria, Op. 52/6 MNER ▲ 22 [ADD] (15.97)

E. Schwarzkopf (sop) *(rec London, 1968)* ("Recital in Honour of Ernest Newman") † R. Strauss:Songs; H. Wolf:Songs (misc) EKRP ▲ 4 (17.97)

E. Schwarzkopf (sop), G. Parsons (pno)—Der Einsame, D.800; An Silvia, D.891; Romanz aus Rosamunde; Seligkeit, D.433 † W. A. Mozart:Songs; R. Schumann:Gesänge, Op. 31; Myrthen, Op. 25; H. Wolf:Songs (misc); E. Wolf-Ferrari:Preghiera AURC ▲ 123 (5.97)

Singphoniker—Trinklied, D.75; Trinklied, D.148; Trinklied, D.267; Punschlied, D.277; Trinklied, D.356; Beitrag zur fünfzig, D.407; Naturgenuss, D.422; Lachen und Weinen, D.777; Das Dörfchen, D.598; Die Nachtigall, D.724; Frühlingsgesang II, D.740; Geist der Liebe II, D.747; Der Gondelfahrer II, D.809; Bootsgesang, D.835; Widerspruch, D.865a; Mondenschein, D.875; Nachthelle, D.892; Zur guten Nacht, D.903; Im Gegenwärtigen Vergangenes, D.710; Das Leben, D.269a *(rec Nov 1995)* ("Complete Part Songs for Male Voices, Vol. 1") CPO ▲ 999397 [DDD] (14.97)

M. Stader (sop), W. Kapell (pno) *(rec 1940-53)* † Beethoven:Con 2 Pno, Op. 19; Chopin:Polonaises Pno; Preludes (24) Pno, Op. 28; S. Rachmaninoff:Rhap on a Theme of Paganini, Op. 43 PHS ▲ 9194 (17.97)

T. Takács (mez), J. Jandó (pno)—An die Musik, D.547; Heidenröslein, D.257; Die Forelle, D.550; Auf dem Wasser zu singen, D.774; Du bist die Ruh; Im Frühling, D.882; Wandrers; Nacht und Träume, D.827; Der Zwerg, D.771; Gretchen am Spinnrade, D.118; Die junge Nonne, D.828; Lied der Mignon I; Lied der Mignon II; Lied der Mignon III; Suleika I, D.720; Suleika II, D.717; Der Tod und das Mädchen, D.531; Erlkönig, D.328 *(rec Oct 8-11, 1991)* NXIN ▲ 550476 [DDD] (5.97)

B. Terfel (b-bar), M. Martineau (pno)—Gruppe aus dem Tartarus, D.583; Litenei, D.343; Die Forelle, D.550; An die Leier, D.737; Lachen und Weinen, D.777; Ständchen, D.889; Schwanengesang, D.957 [Das Fischermädchen]; Die Taubenpost, D.965a; Der Wanderer an den Mond, D.870; Erlkönig, D.328; Der Tod und das Mädchen, D.531; Heidenröslein, D.257; Wandrers Nachtlied II, D.768; An die Musik, D.547; Auf der Bruck, D.853; Schäfers Klagelied, D.121; An Silvia, D.891; Du bist die Ruh, D.776; An die Laute, D.905; Rastlose Liebe, D.138; Ganymed, D.544; Der Musensohn, D.764 † Meeres Stille, D.216 DEUT ▲ 45294 [DDD] (16.97)

E. Thallaug (alt), L. Negro (pno) *(An die Musik, D.547)*, M. Schéle (sop), G. Winbergh (ten), E. Hagegard (bass), L. Negro (pno) *(Der Hochzeitsbraten, D.930) (rec Nacka Aula, Sweden, 1976)* ("From Solo to Quartet") † J. Brahms:Duets (4), Op. 28; Mendelssohn (-Bartholdy):Vars sérieuses, Op. 54; R. Schumann:Songs (misc colls); Spanisches Liederspiel, Op. 74 BIS ▲ 77 [AAD] (17.97)

D. Upshaw (sop), R. Goode (pno)—Ganymed, D.544; Versunken, D.715; Gesäng us Wilhelm Meister, D.877; Gretchen am Spinnrade, D.118; Wandrers Nachtlied II, D.768; Suleika I, D.720; An den Mond, D.296; Rastlose Liebe, D.138 ("Goethe Lieder") † R. Schumann:Songs; H. Wolf:Gedichte von Goethe NON ▲ 79317 (16.97)

E. Wiens (sop), R. Jansen (pno) *(An die Musik, D.547; An Silvia, D.891; Ariette der Claudine; Auf dem Wasser zu singen, D.774; Der Einsame, D.800; Fischerweise, D.881; Frühlingsglaube; Heidenröslein, D.257; Die junge Nonne, D.828; Der Jüngling an der Quelle, D.300; Lachen und Weinen, D.777; Liebhaber in allen Gestalten, D.558; Das Lied im Grünen, D.917; Die Mutter Erde, D.788; Nacht und Träume, D.827; Seligkeit, D.433)*, E. Wiens (sop), R. Jansen (pno), J. Valdepeñas (cl) *(Verschworenen (sels) [Romanze])*, E. Wiens (sop), J. Valdepeñas (cl), R. Jansen (pno), J. Valdepeñas (cl) *(Der Hirt auf dem Felsen, D.965)* † Der Hirt auf dem Felsen, D.965 MUVI (Musica Viva) ▲ 1053 [DDD] (16.97)

F. Wunderlich (ten), H. Giesen (pno)—Die Forelle, D.550; Frühlingsglaube, D.686; Heidenröslein, D.257 *(rec Hochschule for Music Munich, Germany, Nov 1965)* † Schöne Müllerin, D.795 DEUT (The Originals) ▲ 47452 [ADD] (11.97)

F. Wunderlich (ten), H. Giesen (pno)—Der Einsame, D.800; Nachtstück, D.672; An die Laute, D.905; Lied eines Schiffers an die Dioskuren, D.360; An Silvia, D.891; Der Musensohn, D.764; Frühlingsglaube, Op. 20/2; An die Musik, D.547 *(rec Mar 24, 1966)* † Beethoven:Songs; R. Schumann:Dichterliebe, Op. 48 MYTO ▲ 93278 (17.97)

F. Wunderlich (ten), H. Giesen (pno)—Der Einsame, D.800; Nachtstück, D.672; An die Laute, D.905; Lied eines Schiffers an die Dioskuren, D.360; An Silvia, D.891; Der Musensohn, D.764; Im Abendrot, D.799; Schöne Müllerin, D.795, (Op. 25) [Ungeduld] *(rec Salzburg, Aug 19, 1965)* † Beethoven:Songs; R. Schumann:Dichterliebe, Op. 48 ORFE (Festspiel Dokumente) ▲ 432961 [ADD] (16.97)

F. Wunderlich (ten), H. Giesen (pno)—An Silvia, D.891; Lied eines Schiffers an die Dioskuren, D.360; Liebhaber in allen Gestalten, D.558; Der Einsame, D.800; Im Abendrot, D.799; Schwanengesang, D.957 [Ständchen]; An die Laute, D.905; Der Musensohn, D.764; An die Musik, D.547 † Beethoven:Songs; R. Schumann:Dichterliebe, Op. 48 DEUT (The Originals) ▲ 449747 [ADD] (11.97)

E. Höngen (cta), artist unknown—Gretchen am Spinnrade, D.118; Auf dem Wasser zu singen, D.774 *(rec Apr 1946 live)* † J. Brahms:Liebeslieder Waltzes Pno 4-Hands, Op. 52a; B. Marcello:Mio bel foco; R. Schumann:Gesänge, Op. 31; Liederkreis, Op. 39; Myrthen, Op. 25; R. Wagner:Wesendonck Songs; H. Wolf:Gedichte von Goethe; Gedichte von Mörike PRE ▲ 90356 (m) (16.97)

Stabat mater (oratorio) in F/f for solo Voices, Orchestra & Chorus, D.383 (1816)

M. Hajossyova (sop), E. Büchner (ten), H. C. Polster (bass), H. Kegel (cnd), Leipzig Radio Orch, Leipzig Radio Chorus † Mass 2, D.167 BER ▲ 9341 (10.97)

G. Zeumer (sop), D. Ellenbeck (ten), E. G. Schramm (bass), R. Bader (cnd), Berlin RSO, Berlin Radio Chorus † C. M. von Weber:Gloria et honore, J.226; In die solemnitatis, J.250 KSCH ▲ 313055 [ADD] (16.97)

Stabat mater in g for solo Voices, Orchestra & Organ, D.175 (1815)

J. E. Gardiner (cnd), Orch Révolutionnaire et Romantique, Monteverdi Choir † Hymnus an den Heiligen Geist, D.948; Mass 5, D.678; Psalm 92 PPHI ▲ 456578 (16.97)

G. D. Reyghere (sop), L. Maertens (mez), T. Spence (ten), J. Van der Crabben (bar), P. Peire (cnd) † Mass 2, D.167; Mass 3, D.324; Salve regina, D.676 RENE ▲ 87140 [DDD] (16.97)

P. Schreier (cnd), Tapiola Sinfonietta, P. Schreier (cnd), Peter Schreier Choir, S. Isokoski (sop), M. Groop (mez), M. Ullman (ten), J. Kotilainen (bass) † Mass 5, D.678; Salve Regina, D.106 ODE ▲ 917 (17.97)

SCHUBERT, FRANZ (cont.)

Die Sterne (song) for Voice & Piano [text Leitner], D.939 (1828)

P. Pears (ten), B. Britten (pno) *(rec Aldeburgh Festival, European Community, 1958-59)* † G. Fauré:Bonne chanson, Op. 61; H. Purcell:Music of Purcell; R. Schumann:Liederkreis, Op. 39 — BBC ▲ 8006 (17.97)

Symphonies (Nos. 1-6, 8 & 9) (complete)

C. Abbado (cnd), CO of Europe † Rosamunde (sels); Son Pno 4-Hands, D.812 — DEUT 5-▲ 23651 [DDD] (80.97)
K. Böhm (cnd), Berlin PO — DGRM 4-▲ 419318 [ADD]
N. Harnoncourt (cnd), (Royal) Concertgebouw Orch ("The Symphonies") — TELC 4-▲ 91184 (67.97)
M. Viotti (cnd), Saarbrücken RSO *(rec 1992-96)* ("Complete Symphonic Works") † Ovs — CLAV 5-▲ 9700 [DDD] (48.97)

Symphony No. 1 in D, D.82 (1813)

H. Blomstedt (cnd), Dresden Staatskapelle † Sym 2 — BER ▲ 9263 (10.97)
R. Freisitzer (cnd), Moscow Orch *(rec GDRZ Moscow, Feb 14-18, 1995)* † Sym 4 — RD ▲ 30001 [DDD] (16.97)
C. Groves (cnd), English Sinfonia † Ovs; Sym 5 — ICC ▲ 6701272 (9.97)
M. Halász (cnd), Failoni Orch *(rec Italian Institute Budapest, Mar 1994)* † Sym 2 — NXIN ▲ 553093 [DDD] (5.97)
Y. Menuhin (cnd), Menuhin Festival Orch *(rec 1966-68)* † Sym 2; Sym 3; Sym 4; Sym 5; Sym 6 — EMIC 2-▲ 73359 [ADD] (16.97)
H. Rilling (cnd), Galicia Real PO † Sym 2 — HANS ▲ 98312 [DDD] (15.97)
T. Vásáry (cnd), Budapest SO † Sym 2 — ICC ▲ 6601132 (16.97)

Symphony No. 2 in B♭, D.125 (1814-15)

H. Blomstedt (cnd), Dresden Staatskapelle † Sym 1, D.82 — BER ▲ 9263 (10.97)
V. Fedoseyev (cnd), Tchaikovsky SO of Radio Moscow *(rec 1974)* † Liszt:Orpheus, S.98; R. Strauss:Con 1 Hn, Op. 11; R. Wagner:Ring des Nibelungen (orch sels) — RELE ▲ 991048 [ADD] (18.97)
C. Groves (cnd), English Sinfonia † Sym 6 — INMP ▲ 6701282 [DDD] (9.97)
M. Halász (cnd), Failoni Orch *(rec Italian Institute Budapest, Mar 1994)* † Sym 1, D.82 — NXIN ▲ 553093 [DDD] (5.97)
D. Joeres (cnd), West German Sinfonia † Voříšek:Sym — INMP ▲ 1052 [DDD] (11.97)
P. Maag (cnd), Philharmonia Hungarica ("The Story of Schubert in Words & Music") † Life & Music of Schubert; Mass 5, D.678; Mass 6, D.950; Sym 4; Sym 6; Sym 8; Sym 9 — MMD (Music Masters) ▲ 8504 [ADD] (3.97) ▮ 8504 [ADD] (2.98)
Y. Menuhin (cnd), Menuhin Festival Orch *(rec 1966-68)* † Sym 1, D.82; Sym 3; Sym 4; Sym 5; Sym 6 — EMIC 2-▲ 73359 [ADD] (16.97)
K. Page (cnd), Orch da Camera † Sym 5 — MER ▲ 84362 (16.97)
H. Rilling (cnd), Galicia Real PO † Sym 1, D.82 — HANS ▲ 98312 [DDD] (15.97)
T. Vásáry (cnd), Budapest SO † Sym 1, D.82 — ICC ▲ 6601132 (16.97)

Symphony No. 3 in D, D.200 (1815)

C. Abbado (cnd), CO of Europe † Sym 4 — DEUT ▲ 23653 [DDD] (16.97)
H. Abendroth (cnd), Leipzig Gewandhaus Orch ("Hermann Abendroth:Gewandhaus Kapellmeister 1944-45") † J. S. Bach:Suite 3 Orch, BWV 1068; J. Brahms:Tragic Ov, Op. 81; G. F. Handel:Concerti grossi, Op. 6; J. Haydn:Sym 88; Sym 96; W. A. Mozart:Sym 29, K.201; R. Schumann:Manfred Ov, Op. 115 — TAHA 2-▲ 106 (34.97)
T. Beecham (cnd), Royal PO *(rec Salle Wagram, Paris, France, 1958-59)* † Sym 5; Sym 6 — EMIC (Great Recordings of the Century) ▲ 66999 [ADD] (11.97)
B. Berezovsky (cnd), New York PO † Fant Pno, D.760; Sym 8 — TELC ▲ 17133 (16.97)
C. Groves (cnd), English Sinfonia † Ovs — INMP ▲ 967 [DDD] (11.97)
C. Groves (cnd), English Sinfonia † Ovs; Sym 4 — INMP (IMP Classics) ▲ 6701292 (9.97)
M. Halász (cnd), Failoni Orch *(rec Italian Institute Budapest, Mar 1994)* † Sym 6 — NXIN ▲ 553094 [DDD] (5.97)
N. Järvi (cnd), Stockholm Sinfonietta † Sym 4 — BIS ▲ 453 [DDD] (17.97)
O. Kabasta (cnd), Vienna SO *(rec 1940-43)* † Sym 5; W. A. Mozart:Sym 41, K.551 — PRE ▲ 90303 (16.97)
C. Kleiber (cnd), Vienna PO † Sym 8 — DEUT (The Originals) ▲ 449745 [ADD] (11.97)
J. Kovács (cnd), Budapest PO † Rosamunde (sels); Sym 8 — LALI ▲ 15823 [DDD] (3.97)
I. Markevitch (cnd), Leipzig Gewandhaus Orch † G. Mahler:Sym 1; P. Tchaikovsky:Sym 4 — TAHA (Markevitch Edition) 2-▲ 282 (34.97)
Y. Menuhin (cnd), Menuhin Festival Orch *(rec 1966-68)* † Sym 1, D.82; Sym 2; Sym 4; Sym 5; Sym 6 — EMIC 2-▲ 73359 [ADD] (16.97)
H. Rilling (cnd), Galicia Real PO † Sym 4 — HANS ▲ 98310 [DDD] (15.97)
H. Schiff (cnd), Northern Sinfonia † Sym 5; Sym 8 — CHN ▲ 7126 (13.97)
A. Scholz (cnd), South German PO † Sym 4 — PC ▲ 267139 [DDD] (2.97)
M. Viotti (cnd), Saarbrücken RSO *(rec Kongresshalle Saarbrücken, 1992-96)* † Ovs — CLAV ▲ 9619 [DDD] (16.97)

Symphony No. 4 in c, D.417, "Tragic" (1816)

C. Abbado (cnd), CO of Europe † Sym 3 — DEUT ▲ 23653 [DDD] (16.97)
R. Freisitzer (cnd), Moscow Orch *(rec GDRZ Moscow, Feb 14-18, 1995)* † Sym 1, D.82 — RD ▲ 30001 [DDD] (16.97)
C. M. Giulini (cnd), Bavarian RSO *(rec Munich, Feb 27-28, 1993)* † Sym 8 — SNYC ▲ 66833 [DDD] (16.97)
C. Groves (cnd), English Sinfonia † Ovs; Sym 3 — INMP (IMP Classics) ▲ 6701292 (9.97)
N. Järvi (cnd), Stockholm Sinfonietta † Sym 3 — BIS ▲ 453 [DDD] (17.97)
E. Jochum (cnd), (Royal) Concertgebouw Orch ("Eugen Jochum Conducts") † R. Schumann:Sym 4; R. Strauss:Don Juan, Op. 20; Till Eulenspiegels lustige Streiche, Op. 28 — TAHA 2-▲ 257 (34.97)
P. Maag (cnd), Philharmonia Hungarica ("The Story of Schubert in Words & Music") † Life & Music of Schubert; Mass 5, D.678; Mass 6, D.950; Sym 2; Sym 6; Sym 8; Sym 9 — MMD (Music Masters) ▲ 8504 [ADD] (3.97) ▮ 8504 [ADD] (2.98)
I. Markevitch (cnd), Berlin PO *(rec Jesus-Christus Church Berlin, Germany, Dec 1954)* † Berwald:Sym 3; Sym 4 — DEUT (The Originals) ▲ 457705 [ADD] (11.97)
Y. Menuhin (cnd), Menuhin Festival Orch *(rec 1966-68)* † Sym 1, D.82; Sym 2; Sym 3; Sym 5; Sym 6 — EMIC 2-▲ 73359 [ADD] (16.97)
E. Ormandy (cnd), Philadelphia Orch *(rec 1962)* † Rosamunde (sels); Sym 5 — SNYC (Essential Classics) ▲ 60267 (7.97) ▮ 60267 (3.98)
A. Ostrowsky (cnd), Helsingborg SO † Sym 8 — DI ▲ 920213 [DDD] (5.97)
H. Rilling (cnd), Galicia Real PO † Sym 3 — HANS ▲ 98310 [DDD] (15.97)
A. Scholz (cnd), South German PO † Sym 3 — PC ▲ 267139 [DDD] (2.97)

Symphony No. 5 in B♭, D.485 (1816)

D. Barenboim (cnd), Berlin PO — SNYC ▲ 39671 [DDD] (11.97)
T. Beecham (cnd), London PO *(rec 1938-39)* † C. Franck:Sym in d, M.48 — IN ▲ 1394 (15.97)
T. Beecham (cnd), London PO *(rec 1937-44)* † Sym 6; Sym 8 — DLAB (Essential Archive) ▲ 5020 (15.97)
T. Beecham (cnd), Royal PO *(rec Salle Wagram, Paris, France, 1958-59)* † Sym 3; Sym 6 — EMIC (Great Recordings of the Century) ▲ 66999 [ADD] (11.97)
L. Bernstein (cnd), New York PO † R. Schumann:Con Vc; Genoveva (ov) — SNYC ▲ 47609 (10.97)
K. Böhm (cnd), Vienna PO *(rec Vienna, Austria, Dec 1979)* † Beethoven:Sym 6 — DEUT ▲ 47433 [ADD] (11.97)
J. Brett (cnd) *(rec Henry Wood Hall London, 1990)* † W. A. Mozart:Sym 40, K.550 — HODU ▲ 3 (16.97)
J. Ferencsik (cnd), Hungarian State Orch *(rec 1979)* † Sym 8 — CLDI ▲ 4036 [ADD] (10.97)
R. Gandolfi (cnd), Prague Virtuosi † Mass 2, D.167 — DI ▲ 920166 [DDD] (5.97)
C. Groves (cnd), English Sinfonia † Ovs; Sym 1, D.82 — ICC ▲ 6701272 (9.97)
J. van Immerseel (pno), Anima Eterna Orch, J. van Immerseel (cnd), Royal Consort † Rosamunde; Buxtehude:Cants; Debussy:Images (6) Pno; Preludes Pno; J. Haydn:7 Last Words of Christ on the Cross — CCL 4-▲ 1098 (36.97)
D. Joeres (cnd), West German Sinfonia — INMP ▲ 1046 [DDD] (11.97)
O. Kabasta (cnd), Vienna SO *(rec 1940-43)* † Sym 3; W. A. Mozart:Sym 41, K.551 — PRE ▲ 90303 (16.97)
R. Kempe (cnd), BBC SO *(rec 1974)* † J. Brahms:Sym 4 — BBC ▲ 4003 (17.97)
I. Kertész (cnd), Vienna PO † Sym 9 — PENG ▲ 460634 (11.97)
C. Lindberg (trbn), N. Järvi (cnd), Stockholm Sinfonietta *(rec Sweden)* ("The Solitary Trombone") † Sym 6; L. Berio:Sequenza V; J. Cage:Solo Sliding Trb; A. Eliasson:Disegno Trbn; M. Kagel:Atem; K. Stockhausen:In Freundschaft; In Freundschaft, No. 46; Xenakis:Keren — BIS ▲ 388 [DDD] (17.97)
J. Lubbock (cnd), St. John's Smith Square Orch † J. Haydn:Sym 49 — INMP ▲ 819 [DDD] (11.97)
Y. Menuhin (cnd), Menuhin Festival Orch *(rec 1966-68)* † Sym 1, D.82; Sym 2; Sym 3; Sym 4; Sym 6 — EMIC 2-▲ 73359 [ADD] (16.97)
K. Page (cnd), Orch da Camera † Sym 2 — MER ▲ 84362 (16.97)
F. Reiner (cnd), Chicago SO † J. Brahms:Sym 3 — RCAV (Gold Seal) ▲ 61793 (11.97)
H. Schiff (cnd), Northern Sinfonia † Sym 3; Sym 8 — CHN ▲ 7126 (13.97)
S. Skrowaczewski (cnd), Minneapolis SO † Rosamunde; Sym 8 — MRCR ▲ 462954 (11.97)
C. Spering (cnd), Das Neue Orch † Sym 8 — OPUS ▲ 30192 (18.97)
A. Toscanini (cnd), NBC SO *(rec New York, NY, March 1953)* † Sym 8; Sym 9; Mendelssohn (-Bartholdy):Sym 4; Sym 5 — RCAV ▲ 59480 (16.97)
S. Végh (cnd), Salzburg Mozarteum Camerata Academia † Sym 6; Sym 8; Sym 9 — CAPO (Schubert-Edition) 2-▲ 490654 [DDD] (16.97)

SCHUBERT, FRANZ (cont.)

Symphony No. 5 in B♭, D.485 (1816) (cont.)

B. Walter (cnd), Columbia SO *(rec Hollywood, CA, Feb 26 & 29, Mar 3, 1960)* † Sym 7; Sym 8; Beethoven:Leonore (ov 3) — SNYC (Bruno Walter: The Edition, Vol. 4) ▲ 64487 [ADD] (10.97)
B. Walter (cnd), Columbia SO † Rosamunde (sels); Sym 4 — SNYC (Essential Classics) ▲ 60267 (7.97) ▮ 60267 (3.98)
artists unknown † Sym 8 — SNYC ▲ 64561 (4.97)
artists unknown † German Dances (16) Pno, D.783; Sym 8; Waltzes, D.969 — PC ▲ 265082 [DDD] (2.97)

Symphony No. 6 in C, D.589 (1817-18)

T. Beecham (cnd), London PO ("Beecham & London PO, 1944-45, Vol. 2") † Beethoven:Sym 4; W. A. Mozart:Entführung aus dem Serail (sels) — BCS ▲ 42 (16.97)
T. Beecham (cnd), London PO *(rec 1937-44)* † Sym 5; Sym 8 — DLAB (Essential Archive) ▲ 5020 (15.97)
T. Beecham (cnd), Royal PO *(rec Abbey Road, London, England, 1958-59)* † Sym 3; Sym 5 — EMIC (Great Recordings of the Century) ▲ 66999 [ADD] (11.97)
M. Bernardi (cnd), CBC Vancouver SO — SMS (SM 5000) ▲ 5070 [DDD] (16.97)
C. Groves (cnd), English Sinfonia † Sym 2 — INMP ▲ 6701282 [DDD] (9.97)
M. Halász (cnd), Failoni Orch *(rec Italian Institute Budapest, Mar 1994)* † Sym 3 — NXIN ▲ 553094 [DDD] (5.97)
J. M. Händler (cnd) † Mass 3, D.324 — DI ▲ 920218 [DDD] (5.97)
N. Järvi (cnd), Stockholm Sinfonietta *(rec Sweden)* ("The Solitary Trombone") † Sym 5; L. Berio:Sequenza V; J. Cage:Solo Sliding Trb; A. Eliasson:Disegno Trbn; M. Kagel:Atem; K. Stockhausen:In Freundschaft; In Freundschaft, No. 46; Xenakis:Keren — BIS ▲ 388 [DDD] (17.97)
P. Maag (cnd), Philharmonia Hungarica ("The Story of Schubert in Words & Music") † Life & Music of Schubert; Mass 5, D.678; Mass 6, D.950; Sym 2; Sym 4; Sym 8; Sym 9 — MMD (Music Masters) ▲ 8504 [ADD] (3.97) ▮ 8504 [ADD] (2.98)
Y. Menuhin (cnd), Menuhin Festival Orch *(rec 1966-68)* † Sym 1, D.82; Sym 2; Sym 3; Sym 4; Sym 5 — EMIC 2-▲ 73359 [ADD] (16.97)
R. Norrington (cnd), London Classical Players — EMIA ▲ 54210 (16.97)
H. Scherchen (cnd), Vienna State Opera Orch † Méhul:Sym 1 — FORL ▲ 16588 (16.97)
H. Schmidt-Isserstedt (cnd), London SO *(rec Watford Town Hall outside London, July 1-2, 1958)* † Sym 9 — MRCR ▲ 34354 (11.97)
S. Végh (cnd), Salzburg Mozarteum Camerata Academia † Sym 5; Sym 8; Sym 9 — CAPO (Schubert-Edition) 2-▲ 490654 [DDD] (16.97)
M. Viotti (cnd), Saarbrücken RSO *(rec Kongresshalle Saarbrücken, Dec 1995 & Mar 1996)* ("Complete Symphonic Works, Vol. 5") † Sym 8 — CLAV ▲ 9703 [DDD] (16.97)

Symphony No. 7 in E [realized by Brian Newbould], D.729 (1821)

G. Samuel (cnd), Cincinnati PO *(rec Apr 1992)* — CENT ▲ 2139 [DDD] (16.97)
B. Walter (cnd), New York PO *(rec Brooklyn, NY, Mar 3, 1958)* † Sym 5; Sym 8; Beethoven:Leonore (ov 3) — SNYC (Bruno Walter: The Edition, Vol. 4) ▲ 64487 [ADD] (10.97)

Symphony No. 8 in b, D.759, "Unfinished" (1822)

T. Beecham (cnd), London PO *(rec 1937-44)* † Sym 5; Sym 6 — DLAB (Essential Archive) ▲ 5020 (15.97)
B. Berezovsky (cnd), New York PO † Fant Pno, D.760; Sym 3 — TELC ▲ 17133 (16.97)
L. Bernstein (cnd), New York PO † Beethoven:Sym 5 — SNYC ▮ 36719 (3.98)
L. Bernstein (cnd), New York PO † Sym 9 — SNYC ▲ 47610 (10.97)
K. Böhm (cnd), Vienna PO † J. Brahms:Sym 1 — MTAL ▲ 48051 (6.97)
K. Böhm (cnd), Vienna PO *(rec 1940)* ("Böhm, Vol. 4") † J. Brahms:Sym 1 — LYS ▲ 407 (17.97)
K. Böhm (cnd), Vienna PO † J. Brahms:Sym 1 — HCO ▲ 37008 (7.97)
K. Böhm (cnd), Vienna PO † J. Brahms:Sym 1 — IMMM ▲ 37008 (6.97)
G. Cantelli (cnd), Philharmonia Orch ("Guido Cantelli: 1951/1955 Releases") † Mendelssohn (-Bartholdy):Sym 4; R. Wagner:Siegfried Idyll — ENT (Palladio) ▲ 4158 [ADD] (13.97)
J. Ferencsik (cnd), Hungarian State Orch *(rec 1979)* † Sym 5 — CLDI ▲ 4036 [ADD] (10.97)
W. Furtwängler (cnd), Berlin PO—1st movt ("A Tribute to Furtwängler") † Sym 9; Beethoven:Sym 3; Sym 5; Sym 6; J. Brahms:Sym 2; A. Dvořák:Slavonic Dances (sels); Mendelssohn (-Bartholdy):Hebriden, Op. 26; R. Schumann:Con Vc; R. Strauss:Till Eulenspiegels lustige Streiche, Op. 28 — TAHA 4-▲ 1008 (35.97)
J. E. Gardiner (cnd), Lyon Opera Orch—Allegro moderato *(rec Montpellier Opera, France, July 1987)* ("The Magic of the Symphony") † Beethoven:Sym 6; Bizet:Sym; J. Haydn:Sym 101; Sym 94; W. A. Mozart:Sym 40, K.550 — ERAT ▲ 94682 (9.97)
C. M. Giulini (cnd), Bavarian RSO *(rec Munich, Apr 24-28, 1995)* † Sym 4 — SNYC ▲ 66833 [DDD] (16.97)
C. M. Giulini (cnd), Chicago SO † A. Dvořák:Sym 9 — DEUT (Galleria) ▲ 23882 [ADD] (9.97)
C. Groves (cnd), English Sinfonia ("Viennese Splendor: An Evening of Concert Favourites") † Joh. Strauss:Radetzky March, Op. 228; Strauss (II):Tritsch-Tratsch-Polka, Op. 214; Unter Donner und Blitz, Op. 324; Waltzes — INMP (Concert Classics) ▲ 1101 (9.97)
C. Groves (cnd), English Sinfonia † Rosamunde — INMP (IMP Classics) ▲ 6700872 (9.97)
M. Halász (cnd), Slovak PO † Rosamunde (sels) — NXIN ▲ 550145 [DDD] (5.97)
M. Halász (cnd), Slovak PO † Beethoven:Sym 5 — NXIN ▲ 550289 [DDD] (5.97)
V. Handley (cnd), Ulster Orch † Sym 3; Sym 5 — CHN ▲ 7126 (13.97)
H. von Karajan (cnd), Berlin PO † Sym 9 — EMIC (Karajan: Berlin Years, Part 1) ▲ 66105 (11.97)
E. Kleiber (cnd) ("Erich Kleiber: The Pre-Wartime Recordings, Part 1") † W. A. Mozart:Sym 38, K.504; R. Strauss:Rosenkavalier (waltzes); C. M. von Weber:Invitation to the Dance Orch — GRM2 ▲ 78609 (13.97)
E. Kleiber (cnd), Berlin PO *(rec 1935)* † A. Dvořák:Sym 9 — GRM2 ▲ 7802 (13.97)
C. Kleiber (cnd), Vienna PO † Sym 3 — DEUT (The Originals) ▲ 449745 [ADD] (11.97)
O. Klemperer (cnd), Bavarian RSO *(rec Munich, Germany, Apr 1966)* † Mendelssohn (-Bartholdy):Sym 3 — EMIC (Klemperer Legacy) ▲ 66868 [ADD] (11.97)
O. Klemperer (cnd), Vienna PO *(rec live, 1968)* ("From Beethoven to Schubert") † Beethoven:Sym 6 — ENT (Palladio) ▲ 4208 [ADD] (13.97)
H. Knappertsbusch (cnd), Bavarian State Orch *(rec 1955-58)* † Komzák:Concert Waltz, Op. 257 — ORFE ▲ 426981 (16.97)
S. Koussevitzky (cnd), Boston SO *(rec 1935-39)* ("Serge Koussevitzky Conducts") † Mendelssohn (-Bartholdy):Sym 4; R. Schumann:Sym 1 — PHS ▲ 9037 [ADD] (17.97)
J. Kovács (cnd), Budapest PO † Rosamunde — LALI ▲ 15527 [DDD] (3.97)
J. Kovács (cnd), Budapest PO † Rosamunde (sels); Sym 3 — LALI ▲ 15823 [DDD] (3.97)
J. Krips (cnd), Vienna PO † Sym 9 — PLON (Classic Sound) ▲ 452892 (11.97)
L. Ludwig (cnd), London SO *(rec Walthamstow Assembly Hall London)* ("Sampler") † A. Dvořák:Sym 9; W. A. Mozart:Con 3 Vn, K.216; Sym 40, K.550; R. Schumann:Con Pno in a, Op. 54 — EVC 2-▲ 9045 [AAD] (19.97)
P. Maag (cnd), Philharmonia Hungarica ("The Story of Schubert in Words & Music") † Life & Music of Schubert; Mass 5, D.678; Mass 6, D.950; Sym 2; Sym 4; Sym 6; Sym 9 — MMD (Music Masters) ▲ 8504 [ADD] (3.97) ▮ 8504 [ADD] (2.98)
L. Maazel (cnd), Vienna PO † Beethoven:Sym 5 — SNYC ▲ 44783 [DDD] (10.97)
C. Mackerras (cnd), Scottish CO *(rec Dundee, Scotland, Mar 10-12, 1998)* † Sym 9 — TEL ▲ 80502 [DDD] (16.97)
F. Mannino (cnd), National Arts Center Canada Orch † R. Strauss:Metamorphosen — SMS (SM 5000) ▲ 5034 [DDD] (16.97)
W. Mengelberg (cnd), (Royal) Concertgebouw Orch *(rec 1935-42)* ("The Rarest Recordings") † J. S. Bach:Con Vns; Borodin:In the Steppes of Central Asia; W. A. Mozart:Kleine Nachtmusik, K.525 — PHS ▲ 9154 [ADD] (17.97)
W. Mengelberg (cnd), (Royal) Concertgebouw Orch *(rec Amsterdam, June 1943)* ("Willem Mengelberg/Franz Schubert") † Sym 9 — 78'S (The 78s) ▲ 78530 [ADD] (13.97)
W. Mengelberg (cnd), Concertgebouw Orch *(rec Amsterdam, Holland, 1939)* ("Mengelberg Live at the Concertgebouw") † Sym 9 — RY (The Radio Years) ▲ 96 (16.97)
E. Mravinsky (cnd), Leningrad PO *(rec Apr 24, 1959)* † P. Tchaikovsky:Sym 4; C. M. von Weber:Euryanthe (ov) — RUS (The Mravinsky Collection) ▲ 10903 [AAD] (12.97)
K. Münchinger (cnd), Stuttgart RSO—Andante con moto ("Another Kiss: More Music for Love & Passion") † Beethoven:Bagatelle Pno in a, WoO 59; Debussy:Suite bergamasque; A. Dvořák:Sym 9; W. A. Mozart:Kleine Nachtmusik, K.525; Smetana:Moldau; P. Tchaikovsky:Serenade Strs, Op. 48 — INTC ▲ 892934 [AAD] (13.97)
A. Nanut (cnd), Ljubljana RSO ("Music for Meditation, Vol. 2") † A. Adam:Giselle (sels); A. Bruckner:Qnt Strs; Chopin:Berceuse, Op. 57; Gounod:Ave Maria; G. Mahler:Sym 5; Massenet:Méditation from Thaïs — ECL ▲ 506 (2.97)
A. Ostrowsky (cnd), Helsingborg SO † Sym 4 — DI ▲ 920213 [DDD] (5.97)
F. Reiner (cnd), Chicago SO † Beethoven:Coriolan Ov, Op. 62; Fidelio (ov); Sym 5 — RCAV (Red Seal) ▲ 5403 (16.97)
C. Schuricht (cnd), French National Orch *(rec 1963)* † G. Mahler:Sym 3 — STRV 2-▲ 10051 (24.97)
S. Skrowaczewski (cnd), Minneapolis SO † Rosamunde; Sym 5 — MRCR ▲ 462954 (11.97)
C. Spering (cnd), Das Neue Orch † Sym 5 — OPUS ▲ 30192 (18.97)
W. Steinberg (cnd), Pittsburgh SO *(rec Pittsburg, United States of America, Feb 9, 1952)* † J. Brahms:Con 1 Pno, Op. 15 — EMIC ▲ 67019 [ADD] (11.97)

▲ = CD ♦ = Enhanced CD △ = MD ▮ = Cassette Tape ▯ = DCC

SCHUBERT, FRANZ (cont.)

Symphony No. 8 in b, D.759, "Unfinished" (1822) (cont.)

G. Szell (cnd), Cleveland Orch *(rec 1960)* † Sym 9 SNYC (Essential Classics) ▲ 48268 [ADD] (7.97) ■ 48268 [ADD] (3.98)
A. Toscanini (cnd), NBC SO ("The Toscanini Collection, Vol. 14") † Sym 9 RCAV (Gold Seal) ▲ 60290 [ADD] (11.97)
A. Toscanini (cnd), NBC SO *(rec New York, NY, March-June 1950)* † Sym 5; Sym 9; Mendelssohn (-Bartholdy):Sym 4; Sym 5 RCAV ▲ 59480 (16.97)
S. Végh (cnd), Salzburg Mozarteum Camerata Academia † Sym 5; Sym 6; Sym 9 CAPO (Schubert-Edition) 2-▲ 490654 [DDD] (16.97)
M. Viotti (cnd), Saarbrücken RSO *(rec Kongresshalle Saarbrücken, Dec 1995 & Mar 1996)* ("Complete Symphonic Works, Vol. 5") † Sym 6 CLAV ▲ 9703 [DDD] (16.97)
B. Walter (cnd) *(rec 1940s)* ("The 1st Recordings in America for Columbia") † Beethoven:Sym 1; Sym 6; Sym 8 GRM2 ▲ 78805 (26.97)
B. Walter (cnd), New York PO *(rec Brooklyn, NY, Mar 3, 1958)* † Sym 5; Sym 7; Beethoven:Leonore (ov 3) SNYC (Bruno Walter: The Edition, Vol. 4) ▲ 64487 [ADD] (10.97)
B. Walter (cnd), Vienna PO † W. A. Mozart:Sym 41, K.551; R. Wagner:Siegfried Idyll ENT (Palladio) ▲ 4169 [ADD] (13.97)
G. Wand (cnd), Berlin PO † Sym 9 RCAV (Red Seal) 2-▲ 68314 [DDD] (16.97)
B. Weil (cnd), Classical Band † Sym 9 SNYC (Vivarte) ▲ 48132 (16.97)
artists unknown † Sym 5 SNYC ▲ 64561 (4.97)
artists unknown † German Dances (16) Pno, D.783; Sym 5; Waltzes, D.969 PC ▲ 265082 [DDD] (2.97)

Symphony No. 9 in C, D.944, "The Great" (?1825-28)

C. Abbado (cnd), CO of Europe † Rosamunde (sels) DEUT ▲ 23656 [DDD] (16.97)
K. Ančerl (cnd), Berlin RSO ("Edition Karl Ančerl Vol 1") † A. Dvořák:Slavonic Dances (comp); J. Haydn:Sym 93; S. Prokofiev:Romeo & Juliet (suites), Op. 64bis; Rimsky-Korsakov:Scheherazade, Op. 35 TAHA 3-▲ 117 (50.97)
L. Bernstein (cnd), (Royal) Concertgebouw Orch DGRM ▲ 427646 [DDD] (17.97)
L. Bernstein (cnd), New York PO † Sym 8 SNYC ▲ 47610 (10.97)
H. Blomstedt (cnd), Dresden Staatskapelle BER ▲ 9314 (10.97)
F. Brüggen (cnd), Orch of the 18th Century DEUT ▲ 39006 (16.97)
W. Furtwängler (cnd), Berlin PO *(rec Jesus-Christus Church Berlin, Germany, Nov-Dec 1951)* † J. Haydn:Sym 88 DEUT (The Originals) ▲ 47439 [ADD] (11.97)
W. Furtwängler (cnd), Berlin PO *(rec 1942)* † Beethoven:Coriolan Ov, Op. 62; C. M. von Weber:Freischütz (ov) MUA ▲ 826 [AAD]
W. Furtwängler (cnd), Berlin PO ("A Tribute to Furtwängler") † Sym 8; Beethoven:Sym 3; Sym 5; Sym 6; J. Brahms:Sym 2; A. Dvořák:Slavonic Dances (sels); Mendelssohn (-Bartholdy):Hebriden, Op. 26; R. Schumann:Con Vc; R. Strauss:Till Eulenspiegels lustige Streiche, Op. 28 TAHA 4-▲ 1008 (35.97)
W. Furtwängler (cnd), Berlin PO † M. Ravel:Daphnis et Chloé (suite 2) MTAL ▲ 48009 (6.97)
W. Furtwängler (cnd), Vienna PO TAHA ▲ 1040 (17.97)
J. E. Gardiner (cnd), Vienna PO † Gesang der Geister über den Wassern, D.714 DEUT ▲ 457648 [DDD] (16.97)
C. Groves (cnd), English Sinfonia ICC ▲ 6701162 (9.97)
M. Halász (cnd), Failoni Orch *(rec Italian Institute Budapest, Mar 1994)* ("Famous Symphonies: Beethoven, Tchaikovsky, Brahms, Schubert") † Beethoven:Sym 3; Sym 8; J. Brahms:Academic Festival Ov, Op. 80; Sym 4; Tragic Ov, Op. 81; P. Tchaikovsky:Francesca da Rimini, Op. 32; Sym 6 NXIN 4-▲ 504012 [DDD] (19.97)
G. Herbig (cnd), BBC PO † C. M. von Weber:Euryanthe (ov) INMP (BBC Radio) ▲ 5691442 (13.97)
H. von Karajan (cnd), Berlin PO EMIC ▲ 64628 (11.97)
H. von Karajan (cnd), Berlin PO † Sym 8 EMIC (Karajan: Berlin Years, Part 1) ▲ 66105 (11.97)
H. von Karajan (cnd), Vienna PO *(rec 1946-47)* ("The Young Karajan, Vol. 10") † W. A. Mozart:Adagio & Fugue Strs, K.546; Divert 17 Hns Strs, K.334 GRM2 ▲ 78770 (13.97)
I. Kertész (cnd), Vienna PO † Sym 5 PENG ▲ 460634 (11.97)
J. Krips (cnd), London SO † Sym 8 PLON (Classic Sound) ▲ 452892 (11.97)
R. Kubelík (cnd), Royal PO † Ovs RYLC ▲ 70122 (8.97)
P. Maag (cnd), Philharmonia Hungarica ("The Story of Schubert in Words & Music") † Life & Music of Schubert; Mass 5, D.678; Mass 6, D.950; Sym 2; Sym 4; Sym 6; Sym 8 MMD (Music Masters) ▲ 8504 [ADD] (3.97) ■ 8504 [ADD] (2.98)
C. Mackerras (cnd), Scottish CO *(rec Dundee, Scotland, Mar 10-12, 1998)* † Sym 8 TEL ▲ 80502 [DDD] (16.97)
J. Mardjani (cnd), Georgian Festival Orch SNYC ▲ 66574 [DDD] (4.97)
W. Mengelberg (cnd), (Royal) Concertgebouw Orch *(rec Amsterdam, Dec 1940)* ("Willem Mengelberg/Franz Schubert") † Sym 8 78'S (The 78s) ▲ 78530 [ADD] (13.97)
W. Mengelberg (cnd), Concertgebouw Orch *(rec Amsterdam, Holland, 1940)* ("Mengelberg Live at the Concertgebouw") † Sym 8 RY (The Radio Years) ▲ 96 (16.97)
R. Muti (cnd), Vienna PO EMIC (Red Line) ▲ 69836 [DDD] (6.97)
A. Rahbari (cnd), Brussels BRTN PO *(rec June 12-15, 1991)* NXIN ▲ 550502 [DDD] (5.97)
W. Rogner (cnd), Erfurt PO † W. A. Mozart:Sym 35, K.385 QUER ▲ 9709 (18.97)
S. Skrowaczewski (cnd), Minneapolis SO *(rec Northrop Memorial Auditorium Univ. of Minnesota, Nov 26, 1961)* † Sym 6 MRCR ▲ 34354 (11.97)
G. Solti (cnd), Vienna PO *(rec 1981)* † R. Wagner:Siegfried Idyll DECC ▲ 460311 (11.97)
G. Szell (cnd), Cleveland Orch *(rec 1957)* † Sym 8 SNYC (Essential Classics) ▲ 48268 [ADD] (7.97) ■ 48268 [ADD] (3.98)
G. Szell (cnd), Cleveland Orch † Beethoven:Sym 7; G. Rossini:Ovs EMIC (Doublefforte) 2-▲ 69364 (16.97)
A. Toscanini (cnd), NBC SO ("The Toscanini Collection, Vol. 14") † Sym 8 RCAV (Gold Seal) ▲ 60290 [ADD] (11.97)
A. Toscanini (cnd), NBC SO *(rec New York, NY, Feb 1953)* † Sym 5; Sym 8; Mendelssohn (-Bartholdy):Sym 4; Sym 5 RCAV ▲ 59480 (16.97)
A. Toscanini (cnd), Philadelphia Orch ("The Toscanini Collection, Vol. 69") RCAV (Gold Seal) ▲ 60313 [ADD] (11.97)
A. Toscanini (cnd), Philadelphia Orch ("The Toscanini Collection, Vols. 67-70") † Berlioz:Roméo et Juliette (sels); Mendelssohn (-Bartholdy):Midsummer Night's Dream (comp); O. Respighi:Feste romane; R. Strauss:Tod und Verklärung, Op. 24 RCAV (Gold Seal) 4-▲ 60328 [ADD] (40.97)
S. Végh (cnd), Salzburg Mozarteum Camerata Academia † Sym 5; Sym 6; Sym 8 CAPO (Schubert-Edition) 2-▲ 490654 [DDD] (16.97)
B. Walter (cnd), Columbia SO † Rosamunde (sels) SNYC (Bruno Walter: The Edition) ▲ 64478 (10.97)
B. Walter (cnd), London SO ("Bruno Walter with the LSO: The Legendary 1938 Recordings") † Beethoven:Coriolan Ov, Op. 62; Smetana:Bartered Bride (ov); Strauss (II):Zigeunerbaron (ov) GRM2 ▲ 78548 (13.97)
G. Wand (cnd), Berlin PO † Sym 8 RCAV (Red Seal) 2-▲ 68314 [DDD] (16.97)
B. Weil (cnd), Classical Band † Sym 8 SNYC (Vivarte) ▲ 48132 (16.97)

Symphony No. 10 in D [sketches], D.936a (?mid-1828)

C. Mackerras (cnd), Scottish CO ("Symphony No. 10 & Other Unfinished Symphonies") HYP ▲ 67000 (18.97)

Tantum ergo in C for Organ, Orchestra & Chorus, D.739 (1814)

M. Haselböck (cnd), Vienna Academy, Hugo Distler Chorus ("Messen") † Deutsche Messe; Mass 2, D.167; Mass 4, D.452; Mass 6, D.950 CAPO (Schubert-Edition) 2-▲ 490807 [DDD] (16.97)

Tantum ergo in E♭ for solo Voices, Orchestra & Chorus, D.962 (1828)

H. Rilling (cnd), Stuttgart Bach Collegium, Stuttgart Gächinger Kantorei † Mass 6, D.950; Offertory:Intende voci, D.963 HANS (Exclusive) ▲ 98172 (15.97)

Trio Movement in E♭ for Piano, Violin & Cello, D.897, (Op. 148), "Notturno" (?1828)

Arion Trio ("The Complete Chamber Music for Piano & Strings") † Adagio & Rondo concertante Vn, D.487; Fant Vn, D.934; Qnt Pno, D.667; Rondo Vn, D.895; Son Arpeggione, D.821; Son Vn, D.574; Sonatinas (3) Vn; Trio Pno, D.28; Trio 1 Pno, D.898; Trio 2 Pno, D.929 BIS 4-▲ 521 [DDD] (137.97)
Atlantis Ensemble *(rec Bloomfield Hills, MI, Oct 1994 & Nov 1995)* ("Music for Piano Trio 1") † Adagio & Rondo concertante Vn, D.487; Trio 1 Pno, D.898 WILD ▲ 9703 [DDD] (16.97)
Beaux Arts Trio † Trio Pno, D.28; Trio Strs, D.471; Trio Strs, D.581; Trio 1 Pno, D.898; Trio 2 Pno, D.929 PPHI 2-▲ 38700 (17.97)
Beethoven Trio Vienna *(rec Vienna, June 24, 1993)* ("The Complete Piano Trios") † Trio Pno, D.28; Trio 1 Pno, D.898; Trio 2 Pno, D.929 CAMA 2-▲ 401 [DDD] (34.97)
Bekova Sisters ("Schubert Piano Trios, Vol. 1") † Trio 2 Pno, D.929 CHN ▲ 9414 [DDD] (16.97)
Catherine Wilson Trio ("The Catherine Wilson Trio Performs the Romantics") † E. Bloch:Nocturnes; G. Fauré:Trio Pno, Op. 120; Widor:Pièces Pno DHR ▲ 71112 [DDD] (14.97)
W. Hink (vn), F. Doležal (vc), J. Stancul (pno) *(rec Vienna, Sept 1996)* † Trio 2 Pno, D.929 CAMA ▲ 457 [DDD] (18.97)
M. Kaplan (vn), C. Carr (vc), D. Golub (pno) † Trio Pno, D.28; Trio 1 Pno, D.898; Trio 2 Pno, D.929 ARA 2-▲ 6580 (32.97)
La Gaia Scienza † Trio 1 Pno, D.898 WNTR (Basic Edition) ▲ 17 (16.97)
La Gaia Scienza ("Complete Piano Trios") † Trio Pno, D.28; Trio 1 Pno, D.898; Trio 2 Pno, D.929 WNTR 2-▲ 18 (32.97)

SCHUBERT, FRANZ (cont.)

Trio Movement in E♭ for Piano, Violin & Cello, D.897, (Op. 148), "Notturno" (?1828) (cont.)

La Scala Orch Soloists † Mendelssohn (-Bartholdy):Octet Strs, Op. 20; R. Schumann:Märchenerzählungen, Op. 132 THY ▲ 101 (17.97)
Mozartean Players HAM ▲ 907094 (18.97)
J. Pospichal (vn), W. Rehm (vc), W. Sawallisch (pno) † Qnt Pno, D.667 CALG ▲ 50988 [DDD] (18.97)
V. Repin (vn), J. Gustafsson (vc), L. O. Andsnes (pno) † A. Pettersson:Vn Music; I. Stravinsky:Divert Vn; Pieces Str Qt KOCC ▲ 316512 (16.97)
Y. Shiokawa (vn), M. Perényi (vc), A. Schiff (pno) † Son Arpeggione, D.821; Trio 1 Pno, D.898; Trio 2 Pno, D.929 TELC ▲ 13151 (33.97)
Stuttgart Piano Trio *(rec May 1988)* † Trio 2 Pno, D.929 NXIN ▲ 550132 [DDD] (5.97)
Suk Trio *(rec Prague, Sept 1964)* ("The Intimate Schubert") † Son Vn, D.574; Trio 1 Pno, D.898 BOSK ▲ 146 [AAD] (15.97)
Trio Concertante ("Complete Works for Piano & Strings") † Adagio & Rondo concertante Vn, D.487; Qnt Pno, D.667; Trio Pno, D.28; Trio 1 Pno, D.898; Trio 2 Pno, D.929 VB2 2-▲ 5033 [ADD] (9.97)
Trio ex Aequo † Trio 1 Pno, D.898 DI ▲ 920110 [DDD] (5.97)

Trio (sonata in 1 movt) in B♭ for Piano, Violin & Cello, D.28 (1812)

Arion Trio ("The Complete Chamber Music for Piano & Strings") † Adagio & Rondo concertante Vn, D.487; Fant Vn, D.934; Qnt Pno, D.667; Rondo Vn, D.895; Son Arpeggione, D.821; Son Vn, D.574; Sonatinas (3) Vn; Trio Movt Pno Trio, D.897; Trio 1 Pno, D.898; Trio 2 Pno, D.929 BIS 4-▲ 521 [DDD] (137.97)
Atlantis Ensemble *(rec Bloomfield Hills, MI, 1994-95)* ("Music for Piano Trio II") † Trio 2 Pno, D.929 WILD ▲ 9704 [DDD] (16.97)
Beaux Arts Trio † Trio Movt Pno Trio, D.897; Trio Strs, D.471; Trio Strs, D.581; Trio 1 Pno, D.898; Trio 2 Pno, D.929 PPHI 2-▲ 38700 (17.97)
Beethoven Trio Vienna *(rec Vienna, June 17, 1995)* ("The Complete Piano Trios") † Trio Movt Pno Trio, D.897; Trio 1 Pno, D.898; Trio 2 Pno, D.929 CAMA 2-▲ 401 [DDD] (34.97)
W. Hink (vn), F. Doležal (vc), J. Stancul (pno) *(rec Apr & June 1995)* † Trio 1 Pno, D.898 CAMA ▲ 342 [DDD] (18.97)
M. Kaplan (vn), C. Carr (vc), D. Golub (pno) † Trio Movt Pno Trio, D.897; Trio 1 Pno, D.898; Trio 2 Pno, D.929 ARA 2-▲ 6580 (32.97)
Karadar-Bertoldi Ensemble † Adagio & Rondo concertante Vn, D.487; Qnt Pno, D.667 STRV ▲ 20 [DDD] (16.97)
La Gaia Scienza † Trio 2 Pno, D.929 WNTR (Basic Edition) ▲ 6 (16.97)
La Gaia Scienza ("Complete Piano Trios") † Trio Movt Pno Trio, D.897; Trio 1 Pno, D.898; Trio 2 Pno, D.929 WNTR 2-▲ 18 (32.97)
Stockholm Arts Trio *(rec June 1996)* † Trio 1 Pno, D.898 OPU ▲ 19601 [AAD] (16.97)
Stuttgart Piano Trio † Trio 1 Pno, D.898 NXIN ▲ 550131 [DDD] (5.97)
Trio Concertante ("Complete Works for Piano & Strings") † Adagio & Rondo concertante Vn, D.487; Qnt Pno, D.667; Trio Movt Pno Trio, D.897; Trio 1 Pno, D.898; Trio 2 Pno, D.929 VB2 2-▲ 5033 [ADD] (9.97)

Trio No. 1 in B♭ for Piano, Violin & Cello, D.898, (Op. 99) (1827)

Arion Trio ("The Complete Chamber Music for Piano & Strings") † Adagio & Rondo concertante Vn, D.487; Fant Vn, D.934; Qnt Pno, D.667; Rondo Vn, D.895; Son Arpeggione, D.821; Son Vn, D.574; Sonatinas (3) Vn; Trio Movt Pno Trio, D.897; Trio Pno, D.28; Trio 2 Pno, D.929 BIS 4-▲ 521 [DDD] (137.97)
Atlantis Ensemble *(rec Bloomfield Hills, MI, Oct 1994 & Nov 1995)* ("Music for Piano Trio 1") † Adagio & Rondo concertante Vn, D.487; Trio Movt Pno Trio, D.897 WILD ▲ 9703 [DDD] (16.97)
Beaux Arts Trio † Trio Movt Pno Trio, D.897; Trio Pno, D.28; Trio Strs, D.471; Trio Strs, D.581; Trio 2 Pno, D.929 PPHI 2-▲ 38700 (17.97)
Beethoven Trio Vienna *(rec Vienna, June 22-24, 1993)* ("The Complete Piano Trios") † Trio Movt Pno Trio, D.897; Trio Pno, D.28; Trio 2 Pno, D.929 CAMA 2-▲ 401 [DDD] (34.97)
V. Beths (vn), A. Blysma (vc), J. van Immerseel (pno) † Trio 2 Pno, D.929 SNYC (Vivarte) ▲ 62695 (16.97)
W. Gieseking (pno), G. Taschner (vn), L. Hoelscher (vc) *(rec 1947)* ("Gieseking, Vol. 3") † Son Pno, D.894 HPC1 ▲ 134 (17.97)
W. Hink (vn), F. Doležal (vc), J. Stancul (pno) *(rec Apr & June 1995)* † Trio Pno, D.28 CAMA ▲ 342 [DDD] (18.97)
J. Kantorow (vn), P. Muller (vc), J. Rouvier (pno) *(rec 1982-83)* † Qnt Pno, D.667 FORL ▲ 16676 (16.97)
M. Kaplan (vn), C. Carr (vc), D. Golub (pno) † Trio Movt Pno Trio, D.897; Trio Pno, D.28; Trio 2 Pno, D.929 ARA 2-▲ 6580 (32.97)
La Gaia Scienza † Trio Movt Pno Trio, D.897 WNTR (Basic Edition) ▲ 17 (16.97)
La Gaia Scienza ("Complete Piano Trios") † Trio Movt Pno Trio, D.897; Trio Pno, D.28; Trio 2 Pno, D.929 WNTR 2-▲ 18 (32.97)
London Mozart Trio † A. Dvořák:Trio 4 Pno, Op. 90 INMP ▲ 1006 [DDD] (11.97)
Myra Hess Trio ("Myra Hess: A Vignette") † Rosamunde (sels); Son Pno, D.664; J. Brahms:Trio 2 Pno, Op. 87; J. Haydn:Son 50 Kbd, H.XVI/37; W. A. Mozart:Con 21 Pno, K.467 APR 2-▲ 7012 [AAD] (38.97)
Odeon Trio † Octet Ww & Strs, D.803; Trio 2 Pno, D.929 CAPO (Schubert-Edition) 2-▲ 490715 [DDD] (16.97)
D. Oistrakh (vn), S. Knushevitsky (vc), L. Oborin (pno) *(rec 1947)* ("The David Oistrakh Collection, Vol. 3") † Trio 2 Pno, D.929 DHR (Legendary Treasures) ▲ 7710 (16.97)
Rembrandt Trio † Mendelssohn (-Bartholdy):Trio 1 Pno, Op. 49 DOR ▲ 90130 [DDD] (16.97)
A. Schneider (vn), P. Casals (vc), E. Istomin (pno) *(rec Perpignan France, Aug 1951)* † Beethoven:Trio 2 Pno, Op. 1/2 SNYC (The Casals Edition) ▲ 58989 [ADD] (10.97)
Y. Shiokawa (vn), M. Perényi (vc), A. Schiff (pno) † Son Arpeggione, D.821; Trio Movt Pno Trio, D.897; Trio 2 Pno, D.929 TELC ▲ 13151 (33.97)
D. Sitkovetsky (vn), D. Geringas (vc), G. Oppitz (pno) NOVA ▲ 150002 (16.97)
I. Stern (vn), L. Rose (vc), E. Istomin (pno) † Trio 2 Pno, D.929 SNYC (Isaac Stern: A Life in Music) 2-▲ 64516 (23.97)
Stockholm Arts Trio *(rec June 1996)* † Trio Pno, D.28 OPU ▲ 19601 [AAD] (16.97)
Stuttgart Piano Trio † Trio Pno, D.28 NXIN ▲ 550131 [DDD] (5.97)
Suk Trio *(rec Prague, July 1964)* ("The Intimate Schubert") † Son Vn, D.574; Trio Movt Pno Trio, D.897 BOSK ▲ 146 [AAD] (15.97)
I. Then-Bergh (vn), C. Hellmann (vc), M. Schäfer (pno) *(rec Studio 3 des BR, Mar 28-31, 1994)* † Trio 2 Pno, D.929 CALG ▲ 50931 [DDD] (19.97)
J. Thibaud (vn), P. Casals (vc), A. Cortot (pno) † R. Schumann:Trio 1 Pno, Op. 63 MTAL ▲ 48020 (6.97)
J. Thibaud (vn), P. Casals (vc), A. Cortot (pno) *(rec 1926-27)* † Mendelssohn (-Bartholdy):Trio 1 Pno, Op. 49 ENT (Strings) ▲ 99343 (16.97)
J. Thibaud (vn), P. Casals (vc), A. Cortot (pno) † Qnt Pno, D.667 MSER ▲ 586
J. Thibaud (vn), P. Casals (vc), A. Cortot (pno) *(rec London, England, 1928)* ("Casals Trio I") † Beethoven:Trio 6 Pno, Op. 97; Mendelssohn (-Bartholdy):Trio 1 Pno, Op. 49; R. Schumann:Trio 1 Pno, Op. 63 MPLY 2-▲ 2005 (m) [ADD] (16.97)
Trio Concertante ("Complete Works for Piano & Strings") † Adagio & Rondo concertante Vn, D.487; Qnt Pno, D.667; Trio Movt Pno Trio, D.897; Trio Pno, D.28; Trio 2 Pno, D.929 VB2 2-▲ 5033 [ADD] (9.97)
Trio ex Aequo † Trio Movt Pno Trio, D.897 DI ▲ 920110 [DDD] (5.97)
P. Zukerman (vn), L. Harrell (vc), V. Ashkenazy (pno) † Trio 2 Pno, D.929 PLON ▲ 455685 (17.97)

Trio No. 2 in E♭ for Piano, Violin & Cello, D.929, (Op. 100) (1827)

Arion Trio ("The Complete Chamber Music for Piano & Strings") † Adagio & Rondo concertante Vn, D.487; Fant Vn, D.934; Qnt Pno, D.667; Rondo Vn, D.895; Son Arpeggione, D.821; Son Vn, D.574; Sonatinas (3) Vn; Trio Movt Pno Trio, D.897; Trio Pno, D.28; Trio 1 Pno, D.898 BIS 4-▲ 521 [DDD] (137.97)
Atlantis Ensemble *(rec Bloomfield Hills, MI, 1994-95)* ("Music for Piano Trio II") † Trio Pno, D.28 WILD ▲ 9704 [DDD] (16.97)
Beaux Arts Trio † Trio Movt Pno Trio, D.897; Trio Pno, D.28; Trio Strs, D.471; Trio Strs, D.581; Trio 1 Pno, D.898 PPHI 2-▲ 38700 (17.97)
Beethoven Trio Vienna *(rec Vienna, Feb 14-17, 1995)* ("The Complete Piano Trios") † Trio Movt Pno Trio, D.897; Trio Pno, D.28; Trio 1 Pno, D.898 CAMA 2-▲ 401 [DDD] (34.97)
Bekova Sisters ("Schubert Piano Trios, Vol. 1") † Trio Movt Pno Trio, D.897 CHN ▲ 9414 [DDD] (16.97)
V. Beths (vn), A. Blysma (vc), J. van Immerseel (pno) † Trio 1 Pno, D.898 SNYC (Vivarte) ▲ 62695 (16.97)
A. Delmoni (vn), N. Rosen (vc), E. Auer (pno) *(rec Dec 1993)* CLT ▲ 1007 (14.97)
W. Hink (vn), F. Doležal (vc), J. Stancul (pno) *(rec Vienna, Sept 1996)* † Trio Movt Pno Trio, D.897 CAMA ▲ 457 [DDD] (18.97)
M. Kaplan (vn), C. Carr (vc), D. Golub (pno) † Trio Movt Pno Trio, D.897; Trio Pno, D.28; Trio 1 Pno, D.898 ARA 2-▲ 6580 (32.97)
La Gaia Scienza † Trio Pno, D.28 WNTR (Basic Edition) ▲ 6 (16.97)
La Gaia Scienza ("Complete Piano Trios") † Trio Movt Pno Trio, D.897; Trio Pno, D.28; Trio 1 Pno, D.898 WNTR 2-▲ 18 (32.97)
London Mozart Trio † A. Dvořák:Trio 1 Pno, Op. 21 INMP (Classics) ▲ 6700132 (9.97)
Odeon Trio † Octet Ww & Strs, D.803; Trio 1 Pno, D.898 CAPO (Schubert-Edition) 2-▲ 490715 [DDD] (16.97)

SCHUBERT, FRANZ (cont.)
Trio No. 2 in E♭ for Piano, Violin & Cello, D.929, (Op. 100) (1827) (cont.)
D. Oistrakh (vn), S. Knushevitsky (vc), L. Oborin (pno) *(rec 1947)* ("The David Oistrakh Collection, Vol. 3") † Trio 1 Pno, D.898 DHR (Legendary Treasures) ▲ 7710 (16.97)
M. Scherzer (vn), K. Schroter (vc), A. Webersinke (pno) BER ▲ 9295 (10.97)
A. Schneider (vn), P. Casals (vc), M. Horszowski (pno) *(rec Prades France, July 5-6, 1952)* † Beethoven:Trio 1 Pno, Op. 1/1 SNYC (The Casals Edition) ▲ 58988 [ADD] (10.97)
R. Serkin (pno), Busch String Quartet members *(rec 1931-38)* ("The Complete Schubert Recordings") † Fant Vn, D.934; Qt 14 Strs, D.810; Qt 15 Strs, D.887; Qt 8 Strs, D.112 PHS 2-▲ 9141 [ADD] (33.97)
Y. Shiokawa (vn), M. Perényi (vc), A. Schiff (pno) † Son Arpeggione, D.821; Trio Movt Pno Trio, D.897; Trio 1 Pno, D.898 TELC ▲ 13151 (33.97)
D. Sitkovetsky (vn), D. Geringas (vc), G. Oppitz (pno) NOVA ▲ 150003 (16.97)
I. Stern (vn), L. Rose (vc), E. Istomin (pno) † Trio 1 Pno, D.898
SNYC (Isaac Stern: A Life in Music) 2-▲ 64516 (23.97)
Stuttgart Piano Trio *(rec May 1988)* † Trio Movt Pno Trio, D.897 NXIN ▲ 550132 [DDD] (5.97)
I. Then-Bergh (vn), C. Hellmann (vc), M. Schäfer (pno) *(rec Studio 3 des BR, Mar 28-31, 1994)* † Trio 1 Pno, D.898 CALG ▲ 50931 [DDD] (19.97)
Trio Concertante ("Complete Works for Piano & Strings") † Adagio & Rondo concertante Vn, D.487; Qnt Pno, D.667; Trio Movt Pno Trio, D.897; Trio Pno, D.28; Trio 1 Pno, D.898 VB2 2-▲ 5033 [ADD] (9.97)
Villa Musica Ensemble † Qnt in C Strs, D.956 NXIN ▲ 550388 [DDD] (5.97)
P. Zukerman (vn), L. Harrell (vc), V. Ashkenazy (pno) † Trio 1 Pno, D.898 PLON ▲ 455685 (17.97)
Trio in B♭ for Strings [1st movt & 2nd movt fragment], D.471 (1816)
Grumiaux Piano Trio † Trio Movt Pno Trio, D.897; Trio Pno, D.28; Trio Strs, D.581; Trio 1 Pno, D.898; Trio 2 Pno, D.929 PPHI 2-▲ 38700 (17.97)
Israel Flute Ensemble ("Flute Serenade") † Beethoven:Serenade Fl, Vn & Va, Op. 25; F. A. Hoffmeister:Qt Fl; W. A. Mozart:Qt Fl in D, K.285 CACI ▲ 210018 (5.97)
L'Archibudelli *(rec June 8-9, 1993)* † Qt 10 Strs; Trio Strs, D.581 SNYC (Vivarte) ▲ 53982 [DDD] (16.97)
Locrian Ensemble † Qnt in C Strs, D.956 ASVQ ▲ 6207 (10.97)
New Leipzig String Quartet members † Qt Strs, D.2c; Qt 15 Strs, D.887 MDG ▲ 3070601 [DDD] (17.97)
R. Pasquier (vn), B. Pasquier (va), R. Pidoux (vc) † Son Arpeggione, D.821; Trio Strs, D.581 HAM ▲ 901035 (18.97)
Raphael Ensemble † Qnt in C Strs, D.956 HYP ▲ 66724 (18.97)
Trio in B♭ for Strings, D.581 (1817)
Dresden String Trio † W. A. Mozart:Divert Str Trio, K.563 QUER ▲ 9901 (18.97)
Grumiaux Piano Trio † Trio Movt Pno Trio, D.897; Trio Pno, D.28; Trio Strs, D.471; Trio 1 Pno, D.898; Trio 2 Pno, D.929 PPHI 2-▲ 38700 (17.97)
L'Archibudelli *(rec June 8-9, 1993)* † Qt 10 Strs; Trio Strs, D.471 SNYC (Vivarte) ▲ 53982 [DDD] (16.97)
R. Pasquier (vn), B. Pasquier (va), R. Pidoux (vc) † Son Arpeggione, D.821; Trio Strs, D.471 HAM ▲ 901035 (18.97)
Vienna PO Trio *(rec Vienna, Sept 1995)* † W. A. Mozart:Trio Vn, K.563 CAMA ▲ 417 [DDD] (18.97)
Ungarische Melodie in b for Piano, D.817 (1824)
S. Knauer (pno) *(rec Germany, 1997-98)* † Allegretto Pno, D.915; Impromptus (4) Pno; Son in c Pno, D.958
BER ▲ 1190 [DDD] (16.97)
F. Levy (pno) † Allegretto Pno, D.915; German Dances Pno, D.790; Son Pno, D.959; Liszt:Trans, Arrs & Paraphrases PALE ▲ 504 (17.97)
Valses sentimentales (34) for Piano, D.779 (ca 1823)
P. Katin (pno) † Moments musicaux, D.780; Pieces Pno, D.946 ATH ▲ 7 [DDD]
Variations on a French Song (8) in e for Piano 4-Hands, D.624 (1818)
Tal & Groethuysen Duo ("Piano Music for 4-Hands, Vol. 2") † Allegro Pno 4-Hands, D.947; Divert sur des motifs originaux français, D.823; Grandes marches, D.819; Polonaises Pno, D.599; Rondo Pno 4-Hands, D.951
SNYC 2-▲ 66256 (31.97)
N. Walker (pno), A. Farmer (pno) *(rec Concert Hall of the Nimbus Foundation, Dec 14-16, 1994)* ("The Piano Duets, Vol. 1") † Polonaises Pno, D.599; Rondo Pno 4-Hands, D.608; Son Pno 4-Hands, D.617
NIMB ▲ 5443 [DDD] (16.97)
Variations on an Original Theme (8) in A for Piano 4-Hands, D.813 (1824)
L. van Doeselaar (pno), W. Jordans (pno) † Fant Pno, D.940; Marches caractéristiques, D.886; Rondo Pno 4-Hands, D.951 GLOE ▲ 5049 [DDD] (16.97)
C. Ivaldi (pno), N. Lee (pno) † Allegro Pno 4-Hands, D.947; Divert sur des motifs originaux français, D.823; Ländler Pno, D.814; Ov Pno, D.675; Son Pno 4-Hands, D.812 ARN 2-▲ 268038 [AAD] (32.97)
K. Mrongovius (pno), B. Uriarte (pno) ("Franz Schubert: Original Works for Piano 4-Hands") † Allegro Moderato Pno 4-Hands, D.968; Divert sur des motifs originaux français, D.823; Fant Pno, D.940; Ländler Pno, D.814; Marches militaires, D.733 CALG ▲ 50950 [DDD] (19.97)
N. Palmier (pno), J. Rigal (pno) *(rec July 1997)* ("4-Hand Piano Music: The Final Masterpieces") † Allegro Pno 4-Hands, D.947; Divert à l'hongroise, D.818; Fant Pno, D.940 LIDI ▲ 103053 [DDD] (16.97)
Schnabel Piano Duo † Son Pno 4-Hands, D.812 TOWN ▲ 37 (17.97)
Variations (10) in F for Piano, D.156 (1815)
J. Lisney (pno) † Son Pno, D.157; Son Pno, D.960 OLY ▲ 560 [DDD] (16.97)
Variations (13) on a Theme by Anselm Hüttenbrenner in a for Piano, D.576 (1817)
D. Joeres (pno) *(rec Feb 1994)* † Andante Pno, D.604; Impromptu (4) Pno; Moments musicaux, D.780
INMP ▲ 6701832 (9.97)
Variations (8) on a Theme from Hérold's *Marie* in C for Piano 4-Hands, D.908, (Op. 82/1) (1827)
C. Biagini (pno), M. Marzocchi (pno) † Czerny:Son 1 Pno 4-Hands, Op. 10; I. Stravinsky:Pétrouchka (pno reduction) PHEX ▲ 98424 (16.97)
J. Jandó (pno), Z. Kollár (pno) *(rec Budapest, Hungary, Nov 2-5, 1994)* ("Piano Works for 4 Hands, Vol. 2") † Allegro Moderato Pno 4-Hands, D.968; Fant Pno 4-Hands, D.9; Marches militaires, D.733; Ov Pno, D.668; Polonaises Pno, D.599 NXIN ▲ 8553441 [DDD] (5.97)
J. Rowland (pno), K. U. Schnabel (pno) † Divert sur des motifs originaux français, D.823; W. A. Mozart:Son Pno 4-Hands, K.497 TOWN ▲ 41 (17.97)
Variations on a Waltz by Diabelli in c for Piano, D.718 (1821)
F. Ts'ong (pno) ("Fou Ts'ong in Concert") † Allegretto Pno, D.915; German Dances Pno, D.790; German Dances, D.769; German Dances, D.841; Son Pno, D.960; Waltzes (20) Pno, D.146 MER ▲ 84390 (16.97)
Die Verschworenen [The Conspirators] (singspiel in 1 act) [lib Ignaz Castelli after Aristophanes], D.787, "Der häusliche Krieg" (1823)
C. Spering (cnd), Das Neue Orch, Cologne Chorus Musicus OPUS ▲ 30167 (18.97)
Der vierjährige Posten (singspiel in 1 act) [lib T. Körner], D.190 (1815)
P. Maag (cnd), Mediterranea PO, E. Di Pietro (cnd), Solisti Cantori, M. Gonzáles (sop—Käthchen), H. Schmid (ten—Duval), C. Lau (ten—Veit), R. Knös (ten—Il Capitano), S. Morbach (bar—Walther), M. Schaltezky (spkr—Il Generale) [ITA] *(rec Teatro Rendano, Cosenza, Italy, Nov 15-16, 1997) ([ENG,GER,ITA] lib text)*
BONG ▲ 2229 (live) [DDD] (16.97)
Waltzes for Piano
A. Ader (pno)—Valses sentimentales † Ländler Pno; Waltzes, D.969 HMA ▲ 1905233 (9.97)
A. Adler (pno) † Ländler Pno; Son Arpeggione, D.821; J. Brahms:Sextet Strs, Op. 18; Trio 3 Pno, Op. 101; Mendelssohn (-Bartholdy):Son 1 Vc, Op. 45; Son 2 Vc, Op. 58 HMA 3-▲ 290882 (17.97)
K. Betz (pno)—34 sels from 12 Waltzes D.145, 34 Valses sentiment; Ländler, D.366 [No. 3] † German Dances Pno, D.790 KSCH ▲ 310066 [ADD] (16.97)
G. Muntoni (pno)—Originaltänze, D.365; Valses sentimentales, D.779 *(rec May 8-9, 1995)* ("99 Waltzes") † Deutsche Pno, D.973; Deutsche Pno, D.974; Grazer Walzer, D.924; Waltzes, D.969 AART ▲ 47362 [DDD] (10.97)
Waltzes (20) for Piano, D.146, "Letzte Walzer" (1815)
R. Burnett (pno)—No. 1; No. 20 † Dances (42), Op. 18; Ecossaises (6), D.421; Chopin:Andante Spianato & Grand Polonaise, Op. 22; Czerny:Vars on "La Ricordanza", Op. 33; J. N. Hummel:Vars on a theme from Gluck's Armide, Op. 57; R. Schumann:Kinderszenen Pno, Op. 15 AMON ▲ 7 (16.97)
F. Ts'ong (pno)—No. 15; No. 16; No. 17; No. 18 ("Fou Ts'ong in Concert") † Allegretto Pno, D.915; German Dances Pno, D.790; German Dances, D.769; German Dances, D.841; Son Pno, D.960; Vars on a Waltz by Diabelli, D.718
MER ▲ 84390 (16.97)
Waltzes (12) for Piano, D.969, "Valses nobles" (by 1826)
A. Ader (pno) † Ländler Pno; Waltzes Pno HMA ▲ 1905233 (9.97)
M. Bamert (cnd), Berlin German SO [orchd Fortner] ("Hommage à Schubert") † German Dances Pno, D.820; Heuberger:Vars Schubert KSCH (Replay) ▲ 367042 (10.97)
F. Di Nitto (pno) † Pno Music (misc colls) RENE ▲ 87031 [DDD] (16.97)
D. Joeres (pno) *(rec Mar 1993)* † German Dances Pno, D.820; J. Brahms:Waltzes Pno, Op. 39; A. Dvořák:Waltzes Pno, Op. 54 INMP ▲ 6701742 (9.97)

SCHUBERT, FRANZ (cont.)
Waltzes (12) for Piano, D.969, "Valses nobles" (by 1826) (cont.)
L. Kraus (pno) *(rec 1938)* † Dances (42), Op. 18; B. Bartók:Romanian Folk Dances Pno, Sz.56; Rondos on Folk Tunes, Sz.84; Beethoven:Vars & Fugue Pno, Op. 35; Chopin:Impromptu in F♯, Op. 36; Preludes (24) Pno, Op. 28; J. Haydn:Andante with Vars Pno, H.XVII/6 PHS (Piano Masters) ▲ 55 (17.97)
G. Muntoni (pno) *(rec May 8-9, 1995)* ("99 Waltzes") † Deutsche Pno, D.973; Deutsche Pno, D.974; Grazer Walzer, D.924; Waltzes Pno AART ▲ 47362 [DDD] (10.97)
G. Schuchter (pno) ("Vol. 1") † Moments musicaux, D.780; Pno Music (comp solo); Son Pno, D.459; Son Pno, D.625; Son Pno, D.840; Son Pno, D.845 TUD 3-▲ 741 [ADD] (47.97)
artist unknown † German Dances (16) Pno, D.783; Sym 5; Sym 8 PC ▲ 265082 [DDD] (2.97)
Winterreise (cycle of 24 songs) for solo Male Voice & Piano [text Wilhelm Müller], D.911, (Op. 89) (1827)
T. Allen (bar), R. Vignoles (pno) *(rec 1990)* † Songs (misc colls); Yradier:Songs (misc colls)
VCL 2-▲ 61457 [DDD] (11.97)
P. Anders (ten), M. Raucheisen (pno)—Der Lindenbaum; Frühlingstraum; Der Wegweiser *(rec 1943-45)* ("Peter Anders Sings Schubert") † Schwanengesang, D.957; Songs (misc colls) MYTO ▲ 973163 (17.97)
P. Anders (ten), M. Raucheisen (pno) *(rec 1943-52)* ("The Unforgettable Voice of Peter Anders") † Beethoven:An die ferne Geliebte, Op. 98; R. Strauss:Four Last Songs, AV150 TAHA 2-▲ 201 (34.97)
P. Anders (ten), M. Raucheisen (pno) *(rec Berlin, Germany, 1945) ([GER] texts)*
MYTO (Historical Line) ▲ 82014 (17.97)
J. Baird (sop), A. Willis (pno)—Gute Nacht; Die Wetterfahne; Gefrorene Tränen; Erstarrung; Der Lindenbaum; Wasserflut; Auf dem Flusse; Rückblick; Irrlicht; Rast; Frühlingstraum; Einsamkeit *(rec Ambler, PA, Spring 1996)* † Moments musicaux, D.780 NPT ▲ 85614 [DDD] (16.97)
W. Bennett (fl), C. Benson (pno)—Gute Nacht; Der Lindenbaum † Schwanengesang, D.957; Son Arpeggione, D.821; Son Vn, D.574 CAMA ▲ 14 [DDD] (18.97)
V. Braun (bar), A. Kubalek (pno) [GER] DOR ▲ 90145 [DDD] (16.97)
T. Duis (pno) [12 sels arr Liszt for pno] ("Liszt/Schubert Piano Transcriptions") † Ave Maria, Op. 52/6; Meeres Stille, D.216; Pno Music (misc colls) CAPO ▲ 10771 [DDD] (10.97)
D. Fischer-Dieskau (bar), J. Demus (pno) *(rec 1965)* DEUT (The Originals) ▲ 47421 [ADD] (11.97)
D. Fischer-Dieskau (bar), G. Moore (pno) [GER] DEUT ▲ 15187 [ADD] (16.97)
D. Fischer-Dieskau (bar), G. Moore (pno) [GER] *(rec 1955)* † Schwanengesang, D.957; Schöne Müllerin, D.795
EMIC (Studio) 3-▲ 63559 [ADD] (31.97)
I. Gáti (bar), D. Ránki (pno)—Der Lindenbaum; Frühlingstraum; Die Post † Qnt Pno, D.667; Schwanengesang, D.957; Songs (misc colls) HUN ▲ 31683 [DDD] (16.97)
S. Gehrman (bass) † Music of Schubert; Qt 13 Strs, D.804; Qt 14 Strs, D.810; Qt 15 Strs, D.887; Schöne Müllerin, D.795 NIMB 12-▲ 1766 [ADD] (29.97)
T. Hampson (bar), W. Sawallisch (pno) *(rec Munich, Mar 1997)* EMIC ▲ 56445 [DDD] (16.97)
W. Holzmair (bar), I. Cooper (pno) PPHI ▲ 46407 (16.97)
H. Hotter (bass) *(rec 1942-48)* † M. Glinka:Russlan & Ludmilla; Janáček:Jenůfa; J. Offenbach:Contes d'Hoffmann; Schillings:Mona Lisa; R. Strauss:Frau ohne Schatten, Op. 65; R. Wagner:Arias & Scenes; Wesendonck Songs
VL 3-▲ 2000 (30.97)
H. Hotter (bar), G. Moore (pno) *(rec Abbey Road, London, England, 1954)* EMIC ▲ 67000 (m) [ADD] (11.97)
H. Hotter (b-bar), M. Raucheisen (pno) *(rec 1942-44)* † Songs (misc) VOCA (Vocal Archives) 2-▲ 1166 (26.97)
G. Hüsch (bar), H. U. Müller (pno) [GER] *(rec 1933 for HMV)* PHS ▲ 9469 [AAD] (18.97)
G. Hüsch (bar), H. U. Müller (pno) [GER] *(rec 1933 for HMV)* † Schöne Müllerin, D.795; Beethoven:An die ferne Geliebte, Op. 98 PRE (Lebendige Vergangenheit) 2-▲ 89202 [AAD] (31.97)
R. Lang (cta), W. Rieger (pno) *(rec Festhalle Viersen, Oct 30 & Nov 4, 1994)* DSB ▲ 1061 [DDD] (16.97)
L. Lehmann (sop), P. Ulanowsky (pno) *(rec 1940-41)* VOCA (Vocal Archives) ▲ 1173 (13.97)
L. Lehmann (sop), P. Ulanowsky (pno) *(rec 1940-41)* PHS ▲ 33 (17.97)
S. Lorenz (bar), N. Shelter (pno) BER ▲ 9316 (10.97)
C. Ludwig (mez), J. Levine (pno) DEUT (Masters) ▲ 45521 [DDD] (9.97)
L. Marshall (sop), A. Kuerti (pno) *(rec Univ of Toronto Ontario, Nov 1976)* CBC (Perspective) ▲ 2011 [ADD] (16.97)
P. Mason (bar), P. East (pno) *(rec Rockefeller Performing Arts Center SUNY College, F, Jan 1993)*
BRID ▲ 9053 [DDD] (17.97)
K. Moll (bass), C. Garben (pno) [GER] ORF 2-▲ 42832 (36.97)
L. Polgár (bass), J. Schultz (pno) HUN ▲ 31750 (16.97)
C. Prégardien (ten), A. Staier (pno) [period instr] TELC ▲ 18824 (16.97)
H. Rehkemper (bar), M. Gurlitt (pno)—Gute Nacht; Der Lindenbaum; Auf dem Flusse; Die Post; Die Krähe; Die Nebensonnen; Der Leiermann *(rec 1924-28)* † Schwanengesang, D.957; Songs (misc colls)
PRE (Lebendige Vergangenheit) ▲ 89058 [AAD] (16.97)
M. Shirai (mez), H. Höll (pno) † Schöne Müllerin, D.795 CAPO (Schubert-Edition) 2-▲ 490777 [DDD] (16.97)
M. Talvela (bass), R. Gothóni (pno) [GER] BIS ▲ 253 [DDD] (17.97)
R. Tauber (ten), M. Spoliansky (pno)—Gute Nacht; Der Lindenbaum; Wasserflut; Rückblick; Frühlingstraum; Die Post; Die Krähe; Der stürmische Morgen; Der Wegweiser; Das Wirtshaus; Das Wirtshaus; Mut; Der Leiermann *(rec June 20, 1927)* † R. Schumann:Songs PHS ▲ 9370 [AAD] (17.97)
R. Tear (ten), P. Ledger (pno) ASVQ ▲ 6085 [ADD] (10.97)
J. Vickers (ten), P. Schaaf (pno) [GER] *(rec live, Oct 2, 1983)* VAIA 2-▲ 1007 [ADD] (20.97)
Die Zauberharfe [The Magic Harp] (melodrama in 3 acts) [lib G. von Hofmann], D.644 (1820)
T. Moser (ten—Palmerin), J. Németh (bar—cavaliere), O. Edelmann (nar—Alf/Folko/Ryno), C. Ostermayer (nar—Melinde), R. Dierk (nar—Ida), W. Schwickerath (nar—Arnulf), K. Schossmann (nar—Sutur), T. Gotti (cnd), Szeged National Theater PO, Szeged National Theater Chorus *(rec live, 1983) (E,G,I lib texts)*
BONG 2-▲ 2019 [ADD] (32.97)
Die Zauberharfe:Overture (1820)
W. Boskovsky (cnd), Dresden State Opera Orch † Rosamunde BER ▲ 9004 [ADD] (10.97)
R. Krečmer (cnd), Czech Chamber PO † Rosamunde (sels); A. Dvořák:Czech Suite, Op. 39 DI ▲ 920520 (5.97)
Die Zwillingsbrüder (singspiel in 1 act) [lib G. von Hofmann], D.647 (1819)
P. Maag (cnd), Mediterranea PO, E. Di Pietro (cnd), Solisti Cantori, P. Labitzke (sop—Lieschen), H. Schmid (ten—Anton), S. Morbach (bar—Franz & Friedrich), M. Schaltezky (bass—Der Amtmann), G. Heckel (bass—Der Schulze) [ITA] *(rec Teatro Rendano, Cosenza, Italy, Nov 15-16, 1997) ([ENG,GER,ITA] lib text)*
BONG ▲ 2225 (live) [DDD] (16.97)

SCHULHOFF, ERWIN (1894-1942)
Bartipanu (ballet scenes) for Orchestra [for Molière's Le Bourgeois Gentilhomme] (1926)
W. Herbers (cnd) ("Ensemble Works, Vol. 1") CCL ▲ 6994 [DDD]
Bass Nightingale for Contrabassoon (1922)
L. Fait (dbl bn) † Concertino Fl; Divert Ob; Son erotica; Sym germanica SUR ▲ 112170 [DDD]
Concertino for Flute, Viola & Double Bass (1925)
P. Perina (va), E. Kumpera (db), P. Foltyn (fl) † Bass Nightingale; Divert Ob; Son erotica; Sym germanica
SUR ▲ 112170 [DDD]
Winnipesaukee Chamber Players † A. Dvořák:Qts Pno, Opp. 23 & 87; C. Ives:Son 5 Vn RUS ▲ 10029 [DDD] (11.97)
Concerto for Piano & Small Orchestra (1922)
A. Madžar (pno), A. Delfs (cnd), German CO *(rec Freie Waldorfschule Bremen, Germany, Oct 1994)* ("Concertos alla Jazz: Entartete Musik") † Con Str Qt; Double Con Fl; Esquisses de Jazz; Jazz Etudes Pno; Rag Music, Op. 41
PLON ▲ 44819 [DDD] (16.97)
M. Rische (pno), G. Schuller (cnd), Cologne RSO † Sym 5 KSCH ▲ 315972 [DDD] (16.97)
Concerto for String Quartet & Winds (1930)
A. Delfs (cnd), German CO, Hawthorne String Quartet *(rec Freie Waldorfschule Bremen, Germany, Oct 1994)* ("Concertos alla Jazz: Entartete Musik") † Con Pno; Double Con Fl; Esquisses de Jazz; Jazz Etudes Pno; Rag Music, Op. 41 PLON ▲ 44819 [DDD] (16.97)
Z. Košler (cnd), Czech PO ("Erwin Schulhoff:Concertante And Ballet Music") † Double Con Fl; Ogelala
PANT ▲ 811308 [AAD] (11.97)
Divertimento for String Quartet, Op. 14
Kocian String Quartet † Duo Vn & Vc; Sxt Strs SUR ▲ 112167 [DDD]
Divertissement for Oboe, Clarinet & Bassoon (1926)
Novak Trio † Bass Nightingale; Concertino Fl; Son erotica; Sym germanica SUR ▲ 112170 [DDD]
Double Concerto for Flute, 2 Horns, Piano & Strings (1927)
J. Válek (fl), J. Hála (pno), V. Válek (cnd), Dvořák CO ("Erwin Schulhoff:Concertante And Ballet Music") † Con Str Qt; Ogelala PANT ▲ 811308 [AAD] (11.97)
B. Wild (fl), A. Madžar (pno), A. Delfs (cnd), German CO *(rec Freie Waldorfschule Bremen, Germany, Oct 1994)* ("Concertos alla Jazz: Entartete Musik") † Con Pno; Con Str Qt; Esquisses de Jazz; Jazz Etudes Pno; Rag Music, Op. 41 PLON ▲ 44819 [DDD] (16.97)

SCHULHOFF, ERWIN (cont.)

Duo for Violin & Cello (1925)
R. Barton (vn), W. Warner (vc) *(rec Chicago, IL, Dec 1-10, 1998)* ("Double Play") † Kodály:Duo Vn & Vc, Op. 7; Martinů:Duo 2 Vn & Vc; M. Ravel:Son Vn & Vc CED ▲ 47 [DDD] (16.97)
Kocian String Quartet members † Divert Str Qt, Op. 14; Sxt Strs SUR ▲ 112167 [DDD]
O. Krysa (vn), T. Thedéen (vc) *(rec 1994-97)* ("Duos for Violin & Cello") † Honegger:Sonatina Vns & Vc; Martinů:Duo 1 Vn & Vc, H.157; M. Ravel:Son Vn & Vc BIS ▲ 916 [DDD] (17.97)
O. Krysa (vn), T. Thedéen (vc) *(rec Malmö Concert Hall, Sweden, May 12, 1994)* † Son Vc; Son Vn; Son 1 Vn, Op. 7 BIS ▲ 679 [DDD] (17.97)
G. Süssmuth (vn), H. Eschenburg (vc) *(rec Berlin, June 6-8 & Nov 7-8, 1994)* ("Kammermusik für Streicher") † Qt 1 Strs; Son Vn; Sxt Strs CAPO ▲ 10539 [DDD] (11.97)

Esquisses de Jazz [Jazz Sketches] (6) for Piano, "To My Little Friend Jim Clark" (1927)
E. Schulhoff (pno) *(rec Berlin, 1928)* ("Concertos alla Jazz: Entartete Musik") † Con Pno; Con Str Qt; Double Con Fl; Jazz Etudes Pno; Rag Music, Op. 41 PLON ▲ 44819 [DDD] (16.97)

The Flames [Plameny] (opera in 2 acts) [lib Beneš & Brod] (1927-28)
J. Eaglen (sop—Donna Anna/Marguerite/Nun/Woman), C. Höhn (sop—Shadow), R. Schudel (sop—Shadow), C. Lindsley (sop—Shadow), I. Vermillion (mez—La Morte), C. Berggold (alt—Shadow), K. Borris (alt—Shadow), E. Dressen (alt—Shadow), K. Westi (ten—Don Juan), G. Wolf (bass—Harlequin), J. Prein (bass—Commendatore), J. Mauceri (cnd), Berlin German SO, Berlin RIAS Chamber Choir *(rec Jesus-Christus Church Berlin Dahlem, Oct 1993 & Apr 1994) (lib)* PLON 2-▲ 44630 [DDD] (32.97)

Folk Songs & Dances (3) from the Tesin Region for Voice & Piano
O. Černá (mez), F. Kůda (pno) ("Songs") † Mood Pictures, Op. 12; Songs SUR ▲ 3196 (16.97)

Hot Sonata for Alto Saxophone & Piano (1930)
D. Bensmann (a sax), M. Rische (pno) ("The Saxophone") † Glazunov:Con A Sax, Op. 109; Moulaert:Andante, Fugue & Finale; Schaeuble:Duke Ellington Medley KSCH ▲ 313352 [DDD] (16.97)
S. Koutnik (a sax), J. Čech (pno) † Son Fl; Son Vc SUR ▲ 112169 [DDD]

Jazz Etudes (5) for Piano (1926)
E. Schulhoff (pno) *(rec Berlin, Germany, 1928)* ("Concertos alla Jazz: Entartete Musik") † Con Pno; Con Str Qt; Double Con Fl; Esquisses de Jazz; Rag Music, Op. 41 PLON ▲ 44819 [DDD] (16.97)

Melody for Violin & Piano
I. Ženatý (vn), J. Hála (pno) † Son 1 Vn, Op. 7; Son 2 Vn; Suite Vn SUR ▲ 112168 [DDD]

Die Mondsuchtige [Sleepwalking] (ballet) for Orchestra [from Jazz Suite, 1921]
L. Zagrosek (cnd), Leipzig Opera Orch ("Entartete Musik: Music Surpressed by the 3rd Reich") † P. Hindemith:Dämon, Op. 28; Schreker:Geburtstag der Infantin (suite) PLON ▲ 44182 (16.97)

Mood Pictures (3) for Soprano, Violin & Piano, Op. 12
O. Černá (mez), F. Kůda (pno) ("Songs") † Folk Songs & Dances from the Tesin Region; Songs SUR ▲ 3196 (16.97)

Music of Schulhoff
W. Herbers (cnd) —Wolkenpumpe; Bassnachtigall; Sym germanica; Son erotica; 10 Little Pno Pieces; Hot Son; Orinoco; Kassandra; Syncopated Peter; Susi; The Beggar; Die Wolkenpumpe ("Ensemble Works, Vol. 2") CCL ▲ 9997 (18.97)

Ogelala (ballet suite) for Orchestra (1923)
M. Jurowski (cnd), Rhineland-Palatinate State PO † B. Goldschmidt:Comedy of Errors; Greek Suite CPO ▲ 999323 (14.97)
L. Pešek (cnd), Czech PO ("Erwin Schulhoff:Concertante And Ballet Music") † Con Str Qt; Double Con Fl PANT ▲ 811308 [AAD] (11.97)

Piano Music
T. Víšek (pno)—5 Pittoresken; Partita für Klavier; Jazz Etudes (5); Hot Music; Zehn synkopierte Etüden; Suite dansante en jazz pour pno SUR ▲ 111870 [DDD]
T. Víšek (pno)—Esquisses de Jazz; Ostinato; Music für Klavier, Op. 35; Inventionen (11); Klavierstücke (10), Op. 30; Studien (2) Pno *(rec June-Dec 1997)* ("Piano Cycles, 1919-39") SUR ▲ 2171 [DDD] (16.97)

Pieces (5) for String Quartet (1923)
Kocian String Quartet † Qt 1 Strs; Qt 2 Strs SUR ▲ 112166 [DDD]
Petersen String Quartet ("Portrait") † Qt Strs, Op. 25; Beethoven:Quartets for Strings (miscellaneous collections); E. Grieg:Qt Strs, Op. 27; W. A. Mozart:Qt 22 Strs, K.589; F. Schubert:Qnt Strs, D.956; R. Schumann:Qts Strs, Op. 41 CAPO ▲ 14862 [DDD] (10.97)
Schoenberg String Quartet † Qt 1 Strs; Qt 2 Strs; Sxt Strs KSCH ▲ 312332 [DDD] (16.97)

Quartet in G for Strings, Op. 25 (1918)
Petersen String Quartet ("Portrait") † Pieces Str Qt; Beethoven:Quartets for Strings (miscellaneous collections); E. Grieg:Qt Strs, Op. 27; W. A. Mozart:Qt 22 Strs, K.589; F. Schubert:Qnt Strs, D.956; R. Schumann:Qts Strs, Op. 41 CAPO ▲ 14862 [DDD] (10.97)

Quartet No. 1 for Strings (1924)
Brandis String Quartet *(rec Oct 12-14, 1992)* † P. Hindemith:Qt 3 Strs, Op. 22; K. Weill:Qt Strs NIMB ▲ 5410 [DDD] (16.97)
Colorado Chamber Players *(rec LSU Baton Rouge, Apr 1995)* ("Uplifting Discoveries from a Generation Lost: Music of Composers Who Died in the Holocaust") † G. Klein:Trio Vn; Krása:Theme & Vars Str Qt; V. Ullmann:Qt 3 Strs, Op. 43 CENT ▲ 2342 [DDD] (16.97)
Kocian String Quartet † Pieces Str Qt; Qt 2 Strs SUR ▲ 112166 [DDD]
Petersen String Quartet *(rec Berlin, June 6-8 & Nov 7-8, 1994)* ("Kammermusik für Streicher") † Duo Vn & Vc; Son Vn; Sxt Strs CAPO ▲ 10539 [DDD] (11.97)
Schoenberg String Quartet † Pieces Str Qt; Qt 2 Strs; Sxt Strs KSCH ▲ 312332 [DDD] (16.97)

Quartet No. 2 for Strings (1925)
Kocian String Quartet † Pieces Str Qt; Qt 1 Strs SUR ▲ 112166 [DDD]
Schoenberg String Quartet † Pieces Str Qt; Qt 1 Strs; Sxt Strs KSCH ▲ 312332 [DDD] (16.97)

Rag Music for Piano, Op. 41, "To Arthur Bliss" (1922)
E. Schulhoff (pno) *(rec Berlin, Germany, 1928)* ("Concertos alla Jazz: Entartete Musik") † Con Pno; Con Str Qt; Double Con Fl; Esquisses de Jazz; Jazz Etudes Pno PLON ▲ 44819 [DDD] (16.97)

Sextet for Strings (1924)
R. J. Kimstedt (va), M. Sanderling (vc), Petersen String Quartet *(rec Berlin, June 6-8 & Nov 7-8, 1994)* ("Kammermusik für Streicher") † Duo Vn & Vc; Qt 1 Strs; Son Vn CAPO ▲ 10539 [DDD] (11.97)
Kocian String Quartet † Divert Str Qt, Op. 14; Duo Vn & Vc SUR ▲ 112167 [DDD]
J. E. van Regteren (va), T. Kooistra (vc), Schoenberg String Quartet † Pieces Str Qt; Qt 1 Strs; Qt 2 Strs KSCH ▲ 312332 [DDD] (16.97)

Sonata for Cello & Piano, Op. 17 (1915)
J. Barta (vc), J. Čech (pno) † Hot Son; Son Fl SUR ▲ 112169 [DDD]
T. Thedéen (vc), S. Bojsten (pno) *(rec Danderyd Grammar School, Sweden, May 11, 1996)* † Duo Vn & Vc; Son Vn; Son 1 Vn, Op. 7 BIS ▲ 679 [DDD] (17.97)

Sonata erotica for Müttertrompette
D. Stone (müttertrompette) † Bass Nightingale; Concertino Fl; Divert Ob; Sym germanica SUR ▲ 112170 [DDD]

Sonata for Flute & Piano (1927)
P. Foltyn (fl), J. Čech (pno) † Hot Son; Son Vc SUR ▲ 112169 [DDD]
C. Thorspecken (fl), C. Hacke (pno) *(rec Sandhausen, Germany, 1995-96)* ("The Lost Generation") † J. Alain:Movts Fl; P. Haas:Suite Pno, Op. 13; Laparra:Suite Fl; L. Smit:Son Fl BAYE ▲ 100259 [DDD] (17.97)

Sonata No. 1 for Piano (1918)
T. Víšek (pno) ("Sonatas & Suites for Piano") † Son 2 Pno; Son 3 Pno; Suite 2 Pno; Suite 3 Pno SUR ▲ 112172

Sonata No. 2 for Piano (1924)
T. Víšek (pno) ("Sonatas & Suites for Piano") † Son 1 Pno; Son 3 Pno; Suite 2 Pno; Suite 3 Pno SUR ▲ 112172

Sonata No. 3 for Piano (1927)
N. Petrov (pno) ("20th Century Piano Sonatas") † S. Prokofiev:Son 6 Pno, Op. 82; I. Stravinsky:Son Pno OLY ▲ 280 [DDD] (16.97)
T. Víšek (pno) ("Sonatas & Suites for Piano") † Son 1 Pno; Son 2 Pno; Suite 2 Pno; Suite 3 Pno SUR ▲ 112172

Sonata for solo Violin (1926)
O. Krysa (vn) *(rec Danderyd Grammar School, Sweden, Dec 10-11, 1994)* † Duo Vn & Vc; Son Vc; Son 1 Vn, Op. 7 BIS ▲ 679 [DDD] (17.97)
C. Muck (vn) *(rec Berlin, June 6-8 & Nov 7-8, 1994)* ("Kammermusik für Streicher") † Duo Vn & Vc; Qt 1 Strs; Sxt Strs CAPO ▲ 10539 [DDD] (11.97)

Sonata No. 1 for Violin & Piano, Op. 7 (1913)
O. Krysa (vn), T. Tchekina (pno) *(rec Danderyd Grammar School, Sweden, Dec 10-11, 1994)* † Duo Vn & Vc; Son Vc; Son Vn BIS ▲ 679 [DDD] (17.97)
I. Ženatý (vn), J. Hála (pno) † Melody Vn; Son 2 Vn; Suite Vn SUR ▲ 112168 [DDD]

SCHULHOFF, ERWIN (cont.)

Sonata No. 2 for Violin & Piano (1927)
G. Kremer (vn), O. Masienberg (pno) † B. Bartók:Son 2 Vn & Pno, Sz.76; Enescu:Impressions d'enfance, Op. 28 TELC ▲ 13597 (16.97)
I. Ženatý (vn), J. Hála (pno) † Melody Vn; Son 1 Vn, Op. 7; Suite Vn SUR ▲ 112168 [DDD]

Songs
O. Černá (mez), F. Kůda (pno)—Songs (3), Op. 14; Songs (3), "Das Lied vom Kinde"; Song, "Die Garbe" ("Songs") † Folk Songs & Dances from the Tesin Region; Mood Pictures, Op. 12 SUR ▲ 3196 (16.97)
P. Matuszek (bar) † P. Haas:Songs; Krása:Songs SUR ▲ 3334

Suite No. 2 for Piano
T. Víšek (pno) ("Sonatas & Suites for Piano") † Son 1 Pno; Son 2 Pno; Son 3 Pno; Suite 3 Pno SUR ▲ 112172

Suite No. 3 for Piano
T. Víšek (pno) ("Sonatas & Suites for Piano") † Son 1 Pno; Son 2 Pno; Son 3 Pno; Suite 2 Pno SUR ▲ 112172

Suite for Violin & Piano
I. Ženatý (vn), J. Hála (pno) † Melody Vn; Son 1 Vn, Op. 7; Son 2 Vn SUR ▲ 112168 [DDD]

Symphonia germanica for Singing Pianist
T. Víšek (pno) † Bass Nightingale; Concertino Fl; Divert Ob; Son erotica SUR ▲ 112170 [DDD]

Symphony No. 1 (1924-25)
G. A. Albrecht (cnd), Philharmonia Hungarica † Sym 2; Sym 3 CPO ▲ 999251 [DDD] (14.97)
V. Válek (cnd), Prague RSO † Sym 2 SUR ▲ 112160

Symphony No. 2 (1932)
G. Albrecht (cnd), Czech PO *(rec May 3-4 & June 2-3, 1993)* ("Musica Rediviva") † P. Haas:Study; G. Klein:Partita Strs; V. Ullmann:Sym 2 ORF ▲ 337941 [DDD] (18.97)
G. A. Albrecht (cnd), Philharmonia Hungarica † Sym 1; Sym 3 CPO ▲ 999251 [DDD] (14.97)
V. Válek (cnd), Prague RSO † Sym 1 SUR ▲ 112160

Symphony No. 3 (1935)
G. A. Albrecht (cnd), Philharmonia Hungarica † Sym 1; Sym 2 CPO ▲ 999251 [DDD] (14.97)
V. Válek (cnd), Prague RSO † Sym 5 SUR ▲ 112161

Symphony No. 4 for Baritone & Orchestra, "Spanish" (1936-37)
R. Janál (bar), V. Válek (cnd), Prague RSO *(rec Prague, June 2-7, 1997)* † Sym 6 SUR ▲ 112162 [DDD]

Symphony No. 5 (1938)
G. Schuller (cnd), Cologne RSO † Con Pno KSCH ▲ 315972 [DDD] (16.97)
V. Válek (cnd), Prague RSO † Sym 3 SUR ▲ 112161

Symphony No. 6 for Orchestra & Chorus, "Symphony of Freedom" (1941)
V. Válek (cnd), Prague RSO, P. Kühn (cnd), Kühn Mixed Choir *(rec Prague, June 2-7, 1997)* † Sym 4 SUR ▲ 112162 [DDD]

Themen (10) for Piano (1918)
G. Bouwhuis (pno) CCL ▲ 1993 (22.97)

SCHULLER, GUNTHER (1925-

An Arc Ascending for Orchestra (1996)
G. Schuller (cnd), Hanover Radio PO *(rec Hanover, Germany, Dec 1996)* ("Orchestral Works") † Meditation; Studies on Themes of Paul Klee; Vertige d'Eros GMR ▲ 2059 (16.97)

Chamber Symphony (1989)
G. Schuller (cnd), Cleveland Chamber SO *(rec Cleveland, OH)* ("Sound Encounters III") † P. Cooper:Love Songs & Dances; W. Lutoslawski:Paroles tissées GMR ▲ 2058 (16.97)

Choral Music
M. Best (cnd), Corydon Orch, Corydon Singers—Studies on Themes of Paul Klee † A. Bruckner:Choral Music HYP 3-▲ 44071 (36.97)

Concerto for Bassoon & Orchestra
K. Pasmanick (bn), G. Schuller (cnd), Saarbrücken RSO ("Three Concertos") † Con Pno; Con 1 Hn GMR ▲ 2044 (16.97)

Concerto No. 1 for Horn & Orchestra (1944)
R. Todd (hn), G. Schuller (cnd), Saarbrücken RSO ("Three Concertos") † Con Bn; Con Pno GMR ▲ 2044 (16.97)

Concerto for Organ & Orchestra (1994)
J. Diaz (org), M. Bernardi (cnd), Calgary PO *(rec Jack Singer Concert Hall Calgary, Alberta, Oct 14, 1994)* ("Of Reminiscences & Reflections") † Of Reminiscences & Reflections; Past is the Present NWW ▲ 80492 (16.97)

Concerto for Piano & Orchestra (1962)
J. R. Kirstein (pno), M. Rudolf (cnd), Cincinnati SO ("Three Concertos") † Con Bn; Con 1 Hn GMR ▲ 2044 (16.97)

Duologue (4 characteristic pieces) for Violin & Piano (1983)
R. Druian (vn), B. Pasternack (pno) † Paine:Son Vn GMR ▲ 2021 (16.97)

Fantasia for Cello (1960)
S. Kluksdahl (vc) *(rec Esther Boyer College of Music Temple Univ)* ("Lines for Solo Cello") † Broadhead:Lament; D. Martino:Parisonatina Al'dodecafonia; R. Shapey:Krosnick Soli; A. R. Thomas:Spring Song; R. Wernick:Cadenzas & Vars 3 CRI ▲ 762 [DDD] (16.97)

Fantasy for Cello, Op. 19 (1951)
C. Carr (vc) *(rec Oct 1990)* † B. Britten:Suite 3 Vc, Op. 87; G. Crumb:Son Vc; Kodály:Son Vc, Op. 8 GMR ▲ 2031 [DDD] (16.97)
S. Honigberg (vc) ("American Music for Cello") † S. Barber:Son Vc, Op. 6; L. Bernstein:Meditations Vc & Pno; D. Diamond:Kaddish; L. Foss:Capriccio ALBA ▲ 82 [DDD] (16.97)

Eine kleine Posaunenmusik for Trombone & Wind Ensemble (1980)
C. Lindberg (trbn), J. DePreist (cnd), Malmö SO *(rec 1993)* ("American Trombone Concertos") † Creston:Fant Trbn, Op. 42; G. Walker:Con Trbn; E. T. Zwilich:Con Trbn BIS ▲ 628 [DDD] (17.97)

Meditation (symphonic study) for Orchestra (1947)
G. Schuller (cnd), Hanover Radio PO *(rec Hanover, Germany, Dec 1996)* ("Orchestral Works") † Arc Ascending; Studies on Themes of Paul Klee; Vertige d'Eros GMR ▲ 2059 (16.97)

Of Reminiscences & Reflections for Orchestra (1993)
G. Schuller (cnd), Hanover Radio PO *(rec Hannover Germany, Nov 21-22, 1994)* ("Of Reminiscences & Reflections") † Con Org; Past is the Present NWW ▲ 80492 (16.97)

The Past Is in the Present for Orchestra (1994)
G. Schuller (cnd), Hanover Radio PO *(rec Hannover Germany, Nov 21-22, 1994)* ("Of Reminiscences & Reflections") † Con Org; Of Reminiscences & Reflections NWW ▲ 80492 (16.97)

Pieces (5) for 5 Horns (1952)
B. Tuckwell (hn), G. Schuller (cnd), NFB Horn Quartet *(rec Westin, MA, May 1993)* ("Hornithology") † M. Tippett:Son Hns; Wadenpfuhl:Textures GMR ▲ 2062 (13.97)

Quartet No. 2 for Strings (1966)
Emerson String Quartet † H. Cowell:Qt Euphometric; R. Harris:Qt 2 Strs; Imbrie:Qt 4 Strs; A. Shepherd:Triptych NWW ▲ 80453 (16.97)

Quintet No. 2 for Brass (1993)
American Brass Quintet *(rec SUNY College, Purchase, NY)* ("Premier!") † J. Bach:Triptych; D. Sampson:Distant Voices; Welcher:Qnt Brass SUMM ▲ 187 [DDD] (16.97)

Recitative & Rondo for Violin & Piano (1954)
R. Davidovici (vn), A. D. Groote (pno) † H. Aitken:Partita Vn; A. Copland:Nocturne; Piston:Sonatina Vn; P. Schoenfield:Country Fiddle Pieces NWW ▲ 334 [DDD] (16.97)

Romantic Sonata for Clarinet, Horn & Piano
L. Combs (cl), G. Williams (hn), M. A. Covert (pno) † Rochberg:Trio Cl; M. Rózsa:Sonatina Cl CRYS ▮ 731 (9.98)

Studies (7) on Themes of Paul Klee for Orchestra (1959)
A. Dorati (cnd), Minneapolis SO † E. Bloch:Sinfonia breve; A. Copland:Rodeo; G. Gershwin:American in Paris MRCR ▲ 34329 [ADD] (11.97)
G. Schuller (cnd), Hanover Radio PO *(rec Hanover, Germany, Dec 1996)* ("Orchestral Works") † Arc Ascending; Meditation; Vertige d'Eros GMR ▲ 2059 (16.97)

Suite for Woodwind Ensemble (1958)
Aulos Wind Quintet *(rec 1989-90)* ("The Aulos Wind Quintet Plays Music by American Composers, Vol. 1") † S. Barber:Summer Music, Op. 31; J. Cage:Music for Ww; E. Carter:Etudes & Fant; Qnt Ww KSCH ▲ 311532 [DDD] (16.97)

Suite for Woodwind Quintet (1945)
Berlin Philharmonic Wind Quintet *(rec Apr 1998)* ("Summer Music") † S. Barber:Summer Music, Op. 31; E. Carter:Qnt Ww; Machala:American Folk Suite; Medaglia:Suite "Belle Epoque"; Suite popular brasileira; Pitombeira:Ajubete; H. Villa-Lobos:Qnt forme de chôros BIS ▲ 952 [DDD] (17.97)
Reykjavik Wind Quintet *(rec Suffolk, England, July 1992)* ("Barber:Summer Music, Beach:Pastorale & Other American Works Performed by the Reykjavik Wind Quintet") † S. Barber:Summer Music, Op. 31; Beach:Pastorale; I. Fine:Partita; J. Harbison:Qnt Winds; H. Villa-Lobos:Qnt forme de chôros CHN ▲ 9174 [DDD] (16.97)

SCHULLER, GUNTHER (cont.)
Suite for Woodwind Quintet (1945) (cont.)
Sierra Wind Quintet † E. Carter:Etudes & Fant; D. Diamond:Partita Ob, Bn & Pno; Piston:Qnt Ww CMB ▲ 1091 [DDD] (16.97)
Westwood Wind Quintet *(rec May 1992 & Jan 1993)* † Bergsma:Con Ww Qnt; J. Biggs:Scherzo Ww Qnt; E. Carter:Qnt Ww; A. Plog:Animal Ditties; Rochberg:To the Dark Wood; W. Schuman:Dances Ww Qnt CRYS ▲ 752 (15.97)
Symbiosis for Violin, Piano & Percussion (1957)
A. Ajemian (vn), M. Ajemian (pno) *(rec NY, Oct 1962)* † T. O. Lee:Mad Frog!; Qt 3 Strs GMR ▲ 2007 (16.97)
Symphony for Brass & Percussion, Op. 16 (1950)
Summit Brass † J. Cheetham:Keystone Celebration; D. Erb:Sonneries; D. Sampson:Reflections on a Dance; J. Stevens:Moondance SUMM ▲ 127 [DDD] (16.97)
Trio Setting for Violin, Clarinet & Piano (1990)
Verdehr Trio ("The Making of a Medium, Vol. 3") † Averitt:Tripartita; N. Currier:Adagio & Vars CRYS ▲ 743 [DDD] (15.97)
Vertige d'Eros for Orchestra (1945)
G. Schuller (cnd), Hanover Radio PO *(rec Hanover, Germany, Dec 1996)* ("Orchestral Works") † Arc Ascending; Meditation; Studies on Themes of Paul Klee GMR ▲ 2059 (16.97)

SCHULTZ, ANDREW (1960-
Barren Grounds for Chamber Ensemble
Perihelion Ensemble † R. Davidson:Tapestry; B. Sabaneyev:Inner-City Counterpoints VOXA ▲ 14 (18.97)
Collide for Bass Clarinet & Percussion (1990)
Duo Contemporain ("Tube Makers: Music by Australian Composers") † G. Brophy:we bOp; S. Cronin:Even Love Can Wield a Stealthy Blade; R. Edwards:Enyato IV; A. Ford:Getting Blue; Sculthorpe:Simori; Smetanin:Tube Makers GLOE ▲ 5176 [DDD] (16.97)
Dead Songs for Soprano, Clarinet, Cello & Piano (1991)
M. Schindler (sop), Perihelion Ensemble members *(rec Music Dept Univ of Queensland, Australia, Dec 1994)* ("Chamber Music") † Mephisto; Sea-Change; Stick Dance II TALP ▲ 65 [DDD] (18.97)
Mephisto for Flute, Clarinet, Violin, Viola, Double Bass & Guitar (1990)
B. Kendall-Smith (bass), M. Walsh (vn), K. Schaupp (gtr), S. Croucher (fl), G. Roberts (cnd) , G. Roberts (cnd), Perihelion Ensemble members *(rec Music Dept Univ of Queensland, Australia, Dec 1994)* ("Chamber Music") † Dead Songs; Sea-Change; Stick Dance II TALP ▲ 65 [DDD] (18.97)
Sea-Change for Piano (1987)
J. Flemming (pno) *(rec Music Dept Univ of Queensland, Australia, Dec 1994)* ("Chamber Music") † Dead Songs; Mephisto; Stick Dance II TALP ▲ 65 [DDD] (18.97)
The Song of Songs (selections)
R. Peelman (cnd), Song Company ("The Laughter of Mermaids") † S. Cronin:Carmina Pu!; A. Ford:Laughter of Mermaids; G. Whitehead:Virgin & the Nightingale; Whiticker:As Water Bears Salt VOXA ▲ 16 (18.97)
Stick Dance II for Clarinet, Viola & Piano (1989)
Perihelion Ensemble members *(rec Music Dept Univ of Queensland, Australia, Dec 1994)* ("Chamber Music") † Dead Songs; Mephisto; Sea-Change TALP ▲ 65 [DDD] (18.97)

SCHULTZ, ARTHUR (20th cent)
Dragons in the Sky for French Horn, Percussion & Electronic Tape (1989)
T. Bacon (hn), R. Brown (elec/perc) † T-Rex; A. Gottschalk:Section for 4 Hns; Leclaire:Qt Hns; Pinkston:Qt for 4 Hns SUMM ▲ 135 [DDD] (16.97)
T-Rex for French Horn & Piano (1989)
T. Bacon (hn), B. Connelly (pno) † Dragons in the Sky; A. Gottschalk:Section for 4 Hns; Leclaire:Qt Hns; Pinkston:Qt for 4 Hns SUMM ▲ 135 [DDD] (16.97)

SCHULTZ, ROBERT (20th cent)
Piano Music
T. Faigen (pno)—Visions of Dunbar, Op. 25; Montage, Op. 20; Reminiscences, Op. 24/1-8; Ballade, Op. 17; Impromtus, Op. 23/3-5 *(rec Atlanta, GA, June 24-27, 1993)* ("Visions of Dunbar") † Trans Pno ACAD ▲ 20026 (16.97)
Transcriptions for Piano
T. Faigen (pno)—Gluck's Dance of the Blessed Spirits; Fauré's Pavane, Op. 50; Rachmaninoff's Vocalise, Op. 34/14 *(rec Atlanta, GA, June 24-27, 1993)* ("Visions of Dunbar") † Pno Music ACAD ▲ 20026 (16.97)
T. Faigen (pno)—Albinoni:Adagio in g; Gluck:Dance of the Blessed Spirits; Mozart:Soave sia il vento; Bruch:Kol Nidre, Op. 47; Fauré:Pavane, Op. 50; Bach:Air [from Suite 3 Orch]; Con 5 Hpd [Largo]; Giordano:La Mamma morta [from Andrea Chénier]; Rachmaninoff:Vocalise, Op. 34/14; Saint-Saëns:Le cygne; Mascagni:Intermezzo [from Cavalleria rusticana]; Massenet:Meditation [from Thaïs]; Boccherini:Qnt Strs, Op. 13/5 [Minuet & Trio]; Pachelbel:Canon in D *(rec 1993-95)* ("Tina Faigen Plays Schultz Piano Transcriptions") ACAD ▲ 20051 [DDD] (16.97)

SCHULTZ, SVEND SIMON (1913-1998)
Divertimento for Wind Octet (1961)
Danish Wind Octet *(rec Copenhagen, Jan 20, Mar 20 & Apr 10, 1994)* † A. L. Christiansen:Octet Winds, Op. 34; Graugaard:Summerscapes; H. D. Koppel:Music for Ww Octet, Op. 123; S. E. Werner:Catch MARC ▲ 8224002 [DDD] (13.97)

SCHULZ, JOHANN ABRAHAM PETER (1747-1800)
Christi død [Death of Christ] (oratorio) for solo Voices, Orchestra & Chorus [text J. Baggesen] (1792)
I. Dam-Jensen (sop), E. Halling (cta), M. Zachariassen (ten), J. Mannov (bass), C. Hogwood (cnd), Danish National RSO, Danish National Radio Choir *(rec Danish Radio Concert Hall, Oct 3 & 6-7, 1995 & July 23, 1996)* † Dank ich Gott; Høstgildet (ov); Pno Music; Songs CHN ▲ 9553 [DDD] (16.97)
Dank ich Gott an deine Güte (cantata) for solo Voices, Orchestra & Chorus [arr from 2nd movt of Haydn's Symphony No. 104] (1811)
I. Dam-Jensen (sop), E. Halling (cta), C. Hogwood (cnd), Danish National RSO, Danish National Radio Choir *(rec Danish Radio Concert Hall, Oct 3 & 6-7, 1995 & July 23, 1996)* † Christi død; Høstgildet (ov); Pno Music; Songs CHN ▲ 9553 [DDD] (16.97)
Høstgildet:Overture
C. Hogwood (cnd), Danish National RSO *(rec Danish Radio Concert Hall, Oct 3 & 6-7, 1995 & July 23, 1996)* † Christi død; Dank ich Gott; Pno Music; Songs CHN ▲ 9553 [DDD] (16.97)
Largo for Glass Armonica (1799-1800)
B. Hoffmann (g ar) † W. A. Mozart:Adagio & Rondo, K.617; J. G. Naumann:Qt Glass Armonica; Reichardt:Rondeau; Röllig:Qnt Glass Armonica ALLO ▲ 8174 [ADD] (3.97)
Piano Music
C. Hogwood (pno)—Allegretto in C; Andante sostenuto in A, Op. 1/2 *(rec Danish Radio Concert Hall, Oct 3 & 6-7, 1995 & July 23, 1996)* † Christi død; Dank ich Gott; Høstgildet (ov); Songs CHN ▲ 9553 [DDD] (16.97)
Songs
I. Dam-Jensen (sop), J. Mannov (bass), C. Hogwood (pno), Danish National Radio Choir—An die Natur [To Nature]; Abendlied [Evening Song]; Neujahrslied [New Year's Song]; Mailied [May Song] *(rec Danish Radio Concert Hall, Oct 3 & 6-7, 1995 & July 23, 1996)* † Christi død; Dank ich Gott; Høstgildet (ov); Pno Music CHN ▲ 9553 [DDD] (16.97)

SCHULZ-EVLER, ANDREI (1854-1905)
Arabesque on Themes from Johann Strauss' *The Beautiful Blue Danube* for Piano
M.-A. Hamelin (pno) † Chopin:Son Pno in b♭, Op. 35; S. Rachmaninoff:Son 2 Pno, Op. 36; H. Villa-Lobos:Rudepoema PTRY ▲ 2204 (17.97)
T. Labé (pno) ("Virtuoso Johann Strauss: Paraphrases & Arrangements of Favorite Strauss Melodies by Rosenthal, Tau") † L. Godowsky:Symphonic Metamorphosis of Die Fledermaus; Symphonic Metamorphosis of Wein, Weib und Gesang; M. Rosenthal:Carnaval de Vienne Pno; Strauss (II):Waltzes; Tausig:Valse-Caprice DOR ▲ 80102 [DDD] (13.97)
J. Lhévinne (pno), J. Smeterlin (pno) *(rec 1928)* ("Virtuoso Piano Transcriptions Played by 9 Legendary Pianists") † L. Godowsky:Symphonic Metamorphosis of Die Fledermaus; Symphonic Metamorphosis of Künstlerleben; Strauss (II):Pno Trans VAIA ▲ 1019 [ADD] (17.97)
K. Oldham (pno) ("The Art of the Piano Transcription") † Liszt:Fant & Fugue on "Ad nos" Org, S.259; F. Schubert:Pno Music (misc colls) VAIA ▲ 1104 (17.97)

SCHULZE, WERNER (1952-
Beamtensymphonie in Moll-Dur for 3 Singers & Chamber Ensemble (1987)
I. Rainer (cnd), Studio da Camera Ensemble, U. Widmer (sgr), G. Lehner (sgr), B. Schollum (sgr) † L. Dobbins:Fire & Ice; J. J. Gordon:Calaveras; W. Lutoslawski:Little Suite; T. Myers:Configuration VMM (Music from 6 Continents 1993) ▲ 3018 [DDD]

SCHUMAN, WILLIAM (1910-1992)
Carols of Death for Chorus [text Whitman] (1958)
S. Cleobury (cnd), King's College Choir Cambridge *(rec Cambridge, England, June 23-27, 1990)* † L. Bernstein:Chichester Psalms; A. Copland:In the Beginning; C. Ives:Psalm 90; L. Larsen:How It Thrills Us EMIC ▲ 66787 [DDD] (11.97)
H. Rosenbaum (cnd), New York Virtuoso Singers *(rec United States of America)* ("To Orpheus") † Carols of Death; Dallapiccola:Prima serie; Prima serie dei cori di Michelangelo Buonarroti il; Dellaira:Art & Isadora; Art & Isadora Cho; H. W. Henze:Orpheus Behind the Wire; D. Lang:By Fire; Perle:Sonnets to Orpheus; Sonnets to Orpheus Cho *(E text)* CRI ▲ 615 [DDD] (16.97)
G. Smith (cnd), Gregg Smith Singers ("I Hear America Sing") † Esses; Mail Order Madrigals; Orpheus & His Lute; Perceptions; Prelude; Rounds on Famous Words; N. Rorem:Give All To Love; In Time of Pestilence; Letters from Paris; Missa Brevis; Talma:Corona; Leaden Echo; Let's Touch the Sky; Voices of Peace; Wreath of Blessings VB3 (The American Composers) 3-▲ 3037 (14.97)
Colloquies (3) for Horn & Orchestra (1979)
P. Myers (hn), Z. Mehta (cnd), New York PO † G. Crumb:Haunted Landscape NWW ▲ 326 [DDD] (16.97)
Concerto for Piano & Small Orchestra (1938; rev 1942)
R. Tureck (pno), D. Saidenberg (cnd), Saidenberg Little SO *(rec NY, Jan 13, 1943)* ("Rosalyn Tureck: Première Performances") † Dallapiccola:Studi Vn; D. Diamond:Son 1 Pno VAIA ▲ 1124 [ADD] (17.97)
Credendum for Orchestra (1955)
E. Ormandy (cnd), Philadelphia Orch *(rec 1956)* † Gesensway:4 Squares of Philadelphia; Persichetti:Sym 4 ALBA (American Archives) ▲ 276 [AAD] (16.97)
Dances for Woodwind Quintet & Percussion
Westwood Wind Quintet *(rec May 1992 & Jan 1993)* † Bergsma:Con Ww Qnt; J. Biggs:Scherzo Ww Qnt; E. Carter:Qnt Ww; A. Plog:Animal Ditties; Rochberg:To the Dark Wood; G. Schuller:Suite Woodwind Qnt CRYS ▲ 752 (15.97)
Esses: Short Suite for Singers on Words Beginning with S (1982)
R. Rees (sop), L. Dorsey (bass), G. Smith (cnd), Gregg Smith Singers ("I Hear America Sing") † Carols of Death; Mail Order Madrigals; Orpheus & His Lute; Perceptions; Prelude; Rounds on Famous Words; N. Rorem:Give All To Love; In Time of Pestilence; Letters from Paris; Missa Brevis; Talma:Corona; Leaden Echo; Let's Touch the Sky; Voices of Peace; Wreath of Blessings VB3 (The American Composers) 3-▲ 3037 (14.97)
In Praise of Shahn (canticle) for Orchestra (1969)
L. Bernstein (cnd), New York PO † To Thee Old Cause; S. Barber:Adagio Strs; Con Vn SNYC (Bernstein Century) ▲ 63088 (11.97)
O. Mueller (cnd), Juilliard Orch † A. Copland:Connotations; R. Sessions:Black Maskers (suite) NWW ▲ 368 [DDD] (16.97)
In Sweet Music for Chorus
R. Rees (sop), Orpheus Trio † Judith; Night Journey CRI (American Masters) ▲ 791 (16.97)
Judith (ballet) for Orchestra (1949)
Eastman Philharmonia † In Sweet Music; Night Journey CRI (American Masters) ▲ 791 (16.97)
G. Schwarz (cnd), Seattle SO † New England Triptych; Sym 5; Vars on "America" DLS ▲ 3115 [DDD] (14.97)
Mail Order Madrigals for Chorus (1971)
P. Broadbent (cnd), Joyful Company of Singers ("Choral Music") † Perceptions; S. Barber:Choral Music; Let Down the Bars, O Death!, Op. 8/2; B. Bartók:Dirges ASV ▲ 939 (16.97)
G. Smith (cnd), Gregg Smith Singers ("I Hear America Sing") † Carols of Death; Esses; Orpheus & His Lute; Perceptions; Prelude; Rounds on Famous Words; N. Rorem:Give All To Love; In Time of Pestilence; Letters from Paris; Missa Brevis; Talma:Corona; Leaden Echo; Let's Touch the Sky; Voices of Peace; Wreath of Blessings VB3 (The American Composers) 3-▲ 3037 (14.97)
The Mighty Casey (opera in 3 scenes) [lib J. Gury] (1951-53)
R. Rees (sop), T. Bogdan (ten), R. Muenz (b-bar), G. Smith (cnd), Adirondack CO, Gregg Smith Singers, Long Island Choral Association [ENG] ("Three American One-Act Operas") † S. Barber:Hand of Bridge, Op. 35; Blitzstein:Harpies PREM ▲ 1009 [ADD] (16.97)
New England Triptych for Orchestra (1956)
H. Hanson (cnd), Eastman-Rochester Orch † C. Ives:Sym 3; Three Places in New England; Mennin:Sym 5 MRCR ▲ 32755 [ADD] (11.97)
A. Litton (cnd), Dallas SO *(rec Morton H. Meyerson Symphony Center Dallas, TX, TX, May 1995)* ("An American Tapestry") † Griffes:White Peacock; A. Hovhaness:Sym 2; C. Ives:Three Places in New England; Piston:Incredible Flutist DOR ▲ 90224 [DDD] (16.97)
G. Schwarz (cnd), Seattle SO † Judith; Sym 5; Vars on "America" DLS ▲ 3115 [DDD] (14.97)
J. Sedares (cnd), Phoenix SO † B. Herrmann:Sym 1 KOCH ▲ 7135 [DDD] (10.97)
Night Journey (ballet) for Orchestra (1947)
Endymion Ensemble † In Sweet Music; Judith CRI (American Masters) ▲ 791 (16.97)
Orpheus & His Lute for Voice & Piano [text Shakespeare] (1944)
H. Cheifetz (vc), B. Johanson (gtr) [arr Johanson] *(rec Lincoln Hall Auditorium, Portland State Univ., OR, Mar 1997)* ("Affinity") † Debussy:Preludes Pno; M. de Falla:Canciones populares españolas; B. Johanson:Elegy; Fant on a Plainchant; Homemade Music; In Amber Light; M. Ravel:Pavane pour une infante défunte; D. Shostakovich:Dances of the Dolls GAGR ▲ 604 [DDD] (14.97)
R. Rees (sop), D. Holroyd (pno), G. Smith (cnd), Gregg Smith Singers ("I Hear America Sing") † Carols of Death; Esses; Mail Order Madrigals; Perceptions; Prelude; Rounds on Famous Words; N. Rorem:Give All To Love; In Time of Pestilence; Letters from Paris; Missa Brevis; Talma:Corona; Leaden Echo; Let's Touch the Sky; Voices of Peace; Wreath of Blessings VB3 (The American Composers) 3-▲ 3037 (14.97)
Perceptions for Chorus (1982)
P. Broadbent (cnd), Joyful Company of Singers ("Choral Music") † Mail Order Madrigals; S. Barber:Choral Music; Let Down the Bars, O Death!, Op. 8/2; B. Bartók:Dirges ASV ▲ 939 (16.97)
R. Rees (sop), G. Smith (cnd), Gregg Smith Singers ("I Hear America Sing") † Carols of Death; Esses; Mail Order Madrigals; Orpheus & His Lute; Prelude; Rounds on Famous Words; N. Rorem:Give All To Love; In Time of Pestilence; Letters from Paris; Missa Brevis; Talma:Corona; Leaden Echo; Let's Touch the Sky; Voices of Peace; Wreath of Blessings VB3 (The American Composers) 3-▲ 3037 (14.97)
Prayer in Time of War for Orchestra (1943)
J. Mester (cnd), Louisville Orch *(rec 1971-72)* † Sym 4; J. J. Becker:Symphonia brevis; R. Harris:Epilogue to Profiles in Courage: JFK; When Johnny Comes Marching Home (ov) for Orch ALBA ▲ 27 [ADD] (16.97)
Prelude for Female Chorus (or Mixed Chorus) [text Wolfe] (1939)
R. Rees (sop), G. Smith (cnd), Gregg Smith Singers ("I Hear America Sing") † Carols of Death; Esses; Mail Order Madrigals; Orpheus & His Lute; Perceptions; Rounds on Famous Words; N. Rorem:Give All To Love; In Time of Pestilence; Letters from Paris; Missa Brevis; Talma:Corona; Leaden Echo; Let's Touch the Sky; Voices of Peace; Wreath of Blessings VB3 (The American Composers) 3-▲ 3037 (14.97)
Rounds on Famous Words (5) for Chorus (1956 & 1959)
G. Smith (cnd), Gregg Smith Singers ("I Hear America Sing") † Carols of Death; Esses; Mail Order Madrigals; Orpheus & His Lute; Perceptions; Prelude. N. Rorem:Give All To Love; In Time of Pestilence; Letters from Paris; Missa Brevis; Talma:Corona; Leaden Echo; Let's Touch the Sky; Voices of Peace; Wreath of Blessings VB3 (The American Composers) 3-▲ 3037 (14.97)
Symphony No. 3 (1941)
L. Bernstein (cnd), New York PO † R. Harris:Sym 3 DEUT ▲ 19780 [DDD] (16.97)
L. Bernstein (cnd), New York PO † Sym 5; Sym 8 SNYC (Bernstein Century) ▲ 63163 (10.97)
Symphony No. 4 (1941)
J. Mester (cnd), Louisville Orch *(rec 1968-69)* † Prayer in Time of War; J. J. Becker:Symphonia brevis; R. Harris:Epilogue to Profiles in Courage: JFK; When Johnny Comes Marching Home (ov) for Orch ALBA ▲ 27 [ADD] (16.97)
Symphony No. 5, "Symphony for Strings" (1943)
L. Bernstein (cnd), New York PO † Sym 3; Sym 8 SNYC (Bernstein Century) ▲ 63163 (10.97)
G. Schwarz (cnd), Seattle SO † Judith; New England Triptych; Vars on "America" DLS ▲ 3115 [DDD] (14.97)
Symphony No. 6 (1948)
E. Ormandy (cnd), Philadelphia Orch † R. Harris:Sym 7; Piston:Sym 4 ALBA ▲ 256 [AAD] (16.97)
Symphony No. 7 (1960)
L. Maazel (cnd), Pittsburgh SO † Balada:Steel Sym NWW ▲ 348 [DDD] (16.97)
Symphony No. 8 (1962)
L. Bernstein (cnd), New York PO † Sym 3; Sym 5 SNYC (Bernstein Century) ▲ 63163 (10.97)
To Thee Old Cause (evocation) for Oboe, Brass, Timpani, Strings & Piano (1968)
L. Bernstein (cnd), New York PO † In Praise of Shahn; S. Barber:Adagio Strs; Con Vn SNYC (Bernstein Century) ▲ 63088 (11.97)

SCHUMAN, WILLIAM (cont.)
Undertow (choreographic episodes) for Orchestra [from ballet] (1945)
J. Levine (cnd), Ballet Theater Orch *(rec 1953-54)* † Antheil:Capital of the World; R. D. Banfield:Combat
EMIC ▲ 66548 [ADD] (11.97)
Variations on America for Orchestra [arr Schuman from Ives's organ work] (1963)
G. Schwarz (cnd), Seattle SO † Judith; New England Triptych; Sym 5 DLS ▲ 3115 [DDD] (14.97)
When Jesus Wept for Band [from New England Triptych] (1958)
B. Harbach (hpd) [arr for hpd] † S. Adler:Hymnset GAS ▲ 258 (16.97)
SCHUMANN, CAMILLO (1872-1946)
Sonatas (6) for Organ (1898-after 1910)
R. Kluth (org) *(rec Matthias Kreienbrink Organs, Germany, 1984)* ("Complete Organ Sonatas")
MDG ▲ 6060173 [DDD] (17.97)
SCHUMANN, CLARA (WIECK-) (1819-1896)
Choral Songs (3) for a cappella Mixed Chorus (1848)
G. Kegelmann (cnd), Heidelberg Madrigal Choir [GER] † L. Boulanger:Choral Music; Songs; Mendelssohn (-Hensel):Gartenlieder, Op. 3; Nachtreigen BAYE ▲ 100041 [DDD] (17.97)
Concerto in a for Piano & Orchestra, Op. 7 (1835 or 1836)
A. Cheng (pno), J. Falletta (cnd), Women's Philharmonic † L. Boulanger:D'un matin de printemps Orch; D'un soir triste; Mendelssohn (-Hensel):Ov Orch; Tailleferre:Concertino Hp KOCH ▲ 7169 [DDD]
E. Ciccarelli (pno), F. Layer (cnd), Montpellier Languedoc-Roussillon PO *(rec Le Corum Montpellier, June 14-16, 1995)* † R. Schumann:Con Pno in a, Op. 54 AG ▲ 14 [DDD] (18.97)
V. Jochum (pno), J. Silverstein (cnd), Bamberg SO † Trio Pno, Op. 17 TUD ▲ 788 [DDD] (16.97)
E. Rich (pno), D. Burkh (cnd), Janáček PO *(rec Ostrava Czech Republic, 1995)* † C. M. von Weber:Con 1 Pno, Op. 11; Con 2 Pno, Op. 32 CENT ▲ 2283 [DDD] (16.97)
S. Sugitani (pno), G. Oskamp (cnd), Berlin SO † R. Schumann:Con Pno in a, Op. 54 VRDI ▲ 9233 (13.97)
Lieder (6) for Soprano & Piano, Op. 13 (1842-43)
B. Bonney (sop), V. Ashkenazy (pno) † R. Schumann:Frauenliebe und -leben, Op. 42; Liederkreis, Op. 39; Myrthen, Op. 25 PLON ▲ 452898 (16.97)
Piano Music
K. Eickhorst (pno)—Pièces fugitives, Op. 15; Romancea in a & b, Op. 21/1 & Op. posth.; Scherzos in d & c, Opp. 10 & 14; Soirées musicales, Op. 6; Vars on a Theme of Robert Schumann, Op. 20 CPO ▲ 999132 [DDD] (14.97)
V. Jochum (pno)—Valses romantiques, Op. 4; Soirées musicales, Op. 6; Souvenir de Vienne, Impromptu, Op. 9; Scherzo, Op. 10; Romance, Op. 3; Scherzo, Op. 14; Vars on a Theme of Robert Schumann, Op. 20; Impromptu in E *(rec Apr 1995)* TUD ▲ 7007 (16.97)
T. Laredo (pno)—Romance [from Con 1]; Romance, Op. 5; Soirées Musicales, Op. 6; Valse Capriccio 7; Polonaises, Op. 1; Romance, Op. 11; Scherzo, Op. 14 GALL ▲ 839 (19.97)
C. Ortiz (pno)—Romance in a; Scherzo in d; Scherzo 2 in c, Op. 14; Pieces fugitives; Vars on a theme of R. Schumann; Romance in b; 3 Romances, Op. 11 INMP ▲ 6600292 (16.97)
U. Tschohr (pno)—Le Ballet des Revenants; Toccatina, Op. 6; Andante; 3 Preludes & Fugues; Scherzos, Opp. 10 & 14; Romances, Opp. 3 & 21/1-3; Romance (1856) DI ▲ 920267 [DDD]
Pièces fugitives (4) for Piano, Op. 15 (by 1845)
A. Cheng (pno) *(rec CBC Toronto, Jan 6-8, 1995)* ("Piano Music of Clara & Robert Schumann") † Scherzo Pno, Op. 10; Vars on a Theme by Robert Schumann, Op. 20; R. Schumann:Arabeske Pno, Op. 18; Faschingsschwank, Op. 26; Son Pno, Op. 14 CBC (Musica Viva) ▲ 1087 [DDD] (16.97)
I. M. Witoschynskyj (pno) *(rec Mar 15-17, 1996)* ("Clara Schumann & Her Family") † Romances Pno, Op. 21; Songs; Bargiel:Bagatelles, Op. 4; Characteristic Pieces, Op. 1; Fant Pieces, Op. 9; J. Brahms:Serenade 1 Orch, Op. 11; R. Schumann:Albumblätter, Op. 124; Liederkreis, Op. 39; Studies Canon Form, Op. 56 MDG ▲ 6040729 [DDD] (17.97)
Preludes & Fugues (3) for Piano, Op. 16
C. Rakich (org)—No. 1 in g; No. 2 in B♭; No. 3 in d [trans Da Capo] *(rec St. Justin's Church, Hartfor, CT)* ("Transcriptions from St. Justin's") † S. Barber:Adagio Strs; Mussorgsky:Pictures at an Exhibition; Songs; G. Rossini:Guillaume Tell (ov); Strayhorn:Music of B. Strayhorn; R. Wagner:Tristan und Isolde (sels)
AFK ▲ 541 (16.97)
Romance varié in C for Piano, Op. 3 (1831)
V. Jochum (pno) ("Theme & Variations") † Vars on a Theme by Robert Schumann, Op. 20; J. Brahms:Vars in f♯ on Theme of R. Schumann, Op. 9; R. Schumann:Bunte Blätter, Op. 99; Impromptus on a Theme by Clara Wieck, Op. 5 TUD ▲ 7028 (16.97)
Romances (3) for Piano, Op. 11 (1839)
P. Mazzola (pno) † R. Schumann:Impromptus on a Theme by Clara Wieck, Op. 5; Romances Pno, Op. 28; Son Pno, Op. 14 PANC ▲ 510091 [DDD] (17.97)
Romances (3) for Piano, Op. 21 (1853)
I. M. Witoschynskyj (pno) *(rec Mar 15-17, 1996)* ("Clara Schumann & Her Family") † Pièces fugitives, Op. 15; Songs; Bargiel:Bagatelles, Op. 4; Characteristic Pieces, Op. 1; Fant Pieces, Op. 9; J. Brahms:Serenade 1 Orch, Op. 11; R. Schumann:Albumblätter, Op. 124; Liederkreis, Op. 39; Studies Canon Form, Op. 56 MDG ▲ 6040729 [DDD] (17.97)
Romances (3) for Violin & Piano, Op. 22 (1853)
F. Biondi (vn), L. Di Ilio (pno) [period instrs] ("Robert & Clara Schumann") † R. Schumann:Son 1 Vn, Op. 105; Son 2 Vn, Op. 121 OPUS ▲ 3077 (18.97)
Double Image members ("Secret Whispers") † Songs; Trio Pno, Op. 17; Vars on a Theme by Robert Schumann, Op. 20 MER ▲ 84312 [DDD] (16.97)
H. Schellenberger (ob), R. Koenen (pno) *(rec Berlin, Germany, June 1995)* † R. Schumann:Adagio & Allegro Hn, Op. 70; Fantasiestücke Cl, Op. 73; Klavierstücke, Op. 85; Kreisleriana, Op. 16; Liederkreis, Op. 39; Myrthen, Op. 25; Romances Ob, Op. 94; Romances Pno, Op. 28 CAMM ▲ 130014 [DDD] (16.97)
Scherzo in d for Piano, Op. 10 (by 1839)
A. Cheng (pno) *(rec CBC Toronto, Jan 6-8, 1995)* ("Piano Music of Clara & Robert Schumann") † Pièces fugitives, Op. 15; Vars on a Theme by Robert Schumann, Op. 20; R. Schumann:Arabeske Pno, Op. 18; Faschingsschwank, Op. 26; Son Pno, Op. 14 CBC (Musica Viva) ▲ 1087 [DDD] (16.97)
Songs
Double Image members—6 Lieder aus Jucunde, Op. 23/1-6; Er ist gekommen in Sturm und Regen, Op. 12/2; Liebst du um Schönheit, Op. 12/4; Warum willst du and're fragen, Op. 12/11 ("Secret Whispers") † Romances Vn, Op. 22; Trio Pno, Op. 17; Vars on a Theme by Robert Schumann, Op. 20 MER ▲ 84312 [DDD] (16.97)
G. Fontana (sop), K. Eickhorst (pno) ("Complete Songs") CPO ▲ 999127 [DDD] (14.97)
C. Högman (sop), R. Pöntinen (pno)—Am Strande; Sie liebten sich beide; Beim Abschied; Er ist gekommen in Sturm und Regen; Liebst du um Schönheit; Warum willst du and're fragen; Die gute Nacht, die ich dir sage; Lorelei; Geheimes Flüstern hier und dort; O Lust, o Lust *(rec Stockholm Sweden, May 24-27, 1995)* † Mahler (-Werfel):Songs; Mendelssohn (-Hensel):Songs BIS ▲ 738 [DDD] (17.97)
L. Kolb (sop), D. McMahon (pno)—Ich stand in dunklen Träumen; Sie liebten sich Beide; Liebesgarten; Der Mond kommt still gegangen; Ich hab' in deinem Auge; Die stille Lotosblume † Beach:Songs; Poldowski [Irene Regina Wieniawska]:Songs ALBA ▲ 109 (16.97)
I. Lippitz (sop), D. Richards (pno)—25 Lieder (composed 1834-53)—Walzer; Am Strand; Volkslied; Er ist gekommen; Liebst du um Schönheit; Warum willst du and're fragen; Die gute Nacht; Ich stand in dunklen Träumen; Sie liebten sich beide; Liebeszauber; Der Mond kommt still gegangen; Ich hab' in deinem Auge; Die stille Lotosblume; Loreley; O weh des Scheidens; Beim Abschied; Mein Stern; Der Abendstern; Was weinst du, Blümlein; An einem lichten Morgen; Geheimes Flüstern; Auf einem grünen Hügel; Das ist ein Tag; O Lust, O Lust; Das Veilchen [G] ("The Complete Lieder") BAYE ▲ 100206 [DDD] (17.97)
B. Skovhus (bar), H. Deutsch (pno)—Liebeszauber; Der Mond kommt still gegangen; Die stille Lotosblume; Liebst du um Schönheit; Warum willst du and're fragen; Ich hab' in deinem Auge; Die gute Nacht; Ich stand in dunklen Träumen; Sie liebten sich beide; Volkslied; Lorelei ("The Heart of the Poet") † R. Schumann:Dichterliebe, Op. 48; Liederkreis, Op. 24 SNYC ▲ 62372 (16.97)
K. Uecker (sop), J. Polk (pno)—19 Lieder—Am Strand; Volkslied; Er ist gekommen in Sturm und Regen; Liebst du um Schönheit; Warum willst du and're fragen; Ich stand in dunklen Träumen; Sie liebten sich beide; Liebeszauber; Der Mond kommt still gegangen; Ich hab' in deinem Auge; Die stille Lotosblume; Loreley; O weh des Scheidens; Beim Abschied; Was weinst du, Blümlein; An einem lichten Morgen; Geheimes Flüstern hier und dort; Das ist ein Tag, der klingen mag; Das Veilchen [G] ARA ▲ 6624 [DDD] (16.97)
Songs (6) for Voice & Piano, Op. 13 (1842-43)
I. M. Witoschynskyj (pno) *(rec Mar 15-17, 1996)* ("Clara Schumann & Her Family") † Pièces fugitives, Op. 15; Romances Pno, Op. 21; Bargiel:Bagatelles, Op. 4; Characteristic Pieces, Op. 1; Fant Pieces, Op. 9; J. Brahms:Serenade 1 Orch, Op. 11; R. Schumann:Albumblätter, Op. 124; Liederkreis, Op. 39; Studies Canon Form, Op. 56 MDG ▲ 6040729 [DDD] (17.97)
Trio in g for Piano, Violin & Cello, Op. 17 (by 1846)
Clara Wieck Trio BAYE ▲ 100094 [DDD] (17.97)
Double Image members ("Secret Whispers") † Romances Vn, Op. 22; Songs; Vars on a Theme by Robert Schumann, Op. 20 MER ▲ 84312 [DDD] (16.97)

SCHUMANN, CLARA (WIECK-) (cont.)
Trio in g for Piano, Violin & Cello, Op. 17 (by 1846) (cont.)
Macalester Trio ("Chamber Works by Women Composers") † Beach:Trio Pno, Op. 150; L. Boulanger:Cortège; Nocturne; T. Carreño:Qt Strs; Chaminade:Trio 1 Pno, Op. 11; Mendelssohn (-Hensel):Trio Pno, Op. 11; Tailleferre:Son 1 Vn VB2 2-▲ 5029 [ADD] (9.97)
J. Silverstein (vn), C. Carr (vc), V. Jochum (pno) † Con Pno, Op. 7 TUD ▲ 788 [DDD] (16.97)
Triangulus † Saint-Saëns:Trio 1 for Pno, Op. 18 MER ▲ 84355 (16.97)
Variations on a Theme by Robert Schumann in f♯ for Piano, Op. 20 (1853)
D. Carhart (pno) ("Secret Whispers") † Romances Vn, Op. 22; Songs; Trio Pno, Op. 17 MER ▲ 84312 [DDD] (16.97)
A. Cheng (pno) *(rec CBC Toronto, Jan 6-8, 1995)* ("Piano Music of Clara & Robert Schumann") † Pièces fugitives, Op. 15; Scherzo Pno, Op. 10; R. Schumann:Arabeske Pno, Op. 18; Faschingsschwank, Op. 26; Son Pno, Op. 14
CBC (Musica Viva) ▲ 1087 [DDD] (16.97)
V. Jochum (pno) ("Theme & Variations") † Romance varié, Op. 3; J. Brahms:Vars in f♯ on Theme of R. Schumann, Op. 9; R. Schumann:Bunte Blätter, Op. 99; Impromptus on a Theme by Clara Wieck, Op. 5 TUD ▲ 7028 (16.97)
SCHUMANN, ROBERT (1810-1858)
Adagio & Allegro in A♭ for Horn & Piano (w. Violin or Cello ad lib), Op. 70 (1849)
Algae Trio *(rec Apr 1993)* † Beethoven:Son Hn; J. Brahms:Trio Hn, Op. 40; Cherubini:Sons Hn
PAVA ▲ 7295 [DDD] (10.97)
Y. Bashmet (vn), M. Muntian (pno) † Märchenbilder, Op. 113; Bruch:Kol Nidrei, Op. 47; Enescu:Concertpiece Va & Pno; F. Schubert:Son Arpeggione, D.821 RCAV (Red Seal) ▲ 60112 [DDD] (16.97)
J. Cerminaro (hn), Z. Carno (pno) ("Screamers: Difficult Works for the Horn") † J. Haydn:Divert Hn, H.IV/5; W. Kraft:Evening Voluntaries; H. Lazarof:Intrada; R. Steiger:Hexadecathlon CRYS ▲ 679 (15.97)
J. Cox (hn), K. George (pno) † Chopin:Intro & Polonaise, Op. 3; W. Gieseking:Qnt Hn CENT ▲ 2122 [DDD] (16.97)
K. B. Dinitzen (vc), E. Westenholz (pno) † J. Brahms:Son 1 Vc, Op. 38; R. Strauss:Son Vc, Op. 6
KPT ▲ 32172 [DDD]
D. Finckel (vc), W. Han (pno) *(rec New York, NY, 1996)* † Chopin:Son Vc; E. Grieg:Son Vc ARLD ▲ 19701
V. Grewel (hn), C. Hommel (pno) ("Chamber Music for Winds & Piano") † Fantasiestücke Cl, Op. 73; Qnt Pno, Op. 44; Romances Ob, Op. 94; Stücke im Volkston, Op. 102 ARSM ▲ 1164 [DDD] (17.97)
C. Hermann (vc), C. Herrmann (vc), S. Sasaki (pno) ("Brahms & His Friends, Vol. 2") † J. Brahms:Son 1 Vc, Op. 38; Herzogenberg:Duo Vc; Röntgen:Son Vc, Op. 3 DVX ▲ 29407 (16.97)
P. Jacobsen (hn), E. Westenholz (pno) † Fantasiestücke Cl, Op. 73; Märchenbilder, Op. 113; Romances Ob, Op. 94; Stücke im Volkston, Op. 102 KPT ▲ 32080 [DDD]
J. Kiss (ob), J. Jandó (pno) [arr for ob & pno] *(rec Dec 12-15, 1991)* † Fantasiestücke Cl, Op. 73; Romances Ob, Op. 94; Son 1 Vn, Op. 105; Stücke im Volkston, Op. 102 NXIN ▲ 550599 [DDD] (5.97)
M. Kliegel (vc), K. Merscher (pno) *(rec Dec 14-15, 1991)* † Fantasiestücke Cl, Op. 73; Stücke im Volkston, Op. 102; F. Schubert:Son Arpeggione, D.821 NXIN ▲ 550654 [DDD] (5.97)
L. W. Kuyper (hn), T. Hecht (pno) *(rec Performing Arts Ctr/Purchase College-State Univ of, May 8, 1995)* ("Robert Schumann: The Complete Works for Winds & Piano") † Andante & Vars Hn; Fantasiestücke Cl, Op. 73; Märchenerzählungen, Op. 132; Romances Ob, Op. 94 ELY ▲ 709 [DDD] (16.97)
Y.-Y. Ma (vc), E. Ax (pno) † Con Vc; Fantasiestücke Cl, Op. 73; Stücke im Volkston, Op. 102
SNYC ▲ 42663 [DDD] (16.97)
P. Meyer (cl), E. Le Sage (pno) *(rec Musica Théâtre La Choux-de-Fonds, Apr 9-11, 1993)* ("Märchenbilder") † Fantasiestücke Cl, Op. 73; Märchenbilder, Op. 113; Romances Ob, Op. 94; Stücke im Volkston, Op. 102
DNN ▲ 75960 [DDD] (16.97)
K. Pfister (sax), G. Wyss (pno) [trans for sax & pno] † Fantasiestücke Cl, Op. 73; J. Brahms:Sons Cl
GALL ▲ 931 [DDD] (18.97)
D. Pyatt (hn), M. Jones (pno) ("Recital") † Abbot:Alla caccia; Beethoven:Son Hn; Damase:Berceuse, Op. 19; P. Hindemith:Son Hn; Koechlin:Son Hn; F. Strauss:Nocturne Hn, Op. 7 ERAT ▲ 21632 (16.97)
H. Schellenberger (ob), R. Koenen (pno) *(rec Berlin, Germany, June 1995)* † Fantasiestücke Cl, Op. 73; Klavierstücke, Op. 85; Kreisleriana, Op. 16; Liederkreis, Op. 39; Myrthen, Op. 25; Romances Ob, Op. 94; Romances Pno, Op. 28; C. Schumann:Romances Vn, Op. 22 CAMM ▲ 130014 [DDD] (16.97)
R. Schulte (vn), C. O'Riley (pno) † Fantasiestücke Cl, Op. 73; Märchenbilder, Op. 113; Romances Ob, Op. 94
CENT ▲ 2097 [DAD] (16.97)
W. Thomas-Mifune (vc), C. Piazzini (pno) † Fantasiestücke Cl, Op. 73; Romances Ob, Op. 94; F. Schubert:Son Arpeggione, D.821 CALG ▲ 50949 [DDD]
J. Wang (vc), C. Rosenberger (pno) † S. Barber:Son Vc, Op. 6; Chopin:Intro & Polonaise, Op. 3; Son Vc
DLS ▲ 3097 [DDD] (14.97)
P. V. Zelm (hn), L. V. Doeselaar (pno) *(rec Hilversum, Netherlands, Jan 1997)* ("From Fanfare to Cantilena: 19th Century Horn Music") † Beethoven:Son Hn; Krufft:Son Hn in F; Rheinberger:Son Hn ETC ▲ 1210 [DDD] (17.97)
Z. Zuk (hn), M. Holtzel (cnd), Cracow RSO [orchd Ernest Ansermet] ("Horn Romantics") † C. A. Kiel:Con Hn; R. Strauss:Con 1 Hn, Op. 11; C. M. von Weber:Con Hn ZUK ▲ 100955 (10.97)
Album für die Jugend (43 pieces) for Piano, Op. 68 (1848)
R. Lindblom (pno) ("Lindblom Plays Schumann") † Symphonic Etudes, Op. 13; Waldscenen, Op. 82
PRPI ▲ 9159 (17.97)
N. Shelter (pno) [27 sels] BER ▲ 9350 (10.97)
L. H. Stevens (mar)—No. 02, Soldatenmarsch; No. 08, Wilder Reiter ("Marimba When") † Debussy:Children's Corner; A. Khachaturian:Album of Children's Pieces; P. Tchaikovsky:Album pour enfants Pno, Op. 39 DLS ▲ 3142 [DDD]
G. Tozer (pno) *(rec Sydney Australia, Feb 1988)* ("For Children") † J. S. Bach:Anna Magdalena Bach Notebook (sels); B. Bartók:For Children (1945 revision), Sz.42; Little Pieces, Sz.82; Mikrokosmos, Sz.107; W. A. Mozart:Pno Music (misc colls); S. Prokofiev:Music for Children, Op. 65; F. Schubert:Scherzos Pno, D.593; P. Tchaikovsky:Album pour enfants Pno, Op. 39 TALP ▲ 1 [DDD]
A. Weissenberg (pno) RYLC ▲ 70097
Albumblätter (20 pieces) for Piano, Op. 124 (1832-45)
J. Demus (pno) ("Complete Piano Works, Vol. 2") † Arabeske Pno, Op. 18; Canon on "An Alexis"; Carnaval, Op. 9
NUO ▲ 7312 (16.97)
D. Várjon (pno) *(rec Budapest, Jan 17-20, 1994)* ("Schumann, Piano Works") † Impromptus on a Theme by Clara Wieck, Op. 5; Intermezzos, Op. 4; Romances Pno, Op. 28 NXIN ▲ 550849 [DDD] (5.97)
S. Vladar (pno) † Arabeske Pno, Op. 18; Symphonic Etudes, Op. 13 NXIN ▲ 550144 [DDD] (5.97)
P. Wallfisch (pno)—No. 16, Schlummerlied; No. 08, Lied ohne Ende ("Daydreams") † Beethoven:Son 1 Pno, Op. 2/1; Son 14 Pno, Op. 27/2; J. Brahms:Chorale Preludes Org, Op. 122; Fants Pno, Op. 116; Pieces (6) Pno, Op. 118; Chopin:Etudes Pno; J. Field:Nocturnes Pno; Liszt:Etudes de concert (3), S.144; Hungarian Rhaps, S.244; Vivaldi:Cons Vn Strs, Op. 8/1-4 CHN ▲ 6537 [DDD] (12.97)
I. M. Witoschynskyj (pno)—No. 16, Schlummerlied [w. unpublished prelude by C. Schumann] *(rec Mar 15-17, 1996)* ("Clara Schumann & Her Family") † Liederkreis, Op. 39; Studies Canon Form, Op. 56; Bargiel:Bagatelles, Op. 4; Characteristic Pieces, Op. 1; Fant Pieces, Op. 9; J. Brahms:Serenade 1 Orch, Op. 11; C. Schumann:Pièces fugitives, Op. 15; Romances Pno, Op. 21; Songs MDG ▲ 6040729 [DDD] (17.97)
Allegro in b for Piano, Op. 8 (1831)
R. Brautigam (pno) † Fantasiestücke, Op. 111; Gesänge der Frühe, Op. 133; Novelettes, Op. 21
OLY ▲ 436 [DDD] (16.97)
A. Skoumal (pno) *(rec Aug 1996)* ("Carnaval") † Carnaval, Op. 9; Toccata Pno, Op. 7 STMA ▲ 36 [DDD] (18.97)
Andante & Variations in B♭ for Horn, 2 Cellos & 2 Pianos [original version of Op. 46 for 2 Pianos] (1843)
R. Pidoux (vc), M. François (vc), H. Joulain (hn), M. Jude (pno), L. Cabasso (pno) † J. Brahms:Trio Hn, Op. 40
HAM (Les Nouveaux Interprètes) ▲ 911559 (12.97)
A. Stepansky (vc), G. Appleman (vc), T. Hecht (pno), S. Shapiro (pno) *(rec Performing Arts Ctr/Purchase College-State Univ of, May 8, 1995)* ("Robert Schumann: The Complete Works for Winds & Piano") † Adagio & Allegro Hn, Op. 70; Fantasiestücke Cl, Op. 73; Märchenerzählungen, Op. 132; Romances Ob, Op. 94 ELY ▲ 709 [DDD] (16.97)
Andante & Variations in B♭ for 2 Pianos [arr from Andante & Variations for Horn, 2 Cellos & Piano], Op. 46 (1843)
M. Hambourg (pno), M. Hambourg (pno) *(rec 1934)* ("The Hambourg Legacy") † Kreisleriana, Op. 16; Beethoven:Son 12 Pno, Op. 26; Chopin:Andante Spianato & Grand Polonaise, Op. 22; Debussy:Prélude à l'après-midi d'un faune; Liszt:Légendes, S.175 ARBT ▲ 109 [ADD] (16.97)
Arabeske in C for Piano, Op. 18 (1838)
L. O. Andsnes (pno) † Fant Pno, Op. 17; Son 1 Pno, Op. 11 EMIC ▲ 56414 (16.97)
A. Arad (pno) *(rec American Academy & Inst of Arts & Letters, NYC, NY, Mar 1998)* † Fant Pno, Op. 17; Kreisleriana, Op. 16 MUSC ▲ 1001 [DDD] (16.97)
A. Cheng (pno) *(rec CBC Toronto, Jan 6-8, 1995)* ("Piano Music of Clara & Robert Schumann") † Faschingsschwank, Op. 26; Son Pno, Op. 14; C. Schumann:Pièces fugitives, Op. 15; Scherzo Pno, Op. 10; Vars on a Theme by Robert Schumann, Op. 20 CBC (Musica Viva) ▲ 1087 [DDD] (16.97)
A. Cohen (pno) † Fant Pno, Op. 17; J. Brahms:Vars & Fugue on a Theme by Handel, Op. 24 VOXC ▲ 7539 (5.97)
A. Cohen (pno) † Fant Pno, Op. 17; A. Dvořák:Serenade Strs, Op. 22 VOXC ▲ 7540 (5.97)
J. Demus (pno) ("Complete Piano Works, Vol. 2") † Albumblätter, Op. 124; Canon on "An Alexis"; Carnaval, Op. 9
NUO ▲ 7312 (16.97)

SCHUMANN, ROBERT (cont.)

Arabeske in C for Piano, Op. 18 (1838) (cont.)

F. Gevers (pno) *(rec Barcelona, Sept 1995)* ("Oeuvre pour Piano") † Blumenstück, Op. 19; Fant Pno, Op. 17; Kinderszenen Pno, Op. 15; Romances Pno, Op. 28 EAM ▲ 6134 [DDD] (17.97)
Em. Gilels (pno) *(rec 1959-78)* ("Emil Gilels III") † J. Brahms:Con 2 Pno, Op. 83; Chopin:Études Pno; Son Pno in b, Op. 58; Son Pno in b♭, Op. 35; M. Clementi:Son Pno; E. Grieg:Lyric Pieces; F. Schubert:Fant Pno, D.940 PPHI (Great Pianists of the 20th Century) 2-▲ 456799 (22.97)
V. Horowitz (pno) *(rec 1968)* † Blumenstück, Op. 19; Kinderszenen Pno, Op. 15; Kreisleriana, Op. 16; Toccata Pno, Op. 7 SNYC ▲ 42409 [AAD] (16.97)
V. Horowitz (pno) *(rec Jan 2-Feb 1, 1968)* ("The Legendary Masterworks Recordings, 1962-1973, Vol. 4") † Kinderszenen Pno, Op. 15; Chopin:Polonaise 5 Pno, Op. 44; V. Horowitz:Vars Theme from Bizet's Carmen; D. Scarlatti:Sons Kbd SNYC ▲ 53465 [ADD] (16.97)
V. Horowitz (pno) † Fantasiestücke Pno, Op. 12; Toccata Pno, Op. 7; Beethoven:Vars Pno on Original Theme, WoO 80; Debussy:Etudes (12) Pno; J. Haydn:Son 62 Kbd, H.XVI/52; D. Scarlatti:Sons Kbd ENT (Sirio) ▲ 530026 (13.97)
P. Huybregts (pno) † Blumenstück, Op. 19; Carnaval, Op. 9 CENT ▲ 2135 [DDD] (16.97)
F. Kempf (pno) *(rec Stockholm, Sweden, Jan 1999)* † Carnaval, Op. 9; Humoreske Pno, Op. 20; Toccata Pno, Op. 7 BIS ▲ 960 [DDD] (17.97)
W. Kempff (pno) † Bunte Blätter, Op. 99; Carnaval, Op. 9; Davidsbündlertänze, Op. 6; Fant Pno, Op. 17; Humoreske Pno, Op. 20; Kinderszenen Pno, Op. 15; Kreisleriana, Op. 16; Nachtstücke, Op. 23; Papillons Pno, Op. 2; Romances Pno, Op. 28; Son 2 Pno, Op. 22; Symphonic Etudes, Op. 13; Waldscenen, Op. 82 DEUT 4-▲ 35045 [ADD] (26.97)
W. Kempff (pno) *(rec 1951)* ("Wilhelm Kempff") † Kreisleriana, Op. 16; J. Brahms:Ballades (4), Op. 10; Fants Pno, Op. 116; Intermezzos (3) Pno, Op. 117; Pieces (4) Pno, Op. 119; Pieces (6) Pno, Op. 118; Pieces (8) Pno, Op. 76 PPHI (Great Pianists of the 20th Century) 2-▲ 456862 (22.97)
E. Kissin (pno) ("Ich liebe dich, Op. 41/3") † E. Grieg:Pictures from Life in the Country, Op. 19; Pno Music (misc); G. F. Malipiero:I fantisimi; F. Schubert:Qnt Pno, D.667 SNYC ▲ 52567 (16.97)
S. Lindgren (pno) † Chopin:Son Pno in b, Op. 58; Liszt:Mephisto Waltz 1 Pno, S.514; S. Rachmaninoff:Prelude in c♯, Op. 3/2; A. Scriabin:Fant Pno, Op. 28 OPU ▲ 9202
C. Okashiro (pno) † Symphonic Etudes, Op. 13 PPR ▲ 224501 (16.97)
M. Pollini (pno) † Con Pno in a, Op. 54; Symphonic Etudes, Op. 13 DEUT (Masters) ▲ 45522 [DDD] (9.97)
M. Pollini (pno) *(rec 1983)* ("Maurizio Pollini") † Son 1 Pno, Op. 11; Chopin:Scherzos Pno; Debussy:Etudes (12) Pno; Liszt:Son Pno, S.178; F. Schubert:Pieces Pno, D.946; I. Stravinsky:Scenes (3) Pno; Webern:Vars Pno, Op. 27 PPHI (Great Pianists of the 20th Century) ▲ 456937 (22.97)
A. Rubenstein (pno) *(rec 1928-47)* † Kinderszenen Pno, Op. 15; Myrthen, Op. 25; Romances Pno, Op. 28; J. Brahms:Pieces (8) Pno, Op. 76; Songs (5), Op. 49; Liszt:Liebesträume, S.541; F. Schubert:Impromptus (4) Pno; P. Tchaikovsky:Con 1 Pno, Op. 23 GRM2 ▲ 78783 (13.97)
A. Schiff (pno) † Humoreske Pno, Op. 20; Papillons Pno, Op. 2 DNN ▲ 7573 [DDD] (10.97)
N. Shelter (pno) † Blumenstück, Op. 19; Kinderszenen Pno, Op. 15; Romances Pno, Op. 28 BER ▲ 9328 (10.97)
A. Simon (pno) † Kinderszenen Pno, Op. 15; Kreisleriana, Op. 16; Vars on A-B-E-G-G, Op. 1 DANT ▲ 9649 (17.97)
N. Sivelöv (pno) † Kreisleriana, Op. 16; Son Pno, Op. 14; Son 2 Pno, Op. 22 CAPA ▲ 21518 (16.97)
J. Thibaudet (pno) *(rec London, England, July 1994)* † Symphonic Etudes, Op. 13; J. Brahms:Vars on a Theme by Paganini, Op. 35 PLON ▲ 44338 [DDD] (16.97)
F. Ts'ong (pno) *(rec Warsaw, Poland)* † Davidsbündlertänze, Op. 6; Kinderszenen Pno, Op. 15; Kreisleriana, Op. 16; Papillons Pno, Op. 2; Waldscenen, Op. 82 ICC ▲ 6601127 (32.97)
S. Vladar (pno) † Albumblätter, Op. 124; Symphonic Etudes, Op. 13 NXIN ▲ 550144 [DDD] (5.97)
E. Wirssaladze (pno) *(rec Mar 4, 1995)* † Fant Pno, Op. 17; Son 1 Pno, Op. 11 LV ▲ 352 [DDD] (17.97)

Ballszenen (9 dances) for Piano 4-Hands, Op. 109 (1851)

C. Argelli (pno), P. Dirani (pno) † Bilder aus Osten, Op. 66; Kinderball, Op. 130; Klavierstücke, Op. 85; Polonaises Pno 4-Hands FON 2-▲ 9708 (20.97)

Bilder aus Osten (6 impromptus) for Piano 4-Hands, Op. 66 (1848)

C. Argelli (pno), P. Dirani (pno) † Ballszenen, Op. 109; Kinderball, Op. 130; Klavierstücke, Op. 85; Polonaises Pno 4-Hands FON 2-▲ 9708 (20.97)
P. Komen (pno), P. Verhagen (pno) *(rec Nov 1998)* † J. Brahms:Vars in E♭ on Theme of R. Schumann Pno 4-Hands, Op. 23; A. Dietrich:Son Pno 4-Hands, Op. 19; H. Goetz:Son Pno 4-Hands, Op. 17 GLOE ▲ 5188 [DDD] (16.97)

Blumenstück in D♭ for Piano, Op. 19 (1839)

F. Gevers (pno) *(rec Barcelona, Sept 1995)* ("Oeuvre pour Piano") † Arabeske Pno, Op. 18; Fant Pno, Op. 17; Kinderszenen Pno, Op. 15; Romances Pno, Op. 28 EAM ▲ 6134 [DDD] (17.97)
P. Gulda (pno) *(rec Oct 26-29, 1990)* † Kreisleriana, Op. 16 NXIN ▲ 550401 [DDD] (5.97)
V. Horowitz (pno) *(rec 1966)* † Arabeske Pno, Op. 18; Kinderszenen Pno, Op. 15; Kreisleriana, Op. 16; Toccata Pno, Op. 7 SNYC ▲ 42409 [AAD] (16.97)
P. Huybregts (pno) † Arabeske Pno, Op. 18; Carnaval, Op. 9 CENT ▲ 2135 [DDD] (16.97)
L. Lortie (pno) † Bunte Blätter, Op. 99; J. Brahms:Vars in f♯ on Theme of R. Schumann, Op. 9 CHN ▲ 9289 [DDD] (16.97)
N. Shelter (pno) † Arabeske Pno, Op. 18; Kinderszenen Pno, Op. 15; Romances Pno, Op. 28 BER ▲ 9328 (10.97)

Bunte Blätter (14 pieces) for Piano, Op. 99 (1838-51)

C. Haskil (pno) ("The Clara Haskil Legacy") † J. S. Bach:Toccatas Hpd; J. Haydn:Son 50 Kbd, H.XVI/37; F. Schubert:Son Pno in B♭, D.960 TAHA ▲ 291 (17.97)
V. Jochum (pno) [5 sels] ("Theme & Variations") † Impromptus on a Theme by Clara Wieck, Op. 5; J. Brahms:Vars in f♯ on Theme of R. Schumann, Op. 9; C. Schumann:Romance varié, Op. 3; Vars on a Theme by Robert Schumann, Op. 20 TUD ▲ 7028 (16.97)
W. Kempff (pno)—No. 9, Novellette † Arabeske Pno, Op. 18; Carnaval, Op. 9; Davidsbündlertänze, Op. 6; Fant Pno, Op. 17; Humoreske Pno, Op. 20; Kinderszenen Pno, Op. 15; Kreisleriana, Op. 16; Nachtstücke, Op. 23; Papillons Pno, Op. 2; Romances Pno, Op. 28; Son 2 Pno, Op. 22; Symphonic Etudes, Op. 13; Waldscenen, Op. 82 DEUT 4-▲ 35045 [ADD] (26.97)
L. Lortie (pno) † Blumenstück, Op. 19; J. Brahms:Vars in f♯ on Theme of R. Schumann, Op. 9 CHN ▲ 9289 [DDD] (16.97)
D. Paperno (pno)—Nos. 1-8 *(rec 1980-95)* ("Paperno Live") † J. Brahms:Intermezzos (3) Pno, Op. 117; J. Haydn:Sonatas for Piano; Liszt:Années de pèlerinage 2, S.161; Trans, Arrs & Paraphrases; Medtner:Forgotten Melodies 1, Op. 38; S. Rachmaninoff:Moments musicaux, Op. 16; P. Tchaikovsky:Dumka CED ▲ 44 [DDD] (16.97)
S. Richter (pno) ("The Richter Collection, Vol. 2") † Symphonic Etudes, Op. 13; Beethoven:Son 27 Pno, Op. 90; Son 3 Pno, Op. 2/3; Son 4 Pno, Op. 7; Vars & Fugue Pno, Op. 35; Vars Pno on Original Theme, Op. 34; Vars Pno on Original Theme, Op. 76; J. Brahms:Son 1 Vn, Op. 78; Chopin:Scherzos Pno; J. Haydn:Son 39 Kbd, H.XVI/24; S. Rachmaninoff:Etudes-tableaux Pno; Preludes Pno; D. Shostakovich:Son Vn OLY 5-▲ 5013 [DDD] (64.97)
U. Tsachor (pno) † Humoreske Pno, Op. 20 DI ▲ 920185 (5.97)

Canon on H.F. Himmel's "An Alexis send ich dich" in A♭ for Piano (pubd 1859)

J. Demus (pno) ("Complete Piano Works, Vol. 2") † Albumblätter, Op. 124; Arabeske Pno, Op. 18; Carnaval, Op. 9 NUO ▲ 7312 (16.97)

Carnaval (21 pieces) for Piano [4 pieces orchd Ravel, ca 1914], Op. 9 (1833-35)

E. Ansermet (cnd), London PO, E. Ansermet (cnd), Straram Concerts Orch, E. Ansermet (cnd), Diaghilev Ballets Russes Orch, E. Ansermet (cnd), London Philharmonic Choir *(rec 1916-47)* ("Ansermet, Vol. 1") † Chopin:Sylphides (arr); Rimsky-Korsakov:Scheherazade, Op. 35; Snow Maiden (suite); I. Stravinsky:Capriccio Pno; Firebird Suite 1; Pétrouchka Suite; Sym of Psalms; N. Tcherepnin:Pavillon d'Armide LYS1 2-▲ 451
C. Arrau (pno) *(rec 1939)* † Busoni:Sonatina 6 Pno; Chopin:Pno Music (misc colls); Liszt:Années de pèlerinage 3, S.163 PHS ▲ 9928 [AAD] (17.97)
C. Arrau (pno) † Kinderszenen Pno, Op. 15; Waldscenen, Op. 82 PPHI (Silver Line) ▲ 20871 [ADD] (9.97)
C. Arrau (pno) *(rec 1928; 1929; 1939)* † Bizet:Carmen Fantasie; Chopin:Ballade 3 Pno, Op. 47; Scherzos Pno; Debussy:Danse Pno; Estampes; Liszt:Années de pèlerinage 3, S.163 MTAL ▲ 48044 (6.97)
C. Arrau (pno) † Con Pno in a, Op. 54; Chopin:Études Pno; Ballade 3 Pno, Op. 47; Preludes (24) Pno, Op. 28; Tarentelle, Op. 43 ENPL ▲ 287 (13.97)
A. Cortot (pno) *(rec 1928 for HMV)* † Symphonic Etudes, Op. 13; Trio 1 Pno, Op. 63 BPS ▲ 4 [ADD] (16.97)
A. Cortot (pno), C. Arrau (pno), M. Hess (pno) [3 versions] ("Performers in Comparison 3") ENPL (The Piano Library) ▲ 296 (14.97)
J. Demus (pno) ("Complete Piano Works, Vol. 2") † Albumblätter, Op. 124; Arabeske Pno, Op. 18; Canon on "An Alexis" NUO ▲ 7312 (16.97)
M. Deyanova (pno) *(rec Nimbus Foundation Concert Hall, Apr 28-May 2, 1997)* † Fantasiestücke, Op. 111; Faschingsschwank, Op. 26 NIMB ▲ 5545 [DDD] (16.97)
B. Engerer (pno) † Kinderszenen Pno, Op. 15; Liszt:Fant & Fugue on the name B-A-C-H, S.529; Trans, Arrs & Paraphrases HAM ▲ 901600 (18.97)
J. Fennimore (pno) ("Joseph Fennimore in Concert") † Griffes:Son Pno; White Peacock; Liadov:Pieces Pno, Op. 11; A. Scriabin:Etudes (8) Pno, Op. 42; Sgambati:Melodie ALBA ▲ 102 [ADD] (16.97)
W. Gieseking (pno) *(rec 1942-43)* † Kreisleriana, Op. 16; Son 1 Pno, Op. 11 ENPL (Piano Library) ▲ 224 (13.97)

SCHUMANN, ROBERT (cont.)

Carnaval (21 pieces) for Piano [4 pieces orchd Ravel, ca 1914], Op. 9 (1833-35) (cont.)

W. Gieseking (pno) † Davidsbündlertänze, Op. 6; Fant Pno, Op. 17; Kreisleriana, Op. 16; Son 1 Pno, Op. 11 GRM2 2-▲ 78796 (26.97)
L. Godowsky (pno) *(rec 1926-30)* † Beethoven:Son 26 Pno, Op. 81a; Chopin:Études Pno; Nocturnes Pno; Scherzos Pno; Son Pno in b♭, Op. 35; L. Godowsky:Transcriptions & Paraphrases; E. Grieg:Ballade Pno, Op. 24; Liszt:Paraphrase on Verdi PPHI (Great Pianists of the 20th Century, Vol. 37) 2-▲ 456805 (22.97)
M. Hess (pno) *(rec 1942)* ("Myra Hess") † W. A. Mozart:Con 21 Pno, K.467 ENPL (Piano Library) ▲ 231 (13.97)
P. Huybregts (pno) † Arabeske Pno, Op. 18; Blumenstück, Op. 19 CENT ▲ 2135 [DDD] (16.97)
R. Irving (cnd), Philharmonia Orch ("Great Ballet Music II") † Delibes:Coppélia; Sylvia RYLC ▲ 70118 (8.97)
J. Jandó (pno) *(rec Nov 1992)* ("Schumann: Piano Works") † Kinderszenen Pno, Op. 15; Papillons Pno, Op. 2 NXIN ▲ 550784 [DDD] (5.97)
E. L. Kaplan (pno) *(rec First Congregational Church Los Angeles, CA, Sept 1992)* † Chopin:Fantaisie Pno, Op. 49; Mazurkas Pno CMB ▲ 1089 [DDD] (16.97)
E. L. Kaplan (pno) *(rec Los Angeles, CA, Sep 1992)* † Chopin:Fantaisie Pno, Op. 49; Mazurkas Pno; Nocturnes Pno; Waltzes Pno CMB ▲ 1098 (16.97)
A. Karis (pno) † E. Carter:Night Fants; Chopin:Fantaisie Pno, Op. 49 BRID ▲ 9001 (17.97)
F. Kempf (pno) *(rec Stockholm, Sweden, Jan 1999)* † Arabeske Pno, Op. 18; Humoreske Pno, Op. 20; Toccata Pno, Op. 7 BIS ▲ 960 [DDD] (17.97)
W. Kempff (pno) † Arabeske Pno, Op. 18; Bunte Blätter, Op. 99; Davidsbündlertänze, Op. 6; Fant Pno, Op. 17; Humoreske Pno, Op. 20; Kinderszenen Pno, Op. 15; Kreisleriana, Op. 16; Nachtstücke, Op. 23; Papillons Pno, Op. 2; Romances Pno, Op. 28; Son 2 Pno, Op. 22; Symphonic Etudes, Op. 13; Waldscenen, Op. 82 DEUT 4-▲ 35045 [ADD] (26.97)
A. Kubalek (pno) † Fantasiestücke, Op. 111; Gesänge der Frühe, Op. 133; Kinderszenen Pno, Op. 15 DOR ▲ 90116 [DDD] (16.97)
A. Kuerti (pno) *(rec 1979)* † Humoreske Pno, Op. 20; Vars on an Original Theme FL ▲ 23043 [DDD] (16.97)
M. Kwok (pno), P. Freeman (cnd), Slovakia National Orch † Con Pno in a, Op. 54 HALM ▲ 35077 (6.97)
A. B. Michelangeli (pno) *(rec 1960-73)* ("Michelangeli in Recital") † J. Brahms:Ballades (4), Op. 10; Vars on a Theme by Paganini, Op. 35; Busoni:Chaconne Pno; Chopin:Fantaisie Pno, Op. 49; Waltzes Pno; M. Ravel:Gaspard de la nuit MUA 2-▲ 817 [AAD] (31.97)
A. B. Michelangeli (pno) *(rec Royal Albert Hall London, 1957)* † Faschingsschwank, Op. 26; Chopin:Ballade 1 Pno, Op. 23; Fantaisie Pno, Op. 49; Debussy:Images (6) Pno; Mompou:Cançons i dansas Pno TES 2-▲ 2088 (33.97)
B. Moiseiwitsch (pno) ("In Recital") † Kreisleriana, Op. 16; Symphonic Etudes, Op. 13; Beethoven:Andante Pno, WoO 57; Chopin:Etudes Pno; Fant-Impromptu, Op. 66; Son Pno in b, Op. 58; Mussorgsky:Pictures at an Exhibition; Palmgren:West Finnish Dance PHS 2-▲ 9192 (33.97)
M. O'Rourke (pno) † Kreisleriana, Op. 16 CHN ▲ 9388 [DDD] (16.97)
D. Pollack (pno)—No. 11, Chiarina; No. 12, Chopin ("First Kiss") † Kinderszenen Pno, Op. 15; Chopin:Nocturnes Pno; Debussy:Arabesques Pno; Fille aux cheveaux de lin (song); Liszt:Études de concert (3), S.144; Consolations (6), S.172; M. Ravel:Pavane pour une infante défunte; P. Tchaikovsky:Saisons FWIN ▲ 3002 (13.97)
S. Rachmaninoff (pno) *(rec 1928-29)* † E. Grieg:Son 3 Vn, Op. 45; F. Schubert:Son Vn, D.574 ENPL (Piano Library) ▲ 280 (13.97)
S. Radic (pno) † Con Pno in a, Op. 54 PC ▲ 267148 [DDD] (2.97)
J. Reynolds (cnd), European CO Per Musica—No. 1, Préambule; No. 16, Valse allemande *(rec Amsterdam, Netherlands, Nov 1985)* † Chabrier:Pièces pittoresques; Debussy:Danse Pno; Pour le piano; M. Ravel:Ma mère l'oye GLOE ▲ 6034 [DDD] (16.97)
J. Robilette (pno) † Con Pno in a, Op. 54 PRA ▲ 3464 (14.97)
J. Rowland (pno) *(rec Santa Monica, CA, Apr 27-29, 1993)* † Fant Pno, Op. 17; Presto passionato; Waldscenen, Op. 82 TOWN ▲ 43 (17.97)
A. Rubinstein (pno) † Fantasiestücke Pno, Op. 12; Romances Pno, Op. 28; Waldscenen, Op. 82 RCAV (Red Seal) ▲ 5667 [ADD] (16.97)
H. Shelley (pno) † Kinderszenen Pno, Op. 15 CHN ▲ 8814 [DDD] (16.97)
A. Skoumal (pno) *(rec Aug 1996)* ("Carnaval") † Allegro Pno, Op. 8; Toccata Pno, Op. 7 STMA ▲ 36 [DDD] (18.97)
Solomon (pno) *(rec London, 1952)* † J. Brahms:Son 3 Pno, Op. 5; Liszt:Études de concert (3), S.144; Album d'un voyageur, S.156; Rákóczy March Orch, S.117 TES ▲ 1084 (17.97)
P. Spada (pno) *(rec Roma Italy, May 1991)* † Kreisleriana, Op. 16 AART ▲ 47125 [DDD] (17.97)
M. Uchida (pno) † Kreisleriana, Op. 16 PPHI ▲ 42777 (16.97)
L. Vassiliadis (pno) † J. Brahms:Vars on a Theme by Paganini, Op. 35 DI ▲ 920257 [DDD] (5.97)
P. Yegorov (pno) † Kinderszenen Pno, Op. 15 SNYC ▲ 57264 [DDD] (4.97)

Choral Music

F. Rasmussen (cnd), Canzone Choir—Gesänge Chorus, Op. 59; Lieder, Op. 55; Romanzen und Balladen, Op. 67; Romanzen und Balladen, Op. 75; Romanzen und Balladen, Op. 145; Romanzen und Balladen, Op. 146 ("Complete Works for Mixed Choir a cappella") KPT ▲ 32076 [ADD]

Concert sans orchestra in f for Piano, Op. 14 (1835-36)

A. R. Bacha (pno) † Son 2 Pno, Op. 22; Waldscenen, Op. 82 FORL ▲ 16722 [DDD] (16.97)
B. Janis (pno) *(rec 1960-63)* ("Byron Janis II") † Romances Pno, Op. 28; Liszt:Con 1 Pno, S.124; S. Prokofiev:Con 3 Pno, Op. 26; Toccata Pno, Op. 11; S. Rachmaninoff:Con 1 Pno, Op. 1; Con 2 Pno, Op. 18; P. Tchaikovsky:Con 1 Pno, Op. 23 PPHI (Great Pianists of the 20th Century) 2-▲ 456850 (22.97)

Concerto in a for Cello & Orchestra, Op. 129 (1850)

E. Baeyens (vc), F. Terby (cnd), Brussels BRTN PO *(rec Belgian Radio-TV Concerthall, May 1978)* ("Homage to Edmond Baeyens") † Boeck:Cantilena; A. Dvořák:Con Vc PHA ▲ 492002 [DDD] (13.97)
E. Bertrand (vc), S. Denève (cnd), Monte Carlo PO † Lalo:Con Vc; Namouna (suites 1 & 2) ARN ▲ 68458 (16.97)
P. Casals (vc), E. Ormandy (cnd), Prades Festival Orch *(rec Prades France, May 28-29, 1953)* † Stücke im Volkston, Op. 102; Trio 1 Pno, Op. 63 SNYC (The Casals Edition) ▲ 58993 [ADD] (10.97)
C. Coin (vc), P. Herreweghe (cnd), Champs Élysées Orch † Sym 4 HAM ▲ 901598 (18.97)
P. Fournier (vc) *(rec live, 1957-78)* † Martinů:Con 1 Vc; D. Shostakovich:Con 1 Vc, Op. 107 CASC ▲ 2009 (16.97)
P. Fournier (vc), W. Furtwängler (cnd), Berlin PO [excerpts] ("A Tribute to Furtwängler") † Beethoven:Sym 3; Sym 5; Sym 6; J. Brahms:Sym 2; A. Dvořák:Slavonic Dances (sels); Mendelssohn (-Bartholdy):Hebriden, Op. 26; F. Schubert:Sym 8; Sym 9; R. Strauss:Till Eulenspiegels lustige Streiche, Op. 28 TAHA 4-▲ 1008 (35.97)
J. Gamard (vc), P. Kuentz (cnd), Paul Kuentz Orch † Saint-Saëns:Allegro appassionato, Op. 43; Con 1 Vc, Op. 33 PVY ▲ 730053 [DDD] (12.97)
M. Kliegel (vc), A. Constantine (cnd), Irish National SO *(rec National Concert Hall Dublin, May 16-17, 1994)* † J. Brahms:Con Vn & Vc, Op. 102 NXIN ▲ 550938 [DDD] (5.97)
Y.-Y. Ma (vc), C. Davis (cnd), Bavarian RSO † Adagio & Allegro Hn, Op. 70; Fantasiestücke Cl, Op. 73; Stücke im Volkston, Op. 102 SNYC ▲ 42663 [DDD] (16.97)
Y.-Y. Ma (vc), C. Davis (cnd), Bavarian RSO † A. Dvořák:Con Vc; E. Elgar:Con Vc; J. Haydn:Con 2 Vc; Saint-Saëns:Con 1 Vc, Op. 33 SNYC 2-▲ 44562 [ADD] (31.97)
A. Navarra (vc), K. Ančerl (cnd), Czech PO † E. Bloch:Schelomo; O. Respighi:Adagio con variazioni Vc Orch SUR ▲ 111940 [AAD]
G. Piatigorsky (vc), J. Barbirolli (cnd), London PO *(rec 1934)* † Beethoven:Son 2 Vc, Op. 5/2; J. Brahms:Son 1 Vc, Op. 38 PHS ▲ 9447 [AAD] (18.97)
J. D. Pré (vc), D. Barenboim (cnd), New Philharmonia Orch † Con Pno in a, Op. 54; Intro & Allegro, Op. 134 EMIC ▲ 64626 (11.97)
L. Rose (vc), L. Bernstein (cnd), New York PO † Genoveva (ov); F. Schubert:Sym 5 SNYC ▲ 47609 (10.97)
M. Rostropovich (vc), H. von Karajan (cnd), French National Orch *(rec Paris, France, Nov 1976)* † R. Strauss:Don Quixote, Op. 35 EMIC (Great Recordings of the Century) ▲ 66965 [ADD] (11.97)
D. Shafran (vc), K. Kondrashin (cnd), Russian State Orch † M. de Falla:Amor brujo (Ritual Fire Dance); Suite populaire espagnole; J. Haydn:Divert Vc; Kabalevsky:Con 1 Vc, Op. 49 VC ▲ 1026 [ADD] (13.97)
N. Shakhovskaya (vc), L. Markiz (cnd) *(rec 1976)* ("Natalia Shakhovskaya: Russian Performing School") † Boccherini:Con Vc, G.482; P. Tchaikovsky:Vars on a Rococo Theme, Op. 33 RD ▲ 16203 [ADD] (16.97)
J. Starker (vc), S. Skrowaczewski (cnd), London SO † Lalo:Con Vc; Saint-Saëns:Con 1 Vc, Op. 33 MRCR ▲ 32010 [ADD] (11.97)
J. Storgårds (vn), L. Segerstam (cnd), Tampere PO [arr composer for vn & orch] † Con Vn ODE ▲ 879 (17.97)
T. Thedéen (vc), L. Markiz (cnd), Malmö SO † E. Elgar:Con Vc BIS ▲ 486 [DDD] (17.97)
P. Wispelwey (vc) † Fantasiestücke Cl, Op. 73; P. Hindemith:Pieces Vc, Op. 8 CCL ▲ 11097 (18.97)

Concerto in a for Piano & Orchestra, Op. 54 (1st movt, 1841; 2nd & 3rd movts, 1845)

E. Ansermet (cnd), Royal PO, E. Ansermet (cnd), Paris Conservatory Société des Concerts Orch, E. Ansermet (cnd), Swiss Romande Orch ("Ansermet, Vol. 5") † Genoveva (sels); J. Haydn:Sym 101 LYS1 ▲ 456
M. Argerich (pno), N. Harnoncourt (cnd), CO of Europe *(rec Graz Germany, July 1992)* † Con Vn TELC ▲ 90696 [DDD] (16.97)
C. Arrau (pno), K. Krüger (cnd), Detroit SO † Carnaval, Op. 9; Chopin:Études Pno; Ballade 3 Pno, Op. 47; Preludes (24) Pno, Op. 28; Tarentelle, Op. 43 ENPL ▲ 287 (13.97)

▲ = CD ♦ = Enhanced CD △ = MD ▮ = Cassette Tape ▯ = DCC

SCHUMANN, ROBERT (cont.)

Concerto in a for Piano & Orchestra, Op. 54 (1st movt, 1841; 2nd & 3rd movts, 1845) (cont.)

W. Backhaus (pno), K. Böhm (cnd), Vienna PO † Beethoven:Con 5 Pno, Op. 73; J. Brahms:Con Vn & Vc, Op. 102; W. A. Mozart:Con 21 Pno, K.467 STRV 2-▲ 12305 [ADD] (25.97)
D. Barenboim (pno), D. Fischer-Dieskau (cnd), London PO † Con Vc; Intro & Allegro, Op. 134 EMIC ▲ 64626 (11.97)
F. Blumenthal (pno), H. Swarowsky (cnd), Vienna Pro Musica Orch *(rec 1958)* † S. Rachmaninoff:Con 2 Pno, Op. 18 TUXE ▲ 1045 [ADD] (10.97)
A. Brendel (pno), K. Sanderling (cnd), Philharmonia Orch † Fant Pno, Op. 17 PPHI ▲ 462321 (16.97)
E. Ciccarelli (pno), F. Layer (cnd), Montpellier Languedoc-Roussillon PO *(rec Le Corum Montpellier, June 14-16, 1995)* † C. Schumann:Con Pno, Op. 7 AG ▲ 14 [DDD] (18.97)
V. Cliburn (pno), F. Reiner (cnd), Chicago SO † MacDowell:Con 2 Pno, Op. 23; Woodland Sketches, Op. 51 RCAV (Gold Seal) ▲ 60420 [ADD] (11.97)
V. Cliburn (pno), F. Reiner (cnd), Chicago SO *(rec 1960)* † S. Prokofiev:Con 3 Pno, Op. 26 RCAV (Living Stereo) ▲ 62691 [ADD] (11.97)
A. Cortot (pno), L. Ronald (cnd), London SO *(rec 1927 for HMV)* † Davidsbündlertänze, Op. 6; Papillons Pno, Op. 2 BPS ▲ 3 [ADD] (16.97)
S. Costa (pno), S. Gunzenhauser (cnd), Lisbon Gulbenkian Foundation Orch † Intro & Allegro appassionato, Op. 92; Intro & Allegro, Op. 134 NXIN ▲ 550277 [DDD] (5.97)
M. Dalberto (pno), E. Inbal (cnd), Vienna SO *(rec Vienna, Austria, June 1993)* ("Romantic Piano Concertos") † Chopin:Con 1 Pno, Op. 11; S. Rachmaninoff:Con 2 Pno, Op. 18; P. Tchaikovsky:Con 1 Pno, Op. 23 DNN 2-▲ 17013 (16.97)
M. Frager (pno), J. Horenstein (cnd), Royal PO *(rec Walthamstow Town Hall London, Feb 2, 1967)* † Beethoven:Con Vn CHSK ▲ 52 [ADD] (16.97)
N. Freire (pno), R. Kempe (cnd), Munich PO *(rec 1968)* † E. Grieg:Con Pno, Op. 16 SNYC ▲ 46269 [AAD] (7.97)
W. Gieseking (pno), W. Furtwängler (cnd), Berlin PO *(rec Berlin, Mar 1-3, 1942)* ("Wartime German Radio Recordings") † Beethoven:Con 5 Pno, Op. 73 MUA ▲ 815 [AAD] (16.97)
W. Gieseking (pno), W. Furtwängler (cnd), Berlin PO ("Walter Gieseking: World War II Performances") † Liszt:Con 1 Pno, S.124 ENPL (The Piano Library) ▲ 202 (13.97)
W. Gieseking (pno), R. Heger (cnd), Berlin PO *(rec July 1944)* ("Art of Walter Gieseking") † E. Grieg:Con Pno, Op. 16 TAHA ▲ 195 (17.97)
C. M. Giulini (cnd), Chicago SO ("Basic 100, Vol. 48") † E. Grieg:Con Pno, Op. 16 RCAV ▲ 62677 (10.97)
W. Goehr (cnd) † C. Franck:Symphonic Vars, M.46; E. Grieg:Con Pno, Op. 16 AVID ▲ 593 (16.97)
H. Grimaud (pno), D. Zinman (cnd), Berlin German SO *(rec Paris, 1995)* † R. Strauss:Burleske, AV85 ERAT ▲ 11727 [DDD] (16.97)
E. Gröschel (pno), H. Gmür (cnd), North German PO † Carnaval, Op. 9 PC ▲ 267148 [DDD] (2.97)
E. Istomin (pno), B. Walter (cnd), Columbia SO *(rec Hollywood, CA, Jan 20 & 25, 1960)* † Beethoven:Con 5 Pno, Op. 73 SNYC (Bruno Walter: The Edition, Vol. 4) ▲ 64489 [ADD] (10.97)
J. Jandó (pno), A. Ligeti (cnd), Budapest SO † E. Grieg:Con Pno, Op. 16 NXIN ▲ 550118 [DDD] (5.97)
B. Janis (pno), S. Skrowaczewski (cnd), Minneapolis SO † P. Tchaikovsky:Con 1 Pno, Op. 23 MRCR ▲ 32011 [ADD] (11.97)
P. Katin (pno), E. Goossens (cnd), London SO *(rec Walthamstow Assembly Hall London)* ("Sampler") † A. Dvořák:Sym 9; W. A. Mozart:Con 3 Vn, K.216; Sym 40, K.550; F. Schubert:Sym 8 EVC 2-▲ 9045 [AAD] (19.97)
M. Kwok (pno), P. Freeman (cnd), Slovakia National Orch † Carnaval, Op. 9 HALM ▲ 35077 (6.97)
M. Lapansky (pno), B. Rezucha (cnd), Slovak PO † E. Grieg:Con Pno, Op. 16 OPP ▲ 1279 (12.97)
M. Lapansky (pno), B. Rezucha (cnd), Slovak PO † Davidsbündlertänze, Op. 6; Dichterliebe, Op. 48; Kinderszenen Pno, Op. 15; Phantasiestücke Vn, Op. 88; Qts Strs, Op. 41; Sym 3 INTC (Art of Classics) ▲ 885921
L. Lortie (pno), N. Järvi (cnd), Philharmonia Orch † Chopin:Con 2 Pno, Op. 21 CHN ▲ 9061 [DDD] (16.97)
I. Margalit (pno), B. Thomson (cnd), London PO ("Romantic Piano Concertos") † J. Brahms:Con 1 Pno, Op. 15; Mendelssohn (-Bartholdy):Capriccio brillante, Op. 22; Saint-Saëns:Con 2 Pno, Op. 22 CHN 2-▲ 7070 (26.97)
A. B. Michelangeli (pno), A. Galliera (cnd), La Scala Orch *(rec 1942)* † E. Grieg:Con Pno, Op. 16 MTAL ▲ 48058 (6.97)
A. B. Michelangeli (pno), G. Gavazzeni (cnd), Rome RAI SO *(rec 1962)* ("The Vatican Recordings") † Beethoven:Con 5 Pno, Op. 73; Son 3 Pno, Op. 2/3; Chopin:Andante Spianato & Grand Polonaise, Op. 22; Debussy:Images (6) Pno; Preludes Pno; Liszt:Totentanz Pno & Orch, S.126; M. Ravel:Gaspard de la nuit APS 4-▲ 999001 (51.97)
A. B. Michelangeli (pno), D. Lipatti (pno) [2 renditions] *(rec 1942 & 1948)* ("Performers in Comparison 1") ENPL (The Piano Library) ▲ 291 (13.97)
A. B. Michelangeli (pno), D. Mitropoulos (cnd), New York PO *(rec 1948)* ("The American Debut") † J. S. Bach:Sons & Partitas Vn; J. Brahms:Vars on a Theme by Paganini, Op. 35 ENPL (Piano Library) ▲ 272 (13.97)
A. B. Michelangeli (pno), A. Pedrotti (cnd), La Scala Orch † E. Grieg:Lyric Pieces; Tomeoni:Allegro Pno ENPL (Piano Library) ▲ 211 (13.97)
A. B. Michelangeli (pno), A. Pedrotti (cnd), La Scala Orch † E. Grieg:Con Pno, Op. 16 IMMM (Magic Master series) ▲ 37050 (6.97)
I. Moravec (pno), E. Mata (cnd), Dallas SO † J. Brahms:Con 1 Pno, Op. 15 DOR ▲ 90172 (16.97)
Y. Nat (pno), E. Bigot (cnd) † Fantasiestücke Pno, Op. 12; Faschingsschwank, Op. 26; Kinderszenen Pno, Op. 15 ENPL (The Piano Library) ▲ 181 (13.97)
C. Ortiz (pno), L. Foster (cnd), Royal PO † Chopin:Con 2 Pno, Op. 21 RPO ▲ 5004 [DDD] (11.97)
C. Ortiz (pno), L. Foster (cnd), Royal PO † Chopin:Con 2 Pno, Op. 21 ICC ▲ 6701172 (9.97)
J. F. Osorio (pno), E. Bátiz (cnd), Royal PO † C. Franck:Symphonic Vars, M.46; M. Ravel:Con Pno (left hand); Saint-Saëns:Wedding Cake, Op. 76 ASVQ ▲ 6092 [DDD] (11.97)
J. Panenka (pno), K. Ančerl (cnd), Czech PO † P. Tchaikovsky:Con 1 Pno, Op. 23 PRAG ▲ 256000 (18.97)
M. Perahia (pno), C. Abbado (cnd), Berlin PO † Intro & Allegro appassionato, Op. 92; Intro & Allegro, Op. 134 SNYC ▲ 64577 (16.97)
M. Perahia (pno), C. Davis (cnd), Bavarian RSO † E. Grieg:Con Pno, Op. 16 SNYC ▲ 44899 [DDD] (16.97)
M. Pollini (pno), C. Abbado (cnd), Berlin PO † Arabeske Pno, Op. 18; Symphonic Etudes, Op. 13 DEUT (Masters) ▲ 45522 [DDD] (9.97)
S. Richter (pno), W. Rowicki (cnd), Warsaw PO *(rec National Philharmonic Warsaw, Poland, Oct 1958)* † Intro & Allegro, Op. 134; Novelettes, Op. 21; Toccata Pno, Op. 7; Waldscenen, Op. 82 DEUT (The Originals) ▲ 47440 [ADD] (11.97)
J. Robilette (pno), P. Freeman (cnd), St. Petersburg PO † Carnaval, Op. 9 PRA ▲ 3464 (14.97)
P. Rösel (pno), K. Masur (cnd), Leipzig Gewandhaus Orch † P. Tchaikovsky:Con 1 Pno, Op. 23 BER ▲ 9308 (10.97)
A. Rubinstein (pno), J. Krips (cnd), RCA Victor SO *(rec 1958)* † Chopin:Con 2 Pno, Op. 21; E. Grieg:Con Pno, Op. 16; Saint-Saëns:Con 2 Pno, Op. 22; P. Tchaikovsky:Con 1 Pno, Op. 23 PPHI (Great Pianists of the 20th Century, Vol. 86) 2-▲ 456958 (22.97)
A. Rubinstein (pno), E. Leinsdorf (cnd), Boston SO † P. Tchaikovsky:Con 1 Pno, Op. 23 RCAV (Basic 100) ▲ 68454 (10.97) ▮ 68454 (5.98)
A. Rubinstein (pno), W. Steinberg (cnd), RCA Victor SO *(rec 1947)* ("Rubinstein, Vol. 5") † E. Grieg:Con Pno, Op. 16; Liszt:Con 1 Pno, S.124 HPC ▲ 148 (17.97)
E. von Sauer (pno), W. Mengelberg (cnd), (Royal) Concertgebouw Orch *(rec live, 1940)* † Fantasiestücke Pno, Op. 12; Chopin:Bolero; E. von Sauer:Son 1 Pno; F. Schubert:Impromptus (4) Pno; Sgambati:Minuetto vecchio, Op. 18/3 ARBT ▲ 114 (16.97)
G. Schwarz (cnd), Seattle SO *(rec Seattle Opera House, WA, Sept 1988-Feb 1992)* ("The Schumann Edition") † Konzertstück Hns, Op. 86; Manfred Ov, Op. 115; Ov, Scherzo & Finale, Op. 52; Sym 1; Sym 2; Sym 3; Sym 4; Symphonic Etudes, Op. 13 DLS 4-▲ 3146 [DDD] (30.97)
R. Serkin (pno), E. Ormandy (cnd), Philadelphia Orch † Qnt Pno, Op. 44 SNYC ▲ 37256 [ADD] (9.97)
R. Serkin (pno), E. Ormandy (cnd), Philadelphia Orch † Intro & Allegro appassionato, Op. 92; E. Grieg:Con Pno, Op. 16 SNYC (Essential Classics) ▲ 46543 [ADD] (7.97) ▮ 46543 [ADD] (3.98)
R. Shamvill (pno), A. Manzano (cnd), Ecuador National SO *(rec Sucre National Theater Quito, Ecuador, May 20, 1994)* † Manfred Ov, Op. 115 GALL ▲ 859 [DDD] (19.97)
A. Staier (pno), P. Herreweghe (cnd), Champs Élysées Orch [J. B. Streicher fortepno, ca 1850] † Sym 2 HAM ▲ 901555 (18.97)
S. Sugitani (pno), G. Oskamp (cnd), Berlin SO † C. Schumann:Con Pno, Op. 7 VRDI ▲ 9233 (13.97)
I. Uryash (pno), A. Titov (cnd), St. Petersburg New PO † E. Grieg:Con Pno, Op. 16 SNYC ▲ 57227 [DDD] (4.97)
K. Zimerman (pno), H. von Karajan (cnd), Berlin SO *(rec Sept 1981)* † E. Grieg:Con Pno, Op. 16 DEUT (Karajan Gold) ▲ 39015 [DDD] (16.97)

Concerto in d for Piano & Orchestra [incomplete; only first draft of first movement exists] (1839)

J. Eley (pno), S. Stone (cnd), English CO *(rec Roslyn Hill Chapel, London, England)* † Mendelssohn (-Hensel):Jahr (sels); Mendelssohn (-Bartholdy):Pno Music (misc) KOCH ▲ 7197 (16.97)

Concerto in d for Violin & Orchestra, Op. posth (1853)

G. Kremer (vn), N. Harnoncourt (cnd), CO of Europe *(rec Graz Germany, July 1994)* † Con Pno in a, Op. 54 TELC ▲ 90696 [DDD] (16.97)

SCHUMANN, ROBERT (cont.)

Concerto in d for Violin & Orchestra, Op. posth (1853) (cont.)

G. Kremer (vn), R. Muti (cnd), Philharmonia Orch ("Gidon Kramer Plays Great Violin Concertos") † J. Brahms:Con Vn; P. Hindemith:Son Vn & Pno, Op. 11/1; A. Schnittke:Son 2 Vn; Sibelius:Con Vn; C. M. von Weber:Grand Duo Concertant, J.204 EMIC 2-▲ 69334 (16.97)
G. Kulenkampff (vn), H. Schmidt-Isserstedt (cnd), Berlin PO *(rec December 20, 1937)* † Beethoven:Con Vn; W. A. Mozart:Adagio Vn, K.261 DLAB (Essential Archive) ▲ 5018 [ADD] (15.97)
P. Rybar (vn), V. Desarzens (cnd), Lausanne SO *(rec 1951)* † Sibelius:Con Vn DORO (Legendary Artists) ▲ 4009 [ADD] (16.97)
J. Storgårds (vn), L. Segerstam (cnd), Tampere PO † Con Vc ODE ▲ 879 (17.97)
T. Wanami (vn), A. Leaper (cnd), London PO † J. Brahms:Con Vn ICC ▲ 6700732 [DDD] (9.97)

Davidsbündlertänze (18 character pieces) for Piano, Op. 6 (1837)

B. Berezovsky (pno) † Son 2 Pno, Op. 22 TELC ▲ 77476 (16.97)
A. Cortot (pno) *(rec 1937 for HMV)* † Con Pno in a, Op. 54; Papillons Pno, Op. 2 BPS ▲ 3 [ADD] (16.97)
A. Cortot (pno) † Papillons Pno, Op. 2; Symphonic Etudes, Op. posth; Symphonic Etudes, Op. 13 MTAL ▲ 48069 (6.97)
J. Demus (pno) † Con Pno in a, Op. 54; Dichterliebe, Op. 48; Kinderszenen Pno, Op. 15; Phantasiestücke Vn, Op. 88; Qts Strs, Op. 41; Sym 3 INTC (Art of Classics) ▲ 885921
J. Demus (pno) ("Piano Works, Vol. 1") † Fantasiestücke, Op. 111; Gesänge der Frühe, Op. 133; Klavierstücke, Op. 32 NUO ▲ 7311 (16.97)
B. Frith (pno) *(rec Nov 27-29, 1991)* † Fantasiestücke Pno, Op. 12 NXIN ▲ 550493 [DDD] (5.97)
W. Gieseking (pno) *(rec 1953)* † Kreisleriana, Op. 16; J. S. Bach:English Suites FORL ▲ 16590 [AAD] (16.97)
W. Gieseking (pno) *(rec 1938-47)* † Fant Pno, Op. 17; Kinderszenen Pno, Op. 15 ENPL (Piano Library) ▲ 244 (13.97)
W. Gieseking (pno) † Carnaval, Op. 9; Fant Pno, Op. 17; Kreisleriana, Op. 16; Son 1 Pno, Op. 11 GRM2 2-▲ 78796 (26.97)
A. Haefliger (pno) † Waldscenen, Op. 82 SNYC ▲ 48036 (11.97)
W. Kempff (pno) † Arabeske Pno, Op. 18; Bunte Blätter, Op. 99; Carnaval, Op. 9; Fant Pno, Op. 17; Humoreske Pno, Op. 20; Kinderszenen Pno, Op. 15; Kreisleriana, Op. 16; Nachtstücke, Op. 23; Papillons Pno, Op. 2; Romances Pno, Op. 28; Son 2 Pno, Op. 22; Symphonic Etudes, Op. 13; Waldscenen, Op. 82 DEUT 4-▲ 35045 [ADD] (26.97)
A. Malling (pno) *(rec 1994)* † Humoreske Pno, Op. 20 KPT ▲ 32201
M. Perahia (pno) † Fantasiestücke Pno, Op. 12 SNYC ▲ 32299 [ADD] (16.97)
C. C. Sager (pno) *(rec Netherlands, Oct 11-12, 1996)* HANS ▲ 98135 [DDD] (15.97)
F. Ts'ong (pno)—No. 14, Zart und singend *(rec Warsaw, Poland)* † Arabeske Pno, Op. 18; Kinderszenen Pno, Op. 15; Kreisleriana, Op. 16; Papillons Pno, Op. 2; Waldscenen, Op. 82 ICC ▲ 6601127 (32.97)

Dichterliebe (cycle of 16 songs) for Voice & Piano [text Heine], Op. 48 (1840)

J. Benton (bar), G. Kirkland (pno) [ENG] † Beethoven:An die ferne Geliebte, Op. 98; G. Mahler:Lieder eines fahrenden Gesellen SYMP ▲ 1221 [DDD] (18.97)
I. Bostridge (ten), J. Drake (pno) *(rec July 1997)* ("Bostridge Sings Schumann") † Liederkreis, Op. 24; Songs *(E,G texts)* EMIC ▲ 56575 [DDD] (16.97)
D. Fischer-Dieskau (bar), A. Brendel (pno) [GER] † Liederkreis, Op. 39 PPHI ▲ 16352 [DDD] (16.97)
M. Goerne (bar), V. Ashkenazy (pno) † Liederkreis, Op. 24 PLON ▲ 458265 (16.97)
W. Grönroos (bar), R. Gothóni (pno) *(rec 1977)* † Liederkreis, Op. 24 BIS ▲ 92 [AAD] (17.97)
W. Hollweg (ten), H. Giesen (pno) † Con Pno in a, Op. 54; Davidsbündlertänze, Op. 6; Kinderszenen Pno, Op. 15; Phantasiestücke Vn, Op. 88; Qts Strs, Op. 41; Sym 3 INTC (Art of Classics) ▲ 885921
W. Holzmair (bar), I. Cooper (pno) *(rec Esterházy Palace Eisenstadt, Austria, June 27-30, 1994)* † Gesänge, Op. 142; Liederkreis, Op. 24; Myrthen, Op. 25; Romanzen und Balladen, Op. 53; Romanzen und Balladen, Op. 64 PPHI ▲ 46086 (16.97)
H. Hotter (b-bar), H. Altmann (pno) [GER] *(rec 1954)* PRE ▲ 93145 [AAD]
G. Hüsch (bar), H. U. Müller (pno) *(rec 1936)* ("Legendary Song Cycle Recordings") PHS ▲ 9119 [ADD] (17.97)
L. Lehmann (sop), B. Walter (pno) *(rec 1941)* † Frauenliebe und -leben, Op. 42 VOCA (Vocal Archives) ▲ 1158 (13.97)
K. McMillan (bar), M. McMahon (pno) *(rec Canada)* ("Lieder on Poems of Heinrich Heine") † J. Brahms:Songs; Liszt:Songs; Mendelssohn (-Bartholdy):Songs; F. Schubert:Schwanengesang, D.957 *(E, F, text)* MUVI ▲ 1052 [DDD] (16.97)
K. Olli (bar), U. Koneffke (pno) ("Art Songs") † Sibelius:Songs; R. Wagner:Wesendonck Songs BRIO ▲ 103 (16.97)
C. Panzéra (bar), A. Cortot (pno) *(rec 1934 for HMV)* † G. Fauré:Bonne chanson, Op. 61; Songs PHS ▲ 9919 [AAD] (17.97)
C. Panzéra (bar), A. Cortot (pno) *(rec 1934 for HMV)* † Fantasiestücke Pno, Op. 12; Kinderszenen Pno, Op. 15; Kreisleriana, Op. 16 BPS ▲ 5 [ADD] (16.97)
H. Prey (bar), L. Hokanson (pno) [GER] DNN ▲ 7720 [DDD]
T. Quasthoff (bar), R. Szidon (pno) [GER] † Liederkreis, Op. 39; Songs RCAV (Red Seal) ▲ 61225 (16.97)
H. Schlusnus (bar), F. Rupp (pno)—No. 07, Ich grolle nicht *(rec 1919-27)* † Beethoven:Adelaide, Op. 46; J. Brahms:Songs (6), Op. 86; Songs (9), Op. 32; F. Schubert:Songs (misc colls); R. Strauss:Songs; H. Wolf:Songs (misc) PRE (Lebendige Vergangenheit) ▲ 89188 (m) (16.97)
B. Skovhus (bar), H. Deutsch (pno) ("The Heart of the Poet") † Liederkreis, Op. 24; C. Schumann:Songs SNYC ▲ 62372 (16.97)
C. P. Trakas (bar), M. J. Zebrowski (pno) † Zebrowski:Leaving Alexandria TIT ▲ 253 [DDD] (16.97)
J. Vickers (ten), R. Woitach (pno) *(rec live New York, Apr 30, 1967)* ("Jon Vickers in Concert") † A. Dvořák:Zigeunermelodien, Op. 55; G. F. Handel:Messiah (sels); H. Purcell:Pausanias (sels); Songs; A. Scarlatti:Cants & Duets VAIA ▲ 1032 [ADD]
G. Vinogradov (ten) † Gedichte, Op. 90; Liederkreis, Op. 24; Myrthen, Op. 25; S. Rachmaninoff:Songs (14), Op. 34; Rimsky-Korsakov:Songs, Op. 51; A. Rubinstein:Songs; P. Tchaikovsky:Songs PRE ▲ 89118 (16.97)
F. Wunderlich (ten), H. Giesen (pno) [GER] *(rec live, Sept 17, 1966)* ("Last Recital") MYTO ▲ 89011 [ADD] (17.97)
F. Wunderlich (ten), H. Giesen (pno) *(rec live Salzburg, Aug 19, 1965)* † C. W. Gluck:Iphigénie en Tauride MYTO 2-▲ 91544 [ADD] (34.97)
F. Wunderlich (ten), H. Giesen (pno) [GER] *(rec Mar 24, 1966)* † Beethoven:Songs; F. Schubert:Songs (misc colls) MYTO ▲ 93278 (17.97)
F. Wunderlich (ten), H. Giesen (pno) *(rec Salzburg, Aug 19, 1965)* † Beethoven:Songs; F. Schubert:Songs (misc colls) ORFE (Festspiel Dokumente) ▲ 432961 [ADD] (16.97)
F. Wunderlich (ten), H. Giesen (pno) *(rec Hochschule for Music Munich, Germany, Oct-Nov 1965)* † Beethoven:Songs; F. Schubert:Songs (misc colls) DEUT (The Originals) ▲ 449747 [ADD] (11.97)

Fantasia in C for Piano, Op. 17 (1836-38)

D. Achatz (pno) *(rec Nacka Sweden, June 12-13, 1979)* † Kinderszenen Pno, Op. 15; Liszt:Son Pno, S.178 BIS ▲ 144 [AAD] (17.97)
L. O. Andsnes (pno) † Arabeske Pno, Op. 18; Son 1 Pno, Op. 11 EMIC ▲ 56414 (16.97)
A. Arad (pno) *(rec American Academy & Inst of Arts & Letters, NYC, NY, Mar 1998)* † Arabeske Pno, Op. 18; Kreisleriana, Op. 16 MUSC ▲ 1001 [DDD] (10.97)
C. Arrau (pno) † Beethoven:Son 23 Pno, Op. 57; Chopin:Études Pno; Debussy:Pour le piano AURC ▲ 157 (5.97)
A. Brendel (pno) *(rec Vienna, Austria, 1966)* † Symphonic Etudes, Op. 13 VC ▲ 117 [AAD] (13.97)
A. Brendel (pno), K. Sanderling (cnd), Philharmonia Orch † Con Pno in a, Op. 54 PPHI ▲ 462321 (16.97)
A. Cohen (pno) † Arabeske Pno, Op. 18; J. Brahms:Vars & Fugue on a Theme by Handel, Op. 24 VOXC ▲ 7539 (5.97)
A. Cohen (pno) † Arabeske Pno, Op. 18; A. Dvořák:Serenade Strs, Op. 22 VOXC ▲ 7540 (5.97)
C. Curzon (pno) *(rec Aug 24, 1974)* † F. Schubert:Son Pno, D.960 ORFE (Festspiel Dokumente) ▲ 401951 (16.97)
A. Delle-Vigne (pno), A. D. Vigne (pno) † Liszt:Son Pno, S.178 DI ▲ 920316 [DDD] (5.97)
Y. Egorov (pno) *(rec May 1979)* † J. S. Bach:Chromatic Fant & Fugue, BWV 903; Chopin:Fantaisie Pno, Op. 49; W. A. Mozart:Fant Pno, K.475 GLOE ▲ 6015 [ADD] (16.97)
N. Freire (pno) *(rec Toronto)* ("Nelson Freire in Concert") † Debussy:Images (6) Pno; W. A. Mozart:Son 12 Pno, K.332; A. Scriabin:Son 4 Pno, Op. 30; H. Villa-Lobos:A Lenda do Caboclo; As tres Marias ALPE ▲ 9502003
F. Gevers (pno) *(rec Barcelona, Sept 1995)* ("Oeuvre pour Piano") † Arabeske Pno, Op. 18; Blumenstück, Op. 19; Kinderszenen Pno, Op. 15; Romances Pno, Op. 28 EAM ▲ 6134 [DDD] (17.97)
W. Gieseking (pno) *(rec 1938-47)* † Davidsbündlertänze, Op. 6; Kinderszenen Pno, Op. 15 ENPL (Piano Library) ▲ 244 (13.97)
W. Gieseking (pno) † Carnaval, Op. 9; Davidsbündlertänze, Op. 6; Kreisleriana, Op. 16; Son 1 Pno, Op. 11 GRM2 2-▲ 78796 (26.97)
R. Goode (pno) † Humoreske Pno, Op. 20 NON ▲ 79014 [DDD] (9.97)
W. Kempff (pno) † Arabeske Pno, Op. 18; Bunte Blätter, Op. 99; Carnaval, Op. 9; Davidsbündlertänze, Op. 6; Humoreske Pno, Op. 20; Kinderszenen Pno, Op. 15; Kreisleriana, Op. 16; Nachtstücke, Op. 23; Papillons Pno, Op. 2; Romances Pno, Op. 28; Son 2 Pno, Op. 22; Symphonic Etudes, Op. 13; Waldscenen, Op. 82 DEUT 4-▲ 35045 [ADD] (26.97)

SCHUMANN, ROBERT (cont.)

Fantasia in C for Piano, Op. 17 (1836-38) (cont.)

W. Kempff (pno) † Symphonic Etudes, Op. 13 DGRM (Dokumente) ▲ 447977 [ADD] (13.97)

E. Kissin (pno) *(rec Freiburg Germany, Aug 22-25, 1995)* † Liszt:Études d'exécution transcendante (12), S.139 RCAV (Red Seal) ▲ 68262 (16.97)

A. D. Larrocha (pno) *(rec 1993-94)* † Humoreske Pno, Op. 20 RCAV (Red Seal) ▲ 68657 [DDD] (16.97)

N. Magaloff (pno) † Studien nach Capricen von Paganini, Op. 3 FON ▲ 8501 [ADD]

C. F. Miller (pno) *(rec Portsmouth, NH, May 13 & 26, 1995)* † J. Haydn:Trio Strs; Paulus:Miniatures; S. Rachmaninoff:Prelude in c#, Op. 3/2; Preludes Pno; M. Ravel:Alborada del gracioso; Jeux d'eau; D. Scarlatti:Sons Kbd; H. Villa-Lobos:Trio Strs TIT ▲ 231 [DDD]

E. Mursky (pno) † Toccata Pno, Op. 7; Beethoven:Son 13 Pno, Op. 27/1; Son 14 Pno, Op. 27/2 HANS ▲ 98178 (15.97)

M. Perahia (pno) † F. Schubert:Fant Pno, D.760 SNYC ▲ 42124 [DDD] (16.97)

M. Pollini (pno) *(rec Residenz Munich, Germany, Apr 1973)* † F. Schubert:Fant Pno, D.760 DEUT (The Originals) ▲ 47451 [ADD] (11.97)

S. Richter (pno) † Symphonic Etudes, Op. 13 PRAG ▲ 254033 (18.97)

J. Rowland (pno) *(rec Santa Monica, CA, Apr 27-29, 1993)* † Carnaval, Op. 9; Presto passionato; Waldscenen, Op. 82 TOWN ▲ 43 (17.97)

J. Swann (pno) *(rec Fort Worth, TX, 1977)* ("Van Cliburn Retrospective Series, Vol. 2") † S. Barber:Ballade Pno, Op. 46; B. Bartók:Out of Doors, Sz.81; Chopin:Scherzos Pno; Liszt:Vars on "Weinen, Klagen, Sorgen, Zagen" Pno, S.180; I. Stravinsky:Scenes (3) Pno VAIA ▲ 1146 [ADD] (16.97)

E. Wirssaladze (pno) *(rec June 11, 1994)* † Arabeske Pno, Op. 18; Son 1 Pno, Op. 11 LV ▲ 352 [DDD] (17.97)

Fantasiestücke for Clarinet & Piano (w. Violin or Cello ad lib), Op. 73 (1849)

A. Carbonare (cl), A. Dindo (pno) † Märchenbilder, Op. 113; Märchenerzählungen, Op. 132; Romances Ob, Op. 94 AG ▲ 43 (18.97)

J. Cohler (cl) ("More Cohler on Clarinet") † J. Brahms:Son 2 Cl; D. Milhaud:Sonatina Cl, Op. 100; F. Poulenc:Son Cl & Pno; I. Stravinsky:Pieces Cl ONGA ▲ 102 (16.97)

G. Dembinsky (cl), J. Zak (pno) ("Clarinet Fantasy") † G. Rossini:Fant Cl; C. M. von Weber:Grand Duo Concertant, J.204; Vars on a Theme from *Silvana*, Op. 33 CACI ▲ 210014 (5.97)

S. Drucker (cl), S. Shapiro (pno) *(rec Performing Arts Ctr/Purchase College-State Univ of, May 8, 1995)* ("Robert Schumann: The Complete Works for Winds & Piano") † Adagio & Allegro Hn, Op. 70; Andante & Vars Hn; Märchenerzählungen, Op. 132; Romances Ob, Op. 94 ELY ▲ 709 [DDD] (16.97)

Y. Hanani (vc), M. Levin (pno) ("Schubert/Schumann for Cello & Piano") † Stücke im Volkston, Op. 102; F. Schubert:Son Arpeggione, D.821; Sonatinas (3) Vn ECO ▲ 9

P. Hörr (vc), J. Alexander (pno) [trans Friedrich Grützmacher for vc & pno] ("Brahms & His Friends, Vol. 5") † J. Brahms:Sons Cl DVX ▲ 29609 (16.97)

W. Ifrim (cl), C. Hommel (pno) ("Chamber Music for Winds & Piano") † Adagio & Allegro Hn, Op. 70; Qnt Pno, Op. 44; Romances Ob, Op. 94; Stücke im Volkston, Op. 102 ARSM ▲ 1164 [DDD] (17.97)

E. Johnson (cl), G. Back (pno) ("A Clarinet Celebration") † N. Burgmüller:Duo Cl; Giampieri:Carnevale di Venezia; Lovreglio:Fant da concerto on Motifs of Verdi's La tra; C. M. von Weber:Grand Duo Concertant, J.204; Vars on a Theme from *Silvana*, Op. 33 ASV ▲ 732 (16.97)

S. Kam (cl), I. Golan (pno) † Debussy:Première rapsodie Cl; J. Françaix:Theme & Vars Cl; F. Poulenc:Son Cl & Pno TELC ▲ 11022 (16.97)

S. Kanoff (cl), C. Collard (pno) ("Clarinet Music of the 19th & 20th Century") † A. Berg:Pieces Cl, Op. 5; J. Cage:Son Cl; Messiaen:Abîme des oiseaux; F. Poulenc:Son Cl & Pno; I. Stravinsky:Pieces Cl DORO ▲ 3014 [ADD] (16.97)

M. Karr (bn), J. Jamner (pno) [trans Karr from Schumann's version for vc] *(rec Louisville, 1996)* ("A Bassoonist's Voice") † J. S. Bach:Partita Fl, BWV 1013; Cervetto:Sicilienne Bn; Dunhill:Lyric Suite Bn & Pno, Op. 96; J. Françaix:Divert Bn; H. Villa-Lobos:Bachiana brasileira 6 CENT ▲ 2330 [DDD] (16.97)

J. Kiss (ob), J. Jandó (pno) [arr for ob & pno] *(rec Dec 12-15, 1991)* † Adagio & Allegro Hn, Op. 70; Romances Ob, Op. 94; Son 1 Vn, Op. 105; Stücke im Volkston, Op. 102 NXIN ▲ 550599 [DDD] (5.97)

M. Kliegel (vc), K. Merscher (pno) [arr for vc & pno] *(rec Dec 14-15, 1991)* † Adagio & Allegro Hn, Op. 70; Stücke im Volkston, Op. 102; F. Schubert:Son Arpeggione, D.821 NXIN ▲ 550654 [DDD] (5.97)

I.-S. Lee (cl), R. Garten (pno) ("Presenting Im-Soo Lee") † Romances Ob, Op. 94; L. Bassi:Fant di concerto on Verdi's Rigoletto; S. Paik:PAN I; L. Weiner:Pereg Recruiting Dance, Op. 40 SUMM ▲ 235 (16.97)

K. Leister (cl) ("Pieces for Clarinet & Piano") † Romances Ob, Op. 94; Klosé:Little Fant; Kroepsch:Fant on Themes of Weber; Küffner:Intro, Theme & Vars; C. M. von Weber:Grand Duo Concertant, J.204; Vars on a Theme from *Silvana*, Op. 33 CAMA 2-▲ 329 [DDD] (31.97)

K. Leister (cl), F. Bognár (pno) *(rec Berlin, Sept 1992)* † Romances Ob, Op. 94; P. Hindemith:Son Cl; W. Lutoslawski:Dance Preludes Cl & Pno CAMA ▲ 30320 [DDD] (18.97)

W. Ludwig (bn), A. Epperson (pno) [bn & pno trans] † J. Brahms:Son 1 Cl; S. Prokofiev:Son Fl CENT ▲ 2130 (16.97)

Y.-Y. Ma (vc), E. Ax (pno) † Adagio & Allegro Hn, Op. 70; Con Vc; Stücke im Volkston, Op. 102 SNYC ▲ 42663 [DDD] (16.97)

Melos Ensemble *(rec 1964-70)* † Märchenerzählungen, Op. 132; Beethoven:Duos Cl, WoO 27; March Cls, WoO 29; Qnt Pno, Op. 16; Rondino Ww, WoO 25; Sxt Hns; J. Brahms:Qnt Cl; W. A. Mozart:Qnt Pno, K.452 EMIC 2-▲ 72643 [ADD] (16.97)

P. Meyer (cl), E. Le Sage (pno) *(rec Musica Théâtre La Choux-de-Fonds, Apr 9-11, 1993)* ("Märchenbilder") † Adagio & Allegro Hn, Op. 70; Märchenbilder, Op. 113; Romances Ob, Op. 94; Stücke im Volkston, Op. 102 DNN ▲ 75960 [DDD] (16.97)

H. Ni (vc), H. Jeanney (pno) *(rec Turku Finland, June 2-4, 1997)* ("Cello Recital") † Beethoven:Vars Vc on "Bei Männern", WoO 46; Mendelssohn (-Bartholdy):Son 2 Vc, Op. 58; Popper:Elfentanz Vc; F. Schubert:Son Arpeggione, D.821 NXIN ▲ 8554356 [DDD] (5.97)

G. Peyer (cl), G. Pryor (pno) † Romances Ob, Op. 94; F. Schubert:Son Arpeggione, D.821; C. M. von Weber:Vars on a Theme from *Silvana*, Op. 33 CHN ▲ 8506 [DDD] (16.97)

K. Pfister (sax), G. Wyss (pno) [trans for sax & pno] † Adagio & Allegro Hn, Op. 70; J. Brahms:Sons Cl GALL ▲ 931 [DDD] (18.97)

N. Rosen (vc), D. Stevenson (pno) ("Rosen Plays Brahms") † J. Brahms:Sons Vc (comp); Mendelssohn (-Bartholdy):Lied Vc JMR ▲ 5 [DDD] (16.97)

H. Schellenberger (ob d'amore), R. Koenen (pno) *(rec Berlin, Germany, June 1995)* † Adagio & Allegro Hn, Op. 70; Klavierstücke, Op. 85; Kreisleriana, Op. 16; Liederkreis, Op. 39; Myrthen, Op. 25; Romances Ob, Op. 94; Romances Pno, Op. 28; C. Schumann:Romances Vn, Op. 22 CAMM ▲ 130014 [DDD] (16.97)

P. Schmidl (cl), B. Canino (pno) † A. Berg:Pieces Cl, Op. 5; J. Brahms:Sons Cl CAMA ▲ 454 [DDD] (18.97)

R. Schulte (vn), C. O'Riley (pno) [vn & pno arrs] † Adagio & Allegro Hn, Op. 70; Märchenbilder, Op. 113; Romances Ob, Op. 94 CENT ▲ 2097 [DAD] (16.97)

F. Sellheim (vc), E. Sellheim (pno) [vc & pno] *(rec 1978)* † Stücke im Volkston, Op. 102; Mendelssohn (-Bartholdy):Vars concertantes, Op. 17; F. Schubert:Son Arpeggione, D.821 SNYC (Essential Classics) ▲ 48171 (7.97) ▮ 48171 (3.98)

D. Shifrin (cl), C. Rosenberger (pno) † J. Brahms:Sons Cl DLS ▲ 3025 [DDD] (14.97)

W. Thomas-Mifune (vc), C. Piazzini (pno) † Adagio & Allegro Hn, Op. 70; Romances Ob, Op. 94; F. Schubert:Son Arpeggione, D.821 CALG ▲ 50949 [DDD]

N. Thomsen (cl), E. Westenholz (pno) † Adagio & Allegro Hn, Op. 70; Märchenbilder, Op. 113; Romances Ob, Op. 94; Stücke im Volkston, Op. 102 KPT ▲ 32080 [DDD]

J. Vogler (vc), B. Camino (pno) ("Vol. 2") † Beethoven:Son 3 Vc, Op. 69; Vars Vc on "Bei Männern", WoO 46; Vars Vc on "Ein Mädchen oder Weibchen", Op. 66; Vars Vc, WoO 45 BER ▲ 1167 (16.97)

P. Wispelwey (vc) † Con Vc; P. Hindemith:Pieces Vc, Op. 8 CCL ▲ 11097 (18.97)

H. Wright (cl), P. Serkin (pno) *(rec Aug 1992)* † J. Brahms:Sons Cl BOST ▲ 1005 (15.97)

Fantasiestücke (8) for Piano, Op. 12 (1837)

W. Backhaus (pno) *(rec 1954)* ("Wilhelm Backhaus") † Beethoven:Son 17 Pno, Op. 31/2; Son 25 Pno, Op. 79; Son 26 Pno, Op, 81a; Son 32 Pno, Op. 111; Son 8 Pno, Op. 13; J. Brahms:Con 2 Pno, Op. 83; Pieces (4) Pno, Op. 119; Chopin:Etudes Pno; Liszt:Trans, Arrs & Paraphrases; F. Schubert:Impromptus (4) PPHI (Great Pianists of the 20th Century) ▲ 456718 (22.97)

H. Bauer (pno)—No. 5, In der Nacht † Pno Music (misc colls); E. Grieg:Album Leaves (4) Pno, Op. 28; Lyric Pieces; Pictures from Life in the Country, Op. 19; Liszt:Études de concert (2), S.145; Études de concert (3), S.144 BPS ▲ 11 (16.97)

A. Brendel (pno) *(rec 1982)* ("Alfred Brendel") † J. Haydn:Sonatas for Piano; W. A. Mozart:Fant Pno, K.475; F. Schubert:Impromptus (4); Impromptus (4) Pno PPHI (Great Pianists of the 20th Century) ▲ 456727 (22.97)

A. Cortot (pno)—No. 1, Des Abends *(rec 1937 for HMV)* † Dichterliebe, Op. 48; Kinderszenen Pno, Op. 15; Kreisleriana, Op. 16 BPS ▲ 5 [ADD] (16.97)

B. Frith (pno) *(rec Nov 27-29, 1991)* † Davidsbündlertänze, Op. 6 NXIN ▲ 550493 [DDD] (5.97)

V. Horowitz (pno) † Arabeske Pno, Op. 18; Toccata Pno, Op. 7; Beethoven:Vars Pno on Original Theme, WoO 80; Debussy:Etudes (12) Pno; J. Haydn:Son 62 Kbd, H.XVI/52; D. Scarlatti:Sons Kbd ENT (Sirio) ▲ 530026 (13.97)

SCHUMANN, ROBERT (cont.)

Fantasiestücke (8) for Piano, Op. 12 (1837) (cont.)

Y. Nat (pno) † Con Pno in a, Op. 54; Faschingsschwank, Op. 26; Kinderszenen Pno, Op. 15 ENPL (The Piano Library) ▲ 181 (13.97)

I. J. Paderewski (pno)—No. 1, Des Abends; No. 2, Aufschwung; No. 3, Warum? *(rec 1911-37)* † Nachtstücke, Op. 23; J. Brahms:Hungarian Dances Pno; Chopin:Etudes (24) Pno, Opp. 10 & 25; Polonaise 6 Pno, Op. 53; Mendelssohn (-Bartholdy):Lieder ohne Worte; A. Rubinstein:Valse-Caprice Pno ENPL (The Piano Library) ▲ 182 (13.97)

M. Perahia (pno) † Davidsbündlertänze, Op. 6 SNYC ▲ 32299 [ADD] (16.97)

S. Richter (pno) † Humoreske Pno, Op. 20; C. Franck:Prélude, choral et fugue, M.21 MON ▲ 72022 (11.97)

S. Richter (pno)—No. 2, Aufschwung; No. 3, Warum?; No. 7, Traumes Wirren *(rec Moscow, Russia, 1955 & 57)* ("Sviatoslav Richter in the 50's, Vol. 2") † Humoreske Pno, Op. 20; Vars on A-B-E-G-G, Op. 1; Mussorgsky:Pictures at an Exhibition; A. Scriabin:Son 2 Pno, Op. 19; Son 6 Pno, Op. 62; P. Tchaikovsky:Con 1 Pno, Op. 23 PACD 2-▲ 96003 (29.97)

S. Richter (pno)—No. 5, In der Nacht; No. 7, Traumes Wirren *(rec Japan, Feb-Mar 1979)* † Novelettes, Op. 21; Chopin:Preludes (24) Pno, Op. 28 OLY ▲ 287 (16.97)

A. Rubinstein (pno) † Carnaval, Op. 9; Romances Pno, Op. 28; Waldscenen, Op. 82 RCAV (Red Seal) ▲ 5667 [ADD] (16.97)

E. von Sauer (pno)—No. 7, Traumes Wirren *(rec 1940)* † Con Pno in a, Op. 54; Chopin:Bolero; E. von Sauer:Son 1 Pno; F. Schubert:Impromptus (4) Pno; Sgambati:Minuetto vecchio, Op. 18/3 ARBT ▲ 114 (16.97)

S. Tiempo (pno) ("Romantic Recital") † Chopin:Pno Music (misc colls) VRDI ▲ 6806

P. Vairo (pno)—No. 3, Warum? *(rec May 1992)* † Beethoven:Son 12 Pno, Op. 26; E. Grieg:Lyric Pieces; Piano Music (selections); A. Khachaturian:Toccata; Liszt:Liebesträume, S.541; S. Rachmaninoff:Morceaux de salon, Op. 10 STRV ▲ 102 [DDD] (16.97)

E. Wirssaladze (pno) † Kreisleriana, Op. 16 LV ▲ 311 (17.97)

Fantasiestücke (3) for Piano, Op. 111 (1851)

R. Brautigam (pno) † Allegro Pno, Op. 8; Gesänge der Frühe, Op. 133; Novelettes, Op. 21 OLY ▲ 436 [DDD] (16.97)

J. Demus (pno) ("Piano Works, Vol. 1") † Davidsbündlertänze, Op. 6; Gesänge der Frühe, Op. 133; Klavierstücke, Op. 32 NUO ▲ 7311 (16.97)

M. Deyanova (pno) *(rec Nimbus Foundation Concert Hall, Apr 28-May 2, 1997)* † Carnaval, Op. 9; Faschingsschwank, Op. 26 NIMB ▲ 5545 [DDD] (16.97)

V. Horowitz (pno) † Humoreske Pno, Op. 20; Son Pno, Op. 14 RCAV (Gold Seal) ▲ 6680 [ADD] (11.97)

A. Kubalek (pno) † Carnaval, Op. 9; Gesänge der Frühe, Op. 133; Kinderszenen Pno, Op. 15 DOR ▲ 90116 [DDD] (16.97)

Fantasy in C for Violin & Orchestra, Op. 131 (1853)

O. Kagan (vn), A. Tchistiakov (cnd), Moscow State SO *(rec 1986)* ("Oleg Kagan Edition, Vol. XIII") † S. Prokofiev:Con 1 Vn, Op. 19; M. Ravel:Tzigane; Saint-Saëns:Intro & Rondo capriccioso, Op. 28 LV ▲ 173 [ADD] (17.97)

A.-S. Mutter (vn), K. Masur (cnd), New York PO *(rec Avery Fisher Hall, NY, July 1997)* † J. Brahms:Con Vn PPHI ▲ 457075 [DDD] (16.97)

Faschingsschwank aus Wien (5 pieces) for Piano, Op. 26 (1839-40)

A. Cheng (pno) *(rec CBC Toronto, Jan 6-8, 1995)* ("Piano Music of Clara & Robert Schumann") † Arabeske Pno, Op. 18; Son Pno, Op. 14; C. Schumann:Pièces fugitives, Op. 15; Scherzo Pno, Op. 10; Vars on a Theme by Robert Schumann, Op. 20 CBC (Musica Viva) ▲ 1087 [DDD] (16.97)

M. Deyanova (pno) *(rec Nimbus Foundation Concert Hall, Apr 28-May 2, 1997)* † Carnaval, Op. 9; Fantasiestücke, Op. 111 NIMB ▲ 5545 [DDD] (16.97)

A. B. Michelangeli (pno) *(rec Royal Albert Hall London, 1957)* † Carnaval, Op. 9; Chopin:Ballade 1 Pno, Op. 23; Fantaisie Pno, Op. 49; Debussy:Images (6) Pno; Mompou:Cançons i dansas Pno TES 2-▲ 2088 (33.97)

P. Moss (pno) † A. Blank:Poems; A. Roussel:Poèmes de Ronsard, Op. 26; L. Spohr:German Songs, Op. 103; Starer:Songs of Youth & Age; H. Villa-Lobos:Bachiana brasileira 6 CENT ▲ 2106 [DDD] (16.97)

Y. Nat (pno) † Con Pno in a, Op. 54; Fantasiestücke Pno, Op. 12; Kinderszenen Pno, Op. 15 ENPL (The Piano Library) ▲ 181 (13.97)

M. Perahia (pno) ("The Aldeburgh Recital, 1990") † Beethoven:Vars Pno on Original Theme, WoO 80; Liszt:Consolations (6), S.172; Hungarian Rhaps, S.244; S. Rachmaninoff:Études-tableaux Pno SNYC ▲ 46437 [DDD] (16.97)

S. Richter (pno) *(rec Aug 25, 1976)* ("Richter in Helsinki") † Beethoven:Son 7 Pno, Op. 10/3; Chopin:Polonaises-fant, Op. 61 MUA ▲ 1020 [ADD] (16.97)

Frauenliebe und -leben (song cycle) for solo Female Voice & Piano [text Chamisso], Op. 42 (1840)

J. Baker (mez), D. Barenboim (pno) † J. Brahms:Duets (4), Op. 28; Ernste Gesänge, Op. 121; Songs (2), Op. 91; E. Chausson:Poème de l'amour et de la mer, Op. 19; M. Ravel:Shéhérazade Mez EMIC (Doublefforte) 2-▲ 68667 (16.97)

B. Bonney (sop), V. Ashkenazy (pno) † Liederkreis, Op. 39; Myrthen, Op. 25; C. Schumann:Lieder PLON ▲ 452898 (16.97)

J. DeGaetani (mez), L. Luvisi (pno) [GER] *(rec Aspen Music Festival, July 7, 1983)* ("Jan DeGaetani In Concert, Vol. 2") † J. Brahms:Gypsy Songs (8); Songs BRID ▲ 9025 [ADD] (17.97)

M. Horne (mez), F. von Stade (mez), M. Katz (pno) [sung as duet] RCAV (Red Seal) ▲ 61681

L. Lehmann (sop), B. Walter (pno) *(rec 1941)* † Dichterliebe, Op. 48 VOCA (Vocal Archives) ▲ 1158 (13.97)

J. Norman (sop), I. Gage (pno) [GER] † Liederkreis, Op. 39 PPHI ▲ 20784 [ADD] (16.97)

A. S. von Otter (mez), B. Forsberg (pno) † Lieder DEUT ▲ 45881 [DDD] (16.97)

M. Price (sop), J. Lockhart (pno) [GER] ORF ▲ 31821 [DDD] (18.97)

M. Price (sop), M. Price (sop), T. Dewey (pno), T. Dewey (pno) † Gedichte, Op. 36; Lieder-Album für die Jugend, Op. 79; Myrthen, Op. 25; Songs FORL ▲ 16711 [DDD] (16.97)

C. Robbin (mez), M. McMahon (pno) [GER] † Liederkreis, Op. 24 MUVI (Musica Viva) ▲ 1050 [DDD] (16.97)

I. Seefried (sop), E. Werba (pno) *(rec Aug 18, 1960)* † Liederkreis, Op. 39; Myrthen, Op. 25; Songs; J. Brahms:Songs ORFE (Festspiel Dokumente) ▲ 398951 (16.97)

M. Shirai (mez), H. Höll (pno) *(rec Japan, July 1982)* † Liederkreis, Op. 39 CAMA ▲ 2516 [DDD] (18.97)

S. Süssman (mez), D. Baldwin (pno) ("Melodies") † J. Brahms:Gypsy Songs (8); G. Fauré:Chanson d'Eve, Op. 95 DI ▲ 920190 [DDD] (5.97)

T. Takács (mez), J. Jandó (pno) [GER] *(rec 1989)* † J. Brahms:Ernste Gesänge, Op. 121; R. Wagner:Wesendonck Songs NXIN ▲ 550400 [DDD] (5.97)

N. Vallin (sop), G. Andolfi (pno) [Fr trans Jules Barbier] *(rec 1920)* ("Ninon Vallin: Canciones, Leider and Peruvian Folk Songs") † Liederkreis, Op. 39; M. de Falla:Amor brujo (sels); Canciones populares españolas; J. Nin:Songs; R. Strauss:Songs VAIA ▲ 1127 [ADD] (17.97)

Fugues (6) on B-A-C-H for Organ, Op. 60 (1845)

C. Crozier (org)—No. 1, Langsam; No. 5 † Liszt:Prelude & Fugue on the name B-A-C-H, S.260; Reubke:Son on 94th Psalm Org DLS ▲ 3090 [DDD] (14.97)

R. Innig (org) † Sketches, Op. 58; Studies Canon Form, Op. 56 MDG ▲ 3170619 (17.97)

G. Metz (org) † Studies Canon Form, Op. 56 BER ▲ 9285 (10.97)

D. Modersohn (org) ("Historic Organ of St. Gertraudkirche in Frankfurt on Oder") † M. Reger:Pieces (12) Org, Op. 59; S. Rousseau:Org Music THOR ▲ 2285 [DDD] (16.97)

Gedichte (3) for Voice & Piano [text Geibel], Op. 30 (1840)

N. Stutzmann (cta), I. Södergren (pno) † Lieder; Lieder-Album für die Jugend, Op. 79 RCAV ▲ 61799 [DDD] (16.97)

Gedichte (12) for Voice & Piano [text Kerner], Op. 35 (1840)

D. Lichti (b-bar), J. Fialkowska (pno) *(rec Waterloo, Ontario, Canada, Mar 8-10, 1997)* ("Daniel Lichti Sings Brahms & Schumann") † J. Brahms:Ernste Gesänge, Op. 121; Songs (5), Op. 94 *([ENG,FRE,GER] text)* ODRE ▲ 9311 (16.97)

M. Price (sop), G. Johnson (pno) † Liederkreis, Op. 39 HYP ▲ 55011 (9.97)

N. Stutzmann (cta), I. Södergren (pno) *(rec Munich, Oct 1994)* † Gedichte aus 'Liebesfrühling', Op. 37; Minnespiel, Op. 101 RCAV (Red Seal) ▲ 61798 [DDD] (16.97)

Gedichte (6) for Voice & Piano [text Reinick], Op. 36 (1840)

M. Price (sop), M. Price (sop), T. Dewey (pno), T. Dewey (pno) † Frauenliebe und -leben, Op. 42; Lieder-Album für die Jugend, Op. 79; Myrthen, Op. 25; Songs FORL ▲ 16711 [DDD] (16.97)

Gedichte (12) aus 'Liebesfrühling' for Voice & Piano [text Rückert; Nos. 2, 4 & 11 by Clara Schumann], Op. 37 (1840)

N. Stutzmann (cta), I. Södergren (pno) *(rec Munich, Oct 1994)* † Gedichte, Op. 35; Minnespiel, Op. 101 RCAV (Red Seal) ▲ 61798 [DDD] (16.97)

Gedichte (7) for Voice & Piano [text N. Lenau], Op. 90 (1850)

G. Vinogradov (ten), G. Orentlicher (pno) † Dichterliebe, Op. 48; Liederkreis, Op. 24; Myrthen, Op. 25; S. Rachmaninoff:Songs (14), Op. 34; Rimsky-Korsakov:Songs, Op. 51; A. Rubinstein:Songs; P. Tchaikovsky:Songs PRE ▲ 89118 (16.97)

Genoveva (opera in 4 acts) [lib R. Reinick after L. Tieck & C. F. Hebbel], Op. 81 (1847-49)

R. Behle (sop—Margaretha), J. Faulkner (sop—Genoveva), K. Lewis (ten—Golo), A. Titus (bar—Siegfried), H. Stamm (bass—Caspar/Hidulfus), J. Tilli (bass—Balthasar), G. Albrecht (cnd), Hamburg State PO, Hamburg State Opera Chorus [GER] *(rec 1992)* ORF 2-▲ 289932 [DDD] (36.97)

SCHUMANN, ROBERT (cont.)

Genoveva (opera in 4 acts) [lib R. Reinick after L. Tieck & C. F. Hebbel], Op. 81 (1847-49) (cont.)
E. Moser (sop), P. Schreier (ten), D. Fischer-Dieskau (bar), S. Lorenz (bar), K. Masur (cnd), Leipzig Gewandhaus Orch, Berlin Radio Chorus BER (Eterna) 2-▲ 2056 [ADD]
R. Ziesak (sop—Genoveva), M. Lipovšek (mez—Margaretha), D. Walt (ten—Golo), T. Quasthoff (bar—Drago), R. Gilfry (bar—Hidulfus), O. Widmer (bass—Siegfried), N. Harnoncourt (cnd), CO of Europe, Arnold Schoenberg Choir TELC 2-▲ 13144 (33.97)

Genoveva (selections)
E. Ansermet (cnd), Royal PO, E. Ansermet (cnd), Paris Conservatory Société des Concerts Orch, E. Ansermet (cnd), Swiss Romande Orch ("Ansermet, Vol. 5") † Con Pno in a, Op. 54; J. Haydn:Sym 101 LYS1 ▲ 456

Genoveva:Overture
L. Bernstein (cnd), New York PO † Con Vc; F. Schubert:Sym 5 SNYC ▲ 47609 (10.97)
N. Järvi (cnd), London SO † Julius Caesar, Op. 128; Manfred (incidental music), Op. 115; Ov, Scherzo & Finale, Op. 52 CHN (Collect) ▲ 6548 [DDD] (12.97)
R. Leppard (cnd), Indianapolis SO † Ov, Scherzo & Finale, Op. 52; Sym 1 KOSS ▲ 2213 (17.97)

Gesänge der Frühe (5) for Piano, Op. 133 (1853)
R. Brautigam (pno) † Allegro Pno, Op. 8; Fantasiestücke, Op. 111; Novelettes, Op. 21 OLY ▲ 436 [DDD] (16.97)
J. Demus (pno) ("Piano Works, Vol. 1") † Davidsbündlertänze, Op. 6; Fantasiestücke, Op. 111; Klavierstücke, Op. 32 NUO ▲ 7311 (16.97)
A. Kubalek (pno) † Carnaval, Op. 9; Fantasiestücke, Op. 111; Kinderszenen Pno, Op. 15 DOR ▲ 90116 [DDD] (16.97)
A. Schiff (pno) † Kreisleriana, Op. 16; Nachtstücke, Op. 23 TELC ▲ 14566 (16.97)

Gesänge (4) for Double Chorus, Op. 141 (1849)
U. Gronostay (cnd), Netherlands Chamber Choir *(rec Arts Music Recording, Amsterdam, Netherlands, Nov 1995)* † Draeseke:Grosse Messe, Op. 85 GLOE ▲ 5147 [DDD] (16.97)

Gesänge (5) for 4 Male Voices & Horn Quartet ad lib [text H. Laube], Op. 137 (1849)
Michael Thompson Horn Quartet, King's Singers *(rec London, July-Nov 1996)* ("Nightsong") † J. Brahms:Choral Music; M. Reger:Geistliche Gesänge, Op. 138; Rheinberger:Geistliche Gesänge, Op. 69; F. Schubert:Choral Music RCAV (Red Seal) ▲ 68646 [DDD] (16.97)

Gesänge (6) for Voice & Piano, Op. 107 (1851-52)
J. Banse (sop), Cherubini String Quartet [arr Aribert Reimann] TUD ▲ 7063 (16.97)
K. Wakao (ob), C. Eschenbach (pno)—No. 6, Abendlied † Romances Ob, Op. 94; S. Barber:Canzonetta; W. A. Mozart:Son 32 Vn & Pno, K.454 DNN ▲ 18090 (16.97)

Gesänge (4) for Voice & Piano [texts by Bernard, Heine & Kerner], Op. 142 (1840)
W. Holzmair (bar), I. Cooper (pno)—No. 2, Lehn deine Wang; No. 4, Mein Wagen rollet langsam *(rec Esterházy Palace Eisenstadt, Austria, June 27-30, 1994)* † Dichterliebe, Op. 48; Liederkreis, Op. 24; Myrthen, Op. 25; Romanzen und Balladen, Op. 53; Romanzen und Balladen, Op. 64 PPHI ▲ 46086 (16.97)

Gesänge (3) for Voice & Piano, Op. 31 (1840)
E. Höngen (cta), H. Zipper (pno)—No. 2, Die Kartenlegerin *(rec Nov 1946)* † Liederkreis, Op. 39; Myrthen, Op. 25; J. Brahms:Liebeslieder Waltzes Pno 4-Hands, Op. 52a; B. Marcello:Mio bel foco; F. Schubert:Songs (misc colls); R. Wagner:Wesendonck Songs; H. Wolf:Gedichte von Goethe; Gedichte von Mörike PRE ▲ 90356 (m) (16.97)
E. Schwarzkopf (sop), G. Parsons (pno)—No. 2, Die Kartenlegerin † Myrthen, Op. 25; W. A. Mozart:Songs; F. Schubert:Songs (misc colls); H. Wolf:Songs (misc); E. Wolf-Ferrari:Preghiera AURC ▲ 123 (5.97)

Humoreske in B♭ for Piano, Op. 20 (1838)
D. Golub (pno) *(rec Purchase Conservatory of Music Recital Hall, Sept 14-16, 1996)* ("Humoresque") † A. Dvořák:Humoresques, Op. 101; S. Rachmaninoff:Morceaux de salon, Op. 10; J. Suk:Humoreska; P. Tchaikovsky:Morceaux (2) Pno, Op. 10 ARA ▲ 6706 [DDD] (16.97)
R. Goode (pno) † Fant Pno, Op. 17 NON ▲ 79014 [DDD] (9.97)
W. Harden (pno) † M. Reger:Vars & Fugue on a Theme of J. S. Bach, Op. 81 NXIN ▲ 550469 [DDD] (5.97)
V. Horowitz (pno) † Fantasiestücke, Op. 111; Son Pno, Op. 14 RCAV (Gold Seal) ▲ 6680 [ADD] (11.97)
F. Kempf (pno) *(rec Stockholm, Sweden, Jan 1999)* † Arabeske Pno, Op. 18; Carnaval, Op. 9; Toccata Pno, Op. 7 BIS ▲ 960 [DDD] (17.97)
W. Kempff (pno) † Arabeske Pno, Op. 18; Bunte Blätter, Op. 99; Carnaval, Op. 9; Davidsbündlertänze, Op. 6; Fant Pno, Op. 17; Kinderszenen Pno, Op. 15; Kreisleriana, Op. 16; Nachtstücke, Op. 23; Papillons Pno, Op. 2; Romances Pno, Op. 28; Son 2 Pno, Op. 22; Symphonic Etudes, Op. 13; Waldscenen, Op. 82 DEUT 4-▲ 35045 [ADD] (26.97)
A. Kuerti (pno) *(rec 1979)* † Carnaval, Op. 9; Vars on an Original Theme FL ▲ 23043 [DDD] (16.97)
A. D. Larrocha (pno) *(rec 1993-94)* † Fant Pno, Op. 17 RCAV (Red Seal) ▲ 68657 [DDD] (16.97)
R. Lupu (pno) *(rec Corseaux Switzerland, Jan 1993)* † Kinderszenen Pno, Op. 15; Kreisleriana, Op. 16 PLON ▲ 40496 [DDD] (16.97)
A. Malling (pno) *(rec 1994)* † Davidsbündlertänze, Op. 6 KPT ▲ 32201
S. Richter (pno) † Fantasiestücke Pno, Op. 12; C. Franck:Prélude, choral et fugue, M.21 MON ▲ 72022 (11.97)
S. Richter (pno) *(rec Moscow, 1955 & 57)* ("Sviatoslav Richter in the 50's, Vol. 2") † Fantasiestücke Pno, Op. 12; Vars on A-B-E-G-G, Op. 1; Mussorgsky:Pictures at an Exhibition; A. Scriabin:Son 2 Pno, Op. 19; Son 6 Pno, Op. 62; P. Tchaikovsky:Con 1 Pno, Op. 23 PACD 2-▲ 96003 (29.97)
A. Schiff (pno) † Arabeske Pno, Op. 18; Papillons Pno, Op. 2 DNN ▲ 7573 [DDD] (10.97)
U. Tsachor (pno) † Bunte Blätter, Op. 99 DI ▲ 920185 (5.97)

Impromptus (10) on a Theme by Clara Wieck for Piano, Op. 5 (1833)
I. Hobson (pno) † Presto passionato; Son Pno, Op. 14; Son 1 Pno, Op. 11; Son 2 Pno, Op. 22; Vars on A-B-E-G-G, Op. 1 ARA 2-▲ 6621 [DDD] (32.97)
B. Janis (pno) *(rec New York, Jan 24, 1964)* † Mendelssohn (-Bartholdy):Lieder ohne Worte; S. Prokofiev:Con 3 Pno, Op. 26; Toccata Pno, Op. 11; S. Rachmaninoff:Con 1 Pno, Op. 1 MRCR ▲ 34333 (11.97)
V. Jochum (pno) ("Theme & Variations") † Bunte Blätter, Op. 99; J. Brahms:Vars in f# on Theme of R. Schumann, Op. 9; C. Schumann:Romance varié, Op. 3; Vars on a Theme by Robert Schumann, Op. 20 TUD ▲ 7028 (16.97)
P. Mazzola (pno) † Romances Pno, Op. 28; Son Pno, Op. 14; C. Schumann:Romances Pno, Op. 11 PANC ▲ 510091 [DDD] (17.97)
D. Várjon (pno) *(rec Budapest, Jan 17-20, 1994)* ("Schumann, Piano Works") † Albumblätter, Op. 124; Intermezzos, Op. 4; Romances Pno, Op. 28 NXIN ▲ 550849 [DDD] (5.97)

Intermezzos (6) for Piano, Op. 4 (1832)
J. Buskirk (pno) *(rec Smith College, Aug 1994)* † Papillons Pno, Op. 2; Studien nach Capricen von Paganini, Op. 3; Vars on A-B-E-G-G, Op. 1 NPT ▲ 85611 [DDD] (16.97)
D. Várjon (pno) *(rec Budapest, Jan 17-20, 1994)* ("Schumann, Piano Works") † Albumblätter, Op. 124; Impromptus on a Theme by Clara Wieck, Op. 5; Romances Pno, Op. 28 NXIN ▲ 550849 [DDD] (5.97)

Introduction & Allegro appassionato in G for Piano & Orchestra, Op. 92, "Concertstück" (1849)
S. Costa (pno), S. Gunzenhauser (cnd), Lisbon Gulbenkian Foundation Orch † Con Pno in a, Op. 54; Intro & Allegro, Op. 134 NXIN ▲ 550277 [DDD] (5.97)
E. Erdmann (pno) *(rec 1928-45)* ("Erdmann: The Vinyl Recordings") † Beethoven:Con 3 Pno, Op. 37; J. Brahms:Intermezzos (3) Pno, Op. 117; Debussy:Preludes Pno; J. Haydn:Son Kbd; F. Schubert:German Dances Pno, D.790 BAYE 2-▲ 200044 (34.97)
J. Jandó (pno), A. Rahbari (cnd), Brussels BRTN PO *(rec June 3-4, 1992)* † J. Brahms:Con 2 Pno, Op. 83 NXIN ▲ 550506 [DDD] (5.97)
M. Perahia (pno), C. Abbado (cnd), Berlin PO † Con Pno in a, Op. 54; Intro & Allegro, Op. 134 SNYC ▲ 64577 (16.97)
R. Serkin (pno), E. Ormandy (cnd), Philadelphia Orch † Con Pno in a, Op. 54; E. Grieg:Con Pno, Op. 16 SNYC (Essential Classics) ▲ 46543 [ADD] (7.97) ▮ 46543 [ADD] (3.98)

Introduction & Allegro in d & D for Piano & Orchestra, Op. 134 (1853)
D. Barenboim (pno), D. Fischer-Dieskau (cnd), London PO † Con Pno in a, Op. 54; Con Vc EMIC ▲ 64626 (11.97)
S. Costa (pno), S. Gunzenhauser (cnd), Lisbon Gulbenkian Foundation Orch † Con Pno in a, Op. 54; Intro & Allegro appassionato, Op. 92 NXIN ▲ 550277 [DDD] (5.97)
M. Perahia (pno), C. Abbado (cnd), Berlin PO † Con Pno in a, Op. 54; Intro & Allegro appassionato, Op. 92 SNYC ▲ 64577 (16.97)
S. Richter (pno), S. Wislocki (cnd), Warsaw PO *(rec National Philharmonic Warsaw, Poland, Apr 1959)* † Con Pno in a, Op. 54; Novelettes, Op. 21; Toccata Pno, Op. 7; Waldscenen, Op. 82 DEUT (The Originals) ▲ 47440 [ADD] (11.97)
R. Serkin (pno), E. Ormandy (cnd), Philadelphia Orch *(rec 1968)* † J. Brahms:Con 1 Pno, Op. 15; Mendelssohn (-Bartholdy):Capriccio brillante, Op. 22 SNYC (Essential Classics) ▲ 48166 (7.97) ▮ 48166 (3.98)

Julius Caesar (concert overture) in f for Orchestra, Op. 128 (1851)
N. Järvi (cnd), London SO † Genoveva (ov); Manfred (incidental music), Op. 115; Ov, Scherzo & Finale, Op. 52 CHN (Collect) ▲ 6548 [DDD] (12.97)

Kinderball (6 Pieces) for Piano 4-Hands, Op. 130 (1853)
C. Argelli (pno), P. Dirani (pno) † Ballszenen, Op. 109; Bilder aus Osten, Op. 66; Klavierstücke, Op. 85; Polonaises Pno 4-Hands FON 2-▲ 9708 (20.97)

SCHUMANN, ROBERT (cont.)

Kinderball (6 Pieces) for Piano 4-Hands, Op. 130 (1853) (cont.)
J. J. Gutiérrez (pno), M. R. Briá (pno) *(rec 1996)* ("Danses romantiques") † A. Dvořák:Slavonic Dances (sels); E. Grieg:Norwegian Dances, Op. 35; Moszkowski:Spanische Tänze, Op. 12 LAMA (Ars Harmonica) ▲ 20 [DDD] (17.97)

Kinderszenen (13 pieces) for Piano, Op. 15 (1838)
D. Achatz (pno) *(rec Nacka Sweden, Apr 30, 1980)* † Fant Pno, Op. 17; Liszt:Son Pno, S.178 BIS ▲ 144 [AAD] (17.97)
M. Argerich (pno) † Kreisleriana, Op. 16 DEUT ▲ 10653 [DDD] (16.97)
C. Arrau (pno) † Carnaval, Op. 9; Waldscenen, Op. 82 PPHI (Silver Line) ▲ 20871 [ADD] (9.97)
H. Bauer (pno)—Von fremden Ländern und Menschen; Curiose Geschichte; Hasche-Mann; Bittendes Kind; Glückes genug; Wichtige Begebenheit; Träumerei; Am Camin; Ritter vom Steckenpferd; Kind im Einschlummern † Novelettes, Op. 21; Chopin:Music of Chopin NIMB ▲ 8817 [DDD] (11.97)
J. Bovet (pno) † Waldscenen, Op. 82; Debussy:Children's Corner GALL ▲ 746 [AAD]
R. Burnett (pno) † Chopin:Andante Spianato & Grand Polonaise, Op. 22; Czerny:Vars on "La Ricordanza", Op. 33; J. N. Hummel:Vars on a theme from Gluck's Armide, Op. 57; F. Schubert:Dances (42), Op. 18; Ecossaises (6), D.421; Waltzes (20) Pno, D.146 AMON ▲ 7 (16.97)
J. Coop (pno)—Träumerei *(rec Toronto, Canada)* ("The Romantic Piano") † J. Brahms:Pieces (6) Pno, Op. 118; Waltzes (16) Pno, Op. 39; Chopin:Etudes (24) Pno, Op. 10 & 25; Mazurkas Pno; Nocturnes Pno; Debussy:Isle joyeuse; Suite bergamasque; Liszt:Etudes de concert (3), S.144; Liebesträume, S.541; Mendelssohn (-Bartholdy):Pno Music (misc); S. Rachmaninoff:Etudes-tableaux Pno, Opp. 33 & 39; Preludes (23) Pno, Opp. 23 & 32 MUVI ▲ 1015 [DDD] (16.97)
A. Cortot (pno)—Von fremden Ländern und Menschen † Kreisleriana, Op. 16; Symphonic Etudes, Op. 13 GRM2 ▲ 78819 (13.97)
A. Cortot (pno) *(rec 1935 for HMV)* † Dichterliebe, Op. 48; Fantasiestücke Pno, Op. 12; Kreisleriana, Op. 16 BPS ▲ 5 [ADD] (16.97)
J. Demus (pno) † Con Pno in a, Op. 54; Davidsbündlertänze, Op. 6; Dichterliebe, Op. 48; Phantasiestücke Vn, Op. 88; Qts Strs, Op. 41; Sym 3 INTC (Art of Classics) ▲ 885921
E. Dubourg (pno)—Von fremden Ländern und Menschen ("Piano Dreams") † Waldscenen, Op. 82; Chopin:Barcarolle Pno, Op. 60; Liszt:Années de pèlerinage 2, S.161; W. A. Mozart:Son 11 Pno, K.331; F. Schubert:Impromptus (4); Impromptus (8) Pno, D.899 & 935; P. Tchaikovsky:Con 1 Pno, Op. 23 LALI ▲ 14224 (3.97)
B. Engerer (pno) † Carnaval, Op. 9; Liszt:Fant & Fugue on the name B-A-C-H, S.529; Trans, Arrs & Paraphrases HAM ▲ 901600 (18.97)
F. Gevers (pno) *(rec Barcelona, Sept 1995)* ("Oeuvre pour Piano") † Arabeske Pno, Op. 18; Blumenstück, Op. 19; Fant Pno, Op. 17; Romances Pno, Op. 28 EAM ▲ 6134 [DDD] (17.97)
W. Gieseking (pno)—Träumerei *(rec 1938-47)* † Davidsbündlertänze, Op. 6; Fant Pno, Op. 17 ENPL (Piano Library) ▲ 244 (13.97)
I. Haebler (pno)—Fast zu ernst ("Shine: The Complete Classics") † Beethoven:Sym 9; Chopin:Polonaise 6 Pno, Op. 53; Preludes (24) Pno, Op. 28; Liszt:Études d'exécution transcendante (6), S.140; Études de concert (3), S.144; Hungarian Rhaps, S.244; S. Rachmaninoff:Con 3 Pno, Op. 30; Prelude in c#, Op. 3/2; Rimsky-Korsakov:Tale of Tsar Saltan (orch sels); Vivaldi:Gloria; Nulla in mundo pax, RV.630 PPHI 2-▲ 456403 (17.97)
V. Horowitz (pno)—Träumerei *(rec Jan 2-Feb 1, 1968)* ("The Legendary Masterworks Recordings, 1962-1973, Vol. 4") † Arabeske Pno, Op. 18; Chopin:Polonaise 5 Pno, Op. 44; V. Horowitz:Vars Theme from Bizet's Carmen; D. Scarlatti:Sons Kbd SNYC ▲ 53465 [ADD] (16.97)
V. Horowitz (pno) † Kreisleriana, Op. 16; Novelettes, Op. 21 DGRM (Masters) ▲ 445599 [DDD]
V. Horowitz (pno) † Arabeske Pno, Op. 18; Blumenstück, Op. 19; Kreisleriana, Op. 16; Toccata Pno, Op. 7 SNYC ▲ 42409 [AAD] (16.97)
V. Horowitz (pno) ("Horowitz In London") † Chopin:Polonaises-fant, Op. 61 RCAV (Gold Seal) ▲ 61414 (11.97)
P. Huybregts (pno) † Papillons Pno, Op. 2 CENT ▲ 2065 [ADD] (16.97)
J. Jandó (pno) *(rec Nov 1992)* ("Schumann: Piano Works") † Carnaval, Op. 9; Papillons Pno, Op. 2 NXIN ▲ 550784 [DDD] (5.97)
D. Joeres (pno) *(rec Nov 1991)* ("Schumann & His Friends") † J. Brahms:Ballades (4), Op. 10; N. W. Gade:Akvareller, Op. 19; Idyller, Op.34; S. Heller:Traumbilder, Op. 79; T. Kirchner:Nachtbilder, Op. 25 INMP ▲ 1044 [DDD] (11.97)
W. Kapell (pno)—Von fremden Ländern und Menschen † Chopin:Mazurkas Pno; Nocturnes Pno; Polonaises-fant, Op. 61; A. Copland:Son Pno; Mussorgsky:Pictures at an Exhibition; D. Scarlatti:Sons Kbd RCAV ▲ 68997 [ADD] (16.97)
W. Kempff (pno) † Arabeske Pno, Op. 18; Bunte Blätter, Op. 99; Carnaval, Op. 9; Davidsbündlertänze, Op. 6; Fant Pno, Op. 17; Humoreske Pno, Op. 20; Kreisleriana, Op. 16; Nachtstücke, Op. 23; Papillons Pno, Op. 2; Romances Pno, Op. 28; Son 2 Pno, Op. 22; Symphonic Etudes, Op. 13; Waldscenen, Op. 82 DEUT 4-▲ 35045 [ADD] (26.97)
A. Kubalek (pno) † Carnaval, Op. 9; Fantasiestücke, Op. 111; Gesänge der Frühe, Op. 133 DOR ▲ 90116 [DDD] (16.97)
R. Lupu (pno) *(rec Corseaux Switzerland, Jan 1993)* † Humoreske Pno, Op. 20; Kreisleriana, Op. 16 PLON ▲ 40496 [DDD] (16.97)
R. Lupu (pno) *(rec 1993)* ("Radu Lupu") † Beethoven:Son 14 Pno, Op. 27/2; Vars Pno on Original Theme, WoO 80; J. Brahms:Intermezzos (3) Pno, Op. 117; Theme & Vars Pno; E. Grieg:Con Pno, Op. 16; F. Schubert:Moments musicaux, D.780; Son Pno, D.784 PPHI (Great Pianists of the 20th Century) ▲ 456895 (22.97)
Y. Nat (pno) † Con Pno in a, Op. 54; Fantasiestücke Pno, Op. 12; Faschingsschwank, Op. 26 ENPL (The Piano Library) ▲ 181 (13.97)
E. Ney (pno) ("The Art of the Piano, Vol. 1") † J. Brahms:Trio 1 Pno, Op. 8; M. Reger:Suite Vn Pno, Op. 103a; F. Schubert:Son Arpeggione, D.821 ACLR ▲ 39 (17.97)
D. Pollack (pno)—Träumerei ("First Kiss") † Carnaval, Op. 9; Chopin:Nocturnes Pno; Debussy:Arabesques Pno; Fille aux cheveaux de lin (song); Liszt:Études de concert (3), S.144; Consolations (6), S.172; M. Ravel:Pavane pour une infante défunte; P. Tchaikovsky:Saisons FWIN ▲ 3002 (13.97)
A. Rubenstein (pno)—Träumerei *(rec 1928-47)* † Arabeske Pno, Op. 18; Myrthen, Op. 25; Romances Pno, Op. 28; J. Brahms:Pieces (8) Pno, Op. 76; Songs (5), Op. 49; Liszt:Liebesträume, S.541; F. Schubert:Impromptus (4) Pno; P. Tchaikovsky:Con 1 Pno, Op. 23 GRM2 ▲ 78783 (13.97)
A. Schnabel (pno) *(rec London, England, 1946-47)* ("The 1946-47 HMV Solo Recordings") † J. Brahms:Fants Pno, Op. 116; Intermezzos (3) Pno, Op. 117; Rhaps (2) Pno, Op. 79; W. A. Mozart:Rondo Pno, K.511; Son 12 Pno, K.332; C. M. von Weber:Invitation to the Dance Pno, J.260 APR ▲ 5526 (mono) [ADD] (18.97)
H. Shelley (pno) † Carnaval, Op. 9 CHN ▲ 8814 [DDD] (16.97)
N. Shelter (pno) † Arabeske Pno, Op. 18; Blumenstück, Op. 19; Romances Pno, Op. 28 BER ▲ 9328 (10.97)
A. Simon (pno) † Arabeske Pno, Op. 18; Kreisleriana, Op. 16; Vars on A-B-E-G-G, Op. 1 DANT ▲ 9649 (17.97)
F. Ts'ong (pno) *(rec Warsaw, Poland)* † Arabeske Pno, Op. 18; Davidsbündlertänze, Op. 6; Kreisleriana, Op. 16; Papillons Pno, Op. 2; Waldscenen, Op. 82 ICC ▲ 6601127 (32.97)
O. Volkov (pno)—Träumerei *(rec Moscow, Russia, May 22, 1994)* ("Live From Moscow") † F. Kreisler:Vn Pieces; Liszt:Études de concert (2), S.145; S. Prokofiev:Sarcasms Pno, Op. 17; F. Schubert:Impromptus (4) Pno; Moments musicaux, D.780; Son Pno, D.537; A. Scriabin:Preludes (24) Pno, Op. 11; Preludes (5) Pno, Op. 16 BRIO ▲ 106 (16.97)
P. Volpe (pno) † F. Schubert:Son Pno, D.960 DI ▲ 920305 [DDD] (5.97)
A. Walter (cnd), Slovak State PO Košice—Träumerei [trans Josef Strauss] *(rec House of Arts Košice, Slovak Republic, Apr 25-28, 1994)* ("Josef Strauss: Edition, Vol. 2") † Jos. Strauss:Music of Jos. Strauss MARC ▲ 8223562 [DDD] (13.97)
P. Yegorov (pno) † Carnaval, Op. 9 SNYC ▲ 57264 [DDD] (4.97)

Klavierstücke (4) for Piano, Op. 32 (1838-39)
J. Demus (pno) ("Piano Works, Vol. 1") † Davidsbündlertänze, Op. 6; Fantasiestücke, Op. 111; Gesänge der Frühe, Op. 133 NUO ▲ 7311 (16.97)

Klavierstücke (12) for Piano 4-Hands, Op. 85 (1849)
C. Argelli (pno), P. Dirani (pno) † Ballszenen, Op. 109; Bilder aus Osten, Op. 66; Kinderball, Op. 130; Polonaises Pno 4-Hands FON 2-▲ 9708 (20.97)
F. Renggli (fl), J. Schultz (pno)—No. 12, Abendlied [arr for fl & pno] ("Romantic Flute Sonatas") † Romances Ob, Op. 94; Son 1 Vn, Op. 105; Mendelssohn (-Bartholdy):Son Vn (1820); Son Vn, Op. 4 DI ▲ 920400 [DDD] (5.97)
H. Schellenberger (ob), R. Koenen (pno)—No. 12, Abendlied; No. 6, Trauer [arr for pno & ob] *(rec Berlin, Germany, June 1995)* † Adagio & Allegro Hn, Op. 70; Fantasiestücke Cl, Op. 73; Kreisleriana, Op. 16; Liederkreis, Op. 39; Myrthen, Op. 25; Romances Ob, Op. 94; Romances Pno, Op. 28; C. Schumann:Romances Vn, Op. 22 CAMM ▲ 130014 [DDD] (16.97)
A. Spalding (vn), A. Benoist (pno)—No. 12, Abendlied [arr for vn & pno] ("The Art of the Violin, Vol. 3") † J. Brahms:Son 3 Vn, Op. 108; C. Franck:Son Vn, M.8; G. F. Handel:Son Vn; Tartini:Son Vn & Pno ACLR ▲ 42 (17.97)

Konzert-Etüden (6) nach Capricen von Paganini for Piano, Op. 10 (1833)
L. D. Alvanis (pno) ("The Complete Etudes for Solo Piano") † Studien nach Capricen von Paganini, Op. 3; Symphonic Etudes, Op. 13 MER ▲ 84336 [DDD] (16.97)
J. Martin (pno) † Nachtstücke, Op. 23; Studien nach Capricen von Paganini, Op. 3 ARN ▲ 68226 [DDD] (16.97)

SCHUMANN, ROBERT (cont.)

Konzertstück in F for 4 Horns & Orchestra, Op. 86 (1849)

M. Bernardi (cnd), Calgary PO SMS (SM 5000) ▲ 5092 [DDD] (16.97)

R. Bonnevie (hn), G. Schwarz (cnd), Seattle SO † Ov, Scherzo & Finale, Op. 52 DLS ▲ 3084 [DDD] (14.97)

M. Buder (cnd), Bamberg SO † P. Coenen:Vars for 4 French Hns, Op. 69; Genzmer:Con for 4 Hns KSCH ▲ 311021 [DDD] (16.97)

P. Damm (hn), S. Kurz (cnd), Dresden Staatskapelle ("Romantic Horn Concerti") † Lortzing:Konzertstück Hn; Saint-Saëns:Morceau de concert Hn, Op. 94; C. M. von Weber:Con Hn BER ▲ 9324 (10.97)

S. Dent (hn), G. Edwards (hn), R. Maskell (hn), R. Montgomery (hn), J. E. Gardiner (cnd), Orch Révolutionnaire et Romantique *(rec The Colosseum Watford, Oct 1997)* ("The Complete Symphonies") † Ov, Scherzo & Finale, Op. 52; Sym in g PARC 3-▲ 457591 [DDD] (48.97)

J. Justafré (hn), J. Barro (hn), A. Courtois (hn), J. Gantiez (hn) ("The Magic of the French Horn") † N. C. Bochsa:Andante sostenuto; Dauprat:Son Hn & Hp; Dukas:Villanelle; W. A. Mozart:Con 4 Hn, K.495; Rondo Hn, K.371 ERAT ▲ 94801 (9.97)

G. Schwarz (cnd), Seattle SO *(rec Seattle Opera House, WA, Sept 1988-Feb 1992)* ("The Schumann Edition") † Con Pno in a, Op. 54; Manfred Ov, Op. 115; Ov, Scherzo & Finale, Op. 52; Sym 1; Sym 2; Sym 3; Sym 4; Symphonic Etudes, Op. 13 DLS 4-▲ 3146 [DDD] (30.97)

C. Thielemann (cnd), Philharmonia Orch *(rec All Hallows London, England, July 1996)* † Manfred Ov, Op. 115; Sym 2 DEUT ▲ 453482 [DDD] (16.97)

Kreisleriana (8 fantasies) for Piano, Op. 16 (1838; rev 1850)

V. Afanassiev (pno) DNN ▲ 75714 (16.97)

A. Arad (pno) *(rec American Academy & Inst of Arts & Letters, NYC, NY, Mar 1998)* † Arabeske Pno, Op. 18; Fant Pno, Op. 17 MUSC ▲ 1001 [DDD] (10.97)

M. Argerich (pno) † Kinderszenen Pno, Op. 15 DEUT ▲ 10653 [DDD] (16.97)

S. Blet (pno)—Intermezzo ("Favorite Encores") † Blet:Prélude Pno, Op. 5/1; Chopin:Preludes (24) Pno, Op. 28; Liszt:Pno Music (misc); Satie:Piccadilly; D. Scarlatti:Sons Kbd; I. Stravinsky:Studies Pno, Op. 7 FORL ▲ 16752 [DDD] (16.97)

L. Bustani (pno) *(rec Maria Minor Church, Utrecht, Netherlands, Oct 1998)* † Chopin:Fantaisie Pno, Op. 49; Nocturnes Pno; Scherzos Pno CSOC ▲ 4230

S. Cherkassky (pno) *(rec May 13-14 & June 10, 1985)* † Symphonic Etudes, Op. 13; C. Franck:Prélude, choral et fugue, M.21 NIMB ▲ 7705 [DDD] (11.97)

A. Cortot (pno) *(rec 1935 for HMV)* † Dichterliebe, Op. 48; Fantasiestücke Pno, Op. 12; Kinderszenen Pno, Op. 15 BPS ▲ 5 [ADD] (16.97)

A. Cortot (pno) † Kinderszenen Pno, Op. 15; Symphonic Etudes, Op. 13 GRM2 ▲ 78819 (13.97)

M. Gambaryan (pno) *(rec 1971-84)* ("Russian Piano School: Gambaryan") † Son Pno, Op. 14; Beethoven:Son 11 Pno, Op. 22; Liszt:Trans, Arrs & Paraphrases RD (Talents of Russia) ▲ 16299 [ADD] (16.97)

W. Gieseking (pno) *(rec 1953)* † Davidsbündlertänze, Op. 6; J. S. Bach:English Suites FORL ▲ 16590 [AAD] (16.97)

W. Gieseking (pno) *(rec 1942-43)* † Carnaval, Op. 9; Son 1 Pno, Op. 11 ENPL (Piano Library) ▲ 224 (13.97)

W. Gieseking (pno) † Carnaval, Op. 9; Davidsbündlertänze, Op. 6; Fant Pno, Op. 17; Son 1 Pno, Op. 11 GRM2 2-▲ 78796 (26.97)

H. Grimaud (pno) † J. Brahms:Son 2 Pno, Op. 2 DNN ▲ 73336 [DDD] (16.97)

P. Gulda (pno) *(rec Oct 26-29, 1990)* † Blumenstück, Op. 19 NXIN ▲ 550401 [DDD] (5.97)

M. Hambourg (pno) *(rec 1995)* ("The Hambourg Legacy") † Andante & Vars Pnos, Op. 46; Beethoven:Son 12 Pno, Op. 26; Chopin:Andante Spianato & Grand Polonaise, Op. 22; Debussy:Prélude à l'après-midi d'un faune; Liszt:Légendes, S.175 ARBT ▲ 109 [ADD] (16.97)

V. Horowitz (pno) *(rec New York, NY, 1985)* ("The Studio Recordings") † Liszt:Impromptu, S.191; Valses oubliées (4), S.215; D. Scarlatti:Sons Kbd; F. Schubert:Impromptus (4); Marche militaire, D.733; A. Scriabin:Etudes (12) Pno, Op. 8 DEUT ▲ 19217 [DDD] (11.97)

V. Horowitz (pno) † Kinderszenen Pno, Op. 15; Novelettes, Op. 21 DGRM (Masters) ▲ 445599 [DDD]

V. Horowitz (pno) *(rec 1969)* † Arabeske Pno, Op. 18; Blumenstück, Op. 19; Kinderszenen Pno, Op. 15; Toccata Pno, Op. 7 SNYC ▲ 42409 [AAD] (16.97)

V. Horowitz (pno) *(rec New York, NY, Dec 1, 1969)* ("The Complete Masterworks Recordings, Vol. VII: Early Romantics") † Son Pno, Op. 14; Chopin:Pno Music (misc colls) SNYC 2-▲ 53468 (31.97)

P. Jegorov (pno) † Symphonic Etudes, Op. 13 SNYC ▲ 66726 [DDD] (4.97)

W. Kempff (pno) † Arabeske Pno, Op. 18; Bunte Blätter, Op. 99; Carnaval, Op. 9; Davidsbündlertänze, Op. 6; Fant Pno, Op. 17; Humoreske Pno, Op. 20; Kinderszenen Pno, Op. 15; Nachtstücke, Op. 23; Papillons Pno, Op. 2; Romances Pno, Op. 28; Son 2 Pno, Op. 22; Symphonic Etudes, Op. 13; Waldscenen, Op. 82 DEUT 4-▲ 35045 [ADD] (26.97)

W. Kempff (pno) *(rec 1956)* ("Wilhlem Kempff") † Arabeske Pno, Op. 18; J. Brahms:Ballades (4), Op. 10; Fants Pno, Op. 116; Intermezzos (3) Pno, Op. 117; Pieces (4) Pno, Op. 119; Pieces (6) Pno, Op. 118; Pieces (8) Pno, Op. 76 PPHI (Great Pianists of the 20th Century) ▲ 456862 (22.97)

E. Kissin (pno) † Beethoven:Rondo a capriccio Pno, Op. 129; Rondos Pno, Op. 51; Busoni:Chaconne Pno RCAV ▲ 68911 [DDD] (16.97)

A. Kuerti (pno) *(rec Massey Hall Toronto, Mar 1969)* † Son Pno, Op. 14; Toccata Pno, Op. 7 CBC ▲ 2012 [ADD] (16.97)

R. Lupu (pno) *(rec Corseaux Switzerland, Jan 1993)* † Humoreske Pno, Op. 20; Kinderszenen Pno, Op. 15 PLON ▲ 40496 [DDD] (16.97)

B. Moisejwitsch (pno) ("In Recital") † Carnaval, Op. 9; Symphonic Etudes, Op. 13; Beethoven:Andante Pno, WoO 57; Chopin:Études Pno; Fant-Impromptu, Op. 66; Son Pno in b, Op. 58; Mussorgsky:Pictures at an Exhibition; Palmgren:West Finnish Dance PHS 2-▲ 9192 (33.97)

H. Neuhaus (pno)—No. 1, Äusserst bewegt; No. 2, Sehr innig und nicht zu rasch *(rec 1951)* ("Russian Piano School: Neuhaus") † J. Brahms:Pieces (4) Pno, Op. 119; Pieces (8) Pno, Op. 76 RD (Talents of Russia) ▲ 16246 [ADD] (16.97)

M. O'Rourke (pno) † Carnaval, Op. 9 CHN ▲ 9388 [DDD] (16.97)

M. Perahia (pno) † Son 1 Pno, Op. 11 SNYC ▲ 62786 (16.97)

H. Schellenberger (ob), R. Koenen (pno)—Intermezzo [arr for pno & ob] *(rec Berlin, Germany, June 1995)* † Adagio & Allegro Hn, Op. 70; Fantasiestücke Cl, Op. 73; Klavierstücke, Op. 85; Liederkreis, Op. 39; Myrthen, Op. 25; Romances Ob, Op. 94; Romances Pno, Op. 28; C. Schumann:Romances Vn, Op. 22 CAMM ▲ 130014 [DDD] (16.97)

A. Schiff (pno) † Gesänge der Frühe, Op. 133; Nachtstücke, Op. 23 TELC ▲ 14566 (16.97)

R. Shamvili (pno) ("Shamvili Plays Schumann & Glinka") † M. Glinka:Pno Music (misc) GALL ▲ 903 [DDD] (18.97)

A. Simon (pno) † Arabeske Pno, Op. 18; Kinderszenen Pno, Op. 15; Vars on A-B-E-G-G, Op. 1 DANT ▲ 9649 (17.97)

N. Sivelöv (pno) † Arabeske Pno, Op. 18; Son Pno, Op. 14; Son 2 Pno, Op. 22 CAPA ▲ 21518 (16.97)

P. Spada (pno) *(rec Roma Italy, May 1991)* † Carnaval, Op. 9 AART ▲ 47125 [DDD] (10.97)

F. Ts'ong (pno) *(rec Warsaw, Poland)* † Arabeske Pno, Op. 18; Davidsbündlertänze, Op. 6; Kinderszenen Pno, Op. 15; Papillons Pno, Op. 2; Waldscenen, Op. 82 ICC ▲ 6601127 (32.97)

M. Uchida (pno) † Carnaval, Op. 9 PPHI ▲ 42777 (16.97)

L. Vosgerchian (pno) † F. Schubert:Son Pno, D.960 TIT ▲ 210 [DDD]

G. Walker (pno) † J. S. Bach:Wohltemperirte Clavier; Chopin:Études (24) Pno, Opp. 10 & 25; F. Poulenc:Pièces Pno ALBA ▲ 252 [DDD] (16.97)

E. Wirssaladze (pno) † Fantasiestücke Pno, Op. 12 LV ▲ 311 (17.97)

Lieder (5) for Voice & Piano, Op. 40 (1840)

A. S. von Otter (mez), B. Forsberg (pno) † Frauenliebe und -leben, Op. 42 DEUT ▲ 45881 [DDD] (16.97)

N. Stutzmann (cta), I. Södergren (pno) [GER] † Gedichte, Op. 30; Lieder-Album für die Jugend, Op. 79 RCAV ▲ 61799 [DDD] (16.97)

Lieder-Album für die Jugend (song cycle) for Voice & Piano, Op. 79 (1849)

S. Daneman (sop), J. Drake (pno)—No. 13, Marienwörmchen; No. 12, Der Sandmann; No. 26, Schneeglöckchen; No. 23, Er ist's *(rec East Woodhay, England, Apr & June 1997)* † Lieder-Album für die Junged, Op. 79; Liederkreis, Op. 39; Songs EMIC (Debut) ▲ 72828 [DDD] (6.97)

M. Price (sop), M. Price (sop), T. Dewey (pno), T. Dewey (pno)—No. 12, Der Sandmann; No. 13, Marienwörmchen; No. 7b, Zigeunerliedchen: Jeden Morgen; No. 17, Die wandelnde Glocke; No. 26, Schneeglöckchen; No. 23, Er ist's † Frauenliebe und -leben, Op. 42; Gedichte, Op. 36; Myrthen, Op. 25; Songs FORL ▲ 16711 [DDD] (16.97)

N. Stutzmann (cta), I. Södergren (pno) † Gedichte, Op. 30; Lieder RCAV ▲ 61799 [DDD] (16.97)

Liederkreis (cycle of 9 songs) for Voice & Piano [text Heine], Op. 24 (1840)

I. Bostridge (ten), J. Drake (pno) *(rec July 1997)* ("Bostridge Sings Schumann") † Dichterliebe, Op. 48; Songs *(E,G texts)* EMIC ▲ 56575 [DDD] (16.97)

V. Braun (bar), A. Kubalek (pno) [GER] † Liederkreis, Op. 39; J. Brahms:Ernste Gesänge, Op. 121 DOR ▲ 90132 [DDD] (16.97)

M. Goerne (bar), V. Ashkenazy (pno) † Dichterliebe, Op. 48 PLON ▲ 458265 (16.97)

W. Grönroos (bar), R. Gothóni (pno) *(rec 1977)* † Dichterliebe, Op. 48 BIS ▲ 92 [AAD] (17.97)

T. Hampson (bar), W. Sawallisch (pno) ("Heine Lieder") † Romanzen und Balladen, Op. 53 EMIC ▲ 55598 (16.97)

SCHUMANN, ROBERT (cont.)

Liederkreis (cycle of 9 songs) for Voice & Piano [text Heine], Op. 24 (1840) (cont.)

W. Holzmair (bar), I. Cooper (pno) *(rec Esterházy Palace Eisenstadt, Austria, June 27-30, 1994)* † Dichterliebe, Op. 48; Gesänge, Op. 142; Myrthen, Op. 25; Romanzen und Balladen, Op. 53; Romanzen und Balladen, Op. 64 PPHI ▲ 46086 (16.97)

C. Robbin (mez), M. McMahon (pno) [GER] † Frauenliebe und -leben, Op. 42 MUVI (Musica Viva) ▲ 1050 [DDD] (16.97)

B. Skovhus (bar), H. Deutsch (pno) ("The Heart of the Poet") † Dichterliebe, Op. 48; C. Schumann:Songs SNYC ▲ 62372 (16.97)

T. Spence (ten), I. Brown (pno) † R. Holloway:Fant-Pieces on Schumann; Serenade HYP ▲ 66930 (18.97)

G. Vinogradov (ten), G. Orentlicher (pno) † Dichterliebe, Op. 48; Gedichte, Op. 90; Myrthen, Op. 25; S. Rachmaninoff:Songs (14), Op. 34; Rimsky-Korsakov:Songs, Op. 51; A. Rubinstein:Songs; P. Tchaikovsky:Songs PRE ▲ 89118 (16.97)

Liederkreis (cycle of 12 songs) for Voice & Piano [text Eichendorff], Op. 39 (1840)

B. Bonney (sop), V. Ashkenazy (pno)—No. 3, Waldesgespräch; No. 5, Mondnacht † Frauenliebe und -leben, Op. 42; Myrthen, Op. 25; C. Schumann:Lieder PLON ▲ 452898 (16.97)

V. Braun (bar), A. Kubalek (pno) [GER] † Liederkreis, Op. 24; J. Brahms:Ernste Gesänge, Op. 121 DOR ▲ 90132 [DDD] (16.97)

S. Daneman (sop), J. Drake (pno) *(rec East Woodhay, England, Apr & June 1997)* † Lieder-Album für die Jugend, Op. 79; Lieder-Album für die Junged, Op. 79; Songs EMIC (Debut) ▲ 72828 [DDD] (6.97)

P. Dombrecht (ob), J. van Immerseel (pno)—No. 5, Mondnacht † Romances Ob, Op. 94; Kalliwoda:Morceau de Salon, Op. 228; Pixis:Grand Son Ob, Op. 35 ACCE ▲ 78330 (17.97)

D. Fischer-Dieskau (bar), A. Brendel (pno) [GER] † Dichterliebe, Op. 48 PPHI ▲ 16352 [DDD] (16.97)

J. Norman (sop), I. Gage (pno) [GER] † Frauenliebe und -leben, Op. 42 PPHI ▲ 20784 [ADD] (16.97)

P. Pears (ten), B. Britten (pno) *(rec Aldeburgh Festival, European Community, 1958-59)* † G. Fauré:Bonne chanson, Op. 61; H. Purcell:Music of Purcell; F. Schubert:Die Sterne, D.939 BBC ▲ 8006 (17.97)

M. Price (sop), G. Johnson (pno) † Gedichte, Op. 35 HYP ▲ 55011 (9.97)

T. Quasthoff (bar), R. Szidon (pno) [GER] † Dichterliebe, Op. 48; Songs RCAV (Red Seal) ▲ 61225 (16.97)

H. Schellenberger (ob), R. Koenen (pno)—No. 3, Waldesgespräch; No. 5, Mondnacht [arr for pno & ob] *(rec Berlin, Germany, June 1995)* † Adagio & Allegro Hn, Op. 70; Fantasiestücke Cl, Op. 73; Klavierstücke, Op. 85; Kreisleriana, Op. 16; Myrthen, Op. 25; Romances Ob, Op. 94; Romances Pno, Op. 28; C. Schumann:Romances Vn, Op. 22 CAMM ▲ 130014 [DDD] (16.97)

I. Seefried (sop), E. Werba (pno)—No. 8, In der Fremde; No. 3, Waldesgespräch; No. 4, Die Stille; No. 10, Zwielicht *(rec Aug 18, 1960)* † Frauenliebe und -leben, Op. 42; Myrthen, Op. 25; Songs; J. Brahms:Songs ORFE (Festspiel Dokumente) ▲ 398951 (16.97)

M. Shirai (mez), H. Höll (pno) [GER] † Songs CAPO ▲ 10099 [DDD] (11.97)

M. Shirai (mez), H. Höll (pno) *(rec Japan, July 1982)* † Frauenliebe und -leben, Op. 42 CAMA ▲ 2516 [DDD] (18.97)

N. Vallin (sop), G. Andolfi (pno)—No. 1, In der Fremde *(rec 1931)* ("Ninon Vallin: Canciones, Leider and Peruvian Folk Songs") † Frauenliebe und -leben, Op. 42; M. de Falla:Amor brujo (sels); Canciones populares españolas; J. Nin:Songs; R. Strauss:Songs VAIA ▲ 1127 [ADD] (17.97)

I. M. Witoschynskyj (pno)—No. 5, Mondnacht; No. 6, Schöne Fremde; No. 12, Frühlingsnacht [arr C. Schumann for Pno] *(rec Mar 15-17, 1996)* ("Clara Schumann & Her Family") † Albumblätter, Op. 124; Studies Canon Form, Op. 56; Bargiel:Bagatelles, Op. 4; Characteristic Pieces, Op. 1; Fant Pieces, Op. 9; J. Brahms:Serenade 1 Orch, Op. 11; C. Schumann:Pièces fugitives, Op. 15; Romances Pno, Op. 21; Songs MDG ▲ 6040729 [DDD] (17.97)

E. Höngen (cta), artist unknown—No. 3, Waldesgespräch *(rec Apr 1946 live)* † Gesänge, Op. 31; Myrthen, Op. 25; J. Brahms:Liebeslieder Waltzes Pno 4-Hands, Op. 52a; B. Marcello:Mio bel foco; F. Schubert:Songs (misc colls); R. Wagner:Wesendonck Songs; H. Wolf:Gedichte von Goethe; Gedichte von Mörike PRE ▲ 90356 (m) (16.97)

Life & Music of Schumann

J. Perlea (cnd), Bamberg SO *(Sym 4, Op. 120; Andante & Vars Pnos, Op. 46; Symphonic Etudes, Op. 13; Toccata Pno, Op. 7; Kreisleriana, Op. 16; Con Pno in a, Op. 54; Carnaval, Op. 9; Myrthen, Op. 25 [No. 1, Widmung; No. 3, Der Nussbaum]; Papillons Pno, Op. 2; Qnt Pno, Op. 44; Album für die Jugend, Op. 68; Kinderszenen Pno, Op. 15; Con Vc, Op. 129)*, *(Sym 3, Op. 97)* ("The Stories of Schumann & Grieg in Words and Music") † E. Grieg:Con Pno, Op. 16; Life & Music of Grieg; Lyric Pieces; Lyric Suite, Op. 54/1-4; Norwegian Dances, Op. 35 MMD (Music Masters) ▲ 8505 [ADD] (3.97) ▮ 8505 [ADD] (2.98)

Mädchenlieder for Soprano & Alto (or 2 Sopranos), Op. 103 (1851)

R. Follman (sop), L. D. Mills (mez), R. MacNeil (ten), P. Atherton (b-bar), S. McCune (pno), T. Fleischer (pno), W. Hall (cnd), Master Chorale of Orange County—No. 3, An die Nachtigall *(rec Chapman University, Salmon Recital Hall, Orange, CA)* † Spanische Liebeslieder, Op. 138; Spanisches Liederspiel, Op. 74; Zweistimmige Lieder, Op. 43; J. Brahms:Duets (3), Op. 20; Duets (4), Op. 61; Liebeslieder Waltzes, Op. 52; Qts (3) SATB, Op. 31; Qts (3) SATB, Op. 64 KLAV ▲ 11092 [DDD] (18.97)

Manfred (incidental music) [text Lord Byron translated K.A. Suckow], Op. 115 (1848-49)

N. Järvi (cnd), London SO † Genoveva (ov); Julius Caesar, Op. 128; Ov, Scherzo & Finale, Op. 52 CHN (Collect) ▲ 6548 [DDD] (12.97)

Manfred Overture in e♭ for Orchestra, Op. 115 (1848-49)

H. Abendroth (cnd), Leipzig Gewandhaus Orch ("Hermann Abendroth:Gewandhaus Kapellmeister 1944-45") † J. S. Bach:Suite 3 Orch, BWV 1068; J. Brahms:Tragic Ov, Op. 81; G. F. Handel:Concerti grossi, Op. 6; J. Haydn:Sym 88; Sym 96; W. A. Mozart:Sym 29, K.201; F. Schubert:Sym 3 TAHA 2-▲ 106 (34.97)

C. M. Giulini (cnd), Los Angeles PO *(rec Shrine Auditorium, Los Angeles, CA, Dec 1980)* † Beethoven:Sym 3 DEUT (The Originals) ▲ 47444 [ADD/DDD] (11.97)

R. Kubelík (cnd), Bavarian RSO *(rec 1978)* † Sym 3; Sym 4 SNYC (Essential Classics) ▲ 48270 [ADD] (7.97) ▮ 48270 [ADD] (3.98)

R. Leibowitz (cnd), Royal PO *(rec Jan 9, 1962)* † Sym 3; Liszt:Mephisto Waltz 1 Orch, S.110; R. Wagner:Tannhäuser (ov) CHSK ▲ 96 [ADD] (16.97)

A. Manzano (cnd), Ecuador National SO *(rec Sucre National Theater Quito, Ecuador, May 20, 1994)* † Con Pno in a, Op. 54 GALL ▲ 859 [DDD] (19.97)

P. Paray (cnd), Detroit SO † Sym 1; Sym 2; Sym 3; Sym 4 MRCR (Living Presence) 2-▲ 462955 (22.97)

G. Schwarz (cnd), Seattle SO *(rec Seattle Opera House, WA, Sept 1988-Feb 1992)* ("The Schumann Edition") † Con Pno in a, Op. 54; Konzertstück Hns, Op. 86; Ov, Scherzo & Finale, Op. 52; Sym 1; Sym 2; Sym 3; Sym 4; Symphonic Etudes, Op. 13 DLS 4-▲ 3146 [DDD] (30.97)

G. Szell (cnd), Cleveland Orch *(rec Jan 21, 1959)* † Syms (comp) SNYC (Masterworks Heritage) 2-▲ 62349 [ADD] (25.97)

C. Thielemann (cnd), Philharmonia Orch *(rec All Hallows London, England, July 1996)* † Konzertstück Hns, Op. 86; Sym 2 DEUT ▲ 453482 [DDD] (16.97)

A. Toscanini (cnd), NBC SO ("The Toscanini Collection, Vol. 16") † Sym 3; C. M. von Weber:Ovs RCAV (Gold Seal) ▲ 60292 (11.97)

Märchenbilder (4) for Viola (or Violin ad lib) & Piano, Op. 113 (1851)

Y. Bashmet (vn), M. Muntian (pno) † Adagio & Allegro Hn, Op. 70; Bruch:Kol Nidrei, Op. 47; Enescu:Concertpiece Va & Pno; F. Schubert:Son Arpeggione, D.821 RCAV (Red Seal) ▲ 60112 [DDD] (16.97)

S. Braconi (va), A. Dindo (pno) † Fantasiestücke Cl, Op. 73; Märchenerzählungen, Op. 132; Romances Ob, Op. 94 AG ▲ 43 (18.97)

P. Coletti (va), L. Howard (pno) † Beethoven:Notturno Va; Mendelssohn (-Bartholdy):Son Va HYP ▲ 66946 (18.97)

S. Collot (va), K. Toyama (pno) *(rec 1993-97)* ("The Art of the Viola") † Debussy:Son Fl; M. Glinka:Son Va; D. Milhaud:Son 2 Va, Op. 244 CAMA ▲ 30462 [DDD] (18.97)

K. Dreyfus (va), R. McDonald (pno) † Bruch:Romanze Va, Op. 85; Debussy:Beau soir; M. de Falla:Suite populaire espagnole; P. Hindemith:Son Va BRID ▲ 9016 [DDD] (17.97)

T. Frederiksen (va), E. Westenholz (pno) † Adagio & Allegro Hn, Op. 70; Fantasiestücke Cl, Op. 73; Romances Ob, Op. 94; Stücke im Volkston, Op. 102 KPT ▲ 32080 [DDD]

N. Imai (va), R. Vignoles (pno) † J. Brahms:Sons Cl CHN ▲ 8550 [DDD] (16.97)

P. Meyer (cl), E. Le Sage (pno)—No. 1, Mailied; No. 3, An die Nachtigall *(rec Musica Théâtre La Choux-de-Fonds, France, Apr 9-11, 1993)* ("Märchenbilder") † Adagio & Allegro Hn, Op. 70; Fantasiestücke Cl, Op. 73; Romances Ob, Op. 94; Stücke im Volkston, Op. 102 DNN ▲ 75960 [DDD] (16.97)

B. Pasquier (va), J. Heisser (pno) † Berlioz:Harold en Italie, Op. 16 HMA ▲ 1901246 (9.97)

R. Schulte (vn), C. O'Riley (pno) † Adagio & Allegro Hn, Op. 70; Fantasiestücke Cl, Op. 73; Romances Ob, Op. 94 CENT ▲ 2097 [DAD] (16.97)

R. Verebes (va), S. Blondin (pno) *(rec Montreal)* † F. Schubert:Son Arpeggione, D.821; H. Vieuxtemps:Son Va SNE ▲ 580 (16.97)

Wallfisch Duo ("Duo Wallfisch at Prades Festival") † J. Brahms:Son 1 Cl; Mendelssohn (-Bartholdy):Son Va BAYE ▲ 200050 [AAD] (17.97)

SCHUMANN, ROBERT (cont.)

Märchenerzählungen for Clarinet, Viola & Piano (w. Violin ad lib), Op. 132 (1853)

S. Braconi (va), A. Carbonare (cl), A. Dindo (pno) † Fantasiestücke Cl, Op. 73; Märchenbilder, Op. 113; Romances Ob, Op. 94 AG ▲ 43 (18.97)

N. Imai (va), J. Hilton (cl), R. Vignoles (pno) † Bruch:Pieces Cl, Op. 83; W. A. Mozart:Trio Cl, K.498 CHN ▲ 8776 [DDD] (16.97)

La Scala Orch Soloists † Mendelssohn (-Bartholdy):Octet Strs, Op. 20; F. Schubert:Trio Movt Pno Trio, D.897 THY ▲ 101 (17.97)

Melos Ensemble *(rec 1964-70)* † Fantasiestücke Cl, Op. 73; Beethoven:Duos Cl, WoO 27; March Cls, WoO 29; Qnt Pno, Op. 16; Rondino Ww, WoO 25; Sxt Hns; J. Brahms:Qnt Cl; W. A. Mozart:Qnt Pno, K.452 EMIC 2-▲ 72643 [ADD] (16.97)

D. Rence (va), S. Drucker (cl), S. Shapiro (pno) *(rec Performing Arts Ctr/Purchase College-State Univ of, May 8, 1995)* ("Robert Schumann: The Complete Works for Winds & Piano") † Adagio & Allegro Hn, Op. 70; Andante & Vars Hn; Fantasiestücke Cl, Op. 73; Romances Ob, Op. 94 ELY ▲ 709 [DDD] (16.97)

Trio Apollon † J. Brahms:Trio Hn, Op. 40 DI ▲ 920363 [DDD] (5.97)

Mass in c for solo Voices, Orchestra & Chorus, Op. 147 (1852-53)

P. Neumann (org), Cologne Chamber Choir † J. Brahms:Fugue Org; Missa Canonica MDG ▲ 3320598 [DDD] (17.97)

Minnespiel (8) for Voice & Piano [text Rückert], Op. 101 (1849)

N. Stutzmann (cta), I. Södergren (pno)—No. 2, Liebster, deine Worte stehlen; No. 4, Mein schöner Stern; No. 6, O Freund, mein Schirm, mein Schutz! *(rec Munich, Oct 1994)* † Gedichte aus 'Liebesfrühling', Op. 37; Gedichte, Op. 35 RCAV (Red Seal) ▲ 61798 [DDD] (16.97)

Music of Schumann

Helicon Ensemble—Son 2 Vn, Op. 121; Son 2 Vn, Op. 121; Romances Ob, Op. 94; Duette, Op. 34 [No. 4, Familien-Gemälde; Lelse, elnfach; Bewegt]; Duette, Op. 78 [No. 1, Tanzlied; No. 4, Wiegenlied]; Spanisches Liederspiel, Op. 74 [No. 4, In der Nacht]; Minnespiel, Op. 101 [No. 7, Die tausend Grüsse] *(rec New York, NY, July & Oct 1994)* ("A Schumann Salon Concert") HEL ▲ 1018 (10.97)

Myrthen (cycle of 26 songs) for Voice & Piano, Op. 25 (1840)

B. Bonney (sop), V. Ashkenazy (pno)—No. 1, Widmung; No. 3, Der Nussbaum; No. 7, Die Lotosblume; No. 9, Lied der Suleika † Frauenliebe und -leben, Op. 42; Liederkreis, Op. 39; C. Schumann:Lieder PLON ▲ 452898 (16.97)

L. Dawson (sop), I. Partridge (ten), J. Drake (pno) † Songs CHN ▲ 9307 [DDD] (16.97)

M. Dittrich (cnd), Slovak RSO Bratislava—No. 1, Widmung [orchd Joh. Strauss (II)] *(rec Bratislava Slovak Radio Concert Hall, Slovak Republic, June 4-7, 1993)* ("Vol. 46") † Strauss (II):Orchestral Music (comp); Pizzicato-Polka; Vaterländischer Marsch MARC ▲ 8223246 [DDD] (13.97)

W. Holzmair (bar), I. Cooper (pno)—No. 24, Du bist wie eine Blume; No. 7, Die Lotosblume; No. 21, Was will die einsame Träne? *(rec Esterházy Palace Eisenstadt, Austria, June 27-30, 1994)* † Dichterliebe, Op. 48; Gesänge, Op. 142; Liederkreis, Op. 24; Romanzen und Balladen, Op. 53; Romanzen und Balladen, Op. 64 PPHI ▲ 46086 (16.97)

M. Price (sop), M. Price (sop), T. Dewey (pno), T. Dewey (pno)—No. 12, Lieder der Braut aus dem Liebesfrühling II; No. 1, Widmung; No. 25, Aus den östlichen Rosen, Op. 25/25; No. 11, Lieder der Braut aus dem Liebesfrühling I † Frauenliebe und -leben, Op. 42; Gedichte, Op. 36; Lieder-Album für die Jugend, Op. 79; Songs FORL ▲ 16711 [DDD] (16.97)

A. Rubenstein (pno)—No. 1, Widmung *(rec 1928-47)* † Arabeske Pno, Op. 18; Kinderszenen Pno, Op. 15; Romances Pno, Op. 28; J. Brahms:Pieces (8) Pno, Op. 76; Songs (5), Op. 49; Liszt:Liebesträume, S.541; F. Schubert:Impromptus (4) Pno; P. Tchaikovsky:Con 1 Pno, Op. 23 GRM2 ▲ 78783 (13.97)

H. Schellenberger (ob), R. Koenen (pno)—No. 24, Du bist wie eine Blume [arr for pno & ob] *(rec Berlin, Germany, June 1995)* † Adagio & Allegro Hn, Op. 70; Fantasiestücke Cl, Op. 73; Klavierstücke, Op. 85; Kreisleriana, Op. 16; Liederkreis, Op. 39; Romances Ob, Op. 94; Romances Pno, Op. 28; C. Schumann:Romances Vn, Op. 22 CAMM ▲ 130014 [DDD] (16.97)

E. Schwarzkopf (sop), G. Parsons (pno)—No. 9, Lied der Suleika; No. 17, Venetianische Lieder 1; No. 18, Venetianische Lieder 2; No. 3, Der Nussbaum † Gesänge, Op. 31; W. A. Mozart:Songs; F. Schubert:Songs (misc colls); H. Wolf:Songs (misc); E. Wolf-Ferrari:Preghiera AURC ▲ 123 (5.97)

I. Seefried (sop), E. Werba (pno)—No. 1, Widmung; No. 7, Die Lotosblume; No. 3, Der Nussbaum *(rec Aug 18, 1960)* † Frauenliebe und -leben, Op. 42; Liederkreis, Op. 39; Songs; J. Brahms:Songs ORFE (Festspiel Dokumente) ▲ 398951 (16.97)

G. Vinogradov (ten), G. Orentlicher (pno) † Dichterliebe, Op. 48; Gedichte, Op. 90; Liederkreis, Op. 24; S. Rachmaninoff:Songs (14), Op. 34; Rimsky-Korsakov:Songs, Op. 51; A. Rubinstein:Songs; P. Tchaikovsky:Songs PRE ▲ 89118 (16.97)

E. Höngen (cta), artist unknown—No. 3, Der Nussbaum *(rec Apr 1946 live)* † Gesänge, Op. 31; Liederkreis, Op. 39; J. Brahms:Liebeslieder Waltzes Pno 4-Hands, Op. 52a; B. Marcello:Mio bel foco; F. Schubert:Songs (misc colls); R. Wagner:Wesendonck Songs; H. Wolf:Gedichte von Goethe; Gedichte von Mörike PRE ▲ 90356 (m) (16.97)

Nachtlied for Chorus & Orchestra [text Hebbel], Op. 108 (1849)

J. E. Gardiner (cnd), Orch Révolutionnaire et Romantique, Monteverdi Choir † Paradies und die Peri, Op. 50; Requiem für Mignon, Op. 98b PARC 2-▲ 457660 (32.97)

Nachtstücke (4) for Piano, Op. 23 (1839)

W. Kempff (pno) † Arabeske Pno, Op. 18; Bunte Blätter, Op. 99; Carnaval, Op. 9; Davidsbündlertänze, Op. 6; Fant Pno, Op. 17; Humoreske Pno, Op. 20; Kinderszenen Pno, Op. 15; Kreisleriana, Op. 16; Papillons Pno, Op. 2; Romances Pno, Op. 28; Son 2 Pno, Op. 22; Symphonic Etudes, Op. 13; Waldscenen, Op. 82 DEUT 4-▲ 35045 [ADD] (26.97)

J. Martin (pno) † Konzert-Etüden nach Capricen von Paganini, Op. 10; Studien nach Capricen von Paganini, Op. 3 ARN ▲ 68226 [DDD] (16.97)

I. J. Paderewski (pno) *(rec 1911-37)* † Fantasiestücke Pno, Op. 12; J. Brahms:Hungarian Dances Pno; Chopin:Etudes (24) Pno, Opp. 10 & 25; Polonaise 6 Pno, Op. 53; Mendelssohn (-Bartholdy):Lieder ohne Worte; A. Rubinstein:Valse-Caprice Pno ENPL (The Piano Library) ▲ 182 (13.97)

A. Schiff (pno) † Gesänge der Frühe, Op. 133; Kreisleriana, Op. 16 TELC ▲ 14566 (16.97)

Novelettes (8) for Piano, Op. 21 (1838)

H. Bauer (pno)—No. 1, in F; No. 2, in D † Kinderszenen Pno, Op. 15; Chopin:Music of Chopin NIMB ▲ 8817 [DDD] (11.97)

R. Brautigam (pno) † Allegro Pno, Op. 8; Fantasiestücke, Op. 111; Gesänge der Frühe, Op. 133 OLY ▲ 436 [DDD] (16.97)

V. Horowitz (pno)—No. 1, in F † Kinderszenen Pno, Op. 15; Kreisleriana, Op. 16 DGRM (Masters) ▲ 445599 [DDD]

S. Richter (pno)—No. 1, in F *(rec National Philharmonic, Warsaw, Poland, May 1959)* † Con Pno in a, Op. 54; Intro & Allegro, Op. 134; Toccata Pno, Op. 7; Waldscenen, Op. 82 DEUT (The Originals) ▲ 47440 [ADD] (11.97)

S. Richter (pno)—No. 2, in D; No. 4 in D; No. 8 in f# *(rec Japan, Feb-Mar 1979)* † Fantasiestücke Pno, Op. 12; Chopin:Preludes (24) Pno, Op. 28 OLY ▲ 287 (16.97)

S. Richter (pno) ("Classic Richter") † Beethoven:Son 27 Pno, Op. 90; Chopin:Scherzos Pno; S. Rachmaninoff:Preludes Pno; F. Schubert:Son Pno, D.625; P. Tchaikovsky:Morceaux (6) Pno, Op. 51; Saisons OLY ▲ 580 [ADD] (16.97)

E. Wirssaladze (pno) † Son 1 Vn, Op. 105; Trio 1 Pno, Op. 63 LV ▲ 182 (17.97)

Overtures

J. Wildner (cnd), Polish National RSO Katowice—Ov, Scherzo & Finale, Op. 52; Genoveva (ov); Die Braut von Messina, Op. 100; Julius Caesar, Op. 128; Hermann und Dorothea, Op. 136; Szenen aus Goethes Faust; Manfred Ov, Op. 115 *(rec Jan 24-26 & Apr 25-26, 1992)* ("Schumann Overtures") NXIN ▲ 550608 [DDD] (5.97)

Overture, Scherzo & Finale in e/E for Orchestra, Op. 52 (1841; last movt rev 1845)

J. Barnett (cnd), National Orch Alumni Association members *(rec Manhattan Center, NY, Nov 20-22, 1961)* † Chopin:Con 1 Pno, Op. 11 VC ▲ 60 [AAD] (13.97)

M. Bernardi (cnd), Calgary PO † Sym 2 SMS (SM 5000) ▲ 5067 [DDD] (16.97)

J. E. Gardiner (cnd), Orch Révolutionnaire et Romantique *(rec The Colosseum Watford, May 1997)* ("The Complete Symphonies") † Konzertstück Hns, Op. 86; Sym in g PARC 3-▲ 457591 [DDD] (48.97)

N. Järvi (cnd), London SO † Genoveva (ov); Julius Caesar, Op. 128; Manfred (incidental music), Op. 115 CHN (Collect) ▲ 6548 [DDD] (12.97)

D. Joeres (cnd), Royal PO † N. W. Gade:Echoes of Ossian, Op. 1; Mendelssohn (-Bartholdy):Hebriden, Op. 26; Sterndale-Bennett:Naiads INMP (Classics) ▲ 6700152 (9.97)

R. Leppard (cnd), Indianapolis SO † Genoveva (ov); Sym 1 KOSS ▲ 2213 (17.97)

N. Marriner (cnd), Stuttgart RSO CAPO ▲ 10063 [DDD] (11.97)

G. Schwarz (cnd), Seattle SO † Konzertstück Hns, Op. 86 DLS ▲ 3084 [DDD] (14.97)

G. Schwarz (cnd), Seattle SO *(rec Seattle Opera House, WA, Sept 1988-Feb 1992)* ("The Schumann Edition") † Con Pno in a, Op. 54; Konzertstück Hns, Op. 86; Manfred Ov, Op. 115; Sym 1; Sym 2; Sym 3; Sym 4; Symphonic Etudes, Op. 13 DLS 4-▲ 3146 [DDD] (30.97)

Papillons for Piano, Op. 2 (1829-31)

J. Buskirk (pno) *(rec Smith College, Aug 1994)* † Intermezzos, Op. 4; Studien nach Capricen von Paganini, Op. 3; Vars on A-B-E-G-G, Op. 1 NPT ▲ 85611 [DDD] (16.97)

A. Cortot (pno) *(rec 1935 for HMV)* † Con Pno in a, Op. 54; Davidsbündlertänze, Op. 6 BPS ▲ 3 [ADD] (16.97)

SCHUMANN, ROBERT (cont.)

Papillons for Piano, Op. 2 (1829-31) (cont.)

A. Cortot (pno) † Davidsbündlertänze, Op. 6; Symphonic Etudes, Op. posth; Symphonic Etudes, Op. 13 MTAL ▲ 48069 (6.97)

P. Huybregts (pno) † Kinderszenen Pno, Op. 15 CENT ▲ 2065 [ADD] (16.97)

J. Jandó (pno) *(rec Nov 1992)* ("Schumann: Piano Works") † Carnaval, Op. 9; Kinderszenen Pno, Op. 15 NXIN ▲ 550784 [DDD] (5.97)

P. Jegorov (pno) † Waldscenen, Op. 82; F. Schubert:Impromptus (4) Pno SNYC ▲ 64386 [DDD] (4.97)

W. Kempff (pno) † Arabeske Pno, Op. 18; Bunte Blätter, Op. 99; Carnaval, Op. 9; Davidsbündlertänze, Op. 6; Fant Pno, Op. 17; Humoreske Pno, Op. 20; Kinderszenen Pno, Op. 15; Kreisleriana, Op. 16; Nachtstücke, Op. 23; Romances Pno, Op. 28; Son 2 Pno, Op. 22; Symphonic Etudes, Op. 13; Waldscenen, Op. 82 DEUT 4-▲ 35045 [ADD] (26.97)

K. Lifschitz (pno) *(rec Moscow Conservatory, May-June 1990)* † J. S. Bach:Partita Hpd, BWV 831; Medtner:Fairy Tales, Op. 26; Fairy Tales, Op. 34; Morceaux, Op. 31; A. Scriabin:Mazurkas (10) Pno, Op. 3 DNN ▲ 78907 [DDD] (16.97)

M. Perahia (pno) † Symphonic Etudes, Op. 13 SNYC ▲ 34539 [ADD] (16.97)

M. Perahia (pno), M. Perahia (pno) *(rec New York City, United States of America, 1976)* ("A Portrait of Murray Perahia") † Beethoven:Son 23 Pno, Op. 57; Chopin:Fant-Impromptu, Op. 66; Preludes (24) Pno, Op. 28; Mendelssohn (-Bartholdy):Rondo capriccioso, Op. 14; W. A. Mozart:Rondo Pno & Orch, K.382; Rondo Pno Orch, K.382; F. Schubert:Impromptus (4) Pno SNYC ▲ 42448 [AAD/DDD] (11.97)

A. Schiff (pno) † Arabeske Pno, Op. 18; Humoreske Pno, Op. 20 DNN ▲ 7573 [DDD] (10.97)

V. Sofronitsky (pno) *(rec 1946-53)* ("Russian Piano School: Vladimir Sofronitsky") † Beethoven:Andante Pno, WoO 57; F. Schubert:Impromptus (4) Pno; Schöne Müllerin, D.795 RD (Talents of Russia) ▲ 16288 [ADD] (16.97)

F. Ts'ong (pno) *(rec Warsaw, Poland)* † Arabeske Pno, Op. 18; Davidsbündlertänze, Op. 6; Kinderszenen Pno, Op. 15; Kreisleriana, Op. 16; Waldscenen, Op. 82 ICC ▲ 6601127 (32.97)

Das Paradies und die Peri (oratorio) for solo Voices, Orchestra & Chorus [text T. Moore], Op. 50 (1843)

J. E. Gardiner (cnd), Orch Révolutionnaire et Romantique, Monteverdi Choir, B. Bonney (sop), A. Coku (sop), B. Fink (mez), C. Prégardien (ten), N. Archer (ten), W. Dazeley (bar), G. Finley (bar), C. Hauptmann (bass) † Nachtlied, Op. 108; Requiem für Mignon, Op. 98b PARC 2-▲ 457660 (32.97)

C. Nossek (sop), R. Lang (cta), C. Vogel (ten), H. C. Polster (bass), W. Hauschild (cnd), Leipzig RSO, Leipzig Radio Chorus BER 2-▲ 9188 (21.97)

Phantasiestücke (4) for Violin, Cello & Piano, Op. 88 (1842)

Abegg Trio † Con Pno in a, Op. 54; Davidsbündlertänze, Op. 6; Dichterliebe, Op. 48; Kinderszenen Pno, Op. 15; Qts Strs, Op. 41; Sym 3 INTC (Art of Classics) ▲ 885921

Borodin Trio CHN 2-▲ 8832 [DDD] (33.97)

Trio Italiano † Trio 3 Pno, Op. 110 AART ▲ 47527 (10.97)

Piano Music (miscellaneous collections)

H. Bauer (pno)—Fantasiestücke Pno, Op. 12 [No. 5, In der Nacht]; Novelettes, Op. 21 [No. 2, in D] † Fantasiestücke Pno, Op. 12; E. Grieg:Album Leaves (4) Pno, Op. 28; Lyric Pieces; Pictures from Life in the Country, Op. 19; Liszt:Etudes de concert (2), S.145; Etudes de concert (3), S.144 BPS ▲ 11 (16.97)

A. Brendel (pno), H. Holliger (cnd), Berlin PO, H. Holliger (cnd), London SO *(Gesänge, Op. 107 [No. 6, Abendlied]; Adagio & Allegro Hn, Op. 70; Con Pno in a, Op. 54; Fant Pno, Op. 17; Fantasiestücke Pno, Op. 12; Kinderszenen Pno, Op. 15; Stücke im Volkston, Op. 102; Romances Pno, Op. 28; Symphonic Etudes, Op. 13)*, A. Brendel (pno) *(Kreisleriana, Op. 16)* ("The Art of Arthur Brendel") † Beethoven:Pno Music (misc); J. Brahms:Pno Music (misc colls); J. Haydn:Pno Music; Liszt:Pno Music (misc); W. A. Mozart:Pno Music (misc colls); F. Schubert:Allegretto Pno, D.915; Pno Music (misc colls) PPHI 25-▲ 46920 (294.62)

A. Cortot (pno) *(Con Pno in a, Op. 54; Papillons Pno, Op. 2; Davidsbündlertänze, Op. 6; Carnaval, Op. 9; Symphonic Etudes, Op. 13; Kinderszenen Pno, Op. 15; Kreisleriana, Op. 16)*, P. Casals (pno), A. Cortot (pno), J. Thibaud (pno) *(Trio 1 Pno, Op. 63) (rec 1927-37)* ("The Schumann Recordings") ENPL (Piano Library) 3-▲ 259 (39.97)

V. Horowitz (pno)—Toccata Pno, Op. 7; Arabeske Pno, Op. 18; Fantasiestücke, Op. 111; Presto passionato; Kreisleriana, Op. 16; Humoreske Pno, Op. 20; Concert sans orch, Op. 14; Novelettes, Op. 21 [No. 1, in F]; Kinderszenen Pno, Op. 15 *(rec 1934)* ("Vladimir Horowitz") PPHI (Great Pianists of the 20th Century) ▲ 456838 (22.97)

I. J. Paderewski (pno)—Fantasiestücke Pno, Op. 12; Nachtstücke, Op. 23; Waldscenen, Op. 82 *(rec 1911-37)* ("Paderewski Portrait") † J. Brahms:Hungarian Dances Pno; Chopin:Pno Music (misc colls); Mendelssohn (-Bartholdy):Lieder ohne Worte; A. Rubinstein:Valse-Caprice Pno IN ▲ 1366 [ADD] (15.97)

Polonaises (8) for Piano 4-Hands (1828)

C. Argelli (pno), P. Dirani (pno) † Ballszenen, Op. 109; Bilder aus Osten, Op. 66; Kinderball, Op. 130; Klavierstücke, Op. 85 FON 2-▲ 9708 (20.97)

Presto passionato in g for Piano (?1833)

I. Hobson (pno) † Impromptus on a Theme by Clara Wieck, Op. 5; Son Pno, Op. 14; Son 1 Pno, Op. 11; Son 2 Pno, Op. 22; Vars on A-B-E-G-G, Op. 1 ARA 2-▲ 6621 [DDD] (32.97)

J. Rowland (pno) *(rec Santa Monica, CA, Apr 27-29, 1993)* † Carnaval, Op. 9; Fant Pno, Op. 17; Waldscenen, Op. 82 TOWN ▲ 43 (17.97)

Quartet in c for Piano & Strings (1828-30)

Schubert Ensemble of London † Qnt Pno, Op. 44; J. N. Hummel:Qnt Pno, Op. 87; F. Schubert:Qnt Pno, D.667 HYP 2-▲ 22008 (18.97)

Quartet in E♭ for Piano & Strings, Op. 47 (1842)

E. Ax (pno), Cleveland String Quartet † Qnt Pno, Op. 44 RCAV (Red Seal) ▲ 6498 [DDD] (16.97)

R. Burnett (pno), Fitzwilliam String Quartet members [period instrs] † Qnt Pno, Op. 44; Son 1 Vn, Op. 105 AMON ▲ 54 [DDD] (16.97)

G. Gould (pno), Juilliard String Quartet members † J. Brahms:Qnt Pno, Op. 34 SNYC ▲ 52684 (16.97)

Mozart Piano Quartet † Draeseke:Qnt Pno, Op. 48 MDG ▲ 6150673 (17.97)

M. Pressler (pno), Emerson String Quartet † Qnt Pno, Op. 44 DEUT ▲ 45848 [DDD] (16.97)

S. Rhodes (va), Beaux Arts Trio † Qnt Pno, Op. 44; Trios Pno (comp) PPHI (Duo) 2-▲ 456323 (17.97)

I. Stern (vn), J. Laredo (va), Y.-Y. Ma (vc), E. Ax (pno) *(rec Mar 9-12, 1992)* † Beethoven:Qt Pno in E♭ SNYC ▲ 53339 [DDD] (16.97)

Quartets (3) for Strings, Op. 41 (1842)

Athenaeum Enesco String Quartet—No. 1 in a † Qnt Pno, Op. 44 PVY ▲ 797081 (16.97)

Capet String Quartet—No. 1 in a *(rec 1927-28)* ("The Capet Quartet in Romantic Works") † Debussy:Qt Strs, Op. 10; C. Franck:Qnt Pno, M.7; M. Ravel:Qt Strs; F. Schubert:Qt 14 Strs, D.810 BID 2-▲ 133 [ADD] (31.97)

Flonzaley String Quartet—No. 1 in a *(rec Dec 22-23, 1927)* † Qnt Pno, Op. 44; J. Brahms:Qnt Pno, Op. 34; Qt 3 Strs, Op. 67; Mendelssohn (-Bartholdy):Qt 1 Strs, Op. 12; F. Schubert:Qt 15 Strs, D.887 BID 2-▲ 72 [ADD]

Hagen String Quartet—No. 2 in F; No. 3 in A DGRM ▲ 449214 [DDD]

Hagen String Quartet—No. 1 in a † Qnt Pno, Op. 44 DGRM ▲ 447111 [DDD] (18.97)

Lark String Quartet—No. 1 in a; No. 3 in A ARA ▲ 6696 (16.97)

M. Peckham (cnd), Cavani String Quartet—No. 1 in a *(rec Cleveland, United States of America, Aug 28-31, 1994)* † A. Dvořák:Qt 12 Strs, Op. 96 AZI ▲ 71203 [DDD] (15.97)

Petersen String Quartet—No. 1 in a ("Portrait") † Beethoven:Quartets for Strings (miscellaneous collections); E. Grieg:Qt Strs, Op. 27; W. A. Mozart:Qt 22 Strs, K.589; F. Schubert:Qnt Strs, D.956; Schulhoff:Pieces Str Qt; Qt Strs, Op. 25 CAPO ▲ 14862 [DDD] (10.97)

Robert Schumann String Quartet—No. 3 in A † Con Pno in a, Op. 54; Davidsbündlertänze, Op. 6; Dichterliebe, Op. 48; Kinderszenen Pno, Op. 15; Phantasiestücke Vn, Op. 88; Sym 3 INTC (Art of Classics) ▲ 885921

St. Lawrence String Quartet *(rec American Academy of Arts & Letters, NY, 1998)* EMIC ▲ 56797 [DDD] (16.97)

Takács String Quartet † F. Schubert:Qnt Pno, D.667 HUN 2-▲ 12918 (32.97)

Voces Intimae String Quartet—No. 3 in A † Sibelius:Qt Strs in d, Op. 56 BIS ▲ 10 (17.97)

Quintet in E♭ for Piano & Strings, Op. 44 (1842)

V. Aller (pno), Hollywood String Quartet *(rec Hollywood, May 13-16, 1955)* † J. Brahms:Qnt Pno, Op. 34; Qt 2 Strs, Op. 51/2; Qts Pno (comp) TES 3-▲ 3063 [ADD] (49.97)

E. Ax (pno), Cleveland String Quartet † Qt Pno in E♭, Op. 47 RCAV (Red Seal) ▲ 6498 [DDD] (16.97)

D. Bettelheim (vn), S. Rhodes (va), Beaux Arts Trio † Qt Pno in E♭, Op. 47; Trios Pno (comp) PPHI (Duo) 2-▲ 456323 (17.97)

S. Bradbury (pno), Silvestri String Quartet † B. Bartók:Qnt Pno & Strs, DD 77 ASVQ ▲ 6217 (10.97)

R. Burnett (pno), Fitzwilliam String Quartet [period instrs] † Qt Pno in E♭, Op. 47; Son 1 Vn, Op. 105 AMON ▲ 54 [DDD] (16.97)

V. Coq (pno), Manfred String Quartet † J. Brahms:Qt 3 Strs, Op. 67 PVY ▲ 798012 (16.97)

P. Frankl (pno), Lindsay String Quartet † J. Brahms:Qnt Pno, Op. 34 ASV ▲ 728 [DDD] (16.97)

O. Gabrilovich (pno), Flonzaley String Quartet *(rec Dec 21, 1927)* † Qts Strs, Op. 41; J. Brahms:Qnt Pno, Op. 34; Qt 3 Strs, Op. 67; Mendelssohn (-Bartholdy):Qt 1 Strs, Op. 12; F. Schubert:Qt 15 Strs, D.887 BID 2-▲ 72 [ADD]

O. Gabrilowitsch (pno), Flonzaley String Quartet [abridged version] *(rec 1923-24)* VAIA ▲ 1018 [ADD] (17.97)

P. Gulda (pno), Hagen String Quartet † Qts Strs, Op. 41 DGRM ▲ 447111 [DDD] (18.97)

SMITH, CLAUDE T. (1932-1987)
Festival Variations for Orchestra
N. Nozy (cnd), Belgian Guides Symphonic Band ("Nuts") † L. Bernstein:Candide (ov); On the Town (sels); A. Copland:Fanfare for the Common Man; G. Gershwin:Rhap in Blue; M. Gould:Jericho Rhap RENE ▲ 87076 [DDD] (16.97)

SMITH, GREGG (1931-
The Continental Harmonist Ballet for Orchestra & Chorus [based upon themes of William Billings]
G. Smith (cnd), Adirondack CO, Gregg Smith Singers † Billings:Anthems & Fuguing Tunes PREM ▲ 1008 [ADD]
Magnificat for Soprano, Orchestra & Chorus (1961; rev 1980-81)
R. Rees (sop), G. Smith (cnd), Adirondack CO, Gregg Smith Singers, Adirondack Festival Chorus † Prayer for Peace; Vars on Bach Chorale PREM (Composer) ▲ 1020 [ADD] (16.97)
Prayer for Peace for Orchestra, Chorus & Children's Choir (1986)
G. Smith (cnd), Adirondack CO, Gregg Smith Singers, Adirondack Festival Chorus, Adirondack Children's Choir † Magnificat; Vars on Bach Chorale PREM (Composer) ▲ 1020 [ADD] (16.97)
Variations on a Bach Chorale for Orchestra & Chorus (1968)
G. Smith (cnd), Adirondack CO, Gregg Smith Singers, Adirondack Festival Chorus † Magnificat; Prayer for Peace PREM (Composer) ▲ 1020 [ADD] (16.97)

SMITH, HALE (1925-
Expansions for Symphonic Band (1967)
J. P. Paynter (cnd) ("Winds of Change") † R. R. Bennett:Sym Songs; H. Brant:Verticals Ascending; Finney:Con A Sax; Persichetti:Pageant, Op. 59 NWW ▲ 80211 [AAD] (16.97)
Faces of Jazz for Flute & Piano
Aguilar-Delgado Duo † Doran:Poem Fl; P. Juon:Son Fl; Kuhlau:Sons Fl, Op. 83; A. Molina:Gigue; Sarabande PROT ▲ 2201 [DDD] (19.97)
Innerflexions for Orchestra (1977)
A. Nanut (cnd), Slovenian SO † J. Hoffman:Duo Vn & Pno; S. Silver:Son Vc CRI ▲ 590 [DDD] (17.97)

SMITH, HAZEL (20th cent)
Simultaneity for Speaker & Samples (1991)
austraLYSIS members *(rec Sydney, 1993)* ("austraLYSIS: Windows in Time") † Bright:Night Db; L. Cresswell:Organic Music; Soliloquy on a Lambent Tailpiece; R. T. Dean:TimeStrain; R. Rue:Nocturnal Windows; Xenakis:Morsima-Amorsima TALP ▲ 39 [DDD] (18.97)

SMITH, HOWIE (20th cent)
Song for the Children for Alto Saxophone, MIDI Wind Controller, 2 Synthesizers, Organ & Strings (1986)
H. Smith (a sax/elec), E. London (cnd), Cleveland Chamber SO *(rec Drinko Hall, Cleveland State University, OH)* ("The New American Scene") † J. Eaton:Songs of Desperation & Comfort; E. London:novella della sera primavera; R. Perera:Music Fl ALBA ▲ 298 [DDD] (16.97)

SMITH, JOHN STAFFORD (1750-1836)
The Star-Spangled Banner (march) for Orchestra (ca 1780)
A. Toscanini (cnd), NBC SO ("The Toscanini Collection, Vol. 38: All-American Program") † S. Barber:Adagio Strs; G. Gershwin:American in Paris; Grofé:Grand Canyon Suite; J. P. Sousa:Marches & Dances RCAV (Gold Seal) ▲ 60307 (11.97)

SMITH, LARRY ALAN (1955-
The Scrolls for Tenor, Flute, Viola & Clarinet (1982)
Voices of Change ("American Contemporary Chamber Music") † W. Kraft:Melange; R. X. Rodriguez:Chronies; Meditation Fl; Sonatina d'Estate; Welcher:Evening Scenes CRYS ▲ 740 (15.97) ▮ 740 (9.98)
Songs of the Silence for Voice & Piano (1983)
P. Sperry (ten), I. Vallecillo (pno) *(rec Bedford, NY, 1990)* ("Paul Sperry Sings American Cycles & Sets") † R. Beaser:7 Deadly Sins; C. Berg:Six Poems of Frank O'Hara; L. Gruenberg:Animals and Insects, Op. 22; Talma:Terre de France; R. Wilson:Three Painters *(E text)* ALBA ▲ 58 [DDD] (16.97)

SMITH, LINDA CATLIN (1957-
The Surroundings for Piano (1995)
B. Pritchard (pno) *(rec Mar 1998)* ("The View from Here") † View from Here; B. M. Feldman:The I and Thou; Genge:Dream Waltz; Hatch:Fragments of an Unknown Teaching; Rea:Portrait of a Man in Elysian Fields; J. Rolfe:Idiot Sorrow CTR ▲ 6298 [DDD] (16.97)
The View from Here for Piano (1992)
B. Pritchard (pno) *(rec Mar 1998)* ("The View from Here") † Surroundings; B. M. Feldman:The I and Thou; Genge:Dream Waltz; Hatch:Fragments of an Unknown Teaching; Rea:Portrait of a Man in Elysian Fields; J. Rolfe:Idiot Sorrow CTR ▲ 6298 [DDD] (16.97)

SMITH, PETER (1954-
Mare a'440 for Marimba & Live Electronics (1991)
Percussion Group The Hague † J. Cage:Qt for 4 Perc; R. Ford:Wanne mine eyhnen misten; Tsubonoh:Fantom Fire GLOE ▲ 5072 [DDD] (16.97)

SMITH, STUART SAUNDERS (1948-
Family Portraits (3) for Piano [Sylvia; Ivy; Earle] (1992)
T. Moore (pno) ("Crux") † Here & There; Notebook; Tunnels OOD ▲ 11 [DDD] (16.97)
Here & There for Flute, Shortwave Radio & Piano Interior (1971)
J. Fonville (fl), D. Savage (bn), D. Yoken (pno) ("Crux") † Family Portraits; Notebook; Tunnels OOD ▲ 11 [DDD] (16.97)
Music of S. S. Smith
J. Ostryniec (ob) *(Hawk)*, T. Moore (pno) *(Family Portraits:Brenda)*, P. Hoffmann (pno) *(Notebook; Gifts; Pinetop; In Bingham; Aussie Blue)*, S. Smith (voc), S. Smith (elec) *(California Driving)*, J. Whybron (voc), J. Whybron (perc/rcr) *(Wind in the Channel)* ("Wind in the Channel") OOD ▲ 31 [DDD] (16.97)
Notebook for Flute, Trumpet, Piano & Double Bass (1980)
B. Turetzky (db), J. Fonville (fl), E. Harkins (tpt), P. Hoffmann (pno) ("Crux") † Family Portraits; Here & There; Tunnels OOD ▲ 11 [DDD] (16.97)
Tunnels for Percussion (1982)
T. Goldstein (perc) ("Crux") † Family Portraits; Here & There; Notebook OOD ▲ 11 [DDD] (16.97)

SMITH, WADADA LEO (20th cent)
Music of Wadada Smith
K. E. Bakunin (va), W. L. Smith (tpt), California EAR Unit, N'Da Kulture, New Century Players—Moths, Flames & the Giant Sequoia Trees; Hetep; Multiamerica; Nur; Thousand Cranes TZA ▲ 7046 (16.97)
R. Lorentz (vn), E. Duke (vc), D. Stone (fl/pic), M. Walker (cl), W. L. Smith (bells/flgl/tpt), V. Ray (cel/pno), M. Noda (bells/timp/vib), D. Philipson (bells/perc)—Another Wave More Waves; Double Thunderbolt; Tao-Njia; others ("Tao-Njia") TZA (Composer) ▲ 7017 [DDD] (16.97)

SMITH BRINDLE, REGINALD (1917-
Chaconne & Interludes for 2 Guitars, "The Instruments of Peace III"
Gruber & Maklar Guitar Duo ("Contemporary Works for 2 Guitars") † Absil:Suite for 2 Gtrs, Op. 135; L. Aubert:Improvisation; Bogdanović:Son Fant; Bons:Attacca; Jolivet:Sérénade for 2 Gtrs SIGM ▲ 6800 [DDD] (17.97)
Sketches (5) for Violin & Guitar (ca 1959)
Duo Nova ("Duo Nova") † L. von Call:Serenade Vn Gtr, Op. 84; A. Corelli:Sons Vn, Op. 5; Paganini:Centone di sonate, M.S. 112; Sarasate:Serenata andaluza, Op. 28; F. Schubert:Originaltänze, D.365 GALL ▲ 936 [DDD] (18.97)

SMYTH, ETHEL (1858-1944)
Concerto for Violin, Horn & Orchestra (1927)
S. Gawriloff (vn), U. Mayer (cnd), Hanover Radio PO ("Horn Concertos") † Koechlin:Poème; O. Schoeck:Con Hn KSCH ▲ 364122 (16.97)
S. Langdon (vn), R. Watkins (hn), O. D. Martinez (cnd), BBC PO † Serenade CHN ▲ 9449 (16.97)
Piano Music (complete)
L. Serbescu (pno)—4 4-part Dances; Sons 1-3 for Pno; 2 Canons; Invention in D; Suite in E; To Youth!; Pno Piece in E; Vars in D on an Original Theme; 2 Preludes & Fugues ("Complete Piano Works") CPO ▲ 999327 [DDD] (27.97)
Serenade in D for Orchestra (1890)
O. D. Martinez (cnd), BBC PO † Con Vn & Hn CHN ▲ 9449 (16.97)
Short Choral Preludes for Organ
C. Rakich (org) ("Deferred Voices: Organ Music by Women") † Beach:Prelude on an Old Folk Tune; Borroff:Passacaglia; Demessieux:Chorale Preludes on Gregorian Themes, Op. 8; Diemer:Fant Org; Wieruszowski:Chorale Preludes AFK ▲ 527
Sonata in a for Cello & Piano, Op. 5 (1887)
Chagall Trio members ("Impressions That Remain") † Son Vn, Op. 7; Trios Vn MER ▲ 84286 [DDD] (16.97)
Sonata in a for Violin & Piano, Op. 7 (1887)
Chagall Trio members ("Impressions That Remain") † Son Vc, Op. 5; Trios Vn MER ▲ 84286 [DDD] (16.97)

SMYTH, ETHEL (cont.)
Trios (2) for Violin, Oboe & Piano (1927)
Chagall Trio ("Impressions That Remain") † Son Vc, Op. 5; Son Vn, Op. 7 MER ▲ 84286 [DDD] (16.97)
The Wreckers:Overture
A. Gibson (cnd), Royal Scottish National Orch ("Music of the Four Countries") † E. German:Welsh Rhap Orch; H. Harty:With the Wild Geese; MacCunn:Land of the Mountain & the Flood, Op. 8 CFP ▲ 4635 [ADD] (12.97)

SNELL, HOWARD (dates unknown)
Fantasy for Cornet & Brass Band
M. P. Parkes (cnd), Grimethorpe Colliery Band ("From Sonnets to Jazz") † A. van Allan:Refrains & Cadenzas; P. E. Fletcher:Epic Sym; J. McCabe:Salamander; P. Wilby:Jazz; Unholy Sonnets CHN ▲ 4549 (16.97)

SNOW, DAVID (1954-
Dance Movements for Brass Quintet (1981)
American Brass Quintet *(rec Mar 1991)* † Adolphe:Triskelion; R. Dennis:Blackbird Vars; Ewazen:Colchester Fant; D. Sampson:Morning Music SUMM ▲ 133 [DDD] (16.97)

SNYDER, RANDALL (1944-
Double for 2 Pianos & Orchestra
B. Poindefert (cnd), Paris Conservatory Société des Concerts Orch, Clinton-Narboni Duo *(rec Paris, France, June 1997)* † F. Poulenc:Con for 2 Pnos; Tailleferre:Con grosso ELAN ▲ 82298 [DDD] (16.97)
Namdaemun for Orchestra (1993)
R. Silva (cnd), Moravian PO ("Music from 6 Continents 1995") † J. M. Kennedy:Portrait...; D. Patterson:Hermit's Blue; Rabushka:Con Hp; Winges:Aural Colors VMM ▲ 3032 [DDD]
Polemics for Clarinet & Piano
J. Russo (cl), L. W. Ignacio (pno) *(rec PA, United States of America)* ("Masterworks for Clarinet & Piano") † J. Beck:Son Cl; Bremer:Son Cl; Son Clt; S. Chandler:Tune & Chase with Quickstep Dirge; H. Cowell:Six Casual Developments; Rochberg:Dialogues; J. Russo:Preludes (3); Studies (2) *(E text)* CRSR ▲ 9561
Portals for 2 Pianos & Percussion
R. Atherholt (E hn/ob), C. Schubert (b cl/cl), J. Vassalo (tpt) *(rec Shepherd School of Music, Rice University, Houston, United States of America, July 6, 1998)* † B. Bartók:Son 2 Pnos & Perc, Sz.110; P. Bowles:Con for 2 Pnos; Tailleferre:Hommage à Rameau ELAN ▲ 82404 [DDD] (16.97)
Shalimar for Flute, Viola, Cello & Piano
R. Snyder (cnd) ("Silhouettes") † Bulow:Lines; M. Lifchitz:Transformations 3; Meneely-Kyder:Weep; Schiffman:Sestetto Concertato NSR ▲ 1013 [DDD] (15.97)
Shamanic Dances for Orchestra (1991)
M. Machek (cnd), Bohuslav Martinů PO † B. Hobson:Three; Konowalski:Brewerie; Loeb:Suite Concertante; T. Myers:Concertino Orch; K. Steen:Metastasis; G. W. Yasinitsky:Into a Star VMM (Music from 6 Continents 1993) ▲ 3017 [DDD]
Sonata for Oboe & Piano (1993)
W. McMullen (ob), C. Herbener (pno) ("Music in Mixed Accents") † Rabushka:Canzona e Scherzo Capriccioso, Op. 4; Etude Fantasque Pno, Op. 7; Suite Va, Op. 23; Sukegawa:Komoriuta; Trojanowski:Treatment; G. W. Yasinitsky:Music of Wood, Silver & Ivory; On Wings of Angels VMM ▲ 2012 [DDD]

SÖDERLIND, RAGNAR (1945-
Concerto for Violin & Orchestra, Op. 46 (1986)
I. Ragin (vn), D. Burkh (cnd), Janáček PO *(rec Wales, Dec 1995)* † Kvandal:Con Vn CENT ▲ 2336 [DDD] (16.97)

SÖDERLUNDH, LILLE BROR (1912-1957)
Concertino for Oboe & Strings (1944)
A. Nilsson (ob), E. Salonen (cnd), Stockholm Sinfonietta † L.-E. Larsson:Little Serenade, Op. 12; Lidholm:Musik; D. Wirén:Serenade Strs, Op. 11 BIS ▲ 285 [DDD] (17.97)
Concerto for Violin & Orchestra
L. Spierer (vn), A. Jansons (cnd), Stockholm PO † H. Rosenberg:Con 2 Vn CAPA ▲ 21367 [DDD] (16.97)
Petite Suite for Clarinet & Piano
C. Stjernström (cl), M. Kanarva (pno) *(rec Academy of Music of Malmö, Rosenbergssalen, Sweden, July 1996)* † Bozza:Aria Cl; Debussy:Petite pièce Cl; Première rapsodie Cl; Gäfvert:Fant Cl; L.-E. Larsson:Pieces Cl, Op. 61; Saint-Saëns:Son Cl ITIM ▲ 53 (16.97)

SÖDERMAN, AUGUST (1832-1876)
Catholic Mass (missa solemnis) for solo Voices, Orchestra & Chorus (1875)
P. Borin (cnd), Stockholm State Academy of Music Orch, Stockholm State Academy of Music Chamber Choir, Stockholm State Academy of Music Chorus, A. Biel (sop), B. Svendén (mez), C. H. Ahnsjö (ten), C. Appelgren (bass) *(rec 1985-86)* ("Söderman, Vol. 1") † Wallfahrt nach Kevlaar STRL ▲ 1030 [DDD] (15.97)
The Devil's First Tentative Efforts [Hin ondes lärospan] for Orchestra
S. Westerberg (cnd), Stockholm Royal Opera Orch *(rec 1985 & 1995)* ("Overtures at the King's Theater") † Berwald:Dressmaker; I Enter a Monastery; Foroni:Ov 3 Orch; J. M. Kraus:Prosperin; L. Norman:Festive Ov, Op 60; Randel:People from Värmland STRL ▲ 1009 [AAD] (15.97)
King Heimer & Aslog [Kung Heimer och Aslög] for solo Voice & Orchestra [text Hedberg] (ca 1870)
S. Svanholm (ten) ("Set Svanholm: Stockholm Recordings, 1943-58") † G. Rossini:Barbiere di Siviglia (sels); R. Strauss:Ariadne auf Naxos (sels); Verdi:Otello (sels); R. Wagner:Arias & Scenes; C. M. von Weber:Freischütz (sels) BLUB ▲ 58 [ADD] (18.97)
I. Wixell (bar), J. Arnell (cnd), Stockholm PO [SWE] ("Swedish Ballads") † Peterson-Berger:Songs; Rangström:Songs; Stenhammar:Songs MSV ▲ 617 [DDD] (16.97)
Marshal Stig's Daughters [Marsk Stigs döttrar] (incidental music) [text L. Josephson] (1866)
H. Frank (cnd), Helsingborg SO, Mikaeli Chamber Choir, Helsingsborg Concert Choir, Medlemmar Concert Choir [SWE] MSV ▲ 513 (16.97)
Spiritual Songs [Andliga sanger] for Organ & Chorus (1872)
Malmö Chamber Choir *(rec Mar 28-29, 1981)* † Peterson-Berger:Album of 8 Songs, Op. 11; Ryelandt:Missa 6 vocibus, Op. 111 BIS ▲ 181 [AAD] (17.97)
Swedish Festival
S. Westerberg (cnd), Swedish RSO *(rec Berwald Hall, Stockholm, Sweden, May 7, 1986)* ("Swedish Highlights") † Alfvén:Bergakungen (sels); Festspel, Op. 25; Gustav II Adolph, Op. 49; Prodigal Son, Op. 217; Swedish Flag; Swedish Rhap 1, Op. 19; L.-E. Larsson:Pastoralsvit, Op. 19; O. J. Lindblad:Royal Anthem; Stenhammar:Ett folk, Op. 22; Sången, Op. 44; Traditional:Du Gamla, Du Fria; D. Wirén:Serenade Strs, Op. 11 CAPA ▲ 21340 [DDD] (16.97)
Die Wallfahrt nach Kevlaar [Pilgrimage to Kevlaar] for Baritone, Orchestra & Chorus (1859-66)
P. Borin (cnd), Stockholm State Academy of Music Orch, Stockholm State Academy of Music Chorus, P. Wahlgren (bar) *(rec 1985-86)* ("Söderman, Vol. 1") † Catholic Mass STRL ▲ 1030 [DDD] (15.97)

SOJO, VICENTE EMILIO (1887-1974)
Pieces from Venezuela (5) for Guitar
D. Blanco (gtr) *(rec Castle Wik, Sweden, May 25, 1979)* ("Popular Guitar Music") † A. Barrios:Gtr Music; Lauro:Valses Venezolanos Gtr; Sor:Fants Gtr; Grand Solo Gtr, Op. 14; Gtr Music; Son Gtr; Vars Mozart, Op. 9 *(E, F, G text)* BIS ▲ 133 [AAD] (17.97)
Y. Storms (gtr) ("A Touch of Latin") † A. Barrios:Gtr Music; L. Brouwer:Gtr Music; J. Cardoso:Gtr Music; J. Guimarães:Sons de Carrilhões; Lauro:Gtr Music; H. Villa-Lobos:Chôro 1 SYRX ▲ 94106 [DDD] (16.97)

SOLAGE (fl 1370-1390)
Hélas, je voy mon cuer (ballade) for 4 Voices
L. Meeuwsen (mez), Little Consort [ITA] *(rec Sovana, Italy, June 1988)* ("Johannes Ciconia & His Time") † Anonymous:Lamento di Tristano; Caserta:En remirant vo douce pourtaiture; Casia:Lucida pecorella son; Ciconia:Vocal & Instrumental Consort Music *([ITA] text)* CCL ▲ 290 [DDD]

SOLBIATI, ALESSANDRO (1956-
Pezzi (3) for Guitar [2nd version] (1986-87)
F. Halász (gtr) *(rec Sweden, July 1996)* ("Canzoni") † N. D. Angelo:Canzoni Lidie; Magie; L. Berio:Sequenza XI; Petrassi:Nunc; Suoni Notturni BIS ▲ 823 [DDD] (17.97)

SOLDIER, DAVE (20th cent)
Music of Soldier
various artists—Dum Caupona Verterem; Ad Puerum Anglicum; Odalisque in the Seraglio; Miser, Miser; Graffiti from a 19th Century Manuscript; Quodlibet; Parisiue Pardi; Letter to Ausonius; Matarile ("Smut") AVAK ▲ 19 (21.97)
Ultraviolet Railroad (concerto) for Violin, Cello & Orchestra (1992)
M. Feldman (vn), E. Frielander (vc), N. Kirkwood (pno), R. A. Clark (cnd), Manhattan CO ("Dave Soldier: War Prayer") † War Prayer NPT ▲ 85589 [DDD] (16.97)
War Prayer (cantata) for Alto, Tenor, Bass, Gospel Singers & Orchestra [after Mark Twain] (1993)
D. Freeney (alt), J. White (ten), W. Pauley (bass), R. A. Clark (cnd), Manhattan CO, Gospel Singers ("Dave Soldier: War Prayer") † Ultraviolet Railroad NPT ▲ 85589 [DDD] (16.97)

SOLER, JOSEP (1935-
Coronación de espinas [Crowning with Thorns] for 2 Pianos (1993)
K. Mrongovius (pno), B. Uriarte (pno) *(rec Madrid, Spain, Apr 1, 1998)* † Barce:Nuevas Polifonias; Guinjoan:Flamenco; T. Marco:Fandangos; Glasperlenspiel WER ▲ 6634 [DDD]
SOLER, MATTHEW (ca 1720-1799)
Sonata in C for Bassoon & Continuo
Barcelona Consort *(rec Barcelona, Sept 1994)* ("Affetti Musicali") † Castello:Sonate concertate in stil moderno; Mariner:Toccata; Oliver y Astorga:Sons Fls, Op. 3; Pla:Trio Son 12; Telemann:Essercizii Musici; Musique de Table LAMA ▲ 2020 [DDD] (17.97)
SOLER, PADRE ANTONIO (1729-1783)
Andaluz for Chorus & Orchestra
P. Baxa (cnd), Prague Virtuosi, Prague Chamber Choir ("Music for the King of Spain") † Peris:Jubilate Domino; Te Deum; D. Scarlatti:Missa quatour vocum DI ▲ 920300 [DDD] (5.97)
Concertos (6) for 2 Keyboards
F. Bohme (org), F. Werner (org) [sels] † J. Alain:Org Music (misc); G. Guami:Org Music; Mieg:Org Music; M. Reger:Org Music (misc colls) QUER ▲ 9811 (18.97)
E. Elizondo (org), B. Brauchli (org)—Nos. 1 & 2 [2 clvds]; Nos. 3 & 6 [hpd & org]; Nos. 4 & 5 [2 orgs] TIT ▲ 152 [DDD] (16.97)
A. Goldstone (pno), C. Clemmow (pno) OLY ▲ 636 (16.97)
Fandango for Keyboard, M.1A
Falla Trio [arr for 3 gtrs] † I. Albéniz:Suite española 1, Op. 47; W. Boyce:Syms; A. A. Corea:Spain; M. de Falla:Amor brujo (sels) ERTO ▲ 42011 (14.97)
I. Kipnis (hpd) *(rec May 30, 1967)* † Sons Kbd; Blasco de Nebra:Sons Hpd, Op. 1; M. de Falla:Con Hpd; D. Scarlatti:Sons Kbd SNYC ▲ 53264 (7.97)
J. Novacek (pno) *(rec St. John Vianney Church, Juanita, WA, Aug 1994)* ("Spanish Rhapsody") † I. Albéniz:Pno Music (misc); Ginastera:Danzas argentinas, Op. 2; E. Granados:Goyescas (sels); Liszt:Rhap espagnole, S.254; M. Ravel:Alborada del gracioso AMBA ▲ 1014 [DDD] (16.97)
M. Raskin (hpd) PVY ▲ 796061 [DDD] (16.97)
D. Schrader (hpd) CED ▲ 4 [DDD] (16.97)
S. Yates (hpd) *(rec Sommerset, England, Aug 1997)* ("Fandango-Scarlatti in Iberia") † Larrañaga:Son Pno in d; Son Pno in D; D. Scarlatti:Sons Kbd; Seixas:Sons Kbd CHN ▲ 635 [DDD] (16.97)
Quintet No. 1 in C for Harpsichord & Strings (1776)
C. Verrette (vn), M. Shelton (vn), P. Slowik (va), J. M. Rozendaal (vc), D. Schrader (hpd) *(rec Oct & Dec 1992)* † Qnt 2 Hpd; Qnt 3 Hpd CED ▲ 13 [DDD] (16.97)
Quintet No. 2 in F for Harpsichord & Strings (1776)
C. Verrette (vn), M. Shelton (vn), P. Slowik (va), J. M. Rozendaal (vc), D. Schrader (hpd) *(rec Oct & Dec 1992)* † Qnt 1 Hpd; Qnt 3 Hpd CED ▲ 13 [DDD] (16.97)
Quintet No. 3 in G for Harpsichord & Strings (1776)
C. Verrette (vn), M. Shelton (vn), P. Slowik (va), J. M. Rozendaal (vc), D. Schrader (hpd) *(rec Oct & Dec 1992)* † Qnt 1 Hpd; Qnt 2 Hpd CED ▲ 13 [DDD] (16.97)
Quintet No. 4 in a for Harpsichord & Strings (1776)
D. Schrader (hpd), Chicago Baroque Ensemble *(rec WFMT Chicago, May 1996)* ("Vol. 2") † Qnt 5 Hpd; Qnt 6 Hpd CED ▲ 30 [DDD] (16.97)
Quintet No. 5 in D for Harpsichord & Strings (1776)
D. Schrader (hpd), Chicago Baroque Ensemble *(rec WFMT Chicago, May 1996)* ("Vol. 2") † Qnt 4 Hpd; Qnt 6 Hpd CED ▲ 30 [DDD] (16.97)
Quintet No. 6 in g for Harpsichord & Strings (1776)
D. Schrader (hpd), Chicago Baroque Ensemble *(rec WFMT Chicago, May 1996)* ("Vol. 2") † Qnt 4 Hpd; Qnt 5 Hpd CED ▲ 30 [DDD] (16.97)
Sonatas for Keyboard
E. Bátiz (cnd), Mexico City PO ("Música Mexicana: Volume 5") † Buxtehude:Org Music (misc colls); R. Halffter:Obertura Festiva, Op. 21; Tripartita, Op. 25; M. Ponce:Estrellita; Revueltas:Janitzio; Ocho; Sensemayá; F. Villanueva:Vals Poético ASV (Música Mexicana) ▲ 894 (16.97)
P. Cohen (pno) ("Complete Sonatas, Vol 1") GLSS (Los Siglos de Oro) ▲ 920502 (18.97)
P. Cohen (pno) ("Complete Sonatas, Vol. II") GLSS ▲ 920509 (18.97)
C. Haskil (pno) [one sonata] † Beethoven:Con 4 Pno, Op. 58; J. Haydn:Vars (6) Kbd, H.XVII/5; Pescetti:Kbd Music; R. Schumann:Waldscenen, Op. 82 HPC ▲ 154 (17.97)
I. Kipnis (hpd)—Son d Kbd, M. 8; in B, M.13 *(rec May 25, 1967)* † Fandango, M.1A; Blasco de Nebra:Sons Hpd, Op. 1; M. de Falla:Con Hpd; D. Scarlatti:Sons Kbd SNYC ▲ 53264 (7.97)
A. D. Larrocha (pno) [3 sons] *(rec 1974-79)* † I. Albéniz:Iberia Suite; Navarra; M. P. de Albéniz:Son Pno; E. Granados:Danzas españolas (10) Pno; Goyescas (sels); E. Halffter:Danzas (2) Pno; Mompou:Cançons i dansas Pno PPHI (Great Pianists of the 20th Century) ▲ 456883 (22.97)
C. C. Rodriguez (pno)—Son D Kbd, R.84; Son in F#, R.90 *(rec Fairfax, VA, Dec 1997)* ("España en el Corazón:Portrait of Spain") † I. Albéniz:Iberia Suite; M. de Falla:Amor brujo (sels); Vida breve (sels); E. Granados:Danzas españolas (10) Pno; Goyescas (sels) BRIO ▲ 118 [DDD] (16.97)
Versos para Te Deum for Organ
E. Elizondo (org) *(rec La Valenciana Org, Apr 1991)* ("The Organs of Guanajuato, Mexico") † De Gamarra:Son in Tone 8; Versos; N. Ledesma:Son 6 Org; Oxinaga:Fugues Org TIT ▲ 201 [DDD]
SOLLBERGER, HARVEY (1938-
Angel & Stone for Flute & Piano (1981)
H. Sollberger (fl), A. Karis (pno) *(rec New York, Jan 1982)* † Chamber Vars; Divert Fl; Riding the Wind I CRI (American Master) ▲ 743 [ADD] (16.97)
Chamber Variations for Conductor & 12 Instruments (1964)
G. Schuller (cnd), Group for Contemporary Music *(rec Steinway Hall NYC, May 1964)* † Angel & Stone; Divert Fl; Riding the Wind I CRI (American Master) ▲ 743 [ADD] (16.97)
Divertimento for Flute, Cello & Piano (1970)
F. Sherry (vc), H. Sollberger (fl), C. Wuorinen (pno) † Angel & Stone; Chamber Vars; Riding the Wind I CRI (American Master) ▲ 743 [ADD] (16.97)
Double Triptych for Flute & Percussion (1984)
R. Rudich (fl), K. Grossman (perc) † L. Harrison:Ariadne; Con 1 Fl; Sueyoshi:Correspondence V; Trombly:Duo Fl & Perc; Trio in 3 Movts CRI ▲ 568 [DDD] (16.97)
Grand Quartet for Flutes (1961)
Flute Force *(rec NYC, NY, 1989)* † P. Bacchus:Quartet Diverse Fl; I. Dahl:Serenade Fls; D. E. Jones:Tibiae; R. Reynolds:Etudes (4) Fl; Trombly:Cantilena CRI ▲ 581 [DDD] (16.97)
H. Sollberger (fl), S. Sollberger (fl), D. Gilbert (fl), T. Nyfenger (fl) † E. Dugger:Music for Syn; R. Erickson:Ricercar à 5 Trbns; P. Rhodes:Duo Vn & Vc; Westergaard:Vars for 6 Players NWW ▲ 80563 [ADD] (16.97)
Killapata/Chaskapata for solo Flute & Flute Choir
Members of the New York Flute Club ("A Tribute to Otto Luening") † Goeb:Divertimenti; Heiss:Etudes Fl; U. Kay:Suite Fl & Ob; E. Laderman:June 29th; Luening:Canons; Canons 2 Fls; Suite 2 Fl; Trio Fls; Trio 3 Fls CRI ▲ 561 [DDD] (16.97)
Life Study for Soprano, Flute & Harp (1985)
Jubal Trio *(rec Music Division SUNY, Purchase, NY, May 29-30, June 14 & Nov 13, 1995)* ("Jubal Songs") † G. Crumb:Federico's Little Songs; D. W. Freund:Backyard Songs; T. León:Journey; E. Stokes:Song Circle CRI ▲ 738 [DDD] (16.97)
Riding the Wind I for Flute & Chamber Ensemble (1973)
P. Spencer (fl), H. Sollberger (cnd) , H. Sollberger (cnd), Da Capo Chamber Players *(rec Oct 1975)* † Angel & Stone; Chamber Vars; Divert Fl CRI (American Master) ▲ 743 [ADD] (16.97)
Riding the Wind II, III, IV for Flute
H. Sollberger (fl) ("New Music Series, Vol. 3") † R. Carl:Time/Memory/Shadow; E. Carter:Riconoscenza; Delio:contrecoup; Escot:Visione NEU ▲ 45081 (16.97)
The Two & The One for 2 Percussionists & Amplified Cello (1972)
New Music Consort † J. Cage:Double Music; Second Construction; Third Construction; H. Cowell:Pulse; L. Foss:Qt Perc NWW ▲ 80405 [AAD] (16.97)
SOLLIMA, GIOVANNI (1962-
Violincelles Vibrez! (ballata) for 2 Cellos & Orchestra
M. Brunello (vc), M. Brunello (cnd), Italian String Orch † P. Hindemith:Trauermusik; A. Piazzolla:Adiós Nonino; G. Rossini:Péchés de vieillesse (sels); Takemitsu:Scene Vc; P. Tchaikovsky:Andante cantabile; Nocturne Vc AG ▲ 155 (18.97)

SOMARY, JOHANNES (1935-
A Ballad of God & His People (dramatic cantata) for Soprano, Tenor, Orchestra & Chorus (1987)
Hewes (sgr), MacMaster (sgr), J. Somary (cnd), Amor Artis Orch, Amor Artis Chorale *(rec live)* † Saint-Saëns:Requiem, Op. 54 PREM ▲ 1025 [DDD] (16.97)
Songs of Innocence for Soprano, Baritone, Cello, Winds & Double Bass
A. Matthews (sop), Z. Zhou (bar), J. Somary (cnd) ("Three is Company") † 3 Is Company; A. Bird:Suite Ww, Op. 29; J. Freeman:Suite Org PREM ▲ 1042 [DDD] (16.97)
Three Is Company for Flute, Clarinet & Bassoon (1994)
J. Somary (cnd) ("Three is Company") † Songs of Innocence; A. Bird:Suite Ww, Op. 29; J. Freeman:Suite Org PREM ▲ 1042 [DDD] (16.97)
SOMERS, HARRY (1925-
Chansons de la Nouvelle-France (3) for Orchestra & Chorus (1975)
E. Iseler (cnd), CBC Vancouver SO, Elmer Iseler Singers [FRE] † Coulthard:Quebec May; S. I. Glick:Sing Unto the Lord a New Song; D. Holman:Night Music SMS (SM 5000) ▲ 5115 [DDD] (16.97)
Kyrie for SATB Soloists, 8 Instruments, Percussion, Tape & Chorus (1972)
R. Roslak (sop), S. Cooper (mez), R. Missen (ten), N. Lohnes (bass), T. Cadan (bass), E. Iseler (cnd) , Elmer Iseler Singers *(rec Flora McRae Eaton Memorial Auditorium & St. Anne's)* ("Sacred & Profane Somers") † Limericks; Songs from Newfoundland Outports CTR ▲ 5495 [DDD] (16.97)
Limericks (3) for Vocal Soloist, Chamber Orchestra & Chorus (1980)
P. Kern (mez), E. Iseler (cnd) , Elmer Iseler Singers *(rec Flora McRae Eaton Memorial Auditorium & St. Anne's)* ("Sacred & Profane Somers") † Kyrie; Songs from Newfoundland Outports CTR ▲ 5495 [DDD] (16.97)
Lyric for Orchestra (1960)
V. Feldbrill (cnd), National Arts Center Canada Orch *(rec St. Joseph's Church Ottawa, July 6-7, 1995)* ("The Spring of Somers") † North Country; Suite Hp; Sym 1 SMS ▲ 5162 [DDD] (16.97)
Miniatures (11) for Oboe & Piano (1992)
L. Cherney (ob), W. Aide (pno) *(rec St Martin-in-the-Fields Church Toronto, July 1995)* ("The Charmer") † Chan Ka Nin:Charmer; B. Cherney:River of Fire; C. P. Harman:Poem; Hui:San Rocco; Mather:Vouvray CTR ▲ 5395 [DDD] (16.97)
North Country for Orchestra (1948)
V. Feldbrill (cnd), National Arts Center Canada Orch *(rec St. Joseph's Church Ottawa, July 6-7, 1995)* ("The Spring of Somers") † Lyric; Suite Hp; Sym 1 SMS ▲ 5162 [DDD] (16.97)
Picasso Suite:Light Music for Small Orchestra (1964)
M. Bernardi (cnd), CBC Vancouver SO *(rec Vancouver B.C., Mar 6-7, 1992)* † I. Stravinsky:Apollon Musagète; Pulcinella Suite SMS ▲ 5161 [DDD] (16.97)
Songs from the Newfoundland Outports (5) for Piano & Chorus (1969)
B. Ubukata (pno), E. Iseler (cnd), Elmer Iseler Singers *(rec Flora McRae Eaton Memorial Auditorium & St. Anne's)* ("Sacred & Profane Somers") † Kyrie; Limericks CTR ▲ 5495 [DDD] (16.97)
Suite for Harp & Chamber Orchestra (1949)
J. Swartz (hp), V. Feldbrill (cnd), National Arts Center Canada Orch *(rec St. Joseph's Church Ottawa, July 6-7, 1995)* ("The Spring of Somers") † Lyric; North Country; Sym 1 SMS ▲ 5162 [DDD] (16.97)
Symphony No. 1 (1951)
V. Feldbrill (cnd), National Arts Center Canada Orch *(rec St. Joseph's Church Ottawa, July 6-7, 1995)* ("The Spring of Somers") † Lyric; North Country; Suite Hp SMS ▲ 5162 [DDD] (16.97)
SOMMERFELDT, ØYSTEIN (1919-
Divertimento for solo Oboe, Op. 41
B. Hoff (ob) ("The Contemporary Oboe") † Karlsen:Sonatina Ob, Op. 44; T. Madsen:Son Ob; F. Mortensen:Son Ob; S. Olsen:Poems; Strømholm:Con minimo Ob NORW ▲ 1005 (17.97)
Spring Tunes [Vårlåter] for Flute, Op. 44 (arr 1976)
P. Øien (fl) *(rec Oslo, Norway, Feb 1-4, 1978)* ("The Norwegian Flute") † S. Bergh:Pan; Groven:Sunlight Mood; F. Mortensen:Son Fl, Op. 6; S. Olsen:Poem Fl; Serenade Fl, Op. 45; Ørbeck:Pastorale & Allegro Fl BIS ▲ 103 [AAD] (17.97)
SONDHEIM, STEPHEN (1930-
Songs
M. Heller (ten), M. Ormandy (vc), A. Heller (pno)—The Hills of Tomorrow; Take Me to the World; Another 100 People; Not While I'm Around; You Must Meet My Wife; Send in the Clowns; Comedy Tonight; Love I Hear; Later; Anyone Can Whistle; Pretty Women; Follies (sels) [Losing my mind]; Johanna; Good Thing Going; Silly People; Ev'rybody Says Don't; Loving You; Green Finch & Linnet Bird; Being Alive; 1 More Kiss; Sunday ("Take Me to the World") ETC ▲ 1185 (17.97)
SONNINEN, AHTI (1914-1984)
El amor pasa for Soprano, Flute & Orchestra, Op. 40 (1953)
S. Faringer (sop), G. von Bahr (fl), S. Westerberg (cnd) *(rec Stockholm Concert Hall Sweden, Sept 17, 1974)* ("Finnish Wind Music") † Bashmakov:Bagatelles; Con da camera; Kokkonen:Qnt Ww; L. Segerstam:Nnnnooooowwws BIS ▲ 11 [AAD] (17.97)
SONSTEVOLD, GUNNAR (1912-1991)
Sonatina for Bassoon & Piano
R. Rønnes (bn), E. Knardahl (pno) ("The Contemporary Norwegian Bassoon") † Bibalo:Son Bn; Kvandal:Légende, Op. 61b; Lerstad:Son 2 Bn, Op. 192; W. Plagge:Son Bn; H. Saeverud:Autumn SIMX ▲ 1077 [DDD] (18.97)
SOPHRONIOS (7th cent)
Oûtos ho theós (ca 634-38)
Ensemble Diferencias *(rec Waldenburg, Switzerland, Jan 17-18, 1996)* ("Cantio Triplex") † Anonymous:Gospodi Wozzwach; Heilige Dreifaltigkeit; Polielej, utrenja; Dufay:Music of Dufay; Kreta:Kanon DVX ▲ 79610 [DDD] (16.97)
SOPRONI, JÓZSEF (1930-
Sonata No. 1 for Violin & Piano (1979)
E. Perényi (vn), G. Kiss (pno) ("Dedicated to Eszter Perényi") † F. Farkas:Son solo Vn; M. Kocsár:Son solo Vn; Togobickij:Son solo Vn; J. Vajda:Duet Vn & Vc HUN ▲ 31784 (16.97)
SOR, FERNANDO (1778-1839)
Airs (6) choisis de Mozart's *Die Zauberflöte* for Guitar, Op. 19
M. Barrueco (gtr) † Grand Solo Gtr, Op. 14; Vars Mozart, Op. 9; W. A. Mozart:Son 18 Pno, K.576; Son 5 Pno, K.283 EMIC ▲ 66578 [DDD] (11.97)
M. Escarpa (gtr) † Gtr Music NXIN (Guitar Collection) ▲ 8554197 [DDD] (5.97)
Divertissement for Guitar, Op. 23
A. Holzman (gtr) *(rec Newmarket Canada, Dec 17-20, 1994)* ("Guitar Music") † Short Pieces (8) Gtr, Op. 24; Son Gtr, Op. 25 NXIN ▲ 553340 [DDD] (5.97)
Divertissments (6) for Guitar, Op. 2
J. M. Moreno (gtr)—No. 3 *(rec Villa Consuelo, Spain, June 1996)* ("La Guitarra Española II 1818-1918") † Intro & Vars on "Malborough", Op. 28; Llobet:Gtr Music; Mertz:Song without Words; F. Schubert:Music of Schubert; Tárrega:Gtr Music GLSS ▲ 920105 [DDD] (18.97)
Duos for Guitar
R. Kukbica (gtr), W. Berkel (gtr)—Bolero Gtrs, Op. 53; Fant Gtrs, Op. 54bis; Duos Gtr, Op. 55; Divertissements, Op. 61; Divert Gtrs, Op. 62; Souvenir de Russie, Op. 63 *(rec Newmarket, Canada, Apr 19-25, 1995)* ("Complete Guitar Duets Vol 2") NXIN ▲ 8553418 [DDD] (5.97)
Etudes for Guitar
R. Smits (gtr)—Studies (12) Gtr, Op. 6; Studies (24) Gtr, Op. 35; Studies (24) Gtr, Op. 31 [No. 12] *(rec Dec 1991)* † Vars Mozart, Op. 9; N. Coste:Gtr Music ACCE 2-▲ 9182 [DDD] (17.97)
Fantaisie for Guitar, Op. 59, "Elégiaque"
S. Fukuda (gtr) *(rec Fukushima City Music Hall, May 9-12, 1995)* ("Schubertiana") † N. Coste:Grande sérénade, Op. 30; Source de Lyson, Op. 47; Mertz:Gtr Music DNN ▲ 78978 [DDD] (16.97)
R. Porroni (gtr) *(rec Feb 1992)* ("The 19th Century Guitar") † Mertz:Gtr Music; F. Schubert:Songs (misc colls) STRV ▲ 23 (16.97)
Fantasies for Guitar
D. Blanco (gtr)—Intro and Vars on "Ye Banks and Braes", Op. 40 *(rec Castle Wik, Sweden, May 25, 1979)* ("Popular Guitar Music") † Grand Solo Gtr, Op. 14; Gtr Music; Son Gtr; Vars Mozart, Op. 9; A. Barrios:Gtr Music; Lauro:Valses Venezolanos Gtr; Sojo:Pieces Venezuela (5) Gtr BIS ▲ 133 [AAD] (17.97)
P. Pieters (gtr), M. Dumortier (gtr)—Divert Gtrs, Op. 34; Fant Gtr, Op. 41; Fant Gtrs, Op. 54bis *(rec Belgium, June 1995)* ("Duets for 2 Guitars") † Souvenir de Russie, Op. 63 RENE ▲ 92027 [DDD] (16.97)
A. Ramirez (gtr)—Fant Gtr, Op. 59; Fant Gtr, Op. posth *(rec Stadthalle Meinerzhagen, Germany, Oct 4-6, 1994)* ("Compositions for Guitar") † Grand Solo Gtr, Op. 14; Intro & Vars on "Malborough", Op. 28 DNN ▲ 78975 [DDD] (16.97)

▲ = CD ♦ = Enhanced CD △ = MD ▮ = Cassette Tape ▯ = DCC

SOR, FERNANDO (cont.)

Grand Solo for Guitar, Op. 14

M. Barrueco (gtr) † Airs choisis Mozart, Op. 19; Vars Mozart, Op. 9; W. A. Mozart:Son 18 Pno, K.576; Son 5 Pno, K.283 EMIC ▲ 66578 [DDD] (11.97)

D. Blanco (gtr) [D. Blanco] *(rec Castle Wik, Sweden, May 25, 1979)* ("Popular Guitar Music") † Fants Gtr; Gtr Music; Son Gtr; Vars Mozart, Op. 9; A. Barrios:Gtr Music; Lauro:Valses Venezolanos Gtr; Sojo:Pieces Venezuela (5) Gtr *(E, F, G text)* BIS ▲ 133 [AAD] (17.97)

G. Fierens (gtr) *(rec London, England)* ("Spanish Guitar Music") † I. Albéniz:Suite española 1, Op. 47; Castelnuovo-Tedesco:Capriccio diabolico Gtr, Op. 85; Son D Gtr, Op. 77; M. Ponce:Preludio, Balletto & Giga; J. Turina:Fandanguillo, Op. 36; H. Villa-Lobos:Preludes Gtr ASLE ▲ 6190 [DDD] (8.97)

A. Ramírez (gtr) *(rec Stadthalle Meinerzhagen Germany, Oct 4-6, 1994)* ("Compositions for Guitar") † Fants Gtr; Intro & Vars on "Malborough", Op. 28 DNN ▲ 78975 [DDD] (16.97)

M. Rost (gtr), J. Rost (gtr) *(rec Leipzig, Germany, Nov 1979)* † L. Brouwer:Micro piezas Gtr; F. Carulli:Little Duet Gtr, Op. 34/2; F. Martin:Pièces brèves Gtr; Narváez:Diferencias sobre Gtr; Guárdame las vacas Gtr; Seys libros del delphin (sels); J. Rodrigo:Invocación y danza BER ▲ 9331 [ADD] (10.97)

Guitar Music

D. Blanco (gtr)—Intro & Vars on "Malborough", Op. 28; Theme & vars, woO *(rec Castle Wik, Sweden, May 25, 1979)* ("Popular Guitar Music") † Fants Gtr; Grand Solo Gtr, Op. 14; Son Gtr; Vars Mozart, Op. 9; A. Barrios:Gtr Music; Lauro:Valses Venezolanos Gtr; Sojo:Pieces Venezuela (5) Gtr BIS ▲ 133 [AAD] (17.97)

L. Brabec (gtr)—Intro & Vars on "Malborough", Op. 28; Allegretto; Grand Solo Gtr, Op. 14; Son Gtr, Op. 25 [Andante Largo]; Studies Gtr [Sels]; Fant Gtr, Op. 7 ("Grand Solo") † Vars Mozart, Op. 9 SUR ▲ 4 [DDD] (16.97)

R. Burley (gtr)—Fant Gtr, Op. 7 † Vars Mozart, Op. 9 ASVQ ▲ 6223 (10.97)

M. Escarpa (gtr)—Waltzes, Op. 17; Air varié; Waltzes, Op. 18; Vars Gtr, Op. 20; Fant Gtr, Op. 21 † Airs choisis Mozart, Op. 19 NXIN (Guitar Collection) ▲ 8554197 [DDD] (5.97)

S. Fukuda (gtr)—Studies (12) Gtr, Op. 6 [No. 12 in A]; Studies (12) Gtr, Op. 29 [No. 17 in C]; Studies (24) Gtr, Op. 35 [No. 22 in e]; Studies (24) Gtr, Op. 31 [No. 23]; Short Pieces (6) Gtr, Op. 32 [No. 2 Valse in E] *(rec Chichibu Muse Park, Japan, Nov 24-26, 1994)* ("Shin-ichi Fukuda Plays 19th Century Guitar") † Vars Mozart, Op. 9; N. Coste:Gtr Music; Mertz:Gtr Music DNN ▲ 78950 [DDD] (16.97)

N. Goluses (gtr)—Fant Gtr, Op. 58; Fant Gtr, Op. 59; Studies (25) Gtr, Op. 60 *(rec Newmarket Canada, May 15-20, 1995)* NXIN ▲ 553342 [DDD] (5.97)

A. Holzman (gtr)—Fant Gtr; Fant Gtr, Op. 52; Morceau de Concert, Op. 54; Souvenirs d'une soirée à Berlin, Op. 56; Waltzes (6) Gtr, Op. 51 *(rec Newmarket, Canada, June 1995)* ("Guitar Collection") NXIN ▲ 553450 [DDD] (5.97)

T. Hoppstock (gtr)—Bagatelles, Op. 43 [Bagatelle in A]; Salon Pieces Gtr, Op. 33 [No. 3a Sicilienne; No. 1 Allegretto]; Vars Gtr, Op. 16; Studies (24) Gtr, Op. 35 [No. 17 in D] ("Werke für Gitarre") † Vars Mozart, Op. 9 SIGM ▲ 1400 [DDD] (17.97)

T. Hoppstock (gtr)—Studies Gtr, Op. 60 [No. 23; No. 22 in e]; Studies (24) Gtr, Op. 35 [No. 05 in G; No. 11 in d; No. 19 in C; No. 18 in e; No. 12 in F]; Studies (24) Gtr, Op. 31 [No. 18 in b; No. 13]; Studies (25) Gtr, Op. 60 [No. 14]; Studies (12) Gtr, Op. 29 [No. 21 in D]; Short Pieces (8) Gtr, Op. 24 [No. 6 Menuett (Andante); No. 7 Allegretto]; Short Pieces (6) Gtr, Op. 5 [No. 3 Minuet; No. 4 Allegro]; Minuets (12) Gtr, Op. 11/2 [Minuet No. 2]; Minuets (12) Gtr, Op. 11/3 [Minuet No. 3]; Minuets (12) Gtr, Op. 11/6 [Minuet No. 6]; Minuets (12) Gtr, Op. 11/7 [Minuet No. 7]; Minuets (12) Gtr, Op. 11/8 [Minuet No. 8]; Minuets (12) Gtr, Op. 11/9 [Minuet No. 9]; Minuets (12) Gtr, Op. 11/10 [Minuet No. 10] *(rec Darmstadt, 1995-96)* ("Werke für Gitarre") † H. A. Marschner:Bagatelles Gtr, Op. 4; Werthmüller:Son Pno, Op. 17 SIGM ▲ 7500 [DDD] (17.97)

J. McFadden (gtr)—Intro & Vars on "Que ne suis-je la fougère", Op. 26; Intro & Vars on "Gentil Housard", Op. 27; Intro & Vars on "Malborough", Op. 28; Studies (12) Gtr, Op. 29; Fant Gtr, Op. 30 *(rec Newmarket Canada, June 1995)* ("Complete Guitar Music, Vol. 7") NXIN ▲ 8553451 [DDD] (5.97)

J. Richards (gtr)—Short Pieces (6) Gtr, Op. 5 [No. 5]; Intro and Vars on "Ye Banks and Braes", Op. 40; Minuets (12) Gtr, Op. 11 [Sels]; Airs choisis Mozart, Op. 19 [No. 1, Marche religieuse]; Meditación; Divert Gtr, Op. 2; Intro & Vars on "Malborough", Op. 28; Studies (12) Gtr, Op. 29; Fant Gtr, Op. 59 MER ▲ 84346 [DDD] (16.97)

C. M. Ros (gtr), M. G. Ferrer (gtr)—Divert Gtrs, Op. 34; Divert Gtrs, Op. 38; Waltzes Gtrs, Op. 39; Fant Gtr, Op. 41; Divert militaire, Op. 49; Bolero Gtrs, Op. 53; Fant Gtrs, Op. 54bis; Duos Gtr, Op. 55; Divertissements, Op. 61; Divert Gtrs, Op. 62; Souvenir de Russie, Op. 63 ("Complete Works for 2 Guitars") † Waltzes Gtrs, Op. 44bis OTR 2-▲ 1008 (36.97)

A. Segovia (gtr)—Rondo Gtr; Minuet in A † I. Albéniz:Gtr Music; Castelnuovo-Tedesco:Gtr Music; M. Ponce:Gtr Music; Son Mexicana; Tansman:Berceuse et Danse; H. Villa-Lobos:Etudes Gtr; Preludes Gtr; S. L. Weiss:Lt Music AURC ▲ 115

D. Starobin (gtr)—Minuets (12) Gtr, Op. 11/12 [Minuet No. 12]; Studies (12) Gtr, Op. 6 [No. 09]; Septième fant et vars brillantes, Op. 30; Studies (24) Gtr, Op. 35 [No. 03 in a]; Studies (24) Gtr, Op. 31; Souvenirs d'une soirée à Berlin, Op. 56 *(rec Nov 1992)* † N. Coste:Gtr Music; Regondi:Intro et caprice, Op. 23 GHA ▲ 126022 (17.97)

M. Teicholz (gtr)—Pièces de société, Op. 36; Sérénade, Op. 37; Intro and Vars on "Ye Banks and Braes", Op. 40; Short Pieces (6) Gtr, Op. 42 *(rec Newmarket, Canada, Dec 16-22, 1995)* ("Complete Guitar Music, Vol. 9") NXIN ▲ 8553722 [DDD] (5.97)

Introduction & Variations on "Gentil Housard", Op. 27

A. Leonard (gtr) *(rec Cambridge, MA, May 1996)* ("Music of the Ages") † Intro & Vars on "Malborough", Op. 28; J. S. Bach:Sons & Partitas Vn; Suites Vc; J. Dowland:Lt Music; A. Piazzolla:Milonga del angel; Muerte del angel; A. York:Sunburst ACTR ▲ 60101 [DDD] (16.97)

Introduction & Variations on "Malborough s'en va-t-en guerre" for Guitar, Op. 28

A. Leonard (gtr) *(rec Cambridge, MA, May 1996)* ("Music of the Ages") † Intro & Vars on "Gentil Housard", Op. 27; J. S. Bach:Sons & Partitas Vn; Suites Vc; J. Dowland:Lt Music; A. Piazzolla:Milonga del angel; Muerte del angel; A. York:Sunburst ACTR ▲ 60101 [DDD] (16.97)

J. M. Moreno (gtr) *(rec Villa Consuelo, Spain, June 1996)* ("La Guitarra Española II 1818-1918") † Divert Gtr, Op. 2; Llobet:Gtr Music; Mertz:Song without Words; F. Schubert:Music of Schubert; Tárrega:Gtr Music GLSS ▲ 920105 [DDD] (18.97)

A. Ramírez (gtr) *(rec Stadthalle Meinerzhagen, Germany, Oct 4-6, 1994)* ("Compositions for Guitar") † Fants Gtr; Grand Solo Gtr, Op. 14 DNN ▲ 78975 [DDD] (16.97)

Minuets (12) for Guitar, Op. 11/6 (1821-22)

N. Kraft (gtr) *(rec Aug 1993)* ("19th Century Guitar Favourites") † Aguado:Gtr Music; Tárrega:Gtr Music NXIN ▲ 553007 [DDD] (5.97)

Morceau de Concert for Guitar, Op. 54

F. Moretti (gtr) † Son Gtr; Son Gtr, Op. 22; Son Gtr, Op. 25 STRV ▲ 33475 (16.97)

Salon Pieces (3) for Guitar, Op. 33

S. Novacek (gtr) *(rec Newmarket, Canada, Jan 22-26, 1995)* NXIN ▲ 553341 [DDD] (5.97)

Short Pieces (8) for Guitar, Op. 24

A. Holzman (gtr) *(rec Newmarket Canada, Dec 17-20, 1994)* ("Guitar Music") † Divert Gtr, Op. 23; Son Gtr, Op. 25 NXIN ▲ 553340 [DDD] (5.97)

Sonata in C for Guitar, Op. 15b, "Sonata seconda"

D. Blanco (gtr) [D. Blanco] *(rec Castle Wik, Sweden, May 25, 1979)* ("Popular Guitar Music") † Fants Gtr; Grand Solo Gtr, Op. 14; Gtr Music; Vars Mozart, Op. 9; A. Barrios:Gtr Music; Lauro:Valses Venezolanos Gtr; Sojo:Pieces Venezuela (5) Gtr BIS ▲ 133 [AAD] (17.97)

F. Moretti (gtr) † Morceau de Concert, Op. 54; Son Gtr, Op. 22; Son Gtr, Op. 25 STRV ▲ 33475 (16.97)

C. Romero (gtr) † Son Gtr, Op. 22; Vars Mozart, Op. 9; M. Giuliani:Grand Ov, Op. 61; Vars on a Theme by Handel; Tárrega:Gtr Music DLS ▲ 1004 [AAD] (10.97)

M. Rost (gtr), J. Rost (gtr) † Son Gtr, Op. 22; M. de Falla:Homenaje tombeau de Debussy; Spanish Dance; E. Granados:Danzas españolas (10) Pno; J. Rodrigo:Con de Aranjuez LALI ▲ 15602 [DDD] (3.97)

Sonata in C for Guitar, Op. 22, "Grand Sonata I"

F. Moretti (gtr) † Morceau de Concert, Op. 54; Son Gtr; Son Gtr, Op. 25 STRV ▲ 33475 (16.97)

C. Romero (gtr) † Son Gtr; Vars Mozart, Op. 9; M. Giuliani:Grand Ov, Op. 61; Vars on a Theme by Handel; Tárrega:Gtr Music DLS ▲ 1004 [AAD] (10.97)

M. Rost (gtr), J. Rost (gtr) † Son Gtr; M. de Falla:Homenaje tombeau de Debussy; Spanish Dance; E. Granados:Danzas españolas (10) Pno; J. Rodrigo:Con de Aranjuez LALI ▲ 15602 [DDD] (3.97)

Sonata in C for Guitar, Op. 25, "Grand Sonata II"

A. Holzman (gtr) *(rec Newmarket Canada, Dec 17-20, 1994)* ("Guitar Music") † Divert Gtr, Op. 23; Short Pieces (8) Gtr, Op. 24 NXIN ▲ 553340 [DDD] (5.97)

F. Moretti (gtr) † Morceau de Concert, Op. 54; Son Gtr; Son Gtr, Op. 22 STRV ▲ 33475 (16.97)

Songs for Voice & Guitar

M. Almajano (sop), J. M. Moreno (gtr)—Mouvement prière religieuse; Ariettas [Povero cor t'inganni; Lagrime mie d'affanno; Io mentitor!; Perduta l'anima]; Nel cor piu mi sento; Seguidillas [Muchacha y la vergüenza; Si dices que mis ojos; Los canónigos, madre; Las mujeres y cuerdas; Mis descuidados ojos] ("Las mujeres y cuerdas: Canciones y piezas para guitarra") † F. Carulli:Andante affettuoso; M. Giuliani:Songs; Mertz:Song without Words GLSS ▲ 920202 (18.97)

SOR, FERNANDO (cont.)

Songs for Voice & Guitar (cont.)

Elanara—Seguidillas [Cesa de atormentarme; De amor en las prisiones; ¿Cómo ha de resolverse?; Si dices que mis ojos; El que quisiera amando; Muchacha y la vergüenza] ("Mosaic d'España: Spanish & Sephardic Songs") † A. Anderson:Songs; R. Gerhard:Songs; E. Granados:Songs; F. Moretti:Songs; Sutton-Anderson:Songs MER ▲ 84334 [DDD] (16.97)

C. Högman (voc), J. Lindberg (gtr)—Seguidillas [Cesa de atormentarme; De amor en las prisiones; Acuérdate bien mó; Prepárame la tumba; ¿Cómo ha de resolverse?; Muchacha y la vergüenza; Si dices que mis ojos; El que quisiera amando; Las mujeres y cuerdas; Mis descuidados ojos]; Studio 9 para la guitarra; Studio 17; Studio 22 *(rec Sweden, June 28&30, 1985)* ("Songs for the Guitar") † M. Giuliani:Songs; F. Schubert:Songs; L. Spohr:Songs Voice Gtr; C. M. von Weber:Songs Voice Gtr BIS ▲ 293 [DDD] (17.97)

Souvenir de Russie for 2 Guitars, Op. 63

P. Pieters (gtr), M. Dumortier (gtr) *(rec Belgium, June 1995)* ("Duets for 2 Guitars") † Fants Gtr RENE ▲ 92027 [DDD] (16.97)

Studies (12) for Guitar, Op. 29

A. Prevost (gtr) ("Guitar Works, Vol. 3: Complete Etudes") DPV ▲ 9126 (15.97)

Variations on a Theme of Mozart for Guitar, Op. 9

M. Barrueco (gtr) † Airs choisis Mozart, Op. 19; Grand Solo Gtr, Op. 14; W. A. Mozart:Son 18 Pno, K.576; Son 5 Pno, K.283 EMIC ▲ 66578 [DDD] (11.97)

D. Blanco (gtr) [D. Blanco] *(rec Castle Wik, Sweden, May 25, 1979)* ("Popular Guitar Music") † Fants Gtr; Grand Solo Gtr, Op. 14; Gtr Music; Son Gtr; A. Barrios:Gtr Music; Lauro:Valses Venezolanos Gtr; Sojo:Pieces Venezuela (5) Gtr BIS ▲ 133 [AAD] (17.97)

L. Brabec (gtr) ("Grand Solo") † Gtr Music SUR ▲ 4 [DDD] (16.97)

R. Burley (gtr) † Gtr Music ASVQ ▲ 6223 (10.97)

A. D. Forno (gtr) *(rec live)* ("In Concert Part I") † A. Lara:Granada; H. Villa-Lobos:Chôro 1 JST ▲ 1078 (10.97)

S. Fukuda (gtr) *(rec Chichibu Muse Park, Japan, Nov 24-26, 1994)* ("Shin-ichi Fukuda Plays 19th Century Guitar") † Gtr Music; N. Coste:Gtr Music; Mertz:Gtr Music DNN ▲ 78950 [DDD] (16.97)

T. Hopstock (gtr) ("Werke für Gitarre") † Gtr Music SIGM ▲ 1400 [DDD] (17.97)

C. Marcotulli (gtr) ("The Guitar in Opera") † M. Giuliani:Rossiniana; Mertz:Gtr Music OTR ▲ 1007 [DDD] (18.97)

C. Romero (gtr) † Son Gtr; Son Gtr, Op. 22; M. Giuliani:Grand Ov, Op. 61; Vars on a Theme by Handel; Tárrega:Gtr Music DLS ▲ 1004 [AAD] (10.97)

R. Smits (gtr) *(rec Dec 1991)* † Etudes Gtr; N. Coste:Gtr Music ACCE 2-▲ 9182 [DDD] (17.97)

I. Suzuki (gtr) *(rec House St. Gregorius, Oct 14-15, 1980)* ("Guitar Recital") † B. Britten:Nocturnal, Op. 70; Castelnuovo-Tedesco:Con 1 Gtr, Op. 99; H. Hayashi:Hamon; Moreno Torroba:Pieces caractéristiques CAMA ▲ 413 [AAD] (18.97)

Waltzes (6) for 2 Guitars, Op. 44bis

J. Moser (gtr), F. Rahm (gtr) ("Musique espagnole pour deux guitares") † I. Albéniz:Suite española 1, Op. 47; Tango Español; A. de Cabezón:Obras de música (sels); Froelicher:Muleta; E. Granados:Goyescas:Intermezzo GALL ▲ 881 [DDD] (19.97)

C. M. Ros (gtr), M. G. Ferrer (gtr) ("Complete Works for 2 Guitars") † Gtr Music OTR 2-▲ 1008 (36.97)

SORABJI, KAIKHOSRU SHAPURJI (1892-1988)

Fantaisie Espagnole for Piano (1919)

D. Amato (pno) ALTA ▲ 9022 (14.97)

Le Jardin parfumé for Piano (1923)

Y. Solomon (pno) ALTA ▲ 9037 (14.97)

Pastiches (3) for Piano (1922)

C. Grante (pno)—No. 2 [after the Habanera from Bizet's Carmen] † Busoni:Sonatina 6 Pno; Liszt:Réminiscences de Don Juan Pno, S.418; Trans, Arrs & Paraphrases ALTA ▲ 9098 (19.97)

Piano Music

D. Amato (pno)—Quære reliqua hujus materiei inter secretiora; St. Bertrand de Comminges; Toccatinetta sopra C.G.F. (1929); Sutra sul nome dell'amico Alexis (1981); Sutra "Per il caro amico quasi Nipote - Alexis"; Passeggiata arlecchinesca sopra un frammento... *(rec 1981-82)* ("Rondò arlecchinesco") ALTA ▲ 9025 (19.97)

Sonata No. 1 for Piano (1919)

M. Hamelin (pno) ALTA ▲ 9050

Variazione maliziosa e perversa on Grieg's "La morte d'Ase" for Piano

D. Amato (pno) † A. Hinton:Vars & Fugue on a Theme of Grieg; R. Stevenson:Pno Music ALTA ▲ 9021

SØRENSEN, BENT (1958-

Adieu for String Quartet (1986)

Arditti String Quartet ("From Scandanavia") † Alman; Angel's Music; M. Lindberg:Qnt Cl; Saariaho:Nymphea; Tiensuu:Arsenic & Old Lace DISQ ▲ 782033 (18.97)

Alman for String Quartet (1983-84)

Arditti String Quartet ("From Scandanavia") † Adieu; Angel's Music; M. Lindberg:Qnt Cl; Saariaho:Nymphea; Tiensuu:Arsenic & Old Lace DISQ ▲ 782033 (18.97)

Angel's Music for String Quartet (1987-88)

Arditti String Quartet ("From Scandanavia") † Adieu; Alman; M. Lindberg:Qnt Cl; Saariaho:Nymphea; Tiensuu:Arsenic & Old Lace DISQ ▲ 782033 (18.97)

Clairobscur for Chamber Ensemble

J. V. Hessen (cnd), Esbjerg Ensemble † Deserted Churchyards; Minnewater; Shadowland; Sirenengesang DCAP ▲ 8224075 (13.97)

Concerto for Violin & Orchestra, "Decaying Garden" (1992-93)

R. Hirsch (vn), L. Segerstam (cnd), Danish National RSO *(rec live Danish Radio Concert Hall, 1992 & 1994)* † Echoing Garden MARC ▲ 8224039 [DDD] (13.97)

The Deserted Churchyards for Chamber Ensemble (1990)

J. V. Hessen (cnd), Esbjerg Ensemble † Clairobscur; Minnewater; Shadowland; Sirenengesang DCAP ▲ 8224075 (13.97)

D. Starobin (cnd) *(rec American Academy of Arts & Letters, NYC, NY, Apr 1994)* ("Speculum Musicae Plays the New Danes") † Abrahamsen:Winternacht; J. S. Bach:Sons & Partitas Vn; K. A. Rasmussen:Movements on a Moving Line; Ruders:Bells BRID ▲ 9054 [DDD] (17.97)

The Echoing Garden for solo Voices, Orchestra & Chorus (1990-92)

AS. Bäverstam (sop), M. Hill (ten), L. Segerstam (cnd), Danish National RSO, Danish National Radio Choir *(rec live Danish Radio Concert Hall, 1992 & 1994)* † Con Vn MARC ▲ 8224039 [DDD] (13.97)

Minnewater for Chamber Ensemble

J. V. Hessen (cnd), Esbjerg Ensemble † Clairobscur; Deserted Churchyards; Shadowland; Sirenengesang DCAP ▲ 8224075 (13.97)

Shadowland for Chamber Ensemble

J. V. Hessen (cnd), Esbjerg Ensemble † Clairobscur; Deserted Churchyards; Minnewater; Sirenengesang DCAP ▲ 8224075 (13.97)

Sirenengesang for Chamber Ensemble

J. V. Hessen (cnd), Esbjerg Ensemble † Clairobscur; Deserted Churchyards; Minnewater; Shadowland DCAP ▲ 8224075 (13.97)

The Songs of the Decaying Garden for Clarinet (1992)

J. Kruse (cl) *(rec Det Fynske Musikkonservatorium, 1993)* ("Contemporary Danish Works for Clarinet") † Troll-Playing; N. V. Bentzon:Qt Cl; Son Cl; H. D. Koppel:Variazioni Libère, Op. 98; Vars Cl & Pno, Op. 72; Ruders:Tattoo for 1; Throne PLAL ▲ 78 [DAD] (18.97)

Troll-Playing for Clarinet (1982)

J. Kruse (cl) *(rec Det Fynske Musikkonservatorium, 1993)* ("Contemporary Danish Works for Clarinet") † Songs of the Decaying Garden Cl; N. V. Bentzon:Qt Cl; Son Cl; H. D. Koppel:Variazioni Libère, Op. 98; Vars Cl & Pno, Op. 72; Ruders:Tattoo for 1; Throne PLAL ▲ 78 [DAD] (18.97)

SÖRENSON, TORSTEN (1908-1992)

Sonatina for Guitar (1976)

J. Holeček (gtr) *(rec Djursholm Sweden, Jan 30-31, 1982)* ("Romantic Guitar Music") † Castelnuovo-Tedesco:Son Gtr, Op. 77; J. Holeček:Aquarelles; Serenade; Smoke Rings; Swedish Romance; E. von Koch:Monologue 10 BIS ▲ 203 [AAD] (17.97)

SOROZÁBAL, PABLO (1897-1988)

Operetta Arias

A. Arteta (sop), E. G. Asensio (cnd), RTVE SO—Del Manojo de Sosas (sels) † Chapí:Operetta Arias; Chueca:Operetta Arias; Guridi:Operetta Arias; Torroba:Operetta Arias; Vives:Operetta Arias RTVE ▲ 65095 (16.97)

La Tabernera del Puerto (zarzuela) for Voices & Orchestra (1936)

M. Bayo (sop), P. Domingo (ten), J. Pons (bar), V. P. Pérez (cnd), Galicia SO VAL (Zarzuela Collection) ▲ 4766 (18.97)

SOUSA, JOHN PHILIP (1854-1932)
The Belle of Chicago (1892)
R. Bernat (cnd), River City Brass Band † El Capitan (sels); Liberty Bell; Manhattan Beach; Semper Fidelis; Stars & Stripes Forever; Washington Post; E. Bowman:12th St. Rag; H. Fillmore:Marches (misc); S. Joplin:Maple Leaf Rag; G. Rossini:Guillaume Tell (ov) RCBB ▲ 192
The Bride Elect (selections)
K. Brion (cnd), Razumovsky SO—Waltzes; Tarantella: The Dancing Girl *(rec Bratislava, Slovak Republic, Oct 27 & 30, 1995)* ("Vol. 1, On Stage") † El Capitan (sels); Our Flirtations (sels); People Who Live in Glass Houses (sels) NXIN (American Classics) ▲ 8559008 [DDD] (5.97)
El Capitan (operetta in 3 acts)[lib C. Klein, T. Frost & Sousa](selections) (1895)
R. Bernat (cnd), River City Brass Band—March † Belle of Chicago; Liberty Bell; Manhattan Beach; Semper Fidelis; Stars & Stripes Forever; Washington Post; E. Bowman:12th St. Rag; H. Fillmore:Marches (misc); S. Joplin:Maple Leaf Rag; G. Rossini:Guillaume Tell (ov) RCBB ▲ 192
P. La Garde (tpt), K. Brion (cnd), Razumovsky SO—O Warrior Grim; Waltzes; March *(rec Bratislava, Slovak Republic, Oct 27 & 30, 1995)* ("Vol. 1, On Stage") † Bride Elect (sels); Our Flirtations (sels); People Who Live in Glass Houses (sels) NXIN (American Classics) ▲ 8559008 [DDD] (5.97)
Désirée (operetta in 2 acts) [collaborated w. Edward M. Taber] (1882-83)
J. K. Applebaum (sop), K. Brunssen (mez), M. Thorburn (mez), D. Price (ten), G. Bass (bass), R. Lissemore (bass), J. Fisher (cnd), Pocono Pops Orch, Pocono Pops Chorus *(rec East Stroudsburg, PA, Aug 1993)* ("America's First Comic Opera") AMDE ▲ 101 [DDD] (16.97)
The Dwellers in the Western World (suite) for Orchestra (1910)
R. Kapp (cnd) ("Sousa for Orchestra") † Three Quotations (suite) ESSY ▲ 1003 [DDD] (16.97)
Invictus (march)
R. Bernat (cnd), River City Brass Band † Nobles of the Mystic Shrine; Thunderer; H. Fillmore:Marches (misc); E. F. Goldman:On the Mall; Langford:Carnival Day; E. Tomlinson:Best Foot Forward; M. Wilson:British Grenadiers; Men of Harlech; Seventy-Six Trombones; H. C. Work:Colonel Bogey March; Marching through Georgia RCBB ▲ 191
The Liberty Bell (march) for Band (1893)
R. Bernat (cnd), River City Brass Band † Belle of Chicago; El Capitan (sels); Manhattan Beach; Semper Fidelis; Stars & Stripes Forever; Washington Post; E. Bowman:12th St. Rag; H. Fillmore:Marches (misc); S. Joplin:Maple Leaf Rag; G. Rossini:Guillaume Tell (ov) RCBB ▲ 192
Life & Music of Sousa
A. Hannes (nar), M. Diesenroth (cnd), Musikkorps des Wachtbataillons—Stars & Stripes Forever; Crusader; Belle of Chicago; Gladiator; Semper Fidelis; Washington Post; High School Cadets; Thunderer; Hands across the Sea; El Capitan (sels) [March] ("The Stories of Foster & Sousa in Words & Music") † S. C. Foster:Music of Foster MMD (Music Masters) ▲ 8515 [ADD] (3.97) ▮ 8515 [ADD] (2.98)
Manhattan Beach (march) for Band (1893)
R. Bernat (cnd), River City Brass Band † Belle of Chicago; El Capitan (sels), Liberty Bell, Semper Fidelis, Stars & Stripes Forever; Washington Post; E. Bowman:12th St. Rag; H. Fillmore:Marches (misc); S. Joplin:Maple Leaf Rag; G. Rossini:Guillaume Tell (ov) RCBB ▲ 192
Marches & Dances
R. Bashford (cnd), Grenadier Guards Band ("Stirring Marches of the USA Services") PLON (Phase 4 Stereo) ▲ 48957 (9.97)
K. Brion (cnd), New Sousa Band—Glory of the Yankee Navy; New York Hippodrome; Solid Men to the Front!; Sabre & Spurs; U.S. Field Artillery; Pride of Pittsburgh; Free Lance; Semper Fidelis; Royal Welch Fusiliers; Untitled March; Nobles of the Mystic Shrine; Jack Tar; Stars & Stripes Forever ("The Original All-American Sousa!") DLS ▲ 3102 [DDD] (14.97)
K. Brion (cnd), New Sousa Band ("The Sousa Legacy, Vol. 1") BAIN ▲ 6250
K. Brion (cnd), Razumovsky SO—Gladiator; Gliding Girl; Federal; Presidential Polonaise; Irish Dragoon [Circus Galop]; Sandalphon Waltzes; Belle of Chicago; Silver Spray Schottische; Peaches & Cream; Myrrha Gavotte; Fairest of the Fair; Coquette; On the Wings of Lightning; King of France; I, Too, Was Born in Acadia; In Africa; Venus; Hail to the Spirit of Liberty NXIN ▲ 8559029 (5.97)
E. Hills (cnd), Grenadier Guards Band—Stars & Stripes Forever; Hands across the Sea; Power & Glory; Belle of Chicago; Fairest of the Fair ("Hands Across the Sea - Sousa Marches") TELC ▲ 96061 (16.97)
L. Hoskins (cnd), Her Majesty's Royal Marines Band ("Great American Marches I") ANGL ▲ 64671 (11.97)
L. Hoskins (cnd), Her Majesty's Royal Marines Band ("Great American Marches II") ANGL ▲ 64672 (11.97)
E. Howarth (cnd) PLON ▲ 10290 [DDD] (16.97)
D. Hunsberger (cnd) —Semper Fidelis; High School Cadets; Washington Post; Jack Tar; Lloyd Legion; Anchor & Star; Stars & Stripes Forever; El Capitan (sels) [March]; Liberty Bell; Comrades of the Legion; Corcoran Cadets; King Cotton; Hail to the Spirit of Liberty; Thunderer ("Sousa Spectacular") PHOE ▲ 132 (15.97)
T. Kelly (cl), J. Wallace (cnd) *(Stars & Stripes Forever; Washington Post; Semper Fidelis; Chariot Race; Reine de la mer (waltzes); Liberty Bell; Hail to the Spirit of Liberty; Jack Tar; Coquette; Under the Cuban Flag [from Cubaland]; King Cotton; With Pleasure; Manhattan Beach; El Capitan (sels) [March])*, T. Kelly (cl), J. Wallace (cnd) , J. Wallace (cnd), Wallace Collection *(Thunderer)* ("Whad'ya Know AboutSousa") NIMB ▲ 4006 (11.97)
C. MacDonally (cnd), West Point Military Band—Gladiator; U.S. Field Artillery; Bride Elect; King Cotton ("Sousa & American Marches") † Stars & Stripes Forever TUXE ▲ 5032 (10.97)
P. Parkes (cnd), Williams Fairey Band—Semper Fidelis; Crusader; El Capitan (sels) [March]; Invincible Eagle; King Cotton; Hands across the Sea; Manhattan Beach; Our Flirtations; Picadore; Gladiator; Free Lance; Washington Post; Beau Ideal; High School Cadets; Fairest of the Fair; Thunderer; Occidental; Liberty Bell; Corcoran Cadets; National Fencibles; Black Horse Troop; Gridiron Club; Directorate; Belle of Chicago ("From Maine to Oregon: The Williams Fairey Band Plays Sousa Marches") CHN ▲ 4535 [DDD] (16.97)
J. P. Sousa (cnd), Philadelphia Rapid Transit Company Band, J. P. Sousa (cnd), Sousa Band—Washington Post; Stars & Stripes Forever ("Under the Double Eagle") PHS ▲ 9249 (17.97)
A. Toscanini (cnd), NBC SO—El Capitan (sels) [March]; Stars & Stripes Forever ("The Toscanini Collection, Vol. 38: All-American Program") † S. Barber:Adagio Strs; G. Gershwin:American in Paris; Grofé:Grand Canyon Suite; J. S. Smith:Star-Spangled Banner RCAV (Gold Seal) ▲ 60307 (11.97)
United States Marine Band—Semper Fidelis; Presidential Polonaise; Manhattan Beach; Comrades of the Legion; Sabre & Spurs; Gridiron Club; King Cotton; Easter Monday; Who's Who in Navy Blue; Invincible Eagle; Washington Post ("President's Own-United States Marine Band-Sousa Original") ALSM ▲ 5558 [DDD] (16.97)
P. Urbanek (cnd), Czech Brass Orch NON ▲ 71266 [ADD] (9.97)
various artists—Stars & Stripes Forever; Invincible Eagle; High School Cadets; Picadore; Semper Fidelis; El Capitan (sels) [March]; Manhattan Beach; King Cotton; Washington Post; Liberty Bell PLON (Weekend Classics) ▲ 30211 [AAD] (7.97)
Nobles of the Mystic Shrine (march) for Band (1923)
R. Bernat (cnd), River City Brass Band † Invictus; Thunderer; H. Fillmore:Marches (misc); E. F. Goldman:On the Mall; Langford:Carnival Day; E. Tomlinson:Best Foot Forward; M. Wilson:British Grenadiers; Men of Harlech; Seventy-Six Trombones; H. C. Work:Colonel Bogey March; Marching through Georgia RCBB ▲ 191
Our Flirtations (selections)
M. Betko (fl), K. Brion (cnd), Razumovsky SO—Ov; March *(rec Bratislava, Slovak Republic, Oct 27 & 30, 1995)* ("Vol. 1, On Stage") † Bride Elect (sels); El Capitan (sels); People Who Live in Glass Houses (sels) NXIN (American Classics) ▲ 8559008 [DDD] (5.97)
People Who Live in Glass Houses (selections)
K. Brion (cnd), Razumovsky SO—The Champagnes; The Rhine Wines; White Rock & Psyches; The Whiskies-Scotch, Irish, Bourbon & Rye; Convention of the Cordials, Wines & Whiskies; March *(rec Bratislava, Slovak Republic, Oct 27 & 30, 1995)* ("Vol. 1, On Stage") † Bride Elect (sels); El Capitan (sels); Our Flirtations (sels) NXIN (American Classics) ▲ 8559008 [DDD] (5.97)
Piano Music
A. Mandel (pno)—Presidential Polonaise; Moonlight on the Potomac Waltzes, Op. 3 (1901)—se PREM ▲ 1021 [DDD] (16.97)
Semper Fidelis (march) for Band (ca 1888)
R. Bernat (cnd), River City Brass Band † Belle of Chicago; El Capitan (sels); Liberty Bell; Manhattan Beach; Stars & Stripes Forever; Washington Post; E. Bowman:12th St. Rag; H. Fillmore:Marches (misc); S. Joplin:Maple Leaf Rag; G. Rossini:Guillaume Tell (ov) RCBB ▲ 192
S. Koussevitzky (cnd), Boston SO *(rec 1946)* ("Koussevitzky Conducts American Music") † Stars & Stripes Forever; A. Copland:Appalachian Spring (suite); Lincoln Portrait; Salón México; R. Thompson:Testament of Freedom BCS ▲ 50 [ADD] (16.97)
Songs
J. Guyer (sop), M. Wilson (sgr), D. Buck (sgr)—I've made my plans for the summer; Love that lives forever; Valse song; Oh, ye lilies white; Girls who have loved; There's a merry brown thrush; Fighting race; Serenade in Seville; My own, my Geraldine; Sweet Miss Industry; I wonder; You cannot tell how old they are by looking at...; Forever & a day; Sweetheart, I'm waiting; Blue Ridge, I'm coming back to you (1917); Love's radiant hour; Rare old fellow; Stars & Stripes Forever ("Concert, Theater & Parlor Songs") PREM ▲ 1011 [DDD] (16.97)

SOUSA, JOHN PHILIP (cont.)
Stars and Stripes Forever (march) for Band (1897)
R. Bernat (cnd), River City Brass Band † Belle of Chicago; El Capitan (sels); Liberty Bell; Manhattan Beach; Semper Fidelis; Washington Post; E. Bowman:12th St. Rag; H. Fillmore:Marches (misc); S. Joplin:Maple Leaf Rag; G. Rossini:Guillaume Tell (ov) RCBB ▲ 192
K. Brion (cnd) ("The Only American Album You'll Ever Need") † A. Copland:Appalachian Spring (suite); Fanfare for the Common Man; Rodeo (sels); G. Gershwin:American in Paris; Rhap in Blue; Grofé:Grand Canyon Suite DLS ▲ 1606 [DDD] (10.97)
H. Hanson (cnd), Eastman-Rochester Orch *(rec Rochester, NY, May 8, 1962)* † G. Gershwin:Con Pno; Cuban Ov; Rhap in Blue MRCR ▲ 34341 (11.97)
V. Horowitz (pno) [arr V. Horowitz for pno] *(rec 1945)* † Liszt:Liebesträume, S.541; Moszkowski:Etude de virtuosité, Op. 72; D. Scarlatti:Sons Kbd; P. Tchaikovsky:Con 1 Pno, Op. 23 RY (Radio Years) ▲ 92 (16.97)
S. Koussevitzky (cnd), Boston SO *(rec 1946)* ("Koussevitzky Conducts American Music") † Semper Fidelis; A. Copland:Appalachian Spring (suite); Lincoln Portrait; Salón México; R. Thompson:Testament of Freedom BCS ▲ 50 [ADD] (16.97)
C. MacDonally (cnd), West Point Military Band ("Sousa & American Marches") † Marches & Dances TUXE ▲ 5032 (10.97)
Three Quotations (suite) for Orchestra (1895)
R. Kapp (cnd) ("Sousa for Orchestra") † Dwellers in the Western World ESSY ▲ 1003 [DDD] (16.97)
The Thunderer (march) for Band (1889)
R. Bernat (cnd), River City Brass Band † Invictus; Nobles of the Mystic Shrine; H. Fillmore:Marches (misc); E. F. Goldman:On the Mall; Langford:Carnival Day; E. Tomlinson:Best Foot Forward; M. Wilson:British Grenadiers; Men of Harlech; Seventy-Six Trombones; H. C. Work:Colonel Bogey March; Marching through Georgia RCBB ▲ 191
The Washington Post (march) for Band (1889)
R. Bernat (cnd), River City Brass Band † Belle of Chicago; El Capitan (sels); Liberty Bell; Manhattan Beach; Semper Fidelis; Stars & Stripes Forever; E. Bowman:12th St. Rag; H. Fillmore:Marches (misc); S. Joplin:Maple Leaf Rag; G. Rossini:Guillaume Tell (ov) RCBB ▲ 192
SOUSTER, TIM (1943-
Echoes for Brass Band & Live Electronics
A. Barclay (perc), A. Powell (elec), J. Wallace (cnd), Desford Colliery Caterpillar Band, J. Wallace (cnd), Wallace Collection † Equalisation; Heavy Reductions; La Marche; Rabbit Heaven DOY ▲ 73 (16.97)
Equalisation for Brass Quintet & Live Electronics
A. Powell (elec), J. Wallace (cnd), Desford Colliery Caterpillar Band, J. Wallace (cnd), Wallace Collection † Echoes; Heavy Reductions; La Marche; Rabbit Heaven DOY ▲ 73 (16.97)
Heavy Reductions for Tuba, Voice & Tape
R. Haggart (tuba) † Echoes; Equalisation; La Marche; Rabbit Heaven DOY ▲ 73 (16.97)
La Marche for Brass Quintet
J. Wallace (cnd), Desford Colliery Caterpillar Band, J. Wallace (cnd), Wallace Collection † Echoes; Equalisation; Heavy Reductions; Rabbit Heaven DOY ▲ 73 (16.97)
Rabbit Heaven for Brass Quintet & Percussion
A. Barclay (perc), A. Powell (elec), J. Wallace (cnd), Desford Colliery Caterpillar Band, J. Wallace (cnd), Wallace Collection † Echoes; Equalisation; Heavy Reductions; La Marche DOY ▲ 73 (16.97)
SOWANDE, FELA (1905-1987)
African Suite for Strings (1944)
M. Bernardi (cnd), CBC Vancouver SO † M. Forsyth:Sketches from Natal; P. Maurice:Tableaux de Provence; D. Milhaud:Globe-trotter, Op. 358 CBC (SM 5000) ▲ 5135 [DDD] (16.97)
SOWASH, RICK (1950-
Anecdotes & Reflections for Violin, Clarinet, Cello & Piano
C. Olzenak (cl), Mirecourt Trio † Daweswood Suite; Street Suite GAS ▲ 285 (16.97)
Daweswood Suite for Violin, Clarinet, Cello & Piano
C. Olzenak (cl), Mirecourt Trio † Anecdotes & Reflections; Street Suite GAS ▲ 285 (16.97)
Fantasia on "Shenandoah" for Guitar & String Quartet (1990)
J. Pell (gtr), Shelburne String Quartet † MacDowell:Con 2 Pno, Op. 23; New England Idyls, Op. 62; V. Weigl:New England Suite GAS ▲ 236 (16.97)
Piano Trios
Mirecourt Trio—No. 1, "4 Seasons in Bellville" (1977); No. 2, "Orientale & Galop" (1980); No. 3, "A Christmas Divert" (1983); No. 4; rev 1989 GAS ▲ 254 (16.97)
Street Suite for Violin & Clarinet (1976)
K. Goldsmith (vn), C. Olzenak (cl) † Anecdotes & Reflections; Daweswood Suite GAS ▲ 285 (16.97)
SOWERBY, LEO (1895-1968)
All on a Summer's Day (tone poem) for Orchestra, H.325 (1954)
P. Freeman (cnd), Czech National SO *(rec 1996-97)* † Concert Ov, H.251; Passacaglia, Interlude & Fugue, H.207; Sym 2 CED ▲ 39 [DDD] (16.97)
American Pieces (2) for Violin & Piano, H.174 (1923)
R. Murray (vn), G. Quillman (pno) *(rec Richmond, VA, Aug & Oct 1994)* ("Leo Sowerby: Music for Violin & Piano") † Folksong Arrs; Son Vn; Son Vn (1922), H.165; Son Vn (1959), H.367 PREM ▲ 1049 [DDD] (16.97)
Canon, Chacony & Fugue for Organ (1949)
D. Chalmers (org) ("Leo Sowerby: American Master of Sacred Song") † Choral Music; Festival Musick; Org Music GLRI 2-▲ 16 [DDD] (30.97)
Choral Music
D. Chalmers (org), J. Jordan, Jr. (org), E. C. Patterson (cnd) , Gloriae Dei Cantores—Great Is the Lord; Hear My Cry, O God; The Lord Is My Shepherd; How Long Wilt Thou Forget Me; Turn Thou to Thy God; Whoso Dwelleth; An Angel Stood by the Altar ("Leo Sowerby: American Master of Sacred Song") † Canon, Chacony & Fugue; Festival Musick; Org Music GLRI 2-▲ 16 [DDD] (30.97)
L. King (org), L. King (cnd) , Trinity Church Choir Broadway & Wall Street—I Will Lift Up Mine Eyes; I was glad; O Light, from age to age; Benedicte Omnia Opera; Thy word is a lantern; Magnificat & Nunc Dimittis in D; And they drew nigh; Come, Holy Ghost; Eternal light; Org Works—Arioso; Requiescat in Pace GOT ▲ 49034 [DDD] (17.97)
T. Weisflog (org), W. Ferris (cnd), William Ferris Chorale—Throne of God, H.341 [w. Composer Festival Orch]; Interlude Org, H.303; Fanfare No. 3, H.335/3; Thy Word Is a Lantern unto My Feet, H.405; Ad te levavi animeam meam, H.356; God Mounts His Throne, H.436; Come, Risen Lord, H.398 *(rec live, 1986-95)* ("The Throne of God") ALBA ▲ 232 [DDD] (16.97)
Concert Overture for Orchestra, H.251 (1941)
P. Freeman (cnd), Czech National SO *(rec 1996-97)* † All on a Summer's Day, H.325; Passacaglia, Interlude & Fugue, H.207; Sym 2 CED ▲ 39 [DDD] (16.97)
Concerto for Harp & Small Orchestra (1916-19)
S. Hartman (hp), J. Bolle (cnd), Monadnock Music Festival Orch † Rhap; Serenade Str Qt; Songs; Songs of Resignation GAS ▲ 315 [DDD] (16.97)
Concerto for Organ & Strings, "Classic" (1944)
D. Mulbury (org), J. Welsh (cnd), Fairfield Orch *(rec St. Bartholomew's Church New York City, May 3-5, 1994)* ("Works for Organ & Orchestra") † Festival Musick; Medieval Poem; Pageant of Autumn Org MARC ▲ 8223725 [DDD] (13.97)
Dialogue for Piano & Organ (1967)
J. Culp (pno), L. Maycher (org) *(rec 1st Presbyterian Church Kilgore, TX, Oct 21, 1994)* ("Organ Music of Leo Sowerby") RAVN ▲ 310 [DDD] (17.97)
Fantasy for Flute Stops for Organ
C. Crozier (org) † Requiescat in pace; Sym Org DLS ▲ 3075 [DDD] (14.97)
Festival Musick for 2 Trumpets, 2 Trombones, Timpani & Organ (1953)
C. Albach (tpt), S. Radcliff (tpt), T. Hutchinson (trbn), J. Caswell (trbn), D. Mulbury (org), D. Haskins (timp), J. Welsh (cnd), Fairfield Orch *(rec St. Bartholomew's Church New York City, May 5, 1994)* ("Works for Organ & Orchestra") † Con Org; Medieval Poem; Pageant of Autumn Org MARC ▲ 8223725 [DDD] (13.97)
J. Jordan, Jr. (org), Gloriae Dei Brass Ensemble ("Leo Sowerby: American Master of Sacred Song") † Canon, Chacony & Fugue; Choral Music; Org Music GLRI 2-▲ 16 [DDD] (30.97)
Folksong Arrangements
R. Murray (vn), G. Quillman (pno) ("Leo Sowerby: Music for Violin & Piano") † American Pieces, H.174; Son Vn; Son Vn (1922), H.165; Son Vn (1959), H.367 PREM ▲ 1049 [DDD] (16.97)
Forsaken of Man (cantata) for solo Voices, Organ & Chorus (1939)
W. Ferris (cnd), William Ferris Chorale, A. Clark (sop), J. Compton (alt), T. Potter (bass), P. Grizzell (bass), M. Greenberg (bass), B. Hall (sgr), J. Vorassi (sgr), T. Weisflog (org) *(rec St. Thomas the Apostle Church Chicago, IL, June 1990)* NWW ▲ 80394 [AAD] (16.97)

SOWERBY, LEO (cont.)

Medieval Poem for Organ & Orchestra (1926)
D. Craighead (org), J. Welsh (cnd), Fairfield Orch *(rec St. Bartholomew's Church New York City, May 3-5, 1994)* ("Works for Organ & Orchestra") † Con Org; Festival Musick; Pageant of Autumn Org
MARC ▲ 8223725 [DDD] (13.97)

Music of Sowerby
Roberts Wesleyan Brass Ensemble *(Fanfares, H.335/1-3)*, P. Shewan (tpt), J. Bobb (org) *(Fant Tpt & Org, H.380)*, R. Shewan (cnd), Roberts Wesleyan College Chorale *(Come, Risen Lord, H.398B; Psalm 84, H.412; A Liturgy of Hope, H.135; Psalm 124, H.463 [w. James Bobb (org)]; Psalm 121, H.147; The Risen Lord, H.144; The Ark of the Covenant)* ("I Will Lift up Mine Eyes")
ALBA ▲ 238 [DDD] (16.97)

Organ Music
D. Chalmers (org)—Carillon; Arioso; Prelude, "Were You There?"; Bright, Blithe & Brisk *(rec Worcester, MA)* ("Leo Sowerby: American Master of Sacred Song") † Canon, Chacony & Fugue; Choral Music; Festival Musick
GLRI 2-▲ 16 [DDD] (30.97)

Pageant of Autumn for Organ (1931)
D. Craighead (org) *(rec St. Bartholomew's Church New York City, May 4, 1994)* ("Works for Organ & Orchestra") † Con Org; Festival Musick; Medieval Poem
MARC ▲ 8223725 [DDD] (13.97)

Passacaglia, Interlude & Fugue for Orchestra, H.207 (1931-32)
P. Freeman (cnd), Czech National SO *(rec 1996-97)* † All on a Summer's Day, H.325; Concert Ov, H.251; Sym 2
CED ▲ 39 [DDD] (16.97)

Passacaglia for Piano (1942)
G. Quillman (pno) † Son Pno; Suite Pno
NWW ▲ 376 [AAD] (16.97)

Piano Music
M. Halliday (pno)—Folk-tunes (3) from Somerset, H.113; Florida Suite, H.197; From the Northland, H.167; Money Musk, H.145A; Fisherman's Tune, H.161; The Irish Washerwoman, H.115A; L'Amor di quei due, H.168 *(rec New York, Oct 1995)* ("Piano Music of Leo Sowerby")
ALBA ▲ 226 [DDD] (16.97)

Requiescat in pace for Organ (1920)
C. Crozier (org) † Fant for Fl Stops; Sym Org
DLS ▲ 3075 [DDD] (14.97)

Rhapsody for Chamber Orchestra (1922)
J. Bolle (cnd), Monadnock Music Festival Orch † Con Hp; Serenade Str Qt; Songs; Songs of Resignation
GAS ▲ 315 [DDD] (16.97)

Serenade in G for String Quartet (1917)
Amernet String Quartet † Con Hp; Rhap; Songs; Songs of Resignation
GAS ▲ 315 [DDD] (16.97)

Sonata for Piano (1948; rev 1963)
G. Quillman (pno) † Passacaglia Pno; Suite Pno
NWW ▲ 376 [AAD] (16.97)

Sonata in B♭ for Violin & Piano, H.165 (1922)
R. Murray (vn), G. Quillman (pno) *(rec Richmond, VA, Aug & Oct 1994)* ("Leo Sowerby: Music for Violin & Piano") † American Pieces, H.174; Folksong Arrs; Son Vn; Son Vn (1959), H.367
PREM ▲ 1049 [DDD] (16.97)

Sonata in D for Violin & Piano, H.367 (1959)
R. Murray (vn), G. Quillman (pno) *(rec Richmond, VA, Aug & Oct 1994)* ("Leo Sowerby: Music for Violin & Piano") † American Pieces, H.174; Folksong Arrs; Son Vn; Son Vn (1922), H.165
PREM ▲ 1049 [DDD] (16.97)

Sonata in A for Violin & Piano, "Fantasy Sonata" (1944)
R. Murray (vn), G. Quillman (pno) ("Leo Sowerby: Music for Violin & Piano") † American Pieces, H.174; Folksong Arrs; Son Vn (1922), H.165; Son Vn (1959), H.367
PREM ▲ 1049 [DDD] (16.97)

Sonatina for Organ (1944)
B. K. Tidwell (org) *(rec 100 Rank Schantz Organ, Cleveland Heights, OH)* † Sym 4; G. Bales:Petite Suite; Hollins:Trumpet Minuet; H. Howells:Siciliano; Paine:Concert Vars Austrian Hymn; Roger-Ducasse:Pastoral Org; Vierne:Pièces de fantaisie
ARK ▲ 6157 [DDD] (16.97)

Songs
D. Fortunato (mez), V. Macchia-Kadlubkiewicz (vn), T. Buskirk (vn), V. Christensen (va), M. Curry (vc)—Premonition; Kisses; Midnight; Reassurance; Adventure [all texts L. E. Thomas] † Con Hp; Rhap; Serenade Str Qt; Songs of Resignation
GAS ▲ 315 [DDD] (16.97)

R. Osborne (b-bar), M. Halliday (pno)—Songs on Poems of John Masefield (3); Songs on Poems of John Galsworthy (3); American Folksong Arrs (3); Songs for Donna Harrison (3); British Folksong Arrs (2); Songs on Poems of Jeanne Delamarter (2); Late Songs; From the Hillcrest (2) *(rec NY, Mar 1995)* ("Songs of Leo Sowerby")
ALBA ▲ 196 [DDD] (16.97)

Songs of Resignation for Mezzo-Soprano, Violin, Clarinet & Piano [text Chinese 8th cent B.C.] (1948)
D. Fortunato (mez), V. Macchia-Kadlubkiewicz (vn), S. Jackson (cl), A. D. Mare (pno) † Con Hp; Rhap; Serenade Str Qt; Songs
GAS ▲ 315 [DDD] (16.97)

Suite for Piano (1959)
G. Quillman (pno) † Passacaglia Pno; Son Pno
NWW ▲ 376 [AAD] (16.97)

Symphony No. 2 in b, H.188 (1927-28)
P. Freeman (cnd), Chicago Sinfonietta *(rec 1996-97)* † All on a Summer's Day, H.325; Concert Ov, H.251; Passacaglia, Interlude & Fugue, H.207
CED ▲ 39 [DDD] (16.97)

Symphony No. 4 in G (1931)
B. K. Tidwell (org) *(rec 100 Rank Schantz Organ, Cleveland Heights, OH)* † Sonatina for Org; G. Bales:Petite Suite; Hollins:Trumpet Minuet; H. Howells:Siciliano; Paine:Concert Vars Austrian Hymn; Roger-Ducasse:Pastoral Org; Vierne:Pièces de fantaisie
ARK ▲ 6157 [DDD] (16.97)

Symphony in G for Organ (1930)
C. Crozier (org) † Fant for Fl Stops; Requiescat in pace
DLS ▲ 3075 [DDD] (14.97)

Tone Poems
P. Freeman (cnd), Czech National SO—Comes Autumn Time; Prairie; Theme in Yellow; From the Northland *(rec Prague, Oct 1996)* ("Prairie: Tone Poems by Leo Sowerby")
CED ▲ 33 [DDD] (16.97)

Trio in c# for Piano, Violin & Cello (1911)
La Musica Gioiosa Trio † Trio Pno (1953)
NWW ▲ 365 [AAD] (16.97)

Trio for Piano, Violin & Cello (1953)
La Musica Gioiosa Trio † Trio Pno (1911)
NWW ▲ 365 [AAD] (16.97)

SPADINA, ANTONIO (1822-?)

Duetto Concertante on Motifs from Bellini's *Norma* for Clarinet & Piano
B. Röthlisberger (cl), S. Andres (pno) ("Il Clarinetto all'Opera") † L. Bassi:Divertimento on themes from Donizetti's La F; Cavallini:Adagio sentimentale; Fant on Motifs; Labanchi:Fant on Verdi's Aida; Lovreglio:Fant da concerto on Motifs of Verdi's La tra; G. Panizza:Ballabile
GALL ▲ 916 [DDD] (18.97)

SPAHLINGER, MATHIAS (1944-

Apo Do for String Quartet, "von hier" (1982)
Arditti String Quartet ("From Germany") † Y. Höller:Antiphon; R. H. Platz:Qt Strs, "Zeitstrahl"; W. Zimmermann:Festina lente
DISQ ▲ 782036 [DDD] (18.97)

SPARKE, PHILIP (1951-

Between the Moon & Mexico for Brass Ensemble
A. Withington (cnd), Brighouse & Rastrick Band † Miniatures Brass Band; M. Ball:Midsummer Music; Downie:Capriccio; Fernie:Caledonian Journey; Finnegan:Volga Boatman; N. Hefti:L'il Darlin'; Prima:Music of Prima
DOY 2-▲ 87 (24.97)

Dance Movements (4) for Wind Orchestra (1996)
E. Corporon (cnd), North Texas Wind Sym *(rec Univ of Georgia, Feb 1997)* ("Wind Dances") † J. Harbison:Olympic Dances; P. Hart:Circus Ring; McTee:Soundings; Schwantner:In Evening's Stillness
KLAV (Wind Recording Project) ▲ 11084 [DDD] (18.97)

Harmony Music for Brass Ensemble
H. Snell (cnd), Manger Musikklag † London Ov; Pantomine; Partita; Vars on an Enigma; Vikings
DOY ▲ 49 (16.97)

London Overture for Brass Ensemble
H. Snell (cnd), Manger Musikklag † Harmony Music; Pantomine; Partita; Vars on an Enigma; Vikings
DOY ▲ 49 (16.97)

Miniatures (3) for Brass Band
A. White (cnd), Oldham Brass 97 † Between the Moon & Mexico; M. Ball:Midsummer Music; Downie:Capriccio; Fernie:Caledonian Journey; Finnegan:Volga Boatman; N. Hefti:L'il Darlin'; Prima:Music of Prima
DOY 2-▲ 87 (24.97)

Pantomine for Brass Ensemble
H. Snell (cnd), Manger Musikklag † Harmony Music; London Ov; Partita; Vars on an Enigma; Vikings
DOY ▲ 49 (16.97)

Partita for Brass Ensemble
B. Sagstad (cnd), Fodens Band † Harmony Music; London Ov; Pantomine; Vars on an Enigma; Vikings
DOY ▲ 49 (16.97)

SPARKE, PHILIP (cont.)

A Pittsburgh Symphony
D. Colwell (cnd), River City Brass Band † R. Bernat:Dunlap's Creek; J. Curnow:River City Suite; J. W. Jenkins:Gateway West; Heartland
RCBB ▲ 198 (16.97)

Variations on an Enigma for Brass Ensemble
B. Sagstad (cnd), Manger Musikklag † Harmony Music; London Ov; Pantomine; Partita; Vikings
DOY ▲ 49 (16.97)

Vikings for Brass Ensemble
B. Sagstad (cnd), Manger Musikklag † Harmony Music; London Ov; Pantomine; Partita; Vars on an Enigma
DOY ▲ 49 (16.97)

SPASSOV, IVAN (1934-1996)

Ashinka for Chorus
artists unknown *(rec Sofia Bulgaria, 1995)*
ERTO ▲ 42034 [DDD] (16.97)

Easter Music for Christ's Sufferings, Death & Resurrection for solo Voices, Choir & Organ (1994)
K. Zhekova (sop), G. Lazarov (bass), S. Byulbyulian (spkr), A. Toromanova (org), Women's Chamber Choir *(rec Apr 17, 1995)* ("Contemporary Bulgarian Composers, Vol. 1") † Miserere; Sanctification of the Heavenly Space
GEGA ▲ 251 (live) (16.97)

Miserere for solo Voices, Orchestra & Chorus [after Latin cult text]
T. Genova (sop), D. Lozanova (sop), L. Ilieva (sop), V. Mircheva (mez), P. Parvanov (cnd), Plovdiv Secondary School of Music CO, I. Dimitrov (cnd), Polyphonia Chamber a Cappella Choir *(rec Apr 21, 1997)* ("Contemporary Bulgarian Composers, Vol. 1") † Easter Music for Christ's Sufferings; Sanctification of the Heavenly Space *([LAT] text)*
GEGA ▲ 251 (live) (16.97)

Sanctification of the Heavenly Space for Orchestra (1994)
B. Papazian (cnd), Orchestral Ensemble *(rec Apr 9, 1995)* ("Contemporary Bulgarian Composers, Vol. 1") † Easter Music for Christ's Sufferings; Miserere
GEGA ▲ 251 (live) (16.97)

Triptych (songs) for Chorus [texts by Nikolai Liliev]
T. Pavlovitch (cnd), Sofia Chamber Choir † K. Iliev:Quiet Songs; Kolarov:Autumn Was Coming; Winter; Pipkov:Subdued Songs; T. Popov:Winter Reflections; A. Tanev:Let the Maiden Be Mine; Our Father; We Sing Thee; Tekeliev:Dostonio est; Reverie *([ENG,BUL] texts)*
GEGA ▲ 125 (16.97)

SPASSOV, THEODOSII (20th cent)

Music of Spassov
T. Spassov (sgr), S. Yankulov (dr) *(Old Wives' Tales) (rec Jan 1998)*, T. Spassov (sgr), M. Leviev (pno) *(Paleontologomania) (rec June 1993)*, T. Spassov (fl), S. Yankulov (perc) *(Gyurkata) (rec Jan 1998)*, T. Spassov (fl), A. Donchev (pno), H. Yotsov (dr) *(Little Something out of Nothing) (rec Mar 1992)*, T. Spassov (fl), G. Donchev (db), R. Toskov (pno), S. Yankulov (dr) *(For Nicky) (rec Feb 1997)*, S. Onikian (sgr), T. Spassov (fl), N. Dragnev (gtr), D. Shanov (b gtr) *(Christmas Eve with Bells)* ("Bratimene") † Anonymous:Pendata; Rada; Barnev:Horo with Kaval; Samba Rachenitsa; Ellington:Satin Doll; V. Nikolov:Song About the Couscous; Toskov:Songs
GEGA ▲ 132 [DDD] (16.97)

SPEER, DANIEL (1636-1707)

Grund-richtiger ... Unterricht der musicalischen Kunst (selections) (1687)
G. Kent (org), E. H. Tarr (cnd), Eklund's Baroque Ensemble [period instr] *(rec Gothenburg, Sweden, Jul 14-16, 1980)* ("Courtly trumpet ensemble music by Diabelli, Speer, Biber, Keller and Anonymous") † Musikalisch-türkischer Eulenspiegel (sels); Anonymous:Charamela real (sels), No. 51; Charamela real (sels), No. 52; Charamela real (sels), No. 54; H. I. Biber:Son Sancti Polycarpi, KRa; Diabelli:Aufzüge (processional fanfares) (sels); Keller:Processional Fanfares (6)
BIS ▲ 217 [AAD] (17.97)

Musikalisch-türkischer Eulenspiegel (selections) (1688)
G. Kent (org), E. H. Tarr (cnd), Eklund's Baroque Ensemble [period instr] *(rec Gothenburg, Sweden, Jul 14-16, 1980)* ("Courtly trumpet ensemble music by Diabelli, Speer, Biber, Keller and Anonymous") † Grund-richtiger ... Unterricht (sels); Anonymous:Charamela real (sels), No. 51; Charamela real (sels), No. 52; Charamela real (sels), No. 54; H. I. Biber:Son Sancti Polycarpi, KRa; Diabelli:Aufzüge (processional fanfares) (sels); Keller:Processional Fanfares (6)
BIS ▲ 217 [AAD] (17.97)

SPELLER, FRANK (1938-

Choral Music
F. Speller (org), P. Gardner (cnd) , Univ of Texas Concert Chorale—Mass of St. Louis; Gloria Patri [both chorus & org]; Hail Mary [chorus a cappella] † Org Music
ALBA ▲ 49 [DDD] (9.97)

Organ Music
F. Speller (org)—Toccata, "The Majesty of Christ"; 4 Chorale Preludes; Prelude & Fugue in A, "Ecumenical"; Psalm 19, "The heavens declare the glory of God"; 4 Biblical Dances; Te Deum *(rec Visser-Rowland tracker Org Univ of TX-Austin)* † Choral Music
ALBA ▲ 49 [DDD] (9.97)

SPERGER, JOHANN (1750-1812)

Concertino for Flute, Viola & Double Bass, T.4
H. Fukai (va), K. Trumpf (db), A. Jonet (fl), R. Bader (cnd), Kusatsu Festival Orch ("Selected Works") † Qt Db
CAMA ▲ 2064 [DDD] (18.97)

Concerto in D for Trumpet, 2 Oboes, 2 Horns, Strings & Continuo (1779)
L. Güttler (tpt), C. Schornsheim (hpd), M. Pommer (cnd), Leipzig New Bach Collegium Musicum *(rec Dresden, Germany, May 1986)* ("Classical Trumpet Concertos") † Molter:Con 3 Tpt; L. Otto:Con Tpt; F. X. Richter:Con Tpt
CAPO ▲ 10051 [DDD] (11.97)

Quartet in D for Double Bass, Flute, Viola & Cello
J. Gutmann (va), K. Segoe (vc), K. Trumpf (db), C. K. Kim (fl) ("Selected Works") † Con Fl Va, T.4
CAMA ▲ 2064 [DDD] (18.97)

Sonatas for Viola & Double Bass
F. Beyer (va), P. Breuer (db)—No. 1 in D; No. 3 in D *(rec Munster, Germany, Sept 8-9, 1975)* † Dittersdorf:Son Va
ADG ▲ 91009 [ADD] (11.97)

H. Fukai (va), G. Dzwiza (db) ("Rarities for Bass Strings, Vol. 2") † Beethoven:Duet Va Vc, WoO 32; M. Haydn:Divert for Va, Vc & Db; B. Romberg:Trios Va, Op. 38; G. Rossini:Duet Vc & Db
SIGM ▲ 4600 [ADD] (17.97)

SPETH, JOHANNES (1664-ca 1720)

Organ Music
R. G. Freiberger (org), I. Melchersson (org) ("Complete Organ Works")
MDG 2-▲ 6060727 (35.97)

SPIEGEL, LAURIE (1945-

Electronic Music
artists unknown—Cavis Muris ("CDCM Computer Music Series, Vol. 13") † L. Austin:Barbara:The Name, The Sounds, The Music; J. La Barbara:Albero della foglie azzure; Pope:Kombination XI
CENT ▲ 2166 (16.97)

artists unknown—Appalachian Grove *(rec Murray Hill, NJ)* ("Women in Electronic Music - 1977") † R. Anderson:Electronic Music; L. Anderson:Electronic Music; J. M. Beyer:Electronic Music; A. Lockwood:Electronic Music; P. Oliveros:Electronic Music; M. Roberts:Electronic Music
CRI ▲ 728 [ADD] (16.97)

SPIERS, COLIN (20th cent)

Elegy & Toccata for Piano (1980)
J. Carrigan (pno) *(rec Univ of Queensland, Australia)* ("But I Want the Harmonica: Australian Contemporary Piano Music") † Broadstock:Aureole 4; Conyngham:ppp; S. Greenbaum:But I Want the Harmonica; Hiscocks:Piper at the Gates of Dawn; Kats-Chernin:Purple Prelude; Sabin:Another Look at Autumn
VOXA ▲ 23 [DDD] (18.97)

SPIES, CLAUDIO (1925-

Music of Spies
N. Watson (bar), M. Kampmeier (pno) *(Dylan Thomas' Lament & a Complementary Envoi)*, A. May (vn), E. McNutt (fl) *(Insieme [1994])*, A. Feinberg (pno) *(Bagatelle; 4 Dādivas [1977-80])*, C. Whittlesey (sop), J. Arnold (alt), D. Ronis (ten), J. Opalach (bass), H. Martin (pno), C. Spies (cnd) *(5 Sonnet-Settings [1976-77]; Animula Vagula, Blandula [1964])*, B. Greene (E hn/ob), M. Sullivan (E hn/ob) *(Beisammen [1995])*, S. Rhodes (va), R. Miller (hpd/pno) *(Viopiacem Duo for Va & Kbd Instrs [1965])*, R. Miller (pno) *(Impromptu for Pno [1963])*, C. Whittlesey (sop) *(Songs (3) on Poems by May Swenson [1969]) (rec New York, 1979-80)*
CRI ▲ 718 [ADD] (16.97)

SPINACINO, FRANCESCO (fl 1507)

Lute Music
C. Wilson (lt)—Ricercares; Fants; plus others ("Fantasia de mon triste: Renaissance Lute Virtuosi") † Capriola:Lt Music; Francesco Canova da Milano:Lt Music
MENO ▲ 1025 (20.97)

Ricercare for Chamber Ensemble
Circa 1500 Ensemble [ITA] *(rec North Finchley, London, England, Sept 1983)* ("Renaissance Music from the Courts of Mantua & Ferrara") † Anonymous:Calata; Chui dicese non l'amare; Pavana, La cornetta; Saltarello, Baxela un tratto; Saltarello, El marchese di Saluzzo; Se mai per maraveglia; Cara:Songs; Cato:Vocal Music; E. Romano:Cantus cum tenor; Tromboncino:Music of Tromboncino
CHN ▲ 524 [DDD] (16.97)

SPIVAKOVSKY, MICHAEL (1920-1983)

Concerto for Harmonica & Orchestra
T. Reilly (hmc), C. Gerhardt (cnd), Munich RSO † M. Arnold:Con Hmc, Op. 46; R. Farnon:Prelude & Dance; J. Moody:Toledo; H. Villa-Lobos:Con Hmc
CHN ▲ 9248 [DDD] (16.97)

SPOHR, LOUIS [LUDWIG] (1784-1859)

Adagio in F for Cello & Piano, Op. 115
Pallas Trio *(rec Alter Reistadel, Neumarkt, Germany, Aug 29-Sept 1, 1995)* ("Piano Chamber Music") † Rondo brillant Vn, Op. 51; Trio 2 Pno, Op. 123; Trio 5 Pno, Op. 142 MPH ▲ 56822 [DDD] (15.97)

Concerto No. 1 in c for Clarinet & Orchestra, Op. 26 (1808)
E. Brunner (cl), H. Stadlmair (cnd), Bamberg SO † Con 2 Cl, Op. 57; Vars on a Theme from Alruna TUD ▲ 7009 (16.97)
E. Johnson (cl), G. Schwarz (cnd), English CO † Crusell:Con 3 Cl, Op. 11; C. M. von Weber:Con 2 Cl, Op. 74 ASV ▲ 659 (16.97)
K. Leister (cl), R. Frühbeck de Burgos (cnd), Stuttgart RSO † Con 4 Cl ORF ▲ 88101 (18.97)
E. Ottensamer (cl), J. Wildner (cnd), Slovak State PO Košice *(rec House of Arts Košice, Sept 16-19, 1991)* † Con 3 Cl; Potpourri, Op. 80 NXIN ▲ 550688 [DDD] (5.97)

Concerto No. 2 in E♭ for Clarinet & Orchestra, Op. 57 (1810)
E. Brunner (cl), H. Stadlmair (cnd), Bamberg SO † Con 1 Cl, Op. 26; Vars on a Theme from Alruna TUD ▲ 7009 (16.97)
K. Leister (cl), R. Frühbeck de Burgos (cnd), Stuttgart RSO † Con 3 Cl ORF ▲ 88201 (18.97)
E. Ottensamer (cl), J. Wildner (cnd), Slovak RSO Bratislava *(rec Concert Hall of the Slovak Radio Bratislava, Jan 31-Feb 4, 1994)* † Con 4 Cl; Fant & Vars on Danzi, Op. 81 NXIN ▲ 550689 [DDD] (5.97)
W. Pencz (cl), H. Schneidt (cnd), Southwest German RSO Baden-Baden † S. Mayr:Con bergamasco AMAT ▲ 9102 [DDD] (17.97)

Concerto No. 3 in f for Clarinet & Orchestra (1821)
E. Brummer (cl), H. Stadlmair (cnd), Bamberg SO † Con 4 Cl; Potpourri, Op. 80 TUD ▲ 7043 (16.97)
J. Denman (cl), R. Bernhardt (cnd), Royal PO † Con 4 Cl; Potpourri, Op. 80; Vars on a Theme from Alruna IMAS (Masters) ▲ 6600082 (16.97)
K. Leister (cl), R. Frühbeck de Burgos (cnd), Stuttgart RSO † Con 2 Cl, Op. 57 ORF ▲ 88201 (18.97)
E. Ottensamer (cl), J. Wildner (cnd), Slovak State PO Košice *(rec House of Arts Košice, Sept 16-19, 1991)* † Con 1 Cl, Op. 26; Potpourri, Op. 80 NXIN ▲ 550688 [DDD] (5.97)

Concerto No. 4 in e for Clarinet & Orchestra (1828)
E. Brummer (cl), H. Stadlmair (cnd), Bamberg SO † Con 3 Cl; Potpourri, Op. 80 TUD ▲ 7043 (16.97)
J. Denman (cl), R. Bernhardt (cnd), Royal PO † Con 3 Cl; Potpourri, Op. 80; Vars on a Theme from Alruna IMAS (Masters) ▲ 6600082 (16.97)
T. King (cl), A. Francis (cnd), English CO † W. A. Mozart:Con Cl, K.622 MER ▲ 84022 (16.97)
K. Leister (cl), R. Frühbeck de Burgos (cnd), Stuttgart RSO † Con 1 Cl, Op. 26 ORF ▲ 88101 (18.97)
E. Ottensamer (cl), J. Wildner (cnd), Slovak RSO Bratislava *(rec Concert Hall of the Slovak Radio Bratislava, Jan 31-Feb 4, 1994)* † Con 2 Cl, Op. 57; Fant & Vars on Danzi, Op. 81 NXIN ▲ 550689 [DDD] (5.97)

Concerto in a for String Quartet & Orchestra, Op. 131 (1845)
J. LeRoux (cnd), San Francisco Ballet Orch, Lark String Quartet *(rec Marin County, CA, May 12-14, 1998)* † E. Elgar:Intro & Allegro, Op. 47; G. F. Handel:Concerti grossi, Op. 6; Schoenberg:Con Str Qt ARA ▲ 6723 [DDD] (16.97)

Concerto No. 2 in d for Violin & Orchestra, Op. 2 (1804)
U. Hoelscher (vn), C. Fröhlich (cnd), Berlin RSO † Con 5 Vn, Op. 17 CPO ▲ 999067 [DDD] (14.97)

Concerto No. 3 in C for Violin & Orchestra, Op. 7 (1806)
U. Hoelscher (vn), C. Fröhlich (cnd), Berlin RSO † Con 12 Vn, Op. 79; Con 6 Vn, Op. 28 CPO ▲ 999145 [DDD] (14.97)

Concerto No. 4 in b for Violin & Orchestra, Op. 10 (1805)
U. Hoelscher (vn), C. Fröhlich (cnd), Berlin RSO † Con 11 Vn, Op. 70 CPO ▲ 999196 [DDD] (14.97)

Concerto No. 5 in E♭ for Violin & Orchestra, Op. 17 (1807)
U. Hoelscher (vn), C. Fröhlich (cnd), Berlin RSO † Con 2 Vn, Op. 2 CPO ▲ 999067 [DDD] (14.97)

Concerto No. 6 in G for Violin & Orchestra, Op. 28 (1809)
U. Hoelscher (vn), C. Fröhlich (cnd), Berlin RSO † Con 12 Vn, Op. 79; Con 3 Vn, Op. 7 CPO ▲ 999145 [DDD] (14.97)

Concerto No. 7 in e for Violin & Orchestra, Op. 38 (1814)
U. Hoelscher (vn), C. Fröhlich (cnd), Berlin RSO † Con 10 Vn, Op. 62; Con 9 Vn, Op. 55 CPO ▲ 999232 [DDD] (14.97)
T. Nishizaki (vn), L. Pešek (cnd), Bratislava Philharmonic CO † Con 12 Vn, Op. 79 MARC ▲ 8220406 [DDD] (13.97)

Concerto No. 8 in a for Violin & Orchestra, Op. 47, "Gesangsszene" (1816)
A. Adorján (fl), D. Shallon (cnd), Stuttgart RSO † Mendelssohn (-Bartholdy):Con Vn & Orch, Op. 64 ORF ▲ 46831 [DDD] (18.97)
U. Hoelscher (vn), C. Fröhlich (cnd), Berlin RSO † Con 12 Vn, Op. 79; Con 13 Vn, Op. 92 CPO ▲ 999187 [DDD] (14.97)
A. Spalding (vn), E. Ormandy (cnd), Philadelphia Orch *(rec 1938-41)* † Mendelssohn (-Bartholdy):Con Vn & Orch, Op. 64 ENT (Strings) ▲ 99349 (16.97)
E. Wallfisch (vn), R. Goodman (cnd), Brandenburg Orch ("Violin Concertos") † F. Schubert:Rondo Vn, D.438; G. B. Viotti:Con 22 Vn, G.97 HYP ▲ 66840 (18.97)

Concerto No. 9 in d for Violin & Orchestra, Op. 55 (1820)
U. Hoelscher (vn), C. Fröhlich (cnd), Berlin RSO † Con 10 Vn, Op. 62; Con 7 Vn, Op. 38 CPO ▲ 999232 [DDD] (14.97)
E. Morini (vn), F. Waldman (cnd), Musica Aeterna Ensemble *(rec 1962-68)* † Bruch:Con 1 Vn, Op. 26; Wieniawski:Con 2 Vn, Op. 22 ARBT ▲ 106 (16.97)

Concerto No. 10 in A for Violin & Orchestra, Op. 62 (1810)
U. Hoelscher (vn), C. Fröhlich (cnd), Berlin RSO † Con 7 Vn, Op. 38; Con 9 Vn, Op. 55 CPO ▲ 999232 [DDD] (14.97)

Concerto No. 11 in G for Violin & Orchestra, Op. 70 (1825)
U. Hoelscher (vn), C. Fröhlich (cnd), Berlin RSO † Con 4 Vn, Op. 10 CPO ▲ 999196 [DDD] (14.97)

Concerto No. 12 in A for Violin & Orchestra, Op. 79 (1828)
U. Hoelscher (vn), C. Fröhlich (cnd), Berlin RSO † Con 3 Vn, Op. 7; Con 6 Vn, Op. 28 CPO ▲ 999145 [DDD] (14.97)
U. Hoelscher (vn), C. Fröhlich (cnd), Berlin RSO † Con 13 Vn, Op. 92; Con 8 Vn, Op. 47 CPO ▲ 999187 [DDD] (14.97)
T. Nishizaki (vn), L. Pešek (cnd), Bratislava Philharmonic CO † Con 7 Vn, Op. 38 MARC ▲ 8220406 [DDD] (13.97)

Concerto No. 13 in E for Violin & Orchestra, Op. 92 (1835)
U. Hoelscher (vn), C. Fröhlich (cnd), Berlin RSO † Con 12 Vn, Op. 79; Con 8 Vn, Op. 47 CPO ▲ 999187 [DDD] (14.97)

Concerto in C for Violin, Cello & Orchestra (1803)
A. Weithaas (vn), M. Sanderling (vc), H. Breuer (cnd), Thüringian SO ("Music at the Court of Gotha") † Con 1 for 2 Vns, Op. 48; Potpourri Vn Vc, Op. 64 ESDU ▲ 2029 (17.97)

Concerto No. 1 in A for 2 Violins & Orchestra, Op. 48 (1808)
A. Weithaas (vn), M. Georgieva (vn), H. Breuer (cnd), Thüringian SO ("Music at the Court of Gotha") † Con Vn & Vc; Potpourri Vn Vc, Op. 64 ESDU ▲ 2029 (17.97)

Double Quartet No. 1 in d for Strings, Op. 65 (1823)
Academy of St. Martin in the Fields Chamber Ensemble † Double Qt 2 Strs, Op. 77; Double Qt 3 Strs, Op. 87; Double Qt 4 Strs, Op. 136 HYP (Dyad) 2-▲ 22014 (18.97)
Smithsonian Chamber Players *(rec Jan 21-24, 1993)* † Qnts Strs, Op. 33; Sxt Strs, Op. 140 SNYC ▲ 53370 [DDD] (16.97)

Double Quartet No. 2 in E♭ for Strings, Op. 77 (1827)
Academy of St. Martin in the Fields Chamber Ensemble † Double Qt 1 Strs, Op. 65; Double Qt 3 Strs, Op. 87; Double Qt 4 Strs, Op. 136 HYP (Dyad) 2-▲ 22014 (18.97)

Double Quartet No. 3 in e for Strings, Op. 87 (1832-33)
Academy of St. Martin in the Fields Chamber Ensemble † Double Qt 1 Strs, Op. 65; Double Qt 2 Strs, Op. 77; Double Qt 4 Strs, Op. 136 HYP (Dyad) 2-▲ 22014 (18.97)

Double Quartet No. 4 in g for Strings, Op. 136 (1847)
Academy of St. Martin in the Fields Chamber Ensemble † Double Qt 1 Strs, Op. 65; Double Qt 2 Strs, Op. 77; Double Qt 3 Strs, Op. 87 HYP (Dyad) 2-▲ 22014 (18.97)

Duets (3) for 2 Violins, Op. 39 (1816)
V. Szabadi (vn), P. Csaba (vn) HUN ▲ 31866 [DDD] (16.97)

Duets for 2 Violins, Op. 67 (1824)
D. Oistrakh (vn), I. Oistrakh (vn) *(rec 1960)* ("David Oistrakh Collection, Vol. 4") † Beethoven:Con Vn, Vc, Pno, Op. 56; Romances Vn DHR (Legendary Treasures) ▲ 7714 (16.97)
H. Schunk (vn), U. Petersen (vn) CPO ▲ 999343 [DDD] (14.97)

Fantasie & Variations on a Theme of Danzi in B♭ for Clarinet & Strings, Op. 81 (1814)
D. Klöcker (cl), Consortium Classicum † Notturno Ww, Op. 34; Bärmann:Qnt 3 Cl & Str Qt, Op. 23; Busoni:Intro & Elegy; Meyerbeer:Qnt Cl ORF ▲ 213901 [DDD] (18.97)
J. Manasse (cl), Shanghai String Quartet *(rec Oct 1993)* ("Jon Manasse Plays Clarinet Music from 3 Centuries") † J. Cohn:Con Cl; G. Gershwin:Preludes Pno; W. A. Mozart:Qnt Cl, K.581 XLNT ▲ 18009 [DDD]

SPOHR, LOUIS [LUDWIG] (cont.)

Fantasie & Variations on a Theme of Danzi in B♭ for Clarinet & Strings, Op. 81 (1814) (cont.)
E. Ottensamer (cl), J. Wildner (cnd), Slovak RSO Bratislava *(rec Concert Hall of the Slovak Radio Bratislava, Feb 20, 1994)* † Con 2 Cl, Op. 57; Con 4 Cl NXIN ▲ 550689 [DDD] (5.97)

Fantasie No. 2 in c for Harp, Op. 35 (1807)
C. Antonelli (hp) *(rec Rome, Italy, 1987)* ("Harp Festival") † C.P.E. Bach:Son Hp, H.563; B. Britten:Suite Hp, Op. 83; G. Fauré:Impromptu Hp, Op. 86; Saint-Saëns:Fant Hp, Op. 95; G. B. Viotti:Son Hp AART ▲ 47202 [DDD] (10.97)

Faust (opera in 2 acts) [lib J. K. Bernhard] (1813; rev in 3 acts, 1852)
C. Taha (sop), M. Vier (bar), E. von Jordis (bass), G. Moull (cnd), Bielefeld PO, Bielefeld Opera Chorus [1852 version] *(rec live, June 1993)* CPO 2-▲ 999247 [DDD] (27.97)

Faust (selections)
E. Ritchie (sop), V. Soames (cl), J. Purvis (pno) † Vars on a Theme from Alruna; W. A. Mozart:Clemenza di Tito (sels); I. Müller:Qt 2 Cl; F. Paer:Una voce CLCL ▲ 6 [ADD] (17.97)

Faust (overture)
A. Walter (cnd), Budapest SO † Jessonda (ov); Sym 4 MARC ▲ 8223122 [DDD] (13.97)

German Songs (6) for Soprano, Clarinet & Piano, Op. 103
Scarborough Chamber Players † A. Blank:Poems; A. Roussel:Poèmes de Ronsard, Op. 26; R. Schumann:Faschingsschwank, Op. 26; Starer:Songs of Youth & Age; H. Villa-Lobos:Bachiana brasileira 6 CENT ▲ 2106 [DDD] (16.97)
J. Varady (sop), H. Schöneberger (cl), H. Höll (pno) [GER] † Songs Bar, Op. 154 ORF ▲ 103841 [DDD] (18.97)

Jessonda (opera in 3 acts) [lib E. Gehe after A. M. Lemierre], Op. 63 (1823)
J. Varady (sop), R. Behle (sop), T. Moser (ten), D. Fischer-Dieskau (bar), K. Moll (bass), G. Albrecht (cnd), Hamburg State PO, Hamburg State Opera Chorus [GER] ORF 2-▲ 240912 [DDD] (36.97)

Jessonda (selections)
E. Lear (sop), H. Hollreiser (cnd), Berlin RSO *(rec 1959)* ("The Art of Evelyn Lear") † A. Berg:Orchesterlieder, Op. 4; Berlioz:Nuits d'été, Op. 7; R. Strauss:Four Last Songs, AV150 VAIA ▲ 1159 [ADD] (16.97)

Jessonda (overture)
A. Walter (cnd), Budapest SO † Faust (ov); Sym 4 MARC ▲ 8223122 [DDD] (13.97)

Mass in C for 5 Vocal Soloists & Double Chorus, Op. 54 (1820)
Berlin Radio Chorus † Psalms CPO ▲ 999149 [DDD] (14.97)
J. Brych (cnd), Prague Philharmonic Choir † Psalms; Mendelssohn (-Bartholdy):Psalms (3), Op. 78 PRAG ▲ 250117 (18.97)

Nonet in F for Strings & Winds, Op. 31 (1813)
Gaudier Ensemble † Octet HYP ▲ 66699 [DDD] (18.97)
D. Klöcker (cnd) † Notturno Ww, Op. 34 ORF ▲ 155871 [DDD] (18.97)
Nash Ensemble † Octet CRD ▲ 3354 (17.97)
Stanislas Ensemble † G. Rossini:Andante e tema con variazioni Fl; Andante e tema con variazioni Va; Serenade Fl GALL ▲ 721 [DDD] (19.97)

Notturno in C for Winds & Turkish Band, Op. 34 (1815)
D. Klöcker (cnd) † Nonet Strs & Ww, Op. 31 ORF ▲ 155871 [DDD] (18.97)
D. Klöcker (cl), Consortium Classicum † Fant & Vars on Danzi, Op. 81; Bärmann:Qnt 3 Cl & Str Qt, Op. 23; Busoni:Intro & Elegy; Meyerbeer:Qnt Cl ORF ▲ 213901 [DDD] (18.97)

Octet in E for Strings & Winds, Op. 32 (1814)
Consortium Classicum *(rec July 1995)* † Qnt Fl ORF ▲ 410961 [DDD] (18.97)
Gaudier Ensemble † Nonet Strs & Ww, Op. 31 HYP ▲ 66699 [DDD] (18.97)
Nash Ensemble † Nonet Strs & Ww, Op. 31 CRD ▲ 3354 (17.97)

Overtures
C. Fröhlich (cnd), Berlin RSO—Macbeth; Die Prüfung; Alruna; Die Eulenkönigin; Faust; Jessonda; Der Berggeist; Pietro von Abano; Der Alchymist CPO ▲ 999093 [DDD] (14.97)

Potpourri in F for Clarinet & Orchestra [on themes by P. von Winter], Op. 80 (1811)
E. Brummer (cl), H. Stadlmair (cnd), Bamberg SO † Con 3 Cl; Con 4 Cl TUD ▲ 7043 (16.97)
J. Denman (cl), R. Bernhardt (cnd), Royal PO † Con 3 Cl; Con 4 Cl; Vars on a Theme from Alruna IMAS (Masters) ▲ 6600082 (16.97)
E. Ottensamer (cl), J. Wildner (cnd), Slovak RSO Bratislava *(rec House of Arts Košice, Sept 16-19, 1991)* † Con 1 Cl, Op. 26; Con 3 Cl NXIN ▲ 550688 [DDD] (5.97)

Potpourri No. 2 in B♭ for Violin [on themes by Mozart], Op. 22
New Haydn Quartet † Qnt Strs, Op. 144; Sxt Strs, Op. 140 MARC ▲ 8223600 [DDD] (13.97)
K. Sillito (vn) † Qnt Strs, Op. 91; Sxt Strs, Op. 140 CHN ▲ 9424 (16.97)

Potpourri in A for Violin, Cello & Orchestra [on themes from the opera *Jessonda*], Op. 64 (ca 1824)
A. Weithaas (vn), M. Sanderling (vc), H. Breuer (cnd), Thüringian SO ("Music at the Court of Gotha") † Con Vn & Vc; Con 1 for 2 Vns, Op. 48 ESDU ▲ 2029 (17.97)

Psalms (3) for Vocal Soloists & Double Chorus, Op. 85 (1932)
Berlin Radio Chorus † Mass in C, Op. 54 CPO ▲ 999149 [DDD] (14.97)
J. Brych (cnd), Prague Philharmonic Choir † Mass in C, Op. 54; Mendelssohn (-Bartholdy):Psalms (3), Op. 78 PRAG ▲ 250117 (18.97)

Quintet in c for Flute, Clarinet, Horn, Bassoon & Piano, Op. 52 (1820)
W. Genuit (pno), Consortium Classicum *(rec July 1995)* † Octet ORF ▲ 410961 [DDD] (18.97)
Nash Ensemble † Spt Fl CRD ▲ 3399 (17.97)

Quintets (2) in E♭ & G for Strings, Op. 33 (1813-14)
S. Papp (va), Danubius String Quartet *(rec Budapest, Feb 16-18 & Mar 18-19, 1993)* MARC ▲ 8223597 [DDD] (13.97)
Smithsonian Chamber Players *(rec Jan 21-24, 1993)* † Double Qt 1 Strs, Op. 65; Sxt Strs, Op. 140 SNYC ▲ 53370 [DDD] (16.97)

Quintet in a for Strings, Op. 91 (1833-34)
Academy of St. Martin in the Fields Chamber Ensemble † Potpourri 2, Op. 22; Sxt Strs, Op. 140 CHN ▲ 9424 (16.97)

Quintet No. 7 in g for Strings, Op. 144 (1850)
New Haydn Quartet † Potpourri 2, Op. 22; Sxt Strs, Op. 140 MARC ▲ 8223600 [DDD] (13.97)

Rondo brillant for Violin & Piano, Op. 51
Pallas Trio *(rec Alter Reistadel, Neumarkt, Germany, Aug 29-Sept 1, 1995)* ("Piano Chamber Music") † Adagio Vc, Op. 115; Trio 2 Pno, Op. 123; Trio 5 Pno, Op. 142 MPH ▲ 56822 [DDD] (15.97)

Septet in a for Flute, Clarinet, Horn, Bassoon, Violin, Cello & Piano, Op. 147 (1853)
Nash Ensemble † Qnt Fl CRD ▲ 3399 (17.97)

Sextet in C for Strings, Op. 140 (1848)
Academy of St. Martin in the Fields Chamber Ensemble † Potpourri 2, Op. 22; Qnt Strs, Op. 91 CHN ▲ 9424 (16.97)
New Haydn Quartet † Potpourri 2, Op. 22; Qnt Strs, Op. 144 MARC ▲ 8223600 [DDD] (13.97)
Smithsonian Chamber Players *(rec Jan 21-24, 1993)* † Double Qt 1 Strs, Op. 65; Qnts Strs, Op. 33 SNYC ▲ 53370 [DDD] (16.97)

Sonata No. 1 in c for Violin & Harp (1805)
M. Grauwels (fl), C. Michel (hp) [arr for fl & hp] † Chopin:Vars on Rossini; Donizetti:Larghetto & Allegro; L. Drouet:Intro & Vars on an English Theme; G. Rossini:Andante e tema con variazioni Va MARC ▲ 8220441 [DDD] (13.97)
J. Suk (vn), K. Englichová (hp) ("Meditation") † Massenet:Méditation from Thaïs; G. Pierné:Impromptu-Caprice Hp, Op. 9; O. Respighi:Siciliana; G. Rossini:Andante e tema con variazioni Va; Saint-Saëns:Fant Vn DI ▲ 920318 [DDD] (5.97)

Sonata No. 2 in B♭ for Violin & Harp, Op. 16 (1806)
J. Suk (vn), K. Englichová (hp) ("Golden Strings") † J. L. Dussek:Sons Vn, Op. 2; Massenet:Méditation from Thaïs; O. Respighi:Siciliana; G. Rossini:Andante e tema con variazioni Va; Saint-Saëns:Cygne; Fant Vn LT ▲ 38 [DDD] (16.97)

Sonata No. 3 in E♭ for Violin & Harp, Op. 113 (1806)
R. Aitken (fl), E. Goodman (hp) [trans fl & hp] *(rec Castle Wik Sweden, June 2-4, 1979)* ("Flute & Harp") † Son 4 Vn & Hp, Op. 114; Son 5 Vn & Hp, Op. 115; Donizetti:Son Fl & Hp; A. Hovhaness:Garden of Adonis, Op. 245; Krumpholtz:Son Fl & Hp BIS ▲ 143 [AAD] (17.97)
P. Naegele (vn), G. Herbert (hp) † Son 5 Vn & Hp, Op. 115 BAYE ▲ 100264 [DDD] (17.97)

Sonata No. 4 in A♭ for Violin & Harp, Op. 114 (1809)
R. Aitken (fl), E. Goodman (hp) [trans fl & hp] *(rec Castle Wik Sweden, June 2-4, 1979)* ("Flute & Harp") † Son 3 Vn & Hp, Op. 113; Son 5 Vn & Hp, Op. 115; Donizetti:Son Fl & Hp; A. Hovhaness:Garden of Adonis, Op. 245; Krumpholtz:Son Fl & Hp BIS ▲ 143 [AAD] (17.97)

SPOHR, LOUIS [LUDWIG] (cont.)

Sonata No. 5 in E♭ for Violin & Harp, Op. 115 (1811)

R. Aitken (fl), E. Goodman (hp) [trans fl & hp] *(rec Castle Wik Sweden, June 2-4, 1979)* ("Flute & Harp") † Son 3 Vn & Hp, Op. 113; Son 4 Vn & Hp, Op. 114; Donizetti:Son Fl & Hp; A. Hovhaness:Garden of Adonis, Op. 245; Krumpholtz:Son Fl & Hp BIS ▲ 143 [AAD] (17.97)

P. Naegele (vn), G. Herbert (hp) † Son 3 Vn & Hp, Op. 113 BAYE ▲ 100264 [DDD] (17.97)

A. Stein (vc), F. Stein (hp) *(rec Neumünster Church, Zurich, Switzerland, May 12-14, 1982)* ("Court Music for Cello & Harp") † Boccherini:Son 7 Vc & Hp; J.-L. Duport:Nocturne concertant 3 DORO ▲ 3025 [ADD] (16.97)

Songs

M. Patterson (sop), D. Sarge (pno)—Lied des verlassenen Mädchens, WoO 90; Nachgefühl, WoO 91 *(rec July 24-25 & 27, 1995)* † Songs; Songs (6), Op. 41 MARC ▲ 8223869 [DDD] (13.97)

C. Prégardien (ten), T. Hoppstock (gtr) ("Lieder on Love & Death") † J. Brahms:Songs; F. Schubert:Songs (misc) SIGM ▲ 9500 (17.97)

Songs (6) for solo Voice & Piano, Op. 25 (1810)

M. Patterson (sop), D. Sarge (pno) *(rec Clara Wieck Auditorium Sandhausen, July 24-25 & 27, 1995)* † Songs; Songs (6), Op. 41 MARC ▲ 8223869 [DDD] (13.97)

Songs (6) for solo Voice & Piano, Op. 37 (1816)

M. Patterson (sop), D. Sarge (pno) *(rec Clara Wieck Auditorium Sandhausen, July 24-25 & 27, 1995)* † Songs; Songs (6), Op. 41 MARC ▲ 8223869 [DDD] (13.97)

L. Rizzi (sop), F. Zigante (gtr) ("Songs with Guitar") † Songs; Songs (6), Op. 41; Zemire und Azor (sels) STRV ▲ 33371 (16.97)

Songs (6) for solo Voice & Piano, Op. 41 (1818)

M. Patterson (sop), D. Sarge (pno) *(rec Clara Wieck Auditorium Sandhausen, July 24-25 & 27, 1995)* † Songs MARC ▲ 8223869 [DDD] (13.97)

L. Rizzi (sop), F. Zigante (gtr) ("Songs with Guitar") † Songs; Songs, Op. 37; Zemire und Azor (sels) STRV ▲ 33371 (16.97)

Songs (6) for solo Voice & Piano, Op. 72 (1826)

M. Patterson (sop), D. Sarge (pno) *(rec Clara Wieck Auditorium Sandhausen, July 24-25 & 27, 1995)* † Songs; Songs (6), Op. 41 MARC ▲ 8223869 [DDD] (13.97)

L. Rizzi (sop), F. Zigante (gtr) ("Songs with Guitar") † Songs (6), Op. 41; Songs, Op. 37; Zemire und Azor (sels) STRV ▲ 33371 (16.97)

Songs for Voice & Guitar

C. Högman (voc), J. Lindberg (gtr)—Mignon's Lied, Op. 37/1; Getrennte Liebe, Op. 37/5; Lied beim Rundetanz, Op. 37/6 *(rec Sweden, June 28/30, 1985)* ("Songs for the Guitar") † M. Giuliani:Songs; F. Schubert:Songs; Sor:Songs Voice Gtr; C. M. von Weber:Songs Voice Gtr BIS ▲ 293 [DDD] (17.97)

Songs (6) for Baritone, Violin & Piano, Op. 154 (1856)

D. Fischer-Dieskau (bar), D. Sitkovetsky (vn), H. Höll (pno) [GER] † German Songs, Op. 103 ORF ▲ 103841 [DDD] (18.97)

Symphony No. 1 in E♭, Op. 20 (1811)

A. Walter (cnd), Czech-Slovak State PO † Sym 5 MARC ▲ 8223363 [DDD] (13.97)

Symphony No. 2 in d, Op. 49 (1820)

C. Hoey (cnd), Singapore SO † F. P. Lachner:Sym 1 MARC ▲ 8220360 [DDD] (13.97)

A. Walter (cnd), Slovak State PO Košice † Sym 9 MARC ▲ 8223454 (13.97)

Symphony No. 3 in c, Op. 78 (1828)

A. Walter (cnd), Czech-Slovak State PO *(rec Nov 12-16, 1991)* † Sym 6; Sym 9 MARC ▲ 8223439 [DDD] (13.97)

Symphony No. 4 in F, Op. 86, "Die Weihe der Töne" (1832)

A. Walter (cnd), Budapest SO † Faust (ov); Jessonda (ov) MARC ▲ 8223122 [DDD] (13.97)

Symphony No. 5 in c, Op. 102 (1837)

A. Walter (cnd), Czech-Slovak State PO † Sym 1 MARC ▲ 8223363 [DDD] (13.97)

Symphony No. 6 in G, Op. 116, "Historical" (1840)

K. A. Rickenbacher (cnd), Bavarian RSO † Sym 9 ORF ▲ 94841 [DDD] (18.97)

A. Walter (cnd), Czech-Slovak State PO *(rec Nov 12-16, 1991)* † Sym 3; Sym 9 MARC ▲ 8223439 [DDD] (13.97)

Symphony No. 9 in b, Op. 143, "The Seasons" (1850)

K. A. Rickenbacher (cnd), Bavarian RSO † Sym 6 ORF ▲ 94841 [DDD] (18.97)

A. Walter (cnd), Czech-Slovak State PO *(rec Nov 12-16, 1991)* † Sym 3; Sym 6 MARC ▲ 8223439 [DDD] (13.97)

A. Walter (cnd), Slovak State PO Košice † Sym 2 MARC ▲ 8223454 (13.97)

Trios (5) for Piano & Strings (complete)

Beethoven Trio Ravensberg CPO 3-▲ 999246 [DDD] (27.97)

Trio No. 1 in e for Piano, Violin & Cello, Op. 119 (1841)

New Munich Piano Trio ("The Piano Trios") † Trio 2 Pno, Op. 123; Trio 3 Pno, Op. 124; Trio 4 Pno, Op. 133; Trio 5 Pno, Op. 142 ORF 2-▲ 352952 [DDD] (36.97)

Trio No. 2 in F for Piano, Violin & Cello, Op. 123 (1842)

Hartley Piano Trio *(rec St Martin's Church East Woodhay, Oct 13-14, 1994)* † Trio 4 Pno, Op. 133 NXIN ▲ 553205 [DDD] (5.97)

New Munich Piano Trio ("The Piano Trios") † Trio 1 Pno, Op. 119; Trio 3 Pno, Op. 124; Trio 4 Pno, Op. 133; Trio 5 Pno, Op. 142 ORF 2-▲ 352952 [DDD] (36.97)

Pallas Trio *(rec Alter Reistadel, Neumarkt, Germany, Aug 29-Sept 1, 1995)* ("Piano Chamber Music") † Adagio Vc, Op. 115; Rondo brillant Vn, Op. 51; Trio 5 Pno, Op. 142 MPH ▲ 56822 [DDD] (15.97)

Trio No. 3 in a for Piano, Violin & Cello, Op. 124 (1842)

Borodin Trio † Trio 4 Pno, Op. 133 CHN ▲ 9372 [DDD] (16.97)

New Munich Piano Trio ("The Piano Trios") † Trio 1 Pno, Op. 119; Trio 2 Pno, Op. 123; Trio 4 Pno, Op. 133; Trio 5 Pno, Op. 142 ORF 2-▲ 352952 [DDD] (36.97)

Trio No. 4 in B for Piano, Violin & Cello, Op. 133 (1846)

Borodin Trio † Trio 3 Pno, Op. 124 CHN ▲ 9372 [DDD] (16.97)

Hartley Piano Trio *(rec St Martin's Church East Woodhay, Oct 13-14, 1994)* † Trio 2 Pno, Op. 123 NXIN ▲ 553205 [DDD] (5.97)

New Munich Piano Trio ("The Piano Trios") † Trio 1 Pno, Op. 119; Trio 2 Pno, Op. 123; Trio 3 Pno, Op. 124; Trio 5 Pno, Op. 142 ORF 2-▲ 352952 [DDD] (36.97)

Trio No. 5 in g for Piano, Violin & Cello, Op. 142 (1849)

New Munich Piano Trio ("The Piano Trios") † Trio 1 Pno, Op. 119; Trio 2 Pno, Op. 123; Trio 3 Pno, Op. 124; Trio 4 Pno, Op. 133 ORF 2-▲ 352952 [DDD] (36.97)

Pallas Trio *(rec Alter Reistadel, Neumarkt, Germany, Aug 29-Sept 1, 1995)* ("Piano Chamber Music") † Adagio Vc, Op. 115; Rondo brillant Vn, Op. 51; Trio 2 Pno, Op. 123 MPH ▲ 56822 [DDD] (15.97)

Variations in B♭ on a Theme from Alruna for Clarinet & Piano (or Orchestra) (1809)

E. Brunner (cl), H. Stadlmair (cnd), Bamberg SO † Con 1 Cl, Op. 26; Con 2 Cl, Op. 57 TUD ▲ 7009 (16.97)

J. Denman (cl), R. Bernhardt (cnd), Royal PO † Con 3 Cl; Con 4 Cl; Potpourri, Op. 80 IMAS (Masters) ▲ 6600082 (16.97)

V. Soames (cl), J. Purvis (pno) † Faust (sels); W. A. Mozart:Clemenza di Tito (sels); I. Müller:Qt 2 Cl; F. Paer:Una voce CLCL ▲ 6 [ADD] (17.97)

Zemire und Azor (opera in 2 acts) [lib J. J. Ihlee after Marmontel] (1818-19)

S. Blanchard (sop—Lisbe), B. Roth (sop—Zemire), G. Zamfirescu (mez—Fatme), M. Howard (ten—Azor), H. Schöpflin (ten—Ali), J. Schwärsky (bass—Sander), S. von der Schulenburg (spkr—eine Fee), A. Kolar (cnd), Sondershausen Loh Orch, A. Kolar (cnd), Max Bruch Philharmonie, Theater Nordhausen Chorus *(rec Nordhausen, Aug 1996)* DSB 2-▲ 1064 [DDD]

Zemire und Azor (selections)

L. Rizzi (sop), F. Zigante (gtr) ("Songs with Guitar") † Songs; Songs (6), Op. 41; Songs, Op. 37 STRV ▲ 33371 (16.97)

SPONTINI, GASPARE (1774-1851)

Agnes von Hohenstaufen (opera in 3 acts) (1829)

R. Muti (cnd) , M. Caballé (sop), A. Stella (sop) *(rec 1970)* ODRO ▲ 1187 (9.97)

Divertimento for Horn & Harp

S. Hermansson (hn), E. Goodman (hp) *(rec Ontario, Canada, Sept 20-23, 1993)* ("Horn & Harp Soirée - 19th Century French & Italian Duos") † N. C. Bochsa:L'écho (Nocturne 2) Hn & Hp; Boieldieu:Solo Hn & Hp; Chaussier:Elegy Hn & Hp; Dauprat:Air Ecossais Var Hn & Hp, Op. 22; Son Hn & Hp; F. Duvernoy:Nocturne 2 Hn & Hp; Paisiello:Andante Hn & Hp BIS ▲ 648 [DDD] (17.97)

Notturno concertato for Orchestra (1795)

M. Mercelli (fl), P. Pollastri (ob), M. Zuccarini (cnd), Perusina Sinfonia *(rec 1995)* † Cambini:Sinf Fl Ob BONG ▲ 5576 [DDD] (16.97)

Olympia (opera in 3 acts) [lib Dieulafoy & Briffaut] (Italian version, 1819; Paris version, 1821)

J. Varady (sop), S. Toczyska (mez), F. Tagliavini (ten), D. Fischer-Dieskau (bar), J. Becker (bass), G. Fortune (bass), G. Albrecht (cnd), Berlin RSO, Berlin Radio Chorus [Paris version] ORF 2-▲ 137862 [DDD] (36.97)

SPONTINI, GASPARE (cont.)

Li puntigli delle donne [The Stubborness of Women] (farsetta in 2 acts) (1796)

A. Ruffini (sop), S. Rigacci (sop), S. Anselmi (sop), E. Palacio (ten), N. Ulivieri (ten), G. Ruggeri (sgr), M. Zeffiri (sgr), A. Zedda (cnd), Spontini Classic Orch DYNC 2-▲ 189 [DDD] (34.97)

Songs

V. Esposito (sop), L. Gorla (pno)—La petite sorcière; Rêve de l'orient; Le riens d'amour; Le chant de Mignon; Être aimé; L'inconstance; L'adieu; Il faut mourir; Il reviendra; Sentiments d'amour 1; Sentiments d'amour 2; Le départ; L'hereux gondolier; Sul ciglio tuo severo *(rec Genova, Italy, Dec 1997)* ("Chamber Songs") DYNC ▲ 2012 [DDD] (13.97)

Il Teseo riconosciuto (opera in 2 acts) [lib Cosimo Giotti] (1798)

C. Bosi (ten—Evandro), C. Allemano (ten—Egeo), D. D. Auria (ten—Testo), S. Rinaldi-Miliani (bar—Connida), S. Visentin (sgr—Asteria), P. Marrocu (sgr—Medea), D. Piccini (sgr—Leucippe), P. Borromei (sgr—Ombra d'Etra), A. Zedda (cnd), Marchigiano PO, Marchigiano Vincenzo Bellini Lyric Chorus *(rec Teatro Comunale G. B. Pergolesi, Oct 13-15, 1995)* BONG 2-▲ 2193 [DDD] (32.97)

La vestale (opera in 3 acts) [lib Etienne de Jouy] (1807)

K. Huffstodt (sop—Julie), D. Graves (mez—La Grande Vestale), P. Raftery (ten—Cinna), A. Michaels-Moore (bar—Licinius), R. Muti (cnd), La Scala Orch, La Scala Chorus SNYC 3-▲ 66357 (51.97)

R. Plowright (sop), G. Pasino (mez), P. Lefèbvre (ten), F. Araiza (ten), A. Cauli (bar), F. De Grandis (bass), G. Kuhn (cnd), Munich RSO, Munich Radio Chorus [FRE] ORF 2-▲ 256922 [DDD] (36.97)

La vestale (selections)

M. Callas (sop), T. Serafin (cnd), La Scala Orch *(rec Teatro alla Scala Milan, June 1955)* ("Callas at La Scala") † V. Bellini:Sonnambula (sels); Cherubini:Médée (sels) *(E,I lib texts)* EMIC (Callas Edition) ▲ 66457 [ADD] (11.97)

L. Christensen (gtr), M. Kammerling (gtr)—Ov [arr for 2 gtrs] † V. Bellini:Pirata (sels); W. A. Mozart:Clemenza di Tito (ov); G. Rossini:Ovs PLAL ▲ 54 (18.97)

SPRATLAN, LEWIS (1940-

Night Music for Violin, Clarinet & Percussion (1990)

V. Kadlubkiewicz (vn), M. Sussman (cl), J. Kelley (perc) *(rec July 1992)* † S. Macchia:Chamber Con 3; R. Stern:Fant Etude Vn; Wheelock:Partita Vn GAS ▲ 226 [DDD] (16.97)

SPRATLING, HUW (1949-

Choral Music

S. Bullock (sop), T. Chadwell (sop), J. Dyball (hp), H. Tunstall (hp), J. Hatton (org), J. Rennert (cnd) , Spratling Choir—Mass of the Holy Spirit; O Salutaris Hostia; Tantum Ergo; Sinf Str Orch; Son Hp; O Magnum Mysterium; In Paradisum *(rec St. Mary Magdelene Paddington, May 15-17, 1988)* SOMM ▲ 206 [ADD] (17.97)

SREBOTNJAK, ALOJZ (1931-

Macedonian Dances for 2 Oboes, 2 Clarinets, 2 Bassoons & Percussion (1975)

J. Lacombe (cnd) *(rec Montreal, Mar 1995)* ("Chanson et Danses") † F. Farkas:Contrafacta Hungarica; Indy:Chanson et Danses, Op. 50; A. Prinz:Danzas; Regner:Ländler; A. Uhl:Dances CBC (Musica Viva) ▲ 1105 [DDD] (16.97)

STÄBLER, GERHARD (1949-

Traum 1/9/92 for Chamber Ensemble

Musikfabrik NRW † Bruttger:Monolith; N. A. Huber:An Hölderlins Umnachtung; Kalitzke:Salto. Trapez. Ikarus CPO ▲ 999259 [DDD] (14.97)

STACHOWICZ, DAMIAN (1658-1699)

Veni Consolator for 1 Voice, Trumpet & Continuo (or Organ)

B. Jaskulska (sop), R. Gryń (tpt), Tutti e solo *(rec Rydzyna Castle Poland, Sept 1994)* ("Jewels of the Polish Baroque") † Jarzebski:Music of Jarzebski; Mielczewski:Canzona prima a 2; Milwid:Semper mi Iesu; Rohaczewski:Canzon a 4; Sieprawski:Justus germinavit; Szarzyński:Jesu spes mea; Son Vns; Veni Sancte Spiritus DORD ▲ 80136 [DDD] (13.97)

STACHOWSKI, MAREK (1936-

Pezzo grazioso for Wind Quintet (1982)

Warsaw Wind Quintet ("Da camera") † Bargielski:Butterfly Cage; Kurtlewicz:Blow the Wind; Malecki:Suite Ww Qnt; P. Moss:Retours; Palester:Trio d'anches PROV ▲ 182 [DDD] (18.97)

STADLER, ANTON (1753-1812)

Caprices (3) for solo Clarinet (after 1824)

C. Lawson (cl) ("A Grand Duo: The Clarinet & the Early Romantics") † N. Burgmüller:Duo Cl; F. Danzi:Son Cl; C. Loewe:Schottische Bilder, Op. 112; C. M. von Weber:Grand Duo Concertant, J.204 CLCL ▲ 15 [DDD] (17.97)

Trios (18) for 3 Basset Horns

New World Basset Horn Trio ("Music for Basset Horns") † W. A. Mozart:Diverts Bas Hns, K.Anh.229; Duos Hns, K.487 HAM ▲ 1907017 (9.97)

STAEPS, HANS ULRICH (1909-1988)

Sonata in c for Treble Recorder & Piano, "In modo preclassico"

C. Pehrsson (rcr), T. Schuback (pno) *(rec Sweden, May 11-13, 1981)* † Burkhart:Adventslieder; Hovland:Cantus II; Kukuck:Brücke; H.-M. Linde:Amarilli, mia bella; L. Lundén:Little Toe & Nine More; M. Shinohara:Fragmente Rcr BIS ▲ 202 [AAD] (17.97)

STAHMER, KLAUS HINRICH (1941-

Music of Stahmer

W. Heider (cnd) —I Can Fly; Dreamscape; Commentaries; Rotations; plus others THOR ▲ 2210 (16.97)

STAIGERS, DEL (1899-1950)

Carnival of Venice for Cornet

P. McCann (cnt), P. Parkes (cnd), Black Dyke Mills Band *(rec England, Mar 11, 1979)* ("Kings of Brass") † Borodin:Sym 2; D. Bourgeois:Serenade; R. Drigo:Serenata; Lalo:Roi d'Ys (sels); Liszt:Hungarian Rhaps, S.244; R. Strauss:Con 1 Hn, Op. 11 *([ENG] text)* CHN ▲ 4517 [ADD] (16.97)

STAINER, JOHN (1840-1901)

The Crucifixion (oratorio) for Tenor, Bass, Organ & Mixed Chorus (1887)

M. Davies (ten), D. Wilson-Johnson (bar), A. Lucas (org), J. Scott (cnd), St. Paul's Cathedral Choir, J. Scott (cnd), St. Paul's Cathedral Special Choir † Goss:O Saviour of the World CONI ▲ 51193 [DDD] (16.97)

J. Griffett (ten), M. George (bass), A. Newberry (vc), S. Vann (cnd), Peterborough Cathedral Choir ASVQ ▲ 6100 [ADD] (10.97)

M. Hill (ten), M. George (bass), M. Phillips (org), B. Kay (cnd), BBC Singers, B. Kay (cnd), Leth Hill Festival Singers CHN ▲ 9551 (16.97)

STALTERI, ARTURO (20th cent)

Piano Music

A. Stalteri (pno)—Scarlett; Notturno; Théoden e i ricordi; Mulini; Ultima luci de Brea ("Flowers") † A. A. Corea:Fiesta; Debussy:Preludes Pno; P. Glass:Metamorphosis 1-5; R. Sakamoto:Merry Christmas Mr. Lawrence; Sheltering Sky MASO ▲ 90071 [DDD] (16.97)

STALVEY, DORRANCE (1930-

Quartet for Strings (1989)

Arditti String Quartet *(rec Touting England)* ("California Composers") † S. Cohn:Eye of Chaos; D. Davis:Bleeding Particles; B. Goldstein:Aspen Qt ALBA ▲ 159 [DDD] (16.97)

STAMIC, JAN VÁCLAV (1717-1757)

Concerto No. 1 in D for Organ & Orchestra

A. Veselá (org), F. X. Thuri (hpd), V. Válek (cnd), Dvořák CO *(rec St. Mary of Týn Church Prague, Czech Republic, June 22-25, 1982)* ("Mannheim Organ Concertos") † Con 2 Org; Con 3 Org; Con 4 Org; J. W. A. Stamitz:Cons Org SUR ▲ 3094 [AAD]

Concerto No. 2 in C for Organ & Orchestra

A. Veselá (org), F. X. Thuri (hpd), V. Válek (cnd), Dvořák CO *(rec St. Mary of Týn Church Prague, Czech Republic, May 11-28, 1984)* ("Mannheim Organ Concertos") † Con 1 Org; Con 3 Org; Con 4 Org; J. W. A. Stamitz:Cons Org SUR ▲ 3094 [AAD]

Concerto No. 3 in B♭ for Organ & Orchestra

A. Veselá (org), F. X. Thuri (hpd), V. Válek (cnd), Dvořák CO *(rec St. Mary of Týn Church Prague, Czech Republic, May 11-28, 1984)* ("Mannheim Organ Concertos") † Con 1 Org; Con 2 Org; Con 4 Org; J. W. A. Stamitz:Cons Org SUR ▲ 3094 [AAD]

Concerto No. 4 in E♭ for Organ & Orchestra

A. Veselá (org), F. X. Thuri (hpd), V. Válek (cnd), Dvořák CO *(rec St. Mary of Týn Church Prague, Czech Republic, May 11-28, 1984)* ("Mannheim Organ Concertos") † Con 1 Org; Con 2 Org; Con 3 Org; J. W. A. Stamitz:Cons Org SUR ▲ 3094 [AAD]

STAMITZ, ANTON (1750-? after 1796)

Concerto in G for 2 Flutes & Orchestra

H. Giegle (fl), P. Kapun (fl), E. Duvier (cnd), Camerata Romana † C. Stamitz:Con Cl & Bn PC ▲ 267186 [DDD] (2.97)

C. Nicolet (fl), A. Nicolet (fl), J. Faerber (cnd), Württemberg CO † F. Danzi:Concertante Fl, Op. 41; G. Rossini:Intro, Theme & Vars Cl TUD ▲ 702 [ADD] (16.97)

STAMITZ, ANTON (cont.)

Concerto in G for 2 Flutes & Orchestra (cont.)
J. Rampal (fl), S. Kudo (fl), J. Rampal (cnd), Salzburg Mozarteum Orch † Cimarosa:Con Fls; W. A. Mozart:Concertone Vns, K.190; Vivaldi:Con Fls, RV.533 SNYC ▲ 45930 [DDD] (16.97)

Concerto No. 8 in G for Violin & Orchestra
W. Kohlhaussen (vn), W. Kohlhaussen (cnd), Fonte di Musica CO ("The Stamitz Family") † C. Stamitz:Qt Orch; J. W. A. Stamitz:Sinfs ARS ▲ 368307 (15.99)

STAMITZ, CARL (1745-1801)

Concerto in F for Bassoon & Orchestra
Y. Nakanishi (bn), N. Cleobury (cnd), London Mozart Players ("Bassoon Concertos") † J. N. Hummel:Con Bn; C. M. von Weber:Andante & Rondo ungarese Bn; Con Bn ASVQ ▲ 6159 (10.97)

Concerto No. 1 in G for Cello & Orchestra
C. Benda (vc), C. Benda (cnd), Prague CO *(rec Jan 1993)* ("Carl Stamitz: Cello Concertos") † Con 2 Vc; Con 3 Vc NXIN ▲ 550865 [DDD] (5.97)

Concerto No. 2 in A for Cello & Orchestra
C. Benda (vc), C. Benda (cnd), Prague CO *(rec Jan 1993)* ("Carl Stamitz: Cello Concertos") † Con 1 Vc; Con 3 Vc NXIN ▲ 550865 [DDD] (5.97)

Concerto No. 3 in C for Cello & Orchestra
C. Benda (vc), C. Benda (cnd), Prague CO *(rec Jan 1993)* ("Carl Stamitz: Cello Concertos") † Con 1 Vc; Con 2 Vc NXIN ▲ 550865 [DDD] (5.97)

Concertos for Clarinet & Orchestra
E. Brunner (cl), H. Stadlmair (cnd), Munich CO—in B for Vn & Cl; in B for Cl & Bn; No. 6 in B; No. 10 in B TUD ▲ 7004 [DDD] (16.97)
S. Meyer (cl), I. Brown (cnd), Academy of St. Martin in the Fields *(rec Concert Halls Blackheath, Country Unknown, Nov 1992)* ("Clarinet Connection: Sabine Meyer") † W. A. Mozart:Con Cl, K.622; Serenade; C. M. von Weber:Con 1 Cl, Op. 73 EMIC ▲ 55155 [DDD] (16.97)

Concerto No. 3 in B♭ for Clarinet & Orchestra
C. Faucomprez (cl), C. Traunfellner (cnd), Vienna Chamber PO *(rec Vienna, 1990)* ("Clarinet Concertos") † Con Cl & Bn; Con 11 Cl CAMA ▲ 167 [DDD] (18.97)

Concerto No. 11 in E♭ for Clarinet & Orchestra
C. Faucomprez (cl), C. Traunfellner (cnd), Vienna Chamber PO *(rec Vienna, 1990)* ("Clarinet Concertos") † Con Cl & Bn; Con 3 Cl CAMA ▲ 167 [DDD] (18.97)

Concerto in B♭ for Clarinet, Bassoon & Orchestra
K. Etti (cnd), Austrian RSO † A. Stamitz:Con Fls PC ▲ 267186 [DDD] (2.97)
C. Faucomprez (cl), I. Magome (bn), C. Traunfellner (cnd), Vienna Chamber PO *(rec Vienna, 1990)* ("Clarinet Concertos") † Con 11 Cl; Con 3 Cl CAMA ▲ 167 [DDD] (18.97)

Concerto in B♭ for 2 Clarinets & Orchestra
N. Bulfone (cl), D. Pacitti (cl), W. Themel (cnd), Udine CO *(rec Oct 14-15, 1995)* † J. G. Backofen:Con for 2 Cls, Op. 10; F. Devienne:Sinf concertante Cls, Op. 25 AG ▲ 39 [DDD] (18.97)

Concerto in G for Flute & Orchestra, Op. 29
A. Daboncourt (fl), L. Gorelik (cnd), Kharkov PO † J. Haydn:Con Fl & Orch, H.VIIf/1; F. A. Hoffmeister:Con 15 Fl DPV ▲ 9127 (15.97)
M. Helasvuo (fl), J. Saraste (cnd), Helsinki CO † F. Benda:Cons (4) Fl BIS ▲ 268 [DDD] (17.97)
B. Kuijken (trns fl), J. Lamon (cnd), Tafelmusik † C. W. Gluck:Orfeo ed Euridice (dance); J. Haydn:Con Fl [attrib], H.VIIf/D1 SNYC (Vivarte) ▲ 48045 (16.97)
C. Lardé (fl), J. Berlingen (cnd) *(rec Kusatsu Concert Hall, Nov 2-3, 1991)* † J. S. Bach:Con 1 for 2 Hpds, BWV 1060; W. A. Mozart:Sym 29, K.201 CAMA ▲ 284 [DDD] (18.97)
P. Racine (fl), P. Fournillier (cnd), English CO † Con Fl in D; W. A. Mozart:Andante Fl, K.315; Rondo Vn, K.373 NOVA ▲ 150131 [DDD] (16.97)
S. S. Syrinx (pan fl), J. Berlingen (cnd), Normandy Orchestral Ensemble [arr Syrinx] *(rec Oct 1994)* † Albinoni:Cons Ob, Op. 9; B. Bartók:Romanian Folk Dances Vn & Pno; Cimarosa:Con Fls; Con Ob; Vivaldi:Con Fls, RV.533 CASC ▲ 65127

Concerto in D for Flute & Orchestra (1777)
P. Racine (fl), P. Fournillier (cnd), English CO † Con Fl in G, Op. 29; W. A. Mozart:Andante Fl, K.315; Rondo Vn, K.373 NOVA ▲ 150131 [DDD] (16.97)
E. Zukerman (fl), B. Warchal (cnd), Slovak CO † F. Benda:Cons (4) Fl OPP ▲ 2088

Concerto in D for Viola & Orchestra
M. Defant (va), Zandonai Ensemble ("Defant Plays Viola Concertos") † Dittersdorf:Con Va; F. A. Hoffmeister:Con Va SYMO ▲ 106

Duo in D for Violin & Viola, Op.1/2
Zephyrus *(rec Faith Lutheran Church Bloomington, England, July 5-7, 1994)* ("Mozart in Mannheim") † F. Danzi:Petits Duos, Op. 64; Holzbauer:Qnt 1; F. Lebrun:Sons Vn, Op. 1; W. A. Mozart:Qt Fl in C; Toeschi:Quartetto FOCU ▲ 945 [DDD] (16.97)

Octets (Nos. 1 & 2 in B & No. 2 in E♭) & Partitas (in E♭ & No. 1 in B) for Wind Instruments
Consortium Classicum CPO ▲ 999081 [DDD] (14.97)

Quartet for Bassoon & Strings, Op. 19/6
F. Pollet (bn), Eugene Ysaÿe String Trio † F. Devienne:Qts Bn; W. A. Mozart:Duo Bn Vc, K.292; J. C. Vogel:Qts Bn SYRX ▲ 93103 [DDD] (16.97)

Quartets concertantes (6) for Violin, 2 Violas & Cello, Op. 15
C. Straka (cnd), Zeljko Musica—Quartetto Concertante in G † W. A. Mozart:Divert 7 Hns, K.205; Vivaldi:Con Strs, RV.151; Cons Vn(s) Strs, Op. 3/1-12 BER ▲ 9349 (10.97)

Quartet in F for Orchestra
W. Kohlhaussen (cnd), Fonte di Musica CO ("The Stamitz Family") † A. Stamitz:Con 8 Vn; J. W. A. Stamitz:Sinfs ARS ▲ 368307 (15.99)

Quartets (6) for Strings [including 2 for Orchestra], Opp. 4, 11 & 14
L. van Marcke (hn), Apos String Quartet *(rec Berlin, Feb 1996)* ("Chamber Music with Hn") † Hauff:Qnt Hn; F. A. Hoffmeister:Qnt Hn; Küffner:Qnt Hn; W. A. Mozart:Qnt Hn; A. Reicha:Qnt Hn PAVA ▲ 7363 [DDD] (10.97)

Sinfonia Concertante in D for Violin, Viola & Orchestra
R. Krečmer (cnd), Prague Virtuosi † Dittersdorf:Sinf Concertante; J. Haydn:Sinf concertante, H.I/105 DI ▲ 920274 [DDD] (5.97)

Sonata in B♭ for Viola & Piano, Op. 6 (1778)
R. Verebes (va), M. Lagacé (pno) *(rec Montreal)* ("Classical Sonatas") † Dittersdorf:Son Va; J. N. Hummel:Son Va; Vanhal:Son Va SNE ▲ 569 (16.97)

Symphony in D, "La Chasse" (1772)
M. Bamert (cnd), London Mozart Players ("4 Symphonies") † Syms CHN (Contemporaries of Mozart) ▲ 9358 [DDD] (16.97)

Symphonies (6), Op. 13 [also as Op. 16] (1777)
M. Bamert (cnd), London Mozart Players ("4 Symphonies") † Sym in D CHN (Contemporaries of Mozart) ▲ 9358 [DDD] (16.97)

STAMITZ, JOHANN WENZEL ANTON (1717-1757)

Concerto in B♭ for Clarinet & Orchestra
E. Brunner (cl), H. Stadlmair (cnd), Munich CO † F. A. Hoffmeister:Con 2 Cl; F. X. Pokorny:Cons Cl TUD ▲ 7008 [DDD] (16.97)

Concertos (4) for Organ & Orchestra
A. Veselá (org), F. X. Thuri (hpd), V. Válek (cnd), Dvořák CO ("Mannheim Organ Concertos") † J. V. Stamic:Con 1 Org; Con 2 Org; Con 3 Org; Con 4 Org SUR ▲ 3094 [AAD]

Divertimenti (2) in 2 Parts for solo Violin (1762)
S. Staryk (vn) *(rec Montreal, Aug 1964)* ("Sonatas for Solo Violin") † P. Hindemith:Son Vn; Papineau-Couture:Aria Vn; Pisendel:Son solo Vn; S. Prokofiev:Son Vc ORIO ▲ 7809 (13.97)

Litaniae Lauretanae for Soloists, 2 Violins, Bass Instrument & Organ
M. Frimmer (sop), S. Schlüter (alt), H. V. Berne (ten), T. Sol (bass), W. Helbich (cnd), Bremen Baroque Orch, Alsfelder Vocal Ensemble *(rec Unser Lieben Frauen Church Bremen, Germany, May 1997)* † Missa Solemnis; Offertorium CPO ▲ 999471 [DDD] (15.97)

Mass in D for Soloists, Chorus, Orchestra & Organ
W. Helbich (cnd), Bremen Baroque Orch, Alsfelder Vocal Ensemble, M. Frimmer (sop), S. Schlüter (alt), H. V. Berne (ten), T. Sol (bass) *(rec Unser Lieben Frauen Church Bremen, Germany, May 1997)* † Litaniae Lauretanae; Offertorium CPO ▲ 999471 [DDD] (15.97)

Offertorium [Motetto] de venerabili sacramento for Soloists, Orchestra & Organ
W. Helbich (cnd), Bremen Baroque Orch, Alsfelder Vocal Ensemble, M. Frimmer (sop), S. Schlüter (alt), H. V. Berne (ten), T. Sol (bass) *(rec live, Unser Lieben Frauen Church Bremen, Germany, May 3-4, 1997)* † Litaniae Lauretanae; Missa Solemnis CPO ▲ 999471 [DDD] (15.97)

STAMITZ, JOHANN WENZEL ANTON (cont.)

Orchestral Trios (6 sonates à 3 parties concertantes) for 2 Violins & Continuo, Op. 1
artists unknown ARN ▲ 68322 (16.97)

Sinfonias (3) in A, B & G for Orchestra
W. Kohlhaussen (cnd), Fonte di Musica CO ("The Stamitz Family") † A. Stamitz:Con 8 Vn; C. Stamitz:Qt Orch ARS ▲ 368307 (15.99)

STAMP, JACK (1954-

Be Thou My Vision (chorale prelude) for Wind Band
T. O'Neal (cnd), Arizona State Univ Symphonic Band *(rec Fisher Auditorium & Waller Hall IUP Campus, May 1994 & Jan-Feb 1995)* ("Celebrations") † Camphouse:Movement for Rosa; P. Grainger:Folk Song Settings; H. Hanson:Chorale & Alleluia; March Carillon; Melillo:Escape from Plato's Cave; Persichetti:Celebrations; F. Tull:Variants on an Advent Hymn CIT ▲ 88111 [DDD] (15.97)

Divertimento in "F" for Wind Ensemble
J. Stamp (cnd) *(rec Jan 14-16, 1995)* ("Divertimento: Wind Music of American Composers") † D. Diamond:Ceremonial Fanfare; Tantivy; Tower:Stepping Stones (sels); F. Tull:Sketches on a Tudor Psalm; R. Washburn:Sym Band CIT ▲ 88108 [DDD] (15.97)

Gavorkna Fanfare for Wind Symphony (1990)
E. Corporon (cnd), Cincinnati College Conservatory of Music Wind Sym *(rec Univ of Missouri Kansas City, Feb 23, 1991)* ("In Concert") † P. Grainger:Folk Song Settings; In a Nutshell; Skalkottas:Greek Dances, A/K.11; I. Tcherepnin:Statue; M. Tippett:Mosaic; M. Weinstein:Con Ww KLAV ▲ 11067 [DDD] (18.97)

Maryland Songs (4) for Soprano & Wind Orchestra (1995)
T. M. Gomez (sop), E. Corporon (cnd), North Texas Wind Sym *(rec Texas Women's Univ, Nov 1996)* ("Dialogues & Entertainments") † Bremer:Early Light; Corigliano:Gazebo Dances for Band; W. Kraft:Dialogues; Mailman:For Precious Friends; Toch:Miniature Ov KLAV (Wind Recording Project) ▲ 11083 [DDD] (18.97)

Music of Stamp
IUP Wind Ensemble *(Cenotaph; Chorale & Tocata; Antithigram)*, R. Fischer (cnd), Concordia Univ. Wind Sym *(Past the Equinox; The Melting of the Winter's Snow; Fanfare for the Great Hall; Remembrance of Things to Come; Elegy for E Hn & Band [w. M. A. Fasold (E hn)])*, E. Corporon (cnd), CCM Wind Sym *(Canticle; Gavorkna Fanfare; Journey Past the Unicorn; Daybreak for Mar Ensemble; Love's Philosophy; O-Zone [both w. [cnd:G. Olmstead] IUP Perc Ensembl; Jigsaw)* ("Past The Equinox") CIT ▲ 88105 [DDD] (15.97)

STANFORD, CHARLES VILLIERS (1852-1924)

Characteristic Pieces (5) for Violin (or Cello) & Piano, Op. 93 (1905)
P. Barritt (vn), C. Edwards (pno) † Irish Fants Vn, Op. 54; Son 1 Vn, Op. 11; Son 3 Vn, Op. 70 HYP ▲ 67024 (18.97)

Choral Music
S. Farr (org), D. Hill (cnd), Winchester Cathedral Choir—Magnificat & Nunc dimittis in B; The Lord is my Shepherd; Motets, Op. 38; Magnificat & Nunc dimittis in A; If Thou Shalt Confess with thy Mouth; Magnificat & Nunc dimittis in F; And I Saw Another Angel; Pater noster; Magnificat & Nunc dimittis in E; Jubilate in B; Te Deum in B ("Sacred Choral Music, Vol. 1") HYP ▲ 66964 (18.97)
S. Farr (org), D. Hill (cnd), Winchester Cathedral Choir—Bible Songs, Op. 113; Evening Service in G; Morning Service in C ("Sacred Choral Music, Vol. 2") HYP ▲ 66965 (18.97)
D. Hill (cnd), Winchester Cathedral Choir—For Lo, I Raise Up, Op. 145; St. Patrick's Breastplate; Lighten our darkness; Magnificat; other works ("Sacred Choral Music, Vol. 3: The Georgian Years") HYP ▲ 66974 (18.97)
A. Johnstone (org), M. Duley (cnd), Christ Church Cathedral Choir Dublin—For Lo, I Raise Up, Op. 145; The Queen's Service; Festal Communion Service in B; Magnificat & Nunc Dimittis in E; Motets, Op. 135 ("Complete Morning & Evening Services & Offices for Holy Communion, Vol. 3") PRIO ▲ 602 (16.97)
P. Trepte (cnd), Ely Cathedral Choir—Jubilates in A & C; Magnificat in B; Nunc Dimittis in B; Te Deums in A & C ("The Stanford Canticles from Ely") † F. Jackson:Benedictine; T. Noble:Choral Music GILD ▲ 7116 [DDD] (16.97)

Church Music
F. Grier (cnd), Christ Church Cathedral Choir, Oxford, C. Daniels (vc), H. Bicket (org)—Anthem, Op. 145; Blessed Is He Who Is Upright, Op. 38; Evening Service in A, Op 12 *(rec Christ Church Cathedral, Oxford, England)* ("O For the Wings of a Dove") † Anonymous:Church Music; J. S. Bach:Cant 147; Mendelssohn (-Bartholdy):Choral Music; W. A. Mozart:Ave verum corpus, K.618; C. Wood:Hail Gladdening Light ASVQ ▲ 6019 [ADD] (10.97)
E. Higginbottom (cnd), New College Choir Oxford ("Anthems & Motets") CRD ▲ 3497 (17.97)

Concert Piece for Organ & Orchestra, Op. 181 (1921)
G. Weir (org), V. Handley (cnd), Ulster Orch † Irish Rhap 3, Op. 137 CHN ▲ 8861 [DDD] (16.97)

Concert Variations upon an English Theme ("Down among the Dead Men") for Piano & Orchestra, Op. 71 (1898)
M. Fingerhut (pno), V. Handley (cnd), Ulster Orch *(rec Belfast, Ireland, Feb 19-23, 1989)* † Con 2 Pno, Op. 126; Concert Vars upon an English Theme, Op. 71 CHN ▲ 7099 [DDD] (13.97)

Concerto in a for Clarinet & Orchestra, Op. 80 (1902)
J. Hilton (cl), V. Handley (cnd), Ulster Orch † Sym 2 CHN ▲ 8991 [DDD] (16.97)
E. Johnson (cl), C. Groves (cnd), Royal PO † Intermezzi, Op. 13; G. Finzi:Bagatelles Cl, Op. 23; Con Cl ASV ▲ 787 [DDD] (16.97)

Concerto No. 2 in c for Piano & Orchestra, Op. 126 (1911)
M. Fingerhut (pno), V. Handley (cnd), Ulster Orch *(rec Belfast, Ireland, Feb 19-23, 1989)* † Concert Vars upon an English Theme, Op. 71; Concert Vars, Op. 71 CHN ▲ 7099 [DDD] (13.97)

For Lo, I Raise Up (anthem) for Organ & Chorus, Op. 145 (1914)
R. Seal (org), Salisbury Cathedral Choir [ENG] † Song of Peace; J. S. Bach:Fant Org, BWV 572; C. Franck:Prélude, fugue et var, Op. 18; Liszt:Prelude & Fugue on the name B-A-C-H, S.260; T. A. Walmisley:Remember, O Lord; S. S. Wesley:Thou Wilt Keep Him in Perfect Peace MER ▲ 84140 (16.97)

Hymns (6) for Voice & Organ, Op. 113 (1910)
S. Varcoe (bass), I. Watson (org) † Stabat Mater, Op. 96; Te Deum, Op. 66 CHN ▲ 9548 (16.97)

Intermezzi (3) for Clarinet & Piano, Op. 13
E. Johnson (cl), M. Martineau (pno) † Con Cl; G. Finzi:Bagatelles Cl, Op. 23; Con Cl ASV ▲ 787 [DDD] (16.97)

Irish Dances (4) for Piano, Op. 89 (1903)
P. Grainger (pno) [arr Grainger] *(rec 1908-48)* ("Percy Grainger, Vol. 2") † Chopin:Son Pno in b, Op. 58; Son Pno in b♭, Op. 35; R. Schumann:Romances Pno, Op. 28; Symphonic Etudes, Op. 13 PHS ▲ 9013 [AAD] (18.97)

Irish Fantasies for Violin & Piano, Op. 54 (1894)
P. Barritt (vn), C. Edwards (pno)—No. 1, Caoine (A Lament) † Characteristic Pieces Vn, Op. 93; Son 1 Vn, Op. 11; Son 3 Vn, Op. 70 HYP ▲ 67024 (18.97)

Irish Rhapsodies (6) for Orchestra [No. 3 for Cello & Orchestra; No. 6 for Violin & Orchestra] (complete)
L. Mordkovitch (vn), R. Wallfisch (vc), V. Handley (cnd), Ulster Orch † Oedipus tyrannus (prelude) CHN 2-▲ 7002 [DDD] (26.97)

Irish Rhapsody No. 1 in d for Orchestra, Op. 78 (1901)
V. Handley (cnd), Ulster Orch † Sym 6 CHN ▲ 8627 [DDD] (16.97)

Irish Rhapsody No. 2 in f for Orchestra, Op. 84, "The Lament for the Son of Ossian" (ca 1903)
V. Handley (cnd), Ulster Orch † Sym 1 CHN ▲ 9049 [DDD] (16.97)

Irish Rhapsody No. 3 for Cello & Orchestra, Op. 137 (ca 1915)
R. Wallfisch (vc), V. Handley (cnd), Ulster Orch † Concert Piece Org, Op. 181 CHN ▲ 8861 [DDD] (16.97)

Irish Rhapsody No. 4 for Orchestra, Op. 141 (1914)
V. Handley (cnd), Ulster Orch † Sym 5 CHN ▲ 8581 [DDD] (16.97)

Irish Rhapsody No. 5 in g for Orchestra, Op. 147 (1917)
V. Handley (cnd), Ulster Orch † Sym 3 CHN ▲ 8545 [DDD] (16.97)

Irish Rhapsody No. 6 for Violin & Orchestra, Op. 191 (ca 1923)
L. Mordkovitch (vn), V. Handley (cnd), Ulster Orch † Oedipus tyrannus (prelude); Sym 4 CHN ▲ 8884 [DDD] (16.97)

Oedipus tyrannus:Prelude
V. Handley (cnd), Ulster Orch † Irish Rhaps CHN 2-▲ 7002 [DDD] (26.97)
V. Handley (cnd), Ulster Orch † Irish Rhap 6, Op. 191; Sym 4 CHN ▲ 8884 [DDD] (16.97)

Organ Music
artist unknown—Postlude in G; Preludes in E & F [all from Op. 101]; Son 4 Org, Op. 153; Prelude in the Form of a Toccata, Op. 88/3; Postlude in d [from Op. 105] ("Organ Music from the Island of Ireland") † J. S. Bach:Toccata & Fugue Org, BWV 565; J. Dexter:Londonderry Air; Kitson:Communion on an Irish Air; C. S. Lang:Tuba Tune, Op. 15; Widor:Sym 5 Org, Op. 42/1; C. Wood:Preludes Org GILD ▲ 7122 [ADD] (16.97)

Preludes in all the Keys (Nos. 25-48) for Piano, Op. 179 (1921)
P. Jacobs (pno) [Nos. 25-48] † Rhaps from Dante Pno, Op. 92 OLY ▲ 638 (16.97)

Requiem for Voices, Orchestra & Chorus, Op. 63 (1896)
A. Leaper (cnd), Ireland National SO, C. Pearce (cnd) , RTE Philharmonic Choir, V. Kerr (sop) † Veiled Prophet of Khorassan (sels) MARC 2-▲ 8223580 [DDD] (27.97)

Rhapsodies from Dante (3) in a, B & C for Piano, Op. 92 (1875)
P. Jacobs (pno) † Preludes in all the Keys Pno, Op. 179 OLY ▲ 638 (16.97)

▲ = CD ♦ = Enhanced CD △ = MD ▮ = Cassette Tape ▯ = DCC

STANFORD, CHARLES VILLIERS (cont.)

Sonata No. 2 for Cello & Piano
J. L. Webber (vc), J. McCabe (pno) † F. Bridge:Elégie; Scherzetto Vc; J. Ireland:Son Vc ASV ▲ 807 (16.97)

Sonata for Clarinet & Piano, Op. 129 (ca 1912)
E. Jóhannesson (cl), P. Jenkins (pno) *(rec Cambridge, England, Sept 1991)* ("British Music for Clarinet and Piano") † M. Arnold:Son Cl; A. Bliss:Pastoral Cl, Op.posth.; Dunhill:Fant Suite Cl & Pno, Op. 91; H. Ferguson:Short Pieces Cl, Op. 6; Hurlstone:Characteristic Pieces Cl; Stoker:Sonatina Cl, Op. 5 CHN ▲ 9079 (16.97)
E. Johnson (cl), M. Martineau (pno) *(rec London, England)* ("Pastoral - Emma Johnson Plays British Clarinet Mus") † A. Bax:Son Cl; A. Bliss:Nursery Rhymes (2) Cl & Pno, T.20; Pastoral; J. Ireland:Fant-Son Cl; Vaughan Williams:Studies in English Folk-Song; Vocalises Sop & Cl ASV ▲ 891 [DDD] (16.97)
V. Soames (cl), J. Flinders (pno) ("On the Wings of English Melody") † M. Arnold:Son Cl; A. Bliss:Pastoral Cl, Op.posth.; G. Finzi:Bagatelles Cl, Op. 23; J. Ireland:Fant-Son Cl; Vaughan Williams:Studies in English Folk-Song CLCL ▲ 25 [DDD] (17.97)

Sonata No. 2 in G for Organ, Op. 151, "Eroica" (1917)
J. Payne (org) *(rec Fort Worth, TX, June 9, 1994)* ("Sonatas for Organ") † Son 3 Org, Op. 152; Son 4 Org, Op. 153 MARC ▲ 8223754 [DDD] (13.97)

Sonata No. 3 in D for Organ, Op. 152, "Britannica" (1917)
J. Payne (org) *(rec Fort Worth, TX, June 9, 1994)* ("Sonatas for Organ") † Son 2 Org, Op. 151; Son 4 Org, Op. 153 MARC ▲ 8223754 [DDD] (13.97)

Sonata No. 4 in C for Organ, Op. 153, "Celtica" (1918)
J. Payne (org) *(rec Fort Worth, TX, June 9, 1994)* ("Sonatas for Organ") † Son 2 Org, Op. 151; Son 3 Org, Op. 152 MARC ▲ 8223754 [DDD] (13.97)

Sonata No. 1 in D for Violin & Piano, Op. 11 (ca 1880)
P. Barritt (vn), C. Edwards (pno) † Characteristic Pieces Vn, Op. 93; Irish Fants Vn, Op. 54; Son 3 Vn, Op. 70 HYP ▲ 67024 (18.97)

Sonata No. 3 in G for Violin & Piano, Op. 70 (ca 1898)
P. Barritt (vn), C. Edwards (pno) † Characteristic Pieces Vn, Op. 93; Irish Fants Vn, Op. 54; Son 1 Vn, Op. 11 HYP ▲ 67024 (18.97)

A Song of Peace (anthem) for Chorus & Organ
R. Seal (org), Salisbury Cathedral Choir [ENG] † For Lo, I Raise Up, Op. 145; J. S. Bach:Fant Org, BWV 572; C. Franck:Prelude, fugue et var, Op. 18; Liszt:Prelude & Fugue on the name B-A-C-H, S.260; T. A. Walmisley:Remember, O Lord; S. S. Wesley:Thou Wilt Keep Him in Perfect Peace MER ▲ 84140 (16.97)

Stabat Mater for solo Voices, Orchestra & Chorus, Op. 96 (1907)
I. Attrot (sop), P. H. Stephens (mez), N. Robson (ten), S. Varcoe (bass), D. Battiwalla (org), R. Hickox (cnd), BBC PO, BBC Phil Chorus † Hymns; Te Deum, Op. 66 CHN ▲ 9548 (16.97)

Symphonies (7) (complete)
V. Handley (cnd), Ulster Orch CHN 4-▲ 9279 [DDD] (48.97)

Symphony No. 1 in B♭ (1876)
V. Handley (cnd), Ulster Orch † Irish Rhap 2, Op. 84 CHN ▲ 9049 [DDD] (16.97)

Symphony No. 2 in d, "Elegiac" (1882)
V. Handley (cnd), Ulster Orch † Con Cl CHN ▲ 8991 [DDD] (16.97)

Symphony No. 3 in f, Op. 28, "Irish" (1887)
V. Handley (cnd), Ulster Orch † Irish Rhap 5, Op. 147 CHN ▲ 8545 [DDD] (16.97)

Symphony No. 4 in F, Op. 31 (1889)
V. Handley (cnd), Ulster Orch † Irish Rhap 6, Op. 191; Oedipus tyrannus (prelude) CHN ▲ 8884 [DDD] (16.97)

Symphony No. 5 in D, Op. 56, "L'allegro ed il penseroso" (1894)
V. Handley (cnd), Ulster Orch † Irish Rhap 4, Op. 141 CHN ▲ 8581 [DDD] (16.97)

Symphony No. 6 in E♭, Op. 94, "In memoriam George Frederick Watts" (1905)
V. Handley (cnd), Ulster Orch † Irish Rhap 1, Op. 78 CHN ▲ 8627 [DDD] (16.97)

Te Deum for solo Voices, Orchestra & Chorus, Op. 66 (1898)
I. Attrot (sop), P. H. Stephens (mez), N. Robson (ten), S. Varcoe (bass), D. Battiwalla (org), R. Hickox (cnd), BBC PO, BBC Phil Chorus † Hymns; Stabat Mater, Op. 96 CHN ▲ 9548 (16.97)

The Veiled Prophet of Khorassan (selections)
V. Kerr (sop), A. Leaper (cnd), Ireland National SO, C. Pearce (cnd) , RTE Philharmonic Choir † Requiem, Op. 63 MARC 2-▲ 8223580 [DDD] (27.97)

STANGO, JULIETTE (1962-

Sol' per Dirti Addio [Only to Tell You Goodbye] for Orchestra (1992)
R. Black (cnd), Slovak RSO Bratislava † Althans:Valse Excentrique; M. Kessler:Con Pno; Leclaire:Haiku; W. T. McKinley:Andante & Scherzo; Rahbee:Tapestry 1; Rendelman:Chorale & Toccata MASM ▲ 2009 [DDD] (16.97)

STANHOPE, DAVID (20th cent)

Concerto for Band
R. Hower (cnd), Elder Conservatorium Wind Ensemble *(rec Univ of Adelaide Australia, 1995-96)* ("Little Ripper") † E.G.B.D.S.; Folk Song Suites; Little Ripper TALP ▲ 107 [DDD] (18.97)

E.G.B.D.S. [Edvard Grieg By David Stanhope] for Band
R. Hower (cnd), Elder Conservatorium Wind Ensemble *(rec Univ of Adelaide Australia, 1995-96)* ("Little Ripper") † Con Band; Folk Song Suites; Little Ripper TALP ▲ 107 [DDD] (18.97)

Folk Song Suites (3) for Band
R. Hower (cnd), Elder Conservatorium Wind Ensemble *(rec Univ of Adelaide Australia, 1995-96)* ("Little Ripper") † Con Band; E.G.B.D.S.; Little Ripper TALP ▲ 107 [DDD] (18.97)

Little Ripper for Band (1988-89)
R. Hower (cnd), Elder Conservatorium Wind Ensemble *(rec Univ of Adelaide Australia, 1995-96)* ("Little Ripper") † Con Band; E.G.B.D.S.; Folk Song Suites TALP ▲ 107 [DDD] (18.97)

STANKOVICH, EVGENY (1942-

Chamber Symphony No. 2 for Chamber Orchestra
F. Glushchenko (cnd), Ukrainian CO *(rec 1982)* † Night Before Christmas; Sym of Pastorals CSN ▲ 810006 [AAD] (16.97)

The Night Before Christmas (music for the radio play) for Orchestra
F. Glushchenko (cnd), Ukrainian State SO *(rec 1983)* † Chamber Sym 2; Sym of Pastorals CSN ▲ 810006 [AAD] (16.97)

Rasputin (ballet) for Orchestra (1989)
H. Earle (cnd), Odessa PO † Glière:Taras Bul'ba ASV (Music of Ukraine) ▲ 988 (16.97)

Symphony No. 1, "Sinfonia larga" (1973)
T. Kuchar (cnd), Ukrainian National SO *(rec Ukrainian Radio Concert Hall, Jan 27-31, 1995)* † Sym 2; Sym 4 MARC ▲ 8223792 [DDD] (13.97)

Symphony No. 2, "Heroic" (1975)
T. Kuchar (cnd), Ukrainian National SO *(rec Ukrainian Radio Concert Hall, Jan 27-31, 1995)* † Sym 1; Sym 4 MARC ▲ 8223792 [DDD] (13.97)

Symphony No. 4, "Sinfonia lirica" (1977)
T. Kuchar (cnd), Ukrainian State SO *(rec Ukrainian Radio Concert Hall, Jan 27-31, 1995)* † Sym 1; Sym 2 MARC ▲ 8223792 [DDD] (13.97)

Symphony of Pastorals in d for Orchestra (1977)
F. Glushchenko (cnd), Ukrainian State SO *(rec 1982)* † Chamber Sym 2; Night Before Christmas CSN ▲ 810006 [AAD] (16.97)

STANLEY, JOHN (1713-1786)

Concertos (6) for Organ (or Harpsichord or Piano), Op. 10
G. Gifford (org), G. Gifford (cnd), Northern Sinfonia of England CRD ▲ 3365

Concertos (6) for Strings [arr Organ & Strings], Op. 2
S. Standage (cnd), Collegium Musicum 90 CHN ▲ 638 (16.97)

Voluntaries (30) for Organ
R. Hobson (org) *(rec Mayfair England)* † Guilain:Pièces d'orgue pour le Magnificat; Mendelssohn (-Bartholdy):Sons Org, Op. 65 HER ▲ 156

STARCK, ARNO (1886-1960)

Concerto for Mandolin & Orchestra
G. Tröster-Weyhofen (mand), G. Vogt (cnd), Bavarian State Youth Plucked Instrument Orch † H. Baumann:Con Capriccioso; S. Behrend:Serenade Mand; Tober-Vogt:Carnival of Venice; Vivaldi:Con Mand, RV.425 THOR ▲ 2146 [DDD] (16.97)

STARER, ROBERT (1924-

Anna Margarita's Will for Soprano & Chamber Ensemble [text Gail Godwin] (1979)
P. Bryn-Julson (sop), S. Kates (vc), K. Kraber (fl), P. Ingraham (hn), D. Sutherland (pno) *(rec 1980)* † Ariel; Con Cl CRI ▲ 612 [ADD] (17.97)

STARER, ROBERT (cont.)

Annapolis Suite for Harp & Brass Quintet (1983)
N. Allen (hp), American Brass Quintet † Con Ob; Kli Zemer; Samson Agonistes MASM ▲ 2048 [DDD] (16.97)

Ariel, Visions of Isaiah for Soprano, Baritone, Orchestra & Chorus [text from Book of Isaiah] (1959)
R. Peters (sop), J. Patrick (bar), A. Kaplan (cnd), Camerata Orch, A. Kaplan (cnd), Camerata Singers *(rec 1972)* † Anna Margarita's Will; Con Cl CRI ▲ 612 [ADD] (17.97)

At Home Alone for Piano (1980)
G. Berthiaume (pno) ("Excursions for a Pianist") † Caprices Pno; Electric Church; Excursions; Israeli Sketches; Sketches in Color; Son 1 Pno ALBA ▲ 205 [DDD] (16.97)

Caprices (5) for Piano (1948)
G. Berthiaume (pno) ("Excursions for a Pianist") † At Home Alone; Electric Church; Excursions; Israeli Sketches; Sketches in Color; Son 1 Pno ALBA ▲ 205 [DDD] (16.97)

Concerto a 3 for Clarinet, Trumpet, Trombone & Strings (1954)
J. Rabbai (cl), G. Schwarz (tpt), P. Brevig (trbn), A. Kaplan (cnd), Camerata String Orch *(rec 1972)* † Anna Margarita's Will; Ariel CRI ▲ 612 [ADD] (17.97)

Concerto a 4 for Oboe, Clarinet, Bassoon, Horn & Orchestra (1983)
B. Shapiro (ob), C. Sereque (cl), S. Krimsky (bn), J. Cerminaro (hn), G. Schwarz (cnd), Seattle SO † Annapolis Suite; Kli Zemer; Samson Agonistes MASM ▲ 2048 [DDD] (16.97)

Concerto for Cello & Orchestra (1988)
J. Starker (vc), L. Botstein (cnd), Boston Pro Arte CO *(rec Feb 17, 1991)* † R. Wernick:Con Va; R. Wilson:Con Pno CRI ▲ 618 [DDD] (17.97)

Concerto for Viola, Strings & Percussion (1958)
M. Berger (va), J. Snashall (cnd), English CO *(rec 1965)* ("American Concertos") † Bergsma:Con Vn; Colgrass:Concert Masters; L. Harrison:Con Vn; Kupferman:Con Vc, Tape & Orch; B. Lees:Con Vn; Piston:Concertino Pno VB2 (The American Composers) 2-▲ 5158 (9.97)

Duo for Violin & Piano (1988)
W. Terwilliger (vn), A. Cooperstock (pno) ("Chamber Works") † Elegy for a Woman Who Died Too Young; Episodes Va; Qnt Cl ALBA ▲ 152 [DDD] (16.97)

Electric Church for Piano (1991)
G. Berthiaume (pno) ("Excursions for a Pianist") † At Home Alone; Caprices Pno; Excursions; Israeli Sketches; Sketches in Color; Son 1 Pno ALBA ▲ 205 [DDD] (16.97)

Elegy for a Woman Who Died Too Young for Violin & Cello (1990)
C. Cowan (vn), S. Seligman (vc) ("Chamber Works") † Duo Vn & Pno; Episodes Va; Qnt Cl ALBA ▲ 152 [DDD] (16.97)
J. Stewart (vn), S. Honigberg (vc) ("Darkness & Light") † Ben-Haim (Frankenburger):Sonatina Pno; Berlinski:From the World of My Father; Perle:Hebrew Melodies; M. Vainberg:Trio Pno, Op. 24 ALBA ▲ 157 [DDD] (16.97)

Episodes for Viola, Cello & Piano
L. Martin (va), H. Clark (vc), S. Schuldmann (pno) ("Chamber Works") † Duo Vn & Pno; Elegy for a Woman Who Died Too Young; Qnt Cl ALBA ▲ 152 [DDD] (16.97)

Evanescence for Brass Quintet (1980)
American Brass Quintet † Hudson Valley Suite; F. Thorne:Simultaneities; Sym 7 ALBA ▲ 244 [ADD] (16.97)

Excursions for a Pianist for Piano (1991)
G. Berthiaume (pno) ("Excursions for a Pianist") † At Home Alone; Caprices Pno; Electric Church; Israeli Sketches; Sketches in Color; Son 1 Pno ALBA ▲ 205 [DDD] (16.97)

Hudson Valley Suite for Orchestra (1983)
D. A. Miller (cnd), Albany SO † Evanescence; F. Thorne:Simultaneities; Sym 7 ALBA ▲ 244 [ADD] (16.97)

Israeli Sketches (3) for Piano (1957)
G. Berthiaume (pno) ("Excursions for a Pianist") † At Home Alone; Caprices Pno; Electric Church; Excursions; Sketches in Color; Son 1 Pno ALBA ▲ 205 [DDD] (16.97)

Kli Zemer [Instrument of Song] (concerto) for Clarinet & Orchestra
O. Orbach (cl), S. Sperber (cnd), Haifa SO † Annapolis Suite; Con Ob; Samson Agonistes MASM ▲ 2048 [DDD] (16.97)

Light & Shadow for Saxophone Quartet (1978)
Raschèr Saxophone Quartet *(rec 1997-98)* ("America") † S. Adler:Line Drawings; S. Corbett:Vars Saxes; C. Florio:Qt Saxes; W. Peterson:Windup; C. Wuorinen:Qt Saxes BIS ▲ 953 [DDD] (17.97)

Night Thoughts for Soprano, Mezzo-Soprano, Tenor, Baritone & Piano Duet
T. Santiago (sop), J. Hines (mez), A. Griffey (ten), N. Michaels (bar), A. Roberts (pno), E. Roberts (pno) ("Vocal Works") † Remembering Felix; To Think of Time ALBA ▲ 151 [DDD] (16.97)

Piano Music
J. Kolb (pno)—Son 3 Pno; Sketches in Color, Set 2:Khaki, Aquamarine, Silver; Prelude & Toccata; The Ideal Self; Twilight Fants; The Contemporary Virtuoso ("Solo Piano Music, 1946-96") ALBA ▲ 228 [DDD] (16.97)

Preludes (5) for Piano
R. Rust (pno) ("Three American Premieres") † Noon:Etudes Pno, Op. 69; S. Prokofiev:Son 6 Pno, Op. 82; E. Siegmeister:Studies Pno PROT ▲ 1110 [ADD] (18.97)

Preludes (3) for Trumpet & Organ
K. Benjamin (tpt), M. Turnquist (org) ("Clarion: New Music for Trumpet & Organ") † W. Albright:Jericho; P. Eben:Okna; P. Hamelin:Sonata ben melodico; Nelhybel:Metamorphosis GOT ▲ 49067 [DDD] (18.97)

Quintet for Clarinet & Strings
Music in the Mountains Festival Chamber Players ("Chamber Works") † Duo Vn & Pno; Elegy for a Woman Who Died Too Young; Episodes Va ALBA ▲ 152 [DDD] (16.97)

Remembering Felix for Narrator, Cello & Piano
R. J. Lurtsema (nar), H. Clark (vc), S. Schuldmann (pno) ("Vocal Works") † Night Thoughts; To Think of Time ALBA ▲ 151 [DDD] (16.97)

Samson Agonistes (symphonic portrait) for Orchestra (1963)
V. Válek (cnd), Czech RSO † Annapolis Suite; Con Ob; Kli Zemer MASM ▲ 2048 [DDD] (16.97)

Sketches in Color (7) for Piano (1964)
G. Berthiaume (pno) ("Excursions for a Pianist") † At Home Alone; Caprices Pno; Electric Church; Excursions; Israeli Sketches; Son 1 Pno ALBA ▲ 205 [DDD] (16.97)

Sonata No. 1 for Piano (1950)
G. Berthiaume (pno) ("Excursions for a Pianist") † At Home Alone; Caprices Pno; Electric Church; Excursions; Israeli Sketches; Sketches in Color ALBA ▲ 205 [DDD] (16.97)

Songs of Youth & Age for Ensemble
Scarborough Chamber Players † A. Blank:Poems; A. Roussel:Poèmes de Ronsard, Op. 26; R. Schumann:Faschingsschwank, Op. 26; L. Spohr:German Songs, Op. 103; H. Villa-Lobos:Bachiana brasileira 6 CENT ▲ 2106 [DDD] (16.97)

To Think of Time for Soprano & String Quartet
A. K. Donaldson (sop), Mariani String Quartet ("Vocal Works") † Night Thoughts; Remembering Felix ALBA ▲ 151 [DDD] (16.97)

STAROBIN, MICHAEL (1956-

Chase for Amplified Guitar & Computer-Generated Tape (1987)
D. Starobin (gtr) ("New Music with Guitar, Vol. 4") † T. Machover:Bug-Mudra; Roxbury:Songs of Walt Whitman; Saxton:Night Dance Gtr; Searle:2 Practical Cats BRID ▲ 9022 [DDD] (17.97)

STARZER, JOSEPH (FRANZ) (1726-1787)

Divertimento in a for String Quartet
Russian Baroque Ensemble *(rec Nov 1996)* ("Russian Baroque") † P. Baillot:Air russe varié, Op. 11; M. Berezovsky:Son Vn; Vars on a Russian Folksong; Steibelt:Vars on 2 Russian Folksongs; Titz:Qt Strs in G; Son Vn in f♯ ARNO 2-▲ 51626 [DDD] (9.97)

STAUDE, CHRISTOPH (1965-

Obduktion for Saxophone & Ensemble
J. Ernst (sax), Hirsch (cnd) ("New Saxophone Chamber Music") † Kyburz:Cells; Mundry:Komposition Sax; W. Zimmermann:Fragmente der Liebe COLG ▲ 31890 (18.97)

STAVENHAGEN, BERNHARD (1862-1914)

Concerto (No. 1) in b for Piano & Orchestra, Op. 4
R. Keller (pno), J. Faerber (cnd), Berlin SO *(rec 1978)* ("The Romantic Piano Concerto, Vol. 4") † E. D. Albert:Con 2 Pno, Op. 12; Bronsart Von schellendorf:Con Pno, Op. 10; Liszt:Malédiction, S.121; Mosonyi:Con Pno; Raff:Con Pno VB2 2-▲ 5067 [ADD] (9.97)
A. Pistorius (pno), D. Salomon (cnd), Vogtland PO Greiz/Reichenbach † Pieces Pno, Op. 10; Pieces Pno, Op. 2; Pieces Pno, Op. 5 ARS ▲ 368354 [DDD] (15.99)

Concerto No. 2 in A for Piano & Orchestra [newly orchd Joachim-Dietrich Link from surviving piano reduction score] (1912)
V. Lehmann (pno), H. Förster (cnd), Vogtland PO Greiz/Reichenbach † Songs EBS ▲ 6079 [DDD] (17.97)

STAVENHAGEN, BERNHARD (cont.)

Pieces (3) for Piano, Op. 2 (1894-1906)
A. Pistorius (pno) † Con 1 Pno, Op. 4; Pieces Pno, Op. 10; Pieces Pno, Op. 5 ARS ▲ 368354 [DDD] (15.99)

Pieces (3) for Piano, Op. 5 (1894-1906)
A. Pistorius (pno) † Con 1 Pno, Op. 4; Pieces Pno, Op. 10; Pieces Pno, Op. 2 ARS ▲ 368354 [DDD] (15.99)

Pieces (3) for Piano, Op. 10 (1894-1906)
A. Pistorius (pno) † Con 1 Pno, Op. 4; Pieces Pno, Op. 2; Pieces Pno, Op. 5 ARS ▲ 368354 [DDD] (15.99)

Songs (3) for Voice & Piano [arr Joachim-Dietrich Link for voice & orchestra]
H. Spatzek (sop), T. Pfeiffer (bar), H. Förster (cnd), Vogtland PO Greiz/Reichenbach † Con 2 Pno EBS ▲ 6079 [DDD] (17.97)

STEEN, KEN (1958-

Metastasis for Orchestra (1992)
S. Kawalla (cnd), Slovak RSO Bratislava † B. Hobson:Three; Konowalski:Brewerie; Loeb:Suite Concertante; T. Myers:Concertino Orch; R. Snyder:Shamanic Dances; G. W. Yasinitsky:Into a Star VMM (Music from 6 Continents 1993) ▲ 3017 [DDD]

Shadows & Light for Electronic Cello & Electronics (1989)
J. Krieger (vc) *(rec Glastonbury, CT)* † J. Berger:Lead Plates of the Rom Press; J. Cage:Ryoanji Fl; Gwiazda:themythofAcceptAnce; Knehans:Night Chains CRI ▲ 680 [DDD] (16.97)

While Conscience Slept for Flute, Clarinet, Electric Cello & MIDI Keyboards (1989)
J. Krieger (elec vc), G. Shearer (fl), R. Krentzman (cl), I. B'Racz (kbd), M. Ersevim (cnd) ("Spectra: Connecticut Composers") † R. Dix:Lyric Qt; Gryc:American Portraits; W. Penn:Chamber Music II; Welwood:Breath inside the Breath CPS ▲ 8650 [ADD] (16.97)

STEENHOVEN, KAREL VAN (20th cent)

La chanteuse et le bois sauvage for Recorder Quartet (1993)
Amsterdam Loeki Stardust Quartet ("Pictured Air") † B. De Kemp:Lieto; Keuris:Passeggiate; Koomans:Jogger; C. Meijering:Een Paard Met Vijf Poten; Sitting Ducks; P. J. Wagemans:Kwartet Rcrs CCL ▲ 8996

STEFFANI, AGOSTINO (1654-1728)

Sonata in d for Chamber Ensemble, Sibley 8
Trio Basiliensis *(rec Freiburg, Germany, Apr 1996)* ("Concerning Babell & Son") † Babell:Son 2 Rcr; A. Corelli:Son 5 Va da Gamba, Op. 5; P. A. Fiocco:Son in C; G. F. Handel:Rinaldo (sels); Paisible:Son Rcr in F, Sibley 9; Rosier:Son in g ARSM ▲ 1167 [DDD] (17.97)

Vocal Music
R. Bertini (sop), C. Cavina (alt), A. Cremonesi (cnd) —Begl'occhi, Oh Dio, Non Più; Porto L'alma Incenerita; Dimmi, Dimmi Cupido; Occhi, Perchè Piangete?; Crudo Amor, Morir Mi Sento; Sol Negl'occhi Del Mio Bene; Placidissime Catene *(rec June 1994)* ("Duetti da Camera") GLSS ▲ 920902 (18.97)
The Musicke Companye—Che volete o crude pene; Son erede di tormenti *(rec St. Mary's Church Essex, May 1997)* ("Handel & Companye") † G. Bononcini:Cant o duetti; Gominiani:Sono Vc & Continuo, Op. 5; G. F. Handel:Harmonious Blacksmith ITIM ▲ 54 [DDD] (16.97)

STEIBELT, DANIEL (1765-1823)

Sonata in F for Piano 4-Hands
A. Bakhchiev (pno), Y. Sorokina (pno) ("Music from the Pushkin Epoch") † L. W. T. von Ferguson:Son Pno 4-Hnds; J. Field:Grand valse, H.19; Rondeau, H.43; Vars Russian Air, H.10; J. W. Hässler:Grand Son; C. Mayer:Galop militaire; Grand Ov; Mazurka-Caprice; Nocturne CHN ▲ 9418 (16.97)

Variations on 2 Russian Folksongs for Piano
I. Ermakova (pno) *(rec Nov 1996)* ("Russian Baroque") † P. Baillot:Air russe varié, Op. 11; M. Berezovsky:Son Vn; Vars on a Russian Folksong; Starzer:Divert Str Qt; Titz:Qt Strs in G; Son Vn in f# ARNO 2-▲ 51626 [DDD] (9.97)

STEIGER, RAND (1957-

Double Concerto for Piano, Percussion & Orchestra (1986)
A. Karis (pno), S. Schick (perc), R. Steiger (cnd) *(rec 1992)* † Ferneyhough:Prometheus; R. Reynolds:Not only Night; J. Yuasa:Mutterings CRI ▲ 652 [DDD] (17.97)

Hexadecathlon for Horn & Instrumental Ensemble
J. Cerminaro (hn), S. Mosko (cnd) ("Screamers: Difficult Works for the Horn") † J. Haydn:Divert Hn, H.IV/5; W. Kraft:Evening Voluntaries; H. Lazarof:Intrada; R. Schumann:Adagio & Allegro Hn, Op. 70 CRYS ▲ 679 (15.97)

Thirteen Loops for Electro-Acoustic Ensemble
R. Black (cnd), New York New Music Ensemble *(rec 1991-94)* ("New Electro-Acoustic Music") † Primosch:Sacra Conversazione; C. B. Rulon:Res Facta CENT ▲ 2338 [DDD] (16.97)

Trio In Memoriam for Piano, Cello & Percussion
Aequalis † M. Brody:Commedia; Davidovsky:Synchronism 6; Gideon:Son Vc & Pno; Ung:Spiral NWW ▲ 80412 [DDD] (16.97)

Woven Serenade for Clarinet & String Quartet
D. Crockett (cnd), Los Angeles CO *(rec Simi Valley, CA, Sept 29-30, 1993)* ("Für Wolfgang Amadeus") † Crockett:Celestial Mechanics; Hartke:Wir küssen ihnen tausendmal die Hände; L. Larsen:Schoenberg, Schenker & Schillinger CRI ▲ 669 [DDD] (16.97)

STEIN, LEON (1910-

Introduction & Rondo for Flute & Percussion (1960)
D. Peck (fl), J. Ross (perc) ("The Flute Heard Round the World") † Caplet:Improvs Fl; Casella:Barcarola et scherzo, Op. 4; P. Gaubert:Son 1 Fl; Ibert:Entracte Fl; Rieti:Sonatina Fl; A. Wilder:Air Fl BOST ▲ 1027 [DDD] (15.97)

STEINBERG, BEN (dates unknown)

Songs
J. Batt (org), B. Steinberg (cnd), Philadelphia Voces Novae et Antiquae—Prelude Org; Come, My Beloved; Blessing of the Sabbath Candles; Call to Worship; Hear, O Israel; You Shall Love the Lord Your God; Who is Like You, O God; Children of Israel Shall Keep the Sabbath; Blessed Are You, O God; Those Who Keep the Sabbath; You Are One and Your Name is One; Prayer for Peace; May the Words of My Mouth; Blessing Over Wine; At the Dawn I Seek You; This is Israel's Day; Guardian of Israel; Adoration; Benediction *(rec Elkins Park, PA, 1993)* ("Shomeir Yisrael - A Musical Service for Friday Evening for Solo, Choir, Organ & Instruments") ARK (Artists Series) ▲ 6126 [DDD] (16.97)

STEINER, MAX (1888-1971)

The Beast with Five Fingers (film music) for Orchestra (1947)
W. T. Stromberg (cnd), Moscow SO [arr John Morgan] *(rec Mosfilm Studio, Oct 1995)* † Lost Patrol; Virginia City MARC ▲ 8223870 [DDD] (13.97)

The Charge of the Light Brigade (film music) for Orchestra (1936)
R. Kaufman (cnd), Brandenburg PO *(rec Berlin, Germany, Apr 14-16 & June 15-21, 1994)* ("Classical Film Music by Korngold, Newman, Steiner") † Korngold:Devotion; Juarez; A. Newman:Gunga Din MARC ▲ 8223608 [DDD] (13.97)

Film Music
B. Kolman (cnd), Slovak State PO ("Film Scores by Max Steiner") CENT ▲ 2367 (16.97)

Four Wives (selections)
E. Wild (cel/pno), E. Hammerstein (cnd), RCA SO *(rec London, England, Apr 1965)* ("Earl Wild Goes to the Movies") † Chopin:Andante Spianato & Grand Polonaise, Op. 22; Liszt:Etudes de concert (3), S.144; W. A. Mozart:Con 21 Pno, K.467; R. Rodgers:Slaughter on Tenth Avenue Orch; M. Rózsa:Spellbound IVOR ▲ 70801 [ADD] (16.97)

King Kong (film music) for Orchestra (1933)
W. J. Stromberg (cnd), Moscow SO *(rec Mosfilm Studio, Oct 1996)* MARC ▲ 8223763 [DDD] (13.97)

The Lost Patrol (film music) for Orchestra (1934)
W. T. Stromberg (cnd), Moscow SO [arr John Morgan] *(rec Mosfilm Studio, Oct 1995)* † Beast with Five Fingers; Virginia City MARC ▲ 8223870 [DDD] (13.97)

Now, Voyager (film music) for Orchestra (1942)
C. Gerhardt (cnd), National PO London, Ambrosian Singers ("Now, Voyager:Classic Film Scores of Max Steiner") RCAV ▲ 136 [ADD] (11.97)

The Three Musketeers (film score) for Orchestra (1935)
R. Kaufman (cnd), Brandenburg PO [arr John Morgan] *(rec Jesus Christ Church Berlin, Germany, 1994)* ("Captain Blood") † Korngold:Captain Blood; M. Rózsa:King's Thief; V. Young:Scaramouche MARC ▲ 8223607 [DDD] (13.97)

Virginia City (film music) for Orchestra (1940)
W. T. Stromberg (cnd), Moscow SO [arr John Morgan] *(rec Mosfilm Studio, Oct 1995)* † Beast with Five Fingers; Lost Patrol MARC ▲ 8223870 [DDD] (13.97)

STEINHARDT, VICTOR (20th cent)

Music of Steinhardt
artists unknown TOWN ▲ 52 (17.97)

STEINKE, GREG A. (1942-

Native American Notes for String Quartet (1990)
Coolidge String Quartet † B. Britten:Qt 1 Strs, Op. 25; A. Koppel:Qt 1 Strs CLSO ▲ 251 (15.97)

STEINMETZ, WERNER (1959-

Solo & Kammermusik for Violin, Piano, Percussion & String Orchestra
S. Windbacher (vn), E. Theis (cnd), Austrian Chamber Sym † Martinů:Con da camera; Concertino Vc MPH ▲ 56821 [DDD] (15.97)

STELLA, SCIPIONE (ca 1559-1610/30)

O Vos Omnes (motet) for Chorus
G. Place (cnd), Gesualdo Consort, G. Fisher (sop), A. Place (mez), S. Gay (ct), G. Place (ten), S. Birchall (bass) *(rec London, England, 1982-95)* ("Madrigals & Motets from Renaissance Naples") † Gesualdo:Madrigals; Luzzaschi:O dolcezza; Nenna:Madrigals & Songs; Nola:Chi chilichi ASVQ ▲ 6210 [DDD] (10.97)

STENHAMMAR, WILHELM (1871-1927)

Chitra (concert suite in 3 movements) for Orchestra [adapted Hilding Rosenberg 1959 from Stenhammar's incidental music for Rabindranath Tagore's play], Op. 43 (1921)
N. Järvi (cnd), Gothenburg SO † Con 2 Pno, Op. 23 BIS ▲ 476 [DDD] (17.97)

Concerto No. 2 in d for Piano & Orchestra, Op. 23 (1904-07)
G. Erikson (pno), E. Svetlanov (cnd), Swedish RSO † T. Aulin:Con 3 Vn, Op. 14 MSV ▲ 622 (16.97)
C. Ortiz (pno), N. Järvi (cnd), Gothenburg SO † Chitra BIS ▲ 476 [DDD] (17.97)

Excelsior! (symphonic overture) for Orchestra, Op. 13 (1896)
N. Järvi (cnd), Gothenburg SO † Sibelius:Romance Strs, Op. 42; Sym 2 BIS ▲ 252 [DDD] (17.97)

Florez och Blanzeflor (ballad) for Baritone & Orchestra [text Levertin], Op. 3 (1891)
P. Mattei (bar), P. Järvi (cnd), Malmö SO [SWE] † Sentimental Romances, Op. 28 BIS ▲ 550 [DDD] (17.97)

Ithaka for Baritone & Orchestra [text Levertin], Op. 21
H. Hagegård (bar), K. Ingebretsen (cnd), Swedish RSO † Sången, Op. 44; Sentimental Romances, Op. 28 CAPA ▲ 21358 (16.97)

Late Summer Nights [Sensommarnätter] for Piano, Op. 33 (1914)
I. Mannheimer (pno) STRL ▲ 1004 (15.97)

Lodolezzi Sings (incidental music) for Orchestra, Op. 39 (1919)
N. Järvi (cnd), Gothenburg SO † Mellanspel; Mid-Winter, Op. 24 BIS ▲ 438 [DDD] (17.97)

Mellanspel (interlude) for Orchestra [from Sången] (1921)
N. Järvi (cnd), Gothenburg SO † Lodolezzi Sings, Op. 39; Mid-Winter, Op. 24 BIS ▲ 438 [DDD] (17.97)

Mid-Winter (Swedish rhapsody) for Orchestra & Chorus, Op. 24 (1907)
N. Järvi (cnd), Gothenburg SO, Gothenburg Sym Chorus [SWE] † Lodolezzi Sings, Op. 39; Mellanspel BIS ▲ 438 [DDD] (17.97)
E. Salonen (cnd), Swedish RSO MSV ▲ 626 [DDD] (16.97)

Music of Stenhammar
N. Järvi (cnd), Gothenberg SO *(Syms 1 & 2; Suite, Op. 39; Interlude from the Song, Op. 44; Midwinter, Op. 24, Snöfrid, Op. 5, Con 2 Pno [w. Cristina Ortiz (pno)]; Excelsior!, Op. 13; Serenade, Op. 31)*, P. Järvi (cnd), Malmö SO *(Ballad Bar & Orch [w. Peter Mattei (bar)]; Sentimental Romances (2), Op. 28; Con 1 Pno [w. Love Derwinger (pno)])* ("Orchestral Music") BIS 4-▲ 714 [DDD] (51.97)
A. S. von Otter (mez), H. Hagegård (bar), I. Wixell (bar), M. Widlund (pno), Swedish Radio Chorus—Fant 1; Fylgia; Till en ros; Melodi; Sången [Interlude]; Florez och Blanzeflor; Con 2 Pno [Adagio]; September; I Seraillets Have; Son Vn in a [Allegro]; Lycklandsresan; Jungfru Blond och Jungfru Brunett; Ballata [Allegro scherzando]; Sverige; Serenade, Op. 31 [Finale] ("Wilhelm Stenhammar: A Musical Portrait") MSV ▲ 906 (11.97)

One People [Ett folk] (cantata) for Baritone, Orchestra & Chorus [text V. von Heidenstam], Op. 22 (1904-05)
K. Fredriksson (bar), G. Sjökvist (cnd), Swedish RSO, Swedish Radio Chorus, Storkyrkan Choir *(rec 1991 & 1996)* ("Cantatas") † Stockholm Exhibition Cant STRL ▲ 1023 [DDD] (15.97)
S. Westerberg (cnd), Swedish RSO, Swedish Radio Choir *(rec Berwald Hall, Stockholm, Sweden, May 7, 1986)* ("Swedish Highlights") † Sången, Op. 44; Alfvén:Bergakungen (sels); Festspel, Op. 25; Gustav II Adolph, Op. 49; Prodigal Son, Op. 217; Swedish Flag; Swedish Rhap 1, Op. 19; L.-E. Larsson:Pastoralsvit, Op. 19; O. J. Lindblad:Royal Anthem; Söderman:Swedish Festival; Traditional:Du Gamla, Du Fria; D. Wirén:Serenade Strs, Op. 11 CAPA ▲ 21340 [DDD] (16.97)

Piano Music (complete solo works)
L. Negro (pno)—3 Fants, Op. 11; Intermezzo; 3 Small Pno Pieces; Impromptu; Impromptu-Vals; Allegro con moto ed appassionato; Sensommarnätter (Late Summer Nights), Op. 33 ("The Complete Solo Piano Music, Vol. 1") BIS ▲ 554 [DDD] (17.97)
L. Negro (pno)—Sons 1-4 Pno; Fant in a ("Complete Solo Piano Music, Vol. 2") BIS ▲ 634 [DDD] (17.97)
L. Negro (pno)—Son Pno, Op. 12; Son Vn, Op. 19 [w. Tale Olsson (vn)]; Allegro ma non tanto; Allegro brillante *(rec Sweden, 1995)* ("The Complete Solo Piano Music, Vol. 3: Chamber Music with Piano") BIS ▲ 764 [DDD] (17.97)

Quartet No. 6 in d for Strings, Op. 35 (1916)
Zetterqvist String Quartet *(rec Apr-May 1997)* ("Zetterqvist String Quartet") † M. Edlund:brains & dancin'; S.-D. Sandström:Qt 3 Strs OPU ▲ 19702 [DDD] (16.97)

SÅngen for Vocal Soloists, Orchestra & Chorus, Op. 44 (1921)
I. Sörenson (sop), A. S. von Otter (mez), S. Dahlberg (ten), P. Wahlgren (bar), H. Blomstedt (cnd), Swedish RSO, Adolf Fredriks Music School Children's Choir † Ithaka; Sentimental Romances, Op. 28 CAPA ▲ 21358 (16.97)
S. Westerberg (cnd), Swedish RSO—Interlude *(rec Berwald Hall, Stockholm, Sweden, May 7, 1986)* ("Swedish Highlights") † Ett folk, Op. 22; Alfvén:Bergakungen (sels); Festspel, Op. 25; Gustav II Adolph, Op. 49; Prodigal Son, Op. 217; Swedish Flag; Swedish Rhap 1, Op. 19; L.-E. Larsson:Pastoralsvit, Op. 19; O. J. Lindblad:Royal Anthem; Söderman:Swedish Festival; Traditional:Du Gamla, Du Fria; D. Wirén:Serenade Strs, Op. 11 CAPA ▲ 21340 [DDD] (16.97)

Sentimental Romances (2) [Sentimentala Romanser] in f & A for Violin & Orchestra, Op. 28 (1910)
S. Stahlhammer (vn), L. Derwinger (pno) *(rec Stockholm, Sweden, Jul 1997)* † Rangström:Capriccio amoroso; Poem; E. Sjögren:Contrabandist; Lyrical Pieces Vn; Songs (3); Valentin:Adagio; Son Vn; Wachtmeister:På vattnet NSAG ▲ 33 (16.97)
A. Tellefsen (vn), S. Westerberg (cnd), Swedish RSO † Ithaka; Sången, Op. 44 CAPA ▲ 21358 (16.97)
U. Wallin (vn), P. Järvi (cnd), Malmö SO † Florez och Blanzeflor, Op. 3 BIS ▲ 550 [DDD] (17.97)

Songs
H. Hagegård (bar), W. Jones (pno)—Prins Aladin av Lampan, Op. 26/10; Adagio, Op. 20/5; Stjärnöga, Op. 20/1; Florez och Blanzeflor, Op. 3 † J. Brahms:Ernste Gesänge, Op. 121; Songs (5), Op. 105; Sibelius:Songs RCAV (Red Seal) ▲ 68097 (16.97)
P. Mattei (bar), B. Lundin (pno)—Thoughts of Solitude, Op. 7; Songs (5) to Texts by J. L. Runeberg, Op. 8; Swedish Songs (4), Op. 16; Songs (5) of Bo Bergman, Op. 20; Songs & Moods, Op. 26; Late Harvest BIS ▲ 654 [DDD] (17.97)
M. Mørkve (sop), P. A. Frantzen (pno) † Heise:Songs; Rangström:Songs (3) SIMX ▲ 9036 (18.97)
I. Wixell (bar), J. Arnell (cnd), Stockholm PO—En positivvisa; Florez och Blanzeflor; I en skogskbacke; Kväll i Klara; Mellan broarna [Sw] *(rec June 1990)* ("Swedish Ballads") † Peterson-Berger:Songs; Rangström:Songs; Söderman:King Heimer & Aslog MSV ▲ 617 [DDD] (16.97)

Stockholm Exhibition Cantata for solo Voices, Orchestra & Chorus (1897)
B. Rydholm (sop), A. Hudak (alt), J. Christensson (ten), M. Persson (bar), T. Dausgaard (cnd), Swedish RSO, Swedish Radio Chorus *(rec 1991 & 1996)* ("Cantatas") † Ett folk, Op. 22 STRL ▲ 1023 [DDD] (15.97)

Symphony No. 2 in g, Op. 34 (1911-15)
S. Westerberg (cnd), Stockholm PO CAPA ▲ 21151 [AAD] (16.97)

Symphony No. 3 [unfinished] (1818-19)
G. Rozhdestvensky (cnd), Royal Stockholm PO CHN ▲ 9074 [DDD] (16.97)

STENIUS, TORSTEN (1918-1964)

Partita on a Finnish Sacred Folk-Tune for Organ
F. Forsman (org) *(rec Helsinki Finland, Nov 17, 1973)* ("Contemporary Finnish Music") † E. Bergman:Midnight, Op. 83; P. Heininen:touching, Op. 40; P. H. Nordgren:Butterflies, Op. 39; Nummi:Wilderness BIS ▲ 207 [AAD] (17.97)

ŠTĚPÁN, JOSEF ANTONIN (1726-1797)

Capriccios (5) for Keyboard
R. Hill (pno) † Son 2 Kbd; Son 5 Kbd MDG ▲ 6200870 (17.97)

Sonata No. 2 for Keyboard
R. Hill (pno) † Capriccios; Son 5 Kbd MDG ▲ 6200870 (17.97)

Sonata No. 5 for Keyboard
R. Hill (pno) † Capriccios; Son 2 Kbd MDG ▲ 6200870 (17.97)

STEPOVOY, YAKOV (1883-1965)

Cossack's Song for Piano
T. Riabchikova (pno) *(rec Tsai Performance Center Boston)* ("Gutzul Watercolors: Ukrainian Music of the 20th Century") † Lullaby Pno; Liatoshinsky:Preludes Pno (misc); Shamo:Gutzul Watercolors; Humoresque Pno; Pno Music; Prelude Pno; Silvestrov:Pieces Pno SO ▲ 22571 [DDD] (16.97)

STEPOVOY, YAKOV (cont.)
Lullaby for Piano
T. Riabchikova (pno) *(rec Tsai Performance Center Boston)* ("Gutzul Watercolors: Ukrainian Music of the 20th Century") † Cossack's Song; Liatoshinsky:Preludes Pno (misc); Shamo:Gutzul Watercolors; Humoresque Pno; Pno Music; Prelude Pno; Silvestrov:Pieces Pno SO ▲ 22571 [DDD] (16.97)
STEPTOE, ROGER (1952-
Elegy on the Death of Cock Robin for Voice & Ensemble
J. Bowman (ct), P. Ash (cnd) [ENG] † H. Howells:Songs; A. Ridout:Songs Ct; Vaughan Williams:Songs; Warlock:Songs MER ▲ 84158 (16.97)
STERN, ADAM (1955-
The Fairy's Gift (fairy tale) for Narrator & Ensemble [after Perrault]
A. Grebner (spkr), A. Stern (cnd) † G. Kubik:Gerald McBoing Boing; B. Rogers:Musicians of Bremen DLS ▲ 6001 [DDD] (14.97)
STERN, ROBERT (1934-
Blood & Milk for Soprano & Chamber Ensemble (1980)
E. Fulford (sop), D. Kraus (mez), S. Hodkinson (cnd), Eastman Musica Nova Ensemble ("Eastman American Music Series-Vol. 6") † B. Israel:In Praise of Practically Nothing; G. Levinson:In Dark; Noon:Chansons, Op. 32 ALBA ▲ 277 [ADD] (16.97)
Fantasy Etude for Violin (1984)
V. Kadlubkiewicz (vn) *(rec July 1992)* † S. Macchia:Chamber Con 3; Spratlan:Night Music; Wheelock:Partita Vn GAS ▲ 226 [DDD] (16.97)
STERNDALE-BENNETT, WILLIAM (1816-1875)
The Naiads (overture) for Orchestra, Op. 15 (1836)
D. Joeres (cnd), Royal PO † N. W. Gade:Echoes of Ossian, Op. 1; Mendelssohn (-Bartholdy):Hebriden, Op. 26; R. Schumann:Ov, Scherzo & Finale, Op. 52 INMP (Classics) ▲ 6700152 (9.97)
Piano Music
I. Prunyi (pno)—The Maid of New Orleans; Allegro Grazioso; 4 pieces; 3 Musical Sketches; Geneviève; Scherzo; Rondo Piacevole ("Piano Works, Vol. 1") † W. S. Bennett:Pno Music MARC ▲ 8223512 (13.97)
STERNEFELD, DANIEL (1905-1986)
Mater Dolorosa (opera) (1936)
F. Devreese (cnd), Moscow SO *(rec Mosfilm Studio, Oct 1995)* † Rossiniazata; Sym 1 MARC ▲ 8223813 [DDD] (13.97)
G. Llewellyn (cnd), Royal Flanders PO, Zeffiretti Choir of Antwerp, Flemish Radio Choir, M. T. Letorney (sop—Mother), C. Vandevelde (sop—1st Water-Nymph), B. Haveman (sop—2nd Water-Nymph), L. Van Deyck (cta—Night), T. Sol (bar—Death), E. Crommen (spkr—Mother) *(rec live, Antwerp, Belgium, Apr 11, 1997) ([DUT,ENG] lib text)* MARC 2-▲ 8225068 [DDD] (27.97)
Rossiniazata (suite) for Orchestra [after Rossini's piano music] (1981)
F. Devreese (cnd), Moscow SO *(rec Mosfilm Studio, Oct 1995)* † Mater Dolorosa; Sym 1 MARC ▲ 8223813 [DDD] (13.97)
Symphony No. 1 in C for Orchestra (1944)
F. Devreese (cnd), Moscow SO *(rec Mosfilm Studio, Oct 1995)* † Mater Dolorosa; Rossiniazata MARC ▲ 8223813 [DDD] (13.97)
STEUERMANN, EDWARD (1892-1964)
Trio for Piano, Violin & Cello (1954)
Ravinia Trio *(rec Aug 1992)* † Schoenberg:Verklärte Nacht, Op. 4 DVX ▲ 29107 [DDD] (16.97)
STEVEN, DONALD (dates unknown)
Sapphire Song for Clarinet
J. Boisvert (cl) † Boucourechliev:Nocturnes; Pennycook:Praescio IV; K. Stockhausen:Tierkreis Cl SNE ▲ 586 (16.97)
STEVENS, BERNARD (1916-1983)
Aria for Piano
J. Filsell (pno) [original version] † Fant on Giles Farnaby; Son Pno in 1 Movt, Op. 25; H. Howells:Gadabout; Pieces Pno; Sonatina Pno GILD ▲ 7119 [DDD] (16.97)
Concerto for Cello & Orchestra, Op. 18 (1952)
A. Baillie (vc), E. Downes (cnd), BBC PO † Sym of Liberation, Op. 7 MER ▲ 84124 (16.97)
Concerto for Violin & Orchestra, Op. 4 (1943)
E. Kovacic (vn), E. Downes (cnd), BBC PO † Sym 2 MER ▲ 84174 (16.97)
Fantasy on Giles Farnabys Dreame for Piano
J. Filsell (pno) † Aria Pno; Son Pno in 1 Movt, Op. 25; H. Howells:Gadabout; Pieces Pno; Sonatina Pno GILD ▲ 7119 [DDD] (16.97)
Mass for Double Choir (1939)
P. Spicer (cnd), Finzi Singers [LAT] † H. Howells:Choral Music; Mass in the Dorian Mode CHN ▲ 9021 [DDD] (16.97)
Sonata in 1 Movement for Piano, Op. 25 (1954)
J. Filsell (pno) † Aria Pno; Fant on Giles Farnaby; H. Howells:Gadabout; Pieces Pno; Sonatina Pno GILD ▲ 7119 [DDD] (16.97)
Symphony No. 2, Op. 35 (1964)
E. Downes (cnd), BBC PO † Con Vn, Op. 4 MER ▲ 84174 (16.97)
Symphony of Liberation, Op. 7 (1945)
E. Downes (cnd), BBC PO † Con Vc MER ▲ 84124 (16.97)
STEVENS, HALSEY (1908-1989)
Campion Suite for Chorus
P. Rutenberg (cnd), Los Angeles Chamber Singers ("Shenandoah: An American Chorister 1890-1990") † S. Barber:Songs; MacDowell:Northern Songs, Op. 43; Mechem:5 Centuries of Spring; Rutenberg:Ballad of the Buffalo Skinners KLAV ▲ 11052 [DDD] (18.97)
Elizabethan Madrigals (3) for Chorus
P. Rutenberg (cnd), Los Angeles Chamber Singers ("Romancero Gitano") † S. Barber:Songs; Castelnuovo-Tedesco:Romancero gitano, Op. 152; Chorbajian:Bitter for Sweet; M. Lauridsen:Chansons des roses; R. Thompson:Odes to Horace RCMM ▲ 19802 (16.97)
Sonata for Trumpet & Piano (1953-56)
J. Harjanne (tpt), J. Lagerspetz (pno) ("American Trumpet Sonatas") † Antheil:Son Tpt Pno; Jolson:Son Tpt; Kennan:Son Tpt FNL ▲ 17691 (16.97)
A. Plog (tpt), Davis (pno) † F. Campo:Studies Tpt; R. Erickson:Kryl; P. Hindemith:Son Tpt; Petrassi:Fanfare for 3 Tpts; A. Plog:Animal Ditties 2; F. Tull:Profiles Tpt CRYS ▲ 663 [DDD] (15.97)
Sonatina for Tuba & Piano (1960)
D. Randolph (tuba), P. Randolph (pno) *(rec Georgia State Univ., Atlanta, GA, July & Aug 1991)* ("Contrasts in Contemporary Music") † C. Baker:Omaggi; T. R. George:Son Tuba; J. Takács:Son Capricciosa, Op. 81 ACAD ▲ 20018 (16.97)
STEVENS, JOHN (1951-
Fabrics for Brass Quintet (1989)
Wisconsin Brass Quintet † Seasons; V. Reynolds:Qnt Brass SUMM ▲ 164 [DDD] (16.97)
Moondance for Brass (1989)
Summit Brass † J. Cheetham:Keystone Celebration; D. Erb:Sonneries; D. Sampson:Reflections on a Dance; G. Schuller:Sym Brass, Op. 16 SUMM ▲ 127 [DDD] (16.97)
Seasons for Brass Quintet (1986)
Wisconsin Brass Quintet † Fabrics; V. Reynolds:Qnt Brass SUMM ▲ 164 [DDD] (16.97)
STEVENS, THOMAS (1938-
Triangles IV for English Horn & 3 pre-recorded (or live) Oboes (1994)
C. Hove (E hn/ob) *(rec Little Bridges Auditorium Pomona College, Dec 1994 & Jan 1996)* † E. Carter:Pastorale E Hn; P. Hindemith:Son E Hn; J. Marvin:Pieces E hn & Pno; Persichetti:Parable XV, Op. 128; E.-P. Salonen:2nd Meeting CRYS ▲ 328 [DDD] (15.97)
STEVENSON, RONALD (1928-
Passacaglia on DSCH for Piano (1960-62)
R. Clarke (pno) *(rec London, Feb 20, 1993)* MARC ▲ 8223545 [DDD] (13.97)
R. Stevenson (pno) † Prelude, Fugue & Fant on Busoni; Recitative & Air ALTA ▲ 9091
Piano Music
D. Amato (pno)—Den Bergtekne [Taken into the Mountains]; Norse Elegy for Ella Nygaard; Beltane Bonfire † A. Hinton:Vars & Fugue on a Theme of Grieg; Sorabji:Variazione maliziosa e perversa ALTA ▲ 9021
J. Banowetz (pno)—Fugue on a fragment of Chopin; 20th Century Music Diary; Symphonic Elegy for Liszt; A Scottish Tryiptych; Motus perpetuus temporibus fatalibus ALTA ▲ 9089

STEVENSON, RONALD (cont.)
Piano Music (cont.)
M. McLachlan (pno)—Beltane Bonfire; 2 Scottish Ballads ("Piano Music from Scotland") † Center:Bagatelles, Op. 3; Children at Play; Son Pno; F. G. Scott:Songs Pno OLY ▲ 264 [DDD] (16.97)
Prelude & Fugue on a Theme by Liszt for Organ (1961)
K. Bowyer (org) *(rec Org of St. Mary Redcliffe Bristol)* † Sonatina 1 Pno; Busoni:Elegien Pno; Fant contrappuntistica Pno; Fant nach J. S. Bach; A. Hinton:Pansophiae for John Ogdon; J. Ogdon:Dance Suite ALTA 2-▲ 9063 (38.97)
Prelude, Fugue & Fantasy on Themes from Busoni's *Doktor Faust* for Piano
R. Stevenson (pno) ("The Essence of Busoni") † Busoni:Pno Music (original & arrs); Prelude & Etude in Arpeggios; Toccata Pno ALTA ▲ 9041 (19.97)
R. Stevenson (pno) † Passacaglia on DSCH; Recitative & Air ALTA ▲ 9091
Recitative & Air for Piano
R. Stevenson (pno) † Passacaglia on DSCH; Prelude, Fugue & Fant on Busoni ALTA ▲ 9091
Sonatina No. 1 for Piano
J. Ogdon (pno) † Prelude & Fugue on Liszt; Busoni:Elegien Pno; Fant contrappuntistica Pno; Fant nach J. S. Bach; A. Hinton:Pansophiae for John Ogdon; J. Ogdon:Dance Suite ALTA 2-▲ 9063 (38.97)
Transcriptions for Piano
R. Stevenson (pno)—transcriptions & fants from: Busoni:Doktor Faust; Berg:Wiegenlied aus Wozzeck; Bush:Minstrel's Lay; Britten:Peter Grimes ("20th Century Operatic Fantasias") † P. Grainger:Rosenkavalier-Ramble ALTA ▲ 9042 (19.97)
STEWART, RAYMOND G. (1962-
KOHS-Ska for Brass Quintet (1995)
Meridian Arts Ensemble *(rec Amsterdam, Holland, Feb 1996)* ("Anxiety of Influence") † Okay Chorale; S. Barber:Semahane; Debussy:Pour le piano; D. Grabois:Zen Monkey; S. Silverman:Vars on a Theme of Weill; Traditional:Solitario; F. Zappa:Music of F. Zappa CCL ▲ 9796 [DDD] (18.97)
Okay Chorale for Brass Quintet (1994)
Meridian Arts Ensemble [ard] *(rec Amsterdam, Holland, Feb 1996)* ("Anxiety of Influence") † KOHS-Ska; S. Barber:Semahane; Debussy:Pour le piano; D. Grabois:Zen Monkey; S. Silverman:Vars on a Theme of Weill; Traditional:Solitario; F. Zappa:Music of F. Zappa CCL ▲ 9796 [DDD] (18.97)
STEWART, ROBERT (1918-
Idyll for Strings
C. Kendall (cnd) ("American Chamber Music") † J. D. Goodman:Montségur Suite; M. B. Nelson:Song of the Goddesses; T. Sleeper:Qt Pno; Tepper:Con Ob MASM (Chamber Music) ▲ 2010 (16.97)
STICH [OR STICH-PUNTO], JAN VACLAV (1746-1803)
Concerto No. 5 in F for Horn & Orchestra
P. Francomb (hn), H. Griffiths (cnd), Northern Sinfonia of England † C. Förster:Con Hn PANC ▲ 510095 [DDD] (20.97)
Quartet in F for Horn & Strings, Op. 8/1
L. Bergé (hn), Arriaga String Quartet ("Kamermuziek voor hoorn") † Amon:Qt Hn; F. A. Hoffmeister:Qnt Hn; W. A. Mozart:Qnt Hn EUFO ▲ 1207 [DDD] (19.97)
STILL, WILLIAM GRANT (1895-1978)
Choral Music
J. Groh (cnd), Univ of Arkansas Schola Cantorum—Lord I Looked Down the Road; Hard Trials; Holy Spirit Don't You Leave Me; I Feel Like My Time Ain't Long ("A Festive Sunday with William Grant Still") † Festive Ov; Folk Suites; Romance; Sym 3 CMB ▲ 1060 [ADD] (16.97)
Danzas de Panama (suite) for Strings (1948)
L. A. Craft (hp), Kaufman String Quartet † Ennanga; E. Bloch:Son 1 Vn; Q. Porter:Son 1 Vn MUA ▲ 4638 (10.97)
I. Jackson (cnd), Berlin SO † Guiablesse; Instrumental Music KOCH ▲ 7154 [DDD] (10.97)
Darker America (symphonic poem) for Orchestra (1924)
S. Landau (cnd), Westchester SO *(rec 1973)* ("The Incredible Flutist") † From the Black Belt; Coolidge:Blue Planet; New England Autumn; Pioneer Dances; Rhap Hp; Spirituals in Sunshine & Shadow; U. Kay:Dances; D. G. Mason:Prelude & Fugue, Op. 20; Piston:Incredible Flutist VB2 (The American Composers) 2-▲ 5157 (9.97)
Dismal Swamp (symphonic poem) for Piano & Orchestra (1933)
J. Cai (cnd), Cincinnati PO *(rec Univ of Cincinnati, OH, Oct 1995)* † Kaintuck'; Sym 1; O. Wilson:Expansions III CENT ▲ 2331 [DDD] (16.97)
Ennanga for Harp, Piano & String Quartet (1956)
L. A. Craft (hp), Kaufman String Quartet † Danzas de Panamá; E. Bloch:Son 1 Vn; Q. Porter:Son 1 Vn MUA ▲ 4638 (10.97)
Videmus † Instrumental Music; Songs; Songs of Separation; Suite Vn NWW ▲ 80399 [DDD] (16.97)
Festive Overture for Orchestra (1944)
A. B. Lipkin (cnd), Royal PO ("A Festive Sunday with William Grant Still") † Choral Music; Folk Suites; Romance; Sym 3 CMB ▲ 1060 [ADD] (16.97)
Folk Suites (4) for Flute, Clarinet, Oboe, Bassoon, Piano & Strings (1962)
S. Magill (vc), L. Garrison (fl), R. Umiker (cl), A. Tollefson (pno) ("A Festive Sunday with William Grant Still") † Choral Music; Festive Ov; Romance; Sym 3 CMB ▲ 1060 [ADD] (16.97)
M. Steer (db), A. Still (fl), S. De Witt Smith (pno), New Zealand String Quartet † Instrumental Music; Music of Still; Pastorela Vn; Preludes Fl; Suite Vn KOCH ▲ 7192 [DDD] (16.97)
From the Black Belt (suite) for Orchestra (1926)
S. Landau (cnd), Westchester SO *(rec 1973)* ("The Incredible Flutist") † Darker America; Coolidge:Blue Planet; New England Autumn; Pioneer Dances; Rhap Hp; Spirituals in Sunshine & Shadow; U. Kay:Dances; D. G. Mason:Prelude & Fugue, Op. 20; Piston:Incredible Flutist VB2 (The American Composers) 2-▲ 5157 (9.97)
La Guiablesse (ballet) for Orchestra (1927)
I. Jackson (cnd), Berlin SO † Danzas de Panama; Instrumental Music KOCH ▲ 7154 [DDD] (10.97)
Instrumental Music
M. Steer (db), A. Still (fl), S. De Witt Smith (pno), New Zealand String Quartet—Quit Dat Fool'nish; Summerland † Music of Still; Pastorela Vn; Preludes Fl; Suite Vn KOCH ▲ 7192 [DDD] (16.97)
A. Still (fl), S. De Witt Smith (pno)—Quit Dat Fool'nish; Summerland † Danzas de Panama; Guiablesse KOCH ▲ 7154 [DDD] (10.97)
Videmus—Summerland; Out of the Silence (1940); Incantation & Dance (1942) † Ennanga; Songs; Songs of Separation; Suite Vn NWW ▲ 80399 [DDD] (16.97)
Kaintuck' (symphonic poem) for Piano & Orchestra (1935)
J. Cai (cnd), Cincinnati PO *(rec Univ of Cincinnati, OH, Oct 1995)* † Dismal Swamp; Sym 1; O. Wilson:Expansions III CENT ▲ 2331 [DDD] (16.97)
Lenox Avenue (ballet) for Orchestra (1937)
L. Kaufman (vn), B. Herrmann (cnd), Columbia SO ("Pan-Americana: The Violin Artistry of Louis Kaufman") † R. R. Bennett:Con Vn; Song Son; C. M. Guarnieri:Son 2 Vn; E. Helm:Comment on 2 Spirituals; Mcbride:Aria & Toccata in Swing; D. Milhaud:Saudades do Brasil, Op. 67; Triggs:Danza Braziliana Pnos CMB (Historical) ▲ 1078 [ADD]
Miniatures for Flute, Oboe & Piano
G. Shanley (fl), P. Christ (ob), S. Davis (pno) † Ginastera:Duo Fl & Ob, Op. 13; Persichetti:Parable III; W. Schmidt:Sparrow and The Amazing Mr. Avaunt; R. Thompson:Suite Ob CRYS ▲ 321 (15.97) ▮ 321 (9.98)
Music of Still
M. Astrup (sop), R. A. Clark (cnd), Manhattan CO—American Scene:The Southwest; From the Hearts of Women; Mother & Child; American Scene:The Far West; Citadel; Phantom Chapel; Golden Days; Serenade; American Scene:The East ("The American Scene") NPT ▲ 85596 [DDD] (16.97)
Z. Schiff (vn), C. Grant (pno)—Here's One; Vignettes (2) Vn Pno; Summerland; Blues; arr L. Kaufman; Quit dat Fool'nish *(rec Purchase, NY, Mar 1994)* ("Here's One") † A. Copland:Pieces Vn; Rodeo (sels); H. Cowell:Son 1 Vn; Hoiby:Son Vn, Op. 5; F. Price:Deserted Garden 4TAY ▲ 4005 [DDD] (17.97)
Sierra Winds—Miniatures; Folk Suite Nos. 2-4; Incantation & Dance (1942); Quit dat Fool'nish; Summerland; Romance; Vignettes; Get on Board *(rec Las Vegas Nevada)* ("Get on Board: Music of William Grant Still") CMB ▲ 1083 [DDD] (16.97)
M. Steer (db), A. Still (fl), S. De Witt Smith (pno), New Zealand String Quartet—Quit dat Fool'nish; Pastorela; Folk Suite 1; Suite for Vn & Pno [movts I & II]; Prelude for Fl, Str Qnt & Pno *(rec May 1993)* † Folk Suites; Instrumental Music; Pastorela Vn; Preludes Fl; Suite Vn KOCH ▲ 7192 [DDD] (16.97)
Pastorela for Violin & Piano (1946)
M. Steer (db), S. De Witt Smith (pno) † Folk Suites; Instrumental Music; Music of Still; Preludes Fl; Suite Vn KOCH ▲ 7192 [DDD] (16.97)
Piano Music
D. Oldham (pno)—Bells; 7 Traceries; Blues from "Lenox Avenue"; Swanee River; 5 Preludes; Summerland from "3 Visions"; Africa KOCH ▲ 7084 [DDD] (10.97)

STILL, WILLIAM GRANT (cont.)

Piano Music (cont.)

D. Oldham (pno)—Dark Horseman [3 Visions, No. 1]; Radiant Pinnacle [3 Visions, No. 3]; Marionette; Dance [from Costaso]; Rising Tide; Quit dat Fool'nish; Entrance of the Porteuses [from La Guiablesse]; A Deserted Plantation † Dett:Pno Music ALTA ▲ 9013 (19.97)

Preludes for Flute, Piano & Strings (1962)

M. Steer (db), A. Still (fl), S. De Witt Smith (pno), New Zealand String Quartet † Folk Suites; Instrumental Music; Music of Still; Pastorela Vn; Suite Vn KOCH ▲ 7192 [DDD] (16.97)

Romance for Saxophone & Piano (1966)

L. Gwozdz (sax), S. Hass (sax), K. Trevor (cnd), Bohuslav Martinů PO *(rec Zlín, Czech Republic, June 12-14, 1998)* † W. Benson:Aeolian Song; K. Husa:Elegie et Rondeau; Wirth:Inglewood Concerto; Jephthah; J. C. Worley:Claremont Concerto ALBA ▲ 331 [DDD] (16.97)

B. Perconti (a sax), J. March (pno) *(rec Clapp Recital Hall, Univ of Iowa, IA, 1996)* † Derr:I Never Saw Another Butterfly; J. Françaix:Danses exotiques Sax; Heiden:Son Sax; B. Kolb:Related Characters; F. Tull:Concerto da Camera; Threnody CENT ▲ 2345 [DDD] (16.97)

R. Umiker (a sax), A. Tollefson (pno) ("A Festive Sunday with William Grant Still") † Choral Music; Festive Ov; Folk Suites; Sym 3 CMB ▲ 1060 [ADD] (16.97)

Sahdji (ballet) for Orchestra (1930)

N. Hinderas (pno) ("Piano Music by African-American Composers") † Dett:In the Bottoms; T. R. Hakim:Sound Gone; G. Walker:Son 1 Pno; O. Wilson:Pno Piece; J. W. Work:Scuppernong CRI 2-▲ 629 [ADD] (31.97)

Songs

Videmus—Here's 1 (1941); Song for the Lonely (1953); Citadel; Lift Every Voice & Sing [E] † Ennanga; Instrumental Music; Songs of Separation; Suite Vn NWW ▲ 80399 [DDD] (16.97)

Songs of Separation (cycle of 5 songs) for Soprano & Piano Quintet [set to texts of black poets] (1949)

Videmus [ENG] † Ennanga; Instrumental Music; Songs; Suite Vn NWW ▲ 80399 [DDD] (16.97)

Suite for Violin & Piano (1943)

F. Gearhart (vn), P. Tardiff (pno) ("American Music") † A. Copland:Duo Fl; H. Cowell:Suite Vn; Joio:Vars & Capriccio KOCH ▲ 7268 (10.97)

M. Steer (db), S. De Witt Smith (pno), New Zealand String Quartet † Folk Suites; Instrumental Music; Music of Still; Pastorela Vn; Preludes Fl KOCH ▲ 7192 [DDD] (16.97)

Videmus members † Ennanga; Instrumental Music; Songs; Songs of Separation NWW ▲ 80399 [DDD] (16.97)

Symphony No. 1, "Afro-American" (1930)

J. Cai (cnd), Cincinnati PO *(rec Univ of Cincinnati, OH, Oct 1995)* † Dismal Swamp; Kaintuck'; O. Wilson:Expansions III CENT ▲ 2331 [DDD] (16.97)

N. Järvi (cnd), Detroit SO *(rec Sept 29 & Oct 3, 1992)* † Ellington:River (suite) CHN ▲ 9154 [DDD] (16.97)

K. Krueger (cnd), Royal PO † Beach:Sym 1 BRID ▲ 9086 (17.97)

Symphony No. 2 in g, "Song of a New Race" (1937)

N. Järvi (cnd), Detroit SO ("American Series, Vol. 5") † W. L. Dawson:Negro Folk Sym; Ellington:Harlem CHN ▲ 9226 [DDD] (16.97)

Symphony No. 3, "The Sunday Symphony" (1958)

C. Woods (cnd), North Arkansas SO ("A Festive Sunday with William Grant Still") † Choral Music; Festive Ov; Folk Suites; Romance CMB ▲ 1060 [ADD] (16.97)

Three Visions for Piano (1936)

A. Waites (pno) *(rec July 25 & Aug 6, 1990)* † E. Bland:Sketches Set 7; Bonds:Troubled Water; F. Price:Cotton Dance; Dances in the Canebrakes; Old Boatman; Son Pno CMB ▲ 1097 [DDD]

STILLER, ANDREW (1946-

Chamber Symphony for Saxophone Quartet

C. Schadeberg (sop), Amherst Saxophone Quartet *(rec United States of America)* † L. Lustig:Lament on the Death of Music; C. K. Nin:Qt Sax; A. Perry:Qt Sax INNO ▲ 516 (14.97)

A Descent into the Maelstrom for 3 Percussionists (1985)

Maelström Percussion Ensemble † Mouse Singer; Periodic Table of the Elements; Sonata a 3 pulsatoribus; Water Is Wide, Daisy Bell MASM ▲ 2014 (16.97)

The Mouse Singer for Piccolo & String Quartet (1982)

J. Freeman (cnd) † Descent into the Maelstrom; Periodic Table of the Elements; Sonata a 3 pulsatoribus; Water Is Wide, Daisy Bell MASM ▲ 2014 (16.97)

A Periodic Table of the Elements for Chamber Orchestra (1988)

J. Freeman (cnd), Orch 2001 † Descent into the Maelstrom; Mouse Singer; Sonata a 3 pulsatoribus; Water Is Wide, Daisy Bell MASM ▲ 2014 (16.97)

Sonata a 3 pulsatoribus for 3 Percussionists (1986)

Maelström Percussion Ensemble † Descent into the Maelstrom; Mouse Singer; Periodic Table of the Elements; Water Is Wide, Daisy Bell MASM ▲ 2014 (16.97)

The Water Is Wide, Daisy Bell for Piano (1987)

J. Freeman (pno) † Descent into the Maelstrom; Mouse Singer; Periodic Table of the Elements; Sonata a 3 pulsatoribus MASM ▲ 2014 (16.97)

STOCK, DAVID (1939-

Night Vision for Chamber Ensemble (1989)

D. Stock (cnd) *(rec 1995-96)* ("MMC Chamber Music, Vol. IV") † Ellison:Before All Beginning; J. Hill:Tholos; W. T. McKinley:Curtain Up; E. M. McKinley:Summer Portraits MASM ▲ 2061 [DDD] (16.97)

STOCK, JEFFREY (20th cent)

Lulie the Iceberg (children's tale) for Narrator, Violin, Cello, Saxophone, Orchestra & Chorus [based on story by Princess Hisako of Takamodo]

S. Waterston (nar), P. Frank (vn), Y.-Y. Ma (vc), P. Winter (sax), Choral Associates, D. Inouye (cnd), Orchestra of St. Luke's SNYC ▲ 61665 (16.97)

STOCKHAUSEN, KARLHEINZ (1928-

In Freundschaft for solo Instrument, No. 46 (1977)

C. Delangle (s sax) ("The Solitary Saxophone") † L. Berio:Sequenza IXb; Sequenza VIIb; Jolas:Episode Quatrième; Scelsi:Ixor; Maknongan; Pezzi S Sax; Takemitsu:Distance BIS ▲ 640 [DDD] (17.97)

C. Lindberg (trbn) *(rec Sweden, 1988)* ("The Solitary Trombone") † In Freundschaft; L. Berio:Sequenza V; J. Cage:Solo Sliding Trb; A. Eliasson:Disegno Trbn; M. Kagel:Atem; F. Schubert:Sym 5; Sym 6; Xenakis:Keren BIS ▲ 388 [DDD] (17.97)

Klavierstück I-XI for Piano (I-IV 1952-53; V-X 1954-55; IX-X rev 1961; XI 1956)

H. Henck (pno) WER 2-▲ 60135 [DDD]

Mantra for 2 Pianos + Woodblock + Crotales & 2 Ring Modulators, No. 32 (1969-70)

A. Grau (pno), G. Schumacher (pno) WER ▲ 6267 (19.97)

Y. Mikhashoff (pno), R. Bevan (pno), O. Orsted (elec) NALB ▲ 25 (16.97)

Setzt die Segel zur Sonne for Ensemble [from Aus den sieben Tagen]

D. Masson (cnd) HMA ▲ 190795 (9.97)

Spiral for Soloist (1968)

J. Celli (instr) † J. Celli:Sky: S for J; M. Goldstein:Summoning of Focus; E. Schwartz:Extended Ob OOD ▲ 1 [AAD] (16.97)

Stimmung for 6 Vocalists (1968)

P. Walmsley-Clark (sop), K. Flowers (sop), R. Covey-Crump (ten), P. Hillier (bass), P. Rose (bass), Long (sgr) HYP ▲ 66115 (18.97)

Tierkreis [Zodiac] for Clarinet & Piano

J. Boisvert (cl), L. Baril (pno) † Boucourechliev:Nocturnes; Pennycook:Praescio IV; D. Steven:Sapphire Song SNE ▲ 586 (16.97)

Tierkreis [Zodiac] for Piano & Celesta (1975)

J. Mazánek (sitar), R. Dašek (banjo/gtr), J. Boušková (hp), P. Drešer (acc), J. Hála (cel/hpd/pno), A. Bárta (org), D. Mikolášek (bells/cym/mar/vib) ARTA ▲ 30

Zyklus for Percussion (1959)

S. Yoshihara (perc) *(rec Iruma Shimin Kaikan Japan, Feb 1979)* ("Sound Space of Percussion II") † M. Ishii:Search in Grey, Op. 37; NørgÅrd:Waves CAMA ▲ 313 [AAD] (18.97)

STÖHR, RICHARD (1874-1967)

Sonata for Flute & Piano, Op. 61

D. Shostac (fl), A. Perry (pno) ("Masterpieces Rediscovered") † Graener:Suite Fl, Op. 63; Jadassohn:Notturno, Op. 133; Rheinberger:Rhap Fl; Shevchenko:Fant Fl, Op. 1 HRM ▲ 3002 [DDD] (14.97)

STOKER, RICHARD (1938-

Jazz Preludes (2) for Piano, Op. 63 (1980)

E. Parkin (pno) † Poet's Notebook Pno, Op. 19; Regency Suite, Op. 15; Serenade Pno, Op. 17; Son 1 Pno, Op. 26; Son 2 Pno, Op. 71; Vars Pno, Op. 45; Zodiac Vars Pno, Op. 22 PRIO ▲ 659 (16.97)

STOKER, RICHARD (cont.)

A Poet's Notebook for Piano, Op. 19 (1969)

E. Parkin (pno) † Jazz Preludes Pno, Op. 63; Regency Suite, Op. 15; Serenade Pno, Op. 17; Son 1 Pno, Op. 26; Son 2 Pno, Op. 71; Vars Pno, Op. 45; Zodiac Vars Pno, Op. 22 PRIO ▲ 659 (16.97)

Regency Suite for Piano, Op. 15 (1952-59)

E. Parkin (pno) † Jazz Preludes Pno, Op. 63; Poet's Notebook Pno, Op. 19; Serenade Pno, Op. 17; Son 1 Pno, Op. 26; Son 2 Pno, Op. 71; Vars Pno, Op. 45; Zodiac Vars Pno, Op. 22 PRIO ▲ 659 (16.97)

Serenade for Piano, Op. 17 (1962)

E. Parkin (pno) † Jazz Preludes Pno, Op. 63; Poet's Notebook Pno, Op. 19; Regency Suite, Op. 15; Son 1 Pno, Op. 26; Son 2 Pno, Op. 71; Vars Pno, Op. 45; Zodiac Vars Pno, Op. 22 PRIO ▲ 659 (16.97)

Sonata No. 1 for Piano, Op. 26 (1967)

E. Parkin (pno) † Jazz Preludes Pno, Op. 63; Poet's Notebook Pno, Op. 19; Regency Suite, Op. 15; Serenade Pno, Op. 17; Son 2 Pno, Op. 71; Vars Pno, Op. 45; Zodiac Vars Pno, Op. 22 PRIO ▲ 659 (16.97)

Sonata No. 2 for Piano, Op. 71 (1992)

E. Parkin (pno) † Jazz Preludes Pno, Op. 63; Poet's Notebook Pno, Op. 19; Regency Suite, Op. 15; Serenade Pno, Op. 17; Son 1 Pno, Op. 26; Vars Pno, Op. 45; Zodiac Vars Pno, Op. 22 PRIO ▲ 659 (16.97)

Sonatina for Clarinet & Piano, Op. 5

E. Jóhannesson (cl), P. Jenkins (pno) *(rec Cambridge, England, Sept 1991)* ("British Music for Clarinet and Piano") † M. Arnold:Son Cl; A. Bliss:Pastoral Cl, Op.posth.; Dunhill:Fant Suite Cl & Pno, Op. 91; H. Ferguson:Short Pieces Cl, Op. 6; Hurlstone:Characteristic Pieces Cl; Stanford:Son Cl CHN ▲ 9079 (16.97)

Variations for Piano, Op. 45 (1973)

E. Parkin (pno) † Jazz Preludes Pno, Op. 63; Poet's Notebook Pno, Op. 19; Regency Suite, Op. 15; Serenade Pno, Op. 17; Son 1 Pno, Op. 26; Son 2 Pno, Op. 71; Zodiac Vars Pno, Op. 22 PRIO ▲ 659 (16.97)

Zodiac Variations for Piano, Op. 22 (1965)

E. Parkin (pno) † Jazz Preludes Pno, Op. 63; Poet's Notebook Pno, Op. 19; Regency Suite, Op. 15; Serenade Pno, Op. 17; Son 1 Pno, Op. 26; Son 2 Pno, Op. 71; Vars Pno, Op. 45 PRIO ▲ 659 (16.97)

STOKES, ERIC (NORMAN) (1930-

Brazen Cartographies for Brass Quintet (1988)

Chestnut Brass Company *(rec Mar & May 1996)* ("Brazen Cartographies") † Bassett:Qnt Brass; Greatbatch:Scenes from the Brothers Grimm; Krzywicki:Deploration; R. Wernick:Musica Ptolemica ALBA ▲ 233 [DDD] (16.97)

Song Circle for Soprano, Flute & Harp (1993)

Jubal Trio *(rec Music Division SUNY, Purchase, NY, May 29-30, June 14 & Nov 13, 1995)* ("Jubal Songs") † G. Crumb:Federico's Little Songs; D. W. Freund:Backyard Songs; T. León:Journey; H. Sollberger:Life Study CRI ▲ 738 [DDD] (16.97)

STOKES, HARVEY J. (20th cent)

Quartet No. 1 for Strings (1990)

Oxford String Quartet ("The String Quartets") † Qt 2 Strs; Qt 3 Strs ALBA ▲ 288 [DDD] (16.97)

Quartet No. 2 for Strings (1992)

Oxford String Quartet ("The String Quartets") † Qt 1 Strs; Qt 3 Strs ALBA ▲ 288 [DDD] (16.97)

Quartet No. 3 for Strings (1995)

Oxford String Quartet ("The String Quartets") † Qt 1 Strs; Qt 2 Strs ALBA ▲ 288 [DDD] (16.97)

STOKOWSKI, LEOPOLD (1882-1977)

Transcriptions for Orchestra

M. Bamert (cnd), BBC PO—Bach:Toccata & Fugue in d; Air on the G String; Little Fugue in g; Sheep may safely graze; Prelude in b; Passacaglia & Fugue in c; Komm süsser Tod; Wir glauben all' an Einen Gott; Siciliano; Mein Jesu CHN ▲ 9259 [DDD] (16.97)

M. Bamert (cnd), BBC PO—Wagner:Tristan and Isolde [Symphonic Synthesis]; Wagner:Die Walküre [Wotan's Farewell; Magic Fire Music]; Wagner:Parsifal [Symphonic Synthesis, Act 3] CHN ▲ 9686 (16.97)

L. Stokowski (cnd), Houston SO—Chopin:Mazurka in a, Op. 17/4; Prelude in d, Op. 28/24; Waltz in c♯, Op. 64/2 *(rec Houston Civic Center, NY, 1961)* † Amirov:Azerbaijan Mugam; S. Prokofiev:Peter & the Wolf (suite); Peter & the Wolf, Op. 67 EVC ▲ 9048 [ADD] (13.97)

L. Stokowski (cnd), Leopold Stokowski SO—Bach:Prelude & Fugue in c, BWV 582; Komm, süsser Tod, BWV 478; English Suite 2, BWV 807 [Bourée]; Partita 1 Vn, BWV 1002 [Sarabande]; Ein feste Burg ist unser Gott; Christmas Oratorio [Shepherd's Song]; Little Fugue in g, BWV 578; Air on the G String; Mein Jesu, was für Seelenweh befält dich; Partita 3 Vn, BWV 1006 [Preludio]; Toccata & Fugue in d, BWV 565 ("Bach by Stokowski") EMIC ▲ 66385 (11.97)

L. Stokowski (cnd), Philadelphia Orch—Bach:Passacaglia & Fugue in c; Great Fugue in g; Chaconne in d; Toccata & Fugue in d; Ein feste Burg ist unser Gott; selected Chorale Preludes & shorter works *(rec 1927-40)* PHS 2-▲ 9098 [ADD] (33.97)

STOLARCZYK, WILLY (1945-

Café Central (suite) for Piano, Op. 73 (1997)

J. Ribera (pno) *(rec 1998)* ("Café Central") † China House Fl, Op. 39A; Flowers & Harpoons, Op. 71; Little Mermaid, Op. 60; Miniatures avec flageolettes, Op. 31; Ornithological Recitative & Toccata, Op. 8; Son solo Fl, Op. 27; Sonatine Pno, Op. 45A; Van Carmen Vita, Op. 24 DANI ▲ 8196 [DDD] (18.97)

China House (6 course banquet) for Flute & Piano, Op. 39A (1988; rev 1993)

L. Stolarczyk (fl), W. Stolarczyk (pno) *(rec 1998)* ("Café Central") † Café Central, Op. 73; Flowers & Harpoons, Op. 71; Little Mermaid, Op. 60; Miniatures avec flageolettes, Op. 31; Ornithological Recitative & Toccata, Op. 8; Son solo Fl, Op. 27; Sonatine Pno, Op. 45A; Van Carmen Vita, Op. 24 DANI ▲ 8196 [DDD] (18.97)

Earth-Air-Fire-Water (symphony) for 96 Pianos & Percussion (1996)

E. Bach (pno), A. Malling (pno), P. Rosenbaum (pno), J. Ferencsik (pno), A. Riber (pno), S. Larsen (pno), J. Damgaard (pno), E. Kaltoft (pno), R. Bevan (pno), A. Øland (pno), R. Llambias (pno), T. Teirup (pno), F. Gürtler (pno), B. Horn-Ribera (pno), E. Sigurdsson (pno), T. Tronheim (pno), E. Broderson (pno), J. H. Nielsen (pno), A. Gilemann (pno), B. Kjær (pno), J. Thomsen (pno), G. Donslund (pno), H. B. Hansen (pno), L. Karlsson (pno), E. Fessel (pno), L. Nilsson (pno), A. Momme (pno), A. D. Cros Dich (pno), S. M. Slot (pno), H. B. Buhl (pno), L. Olesen (pno), S. Carlsson (pno), U. Erml (pno), V. Sørensen (pno), L. Greibe (pno), B. Krogh (pno), K. Ottosen (pno), I. Bergenholz (pno), K. Gylendorf (pno), B. Elkjær (pno), J. B. Jensen (pno), J. Kaad (pno), A. M. Hjelm (pno), C. U. Munk Andersen (pno), P. Lumbye (pno), O. H. Nielsen (pno), J. Olsson (pno), P. P. Ramsøe Jacobsen (pno), A. Pollmann (pno), J. Borsch (pno), K. Karlshøj (pno), M. T. Assing (pno), A. D. Hansen (pno), J. Hugossen (pno), T. F. Pederson (pno), A. J. Fæø (pno), A. Høgsted (pno), A. S. Parbo (pno), I. Lindmark (pno), T. D. Stathakis (pno), A. R. Ferenczi (pno), I. Hasager (pno), Y. Ichikawa (pno), B. Baur (pno), M. Thastum (pno), J. E. Rasmussen (pno), B. Zielke (pno), C. Zielke (pno), S. Kasch (pno), B. Qiao (pno), I. J. Teirup (pno), L. Rosborg (pno), L. Heininen (pno), D. Højer (pno), E. Refstrup (pno), T. K. Søorensen (pno), E. Kure (pno), M. Rauff (pno), J. B. Eriksson (pno), T. Zapolski (pno), V. Skagbo (pno), P. E. Lindtner (pno), H. Sul (pno), B. Palko (pno), I. Kesseler (pno), A. M. Meineche (pno), K. P. Bach (pno), E. Eliseo (pno), O. Magieres (pno), C. E. Kühl (pno), T. B. Nielsen (pno), V. Zanini (pno), L. Stenhoft (perc), D. Boel (perc), W. Dahlgren (perc), S. Vind (perc), C. Byrith (elec), A. M. Storm (elec), J. Ribera (cnd) *(rec Koldinghaus Castle Denmark, May 2, 1996)* DANI ▲ 1996 (11.97)

Flowers & Harpoons for Flute & Piano, Op. 71 (1997)

L. Stolarczyk (fl), W. Stolarczyk (pno) *(rec 1998)* ("Café Central") † Café Central, Op. 73; China House Fl, Op. 39A; Little Mermaid, Op. 60; Miniatures avec flageolettes, Op. 31; Ornithological Recitative & Toccata, Op. 8; Son solo Fl, Op. 27; Sonatine Pno, Op. 45A; Van Carmen Vita, Op. 24 DANI ▲ 8196 [DDD] (18.97)

The Little Mermaid [Den Lille Havfrue] (suite) for Flute & Piano, Op. 60 (1991)

L. Stolarczyk (fl), W. Stolarczyk (pno) *(rec 1998)* ("Café Central") † Café Central, Op. 73; China House Fl, Op. 39A; Flowers & Harpoons, Op. 71; Miniatures avec flageolettes, Op. 31; Ornithological Recitative & Toccata, Op. 8; Son solo Fl, Op. 27; Sonatine Pno, Op. 45A; Van Carmen Vita, Op. 24 DANI ▲ 8196 [DDD] (18.97)

Miniatures avec flageolettes (3) for Flute & Piano, Op. 31 (1987)

L. Stolarczyk (fl), W. Stolarczyk (pno) *(rec 1998)* ("Café Central") † Café Central, Op. 73; China House Fl, Op. 39A; Flowers & Harpoons, Op. 71; Little Mermaid, Op. 60; Ornithological Recitative & Toccata, Op. 8; Son solo Fl, Op. 27; Sonatine Pno, Op. 45A; Van Carmen Vita, Op. 24 DANI ▲ 8196 [DDD] (18.97)

Ornithological Recitative & Toccata for Flute & Prepared Piano, Op. 8 (1980)

L. Stolarczyk (fl), W. Stolarczyk (prepared pno) *(rec 1998)* ("Café Central") † Café Central, Op. 73; China House Fl, Op. 39A; Flowers & Harpoons, Op. 71; Little Mermaid, Op. 60; Miniatures avec flageolettes, Op. 31; Son solo Fl, Op. 27; Sonatine Pno, Op. 45A; Van Carmen Vita, Op. 24 DANI ▲ 8196 [DDD] (18.97)

Sonata for solo Flute, Op. 27 (1986)

L. Stolarczyk (fl) *(rec 1998)* ("Café Central") † Café Central, Op. 73; China House Fl, Op. 39A; Flowers & Harpoons, Op. 71; Little Mermaid, Op. 60; Miniatures avec flageolettes, Op. 31; Ornithological Recitative & Toccata, Op. 8; Sonatine Pno, Op. 45A; Van Carmen Vita, Op. 24 DANI ▲ 8196 [DDD] (18.97)

Sonatine for Piano, Op. 45A (1990; rev 1998)

W. Stolarczyk (pno) *(rec 1998)* ("Café Central") † Café Central, Op. 73; China House Fl, Op. 39A; Flowers & Harpoons, Op. 71; Little Mermaid, Op. 60; Miniatures avec flageolettes, Op. 31; Ornithological Recitative & Toccata, Op. 8; Son solo Fl, Op. 27; Van Carmen Vita, Op. 24 DANI ▲ 8196 [DDD] (18.97)

STOLARCZYK, WILLY (cont.)

Van Carmen Vita (4 pieces) for Piano, Op. 24 (1985)

W. Stolarczyk (pno) *(rec live, 1986)* ("Café Central") † Café Central, Op. 73; China House Fl, Op. 39A; Flowers & Harpoons, Op. 71; Little Mermaid, Op. 60; Miniatures avec flageolettes, Op. 31; Ornithological Recitative & Toccata, Op. 8; Son solo Fl, Op. 27; Sonatine Pno, Op. 45A DANI ▲ 8196 [DDD] (18.97)

STOLET, JEFFREY (1955-

Simple Requests for Cello Choir

L'Octuor De Violoncelles ("Simple Requests: New American Music for Computers & Live Performers") † E. Chambers:Rothko-Tobey Continuum; Kothman:Interrupted Dances; R. Lyons:Electronique; Gigue Vn; Ice Cream Truck from Hell; R. Oakes:Blues Danube; S. Sung:Mobiles; P. Terry:Aria & Accidental Music CMB ▲ 1088 (16.97)

STOLTZER, THOMAS (ca 1480/85-early 1526)

Missa duplex per totum annum for 4 Voices

M. Cordes (cnd), Weser-Renaissance CPO ▲ 999295 (14.97)

STOLZ, ROBERT (1880-1975)

Arias

I. Kirtesi (sop), Z. Csonka (sop), J. Berkes (ten), L. Kovács (cnd), Hungarian Operetta Orch—Ich liebe dich! [from Zauber der Bohème]; Zwei Herzen im Dreiviertaltakt; Du sollst der Kaiser meiner Seele sein; Adieu, mein kleiner Gardeoffizer *(rec Budapest, Jan 1996)* ("Best of Operetta, Vol. 3") † I. Kálmán:Gräfin Mariza (sels); F. Lehár:Paganini (sels); Strauss (II):Fledermaus (sels); Nacht in Venedig (sels); C. Zeller:Vogelhändler (sels) NXIN ▲ 8550943 [DDD] (5.97)

Der Favorit (selections)

G. Fontana (sop), P. Guth (cnd), Strauss Festival Orch Vienna—Du sollst der Kaiser meiner Seele sein *(rec Ludwigshafen am Rhein, Germany, Oct 1997)* ("Wine, Women & Song") † Venus in Seide (sels); I. Kálmán:Gräfin Mariza (sels); F. Lehár:Eva (sels); Giuditta (sels); Waltzes; Strauss (II):Fledermaus (sels); Nacht in Venedig (ov); Nacht in Venedig (sels); Prinz Methusalem (sels); Waltzes; Jos. Strauss:Ohne Sorgen, Op. 271; Ziehrer:Waltzes & Other Dances DI ▲ 920532 [DDD] (5.97)

Music of Stolz

I. Kertesi (sop), Z. Csonka (sop), J. Berkes (ten), L. Kovács (cnd), Hungarian Operetta Orch—Mein Liebeslied muss ein Walzer sein; Ob blond, ob braun [from Ich liebe alle Frau'n] *(rec Budapest, Jan 1995)* ("Best of Operetta, Vol. II") † I. Kálmán:Operetta Arias; F. Lehár:Graf von Luxemburg (sels); Lustige Witwe (sels); Paganini (sels); Zarewitsch (sels); Zigeunerliebe (sels); Strauss (II):Nacht in Venedig (ov) NXIN ▲ 8550942 [DDD] (5.97)

R. Stolz (cnd), Vienna SO—Gruss aus Wien (marsch); Melodien; Uno-Marsch; Wiener Café; Frühjahrsparade (marschlied) *(rec 1969)* ("The Genius of Robert Stolz") † Komzák:Badener Madeln; F. Lehár:Gold & Silver, Op. 79; Strauss (II):Annen-Polka, Op. 117; Fledermaus (ov); Zigeunerbaron (ov) TUXE ▲ 1023 (10.97)

artists unknown *(Ein Abend mit Robert Stolz), (A klane Drahrerei; Hysterie; Türkischer Marsch; Träume an der Donau; Tief berauscht mich dein Haar; Spiel auf deiner Geige; Fünf-Uhr-Tee bei Robert Stoltz; Ungeküsst sollst du nicht schlafen geh'n; Oft genügt ein Gläschen Sekt; O süsse Señorita, sag' nicht nein)* ("Musik von Robert Stolz") ARSM ▲ 8006 [DDD] (17.97)

Songs

A. Girardi (sgr) *(Der Herrgott, der hat viel zu tun; Das Glükerl)*, R. Tauber (ten) *(Im Prater blüh'n wieder die Bäume; In Wien hab' ich einmal ein Mädel geliebt)*, V. Schwarz (sop) *(Du sollst der Kaiser meiner Seele sein)*, M. Weber (sgr) *(Warum gehört dein roter Mund nicht mir allein)*, L. Frank (sgr) *(2 Herzen im Dreivierteltakt)*, I. Eisinger (sop) *(Auch du wirst mich einmal betrügen; In Wien, wo der Wein und der Walzer blüht)*, L. Haid (sgr) *(Adieu, mein kleiner Gardeoffizier)*, M. Wittrisch (ten) *(Das Lied ist aus [Frag nicht, warum ich gehe]; Mein Liebeslied muss ein Walzer sein; Mir sagt dein Blumenstrauss)*, S. Arno (sgr) *(Ich hab' bei der Trude das Küssen studiert)*, O. K. Weis (sgr) *(Du bist meine Greta Garbo)*, W. Forst (sgr) *(Warum lächelst du, Mona Lisa; Du dummer, kleiner Korporal)*, M. Eggerth (sgr) *(Nur um dich zu lieben, möcht' ich ewig leben; Ein Lied, ein Kuss, ein Mädel)*, H. E. Groh (ten) *(Du, du, du, schliess deine Augen zu)*, C. Kullman (ten) *(Ich sing' mein Lied heut nur für dich)*, W. Domgraf-Fassbaender (bar) *(Vor meinem Vaterhaus steht eine Linde)* ("Various Artists Sing Robert Stolz") BLAG ▲ 103007 (15.97)

Venus in Seide (selections)

G. Fontana (sop), P. Guth (cnd), Strauss Festival Orch Vienna—Spiel auf deiner Geige das Lied von Leid und Lust *(rec Ludwigshafen am Rhein, Germany, Oct 1997)* ("Wine, Women & Song") † Favorit (sels); I. Kálmán:Gräfin Mariza (sels); F. Lehár:Eva (sels); Giuditta (sels); Waltzes; Strauss (II):Fledermaus (sels); Nacht in Venedig (ov); Nacht in Venedig (sels); Prinz Methusalem (sels); Waltzes; Jos. Strauss:Ohne Sorgen, Op. 271; Ziehrer:Waltzes & Other Dances DI ▲ 920532 [DDD] (5.97)

STÖLZEL, GOTTFRIED HEINRICH (1690-1749)

Der Für die Sünde der Welt gemarterte und sterbende Christus (passion oratorio after B. H. Brockes) (1725)

C. Backes (sop), D. Mields (sop), H. Voss (alt), A. Post (ten), K. Schoch (ten), K. Mertens (bass), F. Mehltretter (bass), L. Rémy (cnd), Telemann CO, Michaelstein Chamber Chorus *(rec St. Bartholomäuskirche Blankenburg, Oct 25-31, 1997)* ("Brockes Passion") *(G, E texts)* CPO ▲ 999560 [DDD] (15.97)

STORACE, BERNARDO (fl late 17th cent)

Keyboard Music

S. Henstra (hpd)—Ciaccona in C; Passacaglia in a ("Toccate, partite et passacagli") † Frescobaldi:Hpd Music; A. Gabrieli:Kbd Music; Merula:Kbd Music; G. Picchi:Kbd Music RICE ▲ 167136 (17.97)

Organ Music

A. Marcon (org) ("The Heritage of Frescobaldi, Vol. 1") † B. Pasquini:Org Music; G. Salvatore:Org Music; G. Strozzi:Org Music APS (Historic Organ) ▲ 79405 [DDD] (16.97)

STOVER, HAROLD (1946-

Neumark Variations for Organ & Piano (1987)

J. Morrison (pno), A. Morrison (org) *(rec Morrow, GA, Nov 19, 1995)* ("Festive Duo") † M. Dupré:Prélude, fugue et var, Op. 18; Sinf Pno, Op. 42; Grasse:Festival Ov, Op. 5; S. Rachmaninoff:Con 2 Pno, Op. 18; Preludes Pno ACAD ▲ 20050 (16.97)

Rag, Pastorale & Carillon for 2 Pianos

J. Rogers (pno), J. Morrison (pno) *(rec Morrow, GA, United States of America, June 8-9, 1993)* ("A Virtuoso Duo-Piano Showcase") † J. Brahms:Vars on a Theme by Haydn; J. Costa:Flying Fingers 2 Pnos; E. von Dohnányi:Suite en valse 2 Pnos, Op. 39a; J. B. Duvernoy:Feu roulant, Op. 256; W. Lutoslawski:Vars Theme Paganini 2 Pnos ACAD ▲ 20023 (16.97)

STOYANOV, LOZKO (1934-

Liturgia Solemnis for Bass, Orchestra & Chorus (1980)

A. Vassilev (bass), M. Mtakiev (cnd), Varna PO, Slavonic Voices Male Chamber Choir [Slavonic] KOCH ▲ 7033 [DDD]

STRADELLA, ALESSANDRO (1644-1682)

Cantatas

C. Brandes (sop), I. Matthews (vn), M. Springfels (va da gamba), P. O'Dette (archlt), B. Weiss (hpd)—Fuor della Stigia sponda; Non havea il sole ancora; Frena, ò Filli; Si salvi chi può; Ferma il corso e torna al lido ("Cantatas") † Sinfonias HAM ▲ 907192 (18.97)

R. Giua (sop), C. Miatello (sop), R. Balconi (ct), G. Fagotto (ten), A. Abete (sgr), L. Bertotti (sgr), S. Balestracci (cnd), Santo Spirito Academy Orch, Santo Spirito Academy Chorus—for 5 w. vns [For Holy Christmas]; for 5 w. instrs [For the Souls in Purgatory] STRV ▲ 33392 [DDD] (16.97)

The Crucifixion & Death of our Lord Jesus Christ for Orchestra & Chorus

M. Schneider (cnd), La Stagione, Frankfurt Vocal Ensemble † Lamentation for Wednesday Holy Week; A. Scarlatti:Passion Oratorio CAPO 2-▲ 10411 (17.97)

Lamentation for Wednesday the Holy Week for Orchestra & Chorus

M. Schneider (cnd), La Stagione, Frankfurt Vocal Ensemble † Crucifixion & Death of Our Lord; A. Scarlatti:Passion Oratorio CAPO 2-▲ 10411 (17.97)

Music of Stradella

Convivium ("Early Italian Violin Sonatas") † Castello:Sonate concertate in stil moderno; Cima:Music of; B. Marini:Sons, Syms & Retornelli, Op. 8; Uccellini:Music of HYP ▲ 66985 (18.97)

Sinfonias

I. Matthews (vn), M. Springfels (va da gamba), P. O'Dette (archlt), B. Weiss (hpd)—Sinf 22; Sinf 12 ("Cantatas") † Cants HAM ▲ 907192 (18.97)

Sinfonia alla Serenata for Trumpet, Strings & Continuo, "Il barcheggio"

B. Kratzer (tpt), M. Nuber (org) *(rec Münster zu Villingen, Germany, Feb 1990)* ("Virtuoso Trumpet Music of the Baroque") † Albinoni:Cons Tpt & Org; G. B. Martini:Son al'Postcommunio; Toccata; H. Purcell:Cons Tpt & Org; Telemann:Qnt Tpt; Torelli:Con Tpt; J. G. Walther:Cons Tpt & Org FERM ▲ 20001 [DDD] (16.97)

Y. Waldman (vn), J. Cueto (vn), J. Rende (va), G. Kruvand (db), Maryland Bach Aria Group members ("The Italian Voyage") † J. S. Bach:Cant 110; Cant 20; B. Marcello:Salmo Decimoquinto; Son 2 Vls; Torelli:Son Tpt, G.1 CRYS ▲ 705 [DDD] (15.97)

Susanna (oratorio) for 5 Voices, 2 Violins & Continuo (1681)

S. Piccollo (sop), L. Bertotti (sop), M. Lazzara (ct), M. Nuvoli (ten), M. Perrella (bass), E. Velardi (cnd), Camerata Ligure [period instrs] BONG 2-▲ 2121 [DDD] (32.97)

STRAESSER, JOEP (1934-

Chamber Music

Duo Fusion Moderne *(Intersections V-2 for B Cl & Pno) (rec Concertgebouw Amsterdam)*, H. Sparnaay (b cl), D. Porcelijn (cnd), Ensemble M *(Signals & Echoes for 11 Players & B Cl)*, R. D. Reede (fl) *(A Solo for Alkaios [rec June 9, 1986])* † Gedanken der Nacht; Ramasasiri; Sightseeing V; Sym 3 CV ▲ 44 (19.97)

Gedanken der Nacht (5 songs) for Mezzo-Soprano, 3 Clarinets & Percussion [poems by Rilke] (1992)

A. Goud (mez), J. Sligter (cnd) *(rec Vredenburg Utrecht, Jan 17, 1993)* † Chamber Music; Ramasasiri; Sightseeing V; Sym 3 CV ▲ 44 (19.97)

Ramasasiri [Traveling Song] for Soprano & 5 Instruments [text in Papaun language] (1967-68)

D. W. Prins (sop), A. V. Beek (cnd) *(rec June 26, 1981)* † Chamber Music; Gedanken der Nacht; Sightseeing V; Sym 3 CV ▲ 44 (19.97)

Sightseeing V for String Quartet (1971)

Gaudeamus String Quartet *(rec July 2, 1974)* † Chamber Music; Gedanken der Nacht; Ramasasiri; Sym 3 CV ▲ 44 (19.97)

Symphony No. 3 (1991-92)

E. Waart (cnd), Netherlands Radio PO *(rec Concertgebouw Amsterdam, Feb 20, 1993)* † Chamber Music; Gedanken der Nacht; Ramasasiri; Sightseeing V CV ▲ 44 (19.97)

STRANDBERG, NEWTON (1921-

The Legend of Emmeline Labiche (interlude) for String Orchestra (1952)

J. E. Suben (cnd), Slovak RSO Bratislava ("The Orchestra According to the Seven") † F. D. Angeli:Pieces Orch; Dellaira:Three Rivers; Kenessey:Wintersong, Op. 44; P. Krumm:Con B Cl; Sichel:3 Places in New Jersey; Van Appledorn:Cycles of Moons & Tides OPS1 ▲ 170 [DDD]

Preludes (4) for Orchestra (1961)

J. Swoboda (cnd), Kraków PO † J. Caldwell:Elegy; D. Kowalski:Double Helix; Lomon:Terra Incognita; Olmstead:Sinfonia Borealis; Womack:Pentacle MASM (MMC New Century: Volume XI) ▲ 2069 [DDD] (16.97)

STRANGE, ALLEN (1943-

Shaman: Sisters of Dreamtime for amplified Violin & Electronics (1994)

P. Strange (vn), A. Strange (elec) *(rec Modesto, CA, Nov 1997)* ("Music for Players & Digital Media") † Belet:[Mute]ation; Frengel:Three Short Stories; P. Furman:Synergy; M. Helms:Whispering Modulations; D. Michael:Extensions #1; Wyman:Through the Reed CENT ▲ 2404 (live) [DDD] (16.97)

STRASFOGEL, IGNACE (1909-1996)

Piano Music

K. Lessing (pno) PLON (Entartete Musik) ▲ 455359 (16.97)

STRAUS, OSCAR (1870-1954)

The Merry Nibelungs (burlesque operetta in 3 acts) [lib Rideamus]

L. Griffith (sop—Kriemhild), G. Volkert (sop—Brunhilde), D. Evangelatos (cta—Ute), H. Heidbüchel (ten—Volker), M. Gantner (ten—Gunther), C. Mann (sgr—Vogel), G. Grochowski (sgr—Dankwart), M. Nowak (sgr—Siegfried), G. Henkel (sgr—Giselher), J. Otten (sgr—Hagen), S. Köhler (cnd), Cologne RSO, Cologne Radio Chorus *(rec Cologne, Jan 31-Feb 17, 1995)* CAPO ▲ 10752 [DDD] (17.97)

Music of Straus

A. Walter (cnd), Budapest Strauss SO—Rund um die Liebe:Ov.; Einzugs March; Walzerträume Waltz; G'stellte Mädl'n Polka; Alt-Weiner Reigen, Op. 45; Komm, komm, Held meiner Träme Waltz & L'amour; Bulgaren Marsch; Didi Marsch; Die Schlossparade Marsch; Valse lente; Menuett à la cour; Tragant Waltz; Eine Ballnacht Waltz; Der Reigen Concert Waltz *(rec Apr 1-4, 1993)* MARC ▲ 8223596 [DDD] (13.97)

Der tapfere Soldat (The Chocolate Soldier) (operetta in 3 acts) [lib after Shaw's *Arms & the Man*]

J. L. Thompson (cnd), Ohio Light Opera Orch, Ohio Light Opera Chorus *(rec College of Wooster, OH)* NPT 2-▲ 85650 [DDD] (32.97)

Ein Walzertraum (selections)

E. Liebesberg (sop), R. Holm (sop), D. Hermann (mez), H. Brauner (cta), R. Christ (ten), H. Prikopa (bar), F. Bauer-Theussl (cnd), Vienna Volksoper Orch, Vienna Volksoper Chorus [GER] ("Golden Operetta, Vol. 1") † F. Lehár:Graf von Luxemburg (sels) KOCP ▲ 399223 [AAD] (8.97)

M. Muszely (sop), L. Otto (sop), R. Schock (ten), B. Fritz (bar), W. Schüchter (cnd), Berlin Orch, Berlin Chorus † Strauss (II):Zigeunerbaron (sels) EMPE ▲ 86346 (11.97)

STRAUSS, CHRISTOPH (ca 1575-1631)

Missa Maria Concertata for 9 Voices

Concerto Palatino † Motets HAM ▲ 905243 (18.97)

Motets

Concerto Palatino—Rex Gloriae; Expectans expectavi Dominum; Eripe me Domine; Deus laudem meam; Amen dico vobis; O sapienta; Anima mea cessa; Hodie completi sunt; Exurge domine; Beati omnes; Paratum cor meum † Missa Maria HAM ▲ 905243 (18.97)

STRAUSS, EDUARD (1835-1916)

Bahn frei (polka) for Orchestra, Op. 45 (1869)

P. Guth (cnd), Strauss Festival Orch Vienna *(rec Golden Musikvereinssaal Vienna, Austria)* ("Strauss Dynasty") † Joh. Strauss:Fortuna-Galopp, Op. 69; Radetzky March, Op. 228; Strauss (II):Carneval in Rom (sels); Polkas; Prinz Methusalem (ov); Waltzes; Zigeunerbaron (sels); Jos. Strauss:Feuerfest, Op. 269 DI ▲ 920149 (5.97)

K. Jeitler (cnd), Vienna Young Brass-Philharmonic [arr Apollo 356] *(rec Vienna, Austria, Dec 1989)* ("Radetzky-Marsch: Favorite Showpieces for Brass") † Fučík:Florentine March, Op. 214; Mühlberger:Mir sein die Kaiserjäger; Joh. Strauss:Radetzky March, Op. 228; Strauss (II):Polkas; Waltzes; Jos. Strauss:Mein Lebenslauf ist Lieb und Lust, Op. 263; Moulinet, Op. 57; Ziehrer:Fesche Geister (ov) CAMA ▲ 140 [DDD] (18.97)

Greeting Valse, on English Airs for Orchestra (1885)

J. Georgiadis (cnd), London SO ("Johann Strauss & Family in London") † Old England for ever, Op. 239; Strauss (II):Erinnerung an Covent-Garden, Op. 329; Potpourri-Quadrille; Strauss (III):Krönungs-Walzer, Op. 40 CHN ▲ 8739 [DDD] (16.97)

Mit Chic (polka) for Orchestra, Op. 221

L. Maazel (cnd), Vienna PO ("New Year's Concert 1994") † Lanner:Schönbrunner, Op. 200; Joh. Strauss:Radetzky March, Op. 228; Strauss (II):An der schönen blauen Donau, Op. 314; Fledermaus (sels); Geschichten aus dem Wienerwald, Op. 325; Music of Joh. Strauss, Jr.; Jos. Strauss:Music of Jos. Strauss SNYC ▲ 46694 [DDD] (16.97)

Mit Vergnügen (polka) for Orchestra, Op. 228

L. Maazel (cnd), Vienna PO *(rec live Vienna, Austria, Jan 1, 1996)* ("New Year's Concert 1996") † Joh. Strauss:Radetzky March, Op. 228; Strauss (II):Music of Joh. Strauss, Jr.; Polkas; Waltzes; Jos. Strauss:Jokey-Polka, Op. 278; Nasswalderin, Op. 267; Tanzende Muse, Op. 266; Ziehrer:Wiener Bürger, Op. 419 RCAV (Red Seal) 2-▲ 68421 (16.97)

Music of Eduard Strauss

P. Angerer (cnd), Vienna CO—Schneesternchen, Op. 157; Fesche Geister, Op. 75; Bahn frei, Op. 45 ("Strauss Family Masterworks") † Joh. Strauss:Music of Joh. Strauss, Sr.; Radetzky March, Op. 228; Strauss (II):An der schönen blauen Donau, Op. 314; Kaiser-Walzer, Op. 437; Music of Joh. Strauss, Jr.; Jos. Strauss:Music of Jos. Strauss INTC 3-▲ 885918 [DDD] (16.97)

W. Boskovsky (cnd), Vienna PO—Fesche Geister, Op. 75; Bahn frei, Op. 45; Mit Extrapost, Op. 259 † Joh. Strauss:Music of Joh. Strauss, Sr.; Strauss (II):Music of Joh. Strauss, Jr.; Pizzicato-Polka; Schützen-Quadrille; Jos. Strauss:Music of Jos. Strauss PLON (Budget Box) 6-▲ 455254 (40.97)

J. Rothstein (cnd), Johann Strauss Orch—Blüthenkranz, Op. 292; Saat und Ernte, Op. 159; Weyprecht-Payer-Marsch, Op. 120; Mädchenlaune, Op. 99; Abonnenten, Op. 116 *(rec Morden, England)* ("Vienna Première: Volume 2") † Strauss (II):Klug Gretelein, Op. 462; Lustige Krieg Quadrille, Op. 402; Nacht in Venedig (sels); Strauss (III):Schlau-Schlau, Op. 6; Jos. Strauss:For ever, Op. 193; Music of Jos. Strauss CHN ▲ 8527 [DDD] (16.97)

Old England for ever (polka) for Orchestra, Op. 239

J. Georgiadis (cnd), London SO ("Johann Strauss & Family in London") † Greeting Valse, on English Airs; Strauss (II):Erinnerung an Covent-Garden, Op. 329; Potpourri-Quadrille; Strauss (III):Krönungs-Walzer, Op. 40 CHN ▲ 8739 [DDD] (16.97)

Pfeilschnell (polka) for Orchestra, Op. 179

P. Guth (cnd), Strauss Festival Orch Vienna † Joh. Strauss:Chineser-Galop, Op. 20; Strauss (II):Champagner-Polka, Op. 211; Kaiser-Walzer, Op. 437; Spitzentuch der Königin (sels); Jos. Strauss:Dorfschwalben aus Österreich, Op. 164; Libelle DI ▲ 920240 (5.97)

Polkas & Waltzes

A. Fiedler (cnd), Boston Pops Orch—Bahn frei, Op. 45; Doktrinen, Op. 79 ("Strauss Family Waltzes") † Strauss (II):Pizzicato-Polka; Polkas; Waltzes; Jos. Strauss:Music of Jos. Strauss RCAV (Living Stereo) ▲ 61688 (11.97)

O. Kamu (cnd), Swedish RSO—Souvenir de Bade, Op. 146; Myrthen-Sträusschen, Op. 87; Mit der Strömung, Op. 174 *(rec Oct 4-6, 1993)* ("Strāuse aus Wien") † Strauss (II):Alexandrinen-Polka, Op. 198; Cagliostro in Wien (sels); Carnevals-Spektakel-Quadrille, Op. 152; Göttin der Vernunft (ov); Ritter Pásmán (sels); Simplicius (sels) BIS ▲ 645 [DDD] (17.97)

TAKEMITSU, TORU (cont.)

Piano Distance for Piano (1961)

M. Matsuya (pno) *(rec Japan, Sept 1993)* ("Light Colored Album for Piano - Midori Matsuya plays Japanese Contemporary Pieces") † Hachimura:Vision of Higanbana; Matsumura:Berceuses; A. Miyoshi:Hommage; Ogura:Sonatina; T. Sato:August Laying to Rest; Carpet of Bamboo Leaves Falling onto Northern Sea; Scenery with Tea Gardens; Season of Yellow and Black; Yoshimatsu:Pleiades Dances CAMA ▲ 318 [DDD] (18.97)

Piano Music

N. Ogawa (pno)—Litany (1950/1989); Pause interrompue (1952-59); Pno Distance (1961); For Away (1973); Les Yeux clos (1979); Les Yeux clos II (1988); Rain Tree Sketch (1982); Rain Tree Sketch II (1992) *(rec Danderyd Grammar School Sweden, July 11-12, 1996)* ("The Complete Solo Piano Music") BIS ▲ 805 [DDD] (17.97)

I. Tateno (pno)—Uninterrupted Rests; Pno Distance (1961); For Away (1973); Les Yeux clos (1979); Les Yeux clos II (1988); Rain Tree Sketch (1982); Rain Tree Sketch II (1992) ("Piano Distance") FNL ▲ 15245 (16.97)

Quatrain II for Clarinet, Violin, Cello & Piano (1976)

R. Stoltzman (cl), T. Otaka (cnd), BBC Welsh SO † Fantasma Cantos; Waterways; Waves RCAV (Red Seal) ▲ 62537 (16.97)

Quotation of Dream for 2 Pianos & Orchestra

P. Serkin (pno), P. Crossley (pno), O. Knussen (cnd), London Sinfonietta † Archipelago S.; Dream/Window; How Slow the Wind; Signals from Heaven; Twill by Twilight DEUT (20/21: Music of Our Time) ▲ 453495 [DDD] (16.97)

Rain Tree for 3 Percussionists (or 3 Keyboard Players) (1981)

Kroumata Percussion Ensemble † Matsushita:Airscope II; M. Miki:Mar Spiritual; A. Miyoshi:Rin-sai; Nishimura:Kala BIS ▲ 462 [DDD] (17.97)

Rain Tree Sketch for Piano (1981)

Y. Nagai (pno) *(rec tion Stockholm, Sweden, Dec 1995)* ("Poésie: Yukie Nagai Plays Japanese Piano Music") † For Away; T. Ichiyanagi:Cloud Atlas; Kako:Poésie; A. Miyoshi:Diary of the Sea; Y. Takahashi:Kwanju, May 1980; Yashiro:Son Pno BIS ▲ 766 [DDD] (17.97)

Requiem for String Orchestra (1957)

K. Koizumi (cnd), Winnipeg SO † Debussy:Danse Pno; A. Louie:Songs of Paradise; Mendelssohn (-Bartholdy):Meeresstille und glückliche Fahrt, Op. 27; O. Respighi:Trittico botticelliano SMS (SM 5000) ▲ 5080 [DDD] (16.97)

C. St. Clair (cnd), Pacific SO † From Me Flows What You Call Time; Twill by Twilight SNYC ▲ 63044 (16.97)

Rocking Mirror Daybreak for 2 Violins (1983)

Kaï Ensemble ("Chamber Music") † A Way a Lone; Between Tides; Distance de fée; Hika; Landscape I BIS ▲ 920 [DDD] (17.97)

Scene for Cello & Strings

M. Brunello (vc), M. Brunello (cnd), Italian String Orch † P. Hindemith:Trauermusik; A. Piazzolla:Adiós Nonino; G. Rossini:Péchés de vieillesse (sels); Sollima:Violincelles Vibrez!; P. Tchaikovsky:Andante cantabile; Nocturne Vc AG ▲ 155 (18.97)

Signals from Heaven (2) for Chamber Ensemble (1987)

O. Knussen (cnd), London Sinfonietta † Archipelago S.; Dream/Window; How Slow the Wind; Quotation of Dream; Twill by Twilight DEUT (20/21: Music of Our Time) ▲ 453495 [DDD] (16.97)

Spirit Garden for Orchestra (1994)

H. Wakasugi (cnd), Tokyo Metropolitan SO *(rec Tokyo Metropolitan Art Space, July 25-29, 1994)* † Dream/Window; Gémeaux DNN ▲ 78944 [DDD] (16.97)

Star-Isle for Orchestra (1982)

T. Otaka (cnd), BBC National Orch Wales *(rec Swansea Wales, Nov 7-8, 1995)* † Dreamtime; Flock Descends into the Pentagonal Garden; Orion & Pleiades BIS ▲ 760 [DDD] (17.97)

Toward the Sea II for Alto Flute, Harp & String Orchestra (1981)

F. Hendrickx (a fl), A. Bertrand (hp), R. Werthen (cnd), I Fiamminghi CO *(rec Gent Belgium, Sept 15-18, 1997)* ("Music of Takemitsu") † A Way a Lone; Entre-temps; Film Music; Nostalgia TEL ▲ 80469 (16.97)

Toward the Sea III for Alto Flute & Harp (1989)

R. Aitken (fl), E. Goodman (hp) *(rec Ontario Canada, Sept-Oct 1993)* ("Toward the Sea: Music for Flute & Harp") † Damase:Son Fl & Hp; Inghelbrecht:Sonatina en trois parties; Lauber:Medieval Dances, Op. 45; Petra-Basacopol:Son Fl Hp BIS ▲ 650 [DDD] (17.97)

G. Collins (fl), A. Giles (hp) *(rec ABC Sydney, Jan 1993)* ("Enchanted DreamsExotic Dances") † C. Brumby:Exotic Dances; J. Jongen:Danse lente, Op. 66; A. Piazzolla:Histoire du tango; Rochberg:Slow Fires of Autumn; R. Shankar:Aube enchantée TALP ▲ 31 [DDD] (18.97)

Tree Line for Chamber Orchestra (1988)

O. Underhill (cnd) *(rec Vancouver B.C., Mar 7-9, 1995)* ("Tree Line: Music from Canada & Japan") † Bushnell:Night's Swift Dragons; C. Butterfield:Jappements; J. Kondo:Still Life; A. Louie:Winter Music; M. O'Neill:Ur Og & Aji CBC (Musica Viva) ▲ 1109 [DDD] (16.97)

Twill by Twilight [In Memory of Morton Feldman] for Orchestra (1988)

O. Knussen (cnd), London Sinfonietta † Archipelago S.; Dream/Window; How Slow the Wind; Quotation of Dream; Signals from Heaven DEUT (20/21: Music of Our Time) ▲ 453495 [DDD] (16.97)

R. Numajiri (cnd), Tokyo Metropolitan SO *(rec July 22-26, 1996)* ("Autumn") † A Way a Lone; Autumn; I Hear the Water Dreaming DNN ▲ 18032 [DDD] (16.97)

T. Otaka (cnd), Yomiuri Nippon SO † Matsumura:Con 2 Pno; A. Miyoshi:Noesis; Yoshimatsu:Threnody to Toki, Op. 12 ASV ▲ 1021 (16.97)

C. St. Clair (cnd), Pacific SO † From Me Flows What You Call Time; Requiem SNYC ▲ 63044 (16.97)

Uninterrupted Rests for Piano

M. Yuguchi (pno) *(rec Jan 1996)* ("Contemporary Japanese Piano Music") † Litany Pno; T. Ichiyanagi:Cloud Atlas; H. Otaka:Sonatine Pno; Terauchi:Phoenix Hall and 8 Putto-Figures; Yashiro:Son Pno THOR ▲ 2324 [DDD] (16.97)

Waterways for Piano, Clarinet, Violin, Cello, 2 Harps & 2 Vibraphones (1977)

R. Stoltzman (cl), T. Otaka (cnd), BBC Welsh SO † Fantasma Cantos; Quatrain II; Waves RCAV (Red Seal) ▲ 62537 (16.97)

Waves for Clarinet, Horn, 2 Trumpets & Percussion (1976)

R. Stoltzman (cl), T. Otaka (cnd), BBC Welsh SO † Fantasma Cantos; Quatrain II; Waterways RCAV (Red Seal) ▲ 62537 (16.97)

A Way a Lone for String Quartet, "String Quartet No. 1" (1981; orchd)

Kaï Ensemble ("Chamber Music") † Between Tides; Distance de fée; Hika; Landscape I; Rocking Mirror Daybreak BIS ▲ 920 [DDD] (17.97)

R. Numajiri (cnd), Tokyo Metropolitan SO *(rec July 22-26, 1996)* ("Autumn") † Autumn; I Hear the Water Dreaming; Twill by Twilight DNN ▲ 18032 [DDD] (16.97)

R. Werthen (cnd), I Fiamminghi CO *(rec Gent Belgium, Sept 15-18, 1997)* ("Music of Takemitsu") † Entre-temps; Film Music; Nostalgia; Toward the Sea II TEL ▲ 80469 (16.97)

TAKI, RENTARO (1879-1903)

Hana for Flute & Harp

J. Rampal (fl), L. Laskine (hp) *(rec New York, NY)* ("Japanese Melodies for Flute & Harp") † Kojo-No-Tsuki; Konoe:Chin-Chin Chidori; Miyagi:Haru no Umi; Sugiyama:Defune; Hanayome Ningyo; Traditional:Nambu Ushi Oi Uta; Sakura; K. Yamada:Aka Tombo; Chugoku-Chiho-No-Komoriuta; Kono Michi; Yanada:Jogashima No Ame SNYC ▲ 34568 (16.97)

Kojo-No-Tsuki (Moon over the Ruined Castle) for Flute & Harp (1901)

H. Naka (db), M. Nakagawa (fl), P. Zander (hpd), S. Yoshiwara (perc), M. Mamiya (cnd), Pro Musica Nipponia [arr Mamiya] *(rec Japan)* ("Japanese Melodies") † Anonymous:Chiran-Bushi; Matsushime-Ondo; Oroku-Musume; Zui-Zui-Zukkorobashi; Hirai:Nara-Yama; Konoe:Chin-Chin Chidori; Sugiyama:Defune; Traditional:Sakura, Sakura; K. Yamada:Chugoku-Chiho-No-Komoriuta SNYC ▲ 39703 (16.97)

J. Rampal (fl), L. Laskine (hp) *(rec New York, NY)* ("Japanese Melodies for Flute & Harp") † Hana; Konoe:Chin-Chin Chidori; Miyagi:Haru no Umi; Sugiyama:Defune; Hanayome Ningyo; Traditional:Nambu Ushi Oi Uta; Sakura; K. Yamada:Aka Tombo; Chugoku-Chiho-No-Komoriuta; Kono Michi; Yanada:Jogashima No Ame SNYC ▲ 34568 (16.97)

TAKTAKISHVILI, OTAR (1924-1989)

Concerto No. 2 for Violin & Chamber Orchestra (1987)

L. Issakadze (vn) † Gabunija:Sinf Gioconda; Nasidze:Con Vn; Zinzadse:Phantasie Vn ORF ▲ 304921 [DDD] (18.97)

Sonata for Flute & Piano (1968)

J. Baxtresser (fl), P. Muzijevic (pno) *(rec Bronxville, NY, 1996)* ("New York Legends") † Amirov:Pieces Fl; Debussy:Prélude à l'après-midi d'un faune; P. Gaubert:Three Water Colours; W. Gieseking:Sonatine Fl; F. Martin:Ballade Fl CAL ▲ 512 [DDD] (15.97)

M. Bellavance (fl), M. Bourdeau (pno) † B. Bartók:Hungarian Peasant Songs, Sz.71; Martinů:Son Fl & Pno; S. Prokofiev:Son Fl BRIO ▲ 121 (16.97)

C. Delafontaine (fl), M. Mourtazine-Chapochnikova (pno) ("Decouvertes Transcaucasiennes") † Amirov:Pieces Fl; Glière:Pieces various instrs, Op. 35; Liadov:Prelude Fl & Pno; S. Rachmaninoff:Vocalise GALL ▲ 894 [DDD] (19.97)

TAKTAKISHVILI, OTAR (cont.)

Sonata for Flute & Piano (1968) (cont.)

L. Mironovich (fl), E. Mironovich (pno) *(rec Boston, MA)* ("Magic of the Russian Flute") † E. Denisov:Son Fl; Gubaidulina:Allegro rustico; Nagovitzin:Son Fl; Sinisalo:Miniatures Fl; Vasilenko:Spring Suite, Op. 138 SO ▲ 22567 [DDD] (16.97)

M. Wiesler (fl), R. Pöntinen (pno) † Amirov:Pieces Fl; E. Denisov:Pieces Fl; Son Fl; S. Prokofiev:Son Fl BIS ▲ 419 [DDD] (17.97)

TALLIS, THOMAS (ca 1505-1585)

Church Music

T. Brown (cnd), Clare College Choir Cambridge—Te lucis; In manus tuas *(rec St. George's Church Chesterton, June 26-27, 1991)* ("Compline Service with Anthems & Motets") † W. Byrd:Anthems; Church Music; J. Sheppard:Church Music; Sacred Choral Music; R. White:Sacred Music GILD ▲ 7108 [DDD] (16.97)

H. Christophers (cnd), The Sixteen Chorus—Te lucis ante terminum; O nata lux; O sacrum convivium; Jesu salvator saeculi; Salvator mundi, salva nos; Loquebantur variis linguis [L] † Gaude gloriosa Dei Mater; Lamentations of Jeremiah; Spem in alium CHN (Chaconne) ▲ 513 [DDD] (16.97)

A. Deller (cnd), Deller Consort—Jam lucis orto sidere; Salvator mundi Domine; Deus tuorum militum; Iste confessor; Sermone blando angelus; Jam Christus astra ascenderat; Ex more docti mistico; Te lucis ante terminum [L] † Lamentations of Jeremiah HMA ▲ 190208 [ADD] (9.97)

D. Douglass (cnd), King's Noyse, P. Hillier (cnd), Theater of Voices—Cantiones Sacrae; Audivi vocem de caelo; Derelinquit impius; Benedictus; In ieiunio et fletu; Te lucis ante terminum; If ye love me; Why fum'th in sight ("Lamentations, Motets, String Music") † Lamentations of Jeremiah HAM ▲ 907154 (18.97)

D. Flood (org), Canterbury Cathedral Choir—Ave Dei patris filia; Ave rosa sine spinis; Salve intermerata virgo *(rec Canterbury Cathedral nave)* ("The Canterbury Years") † Mass "Salve intemerata" MENO ▲ 1014 [DDD] (20.97)

E. Higginbottom (cnd), New College Choir Oxford—Gaude gloriosa; Nunc dimittis [from Magnificat]; Cantiones Sacrae [motets] CRD ▲ 3429 [DDD] (17.97)

L. Mortensen (hpd), B. Holten (cnd), Ars Nova Vocal Ensemble—Videte miraculum; Felix namque (I & II); Salvator mundi (I); O Nata lux [L] † Lamentations of Jeremiah KPT ▲ 32003 [DDD]

Oxford Camerata—Loquebantur variis linguis; Salvator mundi; O sacrum convivium; Audivi vocem; Sancte Deus; Videte miraculum; Te lucis ante terminum; In manus tuas Domine *(rec June 29-July 1, 1992)* † Mass 4 Voc NXIN ▲ 550576 [DDD] (5.97)

P. Phillips (cnd), Tallis Scholars—Gaude gloriosa; Loquebantur variis linguis; Miserere nostri; Salvator mundi; Sancte Deus [L] † Spem in alium GIME ▲ 54906 [DDD] (16.97)

P. Phillips (cnd), Tallis Scholars—Salve Intermerata Virgo (antiphon); Absterge Domine; Derelinquat impius; Mihi autem nimis; O sacrum convivum; In ieiunio et fletu; O salutaris hostia; In manus tuas; O nata lux (all motets) † Lamentations of Jeremiah GIME ▲ 54925 [DDD] (16.97)

P. Phillips (cnd), Tallis Scholars—English Anthems; Gaude gloriosa; Loquebantur variis linguis; Miserere nostri; Salvator mundi, salva Nos I & II; Spem in alium ("A Tudor Collection") † W. Byrd:Mass 3 Voc; Mass 4 Voc; Mass 5 Voc; Motets; Cornysh:Sacred & Secular Choral Music; Taverner:Sacred Music PPHI 4-▲ 454895 [DDD] (45.97)

Tallis Scholars—Audivi vocem; Magnificat; Ave Die Patris filia † Messe "Puer natus est" GIME ▲ 454934 (16.97)

R. Woolley (org) *(Gloria tibi Trinitas; Iste confessor Domini sacratus; Ex more docti mistico; Ecce tempus idoneum I & II; Veni Redemptor gentium I & II; Clarifica me pater I-III; A Point; Natus est nobis hodie) (rec Ploujean ge, France, Sept 16-18, 1993)*, C. Robinson (cnd), St. John's College Choir Cambridge *(Jam lucis orto sidere; Laudate Dominum; Jesu salvator saeculi; Salvator mundi; Videte miraculum; Jam Christus astra ascenderat; Quod chorus vatum; O nata lux de lumine) (rec Jesus College Chapel Cambridge, England, July 21-23)* ("Choral & Organ Works") CHN (Chaconne) ▲ 588 (16.97)

D. Wulstan (cnd), Clerkes of Oxenford—O nata lux de lumine; Ecce tempus idoneum; Loquebantur variis linguis; Gaude gloriosa † Spem in alium; J. Sheppard:Sacred Choral Music CFP ▲ 4638 [ADD] (12.97)

Complete Works of Tallis

A. Dixon (cnd), Chapelle du Roi—Ave Dei patris fila; Ave rosa sine spinis alleluia; Ora Pro Nobis; Euge celi porta; Kyrie Deus creator; Mass salve intemerata; Salve intemerata ("Complete Works, Vol. 1") SIUK ▲ 1 (16.97)

A. Dixon (cnd), Chapelle du Roi—Magnificat; Nunc dimitis; Sancte Deus; Conditor kyrie; Mass 4 Voc; Remember, No, O Lord God; Hear the Voice of Prayer; If Ye Love Me; A New Commandment; Benedictus; Te deum for Meanes ("Complete Works, Vol. 2") SIUK ▲ 2 (16.97)

A. Dixon (cnd), Chapelle du Roi—Beati immaculati; Introit:Puer natus est nobis; Kyrie; Deus creator; Mass:Puer natus est nobis; Gloria; Gradual; Viderunt omnes (2); Sequence; Celeste organum; Communion; Suscipe quaeso; Gaude gloriosa ("Complete Works, Vol. 3") SIUK ▲ 3 (16.97)

English Anthems (complete)

P. Phillips (cnd), Tallis Scholars—If Ye Love Me; Hear the Voice & Prayer; A New Commandment; O Lord, Give thy Holy Spirit; Purge Me, O Lord; Verily, Verily I Say unto You; Remember Not, O Lord God; 9 Tunes for Archbishop Parker's Psalter; Out from the Deep; O Lord, in Thee is All My Trust; Christ Rising Again; Blessed are Those That be Undefiled [E] GIME ▲ 54907 [DDD] (16.97)

Gaude gloriosa Dei mater (votive antiphon) for 6 Voices

H. Christophers (cnd), The Sixteen Chorus [LAT] † Church Music; Lamentations of Jeremiah; Spem in alium CHN (Chaconne) ▲ 513 [DDD] (16.97)

P. Phillips (cnd), Tallis Scholars † Psalm Tunes; Salvator mundi I; G. Allegri:Miserere; W. Byrd:Mass 4 Voc; Cornysh:Salve regina; Josquin Desprez:Missa, "L'homme armé sexti toni" GIME ▲ 54999 [AAD/DDD] (16.97)

The Lamentations of Jeremiah for Chorus

M. Brown (cnd), Pro Cantione Antiqua † Spem in alium ICC ▲ 6600952 (16.97)

H. Christophers (cnd), The Sixteen Chorus [LAT] † Church Music; Gaude gloriosa Dei Mater; Spem in alium CHN (Chaconne) ▲ 513 [DDD] (16.97)

A. Deller (ct), W. Brown (ten), G. English (ten), M. Bevan (bar), J. Frost (bass) *(rec Walthamstow Hall London, 1960)* † F. Couperin:Leçons (3) de Ténèbres VC (The Bach Guild) ▲ 2525 [ADD] (13.97)

A. Deller (cnd), Deller Consort [LAT] † Church Music HMA ▲ 190208 [ADD] (9.97)

D. Douglass (cnd), King's Noyse, P. Hillier (cnd), Theater of Voices ("Lamentations, Motets, String Music") † Church Music HAM ▲ 907154 (18.97)

B. Holten (cnd), Ars Nova Vocal Ensemble [LAT] † Church Music KPT ▲ 32003 [DDD]

A. Mackay (cnd), Sarum Consort † Motets; W. Byrd:Infelix ego; Mass 5 Voc ASVQ ▲ 6185 (10.97)

P. Phillips (cnd), Tallis Scholars ("Lamenta") † A. I. Ferrabosco:Lamentations; R. White:Lamentations of Jeremiah GIME ▲ 454996 (16.97)

P. Phillips (cnd), Tallis Scholars † Church Music GIME ▲ 54925 [DDD] (16.97)

Mass for 4 Voices (?1554)

Oxford Camerata *(rec June 29-July 1, 1992)* † Church Music NXIN ▲ 550576 [DDD] (5.97)

Mass for 5 Voices, "Salve intemerata"

D. Flood (org), Canterbury Cathedral Choir *(rec Canterbury Cathedral nave)* ("The Canterbury Years") † Church Music MENO ▲ 1014 [DDD] (20.97)

Messe "Puer natus est"

Tallis Scholars † Church Music GIME ▲ 454934 (16.97)

Motets

H. Chaney (cnd), St. Ignatius of Antioch Choir—Audivi vocem *(rec New York, NY, Jun 14, 1992)* † Certon:Missa 'Sus le pont d'Avignon'; Dunstable:Sancta Maria; Duruflé:Mass, "Cum jubilo", Op. 11; Victoria:Cum beatus Ignatius; C. Wuorinen:Missa Brevis MUA ▲ 4798 [DDD]

A. Mackay (cnd), Sarum Consort—O sacrum convivium; Sancte Deus † Lamentations of Jeremiah; W. Byrd:Infelix ego; Mass 5 Voc ASVQ ▲ 6185 (10.97)

Psalm Tunes (9) for M. Parker for 4 Voices

P. Phillips (cnd), Tallis Scholars † Gaude gloriosa Dei Mater; Salvator mundi I; G. Allegri:Miserere; W. Byrd:Mass 4 Voc; Cornysh:Salve regina; Josquin Desprez:Missa, "L'homme armé sexti toni" GIME ▲ 54999 [AAD/DDD] (16.97)

Salvator mundi I (antiphon) for 5 Voices

P. Phillips (cnd), Tallis Scholars † Gaude gloriosa Dei Mater; Psalm Tunes; G. Allegri:Miserere; W. Byrd:Mass 4 Voc; Cornysh:Salve regina; Josquin Desprez:Missa, "L'homme armé sexti toni" GIME ▲ 54999 [AAD/DDD] (16.97)

Songs

F. C. Fitch (vir)—Like as the doleful dove; O ye tender babes *(rec Berkeley, CA)* ("O Ye Tender Babes") † J. Bull:Kbd Music; W. Byrd:Kbd Music; O. Gibbons:Kbd Music; Inglott:Leaves bee greene; P. Philips:Kbd Music; T. Tomkins:Barafostus' Dreame; Pavan & Galliard WILD ▲ 9507 [DDD] (16.97)

King's Singers ("English Renaissance") † W. Byrd:Songs RCAV (Red Seal) ▲ 68004 (16.97)

Spem in alium [Sing & Glorify] for 40 Voices

M. Brown (cnd), Pro Cantione Antiqua † Lamentations of Jeremiah ICC ▲ 6600952 (16.97)

H. Christophers (cnd), The Sixteen Chorus [LAT] † Church Music; Gaude gloriosa Dei Mater; Lamentations of Jeremiah CHN (Chaconne) ▲ 513 [DDD] (16.97)

Kronos Quartet [multi-tracked str qt arr] † G. Crumb:Black Angels (Images I); C. Ives:They Are There!; Martá:Doom. A Sigh; D. Shostakovich:Qt 8 Strs, Op. 110 NON ▲ 79242 (16.97)

TALLIS, THOMAS (cont.)
Spem in alium [Sing & Glorify] for 40 Voices (cont.)
P. van Nevel (cnd), Huelgas Ensemble † G. Gabrieli:Exaudi me Domine; Josquin Desprez:Qui habitat in adjutorio Altissimi; Manchicourt:Laudate Dominum; Ockeghem:Deo gratias; C. Porta:Masses; Striggio:Ecce beatam lucem SNYC (Vivarte) ▲ 66261 (16.97)
P. Phillips (cnd), Tallis Scholars [LAT] † Church Music GIME ▲ 54906 [DDD] (16.97)
D. Willcocks (cnd), King's College Choir Cambridge ("Great Choral Classics from King's") † G. Allegri:Miserere; J. S. Bach:Cant 41; G. F. Handel:Coronation Anthems for George II, HWV 258-61; Palestrina:Stabat mater; Vivaldi:Gloria (& Intro), RV.588 PLON 2-▲ 452949 (17.97)
D. Wulstan (cnd), Clerkes of Oxenford † Church Music; J. Sheppard:Sacred Choral Music CFP ▲ 4638 [ADD] (12.97)

TALLIS, THOMAS (ca 1505-1585)**& JOHN SHEPPARD** (ca 1516-ca 1560)
Church Music
Oxford Camerata—Loquebantur variis linguis; Salvator mundi; O sacrum convivium; Audivi vocem; Sancte Deus; Videte miraculum; Te lucis ante terminum; In manus tuas Domine *(rec June 29-July 1, 1992)* † Mass 4 Voc NXIN ▲ 550576 [DDD] (5.97)
P. Phillips (cnd), Tallis Scholars—Gaude gloriosa; Loquebantur variis linguis; Miserere nostri; Salvator mundi; Sancte Deus [L] † Spem in alium GIME ▲ 54906 [DDD] (16.97)
R. Woolley (org) *(Gloria tibi Trinitas; Iste confessor Domini sacratus; Ex more docti mistico; Ecce tempus idoneum I & II; Veni Redemptor gentium I & II; Clarifica me pater I-III; A Point; Natus est nobis hodie) (rec Ploujean ge, France, Sept 16-18, 1993)*, C. Robinson (cnd), St. John's College Choir Cambridge *(Jam lucis orto sidere; Laudate Dominum; Jesu salvator saeculi; Salvator mundi; Videte miraculum; Jam Christus astra ascenderat; Quod chorus vatum; O nata lux de lumine) (rec Jesus College Chapel Cambridge, England, July 21-23)* ("Choral & Organ Works") CHN (Chaconne) ▲ 588 (16.97)

TALMA, LOUISE (1906-1996)
La Corona for Chorus [after holy sonnets of John Donne] (1955)
G. Smith (cnd), Gregg Smith Singers ("I Hear America Sing") † Leaden Echo; Let's Touch the Sky; Voices of Peace; Wreath of Blessings; N. Rorem:Give All To Love; In Time of Pestilence; Letters from Paris; Missa Brevis; W. Schuman:Carols of Death; Esses; Mail Order Madrigals; Orpheus & His Lute; Perceptions; Prelude; Rounds on Famous Words VB3 (The American Composers) 3-▲ 3037 (14.97)
Diadem (song cycle) for Tenor & Piano (or 5 Instruments) (1978-80)
P. Sperry (ten), Da Capo Chamber Players ("Voices from Elysium") † A. Copland:As It Fell upon a Day; H. Cowell:Vocalise; Crawford (Seeger):Songs (3); Gideon:Voices from Elysium NWW ▲ 80543 (16.97)
P. Sperry (ten), J. Freeman (cnd), Orch 2001 members, Orch 2001 members *(rec Swarthmore College, PA, Oct 29, 1995)* ("Music of Our Time for Mixed Ensemble, Vol. 2") † G. Crumb:Night of the 4 Moons; Greatbatch:Clockwork Legend; G. Levinson:In Dark; Reise:Chesapeake Rythyms CRI ▲ 760 [DDD] (16.97)
The Leaden Echo & the Golden Echo for Chorus
E. Clark (sop), J. Sherry (pno), G. Smith (cnd), Gregg Smith Singers ("I Hear America Sing") † Corona; Let's Touch the Sky; Voices of Peace; Wreath of Blessings; N. Rorem:Give All To Love; In Time of Pestilence; Letters from Paris; Missa Brevis; W. Schuman:Carols of Death; Esses; Mail Order Madrigals; Orpheus & His Lute; Perceptions; Prelude; Rounds on Famous Words VB3 (The American Composers) 3-▲ 3037 (14.97)
Let's Touch the Sky (3 poems) for Flute, Oboe, Basson & Chorus [after Cummings] (1952)
R. Troxler (fl), G. Reuter (ob), P. Simmons (bn), G. Smith (cnd), Gregg Smith Singers ("I Hear America Sing") † Corona; Leaden Echo; Voices of Peace; Wreath of Blessings; N. Rorem:Give All To Love; In Time of Pestilence; Letters from Paris; Missa Brevis; W. Schuman:Carols of Death; Esses; Mail Order Madrigals; Orpheus & His Lute; Perceptions; Prelude; Rounds on Famous Words VB3 (The American Composers) 3-▲ 3037 (14.97)
Sonata No. 1 for Piano (1943)
R. Rudnytsky (pno) ("Pianistic Portraits") † Liszt:Légendes, S.175; S. Rachmaninoff:Preludes Pno; Rollin:Night Thoughts II; A. Rudnytsky:Vars Pno, Op. 38 ARUN ▲ 3059 (16.97)
Sonata for Violin & Piano (1962)
C. Tait (vn), B. Snyder (pno) ("American Women Composers") † Crawford (Seeger):Son Vn & Pno; Mamlok:Designs; From My Garden; Son Vn; E. T. Zwilich:Son Vn in 3 Movts GAS ▲ 300 (16.97)
Terre de France for Voice & Orchestra
P. Sperry (ten), I. Vallecillo (pno) *(rec Bedford, NY, 1990)* ("Paul Sperry Sings American Cycles & Sets") † R. Beaser:7 Deadly Sins; C. Berg:Six Poems of Frank O'Hara; L. Gruenberg:Animals and Insects, Op. 22; L. A. Smith:Songs of the Silence; R. Wilson:Three Painters *(E text)* ALBA ▲ 58 [DDD] (16.97)
Voices of Peace for Voices & Strings (1973)
R. Rees (sop), S. Whittaker (ten), C. R. Stevens (bar), G. Smith (cnd), Adirondack CO, Gregg Smith Singers ("I Hear America Sing") † Corona; Leaden Echo; Let's Touch the Sky; Wreath of Blessings; N. Rorem:Give All To Love; In Time of Pestilence; Letters from Paris; Missa Brevis; W. Schuman:Carols of Death; Esses; Mail Order Madrigals; Orpheus & His Lute; Perceptions; Prelude; Rounds on Famous Words VB3 (The American Composers) 3-▲ 3037 (14.97)
A Wreath of Blessings for Chorus
G. Scaggs (sop), A. Lindevald (mez), D. Martin (ten), L. Dorsey (bass), G. Smith (cnd), Gregg Smith Singers ("I Hear America Sing") † Corona; Leaden Echo; Let's Touch the Sky; Voices of Peace; N. Rorem:Give All To Love; In Time of Pestilence; Letters from Paris; Missa Brevis; W. Schuman:Carols of Death; Esses; Mail Order Madrigals; Orpheus & His Lute; Perceptions; Prelude; Rounds on Famous Words VB3 (The American Composers) 3-▲ 3037 (14.97)

TAN DUN (1957-
Circle with 4 Trios, Conductor & Audience (1992)
New Ensemble *(rec May 13, 1992)* ("eXchange series") † Eight Colors; Elegy: Snow in June; In Distance; Silk Road CRI ▲ 655 [DDD] (16.97)
Death & Fire [Dialogue with Paul Klee] for Orchestra (1992)
M. Tang (cnd), Helsinki PO † Orchestral Theater II; Out of Peking Opera ODE ▲ 864 (17.97)
Eight Colors for String Quartet (1986-88)
Arditti String Quartet *(rec Feb 28, 1992)* ("eXchange series") † Circle; Elegy: Snow in June; In Distance; Silk Road CRI ▲ 655 [DDD] (16.97)
Elegy: Snow in June for Cello & Percussion (1991)
A. Karttunen (vc), Talujon Percussion Quartet *(rec June 4, 1992)* ("eXchange series") † Circle; Eight Colors; In Distance; Silk Road CRI ▲ 655 [DDD] (16.97)
Ghost Opera for Pipa & String Quartet with Water, Stones, Paper & Metal (1994)
W. Man (pipa/paper/Tibetan b), Kronos Quartet *(rec Skywalker Ranch, CA, Jan 1996) (E text)* NON ▲ 79445 (9.97)
In Distance for Piccolo, Harp & Bass Drum (1987)
K. Wilson (pic), G. Benet (pno), T. Dun (dr) *(rec June 4, 1992)* ("eXchange series") † Circle; Eight Colors; Elegy: Snow in June; Silk Road CRI ▲ 655 [DDD] (16.97)
Intermezzo for Orchestra & 3 Tone Colors (1985)
K. Schermerhorn (cnd), Hong Kong PO *(rec Lyric Theatre of the Hong Kong Academy for Perform, June 28, 1986)* ("First Contemporary Chinese Composers Festival 1986") † W. W. Chan:Sym 3; A. Huang:Con Pno; Qu:Mong Dong; J. Tang:Sym 3; Ye:Moon over the West River MARC (Chinese Contemporary) ▲ 8223915 [DDD] (13.97)
Marco Polo (opera) [lib Paul Griffiths] (1996)
S. Chen (sop), S. Botti (sop), D. Bryant (sop), N. Warren (sop), A. Montano (mez), T. Young (ten), Gong (sgr), T. Dun (cnd), Netherlands Radio CO, Capella Amsterdam SNYC 2-▲ 62912 (32.97)
Music of Tan Dun
T. Dun (cnd), BBC Scottish SO—On Taoism; Orchestral Theatre I; Death & Fire KSCH ▲ 312982 [DDD]
Orchestral Theater II: RE for Orchestra
M. Tang (cnd), Helsinki PO † Death & Fire; Out of Peking Opera ODE ▲ 864 (17.97)
Out of Peking Opera (concerto) for Violin & Orchestra
C. Lin (vn), M. Tang (cnd), Helsinki PO † Death & Fire; Orchestral Theater II ODE ▲ 864 (17.97)
Silk Road for Soprano & Percussion (1989)
S. Botti (sop), P. Guerguerian (perc) *(rec June 4, 1992)* ("eXchange series") † Circle; Eight Colors; Elegy: Snow in June; In Distance CRI ▲ 655 [DDD] (16.97)

TANAKA, KAREN (1961-
Initium for Orchestra & Live Electronics (1992-93)
K. Akiyama (cnd), Tokyo SO *(rec Tokyo Metropolitan Theater Large Hall, June 23, 1993)* † Mamiya:Con III Pno; Nishimura:Mantra of the Light CAMA ▲ 319 [DDD] (18.97)
Prismes for Orchestra (1984)
J. Hirokami (cnd), Malmö SO *(rec (Konserthus), Sweden, June 1990)* ("Japanese Orchestral Music") † Ifukube:Ballata Sinfonica; A. Otaka:Image Orch; Y. Toyama:Matsura Orch; Wada:Folkloric Dance Suite; Folkloric Dance Suite Orch *(E, F, G text)* BIS ▲ 490 [DDD] (17.97)

TANAKA, NORIYASU (20th cent)
Chamber Music
T. Takeda (cl), G. Matsuyama (pno), Y. Yamaguchi (perc) *(Ko-Oh [1989])*, H. Horino (sop), T. Takeda (cl), G. Matsuyama (pno) *(Requiem "Soothing Souls in the Sea" [1988])*, A. Yasuda (vn), K. Chomli (vc), T. Takeda (cl) *(Divert [1994])*, A. Yasuda (vn), K. Chomli (vc), T. Takeda (cl), G. Matsuyama (pno) *(Fragment I [1981])*, A. Yasuda (vn), K. Chomli (vc), G. Matsuyama (pno) *(Dialogue [1993])* ("Chamber Music, Vol. 1") VMM ▲ 2011 [DDD]

TANAKA, TOSHIMITSU (1930-
Movements (2) for Percussion
M. Leoson (perc) † B. T. Andersson:Apollo Con; Donatoni:Omar; Fukushi:Ground; D. Milhaud:Con Mar; Xenakis:Rebonds Perc CAPA ▲ 21466 (16.97)

TANEV, ALEXANDER (1927-1996)
Let the Maiden Be Mine (song) for Chorus
T. Pavlovitch (cnd), Sofia Chamber Choir † Our Father; We Sing Thee; K. Iliev:Quiet Songs; Kolarov:Autumn Was Coming; Winter; Pipkov:Subdued Songs; T. Popov:Winter Reflections; I. Spassov:Triptych; Tekeliev:Dostonio est; Reverie *([ENG,BUL] texts)* GEGA ▲ 125 (16.97)
Our Father for Chorus
T. Pavlovitch (cnd), Sofia Chamber Choir † Let the Maiden Be Mine; We Sing Thee; K. Iliev:Quiet Songs; Kolarov:Autumn Was Coming; Winter; Pipkov:Subdued Songs; T. Popov:Winter Reflections; I. Spassov:Triptych; Tekeliev:Dostonio est; Reverie *([ENG,BUL] texts)* GEGA ▲ 125 (16.97)
We Sing Thee (Tebe poem) for Chorus
T. Pavlovitch (cnd), Sofia Chamber Choir † Let the Maiden Be Mine; Our Father; K. Iliev:Quiet Songs; Kolarov:Autumn Was Coming; Winter; Pipkov:Subdued Songs; T. Popov:Winter Reflections; I. Spassov:Triptych; Tekeliev:Dostonio est; Reverie *([ENG,BUL] texts)* GEGA ▲ 125 (16.97)

TANEYEV, ALEXANDER (1850-1918)
John of Damascus (cantata) for Orchestra & Chorus, Op. 1 (1884)
V. Polianski (cnd), Russian State SO, Russian State Sym Capella † P. Tchaikovsky:Sym 4 CHN ▲ 9608 [DDD] (16.97)
Quartet No. 1 in G for Strings, Op. 25
Talan String Quartet † Qt 2 Strs, Op. 28; Qt 3 Strs, Op. 30 OLY ▲ 543 [DDD] (16.97)
Quartet No. 2 in C for Strings, Op. 28
Talan String Quartet † Qt 1 Strs, Op. 25; Qt 3 Strs, Op. 30 OLY ▲ 543 [DDD] (16.97)
Quartet No. 3 in A for Strings, Op. 30
Talan String Quartet † Qt 1 Strs, Op. 25; Qt 2 Strs, Op. 28 OLY ▲ 543 [DDD] (16.97)

TANEYEV, SERGEI (1856-1915)
At the Reading of a Psalm [Po prochtenii psalma] (cantata) for solo Voices, Orchestra & Chorus, Op. 36 (1915)
Y. Antonov (sgr), Y. Belokrynkin (sgr), R. Kotova (sgr), A. Kozlova (sgr), E. Svetlanov (cnd), USSR SO, Yurlov State Choir RUS ▲ 10044 [AAD] (12.97)
Canzona for Clarinet & Strings (1883)
D. Ashkenazy (cl), C. Mueller (cnd), Cincinnati PO † J. Françaix:Con Cl; R. Moser:Con Cl; Rimsky-Korsakov:Concertstück Cl PANC ▲ 510082 [DDD] (17.97)
Duet for Romeo & Juliet for Soprano, Tenor & Orchestra [completion & orchestration of Tchaikovsky's Romeo & Juliet Duet] (1894)
S. Murphy (sop), K. Lewis (ten), N. Järvi (cnd), Royal Scottish National Orch [RUS] † S. Rachmaninoff:Bells; Vocalise; P. Tchaikovsky:Festival Coronation March CHN ▲ 8476 [DDD] (16.97)
S. Zambalis (sop), J. Daniecki (ten), P. Tiboris (cnd), Moscow Radio-TV SO † Sym 4 BRID ▲ 9034 [DDD] (17.97)
The Oresteia:Overture
N. Järvi (cnd), Philharmonia Orch † Sym 4 CHN ▲ 8953 [DDD] (16.97)
Prelude & Fugue in g# for Piano, Op. 29 (1910; arr for 2 pianos, 1914)
I. Elkina (pno), J. Elkina (pno) ("Cinderella: The Sisters' Version & Other Stories for Duo Piano") † B. Britten:Intro & Rondo alla burlesca; Chopin:Rondos (4) Pnos; Liszt:Paraphrase on Verdi; S. Prokofiev:Cinderella Suite No. 3, Op. 109; P. Schoenfield:Taschyag DNC ▲ 1020 (16.97)
Quintet in g for Piano & Strings, Op. 30 (1911)
Y. Kamei (vn), P. Rosenthal (vn), M. Thompson (va), S. Kates (vc), J. Lowenthal (pno) ARA ▲ 6539 [DDD] (16.97)
Sonata in a for Violin & Piano
I. Politkovsky (vn), E. Epstein (pno) *(rec 1982)* ("Igor Politkovsky: Russian Violin School") † Balakirev:Impromptu Vn; A. Dvořák:Zigeunermelodien, Op. 55; S. Rachmaninoff:Romance Vn & Pno, Op. 6/1; A. Rubinstein:Son 1 Vn, Op. 13; P. Tchaikovsky:Souvenir d'un lieu cher, Op. 42 RD (Talents of Russia) ▲ 16279 [ADD] (16.97)
Symphony No. 2 in B♭ [comp by Vladimir Blok] (1875-78)
V. Fedoseyev (cnd), USSR Radio-TV Large SO † Sym 4; Miaskovsky:Sym 1; Sym 19 RUS ▲ 11008 [AAD] (12.97)
Symphony No. 4 in c, Op. 12 (1898)
N. Järvi (cnd), Philharmonia Orch † Oresteia (ov) CHN ▲ 8953 [DDD] (16.97)
A. Katz (cnd), Novosibirsk PO † Sym 2; Miaskovsky:Sym 1; Sym 19 RUS ▲ 11008 [AAD] (12.97)
P. Tiboris (cnd), Moscow Radio-TV SO † Duet for Romeo & Juliet BRID ▲ 9034 [DDD] (17.97)
Trio in D for Piano, Violin & Cello, Op. 22 (1907)
Borodin Trio CHN ▲ 8592 [DDD] (17.97)
Röhn Trio *(rec Studio 2 of the Bavarian Radio, Sept 19, 1995)* ("Klaviertrios") † P. Tchaikovsky:Trio Pno, Op. 50 CALG ▲ 50951 [DDD] (19.97)

TANG, JORDAN (1948-
Symphony No. 3 (1985)
J. Tang (cnd), Hong Kong PO *(rec Lyric Theatre of the Hong Kong Academy for Perform, June 28, 1986)* ("First Contemporary Chinese Composers Festival 1986") † W. W. Chan:Sym 3; A. Huang:Con Pno; Qu:Mong Dong; Tan Dun:Intermezzo; Ye:Moon over the West River MARC (Chinese Contemporary) ▲ 8223915 [DDD] (13.97)

TANGUY, ERIC (1968-
Music of Tanguy
B. T. Andersson (cnd) ("KammarensebleN Live") † P. Boulez:Le Marteau sans maître; Varèse:Octandre; Xenakis:Jalons CAPA ▲ 21581 (16.97)

TANN, HILARY (1947-
The Cresset Stone for Violin (1993)
Concord Ensemble Ireland ("Celtic Connections") † Of Erthe & Air; Lefanu:Trio 1 Fl; J. O'Leary:Duo Vn; Silenzio della Terra CPS ▲ 8640 [DDD] (16.97)
Of Erthe & Air for Flute, Clarinet & Percussion (1990)
Concord Ensemble Ireland ("Celtic Connections") † Cresset Stone; Lefanu:Trio 1 Fl; J. O'Leary:Duo Vn; Silenzio della Terra CPS ▲ 8640 [DDD] (16.97)

TANNENBAUM, ELIAS (1924-
Last Letters from Stalingrad for Baritone, Guitar, Viola, Piano & Percussion (1981)
R. Osborne (b-bar), T. Pelikan (va), D. Tannenbaum (gtr/pno), B. Trigg (perc) ("Chamber Music of Elias Tannenbaum") † Reflected Images; Shadows ALBA ▲ 247 [DDD] (16.97)
Reflected Images for Flute & Guitar (1988)
D. Tanenbaum (gtr), A. Hersh (fl) ("Chamber Music of Elias Tannenbaum") † Last Letters; Shadows ALBA ▲ 247 [DDD] (16.97)
Shadows for Guitar & String Quartet (1987)
D. Tanenbaum (gtr), Chester String Quartet ("Chamber Music of Elias Tannenbaum") † Last Letters; Reflected Images ALBA ▲ 247 [DDD] (16.97)

TANNER, JERRÉ (1939-
Boy with Goldfish for solo Voices, Orchestra & Chorus
L. Siu (sgr), M. Elliott (sgr), L. Holdridge (cnd), London SO, Nigel Brooks Chorale ALBA ▲ 53 [DDD] (10.97)
The Kona Coffee Cantata (chamber opera in 1 act) for Soprano, Tenor, Baritone, Flute, Strings, Hawaiian Percussion & Continuo [lib Harvey Hess] (1983-86)
T. Rolek (cnd), Prague CO, M. Taylor (sop—Kolea), W. Livingston (ten—Kimo), D. Small (bar—Mr. Kua), K. Stadherr (vn), P. Bělousek (vc), V. Kunt (fl), L. Chermáková (hpd), J. Krob (perc) *([ENG] lib text)* ALBA ▲ 313 [DDD] (16.97)

TANSMAN, ALEXANDRE (1897-1986)
Berceuse et Danse for Guitar
A. Segovia (gtr) † I. Albéniz:Gtr Music; Castelnuovo-Tedesco:Gtr Music; M. Ponce:Gtr Music; Son Mexicana; Sor:Gtr Music; H. Villa-Lobos:Etudes Gtr; Preludes Gtr; S. L. Weiss:Lt Music AURC ▲ 115
Capriccio for Orchestra (1955)
A. De Almeida (cnd), Moscow SO *(rec Moscow Russia, July 1994)* † Con Orch; Etudes MARC ▲ 8223757 [DDD] (13.97)
Cavatina (suite) for Guitar (1950)
R. Aussel (gtr) † Ginastera:Son Gtr, Op. 47; Kleynjans:A l'aube du dernier jour; M. Ponce:Sonatina meridional Gtr; J. Rodrigo:Gtr Music GHA ▲ 126007 (17.97)

TANSMAN, ALEXANDRE (cont.)

Cavatina (suite) for Guitar (1950) (cont.)

S. Grondona (gtr) ("Novecento") † José Martinez Palacios:Son Gtr; Krenek:Suite Gtr; F. Martin:Pièces brèves Gtr; E. Morricone:Pieces Gtr PHEX ▲ 98419 (16.97)

S. Robinson (gtr) † Castelnuovo-Tedesco:Son Cl; Moreno Torroba:Castillos de España; M. Ponce:Son 3 Gtr CENT ▲ 2056 [DDD] (16.97)

Cello & Piano Music

M. K. Jones (vc), G. Jackson (pno) ("Infrequent Music for Cello & Piano") † Arpe:Music Vc; M. de Falla:Melodia; Romanza; H. Villa-Lobos:Vc & Pno Music EMEC ▲ 10 (16.97)

Concerto for Orchestra (1954)

A. De Almeida (cnd), Moscow SO *(rec Moscow Russia, July 1994)* † Capriccio; Etudes MARC ▲ 8223757 [DDD] (13.97)

Etudes (6) for Orchestra (1962)

A. De Almeida (cnd), Moscow SO *(rec Moscow Russia, July 1994)* † Capriccio; Con Orch MARC ▲ 8223757 [DDD] (13.97)

Mazurka for Guitar (1926)

S. Rottersman (gtr) ("Sherri Rottersman: The Sensual Guitar") † I. Albéniz:Suite española 1, Op. 47; Anonymous:Renaissance Pieces Lt; J. S. Bach:Sons & Partitas Vn; E. Granados:Danzas españolas (10) Pno; J. Rodrigo:Ecos de Sefarad; Tárrega:Capricho árabe AURR ▲ 23446 [ADD] (16.97)

Mazurkas (36) for Piano [in 4 books] (1918-41)

D. Andersen (pno) TLNT ▲ 39 (15.97)

Preludes in the Form of Blues (3) for Piano

I. Vaglenova (pno) † Sonatine transatlantique; Sonatine Bn; Suite Bn; Suite Reed Trio ARN ▲ 55401 (13.97)

Septet for Oboe, Clarinet, Bassoon, Horn, Viola, Cello & Double Bass (1930)

A. Jordan (cnd) *(rec Oct 1992)* ("L'Ecole de Paris") † T. Harsányi:Nonet; Martinů:Nonet Ww, Strs & Db GALL ▲ 729 [DDD] (19.97)

Sonatine for Bassoon & Piano (1952)

J. Alhaits (bn), I. Vaglenova (pno) † Preludes in the Form of Blues; Sonatine transatlantique; Suite Bn; Suite Reed Trio ARN ▲ 55401 (13.97)

S. Canuti (bn), U. Fanni (pno) ("Il Salotto Virtuoso") † Cavallini:Adagio & Tarantella; Mendelssohn (-Bartholdy):Con Piece 1, Op. 114; Con Piece 2, Op. 113; Ponchielli:Capriccio Ob & Pno; F. Poulenc:Trio Ob FON ▲ 9505 [DDD] (13.97)

M. Monguzzi (bn), G. Brollo (pno) *(rec May 1995)* ("20th Century Bassoon") † Suite Bn; U. Bertoni:Con Bn; Bozza:Fant Bn; Récit, Sicilienne & Rondò; Dutilleux:Sarabande et Cortège; P. Hindemith:Son Bn; Saint-Saëns:Son Bn BONG ▲ 5565 [DDD] (16.97)

K. Søonstevold (bn), E. Knardahl (pno) *(rec Nacka, Sweden, Apr 1978)* ("The Virtuoso Bassoon") † M. Arnold:Fant Bn, Op. 86; Beethoven:Trio Fl, WoO 37; Blomdahl:Liten svit; R. Boutry:Interferences; E. von Koch:Monologue 5; Morthenson:Unisono BIS ▲ 122 [AAD] (17.97)

Sonatine for Flute & Piano

R. Sherman (fl), R. Votapek (pno) † J. Feld:Son Fl; J. Françaix:Son Fl; F. Poulenc:Vocalise; Tailleferre:Forlane Fl; Son 2 Vn SUMM ▲ 232 (16.97)

Sonatine transatlantique for Piano (1930)

I. Vaglenova (pno) † Preludes in the Form of Blues; Sonatine Bn; Suite Bn; Suite Reed Trio ARN ▲ 55401 (13.97)

Suite for Bassoon & Piano (1960)

J. Alhaits (bn), I. Vaglenova (pno) † Preludes in the Form of Blues; Sonatine transatlantique; Sonatine Bn; Suite Reed Trio ARN ▲ 55401 (13.97)

M. Monguzzi (bn), G. Brollo (pno) *(rec May 1995)* ("20th Century Bassoon") † Sonatine Bn; U. Bertoni:Con Bn; Bozza:Fant Bn; Récit, Sicilienne & Rondò; Dutilleux:Sarabande et Cortège; P. Hindemith:Son Bn; Saint-Saëns:Son Bn BONG ▲ 5565 [DDD] (16.97)

Suite for 2 Pianos & Orchestra

J. Pierce (pno), D. Jonas (pno), D. Amos (cnd), Slovak State PO Košice † Lopatnikoff:Con for 2 Pnos; G. F. Malipiero:Dialogo 7 CENT ▲ 2269 (16.97)

Suite for Reed Trio

A. Beaudoin (ob), J. Bernaud (cl), J. Alhaits (bn) † Preludes in the Form of Blues; Sonatine transatlantique; Sonatine Bn; Suite Bn ARN ▲ 55401 (13.97)

Chicago Chamber Musicians *(rec Chicago, IL, 1997)* ("20th Century French Wind Trios") † G. Auric:Trio Ob; Canteloube:Rustiques; J. Françaix:Divert Ob, Cl, Bn; Ibert:Pièces (5) en trio; D. Milhaud:Pastorale Ob, Op. 147; Suite d'après Corrette, Op. 161; P. Pierné:Bucolique variée CED ▲ 40 [DDD] (16.97)

TAPRAY, JEAN FRANÇOIS (1738-ca 1819)

Concertos (6) for Harpsichord (or Organ), Strings & Continuo, Op. 1 (1758)

D. Ferran (org), G. Bezzina (cnd) K617 ▲ 7079 (18.97)

Quartet concertant for Harpsichord (or Piano), Flute (or Violin), Viola & Bassoon (or Cello), [also as No. 6 in Journal de clavecin], Op. 19 (1784)

L'Academie Royale de Musique de Paris *(rec Oct 1996)* † Qts Hpd; Sons Vn, Op. 23 K617 ▲ 7073 [DDD] (18.97)

Quartets (2) for Harpsichord (or Piano), Clarinet (or Violin), Viola & Bass (or Cello), Op. 18 [sometimes listed as Op. 17 or 21] (1784)

L'Academie Royale de Musique de Paris *(rec Oct 1996)* † Qt concertant, Op. 19; Sons Vn, Op. 23 K617 ▲ 7073 [DDD] (18.97)

Sonatas (2) for Violin, Cello & Harpsichord (or Piano), Op. 23 (1788)

L'Academie Royale de Musique de Paris *(rec Oct 1996)* † Qt concertant, Op. 19; Qts Hpd K617 ▲ 7073 [DDD] (18.97)

TARP, SVEND ERIK (1908-

Battle of Jericho (symphonic poem) for Orchestra (1949)

M. Schønwandt (cnd), Danish National RSO *(rec Nov 14, 1990)* † Con Pno, Op. 39; Sym 7; Te Deum, Op. 33 DCAP ▲ 9005 [DDD] (13.97)

Concerto in C for Piano, Op. 39 (1942-43)

P. Salo (pno), M. Schønwandt (cnd), Danish National RSO *(rec Sept 7, 1990)* † Battle of Jericho; Sym 7; Te Deum, Op. 33 DCAP ▲ 9005 [DDD] (13.97)

Symphony No. 7, Op. 81 (1977)

O. Schmidt (cnd), Danish National RSO *(rec Sept 5, 1986)* † Battle of Jericho; Con Pno, Op. 39; Te Deum, Op. 33 DCAP ▲ 9005 [DDD] (13.97)

Taffelmusik for Woodwind Trio (1932)

Trio Divertimento ("New Danish Woodwind Music") † B. Andersen:Invocation; Serenade; J. Bentzon:Sonatina, Op. 7; F. Friis:November; G. Lund:Talks; F. Weis:Music Fl, Cl & Bn PLAL ▲ 94 [DAD] (18.97)

Te Deum for Orchestra & Chorus, Op. 33 (1938)

J. Nelson (cnd), Danish National RSO, Danish National Radio Choir *(rec Sept 14, 1988)* † Battle of Jericho; Con Pno, Op. 39; Sym 7 DCAP ▲ 9005 [DDD] (13.97)

TÁRREGA, FRANCISCO (1852-1909)

Capricho árabe for Guitar

S. Mentzer (mez), S. Isbin (gtr) † E. Granados:Spanish Dance 5; P. Lansky:Wayfaring Stranger; J. P. A. Martini:Plaisir d'Amour; J. J. Niles:Black is the color; Go 'way from my window; J. Rodrigo:Aranjuez ma penses; F. Schubert:Songs (misc colls) ERAT ▲ 23419 (16.97)

S. Rottersman (gtr) ("Sherri Rottersman: The Sensual Guitar") † I. Albéniz:Suite española 1, Op. 47; Anonymous:Renaissance Pieces Lt; J. S. Bach:Sons & Partitas Vn; E. Granados:Danzas españolas (10) Pno; J. Rodrigo:Ecos de Sefarad; Tansman:Mazurka Gtr AURR ▲ 23446 [ADD] (16.97)

Guitar Music

D. Azabagić (gtr)—Vars on El Carnaval de Venicia; Preludes Gtr 21, 22 & 28 † Asencio:Collectici Intim; J. M. Fernández:Azaroa; Moreno Torroba:Aires de la Mancha; J. Rodrigo:Invocación y danza OTR ▲ 1021 (18.97)

D. Blanco (gtr)—Maria; Alborada *(rec Djursholm, Sweden, 1983)* ("Favorite Guitar Music") † Recuerdos de la Alhambra; I. Albéniz:Gtr Music; S. Myers:Gtr Music; H. Villa-Lobos:Chôro 1; Suite populaire brésilienne; Yocoh:Gtr Music BIS ▲ 233 [DDD] (17.97)

E. Catemario (gtr)—Capricho árabe; Mazurka en Sol; Recuerdos de la Alhambra *(rec Monteggiori, Italy, Sept 1993)* ("Spanish Guitar Music") † I. Albéniz:Gtr Music; E. Granados:Gtr Music; Moreno Torroba:Sonatina Gtr AART ▲ 47145 [DDD] (10.97)

L. Christensen (gtr)—Preludes 2 & 5; Mazurkas [Mazurka in g]; transciptions by Albéniz *(rec Fruering Kirke Denmark, Oct 1987)* † Llobet:Gtr Music PLAL ▲ 59 [AAD] (18.97)

Z. Dukic (gtr)—Capricho árabe; Rosita † J. S. Bach:Sons & Partitas Vn; José Martinez Palacios:Son Gtr; Takemitsu:All in Twilight OTR ▲ 1023 [DDD] (18.97)

S. Grondona (gtr)—Danza mora; Minueto; Preludes Gtr; Capricho árabe † Llobet:Gtr Music DVX ▲ 29701 (16.97)

TÁRREGA, FRANCISCO (cont.)

Guitar Music (cont.)

N. Kraft (gtr)—Rosita; Mazurkas; Estudios [Estudio Brillante de Alard]; Gran Vals; Preludes Gtr [Prelude in d; Prelude in E]; Alborada; Recuerdos de la Alhambra; Maria; Preludios 1 & 11 *(rec Aug 1993)* ("19th Century Guitar Favourites") † Aguado:Gtr Music; Sor:Minuets (12) Gtr, Op. 11/6 NXIN ▲ 553007 [DDD] (5.97)

J. M. Moreno (gtr)—Andante sostenuto; Preludes Gtr [Prelude in E; Prelude in d]; Mazurka en Sol; Valse; Mazurkas [Mazurka in g; Sueño]; Pavana *(rec Villa Consuelo, Spain, June 1996)* ("La Guitarra Española II 1818-1918") † Llobet:Gtr Music; Mertz:Song without Words; F. Schubert:Music of Schubert; Sor:Divert Gtr, Op. 2; Intro & Vars on "Malborough", Op. 28 GLSS ▲ 920105 [DDD] (18.97)

C. Romero (gtr)—Recuerdos de la Alhambra; Valse [Las dos Hermanitas]; Tango † M. Giuliani:Grand Ov, Op. 61; Vars on a Theme by Handel; Sor:Son Gtr; Son Gtr, Op. 22; Vars Mozart, Op. 9 DLS ▲ 1004 [AAD] (10.97)

C. Trepat (gtr)—Valse [Las dos Hermanitas]; Pavana; Preludes 1 & 7; Mazurkas [Mazurka in g] † Arcas:Gtr Music; R. Gerhard:Gemini; Son Vc; Trio Pno; José Martinez Palacios:Son Gtr; Llobet:Gtr Music LAMA ▲ 2021 [DDD] (17.97)

F. Zanon (gtr)—Preludes in A, D & E; Estudios [Estudio Brillante de Alard]; Mazurkas in G & C; Preludes Gtr [Prelude in d]; Maria *(rec Holy Trinity Parish Church, Weston Hertfordshire, England, Aug 1997)* † Faria:Eyes of Recollections; Mertz:Opern-Revue (sels); M. Ponce:Thème, varié et finale NXIN ▲ 8554431 [DDD] (5.97)

Preludes (16) for Guitar

R. Iturri (gtr) PAVA ▲ 7214 [DDD] (10.97)

Recuerdos de la Alhambra for Guitar

D. Blanco (gtr) *(rec Djursholm, Sweden, 1983)* ("Favorite Guitar Music") † Gtr Music; I. Albéniz:Gtr Music; S. Myers:Gtr Music; H. Villa-Lobos:Chôro 1; Suite populaire brésilienne; Yocoh:Gtr Music BIS ▲ 233 [DDD] (17.97)

P. Skareng (gtr) ("El Colibri") † J. S. Bach:Sons & Partitas Vn; Carlstedt:Swedish Dances; Frumerie:Vars on a Swedish Folk Tune, Op. 69a; M. Giuliani:Rossiniana; Lauro:Gtr Music; Sagreras:El Colibri CAPA ▲ 21392 [AAD] (16.97)

TARTINI, GIUSEPPE (1692-1770)

L'arte del arco for Violin, Op. 5/10

G. Colliard (vn) *(rec June 29-30, 1992)* DORO ▲ 3007 [DDD] (16.97)

Concertino for Clarinet & Orchestra

E. Johnson (cl), Y. P. Tortelier (cnd), English CO [arr Gordon Jacobs] † Crusell:Intro, Theme & Vars on a Swedish Air, Op. 12; Debussy:Première rapsodie Cl; C. M. von Weber:Con 1 Cl, Op. 73 ASV ▲ 585 [DDD] (16.97)

Concerto in A for Cello & Strings

M. Rostropovich (vc), G. Rozhdestvensky (cnd), London SO *(rec live Carnegie Hall, 1967)* † O. Respighi:Adagio con variazioni Vc Orch ING ▲ 766 [ADD]

Concerto in D for Cello & Strings

P. Casals (vc) *(rec 1927-36)* ("Pablo Casals: A Baroque Festival") † J. S. Bach:English Suites; Music of Bach; Sons & Partitas Vn; Toccata, Adagio & Fugue Org, BWV 564; Boccherini:Con Vc, G.482; Sons Vn, Op. 5; G. Valentini:Sons Vn, Op. 8 ENT (Strings) ▲ 99320 (16.97)

Concerto in D for Cello, Strings & Continuo

Y. Turovsky (vc) [arr Louis Delune] † Boccherini:Adagio & Allegro, G.6; G. Cassadó:Con Vc, K.447; J. Haydn:Divert Vc CHN ▲ 8768 [DDD] (16.97)

Concerto in G for Flute & Strings [dubious]

J. Galway (fl), C. Scimone (cnd) † Galuppi:Con Fl; Pergolesi:Con Fl; Piacentino:Con Fl RCAV (Red Seal) ▲ 61164 (16.97)

M. Jurkovic (fl), B. Warchal (cnd), Slovak CO ("Flute Concertos") † Pergolesi:Con Fl; Telemann:Cons & Suites Fl OPP ▲ 2621 (10.97)

N. McLaren (fl), J. H. Jones (cnd), Cambridge Baroque Camerata [period instrs] ("Rare Baroque Flute Concertos") † F. Benda:Cons (4) Fl; Quantz:Con in e Fl AMON ▲ 52 [DDD] (16.97)

P. Øien (fl), T. Tønnesen (cnd), Norwegian CO *(rec Sept 2-3, 1978)* † Blavet:Con Fl; Quantz:Con in G Fl; Vivaldi:Con Rcr, RV.441 BIS ▲ 118 [AAD] (17.97)

Concerto in D for Trumpet & Orchestra

R. Smedvig (tpt), J. Ling (cnd), Scottish CO † V. Bellini:Con Ob; J. Haydn:Con Tpt; J. N. Hummel:Con Tpt in E♭, S.49; Torelli:Con Tpt TEL ▲ 80232 [DDD] (16.97)

B. Soustrot (tpt), M. Tardue (cnd) *(rec Oct 1992)* ("6 Italian Concertos for Trumpet & Strings") † B. Marcello:Con Tpt; Torelli:Con Tpt FORL ▲ 16682 [DDD] (16.97)

Concerto in C for Violin & Ensemble, D.1

L'Arte dell'Arco *(rec Villa Cordellina, Montecchio, Italy, Oct 13-15, 1998)* † Con Vn, D.118; Con Vn, D.43; Con Vn, D.61 DYNC ▲ 239 [DDD] (17.97)

Concerto in B♭ for Violin & Ensemble, D.118

L'Arte dell'Arco *(rec Villa Cordellina, Montecchio, Italy, Oct 13-15, 1998)* † Con Vn, D.1; Con Vn, D.43; Con Vn, D.61 DYNC ▲ 239 [DDD] (17.97)

Concerto in d for Violin & Ensemble, D.43

L'Arte dell'Arco *(rec Villa Cordellina, Montecchio, Italy, Oct 13-15, 1998)* † Con Vn, D.1; Con Vn, D.118; Con Vn, D.61 DYNC ▲ 239 [DDD] (17.97)

Concerto in F for Violin & Ensemble, D.61

L'Arte dell'Arco *(rec Villa Cordellina, Montecchio, Italy, Oct 13-15, 1998)* † Con Vn, D.1; Con Vn, D.118; Con Vn, D.43 DYNC ▲ 239 [DDD] (17.97)

Concertos (135) for Violin & Strings (miscellaneous)

B. Antonioni (vn), S. Frontalini (cnd), Kaunas CO—Con Vn, D.12; Cons Vn, Op. 1; Con Vn, D.78 *(rec Kaunas Lithuania, 1993)* BONG ▲ 2177 [DDD] (16.97)

F. Ayo (vn), F. Ayo (cnd) —Con Vn, D.12; Con Vn, D.67; Con Vn, D.78 *(rec Rome Italy, Apr 1-3, 1996)* ("Violin Concertos, Vol 3") DYNC ▲ 163 [DDD] (17.97)

F. Ayo (vn), F. Ayo (cnd), Perusina Sinfonia—Cons Vn, Op. 1 [No. 4 in D]; Con Vn, D.56; Con Vn, D.125 *(rec St. Antonio Abate Church Deruta, July 28-31, 1994)* ("Vol. 2") DYNC ▲ 131 [DDD] (17.97)

F. Ayo (vn), F. Ayo (cnd), Pesaro Rossini Orch—Con Vn, D.96; Con Vn, D.45; in E *(rec Mar 5-7, 1993)* † Sinf Strs in A DYNC ▲ 92 [DDD] (17.97)

C. Chiarappa (vn), C. Chiarappa (cnd), Accademia Bizantina—Con Vn, D.56; Con Vn, D.78; Con Vn, D.96; Con Vn, D.125 *(rec Presso Museo S. Vitale Revenna, Italy, Oct 1-4, 1993)* ("Violin Concertos") DNN ▲ 78969 [DDD] (16.97)

T. Füri (cnd), Bern Camerata—Con Vn, D.56; Con Vn, D.86 *(rec Dec 1992)* † Con Vn, D.45 NOVA ▲ 150092 [DDD] (16.97)

A. Gertler (vn), E. D. Stoutz (cnd), Zurich CO—Con Vn, D.24; Con Vn, D.30; Con Vn, D.68; Con Vn, D.83; Con Vn, D.95 *(rec 1962-63)* HUN ▲ 31529 [ADD] (16.97)

G. Gugliemo (vn), L'Arte dell'Arco *(Con Vn, D.56)*, F. Gugliemo (vn), L'Arte dell'Arco *(Con Vn, D.4; Con Vn, D.75)*, C. Lazari (vn), L'Arte dell'Arco *(Con Vn, D.63)* ("Violin Concertos, Vol. 4") DYNC ▲ 220 [DDD] (17.97)

G. Nikolitch (vn), A. V. Beek (cnd), Auvergne Orch—Cons Vn, Op. 1 [No. 4 in D]; Con Vn, D.78; Con Vn, D.123; Con Vn, D.80; Con Vn, D.115 ("Violin Concertos, Vol. 1") OLY ▲ 475 [DDD] (16.97)

G. Nikolitch (vn), A. V. Beek (cnd), Auvergne Orch—Con Vn, D.117; Con Vn, D.45; Con Vn, D.12; Con Vn, D.51 *(rec 1996)* ("Violin Concertos, Vol. 2") OLY ▲ 476 (16.97)

Concerto in a for Violin & Strings, D.113

Interpreti Veneziani † Con Vn, D.115; Con Vn, D.80 RIVO ▲ 9805 (16.97)

Concerto in a for Violin & Strings, D.115

Interpreti Veneziani † Con Vn, D.113; Con Vn, D.80 RIVO ▲ 9805 (16.97)

Concerto in B♭ for Violin & Strings, D.117

Interpreti Veneziani † Con Vn, D.45; Con Vn, D.67; Con Vn, D.83 RIVO ▲ 9807 (16.97)

Concerto in d for Violin & Strings, D.45

T. Füri (cnd), Bern Camerata *(rec Dec 1992)* † Cons (135) Vn (misc) NOVA ▲ 150092 [DDD] (16.97)

Interpreti Veneziani † Con Vn, D.117; Con Vn, D.67; Con Vn, D.83 RIVO ▲ 9807 (16.97)

J. Szigeti (vn), W. Goehr (cnd), New Friends of Music Orch *(rec 1937)* † J. S. Bach:Arioso Ob; Con 1 Hpd, BWV 1052; W. A. Mozart:Divert 15 Hns & Strs, K.287 BID ▲ 64 [ADD]

Concerto in F for Violin & Strings, D.67

Interpreti Veneziani † Con Vn, D.117; Con Vn, D.45; Con Vn, D.83 RIVO ▲ 9807 (16.97)

Concerto in G for Violin & Strings, D.80

Interpreti Veneziani † Con Vn, D.113; Con Vn, D.115 RIVO ▲ 9805 (16.97)

Concerto in G for Violin & Strings, D.83

Interpreti Veneziani † Con Vn, D.117; Con Vn, D.45; Con Vn, D.67 RIVO ▲ 9807 (16.97)

Concertos (6) for Violin, Strings & Continuo, Op. 2 [D. 73, 2, 124, 62, 3 & 46] (ca 1734)

G. Gugliemo (vn) *(rec June 1997)* ("Violin Concertos, Vol. 2") DYNC 2-▲ 190 [DDD] (34.97)

Concerto in D for Violin, Strings & Continuo, D.21, "Il Crudel"

G. Gugliemo (vn), L'Arte dell'Arco [2 versions of movt 2 [Grave]] *(rec Oct 1997)* ("Violin Concertos, Vol. 3") † Con Vn, D.112; Con Vn, D.72; Con Vn, D.86 DYNC ▲ 196 [DDD] (17.97)

TARTINI, GIUSEPPE (cont.)

Concerto in a for Violin, Strings & Continuo, D.112
G. Gugliemo (vn), L'Arte dell'Arco [ve]] *(rec Oct 1997)* ("Violin Concertos, Vol. 3") † Con Vn, D.21; Con Vn, D.72; Con Vn, D.86 DYNC ▲ 196 [DDD] (17.97)

Concerto in G for Violin, Strings & Continuo, D.72
C. Lazari (vn), L'Arte dell'Arco [ve]] *(rec Oct 1997)* ("Violin Concertos, Vol. 3") † Con Vn, D.112; Con Vn, D.21; Con Vn, D.86 DYNC ▲ 196 [DDD] (17.97)

Concerto in g for Violin, Strings & Continuo, D.86
F. Gugliemo (vn), L'Arte dell'Arco [ve]] *(rec Oct 1997)* ("Violin Concertos, Vol. 3") † Con Vn, D.112; Con Vn, D.21; Con Vn, D.72 DYNC ▲ 196 [DDD] (17.97)

Concertos (12) for Violin, Strings & Continuo [D.85,55,60,15,58,89,111,91,59,71,88 & 18], Op. 1 (1728-34)
L'Arte dell'Arco *(rec Altavilla Vicentia, Feb 1996)* DYNC 3-▲ 160 [DDD] (34.97)

Music of Tartini
D. Amodio (vc), Interpreti Veneziani—Con Vc † G. Rossini:Une Larme; Vivaldi:Con Vc RIVO ▲ 9814 (16.97)

Sinfonia in A for Strings
F. Ayo (cnd), Pesaro Rossini Orch *(rec Mar 5-7, 1993)* † Cons (135) Vn (misc) DYNC ▲ 92 [DDD] (17.97)

Sonatas (miscellaneous)
Accademia Farnese—6 for Fl, Ob, Bn & Bc; 1 for Ob & Bc; 1 for Fl & Hpd MONM (Il grande barocco italiano) ▲ 96018 (18.97)

Sonatas (12) & Pastorale for Violin, Op. 1 (1734)
Locatelli Trio—No. 2 in F; No. 8 in c; No. 12 in F; No. 9 in A; No. 10 in g ("Sonatas, Vol. 1") † Sonatas for Violin & Continuo HYP ▲ 66430 [DDD] (18.97)

Sonatas for Violin & Continuo
F. Biondi (vn), M. Naddeo (vc), P. Monteilhet (thb), R. Alessandrini (hpd)—(5): in g (B g11); in B (B b3); Sons & Pastorale Vn, Op. 1 [No. 10 in g; No. 9 in A]; in G (B G17) OPUS ▲ 599205 [DDD] (18.97)
Locatelli Trio—Sons & Pastorale Vn, Op. 1 [No. 2 in F; No. 12 in F; No. 9 in A; No. 10 in g]; in D, "Sona Autografica" ("Sonatas, Vol. 1") † Sons & Pastorale Vn, Op. 1 HYP ▲ 66430 [DDD] (18.97)
Locatelli Trio—in A (B A4); in B (B B1); Sons Vn, Op. 5 [No. 6 in B♭]; in D, "Sona Autografica" ("Sonatas, Vol. 2") HYP ▲ 66485 [DDD] (18.97)

Sonata in g for Violin & Continuo, Op. 1/10, "Didone abandonata"
G. Barinova (vn), L. Royzman (org) *(rec 1961)* ("Russian Violin School: Galina Barinova") † J. S. Bach:Son Vn Bc, BWV 1021 RD (Talents of Russia) ▲ 16223 [ADD] (16.97)
I. Stern (vn), A. Zakin (pno) ("Isaac Stern: A Life In Music: Vol. 23") † J. S. Bach:Son Vn; Son Vn Bc, BWV 1023; G. F. Handel:Son Vn SNYC ▲ 68361 [ADD] (10.97)

Sonata in g for Violin & Piano [trans M. O. Dupin for Violin & Orchestra], "Devil's Trill"
S. Accardo (vn), L. Manzini (pno) ("Violinist Composers") † Paganini:Cantabile, M.S. 109; Sarasate:Fant on Carmen, Op. 25; T. A. Vitali:Chaconne Vn; Wieniawski:Légende Vn, Op. 17; Polonaise 2, Op. 21 FON ▲ 9602 [DDD] (13.97)
D. Chan (vn), R. Koenig (pno) *(rec Aspen, CO, May 1995)* † G. Gershwin:Songs; Paganini:Con 2 Vn, M.S. 48; Saint-Saëns:Son 1 Vn, Op. 75; P. Tchaikovsky:Souvenir d'un lieu cher, Op. 42; Valse-Scherzo Vn, Op. 34; Ysaÿe:Sons Vn, Op. 27 AMBA ▲ 1017 [DDD] (16.97)
C. Funke (vn), P. Rösel (pno) ("Virtuoso Violin Sonatas") † C. Franck:Son Vn, M.8 BER ▲ 9149 (10.97)
I. Gregoletto (cembalo) † Paganini:Cantabile & Waltz, M.S. 45; Carnevale di Venezia, M.S. 59; Polacca; Streghe RIVO ▲ 9813
A. Manze (vn) [original version for solo vn] HAM ▲ 907213 (18.97)
N. Milstein (vn), L. Mittman (pno) *(rec 1936-40)* ("The Baroque & Romantic Repertoire") † Pergolesi:Son 12 Vn; P. Tchaikovsky:Con Vn; Vivaldi:Sons Vn ENT (Strings) ▲ 99331 (16.97)
N. Milstein (vn), L. Mittman (pno) BID ▲ 55 [ADD]
N. Milstein (vn), L. Pommers (pno) *(rec 1954-59)* ("Italian Sonatas") † A. Corelli:Son Vn, Op. 5/12, "La Follia"; Geminiani:Sons Vn, Op. 4; N. Milstein:Paganiniana; Pergolesi:Son 12 Vn; T. A. Vitali:Chaconne Vn; Vivaldi:Sons Vn EMIC ▲ 66873 (m) [ADD] (11.97)
D. Oistrakh (vn), V. Yampolsky (pno) † F. Schubert:Octet Ww & Strs, D.803 TES ▲ 1114 (17.97)
A. Spalding (vn), A. Benoist (pno) ("The Art of the Violin, Vol. 3") † J. Brahms:Son 2 Vn, Op. 100; C. Franck:Son Vn, M.8; G. F. Handel:Son Vn; R. Schumann:Klavierstücke, Op. 85 ACLR ▲ 42 (17.97)
various artists [excerpt] † J. S. Bach:Sons & Partitas Vn; Beethoven:Son 9 Vn, Op. 47; Mendelssohn (-Bartholdy):Con Vn & Orch, Op. 64; W. A. Mozart:Con 3 Vn, K.216; P. Tchaikovsky:Con Vn MTAL ▲ 48099 (6.97)

Trio Sonatas (6) for 2 Violins & Continuo, Op. 8 (1745-49)
J. Suk (vn), S. Ishikawa (vn), J. Vlasankova (vc), J. Hála (hpd)—No. 1 in E♭; No. 3 in E♭ *(rec Czech Republic, August 1995)* ("Baroque Sonatas") † Trio Sons; G. A. Benda:Sons for 2 Vns; Locatelli:Sons Vn, Op. 8 LT ▲ 27 [DDD] (16.97)

Trio Sonatas (40) for 2 Violins & Continuo (1745-49)
J. Suk (vn), S. Ishikawa (vn), J. Vlasankova (vc), J. Hála (hpd)—Op. 3/2 *(rec Czech Republic, August 1995)* ("Baroque Sonatas") † Trio Sons, Op. 8; G. A. Benda:Sons for 2 Vns; Locatelli:Sons Vn, Op. 8 LT ▲ 27 [DDD] (16.97)

TATE, JEROD (20th cent)

Iyaaknasha': The Little Helper for Double Bass & Orchestra
J. Vandermark (db), T. Russell (cnd), Pro Musica CO † Clingan:Circle of Faith DNC ▲ 1029 (16.97)

TATE, PHYLLIS (1911-1987)

Quartet in F for Strings (1952)
English String Quartet *(rec May 1992)* † Rubbra:Qt 2 Strs, Op. 73; P. Wishart:Qt Strs, Op. 22 RD ▲ 26002 (16.97)

TAURO, ERNA (fl 1916)

Songs
E. Söderström (sop), C. Pehrsson (s rcr), H. Sund (pno) *(Misans klagolåt)*, E. Söderström (sop), C. Pehrsson (a rcr), H. Sund (pno) *(Teaterråttan Emmas visdomsord) (rec Djursholm, Sweden, June 15-18, 1981)* ("Orhängen") † Anonymous:Viktoria; R. Davidson:Gudlös bön; Norlén:Visa vid midsommartid; Olrog:Såna Metoder; Traditional:Ekovisan; Godmorgon, min docka; Vallåt; Vinden drar; Wennerberg:Man borde inte sofva BIS ▲ 187 [AAD] (17.97)

TAUSCH, FRANZ WILHELM (1762-1817)

Concertante No. 2 in B♭ for 2 Clarinets & Orchestra, Op. 26
T. King (cl), N. Bucknall (cl), L. Hager (cnd), English CO † Con 1 Cls; Süssmayr:Con Movt HYP ▲ 66504 (18.97)

Concerto No. 1 in B♭ for 2 Clarinets & Orchestra (1797)
T. King (cl), N. Bucknall (cl), L. Hager (cnd), English CO † Concertante 2, Op. 26; Süssmayr:Con Movt HYP ▲ 66504 (18.97)

TAUSIG, CARL (1841-1871)

Fantasy on Themes of Moniuszko's "Halka" for Piano
M. Ponti (pno) *(rec ca 1973)* † Trans & Arrs Pno; Brassin:Trans Pno; Liszt:Réminiscences de Don Juan Pno, S.418; Trans, Arrs & Paraphrases; Moszkowski:Operatic Paraphrases & Trans Pno; P. Pabst:Concert Paraphrase on Tchaikovsky's Eugen On; Thalberg:Fants & Vars on Opera Themes Pno VB2 2-▲ 5047 [ADD] (9.97)

Transcriptions & Arrangements for Piano
M. Ponti (pno)—Wagner:Ride of the Valkyries; see "Collections, Piano: Ponti" *(rec ca 1973)* † Fant on Themes of Moniuszko; Brassin:Trans Pno; Liszt:Réminiscences de Don Juan Pno, S.418; Trans, Arrs & Paraphrases; Moszkowski:Operatic Paraphrases & Trans Pno; P. Pabst:Concert Paraphrase on Tchaikovsky's Eugen On; Thalberg:Fants & Vars on Opera Themes Pno VB2 2-▲ 5047 [ADD] (9.97)
K. Scherbakov (pno)—Valse-Caprice *(rec Abbey Road Studio 1, England, Nov 1995)* ("Piano Transcriptions") † M. Reger:Improv on "Blue Danube"; M. Rosenthal:Fant on Themes of Joh. Strauss; Schütt:Paraphrase on "G'Schichten aus dem Wienerwald"; Paraphrase on "Rosen aus dem Süden"; Strauss (II):Pno Trans EMCD (Debut) ▲ 69704 [DDD] (6.97)
E. Wild (pno)—Weber:Invitation to the Dance; Schubert:Marche Militaire † S. Rachmaninoff:Con 2 Pno, Op. 18; Isle of the Dead, Op. 29 CHSK ▲ 2 (16.97)

Valse-Caprice in A for Piano [after Joh. Strauss (II)]
T. Labé (pno) ("Virtuoso Johann Strauss: Paraphrases & Arrangements of Favorite Strauss Melodies by Rosenthal, Tau") † L. Godowsky:Symphonic Metamorphosis of Die Fledermaus; Symphonic Metamorphosis of Wein, Weib und Gesang; M. Rosenthal:Carnaval de Vienne Pno; Schulz-Evler:Arabesque Pno; Strauss (II):Waltzes DOR ▲ 80102 [DDD] (13.97)

TAUSKY, VILEM (1910-

Concertino for Harmonica & Orchestra
T. Reilly (hmc), N. Marriner (cnd), Academy of St. Martin in the Fields † G. Jacob:Pieces Hmc; J. Moody:Little Suite; Vaughan Williams:Romance Hmc CHN ▲ 8617 [AAD/ADD] (16.97)

TAVENER, JOHN (1944-

Akathist of Thanksgiving for 2 Countertenors, Organ, Orchestra & Chorus
J. Bowman (ct), T. Wilson (ten), M. Baker (org), M. Neary (cnd), BBC SO, BBC Singers, Westminster Abbey Choir *(rec Jan 21, 1994)* SNYC ▲ 64446 [DDD] (16.97)

TAVENER, JOHN (cont.)

Akhmatova Songs for Soprano & Cello [text Anna Akhmatova] (1993)
P. Rozario (sop), S. Isserlis (vc) *(rec London, Sept 1996)* ("Svyati: Steven Isserlin Plays John Tavener") † Chant Vc; Eternal Memory; Hidden Treasure; Svyati RCAV (Red Seal) ▲ 68761 [DDD] (16.97)

Annunciation for Chorus (1992)
M. Neary (cnd), Westminster Abbey Choir *(rec Westminster Abbey, July 19-22, 1994)* ("John Tavener: Innocence") † Hymns to the Mother of God; Innocence; Lamb; Little Requiem; Song for Athene; Tyger SNYC ▲ 66613 [DDD] (16.97)

Chant for Cello (1995)
S. Isserlis (vc) *(rec London, Sept 1996)* ("Svyati: Steven Isserlin Plays John Tavener") † Akhmatova Songs; Eternal Memory; Hidden Treasure; Svyati RCAV (Red Seal) ▲ 68761 [DDD] (16.97)

...Depart in Peace for Soprano, Violin & Strings (1997)
P. Rozario (sop), C. Gould (vn), C. Gould (cnd), BT Scottish Ensemble † My Gaze is Ever upon You; Tears of the Angels LINN ▲ 85 (16.97)

Elis Thanaton (dramatic cantata) for Soprano, Bass & Orchestra (1987)
R. Hickox (cnd), City of London Sinfonia, P. Rozario (sop), S. Richards (bass) † Theophany CHN ▲ 9440 (16.97)

Eternal Memory for Cello & String Orchestra (1991)
S. Isserlis (vc), V. Spivakov (cnd), Moscow Virtuosi *(rec London, May 1993)* ("Svyati: Steven Isserlin Plays John Tavener") † Akhmatova Songs; Chant Vc; Hidden Treasure; Svyati RCAV (Red Seal) ▲ 68761 [DDD] (16.97)

Eternity's Sunrise for Soprano & Baroque Chamber Orchestra (1998)
artists unknown HAM ▲ 907231 (18.97)

Funeral Ikos for Chorus (1981)
S. Cleobury (cnd), King's College Choir Cambridge ("Ikos") † Magnificat; Górecki:Amen; Totus tuus; Pärt:Beatitudes; Magnificat for Chorus EMIC ▲ 55096 (16.97)
P. Phillips (cnd), Tallis Scholars † Ikon of Light; Lamb GIME ▲ 54905 [DDD] (16.97)

The Hidden Treasure for String Quartet (1989)
D. Phillips (vn), K. B. Feeney (vn), T. Phillips (va), S. Isserlis (vc) *(rec New York City, Oct 1996)* ("Svyati: Steven Isserlin Plays John Tavener") † Akhmatova Songs; Chant Vc; Eternal Memory; Svyati RCAV (Red Seal) ▲ 68761 [DDD] (16.97)

Hymns to the Mother of God (2) for Chorus (1985)
M. Neary (cnd), Westminster Abbey Choir *(rec Westminster Abbey, May 1-5, 1995)* ("John Tavener: Innocence") † Annunciation; Innocence; Lamb; Little Requiem; Song for Athene; Tyger SNYC ▲ 66613 [DDD] (16.97)

Ikon of Light for Strings & Chorus (1984)
Chilingirian String Quartet members, P. Phillips (cnd), Tallis Scholars † Funeral Ikos; Lamb GIME ▲ 54905 [DDD] (16.97)

Innocence for Soprano, Tenor, Bass, Cello, Bells, Organ & Chorus (1995)
P. Rozario (sop), L. Nixon (ten), G. Titus (bass), A. Neary (vc), M. Baker (org), C. Fullbrook (bells), M. Neary (cnd), Westminster Abbey Choir *(rec Westminster Abbey, May 1-5, 1995)* ("John Tavener: Innocence") † Annunciation; Hymns to the Mother of God; Lamb; Little Requiem; Song for Athene; Tyger SNYC ▲ 66613 [DDD] (16.97)

The Lamb for Chorus [text William Blake] (1982)
M. Neary (cnd), Westminster Abbey Choir *(rec Westminster Abbey, May 1-5, 1995)* ("John Tavener: Innocence") † Annunciation; Hymns to the Mother of God; Innocence; Little Requiem; Song for Athene; Tyger SNYC ▲ 66613 [DDD] (16.97)
P. Phillips (cnd), Tallis Scholars † Funeral Ikos; Ikon of Light GIME ▲ 54905 [DDD] (16.97)

The Last Sleep of the Virgin for Handbells & Orchestra (1992)
C. Willems (bells), R. Werthen (cnd), Orch of Flanders *(rec Belgium, Sept 15-18, 1997)* † Protecting Veil TEL ▲ 80487 [DDD] (16.97)

Little Requiem for Father Malachy Lynch for Chamber Orchestra & Chorus (1972)
M. Neary (cnd), English CO, Westminster Abbey Choir *(rec Westminster Abbey, Oct 6, 1994)* ("John Tavener: Innocence") † Annunciation; Hymns to the Mother of God; Innocence; Lamb; Song for Athene; Tyger SNYC ▲ 66613 [DDD] (16.97)

Magnificat & Nunc dimittis for Chorus
S. Cleobury (cnd), King's College Choir Cambridge ("Ikos") † Funeral Ikos; Górecki:Amen; Totus tuus; Pärt:Beatitudes; Magnificat for Chorus EMIC ▲ 55096 (16.97)

Music of Tavener
King's Singers—Funeral Ikos; Lamb *(rec Salisbury Cathedral, England, Feb 21-23, 1995)* † R. R. Bennett:Sermons & Devotions; Górecki:Totus tuus; G. Poole:Wymondham Chants; I. Stravinsky:Blessed Virgin; Our Father; Tormis:Bishop & the Pagan RCAV (Red Seal) ▲ 68255 [DDD] (16.97)
P. Rozario (sop), P. Goodwin (cnd), Academy of Ancient Music *(Eternity's Sunrise; Sappho:Lyrical Fragments; Funeral Canticle; Petra: a ritual dream)*, P. Rozario (sop), A. Manze (vn) *(Song of the Angel)* HAM ▮ 407231 (12.98)

My Gaze is Ever upon You for Violin & Tape (1997)
C. Gould (vn) † ...Depart in Peace; Tears of the Angels LINN ▲ 85 (16.97)

The Protecting Veil for Cello & Orchestra (1987)
Y.-Y. Ma (vc), D. Zinman (cnd), Baltimore SO † Wake Up...And Die SNYC ▲ 62821 [DDD] (16.97) ▮ 62821 [DDD] (10.98) △ 62821 [DDD] (15.97)
F. Springuel (vc), R. Werthen (cnd), Orch of Flanders *(rec Belgium, Sept 15-18, 1997)* † Last Sleep of the Virgin TEL ▲ 80487 [DDD] (16.97)

Sacred Music
B. Turner (cnd), Pro Cantione Antiqua † W. Byrd:Mass 4 Voc; Taverner:Sacred Music ASVQ ▲ 6132 [ADD] (10.97)

Song for Athene for Chorus (1993)
M. Neary (cnd), Westminster Abbey Choir *(rec Westminster Abbey, July 19-22, 1994)* ("John Tavener: Innocence") † Annunciation; Hymns to the Mother of God; Innocence; Lamb; Little Requiem; Tyger SNYC ▲ 66613 [DDD] (16.97)

Svyati [O Holy One] for Cello & Chorus (1995)
S. Isserlis (vc), M. Gobdych (cnd), Kiev Chamber Choir *(rec London, Oct 1995)* ("Svyati: Steven Isserlin Plays John Tavener") † Akhmatova Songs; Chant Vc; Eternal Memory; Hidden Treasure RCAV (Red Seal) ▲ 68761 [DDD] (16.97)

Tears of the Angels for Violin & Strings (1995)
C. Gould (vn), C. Gould (cnd), BT Scottish Ensemble † ...Depart in Peace; My Gaze is Ever upon You LINN ▲ 85 (16.97)

Theophany for Orchestra
R. Hickox (cnd), Bournemouth SO † Elis Thanaton CHN ▲ 9440 (16.97)

Trisagion for Brass Quintet (1981)
Onyx Brass *(rec London, England)* † T. Jackson:Haiku; McBirnie:Son Brass; J. Maynard:Fanfare; A. Ridout:Sark; J. White:Doggerel Machine ITIM ▲ 58 [DDD]

The Tyger for Chorus [text William Blake] (1987)
M. Neary (cnd), Westminster Abbey Choir *(rec Westminster Abbey, May 1-5, 1995)* ("John Tavener: Innocence") † Annunciation; Hymns to the Mother of God; Innocence; Lamb; Little Requiem; Song for Athene SNYC ▲ 66613 [DDD] (16.97)

Wake Up...And Die for Cello Solo & Cello Ensemble
Y.-Y. Ma (vc), D. Zinman (cnd), Baltimore SO members † Protecting Veil SNYC ▲ 62821 [DDD] (16.97) ▮ 62821 [DDD] (10.98) △ 62821 [DDD] (15.97)

We Shall See Him as He Is for Soprano, 2 Tenors, Orchestra & Chorus (1990)
P. Rozario (sop), J. M. Ainsley (ten), A. Murgatroyd (ten), R. Hickox (cnd), BBC Welsh SO, BBC Welsh Chorus [ENG] CHN ▲ 9128 [DDD] (16.97)

The World Is Burning for Chorus
J. E. Gardiner (cnd), Monteverdi Choir London ("Jubilate Deo!") † G. Gabrieli:Canticle Jubilate Deo; Monteverdi:Madrigals Book 8; F. Poulenc:Figure humaine; H. Purcell:Anthems & Services PPHI ▲ 46116 (16.97)

TAVERNER, JOHN (ca 1490-1545)

Gloria tibi Trinitas (mass) for 6 Voices
P. Phillips (cnd), Tallis Scholars † Kyrie 'Leroy'; Western Wynde GIME ▲ 54995 [DDD] (16.97)

In Alium for Soprano, Tape & Orchestra
E. Hulse (sop), T. Yuasa (cnd), Ulster Orch † Protecting Veil NXIN ▲ 8554388 (5.97)

Kyrie 'Leroy' for 4 Voices
P. Phillips (cnd), Tallis Scholars † Gloria tibi Trinitas; Western Wynde GIME ▲ 54995 [DDD] (16.97)

Motets
H. Christophers (cnd), The Sixteen Chorus—O splendor gloriae; Te Deum; Alleluia; Veni, electa mea † Western Wynde HYP ▲ 66507 (18.97)
S. Darlington (cnd), Christ Church Cathedral Choir Oxford—Mater Christi; O Wilhelme, pastor bone [L] NIMB ▲ 5218 [DDD] (16.97)

▲ = CD ♦ = Enhanced CD △ = MD ▮ = Cassette Tape ▯ = DCC

TAVERNER, JOHN (cont.)

The Protecting Veil for Cello & Orchestra

M. Kliegel (vc), T. Yuasa (cnd), Ulster Orch † In Alium NXIN ▲ 8554388 (5.97)

Sacred Music

P. Phillips (cnd), Tallis Scholars—Dum transisset Sabbatum; Leroy Kyrie; Missa Gloria Tibi Trinitas; Western Wind Mass ("A Tudor Collection") † W. Byrd:Mass 3 Voc; Mass 4 Voc; Mass 5 Voc; Motets; Cornysh:Sacred & Secular Choral Music; Tallis:Church Music PPHI 4-▲ 454895 [DDD] (45.97)

B. Turner (cnd), Pro Cantione Antiqua † W. Byrd:Mass 4 Voc; J. Tavener:Sacred Music ASVQ ▲ 6132 [ADD] (10.97)

Village Wedding for Vocal Ensemble

Chanticleer † Z. Long:Words of the Sun; B. Rands:Canti d'Amor; Sametz:in time of; S. Stucky:Cradle Songs; A. R. Thomas:Love Songs; Rub of Love; C. Yi:Tang Poems TELC ▲ 24570 (16.97)

Western Wynde (mass) for 4 Voices

H. Christophers (cnd), The Sixteen Chorus [E,L] † Motets HYP ▲ 66507 (18.97)

P. Phillips (cnd), Tallis Scholars † J. Sheppard:Mass 'The Western Wynde'; Tye:Western Wind Mass GIME ▲ 54927 (16.97)

P. Phillips (cnd), Tallis Scholars † Gloria tibi Trinitas; Kyrie 'Leroy' GIME ▲ 54995 [DDD] (16.97)

D. Willcocks (cnd), King's College Choir Cambridge † W. Byrd:Sacred Music PLON (Double Decker) 2-▲ 452170 (17.97)

TAXIN, IRA (1950-

Quintet for Brass (1973)

Meridian Arts Ensemble *(rec Raphaëlpleinkerk, Amsterdam, Netherlands, Feb 1991)* † A. Arutiunian:Armenian Rhap; J. Bach:Laudes; Etler:Qnt Brass; P. Hindemith:Morgenmusik; W. Lutoslawski:Mini Ov CCSC (Winning Artist's Series) ▲ 2191 [DDD] (18.97)

Meridian Arts Ensemble ("Chaconne; Baroque Lute Recital") † J. S. Bach:Sons & Partitas Vn; Gallot:Folies d'Espagne; T. Satoh:Music of Satoh; Tombeau de Mr. D. Philips; S. L. Weiss:Lt Music CCL ▲ 490 [DDD]

TAYLOR, DEEMS (1885-1966)

Through the Looking Glass for Orchestra, Op. 12 (1921-23)

G. Schwarz (cnd), Seattle SO † Griffes:Bacchanale; Pleasure Dome of Kubla Khan, Op. 8; Poem Fl; Tone-Pictures, Op. 5; White Peacock DLS ▲ 3099 [DDD] (14.97)

TAYLOR, RAYNOR (1747?-1825)

The Ethiop, or The Child of the Desert (opera in 1 act) (1814)

J. Baldoon (cnd), Federal Music Society Opera Company [ed & arr Victor Fell Yellin] † J. Bray:Indian Princess NWW ▲ 80232 (16.97)

TCHAIKOVSKY, BORIS (1925-

Sonata in c for Cello & Piano

A. Vasilieva (vc), B. Tchaikovsky (pno) † M. Vainberg:Sons Vc & Pno RUS ▲ 11026 [ADD] (12.97)

Symphony No. 2 (1967)

K. Kondrashin (cnd), Moscow PO *(rec 1969)* † A. Khachaturian:Funeral Ode in Memory of Lenin; Gayane (sels); Song-Poem RUS ▲ 11063 [AAD] (12.97)

TCHAIKOVSKY, PIOTR (1840-1893)

Album pour enfants (24 easy pieces) for Piano, Op. 39 (1878)

Borodin Trio CHN ▲ 8365 [DDD] (16.97)

I. Heifetz (pno) † S. Prokofiev:Music for Children, Op. 65; D. Shostakovich:Dances of the Dolls SO ▲ 22563 [DDD] (16.97)

I. Heifetz (pno)—Douce rêverie [Sweet Dreams]; A l'église ("The Maiden's Wish") † Morceaux (6) Pno, Op. 19; Liszt:Pno Music (misc); Trans, Arrs & Paraphrases; S. Prokofiev:Pno Music (misc colls); S. Rachmaninoff:Moments musicaux, Op. 16 SO ▲ 22565 [DDD] (16.97)

M. Ponti (pno) ("Complete Solo Piano Music, Vol. 1") † Pno Music; Saisons; Son Pno, Op. 80 VB2 2-▲ 5087 [ADD] (9.97)

L. H. Stevens (mar)—Chant de l'alouette [Song of the Lark]; Prière de matin [Morning Prayer]; Le petit cavalier [Hobby Horse]; Chanson italienne [Italian Song]; Chanson allemande [German Song]; Valse; Chanson napolitaine [Neapolitan Dance-Song]; Mazurka; Enterrement de la poupée [Doll's Burial]; La nouvelle poupée [New Doll]; Conte de la vieille bonne; Douce rêverie [Sweet Dreams] ("Marimba When") † Debussy:Children's Corner; A. Khachaturian:Album of Children's Pieces; R. Schumann:Album für die Jugend, Op. 68 DLS ▲ 3142 [DDD]

G. Tozer (pno)—Le paysan prélude [Song of the Peasant]; L'orgue de barberie [Organ Grinder]; Chanson allemande [German Song] *(rec Sydney, Australia, Feb 1988)* ("For Children") † J. S. Bach:Anna Magdalena Bach Notebook (sels); B. Bartók:For Children (1945 revision), Sz.42; Little Pieces, Sz.82; Mikrokosmos, Sz.107; W. A. Mozart:Pno Music (misc colls); S. Prokofiev:Music for Children, Op. 65; F. Schubert:Scherzos Pno, D.593; R. Schumann:Album für die Jugend, Op. 68 TALP ▲ 1 [DDD]

Y. Turovsky (cnd), Montreal Musici [string orch arr Rostislav Dubinsky & Yuli Turovsky] † L. Mozart:Cassation CHN ▲ 9098 [DDD] (16.97)

Allegro in c for Piano & Orchestra

A. Hoteev (pno), V. Fedoseyev (cnd), Moscow Tchaikovsky SO † Bohemian Melodies; Con 1 Pno, Op. 23; Con 2 Pno, Op. 44; Con 3 Pno, Op. 75; Concert Fant, Op. 56 KSCH 3-▲ 364902 (47.97)

Allegro in f for Piano [incomplete 1st movt of unfinished sonata] (1863-64)

L. Howard (pno) [compd L. Howard as Son Pno in f] ("Piano Sonatas") † Son Pno, Op. 37; Son Pno, Op. 80 HYP ▲ 66939 [DDD] (18.97)

Andante cantabile for Orchestra (or solo Cello & Strings) [from Quartet No. 1 in D for Strings, Op. 11]

L. Bernstein (cnd), New York PO † Qt 1 Strs, Op. 11; S. Barber:Adagio Strs; G. Mahler:Sym 5; Vaughan Williams:Fant on a Theme of Tallis; Fant on Greensleeves SNYC ▲ 38484 [AAD] (9.97) ▮ 38484 [AAD] (3.98)

W. Boughton (cnd), English String Orch *(rec Great Hall, Univ of Birmingham, AL, Aug 1991)* ("Orchestral Favorites, Vol. 2") † Arensky:Vars on a Theme of Tchaikovsky; J. Ireland:Downland Suite; O. Respighi:Ancient Airs & Dances; W. Walton:Pieces Strs; D. Wirén:Serenade Strs, Op. 11 NIMB ▲ 7020 [DDD] (11.97)

M. Brunello (vc), M. Brunello (cnd), Italian String Orch † Nocturne Vc; P. Hindemith:Trauermusik; A. Piazzolla:Adiós Nonino; G. Rossini:Péchés de vieillesse (sels); Sollima:Violincelles Vibrez!; Takemitsu:Scene Vc AG ▲ 155 (18.97)

V. Feigin (vc), N. Järvi (cnd), Estonian State SO *(rec Tallinn, Estonia, 1978)* ("Neeme Järvi: The Early Recordings, Vol. 6") † Nocturne Vc; Pezzo capriccioso, Op. 62; Vars on a Rococo Theme, Op. 33; J. Haydn:Con 2 Vc MELD ▲ 40724 [ADD] (6.97)

D. Ferschtman (vc), L. Markiz (cnd), Amsterdam New Sinfonietta *(rec 1990)* † Elegy Strs; Nocturne Vc; Serenade Strs, Op. 48; Arensky:Vars on a Theme of Tchaikovsky GLOE ▲ 6021 [DDD] (16.97)

M. Freccia (cnd), London PO † Capriccio italien, Op. 45; Con Vn; Marche slave, Op. 31 CHGR ▲ 9012 [DDD] (29.97)

S. Isserlis (vc), J. E. Gardiner (cnd), CO of Europe *(rec Italy)* ("43561490") † Nocturne Vc; Pezzo capriccioso, Op. 62; Vars on a Rococo Theme, Op. 33; E. Bloch:Schelomo; E. Elgar:Con Vc; Kabalevsky:Con 2 Vc, Op. 77; R. Strauss:Don Quixote, Op. 35 VCL 2-▲ 61490 [DDD] (11.97)

J. Judd (cnd), London SO † Con 1 Pno, Op. 23 INMP (LSO Classic Masterpieces) ▲ 893 [DDD] (9.97)

M. Maisky (vc), Orpheus CO *(rec Recital Hall NY State Univ, Purchase, NY, Apr 1996)* † Eugene Onegin (sels); Nocturne Vc; Souvenir de Florence, Op. 70; Vars on a Rococo Theme, Op. 33 DEUT ▲ 453460 [DDD] (16.97)

S. Rolston (vc), M. Bernardi (cnd), Calgary PO *(rec Calgary Centre for the Performing Arts, Canada, Mar 15-16, 1994)* † E. Elgar:Con Vc; Glazunov:Chant du ménestrel, Op. 71; Popper:Hungarian Rhap, Op. 68; Saint-Saëns:Con 1 Vc, Op. 33 CBC (SM 5000) ▲ 5153 [DDD] (16.97)

artists unknown ("Winter Dreams") † Con 1 Pno, Op. 23; Serenade Strs, Op. 48; E. Grieg:Lyric Pieces; Music of Grieg; Sibelius:Swan of Tuonela; Valse triste PPHI (Night Moods) ▲ 453908 [DDD] (9.97)

Andante in B♭ & Finale in E♭ for Piano & Orchestra [unfinished; completed & orchd Taneyev]

B. Glemser (pno), A. Wit (cnd), Polish National RSO Katowice *(rec Polish Radio Concert Hall, Mar 1995)* † Con 1 Pno, Op. 23; Con 3 Pno, Op. 75 NXIN ▲ 550819 [DDD] (5.97)

Arias

S. Aleksashkin (bass), G. Rozhdestvensky (cnd), Philharmonia Orch—Mazeppa (sels); Iolanta (sels); Eugene Onegin (sels) ("Russian Arias, Vol. 2") † Borodin:Prince Igor (sels); Mussorgsky:Boris Godunov (sels); S. Rachmaninoff:Aleko (sels); Rimsky-Korsakov:Arias CHN ▲ 9629 (16.97)

I. Galante (sop), M. Shaguch (sop), A. Fedin (ten), S. Leiferkus (bar), N. Järvi (cnd), Royal Opera House Orch Covent Garden—Iolanta (sels) [Roberto's Aria; Duet of Iolanta & Vaudémont]; Oprichnik (sels) [Natalya's Arioso]; Mazeppa (sels) [Finale]; Maid of Orleans (sels) [Joan's Aria]; Queen of Spades (sels) [Herman's Arioso; Yeletsky's Aria]; Undina (sels) [Undina's Song]; Voyevoda (sels) [Bastryukov's Aria]; Vakula the Smith (sels) [Oksana's Aria]; Eugene Onegin (sels) [Letter Scene (Let me perish)]; Sorceress (sels) [Kuma's Arioso] ("The Tchaikovsky Experience") CONI ▲ 55022 (16.97)

G. Gorchakova (sop), V. Gergiev (cnd), Kirov Theater Orch, Kirov Theater Chorus—Eugene Onegin (sels) [Letter Scene (Let me perish)]; Queen of Spades (sels) [But why these tears? (Zachem eti sl'ozy)]; Sorceress (sels) [Gde zhe ty, moj zjelannyj?]; Oprichnik (sels) [Pachudilis' mne butta galasa] † Verdi:Arias PPHI ▲ 46405 (16.97)

TCHAIKOVSKY, PIOTR (cont.)

Ballet Music

O. Vedernikova (vn), A. Dardyikin (vc), A. Verkholanzeva (hp), A. Vedernikov (cnd), Russian Philharmonia—Swan Lake (suite), Op. 20a; Sleeping Beauty (suite), Op. 66a; Nutcracker Suite, Op. 71a *(rec Moscow Conservatory Large Hall, Russia, Feb 1996)* ("Ballet Suites") AART ▲ 47372 [DDD] (10.97)

Bohemian Melodies for Piano & Orchestra

A. Hoteev (pno), V. Fedoseyev (cnd), Moscow Tchaikovsky SO † Allegro Pno & Orcg; Con 1 Pno, Op. 23; Con 2 Pno, Op. 44; Con 3 Pno, Op. 75; Concert Fant, Op. 56 KSCH 3-▲ 364902 (47.97)

Capriccio italien in A for Orchestra, Op. 45 (1880)

Y. Ahronovitch (cnd), Vienna SO ("Greatest Hits") † J. Brahms:Hungarian Dances Orch; A. Dvořák:Slavonic Dances (sels); Liszt:Préludes, S.97; R. Wagner:Götterdämmerung (sels); Meistersinger (preludes) PRMX ▲ 804 [DDD] (3.97)

K. Ančerl (cnd), Czech PO *(rec 1965-68)* † Mussorgsky:Night on Bare Mountain; Pictures at an Exhibition; Rimsky-Korsakov:Capriccio espagnol, Op. 34 SUR ▲ 111943 [AAD]

D. Barenboim (cnd), Chicago SO † Francesca da Rimini, Op. 32; Ov 1812, Op. 49; Romeo & Juliet DEUT (Masters) ▲ 45523 [DDD] (9.97)

P. Domingo (cnd), Philharmonia Orch † Eugene Onegin (sels); Ov 1812, Op. 49; Romeo & Juliet; Songs (6), Op. 6 CSER (Seraphim) ▲ 73297 [DDD] (6.97)

A. Doráti (cnd), Detroit SO *(rec 1978)* † Fatum; Francesca da Rimini, Op. 32; Hamlet; Marche slave, Op. 31; Ov 1812, Op. 49; Romeo & Juliet; Tempest, Op. 18; Voyevoda, Op. 78 PLON 2-▲ 43003 [ADD] (17.97)

V. Dudarova (cnd), Russian SO † Fatum; Festival Ov, Op. 15; Francesca da Rimini, Op. 32; Hamlet; Ov 1812, Op. 49; Romeo & Juliet; Tempest, Op. 18 OLY ▲ 512 (16.97)

A. Fiedler (cnd), Boston Pops Orch *(rec 1977)* † Rimsky-Korsakov:Capriccio espagnol, Op. 34 LALI ▲ 15312 [DDD] (3.97)

A. Gibson (cnd), London New SO † Andante cantabile; Con Vn; Marche slave, Op. 31 CHGR ▲ 9012 [DDD] (29.97)

V. Kahi (cnd), Georgian Festival Orch ("The Tchaikovsky Album") † Marche slave, Op. 31; Ov 1812, Op. 49; Romeo & Juliet SNYC ▲ 61978 [DDD] (4.97)

K. Kondrashin (cnd), RCA SO † Kabalevsky:Comedians, Op. 26; A. Khachaturian:Masquerade (ballet suite); Rimsky-Korsakov:Capriccio espagnol, Op. 34 RCAV ▲ 63302 (11.97)

K. Labèque (pno), M. Labèque (pno) *(rec London, UK, May 14-19, 1994)* † Marche slave, Op. 31; A. Scriabin:Fant Pnos PPHI ▲ 42778 (16.97)

A. Lazarev (cnd), Bolshoi Theater SO † Eugene Onegin (sels); Nutcracker Suite, Op. 71a; Sleeping Beauty (suite), Op. 66a; Swan Lake (suite), Op. 20a TELC (Ultima) 2-▲ 18965 (16.97)

T. Lønskov (pno), R. Llambias (pno) [arr for pno 4-hands] *(rec 1996)* ("Tchaikovsky, Vol. 2") † Suite 2 Orch, Op. 53 KPT ▲ 32241

L. Maazel (cnd), Bavarian RSO ("Symphonic Battle Scenes") † Ov 1812, Op. 49; Beethoven:Wellington's Victory, Op. 91; Liszt:Battle of the Huns RCAV (Red Seal) ▲ 68471 (16.97)

J. Mardjani (cnd), Georgian Festival Orch † Sym 6 SNYC ▲ 66728 [DDD] (4.97)

Z. Mehta (cnd), Israel PO † Ov 1812, Op. 49; Swan Lake (sels) TELC ▲ 90201 (16.97)

A. Nanut (cnd), Ljubljana SO † Eugene Onegin (sels); Nutcracker (sels); Sleeping Beauty (suite), Op. 66a; Slippers (sels); Souvenir d'un lieu cher, Op. 42; Swan Lake (suite), Op. 20a; Sérénade mélancolique, Op. 26; Valse-Scherzo Vn, Op. 34; Vars on a Rococo Theme, Op. 33 VB3 3-▲ 3026 [ADD]

E. Ormandy (cnd), Philadelphia Orch † Eugene Onegin (sels); Sym 6 SNYC (Essential Classics) ▲ 47657 (7.97) ▮ 47657 (3.98)

E. Ormandy (cnd), Philadelphia Orch † Marche slave, Op. 31; Ov 1812, Op. 49 RCAV (Silver Seal) ▲ 60492 [ADD] (6.97)

E. Ormandy (cnd), Philadelphia Orch † Con Vn; Eugene Onegin (sels); Marche slave, Op. 31; Ov 1812, Op. 49; Romeo & Juliet; Sym 5 SNYC (Essential Classics Take 2) 2-▲ 63281 (14.97)

E. Oue (cnd), Minnesota Orch *(rec Minneapolis, MN, Oct 1-3, 1996)* ("Ports of Call") † Alfvén:Swedish Rhap 1, Op. 19; Borodin:In the Steppes of Central Asia; Chabrier:España; Ibert:Escales; Sibelius:Finlandia, Op. 26; Smetana:Moldau REF ▲ 80 (16.97)

M. Pletnev (cnd), Russian National Orch † Sym 6; Voyevoda, Op. 78 DGRM ▲ 453450 [DDD]

H. Rosbaud (cnd), Berlin Radio Orch *(rec 1940)* † Beethoven:Weihe des Hauses (ov), Op. 124; Liszt:Ce qu'on entend sur la montagne, S.95 IN ▲ 1401 (15.97)

G. Rozhdestvensky (cnd), London SO † Sym 5 INMP (LSO Classic Masterpieces) ▲ 875 [DDD] (9.97)

A. Scholz (cnd), Munich SO ("Masterworks") † Con Vn; Con 1 Pno, Op. 23; Sym 5; Sym 6 INTC 3-▲ 885923 [DDD] (16.97)

L. Stokowski (cnd), Philadelphia Orch *(rec 1928-29)* ("Stokowski Conducts Tchaikovsky") † Romeo & Juliet; Sym 4 PHS ▲ 9120 [ADD] (17.97)

Capriccio in G♭ for Piano, Op. 8 (1870)

M. Pletnev (pno) *(rec 1986/88)* ("Mikhail Pletnev") † Con 2 Pno, Op. 44; Nutcracker Suite, Op. 71a; Romance Pno, Op. 5; Saisons; Sleeping Beauty (sels); Valse-Scherzo Pno, Op. 7 PPHI (Great Pianists of the 20th Century) ▲ 456931 (22.97)

Choral Music

V. Polianski (cnd), USSR State Chamber Choir *(Legend Chorus)*, V. Polianski (cnd), Moscow Conservatory SO, USSR State Chamber Choir *(At Bedtime Chorus)* *(rec Moscow Conservatory Great Hall, Russia, 1987)* ("Russian Conducting School: Valery Poliansky") † Serenade Strs, Op. 48; Arensky:Vars on a Theme of Tchaikovsky RD (Talents of Russia) ▲ 22106 [DDD] (16.97)

V. Popov (cnd), Moscow Academy of Choral Singing—Evening, Op. 46/1; Dawn, Op. 46/6; Legend (When Jesus Christ Was But a Child), Op. 54/5; Autumn, Op. 54/14; Child's Song, Op.54/16; Blessed Is He Who Smiles; Voice of Mirth Grew Silent; Without Time, Without Season; Tis not the Cuckoo in the Damp Pinewood; Nature & Love; At Bedtime Chorus; Golden Cloud Has Slept; Greeting to Anton Rubinstein; Nightingale; Hymn to Sts. Cyril & Methodius; Album pour enfants Pno, Op. 39 [Chanson napolitaine [Neapolitan Dance-Song]] ("Secular Choruses") RUSS ▲ 288156 (18.97)

Concert Fantasia in G for Piano & Orchestra, Op. 56 (1884)

I. Ardašev (pno), L. Svárovský (cnd), Prague SO *(rec Apr 1998)* † S. Prokofiev:Con 2 Pno, Op. 16 SUR ▲ 3382 [DDD] (16.97)

B. Glemser (pno), A. Wit (cnd), Polish National RSO Katowice *(rec Polish Radio Concert Hall Katowice, Mar 20-24, 1995)* † Con 2 Pno, Op. 44 NXIN ▲ 550820 [DDD] (5.97)

A. Hoteev (pno), V. Fedoseyev (cnd), Moscow Tchaikovsky SO † Allegro Pno & Orcg; Bohemian Melodies; Con 1 Pno, Op. 23; Con 2 Pno, Op. 44; Con 3 Pno, Op. 75 KSCH 3-▲ 364902 (47.97)

J. Lowenthal (pno), S. Comissiona (cnd), London SO [original version] † Con 1 Pno, Op. 23 ARA ▲ 6611 (16.97)

M. Pletnev (pno), V. Fedoseyev (cnd), Philharmonia Orch *(rec 1990)* † Con 1 Pno, Op. 23; Con 2 Pno, Op. 44; Con 3 Pno, Op. 75 VCL 2-▲ 61463 [DDD] (11.97)

M. Ponti (pno), R. Kapp (cnd), Prague SO ("Complete Works for Piano & Orchestra") † Con 1 Pno, Op. 23; Con 2 Pno, Op. 44; Con 3 Pno, Op. 75 VB2 2-▲ 5024 [ADD] (9.97)

Concerto No. 1 in b♭ for Piano & Orchestra, Op. 23 (1874-75)

I. Ardašev (pno), J. Bělohlávek (cnd), Czech PO *(rec Mar 1989)* † Pno Music SUR ▲ 110952 [DDD]

M. Argerich (pno), C. Abbado (cnd), Berlin PO *(rec Berlin, Germany, Dec 1994)* † Nutcracker Suite, Op. 71a DEUT ▲ 49816 [DDD] (16.97)

M. Argerich (pno), C. Dutoit (cnd), Royal PO † S. Prokofiev:Con 3 Pno, Op. 26 DEUT ▲ 15062 [AAD/ADD] (16.97)

M. Argerich (pno), K. Kondrashin (cnd), Bavarian RSO *(rec 1980)* † S. Rachmaninoff:Con 3 Pno, Op. 30 PPHI ▲ 46673 (16.97)

D. Baloghova (pno), K. Ančerl (cnd), Czech PO SUR ▲ 111944 [AAD]

J. Banowetz (pno), O. Lenárd (cnd), Czech RSO *(rec Czechoslovak Radio Concert Hall Bratislava, Czech Republic, 1988)* ("Famous Piano Concertos") † Eugene Onegin (sels); Tempest, Op. 18; Beethoven:Con 2 Pno, Op. 19; Con 5 Pno, Op. 73; Chopin:Con 1 Pno, Op. 11; Con 2 Pno, Op. 21; S. Rachmaninoff:Con 2 Pno, Op. 18; Rhap on a Theme of Paganini, Op. 43 NXIN 4-▲ 504011 [DDD] (19.97)

J. Banowetz (pno), O. Lenárd (cnd), Czech-Slovak RSO Bratislava *(rec 1988)* † Eugene Onegin (sels); Tempest, Op. 18 NXIN ▲ 550137 [DDD] (5.97)

S. Cherkassky (pno), L. Ludwig (cnd), Berlin PO † Con 2 Pno, Op. 44 DEUT (Originals) ▲ 457751 (11.97)

V. Cliburn (pno), P. Argento (cnd), Swiss-Italian Radio-TV Orch † Nutcracker, Op. 71; Romeo & Juliet AURC ▲ 108 (5.97)

V. Cliburn (pno), K. Kondrashin (cnd), RCA Victor SO † S. Rachmaninoff:Con 2 Pno, Op. 18 RCAV (Red Seal) ▲ 55912 [ADD] (16.97)

N. Demidenko (pno), A. Lazarev (cnd), BBC SO † A. Scriabin:Con Pno, Op. 20 HYP ▲ 66680 (18.97)

B. Engerer (pno), E. Krivine (cnd), Royal PO *(rec Tooting, England, Nov 1991)* ("Romantic Piano Concertos") † Chopin:Con 1 Pno, Op. 11; S. Rachmaninoff:Con 2 Pno, Op. 18; R. Schumann:Con Pno in a, Op. 54 DNN 2-▲ 17013 (16.97)

V. Feltsman (pno), M. Rostropovich (cnd), National SO Washington D.C. † Con 3 Pno, Op. 75 SNYC ▲ 45756 [DDD] (11.97)

TCHAIKOVSKY, PIOTR (cont.)
Concerto No. 1 in b♭ for Piano & Orchestra, Op. 23 (1874-75) (cont.)
N. Freire (pno), R. Kempe (cnd), Munich PO *(rec 1968)* † Con Vn SNYC ▲ 46268 [ADD] (7.97)
A. Gavrilov (pno), V. Ashkenazy (cnd), Berlin PO † Con Vn CSER (Seraphim) ▲ 73296 [DDD] (6.97)
Em. Gilels (pno), K. Ančerl (cnd), Czech PO † R. Schumann:Con Pno in a, Op. 54 PRAG ▲ 256000 (18.97)
E. Gilels (pno), Z. Mehta (cnd), New York PO † Con Vn SNYC (Essential Classics) ▲ 46339 [ADD] (7.97) ■ 46339 [ADD] (3.98)
E. Gilels (pno), E. Mravinsky (cnd), Leningrad PO ("Mravinsky Live") † Son Pno, Op. 80 RUS ▲ 11170 [ADD] (12.97)
Em. Gilels (pno), F. Reiner (cnd), Chicago SO *(rec 1955)* † Nutcracker (sels) RCAV ▲ 68530 [ADD] (11.97)
B. Glemser (pno), A. Wit (cnd), Polish National RSO Katowice *(rec Polish Radio Concert Hall, Mar 1995)* † Andante & Finale; Con 3 Pno, Op. 75 NXIN ▲ 550819 [DDD] (5.97)
G. Graffman (pno), G. Szell (cnd), Cleveland Orch † S. Rachmaninoff:Preludes Pno SNYC ▲ 37263 [ADD] (9.97)
H. Gutiérrez (pno), D. Zinman (cnd), Baltimore SO † S. Rachmaninoff:Rhap on a Theme of Paganini, Op. 43 TEL ▲ 80193 [DDD] (16.97)
C. Hansen (pno), W. Mengelberg (cnd), Berlin PO *(rec July 11, 1940)* ("Mengelberg Conducts Tchaikovsky") † Sym 5 BCS ▲ 51 [ADD] (16.97)
V. Horowitz (pno), A. Rubinstein (pno), A. Toscanini (cnd), NBC SO, D. Mitropoulos (cnd), Minneapolis SO [2 versions] ("Performers in Comparison 4") ENPL (Piano Library) ▲ 299 (14.97)
V. Horowitz (pno), W. Steinberg (cnd), Hollywood Bowl SO *(rec 1945)* † Liszt:Liebesträume, S.541; Moszkowski:Etude de virtuosité, Op. 72; D. Scarlatti:Sons Kbd; J. P. Sousa:Stars & Stripes Forever RY (Radio Years) ▲ 92 (16.97)
V. Horowitz (pno), A. Toscanini (cnd), NBC SO *(rec Carnegie Hall, Apr 25, 1943)* † Beethoven:Con 5 Pno, Op. 73 RCAV (Gold Seal) ▲ 7992 [ADD] (11.97)
V. Horowitz (pno), A. Toscanini (cnd), NBC SO ("The Toscanini Collection, Vol. 43") † J. Brahms:Con 2 Pno, Op. 83 RCAV (Gold Seal) ▲ 60319 (11.97)
V. Horowitz (pno), A. Toscanini (cnd), NBC SO *(rec 1943, broadcast performance)* ("The Toscanini Collection, Vol. 44") † Mussorgsky:Pictures at an Exhibition RCAV (Gold Seal) ▲ 60321 (11.97)
V. Horowitz (pno), A. Toscanini (cnd), NBC SO † Mussorgsky:Pictures at an Exhibition RCAV (Gold Seal) ▲ 60449 [ADD] (11.97)
V. Horowitz (pno), A. Toscanini (cnd), NBC SO *(rec 1941-47)* † Czerny:Vars on "La Ricordanza", Op. 33; Mendelssohn (-Bartholdy):Vars sérieuses, Op. 54; W. A. Mozart:Son 12 Pno, K.332 ENPL (Piano Library) ▲ 257 (13.97)
V. Horowitz (pno), A. Toscanini (cnd), NBC SO † Mendelssohn (-Bartholdy):Midsummer Night's Dream (sels); S. Rachmaninoff:Con 2 Pno, Op. 18 AVID ▲ 585 (16.97)
V. Horowitz (pno), B. Walter (cnd), New York PO *(rec live, Apr 1948)* ("Horowitz Plays Rachmaninoff & Tchaikovsky") † S. Rachmaninoff:Con 3 Pno, Op. 30 IN ▲ 1398 [ADD] (15.97)
A. Hoteev (pno), V. Fedoseyev (cnd), Moscow Tchaikovsky SO † Allegro Pno & Orcg; Bohemian Melodies; Con 2 Pno, Op. 44; Con 3 Pno, Op. 75; Concert Fant, Op. 56 KSCH 3-▲ 364902 (47.97)
J. Jandó (pno), A. Ligeti (cnd), Budapest PO—Andantino semplice ("Piano Dreams") † Chopin:Barcarolle Pno, Op. 60; Liszt:Années de pèlerinage 2, S.161; W. A. Mozart:Son 11 Pno, K.331; F. Schubert:Impromptus (4); Impromptus (8) Pno, D.899 & 935; R. Schumann:Kinderszenen Pno, Op. 15; Waldscenen, Op. 82 LALI ▲ 14224 (3.97)
J. Jandó (pno), A. Ligeti (cnd), Budapest PO † Con Vn LALI ▲ 15516 [DDD] (3.97)
B. Janis (pno), H. Menges (cnd), London SO † R. Schumann:Con Pno in a, Op. 54 MRCR ▲ 32011 [ADD] (11.97)
B. Janis (pno), H. Menges (cnd), London SO *(rec 1960-63)* ("Byron Janis II") † Liszt:Con 1 Pno, S.124; S. Prokofiev:Con 3 Pno, Op. 26; Toccata Pno, Op. 11; S. Rachmaninoff:Con 1 Pno, Op. 1; Con 2 Pno, Op. 18; R. Schumann:Concert sans orch, Op. 14; Romances Pno, Op. 28 PPHI (Great Pianists of the 20th Century) 2-▲ 456850 (22.97)
E. Kissin (pno), H. von Karajan (cnd), Berlin PO † A. Scriabin:Etudes (8) Pno, Op. 42; Pieces (4) Pno, Op. 51 DEUT ▲ 27485 [DDD] (16.97)
K. Konstantinov (pno), C. Munch (cnd), Paris Conservatory Société des Concerts Orch *(rec 1941-42)* ("Munch, Vol. 6") † W. A. Mozart:Con 20 Pno, K.466; Fant Pno, K.397 LYS ▲ 400 (17.97)
L. Kuzmin (pno), A. Tchistiakov (cnd), Moscow PO † Liszt:Con 1 Pno, S.124 RUS ▲ 10020 [DDD] (12.97)
H. Lang (pno), H. Zanotelli (cnd), North German PO ("Masterworks") † Capriccio italien, Op. 45; Con Vn; Sym 5; Sym 6 INTC 3-▲ 885923 [DDD] (16.97)
J. Lill (pno), J. Judd (cnd), London SO † Andante cantabile INMP (LSO Classic Masterpieces) ▲ 893 [DDD] (9.97)
J. Lill (pno), J. Judd (cnd), London SO ("An Evening of Concert Favourites") † Eugene Onegin (sels); Marche slave, Op. 31; Ov 1812, Op. 49 INMP (Concert Classics) ▲ 1102 (9.97)
J. Lowenthal (pno), S. Comissiona (cnd), London SO [original version] † Concert Fant, Op. 56 ARA ▲ 6611 (16.97)
B. Moiseiwitsch (pno), G. Weldon (cnd), Philharmonia Orch *(rec 1944)* † Con 2 Pno, Op. 44; Morceaux (12) Pno, Op. 40 APR ▲ 5518 [ADD] (18.97)
J. Ogdon (pno), P. Monteaux (cnd), London SO *(rec live Vienna Festival, May 31, 1963)* † Romeo & Juliet; Sym 5 VC 2-▲ 8031 (26.97)
G. Ohlsson (pno), N. Marriner (cnd), Academy of St. Martin in the Fields † S. Rachmaninoff:Con 2 Pno, Op. 18 HANS ▲ 98932 [DDD] (15.97)
H. Paik (pno), H. Paik (pno), B. Zander (cnd), New England Conservatory Youth PO *(rec Teatro Colon Buenos Aires)* † A. Dvořák:Sym 9 CPRO ▲ 329405 [DDD] (16.97)
E. Petri (pno), W. Goehr (cnd), London PO *(rec 1937-38)* † J. Brahms:Vars & Fugue on a Theme by Handel, Op. 24 ENPL (The Piano Library) ▲ 286 (13.97)
M. Petukhov (pno), A. Anissimov (cnd), Buenos Aires PO † Con 2 Pno, Op. 44 PAVA ▲ 7387 [DDD] (10.97)
J. Pierce (pno), P. Freeman (cnd), Slovenia Radio-TV SO † Con 3 Pno, Op. 75; Romeo & Juliet; Sym 4; Sym 6 ICC 3-▲ 6702679 (25.97)
M. Pletnev (pno), V. Fedoseyev (cnd), Philharmonia Orch *(rec 1990)* † Con 2 Pno, Op. 44; Con 3 Pno, Op. 75; Concert Fant, Op. 56 VCL 2-▲ 61463 [DDD] (11.97)
M. Ponti (pno), R. Kapp (cnd), Prague SO ("Complete Works for Piano & Orchestra") † Con 2 Pno, Op. 44; Con 3 Pno, Op. 75; Concert Fant, Op. 56 VB2 2-▲ 5024 [ADD] (9.97)
R. Pöntinen (pno), L. Segerstam (cnd), Bamberg SO † E. Grieg:Con Pno, Op. 16 BIS ▲ 375 (17.97)
R. Pöntinen (pno), L. Segerstam (cnd), Bamberg SO † E. Grieg:Con Pno, Op. 16; G. Pierné:Con Pno, Op. 12; Ramuntcho (suites) BIS (BIS Twins) 2-▲ 375381 (17.97)
V. Postnikova (pno) † Con Vn; Con 2 Pno, Op. 44; Con 3 Pno, Op. 75 PPHI (Double Decker) 2-▲ 448107 (17.97)
S. Richter (pno), K. Ančerl (cnd), Czech PO ("Prague Spring Inspiring") † Beethoven:Sym 9; A. Dvořák:Con Vc; Smetana:Má Vlast SUR 3-▲ 546 [AAD]
S. Richter (pno), K. Ančerl (cnd), Czech PO *(rec 1953)* † S. Prokofiev:Con 1 Pno, Op. 10 SUR (Great Artists) ▲ 110268 [AAD]
S. Richter (pno), H. von Karajan (cnd), Vienna SO † S. Rachmaninoff:Con 2 Pno, Op. 18 DEUT (The Originals) ▲ 47420 [ADD] (11.97)
S. Richter (pno), N. Rachlin (cnd), USSR State SO *(rec Moscow, 1955 & 57)* ("Sviatoslav Richter in the 50's, Vol. 2") † Mussorgsky:Pictures at an Exhibition; R. Schumann:Fantasiestücke Pno, Op. 12; Humoreske Pno, Op. 20; Vars on A-B-E-G-G, Op. 1; A. Scriabin:Son 2 Pno, Op. 19; Son 6 Pno, Op. 62 PACD 2-▲ 96003 (29.97)
S. Rodriguez (pno), E. Tabakov (cnd), Sofia PO † E. Grieg:Con Pno, Op. 16; Liszt:Con 1 Pno, S.124 ELAN ▲ 2228 [DDD] (10.97)
P. Rösel (pno), K. Masur (cnd), Leipzig Gewandhaus Orch † R. Schumann:Con Pno in a, Op. 54 BER ▲ 9308 (10.97)
A. Rubenstein (pno), D. Mitropoulos (cnd), Minneapolis SO *(rec 1928-47)* † J. Brahms:Pieces (8) Pno, Op. 76; Songs (5), Op. 49; Liszt:Liebesträume, S.541; F. Schubert:Impromptu (4) Pno; R. Schumann:Arabeske Pno, Op. 18; Kinderszenen Pno, Op. 15; Myrthen, Op. 25; Romances Pno, Op. 28 GRM2 ▲ 78783 (13.97)
A. Rubinstein (pno) *(rec live New York, NY, 1946-47)* † Chopin:Con 1 Pno, Op. 11 ENPL (Piano Library) ▲ 315 (14.97)
A. Rubinstein (pno), E. Leinsdorf (cnd), Boston SO † R. Schumann:Con Pno in a, Op. 54 RCAV (Basic 100) ▲ 68454 (10.97) ■ 68454 (5.98)
A. Rubinstein (pno), E. Leinsdorf (cnd), Boston SO *(rec 1963)* † Chopin:Con 2 Pno, Op. 21; E. Grieg:Con Pno, Op. 16; Saint-Saëns:Con 2 Pno, Op. 22; R. Schumann:Con Pno in a, Op. 54 PPHI (Great Pianists of the 20th Century, Vol. 86) 2-▲ 456958 (22.97)
G. Sokolov (pno), N. Järvi (cnd), USSR SO *(rec Moscow, 1966)* ("Neeme Järvi: The Early Recordings, Vol. 3") † Saint-Saëns:Con 2 Pno, Op. 22 MELD ▲ 40721 [ADD] (6.97)
Solomon (pno), H. Harty (cnd), Hallé Orch *(rec 1930 for Columbia)* † Chopin:Pno Music (misc colls); Liszt:Etudes de concert (3), S.144; Album d'un voyageur, S.156; Rákóczy March Orch, S.117 PHS ▲ 9478 [AAD] (17.97)
Solomon (pno), H. Harty (cnd), Hallé Orch *(rec 1931)* † Beethoven:Sym 4 PHG ▲ 5015 (14.97)
Solomon (pno), H. Harty (cnd), Hallé Orch *(rec 1931-47)* † J. Brahms:Con 2 Pno, Op. 83 ENPL (Piano Library) ▲ 263 (13.97)
D. Tomic (pno), A. Nanut (cnd), Slovak PO † Romeo & Juliet PC ▲ 267173 [DDD] (2.97)
A. Watts (pno), L. Bernstein (cnd), New York PO *(rec Mar 12, 1973)* ("Leonard Bernstein: The Royal Edition") † S. Rachmaninoff:Con 2 Pno, Op. 18 SNYC ▲ 47630 [ADD] (10.97)
A. Watts (pno), Y. Levi (cnd), Atlanta SO *(rec Woodruff Arts Center Atlanta, GA, Aug 1, 1994)* † Saint-Saëns:Con 2 Pno, Op. 22 TEL ▲ 80386 [DDD] (16.97)

TCHAIKOVSKY, PIOTR (cont.)
Concerto No. 1 in b♭ for Piano & Orchestra, Op. 23 (1874-75) (cont.)
L. Westermayr (pno), E. Simon (cnd), Cluj-Klausenburg Transylvania PO † R. Schumann:Sym 1 STRV ▲ 108 (16.97)
E. Wild (pno), A. Fistoulari (cnd), Royal PO † E. von Dohnányi:Capriccio, Op. 28; Vars on a Nursery Song, Op. 25 CHSK ▲ 13 (16.97)
artists unknown † Saint-Saëns:Con 2 Pno, Op. 22 SNYC ▲ 64560 (4.97)
artists unknown ("Winter Dreams") † Andante cantabile; Serenade Strs, Op. 48; E. Grieg:Lyric Pieces; Music of Grieg; Sibelius:Swan of Tuonela; Valse triste PPHI (Night Moods) ▲ 453908 [DDD] (9.97)
Concerto No. 2 in G for Piano & Orchestra, Op. 44 (1879-80)
S. Cherkassky (pno), R. Kraus (cnd), Berlin PO † Con 1 Pno, Op. 23 DEUT (Originals) ▲ 457751 (11.97)
B. Glemser (pno), A. Wit (cnd), Polish National RSO Katowice *(rec Polish Radio Concert Hall Katowice, Mar 20-24, 1995)* † Concert Fant, Op. 56 NXIN ▲ 550820 [DDD] (5.97)
D. Han (pno), P. Freeman (cnd), St. Petersburg PO PRA ▲ 3441 (14.97)
A. Hoteev (pno), V. Fedoseyev (cnd), Moscow Tchaikovsky SO † Allegro Pno & Orcg; Bohemian Melodies; Con 1 Pno, Op. 23; Con 3 Pno, Op. 75; Concert Fant, Op. 56 KSCH 3-▲ 364902 (47.97)
J. Lowenthal (pno), S. Comissiona (cnd), London SO † Con 3 Pno, Op. 75 ARA ▲ 6583 (16.97)
B. Moiseiwitsch (pno), G. Weldon (cnd), Liverpool PO *(rec 1944)* † Con 1 Pno, Op. 23; Morceaux (12) Pno, Op. 40 APR ▲ 5518 [ADD] (18.97)
B. Moiseiwitsch (pno), G. Weldon (cnd), Liverpool PO *(rec 1944-48)* † Saint-Saëns:Con 2 Pno, Op. 22 HPC ▲ 146 (17.97)
M. Petukhov (pno), A. Anissimov (cnd), Buenos Aires PO † Con 1 Pno, Op. 23 PAVA ▲ 7387 [DDD] (10.97)
M. Pletnev (pno), V. Fedoseyev (cnd), Philharmonia Orch *(rec 1990)* † Con 1 Pno, Op. 23; Con 3 Pno, Op. 75; Concert Fant, Op. 56 VCL 2-▲ 61463 [DDD] (11.97)
M. Pletnev (pno), V. Fedoseyev (cnd), Philharmonia Orch *(rec 1990)* ("Mikhail Pletnev") † Capriccio, Op. 8; Nutcracker Suite, Op. 71a; Romance Pno, Op. 5; Saisons; Sleeping Beauty (sels); Valse-Scherzo Pno, Op. 7 PPHI (Great Pianists of the 20th Century) ▲ 456931 (22.97)
M. Ponti (pno), R. Kapp (cnd), Prague SO ("Complete Works for Piano & Orchestra") † Con 1 Pno, Op. 23; Con 3 Pno, Op. 75; Concert Fant, Op. 56 VB2 2-▲ 5024 [ADD] (9.97)
V. Postnikova (pno) † Con Vn; Con 1 Pno, Op. 23; Con 3 Pno, Op. 75 PPHI (Double Decker) 2-▲ 448107 (17.97)
Concerto No. 3 in E♭ for Piano & Orchestra, Op. 75 (1893)
V. Feltsman (pno), M. Rostropovich (cnd), National SO Washington D.C. † Con 1 Pno, Op. 23 SNYC ▲ 45756 [DDD] (11.97)
B. Glemser (pno), A. Wit (cnd), Polish National RSO Katowice *(rec Polish Radio Concert Hall, Mar 1995)* † Andante & Finale; Con 1 Pno, Op. 23 NXIN ▲ 550819 [DDD] (5.97)
A. Hoteev (pno), V. Fedoseyev (cnd), Moscow Tchaikovsky SO † Allegro Pno & Orcg; Bohemian Melodies; Con 1 Pno, Op. 23; Con 2 Pno, Op. 44; Concert Fant, Op. 56 KSCH 3-▲ 364902 (47.97)
J. Lowenthal (pno), S. Comissiona (cnd), London SO † Con 2 Pno, Op. 44 ARA ▲ 6583 (16.97)
J. Pierce (pno), P. Freeman (cnd), Slovenia Radio-TV SO † Con 1 Pno, Op. 23; Romeo & Juliet; Sym 4; Sym 6 ICC 3-▲ 6702679 (25.97)
J. Pierce (pno), K. Won (cnd), Moscow SO † Sym 7 HALM ▲ 35078 (6.97)
M. Pletnev (pno), V. Fedoseyev (cnd), Philharmonia Orch *(rec 1990)* † Con 1 Pno, Op. 23; Con 2 Pno, Op. 44; Concert Fant, Op. 56 VCL 2-▲ 61463 [DDD] (11.97)
M. Ponti (pno), L. De Froment (cnd), Luxembourg RSO ("Complete Works for Piano & Orchestra") † Con 1 Pno, Op. 23; Con 2 Pno, Op. 44; Concert Fant, Op. 56 VB2 2-▲ 5024 [ADD] (9.97)
V. Postnikova (pno) † Con Vn; Con 1 Pno, Op. 23; Con 2 Pno, Op. 44 PPHI (Double Decker) 2-▲ 448107 (17.97)
G. Tozer (pno), N. Järvi (cnd), London PO *(rec June 7-8, 1991)* † Sym 7 CHN ▲ 9130 [DDD] (16.97)
Concerto in D for Violin & Orchestra (or Piano), Op. 35 (1878)
Y. Bushkov (vn), A. Rahbari (cnd), Slovak Radio New PO † Mendelssohn (-Bartholdy):Con Vn & Orch, Op. 64 DI ▲ 920122 [DDD] (11.97)
A. Campoli (vn), A. Argenta (cnd), London SO *(rec London, England, 1956)* ("Campoli Classics III") † A. Bliss:Con Vn, T.79; Theme & Cadenza Vn BEUL ▲ 310 (m) [ADD] (16.97)
S. Chang (vn), C. Davis (cnd), London SO † J. Brahms:Hungarian Dances Orch EMIC ▲ 54753 (16.97)
R. Chen (vn), P. Kogan (cnd), Hanover Radio PO ("Chen Plays Tchaikovsky") † Souvenir d'un lieu cher, Op. 42; Sérénade mélancolique, Op. 26 BER ▲ 1169 (16.97)
K. Chung (vn) † Con 1 Pno, Op. 23; Con 2 Pno, Op. 44; Con 3 Pno, Op. 75 PPHI (Double Decker) 2-▲ 448107 (17.97)
K. Chung (vn), C. Dutoit (cnd), Montreal SO † Mendelssohn (-Bartholdy):Con Vn & Orch, Op. 64 PLON ▲ 10011 [DDD] (16.97)
K. Chung (vn), A. Previn (cnd), London SO † Sibelius:Con Vn PLON (The Classic Sound) ▲ 25080 (11.97)
A. Dumay (vn), E. Tchakarov (cnd), London SO † Con 1 Pno, Op. 23 CSER (Seraphim) ▲ 73296 [DDD] (6.97)
M. Elman (vn), P. Paray (cnd) † Mendelssohn (-Bartholdy):Con Vn & Orch, Op. 64 MUA ▲ 4868 (10.97)
Z. Francescatti (vn), T. Schippers (cnd), New York PO † Capriccio italien, Op. 45; Eugene Onegin (sels); Marche slave, Op. 31; Ov 1812, Op. 49; Romeo & Juliet; Sym 5 SNYC (Essential Classics Take 2) 2-▲ 63281 (14.97)
C. Funke (vn), H. Vonk (cnd), Dresden Staatskapelle † Romeo & Juliet BER ▲ 9384 (10.97)
I. Gitlis (vn), J. Horenstein (cnd), Vienna SO *(rec ca 1954-57)* † B. Bartók:Con 2 Vn, Sz.112; Son Vn; Bruch:Con 1 Vn, Op. 26; Mendelssohn (-Bartholdy):Con Vn & Orch, Op. 64; Sibelius:Con Vn VOXL (Legends) 2-▲ 5505 [ADD] (9.97)
I. Grubert (vn), V. Sinaisky (cnd), Moscow PO † Souvenir d'un lieu cher, Op. 42; Sérénade mélancolique, Op. 26 RUSS ▲ 788054 (12.97)
J. Heifetz (vn), J. Barbirolli (cnd), London PO *(rec 1934-40)* ("Jascha Heifetz: Concerto Recordings, Vol. 1") † Glazunov:Con Vn; W. A. Mozart:Con 5 Vn, K.219; Sibelius:Con Vn PHS ▲ 9157 [ADD] (33.97)
J. Heifetz (vn), J. Barbirolli (cnd), London PO *(rec 1937 for HMV)* † Glazunov:Con Vn; Sibelius:Con Vn EMIC (Great Recordings of the Century) ▲ 64030 (11.97)
J. Heifetz (vn), J. Barbirolli (cnd), London PO *(rec 1937)* † C. Franck:Son Vn, M.8 ENT (Strings) ▲ 99325 (16.97)
J. Heifetz (vn), J. Barbirolli (cnd), London PO † Sarasate:Zigeunerweisen, Op. 20; H. Vieuxtemps:Con 4 Vn, Op. 31 IMMM ▲ 37063 (6.97)
J. Heifetz (vn), J. Barbirolli (cnd), London PO † W. A. Mozart:Con 5 Vn, K.219 IMMM ▲ 37016 (6.97)
J. Heifetz (vn), F. Reiner (cnd), Chicago SO † Sérénade mélancolique, Op. 26; Mendelssohn (-Bartholdy):Con Vn & Orch, Op. 64 RCAV (Red Seal) ▲ 5933 (16.97)
J. Heifetz (vn), F. Reiner (cnd), Chicago SO *(rec 1955 & 1957)* † J. Brahms:Con Vn RCAV (Gold Seal) ▲ 61495 (11.97)
J. Heifetz (vn), F. Reiner (cnd), Chicago SO *(rec Orch Hall Chicago, Apr 19, 1957)* † Sérénade mélancolique, Op. 26; Mendelssohn (-Bartholdy):Con Vn & Orch, Op. 64 RCAV (Red Seal) ▲ 61743 [ADD] (16.97)
B. Hubermann (vn) † J. S. Bach:Con 2 Vn; Lalo:Sym espagnole, Op. 21 ENT (Strings) ▲ 99369 (16.97)
B. Huberman (vn), E. Ormandy (cnd), Philadelphia Orch *(rec Mar, 1946)* † W. A. Mozart:Con 4 Vn, K.218 MUA ▲ 4299 (10.97)
B. Huberman (vn), W. Steinberg (cnd), Berlin State Opera Orch *(rec 1929)* † Mendelssohn (-Bartholdy):Con Vn & Orch, Op. 64 PHS ▲ 9332 [AAD] (17.97)
V. Hudeček (vn), D. Oistrakh (cnd), Czech PO *(rec live Prague Spring Festival, May 20, 1972)* ("Hudeček & Oistrakh at the Prague Spring Festival") † S. Prokofiev:Romeo & Juliet (sels) SUR ▲ 216 (10.97)
L. Josefowicz (vn), N. Marriner (cnd), Academy of St. Martin in the Fields † Sibelius:Con Vn PPHI ▲ 46131 (16.97)
N. Kennedy (vn), O. Kamu (cnd), London PO † Sibelius:Con Vn EMIC ▲ 54559 [DDD] (16.97)
C. Kim (vn), P. Freeman (cnd), Russian SO *(rec Great Hall of the Moscow Radio Union, Sept 1993)* † Glazunov:Con Vn INSD ▲ 3535 [DDD] (14.97)
G. Kulenkampff (vn), A. Rother (cnd), Berlin State Opera Orch *(rec 1937-39)* ("Georg Kulenkampff, Vol. 2") † A. Dvořák:Con Vn ENT (Strings) ▲ 99352 (16.97)
M. Lubotsky (vn), A. Volmer (cnd), Estonian National SO ("Russian Violin Concertos") † Arensky:Con Vn; Rimsky-Korsakov:Fant on Russian Themes, Op. 33 GLOE ▲ 5174 [DDD] (16.97)
Y. Menuhin (vn), F. Fricsay (cnd), Berlin RIAS SO ("In Memoriam") † Beethoven:Rondo Vn, WoO 41; Son 5 Vn, Op. 24; Son 7 Vn; Son 9 Vn, Op. 47 DEUT (2-Fer) 2-▲ 463175 (17.97)
Midori (vn), C. Abbado (cnd), Berlin PO *(rec Berlin, Germany, 1995-97)* † D. Shostakovich:Con 1 Vn, Op. 99 SNYC ▲ 68338 [DDD] (16.97)
N. Milstein (vn), W. Steinberg (cnd), Pittsburgh SO *(rec Syria Mosque, Pittsburgh, United States of America, Apr 6, 1959)* † J. Brahms:Sym 1 EMIC ▲ 67101 [ADD] (11.97)
N. Milstein (vn), F. Stock (cnd), Chicago SO *(rec 1936-40)* ("The Baroque & Romantic Repertoire") † Pergolesi:Son 12 Vn; Tartini:Son Vn & Pno; Vivaldi:Sons Vn ENT (Strings) ▲ 99331 (16.97)
A.-S. Mutter (vn), H. von Karajan (cnd), Vienna PO *(rec live Salzburg, Austria, 1988)* DEUT ▲ 19241 [DDD] (16.97)
P. Narrato (cnd), Belgium Festival Orch † Serenade Strs, Op. 48 PC ▲ 265064 [DDD] (2.97)
J. Novák (vn), J. Stárek (cnd), Munich SO ("Masterworks") † Capriccio italien, Op. 45; Con 1 Pno, Op. 23; Sym 5; Sym 6 INTC 3-▲ 885923 [DDD] (16.97)
D. Oistrakh (vn), F. Konwitschny (cnd), Dresden Staatskapelle † J. S. Bach:Cons Vn (comp); Beethoven:Romances Vn; J. Brahms:Con Vn DEUT (The Originals) 2-▲ 47427 [ADD] (22.97)

▲ = CD ♦ = Enhanced CD △ = MD ■ = Cassette Tape ▯ = DCC

TCHAIKOVSKY, PIOTR

TCHAIKOVSKY, PIOTR (cont.)
Concerto in D for Violin & Orchestra (or Piano), Op. 35 (1878) (cont.)
D. Oistrakh (vn), S. Samosud (cnd), Bolshoi Theater Orch (*rec 1958-59*) † W. A. Mozart:Con 5 Vn, K.219
 TUXE ▲ 1052 [ADD] (10.97)
D. Oistrakh (vn), E. Ormandy (cnd), Philadelphia Orch † Con 1 Pno, Op. 23
 SNYC (Essential Classics) ▲ 46339 [ADD] (7.97) ■ 46339 [DDD] (3.98)
I. Perlman (vn), E. Ormandy (cnd), Philadelphia Orch † Saint-Saëns:Intro & Rondo capriccioso, Op. 28; Chausson:Poème for Vn & Orch, Op. 25; Sarasate:Carmen Fantasy; Zigeunerweisen, Op. 20; Faurè:Berceuse for Vn, Op. 16; Ravel:Tzigane for Vn & Orch; Saint-Saëns:Havanaise for Vn & Orch, Op. 83; Sarasate:Caprice basque for Vn, Op. 24; Ysaÿe:Extase (poème No. 4); Wieniawski:Scherzo-tarantelle for Vn, Op. 16
 EMIC ▲ 47106 (16.97)
I. Perlman (vn), A. Wallenstein (cnd), London SO (*rec 1960s*) CHSK ▲ 12 (16.97)
I. Perlman (vn), A. Wallenstein (cnd), London SO † Andante cantabile; Capriccio italien, Op. 45; Marche slave, Op. 31 CHGR ▲ 9012 [DDD] (29.97)
R. Ricci (vn), K. Bakels (cnd), Polish National RSO Katowice (*rec June 1997*) ("Ricci: 70 Years of Performing") † Paganini:Con 1 Vn, M.S. 21 DYNC ▲ 203 [DDD] (17.97)
P. Rybar (vn), V. Desarzens (cnd), Vienna Festival Orch ("Mendelssohn & Tchaikovsky: The Great Violin Concertos") † Mendelssohn (-Bartholdy):Con Vn & Orch, Op. 64 DORO ▲ 4005 (16.97)
G. Shaham (vn), G. Sinopoli (cnd), Philharmonia Orch † Sibelius:Con Vn DEUT ▲ 37540 [DDD] (16.97)
T. Spivakovsky (vn), W. Goehr (cnd), London SO (*rec Walthamstow Assembly Hall London*) † Souvenir d'un lieu cher, Op. 42; Sibelius:Con Vn EVC ▲ 9035 [AAD] (13.97)
I. Stern (vn), L. Bernstein (cnd), New York PO (*rec Mar 3, 1975*) ("Leonard Bernstein: The Royal Edition") † Serenade Strs, Op. 48 SNYC ▲ 47637 [ADD] (16.97)
I. Stern (vn), E. Ormandy (cnd), Philadelphia Orch † Mendelssohn (-Bartholdy):Con Vn & Orch, Op. 64
 SNYC ▲ 36724 ■ 36724 (3.98)
I. Stern (vn), E. Ormandy (cnd), Philadelphia Orch † "Isaac Stern: A Life in Music") † Sibelius:Con Vn
 SNYC ▲ 66829 (19.97)
V. Tretyakov (vn), N. Järvi (cnd), Moscow PO (*rec Moscow, 1966*) ("Neeme Järvi: The Early Recordings, Vol. 2") † Paganini:Con 1 Vn, M.S. 21 MELD ▲ 40720 [ADD] (6.97)
E. Verhey (vn), A. Joó (cnd), Budapest SO † Con 1 Pno, Op. 23 LALI ▲ 15516 [DDD] (3.97)
E. Verhey (vn), A. Joó (cnd), Budapest SO † A. Dvořák:Con Vn VRDI ▲ 6804 (10.97)
M. Waiman (vn), G. Rozhdestvensky (cnd), Leningrad Orch † Sym 4 INMP (BBC Radio Classics) ▲ 9134 (13.97)
Xue-Wei (vn), S. Accardo (cnd), Philharmonia Orch † Souvenir d'un lieu cher, Op. 42; Sérénade mélancolique, Op. 26; Valse-Scherzo Vn, Op. 34 ASV ▲ 713 [DDD] (16.97)
P. Zukerman (vn), A. Dorati (cnd), London SO (*rec 1968*) † Con 1 Pno, Op. 23 SNYC ▲ 46268 [ADD] (7.97)
various artists † J. S. Bach:Sons & Partitas Vn; Beethoven:Son 9 Vn, Op. 47; Mendelssohn (-Bartholdy):Con Vn & Orch, Op. 64; W. A. Mozart:Con 1 Vn, K.216; Tartini:Son Vn & Pno MTAL ▲ 48099 (6.97)

Duets
E. Söderström (sop), K. Meyer (mez), J. Eyron (pno)—Dawn, Op. 46/6; Tears, Op. 46/3; In the Garden, near the Ford, Op. 46/4 (*rec Nacka, Sweden, Nov 1 & 3, 1974*) ("Elisabeth Söderström & Kerstin Meyer") † A. Dvořák:Moravian Duets, Opp. 20, 32, 38; Songs; Kodály:Songs; H. Purcell:Come, ye sons of art, away, Z.323; Indian Queen (sels); King Arthur (sels); G. Rossini:Soirées musicales; Songs; Wennerberg:Songs BIS ▲ 17 [AAD] (17.97)

Dumka: Russian Rustic Scene for Piano, Op. 59 (1886)
J. Heifetz (pno) † Morceaux (6) Pno, Op. 19; S. Prokofiev:Son 3 Pno, Op. 28; Toccata Pno, Op. 11; S. Rachmaninoff:Moments musicaux, Op. 16; Morceaux de fant, Op. 3 SO ▲ 22562 (16.97)
K. Jordan (pno) (*rec Waco, TX, Jan 16-20, 1995*) ("Slavic Masterpieces for Piano") † S. Rachmaninoff:Preludes Pno; R. Shchedrin:Pno Music (misc colls); Smetana:Pno Music (misc colls); Szymanowski:Metopes, Op. 29; P. Vladigerov:Pno Music (misc colls) ALBA ▲ 203 [DDD] (16.97)
D. Paperno (pno) (*rec 1980-95*) ("Paperno Live") † J. Brahms:Intermezzos (3) Pno, Op. 117; J. Haydn:Sonatas for Piano; Liszt:Années de pèlerinage 2, S.161; Trans, Arrs & Paraphrases; Medtner:Forgotten Melodies 1, Op. 38; S. Rachmaninoff:Moments musicaux, Op. 16; R. Schumann:Bunte Blätter, Op. 99 CED ▲ 44 [DDD] (16.97)

Elegy in G for Strings (1884)
L. Markiz (cnd), Amsterdam New Sinfonietta (*rec 1990*) † Andante cantabile; Nocturne Vc; Serenade Strs, Op. 48; Arensky:Vars on a Theme of Tchaikovsky GLOE ▲ 6021 [DDD] (16.97)
M. Rachlevsky (cnd), Kremlin CO (*rec Moscow Conservatory Great Hall, Oct-Nov 1991*) ("Music for Strings, Vol. 1") † Qt 1 Strs, Op. 11; Serenade Strs, Op. 48; Souvenir d'un lieu cher, Op. 42 CLAV ▲ 9116 [DDD] (16.97)
J. Serebrier (cnd), Scottish CO † Serenade Strs, Op. 48; Sleeping Beauty (sels); Suite 4 Orch, Op. 61
 ASV ▲ 719 [DDD] (16.97)

Eugene Onegin (opera in 3 acts) [lib Tchaikovsky & Konstantin Shilovsky after Pushkin], Op. 24 (1879)
V. Bak (sop—Tatjana), H. Töpper (mez—Olga), A. Dermota (ten—Lenski), F. Klarwein (ten—Triquet), G. London (b-bar—Eugene), G. Frick (bass—Fürst Gremin), R. Kraus (cnd), Bavarian State Orch, Bavarian Radio Chorus (*rec Munich, 1954*) † G. Mahler:Kindertotenlieder MYTO 2-▲ 00311 (34.97)
L. Chernikh (sop), T. Sinyavskaya (mez), Y. Mazurok (bar), A. Vedernikov (bass), A. Fedin (sgr), V. Fedoseyev (cnd), Moscow SO, V. Fedoseyev (cnd), USSR SO, V. Fedoseyev (cnd), Fernseh SO APC (Legacy Collection) 2-▲ 101751
N. Focile (sop), S. Walker (mez), I. Arkhipova (mez), F. Egerton (ten), D. Hvorostovsky (bar), S. Bychkov (cnd), Orch de Paris PPHI 2-▲ 38235 (32.97)
B. Khaikin (cnd), Bolshoi Theater Orch, Bolshoi Theater Chorus, G. Vishnevskaya (sop), E. Belov (bar), I. Petrov (bass) ODRO 2-▲ 1197 (9.97)
J. Levine (cnd), Dresden Staatskapelle, Leipzig Radio Chorus, M. Freni (sop), A. S. von Otter (mez), N. Shicoff (ten), T. Allen (bar), P. Burchuladze (bass) DEUT 2-▲ 23959 [DDD] (32.97)
A. Tomowa-Sintow (sop), R. Troeva-Mircheva (cta), N. Gedda (ten), Y. Mazurok (bar), N. Ghiuselev (bass), E. Tchakarov (cnd), Sofia Festival Orch, Sofia National Opera Chorus [RUS] SNYC 2-▲ 45539 (32.97)

Eugene Onegin (selections)
J. Banowetz (pno), O. Lenárd (cnd), Czech RSO (*rec Czechoslovak Radio Concert Hall, Bratislava, Czech Republic, 1988*) ("Famous Piano Concertos") † Con 1 Pno, Op. 23; Tempest, Op. 18; Beethoven:Con 5 Pno, Op. 73; Chopin:Con 1 Pno, Op. 11; Con 2 Pno, Op. 21; S. Rachmaninoff:Con 2 Pno, Op. 18; Rhap on a Theme of Paganini, Op. 43 NXIN 4-▲ 504011 [DDD] (19.97)
T. Beecham (cnd), London PO ("Beecham & London PO, 1944-45, Vol. 3") † Berlioz:Troyens (sels); Borodin:Prince Igor (ov); Mendelssohn (-Bartholdy):Sym 5; Rimsky-Korsakov:May Night (ov) BCS ▲ 43 (16.97)
J. Björling (ten), N. Grevillius (cnd), Gothenburg SO—Faint echo of my youth (Lensky's Aria) † Concert Hall Göteborg, Sweden, Aug 5, 1960) ("Jussi Björling's Last Concert") † Alfvén:Songs; Leoncavallo:Pagliacci (sels); G. Puccini:Manon Lescaut (sels); Sibelius:Songs; Verdi:Rigoletto (sels); Trovatore (sels); R. Wagner:Lohengrin (sels) MYTO ▲ 953130 (17.97)
J. Carden (sop), R. Brydon (cnd), Queensland PO † Letter Scene (Let me perish) (*rec 1996*) ("Great Opera Heroines") † B. Britten:Peter Grimes (sels); A. Catalani:Wally (sels); W. A. Mozart:Clemenza di Tito (sels); Cosi fan tutte (sels); G. Puccini:Arias; Verdi:Traviata (sels) WALC ▲ 8026 (16.97)
C. von Dohnányi (cnd), Cleveland Orch † Sym 6 TEL ▲ 80130 (16.97)
P. Domingo (ten), R. Behr (cnd), Philharmonia Orch—Faint echo of my youth (Lensky's Aria) † Capriccio italien, Op. 45; Ov 1812, Op. 49; Romeo & Juliet; Songs (6), Op. 6 CSER (Seraphim) ▲ 73297 [DDD] (6.97)
A. Dorati (cnd), London SO—Waltz; Polonaise † Marche slave, Op. 31; Sym 5 MRCR ▲ 34305 [ADD] (11.97)
A. Carley (sop), J. Serebrier (cnd), Melbourne SO—Letter Scene ("An Evening of Concert Favourites") † Con 1 Pno, Op. 23; Marche slave, Op. 31; Ov 1812, Op. 49 INMP (Concert Classics) ▲ 1102 (9.97)
A. Fiedler (cnd), Boston Pops Orch ("Pops Caviar, Russian Orchestral Fireworks") † Sleeping Beauty (sels); Borodin:In the Steppes of Central Asia; Prince Igor (ov); Prince Igor (sels); E. Elgar:Pomp & Circumstance, Op. 39; A. Khachaturian:Gayane (sels); Masquerade (sels); Rimsky-Korsakov:Russian Easter Overture, Op. 36 RCAV (Living Stereo) ▲ 68132 (11.97)
E. Hannan (sop), S. Edwards (cnd), London PO—Letter Scene (Let me perish) † Sym 5
 CFP (Eminence) ▲ 2187 [DDD] (16.97)
H. Hollreiser (cnd), Bamberg SO † Capriccio italien, Op. 45; Nutcracker (sels); Sleeping Beauty (suite), Op. 66a; Slippers; Souvenir d'un lieu cher, Op. 42; Swan Lake (suite), Op. 20a; Sérénade mélancolique, Op. 26a; Valse-Scherzo Vn, Op. 34; Vars on a Rococo Theme, Op. 33 VB3 3-▲ 3026 [ADD]
P. Koci (bar) † Beethoven:Fidelio (sels); Janáček:From the House of the Dead (sels); W. A. Mozart:Don Giovanni (sels); G. Rossini:Barbiere di Siviglia (sels); Smetana:Kiss (sels); Secret (sels); R. Wagner:Fliegende Holländer (sels); Tannhäuser (sels) GZCL ▲ 303 (6.97)
S. Larin (ten), G. Rozhdestvensky (cnd), Philharmonia Orch, J. McCarthy (cnd), Ambrosian Opera Chorus (*rec London, England, Aug 14-17, 1997*) ("Russian Arias, Vol. 1") † Mazeppa (sels); Queen of Spades (sels); Slippers (sels); Borodin:Prince Igor (sels); Dargomizhsky:Ruslan and Lyudmila (sels); M. Glinka:Ruslan & Ludmilla (sels); S. Rachmaninoff:Boris Godunov (sels); Rimsky-Korsakov:May Night (sels); Sadko (sels) [FRE,GER,RUS,ENG] lib text) CHN ▲ 9603 [DDD] (16.97)
A. Lazarev (cnd), Bolshoi Theater SO—Waltz; Polonaise † Capriccio italien, Op. 45; Nutcracker (suite), Op. 71a; Sleeping Beauty (suite), Op. 66a; Swan Lake (suite), Op. 20a TELC (Ultima) 2-▲ 18965 (16.97)
L. Lehmann (sop) ("Lotte Lehmann in Opera Vol. 1") † W. A. Mozart:Don Giovanni; O. Nicolai:Lustigen Weiber von Windsor (sels); A. Thomas:Mignon (sels); R. Wagner:Arias & Scenes; C. M. von Weber:Freischütz (sels); Oberon (sels)
 NIMB ▲ 7873 [ADD] (11.97)

Eugene Onegin (selections) (cont.)
T. Lemnitz (sop), A. Rother (cnd), Berlin RSO [GER] (*rec 1946*) † W. A. Mozart:Nozze di Figaro (sels); Zauberflöte (sels); R. Strauss:Arabella (sels); Rosenkavalier (sels); Verdi:Trovatore (sels); R. Wagner:Lohengrin (sels); C. M. von Weber:Freischütz (sels) BER (Documents) ▲ 9014 (m) [ADD] (16.97)
O. Lenárd (cnd), Czech-Slovak RSO Bratislava—Waltz; Polonaise (*rec 1988*) † Con 1 Pno, Op. 23; Tempest, Op. 18 NXIN ▲ 550137 [DDD] (5.97)
E. Lindermeier (sop), R. Kempe (cnd), Berlin PO, Berlin German Opera Chorus † Sym 5 TES ▲ 1100 (17.97)
M. Maisky (vc), Orpheus CO—Faint echo of my youth (Lensky's Aria) (*rec Recital Hall NY State Univ, Purchase, NY, Apr 1996*) † Andante cantabile; Nocturne Vc; Souvenir of Florence, Op. 70; Vars on a Rococo Theme, Op. 33 DEUT ▲ 453460 [DDD] (16.97)
U. Mayer (cnd), Edmonton SO (*rec Sherwood Park Alberta, Mar 21-23, 1992*) ("Russian Sketches") † Sleeping Beauty (sels); Borodin:In the Steppes of Central Asia; Ippolitov-Ivanov:Caucasian Sketches, Op. 10; Rimsky-Korsakov:Golden Age Cockerel (suite); D. Shostakovich:Golden Age (ballet suite), Op. 22a SMS ▲ 5169 [DDD] (16.97)
E. Ormandy (cnd), Philadelphia Orch—Waltz; Polonaise † Capriccio italien, Op. 45; Sym 4
 SNYC (Essential Classics) ▲ 47657 (7.97) ■ 47657 (3.98)
E. Ormandy (cnd), Philadelphia Orch—Waltz; Polonaise † Capriccio italien, Op. 45; Ov Con Vn; Marche slave, Op. 31; Ov 1812, Op. 49; Romeo & Juliet; Sym 5 SNYC (Essential Classics Take 2) 2-▲ 63281 (14.97)
A. Pendachanska (sop), N. Ghiaurov (bass), L. Diakovski (sgr), N. Isakov (sgr), Bulgarian National Chorus ("Eugene Onegin Opera Highlights") LALI ▲ 14210 [DDD] (16.97)
B. R. Stees (bn), S. Norris (hp), R. Fusco (pno) [trans for bn, hp & pno] † Donizetti:Elisir d'amore (sels); Lucia di Lammermoor (sels); Hérold:Zampa (ov); W. A. Mozart:Entführung aus dem Serail (sels); G. Rossini:Gazza ladra (sels); Verdi:Trovatore (sels); R. Wagner:Tannhäuser (sels) CLAV ▲ 509815 (16.97)
L. Tjeknavorian (cnd), Armenian PO—Waltz; Polonaise ("A Night on Bare Mountain & Other Russian Favorites") † Romeo & Juliet; Borodin:In the Steppes of Central Asia; Prince Igor (Polovtsian Dances); M. Glinka:Russlan & Ludmilla (ov); Mussorgsky:Night on Bare Mountain; D. Shostakovich:Festive Ov, Op. 96 ASVO ▲ 6180 (13.97)
R. Vargas (ten), M. Viotti (cnd), Munich Radio Orch—Wohin seid ihr entschwunden ("L'amour l'amour") † Donizetti:Arias; Gounod:Roméo et Juliette (sels); Massenet:Manon (sels); Werther (sels); G. Puccini:Bohème (sels); Verdi:Ballo in maschera (sels); Rigoletto (sels) RCAV ▲ 61464 (16.97)
D. Zinman (cnd), Baltimore SO (*rec Baltimore, MD, Nov 22, 1990*) ("Russian Sketches") † Francesca da Rimini, Op. 32; M. Glinka:Russlan & Ludmilla (ov); Ippolitov-Ivanov:Caucasian Sketches, Op. 10; Rimsky-Korsakov:Russian Easter Overture, Op. 36 TEL ▲ 80378 [DDD] (16.97)
various artists—Polonaise † Marche slave, Op. 31; Nutcracker (sels); Ov 1812, Op. 49; Qt 1 Strs, Op. 11; Serenade Strs, Op. 48; Swan Lake (sels); Sym 6 RCAV ▲ 60845 (11.97) ■ 60845 (5.98)
various artists—Letter Scene (Let me perish) † Borodin:Prince Igor (sels); Delibes:Lakmé (sels); P. Mascagni:Cavalleria rusticana (sels); G. Puccini:Turandot (sels); Verdi:Aida (sels); Nabucco (sels); Traviata (sels); R. Wagner:Lohengrin (preludes) HALM ▲ 35029 (6.97)

Fatum (symphonic poem) in c for Orchestra, Op. 77 (1868; destroyed by Tchaikovsky, reconstructed 1896)
A. Doráti (cnd), National SO Washington DC (*rec 1974*) † Capriccio italien, Op. 45; Francesca da Rimini, Op. 32; Hamlet; Marche slave, Op. 31; Ov 1812, Op. 49; Romeo & Juliet; Tempest, Op. 18; Voyevoda, Op. 78
 PLON 2-▲ 43003 [ADD] (17.97)
V. Dudarova (cnd), Russian SO † Capriccio italien, Op. 45; Festival Ov, Op. 15; Francesca da Rimini, Op. 32; Hamlet; Ov 1812, Op. 49; Romeo & Juliet; Tempest, Op. 18 OLY ▲ 512 (16.97)
N. Järvi (cnd), Detroit SO † Storm; Suite 1 Orch, Op. 43 CHN ▲ 9587 (16.97)
M. Pletnev (cnd), Russian National Orch † Ov 1812, Op. 49; Sym 2 DGRM ▲ 453446 [DDD]

Festival Coronation March in D for Orchestra (1883; arr Piano 4-Hands, 1883)
L. Botstein (cnd), American Russian Youth Orch (*rec Tanglewood, MA, June 1997*) ("10th Anniversary: American Russian Youth Orchestra in Concert") † Griffes:Pleasure Dome of Kubla Khan, Op. 8; C. Ives:Washington's Birthday; Paine:As You Like It, Op. 28 TOWN ▲ 53 (17.97)
N. Järvi (cnd), Royal Scottish National Orch † S. Rachmaninoff:Bells; Vocalise; S. Taneyev:Duet for Romeo & Juliet CHN ▲ 8476 [DDD] (16.97)
N. Järvi (cnd), Scottish National Orch (*rec 1988*) ("Russian Masterpieces") † Glazunov:Seasons, Op. 67; A. Khachaturian:Gayane (sels); S. Prokofiev:Love for 3 Oranges (march), Op. 33ter; Romeo & Juliet (sels); Scythian Suite, Op. 20; Rimsky-Korsakov:Little Oak Stick, Op. 62; Mlada (procession); Scheherazade, Op. 35; Tale of Tsar Saltan for Orch, Op. 57; D. Shostakovich:Festive Ov, Op. 96; I. Stravinsky:Firebird (sels) ([ENG,FRE,GER] text) CHN (Collect Series) ▲ 6511 [DDD] (12.97)

Festival Overture in D for Orchestra [on the Danish National Anthem], Op. 15 (1866; arr Piano 4-Hands, 1878)
V. Dudarova (cnd), Russian SO † Capriccio italien, Op. 45; Fatum; Francesca da Rimini, Op. 32; Hamlet; Ov 1812, Op. 49; Romeo & Juliet; Tempest, Op. 18 OLY ▲ 512 (16.97)
R. Llambias (pno), T. Leonskov (pno) † Sym 6 KPT ▲ 32204
M. Pletnev (cnd), Russian National Orch † Marche slave, Op. 31; Sym 1 DGRM ▲ 453445 [DDD] (16.97)
G. Simon (cnd), London SO † Romeo & Juliet; Serenade for N. Rubinstein CHN 2-▲ 8310 (33.97)
G. Simon (cnd), London SO † Serenade for N. Rubinstein CHN ▲ 9190 [DDD] (16.97)

Francesca da Rimini (symphonic fantasy) in e for Orchestra [after Dante], Op. 32 (1876)
D. Barenboim (cnd), Chicago SO † Capriccio italien, Op. 45; Ov 1812, Op. 49; Romeo & Juliet
 DEUT (Masters) ▲ 44523 [DDD] (9.97)
T. Beecham (cnd), London PO ("Beecham Favourites") † Bizet:Arlésienne; Chabrier:España; E. Grieg:Peer Gynt, Op. 23 DLAB (Essential Archives) ▲ 5017 (15.97)
L. Bernstein (cnd), New York PO † Sym 4 DEUT ▲ 29778 [DDD] (16.97)
A. Doráti (cnd), Minneapolis SO † Sym 4; Borodin:Prince Igor (ov) MRCR ▲ 34373 (11.97)
A. Doráti (cnd), National SO Washington D.C. (*rec 1973*) † Capriccio italien, Op. 45; Fatum; Hamlet; Marche slave, Op. 31; Ov 1812, Op. 49; Romeo & Juliet; Tempest, Op. 18; Voyevoda, Op. 78 PLON 2-▲ 43003 [ADD] (17.97)
V. Dudarova (cnd), Russian SO † Capriccio italien, Op. 45; Fatum; Festival Ov, Op. 15; Hamlet; Ov 1812, Op. 49; Romeo & Juliet; Tempest, Op. 18 OLY ▲ 512 (16.97)
S. Edwards (cnd), Royal Liverpool PO † Marche slave, Op. 31; Ov 1812, Op. 49; Romeo & Juliet
 CFP (Eminence) ▲ 2152 [DDD] (16.97)
V. Fedoseyev (cnd), Ostankino Radio-TV Large SO (*rec 1990-91*) † Romeo & Juliet; Tempest, Op. 18; Voyevoda, Op. 78 CSN ▲ 815000 [DDD] (12.97)
N. Järvi (cnd), Detroit SO † Suite 3 Orch, Op. 55 CHN ▲ 9419 (16.97)
I. Markevitch (cnd), London PO † Sym 2; Sym 3 PPHI (Two-Fers) 2-▲ 46148 (17.97)
K. Masur (cnd), Leipzig Gewandhaus Orch † Sym 1 TELC ▲ 44339 [DDD] (16.97)
E. Mravinsky (cnd), Leningrad PO † I. Stravinsky:Baiser de la fée RUS ▲ 11160 [ADD] (12.97)
E. Mravinsky (cnd), Leningrad PO (*rec 1948*) † Serenade Strs, Op. 48 RUS ▲ 15003 [AAD]
E. Mravinsky (cnd), Leningrad PO (*rec Russia, 1983*) † Nutcracker (sels) CONE ▲ 9410 [ADD] (16.97)
C. Munch (cnd), Royal PO (*rec 1963*) † Bizet:Sym CHSK ▲ 7 (16.97)
M. Pletnev (cnd), Russian National Orch † Sym 4 DGRM ▲ 453448 [DDD] (16.97)
A. Rahbari (cnd), Brussels BRTN PO † Sym 6 DI ▲ 920320 [DDD] (5.97)
L. Slatkin (cnd), St. Louis SO (*rec St. Louis, Nov 1991*) † Sym 1 RCAV (Red Seal) ▲ 68662 [DDD] (16.97)
L. Slovak (cnd), Bratislava RSO † A. Dvořák:Symphonic Vars, Op. 78(28) OPP ▲ 642
L. Stokowski (cnd), New York Stadium SO † Hamlet; A. Scriabin:Poème de l'extase, Op. 54
 EVC ▲ 9037 [AAD] (13.97)
E. Svetlanov (cnd), USSR SO (*rec Moscow, 1967-70*) † Sym 1; Sym 2; Sym 3 MELD (2fer) 2-▲ 34163 [ADD] (13.97)
A. Wit (cnd), Polish National RSO Katowice † Polish Radio Concert Hall Katowice, Mar 28-Apr 1, 1993 ("Famous Symphonies: Beethoven, Tchaikovsky, Brahms, Schubert") † Sym 8; J. Brahms:Academic Festival Ov, Op. 80; Sym 4; Tragic Ov, Op. 81; F. Schubert:Sym 9 NXIN 4-▲ 504012 [DDD] (19.97)
A. Wit (cnd), Polish National RSO Katowice † The Maid of Orleans NXIN ▲ 550782 [DDD] (5.97)
D. Zinman (cnd), Baltimore SO (*rec Baltimore, MD, Jan 23, 1990*) ("Russian Sketches") † Eugene Onegin; M. Glinka:Russlan & Ludmilla (ov); Ippolitov-Ivanov:Caucasian Sketches, Op. 10; Rimsky-Korsakov:Russian Easter Overture, Op. 36 TEL ▲ 80378 [DDD] (16.97)

Hamlet (fantasy overture) in f for Orchestra [after Shakespeare], Op. 67 (1888)
M. Abravanel (cnd), Utah SO ("Complete Orchestral Music, Vol. 3") † Romeo & Juliet; Sym 2; Sym 4
 VB2 2-▲ 5006 [ADD]
J. DePreist (cnd), Oregon Ov † Ov 1812, Op. 49; Tempest, Op. 18 DLS ▲ 3081 [DDD] (14.97)
A. Doráti (cnd), National SO Washington D.C. (*rec 1973*) † Capriccio italien, Op. 45; Fatum; Francesca da Rimini, Op. 32; Marche slave, Op. 31; Ov 1812, Op. 49; Romeo & Juliet; Tempest, Op. 18; Voyevoda, Op. 78
 PLON 2-▲ 43003 [ADD] (17.97)
V. Dudarova (cnd), Russian SO † Capriccio italien, Op. 45; Fatum; Festival Ov, Op. 15; Francesca da Rimini, Op. 32; Ov 1812, Op. 49; Romeo & Juliet; Tempest, Op. 18 OLY ▲ 512 (16.97)
A. Leaper (cnd), Polish National RSO Katowice (*rec Concert Hall of the Polish Radio Katowice, Sept 7-12, 1991*) ("Fantasias after Shakespeare") † Romeo & Juliet; Tempest, Op. 18 NXIN ▲ 553017 [DDD] (5.97)
M. Pletnev (cnd), Russian National Orch † Sym 5 DGRM ▲ 453449 [DDD] (18.97)

TCHAIKOVSKY, PIOTR (cont.)

Hamlet (fantasy overture) in f for Orchestra [after Shakespeare], Op. 67 (1888) (cont.)

L. Stokowski (cnd), New York Stadium SO † Francesca da Rimini, Op. 32; A. Scriabin:Poème de l'extase, Op. 54 EVC ▲ 9037 [AAD] (13.97)

Hymn to Sts. Cyril & Methodius for Chorus (1885)

A. Sveshnikov (cnd), USSR State Academic Choir *(rec 1966)* † Vesper Service, Op. 52 CSN ▲ 815003 [AAD/ADD] (12.97)

Iolanta (lyric opera in 1 act) [lib M. Tchaikovsky], Op. 69 (1891)

G. Gorchakova (sop), L. Diadkova (mez), N. Gassiev (ten), G. Grigorian (ten), N. Putilin (bar), D. Hvorostovsky (bar), G. Bezzubenkov (bass), S. Alexashkin (bass), O. Korzhenskaya (sgr), T. Kravtsova (sgr), V. Gergiev (cnd), Kirov Theater Orch, Kirov Theater Chorus *(rec Mariinsky Theatre St. Petersburg)* PPHI 2-▲ 42796 (32.97)

M. Gurevich (sop—Iolanta), J. Miura (sop—Brigitta), T. Tabachuk (mez—Martha), A. Kuhn (mez—Laura), I. Denolfo (ten—Godefroy), K. A. Bolves (ten—Alméric), G. Lehner (bar—Ibn-Hakia), A. Ben (bar—Robert), A. Kotchinian (bass—René), K. Geysen (bass—Bertrand), H. Rotman (cnd), Warsaw PO, ECOV Ensemble members *(rec Ghent Belgium, Aug 28-29, 1993)* CPO 2-▲ 999456 [DDD] (13.97)

E. Kudriavcenko (sop—Iolanta), N. Larionova (sop), T. Erastova (mez), M. Sciutova (mez), T. Erastova (mez—Martha), V. Taraschenko (ten), O. Bektemirov (ten), I. Morozov (bar), V. Redchin (bar), I. Morozov (bar—Robert), V. Redchin (bar—Ibn Hakia), M. Mikhailov (bass), G. Seleznev (bass), G. Seleznev (bass—King René), V. Delman (cnd), Milan RAI Orch, V. Delman (cnd), Milan RAI SO, Milan RAI Chorus *(rec Dec 1989)* BMGR 2-▲ 2017 [DDD] (36.97)

Legend (When Jesus Christ Was But a Child) (song), Op. 54/5

P. Pears (ten), B. Britten (cnd), English CO *(rec 1962)* † Nocturne Vc; Serenade Strs, Op. 48; Suite 4 Orch, Op. 61 BBC (Britten the Performer) ▲ 8002 (17.97)

Liturgy of St. John Chrysostom for Chorus, Op. 41 (1879)

M. Best (cnd), Corydon Singers † Sacred Pieces HYP ▲ 66948 (18.97)

N. Korniev (cnd), St. Petersburg Chamber Choir PPHI ▲ 446685 (16.97)

V. Polianski (cnd), USSR Ministry of Culture Chamber Choir MELD (Russian Choral Music) ▲ 25186 [DDD] (6.97)

Manfred (symphony) in b for Orchestra [after Byron], Op. 58 (1885)

E. Goossens (cnd), London SO *(rec Walthamstow Assembly Hall London)* † Sibelius:Tapiola EVC ▲ 9025 [AAD] (13.97)

K. Koizumi (cnd), Royal PO RPO ▲ 7020 [DDD] (13.97)

R. Leppard (cnd), Indianapolis SO KOSS ▲ 2216 (17.97)

M. Pletnev (cnd), Russian National Orch † Tempest, Op. 18 DEUT ▲ 39891 [DDD] (16.97)

A. Previn (cnd), London SO *(rec 1974)* † Marche slave, Op. 31; Romeo & Juliet; S. Rachmaninoff:Sym 2 EMIC (Doublefforte) 2-▲ 69776 [ADD] (16.97)

C. Silvestri (cnd), Bournemouth SO *(rec 1963)* † O. Respighi:Pini di Roma BBC ▲ 4007 (17.97)

C. Silvestri (cnd), Philharmonia Orch † Liszt:Tasso—Lamento e Trionfo, S.96 TES ▲ 1129 (17.97)

Marche slave in B♭ for Orchestra, Op. 31 (1876)

C. Abbado (cnd), Chicago SO SNYC ▲ 42368 [DDD] (11.97)

C. Abbado (cnd), Chicago SO † Ov 1812, Op. 49; Romeo & Juliet; Tempest, Op. 18 SNYC ▲ 47179 (11.97)

Y. Ahronovitch (cnd), London SO ("Tchaikovsky Spectacular") † Ov 1812, Op. 49; Romeo & Juliet INMP (LSO Classic Masterpieces) ▲ 801 [DDD] (9.97)

J. Barbirolli (cnd) † Qt 1 Strs, Op. 11; Romeo & Juliet; Serenade Strs, Op. 48; Sym 4; Sym 5; Sym 6 RYLC 3-▲ 70403 (20.97)

L. Bernstein (cnd), New York PO SNYC ▲ 36723 (9.97)

L. Bernstein (cnd), New York PO *(rec Jan 21, 1963)* ("Leonard Bernstein: The Royal Edition") † Ov 1812, Op. 49; Sym 5 SNYC ▲ 47634 [ADD] (10.97)

A. Dorati (cnd), Detroit SO † Ov 1812, Op. 49; Romeo & Juliet PLON ▲ 17742 [ADD] (9.97)

A. Doráti (cnd), Detroit SO *(rec 1978)* † Capriccio italien, Op. 45; Fatum; Francesca da Rimini, Op. 32; Hamlet; Ov 1812, Op. 49; Romeo & Juliet; Tempest, Op. 18; Voyevoda, Op. 78 PLON 2-▲ 43003 [ADD] (17.97)

A. Dorati (cnd), London SO † Eugene Onegin (sels); Sym 5 MRCR ▲ 34305 [ADD] (11.97)

C. Dutoit (cnd), Montreal SO † Ov 1812, Op. 49 PLON ▲ 17300 [DDD] (16.97)

S. Edwards (cnd), Royal Liverpool PO † Francesca da Rimini, Op. 32; Ov 1812, Op. 49; Romeo & Juliet CFP (Eminence) ▲ 2152 [DDD] (16.97)

A. Fischer (cnd), Hungarian State Orch † Sym 5 LALI ▲ 15620 [DDD] (3.97)

A. Fischer (cnd), Hungarian State Orch † Souvenir d'un lieu cher, Op. 42; Sym 6 LALI ▲ 15821 [DDD] (3.97)

M. Freccia (cnd), London PO † Andante cantabile; Capriccio italien, Op. 45; Con Vn CHGR ▲ 9012 [DDD] (29.97)

F. Hohman (org) *(rec Augustana Lutheran Church Denver, CO, 1991)* † Romance Pno, Op. 5; Romeo & Juliet; Sym 5 PROO ▲ 7012 [DDD]

H. Ishimaru (cnd), Tokyo Metropolitan SO † Sym 6 DNN ▲ 8085 [DDD]

V. Kahi (cnd), Georgian Festival Orch † Sym 5 SNYC ▲ 57242 [DDD] (4.97)

V. Kahi (cnd), Georgian Festival Orch ("The Tchaikovsky Album") † Capriccio italien, Op. 45; Ov 1812, Op. 49; Romeo & Juliet SNYC ▲ 61978 [DDD] (4.97)

K. Labèque (pno), M. Labèque (pno) [arr A. Batalin] *(rec London, UK, May 14-19, 1994)* † Capriccio italien, Op. 45; A. Scriabin:Fant Pnos PPHI ▲ 42778 (16.97)

N. Nozy (cnd), Belgian Guides Symphonic Band [trans F. Rogister] † Ov 1812, Op. 49; Romeo & Juliet RENE ▲ 87048 [DDD] (16.97)

E. Ormandy (cnd), Philadelphia Orch † Ov 1812, Op. 49; Sym 4 SNYC (Essential Classics) ▲ 46334 [ADD] (7.97) ▮ 46334 [ADD] (3.98)

E. Ormandy (cnd), Philadelphia Orch † Capriccio italien, Op. 45; Ov 1812, Op. 49 RCAV (Silver Seal) ▲ 60492 [ADD] (6.97)

E. Ormandy (cnd), Philadelphia Orch † Capriccio italien, Op. 45; Con Vn; Eugene Onegin (sels); Ov 1812, Op. 49; Romeo & Juliet; Sym 5 SNYC (Essential Classics Take 2) 2-▲ 63281 (14.97)

M. Pletnev (cnd), Russian National Orch † Festival Ov, Op. 15; Sym 1 DGRM ▲ 453445 [DDD] (18.97)

A. Previn (cnd), London SO *(rec 1973)* † Manfred, Op. 58; Romeo & Juliet; S. Rachmaninoff:Sym 2 EMIC (Doublefforte) 2-▲ 69776 [ADD] (16.97)

G. Rozhdestvensky (cnd), London SO † Sym 4 INMP ▲ 867 [DDD] (9.97)

G. Rozhdestvensky (cnd), London SO ("An Evening of Concert Favourites") † Con 1 Pno, Op. 23; Eugene Onegin (sels); Ov 1812, Op. 49 INMP (Concert Classics) ▲ 1102 (9.97)

L. Stokowski (cnd) *(rec 1934-44)* ("Stokowski Conducts Tchaikovsky") † Romeo & Juliet; Sleeping Beauty (suite), Op. 66a; Sym 5 GRM2 2-▲ 78713 (26.97)

L. Stokowski (cnd) † Romeo & Juliet; Songs; G. F. Handel:Messiah (sels) IMMM ▲ 37031 (6.97)

L. Stokowski (cnd), Hollywood Bowl SO *(rec 1945-46)* † Sym 6; S. Rachmaninoff:Isle of the Dead, Op. 29 PHS ▲ 9261 (17.97)

L. Stokowski (cnd), NBC SO *(rec Apr 23, 1942)* ("Stokowski Conducts Tchaikovsky") † Romeo & Juliet; Sym 5 IN ▲ 1367 [ADD] (15.97)

various artists † Eugene Onegin (sels); Nutcracker (sels); Ov 1812, Op. 49; Qt 1 Strs, Op. 11; Serenade Strs, Op. 48; Swan Lake (sels); Sym 6 RCAV ▲ 60845 (11.97) ▮ 60845 (5.98)

Mazeppa (opera in 3 acts) [lib Victor Burenin] (1883)

L. Diadkova (mez—Ljubov), N. Gassiev (ten—Drunken Cossack), N. Putilin (bar—Mazeppa), S. Alexashkin (bass—Vasilij Kocubej), I. Loskutova (sgr—Maria), V. Luhanin (sgr—Orlik), V. Lutsiuk (sgr—Andrei), V. Zhivopistsev (sgr—Iskra), V. Gergiev (cnd), Kirov Opera Orch, Kirov Opera Chorus PPHI 3-▲ 462206 (48.97)

N. Järvi (cnd), Gothenburg SO, Stockholm Royal Opera Chorus, G. Gorchakova (sop), L. Dyadkova (mez), S. Larin (ten), S. Leiferkus (bar), A. Kotscherga (bass) DEUT 3-▲ 39906 [DDD] (48.97)

N. Mitic (bar), Cangalovic (sgr), Bakocevic (sgr), Cakarevic (sgr), O. Danon (cnd), Belgrade National Opera Orch, Belgrade National Opera Chorus [RUS] *(rec live Berlin, Sept 27, 1969)* MYTO 2-▲ 90527 [ADD] (34.97)

Mazeppa (selections)

S. Larin (ten), G. Rozhdestvensky (cnd), Philharmonia Orch, J. McCarthy (cnd), Ambrosian Opera Chorus *(rec London, England, Aug 14-17, 1997)* ("Russian Arias, Vol. 1") † Eugene Onegin (sels); Queen of Spades (sels); Slippers (sels); Borodin:Prince Igor (sels); Dargomyzhsky:Ruslan and Lyudmila (sels); M. Glinka:Russlan & Ludmilla (sels); S. Rachmaninoff:Boris Godunov (sels); Rimsky-Korsakov:May Night (sels); Sadko (sels) *([FRE,GER,RUS,ENG] lib text)* CHN ▲ 9603 [DDD] (16.97)

Morceaux (2) for Piano, Op. 10 (1871)

D. Golub (pno) *(rec Purchase Conservatory of Music Recital Hall, Sept 14-16, 1996)* ("Humoresque") † A. Dvořák:Humoresques, Op. 101; S. Rachmaninoff:Morceaux de salon, Op. 10; R. Schumann:Humoreske Pno, Op. 20; J. Suk:Humoreska ARA ▲ 6706 [DDD] (16.97)

Morceaux (6) for Piano, Op. 19 (1873)

A. Gavrilov (pno) † Balakirev:Islamey; S. Rachmaninoff:Études-tableaux Pno; Morceaux de fant, Op. 3; Pno Music (misc colls); Preludes Pno RYLC ▲ 6471

I. Heifetz (pno)—No. 4, Nocturne in c# † Dumka; S. Prokofiev:Son 3 Pno, Op. 28; Toccata Pno, Op. 11; S. Rachmaninoff:Moments musicaux, Op. 16; Morceaux de fant, Op. 3 SO ▲ 22562 (16.97)

TCHAIKOVSKY, PIOTR (cont.)

Morceaux (6) for Piano, Op. 19 (1873) (cont.)

I. Heifetz (pno) ("The Maiden's Wish") † Album pour enfants Pno, Op. 39; Liszt:Pno Music (misc); Trans, Arrs & Paraphrases; S. Prokofiev:Pno Music (misc colls); S. Rachmaninoff:Moments musicaux, Op. 16 SO ▲ 22565 [DDD] (16.97)

I. Prunyi (pno)—No. 4, Nocturne in c# *(rec Budapest, Hungary, July 13-14, 1988)* † Morceaux (12) Pno, Op. 40; Saisons; Souvenir de Hapsal, Op. 2 NXIN ▲ 550233 [DDD] (5.97)

S. Z. Rutstein (pno)—No. 4, Nocturne in c# ("Rutstein Plays Russian Piano Music") † Morceaux (12) Pno, Op. 40; A. Scriabin:Dances (2) Pno, Op. 73; Preludes (4) Pno, Op. 22; Son 4 Pno, Op. 30; Slonimsky:Choreographic Miniatures; Tishchenko:Son 9 Pno, Op. 114 ALBA ▲ 279 [DDD] (16.97)

Morceaux (12) for Piano, Op. 40 (1879)

B. Moiseiwitsch (pno)—No. 2, Chanson triste in g *(rec 1945)* † Con 1 Pno, Op. 23; Con 2 Pno, Op. 44 APR ▲ 5518 [ADD] (18.97)

I. Prunyi (pno)—No. 2, Chanson triste in g; No. 6, Chant sans paroles *(rec Budapest, Hungary, July 13-14, 1988)* † Morceaux (6) Pno, Op. 19; Saisons; Souvenir de Hapsal, Op. 2 NXIN ▲ 550233 [DDD] (5.97)

S. Z. Rutstein (pno) ("Rutstein Plays Russian Piano Music") † Morceaux (6) Pno, Op. 19; A. Scriabin:Dances (2) Pno, Op. 73; Preludes (4) Pno, Op. 22; Son 4 Pno, Op. 30; Slonimsky:Choreographic Miniatures; Tishchenko:Son 9 Pno, Op. 114 ALBA ▲ 279 [DDD] (16.97)

L. Stokowski (cnd), Philadelphia Orch—No. 6, Chant sans paroles [orchd] ("Stokowski Conducts Tchaikovsky") † Ov 1812, Op. 49; Sym 5 BCS ▲ 15 (16.97)

Morceaux (6) for Piano, Op. 51 (1882)

S. Richter (pno) ("Classic Richter") † Saisons; Beethoven:Son 27 Pno, Op. 90; Chopin:Scherzos Pno; S. Rachmaninoff:Preludes Pno; F. Schubert:Son Pno, D.625; R. Schumann:Novelettes, Op. 21 OLY ▲ 580 [ADD] (16.97)

O. Yablonskaya (pno) *(rec Santa Rosa, CA, May 12-13, 1994)* ("Piano Music, Vol. 1") † Son Pno, Op. 37 NXIN ▲ 553063 [DDD] (5.97)

Moscow [Moskva] (coronation cantata) for Mezzo-Soprano, Baritone, Orchestra & Chorus (1883)

A. Litton (cnd), Dallas SO, Dallas Sym Chorus, S. Furdui (mez), V. Gerello (bar) *(rec Meyerson Center Dallas, TX, Nov 16-18, 1995)* † Ov 1812, Op. 49; Sleeping Beauty (sels); Voyevoda, Op. 78 DLS (Virtual Reality Recording) ▲ 3196 [DDD] (14.97)

Music of Tchaikovsky

S. Comissiona (cnd), Houston SO, S. Comissiona (cnd), London Promenade Orch—Capriccio italien, Op. 45; Nutcracker (sels); Ov 1812, Op. 49 ("Tchaikovsky's Greatest Hits") PRMX ▲ 809 (3.97)

J. Perlea (cnd), Bamberg SO *(Nutcracker Suite, Op. 71a)*, J. Perlea (cnd), Bamberg SO, E. V. Remoortel (cnd), Vienna SO *(Swan Lake (sels))*, E. V. Remoortel (cnd), Vienna SO *(Sleeping Beauty (sels) [Tempo di valse])*, M. Abravanel (cnd), Utah SO *(Sym 4, Op. 36 [Scherzo:Pizzicato ostinato, allegro]; Sym 5, Op. 64 [Andante cantabile, con alcuna licenza]; Ov 1812, Op. 49)*, E. V. Remoortel (cnd), Vienna Musikgesellschaft Orch *(Capriccio italien, Op. 45)*, E. Kunzel (cnd), Cincinnati Pops Orch *(Marche slave, Op. 31; Festival Coronation March; Eugene Onegin (sels) [Waltz])*, M. Ponti (pno) *(Saisons, Op. 37b [June:Barcarolle])*, F. Blumental (pno), M. Gielen (cnd), Vienna Musikgesellschaft Orch *(Con 1 Pno, Op. 23 [Andantino semplice])*, F. Blumental (pno), M. Gielen (cnd), Vienna Musikgesellschaft Orch, M. Munih (cnd), Ljubljana RSO *(Romeo & Juliet)*, M. Munih (cnd), Ljubljana RSO, A. Springer (cnd), Hamburg SO *(Serenade Strs, Op. 48 [Waltz])*, Copenhagen String Quartet *(Qt 1 Strs, Op. 11 [Andante cantabile])*, A. Rosand (vn), L. D. Froment (cnd), Luxembourg Radio Orch *(Con Vn, Op. 35 [Finale (Allegro vivacissimo)])* ("25 Tchaikovsky Favorites") VCC (25 Favorites) ▲ 8816 (3.97)

R. Ricci (vn), C. Höfer (pno)—Valse-Scherzo Vn, Op. 34; Con 2 Pno, Op. 44 [Andante non troppo]; Swan Lake (sels) [Danse russe; Danses des cygnes; Danse des cygnes]; Saisons, Op. 37b [October:Chant d'automne]; Suite 4 Orch, Op. 61; Nocturne Vc; Album pour enfants Pno, Op. 39 [L'orgue de barberie [Organ Grinder; Chanson napolitaine [Neapolitan Dance-Song; Old Nurse's Tale]]]; Morceaux (2) Pno, Op. 10 [No. 2, Humoresque]; Morceaux (6) Pno, Op. 51 [No. 6, Valse sentimentale]; Sérénade mélancolique, Op. 26; Sleeping Beauty (sels) [Aurora's Variation; Act 2 Entr'acte (Andante sostenuto)]; Romance Pno, Op. 5; Souvenir d'un lieu cher, Op. 42; Morceaux (12) Pno, Op. 40 [No. 2, Chanson triste in g]; Lullaby in a Storm, Op. 54/10; Suite 3 Orch, Op. 55; Songs without Words; Qt 3 Strs, Op. 30/3 [Andante] *(rec Mozart Academy, Salzburg, Germany, Feb 5-7, Oct 10-12, 1997)* ("Complete Violin Short Pieces") ONEL 2-▲ 20001 [DDD] (22.97)

V. Spivakov (vn), S. Ozawa (cnd), Philharmonia Orch *(Con Vn, Op. 35) (rec 1981-84)*, S. Ozawa (cnd), Philharmonia Orch *(Capriccio italien, Op. 45) (rec 1981-84)*, S. Ozawa (cnd), Berlin PO *(Francesca da Rimini, Op. 32) (rec 1981-84)*, H. von Karajan (cnd), Berlin PO *(Sym 6, Op. 74) (rec 1971)*, A. Gavrilov (pno), V. Ashkenazy (cnd), Berlin PO *(Con 1 Pno, Op. 23; Con 3 Pno, Op. 75)*, D. Sgouros (pno), W. Weller (cnd), London PO *(Concert Fant, Op. 56)*, A. Previn (cnd), London SO *(Swan Lake (suite), Op. 20a; Sleeping Beauty (suite), Op. 66a; Nutcracker Suite, Op. 71a)* ("Best-Loved Tchaikovsky") EMCD (Seraphim) 4-▲ 69544 [DDD] (14.97)

Y. Temirkanov (cnd), Leningrad PO, Y. Temirkanov (cnd), Leningrad Military Orch *(Eugene Onegin (sels) [Waltz; Polonaise]; Ov 1812, Op. 49)*, I. Perlman (vn), Y. Temirkanov (cnd), Leningrad PO, Y. Temirkanov (cnd), Leningrad Military Orch *(Sérénade mélancolique, Op. 26)*, J. Norman (sop), I. Perlman (vn), Y.-Y. Ma (vc), Y. Temirkanov (cnd), Leningrad PO, Y. Temirkanov (cnd), Leningrad Military Orch *(Valse-Scherzo Vn, Op. 34; Sym 6, Op. 74 [Allegro molto vivace]; Songs (6), Op. 65; Maid of Orleans (sels) [Adieu, forêts])*, Y.-Y. Ma (vc), Y. Temirkanov (cnd), Leningrad PO, Y. Temirkanov (cnd), Leningrad Military Orch *(Vars on a Rococo Theme, Op. 33) (rec live Leningrad, Russia)* ("Tchaikovsky Gala In Leningrad") RCAV (Red Seal) ▲ 60739 (orc) [DDD] (16.97)

artists unknown—Andante cantabile; Swan Lake (sels) [Pas d'action]; Con Vn, Op. 35 [Canzonetta (Andante)]; Sleeping Beauty (sels) [Panorama; Vision of Aurora; Sarabande]; Nutcracker (sels) [Coffee (Arab Dance); Tea (Chinese Dance); Dance of the Mirlitons (Flutes); Dance of the Sugar-Plum Fairy (Var 2)]; Vars on a Rococo Theme, Op. 33 [Final Var]; Sérénade mélancolique, Op. 26; Trio Pno, Op. 50; Con 1 Pno, Op. 23 [Andantino semplice]; Serenade Strs, Op. 48 [Elegy] ("Tchaikovsky at Tea Time") PPHI ▲ 54498 (9.97) ▮ 54498 (5.98)

artists unknown—Sleeping Beauty (sels) [Waltz]; Nutcracker (sels) [Miniature Ov]; Con 1 Pno, Op. 23; Swan Lake (sels) [Dance 4 of the Swans (Danses des petites cygnes); Mazurka]; Eugene Onegin (sels) [Waltz]; Romeo & Juliet; Marche slave, Op. 31; Sym 5, Op. 64 [Valse: Allegro moderato]; Italian Capriccio, Op. 45; Andante cantabile; Ov 1812, Op. 49 ("Favourite Tchaikovsky: Of the Most Popular Tchaikovsky Classics") CFP ▲ 4621 [ADD] (12.97)

artists unknown—Nutcracker Suite, Op. 71a; Swan Lake (suite), Op. 20a; Capriccio italien, Op. 45 ("Classic Hits: Tchaikovsky") PUBM (Majestic) ▲ 1039 (4.97)

various artists—Con Vn, Op. 35 [Allegro moderato]; Con 1 Pno, Op. 23 [Allegro non troppo e molto maestoso]; Swan Lake (sels) [Waltz in A♭ (Corps de Ballet); Scene finale]; Nutcracker (sels) [Waltz of the Flowers; Trépak (Russian Dance)]; Romeo & Juliet; Sleeping Beauty (sels) [Waltz]; Sym 6, Op. 74 [Allegro molto vivace]; Ov 1812, Op. 49 ("Tchaikovsky in Hollywood") RCAV ▲ 68875 (11.97)

Nocturne in c# for Cello & Small Orchestra [trans Tchaikovsky from Morceaux, Op. 19/4] (ca 1888)

M. Brunello (vc), M. Brunello (cnd), Italian String Orch † Andante cantabile; P. Hindemith:Trauermusik; A. Piazzolla:Adiós Nonino; G. Rossini:Péchés de vieillesse (sels); Sollima:Violincelles Vibrez!; Takemitsu:Scene Vc AG ▲ 155 (18.97)

P. Brunt (vn), L. Markiz (cnd), Amsterdam New Sinfonietta *(rec 1990)* † Andante cantabile; Elegy Strs; Serenade Strs, Op. 48; Arensky:Vars on a Theme of Tchaikovsky GLOE ▲ 6021 [DDD] (16.97)

V. Feigin (vc), N. Järvi (cnd), Estonian State SO *(rec Tallinn, 1978)* ("Neeme Järvi: The Early Recordings, Vol. 6") † Andante cantabile; Pezzo capriccioso, Op. 62; Vars on a Rococo Theme, Op. 33; J. Haydn:Con 2 Vc MELD ▲ 40724 [ADD] (6.97)

D. Geringas (vc), D. Geringas (cnd), Southwest German CO Pforzheim † Pezzo capriccioso, Op. 62; Saisons; Vars on a Rococo Theme, Op. 33 EBS ▲ 6033 (17.97)

S. Isserlis (vc), J. E. Gardiner (cnd), CO of Europe *(rec Italy)* ("43561490") † Andante cantabile; Pezzo capriccioso, Op. 62; Vars on a Rococo Theme, Op. 33; E. Bloch:Schelomo; E. Elgar:Con Vc; Kabalevsky:Con 2 Vc, Op. 77; R. Strauss:Don Quixote, Op. 35 VCL 2-▲ 61490 [DDD] (11.97)

M. Kliegel (vc), G. Markson (cnd), Irish National SO *(rec May 17-18, 1993)* † Pezzo capriccioso, Op. 62; Vars on a Rococo Theme, Op. 33; E. Bloch:Schelomo; Bruch:Kol Nidrei, Op. 47 NXIN ▲ 550519 [DDD] (5.97)

M. Maisky (vc), Orpheus CO *(rec Recital Hall NY State Univ, Purchase, NY, Apr 1996)* † Andante cantabile; Eugene Onegin (sels); Souvenir de Florence, Op. 70; Vars on a Rococo Theme, Op. 33 DEUT ▲ 453460 [DDD] (16.97)

M. Rostropovich (vc), B. Britten (cnd), English CO *(rec 1968)* † Legend (When Jesus Christ Was But a Child), Op. 54/5; Serenade Strs, Op. 48; Suite 4 Orch, Op. 61 BBC (Britten the Performer) ▲ 8002 (17.97)

The Nutcracker (ballet in 2 acts) for Orchestra, Op. 71 (1891-92)

E. Ansermet (cnd), Swiss Romande Orch PLON 2-▮ 17055 (8.98)

V. Ashkenazy (cnd), Royal PO † Glazunov:Seasons, Op. 67 PPHI 2-▲ 33000 [DDD] (32.97)

R. Bonynge (cnd), National PO London *(rec Kingsway Hall London, Apr 1974)* † J. Offenbach:Papillon PLON (Double Decker) 2-▲ 44827 [ADD] (17.97)

V. Cliburn (pno), S. Celibidache (cnd), Swiss-Italian Radio-TV Orch † Con 1 Pno, Op. 23; Romeo & Juliet AURC ▲ 108 (5.97)

A. Dorati (cnd), (Royal) Concertgebouw Orch, St. Bavo Cathedral Boys' Choir † Sleeping Beauty (sels) PPHI (Duo) 2-▲ 42562 (17.97)

A. Dorati (cnd), London SO *(rec ca 1962)* † Serenade Strs, Op. 48 MRCR 2-▲ 32750 [ADD] (22.97)

V. Fedotov (cnd), Leningrad PO † Romeo & Juliet MTRC (Russian Legacy) ▲ 8406 (7.97)

▲ = CD ♦ = Enhanced CD △ = MD ▮ = Cassette Tape ▯ = DCC

TCHAIKOVSKY, PIOTR (cont.)

The Nutcracker (ballet in 2 acts) for Orchestra, Op. 71 (1891-92) (cont.)

V. Gergiev (cnd), Kirov Theater Orch PPHI ▲ 462114 (16.97)

C. Mackerras (cnd), London SO TEL 2-▮ 30137 [DDD] (16.98) ▲ 80137 [DDD] (25.97)

C. Mackerras (cnd), London SO TEL ▮ 30140 [DDD] (8.98) ▲ 80140 [DDD] (16.97)

C. Mackerras (cnd), London SO TEL 2-▲ 80137 [DDD] (25.97) ▮ 30137 [DDD] (16.98)

C. Mackerras (cnd), London SO TEL ▲ 80140 [DDD] (16.97) ▮ 30140 [DDD] (8.98)

J. McPhee (cnd), Boston Ballet Orch *(rec live)* BBOR ▲ 10332 [DDD] (17.97)

S. Ozawa (cnd), Boston SO † Sleeping Beauty (suite), Op. 66a DEUT 2-▲ 35619 [DDD] (32.97)

A. Previn (cnd), London SO *(rec May 1-4, 1972)* CFP ▲ 4706 (24.97)

T. Russell (cnd), Naples PO, T. Russell (cnd), Naples FL PO *(rec Naples, FL, Dec 1-2, 1992)* ("The Nutcracker") SUMM 2-▲ 147 [DDD]

G. Solti (cnd), Israel PO † O. Respighi:Boutique fantasque PLON (Weekend Classics) 2-▲ 25509 [AAD] (13.97)

P. Thomas (cnd), Philharmonia Orch † J. Haydn:Con Fl [attrib], H.VIIf/D1; Con Ob; Cons 2 Lire organizzata, H.VIIh/1-5 SNYC 2-▲ 39772 [DDD] (31.97)

The Nutcracker (selections)

H. Adolph (cnd), London Festival Orch—Dance of the Sugar-Plum Fairy (Var 2); Trépak (Russian Dance); Coffee (Arab Dance); Tea (Chinese Dance); Dance of the Mirlitons (Flutes) ("A Night at the Ballet:Highlights from the Nutcracker") † Swan Lake (sels) ECL ▲ 509 (2.97)

C. Dutoit (cnd), Montreal SO † Sleeping Beauty (sels); Swan Lake (sels) PLON ▲ 43555 (16.97)

M. Ermler (cnd), Royal Opera House Orch Covent Garden ("Tchaikovsky Ballet") † Sleeping Beauty (sels); Swan Lake (sels) CONI ▲ 55012 [DDD] (11.97)

D. Jackson (cnd), Royal PO—Miniature Ov; Battle & Transformation Scene; Forest of Fir Trees in Winter (Journey through the Snow) † Capriccio italien, Op. 45; Eugene Onegin (sels); Sleeping Beauty (suite), Op. 66a; Slippers (sels); Souvenir d'un lieu cher, Op. 42; Swan Lake (suite), Op. 20a; Sérénade mélancolique, Op. 26; Valse-Scherzo Vn, Op. 34; Vars on a Rococo Theme, Op. 33 VB3 3-▲ 3026 [ADD]

N. Järvi (cnd), Scottish National Orch—Dance of the Mirlitons (Flutes); Trépak (Russian Dance); Dance of the Sugar-Plum Fairy (Var 2) ("Russian Ballet Masterpieces") † Swan Lake (sels); Glazunov:Raymonda (sels); S. Prokofiev:Romeo & Juliet (sels); D. Shostakovich:Ballet Suite 1; Ballet Suite 2; Ballet Suite 3; I. Stravinsky:Firebird Suite 3 *([ENG,FRE,GER] text)* CHN (Collect Series) ▲ 6512 [DDD] (12.97)

O. Lenárd (cnd), Czech-Slovak State Radio PO *(rec 1989)* † W. A. Mozart:Org Music NXIN ▲ 550514 [DDD] (5.97)

E. Mravinsky (cnd), Leningrad PO—Departure of the Guests-Night; Battle & Transformation Scene; March; Waltz of the Snowflakes; Pas de deux (The Prince & the Sugar-Plum Fairy); Final Waltz *(rec Russia, 1981)* † Francesca da Rimini, Op. 32 CONE ▲ 9410 [ADD] (16.97)

J. Pak (cnd), International SO—Miniature Ov; Coffee (Arab Dance); Tea (Chinese Dance); Trépak (Russian Dance); Pas de deux (The Prince & the Sugar-Plum Fairy); Final Waltz; Apotheosis ECL ▲ 23

A. Previn (cnd), London SO † Sleeping Beauty (sels); Swan Lake (sels) EMIC ▲ 64332 (11.97)

F. Reiner (cnd), Chicago SO—Miniature Ov; Pas de deux (The Prince & the Sugar-Plum Fairy) *(rec 1959)* † Con 1 Pno, Op. 23 RCAV ▲ 68530 [ADD] (11.97)

M. T. Thomas (cnd), Philharmonia Orch—Trépak (Russian Dance); Dance of the Sugar-Plum Fairy (Var 2) ("The Nutcracker: Highlights") SNYC ▲ 62675 (9.97) ▮ 62675 (5.98)

P. Wohlert (cnd), Berlin SO LALI ▲ 15146 (3.97) ▮ 79020 (1.98)

various artists—Pas de deux (The Prince & the Sugar-Plum Fairy); Waltz of the Flowers † Eugene Onegin (sels); Marche slave, Op. 31; Ov 1812, Op. 49; Qt 1 Strs, Op. 11; Serenade Strs, Op. 48; Swan Lake (sels); Sym 6 RCAV ▲ 60845 (11.97) ▮ 60845 (5.98)

Nutcracker Suite for Orchestra, Op. 71a (1892; arr Piano, 1897)

M. Argerich (pno), N. Economou (pno) [arr N. Economou for 2 pnos] *(rec Munich, Germany, Mar 1983)* † Con 1 Pno, Op. 23 DEUT ▲ 49816 [DDD] (16.97)

E. Bátiz (cnd), Royal PO ("Ballet Suites") † Sleeping Beauty (suite), Op. 66a; Swan Lake (suite), Op. 20a ASVQ ▲ 6183 (10.97)

E. Bátiz (cnd), Royal PO † Sleeping Beauty (sels); Sym 5 ALFA ▲ 1007 [DDD]

A. Boult (cnd), New SO London *(rec Walthamstow Town Hall London, July 12-15, 1960)* ("Concert Favorites") † E. Elgar:Pomp & Circumstance, Op. 39; Liszt:Préludes, S.97; Mendelssohn (-Bartholdy):Hebriden, Op. 26; Mussorgsky:Night on Bare Mountain CHSK ▲ 53 [ADD] (16.97)

D. Briggs (org)—Miniature Overture; Waltz of the Flowers ("Popular Organ Music, Vol. 2") † J. Alain:Jardin suspendu, AWV 63; J. S. Bach:Preludes & Fugues (22) Org, BWV 531-552; Preludes & Fugues, BWV 531-552; P. Cochereau:Boléro on a Theme of Charles Racquet; Dukas:L'Apprenti sorcier; C. Franck:Pièces (3) Org, M.37 PRIO ▲ 568 [DDD] (16.97)

S. Celibidache (cnd), London PO *(rec 1948)* † Sym 5 LYS ▲ 432

R. Désormière (cnd), French National SO *(rec Paris, 1953-54)* † Swan Lake (sels) EMIC (Full Dimensional Sound) ▲ 66828 [ADD] (11.97)

A. Dorati (cnd), (Royal) Concertgebouw Orch PPHI ▮ 26177 (4.98)

A. Fiedler (cnd), Boston Pops Orch ("Classics for Children") † S. Prokofiev:Peter & the Wolf, Op. 67; Saint-Saëns:Carnival of the Animals RCAV (Gold Seal) ▲ 6718 [ADD] (11.97) ▮ 6718 [ADD] (6.98)

A. Fiedler (cnd), Boston Pops Orch † Strauss (II):An der schönen blauen Donau, Op. 314; Frühlingsstimmen, Op. 410; Geschichten aus dem Wienerwald, Op. 325; Künstlerleben, Op. 316; Spitzentuch der Königin (sels) PLON (Phase 4 Stereo) ▲ 455154 (9.97)

S. Gorkovenko (cnd), St. Petersburg Radio-TV SO ("Classical Christmas Favorites") † J. S. Bach:Christmas Oratorio (sels); A. Corelli:Con grosso, Op. 6/8; Gounod:Ave Maria; G. F. Handel:Messiah (choruses); F. Schubert:Ave Maria, Op. 52/6 SNYC ▲ 69255 [DDD] (4.97)

D. Jackson (cnd), Royal PO † G. F. Handel:Messiah (sels) SMC 2-▲ 5110 [DDD]

H. von Karajan (cnd), Berlin PO † Sleeping Beauty (suite), Op. 66a; Swan Lake (suite), Op. 20a DEUT ▲ 19175 [ADD] (16.97)

H. von Karajan (cnd), Berlin PO † Romeo & Juliet DEUT (Karajan Gold) ▲ 39021 [DDD] (16.97)

H. von Karajan (cnd), Vienna PO † Sleeping Beauty (suite), Op. 66a; Swan Lake (suite), Op. 20a PLON (The Classic Sound) ▲ 448592 (11.97)

A. Lazarev (cnd), Bolshoi Theater SO † Capriccio italien, Op. 45; Eugene Onegin (sels); Sleeping Beauty (suite), Op. 66a; Swan Lake (suite), Op. 20a TELC (Ultima) 2-▲ 18965 (16.97)

J. Levine (cnd), Vienna PO † Sleeping Beauty (suite), Op. 66a; Swan Lake (suite), Op. 20a DEUT ▲ 37806 [DDD] (16.97)

Los Angeles Guitar Quartet *(rec 1992)* † G. Gabrieli:Gtr Trans; T. Morley:Dances; Warlock:Capriol Suite DLS ▲ 3132 [DDD] (14.97) ▮ 3132 [DDD] (7.98)

I. Markevitch (cnd), Philharmonia Orch † Romeo & Juliet; Swan Lake (suite), Op. 20a; S. Prokofiev:Sym 1 TES ▲ 1107 (17.97)

N. Marriner (cnd), Academy of St. Martin in the Fields † Serenade Strs, Op. 48 PPHI ▲ 11471 [DDD] (16.97)

K. Ono (cnd), Bratislava RSO † Swan Lake, Op. 20 OPP ▲ 2211

E. Ormandy (cnd), Philadelphia Orch † J. S. Bach:Passacaglia & Fugue Org, BWV 582; Pastorale Org, BWV 590; Preludes & Fugues, BWV 531-552; Toccata & Fugue Org, BWV 565; Chopin:Sylphides; Delibes:Coppélia (suite); Sylvia (suite) SNYC (Essential Classics) ▲ 46551 [ADD] (7.97) ▮ 46551 [ADD] (3.98)

S. Pasero (gtr) [trans for gtr] SGO ▲ 8501 [DDD] (16.97)

M. Pletnev (pno) [arr Pletnev] *(rec 1978)* ("Mikhail Pletnev") † Capriccio, Op. 8; Con 2 Pno, Op. 44; Romance Pno, Op. 5; Saisons; Sleeping Beauty (sels); Valse-Scherzo Pno, Op. 7 PPHI (Great Pianists of the 20th Century) ▲ 456931 (22.97)

S. Rohani (cnd), Slovak Radio New PO ("Musica per Tutti, Vol. 9") † Sleeping Beauty (suite), Op. 66a; Swan Lake (suite), Op. 20a; Vivaldi:Domine ad adiuvandum me, RV.593; Gloria; Nisi Dominus, RV.608 DI ▲ 920295 [DDD] (5.97)

M. Rostropovich (cnd), Berlin PO *(rec 1979)* ("Ballet Suites") † Sleeping Beauty (suite), Op. 66a; Swan Lake (suite), Op. 20a DEUT (The Originals) ▲ 449726 [ADD] (11.97)

Shirim [arr Harris & McLaughlin] *(rec Carlisle, MA, Oct 31 & Dec 6, 1997)* ("Klezmer Nutcracker") † J. Brahms:Hungarian Dances Pno 4-Hands; Chopin:Preludes (24) Pno, Op. 28; Enescu:Romanian Rhap 1, Op. 11/1; G. Mahler:Sym 1; Satie:Gnossiennes; Gymnopédies; Traditional:Russian Bulgar; Turk in America NPT ▲ 85640 (16.97)

G. Solti (cnd), Chicago SO † Romeo & Juliet; Swan Lake (suite), Op. 20a PLON (Jubilee) ▲ 30707 [DDD] (9.97)

G. Solti (cnd), Chicago SO ("The Tchaikovsky Album") † Ov 1812, Op. 49; Romeo & Juliet; Swan Lake (suite), Op. 20a; Sym 6 PLON (Double Decker) 2-▲ 455810 (17.97)

J. Sterczyński (pno) *(rec Rzeszow, Mar 7-8, 1993)* ("Piano Works") SELN ▲ 930815 [DDD] (16.97)

L. Stokowski (cnd), Philadelphia Orch *(rec 1927-30)* ("Leopold Stokowski: The Philadelphia Years, Vol. 3") † Berlioz:Damnation de Faust (sels); Saint-Saëns:Samson et Dalila (Bacchanale); Sibelius:Swan of Tuonela GRM2 ▲ 78586 (13.97)

L. Stokowski (cnd), Philadelphia Orch ("Stokowski Conducts Tchaikovsky") † Sym 4 GRM2 (Records of the Century) ▲ 78836 (13.97)

TCHAIKOVSKY, PIOTR (cont.)

Nutcracker Suite for Orchestra, Op. 71a (1892; arr Piano, 1897) (cont.)

A. Titov (cnd), St. Petersburg New Philharmony Orch † Sleeping Beauty (suite), Op. 66a; Swan Lake (sels) SNYC ▲ 57241 [DDD] (4.97)

A. Toscanini (cnd), NBC SO ("The Toscanini Collection, Vol. 18") † Sym 6 RCAV (Gold Seal) ▲ 60297 (11.97)

R. Williams (cnd), London SO *(rec July 7-8, 1987)* † Sleeping Beauty (suite), Op. 66a; Swan Lake (suite), Op. 20a LSO (LSO) ▲ 6900092 (10.97)

Ode to Joy (cantata) for SATB Soloists, Orchestra & Chorus [text Schiller, trans Axakov & others] (1865)

D. Gleeson (cnd), London PO, Geoffrey Mitchell Choir, London Phil Chorus † Romeo & Juliet; S. Prokofiev:Hail to Stalin, Op. 85 IMAS (Masters) ▲ 6600122 (16.97)

Orchestral Music

E. Inbal (cnd), (Royal) Concertgebouw Orch, E. Inbal (cnd), Frankfurt RSO—Fatum, Op. 77; Francesca da Rimini, Op. 32; Hamlet, Op. 67a; Tempest, Op. 18; Storm, Op. 76; Voyevoda, Op. 78; Romeo & Juliet; Ov 1812, Op. 49 PPHI (Duo) 2-▲ 42586 (17.97)

Overture 1812 in E♭ for Orchestra, Op. 49 (1880)

C. Abbado (cnd), Chicago SO † Sym 3 SNYC ▲ 45939 (11.97)

C. Abbado (cnd), Chicago SO † Marche slave, Op. 31; Romeo & Juliet; Tempest, Op. 18 SNYC ▲ 47179 (11.97)

M. Abravanel (cnd), Utah SO ("Complete Orchestral Music, Vol. 1") † Sym 3; Sym 6; Voyevoda, Op. 78 VB2 2-▲ 5004 [ADD]

H. Adolph (cnd), Slovak PO † Sym 4 PC ▲ 267032 [DDD] (2.97)

H. Adolph (cnd), Slovak PO ("Romantic Classics, Vol. 3") † Sym 6; Liszt:Hungarian Rhaps, S.244; W. A. Mozart:Zauberflöte (ov); G. Rossini:Barbiere di Siviglia (ov); Smetana:Bartered Bride (sels) ECL ▲ 502 (2.97)

Y. Ahronovitch (cnd), London SO ("Tchaikovsky Spectacular") † Marche slave, Op. 31; Romeo & Juliet INMP (LSO Classic Masterpieces) ▲ 801 [DDD] (9.97)

Y. Ahronovitch (cnd), London SO ("An Evening of Concert Favourites") † Con 1 Pno, Op. 23; Eugene Onegin (sels); Marche slave, Op. 31 INMP (Concert Classics) ▲ 1102 (9.97)

K. Ančerl (cnd), Czech PO † Berlioz:Carnaval romain, Op. 9; Borodin:In the Steppes of Central Asia; M. Glinka:Russlan & Ludmilla (ov); Liszt:Préludes, S.97; R. Strauss:Till Eulenspiegels lustige Streiche, Op. 28; C. M. von Weber:Invitation to the Dance Orch SUR (Czech Philharmonic) ▲ 111938 [AAD]

D. Barenboim (cnd), Chicago SO † Capriccio italien, Op. 45; Francesca da Rimini, Op. 32; Romeo & Juliet DEUT (Masters) ▲ 45523 [DDD] (9.97)

L. Bernstein (cnd), New York PO *(rec Oct 2, 1962)* ("Leonard Bernstein: The Royal Edition") † Marche slave, Op. 31; Sym 5 SNYC ▲ 47634 [ADD] (10.97)

R. Brydon (org), E. Diazmuñoz (cnd), Mexican State SO † Mussorgsky:Pictures at an Exhibition; Rimsky-Korsakov:Capriccio espagnol, Op. 34 HALM ▲ 35022 (6.97)

I. Buketoff (cnd), New Philharmonia Orch † Beethoven:Wellington's Victory, Op. 91 RCAV (Victrola) ▲ 7731 [DDD] (6.97)

J. DePreist (cnd), Oregon SO † Hamlet; Tempest, Op. 18 DLS ▲ 3081 [DDD] (14.97)

P. Domingo (cnd), Philharmonia Orch † Capriccio italien, Op. 45; Eugene Onegin (sels); Romeo & Juliet; Songs (6), Op. 6 CSER (Seraphim) ▲ 73297 [DDD] (6.97)

A. Dorati (cnd), Detroit SO † Marche slave, Op. 31; Romeo & Juliet PLON ▲ 17742 [ADD] (9.97)

A. Doráti (cnd), Detroit SO *(rec 1978)* † Capriccio italien, Op. 45; Fatum; Francesca da Rimini, Op. 32; Hamlet; Marche slave, Op. 31; Romeo & Juliet; Tempest, Op. 18; Voyevoda, Op. 78 PLON 2-▲ 43003 [ADD] (17.97)

A. Doráti (cnd), Minneapolis SO [Bronze cannon courtesy of U.S. Military Academy, W] † Beethoven:Wellington's Victory, Op. 91 MRCR ▲ 34360 (11.97)

V. Dudarova (cnd), Russian SO † Capriccio italien, Op. 45; Fatum; Festival Ov, Op. 15; Francesca da Rimini, Op. 32; Hamlet; Romeo & Juliet; Tempest, Op. 18 OLY ▲ 512 (16.97)

C. Dutoit (cnd), Montreal SO † Marche slave, Op. 31 PLON ▲ 17300 [DDD] (16.97)

S. Edwards (cnd), Royal Liverpool PO † Francesca da Rimini, Op. 32; Marche slave, Op. 31; Romeo & Juliet CFP (Eminence) ▲ 2152 [DDD] (16.97)

A. Fischer (cnd), Hungarian SO † Sym 6 LALI ▲ 15524 [DDD] (3.97)

V. Gergiev (cnd), Kirov Theater Orch ("White Nights: Romantic Russian Showpieces") † Borodin:Prince Igor (Polovtsian Dances); M. Glinka:Russlan & Ludmilla (ov); A. Khachaturian:Gayane (sels); Spartacus (suite 2) (sels); Liadov:Baba Yaga, Op. 56; Kikimora, Op. 63 PPHI ▲ 42011 (16.97)

A. Gibson (cnd), New SO London *(rec July 1960)* † Sym 6; Smetana:Moldau CHSK ▲ 65 [ADD] (16.97)

N. Järvi (cnd), Gothenburg SO † Borodin:Prince Igor (Polovtsian Dances); Rimsky-Korsakov:Capriccio espagnol, Op. 34; Russian Easter Overture, Op. 36 DEUT ▲ 29984 [DDD] (16.97)

V. Kahi (cnd), Georgian Festival Orch ("The Tchaikovsky Album") † Capriccio italien, Op. 45; Marche slave, Op. 31; Romeo & Juliet SNYC ▲ 61978 [DDD] (4.97)

E. Kunzel (cnd), Cincinnati SO TEL ▮ 30041 [DDD] (8.98) ▲ 80041 [DDD] (16.97)

A. Leaper (cnd), Royal PO † Romeo & Juliet NXIN ▲ 550500 [DDD] (5.97)

A. Litton (cnd), Dallas SO *(rec Meyerson Center Dallas, TX, TX, Nov 16-18, 1995)* † Moscow; Sleeping Beauty (sels); Voyevoda, Op. 78 DLS (Virtual Reality Recording) ▲ 3196 [DDD] (14.97)

L. Maazel (cnd), Bavarian RSO ("Symphonic Battle Scenes") † Capriccio italien, Op. 45; Beethoven:Wellington's Victory, Op. 91; Liszt:Battle of the Huns RCAV (Red Seal) ▲ 68471 (16.97)

Z. Mehta (cnd), Israel PO † Capriccio italien, Op. 45; Swan Lake (sels) TELC ▲ 90201 (16.97)

W. Mengelberg (cnd), (Royal) Concertgebouw Orch ("Willem Mengelberg: A Portrait, 1926-41") † Sym 6; J. S. Bach:Suite 2 Fl, BWV 1067; Beethoven:Egmont (ov); Leonore (ov 3); Sym 3; J. Brahms:Academic Festival Ov, Op. 80; Liszt:Préludes, S.97; R. Wagner:Lohengrin (preludes); Tannhäuser (ov); C. M. von Weber:Freischütz (ov); Oberon (ov) GRM2 3-▲ 78637 (39.97)

W. Mengelberg (cnd), (Royal) Concertgebouw Orch ("Overtures") † Beethoven:Leonore (ov 3); J. Brahms:Academic Festival Ov, Op. 80; Liszt:Préludes, S.97; R. Wagner:Lohengrin (ov); C. M. von Weber:Freischütz (ov) ENT (Sirio) ▲ 530020 (13.97)

N. Nozy (cnd), Belgian Guides Symphonic Band [trans H. Séha] † Marche slave, Op. 31; Romeo & Juliet RENE ▲ 87048 [DDD] (16.97)

E. Ormandy (cnd), Philadelphia Orch † Marche slave, Op. 31; Sym 4 SNYC (Essential Classics) ▲ 46334 [ADD] (7.97) ▮ 46334 [ADD] (3.98)

E. Ormandy (cnd), Philadelphia Orch † Capriccio italien, Op. 45; Marche slave, Op. 31 RCAV (Silver Seal) ▲ 60492 [ADD] (6.97)

E. Ormandy (cnd), Philadelphia Orch † Capriccio italien, Op. 45; Con Vn; Eugene Onegin (sels); Marche slave, Op. 31; Romeo & Juliet; Sym 5 SNYC (Essential Classics Take 2) 2-▲ 63281 (14.97)

E. Ormandy (cnd), Philadelphia Orch, Mormon Tabernacle Choir † Serenade Strs, Op. 48 SNYC ▮ 30447 (10.98)

M. Pletnev (cnd), Russian National Orch † Fatum; Sym 2 DGRM ▲ 453446 [DDD]

F. Reiner (cnd), Chicago SO *(rec Orchestra Hall Chicago, Jan 7, 1956)* † Sym 6; Liszt:Mephisto Waltz 1 Orch, S.110 RCAV (Living Stereo) ▲ 61246 [ADD] (11.97)

H. Scherchen (cnd) † Lt Kijé Suite, Op. 60; Rimsky-Korsakov:Russian Easter Overture, Op. 36; P. Tchaikovsky:Ov 1812, Op. 49; Romeo & Juliet ENT (Palladio) 2-▲ 4167 [ADD] (26.97)

J. Serebrier (cnd), Melbourne SO † G. Holst:Planets, Op. 32; M. Ravel:Boléro ASVQ ▲ 6078 [DDD] (10.97)

L. Slatkin (cnd), St. Louis SO *(rec Powell Symphony Hall, Jan 27, 1993)* † Romeo & Juliet; Sym 2 RCAV (Red Seal) ▲ 68045 [DDD] (16.97)

G. Solti (cnd), Chicago SO ("The Solti Collection, Vol. 10") † Mussorgsky:Pictures at an Exhibition; S. Prokofiev:Sym 1 PLON (Jubilee) ▲ 30446 [DDD] (11.97)

G. Solti (cnd), Chicago SO ("The Tchaikovsky Album") † Nutcracker Suite, Op. 71a; Romeo & Juliet; Swan Lake (suite), Op. 20a; Sym 6 PLON (Double Decker) 2-▲ 455810 (17.97)

L. Stokowski (cnd), Philadelphia Orch ("Stokowski Conducts Tchaikovsky") † Morceaux (12) Pno, Op. 40; Sym 5 BCS ▲ 15 (16.97)

various artists † Eugene Onegin (sels); Marche slave, Op. 31; Nutcracker (sels); Qt 1 Strs, Op. 11; Serenade Strs, Op. 48; Swan Lake (sels); Sym 6 RCAV ▲ 60845 (11.97) ▮ 60845 (5.98)

various artists † J. S. Bach:Air on the G String; Beethoven:Con Vn; Con 3 Pno, Op. 37; J. Brahms:Sym 4; H. Pfitzner:Palestrina (sels); Smetana:Moldau MTAL ▲ 48096 (6.97)

Pezzo capriccioso in b for Cello & Orchestra (or Piano), Op. 62 (1888)

V. Feigin (vc), N. Järvi (cnd), Estonian State SO *(rec Tallinn, 1978)* ("Neeme Järvi: The Early Recordings, Vol. 6") † Andante cantabile; Nocturne Vc; Vars on a Rococo Theme, Op. 33; J. Haydn:Con 2 Vc MELD ▲ 40724 [ADD] (6.97)

M. Fukačová (vc), I. Klánský (pno) [Tchaikovsky's vc & pno version] † A. Dvořák:Rondo; C. Franck:Son Vn, M.8; E. Grieg:Son Vc KPT ▲ 32013 [DDD]

D. Geringas (vc), D. Geringas (cnd), Southwest German CO Pforzheim † Nocturne Vc; Saisons; Vars on a Rococo Theme, Op. 33 EBS ▲ 6033 (17.97)

S. Isserlis (vc), J. E. Gardiner (cnd), CO of Europe *(rec Italy)* ("43561490") † Andante cantabile; Nocturne Vc; Vars on a Rococo Theme, Op. 33; E. Bloch:Schelomo; E. Elgar:Con Vc; Kabalevsky:Con 2 Vc, Op. 77; R. Strauss:Don Quixote, Op. 35 VCL 2-▲ 61490 [DDD] (11.97)

TCHAIKOVSKY, PIOTR (cont.)

Pezzo capriccioso in b for Cello & Orchestra (or Piano), Op. 62 (1888) (cont.)

M. Kliegel (vc), G. Markson (cnd), Irish National SO *(rec May 17-18, 1993)* † Nocturne Vc; Vars on a Rococo Theme, Op. 33; E. Bloch:Schelomo; Bruch:Kol Nidrei, Op. 47 NXIN ▲ 550519 [DDD] (5.97)

R. Wallfisch (vc), G. Simon (cnd), English CO † Songs; E. Bloch:From Jewish Life; A. Dvořák:Polonaise Vc, B.94; Rondo; Silent Woods Vc & Pno, Op. 68/5; Slavonic Dance Vc & Pno, Op. 46/8; Glazunov:Chant du ménestrel, Op. 71 CHN (Collect) ▲ 6552 [DDD] (12.97)

Piano Music

I. Ardašev (pno)—Morceaux (6) Pno, Op. 19 [No. 5, Capriccioso in B♭]; Morceaux (2) Pno, Op. 10 [No. 1, Nocturne in F]; Morceaux (3) Pno, Op. 9 [No. 2, Polka de salon]; Morceaux (18) Pno, Op. 72 [No. 14, Chant élégiaque] † Con 1 Pno, Op. 23 SUR ▲ 110952 [DDD]

I. Hobson (pno)—Songs (6), Op. 16 *(rec Letters, NYC, NY, Nov 16-18, 1991)* ("Hobson's Choice") † J. S. Bach:Toccata, Adagio & Fugue Org, BWV 564; Chopin:Ballade 4 Pno, Op. 52; P. Grainger:Folk Song Settings; Liszt:Réminiscences de Don Juan Pno, S.418; Mendelssohn (-Bartholdy):Rondo capriccioso, Op. 14; M. Rosenthal:Pno Music ARA ▲ 6639 (16.97)

V. Leyetchkiss (pno)—Morceaux (12) Pno, Op. 40 [No. 2, Chanson triste in g; No. 8, Valse in A♭; No. 9, Valse in f#; No. 5, Mazurka in D]; Morceaux (6) Pno, Op. 51; Morceaux (18) Pno, Op. 72 [No. 3, Tendres reproches in c#; No. 10, Scherzo-fantaisie; No. 15, Un poco di Chopin; No. 7, Polacca de concert]; Sym 6, Op. 74 [Allegro molto vivace] ("My Favorite Tchaikovsky") CENT ▲ 2161 [DDD] (16.97)

D. Paperno (pno)—Morceaux (18) Pno, Op. 72 [No. 5, Méditation in D]; Saisons, Op. 37b [August:La Moisson; September:La Chasse; October:Chant d'automne; November:Troika] † Liadov:Vars on a Polish Folk Theme, Op. 51; Medtner:Forgotten Melodies 1, Op. 38; S. Rachmaninoff:Preludes Pno; A. Scriabin:Son 2 Pno, Op. 19 CED ▲ 1 [DDD] (16.97)

M. Ponti (pno)—Morceaux (6) Pno, Op. 51; Morceaux (18) Pno, Op. 72 ("Complete Solo Piano Music, Vol. 1") † Album pour enfants Pno, Op. 39; Saisons; Son Pno, Op. 80 VB2 2-▲ 5087 [ADD] (9.97)

I. Prunyi (pno)—Morceaux (6) Pno, Op. 19 [No. 5, Capriccioso in B♭; No. 1, Rêverie du soir in g]; Morceaux (12) Pno, Op. 40 [No. 10, Danse russe; No. 5, Mazurka in D]; Morceaux (18) Pno, Op. 72 [No. 8, Dialogue in B; No. 12, L'espiègle; No. 7, Polacca de concert; No. 3, Tendres reproches in c#]; Dumka, Op. 59; Morceaux (2) Pno, Op. 10 [No. 2, Humoresque; No. 1, Nocturne in F]; Morceaux (6) Pno, Op. 51 [No. 2, Polka peu dansante; No. 5, Romance in F]; Morceaux (3) Pno, Op. 9 [No. 1, Rêverie in D]; Romance Pno, Op. 5; Souvenir de Hapsal, Op. 2 [No. 2, Scherzo in F] *(rec Jan 11 & 13, 1991)* NXIN ▲ 550504 [DDD] (5.97)

S. Richter (pno)—Morceaux (2) Pno, Op. 10 [No. 1, Nocturne in F; No. 2, Humoresque]; Valse-Scherzo Pno, Op. 7; Morceaux (6) Pno, Op. 19 [No. 5, Capriccioso in B♭; No. 1, Rêverie du soir in g]; Morceaux (12) Pno, Op. 40 [No. 2, Chanson triste in g]; Romance Pno, Op. 5; Morceaux (6) Pno, Op. 51 [No. 5, Romance in F; No. 3, Menuetto scherzoso; No. 1, Valse de salon]; Morceaux (18) Pno, Op. 72 [No. 15, Un poco di Chopin; No. 12, L'espiègle; No. 5, Méditation in D]; Saisons, Op. 37b *(rec 1983)* ("Vol. 4") OLY ▲ 334 [DDD] (16.97)

Quartet in B♭ for Strings [1 movt] (1865)

M. Rachlevsky (cnd), Kremlin CO [arr Rachlevsky] ("Tchaikovsky Music for String Orchestra: Vol III") † Qt 2 Strs, Op. 22; Saisons CLAV ▲ 9414 (16.97)

Quartet No. 1 in D for Strings, Op. 11 (1871)

J. Barbirolli (cnd) —Andante cantabile † Marche slave, Op. 31; Romeo & Juliet; Serenade Strs, Op. 48; Sym 4; Sym 5; Sym 6 RYLC 3-▲ 70403 (20.97)

L. Bernstein (cnd), New York PO † Andante cantabile; S. Barber:Adagio Strs; G. Mahler:Sym 5; Vaughan Williams:Fant on a Theme of Tallis; Fant on Greensleeves SNYC ▲ 38484 [AAD] (9.97) ▮ 38484 [AAD] (3.98)

Borodin String Quartet † Qt 2 Strs, Op. 22; Qt 3 Strs, Op. 30; Souvenir de Florence, Op. 70 TELC 2-▲ 90422 (33.97)

Emerson String Quartet † Borodin:Qt 2 Strs; A. Dvořák:Qt 12 Strs, Op. 96 DEUT (Masters) ▲ 45551 [DDD] (9.97)

Hollywood String Quartet † Borodin:Qt 2 Strs; Glazunov:Novelettes, Op. 15 TES ▲ 1061 [ADD] (17.97)

Kontra String Quartet *(rec 1992)* † Qt 3 Strs, Op. 30 BIS ▲ 642 [DDD] (17.97)

Lafayette String Quartet † D. Shostakovich:Preludes & Fugues Pno, Op. 87; Qt 8 Strs, Op. 110 DOR ▲ 90163 [DDD] (16.97)

Moscow String Quartet † Qt 3 Strs, Op. 30 RUSS ▲ 788101 (12.97)

D. Oistrakh (vn), P. Bondarenko (vn), M. Terian (va), S. Knushevitsky (vc) *(rec 1946)* ("David Oistrakh Collection, Vol. 1") † F. Schubert:Qt 14 Strs, D.810; D. Shostakovich:Trio 2 Pno, Op. 67 DHR (Legendary Treasures) ▲ 7701 (16.97)

E. Ormandy (cnd), Philadelphia Orch [arr T. Frost] † Snow Maiden (sels); Songs; Borodin:Nocturne Str Orch; Chopin:Études Pno; Nocturnes Pno; Liszt:Liebesträume, S.541; Mendelssohn (-Bartholdy):Lieder, Op. 34; S. Rachmaninoff:Sym 2; Vocalise; Rimsky-Korsakov:Sadko (sels); Scheherazade, Op. 35 SNYC ▲ 46355 [ADD/DDD] (9.97)

M. Rachlevsky (cnd), Kremlin CO [arr Rachlevsky] *(rec Moscow Conservatory Great Hall, Oct-Nov 1991)* ("Music for Strings, Vol. 1") † Elegy Strs; Serenade Strs, Op. 48; Souvenir d'un lieu cher, Op. 42 CLAV ▲ 9116 [DDD] (16.97)

Smetana String Quartet † F. Schubert:Qt 10 Strs; R. Schumann:Qnt Pno, Op. 44 TES ▲ 1119 (17.97)

Talich String Quartet *(rec June 1986)* † Borodin:Qt 2 Strs APPR ▲ 6202 [DDD]

various artists—Andante cantabile † Eugene Onegin (sels); Marche slave, Op. 31; Nutcracker (sels); Ov 1812, Op. 49; Serenade Strs, Op. 48; Swan Lake (sels); Sym 6 RCAV ▲ 60845 (11.97) ▮ 60845 (5.98)

Quartet No. 2 in F for Strings, Op. 22 (1874)

Borodin String Quartet † Qt 1 Strs, Op. 11; Qt 3 Strs, Op. 30; Souvenir de Florence, Op. 70 TELC 2-▲ 90422 (33.97)

M. Rachlevsky (cnd), Kremlin CO [arr Rachlevsky] ("Tchaikovsky Music for String Orchestra: Vol III") † Qt in B♭ Strs; Saisons CLAV ▲ 9414 (16.97)

Vermeer String Quartet *(rec May & Oct 1993)* † Souvenir de Florence, Op. 70 CED ▲ 17 [DDD] (16.97)

Quartet No. 3 in e♭ for Strings, Op. 30 (1876)

Borodin String Quartet † Qt 1 Strs, Op. 11; Qt 2 Strs, Op. 22; Souvenir de Florence, Op. 70 TELC 2-▲ 90422 (33.97)

Kontra String Quartet *(rec 1992)* † Qt 1 Strs, Op. 11 BIS ▲ 642 [DDD] (17.97)

Moscow String Quartet † Qt 1 Strs, Op. 11 RUSS ▲ 788101 (12.97)

M. Rachlevsky (cnd), Kremlin CO [arr Rachlevsky] ("Tchaikovsky Music for String Orchestra: Vol II") † Snow Maiden (sels); Snow Maiden, Op. 12; Souvenir de Florence, Op. 70 CLAV ▲ 9317 [DDD] (16.97)

Queen of Spades (opera in 3 acts) [lib M. & P. Tchaikovsky after Pushkin], Op. 68 (1890)

S. Evstatieva (sop), P. Dilova (mez), I. Konsulov (bar), Y. Mazurok (bar), E. Tchakarov (cnd), Sofia Festival Orch, Bulgarian National Chorus [RUS] SNYC 3-▲ 45720 (51.97)

M. Gulegina (sop), O. Borodina (mez), G. Grigorian (ten), V. Gergiev (cnd), Kirov Theater Orch, Kirov Theater Chorus PPHI ▲ 38141 (48.97)

A. Melik-Pashayev (cnd), Bolshoi Theater Orch, G. Nelepp (ten), F. Godovkin (ten), A. Peregudov (ten) *(rec 1949)* LYS1 3-▲ 459 (50.97)

D. Miladinovic (cnd), Belgrade National Opera Orch *(rec live Venice, 1966)* MONM (Teatro La Fenice) 2-▲ 10221 (36.97)

Queen of Spades (selections)

S. Larin (ten), G. Rozhdestvensky (cnd), Philharmonia Orch, J. McCarthy (cnd), Ambrosian Opera Chorus *(rec London, England, Aug 14-17, 1997)* ("Russian Arias, Vol. 1") † Eugene Onegin (sels); Mazeppa (sels); Slippers (sels); Borodin:Prince Igor (sels); Dargomyzhsky:Ruslan and Lyudmila (sels); M. Glinka:Russlan & Ludmilla (sels); S. Rachmaninoff:Boris Godunov (sels); Rimsky-Korsakov:May Night (sels); Sadko (sels) *([FRE,GER,RUS,ENG] lib text)* CHN ▲ 9603 [DDD] (16.97)

C. Lindberg (trbn), R. Pöntinen (pno) [arr Lindberg] *(rec Eskilstuna, Sweden, Jan 4-6, 1990)* ("The Russian Trombone") † E. Denisov:Choral varié; V. Ewald:Mélodie; Goedicke:Improv; Okunev:Adagio & Scherzo Trb & Pno; S. Prokofiev:Romeo & Juliet (sels) BIS ▲ 478 [DDD] (17.97)

Romance in f for Piano, Op. 5 (1868)

F. Hohman (pno) *(rec Augustana Lutheran Church Denver, CO, 1991)* † Marche slave, Op. 31; Romeo & Juliet; Sym 5 PROO ▲ 7012 [DDD]

M. Pletnev (pno) *(rec 1986/88)* ("Mikhail Pletnev") † Capriccio, Op. 8; Con 2 Pno, Op. 44; Nutcracker Suite, Op. 71a; Saisons; Sleeping Beauty (sels); Valse-Scherzo Pno, Op. 7 PPHI (Great Pianists of the 20th Century) ▲ 456931 (22.97)

Romeo & Juliet (fantasy overture) in b for Orchestra [after Shakespeare] (1870)

C. Abbado (cnd), Chicago SO † Sym 4 SNYC ▲ 44911 [DDD] (11.97)

C. Abbado (cnd), Chicago SO † Marche slave, Op. 31; Ov 1812, Op. 49; Tempest, Op. 18 SNYC ▲ 47179 (11.97)

M. Abravanel (cnd), Utah SO ("Complete Orchestral Music, Vol. 3") † Hamlet; Sym 2; Sym 4 VB2 2-▲ 5006 [ADD]

Y. Ahronovitch (cnd), London SO ("Tchaikovsky Spectacular") † Marche slave, Op. 31; Ov 1812, Op. 49 INMP (LSO Classic Masterpieces) ▲ 801 [DDD] (9.97)

J. Barbirolli (cnd) † Marche slave, Op. 31; Qt 1 Strs, Op. 11; Serenade Strs, Op. 48; Sym 4; Sym 5; Sym 6 RYLC 3-▲ 70403 (20.97)

D. Barenboim (cnd), Chicago SO † Capriccio italien, Op. 45; Francesca da Rimini, Op. 32; Ov 1812, Op. 49 DEUT (Masters) ▲ 45523 [DDD] (9.97)

D. Barenboim (cnd), Chicago SO † Sym 4 TELC ▲ 13698 (16.97)

L. Bernstein (cnd), New York PO † Sym 5 DEUT ▲ 29234 [DDD] (16.97)

TCHAIKOVSKY, PIOTR (cont.)

Romeo & Juliet (fantasy overture) in b for Orchestra [after Shakespeare] (1870) (cont.)

L. Bernstein (cnd), New York PO *(rec Jan 28, 1957)* ("Leonard Bernstein: The Royal Edition") † Sym 3 SNYC ▲ 47632 [ADD] (10.97)

J. Buehl (nar), V. Jordania (cnd), Russian Federated Orch [includes narration of Romeo & Juliet story] HEL ▲ 1034 (10.97)

V. Cliburn (pno), L. Stokowski (cnd), Swiss-Italian Radio-TV Orch † Con 1 Pno, Op. 23; Nutcracker, Op. 71 AURC ▲ 108 (5.97)

A. Coates (cnd), London SO *(rec 1928)* ("Tchaikovsky Conducted by Albert Coates") † Sym 6 GSE ▲ 785051 (16.97)

A. Coates (cnd), National SO *(rec London, England, 1945)* ("Coates Conducts Tchaikovsky") † Sym 6 BEUL ▲ 6 (m) [ADD] (16.97)

A. Dmitriev (cnd), Leningrad PO † Nutcracker, Op. 71 MTRC (Russian Legacy) ▲ 8406 (7.97)

P. Domingo (cnd), Philharmonia Orch † Capriccio italien, Op. 45; Eugene Onegin (sels); Ov 1812, Op. 49; Songs (6), Op. 6 CSER (Seraphim) ▲ 73297 [DDD] (6.97)

A. Doráti (cnd), London SO *(rec Watford Town Hall, June 20, 1959)* † Sym 6 MRCR ▲ 34353 (11.97)

A. Dorati (cnd), National SO Washington D.C. † Marche slave, Op. 31; Ov 1812, Op. 49 PLON ▲ 17742 [ADD] (9.97)

A. Doráti (cnd), National SO Washington D.C. *(rec 1974)* † Capriccio italien, Op. 45; Fatum; Francesca da Rimini, Op. 32; Hamlet; Marche slave, Op. 31; Ov 1812, Op. 49; Tempest, Op. 18; Voyevoda, Op. 78 PLON 2-▲ 43003 [ADD] (17.97)

V. Dudarova (cnd), Russian SO † Capriccio italien, Op. 45; Fatum; Festival Ov, Op. 15; Francesca da Rimini, Op. 32; Hamlet; Ov 1812, Op. 49; Tempest, Op. 18 OLY ▲ 512 (16.97)

S. Edwards (cnd), Royal Liverpool PO † Francesca da Rimini, Op. 32; Marche slave, Op. 31; Ov 1812, Op. 49 CFP (Eminence) ▲ 2152 [DDD] (16.97)

V. Fedoseyev (cnd), Ostankino Radio-TV Large SO *(rec 1990-91)* † Francesca da Rimini, Op. 32; Tempest, Op. 18; Voyevoda, Op. 78 CSN ▲ 815000 [DDD] (12.97)

D. Gatti (cnd), Royal PO † S. Prokofiev:Romeo & Juliet (sels) CONI ▲ 51343 [DDD] (16.97)

C. Gerhardt (cnd), National PO London *(rec 1968)* † M. Ravel:Boléro; R. Strauss:Rosenkavalier (suite) CHSK ▲ 35 [ADD] (16.97)

A. Gharabekian (cnd), Ukrainian Radio-TV SO *(rec Kiev, Nov 5-8, 1994)* † S. Prokofiev:Romeo & Juliet (suite 1), Op. 64bis; Romeo & Juliet (suite 2), Op. 64ter RUS ▲ 10090 [DDD] (19.97)

D. Gleeson (cnd), London PO † Ode to Joy; S. Prokofiev:Hail to Stalin, Op. 85 IMAS (Masters) ▲ 6600122 (16.97)

P. Grainger (pno), R. Leopold (pno) [arr Grainger for pno 4-hands] *(rec 1929)* ("Grainger Plays Schumann, Scott, Strauss & Tchaikovsky") † R. Schumann:Romances Pno, Op. 28; Son 2 Pno, Op. 22; Symphonic Etudes, Op. 13; C. Scott:Dances Orch, Op. 22; R. Strauss:Till Eulenspiegels lustige Streiche, Op. 28 KLAV ▲ 11081 [ADD] (18.97)

F. Hohman (org) *(rec Augustana Lutheran Church Denver, CO, 1991)* † Marche slave, Op. 31; Romance Pno, Op. 5; Sym 5 PROO ▲ 7012 [DDD]

A. Joó (cnd), London SO *(rec London, Apr 1983 & June 1986)* † Sym 5 AART ▲ 47241 [DDD] (10.97)

V. Kahi (cnd), Georgian Festival Orch ("The Tchaikovsky Album") † Capriccio italien, Op. 45; Marche slave, Op. 31; Ov 1812, Op. 49 SNYC ▲ 61978 [DDD] (4.97)

V. Kahi (cnd), Georgian Festival Orch † Sym 4 SNYC ▲ 64292 [DDD] (4.97)

I. Karabtchevsky (cnd), Venice Theater Orch *(rec live, 1996)* † A. Dvořák:Sym 9 MONM ▲ 10054 (18.97)

H. von Karajan (cnd), Berlin PO † Nutcracker Suite, Op. 71a DEUT (Karajan Gold) ▲ 39021 [DDD] (16.97)

H. von Karajan (cnd), Vienna PO *(rec 1946)* ("The Young Karajan: The First Recordings, Vol. 7: The Early Recordings with Walter Legge") † Beethoven:Sym 8; W. A. Mozart:German Dances (3), K.605; German Dances (6), K.600; Sym 33, K.319 GRM2 ▲ 78691 (13.97)

K. Koizumi (cnd), Royal PO † Con 1 Pno, Op. 23; Con 3 Pno, Op. 75; Sym 4; Sym 6 ICC 3-▲ 6702679 (25.97)

S. Koussevitzky (cnd) *(rec 1930-44)* † Sym 4; Sym 5; Sym 6 78'S 2-▲ 78550 (m) (26.97)

A. Leaper (cnd), Royal PO † Ov 1812, Op. 49 NXIN ▲ 550500 [DDD] (5.97)

A. Leaper (cnd), Royal PO *(rec Watford Town Hall London, Jan 7-10, 1991)* ("Fantasias after Shakespeare") † Hamlet; Tempest, Op. 18 NXIN ▲ 553017 [DDD] (5.97)

I. Markevitch (cnd), Philharmonia Orch † Nutcracker Suite, Op. 71a; Swan Lake (suite), Op. 20a; S. Prokofiev:Sym 1 TES ▲ 1107 (17.97)

K. Masur (cnd), Leipzig Gewandhaus Orch † Sym 2 TELC ▲ 44943 [DDD] (16.97)

W. Mengelberg (cnd), (Royal) Concertgebouw Orch *(rec 1931)* ("Mengelberg 1928-32 Columbia Recordings") † Sym 4; Sym 5; J. Brahms:Sym 3 GSE 2-▲ 785048 (32.97)

W. Mengelberg (cnd), (Royal) Concertgebouw Orch *(rec 1928-30 & 1941)* † Sym 4; Sym 5; Sym 6 GRM2 2-▲ 78780 (26.97)

W. Mengelberg (cnd), (Royal) Concertgebouw Orch *(rec 1929-30)* ("Mengleberg: Tchaikovsky Vol. 1") † Sym 4 LYS ▲ 132 (17.97)

N. Nozy (cnd), Belgian Guides Symphonic Band [trans M. H. Hindsley] † Marche slave, Op. 31; Ov 1812, Op. 49 RENE ▲ 87048 [DDD] (16.97)

J. Ogdon (pno), P. Monteux (cnd), London SO *(rec live Vienna Festival, May 31, 1963)* † Con 1 Pno, Op. 23; Sym 5 VC 2-▲ 8031 (26.97)

E. Ormandy (cnd), Philadelphia Orch ("Basic 100, Vol. 35") † Sym 5 RCAV ▲ 61853 (10.97)

E. Ormandy (cnd), Philadelphia Orch † Capriccio italien, Op. 45; Con Vn; Eugene Onegin (sels); Marche slave, Op. 31; Ov 1812, Op. 49; Sym 5 SNYC (Essential Classics Take 2) 2-▲ 63281 (14.97)

V. Polianski (cnd), Russian State SO † Sym 5 CHN ▲ 9383 [DDD] (16.97)

A. Previn (cnd), London SO *(rec 1973)* † Manfred, Op. 58; Marche slave, Op. 31; S. Rachmaninoff:Sym 2 EMIC (Doublefforte) 2-▲ 69776 [ADD] (16.97)

A. Rahbari (cnd), Israel SO † Sym 4 DI ▲ 920496 [DDD] (5.97)

H. Scherchen (cnd) † Lt Kijé Suite, Op. 60; Rimsky-Korsakov:Russian Easter Overture, Op. 36; P. Tchaikovsky:Ov 1812, Op. 49; Romeo & Juliet ENT (Palladio) 2-▲ 4167 [ADD] (26.97)

L. Siegel (cnd), London PO ("Bolero") † Liszt:Préludes, S.97; M. Ravel:Boléro; Smetana:Moldau LALI ▲ 15503 [DDD] (3.97)

L. Siegel (cnd), New PO London † Con 1 Pno, Op. 23 PC ▲ 267173 [DDD] (2.97)

G. Simon (cnd), London SO [orig 1869 version] † Festival Ov, Op. 15; Serenade for N. Rubinstein CHN 2-▲ 8310 [DDD] (33.97)

G. Simon (cnd), London SO CHN ▲ 9191 [DDD] (16.97)

G. Sinopoli (cnd), Philharmonia Orch † Sym 6 DGRM ▲ 445601 [DDD]

L. Slatkin (cnd), St. Louis SO *(rec Powell Symphony Hall, Nov 23, 1991)* † Ov 1812, Op. 49; Sym 2 RCAV (Red Seal) ▲ 68045 [DDD] (16.97)

L. Slovák (cnd), Slovak PO † S. Prokofiev:Romeo & Juliet, Op. 64 OPP ▲ 810 (10.97)

G. Solti (cnd), Chicago SO ("The Solti Collection, Vol. 6") † Sym 6 PLON (Jubilee) ▲ 30442 [ADD] (11.97)

G. Solti (cnd), Chicago SO † Nutcracker Suite, Op. 71a; Swan Lake (suite), Op. 20a PLON (Jubilee) ▲ 30707 [DDD] (9.97)

G. Solti (cnd), Chicago SO † Sym 4 PLON (Jubilee) ▲ 30745 [DDD] (9.97)

G. Solti (cnd), Chicago SO ("The Tchaikovsky Album") † Nutcracker Suite, Op. 71a; Ov 1812, Op. 49; Swan Lake (suite), Op. 20a; Sym 6 PLON (Double Decker) 2-▲ 455810 (17.97)

L. Stokowski (cnd) *(rec 1934-44)* ("Stokowski Conducts Tchaikovsky") † Marche slave, Op. 31; Sleeping Beauty (suite), Op. 66a; Sym 5 GRM2 2-▲ 78713 (26.97)

L. Stokowski (cnd) † Marche slave, Op. 31; Songs; G. F. Handel:Messiah (sels) IMMM ▲ 37031 (6.97)

L. Stokowski (cnd), New York City SO *(rec Dec 11, 1944)* ("Stokowski Conducts Tchaikovsky") † Marche slave, Op. 31; Sym 5 IN ▲ 1367 [ADD] (15.97)

L. Stokowski (cnd), Philadelphia Orch *(rec 1928-29)* ("Stokowski Conducts Tchaikovsky") † Capriccio italien, Op. 45; Sym 4 PHS ▲ 9120 [ADD] (17.97)

L. Tjeknavorian (cnd), Armenian PO ("A Night on Bare Mountain & Other Russian Favorites") † Eugene Onegin (sels); Borodin:In the Steppes of Central Asia; Prince Igor (Polovtsian Dances); M. Glinka:Russlan & Ludmilla (ov); Mussorgsky:Night on Bare Mountain; D. Shostakovich:Festive Ov, Op. 96 ASVQ ▲ 6180 (10.97)

A. Toscanini (cnd), La Scala Orch *(rec La Scala, Milan, Italy, Sept 16, 1948)* † Mussorgsky:Pictures at an Exhibition; G. Rossini:Scala di seta (ov); Verdi:Otello (sels) RY (The Radio Years) ▲ 99 (16.97)

A. Toscanini (cnd), NBC SO ("The Toscanini Collection, Vol. 19") RCAV (Gold Seal) ▲ 60298 [ADD] (11.97)

A. Toscanini (cnd), NBC SO *(rec 1946-47)* ("Toscanini Edition, Vol. 2") † Sym 6 GRM2 ▲ 78800 (13.97)

H. Vonk (cnd), Dresden Staatskapelle † Con Vn BER ▲ 9384 (10.97)

B. Walter (cnd), Los Angeles Standard SO *(rec live, 1940-42)* ("Bruno Walter Live, Vol. 2") † Sym 5 LYS ▲ 416 (17.97)

B. Walter (cnd), Los Angeles Standard SO *(rec July 16, 1942)* † A. Dvořák:Sym 9; Smetana:Bartered Bride (ov); Moldau MUA ▲ 4788 (m) [AAD]

W. Weller (cnd), Basel SO † Sym 4 ARSM ▲ 1140 [DDD] (17.97)

P. Wohlert (cnd), Berlin RSO † Sleeping Beauty (suite), Op. 66a; Swan Lake (suite), Op. 20a LALI ▲ 15633 [DDD] (3.97)

TCHAIKOVSKY, PIOTR (cont.)

Romeo & Juliet (fantasy overture) in b for Orchestra [after Shakespeare] (1870) (cont.)

D. Zinman (cnd), Baltimore SO † Sym 4 TEL ▲ 80228 [DDD] (16.97)

Sacred Pieces (9) for unaccompanied Mixed Chorus (1884)

M. Best (cnd), Corydon Singers † Liturgy of St. John Chrysostom, Op. 41 HYP ▲ 66948 (18.97)

N. Kachanov (cnd), New York Russian Chamber Chorus [3 sels] † Vesper Service, Op. 52 KOCH ▲ 7420 (16.97)

Les Saisons [The Seasons] (12 pieces) for Piano, Op. 37b (1875-76)

L. Artymiw (pno) CHN ▲ 8349 [DDD] (16.97)

Y. Bronfman (pno) *(rec Troy, NY, May 21-22, 1998)* † Balakirev:Islamey SNYC ▲ 60689 [DDD] (16.97)

A. Brownridge (pno) *(rec 1994)* † Son Pno, Op. 37 CAL ▲ 88008 [DDD] (12.97)

L. Edlina (pno) † Borodin:Petite Suite Pno CHN ▲ 9309 [DDD] (16.97)

D. Geringas (cnd), Southwest German CO Pforzheim [orchd] † Nocturne Vc; Pezzo capriccioso, Op. 62; Vars on a Rococo Theme, Op. 33 EBS ▲ 6033 (17.97)

N. Järvi (cnd), Detroit SO [arr A. Gauk for orch] † Suite 4 Orch, Op. 61 CHN (Tchaikovsky Suite) ▲ 9514 (16.97)

A. Kubalek (pno) † Kymlicka:Valses Pno DOR ▲ 90102 [DDD] (16.97)

A. Laplante (pno)—October:Chant d'automne *(rec Montreal, Canada, June 1992)* † S. Rachmaninoff:Con 3 Pno, Op. 30; Preludes Pno FL ▲ 23107 [DDD] (16.97)

M. Pletnev (pno) *(rec 1986)* ("Mikhail Pletnev") † Capriccio, Op. 8; Con 2 Pno, Op. 44; Nutcracker Suite, Op. 71a; Romance Pno, Op. 5; Sleeping Beauty (sels); Valse-Scherzo Pno, Op. 7 PPHI (Great Pianists of the 20th Century) ▲ 456931 (22.97)

D. Pollack (pno)—October:Chant d'automne ("First Kiss") † Chopin:Nocturnes Pno; Debussy:Arabesques Pno; Fille aux cheveaux de lin (song); Liszt:Études de concert (3), S.144; Consolations (6), S.172; M. Ravel:Pavane pour une infante défunte; R. Schumann:Carnaval, Op. 9; Kinderszenen Pno, Op. 15 FWIN ▲ 3002 (13.97)

M. Ponti (pno) ("Complete Solo Piano Music, Vol. 1") † Album pour enfants Pno, Op. 39; Pno Music; Son Pno, Op. 80 VB2 2-▲ 5087 [ADD] (9.97)

I. Prunyi (pno) *(rec Budapest, Hungary, July 13-14, 1988)* † Morceaux (12) Pno, Op. 40; Morceaux (6) Pno, Op. 19; Souvenir de Hapsal, Op. 2 NXIN ▲ 550233 [DDD] (5.97)

M. Rachlevsky (cnd), Kremlin CO [suite; arr Rachlevsky] ("Tchaikovsky Music for String Orchestra: Vol III") † Qt in B♭ Strs; Qt 2 Strs, Op. 22 CLAV ▲ 9414 (16.97)

S. Richter (pno) ("Classic Richter") † Morceaux (6) Pno, Op. 51; Beethoven:Son 27 Pno, Op. 90; Chopin:Scherzos Pno; S. Rachmaninoff:Preludes Pno; F. Schubert:Son Pno, D.625; R. Schumann:Novelettes, Op. 21 OLY ▲ 580 [ADD] (16.97)

E. Rivkin (pno) † Son Pno, Op. 37 ACAD ▲ 20054 [DDD] (16.97)

J. Sterczyński (pno) *(rec Rzeszow, Poland, Mar 7-8, 1993)* ("Piano Works") † Chopin:Polonaise 1 Pno, Op. 26/1; Polonaise 2 Pno, Op. 26/2; Polonaise 3 Pno, Op. 40/1; Polonaise 4 Pno, Op. 40/2; Polonaise 5 Pno, Op. 44; Polonaise 6 Pno, Op. 53; Polonaises-fant, Op. 61 SELN ▲ 930916 [DDD] (16.97)

V. Tropp (pno) † S. Rachmaninoff:Morceaux de fant, Op. 3 DNN ▲ 18003 (16.97)

E. Wild (pno) *(rec New York, NY, 1976)* † Medtner:Improv Pno, Op. 31/1; Mussorgsky:Pictures at an Exhibition IVOR ▲ 70903 [ADD] (16.97)

Sérénade mélancolique in b for Violin & Orchestra (or Piano), Op. 26 (1875)

D. Berlinsky (vn), S. Gorakhovich (pno) ("Souvenir d'un lieu cher") † Souvenir d'un lieu cher, Op. 42; Valse-Scherzo Vn, Op. 34; S. Prokofiev:Son 2 Vn; A. Schnittke:Suite in the Old Style; R. Shchedrin:Humoresque Orch; In Imitation of Albéniz HEL ▲ 1015 (10.97)

R. Chen (vn), P. Kogan (cnd), Hanover Radio PO ("Chen Plays Tchaikovsky") † Con Vn; Souvenir d'un lieu cher, Op. 42 BER ▲ 1169 (16.97)

A. Dubeau (vn), I. Blazhkov (cnd), Kiev SO *(rec 1989)* † Kabalevsky:Con Vn; S. Prokofiev:Con 1 Vn, Op. 19 FL ▲ 23036 [DDD] (16.97)

C. Glenn (vn), E. Rachlin (cnd), Cambridge SO † Capriccio italien, Op. 45; Eugene Onegin (sels); Nutcracker (sels); Sleeping Beauty (suite), Op. 66a; Slippers (sels); Souvenir d'un lieu cher, Op. 42; Swan Lake (suite), Op. 20a; Valse-Scherzo Vn, Op. 34; Vars on a Rococo Theme, Op. 33 VB3 3-▲ 3026 [ADD]

I. Grubert (vn), V. Sinaisky (cnd), Moscow PO † Con Vn; Souvenir d'un lieu cher, Op. 42 RUSS ▲ 788054 (12.97)

J. Heifetz (vn) † Con Vn; Mendelssohn (-Bartholdy):Con Vn & Orch, Op. 64 RCAV (Red Seal) ▲ 5933 (16.97)

J. Heifetz (vn) *(rec Hollywood, July 8-10, 1970)* † Con Vn; Mendelssohn (-Bartholdy):Con Vn & Orch, Op. 64 RCAV (Red Seal) ▲ 61743 [ADD] (16.97)

L. Issakadze (vn) *(rec Sept 26-28, 1992)* † Souvenir d'un lieu cher, Op. 42; Souvenir de Florence, Op. 70; Valse-Scherzo Vn, Op. 34 ORF ▲ 307921 [DDD] (18.97)

O. Kagan (vn), V. Lobanov (pno) ("Complete Works for Violin & Piano") † Souvenir d'un lieu cher, Op. 42; Valse-Scherzo Vn, Op. 34 ODE ▲ 733 [DDD] (17.97)

L. Mordkovitch (vn), M. Gusak-Grin (pno) *(rec Frognal, Hampstead, United States of America, Mar 21/22, 1986)* ("Russian Music for Violin & Piano") † Souvenir d'un lieu cher, Op. 42; Valse-Scherzo Vn, Op. 34; Glazunov:Grand Waltz; Raymonda (sels); S. Prokofiev:Mélodies Vn, Op. 35bis; S. Rachmaninoff:Romance Vn & Pno, Op. 6/1; I. Stravinsky:Mavra (sels); Russian Dance *([ENG] text)* CHN ▲ 8500 [DDD] (16.97)

I. Perlman (vn), E. Ormandy (cnd), Philadelphia Orch † Con Vn EMIC ▲ 47106 (16.97)

G. Shaham (vn), Orpheus CO *(rec State Univ of NY Purchase, NY, Dec 1995)* † Beethoven:Romances Vn; A. Dvořák:Romance Vn, Op. 11; E. Elgar:Salut d'amour Orch, Op. 12; F. Kreisler:Vn Pieces (original works & arrs); J. S. Svendsen:Romance Vn, Op. 26 DEUT ▲ 49923 [DDD] (16.97)

I. Stern (vn), E. Ormandy (cnd), Philadelphia Orch ("Isaac Stern: A Life in Music") † Souvenir d'un lieu cher, Op. 42; Bruch:Con 1 Vn, Op. 26; Wieniawski:Con 2 Vn, Op. 22 SNYC ▲ 66830 (10.97)

Xue-Wei (vn), S. Accardo (cnd), Philharmonia Orch † Con Vn; Souvenir d'un lieu cher, Op. 42; Valse-Scherzo Vn, Op. 34 ASV ▲ 713 [DDD] (16.97)

Serenade for Nikolai Rubinstein's Name-Day for Small Orchestra (1872)

G. Simon (cnd), London SO † Festival Ov, Op. 15; Romeo & Juliet CHN 2-▲ 8310 [DDD] (33.97)

G. Simon (cnd), London SO † Festival Ov, Op. 15; Sym 2 CHN ▲ 9190 [DDD] (16.97)

Serenade in C for String Orchestra, Op. 48 (1880)

J. Barbirolli (cnd) † Marche slave, Op. 31; Qt 1 Strs, Op. 11; Romeo & Juliet; Sym 4; Sym 5; Sym 6 RYLC 3-▲ 70403 (20.97)

P. Berglund (cnd), New Stockholm CO † A. Dvořák:Serenade Strs, Op. 22 BIS ▲ 243 [DDD] (17.97)

B. Britten (cnd), English CO *(rec 1968)* † Legend (When Jesus Christ Was But a Child), Op. 54/5; Nocturne Vc; Suite 4 Orch, Op. 61 BBC (Britten the Performer) ▲ 8002 (17.97)

Cicashi Tanaka Ensemble ("Orchestra Plays Adagio") † A. Bruckner:Qt Strs; Sym 2; G. Mahler:Sym 5; Yoshimatsu:Threnody to Toki, Op. 12; Zi:3 Wishes for a Rose CAMA (After Hours Classics) ▲ 423 [DDD] (15.97)

A. Dorati (cnd), Philharmonia Hungarica † Nutcracker, Op. 71 MRCR 2-▲ 32750 [ADD] (22.97)

A. Duczmal (cnd), Amadeus CO † A. Dvořák:Serenade Strs, Op. 22 AART ▲ 47287 [DDD] (10.97)

A. Duczmal (cnd), Polish Radio CO † E. Grieg:Elegiac Melodies, Op. 34; Holberg Suite Pno, Op. 40; J. Suk:Serenade Strs, Op. 6 ASVQ ▲ 6094 [ADD] (10.97)

P. Entremont (cnd), Vienna CO *(rec Feb 1990)* † Souvenir de Florence, Op. 70 NXIN ▲ 550404 [DDD] (5.97)

P. Entremont (cnd), Vienna CO *(rec Brussels, June 1990)* † J. Brahms:Serenade 1 Orch, Op. 11 NXIN ▲ 8553227 [DDD] (5.97)

H. von Karajan (cnd), Berlin PO † A. Dvořák:Serenade Strs, Op. 22 DEUT ▲ 38 [DDD] (16.97)

V. Kazandjiev (cnd), Sofia CO † S. Barber:Adagio Strs; A. Dvořák:Serenade Strs, Op. 22 DNN ▲ 8002 [DDD] (10.97)

L. Markiz (cnd), Amsterdam New Sinfonietta *(rec 1990)* † Andante cantabile; Elegy Strs; Nocturne Vc; Arensky:Vars on a Theme of Tchaikovsky GLOE ▲ 6021 [DDD] (16.97)

N. Marriner (cnd), Academy of St. Martin in the Fields † Nutcracker Suite, Op. 71a PPHI ▲ 11471 [DDD] (16.97)

A. Moglia (vn), A. Moglia (cnd), Toulouse National CO ("Russian Serenades") † Glazunov:Suite Strs, Op. 35 PVY ▲ 730069 (11.97)

E. Mravinsky (cnd), Leningrad PO *(rec 1961)* † Francesca da Rimini, Op. 32 RUS ▲ 15003 [AAD]

P. Narrato (cnd), Belgium Festival Orch † Con Vn PC ▲ 265064 [DDD] (2.97)

G. Octors (cnd), Walloon CO ("Serenades") † A. Dvořák:Serenade Strs, Op. 22; E. Elgar:Serenade Strs, Op. 20 CYPR ▲ 2615 [DDD] (17.97)

E. Ormandy (cnd), Philadelphia Orch † Ov 1812, Op. 49 SNYC ■ 30447 (10.98)

Orpheus CO † E. Grieg:Elegiac Melodies, Op. 34; Holberg Suite Pno, Op. 40 DEUT ▲ 23060 [DDD] (16.97)

V. Polianski (cnd), Belarussian CO *(rec Moscow Conservatory Great Hall, Russia, 1987)* ("Russian Conducting School: Valery Poliansky") † Choral Music; Arensky:Vars on a Theme of Tchaikovsky RD (Talents of Russia) ▲ 22106 [DDD] (16.97)

M. Rachlevsky (cnd), Kremlin CO *(rec Moscow Conservatory Great Hall, Oct-Nov 1991)* ("Music for Strings, Vol. 1") † Elegy Strs; Qt 1 Strs, Op. 11; Souvenir d'un lieu cher, Op. 42 CLAV ▲ 9116 [DDD] (16.97)

A. Scholz (cnd), Slovak PO ("After the Main Course") † W. A. Mozart:Kleine Nachtmusik, K.525; Nozze di Figaro (sels); Qnt Cl, K.581; M. Ravel:Boléro ECL ▲ 515 (2.97)

J. Serebrier (cnd), Scottish CO † Elegy Strs; Sleeping Beauty (sels); Suite 4 Orch, Op. 61 ASV ▲ 719 [DDD] (16.97)

TCHAIKOVSKY, PIOTR (cont.)

Serenade in C for String Orchestra, Op. 48 (1880) (cont.)

L. Slatkin (cnd), St. Louis SO † Borodin:Nocturne Str Orch; J. Pachelbel:Canon & Gigue; Vaughan Williams:Fant on Greensleeves TEL ▲ 80080 [DDD] (16.97)

J. Somary (cnd), English CO *(rec Conway Hall, London, England, 1972)* ("Russian Favorites for Strings") † Arensky:Vars on a Theme of Tchaikovsky; Borodin:Nocturne Str Orch; S. Prokofiev:Sym 1 VC ▲ 37 [AAD] (13.97)

I. Stern (vn), L. Bernstein (cnd), New York PO *(rec Oct 22, 1970)* ("Leonard Bernstein: The Royal Edition") † Con Vn SNYC ▲ 47637 [ADD] (10.97)

E. Svetlanov (cnd), USSR SO *(rec Moscow, 1970)* † Sym 4 MELD ▲ 37878 [ADD] (6.97)

A. Titov (cnd), St. Petersburg Conservatory CO † A. Dvořák:Serenade Strs, Op. 22 SNYC ▲ 57226 [DDD] (4.97)

G. Varga (cnd), Stuttgart CO *(rec Stuttgart, Germany, 1994)* † Arensky:Vars on a Theme of Tchaikovsky; M. Glinka:Divert brillante; S. Rachmaninoff:Pieces Vn Pno, Op. 6 DI ▲ 920323 [DDD] (5.97)

G. Wich (cnd), Southwest German CO Pforzheim—Pezzo in forma di Sonatina ("Another Kiss: More Music for Love & Passion") † Beethoven:Bagatelle Pno in a, WoO 59; Debussy:Suite bergamasque; A. Dvořák:Sym 9; W. A. Mozart:Kleine Nachtmusik, K.525; F. Schubert:Sym 8; Smetana:Moldau INTC ▲ 892934 [AAD] (13.97)

S. Yoo (cnd), Metamorphosen CO *(rec Wellesley, MA, Mar 30-Apr 1, 1997)* † A. Dvořák:Serenade Strs, Op. 22; E. Grieg:Holberg Suite Pno, Op. 40 ACTR ▲ 60105 [DDD] (17.97)

artists unknown ("Winter Dreams") † Andante cantabile; Con 1 Pno, Op. 23; E. Grieg:Lyric Pieces; Music of Grieg; Sibelius:Swan of Tuonela; Valse triste PPHI (Night Moods) ▲ 453908 [DDD] (9.97)

artists unknown † A. Dvořák:Serenade Strs, Op. 22; E. Grieg:Holberg Suite Pno, Op. 40; W. A. Mozart:Kleine Nachtmusik, K.525; R. Strauss:Metamorphosen DNN (Classics Exposed) ▲ 17011 (16.97)

various artists—Waltz † Eugene Onegin (sels); Marche slave, Op. 31; Nutcracker (sels); Ov 1812, Op. 49; Qt 1 Strs, Op. 11; Swan Lake (sels); Sym 6 RCAV ▲ 60845 (11.97) ■ 60845 (5.98)

Sleeping Beauty (ballet) for Orchestra, Op. 66 (1888-89)

A. Doráti (cnd), (Royal) Concertgebouw Orch PPHI (Duo) 2-▲ 46166 (17.97)

V. Gergiev (cnd), Kirov Theater Orch PPHI ▲ 34922 (48.97)

A. Mogrelia (cnd), Czech-Slovak State PO *(rec Mar 18-23 & May 13-25, 1991)* NXIN 3-▲ 550490 [DDD] (15.97)

A. Previn (cnd), London SO EMIC 2-▲ 54814 (32.97)

A. Walachowski (pno), I. Walachowski (pno) [Rachmaninov trans for pno 4-hands] ("Klavierduo Walachowski") † J. Brahms:Vars on a Theme by Paganini, Op. 35; Chopin:Rondos (4) Pnos; W. A. Mozart:Andante & Vars, K.501; M. Ravel:Valse ARS ▲ 368359 [DDD] (15.99)

G. Weldon (cnd), Philharmonia Orch CFP ▲ 4458 [ADD] (24.97)

Sleeping Beauty (selections)

D. Achatz (pno), Y. Nagai (pno) [arr Rachmaninoff for 2 pnos] *(rec Oct 9-12, 1993)* † Swan Lake (sels); Sym 5 BIS ▲ 627 [DDD] (17.97)

E. Bátiz (cnd), Royal PO—Waltz † Nutcracker Suite, Op. 71a; Sym 5 ALFA ▲ 1007 [DDD]

A. Dorati (cnd), (Royal) Concertgebouw Orch, St. Bavo Cathedral Boys' Choir † Nutcracker, Op. 71 PPHI (Duo) 2-▲ 42562 (17.97)

C. Dutoit (cnd), Montreal SO † Nutcracker (sels); Swan Lake (sels) PLON ▲ 43555 (16.97)

M. Ermler (cnd), Royal Opera House Orch Covent Garden ("Tchaikovsky Ballet") † Nutcracker (sels); Swan Lake (sels) CONI ▲ 55012 [DDD] (11.97)

A. Fiedler (cnd), Boston Pops Orch ("Pops Caviar, Russian Orchestral Fireworks") † Eugene Onegin (sels); Borodin:In the Steppes of Central Asia; Prince Igor (ov); Prince Igor (sels); E. Elgar:Pomp & Circumstance, Op. 39; A. Khachaturian:Gayane (sels); Masquerade (sels); Rimsky-Korsakov:Russian Easter Overture, Op. 36 RCAV (Living Stereo) ▲ 68132 (11.97)

V. Gergiev (cnd), Kirov Theater Orch PPHI ▲ 34930 (16.97)

N. Järvi (cnd), Royal Scottish National Orch ["Bluebird" Pas de deux, arr Igor Stravinsky for sm] † I. Stravinsky:Baiser de la fée CHN ▲ 8360 [DDD] (16.97)

G. Kremer (vn), C. Eschenbach (cnd), Philharmonia Orch—La Fée des lilas paraît (finale Act 1); Act 2 Entr'acte (Andante sostenuto) ("Out of Russia") † Lourié:Blackamoor of Peter the Great (sels); Funeral Games in the Honor of Chronos; A. Schnittke:Con 4 Vn; I. Stravinsky:Pastorale Vn TELC ▲ 98440 (16.97)

O. Lenárd (cnd), Czech RSO † Glazunov:Seasons, Op. 67 NXIN ▲ 550079 [DDD] (5.97)

A. Litton (cnd), Dallas SO [9 sels; arr Litton] *(rec Meyerson Center Dallas, TX, TX, Nov 16-18, 1995)* † Moscow; Ov 1812, Op. 49; Voyevoda, Op. 78 DLS (Virtual Reality Recording) ▲ 3196 [DDD] (14.97)

C. Mackerras (cnd), Royal PO † Swan Lake (sels) TEL ▲ 80151 [DDD] (16.97)

U. Mayer (cnd), Edmonton SO *(rec Sherwood Park Alberta, Mar 21-23, 1992)* ("Russian Sketches") † Eugene Onegin (sels); Borodin:In the Steppes of Central Asia; Ippolitov-Ivanov:Caucasian Sketches, Op. 10; Rimsky-Korsakov:Golden Cockerel (suite); D. Shostakovich:Golden Age (ballet suite), Op. 22a SMS ▲ 5169 [DDD] (16.97)

E. Ormandy (cnd), Philadelphia Orch † O. Respighi:Boutique fantasque SNYC (Essential Classics) ▲ 46340 [ADD] (7.97) ■ 46340 [ADD] (3.98)

M. Pletnev (pno) *(rec 1989)* ("Mikhail Pletnev") † Capriccio, Op. 8; Con 2 Pno, Op. 44; Nutcracker Suite, Op. 71a; Romance Pno, Op. 5; Saisons; Valse-Scherzo Pno, Op. 7 PPHI (Great Pianists of the 20th Century) ▲ 456931 (22.97)

A. Previn (cnd), London SO † Nutcracker (sels); Swan Lake (sels) EMIC ▲ 64332 (11.97)

J. Serebrier (cnd), Scottish CO—The Palace Garden; Act 2 Entr'acte (Andante sostenuto) † Elegy Strs; Serenade Strs, Op. 48; Suite 4 Orch, Op. 61 ASV ▲ 719 [DDD] (16.97)

Sleeping Beauty:Ballet Suite, Op. 66a

E. Bátiz (cnd), Royal PO ("Ballet Suites") † Nutcracker Suite, Op. 71a; Swan Lake (suite), Op. 20a ASVQ ▲ 6183 (10.97)

S. Gorkovenko (cnd), St. Petersburg New Philharmony Orch † Nutcracker Suite, Op. 71a; Swan Lake (sels) SNYC ▲ 57241 [DDD] (4.97)

D. Jackson (cnd), Royal PO † Capriccio italien, Op. 45; Eugene Onegin (sels); Nutcracker (sels); Slippers (sels); Souvenir d'un lieu cher, Op. 42; Swan Lake (suite), Op. 20a; Sérénade mélancolique, Op. 26; Valse-Scherzo Vn, Op. 34; Vars on a Rococo Theme, Op. 33 VB3 3-▲ 3026 [ADD]

H. von Karajan (cnd), Berlin PO † Nutcracker Suite, Op. 71a; Swan Lake (suite), Op. 20a DEUT ▲ 19175 [ADD] (16.97)

H. von Karajan (cnd), Vienna PO † Nutcracker Suite, Op. 71a; Swan Lake (suite), Op. 20a PLON (The Classic Sound) ▲ 448592 (11.97)

A. Lazarev (cnd), Bolshoi Theater SO † Capriccio italien, Op. 45; Eugene Onegin (sels); Nutcracker Suite, Op. 71a; Swan Lake (suite), Op. 20a TELC (Ultima) 2-▲ 18965 (16.97)

J. Levine (cnd), Vienna PO † Nutcracker Suite, Op. 71a; Swan Lake (suite), Op. 20a DEUT ▲ 37806 [DDD] (16.97)

New Philharmonia Orch † A. Adam:Giselle (sels); Delibes:Coppélia (suite); Sylvia (suite); M. Ravel:Boléro QUIN ▲ 2100 [DDD] (2.97)

S. Ozawa (cnd), Boston SO † Nutcracker, Op. 71 DEUT 2-▲ 35619 [DDD] (32.97)

S. Rohani (cnd), Slovak Radio New PO ("Musica per Tutti, Vol. 9") † Nutcracker Suite, Op. 71a; Swan Lake (suite), Op. 20a; Vivaldi:Domine ad adiuvandum me, RV.593; Gloria; Nisi Dominus, RV.608 DI ▲ 920295 [DDD] (5.97)

M. Rostropovich (cnd), Berlin PO *(rec 1979)* ("Ballet Suites") † Nutcracker Suite, Op. 71a; Swan Lake (suite), Op. 20a DEUT (The Originals) ▲ 449726 [ADD] (11.97)

L. Stokowski (cnd) *(rec 1934-44)* ("Stokowski Conducts Tchaikovsky") † Marche slave, Op. 31; Romeo & Juliet; Sym 5 GRM2 2-▲ 78713 (26.97)

L. Stokowski (cnd) † Sym 5 IMMM ▲ 37089 (6.97)

L. Stokowski (cnd), Leopold Stokowski SO ("Leopold Stokowski Conducts") † Liadov:Russian Folksongs, Op. 58 ENT (Sirio) ▲ 530010 (13.97)

R. Williams (cnd), London SO *(rec July 7-8, 1987)* † Nutcracker Suite, Op. 71a; Swan Lake (suite), Op. 20a LSO (LSO) ▲ 6900092 (10.97)

P. Wohlert (cnd), Berlin RSO † Romeo & Juliet; Swan Lake (suite), Op. 20a LALI ▲ 15633 [DDD] (3.97)

The Slippers [Cherevichki] (or Les caprices d'Oxane) (comic-fantastic opera in 4 acts) [lib Polonsky after Gogol; rev from Vakula the Smith] (1885)

A. Melik-Pashayev (cnd), Bolshoi Theater Orch, Bolshoi Theater Chorus, E. Kruglikova (sop), E. Antonova (mez), G. Nelepp (ten), V. Shestov (ten), A. Ivanov (bar), I. Ionov (bass) *(rec 1948)* PRE 2-▲ 90350 (m) (31.97)

The Slippers (selections)

S. Köhler (cnd), Philharmonia Hungarica † Capriccio italien, Op. 45; Eugene Onegin (sels); Nutcracker (sels); Sleeping Beauty (suite), Op. 66a; Souvenir d'un lieu cher, Op. 42; Swan Lake (suite), Op. 20a; Sérénade mélancolique, Op. 26; Valse-Scherzo Vn, Op. 34; Vars on a Rococo Theme, Op. 33 VB3 3-▲ 3026 [ADD]

S. Larin (ten), G. Rozhdestvensky (cnd), Philharmonia Orch, J. McCarthy (cnd), Ambrosian Opera Chorus *(rec London, England, Aug 14-17, 1997)* ("Russian Arias, Vol. 1") † Eugene Onegin (sels); Mazeppa (sels); Queen of Spades (sels); Borodin:Prince Igor (sels); Dargomyzhsky:Ruslan and Lyudmila (sels); M. Glinka:Russlan & Ludmilla (sels); S. Rachmaninoff:Boris Godunov (sels); Rimsky-Korsakov:May Night (sels); Sadko (sels) *([FRE,GER,RUS,ENG] lib text)* CHN ▲ 9603 [DDD] (16.97)

TCHAIKOVSKY, PIOTR (cont.)

The Snow Maiden (incidental music) for solo Voices, Small Orchestra & Chorus, Op. 12 (1873)

N. Erassova (sop), A. Arkhipov (ten), N. Vassiliev (ten), A. Tchistiakov (cnd), Bolshoi Theater Orch, Sveshnikov Russian State Choir RUSS ▲ 788090 (12.97)

N. Makarova (nar), C. Rosenberger (pno) DLS ▲ 6004 [DDD] (14.97)

I. Mishura-Lekhtman (mez), V. Grishko (ten), N. Järvi (cnd), Detroit SO, Univ Musical Society Choral Union CHN ▲ 9324 [DDD] (16.97)

E. Okolysheva (mez), A. Mishenkin (ten), I. Golovschin (cnd), Moscow SO, Moscow Capella *(rec Mosfilm Studio, Mar 1996) (E,R texts)* NXIN ▲ 8553856 [DDD] (5.97)

M. Rachlevsky (cnd), Kremlin CO ("Tchaikovsky Music for String Orchestra: Vol II") † Qt 3 Strs, Op. 30; Snow Maiden (sels); Souvenir de Florence, Op. 70 CLAV ▲ 9317 [DDD] (16.97)

The Snow Maiden (selections)

L. Gosman (cnd), Tchaikovsky CO—Melodrama † Qt 1 Strs, Op. 11; Songs; Borodin:Nocturne Str Orch; Chopin:Études Pno; Nocturnes Pno; Liszt:Liebesträume, S.541; Mendelssohn (-Bartholdy):Lieder, Op. 34; S. Rachmaninoff:Sym 2; Vocalise; Rimsky-Korsakov:Sadko (sels); Scheherazade, Op. 35 SNYC ▲ 46355 [ADD/DDD] (9.97)

M. Rachlevsky (cnd), Kremlin CO ("Tchaikovsky Music for String Orchestra: Vol II") † Qt 3 Strs, Op. 30; Snow Maiden, Op. 12; Souvenir de Florence, Op. 70 CLAV ▲ 9317 [DDD] (16.97)

Sonata in G for Piano, Op. 37 (1878)

A. Brownridge (pno) *(rec 1994)* † Saisons CAL ▲ 88008 [DDD] (12.97)

S. Cherkassky (pno) *(rec San Francisco, CA, Apr 18, 1982)* ("The 1982 San Francisco Recital") † Chopin:Polonaises-fant, Op. 61; Waltzes Pno; J. Hofmann:Kaleidoskop, Op. 40; Lully:Suite de pièces; Mendelssohn (-Bartholdy):Scherzo a capriccio IVOR ▲ 70904 [DDD] (16.97)

L. Howard (pno) ("Piano Sonatas") † Allegro Pno; Son Pno, Op. 80 HYP ▲ 66939 [DDD] (18.97)

A. Kuerti (pno) *(rec 1982)* ("Russian Piano Music") † Glazunov:Grande Valse de Concert, Op. 41; Liadov:Pno Music; A. Scriabin:Etudes (3) Pno, Op. 65; Preludes (5) Pno, Op. 74; Son 4 Pno, Op. 30 FL ▲ 23047 [DDD] (16.97)

E. Rivkin (pno) † Saisons ACAD ▲ 20054 [DDD] (16.97)

L. Sirota (pno) *(rec 1955)* ("The Sirota Archives, Vol. 1") † Glazunov:Son 1 Pno, Op. 74; A. Rubinstein:Pno Music ARBT ▲ 110 (16.97)

O. Yablonskaya (pno) *(rec Santa Rosa, CA, May 12-13, 1994)* ("Piano Music, Vol. 1") † Morceaux (6) Pno, Op. 51 NXIN ▲ 553063 [DDD] (5.97)

Sonata in c# for Piano, Op. 80 (1865)

E. Gilels (pno) ("Mravinsky Live") † Con 1 Pno, Op. 23 RUS ▲ 11170 [ADD] (12.97)

L. Howard (pno) ("Piano Sonatas") † Allegro Pno; Son Pno, Op. 37 HYP ▲ 66939 [DDD] (18.97)

M. Ponti (pno) ("Complete Solo Piano Music, Vol. 1") † Album pour enfants Pno, Op. 39; Pno Music; Saisons VB2 2-▲ 5087 [ADD] (9.97)

Songs

J. DeGaetani (mez), G. Kalish (pno)—Not a Word, O My Friend, Op. 6/2; Blue Eyes of Spring; Sleep, Poor Friend, Op. 47/4; Songs (7), Op. 47 [No. 7, Was I Not a Little Blade of Grass?]; Was it the Mother Who Bore Me?, Op. 27/5; Songs (6), Op. 25 [No. 4, The Canary]; It Was in the Early Spring, Op. 38/2; At Bedtime, Op. 27/1; Take My Heart Away; No, Only He Who Has Known, Op. 6/6 *(rec American Academy of Arts & Letters New York, NY, Jan 23-25, 1984)* ("Russian Songs") † Mussorgsky:The Nursery; S. Rachmaninoff:Songs (12), Op. 14; Songs (12), Op. 21; Songs (14), Op. 34; Songs (15), Op. 26; Songs (6), Op. 4 ARA ▲ 6674 [ADD] (16.97)

G. Gorchakova (sop), L. Gergieva (pno)—To Forget So Soon; Songs (6), Op. 28; Songs (6), Op. 16 [No. 1, Cradle Song]; It Was in the Early Spring, Op. 38/2 ("Memories of Love: Russian Romances") † Balakirev:Songs; Dargomyzhsky:Songs; M. Glinka:Songs; S. Rachmaninoff:Songs (12), Op. 14; Songs (12), Op. 21; Songs (6), Op. 8 PPHI ▲ 446720 (16.97)

D. Hvorostovsky (bar), M. Arkadiev (pno)—O, If Only You Could for One Moment, Op. 38/4; Amid the Din of the Ball, Op. 38/3; I Should Like in a Single Word; My Genius, My Angel, My Friend; It Was in the Early Spring, Op. 38/2; I Bless You, Forests, Op. 47/5; Not a Word, O My Friend, Op. 6/2; The Love of a Dead Man, Op. 38/5; On the Golden Cornfields, Op. 57/2; Songs (7), Op. 47 [No. 6, Does the Day Reign?]; We Sat Together, Op. 73/1 ("My Restless Soul") † S. Rachmaninoff:Songs; Songs (12), Op. 14; Songs (12), Op. 21; Songs (6), Op. 8; Rimsky-Korsakov:Songs PPHI ▲ 42536 (16.97)

D. Hvoroststovsky (bar), O. Boshniakovich (pno)—A Tear Trembles, Op. 6/4; No, Only He Who Has Known, Op. 6/6; Reconciliation, Op. 25/1; The Fearful Minute, Op. 28/6; Don Juan's Serenade, Op. 38/1; The Nightingale, Op. 60/4; Exploit, Op. 60/11; I Opened the Window, Op. 63/2; Again, as before, Alone, Op. 73/6 PPHI ▲ 32119 [DDD] (16.97)

L. Kazarnovskaya (sop), L. Orfenova (pno)—Zemfira's Song; Mezza Notte; To Forget So Soon; Songs (6), Op. 16 [No. 1, Cradle Song; No. 2, Wait!]; Take My Heart Away; Songs (6), Op. 25 [No. 2, As O'er the Burning Ashes (words Tennyson)]; Songs (6), Op. 27 [No. 3, Do Not Leave Me]; Songs (6), Op. 28 [No. 4, He Loved Me So Much]; Songs (7), Op. 47 [No. 1, If Only I Had Known; No. 2, Softly the Spirit Flew up to Heaven (words Tolstoy); No. 3, Dusk Fell on the Earth; No. 6, Does the Day Reign?; No. 7, Was I Not a Little Blade of Grass?]; Songs (12), Op. 60 [No. 6, Frenzied Nights [Nochi bezumnïye; No. 7, Gypsy's Song [Pesn' tsïganki; No. 12, The Mild Stars Shone for Us]]] *(rec Aug 18, Sept 3 & Sept 5, 1997)* NXIN ▲ 8554357 [DDD] (5.97)

N. Krasnaya (sop), V. Fedorovtsev (pno)—I Should Like in a Single Word; My Genius, My Angel, My Friend; Zemfira's Song ("Complete Romances, Vol. 1") † Songs (6), Op. 16; Songs (6), Op. 25; Songs (6), Op. 6 RUS ▲ 11078 [DDD] (12.97)

S. Larin (ten), Bekova Sisters—Songs (12), Op. 60 [No. 12, The Mild Stars Shone for Us]; No, Only He Who Has Known, Op. 6/6; Don Juan's Serenade, Op. 38/1; Amid the Din of the Ball, Op. 38/3; Why Did I Dream of You?, Op. 28/3; Mezza Notte; Night, Op. 60/9; Songs (7), Op. 47 [No. 6, Does the Day Reign?]; To Forget So Soon; I Opened the Window, Op. 63/2; Rondel, Op. 65/6; In This Moonlight, Op. 73/3; Déception, Op. 65/2; The Sun Has Set, Op. 73/4; I'll Tell You Nothing, Op. 60/2; Mid Sombre Days, Op. 73/5; Tell Me, What in the Shade of the Branches, Op. 57/1; I Should Like in a Single Word; Not a Word, O My Friend, Op. 6/2; It Was in the Early Spring, Op. 38/2; A Tear Trembles, Op. 6/4; Why?, Op. 6/5; We Sat Together, Op. 73/1; O, If Only You Knew, Op. 60/3; Again, as before, Alone, Op. 73/6 CHN ▲ 9428 [DDD] (16.97)

I. Levinsky (ten), S. Skigin (pno)—Children's Songs, Op. 54; Last Night, Op. 60/1; I'll Tell You Nothing, Op. 60/2; O, If Only You Knew, Op. 60/3; Simple Words, Op. 60/5; Behind the Window in the Shadow, Op. 60/10; Why Did I Dream of You?, Op. 28/3 ("Complete Songs, Vol. III") CONI ▲ 51268 [DDD] (16.97)

N. Makarova (sop), M. Agaffonikova (pno)—Songs (7), Op. 47 [No. 7, Was I Not a Little Blade of Grass?; No. 1, If Only I Had Known; No. 6, Does the Day Reign?]; Amid the Din of the Ball, Op. 38/3; To Forget So Soon; It Was in the Early Spring, Op. 38/2; The Sun Has Set, Op. 73/4; Do Not Believe, My Friend, Op. 6/1 [FRE] † S. Rachmaninoff:Songs (12), Op. 14; Songs (12), Op. 21; Songs (6), Op. 4; Songs (6), Op. 8 MED7 ▲ 9149 [DDD] (18.97)

L. Mkrtchyan (cta), E. Talisman (pno)—I Bless You, Forests, Op. 47/5; Why?, Op. 6/5; Not a Word, O My Friend, Op. 6/2; A Tear Trembles, Op. 6/4; It Was in the Early Spring, Op. 38/2; To Forget So Soon; I Should Like in a Single Word; Do Not Believe, My Friend, Op. 6/1; Songs (7), Op. 47; Reconciliation, Op. 25/1; No, Only He Who Has Known, Op. 6/6; Amid the Din of the Ball, Op. 38/3; I Opened the Window, Op. 63/2; Songs (12), Op. 60; Again, as before, Alone, Op. 73/6; The Nightingale, Op. 60/4; Songs (6), Op. 16 OPUS ▲ 30219 (18.97)

E. Ormandy (cnd), Philadelphia Orch—No, Only He Who Has Known, Op. 6/6 † Qt 1 Strs, Op. 11; Snow Maiden (sels); Borodin:Nocturne Str Orch; Chopin:Études Pno; Nocturnes Pno; Liszt:Liebesträume, S.541; Mendelssohn (-Bartholdy):Lieder, Op. 34; S. Rachmaninoff:Sym 2; Vocalise; Rimsky-Korsakov:Sadko (sels); Scheherazade, Op. 35 SNYC ▲ 46355 [ADD/DDD] (9.97)

M. Pedrotti (bar), S. Ralls (pno)—I Bless You, Forests, Op. 47/5; No, Only He Who Has Known, Op. 6/6; Don Juan's Serenade, Op. 38/1; A Tear Trembles, Op. 6/4 [RUS] † J. Brahms:Songs; Songs (6), Op. 86; Duparc:Songs; Morawetz:Songs; R. Strauss:Songs MUVI (Musica Viva) ▲ 1051 [DDD] (16.97)

L. Stokowski (cnd) —Not a Word, O My Friend, Op. 6/2 † Marche slave, Op. 31; Romeo & Juliet; G. F. Handel:Messiah (sels) IMMM ▲ 37031 (6.97)

G. Vinogradov (ten), G. Orentlicher (pno)—Songs (6), Op. 65; To Forget So Soon; Take My Heart Away; Songs (6), Op. 63 † S. Rachmaninoff:Songs (14), Op. 34; Rimsky-Korsakov:Songs, Op. 51; A. Rubinstein:Songs; R. Schumann:Dichterliebe, Op. 48; Gedichte, Op. 90; Liederkreis, Op. 24; Myrthen, Op. 25 PRE ▲ 89118 (16.97)

R. Wallfisch (vc), G. Simon (cnd), English CO—Songs (7), Op. 47 [No. 7, Was I Not a Little Blade of Grass?]; Legend (When Jesus Christ Was But a Child), Op. 54/5 † Pezzo capriccioso, Op. 62; E. Bloch:From Jewish Life; A. Dvořák:Polonaise Vc, B.94; Rondo; Silent Woods Vc & Pno, Op. 68/5; Slavonic Dance Vc & Pno, Op. 46/8; Glazunov:Chant du ménéstrel, Op. 71 CHN (Collect) ▲ 6552 [DDD] (12.97)

Songs (6) for Voice & Piano, Op. 16 (1872)

N. Krasnaya (sop), V. Fedorovtsev (pno) ("Complete Romances, Vol. 1") † Songs; Songs (6), Op. 25; Songs (6), Op. 6 RUS ▲ 11078 [DDD] (12.97)

Songs (6) for Voice & Piano, Op. 25 (1874-75)

N. Krasnaya (sop), V. Fedorovtsev (pno) ("Complete Romances, Vol. 1") † Songs; Songs (6), Op. 16; Songs (6), Op. 6 RUS ▲ 11078 [DDD] (12.97)

Songs (6) for Voice & Piano, Op. 6 (1869)

P. Domingo (ten), O. Harnoy (vc), R. Behr (cnd), Philharmonia Orch—No. 6, None but the Lonely Heart [arr Doug Riley] † Capriccio italien, Op. 45; Eugene Onegin (sels); Ov 1812, Op. 49; Romeo & Juliet CSER (Seraphim) ▲ 73297 [DDD] (6.97)

TCHAIKOVSKY, PIOTR (cont.)

Songs (6) for Voice & Piano, Op. 6 (1869) (cont.)

N. Krasnaya (sop), V. Fedorovtsev (pno) ("Complete Romances, Vol. 1") † Songs; Songs (6), Op. 16; Songs (6), Op. 25 RUS ▲ 11078 [DDD] (12.97)

Souvenir d'un lieu cher for Violin & Piano [Méditation, Scherzo & Mélodie], Op. 42 (1878)

D. Berlinsky (vn), S. Gorakhovich (pno) ("Souvenir d'un lieu cher") † Sérénade mélancolique, Op. 26; Valse-Scherzo Vn, Op. 34; S. Prokofiev:Son 2 Vn; A. Schnittke:Suite in the Old Style; R. Shchedrin:Humoresque Orch; In Imitation of Albéniz HEL ▲ 1015 (10.97)

B. V. Booren (vn), R. Kofman (cnd), Kiev CO [trans for vn & orch] † J. Brahms:Con Vn VRDI (Masters) ▲ 32278 (13.97)

D. Chan (vn), R. Koenig (pno)—Mélodie [trans for vn & pno] *(rec Aspen, CO, May 1995)* † Valse-Scherzo Vn, Op. 34; G. Gershwin:Songs; Paganini:Con 2 Vn, M.S. 48; Saint-Saëns:Son 1 Vn, Op. 75; Tartini:Son Vn & Pno; Ysaÿe:Sons Vn, Op. 27 AMBA ▲ 1017 [DDD] (16.97)

R. Chen (vn), P. Kogan (cnd), Hanover PO ("Chen Plays Tchaikovsky") † Con Vn; Sérénade mélancolique, Op. 26 BER ▲ 1169 (16.97)

C. Glenn (vn), E. Rachlin (cnd), Cambridge SO [orchd Glazunov] † Capriccio italien, Op. 45; Eugene Onegin (sels); Nutcracker (sels); Sleeping Beauty (suite), Op. 66a; Slippers (sels); Swan Lake (suite), Op. 20a; Sérénade mélancolique, Op. 26; Valse-Scherzo Vn, Op. 34; Vars on a Rococo Theme, Op. 33 VB3 3-▲ 3026 [ADD]

I. Grubert (vn), V. Sinaisky (cnd), Moscow PO † Con Vn; Sérénade mélancolique, Op. 26 RUSS ▲ 788054 (12.97)

A. Haveron (vn), D. Blumenthal (pno)—Mélodie [trans for vn & pno] *(rec July 1997)* † Valse-Scherzo Vn, Op. 34; R. Strauss:Son Vn; I. Stravinsky:Divert Vn; F. Waxman:Carmen Fant; Tristan & Isolde Fant CYPR ▲ 9604 [DDD] (17.97)

L. Issakadze (cnd), Georgian CO *(rec Sept 26-28, 1992)* † Souvenir de Florence, Op. 70; Sérénade mélancolique, Op. 26; Valse-Scherzo Vn, Op. 34 ORF ▲ 307921 [DDD] (18.97)

O. Kagan (vn), V. Lobanov (pno) ("Complete Works for Violin & Piano") † Sérénade mélancolique, Op. 26; Valse-Scherzo Vn, Op. 34 ODE ▲ 733 [DDD] (17.97)

E. Levinson (db), G. Levinson (pno)—Méditation † Beethoven:Son 3 Vc, Op. 69; Bruch:Kol Nidrei, Op. 47; P. Hindemith:Son Db; Koussevitzky:Valse miniature Db, Op. 1/2; S. Rachmaninoff:Trio élégiaque 1; Ranjbaran:Dance of Life CAL ▲ 507 [DDD] (15.97)

L. Mordkovitch (vn), M. Gusak-Grin (pno) *(rec Frognal, Hampstead, United States of America, Mar 21/22, 1986)* ("Russian Music for Violin & Piano") † Sérénade mélancolique, Op. 26; Valse-Scherzo Vn, Op. 34; Glazunov:Grand Waltz; Raymonda (sels); S. Prokofiev:Mélodies Vn, Op. 35bis; S. Rachmaninoff:Romance Vn & Pno, Op. 6/1; I. Stravinsky:Mavra (sels); Russian Dance CHN ▲ 8500 [DDD] (16.97)

I. Perlman (vn), Z. Mehta (cnd), Israel PO—Méditation [arr Glazunov] † A. Khachaturian:Con Vn EMIC ▲ 47087 [DDD] (16.97)

I. Politkovsky (vn), T. Merkoulova (pno)—Mélodie [trans for vn & pno] *(rec 1961)* ("Igor Politkovsky: Russian Violin School") † Balakirev:Impromptu Vn; A. Dvořák:Zigeunermelodien, Op. 55; S. Rachmaninoff:Romance Vn & Pno, Op. 6/1; A. Rubinstein:Son 1 Vn, Op. 13; S. Taneyev:Son Vn RD (Talents of Russia) ▲ 16279 [ADD] (16.97)

M. Rachlevsky (cnd), Kremlin CO—Scherzo [arr Rachlevsky] *(rec Moscow Conservatory Great Hall, Russia, Oct-Nov 1991)* ("Music for Strings, Vol. 1") † Elegy Strs; Qt 1 Strs, Op. 11; Serenade Strs, Op. 48 CLAV ▲ 9116 [DDD] (16.97)

G. Shaham (vn), M. Pletnev (cnd), Russian National Orch [orchd Glazunov] *(rec Great Hall Moscow State Conservatory, Russia, Dec 1996)* ("Meeting in Moscow") † Valse-Scherzo Vn, Op. 34; Glazunov:Con Vn; Kabalevsky:Con Vn DEUT ▲ 457064 [DDD] (16.97)

T. Spivakovsky (vn), W. Goehr (cnd), London SO—Mélodie [arr vn & orch] *(rec Walthamstow Assembly Hall, London, England)* † Con Vn; Sibelius:Con Vn EVC ▲ 9035 [AAD] (13.97)

I. Stern (vn), E. Ormandy (cnd), Philadelphia Orch—Méditation [arr Glazunov] ("Isaac Stern: A Life in Music") † Sérénade mélancolique, Op. 26; Bruch:Con 1 Vn, Op. 26; Wieniawski:Con 2 Vn, Op. 22 SNYC ▲ 66830 (10.97)

H. Udagawa (vn), K. Klein (cnd), London PO † E. Chausson:Poème Vn, Op. 25; Glazunov:Con Vn; Saint-Saëns:Étude Pno, Op. 52/6 INMP (Classics) ▲ 6700312 (9.97)

P. Urbanek (cnd), Prague Festival Orch—Mélodie † Marche slave, Op. 31; Sym 6 LALI ▲ 15821 [DDD] (3.97)

V. Vaidman (vn), E. Krasovsky (pno)—Méditation; Mélodie [arr Glazunov for vn & orch] ("Romantic Strings") † Valse-Scherzo Vn, Op. 34; A. Dvořák:Sonatina Vn, Op. 100; F. Kreisler:Vn Pieces; F. Schubert:Sonatinas (3) Vn CACI ▲ 210004 (5.97)

Xue-Wei (vn), S. Accardo (cnd), Philharmonia Orch—Mélodie [arr vn & orch] † Con Vn; Sérénade mélancolique, Op. 26; Valse-Scherzo Vn, Op. 34 ASV ▲ 713 [DDD] (16.97)

Souvenir de Florence in D for String Sextet, Op. 70 (1890; rev 1891-92)

Academy of St. Martin in the Fields Chamber Ensemble † Glazunov:Qnt Strs, Op. 39 CHN ▲ 9387 [DDD] (16.97)

Arensky Ensemble † Arensky:Qt 2 Strs, Op. 35; Borodin:Sxt Strs MER ▲ 84211 (16.97)

Borodin String Quartet † Qt 1 Strs, Op. 11; Qt 2 Strs, Op. 22; Qt 3 Strs, Op. 30 TELC 2-▲ 90422 (33.97)

I. Brown (cnd), Norwegian CO † R. Strauss:Metamorphosen CHN ▲ 9708 (16.97)

P. Csaba (cnd) *(rec Järvenpää Hall, Aug 1996)* † Janáček:Suite Str Orch ODE ▲ 889 [DDD] (17.97)

P. Entremont (cnd), Vienna CO *(rec Feb 1990)* † Serenade Strs, Op. 48 NXIN ▲ 550404 [DDD] (5.97)

A. Galkovsky (va), V. Feigin (vc), Moscow String Quartet † M. Glinka:Grand Sxt FINE ▲ 9608 (16.97)

L. Issakadze (cnd), Georgian CO *(rec Sept 26-28, 1992)* † Souvenir d'un lieu cher, Op. 42; Sérénade mélancolique, Op. 26; Valse-Scherzo Vn, Op. 34 ORF ▲ 307921 [DDD] (18.97)

J. Klusoň (va), M. Kaňka (vc), Kocian String Quartet † A. Dvořák:Sxt Strs, Op. 48 PRAG ▲ 250116 (18.97)

Lake Winnipesaukee Chamber Players *(rec Rochester, NY, 1997)* † Arensky:Qt 2 Strs, Op. 35 RUS ▲ 10055 [DDD] (11.97)

M. Maisky (vc), Orpheus CO *(rec Recital Hall NY State Univ, Purchase, NY, Apr 1996)* † Andante cantabile; Eugene Onegin (sels); Nocturne Vc; Vars on a Rococo Theme, Op. 33 DEUT ▲ 453460 [DDD] (16.97)

T. Ninič (cnd), Zagreb Solisti † Borodin:Qt 2 Strs ICC ▲ 6701192 (9.97)

Philharmonia Virtuosi members † I. Stravinsky:Apollon Musagète ESSY ▲ 1015 [DDD] (16.97)

M. Rachlevsky (cnd), Kremlin CO [version for str orch] ("Tchaikovsky Music for String Orchestra: Vol II") † Qt 3 Strs, Op. 30; Snow Maiden (sels); Snow Maiden, Op. 12 CLAV ▲ 9317 [DDD] (16.97)

Raphael Ensemble † Arensky:Qt 2 Strs, Op. 35 HYP ▲ 66648 (18.97)

R. Solomonow (va), J. Sharp (vc), Vermeer String Quartet *(rec May-Oct 1993)* † Qt 2 Strs, Op. 22 CED ▲ 17 [DDD] (16.97)

Souvenir de Hapsal (3 pieces) for Piano, Op. 2 (1867)

I. Prunyi (pno)—No. 3, Chant sans paroles *(rec Budapest, Hungary, July 13-14, 1988)* † Morceaux (12) Pno, Op. 40; Morceaux (6) Pno, Op. 19; Saisons NXIN ▲ 550233 [DDD] (5.97)

The Storm (overture) in E for Orchestra [to Ostrovsky's play], Op. 76 (1864)

N. Järvi (cnd), Detroit SO † Fatum; Suite 1 Orch, Op. 43 CHN ▲ 9587 (16.97)

G. Rozhdestvensky (cnd), London SO † Sym 6 INMP ▲ 878 [DDD] (9.97)

A. Wit (cnd), Polish National RSO Katowice *(rec Nov 23-25, 1992)* † Sym 5 NXIN ▲ 550716 [DDD] (5.97)

Suite No. 1 in D for Orchestra, Op. 43 (1878-79)

J. Bělohlávek (cnd), Prague SO † Suite 2 Orch, Op. 53; Suite 3 Orch, Op. 55; Suite 4 Orch, Op. 61; Sym 6; W. A. Mozart:Sym 39, K.543 SUR ▲ 110969 [DDD]

A. Doráti (cnd), New Philharmonia Orch † Suite 2 Orch, Op. 53; Suite 3 Orch, Op. 55; Suite 4 Orch, Op. 61 PPHI 2-▲ 54253 (17.97)

N. Järvi (cnd), Detroit SO † Fatum; Storm CHN ▲ 9587 (16.97)

N. Järvi (cnd), Detroit SO *(rec Detroit, MI, Mar 10-11, 1996)* ("Complete Suites") † Suite 2 Orch, Op. 53; Suite 3 Orch, Op. 55; Suite 4 Orch, Op. 61 CHN 2-▲ 9676 [DDD] (32.97)

S. Sanderling (cnd), Irish National SO *(rec Sept 1992)* † Suite 2 Orch, Op. 53 NXIN ▲ 550644 [DDD] (5.97)

Suite No. 2 in C for Orchestra, Op. 53, "Caractéristique" (1883)

J. Bělohlávek (cnd), Prague SO † Suite 1 Orch, Op. 43; Suite 3 Orch, Op. 55; Suite 4 Orch, Op. 61; Sym 6; W. A. Mozart:Sym 39, K.543 SUR ▲ 110969 [DDD]

A. Doráti (cnd), New Philharmonia Orch † Suite 1 Orch, Op. 43; Suite 3 Orch, Op. 55; Suite 4 Orch, Op. 61 PPHI 2-▲ 54253 (17.97)

N. Järvi (cnd), Detroit SO *(rec Detroit SO Hall, MI, Mar 10-12, 1995)* † Tempest, Op. 18 CHN ▲ 9454 (16.97)

N. Järvi (cnd), Detroit SO *(rec Detroit, MI, Nov 12-13, 1994)* ("Complete Suites") † Suite 1 Orch, Op. 43; Suite 3 Orch, Op. 55; Suite 4 Orch, Op. 61 CHN 2-▲ 9676 [DDD] (32.97)

T. Lønskov (pno), R. Llambias (pno) [arr for pno 4-hands] *(rec 1996)* ("Tchaikovsky, Vol. 2") † Capriccio italien, Op. 45 KPT ▲ 32241

S. Sanderling (cnd), Irish National SO *(rec Sept 1992)* † Suite 1 Orch, Op. 43 NXIN ▲ 550644 [DDD] (5.97)

Suite No. 3 in G for Orchestra, Op. 55 (1884)

H. Bean (vn), A. Doráti (cnd), New Philharmonia Orch † Suite 1 Orch, Op. 43; Suite 2 Orch, Op. 53; Suite 4 Orch, Op. 61 PPHI 2-▲ 54253 (17.97)

J. Bělohlávek (cnd), Prague SO † Suite 1 Orch, Op. 43; Suite 2 Orch, Op. 53; Suite 4 Orch, Op. 61; Sym 6; W. A. Mozart:Sym 39, K.543 SUR ▲ 110969 [DDD]

N. Järvi (cnd), Detroit SO † Francesca da Rimini, Op. 32 CHN ▲ 9419 (16.97)

TCHAIKOVSKY, PIOTR (cont.)
Suite No. 3 in G for Orchestra, Op. 55 (1884) (cont.)
N. Järvi (cnd), Detroit SO *(rec Detroit, MI, Mar 10-12, 1995)* ("Complete Suites") † Suite 1 Orch, Op. 43; Suite 2 Orch, Op. 53; Suite 4 Orch, Op. 61 CHN 2-▲ 9676 [DDD] (32.97)
R. Kempe (cnd), Vienna PO † Sym 6 TES ▲ 1104 (17.97)
K. Kondrashin (cnd), Moscow Philharmonic SO *(rec Concert Hall of Radio Moscow, Russia, Feb 1, 1962)* CONE ▲ 9425 [ADD] (16.97)
N. Marriner (cnd), Stuttgart RSO *(rec Dresden, Germany)* † Suite 4 Orch, Op. 61; Mendelssohn (-Bartholdy):Vom Himmel hoch; Saint-Saëns:Oratorio de Noël, Op. 12; Verdi:Traviata CAPO 2-▲ 10200 [DDD] (11.97)
S. Sanderling (cnd), Irish National SO *(rec Sept 3-4, 1992 & Mar 2-3, 1993)* † Suite 4 Orch, Op. 61 NXIN ▲ 550728 [DDD] (5.97)
E. Svetlanov (cnd), USSR SO—Theme & Vars ("American Ballet Theatre, Vol. 1") † Suite 4 Orch, Op. 61; Bruch:Con 1 Vn, Op. 26; Schoenberg:Verklärte Nacht, Op. 4 RCAV (Red Seal) ▲ 63190 (16.97)
Suite No. 4 in G for Orchestra, Op. 61, "Mozartiana" (1887)
D. Barra (cnd), San Diego CO † M. Glinka:Kamarinskaya; Kabalevsky:Comedians, Op. 26; S. Prokofiev:Summer Day KOCH ▲ 7042 [DDD] (10.97)
H. Bean (vn), C. Bradbury (cl), A. Doráti (cnd), New Philharmonia Orch † Suite 1 Orch, Op. 43; Suite 2 Orch, Op. 53; Suite 3 Orch, Op. 55 PPHI 2-▲ 54253 (17.97)
J. Bělohlávek (cnd), Prague SO † Suite 1 Orch, Op. 43; Suite 2 Orch, Op. 53; Suite 3 Orch, Op. 55; Sym 6; W. A. Mozart:Sym 39, K.543 SUR ▲ 110969 [DDD]
B. Britten (cnd), English CO *(rec 1962)* † Legend (When Jesus Christ Was But a Child), Op. 54/5; Nocturne Vc; Serenade Strs, Op. 48 BBC (Britten the Performer) ▲ 8002 (17.97)
N. Järvi (cnd), Detroit SO † Saisons CHN (Tchaikovsky Suite) ▲ 9514 (16.97)
N. Järvi (cnd), Detroit SO *(rec Detroit, MI, Oct 2, 1995)* ("Complete Suites") † Suite 1 Orch, Op. 43; Suite 2 Orch, Op. 53; Suite 3 Orch, Op. 55 CHN 2-▲ 9676 [DDD] (32.97)
K. Koizumi (cnd), Winnipeg SO † A. Dvořák:Legends Orch, Op. 59; Kodály:Galanta Dances; Morawetz:Carnival Ov SMS (SM 5000) ▲ 5039 [DDD] (16.97)
N. Marriner (cnd), Stuttgart RSO *(rec Dresden, Germany)* † Suite 3 Orch, Op. 55; Mendelssohn (-Bartholdy):Vom Himmel hoch; Saint-Saëns:Oratorio de Noël, Op. 12; Verdi:Traviata CAPO 2-▲ 10200 [DDD] (11.97)
S. Sanderling (cnd), Irish National SO *(rec Sept 3-4, 1992 & Mar 2-3, 1993)* † Suite 3 Orch, Op. 55 NXIN ▲ 550728 [DDD] (5.97)
J. Serebrier (cnd), Scottish CO † Elegy Strs; Serenade Strs, Op. 48; Sleeping Beauty (sels) ASV ▲ 719 [DDD] (16.97)
E. Svetlanov (cnd), USSR SO—Theme & Vars ("American Ballet Theatre, Vol. 1") † Suite 3 Orch, Op. 55; Bruch:Con 1 Vn, Op. 26; Schoenberg:Verklärte Nacht, Op. 4 RCAV (Red Seal) ▲ 63190 (16.97)
H. Zanotelli (cnd), South German PO † Borodin:Prince Igor (Polovtsian Dances); Mussorgsky:Night on Bare Mountain; Rimsky-Korsakov:Capriccio espagnol, Op. 34 PC ▲ 267028 [DDD] (2.97)
Swan Lake (ballet), Op. 20 (1875-76)
E. Ansermet (cnd), Swiss Romande Orch *(rec 1959)* † S. Prokofiev:Romeo & Juliet (suites), Op. 64bis PLON 2-▲ 40630 [ADD] (17.97)
A. Doráti (cnd), Minneapolis SO MRCR 2-▲ 462950 (22.97)
C. Dutoit (cnd), Montreal SO PLON 2-▲ 36212 [DDD] (32.97)
D. Lloyd-Jones (cnd), New London Orch TELC 2-▲ 16451 (33.97)
K. Ono (cnd), Bratislava RSO † Nutcracker Suite, Op. 71a OPP ▲ 2211
J. Silverstein (vn), J. Eskin (vc), A. Ghitalla (tpt), B. Zighera (hp), S. Ozawa (cnd), Boston SO *(rec Sym Hall Boston, MA, Nov 1978)* DEUT 2-▲ 453055 [ADD] (17.97)
E. Svetlanov (cnd), Russian State SO MELD 3-▲ 17082 [DDD] (13.97)
M. T. Thomas (cnd), London SO SNYC 2-▲ 46592 (16.97)
C. Warren-Green (vn), J. Lanchbery (cnd), Philharmonia Orch CFP 2-▲ 4727 [DDD] (24.97)
Swan Lake (selections)
D. Achatz (pno), Y. Nagai (pno) [arr Debussy for 2 pnos] *(rec Oct 9-12, 1993)* † Sleeping Beauty (sels); Sym 5 BIS ▲ 627 [DDD] (17.97)
H. Adolph (cnd), London Festival Orch—Danse des cygnes; Danse hongroise; Danse espagnole; Danse napolitaine ("A Night at the Ballet:Highlights from the Nutcracker") † Nutcracker (sels) ECL ▲ 509 (2.97)
E. Bour (cnd), Southwest German RSO Baden-Baden, T. R. Forrester (cnd), Philharmonia Orch—Lake by Moonlight ("The Kiss: Music for Love and Passion") † Chopin:Con 2 Pno, Op. 21; Fant-Impromptu, Op. 66; Liszt:Hungarian Rhaps, S.244; O. Nicolai:Lustigen Weiber von Windsor (ov); M. Ravel:Boléro; Verdi:Aida (sels); R. Wagner:Tristan und Isolde (orch sels) INTC ▲ 892923 [AAD] (13.97)
R. Désormière (cnd), French National SO—Scene (Moderato) (Act 2 Intro); Waltz in A♭ (Corps de Ballet); Danse espagnole; Danse hongroise; Mazurka; Scene finale *(rec Paris, France, May 1951)* † Nutcracker Suite, Op. 71a EMIC (Full Dimensional Sound) ▲ 66828 [ADD] (11.97)
T. Dokshitzer (tpt), G. Rozhdestvensky (cnd), Bolshoi Theater Orch—Danse napolitaine *(rec 1968)* ("Trumpet Rhapsody") † A. Arutiunian:Con Tpt; H. I. Biber:Son à 6 Tpt; G. Gershwin:Rhap in Blue; Glazunov:Album Leaf; Glière:Con Coloratura Sop; J. N. Hummel:Con Tpt in E♭, S.49 RCAV (Gold Seal) ▲ 32045 [ADD] (11.97)
C. Dutoit (cnd), Montreal SO † Nutcracker (sels); Sleeping Beauty (sels) PLON ▲ 43555 (16.97)
M. Ermler (cnd), Royal Opera House Orch Covent Garden ("Tchaikovsky Ballet") † Nutcracker (sels); Sleeping Beauty (sels) CONI ▲ 55012 [DDD] (11.97)
A. Fiedler (cnd), Boston Pops Orch RCAV (Victrola) ▲ 7879 [ADD] (6.97)
M. Halász (cnd), Slovak PO NXIN ▲ 550050 [DDD] (5.97)
N. Järvi (cnd), Scottish National Orch—Scene (Moderato) (Act 2 Intro); Waltz in A♭ (Corps de Ballet); Dance 4 of the Swans (Danses des petites cygnes); Mazurka ("Russian Ballet Masterpieces") † Nutcracker (sels); Glazunov:Raymonda (sels); S. Prokofiev:Romeo & Juliet (sels); D. Shostakovich:Ballet Suite 1; Ballet Suite 2; Ballet Suite 3; I. Stravinsky:Firebird Suite 3 CHN (Collect Series) ▲ 6512 [DDD] (12.97)
V. Kahi (cnd), Georgian Festival Orch—Mazurka SNYC ▲ 69273 [DDD] (4.97)
C. Mackerras (cnd), Royal PO † Sleeping Beauty (sels) TEL ▲ 80151 [DDD] (16.97)
Z. Mehta (cnd), Israel PO—Suite; Mazurka † Capriccio italien, Op. 45; Ov 1812, Op. 49 TELC ▲ 90201 (16.97)
E. Ormandy (cnd), Philadelphia Orch † A. Adam:Giselle (suite); Meyerbeer:Patineurs (sels) SNYC (Essential Classics) ▲ 46341 [ADD] (7.97) ▮ 46341 [ADD] (3.98)
A. Previn (cnd), London SO † Nutcracker (sels); Sleeping Beauty (sels) EMIC ▲ 64332 (11.97)
G. Solti (cnd), Chicago SO † Sym 5 PLON ▲ 25516 [DDD] (16.97)
A. Titov (cnd), St. Petersburg New Philharmony Orch † Nutcracker Suite, Op. 71a; Sleeping Beauty (suite), Op. 66a SNYC ▲ 57241 [DDD] (4.97)
A. Zhuraitis (cnd), Bolshoi Theater Orch—Waltz in A♭ (Corps de Ballet); Scene (Moderato); Scene (Allegro); Scene (Allegro moderato-Allegro vivo); Assai quasi andante (Act 2); Danse des cygnes; Danse hongroise; Danse russe; Danse espagnole; Pas de deux (Act 3); Scene finale INMP (Classics) ▲ 6700192 (9.97)
A. Zhuraitis (cnd), Bolshoi Theater Orch ("Russian Ballet") † A. Khachaturian:Spartacus (sels); S. Prokofiev:Romeo & Juliet (sels) ICC 3-▲ 6702809 (25.97)
various artists—Dance 1 of the Swans (Waltz in A); Scene finale † Eugene Onegin (sels); Marche slave, Op. 31; Nutcracker (sels); Ov 1812, Op. 49; Qt 1 Strs, Op. 11; Serenade Strs, Op. 48; Sym 6 RCAV ▲ 60845 (11.97) ▮ 60845 (5.98)
Swan Lake:Ballet Suite, Op. 20a
H. Adolph (cnd), London Festival Orch—Scene (Moderato) ("A Night at the Ballet: Great Moments of Ballet Music") † M. Ravel:Boléro; A. Rubinstein:Rêve Angelique; F. Schubert:Rosamunde (sels); Strauss (II):Champagner-Polka, Op. 211; Egyptischer Marsch, Op. 335; Verdi:Aida (sels) ECL ▲ 511 (2.97)
E. Bátiz (cnd), Royal PO † Sym 6 ASVQ ▲ 6091 [DDD] (11.97)
E. Bátiz (cnd), Royal PO ("Ballet Suites") † Nutcracker Suite, Op. 71a; Sleeping Beauty (suite), Op. 66a ASVQ ▲ 6183 (10.97)
A. Boult (cnd), New SO London *(rec London, July 21-22, 1960)* † Sym 5 CHSK ▲ 94 [ADD] (16.97)
A. Fiedler (cnd), Boston Pops Orch RCAV (Gold Seal) ▲ 55233 (11.97)
H. von Karajan (cnd), Berlin PO † Nutcracker Suite, Op. 71a; Sleeping Beauty (suite), Op. 66a DEUT ▲ 19175 [ADD] (16.97)
H. von Karajan (cnd), Vienna PO † Nutcracker Suite, Op. 71a; Sleeping Beauty (suite), Op. 66a PLON (The Classic Sound) ▲ 448592 (11.97)
A. Lazarev (cnd), Bolshoi Theater SO † Capriccio italien, Op. 45; Eugene Onegin (sels); Nutcracker Suite, Op. 71a; Sleeping Beauty (suite), Op. 66a TELC (Ultima) 2-▲ 18965 (16.97)
J. Levine (cnd), Vienna PO † Nutcracker Suite, Op. 71a; Sleeping Beauty (suite), Op. 66a DEUT ▲ 37806 [DDD] (16.97)
I. Markevitch (cnd), Philharmonia Orch † Nutcracker Suite, Op. 71a; Romeo & Juliet; S. Prokofiev:Sym 1 TES ▲ 1107 (17.97)

TCHAIKOVSKY, PIOTR (cont.)
Swan Lake:Ballet Suite, Op. 20a (cont.)
A. Nanut (cnd), Ljubljana SO † Capriccio italien, Op. 45; Eugene Onegin (sels); Nutcracker (sels); Sleeping Beauty (suite), Op. 66a; Slippers (sels); Souvenir d'un lieu cher, Op. 42; Sérénade mélancolique, Op. 26; Valse-Scherzo Vn, Op. 34; Vars on a Rococo Theme, Op. 33 VB3 3-▲ 3026 [ADD]
S. Rohani (cnd), Slovak Radio New PO ("Musica per Tutti, Vol. 9") † Nutcracker Suite, Op. 71a; Sleeping Beauty (suite), Op. 66a; Vivaldi:Domine ad adiuvandum me, RV.593; Gloria; Nisi Dominus, RV.608 DI ▲ 920295 [DDD] (5.97)
M. Rostropovich (cnd), Berlin PO *(rec 1979)* ("Ballet Suites") † Nutcracker Suite, Op. 71a; Sleeping Beauty (suite), Op. 66a DEUT (The Originals) ▲ 449726 [ADD] (11.97)
G. Solti (cnd), Chicago SO † Nutcracker Suite, Op. 71a; Romeo & Juliet PLON (Jubilee) ▲ 30707 [DDD] (9.97)
G. Solti (cnd), Chicago SO ("The Tchaikovsky Album") † Nutcracker Suite, Op. 71a; Ov 1812, Op. 49; Romeo & Juliet; Sym 6 PLON (Double Decker) 2-▲ 455810 (17.97)
R. Williams (cnd), London SO *(rec July 7-8, 1987)* † Nutcracker Suite, Op. 71a; Sleeping Beauty (suite), Op. 66a LSO (LSO) ▲ 6900092 (10.97)
P. Wohlert (cnd), Berlin RSO † Romeo & Juliet; Sleeping Beauty (suite), Op. 66a LALI ▲ 15633 [DDD] (3.97)
Symphonies (6) (complete)
M. Jansons (cnd), Oslo PO CHN 7-▲ 8672 [DDD] (98.97)
H. von Karajan (cnd), Berlin PO DEUT 4-▲ 29675 [ADD] (45.97)
N. Marriner (cnd), Academy of St. Martin in the Fields CAPO ▲ 492481 (44.97)
M. Pletnev (cnd), Russian National Orch *(rec Moscow Conservatory Great Hall, Russia, Apr & Nov 1995)* DEUT 5-▲ 49967 [DDD] (64.97)
Symphony No. 1 in g, Op. 13, "Winter Dreams" (1866; rev 1874)
C. Abbado (cnd), Chicago SO SNYC ▲ 48056 (11.97)
L. Bernstein (cnd), New York PO *(rec Oct 20, 1970)* ("Leonard Bernstein: The Royal Edition") † Sym 2 SNYC ▲ 47631 [ADD] (10.97)
A. Doráti (cnd), London SO † Sym 2; Sym 3; Arensky:Vars on a Theme of Tchaikovsky PPHI 2-▲ 434391 (22.97)
M. Jansons (cnd), Oslo PO CHN ▲ 8402 [DDD] (16.97)
A. Leaper (cnd), Polish National RSO Katowice *(rec Sept 7-12, 1991)* NXIN ▲ 550517 [DDD] (5.97)
I. Markevitch (cnd), London SO † Francesca da Rimini, Op. 32; Sym 2; Sym 3 PPHI (Two-Fers) 2-▲ 46148 (17.97)
K. Masur (cnd), Leipzig Gewandhaus Orch † Francesca da Rimini, Op. 32 TELC ▲ 44939 [DDD] (16.97)
M. Pletnev (cnd), Russian National Orch † Festival Ov, Op. 15; Marche slave, Op. 31 DGRM ▲ 453445 [DDD] (18.97)
G. Schwarz (cnd), Seattle SO *(rec June 7, 1992)* ("Winter Dreams: The Young Tchaikovsky") † Sym 2 DLS ▲ 3087 [DDD] (14.97)
L. Slatkin (cnd), St. Louis SO *(rec St. Louis, Feb 1994)* † Francesca da Rimini, Op. 32 RCAV (Red Seal) ▲ 68662 [DDD] (16.97)
E. Svetlanov (cnd), USSR SO *(rec Moscow, 1967-70)* † Francesca da Rimini, Op. 32; Sym 2; Sym 3 MELD (2fer) 2-▲ 34163 [ADD] (13.97)
Symphony No. 2 in c, Op. 17, "Little Russian" (1872; rev 1879-80)
C. Abbado (cnd), Chicago SO † Tempest, Op. 18 SNYC ▲ 39359 [DDD] (11.97)
M. Abravanel (cnd), Utah SO ("Complete Orchestral Music, Vol. 3") † Hamlet; Romeo & Juliet; Sym 4 VB2 2-▲ 5006 [ADD]
L. Bernstein (cnd), New York PO *(rec Oct 24, 1967)* ("Leonard Bernstein: The Royal Edition") † Sym 1 SNYC ▲ 47631 [ADD] (10.97)
S. Celibidache (cnd), Berlin PO *(rec Berlin, Germany, 1948)* † A. Dvořák:Con Vc URAN ▲ 108 [ADD] (15.97)
A. Doráti (cnd), London SO † Sym 1; Sym 3; Arensky:Vars on a Theme of Tchaikovsky PPHI 2-▲ 434391 (22.97)
M. Jansons (cnd), Oslo PO CHN ▲ 8460 [DDD] (16.97)
A. Leaper (cnd), Polish National RSO Katowice *(rec Mar 23-29, 1991)* † Sym 4 NXIN ▲ 550488 [DDD] (5.97)
I. Markevitch (cnd), London SO † Francesca da Rimini, Op. 32; Sym 1; Sym 3 PPHI (Two-Fers) 2-▲ 46148 (17.97)
K. Masur (cnd), Dresden PO † S. Prokofiev:Sym 1 BER ▲ 2061 [ADD] (11.97)
K. Masur (cnd), Dresden PO † E. Grieg:Con Pno, Op. 16 BER ▲ 9152 (10.97)
K. Masur (cnd), Leipzig Gewandhaus Orch † Romeo & Juliet TELC ▲ 44943 [DDD] (16.97)
M. Pletnev (cnd), Russian National Orch † Ov 1812, Op. 49 DGRM ▲ 453446 [DDD] (18.97)
G. Schwarz (cnd), Seattle SO *(rec May 25, 1993)* ("Winter Dreams: The Young Tchaikovsky") † Sym 1 DLS ▲ 3087 [DDD] (14.97)
G. Simon (cnd), London SO † Festival Ov, Op. 15; Serenade for N. Rubinstein CHN ▲ 9190 [DDD] (16.97)
L. Slatkin (cnd), St. Louis SO *(rec Powell Symphony Hall, Jan 31, 1993)* † Ov 1812, Op. 49; Romeo & Juliet RCAV (Red Seal) ▲ 68045 [DDD] (16.97)
E. Svetlanov (cnd), USSR SO *(rec Moscow, 1967-70)* † Francesca da Rimini, Op. 32; Sym 1; Sym 3 MELD (2fer) 2-▲ 34163 [ADD] (13.97)
Symphony No. 3 in D, Op. 29, "Polish" (1875)
C. Abbado (cnd), Chicago SO † Ov 1812, Op. 49 SNYC ▲ 45939 (11.97)
M. Abravanel (cnd), Utah SO ("Complete Orchestral Music, Vol. 1") † Ov 1812, Op. 49; Sym 6; Voyevoda, Op. 78 VB2 2-▲ 5004 [ADD]
T. Beecham (cnd), London PO *(rec 1934-47)* † Borodin:Prince Igor (sels) GRM2 ▲ 78773 (13.97)
L. Bernstein (cnd), New York PO *(rec Feb 10, 1970)* ("Leonard Bernstein: The Royal Edition") † Romeo & Juliet SNYC ▲ 47632 [ADD] (10.97)
A. Doráti (cnd), London SO † Sym 1; Sym 2; Arensky:Vars on a Theme of Tchaikovsky PPHI 2-▲ 434391 (22.97)
M. Jansons (cnd), Oslo PO CHN ▲ 8463 [DDD] (16.97)
G. Levine (cnd), Royal PO *(rec Henry Wood Hall London, Mar 1996)* † Rimsky-Korsakov:Con Pno, Op. 30 TEL ▲ 80454 [DDD] (16.97)
I. Markevitch (cnd), London SO † Francesca da Rimini, Op. 32; Sym 1; Sym 2 PPHI (Two-Fers) 2-▲ 46148 (17.97)
K. Masur (cnd), Leipzig Gewandhaus Orch TELC ▲ 46322 [DDD] (16.97)
E. Svetlanov (cnd), USSR SO *(rec Moscow, 1967-70)* † Francesca da Rimini, Op. 32; Sym 1; Sym 2 MELD (2fer) 2-▲ 34163 [ADD] (13.97)
A. Wit (cnd), Polish National RSO Katowice *(rec Sept 14-18, 1992)* † Tempest, Op. 18 NXIN ▲ 550518 (5.97)
Symphony No. 4 in f, Op. 36 (1877-78)
C. Abbado (cnd), Chicago SO † Romeo & Juliet SNYC ▲ 44911 [DDD] (11.97)
C. Abbado (cnd), London SO *(rec 1972-76)* ("Les Grandes Symphonies: Nos. 4-6") † Sym 5; Sym 6 DEUT (Double) 2-▲ 37401 (17.97)
M. Abravanel (cnd), Utah SO ("Complete Orchestral Music, Vol. 3") † Hamlet; Romeo & Juliet; Sym 2 VB2 2-▲ 5006 [ADD]
A. Argenta (cnd), Swiss Romande Orch † Beethoven:Son 8 Vn; Sym 3; J. Brahms:Con Vn; Son 2 Vn, Op. 100; Escudero:Concerto Vasco; M. de Falla:Amor brujo; Smetana:Bartered Bride (orch sels); R. Strauss:Till Eulenspiegels lustige Streiche, Op. 28 RTVE 4-▲ 65097 (36.97)
J. Barbirolli (cnd) † Marche slave, Op. 31; Qt 1 Strs, Op. 11; Romeo & Juliet; Serenade Strs, Op. 48; Sym 5; Sym 6 RYLC 3-▲ 70403 (20.97)
D. Barenboim (cnd), Chicago SO † Romeo & Juliet TELC ▲ 13698 (16.97)
E. Bátiz (cnd), Royal Liverpool PO ("Dos Grandes Sinfonias") † A. Dvořák:Sym 8 ALFA ▲ 1001 [DDD] (6.97)
L. Bernstein (cnd), New York PO † Francesca da Rimini, Op. 32 DEUT ▲ 29778 [DDD] (16.97)
L. Bernstein (cnd), New York PO *(rec Apr 28, 1975)* ("Leonard Bernstein: The Royal Edition") SNYC ▲ 47633 [ADD] (10.97)
A. Doráti (cnd), London SO † Francesca da Rimini, Op. 32; Borodin:Prince Igor (ov) MRCR ▲ 34373 (11.97)
H. D. Fuente (cnd), Xalapa SO INMP (Classics) ▲ 6700052 (9.97)
H. de la Fuente (cnd), Xalapa SO † Con 1 Pno, Op. 23; Con 3 Pno, Op. 75; Romeo & Juliet; Sym 6 ICC 3-▲ 6702679 (25.97)
V. Ghiaurov (cnd), Sofia PO LALI ▲ 14014 [DDD] (3.97)
M. Jansons (cnd), Oslo PO CHN ▲ 8361 [DDD] (16.97)
H. von Karajan (cnd), Berlin PO *(rec Philharmonie Berlin, Germany, 1976)* † Sym 5; Sym 6 DEUT 2-▲ 453088 [ADD] (17.97)
H. von Karajan (cnd), Berlin PO ("The Legend") † J. S. Bach:Con 1 Vn; Con 2 Vn; Bizet:Carmen (sels); A. Dvořák:Sym 8; W. A. Mozart:Zauberflöte (sels) DEUT (2-Fers) 2-▲ 445195 (17.97)
S. Koussevitzky (cnd) *(rec 1930-44)* † Romeo & Juliet; Sym 5; Sym 6 78'S 2-▲ 78550 (m) (26.97)
A. Leaper (cnd), Polish National RSO Katowice *(rec Mar 23-29, 1991)* † Sym 2 NXIN ▲ 550488 [DDD] (5.97)
J. Mardjani (cnd), Georgian Festival Orch † Romeo & Juliet SNYC ▲ 64292 [DDD] (4.97)
I. Markevitch (cnd), Leipzig Gewandhaus Orch † G. Mahler:Sym 1; F. Schubert:Sym 3 TAHA (Markevitch Edition) 2-▲ 282 (34.97)
I. Markevitch (cnd), London SO † Sym 5; Sym 6 PPHI 2-▲ 38335 (17.97)
K. Masur (cnd), Leipzig Gewandhaus Orch TELC ▲ 43339 (16.97)
K. Masur (cnd), Leipzig Gewandhaus Orch † Sym 5; Sym 6 TELC 2-▲ 95981 (16.97)

VERDI, GIUSEPPE (cont.)

Il trovatore (selections) (cont.)

S. Ehrling (cnd), Royal Swedish Opera Orchestra, Royal Swedish Opera Chorus *(rec Ytterjärna, Sweden, Oct 1995)* ("The Most Beloved Opera Choruses") † Aida (sels); Nabucco (sels); Traviata (sels); Borodin:Prince Igor (Polovtsian Dances); Donizetti:Maria Stuarda (sels); Gounod:Faust (sels); P. Mascagni:Cavalleria rusticana (sels); R. Wagner:Fliegende Holländer (sels); Lohengrin (sels); Tannhäuser (sels) CAPA ▲ 21520 (16.97)

M. L. Fanelli (sop), B. Franci (bar)—Qual voce! *(rec 1929)* ("Four Italian Baritones of the Past") † Aida (sels); Due Foscari (sels); Falstaff (sels); Otello (sels); Rigoletto (sels); P. Mascagni:Guglielmo Ratcliff (sels); Meyerbeer:Africaine (sels); W. A. Mozart:Don Giovanni (sels); Nozze di Figaro (sels); G. Rossini:Barbiere di Siviglia (sels); Guillaume Tell (sels); R. Wagner:Tannhäuser (sels) PRE ▲ 89962 (m) (16.97)

M. Filippeschi (ten), A. Quadri (cnd), Milan RAI Orch, F. Capuana (cnd), Naples Teatro San Carlo Orch, Naples Teatro San Carlo Chorus *(rec Milan, Italy, 1956)* ("Mario Filippeschi") † Forza del destino (sels); Otello (sels); Vespri siciliani (sels); Meyerbeer:Huguenots (sels); G. Puccini:Fanciulla del West (sels); Turandot (sels); G. Rossini:Guillaume Tell (sels) BONG (Il Mito dell'Opera) ▲ 1059 [ADD] (16.97)

P. Freeman (cnd), National Opera Orch—Tacea la notte; Miserere... ("Opera for Orchestra") † G. Puccini:Tosca (sels); G. Rossini:Barbiere di Siviglia (sels); Gazza ladra (ov) INSD ▲ 3674 (11.97)

L. Gencer (sop), L. Londi (sop), F. Previtali (cnd), Milan RAI SO *(rec 1957)* ("Leyla Gencer, Vol. 2: 1957-58") † Due Foscari (sels); Forza del destino (sels); Donizetti:Anna Bolena (sels); Lucia di Lammermoor (sels); Pizzetti:Assassinio nella cattedrale (sels); G. Puccini:Suor Angelica (sels); Tabarro (sels) MYTO ▲ 973160 (17.97)

B. Heppner (ten), R. Abbado (cnd), Munich RSO, M. Gläser (cnd), Bavarian Radio Chorus—Di quella pira *(rec Residenz Herkulesaal Munich, Sept 27-Oct 3, 1993 & July 4-8, Dec 6-8, 1994)* ("Great Tenor Arias") † Aida (sels); Forza del destino (sels); Luisa Miller (sels); Bizet:Carmen (sels); U. Giordano:Andrea Chénier (sels); Leoncavallo:Bohème (sels); Massenet:Cid (sels); Hérodiade (sels); Meyerbeer:Africaine (sels); G. Puccini:Bohème (sels); Fanciulla del West (sels); Manon Lescaut (sels); Turandot (sels) RCAV (Red Seal) ▲ 62504 [DDD] (16.97)

F. Labò (ten), P. Argento (cnd), Turin Teatro Regio Orch *(rec Bologna, Italy, May 5, 1969)* ("Il Mito Dell'Opera") † Aida (sels); Ballo in maschera (sels); Forza del destino (sels); Macbeth (sels); Simon Boccanegra (sels); Bizet:Carmen (sels); A. Catalani:Loreley (sels); U. Giordano:Andrea Chénier (sels); G. Puccini:Turandot (sels); R. Wagner:Lohengrin (sels) BONG (Il Mito Dell'Opera) ▲ 1068 [ADD] (16.97)

G. Lauri-Volpi (ten), G. Taddei (bar), G. Frazzoni (sgr) ("Gigliola Frazzoni in Concert") † Aida (sels); Bruch:Loreley (sels); P. Mascagni:Cavalleria rusticana (sels); G. Puccini:Madama Butterfly (sels) EKRP ▲ 5 [ADD] (16.97)

T. Lemnitz (sop), K. Schmitt-Walter (bar), A. Rother (cnd), Berlin RSO *(rec Jan 19, 1945)* † W. A. Mozart:Nozze di Figaro (sels); Zauberflöte (sels); R. Strauss:Arabella (sels); Rosenkavalier (sels); P. Tchaikovsky:Eugene Onegin (sels); R. Wagner:Lohengrin (sels); C. M. von Weber:Freischütz (sels) BER (Documents) ▲ 9014 (m) [ADD] (10.97)

J. Luccioni (ten), S. Juyol (sop)—Miserere... ("Il Mito dell'Opera") † Aida (sels); Otello (sels); Bizet:Carmen (sels); Pêcheurs de perles (sels); Gounod:Polyeucte (sels); Reine de Saba (sels); Roméo et Juliette (sels); Leoncavallo:Pagliacci (sels); Massenet:Hérodiade (sels); Manon (sels); Werther (sels); G. Puccini:Bohème (sels); Fanciulla del West (sels); Tosca (sels) BONG ▲ 1127 [ADD/DDD] (16.97)

G. Martinelli (ten), E. Caruso (ten), J. Björling (ten), B. Gigli (ten), G. Lauri-Volpi (ten), A. Cortis (ten), H. Roswaenge (ten), M. Filippeschi (ten), R. Tauber (ten), F. Völker (ten), A. Pertile (ten), J. Biel (ten), F. Tamagno (ten), L. Escalaïs (ten), M. Gilion (ten), A. Paoli (ten), G. Zenatello (ten), J. Sembach (ten), L. Slezak (ten), F. Constantino (ten), B. D. Muro (ten), N. Fusati (ten), N. Piccaluga (ten), E. Bergamaschi (ten), J. O'Sullivan (ten), G. Taccani (ten), V. Lois (ten), H. Lázaro (ten), A. Lindi (ten), F. Merli (ten), J. Kiepura (ten), J. Schmidt (ten), A. Salvarezza (ten), J. Soler (ten)—Di quella pira *(rec 1903-56)* ("Di Quella Pira") BONG ▲ 1051 [AAD] (16.97)

A. Millo (sop), E. Queler (cnd) —D'amor sull'ali rosee *(rec 1988-91)* ("An Operatic Evening") † Otello (sels); Beethoven:Ah, perfido!, Op. 65; A. Dvořák:Rusalka (sels); U. Giordano:Andrea Chénier (sels); G. Rossini:Guillaume Tell (sels) LCD ▲ 215 [ADD] (16.97)

E. Nicolai (mez) *(rec live, 1956)* ("Elena Nicolai in Opera") † Aida (sels) EKLR ▲ 17

M. Olivero (sop), B. Gigli (ten) ("Beniamino Gigli in Opera, 1934-40") † Forza del destino (sels); Cilea:Adriana Lecouvreur (sels); U. Giordano:Andrea Chénier (sels); Gounod:Roméo et Juliette (sels); G. Puccini:Manon Lescaut (sels); Tosca (sels) EKLR ▲ 30

S. Onegin (cta)—Stride la vampa [GER] *(rec 1911-24)* ("Vol. 1: 1911-1914") † Aida (sels); Ballo in maschera (sels); Bizet:Carmen (sels); Donizetti:Lucrezia Borgia (sels); Kienzl:Evangelimann (sels); Saint-Saëns:Samson et Dalila (sels); R. Wagner:Götterdämmerung (sels); Rheingold (sels) NIMB (Prima Voce) ▲ 7898 [ADD] (11.97)

C. Parmentier (cnd) [arr for mands] ("Opera on Mandolins") † Rigoletto (sels); Traviata (sels); V. Bellini:Puritani (sels); Donizetti:Lucia di Lammermoor (sels) PVY ▲ 795042 (16.97)

J. Peerce (ten)—Ah sì, ben mio; Miserere... ("Jan Peerce: A Portrait in His Golden Years 1942-1944") † Traviata (sels); Gounod:Faust (sels); W. A. Mozart:Don Giovanni (sels); G. Puccini:Arias MNER ▲ 19 [ADD]

J. Peerce (ten), J. Björling (ten), K. Thorborg (mez), S. Levin (cnd), RCA Victor Orch, N. Grevillius (cnd) —Ai nostri monti; Ah sì, ben mio; Di quella pira *(rec 1938)* ("Four Famous Met-Tenors of the Past") † Ballo in maschera (sels); Rigoletto (sels); Traviata (sels); Bizet:Carmen (sels); Pêcheurs de perles (sels); Gounod:Faust (sels); Halévy:Juive (sels); Meyerbeer:Africaine (sels); Ponchielli:Gioconda (sels); G. Puccini:Bohème (sels); Tosca (sels) PRE ▲ 89952 (m) (16.97)

L. Price (sop), L. Londi (sop), A. Basile (cnd), Rome Opera Orch—Che più t'arresti; Tacea la notte; Di tale amor; Timor di me?; D'amor sull'ali rosee *(rec 1959-60)* ("Blue Album") † Aida (sels); G. Puccini:Arias RCAV ▲ 68883 [ADD] (11.97)

J. Reynolds (pno), P. Lockwood (pno) [arr Claude Moinette] *(rec Utrecht, Netherlands, Feb 1996)* ("Opera 4-Hands, Vol. 2") † Gounod:Faust (ballet music); Liszt:Réminiscences de Don Juan Pno, S.418; G. Rossini:Guillaume Tell (ov); R. Strauss:Salome (dance of the 7 veils) GLOE ▲ 5153 [DDD] (16.97)

G. Robev (cnd), Sofia PO, Bulgarian National Chorus ("The Most Famous Operatic Choirs, Vol. 1") † Aida (sels); Don Carlos (sels); Forza del destino (sels); Nabucco (sels); Traviata (sels); P. Mascagni:Cavalleria rusticana (sels); G. Puccini:Tosca (sels); R. Wagner:Lohengrin (sels); Tannhäuser (sels); C. M. von Weber:Freischütz (sels) FORL ▲ 16668 [ADD] (16.97)

H. Schymberg (sop), K. Meyer (mez), J. Björling (ten), O. Sivall (ten), H. Hasslo (bar), H. Sandberg (cnd), Royal Opera House Orch Covent Garden, Royal Opera House Covent Garden Chorus—Ah sì, ben mio; Di quella pira; Miserere...; Se m'ami ancor *(rec Royal Opera Stockholm, Sweden, Mar 6, 1960)* ("Jussi Björling's Last Concert") † Rigoletto (sels); Alfvén:Songs; Leoncavallo:Pagliacci (sels); G. Puccini:Manon Lescaut (sels); Sibelius:Songs; P. Tchaikovsky:Eugene Onegin (sels); R. Wagner:Lohengrin (sels) MYTO ▲ 953130 (17.97)

T. Serafin (cnd), La Scala Orch, N. Mola (cnd), La Scala Chorus, G. Modesti (bass)—Vedi! le fosche notturne spoglie (Anvil Chorus); Orco dadi ma fra poco (Soldier's Chorus) *(rec Milan, Italy, June 6-7, 1955)* † Ernani (sels); Giovanna d'Arco (sels); Lombardi (sels); Nabucco (sels); Otello (sels); Requiem Mass; Vespri siciliani (ov) TES 2-▲ 2140 [ADD] (33.97)

B. R. Stees (bn), S. Norris (hp), R. Fusco (pno) [trans for bn, hp & pno; plus others] † Donizetti:Elisir d'amore (sels); Lucia di Lammermoor (sels); Hérold:Zampa (ov); W. A. Mozart:Entführung aus dem Serail (sels); G. Rossini:Gazza ladra (sels); P. Tchaikovsky:Eugene Onegin (sels); R. Wagner:Tannhäuser (sels) CLAV ▲ 509815 (16.97)

E. Stignani (mez) † Aida (sels); Don Carlos (sels); Forza del destino (sels); V. Bellini:Norma (sels); C. W. Gluck:Orfeo ed Euridice (sels); Saint-Saëns:Samson et Dalila (sels); A. Thomas:Mignon (sels) PHG (Great Voices) ▲ 5101 (12.97)

F. Tamagno (ten) *(rec 1903-05)* ("The Mythical Recordings") † Otello (sels); U. Giordano:Andrea Chénier (sels); Massenet:Hérodiade (sels); Meyerbeer:Prophète (sels); G. Rossini:Guillaume Tell (sels); Saint-Saëns:Samson et Dalila VOCA (Vocal Archives) ▲ 1200 (14.97)

K. Te Kanawa (sop), J. Pritchard (cnd), London PO—Timor di me?; D'amor sull'ali rosee † Forza del destino (sels); Otello (sels); W. A. Mozart:Don Giovanni (sels); Ponchielli:Gioconda (sels); G. Puccini:Bohème (sels); Edgar (sels); Madama Butterfly (sels); Manon Lescaut (sels); Suor Angelica (sels); G. Rossini:Cenerentola (sels); R. Wagner:Götterdämmerung (sels); Tristan und Isolde (sels) SNYC ▲ 46288 [ADD] (9.97)

C. Vaness (sop), D. O'Neill (ten), A. Rosner (ten), R. Abbado (cnd), Munich RSO, Bavarian Radio Chorus *(rec Munich, Germany, Apr 13-17, 1993)* ("Carol Vaness Sings Verdi & Donizetti") † Macbeth (sels); Otello (sels); Traviata (sels); Donizetti:Anna Bolena (sels) RCAV (Red Seal) ▲ 61828 [DDD] (16.97)

L. Warren (bar), F. Weissmann (cnd) , Robert Shaw Chorale † Ballo in maschera (sels); Falstaff (sels); Otello (sels); Rigoletto (sels); Bizet:Carmen (sels); Gounod:Faust (sels); Leoncavallo:Pagliacci (sels); J. Offenbach:Contes d'Hoffmann (sels); Ponchielli:Gioconda (sels); G. Rossini:Barbiere di Siviglia (sels) OPIT ▲ 54543 (6.97)

C. Weidinger (sop), M. Polis (mez), R. A. Clark (cnd), Manhattan CO—Tacea la notte *(rec St. Jean Baptiste Church NYC, NY, 1995)* ("Christine Weidinger: Verdi Arias") † Aida (sels); Ballo in maschera (sels); Ernani (sels); Forza del destino (sels); Macbeth (sels); Traviata (sels) NPT ▲ 85581 [DDD] (16.97)

various artists—Di quella pira [plus others] † Rigoletto (sels); Traviata (sels); Donizetti:Elisir d'amore (sels); Lucia di Lammermoor (sels); P. Mascagni:Cavalleria rusticana (sels); G. Puccini:Fanciulla del West (sels); Madama Butterfly (sels); Tosca (sels) PEG ▲ 196 (5.97)

A. Vilumanis (cnd), Latvian National Opera Orch & Chorus, various artists † Ballo in maschera (sels); Nabucco (sels); Bizet:Carmen (sels); Donizetti:Lucia di Lammermoor (sels); Leoncavallo:Pagliacci (sels); P. Mascagni:Cavalleria rusticana (sels); R. Wagner:Lohengrin (sels); Tannhäuser (sels) RIGA ▲ 7 (16.97)

various artists, Radio Bratislava SO—Bohemian Chorus † Aida (sels); Ballo in maschera (sels); Don Carlos (sels); Forza del destino (sels); Nabucco (sels); Rigoletto (sels); Simon Boccanegra (sels); Traviata (sels) GZCL ▲ 57 (6.97)

VERDI, GIUSEPPE (cont.)

I vespri siciliani (opera in 5 acts) [lib Eugène Scribe & Charles Duveyrier] (1855)

M. Callas (sop—Elena), M. Masini (mez—Ninetta), G. Sarri (ten—Danieli), G. K. Bardi (ten—Arrigo), E. Mascherini (bar—Guido), B. Christoff (bass—Giovanni di Procida), M. Frosini (bass—Conte Vaudemont), B. Carmassi (bass—Bethune), E. Kleiber (cnd), Florence Teatro Comunale Orch, Florence Teatro Comunale Chorus *(rec live Florence, 1951)* MELO (Callas Edition Live) 3-▲ 20005 [ADD] (46.97)

A. Cerquetti (sop), M. T. Pace (mez), M. Ortica (ten), C. Tagliabue (bar), B. Christoff (bass), M. Rossi (cnd), Turin RAI SO, Turin RAI Chorus *(rec live Turin, 1955) (E,I lib texts)* MYTO 2-▲ 982184 (34.97)

M. Cunitz (sop), H. Roswaenge (ten), H. Schlusnus (bar), O. von Rohr (bass), K. Schröder (cnd), Hessian RSO, Hesse Radio Chorus *(rec 1951)* † Forza del destino (sels) SIGM 2-▲ 2200 (17.97)

J. Levine (cnd), New Philharmonia Orch, J. Alldis (cnd), John Alldis Choir, M. Arroyo (sop), P. Domingo (ten), S. Milnes (bar), R. Raimondi (bass) RCAV 3-▲ 63492 (34.97)

R. Scotto (sop), G. Raimondi (ten), P. Cappuccilli (bar), R. Raimondi (bass), G. Gavazzeni (cnd), La Scala Orch, La Scala Chorus [ITA] *(rec live, Dec 4 & 10, 1970)* † Vespri siciliani (sels) MYTO 2-▲ 90524 [ADD] (34.97)

I vespri siciliani (selections)

R. Canter (ob), R. Burnett (pno) *(rec Goudhurst, Kent, England, Feb 1985)* † Anonymous:Quinte estampie real; C.P.E. Bach:Son Ob, H.549; Kalliwoda:Morceau de Salon, Op. 228; Marais:Vars on "Les Folies d'Espagne"; Traditional:Alborada; An Dro Nevez; Etenraku; Traditional Turkish; T. A. Walmisley:Sonatina 2 in G Ob & Pno AMON ▲ 22 [DDD] (16.97)

P. Domingo (ten), S. Milnes (bar), A. Guadagno (cnd), London SO *(rec 1970)* ("Domingo: Opera Duets") † Forza del destino (sels); Otello (sels); Bizet:Pêcheurs de perles (sels); Ponchielli:Gioconda (sels); G. Puccini:Bohème (sels); Madama Butterfly (sels); Zandonai:Francesca da Rimini (sels) RCAV (Gold Seal) ▲ 62595 [ADD] (11.97)

M. Favero (sop), R. Tebaldi (sop), M. Stabile (bar), T. Pasero (bass), A. Toscanini (cnd), La Scala Orch, La Scala Chorus *(rec Mar 1946)* ("La Riapertura del Teatro Alla Scala") † Nabucco (sels); Te Deum; Boito:Mefistofele (sels); G. Puccini:Manon Lescaut (sels); G. Rossini:Gazza ladra (sels); Guillaume Tell (sels); Mosè in Egitto (sels) GRM2 2-▲ 78688 (26.97)

M. Filippeschi (ten), G. Guelfi (bar), A. Quadri (cnd), Milan RAI Orch, T. Serafin (cnd), Naples Teatro San Carlo Orch *(rec Milan, Italy, 1956)* ("Mario Filippeschi") † Forza del destino (sels); Otello (sels); Trovatore (sels); Meyerbeer:Huguenots (sels); G. Puccini:Fanciulla del West (sels); Turandot (sels); G. Rossini:Guillaume Tell (sels) BONG (Il Mito dell'Opera) ▲ 1059 [ADD] (16.97)

L. Gencer (sop), G. Casellato-Lamberti (ten), La Scala Chorus † Vespri siciliani MYTO 2-▲ 90524 [ADD] (34.97)

K. Kováts (bass), G. Oberfrank (cnd), Budapest MÁV SO—O tu, Palermo; O patria *(rec Hungary)* ("Kolos Kováts: Verdi Arias") † Arias; Attila (sels); Don Carlos (sels); Ernani (sels); Lombardi (sels); Macbeth (sels); Nabucco (sels); Simon Boccanegra (sels) HUN (Great Hungarian Voices) ▲ 31650 [ADD] (16.97)

O. Lenárd (cnd), Czech-Slovak State Radio PO † Aida (sels); Ovs & Preludes NXIN ▲ 550091 [DDD] (5.97)

J. Lortič (ten), I. Morozov (bar), J. Wildner (cnd), Slovak RSO Bratislava—Quando al mio sen *(rec Slovak Radio Concert Hall Bratislava, Slovak Republic, Feb 15-24, 1994)* ("Operatic Duets for Tenor and Baritone") † Forza del destino (sels); Otello (sels); Bizet:Pêcheurs de perles (sels); Donizetti:Lucia di Lammermoor (sels); G. Rossini:Guillaume Tell (sels) NXIN ▲ 553030 [DDD] (5.97)

P. Plishka (bass), A. Lombard (cnd), Bordeaux-Aquitaine National Orch, Orfeon Pamplones Choir—O patria *(rec Saint-Jean-de-Luz, France, Sept 1989)* † Don Carlos (sels); Macbeth (sels); Nabucco (sels); Mussorgsky:Boris Godunov (sels) FORL ▲ 16613 [DDD] (16.97)

I vespri siciliani:Overture

N. Nozy (cnd), Belgian Guides Symphonic Band *(rec Steurbaut Sound Recording Ctr)* ("Festive Overtures") † Berlioz:Carnaval romain, Op. 9; Lalo:Roi d'Ys (sels); Mendelssohn (-Bartholdy):Ruy Blas, Op. 95; G. Rossini:Gazza ladra (ov); D. Shostakovich:Festive Ov, Op. 96; R. Wagner:Tannhäuser (ov) RENE ▲ 87105 [DDD] (16.97)

V. D. Sabata (cnd), St. Cecilia Academy Orch Rome † Traviata (sels); Beethoven:Sym 6; G. Rossini:Guillaume Tell (ov) GRM2 (Records of the Century) ▲ 78852 (13.97)

T. Serafin (cnd), Philharmonia Orch *(rec London, England, Apr 14, 1961)* † Ernani (sels); Giovanna d'Arco (sels); Lombardi (sels); Nabucco (sels); Otello (sels); Requiem Mass; Trovatore (sels) TES 2-▲ 2140 [ADD] (33.97)

A. Toscanini (cnd), NBC SO *(rec 1939-45)* ("Toscanini Edition Vol. 3") † Aida (sels); Forza del destino (sels); Traviata (sels); G. Rossini:Barbiere di Siviglia (ov); Cenerentola (sels); Gazza ladra (ov); Guillaume Tell (ov); Siège de Corinthe (sels) GRM2 ▲ 78809 (13.97)

VERDU, CARMEN (1962-

Krameria for Ensemble

L. Danceanu (cnd) ("Concert in Bucharest") † Sueño de Neire; Botella:Anihila; Darias:Sunday Suite; Santacreu:Sxt de la Naixenca; Vitae EMEC ▲ 8 (16.97)

Sombra de Ailanto for String Quartet

Floregium String Quartet ("Quattuor at Magistrum") † Botella:Noix; Darias:Miniatura; Relato; Santacreu:Qt de Tardor; Valle:Cants Cordals EMEC ▲ 12 (16.97)

El Sueño de Neire for Ensemble

L. Danceanu (cnd) ("Concert in Bucharest") † Krameria; Botella:Anihila; Darias:Sunday Suite; Santacreu:Sxt de la Naixenca; Vitae EMEC ▲ 8 (16.97)

VERDURMEN, ROB (20th cent)

Pastiche for Ensemble (1993)

Willem Breuker Ensemble *(rec Bellevue Theater, Amsterdam, Netherlands, Dec 28-30, 1993)* † Breuker:For Greetje Bijme; Hand de Vries; New Pillars in the Field of Art; Overtime; Suzuki Violinenlied; Foresythe:Bereceuse for Unwanted Child NMCC ▲ 92042 [DDD] (17.97)

VERESS, SÁNDOR (1907-1992)

Concerto for Clarinet & Orchestra (1981-82)

T. Friedli (cl), H. Holliger (cnd), Bern Camerata † Danze Transilvane; Musica concertante MUSS ▲ 16 [ADD] (17.97)

Danze Transilvane (4) for Strings (1944)

T. Füri (cnd), Bern Camerata † Con Cl; Musica concertante MUSS ▲ 16 [ADD] (17.97)

Hommage à Paul Klee for 2 Pianos & Orchestra

A. Schiff (pno), D. Várjon (pno), H. Holliger (cnd), Budapest Festival Orch TELC ▲ 19992 [DDD] (16.97)

Katica from Térszil [Térszil Katica] (ballet in 1 act) for Orchestra (1942-43)

J. Meszaros (cnd), North Hungarian SO Miskolc † Sym 2 MUSS ▲ 6130 [DDD] (17.97)

Musica concertante for 12 Strings (1965-66)

J. Goritzki (cnd), Neuss German Chamber Academy † Con Cl; Danze Transilvane MUSS ▲ 16 [ADD] (17.97)

Sacred Music

C. Danuser (bar), L. Svetek (bass), J. Meszaros (cnd), North Hungarian SO Miskolc, Budapest Hungarian State Choir—Sancti Augustini Psalmus Contra Partum Donati; Elegie; Das Glasklangespiel MUSS ▲ 6131 (17.97)

Symphony No. 2, "Sinfonia minneapolitana" (1952-53)

J. Meszaros (cnd), North Hungarian SO Miskolc † Katica from Térszil MUSS ▲ 6130 [DDD] (17.97)

VERHEY, THEODOOR (1848-1929)

Concerto in d for Flute & Orchestra, Op. 43

K. Verheul (fl), L. Vis (cnd), Residentie Orch The Hague † Zweers:Sym 3 OLY ▲ 503 [AAD] (16.97)

VERMEULEN, MATTHIJS (1888-1967)

Chamber Music

A. van Baasbank (ten), M. Bon (pno) *(On ne passe pas (1917))*, C. van Tassel (bar), M. van Nieukerken (pno) *(The Soldier (1917), Prélude des origines (195)*, R. Morgan (mez), M. Bon (pno) *(Les filles du roi d'Espagne (1917))*, J. V. Nes (mez), J. Meer (pno) *(La vielle (1917), Le balcon (1944))*, A. Bijlsma (vc), R. De Leeuw (pno) *(Sons Vc 1 & 2 (1918 & 1938))*, V. Beths (vn), J. Kussmaul (va), A. Bijlsma (vc) *(Trio Strs (1923))*, J. Walta (vn), J. Meer (pno) *(Son Vn (1924))*, M. Kweksilber (sop), M. Bon (pno) *(Trois salutations à Notre Dame (1941))*, A. Haenen (mez), T. Hartsuiker (pno) *(Trois chants d'amour (1962))* ("The Complete Matthijs Vermeulen Edition: Chamber Music") CV 3-▲ 39 (55.97)

Orchestral Music

Rotterdam PO *(Sym 1 (1912-14) [w. R. van Driesten (cnd)]; Sym 2 (1919-20) [w. O. Ketting (cnd)]; Sym 6 (1956-58) [w. L. Vis (cnd)])*, Hague PO *(Sym 3 (1921-22) [w. F. Leitner (cnd)]; Sym 4 (1940-41) [w. E. Bour (cnd)])*, Amsterdam PO *(Flying Dutchman:Prologue (1930))*, Netherlands Ballet Orch *(Flying Dutchman:Passacaille et Cortège (1930))*, Utrecht SO *(Flying Dutchman:Interlude (1930); La vielle; arr 1932; both w. O. Ketting (cnd))*, Omroep Orch *(Sym 5 (1941-45) [w. R. van Driesten (cnd)])*, Omroep Radio CO *(Sym 7 (1963-65) [w. R. van Driesten (cnd)])* ("The Complete Matthijs Vermeulen Edition: Orchestral Music") CV 3-▲ 36

VERPLANCK, JOHN (BILLY) (1930-

Petite Suite for Percussion Quartet

Continuum Percussion Quartet † I. Bazelon:Fourscore; J. Cage:Third Construction; L. Harrison:Con Vn; E. Kurtz:Logo I; C. Rouse:Ku-Ka-Ilimoku NWW ▲ 382 [AAD] (16.97)

VERREES, LEON (1893-1947)
O for a Closer Walk with God for Organ (1938)
W. Headlee (org) *(rec live Crouse College, Syracuse, NY, 1989)* † J. S. Bach:Org Music (misc colls); Guilmant:Marche funèbre et chant séraphique, Op. 17/3; D. Johnson:Tpt Tune; D. Milhaud:Preludes Org, Op. 231b; Reubke:Son on 94th Psalm Org RAVN ▲ 440 [DDD] (17.97)
VIADANA, LUDOVICO DA (ca 1560-1627)
Canzonettas (book 1) for 3 Voices
G. B. Columbro (cnd), Cappella Palatina STRV ▲ 33387 [DDD] (16.97)
Concerti ecclesiastici (100) for Voices & Continuo, Op. 12 (1602)
J. Fankhauser (cnd), Vancouver Cantata Singers—Exultate justi † Castello:Sacred Vocal Music; Gesualdo:Sacred Music; Monteverdi:Sacred Vocal Music; M. Neri:Sacred Vocal Music; Sonate da sonarsi, Op. 1; G. Picchi:Sacred Vocal Music; Rigatti:Masses; Motets; Sacred Vocal Music FL ▲ 23097 [DDD] (16.97)
Responsoria ad lamentationes for Voices, Op. 23
artists unknown, artists unknown STRV 2-▲ 33444 [DDD] (32.97)
Sacred Music
J. Canihac (cnd) , R. Vettori (cnd), Vox Hesperia—Missa Solemnis Pro Defunctis; Quinque Absolutionem Post Missam STRV ▲ 33430 [DDD] (16.97)
Sinfonie musicali a 8 for Chamber Ensemble, Op. 18
A. Rasi (cnd) STRV ▲ 33431 (16.97)
Vespri di San Luca for Vocal Soloists, Ensemble & Chorus
S. Pozzer (sop), C. Cavina (alt), J. Benet (ten), M. Bernal (ten), S. Foresti (bass), R. Vettori (cnd), Basso Generale, R. Vettori (cnd), Vox Hesperia, R. Vettori (cnd), Roveretana Accademia di Musica Antica Chorus FON ▲ 9409 (13.97)
Vespri per l'Assunzione della Beata Vergine for Vocal Soloists, Orchestra & Chorus, Op. XXVII (1612)
S. Pozzer (sop), C. Calvino (alt), U. M. Adam (ten), J. Clement (ten), S. Foresti (bass), L'Amaltea Ensemble, Vox Hesperia, San Marco Capella Musicale FON ▲ 9208 [DDD] (13.97)
VIARDOT, PAULINE GARCIA (1821-1910)
Songs
C. Bartoli (mez), M. Chung (pno)—Hai luli; Havanaise; Les Filles de Cadix ("Chant D'Amour") † Berlioz:Songs; Bizet:Songs; Delibes:Filles de Cadix; M. Ravel:Songs PLON ▲ 52667 (16.97) ▮ 52667 (10.98)
K. Ott (sop), C. Keller (pno)—Madrid; Sérénade; Havanaise; Bonjour mon coeur; Grands oiseaux blancs; La petite chevrière; La chêne et le roseau; Chanson de la pluie; L'enfant et la mère; Désespoir; Adieu les beaux jours; Scène d'Hermione; Seize ans; La danse; L'oiselet; Aime-moi; La calandrina; L'espoir renait dans mon âme [F] CPO ▲ 999044 [DDD] (14.97)
VIBERT, MATHIEU (1920-1987)
Du plus loin (3 mélodies cycliques) for Voice & Orchestra [texts Jean-Georges Lossier] (1968)
A. Matthey de l'Etang (mez), J. Meylan (cnd), Swiss Romande Orch † Humana Missa; Lux et Pax; Nocturne; Sym funèbre DORO (Swiss Contemporary Composers) 2-▲ 2001 [ADD] (32.97)
Humana Missa for solo Voices, Orchestra, Chorus & Childrens' Chorus (1971)
J. Meylan (cnd), Swiss Romande Orch, Geneva Grand Théâtre Chorus, Lausanne Oratorio Chorus, Bulle Mixed Choir, E. Brunner (sop), A. Chédel (cta), E. Tappy (ten), E. Bettens (b-bar) † Du plus loin; Lux et Pax; Nocturne; Sym funèbre DORO (Swiss Contemporary Composers) 2-▲ 2001 [ADD] (32.97)
Lux et Pax (prolgue) for Orchestra (1978)
H. Stein (cnd), Swiss Romande Orch † Du plus loin; Humana Missa; Nocturne; Sym funèbre DORO (Swiss Contemporary Composers) 2-▲ 2001 [ADD] (32.97)
Nocturne for English Horn, Oboe & Orchestra (1973)
E. Shann (E hn/ob), A. Gerecz (cnd), Swiss Romande Orch † Du plus loin; Humana Missa; Lux et Pax; Sym funèbre DORO (Swiss Contemporary Composers) 2-▲ 2001 [ADD] (32.97)
Symphonie funèbre for Orchestra (1949)
H. Stein (cnd), Swiss Romande Orch † Du plus loin; Humana Missa; Lux et Pax; Nocturne DORO (Swiss Contemporary Composers) 2-▲ 2001 [ADD] (32.97)

VICTORIA, TOMÁS LUIS DE (ca 1549-1611)
Alma Redemptoris mater for 8 Voices & Organ (1600)
P. Schmidt (cnd), Mixolydian † Surge propera; J. G. de Padilla:Missa "Ego flos campi"; Stabat mater ICC ▲ 6600802 (16.97)
Cum beatus Ignatius (motet) for 5 Voices (1572)
H. Chaney (cnd), St. Ignatius of Antioch Choir *(rec New York, NY, Jun 14, 1992)* † Certon:Missa 'Sus le pont d'Avignon'; Dunstable:Sancta Maria; Duruflé:Mass, "Cum jubilo", Op. 11; Tallis:Motets; C. Wuorinen:Missa Brevis *([ENG,LAT,FRE]text)* MUA ▲ 4798 [DDD]
Duo Seraphim
M. Berry (cnd), Schola Gregoriana of Cambridge *(rec Apr 1998)* ("Angels from the Vatican") † Anonymous:Agnus Dei; Alleluia, assumpta est Maria; Angeli, Archangeli; Angelis suis mandavitde te; Angelus Domini descendit; Ave Maria; Benedicite Dominum; Christe, sanctorum decus Angelorum; Dixit Angelus ad Iacob; Domine Jesu Christe; Exsultet iam Angelica turba caelorum; Facta est cum Angelo; Gloria; Hodie nobis caelorum Rex; In Paradisum; Kyrie; Sanctus; Stetit Angelus; Te laudamus; Te Deum laudamus; Marenzio:Qual mormorio soave; Palestrina:Ave Regina coelorum; Venit Michaël Archangelus; Traditional:Angelus ad pastores ait HER ▲ 220 [DDD] (16.97)
Motets
Copenhagen Schola Cantorum—Eram quasi agnus; Tamquam ad latronem; Cagliaverunt oculi mei; Astiterunt reges terrae; Sepulto Domino; Vere languores; O vos Omnes; Sancta Maria; Senex puerum portabat; Domine, non sum dignus *(rec 1984 & 1987)* † Josquin Desprez:Motets; B. Lewkovitch:Choral Music DANR ▲ 390
J. Savall (cnd), Hespèrion XX, Capella Reial de Catalunya—Ave Maria (a 4); Gaude, Maria virgo (a 5) 1872; Trahe me post te (a 6), 1583; Sancta Maria, succerre miseris (a 4), 1572; Ne timeas, Maria (a 4), 1572; Senex, Puerum portabat (instrumental a 4), 1572; O magnum mysterium (a 4), 1572; Vidi speciosam sicut columbam (a 6), 1572 *(rec Catalogne, Spain, April 1992)* ("Musica Sacra") † Sacred Choral Music; F. Guerrero:Sacred Music; C. de Morales:Sacred Music FONT 3-▲ 9916 [DDD] (36.97)
Officium defunctorum for 6-Part Chorus [includes 2nd Missa pro defunctis] (1605)
D. Hill (cnd), Westminster Cathedral Choir [LAT] HYP ▲ 66250 [DDD] (18.97)
P. McCreesh (cnd), Gabrieli Consort PARC ▲ 47095 [DDD] (16.97)
P. Phillips (cnd), Tallis Scholars [LAT] † A. Lobo:Funeral motet GIME ▲ 54912 [DDD] (16.97)
Sacred Choral Music
H. Christophers (cnd), The Sixteen Chorus—Salve Regina; Alma Redemptoris Mater; Regina caeli; Ave maris stella; Magnificat ("Vol. 1: Devotion to Our Lady") COC ▲ 1501 (16.97)
P. R. Conte (cnd), St. Clement's Choir Philadelphia—Ave Maria (a 4); Vidi aquam; Mass "Laetatus sum"; Motet Laetatus sum; Mess "Ascendens christus in altum"; Motet Ascendens Christus in altum *(rec Paoli, PA, Oct 1995 & Feb 1996)* DORD ▲ 80146 [DDD] (13.97)
S. Darlington (cnd), Christ Church Cathedral Choir, Oxford—Dum complerentur dies Pentecostes; Missa 'Dum complerentur'; Missa 'Simile est regnum coelorum' [LAT] *(rec Oxfordshire, England, July 12-13, 1993)* ("European Choral Music 1525-1751") † J. R. Esteves:Sacred Music; O. de Lassus:Sacred Music; C. de Morales:O sacrum convivium; Palestrina:Sacred Music; Rore:Qual donn'attende NIMB 5-▲ 1758 [DDD] (29.97)
Hespèrion XX, J. Savall (cnd), La Capella Reial de Catalunya Vocal Ensemble—11 Marian works—Ave Maria (a 4); Gaude, Maria virgo (a 5) 1872; Trahe me post te (a 6), 1583; Salve, Regina (a 8), 1572; Ave Regina caelorum (a 5), 1572; Sancta Maria, succerre miseris (a 4), 1572; Ne timeas, Maria (a 4), 1572; Senex, Puerum portabat (instrumental a 4), 1572; O magnum mysterium (a 4), 1572; Vidi speciosam sicut columbam (a 6), 1572; Magnificat Primi toni (a 8), 1600 *(rec 1992)* ("Cantica Beatae Virginis") ASTR ▲ 8767 [DDD] (18.97)
C. Jackson (cnd), Montreal Ancient Music Studio Choir—Ave Maria gratia plena; Omnis pulchritudo Domini; Salve, Regina; Alma Redemptoris Mater † Palestrina:Missa Ut re mi fa sol la; Sacred Choral Music FL ▲ 23120 [DDD] (16.97)
R. Mallavibarrena (cnd), Musica Ficta—Lamentations del jueves Santo; Lamentationes del viernes Santo; Lamentationes del Sábado Santo; In adoratione Crucis *(rec Madrid, 1996)* † Rimonte:De profundis CNTS ▲ 9604 [DDD] (18.97)
J. Savall (cnd), Hespèrion XX, Capella Reial de Catalunya—Salve, Regina (a 8), 1572; Ave Regina caelorum (a 5), 1572; Magnificat Primi toni (a 8), 1600 *(rec Catalogne, Spain, April 1992)* ("Musica Sacra") † Motets; F. Guerrero:Sacred Music; C. de Morales:Sacred Music FONT 3-▲ 9916 [DDD] (36.97)
J. Summerly (cnd), Oxford Camerata—Ave Maria (a 4); Miss O magnum mysterium; Missa O quam gloriosum [L] *(rec Apr 7-8, 1992)* † A. Lobo:Funeral motet NXIN ▲ 550575 [DDD] (5.97)
Surge propera for 5 Voices (1583)
P. Schmidt (cnd), Mixolydian † Alma Redemptoris mater; J. G. de Padilla:Missa "Ego flos campi"; Stabat mater ICC ▲ 6600802 (16.97)
Tenebrae Responsories
D. Hill (cnd), Westminster Cathedral Choir HYP ▲ 66304 (18.97)
P. Phillips (cnd), Tallis Scholars GIME ▲ 54922 [DDD] (16.97)

VICTORIA, TOMÁS LUIS DE (cont.)
Trahe me post te (mass) for Chorus (1592)
J. O'Donnell (cnd), Westminster Cathedral Choir HYP ▲ 66738 (18.97)
VICTORY, GERARD (1921-1995)
Irish Pictures (3) for Orchestra [The Blacksmith; The Irish Hussar; Revel in Reeltime] (1979-80)
P. O. Duinn (cnd), RTE Sinfonietta *(rec UCD Dublin, Sept 28-29, 1994 & Jan 12, 1995)* ("Romantic Ireland") † Duff:Echoes of Georgian Dublin; Larchet:By the Waters of Moyle; P. O'Connor:Introspect; O Riada:Banks of Sullane; A. J. Potter:Rhap under a High Sky MARC (Irish Composer) ▲ 8223804 [DDD] (13.97)
Ultima Rerum (reqium cantata) for Voices, Orchestra & Choir (1975-82)
C. Pearce (cnd), Cór na nÓg, RTE National SO of Ireland, RTE Philharmonic Choir, National Chamber Choir, V. Kerr (sop), B. Greevy (mez), A. Thompson (ten), A. Opie (bar) MARC ▲ 8223532 [DDD] (27.97)
VIEIRA, AMARAL (1952-
Choral-Fantasy for Mezzo-Soprano, Piano, Organ, Harp, 2 Symphonic Bands & Mixed Chorus, Op. 260, "In Nativitate Domini" (1992)
E. Baldin (sop), N. Rodrigues (hp), A. Vieira (pno), S. Asprino (org), R. Farias (cnd), São Paulo State Symphonic Band, L. R. Borges (cnd), Pro Musica Sacra Chorus † Magnificat; Tecladofonia PALS ▲ 11422 [DDD] (16.97)
Concert Paraphrase on La Vie D'Artiste by Johann Strauss for 2 Pianos, Op. 151
M. Brandão (pno), Y. Ferraz (pno) ("La Vie D'Artiste") † H. Goetz:Son Pno 4-Hands, Op. 17; E. Nazareth:Pieces Piano 4-Hands; A. Richardson:On Heather Hill PALS ▲ 11101
Magnificat for Mezzo-Soprano, 2 Symphonic Bands & Mixed Chorus (1990)
E. Baldin (sop), R. Farias (cnd), São Paulo State Symphonic Band, J. F. De Toledo (cnd), Saõ Paulo State Chorus † Choral-Fant, Op. 260; Tecladofonia PALS ▲ 11422 [DDD] (16.97)
Missa pro defunctis for Chorus, Op. 187 (1984)
J. Rozehnal (cnd), Slovak Phil Chorus Chamber Ensemble *(rec Moyzes Hall Bratislava, Jan 1996)* † Stabat Mater, Op. 240 PALS ▲ 11332 [DDD] (16.97)
Requiem in Memoriam for Orchestra & Chorus, Op. 203 (1985)
M. Vach (cnd), Slovak PO, J. Rozehnal (cnd), Slovak Phil Chorus *(rec Slovak Phil Concert Hall Bratislava, Dec 1995)* † Te Deum PALS ▲ 11331 [DDD] (16.97)
Stabat Mater for Vocal Soloists, String Orchestra & Chorus, Op. 240 (1989)
A. Kohútková (sop), D. Slepkovská (mez), S. Somorjai (ten), S. Benačka (bass), V. Kubovčik (bass), M. Vach (cnd), Slovak PO, J. Rozehnal (cnd), Slovak Phil Chorus *(rec Slovak Phil Concert Hall Bratislava, Dec 1995)* † Missa pro defunctis, Op. 187 PALS ▲ 11332 [DDD] (16.97)
Te Deum for Vocal Soloists, Orchestra & Chorus, Op. 181 (1984)
A. Kohútková (sop), D. Slepkovská (mez), S. Somorjai (ten), V. Kubovčik (bass), M. Vach (cnd), Slovak PO, J. Rozehnal (cnd), Slovak Phil Chorus *(rec Slovak Phil Concert Hall Bratislava, Dec 1995)* † Requiem in Memoriam, Op. 203 PALS ▲ 11331 [DDD] (16.97)
Tecladofonia for Keyboard Instruments (2 Pianos, Harpsichord, Celesta, Metalophone, Bells, Toy Piano) & Symphonic Band (1978)
A. Vieira (pno), Y. Ferraz (kbd), R. Farias (cnd), São Paulo State Symphonic Band † Choral-Fant, Op. 260; Magnificat PALS ▲ 11422 [DDD] (16.97)
VIENS, MICHAEL (1953-
ColorScope (song cycle) for Tenor & Piano (1990-92)
B. Fithian (ten), M. C. Viens (pno) ("Song Cycles") † Star Blaze; Sundown Voyager; Voices in the Still MASM ▲ 2040 [DDD] (16.97)
V. Schwarz (bar), R. Stankovský (cnd), Slovak RSO † Insectes Dansants; W. T. McKinley:Dallas: 1963; SinfoNova *([ENG] text)* MASM ▲ 2073 [DDD] (16.97)
Les Insectes Dansants (song cycle) for Piano (1994; orchd)
G. Schwarz (cnd), Seattle SO † ColorScope; W. T. McKinley:Dallas: 1963; SinfoNova MASM ▲ 2073 [DDD] (16.97)
Star Blaze (song cycle) for Tenor & Piano (1990-92)
B. Fithian (ten), M. C. Viens (pno) ("Song Cycles") † ColorScope; Sundown Voyager; Voices in the Still MASM ▲ 2040 [DDD] (16.97)
Sundown Voyager (song cycle) for Tenor & Piano (1990-92)
B. Fithian (ten), M. C. Viens (pno) ("Song Cycles") † ColorScope; Star Blaze; Voices in the Still MASM ▲ 2040 [DDD] (16.97)
Voices in the Still for Baritone (or Mezzo-Soprano) & Piano [text R. Frost] (1990-91)
I. Ganz (mez), M. C. Viens (pno) ("Song Cycles") † ColorScope; Star Blaze; Sundown Voyager MASM ▲ 2040 [DDD] (16.97)
York, Maine (12 études-tableaux) for Piano (1992)
N. Underhill (pno) *(rec Manhattan School of Music)* MASM ▲ 2019 [DDD] (16.97)
VIERK, LOIS V (1951-
Cirrus for 6 Trumpets (1988)
G. Trosclair (tpt) ("Simoom") † Go Gtrs; Simoom XIRE ▲ 102 [ADD]
Go Guitars for 5 Electric Guitars (1981)
S. Josel (elec) ("Go Guitars") † J. Cage:Five; Josel:Solitude Sessions I; Solitude Sessions II; P. Niblock:Gtr Too; Tenney:Spt Gtrs OOD ▲ 36 (16.97)
D. Seidel (gtr) ("Simoom") † Cirrus; Simoom XIRE ▲ 102 [ADD]
Red Shift for Chamber Ensemble (1989)
Bang on a Can members *(rec The Hit Factory New York, Oct 4-8, 1995)* ("Cheating, Lying, Stealing") † Didkovsky:Amalia's Secret; Goshfield:Manufacture of Tangles Ivory; D. Lang:Cheating, Lying, Stealing; Pascoal:Arapua; Rzewski:Piece 4 Pno; Ziporyn:Tsmindao Ghmerto SNYC ▲ 62254 [DDD] (16.97)
Simoom for 8 Cellos
T. Mook (vc) ("Simoom") † Cirrus; Go Gtrs XIRE ▲ 102 [ADD]
Timberline for Chamber Ensemble (1991)
Relâche Ensemble ("Outcome Inevitable") † R. Ashley:Outcome Inevitable; F. W.-H. Ho:Contradiction, Please! The Revenge of Charlie Chan; Hovda:Borealis Music OOD ▲ 17 [DDD] (16.97)
VIERNE, LOUIS (1870-1937)
Carillon de Westminster for Organ [from Pièces de fantaisie], Op. 54/6
F. Houbart (org) PVY ▲ 784041 [DDD] (16.97)
M. H. Long (org) † Méditation Org; Naiades, Op. 55; Stèle pour un enfant, Op. 58; M. Dupré:Sym-Passion, Op. 23; Vars sur un vieux Noël, Op. 20; J. Jongen:Toccata Org, Op. 104; Karg-Elert:Impressions, Op. 72; M. Reger:Pieces (12) Org, Op. 59 KOCH ▲ 7008 [DDD] (16.97)
D. Macomber (org) ("Works of the French Masters") † J. Alain:Litanies, Op. 79; M. Dupré:Vars sur un vieux Noël, Op. 20; Duruflé:Org Music (misc); Prélude et fugue, Op. 7; Roger-Ducasse:Pastoral Org; Widor:Andante sostenuto Org ARK ▲ 6152 [DDD] (16.97)
J. Parker-Smith (org) *(rec London, England)* ("Popular French Romantics, Vol. 1") † Pièces de fantaisie; J. Bonnet:Pièces nouvelles, Op. 7; Gigout:Toccata Org; Guilmant:Son 5 Org, Op. 80; Lefébure-Wély:Org Music; Widor:Sym 1 Org, Op. 13/1; Sym 9 Org, Op. 70 ASV ▲ 539 [DDD] (16.97)
C. Walsh (org) *(rec Lincoln Cathedral, England, 1994)* ("The Organs of Salisbury & Lincoln Cathedrals") † Sur le Rhin; Boëly:Allegretto; Fant & Fugue in B♭; C. Franck:Pastorale, Op. 19; J. Langlais:Adeste Fidelis; Org Music; Triptyque; Tournemire:Improvs (5) PRIO ▲ 648 [DDD] (16.97)
Improvisations (3) for Organ [trans Duruflé]
D. M. Patrick (org) *(rec Coventry Cathedral Org)* † Duruflé:Org Music (comp) ASV ▲ 993 (16.97)
Maestoso in c# for Organ [trans Alexander Schreiner from Kyrie of Messe solennelle]
J. Longhurst (org) *(rec Great Org of Mormon Tabernacle, Salt Lake City, UT)* ("Romantic French Fantasies") † Pièces de fant Org (sels); J. Alain:Org Music (misc); Boëllmann:Ronde Française, Op. 37; Suite 2 Org, Op. 27; M. Dupré:Cortege et Litanie, Op. 19/2; C. Franck:Pièces (3) Org, M.35; Widor:Sym 1 Org, Op. 13/1; Sym 4 Org, Op. 13/4; Sym 5 Org, Op. 42/1 KLAV ▲ 11069 [DDD] (18.97)
March triomphale pour le Centenaire de Napoleon for Organ, 3 Trumpets, 3 Trombones & Timpani, Op. 46 (1921)
D. Di Fiore (org), S. Kershaw (cnd), Auburn SO members ("Les Amoureux de l'Orgue") † C. Franck:Panis angelicus; Gounod:Divine Redeemer; Guilmant:Sym 1; F. Poulenc:Con Org AMBA ▲ 1019 [DDD] (16.97)
Meditation & Prelude for Organ, Op. 31
M. Murray (org) † J. S. Bach:Preludes & Fugues, BWV 531-552; M. Dupré:Org Music; C. Franck:Chorales Org, M.38-40; Org Music; Widor:Sym 6 Org, Op. 42/2 TEL ▲ 80169 [DDD] (16.97)
Méditation for Organ [from Improvisations, 1930]
M. H. Long (org) † Carillon de Westminster, Op. 54/6; Naiades, Op. 55; Stèle pour un enfant, Op. 58; M. Dupré:Sym-Passion, Op. 23; Vars sur un vieux Noël, Op. 20; J. Jongen:Toccata Org, Op. 104; Karg-Elert:Impressions, Op. 72; M. Reger:Pieces (12) Org, Op. 59 KOCH ▲ 7008 [DDD] (16.97)
J. S. Whiteley (org) *(rec Cavaillé-Coll org, St. Ouen, Rouen, France)* † P. Cochereau:Symphonie; M. Dupré:Préludes & Fugues, Op. 36; Vars on Adeste Fidèles; Ibert:Choral sur Justorum animae; Paponaud:Toccata PRIO ▲ 619 [DDD] (16.97)

VIERNE, LOUIS (cont.)

Messe solennelle for Vocal Soloists, Organ, Orchestra & Chorus [unpublished], Op. 16 (1903-05)
M. Bouvard (org), Y. Uyama (org), J. Suhubiette (cnd), Les Eléments *(rec Toulouse/Saint Sernin 1889, Basilica Saint-Sernin, Aug 30 & Sept 2, 1996)* † Widor:Sym 10 Org, Op. 73 TEMR ▲ 316008 [DDD] (18.97)

Naiades for Organ, Op. 55
M. H. Long (org) † Carillon de Westminster, Op. 54/6; Méditation Org; Stèle pour un enfant, Op. 58; M. Dupré:Sym-Passion, Op. 23; Vars sur un vieux Noël, Op. 20; J. Jongen:Toccata Org, Op. 104; Karg-Elert:Impressions, Op. 72; M. Reger:Pieces (12) Org, Op. 59 KOCH ▲ 7008 [DDD] (16.97)

Organ Music
D. Hill (org)—Clair de lune [from Suite 2, Op. 53]; Carillon de Westminster, Op. 54/6 *(rec Trinity Cathedral Portland, OR, May 1994)* ("There Let the Pealing Organ Blow") † J. S. Bach:Toccata & Fugue Org, BWV 565; F. Bridge:Adagio Org; C. Franck:Chorales Org, M.38-40 HER ▲ 190 [DDD] (19.97)

Piano Music (complete)
G. Delvallée (pno)—Suite bourguignonne, Op. 17; Solitude, Op. 44; Ainsi parlait Zarathoustra, Op. 49; Le glas, Op. 39; 2 pièces, Op. 7 ("Complete Piano Works, Vol. 2") ARN ▲ 68312 [DDD] (16.97)
O. Gardon (pno)—Préludes (12), Op. 36; Silhouettes d'enfants, Op. 43; Pièces (2), Op. 7; Le Glas, Op. 39/2; Nocturnes (3), Op. 35; Suite bourguignonne, Op. 17; Solitude, Op. 44 ("L'Oeuvre pour piano") TIMP 2-▲ 2023 [DDD] (36.97)

Pièces de fantaisie for Organ (selections)
N. Hakim (org)—Carillon de Westminster, Op. 54/6; Étoile de soir, Op. 54/3 *(rec Église de Sainte-Trinité, Paris, France, Mar 1997)* ("Canticum: French Organ Music") † C. Franck:Chorales Org, M.38-40; Pièces (3) Org, M.36; N. Hakim:Org Music; J. Langlais:Ave Maria, Ave maris stella; Te Deum; Messiaen:Livre du Saint-Sacrement; Nativité du Seigneur EMIC (Debut) ▲ 72272 [DDD] (6.97)
F. Houbart (org)—Suite No. 2, Op. 53:Hymne au soleil; Clair de lune [from Suite 2, Op. 53]; Toccata PVY ▲ 788013 [DDD] (16.97)
J. Longhurst (org)—Clair de lune [from Suite 2, Op. 53]; Les cloches de Hinckley [from Suite 4, Op. 55] *(rec Great Org of Mormon Tabernacle, Salt Lake City, UT)* ("Romantic French Fantasies") † Maestoso; J. Alain:Org Music (misc); Boëllmann:Ronde Française, Op. 37; Suite 2 Org, Op. 27; M. Dupré:Cortège et Litanie, Op. 19/2; C. Franck:Pièces (3) Org, M.35; Widor:Sym 1 Org, Op. 13/1; Sym 4 Org, Op. 13/4; Sym 5 Org, Op. 42/1 KLAV ▲ 11069 [DDD] (16.97)

Pièces de fantaisie (24 concert pieces) for Organ [in 4 volumes], Opp. 51, 53, 54 & 55 (1926-27)
S. Armstrong-Ouellette (org) *(rec Mission Church, Boston, MA)* ("Musique de la Basilique") † Dupont:Méditation; Gigout:Pièces Org (sels); Guilmant:Son 7 Org, Op. 89; G. Pierné:Pièces Org, Op. 29; Saint-Martin:Toccata de la Libération; Saint-Saëns:Fant 1 Org AFK ▲ 538 (16.97)
G. Baker (org) *(rec Abbatiale Saint-Ouen de Rouen, France, May 24-27, 1994)* SOC 2-▲ 817 (31.97)
G. Kaunzinger (org) *(rec Org of Stiftsbasilika Waldsassen, May 1997)* NOVA 2-▲ 150132 [DDD] (16.97)
B. V. Oosten (org) *(rec Cavaillé-Coll-Organ Saint-Ouen, Rouen, France, June, 1998)* MDG 2-▲ 3160847 [DDD] (32.97)
J. Parker-Smith (org)—Claire de lune *(rec London, England)* ("Popular French Romantics, Vol. 1") † Carillon de Westminster, Op. 54/6; J. Bonnet:Pièces nouvelles, Op. 7; Gigout:Toccata Org; Guilmant:Son 5 Org, Op. 80; Lefébure-Wély:Org Music; Widor:Sym 1 Org, Op. 13/1; Sym 9 Org, Op. 70 ASV ▲ 539 [DDD] (16.97)
B. K. Tidwell (org) *(rec 100 Rank Schantz Organ, Cleveland Heights, OH)* † G. Bales:Petite Suite; Hollins:Trumpet Minuet; H. Howells:Siciliano; Paine:Concert Vars Austrian Hymn; Roger-Ducasse:Pastoral Org; Sowerby:Sonatina for Org; Sym 4 ARK ▲ 6157 [DDD] (16.97)

Pièces (24) en style libre for Organ, Op. 31 (1913)
J. Beck (org) *(rec Bel Air Presbyterian Los Angeles)* † Sym 6 Org, Op. 59 ARK ▲ 6124 (16.97)
M. Stewart (org) † Sym 1 Org, Op. 14 KPT ▲ 32067 [ADD]

Poème for Piano & Orchestra (1926)
F. Kerdoncuff (pno), P. Bartholomée (cnd), Liège PO † Sym in a TIMP ▲ 1036 (18.97)

Poèmes de Baudelaire (5) for Voice & Piano (1924)
M. Delünsch (sop), F. Kerdoncuff (pno) ("Mélodies") † Poèmes grecs; Spleens et détresses TIMP ▲ 1040 (18.97)

Poèmes grecs (4) for Voice, Harp & Piano
M. Delünsch (sop), C. Icart (hp), F. Kerdoncuff (pno) ("Mélodies") † Poèmes de Baudelaire; Spleens et détresses TIMP ▲ 1040 (18.97)

Quintet in c for Piano & Strings, Op. 42 (1917)
A. Globenski (pno), Laval String Quartet † Widor:Qnt Pno, Op. 68 SNE ▲ 610 (16.97)

Rhapsody for Harp (1911)
F. Bartholomée (hp) ("Harp Landscapes") † Debussy:Danses sacrée et profane; Enescu:Allegro de Concert; Koechlin:Nocturne Hp, Op. 33; G. C. Menotti:Cantilena e scherzo Hp; Rohozinski:Suite brève; A. Roussel:Impromptu Hp, Op. 21 CYPR ▲ 1615 [DDD] (17.97)

Silhouettes d'enfants for Piano, Op. 43
G. Delvallée (pno) ARN ▲ 68270 [DDD] (16.97)

Sonata in b for Cello & Piano, Op. 27 (1910)
V. Spanoghe (vc), A. De Groote (pno) *(rec Brussels Royal Conservatory Concert Hall, Belgium, Aug 1995)* ("French Cello Sonatas, Vol. 2") † J. Jongen:Son Vc; Tournemire:Poème Vc, Op. 35 TLNT ▲ 291035 [DDD] (15.97)

Sonata in g for Violin & Piano, Op. 23 (1906)
A. Robert (vn), S. Deferne (pno) † Messiaen:Thème et vars Vn; Ropartz:Son 3 Vn CBC ▲ 1110 [DDD] (16.97)

Spleens et détresses (song cycle) for Voice & Piano [text Verlaine] (1924)
M. Delünsch (sop), F. Kerdoncuff (pno) ("Mélodies") † Poèmes de Baudelaire; Poèmes grecs TIMP ▲ 1040 (18.97)

Stèle pour un enfant défunt for Organ (No. 3 from Triptyque), Op. 58
M. H. Long (org) † Carillon de Westminster, Op. 54/6; Méditation Org; Naiades, Op. 55; M. Dupré:Sym-Passion, Op. 23; Vars sur un vieux Noël, Op. 20; J. Jongen:Toccata Org, Op. 104; Karg-Elert:Impressions, Op. 72; M. Reger:Pieces (12) Org, Op. 59 KOCH ▲ 7008 [DDD] (16.97)

Sur le Rhin for Organ
C. Walsh (org) *(rec Salisbury Cathedral, England, 1984-85)* ("The Organs of Salisbury & Lincoln Cathedrals") † Carillon de Westminster, Op. 54/6; Boëly:Allegretto; Fant & Fugue in B♭; C. Franck:Pastorale, Op. 19; J. Langlais:Adeste Fidelis; Org Music; Triptyque; Tournemire:Improvs (5) PRIO ▲ 648 [DDD] (16.97)

Symphony in a for Orchestra (1907-08)
P. Bartholomée (cnd), Liège PO † Poème Pno TIMP ▲ 1036 (18.97)

Symphony No. 1 in d for Organ, Op. 14 (1899)
M. Brincken-Schuler (org) † Sym 4 Org, Op. 32 MOTE ▲ 11891 (17.97)
H. Fagius (org)—Final *(rec Härnösand Cathedral, Sweden, July 8, 1977)* † J. S. Bach:Cant 147; Toccata & Fugue Org, BWV 565; Boëllmann:Suite gothique Org, Op. 25; O. Lindberg:Music of Lindberg; Mendelssohn (-Bartholdy):Preludes & Fugues Org, Op. 37; Sons Org, Op. 65; Saint-Saëns:Fant 1 Org BIS 2-▲ 156 [AAD] (34.97)
L. Rogg (org) *(rec Victoria Hall Geneva, Switzerland)* † J. Brahms:Vars on a Theme by Haydn; C. Franck:Chorales Org, M.38-40; Widor:Sym 5 Org, Op. 42/1 CASC ▲ 1028 (16.97)
D. Sanger (org) † Sym 2 Org, Op. 20 MER ▲ 84192 (16.97)
M. Stewart (org) † Pièces en style libre, Op. 31 KPT ▲ 32067 [ADD]

Symphony No. 2 in e for Organ, Op. 20 (1903)
P. Cochereau (org)—Cantabile; Scherzo † J. S. Bach:Org Music (misc colls); P. Cochereau:Org Music; F. Couperin:Pièces d'orgue consistantes en deux Messes; Messiaen:Banquet céleste AURC ▲ 180 (5.97)
S. Farrell (org) *(rec Org of St. Edmundsbury Cathedral)* ("French Connections") † J. Jongen:Son heroïca, Op. 94; J. Langlais:Méditations HER ▲ 208 [DDD] (18.97)
D. Sanger (org) † Sym 1 Org, Op. 14 MER ▲ 84192 (16.97)
H. Wilkinson (org) ("Girard: The Definitive Recording") † H. C. Banks:Beyond the Aurora; Karg-Elert:Org Music; Willan:Intro, Passacaglia & Fugue, Op. 149 PROO ▲ 7044 [DDD]

Symphony No. 3 in f# for Organ, Op. 28 (1912)
C. Hamberger (org) *(rec Abteikirche Münsterschwarzach, 1981)* ("Organ Recital in the Münsterschwarzach Abbey Church") † Guilmant:Son 1 Org, Op. 42 CALG ▲ 50494 [ADD] (19.97)
G. Kime (org) *(rec Dec 30-Jan 1, 1997-98)* ("Paris by the Bay") † M. Dupré:Sym-Passion, Op. 23 RAVN ▲ 450 [DDD] (17.97)
B. Mathieu (org) *(rec Nancy France, Dalstein-Haerpfer Org, June 4-5, 1995)* † Sym 6 Org, Op. 59 NXIN (The Organ Encyclopedia) ▲ 553524 [DDD] (5.97)

Symphony No. 4 in g for Organ, Op. 32 (1914)
M. Brincken-Schuler (org) † Sym 1 Org, Op. 14 MOTE ▲ 11891 (17.97)

Symphony No. 6 in B for Organ, Op. 59 (1930)
J. Beck (org) *(rec Bel Air Presbyterian Los Angeles)* † Pièces en style libre, Op. 31 ARK ▲ 6124 (16.97)
D. Craighead (org) † M. Reger:Son 2 Org, Op. 60 DLS ▲ 3096 [DDD] (14.97)
J. Farris (org) † J. Alain:Deuxième fant, AWV 91; M. Dupré:Vars sur un vieux Noël, Op. 20; Duruflé:Prélude et fugue, Op. 7; C. Franck:Pièces (3) Org, M.35; Widor:Sym 6 Org, Op. 42/2 DLS ▲ 3049 [DDD] (14.97)
B. Mathieu (org) [Dalstein-Haerpfer Org, Eglise Saint-Sébastien] *(rec Nancy France, June 4-5, 1995)* † Sym 3 Org, Op. 28 NXIN (The Organ Encyclopedia) ▲ 553524 [DDD] (5.97)

VIERU, ANATOL (1926-

Concerto for Violin, Cello & Orchestra (1979)
O. Kagan (vn), N. Gutman (vc), A. Vieru (cnd), Romanian Radio Orch † Sym 5 OLY ▲ 409 [AAD] (16.97)

Narration II for Saxophone & Orchestra (1986)
D. Kientzy (sax), R. Georgescu (cnd), Timişoara PO ("The Romanian Saxophone") † Marbe:Con for Daniel Kientzy; S. Niculescu:Concertante Sym 3 OLY (Explorer) ▲ 410 [AAD] (16.97)

Symphony No. 5 for Orchestra & Chorus (1985)
L. Baci (cnd), Romanian Radio Orch, Romanian Radio Chorus † Con Vn Vc OLY ▲ 409 [AAD] (16.97)

VIEUXTEMPS, HENRI (1820-1881)

Allegro & Scherzo in B♭ for Viola & Piano [from unfinished Viola Sonata], Op. 60 (1884)
P. Xuereb (va), L. Devos (pno) ("Viola Pieces by Violin Virtuosi") † Hubay:Concertstück Vc, Op. 20; J. Joachim:Vars on a Theme Va, Op. 10; Wieniawski:Rêverie Va & Pno TLNT ▲ 291012 [DDD] (15.97)

Capriccio for Viola, Op. 55/9
R. Verebes (va) ("The Solo Viola") † M. Barnes:Ballade; P. Hindemith:Son Va; K. Penderecki:Cadenza Va; M. Reger:Suites Va, Op. 131d; I. Stravinsky:Elégie Va SNE ▲ 562 (16.97)

Concerto No. 2 in f# for Violin & Orchestra, Op. 19 (1836)
M. Keylin (vn), D. Burkh (cnd), Janáček PO *(rec Ostrava Czech Republic, Apr 1995)* ("Romantic Violin Concertos") † Con 3 Vn, Op. 25 NAB ▲ 211412 [DDD] (11.97)
A. Markov (vn), L. Renes (cnd), Monte Carlo PO † Con 4 Vn, Op. 31; Con 5 Vn, Op. 37 ERAT ▲ 17878 (16.97)

Concerto No. 3 in A for Violin & Orchestra, Op. 25 (1844)
M. Keylin (vn), D. Burkh (cnd), Janáček PO *(rec Ostrava Czech Republic, Apr 1995)* ("Romantic Violin Concertos") † Con 2 Vn, Op. 19 NAB ▲ 211412 [DDD] (11.97)

Concerto No. 4 in d for Violin & Orchestra, Op. 31 (ca 1850)
J. Heifetz (vn), J. Barbirolli (cnd), London PO, E. Goossens (cnd), Cincinnati SO, S. Koussevitzky (cnd), Boston SO *(rec 1935-41)* ("Jascha Heifetz: Concerto Recordings, Vol. 2") † J. Brahms:Con Vn; H. Vieuxtemps:Con 4 Vn, Op. 31; W. Walton:Con Vn; Wieniawski:Con 2 Vn, Op. 22 PHS 2-▲ 9167 [ADD] (33.97)
J. Heifetz (vn), J. Barbirolli (cnd), London PO † Sarasate:Zigeunerweisen, Op. 20; P. Tchaikovsky:Con Vn IMMM ▲ 37063 (6.97)
A. Markov (vn), L. Renes (cnd), Monte Carlo PO † Con 2 Vn, Op. 19; Con 5 Vn, Op. 37 ERAT ▲ 17878 (16.97)
V. Příhoda (vn) † Paganini:Con 1 Vn, M.S. 21; I palpiti, M.S. 77; Sons Vn & Gtr, M.S. 27; Streghe; Wieniawski:Con 2 Vn, Op. 22 BID ▲ 135 (16.97)

Concerto No. 5 in a for Violin & Orchestra, Op. 37, "Grétry" (1861)
S. Chang (vn), C. Dutoit (cnd), Philharmonia Orch *(rec Henry Wood Hall London, Dec 22-23, 1994)* † Lalo:Sym espagnole, Op. 21 EMIC ▲ 55292 [DDD] (16.97)
J. Heifetz (vn), M. Sargent (cnd), New SO London RCAV (Red Seal) ▲ 6214 [ADD] (16.97)
J. Heifetz (vn), M. Sargent (cnd), New SO London *(rec Walthamstow Town Hall London, May 15 & 22, 1961)* † Bruch:Con 1 Vn, Op. 26; Scottish Fant, Op. 46 RCAV (Red Seal) ▲ 61745 [ADD] (16.97)
A. Markov (vn), L. Renes (cnd), Monte Carlo PO † Con 2 Vn, Op. 19; Con 4 Vn, Op. 31 ERAT ▲ 17878 (16.97)
P. Zukerman (vn), C. Mackerras (cnd), London SO *(rec 1969)* † Bruch:Con 1 Vn, Op. 26; Lalo:Sym espagnole, Op. 21 SNYC (Essential Classics) ▲ 48274 [ADD] (7.97) ■ 48274 [ADD] (3.98)

Concerto No. 6 in G for Violin & Orchestra, Op. 47 (1883)
G. Poulet (vn), P. Bartholomée (cnd), Liège PO † Con 7 Vn, Op. 49; Greeting to America, Op. 56 VAL ▲ 4797 (18.97)

Concerto No. 7 in a for Violin & Orchestra, Op. 49 (1883)
G. Poulet (vn), P. Bartholomée (cnd), Liège PO † Con 6 Vn, Op. 47; Greeting to America, Op. 56 VAL ▲ 4797 (18.97)

Duo concertant on themes from Weber's Oberon (No. 2) for Violin & Piano, Op. 14
T. Gilissen (va), J. V. Eynden (pno) [arr va & pno] *(rec Brussels, June 1985)* † Elégie Va, Op. 30; Fant appassionata, Op. 35; Son Va PAVA ▲ 7340 [DDD] (10.97)

Elégie for Viola (or Cello) & Piano, Op. 30
T. Gilissen (va), J. V. Eynden (pno) *(rec Brussels, June 1985)* † Duo concertant 2, Op. 14; Fant appassionata, Op. 35; Son Va PAVA ▲ 7340 [DDD] (10.97)
R. Verebes (va), S. Blondin (pno) ("The Romantic Viola") † E. Bloch:Meditation & Processional; Suite hébraïque; Bruch:Romanze Va, Op. 85; Enescu:Concertpiece Va & Pno; Kodály:Adagio Vn & Pno; Vaughan Williams:Romance Va; Wieniawski:Rêverie Va & Pno SNE ▲ 612 (16.97)

Etudes (36) for Violin, Op. 48 (1882)
M. Guttman (vn), Y. Kikuchi (pno)—No. 18, "Lamento" † Feuilles d'Album, Op. 40; Morceaux de Salon, Op. 22; Romances sans paroles, Op. 7; Son Vn; Voies du coeur, Op. 53 ASVD ▲ 1050 (16.97)

Fantasia appassionata for Violin & Orchestra, Op. 35 (ca 1860)
C. Jongen (vn), G. Cartigny (cnd), Liège SO *(rec Conservatoire Royal de Musique Liège, June 1972)* † Duo concertant 2, Op. 14; Elégie Va, Op. 30; Son Va PAVA ▲ 7340 [DDD] (10.97)

Feuilles d'Album (3) for Violin Piano, Op. 40 (1864)
M. Guttman (vn), Y. Kikuchi (pno)—No. 1, "Romance" † Etudes Vn, Op. 48; Morceaux de Salon, Op. 22; Romances sans paroles, Op. 7; Son Vn; Voies du coeur, Op. 53 ASVD ▲ 1050 (16.97)

Greeting to America for Violin & Piano, Op. 56 (1883)
G. Poulet (vn), P. Bartholomée (cnd), Liège PO † Con 6 Vn, Op. 47; Con 7 Vn, Op. 49 VAL ▲ 4797 (18.97)

Morceaux de salon (6) for Violin & Piano, Op. 22 (1847)
M. Guttman (vn), Y. Kikuchi (pno)—No. 3, "Rêverie" † Etudes Vn, Op. 48; Feuilles d'Album, Op. 40; Romances sans paroles, Op. 7; Son Vn; Voies du coeur, Op. 53 ASVD ▲ 1050 (16.97)

Romances sans paroles for Violin & Piano, Op. 7 (ca 1845)
M. Guttman (vn), Y. Kikuchi (pno)—No. 2 † Etudes Vn, Op. 48; Feuilles d'Album, Op. 40; Morceaux de Salon, Op. 22; Son Vn; Voies du coeur, Op. 53 ASVD ▲ 1050 (16.97)

Sonata in B♭ for Viola & Piano, Op. 36 (1863)
T. Gilissen (va) *(rec Brussels, June 1985)* † Duo concertant 2, Op. 14; Elégie Va, Op. 30; Fant appassionata, Op. 35 PAVA ▲ 7340 [DDD] (10.97)
R. Verebes (va), S. Blondin (pno) *(rec Montreal)* † F. Schubert:Son Arpeggione, D.821; R. Schumann:Märchenbilder, Op. 113 SNE ▲ 580 (16.97)

Sonata in D for Violin & Piano, Op. 12 (ca 1845)
M. Guttman (vn), Y. Kikuchi (pno) † Etudes Vn, Op. 48; Feuilles d'Album, Op. 40; Morceaux de Salon, Op. 22; Romances sans paroles, Op. 7; Voies du coeur, Op. 53 ASVD ▲ 1050 (16.97)

Viola & Piano Music
N. Imai (va), R. Vignoles (pno)—(comp) Capriccio in c, Op. posth.; Elégie, Op. 30; Son in B♭, Op. 36 † C. Franck:Son Vn, M.8 CHN ▲ 8873 [DDD] (16.97)
P. Lénert (va), J. Cohen (pno) ("Complete Music for Viola & Piano") MED7 ▲ 141340 (18.97)

Violin & Piano Music
R. Ricci (vn), M. Vincenzi (pno)—Fant appassionata; Ballade et Polonaise; Chant d'amour; Désespoir; Souvenir; Rondino; Tarantella; Réverie; Romance; Hommage à Paganini; Innocence; Yankee Doodle *(rec Genoa Italy, May 3-5, 1995)* ("A Homage by Ruggiero Ricci") DYNC ▲ 112 [DDD] (17.97)

Voies du coeur (9) for Violin & Piano, Op. 53 (1883)
M. Guttman (vn), Y. Kikuchi (pno)—No. 5, Rêve † Etudes Vn, Op. 48; Feuilles d'Album, Op. 40; Morceaux de Salon, Op. 22; Romances sans paroles, Op. 7; Son Vn ASVD ▲ 1050 (16.97)

VIGELAND, NILS (1950-

Progress for Live & Pre-Recorded Percussion Instruments (1984)
J. Williams (perc), M. Pugliese (perc) *(rec NYC, NY, live, Apr 4, 1989)* ("Perkin' at Merkin") † J. Cage:Music for...; M. Feldman:King of Denmark; H. Mancini:Peter Gunn (sels); Nørgård:Waves; Xenakis:Psappha MODE ▲ 25

VIGIL, MARK (1954-

Music of Vigil
L. Gardiner (pno), Univ of Oregon Orch *(Octet Wildflowers)*, L. Gardiner (pno) *(Fant Pno)*, Metolius Quartet *(Trio Fl, Va & Hp; I Have Cut Bamboo; Trio Vn, Cl & Pno; Qt 1 Strs; Sun & Sunflower; Secret Sky)*, artist unknown *(Interlude)*, D. Burham (va), J. P. s (fl), M. Griffiths (hp), Metolius Quartet *(And Yet There Could Be Love)* ("In Expression: The Music of Mark Vigil") NRTH ▲ 70004 (34.97)

VIITANEN, HARRI (1954-

Firmamentum [The Firmament] (concerto) for Organ & Orchestra (1985-88)
H. Viitanen (org), H. Lintu (cnd), Avanti! CO ("Firmamentum") † Images d'oiseau; Voyager BIS ▲ 887 [DDD] (17.97)

Images d'oiseau for Organ (1992)
H. Viitanen (org) ("Firmamentum") † Firmamentum; Voyager BIS ▲ 887 [DDD] (17.97)

Voyager for Tape (1988; rev 1997)
H. Viitanen (org) ("Firmamentum") † Firmamentum; Images d'oiseau BIS ▲ 887 [DDD] (17.97)

VILLA-LOBOS, HEITOR (1887-1959)

A Lenda do Caboclo for Piano (1920)

I. Ametrano (pno) *(rec 1998)* ("Latino-American Piano Music") † Chôro 5; Ciclo brasilliero; Caba:Aire indio 2; Aire indio 4; Fabini:Estudio arpegiado; Triste 1; Fariñas:Sones sencillos; Ginastera:Danzas argentinas Pno, Op. 2; Malambo, Op. 7; Milonga; F. Mignone:Valsa de esquina 1; Valsa de esquina 2; E. Nazareth:Pno Music MAND ▲ 4930 [DDD] (18.97)

C. Bruinsma (gtr), P. Rueffer (gtr) *(rec Bedford School, England)* ("Brazileira") † Bachiana brasileira 2; Bachiana brasileira 4; Cirandas (16 rondos) Pno; L. Almeida:Brazilliance Gtr; D. Milhaud:Scaramouche; A. Piazzolla:Grand Tango; Wüsthoff:Concerto de Samba; A. York:Rosetta Gtr ASV ▲ 2079 [DDD] (12.97)

N. Freire (pno) ("Nelson Freire in Concert") † As tres Marias; Debussy:Images (6) Pno; W. A. Mozart:Son 12 Pno, K.332; R. Schumann:Fant Pno, Op. 17; A. Scriabin:Son 4 Pno, Op. 30 ALPE ▲ 9502003

D. Halász (pno) ("Complete Piano Music, Vol. 1") † Bachiana brasileira 4; Carnaval das crianças brasileiras; Chôro 5; Rudepoema; Suite floral BIS ▲ 712 (17.97)

Amazonas (symphonic poem) for Orchestra (1917)

E. A. Diemecke (cnd), Bolívar SO *(rec Aula Magna of the Universidad Central de Venezuela, July-Aug 1995)* † Con 2 Vc; Sym 4 DOR ▲ 90228 [DDD] (16.97)

R. Duarte (cnd), Czech-Slovak RSO Bratislava MARC ▲ 8223357 (13.97)

As tres Marias for Piano (1939)

N. Freire (pno) ("Nelson Freire in Concert") † A Lenda do Caboclo; Debussy:Images (6) Pno; W. A. Mozart:Son 12 Pno, K.332; R. Schumann:Fant Pno, Op. 17; A. Scriabin:Son 4 Pno, Op. 30 ALPE ▲ 9502003

Assobio a Jato (The Jet Whistle) for Flute & Cello (1950)

R. Sylvester (vc), S. Baron (fl) ("Music of Latin America") † Chôro 5; Ciclo brasilliero; J. J. Castro:Sonatina española; C. Chávez:Pieces (7) Pno; Ginastera:Duo Fl & Ob, Op. 13; Suite de danzas criollas, Op. 15; Revueltas:Allegro Pno PHOE ▲ 140 [ADD] (15.97)

Bachianas brasileiras (9) (complete)

L. Guimaraes (sop), N. Freire (pno), I. Karabtchevsky (cnd), Brazil SO *(rec June-Sept 1987)* ("Bachianas brasileiras: Complete Edition") IRI 3-▲ 143 [ADD] (47.97)

Bachiana brasileira No. 1 for 8 Cellos (1930)

E. Bátiz (cnd), Royal PO EMIC ▲ 47433 [DDD] (16.97)

Brazilian Guitar Quartet [arr Abreu for gtr quartet] *(rec São Paulo, Brazil, Dec 27-30, 1998)* † Gomes:Son Str Qt; C. M. Guarnieri:Canção sertaneja; Dança brasileira; Dança negra; Ponteios Pno; F. Mignone:Lundu DLS ▲ 3245 [DDD] (14.97)

Cello Octet † P. Boulez:Messagesquisse; Capon:A tempo; Dusapin:Loop; Pärt:Fratres for 8 Vcs; E. Vásquez:Migrations BUD ▲ 13 [DDD] (16.97)

G. Gomiero (sop), M. Brunello (vc), Orch Villa-Lobos [trans 12 vcs] † Bachiana brasileira 5; J. S. Bach:Suite 3 Orch, BWV 1068; Wohltemperirte Clavier; Jobim:Gtr Music AURC ▲ 403 (5.97)

Parisot (cnd) † Bachiana brasileira 5; J. S. Bach:Music of Bach DLS ▲ 3041 (14.97)

L. Stokowski (cnd), New York Stadium SO *(rec Manhattan Center NYC, NY)* † Uirapurú; Debussy:Children's Corner; S. Prokofiev:Ugly Duckling, Op. 18 EVC ▲ 9023 [AAD] (13.97)

H. Villa-Lobos (cnd), French National RSO *(rec Paris, France, Jan 8 & 9, 1958)* † Bachiana brasileira 2; Bachiana brasileira 5; Bachiana brasileira 9 EMIC (Great Recordings of the Century) ▲ 66964 [ADD] (11.97)

Bachiana brasileira No. 2 for Orchestra (1930)

L. Bernstein (cnd), New York PO *(rec 1962)* † Bachiana brasileira 5; C. Chávez:Sym 2; A. Copland:Danzón Cubano; Salón México; O. L. Fernandez:Batuque; C. M. Guarnieri:Dança brasileira; Revueltas:Sensemayá SNYC (Bernstein Century) ▲ 60571 [ADD] (10.97)

C. Bruinsma (gtr), P. Rueffer (gtr)—Toccata (O trenzinho do Caipira) *(rec Bedford School, England)* ("Brazileira") † A Lenda do Caboclo; Bachiana brasileira 4; Cirandas (16 rondos) Pno; L. Almeida:Brazilliance Gtr; D. Milhaud:Scaramouche; A. Piazzolla:Grand Tango; Wüsthoff:Concerto de Samba; A. York:Rosetta Gtr ASV ▲ 2079 [DDD] (12.97)

P. Capolongo (cnd), Orch de Paris † Bachiana brasileira 5; Bachiana brasileira 6; Bachiana brasileira 9 EMIC ▲ 47357 [ADD] (16.97)

E. Goossens (cnd), London SO † Antill:Corroboree (suite); Ginastera:Estancia (suite); Panambí (suite), Op. 1a EVC ▲ 9007 [AAD] (13.97)

J. López-Cobos (cnd), Cincinnati SO *(rec Cincinnati Ohio, Apr 23-24, 1995)* † Bachiana brasileira 4; Bachiana brasileira 8 TEL ▲ 80393 [DDD] (16.97)

E. Mata (cnd), Bolívar SO ("Music of Latin American Masters") † Uirapurú; C. Chávez:Caballos de vapor (suite); Sym 2; Estévez:Mediodía en el Llano; Ginastera:Estancia (sels); Pampeana 3, Op. 24; Orbón:Con grosso; Versiones sinfónicas; Revueltas:Redes; Sensemayá DOR 3-▲ 98102 [DDD] (36.97)

D. Montgomery (cnd), Jena PO ("Orchestral Works") † Dança frenética; Dawn in a Tropical Forest; Mômoprecoce ARNO ▲ 54465 (4.97)

H. Villa-Lobos (cnd), French National RSO *(rec Paris, France, May 10 & 11, 1956)* † Bachiana brasileira 1; Bachiana brasileira 5; Bachiana brasileira 9 EMIC (Great Recordings of the Century) ▲ 66964 [ADD] (11.97)

Bachiana brasileira No. 3 for Piano & Orchestra (1938)

C. Ortiz (pno), V. Ashkenazy (cnd), New Philharmonia Orch *(rec 1976-90)* ("Instrumental & Chamber Works") † Con Gtr; Fant Sax; Mômoprecoce; Pno Music EMIC (Doubleforte) 2-▲ 72670 [ADD] (16.97)

Bachiana brasileira No. 4 for Piano (or Orchestra) (1930-36)

S. Assad (gtr)—Preludio (Introdução) [arr Assad] *(rec Netherlands, May 1995)* ("Saga Dos Migrantes") † S. Assad:Saga Dos Migrantes; Ginastera:Son 1 Pno, Op. 22; Gismonti:Gtr Music; A. Piazzolla:Music of Piazzolla NON ▲ 79365 (16.97)

C. Bruinsma (gtr), P. Rueffer (gtr) *(rec Bedford School, England)* ("Brazileira") † A Lenda do Caboclo; Bachiana brasileira 2; Cirandas (16 rondos) Pno; L. Almeida:Brazilliance Gtr; D. Milhaud:Scaramouche; A. Piazzolla:Grand Tango; Wüsthoff:Concerto de Samba; A. York:Rosetta Gtr ASV ▲ 2079 [DDD] (12.97)

D. Halász (pno) ("Complete Piano Music, Vol. 1") † A Lenda do Caboclo; Carnaval das crianças brasileiras; Chôro 5; Rudepoema; Suite floral BIS ▲ 712 (17.97)

F. Hasaj (cnd), Camerata Bariloche *(rec Troy, NY, Feb 1997)* ("Death of an Angel") † Bachiana brasileira 9; Blauth:Concertino; Ginastera:Con Strs, Op. 33; Pampeana 1, Op. 16; A. Piazzolla:Tangos (misc) DOR (Music of Latin American Masters) ▲ 90249 [DDD] (16.97)

J. López-Cobos (cnd), Cincinnati SO *(rec Cincinnati Ohio, Apr 23-24, 1995)* † Bachiana brasileira 2; Bachiana brasileira 8 TEL ▲ 80393 [DDD] (16.97)

A. Petchersky (pno) † Chôro 5; Ciclo brasilliero; Valsa da dor ASV ▲ 607 [DDD] (16.97)

F. Varani (pno) ("Varani Plays Villa-Lobos") † Carnaval das crianças brasileiras; Ciclo brasilliero; Cirandas (16 rondos) Pno; Danças características africanas PAUI ▲ 12143 (17.97)

Bachiana brasileira No. 5 for Soprano & 8 Cellos (1938-45)

V. D. Angeles (sop), H. Villa-Lobos (cnd), French National RSO *(rec Paris, France, June 7 & 13, 1956)* † Bachiana brasileira 1; Bachiana brasileira 2; Bachiana brasileira 9 *([ENG,POR]text)* EMIC (Great Recordings of the Century) ▲ 66964 [ADD] (11.97)

B. Asawa (ct), N. Marriner (cnd), Academy of St. Martin in the Fields *(rec Henry Wood Hall, England, Nov 1997)* † Canções Típicas Brasileiras; Forest of the Amazon; G. Fauré:Mélodies 'de Venise', Op. 58; Pavane; Songs; Medtner:Songs; S. Rachmaninoff:Songs (12), Op. 14; Songs (6), Op. 38; Songs (6), Op. 4; Vocalise RCAV (Red Seal) ▲ 68903 [DDD] (16.97)

A. Augér (sop), Parisot (cnd) † Bachiana brasileira 1; J. S. Bach:Music of Bach DLS ▲ 3041 (14.97)

H. Cheifetz (vc), B. Johanson (gtr)—Aria (Cantilena) [arr Cheifetz vc & gtr] *(rec Portland, OR, 1989-90)* ("Songs from the Cello") † F. Couperin:Pièces en Concert; Debussy:Son Vc; M. de Falla:Suite populaire espagnole; M. Ravel:Pièce en forme de Habanera; F. Schubert:Songs (misc); R. Schumann:Songs GAGR ▲ 927 [DDD] (14.97)

N. Davrath (sop), C. Stern (vc), L. Bernstein (cnd), New York PO *(rec 1962)* † Bachiana brasileira 2; C. Chávez:Sym 2; A. Copland:Danzón Cubano; Salón México; O. L. Fernandez:Batuque; C. M. Guarnieri:Dança brasileira; Revueltas:Sensemayá SNYC (Bernstein Century) ▲ 60571 [ADD] (10.97)

R. Dyens (gtr)—Aria (Cantilena) [arr Dyens] *(rec France)* ("Nuages") † Dyens:Sols d'lèze; Songe capricorne; Tristemusette; Valse en skaï; Ville d'Avril; Jobim:Felicidade; T. Monk:Round Midnight; D. Reinhardt:Nuages; Satie:Gnossiennes; Villoldo:El choclo GHA ▲ 126043 (17.97)

P. Freund (sop), T. Korhonen (gtr) ("Complete Works for Guitar, Vol. 2") † Chôro 1; Distribução de Flores; Preludes Gtr; Serestas; Suite populaire brésilienne; Sxt mistico ODE ▲ 838 (17.97)

J. Gomez (sop), Pleeth Cello Octet HYP ▲ 66257 [DDD] (18.97)

G. Gomiero (sop), M. Brunello (vc), Orch Villa-Lobos [trans 12 vcs] † Bachiana brasileira 1; J. S. Bach:Suite 3 Orch, BWV 1068; Wohltemperirte Clavier; Jobim:Gtr Music AURC ▲ 403 (5.97)

K. T. Kanawa (sop), L. Harrell (vc) *(rec Walthamstow Town Hall, June 24, 1984)* † Canteloube:Songs of Auvergne PLON (Double Decker) 2-▲ 44995 [DDD] (17.97)

E. Lear (sop) [arr for orch] ("A Celebration of Twentieth-Century Song") † S. Barber:Knoxville: Summer of 1915; A. Berg:Early Songs; M. Ravel:Shéhérazade Mez VAIA ▲ 1049 (17.97)

M. Mesplé (sop), P. Capolongo (cnd), Orch de Paris [POR] † Bachiana brasileira 2; Bachiana brasileira 6; Bachiana brasileira 9 EMIC ▲ 47357 [ADD] (16.97)

VILLA-LOBOS, HEITOR (cont.)

Bachiana brasileira No. 5 for Soprano & 8 Cellos (1938-45) (cont.)

A. Moffo (sop), L. Stokowski (cnd), American SO † Canteloube:Songs of Auvergne (sels); S. Rachmaninoff:Vocalise RCAV (Gold Seal) ▲ 7831 [ADD] (11.97)

A. Moffo (sop), L. Stokowski (cnd), American SO ("Basic 100, Vol. 27") † Preludes Gtr; G. Holst:Planets, Op. 32; J. Rodrigo:Con de Aranjuez; Fant para un gentilhombre; Vaughan Williams:Fant on a Theme of Tallis; Fant on Greensleeves RCAV ▲ 61724 (10.97)

Trio Concertante [db-vc-gtr arr] † B. Bartók:Mikrokosmos, Sz.107 GMR ▲ 2035 (16.97)

Bachiana brasileira No. 6 for Flute & Bassoon (1938)

P. Capolongo (cnd), Orch de Paris † Bachiana brasileira 2; Bachiana brasileira 5; Bachiana brasileira 9 EMIC ▲ 47357 [ADD] (16.97)

A. Griminelli (fl), R. Vernizzi (bn) *(rec Torino Italy, Feb 1987)* ("Wind Music") † Chôro 2; Duo Ob & Bn; Qnt forme de chôros; Qt Fl; Trio Ob AART ▲ 47200 [DDD] (10.97)

K. Karr (fl), M. Karr (bn) *(rec Louisville, 1996)* ("A Bassoonist's Voice") † J. S. Bach:Partita Fl, BWV 1013; Cervetto:Sicilienne Bn; Dunhill:Lyric Suite Bn & Pno, Op. 96; J. Françaix:Divert Bn; R. Schumann:Fantasiestücke Cl, Op. 73 CENT ▲ 2330 [DDD] (16.97)

New York Woodwind Quintet members ("The Best of the New York Woodwind Quintet, Vol. 2") † Duo Ob & Bn; Qnt forme de chôros; I. Fine:Partita; P. Hindemith:Kleine Kammermusik, Op. 24/2; Ibert:Pièces brèves Ww; D. Milhaud:Cheminée du Roi René, Op. 205; Van Vactor:Scherzo Ww Qnt; A. Wilder:Up Tempo BOSK ▲ 139 [AAD] (15.97)

Scarborough Chamber Players † A. Blank:Poems; A. Roussel:Poèmes de Ronsard, Op. 26; R. Schumann:Faschingsschwank, Op. 26; L. Spohr:German Songs, Op. 103; Starer:Songs of Youth & Age CENT ▲ 2106 [DDD] (16.97)

Bachiana brasileira No. 8 for Orchestra (1944)

J. López-Cobos (cnd), Cincinnati SO *(rec Cincinnati Ohio, Apr 23-24, 1995)* † Bachiana brasileira 2; Bachiana brasileira 4 TEL ▲ 80393 [DDD] (16.97)

Bachiana brasileira No. 9 for Strings (1945)

P. Capolongo (cnd), Orch de Paris † Bachiana brasileira 2; Bachiana brasileira 5; Bachiana brasileira 6 EMIC ▲ 47357 [ADD] (16.97)

F. Hasaj (cnd), Camerata Bariloche *(rec Troy, NY, Feb 1997)* ("Death of an Angel") † Bachiana brasileira 4; Blauth:Concertino; Ginastera:Con Strs, Op. 33; Pampeana 1, Op. 16; A. Piazzolla:Tangos (misc) DOR (Music of Latin American Masters) ▲ 90249 [DDD] (16.97)

Y. Turovsky (cnd), Montreal Musici † Evangelista:Airs d'Espagna; Ginastera:Con Strs, Op. 33 CHN ▲ 9434 (16.97)

H. Villa-Lobos (cnd), French National RSO *(rec Paris, France, May 16, 1956)* † Bachiana brasileira 1; Bachiana brasileira 2; Bachiana brasileira 5 EMIC (Great Recordings of the Century) ▲ 66964 [ADD] (11.97)

Bailado infantil for Piano (1911)

D. Halász (pno) *(rec Oct 1997)* ("Complete Piano Music, Vol. 3") † Brinquedo de roda; Francette et Piá; Histórias da Carochinha; Petizada; Pno Music; Suite infantil 2 BIS ▲ 912 [DDD] (17.97)

Brinquedo de roda (6 pieces) for Piano (1912)

D. Halász (pno) *(rec Oct 1997)* ("Complete Piano Music, Vol. 3") † Bailado infantil; Francette et Piá; Histórias da Carochinha; Petizada; Pno Music; Suite infantil 2 BIS ▲ 912 [DDD] (17.97)

Canções Típicas Brasileiras for Voice & Piano (1919-35)

B. Asawa (ct), N. Marriner (cnd), Academy of St. Martin in the Fields—Pálida Madona *(rec Henry Wood Hall, England, Nov 1997)* † Bachiana brasileira 5; Forest of the Amazon; G. Fauré:Mélodies 'de Venise', Op. 58; Pavane; Songs; Medtner:Songs; S. Rachmaninoff:Songs (12), Op. 14; Songs (6), Op. 38; Songs (6), Op. 4; Vocalise RCAV (Red Seal) ▲ 68903 [DDD] (16.97)

Carnaval das crianças brasileiras (8 pieces) for Piano (1919-20)

D. Halász (pno) ("Complete Piano Music, Vol. 1") † A Lenda do Caboclo; Bachiana brasileira 4; Chôro 5; Rudepoema; Suite floral BIS ▲ 712 (17.97)

F. Varani (pno) ("Varani Plays Villa-Lobos") † Bachiana brasileira 4; Ciclo brasilliero; Cirandas (16 rondos) Pno; Danças características africanas PAUI ▲ 12143 (17.97)

Cello & Piano Music

M. K. Jones (vc), G. Jackson (pno) ("Infrequent Music for Cello & Piano") † Arpe:Music Vc; M. de Falla:Melodia; Romanza; Tansman:Vc & Pno Music EMEC ▲ 10 (16.97)

T. Lisboa (vc), M. Braga (pno)—Berceuse, Op. 50; O canto do Cisne Negro; Sonhar, Op. 14; Bachiana brasileira 5 [Aria (Cantilena)]; Prelúdio 2; Divagação; Cap, Op. 49; Elégie; Pequena Suite; Bachiana brasileira 2 MER ▲ 84357 (16.97)

B. Verheij (vc), B. Brackman (pno)—Divagação; Pequena Suite; Son 2 Vc, Op. 66; Prelúdio 2; Sonhar, Op. 14; Cap, Op. 49; Elégie; Berceuse, Op. 50; O canto do Cisne Negro *(rec Amsterdam, 1992-93)* ("Works for Cello & Piano") ERAS ▲ 156 [DDD]

Choral Music

M. Best (cnd), Corydon Orch, Corydon Singers—Missa Sao Sebastiao; Magnificat Alleluia; Bendita sabedoria; Ave Maria; Pater noster; Cor dulce, cor amabile; Panis angelicus; Praesepe; Sub tuum HYP ▲ 66638 (18.97)

Chôro No. 1 for Guitar (1920)

M. Barrueco (gtr) *(rec 1988)* † Preludes Gtr; L. Brouwer:Gtr Music; Orbón:Prelude y danza EMIC ▲ 66576 [DDD] (11.97)

D. Blanco (gtr) *(rec Djursholm, Sweden, 1983)* ("Favorite Guitar Music") † Suite populaire brésilienne; I. Albéniz:Gtr Music; S. Myers:Gtr Music; Tárrega:Gtr Music; Recuerdos de la Alhambra; Yocoh:Gtr Music BIS ▲ 233 [DDD] (17.97)

A. D. Forno (gtr) *(rec live)* ("In Concert Part I") † A. Lara:Granada; Sor:Vars Mozart, Op. 9 JST ▲ 1078 (10.97)

R. Iturri (gtr) † Etudes Gtr; Preludes Gtr; Suite populaire brésilienne RENE ▲ 86011 [AAD] (16.97)

T. Korhonen (gtr) ("Complete Works for Guitar, Vol. 2") † Bachiana brasileira 5; Distribução de Flores; Preludes Gtr; Serestas; Suite populaire brésilienne; Sxt mistico ODE ▲ 838 (17.97)

A. Pierri (gtr) FL ▲ 23051 (16.97)

R. Smits (gtr) † Preludes Gtr; Suite populaire brésilienne; Bilhar:Tira poeira; J. Cardoso:Gtr Music; R. Ojeda:Rasguido Doble; A. Ramirez:Alfonsina ACCE ▲ 96121 [DDD] (17.97)

J. Sommer (gtr) † Distribução de Flores; Preludes Gtr; Suite populaire brésilienne; Sxt mistico CLSO ▲ 186 (15.97)

Y. Storms (gtr) ("A Touch of Latin") † A. Barrios:Gtr Music; L. Brouwer:Gtr Music; J. Cardoso:Gtr Music; J. Guimarães:Sons de Carrilhões; Lauro:Gtr Music; Sojo:Pieces from Venezuela SYRX ▲ 94106 [DDD] (16.97)

A. E. Street (gtr) † Etudes Gtr; Preludes Gtr; Suite populaire brésilienne ARN ▲ 68029 [DDD] (16.97)

M. Tröster (gtr) † Etudes Gtr; Preludes Gtr; Suite populaire brésilienne THOR ▲ 2052 [DDD] (16.97)

Chôro No. 2 for Flute & Clarinet (1924)

A. Griminelli (fl), M. Carulli (cl) *(rec Torino Italy, Feb 1987)* ("Wind Music") † Bachiana brasileira 6; Duo Ob & Bn; Qnt forme de chôros; Qt Fl; Trio Ob AART ▲ 47200 [DDD] (10.97)

Chôro No. 5 for Piano, "Alma brasileira" (1925)

I. Ametrano (pno) *(rec 1998)* ("Latino-American Piano Music") † A Lenda do Caboclo; Ciclo brasilliero; Caba:Aire indio 2; Aire indio 4; Fabini:Estudio arpegiado; Triste 1; Fariñas:Sones sencillos; Ginastera:Danzas argentinas Pno, Op. 2; Malambo, Op. 7; Milonga; F. Mignone:Valsa de esquina 1; Valsa de esquina 2; E. Nazareth:Pno Music MAND ▲ 4930 [DDD] (18.97)

D. Halász (pno) ("Complete Piano Music, Vol. 1") † A Lenda do Caboclo; Bachiana brasileira 4; Carnaval das crianças brasileiras; Rudepoema; Suite floral BIS ▲ 712 (17.97)

A. Petchersky (pno) † Bachiana brasileira 4; Ciclo brasilliero; Valsa da dor ASV ▲ 607 [DDD] (16.97)

H. Somer (pno) ("Music of Latin America") † Assobio a Jato; Ciclo brasilliero; J. J. Castro:Sonatina española; C. Chávez:Pieces (7) Pno; Ginastera:Duo Fl & Ob, Op. 13; Suite de danzas criollas, Op. 15; Revueltas:Allegro Pno PHOE ▲ 140 [ADD] (15.97)

Chôro No. 7 for 8 Instruments, "Settiminio" (1924)

L. Graham (cnd), National Chamber Players ("Nonets & Septets") † Indy:Chanson et Danses, Op. 50; Jaroch:Children's Suite; Martinů:Nonet Ww, Strs & Db; I. Stravinsky:Septet KLAV ▲ 11080 [DDD] (18.97)

J. Stephens (cnd), American Camerata † Krenek:Capriccio Vc; L. Moss:Clouds; Syms Brass; Persichetti:King Lear; Sapieyevski:Mercury Con AMCA ▲ 10305 (18.97)

H. Villa-Lobos (cnd), Sym of the Air *(rec 1959)* † Danças características africanas; Emperor Jones; O Papagio de Moleque; Suite floral; A. Heller:Feliz Anniversario ETC ▲ 1216 (17.97)

Chôro No. 8 for 2 Pianos & Orchestra (1925)

E. Sawyer (pno), S. Muniz (pno), E. D. Carvalho (cnd), Paraiba SO † Fant Vc; Uirapurú; M. Nobre:Convergências DLS ▲ 1017 [DDD] (10.97)

Chôro No. 10 for Orchestra & Chorus

E. Mata (cnd), Bolívar SO † Estévez:Florentino, el que cantó con el diablo DOR ▲ 80101 [DDD] (13.97)

Chôro No. 11 for Piano & Orchestra

R. Gothóni (pno), S. Oramo (cnd), Finnish RSO ODE ▲ 916 (17.97)

▲ = CD ♦ = Enhanced CD △ = MD ▮ = Cassette Tape ▯ = DCC

VILLA-LOBOS, HEITOR (cont.)

Chôros bis (2) for Violin & Cello (1928)
Y. Zhang (vn), T. Lisboa (vc) ("O Violoncello do Villa, Vol. 2") † Son 2 Vc, Op. 66; Trio 1 Pno; J. S. Bach:Wohltemperirte Clavier MER ▲ 84391 (16.97)

Ciclo brasilliero (4 pieces) for Piano (1936)
I. Ametrano (pno) *(rec 1998)* ("Latino-American Piano Music") † A Lenda do Caboclo; Chôro 5; Caba:Aire indio 2; Aire indio 4; Fabini:Estudio arpegiado; Triste 1; Fariñas:Sones sencillos; Ginastera:Danzas argentinas Pno, Op. 2; Malambo, Op. 7; Milonga; F. Mignone:Valsa de esquina 1; Valsa de esquina 2; E. Nazareth:Pno Music MAND ▲ 4930 [DDD] (18.97)
A. Petchersky (pno) † Bachiana brasileira 4; Chôro 5; Valsa da dor ASV ▲ 607 [DDD] (16.97)
H. Somer (pno)—Dansa do Indio Branco ("Music of Latin America") † Assobio a Jato; Chôro 5; J. J. Castro:Sonatina española; C. Chávez:Pieces (7) Pno; Ginastera:Duo Fl & Ob, Op. 13; Suite de danzas criollas, Op. 15; Revueltas:Allegro Pno PHOE ▲ 140 [ADD] (15.97)
F. Varani (pno) ("Varani Plays Villa-Lobos") † Bachiana brasileira 4; Carnaval das crianças brasileiras; Cirandas (16 rondos) Pno; Danças características africanas PAUI ▲ 12143 (17.97)

Ciranda das sete notas (fantasy) for Bassoon & Orchestra (1933)
M. Turkovič (bn), M. Sieghart (cnd), Stuttgart CO † J. Françaix:Divert Bn; G. Gershwin:Porgy & Bess (sels); M. Haydn:Concertino Bn & Orch; W. A. Mozart:Con Bn, K.191 ORF ▲ 223911 [DDD] (18.97)

Cirandas (16 rondos) for Piano (1926)
G. Andreza (perc), Brasil Brass Quintet [3 Cirandas arr José Alberto Kaplan] *(rec João Pessoa Paraíba, Brazil, Mar 22-26, 1995)* ("Brassil Plays Brazil") † Ursicino da Silva:Music of Duda Ursicino da Silva NIMB ▲ 5462 [DDD] (16.97)
C. Bruinsma (gtr), P. Rueffer (gtr) *(rec Bedford School, England)* ("Brazileira") † A Lenda do Caboclo; Bachiana brasileira 2; Bachiana brasileira 4; L. Almeida:Brazilliance Gtr; D. Milhaud:Scaramouche; A. Piazzolla:Grand Tango; Wüsthoff:Concerto de Samba; A. York:Rosetta Gtr ASV ▲ 2079 [DDD] (12.97)
A. Petchersky (pno) ("Piano Music, Vol. 2") † Rudepoema ASV ▲ 959 (16.97)
S. Rubinsky (pno) † Pno Music NXIN ▲ 8554489 [DDD] (5.97)
F. Varani (pno) ("Varani Plays Villa-Lobos") † Bachiana brasileira 4; Carnaval das crianças brasileiras; Ciclo brasilliero; Danças características africanas PAUI ▲ 12143 (17.97)

Concerto No. 2 for Cello & Orchestra (1953)
A. Diaz (vc), E. A. Diemecke (cnd), Bolívar SO *(rec Aula Magna of the Universidad Central de Venezuela, July-Aug 1995)* † Amazonas; Sym 4 DOR ▲ 90228 [DDD] (16.97)

Concerto for Guitar & Orchestra (1951)
J. Bream (gtr), A. Previn (cnd), London SO † J. Rodrigo:Con de Aranjuez RCAV (Gold Seal) ▲ 6525 [ADD] (11.97)
E. Fernández (gtr) † M. Arnold:Con Gtr, Op. 67; M. Giuliani:Con 1 Gtr, Op. 30; M. Ponce:Concierto del sur; J. Rodrigo:Con de Aranjuez; Vivaldi:Con Lt Vns, RV.93 PLON 2-▲ 455364 (17.97)
R. Jimenez (gtr), F. Lozano (cnd), Carlos Chávez SO ("3 Concertos for Guitar") † M. Ponce:Concierto del sur; J. Rodrigo:Con de Aranjuez FORL ▲ 16733 [DDD] (16.97)
R. Jimenez (gtr), F. Lozano (cnd), Carlos Chávez SO ("3 Conciertos for Guitar") † M. Ponce:Concierto del sur; J. Rodrigo:Con de Aranjuez FORL ▲ 16736 [DDD] (16.97)
R. Jimenez (gtr), F. Lozano (cnd), Carlos Chávez SO † M. Ponce:Concierto del sur; J. Rodrigo:Con de Aranjuez FORL ▲ 16757 (16.97)
T. Korhonen (gtr), S. Oramo (cnd), Finnish RSO ("Complete Works for Guitar, Vol. 1") † Etudes Gtr; Intro to the Chôros ODE ▲ 837 [DDD] (17.97)
N. Kraft (gtr), K. Koizumi (cnd), Winnipeg SO † J. Rodrigo:Con de Aranjuez SMS (SM 5000) ▲ 5066 [DDD] (16.97)
N. Kraft (gtr), N. Ward (cnd), Northern CO *(rec Oct 7-9, 1992)* † Castelnuovo-Tedesco:Con 1 Gtr, Op. 99; J. Rodrigo:Con de Aranjuez NXIN ▲ 550729 [DDD] (5.97)
A. Moreno (gtr), E. Bátiz (cnd), Mexico City PO † Bizet:Jeux d'enfants; Castelnuovo-Tedesco:Con 1 Gtr, Op. 99; G. Fauré:Dolly ICC ▲ 6702342 (9.97)
A. Romero (gtr), J. López-Cobos (cnd), London PO *(rec 1976-90)* ("Instrumental & Chamber Works") † Bachiana brasileira 3; Fant Sax; Mômoprecoce; Pno Music EMIC (Doubleforte) 2-▲ 72670 [ADD] (16.97)
M. Tsessos (gtr), V. Altschuler (cnd), St. Petersburg Philharmony CO † Castelnuovo-Tedesco:Con 1 Gtr, Op. 99; Vivaldi:Cons Gtr SNYC ▲ 64335 [DDD] (4.97)
W. Weigl (gtr), P. Schmelzer (cnd) † Castelnuovo-Tedesco:Con 1 Gtr, Op. 99; M. Ponce:Concierto del sur KSCH ▲ 310392 [DDD] (16.97)
J. Williams (gtr), D. Barenboim (cnd), English CO † J. Rodrigo:Con de Aranjuez SNYC ▲ 33208 (16.97)
J. Williams (gtr), D. Barenboim (cnd), English CO † Castelnuovo-Tedesco:Con 1 Gtr, Op. 99; M. Giuliani:Con 1 Gtr, Op. 30; M. Ponce:Concierto del sur; J. Rodrigo:Con de Aranjuez; Fant para un gentilhombre; Vivaldi:Con Lt Vns, RV.93; Cons Mand SNYC 2-▲ 44791 [ADD] (31.97)

Concerto for Harmonica & Orchestra (1955-56)
T. Reilly (hmc), E. Smola (cnd), Southwest German RSO Baden-Baden † M. Arnold:Con Hmc, Op. 46; R. Farnon:Prelude & Dance; J. Moody:Toledo; M. Spivakovsky:Con Hmc CHN ▲ 9248 [DDD] (16.97)

Dança dos mosquitos for Orchestra (1922)
R. Duarte (cnd), Slovak RSO Bratislava *(rec May 10-15, 1993)* † Dança frenética; Danças características africanas; Rudepoema MARC (Latin American Classics) ▲ 8223552 [DDD] (13.97)

Dança frenética for Orchestra (1919)
R. Duarte (cnd), Slovak RSO Bratislava *(rec May 10-15, 1993)* † Dança dos mosquitos; Danças características africanas; Rudepoema MARC (Latin American Classics) ▲ 8223552 [DDD] (13.97)
D. Montgomery (cnd), Jena PO ("Orchestral Works") † Bachiana brasileira 2; Dawn in a Tropical Forest; Mômoprecoce ARNO ▲ 54465 (4.97)

Danças características africanas (3 dances) for Piano (1915; orchd 1916)
R. Duarte (cnd), Slovak RSO Bratislava *(rec May 10-15, 1993)* † Dança dos mosquitos; Dança frenética; Rudepoema MARC (Latin American Classics) ▲ 8223552 [DDD] (13.97)
A. Heller (pno) *(rec 1959)* † Chôro 7; Emperor Jones; O Papagio de Moleque; Suite floral; A. Heller:Feliz Anniversario ETC ▲ 1216 (17.97)
F. Varani (pno) ("Varani Plays Villa-Lobos") † Bachiana brasileira 4; Carnaval das crianças brasileiras; Ciclo brasilliero; Cirandas (16 rondos) Pno PAUI ▲ 12143 (17.97)

Dawn in a Tropical Forest (overture) for Orchestra (1953)
D. Montgomery (cnd), Jena PO ("Orchestral Works") † Bachiana brasileira 2; Dança frenética; Mômoprecoce ARNO ▲ 54465 (4.97)

Distribução de Flores for Flute & Guitar (1937)
P. Freund (sop), T. Korhonen (gtr) ("Complete Works for Guitar, Vol. 2") † Bachiana brasileira 5; Chôro 1; Preludes Gtr; Serestas; Suite populaire brésilienne; Sxt mistico ODE ▲ 838 (17.97)
J. Sommer (gtr), B. Larsen (fl) † Chôro 1; Preludes Gtr; Suite populaire brésilienne; Sxt mistico CLSO ▲ 186 (15.97)

Duo for Oboe & Bassoon (1957)
P. Borgonovo (ob), R. Vernizzi (bn) *(rec Torino Italy, Feb 1987)* ("Wind Music") † Bachiana brasileira 6; Chôro 2; Qnt forme de chôros; Qt Fl; Trio Ob AART ▲ 47200 [DDD] (10.97)
A. Klein (ob), G. Sakakeeny (bn) ("25th Anniversary—International Double Reed Society") † J. Françaix:Trio Ob; A. Previn:Trio Ob; G. Rossini:Barbiere di Siviglia (wind ensemble) CRYS ▲ 870 (15.97)
New York Woodwind Quintet members ("The Best of the New York Woodwind Quintet, Vol. 2") † Bachiana brasileira 6; Qnt forme de chôros; I. Fine:Partita; P. Hindemith:Kleine Kammermusik, Op. 24/2; Ibert:Pièces brèves Ww; D. Milhaud:Cheminée du Roi René, Op. 205; Van Vactor:Scherzo Ww Qnt; A. Wilder:Up Tempo BOSK ▲ 139 [AAD] (15.97)

Emperor Jones (ballet) for Orchestra (1956)
H. Villa-Lobos (cnd), Sym of the Air *(rec 1959)* † Chôro 7; Danças características africanas; O Papagio de Moleque; Suite floral; A. Heller:Feliz Anniversario ETC ▲ 1216 (17.97)

Etudes (12) for Guitar (1929)
A. D. Forno (gtr)—Etude No. 1; Etude No. 8; Etude No. 11; Etude No. 7 *(rec New York, United States of America)* ("Del Forno plays Villa-Lobos") † Preludes Gtr; Suite populaire brésilienne JST ▲ 1080 (18.97)
T. Hoppstock (gtr) ("Werke für Gitarre") † L. Brouwer:Estudios Sencillos; Paganini:Caprices Vn, M.S. 25 SIGM ▲ 4100 [DDD] (17.97)
R. Iturri (gtr)—Etude No. 5; Etude No. 6; Etude No. 8 † Chôro 1; Preludes Gtr; Suite populaire brésilienne RENE ▲ 86011 [AAD] (16.97)
T. Korhonen (gtr) ("Complete Works for Guitar, Vol. 1") † Con Gtr; Intro to the Chôros ODE ▲ 837 [DDD] (17.97)
N. Kraft (gtr)—Etude No. 3; Etude No. 4; Etude No. 11 *(rec Cambridge University, England, Jan 1990)* ("Spanish & South American Works for Guitar") † I. Albéniz:Mallorca, Op. 202; Piezas caracteristicas, Op. 92; Suite española 1, Op. 47; Castelnuovo-Tedesco:Platero y yo, Op. 190; M. de Falla:Homenaje tombeau de Debussy; Sombrero de tres picos (dances); Moreno Torroba:Sonatina Gtr; J. Turina:Homenaje a Tárrega, Op. 69 CHN ▲ 8857 [DDD] (16.97)
A. Ramírez (gtr) *(rec Stadthalle Meinerzhagen Germany, Oct 12-15, 1993)* ("Works by Villa-Lobos & Ginastera") † Preludes Gtr; Ginastera:Son Gtr, Op. 47 DNN ▲ 78931 [DDD] (16.97)

VILLA-LOBOS, HEITOR (cont.)

Etudes (12) for Guitar (1929) (cont.)
P. Riis (gtr) *(rec June 1980-Sept 1982)* ("Classical Guitar") † Preludes Gtr; Suite populaire brésilienne; J. Turina:Homenaje a Tárrega, Op. 69; S. L. Weiss:Lt Music OPU ▲ 8015 [AAD]
A. Segovia (gtr)—Etude No. 1; Etude No. 8 † Preludes Gtr; I. Albéniz:Gtr Music; Castelnuovo-Tedesco:Gtr Music; M. Ponce:Gtr Music; Son Mexicana; Sor:Gtr Music; Tansman:Berceuse et Danse; S. L. Weiss:Lt Music AURC ▲ 115
A. E. Street (gtr)—Etude No. 7; Etude No. 4; Etude No. 8; Etude No. 11 † Chôro 1; Preludes Gtr; Suite populaire brésilienne ARN ▲ 68029 [DDD] (16.97)
M. Tröster (gtr) † Chôro 1; Preludes Gtr; Suite populaire brésilienne THOR ▲ 2052 [DDD] (16.97)

Fantasia for Cello & Orchestra (1945)
J. Starker (vc), F. D. Carvalho (cnd), Paraiba SO † Chôro 8; Uirapurú; M. Nobre:Convergências DLS ▲ 1017 [DDD] (10.97)

Fantasia for Soprano Saxophone & Chamber Orchestra (1948)
G. Banaszak (sax), B. Jarmolowicz (cnd), Polish National CO of Slupsk *(rec Slupsk State Theatre, Poland, Apr 1998)* † P.-M. Dubois:Con A Sax; Glazunov:Con A Sax, Op. 109; Ibert:Con Vc; S. Rachmaninoff:Vocalise CENT ▲ 2400 [DDD] (16.97)
J. Harle (sax), N. Marriner (cnd), Academy of St. Martin in the Fields ("Saxophone Concertos") † R. R. Bennett:Con A Sax; Debussy:Rapsodie Sax; Glazunov:Con A Sax, Op. 109; T. Heath:Out of the Cool; Ibert:Concertino da camera EMIC ▲ 72109 [DDD] (6.97)
J. Harle (s sax), N. Marriner (cnd), Academy of St. Martin in the Fields *(rec 1976-90)* ("Instrumental & Chamber Works") † Bachiana brasileira 3; Con Gtr; Mômoprecoce; Pno Music EMIC (Doubleforte) 2-▲ 72670 [ADD] (16.97)

The Forest of the Amazon (symphonic poem) for Soprano & Orchestra
B. Asawa (ct), N. Marriner (cnd), Academy of St. Martin in the Fields—Canção do Amor *(rec Henry Wood Hall, England, Nov 1997)* † Bachiana brasileira 5; Canções Típicas Brasileiras; G. Fauré:Mélodies 'de Venise', Op. 58; Pavane; Songs; Medtner:Songs; S. Rachmaninoff:Songs (12), Op. 14; Songs (6), Op. 38; Songs (6), Op. 4; Vocalise RCAV (Red Seal) ▲ 68903 [DDD] (16.97)
R. Fleming (sop), A. Heller (cnd), Moscow RSO CSN ▲ 810012 [DDD]

Francette et Pià (10 pieces) for Piano [No. 10 for Piano 4-Hands] (1929)
D. Halász (pno) *(rec Oct 1997)* ("Complete Piano Music, Vol. 3") † Bailado infantil; Brinquedo de roda; Histórias da Carochinha; Petizada; Pno Music; Suite infantil 2 BIS ▲ 912 [DDD] (17.97)

Guitar Music
Y. Storms (gtr)—Etudes Gtr [Etude No. 1; Etude No. 8; Etude No. 11]; Preludes Gtr [No. 1 in e: Andantino espressivo; No. 3; No. 5]; Suite populaire brésilienne [Valsa-choro] *(rec 1991)* † Songs PAVA ▲ 7256 [DDD] (10.97)
F. Zigante (gtr)—Chôro 1; Etudes Gtr; Simples; Preludes Gtr; Suite populaire brésilienne ("Complete Works for Solo Guitar") STRV ▲ 33378 [DDD] (16.97)

Histórias da Carochinha (4 pieces) for Piano (1919)
D. Halász (pno) *(rec Oct 1997)* ("Complete Piano Music, Vol. 3") † Bailado infantil; Brinquedo de roda; Francette et Pià; Petizada; Pno Music; Suite infantil 2 BIS ▲ 912 [DDD] (17.97)

Introduction to the Chôros for Guitar & Orchestra (1929)
T. Korhonen (gtr), S. Oramo (cnd), Finnish RSO ("Complete Works for Guitar, Vol. 1") † Con Gtr; Etudes Gtr ODE ▲ 837 [DDD] (17.97)

Magdalena (musical comedy in 2 acts) (1948)
J. Kaye (sop) *(rec Lincoln Center cast, 1988)* COL ▲ 44945 [DDD] (16.97)

Mômoprecoce (fantasy) for Piano & Orchestra (1929)
M. A. De Almeida (pno), D. Montgomery (cnd), Jena PO ("Orchestral Works") † Bachiana brasileira 2; Dança frenética; Dawn in a Tropical Forest ARNO ▲ 54465 (4.97)
C. Ortiz (pno), V. Ashkenazy (cnd), New Philharmonia Orch *(rec 1976-90)* ("Instrumental & Chamber Works") † Bachiana brasileira 3; Con Gtr; Fant Sax; Pno Music EMIC (Doubleforte) 2-▲ 72670 [ADD] (16.97)

Music of Villa-Lobos
I. Carreno (vn), P. Bournet (gtr)—Serestas [Modinha]; Distribução de Flores *(rec 1994)* ("Café 1930") † I. Carreño:Fant; F. Gonzalez:Music of Gonzalez; C. Machado:Music of Machado; A. Piazzolla:Music of Piazzolla; Tangos (misc) IRI ▲ 269 [DDD] (16.97)

O Papagio de Moleque (episódo sinfônico) for Orchestra (1932)
H. Villa-Lobos (cnd), Sym of the Air *(rec 1959)* † Chôro 7; Danças características africanas; Emperor Jones; Suite floral; A. Heller:Feliz Anniversario ETC ▲ 1216 (17.97)

Petizada (6 pieces) for Piano (1912)
D. Halász (pno) *(rec Oct 1997)* ("Complete Piano Music, Vol. 3") † Bailado infantil; Brinquedo de roda; Francette et Pià; Histórias da Carochinha; Pno Music; Suite infantil 2 BIS ▲ 912 [DDD] (17.97)

Piano Music
L. Ascot (pno)—Chôro 1; Tristorosa; A Lenda do Caboclo; Valsa da dor; Chôro 5 ("Music of Brazil") † E. Nazareth:Pno Music CASC ▲ 1050 (16.97)
D. Halász (pno)—Ciclo brasilliero; Valsa da dor; Cirandas (16 rondos) Pno; Sul América *(rec Feb 1996)* ("Complete Piano Music, Vol. 2") BIS ▲ 812 [DDD] (17.97)
D. Halász (pno)—Suite infantil 1; Cirandinhas *(rec Oct 1997)* ("Complete Piano Music, Vol. 3") † Bailado infantil; Brinquedo de roda; Francette et Pià; Histórias da Carochinha; Petizada; Suite infantil 2 BIS ▲ 912 [DDD] (17.97)
A. Heller (pno)—Bachiana brasileira 4; Chôro 5; New York Skyline; Ibericarabé; Nuvens [Waltz in D]; Valsa da dor; Ondulando; A Lenda do Caboclo; Saudades das Selvas Brasileiras; Poema singelo; Sul América; Fábulas características [O gato e o rato] ("Piano Works, Vol. 1") ETC ▲ 1123 [DDD] (17.97)
A. Heller (pno)—Ciclo brasilliero; Cirandas (16 rondos) Pno ("Piano Works, Vol. 2") ETC ▲ 1159 [DDD] (17.97)
A. Heller (pno)—Carnaval das crianças brasileiras; Simples Coletânea; Francette et Pià; As tres Marias; Homenagem a Chopin; Rudepoema ("Piano Works, Vol. 3") ETC ▲ 1220 [DDD] (17.97)
C. Ortiz (pno)—A próle do bébé; Ciclo brasilliero [Festa no sertão; Impressões seresteiras]; Chôro 5; A Lenda do Caboclo *(rec 1976-90)* ("Instrumental & Chamber Works") † Bachiana brasileira 3; Con Gtr; Fant Sax; Mômoprecoce EMIC (Doubleforte) 2-▲ 72670 [ADD] (16.97)
S. Rubinsky (pno)—A próle do bébé; Homenagem a Chopin † Cirandas (16 rondos) Pno NXIN ▲ 8554489 [DDD] (5.97)
R. Rust (pno)—Ciclo brasilliero; Valsa da dor; Bachiana brasileira 4; Suite floral; Chôro 5; Rudepoema *(rec June 1994)* ("Piano Music of Villa-Lobos") CENT ▲ 2224 (16.97)

Preludes (5) for Guitar (1940)
M. Barrueco (gtr) *(rec 1988)* † Chôro 1; L. Brouwer:Gtr Music; Orbón:Prelude y danza EMIC ▲ 66576 [DDD] (11.97)
J. Bream (gtr) ("Basic 100, Vol. 27") † Bachiana brasileira 5; G. Holst:Planets, Op. 32; J. Rodrigo:Con de Aranjuez; Fant para un gentilhombre; Vaughan Williams:Fant on a Theme of Tallis; Fant on Greensleeves RCAV ▲ 61724 (10.97)
O. Chassain (gtr) *(rec Limoges, France, 1996)* ("Éventail; Masters of the Spanish Guitar") † I. Albéniz:Austrias; Córdoba; M. de Falla:Amor brujo (sels); Sombrero de tres picos (suite 2); M. Ponce:Sonatina Meridional; J. Rodrigo:Fandango; Zarabanda lejana; J. Turina:Son Gtr, Op. 61 MENO ▲ 1022 [DDD] (20.97)
G. Fierens (gtr)—No. 3 *(rec London, England)* ("Spanish Guitar Music") † I. Albéniz:Suite española 1, Op. 47; Castelnuovo-Tedesco:Capriccio diabolico Gtr, Op. 85; Son D Gtr, Op. 77; M. Ponce:Preludio, Balletto & Giga; Sor:Grand Solo Gtr, Op. 14; J. Turina:Fandanguillo, Op. 36 ASLE ▲ 6190 [DDD] (8.97)
A. D. Forno (gtr) *(rec New York, United States of America)* ("Del Forno plays Villa-Lobos") † Etudes Gtr; Suite populaire brésilienne JST ▲ 1080 (18.97)
R. Guthrie (gtr) *(rec Holy Nativity Episcopal Church, Plano, TX, 1995)* † L. Almeida:Gtr Music; J. Guimarães:Gtr Music; Lauro:Gtr Music; M. Ponce:Gtr Music; J. Silva:Gtr Music ENRE ▲ 9509 [DDD] (16.97)
R. Iturri (gtr) † Chôro 1; Etudes Gtr; Suite populaire brésilienne RENE ▲ 86011 [AAD] (16.97)
Y. Kamata (gtr) ("Serie Americana: Guitar Works of Latin America") † Ayala:Serie Americana; Lauro:Suite Venezolano; A. Piazzolla:Pieces (5) Gtr CAMA ▲ 453 [DDD] (18.97)
T. Korhonen (gtr) ("Complete Works for Guitar, Vol. 2") † Bachiana brasileira 5; Chôro 1; Distribução de Flores; Serestas; Suite populaire brésilienne; Sxt mistico ODE ▲ 838 (17.97)
G. Kreplin (gtr) *(rec Broad Creek, MD, Spring 1995)* ("Bach in Brazil") † J. S. Bach:Suite Lt, BWV 995; Lauro:Valses Venezolanos ASCE ▲ 103 [DDD] (15.97)
O. Liebert (gtr) [arr O. Castro-Neves for gtr & orch] ("Leaning into the Night") † O. Liebert:Gtr Music; Mompou:Impresiones intimas; G. Puccini:Gianni Schicchi (sels); M. Ravel:Music of Ravel; Pavane pour une infante défunte; Satie:Gymnopédies COL ▲ 63105 (16.97)
W. Lieske (gtr) † L. Brouwer:Paisaje cubano con campanas; Preludios epigramaticos; A. Piazzolla:Pieces (5) Gtr INTC ▲ 830877 [DDD] (13.97)
A. Ramírez (gtr) *(rec Stadthalle Meinerzhagen Germany, Oct 12-15, 1993)* ("Works by Villa-Lobos & Ginastera") † Etudes Gtr; Ginastera:Son Gtr, Op. 47 DNN ▲ 78931 [DDD] (16.97)

VILLA-LOBOS, HEITOR (cont.)
Preludes (5) for Guitar (1940) (cont.)
P. Riis (gtr) *(rec June 1980-Sept 1982)* ("Classical Guitar") † Etudes Gtr; Suite populaire brésilienne; J. Turina:Homenaje a Tárrega, Op. 69; S. L. Weiss:Lt Music OPU ▲ 8015 [AAD]
A. Segovia (gtr)—No. 3 † Etudes Gtr; I. Albéniz:Gtr Music; Castelnuovo-Tedesco:Gtr Music; M. Ponce:Gtr Music; Son Mexicana; Sor:Gtr Music; Tansman:Berceuse et Danse; S. L. Weiss:Lt Music AURC ▲ 115
R. Smits (gtr) † Chôro 1; Suite populaire brésilienne; Bilhar:Tira poeira; J. Cardoso:Gtr Music; R. Ojeda:Rasguido Doble; A. Ramirez:Alfonsina ACCE ▲ 96121 [DDD] (17.97)
J. Sommer (gtr) † Chôro 1; Distribução de Flores; Suite populaire brésilienne; Sxt mistico CLSO ▲ 186 (15.97)
A. E. Street (gtr) † Chôro 1; Etudes Gtr; Suite populaire brésilienne ARN ▲ 68029 [DDD] (16.97)
M. Tröster (gtr) † Chôro 1; Etudes Gtr; Suite populaire brésilienne THOR ▲ 2052 [DDD] (16.97)
J. Williams (gtr) *(rec London, 1974)* ("John Williams Guitar Recital") † M. Giuliani:Vars on a Theme by Handel; Paganini:Caprices Vn, M.S. 25; D. Scarlatti:Sons Kbd
SNYC (Essential Classics) ▲ 62425 [ADD] (7.97) ▮ 62425 [ADD] (3.98)
Quartet for Flute, Oboe, Clarinet & Bassoon (1928)
A. Griminelli (fl), P. Borgonovo (ob), M. Carulli (cl), R. Vernizzi (bn) *(rec Torino Italy, Feb 1987)* ("Wind Music") † Bachiana brasileira 6; Chôro 2; Duo Ob & Bn; Qnt forme de chôros; Trio Ob AART ▲ 47200 [DDD] (10.97)
Quartet No. 1 for Strings (1915)
Latin American String Quartet *(rec Troy, NY, Apr 1994)* ("String Quartets, Vol. 1") † Qt 17 Strs; Qt 6 Strs
DOR ▲ 90205 [DDD] (16.97)
Quartet No. 2 for Strings (1915)
Cuarteto Latinoamericano *(rec Mexico City, Mexico, Nov & Dec 1998)* ("String Quartets, Vol. 4") † Qt 12 Strs; Qt 16 Strs DOR ▲ 93179 [DDD] (16.97)
Quartet No. 3 for Strings (1916)
Cuarteto Latinoamericano ("String Quartets, Vol. 2") † Qt 13 Strs; Qt 8 Strs DOR ▲ 90220 (16.97)
Danubius String Quartet † Qt 10 Strs; Qt 15 Strs MARC ▲ 8223393 (13.97)
Quartet No. 4 for Strings (1917)
Danubius String Quartet *(rec Apr 18-19, 1991)* † Qt 14 Strs; Qt 6 Strs MARC ▲ 8223391 [DDD] (13.97)
Quartet No. 6 for Strings (1938)
Danubius String Quartet *(rec May 20-23, 1991)* † Qt 14 Strs; Qt 4 Strs MARC ▲ 8223391 [DDD] (13.97)
Hollywood String Quartet † Creston:Qt Strs, Op. 8; Debussy:Danses sacrée et profane; M. Ravel:Intro & Allegro Hp; J. Turina:Oración del torero, Op. 34 TES ▲ 1053 [ADD] (17.97)
Latin American String Quartet *(rec Troy, NY, Apr 1994)* ("String Quartets, Vol. 1") † Qt 1 Strs; Qt 17 Strs
DOR ▲ 90205 [DDD] (16.97)
Quartet No. 7 for Strings (1941)
Cuarteto Latinoamericano ("String Quartets, Vol. 3") † Qt 15 Strs DOR ▲ 90246 (16.97)
Quartet No. 8 for Strings (1944)
Cuarteto Latinoamericano ("String Quartets, Vol. 2") † Qt 13 Strs; Qt 3 Strs DOR ▲ 90220 (16.97)
Quartet No. 10 for Strings (1946)
Danubius String Quartet † Qt 15 Strs; Qt 3 Strs MARC ▲ 8223393 (13.97)
Quartet No. 12 for Strings (1950)
Cuarteto Latinoamericano *(rec Mexico City, Mexico, Nov & Dec 1998)* ("String Quartets, Vol. 4") † Qt 16 Strs; Qt 2 Strs DOR ▲ 93179 [DDD] (16.97)
Quartet No. 13 for Strings (1951)
Cuarteto Latinoamericano ("String Quartets, Vol. 2") † Qt 3 Strs; Qt 8 Strs DOR ▲ 90220 (16.97)
Quartet No. 14 for Strings (1953)
Danubius String Quartet *(rec Apr 22-25, 1991)* † Qt 4 Strs; Qt 6 Strs MARC ▲ 8223391 [DDD] (13.97)
Quartet No. 15 for Strings (1954)
Cuarteto Latinoamericano ("String Quartets, Vol. 3") † Qt 7 Strs DOR ▲ 90246 (16.97)
Danubius String Quartet † Qt 10 Strs; Qt 3 Strs MARC ▲ 8223393 (13.97)
Quartet No. 16 for Strings (1955)
Cuarteto Latinoamericano *(rec Mexico City, Mexico, Nov & Dec 1998)* ("String Quartets, Vol. 4") † Qt 12 Strs; Qt 2 Strs DOR ▲ 93179 [DDD] (16.97)
Quartet No. 17 for Strings (1957)
Latin American String Quartet *(rec Troy, NY, Apr 1994)* ("String Quartets, Vol. 1") † Qt 1 Strs; Qt 6 Strs
DOR ▲ 90205 [DDD] (16.97)
Quintette en forme de chôros for Woodwinds (1928; rev 1953)
A. Griminelli (fl), P. Borgonovo (ob), F. Pomarico (E hn), M. Carulli (cl), R. Vernizzi (bn) *(rec Torino Italy, Feb 1987)* ("Wind Music") † Bachiana brasileira 6; Chôro 2; Duo Ob & Bn; Qt Fl; Trio Ob AART ▲ 47200 [DDD] (10.97)
New York Woodwind Quintet ("The Best of the New York Woodwind Quintet, Vol. 2") † Bachiana brasileira 6; Duo Ob & Bn; I. Fine:Partita; P. Hindemith:Kleine Kammermusik, Op. 24/2; Ibert:Pièces brèves Ww; D. Milhaud:Cheminée du Roi René, Op. 205; Van Vactor:Scherzo Ww Qnt; A. Wilder:Up Tempo BOSK ▲ 139 [AAD] (15.97)
Reykjavik Wind Quintet *(rec Suffolk, England, July 1992)* ("Barber:Summer Music, Beach:Pastorale & Other American Works Performed by the Reykjavik Wind Quintet") † S. Barber:Summer Music, Op. 31; Beach:Pastorale; I. Fine:Partita; J. Harbison:Qnt Winds; G. Schuller:Suite Woodwind Qnt CHN ▲ 9174 [DDD] (16.97)
Scandinavian Wind Quintet † Bozza:Scherzo, Op. 48; Ibert:Pièces brèves Ww; D. Milhaud:Cheminée du Roi René, Op. 205; M. Ravel:Tombeau; Taffanel:Music of Taffanel PLAL ▲ 58 (18.97)
N. Shore (E hn), Berlin Philharmonic Wind Quintet members *(rec Apr 1998)* ("Summer Music") † S. Barber:Summer Music, Op. 31; E. Carter:Qnt Ww; Machala:American Folk Suite; Medaglia:Suite "Belle Epoque"; Suite popular brasileira; Pitombeira:Ajubete; G. Schuller:Suite Woodwind Qnt BIS ▲ 952 [DDD] (17.97)
Rudá (ballet) for Orchestra (1951)
R. Duarte (cnd), Slovak RSO Bratislava [rev R. Duarte] *(rec Slovak Radio Concert Hall Bratislava, Feb 27-Mar 6, 1995)* † Sym 6 MARC ▲ 8223720 [DDD] (13.97)
Rudepoema for Piano (1921-26)
R. Duarte (cnd), Slovak RSO Bratislava [arr for orch] *(rec May 10-15, 1993)* † Dança dos mosquitos; Dança frenética; Danças características africanas MARC (Latin American Classics) ▲ 8223552 [DDD] (13.97)
D. Halász (pno) ("Complete Piano Music, Vol. 1") † A Lenda do Caboclo; Bachiana brasileira 4; Carnaval das crianças brasileiras; Chôro 5; Suite floral BIS ▲ 712 (17.97)
M.-A. Hamelin (pno) † Chopin:Son Pno in b♭, Op. 35; S. Rachmaninoff:Son 2 Pno, Op. 36; Schulz-Evler:Arabesque Pno PTRY ▲ 2204 (17.97)
A. Petchersky (pno) ("Piano Music, Vol. 2") † Cirandas (16 rondos) Pno ASV ▲ 959 (16.97)
Serestas for Voice & Piano (or Orchestra) (1925)
P. Freund (sop), T. Korhonen (gtr) ("Complete Works for Guitar, Vol. 2") † Bachiana brasileira 5; Chôro 1; Distribução de Flores; Preludes Gtr; Suite populaire brésilienne; Sxt mistico ODE ▲ 838 (17.97)
Sexteto mistico for Flute, Oboe, Saxophone, Harp, Celesta & Guitar (1917)
J. Sommer (gtr), B. Larsen (fl) † Chôro 1; Distribução de Flores; Preludes Gtr; Suite populaire brésilienne
CLSO ▲ 186 (15.97)
artists unknown, T. Korhonen (gtr) ("Complete Works for Guitar, Vol. 2") † Bachiana brasileira 5; Chôro 1; Distribução de Flores; Preludes Gtr; Serestas; Suite populaire brésilienne ODE ▲ 838 (17.97)
Sonata No. 2 for Cello & Piano, Op. 66 (1916)
J. Humeston (vc), M. Duphil (pno) † Trio 2 Pno MARC ▲ 8223164 (13.97)
T. Lisboa (vc), M. Braga (pno) ("O Violoncello do Villa, Vol. 2") † Chôros bis; Trio 1 Pno; J. S. Bach:Wohltemperirte Clavier MER ▲ 84391 (16.97)
C. Malich (vc), I. Bambirra (pno) † Ginastera:Pampeana 2, Op. 21; A. Piazzolla:Grand Tango ESDU ▲ 3017 (17.97)
Sonata No. 2 (fantasia) for Violin & Piano (1915)
M. Foster (vn), E. Plawutsky (pno) † C. M. Guarnieri:Coletanea; Miguez:Son Vn; M. Nobre:Desafio III
SNE ▲ 593 (16.97)
Songs
A. D. Brégan (sop), Y. Storms (gtr)—Canção do Poeta; Duas Paisagens; Canção de Cristal; Samba Clássico; Jardim Fanado; Serestas [Vôo; Canção do Carreiro]; Dinga-Donga; Bachiana brasileira 5; Poemas Indígenas [Canidé-Ioune-Sabath] † Gtr Music PAVA ▲ 7256 [DDD] (10.97)
L. Comtois (mez), M. Bourdeau (pno)—Modinhas e Canções 1 [Lundu da Marquesa de Santos; Evocação]; Little Song; Canções Típicas Brasileiras [Adeus Ema]; Serestas [O Anjo da Guarda]; Samba Clássico [POR] ("Songs of the Americas") † S. Barber:Songs (4), Op. 13; L. Bernstein:I Hate Music; Peter Pan (sels); Piccola Serenata; M. Forsyth:Songs from the Q'Appelle Valley; Ginastera:Canciones (2), Op. 3; Canciones populares argentinas, Op. 10; C. Ives:Songs; Mercure:Dissidence BRIO ▲ 112 [DDD] (16.97)
Suite floral (3 pieces) for Piano (1917-18)
D. Halász (pno) ("Complete Piano Music, Vol. 1") † A Lenda do Caboclo; Bachiana brasileira 4; Carnaval das crianças brasileiras; Chôro 5; Rudepoema BIS ▲ 712 (17.97)
A. Heller (pno) *(rec 1959)* † Chôro 7; Danças características africanas; Emperor Jones; O Papagio de Moleque; A. Heller:Feliz Anniversario ETC ▲ 1216 (17.97)

VILLA-LOBOS, HEITOR (cont.)
Suite infantil No. 2 for Piano (1912)
D. Halász (pno) *(rec Oct 1997)* ("Complete Piano Music, Vol. 3") † Bailado infantil; Brinquedo de roda; Francette et Pià; Histórias da Carochinha; Petizada; Pno Music BIS ▲ 912 [DDD] (17.97)
Suite populaire brésilienne for Guitar (1908-12)
D. Blanco (gtr)—Mazurka-choro; Schottisch-choro; Valsa-choro; Gavota-choro; Chorinho *(rec Djursholm, Sweden, 1983)* ("Favorite Guitar Music") † Chôro 1; I. Albéniz:Gtr Music; S. Myers:Gtr Music; Tárrega:Gtr Music; Recuerdos de la Alhambra; Yocoh:Gtr Music BIS ▲ 233 [DDD] (17.97)
A. D. Forno (gtr) *(rec New York, United States of America)* ("Del Forno plays Villa-Lobos") † Etudes Gtr; Preludes Gtr JST ▲ 1080 (18.97)
R. Iturri (gtr) † Chôro 1; Etudes Gtr; Preludes Gtr RENE ▲ 86011 [AAD] (16.97)
T. Korhonen (gtr) ("Complete Works for Guitar, Vol. 2") † Bachiana brasileira 5; Chôro 1; Distribução de Flores; Preludes Gtr; Serestas; Sxt mistico ODE ▲ 838 (17.97)
P. Riis (gtr)—Mazurka-choro *(rec June 1980-Sept 1982)* ("Classical Guitar") † Etudes Gtr; Preludes Gtr; J. Turina:Homenaje a Tárrega, Op. 69; S. L. Weiss:Lt Music OPU ▲ 8015 [AAD]
R. Smits (gtr) † Chôro 1; Preludes Gtr; Bilhar:Tira poeira; J. Cardoso:Gtr Music; R. Ojeda:Rasguido Doble; A. Ramirez:Alfonsina ACCE ▲ 96121 [DDD] (17.97)
J. Sommer (gtr) † Chôro 1; Distribução de Flores; Preludes Gtr; Sxt mistico CLSO ▲ 186 (15.97)
A. E. Street (gtr)—Gavota-choro † Chôro 1; Etudes Gtr; Preludes Gtr ARN ▲ 68029 [DDD] (16.97)
M. Tröster (gtr) † Chôro 1; Etudes Gtr; Preludes Gtr THOR ▲ 2052 [DDD] (16.97)
Symphony No. 4, "A vitória" (1919)
E. A. Diemecke (cnd), Bolivar SO *(rec Aula Magna of the Universidad Central de Venezuela, July-Aug 1995)* † Amazonas; Con 2 Vc DOR ▲ 90228 [DDD] (16.97)
Symphony No. 6, "Sobre a linha das monyanhas do Brasil" (1944)
R. Duarte (cnd), Slovak RSO Bratislava [rev R. Duarte] *(rec Slovak Radio Concert Hall Bratislava, Feb 27-Mar 6, 1995)* † Rudá MARC ▲ 8223720 [DDD] (13.97)
Trio for Oboe, Clarinet & Bassoon (1921)
P. Borgonovo (ob), M. Carulli (cl), R. Vernizzi (bn) *(rec Torino Italy, Feb 1987)* ("Wind Music") † Bachiana brasileira 6; Chôro 2; Duo Ob & Bn; Qnt forme de chôros; Qt Fl AART ▲ 47200 [DDD] (10.97)
Trio No. 1 for Piano, Violin & Cello (1911)
Ahn Trio † M. Ravel:Trio Pno CHSK ▲ 124 (16.97)
M. Braga (pno), Y. Zhang (vn), T. Lisboa (vc) ("O Violoncello do Villa, Vol. 2") † Chôros bis; Son 2 Vc, Op. 66; J. S. Bach:Wohltemperirte Clavier MER ▲ 84391 (16.97)
A. Spiller (vn), J. Humeston (vc), M. Duphil (pno) † Trio 3 Pno MARC ▲ 8223182 (13.97)
Trio No. 2 for Piano, Violin & Cello (1915)
A. Núñez (vn), J. Humeston (vc), M. Duphil (pno) † Son 2 Vc, Op. 66 MARC ▲ 8223164 (13.97)
Trio No. 3 for Piano, Violin & Cello (1918)
A. Spiller (vn), J. Humeston (vc), M. Duphil (pno) † Trio 1 Pno MARC ▲ 8223182 (13.97)
Trio for Strings
Capriccio Ensemble *(rec Portsmouth, NH)* † J. Haydn:Trio Strs; Paulus:Miniatures; S. Rachmaninoff:Prelude in c♯, Op. 3/2; Preludes Pno; M. Ravel:Alborada del gracioso; Jeux d'eau; D. Scarlatti:Sons Kbd; R. Schumann:Fant Pno, Op. 17 TIT ▲ 231 [DDD]
Uirapurú (ballet suite) for Orchestra (1917)
E. D. Carvalho (cnd), Paraiba SO † Chôro 8; Fant Vc; M. Nobre:Convergências DLS ▲ 1017 [DDD] (10.97)
E. Mata (cnd), Bolivar SO *(rec Central Univ. of Venezuela Caracas, July 1994)* ("Latin American Ballets") † C. Chávez:Caballos de vapor (suite); Ginastera:Estancia (sels) DOR ▲ 90211 [DDD] (16.97)
E. Mata (cnd), Bolivar SO ("Music of Latin American Masters") † Bachiana brasileira 2; C. Chávez:Caballos de vapor (suite); Sym 2; Estévez:Mediodia en el Llano; Ginastera:Estancia (sels); Pampeana 3, Op. 24; Orbón:Con grosso; Versiones sinfónicas; Revueltas:Redes; Sensemayá DOR 3-▲ 98102 [DDD] (36.97)
L. Stokowski (cnd), New York Stadium SO *(rec Manhattan Center NYC, NY)* † Bachiana brasileira 1; Debussy:Children's Corner; S. Prokofiev:Ugly Duckling, Op. 18 EVC ▲ 9023 [AAD] (13.97)
Valsa da dor for Piano (1932)
A. Petchersky (pno) † Bachiana brasileira 4; Chôro 5; Ciclo brasilliero ASV ▲ 607 [DDD] (16.97)

VILLANUEVA, FELIPE (1862-1893)
Piano Music
G. R. Weber (pno)—Vals Poético † Armengol:Pno Music; R. Castro:Pno Music; A. Elias:Pno Music; M. Ponce:Pno Music CLME ▲ 3 (13.97)
Vals Poético for Orchestra
E. Bátiz (cnd), Mexico City PO ("Música Mexicana: Volume 5") † Buxtehude:Org Music (misc colls); R. Halffter:Obertura Festiva, Op. 21; Tripartita, Op. 25; M. Ponce:Estrellita; Revueltas:Janitzio; Ocho; Sensemayá; P. A. Soler:Sons Kbd ASV (Música Mexicana) ▲ 894 (16.97)
H. de la Fuente (cnd), Mexico City PO † R. Castro:Intermezzo de Atzimba; Intermezzo Oriental; Minueto; Vals Capricho; M. B. Jiménez:Angelus; Rolon:Festin de los Enamos; Rosas:Sobre las Olas CLMX ▲ 21004 (13.97)

VILLETTE, PIERRE (1926-1969)
Choral Music
R. Allwood (cnd), Rodolfus Choir—Salve, Regina; O magnum mysterium; Attende, Domine; O sacrum convivium; Hymne à la Vierge *(rec Eton College Chapel, Dec 1993)* ("Mater, ora filium: Choral Music by Bax & Villette") † A. Bax:Choral Music HER ▲ 176 [DDD] (19.97)
Motets
D. Bargier (cnd), Rouen Chamber Choir—Hymne a la vierge, Op. 24; Strophes polyphoniques pour le veni creator, Op. 2, Op. 29; Attende domine, Op. 45; O magnum mysterium, Op. 53; Notre père d'aix, Op. 75 † Duruflé:Requiem, Op. 9 SOC ▲ 140 [ADD] (16.97)
D. Hill (cnd), Winchester Cathedral Choir—O salutaris hostia; O magnum mysterium *(rec Winchester Cathedral, England, July 1996)* † G. Fauré:Cantique de Jean Racine, Op. 11; Requiem, Op. 48; Roger-Ducasse:Motets
VCL ▲ 45318 [DDD] (16.97)

VILLOLDO, ANGEL GREGORIO (1868-1919)
El choclo (tango) [text ?Discepolo & Catan]
R. Dyens (gtr) [arr Dyens] *(rec France)* ("Nuages") † Dyens:Sols d'ìèze; Songe capricorne; Tristemusette; Valse en skaï; Ville d'Avril; Jobim:Felicidade; T. Monk:Round Midnight; D. Reinhardt:Nuages; Satie:Gnossiennes; H. Villa-Lobos:Bachiana brasileira 5 GHA ▲ 126043 (17.97)

VINCENT, JOHN (1902-1977)
Symphonic Poem after Descartes for Orchestra (1958-59)
E. Ormandy (cnd), Philadelphia Orch *(rec Apr 1, 1959)* † Sym in D; Joio:Air Power
ALBA (American Archives) ▲ 250 [AAD] (16.97)
Symphony in D for Orchestra, "A Festival Piece in 1 Movement" (1954; rev 1956)
E. Ormandy (cnd), Philadelphia Orch *(rec Apr 14, 1957)* † Sym Poem after Descartes; Joio:Air Power
ALBA (American Archives) ▲ 250 [AAD] (16.97)

VINCI, LEONARDO (ca 1690-1730)
Music of Vinci
A. Florio (cnd) ("Treasures of Naples, Vol. 3: L'Opera Buffa Napoletana") † L. Leo:Music of OPUS ▲ 30184 (18.97)
Z. Soave (fl), E. Di Felice (cnd), Ensemble L'Apothéose—Son 1 Fl; Son 2 Fl ("18th Century Flute Sonatas") † D. N. Sarro:Music of Sarro; A. Scarlatti:Music of A. Scarlatti STRV ▲ 33489 (16.97)
Sonatas (12) for Flute & Continuo
artists unknown, C. Ferrarini (cnd), Accademia Farnese MONM 2-▲ 96015 (36.97)
Li zita 'n galera (opera buffa) [lib B. Saddumene] (1722)
A. Florio (cnd), Cappella de' Turchini OPUS (Treasures of Naples, Vol. 8) 2-▲ 30212 (36.97)

VINDERS, JHERONIMUS (fl 1510-1550)
Klaagliederen op den dood van Josquin for Chorus
J. Summerly (cnd), Oxford Camerata *(rec Oxford, England, Apr 20-21, 1995)* ("Early Music") † Josquin Desprez:Chansons & Motets; Missa, "L'homme armé sexti toni" *([ENG,LAT] text)*
NXIN (Early Music) ▲ 8553428 [DDD] (5.97)

VINE, CARL (1954-
The Battlers (film music) for Orchestra
D. Stanhope (cnd), Tall Poppies Orch TALP ▲ 24 [DDD] (18.97)
Concerto for Oboe & Orchestra (1996)
D. Nuttall (ob), D. Masson (cnd), Australian Youth Orch *(rec Apr 1997)* ("A Garden of Earthly Delights") † Lumsdaine:Garden of Earthly Delights; Sculthorpe:Con Pno TALP ▲ 113 [DDD] (18.97)
Descent (Metropolis: The Workers' View) for Orchestra
D. Harding (cnd), London SO *(rec London, England, Dec 1997)* † Borisova-Ollas:Wings of the Wind; D. Gasparini:Through the Looking Glass; Hartke:Ascent of the Equestrian in a Balloon; Z. Long:Poems from Tang; A. March:Marine-à travers les arbres EMIC (Debut) ▲ 72826 [DDD] (6.97)

▲ = CD ♦ = Enhanced CD △ = MD ▮ = Cassette Tape ▯ = DCC

VINE, CARL (cont.)
Miniature IV for Flute (or Piccolo), Clarinet (or Bass Clarinet), Violin, Viola & Piano (1988)
Australia Ensemble *(rec John Clancy Auditorium Univ of New South Wales, 1993)* ("Samsara") † D. Banks:Divert Fl & Strs; Kerry:Son da Camera; B. Kos:Catena 2; Sitsky:Trio 6 Fl VOXA ▲ 20 [DDD] (18.97)
Sonata for Flute & Piano (1992)
G. Collins (fl), D. Miller (pno) *(rec ABC Ultimo Centre, Jan-Feb 1995)* ("Spinning: New Australian Flute Music") † N. Butterly:Wind Stirs Gently; R. Edwards:Ecstatic Dances Fls; A. Ford:Spinning; Humble:Son Fl; Smalley:Ceremony III; M. Wesley-Smith:Balibo TALP ▲ 69 [DDD]

VINTER, GILBERT (1909-1969)
James Cook—Circumnavigator for Band (1970)
artists unknown ("Epic Brass: British Music for Brass Band") † E. Ball:Sinfonietta; E. Elgar:Severn Suite Brass, Op. 87; P. E. Fletcher:Epic Sym; Rubbra:Vars on "The Shining River", Op. 101 CHN ▲ 4508 [ADD] (16.97)
Miniatures (2) for Wind Quintet
Sundsvall Wind Quartet † Ibert:Pièces brèves Ww; G. Jacob:Sxt Pno & Ww Qnt, Op. 6; Thuille:Sxt Pno, Op. 6 CAPA ▲ 21497 (16.97)
Salute to Youth
P. Parkes (cnd), Black Dyke Mills Band *(rec Dewsbury, England, Jan 21-22, 1986)* ("The Complete Champions") † W. Heaton:Contest Music; G. Lloyd:Royal Parks; J. McCabe:Music of McCabe CHN ▲ 4509 [DDD] (16.97)

VIOTTI, GIOVANNI BATTISTA (1755-1824)
Concerto No. 7 in G for Piano & Orchestra
C. Canziani (pno), Ducale CO *(rec 1998)* † Con 9 Vn BONG ▲ 5092 [DDD] (16.97)
Concertos for Violin & Orchestra
F. Mezzena (vn), F. Mezzena (cnd), Perusina Sinfonia—No. 4 in D; No. 20 in D; No. 27 in C *(rec May 1998)* ("Violin Concertos, Vol. 5") DYNC ▲ 206 [DDD] (17.97)
Concerto No. 4 in D for Violin & Orchestra, G.33 (1782)
G. Rimonda (vn) *(rec Pinerolo, 1997)* † Sym Concertante 1, G.76 BONG ▲ 5567 [DDD] (16.97)
Concerto No. 6 in E for Violin & Orchestra, G.34 (1782)
F. Mezzena (vn), F. Mezzena (cnd), Perusina Sinfonia *(rec Italy, March 3-5, 1999)* † Con 23 Vn, G.98; Con 5 Vn, G.45 DYNC ▲ 238 [DDD] (17.97)
Concerto No. 5 in C for Violin & Orchestra, G.45 (1782)
F. Mezzena (vn), F. Mezzena (cnd), Perusina Sinfonia *(rec Italy, March 3-5, 1999)* † Con 23 Vn, G.98; Con 6 Vn, G.34 DYNC ▲ 238 [DDD] (17.97)
Concerto No. 19 in g for Violin & Orchestra, G.91 (1791; rev 1818)
R. Kussmaul (vn), J. Goritzki (cnd), Neuss German Chamber Academy † Con 22 Vn, G.97 CPO ▲ 999324 (14.97)
Concerto No. 22 in a for Violin & Orchestra, G.97 (ca 1792-97)
L. Bobesco (vn), K. Redel (cnd), Rhineland-Palatinate State PO † Con 23 Vn, G.98 TLNT ▲ 291013 [ADD] (15.97)
R. Kussmaul (vn), J. Goritzki (cnd), Neuss German Chamber Academy † Con 19 Vn, G.91 CPO ▲ 999324 (14.97)
I. Perlman (vn), L. Foster (cnd), Julliard Orchestra *(rec Queens College/City University of New York, United States of America, May 1998)* ("Concertos from my Childhood") † Bériot:Scène de Ballet, Op. 100; Rieding:Con Vn; F. Seitz:Schüler-Konzert 2 Vn, Op. 13 EMIC ▲ 56750 [DDD] (16.97)
O. Shumsky (vn), V. Sokolov (pno) ("Historic Studio Recordings") † M. Ravel:Son Vn & Vc; O. Respighi:Son Vn; Wieniawski:Polonaise 2, Op. 21 BID ▲ 136 [ADD] (16.97)
F. Sommer-Link (vn), L. Graham (cnd), American Promenade Orch ("Premiere Evening") † Busoni:Lustspiel Ov, K. 245; Lalo:Arlequin; O. Nicolai:Lustigen Weiber von Windsor (ov); C. M. von Weber:Drei Pintos (sels) KLAV ▲ 11053 [DDD] (18.97)
E. Wallfisch (vn), R. Goodman (cnd), Brandenburg Orch ("Violin Concertos") † F. Schubert:Rondo Vn, D.438; L. Spohr:Con 8 Vn, Op. 47 HYP ▲ 66840 [DDD] (18.97)
Concerto No. 23 in G for Violin & Orchestra, G.98 (ca 1792-94)
L. Bobesco (vn), K. Redel (cnd), Rhineland-Palatinate State PO † Con 22 Vn, G.97 TLNT ▲ 291013 [ADD] (15.97)
F. Mezzena (vn), F. Mezzena (cnd), Perusina Sinfonia *(rec Italy, March 3-5, 1999)* † Con 5 Vn, G.45; Con 6 Vn, G.34 DYNC ▲ 238 [DDD] (17.97)
Concerto No. 9 in A for Violin & Orchestra (1783-84)
G. Rimonda (vn), Ducale CO *(rec 1998)* † Con 7 Pno BONG ▲ 5092 [DDD] (16.97)
Duos concertantes (6) for 2 Cellos, Op. 6 (ca 1799)
E. Baldini (vn), S. Cavuoto (vn) † Duos concertantes Vns, G.93-95 AG ▲ 56 [DDD] (18.97)
Duos concertantes (3) for 2 Violins, G.93-95, "Hommage à l'amitie" (ca 1802-03)
E. Baldini (vn), S. Cavuoto (vn) † Duos concertantes Vc, Op. 6 AG ▲ 56 [DDD] (18.97)
Deschka Duo *(rec July 1997)* † Sérénades en duos concertants DYNC (2000) ▲ 2008 [DDD] (13.97)
Music of Viotti
L'Arte dell'Arco—2 Trios for 2 Vns & Vc; 3 Serenades for 2 Vns *(rec Genova Italy, Dec 1-3, 1994)* ("Trios and Serenades") DYNC ▲ 101 [DDD] (17.97)
Quartets (3) for Flute & Strings, Op. 22
C. Ferrarini (fl), Salisburg String Quartet members STRV ▲ 33338 [DDD] (16.97)
Mannheim String Quartet † J. Haydn:Qts Fl, Op. 5; Pleyel:Qt Fl TIT ▲ 172 [DDD] (16.97)
G. Petrucci (fl), Kodály String Quartet members ("3 Flute Quartets, Op. 22") TUD ▲ 7021 [DDD] (16.97)
Quartets (3) for Strings, G.112-114
Aira String Quartet *(rec Dynamic's Genoa, Apr 5-7, 1995)* DYNC ▲ 138 [DDD] (17.97)
Sérénades en duos concertants (6) for 2 Violins, G.145-150 (Op. 23) (ca 1807)
Deschka Duo *(rec July 1997)* † Duos concertantes Vns, G.93-95 DYNC (2000) ▲ 2008 [DDD] (13.97)
Sonata in B♭ for Harp
C. Antonelli (hp) *(rec Rome, Italy, 1987)* ("Harp Festival") † C.P.E. Bach:Son Hp, H.563; B. Britten:Suite Hp, Op. 83; G. Fauré:Impromptu Hp, Op. 86; Saint-Saëns:Fant Hp, Op. 95; L. Spohr:Fant 2 Hp, Op. 35 AART ▲ 47202 [DDD] (10.97)
Sonatas for Violin & Piano
F. Ayo (vn), C. De Bernart (pno)—Sons Op. 4/5-6; Nos. 1 & 2 [from Book 2] *(rec Genova Italy, Feb 1997)* ("Complete Sonatas for Violin & Piano, Vol. 2") † Son Vn, G.30, Op. 4/5; Son Vn, G.31, Op. 4/6; Son Vn, G.35, G. 35; Son Vn, G.36, G. 36 DYNC (2000) ▲ 2003 [DDD] (13.97)
Sonata in E♭ for Violin & Piano [from Book I], G.30, Op. 4/5 (ca 1785)
F. Ayo (vn), C. Bernart (pno) *(rec Feb 1997)* ("Complete Sonatas for Violin & Piano, Vol. 2") † Son Vn, G.31, Op. 4/6; Son Vn, G.35, G. 35; Son Vn, G.36, G. 36; Sonatas for Violin & Piano DYNC (2000) ▲ 2003 [DDD] (13.97)
Sonata in b♭ for Violin & Piano [from Book I], G.31, Op. 4/6 (ca 1785)
F. Ayo (vn), C. Bernart (pno) *(rec Feb 1997)* ("Complete Sonatas for Violin & Piano, Vol. 2") † Son Vn, G.30, Op. 4/5; Son Vn, G.35, G. 35; Son Vn, G.36, G. 36; Sonatas for Violin & Piano DYNC (2000) ▲ 2003 [DDD] (13.97)
Sonata in A for Violin & Piano [Book II, No. 1], G. 35 (ca 1785)
F. Ayo (vn), C. Bernart (pno) *(rec Feb 1997)* ("Complete Sonatas for Violin & Piano, Vol. 2") † Son Vn, G.30, Op. 4/5; Son Vn, G.31, Op. 4/6; Son Vn, G.36, G. 36; Sonatas for Violin & Piano DYNC (2000) ▲ 2003 [DDD] (13.97)
Sonata in E♭ for Violin & Piano [Book II, No. 2], G. 36 (ca 1785)
F. Ayo (vn), C. Bernart (pno) *(rec Feb 1997)* ("Complete Sonatas for Violin & Piano, Vol. 2") † Son Vn, G.30, Op. 4/5; Son Vn, G.31, Op. 4/6; Son Vn, G.35, G. 35; Sonatas for Violin & Piano DYNC (2000) ▲ 2003 [DDD] (13.97)
Symphony Concertante in A for 2 Flutes & Orchestra [arr from Concerto for Violin], G.25 (1788)
M. Larrieu (fl), G. Nova (fl), G. Rimonda (cnd), Ducale CO, G. Rimonda (cnd), Camerata Ducale † Boccherini:Sym in D, G.490; Cimarosa:Con for 2 Fls; Con Fls BONG ▲ 5077 [DDD] (16.97)
Symphony Concertante No. 1 for 2 Violins & String Orchestra, G.76 (1787)
G. Rimonda (vn), C. Canziani (pno) [arr Steibelt for vn, pno & orch (ca 1788)] *(rec Pinerolo, 1997)* † Con 4 Vn, G.33 BONG ▲ 5567 [DDD] (16.97)

VISÉE, ROBERT DE (ca 1650/60-after 1720)
Guitar Music
A. Lawrence-King (hp)—La Royalle (allemande); Courante I & II; Sarabande; Gavotte; Chaconne; Mascarade Rondeau [all arr hp] *(rec Toddington England, Jan 23-25, 1996)* ("La Harpe Royale") † F. Couperin:Art de toucher le clavecin; L. Couperin:Hpd Music; F. Couperin:Nations; Pièces de clavecin (sels) DEHA ▲ 77371 [DDD] (16.97)
Guitar Pieces [Books 1 & 2] (selections)
M. Barrueco (gtr) *(rec 1989)* † J. S. Bach:Prelude, Fugue & Allegro Lt, BWV 998; Sons & Partitas Vn EMIC ▲ 66575 [DDD] (11.97)
Livre de pièces pour la guitarre (pubd 1686)
S. Volta (gtr)—Suite No. 9; Suite No. 10; Suite No. 11; Suite No. 12 ARN ▲ 68422 (16.97)
Lute & Guitar Music
J. Lindberg (lt)—Suite in d *(rec Sweden, Mar 9-11, 1986)* ("Baroque Music for Lute & Guitar") † Anonymous:Lt & Gtr Music; J. S. Bach:Fugue Lt; Prelude Lt, BWV 999; D. Kellner:Lt & Gtr Music; Roncalli:Lt & Gtr Music; S. L. Weiss:Lt Music BIS ▲ 327 [DDD] (17.97)

VISÉE, ROBERT DE (cont.)
Pieces for Theorbo & Lute
J. M. Moreno (thb)—Pieces in G; Entrée des Espagnols de M. Lully; Logistille de M. Lully; Chaconne des Harlequins de M. Lully; Pieces in C; Les Sylvains de M. Couperin; Les Bergeries de M. Couperin *(rec San Lorenzo de El Escorial Spain, Nov 1995)* ("Pièces de Théorbe") GLSS ▲ 920104 [DDD] (18.97)
Pieces for Theorbo & Lute (1716)
H. Smith (thb) ("Chamber Music at Versailles") † Machy:Pieces VI ASTR 2-▲ 8668 (18.97)
Suite in e for 2 Theorbos
E. Bellocq (thb), M. Moscardo (thb) † Suite in G Thb; Corbetta:Concert Gtrs; La Guitarre royalle; Sarabande NXIN ▲ 8553745 [DDD] (5.97)
Suite in G for 2 Theorbos
E. Bellocq (thb), M. Moscardo (thb) † Suite in e Thb; Corbetta:Concert Gtrs; La Guitarre royalle; Sarabande NXIN ▲ 8553745 [DDD] (5.97)

VÏSHNEGRADSKY, IVAN (1893-1979)
Music of Vishnegradsky
B. Mather (pno), M. Couroux (pno), F. Couture (pno), P. Helmer (pno), P. LePage (pno), J. Laurendeau (ondes martenot), S. Binet-Audet (ondes martenot), G. Grenier (ondes martenot), E. Lemire (ondes martenot)—Transparences I & II; Composition in Quarter-Tones; Cosmos, Op. 28 ("Hommage à Vïshnegradsky") SNE ▲ 589 (16.97)

VISSOTZKI, VLADIMIR (20th cent)
Lieder Vom Krieg for Voice & Guitar
V. Vissotzki (sgr), V. Vissotzki (gtr) PLAE ▲ 888776

VISVIKIS, DEMIS (20th cent)
Mondes irisés for Saxophone & Piano (1996)
Duo Dilemme *(rec Jan 1998)* ("Nouvelle musique pour saxophone et piano") † M. Angulo:Bisonante Sax; Charrière:Voix meurtrie; Guerandi:Towards; J. A. Lennon:Distances Within Me; M. Nyman:Shaping the Curve DORO ▲ 5011 [DDD] (16.97)

VITALE, WAYNE (20th cent)
Khayalan Tiga for Gamelan Orchestra (1991)
artists unknown ("American Works for Balinese Gamelan Orchestra") † Tenzer:Banyuari; Situ Banda; Ziporyn:Aneh Tapi Nyata; Kekembangan NWW ▲ 80430 (16.97)

VITALI, GIOVANNI BATTISTA (1632-1692)
Music of Vitali
Quartetto Italiano † Boccherini:Qts Strs; Cambini:Qts Strs; Galuppi:Music of; Vivaldi:Sinf Strs in b, RV.169 TES ▲ 1124 (17.97)
Varie partie del passemezo, ciaccona, capricii, e passagalii for 2 Violins & Viol (or Spinet), Op. 7 (1682)
Accademia Farnese MONM (Il grande barocco Italiano) ▲ 96002 (17.97)

VITALI, TOMASO ANTONIO (1663-1745)
Chaconne in g for Violin & Continuo [attrib]
S. Accardo (vn), L. Manzini (pno) ("Violinist Composers") † Paganini:Cantabile, M.S. 109; Sarasate:Fant on Carmen, Op. 25; Tartini:Son Vn & Pno; Wieniawski:Légende Vn, Op. 17; Polonaise 2, Op. 21 FON ▲ 9602 [DDD] (13.97)
H. Lindemann (va), B. Martin (pno) ("Hommage a Primrose") † J. Brahms:Son 1 Cl; J. Joachim:Vars on a Theme Va, Op. 10; Paganini:Caprices Vn, M.S. 25; S. Rachmaninoff:Vocalise; Wieniawski:Etude-caprices Vn, Op. 18 TACE ▲ 45
N. Milstein (vn), A. Balsam (pno) *(rec 1954-59)* ("Italian Sonatas") † A. Corelli:Son Vn, Op. 5/12, "La Follia"; Geminiani:Sons Vn, Op. 4; N. Milstein:Paganiniana; Pergolesi:Son 12 Vn; Tartini:Son Vn & Pno; Vivaldi:Sons Vn EMIC ▲ 66873 (m) [ADD] (11.97)
N. Milstein (vn), J. Blatt (pno) *(rec Coolidge Auditorium Library of Congress, Oct 7, 1946)* ("Nathan Milstein in Recital") † Mendelssohn (-Bartholdy):Con Vn & Orch, Op. 64; N. Milstein:Paganiniana BRID ▲ 9064 (17.97)

VITO-DELVAUX, BERTHE DI (1915-
Music of Vito-Delvaux
L. Di Vito (mez), E. Melon (vn), F. Orval (hn), D. Blumenthal (pno), J. Schills (pno)—Son Vn, Op. 81; Pezzo concertanto; Songs from Opp. 39, 65, 80, 104 & 111; Songs, Op. 202; Son Hn, Op. 109; Caricatures RENE ▲ 87136 (16.97)

VIVALDI, ANTONIO (1678-1741)
All'ombra di sospetto (cantata) for Soprano, Flute & Continuo, RV.678
C. Gasdia (sop), F. Tasini (hpd), C. Ferrarini (cnd), Barocco Veneziano † Lungi dal vago volto, RV.680; Salve Regina, RV.617 MONM 2-▲ 90031 (34.97)
Arias
K. Eckersley (sop), P. Rapson (hpd), P. Rapson (cnd) —Fida Ninfa (sels) [Alma opressa]; Griselda (sels) [Agitata da due venti] † Cons Vn Strs, Op. 8/1-4; Incoronazione di Dario (sels) MER ▲ 84195 (16.97)
E. Kirkby (sop), R. Goodman (cnd), Brandenburg Consort—Ottone in Villa (sels) [Gelosia, tu giá rendi l'alma mia; Loombre, l'aure]; Catone in Utica (sels) [Se mai senti spirati sul volto; Se in campo armato]; Incoronazione di Dario (sels) [Non mi lusinga vana speranza]; Atenaide (sels) [Ferma Teodosio]; Griselda (sels) [Ombre vane, ingiusti orrori; Agitata da due venti]; Tito Manlio (sels) [Non ti lusinghi, la credeltade] ("Opera Arias & Sinfonias") HYP ▲ 66745 (18.97)
Beatus vir (Psalm 112) in C for 2 Choruses, RV.597
M. Burgess (sop), J. Chamonin (sop), C. Watkinson (cta), J. Malgoire (cnd), La Grande Écurie et la Chambre du Roy, Raphaël Passaquet Vocal Ensemble *(rec 1976)* † Gloria; J. S. Bach:Magnificat, BWV 243 SNYC (Essential Classics) ▲ 48280 [ADD] (7.97) ▮ 48280 [ADD] (3.98)
C. Calvi (cta), S. M. von Hase (cta), V. Manno (ten), Bonitatibus (sgr), Trogu (sgr) † Gloria (& Intro), RV.588; Sacred Choral Music AG ▲ 1 [DDD] (18.97)
S. Kralev (cnd) † Gloria GEGA ▲ 199 (16.97)
J. Whitaker (sop), C. Lane (sop), R. Glenton (vc), C. Swain (ob), C. Stokes (org), N. Ward (cnd), Northern CO, Oxford Schola Cantorum *(rec Hale Cheshire, Mar 14, 1994)* † Gloria NXIN ▲ 550767 [DDD] (5.97)
artists unknown ("Vivaldi Glorias") † Dixit Dominus, RV.594; Gloria; Gloria (& Intro), RV.588; Magnificat, RV.611 PLON (Double Decker) 2-▲ 43455 (17.97)
Cantatas
P. M. Bedi (sop), Chicago Baroque Ensemble—All'ombra di sospetto, RV.678; Lungi dal vago volto, RV.680 *(rec Evanston, IL, May-Aug 1995)* ("A Vivaldi Concert") † Motets; Sons Vc CED ▲ 25 [DDD] (16.97)
R. Bertini (sop), F. M. Sardelli (cnd) —Amor hai vinto, RV.683; Elvira, Elvira, anima mia, RV.654; Aure, voi più non siete, RV.652; Nel partir da te mio caro, RV.661; T'intendo si mio cor, RV.668; Seben vivono senz'alma, RV.664 ("The Cantatas, Part 1") TACT ▲ 672207 (16.97)
E. C. Fedi (sop), F. M. Sardelli (cnd) *(All'ombra di sospetto, RV.678; Che giova il sospirar, RV.679; Perché son molli, RV.681; Vengo a voi, luci adorate, RV.682)*, F. M. Sardelli (cnd) *(Lungi dal vago volto, RV.680)* ("Flute Concerti, Part 2") † Con Fl; Fl Music; Son Fl, RV.48 TACT ▲ 672204 [DDD] (16.97)
C. Gasdia (sop), C. Ferrarini (cnd), Barocco Veneziano—Amor hai vinto, RV.683; Seben vivono senz'alma, RV.664; Par che tardo, RV.662; All'or che lo squardo, RV.650; Elvira, Elvira, anima mia, RV.654; T'intendo si mio cor, RV.668; Si, si, luci adorate, RV.666; Si levi dal pensier, RV.665; Indarno cerca la tortorella, RV.659 ("Cantatas for Soprano & Continuo, Vols. 3-4") MONM 2-▲ 90021 (34.97)
R. Invernizzi (sop), Conserto Vago—Sorge vermiglia in ciel, RV.667; All'or che lo squardo, RV.650; Il povero mio cor, RV.653; La farfalletta s'aggira, RV.660; Amor hai vinto, RV.683; Fonti del pianto, RV.656 ("Cantatas, Vol. 1") AG ▲ 101 (18.97)
R. Invernizzi (sop), Conserto Vago—Usignoletto bello, RV.796; Si, si, luci adorate, RV.666; T'intendo si mio cor, RV.668; Scherza di fronda, RV.663; Tra l'erbe, i zeffiri, RV.669; All'ombra di sospetto, RV.678 ("Canatas, Vol. 2") AG ▲ 147 (18.97)
M. Lazzara (ct), A. Plotino (cnd), Genoa CO—Cessate omai cessate, RV.684; Qual in pioggio dorata, RV.686; O mie porpore più belle, RV.685; Amor hai vinto, RV.683 *(rec Mar 1998)* ("Cantatas for Alto") DYNC ▲ 222 [DDD] (17.97)
A. Ruffini (sop), C. Calvi (cta), R. Gini (cnd) —Fonti del pianto, RV.656; Sorge vermiglia in ciel, RV.667; Lungi dal vago volto, RV.680; Perfidissimo cor!, RV.674; Piango, gemo, sospiro, RV.675 ("Cantatas, Vol. 1") NUO (Ancient Music) ▲ 6859 [DDD] (16.97)
R. Wong (ct), E. Blumenstock (vn), P. Hale (vc), L. Miller (fl), M. Dollendorf (bn)—Sorge vermiglia in ciel, RV.667; All'ombra di sospetto, RV.678; Amor hai vinto, RV.683; La farfalletta s'aggira, RV.660; Lungi dal vago volto, RV.680 *(rec Univ of CA Santa Cruz)* ("Antonio Vivaldi: Soprano Cantatas") HEL ▲ 1032 (10.97)
Choral Music
F. Lott (sop), M. Marshall (sop), A. Murray (mez), J. Kowalski (alt), A. Rolfe Johnson (ten), R. Holl (bass), V. Negri (cnd), English CO, V. Negri (cnd), (Royal) Concertgebouw Orch, John Alldis Choir—Gloria, RV.589; Stabat Mater, RV.621; Nulla in mundo pax, RV.630; Beatus vir, RV.597; Jubilate O Amaeni, RV.639; Gloria (& Intro), RV.588; Magnificat, RV.611 ("The Great Choral Masterpieces") PPHI (Duo) 2-▲ 462170 (17.97)

VIVALDI, ANTONIO (cont.)

Concertos for Bassoon & Orchestra

K. Dosaka (bn), Bach-Mozart Ensemble Tokyo *(rec June 22-26, 1992)* † Con Fl Ob, RV.107 DNN ▲ 75198 [DDD] (16.97)

M. Turkovič (bn), Italian Solisti—Con Bn, RV.478; Con Bn, RV.480; Con Bn, RV.484 ("5 Concerti for Bassoon, Strings & Continuo") † Con Bn DNN ▲ 77528 [DDD]

Concerto in e for Bassoon, Strings & Continuo, RV.484

T. Pinnock (cnd), English CO † Con Mands, RV.532; Con Strs, RV.151; Con Vn Ob, RV.548; Con Vns Rcrs Mans, RV.558; Cons Fl, Op. 10/1-6; Cons Vn(s) Strs, Op. 3/1-12 PARC (3D Baroque) ▲ 31710 [DDD] (9.97)

Concerto in a for Bassoon, Strings & Continuo, RV.498

M. Turkovič (bn), Italian Solisti ("5 Concerti for Bassoon, Strings & Continuo") † Con Bn; Cons Bn DNN ▲ 77528 [DDD]

Concerto in B♭ for Bassoon, Strings & Continuo, RV.501, "La Notte II"

M. Turkovič (bn), Italian Solisti ("5 Concerti for Bassoon, Strings & Continuo") † Con Bn; Cons Bn DNN ▲ 77528 [DDD]

Concerto in d for Cello & Orchestra

J. Alexander (vc), Slovak CO ("Classic Hits: Vivaldi") † Con Fl Gtr; Con Gtr; Con 2 Vns, RV.514; Cons Fl, Op. 10/1-6; Cons Vn(s) Strs, Op. 3/1-12 PUBM (Majestic) ▲ 1041 [DDD] (4.97)

Concerto in c for Cello & Orchestra, RV.401

R. Wallfisch (vc), N. Kraemer (cnd), London Sinfonietta *(rec East Finchley & Conway Hall London, England, Apr-May & Sept 1994)* ("Cello Concerti, Vol. 2") † Con Vc; Con Vcs, RV.531; Cons Cello NXIN (Vivaldi Collection) ▲ 550908 [DDD] (5.97)

C. Warren-Green (cnd), London CO *(rec 1988-89)* † Con Tpts, RV.537; Con 3 Vns, RV.551; Cons Diverse Instrs; Cons Vn Strs, Op. 8/1-4; Cons Vn(s) Strs, Op. 3/1-12 VCL 2-▲ 61466 [DDD] (11.97)

Concertos for Cello & Orchestra

O. Harnoy (vc), P. Robinson (cnd), Toronto CO—Con Vc, RV.404; Con Vc, RV.407; Con Vc, RV.411; Con Vc, RV.417; Con Vc, RV.420 ("Vivaldi Concertos, Vol. 3") † Con Vn Vc, RV.544 RCAV (Red Seal) ▲ 61578 (16.97)

R. Wallfisch (vc), N. Kraemer (cnd), London Sinfonietta—Con Vc, RV.408 *(rec East Finchley & Conway Hall London, England, Apr-May & Sept 1994)* ("Cello Concerti, Vol. 2") † Con Vc; Con Vcs, RV.531 NXIN (Vivaldi Collection) ▲ 550908 [DDD] (5.97)

R. Wallfisch (vc), N. Kraemer (cnd), London Sinfonietta—Con Vc, RV.423; Con Vc, RV.402; Con Vc, RV.418; Con Vc, RV.403; Con Vc, RV.407; Con Vc, RV.409 *(rec East Finchley & Conway Hall London, Apr-May & Sept 1994)* ("Cello Concerti, Vol. 3") † Con Vc NXIN (Vivaldi Collection) ▲ 550909 [DDD] (5.97)

R. Wallfisch (vc), N. Kraemer (cnd), London Sinfonietta—Con Vc, RV.416; Con Vc, RV.411; Con Vc, RV.405; Con Vc, RV.420; Con Vc, RV.414; Con Vc, RV.417; Con Vc, RV.421 *(rec East Finchley & Conway Hall London, Apr-May & Sept 1994)* ("Cello Concerti, Vol. 4") NXIN (Vivaldi Collection) ▲ 550910 [DDD] (5.97)

P. Wispelwey (vc), Florilegium—Con Vn, RV.295 [Larghetto]; Con Vn, RV.190 [Largo]; Con Strs, RV.109 [Adagio]; Con Vc, RV.404 [Allegro Vivace]; Con Vn, RV.226 [Largo]; Con Vn, RV.341 [Largo] *(rec Highgate London, Aug 1996)* ("Vivaldi Concerti") † Con Vc; Cons Vn, Op. 4/1-12 CCL ▲ 10097 [DDD] (18.97)

Concerto in C for Cello, Strings & Continuo, RV.400

R. Wallfisch (vc), N. Kraemer (cnd), London Sinfonietta *(rec East Finchley & Conway Hall London, England, Apr-May & Sept 1994)* ("Cello Concerti, Vol. 2") † Con Vc; Con Vcs, RV.531; Cons Cello NXIN (Vivaldi Collection) ▲ 550908 [DDD] (5.97)

Concerto in d for Cello, Strings & Continuo, RV.407

D. Amodio (vc), Interpreti Veneziani † Con Vc; G. Rossini:Une Larme; Tartini:Music of Tartini RIVO ▲ 9814 (16.97)

P. Wispelwey (vc), Florilegium *(rec Highgate London, England, Aug 1996)* ("Vivaldi Concerti") † Con Vc; Cons Cello; Cons Vn, Op. 4/1-12 CCL ▲ 10097 [DDD] (18.97)

Concerto in e for Cello, Strings & Continuo, RV.409

N. Black (ob), J. Brown (ob), T. King (cl), J. L. Garcia (cnd) ("Four Seasons & Other Great Concertos") † Con Fl; Con Flautino, RV.443; Con Mand, RV.425; Con Ob; Con Strs, RV.151; Con Tpts, RV.537; Cons Diverse Instrs; Cons Vn Strs, Op. 8/1-4; Cons Vn(s) Strs, Op. 3/1-12 SNYC (Essential Classics Take 2) 2-▲ 63284 (14.97)

Concerto in F for Cello, Strings & Continuo, RV.410

P. Wispelwey (vc), Florilegium *(rec Highgate London, England, Aug 1996)* ("Vivaldi Concerti") † Con Vc; Cons Cello; Cons Vn, Op. 4/1-12 CCL ▲ 10097 [DDD] (18.97)

Concerto in F for Cello, Strings & Continuo, RV.411

P. Wispelwey (vc), Florilegium *(rec Highgate London, England, Aug 1996)* ("Vivaldi Concerti") † Con Vc; Cons Cello; Cons Vn, Op. 4/1-12 CCL ▲ 10097 [DDD] (18.97)

Concerto in G for Cello, Strings & Continuo, RV.413

D. Amodio (vc), Interpreti Veneziani † Con Vc; G. Rossini:Une Larme; Tartini:Music of Tartini RIVO ▲ 9814 (16.97)

R. Wallfisch (vc), N. Kraemer (cnd), London Sinfonietta *(rec East Finchley & Conway Hall London, England, Apr-May & Sept 1994)* ("Cello Concerti, Vol. 2") † Con Vc; Con Vcs, RV.531; Cons Cello NXIN (Vivaldi Collection) ▲ 550908 [DDD] (5.97)

P. Wispelwey (vc), Florilegium *(rec Highgate London, England, Aug 1996)* ("Vivaldi Concerti") † Con Vc; Cons Cello; Cons Vn, Op. 4/1-12 CCL ▲ 10097 [DDD] (18.97)

Concerto in G for Cello, Strings & Continuo, RV.415

P. Wispelwey (vc), Florilegium *(rec Highgate London, England, Aug 1996)* ("Vivaldi Concerti") † Con Vc; Cons Cello; Cons Vn, Op. 4/1-12 CCL ▲ 10097 [DDD] (18.97)

Concerto in a for Cello, Strings & Continuo, RV.418

D. Amodio (vc), Interpreti Veneziani † Con Vc; G. Rossini:Une Larme; Tartini:Music of Tartini RIVO ▲ 9814 (16.97)

Concerto in a for Cello, Strings & Continuo, RV.421

P. Wispelwey (vc), Florilegium *(rec Highgate London, England, Aug 1996)* ("Vivaldi Concerti") † Con Vc; Cons Cello; Cons Vn, Op. 4/1-12 CCL ▲ 10097 [DDD] (18.97)

Concerto in a for Cello, Strings & Continuo, RV.422

R. Wallfisch (vc), N. Kraemer (cnd), London Sinfonietta *(rec East Finchley & Conway Hall London, England, Apr-May & Sept 1994)* ("Cello Concerti, Vol. 2") † Con Vc; Con Vcs, RV.531; Cons Cello NXIN (Vivaldi Collection) ▲ 550908 [DDD] (5.97)

P. Wispelwey (vc), Florilegium *(rec Highgate London, England, Aug 1996)* ("Vivaldi Concerti") † Con Vc; Cons Cello; Cons Vn, Op. 4/1-12 CCL ▲ 10097 [DDD] (18.97)

Concerto in b for Cello, Strings & Continuo, RV.424

R. Wallfisch (vc), N. Kraemer (cnd), London Sinfonietta *(rec East Finchley & Conway Hall London, England, Apr-May & Sept 1994)* ("Cello Concerti, Vol. 3") † Cons Cello NXIN (Vivaldi Collection) ▲ 550909 [DDD] (5.97)

P. Wispelwey (vc), Florilegium *(rec Highgate London, England, Aug 1996)* ("Vivaldi Concerti") † Con Vc; Cons Cello; Cons Vn, Op. 4/1-12 CCL ▲ 10097 [DDD] (18.97)

Concerto in g for 2 Cellos & Strings, RV.531

A. Aubut (vc), Y. Turovsky (vc), Y. Turovsky (cnd), Montreal Musici—Largo ("Tranquillity") † Con Rcr, RV.444; Con Strs, RV.158; Cons Fl, Op. 10/1-6; Arcus:Vars on Simple Gifts; J. Christian Bach:Con in c; Boccherini:Con Vc, G.482; D. Shostakovich:Con 2 Pno, Op. 102; I. Stravinsky:Con Str Orch; Wassenaer:Concerti Armonici CHN ▲ 8573 [DDD] (16.97)

J. Coe (vc), D. Watkin (vc), S. Standage (cnd), Collegium Musicum 90 † Con Vn Org Ob, RV.554 CHN (Chaconne) ▲ 528 [DDD] (16.97)

C. Coin (vc), Il Giardino Armonico ("Double & Triple Concertos") † Con Vn Vc, RV.544; Con Vn Vcs, RV.561; Con 3 Vns, RV.551; Cons Diverse Instrs TELC (Das alte Werk) ▲ 94552 (16.97)

A. Debrus (vc), G. Boucher (cnd), Arpeggio CO *(rec Studio Métamorphoses d'orphée)* ("Cello Concertos") PAVA ▲ 7352 [DDD] (10.97)

M. Kaňka (vc), A. Bárta (cnd), Prague CO SUR ▲ 112121 [DDD]

M. Naddeo (vc), A. Fantinuoli (vc), F. Biondi (cnd), Europa Galante *(rec Apr 1993)* OPUS ▲ 3086 [DDD] (18.97)

Parisot (vc), J. Starker (vc), E. D. Carvalho (cnd), Paraiba SO † B. Bartók:Con Va; S. Prokofiev:Con 2 Vn, Op. 63; P. Tchaikovsky:Vars on a Rococo Theme, Op. 33 DLS ▲ 1018 [DDD] (10.97)

M. Peters (vc), P. Sigl (vc), M. Haselböck (cnd), Vienna Academy [period instrs] ("Duo Concerti") † Con Fls, RV.533; Con Ob Bn, RV.545; Con Orchs, RV.583; Con Tpts, RV.537; Con Vn Org, RV.542 NOVA ▲ 150074 [DDD] (16.97)

S. Raldugin (vc), Z. Zaliyailo (vc), L. Korkhin (cnd), Renaissance CO ("Great Instrumental Concertos") † Con Mand, RV.425; Con Mands, RV.532 SNYC ▲ 57244 [DDD] (4.97)

P. Tortelier (vc), M. Tortelier (vc), P. Ledger (hpd), P. Ledger (cnd), London Mozart Players ("Best-Loved Vivaldi") † Cons Vn(s) Strs, Op. 3/1-12; Music of Vivaldi EMCD (Seraphim) 4-▲ 69545 [DDD] (14.97)

Y. Turovsky (vc), A. Aubut (vc), Y. Turovsky (cnd), Montreal Musici † Boccherini:Con Vc, G.483 CHN ▲ 8408 [DDD] (16.97)

R. Wallfisch (vc), N. Kraemer (cnd), London Sinfonietta *(rec East Finchley & Conway Hall London, England, Apr-May & Sept 1994)* ("Cello Concerti, Vol. 2") † Con Vc; Cons Cello NXIN (Vivaldi Collection) ▲ 550908 [DDD] (5.97)

Concerto in C for 2 Clarinets, 2 Oboes, Strings & Continuo, RV.559

S. Bliznetzov (ob), S. Blashenov (bn), L. Korkhin (cnd) ("Vivaldi: A Flute Festival") † Con Rcr, RV.108; Con Rcr, RV.441; Cons Fl, Op. 10/1-6 SNYC ▲ 66724 [DDD] (4.97)

VIVALDI, ANTONIO (cont.)

Concertos for Diverse Instruments

L. Auriacombe (cnd), Toulouse CO—(5) for 4 Vns in b; (5) for 4 Vns in b *(rec 1967 & 1969)* EMIC 2-▲ 69143 [ADD] (13.97)

C. Coin (vc), Il Giardino Armonico—Con Vns Vcs, RV.564; Con Vn, RV.552 ("Double & Triple Concertos") † Con Vcs, RV.531; Con Vn Vc, RV.544; Con Vn Vcs, RV.561; Con 3 Vns, RV.551 TELC (Das alte Werk) ▲ 94552 (16.97)

Collegium Pro Musica—Con Vn Ob, RV.92; Con Fl, Vns, Bn & Vc, RV.106; Con Fl Vn Bn, RV.91 *(rec Montevarchi Italy, May 15-17, 1995)* ("Concerti a tre e a quattro") † Con Fl Vn Bn, RV.100; Con Rcr, Ob & Bn, RV.103; Trio Son Fl & Vn, RV.84 DYNC ▲ 156 [DDD] (17.97)

M. Frasca-Colombier (vn), L. Paugam (vn), S. Ochi (mand), T. Ochi (mand), J. Labylle (pic), P. Kuentz (cnd), Paul Kuentz Orch—Con Bn, RV.501; Con Va, RV.394; Con Bn, RV.497 ("6 Rare Concertos") † Con Flautino, RV.443; Con Mands, RV.532; Con Vn PVY ▲ 730052 [DDD] (12.97)

J. L. Garcia (cnd), English CO *(Con Strs, RV.129; Con Vn, RV.234)*, E. Zukerman (fl), P. Zukerman (cnd), English CO *(Cons Fl, Op. 10/1-6 [No. 3 in D, "Il Gardellino"])*, H. Haenchen (cnd), C.P.E. Bach CO, N. Jenkins (cnd), Clarion Music Society *(Cons Vn(s) Strs, Op. 3/1-12 [No. 9 in D])*, N. Jenkins (cnd), Clarion Music Society *(Con Vn, RV.353)* ("Four Seasons & Other Great Concertos") † Con Fl; Con Flautino, RV.443; Con Mand, RV.425; Con Ob; Con Strs, RV.151; Con Tpts, RV.537; Con Vc; Cons Vn Strs, Op. 8/1-4; Cons Vn(s) Strs, Op. 3/1-12 SNYC (Essential Classics Take 2) 2-▲ 63284 (14.97)

L. Güttler (cnd) —Con Vn Ob Rcrs, RV.576 † Con Ob; Con Va Lt, RV.540; Con Vn; Con Vns Rcrs Mans, RV.558; Sinf BER ▲ 1082 [DDD] (16.97)

J. Holloway (vn), S. Comberti (vc), M. Verbruggen (rcr), P. Goodwin (ob), D. Godburn (bn), J. Toll (hpd)—Trio Son Fl & Vn, RV.84; Con Rcr, RV.105 † Con Fl Ob, RV.99; Con Rcr Ob, RV.95; Con Rcr, Ob & Bn, RV.103; Con Rcr, Ob & Vn, RV.94; Trio Son Rcr Bn, RV.86 HAM ▲ 907046 (18.97)

V. Hudeček (vn), L. Brabec (gtr), J. Stivín (rcr), G. Delogu (cnd), Janáček CO, G. Delogu (cnd), Prague CO—Con Va Lt, RV.540 ("Brabec, Stivín & Hudeček Play Vivaldi") † Con Rcr, RV.108; Con Vn Org, RV.542; Con Vns Rcrs Mans, RV.558; Cons Vn(s) Strs, Op. 3/1-12 SUR ▲ 3023 [DDD] (16.97)

R. King (cnd), King's Consort—Con Vn Trbs Obs, RV.574; Con Va Hns Obs, RV.97; Con in D Tpts, RV.781; Con Vns Ob Rcrs, RV.555; Con Vns Rcrs Obs, RV.566 ("Concerti for Diverse Instruments") † Con Vn Ob Vas, RV.579; Con Vn Obs Hns, RV.562 HYP ▲ 67073 [DDD] (18.97)

N. McGegan (cnd), Philharmonia Baroque Orch—Con Vn Obs Hns, RV.569; Con Vn Obs Hns, RV.568; Con Vn Obs Hns, RV.562 *(rec Oakland, CA, Oct 1996)* ("Vivaldi for Diverse Instruments") † Con Obs, RV.535; Con Vn; Con Vn Obs, RV.577 REF ▲ 77 [DDD] (16.97)

Musica Concertiva—Con Rcr, Ob & Bn, RV.103 ("Vivaldi e Il Suo Tempo") † Con Fl, Vns, Bn & Vc, RV.106; Trio Son Rcr Bn, RV.86; A. Lotti:Son Fl; Trio Fl SUR ▲ 3097 [DDD] (16.97)

T. Pinnock (cnd), English Concert—Con Bn, RV.485; Con Strs, RV.156; Con Vn Obs Rcrs Bn, RV 577; Con Vns Vcs, RV.575 ("7 Concerti for Woodwind & Strings") † Con Flautino, RV.444; Con Ob; Con Strs, RV.166 PARC ▲ 45839 [DDD] (16.97)

D. Rix (ct), D. Davis (fl), D. Dobing (fl), C. Hooker (ob), H. McQueen (ob), R. McDowall (cl), J. Graham (bn), C. Steele-Perkins (tpt), M. Meekes (tpt), S. Stirling (hn), T. Caister (hn), N. Kraemer (hpd), N. Kraemer (cnd), London Sinfonietta—Sinf Strs, RV.122; Con Tpts, RV.537; Con Cls Obs, RV.560; Con Hns, RV.538 *(rec All Saints Church East Finchley, Oct 1994 & Jan 1995)* ("Vivaldi: Wind Concerti") † Con Fls, RV.533; Con Hns, RV.539; Con Ob Bn, RV.545 NXIN (Vivaldi Collection) ▲ 553204 [DDD] (5.97)

J. Veilhan (cl), P. Couvert (cnd), St. Cecilia Academy Orch Rome—Con Vns Ob Rcrs, RV.555; Con Obs Rcrs, RV.556; Con Cls Obs, RV.560; Con Vn Obs, RV.577; Con Vn Ob Vas, RV.579; Con Cls Obs, RV.559 *(rec Paris, France, Jan 1996)* ("Concerti con Molti Istromenti") † Con Vns Rcrs Mans, RV.558 K617 ▲ 7062 [DDD] (18.97)

Venice New Quintet—Con Fl Ob Vn, RV.88 ("Concertos without Orchestra") † Con Fl Ob, RV.107; Con Fl Ob, RV.99; Con Rcr, Ob & Bn, RV.103; Con Rcr, Ob & Vn, RV.101; Con Rcr, Ob & Vn, RV.94 TACT ▲ 672205 [DDD] (16.97)

B. Warchal (cnd), Slovak CO ("Instrumental Concertos, Vol. 1") OPP ▲ 2636 (10.97)

C. Warren-Green (cnd), London CO—Con Ob, RV.447; Con Bn, RV.502 *(rec 1988-89)* † Con Tpts, RV.537; Con Vc; Con 3 Vns, RV.551; Cons Vn Strs, Op. 8/1-4; Cons Vn(s) Strs, Op. 3/1-12 VCL 2-▲ 61466 [DDD] (11.97)

A. Watts (bn), Nouveau Quartet—Trio Son Vn Vc, RV.83, F.XVI 1; Con Fl Vn Bn, RV.96; Con Fl Vn Bn, RV.100; Con Fl Vn(s) Bn, RV.106 ("Chamber Concertos") † Con Fl Vn Bn, RV.91; Trio Son Fl & Vn, RV.84 AMON ▲ 47 [DDD] (16.97)

Concerto in C for Flautino, Strings & Continuo, RV.443

G. von Bahr (fl), J. Wedin (cnd) † Con Flautino, RV.444; Con Flautino, RV.445; J. S. Bach:Partita Fl, BWV 1013; C.P.E. Bach:Son Fl, H.562; J. S. Bach:Suite 2 Fl, BWV 1067 BIS ▲ 21 (17.97)

M. Frasca-Colombier (vn), L. Paugam (vn), S. Ochi (mand), T. Ochi (mand), J. Labylle (pic), P. Kuentz (cnd), Paul Kuentz Orch ("6 Rare Concertos") † Con Mands, RV.532; Con Vn; Cons Diverse Instrs PVY ▲ 730052 [DDD] (12.97)

D. Laurin (rcr) *(rec 1991)* ("Recorder Concertos") † Cons Fl, Op. 10/1-6; Cons Rcr BIS ▲ 635 (17.97)

J. Rampal (fl), C. Scimone (cnd) † Con Fl; Con Flautino, RV.444; Con Fls, RV.533; Con Rcr, RV.108; Con Rcr, RV.441; Cons Fl, Op. 10/1-6 SNYC 2-▲ 45623 [ADD] (14.97)

J. Válek (fl), J. Novotny (fl), J. Stivín (flautino) † Con Flautino, RV.444; Con Flautino, RV.445; Con Fls, RV.533; Con Rcr, RV.108 NXIN ▲ 550385 [DDD] (5.97)

J. Veilhan (pic), J. Malgoire (cnd), La Grande Ecurie et la Chambre du Roy ("Four Seasons & Other Great Concertos") † Con Fl; Con Mand, RV.425; Con Ob; Con Strs, RV.151; Con Tpts, RV.537; Con Vc; Cons Diverse Instrs; Cons Vn Strs, Op. 8/1-4; Cons Vn(s) Strs, Op. 3/1-12 SNYC (Essential Classics Take 2) 2-▲ 63284 (14.97)

Concerto in C for Flautino, Strings & Continuo, RV.444

G. von Bahr (fl), J. Wedin (cnd) † Con Flautino, RV.443; Con Flautino, RV.445; J. S. Bach:Partita Fl, BWV 1013; C.P.E. Bach:Son Fl, H.562; J. S. Bach:Suite 2 Fl, BWV 1067 BIS ▲ 21 (17.97)

T. Pinnock (cnd), English Concert ("7 Concerti for Woodwind & Strings") † Con Ob; Con Strs, RV.166; Cons Diverse Instrs PARC ▲ 45839 [DDD] (16.97)

J. Rampal (fl), C. Scimone (cnd) † Con Fl; Con Flautino, RV.443; Con Fls, RV.533; Con Rcr, RV.108; Con Rcr, RV.441; Cons Fl, Op. 10/1-6 SNYC 2-▲ 45623 [ADD] (14.97)

J. Válek (fl), J. Novotny (fl), J. Stivín (flautino) † Con Flautino, RV.443; Con Flautino, RV.445; Con Fls, RV.533; Con Rcr, RV.108 NXIN ▲ 550385 [DDD] (5.97)

Concerto in a for Flautino, Strings & Continuo, RV.445

G. von Bahr (fl), J. Wedin (cnd) † Con Flautino, RV.443; Con Flautino, RV.444; J. S. Bach:Partita Fl, BWV 1013; C.P.E. Bach:Son Fl, H.562; J. S. Bach:Suite 2 Fl, BWV 1067 BIS ▲ 21 (17.97)

S. Gazzelloni (fl) ("Complete Flute Concertos") † Con Fl; Con Flautino, RV.443; Con Fls, RV.533; Con Rcr, RV.441; Cons Fl, Op. 10/1-6 PPHI (Duo) 2-▲ 54256 (17.97)

J. Válek (fl), J. Novotny (fl), J. Stivín (flautino) † Con Flautino, RV.443; Con Flautino, RV.444; Con Fls, RV.533; Con Rcr, RV.108 NXIN ▲ 550385 [DDD] (5.97)

Concertos (6) for Flute & Orchestra, Op. 10/1-6 (RV.428, 433-35, 437 & 439) (ca 1729-30)

B. Cavallo (vn), R. Muti (cnd), La Scala Orch Soloists—No. 2 in g, "La notte (I)" † Con Fl Ob Bn, RV.570; Cons Vn Strs, Op. 8/1-4 CSER ▲ 73298 [DDD] (6.97)

J. Galway (fl) RCAV (Gold Seal) ▲ 61351 (11.97)

S. Gazzelloni (fl) ("Complete Flute Concertos") † Con Fl; Con Flautino, RV.445; Con Fls, RV.533; Con Rcr, RV.108; Con Rcr, RV.441 PPHI (Duo) 2-▲ 54256 (17.97)

C. Hogwood (cnd), Academy of Ancient Music Orch † Cons Vn(s) Strs, Op. 3/1-12 PLON (Double Decker) 2-▲ 458078 (17.97)

T. Hutchins (fl), Y. Turovsky (cnd), Montreal Musici—No. 1 in F, "La Tempesta di mare" [Largo only] ("Tranquillity") † Con Rcr, RV.444; Con Strs, RV.158; Con Vcs, RV.531; Arcus:Vars on Simple Gifts; J. Christian Bach:Con in c; Boccherini:Con Vc, G.482; D. Shostakovich:Con 2 Pno, Op. 102; I. Stravinsky:Con Str Orch; Wassenaer:Concerti Armonici CHN ▲ 8573 [DDD] (16.97)

I Filarmonici *(rec Nov 1994)* ("Le Dodici opera a stampa: Opera X, Sei concerti per flauto ed archi") TACT ▲ 672236 [DDD] (16.97)

Il Giardino Armonico—No. 4 in G ("Vol. 1") † Con Fl Bn, RV.104; Con Fl Ob Vn, RV.98; Con Fl Ob, RV.90; Con Rcr, Ob & Vn, RV.101; Con Rcr, RV.442 TELC ▲ 73267 [DDD] (16.97)

H. von Karajan (cnd), Berlin PO—No. 2 in g, "La notte (I)" † Albinoni:Adagio; J. S. Bach:Suite 3 Orch, BWV 1068; C. W. Gluck:Orfeo ed Euridice (dance); W. A. Mozart:Serenade 6 Orch, K.239; J. Pachelbel:Canon & Gigue DEUT ▲ 13309 [DDD] (16.97)

I. Kipnis (hpd), I. Kipnis (cnd) —No. 3 in D, "Il Gardellino" [period instrs] † Con Hpd, RV.780; Cons Vn Strs, Op. 8/1-4 CHSK ▲ 78 [DDD] (16.97)

A. Kiskatchi (fl), A. Titov (cnd), St. Petersburg New Classical Orch, L. Korchin (cnd), Collegium dell'Arte—No. 2 in g, "La notte (I)"; No. 5 in F ("Vivaldi: A Flute Festival") † Con Cls Obs, RV.559; Con Rcr, RV.108; Con Rcr, RV.441 SNYC ▲ 66724 [DDD] (4.97)

D. Laurin (rcr)—No. 5 in F; No. 2 in g, "La notte (I)" *(rec 1991)* ("Recorder Concertos") † Con Flautino, RV.443; Cons Rcr BIS ▲ 635 (17.97)

VIVALDI, ANTONIO (cont.)

Concertos (6) for Flute & Orchestra, Op. 10/1-6 (RV.428, 433-35, 437 & 439) (ca 1729-30) (cont.)

I. Levin (vn), P. Zukerman (vn), S. Accardo (vn), F. Agostini (vn), H. Szeryng (vn), M. Paris (vl), A. Romero (gtr), C. Romero (gtr), C. Romero (gtr), A. Nicolet (fl), H. Holliger (ob)—No. 3 in D, "Il Gardellino"; No. 2 in g, "La notte (I)" [Cantabile only] ("Vivaldi for Valentines: Romantic Interludes for the One You Love") † Con Vn; Music of Vivaldi PPHI ▲ 54051 (9.97) ▮ 54051 (5.98)

A. Nicolet (fl), C. Jaccottet (hpd), J. Faerber (cnd), Württemberg CO INTC ▲ 820501 (9.97)

T. Pinnock (cnd), English CO—No. 2 in g, "La notte (I)" † Con Bn; Con Mands, RV.532; Con Strs, RV.151; Con Vn Ob, RV.548; Con Vns Rcrs Mans, RV.558; Cons Vn(s) Strs, Op. 3/1-12 PARC (3D Baroque) ▲ 31710 [DDD] (9.97)

J. Rampal (fl), Louis de Froment Chamber Ensemble TUXE ▲ 1063 [ADD] (10.97)

J. Rampal (fl), C. Scimone (cnd) SNYC ▲ 39062 [DDD] (16.97)

J. Rampal (fl), C. Scimone (cnd) † Con Fl; Con Flautino, RV.443; Con Flautino, RV.444; Con Fls, RV.533; Con Rcr, RV.108; Con Rcr, RV.441 SNYC 2-▲ 45623 [ADD] (14.97)

J. See (fl), N. McGegan (cnd), Philharmonia Baroque Orch ("Flute Concertos") † Con Fls, RV.533 HAM ▲ 7905193 [DDD] (12.97)

J. Stivín (rcr), Slovak CO—No. 4 in G ("Classic Hits: Vivaldi") † Con Fl Gtr; Con Gtr; Con Vc; Con 2 Vns, RV.514; Cons Vn(s) Strs, Op. 3/1-12 PUBM (Majestic) ▲ 1041 [DDD] (4.97)

P. Zukerman (fl), P. Zukerman (cnd), English CO—No. 3 in D, "Il Gardellino" [Allegro only] ("Sunday Brunch. Vol 2") † Con Mand, RV.425; Con Mands, RV.532; Cons Vn Strs, Op. 8/1-4; J. S. Bach:Cant 147; Cant 156; Cant 78; Con 5 Hpd, BWV 1056; Suite 2 Fl, BWV 1067; G. F. Handel:Minuet Vc & Pno; Solomon (arrival of the queen of Sheba); Water Music (sels); A. Marcello:Con Ob Strs in d, Op. 1; Mouret:Suite de symphonies; H. Purcell:Abdelazer (sels); Gordian Knot Unty'd (sels); V. Tommasini:Donne di buon umore (sels) SNYC (Dinner Classics) ▲ 46359 [AAD] (9.97)

Concerto in B for Flute

S. Lautenbacher (vn), J. Faerber (cnd), Württemberg CO ("The Stories of Vivaldi & Corelli in Words & Music") † Con Vn Strs Bc, Op. 9/1-12; Cons Vn Strs, Op. 8/1-4; Cons Vn(s) Strs, Op. 3/1-12; Cons Vn, Op. 4/1-12; Life & Music of Vivaldi; A. Corelli:Life & Music of Corelli MMD ▲ 8510 [ADD] (3.97) ▮ 8510 [ADD] (2.98)

Concertos for Flute & Orchestra (miscellaneous)

J. Rampal (fl)—Con Fl, RV.430 *(rec May 10-13, 1992)* † Con Fl; Con Vn Org, RV.541; Cons Vn Strs, Op. 8/1-4 SNYC ▲ 53105 [DDD] (16.97) COL △ 53105 [DDD]

Concerto in g for Flute (or Violin), Bassoon & Strings, RV.104, "La notte (I)"

J. Baker (fl), K. Hoffmann (bn), A. Janigro (cnd) *(rec Baumgarten Hall Vienna, May 5-7, 1962)* ("Julius Baker: The Virtuoso Flute") † W. A. Mozart:Con Fl & Hp, K.299; Telemann:Cons & Suites Fl VC ▲ 42 [AAD] (13.97)

J. Garcia (vn) † Con Fl Ob Bn, RV.570; Cons Vn Strs, Op. 8/1-4 ASVQ ▲ 6148 [DDD]

Il Giardino Armonico ("Vol. 1") † Con Fl Ob Vn, RV.98; Con Fl Ob, RV.90; Con Rcr, Ob & Vn, RV.101; Con Rcr, RV.442; Cons Fl, Op. 10/1-6 TELC ▲ 73267 [DDD] (16.97)

M. Verbruggen (rcr), D. Godburn (bn), N. McGegan (cnd), Philharmonia Baroque Orch † Con Rcr, RV.441; Cons Rcr HAM ▲ 907040 (18.97)

Concerto for Flute & Guitar

J. Zsapka (gtr), D. Zsopkova (fl) ("Classic Hits: Vivaldi") † Con Gtr; Con Vc; Con 2 Vns, RV.514; Cons Fl, Op. 10/1-6; Cons Vn(s) Strs, Op. 3/1-12 PUBM (Majestic) ▲ 1041 [DDD] (4.97)

Concerto in F for Flute, Oboe, Bassoon, Strings & Continuo, RV.570, "La tempesta di mare"

B. Cavallo (vn), A. Negroni (ob), V. Zucchiati (bn), R. Muti (cnd), La Scala Orch Soloists † Cons Fl, Op. 10/1-6; Cons Vn Strs, Op. 8/1-4 CSER ▲ 73298 [DDD] (6.97)

J. Garcia (vn) † Con Fl Bn, RV.104; Cons Vn Strs, Op. 8/1-4 ASVQ ▲ 6148 [DDD]

Concerto in D for Flute (or Violin), Oboe (or Violin), Bassoon (or Cello) & Continuo, RV.90, "Il Gardellino"

Il Giardino Armonico ("Vol. 1") † Con Fl Bn, RV.104; Con Fl Ob Vn, RV.98; Con Rcr, Ob & Vn, RV.101; Con Rcr, RV.442; Cons Fl, Op. 10/1-6 TELC ▲ 73267 [DDD] (16.97)

Concerto in C for Flute, Oboe, Violin, Bassoon & Continuo, RV.88

Il Giardino Armonico ("Vol. 2") † Con Fl Vn Bn, RV.100; Con Rcr Ob, RV.95; Con Rcr, Ob & Bn, RV.103; Con Rcr, Ob & Vns, RV.87; Sons Vns Vl, Op. 1/1-12 TELC ▲ 73268 [DDD] (16.97)

Concerto in F for Flute, Oboe, Violin, Bassoon & Continuo, RV.99

J. Holloway (vn), S. Comberti (vc), M. Verbruggen (rcr), P. Goodwin (ob), D. Godburn (bn), J. Toll (hpd) † Con Rcr Ob, RV.95; Con Rcr, Ob & Bn, RV.103; Con Rcr, Ob & Vn, RV.94; Cons Diverse Instrs; Trio Son Rcr Bn, RV.86 HAM ▲ 907046 (18.97)

Venice New Quintet ("Concertos without Orchestra") † Con Fl Ob, RV.107; Con Rcr, Ob & Bn, RV.103; Con Rcr, Ob & Vn, RV.101; Con Rcr, Ob & Vn, RV.94; Cons Diverse Instrs TACT ▲ 672205 [DDD] (16.97)

Concerto in g for Flute, Oboe, Violin, Bassoon & Continuo, RV.107

Musical Offering † Con Rcr Ob, RV.95; Trio Son Vn Vc, RV.83 NON ▲ 79067 (9.97)

Venice New Quintet ("Concertos without Orchestra") † Con Fl Ob, RV.99; Con Rcr, Ob & Bn, RV.103; Con Rcr, Ob & Vn, RV.101; Con Rcr, Ob & Vn, RV.94; Cons Diverse Instrs TACT ▲ 672205 [DDD] (16.97)

N. Wakamatsu (vn), M. Arita (fl), M. Homma (ob), K. Dosaka (bn), Bach-Mozart Ensemble Tokyo *(rec June 22-26, 1992)* † Cons Bn DNN ▲ 75198 [DDD] (16.97)

Concerto in F for Flute, Oboe, Violin (or Bassoon) & Continuo, RV.98, "La tempesta di mare (I)"

Il Giardino Armonico ("Vol. 1") † Con Fl Bn, RV.104; Con Fl Ob, RV.90; Con Rcr, Ob & Vn, RV.101; Con Rcr, RV.442; Cons Fl, Op. 10/1-6 TELC ▲ 73267 [DDD] (16.97)

Concerto in D for Flute, Strings & Continuo

J. Rampal (fl) *(rec May 10-13, 1992)* † Con Vn Org, RV.541; Cons Fl (misc); Cons Vn Strs, Op. 8/1-4 SNYC ▲ 53105 [DDD] (16.97) COL △ 53105 [DDD]

F. M. Sardelli (cnd) ("Flute Concerti, Part 2") † Cants; Fl Music; Son Fl, RV.48 TACT ▲ 672204 [DDD] (16.97)

Concerto in D for Flute, Strings & Continuo, RV.427

S. Gazzelloni (fl) ("Complete Flute Concertos") † Con Fl; Con Flautino, RV.445; Con Fls, RV.533; Con Rcr, RV.108; Con Rcr, RV.441; Cons Fl, Op. 10/1-6 PPHI (Duo) 2-▲ 54256 (17.97)

Modo Antiquo *(rec Oct 1993)* ("Concerti per Flauto traversiere ed archi") † Con Fl; Con Fls, RV.533 TACT ▲ 672202 [DDD] (16.97)

J. Rampal (fl), C. Scimone (cnd) † Con Fl; Con Flautino, RV.443; Con Flautino, RV.444; Con Fls, RV.533; Con Rcr, RV.108; Con Rcr, RV.441; Cons Fl, Op. 10/1-6 SNYC 2-▲ 45623 [ADD] (14.97)

Concerto in D for Flute, Strings & Continuo, RV.429

S. Gazzelloni (fl) ("Complete Flute Concertos") † Con Fl; Con Flautino, RV.445; Con Fls, RV.533; Con Rcr, RV.108; Con Rcr, RV.441; Cons Fl, Op. 10/1-6 PPHI (Duo) 2-▲ 54256 (17.97)

Modo Antiquo *(rec Oct 1993)* ("Concerti per Flauto traversiere ed archi") † Con Fl; Con Fls, RV.533 TACT ▲ 672202 [DDD] (16.97)

J. Rampal (fl), C. Scimone (cnd) † Con Fl; Con Flautino, RV.443; Con Flautino, RV.444; Con Fls, RV.533; Con Rcr, RV.108; Con Rcr, RV.441; Cons Fl, Op. 10/1-6 SNYC 2-▲ 45623 [ADD] (14.97)

Concerto in e for Flute, Strings & Continuo, RV.431

J. Rampal (fl), C. Scimone (cnd) † Con Fl; Con Flautino, RV.443; Con Flautino, RV.444; Con Fls, RV.533; Con Rcr, RV.108; Con Rcr, RV.441; Cons Fl, Op. 10/1-6 SNYC 2-▲ 45623 [ADD] (14.97)

Concerto in e for Flute, Strings & Continuo, RV.432

J. Rampal (fl), C. Scimone (cnd) † Con Fl; Con Flautino, RV.443; Con Flautino, RV.444; Con Fls, RV.533; Con Rcr, RV.108; Con Rcr, RV.441; Cons Fl, Op. 10/1-6 SNYC 2-▲ 45623 [ADD] (14.97)

Concerto in G for Flute, Strings & Continuo, RV.436

S. Gazzelloni (fl) ("Complete Flute Concertos") † Con Fl; Con Flautino, RV.445; Con Fls, RV.533; Con Rcr, RV.108; Con Rcr, RV.441; Cons Fl, Op. 10/1-6 PPHI (Duo) 2-▲ 54256 (17.97)

Modo Antiquo *(rec Oct 1993)* ("Concerti per Flauto traversiere ed archi") † Con Fl; Con Fls, RV.533 TACT ▲ 672202 [DDD] (16.97)

J. Rampal (fl), C. Scimone (cnd) † Con Fl; Con Flautino, RV.443; Con Flautino, RV.444; Con Fls, RV.533; Con Rcr, RV.108; Con Rcr, RV.441; Cons Fl, Op. 10/1-6 SNYC 2-▲ 45623 [ADD] (14.97)

Concerto in G for Flute, Strings & Continuo, RV.438

J. L. Garcia (cnd), English CO ("Four Seasons & Other Great Concertos") † Con Flautino, RV.443; Con Mand, RV.425; Con Ob; Con Strs, RV.151; Con Tpts, RV.537; Con Vc; Cons Diverse Instrs; Cons Vn Strs, Op. 8/1-4; Cons Vn(s) Strs, Op. 3/1-12 SNYC (Essential Classics Take 2) 2-▲ 63284 (14.97)

S. Gazzelloni (fl) ("Complete Flute Concertos") † Con Fl; Con Flautino, RV.445; Con Fls, RV.533; Con Rcr, RV.108; Con Rcr, RV.441; Cons Fl, Op. 10/1-6 PPHI (Duo) 2-▲ 54256 (17.97)

Modo Antiquo *(rec Oct 1993)* ("Concerti per Flauto traversiere ed archi") † Con Fl; Con Fls, RV.533 TACT ▲ 672202 [DDD] (16.97)

J. Rampal (fl), C. Scimone (cnd) † Con Fl; Con Flautino, RV.443; Con Flautino, RV.444; Con Fls, RV.533; Con Rcr, RV.108; Con Rcr, RV.441; Cons Fl, Op. 10/1-6 SNYC 2-▲ 45623 [ADD] (14.97)

Concerto in a for Flute, Strings & Continuo, RV.440

S. Gazzelloni (fl) ("Complete Flute Concertos") † Con Fl; Con Flautino, RV.445; Con Fls, RV.533; Con Rcr, RV.108; Con Rcr, RV.441; Cons Fl, Op. 10/1-6 PPHI (Duo) 2-▲ 54256 (17.97)

Modo Antiquo *(rec Oct 1993)* ("Concerti per Flauto traversiere ed archi") † Con Fl; Con Fls, RV.533 TACT ▲ 672202 [DDD] (16.97)

VIVALDI, ANTONIO (cont.)

Concerto in a for Flute, Strings & Continuo, RV.440 (cont.)

J. Rampal (fl), C. Scimone (cnd) † Con Fl; Con Flautino, RV.443; Con Flautino, RV.444; Con Fls, RV.533; Con Rcr, RV.108; Con Rcr, RV.441; Cons Fl, Op. 10/1-6 SNYC 2-▲ 45623 [ADD] (14.97)

Concerto in g for Flute, Violin(s), Bassoon, Cello & Continuo, RV.106

Musica Concertiva ("Vivaldi e Il Suo Tempo") † Cons Diverse Instrs; Trio Son Rcr Bn, RV.86; A. Lotti:Son Fl; Trio Fl SUR ▲ 3097 (16.97)

Concerto in D for Flute, Violin, Bassoon & Continuo, RV.91

A. Watts (bn), Nouveau Quartet ("Chamber Concertos") † Cons Diverse Instrs; Trio Son Fl & Vn, RV.84 AMON ▲ 47 [DDD] (16.97)

Concerto in F for Flute, Violin, Bassoon & Continuo, RV.100

Collegium Pro Musica *(rec Montevarchi, Italy, May 15-17, 1995)* ("Concerti a tre e a quattro") † Con Rcr, Ob & Bn, RV.103; Cons Diverse Instrs; Trio Son Fl & Vn, RV.84 DYNC ▲ 156 [DDD] (17.97)

Il Giardino Armonico ("Vol. 2") † Con Fl Ob Vn, RV.88; Con Rcr Ob, RV.95; Con Rcr, Ob & Bn, RV.103; Con Rcr, Ob & Vns, RV.87; Sons Vns Vl, Op. 1/1-12 TELC ▲ 73268 [DDD] (16.97)

J. Krcek (cnd), Chamber Orchestra † Con Lt Vns, RV.93; Con Rcr Vn Bn, RV.92; Con Rcr, RV.108; Con Va Hns Obs, RV.97; Trio Son Fl & Vn, RV.84 GZCL ▲ 246 (6.97)

Concertos (6) for Flute, Violin, Strings & Harpsichord

I. Stern (vn), J. Rampal (fl), J. Rolla (cnd), Franz Liszt CO SNYC ▲ 45867 [DDD] (16.97)

Concerto in C for 2 Flutes & Strings, RV.533

W. Bennett (fl), L. Smith (fl), N. Marriner (cnd), Academy of St. Martin in the Fields † Con Mands, RV.532; Con Ob Bn, RV.545; Con Vn Obs, RV.563 PPHI ▲ 12892 [DDD] (16.97)

E. Duvier (cnd), Camerata Romana † Con Tpts, RV.537 PC ▲ 267039 [DDD] (2.97)

S. Gazzelloni (fl) ("Complete Flute Concertos") † Con Fl; Con Flautino, RV.445, Con Rcr, RV.108; Con Rcr, RV.441; Cons Fl, Op. 10/1-6 PPHI (Duo) 2-▲ 54256 (17.97)

C. Gurtner (fl), L. Brunmayr (fl), M. Haselböck (cnd), Vienna Academy [period instrs] ("Duo Concerti") † Con Ob Bn, RV.545; Con Orchs, RV.583; Con Tpts, RV.537; Con Vcs, RV.531; Con Vn Org, RV.542 NOVA ▲ 150074 [DDD] (16.97)

Modo Antiquo *(rec Oct 1993)* ("Concerti per Flauto traversiere ed archi") † Con Fl TACT ▲ 672202 [DDD] (16.97)

J. Rampal (fl), S. Kudo (fl), J. Rampal (cnd), Salzburg Mozarteum Orch † Cimarosa:Con Fls; W. A. Mozart:Concertone Vns, K.190; A. Stamitz:Con Fls SNYC ▲ 45930 [DDD] (16.97)

J. Rampal (fl), C. Scimone (cnd) † Con Fl; Con Flautino, RV.443; Con Flautino, RV.444; Con Rcr, RV.108; Con Rcr, RV.441; Cons Fl, Op. 10/1-6 SNYC 2-▲ 45623 [ADD] (14.97)

D. Rix (ct), D. Davis (fl), D. Dobing (fl), C. Hooker (ob), H. McQueen (ob), R. McDowall (cl), J. Graham (bn), C. Steele-Perkins (tpt), M. Meekes (tpt), S. Stirling (hn), T. Caister (hn), N. Kraemer (hpd), N. Kraemer (cnd), London Sinfonietta *(rec All Saints Church East Finchley, England, Oct 1994 & Jan 1995)* ("Vivaldi: Wind Concerti") † Con Hns, RV.539; Con Ob Bn, RV.545; Cons Diverse Instrs NXIN (Vivaldi Collection) ▲ 553204 [DDD] (5.97)

J. See (fl), S. Schultz (fl), N. McGegan (cnd), Philharmonia Baroque Orch ("Flute Concertos") † Cons Fl, Op. 10/1-6 HAM ▲ 7905193 [DDD] (12.97)

S. S. Syrinx (pan fl), J. Rampal (trns fl), J. Berlingen (cnd), Normandy Orchestral Ensemble [arr Syrinx] *(rec Oct 1994)* † Albinoni:Cons Ob, Op. 9; B. Bartók:Romanian Folk Dances Vn & Pno; Cimarosa:Con Fls; Con Ob; C. Stamitz:Con Fl in G, Op. 29 CASC ▲ 65127

J. Válek (fl), J. Novotny (fl), J. Stivín (flautino) † Con Flautino, RV.443; Con Flautino, RV.444; Con Flautino, RV.445; Con Rcr, RV.108 NXIN ▲ 550385 [DDD] (5.97)

Concertos for Guitar & Orchestra

P. Romero (gtr) PPHI ▲ 34082 [DDD] (16.97)

M. Tsessos (gtr), V. Altschuler (cnd), St. Petersburg Philharmony CO † Castelnuovo-Tedesco:Con 1 Gtr, Op. 99; H. Villa-Lobos:Con Gtr SNYC ▲ 64335 [DDD] (4.97)

Concerto in C for Guitar & Orchestra

M. Zelenka (gtr), Slovak CO ("Classic Hits: Vivaldi") † Con Fl Gtr; Con Vc; Con 2 Vns, RV.514; Cons Fl, Op. 10/1-6; Cons Vn(s) Strs, Op. 3/1-12 PUBM (Majestic) ▲ 1041 [DDD] (4.97)

various artists † Cons Vn Strs, Op. 8/1-4; Albinoni:Adagio; J. S. Bach:Brandenburg Con 2, BWV 1047; Brandenburg Con 3, BWV 1048; Brandenburg Con 5, BWV 1050; Jesu, bleibet meine Freude; Suite 2 Fl, BWV 1067; Suite 3 Orch, BWV 1068; G. F. Handel:Messiah (sels); Royal Fireworks Music, HWV 351; Serse (sels); Water Music, HWV 348-50; Mouret:Rondeau; J. Pachelbel:Canon & Gigue RCAV ▲ 60840 (10.97) ▮ 60840 (5.98)

Concerto in D for Guitar

various artists—Adagio † Cons Vn Strs, Op. 8/1-4; Albinoni:Adagio; J. S. Bach:Brandenburg Con 2, BWV 1047; Brandenburg Con 3, BWV 1048; Brandenburg Con 5, BWV 1050; Suite 2 Fl, BWV 1067; Suite 3 Orch, BWV 1068; G. F. Handel:Music of Handel; Mouret:Music of Mouret; J. Pachelbel:Canon & Gigue RCAV ▲ 63501 (11.97)

Concerto in A for Harpsichord & Orchestra, [re-constructed Igor Kipnis after Concerto for Violin, Cello & Orchestra, RV.546], RV.780

I. Kipnis (hpd), I. Kipnis (cnd) [period instrs] † Cons Fl, Op. 10/1-6; Cons Vn Strs, Op. 8/1-4 CHSK ▲ 78 [DDD] (16.97)

Concerto in F for 2 Horns, Strings & Continuo, RV.538

Z. Zuk (hn), J. Muzyk (hn), J. Stanienda (cnd), Wroclaw CO Leopoldinum ("Il Corno Italiano") † Con Hns, RV.539; Belloli:Con Hunting Hn; Cherubini:Sons Hn; Mercadante:Con Hn; N. Rota:Castel del Monte ZUK ▲ 160528 (10.97)

Concerto in F for 2 Horns, Strings & Continuo, RV.539

D. Rix (ct), D. Davis (fl), D. Dobing (fl), C. Hooker (ob), H. McQueen (ob), R. McDowall (cl), J. Graham (bn), C. Steele-Perkins (tpt), M. Meekes (tpt), S. Stirling (hn), T. Caister (hn), N. Kraemer (hpd), N. Kraemer (cnd), London Sinfonietta—Allegro *(rec All Saints Church East Finchley, England, Oct 1994 & Jan 1995)* ("Vivaldi: Wind Concerti") † Con Fls, RV.533; Con Ob Bn, RV.545; Cons Diverse Instrs NXIN (Vivaldi Collection) ▲ 553204 [DDD] (5.97)

Z. Zuk (hn), J. Muzyk (hn), J. Stanienda (cnd), Wroclaw CO Leopoldinum ("Il Corno Italiano") † Con Hns, RV.538; Belloli:Con Hunting Hn; Cherubini:Sons Hn; Mercadante:Con Hn; N. Rota:Castel del Monte ZUK ▲ 160528 (10.97)

Concerto in D for Lute (or Guitar), 2 Violins & Continuo, RV.93

G. Antonini (cnd) † Con Mand, RV.425; Con Mands, RV.532; Con Va Lt, RV.540; Con Vns Rcrs Mans, RV.558; Trio Son Vn Lt, RV.82; Trio Son Vn Lt, RV.85 TELC ▲ 91182 (16.97)

D. Benkö (lt), J. Rolla (cnd), Franz Liszt CO † Con Va Lt, RV.540; Trio Son Vn Lt, RV.82; Trio Son Vn Lt, RV.85 HUN ▲ 11978

L. Brabec (gtr), O. Vlček (cnd), Prague CO † Con Mand, RV.425; Con Mands, RV.532; Con Va Lt, RV.540 SUR ▲ 104126 [DDD]

E. Fernández (gtr) † M. Arnold:Con Gtr, Op. 67; M. Giuliani:Con 1 Gtr, Op. 30; M. Ponce:Concierto del sur; J. Rodrigo:Con de Aranjuez; H. Villa-Lobos:Con Gtr PLON 2-▲ 455364 (17.97)

S. Isbin (gtr), L. Foster (cnd), Lausanne CO [solo gtr & str orch arr Emilio Pujol, edited Sharo] † J. Rodrigo:Con de Aranjuez; Fant para un gentilhombre VCL ▲ 59024 [DDD] (16.97)

M. Kraemer (va d'amore/vn), R. Lislevand (gtr/lt), G. Morini (positive org) † Con Va Lt, RV.540; Trio Son Vn Lt, RV.82; Trio Son Vn Lt, RV.85 ASTR ▲ 128587 (12.97)

N. Kraft (gtr), B. Silver (hpd) [arr by the performers for gtr & hpd] † J. Haydn:Qts (6) Strs, H.III/7-12, Op. 2; J. Rodrigo:Fant para un gentilhombre CHN ▲ 8937 [DDD] (16.97)

J. Krcek (cnd), Chamber Orchestra † Con Fl Vn Bn, RV.100; Con Rcr Vn Bn, RV.92; Con Rcr, RV.108; Con Va Hns Obs, RV.97; Trio Son Fl & Vn, RV.84 GZCL ▲ 246 (6.97)

V. Kruglov (mand), Northern Crown Soloists Ensemble *(rec 1992)* ("Mandolin Concertos") † Con Mand, RV.425; Con Mands, RV.532; J. N. Hummel:Con Mand & Strs, S.28 OLY ▲ 582 [DDD] (16.97)

H. Navez (gtr), A. Moglia (cnd), Toulouse National CO † Con Mand, RV.425; Cons Vn Strs, Op. 8/1-4 PVY ▲ 730038 (12.97)

R. Porroni (gtr), Ensemble Duomo ("Una Chitarra per Vivaldi") † Con Va Lt, RV.540; Pastor fido, Op. 13/1-6; Trio Son Vn Lt, RV.82; Trio Son Vn Lt, RV.85 STRV ▲ 43 (16.97)

P. Press (gtr), R. Kapp (cnd) ("The Miraculous Mandolin: Concertos & Sonatas for Mandolin & Guitar") † Con Mand, RV.425; Con Mands, RV.532; Con Va Lt, RV.540; Trio Son Vn Lt, RV.82; Trio Son Vn Lt, RV.85 ESSY ▲ 1004 [DDD] (16.97)

K. Scheit (gtr), W. Boettcher (cnd) *(rec Baumgartner Kasino Vienna, Austria, Jan 12-13 & 18, June 23, 1961)* ("The Virtuoso Guitar, Vol. 2") † Con Va Lt, RV.540; F. Carulli:Con Gtr; J. Dowland:Galliards; Torelli:Con Vn Gtr VC ▲ 1020 [ADD] (13.97)

N. Sparf (vn), T. Galli (va), J. Lindberg (cnd) † Con Va Lt, RV.540; Trio Son Vn Lt, RV.82; Trio Son Vn Lt, RV.85 BIS ▲ 290 [DDD] (17.97)

Tetra Guitar Quartet † Cons Vn Strs, Op. 8/1-4 ICC ▲ 6600692 (16.97)

J. Williams (gtr) † Cons Mand; Castelnuovo-Tedesco:Con 1 Gtr, Op. 99; M. Giuliani:Con 1 Gtr, Op. 30; M. Ponce:Concierto del sur; J. Rodrigo:Con de Aranjuez; Fant para un gentilhombre; H. Villa-Lobos:Con Gtr SNYC 2-▲ 44791 [ADD] (31.97)

J. Williams (gtr) † M. Giuliani:Con 1 Gtr, Op. 30; J. Rodrigo:Con de Aranjuez; Fant para un gentilhombre SNYC (Essential Classics) ▲ 48168 (7.97) ▮ 48168 (3.98)

VIVALDI, ANTONIO (cont.)

Concerto in D for Lute (or Guitar), 2 Violins & Continuo, RV.93 (cont.)

N. Yepes (gtr), P. Kuentz (cnd), Paul Kuentz CO † Con Mand, RV.425; Con Mands, RV.532; Con Va Lt, RV.540 DEUT (Resonance) ▲ 29528 [ADD] (7.97)

Concertos for Mandolin & Strings

C. Schneider (mand), D. Meyer (mand), K. Redel (cnd) —Cons in C & D for Mand & Strs; Con in G for 2 Mands & Strs; Con in C for 2 Mands & Orch FORL ▲ 16548 [AAD] (16.97)

Concerto in A for Mandolin & Strings

J. Williams (gtr) † Con Lt Vns, RV.93; Castelnuovo-Tedesco:Con 1 Gtr, Op. 99; M. Giuliani:Con 1 Gtr, Op. 30; M. Ponce:Concierto del sur; J. Rodrigo:Con de Aranjuez; Fant para un gentilhombre; H. Villa-Lobos:Con Gtr SNYC 2-▲ 44791 [ADD] (31.97)

Concerto in C for Mandolin, Strings & Continuo, RV.425

G. Antonini (cnd) † Con Lt Vns, RV.93; Con Mands, RV.532; Con Va Lt, RV.540; Con Vns Rcrs Mans, RV.558; Trio Son Vn Lt, RV.82; Trio Son Vn Lt, RV.85 TELC ▲ 91182 (16.97)

L. Brabec (gtr), O. Vlček (cnd), Prague CO † Con Lt Vns, RV.93; Con Mands, RV.532; Con Va Lt, RV.540 SUR ▲ 104126 [DDD]

S. Goichberg (mand), E. Earle (hpd), M. Goberman (cnd), New York Sinfonietta ("Sunday Brunch. Vol 2") † Con Mands, RV.532; Cons Fl, Op. 10/1-6; Cons Vn Strs, Op. 8/1-4; J. S. Bach:Cant 147; Cant 156; Cant 78; Con 5 Hpd, BWV 1056; Suite 2 Fl, BWV 1067; G. F. Handel:Minuet Vc & Pno; Solomon (arrival of the queen of Sheba); Water Music (sels); A. Marcello:Con Ob Strs in d, Op. 1; Mouret:Suite de symphonies; H. Purcell:Abdelazer (sels); Gordian Knot Unty'd (sels); V. Tommasini:Donne di buon umore (sels) SNYC (Dinner Classics) ▲ 46359 [AAD] (9.97)

M. Gould (tpt), E. Carrol (tpt), R. Kapp (cnd) —Largo ("Four Seasons & Other Great Concertos") † Con Fl; Con Flautino, RV.443; Con Ob; Con Strs, RV.151; Con Tpts, RV.537; Con Vc; Cons Diverse Instrs; Cons Vn Strs, Op. 8/1-4; Cons Vn(s) Strs, Op. 3/1-12 SNYC (Essential Classics Take 2) 2-▲ 63284 (14.97)

R. Kapp (cnd), Philharmonia Virtuosi, New York—Largo *(rec NYC, NY)* ("Greatest Hits of 1721") † Con Tpts, RV.537; Cons Vn Strs, Op. 8/1-4; J. S. Bach:Cant 147; Cant 208; Suite 2 Fl, BWV 1067; J. Clarke:Prince of Denmark's March; A. Corelli:Con Grosso in g 2 Vns, Vla & Vc, Op. 6/8; G. F. Handel:Water Music, HWV 348-50; A. Marcello:Con Ob Strs in c; J. P. A. Martini:Plaisir d'Amour SNYC ▲ 35821 (9.97)

T. Kostyanaia (mand), L. Korkhin (cnd), Renaissance CO ("Great Instrumental Concertos") † Con Mands, RV.532; Con Vcs, RV.531 SNYC ▲ 57244 [DDD] (4.97)

V. Kruglov (mand), Northern Crown Soloists Ensemble *(rec 1992)* ("Mandolin Concertos") † Con Lt Vns, RV.93; Con Mands, RV.532; J. N. Hummel:Con Mand & Strs, S.28 OLY ▲ 582 [DDD] (16.97)

A. Lizzio (cnd), San Marco Musici † Con Vn; Con Vn Obs Hns, RV.571; Con 2 Vns, RV.524 PC ▲ 265005 [DDD] (2.97)

L. Mayer (mand), B. Glaetzner (ob), Güttler (tpt), K. Sandau (tpt), M. Pommer (cnd), Leipzig New Bach Collegium Musicum, M. Pommer (cnd), Budapest Strings † Con Tpts, RV.537; Cons Vn Strs, Op. 8/1-12; Cons Vn Strs, Op. 8/1-4 LALI ▲ 15518 [DDD] (3.97)

H. Navez (gtr), A. Moglia (cnd), Toulouse National CO † Con Lt Vns, RV.93; Cons Vn Strs, Op. 8/1-4 PVY ▲ 730038 (12.97)

T. Ochi (mand), S. Ochi (mand), P. Kuentz (cnd), Paul Kuentz CO † Con Lt Vns, RV.93; Con Mands, RV.532; Con Va Lt, RV.540 DEUT (Resonance) ▲ 29528 [ADD] (7.97)

P. Press (mand), R. Kapp (cnd) ("The Miraculous Mandolin: Concertos & Sonatas for Mandolin & Guitar") † Con Lt Vns, RV.93; Con Mands, RV.532; Con Va Lt, RV.540; Trio Son Vn Lt, RV.82; Trio Son Vn Lt, RV.85 ESSY ▲ 1004 [DDD] (16.97)

P. Romero (gtr) [arr gtr Romero] ("Moll Flanders") † J. S. Bach:Brandenburg Con 3, BWV 1048; Suite 3 Orch, BWV 1068; G. F. Handel:Water Music, HWV 348-50; Mancina:Moll Flanders; J. Offenbach:Contes d'Hoffmann (sels) PLON ▲ 52485 (16.97)

G. Tröster-Weyhofen (mand), G. Vogt (cnd), Bavarian State Youth Plucked Instrument Orch † H. Baumann:Con Capriccioso; S. Behrend:Serenade Mand; A. Starck:Con Mand; Tober-Vogt:Carnival of Venice THOR ▲ 2146 [DDD] (16.97)

Concerto in G for 2 Mandolins (or 2 Guitars), String & Continuo, RV.532

G. Antonini (cnd) † Con Lt Vns, RV.93; Con Mand, RV.425; Con Va Lt, RV.540; Con Vns Rcrs Mans, RV.558; Trio Son Vn Lt, RV.82; Trio Son Vn Lt, RV.85 TELC ▲ 91182 (16.97)

L. Brabec (gtr), M. Mysliviček (gtr), O. Vlček (cnd), Prague CO † Con Lt Vns, RV.93; Con Mand, RV.425; Con Va Lt, RV.540 SUR ▲ 104126 [DDD]

M. Frasca-Colombier (vn), L. Paugam (vn), S. Ochi (mand), T. Ochi (mand), J. Labylle (pic), P. Kuentz (cnd), Paul Kuentz Orch ("6 Rare Concertos") † Con Flautino, RV.443; Con Vn; Cons Diverse Instrs PVY ▲ 730052 [DDD] (12.97)

A. Ganoci (mand), F. Pavlinek (mand), A. Heiller (org), A. Janigro (cnd), Zagreb Solisti *(rec Baumgartner Hall Vienna, June 1964)* † Con Tpts, RV.537; Cons Vn Strs, Op. 8/1-4 VC ▲ 2536 [ADD] (13.97)

A. Ganoci (mand), F. Pavlinek (mand), A. Janigro (cnd) *(rec 1964)* BG (The Bach Guild) ▲ 2006 [ADD] (13.97)

G. Kessler (gtr), D. Bender (ob)—Andante *(rec England)* ("Trio Sonata - Encore!") † J. S. Bach:Sons & Partitas Vn; Trio Son for 2 Vns; E. Granados:Danzas españolas (10) Pno; Goyescas:Intermezzo; E. Noda:Tanka Fl, Ob & Gtr; Telemann:Essercizii Musici; Fants (12) Fl, TWV40:2-13; T. Tomkins:Instrumental & Vocal Music; Wooldridge:Partita Ww, Op. 38 *(E text)* BOSK ▲ 114 [DDD] (15.97)

T. Kostyanaia (mand), A. Boguk (mand), L. Korkhin (cnd), Renaissance CO ("Great Instrumental Concertos") † Con Mand, RV.425; Con Vcs, RV.531 SNYC ▲ 57244 [DDD] (4.97)

V. Kruglov (mand), Northern Crown Soloists Ensemble *(rec 1992)* ("Mandolin Concertos") † Con Lt Vns, RV.93; Con Mand, RV.425; J. N. Hummel:Con Mand & Strs, S.28 OLY ▲ 582 [DDD] (16.97)

T. Ochi (mand), S. Ochi (mand), P. Kuentz (cnd), Paul Kuentz CO † Con Lt Vns, RV.93; Con Mand, RV.425; Con Va Lt, RV.540 DEUT (Resonance) ▲ 29528 [ADD] (7.97)

T. Pinnock (cnd), English CO † Con Bn; Con Strs, RV.151; Con Vn Ob, RV.548; Con Vns Rcrs Mans, RV.558; Cons Fl, Op. 10/1-6; Cons Vn(s) Strs, Op. 3/1-12 PARC (3D Baroque) ▲ 31710 [DDD] (9.97)

P. Press (mand), S. Kuney (mand), R. Kapp (cnd) ("The Miraculous Mandolin: Concertos & Sonatas for Mandolin & Guitar") † Con Lt Vns, RV.93; Con Mand, RV.425; Con Va Lt, RV.540; Trio Son Vn Lt, RV.82; Trio Son Vn Lt, RV.85 ESSY ▲ 1004 [DDD] (16.97)

A. Saint-Cyr (mand), C. Schneider (mand), J. Malgoire (cnd), La Grande Écurie et la Chambre du Roy—Andante ("Sunday Brunch. Vol 2") † Con Mand, RV.425; Cons Fl, Op. 10/1-6; Cons Vn Strs, Op. 8/1-4; J. S. Bach:Cant 147; Cant 156; Cant 78; Con 5 Hpd, BWV 1056; Suite 2 Fl, BWV 1067; G. F. Handel:Minuet Vc & Pno; Solomon (arrival of the queen of Sheba); Water Music (sels); A. Marcello:Con Ob Strs in d, Op. 1; Mouret:Suite de symphonies; H. Purcell:Abdelazer (sels); Gordian Knot Unty'd (sels); V. Tommasini:Donne di buon umore (sels) SNYC (Dinner Classics) ▲ 46359 [AAD] (9.97)

B. Sztankovits (gtr), Z. Tokos (gtr) *(rec Unitarian Church Budapest, Nov 1991)* ("Famous Baroque Concerti") † Con 2 Vns, RV.523; J. S. Bach:Con 1 for 2 Hpds, BWV 1060; Easter Oratorio, BWV 249; G. F. Handel:Concerti grossi, Op. 6; Solomon (arrival of the queen of Sheba) NXIN ▲ 553028 [DDD] (5.97)

J. Tyler (mand), D. Wootton (mand), N. Marriner (cnd), Academy of St. Martin in the Fields † Con Fls, RV.533; Con Ob Bn, RV.545; Con Vn Obs, RV.563 PPHI ▲ 12892 [DDD] (16.97)

J. Williams (gtr), C. Bonell (gtr), K. Marjoram (b chl), B. Gascoigne (mar), M. Pert (vib)—Allegro; Allegro *(rec NYC, NY)* ("John Williams & Friends") † J. S. Bach:Cant 147; Cons Org; Suites Vc; Trio Son for 2 Vns; Daquin:Pièces de clavecin (sels); W. A. Mozart:Adagio Glass Amc, K.356; Son 11 Pno, K.331; H. Purcell:Sons (12) of 3 Parts for 2 Vns, Z.790-801; Telemann:Bourree alla Polacca SNYC ▲ 35108 [AAD] (16.97)

Concertos for Oboe & Orchestra

B. Glaetzner (ob), H. Haenchen (cnd), Berlin CO *(rec 1978)* ("Oboe Concertos") † Telemann:Con Ob BER ▲ 9210 (10.97)

J. Spinosi (cnd) *(rec Oct 1996)* ("Concerti con Molti Strumenti, Vol. 2") † Cons Rcr PVY ▲ 797012 (16.97)

Concerto in G for Oboe, Bassoon & Strings, RV.545

P. Frankenberg (ob), G. van der Wulp (bn), M. Haselböck (cnd), Vienna Academy [period instrs] ("Duo Concerti") † Con Fls, RV.533; Con Orchs, RV.583; Con Tpts, RV.537; Con Vcs, RV.531; Con Vn Org, RV.542 NOVA ▲ 150074 [DDD] (16.97)

C. Nicklin (ob), G. Sheen (bn), N. Marriner (cnd), Academy of St. Martin in the Fields † Con Fls, RV.533; Con Mands, RV.532; Con Vn Obs, RV.563 PPHI ▲ 12892 [DDD] (16.97)

D. Rix (cl), D. Davis (fl), D. Dobing (fl), C. Hooker (ob), H. McQueen (ob), R. McDowall (cl), J. Graham (bn), C. Steele-Perkins (tpt), M. Meekes (tpt), S. Stirling (hn), T. Caister (hn), N. Kraemer (hpd), N. Kraemer (cnd), London Sinfonietta *(rec All Saints Church East Finchley, England, Oct 1994 & Jan 1995)* ("Vivaldi: Wind Concerti") † Con Fls, RV.533; Con Hns, RV.539; Cons Diverse Instrs NXIN (Vivaldi Collection) ▲ 553204 [DDD] (5.97)

Concerto in C for Oboe, Strings & Continuo [trans from Violin Concerto, Op. 8/12 (RV.178)], RV.449

T. Pinnock (cnd), English Concert ("7 Concerti for Woodwind & Strings") † Con Flautino, RV.444; Con Strs, RV.166; Cons Diverse Instrs PARC ▲ 45839 [DDD] (16.97)

Concerto in D for Oboe, Strings & Continuo, RV.453

J. Anderson (ob), S. Wright (cnd), Philharmonia Orch *(rec St. Jude-on-the-Hill Hampstead, England, Jan 5-6, 1989)* † Con Ob; A. Benjamin:Con Ob Strs; Cimarosa:Con Ob; A. Marcello:Con Ob Strs in d NIMB ▲ 7027 [DDD] (11.97)

VIVALDI, ANTONIO (cont.)

Concerto in F for Oboe, Strings & Continuo, RV.455

J. Anderson (ob), S. Wright (cnd), Philharmonia Orch *(rec St. Jude-on-the-Hill Hampstead, England, Jan 5-6, 1989)* † Con Ob; A. Benjamin:Con Ob Strs; Cimarosa:Con Ob; A. Marcello:Con Ob Strs in d NIMB ▲ 7027 [DDD] (11.97)

L. Güttler (cnd) † Con Va Lt, RV.540; Con Vn; Con Vns Rcrs Mans, RV.558; Cons Diverse Instrs; Sinf BER ▲ 1082 [DDD] (16.97)

Concerto in a for Oboe, Strings & Continuo, RV.461

J. Anderson (ob), S. Wright (cnd), Philharmonia Orch *(rec St. Jude-on-the-Hill Hampstead, England, Jan 5-6, 1989)* † Con Ob; A. Benjamin:Con Ob Strs; Cimarosa:Con Ob; A. Marcello:Con Ob Strs in d NIMB ▲ 7027 [DDD] (11.97)

J. L. Garcia (cnd), English CO ("Four Seasons & Other Great Concertos") † Con Fl; Con Flautino, RV.443; Con Mand, RV.425; Con Strs, RV.151; Con Tpts, RV.537; Con Vc; Cons Diverse Instrs; Cons Vn Strs, Op. 8/1-4; Cons Vn(s) Strs, Op. 3/1-12 SNYC (Essential Classics Take 2) 2-▲ 63284 (14.97)

G. Mattes (ob) *(rec Apr 1994)* ("Oboenkonzerte") † A. Corelli:Con in F Ob; A. Marcello:Con Ob Strs in d, Op. 1 NOVA ▲ 150141 (16.97)

Concerto in C for Oboe, 2 Violins & Strings, RV.554

J. Baird (sop), S. Duvol (ob), B. Fix-Keller (hpd), V. Radu (cnd), Ama Deus Ensemble † J. S. Bach:Lobet den Herrn, alle Heiden, BWV 230; Magnificat, BWV 243; Hammerschmidt:Music of Hammerschmidt; G. F. Handel:Messiah (sels); A. Scarlatti:Music of A. Scarlatti VOXC ▲ 7548 (5.97)

Concerto in d for 2 Oboes, Strings & Continuo, RV.535

N. McGegan (cnd), Philharmonia Baroque Orch *(rec Oakland, CA, Oct 1996)* ("Vivaldi for Diverse Instruments") † Con Vn; Con Vn Obs, RV.577; Cons Diverse Instrs REF ▲ 77 (16.97)

Concertos for Orchestra

A. Ephrikian (cnd) —Con Strs, RV.120; Con Strs, RV.123; Con Strs Bc, RV.152; Con Strs Bc, RV.155 † Con Strs, RV.129; Cons Vn Strs, Op. 12/1-6 HMA ▲ 1901012 [ADD] (9.97)

A. Nanut (cnd), Zagreb Solisti—in A ("Famous Concertos") † Cons Vn(s) Strs, Op. 3/1-12; Sinf PC ▲ 265075 [DDD] (2.97)

Concerto in B♭ for 2 Orchestras & Continuo, RV.583

M. Haselböck (cnd), Vienna Academy [period instrs] ("Duo Concerti") † Con Fls, RV.533; Con Ob Bn, RV.545; Con Tpts, RV.537; Con Vcs, RV.531; Con Vn Org, RV.542 NOVA ▲ 150074 [DDD] (16.97)

Concertos for Recorder & Orchestra

Breuer (rcr) † Telemann:Qts or trios (6) LALI ▲ 15634 [DDD] (3.97)

D. Laurin (rcr)—Cons Fl, Op. 10/1-6 [No. 5 in F]; Con Rcr, RV.441; Con Flautino, RV.444 *(rec 1991)* ("Recorder Concertos") † Con Flautino, RV.443; Cons Fl, Op. 10/1-6 BIS ▲ 635 (17.97)

T. Perrenoud (rcr), Amsterdam Baroque Soloists—Con Rcr, RV.444 ("Sur les Chemins de l'Europe Galante") † Con Rcr; Con Rcr, RV.441; Babell:Con Rcr CLAV ▲ 509706 (16.97)

M. Sandhoff (rcr), C. Breuer (rcr) † Telemann:Essercizii Musici LALI ▲ 14036 [DDD] (3.97)

J. Spinosi (cnd) *(rec Oct 1996)* ("Concerti con Molti Strumenti, Vol. 2") † Cons Ob PVY ▲ 797012 (16.97)

M. Verbruggen (rcr), N. McGegan (cnd), Philharmonia Baroque Orch—(6) in C, RV.443 & in C, RV.444 (sopranino rcr); Cons Fl, Op. 10/1-6 [No. 1 in F, "La Tempesta di mare"; No. 5 in F; No. 4 in G] † Con Fl Bn, RV.104; Con Rcr, RV.441 HAM ▲ 907040 (18.97)

Concerto in g for Recorder, Oboe, Bassoon & Continuo, RV.103

Collegium Pro Musica *(rec Montevarchi, Italy, May 15-17, 1995)* ("Concerti a tre e a quattro") † Con Fl Vn Bn, RV.100; Cons Diverse Instrs; Trio Son Fl & Vn, RV.84 DYNC ▲ 156 [DDD] (17.97)

J. Holloway (vn), S. Comberti (vc), M. Verbruggen (rcr), P. Goodwin (ob), D. Godburn (bn), J. Toll (hpd) † Con Fl Ob, RV.99; Con Rcr Ob, RV.95; Con Rcr, Ob & Vn, RV.94; Cons Diverse Instrs; Trio Son Rcr Bn, RV.86 HAM ▲ 907046 (18.97)

Il Giardino Armonico ("Vol. 2") † Con Fl Ob Vn, RV.88; Con Fl Vn Bn, RV.100; Con Rcr Ob, RV.95; Con Rcr, Ob & Vns, RV.87; Sons Vn Vl, Op. 1/1-12 TELC ▲ 73268 [DDD] (16.97)

Venice New Quintet ("Concertos without Orchestra") † Con Fl Ob, RV.107; Con Fl Ob, RV.99; Con Rcr, Ob & Vn, RV.101; Con Rcr, Ob & Vn, RV.94; Cons Diverse Instrs TACT ▲ 672205 [DDD] (16.97)

Concerto in D for Recorder, Oboe, Violin, Bassoon & Continuo, RV.94

J. Holloway (vn), S. Comberti (vc), M. Verbruggen (rcr), P. Goodwin (ob), D. Godburn (bn), J. Toll (hpd) † Con Fl Ob, RV.99; Con Rcr Ob, RV.95; Con Rcr, Ob & Bn, RV.103; Cons Diverse Instrs; Trio Son Rcr Bn, RV.86 HAM ▲ 907046 (18.97)

S. Reiss (rcr), Hesperus † Con Rcr, RV.444; Babell:Con in d Rcr; Graupner:Con Rcr; Naudot:Con Rcr; Telemann:Son Rcr KOCH ▲ 7454 (16.97)

Venice New Quintet ("Concertos without Orchestra") † Con Fl Ob, RV.107; Con Fl Ob, RV.99; Con Rcr, Ob & Bn, RV.103; Con Rcr, Ob & Vn, RV.101; Cons Diverse Instrs TACT ▲ 672205 [DDD] (16.97)

Concerto in D for Recorder (or Violin), Oboe (or Violin), Violin, Bassoon (or Cello) & Continuo, RV.95

J. Holloway (vn), S. Comberti (vc), M. Verbruggen (rcr), P. Goodwin (ob), D. Godburn (bn), J. Toll (hpd) † Con Fl Ob, RV.99; Con Rcr, Ob & Bn, RV.103; Con Rcr, Ob & Vn, RV.94; Cons Diverse Instrs; Trio Son Rcr Bn, RV.86 HAM ▲ 907046 (18.97)

Il Giardino Armonico ("Vol. 2") † Con Fl Ob Vn, RV.88; Con Fl Vn Bn, RV.100; Con Rcr, Ob & Bn, RV.103; Con Rcr, Ob & Vns, RV.87; Sons Vn Vl, Op. 1/1-12 TELC ▲ 73268 [DDD] (16.97)

Musical Offering † Con Fl Ob, RV.107; Trio Son Vn Vc, RV.83 NON ▲ 79067 (9.97)

Concerto in G for Recorder, Oboe, Violin, Bassoon & Continuo, RV.101

Il Giardino Armonico ("Vol. 1") † Con Fl Bn, RV.104; Con Fl Ob Vn, RV.98; Con Fl Ob, RV.90; Con Rcr, RV.442; Cons Fl, Op. 10/1-6 TELC ▲ 73267 [DDD] (16.97)

Venice New Quintet ("Concertos without Orchestra") † Con Fl Ob, RV.107; Con Fl Ob, RV.99; Con Rcr, Ob & Bn, RV.103; Con Rcr, Ob & Vn, RV.94; Cons Diverse Instrs TACT ▲ 672205 [DDD] (16.97)

Concerto in C for Recorder, Oboe, 2 Violins & Continuo, RV.87

Il Giardino Armonico ("Vol. 2") † Con Fl Ob Vn, RV.88; Con Fl Vn Bn, RV.100; Con Rcr Ob, RV.95; Con Rcr, Ob & Bn, RV.103; Sons Vn Vl, Op. 1/1-12 TELC ▲ 73268 [DDD] (16.97)

Concerto in c for Recorder, Strings & Continuo, RV.441

S. Gazzelloni (fl) ("Complete Flute Concertos") † Con Fl; Con Flautino, RV.445; Con Fls, RV.533; Con Rcr, RV.108; Cons Fl, Op. 10/1-6 PPHI (Duo) 2-▲ 54256 (17.97)

L. Korkhin (cnd) ("Vivaldi: A Flute Festival") † Con Cls Obs, RV.559; Con Rcr, RV.108; Cons Fl, Op. 10/1-6 SNYC ▲ 66724 [DDD] (4.97)

P. Øien (fl), T. Tønnesen (cnd), Norwegian CO *(rec Sept 2-3, 1978)* † Blavet:Con Fl; Quantz:Con in G Fl; Tartini:Con Fl BIS ▲ 118 [AAD] (17.97)

T. Perrenoud (rcr), Amsterdam Baroque Soloists ("Sur les Chemins de l'Europe Galante") † Con Rcr; Cons Rcr; Babell:Con Rcr CLAV ▲ 509706 (16.97)

J. Rampal (fl), C. Scimone (cnd) † Con Fl; Con Flautino, RV.443; Con Flautino, RV.444; Con Fls, RV.533; Con Rcr, RV.108; Cons Fl, Op. 10/1-6 SNYC 2-▲ 45623 [ADD] (14.97)

M. Verbruggen (rcr), N. McGegan (cnd), Philharmonia Baroque Orch † Con Fl Bn, RV.104; Cons Rcr HAM ▲ 907040 (18.97)

Concerto in F for Recorder, Strings & Continuo, RV.442

Il Giardino Armonico ("Vol. 1") † Con Fl Bn, RV.104; Con Fl Ob Vn, RV.98; Con Fl Ob, RV.90; Con Rcr, Ob & Vn, RV.101; Cons Fl, Op. 10/1-6 TELC ▲ 73267 [DDD] (16.97)

Concerto in C for Recorder & Strings, RV.444

T. Hutchins (rcr), Y. Turovsky (cnd), Montreal Musici ("Tranquillity") † Con Strs, RV.158; Con Vcs, RV.531; Cons Fl, Op. 10/1-6; Arcus:Vars on Simple Gifts; J. Christian Bach:Con in c; Boccherini:Con Vc, G.482; D. Shostakovich:Con 2 Pno, Op. 102; I. Stravinsky:Con Str Orch; Wassenaer:Concerti Armonici CHN ▲ 8573 [DDD] (16.97)

S. Reiss (rcr), Hesperus † Con Rcr, Ob & Vn, RV.94; Babell:Con in d Rcr; Graupner:Con Rcr; Naudot:Con Rcr; Telemann:Son Rcr KOCH ▲ 7454 (16.97)

Concerto in D for Recorder, Violin, Bassoon (or Cello) & Continuo, RV.92

J. Krcek (cnd), Chamber Orchestra † Con Fl Vn Bn, RV.100; Con Lt Vns, RV.93; Con Rcr, RV.108; Con Va Hns Obs, RV.97; Trio Son Fl & Vn, RV.84 GZCL ▲ 246 (6.97)

Concerto in a for (Alto) Recorder, 2 Violins & Continuo

T. Perrenoud (rcr), Amsterdam Baroque Soloists ("Sur les Chemins de l'Europe Galante") † Con Rcr, RV.441; Cons Rcr; Babell:Con Rcr CLAV ▲ 509706 (16.97)

Concerto in a for Recorder, 2 Violins & Continuo, RV.108

S. Gazzelloni (fl) ("Complete Flute Concertos") † Con Fl; Con Flautino, RV.445; Con Fls, RV.533; Con Rcr, RV.441; Cons Fl, Op. 10/1-6 PPHI (Duo) 2-▲ 54256 (17.97)

V. Hudeček (vn), L. Brabec (gtr), J. Stivín (rcr), G. Delogu (cnd), Janáček CO, G. Delogu (cnd), Prague CO ("Brabec, Stivín & Hudeček Play Vivaldi") † Con Vn Org, RV.542; Con Vns Rcrs Mans, RV.558; Cons Diverse Instrs; Cons Vn(s) Strs, Op. 3/1-12 SUR ▲ 3023 (16.97)

A. Kiskatchi (fl), L. Korchin (cnd), Collegium dell'Arte ("Vivaldi: A Flute Festival") † Con Cls Obs, RV.559; Con Rcr, RV.441; Cons Fl, Op. 10/1-6 SNYC ▲ 66724 [DDD] (4.97)

J. Krcek (cnd), Chamber Orchestra † Con Fl Vn Bn, RV.100; Con Lt Vns, RV.93; Con Rcr Vn Bn, RV.92; Con Va Hns Obs, RV.97; Trio Son Fl & Vn, RV.84 GZCL ▲ 246 (6.97)

▲ = CD ◆ = Enhanced CD △ = MD ▮ = Cassette Tape ▯ = DCC

VIVALDI, ANTONIO (cont.)

Concerto in a for Recorder, 2 Violins & Continuo, RV.108 (cont.)

J. Rampal (fl), C. Scimone (cnd) † Con Fl; Con Flautino, RV.443; Con Flautino, RV.444; Con Fls, RV.533; Con Rcr, RV.441; Cons Fl, Op. 10/1-6 SNYC 2-▲ 45623 [ADD] (14.97)

J. Válek (fl), J. Novotny (fl), J. Stivín (flautino) † Con Flautino, RV.443; Con Flautino, RV.444; Con Flautino, RV.445; Con Fls, RV.533 NXIN ▲ 550385 [DDD] (5.97)

Concertos for Strings (miscellaneous)

La Pièta—Con Strs, RV.138; Con Strs, RV.159 *(rec Quebec, Oct 1997)* ("Per Archi") † Con Strs, RV.151; Con Strs, RV.156; Con Vn; Cons Vn(s) Strs, Op. 3/1-12; Sinf/Con Strs, RV.146; Sons Vns Vl, Op. 1/1-12 FL ▲ 23128 [DDD] (16.97)

Los Angeles Guitar Quintet—1 Con Grosso *(rec 1993)* ("Aquarelle") † L. Almeida:Los Angeles Aquarelle Suite; Beiderbecke:Pno Music; G. Gershwin:Music of Gershwin; Jobim:Gtr Music; W. A. Mozart:Qnt Cl, K.581 ERTO ▲ 42016 [ADD] (14.97)

Concerto in C for Strings & Continuo, RV.114

B. Labadie (cnd), Les Violons du Roy *(rec Quebec, Canada, June 1998)* ("Concerti for Strings") † Con Strs, RV.120; Con Strs, RV.151; Con Strs, RV.157; Cons Vn(s) Strs, Op. 3/1-12; Sinf Strs in b, RV.169 DOR ▲ 90255 [DDD] (16.97)

Vienna Flautists *(rec Slovak Radio Concert Hall Bratislava, Slovak Republic, June 2-3, 1994)* ("Concertos") † Con Strs, RV.117; Con Strs, RV.143; Con Strs, RV.151; Con Strs, RV.159; Con 3 Vns, RV.551; Cons Vn(s) Strs, Op. 3/1-12; Sinf; Sinf Strs in b, RV.169 DI ▲ 920230 [DDD] (5.97)

Concerto in C for Strings & Continuo, RV.117

Vienna Flautists *(rec June 2-3, 1994)* ("Concertos") † Con Strs, RV.114; Con Strs, RV.143; Con Strs, RV.151; Con Strs, RV.159; Con 3 Vns, RV.551; Cons Vn(s) Strs, Op. 3/1-12; Sinf; Sinf Strs in b, RV.169 DI ▲ 920230 [DDD] (5.97)

Concerto in c for Strings & Continuo, RV.120

B. Labadie (cnd), Les Violons du Roy *(rec Quebec, Canada, June 1998)* ("Concerti for Strings") † Con Strs, RV.114; Con Strs, RV.151; Con Strs, RV.157; Cons Vn(s) Strs, Op. 3/1-12; Sinf Strs in b, RV.169 DOR ▲ 90255 [DDD] (16.97)

Concerto in d for Strings & Continuo, RV.129, "Madrigalesco"

A. Ephrikian (cnd) † Cons Orch; Cons Vn Strs, Op. 12/1-6 HMA ▲ 1901012 [ADD] (9.97)

Purcell Quartet ("Vivaldi in furore") † Con Strs, RV.130; Cons Vn Strs, Op. 12/1-6; Laudate pueri Dominum, RV.601; Sinf Strs in b, RV.169 CHOC (Chaconne) ▲ 613 (16.97)

Concerto in E♭ for Strings & Continuo, RV.130, "Al Santo Sepolcro II"

Purcell Quartet ("Vivaldi in furore") † Con Strs, RV.129; Cons Vn Strs, Op. 12/1-6; Laudate pueri Dominum, RV.601; Sinf Strs in b, RV.169 CHOC (Chaconne) ▲ 613 (16.97)

Concerto in f for Strings & Continuo, RV.143

Vienna Flautists *(rec Slovak Radio Concert Hall Bratislava, Slovak Republic, June 2-3, 1994)* ("Concertos") † Con Strs, RV.114; Con Strs, RV.117; Con Strs, RV.151; Con Strs, RV.159; Con 3 Vns, RV.551; Cons Vn(s) Strs, Op. 3/1-12; Sinf; Sinf Strs in b, RV.169 DI ▲ 920230 [DDD] (5.97)

Concerto in G for Strings & Continuo, RV.151, "Alla rustica"

N. Jenkins (cnd), Clarion Music Society ("Four Seasons & Other Great Concertos") † Con Fl; Con Flautino, RV.443; Con Mand, RV.425; Con Ob; Con Tpts, RV.537; Con Vc; Cons Diverse Instrs; Cons Vn Strs, Op. 8/1-4; Cons Vn(s) Strs, Op. 3/1-12 SNYC (Essential Classics Take 2) 2-▲ 63284 (14.97)

La Pièta *(rec Quebec, Canada, Oct 1997)* ("Per Archi") † Con Strs, RV.156; Con Vn; Cons Strs (misc); Cons Vn(s) Strs, Op. 3/1-12; Sinf/Con Strs, RV.146; Sons Vns Vl, Op. 1/1-12 FL ▲ 23128 [DDD] (16.97)

B. Labadie (cnd), Les Violons du Roy *(rec Quebec, Canada, June 1998)* ("Concerti for Strings") † Con Strs, RV.114; Con Strs, RV.120; Con Strs, RV.157; Cons Vn(s) Strs, Op. 3/1-12; Sinf Strs in b, RV.169 DOR ▲ 90255 [DDD] (16.97)

T. Pinnock (cnd), English CO † Con Bn; Con Mands, RV.532; Con Vn Ob, RV.548; Con Vns Rcrs Mans, RV.558; Cons Fl, Op. 10/1-6; Cons Vn(s) Strs, Op. 3/1-12 PARC (3D Baroque) ▲ 31710 [DDD] (9.97)

C. Straka (cnd), Zeljko Musica † Cons Vn(s) Strs, Op. 3/1-12; W. A. Mozart:Divert 7 Hns, K.205; C. Stamitz:Qts concertantes, Op. 15 BER ▲ 9349 (10.97)

Vienna Flautists *(rec June 2-3, 1994)* ("Concertos") † Con Strs, RV.114; Con Strs, RV.117; Con Strs, RV.143; Con Strs, RV.159; Con 3 Vns, RV.551; Cons Vn(s) Strs, Op. 3/1-12; Sinf; Sinf Strs in b, RV.169 DI ▲ 920230 [DDD] (5.97)

Concerto in g for Strings & Continuo, RV.156

La Pièta *(rec Quebec, Canada, Oct 1997)* ("Per Archi") † Con Strs, RV.151; Con Vn; Cons Strs (misc); Cons Vn(s) Strs, Op. 3/1-12; Sinf/Con Strs, RV.146; Sons Vns Vl, Op. 1/1-12 FL ▲ 23128 [DDD] (16.97)

Concerto in g for Strings & Continuo, RV.157

B. Labadie (cnd), Les Violons du Roy *(rec Quebec, Canada, June 1998)* ("Concerti for Strings") † Con Strs, RV.114; Con Strs, RV.120; Con Strs, RV.151; Cons Vn(s) Strs, Op. 3/1-12; Sinf Strs in b, RV.169 DOR ▲ 90255 [DDD] (16.97)

Concerto in A for Strings & Continuo, RV.158, "Concerto ripieno"

Y. Turovsky (vc), Y. Turovsky (cnd), Montreal Musici—Largo ("Tranquillity") † Con Rcr, RV.444; Con Vcs, RV.531; Cons Fl, Op. 10/1-6; Arcus:Vars on Simple Gifts; J. Christian Bach:Con in c; Boccherini:Con Vc, G.482; D. Shostakovich:Con 2 Pno, Op. 102; I. Stravinsky:Con Str Orch; Wassenaer:Concerti Armonici CHN ▲ 8573 [DDD] (16.97)

Concerto in A for Strings & Continuo, RV.159

Vienna Flautists *(rec June 2-3, 1994)* ("Concertos") † Con Strs, RV.114; Con Strs, RV.117; Con Strs, RV.143; Con Strs, RV.151; Con 3 Vns, RV.551; Cons Vn(s) Strs, Op. 3/1-12; Sinf; Sinf Strs in b, RV.169 DI ▲ 920230 [DDD] (5.97)

Concerto in B♭ for Strings & Continuo, RV.166

T. Pinnock (cnd), English Concert ("7 Concerti for Woodwind & Strings") † Con Flautino, RV.444; Con Ob; Cons Diverse Instrs PARC ▲ 45839 [DDD] (16.97)

Concertos for Trumpet & Orchestra

M. André (tpt), H. von Karajan (cnd), Berlin PO—Con Tpt in A♭ *(rec Berlin, Germany, May 28-29, 1974)* † J. N. Hummel:Con Tpt in E♭, S.49; L. Mozart:Con Tpt; Telemann:Qnt Tpt EMIC (Great Recordings of the Century) ▲ 66961 [ADD] (11.97)

Concerto in C for 2 Trumpets, Strings & Continuo, RV.537

E. Duvier (cnd), Camerata Romana † Con Fls, RV.533 PC ▲ 267039 [DDD] (2.97)

T. Freas (tpt), J. Hamlin (tpt), V. Radu (cnd), Ama Deus Ensemble *(rec Wayne, PA, Fall 1996)* † Gloria; Magnificat, RV.611 NPT ▲ 85617 [DDD] (16.97)

M. Gould (tpt), E. Carrol (tpt), R. Kapp (cnd), Philharmonia Virtuosi ("Four Seasons & Other Great Concertos") † Con Fl; Con Flautino, RV.443; Con Mand, RV.425; Con Ob; Con Strs, RV.151; Con Vc; Cons Diverse Instrs; Cons Vn Strs, Op. 8/1-4; Cons Vn(s) Strs, Op. 3/1-12 SNYC (Essential Classics Take 2) 2-▲ 63284 (14.97)

L. Güttler (tpt), K. Sandau (tpt), M. Pommer (cnd), Leipzig New Bach Collegium Musicum † Con Mand, RV.425; Cons Vn Strs, Op. 8/1-12; Cons Vn Strs, Op. 8/1-4 LALI ▲ 15518 [DDD] (3.97)

D. Hickman (tpt), D. Carlsen (tpt), T. Rolston (cnd) *(rec Aug 1990)* ("Intimate Baroque") † J. S. Bach:Brandenburg Con 2, BWV 1047; Hertel:Con à 6; Telemann:Qnt Tpt SUMM ▲ 118 [DDD] (16.97)

R. Kapp (cnd), Philharmonia Virtuosi, New York—Allegro *(rec NYC, NY)* ("Greatest Hits of 1721") † Con Mand, RV.425; Cons Vn Strs, Op. 8/1-4; J. S. Bach:Cant 147; Cant 208; Suite 2 Fl, BWV 1067; J. Clarke:Prince of Denmark's March; A. Corelli:Con Grosso in g 2 Vns, Vla & Vc, Op. 6/8; G. F. Handel:Water Music, HWV 348-50; A. Marcello:Con Ob Strs in c; J. P. A. Martini:Plaisir d'Amour SNYC ▲ 35821 (9.97)

S. Keavy (tpt), A. Lackner (tpt), M. Haselböck (cnd), Vienna Academy [period instrs] ("Duo Concerti") † Con Fls, RV.533; Con Ob Bn, RV.545; Con Orchs, RV.583; Con Vcs, RV.531; Con Vn Org, RV.542 NOVA ▲ 150074 [DDD] (16.97)

W. Marsalis (tpt), R. Leppard (cnd), English CO † H. I. Biber:Son in A Tpts; M. Haydn:Con Tpt, Hns & Strs; J. Pachelbel:Canon & Gigue; Telemann:Con Tpts SNYC ▲ 42478 [DDD] (16.97) ▮ 42478 [DDD] (10.98)

G. Schwarz (tpt), G. Schwarz (cnd), 92nd St. Y Chamber SO † J. E. Altenburg:Con Tpts; H. I. Biber:Son Tpts; Telemann:Qnt Tpt; Torelli:Sons à 5 Tpts DLS ▲ 3002 [DDD] (14.97)

J. Thompson (tpt), R. Early (tpt), Y. Turovsky (cnd), Montreal Musici † Con Vn Org, RV.542; Con Vns Vcs, RV.575; Cons Vn(s) Strs, Op. 3/1-12 CHN ▲ 8651 [DDD] (16.97)

G. Touvron (tpt), B. Zacharie (tpt) *(rec Jan 1997)* ("Centenary of the Vichy Municipal Wind Band") † A. Arutiunian:Con Tpt; J. B. Chance:Vars on a Korean Theme; J. Offenbach:Orphée aux enfers (ov); A. Reed:Hymn Vars LIDI ▲ 301049 [DDD] (16.97)

C. Warren-Green (cnd), London CO *(rec 1988-89)* † Con Vc; Con 3 Vns, RV.551; Cons Diverse Instrs; Cons Vn Strs, Op. 8/1-4; Cons Vn(s) Strs, Op. 3/1-12 VCL 2-▲ 61466 [DDD] (11.97)

H. Wobisch (tpt), A. Holler (tpt), A. Heiller (hpd), A. Janigro (cnd), Zagreb Solisti *(rec Baumgartner Hall Vienna, May 1961)* † Con Mands, RV.532; Cons Vn Strs, Op. 8/1-4 VC ▲ 2536 [ADD] (13.97)

Concerto in F for Viola d'amore, 2 Horns, 2 Oboes, Bassoon & Continuo, RV.97

J. Krcek (cnd), Chamber Orchestra † Con Fl Vn Bn, RV.100; Con Lt Vns, RV.93; Con Rcr Vn Bn, RV.92; Con Rcr, RV.108; Trio Son Fl & Vn, RV.84 GZCL ▲ 246 (6.97)

VIVALDI, ANTONIO (cont.)

Concerto in d for Viola d'amore, Lute (or Guitar) & Strings, RV.540

P. Angerer (va), K. Scheit (gtr), W. Boettcher (cnd) *(rec Baumgartner Kasino Vienna, Austria, Jan 12-13 & 18, June 23, 1961)* ("The Virtuoso Guitar, Vol. 2") † Con Lt Vns, RV.93; F. Carulli:Con Gtr; J. Dowland:Galliards; Torelli:Con Vn Gtr VC ▲ 1020 [ADD] (13.97)

G. Antonini (cnd) † Con Lt Vns, RV.93; Con Mand, RV.425; Con Mands, RV.532; Con Vns Rcrs Mans, RV.558; Trio Son Vn Lt, RV.82; Trio Son Vn Lt, RV.85 TELC ▲ 91182 (16.97)

L. Bársony (va), D. Benkö (lt), J. Rolla (cnd), Franz Liszt CO † Con Lt Vns, RV.93; Trio Son Vn Lt, RV.82; Trio Son Vn Lt, RV.85 HUN ▲ 11978

M. Frasca-Colombier (vn), N. Yepes (gtr), P. Kuentz (cnd), Paul Kuentz CO † Con Lt Vns, RV.93; Con Mand, RV.425; Con Mands, RV.532 DEUT (Resonance) ▲ 29528 [ADD] (7.97)

L. Güttler (cnd) † Con Ob; Con Vn; Con Vns Rcrs Mans, RV.558; Cons Diverse Instrs; Sinf BER ▲ 1082 [DDD] (16.97)

M. Huggett (vn), J. Lindberg (lt), Drottningholm Baroque Ensemble † Con Lt Vns, RV.93; Trio Son Vn Lt, RV.82; Trio Son Vn Lt, RV.85 BIS ▲ 290 [DDD] (17.97)

M. Kraemer (va d'amore/vn), R. Lislevand (gtr/lt), G. Morini (positive org) † Con Lt Vns, RV.93; Trio Son Vn Lt, RV.82; Trio Son Vn Lt, RV.85 ASTR ▲ 128587 (12.97)

L. Malý (va), L. Brabec (gtr), O. Vlček (cnd), Prague CO † Con Lt Vns, RV.93; Con Mand, RV.425; Con Mands, RV.532 SUR ▲ 104126 [DDD]

A. Manze (cnd), Academy of Ancient Music ("Concert for the Prince of Poland") † Con Vn; Con Vns Rcrs Mans, RV.558; Cons Vn Strs, Op. 8/1-12; Sinf HAM ▲ 907230 (18.97)

R. Porroni (gtr), Ensemble Duomo ("Una Chitarra per Vivaldi") † Con Lt Vns, RV.93; Pastor fido, Op. 13/1-6; Trio Son Vn Lt, RV.82; Trio Son Vn Lt, RV.85 STRV ▲ 43 (16.97)

L. Schulman (va), L. Schulman (vl), P. Press (gtr), P. Press (gtr), R. Kapp (cnd) ("The Miraculous Mandolin: Concertos & Sonatas for Mandolin & Guitar") † Con Lt Vns, RV.93; Con Mand, RV.425; Con Mands, RV.532; Trio Son Vn Lt, RV.82; Trio Son Vn Lt, RV.85 ESSY ▲ 1004 [DDD] (16.97)

Concertos for Violin & Orchestra (miscellaneous)

S. Accardo (vn) † Cons Vn Strs, Op. 8/1-4 RCAV (Silver Seal) ▲ 60542 [ADD] (6.97)

R. Baraldi (vn), A. Martini (cnd), Accademia I Filarmonici—Con Vn, RV.184; Con Vn, RV.241; Con Vn, RV.267; Con Vn, RV.292; Con Vn, RV.329; Con Vn, RV.363 *(rec Verona Italy, June 1995)* ("Dresden Concerti, Vol. 2") NXIN 2-▲ 553793 [DDD] (5.97)

P. Peabody (vn), R. Kapp (cnd) —Con Vn, RV.346; Con Vn, RV.199 *(rec May 2, 1991)* ("Vivaldi's Favorites, Vol. 2") † Con Vn Strs Bc, Op. 9/1-12; Cons Vn Strs, Op. 8/1-12; Cons Vn(s) Strs, Op. 3/1-12 ESSY ▲ 1024 [DDD] (16.97)

C. Rossi (vn), A. Martini (cnd), Accademia I Filarmonici—Con Vn, RV.240; Con Vn, RV.388; Con in E♭ Vn; Con Vn, RV.344; Con Vn, RV.224; Con Vn, RV.219; Con Vn, RV.213 NXIN (The Vivaldi Collection) ▲ 8554310 [DDD] (5.97)

Concerto in F for Violin, Cello, Strings & Continuo, RV.544, "Il Proteo ossia Il mondo al rovescio"

C. Coin (vc), Il Giardino Armonico ("Double & Triple Concertos") † Con Vcs, RV.531; Con Vn Vcs, RV.561; Con 3 Vns, RV.551; Cons Diverse Instrs TELC (Das alte Werk) ▲ 94552 (16.97)

O. Harnoy (vc), P. Robinson (cnd), Toronto CO ("Vivaldi Concertos, Vol. 3") † Cons Cello RCAV (Red Seal) ▲ 61578 (16.97)

Concerto in B♭ for Violin, Cello, Strings & Continuo, RV.547

J. Lamon (cnd), Tafelmusik † Con Vns Vcs, RV.575 SNYC (Vivarte) ▲ 48044 (16.97)

I. Oistrakh (vn), O. Harnoy (vc), P. Robinson (cnd), Toronto CO *(rec Toronto, Feb 1992)* ("Cello Concertos, Vol. 4") RCAV (Red Seal) ▲ 68228 [DDD] (16.97)

Concerto in C for Violin, 2 Cellos, Strings & Continuo, RV.561

C. Coin (vc), Il Giardino Armonico ("Double & Triple Concertos") † Con Vcs, RV.531; Con Vn Vc, RV.544; Con 3 Vns, RV.551; Cons Diverse Instrs TELC (Das alte Werk) ▲ 94552 (16.97)

Concerto in B♭ for Violin, Oboe & Orchestra, RV.548

T. Pinnock (cnd), English CO † Con Bn; Con Mands, RV.532; Con Strs, RV.151; Con Vns Rcrs Mans, RV.558; Cons Fl, Op. 10/1-6; Cons Vn(s) Strs, Op. 3/1-12 PARC (3D Baroque) ▲ 31710 [DDD] (9.97)

Concerto in B♭ for Violin, Oboe, Salmo, 3 Violas, Strings & Continuo, RV.579, "Funebre"

R. King (cnd), King's Consort ("Concerti for Diverse Instruments") † Con Vn Obs Hns, RV.562; Cons Diverse Instrs HYP ▲ 67073 (18.97)

Concerto in F for Violin, 2 Oboes, 2 Horns, Cello, Bassoon, Strings & Continuo, RV.571

A. Lizzio (cnd), San Marco Musici † Con Mand, RV.425; Con Vn; Con 2 Vns, RV.524 PC ▲ 265005 [DDD] (2.97)

Concerto in D for Violin, 2 Oboes, 2 Horns, Strings & Continuo, RV.562

R. King (cnd), King's Consort ("Concerti for Diverse Instruments") † Con Vn Ob Vas, RV.579; Cons Diverse Instrs HYP ▲ 67073 (18.97)

Concerto in g for Violin, 2 Oboes, 2 Recorders, Bassoon, Strings & Continuo, RV.577

N. McGegan (cnd), Philharmonia Baroque Orch *(rec Oakland, United States of America, Oct 1996)* ("Vivaldi for Diverse Instruments") † Con Obs, RV.535; Con Vn; Cons Diverse Instrs REF ▲ 77 (16.97)

Concerto for Violin, 2 Oboes (or 2 Trumpets), Strings & Continuo, RV.563

R. Alessandrini (cnd) † Gloria; Magnificat, RV.611 OPUS ▲ 30195 (18.97)

I. Brown (vn), M. Laird (tpt), W. Houghton (tpt), N. Marriner (cnd), Academy of St. Martin in the Fields † Con Fls, RV.533; Con Mands, RV.532; Con Ob Bn, RV.545 PPHI ▲ 12892 [DDD] (16.97)

Concerto in C for Violin, Organ (or Cello), Oboe, Strings & Continuo, RV.554

S. Standage (vn), M. Comberti (vn), A. Robson (ob), S. Standage (cnd), Collegium Musicum 90 † Con Vcs, RV.531 CHN (Chaconne) ▲ 528 [DDD] (16.97)

Concerto in d for Violin, Organ, Strings & Continuo, RV.541

J. Rampal (fl) *(rec May 10-13, 1992)* † Con Fl; Cons Fl (misc); Cons Vn Strs, Op. 8/1-4 SNYC ▲ 53105 [DDD] (16.97) COL △ 53105 [DDD]

Concerto in F for Violin, Organ, Strings & Continuo, RV.542

V. Hudeček (vn), L. Brabec (gtr), J. Stivín (rcr), G. Delogu (cnd), Janáček CO, G. Delogu (cnd), Prague CO ("Brabec, Stivín & Hudeček Play Vivaldi") † Con Rcr, RV.108; Con Vns Rcrs Mans, RV.558; Cons Diverse Instrs; Cons Vn(s) Strs, Op. 3/1-12 SUR ▲ 3023 (16.97)

I. Kertész (vn), M. Haselböck (org), M. Haselböck (cnd), Vienna Academy [period instrs] ("Duo Concerti") † Con Fls, RV.533; Con Ob Bn, RV.545; Con Orchs, RV.583; Con Tpts, RV.537; Con Vcs, RV.531 NOVA ▲ 150074 [DDD] (16.97)

E. Turovsky (vn), E. Skerjanc (vn), A. Aubut (vc), Y. Turovsky (cnd), Montreal Musici † Con Tpts, RV.537; Con Vns Vcs, RV.575; Cons Vn(s) Strs, Op. 3/1-12 CHN ▲ 8651 [DDD] (16.97)

Concertos for Violin(s), Strings & Continuo, Op. 3/1-12 (RV.549, 578, 310, 550, 519, 356, 567, 522, 230, 580, 565, 265), "L'estro armonico" (1712)

W. Boskovsky (vn), J. Tomasow (vn), P. Matheis (vn), W. Hintermeyer (vn), R. Harand (vc), H. von Nordberg (hpd), M. Rossi (cnd), Vienna State Opera CO *(rec Brahmsaal Vienna, June 1957)* VC 2-▲ 66 [AAD] (26.97)

E. Casazza (vn), F. Biondi (vn), I. Longo (vn), R. Negri (vn), M. Naddeo (vc), F. Biondi (cnd), Europa Galante *(rec Puianello, Reggio Emilio, Italy, 1997-98)* VCL 2-▲ 45315 [DDD] (16.97)

L. Chan (vn), P. Cochand (vn), P. Cochand (cnd) *(rec Oct 19-21, 1992)* † J. Pachelbel:Canon & Gigue; F. X. Richter:Grandes simphonies; Telemann:Don Quichotte (suite) GALL ▲ 723

F. Cipriani (vn), E. Velardi (cnd), Alessandro Stradella Consort BONG 2-▲ 5597 (32.97)

V. Gluz (vn), I. Romanyuk (vn), A. Titov (cnd), St. Petersburg Classical Music Studio Orch—No. 8 in a; No. 11 in d † Cons Vn Strs, Op. 8/1-4 SNYC ▲ 57243 [DDD] (4.97)

H. Haenchen (cnd), C.P.E. Bach CO, N. Jenkins (cnd), Clarion Music Society—No. 9 in D; No. 11 in d ("Four Seasons & Other Great Concertos") † Con Fl; Con Flautino, RV.443; Con Mand, RV.425; Con Ob; Con Strs, RV.151; Con Tpts, RV.537; Con Vc; Cons Diverse Instrs; Cons Vn Strs, Op. 8/1-4 SNYC (Essential Classics Take 2) 2-▲ 63284 (14.97)

C. Hogwood (cnd), Academy of Ancient Music Orch † Cons Fl, Op. 10/1-6 PLON (Double Decker) 2-▲ 458078 (17.97)

V. Hudeček (vn), L. Brabec (gtr), J. Stivín (rcr), G. Delogu (cnd), Janáček CO, G. Delogu (cnd), Prague CO—No. 11 in d ("Brabec, Stivín & Hudeček Play Vivaldi") † Con Rcr, RV.108; Con Vn Org, RV.542; Con Vns Rcrs Mans, RV.558; Cons Diverse Instrs SUR ▲ 3023 (16.97)

Italian Solisti DNN 2-▲ 72719 [DDD] (33.97)

La Pièta—No. 1 in D; No. 11 in d *(rec Quebec, Canada, Oct 1997)* ("Per Archi") † Con Strs, RV.151; Con Strs, RV.156; Con Vn; Cons Strs (misc); Sinf/Con Strs, RV.146; Sons Vns Vl, Op. 1/1-12 FL ▲ 23128 [DDD] (16.97)

J. Lamon (cnd), Tafelmusik—No. 11 in d; No. 11 in d; No. 11 in d [Allegro-Adagio e spicato-Allegro only] *(rec Toronto, Canada)* ("Italian Concerti Grossi") † Sons Vns Vl, Op. 1/1-12; Geminiani:Concerti grossi (12), Op. 6 [arr of Op. 5]; Locatelli:Cons (6) for 4 Vns 2 Vas, Op. 7; A. Scarlatti:Cons (6) in 7 Parts for 2 Vns; Torelli:Concerti grossi (12), Op. 8 SMS ▲ 5099 [DDD] (16.97)

J. Laredo (vn), J. Laredo (cnd), Scottish CO—No. 8 in a; No. 11 in d; No. 10 in b † Con 3 Vns, RV.551 ICC ▲ 6702352 (9.97)

S. Lautenbacher (vn), J. Faerber (cnd), Württemberg CO—No. 10 in b; No. 10 in b ("The Stories of Vivaldi & Corelli in Words & Music") † Con Fl; Con Vn Strs Bc, Op. 9/1-12; Cons Vn Strs, Op. 8/1-4; Cons Vn, Op. 4/1-12; Life & Music of Vivaldi; A. Corelli:Life & Music of Corelli MMD ▲ 8510 [ADD] (3.97) ▮ 8510 [ADD] (2.98)

VIVALDI, ANTONIO (cont.)
Concertos for Violin(s), Strings & Continuo, Op. 3/1-12 (RV.549, 578, 310, 550, 519, 356, 567, 522, 230, 580, 565, 265), "L'estro armonico" (1712) (cont.)
N. Marriner (cnd), Academy of St. Martin in the Fields PLON (Double Decker) 2-▲ 43476 (17.97)
Y. Menuhin (vn), A. Lysy (vn), M. Lee (vn), H. Kun (vn), E. Vassallo (vc), A. Lysy (cnd), Camerata Lysy Gstaad—No. 11 in d; No. 1 in D ("Best-Loved Vivaldi") † Con Vcs, RV.531; Music of Vivaldi EMCD (Seraphim) 4-▲ 69545 [DDD] (14.97)
R. Michelucci (vn) ("L'Estro Armonico, Op. 3: complete") PPHI (Duo) 2-▲ 46169 (17.97)
A. Nanut (cnd), Zagreb Solisti—No. 8 in a; No. 10 in b ("Famous Concertos") † Cons Orch; Sinf PC ▲ 265075 [DDD] (2.97)
Orpheus CO—No. 10 in b † Albinoni:Adagio; J. S. Bach:Jesu, bleibet meine Freude; Suite 3 Orch, BWV 1068; A. Corelli:Con grosso, Op. 6/8; G. F. Handel:Solomon (arrival of the queen of Sheba); J. Pachelbel:Canon & Gigue; H. Purcell:Chacony Strs, Z.730 DEUT ▲ 29390 [DDD] (11.97)
F. Paul (vn), E. Klein (cnd), Hamburg Soloists—No. 11 in d *(rec Hamburg-Rahlstedt, Germany, Apr 1995)* ("Four Seasons & Concerto Grosso") † Cons Vn Strs, Op. 8/1-4 ARNO ▲ 27781 [DDD] (4.97)
P. Peabody (vn), R. Kapp (cnd) —No. 11 in d *(rec May 2, 1991)* ("Vivaldi's Favorites, Vol. 2") † Con Vn Strs Bc, Op. 9/1-12; Cons Vn (misc); Cons Vn Strs, Op. 8/1-12 ESSY ▲ 1024 [DDD] (16.97)
T. Pinnock (cnd), English CO—No. 11 in d; No. 1 in D † Con Bn; Con Mands, RV.532; Con Strs, RV.151; Con Vn Ob, RV.548; Con Vns Rcrs Mans, RV.558; Cons Fl, Op. 10/1-6 PARC (3D Baroque) ▲ 31710 [DDD] (9.97)
M. Sandler (ob), M. Boenau (bn), A. Lawrence-King (hpd), A. Lawrence-King (cnd), Harp Consort—No. 8 in a *(rec June 1995)* † J. S. Bach:Aria variata alla maniera italiana, BWV 989; T. Carolan:Carolan's Con; G. F. Handel:Cons (16) Org DEHA ▲ 77366 [DDD] (16.97)
S. Standage (vn), T. Pinnock (cnd), English Concert PARC 2-▲ 23094 [DDD] (32.97)
L. Stokowski (cnd), Leopold Stokowski SO—No. 11 in d ("The Stokowski Collection, Vol. 1") † J. S. Bach:Cant 147; Cant 208; A. Corelli:Con grosso, Op. 6/8; W. A. Mozart:Serenade VC ▲ 8009 [ADD] (13.97)
C. Straka (cnd), Zeljko Musica—No. 11 in d; No. 8 in a † Con Strs, RV.151; W. A. Mozart:Divert 7 Hns, K.205; C. Stamitz:Qts concertantes, Op. 15 BER ▲ 9349 (10.97)
A. Titov (cnd), St. Petersburg New Classical Orch—No. 1 in D; No. 9 in D; No. 5 in A; No. 3 in G ("Vivaldi: A Violin Festival") † Cons Vns SNYC ▲ 66725 [DDD] (4.97)
A. Toscanini (cnd), NBC SO—No. 11 in d ("Christmas 1937: Toscanini's 1st NBC Concert") † J. Brahms:Sym 1; W. A. Mozart:Sym 40, K.550 RY (The Radio Years) ▲ 13 (16.97)
N. Trotier (vn), J. Triquet (vn), B. Labadie (cnd), Les Violons du Roy—No. 8 in a; No. 9 in D; No. 3 in G; No. 11 in d *(rec Quebec, Canada, June 1998)* ("Concerti for Strings") † Con Strs, RV.114; Con Strs, RV.120; Con Strs, RV.151; Con Strs, RV.157; Sinf Strs in b, RV.169 DOR ▲ 90255 [DDD] (16.97)
E. Turovsky (vn), E. Skerjanc (vn), A. Aubut (vc), Y. Turovsky (cnd), Montreal Musici—No. 11 in d † Con Tpts, RV.537; Con Vn Org, RV.542; Con Vns Vcs, RV.575 CHN ▲ 8651 [DDD] (16.97)
Vienna Flautists—No. 1 in D; No. 4 in e *(rec Slovak Radio Concert Hall Bratislava, Slovak Republic, June 2-3, 1994)* ("Concertos") † Con Strs, RV.114; Con Strs, RV.117; Con Strs, RV.143; Con Strs, RV.151; Con Strs, RV.159; Con 3 Vns, RV.551; Sinf; Sinf Strs in b, RV.169 DI ▲ 920230 [DDD] (5.97)
B. Warchal (cnd), Slovak CO—No. 11 in d ("Classic Hits: Vivaldi") † Con Fl Gtr; Con Gtr; Con Vc; Con 2 Vns, RV.514; Cons Fl, Op. 10/1-6 PUBM (Majestic) ▲ 1041 [DDD] (4.97)
C. Warren-Green (vn), C. Warren-Green (cnd), London CO—No. 8 in a; No. 10 in b *(rec 1988-89)* † Con Tpts, RV.537; Con Vc; Con 3 Vns, RV.551; Cons Diverse Instrs; Cons Vn Strs, Op. 8/1-4 VCL 2-▲ 61466 [DDD] (11.97)
P. Zukerman (vn), K. Sillito (vn), P. Zukerman (cnd), English CO—No. 8 in a; No. 11 in d *(rec 1971)* † J. S. Bach:Cons Vn (comp) SNYC (Essential Classics) ▲ 48273 [ADD] (7.97) ▮ 48273 [ADD] (3.98)

Concertos for Violin, Strings & Continuo, Op. 4/1-12 (RV.383a, 279, 301, 357, 347, 316a, 185, 249, 284, 196, 204, 298), "La stravaganza" (ca 1712-13)
E. Bellotti (org) [6 cons] DCTA ▲ 18
S. Lautenbacher (vn), J. Faerber (cnd), Württemberg CO—No. 01 in B♭; No. 12 in G ("The Stories of Vivaldi & Corelli in Words & Music") † Con Fl; Con Vn Strs Bc, Op. 9/1-12; Cons Vn Strs, Op. 8/1-4; Cons Vn(s) Strs, Op. 3/1-12; Life & Music of Vivaldi; A. Corelli:Life & Music of Corelli MMD ▲ 8510 [ADD] (3.97) ▮ 8510 [ADD] (2.98)
A. Martini (vn), A. Martini (cnd), I Filarmonici CO—No. 07 in C; No. 08 in d; No. 09 in F; No. 10 in c; No. 07 in C; No. 12 in G TACT ▲ 672227 [DDD] (16.97)
A. Martini (vn), A. Martini (cnd), I Filarmonici CO—No. 01 in B♭; No. 02 in e; No. 03 in G; No. 04 in a; No. 05 in A; No. 06 in g TACT ▲ 672226 [DDD] (16.97)
P. Wispelwey (vc), Florilegium—No. 01 in B♭ *(rec Highgate London, England, Aug 1996)* ("Vivaldi Concerti") † Con Vc; Cons Cello CCL ▲ 10097 [DDD] (18.97)
P. Zukerman (vn), P. Zukerman (cnd), English CO—No. 11 in D † Con Vn; Cons Vn Strs, Op. 8/1-12 RCAV (Red Seal) ▲ 68433 (16.97)

Concertos (6) for Violin, Strings & Continuo, Op. 6/1-6 (RV.324, 259, 318, 216, 280, 239) (1716-17)
Italian Solisti *(rec Aug 19-22, 1995)* DNN ▲ 18024 [DDD] (16.97)
A. Martini (cnd), I Filarmonici TACT ▲ 672229 (16.97)

Concertos (12) for Violin, Strings & Continuo [including "The Four Seasons", Nos. 1-4], Op. 8/1-12 (RV.269, 315, 293, 297, 253, 180, 242, 332, 236, 362, 210, 178), "Il cimento dell'armonia e dell'inventione" (ca 1725)
E. Casazza (vn)—No. 5 in E♭, "La tempesta di mare"; No. 6 in C, "Il piacere" *(rec Treviso, Italy, Mar 1996)* † Cons Vn Strs, Op. 8/1-4 AART ▲ 47369 [DDD] (10.97)
C. Chiarappa (cnd), Accademia Bizantina ("Il Cimento Dell'Armonia e Dell'Inventione, Volumes 1 & 2") DNN ▲ 75352 [DDD] (16.97)
A. Harnoncourt (vn), N. Harnoncourt (cnd), Vienna Concentus Musicus—No. 5 in E♭, "La tempesta di mare"; No. 6 in C, "Il piacere" † Cons Vn Strs, Op. 8/1-4 TELC ▲ 91851 (9.97)
I Filarmonici—No. 5 in E♭, "La tempesta di mare"; No. 6 in C, "Il piacere" *(rec Verona, Italy, Nov 1995)* † Cons Vn Strs, Op. 8/1-4 TACT ▲ 672232 [DDD] (16.97)
I Filarmonici—No. 7 in d; No. 8 in g; No. 9 in d, (RV.454 for Ob); No. 10 in B♭, "La caccia"; No. 11 in D; No. 5 in E♭, "La tempesta di mare"; No. 6 in C, "Il piacere" *(rec Verona, Italy, Nov 1994)* TACT ▲ 672233 [DDD]
Interpreti Veneziani RIVO ▲ 9815
Italian Solisti—No. 5 in E♭, "La tempesta di mare"; No. 6 in C, "Il piacere" † Cons Vn Strs, Op. 8/1-4 DNN ▲ 1471 [DDD] (16.97)
A. Manze (cnd), Academy of Ancient Music—No. 5 in E♭, "La tempesta di mare"; No. 6 in C, "Il piacere" ("Concert for the Prince of Poland") † Con Va Lt, RV.540; Con Vn; Con Vns Rcrs Mans, RV.558; Sinf HAM ▲ 907230 (18.97)
L. Mayer (mand), B. Glaetzner (ob), Güttler (tpt), K. Sandau (tpt), M. Pommer (cnd), Leipzig New Bach Collegium Musicum, M. Pommer (cnd), Budapest Strings—No. 9 in d, (RV.454 for Ob) † Con Mand, RV.425; Con Tpts, RV.537; Cons Vn Strs, Op. 8/1-4 LALI ▲ 15518 [DDD] (3.97)
Y. Menuhin (vn), J. Maksymiuk (cnd), Polish CO † Cons Vn Strs, Op. 8/1-4 RYLC ▲ 6461
Y. Menuhin (vn), J. Maksymiuk (cnd), Polish CO—No. 5 in E♭, "La tempesta di mare"; No. 11 in D ("Unforgettable Vivaldi") † Cons Vn Strs, Op. 8/1-4 CFP ▲ 68820 (11.97)
P. Peabody (vn), R. Kapp (cnd) —No. 11 in D *(rec May 2, 1991)* ("Vivaldi's Favorites, Vol. 2") † Con Vn Strs Bc, Op. 9/1-12; Cons Vn (misc); Cons Vn(s) Strs, Op. 3/1-12 ESSY ▲ 1024 [DDD] (16.97)
J. Rolla (cnd), Franz Liszt CO † Donizetti:Don Pasquale HUN 2-▲ 12465 [DDD] (32.97)
R. Thomas (vn), R. Thomas (cnd), Bournemouth Sinfonietta CHN 2-▲ 7124 (26.97)
P. Zukerman (vn), P. Zukerman (cnd), English CO—No. 5 in E♭, "La tempesta di mare"; No. 6 in C, "Il piacere"; No. 9 in d, (RV.454 for Ob); No. 10 in B♭, "La caccia"; No. 11 in D SNYC (Essential Classics) ▲ 53513 (7.97) ▮ 53513 (3.98)
P. Zukerman (vn), P. Zukerman (cnd), English CO—No. 7 in d † Con Vn; Cons Vn, Op. 4/1-12 RCAV (Red Seal) ▲ 68433 (16.97)
artists unknown ("Vivaldi: 12 Concerti, Op. 8") PPHI 2-▲ 38344 (17.97)

Concertos (4) for Violin, Strings & Continuo, Op. 8/1-4 (RV.269, 315, 293, 297), "The Four Seasons"
S. Accardo (vn) RCAV (Victrola) ▲ 7732 [DDD] (6.97)
S. Accardo (vn) † Cons Vn (misc) RCAV (Silver Seal) ▲ 60542 [ADD] (6.97)
Amsterdam Guitar Trio RCAV (Gold Seal) ▲ 61652 (11.97)
L. Artymiw (pno)—No. 3 in F, "Autumn" [Allegro only] ("Daydreams") † Beethoven:Son 1 Pno, Op. 2/1; Son 14 Pno, Op. 27/2; J. Brahms:Chorale Preludes Org, Op. 122; Fants Pno, Op. 116; Pieces (6) Pno, Op. 118; Chopin:Études Pno; J. Field:Nocturnes Pno; Liszt:Études de concert (3), S.144; Hungarian Rhaps, S.244; R. Schumann:Albumblätter, Op. 124 CHN ▲ 6537 [DDD] (12.97)
B. Bánfalvi (vn), K. Botvay (cnd), Budapest Strings † Con Mand, RV.425; Con Tpts, RV.537; Cons Vn Strs, Op. 8/1-12 LALI ▲ 15518 [DDD] (3.97)
F. Biondi (vn) OPUS ▲ 569120 (18.97)
F. Biondi (cnd), Europa Galante OPUS ▲ 912 (7.97)
A. Cappelletti (vn), I. Bolton (cnd), Scottish CO † Con Vn KSCH ▲ 367242 (6.97)
G. Carmignola (vn), Sonatori de la Gioiosa Marca *(rec Treviso Italy, 1993)* ("Le Quattro Stagioni") † Con 3 Vns, RV.551 DVX (Divox Antiqua) ▲ 79404 [DDD] (16.97)

VIVALDI, ANTONIO (cont.)
Concertos (4) for Violin, Strings & Continuo, Op. 8/1-4 (RV.269, 315, 293, 297), "The Four Seasons" (cont.)
D. Carpenter (db), E. Daniels (cl), A. Broadbent (pno), P. Erskine (dr) *(rec Long Beach, CA, Mar 15, 1996)* ("The Five Seasons") SHA ▲ 5017 (17.97)
E. Casazza (vn) *(rec Treviso, Italy, Mar 1996)* † Cons Vn Strs, Op. 8/1-12 AART ▲ 47369 [DDD] (10.97)
C. Chiarappa (vn), Accademia Bizantina † J. S. Bach:Con Vns; Con 1 Vn; Con 2 Vn DNN ▲ 17007 (16.97)
J. Corigliano, Sr. (vn), L. Bernstein (cnd), New York PO SNYC (Bernstein Century) ▲ 63161 (11.97)
C. Ferrarini (fl), L. Fontana (hpd) ("Musica per Flauto e Clavicembalo") † G. F. Handel:Royal Fireworks Music, HWV 351; Water Music, HWV 348-50; J.-J. Rousseau:Printemps du Vivaldi STRV ▲ 33301 [DDD] (16.97)
G. Franzetti (vn), R. Muti (cnd), La Scala Orch Soloists † Con Fl Ob Bn, RV.570; Cons Fl, Op. 10/1-6 CSER ▲ 73298 [DDD] (6.97)
J. Galway (fl), J. Galway (cnd) RCAV (Gold Seal) ▲ 60748 [ADD] (11.97)
J. Garcia (vn) † Con Fl Bn, RV.104; Con Fl Ob Bn, RV.570 ASVQ ▲ 6148 [DDD]
V. Gluz (vn), A. Titov (cnd), St. Petersburg Classical Music Studio Orch † Cons Vn(s) Strs, Op. 3/1-12 SNYC ▲ 57243 [DDD] (4.97)
G. von der Goltz (vn), A. Lawrence-King (cnd), Freiburg Baroque Orch DEHA ▲ 77384 [DDD] (16.97)
Guidantus Ensemble ("L'osservazione musicale") † F. Couperin:Pièces de clavecin (sels) STRV ▲ 80001 [DDD] (12.97)
A. Harnoncourt (vn), N. Harnoncourt (cnd), Vienna Concentus Musicus † Cons Vn Strs, Op. 8/1-12 TELC ▲ 91851 (9.97)
C. Hogwood (cnd), Academy of Ancient Music PLOI ▲ 10126 [DDD] (16.97)
J. Holloway (vn), J. Malgoire (cnd), La Grande Écurie et la Chambre du Roy SNYC (Essential Classics) ▲ 47662 (7.97) ▮ 47662 (3.98)
I Filarmonici *(rec Verona, Italy, Nov 1995)* † Cons Vn Strs, Op. 8/1-12 TACT ▲ 672232 [DDD] (16.97)
Italian Solisti † Cons Vn Strs, Op. 8/1-12 DNN ▲ 1471 [DDD] (16.97)
Italian Solisti ("Seasons") † A. Piazzolla:Cuatro estaciones porteñas DNN ▲ 18036 (16.97)
R. Kapp (cnd), Philharmonia Virtuosi, New York—No. 1 in E, "Spring" [Allegro only] *(rec NYC, NY)* ("Greatest Hits of 1721") † Con Mand, RV.425; Con Tpts, RV.537; J. S. Bach:Cant 147; Cant 208; Suite 2 Fl, BWV 1067; J. Clarke:Prince of Denmark's March; A. Corelli:Con Grosso in g 2 Vns, Vla & Vc, Op. 6/8; G. F. Handel:Water Music, HWV 348-50; A. Marcello:Con Ob Strs in c; J. P. A. Martini:Plaisir d'Amour SNYC ▲ 35821 (9.97)
N. Kennedy (vn), N. Kennedy (cnd), English CO *(rec 1986-89)* EMIC ▲ 56253 [DDD] (16.97)
I. Kipnis (hpd), I. Kipnis (cnd) [period instrs] † Con Hpd, RV.780; Cons Fl, Op. 10/1-6 CHSK ▲ 78 [DDD] (16.97)
D. Kovács (vn), L. Gardelli (cnd), Budapest SO *(rec 1962)* CLDI ▲ 4009 [ADD] (10.97)
M. Kransberg-Talvi (vn), A. Francis (cnd), Northwest CO Seattle † Sinf AMBA ▲ 1010 [DDD]
G. Kremer (vn), C. Abbado (cnd), London SO DEUT (Galleria) ▲ 31172 [ADD] (9.97)
S. Kuijken (vn), F. Brüggen (rcr) ("Vivaldi's Greatest Hits") † Music of Vivaldi PRMX ▲ 816
J. Lamon (vn), J. Lamon (cnd), Tafelmusik † Sinf Strs in b, RV.169 SNYC (Vivarte) ▲ 48251 [DDD] (16.97)
J. Lamon (cnd), Tafelmusik—No. 1 in E, "Spring" [Allegro only] ("Build Your Baby's Brain") † J. S. Bach:Air on the G String; Cant 147; Cant 208; Beethoven:Bagatelle Pno in a, WoO 59; G. F. Handel:Solomon (sels); W. A. Mozart:Kleine Nachtmusik, K.525; Son 11 Pno, K.331; J. Pachelbel:Canon & Gigue; F. Schubert:Qnt Pno, D.667 SNYC ▲ 60815 [DDD] (9.97) ▮ 60815 [DDD] (5.98)
S. Lautenbacher (vn), J. Faerber (cnd), Württemberg CO ("The Stories of Vivaldi & Corelli in Words & Music") † Con Fl; Con Vn Strs Bc, Op. 9/1-12; Cons Vn(s) Strs, Op. 3/1-12; Cons Vn, Op. 4/1-12; Life & Music of Vivaldi; A. Corelli:Life & Music of Corelli MMD ▲ 8510 [ADD] (3.97) ▮ 8510 [ADD] (2.98)
C. Lindberg (trbn), O. Kamu (cnd), New Stockholm CO—No. 4 in f, "Winter" *(rec Sweden, Sep 23-26 & Nov 27, 1987)* ("The Winter Trombone") † L.-E. Larsson:Concertino Trb, Op. 45/7; D. Milhaud:Concertino d'hiver, Op. 327; R. Pöntinen:Blue Winter; Telemann:Con Trb BIS ▲ 348 [DDD] (17.97)
L. Maazel (vn), L. Maazel (cnd), French National Orch SNYC ▲ 39008 [DDD] (16.97)
J. Maksymiuk (cnd), Polish CO ("Unforgettable Vivaldi") † Cons Vn Strs, Op. 8/1-12 CFP ▲ 68820 (11.97)
Y. Menuhin (vn), J. Maksymiuk (cnd), Polish CO † Cons Vn Strs, Op. 8/1-12 RYLC ▲ 6461
A. Moglia (vn), A. Moglia (cnd), Toulouse National CO † Con Lt Vns, RV.93; Con Mand, RV.425 PVY ▲ 730038 (12.97)
A.-S. Mutter (vn), H. von Karajan (cnd), Vienna PO EMIC ▲ 47043 (16.97)
M. J. Newman (cnd), New York Musica Antiqua, Voci Angeli *(rec Presbyterian Church Mt. Kisco NY)* ("Viva Vivaldi!") † Gloria HEL ▲ 1014 (10.97)
T. Nishizaki (vn), S. Gunzenhauser (cnd), Capella Istropolitana NXIN ▲ 550056 [DDD] (5.97)
E. Oliveira (vn), G. Schwarz (cnd), Los Angeles CO DLS ▲ 3007 [DDD] (14.97)
E. Oliveira (vn), G. Schwarz (cnd), Los Angeles CO † G. F. Handel:Water Music, HWV 348-50 DLS 2-▲ 3704 (14.97)
L. Oshavkova (fl), N. Boyadjiev (cnd), Bulgarian Ladies' CO *(rec Sofia, Bulgaria, June 1998)* † G. F. Handel:Concerti grossi, Op. 6 GEGA ▲ 130 [DDD]
F. Paul (vn), E. Klein (cnd), Hamburg Soloists *(rec Hamburg-Rahlstedt, Germany, Apr 1995)* ("Four Seasons & Concerto Grosso") † Cons Vn(s) Strs, Op. 3/1-12 ARNO ▲ 27781 [DDD] (4.97)
P. Peabody (vn), R. Kapp (cnd) ESSY ▲ 1001 [DDD] (16.97)
I. Perlman (vn), Z. Mehta (cnd), Israel PO DEUT ▲ 19214 [DDD] (16.97) ▮ 19214 [DDD] (10.98)
I. Perlman (vn), I. Perlman (cnd), Israel PO EMIC ▲ 47319 [DDD] (16.97)
I. Perlman (vn), I. Perlman (cnd), Israel PO EMIC ▲ 64333 (11.97)
J. Rampal (fl), J. Rampal (cnd), Franz Liszt CO *(rec May 10-13, 1992)* † Con Fl; Con Vn Org, RV.541; Cons Fl (misc) SNYC ▲ 53105 [DDD] (16.97) COL △ 53105 [DDD]
P. Saint-Denis (fl), I. Rechtman (cmpt) *(rec Oct 1992)* ("The New Four Seasons") ORG ▲ 3020 [DDD] (13.97)
N. Salerno-Sonnenberg (vn) EMIC ▲ 49767 [DDD] (16.97)
J. Schroeder (cnd), Concerto Amsterdam HAM ▲ 1905129 (9.97)
M. Schwalbe (vn), H. von Karajan (cnd), Berlin PO † Albinoni:Adagio; A. Corelli:Con grosso, Op. 6/8 DEUT ▲ 15301 [ADD] (16.97)
C. Scimone (cnd) TELC (Ultima) 2-▲ 18968 (16.97)
G. Shaham (vn), Orpheus CO † F. Kreisler:Vn Pieces DEUT ▲ 39933 [DDD] (17.97) ▮ 39933 [DDD] (10.98)
J. Silverstein (vn), S. Ozawa (cnd), Boston SO TEL ▲ 80070 [DDD] (16.97)
S. Standage (vn), T. Pinnock (cnd), English CO CRD ▲ 3325 (17.97)
S. Standage (vn), T. Pinnock (cnd), English Concert PARC ▲ 45 [DDD] (16.97)
I. Stern (vn), I. Stern (cnd), Jerusalem Music Center CO SNYC ▲ 42526 (7.97)
J. Suk (vn), L. Hlaváček (cnd), Prague CO † J. S. Bach:Con Vns SUR ▲ 110281 [AAD]
J. Suk (vn), L. Pešek (cnd), Prague PO *(rec June 1998)* LT ▲ 59 [DDD] (16.97)
Tetra Guitar Quartet † Con Lt Vns, RV.93 ICC ▲ 6600692 (16.97)
J. Tomasow (vn), A. Heiller (hpd), A. Janigro (cnd), Zagreb Solisti *(rec Vienna, June 1957)* † Con Mands, RV.532; Con Tpts, RV.537 VC ▲ 2536 [ADD] (13.97)
Y. Waldman (vn), J. Somary (cnd), Amor Artis Orch † J. S. Bach:Con 1 for 2 Hpds, BWV 1060; A. Corelli:Con grosso, Op. 6/8 ORG ▲ 1013 [DDD] (13.97)
J. Wallez (vn), J. Wallez (cnd) FORL ▲ 16644 [AAD] (16.97)
E. Wallfisch (vn), P. Rapson (hpd), P. Rapson (cnd) † Arias; Incoronazione di Dario (sels) MER ▲ 84195 (16.97)
C. Warren-Green (vn), C. Warren-Green (cnd), London CO *(rec 1988-89)* † Con Tpts, RV.537; Con Vc; Con 3 Vns, RV.551; Cons Diverse Instrs; Cons Vn(s) Strs, Op. 3/1-12 VCL 2-▲ 61466 [DDD] (11.97)
T. Zehetmair (vn), Bern Camerata BER ▲ 1164 (16.97)
I. Ženatý (vn), O. Vlček (cnd), Prague Virtuosi DI ▲ 920219 [DDD] (5.97)
P. Zukerman (fl), P. Zukerman (cnd), English CO—No. 3 in F, "Autumn" [Allegro only] ("Sunday Brunch, Vol 2") † Con Mand, RV.425; Con Mands, RV.532; Cons Fl, Op. 10/1-6; J. S. Bach:Cant 147; Cant 156; Cant 78; Con 5 Hpd, BWV 1056; Suite 2 Fl, BWV 1067; G. F. Handel:Minuet Vc & Pno; Solomon (arrival of the queen of Sheba); Water Music (sels); A. Marcello:Con Ob Strs in d, Op. 1; Mouret:Suite de symphonies; H. Purcell:Abdelazer (sels); Gordian Knot Unty'd (sels); V. Tommasini:Donne di buon umore (sels) SNYC (Dinner Classics) ▲ 46359 [AAD] (9.97)
P. Zukerman (vn), P. Zukerman (cnd), English CO SNYC ▲ 38478 [ADD] (9.97) ▮ 38478 [ADD] (3.98)
P. Zukerman (vn), P. Zukerman (cnd), English CO ("Four Seasons & Other Great Concertos") † Con Fl; Con Flautino, RV.443; Con Mand, RV.425; Con Ob; Con Strs, RV.151; Con Tpts, RV.537; Con Vc; Cons Diverse Instrs; Cons Vn(s) Strs, Op. 3/1-12 SNYC (Essential Classics Take 2) 2-▲ 63284 (14.97)
P. Zukerman (vn), P. Zukerman (cnd), St. Paul CO SNYC ▲ 36710 [DDD] (9.97)
P. Zukerman (vn), P. Zukerman (cnd), St. Paul CO † H. Purcell:Gordian Knot Unty'd (sels); Old Bachelor (sels); Son Tpt, Z.850 SNYC ▲ 44644 [DDD] (10.97)
various artists—No. 1 in E, "Spring"; No. 4 in f, "Winter" [Allegro non molto only] † Con Gtr; Albinoni:Adagio; J. S. Bach:Brandenburg Con 2, BWV 1047; Brandenburg Con 3, BWV 1048; Brandenburg Con 5, BWV 1050; Jesu, bleibet meine Freude; Suite 2 Fl, BWV 1067; Suite 3 Orch, BWV 1068; G. F. Handel:Messiah (sels); Royal Fireworks Music, HWV 351; Serse (sels); Water Music, HWV 348-50; Mouret:Rondeau; J. Pachelbel:Canon & Gigue RCAV ▲ 60840 (10.97) ▮ 60840 (5.98)

 ▲ = CD ♦ = Enhanced CD △ = MD ▮ = Cassette Tape ▯ = DCC

VIVALDI, ANTONIO (cont.)

Concertos (4) for Violin, Strings & Continuo, Op. 8/1-4 (RV.269, 315, 293, 297), "The Four Seasons" (cont.)

various artists—No. 4 in f, "Winter"; No. 1 in E, "Spring" ("Baby Needs Baroque") † J. S. Bach:Brandenburg Con 1, BWV 1046; French Suites; Goldberg Vars, BWV 988; Inventions Hpd; Son Vn; Sons & Partitas Vn; Suite 2 Fl, BWV 1067; G. F. Handel:Water Music, HWV 348-50; J. Pachelbel:Canon & Gigue; Telemann:Qnt Tpt; Son Fl; Torelli:Son 5 No. 1 in D DLS ▲ 1609 [DDD] (10.97) ▮ 1609 [DDD] (8.98)

various artists—No. 1 in E, "Spring"; No. 4 in f, "Winter" † Con in D Gtr; Albinoni:Adagio; J. S. Bach:Brandenburg Con 2, BWV 1047; Brandenburg Con 3, BWV 1048; Brandenburg Con 5, BWV 1050; Suite 2 Fl, BWV 1067; Suite 3 Orch, BWV 1068; G. F. Handel:Music of Handel; Mouret:Music of Mouret; J. Pachelbel:Canon & Gigue RCAV ▲ 63501 (11.97)

artists unknown PC ▲ 265074 [DDD] (2.97)

Concertos (12) for Violin(s), Strings & Continuo (RV.181a, 345, 334, 263a, 358, 348, 359, 238, 530, 300, 198a, 391), Op. 9/1-12, "La cetra II" (1727)

I. Brown (cnd), Academy of St. Martin in the Fields PPHI (Double Decker) 2-▲ 448110 (17.97)

Italian Solisti *(rec 1990)* DNN 2-▲ 79475 [DDD] (33.97)

L'Arte dell'Arco ("La Cetra II") DYNC 2-▲ 147 [DDD] (34.97)

S. Lautenbacher (vn), J. Faerber (cnd), Württemberg CO—No. 2 in A ("The Stories of Vivaldi & Corelli in Words & Music") † Con Fl; Cons Vn Strs, Op. 8/1-4; Cons Vn(s) Strs, Op. 3/1-12; Cons Vn, Op. 4/1-12; Life & Music of Vivaldi; A. Corelli:Life & Music of Corelli MMD ▲ 8510 [ADD] (3.97) ▮ 8510 [ADD] (2.98)

P. Makanowitzky (vn), V. Golschmann (cnd), Vienna State Opera CO *(rec Baumgartner Hall Vienna, Apr 17-24, 1960)* VC 2-▲ 68 [AAD] (26.97)

P. Peabody (vn), R. Kapp (cnd) —No. 3 in g; No. 10 in A *(rec May 2, 1991)* ("Vivaldi's Favorites, Vol. 2") † Cons Vn (misc); Cons Vn Strs, Op. 8/1-12; Cons Vn(s) Strs, Op. 3/1-12 ESSY ▲ 1024 [DDD] (16.97)

Concertos for Violin(s), Strings & Continuo, Op. 11/1-6 (RV.207, 277, 336, 308, 202, 460) (ca1729-30)

E. Pellegrino (vn), G. Bortolato (ob), I Filarmonici CO TACT ▲ 672237 (16.97)

Concertos (6) for Violin(s), Strings & Continuo, Op. 12/1-6 (RV.317, 244, 124, 173, 379, 361) (ca 1729-30)

P. Beznosiuk (vn), C. Hogwood (cnd), Academy of Ancient Music PPHI ▲ 443556 (16.97)

M. Elman (vn), V. Golschmann (cnd), Vienna State Opera CO—No. 1 in g *(rec June 1960)* † Nardini:Con Vn VC ▲ 8033 [ADD] (13.97)

A. Ephrikian (cnd) —No. 3 in D † Con Strs, RV.129; Cons Orch HMA ▲ 1901012 [ADD] (9.97)

Italian Solisti *(rec Pizzola sul Brenta Italy, July 25-29, 1994)* DNN ▲ 78974 [DDD] (16.97)

A. Martini (cnd) ("Works, Volume 12") TACT ▲ 672238 [DDD] (16.97)

Purcell Quartet—No. 3 in D ("Vivaldi in furore") † Con Strs, RV.129; Con Strs, RV.130; Laudate pueri Dominum, RV.601; Sinf Strs in b, RV.169 CHOC (Chaconne) ▲ 613 (16.97)

A. Stang (vn), L. Korkhin (cnd), Renaissance CO—No. 1 in g † J. S. Bach:Con Vns; Con 1 Vn; Con 2 Vn SNYC ▲ 57217 [DDD] (4.97)

Concerto in C for Violin, Strings & Continuo, RV.170

A. Martini (vn), Accademia I Filarmonici *(rec Sala del Morone Verona, Italy, Mar 1995)* ("Dresden Concerti, Vol. 1") † Con Vn NXIN (The Vivaldi Collection) ▲ 8553792 [DDD] (5.97)

Concerto in C for Violin & Strings, RV.187

P. Zukerman (vn), P. Zukerman (cnd), English CO † Con Vn; Cons Vn Strs, Op. 8/1-12; Cons Vn, Op. 4/1-12 RCAV (Red Seal) ▲ 68433 (16.97)

Concerto in C for Violin, Strings & Continuo, RV.195

P. Zukerman (vn), P. Zukerman (cnd), English CO † Con Vn; Cons Vn Strs, Op. 8/1-12; Cons Vn, Op. 4/1-12 RCAV (Red Seal) ▲ 68433 (16.97)

Concerto in c for Violin, Strings & Continuo, RV.197

P. Zukerman (vn), P. Zukerman (cnd), English CO † Con Vn; Cons Vn Strs, Op. 8/1-12; Cons Vn, Op. 4/1-12 RCAV (Red Seal) ▲ 68433 (16.97)

Concerto in c for Violin, Strings & Continuo, RV.199, "Il sospetto"

I. Levin (vn), P. Zukerman (vn), S. Accardo (vn), F. Agostini (vn), H. Szeryng (vn), M. Paris (vl), A. Romero (gtr), C. Romero (gtr), C. Romero (gtr), A. Nicolet (fl), H. Holliger (ob) [Andante only] ("Vivaldi for Valentines: Romantic Interludes for the One You Love") † Con Vn; Cons Fl, Op. 10/1-6; Music of Vivaldi PPHI ▲ 54051 (9.97) ▮ 54051 (5.98)

Concerto in D for Violin, Strings & Continuo, RV.209

P. Zukerman (vn), P. Zukerman (cnd), English CO † Con Vn; Cons Vn Strs, Op. 8/1-12; Cons Vn, Op. 4/1-12 RCAV (Red Seal) ▲ 68433 (16.97)

Concerto in E♭ for Violin, Strings & Continuo, RV.256, "Il ritiro"

A. Lizzio (cnd), San Marco Musici † Con Mand, RV.425; Con Vn Obs Hns, RV.571; Con 2 Vns, RV.524 PC ▲ 265005 [DDD] (2.97)

Concerto in E for Violin, Strings & Continuo, RV.270, "Il riposo, per il Santissimo Natale"

S. Standage (cnd), Collegium Musicum 90 † A. Corelli:Con grosso, Op. 6/8; Manfredini:Cons Vns, Op. 3; A. Scarlatti:Pastorale per nascita di Nostro Signore; Telemann:In dulci jubilo, TWV1: 939 CHN ▲ 634 (16.97)

Concerto in E for Violin, Strings & Continuo, RV.271, "L'amoroso"

A. Dubeau (vn), La Pièta *(rec Quebec, Oct 1997)* ("Per Archi") † Con Strs, RV.151; Con Strs, RV.156; Cons Strs (misc); Cons Vn(s) Strs, Op. 3/1-12; Sinf/Con Strs, RV.146; Sons Vns Vl, Op. 1/1-12 FL ▲ 23128 [DDD] (16.97)

I. Levin (vn), P. Zukerman (vn), S. Accardo (vn), F. Agostini (vn), H. Szeryng (vn), M. Paris (vl), A. Romero (gtr), C. Romero (gtr), C. Romero (gtr), A. Nicolet (fl), H. Holliger (ob) ("Vivaldi for Valentines: Romantic Interludes for the One You Love") † Con Vn; Cons Fl, Op. 10/1-6; Music of Vivaldi PPHI ▲ 54051 (9.97) ▮ 54051 (5.98)

Concerto in G for Violin, Strings & Continuo, RV.314a

A. Cappelletti (vn), I. Bolton (cnd), Scottish CO † Con Vn; Cons Vn Strs, Op. 8/1-4 KSCH ▲ 367242 (6.97)

A. Martini (vn), Accademia I Filarmonici *(rec Sala del Morone Verona, Italy, Mar 1995)* ("Dresden Concerti, Vol. 1") † Con Vn NXIN (The Vivaldi Collection) ▲ 8553792 [DDD] (5.97)

Concerto in g for Violin, Strings & Continuo, RV.319

A. Cappelletti (vn), I. Bolton (cnd), Scottish CO † Con Vn; Cons Vn Strs, Op. 8/1-4 KSCH ▲ 367242 (6.97)

A. Martini (vn), Accademia I Filarmonici *(rec Sala del Morone Verona, Italy, Mar 1995)* ("Dresden Concerti, Vol. 1") † Con Vn NXIN (The Vivaldi Collection) ▲ 8553792 [DDD] (5.97)

Concerto in A for Violin, Strings & Continuo, RV.341

A. Martini (vn), Accademia I Filarmonici *(rec Sala del Morone Verona, Italy, Mar 1995)* ("Dresden Concerti, Vol. 1") † Con Vn NXIN (The Vivaldi Collection) ▲ 8553792 [DDD] (5.97)

Concerto in B♭ for Violin, Strings & Continuo, RV.364

P. Zukerman (vn), P. Zukerman (cnd), English CO † Con Vn; Cons Vn Strs, Op. 8/1-12; Cons Vn, Op. 4/1-12 RCAV (Red Seal) ▲ 68433 (16.97)

Concerto in B♭ for Violin, Strings & Continuo, RV.366, "Il Carbonelli"

A. Martini (vn), Accademia I Filarmonici *(rec Sala del Morone Verona, Italy, Mar 1995)* ("Dresden Concerti, Vol. 1") † Con Vn NXIN (The Vivaldi Collection) ▲ 8553792 [DDD] (5.97)

Concerto in B♭ for Violin, Strings & Continuo, RV.383

A. Martini (vn), Accademia I Filarmonici *(rec Sala del Morone Verona, Italy, Mar 1995)* ("Dresden Concerti, Vol. 1") † Con Vn NXIN (The Vivaldi Collection) ▲ 8553792 [DDD] (5.97)

Concerto in A for Violin, Strings & Continuo, RV.552, "Per eco in Lontana"

M. Frasca-Colombier (vn), L. Paugam (vn), S. Ochi (mand), T. Ochi (mand), J. Labylle (pic), P. Kuentz (cnd), Paul Kuentz Orch ("6 Rare Concertos") † Con Flautino, RV.443; Con Mands, RV.532; Cons Diverse Instrs PVY ▲ 730052 [DDD] (12.97)

L. Güttler (cnd) † Con Ob; Con Va Lt, RV.540; Con Vns Rcrs Mans, RV.558; Cons Diverse Instrs; Sinf BER ▲ 1082 [DDD] (16.97)

N. McGegan (cnd), Philharmonia Baroque Orch *(rec Oakland, CA, Oct 1996)* ("Vivaldi for Diverse Instruments") † Con Obs, RV.535; Con Vn Obs, RV.577; Cons Diverse Instrs REF ▲ 77 (16.97)

A. Manze (cnd), Academy of Ancient Music ("Concert for the Prince of Poland") † Con Va Lt, RV.540; Con Vns Rcrs Mans, RV.558; Cons Vn Strs, Op. 8/1-12; Sinf HAM ▲ 907230 (18.97)

Concertos for 2 Violins & Orchestra

V. Gluz (vn), I. Romanyuk (vn), A. Titov (cnd), St. Petersburg New Classical Orch ("Vivaldi: A Violin Festival") † Cons Vn(s) Strs, Op. 3/1-12 SNYC ▲ 66725 [DDD] (4.97)

P. Kuentz (cnd), Paul Kuentz Orch PVY 2-▲ 730071 (23.97)

J. Schröder (vn), R. Brown (vn), N. TeBrake (vn), S. Ritchie (vn), J. Griffin (va), M. Lutzke (vc), M. Willens (db), A. Fuller (hpd) *(rec June 6-8, 1986)* † Sinf; J. S. Bach:Cons Vn (comp); Trio Son for 2 Vns REF ▲ 23 [DDD] (16.97)

Concerto in G for 2 Violins, 2 Cellos, Strings & Continuo, RV.575

J. Lamon (cnd), Tafelmusik † Con Vn Vc, RV.547 SNYC (Vivarte) ▲ 48044 (16.97)

C. Prévost (vn), L. Hall (vn), A. Aubut (vc), B. Hurtubise (vc), Y. Turovsky (cnd), Montreal Musici † Con Tpts, RV.537; Con Vn Org, RV.542; Cons Vn(s) Strs, Op. 3/1-12 CHN ▲ 8651 [DDD] (16.97)

Concerto in C for 2 Violins, 2 Recorders, 2 Mandolins, 2 Salmos, 2 Theorbos, Cello, Strings & Continuo, RV.558

G. Antonini (cnd) † Con Lt Vns, RV.93; Con Mand, RV.425; Con Mands, RV.532; Con Va Lt, RV.540; Trio Son Vn Lt, RV.82; Trio Son Vn Lt, RV.85 TELC ▲ 91182 (16.97)

VIVALDI, ANTONIO (cont.)

Concerto in C for 2 Violins, 2 Recorders, 2 Mandolins, 2 Salmos, 2 Theorbos, Cello, Strings & Continuo, RV.558 (cont.)

L. Güttler (cnd) † Con Ob; Con Va Lt, RV.540; Con Vn; Cons Diverse Instrs; Sinf BER ▲ 1082 [DDD] (16.97)

V. Hudeček (vn), L. Brabec (gtr), J. Stivín (rcr), G. Delogu (cnd), Janáček CO, G. Delogu (cnd), Prague CO ("Brabec, Stivín & Hudeček Play Vivaldi") † Con Rcr, RV.108; Con Vn Org, RV.542; Cons Diverse Instrs; Cons Vn(s) Strs, Op. 3/1-12 SUR ▲ 3023 (16.97)

A. Manze (cnd), Academy of Ancient Music ("Concert for the Prince of Poland") † Con Va Lt, RV.540; Con Vn; Cons Vn Strs, Op. 8/1-12; Sinf HAM ▲ 907230 (18.97)

T. Pinnock (cnd), English CO † Con Bn; Con Mands, RV.532; Con Strs, RV.151; Con Vn Ob, RV.548; Cons Fl, Op. 10/1-6; Cons Vn(s) Strs, Op. 3/1-12 PARC (3D Baroque) ▲ 31710 [DDD] (9.97)

J. Veilhan (cl), P. Couvert (cnd), St. Cecilia Academy Orch Rome *(rec Paris, France, Jan 1996)* ("Concerti con Molti Istromenti") † Cons Diverse Instrs K617 ▲ 7062 [DDD] (18.97)

Concerto in B♭ for 2 Violins, Strings & Continuo, RV.524

A. Lizzio (cnd), San Marco Musici † Con Mand, RV.425; Con Vn; Con Vn Obs Hns, RV.571 PC ▲ 265005 [DDD] (2.97)

Concerto in F for 3 Violins, Strings & Continuo, RV.551

G. Carmignola (vn), Sonatori de la Gioiosa Marca *(rec Treviso Italy, 1993)* ("Le Quattro Stagioni") † Cons Vn Strs, Op. 8/1-4 DVX (Divox Antiqua) ▲ 79404 [DDD] (16.97)

C. Coin (vc), Il Giardino Armonico ("Double & Triple Concertos") † Con Vcs, RV.531; Con Vn Vc, RV.544; Con Vn Vcs, RV.561; Cons Diverse Instrs TELC (Das alte Werk) ▲ 94552 (16.97)

J. Laredo (vn), J. Laredo (cnd), Scottish CO † Cons Vn(s) Strs, Op. 3/1-12 ICC ▲ 6702352 (9.97)

I. Stern (vn), I. Perlman (vn), P. Zukerman (vn) *(rec NYC, United States of America)* ("60th Anniversary Celebration") † J. S. Bach:Con Vns; W. A. Mozart:Sinf concertante Vn, K.364 *([ENG,FRE,GER] text)* SNYC ▲ 36692 (16.97)

Vienna Flautists *(rec June 2-3, 1994)* ("Concertos") † Con Strs, RV.114; Con Strs, RV.117; Con Strs, RV.143; Con Strs, RV.151; Con Strs, RV.159; Cons Vn(s) Strs, Op. 3/1-12; Sinf; Sinf Strs in b, RV.169 DI ▲ 920230 [DDD] (5.97)

C. Warren-Green (vn), C. Warren-Green (cnd), London CO *(rec 1988-89)* † Con Tpts, RV.537; Con Vc; Cons Diverse Instrs; Cons Vn Strs, Op. 8/1-4; Cons Vn(s) Strs, Op. 3/1-12 VCL 2-▲ 61466 [DDD] (11.97)

Concerto in d for 2 Violins, Strings & Continuo, RV.514

J. Kopelman (vn), P. Hamar (vn) ("Classic Hits: Vivaldi") † Con Fl Gtr; Con Gtr; Con Vc; Cons Fl, Op. 10/1-6; Cons Vn(s) Strs, Op. 3/1-12 PUBM (Majestic) ▲ 1041 [DDD] (4.97)

Concerto in a for 2 Violins, Strings & Continuo, RV.523

B. Sztankovits (gtr), Z. Tokos (gtr) *(rec Unitarian Church Budapest, Hungary, Nov 1991)* ("Famous Baroque Concerti") † Con Mands, RV.532; J. S. Bach:Con 1 for 2 Hpds, BWV 1060; Easter Oratorio, BWV 249; G. F. Handel:Concerti grossi, Op. 6; Solomon (arrival of the queen of Sheba) NXIN ▲ 553028 [DDD] (5.97)

Dixit Dominus in D (Psalm 110) for 2 Choruses, RV.594

J. Bowman (ct), J. Malgoire (cnd), La Grande Écurie et la Chambre du Roy ("Music from the Age of Castratos") † Montezuma (sels); Nisi Dominus, RV.608; G. Allegri:Motets; Broschi:Arias; M.-A. Charpentier:Salve regina à 3 voix pareilles, H.23; C. W. Gluck:Orfeo ed Euridice (sels) ASTR ▲ 8552 [DDD] (16.97)

artists unknown ("Vivaldi Glorias") † Beatus vir, RV.597; Gloria; Gloria (& Intro), RV.588; Magnificat, RV.611 PLON (Double Decker) 2-▲ 43455 (17.97)

Domine ad adiuvandum me in G (Psalm 70.2) for Vocal Soloists, Orchestra & Chorus, RV.593

M. Filová (sop), M. Benačková (mez), T. Strugala (cnd), Prague Virtuosi, J. Pančík (cnd), Prague Chamber Choir ("Musica per Tutti, Vol. 9") † Gloria; Nisi Dominus, RV.608; P. Tchaikovsky:Nutcracker Suite, Op. 71a; Sleeping Beauty (suite), Op. 66a; Swan Lake (suite), Op. 20a DI ▲ 920295 [DDD] (5.97)

J. Skidmore (cnd), Baroque Orch, Ex Cathedra Choir † Sacred Choral Music ASV (Gaudeamus) ▲ 137 [DDD] (16.97)

Il Farnace (opera in 3 acts), RV.711 (1726)

M. D. Bernart (cnd), San Remo SO, M. Dupuy (sop), P. Malakova (mez), D. Dessy (mez), K. Angeloni (mez), L. Rizzi (cta), R. Garazioti (ten) *(rec live, 1982)* AG 2-▲ 88 (25.97)

Filiae mestae (motet) in c for Chorus, RV.638

R. King (cnd) , King's Consort, D. York (sop), C. Denley (mez), J. Bowman (ct) ("Sacred Music, Vol 2") † In furore giustissimae irae, RV.626; Londe mala umbrae terrores, RV.629; Motets; Nulla in mundo pax, RV.630 HYP ▲ 66779 (18.97)

Flute Music

F. M. Sardelli (cnd) —Con Fl, RV.431; Con Fl, RV.432; Sinf in G for Fl & Strs, RV.68; Son Fl, RV.51 ("Flute Concerti, Part 2") † Cants; Con Fl; Son Fl, RV.48 TACT ▲ 672204 [DDD] (16.97)

Gloria (& Introduction) in D for Chorus [last movt arr from Ruggieri's *Gloria*], RV.588

C. Calvi (cta), S. M. von Hase (cta), V. Manno (ten), Bonitatibus (sgr), Trogu (sgr) † Beatus vir, RV.597; Sacred Choral Music AG ▲ 1 [DDD] (18.97)

P. Kwella (sop), E. Priday (sop), C. Wyn-Rogers (cta), A. Carwood (ten), S. Darlington (cnd), Hanover Band, Christ Church Cathedral Choir Oxford † Gloria NIMB ▲ 5278 [DDD] (16.97)

D. Willcocks (cnd), King's College Choir Cambridge ("Great Choral Classics from King's") † G. Allegri:Miserere; J. S. Bach:Cant 41; G. F. Handel:Coronation Anthems for George II, HWV 258-61; Palestrina:Stabat mater; Tallis:Spem in alium PLON 2-▲ 452949 (17.97)

artists unknown ("Vivaldi Glorias") † Beatus vir, RV.597; Dixit Dominus, RV.594; Gloria; Magnificat, RV.611 PLON (Double Decker) 2-▲ 43455 (17.97)

Gloria in D for Chamber Orchestra & Chorus [last movt arr from Ruggieri's *Gloria*], RV.589 (1708)

R. Alessandrini (cnd) , Akademia Vocal Ensemble † Con Vn Obs, RV.563; Magnificat, RV.611 OPUS ▲ 30195 (18.97)

T. Bonner (sop), E. Kirkby (sop), M. Chance (ct), R. Hickox (cnd), Collegium Musicum 90 † J. S. Bach:Magnificat, BWV 243 CHN (Chaconne) ▲ 518 [DDD] (16.97)

M. Burgess (sop), J. Chamonine (sop), C. Watkinson (cta), J. Malgoire (cnd), La Grande Écurie et la Chambre du Roy, Raphaël Passaquet Vocal Ensemble *(rec 1976)* † Beatus vir, RV.597; J. S. Bach:Magnificat, BWV 243 SNYC (Essential Classics) ▲ 48280 [ADD] (7.97) ▮ 48280 [ADD] (3.98)

M. Corboz (cnd) † Magnificat, RV.610 ERAT ▲ 17919 (9.97)

A. Crookes (sop), J. Whitaker (sop), C. Trevor (alt), R. Glenton (vc), C. Swain (ob), C. Stokes (org), N. Ward (cnd), Northern CO, Oxford Schola Cantorum *(rec Hale Cheshire, Dec 3, 1993)* † Beatus vir, RV.597 NXIN ▲ 550767 [DDD] (5.97)

M. Filová (sop), M. Benačková (mez), T. Strugala (cnd), Prague Virtuosi, J. Pančík (cnd), Prague Chamber Choir ("Musica per Tutti, Vol. 9") † Domine ad adiuvandum me, RV.593; Nisi Dominus, RV.608; P. Tchaikovsky:Nutcracker Suite, Op. 71a; Sleeping Beauty (suite), Op. 66a; Swan Lake (suite), Op. 20a DI ▲ 920295 [DDD] (5.97)

L. Güttler (cnd) , Hallenser Madrigal Singers † Magnificat, RV.611 BER ▲ 1003 [DDD]

B. Hendricks (sop), A. Murray (mez), J. Rigby (mez), U. Heilmann (ten), J. Hynninen (bar), N. Marriner (cnd), Academy of St. Martin in the Fields, Academy Chorus † J. S. Bach:Magnificat, BWV 243 EMIC ▲ 54283 (16.97)

P. Jensen (sop), D. Upshaw (sop), M. Simpson (mez), D. Gordon (ten), W. Stone (bar), R. Shaw (cnd), Atlanta SO, Atlanta Chamber Chorus † J. S. Bach:Magnificat, BWV 243 TEL ▲ 80194 [DDD] (16.97)

Z. Kloubová (sop), J. Žigmund (va), J. Krejčí (ob), D. Dimitrov (tpt), V. Roubal (org)—Domine Deus † Motets; J. S. Bach:Cant 51; Cant 92; G. F. Handel:German Arias, HWV 202-10; Joshua (sels); Messiah (sels); J. Haydn:Schöpfung (sels); W. A. Mozart:Ave verum corpus, K.618; Exsultate, jubilate, K.165; Vesperae solennes de confessore, K.339; Saint-Saëns:Ave Maria; F. Schubert:Ave Maria, Op. 52/6 GZCL ▲ 276 (6.97)

S. Kralev (cnd) † Beatus vir, RV.597 GEGA ▲ 199 (16.97)

P. Kwella (sop), E. Priday (sop), C. Wyn-Rogers (cta), A. Carwood (ten), S. Darlington (cnd), Hanover Band, Christ Church Cathedral Choir Oxford † Gloria (& Intro), RV.588 NIMB ▲ 5278 [DDD] (16.97)

R. Muti (cnd), New Philharmonia Orch, N. Balatsch (cnd), New Philharmonia Chorus, T. Berganza (mez), L. V. Terrani (cta) *(rec London, England, 1976-77)* † Magnificat, RV.611 EMIC (Great Recordings of the Century) ▲ 67002 [ADD] (11.97)

V. Negri (cnd), English CO, M. Marshall (sop)—Gloria in excelsis [1st movement-Allegro] ("Shine: The Complete Classics") † Nulla in mundo pax, RV.630; Beethoven:Sym 9; Chopin:Polonaise 6 Pno, Op. 53; Preludes (24) Pno, Op. 28; Liszt:Etudes d'exécution transcendante (6), S.140; Études de concert (3), S.144; Hungarian Rhaps, S.244; S. Rachmaninoff:Con 3 Pno, Op. 30; Prelude in c#, Op. 3/2; Rimsky-Korsakov:Tale of Tsar Saltan (orch sels); R. Schumann:Kinderszenen Pno, Op. 15 PPHI 2-▲ 456403 (17.97)

M. J. Newman (cnd), New York Musica Antiqua, Voci Angeli *(rec Presbyterian Church Mt. Kisco NY)* ("Viva Vivaldi!") † Cons Vn Strs, Op. 8/1-4 HEL ▲ 1014 (10.97)

T. Pinnock (cnd), English CO, English Concert Choir, N. Argenta (sop), I. Attrot (sop), C. Denley (mez) † A. Scarlatti:Dixit Dominus PARC ▲ 23386 [DDD] (16.97)

V. Radu (cnd), Ama Deus Ensemble, Ama Deus Ensemble Chorus, J. Baird (sop), G. Stoleriu (sop), L. Gratis (mez), S. Davol (ob) *(rec Wayne, PA, Fall 1996)* † Con Tpts, RV.537; Magnificat, RV.611 NPT ▲ 85617 [DDD] (16.97)

F. Sailer (sop), M. Bence (cta), M. Couraud (cnd), Stuttgart Pro Musica Orch *(rec 1964)* † Stabat Mater, RV.621 TUXE ▲ 1032 [ADD] (10.97)

E. Vaughan (sop), J. Baker (mez), N. Marriner (cnd), Academy of St. Martin in the Fields, King's College Choir Cambridge † J. Haydn:Mass 11, "Nelsonmesse", H.XXII/11 PLON (Jubilee) ▲ 21146 [ADD] (9.97)

VIVALDI, ANTONIO (cont.)

Gloria in D for Chamber Orchestra & Chorus [last movt arr from Ruggieri's *Gloria*], RV.589 (1708) (cont.)

artists unknown ("Vivaldi Glorias") † Beatus vir, RV.597; Dixit Dominus, RV.594; Gloria (& Intro), RV.588; Magnificat, RV.611 PLON (Double Decker) 2-▲ 43455 (17.97)

Griselda (opera in 3 acts) [lib Zeno, adapted C. Goldoni] (1735)

F. Fanna (cnd), Montpelier-Moscow Soloists, G. Morigi (sop), L. Poleri-Tosi (sop), H. Centner (sgr) AG 3-▲ 91 (18.97)

Griselda (selections)

Les Boréades de Montréal *(rec Church of St. Augustin de Mirabel Quebec, May 5-7, 1997)* ("Théâtre Musical") † G. F. Handel:Acis & Galatea (suite); Rebel:Caractères de la danse (suite); J. H. Schmelzer:Fechtschule ATMM ▲ 22152 [ADD] (15.97)

In furore guistissimae irae (motet) in c for Chorus, RV.626

R. King (cnd) , King's Consort, D. York (sop), C. Denley (mez), J. Bowman (ct) ("Sacred Music, Vol 2") † Filiae mestae, RV.638; Londe mala umbrae terrores, RV.629; Motets; Nulla in mundo pax, RV.630 HYP ▲ 66779 (18.97)

L'incoronazione di Dario (opera) [lib A. Morselli], RV.719 (1717)

I. Poulenard (sop), A. Mellon (sop), H. Ledroit (ct), G. Lesne (ct), D. Visse (ct), J. Elwes (ten), M. Verschaeve (bar), G. Bezzina (cnd) HMA 3-▲ 1901235 (26.97)

L'incoronazione di Dario (selections)

J. Corazolla (cnd), Rhenish CO—Sinfonia ("Symphonies of the Italian Baroque") † Albinoni:Cons Strs, Op. 10; A. Corelli:Concerti grossi, Op. 6; Geminiani:Concerti grossi (6) for 2 Vns, Op. 3; Locatelli:Concerti grossi, Op. 1; G. B. Sammartini:Sinf in A; Sym in G; Torelli:Con musicali, Op. 6 ENTE ▲ 92 [DDD] (10.97)

P. Rapson (hpd), P. Rapson (cnd) † Arias; Cons Vn Strs, Op. 8/1-4 MER ▲ 84195 (16.97)

Juditha triumphans devicta Holofernes barbarie (oratorio) for Soloists, Orchestra & Chorus [text J. Cassetti], RV.645 (1716)

M. Kiehr (sop), A. Murray (mez), J. Rigby (mez), S. Bickley (mez), S. Connolly (cta), R. King (cnd) , King's Consort Choir ("Sacred Music, Vol. 4") HYP 2-▲ 67281 (36.97)

M. László (sop—Abra), Z. Barlay (cta—Juditha), J. Réti (ten—Servo), Z. Bende (bar—Holofernes), J. Dene (bar—Ozias), F. Szekeres (cnd), Hungarian State Orch, G. Czigány (cnd), Budapest Madrigal Choir *(rec 1968)* CLDI ▲ 4022 [ADD] (21.97)

M. Zádori (sop), J. Németh (mez), K. Gémes (mez), G. Banditelli (cta), A. Markert (cta), N. McGegan (cnd), Capella Savaria, Savaria Vocal Ensemble [LAT] HUN 2-▲ 31063 [DDD] (32.97)

Laudate pueri Dominum (Psalm 113) in c for Voice & Chorus, RV.600 (?1717)

K. Gauvin (sop), Les Chambristes de Ville-Marie *(rec May 1997)* ("Motets for Soprano") † Motets *(E,F,L texts)* FL ▲ 23099 [DDD] (16.97)

Laudate pueri Dominum (Psalm 113) in G for Voice & Chorus, RV.601

C. Bott (sop), S. Preston (fl), Purcell Quartet ("Vivaldi in furore") † Con Strs, RV.129; Con Strs, RV.130; Cons Vn Strs, Op. 12/1-6; Sinf Strs in b, RV.169 CHOC (Chaconne) ▲ 613 (16.97)

Life & Music of Vivaldi

S. Lautenbacher (vn), J. Faerber (cnd), Württemberg CO—Cons Vn Strs, Op. 8/1-12 [No. 11 in D]; Gloria, RV.589; The Nymph & the Shepherd ("The Stories of Vivaldi & Corelli in Words & Music") † Con Fl; Con Vn Strs Bc, Op. 9/1-12; Cons Vn Strs, Op. 8/1-4; Cons Vn(s) Strs, Op. 3/1-12; Cons Vn, Op. 4/1-12; A. Corelli:Life & Music of Corelli MMD ▲ 8510 [ADD] (3.97) ▮ 8510 [ADD] (2.98)

Londe mala umbrae terrores in g for Chorus, RV.629

R. King (cnd) , King's Consort, D. York (sop), C. Denley (mez), J. Bowman (ct) ("Sacred Music, Vol 2") † Filiae mestae, RV.638; In furore giustissimae irae, RV.626; Motets; Nulla in mundo pax, RV.630 HYP ▲ 66779 (18.97)

Lungi dal vago volto (canata) for Soprano, Violin & Continuo, RV.680

C. Gasdia (sop), F. Tasini (hpd), C. Ferrarini (cnd), Barocco Veneziano † All'ombra di sospetto, RV.678; Salve Regina, RV.617 MONM 2-▲ 90031 (34.97)

Magnificat in g for Vocal Soloists, Orchestra & Chorus, RV.610

M. Corboz (cnd) † Gloria ERAT ▲ 17919 (9.97)

S. Le Blanc (sop), D. Forget (sop), R. Cunningham (alt), H. Ingram (ten), J. Lamon (cnd), Tafelmusik, Tafelmusik Chamber Choir [LAT] HYP ▲ 66247 [DDD] (18.97)

F. Szekeres (cnd), Budapest Strings, Budapest Madrigal Choir, T. Takács (mez), D. Gulyás (ten), T. Bátor (bass), R. Szücs (bass) † Magnificat, RV.611; Albinoni:Magnificat; Caldara:Magnificat; G. B. Sammartini:Magnificat in B♭ HUN ▲ 31259 [DDD] (16.97)

Magnificat in g for Vocal Soloists, Orchestra & Chorus, RV.611

R. Alessandrini (cnd) , Akademia Vocal Ensemble † Con Vn Obs, RV.563; Gloria OPUS ▲ 30195 (18.97)

L. Güttler (cnd) , Hallenser Madrigal Singers † Gloria BER ▲ 1003 [DDD]

R. Muti (cnd), New Philharmonia Orch, N. Balatsch (cnd), New Philharmonia Chorus, T. Berganza (mez), L. V. Terrani (cta) *(rec London, England, 1976-77)* † Gloria EMIC (Great Recordings of the Century) ▲ 67002 [ADD] (11.97)

V. Radu (cnd), Ama Deus Ensemble, Ama Deus Ensemble Chorus, J. Baird (sop), L. Gratis (mez) *(rec Wayne, PA, Fall 1996)* † Con Tpts, RV.537; Gloria NPT ▲ 85617 [DDD] (16.97)

F. Szekeres (cnd), Budapest Strings, Budapest Madrigal Choir, J. Németh (mez), T. Takács (mez), T. Bátor (bass), Kovács (sgr), Szökefalvi-Nagy (sgr) † Magnificat, RV.610; Albinoni:Magnificat; Caldara:Magnificat; G. B. Sammartini:Magnificat in B♭ HUN ▲ 31259 [DDD] (16.97)

artists unknown ("Vivaldi Glorias") † Beatus vir, RV.597; Dixit Dominus, RV.594; Gloria; Gloria (& Intro), RV.588 PLON (Double Decker) 2-▲ 43455 (17.97)

Montezuma (selections)

D. Visse (ct), J. Malgoire (cnd), La Grande Écurie et la Chambre du Roy—Gl'oltraggidella sorte ("Music from the Age of Castratos") † Dixit Dominus, RV.594; Nisi Dominus, RV.608; G. Allegri:Motets; Broschi:Arias; M.-A. Charpentier:Salve regina à 3 voix pareilles, H.23; C. W. Gluck:Orfeo ed Euridice (sels) ASTR ▲ 8552 [DDD] (16.97)

Motets

P. M. Bedi (sop), Chicago Baroque Ensemble—Nulla in mundo pax, RV.630; Londe mala umbrae terrores, RV.629 *(rec Evanston, IL, May-Aug 1995)* ("A Vivaldi Concert") † Cants; Sons Vc CED ▲ 25 [DDD] (16.97)

K. Gauvin (sop), Les Chambristes de Ville-Marie—Sum in medio tempestatum, RV.632; O qui coeli terraeque, RV.631 *(rec May 1997)* ("Motets for Soprano") † Laudate pueri Dominum, RV.600 FL ▲ 23099 [DDD] (16.97)

Z. Kloubová (sop), J. Žigmund (va), J. Krejčí (ob), D. Dimitrov (tpt), V. Roubal (org)—In turbato mare, RV.627 † Gloria; J. S. Bach:Cant 51; Cant 92; G. F. Handel:German Arias, HWV 202-10; Joshua (sels); Messiah (sels); J. Haydn:Schöpfung (sels); W. A. Mozart:Ave verum corpus, K.618; Exsultate, jubilate, K.165; Vesperae solennes de confessore, K.339; Saint-Saëns:Ave Maria; F. Schubert:Ave Maria, Op. 52/6 GZCL ▲ 276 (6.97)

D. Röschmann (sop), C. Robbin (mez), B. Labadie (cnd) —In furore giustissimae irae, RV.626 † Stabat Mater, RV.621; Pergolesi:Stabat mater DOR ▲ 90196 [DDD] (16.97)

D. York (sop), C. Denley (mez), J. Bowman (ct), R. King (cnd) , King's Consort—Clarae stellae, RV.625; Canta in prato, RV.623 ("Sacred Music, Vol 2") † Filiae mestae, RV.638; In furore giustissimae irae, RV.626; Londe mala umbrae terrores, RV.629; Nulla in mundo pax, RV.630 HYP ▲ 66779 (18.97)

Music of Vivaldi

S. Accardo (vn), S. Accardo (cnd), Naples Weekly International Soloists *(Con Vn, RV.286; Con Vn, RV.243; Con Vn, RV.270; Cons Vn(s), Op. 11/1-6)*, P. Tortelier (vc), P. Ledger (hpd), P. Ledger (cnd), London Mozart Players *(Con Vc, RV.400; Con Vc, RV.424; Con Vc, RV.401)*, J. F. Manzone (vn), P. Tortelier (vc), M. Tortelier (vc), P. Ledger (hpd), P. Ledger (cnd), London Mozart Players *(Con Vn Vcs, RV.561)*, Y. Menuhin (vn), A. Lysy (cnd), Camerata Lysy Gstaad *(Cons Vn Strs, Op. 8/1-4)*, Y. Menuhin (vn), A. Lysy (vn), A. Lysy (cnd), Camerata Lysy Gstaad *(Con 2 Vns, RV.510)*, H. D. Vries (ob), Zagreb Solisti *(Con Ob, RV.461; Con Ob, RV.450; Con Ob, RV.453; Con Ob, RV.454; Con Ob, RV.456; Con Vn (Ob), Op. 7; Con Ob, RV.449)* ("Best-Loved Vivaldi") † Con Vcs, RV.531; Cons Vn(s) Strs, Op. 3/1-12 EMCD (Seraphim) 4-▲ 69545 [DDD] (14.97)

K. Botvay (cnd), Budapest Strings *(Cons Vn Strs, Op. 8/1-4)*, Franz Liszt CO *(Siciliano)*, L. Güttler (tpt), K. Sandau (tpt) *(Con Hns, RV.539 [Allegro])*, B. Glaetzner (ob) *(Con Ob)* ("Masters of Classical Music, Vol. 7: Antonio Vivaldi") † Son Vn, RV.34 LALI ▲ 15807 [DDD] (3.97)

S. Kuijken (vn), F. Brüggen (rcr)—Con Bn, RV.483; Con Bn, RV.504 ("Vivaldi's Greatest Hits") † Cons Vn Strs, Op. 8/1-4 PRMX ▲ 816

I. Levin (vn), P. Zukerman (vn), S. Accardo (vn), F. Agostini (vn), H. Szeryng (vn), M. Paris (vl), A. Romero (gtr), C. Romero (gtr), C. Romero (gtr), A. Nicolet (fl), H. Holliger (ob)—Cons Vn Strs, Op. 8/1-4 [No. 4 in f, "Winter"]; Con in D for Gtr [Largo]; Con in C for Diverse Instrs [Andante molto]; Con Strs [Andante molto]; Con in D for 2 Vns & 2 Vcs [Largo]; Con Ob [Larghetto]; Con Gtr [Largo; Larghetto]; Con in F for 3 Vns [Andante]; Con in F for Fl [Largo]; Con Va [Largo]; Con Vn, RV.270 [Allegro; Larghetto]; Con in G for Ob, Bn & Strs [Largo]; Con in B for Vn & Strs [Largo]; Con in G for Fl [Largo]; Con Obs [Largo]; Con Orch [Largo non molto]; Con in C Ob, RV.554 [Adagio] ("Vivaldi for Valentines: Romantic Interludes for the One You Love") † Con Vn; Cons Fl, Op. 10/1-6 PPHI ▲ 54051 (9.97) ▮ 54051 (5.98)

A. B. Michelangeli (pno)—Allegro † Chopin:Mazurkas Pno; Scherzos Pno; Debussy:Images (6) Pno; Galuppi:Presto; Liszt:Con 1 Pno, S.124 IMMM (Magic Master series) ▲ 37007 (6.97)

VIVALDI, ANTONIO (cont.)

Music of Vivaldi (cont.)

A. B. Michelangeli (pno), M. Rossi (cnd), Turin RAI SO *(rec live La Scala, Nov 24, 1947)* † Beethoven:Con 5 Pno, Op. 73; E. Grieg:Pno Music (misc) RY (Radio Years) ▲ 91 (16.97)

I. Scheerer (vn), J. Geffert (org), Johann Christian Bach Academy—Con Vn Org, RV.541; Con Vn Org, RV.542; Con Vn, RV.170 ("Italienische Orgelkonzerte") † J. Christian Bach:Music of Bach; Lucchesi:Con Org FERM ▲ 20002 [DDD] (16.97)

H. Tims (gtr), H. Visser (gtr), A. Visser (fl), B. Brouwer (hpd)—Con in D; Largo; Allegro; Con in G [Andante]; Son 8 Fl [Prélude] *(rec 1996)* ("Buon Giorno: Visser Meets Italian Masters") † Albinoni:Music of Albinoni; Cimarosa:Music of Cimarosa; D. Scarlatti:Sons Kbd OREA ▲ 5284 [DDD] (11.97)

Nisi Dominus (Psalm 127) in g for Vocal Soloist & Orchestra, RV.608

J. Bowman (ct), J. Malgoire (cnd), La Grande Écurie et la Chambre du Roy—Sicut erat, Amen ("Music from the Age of Castratos") † Dixit Dominus, RV.594; Montezuma (sels); G. Allegri:Motets; Broschi:Arias; M.-A. Charpentier:Salve regina à 3 voix pareilles, H.23; C. W. Gluck:Orfeo ed Euridice (sels) ASTR ▲ 8552 [DDD] (16.97)

M. Chance (ct), T. Pinnock (cnd), English Concert † Sinf Strs in b, RV.169; Stabat Mater, RV.621 DGRM ▲ 453428 [DDD]

M. Filová (sop), M. Benačková (mez), T. Strugala (cnd), Prague Virtuosi, J. Pančík (cnd), Prague Chamber Choir ("Musica per Tutti, Vol. 9") † Domine ad adiuvandum me, RV.593; Gloria; P. Tchaikovsky:Nutcracker Suite, Op. 71a; Sleeping Beauty (suite), Op. 66a; Swan Lake (suite), Op. 20a DI ▲ 920295 [DDD] (5.97)

O. Ryabets (male sop), S. Bezrodnaya (cnd), Vivaldi CO *(rec 1992)* † Pergolesi:Stabat mater OLY ▲ 583 [DDD] (16.97)

Nulla in mundo pax (motet) in E for Vocal Soloist & Ensemble, RV.630

E. Ameling (sop), V. Negri (cnd), English CO ("Shine: The Complete Classics") † Gloria; Beethoven:Sym 9; Chopin:Polonaise 6 Pno, Op. 53; Preludes (24) Pno, Op. 28; Liszt:Études d'exécution transcendante (6), S.140; Études de concert (3), S.144; Hungarian Rhaps, S.244; S. Rachmaninoff:Con 3 Pno, Op. 30; Prelude in c#, Op. 3/2; Rimsky-Korsakov:Tale of Tsar Saltan (orch sels); R. Schumann:Kinderszenen Pno, Op. 15 PPHI 2-▲ 456403 (17.97)

R. King (cnd) , King's Consort, D. York (sop), C. Denley (mez), J. Bowman (ct) ("Sacred Music, Vol 2") † Filiae mestae, RV.638; In furore giustissimae irae, RV.626; Londe mala umbrae terrores, RV.629; Motets HYP ▲ 66779 (18.97)

L'Olimpiade (opera in 3 acts) [lib Metastasio], RV.725 (1734)

R. Clemencic (cnd) , La Cappella, L. Meeuwsen (sop), M. Sluis (sop), A. Christofellis (alt), E. von Magnus (cta), G. Lesne (ct), W. Oberholtzer (bar), A. W. Schultze (bass) [ITA] *(rec live Paris, France, Feb 8-10, 1990)* NUO (Ancient Music) 2-▲ 6932 [DDD] (32.97)

Ottone in Villa (opera in 3 acts) [lib D. Lalli], RV.729 (1713)

N. Argenta (sop), M. Groop (sop), S. Gritton (sop), S. Daneman (mez), M. Padmore (ten), R. Hickox (cnd), Collegium Musicum 90 CHOC (Chaconne) 2-▲ 614 (32.97)

A. M. Ferrante (sop—Tullia), P. Pace (sop—Cleonilla), A. Christofellis (alt—Caio), J. Nirouët (ct—Ottone), L. Petroni (ten—Decio), F. Colusso (cnd) BONG 3-▲ 10016 [DDD] (47.97)

Il pastor fido (6 sonatas) for Flute, Oboe, Violin & Continuo (RV.54, 56, 57, 59, 55, 58), Op. 13/1-6 (ca 1737)

E. Caroli (fl), L. Kawecka (hpd) *(rec July 1991)* STRV ▲ 21 (16.97)

R. Köhnen (vc), R. Fabbriciani (fl), C. Denti (hpd) AART ▲ 47299 (10.97)

C. Lawson (chl), J. Toll (hpd/org) [arr rcr & va bastarda] HAM ▲ 907104 (18.97)

R. Porroni (gtr), Ensemble Duomo [3 sels arr for gtr, vc & hpd] ("Una Chitarra per Vivaldi") † Con Lt Vns, RV.93; Con Va Lt, RV.540; Trio Son Vn Lt, RV.82; Trio Son Vn Lt, RV.85 STRV ▲ 43 (16.97)

B. Re (vl), C. Mendoze (rcr), G. Barbolini (hpd) † J. S. Bach:Sons Fl; A. Corelli:Sons Vn, Op. 5 PVY ▲ 787023 [DDD] (16.97)

Sacred Choral Music

C. Apollonio (sop), E. Andreani (cta), O. Vlček (cnd), Prague Virtuosi, F. Fanna (cnd), Prague Chamber Choir—Dixit Dominus, RV.595; Salve Regina, RV.617 DI ▲ 920203 [DDD] (5.97)

F. Fanna (cnd) , Ambrosian Polyphonic Madrigalists—Jubilate O Amaeni, RV.639 *(rec Nov 1994)* † Beatus vir, RV.597; Gloria (& Intro), RV.588 AG ▲ 1 [DDD] (18.97)

S. Gritton (sop), C. Denley (mez), D. Wilson-Johnson (bar), L. Milne (sgr), L. Atkinson (trbn), R. King (cnd), King's Consort, King's Consort Choir—Magnificat, RV.610; Lauda Jerusalem, RV.609; Kyrie, RV.587; Credo, RV.591; Dixit Dominus, RV.594 ("Sacred Music - 1") HYP ▲ 66769 (18.97)

S. Gritton (sop), C. Wyn-Davies (sop), C. Denley (mez), C. Daniels (ten), N. Davies (bar), M. George (bass), R. King (cnd), King's Consort, King's Consort Choir—Dixit Dominus, RV.595; Beatus vir, RV.598; Domine ad adiuvandum me, RV.593; Beatus vir, RV.597; Credidi propter quod, RV.605 ("Sacred Music — 3") HYP ▲ 66789 (18.97)

J. Skidmore (cnd), Baroque Orch, Ex Cathedra Choir—Beatus vir, RV.597; Stabat Mater, RV.621; Magnificat, RV.610 [Canticle] † Domine ad adiuvandum me, RV.593 ASV (Gaudeamus) ▲ 137 [DDD] (16.97)

Salve Regina in c for 2 Choruses, RV.616

J. Bowman (ct), J. Audoli (cnd) [LAT] † Pergolesi:Con Vn; Concertino 2 Strs; Salve regina Ct in f ARN ▲ 68026 [DDD] (16.97)

R. King (cnd), King's Consort, J. Bowman (ct) † J. S. Bach:Cant 54; Pergolesi:Salve regina Ct in f MER ▲ 84138 (16.97)

Salve Regina (antiphon) in F for Voices, RV.617

C. Gasdia (sop), F. Tasini (hpd), C. Ferrarini (cnd), Barocco Veneziano † All'ombra di sospetto, RV.678; Lungi dal vago volto, RV.680 MONM 2-▲ 90031 (34.97)

Sinfonia in C for Strings & Continuo, RV.116

A. Nanut (cnd), Zagreb Solisti ("Famous Concertos") † Cons Orch; Cons Vn(s) Strs, Op. 3/1-12 PC ▲ 265075 [DDD] (2.97)

J. Schröder (vn), S. Ritchie (vn), J. Griffin (va), M. Lutzke (vc), M. Willens (db), A. Fuller (hpd) *(rec June 6-8, 1986)* † Cons Vns; J. S. Bach:Cons Vn (comp); Trio Son for 2 Vns REF ▲ 23 [DDD] (16.97)

Sinfonia in e for Strings & Continuo, RV.134

M. Kransberg-Talvi (vn), A. Francis (cnd), Northwest CO Seattle † Cons Vn Strs, Op. 8/1-4; Sinf AMBA ▲ 1010 [DDD]

Vienna Flautists *(rec June 2-3, 1994)* ("Concertos") † Con Strs, RV.114; Con Strs, RV.117; Con Strs, RV.143; Con Strs, RV.151; Con Strs, RV.159; Con 3 Vns, RV.551; Cons Vn(s) Strs, Op. 3/1-12; Sinf Strs in b, RV.169 DI ▲ 920230 [DDD] (5.97)

Sinfonia/Concerto in G for Strings & Continuo, RV.146

La Pièta *(rec Quebec, Oct 1997)* ("Per Archi") † Con Strs, RV.151; Con Strs, RV.156; Con Vn; Cons Strs (misc); Cons Vn(s) Strs, Op. 3/1-12; Sons Vns Vl, Op. 1/1-12 FL ▲ 23128 [DDD] (16.97)

Sinfonia in G for Strings & Continuo, RV.149

L. Güttler (cnd) † Con Ob; Con Va Lt, RV.540; Con Vn; Con Vns Rcrs Mans, RV.558; Cons Diverse Instrs BER ▲ 1082 [DDD] (16.97)

M. Kransberg-Talvi (vn), A. Francis (cnd), Northwest CO Seattle † Cons Vn Strs, Op. 8/1-4; Sinf AMBA ▲ 1010 [DDD]

A. Manze (cnd) ("Concert for the Prince of Poland") HAM ▮ 407230 (12.98)

A. Manze (cnd); Academy of Ancient Music ("Concert for the Prince of Poland") † Con Va Lt, RV.540; Con Vn; Con Vns Rcrs Mans, RV.558; Cons Vn Strs, Op. 8/1-12 HAM ▲ 907230 (18.97)

Sinfonia in g for Strings & Continuo, RV.156

M. Kransberg-Talvi (vn), A. Francis (cnd), Northwest CO Seattle † Cons Vn Strs, Op. 8/1-4; Sinf AMBA ▲ 1010 [DDD]

Sinfonia in b for Strings & Continuo, RV.169, "Al Santo Sepolcro (I)"

M. Chance (ct), T. Pinnock (cnd), English Concert † Nisi Dominus, RV.608; Stabat Mater, RV.621 DGRM ▲ 453428 [DDD]

B. Labadie (cnd), Les Violons du Roy *(rec Quebec, Canada, June 1998)* ("Concerti for Strings") † Con Strs, RV.114; Con Strs, RV.120; Con Strs, RV.151; Con Strs, RV.157; Cons Vn(s) Strs, Op. 3/1-12 DOR ▲ 90255 [DDD] (16.97)

J. Lamon (cnd), Tafelmusik † Cons Vn Strs, Op. 8/1-4 SNYC (Vivarte) ▲ 48251 [DDD] (16.97)

Purcell Quartet ("Vivaldi in furore") † Con Strs, RV.129; Con Strs, RV.130; Cons Vn Strs, Op. 12/1-6; Laudate pueri Dominum, RV.601 CHOC (Chaconne) ▲ 613 (16.97)

Quartetto Italiano † Boccherini:Qts Strs; Cambini:Qts Strs; Galuppi:Music of; G. B. Vitali:Music of TES ▲ 1124 (17.97)

Vienna Flautists *(rec June 2-3, 1994)* ("Concertos") † Con Strs, RV.114; Con Strs, RV.117; Con Strs, RV.143; Con Strs, RV.151; Con Strs, RV.159; Con 3 Vns, RV.551; Cons Vn(s) Strs, Op. 3/1-12; Sinf DI ▲ 920230 [DDD] (5.97)

Sonatas (9) for Cello & Continuo (RV.39-47)

P. Carrai (vc), E. Barker (db), M. Kroll (hpd)—in e, RV.40; in F, RV.41; in a, RV.43; in B♭, RV.45; in B♭, RV.46; in B♭, RV.47 [trans Edwin Barker for db & bc] † P. Hindemith:Son Db; F. Schubert:Son Arpeggione, D.821 BOST ▲ 1018 [DDD] (15.97)

Chicago Baroque Ensemble—in B♭, RV.45 *(rec Evanston, IL, May-Aug 1995)* ("A Vivaldi Concert") † Cants; Motets CED ▲ 25 [DDD] (16.97)

O. Harnoy (vc), C. Tilney (hpd)—in e, RV.40; in F, RV.41; in a, RV.43; in B♭, RV.45; in B♭, RV.46; in B♭, RV.47 RCAV (Red Seal) ▲ 60430 (16.97)

880

▲ = CD ♦ = Enhanced CD △ = MD ▮ = Cassette Tape ▯ = DCC

WOLF, HUGO (cont.)
Italienische Liederbücher for Voice & Piano [2 volumes; anon Italian poems trans Heyse] (cont.)
Lieder für eine Frauenstimme (6) for Voice & Piano

T. Lemnitz (sop), M. Raucheisen (pno)—No. 4, Wiegenlied im Sommer; No. 5, Wiegenlied in Winter ("The Hugo Wolf Society Complete Edition-1931-1938") † Über Nacht, UP 48; Alte Weisen; Gedichte nach Heine; Gedichte von Eichendorff; Gedichte von Goethe; Gedichte von Michelangelo; Gedichte von Mörike; Gedichte von Robert Reinick; Gedichte von Scheffel; Gedichte Eichendorff; Italienische Liederbücher; Spanisches Liederbuch (Geistliche Lieder); Spanisches Liederbuch (Weltliche Lieder) EMIC 5-▲ 66640 (m) [ADD] (52.97)

Penthesilea (symphonic poem) for Orchestra [after Kleist] (1883-85)

O. Suitner (cnd), Berlin Staatskapelle † H. Pfitzner:Käthchen von Heilbronn (sels); R. Strauss:Sym Fant from Die Frau ohne Schatten BER ▲ 9026 [ADD] (10.97)

Quartet in d for Strings (1878-84)

Auryn String Quartet † Intermezzo Str Qt; Italian Serenade Str Qt CPO ▲ 999529 (13.97)

Songs (miscellaneous)

E. Ameling (sop), R. Jansen (pno)—Spanisches Liederbuch (Geistliche Lieder) [No. 4, Die ihr schwebet; No. 2, Die du Gott gebarst; No. 6, Ach, des Knaben Augen; No. 7, Mühvoll komm ich und beladen]; Spanisches Liederbuch (Weltliche Lieder) [No. 24, Komm o Tod, von Nacht umgeben; No. 13, Mögen alle bösen Zungen; No. 12, Sagt, seid ihr es, feiner Herr; No. 23, Tief im Herzen trag ich Pein; No. 30, Wer tat deinem Füsslein weh?; No. 25, Ob auch finstre Blicken glitten; No. 11, Herz, verzage nicht geschwind; No. 26, Bedeckt mich mit Blumen; No. 28, Sie blasen zum Abmarsch; No. 34, Geh, Geliebter, geh jetzt]; Gedichte von Mörike [No. 23, Auf ein altes Bild; No. 13, Im Frühling; No. 16, Elfenlied; No. 12, Verborgenheit; No. 7, Das verlassene Mägdlein; No. 38, Lied vom Winde; No. 9, Nimmersatte Liebe] HYP ▲ 66788 (18.97)

K. Flagstad (sop), W. Alme (pno)—Gedichte von Scheffel [No. 6, Zur Ruh, zur Ruh!]; Gedichte von Mörike [No. 28, Gebet; No. 36, Lebe wohl; No. 46, Gesang Weylas]; Gedichte von Eichendorff [No. 1, Der Freund]; Über Nacht, UP 48; Gedichte von Goethe [No. 29, Anakreons Grab]; Italienische Liederbücher [No. 18, Heb auf dein blondes Haupt]; Gedichte von Robert Reinick [No. 2, Morgenstimmung] *(rec Oslo, 1954)* ("Vol. 5: German Lieder, Norwegian Radio 1954") † Beethoven:Songs; J. Brahms:Songs; F. Schubert:Ave Maria, Op. 52/6; Songs (misc colls); R. Schumann:Songs; R. Strauss:Songs SIMX 2-▲ 1825 (39.97)

G. Hartman (sop), J. Whitelaw (pno)—Gedichte von Mörike [No. 24, In der Frühe; No. 34, Peregrina II; No. 39, Denk es, O Seele!; No. 17, Der Gärtner; No. 45, Nixe Binsefuss; No. 2, Der Knabe und das Immlein; No. 18, Zitronenfalter im April; No. 11, An eine Äolsharfe; No. 33, Peregrina I]; Italienische Liederbücher [No. 40, O wär dein Haus durchsichtig; No. 16, Ihr jungen Lente; No. 6, Wer rief dich denn?; No. 8, Nun lass uns Frieden schliessen; No. 19, Wir haben beide lange Zeit geschwiegen; No. 24, Ich esse nun mein Brot; No. 15, Mein Liebster ist so klein; No. 25, Mein Liebster hat zu Tische; No. 12, Nein, junger Herr!]; Spanisches Liederbuch (Geistliche Lieder) [No. 2, Die du Gott gebarst]; Spanisches Liederbuch (Weltliche Lieder) [No. 12, Sagt, seid ihr es, feiner Herr]; Gedichte von Goethe [Lied der mignon] *(rec Apr 1997)* ("Recital") CYPR ▲ 1608 [DDD] (17.97)

A. Kipnis (bass), G. Moore (pno), C. V. Bos (pno), E. V. Wolff (pno)—Gedichte von Goethe [No. 51, Grenzen der Menschheit; No. 14, Cophtisches Lied I]; Gedichte von Mörike [No. 19, Um Mitternacht]; Italienische Liederbücher [No. 33, Sterb ich, so hüllt in Blumen; No. 8, Nun lass uns Frieden schliessen; No. 19, Wir haben beide lange Zeit geschwiegen; No. 14, Geselle, woll'n wir uns in Kutten hüllen; No. 18, Heb auf dein blondes Haupt; No. 37, Wie viele Zeit verlor ich; No. 23, Was für ein Lied soll dir gesungen werden]; Gedichte von Michelangelo; Gedichte von Eichendorff [No. 2, Der Musikant; No. 5, Der Soldat I; No. 9, Der Schreckenberger]; Alte Weisen [No. 6, Wie glänzt der helle Mond] *(rec 1933-35)* † J. Brahms:Ernste Gesänge, Op. 121 PRE 2-▲ 89204 [AAD] (31.97)

L. Lehmann (sop), P. Ulanowsky (pno)—Gedichte von Goethe [No. 28, Frühling übers Jahr]; Gedichte von Mörike [No. 24, In der Frühe; No. 23, Auf ein altes Bild; No. 37, Heimweh; No. 33, Peregrina I]; Italienische Liederbücher [No. 1, Auch kleine Dinge] ("26 Lieder") † J. Brahms:Songs; Songs (9), Op. 32; R. Schumann:Songs; R. Strauss:Songs GSE ▲ 785057

E. Mathis (sop), G. Wyss (pno)—Gedichte von Mörike [No. 27, Zum neuen Jahr; No. 28, Gebet; No. 23, Auf ein altes Bild; No. 30, Neue Liebe; No. 39, Denk es, O Seele!; No. 12, Verborgenheit; No. 51, Bei einer Trauung; No. 7, Das verlassene Mägdlein; No. 8, Begegnung; No. 9, Nimmersatte Liebe; No. 11, An eine Äolsharfe; No. 6, Er ist's]; Lieder für eine Frauenstimme [No. 6, Mausfallensprüchlein] ("Lieder") † R. Strauss:Songs DNN ▲ 18006 [DDD] (16.97)

N. Meel (ten), D. Keuning (pno)—An *, UP 32; Traurige Wege, UP 38; Herbstentschluss, UP 75; Sie haben heut Abend Gesellschaft, UP 47; Ich stand in dunkeln Träumen, UP 49; Das ist ein Brausen und Heulen, UP 50; Aus meinen grossen Schmerzen, UP 52; Mir träumte von einem Königskind, UP 53; Mein Liebchen, wir sassen beisammen, UP 54; Es blasen die blauen Husaren, UP 55; Ernst ist der Frühling, UP 67; Späterbstnebel, UP 66; Wo ich bin, mich rings umdunkelt, UP 51; Du bist wie eine Blume, UP 26; In der Fremde VI, UP 93; Rückkehr, UP 90; Gedichte von Eichendorff [No. 19, Die Nacht; No. 18, Erwartung; No. 4, Ständchen]; Nachruf, UP 81; Wohin mit der Freud?, UP 89; Liebchen, wo bist du?, UP 96; Nachtgruss, UP 92; Frühlingsglocken, UP 94; Liebesbotschaft, UP 95 *(rec Utrecht, Netherlands, Jan 1996)* ("A Selection of Early Songs") GLOE ▲ 5149 [DDD] (16.97)

M. Mödl (sop), R. von Zustrow (pno) ("Liederabende, Vol. 1") † F. Schubert:Songs (misc); R. Wagner:Wesendonck Songs GEBH ▲ 1 (17.97)

H. Schlusnus (bar), B. Seidler-Winkler (pno) *(Gedichte von Eichendorff [No. 1, Der Freund; No. 2, Der Musikant; No. 3, Verschwiegene Liebe]),* H. Schlusnus (bar), F. Rupp (pno) *(Gedichte von Goethe [No. 11, Der Rattenfänger; No. 19, Epiphanias]; Heimweh),* H. Schlusnus (bar), M. Raucheisen (pno) *(Gedichte von Mörike [No. 10, Fussreise; No. 6, Er ist's]) (rec 1919-27)* † Beethoven:Adelaide, Op. 46; J. Brahms:Songs (6), Op. 86; Songs (9), Op. 32; F. Schubert:Songs (misc colls); R. Schumann:Dichterliebe, Op. 48; R. Strauss:Songs PRE (Lebendige Vergangenheit) ▲ 89188 (m) (16.97)

E. Schwarzkopf (sop) *(rec London, 1968)* ("Recital in Honour of Ernest Newman") † F. Schubert:Songs (misc); R. Strauss:Songs EKRP ▲ 4 (17.97)

E. Schwarzkopf (sop), G. Parsons (pno)—Gedichte von Goethe [No. 9, Mignon (Kennst du das Land)]; Gedichte von Mörike [No. 7, Das verlassene Mägdlein]; Spanisches Liederbuch (Geistliche Lieder) [No. 2, Die du Gott gebarst]; Spanisches Liederbuch (Weltliche Lieder) [No. 19, Trau nicht der Liebe]; Italienische Liederbücher [No. 11, Wie lange schon]; Gedichte von Eichendorff [No. 7, Die Zigeunerin] † W. A. Mozart:Songs; F. Schubert:Songs (misc colls); R. Schumann:Gesänge, Op. 31; Myrthen, Op. 25; E. Wolf-Ferrari:Preghiera AURC ▲ 123 (5.97)

F. Wunderlich (ten), J. Müller-Meyen (pno)—Italienische Liederbücher [No. 4, Gesegnet sei, durch den die Welt entstund; No. 13, Hoffärtig seid Ihr, schönes Kind; No. 31, Wie soll ich fröhlich sein; No. 8, Nun lass uns Frieden schliessen; No. 42, Nicht länger kann ich singen] *(rec Bamberg, Germany, 1964)* † G. Mahler:Lied von der Erde MYTO ▲ 975171 (17.97)

Spanisches Liederbuch (Geistliche Lieder) for Voice & Piano (1889-90)

J. Baker (mez), M. Isepp (pno)—No. 3, Nun wandre, Maria; No. 4, Die ihr schwebet; No. 6, Ach, des Knaben Augen; No. 9, Herr, was trägt der Boden hier † D. Argento:From the Diary of Virginia Woolf; Debussy:Songs; Duparc:Songs; G. Fauré:Songs DNC ▲ 1019 [ADD] (16.97)

A. Trianti (sop), E. Rethberg (sop), E. Gerhardt (mez), C. V. Bos (pno)—No. 4, Die ihr schwebet; No. 6, Ach, des Knaben Augen; No. 3, Nun wandre, Maria; No. 9, Herr, was trägt der Boden hier; No. 11, Klinge, klinge, mein Pandero; No. 7, Mühvoll komm ich und beladen [trans Geibel] ("The Hugo Wolf Society Complete Edition-1931-1938") † Über Nacht, UP 48; Alte Weisen; Gedichte nach Heine; Gedichte von Eichendorff; Gedichte von Goethe; Gedichte von Michelangelo; Gedichte von Mörike; Gedichte von Robert Reinick; Gedichte von Scheffel; Gedichte Eichendorff; Italienische Liederbücher; Lieder für eine Frauenstimme; Spanisches Liederbuch (Weltliche Lieder) EMIC 5-▲ 66640 (m) [ADD] (52.97)

Spanisches Liederbuch for Voice & Piano [after Heyse & Geibel] (1889-90)

J. DeGaetani (mez), G. Kalish (pno) [16 sels] *(rec ca 1974)* NON ▲ 79263 (9.97)

E. Schwarzkopf (sop), D. Fischer-Dieskau (bar), G. Moore (pno) *(rec Ufa-Tonstudio Berlin, Germany, Dec 1966 & Jan 1967)* DEUT (The Originals) 2-▲ 457726 [ADD] (22.97)

Spanisches Liederbuch (Weltliche Lieder) for Voice & Piano (1889-90)

A. Trianti (sop), R. Ginster (sop), M. Fuchs (sop), E. Gerhardt (mez), K. Erb (ten), G. Hüsch (bar), H. Janssen (bar), C. V. Bos (pno), H. U. Müller (pno), G. Moore (pno)—No. 2, In dem Schatten meiner Locken; No. 6, Wenn du zu den Blumen gehst; No. 13, Mögen alle bösen Zungen; No. 14, Köpfchen, nicht gewimmert; No. 16, Bitt' ihn, o Mutter; No. 5, Auf dem grünen Balkon; No. 4, Treibe nur mit Lieben Spott; No. 19, Trau nicht der Liebe; No. 28, Sie blasen zum Abmarsch; No. 20, Ach, im Maien war's; No. 11, Herz, verzage nicht geschwind; No. 22, Dereinst, dereinst, Gedanke mein; No. 21, Alle gingen, Herz, zur Ruh; No. 23, Tief im Herzen trag ich Pein; No. 24, Komm o Tod, von Nacht umgeben; No. 34, Geh, Geliebter, geh jetzt [trans Geibel] *(rec London, England, June 15, 1937)* ("The Hugo Wolf Society Complete Edition-1931-1938") † Über Nacht, UP 48; Alte Weisen; Gedichte nach Heine; Gedichte von Eichendorff; Gedichte von Goethe; Gedichte von Michelangelo; Gedichte von Mörike; Gedichte von Robert Reinick; Gedichte von Scheffel; Gedichte Eichendorff; Italienische Liederbücher; Lieder für eine Frauenstimme; Spanisches Liederbuch (Geistliche Lieder) EMIC 5-▲ 66640 (m) [ADD] (52.97)

WOLF, HUGO (cont.)
Über Nacht (song) for Voice & Piano, UP 48

E. Gerhardt (mez), C. V. Bos (pno) *(rec Small Queen's Hall, London, England, June 6, 1931)* ("The Hugo Wolf Society Complete Edition-1931-1938") † Alte Weisen; Gedichte nach Heine; Gedichte von Eichendorff; Gedichte von Goethe; Gedichte von Michelangelo; Gedichte von Mörike; Gedichte von Robert Reinick; Gedichte von Scheffel; Gedichte Eichendorff; Italienische Liederbücher; Lieder für eine Frauenstimme; Spanisches Liederbuch (Geistliche Lieder); Spanisches Liederbuch (Weltliche Lieder) EMIC 5-▲ 66640 (m) [ADD] (52.97)

WOLFE, JULIA (1958-

Four Marys for String Quartet (1991)

Cassatt String Quartet *(rec Jan 1993)* ("Cassatt") † T. Davidson:Cassandra Sings; D. Godfrey:Intermedio; Hovda:Lemniscates; Waggoner:Song:Strophic Vars CRI ▲ 671 [DDD] (16.97)

The Vermeer Room for Chamber Ensemble (1990)

L. Vaillancourt (cnd), Nouvel Ensemble Moderne *(rec United States of America, 1990)* ("Bang on a Can Live, Vol 1") † A. Cameron:Two Bits; Doerrfeld:Evening Chant; M. Gordon:Strange Quiet; T. Johnson:Failing; S. Lindroth:Relations to Rigor; Ziporyn:Luv Time CRI ▲ 628 [DDD] (16.97)

WOLFE, STANLEY (1924-

Canticle for Strings (1957)

P. Freeman (cnd), Mexican State SO † H. Aitken:Rosa de Fuego; Soledades, Cantata VII; D. Riley:Apparitions; D. E. Thomas:Many Happy Returns CRI ▲ 595 [DDD] (17.97)

WOLFF, CHRISTIAN (1934-

Bread & Roses for Piano (1976)

S. Pinkas (pno) ("Bread & Roses: Piano Works, 1976-1983") † Hay una Mujer Desaparecida; Preludes Pno; Song Pno MODE ▲ 43 [DDD] (17.97)

Hay Una Mujer Desaparecida for Piano (1979)

S. Pinkas (pno) ("Bread & Roses: Piano Works, 1976-1983") † Bread & Roses; Preludes Pno; Song Pno MODE ▲ 43 [DDD] (17.97)

Mayday Materials for Electronics

C. Wolff (synclavier) *(rec Dartmouth College, Hanover, NH)* ("CDCM Computer Music Series, Vol. 6") † J. Appleton:Brush Canyon; Degitaru Ongaku; D. E. Jones:Still Life in Wood & Metal; Still Life Dancing; P. Moravec:Devices & Desires CENT ▲ 2052 [DDD] (16.97)

Music of Wolff

Barton Workshop ("I Like to Think of Harriet Tubman") MODE ▲ 69 [DDD] (17.97)

Piano Song for Piano, "I Am a Dangerous Woman" (1983)

S. Pinkas (pno) ("Bread & Roses: Piano Works, 1976-1983") † Bread & Roses; Hay una Mujer Desaparecida; Preludes Pno MODE ▲ 43 [DDD] (17.97)

Preludes (11) for Piano (1981)

S. Pinkas (pno) ("Bread & Roses: Piano Works, 1976-1983") † Bread & Roses; Hay una Mujer Desaparecida; Song Pno MODE ▲ 43 [DDD] (17.97)

WOLFF, SEBASTIAN (1929-

Organ Music

J. Filsell (org)—Fantasia & Fugue; Advent Chorale; O come, O come Emmanuel; Lo, he comes with clouds descending; Prelude on Somerset Carol; Unto us is born a son; Chorale on Orlando Gibbons; Our Father; Nocturne; Come, Holy Ghost; Most ancient of all mysteries; Processional; Adagio & Fugue; O Sacred Head sore wounded; Fanfare for Easter Day; Jesus Christ is risen; At the Lamb's high feast; Christ the Lord; Carillon *(rec Buckfast Abbey org, England, Feb 1999)* HER ▲ 229 [DDD] (18.97)

WOLF-FERRARI, ERMANNO (1876-1948)

Le donne curiose (opera) [lib L. Sugana after Goldoni] (1902-03)

E. Fusco (sop), P. Bottazzo (ten), A. Mariotti (bass), C. Fabris (sgr), Rinaldi (cnd), Venice Theater Orch *(rec Jan 1968)* MONM 2-▲ 10141 (36.97)

Idillio-Concertino in A for Oboe, 2 Horns & String Orchestra, Op. 15 (1933)

S. Dent (ob), W. Rajski (cnd), Polish CO ("Greatest Oboe Concertos, Vol. 2") † J. S. Bach:Con 1 for 2 Hpds, BWV 1060; J. Haydn:Con Ob; A. Marcello:Con Ob Strs in d AMAT ▲ 9502 [DDD] (17.97)

H. Lucarelli (ob), D. Spieth (cnd), Lehigh Valley CO † S. Barber:Canzonetta; R. Strauss:Con Ob, AV144; Vaughan Williams:Con Ob KOCH ▲ 7023 [DDD]

Italian Songbook (21 songs) for Soprano & Piano, Op. 17

Y. Janicke (mez), B. Canino (pno) † Pno Music CPO ▲ 999270 (14.97)

Orchestral Music

J. Serebrier (cnd), Royal PO—I gioielli della Madonna; Quattro rusteghi; La dama boba; L'amore medico; Il campiello; Il segreto di Susanna [from operas] ASV ▲ 861 (12.97)

Overtures & Intermezzi

H. Rögner (cnd), Berlin RSO † Serenade Strs BER ▲ 9177 (10.97)

Piano Music

B. Canino (pno)—Rispetti, Opp. 11 & 12; 3 Impromptus, Op. 13; 3 Pno Pieces, Op. 14 † Italian Songbook, Op. 17 CPO ▲ 999270 (14.97)

Preghiera for Soprano & Piano

E. Schwarzkopf (sop), G. Parsons (pno) † W. A. Mozart:Songs; F. Schubert:Songs (misc colls); R. Schumann:Gesänge, Op. 31; Myrthen, Op. 25; H. Wolf:Songs (misc) AURC ▲ 123 (5.97)

Quintet in D♭ for Piano & Strings, Op. 6 (1900)

W. Sawallisch (pno), Leopolder String Quartet *(rec 1988)* ("Chamber Music") † Qnt Strs, Op. 24; Trio 1 Pno, Op. 5; Trio 2 Pno, Op. 7 MDG 2-▲ 3080310 [DDD] (35.97)

Quintet in C for Strings, Op. 24

F. Ruf (va), Leopolder String Quartet *(rec 1988)* ("Chamber Music") † Qnt Pno, Op. 6; Trio 1 Pno, Op. 5; Trio 2 Pno, Op. 7 MDG 2-▲ 3080310 [DDD] (35.97)

WOLF-FERRARI, ERMANNO (cont.)
Serenade in E♭ for Strings (?1893)
R. Padoin (cnd), Accademia Veneta CO ("Late Romantic Serenades") † E. Elgar:Serenade Strs, Op. 20; R. Fuchs:Serenade 3 Strs, Op. 21 PHEX ▲ 98207 (16.97)
H. Rögner (cnd), Berlin CO † Ovs & Intermezzi BER ▲ 9177 (10.97)
Sinfonia da camera in B♭ for 11 Instruments, Op. 8 (1901)
MiNensemblet *(rec Alter Pfarrsaal Nöttingen, Oct 12-17, 1995)* † E. Bloch:Episodes MARC ▲ 8223868 [DDD] (13.97)
Sly (opera) [lib Forzano after Shakespeare] (1927)
R. Frühbeck de Burgos (cnd) , D. Dessi (sop), J. Carreras (ten), J. Pons (bar) *(rec live Zurich, Switzerland, 1998)* LCD 2-▲ 240 (32.97)
Sonatas (3) for Violin & Piano [No. 1 in g, Op. 1 (1895); No. 2 in a, Op. 10 (1901); No. 3 in E, Op. 27 (1943)]
C. Rossi (vn), M. Vincenzi (pno) DYNC ▲ 68 [DDD] (17.97)
Suite-concertino in F for Bassoon, 2 Horns & Strings, Op. 16
C. Millard (bn), M. Bernardi (cnd), CBC Vancouver SO ("Concerti Italiani") † Donatoni:Con Bn; Nussio:Vars; N. Rota:Con Bn SMS ▲ 5185 (16.97)
Trio No. 1 in D for Piano, Violin & Cello, Op. 5 (before 1898)
Munich Piano Trio *(rec 1988)* ("Chamber Music") † Qnt Pno, Op. 6; Qnt Strs, Op. 24; Trio 2 Pno, Op. 7 MDG 2-▲ 3080310 [DDD] (35.97)
Raphael Trio † Trio 2 Pno, Op. 7 ASV ▲ 935 [DDD] (16.97)
Trio No. 2 in F# for Piano, Violin & Cello, Op. 7 (1900)
Munich Piano Trio *(rec 1988)* ("Chamber Music") † Qnt Pno, Op. 6; Qnt Strs, Op. 24; Trio 1 Pno, Op. 5 MDG 2-▲ 3080310 [DDD] (35.97)
Raphael Trio † Trio 1 Pno, Op. 5 ASV ▲ 935 [DDD] (16.97)

WÖLFL, JOSEPH (1773-1812)
Grand Duo in d for Cello & Piano, Op. 31 (1805)
B. Hampton (vc), N. Schwartz (pno) *(rec Palo Alto, 1978)* † Sons (30) Pno ORIO ▲ 7812 (13.97)
Sonatas (30) for Piano
V. Pleshakov (pno)—in c, Op. 25; in E, Op. 33/3; in d; Op. 33/2 *(rec Pacific Palisades, CA, 1969)* † Grand Duo Vc & Pno, Op. 31 ORIO ▲ 7812 (13.97)

WOLFORD, BILL (20th cent)
Music of Wolford
B. Wolford (elec/instr/tape/elec) ("Bill Wolford's Head") INNO ▲ 518 [DDD] (14.97)

WOLKING, HENRY (1947-
Methenyology for Orchestra (1988)
S. Kawalla (cnd), Koszalin State PO † R. Carl:Wide Open Field; J. Gallagher:Berceuse; I. Heifetz:Raga; Kiraly:Pinocchio (suite 1); T. Myers:Elegy VMM (Music from 6 Continents 1994) ▲ 3030 [DDD]
Pangaea for Orchestra
J. Russo (cl), M. Schatz (cnd), Fairbanks SO *(rec Alaska, United States of America)* ("Virtuoso Works for Clarinet & Orchestra") † Debussy:Première rapsodie Cl; Donizetti:Concertino Cl; Joio:Concertante Cl & Orch; I. Stravinsky:Pieces Cl; Swack:Sym 2 Strs *(E text)* CRSR ▲ 9459
Reaching for Orchestra
L. Poulson (mez), G. Elias (vn), K. Cardon (vc), L. Hammons (cl), T. Cheney (pno), M. Rosenzweig (cnd), Canyonlands *(rec Salt Lake City, UT, 1994-95)* ("New Music from Utah") † Cathey:Bardol Saga; M. Johnson:Nocturne; Quaglia:Quartetto; Roens:Delicate Arch; Invocation; Time & Again; Yao:Drifting About *([ENG] text)* CENT ▲ 2360 [DDD] (16.97)

WOLPE, STEFAN (1902-1972)
Battle Piece for Piano (1943-47)
M. Hamelin (pno) † Bolcom:New Etudes NWW ▲ 354 [DDD] (16.97)
G. D. Madge (pno) † Passacaglia Pno; Pno Music (misc); Toccata in 3 Parts Pno CPO ▲ 999055 [DDD] (14.97)
Cantata for solo Voice, Voices & Instruments [text Hölderlin, Herodotus, Creeley] (1963-68)
L. Bollinger (sop), C. Kallisch (mez), U. Kamps-Paulsen (mez), C. von Schmettow (alt), H. Clemens (spkr), H. C. Ziegler (spkr), J. Kussmaul (cnd), Robert Schumann CO *(rec Köln, Sept 1998)* † Qt Ob, Vc, Pno & Perc; Qt Strs *(E,G texts)* CPO ▲ 999090 [DDD] (14.97)
Form for Piano (1959)
R. Sherman (pno) *(rec Rutgers Presbyterian Church New York City)* ("Form") † Piece in 2 Parts; A. Berger:Pieces Pno; Septet NWW ▲ 80308 (16.97)
Form IV:Broken Sequences for Piano (1969)
P. Serkin (pno) † Passacaglia Pno; Pastorale Pno; Lieberson:Bagatelles Pno; I. Stravinsky:Serenade Pno; Son Pno NWW ▲ 344 [DDD] (16.97)
The Man from Midian (ballet) for Orchestra (1942)
Group for Contemporary Music † Qt Strs; 2nd Piece Vn; Schoenberg:Pieces Orch, Op. 16 KOCH ▲ 7315 (10.97)
Music of Wolpe
J. Castle (mez), A. Korf (cnd) —Musik für Hamlet for Fl, Cl & Vc (1929); To the Dancemaster for Mez, Cl & Pno (1938); Lieder von Bertolt Brecht for Mez & Pno; Qt 1 for Tpt, T Sax, Perc & Pno (1950); Piece in 2 Parts for 6 Players (1962); Piece for 2 Instrumental Units (1962); Solo Piece for Tpt (1966); Piece for Tpt & 7 Instrs (1971) KOCH ▲ 7141 [DDD] (17.97)
D. Holzman (pno) *(rec 1990)* † P. M. Davies:Farewell to Stromness; Son Pno; Yesnaby Ground; Pleskow:Son Pno CENT ▲ 2102 [DDD] (16.97)
Palestinian Notebook for Piano (1939)
D. Holzman (pno) ("Piano Music by Jewish Composers") † Avni:Epitaph; Ben-Haim (Frankenburger):Pieces Pno; E. Bloch:Visions & Prophecies; Schoenberg:Pieces (3) Pno, Op. 11 ALBA ▲ 283 [DDD] (16.97)
Passacaglia (study on an interval row) for Piano (1936; rev 1971)
G. D. Madge (pno) † Battle Piece; Pno Music (misc); Toccata in 3 Parts Pno CPO ▲ 999055 [DDD] (14.97)
P. Serkin (pno) † Form IV:Broken Sequences; Pastorale Pno; Lieberson:Bagatelles Pno; I. Stravinsky:Serenade Pno; Son Pno NWW ▲ 344 [DDD] (16.97)
K. Wolpe (pno) *(rec Sept 30-Oct 1 & Dec 14, 1992)* † Pno Music (misc); Zemach Suite LARG ▲ 5120 [DDD] (16.97)
Pastorale for Piano (1939)
P. Serkin (pno) † Form IV:Broken Sequences; Passacaglia Pno; Lieberson:Bagatelles Pno; I. Stravinsky:Serenade Pno; Son Pno NWW ▲ 344 [DDD] (16.97)
Piano Music (miscellaneous short pieces)
G. D. Madge (pno)—Gesang, weil ich etwas Teures verlassen mich; Stehende Musik (1925); Tango (1927); Rag-Caprice (1927); Marche caractéristique, Op. 10/1 (1928); Dance in Form of a Chaconne (1938); Displaced Spaces (1946); Form IV: Broken Sequences for Pno † Battle Piece; Passacaglia Pno; Toccata in 3 Parts Pno CPO ▲ 999055 [DDD] (14.97)
K. Wolpe (pno)—Early Piece; Studies, Part 1; 2 Studies, Part 2; Form for Pno; Form IV *(rec Sept 30-Oct 1 & Dec 14, 1992)* † Passacaglia Pno; Zemach Suite LARG ▲ 5120 [DDD] (16.97)
Piece in 3 Parts for Piano & 16 Instruments (1960-61)
P. Serkin (pno), O. Knussen (cnd) *(rec Lincoln Center New York City, Mar 15, 1992)* † Qnt w. Voice; Suite im Hexachord BRID ▲ 9043 [DDD] (17.97)
Piece in 2 Parts for Violin (1964)
R. M. Harbison (vn) *(rec Rutgers Presbyterian Church New York City)* ("Form") † Form; A. Berger:Pieces Pno; Septet NWW ▲ 80308 (16.97)
Quartet for Oboe, Cello, Piano & Percussion (1955)
B. Glaetzner (cnd), Hanns Eisler New Music Group Leipzig *(rec Köln, Dec 1989)* † Cant Voc, Vocs & Instrs; Qt Strs *(E,G texts)* CPO ▲ 999090 [DDD] (14.97)
F. Sherry (vc), S. Taylor (ob), A. Karis (pno), D. Kennedy (perc) *(rec Nov 9-10, 1991)* † Son Vn; Trio in 2 Parts Fl KOCH ▲ 7112 [DDD] (16.97)
Quartet for Strings (1968-69)
Group for Contemporary Music members † Man from Midian; 2nd Piece Vn; Schoenberg:Pieces Orch, Op. 16 KOCH ▲ 7315 (10.97)
Juilliard String Quartet † Babbitt:Qt 4 Strs; R. Sessions:Qt 2 Strs CRI ▲ 587 [DDD] (16.97)
Silesian String Quartet *(rec Köln, Apr 1991)* † Cant Voc, Vocs & Instrs; Qt Ob, Vc, Pno & Perc *(E,G texts)* CPO ▲ 999090 [DDD] (14.97)
Quartet for Trumpet, Tenor Saxophone, Percussion & Piano (1954)
A. Weisberg (cnd) † Babbitt:All Set; Rochberg:Serenata d'estate; S. Shifrin:Satires of Circumstance; R. Wernick:Kaddish-Requiem NON ▲ 79222 (16.97)
Quintet with Voice for Baritone, Clarinet, Horn, Cello, Harp & Piano [text H. Morley] (1956-57)
J. Opalach (bass), W. Purvis (cnd), Speculum Musicae, Speculum Musicae [also includes reading by Hilda Morley of her poem] *(rec New York City, Dec 23, 1992)* † Piece in 3 Parts; Suite im Hexachord BRID ▲ 9043 [DDD] (17.97)

WOLPE, STEFAN (cont.)
Second Piece for Violin Alone (1966)
Group for Contemporary Music members † Man from Midian; Qt Strs; Schoenberg:Pieces Orch, Op. 16 KOCH ▲ 7315 (10.97)
P. Zukofsky (vn) *(rec Paul Hall Julliard School of Music, May 21, 1972)* † H. Brant:Quombex; J. Cage:Nocturne; M. Feldman:Vertical Thoughts II; P. Glass:Strung Out; Scelsi:Anahit; Xenakis:Mikka; Mikka S CP2 ▲ 108 [AAD] (19.97)
Solo Piece for Trumpet (1966)
G. Schwarz (tpt) † H. Brant:Con Tpt; E. Carter:Canon for 3; Moryl:Salvos; Whittenberg:Polyphony PHOE ▲ 115 [AAD] (15.97)
Sonata for Oboe & Piano (1938-41)
H. Sargous (ob), L. Ward (pno) ("Architecture & Aria: Three Centuries of Virtuoso Oboe") † J. S. Bach:Sons Fl; A. Mead:Scena; Pasculli:Grand Con Ob CRYS ▲ 327 [DDD] (15.97)
Sonata for Violin & Piano (1949)
J. Fleezanis (vn), G. Ohlsson (pno) *(rec Nov 9-10, 1991)* † Qt Ob, Vc, Pno & Perc; Trio in 2 Parts Fl KOCH ▲ 7112 [DDD] (16.97)
Songs (miscellaneous)
E. Berendsen (mez), D. Bloch (pno)—Lieder (5) on Hölderlein Texts; Onder dem Kinds Wiegele; Es Kimt Gefloigen di Gilderne Pawe; Sim Shalom [from Ballad of the Unknown Soldier]; Rechot; Mazkeret [both from Lieder (4), Op. 29]; Song of Songs [from Songs (6) from the Hebrew]; Lo Nelech Mi Po; Saleinu al K'tefeinu; Tel-Aviv; Apollo & Artemis; The Hour Glass; The Angel; Music for Medium Voice & Piano ("Wild Roses") SYMP ▲ 1216 [DDD] (18.97)
Suite im Hexachord for Oboe & Clarinet (1936)
Speculum Musicae members *(rec Astoria, Jan 12, 1993)* † Piece in 3 Parts; Qnt w. Voice BRID ▲ 9043 [DDD] (17.97)
Symphony for Orchestra (1955-56; rev 1964)
A. Weisberg (cnd), Orch of the 20th Century † R. Sessions:Con Vn CRI ▲ 676 [ADD] (16.97)
Toccata in 3 Parts for Piano (1946)
G. D. Madge (pno) *(rec 1969)* † Battle Piece; Passacaglia Pno; Pno Music (misc) CPO ▲ 999055 [DDD] (14.97)
Trio in 2 Parts for Flute Cello & Piano (1964)
F. Sherry (vc), H. Sollberger (fl), C. Wuorinen (pno) *(rec Nov 9-10, 1991)* † Qt Ob, Vc, Pno & Perc; Son Vn KOCH ▲ 7112 [DDD] (16.97)
Zemach Suite for Piano (1939)
K. Wolpe (pno) *(rec Sept 30-Oct 1 & Dec 14, 1992)* † Passacaglia Pno; Pno Music (misc) LARG ▲ 5120 [DDD] (16.97)

WOMACK, DONALD REID (1966-
Pentacle for Orchestra (1995)
D. Stock (cnd), Silesian PO † J. Caldwell:Elegy; D. Kowalski:Double Helix; Lomon:Terra Incognita; Olmstead:Sinfonia Borealis; N. Strandberg:Preludes for Orchestra MASM (MMC New Century: Volume XI) ▲ 2069 [DDD] (16.97)

WOOD, CHARLES (1866-1926)
Hail Gladdening Light (choral)
F. Grier (cnd), Christ Church Cathedral Choir, Oxford, C. Daniels (vc), H. Bicket (org) *(rec Christ Church Catheral, Oxford, England)* ("O For the Wings of a Dove") † Anonymous:Church Music; J. S. Bach:Cant 147; Mendelssohn (-Bartholdy):Choral Music; W. A. Mozart:Ave verum corpus, K.618; Stanford:Church Music ASVQ ▲ 6019 [ADD] (10.97)
Music of Charles Wood
M. Brewer (cnd), National Youth Choir of Great Britain *(Nights of Music; The Whispering Waves; If Love Be Dead; Song for a Dance; As the Moon's Soft Splendour; The Nymph's Fawn; Music, When Soft Voices Die; How Sweet the Tuneful Bells)*, R. Isaacs (cnd), National Youth Choir of Great Britain *(The Widow Bird; Come, Sleep; When Thou Art Nigh; A Clear Midnight; How Dear to Me; Hence Away, Begone!; Full Fathom Five; When Winds That Move Not) (rec Marlborough College, England, Aug 19-20, 1997)* † Pearsall:Songs PRIO ▲ 622 [DDD] (16.97)
Preludes (16) for Organ
artist unknown ("Organ Music from the Island of Ireland") † J. S. Bach:Toccata & Fugue Org, BWV 565; J. Dexter:Londonderry Air; Kitson:Communion on an Irish Air; C. S. Lang:Tuba Tune, Op. 15; Stanford:Org Music; Widor:Sym 5 Org, Op. 42/1 GILD ▲ 7122 [ADD] (16.97)

WOOD, FREDERIC HERBERT (1880-1963)
Scenes from Kent (4) for Organ, Op. 23 (1923)
D. Liddle (org) *(rec org of St. Ignatius Loyola New York)* † Hollins:Concert Ov 2; Widor:Sym 9 Org, Op. 70 GILD ▲ 7149 [DDD] (16.97)

WOOD, HAYDN (1882-1959)
Orchestral Music
A. Leaper (cnd), Czech-Slovak RSO Bratislava—Apollo Ov; Brown Bird Singing; Joyousness Waltz; London Cameos; Mannin Veen; Rhap Mylecharane; Seafarer; Serenade to Youth; Sketch of a Dandy MARC (British Light Music) ▲ 8223402 [DDD] (13.97)

WOOD, HENRY JOSEPH (1869-1944)
Divertimento for Piano & Orchestra
C. Sorel (pno), E. Buckley (cnd), WNYC Fest Orch *(rec live, Carnegie Hall, NY, 1961)* ("3 American Piano Concertos") † MacDowell:Con 2 Pno, Op. 23; H. Morris:Con Pno EMSO ▲ 8156 (9.97)
Fantasia on British Sea Songs for Orchestra & Chorus
P. Daniel (cnd), English Northern Philharmonia, Leeds Festival Chorus *(rec Town Hall, Leeds, England, 1996)* † M. Arnold:Tam o'Shanter Ov, Op. 51; E. Elgar:Enigma Vars, Op. 36; Pomp & Circumstance, Op. 39; H. Parry:I Was Glad; Jerusalem; W. Walton:Crown Imperial; Orb & Sceptre NXIN ▲ 8553981 [DDD] (5.97)

WOOD, JAMES (1953-
Phainomena for Instruments, Voices & Tape (1994)
J. Wood (cnd) , New London Chamber Choir *(rec 1993-97)* ("Two Men Meet") † Two Men Meet; Venancio Mbande Talking with the Trees NMCC ▲ 44 [DDD] (17.97)
Spirit Festival with Lamentations for Quartertone Marimba & Percussion Quartet (1992)
R. van Sice (mar/perc), Percussive Rotterdam *(rec Gent Belgium, June 26, 1993)* † Village Burial with Fire Mar MODE ▲ 51 [DDD] (17.97)
Two Men Meet, Each Presuming the Other to Be from a Distant Planet (concerto) for Percussionist & 24 Instruments (1995)
S. Schick (perc), J. Wood (cnd) *(rec 1993-97)* ("Two Men Meet") † Phainomena; Venancio Mbande Talking with the Trees NMCC ▲ 44 [DDD] (17.97)
Venancio Mbande Talking with the Trees (concerto) for Quartertone Maribma & 15 Instruments
K. Kato (mar), J. Wood (cnd), Critical Band *(rec 1993-97)* ("Two Men Meet") † Phainomena; Two Men Meet NMCC ▲ 44 [DDD] (17.97)
Village Burial with Fire for Marimba & Percussion Ensemble (1989)
R. van Sice (mar), Percussive Rotterdam *(rec Gent Belgium, June 26, 1993)* † Spirit Festival with Lamentations MODE ▲ 51 [DDD] (17.97)

WOODS, PHIL (1931-
Improvisations (3) for Saxophone Quartet (1978)
Prism Saxophone Quartet † P.-M. Dubois:Qt Sax; M. Levy:Sax Qt Music; R. Peck:Drastic Measures; Singelée:Qt 1 Saxes, Op. 53 KOCH ▲ 7024 [DDD] (16.97)

WOOF, BARBARA (1958-
Soundings for Gamelan (1988)
J. Sligter (cnd) *(rec Singelkerk, Amsterdam, Netherlands, Dec 1995)* † A. Alberts:Haké; Eisma:Mawar Jiwa; T. Leeuw:Gending; Termos:Kendang EMEC ▲ 92062 [DDD]

WOOLDRIDGE, DAVID (20th cent)
Partita for Winds, Op. 38
G. Kessler (gtr), D. Bender (E hn) *(rec Berklee College of Music, Boston, MA)* ("Trio Sonata - Encore!") † J. S. Bach:Sons & Partitas Vn; Trio Son for 2 Vns; E. Granados:Danzas españolas (10) Pno; Goyescas:Intermezzo; E. Noda:Tanka Fl, Ob & Gtr; Telemann:Essercizii Musici; Fants (12) Fl, TWV40:2-13; T. Tomkins:Instrumental & Vocal Music; Vivaldi:Con Mands, RV.532 *(E text)* BOSK ▲ 114 [DDD] (15.97)

WOOLF, RANDALL (1959-
Dancétudes for Piano (1982-83)
K. Supové (pno) *(rec Nov 1992)* ("Figure 88") † M. Epstein:Waterbowls; L. Foss:Solo Pno; D. Lang:While Nailing at Random; Rzewski:North American Ballads CRI (Emergency Music) ▲ 653 [DDD] (17.97)
Ice 9 for Ensemble (1992)
B. Lubman (cnd) *(rec Performing Arts Center SUNY Purchase, June 1995 & Nov 1997)* ("Rock Steady") † New Dancetudes; Quicksilver; Shakedown; Your Name Backwards CRI (Emergency Music) ▲ 777 [DDD] (16.97)

WOOLF, RANDALL (cont.)
New Dancetudes for Piano (1988)
K. Supové (pno) *(rec Music Division SUNY Purchase, Jan 1998)* ("Rock Steady") † Ice 9; Quicksilver; Shakedown; Your Name Backwards CRI (Emergency Music) ▲ 777 [DDD] (16.97)
Nobody Move for Piano
P. Goodson (pno) ("Strange Attractors: New American Music for Piano") † J. Harbison:Occasional Pieces; M. Herman:Arena; S. Jaffe:Impromptu; Kyr:White Tigers; A. R. Thomas:Whites ALBA ▲ 231 [DDD] (16.97)
Quicksilver for Flute & Violin (1992)
L. Chang (vn), J. DeMart (fl) *(rec Performing Arts Center SUNY Purchase, June 1995 & Nov 1997)* ("Rock Steady") † Ice 9; New Dancetudes; Shakedown; Your Name Backwards CRI (Emergency Music) ▲ 777 [DDD] (16.97)
Shakedown for Ensemble (1990)
B. Lubman (cnd) *(rec Performing Arts Center SUNY Purchase, June 1995 & Nov 1997)* ("Rock Steady") † Ice 9; New Dancetudes; Quicksilver; Your Name Backwards CRI (Emergency Music) ▲ 777 [DDD] (16.97)
Your Name Backwards for Voice & Keyboards
Twisted Tutu *(rec Performing Arts Center SUNY Purchase, June 1995 & Nov 1997)* ("Rock Steady") † Ice 9; New Dancetudes; Quicksilver; Shakedown CRI (Emergency Music) ▲ 777 [DDD] (16.97)

WOOLLEN, RUSSELL (1923-
Elegy & Divertimento for Strings (1992)
J. Stephens (cnd) ("From Fantasy to Elegy") † Fant Fl; Qt Fl; Trio Fl AMCA ▲ 10310 [DDD]
Fantasy for Flute & Harpsichord (1968)
J. Stephens (cnd) ("From Fantasy to Elegy") † Elegy & Divert Strs; Qt Fl; Trio Fl AMCA ▲ 10310 [DDD]
Lines of Steven Crane (song cycle) for Voice & Chamber Orchestra [text S. Crane] (ca 1981)
M. Ingham (bar), J. Stephens (cnd), American Camerata *(rec Rockville, MD)* † Madrigals; Songs of Eve; Songs on Poems of Elinor Wylie *([ENG] text)* AMCA ▲ 10311 (16.97)
Madrigals (3) for Voice & Piano [text Elinor Wylie]
K. Krebill (cnd), Musikanten *(rec Rockville, MD)* † Lines of Steven Crane; Songs of Eve; Songs on Poems of Elinor Wylie *([ENG] text)* AMCA ▲ 10311 (16.97)
Quartet for Flute, Oboe, Cello & Piano (1967; rev 1989)
J. Stephens (cnd) ("From Fantasy to Elegy") † Elegy & Divert Strs; Fant Fl; Trio Fl AMCA ▲ 10310 [DDD]
Songs of Eve (song cycle) for Voice & Piano [text L. Pastan] (1988)
L. Mabbs (sop), J. McGinn (pno) *(rec Rockville, MD)* † Lines of Steven Crane; Madrigals; Songs on Poems of Elinor Wylie *([ENG] text)* AMCA ▲ 10311 (16.97)
Songs (3) on Poems of Elinor Wylie for Voice & Piano (1978)
L. Mabbs (sop), J. McGinn (pno) *(rec Rockville, MD)* † Lines of Steven Crane; Madrigals; Songs of Eve *([ENG] text)* AMCA ▲ 10311 (16.97)
Trio for Flute, Clarinet & Piano (1985)
J. Stephens (cnd) ("From Fantasy to Elegy") † Elegy & Divert Strs; Fant Fl; Qt Fl AMCA ▲ 10310 [DDD]

WOOLRICH, JOHN (1954-
Concert Arias (4) for Voices & Orchestra
E. Hulse (sop), A. Eikenes (sop), C. Cairns (mez), J. Lubbock (cnd), St. John's Smith Square Orch † It Is Midnight, Dr. Schweitzer; Leap in the Dark; Theatre Represents a Garden: Night; Ulysses Awakes ASV ▲ 1049 (16.97)
It Is Midnight, Dr. Schweitzer for Orchestra
J. Lubbock (cnd), St. John's Smith Square Orch † Concert Arias (4); Leap in the Dark; Theatre Represents a Garden: Night; Ulysses Awakes ASV ▲ 1049 (16.97)
A Leap in the Dark for Orchestra
J. Lubbock (cnd), St. John's Smith Square Orch † Concert Arias (4); It Is Midnight, Dr. Schweitzer; Theatre Represents a Garden: Night; Ulysses Awakes ASV ▲ 1049 (16.97)
Music of John Woolrich
M. Wiegold (sop), J. Atkins (va), D. Mason (cnd) ("Lending Wings") NMCC ▲ 29 [DDD] (17.97)
Si va Facendo Notte for Clarinet & 11 Solo Strings (1991)
M. Van de Wiel (b cl), J. Clayton (cnd), Chetham's CO ("Mozart Reflections") † Birtwistle:Linoi 1; W. A. Mozart:Con Cl, K.622; Süssmayr:Con Movt OLY ▲ 484 [DDD] (16.97)
The Theatre Represents a Garden: Night for Orchestra
J. Lubbock (cnd), St. John's Smith Square Orch † Concert Arias (4); It Is Midnight, Dr. Schweitzer; Leap in the Dark; Ulysses Awakes ASV ▲ 1049 (16.97)
Ulysses Awakes for Viola & Orchestra
J. Atkins (va), J. Lubbock (cnd), St. John's Smith Square Orch † Concert Arias (4); It Is Midnight, Dr. Schweitzer; Leap in the Dark; Theatre Represents a Garden: Night ASV ▲ 1049 (16.97)

WORK, HENRY CLAY (1832-1884)
Colonel Bogey March for Band
R. Bernat (cnd), River City Brass Band † Marching through Georgia; H. Fillmore:Marches (misc); E. F. Goldman:On the Mall; Langford:Carnival Day; J. P. Sousa:Invictus; Nobles of the Mystic Shrine; Thunderer; E. Tomlinson:Best Foot Forward; M. Wilson:British Grenadiers; Men of Harlech; Seventy-Six Trombones RCBB ▲ 191
Marching through Georgia for Band
R. Bernat (cnd), River City Brass Band † Colonel Bogey March; H. Fillmore:Marches (misc); E. F. Goldman:On the Mall; Langford:Carnival Day; J. P. Sousa:Invictus; Nobles of the Mystic Shrine; Thunderer; E. Tomlinson:Best Foot Forward; M. Wilson:British Grenadiers; Men of Harlech; Seventy-Six Trombones RCBB ▲ 191

WORK, JOHN WESLEY (II) (1901-1967)
Scuppernong for Piano (1951)
N. Hinderas (pno) ("Piano Music by African-American Composers") † Dett:In the Bottoms; T. R. Hakim:Sound Gone; W. G. Still:Sahdji; G. Walker:Son 1 Pno; O. Wilson:Pno Piece CRI 2-▲ 629 [ADD] (31.97)
C. Jackson (pno) ("American Journey") † Dett:In the Bottoms; G. Gershwin:Rhap in Blue; R. Goldmark:Prairie Idylls; R. Harris:American Ballads; Q. Porter:Son Pno DTT ▲ 9807 (17.97)

WORLEY, JOHN C. (1919-1999)
Claremont Concerto for Saxophone & Orchestra (1962)
L. Gwozdz (sax), S. Hass (sax), K. Trevor (cnd), Bohuslav Martinů PO *(rec Zlín, Czech Republic, June 12-14, 1998)* † W. Benson:Aeolian Song; K. Husa:Elegie et Rondeau; W. G. Still:Romance; Wirth:Inglewood Concerto; Jephthah ALBA ▲ 331 [DDD] (16.97)

WOYRSCH, FELIX (1860-1944)
Symphonic Prologue to Dante's Divine Comedy for Orchestra, Op. 40 (1892)
M. A. Gómez-Martínez (cnd), Hamburg SO † Sym 1; A. Reicha:Qnt Fl; Qnt Ob MDG ▲ 3010501 [DDD] (17.97)
Symphony No. 1 in c, Op. 52 (1908)
M. A. Gómez-Martínez (cnd), Hamburg SO † Sym Prologue to Dante's Divine Comedy, Op. 40; A. Reicha:Qnt Fl; Qnt Ob MDG ▲ 3010501 [DDD] (17.97)

WRAGGETT, WES R. D. (20th cent)
Maya for Guitar & Tape (1990)
W. Beauvais (gtr), W. Wraggett (tape) *(rec Toronto, 1989-97)* ("A Bridge Beyond") † Komorous:Amaryllis; Kucharzyk:Impulse; Mozetich:Pieces Gtr; Siddall:Skook's Curiosity; S. Wingfield:Teyata CTR ▲ 6198 [DDD] (16.97)

WRANITZKY, PAUL (1756-1808)
Harmonie in F for Wind Ensemble
T. Oray (ob), K. Kadereit (ob), W. Esch (cl), A. Münten (cl), J. Thomsen (bn), K. Hoffmann (bn), E. Hellrung (hn), G. Reuber (hn) *(rec Jun 1997)* † V. V. Mašek:Serenade; Mysliveček:Octets Ww; Triebensee:Partita ARS ▲ 368357 [DDD] (15.99)

WRIGHT, M. SEARLE (1918-
Introduction, Passacaglia & Fugue for Organ
F. Swann (org) † J. S. Bach:Passacaglia & Fugue Org, BWV 582; C. Franck:Chorales Org, M.38-40 GOT ▲ 49049 [DDD] (17.97)

WRIGHT, MARY (dates unknown)
Lizard Belly Moon for Electric Guitars
M. Stewart (elec gtr), B. Anderson (elec gtr), J. Tamburello (elec gtr), R. Black (elec bass) *(rec NYC, NY, 1991)* ("Bang on a Can - Live, Vol. 3") † L. Bouchard:Lung Ta; Didkovsky:I Kick My Hand; O. J. Garcia:Colores Ultraviolados; B. Marcus:Adam and Eve; P. Reller:Carcass CRI ▲ 672 [DDD] (16.97)

WRIGHT, MAURICE (1949-
Chamber Symphony for Piano & Electronic Sound
M. Hamelin (pno) † Night Watch; Son 2 Pno; Suite Pno CRI ▲ 660 [DDD] (16.97)
Choral Music
P. Schubert (cnd), New Calliope Singers—When As in Silks; Alas This Life; Expiration; My Love in Her Attire *(rec NYC, NY, June 1990)* † Babbitt:Cultivated Choruses; J. Druckman:Corinna's Going A-Maying; Death Be Not Proud; Faery Beam upon You; Madrigals; Shake off Your Heavy Trance; S. Gerber:Saison en enfer; Gideon:Habitable Earth; Monod:Cantus Contra Cantum IV CRI ▲ 638 [DDD] (16.97)

WRIGHT, MAURICE (cont.)
Night Scenes for Orchestra (1989)
G. Rothman (cnd), Riverside SO † Davidovsky:Divert Vc; Korf:Sym 2 NWW ▲ 383 [DDD] (16.97)
Night Watch for Soprano & Piano
J. K. Applebaum (sop), M. Hamelin (pno) † Chamber Sym Pno; Son 2 Pno; Suite Pno CRI ▲ 660 [DDD] (16.97)
Quintet for Brass (1986)
American Brass Quintet † Bolcom:Qnt; J. Druckman:Other Voices; R. Shapey:Qnt Brass NWW ▲ 377 [DDD] (16.97)
Sonata No. 2 for Piano
M. Hamelin (pno) † Chamber Sym Pno; Night Watch; Suite Pno CRI ▲ 660 [DDD] (16.97)
Sonata for Piano (1982)
M. Hamelin (pno) † C. Ives:Son 2 Pno NWW ▲ 378 [DDD] (16.97)
Suite for Piano
M. Hamelin (pno) † Chamber Sym Pno; Night Watch; Son 2 Pno CRI ▲ 660 [DDD] (16.97)

WUORINEN, CHARLES (1938-
Album Leaf for Chamber Ensemble
Group for Contemporary Music † Fortune; Tashi; Vars II Vc; Vars Vn KOCH ▲ 7618 (10.97)
Archaeopteryx for Bass Trombone & 10 Players (1978)
D. Taylor (b trbn), C. Wuorinen (cnd) † Archangel; Five; Hyperion KOCH ▲ 7614 (10.97)
Archangel for Bass Trombone & String Quartet (1977)
D. Taylor (b trbn), C. Wuorinen (cnd) † Archaeopteryx; Five; Hyperion KOCH ▲ 7614 (10.97)
The Blue Bamboula for Piano (1980)
G. Ohlsson (pno) † Fant Vn; Long & the Short; Pieces Vn; Spinoff BRID ▲ 9008 [DDD] (17.97)
Chamber Concerto for Flute & 10 Instruments (1964)
H. Sollberger (fl), C. Wuorinen (cnd), Group for Contemporary Music *(rec Columbia Univ New York)* † Chamber Con Tuba; Con Pno; 2-Part Sym CRI (American Master) ▲ 744 [ADD] (16.97)
Chamber Concerto for Tuba, 12 Winds & 12 Drums (1970)
D. Braynard (tuba), C. Wuorinen (cnd), Group for Contemporary Music † Chamber Con Fl; Con Pno; 2-Part Sym CRI (American Master) ▲ 744 [ADD] (16.97)
Concerto No. 3 for Piano & Orchestra
G. Ohlsson (pno), H. Blomstedt (cnd), San Francisco SO † Golden Dance NON ▲ 79185 [DDD] (16.97)
Concerto for Piano & Orchestra (1966)
C. Wuorinen (pno), J. Dixon (cnd), Royal PO *(rec 1968)* † Chamber Con Fl; Chamber Con Tuba; 2-Part Sym CRI (American Master) ▲ 744 [ADD] (16.97)
Double Solo for Horn Trio
Group for Contemporary Music ("Wuorinen Trios") † Trio Bass Trbn; Trio Hn; Trio Hn Continued; Trio Pno; Trio Trbn KOCH ▲ 7617 (10.97)
Duo for Violin & Piano (1966)
P. Zukofsky (vn), C. Wuorinen (pno) ("The Winds") † Vars Bn; Winds NWW ▲ 80517 (16.97)
Fantasia for Violin & Piano (1974)
B. Hudson (vn), G. Ohlsson (pno) † Blue Bamboula; Long & the Short; Pieces Vn; Spinoff BRID ▲ 9008 [DDD] (17.97)
Fast Fantasy for Cello & Piano (1979)
F. Sherry (vc), C. Wuorinen (pno) † Qt 3 Strs; Son Vn NWW ▲ 385 [DDD] (16.97)
Five (concerto) for Amplified Cello & Orchestra (1987)
F. Sherry (vc), C. Wuorinen (cnd) † Archaeopteryx; Archangel; Hyperion KOCH ▲ 7614 (10.97)
Fortune for Chamber Ensemble
Group for Contemporary Music † Album Leaf; Tashi; Vars II Vc; Vars Vn KOCH ▲ 7618 (10.97)
The Golden Dance for Piano & Orchestra
G. Ohlsson (pno), H. Blomstedt (cnd), San Francisco SO † Con 3 Pno NON ▲ 79185 [DDD] (16.97)
Hyperion for 12 Instruments (1975)
C. Wuorinen (cnd) † Archaeopteryx; Archangel; Five KOCH ▲ 7614 (10.97)
The Long & the Short for Violin (1969)
B. Hudson (vn) † Blue Bamboula; Fant Vn; Pieces Vn; Spinoff BRID ▲ 9008 [DDD] (17.97)
Missa Brevis for Chorus and Organ (1991)
H. Chaney (cnd), St. Ignatius of Antioch Choir, H. Chaney (org) *(rec Casavant Frères org, New York, NY, Feb 23, 1992)* † Certon:Missa 'Sus le pont d'Avignon'; Dunstable:Sancta Maria; Duruflé:Mass, "Cum jubilo", Op. 11; Tallis:Motets; Victoria:Cum beatus Ignatius *([ENG,LAT,FRE]text)* MUA ▲ 4798 [DDD]
Music of Wuorinen
Group for Contemporary Music—Qnt Pno; Lightenings VIII; The Mission of Virgil; Qt Perc KOCH ▲ 7410 (16.97)
Percussion Duo for Piano & Percussion (1979)
New Millennium Ensemble members [plus others] *(rec SUNY, Stonybrook, NY)* ("H.C.E.: Here Comes Everybody") † M. Feldman:I Met Heine in the Rue Fürstenberg; Festinger:Serenade for 6; R. Morris:Broken Consort CRI ▲ 772 [DDD] (16.97)
Percussion Symphony for 24 Percussionists (1976)
C. Wuorinen (cnd) NON ▲ 79150
Piano Music
A. Feinberg (pno)—Bagatelle; Capriccio † Son 3 Pno; M. Feldman:Palais de Mari KOCH ▲ 7308 (10.97)
Pieces (6) for Violin & Piano (1977)
B. Hudson (vn), G. Ohlsson (pno) † Blue Bamboula; Fant Vn; Long & the Short; Spinoff BRID ▲ 9008 [DDD] (17.97)
Quartet for Saxophones (1992)
Raschèr Saxophone Quartet *(rec 1997-98)* ("America") † S. Adler:Line Drawings; S. Corbett:Vars Saxes; C. Florio:Qt Saxes; W. Peterson:Windup; Starer:Light & Shadow BIS ▲ 953 [DDD] (17.97)
Quartet No. 2 for Strings (1979)
Group for Contemporary Music † J. Harvey:Qt 1 Strs; W. Peterson:Qt 1 Strs KOCH ▲ 7615 (10.97)
Quartet No. 3 for Strings (1987)
B. Hudson (vn), C. Zeavin (vn), L. Martin (va), F. Sherry (vc) † Fast Fant Vc; Son Vn NWW ▲ 385 [DDD] (16.97)
A Reliquary for Igor Stravinsky for Orchestra & Chorus (1975)
O. Knussen (cnd), London Sinfonietta † I. Stravinsky:Abraham & Isaac; Flood; Requiem Canticles; Vars 'Aldous Huxley in memoriam' Orch DEUT ▲ 47068 [DDD] (16.97)
Sacred Music
E. Waart (cnd), Minnesota Orch—Mass for the Restoration of St. Luke in the Fields; A Solis Ortu; Ave Christe; Genesis KOCH ▲ 7336 [DDD] (16.97)
Sonata No. 3 for Piano
A. Feinberg (pno) † Pno Music; M. Feldman:Palais de Mari KOCH ▲ 7308 (10.97)
Sonata for Violin & Piano (1988)
B. Hudson (vn), G. Ohlsson (pno) † Fast Fant Vc; Qt 3 Strs NWW ▲ 385 [DDD] (16.97)
Spinoff for Violin, Double Bass & Conga Drums (1983)
B. Hudson (vn), D. Palma (db), J. Passaro (perc) † Blue Bamboula; Fant Vn; Long & the Short; Pieces Vn BRID ▲ 9008 [DDD] (17.97)
Tashi for Chamber Ensemble
Group for Contemporary Music † Album Leaf; Fortune; Vars II Vc; Vars Vn KOCH ▲ 7618 (10.97)
Trio for Bass Trombone, Tuba & Double Bass (1981)
Group for Contemporary Music ("Wuorinen Trios") † Double Solo; Trio Hn; Trio Hn Continued; Trio Pno; Trio Trbn KOCH ▲ 7617 (10.97)
Trio for Horn, Violin & Piano (1981)
Group for Contemporary Music ("Wuorinen Trios") † Double Solo; Trio Bass Trbn; Trio Hn Continued; Trio Pno; Trio Trbn KOCH ▲ 7617 (10.97)
Trio for Horn, Violin & Piano Continued (1985)
Group for Contemporary Music ("Wuorinen Trios") † Double Solo; Trio Bass Trbn; Trio Hn; Trio Pno; Trio Trbn KOCH ▲ 7617 (10.97)
Trio for Piano, Violin & Cello (1983)
Group for Contemporary Music ("Wuorinen Trios") † Double Solo; Trio Bass Trbn; Trio Hn; Trio Hn Continued; Trio Trbn KOCH ▲ 7617 (10.97)
Trio for Trombone, Marimba & Piano (1985)
Group for Contemporary Music ("Wuorinen Trios") † Double Solo; Trio Bass Trbn; Trio Hn; Trio Hn Continued; Trio Pno KOCH ▲ 7617 (10.97)

WUORINEN, CHARLES (cont.)

Two-Part Symphony (1977-78)
D. R. Davies (cnd), American Composers Orch *(rec Alice Tully Hall NYC, Dec 1978)* † Chamber Con Fl; Chamber Con Tuba; Con Pno CRI (American Master) ▲ 744 [ADD] (16.97)

Variations for Bassoon (1971-72)
D. MacCourt (bn), S. Jolles (hp), G. Gottlieb (timp) ("The Winds") † Duo Vn; Winds NWW ▲ 80517 (16.97)

Variations for Violin
Group for Contemporary Music † Album Leaf; Fortune; Tashi; Vars II Vc KOCH ▲ 7618 (10.97)

Variations II for Cello
Group for Contemporary Music † Album Leaf; Fortune; Tashi; Vars Vn KOCH ▲ 7618 (10.97)

The Winds for Chamber Ensemble (1977)
A. Korf (cnd) ("The Winds") † Duo Vn; Vars Bn NWW ▲ 80517 (16.97)

WÜRTZLER, ARISTID VON (1930-

Modern Sketches for Harp
S. Kowalczuk (hp) ("Festival on the Classical Harp") † I. Albéniz:Pno Music (misc); Albrechtsberger:Partita Hp; Grandjany:Rhap Hp, Op. 10; W. A. Mozart:Adagio & Rondo, K.617 HUN ▲ 31577 (16.97)

WÜSTHOFF, KLAUS (1922-

Concerto de Samba
C. Bruinsma (gtr), P. Rueffer (gtr) *(rec Bedford School, England)* ("Brazileira") † L. Almeida:Brazilliance Gtr; D. Milhaud:Scaramouche; A. Piazzolla:Grand Tango; H. Villa-Lobos:A Lenda do Caboclo; Bachiana brasileira 2; Bachiana brasileira 4; Cirandas (16 rondos) Pno; A. York:Rosetta Gtr ASV ▲ 2079 [DDD] (12.97)

WUSTIN, ALEXANDER (1943-

Musique pour l'ange for Tenor Saxophone, Cello & Vibraphone (1995)
V. Westphal (vc), C. Delangle (t sax), J. Geoffroy (vib) *(rec Paris, France, July 1995)* ("The Russian Saxophone") † E. Denisov:Son alt Sax; Son alt Sax & Vc; Gubaidulina:Duo-Son; Karasikov:Casus in terminus; Raskatov:Pas de deux BIS ▲ 765 [DDD] (17.97)

WYATT, SCOTT A. (1951-

Still Hidden Laughs for Synclavier and Yamaha Systems (1988)
S. A. Wyatt (cmpt) *(rec Urbana-Champaign, IL)* ("CDCM Computer Music Series, Vol. 3: University of Illinois") † H. Brün:I toLD You so!; S. Martirano:Everything Goes When the Whistle Blows; J. Melby:Chor der Waisen; C. Scaletti:SunSurgeAutomata; Tipei:Cuniculi CENT ▲ 2045 (16.97)

WYGANOWSKI, TADHE GEISLER (1913-1989)

Music of Wyganowski
J. Morton (vn) *(Pastorale; Cantabile; Danse des Montagnard; Fant Polonaise)*, M. Bezverkhny (vn) *(Souvenir heureux; Térésa Habanera; Gavotta Capricciosa; L'enfant et le coucou; Rêverie; Berecuse; Slow Melody; Chant & Danse Russe; Elégie [all w. Olga Bezverkhny (pno)]; Mélodie juive)* PAVA ▲ 7330 [DDD] (10.97)

WYK, ARNOLD (CHRISTIAN VLOK) VAN (1916-1983)

Primavera for Orchestra (1960)
O. Hadari (cnd), Cape Town SO † Sym 1; Sym 2, "Sinf ricerata" GSE ▲ 1509 [DDD] (16.97)

Symphony No. 1 in a (1941-43)
O. Hadari (cnd), Cape Town SO † Primavera; Sym 2, "Sinf ricerata" GSE ▲ 1509 [DDD] (16.97)

Symphony No. 2, "Sinfonia ricerata" (1952)
O. Hadari (cnd), Cape Town SO † Primavera; Sym 1 GSE ▲ 1509 [DDD] (16.97)

WYLIE, RUTH SHAW (1916-1989)

Mandala for Piano, Op. 33/2
B. D. Salwen (pno) † Preludes Pno, Op. 12; Psychogram, Op. 25; Soliloquy, Op. 23; White Raven, Op. 37/2; Retzel:Line Drawings & Earthen Clay Figures OPS1 ▲ 165 (12.97)

Preludes for Piano, Op. 12 (1949)
B. D. Salwen (pno) † Mandala; Psychogram, Op. 25; Soliloquy, Op. 23; White Raven, Op. 37/2; Retzel:Line Drawings & Earthen Clay Figures OPS1 ▲ 165 (12.97)

Psychogram for Piano, Op. 25 (1968)
B. D. Salwen (pno) † Mandala; Preludes Pno, Op. 12; Soliloquy, Op. 23; White Raven, Op. 37/2; Retzel:Line Drawings & Earthen Clay Figures OPS1 ▲ 165 (12.97)

Soliloquy for Piano Left Hand Alone, Op. 23 (1966)
B. D. Salwen (pno) † Mandala; Preludes Pno, Op. 12; Psychogram, Op. 25; White Raven, Op. 37/2; Retzel:Line Drawings & Earthen Clay Figures OPS1 ▲ 165 (12.97)

The White Raven for Piano, Op. 37/2 (1983)
B. D. Salwen (pno) † Mandala; Preludes Pno, Op. 12; Psychogram, Op. 25; Soliloquy, Op. 23; Retzel:Line Drawings & Earthen Clay Figures OPS1 ▲ 165 (12.97)

WYMAN, DAN (1948-

Through the Reed for Viola d'amore & Electronics (1997)
J. Hansen (va d'amore), D. Wyman (elec) *(rec Los Gatos, CA, Feb 1998)* ("Music for Players & Digital Media") † Belet:[Mute]ation; Frengel:Three Short Stories; P. Furman:Synergy; M. Helms:Whispering Modulations; D. Michael:Extensions #1; A. Strange:Shaman: Sisters of Dreamtime CENT ▲ 2404 (live) [DDD] (16.97)

WYNER, YEHUDI (1929-

Concert Duo for Violin & Piano (1956)
M. Makarski (vn), B. McMunn (pno) † J. Cage:Melodies Vn & Kbd; J. Harbison:Songs of Solitude; Hartke:Oh Them Rats Is Mean in My Kitchen NWW ▲ 80391 [DDD] (16.97)
M. Raimondi (vn), Y. Wyner (pno) † Intermedio; Memorial Music; Passage I; Serenade Fl; Short Fants CRI (American Masters) ▲ 701 [ADD] (16.97)

Intermedio (lyric ballet) for Soprano & Strings (1974)
S. D. Wyner (mez), Y. Wyner (cnd) *(rec Mar 21, 1976)* † Concert Duo Vn; Memorial Music; Passage I; Serenade Fl; Short Fants CRI (American Masters) ▲ 701 [ADD] (16.97)

Memorial Music (in 2 parts) for Soprano & 3 Flutes (1971-73)
S. D. Wyner (mez), M. Posses (fl), J. Drexler (fl), P. Standaart (fl) *(rec Dwight Chapel Yale University, 1975)* † Concert Duo Vn; Intermedio; Passage I; Serenade Fl; Short Fants CRI (American Masters) ▲ 701 [ADD] (16.97)

Passage I for Small Ensemble (1983)
D. Asia (cnd) *(rec SUNY Purchase New York, Oct 1985)* † Concert Duo Vn; Intermedio; Memorial Music; Serenade Fl; Short Fants CRI (American Masters) ▲ 701 [ADD] (16.97)

Serenade for Flute, Trumpet, Horn, Trombone, Viola, Cello & Piano (1958)
Y. Wyner (cnd) *(rec New England Conservatory of Music Boston, Nov 6, 1977)* † Concert Duo Vn; Intermedio; Memorial Music; Passage I; Short Fants CRI (American Masters) ▲ 701 [ADD] (16.97)

Short Fantasies (3) for Piano (1963-71)
R. Miller (pno) † Concert Duo Vn; Intermedio; Memorial Music; Passage I; Serenade Fl CRI (American Masters) ▲ 701 [ADD] (16.97)

WYRE, JOHN (1941-

Connexus for Percussion & Orchestra
P. Bay (cnd), Rochester PO, Nexus *(rec Apr 23, 1992)* ("Voices") † W. Cahn:Birds Perc; Kebjar-Bali; Voices Perc NEXU ▲ 10317 [DDD] (16.97)

Maruba for Tuba & Percussion (1987)
J. Jarvis (tuba), M. Ford (mar) *(rec Wright Auditorium, ECU, NC, Sept 8, 1997)* ("Athletic Conveyances-Music for Tuba & Percussion") † W. S. Hartley:Con Tb; W. Penn:Capriccio; Taggart:Athletic Conveyances ARUN (Contemporary Performer) ▲ 3061 (16.97)

WYSHNEGRADSKY, IVAN (1893-1980)

Chant douloureux et étude for Violin (in 1/3, 1/4, 1/6 & 1/8 tones) & Piano, Op. 6 (1918)
M. Gelland (vn), L. Wallin (pno) *(rec Sweden, 1995)* ("Lyrische Aspekte unseres Jahrhundert") † Chant nocturne, Op. 12 bis; Acker:Son Vn; W. Burkhard:Son Vn; H. Jelinek:Zahme Xenien, Op. 32; A. D. Sapp:And the Bombers Went Home, W.53; O. Schoeck:Son Vn; R. Strauss:Allegretto Vn, AV149 VMM ▲ 2017 [DDD]

Chant nocturne for Violin (in 1/4, 1/6 & 1/8 tones) & 2 Pianos (in 1/4 tones), Op. 12 bis (1923)
M. Gelland (vn), U. Gareis (pno), K. Pohl (pno) *(rec Sweden, 1995)* ("Lyrische Aspekte unseres Jahrhundert") † Chant douloureux et étude, Op. 6; Acker:Son Vn; W. Burkhard:Son Vn; H. Jelinek:Zahme Xenien, Op. 32; A. D. Sapp:And the Bombers Went Home, W.53; O. Schoeck:Son Vn; R. Strauss:Allegretto Vn, AV149 VMM ▲ 2017 [DDD]

WYTON, ALEXANDER FRANCIS (1921-

Music of Wyton
J. Horner (sop), B. Hodges (sop), J. Ullyette (sop), R. Wilshire (sop), D. Timpane (bass), C. Albach (tpt), J. Hamlin (tpt), T. Hutchinson (trbn), M. Johansen (b trbn), M. Keiser (org), O. Burdick (org), S. Lawson (org), M. W. Peterson (org), D. Haskins (timp), O. Burdick (cnd), Trinity Church Choir—Resurrection Suite; Easter Day; Coburn; Kyrie, Gloria, Sanctus & Benedictus & Agnus Dei; Out of the Deep; This Joyful Eastertide; The Vision of Isaiah; Go Ye Therefore; Come, Holy Ghost, Creator Blest; Rowthorn; Fanfare ("Choral & Organ Music of Alec Wyton") GOT ▲ 49088 [DDD] (17.97)

XENAKIS, IANNIS (1922-

A la Mémoire de Witold Lutoslawski for 2 Trumpets & 2 Horns (1994)
C. Z. Bornstein (cnd) ("Ensemble Music 2") † Échange; Akrata; Xas MODE ▲ 56 (17.97)

Aïs for Amplified Baritone, solo Percussion & Large Orchestra (1980)
P. Larson (bar), S. Schick (perc), T. Nee (cnd), La Jolla SO † Gendy3; Taurhiphanie; Thalleïn NEU ▲ 45086 [DDD] (16.97)

Akanthos for 9 Instruments (1977)
C. Z. Bornstein (cnd) *(rec Thread Waxing Space New York, NY, June 21, 1995)* ("Ensemble Music 1") † Eonta; N'shima; Plektó; Rebonds "b" & "a" Perc MODE ▲ 53

Akrata for 8 Winds & 8 Brass (1964-65)
C. Z. Bornstein (cnd) ("Ensemble Music 2") † Échange; A la Mémoire de W. Lutoslawski; Xas MODE ▲ 56 (17.97)

Analogiques A + B for 3 Violins, 3 Cellos, 3 Double Basses & Electronic Tape (1958)
P. D. Miller (elec), C. Z. Bornstein (cnd), ST-X Ensemble ("Xenakis Complete, Vol. 2") † Charisma; Herma; Palimpsest; Thalleïn; Waarg VAND (Iannissimo!) ▲ 3 [DDD] (16.97)

Chamber Music
C. Helffer (pno), Arditti String Quartet—Akea, Qnt for Pno & Strs (1986); À R. (Hommage to Ravel) for Pno (1987); Dikthas for Vn & Pno (1979); Embellie for Va (1981); Evryali for Pno (1973); Herma for Pno (1960-61); Ikhoor for Str Trio (1978); Kottos for Vc (1977); Mists for Pno (1980); Nomos Alpha for Vc (1966); St/4 for Str Qt (1955-62); Tetora for Str Qt (1990); Tetras for Str Qt (1983) ("Chamber Music, 1955-1990") † Mikka; Mikka S DISQ 2-▲ 782005 [DDD] (36.97)

Charisma for Clarinet & Cello (1971)
D. Barrett (vc), M. Suzuki (cl) ("Xenakis Complete, Vol. 2") † Analogiques A + B; Herma; Palimpsest; Thalleïn; Waarg VAND (Iannissimo!) ▲ 3 [DDD] (16.97)

Choral Music
Critical Band, J. Wood (cnd), New London Chamber Choir—A Colonne; Knephas; Medea; Nuits; Serment HYP ▲ 66980 (18.97)

Dämmerschein for Orchestra (1994)
J. P. Izquierdo (cnd), Carnegie Mellon PO *(rec Pittsburgh, PA, Apr 1996)* † Déesse Athéna; Persephassa; Varèse:Amériques MODE ▲ 58 [DDD] (17.97)

La Déesse Athéna for Baritone, Percussion & Chamber Ensemble (1992)
P. Larson (bar), T. Adams (perc), J. P. Izquierdo (cnd), Carnegie Mellon PO *(rec Pittsburgh, PA, Apr 1996)* † Dämmerschein; Persephassa; Varèse:Amériques MODE ▲ 58 [DDD] (17.97)

Dmaathen for Oboe & Percussion (1976)
B. Glaetzner (ob) ("Contemporary Music for Oboe") † L. Berio:Sequenza VII; L. Lombardi:Einklang; F. Schenker:Horstuck; I. Yun:Piri Ob BER ▲ 1172 (16.97)

DOX-ORKH for Violin & Orchestra (1991)
I. Arditti (vn), J. Nott (cnd), Moscow PO *(rec Tchaikovsky Conservatory Great Hall, Moscow, Russia, Mar 1995)* † L. Berio:Corale; Mira Fornés:Desde Tan Tien BIS ▲ 772 [DDD] (17.97)

Échange for Bass Clarinet & Ensemble (1989)
M. Lowenstern (b cl), C. Z. Bornstein (cnd) ("Ensemble Music 2") † A la Mémoire de W. Lutoslawski; Akrata; Xas MODE ▲ 56 (17.97)

Eonta for Piano & Chamber Ensemble (1963-64)
J. Drouin (pno), W. Boudreau (cnd) *(rec Dec 1993)* † Arseneault:Après; L. Berio:Corale; L. Bouchard:Compressions; J. Cage:Daughters of the Lonesome Isle FL ▲ 23111 [DDD] (16.97)
J. Rubin (pno), C. Z. Bornstein (cnd) *(rec Thread Waxing Space New York, NY, June 21, 1995)* ("Ensemble Music 1") † Akanthos; N'shima; Plektó; Rebonds "b" & "a" Perc MODE ▲ 53

Gendy3 for Computer Generated Sound (1991)
soloist unknown (sop) † Aïs; Taurhiphanie; Thalleïn NEU ▲ 45086 [DDD] (16.97)

Herma for Piano (1960-64)
J. Rubin (pno) ("Xenakis Complete, Vol. 2") † Analogiques A + B; Charisma; Palimpsest; Thalleïn; Waarg VAND (Iannissimo!) ▲ 3 [DDD] (16.97)

Jalons for Orchestra (1988)
B. T. Andersson (cnd) ("KammarensebleN Live") † P. Boulez:Le Marteau sans maître; É. Tanguy:Music of; Varèse:Octandre CAPA ▲ 21581 (16.97)

Keren for Trombone (1986)
C. Lindberg (trbn) *(rec Sweden, 1988)* ("The Solitary Trombone") † L. Berio:Sequenza V; J. Cage:Solo Sliding Trb; A. Eliasson:Disegno Trbn; M. Kagel:Atem; F. Schubert:Sym 5; Sym 6; K. Stockhausen:In Freundschaft; In Freundschaft, No. 46 BIS ▲ 388 [DDD] (17.97)

Kraanerg (ballet) for Orchestra & Tape (1968)
DJ Spooky (elec), C. Z. Bornstein (cnd) *(rec live Cooper Union, Nov 19, 1996)* ASP ▲ 975 (15.99)

Le Légende d'Eer for Chamber Ensemble
various artists ("Iannis Xenakis 2") DISQ ▲ 782058 (18.97)

Mikka for Violin (1972)
C. Helffer (pno), Arditti String Quartet ("Chamber Music, 1955-1990") † Chamber Music; Mikka S DISQ 2-▲ 782005 [DDD] (36.97)
P. Zukofsky (vn) *(rec New York City, June 29, 1976)* † Mikka S; H. Brant:Quombex; J. Cage:Nocturne; M. Feldman:Vertical Thoughts II; P. Glass:Strung Out; Scelsi:Anahit; S. Wolpe:2nd Piece Vn CP2 ▲ 108 [AAD] (19.97)

Mikka S for Violin (1976)
C. Helffer (pno), Arditti String Quartet ("Chamber Music, 1955-1990") † Chamber Music; Mikka DISQ 2-▲ 782005 [DDD] (36.97)
P. Zukofsky (vn) *(rec New York City, United States of America, June 29, 1976)* † Mikka; H. Brant:Quombex; J. Cage:Nocturne; M. Feldman:Vertical Thoughts II; P. Glass:Strung Out; Scelsi:Anahit; S. Wolpe:2nd Piece Vn CP2 ▲ 108 [AAD] (19.97)

Morsima-Amorsima for Piano, Violin, Cello & Double Bass (1956-62)
austraLYSIS members *(rec 2MBS-FM, 1993)* ("austraLYSIS: Windows in Time") † Bright:Night Db; L. Cresswell:Organic Music; Soliloquy on a Lambent Tailpiece; R. T. Dean:TimeStrain; R. Rue:Nocturnal Windows; H. Smith:Simultaneity TALP ▲ 39 [DDD] (18.97)

Mycenae-Alpha for Electronics (1978)
artist unknown ("Electro Acoustic Music: Classics") † Babbitt:Philomel; Phonemena Sop & Tape; R. Reynolds:Transfigured Wind IV; Varèse:Poeme électronique NEU ▲ 45074 [ADD]

N'shima for 2 Sopranos & Chamber Ensemble (1975)
C. Aks (sop), A. Lindevald (mez), C. Z. Bornstein (cnd) *(rec Thread Waxing Space New York, NY, June 21, 1995)* ("Ensemble Music 1") † Akanthos; Eonta; Plektó; Rebonds "b" & "a" Perc MODE ▲ 53

Nuits for Mixed Chorus (1967-68)
M. Tranchant (cnd), French Vocal Group † Messiaen:O sacrum convivium!; Rechants ARN ▲ 68084 (16.97)

Okho for 3 Percussionists (1989)
Percussion Group The Hague—see Collections, "Percussion: Percussion Group The Hague" † R. Ford:Trarre; M. Ishii:13 Drums GLOE ▲ 5066 [DDD] (16.97)
D. Vineis (cnd) † Persephassa; Psappha STRV ▲ 40001 (16.97)

Palimpsest for Winds, Strings, Piano & Percussion (1979)
C. Z. Bornstein (cnd), ST-X Ensemble ("Xenakis Complete, Vol. 2") † Analogiques A + B; Charisma; Herma; Thalleïn; Waarg VAND (Iannissimo!) ▲ 3 [DDD] (16.97)

Persephassa for Percussion Ensemble (1969)
J. P. Izquierdo (cnd), Carnegie Mellon PO *(rec Pittsburgh, PA, Apr 1996)* † Déesse Athéna; Dämmerschein; Varèse:Amériques MODE ▲ 58 [DDD] (17.97)
D. Vineis (cnd) † Okho; Psappha STRV ▲ 40001 (16.97)

Pleiades for Percussion Sextet (1979)
A. Loguin (cnd) † Psappha BIS ▲ 482 [AAD] (17.97)
Strasbourg Percussion Ensemble ("Pléiades") HAM ▲ 1905185 (9.97)

Plektó for Chamber Ensemble (1993)
C. Z. Bornstein (cnd) *(rec Thread Waxing Space New York, NY, June 21, 1995)* ("Ensemble Music 1") † Akanthos; Eonta; N'shima; Rebonds "b" & "a" Perc MODE ▲ 53

Psappha for Percussion (1975)
G. Mortensen (perc) † Gudmunsen-Holmgreen:Triptykon; Nørgård:I Ching BIS ▲ 256 [AAD] (17.97)
G. Mortensen (perc) † Pleiades BIS ▲ 482 [AAD] (17.97)
M. Pugliese (perc) *(rec NYC, NY, live, Apr 4, 1989)* ("Perkin' at Merkin") † J. Cage:Music for...; M. Feldman:King of Denmark; H. Mancini:Peter Gunn (sels); Nørgård:Waves; Vigeland:Progress MODE ▲ 25
D. Vineis (cnd) † Okho; Persephassa STRV ▲ 40001 (16.97)

XENAKIS, IANNIS (cont.)
Rebonds for Percussion
M. Leoson (perc) † B. T. Andersson:Apollo Con; Donatoni:Omar; Fukushi:Ground; D. Milhaud:Con Mar; T. Tanaka:Movts Perc CAPA ▲ 21466 (16.97)
Rebonds "b" & "a" for Percussion (1987-89)
R. McEwan (perc) *(rec Thread Waxing Space New York, NY, June 21, 1995)* ("Ensemble Music 1") † Akanthos; Eonta; N'shima; Plektó MODE ▲ 53
Taurhiphanie for Computer Generated Sound (1987-88)
soloist unknown (sop) † Aïs; Gendy3; Thalleïn NEU ▲ 45086 [DDD] (16.97)
Thalleïn for 14 Instruments (1984)
C. Z. Bornstein (cnd), ST-X Ensemble ("Xenakis Complete, Vol. 2") † Analogiques A + B; Charisma; Herma; Palimpsest; Waarg VAND (Iannissimo!) ▲ 3 [DDD] (16.97)
R. Steiger (cnd) † Aïs; Gendy3; Taurhiphanie NEU ▲ 45086 [DDD] (16.97)
Waarg for 13 Instruments (1988)
C. Z. Bornstein (cnd), ST-X Ensemble ("Xenakis Complete, Vol. 2") † Analogiques A + B; Charisma; Herma; Palimpsest; Thalleïn VAND (Iannissimo!) ▲ 3 [DDD] (16.97)
M. Ceccanti (cnd) *(rec Museo Pecci Prato, Italy, Mar 21, 1992)* † L. Berio:Différences; S. Bussotti:Nascosto for Pierre Boulez; Sciarrino:Introduzione all'oscuro AART ▲ 47135 [DDD] (10.97)
Xas for Saxophone Quartet (1987)
C. Z. Bornstein (cnd) ("Ensemble Music 2") † Échange; A la Mémoire de W. Lutoslawski; Akrata MODE ▲ 56 (17.97)

XIMÉNEZ, JOSÉ (1601-1672)
Obra del primer tono de lleno for Keyboard
S. Yates (hpd) *(rec Somerset, England, Dec 1993)* ("Spanish & Portuguese Harpsichord") † Anonymous:Españoleta; Cabanilles:Pasacalles I; Tiento de batalla del octavo tono; H. Cabezón:Dulce memoria glosada; A. de Cabezón:Obras de música (sels); Carreira:Canção a quatro glosada; Coelho:Segunda tento do primeiro tom; Segunda Susana grosada a 4 sobre a de 5 CHN ▲ 560 [DDD] (16.97)

XIMENO, FABIÁN (fl 1650)
Missa sobre el "Beatus Vir de Fray Xacinto" for solo Voices & Chorus
R. Escher (sop), C. Gendron (sop), B. J. Echenique (cnd), Angelicum de Puebla *(rec 1996)* ("México Barroco, Puebla 3") URT ▲ 2006 (16.97)

XIN HUGUANG (1933-
Gada Meilin (symphonic poem) for Orchestra (1956)
K. Jean (cnd), A. Leaper (cnd), Czech-Slovak RSO Bratislava ("Chinese Orchestral Music") † Q. Chen:Dagger Dance; Drum & Song; Fant on a Xinjian Folk Song; S. Ding:Xinjiang Dances; Yin:Yellow River Fant MARC ▲ 8223408 [DDD] (13.97)

YAITCHKOV, DMITRI (dates unknown)
Choral Music
L. Arshavskaya (cnd), Cantus Sacred Music Ensemble—God is With Us; Praise the Lord O My Soul; O Joyous Light; The Lord Our God; others ("A Choral Selection") OLY ▲ 488 [DDD] (16.97)

YAMADA, KOSAKU (1886-1965)
Aka Tombo for Flute & Harp
J. Rampal (fl), L. Laskine (hp) *(rec New York, NY)* ("Japanese Melodies for Flute & Harp") † Chugoku-Chiho-No-Komoriuta; Kono Michi; Konoe:Chin-Chin Chidori; Miyagi:Haru no Umi; Sugiyama:Defune; Hanayome Ningyo; Taki:Hana; Kojo-No-Tsuki; Traditional:Nambu Ushi Oi Uta; Sakura; Yanada:Jogashima No Ame SNYC ▲ 34568 (16.97)
Chanson triste japonaise for Violin & Piano (1921)
S. Numata (vn), A. Tadenuma (pno) *(rec July 1997)* ("Japanese Music for Violin & Piano") † Karatchi no hana; K. Hirao:Son Vn; K. Kishi:Pieces Vn; H. Otaka:Son Vn CAMA ▲ 30477 [DDD] (18.97)
Chugoku-Chiho-No-Komoriuta
H. Naka (db), M. Nakagawa (fl), P. Zander (hpd), S. Yoshiwara (perc), M. Mamiya (cnd), Pro Musica Nipponia [arr Mamiya] *(rec Japan)* ("Japanese Melodies") † Anonymous:Chiran-Bushi; Matsushime-Ondo; Oroku-Musume; Zui-Zui-Zukkorobashi; Hirai:Nara-Yama; Konoe:Chin-Chin Chidori; Sugiyama:Defune; Taki:Kojo-No-Tsuki; Traditional:Sakura, Sakura SNYC ▲ 39703 (16.97)
J. Rampal (fl), L. Laskine (hp) *(rec New York, NY)* ("Japanese Melodies for Flute & Harp") † Aka Tombo; Kono Michi; Konoe:Chin-Chin Chidori; Miyagi:Haru no Umi; Sugiyama:Defune; Hanayome Ningyo; Taki:Hana; Kojo-No-Tsuki; Traditional:Nambu Ushi Oi Uta; Sakura; Yanada:Jogashima No Ame SNYC ▲ 34568 (16.97)
Karatchi no hana for Violin & Piano
S. Numata (vn), A. Tadenuma (pno) *(rec July 1997)* ("Japanese Music for Violin & Piano") † Chanson triste japonaise; K. Hirao:Son Vn; K. Kishi:Pieces Vn; H. Otaka:Son Vn CAMA ▲ 30477 [DDD] (18.97)
Kono Michi
J. Rampal (fl), L. Laskine (hp) *(rec New York, NY)* ("Japanese Melodies for Flute & Harp") † Aka Tombo; Chugoku-Chiho-No-Komoriuta; Konoe:Chin-Chin Chidori; Miyagi:Haru no Umi; Sugiyama:Defune; Hanayome Ningyo; Taki:Hana; Kojo-No-Tsuki; Traditional:Nambu Ushi Oi Uta; Sakura; Yanada:Jogashima No Ame SNYC ▲ 34568 (16.97)
Music of Yamada
S. Numata (vn), A. Tadenuma (pno)—Lullaby [from the Chugoku Area]; Red Dragonfly *(rec Saitama Geijyutsu Gekijo Music Hall, Apr 26, 1995)* † Ikenouchi:Sonatine Vn; A. Miyoshi:Son Vn; T. Noda:In the Garden; Takemitsu:Hika CAMA ▲ 409 [DDD] (18.97)

YAMADA, NORMAN (20th cent)
Music of Yamada
various artists—Being & Time [excerpt 1]; One, Two, Three; Deterioration #1; On the Fetish Character; In Music & the Regression of Listening; Being & Time [excerpt 2] ("Being & Time") TZA (Composer) ▲ 7035 [DDD] (16.97)

YAMAMOTO, HOZAN (1937-
Ichikotsu for Koto & Flute (1966)
K. F. Asawa (fl), K. Kudo (koto) † K. Hirai:Son Koto & Fl; Miyagi:Haru no Umi; Izumi; T. Sawai:Flower CRYS ▲ 316 [DDD] (15.97) ■ 316 [DDD] (9.98)

YAMASH'TA, STOMU (1947-
Sea & Sky for Synthesizers, Percussion & Orchestra
S. Izumi (syn), T. Kobobu (syn), S. Yamashita (perc/syn) KUC ▲ 11072 (16.97) ■ 11072 (10.98)

YANADA, TADASHI (1893-1939)
Jogashima No Ame for Flute & Harp
J. Rampal (fl), L. Laskine (hp) *(rec New York, NY)* ("Japanese Melodies for Flute & Harp") † Konoe:Chin-Chin Chidori; Miyagi:Haru no Umi; Sugiyama:Defune; Hanayome Ningyo; Taki:Hana; Kojo-No-Tsuki; Traditional:Nambu Ushi Oi Uta; Sakura; K. Yamada:Aka Tombo; Chugoku-Chiho-No-Komoriuta; Kono Michi SNYC ▲ 34568 (16.97)

YANNATOS, JAMES (1929-
Concerto for Piano & Orchestra (1992-93)
W. Doppmann (pno), J. Yannatos (cnd), Harvard-Radcliffe Orch † Sym 4 ALBA ▲ 278 [DDD] (16.97)
Ritual Images—A Fantasy for Orchestra & Tape (1974)
J. Yannatos (cnd), Harvard-Radcliffe Orch † A. Copland:Con Cl; Ginastera:Con Hp AFK ▲ 509 (16.97)
Symphony No. 4, "Tiananmen Square" (1989-90)
J. Yannatos (cnd), Harvard-Radcliffe Orch † Con Pno ALBA ▲ 278 [DDD] (16.97)
Trinity Mass for solo Voices, Narrator, Orchestra & Chorus (1983-84)
L. Shelton (sop), M. Vargas (mez), J. Humphrey (ten), S. Sylvan (bar), R. Honeysucker (bass), J. Robards (nar), J. Yannatos (cnd), Harvard-Radcliffe Orch, Harvard Glee Club, Radcliffe Choral Society, Bach Back Bay Chorale, Youth Pro Musica ALBA ▲ 241 [DDD] (16.97)

YANOV-YANOVSKY (20th cent)
Lacrymosa for String Quartet (1991)
Kronos Quartet ("Night Prayers") † Ali-Zade:Mugam Sayagi; Golijov:K'Vakarat; Gubaidulina:Qt 4 Strs; Kancheli:Night Prayers for Str Qt; Tahmizyan:Cool Wind is Blowing NON ▲ 79346 (16.97)

YAO, SHA (1956-
Drifting About
B. Hulse (cnd), Canyonlands *(rec Salt Lake City, UT, 1994-95)* ("New Music from Utah") † Cathey:Bardol Saga; M. Johnson:Nocturne; Quaglia:Quartetto; Roens:Delicate Arch; Invocation; Time & Again; Wolking:Reaching *([ENG] text)* CENT ▲ 2360 [DDD] (16.97)

YARDUMIAN, RICHARD (1917-1985)
Veni, Sancte Spiritus (chorale prelude) for Orchestra (1959)
P. Freeman (cnd), Czech National SO *(rec Prague, Czech Republic, 1996)* ("Paul Freeman Introduces American Music") † W. Logan:Runagate, Runagate; Narrative:Paul Freeman Introduces American Music 1; Rendelman:Oct 9, 1943; P. Saltzman:Walls; J. Williams:Fanfare for Life ALBA (Exploratory Series, Vol. 1) ▲ 312 [DDD] (16.97)

YARED, GABRIEL (1949-
Les Misérables (film music) for Orchestra
artists unknown HOL ▲ 162147 (16.97)

YASHIRO, AKIO (1929-1976)
Quartet for Strings (1954-55)
C. Tanaka (vn), S. Muto (vn), T. Uzuka (va), K. Yasuda (vc) ("Complete Chamber Music, Vol. 2") † Trio Pno CAMA ▲ 51 (18.97)
Sonata for 2 Flutes & Piano (1957)
S. Koide (fl), R. Noguchi (fl), F. Inoue (pno) † Son Pno; Suite Classique CAMA ▲ 50 (18.97)
Sonata for Piano (1961)
I. Endo (pno) † Son Fls; Suite Classique CAMA ▲ 50 (18.97)
Y. Nagai (pno) *(rec tion Stockholm, Sweden, Dec 1995)* ("Poésie: Yukie Nagai Plays Japanese Piano Music") † T. Ichiyanagi:Cloud Atlas; Kako:Poésie; A. Miyoshi:Diary of the Sea; Y. Takahashi:Kwanju, May 1980; Takemitsu:For Away; Rain Tree Sketch BIS ▲ 766 [DDD] (17.97)
M. Yuguchi (pno) *(rec Jan 1996)* ("Contemporary Japanese Piano Music") † T. Ichiyanagi:Cloud Atlas; H. Otaka:Sonatine Pno; Takemitsu:Litany Pno; Uninterrupted Rests; Terauchi:Phoenix Hall and 8 Putto-Figures THOR ▲ 2324 [DDD] (16.97)
Suite Classique for Piano 4-Hands
K. Kanazawa (pno), K. Yasukawa (pno) † Son Fls; Son Pno CAMA ▲ 50 (18.97)
Trio for Piano, Violin & Cello (1948)
C. Tanaka (vn), K. Yasuda (vc), H. Puig-Roget (pno) ("Complete Chamber Music, Vol. 2") † Qt Strs CAMA ▲ 51 (18.97)

YASINITSKY, GREGORY W. (1953-
Into a Star for Orchestra (1993)
S. Kawalla (cnd), Slovak RSO Bratislava † B. Hobson:Three; Konowalski:Brewerie; Loeb:Suite Concertante; T. Myers:Concertino Orch; R. Snyder:Shamanic Dances; K. Steen:Metastasis VMM (Music from 6 Continents 1993) ▲ 3017 [DDD]
Music of Wood, Silver & Ivory for Cello, Flute & Piano (1991)
L. Wharton (vc), A. M. Yasinitsky (fl), G. Berthiaume (pno) ("Music in Mixed Accents") † On Wings of Angels; Rabushka:Canzona e Scherzo Capriccioso, Op. 4; Etude Fantasque Pno, Op. 7; Suite Va, Op. 23; R. Snyder:Son Ob; Sukegawa:Komoriuta; Trojanowski:Treatment VMM ▲ 2012 [DDD]
On Wings of Angels for Flute (1992)
A. M. Yasinitsky (fl) ("Music in Mixed Accents") † Music of Wood, Silver & Ivory; Rabushka:Canzona e Scherzo Capriccioso, Op. 4; Etude Fantasque Pno, Op. 7; Suite Va, Op. 23; R. Snyder:Son Ob; Sukegawa:Komoriuta; Trojanowski:Treatment VMM ▲ 2012 [DDD]

YASUI, BYRON (1941-
Piccola Arietta No. 2 for solo Guitar (1980) [orchd 1996]
C. Barbosa-Lima (gtr), P. Djurov (cnd), Sofia Soloists *(rec Sofia Bulgaria, Mar 1997)* ("O Boto") † Castelnuovo-Tedesco:Capriccio diabolico Gtr, Op. 85; E. Cordero:Con Antillano; Nana para una Negrita; G. F. Handel:Cons (16) Org; Pujol Vilarrubí:Tonadilla ERTO ▲ 42048 [DDD] (16.97)

YE, XIAOGANG (1955-
Moon over the West River for Orchestra (1984)
K. Schermerhorn (cnd), Hong Kong PO *(rec Lyric Theatre of the Hong Kong Academy for Perform, June 28, 1986)* ("First Contemporary Chinese Composers Festival 1986") † W. W. Chan:Sym 3; A. Huang:Con Pno; Qu:Mong Dong; Tan Dun:Intermezzo; J. Tang:Sym 3 MARC (Chinese Contemporary) ▲ 8223915 [DDD] (13.97)

YEGOROV, ALEXANDER (1887-1959)
Bogoroditse Devo for Chorus
N. Korniev (cnd), St. Petersburg Chamber Choir *(rec St. Petersburg, Russia, Apr 1996)* ("Russian Christmas") † Anonymous:Deva dnes'; Dobr'ia vechir Tobi; Nebo i zemlya; Noch' tikha, noch svyata; Nova radist' stala; Pavochka khodit; Rozhdestvo Christovo angel priletel; Rozhdestvo Khristovo ves' mir prazdnuet; Vzglyani syuda; Chesnokov:Sacred Works, Op. 43; Cui:Presvyatїya bogoroditsї, Op. 93; Gretchaninoff:Vokliknite Gospodevi vsya zemlya, Op. 19/2; Liadov:Perelozheniya iz obikhoda; Shvedov:Tebe Poem PPHI ▲ 454616 [DDD] (16.97)

YEKMALIAN, MAKAR (1856-1905)
Armenian Mass for Vocal Solists & Chorus
A. Mansourian (sop), V. Haroutunian (bass), L. Chabanian (cnd), St. Gayané Chapel Armenian Liturgical Choir AB ▲ 1416 (16.97)

YI, CHEN (1953-
As in a Dream (set of 2 songs) for Soprano, Pipa & Zheng [text Li Qing-zhao] (1988; rev 1994)
R. Lan (sop), M. Xiao-Fen (instr), Y. Yi (instr) *(rec New York City, NY, 1997-8)* † Duo Ye; Near Distance; Qi; Shuo; Song in Winter; Sparkle *([CHN,ENG] text)* CRI ▲ 804 [DDD] (16.97)
Duo Ye for Pipa & Voice (1995)
M. Xiao-Fen (pipa) *(rec New York City, NY, 1997-8)* † As in a Dream; Near Distance; Qi; Shuo; Song in Winter; Sparkle CRI ▲ 804 [DDD] (16.97)
Near Distance: Lost in thought about ancient culture & modern civilization (sextet) for Chamber Orchestra (1988)
J. Milarsky (cnd), New York New Music Ensemble *(rec New York City, NY, 1997-8)* † As in a Dream; Duo Ye; Qi; Shuo; Song in Winter; Sparkle CRI ▲ 804 [DDD] (16.97)
Qi for Chamber Orchestra (1997)
New Music Consort *(rec New York City, NY, 1997-8)* † As in a Dream; Duo Ye; Near Distance; Shuo; Song in Winter; Sparkle CRI ▲ 804 [DDD] (16.97)
Shuo for String Orchestra (or String Quintet) (1994)
Manhattan String Quartet members *(rec New York City, NY, 1997-8)* † As in a Dream; Duo Ye; Near Distance; Qi; Song in Winter; Sparkle CRI ▲ 804 [DDD] (16.97)
Song in Winter for Dizi, Zheng, & Harpsichord (1993)
J. Lindorff (hpd), W. Lai-gen (instr), Y. Yi (instr) *(rec New York City, NY, 1997-8)* † As in a Dream; Duo Ye; Near Distance; Qi; Shuo; Sparkle CRI ▲ 804 [DDD] (16.97)
Sparkle for Chamber Orchestra (1992)
C. Heldrich (cnd), New Music Consort *(rec New York City, NY, 1997-8)* † As in a Dream; Duo Ye; Near Distance; Qi; Shuo; Song in Winter CRI ▲ 804 [DDD] (16.97)
Tang Poems for Vocal Ensemble
Chanticleer [sels] † Z. Long:Words of the Sun; B. Rands:Canti d'Amor; Sametz:in time of; S. Stucky:Cradle Songs; Taverner:Village Wedding; A. R. Thomas:Love Songs; Rub of Love TELC ▲ 24570 (16.97)

YIN, CHENG-ZONG (1941-
Yellow River Concerto for Piano & Orchestra
C.-Z. Yin (pno), A. Leaper (cnd), Bratislava RSO MARC ▲ 8223412 [DDD] (13.97)
Yellow River Fantasy for Orchestra [adapted Peter Breiner from Yellow River Concerto]
A. Leaper (cnd), Bratislava RSO ("Chinese Orchestral Music") † Q. Chen:Dagger Dance; Drum & Song; Fant on a Xinjian Folk Song; S. Ding:Xinjiang Dances; Xin Huguang:Gada Meilin MARC ▲ 8223408 [DDD] (13.97)

YOCOH, YUQUIJIRO (1933-
Guitar Music
D. Blanco (gtr)—Sakura, Theme & Vars *(rec Djursholm, Sweden, 1983)* ("Favorite Guitar Music") † I. Albéniz:Gtr Music; S. Myers:Gtr Music; Tárrega:Gtr Music; Recuerdos de la Alhambra; H. Villa-Lobos:Chôro 1; Suite populaire brésilienne BIS ▲ 233 [DDD] (17.97)

YORDANOV, DANKO (dates unknown)
Bonbonnière Fantasy for Flute, Violin, Cello & Piano [after Rossini's Il barbiere di Siviglia]
Academic Chamber Ensemble [cavatina] † Donizetti:Son Fl; J. Haydn:Trio 8 Vns & Bc, H.V/G3; Martinů:Madrigal Son; A. Schnittke:Suite in the Old Style; C. M. von Weber:Trio Fl, Op. 63 GEGA ▲ 103 [DDD] (16.97)

YORK, ANDREW (20th cent)
Rosetta for Guitar
C. Bruinsma (gtr), P. Rueffer (gtr) *(rec Bedford School, England)* ("Brazileira") † L. Almeida:Brazilliance Gtr; D. Milhaud:Scaramouche; A. Piazzolla:Grand Tango; H. Villa-Lobos:A Lenda do Caboclo; Bachiana brasileira 2; Bachiana brasileira 4; Cirandas (16 rondos) Pno; Wüsthoff:Concerto de Samba ASV ▲ 2079 [DDD] (12.97)
Sunburst for Guitar
A. Leonard (gtr) *(rec Cambridge, MA, May 1996)* ("Music of the Ages") † J. S. Bach:Sons & Partitas Vn; Suites Vc; J. Dowland:Lt Music; A. Piazzolla:Milonga del angel; Muerte del angel; Sor:Intro & Vars on "Gentil Housard", Op. 27; Intro & Vars on "Malborough", Op. 28 ACTR ▲ 60101 [DDD] (16.97)
Transilience for Guitar, Flute & Piano
J. Brown (gtr), J. Vinci (fl), A. Alton (pno) ("Five Premieres: Chamber Works With Guitar") † P. Blanchard:Music of Blanchard; Chobanian:Images; V. Fine:Canzones y Dances; A. Holland:Poems Without Words ALBA ▲ 86 [DDD] (16.97)

YORK, WES (1949-

My Heart Is Different for Soprano & Piano
S. Botti (sop), D. Buechner (pno) *(rec Feb 1989)* † Native Songs; Reminiscence 2; Songs from Levertov Scores; Songs on a Poem of Su Tung P'O NWW ▲ 80439 (16.97)

Native Songs (3) for Voices & Ensemble [Where the Wind Is; Someone Somewhere; Today is Mine]
N. Armstrong (sop), S. Sylvan (bar), S. Downey (sgr), R. Woodhouse (sgr), P. Friedland (fl), J. Fischer (pno), J. R. Smith (perc) *(rec May 1987)* † My Heart Is Different; Reminiscence 2; Songs from Levertov Scores; Songs on a Poem of Su Tung P'O NWW ▲ 80439 (16.97)

Reminiscence 2 for Flute, Clarinet & Piano
J. D. Fredericks (fl), I. Greitzer (cl), K. Supové (pno) *(rec May 1987)* † My Heart Is Different; Native Songs; Songs from Levertov Scores; Songs on a Poem of Su Tung P'O NWW ▲ 80439 (16.97)

Songs from the Levertov Scores for Voice, Violin & Marimba [The Presence; Remembering; Stepping Westward]
S. Botti (sop), Marimolin *(rec May 1987)* † My Heart Is Different; Native Songs; Reminiscence 2; Songs on a Poem of Su Tung P'O NWW ▲ 80439 (16.97)

Songs (2) on a Poem of Su Tung P'O for Ensemble [Lament; Ode]
D. Ripley (bass), B. Lancaster (sgr), H. Weinberger (sgr) *(rec May 1987)* † My Heart Is Different; Native Songs; Reminiscence 2; Songs from Levertov Scores NWW ▲ 80439 (16.97)

YOSHIMATSU, TAKASHI (1953-

Around the Round Ground for Guitar
S. Fukuda (gtr) ("Tender Toys") † Short Dream Songs; Tender Toys; Water Color Scalar DNN ▲ 18053 (16.97)

Concerto for Guitar & Orchestra, "Pegasus Effect"
C. Ogden (gtr), S. Fujioka (cnd), BBC PO † Sym 2; Threnody to Toki, Op. 12 CHN ▲ 9438 (16.97)

Concerto for Saxophone, "Cyber-Bird"
N. Sugawa (sax), S. Fujioka (cnd), BBC PO † Sym 3 CHN ▲ 9737 (16.97)

Concerto for Trombone & Orchestra, Op. 55, "Orion Machine" (1992-93)
Y. Hakoyama (trbn), Y. Toyama (cnd), Japan Philharmonic SO *(rec Japan, Apr 1993)* † Kamui-Chikap Sym, Op. 40 CAMA ▲ 30354 [DDD] (18.97)

Kamui-Chikap [Bird-God] Symphony, Op. 40, "Symphony No. 1" (1988-90)
T. Otaka (cnd), Tokyo PO *(rec Tokyo, June 2, 1990)* ("The Min-On Contemporary Music Festival '90") † J. Kondo:In the Woods; T. Suzuki:Hymnos CAMA ▲ 190
T. Otaka (cnd), Tokyo PO *(rec Japan, June 1990)* † Con Trbn, Op. 55 CAMA ▲ 30354 [DDD] (18.97)

Moyura for Koto & Shakahuchi
K. Mitsuhashi (shak), N. Yoshimura (koto) *(rec Iruma City Auditorium, Dec 14, 1990)* † Minami:Coloration-Project III; Nishimura:Nanae; S. Satoh:Kamu-Ogi-Guoto; J. Yuasa:Cosmos Haptic 3 CAMA ▲ 189 [DDD] (18.97)

Music of Yoshimatsu
M. Inoue (cnd), New Japan PO—Threnody to Toki; Chikap; The Age of Birds; Digital Bird Suite; 4 Pieces in Bird Shape; Random Bird Vars; Sym 2 ("The Age of Birds") CAMA 2-▲ 178
K. Tabe (pno), S. Fujioka (cnd), Manchester Camerata—Con Pno, "Memo Flora"; And Birds Are Still; While an Angel Falls into a Dove; Dream Colored Mobile II; White Landscapes CHN ▲ 9652 (16.97)

Nabari for 17-String Koto (1992)
T. Kikuchi (koto) *(rec Saitama Arts Theater Concert Hall, Japan, Apr 1995)* ("Kamunagi") † Ikebe:Kageru; Matsumura:Air of Prayer; Nishimura:Kamunagi; S. Satoh:Tamaogi-Koto CAMA ▲ 267 [DDD] (18.97)

Pleiades Dances (5) for Piano
M. Matsuya (pno) *(rec Japan, Sept 1993)* ("Light Colored Album for Piano - Midori Matsuya plays Japanese Contemporary Pieces") † Hachimura:Vision of Higanbana; Matsumura:Berceuses; A. Miyoshi:Hommage; Ogura:Sonatina; T. Sato:August Laying to Rest; Carpet of Bamboo Leaves Falling onto Northern Sea; Scenery with Tea Gardens; Season of Yellow and Black; Takemitsu:Pno Distance CAMA ▲ 318 [DDD] (18.97)
K. Tabe (pno) DNN ▲ 18002 (16.97)

Short Dream Songs (4) for Guitar
S. Fukuda (gtr) ("Tender Toys") † Around the Round Ground; Tender Toys; Water Color Scalar DNN ▲ 18053 (16.97)

Symphony No. 2, "At Terra"
S. Fujioka (cnd), BBC PO † Con Gtr; Threnody to Toki, Op. 12 CHN ▲ 9438 (16.97)

Symphony No. 3 for Orchestra
S. Fujioka (cnd), BBC PO † Con Sax CHN ▲ 9737 (16.97)

Tender Toys for Guitar
S. Fukuda (gtr) ("Tender Toys") † Around the Round Ground; Short Dream Songs; Water Color Scalar DNN ▲ 18053 (16.97)

Threnody to Toki for Piano & String Orchestra, Op. 12
S. Fujioka (cnd), BBC PO † Con Gtr; Sym 2 CHN ▲ 9438 (16.97)
M. Inoue (cnd), New Japan PO ("Orchestra Plays Adagio") † A. Bruckner:Qt Strs; Sym 2; G. Mahler:Sym 5; P. Tchaikovsky:Serenade Strs, Op. 48; Zi:3 Wishes for a Rose CAMA (After Hours Classics) ▲ 423 [DDD] (15.97)
M. Nojima (pno), T. Otaka (cnd), Yomiuri Nippon SO † Matsumura:Con 2 Pno; A. Miyoshi:Noesis; Takemitsu:Twill by Twilight ASV ▲ 1021 (16.97)

Unicorn Circuit for Bassoon & Orchestra
I. Magome (bn), M. Enkoji (cnd), Sendai PO † Nishimura:Tapas CAMA ▲ 175 (18.97)

Water Color Scalar for Guitar
S. Fukuda (gtr) ("Tender Toys") † Around the Round Ground; Short Dream Songs; Tender Toys DNN ▲ 18053 (16.97)

YOSHIOKA, TAKAYOSHI (1955-

Rhapsody for Marimba, Flute, Clarinet, Double Bass & Drums
C. Laurence (db), E. Beckett (fl), R. Howitt (cl), E. Glennie (mar), R. Salmins (dr) *(rec London, England, Sept 1994)* ("Wind in the Bamboo Grove") † K. Abe:Michi; Vars on Japanese Children's Songs; Wind in the Bamboo Grove; M. Miki:Mar Spiritual; Yuyama:Divert Mar CAT ▲ 68193 [DDD] (16.97)

YOST, MICHEL (1754-1786)**& JOHANN CHRISTOPH VOGEL** (1756-1788)

Concerto No. 7 in B♭ for Clarinet & Orchestra
D. Klöcker (cl) *(rec Mar 1996)* † Con 11 Cl; Con 8 Cl; Con 9 Cl MDG ▲ 3010718 [DDD] (17.97)

Concerto No. 8 in E♭ for Clarinet & Orchestra
D. Klöcker (cl) *(rec Mar 1996)* † Con 11 Cl; Con 7 Cl; Con 9 Cl MDG ▲ 3010718 [DDD] (17.97)

Concerto No. 9 in B♭ for Clarinet & Orchestra
D. Klöcker (cl) *(rec Mar 1996)* † Con 11 Cl; Con 7 Cl; Con 8 Cl MDG ▲ 3010718 [DDD] (17.97)

Concerto No. 11 in B♭ for Clarinet & Orchestra
D. Klöcker (cl) *(rec Mar 1996)* † Con 7 Cl; Con 8 Cl; Con 9 Cl MDG ▲ 3010718 [DDD] (17.97)

YOULL, HENRY (fl 1608)

Songs
Trinity Consort—Only joy, now here you are *(rec 1998)* ("O Sprite Heroic-The life, love & death of Sir Philip Sydney explored") † W. Byrd:Consort Music; A. I. Ferrabosco:Songs; J. Mundy:Songs; Pilkington:Songs; Vautor:Songs; J. Ward:Songs BEUL ▲ 2 [DDD] (16.97)

YOUMANS, VINCENT (1898-1946)

Songs
J. Morris (mez), R. White (ten), W. Bolcolm (pno)—The Carioca; Music Makes Me; Does it Pay to Be a Lady; Love Is Like a Song; Why, Oh Why?; Rise & Shine; You Started Something; I Want a Yes Man; You're Everywhere; Tie a String Around Your Finger; I'm Glad I Waited & others ("The Carioca: Songs of Vincent Youmans, Vol. 2") ARA ▲ 6692 (16.97)

YOUNG, GORDON (1919-

Triptych for Flute & Organ
F. Shelly (fl), S. Egler (org)—Elegy *(rec Wiedemann Recital Hall, Wichita State University, KS)* ("The Dove Descending") † M. Albrecht:Psalms; Berlinski:Adagietto; Ochse:Prelude & Fugue Ft & Org; Roush:Dove Descending; B. W. Sanders:Pieces Fl; J. Weaver:Rhapsody SUMM ▲ 174 [DDD] (16.97)

YOUNG, LA MONTE (1935-

Sarabande for Piano (1959; rev 1991)
J. Schneider (gtr), A. Shulman (hp) [arr J. Schneider for gtr & hp] *(rec KPFK-FM Los Angeles, CA, 1993)* ("Just West Coast") † J. Cage:Dream Pno; In a Landscape; L. Harrison:Suite 2 Gtr; H. Partch:Barstow Gtr; Studies on Ancient Greek Scales BRID ▲ 9041 [DDD] (17.97)

YOUNG, VICTOR (1900-1956)

Film Music
R. Kaufman (cnd), New Zealand SO—For Whom the Bell Tolls; The Quiet Man; Around the World in 80 Days; Samson & Delilah; Shane ("Shane:A Tribute to Victor Young") KOCH ▲ 7365 (16.97)
W. T. Stromberg (cnd), Moscow SO, Moscow SO Chorus—Greatest Show on Earth; Uninvited; Gulliver's Travels; Bright Leaf MARC ▲ 8225063 [DDD] (13.97)

YOUNG, VICTOR (cont.)

Music of Young
R. Mendez (tpt), I. Cisneros (cnd) —Around the World in 80 Days ("Trumpet Showcase") † Louiguy:Songs; R. Mendez:Music of Mendez; G. Rossini:Barbiere di Siviglia (sels); F. Schubert:Ave Maria, Op. 52/6 SUMM ▲ 206 [DDD] (16.97)

Scaramouche (film score) for Orchestra (1952)
R. Kaufman (cnd), Brandenburg PO [reconstructed William Stromberg] *(rec Jesus Christ Church Berlin, Germany, 1994)* ("Captain Blood") † Korngold:Captain Blood; M. Rózsa:King's Thief; M. Steiner:Three Musketeers MARC ▲ 8223607 [DDD] (13.97)

YRADIER, SEBASTIÁN DE (1809-1865)

Songs (miscellaneous collections)
A. Augér (sop), L. Orkis (pno)—Calesera *(rec 1990)* † F. Schubert:Songs (misc colls); Winterreise, D.911 VCL 2-▲ 61457 [DDD] (11.97)

YSAŸE, EUGÈNE (1858-1931)

Poème élégiaque for Violin & Piano
P. Graffin (vn), P. Devoyon (pno) † Rêve d'enfant; Sons Vn, Op. 27 HYP ▲ 66940 (18.97)
V. Hoffman (vn), J. Huntly (pno) ("Le violon de la mort") † Sons Vn, Op. 27; Zieritz:Violon de la mort CRSR ▲ 9665 [DDD]

Rêve d'enfant for Violin & Piano
P. Graffin (vn), P. Devoyon (pno) † Poème élégiaque Vn & Pno; Sons Vn, Op. 27 HYP ▲ 66940 (18.97)

Sonata for Cello, Op. 28
R. Penneys (pno) *(rec Baton Rouge, LA, Mar 1994)* ("Cello Sonatas") † G. Crumb:Son Vc; Kodály:Son Vc, Op. 8 CENT ▲ 2228 [DDD] (16.97)
H. Ruijsenaars (vc) † M. Reger:Suites Vc, Op. 131c CLSO ▲ 177 (15.97)

Sonatas (6) for Violin, Op. 27 (1924)
V. Bolognese (vn) AART ▲ 47175 [DDD] (10.97)
R. Cani (vn) ("Sonatas for Solo Violin") † B. Bartók:Son Vn; E. Bloch:Suite 1 Vn; Suite 2 Vn; S. Prokofiev:Son Vc AG ▲ 106 (18.97)
D. Chan (vn) *(rec Aspen, CO, May 1995)* † G. Gershwin:Songs; Paganini:Con 2 Vn, M.S. 48; Saint-Saëns:Son 1 Vn, Op. 75; Tartini:Son Vn & Pno; P. Tchaikovsky:Souvenir d'un lieu cher, Op. 42; Valse-Scherzo Vn, Op. 34 AMBA ▲ 1017 [DDD] (16.97)
A. Delmoni (vn) ("Ysaÿe-Kreisler-Bach: Solo Violin Works") † J. S. Bach:Sons & Partitas Vn; F. Kreisler:Recitativo & Scherzo-caprice, Op. 6 JMR ▲ 14 (16.97)
P. Graffin (vn) † Poème élégiaque Vn & Pno; Rêve d'enfant HYP ▲ 66940 (18.97)
V. Hoffman (vn) ("Le violon de la mort") † Poème élégiaque Vn & Pno; Zieritz:Violon de la mort CRSR ▲ 9665 [DDD]
L. Josefowicz (vn) † B. Bartók:Son Vn; H. W. Ernst:Roi des aulnes, Op. 26; F. Kreisler:Recitativo & Scherzo-caprice, Op. 6; Paganini:Intro & Vars on Nel cor più non mi sento, M.S. 44 PPHI ▲ 46700 (16.97)
I. Kaler (vn) *(rec Methuen, MA, May 1995)* † P. Hindemith:Son Vn; J. Martinon:Sonatina 5 Vn, Op. 32/1; S. Prokofiev:Son Vc ONGA ▲ 103 [DDD] (16.97)
T. Kato (vn) DNN ▲ 18011 (16.97)
L. Mordkovitch (vn) CHN ▲ 8599 [DDD] (16.97)
O. Shumsky (vn) NIMB ▲ 7715 [DDD] (11.97)
T. Wanami (vn) SOMM ▲ 12 (18.97)
N. Znaider (vn)—No. 2 *(rec Royal Conservatory of Music, Brussels, Belgium, May 20, 1997)* † E. Chausson:Poème Vn, Op. 25; Debussy:Son Vn; Sibelius:Con Vn; Wieniawski:Polonaise 1, Op. 4 CYPR ▲ 9608 [DDD] (17.97)

Variations on Paganini's Caprice No. 24 for Violin
Arte del Suono String Quartet [arr Jacques Ysaÿe for str qt] *(rec Jan 1994)* ("Rare Works for String Quartet") † Boccherini:Qts Strs; G. Puccini:Crisantemi; Minuets PAVA ▲ 7309 [DDD] (10.97)

YTTREHUS, ROLV (1926-

Explorations for Piano (1985)
D. Holzman (pno) *(rec Harvard Univ, Jan 1995)* ("Explorations: New American Piano Music") † Boros:Mnem; Cornicello:Son 2 Pno; M. Greenbaum:Amulet; Pleskow:Son 2 Pno CENT ▲ 2291 [DDD] (16.97)

YU, JULIAN JING-JUN (1957-

Wu-Yu for Orchestra & Chorus
S. Kawalla (cnd), Koszalin State PO, Silesian Univ Choir † J. Fortner:Quadri; H. Nakamura:Litaniae; D. Scott:Arras; Van de Vate:Voices VMM ▲ 3022 [DDD]

YUASA, JOJI (1929-

Cosmos Haptic No. 3 for Koto & Shakahuchi, "Kokuh"
K. Mitsuhashi (shak), N. Yoshimura (koto) *(rec Iruma City Auditorium, Dec 14, 1990)* † Minami:Coloration-Project III; Nishimura:Nanae; S. Satoh:Kamu-Ogi-Guoto; Yoshimatsu:Moyura CAMA ▲ 189 [DDD] (18.97)

Eye on Genesis for UPIC for Computer-Generated Sound (1991)
J. Yuasa (cmpt) † Nine Levels of Ze-Ami; Terms of Temporal Detailing NEU ▲ 45096 [DDD] (16.97)

Koto Uta Basho's 5 Haiku for Koto & Ensemble
T. Sawai (koto), Sawai Koto Ensemble † Matsumura:Fant Koto; Nishimura:Iris of Time; River of Time; Stratums of Time; T. Sawai:Gosechi No Mai CAMA ▲ 92

Mutterings for Soprano & Ensemble (1988)
C. Plantamura (sop), H. Sollberger (cnd) , SONOR Ensemble of Univ of California San Diego members *(rec Oct 1992)* † Ferneyhough:Prometheus; R. Reynolds:Not only Night; R. Steiger:Double Con CRI ▲ 652 [DDD] (17.97)

The Nine Levels of Ze-Ami for 17 Players & Tape (1988)
J. Yuasa (tape), K. Nagano (cnd) † Eye on Genesis for UPIC; Terms of Temporal Detailing NEU ▲ 45096 [DDD] (16.97)

Not I, But the Wind for Amplified Alto Saxophone (1976)
D. Pituch (sax) *(rec Trixi Tonstudio Munich)* ("David Pituch Plays New Compositions for the E Alto Saxophone") † A. Bloch:Notes; B. Fennelly:Con Sax; Tesserae VIII; Palester:Concertino A Sax PROV ▲ 175 [ADD]

Scenes from Basho for Orchestra
T. Otaka (cnd), Tokyo PO *(rec live Tokyo Bunka-Kaikan Large Hall, May 30, 1981)* † Fukushi:Chromosphere; A. Otaka:Image Orch CAMA ▲ 293 [AAD] (18.97)

Terms of Temporal Detailing for Bass Flute, "Homage to David Hockney" (1989)
J. Fonville (b fl) † Eye on Genesis for UPIC; Nine Levels of Ze-Ami NEU ▲ 45096 [DDD] (16.97)

Towards the Midnight Sun for Computer Generated Tape & Amplified Piano (1984)
A. Karis (pno) *(rec American Academy of Arts & Letters, NYC, NY, June 1994)* † Babbitt:Reflections; Davidovsky:Synchronism 6; A. Kreiger:Fant Pno; Primosch:Secret Geometry CRI ▲ 707 [DDD] (16.97)

YUKECHEV, YURI (20th cent)

Sacred Choral Music
M. E. Callahan (sop), N. Kachanov (cnd), New York Russian Chamber Chorus—My Heart Is Ready; O, Beauty; Chant; By Candlelight ("My Heart is Ready: New Age Russian Chant") HEL ▲ 1005 (10.97)

YUN, ISANG (1917-1995)

Concertino for Accordion & String Quartet (1983)
M. Miki (acc), Nomos String Quartet † Qt 3 Strs; Qt 4 Strs; Tapis CPO ▲ 999075 [DDD] (14.97)

Concerto for Cello & Orchestra
S. Palm (vc), H. Zender (cnd), Berlin RSO *(rec Mar 25, 1976)* † Son Ob CAMA ▲ 22 (18.97)

Concerto for Clarinet & Orchestra
E. Brunner (cl), P. Thomas (cnd), Bavarian RSO † Piri Cl & Orch; Riul CAMA ▲ 46 (18.97)

Concerto for Flute & Chamber Orchestra (1977)
R. Staege (fl), H. Zender (cnd), Saarbrücken RSO *(rec Saarbrück Radio Studio, May 1985)* † Gong-Hu; In Balance; Salomo CAMA ▲ 109 [AAD] (18.97)

Contrasts for Violin
L'Art Pour L'Art Ensemble † Duo Vc & Hp; Gagok; Novelette Fl; Sori CPO ▲ 999118 [DDD] (14.97)
A. Tatsumi (vn) *(rec Shibukawa City Auditorium, May 26, 1988)* † Gasa; Königliches Thema; Qnt Cl CAMA ▲ 70 [AAD] (18.97)

Distanzen for Woodwind Quintet & String Quintet (1988)
P. Méfano (cnd) † Kammerkonzerts; Königliches Thema; Music for 7 Instrs 2E2M ▲ 1010 (20.97)

Double Concerto for Oboe, Harp & Small Orchestra (1977)
H. Holliger (ob), U. Holliger (hp), D. R. Davies (cnd), Saarbrücken RSO † Images CAMA ▲ 108 [DDD] (18.97)

Duo for Cello & Harp
L'Art Pour L'Art Ensemble † Contrasts Vn; Gagok; Novelette Fl; Sori CPO ▲ 999118 [DDD] (14.97)

Duo for Viola & Piano (1976; rev 1993)
N. Imai (va), M. Miki (acc) [trans for va & acc] *(rec Apr 1998)* ("Into the Depth of Time") † Hosokawa:Into the Depths of Time; Irino:Suite Va; Y. Takahashi:Ins Tal; Like a Water Buffalo; Like Swans Leaving the Lake BIS ▲ 929 [DDD] (17.97)

YUN, ISANG (cont.)
Exemplum in memoriam Kwangju for Orchestra (1981)
B. Kim (cnd), Korea State SO *(rec in Pyong-Yang, 1986-70)* † Naui Dang, Naui Minjokiyo!
CPO ▲ 999047 [AAD] (14.97)
Festlicher Tanz for Wind Quintet (1988)
Albert Schweitzer Wind Quintet *(rec Dec 1991)* † Movt I; Movt II; Pezzo fantasioso; Rondell; Sori
CPO ▲ 999184 [DDD] (14.97)
Gagok for Voice, Guitar & Percussion (1972)
L'Art Pour L'Art Ensemble † Contrasts Vn; Duo Vc & Hp; Novelette Fl; Sori CPO ▲ 999118 [DDD] (14.97)
Gasa for Violin & Piano (1963)
A. Tatsumi (vn), Y. Takahashi (pno) *(rec Shibukawa City Auditorium, May 26, 1988)* † Contrasts Vn; Königliches Thema; Qnt Cl CAMA ▲ 70 [AAD] (18.97)
Gong-Hu for Harp & Strings (1984)
U. Holliger (hp), H. Holliger (cnd) *(rec Bremen Radio Studio, June 1985)* † Con Fl; In Balance; Salomo
CAMA ▲ 109 [AAD] (18.97)
Images for Flute, Oboe, Violin & Cello (ca 1963)
H. Schneeberger (vn), T. Demenga (vc), A. Nicolet (fl), H. Holliger (ob) † Double Con CAMA ▲ 108 [DDD] (18.97)
In Balance for Harp (1987)
U. Holliger (hp) *(rec Bremen Radio Studio, June 1985)* † Con Fl; Gong-Hu; Salomo CAMA ▲ 109 [AAD] (18.97)
Kammerkonzerts I & II for Chamber Ensemble (1990)
P. Méfano (cnd) † Distanzen; Königliches Thema; Music for 7 Instrs 2E2M ▲ 1010 (20.97)
Königliches Thema for Violin [after Bach] (1976)
P. Méfano (cnd) † Distanzen; Kammerkonzerts; Music for 7 Instrs 2E2M ▲ 1010 (20.97)
A. Tatsumi (vn) *(rec Shibukawa City Auditorium, May 26, 1988)* † Contrasts Vn; Gasa; Qnt Cl
CAMA ▲ 70 [AAD] (18.97)
Monolog for Bassoon (1985)
D. Jensen (bn) *(rec 1997)* † O. Berg:Sonatine Bn; Vertigo; P. Hindemith:Son Bn; Nussio:Vars; O. Schoeck:Son Bn; M. Schoof:Impromptus Bn MDG ▲ 6030831 [DDD] (17.97)
Movement I for Wind Quintet (1991)
Albert Schweitzer Wind Quintet *(rec Dec 1991)* † Festlicher Tanz; Movt II; Pezzo fantasioso; Rondell; Sori
CPO ▲ 999184 [DDD] (14.97)
Movement II for Wind Quintet (1991)
Albert Schweitzer Wind Quintet *(rec Dec 1991)* † Festlicher Tanz; Movt I; Pezzo fantasioso; Rondell; Sori
CPO ▲ 999184 [DDD] (14.97)
Music for 7 Instruments (1959)
P. Méfano (cnd) † Distanzen; Kammerkonzerts; Königliches Thema 2E2M ▲ 1010 (20.97)
Music of Yun
artists unknown—Sym 1; Loyang; Con Vc; Son Ob, Hp & Va; Con Cl; Riul; Piri; Kantata; Exemplum; Königliches; GASA; Con Vn; Muak-Tänzerische; Pièce Concertante; Double Con; Images; Con Fl; Salomo; Gong-fu; In Balance CAMA 10-▲ 231
Naui Dang, Naui Minjokiyo! [My Land, My People] (patriotic/propaganda work) for Soloists, Orchestra & Chorus (1987)
B. Kim (cnd), Korea State SO *(rec in Pyong-Yang, 1986-70)* † Exemplum in memoriam Kwangju
CPO ▲ 999047 [AAD] (14.97)
Novelette for Flute, Harp, Violin & Cello (1980)
L'Art Pour L'Art Ensemble † Contrasts Vn; Duo Vc & Hp; Gagok; Sori CPO ▲ 999118 [DDD] (14.97)
Pezzo fantasioso for 2 Flutes & Cello (1988)
Albert Schweitzer Wind Quintet *(rec Dec 1991)* † Festlicher Tanz; Movt I; Movt II; Rondell; Sori
CPO ▲ 999184 [DDD] (14.97)
Piri for Clarinet & Orchestra
E. Brunner (cl), P. Thomas (cnd), Bavarian RSO † Con Cl; Riul CAMA ▲ 46 (18.97)
Piri for Oboe (or Clarinet) (1971)
E. Brunner (cl) *(rec Bavarian Radio, Nov 25, 1982)* ("The Art of Playing Clarinet") † Qnt Cl; F. Devienne:Son 1 Cl; Son 2 Cl; J. Haydn:Trios Cl, Vn & Vc CAMA ▲ 356 [DDD]
B. Glaetzner (ob) ("Contemporary Music for Oboe") † L. Berio:Sequenza VII; L. Lombardi:Einklang; F. Schenker:Horstuck; Xenakis:Dmaathen BER ▲ 1172 (16.97)
Quartet for Oboe, Violin, Viola & Cello (1994)
K. Sawa (vn), T. Ichitsubo (va), T. Hayashi (vc), H. Shibayama (ob), S. Shinohe (cl), Sawa String Quartet *(rec Niigata, Japan)* ("The Last Works of Isang Yun") † Qnt 2 Cl; Qt 5 Strs CAMA ▲ 30363 [DDD] (18.97)
Quartet No. 3 for Strings (1959)
Nomos String Quartet † Concertino Acc; Qt 4 Strs; Tapis CPO ▲ 999075 [DDD] (14.97)
Quartet No. 4 for Strings (1988)
Nomos String Quartet † Concertino Acc; Qt 3 Strs; Tapis CPO ▲ 999075 [DDD] (14.97)
Quartet No. 5 for Strings (1990)
Sawa String Quartet *(rec Niigata, Japan)* ("The Last Works of Isang Yun") † Qnt 2 Cl; Qt Ob
CAMA ▲ 30363 [DDD] (18.97)
Quartet No. 6 for Strings (1992)
Amati String Quartet *(rec Mar 1996)* † Qnt Cl; Qnt 2 Cl CPO ▲ 999428 [DDD] (13.97)
Quintet for Clarinet & String Quartet (1984)
E. Brunner (cl), Amati String Quartet *(rec Mar 1996)* † Qnt 2 Cl; Qt 6 Strs CPO ▲ 999428 [DDD] (13.97)
E. Brunner (cl), Akiko Tatsumi String Quartet *(rec Maebashi City Auditorium, Aug 31, 1984)* † Contrasts Vn; Gasa; Königliches Thema CAMA ▲ 70 [AAD] (18.97)
E. Brunner (cl), Akiko Tatsumi String Quartet *(rec Maebashi Shimin Bunka Kaikan, Country Unknown, 1984)* ("The Art of Playing Clarinet") † Piri Ob; F. Devienne:Son 1 Cl; Son 2 Cl; J. Haydn:Trios Cl, Vn & Vc CAMA ▲ 356 [DDD]
Quintet No. 2 for Clarinet & String Quartet (1994)
E. Brunner (cl), Amati String Quartet *(rec Mar 1996)* † Qnt Cl; Qt 6 Strs CPO ▲ 999428 [DDD] (13.97)
S. Shinohe (cl), Sawa String Quartet *(rec Niigata, Japan)* ("The Last Works of Isang Yun") † Qt Ob; Qt 5 Strs
CAMA ▲ 30363 [DDD] (18.97)
Riul for Clarinet & Piano (1968)
E. Brunner (cl), A. Kontarsky (pno) † Con Cl; Piri Cl & Orch CAMA ▲ 46 (18.97)
Rondell for Oboe, Clarinet & Bassoon (1975)
C. Dimigen (ob), D. Schneider (cl), E. Hübner (bn) *(rec Dec 1991)* † Festlicher Tanz; Movt I; Movt II; Pezzo fantasioso; Sori CPO ▲ 999184 [DDD] (14.97)
Salomo for Alto Flute (1978)
R. Staege (fl) *(rec Saarbrück Radio Studio, May 1985)* † Con Fl; Gong-Hu; In Balance CAMA ▲ 109 [AAD] (18.97)
Sonata for Oboe, Harp and Viola
H. Fukai (va), H. Holliger (ob), U. Holliger (hp) *(rec Mar 25, 1976)* † Con Vc CAMA ▲ 22 (18.97)
Sori for Flute (1988)
L'Art Pour L'Art Ensemble † Contrasts Vn; Duo Vc & Hp; Gagok; Novelette Fl CPO ▲ 999118 [DDD] (14.97)
A. Tezlaff (fl) *(rec Dec 1991)* † Festlicher Tanz; Movt I; Movt II; Pezzo fantasioso; Rondell
CPO ▲ 999184 [DDD] (14.97)
Symphony No. 1 (1983)
T. Ukigaya (cnd), Pomeranian PO † Sym 3 CPO ▲ 999125 [DDD] (14.97)
Symphony No. 2 (1984)
T. Ukigaya (cnd), Pomeranian PO † Sym 4 CPO ▲ 999147 [DDD] (14.97)
Symphony No. 3 (1985)
T. Ukigaya (cnd), Pomeranian PO † Sym 1 CPO ▲ 999125 [DDD] (14.97)
Symphony No. 4 (1986)
T. Ukigaya (cnd), Pomeranian PO † Sym 2 CPO ▲ 999147 [DDD] (14.97)
Symphony No. 5 for Baritone & Orchestra [after poems by Nelly Sachs] (1987)
R. Salter (bar), T. Ukigaya (cnd), Pomeranian PO CPO ▲ 999148 [DDD] (14.97)
Tapis for String Quintet
Nomos String Quartet † Concertino Acc; Qt 3 Strs; Qt 4 Strs CPO ▲ 999075 [DDD] (14.97)
YUYAMA, AKIRA (1932-
Divertimento for Marimba & Alto Saxophone
J. Harle (a sax), E. Glennie (mar) *(rec London, England, Sept 1994)* ("Wind in the Bamboo Grove") † K. Abe:Michi; Vars on Japanese Children's Songs; Wind in the Bamboo Grove; M. Miki:Mar Spiritual; Yoshioka:Rhap Mar
CAT ▲ 68193 [DDD] (16.97)

ZACH, JAN (1699-1773)
Organ Music
J. Hora (org)—Preludes Org, K A1-3 [K A1, Prelude in c; K A3, Prelude in A♭]; Fugues Org, K A4-5; Fugue in D Org *(rec Prague, Czech Republic, 1997)* ("Complete Organ Works") † Kopřiva:Org Music; Kuchař:Org Music
RD (Vixen) ▲ 10004 [DDD] (16.97)
ZÁDOR, JENŐ (1894-1977)
Christopher Columbus (opera) for Orchestra & Chorus
L. Barrymore (nar), L. Halasz (cnd), American SO, American Concert Choir *(rec 1975)* † Studies
CMB ▲ 1100 [ADD] (16.97)
Studies for Orchestra
P. Freeman (cnd), Westphalian SO *(rec 1975)* † Christopher Columbus CMB ▲ 1100 [ADD] (16.97)
ZAHAB, ROGER (1957-
Verging Lightfall for Violin & Keyboard
R. Zahab (vn), E. Moe (hpd/org/pno) † J. Cage:Harmonies Vn & Kbd KOCH ▲ 7130 [DDD] (10.97)
ZAIDEL-RUDOLPH, JEANNE (1948-
At the End of the Rainbow (symphonic poem) for Orchestra (1988)
A. Stephenson (cnd), South African National SO ("Music of the Spheres") † Fanfare Festival Ov; Masada; Sefirot Sym; Tempus Fugit; Virtuoso I GSE ▲ 1532
Fanfare Festival Overture for Orchestra (1985)
O. Hadari (cnd), South African National SO ("Music of the Spheres") † At the End of the Rainbow; Masada; Sefirot Sym; Tempus Fugit; Virtuoso I GSE ▲ 1532
Masada for Bassoon & String Quartet (1989)
A. Strydom (cnd) , A. Strydom (cnd), CCM Contemporary Music Ensemble ("Music of the Spheres") † At the End of the Rainbow; Fanfare Festival Ov; Sefirot Sym; Tempus Fugit; Virtuoso I GSE ▲ 1532
Sefirot Symphony for Wind, Brass, Percussion & Harp (1992)
O. Hadari (cnd), South African National SO ("Music of the Spheres") † At the End of the Rainbow; Fanfare Festival Ov; Masada; Tempus Fugit; Virtuoso I GSE ▲ 1532
Tempus Fugit for Orchestra (1986)
W. Mony (cnd) ("Music of the Spheres") † At the End of the Rainbow; Fanfare Festival Ov; Masada; Sefirot Sym; Virtuoso I GSE ▲ 1532
Virtuoso I for Piano (1988)
M. Tomas (pno) ("Music of the Spheres") † At the End of the Rainbow; Fanfare Festival Ov; Masada; Sefirot Sym; Tempus Fugit GSE ▲ 1532
ZAIMONT, JUDITH LANG (1945-
A Calendar Set for Piano (1976)
J. Polk (pno) ("Zones") † Trio 1 Pno; Trio 2 Pno ARA ▲ 6683 (16.97)
N. K. Solomon (pno) *(rec Slippery Rock University, PA, 1992)* ("Vive la Différence") † V. Bond:Sandburg Suite; J. Brockman:Character Sketches; T. León:Momentum; M. Richter:Exequy; Fragments; Schonthal:Fiestas Y Danzas; G. Walker:Cantos for the End of Summer LEON ▲ 334 [DDD] (16.97)
Dance/Inner Dance for Flute, Oboe & Cello (1985)
T. Mook (vc), K. Nester (fl), R. Smith (ob) *(rec SUNY Purchase Theatre, NY, 1995)* ("Neon Rhythm: Chamber Music of Judith Lang Zaimont") † Doubles; Hidden Heritage; Sky Curtains ARA ▲ 6667 [DDD] (16.97)
Doubles for Oboe & Piano (1993)
L. Kozenko (ob), D. Burnett (pno) *(rec SUNY Purchase Theatre, NY, 1995)* ("Neon Rhythm: Chamber Music of Judith Lang Zaimont") † Dance/Inner Dance; Hidden Heritage; Sky Curtains ARA ▲ 6667 [DDD] (16.97)
From the Great Land (song cycle) for Mezzo-Soprano, Clarinet & Piano [setting of Frank Buske's Woman's Songs]
American Chamber Ensemble [ENG] † P. Hindemith:Qt Cl; V. Weigl:Songs of Remembrance LEON ▲ 329 (16.97)
Hidden Heritage (dance symphony) for Flute (or Alto Flute), Cello, Piano, Reed Player (Clarinet, Bass Clarinet & Tenor Saxophone) & Percussion (1987)
D. Finkel (vc), K. Moratz (fl), D. Krakauer (b cl/cl/t sax), C. Adams (pno), B. Dove (perc), D. Kosloff (cnd) *(rec SUNY Purchase Theatre, NY, 1995)* ("Neon Rhythm: Chamber Music of Judith Lang Zaimont") † Dance/Inner Dance; Doubles; Sky Curtains ARA ▲ 6667 [DDD] (16.97)
Parable (A Tale of Abram & Isaac) for Narrator, Mixed Voices & Organ (1985)
J. Rice (cnd), Florilegium Chamber Choir [He,E] † Serenade:To Music; Musgrave:Madrigals; Rorate Coeli
LEON ▲ 328 [DDD] (16.97)
Piano Music
J. L. Zaimont (pno) *(Suite Impressions (3); Evening; Calendar Set [June; July; August; September]; Pno Rags (2); Nocturne "La Fin de siécle")*, J. L. Zaimont (pno), D. Kosloff (pno) *(Snazzy Son)* ("Summer Melodies")
4TAY ▲ 4001 [DDD] (17.97)
Serenade: To Music for 6 solo Voices (1981)
J. Rice (cnd), Florilegium Chamber Choir [He,E] † Parable; Musgrave:Madrigals; Rorate Coeli
LEON ▲ 328 [DDD] (16.97)
Sky Curtains for Flute, Clarinet, Bassoon, Viola & Cello (1984)
L. Martin (va), C. Finkel (vc), K. Nester (fl), D. Gilbert (cl), B. Wagner (bn) *(rec SUNY Purchase Theatre, NY, 1995)* ("Neon Rhythm: Chamber Music of Judith Lang Zaimont") † Dance/Inner Dance; Doubles; Hidden Heritage
ARA ▲ 6667 [DDD] (16.97)
Trio No. 1 for Piano, Violin & Cello, "Russian Summer"
P. Winograd (vn), P. Wyrick (vc), J. Polk (pno) ("Zones") † Calendar Set; Trio 2 Pno ARA ▲ 6683 (16.97)
Trio No. 2 for Piano, Violin & Cello, "Zones"
P. Winograd (vn), P. Wyrick (vc), J. Polk (pno) ("Zones") † Calendar Set; Trio 1 Pno ARA ▲ 6683 (16.97)
When Angels Speak (fantasy) for Wind Quintet (1987)
Manhattan Wind Quintet ("When Angels Speak") † Maslanka:Qnt 2 Ww; Susser:Till Drumlin Waves; Wisner:Nocturne Ww ALBA ▲ 246 [DDD] (16.97)
ZAK, MICHAEL PHILLIP (dates unknown)
Trio for Violin, Cello & Piano
G. J. Schenk (vn), H. Jacob (vc), L. W. Ignacio (pno) ("Albumleaf") † Bergsma:Songs (4); Diemer:Quiet, Lovely Piece; E. Pellegrini:Serenata a Tre; M. Reger:Albumblatt & Tarantella; Sons (2) Cl, Op. 49; Wendelburg:Son Cl
CRSR ▲ 9358
ZALUSKI, IWO (1939-
Variations on a Theme of Amelia Zaluska for Piano
I. Zaluski (pno) *(rec St. Ives, Cambridge, England, Jan 1998)* ("Music of the Ogiński Dynasty, Vol. 2") † M. K. Ogiński:Pno Music; F. K. Ogiński:Pno Music; K. O. Ostaszewski:Funeral March in Honour of Marshal Piludski; W. O. Ostaszewski:Turn of the Wave; K. B. Zaluski:Pno Music OLY ▲ 645 [DDD] (16.97)
ZALUSKI, KAROL BERNARD (1834-1919)
Piano Music
I. Zaluski (pno)—Mazurka in c; Mazurka in C; Polonaise in D♭; Lever du soleil *(rec St. Ives, Cambridge, England, Jan 1998)* ("Music of the Ogiński Dynasty, Vol. 2") † M. K. Ogiński:Pno Music; F. K. Ogiński:Pno Music; K. O. Ostaszewski:Funeral March in Honour of Marshal Piludski; W. O. Ostaszewski:Turn of the Wave; I. Zaluski:Vars on a Theme of Amelia Zaluska OLY ▲ 645 [DDD] (16.97)
ZANDONAI, RICCARDO (1883-1944)
Francesca da Rimini (opera in 4 acts) [lib Tito Ricordi] (1914)
E. Filipova (sop), K. Riegel (ten), P. Rouillon (bar), D. Rigosa (bass), F. Kalt (sgr), F. Lusis (cnd), Vienna SO, Vienna Volksoper Chorus *(rec Bergenz Festival, 1994)* KSCH 2-▲ 313682
R. Kabaivanska (sop), P. Domingo (ten), M. Manuguerra (bar), N. Saetta (sgr), E. Queler (cnd) *(rec live, Mar 22, 1973)* SRON 2-▲ 840 [ADD] (25.97)
M. Olivero (sop—Francesca), E. Vincenzi (sop—Garsenda), L. Marimpietri (sop—Biancofiore), P. Perotti (sop—Samaritana), G. Carturan (mez—Smaragdi), B. Casoni (mez—Altichiara), A. M. Rota (cta—Donella), M. del Monaco (ten—Paolo), P. D. Palma (ten—Malatestino), A. Mercuriali (ten—Ser Toldo Berardengo), R. Pelizzoni (ten—Prisoner), A. Cesarini (ten—Archer), G. Malaspina (bar—Gianciotto), D. Mantovani (bar—Jester), E. Campi (bass—Ostasio), G. Morresi (bass—Tower warden), G. Gavazzeni (cnd), La Scala Orch, La Scala Chorus *(rec La Scala Theatre Milan, June 4, 1959)* LCD 2-▲ 107 (16.97)
Francesca da Rimini (selections)
M. Olivero (sop) *(rec 1967-72)* ("The Famous Amsterdam Concerts") † U. Giordano:Fedora (sels); Verdi:Traviata (sels) BELV 2-▲ 7207 (29.97)
K. Ricciarelli (sop), P. Domingo (ten), A. Guadagno (cnd), St. Cecilia Academy Orch Rome *(rec 1972)* ("Domingo: Opera Duets") † Bizet:Pêcheurs de perles (sels); Ponchielli:Gioconda (sels); G. Puccini:Bohème (sels); Madama Butterfly (sels); Verdi:Forza del destino (sels); Otello (sels); Vespri siciliani (sels)
RCAV (Gold Seal) ▲ 62595 [ADD] (11.97)
M. Stabile (bar), G. Nessi (ten)—Chi ha chiuso? *(rec 1928)* † Boito:Nerone (sels); Donizetti:Don Pasquale (sels); U. Giordano:Andrea Chénier (sels); W. A. Mozart:Don Giovanni (sels); Nozze di Figaro (sels); G. Puccini:Tosca (sels); Verdi:Aida (sels); Falstaff (sels); Otello (sels) PRE (Lebendige Vergangenheit) ▲ 89180 (m) (16.97)

ZANETTI, GASPARO (fl 1626-1645)
Il scolaro di Gasparo Zanetti [Zanetti's anthology & arrangement of late 16th & early 17th-century Italian dances]
C. Mendoze (cnd) PVY ▲ 792012 [DDD] (16.97)

ZAPPA, ENRIC ANDREW (1953-
Hydra Sonata for Flute & Piano (1988)
P. Call (fl), M. Graber (pno) ("Excursions") † Bozza:Caprice-Improvisation; Hush:Qt 1 Strs; Son Vc; J. Russo:Pieces Cl; Son 1 Fl; Van Appledorn:Ayre CRSR ▲ 9257
various artists ("Strictly Genteel: A 'Classical' Introduction to Frank Zappa") † F. Zappa:Duke of Prunes; Music of F. Zappa; Uncle Meat RYK ▲ 10578 (16.97)

ZAPPA, FRANK (1940-1993)
Be-Bop Tango for Orchestra
Omnibus Wind Ensemble *(rec 1994-5)* ("Music by Frank Zappa") † Music of F. Zappa; Number 7; Peaches en Regalia; Revised Music for a Low Budget Orch; M. Ravel:Boléro OPU ▲ 19403 [AAD] (16.97)
The Black Page for Piano & Percussion (1977)
Minnesota Contemporary Ensemble ("180° from Ordinary") † Gleck:2 Tpts; Gubaidulina:Chaconne Pno; L. Larsen:Black Roller; A. Piazzolla:4, for Tango; Siskind:Rituale; Trenka:WatchWait INNO ▲ 513 [ADD] (14.97)
Blessed Relief for Chamber Ensemble
Bossini (cnd) ("Prophetic Attitude") † A Pound for a Brown; Cletus Awreetus-Awrightus; Duke of Prunes; King Kong; Music of F. Zappa; Number 6; Peaches en Regalia; Sofa; Uncle Meat; 20 Small Cigars ED ▲ 13071 (18.97)
Bob in Dacron for Orchestra
K. Nagano (cnd), London SO *(rec Jan 1983)* ("Zappa, Vol. 1 & 2") † Bogus Pomp; Mo 'n' Herb's Vacation; Pedro's Dowry; Sad Jane; Strictly Genteel RYK 2-▲ 10540 (19.97)
Bogus Pomp for Orchestra
K. Nagano (cnd), London SO *(rec Jan 1983)* ("Zappa, Vol. 1 & 2") † Bob in Dacron; Mo 'n' Herb's Vacation; Pedro's Dowry; Sad Jane; Strictly Genteel RYK 2-▲ 10540 (19.97)
Cletus Awreetus-Awrightus for Chamber Ensemble
Bossini (cnd) ("Prophetic Attitude") † A Pound for a Brown; Blessed Relief; Duke of Prunes; King Kong; Music of F. Zappa; Number 6; Peaches en Regalia; Sofa; Uncle Meat; 20 Small Cigars ED ▲ 13071 (18.97)
Dog-Breath Variations for Wind Ensemble (1970)
E. Corporon (cnd), Cincinnati College Conservatory of Music Wind Sym *(rec Corbett Auditorium, OH, May 1992)* ("Songs & Dances") † Envelopes; Gillingham:Songs of the Night; B. Gilmore:Folksongs; Persichetti:Mascarade; F. Schmitt:Dionysiaques, Op. 62 KLAV ▲ 11066 [DDD] (18.97)
Duke of Prunes for Chamber Ensemble
Bossini (cnd) ("Prophetic Attitude") † A Pound for a Brown; Blessed Relief; Cletus Awreetus-Awrightus; King Kong; Music of F. Zappa; Number 6; Peaches en Regalia; Sofa; Uncle Meat; 20 Small Cigars ED ▲ 13071 (18.97)
various artists ("Strictly Genteel: A 'Classical' Introduction to Frank Zappa") † Music of F. Zappa; Uncle Meat; E. A. Zappa:Hydra Son RYK ▲ 10578 (16.97)
Dupree's Paradise for Chamber Ensemble (1972)
P. Boulez (cnd) *(rec Paris, France, Jan 1984)* ("Boulez Conducts Zappa: The Perfect Stranger") † Girl in the Magnesium Dress; Jonestown; Love Story; Naval Aviation in Art?; Outside Now Again; Perfect Stranger RYK ▲ 10542 (11.97)
Envelopes for Wind Ensemble (1978)
E. Corporon (cnd), Cincinnati College Conservatory of Music Wind Sym *(rec Corbett Auditorium, OH, May 1992)* ("Songs & Dances") † Dog-Breath Vars; Gillingham:Songs of the Night; B. Gilmore:Folksongs; Persichetti:Mascarade; F. Schmitt:Dionysiaques, Op. 62 KLAV ▲ 11066 [DDD] (18.97)
The Girl in the Magnesium Dress for Chamber Ensemble
Barking Pumpkin Digital Gratification Consort *(rec Utility Muffin Research Kitchen, United States of America, ca 1984)* ("Boulez Conducts Zappa: The Perfect Stranger") † Dupree's Paradise; Jonestown; Love Story; Naval Aviation in Art?; Outside Now Again; Perfect Stranger RYK ▲ 10542 (11.97)
Jonestown for Chamber Ensemble
Barking Pumpkin Digital Gratification Consort *(rec Utility Muffin Research Kitchen, United States of America, ca 1984)* ("Boulez Conducts Zappa: The Perfect Stranger") † Dupree's Paradise; Girl in the Magnesium Dress; Love Story; Naval Aviation in Art?; Outside Now Again; Perfect Stranger RYK ▲ 10542 (11.97)
King Kong for Chamber Ensemble
Bossini (cnd) ("Prophetic Attitude") † A Pound for a Brown; Blessed Relief; Cletus Awreetus-Awrightus; Duke of Prunes; Music of F. Zappa; Number 6; Peaches en Regalia; Sofa; Uncle Meat; 20 Small Cigars ED ▲ 13071 (18.97)
Love Story for Chamber Ensemble
Barking Pumpkin Digital Gratification Consort *(rec Utility Muffin Research Kitchen, United States of America, ca 1984)* ("Boulez Conducts Zappa: The Perfect Stranger") † Dupree's Paradise; Girl in the Magnesium Dress; Jonestown; Naval Aviation in Art?; Outside Now Again; Perfect Stranger RYK ▲ 10542 (11.97)
Mo 'n' Herb's Vacation for Orchestra
K. Nagano (cnd), London SO *(rec Jan 1983)* ("Zappa, Vol. 1 & 2") † Bob in Dacron; Bogus Pomp; Pedro's Dowry; Sad Jane; Strictly Genteel RYK 2-▲ 10540 (19.97)
Music of Frank Zappa
Bossini (cnd) —Strictly Genteel; Black Page; Mr. Green Genes; Idiot Bastard Son; Outside Now Again ("Prophetic Attitude") † A Pound for a Brown; Blessed Relief; Cletus Awreetus-Awrightus; Duke of Prunes; King Kong; Number 6; Peaches en Regalia; Sofa; Uncle Meat; 20 Small Cigars ED ▲ 13071 (18.97)
J. Klibonoff (pno), Meridian Arts Ensemble *(Run Home Slow; Little March; Little House I Used to Live In)*, J. Ferarri (perc), J. Klibonoff (pno), Meridian Arts Ensemble *(Black Page; Black Page) (rec Amsterdam, Holland, Feb 1996)* ("Anxiety of Influence") † S. Barber:Semahane; Debussy:Pour le piano; D. Grabois:Zen Monkey; S. Silverman:Vars on a Theme of Weill; R. G. Stewart:KOHS-Ska; Okay Chorale; Traditional:Solitario CCL ▲ 9796 [DDD] (18.97)
Omnibus Wind Ensemble—Inca Roads; How Could I Be Such a Fool; Black Page No. 2; Igor's Boogie; Alien Orifice; Brown Shoes Don't Make It; Let's Make the Water Turn Black; Sinister Footwear; Dog-Breath Vars; Uncle Meat *(rec 1994-5)* ("Music by Frank Zappa") † Be-Bop Tango; Number 7; Peaches en Regalia; Revised Music for a Low Budget Orch; M. Ravel:Boléro OPU ▲ 19403 [AAD] (16.97)
various artists—Uncle Meat:Main Title Theme; Regyptian Strut; Pedro's Dowry; Outrage at Valdez; Little Umbrellas; Run Home Slow; Dwarf Nebula Processional March; Dupree's Paradise; Aybe Sea; Naval Aviation in Art?; G-Spot Tornado; Dog-Breath Vars; Strictly Genteel; Op. 1/3:Presto; Op. 1-4:Allegro ("Strictly Genteel: A 'Classical' Introduction to Frank Zappa") † Duke of Prunes; Uncle Meat; E. A. Zappa:Hydra Son RYK ▲ 10578 (16.97)
Naval Aviation in Art? for Chamber Ensemble
P. Boulez (cnd) *(rec Paris, France, Jan 1984)* ("Boulez Conducts Zappa: The Perfect Stranger") † Dupree's Paradise; Girl in the Magnesium Dress; Jonestown; Love Story; Outside Now Again; Perfect Stranger RYK ▲ 10542 (11.97)
Number 6 for Chamber Ensemble
Bossini (cnd) ("Prophetic Attitude") † A Pound for a Brown; Blessed Relief; Cletus Awreetus-Awrightus; Duke of Prunes; King Kong; Music of F. Zappa; Peaches en Regalia; Sofa; Uncle Meat; 20 Small Cigars ED ▲ 13071 (18.97)
Number 7 for Chamber Ensemble
Omnibus Wind Ensemble *(rec 1994-5)* ("Music by Frank Zappa") † Be-Bop Tango; Music of F. Zappa; Peaches en Regalia; Revised Music for a Low Budget Orch; M. Ravel:Boléro OPU ▲ 19403 [AAD] (16.97)
Outside Now Again for Chamber Ensemble
Barking Pumpkin Digital Gratification Consort *(rec Utility Muffin Research Kitchen, United States of America, ca 1984)* ("Boulez Conducts Zappa: The Perfect Stranger") † Dupree's Paradise; Girl in the Magnesium Dress; Jonestown; Love Story; Naval Aviation in Art?; Perfect Stranger RYK ▲ 10542 (11.97)
Peaches en Regalia for Chamber Ensemble
Bossini (cnd) ("Prophetic Attitude") † A Pound for a Brown; Blessed Relief; Cletus Awreetus-Awrightus; Duke of Prunes; King Kong; Music of F. Zappa; Number 6; Sofa; Uncle Meat; 20 Small Cigars ED ▲ 13071 (18.97)
Omnibus Wind Ensemble *(rec 1994-5)* ("Music by Frank Zappa") † Be-Bop Tango; Music of F. Zappa; Number 7; Revised Music for a Low Budget Orch; M. Ravel:Boléro OPU ▲ 19403 [AAD] (16.97)
Pedro's Dowry for Orchestra
K. Nagano (cnd), London SO *(rec Jan 1983)* ("Zappa, Vol. 1 & 2") † Bob in Dacron; Bogus Pomp; Mo 'n' Herb's Vacation; Sad Jane; Strictly Genteel RYK 2-▲ 10540 (19.97)
The Perfect Stranger for Chamber Ensemble
P. Boulez (cnd) *(rec Paris, France, Jan 1984)* ("Boulez Conducts Zappa: The Perfect Stranger") † Dupree's Paradise; Girl in the Magnesium Dress; Jonestown; Love Story; Naval Aviation in Art?; Outside Now Again RYK ▲ 10542 (11.97)
A Pound for a Brown for Chamber Ensemble
Bossini (cnd) ("Prophetic Attitude") † Blessed Relief; Cletus Awreetus-Awrightus; Duke of Prunes; King Kong; Music of F. Zappa; Number 6; Peaches en Regalia; Sofa; Uncle Meat; 20 Small Cigars ED ▲ 13071 (18.97)

ZAPPA, FRANK (cont.)
Revised Music for a Low Budget Orchestra
Omnibus Wind Ensemble *(rec 1994-5)* ("Music by Frank Zappa") † Be-Bop Tango; Music of F. Zappa; Number 7; Peaches en Regalia; M. Ravel:Boléro OPU ▲ 19403 [AAD] (16.97)
Sad Jane for Orchestra
K. Nagano (cnd), London SO *(rec Jan 1983)* ("Zappa, Vol. 1 & 2") † Bob in Dacron; Bogus Pomp; Mo 'n' Herb's Vacation; Pedro's Dowry; Strictly Genteel RYK 2-▲ 10540 (19.97)
Sofa for Chamber Ensemble
Bossini (cnd) ("Prophetic Attitude") † A Pound for a Brown; Blessed Relief; Cletus Awreetus-Awrightus; Duke of Prunes; King Kong; Music of F. Zappa; Number 6; Peaches en Regalia; Uncle Meat; 20 Small Cigars ED ▲ 13071 (18.97)
Strictly Genteel for Orchestra
K. Nagano (cnd), London SO *(rec Jan 1983)* ("Zappa, Vol. 1 & 2") † Bob in Dacron; Bogus Pomp; Mo 'n' Herb's Vacation; Pedro's Dowry; Sad Jane RYK 2-▲ 10540 (19.97)
20 Small Cigars for Chamber Ensemble
Bossini (cnd) ("Prophetic Attitude") † A Pound for a Brown; Blessed Relief; Cletus Awreetus-Awrightus; Duke of Prunes; King Kong; Music of F. Zappa; Number 6; Peaches en Regalia; Sofa; Uncle Meat ED ▲ 13071 (18.97)
Uncle Meat for Chamber Ensemble
Bossini (cnd) ("Prophetic Attitude") † A Pound for a Brown; Blessed Relief; Cletus Awreetus-Awrightus; Duke of Prunes; King Kong; Music of F. Zappa; Number 6; Peaches en Regalia; Sofa; 20 Small Cigars ED ▲ 13071 (18.97)
various artists ("Strictly Genteel: A 'Classical' Introduction to Frank Zappa") † Duke of Prunes; Music of F. Zappa; E. A. Zappa:Hydra Son RYK ▲ 10578 (16.97)
Waltz for Guitar (1958)
D. Tanenbaum (gtr) † A. Hovhaness:Sons Gtr; Kernis:Partita Gtr; S. Reich:Nagoya Gtrs; Richmond:Preludes Gtr; T. Riley:Barabas NALB ▲ 95 (16.97)

ZAREBSKI, JULIUSZ (1854-1885)
Grand polonaise in F# for Piano, Op. 6 (1881)
E. Weidner-Zajac (pno) *(rec Sept 1993)* ("Masques: Polish Piano Works") † Pno Music; W. Lutoslawski:Bucolics Pno; Szymanowski:Masques (3), Op. 34; Mazurkas Pno, Op. 50; Preludes Pno, Op. 1 DOR ▲ 80121 [DDD] (13.97)
Piano Music
E. Weidner-Zajac (pno)—Lullaby, Op. 22; Tarantelle, Op. 25 *(rec Sept 1993)* ("Masques: Polish Piano Works") † Grand polonaise Pno, Op. 6; W. Lutoslawski:Bucolics Pno; Szymanowski:Masques (3), Op. 34; Mazurkas Pno, Op. 50; Preludes Pno, Op. 1 DOR ▲ 80121 [DDD] (13.97)

ZAWINUL, JOE (1932-
Stories of the Danube (in 7 movts) for solo Voice, Keyboard, Percussion & Orchestra
B. Ocal (voc), J. Zawinul (kbd), W. Grassman (dr), B. Ocal (perc), C. Richter (cnd), Brno State PO PPHI ▲ 54143 (16.97)

ZBINDEN, JULIEN-FRANÇOIS (1917-
Concerto da camera for Piano, Strings & Orchestra, Op. 16 (1950-51)
C. Dobler (pno), C. Meister (cnd), Prague Brixi CO † E. Bloch:Con grosso 1; J. Meier:Esquisses; W. Vogel:Hörformen II GALL ▲ 728 [DDD] (19.97)

ZEBROWSKI, MARCIN JOZEF (1702-1770)
Leaving Alexandria for Voice & Piano (1997)
C. P. Trakas (bar), M. J. Zebrowski (pno) † R. Schumann:Dichterliebe, Op. 48 TIT ▲ 253 [DDD] (16.97)

ZECCHI, ADONE (1904-
Divertimento for Flute, Harp & Strings (1932)
O. Kudryachov (fl), V. Dulova (hp), M. Terian (cnd), Moscow Conservatory Student Orch Strings *(rec 1961)* ("Vera Dulova - Russian Performing School") † Damase:Sonatine Hp; Debussy:Suite bergamasque; Jolivet:Con Hp; Manino:Canzoni per Arpa; Salzedo:Preludes Hp RD (Talents of Russia) ▲ 16204 [AAD] (16.97)

ZEHAVI, ODED (1961-
Concerto for Violin & Orchestra
M. Guttman (vn), D. Shallon (cnd), London PO ("Israeli Violin Concertos") † Ben-Haim (Frankenburger):Con Vn; Sheriff:Con Vn ASV ▲ 1038 (16.97)

ZEIGER, JOHAN (1904-1961)
Estonian Suite for Winds
Viento Ensemble *(rec Portland, OR, Mar 1992)* ("Music of Eastern Europe: Woodwind Works") † F. Hidas:Qnt 3 Ww; Janáček:Moravian Dances Orch; L. Sabaneyev:Suite Ww Qnt; T. Svoboda:Trio Fl CENT ▲ 2211 [DDD] (16.97)

ZEISL, ERIC (1905-1959)
Sonata for Cello & Piano (1950-51)
M. Moskovitz (vc), D. Shapiro (pno) † Reizenstein:Cantilena, Op. 18; Elegy; Son Vc ASVQ ▲ 6225 (10.97)

ZELENKA, JAN DISMAS (1679-1745)
Capriccios (5) for Chamber Ensemble (1729)
L. Güttler (cnd) *(rec Feb 1988)* ("Concerti a diversi concertanti") BER ▲ 1002 [DDD] (16.97)
J. Sonnentheil (cnd), Neu-Eröffnete Orch ("Complete Orchestral Works, Vol. 1") † Con à 8; Hipocondrie à 7 CPO ▲ 999458 (14.97)
Chwalte Boha sylneho (psalm cycle) in G for Bass & Organ
Prague Madrigalists † Laetatus sum; Memento Domine David; Miserere in c SUR ▲ 112175 [DDD]
Concerto à 8 for Orchestra (?1723)
Collegium 1704 ("Composizione per Orchestra") † Hipocondrie à 7; Ov & Concertanti, ZWV 188; Sinfonia & Concertanti, ZWV 189; Son 3 CO SUR ▲ 9 (16.97)
J. Sonnentheil (cnd), Neu-Eröffnete Orch [period instrs] ("Complete Orchestral Works, Vol. 1") † Capriccios; Hipocondrie à 7 CPO ▲ 999458 (14.97)
Hipocondrie à 7 for Chamber Orchestra (1723)
Collegium 1704 ("Composizione per Orchestra") † Con à 8; Ov & Concertanti, ZWV 188; Sinfonia & Concertanti, ZWV 189; Son 3 CO SUR ▲ 9 (16.97)
R. Kubelík (cnd), Czech PO *(rec Prague, Czech Republic, 1946)* † F. A. Miča:Sinfonia; F. I. A. Tůma:Partita Strs; Vejvanovsky:Sons & Serenades SUR ▲ 3381 (m) [ADD] (10.97)
J. Sonnentheil (cnd), Neu-Eröffnete Orch [period instrs] ("Complete Orchestral Works, Vol. 1") † Capriccios; Con à 8 CPO ▲ 999458 (14.97)
Laetatus sum for 2 Flutes, 2 Violins, Viola, Organ & Chorus
Prague Madrigalists † Chwalte Boha sylneho; Memento Domine David; Miserere in c SUR ▲ 112175 [DDD]
Lamentationes Jeremiae Prophetae for Contralto, Tenor, Baritone & Chorus, ZWV 53 (1722)
U. Groenewold (cta), H. Meens (ten), M. V. Egmond (bass), R. Shaw (cnd), Academy of the Begynhof Amsterdam [LAT] GLOE ▲ 5050 [DDD] (16.97)
Litaniae Omnium Sanctorum for solo Voices, Orchestra & Chorus
J. Jonášová (sop), D. Drobková (cta), M. Kopp (ten), L. Mátl (cnd), Czech PO, Prague Phil Choir *(rec Rudolfinum Prague, Czech Republic, Dec 1983)* ("Magnificat") † Magnificat in D, ZWV 108; Psalmus 129; Salve Regina SUR ▲ 3315 [DDD]
Magnificat in C for solo Voices, Organ, Orchestra & Chorus, ZWV 107
M. Suzuki (cnd), Japan Bach Collegium ("Magnificat") † Magnificat in D, ZWV 108; J. S. Bach:Magnificat, BWV 243; Kuhnau:Magnificat BIS ▲ 1011 [DDD] (17.97)
Magnificat in D for solo Voices, Organ, Orchestra & Chorus, ZWV 108 (1725)
J. Jonášová (sop), M. Mrázová (cta), J. Hora (org), P. Kühn (cnd), Prague CO, Kühn Mixed Choir *(rec Rudolfinum Prague, Czech Republic, July 1982)* ("Magnificat") † Litaniae Omnium Sanctorum; Psalmus 129; Salve Regina SUR ▲ 3315 [DDD]
M. Suzuki (cnd), Japan Bach Collegium ("Magnificat") † Magnificat in C, ZWV 107; J. S. Bach:Magnificat, BWV 243; Kuhnau:Magnificat BIS ▲ 1011 [DDD] (17.97)
Memento Domine David for Ensemble
Prague Madrigalists † Chwalte Boha sylneho; Laetatus sum; Miserere in c SUR ▲ 112175 [DDD]
Miserere (Psalm 50) in c for Chorus & Ensemble, ZWV 57
R. Válek (cnd) , Czech Chamber Choir † Requiem, ZWV 48 SUR ▲ 52 [DDD] (16.97)
Miserere in c for 2 Oboes, Strings, Organ & Chorus (1738)
H. Max (cnd), Das Kleine Konzert, Rhineland Kantorei, Dormagen Boys' Choir ("Miserere") † J. A. Hasse:Miserere in c Orch CAPO ▲ 10557 [DDD] (11.97)
Prague Madrigalists † Chwalte Boha sylneho; Laetatus sum; Memento Domine David SUR ▲ 112175 [DDD]
Missa Circumcisionis Domini Nostri Jesu Christi (1724)
K. Wagner (cnd), Dresden Staatskapelle members, Dresden Church Choir, Anonymous (cnd), Dresden Children's Choir [LAT] † Missa Circumcissionis ENTE ▲ 87 [ADD/DDD] (10.97)

▲ = CD ♦ = Enhanced CD △ = MD ▮ = Cassette Tape ▯ = DCC

ZELENKA, JAN DISMAS (cont.)

Missa Circumcissionis for solo Voices, Orchestra & Chorus (1726)
A. Ihle (sop), B. Pfretzschner (alt), E. Wagner (ten), M. Henneberg (bass), K. Wagner (cnd), Dresden Staatskapelle, Dresden Cathedral Choir, Dresden Boys' Choir *(rec 1983)* † Missa Circumcisionis ENTE ▲ 87 [ADD/DDD] (10.97)

Missa Dei Patris, ZWV 19 (1740)
L. Güttler (cnd), Thüringian Academic Sing Circle BER ▲ 1078 (16.97)

Missa Gratias agimus tibi in D, ZWV 13 (1730)
J. Jonášová (sop), M. Mrázová (cta), V. Dolezal (ten), P. Mikuláš (bass), J. Bělohlávek (cnd), Czech PO, Czech Phil Chorus [LAT] † Responsoria pro Hebdomada Sancta; Sub tuum praesidium 3, ZWV 157 SUR ▲ 110816 [DDD]

Missa Sanctissimae Trinitatis in a for Soloists & Chorus, ZWV 17 (1736)
M. Frimmer (sop), E. Graf (cta), M. Brutscher (ten), W. Wehnert (cnd), Marburg Bach Choir THOR ▲ 2265 (17.97)
A. Hlavenková (sop), L. Moravec (alt), M. Kožená (cta), R. Sporka (ten), S. Předota (ten), M. Pospí II (bass), M. Stryncl (cnd) STMA ▲ 17 [DDD] (18.97)

Missa Votiva in e for SATB solo voices, Orchestra & Chorus, ZWV 18 (1739)
C. Hampe (sop), E. Graf (cta), J. Duske (ten), J. Gebhardt (bass), W. Wehnert (cnd), Hesse Bach Collegium, Marburg Bach Choir [LAT] THOR ▲ 2172 [DDD] (16.97)

Overture & Concertanti (7) in F for Chamber Orchestra, ZWV 188
Collegium 1704 ("Composizione per Orchestra") † Con à 8; Hipocondrie à 7; Sinfonia & Concertanti, ZWV 189; Son 3 CO SUR ▲ 9 (16.97)

Psalmus 129, for solo Voices, Organ, Orchestra & Chorus, "De profundis" (1724)
M. Mrázová (cta), J. Vogt (ten), J. Hora (org), P. Kühn (cnd), Prague CO, Kühn Mixed Choir *(rec Rudolfinum Prague, Czech Republic, July 1982)* ("Magnificat") † Litaniae Omnium Sanctorum; Magnificat in D, ZWV 108; Salve Regina SUR ▲ 3315 [DDD]

Requiem in d for Chorus & Ensemble, ZWV 48 (1721)
R. Válek (cnd), Czech Chamber Choir † Miserere, ZWV 57 SUR ▲ 52 [DDD] (16.97)

Responsoria pro Hebdomada Sancta, ZWV 55/10,11,13,14 & 15
L. Mátl (cnd), Czech Phil Chorus [LAT] † Missa Gratias agimus tibi, ZWV 13; Sub tuum praesidium 3, ZWV 157 SUR ▲ 110816 [DDD]

Sacred Music
M. Lins (sop), K. Wessel (alt), G. Schwarz (bass), Dingel-Chulten (sgr), T. Reuber (cnd), Metamorphosis Baroque Orch, Capella Piccola—Psalm 109, "Dixit Dominus"; Sub Tuum Praesidium; Benedictus Sit Deus Pater; Ave Regina Coelorum; Litaniae Lauretanae; Magnificat ("Sacred Works for Soloists, Orchestra & Chorus") THOR ▲ 2181 (16.97)

Salve Regina for Orchestra & Chorus (1730s)
L. Mátl (cnd), Czech PO, Prague Phil Choir *(rec Rudolfinum Prague, Czech Republic, Jan 3, 1985)* ("Magnificat") † Litaniae Omnium Sanctorum; Magnificat in D, ZWV 108; Psalmus 129 SUR ▲ 3315 [DDD]

Sinfonia & Concertanti (8) in a for Chamber Orchestra, ZWV 189
Collegium 1704 ("Composizione per Orchestra") † Con à 8; Hipocondrie à 7; Ov & Concertanti, ZWV 188; Son 3 CO SUR ▲ 9 (16.97)
P. Rapson (cnd), Fiori Musicali † J. S. Bach:Brandenburg Con 2, BWV 1047; Con 1 Hpd, BWV 1052 MENO ▲ 1019 [DDD] (20.97)

Sonata No. 3 in B♭ for Chamber Orchestra
Collegium 1704 ("Composizione per Orchestra") † Con à 8; Hipocondrie à 7; Ov & Concertanti, ZWV 188; Sinfonia & Concertanti, ZWV 189 SUR ▲ 9 (16.97)

Sub tuum praesidium No. 3 (antiphon) for Chorus, ZWV 157
L. Mátl (cnd), Czech Phil Chorus [LAT] † Missa Gratias agimus tibi, ZWV 13; Responsoria pro Hebdomada Sancta SUR ▲ 110816 [DDD]

Trio Sonatas (6) for Oboes, Bassoon & Continuo
P. Dombrecht (ob), D. Bond (bn) ACCE 2-▲ 8848 (34.97)
H. Holliger (ob), M. Bourgue (ob), T. Zehetmair (vn), K. Stoll (db), J. Rubin (lt), K. Thunemann (bn), C. Jaccottet (hpd) *(rec Salle de Musique, La Chaux-de-Fonds, France, June 1997)* UECM 2-▲ 462542 [DDD] (34.97)
V. Hoskovec (db), J. Brožková (ob), V. Jouza (ob), J. Kubita (bn), F. X. Thuri (hpd)—No. 4 in g; No. 5 in F; No. 6 in c STMA ▲ 9 [DDD]
J. Jouza (vn), V. Hoskovec (db), J. Brožková (ob), V. Jouza (ob), J. Kubita (bn), F. X. Thuri (hpd)—No. 1 in F; No. 2 in g; No. 3 in B *(rec 1993)* STMA ▲ 8 [DDD] (18.97)
Zefiro Ensemble—No. 2 in g; No. 5 in F; No. 6 in c ASTR ▲ 8511 (18.97)

Ultimarum prima dicta Missa Dei Filii in C
H. Rademann (cnd), Dresden Baroque Orch, Dresden Chamber Choir † J. A. Hasse:Miserere in c Orch RAUM ▲ 9702 (17.97)

ZELLER, CARL (JOHANN ADAM) (1842-1898)

Arias
E. Kunz (bar) ("Eric Kunz: Opera, Operetta & Song") † Lortzing:Arias; W. A. Mozart:Arias; Strauss (II):Lustige Krieg (sels); Nacht in Venedig (sels); Zigeunerbaron (sels) TES ▲ 1059 (17.97)

Der Obersteiger (selections)
E. Schwarzkopf (sop), O. Ackermann (cnd), Philharmonia Orch—Sei nicht bös *(rec Kingsway Hall, London, England, July 1957)* † Vogelhändler (sels); Heuberger:Opernball (sels); F. Lehár:Arias; Millöcker:Dubarry (sels); Sieczynski:Wien, du Stadt meiner Träume; Strauss (II):Casanova (sels); Suppé:Boccaccio (sels) *([ENG,GER] text)* EMIC (Great Recordings of the Century) ▲ 67004 [ADD] (11.97)

Vogelhändler (selections)
I. Kirtesi (sop), Z. Csonka (sop), J. Berkes (ten), L. Kovács (cnd), Hungarian Operetta Orch *(rec Budapest, Jan 1996)* ("Best of Operetta, Vol. 3") † I. Kálmán:Gräfin Mariza (sels); F. Lehár:Paganini (sels); R. Stolz:Arias; Strauss (II):Fledermaus (sels); Nacht in Venedig (sels) NXIN ▲ 8550943 [DDD] (5.97)
S. Knittel (sop), C. Gorner (sop), H. Hoppe (ten), F. Gruber (ten), C. Michalski (cnd), Graunke SO † Abrahám:Viktoria und ihr Husar (sels); Suppé:Boccaccio (sels) EMPE ▲ 86351
E. Lind (sop), A. Rost (sop), P. Domingo (ten), J. Carreras (ten), T. Hampson (bar), M. Viotti (cnd), Budapest PO *(rec live Bad Ischl, Austria)* ("A Tribute to Operetta") † I. Kálmán:Csárdásfürstin (sels); Gräfin Mariza (sels); F. Lehár:Arias DEUT ▲ 459658 (16.97)
E. Schwarzkopf (sop), O. Ackermann (cnd), Philharmonia Orch—Ich bin die Christel von der Post; Schenkt man sich Rosen in Tirol *(rec Kingsway Hall, London, England, July 1957)* † Obersteiger (sels); Heuberger:Opernball (sels); F. Lehár:Arias; Millöcker:Dubarry (sels); Sieczynski:Wien, du Stadt meiner Träume; Strauss (II):Casanova (sels); Suppé:Boccaccio (sels) *([ENG,GER] text)* EMIC (Great Recordings of the Century) ▲ 67004 [ADD] (11.97)

ZELTER, CARL FRIEDRICH (1758-1832)

Songs
A. Folan (sop), T. Beghin (pno)—Rastlose Liebe; Einsamkeit; Sonett; Die Braut am Gestade; Lied aus der Ferne; An eine Mutter, deren Tochter als Kind starb; Des Mädchens Klage; An den Mond; Der Verliebte; Margarethe; Wandrers Nachtlied; Gleich und gleich *(rec Ghent, Belgium, July 1998)* † Mendelssohn (-Bartholdy):Songs EUFO ▲ 1286 [DDD] (18.97)
H. Mammel (ten), L. Holtmeier (pno) [Goethe lieder] ("Goethe Lieder") † F. Schubert:Songs (misc) ARSM 2-▲ 1246 (34.97)

ZEMLINSKY, ALEXANDER VON (1871-1942)

Chamber Music
Corda String Quartet—Movts Str Qt; Movts Str Qnt † Schoenberg:Qt Strs in D; Trio Strs, Op. 45 STRV ▲ 33438 (16.97)

Choral Music
M. Mainka (sop), A. Schlüter (cta), Y. Park (ten), S. Kohnke (bass), J. Conlon (cnd), Cologne Gürzenich PO, R. Wipperman (cnd), Düsseldorf Municipal Choral Society *(Psalm 83) (rec Köln, Germany, Apr 1998)*, J. Conlon (cnd), Cologne Gürzenich PO, Mülheimer Kantorei *(Geheimnis; Geheimnis; Aurikelchen) (rec Köln, Germany, June 1998)*, A. Sebald (fl), C. Menke (fl), E. Hellrung (hn), R. Thistle (hn), M. Rohrmus (hp), J. Conlon (cnd), Cologne Gürzenich PO, Mülheimer Kantorei *(Minnelied) (rec Köln, Germany, June 1998)*, L. Blum (ten), R. Giefer (org), J. Conlon (cnd), Cologne Gürzenich PO, Mülheimer Kantorei *(Hochzeitsgesang) (rec Köln, Germany, June 1998)* † Frühlingsbergräbnis; Psalm 13, Op. 24; Psalm 23, Op. 14 EMIC ▲ 56783 [DDD] (16.97)

Cymbeline (incidental music) for Orchestra [after Shakespeare], Op. 14 (1914)
J. Conlon (cnd), Cologne Gürzenich PO *(rec Cologne, Germany, 1996-7)* † Frühlingsbergräbnis; Tanzpoem EMIC ▲ 56474 [DDD] (16.97)

Es War Einmal (selections)
E. Johansson (sop—Prinzessin/Prinzessin/Prinzessin), K. Westi (ten—Prinz/Prinz/Prinz), P. Wahlgren (bar—Kaspar/Kaspar/Kaspar), H. Graf (cnd), Danish National RSO, Danish National Radio Chorus ("German Opera of the 20th Century") † Kreidekreis (sels); König Kandaules (sels); Traumgörge (sels); M. Gurlitt:Wozzeck (sels); F. Schmidt:Notre Dame (sels); Schreker:Ferne Klang (sels); Schatzgräber (sels) CAPO ▲ 10724 [DDD] (10.97)

ZEMLINSKY, ALEXANDER VON (cont.)

Eine florentinische Tragödie (opera) [lib Wilde; translated M. Meyerfeld], Op. 16 (1915-16)
D. Soffel (mez), K. Riegel (ten), G. Sarabia (bar), G. Albrecht (cnd), Berlin RSO [GER] KSCH ▲ 314012 [DDD] (16.97)
I. Vermillion (mez—Bianca), H. Kruse (ten—Guido), A. Dohmen (bar—Simone), R. Chailly (cnd), (Royal) Concertgebouw Orch PLON (Entartete Musik) ▲ 455112 (16.97)
D. Voigt (sop—Bianca), D. Kuebler (ten—Guido), D. R. Albert (bar—Simone), J. Conlon (cnd), Cologne Gürzenich PO *(rec Cologne, Germany, Mar 1997) (E,G lib texts)* EMIC ▲ 56472 [DDD] (16.97)

Frühlingsbegräbnis for SATB, Voices & Orchestra [text P. Heyse] (1896)
J. Conlon (cnd), Cologne Gürzenich PO, R. Wipperman (cnd), Düsseldorf Municipal Choral Society, D. Voigt (sop), D. R. Albert (bar) *(rec Köln, Germany, 1996-97)* † Choral Music; Psalm 13, Op. 24; Psalm 23, Op. 14 *([ENG,FRE,GER] text)* EMIC ▲ 56783 [DDD] (16.97)
E. Mathis (sop), R. Hermann (bar), A. Beaumont (cnd), North German SO, North German Radio Chorus † Maiblumen bluhten uberall; Sym 1; Waldgespräch CAPO ▲ 10740 [DDD] (10.97)
D. Voigt (sop), D. Kuebler (ten), D. R. Albert (bar), J. Conlon (cnd), Cologne Gürzenich PO, Dusseldorf Municipal Choral Society *(rec Cologne, Germany, 1996-7)* † Cymbeline, Op. 14; Tanzpoem *(E,G texts)* EMIC ▲ 56474 [DDD] (16.97)

Das gläserne Herz [The Glass Heart] (ballet suite) for Orchestra (1903)
G. Albrecht (cnd), Hamburg PO † König Kandaules (sels); Symphonische Gesänge, Op. 20 CAPO ▲ 10448 [DDD] (11.97)
L. Rajter (cnd), Czech-Slovak RSO Bratislava † Sym 1 MARC ▲ 8223166 (13.97)

Humoresque (exercises) for Wind Quintet
Aulos Wind Quintet † G. Holst:Qnt Ww; Jolivet:Sérénade Ob; C. Nielsen:Qnt Ww; P. Pierné:Suite pittoresque KSCH ▲ 310100 [DDD] (16.97)
Berlin Philharmonic Wind Quintet *(rec Nov 1992)* † J. B. Foerster:Qnt Ww; Pilss:Serenade Ww; C. Reinecke:Sxt Ww BIS ▲ 612 [DDD] (17.97)
H. Heinzmann (fl), M. Lammers (ob), W. Hermann (cl), B. Groth (bn), B. Künkele (hn)—Rondo *(rec Hamburg, Germany, Oct 5, 1996)* † Hunting Piece; Movts Str Qt; Qt Cl; Songs THOR ▲ 2376 [DDD] (16.97)

Hunting Piece for 2 Horns & Piano (1939)
B. Künkele (hn), T. Schwesig (hn), J. Lamke (pno) *(rec Hamburg, Germany, Oct 5, 1996)* † Humoresque; Movts Str Qt; Qt Cl; Songs THOR ▲ 2376 [DDD] (16.97)

Irmelin Rose und andere Gesänge (4) for Voice & Piano, Op. 7 (ca 1899)
R. Ziesak (sop), I. Vermillion (mez), C. Elsner (ten), C. Garben (pno) CPO ▲ 999455 (14.97)

Kleider machen Leute (musical comedy in 2 acts) [lib Feld after Keller] (ca 1908)
E. Mathis (sop), H. Winkler (ten), V. Vogel (ten), C. Otelli (bar), R. Scholze (bass), H. Franzen (bass), W. Slabbert (sgr), R. Weikert (cnd), Zurich Opera Orch, Zurich Opera House Chorus [GER] *(rec live Zurich Opera House, June 29, 1990)* KSCH 2-▲ 314069 [DDD] (31.97)

Der König Kandaules [King Kandaules] (opera in 3 acts) [lib Zemlinsky after Gide; translated F. Blei] (unfinished; score reconstructed by Antony Beaumont) (ca 1935)
G. Albrecht (cnd), Hamburg State PO, N. Warren (sop—Nyssia), P. Galliard (ten—Syphax), J. O'Neal (ten—König Kandaules), M. Pederson (bar—Gyges), K. Häger (bass—Phedros), S. Yang (bass—Philebos), K. Gysen (sgr—Pharnaces), G. Jentjens (sgr—Archelaos), M. Kwiecien (sgr—Nicomedes), F. Seiler (sgr—Sebas) *(rec Hamburg, Germany, Oct 1996)* CAPO 2-▲ 60071 [DDD] (16.97)

Der König Kandaules [King Kandaules] (selections)
F. Grundheber (bar), G. Albrecht (cnd), Hamburg PO † Gläserne Herz; Symphonische Gesänge, Op. 20 CAPO ▲ 10448 [DDD] (11.97)
M. Pederson (bar—Gyges), G. Albrecht (cnd), Hamburg State PO ("German Opera of the 20th Century") † Es War Einmal (sels); Kreidekreis (sels); Traumgörge (sels); M. Gurlitt:Wozzeck (sels); F. Schmidt:Notre Dame (sels); Schreker:Ferne Klang (sels); Schatzgräber (sels) CAPO ▲ 10724 [DDD] (10.97)

Der Kreidekreis (selections)
R. Behle (sop—Haitang), S. Soltesz (cnd), Berlin RSO ("German Opera of the 20th Century") † Es War Einmal (sels); König Kandaules (sels); Traumgörge (sels); M. Gurlitt:Wozzeck (sels); F. Schmidt:Notre Dame (sels); Schreker:Ferne Klang (sels); Schatzgräber (sels) CAPO ▲ 10724 [DDD] (10.97)

Lyric Symphony for Soprano, Baritone & Orchestra [text Tagore], Op. 18 (1923)
A. Marc (sop), H. Hagegard (bar), R. Chailly (cnd), (Royal) Concertgebouw Orch † Symphonische Gesänge, Op. 20 PLON (Entartete Musik) ▲ 43569 [DDD] (16.97)
E. Söderström (sop), D. Duesing (bar), B. Klee (cnd), Berlin RSO [GER] † Songs to Poems by Maeterlinck, Op. 13 KSCH ▲ 311053 [ADD] (17.97)
D. Voigt (sop), B. Terfel (bar), G. Sinopoli (cnd), Vienna PO DGRM ▲ 449179 [DDD]

Maiblumen blühten überall for Soprano & Strings (ca 1903)
E. Mathis (sop), A. Beaumont (cnd), North German SO † Frühlingsbergräbnis; Sym 1; Waldgespräch CAPO ▲ 10740 [DDD] (10.97)

Movements (2) for String Quartet (1929)
Pražák String Quartet † Qt 1 Strs, Op. 4; Qt 4 Strs, Op. 25 PRAG ▲ 250107 (18.97)
K. Schaitzbach (vn), M. Shimizu (vn), J. Zeijl (va), M. Katzenmeier (vc) *(rec Hamburg, Germany, Oct 5, 1996)* † Humoresque; Hunting Piece; Qt Cl; Songs THOR ▲ 2376 [DDD] (16.97)

Psalm 13 for Orchestra & Chorus, Op. 24 (1935)
R. Chailly (cnd), Berlin RSO, Ernst Senff Chamber Choir † Psalm 23, Op. 14; Seejungfrau PLON (Entartete Musik) ▲ 444969 (16.97)
J. Conlon (cnd), Cologne Gürzenich PO, R. Wipperman (cnd), Düsseldorf Municipal Choral Society *(rec Köln, Germany, Apr 1998)* † Choral Music; Frühlingsbergräbnis; Psalm 23, Op. 14 *([ENG,FRE,GER] text)* EMIC ▲ 56783 [DDD] (16.97)

Psalm 23 for Orchestra & Chorus, Op. 14 (ca 1910)
R. Chailly (cnd), Berlin RSO, Ernst Senff Chamber Choir † Psalm 13, Op. 24; Seejungfrau PLON (Entartete Musik) ▲ 444969 (16.97)
J. Conlon (cnd), Cologne Gürzenich PO, R. Wipperman (cnd), Düsseldorf Municipal Choral Society *(rec Köln, Germany, Apr 1998)* † Choral Music; Frühlingsbergräbnis; Psalm 13, Op. 24 *([ENG,FRE,GER] text)* EMIC ▲ 56783 [DDD] (16.97)

Psalm 83 for Orchestra & Chorus (1900)
R. Chailly (cnd), Vienna PO, R. Chailly (cnd), Slovak Phil Chorus, T. Trotter (org) † Janáček:Glagolitic Mass; Korngold:Passover Psalm PLON ▲ 460213 (16.97)

Quartet for Clarinet & Strings (1938-39)
K. Schaitzbach (vn), J. Zeijl (va), M. Katzenmeier (vc), W. Hermann (cl) *(rec Hamburg, Germany, Oct 5, 1996)* † Humoresque; Hunting Piece; Movts Str Qt; Songs THOR ▲ 2376 [DDD] (16.97)

Quartet No. 1 in A for Strings, Op. 4 (ca 1895)
Artis String Quartet *(rec Dec 1997)* † Qt 2 Strs, Op. 15 NIMB ▲ 5563 [DDD] (16.97)
Pražák String Quartet † Movts Str Qt; Qt 4 Strs, Op. 25 PRAG ▲ 250107 (18.97)
Vienna String Quartet † A. Berg:Qt Strs, Op. 3; Webern:Movts (5) Str Qt, Op. 5 CAMA ▲ 99 (18.97)

Quartet No. 2 for Strings, Op. 15 (1914)
Artis String Quartet *(rec Dec 1997)* † Qt 1 Strs, Op. 4 NIMB ▲ 5563 [DDD] (16.97)
Artis String Quartet † Schoenberg:Qt Strs in D ORF ▲ 194901 [DDD] (18.97)
Schoenberg String Quartet † Qt 3 Strs, Op. 19 KSCH ▲ 310118 [DDD] (16.97)

Quartet No. 3 for Strings, Op. 19 (ca 1923)
Artis String Quartet † Qt 4 Strs, Op. 25; Müller-Hermann:Qt Strs, Op. 6 NIMB ▲ 5604 (16.97)
Schoenberg String Quartet † Qt 2 Strs, Op. 15 KSCH ▲ 310118 [DDD] (16.97)

Quartet No. 4 for Strings, Op. 25 (1936)
Artis String Quartet † Qt 3 Strs, Op. 19; Müller-Hermann:Qt Strs, Op. 6 NIMB ▲ 5604 (16.97)
Lark String Quartet *(rec SUNY Purchase, NY, June 1995)* † Schoenberg:Qt 1 Strs, Op. 7 ARA ▲ 6671 (16.97)
Pražák String Quartet † Movts Str Qt; Qt 1 Strs, Op. 4 PRAG ▲ 250107 (18.97)

Sarema (opera in 3 acts) [lib Adolph von Zemlinszky after R. von Gottschall] (ca 1895)
A. Scheel (bar), Y. Zinovenko (bass), K. Clarke (sgr), N. Herbosch (sgr), N. Kleinhenn (sgr), L. Lukas (sgr), F. Simson (sgr), I. Dénes (cnd), Trier Theater Orch, Trier Theater Chorus KOCC 2-▲ 6467 (31.97)

Sarema:Overture
T. Dausgaard (cnd), Danish National RSO † Seejungfrau; Sinf CHN ▲ 9601 (16.97)

Die Seejungfrau (fantasy) for Orchestra [after Andersen] (ca 1903)
R. Chailly (cnd), Berlin RSO † Psalm 13, Op. 24; Psalm 23, Op. 14 PLON (Entartete Musik) ▲ 444969 (16.97)
J. Conlon (cnd), Cologne Gürzenich PO † Sinf EMIC ▲ 55515 (16.97)
T. Dausgaard (cnd), Danish National RSO † Sarema (ov); Sinf CHN ▲ 9601 (16.97)

Sinfonietta for Orchestra, Op. 23 (1934)
J. Conlon (cnd), Cologne Gürzenich PO † Seejungfrau EMIC ▲ 55515 (16.97)
T. Dausgaard (cnd), Danish National RSO † Sarema (ov); Seejungfrau CHN ▲ 9601 (16.97)

ZEMLINSKY, ALEXANDER VON (cont.)

Songs

D. Hesse (sop), A. Beaumont (pno)—Lieder (6), Op. 22; Ahnung Beatricens; Lieder (4); My Ship & I; Love, I must say goodbye; Circe (sels) [Lied der Circe]; Zwölf Lieder, Op. 27 [No. 1, Entführung [text George; No. 9, Afrikanischer Tanz [text Hughes; No. 7, Elend [text Hughes]]]]; Sechs Lieder, Op. 22 [No. 2, Abendkelch voll Sonnenlicht [text Morgenstern]] *(rec Hamburg, Germany, Oct 5, 1996)* † Humoresque; Hunting Piece; Movts Str Qt; Qt Cl THOR ▲ 2376 [DDD] (16.97)

Songs (6) to Poems by Maurice Maeterlinck for Mezzo-Soprano (or Baritone) & Piano, Op. 13 (1910-13; orchd)

G. Linos (sop), B. Klee (cnd), Berlin RSO [GER] † Lyric Sym, Op. 18 KSCH ▲ 311053 [ADD] (17.97)

A. S. von Otter (mez), J. E. Gardiner (cnd), North German SO *(rec Hamburg, Germany, 1993)* ("Mahler & Zemlinsky Lieder") † G. Mahler:Lieder eines fahrenden Gesellen; Songs from Rückert PPHI ▲ 439928 [DDD] (16.97)

B. Svendén (mez), J. Carewe (cnd), Nice PO [GER] † G. Mahler:Kindertotenlieder FORL ▲ 16642 [DDD] (16.97)

Symphonische Gesänge [Symphonic Songs] for Voice & Orchestra, Op. 20 (1929)

F. Grundheber (bar), G. Albrecht (cnd), Hamburg PO † Gläserne Herz; König Kandaules (sels) CAPO ▲ 10448 [DDD] (11.97)

W. White (bass), R. Chailly (cnd), (Royal) Concertgebouw Orch † Lyric Sym, Op. 18 PLON (Entartete Musik) ▲ 43569 [DDD] (16.97)

Symphony No. 1 in d (1892)

A. Beaumont (cnd), North German SO † Frühlingsbergräbnis; Maiblumen blühten überall; Waldgespräch CAPO ▲ 10740 [DDD] (10.97)

J. Conlon (cnd), Cologne Gürzenich PO *(rec Jan 1996)* ("Symphonien 1 & 2") † Sym 2 EMIC ▲ 56473 [DDD] (16.97)

L. Rajter (cnd), Czech-Slovak RSO Bratislava † Gläserne Herz MARC ▲ 8223166 (13.97)

Symphony No. 2 in B (1897)

J. Conlon (cnd), Cologne Gürzenich PO *(rec Jan 1996)* ("Symphonien 1 & 2") † Sym 1 EMIC ▲ 56473 [DDD] (16.97)

E. Seipenbusch (cnd), Slovak PO *(rec Nov 1985)* MARC ▲ 8220391 [DDD] (13.97)

Ein Tanzpoem [A Dance-Poem] (in 1 act) for Orchestra [after Hofmannsthal] (1901-12)

J. Conlon (cnd), Cologne Gürzenich PO *(rec Cologne, Germany, 1996-7)* † Cymbeline, Op. 14; Frühlingsbergräbnis *(E,G texts)* EMIC ▲ 56474 [DDD] (16.97)

Der Traumgörge (opera) [lib L. Feld] (1904-06)

P. Coburn (sop), J. Martin (sop), G. M. Ronge (sop), B. Calm (mez), J. Protschka (ten), H. Kruse (ten), P. Haage (ten), H. Welker (bar), V. von Halem (bass), M. Blasius (bass), G. Albrecht (cnd), Frankfurt RSO [GER] CAPO 2-▲ 10241 [DDD] (17.97)

Der Traumgörge (selections)

P. Coburn (sop—Grete), J. Protschka (ten—Görge), G. Albrecht (cnd), Frankfurt RSO, Hessian Radio Youth & Figural Choir ("German Opera of the 20th Century") † Es War Einmal (sels); Kreidekreis (sels); König Kandaules (sels); M. Gurlitt:Wozzeck (sels); F. Schmidt:Notre Dame (sels); Schreker:Ferne Klang (sels); Schatzgräber (sels) CAPO ▲ 10724 [DDD] (10.97)

Trio in d for Clarinet (or Viola), Cello & Piano, Op. 3 (1895)

Amici Chamber Ensemble † Beethoven:Trio 7 Pno, Op. 11; Chan Ka Nin:Among Friends SUMM ▲ 151 [DDD] (16.97)

Danish Trio † J. Brahms:Trio Cl PLAL ▲ 52

Ensemble Kontraste † J. Brahms:Trio Cl; Rabl:Qt Cl THOR ▲ 2368 [DDD] (16.97)

D. Geringas (vc), E. Brunner (cl), G. Oppitz (pno) † Schoenberg:Chamber Sym 1, Op. 9 TUD ▲ 717 [DDD] (16.97)

T. Gilissen (va), R. Dieltiens (vc), W. Boeykens (cl), R. Groslot (pno) *(rec 1991)* † Bruch:Pieces Cl, Op. 83 HMA ▲ 1901371 (9.97)

Waldgespräch for Soprano, 2 Horns, Harp & Strings (1895)

E. Mathis (sop), A. Beaumont (cnd), North German SO † Frühlingsbergräbnis; Maiblumen blühten überall; Sym 1 CAPO ▲ 10740 [DDD] (10.97)

Der Zwerg [or Der Geburtstad der Infantin] (opera) [lib G. C. Klaren after Oscar Wilde, *The Birthday of the Infanta*], Op. 17 (1920-21)

I. Nielsen (sop), B. Haldas (sop), K. Riegel (ten), D. Weller (bass), G. Albrecht (cnd), Berlin RSO, Berlin RIAS Women's Chamber Choir [GER] KSCH ▲ 314013 [DDD]

ZEMZARIS, IMANTS (1951-

Organ Music

H. Ericsson (org)—Pastorales for Summer Flute *(rec Sweden, Mar 1992)* ("Baltic Organ Music") † Čiurlionis:Chorale Fugue on 'Aus tiefer Not schrei ich zu...'; Pno Music; Kutavičius:Org Music; Pärt:Annum per annum Org; Süda:Kbd Music; Vasks:Org Music BIS ▲ 561 [DDD] (17.97)

ZENDER, HANS (1936-

Cantata for Alto, Alto Flute, Cello & Harpsichord [text Meister Eckehart] (1980)

H. Aurbacher (alt), Saarbrücken Integration Ensemble members *(rec March 20 1981,))* ("Hans Zender Edition, Vol. 13") † Haiku; Zeitstrome; Scelsi:Pezzi Orch; Pranam CPO ▲ 999485 [ADD] (6.97)

Canto VIII for Voices, Choir, Electronics & Orchestra, "Shir Hashirim-Lied der Lieder"

J. Moffat (sop), M. Hill (ten), R. Staege (fl), U. Dierksen (trbn), U. Löffler (kbd), C. Schulte (elec), H. Zender (cnd), Saarbrücken RSO ("Hans Zender Edition, Vol. 14") CPO ▲ 999486 (6.97)

Haiku (5) for Flute & Strings (1982)

R. Staege (fl), H. Zender (cnd), Saarbrücken RSO *(rec May 20 1983,))* ("Hans Zender Edition, Vol. 13") † Cant; Zeitstrome; Scelsi:Pezzi Orch; Pranam CPO ▲ 999485 [ADD] (6.97)

Zeitstrome for Orchestra (1974)

H. Zender (cnd), Saarbrücken RSO *(rec Nov 22 1974,))* ("Hans Zender Edition, Vol. 13") † Cant; Haiku; Scelsi:Pezzi Orch; Pranam CPO ▲ 999485 [ADD] (6.97)

ZHIVOTOV, ALEXEY (1904-1964)

Fragmenti for Flute, Clarinet, Bassoon, Trumpet & Piano Quintet (1928)

A. Lazarev (cnd) ("Russian Music from the 1920's") † Deshevov:Rails; Knipper:Con Bn; Polovinkin:Suite for 2 Pnos; G. Popov:Chamber Sym, Op. 2; Roslavets:Nocturne MELD (Musica non grata) ▲ 49955 (6.97)

ZHU, JIANER (20th cent)

Festival Overture for Orchestra (1958)

C. Peng (cnd), Shanghai PO *(rec Shanghai, China, Dec 1993)* † Sym 1 MARC (Chinese Composers) ▲ 8223940 [DDD] (13.97)

Sketches in the Mountains of Guizhou (symphonic suite) for Orchestra (1982)

C. Peng (cnd), Shanghai PO *(rec Shanghai, China, Jan 1994)* † Sym Fant; Sym 4 MARC (Chinese Composers) ▲ 8223941 [DDD] (13.97)

Symphonic Fantasia for Orchestra, "In Memory of Martyrs for Truth" (1980)

C. Peng (cnd), Shanghai PO *(rec Shanghai, China, Jan 1994)* † Sketches in the Mountains of Guizhou; Sym 4 MARC (Chinese Composers) ▲ 8223941 [DDD] (13.97)

Symphony No. 1 (1986)

C. Peng (cnd), Shanghai PO *(rec Shanghai, China, Dec 1993)* † Festival Ov MARC (Chinese Composers) ▲ 8223940 [DDD] (13.97)

Symphony No. 4, "6.4.2-1" (1990)

Y. Xunfa (bamboo fl), C. Peng (cnd), Shanghai PO *(rec Shanghai, China, Jan 1994)* † Sketches in the Mountains of Guizhou; Sym Fant MARC (Chinese Composers) ▲ 8223941 [DDD] (13.97)

ZHUKOV, SERGEY (1951-

Concerto Grosso for Violin, Cello, Piano & Orchestra

E. Bekova (vn), A. Bekova (vc), E. Bekova (pno), G. Pehlivanian (cnd), Residentie Orch The Hague † Con Mystery CHN ▲ 9588 (16.97)

Concerto Mystery for Violin, Cello, Piano & Orchestra

E. Bekova (vn), A. Bekova (vc), E. Bekova (pno), G. Pehlivanian (cnd), Residentie Orch The Hague † Con Grosso CHN ▲ 9588 (16.97)

ZI, HANG (dates unknown)

Three Wishes for a Rose for Orchestra

T. Nishizaki (vn), H. Shek (cnd), Gunma SO [arr Akira Nishimura] ("Orchestra Plays Adagio") † A. Bruckner:Qt Strs; Sym 2; G. Mahler:Sym 5; P. Tchaikovsky:Serenade Strs, Op. 48; Yoshimatsu:Threnody to Toki, Op. 12 CAMA (After Hours Classics) ▲ 423 [DDD] (15.97)

ZIEHRER, CARL MICHAEL (1843-1922)

Echt Wienerisch for Orchestra

Strauss-Lanner Ensemble, Schrammel Ensemble, Montréal Trio Kaffeehaus ("Viennese Telegram") † Hoch und Nieder; Lanner:Hans-Jörgel Polka, Op. 194; J. Schrammel:Antoineten Polka; Weana Gmüath Waltz; E. Strauss:Unter der Enns; Joh. Strauss:Jugendfeuer, Op. 90; Wiener Carneval-Walzer, Op. 3; Strauss (II):Lob der Frauen, Op. 315; Telegramme, Op. 318 SNE ▲ 644 (16.97)

ZIEHRER, CARL MICHAEL (cont.)

Fesche Geister (overture) for Orchestra

K. Jeitler (cnd), Vienna Young Brass-Philharmonic [arr Gustav Gaigg] *(rec Vienna, Austria, Dec 1989)* ("Radetzky-Marsch: Favorite Showpieces for Brass") † Fučík:Florentine March, Op. 214; Mühlberger:Mir sein die Kaiserjäger; E. Strauss:Bahn frei, Op. 45; Joh. Strauss:Radetzky March, Op. 228; Strauss (II):Polkas; Waltzes; Jos. Strauss:Mein Lebenslauf ist Lieb und Lust, Op. 263; Moulinet, Op. 57 CAMA ▲ 140 [DDD] (18.97)

Hoch und Nieder (march) for Orchestra

Strauss-Lanner Ensemble, Schrammel Ensemble, Montréal Trio Kaffeehaus ("Viennese Telegram") † Echt Wienerisch; Lanner:Hans-Jörgel Polka, Op. 194; J. Schrammel:Antoineten Polka; Weana Gmüath Waltz; E. Strauss:Unter der Enns; Joh. Strauss:Jugendfeuer, Op. 90; Wiener Carneval-Walzer, Op. 3; Strauss (II):Lob der Frauen, Op. 315; Telegramme, Op. 318 SNE ▲ 644 (16.97)

Loslassen!!!! (polka) for Orchestra, Op. 386 (1887)

Montréal Trio Kaffeehaus, Laferrière-Doane Family Vocal Quintet ("Ragtime in Vienna") † Rendez-vous!; Weaner Mad'ln Waltz, Op. 388; S. Joplin:Music of Joplin (various instrumental & ensemble performances); Strauss (II):Annen-Polka, Op. 117; Morgenblätter, Op. 279; Pizzicato-Polka SNE ▲ 632 (16.97)

Rendez-vous! for Orchestra

Montréal Trio Kaffeehaus, Laferrière-Doane Family Vocal Quintet ("Ragtime in Vienna") † Loslassen!!!!, Op. 386; Weaner Mad'ln Waltz, Op. 388; S. Joplin:Music of Joplin (various instrumental & ensemble performances); Strauss (II):Annen-Polka, Op. 117; Morgenblätter, Op. 279; Pizzicato-Polka SNE ▲ 632 (16.97)

Waltzes & Other Dances

P. Guth (cnd), Strauss Festival Orch Vienna—Fremdenführer (sels) [Liebe, schöne alte Donaustadt (Waltz Song)]; Loslassen!!!!, Op. 386 *(rec Ludwigshafen am Rhein, Germany, Oct 1997)* ("Wine, Women & Song") † I. Kálmán:Gräfin Mariza (sels); F. Lehár:Eva (sels); Giuditta (sels); Waltzes; R. Stolz:Favorit (sels); Venus in Seide (sels); Strauss (II):Fledermaus (sels); Nacht in Venedig (ov); Nacht in Venedig (sels); Prinz Methusalem (sels); Waltzes; Jos. Strauss:Ohne Sorgen, Op. 271 DI ▲ 920532 [DDD] (5.97)

A. Walter (cnd), Razumovsky Sinfonia—Wiener Bürger, Op. 419; Loslassen!, Op. 386; Liebesrezepte, Op. 434; Die Tänzerin, Op. 490; Landstreicher-Quadrille, Op. 496; Clubgeister, Op. 452; Bürgerlich und romantisch, Op. 94; Auersperg-Marsch, Op. 111; Diesen Kuss der ganzen Welt!, Op. 442; Pfiffig, Op. 384; Österreich in Tönen, Op. 373 *(rec Slovak Radio Concert Hall Bratislava, Slovak Republic, Feb 1995)* ("Selected Dances & Marches, Vol. 1") MARC ▲ 8223814 [DDD] (13.97)

Weaner Mad'ln Waltz for Orchestra, Op. 388

Montréal Trio Kaffeehaus, Laferrière-Doane Family Vocal Quintet ("Ragtime in Vienna") † Loslassen!!!!, Op. 386; Rendez-vous!; S. Joplin:Music of Joplin (various instrumental & ensemble performances); Strauss (II):Annen-Polka, Op. 117; Morgenblätter, Op. 279; Pizzicato-Polka SNE ▲ 632 (16.97)

Wiener Bürger for Orchestra, Op. 419

L. Maazel (cnd), Vienna PO *(rec live Vienna, Austria, Jan 1, 1996)* ("New Year's Concert 1996") † E. Strauss:Mit Vergnügen, Op. 228; Joh. Strauss:Radetzky March, Op. 228; Strauss (II):Music of Joh. Strauss, Jr.; Polkas; Waltzes; Jos. Strauss:Jokey-Polka, Op. 278; Nasswalderin, Op. 267; Tanzende Muse, Op. 266 RCAV (Red Seal) 2-▲ 68421 (16.97)

ZIERITZ, GRETE VON (1899-

Triptychon (gypsy-romance) for Violin

M. Boettcher (vn) † Alotin:Sonatina Vn; Beau:Son Vn; L. Boulanger:D'un matin de printemps Fl; M. Danzi:Son 1 Vn, Op. 1; Dinescu:Echos I; Mendelssohn (-Hensel):Adagio BAYE ▲ 100169 [DDD] (17.97)

Le violon de la mort (danses macabres) for Violin & Piano (& Orchestra) (1951-2)

V. Hoffman (vn), J. Huntly (pno) ("Le violon de la mort") † Ysaÿe:Poème élégiaque Vn & Pno; Sons Vn, Op. 27 CRSR ▲ 9665 [DDD]

ZIFFRIN, MARILYN (1926-

Songs (3) of the Trobairitz for Voice & Piano

N. Pilgrim (sop), M. Lifchitz (pno) ("Music at the Crossroads") † A. Brings:Bagatelles; Diemer:Sxt Fl; Rudajev:Petite Suite Parisienne; Toensing:Angels NSR ▲ 1005 (15.97)

Symphony for Voice & Orchestra, "Letters" (1989)

N. Pilgrim (sop), R. Black (cnd), Slovak RSO Bratislava *(rec Slovak National Republic, Slovak Republic, 1993)* ("MMC New Century, Vol. 1") † D. Colson:Searching Schubert; D. Ernst:Crossover; Kidde:Quest; Muncy:Paean; Skupinsky:Wild 'n' Sexy MASM ▲ 2015 [DDD] (16.97)

ZIMBALIST, EFREM (1889-1985)

Slavonic Dances (3) for Violin & Piano

Z. Schiff (vn), C. Eisenberg (pno)—Hebrew Song & Dance † J. Achron:Hebrew Melody, Op. 33; Castelnuovo-Tedesco:Sea Murmurs, Op. 24a; Haym:Sephardic Melody; Hush:Shir Eres; Son Vn; Krein:Caprice Hebraique; M. Lavry:Jewish Dances 4TAY ▲ 4002 (18.97)

ZIMMER, HANS (20th cent)

Crimson Tide (film music) for Orchestra

artists unknown HOL ▲ 62025 (16.97) ▮ 62025 (10.98)

The Power of One (film music) for Orchestra

artists unknown ELE ▲ 61335 (17.97) ▮ 61335 (11.98)

ZIMMERMANN, BERND ALOIS (1918-1970)

Antiphonen for Viola & Small Orchestra (1961-62)

E. Schloifer (va), H. Zender (cnd), Saarbrücken RSO ("Hans Zender Edition, Vol. 10") † Con Vc en forme de pas de trois; Impromptu Orch; Photoptosis CPO ▲ 999482 (6.97)

Concerto en forme de pas de trois for Cello & Orchestra (1965-66)

S. Palm (vc), H. Zender (cnd), Saarbrücken RSO ("Hans Zender Edition, Vol. 10") † Antiphonen; Impromptu Orch; Photoptosis CPO ▲ 999482 (6.97)

Concerto for Oboe & Orchestra (1952)

D. Doherty (ob), O. Henzold (cnd), Lucerne SO ("Oboe Concertos") † J. Haydn:Con Ob; Martinů:Con Ob; W. A. Mozart:Con Ob PANC ▲ 510090 [DDD] (17.97)

T. Indermühle (ob), C. Schnitzler (cnd), Bretagne Orch † Martinů:Con Ob; R. Strauss:Con Ob, AV144; Vaughan Williams:Con Ob CAMA ▲ 346 (18.97)

Dialogue (concerto) for 2 Pianos & Orchestra (1960; rev 1965)

A. Grau (pno), G. Schumacher (pno), B. Kontarsky (cnd), Berlin German SO † Monologue Pnos; Perspektiven; Photoptosis COLG ▲ 20002 (18.97)

Enchiridion (short pieces) for solo Piano (1949-52)

B. Waumbach (pno) † Intercommunicazione Vc; Short Studies Vc; Son Vc CPO ▲ 999198 [DDD] (14.97)

Impromptu for Orchestra (1958)

H. Zender (cnd), Saarbrücken RSO ("Hans Zender Edition, Vol. 10") † Antiphonen; Con Vc en forme de pas de trois; Photoptosis CPO ▲ 999482 (6.97)

Intercommunicazione for Cello & Piano (1967)

M. Bach (vc), B. Waumbach (pno) † Enchiridion; Short Studies Vc; Son Vc CPO ▲ 999198 [DDD] (14.97)

Monologue for 2 Pianos (1964)

A. Grau (pno), G. Schumacher (pno) † Dialogue Pnos; Perspektiven; Photoptosis COLG ▲ 20002 (18.97)

Perspektiven, Music to an Imaginary Ballet for 2 Pianos (1955-56)

A. Grau (pno), G. Schumacher (pno) † Dialogue Pnos; Monologue Pnos; Photoptosis COLG ▲ 20002 (18.97)

Photoptosis (prelude) for Orchestra (1968)

B. Kontarsky (cnd), Berlin German SO † Dialogue Pnos; Monologue Pnos; Perspektiven COLG ▲ 20002 (18.97)

H. Zender (cnd), Saarbrücken RSO ("Hans Zender Edition, Vol. 10") † Antiphonen; Con Vc en forme de pas de trois; Impromptu Orch CPO ▲ 999482 (6.97)

Short Studies (4) for Cello (1970)

M. Bach (vc) † Enchiridion; Intercommunicazione Vc; Son Vc CPO ▲ 999198 [DDD] (14.97)

S. Nimsgern (b-bar), W. Quadflieg (nar), C. Bantzer (nar), G. Boselli (vc), W. Humburg (cnd), Münster SO † Son Va; Son Vc; Son Vn STRV ▲ 33340 (16.97)

Sonata for Cello (1959-60)

M. Bach (vc) † Enchiridion; Intercommunicazione Vc; Short Studies Vc CPO ▲ 999198 [DDD] (14.97)

G. Boselli (vc) † Short Studies Vc; Son Va; Son Vn STRV ▲ 33340 (16.97)

Sonata for Viola (1955)

W. Janssen (va) † Short Studies Vc; Son Vc; Son Vn STRV ▲ 33340 (16.97)

Sonata for Violin

B. Crosta (vn) † Short Studies Vc; Son Va; Son Vc STRV ▲ 33340 (16.97)

ZIMMERMANN, HEINZ WERNER (1930-

Psalmkonzert for Baritone, Trumpets, Vibraphone, Double Bass, Chorus & Boys' Chorus (1957)

B. McDaniel (bar), R. Weiler (db), R. Lsöch (tpt), W. Neumann (tpt), W. Scholz (tpt), L. Schumann (vib), K. M. Ziegler (cnd) , Karlsruhe Christ Church Chorus, Karlsruhe Helmholtz School Boys' Choir ("New Music in the Church") † J. Cage:Souvenir Org; A. Mellnäs:Omnia tempus habent; Schnebel:Lamento di guerra; Schoenberg:De profundis, Op. 50b; Friede auf Erden, Op. 13 CATA ▲ 58009 [ADD] (15.97)

ZIMMERMANN, UDO (1943-
Nouveaux divertissements d' après Jean-Philippe Rameau for Horn & Orchestra
P. Damm (hn) † R. Strauss:Con 1 Hn, Op. 11; Con 2 Hn, AV132 BER ▲ 9180 (10.97)
Die weisse Rose (selections)
G. Fontana (sop), L. Harder (ten), U. Zimmermann (cnd) [scenes for 2 solo voc & instrumental ensemble] ORF ▲ 162871 [DDD] (18.97)

ZIMMERMANN, WALTER (1949-
Festina lente for String Quartet (1990)
Arditti String Quartet ("From Germany") † Y. Höller:Antiphon; R. H. Platz:Qt Strs, "Zeitstrahl"; Spahlinger:Apo Do, "von hier" DISQ ▲ 782036 (18.97)
Fragmente der Liebe for Saxophone, Clarinet, Soprano & String Quartet (1987)
J. Ernst (sax), Hirsch (cnd) ("New Saxophone Chamber Music") † Kyburz:Cells; Mundry:Komposition Sax; Staude:Obduktion COLG ▲ 31890 (18.97)

ZINDARS, EARL (1927-
Trigon for Tuba
F. Cooley (tuba) ("The Romantic Tuba") † J. S. Bach:Sons Fl; J. Brahms:Ernste Gesänge, Op. 121; A. Russell:Suite Concertante CRYS ▲ 120 (15.97) ▮ 120 (9.98)

ZINGARELLI, NICCOLÒ ANTONIO (1752-1837)
Dante:Inferno for Voice & Piano
E. Palacio (ten), S. Pala (pno) *(rec S. Martino Church Tirano, June 30, 1995)* † Passione di Gesù Cristo AG ▲ 18 [DDD] (18.97)
La passione di Gesù Cristo (oratorio) for Vocal Soloists & Orchestra [after Metastasio] (1787)
E. Palacio (ten), S. Alaimo (bar), J. D. Florez (sgr), P. Pelucchi (cnd), Bergamo Collegium Musicum *(rec S. Martino Church Tirano, June 30, 1995)* † Dante:Inferno AG ▲ 18 [DDD] (18.97)

ZINZADSE, SULCHAN (1926-1991)
Phantasie for Violin & Strings (1989)
L. Issakadze (cnd), Georgian CO † Gabunija:Sinf Gioconda; Nasidze:Con Vn; Taktakishvili:Con 2 Vn ORF ▲ 304921 [DDD] (18.97)

ZIPOLI, DOMENICO (1688-1726)
Organ Music
M. Colin (org) *(rec Org of Agati-Cabourdin de la Collegiate-Pancrace d)* ("The Italian Organ") † Davide Da bergamo:Org Music; D. Scarlatti:Org Music EPRO ▲ 9505 (17.97)
Sonate d'intavolatura for Organ (or Harpsichord) (1716)
S. Vartolo (org) TACT ▲ 682602 (16.97)
Suite in b for Piano & Ensemble
L. Koutalari-Ioannou (pno), B. Papazian (cnd), Orchestral Ensemble † Cambini:Cons Hpd, Op.15/3; Galuppi:Sons Hpd (misc); G. B. Grazioli:Sonata in G; L. D. Rossi:Andantino in G GEGA ▲ 53 (16.97)

ZIPORYN, EVAN (1959-
Aneh Tapi Nyata for Voice, Gamelan Orchestra & 11 Western Instruments (1992)
K. Beddall (voc) ("American Works for Balinese Gamelan Orchestra") † Kekembangan; Tenzer:Banyuari; Situ Banda; W. Vitale:Khayalan Tiga NWW ▲ 80430 (16.97)
Kekembangan for Saxophone Quartet & Gamelan Orchestra [after N. Windha's Kembang] (1990)
E. Ziporyn (sax), C. Jonas (sax), R. McKean (sax), D. Plonsey (sax) ("American Works for Balinese Gamelan Orchestra") † Aneh Tapi Nyata; Tenzer:Banyuari; Situ Banda; W. Vitale:Khayalan Tiga NWW ▲ 80430 (16.97)
Luv Time for Percussion Ensemble
E. Ziporyn (b cl), D. Mott (bar sax), B. Elmer (trbn), J. Van Buskirk (pno) *(rec United States of America, 1989)* ("Bang on a Can Live, Vol 1") † A. Cameron:Two Bits; Doerrfeld:Evening Chant; M. Gordon:Strange Quiet; T. Johnson:Failing; S. Lindroth:Relations to Rigor; J. Wolfe:Vermeer Room CRI ▲ 628 [DDD] (16.97)
Tsmindao Ghmerto for Bass Clarinet
E. Ziporyn (b cl) *(rec The Hit Factory New York, Oct 4-8, 1995)* ("Cheating, Lying, Stealing") † Didkovsky:Amalia's Secret; Gosfield:Manufacture of Tangles Ivory; D. Lang:Cheating, Lying, Stealing; Pascoal:Arapua; Rzewski:Piece 4 Pno; Vierk:Red Shift SNYC ▲ 62254 [DDD] (16.97)

ZNOVIEV, B. (dates unknown)
Dieu est parmi nous
Zagorsk Monastery Monks' Choir *(rec Zagorsk Monastery, France, 1989)* † Anonymous:Chant du Monastère du Désert; Chants rituels Noël; Esprit-Saint tu es là; Heureux soit l'élu du Seigneur; Hymne dédié à Saint-Georges; O douce lumière; Péchés sont pardonés; Que Dieu bénisse mon âme; Sous protection anges; Arkhangelsky:Louons la Saint-Vierge; Bortnyansky:Comme les anges; Gloire à Dieu au plus haut des cieux; Ivov:Que ton coeur se réjouisse; Nathaneal (Monk):Justice est en toi musique AB ▲ 1402 [ADD] (16.97)

ZONN, PAUL MARTIN (1939-
Ultimate Nimbus for 3 Clarinets
L. Combs (cl), J. DeRoche (cl), J. B. Yeh (b cl) *(rec Chicago, Feb 16 & 18, 1996)* ("Chicago Clarinet Trio") † Bouffil:Trio 2 for 3 Cls, Op. 8/2; Mihalovici:Son Cls, Op. 35; A. Prinz:Con a Cinque; Sandroff:Joie HEL ▲ 1028 (10.97)

ZORN, JOHN (1953-
Angelus Novus for Wind Octet
Callithumpian Consort ("Angelus Novus") † Carny; Christabel; For Your Eyes Only TZA (Composer) ▲ 7028 [DDD] (16.97)
Aphorias: Requia for 6 Boy Sopranos, Piano & Orchestra
S. Drury (pno), D. R. Davies (cnd), American Composers Orch, Hungarian Children's Radio Choir TZA ▲ 7037 [DDD] (16.97)
Blues Noël for Chamber Ensemble
F. Frith (gtr), B. Frisell (gtr), J. Staley (trbn), C. Emmanuel (hp), A. Coleman (kbd), B. James (kbd), D. Weinstein (kbd), I. Mori (perc), J. Lurie (instr), C. Marclay (instr), D. Hofstra (instr), L. Shioi (instr), R. Foreman (instr), S. Wu (instr), R. Quine (instr), M. Blair (instr) † Godard; Spillane TZA ▲ 7324 (16.97)
The Book of Heads for Guitar
M. Ribot (gtr) † Dark River TZA ▲ 7009 [DDD] (16.97)
Carny for Piano
S. Drury (pno) ("Angelus Novus") † Angelus Novus; Christabel; For Your Eyes Only TZA (Composer) ▲ 7028 [DDD] (16.97)
Cat o' Nine Tails for String Quartet (1988)
M. Feldman (vn), E. Friedlander (vn), L. Martin (va), J. Hammann (vc) *(rec New York City, NY, Dec 1998)* † Dead Man; Kol Nidre; Memento Mori TZA ▲ 7047 [DDD] (16.97)
Christabel for Chamber Ensemble (1972)
Callithumpian Consort ("Angelus Novus") † Angelus Novus; Carny; For Your Eyes Only TZA (Composer) ▲ 7028 [DDD] (16.97)
Dark River for 4 Bass Drums
J. Pugliese (perc) † Book of Heads TZA ▲ 7009 [DDD] (16.97)
The Dead Man (13 Specimen) for String Quartet (1990)
M. Feldman (vn), E. Friedlander (vn), L. Martin (va), J. Hammann (vc) *(rec New York City, NY, Jan 1999)* † Cat o' Nine Tails; Kol Nidre; Memento Mori TZA ▲ 7047 [DDD] (16.97)
Duras for Ensemble
artists unknown ("Duras:Duchamp") † Étant Donnés TZA (Composer) ▲ 7023 [DDD] (16.97)
Elegy for Ensemble
M. Patton (sgr), D. Abel (vn), Scummy (gtr), B. Chaffe (fl), W. Winant (perc) † Kristallnacht TZA ▲ 7302 [ADD] (16.97)
Étant Donnés [69 paroxyms for Marcel Duchamp] for Ensemble
artists unknown ("Duras:Duchamp") † Duras TZA (Composer) ▲ 7023 [DDD] (16.97)
Film Music
J. Jaffe (va), E. Friedlander (vc), M. Ribot (gtr), C. Emanuel (hp), J. Zorn (kbd), A. Coleman (kbd), J. Pugliese (perc), J. Baron (perc), C. Baptista (perc)—Pueblo; Elegant Spanking; Credits Included; Maogai; A Lot of Fun for the Evil One ("Film Works IV: S & M + More") TZA ▲ 7310 (16.97)
For Your Eyes Only (chamber symphony)
Callithumpian Consort ("Angelus Novus") † Angelus Novus; Carny; Christabel TZA (Composer) ▲ 7028 [DDD] (16.97)
Godard for Chamber Ensemble
F. Frith (gtr), B. Frisell (gtr), J. Staley (trbn), C. Emmanuel (hp), A. Coleman (kbd), B. James (kbd), D. Weinstein (kbd), I. Mori (perc), J. Lurie (instr), C. Marclay (instr), D. Hofstra (instr), L. Shioi (instr), R. Foreman (instr), S. Wu (instr), R. Quine (instr), M. Blair (instr) † Blues Noël; Spillane TZA ▲ 7324 (16.97)
Kol Nidre for String Quartet (1992)
M. Feldman (vn), E. Friedlander (vn), L. Martin (va), J. Hammann (vc) *(rec New York City, NY, Apr 1999)* † Cat o' Nine Tails; Dead Man; Memento Mori TZA ▲ 7047 [DDD] (16.97)

ZORN, JOHN (cont.)
Kristallnacht for Instrumental Ensemble
M. Feldman (vn), M. Ribot (gtr), M. Dresser (elec bass), D. Krakauer (b cl/cl), F. London (tpt), A. Coleman (kbd), W. Winant (perc) † Elegy TZA ▲ 7302 [ADD] (16.97)
Memento Mori for String Quartet (1996)
M. Feldman (vn), E. Friedlander (vn), L. Martin (va), J. Hammann (vc) *(rec New York City, NY, May 1999)* † Cat o' Nine Tails; Dead Man; Kol Nidre TZA ▲ 7047 [DDD] (16.97)
Music of Naked City
Naked City—Val de Travers; Une Correspondance; La feé Verte; Fleurs du Mal; Artemisia Absinthium; Notre Dame de L'Oubli [for Olivier Messiaen]; VERLAINE; Rend fou ("Absinthe") AVAK ▲ 4 (21.97)
Music of Zorn
Bar Kokhba Sextet, Masada String Trio—Tahah; Sippur; Karet; Hadashah; Taharah; Mispar; Ratzah; Zebdi; Yatzar; Malkhut; Hodaah; Elilah; Meholalot; Kochot; Lachish; Shidim; Aravot; Moshav; Lilin; Hazor; Kisofim; Khebar; Laylah; Teli; Tevel; Eitan; Ner Tamid; Idalah-Abal; Gevurah ("The Circle Maker") TZA ▲ 7122 [DDD] (22.97)
Z. Jinglin (nar), J. H. Shin (nar), A. Tran (nar), F. Frith (gtr), B. Frisell (gtr), A. Coleman (kbd), W. Horvitz (kbd), J. Baron (dr), S. Bennett (dr)—Hu Die; Hwang Chin-Ee; Que Tran ("New Traditions in East Asian Bar Bands") TZA ▲ 7311 (16.97)
Masada—Gevurah; Nazikin; Mahshav; Rokhev; Abidan; Sheloshim; Hath-Arob; Paran; Mahlah; Socoh; Yechida; Bikkurim; Idalah-Abal; Tannaim; Nefesh; Mo'ed; Maskil; Mishpatim; Sansanah; Shear-Jashub; Mashav; Machin; Karaim ("Bar Kokhba") TZA 2-▲ 7108 [DDD] (22.97)
J. Zorn (a sax) ("Filmworks III: 1990-95") TZA (Tzadik Archival) ▲ 7309 [DDD] (16.97)
various artists—Lacrosse; Hockey; Pool; Archery; plus others ("The Parachute Years, 1977-1980") TZA (Archival) 7-▲ 7316 (96.97)
various artists—Fils des Etoiles; This Way out; Music for Children; Bikini Atoll; Bone Crusher; Dreamer of Dreams; Cycles du Nord; SooKi's Lullaby ("Music Romance Vol. 1: Music for Children") TZA ▲ 7321 (16.97)
Redbird for Harp, Violin, Cello & Percussion
J. Jaffe (va), E. Friedlander (vc), C. Emanuel (hp), J. Pugliese (perc) ("Redbird") TZA ▲ 7008 [DDD] (16.97)
Road Runner for Accordian (1986)
G. Klucevsek (acc) *(rec Church of the Holy Trinity, New York, NY, Mar 1993)* † Duckworth:Slow Dancing in Yugoslavia; F. Frith:Disinformation Polka; Klucevsek:Music of Klucevsek STKL ▲ 207 [DDD] (16.97)
Spillane for Chamber Ensemble
F. Frith (gtr), B. Frisell (gtr), J. Staley (trbn), C. Emmanuel (hp), A. Coleman (kbd), B. James (kbd), D. Weinstein (kbd), I. Mori (perc), J. Lurie (instr), C. Marclay (instr), D. Hofstra (instr), L. Shioi (instr), R. Foreman (instr), S. Wu (instr), R. Quine (instr), M. Blair (instr) † Blues Noël; Godard TZA ▲ 7324 (16.97)

ZORZI, JUAN CARLOS (1936-
Adagio elegíaco for Strings
(rec Troy, NY, Feb 1994) ("Impresiones") † L. Gianneo:Piezas criollas; Ginastera:Impresiones de la Puna; Guastavino:Cantilenas Argentinas y Final; Jeromita Linares DOR ▲ 90202 [DDD] (16.97)

ZUCKERT, LEON (1904-
Music of Zuckert
O. Harnoy (vc), R. Golani (vl), L. Zuckert (cnd), Toronto SO, L. Zuckert (cnd), CBC Orch ("Along Gypsy Trails: A Tribute to Leon Zuckert") DHR 2-▲ 71123 (23.97)

ZUIDAM, ROBERT (1964-
Fishbone for Wind Instruments & Piano [from 3 Mechanisms]
B. Lubman (cnd) † Emmerik:Architektur der Ebene; I. Klein:Iris; Roosendael:Tala; Rossem:Brisk CV ▲ 27 (19.97)

ZUMMO, PETER (20th cent)
Experimenting with Household Chemicals (piece in 6 parts) for Trombone & Electronics [w. optional Ensemble] (1987-91)
P. Zummo (voc), P. Zummo (trbn), A. Russell (kbd/vc), D. Masuzzo (db), J. Gibson (sax), J. Kubera (syn), B. Ruyle (mar), M. Ahmed (perc) XIRE ▲ 116

ZUMSTEEG, JOHANN RUDOLF (1760-1802)
Sonata for Cello & Continuo
J. Baumann (vc), K. Stoll (db), W. Döling (hpd) ("Amazing Duo, Vol. 2") † Boccherini:Adagio & Allegro, G.6; Fesch:Sons Vn & Vc, Op. 8a; Francoeur:Sons Vn & Bc; Pergolesi:Sinf Vc CAMA ▲ 2044 [DDD] (18.97)

ZWEERS, BERNARD (1854-1924)
Symphony No. 3, "To My Fatherland"
H. Vonk (cnd), The Hague PO † T. Verhey:Con Fl OLY ▲ 503 [AAD] (16.97)

ZWILICH, ELLEN TAAFFE (1939-
Celebration for Orchestra (1984)
J. Nelson (cnd), Indianapolis SO † Prologue & Vars Strs; Sym 1 NWW ▲ 336 [DDD] (16.97)
Chamber Symphony (1979)
R. Pittman (cnd), Boston Musica Viva *(rec 1980)* † Qt Strs; Son Vn in 3 Movts; Cory:Apertures; Designs; Profiles CRI ▲ 621 [ADD]
Clarino Quartet for 4 Trumpets (or Clarinets) (1977)
L. Ranger (tpt), D. Flello (tpt), C. Lane (tpt), D. Michaux (tpt) *(rec Univ of Victoria, May 1994)* ("The Trumpet Comes of Age: 1940-1980") † Coulthard:Fanfare Son; Kupferman:Infinities; F. Peeters:Son Tpt, Op. 51; H. Shapero:Son Tpt CRYS ▲ 669 (15.97)
Concerto for Bassoon & Orchestra (1993)
N. Goeres (bn), L. Maazel (cnd), Pittsburgh SO *(rec Pittsburgh, PN, May 1996)* † Balada:Lament; B. Lees:Con Hn NWW ▲ 80503 [DDD] (16.97)
Concerto for Flute & Orchestra (1989)
D. A. Dwyer (fl), J. Sedares (cnd), London SO † L. Bernstein:Halil; Piston:Concertino Pno KOCH ▲ 7142 [DDD] (17.97)
Concerto grosso 1985 for Orchestra [after Handel]
Z. Mehta (cnd), New York PO † Con Tpt; Double Qt Strs; Symbolon NWW ▲ 372 [DDD] (16.97)
J. Sedares (cnd), Louisville Orch ("World Premiere Recordings") † Con Ob; Sym 3 KOCH ▲ 7278 [DDD] (16.97)
Concerto for Oboe & Orchestra
J. Mack (ob), J. Sedares (cnd), Louisville Orch ("World Premiere Recordings") † Con grosso 1985; Sym 3 KOCH ▲ 7278 [DDD] (16.97)
Concerto for Trombone & Orchestra (1988)
C. Lindberg (trbn), J. DePreist (cnd), Malmö SO *(rec 1993)* ("American Trombone Concertos") † Creston:Fant Trbn, Op. 42; G. Schuller:Kleine Posaunenmusik; G. Walker:Con Trbn BIS ▲ 628 [DDD] (17.97)
Concerto for Trumpet & 5 Players (1984)
P. Smith (tpt), Z. Mehta (cnd) † Con grosso 1985; Double Qt Strs; Symbolon NWW ▲ 372 [DDD] (16.97)
Double Quartet for Strings (1984)
E. T. Zwilich (cnd) † Con grosso 1985; Con Tpt; Symbolon NWW ▲ 372 [DDD] (16.97)
Passages for Soprano & Chamber Ensemble (1981)
L. Boucher (sop), A. Carlson (vn), P. Singleton (va), J. Karpf (vc), J. Stone (fl/pic), T. Kerstetter (b cl/cl), F. J. Lozier (pno), J. Parks (perc), S. O'Kelley (perc) *(rec Roswell, GA, 1993)* ("The Voice & the Virtuoso") † L. Nielson:Black Magic; Schoenberg:Pierrot lunaire, Op. 21 ACAD ▲ 20027 (16.97)
Prologue & Variations for String Orchestra (1983)
J. Nelson (cnd), Indianapolis SO † Celebration; Sym 1 NWW ▲ 336 [DDD] (16.97)
S. Yoo (cnd), Metamorphosen CO *(rec Weston, MA, Apr 1994)* ("Metamorphosen Performs Chamber Orchestral Works") † E. Carter:Elegy Va; D. Coleman:Long Ago, This Radiant Day; Corigliano:Voyage Strs; I. Fine:Serious Song; Ruehr:Shimmer ALBA ▲ 194 [DDD] (16.97)
Quartet for Strings (1974)
New York String Quartet *(rec Nov 1986)* † Chamber Sym; Son Vn in 3 Movts; Cory:Apertures; Designs; Profiles CRI ▲ 621 [ADD]
Quintet for Clarinet & String Quartet (1990)
I. Kavafian (vn), A. Kavafian (vn), P. Neubauer (va), F. Sherry (vc), D. Shifrin (cl) *(rec 1994-96)* † Adolphe:At the Still Point, There the Dance Is; Corigliano:Soliloquy Cl; Sheng:Concertino Cl; Tower:Turning Points DLS 2-▲ 3183 [DDD] (14.97)
Sonata in 3 Movements for Violin & Piano (1973-74)
C. Tait (vn), B. Snyder (pno) ("American Women Composers") † Crawford (Seeger):Son Vn & Pno; Mamlok:Designs; From My Garden; Son Vn; Talma:Son Vn GAS ▲ 300 (16.97)
J. Zwilich (vn), J. Gemmell (pno) † Chamber Sym; Qt Strs; Cory:Apertures; Designs; Profiles CRI ▲ 621 [ADD]
Symbolon for Orchestra (1988)
Z. Mehta (cnd), New York PO † Con grosso 1985; Con Tpt; Double Qt Strs NWW ▲ 372 [DDD] (16.97)
Symphony No. 1 [in 3 movts] (1982)
J. Nelson (cnd), Indianapolis SO † Celebration; Prologue & Vars Strs NWW ▲ 336 [DDD] (16.97)

ZWILICH, ELLEN TAAFFE

ZWILICH, ELLEN TAAFFE (cont.)
Symphony No. 3
  J. Sedares (cnd), Louisville Orch ("World Premiere Recordings") † Con grosso 1985; Con Ob
                                              KOCH ▲ 7278 [DDD] (16.97)

Trio for Piano, Violin & Cello (1987)
  Kalichstein-Laredo-Robinson Trio ("Legacies") † L. Kirchner:Trio 2 Pno; Pärt:Adagio; S. Silverman:In Celebration
                                              ARA ▲ 6676 (16.97)

ZYMAN, SAMUEL (1956-
Concerto for Flute & Chamber Orchestra
  M. Canales (fl), B. J. Echenique (cnd), Mexico City CO ("Música Para Flauta de las Américas, Vol. 1") † Son Fl; L. Schifrin:Tangos Fl & Hp
                                           URT ▲ 1 [DDD] (16.97)

Encuentros for Orchestra
  B. J. Echenique (cnd), Orch of the Americas ("México Sinfonico") † Carrasco:Preludio Sinfónico; R. Castro:Minueto; J. M. Chávez:Huerfanita; Galindo:Poema de Neruda; Márquez:Danzón 4; Moncayo Garcia:Huapango; Sinfonieta
                                           URT ▲ 20 (16.97)

Soliloquy for Orchestra
  E. Diazmuñoz (cnd), Mexico City PO † Catán:En un doblez tiempo; Espinosa:Ifegenia Cruel (ov); Lavista:Fiction; A. L. Ponce:Elegy
                                           CLME ▲ 21232 (13.97)

Sonata for Flute & Piano
  M. Canales (fl), A. M. Tradatti (pno) ("Música Para Flauta de las Américas, Vol. 1") † Con Fl; L. Schifrin:Tangos Fl & Hp
                                           URT ▲ 1 [DDD] (16.97)

CONTENTS

COLLECTIONS

Accordion & Concertina	927
Ballet & Dance Music	927
Ballet & Dance Music Collections	927
Bands	927
Bands Collections	930
Baroque Music	930
Baroque Music Collections	932
Bassoon	933
Bassoon Collections	933
Brass & Wind Ensemble	933
Brass & Wind Ensemble Collections	936
Carillon/Church Bells/Handbells	936
Carillon/Church Bells/Handbells Collections	936
CD-Rom	936
CD-Rom Collections	937
Cello	937
Cello Collections	939
Chamber Music	939
Chamber Music Collections	942
Chant	942
Chant Collections	946
Choral	946
Choral Collections	956
Christmas	957
Christmas Collections	965
Clarinet	966
Clarinet Collections	967
Classical Music (Misc.)	967
Classical Music (Misc.) Collections	968
Conductors	976
Crossover	979
Double Bass	979
Dulcimer (& Other Hammered String Instruments)	979
Dulcimer (& Other Hammered String Instruments) Collections	980
Early Music	980
Early Music Collections	989
Electronic Music	990
Electronic Music Collections	990
Film Soundtracks	991
Film Soundtracks Collections	992
Flute & Piccolo	993
Flute & Piccolo Collections	995
Flute & Guitar Duos	995
Flute & Harp Duos	996
Flute & Organ Duos	996
Glass Armonica	996
Guitar	996
Guitar Collections	1001
Harp	1001
Harp Collections	1002
Harpsichord (& Other Early Keyboard Instruments)	1002
Harpsichord (& Other Early Keyboard Instruments) Collections	1003
Horn	1003
Instrumental (Misc.)	1004
Instrumental (Misc.) Collections	1005
Judaica	1005
Judaica Collections	1005
Lute	1005
Lute Collections	1006
Mandolin	1006
Mechanical Music & Music Boxes Collections	1006
Non-Western Classical Music	1006
Non-Western Classical Music Collections	1007
Oboe & English Horn	1007
Opera & Operetta	1007
Opera & Operetta Collections	1008
Orchestral	1009
Orchestral Collections	1016
Organ	1020
Organ Collections	1026
Organ, Brass & Percussion	1027

Percussion	1027
Percussion Collections	1028
Piano	1028
Piano Collections	1036
Recorder	1038
Recorder Collections	1038
Saxophone	1038
String Ensemble	1039
String Ensemble Collections	1040
Trombone	1040
Trumpet	1041
Trumpet Collections	1042
Trumpet & Organ	1043
Trumpet & Organ Collections	1043
Tuba	1043
Viennese Waltzes & Light Music	1043
Viennese Waltzes & Light Music Collections	1044
Viol	1044
Viola	1044
Viola Collections	1044
Violin	1045
Violin Collections	1049
Vocal	1049
Vocal Collections	1082
Vocal Ensemble	1092
Wedding Music	1092
Wedding Music Collections	1093

ACCORDION & CONCERTINA

Davine, Robert (acc)
The Concert Accordion Artistry of Robert Davine, w. Lamont Chamber Players—features works by Lang *(Prelude & Fugue in C)*, Effinger *(Nocturne)*, Creston *(Prelude & Dance, Op. 69)*, Zarlengo *(Suite for Acc, Vc & Pno)*, Volpi *(Preludio, Op. 31)*, Lockwood *(Son-Fant)*, Gart *(Vivo)*, Pino *(Concertino)*, Diamond *(Night Music)*, Seiber *(Intro & Allegro)* CRYS ▲ 160 (15.97)

Hohner Accordian SO [cnd:Rudolph Würthner]
Accordiorama—features works by Liszt *(Hungarian Rhap 2)*, Rossini *(Guillaume Tell Ov)*, Weber *(Invitation to the Dance, Op. 65)*, Ponchielli *(Dance of the Hours [from La Gioconda])*, Dinicu *(Hora Staccato [w. Günther Wertz (chromonica)])*, Brahms *(Hungarian Dances 5 & 6)*, Joh. Strauss II *(Perpetuum Mobile, Op. 25)*, Würthner *(Concert Etude on a Theme of Paganini, "La Campanella" [w. Karl Perenthaler (acc)])* *(rec Baumgarten Hall, Vienna, 1961)* VC ▲ 81 [AAD] (13.97)
Accordiorama, Vol. 2, w. Hohner Accordion SO [cnd:R. Würthner]—features K. Alford *(Colonel Bogey)*, Confrey *(Dizzy Fingers)*, P. Frosini *(Bel Viso)*, Fučík *(Entry of the Gladiators)*, Gounod *(Faust (sels))*, R. Herzer *(Hoch Heidecksburg March)*, Hubay *(Hejre Kati, Op. 32/4)*, F. Loewe *(My Fair Lady (sels))*, H. C. Lumbye *(Champagne Galop, Op. 14)*, T. Mackeben *(Münch'ner G'schichten)*, T. Reilly *(Bavarian Woodpecker)*, Schittenhelm *(Der Ziegenbock; Lustige Polka)*, Schlunk *(Schwarzwälder Polka)*, Strauss (II) *(Annen-Polka, Op. 117)*, E. Waldteufel *(Skaters' Waltz)*, Würthner *(Ländler in Thirds)* VC ▲ 109 [AAD] (13.97)

Hussong, Stefan (acc)
Tango Fantasy—features works by Piazzolla *(Libertango; S'il vous plaît)*, Stravinsky *(Tango [from The Soldier's Tale]; Tango 1940)*, Wolpe *(Tango)*, Albeniz *(Tango [from España])*, Soler *(Sons 45, 47 & 62)*, Tiensuu *(Fantango)*, Rojko *(Alien-Tango)*, Cage *(Perpetual Tango)*, Satie *(Le tango perpetuel [from Sports et divertissements])*, Ishii *(Tango Prism)*, Klein *(Essercizi)* DNN ▲ 78841 [DDD] (16.97)

Jacobs, Helmut C. (acc)
Paganiniana—features works by Baur, Brehme, Haydn, Karg-Elert, Mozart, Reger CPO ▲ 999057 [DDD] (15.97)

Klucevsek, Guy (acc)
Manhattan Cascade *(incl 4 polkas)*—features works by Mary Ellen Childs, Anthony Coleman, Rolf Groesbeck, Aaron Jay Kernis, John King, Guy Klucevsek, Christian Marclay, Lois V Vierk, John Zorn CRI ▲ 626 [DDD] (16.97)

Murray, Owen (acc)
On the Wings of the Wind—features works by Bach *(Prelude & Fugue in d, BWV 554)*, Mozart *(Andante in F, K.616)*, D. Scarlatti *(Son in c, K.11; Son in C, K.159)*, Messiaen *(La Nativité du Seigneur [Nos. 6 & 7])*, McLeod *(The Passage of the Divine Bird)*, Clarke *(On the Wings of the Wind)*, McGuire *(Prelude 12)*, Derbenko *(Little Suite)*, Zolotaryov *(Children's Suite 1)* MER ▲ 84366 (16.97)

BALLET & DANCE MUSIC

Atlantic Sinfonietta [cnd:Andrew Schenck]
More Music for Martha Graham *(see Composer section under Hindemith (Herodiade), Menotti & W. Schuman)* KOCH ▲ 7051 [DDD] (16.97)
Music for Martha Graham: The Original Versions *(see Composer section under Barber (Cave of the Heart) & Copland (Appalachian Spring)* KOCH ▲ 7019 [DDD] (16.97)

Baltimore SO [cnd:David Zinman]
Dance Mix—features works by Adams *(The Chairman Dances)*, Argento *(Tango)*, Bernstein *(Mambo)*, Daugherty *(Desi)*, Harbison *(Remembering Gatsby)*, Kernis *(New Era Dance)*, Larsen *(Collage:Boogie)*, Moran *(Points of Departure)*, Rouse *(Bonham)*, Schiff *(Stomp)*, Torke *(Charcoal)* *(rec Joseph Meyerhoff Symphony Hall, Baltimore, Apr 9-10, 1994)* PLON ▲ 44454 [DDD] (16.97)

Czech-Slovak RSO [cnd:Ondrej Lenárd]
Invitation to the Dance—features works by Adam *(Giselle [sels])*, Delibes *(Lakmé [sels])*, Gounod *(Faust [ballet music])*, Ponchielli *(Dance of the Hours)*, Weber *(Invitation to the Dance)* NXIN ▲ 550081 [DDD] (5.97)

London PO, London SO [cnd:Antál Dorati]
Les Ballets Russes—features works by J. Strauss, Jr. *(The Blue Danube)*, D'Erlanger *(Les Cent Baisers)*, Chabrier *(Cotillon)*, Boccherini *(Scuola Di Ballo)* PHS ▲ 36 (17.97)
Ballet Gala: Pas De Deux—features works by Minkus *(Pas de deux [from Don Quixote])*, Tchaikovsky *(Pas de deux [from Sleeping Beauty], Pas de deux [from The Nutcracker:Act II])*, Minkus *(Pas de deux [from Paquita])*, Drigo *(Pas de deux [from Le Corsaire & Esmerelda])*, Auber *(Pas classique)*, Helsted *(Pas de deux [from Flower Festival in Genzano])* PLON ▲ 33862 [ADD] (11.97)

London SO [cnd:Neeme Järvi], Scottish National Orch
Russian Ballet Masterpieces—features works by Glazunov, Prokofiev, Shostakovich, Stravinsky, Tchaikovsky CHN (Collect) ▲ 6512 [DDD] (12.97)

Philharmonia Orch [cnd:Geoffrey Simon]
French Ballet Music of the 1920s—features collective score by Ravel, Ferroud, Ibert, Roland, Manuel, Delannoy, Roussel, Milhaud, Poulenc, Auric, Schmidt *(L'éventail de Jeanne)*; collective score by Auric, Milhaud, Poulenc, Tailleferre, Honegger *(Les mariés de la Tour Eiffel)* CHN ▲ 8356 [DDD] (16.97)

Quebec SO [cnd:Simon Streatfeild]
A Tribute to Pavlova—features works by Glazunov, Tchaikovsky, A. Rubinstein, Delibes, Minkus, Drigo, Adam, Saint-Saëns SMS (SM 5000) ▲ 5048 [DDD] (16.97)

Ricercar Academy Orch [cnd:Pietro Busca]
Mascharada: 2 Centuries of European Dances & Instrumental Music—features works by Anonimo *(Lamento di Tristano-Rotta; Ils sont biens peles; L'Autre jour)*, Isaac *(Mon père m'a donné Mari)*, Attaignant *(Bransles; Pavane; Gaillarde; Basse danse [La gotta; La brosse])*, Brade *(Allmand; Coranta; Paduana; Galliarda; Türkischintrada; Der andere Mascharada; Courante; Comoedianten Tanz; Des rothschencken Tanz; Der satyrn Tanz; Der pilligrienen Tanz; Ein schottischer Tanz; Hennensein Tanz)*, Praetorius *(Courante de la Volte; Ballet; Bransie simple de novelle)*, Merula *(La Merula; La Monteverde)* STRV ▲ STV 33381 [DDD]

Tango 7 [Daniel Binelli (band), Daniel Zisman (vn), Osvaldo Ciancio (vn), Eduardo Vassallo (vc), Gerardo Vila (pno/fl), Hugo Romero (gtr), Silvio Acosta (db)]
Música de Buenos Aires 2: Tango 7—features works by Piazzolla *(Marrón y azul [arr Ismael Spitalnik]; S.V.P; Bandó; Romance del diablo; Allegro Tangabile)*, De Caro *(Copacabana [arr Daniel Binelli/Hugo Romero])*, Pugliese *(Negracha [arr Astor Piazzolla])*, Mendizabal *(El enterriano)*, Binelli *(Al pintor Aldo Severi; Paris desde aquí)*, Plaza *(Payadora)*, Chiloé *(Mi tentación [arr Astor Piazolla])*, Balcarce *(La bordona [arr Ismael Spitalnik])*, Salgán *(A don Agustin Bardi [arr Ismael Spitalnik])* *(rec Switzerland, Nov 1992)* VOXC ▲ 7528 (5.97)

Trutneva, Natalia (pno)
Ballet Russe—features Réverence (2); Exercises à la barre; Exercises au milleu; Allegro; Exercises aux pointes *(rec Minsk, Dec 1996)* ERAS ▲ 209 [DDD]

BALLET & DANCE MUSIC COLLECTIONS

American Dancer: The American Music Collection, Vol. 4—features works by Bernstein, Copland, Gould, Menotti, Barber, Dello Joio, Griffes, Moross, Still, W. Schuman KOCH ▲ 7600 (10.97)

Boléro & Other Greatest Dance Hits RCAV ▲ 60935 (10.97) ∎ 60935

Can-Can & Other Dances from the Opera—features performances by Czech Republic SO *(Gounod:Ballet Music [from Faust]; Offenbach:Barcarole [from Tales of Hoffmann]; Saint-Saëns:Bacchanale [from Samson & Delilah]; Ponchielli:Dance of the Hours [from La Gioconda]; Tchaikovsky:Dances [from Eugene Onegin]; Falla:Interlude & Dance [from La vida breve])*, Slovak PO *(Smetana:Dances [from The Bartered Bride]; Mussorgsky:Gopak [from Fair at Sorochintsy]; Dance of the Persian Slaves [from Khovanshchina])*, Royal PO *(Borodin:Polovtsian Dances [from Prince Igor])*, Slovak State PO Košice *(Offenbach:Can-Can [from Orpheus in the Underworld])* NXIN ▲ 550924 [DDD] (5.97)

Come & Trip It—features performances of instrumental dance music from 1780-1920 by Federal Music Society members *(Jullien:Prima Donna Waltz; Dodworth:Jenny Lind Polka; Reinagle: Minuet & Gavotte; Grobe:Natalie Polka-Mazurka; Flirt Polka; d'Albert:Flying Cloud Schottische; Johnson:Victoria Gallop; La Sonambula Quadrille No. 2; trad:Country Fiddle Music)*, Schwarz Dance Orch [cnd:Gerard Schwarz] *(Holzmann:Blaza-Away!; Stone:Ma Ragtime Baby; Moret:Hiawatha; Schwartz:Chinatown, My Chinatown; Logatti:El Irresistable; trad/arr de Witt:Eliza Jane McCue)*, Hyman Dance Orch [cnd:Dick Hyman] *(Gumble:At the Mississippi Cabaret; Jerome:Valse da ma Coeur; Bowman:Kansas City Blues; Hickman/Black:Hold Me; Gaskill:Waltzing the Blues; Pinkard:Sweet Man)* NWW ▲ 80293 (16.97)

The Dance Collection, w. Ondrej Lenárd (cnd), Keith Clark (cnd), Stephen Gunzenhauser (cnd), Kenneth Jean (cnd), Barry Wordsworth (cnd), Adrian Leaper (cnd), Johannes Wildner (cnd), Czech RSO, Slovak RSO, Slovak PO, Royal PO, Slovak State PO, CRS SO, Thalia-Schrammeln Quartet—features works by Weber *(Invitation to the Dance, J.260)*, Adam *(Giselle)*, Gounod *(Faust [sels])*, Delibes *(Lakmé (sels); Coppélia:Suite; Sylvia:Suite; La Source:Suite; Le Roi s'amuse [ballet music]; Kassya [Trepak])*, Ponchielli *(Dance of the Hours [from La Gioconda])*, Offenbach *(Can-Can [from Orpheus in the Underworld]; Barcarole [from Tales of Hoffman])*, Smetana *(Polka & Furiant [from The Bartered Bride])*, Saint-Saëns *(Bacchanale [from Samson & Delilah])*, Mussorgsky *(Gopak [from Sorochintsy Fair]; Dance of the Persian Slaves [from Khovanshchina])*, Tchaikovsky *(Polonaise & Waltz [from Eugene Onegin])*, Falla *(Interlude & Dance [from La vida breve])*, Borodin *(Polovtsian Dances [from Prince Igor])*, Lehmann *(Blitzzug-Marsch [arr Josef Mikulas])*, Schubert *(Kleine wiener Walzer [arr Walter Wasservogel])*, Strohmayer *(Veilchen-Polka [arr Anton Pürkner]; Alsergründer-Walzer [arr Lois Böck]; Zepperl-Polka [arr Anton Pürkner]; Ottakringer-Marsch [arr Anton Pürkner])*, Fahbrach *(Im Kahlenbergerdörfl [arr Josef Mikulas])*, Joh. Schrammel *(Frisch gewagt; Sei weider guat [both arr Walter Wassevogel]; In arte voluptas [arr Lois Böck])*, Jos. Schrammer *(Der weana is'all'weil leger, Lied; Nussdorfer-Marsch [arr Lois Böck]; Bei guter Laune [arr Walter Wasservogel]; Antoinetten-Polka [arr Walter Wassevogel])*, Zdobnitzky *(Rummel-Polka [arr Josef Mikulas])*, J. Strauss Jr. *(Liebeslieder Walzer [arr Walter Wassevogel])*, K. & J. Mikulas *(Dressler Tanzweisen)*, anon *(Das picksüsse Hölzl [arr Lois Böck])* *(rec Czechoslovak Radio Concert Hall, Bratislava, Feb 1-4, 1988)* NXIN 4-▲ 504015 [DDD] (19.97)

Incitation to Desire: Tangos for Yvar Mikhashoff, 1945-93—features works by Sahl *(Exiles' Cafe)*, Cage *(Perpetual Canon [Version A]; Perpetual Tango II)*, Rudhyar *(Tango d'Antan)*, Duckworth *(Tango Voices)*, Schimel *(Fromage Dangereux)*, Foss *(Curriculum Vitae Tango)*, Pender *(Ms Jackson Dances for the World)*, Bennett *(Tango after Syrinx)*, Biscardi *(Incitation to Desire)*, Ludova *(Tango Music)*, Bright *(Tango Dreaming)*, Sa'ry *(Tango)*, Nancarrow *(Tango?)*, Hill *(Tango No Tango)*, Raschke *(Tango auf drei Beinum)*, Copland *(Tempo di Tango)*, Jaggard *(Tango)*, Berkman *(Thorn-torn Lips)* *(rec Slee Hall, SUNY, Buffalo, NY, May 22-25, 1992)* NALB ▲ 73

BANDS

Adjutant General's Corps Band [cnd:Capt. M.J. Torrent]
New Horizons—features 18 sels including Gaudeamus Igitur; When You Wish upon a Star; Greensleeves; La Calinda; Molly on the Shore; The Adjutant General BND ▲ 5106 (16.97)

Aldershot Command Searchlight Tattoo
Tattoo—features works by Holzmann *(Blaze Away)*, Alford *(On the Quarter Deck; Colonel Bogey March; The Standard of St. George)*, Schubert *(Land of My Fathers/Sweet Polly Oliver/Marche Militaire [arr Osborne])*, James *(Aldershot Tattoo March)*, Javaloyes *(El Abanicao)*, R. B. Hall *(Officer of the Day March)*, Meister *(Le Grenadier du Caucase)*, Williams *(Blue Devils)*, Sousa *(Stars & Stripes Forever)*, McBain *(Mechanised Infantry)*, Plater *(March of the King's Men)*, Rhodes *(Golden Spurs)*, Adams *(Crown Commenwealth)*, B. Silver *(Royal Review)*, A. Young *(Tournament)*, Friedemann *(Slavonic Rhap)*, plus arrs of trad tunes *(The Skye Gathering/Portree Men/Clachnacuddin/Piper of Drummond; The Border/Newhall Castle/Caledonian Carol; Struy Lodge; Fanfare/Minstrel Boy/The Watchtower)* *(rec 1932-38)* BEUL ▲ 19 (m) [ADD] (16.97)

Americus Brass Band
Music of the Civil War SUMM ▲ 126 [DDD] (16.97) ∎

Artistica Buñol [cnd:Henrie Adams]
Salute from Spain—features works by Padilla *(Valencia [Marche de la bien amada])*, Giménez *(La Torre del Oro [Preludio Sinfónica])*, Chueca y Valverde *(Sel [w. Astrid Crone (sgr); arr P. Marquina])*, Larregla *(Viva Navarra [Jota])*, Soutullo *(Puente Areas [Pasodoble])*, Guridi *(El Caserio [Fant; arr M. San Miguel])*, Breton *(La Dolores [Gran Jota])*, Morera *(La Santa Espina [Sardana])*, Serrano *(Himno a Valencia)* *(rec Monte Carlo Theater, Buñol, Spain)* World Wind ▲ WWM 500 024 [DDD]

Band of the Life Guards [cnd:Maj. Colin J. Reeves]
From the Big Screen—features John Williams's Evening at Pops [We're Looking Ahead; The Cowboys; The Dance of the Witches; Olympic Fanfare & Theme]; This Land; To Die For; Circle of Life; Be Prepared; Can You Feel the Love Tonight?; Hakuna Matata; I Just Can't Wait to Be King [all from The Lion King]; I Have Nothing; I'm Every Woman; I Will Always Love You [all from The Bodyguard]; An Aladdin Fantasy [Arabian Nights; One Jump Ahead; Friend Like Me; Prince Ali; A Whole New World]; Star Trek:Through the Generations [themes from Star Trek, Star Trek:The Next Generation & Star Trek:Deep Space 9]; Themes from E. T.; Robin Hood, Prince of Thieves; Indiana Jones & the Temple of Doom; sels from Jurassic Park BND ▲ 5116 [DDD] (16.97)

Belgian Air Force Royal Symphonic Band [cnd:Alain Crepin]
The Comedians—features works by Kabalevsky *(The Comedians)*, Jay Chattaway, Alain Crepin, James Curnow, et al. RENE ▲ 87036 [DDD] (16.97)
Golden Jubilee of the Belgian Air Force—features works by Mestrez *(March of the Belgian Air Force [2 versions])*, Keyaert *(Jour de Guerre; Jour de Tristesse)*, Davies *(March of the Royal Air Force)*, Beethoven *(Adagio [from Son Pathétique, Op. 13])*, Brosse *(Music for a Celebration)*, Poutoire *(Colonel Chopin)*, Tchaikovsky *(Barcarolle, Op. 37/6 [from Les saisons])*, Crepin *(Aircodos [March of the Air Commandos]; Saxs en Parallèles; The White Bison; Bij ons in Kee Bie; Rhap voor Berlare)*, Legrand *(L'été 42)*, Colpin/Steve *(349 Squadron March)*, Crepin/Harrison *(Tenacity)*, Campenhout *(La brabançonne [Belgian National Anthem])* *(rec Steurbaut Sound Recording Centre)* RENE ▲ 87124 [DDD] (16.97)
Soloists & Composers of the Belgian Air Force Royal Symphonic Band—features works by Quevy *(Looping)*, Ruelle *(Con 1 Tpt [w. André Robette (tpt)])*, Devroye *(Whan an event)*, Nijs *(Explorations)*, Itturalde *(Pequena Czarda [w. Olivier Zbona (sax)])*, Govaere *(Follow Me)*, A. Shaw *(Con Cl [w. William Huybandt (cl)])*, Ceulemans *(Ray Jeans)*, Geeraerts *(Flying Tpts)*, Hefti *(Splanky)*, M. Dubois *(Pioneers Forward)* RENE ▲ 87144 [DDD] (16.97)

Belgian Guides Symphonic Band
Belgian Guides Symphonic Band—features works by J. Absil *(Rites, Op. 79)*, Dukas *(L'apprenti Sorcier)*, Gershwin *(An American in Paris)*, A. Hansotte *(March of the 11th Line Regiment)*, A. Reed *(Praise Jerusalem)*, H. Thijssen *(Limbourg, My Land)* RENE ▲ 87056 [DDD] (16.97)

Belgian Guides Symphonic Band [cnd:Norbert Nozy]
Belgian Military Marches, Vol. 1: Cavalry Marches—features The Charge at Burkel, 20 Marches & 26 Cavalry Trumpet Calls RENE ▲ 87040 [DDD] (16.97)
Belgian Military Marches, Vol. 2: Infantry Marches RENE ▲ 87055 (16.97)
French Military Marches—features works by C. R. de Lisle *(La Marseillaise)*, Lully *(Marches pour la Garde Française [1-2])*, Rosseau *(Marche du Devin du Village)*, Prevost *(Refrains des Régiments de l'Armée de Sambre et Meuse; Marche Historique Française)*, Auber *(March on Themes from Fra Diavolo [arr A. Prevost])*, Gounod *(Marche de 12th Hussards; March on Themes from Le Tribut de Zamora [both arr A. Prevost])*, Voisin *(Marche de 11th Régiment de Zouaves)*, Ganne *(Marche Lorraine)*, Meister *(Le Grenadier du Caucase)*, Petit *(Salut au 85th)*, Delorient *(Marche des Masquisards)*, Clowez *(Marche de la Deuxième D. B.)*, Honegger *(Marche des Ambassadeurs [from Nicolas de Flüe; arr Pierre Dupont])*, Saint-Saëns *(Marche Héroïque, Op. 34 [trans Eugène Mastio])*, Berlioz *(Marche Hongroise [from La Damnation de Faust; trans A. Gironce])*, plus anon marches *(Marche de Soldats de Robert Bruce [arr A. Prevost]; Marche de la Garde Consulaire à Marengo; Marche des Bonnets à Pollis [both arr Jean Furgeot]; Austerlitz [arr J. Vidal])* RENE ▲ 87130 [DDD] (16.97)

Belgian Guides Symphonic Band [cnd:Yvon Ducene]
Works for Symphonic Band—features works by Milhaud, De Boeck, Bizet, Bartók, Granados, et al. RENE ▲ 86018 (16.97)

Besses o' th' Barn Band [cnd:Roy Newsome, Alec Evans]
Hymns & Things—features various artists *(Simple Gifts, Dem Bones, O For the Wings of a Dove, Eventide, plus others)* CHN ▲ 4529 [DDD] (17.97)

Black Dyke Band [cnd:James Watson]

Cathedral Brass—features works by Boyce *(Tpt Voluntary [arr Bennett; w. James Watson (pic), Philip Wilby (org)])*, C. Franck *(Panis angelicus [w. James Watson (tpt), Robert Childs (eup), Philip Wilby (org)])*, Mascagni *(sel from Cavalleria rusticana [arr Gay; w. Kevin Crockford (tpt), Philip Wilby (org)])*, Saint-Saëns *(Sym 3 Org [Finale; arr Cosens; w. Philip Wilby (org), Johnora Hildbrand (pno), Wendy Nightingale (pno)])*, Sullivan *(The Lost Chord [arr Langford; w. Philip Wilby (org)])*, Wagner *(Procession to the Minster [arr Snell; w. Philip Wilby (org)])*, J. Webb *(Share My Yoke [arr Bosanko; w. James Watson (tpt)])*, plus arr Wilby *(Praise My Soul; Alleluiah Sing to Jesus; The Day Thou Gavest; Love Divine; Abide with Me; Morning Has Broken [w. Matthew Baker (cnt)]; Thine Be the Glory) (rec Peel Hall, Nov-Dec 1996)* DOY ▲ 60 [DDD] (16.97)

Great British Marches—features works by Kaye *(Queensbury)*, Hume *(Roll Away, Bet)*, G. Allan *(Battle Abbey; Senator; Imperioso; Raby; Knight Templar)*, C. Anderson *(O.R.B.)*, S. Cope *(Invincible)*, S. Douglas *(Pompous Main)*, Rimmer *(Cossack)*, Verner *(Captain)*, G. Hawkins *(Olympus) (rec Manchester, 1994)* DOY ▲ DOY 039 [DDD]

Revelations—features works by Widor *(Sym 5 Org [Toccata; arr P. Sparke])*, Wilby *(Revelation:Sym for Double Brass)*, Sutton *(Paragon [w. Matthew Baker (cnt)])*, Texidor *(Ampartico Roca [arr A. Winter])*, Heath *(Big Band Set [arr B. Geldard])*, Barry *(Impromptu for Tuba [w. Ken Ferguson (tuba)])*, Schubert *(Ave Maria [arr D. Hughes])*, Camerata *(Carnival of Venice [arr A. Catherall; w. Robert Childs (eup)])*, Respighi *(Pines of Rome:March [arr H. Snell]) (rec Nov 1995)* DOY ▲ DOY 046 [DDD]

Black Dyke Mills Band [cnd:Roy Newsome, Edward Heath]

Morning Cloud—features works by Smetana *(Polka [from The Bartered Bride; arr D. Wright])*, Rossini *(The Thieving Magpie Ov [arr Wright])*, Dvořák *(Rusalka's Song to the Moon [w. Phillip McCann (cnt); arr G. Langford])*, Delibes *(Entry of the Huntresses [arr R. Newsome])*, Tchaikovsky *(Miniature Ov [from The Nutcracker Suite; arr Wright])*, Handel *(Siciliana & Giga [w. K. Wadsworth (hn); arr Langford])*, Langford *(Rhap on Sea Shanties)*, Elgar *(Pomp & Circumstance March 1 [arr J. Ord Home])* CHN ▲ 4534 [ADD] (17.97)

Black Dyke Mills Band [cnd:Maj. Peter Parkes]

Black Dyke Plays Rossini CHN ▲ 4505 [DDD] (16.97)

Champions of Brass *(20th cent works for brass band)*—features works by G. Bailey, G. Bantock, E. Gregson, G. Langford, W. Mathias, R. Vaughan Williams CHN ▲ 4510 [ADD] (16.97)

Classic Brass—features works by E. Ball, Chabrier, Donizetti, E. Gregson, L. Knipper, R. Newsome, Offenbach, Schubert, Joh. Strauss CHN (Collect) ▲ 6539 [ADD] (12.97)

The Complete Champions *(20th cent works for brass band)*—features works by Wilfred Heaton *(Contest Music)*, George Lloyd *(Royal Parks)*, John McCabe *(Cloudcatcher Fells)*, Gilbert Vinter *(Salute to Youth)* CHN ▲ 4509 [DDD] (16.97)

Famous Marches—features Colonel Bogey; Coronation March; Torch of freedom; Spirit of pageantry; Sousa medley; Dambusters March; etc. CHN (Collect) ▲ 6516 [ADD] (12.97)

The John Foster Black Dyke Mills Band Celebrates 150 Years—features works by Bellstedt *(Capriccio Brillante)*, Dvořák *(New World Sym [Finale])*, Ireland *(Downland Suite [Elegy])*, Jämefelt *(Praeludium)*, Gordon Langford *(Famous British Marches [medley]; Serenade [from Son, Serenade & Scherzo])*, Offenbach *(Can-Can)*, Handel Parker *(Deep Harmony [hymn tune])*, J. J. Richards *(Midwest March)*, Rimsky-Korsakov *(Dance of the Tumblers)*, Toselli *(Serenata), Weber (The Ruler of the Spirits [ov])*, G. H. Willcocks *(The Champions [march])*, Windsor/Koenig *(Alpine Echoes & Post Horn Gallop)* CHN ▲ 4516 [DDD] (16.97)

Kings of Brass—features works by Borodin *(Sym 2 [Scherzo])*, D. Bourgeois *(Serenade)*, Drigo *(Serenade, "Les Millions d'Arlequin")*, Lalo *(Le roi d'Ys [ov])*, Liszt *(Hungarian Rhap 2)*, Del Staigers *(Carnival of Venice)*, R. Strauss *(Hn Con 1 [Finale])* CHN ▲ 4517 [ADD] (16.97)

Overtures—features works by Auber *(The Black Domino)*, Donizetti *(Daughter of the Regiment)*, Nicolai *(The Merry Wives of Windsor)*, Rossini *(Italiana in Algeri)*, Suppé *(The Beautiful Galathea; Light Cavalry)*, Verdi *(Forza del destino)*, Weber *(Oberon)* CHN ▲ 4514 [DDD] (17.97)

Russian Festival—features works by Borodin *(Str Qt 2 [Nocturne])*, Glinka *(Russlan & Ludmilla [ov])*, Mussorgsky *(Khovanshchina [Prelude]; Sorochinsky Fair [Gopak])*, Prokofiev *(The Montagus & the Capulets [from Romeo & Juliet])*, Rachmaninoff *(Vocalise)*, Rimsky-Korsakov *(Scheherazade Love Theme)*, Shostakovich *(Festival Ov)*, Tchaikovsky *(Sym 2, "The Little Russian" [Finale])* CHN ▲ 4519 [ADD] (16.97)

Traditionally British—features The Blaydon Races; Drink to me only; The British Grenadiers; Greensleeves; Fant on British Sea Songs; Loch Lomond/Comin' through the rye; etc. CHN (Collect) ▲ 6515 [ADD] (12.97)

World Famous Marches—features works by H. L. Blankenburg, R. B. Hall, W. Rimmer CHN (Collect) ▲ 6565 [ADD] (12.97)

Britannia Building Society Band [cnd:John Pryce-Jones]

The Best of Brass & Voices *(see CHORAL, Halifax Choral Society)*

Canadian Forces Air Command Band [cnd:Terry O'Connor]

Silent Sky—features John Gay Suite [Intrada, Romanza, Intermezzo, Finale]; Gordon Lightfoot Medley [If You Could Read My Mind/Early Morning Rain/Pussy Willows Cat Tails]; Music from "Far & Away"; A Copland Portrait; Music from "Memphis Belle" [Amazing Grace, Steel Lady, Flying Home, The Landing/Memphis Belle]; Silent Sky; Wind Beneath My Wings; Music for a Tattoo [Spitfire Prelude, Dam Busters March, USAF March, Wish Me Luck as You Wave Me Goodbye, The White Cliffs of Dover, Airman's Prayer, RCAF March Past] BND ▲ 5100 [DDD] (16.97)

Canadian Forces Central Band [cnd:Denis Bouchard]

Canada Remembers—features Air Force Ov; Vera Lynn Medley; Je me souviens; Bless 'Em All Medley; Never Again; Normandy Landing; Salute to the Big Bands; Canada Overseas; Nightfall in Camp; Athene; 7 Seas Ov; Lili Marlene; Closer Medley; God Save the Queen; O Canada BND ▲ 5105 [DDD] (16.97)

Coldstream Guards Regimental Band [cnd:Maj. Roger G. Swift]

Marches, Vol. 1 *(British marches)* DNN ▲ 73806 [DDD] (16.97)

Marches, Vol. 2: Music of America & Continental Europe DNN ▲ 73807 [DDD] (16.97)

National Anthems, Vol. 1 *(42 national anthems of Europe, Asia & the USSR)* DNN ▲ 74500 [DDD] (16.97)

National Anthems, Vol. 2 *(41 national anthems of the Americas, Africa, the Middle East & Oceania)* DNN ▲ 74501 [DDD] (16.97)

Coldstream Guards Regimental Band [cnd:Maj. David Marshall], Queen's Own Highlanders Pipes & Drums (Seaforth & Camerons)

Bond of Friendship—features A Fanfare for Our Heroes; Scarlet & Gold; Pibroch O'Donald Dhu; The Crags of Tumbledown; The Duke of York; Hornpipe; HRH The Duke of Cambridge; Band & Pipes Marches; When the Guards Are on Parade; English Airs; Army of the Nile; Ode to Joy; From a Distance; The Magnificent 7; Band & Pipes Medley; Fanfare, Pride of London; March Medley; A Nightingale Sang in Berkeley Square; The Purple Pageant; Bond of Friendship; World War I Medley; The Caissons Go Rolling Along; Pipes & Drums Medley; Sands of Kuwait; Evening Hymn & Last Post; Auld Lang Syne; The Coldstream March; March Off BND ▲ 5073 (16.97)

CWS Glasgow Band [cnd:Howard Snell]

Flower of Scotland—features works by Rimmer *(Australasian)*, Sparke *(Capariccio [w. Gavin Lindsay (sop)])*, Williamson *(Flower of Scotland [arr Ferney])*, Ball *(Softly Sounds the Little Bell; Star Lake)*, Heath *(Frolic for Trbns)*, Rodgers *(You'll Never Walk Alone [arr Snell])*, Borodin *(Polovtsian Dances)*, Cruger *(Now Thank We All Our God)*, Gershwin *(The Man I Love [w. Anne Murphy (bar)])*, Rose *(Holiday for Strings [arr Farr])*, Foster *(Beautiful Dreamer [arr Snell])*, Graham *(Prelude to a New Age)*, Hazell *(Mr Jums [arr Catherall])*, Friedmann *(Slavonic Rhap 2 [arr Wright])* DOY ▲ 5 [DDD] (16.97)

Czech Army Central Band [cnd:Karel Bělohoubek, Viliam Béreš, Jaroslav Šíp]

Majorettes March—features works by Fučik, Kmoch, Štolc, Vačkář, Hančl, R. Nováček, Vejvoda, Kudelásek, Lepič, Brázda, Bažant, Béreš, Spanilý, Slitr, Löffler, J. Pavel & L. Abel *(rec May 1997)* LT ▲ 70 (16.97)

D. C. Hall's New Concert & Quadrille Band

Grand Concert! *(vocal & instrumental music heard in 19th century America) (rec Sept 20-21, 1991)* DOR ▲ 80108 [DDD] (13.97)

Dalewool Auckland Brass [cnd:Nigel Weeks]

Power & Passion—features works by Rossini, Pryor, Gershwin, Vinter, Code, Wilcox, plus others ATOL ▲ 9802 (18.97)

Danish Concert Band

Concert Band Music—features works by Leif Kayser, Rolf Wilheim, Erik Norby, Saint-Saëns, J. S. Bach, John Barnes Chance, Bernstein *(rec 1990)* Rondo Grammofon ▲ RCD 8331 [DDD]

Durham Constabulary Brass Band [cnd:Dennis Noble]

The Gentle Touch—features In Celebration; Where No Man Has Gone Before; Here's That Rainy Day; I Could Be So Good for You; Fascination; Shepherd's Hey; Love Changes Everything; The Lady Detectives; Midnight Reverie; Juliet Bravo; Cagney & Lacey; The Jaguar; La Virgen De La Macarena; Born Free; Sullivan at Sea; World Traveller; St. Clement; Songs of the Quay BND ▲ 5079 [DDD] (16.97)

1st & 2nd Battalion Combined Drum Corps [cnd:Capt. Michael Hall]

Out the Escort—features Out the Escort; Retreat Marches (Lasota; Leconfield; Mandora); Belphegor; The Sentinel; March of the King's Company No. 1; Le Tambour Major; Triplet (Hanover Girl; Charlottenburg; The Views Wood Fifer); Prussian Glory; Captain Nichols; Galanthia; Le Reve Passe; The Girl I Left behind Me; Eagle & Star; Brooklyn Belle; Les Petits Tambours; Slow March: The Old Coldstream March; Vendetta; The Adjutant (Captain Loyd); Regimental March Past in Slow Time: Figaro BND ▲ 5052 [DDD] (16.97)

Funen Military Band [cnd:Erik Hammerbak]

The Last Sundown—features works by F. N. Pedersen *(Dansk Tattoo March)*, Mozart *(Zauberflöte [ov; arr W. Rimmer])*, J. Williams *(Concert March [from 1941; arr S. Sykes]; Indiana Jones & the Temple of Doom [arr R. Farr])*, G. Ø. Hansen *(Trompetina [w. Per Hyttel (tpt), Henrik Hou Jørgensen (tpt)])*, L. Kayser *(Military March 1)*, Lumbye *(Bouquet Royal [arr E. Hammerbak])*, Holm *(Festmusik 1978)*, Widquist *(Under Blågel Fana)*, Nielsen *(Prelude to the 7th Picture of the Mother [arr E. Hammerbak])*, V. Hansen *(Jubilee March of the Danish Life Guard Regiment)*, Grieg *(Funeral March for Richard Nordraak [arr H. Snell])*, J. Bechgård *(The Sun Has Gone Down) (rec Apr 1997)* DANI ▲ 8186 [DDD] (18.97)

Gibbs, Norman (bgl), Her Majesty's Royal Marines Band Corps of Drums [cnd:Capt. Peter Heming]

Portsmouth—features works by Boyce *(Heart of Oak)*, Isaac *(Warship)*, Bashford *(Splice the Mainbrace)*, Hood *(The Nelson Touch)*, Zehle *(Trafalgar; Viscount Nelson)*, Sousa *(Hands across the Sea)*, Dunn *(Under the White Ensign)*, Vaughan Williams *(Sea Songs)*, Heming *(Victory; Salute to the Sovereign)*, Hayward *(Bugle Fanfare)*, Piner *(Drum Display)*, Scholefield *(The Day Thou Gavest Lord Is Ended)*, Wood *(Fant on British Sea Songs)*, Elgar *(Land of Hope & Glory)*, trad *(Portsmouth)* BND ▲ 5020 [DDD]

Goldman Band [cnd:Richard Franco Goldman, Ainslee Cox]

The Golden Age of the American March—features works by Sousa, Victor Herbert, Edwin Franko Goldman, et al. NWW ▲ 80266 [AAD] (16.97)

Gordon Highlanders Drums Pipes & Regimental Band

Cock o' the North—features Long Reveille; Grampian Welcome; Highland Gathering; Rose of Kelvingrove; Pipe Medley; Castlegate to Holborn; Elizabeth of Glamis; Ye Banks & Braes; Cornkisters; Mess Pipers; Drummers Fanfare; Highland Troop; The Garb of Old Gaul; Company Marches; Pipes & Band Medley; Loch Maree; Jacobite Prince; Bonnie Black Isle; Jock's Favorites; Aberdeen Sel; March Off the Colors Tattoo Last Post; Cock o' the North; Lights Out BND ▲ 5077 [DDD] (16.97)

Great American Main Street Band

Under the Big Top ANGL ▲ 54728 (16.97) 54728

Grenadier Guards Band

Stirring Marches of the U.S. Services PLON (Weekend Classics) ▲ 33681 (6.97) ▮ 33681

Grenadier Guards Band [cnd:Maj. Rodney J. Parker], Gordon Highlanders Drums & Pipes

New World Salute—features Fanfare: New World Salute; Stabat Mater; March: Arromanches; Westminster Chimes/Let's All Go down the Strand/London Pride/Maybe It's because I'm a Londoner; 2001: Also sprach Zarathustra/Superman; 633 Squadron; The Green Hills of Tyrol; The Battles O'er/Lochanside; The Scottish Division/The Braes of Mar/Aspin Bank/The Piper of Drummond; See the Conquering Hero Comes/Edinburgh Castle/The Soldier's Return/Crusader's March/The Bonnie Lass of Fyvie; Kumbaya/The Barren Rocks of Aden/Piping Hot, plus others *(rec 1988)* BND ▲ 5019 [DDD] (16.97)

Grenadier Guards Band [cnd:Maj. Phillip E. Hills]

When the Guards Are on Parade—features The Bond of Friendship; When the Guards Are on Parade; Royal Standard; National Emblem; Army of the Nile; The King's Guard; The Mareth Line; Namur; Marche de la Gendarmerie Belge; Glorious Victory; The Old Grenadier; Army & Marine; Royal Salute; Steadfast & True; The Contemptibles; Bravest of the Brave; The Great Little Army; On the Square; Birdcage Walk; Queen's Company; The Inkerman March; The Duke of York's March; The Grenadier's Return; Scipio; The British Grenadiers BND ▲ 5104 [DDD] (16.97)

Grenadier Guards Band [cnd:Maj. S. A. Watts]

On Stage—features Brubeck:A Portrait in Time [Take 5/Blue Rondo a la Turk/Summer Song/Unsquare Dance]; plus Fanfare:Stage Presence; Concert March:Full Speed Ahead [from The Caine Mutiny]; Waltz [from The Grenadiers]; Ov on Themes of Offenbach; Love Changes Everything [from Aspects of Love]; Carnival of Venice; The Debutante; Prelude to Romance; Send in the Clowns; Me & My Girl [sel]; Carmen March; March & Dance of the Comedians; Les Miserables [sel]; Fiesta [Spanish Rhap] BND ▲ 5032 [DDD] (16.97)

Grimethorpe Colliery Band [cnd:Garry Cutt, Maj Peter Parkes]

Grimethorpe—features works by Browne Hall *(Death or Glory)*, Rodrigo *(Concierto de Aranjuez [w. Mark Walters (flgl); Adagio; arr Bolton])*, Downie *(Purcell Vars)*, Clarke *(From the Shores of the Mighty Pacific [w. Richard Marshall (cnt); arr Newsome])*, Weber *(Abu Hassan Ov [arr Langford])*, Respighi *(The Pines of Rome [March; arr Snell])*, Sykes *(Carnival Cocktail [w. Mike Kilroy (eup)])*, Whelan *(Riverdance [arr Farr])*, Porter *(It's Alright [w. Jonathan Beatty (trbn), Andrew Hirst (trbn), Simon Kingsley (trbn), Simon Willis (trbn); arr Brevik])*, King *(Barnum & Bailey's Favorite March [arr Roberts])*, Redhead *(Isaiah 40)*, trad *(The Lark in the Clear Air [arr Langford])* CHN ▲ 4545 (16.97) ▮ BBTD 4545

Grimethorpe Colliery Band [cnd:Maj Peter Parkes]

French Bonbons—features works by Ganne *(Marche lorraine)*, Debussy *(Petite suite; The Girl with the Flaxen Hair)*, Lalo *(Presto [from Rapsodie norvégienne])*, Fauré *(Berceuse [from Dolly Suite])*, Saint-Saëns *(Marche militaire française)*, Satie *(Gymnopédie No. 1)*, Hérold *(Clog Dance [from La Fille mal gardée])*, Langford *(An Offenbach Fant)*, Ravel *(Pavane pour une infante défunte)*, Jessel *(The Parade of the Tin Soldiers)*, Godard *(Berceuse de Jocelyn)*, Gounod *(Marche militaire la ronde)*, Bizet *(Duet [from The Pearlfishers])*, Chabrier *(Joyeuse marche)* CHN (Brass) ▲ 4542 (16.97)

Grimethorpe Colliery Band [cnd:Frank Renton]

Paganini Variations for Brass Band—features works by Rimmer *(Ravenswood)*, Ball *(Journey into Freedom)*, Mozart *(Queen of the Night's Aria [arr A. Smith; w. Kevin Crockford (s cnt)])*, Jagger/Richards *(Ruby Tuesday [arr A. Catherall])*, Morrison *(Buster Strikes Back [w. Alan Morrison (cnt)])*, Saint-Saëns *(Sym 3 Org:Finale)*, German *(President)*, Debussy *(Girl with the Flaxen Hair [arr M. Brand])*, Kneale *(Blue John [w. Simon Kingsley (trbn)])*, Brubeck *(Blue Rondo à la Turk [arr K. Edwards])*, Wilby *(Paganini Vars) (rec BBC Studio 7, Oct 1991)* DOY ▲ DOY 015 [DDD]

Hannaford Street Silver Band [cnd:Howard Cable]

Northern Delights—features works by Ridout *(Fanfare)*, Lavallée *(Ov to The Bridal Rose; O Canada [both arr H. Cable])*, J. P. Clarke *(The Lays of the Maple Leaf)*, Irvine *(Anniversary Ov)*, Cable *(Ontario Pictures; Saturday's Game)*, J. K. Bell *(In the Land of Spirits)*, Curnow *(Jubilation)*, Cowell *(Rollercoaster)*, Campbell, Harron & Moore *(Anne of Green Gables [sels])*, trad *(Carnival of Venice [arr J. Cowell])* ODRE ▲ 9308 [DDD]

Hannaford Street Silver Band [cnd:Stephen Chenette]

Canadian Impressions, w. Curtis Metcalf—features works by Cable, Forsyth, Weinzweig, Kulesha, Irvine, Luedeke CBC (SM 5000) ▲ 5136 [DDD] (16.97)

Her Majesty's Dragoon Guards Band [cnd:Capt. C. C. Gray]

Festivo, w. Royal Scots Dragoon Guards Pipes & Drums—features Regimentsgruss; Namur; Marche Lorraine; Barnum & Bailey's Favorite; The Welshman; A Yorkshire Ov; Rhap on the Minstrel Boy; The Queen Elizabeth March Set; Rhap for Eup; Celtic Folk; Rhosymedre; Finnegan's Wake; Ensign Ewart's Air; 3 Dale Dances; Pipes & Drums Medley; Sicilienne; Festivo; Radetzky March; 3 DGs; Fare Ye Well Inniskilling BND ▲ 5118 [DDD] (16.97)

Her Majesty's Life Guards Concert Band [cnd:Maj. Colin J. Reeves]

The Royal Salute *(music written for or associated with the British monarchy)*—features works by Arne *(Rule Brittania)*, Elgar *(Coronation March; Imperial March; Pomp & Circumstance Marches 1 & 4)*, Handel *(Arrival of the Queen of Sheba; My heart is inditing; The King shall rejoice; Zadok the Priest)*, Holst *(I vow to thee my country)*, Parry *(Jerusalem)*, Walton *(Crown Imperial; Orb & Sceptre)* COL ▲ 48473 (16.97)

Her Majesty's Royal Marines Band [cnd:Lt. Col. G. A. C. Hoskins]

Globe & Laurel—features On Parade; The Globe & Laurel; Officer of the Day; Cavalry of the Steppes; Uncle Sammy; Dad's Army March; Belphegor; The Advance Guard; My Regiment; Brass Buttons; The Gladiators Farewell; Punjab; The Contemptibles; The Voice of the Guns; Robinson's Grand Entree; Dunedin; Vimy Ridge; On the Square BND ▲ 5023 [DDD] (16.97)

Her Majesty's Royal Marines Commandos Band [cnd:Capt. D. C. Cole]

Kaleidoscope, w. Emer McParland (voc), Her Majesty's Royal Marines Commandos Big Band—features March: Royal Buglers; Jubilee Ov; Londonderry Air; Shepherd's Hey; Valdres March; Irish Washerwoman; West Side Story [I Feel Pretty; Maria; Something's Coming; Tonight; One Hand, One Heart; Cool; America]; Can't Buy Me Love; Passion Eyes; Time after Time; All Through the Night; Kaleidoscope [Black Is Black; Lady in Red; Blue Rondo a la Turk; A Whiter Shade of Pale] BND ▲ 5064 (16.97)

Household Cavalry Bands

The Horse Guard—features Royal Salute; The Life Guards Quick March [Milanollo]; The Life Guards Slow March; The Blues & Royals Quick & Slow Marches; Boots & Saddles; Tpt March [Fehrbelliner Reitermarsch]; Quickest & Best; Golden Spurs; The Black Horse; Imperial Life Guards; With Sword & Lance; Agrippa; Horse Guards; Trots Medley; Children of the Regiment; To Your Guard; Royal Standard; The Household Cavalry Musical Ride; The Bands of the Household Cavalry BND ▲ 7005 [DDD] (16.97)

Household Division Massed Bands [cnd:Lt. Col. D. E. Price]

Scarlet & Gold—features Guidon; Scarlet & Gold Fanfare; La rejouissance; Fascinating Rhythm/Embraceable You/Somebody Loves Me/Someone to Watch Over Me/I Got Rhythm; 4 Scottish Dances [Allegretto]; Padstow Lifeboat; Chit Chat Polka; Hogan's Heroes/The Adjutant/Hazelmere/Sospan Fach/God Bless the Prince of Wales; Send in the Clowns; Machine Gun Guards; Regimental Marches [Milanollo/The Blues & Royals Quick March/British Grenadiers/Heilan' Laddie/St. Patrick's Day/The Rising of the Lark]; In the Miller Mood [Little Brown Jug/At Last/Anvil Chorus]; Bond of Friendship; Nessun Dorma; People; Circus Gallop; Festive Ov; National Anthem *(rec Royal Festival Hall, London, Dec 3, 1996)* BND ▲ 5131 (16.97)

Irish Guards Band [cnd:Maj. M. J. Henderson]
Emerald Isle—features Emerald Isle; Come Back Paddy Reilly; Micks' March; The Harp That Once through Tara's Halls; Wild Colonial Boy/Black Velvet Band; Minstrel Boy; Carrickfergus; Phil the Fluter's Ball; The March Hare; Guards Armoured Division; Quis Separabit; Capitalcard; Premier Concertante; Pavane; The Silver Trbn Rag; Symphonic Gershwin; Auld Lang Syne & Last Post; Regimental Marches *(rec Feb 3-5, 1997)* BND ▲ 5134 (16.97)

King's Own Royal Border Regimental Band [cnd:D. J. Milgate]
Battle Honours—features The Battle; Namur; Arnhem; Salamanca; The Standard of St. George; Sambre et Meuse; Le Reve Passe; Sarie Marais; Cavalcade of Martial Songs; Hn of the Hunter; Joe Bowman; Capricious Aloysius [cl solo]; Brass Fever; My Fair Lady: Symphonic Scenario for Concert Band; Post Hn Solo:The Huntsman; Regimental Slow March; Regimental Quick March BND ▲ 5075 [DDD] (16.97)

King's Own Scottish Borderers, Pipes & Drums 1st Battalion, Scottish Division Lowland Band
The Spirit of Scotland—features The Spirit of Scotland; Rose of Kelvinside; Highland Cathedral; Will Ye No Come Back Again; Pipers Spirit; Amazing Grace; Hundred Pipers; Flower of Scotland; The Way Old Friends Do; Cuttin' Bracken; Scottish Fant; Mist-Covered Mountains; Scotland the Brave; Company Marches; The Borderers; Blue Bonnets O'er the Border CDIT ▲ 623 (16.97)

Kirkintilloch Band [cnd:Frank Renton]
Brass o' Scotland—features Moray Firth; Flower of Scotland; The Wee Cooper o' Fyfe; Amazing Grace; Ecossaise; My Love is Like a Red, Red Rose; Loch Lomond; Intrada, Song & Dance; The Wee MacGreegor; The Love of My Life; Scottish Rhapsody; Eriksay Love Lilt; Land of the Mountain & the Flood; Skye Boat Song Medley BND ▲ 5078 [DDD] (16.97)

Kneller Hall All-Star Band
Kneller Hall: A Musical Salute to the Royal Military School of Music—features Regimental Quick March of the Royal Military School of Music; Pineapple Poll; The Great Little Army; 1st Suite in E♭ for Military Band; 3 Humoresques; Toccata Marziale; HRH The Duke of Cambridge; Sir Godfrey Kneller; An Original Suite; Serenade; Celebration BND ▲ 5109 [DDD] (16.97)

Light Division Band & Bugles [cnd:Capt. R. Owen]
A Living Tradition—features Silver Bugles; Zorba's Dance; The Rifle Regiment; Sir John Moore; Let's Face the Music & Dance; Here's That Rainy Day; Triomphale; Con Cl; Symphonic Beatles [A Hard Day's Night, Yesterday, I Want to Hold Your Hand, Michelle, Hey Jude]; Gavorkna Fanfare; Drigo's Serenade; Bill; Sabre Dance; Auld Lang Syne/Last Post; Light Division Marches [Light Infantry, Royal Green Jackets, Light Division] BND ▲ 5123 [DDD] (16.97)

McCann, Phillip (cnt), Black Dyke Mills Band
More of the World's Most Beautiful Melodies—features Your tiny hand is frozen, Celeste Aida, Skye Boat Song, slow movt themes from the Bruch & Mendelssohn Vn Cons, etc. CHN ▲ 4502 [DDD] (16.97)
The World's Most Beautiful Melodies—features Ave Maria, Brahms' Lullaby, The Lost Chord, etc. CHN ▲ 4501 [DDD] (16.97)

Massed Bands [cnd:Harry Mortimer], Black Dyke Mills Band [cnd:Maj. Peter Parkes], Besses o' th' Barn Band [cnd:Roy Newsome], IMI Yorkshire Imperial Band [cnd:James Scott]
The British Bandsman Centenary Concert (1987)—features works by Derek Broadbent *(British Bandsman)*, Elgar *(Pomp & Circumstance March 1)*, Grieg *(Elegiac Melody 2, "Spring")*, Ray Steadman *(Centenary Fanfare)*, Arthur Sullivan *(The Lost Chord; Pineapple Poll [Finale]; Yeomen of the Guard [Ov])*, Eric Ball *(Journey into Freedom)*, Elgar Howarth *(Legends)*, Rimsky-Korsakov *(Flight of the bumble bee)*, Peter Graham *(Brilliante)*, Paganini *(Moto perpetuo)*, Ray Steadman *(The Beacons)* CHN ▲ 4513 [DDD] (16.97)

New Columbian Brass Band [cnd:George Foreman]
A Trip to Coney Island: Descriptive Overtures from America's Golden Age, w. Ed Brand (ten), Andrew Moore (ten), Dan Weeks (ten), Phil Lester (bar), Ron Walton (bar), Nick Lawrence (bass), Shelby Reynolds (bass)—features works by Tobani *(A Trip to Coney Island)*, Reeves *(The Evening Call)*, Herman *(Columbus)*, Barnhouse *(The Battle of Shiloh)*, Rollinson *(The Hunting of the Snark)*, Sweet *(The Battle of San Juan Hill) (rec Newlin Hall, Norton Center for the Arts, Centre College, Danville, KY, Nov 6-8, 1995, May 12 & Nov 22, 1996)* DORD ▲ 80153 [DDD] (13.97)
Thatsum Rag!—features B. R. Anthony *(Fan Tan)*, Barnhouse *(Geo'ge Washin'ton Birthday Pahty)*, Belding *(Good Gravy Rag)*, C. Blake *(That Tired Rag)*, Eno *(African Smile)*, Fuhrer *(Zampede Rag)*, J. B. Gardner *(Sarazan)*, A. Holzmann *(Bunch o' Blackberries)*, K. L. King *(Kentucky Sunrise; Walking Frog)*, J. B. Lampe *(Creole Bells; Watermelon Club)*, Losey *(Warm Doughnuts)*, K. Mills *(At a Georgia Campmeeting)*, Pinard *(Thatsum Rag)*, A. Pryor *(Artful Artie; Kansas; Razzazza Mazzazza)*, Von Tilzer *(Cubanola Glide)*, Wenrich *(Smiler; Sweetmeats)* DOR ▲ 93165 [DDD] (16.97)

Ohio State Univ Marching Band [cnd:Jon Woods]
Hey! Buckeyes!—features works by Mussorgsky *(Night on Bald Mountain)*, Williams *(Robin Hood Medley)*, B. Conti *(Right Stuff (Marines Hymn) [all arr Pfaffman]; Gonna Fly Now [arr McDaniel])*, Kern *(This Song Is You)*, Goldsmith *(Star Trek)*, Lecuona *(Malagueña [all arr Tatgenhorst])*, Jewell *(E Pluribus Unum)*, Wilson *(76 Trombones [arr Tatgenhorst])*, plus Buckeye Battle Cry; Hey! Cheer; Fight the Team; Le Regiment; I Wanna Go Back; Hang on Sloopy; Carmen Ohio; Danger Zone; New York, New York; My Way; Final Countdown; Wooly Bully; Blues in the Night; America the Beautiful; Over There; Glenn Miller Medley; Fat Bottomed Girls; Drum Cadence Coronet ▲ COR 411-2 ▮

Parachute Regiment Bands
The Airborne Soldier—features The Ride of the Valkyries; Pomp & Circumstance March 4; The Red Beret; The Winged Dagger; Freefall; Airborne Warrior; Soldiers from the Skies; A Bridge Too Far; Arnhem; Pegasus; All American Soldier; Canadian Airborne; Marche des Parachutists Belges; Les Gars du bigeard; The Dakota; The Paras; Bruneval Raid; 3 Para Songs; Thunderbirds; Stirling of Kier BND ▲ 7007 [DDD] (16.97)

Paragon Ragtime Orch [cnd:Rick Benjamin]
On the Boardwalk *(ragtime music from the Arthur Pryor library)*—features Chatterbox Rag; Memphis Blues; George M. Cohan Medley; Paragon Rag; Heart of America; Made in America; In the Hills of Old Kentucky; Aggravation Rag; Slippery Hank; On the Level You're a Little Devil; An Operatic Nightmare: Desacration Rag No. 2;Snookums Rag; Mr. Black Man; Kentucky Home; That Epidemic Rag!; Under the Mellow Arabian Moon; That Eccentric Rag; Black & White Rag; Old Timers Waltz Medley; St. Louis Rag; On Jersey Shore NPT ▲ 60039 [DDD] (12.97)
The Whistler & His Dog—features ragtime music from the Arthur Pryor library by Biese/Klickman *(Dynamite Rag)*, Cobb/Alexander *(Bring Me Back My Lovin' Honey Boy)*, Janya *(Aviation Rag)*, Joplin *(Pine Apple Rag)*, L. S. Roberts *(Smiles)*, H. Green *(Triplets [w. Erik Charleston (xyl)])*, A. Pryor *(The Love Kiss; The Whistler & His Dog)*, Lake *(La Belle Parisienne)*, Winkler *(Banana Peel Rag)*, Arndt *(Symphonic Nightmare: Descecration Rag No. 1)*, Handy *(Jogo Blues)*, Oleman *(Winter Garden Rag)*, Losey *(Black Rock)*, Hill *(Oh You Drummer)*, Hirsch *(I Wonder Whether I've Loved You All My Life?)*, Botsford *(Grizzly Bear Rag)*, C. L. Roberts *(Junk Man Rag0*, M. L. Lake *(Old Chestnuts)*, Nat Johnson *(Gold Dust Twins Rag)* NPT ▲ 60069 [DDD] (12.97)

Matthew Phillips Circus Band [cnd:Matthew H. Phillips]
Thoroughbred Thunder: Out of the Gate Galops, Screamers & Patriotic Marches—features works by Jos. Richards *(Con Celetira Galop; Speedway Galop; American Ranger March; Show World March; March, "To the Frontier"; Geneva Galop; Ozark Trails March)*, Karl King *(Home Stretch Galop; Emporia Galop; Excelsior Galop; Prestissimo Galop; Majestic Galop; Walsenburg Galop)*, Guy Holmes *(Challenge March; Winter Sports Galop)*, Russell Alexander *(Shoot the Chutes Galop; Steeplechase; Bastinado Galop; Round-Up)*, Fred Huffer *(Thunderbolt Galop)*, Gordon Newham *(White Horse March)*, Wm. P. Chambers *(Equestrian (Buffalo Bill) March)*, Fr. Jewell *(They're Off Galop; March, "In the Lead")*, Sousa *(Black Horse Troop March; Riders for the Flag March)*, Brockenshire *(Cavalry Soldier March)*, John Taylor *(Contest Winners March; Victory Parade March)* ALBA ▲ 294 [DDD] (16.97)

Regimental Band, Black Watch Pipes & Drums
Royal Highlanders—features Regimental Calls; Company; Pipes & Drums Set; Impression on a Scottish Air; Slow & Quick Marches; Royal Highlanders; Pipes & Drums & Marches; Marches; Hebrides Suite; The Ceilidh Band; Pipes & Drums Medley [Andy's Lullaby; Archie MacKenzie of Dumbarton]; March: Army of the Nile; Scots Wha Hae; Medley [Dark Island; Itchy Fingers; The Clumsy Lover]; Distant Hills; The Day Thou Gavest Lord Is Ended; Last Post/Auld Lang Syne; Regimental Lament: Sleep Dearie Sleep; March Off BND ▲ 5069

Rhythm & Bluefield Band [David Bluefield (pno), Chris Bank (sax), Howard Arthur (gtr), Kirwan Brown (elec bass), Tom Hills (dr/perc), Brian Savage (fl), Tim Fox (tpt), Steve Cole (cl)]
Reclassified: Clazzual Sax 2—features works by Schumann *(Träumerei; Ich grolle nicht)*, Chopin *(Nocturne in f, Op. 55/1)*, Sousa *(Washington Post)*, Brahms *(Sym 4 in e)*, Tchaikovsky *(Dance of the Sugar Plum Fairy)*, Debussy *(Reverie)*, Villa-Lobos *(Etude 1 in e)*, Puccini *(Vissi D'arte [from Tosca])*, Grieg *(Hall of the Mtn Ring [from Peer Gynt])*, Beethoven *(Son 8 for Pno)* 84166 ▲ 2345

River City Brass Band
Concert in the Park—features works by Sousa *(El Capital; The Belle of Chicago; Semper Fidelis; Manhattan Beach; The Washington Post; The Liberty Bell; The Stars & Stripes Forever)*, Joplin *(Maple Leaf Rag)*, Fillmore *(Lassus Trombone)*, Bowman *(12th Street Rag)*, plus William Tell Ov; Grand Duchess Galop; The Lost Chord; Love's Old Sweet Song; The Fireman's Polka; plus others RCBB ▲ 192 (14.97)
Footlifters—features Colonel Bogey; Marching through Georgia; Men of Harlech; The British Grenadiers; 76 Trombones; Americans We; The Footlifter; Invictus; The Thunderer; Nobles of the Mystic Shrine; Best Foot Forward; Carnival Day; On the Mall; plus others RCBB ▲ 191 (14.97)
Pittsburgh on Parade—features works by Rogers *(A Mister Roger's Neighborhood Medley)*, Strayhorn *(Chelsea Bridge; Satin Doll)*, Garner *(Misty)*, Mancini *(The Pink Panther Theme)*, Herbert *(Indian Summer; March of the Toys)*, Nestico *(Vaquero)*, Haberman *(Tin-Lizzy Rag)*, plus A Stephen Foster Fant; Pittsburgh Fight Songs; plus others RCBB ▲ 193 (14.97)

Romanian Central Military Band [cnd:I. Croitoru, C. Coman]
Salute from Romania—features works by Vulpe *(Marşul Tineretului)*, Eremia *(Marşul Marinei)*, Ardeleanu *(Sunetul Fanfarei)*, Andreoiu *(Marş Aniversar)*, Paiu *(Victoria)*, plus folksongs *(Hora Pe Loc; Dans Din Oaş; Sîrba Din Gorj; Bănăţeana; Bătuta Moldovenească; Joc De Doi; Invîrtită Şi Haţegană; Intoarsa De La Săceni; Hor Unu Şi Doi; Marş Aniversar; Sanie Cu Zurgălăi [w. Florina Cupsa (sop)]; Perle Româneşti; Geamparale Moldoveneşti; Sîrba Fetiţelor [w. Belu Viorel (pan fl)]; Joc De Doi [w. Belu Viorel (pan fl), Băltăreţu George (sax)] Ciocârlia; Sârba Lui Banu; Deştoapta-t Române) (rec Bucureşti, Romania, May 1996)* World Wind ▲ WWM 500 017 [DDD]

Royal Air Force Cranwell College Band [cnd:D. Stephens]
633 Squadron—features E. Coates *(Dambusters March)*, H. W. Davies *(Royal Air Force March Past)*, Fučík *(Entry of the Gladiators)*, R. Goodwin *(Luftwaffe March; Those Magnificent Men; 633 Squadron)*, Graham *(Champion)*, A. Holzmann *(Blaze Away)*, Javaloyes *(Abanico)*, Knipper *(Cossack Patrol)*, Langford *(Battle of Britain March)*, Latann *(Light of Foot)*, Lockyer *(Pathfinders March)*, Sousa *(Liberty Bell; Washington Post)*, Starke *(With Sword & Lance)*, J. Strauss *(Radetzky March, Op. 228)*, J. F. Wagner *(Under the Double Eagle)*, W. Walton *(Spitfire Prelude)* CHN ▲ 6585 [ADD] (13.97)

Royal Air Force Regiment Band [cnd:Lt. D. W. Compton]
Stage to Screen—features Olympic Fanfare & Theme; Out of Africa; Riverdance; 633 Squadron; Soldier, Soldier; Miss Saigon [sels]; La Callifa/Gabriel's Oboe [from The Mission]; Ad Astra; Last of the Summer Wine; Battle of Britain Suite [sels]; Superman; Star Wars; The Brittas Empire; The Dambusters March BND ▲ 5122 [DDD] (16.97)

Royal Air Force Western Band, Western Big Band [cnd:Lt. D. J. G. Stubbs]
Songs of the West—features March [from Little Suite]; Volga Boat Song; Puzta [from 4 Gypsy Dances]; Weep No More; March: Barnum & Bailey's Favorite; Auld Lang Syne; Songs of the West; The Stars & Stripes Forever; March of the Pacemakers; Scarborough Fair; Wookey Hole [from Mendip Suite]; Is You Is or Is You Ain't My Baby; Cygnus; Swing Low Sweet Chariot BND ▲ 5062 [DDD]

Royal Artillery Band [cnd:Maj. T.S. Davis]
Marches for Europe—features 24 sels including Imperial Echoes; Marche Militaire; Father Rhine; Red Square Review; Rakoczy March; Valdres March; Under Freedom's Banner BND ▲ 5080
Overture!—features Light Cavalry Ov; Hampton Court Ov; Candide Ov; Bronze Horse Ov; A Festive Ov; Zampa Ov; Music for a Festival Ov; The Marriage of Figaro Ov; The Drum Major's Daughter Ov; Colas Bregnon Ov BND ▲ 5121 [DDD] (16.97)

Royal Artillery Band [cnd:Maj. S. V. Hays], Herald Trumpeters
The Queen's Birthday Salute—features works by Curzon *(The Royal Regiment)*, Young *(Royal Birthday; 21-Gun Salute)*, Millman *(Hark, the Bonny Christchurch Bells)*, Kaps *(The Screw Guns)*, Koenig *(The Post Horn Galop)*, Catalinet *(Fanfare Militaire)*, Sullivan *(March of the Peers [from Iolanthe])*, Bliss *(Fanfare for a Jubilant Occasion)*, Elgar *(Land of Hope & Glory)*, trad *(The Royal Artillery Slow March; The Keel Row; Bonnie Dundee; The British Grenadiers; Greensleeves) (rec live, Hyde Park, London, June 13, 1957)* VC ▲ 51 [AAD] (13.97)

Royal Corps of Signals Band [cnd:Maj. D. F. Wall]
The Signaller—features Begone Dull Care; The Signaller; Swift & Sure; HRH The Princess Royal; On Richmond Hill Baht'at; The Donkey Serenade; Lassus Tombone; Vimy Ridge; The Master; Jubilee Ov; Londonberry Air; Largo al Factotum; Blandford Suite; Nessun Dorma; Rondo for Hns; The Carnival of Venice; Con for Drum Set; Farandole; The History of the Royal Corps of Signals BND ▲ 5114 [DDD] (16.97)

Royal Dragoon Guards Regimental Band [cnd:R. Pennington]
Fame & Renown—features Dettingen Fanfare; Norma; Soldiers Chorus/Sprig of Shillelagh; St. Patrick's Day; God Bless the Prince of Wales; Regimental Slow March of the Royal Dragoon Guards; Regimental Quick March of the Royal Dragoon Guards; Killaloe; Irish Rhap; Yorkshire Relish; Nessun Dorma; Les Miserables; 1 Moment in Time; I Know Him So Well; That's What Friends Are For; Highland Cathedral; Post Horn Galop; Londonderry Air; Echoes of an Era [Beatles Medley]; Regimental Quick March of the Royal Dragoon Guards [reprise] BND ▲ 5110 [DDD] (16.97)

Royal Electrical & Mechanical Engineers Corps Band [cnd:Maj. Kevin C. Lamb]
An Operatic Festival—features works by Wagner *(March [from Der Ring des Nibelungen])*, Lalo *(Le Roi d'Ys [Ov])*, Puccini *(Vissi d'arte [from Tosca])*, Mascagni *(Easter Hymn [from Cavalleria rusticana])*, Delibes *(Flower Duet [from Lakmé])*, Bizet *(Carmen [suite])*, Mozart *(Le nozze di Figaro [Ov])*, Bizet *(Deep inside the Sacred Temple [from Les Pêcheurs de perles])*, Cimarosa *(L'impresario in angustie [Ov])*, Verdi *(Slave's Chorus [from Nabucco])*, Rossini *(Una voce poco fa [from Il barbiere di Siviglia])*, Mussorgsky *(Coronation Scene [from Boris Godunov])* BND ▲ 5129

Royal Engineers Corps Band [cnd:Lt. Col. P. R. Evans]
Quality Plus—features March: Quality Plus; Stage Centre; Michael! [Bad; I Just Can't Stop Loving You; The Way You Make Me Feel; Man in the Mirror]; Stardust; Arnhem; John Williams's Evening at Pops [We're Looking Good; The Cowboys; The Dance of the Witches; Olympic Fanfare & Theme]; Corps March: Wings; Les Miserables; Theme for Zara; The Sapper Patrol; Jubilee Ov; Europe United; Reflective Mood; Robin Hood, Prince of Thieves BND ▲ 5068 (16.97)

Royal Highland Fusiliers Regimental Band Pipes & Drums
Afore Ye Go—features Royal Highland Fusiliers; The Cross of St. Andrew; Song for Suzanne; Birkenhead; Pipe Dreams; Be Ye Also Ready; Scottish Serenade; Victory Salute; Oft in the Stilly Night; Pipe Set; Bays of Harris; Sunset Salute; 79th Farewell to Gibralter; My Own Land; 10th H.L.I. Crossing the Rhine; Misty Morn; Assaye; Afore Ye Go; 74th Officers Mess Call; Company Marches; Regimental Marches; Regimental Slow March; Regimental Quick March; March Medley BND ▲ 5102 [DDD] (16.97)

Royal Irish Regiment Band Bugles Pipes & Drums [cnd:Capt. C. C. Attrill]
Reflections—features Fanfare "Blackthorn"; General Salute "Let Erin Remember"; Green Glens of Antrim/Star of the County Down; Ulster Division; O'Donnell Abu; Paddy Carey; Eileen Allanagh; Let Erin Remember; Willow Tree; March Off; Kerry March; 7 Towers March; A Caubeen Trimmed with Blue; Faugh-a-Ballagh; Bugle March Medley; Fanfare:Hillsborough; Reflections; The Last of the Great Whales; Loose Canon Marches; South Down Militia; Nora Creina/Barrossa; Off, Off Said the Stranger; Killaloe BND ▲ 5133 (16.97)

Royal Lancers Band [cnd:Capt. D. Burton]
Days of Glory—features Days of Glory; God Bless the Prince of Wales; Stable Jacket; Mack & Mabel [Ov]; Reilly Ace of Spies; Salute to Glory; Feelin' Free; Casterbridge; Song for Ina; In Celebration; Lonely Bugler; Summer's Lease; Roar of Armour; Lancer's Farewell; Strike up the Band; The Galloping Major; Cornish Ov; Midway March; Suo Gan & Cavalry Last Post BND ▲ 5137 (16.97)

Royal Welsh Fusiliers Regimental Band [cnd:Paul Goodwin]
We'll Keep a Welcome—features Castell Conwy; Namur; The Vanished Army [They Never Die]; The Royal Welch Fusiliers; March of the Royal Welch Fusiliers; Salute the Prince of Wales; The Prince of Wales; Bond of Friendship; My Congratulations; The Flash & Hackle; Castell Coch; Men of Harlech; Southfield; The Princess of Wales; Serenade; A Nightingale Sang in Berkeley Square; That's Entertainment; We'll Keep a Welcome; Saint David; National Anthem; Of Noble Anthem; Of Noble Race Was Shenkin; Jenny Jones; The British Grenadiers; For They Are Jolly Good Fellows; The Regimental Slow March; The Regimental Quick Marches BND ▲ 5107 [DDD] (16.97)

Sarpsburg Symphonic Wind Band *(also known as the HV-01 Home Guard Band)* [cnd:Lt. Col. Christer O. Johannesen]
Overalt-Alltid!—features works by Damberg *(Heimevernsmarsj)*, Johansen *(Frigjøringsmarsj)*, Rydberg *(Italia Konsertmarsch 2)*, Chernetsky *(March of the Minesweepers)*, Thingnæs *(Norsk Politimarsj; Luftforsvarets Jubileumsmarsj)*, Zeman/Olbert *(Prager Gassen [Zástavská] march)*, Alford *(Thin Red Line)*, Fillmore *(His Honor)*, Kent *(White Cliffs of Dover)*, Widquist *(Chefsmarsch)*, Williams *(Symphonic Marches)*, King *(We'll Meet Again)*, F. W. Schubert *(Göta Livgardes marsch)* Great Lakes Music Enterprises Inc ▲ HV01

Scottish Division Lowland Band & Pipers [cnd:Capt. G. O. Jones]
Edinburgh Castle—features March: Scotland the Brave; Bonnie Black Isle; March: Holyrood; Will Ye No Come Back Again?; March: Pentland Hills; Festoso [from Caledonia]; March: Edinburgh Castle; Pipes Set: 3/4 Marches [Colin's Cattle, Bloody Fields of Flanders, The Shoals of Herring]; March: The Cross of St. Andrew; Hebrides Suite [The Peat Fire Flame, An Eriskay Love Lilt, The Road to the Isles]; Ye Banks & Braes; Misty Morn; Dunedin; Pipes Set: 6/8 Marches [Balmoral Highlanders, Cameronian Rant, Mrs. McPherson of Inveran]; Regimental Slow March: The Garb of Old Gaul; Regimental March of the Royal Scots (The Royal Regiment): Dumbarton Drums; Regimental March of the Royal Highland Fusiliers: Whistle O'er the Lave O't/British Grenadiers, plus others BND ▲ 5115 [DDD] (16.97)

Sellers Engineering Band
Legend in Brass—features works by J. Curnow, C. Jenkins, E. Leidzen, E. Ball, R. Newton, R. Redhead CHN ▲ 4531 [DDD] (17.97)
We Love a Parade—features works by Fucik, M. Wilson, Coates, Bizet, Schubert, Jessel, Tchaikovsky, Mozart, Meyerbeer CHN ▲ 4527 [DDD] (17.97)
The World of Brass—features works by Delibes *(Lakmé [Flower Duet])*, Dvořák *(New World Sym [Largo])*, Alan Fernie *(Scottish Rhap)*, Grieg *(The Last Spring)*, Gordon Langford *(An Australian Fant; A Russian Fant; 3 Tenors Fant)*, Rimsky-Korsakov *(Capriccio Espagnole [sels])*, Sousa *(The Stars & Stripes Forever)*, Joh. Strauss *(Blue Danube Waltz)*, trad *(The Ash Grove; Blaydon Races; The Rose of Tralee)* CHN ▲ 4511 [DDD] (16.97)

Soncino Civic Band [cnd:Giancarlo Locatelli]
Rhapsody in Band—features works by Holst *(Suite in F, Op. 28/2)*, Brossè *(Music for a Celebration; 7 Inch-Framed)*, de Meij *(Aquarium, Op. 5)*, Grundman *(American Folk Rhap No. 3)*, van der Roost *(Canterbury Choral)*, Cesarini *(Convergentes)*, Lennon/McCartney *(Yellow Submarine [arr Reijiko Koroku]) (rec Dec 1995 & Mar 1996)* STRV ▲ 80002 [DDD] (12.97)

Stadacona Band of Maritime Forces Atlantic [cnd:Lt. Peter Van der Horden]
On the Quarter Deck—features On the Quarter Deck; Parade of the Tall Ships; Helen Creighton Folk Songs; The Vedette; Ov to an Unwritten Comedy; Concertino for Fl; 7 Seas Ov; Les Arrivants; The Gladiator's Farewell; Anne Murray Medley; Procession of the Nobles; A Nova Scotia Farewell; Barrett's Privateers; Navy Medley; H. M. Jollies; Heart of Oak BND ▲ 5113 [DDD] (16.97)

U.S. Military Band
American Military Marches—features Stars & Stripes Forever; The Thunderer; El Capitán; Semper Fidelis; High School Cadets; Rifle Regiment; Washington Post March; Manhattan Beach March; The Liberty Bell; The Picador; Hands Across the Sea; Departure of the Gladiators; The Bridge over the River Kwai ["Colonel Bogey"]; Florentine March; The Spirit of Liberty; The Conqueror; National Emblem; Washington Grays; Diplomat March; Pomp & Circumstance; Radetzky March ACCO ▲ 300132 [AAD]

Virginia Grand Military Band [cnd:Loras John Schissel]
Marching Along—features works by Hughes *(Acropolis)*, Sousa *(The Welch Fusilier; Sabre & Spurs; Homeward Bound)*, L. B. Smith *(The March King)*, Klohr *(The Billboard)*, Fillmore *(His Excellency; Men of Ohio)*, Alexander *(Olympia Hippodrome)*, K. L. King *(Barnum & Bailey's Favorite; Tiger Triumph)*, Cupero *(Honey Boys on Parade)*, Green *(The Viator)*, Holzmann *(Blaze Away!)*, Barnhouse *(Idaho)*, Morris *(The Kilties) (rec Bishop Denis J. O'Connell High School, Arlington, VA, Sept 27, 1997)* Walking Frog ▲ WFR 430

Welsh Guards Band [cnd:Maj. P. Hannam]
Music from the Changing of the Guard—features Marching to the Palace:To Your Guard, The Empire, Birdcage Walk, The Guardsman; Advance in Slow Time:Long Live Elizabeth; Incidental Music:Royal Review, Oxford Street, Music of the Night, Waterloo March, Welsh Airs & Fancies, Children's Patrol, Gold & Silver Waltz, The Spirit of Pageantry, Welsh Rhap, Great & Glorious; Return to the Barracks:Guards Parade, Lord Rothermere's March, Guards Armoured Division, The King's Guard, The Welshman BND ▲ 5045 [DDD] (16.97)

West Point Military Band [cnd:Capt. MacDonally]
Sousa & American Marches—features marches by Sousa & Sweet, Lighten, Beethoven, Seitz & Klohr † Sousa:Marches & Dances; Stars & Stripes Forever TUXE ▲ 5032 (10.97)

Williams Fairey Band [cnd:James Gourlay, Bryan Hurdley]
Bone Idyll, w. Brett Baker (trbn)—features works by Dewhurst *(Brasilia)*, Saint-Saëns *(Cavatine)*, Bourgeois *(Bone Idyll)*, Langford *(Rhap)*, Sparke *(Prelude & Scherzo)*, Henley/Silbar *(The Wind beneath My Wings)*, Guilmant *(Morceau symphonique)*, Godard *(Berceuse de Jocelyn)*, David *(Concertino)*, trad *(Annie Laurie; Nobody Knows the Trouble I See)* CHN (Brass) ▲ 4543 (16.97)

Spanish Impressions—features works by Texidor *(Amparito Roca; Bonds of Friendship-Spanish March [all arr A. Winter])*, Ravel *(Alborada del gracioso [arr D. Bourgeois])*, Delibes *(Maids of Cadiz [w. Brian Taylor (cnt); arr G. Langford])*, Falla *(Ritual Fire Dance [arr A. Street])*, Bizet *(Carmen Fant [arr G. Langford])*, Granados *(Andalucia [w. Simon Stonehouse (flgl); arr H. Snell])*, Giménez *(La boda de Luis Alonso [arr J. Gourlay])*, Ellerby *(Evocations)*, Newton *(4 Spanish Impressions)* CHN ▲ 4544 (16.97) ▮

BANDS COLLECTIONS

Bands & Pipes from the Borders: Berwick Military Tattoo 1996, w. King's Division Waterloo Band, Northumbria Police Band, Northumberland Royal Regiment of Fusiliers Band, Scottish Division Highland Band, Massed Military Bands—features Opening Fanfare; Pipes & Drums Medley; Finale—Pipes, Drums & Bands BND ▲ 5130 (16.97)

Famous Arrangements by Johan de Meij—features performances by Royal Military Band of Holland [cnd:Pierre Kuijpers] *(Steffaro:March to Mars; Tchaikovsky:Mazeppa [Berceuse]; Williams:Star Wars Saga; Shanklin:Chanson d'Amour [w. F. H. A. Hendrix (ten sax)])*, Royal Airforce Band of Holland [cnd:Johan de Meij] *(Ulvaeus/Andersson:Chess [Highlights])*, Amsterdam Wind Orch [cnd:Heinz Friesen] *(Barry:Out of Africa)*, Brabant Conservatory Sym Windband [cnd:Jan Cober] *(C. M. Schönberg:Miss Saigon [Sym Portrait])*, Royal Military Band of Holland [cnd:Jan van Ossenbruggen] *(W. Faust:Honky Tonk Ragtime; Crewe/Gaudio:Can't Take My Eyes Off You)* World Wind ▲ WWM 500 016 [DDD]

The Great Marches
Vol. 1—features Colonel Bogey; Blaze Away; On the Quarterdeck; Liberty Bell; Washington Grays; Army of the Nile; Berliner Luft; Great Little Army; Radetzky March; With Sword & Lance; National Emblem; Holyrood; Semper Fidelis; Boots & Saddles; La Reve Passe; Scarlet & Gold; The Thunderer; Coburg; The Thin Red Line; Anchors Aweigh; Old Comrades; The Standard of St. George BND ▲ 5006 [DDD] (16.97)

Vol. 2—features Hands across the Sea; Fame & Glory; Marche Lorraine; General Mitchell; Children of the Regiment; High School Cadets; Through Bolts & Bars; Sons of the Brave; Preobrajensky March; Sarafand; Invincible Eagle; Staffordshire Knot; To Your Guard; Le Pere la Victoire; The Skywriter; Waldmere; Triumph of Right; Arromanches; Ridgewood; Steafast & True; Glorius Victory; El Abanico; Marche Militaire BND ▲ 5018 [DDD] (16.97)

Vol. 3—features Voice of the Guns; Golden Spurs; Wings; Royal Air Force March Past; Black Horse Troop; The Gunners; Barvada; Officer of the Day; The Mad Major; Red Cloak; Down the Mall; Iron Regiment; The Trombone King; Cavalry of the Clouds; Imperial Life Guards; The Tpt Major; Grid Iron Club; My Congratulations; Royal Standard; The Purple Pageant; Marche des Parachutists Belges; Chief of Staff; Inkerman; Pentland Hills; Imperial March BND ▲ 5029 [DDD] (16.97)

Vol. 4—features Dunedin; Under the Double Eagle; Arnhem; Fearless & True; Crown of Joy; San Lorenzo; Eagle Squadron; Sambre et Meuse; Punjaub; The Queen's Company; Trafalgar; Guard's Armoured Division; Belphegor; Out of the Blue; Secundrabad; Old Panama; Nijmegen; The Black Horse; The Middy; The Drum Majorette; Mechanised Infantry; Birdcage Walk; Fehrbelliner Reitermarsch; New Colonial; The Star of St. Patrick BND ▲ 5053 [DDD] (16.97)

Vol. 5—features The Contemptibles; On the Square; Aces High; The King's Guard; Hoch und Deutschmeister; The Vedette; Cavalry Walk; Carmen March; H.M. Jollies; Alma; Sounding Brass; B.B. & C.F.; March of the Royal British Legion; British 8th; Barnum & Bailey's Favourite; Guard's Parade; The Old Gray Mare; Grandioso; Flying Eagle; Cavalry of the Steppes; Through Night to Light; Blue Devils; Marche Americaine; My Regiment BND ▲ 5060 [DDD] (16.97)

Vol. 6—features The Guardsman; Valdres March; Europe United; Parade of the Champions; Namur; Century of Progress; On Parade; Light of Foot; The Jolly Airman; The Crusader; Nairn; Wembley Way; The Watch Tower; Wings; Death or Glory; The Prince; The Captain General; Sabre & Spurs; Light Division; The Advance Guard; Spanish March; Royal Welch Fusiliers; Schoenfeld March; Les Clarions Anglais; Princess of Wales March; Pathfinders BND ▲ 5074 [DDD] (16.97)

Vol. 7—features Adjutant General's Corps Band [cnd:M. Torrent] *(Safroni:Imperial Echoes)*, Corps of Royal Engineers Band [cnd:P. Evans] *(F. Jewell:Quality Plus)*, Grenadier Guards Band [cnd:D. Kimberley] *(Dunkler:Grenadier Mars; Zehle:Army & Marine)*, H.M. Royal Marines Band [cnd:G. Hoskins], H.M. Royal Marines School of Music Band [cnd:G. Hoskins] *(T. Bidgood:Vimy Ridge)*, H.M. Royal Marines Band [cnd:P. Heming] *(F. V. Dunn:Under the White Ensign)*, H.M. Royal Marines Commandos Band [cnd:D. Cole] *(W. J. Adams:Royal Buglers)*, H.M. Royal Marines School of Music Band [cnd:G. Hoskins] *(H. L. Blankenburg:Gladiator's Farewell)*, King's Own Royal Border Regimental Band [cnd:D. Milgate] *(F. V. Dunn:Sarie Marais)*, Regimental Band of the Black Watch [cnd:T. Calton] *(Calton:Royal Highlanders)*, Regimental Band of the 13th/18th Royal Hussars [cnd:A. Chatburn] *(Traditional:Ca ira)*, Regimental Band of the 14th/20th Kings Hussars [cnd:R. Sands] *(Traditional:Gardes de la Reine)*, Regimental Band of the 16th/5th Queen's Royal Lancers [cnd:R. Bashford] *(R. Bashford:Stable Jacket; G. O. Jones:Forward of the Line; Thundering Guns)*, Royal Air Force Central Band [cnd:H. Hingley] *(G. Richards:Jaguar)*, Royal Air Force Cranwell College Band [cnd:D. Davison] *(Sousa:Stars & Stripes Forever)*, Royal Air Force German Band [cnd:H. Hingley] *(Hingley:Tornado)*, Royal Artillery Band [cnd:T. Davis] *(Lincke:Father Rhine; Nowotny:Under Freedom's Banner)*, Royal Artillery Orch [cnd:F. Renton] *(V. Herbert:March of the Toys)*, Royal Corps of Transport Band [cnd:T. Kenny] *(Traditional:Wait for the Wagon)*, St. George's Royal Regiment of Fusiliers Band [cnd:C. Attrill] *(A. Prévost:Marche de la Gendarmerie National Belge)*, Welsh Guards Band [cnd:P. Hannam] *(Tulip:Empire)* BND ▲ 5112 [DDD] (16.97)

Vol. 8, w. Coldstream Guards Regimental Band, Royal Scots Dragoon Guards Regimental Band, Her Majesty's Royal Marines Band, Royal Air Force Massed Bands, et al.—features Bond of Friendship; The 3 D. G.'s; Washington Post; Fortune Favours the Bold; Chimes of Liberty; Salamanca; Queen's Division; The Rifle Regiment; Quickest & Best; Battleaxe Company; El Capitan; Cockney Cocktail; Viscount Nelson; Red Square Review; Regimentsgruss; Swift & Sure; Under the Allied Banner; Blow Away the Morning Dew; Marche Vanier; Ship to Shore; All American Soldier; Agrippa; First Post; Pride of Lions; St. Louis Blues March BND ▲ 5128 (16.97)

Into History—features performances by Regimental Band *(Colonel in Chief; Royal Fireworks Ov; I Vow to Thee My Country; Bolero; Intrada & Ov [from Music for a Festival]; Con for 2 Tpts; Southerlands Ov; The Battle of Aliwal; Punjaub; Jerusalem; Forward of the Line; The Allies; Scarlet Lancers; Fant Prelude on Crimond)*, 5th Royal Irish Lancers *(St. Patrick's Day; Slow March)*, Queen's Royal Lancers *(Slow March; Scarlet & Green; Queen Charlotte; Stable Jacket; Slow March)* BND ▲ 5082 [DDD] (16.97)

Marsz, Marsz Polonia, w. Krakow Garrison Military Band, Polish Air Force Band, Polish Army Band, Polish Navy Band, Pomeranian Military District Band, Silesian Military District Band, Warsaw Military District Band—features works by Wybicki *(Hymn Polski [arr Rezler])*, Melcer & Rezler *(Marsz Generalski)*, Kurpiński *(Warszawianka [arr Pawlowski])*, Sledziński *(Marsz I Brygady)*, Nowowiejski *(Pod Sztandarem Pokoju)*, Kolakowski *(Strzelcy Maszerują)*, Kuczera *(Bohater)*, Maj *(Na Falach Eteru; P O S)*, Lewacki *(Marsz No. 7; Marsz-Krakowiak No. 2)*, Zieliński *(Serce W Plecaku [arr Wiśniewski])*, Kwiatkowski *(Podniebne Orly)*, Landowski *(Marsz Wiwat; Marsz Eskadra)*, Szabat *(Slawa Zolnierza Polskiego)*, Dulin *(Marsz Floty Polskiej)*, Rzepus *(Polskim Kombatantom; Orp Blyskawica [both arr Kwiatkowski])*, Karaś *(Vivat Polonia)*, Gajdeczka *(Pancerniak)*, Latwis *(Marsz Lotnikow [arr Schubert])*, anon *(Marsz, Marsz Polonia [arr Szulia]; Szara Piechota [arr Waliszewski]; Wesola Marynarska Wiara; Marszowe Melodie Morskie [both arr Stromski]; Marsz Kozietulskiego [arr Kwiatkowski])* POLN ▲ ECD 064 [DDD]

Music from the 1991 Royal Tournament—features performances by Fanfare Trumpeters, Band & Organ *(The Tournament)*, Massed Bands *(A Mozart Pageant; Grand Finale)*, King's Troop Royal Horse Artillery *(Musical Drive)*, Royal Horse Guards & 1st Dragoons *(The Mounted Band of the Blues & Royals; The Household Cavalry Musical Band)*, Royal Corps of Signals Band *(The Royal Air Force Police Dogs; Interval Music; Music for the Royal Navy Field Gun Competition; The American Civil War)*, 1st Battalion Scots Guard Pipes & Drums *(Pipes & Drums)* BND ▲ 5091 (16.97)

Music from the 1992 Royal Tournament—features performances by Royal Air Force Massed Bands *(Mahler:Sym 5 [sels]; Sym 7 [Rondo]; Elgar:Sym 1 [sels]; plus Battle in the Air; Song That Saw Us Through; The Dam Busters March; Strike up the Band; Rhap in Blue; Ad Astra; Lords of the Air; God Save the Queen; RAF March Past)*, Corps Royal Electric & Mechanical Engineers Staff Band *(Bonnie Dundee; Old Towler; Gary Owen; Hunting the Hare; 'Round the Marble Arch; Come Lasses & Lads; The Galloping Major; Light Cavalry; Post Horn Galop; John Peel; The Campbells Are Coming; Royal Artillery Slow March; The Keel Row; RAF Regiment March "Holyrood"; Fanfare)*, plus others BND ▲ 5092 [DDD] (16.97)

Music from the 1993 Royal Tournament—features performances by Her Majesty's Royal Marines Massed Bands *(The Opening; Window Ladder Display & Cutlass Display; The Finale/Victory/The Battle of Trafalgar; The Celebration [Mast Manning]; Commemoration of the Battle of the Atlantic 1943; National Anthem)*, Royal Artillery Band *(The Musical Drive of the King's Troop; Royal Horse Artillery; Mountain Rescue; Army Dog Display; The Royal Signals Motor Cycle Display Team [The White Helmets]; Interval Music; Music for the Royal Navy Field Gun Competition)*, Russian Navy Band *(The Russian Navy Band & Dancers; March Off)* BND ▲ 5093 [DDD] (16.97)

Music from the 1994 Royal Tournament, w. Coldstream Guards Band, Grenadier Guards Band, Irish Guards Band, Life Guards Band, Welsh Guards Band, et al.—features Jupiter [I Vow to Thee My Country]; Fanfare & Prelude [from Götterdämmerung]; The Ride of the Valkyries; The World in Union; Musical Drive of the King's Troop, Royal Horse Artillery; The Royal Engineers in Action; The Ark [Animals Who Have Served]; Allied Rapid Reaction Corps; Worcester Castle/Crown of State/Pomp & Circumstance No. 4; Salut d'amour; Pomp & Circumstance No. 1; Interval Music [Music of the Adjutant General's Corps]; Music for the Royal Navy Field Gun Race; Music for the Royal Air Force Dog Display; Grand Inaugural March; Birdland; Pipes & Drums [Highland Laddie; 79th Farewell to Gibraltar]; others BND ▲ 5094 [DDD] (16.97)

Music from the 1997 Royal Tournament, w. Blues & Royals Band, Household Division Massed Bands, Hussars & Light Dragoons Band, Massed Pipes & Drums, New Zealand Armed Forces Maori Warriors & Maidens—features 17 sels including Opening Fanfare; March Off; Ov 1812; How Much is the Doggie in the Window? BND ▲ 5097 (16.97)

Musical Traditions in Blue & Gold—features performances by United States Naval Academy Band *(Wagner:Meistersinger [Ov]; Naval Academy March; Chester; Henry Mancini Medley; America 1st; American Salute; America, the Dream Goes On; Sea Medley; Hands Across the Sea; Marine Medley)*, United States Naval Academy Glee Club *(Tho' We Roam the Seas; Boston Harbor; Spanish Ladies; Must Jesus Bear the Cross Alone?; Were You There?; Zion's Walls)*, Naval Academy Band, Naval Academy Glee Club *(Annapolis Medley)* Richardson ▲ 3297700172

Nationale Taptoe Breda 1997—features performances by Koninklijke Militaire Kapel [cnd:P. J. P. M. Jansen] *(R. Strauss:Festmusik der Stadt Wien; Rosza:Ben Hur [Parade of the Charioteers]; Rosenman:Star Trek [The Voyage Home]; Conti:North & South; Mars/Grevenbroek:Ondersteunen Is Onze Missie)*, Bereden Wapens Trompetterkorps [cnd:J. W. Schoonhoven] *(H. Fillmore:Greased Lightning; Rolling Thunder)*, Johan Willem Friso Kapel [cnd:W. A. M. E. Schillings] *(Oh When the Saints; Gershwin:Strike up the Band [w. Cindy Oudshoorn (sgr)]; Sousa:Stars & Stripes Forever [w. G. Flik (pic)])*, Regio-Orkest [cnd:A. G. van Dun] *(Reijnhoudt:Defileermars der Koninklijke Marechaussee)*, Fanfara a Cavallo del Reggimento dei Carabinieri a Cavallo [cnd:Maresciallo D. Antonucci] *(Williams:Jhons; Di Martino:Diana; A. Lanciani:Principe Eugenio)*, Koninklijke Luchtmacht Kapel [cnd:J. Pommer] *(Schifrin:Mission Impossible Theme; Broughton:Jag Theme; Hermans:De Wandelclub; Böhmer:Mars van de Koninklijke Militaire School Luchtmacht)*, His Majesty the King's Guard Band [cnd:I. Andresen] *(Hvam:Gardemarsj; Caspersen:Bøygen; Svendsen:Fest-Polonaise, Op. 12; Schiolberg:Gammel Jegermarsj)*, Koninklijke Marine Marinierskapel [cnd:M. W. M. Hamers] *(Goldsmith:The Wind & the Lion; Jarre:Lawrence of Arabia Theme; Shostakovich:Jazz Suite 2 [Dance 1]) (rec Aug 21-30, 1997)* World Wind ▲ WWM 500 028 [DDD]

One Hundred Thousand Welcomes, w. Black Watch Pipes & Drums, Blues & Royals Band, Life Guards Band—features 19 sels including Amazing Grace; Auld Lang Syne; Scotland the Brave; Bluebells of Scotland; Ode to Joy BND ▲ 5136 (16.97)

Pass in Review—features performances by United States Marine Band *(Sousa:Semper Fidelis; Stars & Stripes Forever; Hail to the Spirit of Liberty; Hands Across the Sea; Jack Tar; Beau Ideal; Anderson:Bugler's Holiday; Barber:Commando March; Goldman:Chimes of Liberty; Meacham:American Patrol; Grafulla:Washington Grays; Reeves:2nd Regiment Connecticut National Guard; Wagner:Walkure Fant)*, *(plus Marines' Hymn; March of the Women Marines; March of the Olympians; Americal the Beautiful; La Marseillaise; Star Spangled Banner; Armed Forces Medley; American Pageant)*, Symphony Arts Orch *(Rodgers:Victory at Sea (suite))*, United States Naval Academy Men's Glee Club *(Eternal Father; Taps)* Richardson 2-▲ 3297700222

Set Sail—features performances by Naval Academy Glee Club *(Anchors Aweigh; A-Roving; Blow the Man Down; Lowlands; What Shall We Do with a Drunken Sailor?; Farewell to Grog; Old Man Noah; Shenandoah; High Barbary; Navy Blue & Gold; We Saw the Sea; We Are from Crabtown/We Are the Old Nyvee/ Don't give up the Ship; Down, Down, Underneath the Ocean; Bless 'em All; Eyes of the Fleet/Navy Victory March/Up & at e'm Navee; America the Beautiful; Eternal Father; Star-Spangled Banner)*, Naval Drum & Bugle Corps *(Battle; Spirit of America; Thunderer)*, Full Sail Trio *(Song of the Fishes; Rhyme of the Chivalrous Shark)*, Naval Academy Band *(Anchors Aweigh [2 versions]; Marines' Hymn; Nobel Men; Footlifter; American Legion; Christopher Columbus; Army of the Nile)* Richardson ▲ 3297700072

WMC 1997 Highlights:Brassband—features performances by Rupelmonde Mercator Brass [cnd:Patrick van der Meiren] *(Sparke:Triptych for Brassband)*, Bakkeveen Spijkerpakkenband [cnd:Sijtze van der Hoek] *(Haan:Inspiration)*, Buizingen Brass Band Union [cnd:Luc Vertommen] *(Graham:The Dawning)*, Leicester Ratby Cooperative Brass Band [cnd:Kevin Steward] *(Aagard-Nilsen:The Binding of the Wolf)*, Wealdstone Desford Colliery Band [cnd:Frank Renton] *(Wilby:Paganini Vars)*, Stef Pillaert (eup), Willebroek Brass Band [cnd:Frans Violet] *(Symphonic variants for Eup & Band) (rec live, Roda Hall, Kerkrade, July 1997)* World Wind ▲ WWM 500031 [DDD]

WMC 1997 Highlights:Fanfare—features performances by Andels Fanfare Corps [cnd:Danny Oosterman] *(Goorhuis:La Forza Della Loro Vita)*, Koninklijke Fanfare Eensgezindheid Maasbracht-Beek [cnd:Fried Dobbelstein] *(Wagner:Elsa's Procession [from Lohengrin])*, Koninklijke Fanfare St. Caecilia, Puth [cnd:Frenk Rouschop] *(Roost:Avalon)*, Fanfare St. Wiro 't Reutje St. Odiliënberg [cnd:R. Schrader] *(Toebosch:16'85)*, Gelders Fanfare Orkest [cnd:Tijmen Botma] *(Jong:Omaggio a Kristina D.)*, Kempisch Jeugd Fanfareorkest, Herentals [cnd:Manu Mellaerts] *(Roost:Con Grosso Tpt, Trbn & Orch)*, Koninklijke Fanfare De Vriendenkring Kessenich [cnd:Laurens Hendrikx] *(Goorhuis:Innocent Condemned)*, Koninklijke Erkende Fanfare St. Cecilia, Bocholtz [cnd:Jos Stoffels] *(Brand:Dreams & Fancies)*, Chr. Muziekvereniging Oranje, Minnertsga [cnd:Jouke Hoekstra] *(Mertens:Aragorn)*, Koninklijke Fanfare Eensgezindheid Maasbracht-Beek [cnd:Fried Dobbelstein] *(Dikker:Wind & Water in Triple Movt)*, Fanfare St. Caecilia Schinnen [cnd:Harry Dieteren] *(Vliex:Tintagel Castle) (rec live, Roda Hall, Kerkrade, July 1997)* World Wind 2-▲ WWM 500030 [DDD]

WMC 1997 Highlights:Symphonic Wind Orchestra—features performances by RUM Blasersymfonikar [cnd:Lars Benstrop] *(Hovland:Fanfare & Chorale)*, Thorn Koninklijke Harmonievan [cnd:Jan Cober] *(Zacares Fort:Diptic Symfonic)*, Tilburg Koninklijke Harmonie Orpheus [cnd:Hennie Ramaekers] *(Absil:Danses Bulgares, Op. 103)*, Koninklijke Harmonie Ste. Cécile Eijsden [cnd:Jan Cober] *(Kodály:Vars on a Hungarian Folk Song, "The Peacock")*, Agrupacion Musical de Manuel [cnd:Azael Tormo Muñoz] *(Woolfenden:Gallimaufry)*, Eijsden Koninklijke Oude Harmonie [cnd:Ben Essers] *(Weiner:Ungarische Volkstänze)*, Harmonie De Volksgalm Zichen Zussen Bolder [cnd:Sandro Moretti] *(Holst:Songs of the West)*, Klaawaals Symfonisch Blaasorkest N. L. S. [cnd:Wim Steinmann] *(Sparke:Dance Movt)*, RK Gildenbondsharmonie Boxtel [cnd:Frenk Rouschop] *(Shostakovitch:The Bolt Suite [Ov; General Dance & Apotheosis])*, Banda del Associazione Musicale Lao Silesu Samassi [cnd:Pittau Francesco] *(Mertens:Xenia Sarda) (rec live, Roda Hall, Kerkrade, July 1997)* WWIN 2-▲ 500029 [DDD]

BAROQUE MUSIC

Academy of Ancient Music Orch [cnd:Christopher Hogwood]
Academy of Ancient Music—features works by Pachelbel, Vivaldi, Gluck, Handel PLOI ▲ 10553 (16.97) ▮ 10553

Adams, Piers (rcrs), Howard Beach (hpd/pno), D. Watkin (vc)
The English Nightingale—features works by Bach *(Son in g, BWV 1034)*, Van Eyck *(Vars on Engels Nachtegaeltje; Vars on Wat Zal Men Op Den Avond Doen)*, Telemann *(Fants 1 & 12)*, Corelli *(Son in F, Op. 5/4)*, G. Bassano *(Divisions on Onques Amour)*, W. Croft *(Son in G)*, E. Krähmer *(Concert Polonaise; Rondeau Hongrois)*, D. Castello *(Son Prima)* ALBA ▲ 88 [DDD]

Agrupación Música [cnd:Enzo Gieco]
Peru—Guatemala: Music of the Latin American Cathedrals, 16th through 18th Century Baroque Music from Unpublished Manuscripts—features works by Tomás Pascual *(3 Villancicos)*, Roque Ceruti *(A cantar un villancico)*, Jose de Orejón y Aparicio *(Ah del dia)*, Frere Esteban Ponce de Leon *(Venid, venid, deidades)*, anon *(Hanac Pachap; Un juguetico de fuego)* AB ▲ 1425 (13.97)

Almajano, Marta (sop), Al Ayre Español [cnd:Eduardo Lopez Banzo]
Barroco Español, Vol. 1—features works by Literes, Galán, Torres, Valls, Iribarran CONI ▲ 75605-77325-2 [DDD]

Arita, Masahiro (trns fl), Tetsuya Nakano (vl), Chiyoko Arita (hpd), Bach-Mozart Ensemble Tokyo
Italian Baroque Flute Music—features works by Tartini *(Con in G, D.105)*, Locatelli *(Son in g, Op. 2/6)*, Marcello *(Son in b, Op. 2/2)*, Vivaldi *(Son in C, RV.48)*, Veracini *(Son in a, Op. 1/1)*, Corelli *(Son in e, "La Follia", Op. 5/12)*, Pergolesi *(Con in G)* DNN (Aliare) ▲ 18013 (16.97)

▲ = CD ♦ = Enhanced CD △ = MD ▮ = Cassette Tape ▯ = DCC

Assad, Sérgio (gtr), Odair Assad (gtr)
Sergio & Odair Assad—features works by Scarlatti *(Son in C, K.251)*, Rameau *(Pièces de clavecin [sels])*, Couperin *(Pièces de clavecin [sels])*, J. S. Bach *(Das wohltemperierte Klavier, Book 1)* 75597 ▲ 79292 ▮ 79292-4

Baroque CO [cnd:Ettore Stratta]
Pachelbel's Canon, Albinoni's Adagio & Other Baroque Favorites RCAV ▲ 7821 [ADD] (6.97) ▮ 7821

Berlin Baroque Company
Musik aus Sanssouci [Music from Sanssouci]—features works by C.P.E. Bach *(Duo in C for Violin & Clavier, W.73; Son. in C for Viol, W.136)*, Schaffrath *(Duet in d for 2 Viols)*, Janitsch *(Quadro in G for Flute, Oboe, Violin & Continuo)*, Benda *(Son. in E♭ Violin)*, Frederick II CAPO ▲ 10477 [DDD] (11.97)

Bern Camerata [cnd:Thomas Füri]
Baroque Festival—features works by Albinoni, Bach, Handel, Manfredini, Pachelbel, Purcell, Vivaldi NOVA ▲ 150004 [DDD] (16.97)

Boston Camerata [cnd:Joel Cohen]
Musique Judéo-Baroque—features works by Saladin *(Canticum hebraicum)*, Grossi *(Cantata Ebraica)*, S. Rossi *(Songs of Solomon)* HMA ▲ 1901021 [ADD] (9.97)

Budapest Strings
Famous Baroque Concerti—features works by Handel *(Arrival of the Queen of Sheba; Con Grosso in G, Op. 6/1)*, Vivaldi *(Cons in G, RV.516 [w. Béla Bánfalvi (vn), Zsuzsa Németh (vn)], in a, RV.461 [w. Emilia Csánky (ob)] & in G, RV.532 [w. Béla Sztankovits (gtr), Zoltán Tokos (gtr)])*, J. S. Bach *(Adagio [from Easter Oratorio, BWV 249]; Con in c, BWV 1060 [w. Emilia Csánky (ob), Béla Bánfalvi (vn)]) (rec Unitarian Church, Budapest, Nov 1991)* NXIN ▲ 553028 [DDD] (5.97)

Buffalo Guitar Quartet [James Piorkowski (gtr), Richard Falkenstein (gtr), Len Biszkont (gtr), John Sawers (gtr)]
Gypsy's Round—features Baroque & Renaissance transcriptions for gtr qt by Byrd *(Coranto; Pavane; Galliard; Fant [all arr Sawers]; Gypsy's Round [arr Piorkowski])*, Praetorius *(Terpsichore Dances:Ballet; Spagnoletta; 3 Bransels doubles [all arr Sawyers]; Courante; La Bource [both arr Sparks])*, Telemann *(Son in G [arr Sawyers])*, Dowland *(Lachrimae Antiquae Pavan; M. Bucton's Galliard; Sir John Souch, His Galliard; Captain Digorie Piper, His Galliard [all arr Sawyers])*, Bull *(Galiarda [arr Piorkowski]; The King's Hunt [arr Sparks])*, Vivaldi *(Son in g [arr Sawyers/Falkenstein]) (rec Chautaqua, NY, June-July 1995)* CENT ▲ 2294 [DDD] (16.97)

Butler, Barbara (tpt), Charles Geyer (tpt)
With Clarion Voice: Trumpets of the Baroque, w. Music of the Baroque Orch [cnd:Thomas Wikman]—features works by Telemann *(Con 1 for 3 Clarini)*, Lassus *(Sicut rosa; Fulgebunt justi)*, Purcell *(Sym [from The Fairy Queen, Act IV]; Sym [from King Arthur, Act V])*, Franceschini *(Son in D for 2 Tpts)*, Torelli *(Sinf à 4, G.33)*, Praetorius *(Gelobet seist du Jesu Christ; Von Himmel hoch)*, Vierdanck *(Capriccii IV & V à 3 Cornetti)*, Vivaldi *(Con in C for 2 Tpts) (rec Notre Dame de Chicago, Chicago, IL & Walk Festival Hall, Grand Teton Music Festival, Teton Village, WY)* DNC ▲ 1026 [DDD] (16.97)

Cambridge Baroque Camerata
A Golden Treasury of Baroque Music—features works by A. Scarlatti, Tartini, Locatelli, Telemann, Quantz, D. Scarlatti, Bach, Arne, plus others AMON ▲ 68 (16.97)

Capella Cisplatina, Elyma Ensemble, Luis Berger Ensemble [cnd:Gabriel Garrido], Cordoba Children's Choir [cnd:Emma Sanchez]
Baroque Music at the Royal Audience of Charcas—features works by Araujo *(Aquí, aquí, valentones)*, Ceruti *(Hoy que Francisco reluce; Segun veo el aparato; En la rama frondosa)*, Durán de la Motta *(Llegan las luces)*, Tardio & Guzmán *(Entre obeliscos nevados; Alarma, alarma, afectos; Todos los cuatro elementos)*, Chavarría, Tardio & Ceruti *(Afuela, apalta)*, Chavarría *(Con tan tierno llanto)*, Flores *(Afuera nuves)*, Ceruti & Tardio *(Naced antorcha brillante) (rec Apr 19-24, 1996)* K617 ▲ 7064 [DDD] (18.97)

Capella Istropolitana [cnd:Richard Edlinger]
Baroque Favorites—features works by Bach, Handel, Praetorius, D. Scarlatti, Torelli, Vivaldi NXIN ▲ 550102 [DDD] (5.97)
Best of Baroque Music—features works by Albinoni, Bach, Corelli, Handel, A. Marcello, Telemann, Vivaldi NXIN ▲ 550014 [DDD] (5.97)

Capella Istropolitana [cnd:Jaroslav Krček]
Italian Concerti Grossi—features works by Sammartini, Albinoni, Vivaldi, Locatelli, Manfredini, Corelli, Geminiani, A. Scarlatti *(rec Mar 1993)* NXIN ▲ 550877 [DDD] (5.97)

Caroli, Enzo (fl), Livio Caroli (ob), Paola Frezzato (bn), Lidia Kawecka (hpd)
Italian Baroque Sonatas & Trio Sonatas—features works by Vivaldi, Sammartini, Vinci, Besozzi, Locatelli STRV ▲ 42 (16.97)
Italian Baroque Trio Sonatas—features works by Vivaldi, Galuppi, Jommelli, Nardini & Platti STRV ▲ 39 (16.97)

City Waites
Music from the Time of Charles II—features works by M. Locke *(Ayre, Saraband, Courante, Allemand; Broken Consort in C)*, W. Lawes *(Oh My Clarissa; Among Thy Fancies; Gather Your Rosebuds)*, H. Lawes *(This Mossy Bank They Prest)*, Corbetta *(Alleman, Minuet, Fanfare [from La Chittara Royale])*, J. Wilson *(In the Merry Month of May)*, Playford *(The King's Jig; The 29th of May [both from Playford's Complete Dancing Master])*, Paisable *(Ov & Gavotte)*, Saville *(Here's a Health unto His Majesty)*, Pelegrini *(Balletto Primo, Corrente Festa [from Armonia Concerti Sopra Chittare Espanola])*, Mateis *(Suite:Adagio, Fuga, Adagio, Burlesca-Allegro)*, Lully *(Le Bourgeois Gentilhomme:Ov)*, D'Urfey *(The Wanton Trick)*, Sanz *(Matachia, Espanleta, Pavana, Forneo, Canarios)*, S. Ives *(Shepard Well Met)*, J. Blow *(Ah Heav'n! What Is't I Hear?)*, Tompkins *(Fine Young Folly)*, Reynolds *(Dialogue between a Lover & His Friend)*, anon *(Long Look't for Now May Come at Last)* SALM (Famous Name) ▲ 302 [DDD] (14.97)
Music of the Stuart Age—features music from 17th cent England by Purcell *(Tpt Tune; Air; 1st Act Tune; Fairest Isle; Harvest Home; How Blest Are the Shepheards; Song Tune [all from King Arthur]; Sefuchi's Farewell)*, Playford *(The Chirping of the Lark; Parson's Farewell; Newcastle; Cuckolds All in a Row; Grimstock; Heartsease; Jenny Pluck Pears; Maiden Lane; Lavena [all from Complete Dancing Master])*, Ravencroft *(Tomorrow the Fox Will Come to Town)*, Blow *(Mortlack's Ground)*, Jenkins *(Fant Suite à 5; Aire)*, trad *(Martin Said to His Man)* SALM (Music Treasury) ▲ 105 (14.97)

City Waites, Noise of Minstrels
Lads & Lasses: Music of the English Countryside—features works by D'Urfey *(You Lasses & Lads; The Country Lass)*, Playford *(The Chirping of the Lark/Parson's Farewell; Newcastle; The Spanish Gypsy; Millfield/Argeers/Nonsuch; The Great Booby; Maiden Lane; 1 Misty Moisty Morning; The Merry, Merry Milkmaids; All in a Garden Green; Stanes Morris; Blue Cap; 9 Pins; Paul's Wharf; Heart's Ease [all from Playford's Dancing Master/Playford Collection])*, plus anon/trad songs & dances *(Branles; The Couple of Pigeons/The Parson in Boots; Ward's Brae; Sellinger's Round/Wilson's Wilde/Hulichan's Jig)* SALM (Popular Past) ▲ 403 (14.97)

Clarion Ensemble
Clarion Ensemble—features works by Arban, Bishop, Clarke, Donizetti, Enescu, Fantini, Frescobaldi, Koenig, Monteverdi, Purcell, A. Scarlatti AMON ▲ 30 [DDD] (16.97)

Collegium Aureum, Leonhardt Ensemble, La Petite Bande, et al.
Greatest Hits of 1750—features Bach *(Air on the G String)*, Pachebel *(Canon)*, Vivaldi *(4 Seasons, etc.)* PRMX ▲ 817 (3.97) 817 (4.98)

Cologne Musica Antiqua [cnd:Reinhard Goebel]
Baroque Chamber Music—features works by Dietrich Becker, Louis-Antoine Dornel, Johann Caspar Kerll, Monsieur Nadot, Johann Heinrich Schmelzer *(rec 1974-75)* KSCH ▲ 310612 [ADD] (16.97)
Chaconne—features works by Lully *(Chaconne in G)*, Marini *(Passacaglio in g, Op. 22)*, Corelli *(Ciacona in G)*, Purcell *(Chaconies (2) in g, Z.730 & 807)*, Blow *(Chacony in G)*, Mayr *(Passacaglia-Grave in B♭)*, Pezel *(Son-Ciacona in B♭)*, Muffat *(Chaconne in G)* PARC ▲ 453418 [DDD] (16.97)
Italian Baroque Concerti—features works by Leo, Locatelli, Mossi, Torelli, Valentini PARC ▲ 435393-2 [DDD]

Concert des Nations, Hespèrion XX [cnd:Jordi Savall]
Meslanges Royaux: Music at the Time of Louis XIII & XIV—features works by Sainte-Colombe, Marais, Couperin, Lully, Charpentier, plus others FONT ▲ 9914 (16.97)

Concerto Palatino [Bruce Dickey (cnt), Doron Sherwin (cnt), Charles Toet (trbn), Wim Becu (trbn), Stephen Stubbs (chit), Klaus Eichhorn (org)]
Effetti e Stravaganze: Affect & Effect in 17th Century Instrumental Music—features works by Picchi *(Canzon unidecima à 4)*, Corradini *(La Sincoapta; Son in risposta La golfreramma)*, Piccinini *(Toccata chromatica)*, Marini *(Son decima terza senza candenza)*, Trolio *(Canzon à 4)*, Selma y Salaverde *(Canzon à 2 tenori)*, Fontana *(Son 11 à 2 canti)*, Uccellini *(Son XI à 2 Vn & 2 Db; Aria nona à 3 L'Emenfrodito)*, Merula *(Canzon La Gallina à 2)*, Viadana *(Canzon francese in riposta)*, Kempis *(Sinf 1)*, Ré *(Canzon à 4 un risposta)*, Riccio *(Canzon La Moceniga in ecco) (rec Brussels, Feb 1994)* ACCE ▲ 94102 [DDD] (17.97)

Les Concerts du Monde [cnd:Keith Clark]
Movies Go Baroque *(works by Baroque masters from 13 films)*—features works by Lully *(Marche [from Tous les matins du monde])*, Handel *(Entrance of the Queen of Sheba [from Heartburn]; Largo from Xerxes; Allegro from Con 13 for Org [both from Dangerous Liaisons]; Sarabande [from Barry Lyndon])*, Pachelbel *(Canon & Gigue in D [from Ordinary People])*, Marais *(The Bells of Ste. Geneviève [from Tous les matins du monde])*, Marcello *(Adagio from Con for Ob & Strs [from Lorenzo's Oil])*, J. S. Bach *(Allegro from Con in D for Hpd; Presto from Brandenburg Con 4 [both from Slaughterhouse 5]; Largo from Con in f for Hpd [from Hanah & Her Sisters])*, Charpentier *(Te Deum [from Valmont])*, Albinoni *(Adagio [from Galipoli])*, Vivaldi *(Allegro from Con in C for 2 Tpts [from 4 Seasons]; Largo from Con for Gtr [from The Cowboys]; Allegro from Con in C for Mand & Strs [from Kramer vs. Kramer]) (rec June 7-9, 1993)* TEL ▲ 80336 [DDD] (15.97) ▮

Datura Trombone Quartet [U. Schrodl (trbn), S. Geiger (trbn), O. Siefert (trbn), V. Stoll (trbn)], Anton Scharinger (db), Clemens Weigel (baroque vc), T. Strauss (org), J. Gagelmann (perc), R. Haeger (perc)
Barockmusik für Posaunen und Gesang—features works by Mainero *(Vier italienische Tänze)*, Schütz *(Fili mi, Absalon, SWV 270; Attendite, populе meus, SWV 270)*, Ahle *(Herr, nun lässt Du Deinen Diener)*, Kuhnau *(Biblische Son 1, "David und Goliath")*, Selle *(Domine, exaudi orationem meam)*, Byrd *(The Earl of Salisbury's Pavane)*, Corelli *(Son da chiesa, Op. 3/7)*, Praetorius *(Vier Tänze aus "Terpsichore")* ARSM ▲ 1094 [DDD] (17.97)

Dieltiens, Roel (vc), Richte van der Meer (vc), K. Junghänel (thb), R. Kohnen (hpd)
Italian Cello Music—features works by Bononcini, Willem De Fesch & D. Gabrieli ACCE ▲ 9070 [DDD] (17.97)

English CO [cnd:Raymond Leppard]
Pachelbel's Canon in D & Other Baroque Favorites—features works by Bach, M.-A. Charpentier, Gluck, Handel, A. Marcello, Purcell, Vivaldi COL ▲ 44650 [DDD] (10.97) ▮ 44650 (5.98)

English CO [cnd:James Levine], James Galway (fl), Vladimir Spivakov (vn), Pinchas Zukerman (vn), Canadian Brass, et al.
The Bells of St. Genevieve & Other Baroque Favorites—features works by Marias *(The Bells of St. Genevieve)*, Bach, Handel, Pachelbel, Vivaldi, et al. RCAV ▲ 61002 [DDD] (16.97) ▮ 61002 (9.98) □ 09026-61002-5

English CO [cnd:Raymond Leppard], Grande Écurie [cnd:Jean-Claude Malgoire], Philharmonia Virtuosi [cnd:Richard Kapp], et al.
Great Baroque Favorites—features works by Bach, Charpentier, Handel, A. Marcello, Pachelbel, Purcell, Vivaldi, Albinoni, Clarke, Mouret COL ▲ 38482 (9.97) ▮ 38482 (3.98)

English CO [cnd:Johannes Somary], Leopold Stokowski Orch [cnd:Leopold Stokowski], Zagreb Solisti [cnd:Antonio Janigro], et al.
Solid Gold Baroque—features works by Albinoni, Bach, Clarke, Corelli, Gluck, Handel, Pachelbel, Telemann, Vivaldi VC ▲ 4021 [ADD] (13.97)

English Concert [cnd:Trevor Pinnock]
Best of Baroque, Vol. 1—features works by Bach, Handel, Pachelbel, Vivaldi PARC ▲ 419410-2 [DDD/ADD]
Best of Baroque, Vol. 2—features works by Albinoni, Handel, Purcell, Vivaldi PARC ▲ 423197-2 [DDD]

French Instrumental Ensemble
Albinoni's Adagio—features works by Albinoni *(Adagio)*, Bach, Boccherini, Handel, Haydn, Mozart, Pachelbel, Vivaldi FORL ▲ 16527 [DDD] (16.97)

La Follia Ensemble Salzburg
Music in Austria before Mozart: Late 17th-Early 18th Century—features works by Stefano Bernardi *(3 Canzonas for Strs & Bc)*, Heinrich Biber *(Mensa Sonora, Pars III)*, Antonio Caldara *(Sinf 4, "Morte e sepultara di Christo")*, Johann Joseph Fux *(Concentus-Musico-Instrumentalis, VI)*, Johann Heinrich Schmelzer *(Fechtschule; Lament on the Death of Ferdinand III) (rec 1992)* VTL-The Vital Sound ▲ VTLCLAS001 [DDD]

Gabrieli Consort, Gabrieli Players [cnd:Paul McCreesh]
Venetian Vespers—features works by Monteverdi, Rigatti, Grandi, Cavalli, et al. PARC ▲ 37552 (32.97)

Galway, James (fl)
Pachelbel Canon & other Baroque Favorites—features works by Pachelbel *(Canon in D)*, Vivaldi *(Con, Op. 10/3 [Allegro]; Cantabile; Allegro [from* Spring of 4 Seasons*])*, Telemann *(Suite for Fl & Strs; Réjouissance; Polonaise)*, Handel *(Son Op. 1/4 [Allegro]; Arrival of the Queen of Sheba; Son, Op. 1/11 [Siciliana & Allegro]; Messiah [Pastoral Sym]; Xerxes [Largo])*, Bach *(Air on the G String; Suite 2, BWV 1067; Menuet & Badinerie; Son 4 [Allegro]; Son 2 [Siciliano]; Con, BWV 1059 [Presto])*, Albinoni *(Adagio)*, Marais *(Le basque)*, Quantz *(Con in C [Presto])* RCAV (Red Seal) ▲ 61928 [DDD] (16.97) ▮ 61928 (9.98)

Geneva Baroque Duo [Jonathan Rubin (lt), Sharyn Rubin (b vl)]
Geneva Baroque Duo—features works by Dalza, Capirola/Cara, Ortiz, Ballard, Attaignant, de Rippe/Lupus or Cadéac, le Roy, Byrd, Dowland, Farnaby, Cutting, anon *(rec Dec 1987)* GALL ▲ CD 540 [DDD]

German Bach Soloists [cnd:Helmut Winschermann]
Baroque Treasures, Vol. 2: Bach—features works by Bach *(Brandenburg Cons 1-4)* LALI ▲ 15657 [DDD] (3.97)
Baroque Treasures, Vol. 5: Bach—features works by Bach *(Suites Orch 1-3)* LALI ▲ 15660 [DDD] (3.97)
Baroque Treasures, Vol. 8: Bach—features works by Bach *(Vn Cons, BWV 1041 & 1042; Con for 2 Vns, BWV 1043; Con for 3 Vns, BWV 1063)* LALI ▲ 15663 [DDD] (3.97)

Gervasio Duo [Carmen Schultz (baroque mand), Jürgen Thiergärtner (baroque gtr)]
Baroque Mandolin & Guitar—features works by Vivaldi *(Son in C, RV.82)*, D. Scarlatti *(Son 53, K.88)*, Castello *(Due sonate a soprano solo)*, Capponi *(Son 12 in G)*, anon *(Son 5)* 5422 ▲ 999226 [DDD]

Il Giardino Armonico Ensemble
Christmas Concertos—features works by Antonacci, Coreli, Manfredini, Pez, Torelli, Vivaldi ELEC ▲ 46013

Grupo Fontegara
Baroque Music from the New Spain SPT ▲ 21011

Hannan, Peter (rcr), Colin Tilney (hpd), Christel Thielmann (vl)
Baroque Sonatas & Canzonas for Recorder, Harpsichord & Viol—features works by Bassano, Cima, Frescobaldi, A. Gabrieli, Handel, Telemann SMS (SM 5000) ▲ 5049 [DDD] (16.97)

Helicon [cnd:Albert Fuller] [Jaap Schröder (vn), Stanley Ritchie (vn), Linda Quan (vn)]
Vivaldi/Bach—features works by Bach *(2-Vn Con, Prelude in C, Trio Son in C)*, Vivaldi *(Con in E♭, Sinf in C, Trio Son in g)* Reference ▲ RR 23CD [DDD]

Hollowy, John (vn), Stanley Ritchie (vn), Andrew Manze (vn), Mary Springfels (vl), Nigel North (lt), John Toll (hpd/org)
Three Parts upon a Ground—features works by Pachelbel, Buonamente, Gabrieli, Marini, Uccellini, Fontana, Constantin, Schmelzer, Hacquart, Rosier HAM ▲ 907091

Humphreys, Wendy (sop), Daniel Lichti (b-bar), Stuart Laughton (tpt/nat tpt/cnt), William O'Meara (org), David Campion (timp/perc)
Baroque Banquet *(see Composer section:Susato, Franceschini, Bach, Handel, A. Scarlatti, Telemann, J. Clarke)* OPDR ▲ 9303 (16.97)

In Stil Moderno [Mimi Mitchell (vn), Heidi Erbrich (vn), Timothy Dowling (trbn), Cas Gevers (trbn), Vincent Rombouts (b trbn), Stephen Taylor (org)]
Musica Polonica—Eastern European music of the 17th century featuring works by Buonamente *(Canzona a 5; Son a 5)*, Mielczewski *(Canzons I-II)*, Jelich *(O pretiosum; Domine Deus meus; Domine Dominus)*, Rohaczewski *(Canzon a 4)*, Jarzebski *(Canzon III; Son Chromatica; Con primo)*, Speer *(Sons (4))*, Szarzyński *(Son)*, Merula *(Capriccio cromatico)*, plus anon piece *(Duma) (rec Walloon Church, Amsterdam, July 1995)* CNTS ▲ 9611 [DDD] (18.97)

King's Consort [cnd:Robert King]
Baroque Collection—features works by Bach, Gabrieli, Handel, Purcell, Vivaldi, Telemann HYP ▲ 4 (7.97)

Köhler, Axel (alt)
Jubilate Domino, w. Lautten Compagney—features works by Franck *(Cant, "Weil Jesu, ich in meinem Sinn")*, Rosenmüller *(Psalm 134)*, Buxtehude *(Jubilate Domino)*, Kühnel *(Aria solo for Vl)*, Schmelzer *(Sons VIII & IX)*, J. M. Bach *(Cant, "Auf, lässt uns den Herren loben")*, Tunder *(Salve mi Jesu)*, Bernhard *(Was betrübst du dich meine Seele)* CAPO ▲ 10478 [DDD] (11.97)

Kol, B. (rcr), Amy Brodo (vc), David Shemer (hpd)
Baroque Favorites—features works by Cima, Corelli, Fontana, Handel, Telemann, Van Eyck, Vivaldi PWK ▲ 1138 [DDD]

Lanterly Ensemble, Mona Spagele (sop), Werner Buchin (alt), Albrecht Pohl (bass)
Luneburg 1647—features works by Monteverdi, Ghizzolo, Merula, Werner, G. Weber MDG ▲ 6050647 (16.97)

Lewin, Michael (lt), Marilyn Sansom (vc), Alastair Ross (org)
Music of the "Chapels Royal" of England, w. J. E. Gardiner (cnd), English Baroque Soloists, Monteverdi Choir—features works by Blow, Locke, Purcell, Humfrey ERAT ▲ 45987

London Brass
Gabrieli in Venice—features works by Giovanni Gabrieli, Andrea Gabrieli, Frescobaldi, Marini TELC ▲ 90856 (16.97)

Machamer, Steven (vib), Gerald Ranck (pno), Eric Wyrick (vn)
Vibrant Baroque *(see COMPOSERS section:Bach, Handel, Leclair)* Ashlar Records ▲ 1009

Mainz CO, Württemberg CO
The Pachelbel Canon & Other Baroque Favorites, w. various soloists—features works by Pachelbel, Vivaldi *(Con in C for 2 Tpts)*, Albinoni *(Adagio for Org & Strs)*, Bach *(Brandenburg Con 5)* ALLO ▲ 8098 [ADD] (3.97) ▮ 8098

Maryland Bach Aria Group members [Larry E. Vote (bar), Jeffrey Silberschlag (tpt), Deborah Greitzer (bn), Jeanne Fryberger Vote (hpd)]
The Maryland Bach Aria Group, w. ob & str—features works by Bach, Fasch, Handel, Telemann CRYS ▲ 704 (15.97) ▮ 704

Matthews, Ingrid (baroque vn), Byron Schenkman (hpd)
In Stil Moderno—features music by Castello *(Son prima; Son seconda)*, Fontana *(Son seconda)*, Frescobaldi *(Toccata [from Berlin manuscript]; Toccata I [bk 1]; Toccata II [bk 2]; Cento Partite sopra Passacagli)*, Leonarda *(Son duodecima)*, Marini *(Romanesca; Son quatra)*, Uccelini *(Son seconda)*, Caccini *(Aria sopra la Romanesca; Amarilli mia bella)*, Picchi *(Toccata) (rec Shrine to Music Museum, Vermillion, SD, Jan 1995)* WILD ▲ 9512 [DDD] (15.97)

BAROQUE MUSIC

Minstrelsey [Nancy Froseth (va/rcr), David Hays (baroque vn), David Livingston (rcr), Phillip Rukavina (thb/lt/cittern)]

A Bit 'O the Beggar & Tunes 'O the Isles, w. Lisa Habeck (sop)—features works by Pepusch *(Allegro in g)*, Packington *(Thus Gamesters United [from Beggars Opera])*, Purcell *(The Modes of the Court; Virgins Are Like the Fair Flower; When Young at the Bar [all from Beggar's Opera]; If Love's a Sweet Passion; Chaconne)*, Adson *(Adson's Masque)*, Kapsberger *(Kapsberger)*, anon/trad *(Through All the Employments of Life; Youth's the Season Made for Joy; Come Sweet Lass; The Turtle Thus; I'm Like a Skiff on the Ocean Tossed; O What Pain It Is to Part; Cease Your Funning; Were I Laid on Greenland's Coast [all from Beggar's Opera]; Coleraine; Arran Boat, the Chapel Bell; Morning Dew; Sally Gardens; The Swallow's Tail Reel, the Swallow's Tail Jig [all trad Irish]; The Black Nag; Love's Triumph; Sir Francis Bacon's Masque; Sir Francis Bacon's 2nd Masque; Cupararee; The 2nd of Grey's Inn; The Mountebanks Dance at Gray's Inn; The Standing Masque; Mrs. Sparks Maggot; Wilson's Love; The King's Mistress; A Trip to Paris, St. Martins Nonesuch) (rec Nov 21, 23-24, 1996)* LYR (Early Music Series) ▲ 8032 [DDD] (16.97)

Mule, Marcel (sax)

Le Patron of the Saxophone-Encore!—features works by Vellones, Saint-Saëns, Schumann, Pierné, Boccherini, plus others CLCL ▲ 21 (17.97)

I Musici

Baroque Favorites—features works by Pachelbel *(Canon in D)*, Albinoni *(Adagio in g)*, Handel *(Con. in B♭ for Harp & Orch., Op. 4/6)*, Corelli *(Con. grosso in g, Op. 6/8)*, J.S. Bach *(Suite No. 2 in b, BWV 1067 & others)* PPHI (Solo) ▲ 42396

New York Kammermusiker Double Reed Ensemble [cnd:Ilonna Pederson]

A Baroque Celebration—features works by Lully *(Suite from Le mariage forcé; Air des hautbois; Air des hautbois; Marche de mousquetaires du roy de France)*, Purcell *(Suite from The Fairie Queen; Down, Down with Bacchus)*, Philidor *(Air des hautbois)*, Jenkins *(6 Airs)*, Handel *(3 Short Trios from Almina; Suite from the Water Music)*, J.S. Bach *(Contrapuntus I from Art of the Fugue) (rec June 1993)* DOR ▲ 90189 [DDD] (16.97)

Northwest German Chamber Soloists

Barrock on the Rocks: Musical Amusements from Bach to the Beatles—features works by Mozart, Spencer Williams, Lennon/McCartney, Fučik, Gade, Scott Joplin, Sidney Bechet, Gershwin, J. P. Johnson, Harry Warren, P. Desmond, Original Dixieland Jazz Band, T. Wright (Fats) Waller/Clarence Williams, Joachim Klemm, and themes based on works by Bach, Prokofiev, Saint-Saëns, Sibelius, Tchaikovsky, Wagner *(rec Oct 1991)* MDG ▲ 3442 [DDD]

Novus Brass Ensemble

Taffel Consort, w. Ursula Dütschler (hpd), Laurent De Ceunick (perc)—features works by Simpson *(Almande; Canzon; Volta; Ricercar on "Bonny Sweet Robin"; Paduan; Ballet)*, Dowland *(Paduan; Aria (Mistresse Nichols Almand); 2 Voltas; Courant)*, M. Webster *(Galliard; Mascarada)*, C. Töpffer *(Volta; Paduan; Almande; Ballet)*, Farnaby *(A Maske [from the Fitzwilliam Virginal Book])*, J. Grabbe *(Canzon; Intrada)*, R. Johnson *(Satyr's Dance)*, Bleyer *(Paduan; Courant; Ballet)*, Ferrabosco II *(Aria)*, Sherly *(Courant)*, Krosch *(Courants (2))*, R. Bateman *(Aria) (rec Sornetan Church, Jura; Feb 1995)* CLAV ▲ 9510 [DDD]

Orpheus CO

Orpheus Chamber Orchestra—features works by Albinoni *(Adagio)*, J.S. Bach *(Jesu bleibet meine Freude; Overture No. 3)*, Corelli *(Christmas Concerto)*, Handel *(Arrival of the Queen of Sheba; Largo)*, Purcell *(Chaconne in g)*, Vivaldi *(Concerto Op. 3, No. 10)* DEUT ▲ 29390 [DDD] (16.97)

Jean-François Paillard CO [cnd:Jean-François Paillard]

The Pachelbel Canon, Albinoni Adagio & Other Baroque Melodies—features works by Bach, Clarke, Corelli, Handel, Marcello, Molter, Rameau, Vivaldi, Zipoli RCAV (Red Seal) ▲ 65468 [DDD] (16.97) ▮ 65468 (9.98)

Parley of Instruments [cnd:Roy Goodman, Peter Holman]

German Consort Music 1660-1710—features works by G. Böhm, J.C.F. Fischer, J. Rosenmüller, H. Schmelzer, Telemann HYP ▲ 66074 [DDD] (18.97)

Prague Musica Antiqua [cnd:Pavel Klikar]

Baroque Music from the Kromeríz Archives—features works by H. A. Brückner, W. Ebner, J. J. Flixius, V. Lamb, J. H. Schmelzer SUR ▲ 111416 [DDD]

Italian Music of Early Baroque—features works by Uccellini *(Sinfs 2 & 19)*, Donati *(In te domine speravi; Gaude Maria virgo)*, Turini *(Son 1; Desidero te millies)*, Merula *(Ego flos campi)*, Picchi *(Canzoni 4 & 5)*, Mariani *(Canzon "La guaralda")*, Tarditi *(Jesu care)*, Arrigoni *(Vulnerasti cor meum)*, Cima *(Capriccio)*, Rossi *(Son detta la Viena), Marini (Sinf la matinenga), Capuana (Ecce panis)* SUR ▲ 111816 [DDD]

Prague Musici

Baroque Music in France PVY (Favourites) ▲ 730013 [DDD]

Puirt a Baroque [David Greenberg (vns), Terry McKenna (gtrs), David Sandall (hpd)]

Kinloch's Fantasy: A Curious Collection of Scottish Sonatas & Reels MARQ ▲ 211 (16.97)

Renaissance CO [cnd:Leo Korchin]

A Baroque Festival—features works by Boccherini *(Qnt in E for Strs, Op. 13/5 [Minuetto])*, Albinoni *(Sinf in G)*, Gluck *(Dance)*, Marcello *(Con 2 in c for Ob & Str Orch [w. C. Oshinakaev])* 7464 ▲ 57253 [DDD]

Rhine Bach Collegium

The Marriage of the Hen & the Cuckoo: Program Music of the Baroque Period—features works by J. G. Ahle *(Unstrutische Nachtigall)*, C. Harst *(The Great Storm for Hpd)*, N. a Kempis *(Symphonia 4 a 4 supra Cucuc)*, L. Mozart *(Frog Partie)*, J. H. Schmelzer *(Son "Cucu")*, M. Uccelini *(The Marriage of the Hen & the Cuckoo)*, G. J. Werner *(16 sels from Musikalischer Instrumental-Kalender)* 5422 ▲ 999083 [DDD]

Ricercar Consort

Compendium of Baroque Musical Instruments—features works by Pohle, Schmelzer, Hammerschmidt, Scheidt, Correa de Arauxo, Landi, de Selma y Salaverde, de Ribayaz, Frescobaldi, Trabacci, Bartolotti, Jenkins, Krausen, Greeting, Farnaby, Philidor, Raison, Marais, Gaultier, Visee, F. Couperin, N. Chedeville, Löwen, Walther, Weckman, Bruhns, Keller, Kosteletztki, J. S. Bach, Pachelbel, Handel, Vivaldi, Fontanelli, Geminiani, Graun, Telemann, C. P. E. Bach, Graupner, E. P. Chedeville, Mozart, W. F. Bach, Tuma, Gretry RICE 3-▲ 93001 [DDD] (34.97)

Ricercar Consort [cnd:Philippe Pierlot]

German Baroque Chamber Music—features works by Bertali, Biber, Hammerschmidt, Pachelbel, Schein, Schmelzer, Stadlmayr, Stephani, Turini RICE ▲ 78060 [DDD] (17.97)

St. Andrew Camerata [cnd:Leonard Friedman]

17 Jewels in the Crown of the Baroque—features works by Albinoni *(Adagio)*, Bach *(Jesu, joy; Sheep may safely graze; etc.)*, Gluck *(Dance of the blessed spirits)*, Handel *(Entrance of the Queen of Sheba; Largo from Xerxes; etc.)*, Mouret *(Fanfare [Masterpiece Theatre theme])*, Pachelbel *(Kanon)*, Telemann *(Réjouissance)*, Vivaldi *(Winter, from the Four Seasons; etc.)* ORG ▲ 1002 [DDD] (13.97)

St. James' Baroque Players [cnd:Ivor Bolton]

Baroque Music of Bologna—features works by Torelli, Franceschini, Gabrielli TELC ▲ 91192

St. Paul CO [cnd:Pinchas Zukerman]

Baroque Music—features works by Handel, Pachelbel, Purcell, Rameau, Telemann, Vivaldi PPHI ▲ 12215 [DDD] (16.97) 12215

Scaramouche [Andrew Manze (vn), Caroline Balding (vn), Ulrike Wild (hpd/org), Jaap ter Linden (b vl)]

Henry Purcell & His Times: 17th Century English Chamber Music—features works by Purcell, M. Locke, W. Lawes, J. Jenkins, C. Simpson *(rec Jan 1992)* CCL ▲ 4792 [DDD] (17.97)

Scholl, Andreas (ct), Alix Verzier (vc), Markus Markl (hpd), Karl Ernst Schröder (lt), Friederike Heumann (va), Juan Manuel Quintana (va), Stephanie Pfister (vn), Pablo Valetti (vn)

Deutsche Barocklieder—features works by Nauwach *(Jetzund kompt die Nacht herbey; Ach Liebste, lass uns eilen)*, Albert *(Turpe senex miles, turpe senilis amor; Veneris miseras resonare querelás)*, Fischer *(Praeludium & Chaconne VIII)*, A. Krieger *(Die Liebesgluth verkehrt den Muth; Ihr bleibet nicht Bestand verpflicht; Der Liebe Macht herrscht Tag und Nacht; Der Rheinische Wein)*, J. P. Krieger *(Son a doi; Violine e Viola da Gamba; Schmilz, hartes Herz; Verliebtes Weinen und Lachen; Die Heissverliebte; An die Einsamkeit; Die holde Nacht)*, Hammerschmidt *(Kunst des Küssens)*, Hagen *(Menuetto con variazioni di Locatelli)*, Görner *(Die Nacht, An den Schlaf)* HAM ▲ 901505 (17.97)

Scottish CO [cnd:Jaime Laredo], City of London Sinfonia [cnd:R. Hickox], E. Ritchie (sop), Bowman (ct), J. Purvis (pno)

Baroque Beauties—features works by Handel *(Arrival of the Queen of Sheba [from Solomon]; Water Music)*, J. S. Bach *(Sheep May Safely Graze; Bandenburg Con 3; Air on the G String)*, Albinoni *(Adagio & others)* POS (The Orchid) ▲ 11010

Sóliles, Jérôme (vl/sgr)

Caminando, w. Haim Shazar (lts)—features works by C. de Sermisy *(Languir me fais)*, D. Ortiz *(Recercada 1-3 & 8 in Trattato de Glosas; Recercada 1 sobre "Doulce memoire")*, Whitfelde *(The English Huntsuppe)*, Regnault *(Doulce memoire)*, A. L. de Milan *(Pavan & Gaillarde)*, Kapsberger *(Toccata II)*, Handel *(Camminando, in Vedendo Amor)*, Kellner *(Pièces in D)*, anon *(3 Morillas m'anamoran)* GALL ▲ 961 [DAD] (18.97)

Steger, Maurice (rcr)

An English Collection, w. Continuo Consort [cnd:Naoki Kitaya]—features work by Handel *(Son II & XI in e & F)*, Hilton *(3 Fants in 3 Parts)*, Locke *(Suite IV in e)*, Sammartini *(Son VI in a, Op. 2)*, H. Purcell *(A New Ground)*, anon *(A Jacobean Masque, Parts I & II) (rec Tibor Varga Foundation Hall, Sion, Switzerland; May 11-15, 1996)* CLAV ▲ 9614 [DDD] (16.97)

Stuttgart CO [cnd:Karl Münchinger]

Stuttgart CO—features works by Pachelbel, L. Mozart, Bach, Albinoni, Boccherini, Gluck, Handel PLON ▲ 11973 [DDD] (16.97)

Summit Brass

Delights—features works by Handel *(Royal Fire Music (Ov); Water Music)*, Bernstein *(West Side Story:Suite)*, Mussorgsky *(Pictures at an Exhibition)*, Scheidt *(Gagliarda Battaglia)*, Stratton *(2 Quicksteps)* SUMM ▲ 138 [DDD] (16.97) ▮

Tafelmusik [cnd:Jeanne Lamon]

Italian Concerti Grossi—features works by Geminiani, Locatelli, A. Scarlatti, Torelli, Vivaldi SMS (SM 5000) ▲ 5099 [DDD] (16.97) ▮ SMC 5099 (D)

Popular Masterworks of the Baroque—features works by Pachelbel *(Canon)*, Handel, Bach, Purcell, Vivaldi, Telemann [period instrs] Reference ▲ RR 13CD [ADD]

Toronto CO [cnd:Andrew Davis]

The Baroque Album, w. Jeanne Baxtresser (fl), John Cowell (tpt), Ofra Harnoy (vc), Andrew Davis (hpd/org)—features works by Handel *(Arrival of the Queen of Sheba; The Harmonius Blacksmith)*, Pachelbel *(Canon in D)*, Bach *(Prelude & Fugue 5; Air on a G String; Son Fl, BWV 1030)*, Clarke *(Tpt Voluntary)*, Purcell *(A New Irish Tune/Abdelazer)*, Corelli *(Gigue)*, D. Scarlatti *(Son Hpd, K.209)*, Albinoni *(Adagio)* ICC ▲ 6701692 (8.97)

Trio Rococo [Niels Eje (ob), Inge Mulvad Eje (vc), Lillian Törnqvist (hp)]

Trio Rococo Plays Rococo Trios—features works by C. P. E. Bach, Hertel, Molter, von Paradis, Krumpholz, Rust DANR ▲ 350 [DDD]

Veilhan, Jean-Claude (chl)

The Baroque Chalumeau, w. Eric Lorho, Mensa Sonora Ensemble [cnd:Jean Maillet]—features works by Paganelli, Telemann, Fasch, Graupner, Hoffmeister PVY ▲ 796103 [DDD] (16.97)

Venice Solisti [cnd:Claudio Scimone]

Baroque in Italy—features works by Albinoni, Geminiani, Locatelli, Marcello, Scarlatti, Vivaldi COL (Essential Classics) ▲ 46547 [ADD] (7.97) ▮ 46547 (3.98)

Vittorio, Pino de, Cappella della Pietà de Turchini

Oh Cielo, Oh Ammore: Baroque Neopolitan Cantatas, Vol. 1 SYM ▲ 9 [DDD]

Walsingham Ensemble

Artus Aux-Cousteaux de la Musique du Roy—features works by Aux-Cousteaux *(Ouverz, Prince du ciel; Grand Roy pour qui le ciel; Beaux yeux, ne versez plus de larmes; Madrigalle à 4; Nous ne sommes pas nez; La terre s'esmaille de vert)*, Picard *(Branle à mencer)*, Van Eyck *(Praeludium)*, Hotman *(Pièces de viole in d)*, Racan/Aux-Cousteaux *(Tirsis, il faut penser)*, J. Henry *(Fant)*, Lazarin *(Gigue)*, Mathieu/Aux-Cousteaux *(Quatrains (2) à 3)*, Gallot/anon *(Pièces de Guiterre in d)*, M. de la Pierre *(Gaillarde in G.ré.sol)*, Desportes/Aux-Cousteaux *(Douce liberté désirée)*, Mésangeau *(Pièces de Luth in g)*, Guérdon/Van Eyck *(Courante Mars)*, plus anon piece *(Allemande in A.mi.la) (rec Mayenne, France, May 1997)* CYPR ▲ 1604 [DDD] (17.97)

Windsor Box & Fir Company [Jenny Thomas (fl), Michael Sanderson (vn/ten), Ian Gammie (b vl), Katharine May (hpd)]

Music for Love & Marriage, w. Elinor Bennett (hp), Martin Souter (org)—features works by J. Christi. Bach *(Trio in G)*, C. F. Abel *(Son for Gamba in A)*, Stanley *(Son Fl, Op. 4/3; Voluntaries, Opp. 5/8 & 7/1, 5-6)*, Earl of Abingdon *(Fops Alley; Hop Tops; La Bella Donna; Capriccio 1)*, J. Hook *(Lass of Richmond Hill)*, Sancho *(The Complaint)*, Dussek *(Son in E♭)*, Mozart *(Air w. Vars; Rondo Pastorale)* ISIS ▲ 26 [DDD] (16.97)

Zagreb Solisti

Baroque Treasures—features works by Albinoni, Corelli, Locatelli, Vivaldi PMG (Vienna Masters) ▲ CD 160105 [DDD]

BAROQUE MUSIC COLLECTIONS

And the Angels Sing *(Baroque-style arrangements of over 20 classic Christmas carols & hymns, performed by period instr ensemble—strs, hp, brass, hpd, etc.—made up of New England-based musicians specializing in early & baroque music performance)* NOR ▲ 35 [DDD] 35

Baroque—features performances by Grande Écurie & la Chambre du Roy [cnd:Jean-Claude Malgoire] *(Pergolesi:Stabat Mater Dolorosa [w. Isabelle Poulenard (sop), Jean-Louis (ct)]; Handel/Mozart:Alleluia [from Messiah])*, Rolf Lislevand (thb) *(Kapsberger:Bergamasca)*, Le Concert Français [cnd:Pierre Hantai] *(Telemann:B♭ Trio Son for Rcr, Hpd, Obligato & Bc)*, Rare Fruits Council *(Biber:Passacaglia Part V)*, La Maîtrise Boréale *(Vivaldi:In éxitu Israël)*, L'armonia e l'inventione [cnd:Alfredfo Bernardini] *(Vivaldi:Largo [from Con for Ob, Strs & Bc])*, Blandine Verlet (hpd) *(Couperin:Les Baricades Mistérieuses)*, Limoges Baroque Ensemble [cnd:Christophe Coin] *(J. S. Bach:Sinf [from Cant, BWV 49; w. William Jansen (org)]; Allegro [from Con in a BVW 593; w. Michael Chapuis (org)])*, Andrew Lawrence-King (hp), Hile Perl (gamba) *(Purcell:Suite in a, Round-O)*, Fitzwilliam Ensemble *(Passacaglia:Suite in e)*, Hopkinson Smith (bar lt/thb) *(De Visée:Gigue; Soler:De Clarines Son [w. Bob Van Asperen (hpd)])*, Les Talens Lyriques [cnd:Christophe Rousset] *(Handel:Lascia ch'io pianga [from Rinaldo; w. Ewa Mallas-Godlweska (sop), Derek Lee Ragin (ct)])* ASTR ▲ 8593 (16.97)

Baroque at Bathtime: A Relaxing Serenade to Wash Your Cares Away—features sels from works by Vivaldi *(Con in D for Gtr, Strs & Bc [Largo]; Con 3 in D for Fl, Strs & Bc [Il gardellino]; Con in G for 2 Gtrs, Strs & Bc [Adagio]; Winter [from The 4 Seasons]; Con in a for Gtr, Strs & Bc [L'estro armonico])*, Bach *(Con in d for Ob, Strs & Bc [Siciliano])*, Marcello *(Con in d for Ob, Strs & Bc [Adagio])*, Pachelbel *(Canon in D)*, Telemann *(Con in G fo Ob d'amore, Strs & Bc [Adagio]; Con in A [Sicilienne]; Con in D for Ob, Strs & Bc [Grazioso])*, Quantz *(Con in G for Fl [Arioso])*, Cimarosa *(Con in C for Ob & Strs [Siciliana & Introduzione])*, Handel *(Suite 1 in F [Air]; Con 1 in B♭ for Ob, Strs & Bc [Adagio & Largo]; Con 2 in B♭ for Ob, Strs & Bc [Andante])*, Marelli *(Suite 1 [Andante])*, Corelli/Barbirolli *(Con in F [Preludio])* PPHI ▲ 46764 (11.97) ▮ 46764 (5.98)

Baroque Classics, Vol. 1—features works by Albinoni, Bach, Handel, et al. PPHI (Miniature) ▲ 422271-2

A Baroque Collection—features works by Purcell *(Suite 1)*, Vivaldi *(Con for 3 Vns)*, Couperin *(Piece en concert)*, Bach *(Brandenburg Con 2)*, plus others PUBM (Majestic) ▲ 1042 (4.97)

A Baroque Festival—features performances by Renaissance CO [cnd:Leo Korchin] *(Boccherini:Minuetto [from Qnt in E for Strs, Op. 13/5]; Albinoni:Sinf in G; Marcello:Con 2 in c for Ob & Strs [w. Chanjafi Oshinakaev (ob)]; Gluck:Dance of the Blessed Spirits [from Orfeo ed Euridice; w. Alexander Kiskachi (fl)]; Vivaldi:Con in A for Strs & Bc, RV.159; Con in F for Fl, Strs & Bc, RV.433 [w. Alexander Kiskachi (rcr)]; Handel:Ombra mai fu [Largo from Serse])*, Pavlovsk SO [cnd:Vladimir Rylov] *(Handel:Passacaglia [from Suite 7 in g]; Purcell:Pavane & Chaconne)*, New Classical Orch (St Petersburg) [cnd:Alexander Titov] *(Corelli:Con grossos, Op. 6/1-4, 8 & 9; Vivaldi:Con in D for 4 Vns & Strs, Op. 3/1 [RV.549]; Con in G for Vn & Strs, Op. 3/3 [RV.310; w. Igor Romanyuk (vn)]; Con in D for Vn & Strs, Op. 3/9 [RV.230]; Con in D for Vn & Strs, RV.234 [both w. Vladislav Gluz (vn)]; Con in A for 2 Vns & Strs, Op. 3/5 [RV.519]; Con in A for 2 Vns & Strs, RV.523 [both w. Vladislav Gluz (vn), Igor Romanyuk (vn)])*, Classic Music Studio Orch (St Petersburg) [cnd:Alexander Titov] *(Bach:Cons 3, 4 & 6 in G, G & B♭, BWV 1048, 1049 & 1051; Con in d for Pno, BWV 1052 [w. Pavel Jegorov (pno)]; Con in D for Pno, BWV 1054; Con in f for Pno, BWV 1056 [both w. Oleg Malov (pno)]; Con 1 in c for 2 Pnos, BWV 1060 [w. Alla Kustariova (pno), Oleg Malov (pno)])* 7464 5-▲ 61992 [DDD]

Baroque Festivities—features Works for Musette; Masques & Fantasies; plus Kapsberger *(Works for Thb, Book IV)*, Zelenka *(Ob & Bn Sons)*, Falconieri *(Fants; Dances; Villanelles; Arias)* ASTR 5-▲ 8584 (54.97)

Baroque for Dummies EMIC (Classical Music for Dummies) ♦ CDU 66400

Baroque Treasures

Vol. 1: Vivaldi—features works by Vivaldi *(The 4 Seasons; Mand Con, RV.425; Ob Con, RV.454; Con for 2 Tpts, RV.537)* LALI ▲ 15656 [DDD] (3.97)

Vol. 3: Handel—features works by Handel *(Con Grosso, Op. 3/3; Water Music Suites 1-3)* LALI ▲ 15658 [DDD] (3.97)

Vol. 4: Telemann—features works by Telemann *(Tpt Con in D; Ov in F; 2 Tpt Suites in D; Suite in D for 3 Tpts)* LALI ▲ 15659 [DDD] (3.97)

Vol. 6: Handel—features works by Handel *(Handelerform Con Grosso, Op. 3/2, 4 & 6, Op. 6/4; Royal Fireworks Suite)* LALI ▲ 15661 [DDD] (3.97)

Vol. 7: Corelli—features works by Corelli *(Con Grosso, Op. 6/5-8; Tpt Son in D)* LALI ▲ 15662 [DDD] (3.97)

Vol. 9: Handel—features works by Handel *(Org Cons, Op. 4/2, 4 & 5, Op. 7/4; sels from Jeptha, Messiah, Samson)* LALI ▲ 15664 [DDD] (3.97)

Vol. 10: Baroque Highlights—features works by Albinoni, Bach, Gluck, et al. LALI ▲ 15665 [DDD] (3.97)

Best of Baroque—features works by Bach, Albinoni, Pachelbel, Handel & others CSER (Seraphim) ▲ 69586 (3.97)

The Best of Baroque—features works by Albinoni *(Adagio [w. Maria Teresa Garatti (org), I Musici])*, Vivaldi *(Cons Vn, Op. 8/1-4, "4 Seasons" [w. Szymon Goldberg (vn), Szymon Goldberg (cnd), Netherlands CO]; Con for 2 Mands, RV.532 [rev F. Giegling; w. Gino del Vescovo (mand), Tommaso Ruta (mand), I Musici]; Con for 2 Tpts, RV.537 [rev F. Giegling; w. Henry Adelbrecht (tpt), Jean-Pierre Mathez (tpt), I Musici])*, Handel *(Water Music [Suite 1] [w. Academy of St. Martin in the Fields, Neville Marriner (cnd)]; Messiah:Hallelujah Chorus [w. London SO, Colin Daivs (cnd), London Sym Choir]; Con in B♭ for Hp, HWV 294 [w. Ursula Holliger (hp), André Pépin (fl), Jean-Claude Hermanjat (fl), I Musici])*, Pachelbel *(Canon & Gigue in D [w. I Musici])*, J. S. Bach *(Suite Orch 3:Air [w. Academy of St. Martin in the Fields, Neville Marriner (cnd)]; Brandenburg Con 2 [w. Henryk Szeryng (vn), Michala Petri (rcr), Heinz Holliger (ob), André Bernard (tpt), Academy of St. Martin in the Fields, Neville Marriner (cnd)]; Con in d, BWV 1043 [w. Henryk Szeryng (vn), Maurice Hasson (vn), Academy of St. Martin in the Fields, Neville Marriner (cnd)])* PPHI (2-fers) 2-▲ 456049 (17.97)

Best of the Baroque—features performances by Collegium Aureum *(Mouret:Fanfare [Masterpiece Theatre Theme]; Pachelbel:Canon in D)*, Salzburg Camerata Academica *(Vivaldi:4 Seasons [Allegro from "The Spring"])*, London Festival Orch *(Handel:Water Music Suite [Alla Hornpipe])*, Camerata Romana *(Bach:Brandenburg Con 2)*, Royal PO *(Bach:Orchestral Suite No. 3 [Air on the G String]; Handel:Hallelujah! [from Messiah; w. Royal Philharmonic Choral Society])*, Toronto SO *(Handel:Arrival of the Queen of Sheba)*, Bamburg PO *(Handel:Royal Fireworks Music [La réjouissance])*, Christiane Jaccottet (hpd) *(Bach:Prelude & Fugue in C)*, Chicago Chamber Brass *(Gabrieli:Canzona per sonare No. 2)*, Cathedral Brass *(Purcell:Sym [from The Fairy Queen])* [some printed scores included] INSD ♦ CD 1253

The English Orpheus, 1600-1800—features works by Locke *(Curtain Tune in C; Jesu acctor clementie)*, Croft *(Sym; Verse & Chorus [from Jubilate in D])*, D. Johnson-Simpson *(The Satyrs' Dance [from Oberon])*, Blow *(Morlake ground; Salvator mundi salva nos)*, Shield *('Tis only no harm to know it, you know)*, Bond *(Con 6 in B♭ [Affettuoso]; Solo in E)*, Dibdin *(So there she lies upon the floor; If I was a wife [from The Ephesian Matron])*, Purcell *(Cibell in C)*, Peter Philips *(Tu es Petrus; Aria del Gran Duca)*, Gibbons *(Fant a 4 No. 1, "For the great double bass")*, Jenkins *(Fant Suite 2 in a)*, Stanley *(Con 2 in b [Allegro])*, Roseingrave *(Voluntary in g)*, Bassano *(Pavan & Galliard)*, Weelkes *(O Jonathan, woe is me)*, Clarke (And see, Apollo has unstrung his lyre; Mr. Purcell's Farewell [from Come, come along for a dance & song]) HYPD ▲ 1 (7.97)

Favorite Baroque—features works by Handel *(Solomon:Arrival of the Queen of Sheba)*, Albinoni *(Adagio in g)*, Vivaldi *(Fl Con, Op. 10/3 [Allegro])*, Purcell *(Ritornello, Verse & Chorus Come Ye Sons of Art)*, Pachelbel *(Canon in D)*, Vivaldi *(The 4 Seasons, Op. 8/1)*, Bach *(Suite 3 in D [Air]; Brandenburg Con 2 [Allegro])*, Handel *(Water Music Suite 2)*, Gluck *(Orfeo & Eurydice [Dance of the Blessed Spirits])*, Corelli *(Christmas Con, Op. 6/8 [Largo])*, Purcell *(Dido & Aeneas, Act 3:When I am Laid in Earth)*, Mozart*(Allegro, Serenade, K.525)* CFP ▲ 4620 [DDD] (12.97)

Flow My Tears: Larmes Baroque—features performances by Jean-Loup (ct), Les Passions de l'Âme *(J. C. Bach:Lamento "Ach, dass ich Wassers..."; F. Couperin:Plorant, ploravit...; Dowland:Flow my tears; Come heavy sleep; Dubuisson:Plainte sur la mort de M. Lambert; Handel:A languir ed a penar; J. La Barre:Tristes enfans de mes déşirs; Lambert:Laisse-moy soupirer; Purcell:The plaint (Fairy Queen); Vivaldi:Piango, gemo, sospiro e peno)*, Les Passions de l'Âme [Mauricio Buraglia (lt/thb), Pierre Trocellier (org/hpd), Nima Ben David (b vl/pardessus de vl), Adrian Lhomme (t vl), Caroline Howald (b vl), Alice Cota (b vl), Rudolf Kowall (vle/contrebass)] *(Gaultier:La Pleureuse; Les larmes de Mousieur Boisset; Hume:Captain Humes Pavan; Rameau:Les tendres plaintes)* ASTR ▲ 8634 [DDD] (18.97)

Forms & Figures in Baroque Music
HAM (Discovery) 2-▲ 595001 (35.97)

[Editor's Note]: also includes instructional book

Greatest Baroque Hits—features works by Pachelbel *(Canon in D)*, Handel *(Harmonious Blacksmith [Bk 1, HWV 430/4; w. Igor Kipnis (hpd)], (plus works by Albinoni, Bach, Mouret, Vivaldi)* 39014 ▮ COL (7.98)

Greatest Hits: Baroque—features performances by Kipnis (hpd) *(Clarke:Prince of Denmark's March)*, plus other sels
COL ▲ 66706 (9.97) 66706 (5.98)

Music in Cremona at the Time of Monteverdi, w. Gemma Bertagnolli (sop), Cremona Solisti [cnd:Marco Fracassi]—features music by Monteverdi, Merula, Corradini LBD ▲ 1 (16.97)

Music in England in the Time of Hogarth, w. Philharmonia Baroque, Broadside Band, et al. HAM ▲ 986002 (14.97)

A Musical Celebration at Versailles, w. various artists ASTR ▲ 8628 (16.97)

A Musical Landscape *(Music from the French & Italian Baroque to celebrate Nicolas Poussin)*—features performances by London Oboe Band [cnd:Paul Goodwin] *(Lully:Le Bourgeois Gentilhomme)*, Les Arts Florissants [cnd:William Christie] *(Lully:Atys; Lambert:Tout l'univers obéit à l'amour; Ombre de mon amant; Charpentier:David et Jonathas; Rossini:Orfeo)*, Chapelle Royale Orch [cnd:Philippe Herreweghe] *(Lully:Armide [Act II, scene 5])*, Concerto Vocale [cnd:René Jacobs] *(Monterverdi:Il Ritorno d'Ulisse in Patria; Troppo ben puo; Cavalli:Giasone)*, Philharmonia Baroque Orch [cnd:Nicholas McGegan] *(Handel:La Resurrezione)* HAM ▲ 90613

Offrandes à la Mére du Baroque Universal—features works dedicated to Mary from Palermo & Mexico in performaces by Compañia Musical de las Americas [cnd:Josep Cabré] *(Messe de l'Assomption de la Vierge)*, La Grande Ecurie et la Chambre du Roy, Compañia Muisical de las Americas, Versailles Maîtrise Nationale [cnd:Jean-Claude Malgoire] *(Vêpres de l'Assomption)*, Musica Antica Studio Vocal Ensemble, Antonio Il Verso, Palestrina Choir, Euphonia Ensemble, Mille Regretz Ensemble, Les Rossignols de Poznan, Elyma Ensemble [cnd:Gabriel Garrido] *(Vespro per lo Stellano della Beata Virgine)* K617 ▲ 7074

Pachelbel, w. Jean-Pierre Rampal (fl), Igor Kipnis (hpd), Raymond Leppard (cnd), John Williams (gtr), Canadian Brass, Edward Power Biggs (org), et al.—features works by Pachelbel *(Canon & Gigue in D)*, Albinoni *(Adagio)*, Handel *(Water Music (sels))*, Vivaldi *(Cons for Vn & Strs, Op. 8/1-4, "The 4 Seasons")*, Bach *(Jesu Joy of Man's Desiring)*, plus others
COL (Greatest Hits) ▲ 62680 (9.97) ▮ 62680 (5.98)

Pachelbel Canon—features works by Albinoni, Bach, Handel, et al. PLON (Jubilee) ▲ 17781 [ADD] (11.97)

Pachelbel Canon: Baroque Favorites—features works by Bach, Handel, Telemann, et al. LALI ▲ 15613 [DDD] (3.97)

Pathways of Baroque Music: Cathedrals & Chapels, w. various artists HAM 5-▲ 2908006 (52.97)

Pathways of Baroque Music: Instrumental Music, w. various artists HAM 5-▲ 2908011 (52.97)

Pathways of Baroque Music: The Secular Voice, w. various artists HAM 5-▲ 2908001 (52.97)

Splendor & the Brass: Festive Music of the Baroque—features performances by Nick Norton (tpt), Anthony Plog (tpt), Michael Soachs (tpt), James Thompson (tpt) *(Zelenka:3 Fanfares)*, Summit Brass *(Handel:Water Music [sels]; Royal Fireworks Ov)*, David Hickman (tpt), Douglas Carlsen (tpt), Banff Festival Strings [cnd:Thomas Rolston] *(Vivaldi:Con in C for 2 Tpts, Op. 46/1)*, Atlantic Brass Quintet *(Holborne:3 Elizabethan Dances; Praetorius:Terpsichore Suite)*, David Hickman (tpt), Banff Festival Strings [cnd:Thomas Rolston] *(Bach:Brandenburg Con 2 in F)*, St. Louis Brass Quintet *(Scheidt:Gailliard Battaglia)*, James Thompson (tpt), Michael Sachs (tpt), George Recker (tpt), Patrick Kunkee (tpt), Nick Norton (tpt), Anthony Plog (tpt) *(anon:Charamela Real)* SUMM ▲ 189 [DDD] (10.97)

25 Baroque Favorites—features performances by London SO [cnd:Philip Gibson] *(Pachelbel:Canon; Handel:Ombra mai fu [Handel's Largo])*, A. Caroldi (ob), A. Alvarosi (ob), Milano Virtuosi [cnd:Piero Santi] *(Vivaldi:Con in d for 2 Obs & Strs [Largo])*, Chicago CO [cnd:Dieter Kober] *(Handel:Water Music [Minuet])*, Heinz Zickler (tpt), Mainz CO [cnd:Günter Kehr] *(Purcell:Tpt Con in D [Adagio]; Telemann:Con in D for Tpt & Strs [Grave]; Torelli:Con in D for Tpt, 2 Vns, Va, Basso & Bc [Allegro]; Fasch:Con in D for Tpt, 2 Obs, Strs & Bc [Allegro])*, I Musici di Zagreb *(Corelli:Sarabande; Vivaldi:Con Grosso in d [Allegro])*, Helmut Hucke (ob), Southwest German CO [cnd:Paul Angerer] *(Marcello:Ob Con in d [Adagio])*, Royal PO [cnd:Frank Shipway] *(Bach:Air on the G String)*, Douglas Haas (org), Württemberg CO [cnd:Jörg Faerber] *(Albinoni:Adagio for Strs in g)*, Alexander Permovalsky (vn), Baroque Festival Orch [cnd:Alberto Lizzio] *(Vivaldi:The 4 Seasons [Spring, Largo])*, Philharmonia Slavonica [cnd:Karel Brazda] *(Bach:Brandenburg Con 4 in G [Andante])*, Helmut Schneidewind (tpt), Wolfgang Pasch (tpt), Württemberg CO [cnd:Jörg Faerber] *(Manfredini:Con in D for 2 Tpts & Strs [Largo])*, Helmut Schneidwind (tpt), Heinz Zickler (tpt), Wolfgang Pasch (tpt), Walter Schetsche (tpt), Wilhelm Ackerman (tpt), Otto Jahn (tpt), Württemberg CO [cnd:Jörg Faerber] *(Stoelzel:Con in D for 6 Tpts & Strs)*, Edward Carroll (tpt), Concerto Rotterdam *(Baldassare:Tpt Son 1 in F [Grave])*, Alois Spach (ob), Alfred Sous (ob), Hans Bogacchi (ob), Mainz CO [cnd:Günter Kehr] *(Telemann:Suite in F for Hn, 2 Obs & Strs [Der Alster Echo])*, Ulrich Koch (va pomposa), Southwest German Orch [cnd:Paul Angerer] *(Sammartini:Con in C for Va Pomposa & Strs [Andante])*, Christianne Jaccottet (hpd), Württemberg CO [cnd:Jörg Faerber] *(Bach:Hpd Con in g [1st movt])*, Herman Sauter (tpt), Southwest German CO [cnd:Paul Angerer] *(Stradella:Son for Tpt & Strs [Allegro])*, Southwest German CO [cnd:Paul Angerer] *(Handel:Con Grosso No. 5 in D [Larghetto]; Corelli:Con Grosso in g [Allegro])*, Salzburg Soloists *(Clarke:Tpt Voluntary)* VCC (25 Favorites) ▲ 8820 ▮ 8820

The Ultimate Baroque Collection—features works by Albinoni, Bach, Handel, Pachelbel, Purcell, Telemann, Vivaldi
ERAT ▲ 92876 [DDD] (9.97)

BASSOON

Caliban Quartet [Fraser Jackson (bn), Nadina Mackie Jackson (bn), Kathleen McLean (bn), Michael Sweeney (bn)]
Bassoonatics! *(arr by F. Jackson & M. Sweeney)*, w. Mark Duggan (perc)—features works by Gershwin *(3 Preludes; I Got Rhythm)*, Brahms *(8 Waltzes [from 16 Waltzes, Op. 39])*, Sibelius *(Little Suite [from The Tempest, Op. 109]; Sonatine, Op. 67)*, Hahn *(3 Postcards)*, Mitchell Clarke *(Madrigal)*, Mozart *(Gigue, K.574)*, Anderson *(Bassoonist's Holiday)*, McHugh & Fields/Tatum *(I'm in the Mood for Love)*, Ellington *(Caravan)*, Lennon & McCartney *(Oh! Darling)*, Stravinsky *(Tango)*, Welsh *(Tango)*, Weill *(Youkali)*, Piazzolla *(Tango)*, Douglas *(Azure) (rec Glenn Gould Studio, Toronto, June 7 & 13, 1996)*
CBC (Musica Viva) ▲ 1116 [DDD] (16.97)

Janota, Gábor (bn)
Contemporary Hungarian Music for Bassoon, w. Zoltán Kocsis (pno/cym/hpd/prepared pno/harm/org/perc), Klára Körmendi (pno)—features works by Bozay *(Episodi 2)*, Petrovics *(Passacaglia in Blues)*, Dubrovay *(Scherzo; Pezzi (5))*, Sári *(Meditazione)*, Vidovszky *(Solo w. obbligato accompaniment)*, Kalmár *(Monologo 7/a)*, Sáry *(The Echoing Green)*, Lendvay *(Movts (3) Bn & Pno)* HUN ▲ 31725 [AAD/DDD] (16.97)

Loubry, Luc (bn)
The Golden Age of the Harp & French Bassoon—features works by Debussy, Labarre, Naderman, Saint-Saëns
ARCB ▲ SBCD 1511

McGill, David (bn)
Orchestral Excerpts for Bassoon—features sels. from works by Mozart *(Le nozze di Figaro)*, Beethoven *(Syms 4 & 9; Cons 1-3 for Vn)*, Berlioz *(Sym fantastique)*, Rossini *(La Gazza Ladra)*, Donizetti *(Una furtiva lagrima)*, Tchaikovsky *(Syms 4-6)*, Rimsky-Korsakov *(Scheherazade)*, R. Strauss *(Till Eulenspiegels lustige Streiche; Ein Heldenleben)*, Ravel *(Bolero; Alborada del grazioso; Rapsodie Espanol; Con in G for Pno)*, Stravinsky *(Firebird; La sacre du printemps)*, Bartók *(Con for Orch)*, Shostakovich *(Syms 1 & 9) (rec Plymouth Church Chapel, Shaker Heights, OH, Dec 13, 1993 & July 26, 1994)*
SUMM ▲ 162 [DDD] (16.97)

Marchese, Catherine (bn)
Bassoon Recital, w. Emile Naoumoff (pno)—features works by Devienne *(Son., Op. 24/5)*, Saint-Saëns *(Son., Op. 168; Romance, Op. 36)*, Ravel *(Habanera)*, Petit *(Guilledoux)*, Tansman *(Aria)*, Boulanger *(Nocturne)*, Naoumoff *(Intense et doux; Lyrique mais sobre; Mélancolique et "Slave")*, David *(Concertino, Op. 12)*, Weber *(Andante et Rondo ungarese, J.158)*, Spohr *(Adagio, Op. 115), J.S. Bach (),)* GEGA ▲ 162 [DDD] (16.97)

Millard, Christopher (bn)
Mélange: French Music for Bassoon, w. Kenneth Broadway (pno), Camille Churchfield (fl)—features works by Paul Bonneau, Henri Büsser, Dutilleux, Pierre Gabaye, Gabriel Grovlez, Paul Jeanjean, Charles Koechlin, G. Pierné, H. Sauguet, A. Tansman SUMM ▲ 128 [DDD] (16.97) ▮
Orchestral Excerpts for Bassoon, Vol. 2—features 37 excerpts SUMM (OrchestraPro) ▲ 220 (16.97)

Nigro, Susan (ctbn)
Little Tunes for the Big Bassoon, w. Mark Lindeblad (pno)—features works by Cherubini *(Morceau pour le Basson)*, Corelli *(Suite from Vars on Themes of Tortini [arr Dishinger])*, Geminiani *(Con Grosso, Op. 3/2 [Allegro; arr Dishinger])*, Debussy *(Jimbo's Lullaby [arr Fitzgerald])*, Bozza *(Burlesque)*, Gipps *(Honey-Colored Cow, Op. 3d; Leviathan, Op. 59; The Ox & the Ass, Op. 71)*, B. Phillips *(Concert Piece)*, Laudenslager *(Little Suite, Op. 23 [arr Friedman])*, Organn *(Romance)*, Desmond *(Take 5 [arr Keller])*, Hagen *(Harlem Nocturne [arr Haring])*, H. Mancini *(Pink Panther [arr Frackenpohl])*, W. Davis *(Vars on a Theme of R. Schumann)*, Del Negro *(Down in the Deep Cellar [arr Margolis])*, Fucik *(Der Alte Brummbar, Op. 21)*, plus trad songs *(Cl Polka [arr Hummel]; Tarantell Napoletano [arr Nigro])* CRYS ▲ 348 (15.97)

Perkins, Laurence (bn)
Serenade for Susan: A Musical Tribute, w. Manchester Camerata Orch—features works by Glère, Perkins, Fauré, Grovlez, Michael Legrand, Weissenborn, Milde, Rachmaninoff, Vinter, Elgar, Albert, McLeod, Dorff-Herbstritt-Sklenov-Lloyd *(rec Sept 8 & 11-12, 1989 & Aug 11, 1990)* INMP ▲ 1031 [DDD] (10.97)

Smith, Daniel (bn)
Bassoon Bon-Bons, w. Royal PO [cnd:Ettore Stratta], English CO [cnd:Philip Ledger], Coull String Quartet, Roger Vignoles (pno)—features works by Bach, Chopin, Corelli, Debussy, Kreisler, Martini, Rachmaninoff, Schubert, Tchaikovsky, Verdi, Vivaldi, Henry Hargrave, Gordon Jacob, Arne, Dunhill, Elgar, Gordon Jacob, Vaughan William, plus The Londonderry Air ASV ▲ 2052 [DDD] (12.97)
Bravo Bassoon, w. Jonathan Still (pno), Caravaggio Ensemble—features Träumerei; Melody in F; Après un rêve; Smoke Gets in Your Eyes; Largo al factotum ASV ▲ 2078 [DDD] (12.97)
English Music for Bassoon & Piano, w. Roger Vignoles (pno)—features works by Arne, Avison, Dunhill, Elgar, Hurlstone, Jacob, Vaughan Williams, & others ASV ▲ 535 (17.97)

Sønstevold, Knut (bn)
The Virtuoso Bassoon—features works by M. Arnold *(8 English Dances, Opp. 27 & 33)*, Beethoven *(Trio in G for Fl, Bn & Pno, WoO 37 [w. G. von Bahr & L. Negro])*, Blomdahl *(Liten svit for Bn & Pno)*, Koch *(Monolog 5)*, Jan Morthenson *(Unisono for Bn, Live Electronics & Hpd [w. E. Nordwall])*, Tansman *(Sonatina for Bn & Pno [w. Knardahl])*, Boutry *(Interfénces for Bn & Pno [w. Knardahl])* BIS ▲ 122 [AAD] (17.97)

Tanaka, Masahito (bn)
Bassoon Fantasia—features works by Albéniz, Bloch, Chopin/Glazunov, G. Dinicu/J. Heifetz, Elgar, de Falla, P. A. Genin, F. Kreisler, C. Lenom, Rachmaninoff, Saint-Saëns, J. Weissenborn PAVA ▲ 7252 [DDD] (10.97)
French Music for Bassoon, w. Kazue Kojima (pno), Shigeko Tojo (fl), Erika Inoue (hp)—features works by Pierné *(Solo de Concert, Op. 35)*, Saint-Saëns *(Son Bn, Op. 168)*, Gallon *(Récit & allegro)*, Dutilleux *(Sarabande & Cortège)*, Allard *(Vars sur un thème de Paganini)*, Gabaye *(Sonatine Fl & Bn)*, Jolivet *(Pastorales de Noël) (rec Oct 1995)*
PAVA ▲ 7349 [DDD] (10.97)
The Magic Bassoon, w. Seiko Sumi (pno)—features works by Jacqueline Fontyn *(Zephyr [w. Sumi])*, Hindemith *(Son [w. Sumi])*, Choji Kaneta *(Ambivalence IV)*, Mercadante *(Cavatine di Donna Caritea, Op. 60)*, Saint-Saëns *(Son, Op. 168 [w. Sumi])*, Jean-Louis Tulou *(Grand Solo No. 13, Op. 96)*, Weber *(Andante e Rondo ongarese, Op. 35 [w. Sumi])*, Isang Yun *(Monologue)* THOR ▲ 2099 [DDD] (16.97)

BASSOON COLLECTIONS

United Sounds of Bassoon, w. various artists—features works by Prokofiev, DesPrez, Corrette, Schiffelholz, Mozart, Bizet, Stravinsky, Hindemith, Schickele & others KSCH ▲ 313742 [DDD] (16.97)

BRASS & WIND ENSEMBLE

American Brass Quintet [Raymond Mase (tpts/flgl), Chris Gekker (tpts/flgl), David Wakefield (hn), Michael Powell (trbns), John D. Rojak (b trbn)]
American Brass Quintet—features works by Bach, Coperario, Dowland, Ferrabosco, A. Gabrieli, G. Gabrieli, Holborne, Morley, Scheidt, Simpson, Speer, Storl, Weelkes DLS ▲ 3003 [DDD]
The Yankee Brass Band *(popular music from mid-19th cent America on period instrs)* NWW ▲ 312 [ADD] (16.97)

Annapolis Brass Quintet, Berlin Brass Quintet, Dallas Brass Quintet, Metropolitan Brass Quintet, New York Brass Quintet, 1-5 Brass Quintet, St. Louis Brass Quintet
Brass Bonanza—features works by Malcolm Arnold, Horovitz, Hovhaness, et al. CRYS ▲ 200 [ADD/DDD] (15.97)

Aquitaine Brass, London Brass [cnd:Richard Harvey]
Fanfare for the Common Man—features works by Lully, Copland, Adson, Gesualdo, Gabrieli, Viadana, Purcell, Richard Harvey ASV ▲ 870 [DDD] (16.97)

Aria en Harmonie Quartet
Le Bal du kiosque à musique *(19th & early 20th century dance music)*—featuring works by Metra *(Les lanciers; Les roses; Brise du soir; Blanche Marguerite)*, Bosc *(Big Boot Dance)*, Desmarquoy *(La berline française)*, Ganne *(Les saltimbangues [quadrille & polk]; L'auvergnate)*, Peschini *(Danse des patineurs)*, Offenbach *(Orphée aux enfers [arr I. Strauss])*, Borel-Clerc *(La matchiche)*, Cairanne *(Le bouquet final) (rec Dec 1989)* FMD ▲ 183 [DDD]

Aries Brass Quintet
Aries Brass Quintet—features works by Bach, Byrd, Debussy, Grainger, Handel, Mahler, Mouret, Pachelbel
CENT ▲ 2083 [DDD] (16.97)

Arnold Quintet
Arnold Quintet—features works by Berio *(Ricorrenze)*, Sciarrino *(Qnt 2 Ww)*, Francesconi *(Attesa)*, Einaudi *(Ai margini dell'aria)*, Gentilucci *(Chile, 1973)*, Ghendi *(Qnt 1 Ww)* BMGR ▲ 1010 (18.97)

Atlantic Brass Quintet [Joseph Foley (tpt), Jeffrey Luke (tpt), R. Rasmussen (hn), John Faieta (trbn), John Manning (tuba)]
A Musical Voyage—features works by Telemann *(Con in B♭ [arr J. Foley])*, Holborne *(3 E.an Dances [arr ABQ])*, Peuerl *(Canzon I [arr B. Fitzgerald])*, Praetorius *(Terpsichore [Suite; arr ABQ])*, J. S. Bach *(Contrapunctus IV [arr Glasel])*, Ewald *(Qnt in D♭ No. 3, Op. 11)*, Satie *(3 Pieces [arr R. Rasmussen])*, Arutunian *(Armenian Scenes [1984])*
SUMM ▲ 119 [DDD] (16.97) ▮

Avena Trio [Jan de Maeyer (ob), Nestor Janssens (cl), Luc Loubry (bn)]
Recital of French Music—features works by D. Dondeyne, Françaix, Ibert, Tomasi ARCB ▲ SBCD 2500 [DDD]

Bavarian Brass Soloists of Munich [cnd:Gerd Zapf]
5 Centuries of Music for Brass Ensemble—features works by Boyce, Bruckner, Diabelli, C. Gervaise, G. Gabrieli, Handel, Lassus, Mouret, Orff, Purcell, et al. CALG ▲ CAL 50837 [DDD]

Bayreuth Festival Horns
Es blies ein Jäger wohl in sein Horn Acanta ▲ 43469
Fantasies for 8 Horns—features works by Wagner *(Lohengrin-Fant)*, Karl Stiegler *(Rheingold-Fant)*, Manfred Klier *(Siegfried- & Tristan und Isolde-Fants)* Acanta ▲ 43800

Belgian National Orchestra Clarinet Quartet
4 Clarinets—features works by Mortier, Bernstein, Gershwin, Thompson, Botsford, Rogers, Pleckmans, et al.
SYRX ▲ 97101 (16.97)

BRASS & WIND ENSEMBLE

Berlin Brass

Berlin Brass *(members of Berlin German Opera Orch & Berlin PO)*—features works by Clarke *(The Prince of Denmark's March)*, Horovitz *(Music Hall Suite [Soubrette Song; Trick-cyclists; Adagio-Team; Soft Shoe Shuffle; Les Girls])*, Farnaby *(Fancies, Toyes & Dreames [The Old Spagnoletta; His Rest; Tell Mee Daphne; A Toye; His Dreame; The New Sa-Hoo])*, Gershwin *(Porgy & Bess [sels])*, Scheidt *(Canzon Bergamasque)*, Banchieri *(Son)*, Pollack *(That's A Plenty)*, Stevens *(Triangels)*, Khachaturian *(Säbeltanz)*, trad *(Frère Jacques; Just a Closer Walk)*, anon *(Intrada)*, plus Salute to Glenn Miller [American Patrol; Moonlight Serenade; arr Bill Holcombe] Binaural Source-Audio Electronics ▲ C-5

Boehme Wind Quintet [Sheryl Heinze (fl), P. Lanini (ob), S. Hartmann (cl), J. Anderer (hn), R. Wagner (bn)]

American Winds, Vol. 2: Jam Session—features works by Mayer *(Yankee Doodle Fanfare)*, Cowell *(Ballad for Wind Qnt)*, Amram *(Qnt for Winds)*, Fine *(Romanza)*, Hoiby *(Diversions for Wind Qnt)*, N. Dello Joio *(Vars on an Orginal Christmas Tune)*, McBride *(Jam Session)* PREM ▲ 1023 [DDD] (16.97)

Borealis Wind Quintet

Discoveries—features works by Wazen, Steinmetz, DelAguila HEL ▲ 1030 (10.97)

Brass Ring

Brass Ring—features works by Bach, Berio, V. Ewald, G. Gabrieli, Bryan Kelly, Praetorius CRYS ▲ 561 (15.97) ▮ 561

Brass Septet of the Prague Castle

Festival Music of Rudolphian Prague—features Demantius *(Conviviorum deliciae)*, M. Franck *(Neue Musicalische Intraden)*, H. L. Hassler *(Lustgarten (suite))*, Orologio *(Intradae Alexandri Orologii)*, V. Otto *(Newe Paduanen (suite))*, M. Praetorius *(Terpsichore)*, J. H. Schein *(Venus Kräntzlein)*, Vodňanský *(Psalmi poenitentiales)* MUL ▲ 310380 [DDD] (10.97)

California Wind Orch

A Slice of America—features 17 anthems & marches including The Star Spangled Banner; The Marines' Hymn; Semper Fidelis; Anchors Aweigh; Semper Paratus; America the Beautiful; Stars & Stripes Forever SUMM ▲ 215 (10.97)

Canadian Brass [Fred Mills (tpt), Ronald Romm (tpt), David Ohanian (hn), Eugene Watts (trbn), Charles Daellenbach (tuba)]

Basin Street—features works by George Segal (banjo & vocals on 4 sels) & trad New Orleans jazz tunes COL ▲ 42367 [DDD] (9.97) 42367

Best of the Canadian Brass *(19 classical, popular & sacred music sels from previous CBS Masterworks releases)* COL ▲ 45744 [DDD] (16.97) ▮ 45744 (10.98)

Bolero & Other Blockbusters—features Also sprach Zarathustra; Con for 2 Tpts; Sarabande; Bolero; Turkish March; Jesu, Joy of Man's Desiring; Rondeau; Royal Fireworks; Gloria; Largo; Minute Waltz; Toreador Song; Turkish Rondo; Cor Royale; Waltz of the Flowers; Dance of the Hours; Glow-Worm; Hall of the Mountain King; Can-Can; Jerusalem; La Virgen de la Macarena; Grand March [from Aida]; Gaudeamus Igitur; Ov to H.M.S. Pinafore; Golyardes' Grounde; Farewell Anthem RCAV ▲ 68109 (10.97) ▮ 68109 (6.98)

Brass Busters, w. New York PO Brass, Boston Sym Brass RCAV ▲ 68076 (16.97) ▮ 68076

Brass on Broadway, w. Luther Henderson (kbd), Edward Metz (perc), Star of Indiana Drummers—features works by Gershwin *(I Got Rhythm; Bess, You Is My Woman Now; Strike up the Band)*, Loesser *(Fugue for Tin Hns)*, Lloyd-Webber *(Memory; The Race; Music of the Night)*, Rodgers *(Carousel Waltz; Slaughter on 10th Avenue)*, Sondheim *(Send in the Clowns)*, Sullivan *(Let the Tpts Bray)*, Styne *(Bye Bye Baby)*, Ellington *(In a Sentimental Mood; It Don't Mean a Thing If It Ain't Got That Swing)*, Wilson *(76 Trombones)* PPHI ▲ 42133 (16.97)

Canadian Brass Live!—features works by Gabrieli, Mozart, Pachelbel, Vivaldi, et al. COL ▲ 39515 (9.97) 39515

Champions *(covers of pop/rock hits by The Beatles, Simon & Garfunkel, Billy Joel, Elton John, et al.)* COL ▲ 37797 ▮ PMT 37797

Christmas with the Canadian Brass, w. John Grady (org) org of St. Patrick's Cathedral RCAV (Gold Seal) ▲ 4132 ▮ 4132

Encore *(classical, ragtime, etc.)* MUVI (Musica Viva) ▲ 1011 [ADD] (16.97)

The Essential Canadian Brass—features Also sprach Zarathustra (opening); The Well-Tampered Bach; Tuba Tiger Rag; Flight of the Tuba Bee; etc. PPHI ▲ 32571 [DDD] (16.97) ▮ 32571 ▯ 432571-5

Greatest Hits—features works by Bach *(Toccata & Fugue Org, BWV 565)*, Pachelbel *(Canon)*, Handel, Mouret, Sousa, et al RCAV (Red Seal) ▲ 4733 (16.97) ▮ 4733 (9.98)

High, Bright, Light & Clear: The Glory of Baroque Brass—features works by Purcell, Scheidt, Clarke, Reiche, Mouret, Bach, Boyce RCAV (Red Seal) ▲ 4574 [DDD] (16.97) ▮ 4574

In Berlin—features works by Pachelbel, Lassus, Bach, Gibbons, Palestrina, Gabrieli, Albinoni COL ▲ 39035 [DDD] (11.97) 39035

More Greatest Hits—features works by Bach, Barber, Bizet, Debussy, Gershwin, Khachaturian, Rossini, Scheidt, Jelly Roll Morton, Fats Waller, James P. Johnson, et al. RCAV (Red Seal) ▲ 5628 [DDD] (16.97) ▮ 5628

Plays Great Baroque Music—features works by Bach *(Passacaglia & Fugue Org; Sheep May Safely Graze; Toccata & Fugue Org, BWV 565)*, Pachelbel *(Canon)*, Handel *(Water Music (suites))* RCAV (Gold Seal) ▲ 3554 (16.97) 3554

Red, White & Brass, w. Boston SO members, New York PO—features Voluntary On Old Hundredth, American Patrol, Cohan on Broadway, Salute to Sousa, Alexander's Ragtime Band, Grand Circus Fantasia, etc. PPHI ▲ 34276 [DDD] (11.97) ▮ 34276

Toccata, Fugues & Other Diversions—features works by Bach *(Toccata & Fugue in d, BWV 565; "Little" Fugue in g, BWV 578)*, Howard Cable *(Songs of Newfoundland)*, Jelly Roll Morton *(Grandpa's Spells)*, Purcell *(Son in D for Tpt & Org)*, Norman Symonds *(A Diversion)*, trad/arr Don Gillis *(Just a closer walk with thee)* ORG ▲ 3014 [ADD] (13.97)

The Village Band—features works by Sousa, Stephen Foster, Suppé, Rossini, et al. RCAV (Red Seal) ▲ 4436 (16.97) ▮ 4436

Center City Brass

Street Song—features works by Bernstein, Ewazen, Previn, Tilson Thomas DNC ▲ 1030 (16.97)

Chamber Opera Quintet [Theo Mertens, François van Kerckhoven, Alex van Aeken, José Schyns, Gerard Peeters]

Virtuoze Miniaturen—features works by Susato, Holborne, Le Jeune, Schöggl, Poulenc, Granados, Bartók, van Lijnschooten, Meyers, van der Roost, de Meester, Grainger, Renwick, Devreese, Cabus, Celis, Verschueren *(rec Oct-Dec 1987)* EUFO ▲ EUF 1122 [DDD]

Chestnut Brass Company

The Music of Francis Johnson & his Contemporaries: Early 19th-Century Black Composers *(concert band marches & dance music)*—features works by Francis Johnson, plus 10 works by others MUMA ▲ 7029 [DDD] (10.97)

Pastime with Good Company *(Renaissance, Baroque & 19th-20th Cent Music, on historical & modern instrs)* CRYS ▲ 562 (15.97) ▮ 562

Chicago Brass Quintet

Chicago Brass Quintet—features works by Bartók *(Folk Song Suite)*, Falla *(El Amor Brujo Suite; Miller's Dance)*, E. Haines *(Toccata)*, J. Hopkins *(Brass Qnt 1)*, J. Mattern *(Son Breve)*, Mussorgsky *(Hopak)* CRYS ▮ 211

Chicago Chamber Brass

Fireworks for Brass—features works by Bach, Handel, Sousa, Tchaikovsky, et al. PRMX ▲ 805 (3.97) ▮ 805 (6.98)

Chicago Chamber Brass [cnd:Howard Dunn], Dallas Wind Sym

The Brass & the Band CRYS ▲ 431 [DDD] (15.97) ▮ 431

Cleveland Sym Winds [cnd:Frederick Fennell]

Stars & Stripes *(Marches, Fanfares & Wind Band Spectaculars)*—features works by Barber, Fucik, King, Vaughan Williams, Sousa, et al. † Arnaud:Fanfares; Grainger:Lincolnshire; Vaughan Williams:English Folk Suite TEL ▲ 80099 [DDD] (15.97)

Les Cuivres Français [cnd:Thierry Caens]

Fanfares for the Kings of France—features works by Mouret, Gervaise, Lully, Rameau, Marais, Couperin, Josquin Desprez & Lalande PVY ▲ 730080 (16.97)

Dallas Wind Sym [cnd:Howard Dunn]

Fiesta! Reference ▲ RR 38CD [DDD]

Dallas Wind Sym [cnd:Frederick Fennell]

Fennell Favorites!—features works by Bach, Brahms, Goldmark, Halvorsen, MacDowell, Prokofiev Reference ▲ RR 43CD [DDD]

Marches I've Missed—features works by Alford *(On the Quarterdeck)*, Belsterling *(March of the Steel Men [arr Alford])*, W. P. Chambers *(Chicago Tribune March)*, R. Crawford *(U.S. Air Force March)*, H. Fillmore *(Footlifter; Men of Ohio)*, G. Gates *(Sol y Sombra)*, R. B. Hall *(New Colonial March)*, Javaloyes *(El Albanico)*, Jessel *(Parade of the Wooden Soldiers [arr Morrissey])*, K. L. King *(Rough-Riders [arr Swearington])*, P. Lavalle *(Band of America)*, Lithgow *(Invercargill [arr Laurendeau])*, S. E. Morris *(Kilties)*, Olivadoti *(Hall of Fame)*, Sbraccia *(La Banda Nascente)*, Sousa *(Gladiator March; Northern Pines) (rec Meyerson Symphony Center, Dallas, TX, July 15, 1998)* REF ▲ 85 (16.97)

Le Débuché de Paris

The Art of the Hunting Horn ARN ▲ 60353 (13.97)

Denmark Royal Guards Brass Ensemble

The Court of Queen Margrethe II—features works by LaLande *(Fanfare)*, Purcell *(Tpt Tune & Air)*, Stöerl *(Sons 2, 4 & 5)*, Bach *(Contrapunctus IX)*, Franck *(Panis Angelicus)*, Henriques *(Bryllupsmarch)*, Langgaard *(Ribe Tildig Morgen)*, Wilm *(Intermezzo)*, Kreisler *(Liebeslied)*, Giraud *(Sous le Ciel de Paris)*, Olivieri *(Au revoir)*, S. Joplin *(The Crysanthemum)*, Lennon/McCartney *(Hey Jude; Penny Lane)*, J. Clarke *(Tpt Voluntary)* CLSO ▲ CLASSCD 164

Denver Brass [cnd:Kenneth Singleton]

Elegant Classics for Brass—features works by Rossini *(Barber of Seville Ov)*, Grainger *(Colonial Song; Shepherd's Hey)*, Shostakovich *(Concertino, Op. 94)*, Schmeltzer *(Son a VII)*, Byrd *(Suite)*, Delinger *(Paradox)*, Debussy *(Suite from the Preludes)*, Pachelbel *(Ciacona in f) (rec Bethany Lutheran Church, Englewood, CO, June 17-19, 1991)* CENT ▲ 2261 [DDD] (16.97)

Detmold Hornists

Horn Quartets—features works by Jean Désiré Artôt *(Allegro No. 11 [from 12 Qts])*, E. Bozza *(Suite in F for 4 Hns)*, Constantin Homilius *(Qt in B♭, Op. 38)*, Herman Jeurissen *(Lustige Streiche)*, Molter *(Sinf in C)*, Rimsky-Korsakov *(Notturno)*, Franz Strauss *(3 Qts)*, Anton Wunderer *(Aufbruch zur Jagd und Hallali; Ländler; Waldruhe)* MDG ▲ 3324 [DDD] (16.97)

Dutch Tuba Quartet [Hugo Verweij (eup), Arjen Bos (eup), Jan van de Sanden (tuba), Ron Antens (tuba)]

Four Keen Guys—features works by Frackenpohl *(Pop Suite)*, Jacob *(Pieces (4) Tuba Qt)*, Gillis *(Four Kuehn ("Keen") Guys)*, Beal *(Movts (3) for 4 Tubas)*, Berlioz/Werden *(Hungarian March)*, Stevens *(Manhattan Suite)*, Joplin/Werden *(Easy Winners)*, Mertens *(Scyths)*, Handy/Holcombe *(St. Louis Blues) (rec Loosdrecht, Jan 1996)* World Wind ▲ WWM 500 023 [DDD]

Eastern Brass Quintet

Classical Brass—features works by Arnold, Schein, Clavert, Hindemith, C. Monteverdi, J. S. Bach, F. Couperin, G. Gabrieli, Cheetham, Holborne, Charles Ives KLAV ▲ 11025 [ADD]

Eastern Brass Quintet, w. Mary Binney Montgomery (pno), C. Lytle (pno), W. N. Roberts (hpd)—features works by Joplin, A. Marshall, J. Lamb, W. Krell, J. Morton, C. Hunter, K. King, R. Griffith, G. Gershwin KLAV ▲ KCD 11009 [ADD]

Eastman Wind Ensemble [cnd:Frederick Fennell]

Ballet for Band/Wagner for Band *(includes entire "Ballet for Band" LP, plus 1 side of the original Wagner LP)*—features works by Gounod *(Faust Ballet Music)*, Respighi *(La boutique fantasque)*, Sullivan *(Pineapple Poll Suite)*, Wagner *(Lohengrin [Act III Prelude & Bridal Chorus]; Rheingold [Entry of the Gods into Valhalla])* MRCR ▲ 34322 [ADD] (11.97)

British & American Band Classics—features performances by R. R. Bennett, Holst, Jacob, Walton, C. Williams MRCR ▲ 32009 (11.97)

The Civil War: Its Music & Sounds MRCR 2-▲ 32591 (22.97)

Hands across the Sea: Marches from around the World—features The Golden Ear; Hands across the Sea; Father of Victory; Old Comrades March; Valdres March; Inglesina; Knightsbridge March; The U.S. Field Artillery; The Thunderer; Washington Post; King Cotton; El Capitan; American Patrol; On the Mall; Lights Out; Barnum & Bailey's Favorite; Colonel Bogey; The Billboard; The Stars & Stripes Forever MRCR ▲ 34334 (11.97)

Screamers (Circus Marches) & March Time—features works by Goldman & others MRCR ▲ 32019 [ADD] (11.97)

20th Century Works for Wind Band MRCR ▲ 32754 [ADD] (11.97)

Eastman Wind Ensemble members [cnd:Frederick Fennell]

The Spirit of '76 & Ruffles & Flourishes MRCR ▲ 434386 (11.97)

Edmonton Wind Ensemble [cnd:Harry Pinchin]

Concert in the Park—features works by Howard Cable, John Barnes Chance, Robert Farnon, Arthur Sullivan, Weber, Weinberger, et al. SMS (SM 5000) ▲ 5079 [DDD] ▮ SMC 5079 (D)

Snake Fence Country—features M. Arnold *(Little Suite 1 Brass, Op. 80 [1. Prelude; 2. Siciliano; 3. Rondo])*, H. Cable *(Quebec Folk Fant; Snake Fence County)*, Chatman *(Grouse Mountain Lullaby)*, P. Grainger *(Folk Song Settings [Irish Tune from County Derry; Shepherd's Hey])*, G. Holst *(Suite 2 Band, Op. 28/2)*, Leemans *(Marche des Parachutists Belges)*, Mercure *(Pantomime)*, D. Milhaud *(Suite française, Op. 248)*, G. Ridout *(Tafelmusik)* SMS ▲ 5165 [DDD] (16.97)

Empire Brass Quintet [R. Smedvig (tpt), J. Curnow (tpt), E. Ruske (hn), R. Douglas Wright (trbn), K. Amis (tuba)]

Braggin' in Brass—features works by Duke Ellington, Fats Waller, Jelly Roll Morton, Cole Porter, et al. TEL ▲ 80249 [DDD] (15.97) ▮

Class Brass: Classical Favorites for Brass—features works by Bizet, Borodin, Brahms, Copland, Dvořák, Fauré, Ginastera, Grieg, Mussorgsky, Prokofiev, Ravel, Rimsky-Korsakov, Smetana, Tchaikovsky, Verdi TEL ▲ 80220 [DDD] (15.97) ▮

Class Brass II: On the Edge—features works by Shostakovich, Khachaturian, Saint-Saëns, Bizet, Fauré, Bernstein, Enesco, Stravinsky, Offenbach, Copland TEL ▲ 80305 (15.97) ▮

Empire Brass: Greatest Hits—features works by Gabrieli *(Sacrae symphoniae [Canzon septimi toni 2])*, Scheit *(Canzona bergamasca)*, R. Strauss *(Feierlicher Einzug)*, Mozart *(Impresario [ov])*, Debussy *(Suite bergamasque [Prélude])*, Enesco *(Romanian Rhap 1)*, Tchaikovsky *(Nutcracker Suite [Arabian Dance])*, Caccini *(Amarilli mia bella)*, Susato *(Basse Danse Bergeret)*, Weck/de la Torre *(Hopper Dance)*, Smetana *(Bartered Bride [Dance of the Comedians])*, Gershwin *(Summertime [from Porgy and Bess])*, Coleman/Fields *(Sweet Charity [Big Spender])*, plus trad *(When the Saints Go Marching In)* TEL ▲ 80438 [DDD] (15.97)

Empire Brass on Broadway TEL ▲ 80303 [DDD] (15.97) ▮ CS 30303 (D)

Passage, 138 B.C.-A.D. 1611, w. Laurie Monahan (mez), Michael Collver (ct), Pete Maunu (acoustic/elec/12string gtr), Doug Lunn (fretless bass), David Goldblatt (kbd), K. Wortman (elec/acoustic perc)—features Haec Dies; Spritual Dance; Minimal; Sibley Sanctus Lydian; De profundis; Hopper Dance; Instrumental; Sy Dolce; Factus est repente; Sun Credo; Scandinavian Chant; 1st Delphic Hymn; Dilectus meus; Peccatem em quotidie; Lydian; The Melancholy of Departure *(rec Lenox, MA & Los Angeles, CA May 27-29 & June 28-July 2, 1994)* TEL ▲ 80355 [DDD] (15.97) ▮

Romantic Brass: Music of France & Spain—features works by Albéniz, Debussy, Falla, Granados, Ravel, Rodrigo, Turina TEL ▲ 80301 [DDD] (15.97) ▮

Royal Brass: Music from the Renaissance & Baroque—features works by Mouret *(Masterpiece Theatre theme)*, Albinoni, Bach, Handel, Holborne, Palestrina, et al. TEL ▲ 80257 [DDD] (15.97) ▮

Epsilon Brass Ensemble

Musique Française pour quintette de cuivres et harmonie, w. Republican Guard Orch of Harmony [cnd:Roger Boutry]—features works by R. Boutry, P.-M. Dubois, S. Lancen, J.-C. Naude, F. Rauber FORL ▲ 16646 [DDD] (16.97)

Fine Arts Brass Ensemble [Bryan Allen (tpt), Andy Culshaw (tpt), Stephen Roberts (hn), Simon Hogg (trbn), Richard Sandland (tuba)]

Best of the Fine Arts Brass Ensemble—features works by Sousa *(Stars & Stripes Forever)*, Waller *(Smashin' 3rds/Valentine Stomp)*, Rocca *(Tiger Rag)*, Mascagni *(Cavalleria rusticana [Intermezzo; arr S. Hogg])*, J. Strauss *(Thunder & Lightning Polka)*, Pachelbel *(Canon)*, Porter *(Another Openin', Another Show)*, Vivaldi *(4 Seasons [Winter])*, Berlin *(Not for All the Rice in China)*, Williams *(Devil's Gallop [arr S. Hogg])*, Maschwitz/Sherwin *(Nightingale Sang in Berkeley Square)*, Yellen/Ager *(Ain't She Sweet)*, Bratton *(Teddy Bear's Picnic)*, Coots/Klages *(Doin' the Raccoon)* [all arr S. Roberts except where noted] DOY ▲ DOY 010 [DDD]

The Lighter Side of the Fine Arts Brass Ensemble—features works by Bach, Irving Berlin, Charpentier, Elgar, Fauré, Rossini, Sousa, Tchaikovsky, Robin Holloway *(Brass Qnt; Divert 5, Op. 67)* SAY ▲ 381 [DDD] (16.97)

French Brass

Alla Francese—features works by Poulenc *(Son for Hn, Tpt & Trbn)*, Saint-Saëns *(Cavatine for T Trbn & Pno, Op. 144)*, Dukas *(Villanelle for Hn & Pno)*, Ibert *(Impromptu for Tpt & Pno)*, Dutilleux *(Choral, cadence et fugato for Trbn & Pno)*, Françaix *(Divert for Hn & Pno)*, Hubeau *(Son for Chromatic Tpt & Pno)*, Gabaye *(Récréation for Tpt, Hn, Trbn & Pno)* PVY ▲ 793041 [DDD] (16.97)

Gerhard Meinl Tuba Sextet

Tuba!: A 6 Tuba Musical Romp—features works by Bach *(Fugue in g)*, Couperin *(Les Mysterieueses)*, Gabrieli *(Canzone)* ANGL ▲ 54729 (16.97) ▮ 54729

Gothenburg Brass Band [cnd:Bengt Eklund]

Versatile Reality—features works by Shostakovich *(Festival Ov, Op. 96)*, Roman *(The Royal Wedding Music of Drottingholm)*, Bellini *(Con Hn in E♭)*, Johansson *(Anniversary Ov)*, Hylander *(Strawberry Prelude)*, Rossini *(Guillaume Tell Ov for Cowbells & Xyl)*, Aagaard-Nilsen *(Circius-Wind of the North)*, Sparke *(Mountain Song)*, Gregson *(Dances & Arias)*, plus Music from the Elisabethan Court [arr Howarth] IGC ▲ 62 (16.97)

Greater Bendigo Concert Brass [cnd:Mark Ford]

Hot Brass—features Rock Music III; Ticket to Ride; Born Free; Heal the World; Aladdin; Manhattan Skyline; With One Look; A World of Our Own; Jurassic Park; Schindler's List; Say You, Say Me; Robin Hood—Prince of Thieves; I Will Always Love You; Lil' Darlin'; Adventures in Brass WALC ▲ 9001 [DDD]

Grimethorpe Colliery Band [cnd:Peter Parkes]

The Melody Shop—features The Melody Shop; Slaughter on 10th Avenue; Doretta's Aria [from La rondine]; Lezghinka; The Debutante; Prelude to Act 3 [from Lohengrin]; Every Time We Say Goodbye; Rhap España; Tpt Blues & Cantabile; Adagio; Gallop [from Guillaume Tell]; McArthur Park; 18th Paganini Var; Punchinello; Ave Maria; Light Walk; One Day in Your Life; Toccata CHN ▲ 4552 (16.97)

Hickman, David (cnt), Mark H. Lawrence (trbn)

The Golden Age of Brass: Virtuoso Solos, Vol. 1, w. American Serenade Band [cnd:Henry Charles Smith]—features works by J. C. Bartlett, Herman Bellstedt, Herbert L. Clarke, John Hartmann, Arthur Pryor, Rossini, Tchaikovsky, Verdi, Leo Zimmermann SUMM ▲ 114 [DDD] (16.97) ▮

The Golden Age of Brass: Virtuoso Solos, Vol. 2—features works by Theresa Del Riego, Frederick Innes, Jules Levy, Alessandro Liberati, Tito Mattei, Arthur Pryor, Saint-Saëns, Thomas Short, Frank Simon, Tchaikovsky SUMM ▲ 121 [DDD] (16.97) ▮

HR Brass [cnd:Lutz Köhler]

HR Brass *(Brass Ensemble of the Frankfurt RSO)*—features works by Bach *(Brandenburg Con 3)*, Barber *(Mutations from Bach)*, Copland *(Fanfare for the Common Man)*, Elliott Carter *(Fant upon 1 note from Purcell)*, Handel *(Royal Fireworks Music)*, Purcell *(Fant upon 1 note; Fant in Nomine à 6)* CAPO ▲ 10361 [DDD] (11.97)

934 ▲ = CD ♦ = Enhanced CD △ = MD ▮ = Cassette Tape ▯ = DCC

Hungarian Army Central Wind Orch [cnd:László Marosi, László Dohos, László Geiger]
Marches from the Hungarian History—features works by Doppler, Druschetzky, Gungl, Haydn, Hertelendi, Kisfaludy, de Loiseau, Massák, Proszt, Rezniček, Siposs, Starke, Tasner, Zaitz HUN ▲ 31447 [DDD] (16.97)

Israeli Wind Virtuosi
Israeli Wind Virtuosi—features works by Bach, Beethoven, Haydn, Mozart, Rameau, Scarlatti KOCH ▲ 7309 (16.97)

Israeli Wind Virtuosi [Eli Heifetz (cl), Mordechai Rechtman (bn)]
Israeli Wind Virtuosi & Friends, w. Menahem Breuer (vn), Gad Lewertoff (va), Avshalom Sarid (va), Yoram Alperin (vc)—features works by Beethoven & Mozart KOCH ▲ 7401 (16.97)

Philip Jones Brass Ensemble
PJBE Finale: Music Written for Philip Jones—features works by M. Berkeley, et al. CHN ▲ 8490 [DDD] (16.97)
Weekend Brass—features works by Clarke, G. Gabrieli, Handel, etc. PLON (Weekend Classics) ▲ 21633

Keystone Wind Ensemble [cnd:Jack Stamp]
Pageant: American Music for Symphonic Band—features works by Persichetti *(Pageant)*, Dello Joio *(Scenes from the Louvre)*, Robert R. Bennett *(Symphonic Songs)*, Barber *(Commando March)*, J. B. Chance *(Incantation & Dance)*, W. Schuman *(Newsreel in 5 Shots)*, J. W. Jenkins *(American Ov)*, F. Werle *(Concertino)*, Stamp *(Cheers)* CIT ▲ 88132 [DDD] (15.97)
Songs of Abelard & Other World Premieres—features works by M. Gould *(Fanfare for Freedom)*, Mennin *(Canzona)*, Dello Joio *(Songs of Abelard [w. Curt Scheib (bar)])*, Creston *(Celebration Ov)*, Persichetti *(Bagatelles)*, Camphouse *(Watchman Tell Us of the Night)*, Bergsma *(March with Tpts)*, T. Mahr *(Fant in G)* CIT ▲ 88128 [DDD] (15.97)

Lieurance Woodwind Quintet
Lieurance Woodwind Quintet: Debut Recording—features works by Carter *(Woodwind Qnt)*, Fine *(Partita for Wind Qnt)*, Berger *(Qt in C)*, Persichetti *(Pastoral, Op. 21)*, Barrows *(March)*, Barber *(Summer Music, Op. 31)* SUMM ▲ 149 [DDD] (16.97)

Locke Brass Consort [cnd:James Stobart]
Fanfare: British Music for Symphonic Brass Ensemble—features works by Arthur Benjamin, Arthur Bliss, Havergal Brian, Elgar, Gordon Jacob, Edmund Rubbra, Robert Simpson, Michael Tippett, William Walton CHN (Collect) ▲ 6573 [ADD] (12.97)

London Brass
Baroque & Brass—features works by Bach, Couperin, Handel, Purcell, Rameau, Stanley, et al. TELC (Digital Experience) ▲ 77604 [DDD] ▮
Christmas with London Brass ELEC ▲ 46443 [DDD] ▮ 46443
I Got Rhythm *(Songs from the Shows)—features works by George Gershwin, Jerome Kern, Cole Porter, Richard Rodgers, et al.* ELEC ▲ 46444
Impressions of Brass—features works by Ravel *(Bolero)*, Fauré *(Pie Jesu)*, Debussy *(Golliwog's Cake Walk; Clair de lune)*, Bizet *(Suite [from Carmen])*, plus others ICC ▲ 6701982 (8.97)
International Folk Songs: Around the World with London Brass ELEC ▲ 73270
¡Viva España! ELEC ▲ 76990

London Brass Players [cnd:Joshua Rifkin]
Baroque Fanfares & Sonatas Elektra/Nonesuch ▮ 71145-4

London Gabrieli Brass Ensemble
From the Steeples & the Mountains *(20th-cent music for brass in various combinations, some w. org)*—features works by Barber *(Mutations from Bach)*, Cowell *(Grinnel Fanfare; Hymn & Fuguing Tune 12; Rondo; Tall tale)*, Elliott Carter *(Fant upon 1 note from Purcell)*, Glass *(Brass Sxt)*, Harris *(Chorale for Org & Brass)*, Ives *(From the steeples & the mountains; Processional:Let there be light)*, Ruggles *(Angels)*, Thomson *(Family Portrait)* HYP ▲ 66517
The Splendour of Baroque Brass—features works by Bach, M.-A. Charpentier, Clarke, G. Gabrieli, Holborne, Locke, Pezel, Purcell, Scheidt, Stanley, Susato, Anon. ASVQ ▲ 6013 [ADD] (10.97)

London Gabrieli Brass Ensemble, London Gabrieli Chorus
A Heralding of Battles & Ceremonies *(Brass Music of the Baroque)* Elektra/Nonesuch ▮ 71414-4

London SO Brass [cnd:Eric Crees]
London Symphony Brass—features works by Barber *(Mutations from Bach)*, Bernstein *(Prelude, Fugue & Riffs; West Side Story Suite)*, Copland *(Ceremonial Fanfare; Fanfare for the Common Man; El Salón México)*, Cowell *(Fanfare for the Latin American Allies)*, Ives *(Variations on "America")* COC ▲ 1288 [DDD] (16.97)

Los Angeles PO members [cnd:Akira Endo], Crystal CO
Music for Double-Reed Ensemble, w. Bert Gassman (ob)—features works by Bach *(Ricercar a 6)*, Lukas Foss *(Oboe Concerto)*, Handel *(2 Pieces)*, George Heussenstamm *(Set for Double Reeds)*, Boris Pillin *(3 Pieces for Double-Reed Septet)* CRYS ▲ 871 (15.97)

Ludwig Güttler Wind Ensemble
All the World Praise God—features works by Schütz, Gabrieli and Praetorius CAPO ▲ 10068 [DDD]
Dresden, City of Music—features works by Fantini, Fasch, Handel, Heinichen, Monteverdi, Pezel, Pisendel, Schütz, Vivaldi, Zelenka CAPO ▲ 10 395 [DDD]

Mainz CO [cnd:Günter Kehr, Jörg Faerber], Württemberg CO
The Virtuoso French Horn, w. various soloists—features works by Telemann *(Suite in F for Horns, 2 Oboes & Strings)*, Vivaldi's *(Concerto in F for 2 Horns & Strings)*, Rosetti *(Horn Concerto in d)* ALLO ▲ 8144 [ADD] ▮ 8144

Make Believe Brass
18 Wild, Wacky & Winsome Works for Brass Quintet *(a modern recreation of a turn-of-the-century American brass band concert by Disneyland's brass quintet-in-residence)*—features music by Beethoven, Delibes, Haydn, Kabalevsky, Ketèlby, Khachaturian, Meyerbeer, Ponchielli, Rossini, Sousa, Tchaikovsky, Weill; plus various American pop standards CRYS ▲ 432 [DDD] (15.97) ▮ 432

Mélodia Brass Ensemble [cnd:Pierre-Alain Bidaud]
The European—features works by James Curnow, Gordon Langford, François Margot, Goff Richards and G.H. Willcocks; eight transcriptions of works by Ernest Ansermet, Paul Dukas, Sam Fonteyn, Harry James, LaRocca & Shields, John Scott, Shostakovich, Wagner GALL ▲ CD 624 [ADD]
Opera Fantasies, w. Stefan Vladar [pno]—features works by Bizet *(Fantaisie brillante on Themes from Carmen for Flute & Piano, arr. Borne)*, Weber *(Der Freischütz Fantasy for Clarinet & Piano, arr. Fritz Kroepsch)*, Gershwin *(Songs from Porgy & Bess for Bassoon & Piano, arr. Heinze Czadek)*, Verdi *(Rigoletto Concert Paraphrase for solo Piano, arr. Liszt)*, Wagner *(Der Ring des Nibelungen Fantasy for Horn & Piano, arr. R. Horvath)*, Donizetti *(Concerto sopra motivi dell'opera La Favorita for Oboe & Piano, arr. Pasculli)* COL ▲ 52564

Meridian Arts Ensemble
Anxiety of Influence—features works by Zappa *(Run Home Slow; The Little March; Little House I Used to Live In; Black Page)*, Barber *(Semahane [Whirling Wind])*, Debussy *(Pour Invoquer Pan; Sarabande)*, Grabois *(Zen Monkey)*, Silverman *(Vars on a theme of Kurt Weill)*, Stewart *(KOHS-Ska; Okay Chorale)* CCL ▲ 9796 (17.97)

Meridian Arts Ensemble [John Nelson (tpt), Daniel Grabois (hn), Josef Burgstaller (tpt), Benjamin Herrington (trbn), Raymond G. Stewart (tuba), John Ferrari (perc)]
Ear Mind I—features works by Zappa *(King Kong [arr Burgstaller]; The Black Page [arr Newman & Nelson]; Lumpy Gravy; Marqueson's Chicken; Pygmy Twylyte; Hungry Freaks Daddy [all arr Nelson])*, J. Forsythe *(Sanctity)*, Su Lian Tan *(Moo Shu Wrap Rap)*, J. Nelson *(Fanfare for Nothingness; Sleepless)*, J. Ferrari *(MAE We Strut?; Crunch)*, T. Pierson *(Brass Qnt)*, J. Burgstaller *(Lullaby; Dr. J. Geyser)*, R. Brecker *(Some Skunk Funk [arr Herrington])* CCL ▲ 11898 [DDD] (17.97)
Smart Went Crazy, w. Mo Roberts (perc)—features works by Frank Zappa, J. Halle, Phillip Johnston, Billy Strayhorn, Kirk Nurock, Norman Yamada, Jimi Hendrix, Traditional Afro/Cuban *(rec Mar 1993)* CCSC ▲ 4192 [DDD] (17.97)
Winning Artists Series—features works by Arutiunian *(Armenian Scenes)*, Jan Bach *(Laudes)*, Etler *(Quintet for Brass)*, Hindemith *(Morgenmusik)*, Lutoslawski *(Mini Overture)*, Taxin *(Brass Quintet) (rec Feb 1991)* CCSC ▲ 2191 [DDD] (17.97)

Mighty Tubadours
Mighty Tubadours Merry Christmas Album CRYS ▮ C422
Music Performed by Tuba Quartet—features works by A. Bartles, V. Herbert, R. Vaughan, et al. CRYS ▲ 420 (15.97)
The Tubadours *(Disneyland's tuba quartet-in-residence)* CRYS ▮ C421

Millar Brass Ensemble [cnd:Bruce Briney]
A Chicago Brass Tradition—features works by Berner, Franzetti, Hornoff, Plog, Rautavaara, Wilbye KOSS ▲ 1011 [DDD] (17.97)
Millar Brass Ensemble—features works by Bach, Brahms, Tomasi, Tull, Wagner CRYS ▲ 433 (15.97) ▮ 433

Millar Brass Ensemble [cnd:Vincent Cichowicz]
Brass Surround—features works by Prokofiev *(March, Op. 99; March [from The Love for 3 Oranges])*, Susato *(6 Dances [from La Danserie]; La Mourisque; Bransle 4 Bransle; Ronde; Basse Danse Bergeret; Ronde—Mon Amy; Pavane Battaille)*, Grieg *(Funeral March)*, Mouret *(Rondeau)*, Morley *(Now is the Month of Maying)*, Gabrieli *(Son pian' e forte; Canzona septimi toni, No. 2)*, Chesnokov *(Salvation is Created)*, Pachelbel *(Magnificat)*, Britten *(Russian Funeral)*, Bach *(Suite de danses; Sarabande; Bourée; Sicilienne; Badinerie) (rec Alice Millar Chapel, Northwestern University, Evanston, IL, May 8-10 & 12, 1995)* DLS ▲ 3171 [DDD]

Missouri Brass Quintet [Keith Benjamin (tpt), Jay Sollenberger (tpt), Ann Ellsworth (hn), John Leisenring (trbn), Daniel Burdick (tuba)], John Obetz (org)
Festival of Organ & Brass, w. Jon Donald (perc)—features works by Peeters *(Entrada Festiva)*, J. S. Bach *(Nun danket alle Gott; Jesu, nun sei gepreistet)*, Pinkham *(Gloria)*, Gabrielli *(Son Pian'e Forte; Canzon Duodecimi Toni; Canzon Noni Toni)*, Karl-Elert *(Marche Triomphale)*, Purcell *(Music for the Funeral of Queen Mary)*, Praetorius *(In Dulci Jubilo)*, R. Strauss *(Feirlicher Einzug der Ritter des Johannitzordens)*, Pfautsch *(If Thou but Suffer God to Guide Thee)*, Widor *(Salvum Fac Populum Tuum)* [RLDS Peace Temple Casavant Org] *(rec RLDS Peace Temple, Independence, MO)* RBW ▲ RBWCD 008

Munich Brass
Munich Brass—features works by Malcolm Arnold *(Quintet)*, Victor Ewald *(Quintet No. 2, Op. 6)*, Richard Roblee *(American Images)*, Gershwin *(Gershwin in Brass)*, et al. ORF ▲ 166881 [DDD] (18.97)

New Mexico Brass Quintet
Baroque & 20th Century Works—features works by Bach, M. Brouwer, Handel, W. Hutchison, M. Lamb, Scheidt CRYS ▲ 563 (15.97) ▮ 563
New Mexico Brass Quintet—features works by Arban *(Fantaisie on "Ma la sola, ahime!...Ah! la pena in lor piombo" from Bellini's* Beatrice di Tenda *for Cornet & Piano)*, Beveridge *(Magic Flute Fantasy [after Mozart])*, Cheetham *(A Brass Menagerie)*, Handel *(Judas Maccabaeus:Sound an Alarm)*, Luedeke *(Quintet, "Complexities & Contradictions")*, Morton *(Dead Man Blues)* CRYS ▲ 560 [DDD] (15.97) ▮ 560

New York Brass Quintet
Baroque Brass 9538 ▮ RCAV

New York Philomusica Chamber Ensemble, Dorian Quintet, et al.
Winds: 20th Century Music for Woodwinds—features works by Messiaen *(Quartet for the End of Time; Le merle noir for Flute & Piano)*, Barber *(Summer Music for Woodwind Quintet)*, Poulenc *(Sextuor for Piano & Woodwind Quintet [w. Jean Casadesus (piano)])*, Ibert *(Troispièces brèves)*, Bozz *(Scherzo for Woodwind Quintet)*, Françaix *(Quintet for Woodwinds)*, Fine *(Partita for Wind Quintet)* VB2 2-▲ 5083 [ADD] (9.97)

New York Woodwind Quintet
Best of the New York Woodwind Quintet, Vol. 1, w. Ronald Roseman (ob), Jerome Roth (ob), Ralph Froelich (hn)—features works by Barber *(Summer Music)*, Carter *(Etudes (8) & Fant)*, Sweelinck *(Vars on a Folk Song)*, Reicha *(Qnt Ww, Op. 88/2 [Finale])*, Pierne *(Pastorale variée)*, Barrows *(March)*, Nielsen *(Qnt, Op. 43)* BOSK ▲ 137 [AAD] (15.97)

Niagara Brass Ensemble [cnd:James Tinsley]
Baroque Brass—features works by J. S. Bach *(O Haupt voll Blut und Wunden; Contrapunctus I; Jesus bleibet meine Freude; Prelude & Fugue in e; Nun komm, der Heiden Heiland; In dulci jubilo; Christ lag in Todesbanden; Nun danket alle Gott; Komm süsser Tod; Fugue in C; Hilf, Herr Jesu, lass gelingen; Prelude & Fugue; Aria:Bist du bei mir; Ein feste Burg ist unser Gott; Auf, Schmetternde Töne muntern Trompeten; Fant on Prelude & Contrapunctus IX)*, Desprez *(Heth Sold ein Meisken Garn Om Win)*, Holborne *(English Dances (6))*, Gibbons *(Silver Swan)*, Clark *(Trumpet Voluntary)*, Mouret *(Rondeau [from Sinf of Fanfares])*, Anon *(2 16th century fanfares:Ich sag ade; Als ich anschau das frölich Gsicht)* FL ▲ 23087 [DDD] (11.97)

North Texas College of Music Wind Sym [cnd:Eugene Corporon]
Tributes—features works by Jack Stamp *(Aubrey Fanfare)*, Fisher Tull *(Sketches on a Tudor Psalm)*, Donald Grantham *(Bum's Rush)*, Morton Gould *(Ballad)*, Roger Cichy *(Divert)*, Gustav Holst *(Hammersmith, Op. 52)*, Cindy McTee *(California Counterpoint [The Twittering Machine])*, Dan Welcher *(Zion) (rec Univ. of North Texas Concert Hall, Apr 28-May 1, 1995)* KLAV ▲ 11070 [DDD] (17.97)

Nothing But Valves [William Adcock (tpt), Andrew Wilson (tpt), Samuel Compton (hn), Lance LaDuke (eup)]
Nothing But Valves—features works by Haines *(Toccata)*, Frackenpohl *(Qt)*, Hartley *(Solemn Music)*, S. Scott *(Qt for Brass)*, MacDowell *(Pieces (3) [arr Dave Thomas])*, P. Graham *(Timepiece)*, Sander *(Anecdotes)*, Ramsoe *(Qt No. 5)*, Dowland *(Come Again, Sweet Love) (rec Fredrick, MA)* ERCR ▲ 3003 (17.97)

Odyssée Ensemble
XX—features works by Dusapin *(Stanze)*, Amy *(Syms Strs)*, Darasse *(Antagonisme IV)*, Landowski *(Blanc et feu)*, Miereanu *(Musiques élémentaires pour la messe)*, Levinas *(Clov et hamm)*, Serre *(Memoire d'anges)* CHMD ▲ 5642 (16.97)

Parforce Horn Corps Norderstedt
Musique de chasse—features works by various artists *(The Hunter's Joy; Hunting Fanfares; St Hubert's Mass)* NOVA ▲ 150051 [DDD] (16.97)

Parforce Horn Players Munich
Hunting Music—features works by Cantin, Deisenroth & Rossini ORF ▲ 34821 [DDD] (18.97)

Pioneer Brass
Acres of Clams—features works by Balfe, Bellini, E.K. Eaton, Henry Filmore, Stephen Foster, Samuel J. Gilbert, Alice Hawthorne, Scott Joplin, et al. *(rec 1991)* CENT ▲ 2131 [DDD] (16.97)

Proteus 7
For Your Ears Only—features works by Mancini *(The Pink Panther [arr P. Ferguson])*, Schifrin *(Mission:Impossible [arr K. Kugler])*, Sloan & Barri *(Secret Agent Man [arr K. Kugler])*, DiLorenzo *(Private Eye; Proteack Attack)*, Bacharach *(Scenes from Casino Royale [arr F. F. Zweifel])*, Szathmary *(Get Smart [arr D. Sorenson])*, Barry, Brown, DiLorenzo, Norman & Conti *(Bond, License to Thrill [suite; arr A. DiLorenzo]) (rec Troy Savings Bank Music Hall, Troy, NJ, Oct 1997)* DOR ▲ 90258 [DDD] (16.97)

Prunes [Frøydis Ree Werke (hn), Roger Bobo (tuba/b hn)]
Music for Horn, Tuba & Bass Horn—features works by Bach, Cui, Kellaway, Schubert & Sinigaglia CRYS ▮ 126

QuintEssential Sackbut & Cornett Ensemble
In Venetia—features works by G. Gabrieli, A. Gabrieli, Priuli, Picchi, Merula, Merulo MER ▲ 84367 (16.97)

Quintet of the Americas [Marco Granados (fl), Matthew Sullivan (ob), Christopher Jepperson (cl), Thomas Novak (bn), Barbara Oldham (hn)]
Souvenirs: 20 Musical Mementos from the New World—features works by Ballard *(The Soul, from Ritmo Indio)*, Barber *(Summer Music)*, Bernstein *(Candide Overture)*, Cohn *(Strutting butterflies)*, Gershwin *(Summertime)*, Gottschalk *(Souvenir de Porto Rico; Tournament galop)*, J. P. Johnson *(Carolina shout)*, Joplin *(The ragtime dance)*, Ory *(Muskrat ramble)*, Schuller *(Blues, from Suite for Wind Quintet)*, Trad.*(Goin' home; Shenandoah)*, Castilla *(Bunde Tolimense)*, Matos *(La Cumparsita)*, E. Nazareth *(Apanhei-Te Cavaquinho [Pick up your ukulele])*, Olaya-Muñoz *(Semblanzas [Aspects])*, Trad.*(Tonada)*,Villa-Lobos *(A Pombinha voou [Away the little pigeon flew]; Os Pombinhos [The little pigeons])* XLNT ▲ [DDD]

Rascher Saxophone Ensemble
The Rascher Saxophone Ensemble—features works by Wirth *(Portals:A Prelude for Saxes)*, Kastner *(Sextour)*, Hartley *(Octet)*, plus arrs by Patrick *(Bach:Wie schön leuchtet der Morgenstern; Wachtet Auf!; If Thou Be Near; Husa:Chanson Melancholique Ov; Bellman:Mark Hur Var Skugga; Vivaldi:Con "Alla Rustica", RV.151; Grieg:Sailor's Song; Mendelssohn: Lieder ohne Worte [Trauermarsch])*, Koulman *(Bach:Fugue 22)*, Heyburn *(The Turtle Dove; Bach:Cant 99 [Opening Chorus])*, Worley *(Grieg:Last Spring; Holberg Suite)*, Rex *(Handel:Con grosso in C)*, Grainger *(Ye Banks & Braes O' Bonnie Doon)*, Hunt *(Beethoven:The Heavens Resound) (rec Coronet Recording Co, Columbus, OH; Union College, Schenectady, NY; 1974; July 2 & 3, 1975)* Coronet ▲ COR 401-0

Renn Brass Quintet [Uwe Zaiser (tpt), Peter Leiner (tpt), Sjön Scott (hn), Jochen Scheerer (trbn), Ralf Rudolph (tuba)]
Faites vos jeux!—features works by Sherman *(King Louie's Song [arr R. Rudolph])*, Handy *(Beale Street Blues [arr L. Henderson])*, G. Miller *(Tuxedo Junction [arr P. Nagle])*, Bizet *(Carmen Suite [arr F. Mills])*, J. S. Bach *(Prelude & Fugue, BWV 532 [arr J. Pfiester];)*, Jobim *(Brazilian Medley (Girl from Ipanema; 1 Note Samba) [arr R. Rudolph])*, Gershwin *(4 Hits for 5)*, Barker *(Chinesische Suite [arr R. Rudolph])*, Arp *(Tuba Blues)*, Lennon/McCartney *(Honey Pie [arr R. Willis])*, Rudolph *(Saint's Hallelujah)*, C. Parker *(Au privave [arr K. Roggors])*, plus *(Kïniglich Bayrische Amtsgerichtspolka [arr R. Rudolph]) (rec 1996)* BAYE ▲ 150017 [DDD] (17.97)

Reykjavik Wind Quintet [Bernhardur Wilkinson (fl), Einar Jóhannesson (cl), Dadi Kolbeinsson (ob), Joseph Ognibene (hn), Hafsteinn Gudmundsson (bn)]
Barber, Beach & Other American Works—features works by Barber, Fine, Schuller, Harbison, Beach, Villa-Lobos CHN ▲ 9174 [DDD] (16.97)
French Wind Music—features works by Ibert *(3 Pièces Brèves)*, Françaix *(Qnt. No. 1)*, Milhaud *(Le Cheminée du Roi René, Op. 205)*, Damase *(17 Vars.)*, Pierné *(Pastorale, Op. 14/1)*, Poulenc *(Novelette No. 1)*, Fauré *(Berceuse [from Dolly Suite, Op. 56/1])*, Debussy *(Le petit nègre)* CHN ▲ 9362 [DDD] (16.97)

Royal Danish Brass
BBC: The British Brass Connection—features works from Scotland, Wales, Ireland & England by Britten *(Serenade, Op. 31 [Prologue & Epilogue]; Fanfare for St. Edmundsbury)*, Purcell *(Music for Queen Mary II)*, Dowland *(Semper Dowland Semper Dolens)*, Henry VIII *(Pastime with Good Company)*, Clarke *(Tpt Voluntary [all arr M. Andersen])*, Byrd *(The Erle of Oxford's March [arr E. Howarth])*, Handel/Hume *(Harmonius Blacksmith [arr M. Andersen])*, Elgar *(Enigma Vars [Nimrod])*, Premru *(Felicity)*, P. McCartney *(Wanderlust [arr M. Andersen])*, Hearne *(Sarn Helen)*, Boydell *(Viking Lip-Music, Op. 91)*, plus anon pieces *(The Page's Masque; Amazing Grace [both arr M. Andersen])* ROND ▲ 8358 [DDD] (18.97)

BRASS & WIND ENSEMBLE

Royal Danish Brass [Jonas Wiik (tpt), Niels-Jørn Jessen (tpt), Niels Vind (tpt), Thomas Jensen (tpt), Henning Hansen (hn), Ola Nilsson (hn), Torbjörn Kroon (trbn), Keld Jørgensen (trbn), Jan Mortensen (b trbn), Mogens Andresen (eup), Jens Bjørn-Larsen (tuba)]
Brass Ability—features works by Handel *(Music for the Royal Fireworks)*, Schildt *(Gleich wie das Feuer)*, Bach *(Fugue in g)*, Lumbye *(Salute for August Bournonville)*, Grieg *(Hyldingsmarch)*, Bellstedt *(Napoli)*, Schmidt *(Dansk-Faerosk Fanfare)*, Helweg *(Interference)*, Laumann *(Song for Oliver; Live and Let Live)*, Lennon/McCartney *(Blackbird)*, Asmussen *(Oh, What A Day!)*, Zawinul *(Birdland)* ROND ▲ 8344 (19.97)
Cascade, w. Søren Monrad (perc), Per Jensen (perc)—features works of Ørvad *(Cascade)*, Gabrielli *(Son 4 Trbns; Son Pian'e Forte)*, Lorentzen *(Fanfare I, Fanfare II)*, Marini *(Canzoni 4 Trbns)*, Pezel *(Son 22)*, Speer *(Son 4 Trbns)*, Holmboe *(Notes; Qt Brass)*, Deprez *(Vive le Roi)*, Holten *(Vive le Roi)*, Andresen *(Good Morning [w Søren Monrad (perc), Per Jensen (perc)]) (rec 1996)* ROND ▲ 8352 (19.97)
Masterpieces for Brass & Encores!, Vol. II—features works by Orologio, Dowland, arr. Mogens Andresen, Clarke, J.S. Bach, Anon., Pachelbel, Mozart, Dvorak, Hindemith, Kellaway, Mancini, Normann, Premru Rondo Grammofon ▲ RCD 8333

Royal Danish Brass [Jonas Wiik (tpt), Niels-Jørn Jessen (tpt), Niels Vind (tpt), Thomas Jensen (tpt), Henning Hansen (hn), Ola Nilsson (hn), Torbjörn Kroon (trbn), Keld Jørgensen (trbn), Jan Mortensen (b trbn), Mogens Andresen (eup), Jens Bjørn-Larsen (tuba)], Danish Concert Band
Band Solos—features works by Mel Brolles, Launy Grandahl, David Bennett, Arcady Dubensky, Del Staigers, Dmitri Shostakovich, Harold L. Walters, Arthur Pryor, Leroy Anderson, Frank/Hafner, David Rose Rondo Grammofon ▲ RCD 8324

St. Louis Brass Quintet
Baroque Brass—features works by Albinoni, Bach, Fux, Praetorius, Scheidt, Vivaldi, Anon. SUMM ▲ 118 [DDD] (16.97) ▮
Fascinating Rhythms—features works by Falla, Gershwin, Plog, plus others SUMM ▲ SMT 195

Scandinavian Brass Ensemble [cnd:Jorma Panula]
Brass Festival—features works by C. Danielsson *(Suite 3)*, V. Holmboe *(Con Brass)*, T. Madesen *(Divert Brass & Perc)*, plus B. Hallberg, Grieg, A. Almila BIS ▲ 265 [DDD] (17.97)

Selandia Wind Ensemble
Wind Chamber Music I—features works by Bentzon *(Racconto 3 for Ob, Cl & Bn, Op. 31)*, Bozza *(Pièces pour une musique de nuit (3) for Fl, Ob, Cl & Bn)*, Debussy *(Petite Suite; Syrinx)*, Françaix *(Qt for Fl, Ob, Cl & Bn)*, Pierné *(Pastorale Ww)*, Riisager *(Divert for Fl, Bn & Hn, Op. 42)*, plus Hoffding KPT ▲ 32032 [DDD]

Solid Brass
Christmas with Solid Brass *(carols & songs arranged for brass & percussion)* DOR ▲ 90114 [DDD] (16.97)
Gershwin to Sousa—features works by Anderson *(Bugler's Holiday)*, Parker *(Radio City; Echos of Harlem; Tuxedo Junction)*, Ellington *(I'm Just a Lucky So & So)*, Gershwin *(Prelude; Rialto Ripples)*, Joplin *(Solid's Joplin [The Ragtime Dance])*, Copland *(Zion; Hoe Down; Canzona)*, Leinbach *(Cheer Boys Cheer-Listen to the Mockingbird; Luto Quick Step; Dixie & Bonnie Blue Flag)*, Sousa *(Sempre Fidelis; U.S.A Hooray; Stars & Stripes Forever)* Binaural Source-Joseph Grado Signature ▲ C-19
Solid Brass at the Opera—features selections from Carmen, Don Giovanni, The Magic Flute, King Arthur, The Fairy Queen, Rigoletto, Lohengrin DOR ▲ 90108 [DDD] (16.97)

Stockholm Chamber Brass
Heavy Metal—features works by Jan Bach, Henze, Jevtic, Nilsson), Hindemith *(Morgenmusik)*, Lundquist *(Scandinavian Music)*, Lutoslawski *(Mini Overture)*, Rabe *(Escalations)*, Sandström *(Heavy Metal)* BIS ▲ 544 [DDD] (17.97)

Stockholm Philharmonic Brass Ensemble
Music for Brass: Through Time & Space—features works by Praetorius, Gabrielli, Lutoslawski, Arnold, Poulenc, Dubois, Turpin, Arlen & Blake CAPA ▲ 21258 [DDD] (16.97)

Stockholm Philharmonic Brass Ensemble, Malmö Brass Ensemble
Music for Brass Ensemble from the 16th-18th Centuries—features works by Pezel *(Suite of Dances)*, Roman *(Drottningholmsmusiken [sel])*, Byrd *(English Dances)*, Howarth *(English Dances)*, Düben *(Swedish Dances)*, Gervaise *(Pavanne d'Angleterre)*, Claude *(Revecy venir du printans)*, anon *(Son from "Die Bänkelsängerlieder")*, Locke *(Music for His Majesty's Sackbuts & Cornetts)*, Scheidt *(Canzon a 5 voc. ad imitationem Bergamas Angl.)*,Gabrieli *(Canzon spetimi toni No. 1 Sacrae Simphoniae-Venice) (rec June 1974 & Nov 22-23, 1982)* BIS ▲ 223 [ADD/DDD] (17.97)

Summit Brass
American Tribute—features works by J. Cheetham *(Keystone Celebration)*, D. Erb *(Sonneries)*, D. Sampson *(Reflections on a Dance)*, G. Schuller *(Symphony for Brass & Percussion)*, J. Schwantner *(Fanfare for D.H.)*, D. Welcher *(Castle Creek Fanfare)* SUMM ▲ 127 [DDD] (16.97) ▮
Paving the Way—features works by Holst *(Mars [from The Planets; trans. Ralph Sauer])*, Ewazen *(Sym. in Brass)*, Tomasi *(Fanfares Liturgiques)*, Shostakovich *(Concertino, Op. 94 [trans. Kenneth Singleton])*, Ives *(Vars. on America [trans. Carl Topilow])*, Copland *(Hoe-Down [from Rodeo; C. Topilow]) (rec Centre College, Danville, KT, June 20-21, 1994)* SUMM ▲ 171 [DDD] (16.97)
Spirits of Fire—features works by Holst *(The Perfect Fool)*, Koetsier *(Sym for Brass)*, Casals *(O Vos Omnes)*, Barber *(Mutations from Bach)*, Lazarof *(Summit Concertante)*, Plog *(Scherzo)*, plus others SUMM ▲ 218 (16.97)
Toccata & Fugue—features works by Bach & Gabrieli SUMM ▲ 101 [DDD] (16.97) ▮

Swiss Brass Quintet [Gérard Métrailler (tpt), Jean-Pierre Bourquin (tpt), Isabelle Bourgeois (hn), Pascal Emonet (trbn), Germain Buscaglia (tuba)]
Brilliant Brass—features works by Barboteu *(Chansonnerie)*, Farkas *(Danses hongroises du 17ème siècle)*, Gay *(5 for 5)*, Joplin *(Paragon Rag [arr Pilafian])*, Massy *(Twel 2; Autour de Twel 2)*, Seidel *(When the Brass "Bend"; Jazzons un peu)*, Sturzenegger *(Ricercar)*, Verdi *(Nabucco (ov) [arr Chappot]) (rec Salle Patino, Geneva, Switzerland, June 28-30, 1997)* DIDC ▲ 20 [DDD] (16.97)

Swiss Romande Brass Ensemble
10th Anniversary CASC ▲ 1039 (16.97)

Swiss Romande Horns [cnd:André Besançon]
Festive Brass—features works by Phalèse *(Danserye du Premier livre)*, Mouret *(Sym de fanfare)*, Philidor *(Grandes fanfares de la chambre)*, Lully *(Danses nobles)*, Attaingnant *(Au bois joli)*, Charpentier *(Te Deum [Prelude])*, Cherubini *(Marches 1, 2, 4 & 6)*, Rameau *(Dardanus [Ov])*, Dukas *(Fanfare [from La Péri])*, Gounod *(Finale [from Faust])* CASC ▲ 1015 (16.97)

Taffanel Wind Quintet
Works for Wind Ensemble—features works by Reicha *(Qnt., Op. 88/2)*, Rossini *(Qt. 6)*, Danzi *(Qnt., Op.56/2)*, Françaix *(Qnt.)*, Hindemith *(Kleine Kammermusik, Op. 24/2)* DNN ▲ 8004 [DDD]

Tower Brass Quintet
At Play—features works by Reiche *(Abblasen)*, J.S. Bach *(Tpt Fugue; Fant)*, Lejeune *(Revecy venir du printemps)*, Marenzio *(Già torna a rallegrar)*, Koestler *(Kinderzirkus)*, Lully *(Ov to Alceste)*, Hidas *(Play)*, Gershwin *(Suite from Porgy & Bess; 3 Preludes)* CPS ▲ 8061 [ADD]

Trio Armin Rosin
Masterworks for Brass—features works by Boris Blacher *(Divertimento)*, Dario Castello *(Quinta Sonata à 2)*, Jean-Michel Damase *(Trio)*, Scott Joplin *(The Entertainer)*, Jan Koetsier *(Gran Trio)*, Mozart *(Rondo alla turca)*, G.B. Riccio *(3 Canzonen)* HANS ▲ 98557 [DDD] (15.97)

True North Brass [Stuart Laughton (tpt), Raymond Tizzard (tpt), Joan Watson (hn), Alastair Kay (trbn), Scott Irvine (tuba)]
True North Brass—features works by Monti *(Czardas)*, Irvine *(Ceremonial Fanfare; Morning Song; The True North)*, Lavallée *(La rose nuptiale)*, Bach *(St. Anne's Fugue)*, Ellington *(Don't Get Around Much Anymore)*, Carmichael *(Stardust)*, Cable *(Ontario Pictures)*, Kulesha *(Divert)*, H. L. Clarke *(Cousins)*, trad *(Ho Ro My Nut Brown Maiden; Cl Polka) (rec Port Nelson Church, Burlington, Ontario Sept & Oct 1997)* ODRE ▲ 9313 (16.97)

Wallace Collection
The Origin of the Species—features Victorian brass music from Cyfarthfa Castle, Wales NIMB ▲ NIM 5470

Washington Winds [cnd:Edward Peterson]
Classics!—features works of Denza *(Funiculi, funicula [arr Reed])*, Dvořák *(Slavonic Dance No. 8 [arr Longfield])*, J. S. Bach *(Jesu, Joy of Man's Desiring [arr Reed])*, Padilla *(El Relicario [arr Longfield])*, J. Strauss *(Radetzky March [arr Reed])*, Franck *(Panis Angelicus)*, Tchaikovsky *(Chanson Triste [arr Reed]; Nutcracker Suite (sels) [arr Longfield])*, Brahms *(Hungarian Dance No. 5 [arr Longfield])*, Monterde *(Macarena [arr Reed])*, Lehar *(Vilia [arr Reed])*, Bizet *(Farandole [arr Longfield])*, Schumann *(Traumerei [arr Longfield])*, Wagner *(Pilgrim's Chorus from Tannhauser [arr Reed])*, Handel *(Hallelujah Chorus [arr Longfield] (rec Omega Studios, Rockville, MD)* Walking Frog ▲ WFR 129 [DDD]

Western Wind
An Old-Fashioned Christmas: Caroling with the Western Wind 75597 ▲ 79053 ▮ 79053-4

Wizards! [Blake Duncan (E hn), Andrea Gullickson (ob/ob d'amore/E hn), Mark Weiger (ob/ob d'amore/E hn), Sally Bennet Faulconer (ob), Robert Barris (bn), Greg Morton (bn)]
Fantasy for Wizards!—features works by Morton *(Fant for Wizards!)*, Curtis *(Klezmer Wedding)*, Kibbe *(Divert, Op. 39)*, Chopin *(Waltz Brilliante, Op.34/2 [arr Greg Morton])*, Corina *(Suite for Double Reed Qnt)*, Constantinides *(Transformations Ob)*, Gottschalk *(Danza, Op. 33 [arr Greg Morton])*, Bartók *(Romanian Folk Dances [6; arr Morton/Miller])*, Wenth *(Qt Concertante) (rec St. Bridget's Church, Morse, IA, 1995-96)* CRYS ▲ 872 (15.97)

BRASS & WIND ENSEMBLE COLLECTIONS

The Sounds of Trinity—features works by Bach, A. Campra, J. Clarke, Fauré, Handel, Howells, Karg-Elert, MacDowell, Mouret, Horatio Parker, Purcell, Satie, R. Strauss, Tchaikovsky, Vierne [arr for org, brass & timp ensemble] *(rec Trinity Church, Boston, Mass., 1991)* ARK ▲ 6116 [DDD] (16.97)

CARILLON/CHURCH BELLS/HANDBELLS

Bruges Belfry Bells
Four Centuries of Chimes Music *(several original Flemish pieces for chimes; plus arrangements of 15 works by 16th-20th cent. composers)*—features works by Vivaldi, Mozart, Rossini, Satie, et al. RENE ▲ 88904 [DDD] (16.97)

Deya Marshall Handbell Ensemble
Deya Marshall Handbell Ensemble—features Noël des cloches; Venez, bergers; What Child Is This?; On entend partout carillon; Menuet; Air & Noël; Quodlibet; Done nobis pacem; La Caroline; Petite sonnerie de soir; A Voluntary on a Flight of Angels; De Spirito Sancto; Les clochettes; Recercadas 1 & 2; The Willow Song; Americana; Gnossienne No. 3; La complainte de Quasimodo STUD ▲ 2575 (18.97)

Hollander, Geert d' (car)
Carillon of the Antwerp Cathedral—features works by Peter Benoit, Willem De Fesch, Geert D'hollander, Jos D'hollander, Bizet *(melodies from Carmen)*, Strauss *(Pizzicato-polka)*, et al. RENE ▲ 88902 [DDD] (16.97)

Hollander, Geert d' (car), Jos d' Hollander (car)
Carillon of the Belfry of Ghent—features works by Peter Benoit, Joost Boutmy, Johan Destoop, et al. RENE ▲ 88901 [DDD] (16.97)

Hollander, Geert d' (car), Jos d' Hollander (car), Eddy Marien (car), Carlo van Luft (car)
The Carillon of the St. Rombouts Cathedral at Malines—features works by Jef Denijn, Benoit Franssen, Frans Geysen, Borodin, Rimsky-Korsakov & Schubert RENE ▲ 88903 [DDD] (16.97)

Lannoy, Jacques (car)
The Art of the Carillon—features works by Desmarets *(Rigaudon [from Circé])*, Montéclair *(Musette [from Les festes de l'été])*, Lacoste *(Sarabande [from Philomène])*, Aubert *(Forlane [from La reine des Péris])*, Mouret *(Bourrée [from Les Amours de Ragonde]; Forlane [from Les Amours des Dieux]; Air pour trompettes et fifres)*, Lully *(Marche française; Gavotte [from Atys])*, d'Andrieu *(Le timpanon)*, Couperin *(3 Pieces Hpd; Gigue)*, Exaudet *(Menuet)*, Rameau *(Le tambourin)*, Daquin *(Le coucou)* [Douai Belfry car; all works trans J. Lannoy] ARN ▲ 60349 [AAD] (13.97)

Sonos Handbell Ensemble [cnd:James Meredith]
Classical Sonos—features works by Bach *(Nun freut euch lieben Christen g'mein, BWV 734; Von Gott will ich nicht lassen, BWV 658; O Mensch, bewein' dein' Sünde gross, BWV 622; Toccata & Fugue in d, BWV 565; Toccata in G, BWV 916; Jesus bleibet meine Freude [chorale from BWV 147])*, Vivaldi *(Con in a [from Con for 2 Vns, Op. 3/8, RV.522])*, Mozart *(Adagio & Rondo in C, K.617; Rondo alla Turca, K.331 [from Son 11 in A])* WETE ▲ 5182 [DDD] (16.97)
Sonos Handbell Ensemble—features works by Tchaikovsky *(Trépak)*, Tucker *(Rustic Dance)*, Buckwalter *(Nocturne in a)*, Albéniz *(Leyenda)*, J.S. Bach *(Toccata in G, BWV 916 [Adagio])*, Khachaturian *(Sabre Dance [from Gayane])*, Debussy *(Arabesque)*, Lowry *(Shall We Gather at the River?)*, Berlin *(Alexander's Ragtime Band)*, Copland *(Saturday Night Dance; Hoe-Down [both from Rodeo])*, trad. *(Aka Tonbo [Red Dragonfly]; Hava Nageela; Le P'ing; Shenandoah; Greensleeves; J. Fit the Battle of Jericho)* WETE ▲ 5170 [DDD] (16.97)

Sound in Brass Handbells, Launton Handbell Ringers, Four in Hand Grosmont Handbell Ringers, Change Ringing Handbell Group
Ringing Clear: The Art of Handbell Ringing—features A Stephen Foster medley; Isle of Capri; Silver threads among the gold; Bells of St. Mary's; plus melodies by Leroy Anderson, Brahms, Debussy, et al. SAY ▲ 333 [AAD] (16.97)

Westminster Concert Bell Choir [cnd:Donald E. Alfred]
Westminster Bell Choir *(14 selections performed on a seven and one-half octave set of Malmark Handbells)*—features Sleepers, awake; Greensleeves; The stars and stripes forever; etc. GOT ▲ 49042 (16.97)

CARILLON/CHURCH BELLS/HANDBELLS COLLECTIONS

Bells in Russia *(orginal recordings from famous churches and cloisters)*—features Cathedral of St. Aleksandr, Tallin *(Ringing during the Liturgy)*, Pskovo-Pečora *(The funeral bells; Ringing during the Great Doxology; Ringing during Holy Week)*, Püchti *(The funeral bells)*, Monastry in the Caves, Pskovo *(Polyeleon bell)*, Convent of the Defunction of Mary, Püchti *(Feast ringing)*, Trinity Church, Zales'e *(Feast ringing)*, Monastry, Pečora *(Feast ringing)*, Church of the Forty Martyrs, Pečora *(Feast bells)*, Belfry of Lavra, Zagorsk *(Feast ringing)*, Convent of the New Virgins, Moscow *(Feast bells)* CHR ▲ 74553 (17.97)

CD-ROM

Bach, Johann Sebastian
Brandenburg Concertos 1-3, BWV 1046-48 *[WIN]*, w. German Bach Soloists [cnd:Helmut Winschermann]—features complete scores synchronized to music [w. zoom capabilities]; composer biography; notes on the compositions; video clips of composer's native country; complete print-out capabilities LALI ♦ 90013 [DDD]
Brandenburg Concertos 4-6, BWV 1049-51 *[WIN]*, w. German Bach Soloists [cnd:Helmut Winschermann]—features complete scores synchronized to music [w. zoom capabilities]; composer biography; notes on the compositions; video clips of composer's native country; complete print-out capabilities LALI ♦ 90014 [DDD]
Music of Johann Sebastian Bach *[WIN]*, w. Leipzig New Bach Collegium Musicum [cnd:Max Pommer]—features *(Toccata & Fugue in d for Organ, BWV 538; Brandenburg Concerto No. 2 in F, BWV 1047 [Allegro]; Concerto No. 2 in E for Violin, BWV 1042 [Adagio]; Prelude in c; Suite No. 1 in C, BWV 1066 [Passepied]; Suite No. 2 in b for Flute & Strings, BWV 1067 [Badinerie]; Suite No. 3 in D, BWV 1068 [Air]; Suite No. 4 in D, BWV 1069 [Rejouissance]; plus others)*, complete scores synchronized to music [w. zoom capabilities]; composer biography; notes on the compositions; video clips of composer's native country; complete print-out capabilities LALI ♦ 90025 [DDD]
Suites Nos. 1 & 2 in C & b for Orchestra *[WIN]*, w. German Bach Soloists [cnd:Helmut Winschermann]—features complete scores synchronized to music [w. zoom capabilities]; composer biography; notes on the compositions; video clips of composer's native country; complete print-out capabilities LALI ♦ 90034 [DDD]

Beethoven, Ludwig van
Music of Beethoven *[WIN]*, w. Sofia PO [cnd:Emil Tabakov], London SO [cnd:Alfred Scholz]—features *(Concerto No. 2 in B♭ for Piano, Op. 19 [Adagio]; Romance No. 2 in F for Violin, Op. 50; Bagatelle in a for Piano, WoO 59, "Für Elise"; Sonata No. 14 in c# for Piano, Op. 27/2, "Moonlight Sonata" [Adagio sosenuto]; Egmont:Overture; Coriolan Overture in c, Op. 62)*; complete scores synchronized to music [w. zoom capabilities]; composer biography; notes on the compositions; video clips of composer's native country; complete print-out capabilities LALI ♦ 90026 [DDD]
Symphonies (9) (complete) *[WIN]*, w. Dresden PO [cnd:Herbert Kegel]—features complete scores synchronized to music [w. zoom capabilities]; composer biography; notes on the compositions; video clips of composer's native country; complete print-out capabilities LALI 10-♦ 33001 [DDD]
Symphony No. 1 in C, Op. 21 (1800) *[WIN]*, w. Dresden PO [cnd:Herbert Kegel]—features complete score synchronized to music [w. zoom capabilities]; composer biography; notes on the composition; video clips of composer's native country; complete print-out capabilities LALI ♦ 90003 [DDD]
Symphony No. 2 in D, Op. 36 (1801-02) *[WIN]*, w. Dresden PO [cnd:Herbert Kegel]—features complete score synchronized to music [w. zoom capabilities]; composer biography; notes on the composition; video clips of composer's native country; complete print-out capabilities LALI ♦ 90004 [DDD]
Symphony No. 3 in E♭, Op. 55, "Eroica" (1803) *[WIN]*, w. Dresden PO [cnd:Herbert Kegel]—features complete score synchronized to music [w. zoom capabilities]; composer biography; notes on the composition; video clips of composer's native country; complete print-out capabilities LALI ♦ 90005 [DDD]
Symphony No. 4 in B♭, Op. 60 (1806) *[WIN]*, w. Dresden PO [cnd:Herbert Kegel]—features complete score synchronized to music [w. zoom capabilities]; composer biography; notes on the composition; video clips of composer's native country; complete print-out capabilities LALI ♦ 90006 [DDD]
Symphony No. 5 in c, Op. 67 (1807-08) *[WIN]*, w. Dresden PO [cnd:Herbert Kegel]—features complete score synchronized to music [w. zoom capabilities]; composer biography; notes on the composition; video clips of composer's native country; complete print-out capabilities LALI ♦ 90007 [DDD]

▲ = CD ♦ = Enhanced CD △ = MD ▮ = Cassette Tape ▯ = DCC

Beethoven, Ludwig van (cont.)

Symphony No. 6 in F, Op. 68, "Pastorale" (1808) *[WIN]*, w. Dresden PO [cnd:Herbert Kegel]—features complete score synchronized to music [w. zoom capabilities]; composer biography; notes on the composition; video clips of composer's native country; complete print-out capabilities LALI ♦ 90008 [DDD]

Symphony No. 7 in A, Op. 92 (1811-12) *[WIN]*, w. Dresden PO [cnd:Herbert Kegel]—features complete score synchronized to music [w. zoom capabilities]; composer biography; notes on the composition; video clips of composer's native country; complete print-out capabilities LALI ♦ 90009 [DDD]

Symphony No. 8 in F, Op. 93 (1812) *[WIN]*, w. Dresden PO [cnd:Herbert Kegel]—features complete score synchronized to music [w. zoom capabilities]; composer biography; notes on the composition; video clips of composer's native country; complete print-out capabilities LALI ♦ 90010 [DDD]

Symphony No. 9 in d, Op. 125, "Choral Symphony" (1822-24) *[WIN]*, w. Dresden PO [cnd:Herbert Kegel]—features complete score synchronized to music [w. zoom capabilities]; composer biography; notes on the composition; video clips of composer's native country; complete print-out capabilities LALI ♦ 90011 [DDD]

Chopin, Frédéric

Concerto No. 1 in e for Piano & Orchestra, Op. 11 (1830) *[WIN]*, w. Sandor Falvai (pno), Budapest PO [cnd:András Kórodi]—features complete score synchronized to music [w. zoom capabilities]; composer biography; notes on the composition; video clips of composer's native country; complete print-out capabilities LALI ♦ 90016 [DDD]

Concerto No. 2 in f for Piano & Orchestra, Op. 21 (1829-30) *[WIN]*, w. Adam Harasiewicz (pno), Warsaw PO [cnd:Kazimierz Kord]—features complete score synchronized to music [w. zoom capabilities]; composer biography; notes on the composition; video clips of composer's native country; complete print-out capabilities LALI ♦ 90017 [DDD]

Music of Chopin *[WIN]*—features Krzystof Jablonski (pno) *(Études, Op. 10/5 & Op. 25/10)*, Jean-Marc Luisada (pno) *(Mazurkas (4), Op. 24; Waltz in E♭, Op. 18)*, Stanislav Bunin (pno) *(Preludes, Op 28/13-18)*, Evelyne Dubourg (pno) *(Scherzo No. 2 in b♭, Op. 31)*, Yuval Fichman (pno) *(Nocturne in C#)*; complete scores synchronized to music [w. zoom capabilities]; composer biography; notes on the compositions; video clips of composer's native country; complete print-out capabilities LALI ♦ 90031 [DDD]

Dvořák, Antonín

Symphony No. 9 in e, Op. 95, "From the New World" (1893) *[WIN]*, w. New World SO [cnd:Pavel Urbanek]—features complete score synchronized to music [w. zoom capabilities]; composer biography; notes on the composition; video clips of composer's native country; complete print-out capabilities LALI ♦ 90015 [DDD]

Hindemith, Paul

Life & Music of Hindemith *[MAC; WIN]*—features over 1000 photos & illustrations, historical film clips, 120 minutes of musical excerpts & spoken documents, list of works, bibliography, discography, comprehensive text section & index of subjects & people [E,G] WER ♦ MV 0802-0

Liszt, Franz

Concerto No. 2 in A for Piano & Orchestra, S.125 (1839; rev 1849-61) *[WIN]*, w. Jenö Jandó (pno), Budapest SO [cnd:András Ligeti]—also features *(Fantasy on Hungarian Folk Tunes, S.123; Polonaise brillante [after Weber, Op. 72], S.367)*; complete scores synchronized to music [w. zoom capabilities]; composer biography; notes on the compositions; video clips of composer's native country; complete print-out capabilities LALI ♦ 90021 [DDD]

Mozart, Wolfgang Amadeus

Eine kleine Nachtmusik in G for Strings & Continuo, K.525 (1787) *[WIN]*, w. Vienna Mozart Ensemble [cnd:Herbert Kraus]—also features Salzburg Camerata Academica [cnd:Sándor Vegh] *(Divertimentos (3) in D, B♭ & F, K.136-138/125 a-c)*; complete scores synchronized to music [w. zoom capabilities]; composer biography; notes on the compositions; video clips of composer's native country; complete print-out capabilities LALI ♦ 90018 [DDD]

Music of Mozart *[WIN]*, w. Franz Liszt CO [cnd:János Rolla], Vienna Mozart Ensemble [cnd:Herbert Kraus], Camerata Academica Salzburg [cnd:Sándor Vegh]—features *(Concerto in A for Clarinet, K.622 [Adagio]; Eine kleine Nachtmusik in G, K.525 [Allegro]; Divertimento in D for Horns & Strings, K.344/320b [Menuetto]; Turkish March; Concerto No. 2 in D for Flute, K.314/285d [Allegro]; Serenade in E♭ for Winds, K.375 [Menuetto]; Concerto No. 3 in G for Violin, K.216 [Allegro]; Concerto No. 3 in E♭ for Horn, K.447 [Allegro])*; complete scores synchronized to music [w. zoom capabilities]; composer biography; notes on the compositions; video clips of composer's native country; complete print-out capabilities LALI ♦ 90024 [DDD]

Symphony No. 40 in g, K.550 (1788) *[WIN]*, w. Salzburg Mozarteum Orch [cnd:Hans Graf]—features complete score synchronized to music [w. zoom capabilities]; composer biography; notes on the composition; video clips of composer's native country; complete print-out capabilities LALI ♦ 90001 [DDD]

Symphony No. 41 in C, K.551, "Jupiter" (1788) *[WIN]*, w. Salzburg Mozarteum Orch [cnd:Hans Graf]—features complete score synchronized to music [w. zoom capabilities]; composer biography; notes on the composition; video clips of composer's native country; complete print-out capabilities LALI ♦ 90002 [DDD]

Prokofiev, Sergei

Peter & the Wolf for Narrator & Orchestra, Op. 67 (1936) *[WIN]*, w. Jack Lemmon (nar), Prague Festival Orch [cnd:Pavel Urbanek]—features complete score synchronized to music [w. zoom capabilities]; composer biography; notes on the composition; video clips of composer's native country; complete print-out capabilities LALI ♦ 90035 [DDD]

Puccini, Giacomo

Tosca (opera in 3 acts) [lib Giuseppe Giacosa & Luigi Illica after Sardou] (1898-99), w. Maria Callas (sop), Giuseppe di Stefano (ten), Tito Gobbi (bar), La Scala Orch [cnd:Victor de Sabata], La Scala Chorus—features pictures of a Covent Garden Tosca production, artists & producers; on-screen lib [E,F,G,I]; synopsis & biographies; Callas discography & video excerpts of stage performances *(rec live, La Scala, 1953)* EMIC (m) ♦ ARIR 91472 [MAC]; ARIR 91788 [PC] [ADD]

Schubert, Franz

Music of Schubert *[WIN]*, w. Jenö Jandó (pno), Budapest PO [cnd:János Kovács], Colorado String Quartet—features *(Quintet in A for Piano & Strings, D.667, "Trout Quintet" [Tema con Variazioni]; Entr'acte; Ballet Music [both from Rosamunde]; Moments musicaux in a; Symphony No. 8 in b, D.759, "Unfinished" [Allegro moderato])*; complete scores synchronized to music [w. zoom capabilities]; composer biography; notes on the compositions; video clips of composer's native country; complete print-out capabilities LALI ♦ 90032 [DDD]

Strauss (II), Johann

Music of Johann Strauss (II) *[WIN]*, w. Luxembourg RSO [cnd:Kurt Redel], Vienna Strauss Orch [cnd:Joseph Francek]—features *(The Blue Danube; Vienna Blood; Tritch Tratsch Polka; Die Fledermaus (selections); Introduction [from Der Zigeunerbaron])*; complete scores synchronized to music [w. zoom capabilities]; composer biography; notes on the compositions; video clips of composer's native country; complete print-out capabilities LALI ♦ 90027 [DDD]

Tchaikovsky, Piotr

Ballet Suites *[WIN]*, w. Berlin SO [cnd: Peter Wohlert]—features *(Sleeping Beauty:Ballet Suite, Op. 66a; Swan Lake:Ballet Suite, Op. 20a)*; complete scores synchronized to music [w. zoom capabilities]; composer biography; notes on the compositions; video clips of composer's native country; complete print-out capabilities LALI ♦ 90022 [DDD]

Music of Tchaikovsky *[WIN]*, w. Bavarian RSO [cnd:Hans Vonk], Vienna SO [cnd:Yuri Ahronovitch], Budapest SO [cnd:András Ligeti]—features *(Sleeping Beauty:Ballet Suite; Capriccio italien in A, Op. 45; Serenade in C for Strings, Op. 48 [Waltz]; Scene No. 10; Waltz [both from Swan Lake]; Polonaise [from Eugene Onegin]; Concerto in D for Violin, Op. 35 [Andante])*; complete scores synchronized to music [w. zoom capabilities]; composer biography; notes on the compositions; video clips of composer's native country; complete print-out capabilities LALI ♦ 90029 [DDD]

Nutcracker (selections) *[WIN]*, w. Berlin RSO [cnd:Peter Wohlert]—features complete score synchronized to music [w. zoom capabilities]; composer biography; notes on the composition; video clips of composer's native country; complete print-out capabilities LALI ♦ 90023 [DDD]

Symphony No. 5 in e, Op. 64 (1888) *[WIN]*, w. Prague Festival Orch [cnd:Pavel Urbanek]—features complete score synchronized to music [w. zoom capabilities]; composer biography; notes on the composition; video clips of composer's native country; complete print-out capabilities LALI ♦ 90019 [DDD]

Verdi, Giuseppe

Music of Verdi *[WIN]*, w. Sofia PO [cnd:Vassil Stefanov], Svetoslav Obretenov Bulgarian National Choir—features *(Overture [from Nabucco]; Prelude [from Aida]; Prelude; Libiano ne'lieti calici; Di Madride noi siam mattadori [all from La traviata]; Vedi! le fosche notturne (Gypsies Chorus); Or co'daddi, ma fra poco (Soldiers' Chorus) [both from Il trovatore]; Overture [from Aroldo])*; complete scores synchronized to music [w. zoom capabilities]; composer biography; notes on the compositions; video clips of composer's native country; complete print-out capabilities LALI ♦ 90033 [DDD]

Vivaldi, Antonio

Concertos (4) for Violin, Strings & Continuo, Op. 8/1-4 (RV.269, 293, 297, 315), "The Four Seasons" *[WIN]*, w. Budapest Strings [cnd:Károly Botvay]—features complete score synchronized to music [w. zoom capabilities]; composer biography; notes on the composition; video clips of composer's native country; complete print-out capabilities LALI ♦ 90012 [DDD]

Music of Vivaldi *[WIN]*—features Bela Banfalvi (vn), Budapest Strings [cnd:Karoly Botvay] *(Spring; Autumn [both from Concertos for Violin, Strings & Continuo, Op. 8/1-4 (RV.269, 293, 297, 315), "The Four Seasons"])*, Burkhart Glaetzner (ob), Leipzig New Bach Collegium Musicum [cnd:Max Pommer] *(Concerto in g for Oboe; Sonata in B♭ for Oboe)*; complete scores synchronized to music [w. zoom capabilities]; composer biography; notes on the compositions; video clips of composer's native country; complete print-out capabilities LALI ♦ 90030 [DDD]

Wagner, Richard

Music of Wagner *[WIN]*, w. Budapest SO [cnd:György Lehel], Sofia RSO [cnd:Vassil Kazandjiev]—features *(Overture; Arrival of the Guests at Wartburg [both from Tannhäuser]; Dance of the Prentices; Prelude to Act 3; Procession of the Masters [all from Die Meistersinger von Nürnberg]; Prelude & Liebestod [from Tristan und Isolde])*; complete scores synchronized to music [w. zoom capabilities]; composer biography; notes on the compositions; video clips of composer's native country; complete print-out capabilities LALI ♦ 90028 [DDD]

Wagner, Richard (cont.)

Der Ring des Nibelungen [Das Rheingold, Die Walküre, Siegfried, Götterdämmerung] (1876) (complete) *[WIN]*, w. R. Crespin (sop), K. Flagstad (sop), B. Nilsson (sop), C. Watson (sop), C. Ludwig (mez), J. Madeira (mez), J. King (ten), G. Stolze (ten), S. Svanholm (ten), W. Windgassen (ten), D. Fischer-Dieskau (bar), G. London (bar), H. Hotter (b-bar), G. Neidlinger (b-bar), G. Frick (bass), Vienna PO [cnd:Georg Solti]—features complete recording, complete vocal score, German & English libretto, 100 articles, photographic scenes from stage productions MCP 1001 (68.97) ♦ MED 1001

CD-ROM COLLECTIONS

Baroque Highlights *[WIN]*—features J. S. Bach *(Suite No. 4 in D, BWV 1069 [Rejouissance]; Suite No.3 in D, BWV 1068 [Air])*, Vivaldi *(Concerto in g for Oboe)*, Pachelbel *(Canon & Gigue in D for 3 Violins & Continuo)*, Handel *(Concerto grosso, Op. 6/5 [Allegro]; Concerto grosso, Op. 6/4 [Allegro]; Concerto grosso, Op. 6/8 [Andante allegro])*, Haydn *(Concerto in E♭ for Trumpet, H.VIIe/1)*; complete scores synchronized to music [w. zoom capabilities]; composer biography; notes on the compositions; video clips of composer's native country; complete print-out capabilities LALI ♦ 90020 [DDD]

The Guide to Classical Music *[WIN]*—features biographies of over 60 composers; audio excerpts from over 200 pieces; video performances Cambrix ♦ 065

Guide to the Orchestra *[WIN]*, w. City of Birmingham SO [cnd:Simon Rattle]—features video interviews of orchestra musicians; interview with Simon Rattle; works by various composers including Henry Purcell, Benjamin Britten, Judith Weir Cambrix ♦ CPO 70

The Hutchinson Encyclopedia of Music *[WIN]*—features performers from all periods; music clips; timeline; suggested recordings; biographies [originally published as Everyman Dictionary of Music] Cambrix ♦ CP 134

CELLO

Bengtsson, Erling Bløndal (vc)

Erling Blöndal Bengtsson, w. Ingolf Olsen (gtr)—features works by Boccherini, Haydn, Brahms Bach, Gounod, Villa-Lobos, Prokofiev, Martini, Sor, J.S. Bach, Corelli, Valentini, Mozart, Ponce, Handel, Henriques, Ibert, Schubert *(rec Sept 22-25, 1986)* DANR ▲ 335

Bloemendal, Coenraad (vc)

The Cantorial Voice of the Cello, w. Valerie Tryon (pno), Andrés Diaz (vc), Andrew Mark (vc)—features works by Mendelssohn *(Son. No. 2 in D, Op. 58)*, Offenbach *(Grand Duo Concertant for 2 Vcs, Op. 43 [Andante])*, Popper *(Requiem for 3 Vcs & Pno, Op. 66; Wie einst in schöner'n Tagen, Op. 64)*, Bruch *(Kol Nidrei, Op. 47)*, Glantz *(Tal for solo Vc)*, Bloch *(From Jewish Life [Prayer No. 1])*, Ravel *(Deux mélodies hébraïques [No. 1, "Kaddisch"])*, Ben-Haim *(3 Songs without Words)*, Glick *(Prayer & Dance) (rec Troy Savings Bank Music Hall, Troy, NY, May 1994)* DOR ▲ 90208 [DDD] (16.97)

Peter Buck Cello Ensemble

Rondo Violoncello—features works by Villa-Lobos *(Bachianas Brasileiras 1)*, Bernstein *(West Side Story [sels])*, Wagner *(Tristan und Isolde [ov])*, Bach *(A Musical Offering [Ricercar])*, Funck *(Suite in D)*, Klengel *(Hymnus)*, Lamb *(Bohemia Rag)* HAM ▲ 905240 (17.97)

Casals, Pablo (vc)

Bow & Baton: Complete 1929-30 HMV Singles & 1928 London Symphony Recordings, w. Blas-Net (pno), Otto Schulhof (pno)—features works by Brahms *(Haydn Vars.)*, Beethoven *(Corolian Ov.)*, Mendelssohn, Rimsky-Korsakov, Boccherini, Tartini, J.S. Bach, Dvořák, others PHS ▲ 9128 [ADD] (17.97)

Casals *(4-CD boxed set)*—features works by Beethoven *(Complete Cello Sonatas)*, Dvořák *(Cello Concerto, Bruch—Kol Nidrei & Boccherini—Cello Concerto in B♭)*, et al. PHS 4-▲ 9935 (m) [AAD] (49.97)

Casals Festivals at Prades, Vol. 1 (1953-1959)—features works by Brahms *(Piano Trio No. 3, Op. 101)*, et al. MUA 4-▲ 688 (m) [AAD] (63.97)

Casals Festivals at Prades, Vol. 2 (1953-1959)—features works by Brahms *(Piano Trio No. 1, Op. 8)*, et al. MUA 4-▲ 689 (m) [AAD] (63.97)

The Complete Acoustic Recordings 1915-25, Vol. 1—features works by Elgar *(Salut d'amour)*, Handel *(Largo [from Serses])*, Rubinstein *(Melody in F)*, Tartini *(Con Vc in d [Adagio])*, Bruch *(Kol Nidre)*, Popper *(Spanish Serenade, Op. 11/3; Mazurka in g)*, Saint-Saëns *(Le Cygne)*, Campagnoli *(Romance)*, Fauré *(Apres un rêve)*, Schumann *(Träumerei)*, Liszt *(Liebestraum)*, Bach *(Suite 3 Vc) (rec 1915-16)* BID ▲ 141 [ADD] (16.97)

The Complete Acoustic Recordings 1915-25, Vol. 2—features works by Schumann *(Abendlied; Träumerei)*, Mozart *(Qnt Cl [Larghetto])*, Kreisler *(Chanson Louis XIII & Pavane)*, Saint-Saëns *(Allegro Appassionato; Le Cygne)*, Handel *(Largo [from Serse])*, Rubinstein *(Melody in F)*, Liszt *(Liebestraum)*, Wagner *(Abendstern)*, Lassen *(Thine Eyes So Blue)*, Bach *(Suite 3 Vc [Air])*, Chopin *(Nocturne in E♭ [arr Popper]) (rec 1916-20)* BID ▲ 142 [ADD] (16.97)

The Complete Acoustic Recordings 1915-25, Vol. 3—features works by Crouch *(Kathleen Mavoureen)*, Moore *(Believe Me if All Those Endearing Young Charms)*, Popper *(Gavotte in D, Op. 23)*, Elgar *(Salut d'amour)*, Hinkson *(Would God I Were the Tender Apple Blossom)*, Rubinstein *(Romance in E♭)*, Sgambati *(Serenata Napoletana)*, MacDowell *(To a Wild Rose)*, Del Riego *(Oh, Dry Those Tears)*, Bruch *(Kol Nidre)*, Glazunov *(Mélodie Arabe, Op. 20/1)*, Haydn *(Con Vc in D [Adagio])*, Mendelssohn *(Serenade, Op. 67/6)*, Brahms *(Sapphische Ode)*, Handel *(Minuet)*, Tchaikovsky *(Mélodie; Autumn Song, Op. 37/10)*, Cui *(Berceuse, Op. 20/18)*, Bach *(Adagio [arr Siloti])*, Granados *(Goyescas [Intermezzo; arr Cassado]) (rec 1920-25)* BID ▲ 143 [ADD] (16.97)

Encores, w. Charles Baker (pno), Eugene Istomin (pno)—features works by Bach *(Prelude; Sarabande [both from Suite No. 3 in C for Vc, BWV 1009]; Aria [from Pastorale in F for Org, BWV 590]; Recitative [from Con No. 3 for Org, BWV 594])*, Handel *(Largo [from Xerxes])*, Saint-Saëns *(The Swan)*, Popper *(Spanish Dance No. 2)*, Campagnoli *(Romanza)*, Schumann *(Träumerei [from Kinderscenen; arr Pablo Casals])*, Boccherini *(Allegro [from Son in A for Vc])*, Haydn *(Adagio [from Son No. 19 in D for Pno, Hob.XVII9])*, Falla *(Nana [No. 5 from 7 Canciones populares Españolas])*, anon. *(El Cant dels Ocells [Folklore Catalan]) (rec 1915-54)* COL (Casals Edition) ▲ 66573 [ADD] (10.97)

Encores—features works by Boccherini *(Adagio and Allegro from Sonata No. 6 in A (Rec. 1929))*, Haydn *(Tempo di Minuetto from Sonata No. 1 in C (Rec. 1936))*, Brahms *(Violin-Cello Con.; Cello Son. 2)* PHS ▲ 9363 [AAD] (17.97)

Legendary Performers: Casals Early Recordings, 1925-28—selections include works by J.S. Bach, Granados, Popper, Macdowell & others *(rec 1925-28)* RCAV (Gold Seal) ▲ 61616 (10.97)

The Victor Recordings (1926-1928), w. Nikolai Mednikoff (pno)—features works by Bach, Bruch, Chopin, Debussy, Fauré, Godard, Granados, Hillemacher, Popper, Rubinstein, Saint-Saëns, Schubert, Schumann, Sgambati, Wagner BID ▲ 17 [ADD]

Cassado, Gaspar (vc)

Gaspar Cassado Performs Cello Masterpieces, w. Jonel Perlea (cnd)—features performances with Bamberg SO *(Schubert/Cassado:Vc Con [arrangement of the Arpeggione Sonata, D.821]; Schumann:Vc Con)*, Pro Musica Orch *(Dvořák:Vc Con, Op. 104; Rondo in G; Silent Woods; Respighi:Adagio & Vars for Vc & Orch; Tchaikovsky:Vars on a Rococo Theme) (rec mid-late 1950s)* VOXL 2-▲ 5502 [ADD]

CELLO [Laura Bontrager (vc), Maria Kitsopoulos (vc), Maureen McDermott (vc), Caryl Paisner (vc)]

Subliminal Blues & Greens—features works by Bisharat *(Lying in Wait)*, M. Weber *(Walking Man; Jommin' Mon)*, Beal *(6 Mile Creek; Bela in Blue)*, Pilley *(Snow Pony)*, Scharnberg *(Subliminal Blues & Greens; Goodnight (for Home))*, Thatcher *(Suite for Transient Minds)*, Baun *(Street Mapping)*, Chipkin *(Funk by Proxy)*, Werking *(Folk Prayer)*, Rizzo *(Cadillactica) (rec Troy Savings Bank Music Hall, Troy, NY)* DNC ▲ 1011 [DDD] (16.97)

Cheifetz, Hamilton (vc)

Jubilatum, w. Bryan Johanson (gtr), Harold Gray (pno)—features works by Francoeur *(Son in E Vn [Largo cantabile; Allegro vivo; both arr Trowell])*, Franz *(Out of My Great Sorrows [arr Cheifetz])*, Reger *(Forest Solitude [arr Cheifetz])*, Frescobaldi *(Toccata [arr Cassadó])*, Saint-Saëns *(Le Cygne)*, Haydn *(Divert [Adagio; Tempo di minuetto; Allegro di molto; all arr Piatigorsky])*, Bach *(Suite 3 Vc)*, Johanson *(Berceuse Vc Gtr; Jubilatum) (rec Lincoln Performance Hall, Portland, OR, Jan 5-7, 1993)* GAGR ▲ 929 [DDD] (14.97) 929 (9.98)

Chung-oo (vc)

Invitation To Romance—features works by Kosma & Mercer *(Autumn Leaves)*, Raskin *(Laura)*, Mancini *(Charade)*, Lloyd Webber *(Memory)*, Garner *(Misty)*, Gagnon & Voisine *(Am I Wrong?)*, Hamlisch *(The Way We Were)*, Ellington *(Ellington Medley)*, Kern *(Smoke Gets in Your Eyes)*, Sondheim *(Send in the Clowns)*, Legrand *(What Are You Doing the Rest of Your Life?)*, Rodgers *(If I Loved You)*, plus trad *(Danny Boy)* OPNI ▲ 9801 (16.97)

Claret, Lluís (vc)

In Memoriam Pablo Casals, w. Seon-Hee Myong (pno), Barcelona Cello Ensemble—features works by J.S. Bach *(Pastorale in f for Org)*, Cervelló *(Un Cant a Pau Casals)*, P. Casals *(Sant Martí del Canigó)*, E. Casals *(El cant dels Ocells; Suite en ré)*, Fauré *(Après un rêve)*, Granados *(Intermezzo de Goyescas)*, Cassadó *(Requiebros)*, Falla *(Nana)*, Schubert *(L'abeille)* VAL ▲ 4733

Cologne Philharmonic Cellists

Cellicatissimo: Light Tunes For Serious Cellists—features works by Leroy Anderson, Arthur Benjamin, Faure, Françaix, Gretchaninov, Louis de Caix d'Hervelois, Wilfried Hiller, Offenbach, Rimsky-Korsakov, Saint-Saëns, Stravinsky, Stanley Weiner KSCH ▲ 311522 [DDD] (16.97)

Conjunto Ibérico Cello Octet [cnd:Elias Arizcuren]

Conjunto Ibérico Cello Octet, w. Clara McFadden (sop)—features works by Pablo Casals *(Adoracion de los Reyes Magos [from oratorio El Pesebre]; El Cant dells ocells—transcriptions for cello ensemble)*, Juana Garcia *(Cuatro Bagatelas for Cello Ensemble)*, Alberto Ginastera *(Cancion al arbol del olvido; Pampanea No. 2—transcriptions for cello ensemble)*, Xavier Montsalvatge *(Cinco Canciones Negras—transcribed for soprano & 8 cellos)*, Enric Morera *(Melangia for cello ensemble)*, Villa-Lobos *(Bachiana brasiliera No. 5 for Soprano & Cello Ensemble) (rec 1992)* CCL ▲ 9323 [DDD]

12 hommages à Paul Sacher pour violoncelle—features works by Ginastera *(Puneña No. 2, Op. 45)*, W. Fortner *(Zum Spielen für den 70. Gerburtstag [theme & var])*, Henze *(Capriccio)*, Beck *(Für Paul Sacher 3 Epigramme)*, Halffter *(Variationen über das Thema eSACHERe)*, Huber *(Transpositio ad infinitum) (rec Switzerland, June 1993)* † Berio:Mots sont allés; Boulez:Messagesquisse; Britten:Tema "Sacher"; Dutilleux:Strophes sur le nom; Holliger:Chaconne; Lutoslawski:Sacher Variationen ECM 2-▲ 21520 [DDD] (30.97)

Diaz, Andrés (vc)

Russian Romantics for Cello & Piano, w. Samuel Sanders (pno)—features works by Tchaikovsky *(Romance, Op. 51/5; Song without Words, Op. 2/3; Sad Song, Op 40/2; Méditation, Op. 72/5; Neapolitan Song, Op. 39/18; Lullaby, Op. 16/1; Barcarolle, Op. 37/6;Valse sentimentale, OP. 51/6; Pezzo capriccioso, Op. 62; Nocturne, Op. 19/4)*, Scriabin *(Étude, Op. 8/11; Poème, Op. 32/1)*, Rachmaninoff *(Méldie, Op. 3/3)*, Chopin *(Étude, Op. 25/7 [arr. Glazunov)*, Glazunov *(Chant du ménéstrel, Op. 71)*, Liadov *(Russian Dance)*, Stravinsky *(Russian Maiden Song [Chanson russe]) (rec Apr 1993)* DOR ▲ 90188 [DDD] (16.97)

Drinkall, R. (vc)

Duo, w. Dian Baker (pno)—features works by Bach *(Arioso)*, Bruch *(Kol Nidre)*, Rachmaninoff *(Vocalise)*, Fauré *(Sicilienne; Après un rêve; Pavane)*, Falla *(Jota; Nana)*, Ravel *(Habanera)*, Schumann *(Fantasy)*, Saint-Saëns *(The Swan)*, Paradis *(Sicilienne)*, Nibley *(Elegy)*, Corelli *(Adagio)*, Mendelssohn *(Song without words)*, Squire *(Tarantella)*, Chopin *(Largo)* KLAV ▲ 11043 [DDD]

Du Pré, Jacqueline (vc)

The Columbia Recordings, Vol. 2, w. Michael Taube (pno), Theo Van der Pas (pno), Gerald Moore (pno), Wolfgang Rebner (pno)—features works by Bach/arr. Gounod *(Ave Maria)*, Beethoven *(Trio [Serenade] in D for Violin, Viola & Cello, Op. 8—Szymon Goldberg, Paul Hindemith, Emanuel Feuermann)*, Brahms *(Cello Sonata No. 1 in e, Op. 38)*, Cui *(Orientale, w.)*, Drigo *(Serenade)*, Mendelssohn *(Spring Song)*, Reger *(Suite in G for Solo Cello, Op. 131c/1)*, Rimsky-Korsakov *(Hindoo Song)*, Schumann *(Träumerei) (rec 1930-39)* PHS ▲ 9443 (m) [AAD] (17.97)

The Columbia Recordings, Vol. 3, w. Gerald Moore (pno), Myra Hess (pno), Paul Hindemith (va/cnd), Szymon Goldberg (cnd)—features works by Albéniz *(Tango)*, Beethoven *(Cello Sonata No. 3 in A, Op. 69)*, Hindemith *(Sonata for Solo Cello, Op. 25/3; Scherzo for Viola & Cello; String Trio No. 2 [1933])*, Saint-Saëns *(Le cygne [The Swan])*, Weber *(Andantino from Konzertstück, Op. 79, w. Gerald Moore) (rec 1930-39)* PHS ▲ 9446 (m) [AAD] (17.97)

Early German Parlophone Recordings—features works by Saint-Saëns, Sarasate, Granados, Giordani, Valensin, Dvořák *(Con. in b, Op. 104)*, Bruch *(Kol Nidre, Op. 47)*, Haydn *(Con. in D, H.VIIb/2)*, Popper *(Serenade) (rec 1921-30)* PHS ▲ 9077 [AAD] (17.97)

Les introuvables de Jacqueline Du Pré—features performances with London SO [cnd:John Barbirolli] *(Elgar:Con. in e; Monn:Con. in g; Haydn:Con. in D)*, Royal PO [cnd:Malcolm Sargent] *(Delius:Con. Vc)*, New Philharmonia Orch. [cnd:Daniel Barenboim] *(Saint-Saëns:Con. No. 1 in a; Schumann:Con. in a, Op. 129)*, Chicago SO [cnd:Daniel Barenboim] *(Dvořák:Con. in b, Op. 104; Waldesruhe, Op. 68)*, English CO [cnd:Daniel Barenboim] *(Haydn:Con. in D)*, Daniel Barenboim (pno) *(Chopin:Son. in g; Franck:Son. in A; Beethoven:3 Vars. [on See, the Conqu'ring Hero Comes; Bei Männern, welche Liebe fühlen; Ein Mädchen oder Weibchen])*, Gerald Moore (pno) *(Fauré:Elégie; Bruch:Kol nidrei)*, Ernest Lush (pno) *(Handel:Son. in g)*, Stephen Bishop (pno) *(Beethoven:Sons. No. 3 in A & No. 5 in D)*, solo performance of Bach *(Suites Nos. 1 in G & 2 in d)* EMIC 6-▲ 68132 [ADD] (39.97)

Feuermann, Emanuel (vc)

The Columbia Recordings, Vol. 1, w. Theo Van der Pas (pno), Malcolm Sargent (cnd), *(orch unknown)*—features works by Beethoven *(Variations on Mozart's "Bei Männern,")*, Chopin *(Nocturne in E♭, Op. 9/2 & Waltz in a, Op. 34/2)*, Gluck *(Melodie from Orphée)*, Haydn *(Cello Concerto in D, Op. 101)*, Schubert *(Arpeggione Sonata; w. Gerald Moore (pno))*, Sgambati *(Serenata Napoletanata)) (rec 1934-37)* PHS ▲ 9442 (m) [AAD] (17.97)

Emanuel Feuermann, w. Michael Taube (cnd), Gerald Moore (pno), Wolfgang Rebner (pno), Michael Taube (pno)—features works by Brahms *(Son 1 in e, Op. 38)*, Popper *(Serenade; Hungarian Rhap, Op. 68)*, plus Mendelssohn, Rimsky-Korsakov, Drigo, Saint-Saëns, Cui, Grandaos, Sarasate, Bach/Gounod, Giordani, Valensin *(rec 1926; 1927; 1929; 1930; 1934; 1936; 1939)* MTAL ▲ 48025 (6.97)

Encores—features works by Bach [arr Gounod], Saint-Saëns, Sarasate, Granados, Giordani, Popper, Mendelssohn, Schumann, Valensin, Albéniz, Weber *(rec 1924-39)* ENT (Strings) ▲ 99354 (16.97)

Fournier, Pierre (vc)

Fournier, Vol. 2—features works by Fauré *(Elegie)*, Ravel *(Habanera)*, Debussy *(Prelude)*, Stravinsky *(Russian Maiden Song)*, Bloch *(Nigun)*, Francoeur *(Largo & Allegro)*, J. S. Bach *(Choral [arr Fournier])*, Haydn *(Minuet)*, Weber *(Polonaise)*, Albéniz *(Malaguena)*, Nin *(Granada)*, Chopin *(Polonaise)* ARL ▲ 193 (15.97)

Gastinel, Anne (vc)

Debut Recital, w. Suzy Bossard (pno)—features works by Debussy *(Sonata No. 1)*, Fauré *(Élégie; Cello Sonata Op. 117)*, Gastinel, Marais & Merlet OTT ▲ OTT 79032 [DDD]

Geringas, David (vc)

Homages to Paul Sacher—features works by Britten; Halffter; Henze; Lutoslawski; Berio; Boulez; Ginastera; Beck; Huber; Holliger; Dutilleux ESDU ▲ 2020 (17.97)

Solo for Tatjana—features works by Ligeti, Scheidt, Suslin, Meyer, Hindemith, Casals, plus others ESDU ▲ 2019 (17.97)

Gorokhov, Leonid (vc)

Russian Discoveries, w. Colin Stone (pno)—features works by Fitzenhagen *(Perpetuum mobile; Notturno)*, Davydov *(Waltz; Sunday Morning; Adieu; Solitude; In the Morning; By the Fountain)*, Cui *(Barcarolle; Cantabile)*, Tchaikovsky *(Pezzo capriccioso)*, Arensky *(Chant triste; Oriental Melody; Humoresque; Little Ballad; Capriccioso Dance)*, Gretchaninov *(Nocturne [from Suite Vc, Op. 86]; Lullaby)*, Glazunov *(Minstrel's Song)*, Blumenfeld *(Elegy; Capriccioso)*, Sokolov *(Prelude, Op. 26/1)*, Rachmaninoff *(Oriental Dance; Vocalise)* OLY ▲ 641 (16.97)

Gregor-Smith, Bernard (vc)

Cello Romance, w. Yolande Wrigley (pno)—features works by Borodin, Debussy, Fauré, Glazunov, Gliere, Granados, Leighton, Rachmaninoff, Ravel, Rimsky-Korsakov, Rubinstein, Saint-Saëns, Shostakovich & Tchaikovsky ASV ▲ 2103 (12.97)

Gron, Anders (vc)

Cello Favorites, Vol. 3, w. J. Nielsen (pno)—features works by Schumann *(Adagio & Allegro, Op. 70; Fantasiestücke, Op. 73)*, Martinu *(Vars. on a Theme of Rossini)*, Ravel *(Pièce en forme de habanera)*, Villa-Lobos *(The Song of the Black Swan)*, Ginastera *(Pampeana No. 2)*, Chopin *(Son. for Cello & Piano, Op. 65)* DANI ▲ 8158

Gruber, Emanuel (vc)

Heart of the Cello, w. Herut Israeli (pno)—features works by Haydn *(Divertimento)*, Rachmaninoff *(Vocalise)*, Rimsky-Korsakov *(Flight of the Bumble Bee)*, Saint-Saëns *(Allegro Appassionato; The Swan from "Carnival of the Animals")*, Schubert *(Arpeggione Sonata)*, Schumann *(5 Stücke im Volkston)*, Tchaikovsky *(Valse Sentimentale)* PWK ▲ 1135 [DDD]

Gylfadóttir, Bryndís Halla (vc)

Cello, w. Snorri Sigfús Birgisson (pno), Marta Guthrún Halldórsdóttir (sop)—features works by Másson *(Hrím)*, Tómasson *(Eter)*, Sveinsson *(Dal regno del silenzio)*, Hauksson *(Psychomachia)*, Sigurbjörnsson *(Flakk)*, Nordal *(Pictures on a Panel Wall)* MFIC ▲ 804

Harnoy, Ofra (vc)

Bach to Offenbach, w. Maureen Forrester (cta), Andrew Davis (pno), Canadian Piano Trio, et al.—features works by Saraste *(Spanish Dance)*, Gershwin *(I Got Rhythm)*, Bach *(Suite 3 Vc [Bourée])*, Chopin *(Nocturne in c#)*, Lennon & McCartney *(Hey Jude)*, plus others INMP ▲ 6600672 (16.97)

An Evening with Ofra Harnoy, w. Orford String Quartet—features music by Boccherini *(Sonata No. 6)*, Casals *(Song of the Birds)*, Dvořák *(Waltz, Op. 54/1)*, Schubert *(Quintet, D.956)* PRA ▲ 418 [DDD]

Ofra Harnoy & Friends: Duets—features works by Tchaikovsky *(Sentimental Waltz, Op. 51)*, Schubert *(Allegro [from Qnt in C, D.956])*, Dvořák *(Waltz, Op. 54/1)*, Massenet *(Elegie)*, Danzi *(Duo No. 2, Op. 64)*, Rimsky-Korsakov *(Flight of the Bumblebee)*, Gershwin *(Summertime; Vars on Summertime; Vars on I Got Rhythm; Stairway to Paradise)*, Harrison *(Here Comes the Sun)*, Bozza *(Duet for Vc & Ob)*, Stevens *(Andante for 2 Vcs)* INMP (Classics) ▲ 6700622 (8.97)

Ofra Harnoy & Friends, w. Orford String Quartet, J. Baxtresser (fl), M. Forrester (cta), P. Brodie (sax), M. Dussek (pno), et al.—features works by Danzi, Falla, Foss, Gershwin, et al. PRA ▲ 552 [DDD]

Ofra Harnoy Collection, Vol. 4, w. William Aide (pno)—features works by Rimsky-Korsakov *(The Flight of the Bumblebee [from Tsar Saltan])*, Chopin *(Intro & Polonaise brillante, Op. 3)*, Stravinsky *(Russian Maiden's Song)*, Falla *(Ritual Fire Dance [from El Amor brujo]; Danza española [from La Vida breve])*, Tchaikovsky *(Autumn Song)*, Paganini *(Caprice, Op. 1/24)*, Martini *(Plaisir d'amour)*, Popper *(Serenade, Op. 54/2)*, Piatti *(Caprice, Op. 25/7)*, Zuckert *(N'ilah)*, Tsintsadze *(Chonguri)*, Gershwin *(Summertime [from Porgy & Bess]) (rec Timothy Eaton Memorial Church, Toronto, Canada, 1982)* RCAV (Gold Seal) ▲ 68369 [ADD] (10.97)

Salut d'Amour, w. Helena Bowkun (pno), Michael Dussek (pno), Catherine Wilson (pno)—features works by Bloch, Debussy, Elgar, Falla, Fauré, Gershwin, Popper, et al. RCAV (Red Seal) ▲ 60697 [AAD/DDD] 60697

Heled, Simca (vc)

Rare Cello Music, w. Daniel Edni (pno), Jonathan Feldman (pno), Michael Levin (pno), Alexander Peskanov (pno), Jonathan Zak (pno)—features works by Rodrigo *(Sicilienne)*, Ries *(Grand Son, Op. 20)*, Bazelaire *(Suite Française, Op. 114)*, Bréval *(Son in C)*, Mendelssohn *(Songs without Words, Op. 109)*, Weber *(Rondo)*, Tcherepnin *(Son in D)*, Rimsky-Korsakov *(Flight of the Bumble Bee) (rec 1976, 1982-83, 1985, 1989, 1991)* CLSO ▲ 153 (14.97)

Janigro, Antonio (vc)

Cello Favorites, w. Antonio Beltrami (pno)—features works by Granados *(Intermezzo [from Goyescas])*, Paradies *(Sicilienne)*, Bach *(Andante)*, Fauré *(Après un rêve; Elégie in c, Op. 24)*, Popper *(Chanson villageoise; Papillon)*, Dvořák *(Songs My Mother Taught Me)*, Falla *(Ritual Fire Dance [from El Amor Brujo; arr P. Kochanski])*, Saint-Saëns *(The Swan)*, Rubinstein *(Mélodie in F [arr Popper])*, Chopin *(Nocturne [arr Piatigorsky])*, Nin *(Granadina [arr Kochanski])*, Ravel *(Pièce en forme de Habanera [arr Bazelaire])*, Rimsky-Korsakov *(Flight of the Bumblebee [arr Strimer])*, Senaillé *(Allegro spiritoso [arr J. Salmon])*, Ravel *(Pièce en forme de Habanera [arr Bazelaire]) (rec Baumgarten Hall, Vienna, 1961)* VC ▲ 80 [AAD] (13.97)

King, Terry (vc)

Cello America, Vol. 1—features works by Barber, Cooper, Harris & Reale MUA ▲ 603 [DDD]

Cello America, Vol. 2—features works by Cowell, Creston, Drew, Foss & Riegger MUA ▲ 685 [DDD]

Kliegel, Maria (vc)

Le Grand Tango & Other Dances for Cello & Piano, w. Bernd Glemser (pno)—features works by Tagell, Cassadó, de Falla, Rachmaninoff, Popper, Tchaikovsky, Piazzolla *(rec May 3-4, 1993)* NXIN ▲ 550785 [DDD] (5.97)

The Love Collection, w. Bernd Glemser (pno)—features works by Tagell *(Flamenco)*, Cassadó *(Suite for Vc)*, Falla *(Spanish Dance [arr G. Pekkera]; Ritual Fire Dance [arr Gregor Piatigorsky])*, Rachmaninov *(Oriental Dance, Op. 2/2 [arr Leonard Rose])*, Popper *(Gnomentanz, Op. 50/2; Mazurka, Op. 11/3; Gavotte, Op. 23; Menuetto, Op. 65/2; Tarantella, Op. 33)*, Tchaikovsky *(Valse sentimentale in f, Op. 51/6 [arr Leonard Rose])*, Piazzolla *(Le Grand Tango) (rec Clara Wieck Auditorium, Heidelberg, May 3-4, 1993)* † OPERA & ORATORIO COLLECTIONS:Love Collection; ORCHESTRAL COLLECTIONS:Love Collection NXIN 4-▲ 504004 [DDD] (19.97)

Virtuoso Cello Encores, w. Raymund Havenith (pno)—features works by Bach, S. Barchet, G. Cassadó, Debussy, Gershwin, Granados, Offenbach, Popper, Rachmaninoff, Ravel, Schubert, J.B. Senaillé, Shostakovich, Vieuxtemps MARC ▲ 8223403 [DDD] (14.97)

Kuijken, Wieland (vc)

Viol Solo Recital—features works by Abel, Ortiz, Schenck, Telemann, Simpson & Hume DNN ▲ 75659 [DDD] (16.97)

Lavotha, Elemér (vc)

Popular & Serious Music for Cello & Piano, w. Kerstin Aberg (pno)—features works by Martinu *(Son 1 Vc)*, plus Bach/arr Gounod, Chopin, Fauré, Granados, Kodály, Ingvar Lidholm, Popper, Rachmaninoff, Ravel, Saint-Saëns, Tchaikovsky, Ernst Toch BIS ▲ 72 [AAD] (17.97)

Leonard, Ronald (vc)

Orchestral Excerpts for Cello—features sels from works by Rossini *(Guillaume Tell [Ov])*, Brahms *(Syms 1-3)*, R. Strauss *(Don Juan; Ein Heldenleben; Don Quixote)*, Beethoven *(Syms 5, 8 & 9)*, Debussy *(La Mer)*, Verdi *(Requiem)*, Mozart *(Le nozze di Figaro; Sym 40)*, Mendelssohn *(A Midsummer Night's Dream)*, Tchaikovsky *(Syms 4 & 6)*, Dvořák *(Sym 8)*, plus others SUMM (OrchestraPro) ▲ 196 (16.97)

Lewis, Dorothy (vc)

Music by Southern Composers for Cello & Piano, w. C. Lewis (pno)—features works by Boury, Bryant, Gerschefski, Knox, Presser, & Robertson GAS ▲ 274 (16.97) ▮ GAS 274

Romances, w. C. Lewis (pno)—features works by M. Enrico Bossi, Debussy, Jean Gabriel-Marie, Walter Golz, Hans Huber, Joseph Malkin, Rachmaninoff, Reger, Rubinstein, Saint-Saëns, Sibelius, Christian Sinding, Scriabin, Johann Svendsen, Francis Thome ACAD ▲ 20013 (16.97)

Lidström, Mats (vc)

Swedish Cello Sonatas, w. Bengt Forsberg (pno)—features works by Roman *(Largo)*, Berwald *(Duo)*, Rosenberg *(Son Vc)*, Mankell *(Nocturne)*, Melchers *(Movements I, II & III)*, Lidström *(Tango) (rec Royal Academy of Music, Stockholm, Nov 1995)* CAPA ▲ 21460 (16.97)

Lloyd Webber, Julian (vc)

Cradle Song, w. Pamela Chowhan (pno), John Lenehan (pno), Richard Rodney Bennett (pno)—features works by Brahms *(Wiegenlied, Op. 49/4)*, Canteloube *(Songs of the Auvergne [Brezairola])*, Dvořák *(Wiegenlied; Gypsy Melodies, Op. 55 [Songs My Mother Taught Me])*, Fauré *(Berceuse)*, D. Heath *(Gentle Dreams)*, T. Hewitt *(Shepherd's Lullaby [arr P. Chowhan])*, Khachaturian *(A Little Song)*, J. Lenehan *(Alice)*, J. Lloyd Webber *(Song for Baba [arr P. Chowhan])*, W. Lloyd Webber *(Slumber Song)*, Montsalvatge *(Canción de cuna para dormir a un negrito)*, Poulenc *(Lent et mélancholique [from Babar the Elephant]*, Quilter *(Slumber Song; Where Go the Boats)*, J. Rutter *(Mary's Lullaby [arr D. Willcocks])*, Schubert *(Wiegenlied, Op. 98/2)*, R. Schumann *(Kinderszenen, Op. 15 [Träumerei])*, C. Scott *(Lullaby, Op. 57/2)*, plus other sels *(Nursery Suite (Rock-a-bye Baby/Golden Slumbers/Rocking Carol) [arr P. Chowhan]; Film Medley (Baby Let Me Take You Dreaming/Welcome to My Dream/Sleepyhead) [arr R. Rodney Bennett]) (rec Henry Wood Hall, London, Oct 26-28, 1993)* PPHI ▲ 42426 (16.97)

English Idyll, w. Academy of St. Martin in the Fields [cnd:Neville Marriner]—features works by Vaughan Williams *(Romanza)*, Elgar *(Romance in d, Op. 62; Une Idylle, Op. 4/1 [w. John Birch (org)])*, Delius *(2 Pieces for Vc & Chamber Orch.)*, Grainger *(Youthful Rapture; Brigg Fair)*, Dyson *(Fant.)*, Ireland *(The Holy Boy)*, Davies *(Solemn Melody [w. John Birch (org)])*, Holst *(Invocation)*, Scott *(Pastoral & Reel [w. John Lenehan (pno)])* PPHI ▲ 42530 (16.97)

Romantic Cello, w. Yitkin Seow (pno)—features works by Chopin, Delius, Elgar, Fauré, Mendelssohn, Popper, Rachmaninoff, Saint-Saëns ASVQ ▲ 6014 [ADD] (10.97)

Ma, Yo-Yo (vc)

Anything Goes, w. Stéphane Grappelli (vn)—features works by Cole Porter COL ▲ 45574 [DDD] 45574

Hush, w. Bobby McFerrin (sgr)—features works by McFerrin, Bach, Rachmaninoff, Rimsky-Korsakov, Vivaldi, et al. COL ▲ 48177 (16.97) △ SM 48177 ▮ 48177 (10.98)

Portrait of Yo-Yo Ma—features works by Bach, Beethoven, Dvořák-Kreisler, Haydn, Kreisler, Paganini, Saint-Saëns COL ▲ 44796 [DDD/ADD] (16.97) 44796

Maisky, Mischa (vc)

Adagio, w. Orch de Paris [cnd:S. Bychkov]—features works by Bruch, Dvořák, Fauré, Glazunov, Haydn, Respighi, Saint-Saëns, R. Strauss, Tchaikovsky DEUT ▲ 35781 [DDD] (16.97)

Cellissimo, w. D. Hovora (pno)—features works by Bach, Handel, Boccherini, Schubert, Schumann, Chopin, Bloch, Saint-Saëns & Debussy DEUT ▲ 39863 (16.97)

Maréchal, Maurice (vc)

The Art of Maurice Maréchal, Book 1 (1929-1937), w. *(various pianists)*—features works by Rameau, J.S. Bach, C.P.E. Bach, Boccherini, Schumann, Chopin, Liszt, Gounod, Saint-Saëns, Grieg, Fauré, Granados & Ravel *(rec 1929-37)* ENT (Strings) ▲ 99301 (16.97)

The Art of Maurice Maréchal, Book 2, w. *(various pianists)* ENT (Strings) ▲ 99316 (16.97)

Maurice Maréchal: Book 3—features works by J. C. Bach *(Con Vc)*, Desplanes *(Intrada)*, Massenet *(Les Erinnyes [sels])*, Mussorgsky *(Gopak)*, Dvořák *(Indian Lament)*, Fauré *(Élégie)*, Boëllman *(Vars Symphoniques, Op. 23)*, Falla *(7 Canciones Populares Españolas)*, Ibert *(Histoires) (rec 1928-48)* ENT (Strings) ▲ 99356 (16.97)

Mariscal, Ignacio (vc)

Mexico & the Violoncello, w. Carlos Alberto Pecero (pno)—features works by Montiel *(Cantinela)*, Rolon *(Lied)*, Lavista *(Cuaderno de Viaje)*, Sandi *(Sonatina Vc Pno)*, Hernandez *(Son Vc Pno)*, Toussaint *(Pieza Vc)*, Galindo *(Son Vc Pno)*, Cuen *(Canto para las Animas)* SPT ▲ 21016 [DDD] (16.97)

Navarra, André (vc)

Eight Japanese Melodies, w. Annie d' Arco (pno) † Saint-Saëns:Cello Sonatas CALL ▲ 9818 [ADD]

Niculescu, Anton (vc)

Gaspar Cassadó, w. Barbara Lolé (pno)—features works by Cassadó *(Requiebros; Sérénade pour M.me la Princesse; Danse du diable vert)*, Frescobaldi *(Toccata)*, Couperin *(Pastorale)*, Schubert *(Allegretto grazioso)*, Crescenzo *(Prima carezza)*, Popper *(Elfentanz)*, Granados *(Intermezzo)*, Liszt *(Liebesträume)*, Borodin *(Serenata alla spagnola)*, Paderewski *(Minuet, Op. 14/1)* [all works by other composers arr Cassadó for vn & pno] *(rec Mar 1986)* STRV ▲ 11 (16.97)

Noras, Arto (vc)

Masterpieces for Cello, w. Tapani Valsta (pno/org)—features works by Saint-Saëns, Sibelius, von Weber, Schubert, de Sarasate, Paganini, Frescobaldi, Ginastera, Handel, Schumann, J.S. Bach, Rachmaninoff ELEC ▲ 95883 [AAD]

Orloff, Vladimir (vc)

The Art of Vladimir Orloff, w. George Enescu PO [cnd:Eugene Goossens], Hallé SO [cnd:John Barbirolli], Vienna SO [cnd:Wolfgang Sawallisch], Vienna Tonkünstler Orch [cnd:Walter Weller], et al.—features works by Schumann *(Con Vc)*, Vieru *(Con Vc)*, Elgar *(Con Vc in e)*, Boccherini *(Son 6 Vc)*, Haydn *(Con Vc in c)*, Brahms *(Double Con in a, Op. 102 [w. Josef Sivo (vn)])*, Locatelli *(Son Vc in D)*, Saint-Saëns *(Con Vc in a)*, Khachaturian *(Con Vc in e)*, Shostakovich *(Con 1 Vc) (rec 1949-76)* DHR (Legendary Treasures) 3-▲ 7711 (47.97)

Patterson, Louise (vc)

Cello und Klavier: Chamber Music from Bohemia, w. Jiří Neidoba (pno)—features works by Suk, Dvořák, Janáček, Martinů, plus others QUER ▲ 9606 (18.97)

Pereira, David (vc)
Cello Dreaming—features contemporary Australian works by D. Banks *(Sequence)*, Lumsdaine *(blue upon blue)*, Sculthorpe *('Cello Dreaming)*, R. Edwards *(Monos I)*, Hannan *(Rajas)*, Sitsky *(Improv & Cadenza)*, Butterly *(Of Wood)*, Finsterer *(Tract) (rec 1993 & 1995)* TALP ▲ 75 [DDD] (18.97)
Evocations: The Poet, w. David Bollard (cl)—features works by Jardanyi, Koch, Kramer, Martinu, Dvorák, Glazunov, Fauré, Nin, Delius, Kodály, Farkas TALP ▲ TP 10 [DDD]

Perényi, Miklós (vc)
Miklós Perényi & Zoltán Kocsis in Concert, w. Zoltán Kocsis (pno/harm)—features works by J. S. Bach *(Prelude & Fugue, BWV 853 [trans Kodály])*, Chopin *(Etude, Op. 25/7 [trans Glazunov])*, Liszt *(Valse oubliée 1 [trans Busoni]; La lugubre gondola)*, Popper *(Elfentanz)*, Sibelius *(Valse triste [arr Kocsis])*, Debussy *(La plus que lente [trans Kocsis]; Son [w. János Pilz (vn), András Keller (vn)])*, Dvořák *(Bagatelles, Op. 47 [w. János Pilz (vn), András Keller (vn)]) (rec 1989-95)* HUN ▲ 31673 [AAD/DDD] (16.97)

Piatigorsky, Gregor (vc)
Gregor Piatigorsky—features works by Boccherini *(Son 2 Vc)*, Haydn *(Divert in D)*, Schumann *(Fantasiestücke)*, Chopin *(Intro & Polonaise brilliante)*, Fauré *(Tarantelle)*, Saint-Sa(uml)ens *(The Swan)*, Debussy *(Romance)*, Ravel *(Piece en forme d'habanera)*, Granados *(Orientale)*, Prokofiev *(Masques from Romeo & Juliet)*, Shostakovich *(Son Vc, Op. 40)*, Rubenstein *(Melody in F)* BID ▲ 117
His Best Pre-War 78s—features works by Beethoven *(Cello Sonata No. 2)*, Brahms *(Cello Sonata No. 1)*, Schumann *(Cello Concerto)*, plus short pieces by Mendelssohn, Moszkowski & Tchaikovsky *(rec 1927-34)* MUA ▲ 674 [AAD] (16.97)

Prieto, Carlos (vc)
Espejos, w. Edison Quintana (pno)—features works by Falla *(Suite popular Española)*, E. Halffter *(Canzona e Pastorella)*, Marco *(Primer Espejo de Falla)*, Lavista *(Tres Danzas Seculares)*, Heras *(Canción en el Puerto)*, Castillo *(Alborada)*, R. Halffter *(Son Vc, Op. 26)* URT ▲ 15 (16.97)
Le Grand Tango, w. Edison Quintana (pno)—features works by Piazzolla *(Le Grand Tango; Milonga; Michelangelo 70; Balada para mi muerte)*, Ginastera *(Triste)*, Villa-Lobos *(Aria [from Bachiana Brasileira 5])*, Ibarra *(Son Vc)*, Rodriguez *(Lulla-a-Bear)*, Enriquez *(Fant)* URT ▲ 14 (16.97)

Rautio, Erkki (vc)
Finnish Miniatures for Cello, w. Izumi Tateno (pno)—features works by Mielck, Sohlström, Järnefelt, Merikanto, Kuula, Melartin, Sibelius, Kuusisto, Sonninen, Marttinen, Salmenhaara, Saikkola, Johansson, Sallinen *(rec Jan 3 & 7, 1991)* ELEC ▲ 95871 [DDD]

Rosa, William de (vc)
Cellist's Holliday, w. Noreen Cassidy-Polera (pno)—features works by Frescobaldi/Cassado *(Toccata)*, Bach/Siloti *(Adagio)*, Chopin/Rose *(Intro & Polonaise brilliante, Op. 3)*, Paganini/Silva *(Vars on a theme from Rossini's "Moses")*, Fauré *(Elegy, Op. 24; Après un rêve [arr Casals])*, Debussy *(La fille aux cheveux de Lin)*, Tchaikovsky *(Pezzo capriccioso, Op. 62; Nocturne, Op. 19/4)*, Rimsky-Korsakov *(Flight of the Bumble Bee)*, Rachmaninoff *(Vocalise, Op. 34/14)*, Davidoff *(At the Fountain, Op. 20/2)* AUDO ▲ 72046 (16.97)

Rose, Leonard (vc)
The Memorial Edition—features works by Bach, Bloch, Haydn, Sammartini, Brahms, Debussy & Tchaikovsky *(rec 1945-47)* PHS 2-▲ 9273 (33.97)

Rosen, Nathaniel (vc)
Orientale: Romantic Music for Cello, w. Doris Stevenson (pno), Arturo Delmoni (vn)—features works by Debussy, Elgar, Falla, Granados, Haydn, Martinu, Popper, Saint-Saëns, Sarasate, Schubert, Tchaikovsky, Piatigorsky, Prokofiev and Kreisler NOR ▲ 27
Reverie: Romantic Music for Quiet Times, w. Kaaren Erickson (sop), Doris Stevenson (pno), Arturo Delmoni (vn)—features works by Mendelssohn *(A May Breeze)*, Boccherini/Kreisler *(Allegretto)*, Beethoven/Kreisler *(Andante)*, Lalo *(Chants russes)*, Fauré *(Elegie)*, Satie *(Gymnopédie No. 1)*, Bizet *(Intermezzo)*, Desplanes *(Intrada)*, Bach *(Jesus Christ, I Implore Thee)*, Ravel/Castelnuovo-Tedesco *(La Vallee des cloches)*, Schumann *(Langsam)*, Chopin *(Largo)*, Rachmaninoff *(Lied)*, R. Strauss *(Morgen)*, Casella *(Notturno)*, Brahms *(O Tod, Wie Bitter Bist Du)*, Debussy *(Romance)*, Elgar *(Sospiri)* 23807 ▲ 10

Rostropovich, Mstislav (vc)
Les Chefs-d'Oeuvre du Violoncelle, w. Berlin PO [cnd:Herbert von Karajan], Israel PO [cnd:Leonard Bernstein]—features works by Vivaldi, Tartini, Boccherini, Tchaikovsky, Glazunov, Shostakovich & Bernstein DEUT (Double) 2-▲ 37952 (17.97)
The Russian Years 1950-74—features works by Honegger, Stravinsky, Scriabin, Milhaud, de Falla, Dvořák, R. Strauss, Fauré, Debussy, Schubert, Prokofiev, Handel, Britten, Shostakovich, Tchaikovsky, Villa-Lobos, Respighi & Kabelevsky *(rec Moscow, 1960's)* EMIC 13-▲ 72016 (86.97)

Rudiakov, Michael (vc)
Cello Charms, w. R. Levy (pno)—features works by Moszkowski *(Guitarre)*, Weber *(Adagio & Allegro for Violin [trans. Gregor Piatigorsky])*, J.S. Bach *(Aria [from Orchestral Suite; trans. Joachim Stutchewski])*, Mendelssohn *(Song without Words, Op. 109; Song without Words in A for Piano [trans. Chanan Winternitz for cello])*, Schubert *(The Bee [trans. P. Casals])*, Foss *(Capriccio)*, Rochberg *(Ricordanza)*, Perkinson *(Calvary Ostinato; Perpetual Motion)*, Granados *(Intermezzo [from Goyescas; arr. Gaspar Cassado])*, Ravel *(Habanera [trans. Bazelaire])*, Paradis *(Sicilenne)*, Achron *(Sher)*, Stutchewski *(Kadish; Hassidic Dance) (rec Marlboro, VT, May 1993)* CENT ▲ 2192 [DDD] (16.97)

Schilders, Beatrijs (vc)
Belgian Composers of the Antwerp Conservatory, w. Urbain Boodts (pno)—features works by Callaerts *(Gavotte, Op. 20)*, Wambach *(Andante appasionato)*, Gilson *(Suite)*, Blockx *(Serenade de Milenka)*, Van den Broeck *(Poema)*, Durlet *(De Toevlucht)*, D'Haeyr *(Sarabande)* RENE ▲ 87135 (16.97)

Schuback, Peter (vc)
Violoncello Con Forza—features works by Rosell *(Nattens Träd [Tree of Night])*, Maros *(Schattierungen)*, Börtz *(Monologhi 8)*, Glaser *(Lettre a Une Âme [Letter to a Soul])*, Sandberg *(For-Ofog)*, Franzén *(Gryningsmusik [Dawn Music])*, Schuback *(Devant Le Fin [Approaching the End])* PHNS ▲ 45 [DDD] (16.97)

Sollima, Giovanni (vc)
Aquilarco: Dynamic Cello Music POIN ▲ 462546 (16.97)

Starker, János (vc)
Janos Starker Plays, w. Gyorgy Sebok (pno)—features works by Boccherini *(excerpt from Son. in A)*, Vivaldi *(Son. in e)*, Corelli *(Son. in d)*, Locatelli *(Son. in D [arr. A. Piatti])*, Valentini *(Son. in E [w. S. Swedish (piano); arr. Piatti])*, J.S. Bach *(Son. in g, BWV 1029) (rec Apr 16-17, 1963-June 6-7, 1966)* MRCR ▲ 34344 (11.97)
The Road to Cello Playing—features works by Hindemith *(Son solo Vc, Op. 25/3)*, Heiden *(Vars on Lilibulero)*, Cassado *(Suite solo Vc)*, plus works by Lee, Schroder, Dotzauer, J. L. & J. P Duport, Piatti, Popper, Grutzmacher & Paganini PACD ▲ 97008 (14.97)
Starker Encore Album—features works by Schubert, Saint-Saëns, Bloch, Bartók, et al. DNN ▲ 8117 [DDD] (11.97)
Virtuoso Music for Cello—features works by Paganini, Popper, Fauré, Debussy, Ravel, et al. DNN ▲ 8118 [DDD] (11.97)

Thedéen, Torleif (vc)
Russian Cello Music, w. Roland Pöntinen (pno)—features works by Schnittke, Shostakovich, Stravinsky BIS ▲ 336 (17.97)

Thomas-Mifune, Werner (vc)
Harmonies Du Soir: Virtuoso Romantic Cello Music, w. Munich CO [cnd:Hans Stadlmair]—features works by Fauré, Françaix, Offenbach, David Popper, Paganini, Sarasate, Schubert, Wagner ORF ▲ 131851 [DDD] (18.97)
Magic Cello—features works of J.S. Bach *(Air on the G String)*, Schubert *(Ave Maria)*, Chopin *(Waltz in c#; Etude in c)*, Schumann *(Kinderszenen)*, Liszt *(Leibstraum)*, Wagner *(Tannhäuser:Pilgrim's Chorus)*, Dvořák *(Slavic Dance in e)*, Sibelius *(Valse triste)*, Fucik *(Florentiner March)* [all arr Thomas-Mitfune for vc or vcs] CALG ▲ 50967 [ADD] (19.97)
Salut d'amour, w. Carmen Piazzini (pno)—features works by Shostakovich *(Romanze)*, Tchaikovsky *(Valse sentimantale; Arie des Lenski [from Eugene Onegin]; Neapolitanisches Lied)*, Chopin *(Nocturne)*, Bizet *(Andantino [from Carmen])*, Bruch *(Kol Nidrei, Op. 47)*, Mendelssohn *(Lied ohne Worte)*, Dvořák *(Rondo)*, Elgar *(Salut d'amour)*, Paradis *(Sicilienne)*, Wagner *(Träume [from Wesendock-Lieder])*, Tanejew *(Suite de concert [Andante])*, Casals *(Gesang der Vögel)*, Handel *(Serse [Largo])*, J. S. Bach *(Arioso in f)*, Rachmaninoff *(Vocalise)*, Park *(Love Gone with Autumn Behind)* ORF ▲ 443961 [DDD] (18.97)

Ullner, Niels (vc)
Cello Favorites DANR ▲ DAN 330

Varshavsky, Mark (vc)
A Century of Italian Music from Scarlatti to Paganini, w. Christine Lacoste (vc) DUC ▲ 19 [DDD]

Wang, Jian (vc)
Presenting Jian Wang, w. Carol Rosenberger (pno)—features works by Samuel Barber *(Cello Sonata)*, et al. DLS ▲ 3097 [DDD]

Wispelwey, Pieter (vc)
Styles, w. Paul Komen (pno), Lois Shapiro (pno), Florilegium—features works by Bach *(Prelude; Courante [both from Suite No. 1 in G]; Allemande [from Suite No. 6 in D])*, Ligeti *(Capriccio [from Son for Vc])*, Hindemith *(Son, Op. 25/3 [1st movt])*, Brahms *(Allegro Vivace [from Son for Vc & Pno, Op. 99])*, Sessions *(Berceuse; Epilogue [both from 6 Pieces for Vc])*, Beethoven *(Adagio Cantabile; Allegro Vivace [both from Son in A, Op. 69]; Rondo [from Son in F, Op. 17])*, Vivaldi *(Preludio; Allemande [both from Son No. 6 in B♭])*, Britten *(Suite No. 1, Op. 72 [6th movt])*, Kodály *(Allegro Molto Vivace [from Son for Vc, Op. 8])*, Haydn *(Allegro Molto [from Con in C for Vc])* CCL ▲ 395 (7.97)

CELLO COLLECTIONS

Cello Concertos
HAM ▲ 901655 (17.97)

The Magic of the Cello—features performances by Frédéric Lodeon *(Haydn:Allegro [from Con, Op. 101]; Boccherini:Rondo Allegro [from Con No. 9] [both w. Theodor Guschlbauer (cnd), Bournemouth Sinfonietta Orch]; Duport:Romance [from Con No. 2]; Adagio-Presto [from Duo for Vcs, Op. 1/3; w. Xavier Gagnepain (vc)] [both w. Jean-Pierre Wallez (cnd), Paris Orchestral Ensemble]; Chopin:Largo [from Son for Vc & Pno, Op. 65; w. François-René Duchable (pno)])*, Paul Tortelier *(Vivaldi:Allegro [from Son No. 1 for Vc & Hpd, R.47]; Largo [from Son No. 4 for Vc & Hpd, R.45] [w. Robert Veyron-Lacroix])*, André Navarra *(Saint-Saëns:Allegro non troppo [from Con No. 1, Op. 33]; Lalo:Intermezzo [from Con] [both w. Charles Munch (cnd), Robert Lamoureux Concert Association])*, Yvan Chiffoleau *(Debussy:Finale [from Son for Vc & Pno; w. Jean Hubeau])*, Roland Pidoux *(Saint-Saëns:Romance for Vc & Pno, Op. 36; w. Jean Hubeau (pno)]; Fauré:Andante [Son No 1 for Vc & Pno, Op. 109]; Elegie for Vc & Pno, Op. 24 [both w. Jean-Claude Pennetier (pno)])* ERAT ▲ 94689 (9.97)

The Recorded Cello: The History of Cello on Record, Vol. 1—features DISC ONE: EUROPEAN TRADITIONS: recordings by Pablo Casals, Gaspar Cassadó, Tibor de Machula, Enrico Mainardi, Vilmos Palotai, Milos Sádlo, Hermann Sandby, František Smetana, Guilhermina Suggia, Alexandr Večtomov, Ladislav Zelenka; DISC TWO: THE RUSSIAN TRADITION—recordings by Radu Aldulescu, Alexander Barjansky, Sviatoslav Knushevitzky, Mstislav Rostropovich, Daniel Shafran, A.V. Wierzbilowicz; DISC THREE: THE AMERICAN TRADITION—recordings by Ennio Bolognini, Paolo Gruppe, Victor Herbert, Samuel Mayes, Frank Miller, Gregor Piatigorsky, Leonard Rose, Felix Salmond, Luigi Silva, Alfred Wallenstein *(rec 1904-60)* PHS 3-▲ PEA 9981 (m) [AAD]

The Recorded Cello: The History of Cello on Record, Vol. 2—features performances by DISC ONE: THE ENGLISH TRADITION—recordings by Philipp Abbas, John Barbirolli, Auguste van Biene, Maurice Eisenberg, Beatrice Harrison, Keith Harvey, Lauri Kennedy, Edmund Kurtz, Ludwig Lebell, Jacques van Lier, Peter Muscant, Alfred Newberry, Anthony Pini, William Pleeth, Antoni Sala, Cedric Sharpe, W.H. Squire, W.E. Whitehouse; DISC TWO: THE GERMAN TRADITION—recordings by Hugo Becker, Friedrich Buxbaum, Gutia Casini, Emanuel Feuermann, Arnold Földesy, Carl Fuchs, Paul Grümmer, Heinrich Grünfeld, Anton Hekking, Ludwig Hoelcher, Joseph Hollman, Hans Kindler, Julius Klengel, Hugo Kreisler, Heinrich Kruse, Beatrice Reichert; DISC THREE: THE FRANCO-BELGIAN TRADITION—recordings by Paul Bazelaire, Umberto Benedetti, Iwan D'Archambeau, Pierre Fournier, Adolphe Frézin, Gérard Hekking, Robert Maas, Gaston Marchésini, Maurice Maréchal, André Navarra, Claude Paschal, Etienne Pasquier, Paul Tortelier, Joseph Tzipine *(rec 1904-60)* PHS 3-▲ PEA 9984 (m) [AAD]

12 Hommages a Paul Sacher pour violincelle—features performances by Patrick Demenga *(Ginastera:Puneña No. 2, Op. 45; Fortner:Zum Spielen für den 70. Geburtstag [Theme & Vars.]; Henze:Capriccio; Beck:Für Paul Sacher 3 Epigramme; Dutilleux:3 Strophes sur le nom de Sacher)*, Thomas Demenga *(Lutoslawski:Sacher-Variationen; Berio:Les mots sont allés; Halffter:Variationen über das Thema eSACHERe; Britten:Tema eSACHERe; Huber:Transpositio ad infinitum für ein virtuoses Solocello; Holliger:Chaconne)*, Beat Feigenwinter, Michael Keller, Barbara Lichter, Anna Loudos, Françoise Schiltknecht & Pierpaolo Toso [cnd:Jürg Wyttenbach] *(Boulez:Messagesquisse for 7 vc) (rec June 1993)* ECM 2-▲ 21520 [DDD] (30.97)

Virtuoso Cello Music—features performances by Ememér Lavotha (vc) *(C. P. E. Bach:Con Vc in A, W.172; Couperin:Pièces en concert; Boccherini:Con Vc in D [all w. [cnd:Jan-Olav Wedin] Kalmar Läns CO])*, Bengt Ericson (vc) *(Saint-Saëns:Le Cygne; Cassado:Serenade; Faueé:Sicilienne, Op. 78; Massenet:Elégie; Kreisler:Liebeslied; Tournier:Nocturne [all w. Karin Langebo (hp)])* BIS ▲ 224 [DDD/ADD] (17.97)

CHAMBER MUSIC

Academy of St. Martin in the Fields Chamber Ensemble
Academy Classics—features works by Mozart *(Divert. in D, K334/320b [Minuet & Trio]; Ein musikalischer Spass, K.522 [Finale])*, Dvořák *(Humoresque, Op. 101/7)*, Tchaikovsky *(Souvenir de Florence, Op. 78 [Movt 3])*, Grieg *(At the Cradle [from* Lyric Suite, Op. 68/5*]; Elegiac Melodies [2], Op. 34)*, Ravel *(Pavane pour une infante défunte)*, Elgar *(Salut d'amour, Op. 12)*, Walton *(Touch her soft lips and part [from Henry V])*, Gershwin *(Summertime)*, Pachelbel *(Kanon)*, Rachmaninoff *(Vocalise, Op.34/14)*, Debussy *(Clair de lune)* CHN ▲ 9216 [DDD] (16.97)

Amazing Orch [cnd:Thomas Jäderlund] [Thomas Jäderlund (a sax), Thomasz Stanko (tpt), Stein-Erik Tafjord (tuba), Christy Doran (gtr), Svante Henryson (vc/elec bass), Guy Klucevsek (acc), Johnny Axelsson (perc)]
Nordic Meeting 1994-95 CAPA 2-▲ 22045 (31.97)

Anderson, John (ob), Simon Wynberg (gtr)
Summertime: Music for Oboe & Guitar—features arrangements for oboe & guitar or solo guitar of music by Bach, Coste, Gershwin, Ibert, Mertz, Satie, Sor, Villa-Lobos, Wanhal CHN (Collect) ▲ 6581 [DDD] (12.97)

Antidogma Musica
The 11th Antidogma Musica Festival—features works by Scelsi *(Ko-Tha)*, Miereanu *(Rumore—Come nebbia al vento)*, Correggia *(L'ab' me évanoui)*, Macias *(Les adieux) (rec Turin, 1988)* ADDA ▲ 581157

Apap, Gille (vn), Jean-Marc Apap (va), Chris Judge (gtr), Brendan Statom (db)
Gilles Apap & the Transylvanian Mountain Boys—features works by Falla *(Spanish Dance No. 1 [from La vida breve, Act II])*, Dinicu *(Zella Zella)*, Monti *(The Whistle; Hora in b [Csárdas])*, Prokofiev *(March [from The Love for 3 Oranges])*, Ferencz *(Valse Triste)*, Lakatos *(Wunderbar Violin)*, Privat *(Java Manouche)*, Khachaturian *(Sabre Dance [from Gayane])*, trad *(2 Guitars; Hora Romanesca; Desire; Zina's Tune; Youri, You're In; Hora Presta; Gypsy Medley)* COL ▲ 62374 (16.97)

Apollo [Carey Domb (gtr), Daniel Domb (vc)]
Apollo—features works by Bach *(Ariosa)*, Tartini *(Vars on a Theme of Corelli, Nos. 11, 26, 27 & 45)*, Casals *(Song of the Birds)*, Schubert *(Serenade; Ave Maria)*, Ibert *(The Little White Donkey)*, Saint-Saëns *(The Swan)*, Paganini *(Moses Fant Vars)*, Puccini *(O Mio Babbino Caro [from Gianni Schicchi])*, Verdi *(Addio, Del Passato [from La traviata])*, Donizetti *(Una Furtiva Lagrima [from L'elisir d'amore])*, Rota *(Speak Softly Love [from The Godfather])*, de Curtis *(Torna a Surriento)*, Massenet *(Meditation [from Thaïs])*, trad *(Danny Boy; Amazing Grace)* OASI ▲ 2390 (16.97)

Argenta, Nancy (sop), Trio Sonnerie [Monica Huggett (vn), Sarah Cunningham (strs), Mitzi Meyerson (kbd)]
A Portrait of Love HAM (Suite) ▲ 7907081 (12.97)

Arita, Masahiro (fl), Chiyoko Arita (hpd), Tetsuya Nakano (vl)
18th Century "New Generation" German Flute Music—features works by Müthel, Friedrich II, Benda, C.P.E. Bach, Abel, Kleinknecht *(rec Nov 11-12, 1991 & Feb 26-28, 1992)* DNN ▲ 75025 [DDD] (16.97)

Artela, Ainhoa (sop), Michael Long (gtr), Richard Bock (vc)
Music from the Royal Courts of Europe—features 15th-18th cent music by Gastoldi *(La Sdegnato)*, V. Galilei *(Bianco Fiore; Se Lo M'Accorgo)*, Praetorius *(Balletto)*, Bottegari *(Monicella mi Farei)*, Dowland *(My Lady Hunssdon's Puffe)*, Sanz *(Passacalle; Marisapalos)*, Mudarra *(Triste estava el Rey David)*, R. de Visse *(Minuet)*, M. de Fuenllana *(De antequera sale el moro)*, plus trad songs *(Noches, Noches [3 versions]; Los Bilbilicos; Una Matica de Ruda [all from Spain]; Con que la lavare; Une jeune fillette [both from France]; Danza [from Germany])* HEL ▲ 1023 (10.97)

Atlanta Chamber Players
Soirée Sweets—features Barili *(Cradle Song, Op. 18)*, J. Brahms *(Hungarian Dances Orch [No. 6 in D])*, G. Finzi *(Bagatelles (5), Op. 23 [Romance; Forlana])*, B. Godard *(Suite de trois morceaux, Op. 116 [Valse])*, Ibert *(Interludes [Andante espressivo; Allegro vivo])*, F. Kreisler *(Farewell to Cucullain; Miniature Viennese March; Syncopation; Tempo di Minuetto)*, Massenet *(Méditation from Thaïs)*, W. A. Mozart *(Trio Cl, K.498 [3. Rondo: allegretto])*, Quantz *(Trio Son [Allegro; Allegro])*, Saint-Saëns *(Cygne)*, F. Schubert *(Schwanengesang, D.957 [Das Fischermädchen; Ständchen])* ACAD ▲ 20063 (16.97)

Aubier, Eric (tpt), Baermann Clarinet Sextet
Recontre—features works by Albinoni *(ConTpt. "St. Mark")*, Ponchielli *(Il covenio)*, Lancen *(Con à 6)*, Loucheur *(Concertino)*, Chebrou *(Polyton)*, Charbrier *(Cortege burlesque)*, Faillenot *(Tryptique)* MGU ▲ 519282

Aurora Ensemble [Enrico Gatti (vn), Odile Edouard (vn), Alain Gervreau (vc), Guido Morini (org/hpd)], Adriana Egivi (sgr), Sigrid Lee (sgr), Stefano Pilati (perc/sgr)]
The Art of the Violin in Italy During the 17th & 18th Centuries, Vol. 1—features works by Tarquinio Merula, Nicola Matteis, Agostino Guerrieri, Carlo Mannelli, Giovanni Pandolfi Mealli, Marco Uccellini, Giovanni Buinaventure Viviani, Angelo Berardi & Pierto Degli Antoni SYM ▲ 2 [DDD]
L'Arte del Violino—features works by Uccellini *(Aria XI sopra il Caporal Simon; Son. XXVI a 3 sopra La Prosperina)*, Torelli *(Perfidia a due violini)*, Colombi Jacchini *(Son. VII a 3)*, Bononcini *(Corrente La Pegolotta; Allemanda La Guelfa; Corrente L'incognita; Son. da chiesa No. 10, Op. VI)*, Vitali *(Son. La Guidoni; Son. da chiesa No. 12, Op. II)*, Uccellini *(Aria XIII sopra Questa bella sirena; Son. XXVII a3; Aria XV sopra La Scatola dagli agghi)*, Colombi *(Scordatura for solo Vn [Ciacona]; Vars. a 2 sull' Aria di Bergamasca)*, Gabrielli *(Ricercare for solo Vc)*, Cazzati *(Son. a 2 La Gaetana)* SYM ▲ SY 91S11 [DDD]

Avena Trio [Jan de Maeyer (ob), Nestor Janssens (cl), Luc Loubry (bn)]
Festival of French Music—features works by Tomasi, Ibert, Françaix, Dondeyne, Ropartz & Canteloube DI ▲ 920181 [DDD] (5.97)

Rachmaninoff's Rhapsody *(with the sound of soft rain)*—features works by Rachmaninoff *(Rhap on a Theme of Paganini (18th var))*, Bach *(Suite No. 3)*, Pachelbel *(Canon)*, Debussy *(Prélude à l'après-midi d'un faune)*, Mozart *(Adagio non troppo [from Con No. 1 for Flute])*, Beethoven *(Larghetto [from Con in D for Violin])*, Vaughan Williams *(Fant on a Theme by Thomas Tallis)*, Fauré *(Sicilienne [from Pelleas et Melisande])*, Brahms *(Poco Allegretto [from Sym No. 3])*
SMC ("Gentle Persuasion For Relaxation & Meditation") ▲ 5213 5213

Reference Classics—features works by Copland, Pachelbel, Walton, Liszt, Respighi, Britten, Weill, Rameau, Rutter, Chihara, Stravinsky, Berloiz Reference ▲ RR S1CD

Relax with the Classics

(4 vol series of over 50 Baroque works for chamber orchestra "scientifically selected from over 400 carefully auditioned pieces by Dr. Charles Schmid of the LIND Institute...The music has a perceptible tempo of between 50 and 70 beats per minute, mirroring the rate of the human heart at rest. Listening to music at this tempo invites and enhances relaxation.")

Vol. 1, Largo—features works by Pachelbel *(Kanon)*, Albinoni, Caudioso, Delalande, Gluck, Handel, Molter, Mozart, Scarlatti, Vivaldi Lind ▲ * ▮ LI 501

Vol. 2, Adagio—features works by Albinoni, Corelli, Gluck, M. Haydn, Mozart, Salieri, Scarlatti, Telemann, Vivaldi Lind ▲ * ▮ LI 502

Vol. 3, Pastorale—features works by Albinoni, Bach, Corelli, Gluck, Vivaldi, Zipoli Lind ▲ * ▮ LI 503

Vol. 4, Andante—features works by Albinoni, Durante, Giuliani, Handel, Manfredini, Paisiello, Pergolesi, Porpora, Tartini, Vivaldi Lind ▲ * ▮ LI 504

Relaxing Classics—features works by Mozart *(Adagio [from Con in A for Cl, K. 622]; Andante [from Con No. 2 in E♭ for Hn, K.417])*, Bach *(Air [from Suite No. 3 in D, BWV 1068])*, Gluck *(Dance of the Blessed Spirits [from Orfeo ed Euridice])*, Vivaldi *(Largo from Winter [from the Four Seasons])*, Elgar *(Larghetto [from Serenade in e, Op. 20])*, Dvořák *(Largo [from Sym No. 9])*, Tchaikovsky *(Andante Cantabile)*, Vaughan Williams *(Fant on Greensleeves)*, Saint-Saëns *(The Aquarium [from Carnival of the Animals])*, Satie *(Gymnopédies Nos. 1 & 3)*, Beethoven *(Andante molto mosso [from Sym No. 6 in F, Op. 68])*
CFP (Relaxing) ▲ 4665 (12.97)

Revelations—features little known music by Blake, Damase, Bliss, Daniel-Lesur, Ginastera, Goldmark, Headington, Howells, Koechlin, Martucci, Moliero, Ponce, Raff, Paisiello, Rubbra & Wolf-Ferrari ASV ▲ 1001 [DDD] (7.97)

Romance—features performances by Londonfestival Orch [cnd:A. Scholz] *(Brahms:Hungarian Dance 1 [Allegro molto])*, I. Kalcina (gtr) *(Albeniz:Austurias; Tarrega:Réquerdos de la Allehambra)*, London PO [cnd:A. Scholz] *(Schubert:Sym 5 [Andante con moto])*, Ljubljana RSO [cnd:A. Nanut] *(Bizet:L'Arlésianne Suite 2)*, London SO [cnd:A. Scholz] *(Mendelssohn:Sym 4 [Allegro Vivace])*, J. P. Santos (pno) *(Satie:Gymnopiéde 1)*, New PO [cnd:M. Pohronec] *(Bruch:Con 1 Vn [w. J. Spitkova (vn)])*, North German PO [cnd:H. Zanitelli] *(Handel:Christmas Con)*, ORTF SO [cnd:M. Horvath (cnd)] *(Dvořák:Slavonic Dance, Op. 46/2)* UNIN ▲ 8010 (5.97) 8010 (3.98)

The Romantic Approach, Vol. 2: A Special Collection of Classical Music from Italy & France—features performances by Czecho-Slovak RSO (Bratislava) *(Mascagni:Intermezzo [from Cavalleria Rusticana; w. Alexander Rahbari (cnd)]; Debussy:Clair de lune; Fauré:Berceuse [w. Keith Clark (cnd)]; Satie:Gymnopedie No. 1 [w. Ondrej Lenárd (cnd)])*, Transylvanica Camerata [cnd:György Selmeczi] *(Francaix:Prelude No. 5 for Strs; Vivaldi:Largo for Man & Strs [from Con in c, R.425; w. Gèza Imre (man)]; Respighi:Nocturne [from La boutique fantasque]; Massenet:Méditation for Vn & Orch [from Thaïs; w. János Selmeczi (vn)])*, Rossini Ensemble (Budapest) [cnd:Andras Kiss] *(Rossini:Son No. 1 for Strs [2nd movt])*, Failoni Orch [cnd:Gèza Oberfrank] *(Puccini:Crisantemi; Verdi:Qt for Strs [2nd movt])*, Czecho-Slovak State PO (Košice) [cnd:Johannes Wildner] *(Martucci:Notturno, Op. 70/1)*, Kodály String Quartet *(Debussy:Qt for Strs [3rd movt]; Ravel:Qt for Strs [3rd movt])* CEHA ▲ 13101 (15.97)

Romantic Classics, Vol. 1—features performances by Svetlana Stanceva (pno), Mozart Festival Orch [cnd:Alberto Lizzio] *(Mozart:Con 20 Pno [Romance]; Con 21 Pno [Andante])*, José Maria Pérez (ten), Nuremberg SO [cnd:Hanspeter Gmür] *(Leoncavallo:Vesti la giubba [I Pagliacci], Verdi:Celeste Aida [Aida])*, London PO [cnd:Lawrence Siegel] *(Tchaikovsky:Romeo & Juliet)*, Slovak PO [cnd:Alberto Lizzio] *(Grieg:Peer Gynt Suite 1 [Morning Mood])*, London Festival Orch [cnd:Henry Adolph] *(Nutcracker Suite [Arabian Dance])*, South German PO [cnd:Alberto Lizzio] *(Saint-Saëns:Le Cygne)*, Camerata Slavonica [cnd:Alfred Scholz] *(Mozart:Kleine Nachtmusik [Andante])*, Dobravka Tomšič (pno) *(Beethoven:Son 14 Pno [Adagio sostenuto])*, Dieter Goldmann (pno), Munich SO [cnd:Henry Adolph] *(Rachmaninoff:Con 2 Pno [Adagio sostenuto])* ECL ▲ 500 (2.97)

Romantic Dinner for Two—features performances by San Marco Musici [cnd:Alberto Lizzio] *(Vivaldi:Cons Vn, Op. 8/1-4 [Autumn])*, North German PO [cnd:Robert Hala] *(Handel:Water Music Suite 1)*, Stuttgart CO [cnd:Bernhard Güller] *(Pachelbel:Canon in D)*, Royal PO [cnd:Frank Shipway] *(Offenbach:Contes d'Hoffman [Barcarolle])*, London SO [cnd:Alfred Scholz] *(Gounod:Faust [Moderato con moto])*, Dieter Goldmann (pno) *(Debussy:Clair de Lune)*, Camerata Romana [cnd:Eugen Duvier] *(Vivaldi:Con Mand, RV.425 [Allegro])*, Vienna Volksoper Orch [cnd:Alfred Scholz] *(Joh. Strauss (II):Emperor Waltz, Op. 437)*, Svetlana Stanceva (pno), Mozart Festival Orch [cnd:Alberto Lizzio] *(Mozart:Con 21 Pno [Andante])*, Hugo Steurer (pno) *(Beethoven:Bagatelle, WoO 59)* ECL ▲ 513 (2.97)

Romeo & Juliet: Music for the World's Greatest Lovers—features works by Tchaikovsky, Delius, Prokofiev, Ravel, Fauré, Sibelius, Gershwin & Wagner ASVQ ▲ 6126 (10.97)

Russian Orchestral Favorites—features works by Glinka, Mussorgsky, Tchaikovsky, et al. LALI ▲ 15636 (3.97)

Sabre Dance—features works by Khatchaturian, Ponchielli, Rossini, et al. LALI ▲ 15504 (3.97)

Sampler Three—features performances by La Follia Salzburg *(Schmelzer:Fechtschule; Biber:Mensa sonora, Part II)*, G. Hecher (piano) *(Liszt:Invocation)*, A. Greenbaum (flute), A. Leiser (piano) *(Ives:On the Counter; Schickele:Spring Serenade Finale 5)*, F. Zebinger (harpsichord) *(Fux:Parthia in A, K. 405 [Menuet & Rondo]; Ciaconna in D, K.403)*, M. Rose (piano) *(Mozart:Son. No. 14 in c, K.457 [Molto allegro])*, New York Consort of Viols *(Byrd:Fants. a 4 in G & D; Ye Sacred Muses)*, Bruce Brubaker (piano) *(Brahms:Fants, Op. 116 [sels.])* VITL ▲ VS 003

Schroeder's Greatest Hits—features The Peanuts Theme; Chopin's Minute Waltz; Beethoven's Für Elise; etc.
RCAV ▲ 61240 (10.97) ▮ 61240 (5.98)

Schubertiade: Rétrospective, w. Sine Nomine String Quartet, Lausaunne Trio, C. Homberger (ten), S. Kanoff (pno), C. Favre (pno), Choeur des XVI de Fribourg, et al.—features works by Beethoven *(Trio No. 3 for Pno, Vn & Vc, Op. 1/3 [Allegro con brio movt])*, Antoine de Bertrand *(Beauté dont la douceur pourrait vaincre les Rois for chorus a cappella)*, Brahms *(3 Choral Songs; 2 Pno Pieces; Qnt. for Cl & Strs [Allegro movt])*, J.L.P. Gluck *(Chant d'été)*, Mendelssohn *(Son. in D for Vc & Pno, Op. 58 [2 movts])*, Schubert *(In der Ferne; Abschied [both from Schwanengesang]; Das Dörfchen for Chorus)*
GALL ▲ CD 631 [AAD]

Scotland's Music, w. various artists—features sels surveying the history of Scottish music from the 9th century to the present LINN 2-▲ 8 (24.97)

Seasons of Love, w. Academy of Saint Martin in the Fields, London Consort, London PO, London SO, Philharmonia Orch, et al.—features works by Albinoni, Barber, Beethoven, et al. COC 2-▲ 1609 (16.97)

Sensual Classics—features works by Rachmaninoff *(Piano Concerto No. 2:Adagio [excerpt]; Symphony No. 2:Adagio [excerpt])*, Bizet *(Carmen Act 3:Entracte)*, Vivaldi *(Mandolin concerto in d:Adagio)*, Borodin *(String Quartet:Notturno [excerpt])*, Beethoven *(Sonata No. 14:Adagio Sostenuto)*, Albinoni *(Oboe Concerto No. 2:Adagio)*, Khachaturian *(Spartacus:Adagio [excerpt])*, Ravel *(Lever du jour; Bolero [excerpt])*, Mahler *(Symphony No. 5:Adagio [excerpt])*, Saint-Saëns *(The Swan)*, Chopin *(Prelude No. 4 in e)*, Stravinsky *(The Firebird:Berceuse)* Schumann *(Kinderscenen:Traumen)*, J.S. Bach *(Suite in d:Air)* 45098 ▲ 90055 ▮ 90055-4

Sensual Classics II, w. A. Sultanov (pno), C. Katsaris (pno), Brodsky String Quartet, London SO [cnd:M. Shostakovich], New York PO [cnd:Z. Mehta], BBC SO [cnd:A. Davis], Leipzig Gewandhaus Orch [cnd:K. Masur], 12 Cellos of the Berlin PO [cnd:A. Jordan, E. Inbal], et al.—features works by Brahms, Prokofiev, Tchaikovsky, Bernstein, Satie, Chopin, Rachmaninoff, Elgar, Debussy & others TELC ▲ 92014 (16.97) ▮

Sensual Classics, Too—features performances by Aleksei Sultanov (pno), London SO [cnd:M. Shostakovich] *(Tchaikovsky:Con. No. 1 for Pno [Andantino])*, Cleveland Orch. [cnd:C.von Dohnányi] *(Brahms:Sym. No. 3 [Allegretto])*, St. Paul CO [cnd:H.Wolff] *(Shostakovich:Con. No. 2 for Pno [Andante; w. Elisabeth Leonskaja (pno)]; Bizet:Sym. in C [Adagio]; Ravel:Pavane pour une infante defunte)*, Rudolf Buchbinder (pno) *(Beethoven:Son. No. 8 for Pno, "Pathétique" [Adagio cantabile]; Schubert:Impromptu, Op. 90/3 [Andante])*, German Chamber PO [cnd:T. Zehetmair] *(Beethoven:Romance, Op. 50)*, Elisabeth Leonskaja (pno) *(Chopin:Nocturne No. 1)*, New York PO [cnd:K. Masur] *(Dvořák:Slavonic Dance, Op. 72/2)*, Dieter Klöcker (cl), MOS [cnd:L. Hager] *(Mozart:Con. for Cl, K.622 [Adagio])* TELC ▲ 98724-2 ▮

Sensual Moments: Classics for Lovers—features performances by Georgian Festival Orch *(Tchaikovsky:Love Theme [from Romeo & Juliet; w. Vato Kahi (cnd)]; Rachmaninoff:Adagio [from Sym No. 2]; Ravel:Bolero [both w. Jahni Mardjani (cnd)])*, Nelly Lee (sop), Novosibirsk PO [cnd:Arnold Kaz] *(Rachmaninoff:Vocalise, Op. 34/14)*, New Classical Orch [cnd:Alexander Titov] *(Dvořák:Larghetto [from Serenade for Strs, Op. 22]; Prokofiev:Larghetto [from Sym No. 1, Op. 25])*, Vladimir Shakin (pno) *(Chopin:Barcarolle in F#, Op. 60)*, Marcos Tsessos (gtr), St Petersburg Philharmonic CO [cnd:Vladimir Altschuler] *(Castelnuovo-Tedesco:Andante alla romanza [from Con No. 1 for Gtr, Op. 99])*, Nodar Gabunia (pno) *(Beethoven:Adagio sostenuto [from Son No. 14 for Pno, Op. 27/2])* 7464 ▲ 61976 [DDD]

The Sensuous Baroque—features Concerti grossi and Concerto movements by Bach, F. Couperin, Geminiani, Handel, Locatelli, Lully, A. Marcello, Rameau, Telemann, Torelli, Vivaldi VCC (Cameo Classics) ▲ 8703 [ADD] ▮ 8703

Serenade—features works for string orchestra by Mozart, Elgar, Tchaikovsky VCC (Cameo Classics) ▲ 8711 (3.97) ▮ 8711

Serenade—features works by Brahms, Haydn, Schubert, et al. LALI ▲ 15505 (3.97)

78 Classics-Vol. 2—features (Royal) Concertgebouw Orch [cnd:W. Mengelberg] *(Strauss (II):Perpetuum mobile, Op. 257)*, Berlin PO [cnd:S. Ochs], Berlin Philharmonic Choir [cnd:S. Ochs], U. v. Diemen (sgr) *(W. A. Mozart:Vesperae solennes de confessore, K.339 [05. Laudate Dominum])*, Berlin State Opera Orch [cnd:E. Orthmann], A. Kipnis (ten) *(W. A. Mozart:Entführung aus dem Serail (sels) [Wer ein Liebchen hat gefunden])*, BBC SO [cnd:A. Boult] *(E. Elgar:Imperial March, Op. 32)*, Hallé Orch [cnd:H. Harty], Manchester Children's Choir [cnd:H. Harty] *(H. Purcell:Libertine (sels) [Nymphs & shepherds, come away])*, London PO [cnd:T. Beecham] *(Chabrier:España)*, London SO [cnd:G. Toye] *(Delius:Walk to the Paradise Garden)*, London SO [cnd:H. Wood], I. Scharrer (pno) *(Litolff:Con Symphonique 4 Pno & Orch, Op. 102 [Scherzo])*, London SO [cnd:J. Barbirolli], L. Melchior (ten) *(R. Wagner:Meistersinger (sels) [Morgenlich leuchtend (Prize Song)])*, London SO [cnd:A. Coates], H. Dawson (org) *(G. F. Handel:Cons Org [No. 13 in F, HWV 295 ("The Cuckoo & the Nightingale")])*, E. Schumann (sop) *(Smetana:Kiss (sels) [Cradle Song])*, BBC Wireless Military Band [cnd:B. O'Donnell] *(G. Rossini:Tancredi (ov))*, E. Caruso (ten) *(A. Sullivan:The Lost Chord)*, A. Segovia (gtr) *(Moreno Torroba:Sonatina Gtr)*, C. Draper (cl) *(J. Mohr:Air Varié)*, I. Friedman (pno) *(A. Rubinstein:Soirées à Saint-Pétersbourg [Romance in E♭])*
BEUL ▲ 24 (m) (16.97)

75 Years of the Donaueschinger Music Festival, 1921-96—features works by Webern, Berg, Messiaen, Hindemith, Penderecki, Zender, Halffter, Krenek, Hartmann, Lachenmann, Ferneyhough, plus others COLG 12-▲ 31899 (181.97)

Soft Lights, Sweet Music: 33 Classical Favorites for After-Dinner Relaxation—features works by Bach, Vivaldi, Mozart, Gluck, Schumann, Elgar, Grainger, Ravel, Mendelssohn, Debussy, Gaubert, others ASV 2-▲ 258 [DDD/ADD]

Sound & Vision—features various artists performing orchestral & instrumental works by *(Bach, Beethoven, Dvořák, Elgar, Handel, Mozart, Mussorgsky, Pachelbel, Ravel, Saint-Saëns, Satie, Vivaldi)* INMP ▲ 7 [DDD] (8.97)

The Sound of Everest—features performances by London SO [cnd:E. Jorda] *(de Falla:El sombrero de tres picos [Intro., Afternoon])*, London SO [cnd:W. Susskind] *(Gould:Proclamation; Little Bit of Sin)*, London PO [cnd:A. Boult] *(Vaughan Williams:The Wasps [Ov.])*, London SO [cnd:E. Goossens] *(Ginastera:Panambi [ballet suite], Op. 1a; Berloiz:Symphonie Fantastique)*, London SO [cnd:A. Fistoulari] *(Khachaturian:Gayane)*, New York Stadium SO [cnd:L. Stokowski] *(Prokofiev:Cinderella)*, London SO [cnd:M. Sargent] *(Mussorgsky:Pictures at an Exhibition)* EVC ▲ 9050 [AAD] (9.97)

Special 20th Anniversary Celebration Disc—features performances by Eric Westberg Vocal Ensemble *(Jansson: To the Mothers of Brazil)*, Omnibus Wind Ensemble *(Zappa:Inca Roads)*, Stockholm Sinf *(Beethoven:Sym 1 [Finale])*, Stefan Lindgren *(Chopin:Son 3 Pno [Scherzo])*, Stockholm Arts Trio *(Schubert:Trio 1 Pno [Allegro & Scherzo])*, Sören Hermansson *(Lindberg:Gammal Fäbodspsalm)*, Kjell Fagéus *(Arnold:Fant Cl)*, Bob Bernard *(Oliver/Williams:West End Blues)*, Lars Erstrand *(Hawkins:Stuffy)*, Sweedish Jazz Kings *(Austin/Bergere:How Come You Do Me)*, Kjell Öhman *(Summerwind)*, Kenneth Arnström *(Gonsalves:Solitariness)*, Eric Bibb *(trad:Needed Time)*, Manolo Yglesias *(Jansson:Latina-Rumba Flamenco)* OPU ▲ 19692 (13.97)

Spiritus: Great Sacred Music through the Ages—features performances by H. Hennig (cnd), London Baroque, Hannover Boys' Choir, Hilliard Ensemble *(Schütz:Meine Seele erhebet den Herren [from Magnificat, SVW 494])*, E. Jochum (cnd), Bavarian RSO, Bavarian Radio Sym Chorus *(Bach:Crucifixus-Et resurrexit [w. H. Donath (sop), B. Fassbaender (mez), C. Ahnsjö (ten), R. Hermann (bar), R. Holl (bass); from Mass in b]; Mozart:Laudate Dominum [w. E. Moser (sop), J. Hamari (mez), N. Gedda (ten), D. Fischer-Dieskau (bar); from Vesperae solennes])*, R. Muti (cnd), Berlin PO, Stockholm Chamber Choir, Swedish Radio Chorus *(Mozart:Ave verum corpus, K.618)*, M. Marshall (sop), C. Schönknecht (sop), C. Watkinson (cta), K. Lewis (ten), R. Holl (bass), H. Scholze (org), N. Marriner (cnd), Dresden Staatskapelle, Leipzig Radio Choir *(Haydn:Kyrie [from Nelsonmesse, H.XXII:11])*, E. Ameling (sop), J. Baker (mez), T. Altmeyer (ten), M. Rintzler (bass), C. M. Giulini (cnd), New Philharmonia Orch, New Philharmonia Chorus *(Beethoven:Agnus Dei [from Mass, Op. 86])*, L. Popp (sop), B. Fassbaender (mez), A. Dallapozza (ten), D. Fischer-Dieskau (bar), W. Sawallisch (cnd), Bavarian RSO, Bavarian Radio Sym Chorus *(Schubert:Credo [from Mass 3])*, E. Speiser (sop), H. Watts (cta), K. Equiluz (ten), S. Nimsgern (bass), G. Wilhelm (cnd), Werner Keltsch Instrumental Ensemble, Stuttgart Hymnus Boys' Choir *(Weber:Sanctus [from Missa sancta 2])*, H. Bramma (org), C. Robinson (cnd), Worcester Cathedral Choir *(Elgar:Ave Maria, Op. 2/2)*, D. Willcocks (cnd), King's College Choir Cambridge *(Vaughan Williams:Gloria [from Mass in g]; Britten:Missa brevis, Op. 63)*, J. Baker (mez), S. Roberts (bar), T. Hugh (vc), J. Butt (org), P. Ledger (cnd), King's College Choir Cambridge *(Duruflé:Sanctus [from Requiem, Op. 9])*, B. Hendricks (sop), G. Prêtre (cnd), French National Orch, French Radio Chorus *(Poulenc:Laudamus te [from Gloria])*, S. Cleobury (cnd), King's College Choir Cambridge *(Tavener:Magnificat)* EMIC ▲ 69748 [ADD/DDD] (6.97)

The Splendid Rebirth of Italian Music—features performances by Europa Galante *(Vivaldi:4 Seasons; Con. in e for Strings, R.133; Tartini:Son. in G♭; Pergolesi:Salve Regina in a:Castello:Son. No. 10; Boccherini:Qnt. in g, Op. 46/4; A. Scarlotti:Maddalena)*, Concerto Italiano *(Monteverdi:Madrigals, Book 4; Frescobaldi:Arie Musicali)*, Alla Francesca *(Landini:Ecco la primavera)*, Europa Galante & Concerto Italiano *(A. Scarlatti:Cain, or the First Murder)*, Fabio Biondi *(Respighi:Aubade)*, Le Parlement de Musiqe *(D. Scarlatti:Lamentations for Holy Week)* OPUS ▲ 30108

Spring Classics, w. Richard Stoltzman (cl), Pinchas Zukerman (vn), Boston Pops Orch [cnd:Arthur Fiedler], Philadelphia Orch [cnd:James Levine], St. Louis SO [cnd:Leonard Slatkin], Boston SO [cnd:Charles Munch], Munich RSO [cnd:Roberto Abbado], Philharmonia Virtuosi [cnd:Richard Kapp], Guildhall String Ensemble, et al.—features works by Ashmore *(4 Seasons [Spring])*, Beethoven *(Son 5 Vn, "Spring" [Rondo])*, Copland *(Appalachian Spring [Simple Gifts])*, Debussy *(Rondes du printemps [from Images])*, Grieg *(The Last Spring)*, Mendelssohn *(Spring Song)*, Schumann *(Sym 1 [Andante un poco maestoso; Allegro molto vivace])*, Stravinsky *(Soring Rounds; Ritual of the Rival Tribes; Procession of the Sage [all from Le sacre du printemps])*, Tchaikovsky *(Seasons [Spring])*, Verdi *(Spring [from I vespri siciliani])*, Vivaldi *(4 Seasons [Spring:Allegro; Largo])* RCAV (Greatest Hits) ▲ 63152 (10.97) ▮ 63152 (5.98)

The Stereo Morning Collection: Peter Togni's Favourite CBC Records—features performances by CBC Vancouver Orch [cnd:Arthur Polson] *(Togni:Shimmeree I - III (theme from Stereo Morning) [w Jane Coop (pno)])*, Calgary PO [cnd:Mario Bernardi] *(Prokofiev:Con 1 Pno Orch (1st movt) [w Jane Coop (pno)]; Schumann:Sym 3 (5th movt))*, Sym Nova Scotia [cnd:Georg Tinter] *(Delius:Dance from Koanga)*, Kitchener-Waterloo Sym [cnd:Raffi Armenian] *(Mahler:Ging heut' morgen übers Feld [w Catherine Robbin (mez)]; Poulenc:Con Pnos Orch (2nd movt) [w James Anagnoson (pno), Leslie Kinton (pno)])*, Vancouver Chamber Choir [cnd:Jon Washburn] *(Raminsh:Ave, verum corpus)*, Moshe Hammer (vn), William Beauvais (gtr) *(Wingfield:Bulgarian Dance 3)*, CBC Vancouver Orch [cnd:Mario Bernardi] *(Mozart:Con 9 Pno [w Angela Cheng (pno)]; Respighi:Aria - Campanae parisienes; Coulthard:Mademoiselle Québécoise)*, New World Consort *(anon:Ballade-Ring out Your Bells [w Suzie LeBlanc (sop)])*, New Music Consorts [cnd:Robert Aitken] *(McPhee:Pemoengkah)*, Tafelmusik Baroque Orch [cnd:Jeanne Lamon] *(Avison:Con Grosso 12 (2nd movt))*, Toronto SO [cnd:Andrew Davis] *(Strauss:Di rigori armato il seno (from Der Rosenkavalier) [w Ben Heppner (ten)])*, Robert Silverman (pno) *(Brahms:Intermezzo Op. 118)* SMS ▲ 96 (12.97)

Stradivari Sampler

Discover the Classics, Vol. 1—features works by Bach, Beethoven, Berlioz, Chopin, Handel, Liszt, Mozart, Joh. Strauss, Tchaikovsky STRD ▲ 6031 [DDD] ▮ 6031

Discover the Classics, Vol. 2—features works by Bach, Brahms, Chopin, Mahler, Mozart, Rachmaninoff, Rimsky-Korsakov, Joh. Strauss, Tchaikovsky STRD ▲ 6032 [DDD] ▮ 6032

Stress Busters (Music for a Stress-Less World), Vol. 1
RCAV ▲ 60710 [ADD] (10.97) ▮ 60710 (5.98)

Stress Busters, Vol. 2: More Stress Busters
RCAV ▲ 60711 [ADD] (10.97) ▮ 60711 (5.98)

Summerdays: From the Musical Masterworks Festival at Old Lyme Sheir Greenwald (sop), Beverly Hoch (sop), John Koch (ten), Aloysia Friedman (vn), Michele Sidener (va), Norman Krieger (cnd), Norman Krieger (pno)—features works by Mozart *(Das Veilchen, K.476l Abendempfindung, K.523; Schon lachy der holde Frühling, K.580; An Chloë, K.524; Warnung, K.433)*, Berg *(Schiflied; Die Nachtigall [both from 7 Early Songs])*, Lehár *(Meine Lippen Sie Küssen So Heiss)*, Barber *(The Secrets of the Old, Op. 13/2; With Rue My Heart Is Laden, Op. 2/2; Bessie Bobtail, Op. 2/3; Sure on This Shining Night, Op.13/3; The Daisies, Op. 2/1)*, Glazunov *(Elegie Va, Op. 17)*, Bernstein *(Maria [from West Side Story])*, Gershwin *(Stairway to Paradise)* WETE ▲ 5173 [DDD] (16.97)

The Sunday Brunch Album—features English CO, Philadelphia Orch., John Williams, Pablo Casals, Pinchas Zukerman, et al. performing *(baroque music by Albinoni, Bach, Corelli, Handel, Pachelbel, Purcell, Vivaldi)*
COL (Dinner Classics) ▲ 45547 (9.97) ▮ 45547 (5.98)

Sunday Brunch, Vol. 2—features various artists performing *(baroque orchestral music by Bach, Handel, Mouret Purcell, Vivaldi)* COL (Dinner Classics) ▲ 46359 [AAD] (9.97) 46359

The Symphonic Sound Stage

Vol. 1 *[Delos Records orchestral music sampler ("a listener's guide to the art & science of recording the orchestra")]*—features works by Falla, Haydn, Lutoslawski, Prokofiev, Respighi, R. Strauss, Stravinsky DLS ▲ 3502 [DDD]

Vol. 2 (Second Stage)—features works by Bartók, Hanson, Haydn, Kodály, Piston, Rachmaninoff, Rimsky-Korsakov, Shostakovich, R. Strauss, Stravinsky, et al. DLS ▲ 3504 [DDD]

The Telarc Collection, Vols. 1 & 2 *(selections from the Telarc classical, pops & jazz catalog; available singly, each disc contains over 60 minutes of music and carries a suggested retail price of $5.99)* TEL ▲ 89101 [DDD] (5.97)

This Is My Country—features works by Grofé *(Grand Canyon Suite)*, Howe/Steffe *(Battle Hymn of the Republic)*, Ives *(Vars on America)*, Smith/Key *(Star Spangled Banner)*, Berlin *(God Bless America)*, plus other sels
RCAV (Greatest Hits) ▲ 61545 (10.97) ▮ 61545 (5.98)

A Time of Healing: Music from the Oklahoma City Memorial Service—features performances by Oklahoma City PO [cnd:Joel Levine] *(Beethoven:Sym No. 7 [Movt II]; Bach:Air; Sheep May Safely Graze [w. Susan Powell (sgr)]; Ravel:Pavane for a Dead Princess; Joncas:On Eagle's Wings [orchd Jerry Neil Smith; w. Susan Powell (sgr)]; trad:Amazing Grace [arr O'Connor; w. Mark O'Connor (vn)]; Rachmaninoff:Sym No. 2 [Movt III]; Berlin:God Bless America [w. Ernestine Dillard (sgr)])*, Children's Choral Society of Oklahoma, CCSO String Quartet [cnd:Judith Burns] *(Bach:Bist du bei mir; trad:Soli deo Gloria)*, Canterbury Choral Society [cnd:Dennis Shrock] *(Manual:Alleluia)*, Kim Boyce (instr unknown) *(Lacy/Siler:Not Too Far From Here) (rec Oklahoma City, June 2, 1995)* Warner Bros. ▲ 9 46062-2

Titanic: Melodies from the White Star Music Book, w. Alfredo Campoli (vn), Albert Sandler (vn), William Primrose (va), Victor Concert Orch, et al.—features selections from Faust; Orpheus in the Underworld; The Mikado; El Capitan; Salut d'amour; God Save the King; plus others *(rec 1926-41)* PEFL (Flapper) ▲ 7822 (17.97)

Top Ten of Classical Music, Vol. 1: Romantic—features works by Massenet, R. Strauss, Tchaikovsky, et al. LALI ▲ 15638 [DDD] (3.97)

Top Ten of Classical Music, Vol. 2: Classical—features works by Beethoven, Haydn, Mozart, et al. LALI ▲ 15639 [DDD] (3.97)

Top Ten of Classical Music, Vol. 3: Baroque—features works by Albinoni, Bach, Pachelbel, et al. LALI ▲ 15640 [DDD] (3.97)

Top Ten Reasons to Listen to Classical Music—features works by Pachelbel *(Canon)*, Vivaldi *(4 Seasons:Spring [Movt. I])*, Bach *(Air on the G String)*, Mozart *(Eine kleine Nachtmusik [Movt. I])*, Beethoven *(Sym. 5 [Movt. I])*, Rossini *(William Tell Ov.:Finale)*, J. Strauss II *(Blue Danube Waltz)*, Debussy *(Clair de lune)*, Ravel *(Bolero)*, Tchaikovsky *(1812 Ov.)* RCAV (60+) ▲ 68136 (10.97) ▮ 68136 (5.98)

Treasures of Russia OPUS ▲ 1009 (7.97)

The Tsar, w. Philadelphia Orch [cnd:Eugene Ormandy], André Kostelanetz (cnd), Jennie Tourel (mez), Claudio Abbado (cnd), Chicago SO, et al.—features works by Rimsky-Korsakov *(Flight of the Bumblebee [from Tale of Tsar Saltan])*, Tchaikovsky *(1812 Ov; Russian Dance [from Nutcracker])*, Glière *(Russian Sailor's Dance)*, Borodin *(Nocturne)*, Mussorgsky *(Great Gate of Kiev)*, trad *(Dark Eyes; 2 Guitars)*, plus others COL (Greatest Hits) ▲ 62683 (9.97) ▮ 62683 (5.98)

Tune Your Brain:Music to Manage Your Mind, Body & Mood—features works by Chopin *(Nocturne in b♭, Op. 9/1 [w. Tamás Vásáry (pno)])*, Mozart *(Con 17 in G for Pno, K.453 [Allegretto; w. Géza Anda (pno/cnd), Salzburg Mozarteum Camerata Academica])*, Bach *(Prelude & Fugue 1 in C [from The Well-Tempered Clavier; w. Trevor Pinnock (hpd)])*, Dalza *(Piva [w. Piffaro])*, Handel *(Music for the Royal Fireworks [La Réjouissance:Allegro; w. Orpheus CO])*, Haydn *(Singt dem Herren, alle Stimmen [from Die Schöpfung; w. Monteverdi Choir, English Baroque Soloists, John Eliot Gardiner (cnd)])*, Korngold *(Con in D for Vn [Moderato nobile; w. Gil Shaham (vn), London SO, André Previn (cnd)])*, Holst *(Mars [from The Planets; w. Philharmonia Orch, John Eliot Gardiner (cnd)])*, Debussy *(Prélude à l'après-midi d'un faune [w. Cleveland Orch, Pierre Boulez (cnd)])*, Schubert *(Ave Maria [w. Cheryl Studer (sop), London SO, Ion Marin (cnd)])*, Wagner *(The Ride of the Valkyries [from Die Walküre; w. Metropolitan Opera Orch, James Levine (cnd)])*, Bizet *(March of the Toreadors [from Carmen; w. Bastille Opera Orch, Myung-Whun Chung (cnd)])* PPHI ▲ 457356 (11.97) ▮ 457356 (5.98)

TV Classics RCAV ▲ 60935 (10.97) ▮ 60935

20 Gramophone All-time Greats, Vol. 2—features performances by F. Kreisler, Tita Ruffo, L. Tetrazzini, Ignaz Paderewski, E. Caruso, Pablo Casals, Dame Nellie Melba, T. Schipa, L. Tibbett, J. Heifetz & others *(rec 1912-39)* ASLE ▲ 5133 [ADD] (12.97)

20 Gramophone All-Time Greats, Vol. 3—features performances by Jussi Björling (ten), Beniamino Gigli (ten), Giuseppe de Luca (bar), Alexander Kipnis (bass), Pablo Casals (vc), Alfred Cortot (pno), George Gershwin (pno), Percy Grainger (pno), Yehudi Menuhin (vn), Arthur Fiedler (cnd), others *(sels unknown) (rec 1925-44)* ASV ▲ 5155 [ADD] (13.97)

20 Gramophone All-Time Greats, Vol. 4—features Marian Anderson (cta) *(Were You There)*, Enrico Caruso (ten) *(O Sole Mio)*, Kirsten Flagstad (sop) *(Liebestod)*, Beniamino Gigle (ten) *(Che Gelida Manina)*, Lotte Lehmann (sop) *(Czárdás)*, Jascha Heifetz (vn) *(Hora Staccato)*, Edward Elgar (cnd) *(Pomp & Circumstance)*, plus others ASLE ▲ 5209 (12.97)

20 Gramophone All-Time Greats, Vol. 5—features performances by Lotte Lehmann (sop), Rosa Ponselle (sop), Elisabeth Schumann (sop), Maggie Teyte (sop), Maria Olczewska (mez), Conchita Supervia (mez), Clara Butt (cta), Tito Schipa (ten), Richard Tauber (ten), Feodor Chaliapin (bass), Pablo Casals (vc), Vladimir Horowitz (pno), Benno Moiseiwitsch (pno), Ignace Jan Paderewski (pno), John Philip Sousa (cnd), Vienna PO [cnd:Clemens Krauss], plus others *(rec 1923-45)* ASLE ▲ 5215 (12.97)

The Victrola Sampler

Vol. 1—features works by Bach, Beethoven, Berlioz, Chopin, Dukas, Rimsky-Korsakov, Joh. Strauss, Tchaikovsky, Vivaldi RCAV ▲ 7818 [ADD] 7818

Vol. 2—works by Bach, Beethoven, Brahms, Handel, Mussorgsky, Offenbach, Pachelbel, Saint-Saëns, Tchaikovsky, Wagner RCAV ▲ 7876 [ADD] 7876

The Viennese Album—features I. Cohen (vn), F. Galimir (vn), Alexander Schneider Quintet, M. Tree (va), J. Levine (db) *(J. Strauss:Radetzky March, Op. 228; Strauss (II):An der schönen blauen Donau, Op. 314)*, Columbia SO [cnd:M. Katims], I. Stern (vn) *(F. Kreisler:Liebesleid)*, F. Galimir (vn), P. Wolfe (vn), Alexander Schneider Quintet, W. Trampler (va), J. Levine (db) *(J. Strauss:Mein Lebenslauf ist Lieb und Lust, Op. 263; Strauss (II):Wiener Blut (waltz), Op. 354)*, Members of the Cleveland Orch [cnd:G. Szell], R. Casadesus (pno) *(W. A. Mozart:Con 21 Pno, K.467)*, Philadelphia Orch [cnd:E. Ormandy] *(Beethoven:Bagatelle in a, WoO 59; Mendelssohn (-Bartholdy):Preludes & Fugues (3), Op. 37 [No. 2 in G]; F. Schubert:Ständchen, Op. 135; Strauss (II):Kaiser Walzer, Op. 437)*, I. Stern (vn), M. Rostropovich (vc), J. Rampal (fl) *(J. Haydn:Son 1 in C [03. Finale, vivace])*, Tchaikovsky CO [cnd:L. Gosman] *(J. Haydn:Qts (6) Strs, Op. 3 [No. 5 in F]; W. A. Mozart:Petits riens (sels) [Pantomime])*, London Symphonic Band members [cnd:J. Snashall] *(W. A. Mozart:Don Giovanni (sels) [Minuet]; Nozze di Figaro (sels) [Voi, che sapete che cosa è amor]; Zauberflöte (sels) [Der Vogelfänger bin ich ja; Ein Mädchen oder Weibchen])*, Tokyo Akademiker Ensemble [cnd:F. Asazuma], P. Robison (fl) *(F. Kreisler:Schön Rosmarin)* COL ▲ 45545 [ADD/DDD] (9.97) ▮ 45545 [ADD/DDD] (5.98)

Visions of Heaven—features performances by Mark Kruczek (org), Voices of Ascension Orch, Voices of Ascension Choir [cnd:Dennis Keene] *(Palestrina:Jesu Rex admirabilis; Duruflé:Kyrie & Sanctus [from Requiem, Op. 9]; Holst:Ave Maria; Victoria:Ave Maria; Farrant:Lord, for Thy Tender Mercy's Sake; Byrd:Rejoice, rejoice; Justorum animae; Bruckner: Os justi (Gradual) [from The Mouth of the Righetous])*, Eric Plutz (org), St. John's Episcopal Cathedral Choir [cnd:Donald Pearson] *(Invitation to Prayer; Barber:Angus Dei [trans from Adagio, Op. 11]; Hallock:Let My Prayer Come Up as the Incense)*, Westminster Choir [cnd:Joseph Flummerfelt] New Jersey Symphony [cnd:Zdenek Macal] *(Dvořák:Tue nati vulnerati [from Sabat Mater, Op. 58])*, Todd Wilson (org) *(Bach:Jesu, Joy of Man's Desiring [from Cantata 147]; Brahms:Chorale Prelude, Schmücke dich, o liebe Seele, Op. 122/5; Harris:Prelude in E♭; Bach:Air on the G String [arr Barnes from Suite in D])*, Robert Noehren (org) *(Brahms:O wie selig sied ihr doch, ihr Frommen)*, Vinson Cole (ten), Patrick Stephens (pno) *(Bach:Ave Maria [arr Gounod])*, Arleen Auger (sop), Mostly Mozart Orch [cnd:Gerard Schwarz] *(Handel:He Shall Feed His Flock [from Messiah])* DLS ▲ 3227 [DDD] (14.97)

Walking Frog Records Sampler Volume 1—features performances by Washington Winds *(King:Barnum & Bailey's Favorite; Huckeby:Explorations; Angela's Song; Swearingen:Let the Spirit Soar; Legacy; Denza:Funiculi, Funicula; Sheldon:West Highlands Sojurn; Danse Celestiale; Sousa:Fugue on Yankee Doodle; Baker (arr.):Danny Boy; Shaffer:Flight of the Peagasus; Brahms:Hungarian Dance 5)*, Dixie Power Trio *(Fidgety Feet)*, Buffalo Bill's Cowboy Band *(Buffalo Bill's Farewell March & 2-step)*, Senzoku Gakuen Wind Orch *(Reed:Khoomar)*, Dominic Spera Big Band *(Spera:Knight's Court)* Walking Frog ▲ WFR 139 [DDD]

Wergo Collection: Music of Our Century—features works by Ligeti *(Le Grand macabre [Scenes & Interludes]; Etude No. 1 for Pno)*, Hindemith *(Der Dämon [Prelude Act 2; Finale])*, Stockhausen *((Klavierstuck 1),)*, Cage *((Music of Changes [Book 1]; A Room for Pno & for Prepared Pno),)*, Berberian *((MagnifiCathy [A ticket to Rice]),)*, Scelsi *((Canti del Capricorno [No. 1]),)*, Henze *((Qt 5 Strs [4th movt]),)*, Penderecki *((Stabat Mater),)*, M. Monk *((Our Lady of Late [Sigh]),)*, H. Weiss *((Arche [sels]),)*, Ives *(Pno Pieces [Study No. 21])*, Brouwer *(Vars. 4 & 5)*, Hiller *(Mix or Match; Cleaning up the Mess)* WER ▲ 60200 [ADD] (7.97)

Winter Classics—features various artists performing works by Ashmore *(4 Seasons [Winter])*, Debussy *(Snowflakes Are Falling; Footprints in the Snow [from Preludes Book 1])*, Mozart *(Musical Sleigh Ride)*, Tchaikovsky *(Sym 1 [Adagio cantabile]; The Seasons [Dec, Jan, Feb])*, Vaughan Williams *(Sinf Antarctica [Landscape])*, Vivaldi *(Con Vn, Op. 8/4, "Winter")*, Waldteufel *(Skater's Waltz)* ons +0 RCAV ▲ 68984 (10.97) ▮ 68984 (5.98)

Witches' Brew—features performances by J. Toth (vn), Mexican State SO [cnd:E. Bátiz] *(Saint-Saëns:Danse Macabre; Dukas:L'Apprenti sorcier)*, Sydney SO [cnd:J. Serebrier] *(Mussorgsky:A Night on the Bare Moun)*, Mexico City PO [cnd:E. Bátiz] *(Liadov:2 Russian Witches)*, Royal PO [cnd:E. Bátiz] *(Berlioz:Dream of the Witches' Sabbath [from Sym fantastique])*, Orch of St. John's, Smith Square [cnd:J. Lubbock] *(Mendelssohn:A Midsummer Night's Dream [Scherzo])*, G. Fergus-Thompson (pno) *(Debussy:The Dance of Puck [from Preludes, Book 1])*, Royal PO [cnd:Yondani Butt] *(Grieg:March of the Dwarves [from Lyric Suite])*, Melbourne SO [cnd:J. Serebrier] *(Holst:Uranus, the Magician [from The Planets])*, Marisa Robles (hp), C. Hyde-Smith, Marisa Robles Harp Ensemble *(Robles:The Narnia Suite)*, S. Mayer (pno), London SO [cond:Tamás Vásáry] *(Liszt:Totentanz)* ASVQ ▲ 6117 [ADD/DDD] (10.97)

Women Composers & Their Music: An Historical Sampling from the Middle Ages to the Present

Vol. 1—features works by Elisabeth Jacquet de la Guerre, Louise Reichardt, Louise Farrenc, Ellen Taaffe Zwilich, Rebecca Clarke, Lili Boulanger, Ruth Schonthal, Katherine Hoover, Francesca Caccini, Alma Mahler, Fanny Mendelssohn, Settimia Caccini, Barbara Kolb, Barbara Strozzi, Marga Richter LEON * ▮ LPI 1

Women of Note, w. various artists—features works by Beach, L. Boulanger, N. Boulanger, Clarke, Gubaidulina, Larsen, Fanny Mendelssohn, Monk, Musgrave, Ran, C. Schumann, plus other women composers KOCH ▲ 7603 (10.97)

World of Classics: The Great History of Austrian Classical Music, w. various artists—features works by Bruckner, Czerny, Haydn, Milloecker, Mozart, et al. CREG 5-▲ 1165 (22.97)

World of Classics: The Great History of Belgian & Dutch Classical Music, w. various artists—features works by Gombert, Lassus, Sweelinck, Franck, Vieuxtemps, et al. CREG 5-▲ 1170

World of Classics: The Great History of English Classical Music, w. various artists—features works by Gibbons, Byrd, Purcell, Elgar, Holst, et al. CREG 5-▲ 1171 (22.97)

World of Classics: The Great History of French Classical Music, w. various artists—features works by Bizet, Couperin, Rameau, Berlioz, Fauré, Debussy, et al. CREG 5-▲ 1166 (22.97)

World of Classics: The Great History of German Classical Music, w. various artists—features works by Bach, Beethoven, Brahms, Handel, Schumann, Wagner, et al. CREG 5-▲ 1164 (22.97)

World of Classics: The Great History of Russian Classical Music, w. various artists—features works by Glinka, Tchaikovsky, Borodin, Mussorgsky, Rimsky-Korsakov, Scriabin, et al. CREG 5-▲ 1168 (22.97)

World of Classics: The Great History of Scandinavian Classical Music, w. various artists—features works by Sibelius, Grieg, Dueben, Svendsen, Sinding CREG 5-▲ 1169 (22.97)

World of Classics: The Great History of Spanish Classical Music, w. various artists—features works by Victoria, Guerrero, Cabezón, Sor, Sarasate, Turina, et al. CREG 5-▲ 1167 (22.97)

The World's Best Known Classics—features performances by [Vol. 1] Royal PO [cnd:F. Shipway] *(Clarke:Trumpet Voluntary)*, D. Tomšič (piano) *(D. Scarlatti:Son. in d, L.413)*, W. Basch (trumpet), W. Rubsam (organ) *(Telemann:La Vaillance; La Grace)*, I Solisti Zagreb *(Albinoni:Con. in B♭)*, H.-C. Becker-Foss (organ) *(Toccata & Fugue in d, BWV 565)*, A. Miyazashi (flute), T. Ozawa (harp), Belgian Festival Orch. [cnd:P. Narrato] *(Mozart:Con. in C, K.299 [Allegro])*, Berlin SO [cnd:C.-A. Bünte] *(Schubert:German Dance No. 1 in D)*, B. Hoffmann (glass harmonica) *(Haydn:Musical Clock [Allegro])*, London SO [cnd:A. Scholz] *(Beethoven:Sym. No. 2 [Scherzo])*, H. Gàl (piano) *(Schubert:Moment Musical in f)*, Mozart Festival Orch. [cnd:W. Patzek] *(Mozart:Sym. No. 38, "Prague" [Adagio-Allegro])*; [Vol. 2] Ljubljana RSO [cnd:A. Nanut] *(de Falla:Fire Dance [from* El amor bujo*]; Addinsell:Warshaw Con.)*, W. Basch (trumpet), W. Rubsam (organ) *(Bach:Aria of the Postillon, BWV 992)*, Stuttgart PO Soloists *(Beethoven:Septet, Op. 20 [Menuet])*, Paris RSO [cnd:L. Bertrand] *(Bizet:Song of the Toreador [from* Carmen*])*, London PO [cnd:L. Siegel] *(Borodin:Polovtzian Dance [from* Prince Igor*])*, H. Gàl *(Brahms:Waltz in A♭, Op. 39)*, H. Spitkova (violin), Philharmonia Slavonica [cnd:A. Lizzio] *(Bruch:Con. No. 1 for Violin, Op. 26 [Adagio])*, D. Tomšič *(Chopin:Fant.-Impromptu, Op. 66)*, London SO [cnd:A. Scholz] *(Dvořák:Slavonic Dance, Op. 72/2)*, P. Schmallfuss (piano) *(Debussy:Clair de lune [from* Suite bergamasque*])*, Slovak National PO [cnd:L. Pešek] *(Grieg:Solveig's Song [from* Peer Gynt*])*, Bratislava CO [cnd:O. von Dohnányi] *(Handel:Hornpipe [from* Water Music*])*, Stuttgart Wind Quintet *(Haydn:Divert. No. 1, "St. Antoni")*, R. Ricci (violin), B. Kontarsky (piano) *(Kreisler:Caprice viennoise)*, London Festival Orch. [cnd:A. Scholz] *(Khatchaturian:The Sabre Dance [from* Gayaneh*])*; [Vol. 3] London Festival Orch. [cnd:K. Schlegel] *(Beethoven:Ov. [from* Creatures of Prometheus, Op. 43*])*, A. Myazashi (flute), T. Ozawa (harp), Belgian Festival Orch. [cnd:P. Narrato] *(Mozart:Con. in C, K.299 [Allegro])*, Quartetto di San Marco *(Haydn:Qt. in D, Op. 64/5, "The Lark" [Allegro moderato])*, Camierata Academica Salzburg [cnd:A. von Pitamic] *(Mozart:Eine kleine Nachtmusik, K.525 [Allegro])*, S. Capova (piano) *(Schubert:Impromptu in A♭, Op. 142/2)*, M. Bergreich (piano), Philharmonic Fest. Orch. [cnd:V. Petroschoff] *(Beethoven:Con. No. 5 for Piano, Op. 73 [Allegro])*, R. Schweizer (organ) *(Haydn:Minuet [from* The Musical Clock*])*, J. Dokupil (horn), Mozart Festival Orch. [cnd:W. Patzek] *(Mozart:Con. No. 2 for Horn, K.417 [Andante])*, London SO [cnd:A. Scholz] *(Beethoven:Sym. No. 2 [Scherzo])*, H. Gàl *(Schubert:Moment Musical in f)*; [Vol. 4] Royal PO [cnd:F. Shipway] *(Massenet:Meditation [from* Thaïs*])*, Philharmonia Orch. London [cnd:A Scholz] *(Adam:Apothéose [from* Giselle*])*, Philharmonia Orch. [cnd:L. Siegel] *(Tchaikovsky:Pas d'action [from* Sleeping Beauty*])*; P. Schmallfuss (piano) *(Debussy:Clair de lune)*, Slovak PO [cnd:L. Pešek] *(Grieg:Suite 1 [from* Peer Gynt*])*, Stuttgart RSO [cnd:G. Navarra] *(Albinoni:Adagio in g)*, J. Bulva (piano) *(Liszt:Love Dream No. 3 in A♭)*, A. Pervomaisky (violin), London Fest. Orch. [cnd:A. Lizzio] *(Vivaldi:Winter [from* 4 Seasons*])*, London Fest. Orch. [cnd:V. Petroschoff] *(Tchaikovsky:Sea in the Moonlight [from* Swan Lake*])*, S. Stanceva (piano), Mozart Fest. Orch. [cnd:A. Lizzio] *(Mozart:Con. No. 21 for Piano [Movt. 2, Andante])*, P. Schaeffer (violin), Belgian Fest. Orch. [cnd:L. Bertrand] *(Bruch:Con. in g for Violin [Adagio])*, Joze Ostranc (clarinet), Mozart Fest. Orch. [cnd:A. Lizzio] *(Mozart:Con. in A for Clarinet [Adagio])* 2272 4-▲ 3173 [DDD]

World's Greatest Love Themes—features works by Barber *(Adagio for Strings)*, Beethoven *("Moonlight" Sonata—1st movement)*, Debussy *(Clair de lune)*, Mascagni *(Cavalleria Rusticana—Intermezzo)*, Ravel *(Daphnis et Chloé Suite)*, Tchaikovsky *(Romeo and Juliet [fantasy overture])*, Wagner *(Tristan und Isolde—Prelude)* PRMX (Maxiplay) ▲ 879 [DDD] (3.97) 879

The Yellow Guide Classical Music, w. Mirella Freni (sop), Gil Shaham (vn), Martha Argerich (pno), Krystian Zimerman (pno), Claudio Abbado (cnd), Pierre Boulez (cnd), John Eliot Gardiner (cnd), Herbert von Karajan (cnd), James Levine (cnd), Trevor Pinnock (cnd), Mikhail Pletnev (cnd)—features works by Dvořák *(Sym 9 [Largo])*, Grieg *(In the Hall of the Mountain King [from Peer Gynt])*, Handel *(Hallelujah Chorus [from Messiah])*, Mussorgsky *(Pictures at an Exhibition [The Great Gate of Kiev])*, Puccini *(Un bel di [from Madama Butterfly])*, Rossini *(Guillaume Tell Ov)*, Saint-Saëns *(Le Cygne)*, J. Strauss II *(An der schönen blauen Donau, Op. 314)*, R. Strauss *(Also sprach Zarathustra)*, Vivaldi *(Cons Vn, Op. 8/1-4 [Winter])*, Wagner *(Ride of the Valkyries [from Die Walküre])* DEUT 3-▲ 457440 (34.97)

You Are There!—features works by Coates *(Halcyon Days)*, Gounod *(Furneral March of a Marionette)*, Tchaikovsky *(Vars. on a Rococo Theme [sels.])*, Stravinsky *(Scherzo a la Russe)*, Soloviev/Sedoy *(Midnight in Moscow)*, Bizet *(Danse bohème)*, de Lisle *(La Marseillaise)*, Khachaturian *(Dance of the Rose Maidens)*, Brahms *(Hungarian Dance No. 7 in A; Con. in D for Vn [sel.])*, Liszt *(Con. No. 2 in A for Pno [Allegro animato])*, Prokofiev *(March)*, Copland *(Appalachian Spring)*, Vardell *(Joe Clark Steps out)*, Sousa *(The Liberty Bell)*, Saint-Saëns *(Sym. No. 3 for Org [sel,])*, J.S. Bach *(Suite No. 6 in D [Gavottes])*, Mendelssohn *(Song without Words, Op. 62/1)*, Anderson *(The Syncopated Clock)*, Respighi *(Ancient Airs & Dances for Lt [Suite No. 2])*, Chabrier *(Joyeuse Marche)*, Hanson *(Sym. No. 2 [Allegro con brio])* PPHI ▲ 42541

Your Favorite Classics—features works by Albinoni *(Adagio)*, Alfvén *(Swedish Rhap.)*, Bach *(Air; Badinerie; Toccata; others)*, Beethoven *(Für Elise; Moonlight Son.)*, Boccherini *(Minuet)*, Dvořák *(Slavonic Dance No. 8)*, Debussy *(Clair de lune; others)*, Elgar *(Con. for Vc)*, Gluck *(Dance of the Blessed Spirits)*, Grieg *(To Spring; Con. for Pno; others)*, Larsson *(Pastoral Suite)*, Mozart *(Elvira Madigan Con.; Eine kleine Nachtmusik)*, Nielsen *(The Fog is Lifting)*, Pachelbel *(Canon)*, Schumann *(Träumerei)*, Sibelius *(Valse Triste; others)*, Stravinsky *(Rite of Spring)*, Vivaldi *(Spring; Con. for Pic; others)* BIS 3-▲ 750 (17.97)

Your Overture Favorites—features works by Brahms, Mendelssohn, Mozart, etc. PWK ▲ 1126 [AAD]

Women Composers & Their Music: An Historical Sampling from the Middle Ages to the Present

Vol. 2—features works by Clara Schumann, Ruth Schonthal, Josephine Lang, Ludmila Ulehla, Pauline Viardot-Garcia, Judith Lang Zaimont, Priaulx Rainier, Rebecca Clarke, Julie Kabat, Sarah Aderholdt, Katherine Hoover, Germaine Tailleferre, Fanny Mendelssohn, Lili Boulanger, Louise Farrenc, Lucie Vellère, Isabella Leonarda, Amy Beach, Hildegard von Bingen LEON * ▮ LPI 2

CONDUCTORS

Abbado, Claudio (cnd)

The Abbado Edition *(a retrospective of Abbado's 25-year recording career with Deutsche Grammophon, this 25-CD midpriced set includes orchestral and operatic recordings Abbado has made for DG with the Berlin PO, Boston SO, Chicago SO, London SO, Vienna PO, La Scala Orch., and CO of Europe)*—features works by Bartók *(Miraculous Mandarin [w. London SO & Ambrosian Singers])*, Beethoven *(Syms 3, 5, 6 & 7; Consecration of the House; Coriolan Ov; Egmont Ov; King Stephen Ov; Leonore Ovs 2 & 3; Calm Sea & Prosperous Voyage [w. Vienna PO])*, Berg *(Altenberg Lieder; Lulu Suite; 3 Orchestral Pieces [w. M. Price, London SO])*, Bizet *(L'Arlésienne Suites [w. London SO]; Carmen sels [w. Berganza, Domingo, London SO])*, Brahms *(Academic Festival Ov; Sym 2 [w. Boston PO]; 12 Hungarian Dances [w. Vienna PO])*, Debussy *(Nocturnes [w. Boston SO]; Prélude à l'après-midi d'un faune [w. London SO])*, Haydn *(Syms 96 & 101 [w. CO of Europe])*, Mahler *(Sym 4 [w. Von Stade, Vienna PO])*, Mendelssohn *(Syms 3, 4 & 5; Hebrides; Midsummer Night's Dream; Fair Melusina [w. London SO])*, Mozart *(Cons 17 & 21 for Pno [w. Serkin, Vienna PO or London SO]; Cons 20 & 27 for Pno [w. Gulda, Vienna PO])*, Mussorgsky *(Pictures at an Exhibition; Prelude to Khovanshchina [w. London SO])*, Prokofiev *(Lt. Kijé Suite [w. unknown SO])*, Ravel *(Alborada del gracioso; Boléro; Ma Mère l'Oye; La Valse [w. London SO])*, Rossini *(Barber of Seville sels [w. Berganza, Alva, Prey, London SO])*, Schubert *(Syms 8 & 9; Rosamunde sels; Fierrabras Ov [w. Co of Europe])*, Scriabin *(Poem of Ecstasy [w. Boston SO])*, Johann & Josef Strauss *(Waltzes & Polkas)*, Stravinsky *(Firebird Suite; Pétrouchka; Sacre du printemps [w. London SO]; Pulcinella sels [w. Berganza, Davies, Shirley-Quirk, London SO])*, Tchaikovsky *(Con Vn [w. Milstein, Vienna PO]; Sym 6 [w. Vienna PO])*, Verdi *(Aida sels [w. Ricciarelli, Domingo, Nucci, Ghiaurov, La Scala Orch & Chorus]; Ovs & Choruses from Aida, Ballo in maschera, Don Carlos, Ernani, Macbeth, Nabucco, Requiem, Simon Boccanegra, Trovatore [w. La Scala Orch & Chorus])* PPHI 25-▲ 37000 (294.62)

Abbado, Claudio (cnd), Karl Böhm (cnd), Wilhelm Furtwängler (cnd), Carlo Maria Giulini (cnd), Herbert von Karajan (cnd), Lorin Maazel (cnd)

Great Conductors at RAI—features works by Boccherini, Beethoven, Ravel, Bach, Tchaikovsky & Wagner DIMA (Diamante) 3-▲ 2054 (36.97)

Albert, Werner Andreas (cnd)

Discover New Worlds, w. Bamberg SO, Hanover Radio PO, North German RSO, Northwest German PO, Queensland SO, Rhineland-Palatinate State PO, Sydney SO, D. Geringas (vc)—features Busoni *(Lustspiel Ov, Op. 38)*, Frankel *(May Day Ov, Op. 22)*, H. Goetz *(Sym in F, Op. 9)*, P. Hindemith *(Grabelung)*, Korngold *(Sym, Op. 40)*, H. Pfitzner *(Con 2 a Vc & Orch)*, Volkmann *(Sym 1)*, S. Wagner *(Die heilige Linde Ov)* CPO ▲ 999310 [ADD] (16.97)

Alessandrini, Rinaldo (cnd)

Viva Alessandrini, w. Concerto Italiano OPUS ▲ 1004 (7.97)

Ansermet, Pierre (cnd)

The Ansermet Edition, Vol. 1—features works by Debussy *(La Mer)*, etc. *(see Composer section)* PLON ▲ 33711

976 ▲ = CD ♦ = Enhanced CD △ = MD ▮ = Cassette Tape ▯ = DCC

Arnold, Malcolm (cnd)
The Composer, The Conductor: A 75th Birthday Tribute—features performances of Arnold's works by BBC SO *(Peterloo Ov, Op. 97; Fair Field (ov), Op. 110)*, Phyllis Sellick (pno), Cyril Smith (pno), BBC SO *(Con for 2 Pnos [3 hands])*, Ambrosian Singers, Ambrosian Soloists, English CO *(Song of Simeon (Nativity Masque), Op. 69)*, Roger Best (va), Northern Sinf *(Con Va, Op. 108)*, London PO *(4 Cornish Dances)*, Alan Loveday (vn), Frances Mason (vn), London PO *(Con for 2 Vns, Op. 77)*, Osian Ellis (hp) *(Fant for Hp, Op. 117)*, English CO *(Sinfonietta 1, Op. 48)*, Alan Civil (hn), English CO *(Con 2 Hn, Op. 58)*, Pamela Bowden (cta), BBC Northern Orch *(5 Blake Songs) (rec BBC Archives)* INMP (BBC Radio Classics) 2-▲ 5691817 (25.97)

Barbirolli, John (cnd)
Viennese Night, w. Hallé Orch—features works by Joh. Strauss II & Lehár, plus others *(rec 1954-57)* DLAB ▲ 1010 (17.97)

Barenboim, Daniel (cnd)
Daniel Barenboim: The Maestro, w. English CO; Paris Orch; London PO—features works by Beethoven *(Son 14 Pno, "Moonlight" [w. Barenboim (pno)])*, Bizet *(L'Arlesienne Suite No. 1)*, Dvořák *(Serenade in E for Strs)*, Fauré *(Pavane for Orch, Op. 50; Requiem [w. Armstrong (sop), Fischer-Dieskau (bar)])*, Haydn *(Con 1 Vc [w. Du Pré (vc)])*, Mozart *(Con 21 Pno [w. Barenboim (pno)]; Sym 41, "Jupiter")*, Schumann *(Con in a for Pno [w. Barenboim (pno)])* RYLC 3-▲ 70312 (20.97)

Beecham, Thomas (cnd)
Beecham Conducts Favourite Overtures, Vol. 2, w. London PO—features works by Mozart, Weber, Brahms, Wagner, Berlioz, Rossini *(rec between 1933 & 1940)* DLAB ▲ 7009 [ADD]
Sir Thomas Beecham *(a selection of early recordings and live performances and a broadcast from Radio Luxembourg)*, w. Beecham SO, London PO—features works by J. Strauss, Rossini, de Missa, Mascagni, Mendelssohn, Weber, Mozart, Massenet, R. Strauss, Tchaikovsky, Stravinsky, Gounod, Lully, Debussy, Dvorak, Beethoven, Brahms, Schubert *(rec 1910, 1912, 1916, 1918, 1936 & 1939)* SYMP 2-▲ SYM 1096/97
Sir Thomas Beecham: American Columbia Recordings, 1942-52—features works by Mendelssohn *(Sym 4)*, Tchaikovsky *(Capriccio Italien [2 versions: w. Columbia SO & w. orch unknown])*, Sibelius *(Pelléas et Mélisande [Mélisande; w. New York PO 1942]; Sym 7)*, Nicolai *(Merry Wives of Windsor [ov; w. Columbia SO 1949])*, Ponchielli *(La Gioconda [Dance of the Hours])*, Bizet *(Carmen Suites [sels])*, Rimsky-Korsakov *(Le Coq d'Or Suite [sels; w. New York PO 1942])*, Rossini *(Semiramide [ov; w. Philadelphia Orch 1952])* COL (Masterworks Heritage) 2-▲ 63366 (25.97)
Vintage Beecham—features works by Handel, Dvořák, Offenbach, Bizet, Delius, Mendelssohn, J. Strauss II, Borodin *(rec between 1933 & 1939)* DLAB ▲ 7003 [ADD] (17.97)

Bernstein, Leonard (cnd)
Bernstein Conducts Bernstein: The Concert Works Sym. No. 2, "The Age of Anxiety" [w. Philippe Entremont]; Sym. No. 3, "Kaddish" [w. Jennie Tourel]; Chichester Psalms [w. Camerata Singers]; Prelude, Fugue & Riffs [w. Benny Goodman, Columbia Jazz Combo]; Serenade after Plato's "Symposium" [w. Zito Francescatti (vn), New York PO] 7 COL 3-▲ 47162
Bernstein Conducts Bernstein: The Theatre Works, Vol. 1, w. New York PO, Columbia Wind Ensemble, various soloists—features Fancy Free; Facsimile; On the Town (complete); Three Dance Episodes from On the Town; Overture to Candide; Symphonic Dances from West Side Story; Trouble in Tahiti COL 3-▲ 47154
Bernstein: Nocturne, w. New York PO—features works by Offenbach *(Barcarolle [from Gaîté Parisienne; orchd Rosenthal])*, Humperdinck *(Children's Prayer [from Hänsel und Gretel, Act II])*, Bizet *(Nocturne (Micaëla's Aria) [from Carmen:Suite 2]; Adagio [from L'Arlésienne:Suite 1])*, Barber *(Adagio for Strs)*, Grieg *(Morning Mood [from Peer Gynt:Suite 1])*, Vaughan Williams *(Fant on "Greensleeves")*, Ravel *(Pavane pour une infante défunte)*, Tchaikovsky *(Andante cantabile)*, Rachmaninoff *(Var 18:Andante cantabile [from Rhap on a Theme of Paganini])*, Mozart *(Andante [from Eine kleine Nachtmusik])*, Sibelius *(Valse triste)*, Vivaldi *(Largo [from "Winter" from Cons, Op. 8/1-4])*, Copland *(Corral Nocturne [from Rodeo])* COL ▲ 62617 (9.97) ▮ 62617 (5.98)
Bernstein Plays & Conducts—features works by Beethoven *(Con. No. 1 for Pno [with Israel PO])*, Gershwin *(Rhap. in Blue [with Columbia SO])*, Mozart *(Con. No. 25 for Pno [with Israel PO]; Qt for Pno & Strs, K.478 [with Juilliard Str Qt])*, Ravel *(Con. for Pno in G [with Columbia SO])*, Schumann *(Qnt for Pno & Strs, Op. 44 [with Juilliard Str Qt])*, Shostakovich *(Con. No. 2 for Pno [with New York PO])* COL 3-▲ 47166
Favorite Overtures, w. New York PO *(see Composer section—Rossini:Overtures, etc.)* COL ▲ 37240 [AAD] (9.97) 37240 (3.98)
The Joy of Bernstein, w. New York PO, Vienna PO, Los Angeles PO, Israel PO—features works by Bernstein, Copland, Gershwin, Beethoven, Haydn, Mahler & Stravinsky DEUT ▲ 45486 (16.97)
Mahler Songs—features Des Knaben Wunderhorn; Rückert Lieder; Lieder und Gesänge (sels); Songs of a Wayfarer [with Christa Ludwig, Walter Berry, Dietrich Fischer-Dieskau, Bernstein (pno)] COL 2-▲ 47170
Nocturne II, w. New York PO—features works by Beethoven *(Con 5 Pno, Op. 73 "Emperor" [Adagio un poco moto; w. Rudolf Serkin (pno)])*, Bizet *(L'Arlésienne Suite No. 1 [Adagietto])*, Borodin *(In the Steppes of Central Asia)*, Gounod *(Faust [Adagio—animato])*, Grieg *(Peer Gynt Suite 2, Op. 55 [Solvejg's Song])*, Rachmaninoff *(Con 2 Pno [Adagio sostenuto; w. Gary Graffman (pno)])*, Rimsky-Korsakov *(Shéhérazade, Op. 35 [Young Prince & Young Princess; w. John Corigliano (vn)])*, Tchaikovsky *(Serenade for Strings, Op. 48 [Élégie])*, Villa-Lobos *(Bachiana Brasileria No. 5 [w. Netania Davrath (sop), Carl Stern (vc)])*, Vivaldi *(Con Ob, RV.454 [Largo; w. Harold Gomberg (ob)])* COL ▲ 63076 (9.97) ▮ 63076 (5.98)
Romantic Favorites for Strings, w. New York PO *(see Composer section—Barber:Adagio, etc.)* COL ▲ 38484 [AAD] (9.97) 38484 (3.98)

Böhm, Karl (cnd)
The Dresden Years, w. Saxon State Orch—features ovs, intermezzos & complete scenes from Oberon; The Bartered Bride; Die Fledermaus; Donna Diana; Hänsel und Gretel; Salome; Der Rosenkavalier; Der Freischütz; Le nozze di Figaro; Lohengrin; Tannhäuser; Die Meistersinger von Nürnberg; Der fliegende Holländer; Kaiserwalzer; Die Entführung aus dem Serail; Aida; Otello; Cavalleria rusticana; Pagliacci *(rec 1938-40)* GRM2 2-▲ 78734 (25.97)

Boult, Adrian (cnd)
Colonel Bogey: The Great Military Marches, w. London PO 60318 ▮ COL
Concert Favorites, w. New SO London *(see Composer Section under Mussorgsky—Night On Bare Mountain, Tchaikovsky—Nutcracker Suite, etc.) (all rec Walthamstow Town Hall, London July 12-15, 1960)* CHSK ▲ 53 [ADD] (15.97)
Sir Adrian Boult Conducts English Music—features performances by A. Boult, BBC Orch. *(Walton:Portsmouth Point; Crown Imperial; Vaughan Williams:Fant. on a Theme by Thomas Tallis; Bliss:Music for Strings; Elgar:Intro. & Allegro, Op. 47; Dream of Gerontius, Op. 38; Imperial March, Op. 32; Sospiri, Op. 70; Enigma Vars., Op. 36)*, A. Boult, Hallé Orch. *(Butterworth:A Shropshire Lad Rhap.) (rec 1936-42)* VAIA 2-▲ 1067 (m) [ADD] (31.97)

Cotte, Roger (cnd)
Ritual Music of the 18th Century Free Masons—features works by Beethoven, F. Giroust, F.-H. Himmel, Mozart, H.-J. Taskin ARN ▲ 68134 [AAD] (16.97)

Delerue, Georges (cnd)
Chansons de théâtre par Marc et André, 1920-1960—features works by Weill *(Le chant des canons [from L'opera de quat'sous])*, Jarre *(Chanson de l'etoile [from Les caprices de marianne]; Chanson de nucléa)*, Kosma *(Rue des blancs-manteaux [from Huis-clos])*, Delerue *(Roses rouges pour moi)*, Auric *(A droite, alignement!... [from Les oiseaux])*, Jaubert *(Chanson de tessa)*, Wiener *(Tu s'ras putain, ma fille [from Les mysteres de paris])*, Parys *(Voulez-vous jouer avec moi?; Marche des polytechniciens [from La Tour eiffel qui tue])*, Bischoff *(Complainte de punch [from La famille arlequin])*, Dutilleux *(Usez mieux, ô beautés fières [from Princesse d'elide])*, Hahn *(Ne soupirez plus [from Beaucoup de bruit pour rien])*, plus others ADES ▲ 132192

Dorati, Antál (cnd)
Wiener Walzer—features performances by Philharmonia Hungarica *(works by Lehár, Kálmán, Josef Strauss, Dohnányi, Waldteufel, Lanner)*, Minnesota Orch. (aka Minneapolis SO) *(works by J. Strauss II, Josef Strauss, E. Strauss) (rec Nov 1956-June 1958)* MRCR ▲ 34338 (11.97)

Fennell, Frederick (cnd)
Frederick Fennell Conducts Cole Porter & George Gershwin: The Studio Recordings—features 24 Porter and Gershwin songs in pop orchestral arrangements MRCR ▲ 34327 [ADD] (11.97)

Fiedler, Arthur (cnd), Erich Leinsdorf (cnd), Fritz Reiner (cnd)
Classics: The Greatest Hits—features works by Pachelbel *(Canon)*, Tchaikovsky *(1812 Overture)*, Vivaldi *(The Four Seasons)* RCAV ▲ 60836 (10.97) ▮ 60836 (5.98)

Fiedler, Arthur (cnd), James Levine (cnd), Erich Leinsdorf (cnd), Fritz Reiner (cnd)
Mozart in Hollywood RCAV ▲ 60933 (10.97) ▮ 60933
Mozart: Greatest Hits—features Eine kleine Nachtmusik; Elvira Madigan Theme; Rondo alla turca; etc. RCAV ▲ 60829 (10.97) ▮ 60829 (5.98)

Fiedler, Arthur (cnd), Eugene Ormandy (cnd)
Wagner: Greatest Hits, w. Robert Shaw Chorale—features Ride of the Valkyries, Bridal Chorus, etc. RCAV ▲ 60847 (10.97) ▮ 60847 (5.98)

Fiedler, Arthur (cnd), Eugene Ormandy (cnd), Aaron Copland (cnd)
Copland: Greatest Hits—features Appalachian Spring, Billy the Kid Suite, Hoedown, The Tender Land, etc. RCAV ▲ 60837 (10.97) ▮ 60837 (5.98)

Fiedler, Arthur (cnd), Eugene Ormandy (cnd), Fritz Reiner (cnd)
Tchaikovsky: Greatest Hits—features Swan Lake, Nutcracker, Overture 1812, Marche slave RCAV ▲ 60845 (10.97) ▮ 60845 (5.98)

Fiedler, Arthur (cnd), Leopold Stokowski (cnd)
Pachelbel Canon & Other Baroque Hits, w. James Galway (fl), et al.—features Four Seasons, Water Music, Fireworks Music, Masterpiece Theater Theme, etc. RCAV ▲ 60840 (10.97) ▮ 60840 (5.98)

Fischer, Edwin (cnd)
The Art of Edwin Fischer, Vol. 1—features works by Bach *(Brandenburg Concerto No. 2)*, Beethoven & Brahms *(see Composer section) (rec 1939-41)* KOCH ▲ 7701 [AAD]

Furtwängler, Wilhelm (cnd)
Chronological Edition of the Recordings from 1926-45, Vol. 2, w. Berlin PO, Vienna PO—features works by Bach, Brahms, Beethoven, Dvořák, Mozart, Rossini, J. Strauss, Wagner & Weber *(rec 1930-37)* ENT (Idis) 2-▲ 277 (25.97)
Chronological Recordings, Vol. 1: 1926-1945, w. Berlin PO—features works by Weber, Beethoven, Mendelssohn, Bach, Schubert, Wagner, R. Strauss & Berlioz *(rec 1926-30)* ENT (Istituto Discografico Italiano) 2-▲ 272 (25.97)
Early Studio Recordings 1929-43, w. Berlin PO, Vienna PO—features works by Beethoven, Brahms, Bruckner, Wagner, Mozart, Tchaikovsky, Bach, Rossini, Gluck, Furtwängler MUA 4-▲ 954 (47.97)

Gould, Morton (cnd)
Brass & Percussion, Symphonic Band—features music by Sousa *(The Star and Stripes Forever; On Parade; Semper Fidelis; Hands Across the Sea; The Thunderer; Washington Post; The Gladiator; El Capitan; The U.S. Field Artillery March; The High School Cadets; Sound Off; The Corcoran Cadets March; Manhattn Beach; National Fencibles March)*, Goldman *(Jubilee; On The Mall;The Chimes of Liberty; Happy Go Lucky)*, Gould *(Parade; Fourth of July; Battle Hymn; American Youth March)*, Bagley *(National Emblem)*, Meacham *(American Patrol)*, Emmett *(Dixie)*, Traditional *(Yankee Doodle) (rec 1956 & 1959)* RCAV (Living Stereo) ▲ 61255 (10.97) ▮ 61255

Hayman, Richard (cnd)
World Famous Marches, w. Richard Hayman SO—features American Salute, Look Sharp, When the Saints Go Marching In, etc. *(rec Apr 1989)* NXIN ▲ 990010 [DDD] (5.97)

Herreweghe, Philippe (cnd)
Portrait *(sels from previous Harmonia Mundi releases)*—features selections from works by J. S. Bach *(St. Matthew Passion; Easter Oratorio)*, Rameau *(Les Indes Galantes)*, Bruckner *(Ave Maria)*, Weill *(Berliner Requiem)*, Beethoven *(Missa solemnis)*, Mendelssohn *(Elijah; Paulus; Midsummer Night's Dream)*, Schoenberg *(Pierrot Lunaire)*, Fauré *(Requiem)*, Berlioz *(Nuit d'Été)*, Mahler *(Das lied von der Erde)*, Schumann *(Sym 2)*, plus others HAM ▲ 2901636 (7.97)

Hickox, Richard (cnd)
The Best of Richard Hickox, w. London SO, London Sym Chorus, Penelope Walmsley-Clark (sop), John Graham-Hall (ten), D. Maxwell (bar), Southend Boys' Choir, London Voices—features works by Orff, Holst, Verdi, Gounod, Borodin INMP 3-▲ 1073 [DDD]
Classic Widows: British Music of the 20th Century—features performances by City of London Sinf. *(Walton:Long Steel Grass; Old Sir Faulk [both w. Susana Walton (nar)]; Gloria [from Christopher Columbus; w. Arthur Davies (ten), Westminster Singers]; Alwyn:Lyra Angelica [movt. 1; w. Rachel Masters (hp)])*, Bournemouth SO *(B. Stevens:Mark of Cain [sels.; arr. A. Williams]; A Sym. of Liberation [movt. 2]; Frankel:Sym. 5 [movt. 1]; Carriage & Pair; Searle:Sym. 2 [movt. 1]; Walton:Touch her soft lips & part [from Henry V])*, London SO *(Alwyn:Odd Man Out [Prelude]; Vaughan Williams:The Lark Ascending [w. Michael Davies (vn), Bryden Thomson (cnd)])*, Northern Sinf. *(Bliss:The Pigeon Son [w. Della Jones (mez)])*, Royal Scottish National Orch. *(Sym. No. 3, Op. 90, "Laudes musicae" [movt. 3; w. Neil Mackie (ten)])* CHN ▲ 7008 [DDD]

Karajan, Herbert von (cnd)
The Adagio Box, w. Berlin PO—features works by Albinoni *(Adagio)*, Bach *(Suite No 3 for Orch [Air])*, Beethoven *(Sym 7 [Allegretto]; Sym 6 [Scene by the Brook])*, Bizet *(Adagietto [from L'Arlésienne]; Entr'acte III [from Carmen])*, Brahms *(Sym 3 [Andante])*, Chopin *(Nocturne [from Les Sylphides])*, Debussy *(Prélude à l'après-midi d'un faune)*, Delibes *(Ballad [from Coppelia])*, Dvořák *(Sym 9 [Largo]; Serenade for Strs [Moderato])*, Gluck *(Dance of the Blessed Spirits [from Orfeo ed Euridice])*, Grieg *(Aase's Death [from Peter Grimes]; Solveig's Song [from Peer Gynt]; Sarabande [from Holberg's Time])*, Handel *(Con grosso, Op. 6/12)*, Haydn *(Sym 87 [Adagio])*, Holst *(Planets [Venus])*, Mahler *(Sym 5 [Adagietto])*, Mascagni *(Intermezzo [from Cavalleria rusticana])*, Massenet *(Meditation [from Thaïs])*, Mozart *(Diverts, K.287 [Adagio] & 334 [Adagio]; Adagio, K.546; Eine kleine Nachtmusik [Romance]; Sym 38 [Andante])*, Offenbach *(Barcarolle [from Contes d'Hoffman])*, Pachelbel *(Canon & Gigue)*, Ravel *(Pavane pour une infante défunte; Rapsodie espagnole [Prelude to the Night; Habanera])*, Respighi *(Ancient Airs & Dances [Suite 3]; Fontane [Valle Guilia Fountain at Daybreak; Villa Medici Fountain at Sunset])*, Sibelius *(Valse Triste; Swan of Tuonela)*, Smetana *(Má Vlast [The Moldau])*, Rimsky-Korsakov *(The Young Prince & the Young Princess [from Scheherazade])*, Tchaikovsky *(Serenade Strs [Elegy]; Love Theme [from Romeo & Juliet])*, Vivaldi *(Sinf in b [Adagio molto]; Con in a for 2 Vns, RV.523; 4 Seasons [Winter:Largo])*, Wagner *(Isolde's Love Death [from Tristan und Isolde])* DEUT 4-▲ 453834 (47.97)
Arias, Overtures & Intermezzi, w. Philharmonia Orch—features works by Offenbach *(Orphée aux enfers [ov]; Les contes d'Hoffmann [Barcarolle])*, Gounod *(Vous qui faites l'endormie [w. Boris Christoff (bass); from Faust])*, Ponchielli *(La Gioconda [Dance of the Hours])*, Leoncavallo *(I Pagliacci [Intermezzo])*, Mascagni *(Cavalleria rusticana [Intermezzo]; L'amico Fritz [Intermezzo])*, Mussorgsky *(Khovanshchina [Entr'acte 4; Dance of the Persian Slaves]; In the Town of Kazan [w. Boris Christoff (bass); from Boris Godunov])*, Puccini *(Manon Lescaut [Intermezzo act 3])*, Verdi *(La traviata [Prelude act 3]; Aida [Ballet Music]; Elle gaimmia m'amo; Dormirò sol [both w. Boris Christoff (bass); both from Don Carlo]) (rec 1950-56)* EMIC (Karajan:The London Years) ▲ 66603 (m) [ADD] (11.97)
The Artist's Album—features works by Mozart *(Die Zauberflöte (ov))*, Beethoven *(Sym 3 [Scherzo])*, Wagner *(Rheingold [closing scene])*, Verdi *(Otello [ballet music])*, Webern *(Passacaglia, Op. 1)*, Mendelssohn *(Con Vn, Op. 64 [Finale])*, R. Strauss *(Rosenkavalier [presentation of the silver rose])*, Bruckner *(Sym 7 [Scherzo])*, Joh. Strauss (II) *(Zigeunerbaron (ov); Perpetuum mobile) (rec 1938-89)* DEUT ▲ 457689 (16.97)
Baroque Music, w. Berlin PO—features works by Albinoni, Bach, Gluck, Mozart, Pachelbel, Vivaldi DEUT ▲ 13309 [DDD] (16.97) 13309
The First Recordings, 1938-44—features works by Beethoven, Brahms, Cherubini, Dvořák, Mozart, Rossini, Smetana, Joh. Strauss II, R. Strauss, Tchaikovsky, Verdi, Wagner & Weber GRM2 6-▲ 78026 (77.97)
Italian Opera Arias, w. Irmgard Seefried (sop), Maria Cebotari (sop), Elisabeth Schwarzkopf (sop), Ljuba Welitsch (sop), Erich Kunz (bar), Vienna PO—features arias from Mozart *(Don Giovanni; Le nozze di Figaro)*, Mascagni *(Cavalleria rusticana)*, Puccini *(Manon Lescaut; La bohème; Gianni Schicchi)* VCL (Karajan:The Vienna Years) ▲ 66393 (11.97)
Karajan Adagio, w. Berlin PO—features works by Albinoni *(Adagio)*, Bach *(Air [from Suite No. 3 for Orch.])*, Beethoven *(Allegretto [from Sym. 7])*, Brahms *(Andante [from Sym. 3])*, Grieg *(Aase's Death [from Peer Gynt])*, Mahler *(Adagietto [from Sym. 5])*, Massenet *(Meditation [from Thaïs])*, Mozart *(Adagio [from Divert. in B♭, K.287])*, Pachelbel *(Canon & Gigue)*, Sibelius *(Valse triste)*, Vivaldi *(Adagio molto [from Sinf. in b])* DEUT ▲ 45282 (16.97) 45282 (10.98)
Karajan Adagio 2, w. Berlin PO—features works by Respighi *(Suite 3 [from Ancient Airs & Dances])*, Grieg *(Solveig's Song [from Peer Gynt])*, Ravel *(Pavane pour une infante défunte)*, Dvořák *(Largo [from Sym No. 9])*, Sibelius *(Swan of Tuonela)*, Bizet *(Adagietto [from L'Arlésienne])*, Tchaikovsky *(Elegy [from Serenade for String Orchestra])*, Vivaldi *(Con in a for 2 Violins, R.523; Largo [from "Winter" from Cons, Op. 8/1-4])*, Handel *(Con grosso, Op. 6/12)*, Gluck *(Dance of the Blessed Spirits [from Orfeo ed Euridice])*, Mozart *(Adagio, K.546) (rec Church of Jesus Christ, Berlin; Victoria Room, St. Moritz; French Church, St. Moritz; Philharmonie, Berlin; Mar 1964, Aug 1966, Aug 1969, Aug & Dec 1970, Aug 1972, Sept 1980, Feb 1982, Sept 1983, Feb 1984 & Feb 1986)* DEUT ▲ 49515 [ADD/DDD] (16.97) 49515 (10.98)
Opera Arias, w. Hilde Konetzni (sop), Maria Cebotari (sop), Elisabeth Schwarzkopf (sop), Ljuba Welitsch (sop), Josef Witt (ten), Erich Kunz (bar), Vienna PO—features arias from Mozart *(Die Zauberflöte; Die Entführung aus dem Serail)*, Joh. Strauss (II) *(Die Zigunerebaron)*, R. Strauss *(Der Rosenkavalier; Salome; Ariadne auf Naxos)*, Smetana *(The Bartered Bride)* VCL (Karajan:The Vienna Years) ▲ 66394 (11.97)
Opera Intermezzi—features sels. from Adriana Lecouvreur, Fedora, Amico Fritz, Thaïs, Manon Lescaut, Suor Angelica, Notre Dame, Traviata, Gioielli della Madonna † Leoncavallo; Mascagni *(see Composer section)* 42300 3-▲ 19257 [ADD]
Orchestral Favorites, Vol. 1, w. Berlin PO, Philharmonia Orch—features works by Mozart *(Eine kleine Nachtmusik; German Dance No. 3)*, Handel *(Water Music Suite [arr H. Harty])*, Smetana *(Die Moldau [from Má Vlast])*, Weber *(Invitation to the Dance [arr Berlioz])*, Berlioz *(Royal Hunt & Storm [from Les Troyens]; March Hongroise [from Faust])*, Waldteufel *(Les Patineurs Waltz, Op. 183)*, Tchaikovsky *(Ov 1812)*, Mendelssohn *(Hebrides Ov, Op. 26)*, Suppe *(Light Calvalry Ov)*, Offenbach *(Carnival Romain Ov; Tales of Hoffmann:Baracolle)*, Respighi *(Pines of Rome)*, Sibelius *(Finlandia; Valse triste)*, Charbrier *(Espana Rhap; Marche joyeuse)*, Granados *(Goyescas:Intermezzo)*, J. Strauss *(Radetzky-March)*, Weinberger *(Polka [from Schwanda the Bagpiper])*, Verdi *(Traviata:Prelude Act III)*, Puccini *(Manon:Intermezzo)*, Bizet *(Carmen Suite 1)* RYLC 3-▲ 70006 (20.97)
Spectacular DEUT ▲ 457496 (16.97)

Kempe, Rudolf (cnd)
Vienna Philharmonic "On Holiday", w. Vienna PO TES ▲ 1127 (17.97)

Kleiber, Erich (cnd)
Erich Kleiber Conducts Waltzes & Overtures 1923-33 ARCH ▲ ARC 102
The Pre-Wartime Recordings, Part 2, w. various orchs—features works by Mozart *(Eine kleine Nachtmusik)*, Liszt *(Les Préludes)*, Mendelssohn *(A Midsummer Night's Dream [sels])*, Smetana *(The Moldau; The Bartered Bride [Ov])*, Bizet *(Carmen [Preludes])*, Reznicek *(Donna Diana [Ov])*, Nicolai *(Die lustigen Weiber von Windsor [Ov]) (rec 1927-36)* GRM2 ▲ 78778 (13.97)

Klemperer, Otto (cnd)
Otto Klemperer, w. Berlin Staatskapelle—features works by Beethoven, Wagner, Brahms, Strauss, Ravel, Debussy, Auber & Offenbach *(rec 1926-31)* GRM2 2-▲ 78682 (25.97)

Klemperer, Otto (cnd) (cont.)
Otto Klemperer: The Maestro, w. Philharmonia Orch, New Philharmonia Orch—features works by Beethoven *(Sym 6, "Pastorale"; Fant in C for Pno, Orch & Chorus [w. Barenboim (pno), John Alldis Choir])*, J. S. Bach *(Brandenburg Con 2)*, Brahms *(Academic Festival Ov; Tragic Ov)*, Haydn *(Sym 101, "The Clock")*, Mendelssohn *(Sym 4, "Italia")*, Mozart *(Sym 36, "Linz")*, Schubert *(Sym 8, "Unfinished")*, Wagner *(Parsifal:Prelude to Act 1)* RYLC 3-▲ 70308 (20.97)

Krauss, Clemens (cnd)
Clemens Krauss Directs, Vol. 2, w. Vienna PO—features works by de Falla, Joh. Strauss, Jos. Strauss & R. Strauss *(rec 1940-41)* PRE ▲ 90291 (16.97)

Kunzel, Erich (cnd)
Erich Kunzel Conducts see Cincinnati Pops and Winnipeg Symphony Orchestras

Maazel, Lorin (cnd)
Lorin Maazel: The Maestro, w. Berlin PO, Philharmonia Orch, New Philharmonia Orch, Paris Orch—features works by Brahms *(Con 2 Pno [w. Sviatoslav Richter (pno)])*, Dvořák *(Slavonic Dances (8))*, Mussorgsky *(Pictures at an Exhibition)*, Ravel *(Alborado del gracioso; Pavane pour une enfante défunte; Boléro)*, R. Strauss *(Till Eulenspiegels lustige Streiche)*, Tchaikovsky *(Con 1 Pno [w. Emil Gilels (pno)]; Con in D for Vn [w. Frank Peter Zimmerman (vn)])* RYLC 3-▲ 70304 (20.97)

Markevitch, Igor (cnd)
Igor Markevitch: Homage to Diaghilev, w. Philharmonia Orch—features works by Markevitch, Debussy, Ravel, Weber, plus others TES ▲ 1105 (17.97)

Mehta, Zubin (cnd), Erich Leinsdorf (cnd), Arthur Fiedler (cnd), et al.
Beethoven: Greatest Hits—features excerpts from Symphonies 3,5 & 9; Moonlight Sonata; Für Elise; etc. RCAV ▲ 60831 (10.97) ▮ 60831 (5.98)

Monteux, Pierre (cnd)
Highlights from the Pierre Monteux Edition, w. San Francisco SO, Chicago SO, Boston SO—features works by Strauss *(Ein Heldenleben)*, Beethoven *(Sym. 8 [movt 2])*, Charbrier *(Le Roi malgre lui:Fête Polonaise)*, Ravel *(Daphnis et Chloé:Suite 1 [Danse guerriere])*, Stravinsky *(Pétrouchka:Tableau II)*, Brahms *(Sym. 2 [movt 4])*, Berlioz *(Symphonie fantastique:March to the Scaffold)*, Franck *(Sym. in d [movt 3])*, Rimsky-Korsakov *(Scheherazade [movt 3])*, Debussy *(Nocturnes:Fête)*, Tchaikovsky *(Sym. 4 [movt 1])*, Delibes *(Sylvia:Procession of Bacchus)* RCAV (Gold Seal) ▲ 61978 (6.97)
The Pierre Monteux Edition, w. San Francisco SO, RCA Victor Orch, Boston SO, Chicago SO—features works by [Disc 1] *(Beethoven & Bach)* [Disc 2] *(Berlioz)* [Disc 3] *(Brahms & Mahler)* [Disc 4] *(Chausson & Chabrier,)* [Disc 5] *(Debussy,)* [Disc 6] *(Franck & d'Indy,)* [Disc 7] *(d'Indy,)* [Disc 8] *(Ravel, Lalo & Ibert,)* [Disc 9] *(Rimsky-Korsakov,)* [Disc 10] *(R. Strauss,)* [Disc 11] *(Stravinsky)* [Discs 12 & 13] *(Tchaikovsky)* [Disc 14] *(Liszt, Scriabin & Debussy)* [Disc 15] Delibes & Gounod RCAV (Gold Seal) 15-▲ 61893 (153.97)
Sunday Evenings with Pierre Monteux: Broadcast Performances from San Francisco, 1941-52, w. various orchs—features works by Beethoven *(Die Weihe des Hauses [Ov]; Sym 5; Die Geschöpfe de Prometheus [Adagio]; Egmont [Ov]; Fidelio [Ov]; Leonore [3rd Ov])*, Mozart *(Don Giovanni [Ov]; Sym 35; Con 12 Pno [w. William Kapell (pno)]; Die Zauberflöte [Ov]; Die Entführung aus dem Serail [Ov])*, Gluck *(Iphigénie en Aulide [Ov])*, Haydn *(Sym 88)*, R. Strauss *(Don Juan; Tod und Verklärung; Till Eulenspiegels lustige Streiche; Der Rosenkavalier [Suite])*, Wagner *(Parsifal [Prelude & Gurnemanz final scene]; Die Meistersinger von Nürnberg [Prelude, Act 1; Prelude, Act 3; Dance of the Apprentices; Procession of the Masters]; Der fliegende Holländer [Ov]; Tristan und Isolde [Prelude & Liebestod]; Die Walküre [Wotan's Farewell & Magic Fire Music]; Siegfried [Forest Murmurs]; Götterdämmerung [Siegfried's Rhine Journey]; Rienzi [Ov])*, Liszt *(Les Préludes; Hungarian Rhap 2)*, Berlioz *(Le Carnaval romain; Les Troyens [Prelude]; L'Enfance du Christ [La Fuite en Egypt Ov; Trio for 2 Fls & Hp]; Le Damnation de Faust [Minuet des Follets; Ballet des Sylphes; Marche Hongroise]; Roméo et Juliette [Combat; Tumult; Romeo Alone; Fête at the Capulets; Love Scene]; Le Corsaire)*, Mendelssohn *(Die Hebriden; Sym 4; Ruy Blas)*, Tchaikovsky *(Romeo & Juliet)*, Brahms *(Waltzes, Op. 39/1, 2, 11, 14, 15; Sym 1; Tragic Ov)*, Rossini *(L'italiana in Algeri [Ov])*, Thomas *(Mignon [Ov])*, Dukas *(L'Apprenti sorcier)*, Messiaen *(L'Ascension [3 Mediations])*, Sibelius *(Valse triste)*, Weber *(Euryanthe [Ov])*, Sousa *(Stars & Stripes Forever)*, Borodin *(Prince Igor [Polovtsian Dances])*, Rimsky-Korsakov *(Christmas Eve [Suite]; Russian Easter Festival; Capriccio espagnol)*, Glazunov *(Scènes de ballet)*, Rachmaninoff *(Sym 2)*, Franck *(Prélude, choral et fugue [orchd Pierné]; Redémption; Psyche [Suite]; Sym in d)* MUA 10-▲ 978 [AAD] (125.97)

Mravinsky, Evgeny (cnd)
Volumes 11-20, w. Leningrad PO—features works by Beethoven *(Sym No. 5 in c, Op. 67; Sym No. 7 in A, Op. 92)*, Brahms *(Sym No. 3 in F, Op. 90; Sym No. 4 in e, Op. 98)*, Bruckner *(Sym No. 8 in c)*, R. Strauss *(Con No. 1 in E♭ for Hn, Op. 11; An Alpine Sym, Op. 64)*, Ovsyaniko-Kulikovsky *(Sym No. 21 in g)*, Shostakovich *(Sym No. 5 in d, Op. 47; Sym No. 7 in C, Op. 60, "Leningrad"; Sym No. 8 in c, Op. 65)*, Glazunov *(Sym No. 4 in E♭, Op. 48)*, Tchaikovsky *(Sym No. 4 in f, Op. 36; Sym No. 6 in b, Op. 74, "Pathétique"; Francesca da Rimini, Op. 32; Serenade for String Orch in C, Op. 48; Capriccio italien, Op. 45)*, Rimsky-Korsakov *(Tale of the Invisible City of Kitezh) (rec 1947-73)* MELD (Mravinsky Edition) 10-▲ 29459 [ADD] (60.97)

Munch, Charles (cnd)
Hommage à Charles Munch, w. French National Orch—features works by Beethoven *(Die Weihe des Hauses (ov); Syms 4 & 7)*, Berlioz *(Symphonie fantastique; Le Corsaire; Benvenuto Cellini (ov))*, Brahms *(Sym 2)*, Debussy *(Images for Orch; Fant for Pno; La Mer)*, Dutilleux *(Sym 2)*, Fauré *(Pelléas et Mélisande)*, Franck *(Sym in d)*, Honegger *(Syms 1, 2 & 5; Le Chant de Nigamon; Pastorale d'été)*, Roussel *(Bacchus et Ariane (suite 2); Syms 3 & 4)*, R. Schumann *(Sym 4)*, Sibelius *(Swan of Tuonela; Return of Lemminkaïnen [both from 4 Legends])* VAL 10-▲ 4822 [ADD] (91.97)

Neumann, Václav (cnd)
Václav Neumann Conducts *see* Czech Philharmonic Orchestra [above]

Ormandy, Eugene (cnd), Seiji Ozawa (cnd), Arthur Fiedler (cnd), Fritz Reiner (cnd)
Classics at the Movies—features classical selections from *Apocalypse Now, Amadeus, Die Hard, Platoon*, others RCAV ▲ 60833 (10.97) ▮ 60833

Previn, André (cnd)
André Previn: The Maestro, w. London SO, Pittsburgh SO, Vienna PO—features works by Haydn *(Sym 104, "London")*, Mozart *(Con 20 Pno, K.466 [w. André Previn (pno)])*, Berlioz *(La carnaval romain)*, Tchaikovsky *(Romeo & Juliet (fantasy ov); Swan Lake (sels))*, Ravel *(La Valse)*, Dukas *(L'Apprenti sorcier)*, Debussy *(Prélude à l'après-midi d'un faune)*, Gershwin *(Rhap in Blue [w. André Previn (pno)]; Porgy & Bess (symphonic picture))*, Barber *(Adagio)*, R. Strauss *(Don Juan)*, Rodrigo *(Concierto de Aranjuez [w. Angel Romero (gtr)])* RYLC 3-▲ 70300 (20.97)

Rieu, André (cnd)
André Rieu in Concert—features works by Lehár, Mozart, Schubert, Strauss PPHI ▲ 534266 (17.97) ▮ 534266 (10.98)
The Christmas I Love *(see CHRISTMAS section:Johann Strauss Orch)*

Sabajno, Carlo (cnd)
Portrait of Carlo Sabajno, Vol. 1—features works by Wagner, Verdi, Mozart, Leoncavallo, Mascagni, Ponchielli, Mendelssohn, Catalani *(rec 1905-20)* ENT (Idis) ▲ 305 (13.97)

Sabata, Victor de (cnd)
Victor de Sabata—features works by Beethoven *(Sym 3)*, Brahms *(Sym 4)*, Strauss *(Tod und Verklärung)*, Berlioz *(Le carnaval romain)*, Wagner *(Ride of the Valkyries [from Die Walküre]; Prelude to Act 1 [from Tristan und Isolde])*, Sibelius *(Valse triste) (rec 1939-46)* GRM2 2-▲ 78686 (25.97)

Sacher, Paul (cnd)
Paul Sacher Und Die Neue Musik, w. Basel CO, Basel SO members, A. Nunez (vn), Zurich Collegium Musicum, Sterk'scher Private Choir, Basel Percussion Ensemble, E. Strauss (vc), F. Manz (fl), A. Morf (cl), F. Vlasak (tpt), B. Gutknecht (trbn), G. Wyss (pno), K. Jacobi (org), R. Scheidegger (org), P. Solomon (org) Giebel, Agnes (sop), Julia Juon (mez), Elsa Cavelti (alt), Heiner Hopfner (ten), Peter Pears (ten), Heinz Rehfuss (bass), Pierre Fournier (vc), Heinz Holliger (ob), Ursula Holliger (hp), Matthias Würsch (cym), Phyllis Bryn-Julson (sop), Pierre Béboux (perc), Günther (perc), Fithjof Koch (perc), Daniel Zoller (perc)—features C. Beck *(Hommages)*, B. Britten *(Cant academica, Op. 62)*, Chávez *(Tambuco)*, Döhl *(Conductus)*, Dutilleux *(Mystère de l'Instant)*, W. Fortner *(Vars)*, H. W. Henze *(Double Con)*, Kelterborn *(Visions Sonores)*, F. Martin *(Con Vc)*, Moret *(Visitations)*, Rihm *(Dunkeles Spiel)*, W. Vogel *(Composition CO)* ARSM 3-▲ 1155 [DDD] (57.97)

Sargent, Malcolm (cnd)
Sir Malcolm Sargent Conducts Favourite Choral Music, w. Royal Choral Society, various London orchs—features works by Elgar, Handel, Haydn, Mendelssohn, Parry, Sullivan, et al. *(rec 1926-32)* PHS ▲ 9380 (m) [AAD] (17.97)

Scherchen, Hermann (cnd)
A Tribute to Hermann Scherchen—features performances by Vienna SO *(Bach:A Musical Offering, BWV 1079)*, Hessian Radio Orch *(Bach:Prelude & Fugue in E♭, BWV 552 [orchd Schoenberg])*, Swedish Radio Orch *(Bartók:Music for Strs, Perc & Cel; Schoenberg:Chamber Sym 1)*, Lugano Radio-TV Orch *(Beethoven:Sym 8; Sym 9 [w. M. Lászlo (sop), L. Devallier (cta), P. Monteanu (ten), R. Arié (bass), Lugano Radio-TV Chorus])*, Paris Conservatory *(Berlioz:Entrée des construceurs; Entrée des matelots; Entrée des laboureurs [all from Les Troyens])*, Czech PO *(Kallinikov:Sym 1)*, Stuttgart RSO *(Prokofiev:Lieutenant Kijé Suite)*, Darmstadt Landestheater Orch *(Schoenberg:Golden Calf Scene [from Moses und Aaron; w. Darmstadt Landestheater Chorus])*, Herford PO *(Verdi:Nabucco (ov))*, orch unknown *(Krenek:Sym 1)* TAHA 5-▲ 185 (50.97)

Solti, Georg (cnd)
Sir Georg Solti: Grammy Champion *(A survey covering the entire chronology, 1967-1991, of Solti's Grammy award-winning recordings; 13 selections, over 73 minutes of music, plus a 132-page book highlighting Solti's career. This budget-priced compilation includes selections from award-winning orchestral and operatic recordings he has made for London Records with the Chicago SO, London PO and Vienna PO.)*—features works by Bach, Beethoven, Berlioz, Brahms, Haydn, Liszt, Mahler, Mozart, Verdi, Wagner PPHI ▲ 36779 [ADD/DDD]

Solti, Georg (cnd) (cont.)
The Solti Collection *(a selection of Sir Georg Solti's major recordings in a special midpriced series, available as twelve individual cds)*—for details, see Composer Section under Beethoven, Berlioz, Brahms, Holst, Mahler, Mozart, Ravel, Schubert, R. Strauss, Tchaikovsky, Wagner PLON (Jubilee) 12-▲ 30437 [ADD/DDD]
The Solti Edition *(in commemoration of Solti's 80th birthday on 21 October 1992, this 25-CD midpriced set includes orchestral and operatic recordings he has made for London Records)*, w. Chicago SO, London PO, London SO, Vienna PO, New Philharmonia Orch, Royal Opera House Orch, CO of Europe—features works by Bartók *(Concerto for Orchestra; Dance Suite; Miraculous Mandarin Suite—LSO)*, Beethoven *(Piano Concerti 2 & 5—Vladimir Ashkenazy, CSO; Symphonies 4 & 5—CSO)*, Berlioz *(Symphonie fantastique; Les Francs-juges—CSO)*, Bizet *(Carmen:Scenes & Arias—Te Kanawa, Troyanos, Domingo, LPO)*, Brahms *(Symphony No. 4; Haydn Variations—CSO; Deutsches Requiem—Te Kanawa, Weikl, CSO & Chorus)*, Bruckner *(Symphony No. 7—CSO)*, Dvořák *(Symphony No. 9—CSO)*, Handel *(Messiah:Arias & Choruses—Te Kanawa, Gjevang, Lewis, Howell, CSO & Chorus)*, Haydn *(Symphonies 94 & 100—LPO)*, Mahler *(Symphony No. 4—Te Kanawa, CSO; Symphony No. 5—CSO)*, Mendelssohn *(Symphonies 3 & 4—CSO)*, Mozart *(Magic Flute highlights—Jo, Ziesak, Heilmann, Kraus, Moll, VPO; Requiem—Auger, Bartoli, Cole, Pape, VPO; Symphonies 40 & 41—COE)*, Puccini *(Tosca highlights—Te Kanawa, Aragall, Nucci, NPO)*, Schubert *(Symphonies 5 & 8—VPO)*, R. Strauss *(Also sprach Zarathustra; Don Juan; Till Eulenspiegel—CSO)*, Tchaikovsky *(1812 Overture; Nutcracker Suite; Romeo & Juliet—CSO)*, Verdi *(Aida: Scenes & Arias—L. Price, Gorr, Vickers, ROHO; Ballo in maschera highlights—M. Price, Pavarotti, Bruson, NPO)*, Wagner *(orchestral excerpts from The Ring—VPO; Lohengrin highlights—Norman, Domingo, Randová, Sotin, VPO)* PLON 25-▲ 36600

Stock, Frederick (cnd)
Frederik Stock, w. Chicago SO—features works by Bach, Enesco, Sibelius, Reznicek, Glière, Ponchielli, Paganini, Glazunov, plus others *(rec 1930-40)* LYS 2-▲ 42 (30.97)

Stokowski, Leopold (cnd)
Bach Transcriptions, w. Leopold Stokowski Orch RCAV (Gold Seal:Legendary Performers) ▲ 60922 (10.97)
Fantasia *(soundtrack to the Disney film)*, w. Leopold Stokowski Orch—features works by Beethoven *(Sym. 6)*, Stravinsky *(Le sacre du printemps)*, Tchaikovsky *(Nutcracker Suite)*, J.S. Bach *(Toccata & Fugue in d [trans. Stowkowski])*, Dukas *(L'apprenti sorcier)*, Ponchielli *(La Gioconda:Dance of the Hours)*, Mussorgsky *(Night on Bald Mountain)*, Schubert *(Ave Maria)* DBV 2-▲ 60007 (22.97) 60007
Great Recordings with the Philadelphia Orchestra, w. Philadelphia Orch—features works of Sibelius, Wagner, Saint-Saëns, Gliere, J. S. Bach, Ippolitov-Ivanov, Berlioz, Mussorgsky, Liszt, Schönberg *(rec 1927 & 1940)* PHG 2-▲ 5025 (28.97)
Leopold Stokowski, w. Philadelphia Orch—features works by Sibelius *(Finlandia; Swan of Tuonela)*, Berlioz *(Marche hongroise)*, Liszt *(Hungarian Rhap 2)*, A. Thomas *(Gavotte [from Mignon])*, Wagner *(Magic Fire Music [from Die Walküre]; Closing Scene [from Götterdämmerung])*, Glière *(Red Poppy (suite), "The Russian Sailors' Dance")*, Ippolitov-Ivanov *(Caucasian Sketches)*, Satie *(Gymnopédies 1 & 2)*, Schoenberg *(Prelude & Interlude [from Gurrelieder])* MTAL ▲ 48015 (6.97)
The Orchestra Landmarks of a Distinguished Career, w. Leopold Stokowski Orch—features works by Barber, Dukas, Debussy, Farberman, Mussorgsky, Persichetti, Sibelius, J. Strauss II, R. Strauss, Tchaikovsky, Vaughan Williams EMIC ▲ 65614 (11.97)
The Stokowski Collection, Vol. 1 *see Composer section: Mozart—Serenade No. 10; etc*, w. Leopold Stokowski Orch VC ▲ 8009 [ADD] (13.97)
A Stokowski Fantasia *(a collection of the five major works included in Walt Disney's film "Fantasia," as originally recorded by Stokowski and the Philadelphia Orchestra for Victor Records between 1926 and 1940)*, w. Philadelphia Orch—features works by Bach *(Toccata & Fugue in d, BWV 565, orchestrated by Stokowski; rec. 1927)*, Dukas *(The Sorcerer's Apprentice, rec. 1937)*, Mussorgsky/arr. Stokowski *(A Night on the Bare Mountain; rec. 1940)*, Stravinsky *("Adoration of the Earth" and "The Sacrifice" from The Rite of Spring; rec. 1929 and 1930)*, Tchaikovsky *(Nutcracker Suite; rec. 1926)* PHS ▲ 9488 [AAD] (17.97)
Stokowski Plays De Falla, Strauss, etc, w. Philadelphia Orch, NBC SO, New York SO—features works by Falla *(Spanish Dance [from La vida breve])*, R. Strauss *(Dance of the 7 Veils [from Salome])*, Tchaikovsky *(Marche slave; Romeo & Juliet (fantasy ov); Solitude)*, Schubert *(Tyrolean Dance)*, Scriabin *(Etude in c#)*, Joaquín Turina *(Gypsy Dance)*, Handel *(Pastoral Sym [from Messiah])*, Sousa *(Manhattan Beach; El Capitan)*, Foster *(Oh, Susannah!)* MTAL ▲ 48033 (6.97)
The Stokowski "Pops" Collection, w. Philadelphia Orch—features works by Weber *(Invitation to the Dance)*, J. Strauss, Jr. *(Blue Danube; Tales from the Vienna Woods)*, Brahms *(Serenade 1:Minuet)*, Sibelius *(Swan of Tuonela; Finlandia)*, Albéniz *(Iberia:Festival in Seville)*, Falla *(Danse espagnole [from La vida breve])*, Novacek *(Perpetuum mobile [arr Stokowski])*, Tchaikovsky *(Nutcracker:Suite)* BCS ▲ 47 [AAD] (16.97)
Stokowski Stereo Collection—features works by J. S. Bach *(Toccata & Fugue, BWV 565 [includes rehearsal, w. London SO]; Chaconne [from Partita 2]; Preludio [from Partita 3]; Air on the G String; Ein feste Burg; Fugue in g, BWV 578; Arioso [from Cant 156]; Sleepers, Awake; Komm süsser Tod [all trans Stokowski, w. London SO]; Jesu, Joy of Man's Desiring; Sheep May Safely Graze [both w. New SO, Norman Luboff Choir])*, Wagner *(Rienzi:Ov [includes 2 endings & rehearsal, w. Royal PO]; Meistersinger:Act III Prelude; Dance of the Apprentices; Procession of the Meistersingers [all w. London SO]; Tristan & Isolde:Prelude [w. London SO]; Act III Prelude [w. Royal PO]; Götterdämmerung:Siegfried's Rhine Journey & Funeral March; Brünnhilde's Immolation [all w. London SO]; Walküre:Ride of the Valkeries; Magic Fire Music [both w. Royal PO]; Rheingold:Entrance of the Gods [w. Royal PO]; Tannhäuser:Ov & Venusberg Music [w. Royal PO]; Pilgrim's Chorus [w. New SO, Norman Luboff Choir])*, Beethoven *(Sym 6:movts IV & V (excerpts) [w. NBC SO]; Sym 3; Coriolan Ov [both w. London SO]; The Heav'ns Are Telling [w. New SO, Norman Luboff Choir])*, Mahler *(Sym 2:movts III-V (rehearsal excerpts) [w. London SO]; Sym 2 [comp, w. B. Fassbaender (mez), Margaret Price (sop), London SO, London Sym Chorus])*, Brahms *(Sym 4; Academic Festival Ov [both w. New Philharmonia Orch])* Handel *(Royal Fireworks Music; Water Music:Suite [both w. RCA Victor SO]; Largo [w. New SO, Norman Luboff Choir])*, Rimsky-Korsakov *(Scheherazade [w. Royal PO]; Russian Easter Ov [w. Chicago SO])*, Tchaikovsky *(Sym 6 [w. London SO]; Pater Noster [w. New SO, Norman Luboff Choir])*, Enesco *(Romanian Rhap 1, Op. 11 [w. RCA Victor SO])*, Liszt *(Hungarian Rhap 2 [w. RCA Victor SO])*, Dvořák *(Sym 9 [w. New Philharmonia Orch])*, Smetana *(The Moldau [w. RCA Victor SO])*, Canteloube *(Chants d'Auvergne [w. American SO])*, Villa-Lobos *(Bachianas brasilerias 5 [w. American SO])*, Rachmaninoff *(Vocalise, Op. 34/14 [w. Anna Moffo (sop), American SO])*, Prokofiev *(Romeo & Juliet (sels) [w. NBC SO])*, Menotti *(Sebastian:Suite [w. NBC SO])*, Shostakovich *(Sym 6; Age of Gold:Suite [both w. Chicago SO])*, A. Khachaturian *(Sym 3 [w. Chicago SO])*, Humperdinck *(Evening Prayer [w. New SO, Norman Luboff Choir])*, Gluck *(O Savior, Hear Me [w. New SO, Norman Luboff Choir]) (rec 1954-75)* RCAV (Gold Seal) 14-▲ 68443 (143.97)

Toscanini, Arturo (cnd)
Arturo Toscanini: The 1st Recordings, 1920-26, w. La Scala Orch, New York PO—features works by Galilei *(Suites Nos. 1 & 2 [from Ancient Dances & Airs; arr Respighi])*, Mozart *(Sym no. 39 [Minuetto & Finale])*, Beethoven *(Sym No. 1 [Finale]; Sym No. 5 [Finale])*, Donizetti *(Don Pasquale Ov)*, Berlioz *(Marche hongroise [from La damnation de Faust])*, Mendelssohn *(Scherzo; Wedding March; Nocturne [all from A Midsummer Night's Dream])*, Bizet *(L'Arlésienne Suite No. 2 [Farandole]; Carmen [Prelude to Act IV])*, Massenet *(Fête Bohème [from Scènes pittoresque])*, Wolf-Ferrari *(I Gioielli della Madonna Ov)*, Pizzetti *(Le Quai du Port de Famagoust [from La Pisanelle])* SYMP ▲ 1189 (17.97)
His Later Years in America, Vol. 1: 1929-1946, w. NBC SO, New York PO—features works by Rossini, Verdi, Smetana, Bizet, Thomas, Weber, Suppé, Bach, Waldteufel, Mozart, Berlioz & Cimarosa ENT (Istituto Discografico Italiano) 2-▲ 270 (25.97)
Mature Years in America, Vol. 2, w. NBC SO, New York PO, Philadelphia Orch—features works by Bizet, Glinka, Gluck, Mendelssohn, Paganini, Rossini, Schumann, J. Strauss II & Wagner *(rec 1929-46)* ENT (Idis) 2-▲ 284 (25.97)
Toscanini At La Scala (1946 & 1948): Concert to Inaugurate the Re-Built Theater—features works by Boito, Puccini, Rossini, Verdi, *("Arrigo Boito Memorial Concert" (Rec. live, 6/10/48)—selections from Boito's Mefistofele)* SRON 3-▲ SRO 802-3 (m) [ADD]
The Toscanini Collection
Vols. 1-5 (*seeComposer section: Beethoven—Symphonies, complete)*
Vols. 6-9 *(available singly or boxed; see Composer section: Brahms—Symphonies, complete; etc.)*
Vol. 10 (*see* Composer section: Mozart—Symphony No. 35, etc.)
Vol. 11 (*see* Composer section: Mozart—Symphonies 39-41)
Vol. 12 (*see* Composer section: Haydn—Symphonies 88, 94, 98)
Vol. 13 (*see* Composer section: Haydn—Symphonies 99 & 101, etc.)
Vol. 14 (*see* Composer section: Schubert—Symphony Nos. 8 & 9)
Vol. 15 (*see* Composer section: Schubert—Symphonies 5 & 9)
Vol. 16 (*see* Composer section: Schumann—Symphony No. 3 & Manfred Overture; Weber—Overtures)
Vol. 17 (*see* Composer section: Mendelssohn—Symphony Nos. 4 & 5; etc.)
Vol. 18 (*see* Composer section: Tchaikovsky—Symphony No. 6 & Nutcracker Suite)
Vol. 19 (*see* Composer section: Tchaikovsky—Manfred Symphony & Romeo and Juliet)
Vol. 20 (*see* Composer section: Franck—Symphony in d; Saint-Saëns—Symphony No. 3)
Vol. 21 (*see* Composer section: Sibelius—Symphony No. 2, etc.)
Vol. 22 (*see* Composer section: Shostakovich—Symphony No. 7)
Vol. 23 (*see* Composer section: Beethoven—Symphonies 3 & 8)
Vol. 24 (*see* Composer section: Dvořák—Symphony No. 9; etc.)
Vol. 25 (*see* Composer section: Beethoven—Symphony No. 5, etc.)
Vol. 26 (*see* Composer section: Brahms—Symphony No. 1, etc.)
Vol. 27 (*see* Composer section: Cherubini—Symphony in D & Overtures; Cimarosa—Overtures)

978 ▲ = CD ♦ = Enhanced CD △ = MD ▮ = Cassette Tape ▯ = DCC

Toscanini, Arturo (cnd) (cont.)
Vol. 28: All-Russian Program (*see* Composer section: Prokofiev—Symphony No. 1, Shostakovich—Symphony No. 1, etc.)
Vol. 29 (*see* Composer section: Beethoven—Symphony No. 3; Mozart—Symphony No. 40)
Vol. 30 (*see* Composer section: R. Strauss—Death and Transfiguration; Don Quixote)
Vol. 31 (*see* Composer section: R. Strauss—Don Juan, Till Eulenspiegel, etc.; Wagner—Siegfried Idyll, etc.)
Vol. 32 (*see* Composer section: Respighi—Fountains of Rome; Pines of Rome; Feste Romane)
Vol. 33 (*see* Composer section: Berlioz—Harold in Italy, etc.)
Vol. 34 (*see* Composer section: Berlioz—Roméo et Juliette; Bizet—L'Arlésienne & Carmen Suites)
Vol. 35 (*see* Composer section—Elgar:Enigma Variations; Mussorgsky:Pictures at an Exhibition)
Vol. 36 (*see* Composer section: Mendelssohn—Midsummer Night's Dream & Octet)
Vol. 37 (*see* Composer section—Debussy:La Mer, etc.)
Vol. 38: All-American Program (*see* Composer section: Barber—Adagio, Gershwin—American in Paris, Grofé—Grand Canyon Suite, etc.)
Vol. 39: All-French Program (*see* Composer section: Berlioz—Overtures, Dukas—Apprenti sorcier, Saint-Saëns—Danse macabre, etc.)
Vol. 40—features works by Bach (*Air on the G String*), Glinka (*Jota argonesa*), Leopold Mozart (*The Toy Symphony*), Paganini (*Moto perpetuo*), Ponchielli (*Dance of the Hours*), Joh. Strauss II (*An der schönen, blauen Donau; Tritsch-Tratsch Polka*), Suppé (*Poet and Peasant Overture*), Waldteufel (*The Skater's Waltz*), Weber (*Invitation to the Dance*) RCAV (Gold Seal) ▲ 60308 (m) [ADD] (10.97) 60308
Vol. 41 (*see* Composer section: Beethoven—Piano Concerto No. 3; Violin Concerto)
Vol. 42 (*see* Composer section: Beethoven—Piano Concerti 1 & 4)
Vol. 43 (*see* Composer section: Brahms—Piano Concerto No. 2; Tchaikovsky—Piano Concerto No. 1 [Horowitz])
Vol. 44 (*see* Composer section: Mussorgsky—Pictures; Tchaikovsky—Piano Concerto No. 1 [Horowitz])
Vol. 45 (*see* Composer section: Beethoven—Overtures)
Vol. 46 (*see* Composer section: Gluck—Orfeo ed Euridice, excerpts; etc.)
Vol. 47 (*see* Composer section: Rossini—Overtures)
Vol. 48 (*see* Composer section: Wagner—Faust Overture, etc.)
Vol. 49 (*see* Composer section: Wagner—orchestral excerpts from Götterdämmerung, Lohengrin, Tannhäuser, Tristan, Walküre)
Vol. 50: Music From Italian Opera (*see* Composer section: Verdi—Overtures and Preludes, etc.)
Vol. 51: Overtures—features works by Hérold (*Zampa*), Humperdinck (*Hansel und Gretel*), Kabalevsky (*Colas Breugnon*), Mozart (*Magic Flute*), Rossini (*William Tell*), Smetana (*Bartered Bride*), Thomas (*Mignon*), Verdi (*Forza del destino*), Weber (*Der Freischütz*) RCAV (Gold Seal) ▲ 60310 (10.97) 60310
Vol. 52 (*see* Composer section—Wagner:Siegfried Idyll, etc.)
Vol. 53 (*see* Composer section: Wagner—Götterdämerung & Siegfried excerpts)
Vol. 54 (*see* Composer section: Beethoven—Fidelio)
Vol. 55 (*see* Composer section—Puccini:La Bohème)
Vol. 56 (*see* Composer section: Verdi—Aida)
Vol. 57 (*see* Composer section: Verdi—Falstaff)
Vol. 58 (*see* Composer section: Verdi—Otello)
Vol. 59 (*see* Composer section—Verdi:Ballo in maschera)
Vol. 60 (*see* Composer section: Verdi—Traviata)
Vol. 61 (*see* Composer section—Beethoven (Missa Solemnis) & Cherubini)
Vol. 62 (*see* Composer section—Verdi (Rigoletto:Act 4), etc.
Vol. 63 (*see* Composer section: Verdi—Requiem Mass, etc.)
Vols. 64-66: The New York Philharmonic Recordings RCAV (Gold Seal) 3-▲ 60329 [ADD] (30.97) 60329
Vol. 64 (*see* Composer section: Beethoven—Symphony No. 7; etc.)
Vol. 65 (*see* Composer section: Brahms—Haydn Variations; Mozart—Symphony No. 35; etc.)
Vol. 66 (*see* Composer section: Rossini—Overtures; etc.)
Vols. 67-70: The Philadelphia Orchestra Recordings (*see* Composer section—Debussy (La mer), etc.
Vol. 67 (*see* Composer section: Debussy—La Mer; Respighi—Feste Romane)
Vol. 68 (*see* Composer section: R. Strauss—Death and Transfiguration; Tchaikovsky—Symphony No. 6)
Vol. 69 (*see* Composer section: Schubert—Symphony No. 9)
Vol. 70 (*see* Composer section: Berlioz—Roméo et Juliette [Queen Mab's Scherzo]; Mendelssohn—Midsummer Night's Dream)
Vol. 71: La Scala Orchestra Acoustic Recordings: 1920-21—features works by Beethoven (*Symphony No. 1—4th movt.; Symphony No. 5—4th movt.*), Berlioz (*Rakoczy March*), Bizet (*L'Arlésienne Suite No. 2—Farandole; Carmen—Act 4 Entr'acte, Aragonaise*), Donizetti (*Don Pasquale—Overture*), Massenet (*Fête bohème*), Mendelssohn (*Scherzo & Wedding March*), Mozart (*Symphony No. 39—Menuetto & Finale*), Pizzetti (*Le quai du porte de Famagouste—Act 1 Prelude*), Respighi (*Gagliarda*), Wolf-Ferrari (*Il segreto di Susanna—Overture*) RCAV (Gold Seal) ▲ 60315 (10.97) 60315
The Toscanini Collection: The Limited Edition RCAV (Gold Seal) 82-▲ 60250
[Editor's Note]: Limited to 5,000 sets worldwide, this edition consists of the 71 individual volumes housed in a special three-shelf hardwood case with a gold-embossed glass dust cover. To authenticate ownership, an individually-numbered 123-page commemorative guide to the collection is included with each set.
Toscanini Conducts Italian Rarities—features works by Busoni, Tommasini, Scarlatti, Verdi, Bossi, Bazzini, Rieti, Wolf-Ferrari, plus others Archive Documents 2-▲ ATCD 100
The Toscanini Sampler (*limited edition budget-priced 69-minute selection from the ongoing Toscanini series*)—features works by Beethoven, Berlioz, Brahms, Puccini, Rossini, Smetana, Verdi, Wagner RCAV (Gold Seal) ▲ 60340 [ADD] (6.97)

Wood, Henry (cnd)
The Best of Sir H. J. Wood, w. Irene Scharrer (pno)—features works by Haydn, Schubert, Litolff, Bruckner, Beethoven, Brahms, J.S. Bach, Rachmaninoff, Dvořák (*rec 1932-37*) DLAB 2-▲ 2002 [ADD]
Sir H. J. Wood Conducts Proms Favourites, w. Queen's Hall Orch, British SO, London PO, London SO—features works by Coates, Grainger, Wagner; Berlioz, Gounod, Elgar; Järnefelt (*rec Nov 1929-Mar 1940*) DLAB ▲ 8008 [ADD]

Zender, Hans (cnd)
Hans Zender Edition, w. Saarbrücken RSO—features works by Mozart (*Syms 32, 36 & 41*), Beethoven (*Syms 1 & 6; Con Vn, Op. 61*), Schumann (*Syms 2 & 4*), Debussy (*Images Orch; Jeux; Mer*), Mahler (*Syms 6, 7 & 9; Knaben Wunderhorn (sels)*), Reger (*Nonnen; Romantische Suite*), Schoenberg (*Begleitmusik; Orch Pieces, Op. 16; Survivor*), Messiaen (*Poèmes; Hymne*), Zimmermann (*Antiphonen; Impromptu; Photoptosis; Con Vc*), Feldman (*Fl & Orch; Vc & Orch; Ob & Orch; Pno & Orch*), Boulez (*Rituel*), Lachenmann (*Harm*), Riehm (*Gewidmet*), Scelsi (*Pezzi Orch; Pranam*), Zender (*Haiku; Cant; Zeitstrome; Canto VIII*) CPO 14-▲ 999534 (87.97)

CROSSOVER

Die Knödel
Die Noodle!—features works by Dienz, Algibut, Haller, Rüegg, plus others KOCR ▲ 7923 (16.97)
Overcooked Tyroleans KOCR ▲ 7908 (16.97)

Trio Rococo [Niels Eje (ob), Inge Mulvad Eje (vc), Lillian Törnqvist (hp)]
Norwegian Wood: A Classical Take on Beatles Classics—features Eleanor Rigby; Yesterday; Here Comes the Sun; Because; Day Tripper; Michelle; And I Love Her; Blackbird; In My Life; For No One; All My Loving; Here, There & Everywhere; I Am the Walrus; She's Leaving Home; The Fool on the Hill; Norwegian Wood RCAV ▲ 22488 (16.97) ▮ 22488 (9.98)

Turtle Island String Quartet [Darol Anger (vn), Tracy Silverman (vn), Danny Seidenberg (va), Mark Summer (vc)], Detroit SO [cnd:Neeme Järvi]
A Night in Tunisia, A Week in Detroit—features works by David Balakrishnan (*Spider Dreams [Suite]*), Jeff Beal (*Interchange*), Dizzy Gillespie (*A Night in Tunisia [arr. Vince Mendoza]*), Miles Davis (*7 Steps to Heaven [arr. Turtle Island String Quartet]*), Turtle Island String Quartet (*Bach's Lunch*), Tower of Power (*Who Do You Think You Are? [arr. Danny Seidenberg]*) CHN (New Direction) ▲ 9331 [DDD] (16.97)

DOUBLE BASS

Berlin PO Double Bass Quartet [Klaus Stoll (db), Friedrich Witt (db), Erich Hartmann (db), Wolfgang Kohly (db)]
Kontrabassquartett der Berliner Philharmoniker—features works by Funck (*Adagio & Allemande Db Qt*), B. Alt (*Suite for 4 Dbs*), Findeisen (*Prelude for 4 Dbs*), Mozart (*Ave verum corpus, K.618 [arr db qt]*), Jorns (*Mobile perpetuum*), Chihara (*Logs*), E. Hartmann (*Qt Dbs*) CAMA ▲ 2562 [DDD] (17.97)

Bradetich, Jeff (db)
Classics for All to Hear (*recordings especially arranged and acoustically prepared for the hard of hearing*), w. Judi Rockey Bradetich (pno)—features works by Bach, Schubert, Dvořák, Gershwin, S. Foster, Handel, Chopin, Massenet, Humperdinck, Copland, Sibelius, Kreisler Music for All to Hear ▲ 9101 ▮ 9101

Brussels Double Bass Quartet
Brussels Double Bass Quartet—features works by Alt, Bottesini, Joplin, Prokofiev, Vanherenthals, and arrangements of 10 Spirituals PAVA ▲ 7254 (10.97)

Canonici, Corrado (db)
Contrabass—features works by Ghezzo (*5 Corrado Songs*), Berio (*Psy*), Macchi (*Anafora*), Giraud (*Bleu et ombre [w. Ombretta Macchi (voc)]*), Kessner (*Circle Music I-B [w. Paolo Zannini (pno)]*), Scelsi (*Maknongan*), Cage (*Music for 2 [w. Guido Arbonelli (cl)]*), Mazurek (*Cries of the Innocent*) CPS ▲ 8628 [DDD] (16.97)

Coppieters, Frank (db)
Salon-Music for a Double Bass, w. H. Eeman (pno)—features works by Misek (*Son., Op. 6/2*), Bottesini (*Elegie in D; Tarantella*), Koussevitzky (*Chanson triste, Op. 2; Valse miniature, Op. 1/2; Humoresque*), Lorenziti (*Gavotte [arr. Edouard Nany]*), van Rossum (*Reminiscenze, Op. 17*), Coryn (*Thoughts on a Theme for solo Double Bass*) RENE ▲ 86006 [ADD] (16.97)

Drew, Lucas (db)
Double Bass Sampler, w. Warren Broome (kbd)—features works by J. S. Bach (*Suite 1 Vc*), Boda (*Fant Db & Bass Qt [w. Univ of Miami Bass Quartet]*), Capuzzi (*Con in F*), Cimador (*Con in G*), L. Drew (*Sound Study for 8 Dbs [w. Univ of Miami Bass Ensemble]*), E. B. Fardig (*Scherzo*), K. Hiatt (*Hyperduo for Fl, Db & Synthesized Samples [w. Christine Nield (fl)]*), B. Marcello (*Son in e*), Pergolesi (*Sinf in F*), Sandby (*Solopiece [pno reduction]*), Sevitzky (*Nocturne*) Coronet ▲ COR 401-1

Frankfurt Contra Bass Quartet
Quattro Contra Bassi—features works for 1-4 double basses by Alm Peña, Telemann, Tabakov, Brumby, Haydn, Venherenthals MDG ▲ 6030634 (16.97)

Fuller, Jerry (db)
Duets *see* Composer section under Dittersdorf, et al. for contents Musical Arts Society ▲ CD 41592 [DDD] ▮ CS 41592 (D)
Songs, Dances & Fantasy, w. Frederick Ockwell (pno), Kenneth Dorsch (hpd), William Ferris (pno), Steve Hartman (hp), Thomas Potter (bass), John Vorrasi (ten), Anne Waller (gtr)—features works by William Ferris, Tibor Freso, Nicolo Porpora, Borodin, Glinka, Grétry, Handel Musical Arts Society ▲ CD 41589 [AAD] ▮ CS 41589

Giorgi, Massimo (db)
Il Contrabasso Italiano, w. Aquilani Solisti [cnd:Vittorio Antonellini]—features works by Dragonetti, Bottesini, Eccles, Cimador & Bloch KSCH ▲ 314242 (16.97)

Goïlav, Yoan (db)
Les Plus belles transcriptions pour contrebass et piano, w. Heinz Börlin (pno)—features works by Brahms (*Cello Sonata, Op. 38*), Chopin (*Etude No. 7*), Gabriel-Marie (*La cinquantaine*), Schumann (*3 Fantasie Stücke*), Tchaikovsky (*Valse sentimentale*) GALL ▲ CD 675 [DDD]

Guettler, Knut (db)
Miracle Contrabass—features works by J. S. Bach (*Son VI Hpd, BWV 1028*), Rachmaninoff (*Vocalise*), Granados (*Goyescas:Intermezzo*), Bloch (*Prayer*), Koussevitzky (*Chanson triste, Op. 2:Con tristezza*), London (*Almost Spring [all w. Keiko Ogura (pno)]*), Hoffmeister (*Db Qt No. 2 [w. Yu Kazaoka (vn), Shusuke Nishikawa (va), Ken Segoe (vc)]*), Guettler (*Vars on Greensleeves for solo Db*) CAMA ▲ 2063 [DDD] (17.97)

Hanskov, Mette (db)
Lady Plays the Bass, w. T. Lønskov (pno), Niels Erik Aggesea (org)—features works by Glière, Granados, Bottesini, Frantisek Cerny, V. Kuschynska, plus various Danish folksongs (*rec Apr 1991*) DANR ▲ 378 [DDD]

Karr, Gary (db)
The Spirit of Koussevitzky, w. Harmon Lewis (pno)—features works by Glière (*Intermezzo & Tarantella, Op. 9/1 & 2; Prelude & Scherzo, Op. 32/1 & 2*), Serge Koussevitzky (*Andante & Valse miniature, Op. 1/1 & 2; Chanson triste, Op. 2; Humoresque, Op. 4*), Rachmaninoff (*Vocalise*), Scriabin (*Preludes, Etudes & Albumleaf, from Opp. 2,9,16,22,42 & 45*) VQR Digital ▲ VQR 2031 [DDD]

Katrama, Jorma (db)
Contrabbasso con bravura, w. Margit Rahkonen (pno)—features works by Sibelius, Sallinen, Bottesini, Koussevitzsky, Sanit-Saëns, Rimsky-Korsakov, Monti, Paganini, Popper (*rec Mar 1989*) FNL ▲ 95864 [DDD]

Léandre, Joëlle (db)
Works for Double Bass & Accordian, w. Pascal Contet (acc)—features Die grosse Sonate; Danses musettes; Parcours 1; Ecsale; Parcours six feux de characters; plus other pieces MDA7 ▲ 1 (18.97)

New Colophonium Bass Quartet
What a Wonderful Contrabass World!, w. Berlin PO, Contrabass Quartet—features works by Runswick (*Strauss in the Doghouse; American Basses*), Brumby (*Suite*), Koussevitzky (*Chanson Triste*), Bottesini (*Gavotto in G; Polacca; Passione Amerosa*), Gounod (*Petit Scherzo*), Sperger (*Finale [from Son. for Viola & Contrabass in D]*), Mozart (*Ave Verum Corpus*), J.S. Bach (*Sarabande, BWV 1008*) CAMA ▲ 60 (17.97)

Rollez, Jean-Marc (db)
Encores! Bis!: Works for Double Bass, w. Angeline Pondepeyre (pno)—features works by Cassado (*Requiebros*), Shostakovich (*Adagio*), Guidi (*Prière*), Bottesini (*2 Arias [from Bellini's Norma]; Elégie in D*), Popper (*Rhapsodie Hongroise, Op. 68*), Glazunov (*Sérénade Espagnole*), Fauré (*Elégie*), Mendelssohn, Rimsky-Korsakov, Massenet, others MGU ▲ 350507

Sanderling, Barbara (db)
Double Bass Rarities, w. Konrad Other (vn), Helmut Löchel (va), Rolf Döhler (vc/vl)—features works by Rossini (*Duet Vc Db*), Haydn, Couperin, Vanhal BER ▲ 9355 (10.97)

Scodanibbio, Stefano (db)
Voyage That Never Ends (*rec Modena, Italy, Nov 18-19, 1997*) NALB ▲ 101 (16.97)

Stoll, Klaus (db)
Virtuosity Contrabass—features works by Giovannino (*Son in F*), Handel (*Con Db in a*), Bottesini (*Elegia in D; Gavotta in G*), Shostakovich (*Romanze*), Koussevitzky (*Chanson triste, Op. 2 [all w. Keiko Ogura (pno)]*), Mozart (*Son Vc, K.292:Rondo*), Rossini (*Duo Vc Db:Allegro [both w. Jörg Baumann (vc)]*), Eccles (*Son in g [w. Noyuri Ariga (hpd)]*), Abel (*Son solo Db in D*) CAMA ▲ 2061 [DDD] (17.97)

Streicher, Ludwig (db)
Encores, w. Astrid Spitznagel (pno)—features works by Albéniz, Boccherini, Debussy, Glazunov, Granados, Ludwig Streicher, Eduardo Toldrá, Turina, Pedro Valls ORF ▲ 225911 [DDD] (18.97)

DULCIMER (& OTHER HAMMERED STRING INSTRUMENTS)

Duo Salterio
A Touch of Spring: Peaceful Poetic Music for Dulcimer & Guitar—features works by Bach, Fauré, Satie, Stravinsky, Tansman, Field, Schumann, Bartók, others CLSO ▲ 117

Koenig, Carole (ham dlc)
After Shadows: Classics for Quiet Moods—features works by Debussy, Ravel, Satie, et al.), w. harp, clarinet, violin, viola & flute Carole Koenig Music ▲ CCD 1007 [ADD] ▮ CC 1007 (CrO2)
Encore!: Renaissance & Baroque Music on the Hammered Dulcimer, w. gtr, fl, vn, va, kbd, perc—features works by Bach, Handel, et al. Carole Koenig Music ▲ CCD 1006 [ADD] ▮ CC 1006 (CrO2)
Gala: Classics from a Romantic Era (*instrumental classics of Victorian America*), w. vn, va, pno Carole Koenig Music ▲ CCD 1008 [ADD] ▮ CC 1008 (CrO2)
Palace Act: Baroque Music on the Hammered Dulcimer, w. vn, va, kbd, perc—features selections from symphonies by William Boyce Carole Koenig Music ▲ CCD 1003 [ADD] ▮ CC 1003 (CrO2)
Past Times Present: Medieval & Renaissance Music on the Hammered Dulcimer, w. vn, va, kbd, perc—features selections from Praetorius's Terpsichore dances; etc. Carole Koenig Music ▲ CCD 1004 [ADD] ▮ CC 1004 (CrO2)

Kolodner, Ken (ham dlc)
Walking Stones: A Celtic Sojourn, w. Laura Risk (fid), Robin Bullock (gtr/cittern) DOR ▲ 90248 (16.97)

Schickhaus, Karl-Heinz (ham dlc)
Piezas de Salterio: Spanish Dulcimer Music—features 3 sonatas & a divertimento from the anonymous 1754 manuscript *Piezas de Salterio* TUD ▲ 738 [DDD] (16.97)

Wilkinson (dlc)
Elizabethan Music for Dulcimer, w. Bruce Harrel (rcr), Saundra Nelson (vc), Frederick Road (lt), Cyntia Smith (dlc), Michael Stromberg (gtr)—features works by R. Johnson (*Hit and Take It Alman/Untitled Alman*), J. Johnson (*The Flatt Pavin*), Byrd (*Fortune My Foe; The Woods Soe Wylde; The Earle of Salisbury Pavan*), Dowland (*Goe from My Window; Untitled Air/Lady Hammond's Alman; Lesson for 2 Fls; Tarleton's Resurrection/The Parlement*), plus (*Lord Willoughby's Welcome Home; Bonnie Sweet Robin; Pakington's Pownde*) KM ▲ 3907 (15.97)

DULCIMER (& OTHER HAMMERED STRING INSTRUMENTS) COLLECTIONS

Sonatas for Dulcimer & Harpsichord—features works by P. Beretta, M. Chiesa, A. Conti, C. Monza *(see Composer section)* TUD ▲ 736 [DDD] (16.97)

EARLY MUSIC

A Capella Portugesa [cnd:Owen Rees]
Masters of the Royal Chapel, Lisbon, w. Stephen Farr (org)—features works by Carriera, Coelho, Guerrero, Alvarado, de Brito & de Magalhães HYP ▲ 66725 (17.97)
Music from Renaissance Coimbra—features works by de Cristo, Fernandez, Pirez, de Paiva, da Esperana, Rebelo HYP ▲ 66735 (17.97)
Academy of Ancient Music Orch [cnd:Christopher Hogwood]
Music from the Time of Elizabeth I PLOI ▲ 33193
Accademia del Ricercare [cnd:Pietro Busca]
Chenonceau: Music of the Court of Caterina de Medici—features 31 pavanes, galiards, branles & saltarellos STRV ▲ 33479 (16.97)
Accademia Monteverdiana Orch [cnd:Denis Stevens]
Music in Honor of St. Thomas of Canterbury Elektra/Nonesuch ▮ 71292-4
Accentus Ensemble [cnd:Thomas Wimmer]
Cancionero Musical de Palacio [Music of the Spanish Court]—features works by Anchieta *(Con amores, mi madre)*, Enzina *(Pues que jamás olvidaros; Si abrá en este baldrés; Levanta Pascual; Todos los bienes del mundo; Fata la parte; Pedro, i bien te quiero; Qu'es de ti, desconsolado?; Hoy comamos y bebamos)*, Alonso *(Tir'allá, que non quiero; La tricotea)*, Baena *(Todo quanto yo servi)*, Badajos *(Malos adalides fueron)*, Millán *(Durandarte)*, Torre *(Danza alta)*, Ponce *(Como está sola mi vida)*, Anonymous *(Rodrigo Martinez; Si d'amour pena sentis; Ay triste, que vengo; So ell enzina; O voy; Tres morillas m'enamoran) (rec Lutheran Stadtpfarrkirche A. B., Vienna, May 9-12, 1995)* NXIN (Early Music) ▲ 553536 [DDD] (5.97)
Sephardic Romances—features Avrix mi galancia; La Serena; Sa'dâwî; Partos trocados; Yo m'enamorai d'un aire/Las estrellas de los cielos; Si verias; A la nana; Omorfoula; El rey que muncho madruga; Páxaro d'hermozura; Esta montaña d'enfrente; Kavaldulka; Por la tu puerta yo pasi; Hija mia mi querida; Nani, nani; Ya viene el cativo; Rahelica baila *(rec W.A.R. Studio, Vienna, Sept 1995)* NXIN ▲ 8553617 [DDD] (5.97)
Sephardic Romances: Music of the Spanish Jews from 1500 PRE ▲ 90161 [DDD] (16.97)
Alba Musica Kyo Ensemble [cnd:Toyohiko Satoh]
Music of Shakespeare—features works by Morley, Byrd, Jones, Wilson, Johnson CCL ▲ 11497 (17.97)
Alegria Ensemble
Carmina Burana XII *(music from the 13th-century Codex burana)* PVY ▲ 791092 [DDD] (16.97)
Alia Musica [cnd:Miguel Sanchez]
Andalucia in Judeo-Spanish Music—features El Cautive del Renegado; Et Sa Are Rason; Dodi Yarad Legano; 9 other sels AL ▲ 111 (18.97)
Alla Francesca
Llibre Vermell de Montserrat—features In virgulto gracie; Tanto son da groriosa; A Madre de Jhesu-Cristo; Mui grandes noit'e dia; Casta catolica; O virgo splendens; Stella splendens in montre; Laudemus virginem; Los set goytx; Cuncti simus; Polorum regina; Inperayritz de la ciutat joyosa; Mariam matrem virginem; Inperayrita de la ciutat joyosa; Ad mortem festinamus OPUS ▲ 30131 (17.97)
Alla Francesca, Alta
Armes, Amours—features works by Andrieu, Binchois, Busnoy, Grimace, Morton OPUS ▲ 30221 (17.97)
Almquist, N. (sgr), John Arnold (sgr), T. Chancey, E. Bulkely (instr)
For Citizens & Peasants: Popular Tunes from Old Norwegian Music Books *(A Medieval Tapestry, Instrumental & Vocal Music from the 12th-14th Centuries)*—features works by Raimbaut de Vaqueras, Thibaut, Roi de Navarre, Moniot D'Arras, Jehannot de L'escurel, Hildegard von Bingen, Anon., Guillaume le Vinier FOLG ▲ BDCD 9003 [DDD]
Altramar Medieval Music Ensemble [Jann Cosart (vih/rebec), Angela Mariani (voc/hp/lira/perc), Chris Smith (vih/lt/oud/perc), David Stattelman (voc/perc)]
Crossroads of the Celts—features Anonymous *(A vous amours ains c'a nului; Adest dies leticie; Amra; Brigit bé bithmaith; Cristo canamus gloriam; Ecce fulget; May Song; O Columba insignis signifer; Stantipe Smarmore; The Lay of the Forge; Winter; Ysgolan)* DOR ▲ 93177 [DDD] (16.97)
Iberian Garden: Jewish, Christian & Muslim Music in Medieval Spain, Vol. 1, w. Timothy G. Johnson (shawm), Allison Zelles (voc/hp/perc)—features works by Levi Ibn al-Tabban *(Lababi ya ireni kaso el lasaharah)*, Yehuda ha-Levi *(Rase am et hitassef)*, Ibn Zuhr *(Ma li-l-muwallah)*, Berenguer de Palol *(Dona si totz temps vivia)*, Martim Codax *(Eno sagrado en Vigo)*, anon *(Dum pater familias [from Codex Calixtinus]; Rosa das Rosas [from Cantigas de Santa Maria]) (rec Church of the Immaculate Conception, St. Mary-of-the-Woods, IN, Dec 1994 & Nov 1995)* DORD ▲ 80151 [DDD] (13.97)
Iberian Garden: Jewish, Christian & Muslim Music in Medieval Spain, Vol. 2, w. Timothy G. Johnson (shawm), Allison Zelles (voc/hp/perc)—features works by Ibn Quzman *(Yâhni-kúm, Yahni-kum!)*, Abraham ibn Ezra' *('Ahalay yikkonu darakay)*, Al-Amâ or Ibn Baqi *(Adir la-na 'akwab)*, Altramar *(Ball de la Mort; Canción del Shofar)*, anon *(Plange Castella misera; La Afrenta de Corpes) (rec Church of the Immaculate Conception, St. Mary-of-the-Woods, IN Dec 1994 & Nov 1995)* DORD ▲ 80158 [DDD] (13.97)
Altramar Medieval Music Ensemble [Angela Mariani (hp/voc), Allison Zelles (sgr/voc), Jann Cosart (vielle/rebec), Chris Smith (gittern/oud), David Stattleman (perc/voc)]
St. Francis & the Minstrels of God—features Canticum creatorum; Fami cantar l'amor di la beata; Sia laudato San Francesco; Francesco; Cristo è nato; Saltarello Sancto Antonio; Laudar vollio per amore; Spirito sancto da servire *(rec St. Bridget's Catholic Church, Nolan Settlement, IA, Mar 1994)* DOR ▲ 80143 [DDD] (13.97)
Amaryllis Consort [cnd:Charles Brett]
English Madrigals, w. Robert Aldwinckle (hpd)—features Fyer! Fyer!; The King's Morisco; My Bonnie Lass; Sleep Fleshly Birth; Poor is the Life; The Silver Swan; A Ground; What is Our Life?; All Creatures Now; Hark! All Ye Lovely Saints Above; The Primrose; There is a Lady; Come Sable Night; Retire, My Troubled Soul; Fair Phyllis; Oyez! Has Anyone Found a Lad?; Though Amaryllis Dance in Green; The Earl of Salisbury [Pavan]; Come Away, Sweet Love; Weep, Weep Mine Eyes; Fain Would I Wed; Draw On, Sweet Night; Adieu, Sweet Amaryllis *(rec Apr 2-3, 1987)* ICC ▲ 6701752 (8.97)
Italian Madrigals—features works by Arcadelt, G. Caimo, P. de Monte, A. Gabrieli, G. Gastoldi, Gesualdo, Lassus, G. Mainerio, L. Marenzio, Monteverdi, M. Negri, O. Vecchi, G. Wert ICC ▲ 6702082 [DDD] (8.97)
American Brass Quintet [Raymond Mase (tpts/flgl), Chris Gekker (tpts/flgl), David Wakefield (hn), Michael Powell (trbns), John D. Rojak (b trbn)]
Fyre & Lightning: Consort Music of 1600—features works by Adson *(Masquing Ayre)*, Weelkes *(Strike it up Tabor)*, Morley *(Fyre & Lightning; Lady Those Eyes)*, Wilbye *(Sweet Honey Sucking Bees)*, Guami *(Canzon 19)*, Merulo *(Canzon 23)*, Gabrieli *(Ricercar del sesto tuono; Canzoni e Son.)*, Chilese *(Canzon 22)*, Monteverdi *(3 Madrigals; La Tral)*, Marenzio *(A mi tirsi)*, Vecchi *(Clorinda)*, Simpson *(Intrada; Galliard; Pavane)*, Brade *(Pavane; Galliard)*, Ward *(Fancy à 6)*, Holborne *(Fancy à 3)*, Coperario *(Fancy à 5)*, Giamberti *(Solfeggiamento)*, Coperario *(Fancy à 6)*, anon. *(A Toy; Strawberry Leaves) (rec Joan & Irving Harris Concert Hall, Aspen Music Festival, Aspen, CO, Aug 1994)* SUMM ▲ 181 [DDD] (16.97)
Amsterdam Loeki Stardust Quartet [Daniel Brüggen (rcr), Bertho Driever (rcr), Paul Leenhouts (rcr), Karel van Steenhoven (rcr)]
Consort Songs, w. Connor Burrowes (trb), David Miller (lt/gtr)—features works by Dowland *(Sorrow, Come [arr Wigthorpe]; Courant; Aria)*, Byrd *(Wretched Albinus; With Lilies White)*, Tallis *(When Shall My Sorrowful Sighing)*, Nicholson *(In a Merry May Morn)*, Simpson *(Male-Content; Paduan; Volta)*, Cobbold *(Ye Mortal Wights)*, Mando *(Like as the Day)*, Jenkins *(Fant VII)*, Ferrabosco II *(4-note Pavan)*, anon *(Complain with Tears; When May Is in His Prime; This Merry Pleasant Spring; How Can the Tree)* CCL ▲ 9196 (17.97)
Ancient Consort Singers [cnd:John Alexander], Ancient Instrumental Ensemble [cnd:Ron Purcell]
Spanish Renaissance Music from the Old & New World—features works by Gaspar Fernandes, Juan Guitierrez de Padilla, Antonio de Salazar, Fray Geronimo Gonzalez, Enriques de Valderrabano, Luys de Narvaez, Juan Ponce, Juan Vasquez, Pedro Rimonte, Anon. *(rec 1980)* ENTE ▲ 7 [ADD] (10.97)
Anonymous 4
A Lammas Ladymass—features 13th & 14th century English chant & polyphony HAM ▲ 907222 (17.97) ▮
Anonymous 4 [Ruth Cunningham (sgr), Marsha Genensky (sgr), Susan Hellauer (sgr), Johanna Rose (sgr)]
The Lily & the Lamb: Chant & Polyphony from Medieval England—features O gloriosa domina; Pe milde lomb isprad o rode; Ave Maria gracia plena; O Maria stella maris; Stabat iuxta Christi crucem; Stillat in stellam radium; Salve virgo singularis; Stond wel, moder, under roode; O Maria virgo pia; In te concipitur; Jesu Cristes milde moder; Veni mater gracie; Dou way, Robin; O mors moreris; O vita vera; Mors; Salve virgo tonantis solium; Miserere miseris; Ave Maria salus hominum; Memor esto tuorum; Ave regina coelorum HAM ▲ 907125 (17.97) ▮
Anonymous 4 (cont.)
Love's Illusion: Courtly Love Songs of Medieval France from the Montpellier Codex HAM ▲ 907109 (17.97) ▮
Miracles of Sant'Iago: Medieval Chant & Polyphony from the Codex Calixtinus HAM ▲ 2907156 (7.97)
Portrait *(sels from previous Harmonia Mundi releases)*—features Venite omnes cristicole; Ad superni regis decus; Portum in ultimo; O Maria stella maris; Stabat iuxta Christi crucem; Stillat in stellam radium; Primo tempore alleviata; Specious forma; Mi Atyánk Atya Isten; Puisque bele dame m'eime; Ne sai, que je die; Amor potest conqueri; Quant yver la bise ameine; On doit fin[e] amor; Edi beo thu hevene quene; Ave maris stella; Salve virgo virginum; Ther is no rose of swych virtu; Prolis eterne genitor; Ecce quod natura; Spiriti sancto HAM ▲ 2907210 (7.97)
Anonymus Ensemble [cnd:Claude Bernatchez]
Llibre Vermell: La Route des pèlerins de Montserrat *(14th cent pilgrimage songs & dances from Catalonia)*—features O virgo splendes (fanfare); Improvisation sur Ad Mortem festinamus Stella splendens; Imperaytrita de la ciutat joyosa; Laudemus Viginenem; Splendens ceptigera; Danse en rond; Los set goyts; Cuncti simus concanentes; Improvisations sur Los set goyts:Polorum regina; Splendens ceptigera:Mariam matrem viginem; Laudemus virginem:Imperaytritz de la ciutat joyosa; Stella splendens:Ad mortem festinamus/Danse macabre; O virgo splendes (fanfare) *(rec Nov 1993)* ANAL ▲ 28001
Rue des jugleors: Instrumental & Vocal Music from the 12th to 14th Centuries—features Danse; Istanpitta Chominciamento di gioia; On parole/A Paris/Frese nouvele; La uitime estampie real; Sire Cuens, j'ai vielé; Istanpitta Isabella; La Seconde estampie roial; Retrove; Souvent souspire; Stantipes; Retrove Petrone; Homo quo vigeas vide/Et gaudebit; Improvisation; Curritur ad vocem; Procurans odium; Dic Christi veritas; Bella fulminante; Tempus est iocundum *(rec Eglise Saint-Dominique, Quebec, Nov 1993)* FL (Fleur de Lys) ▲ 23056 [DDD] (12.97)
Ars Italica
Music from 15th Century Italy TACT ▲ 400201 (16.97)
Augsburg Early Music Ensemble
Hildegard von Bingen & Her Time: Sacred Music of the 12th Century—features works by von Bingen, Abaelardus, Anon. CHR ▲ 74584 [DDD] (17.97)
Loves & Desires: Songs of the Trouvères—features works by D'Arras, Nesle, Bodel, Muset, Erart, Champagne, et al. *(rec Dec 1991)* CHR ▲ 77117 [DDD] (17.97)
Mysterium Mariae—features Marian songs of the late Middle Ages *(Wer ist die da durchleuchtet; Ave mater o Maria; Miadleich pluem; Mutato modo geniture; Maria keusche muter zart; Ave gloriosa mater salvatoris; Stella maris illustrans omnia; Salve regina; Maria pis gegrüsset; Imperayritz da la ciutat joyosa; Polorum regina; Ave pulcherrima regina; O Maria rogatrix)* CHR ▲ 77188 [DDD] (17.97)
Troubadours, Trouvères & Minnesingers *(songs & dances of the Middle Ages)* CHR ▲ 74519 (17.97)
Aurora Ensemble [cnd:Enrico Gatti]
Music in the Time of Guido Reni—features works by Frescobaldi, Palestrina, Marini, de Selma, de Rore, Castello, Rossi, Montalbano & Pesenti TACT ▲ 560001 (16.97)
Azéma, Anne (sop), Cheryl Ann Fulton (hps), Shira Kammen (rebec/vielle/hp), Jesse Lepkoff (fl)
The Unicorn: Myth & Mystery in Medieval France (1200-1300) ERAT ▲ 94830 [DDD] (16.97)
Azéma, Anne (sop), Ellen Hargis (sop), Henri Ledroit (ct), William Hite (ten), Richard Morrison (bass), Andrea von Ramm (sgr), Boston Camerata [cnd:Joel Cohen]
Tristan et Iseult: A Medieval Romance in Music & Poetry ERAT ▲ 98482 (9.97)
Baird, Julianne (sop), Ronn McFarlane (lt)
The English Lute Song—features works by Anon., T. Brewer, Campion, Ferrabosco, R. Johnson, N. Lanier, Morley, W. Webb, J. Wilson; plus lute solos by Anon., Johnson DOR ▲ 90109 [DDD] (16.97)
The Italian Lute Song—features works by Monteverdi *(Laudate Dominum; Maledetto; Eri già tutta mia; Si dolce è'l tormento)*, Frescobaldi *(Se l'aura spira; Così mi disprezzate; Dunque dovrò)*, Negri *(Bianco Fiore; Bizziaria d'Amore; Cesarino; Bassa delle Ninse; Pavaniglia; Brando Gentile)*, Biabo *(Fuggi, fuggi, fuggi)*, Bossinensi *(Ricercar)*, Cara *(Non è tempo)*, Josquin des Prez *(In te domine speravi)*, Tromboncino *(Ostinato vo' seguire)*, Borrono *(Pavana chiamata la Milanesa; Saltarello; Saltarello chiamato Rose Viole; Saltarello chiamato bel Fiore; Tochata da sonare nel fine del ballo)*, Caccini *(Amarilli mia bella; Dolcissimo sospiro; Belle rose porporine)*, anon *(O bella più)*, Kapsberger *(Toccata 5; Gagliarda 10; Corrente 7)*, Gagliano *(Bontà del Ciel eterna; Pastor, levate Sù)*, Carissimi *(Apritevi inferni) (rec Troy Savings Bank Music Hall, Troy, NY, Oct 1995 & Feb 1996)* DOR ▲ 90236 [DDD] (16.97)
Baltimore Consort [Custer LaRue (sop), Chris Norman (wooden fl/bgp), Ronn McFarlane (lt), Mark Cudek (cittern/t vl/b vl), Mary Anne Ballard (trb vl), Larry Lipkis (b vl/rcr)], Merry Companions
The Art of the Bawdy Song *(Elizabethan songs with explicit texts about sex and/or drinking)*—features works by Aldridge, Anonymous, Blow, Church, Cranford, D'Urfey, Eccles, Ellis, Isum, Jones, Purcell, Weelkes *(rec Oct 1990)* DOR ▲ 90155 [DDD] (11.97) ▮ 90155 (13.98)
Baltimore Consort [Custer LaRue (sop), Chris Norman (fl), Mary Anne Ballard (vl), Mark Cudek (cittern/vl), Larry Lipkis (vl/rcr), Ronn McFarlane (lt)]
The Ladyes Delight: Entertainment Music of Elizabethan England, w. William Simms (bandora)—features works by Reade *(A Jigge ye Firste)*, Johnson *(Chi Passa)*, Ravenscroft *(Yonder Comes a Curteous Knight)*, Allison *(The Batchelars Delight)*, Marston *(The Darke is my Delight [from The Dutch Courtesan])*, Bachiler *(The Widdowes Mite)*, Holmes *(Robin is to the Greenwood Gone; Ye French Volta)*, Conversi *(Sola Soletta [from Consort Lessons])*, Byrd *(My Lord of Oxenfords Maske)*, anon *(Lavolto; La Coronto; The Lord Souches Maske; O Mistris Mine [all from Consort Lessons]; The Shaking of the Sheets [from The English Dancing Master]; The Queen's Treble [from Jane Pickering Lute Book]; The Knot [from The Dancing Master]; Light o'Love [from New Lessons for the Cittern]; The Ladyes Delight; Jumpe at my Cozen; Howells Delight; Balow, My Babe] (rec Troy Savings Bank Music Hall, Troy, NY, Apr-May & Dec 1997)* DOR ▲ 90252 [DDD] (16.97)
On the Banks of Helicon: Early Music of Scotland DOR ▲ 90139 [DDD] (11.97) 90139 (13.98)
La Rocque 'n' Roll: Popular Music of Renaissance France—features works by Adrian Le Roy, Praetorius, Jehan Chardavoine, Giovanni Bassano, Pierre Phalèse, Jehan Planson, Loys Bourgeois, Strassbourg Psalter, Thomas Champion, Claude Goudimel, Pierre Attaingnant, Claudin De Sermisy, Pierre Certon, Robert Ballard, Daniel Bachelar, Eustach du Caurroy, Jacques Mangeant DOR ▲ 90177 [DDD] (16.97)
A Trip to Killburn: Playford Tunes & Their Ballads—features All in a Garden Green; Parsons Farewell; Beggar Boy; John Come Kiss Me Now; Newcastle; The French Report; The Mulberry Garden; A Scots Rant; A Trip to Killburn; The Broom of Cowdenknows; The Joviall Broome Man; Lull Me Beyond Thee; An Italian Rant; The Famous Ratcatcher; Jenny Pluck Pears; Bobbing Joe; Merry, Merry Milkmaids; The Beautiful Shepherdess of Arcadia *(rec Troy Savings Bank Music Hall, Troy, NY, Jan 1996)* DOR ▲ 90238 [DDD] (11.97) 90238 (13.98)
Tunes from the Attic—features works by Morley *(Joyne Hands)*, Akeroyde *(Jenny, My Blithest Maid)*, Playford *(Johnny Cock Thy Beaver [from The Division Vn]; The Northern Lasse's Lamentation [from The English Dancing Master]; Well Hall [from Dancing Master])*, Wode *(Pavan; Come Love, Let's Walk [from Thomas Wode's Partbooks])*, Nicholson *(The Jewes Dawnce)*, Johnson *(Green Garters)*, Purcell *(Oh! How Happy's He [from Dioclesian])*, Ballet *(Callino [from William Ballet's MS Lt Book])*, Stirling *(Joy to the Person of My Love [from William Stirling's Cantus Partbook])*, anon *(You Lasses & Lads [from Wit & Mirth, or Pills to Purge Melancholy]; Galliard [Dublin Vir]; The Mermaid's Song; The Old Maid of the Dust Mill; The Irish Ho-Hoane; The Irishe Dumpe [both Fitzwilliam Virs]) (rec Troy Savings Bank Music Hall, Troy, NY, Oct 1995 & June 1996)* DOR ▲ 90235 [DDD] (16.97)
Watkins Ale: Music of the English Renaissance DOR ▲ 90142 [DDD] (16.97)
La Bande des Hautbois du Roi [cnd:Paolo Tognon]
Ceremonial Court Music in the XVII & XVIII Centuries—features works by J. B. Lully, Krieger, L. Lully, J. C. Pez & Philidor NUO (Ancient Music) ▲ NUO 7286
Banditelli, Gloria (cta), Tiziano Bagnati (thb), Massimo Lonardi (baroque gtr), Flavio Bonizzoni (hpd)
Arie e Lamenti—features works by d'India *(Voi ch'ascoltate; Intenerite voi; Lamento d'Olimpia; Apertamente dice la gente; Piangono al pianger mio; Da l'onde del mio pianto; Donna lo vorrei dir molto; Tu parti, ahi lasso; Piange Madonna; La tra le selve; Misera non credea; Ma che? Squallido e oscuro; O che gradita; Infelice didone; Torna il sereno zefiro)*, Kapsberger *(Preludi e Canzona prima)*, Frescobaldi *(Balletto, corrente e passacagli) (rec Nov 1995)* STRV ▲ 33419 [DDD] (16.97)
Barcelona Ars Musica [cnd:Enric Gispert]
Le Moyen Age Catalan HMA ▲ 190051 (9.97)
Basel Madrigalists [cnd:Fritz Näf], Basel Ensemble Galliarda
Gesellige Zeit: German Songs, Madrigals & Instrumental Music from the 16th & 17th Centuries—features works by Senfl *(Mit Lust tritt ich an diesen Tanz; Mir ist ein rot Goldringelein; Unsäglich Schmerz)*, Melchior Franck *(Kommt, ihr G'spielen; Galliarada à 5)*, Hassler *(Feinslieb, du hast mich g'fangen; Septima Intrada; Nun fanget an ein guts Liedlein zu singen; Tertia Intrada à 6; Quarta Intrada à 6)*, Lechner *(Ein edler Jäger wohlgemut; Gott b'hüte dich—Ritornell)*, von Bruck *(So trinken wir alle)*, Zirler *(Die Sonn, die ist verblichen)*, Hausmann *(Paduan à 6; Galliarada à 6)*, Isaac *(Tmeiskin uas iunch; Zwischen Berg und tiefem Tal; Der Welte Fundt)*, Hofhaimer *(Meins Traurens ist)*, Lichtlein *(Cappricio à 6)*, Demantius *(Tanz à 5)*, Eccard *(Fröhlich will ich singen)*, anon. *(Ich sag ade) (rec Reformed Church, CH-Arlesheim, Feb 13-15, 1987)* MPH ▲ 56803 (14.97)
Becker, Peter (bar)
Songs of the Troubadours & Trouvères, w. Robert Eisenstein (medieval fid)—12th-13th century songs featuring works by Marcabru *(Pax in nomine Domini!)*, Bernart de Ventadorn *(Non es meravelha s'eu chan)*, Vidal *(Anc no mori per amor ni per al)*, Miraval *(Bel m'es q'ieu chant e coindei)*, Riquier *(Pus asters no m'es donatz)*, Chatelain de Coucy *(La douce voiz du rosignol sauvage)*, Guiot de Dijon *(Chanterai por mon corage)*, Vinier/Champagne *(Sire, ne me celez mie)*, Champagne *(J'aloie l'autrier errant)*, Erart *(Nus chanters mais le mein cuer ne leeche)*, plus anon pieces *(A l'entrade del tens clar; Pensis, chief enclin; Estampies (2); Bein m'ont Amours entrepris) (rec Mt. Holyoke College, May 1995) ([F,E] texts)* FOLG ▲ 9711 [DDD] (16.97)

▲ = CD ♦ = Enhanced CD △ = MD ▮ = Cassette Tape ▯ = DCC

Bellini, Mikael (alt), Lennart Löwgren (ct), Carl Unander-Scharin (ten), Lars Arvidson (bass), Sven-Anders Benktsson (bass), Sven Aberg (lt), Hortus Musicus, Tallinn [cnd:Andres Mustonen]
The Royal Court of the Vasa Kings, 1523-1611 *(music from the Swedish court)* MSV ▲ 202 [DDD] (16.97)

Martin Best Consort
Amor de Lonh: The Distant Love of Troubadors—features works by Guiraut de Bornelh *(Sius quer conselh, bel ami Alamanda; Canso melody)*, Perotin *(Beata Viscera)*, Jaufre Rudel de Blaye *(Can lo rossinhols el folhos; Can lo rius de la fontana)*, St. Yrieux Gradual *(O Maria lesse Virga)*, Bernart de Ventadorn *(Ab joi mou lo vers el comens; Tant ai mo cor ple de joya; Can par la flors jostal vert folh)*, Cluny *(Venit dilectus)*, Hermanus Contractus *(Alma redemptoris mater)*, St. Maur-les-Fosses *(Paradisi porta)*, Montier-la-Celle *(Anima mea liquefacta est)*, anon *(2 Saltarellos; Danse Royale; Ductia; Lamento di Tristan; Rotta) (rec Nimbus Foundation Concert Hall, July 15-17, 1996)* NIMB ▲ 5544 [DDD] (16.97)

Martin Best Mediaeval Ensemble [cnd:Martin Best]
Cantigas of Santa Maria of Alfonso X *(13th-cent. Spanish songs in praise of the Virgin)* NIMB ▲ 5081 [DDD] (16.97)
Dante Troubadours—features works by Guiraut de Bornelh, Bertran de Born, Arnaut Daniel, Bernart de Ventadorn, Piere Vidal, et al. NIMB ▲ 5002 (16.97)
Forgotten Provence: Music-Making in the South of France, 1150-1550 NIMB ▲ 5445 (16.97)
The Last of the Troubadours: The Art & Times of Guiraut Riquier, 1230-1292 NIMB ▲ 5261 [ADD] (16.97)
Songs of Chivalry—features works by Guilhelm IX, Huon D'oisy, Thibaut de Navarre, Marcabru, Blondel de Nesle, Moniot d'Arras, Bernart de Ventadorn, etc. NIMB ▲ 5006 (16.97)

Bimbetta [Andrea Fullington (sop), Sonja Rasmussen (sop), Allison Zeles (sop), Shelley Taylor (vc), Katherine Shao (hpd)]
War of Love—features works by d'India *(Alla guerra d'amore)*, Purcell *(What Can We Poor Females Do?; No, Resistance is but Vain; From Rosy Bowers; Ah! How Pleasant 'tis to Love; O Let Me Weep!)*, Monteverdi *(Occhi miei; Non voglio amare; Zefiro torna)*, Strozzi *(Begli occhi)*, Frescobaldi *(Toccata terza)*, Gabrielli *(Ricercar V)*, Amos *(Leather)*, Peri *(Tu dormi)*, Lanier *(Though I Am Young) (rec Pony Tracks Ranch, Portola Valley, CA, Nov 1995)* DNC ▲ 1023 [DDD] (16.97)

Gilles Binchois Ensemble [cnd:Dominique Vellard]
Music & Poetry at Saint-Gall: 9th Century Sequences & Tropes HAM ▲ 905239 (17.97)

Bob, Frank & Zussen
A Ricolta Bubu: Medieval & Renaissance Music—features works by Laurentius de Florentina *(A ricolta bubu)*, Dowland *(Fine Knacks for Ladies; Mrs. Nichols Alamand)*, Gervaise *(A Paris)*, Stefani *(I senti' matutino)*, Foster *(Hard Times)*, Juan del Encina *(Ay triste que vengo!)*, Gardani *(Salttarello del Re)*, Isaac *(Innsbruck, ich muss dich lassen)*, Claessens *(My Papa's Waltz; Balamando)*, plus trad/anon pieces *(Cancion Nina y vina; Brasilia; Hadju; Cil s'entrement; When a Knight; Las morillas de Jaen) (rec Studio The Grove, Schelle, 1997)* PAVA ▲ 7391 [DDD] (10.97)

Les Boréades Montréal
Private Musick: English Chamber Music in the Time of the Stuarts ATMM ▲ 22132 (14.97)

Boston Baroque Orch [cnd:Martin Pearlman], Boston Baroque Chorus
Lost Music of Early America: Music of the Moravians, w. Cyndia Sieden (sop), Sharon Baker (sop)—features works by Peter *(Der Herr ist mein Theil; Es ist ein köstlich Ding; Ich will immer harren; Ich danke Dir ewiglich; Ich will dir ein Freudenopfer)*, Dencke *(Meine Seele erhebet den Herrn; Gesegnet bist du, sein Volk; Mein Herz dichet ein feines Lied)*, Michael *(Hail Infant Newborn)*, Antes *(Loveliest Immanuel)*, Peter *(Ich will euch wie ein Thau seyn; Siehe meine Knechte)*, Schulz *(Thou Child Divine)*, Kellner *(Ach Schönster [arr Gregor])*, Herbst *(Suchet sein Antlitz; Ich gehe einher in der Kraft des Herrn)*, Gambold *(Die mit Thränen säen; Rondo for Pno)*, Geisler *(O lieblicher Heiland, du mein Versöhner; Die Frucht des Geistes ist Liebe)*, Gregor *(Das ist ein Tag)*, Müller *(O Sing, all ye Redeemed)*, anon hymns *(Freuen wir uns; Join We All with One Accord; Zeige mir dein Angesicht; Heiliger Herre Gott; Lob Gott getrost mir Singen; Herz und Herz vereint zusammen; Kommt, danket dem Helden; Sing Hallelujah; Herr und Ältster deiner Kreuzgemeine; Jesus Makes My Heart Rejoice) (rec Mechanics Hall, Worchester, MA, Nov 3-4, 1997)* TEL 2-▲ 80482 [DDD] (15.97)

Boston Camerata [cnd:Joel Cohen]
The American Vocalist: Spirituals & Folk Hymns, 1850-1870 ERAT ▲ 45818 (16.97) ▮ 45818
Angels: Voices from Eternity, w. Tod Machover (syn)—features music from diverse eras & cultures on theme of angels ERAT ▲ 14773 (16.97)
Carmina Burana—features medieval songs from the Benediktbeuren manuscript (ca 1230) [not Orff's version] *(rec Weston, MA, June 28-July 3, 1996)* ERAT ▲ 14987 (16.97)
New Britain: The Roots of American Folksong—features music of French, German and Scottish immigrants; wandering songs and ballads of early New England; music of the Sacred Harp tradition; and popular folk standards ERAT ▲ 45474 [DDD] (16.97)
Nueva España: Close Encounters in the New World (1590-1690) *(Latin American spirituals and instrumental dances)*, w. Boston Shawn and Sackbut Ensemble, Women's Choir of the Church Les Amis de la Sagesse, Schola Cantorum of Boston—features works by Azéma, Hanchard, Ragin, Duguay, McCabe ERAT ▲ 45977 (16.97) 45977
The Sacred Bridge *(Jewish and Christian liturgical music of medieval Europe)* ERAT ▲ 45513 [DDD] (16.97)
Sing We Noël: Christmas Music From England & Early America 75597 ▲ 71354
Tristan & Iseult *(a medieval romance in music and poetry)* ELEC ▲ 45348

Boston Camerata [cnd:Joel Cohen], Schola Cantorum of Boston [cnd:Frederick Jodry]
Lamentations—features works by Bouzignac *(Heu! Unus ex vobis me tradet hodie; Ha! Plange)*, La Ceppede *(Mais qui vous meut, Seigneur)*, Genet dit Carpentras *(Vexilla regis)*, Gilles *(1st Lamentations [3] for Mercredy Saint au Soir, Jeudy Saint au Soir & Vendredy Saint au Soir)*, Vitré *(Comme Trois Forgerons)*, Godolin *(Sur l'Albre de la Crotz)*, trad. *(Ne avertas faciem tuam) (rec Campion Center, Boston, Apr 1994)* 70633 ▲ 98480 [DDD]

Bott, Catherine (sop)
Sweet Is The Song—features unaccompanied songs from the 12th & 13th cent PLOI ▲ 448999 (16.97)

Bott, Catherine (sop), Philip Pickett & Friends
Alchemist—features works by Monteverdi *(Introit & Hymn [from Vespers of 1610]; Orfeo)*, Du Prez *(Bacchanalia; Celtic Dawn; Adoremus Dominum)*, Ortiz *(Renaissance Rip)*, Mainerio *(Balkan Trilogy; Dodo Brasserie Sextet; Ruff Music)*, Daman *(Harmony of the Spheres)*, Le Jeune *(Pandora's Music Box)*, anon *(The King Is Dead)* LINN ▲ 31 (16.97)

Julian Bream Consort
Fantasies, Ayres & Dances: Elizabethan & Jacobean Consort Music RCAV (Red Seal) ▲ 7801 [DDD] (16.97) 7801

Broadside Band [cnd:Jeremy Barlow]
Il Ballarino *(Italian Dances, ca. 1600)*—features music from four Italian dance treatises of the late 16th-early 17th cents. by Fabritio Caroso, Cesare Negri & Livio Lupi da Caravaggio HYP ▲ 66244 [DDD] (17.97)
Danses populaires françaises *(from Arbeau's "Orchésographie", 1588)* HAM ▲ 901152
English Country Dances *(22 country dance tunes selected from the 1st-12th editions of John Playford's Dancing Master, 1651-1703, arranged by Jeremy Barlow for various instrumental combinations of recorder, flute, hurdy-gurdy, violin, viols, lute, dulcimer, harpsichord, regal, etc.)* SAY ▲ 393 [DDD] (16.97)
John Playford's Popular Tunes *(17th cent. English airs & dances)* AMON ▲ 28 (16.97)
Popular Tunes in 17th Century England—features Hyde Park; Maiden Lane; Gray's Inn; Cuckolds all in a row; Merry milkmaids we; etc. HMA ▲ 1901039 (9.97)

Calliope [Lucy Bardo (vl), Lawrence Benz (trbn), Allan Dean (tpt), Frederic Hand (gtr), Ben Harms (perc)]
Calliope Dances: A Renaissance Revel 75597 ▲ 79039 [DDD] ▮ 79039-4 (D)
Calliope: Diversions—features twenty 14th-16th cent. instrumental works by Binchois, Cabezon, Dowland, Dufay, Susato, et al. SUMM ▲ 112 [DDD] (16.97) ▮
Calliope Festival: An Italian Renaissance Revel Elektra/Nonesuch ▮ 79069-4 (D)

La Camerata de Paris [Elena Polonska (hps/perc), John McLean (fls/guimbarde/psaltery/perc), Isabelle Quellier (vls/rebec/fl/perc), Radmille (gtr/voc)]
Sur le chemin de Compostelle—music from pilgrims' treks to Compostelle in the Middle Ages featuring O ciego adante; Muineira de Paya; A vida; Cande Alario; Muineira de Pontevedra; Durme, durme; El alma; Pasacalla marcha; Paso doble de los gigantes; Alalà I-III; Danze de los palilos; Gerineldo; Canto procesional; Muito devemos; Accorrer; Maravilosos; Virgen Gloriosa AB ▲ 291822 (13.97)

Camerata Mediterranea [cnd:Joel Cohen]
Lo Gai Saber: Troubadours and Minstrels, 1100-1300, w. Anne Azéma (sop), François Harismendy (voc), Jean-Luc Madier (voc), Cheryl Ann Fulton (hp), Jöel Cohen (instr), Shira Kammen (instr)—features works by Peire Vidal, Gaucelm Faidit, Sordello di Mantova, Bertrand de Born, Comtessa de Dia, Raimon d'Avignon, et al. ERAT ▲ 45647 [DDD] (16.97)

Canadian Brass [Fred Mills (tpt), Ronald Romm (tpt), David Ohanian (hn), Eugene Watts (trbn), Charles Daellenbach (tuba)]
The Canadian Brass Go for Baroque!—features Air pour les trompettes; Tpt Voluntary; Kanon; Fant. in C; We Hasten with Eager Footsteps; Fant. & Fugue in d; My Heart Ever Faithful; Tocatta & Fugue in d; Fugue in g; Tpt Voluntary; Contrapunctus I; Tpt Tune & Ayre; Galliard Battaglia; Canzon Aechiopican; Son in 3 Movts for Tpts; Where'er You Walk; Hallelujah, Amen; Madrigal RCAV ▲ 68107 (10.97) ▮ 68107 (6.98)
Renaissance Men—features Renaissance Suite; Canzon Septimi toni a 8; Pezel Brass Dance; Royal Fanfare; 2 Dances; Canzon; Tudor Suite; Intrada; Revecy Venir du Printans; Hodie, Christus natus est; 3 Elizabethan Madrigals; Hosanna to the Son of God; Hosanna; Canzona Prima a 5; 7 Renaissance Dances; Canzona per Sonare II; Ave maris stella; Orfeo Fanfare RCAV ▲ 68108 (10.97) ▮ 68108 (6.98)

Cantilena Antiqua Ensemble [cnd:Stefano Albarello]
Canticum Canticorum [The Song of Songs]: The Sacred Symbol of Love in Medieval Musical Tradition—features love songs from the 12-13th centuries SYM ▲ 95135 (18.97)
Ondas do Mar: Love Songs from the Mediterranean in the 13th Century SYM ▲ 98157 (18.97)

Cantus Cologne [cnd:Konrad Junghänel]
Il Pastor Fido—features 17th cent. madrigal settings by various composers to texts from G. Battista Guarini's pastoral tragicomedy "Il pastor fido" DEHA ▲ 77240

Capella Alamire [cnd:Peter Urquhart]
Motets, 1450-1550—features works by Franco-Flemish composers Antoine Busnoys, Nicolas Gombert, Josquin Des Prez TIT ▲ 202

Capella Antiqua Munich
Voices of the Middle Ages [G,I,L] *(rec Sept 1967)* Elektra/Nonesuch ▮ 71171-4

Capella Rudolphina [cnd:Petr Daněk], Duodena Cantitans
Felix Austriae Domus: Music in the 16th Cent Habsburg Empires—features works by Handl-Gallus *(Missa quinque vocum super Adesto dolori meo; Resonet in laudibus)*, Clemens non Papa *(Adesto dolori meo)*, Flecha *(Di di in di vo cangiando; El fuego)*, Orologio *(Ahimè partito e'l mio bel; Tutta vezzosa e bella; O fortunata milla)*, Melli *(Capriccio detto il gran Matias)*, Willaert *(Haud aliter pugnans)*, Gombert *(Felix Austriae domus)*, Lobo *(Versa est in luctum)*, Gastoldi & Lerchenfels *(Victoriosi duces, concelebrate luces)*, anon *(Dass Klaglied von dem volzognen Urthel und Sententz wider die Rebellen ihro Kays. Mtt. Ferdinandi II) (rec Prayer Hall, Korunni Street, Prague, Jan 9-12, 1997)* SUR ▲ 3326 [DDD]

Capilla Flamenca
Renaissance-polyfonie in Brugge: The Songbook of Zeghere van Male EUFO ▲ EUF 1155 [DDD]

Cappella Figuralis [cnd:Jos van Veldhoven], Netherlands Bach Society
Saints & Sinners:Latin Musical Dialogues from the 17th Century CCL ▲ 12498 (17.97)

Cappella Nova [cnd:Alan Tavener]
The Miracles of St. Kentigern: Scottish Medieval Plainchant—features music from the 1st Vespers, Matins & 2nd Vespers for the feast of St. Kentigern ASV ▲ 169 (16.97)

Cappella Pietà de Turchini
A Neapolitan Vespers of the Blessed Virgin Mary, 1632 not advised of composers or selections SYM ▲ 4 [DDD]

Capriccio Stravagante [cnd:Skip Sempé]
Capriccio Stravagante—features works by Monteverdi, Farina, Mussi, Verso, Zanetti DEHA ▲ 77190
Monteverdi & His Time, w. Guillemette Laurens (mez)—features works by Castello, Frescobaldi, Malvezzi, Marini, Merula, Monteverdi, Riccio DEHA ▲ 05472-77200-2 [DDD]

Carrier, James (shm/rcrs/oud/hp/gemshn), Hazel Ketchum (sgr/saz-lt/perc), J. Holenko (oud/chitarra/psaltery/saz-lt/perc), Will Mason (saz-lt/chitarra/vih/ham dlc/perc)
Sonus Chanterai: Music of Medieval France—features Penser ne doit vilenie; Gaite de la tor; Chanterai pour mon coraige; Quan je voy le duc; Non es meravelha s'eu chan; Souvent souspire; Quant je suis; Je puis trop bien; De bonté, de valour; Ma fin est ma commencement; Gaite de la tor; Reis glorios; Estampie real *(rec St. John's Episcopal Church, Columbia, MD, Sept 1993)* DOR ▲ 80123 [DDD] (13.97)

Chance, Michael (ct), David Cordier (ct), Tragicomedia
A Musicall Dreame *(see Composer section under Robert Jones)* HYP ▲ 66335 [DDD]

Charivari Agréable
Chamber Music for the King—features works by Couperin, D'Hervelois, Forqueray & Siret ASV ▲ 159 (16.97)

Chiaroscuro Ensemble [cnd:Nigel Rogers]
Chiaroscuro Ensemble—features works by Dufay *(Missa "Se la face ay pale" and 3 chansons)*, Isaac *(Ich stunden einem Morgen)*, Lassus *(Salmi penitenziali No. 1, "Domine, ne in furore tuo" & No. 6, "De Profundis")*, Senfl *(Ich stund en einem Morgen, 2 versions)* NUO ▲ NUO 6741 [DDD]

Christensen, Agnethe (alt)
Alba: Songs of Longing & Lustful Tunes, w. Poul Høxbro (pipe/perc)—music from medieval Spain & France featuring Reis glorios; La seconde Estampie Royal; Cantigas de Amigo; La quinte Estampie Royal; La septieme Estampie Royal; La tierche Estampie Royal; La seste Estampie Royal; La ultime Estampie Royal; La quarte Estampie Royal; Virgen Madre CLSO ▲ 170 (14.97)

I Ciarlatani
Codex Manesse: The Great Heidelberg Song Manuscript—features works by Horheim *(Nv enbeis ich doch des frankes nie)*, Ventadorn *(Can l'erba fresch)*, Aist *(Der winter were mir ein zit)*, Rugge *(Habe ich friunt die wünschen ir)*, Vaqueiras *(Kalenda maia)*, Steinach *(Er fvnde gvoten kovf an minen laren)*, Vidal *(Baros de mon dan covit)*, Vogelweide *(Alrerst lebe ich mir werde)*, Hausen *(Min herze vnde min lip die wellent scheiden)*, Tanhuser *(Steter dienest der ist gvot; Ich lobe ein wib)*, Wimpfener Fragmente *(Ave gloriosa)*, Der Wilde Alexander *(Owe daz nach liebe ergat)*, Borneill *(Reis glorios)*, Peirol *(D'eisa la razon)*, Reuental *(Owe dirre not; Ich het an si gewendet; So blossen wir den anger nie gesahen)*, Cantigas de Santa Maria *(Razon an os diabos; Como poden per sas culpas)*, anon. *(A l'entrada del tens clar; Drei Instrumentalstücke)* CHR ▲ 77192 [DDD] (17.97)
Fly Cheerful Voices *(music composed & performed for the marriage of Psalzgraf Friedrich V & Elizabeth Stuart, 1613)*—features works by Dowland, Coperario, R. Johnson, Byrd, Campion, plus others CHR ▲ 77214 (17.97)
O Maria, Maris Stella—features 13th century motets from the Wimpfen Fragments CHR ▲ 77215 (17.97)
Renaissance Music at the Court in Heidelberg—features Gen haidelwerg rait ich; Ich michel beham/Drakul; Tandernaken; Wer gnad durch klaff; Maria zart; Pete quid vis; Ascendo ad patrem meum; Die sonn die ist verblichen; Ein gutes nerrisch tentzlein; Der gutzgauch auff dem zaune sass; Der heylig herr sant Matheis; Wem wöl wir disen rebner bringen; La bona nocte; Fraw ich bin euch von hertzen hold; Die aller holdtseligst auff erden; Es hett ein bidermann ein weib; La gambetta; Herr Gott du lieber Vatter mein; Ich stieg, ich stieg; Pauan XXI/Galliard XXII; Volta; Hertzlich thut mich erfrewen; Pavana del povero soldato; So wünsch ich ir ein gute Nacht; Courant; The 1st of the Lords'; Wooe Her & Win Her; The Queenes Command; Mascarada; Che fera fed al cielo; The Maypole CHR ▲ 77184 [DDD] (17.97)

Circa 1500 Ensemble
The Flower of All Ships: Tudor Court Music from the Time of the Mary Rose [E,F] CRD ▲ 3448 [DDD] (17.97)

Circa 1500 Ensemble [cnd:Nancy Hadden]
A Handefull of Pleasant Delites, w. Mhairi Lawson (sop), Nancy Hadden (fl)—features In a Garden so Greene; The Frog Galliard; All in a Garden Grene; What Mightie Motion; Passymeasures & the Lady; Greensleeves; plus others ASV ▲ 163 (16.97)
Music from the Spanish Kingdoms *(30 15th/16th-cent instrumental/vocal works)*—features works by Marchetto Cara, Juan del Encina, Alonso Hernandez, Josquin Des Prez, Adrian Willaert, Anon., et al. CRD ▲ 3447 [DDD] (17.97)
Renaissance Music from the Courts of Mantua & Ferrara—features works by M. Cara, Diomedes, E. Romano, F. Spinacino, B. Tromboncino [I] CHN (Chaconne) ▲ 524 [DDD] (16.97)

Circa 1500 Ensemble [cnd:Nancy Hadden], Redbyrd
New Fashions: Cries & Ballads of London *(21 E.an and Jacobean ballads and rounds)*—features works by T. Ravenscroft *(New oysters; Three blind mice; Three country dances in one; Well fare the nightingale; Come follow me; Browning)*, John Dowland *(Fine knacks for ladies)*, A. Holborne *(The voyce of the ghost)*, Clement Woodcock *(Browning my dear)*, C. Tye *(In nomine Crye)*, T. Weelkes *(Cries of London)*, T. Ford *(Cate of Brady)*, Anon. *(Nutmegs and ginger; Grimstock; Greensleeves)* CRD ▲ 3487 [DDD] (17.97)

City Waites
Music from the Time of Henry VIII—features works by Susato *(Nachtanz das ist ein Scheiden; Schafertanz; Ronde 'Mein Freund'; Ronde 'Wo bist du')*, Henry VIII *(Whereto I Should Express; If Love Now Reigned; En Vray Amoure; Helas Madame; Gentil Prince)*, Attaignant *(Bransle de Bourgogne)*, Cornish *(Fa La Sol; Blow Thy Horn Hunter)*, Sermisy *(O doulce amour; En esperant; De vous servir; Amour me Poingt)*, plus anon works *(England Be Glad; Madame d'Amours; I Am a Jolly Foster; And I Were A Maiden; Why Shall Not I; Si Fortune; I Have Been A Foster [all from the Court Song Book]; In Wilderness [from the Ritson Mss]; La Spagna; Scarmella; Time to Pass with Goodly Sort/Taunder Naken; Hola Hey! Pl la Vertu Goy; Vive le Roy)* SALM (Famous Name) ▲ 301 [DDD] (14.97)

Claude-Gervaise Ensemble [cnd:Giles Plantes]
Music in the Age of Leonardo Da Vinci *(instrumental & vocal music)*—features works by G. Ambrosio, M. Cara, J.-A. Dalza, Domenico, G. Fogliano, Gulielmus, Josquin, J. Mouton, M. Pesenti, A. Stringari, Anon. MUVI (Musica Viva) ▲ 1022 [DDD]

Clemencic Consort [cnd:René Clemencic] [René Clemencic (fl), Luigi Mangiocavallo (vn), Edward Smith (hpd), Luciano Contini (lt), Claudio Ronco (vc)]
Carmina Burana HAM ▲ 90335 (17.97)
Carmina Burana—this is a complete recording of the original, early 13th-century manuscript, the Carmina Burana, a collection of sacred and secular vocal and instrumental works from many European countries [period instrs] *(rec mid 1970s)* HMA 3-▲ 190336 (17.97)
Danses anciennes de Hongrie et de Transylvanie HMA ▲ 1901003 (9.97)
La Fête de L'âne: Traditions du moyen âge HAM (Suite) ▲ 7901036 (12.97)
Motetus: Music at the Time of Notre-Dame in Paris, w. Dominique Visse (ct), Eric Mentzel (ten), Colin Mason (bar), Edmund Brownless (sgr)—features Organum-Clausula-Matetus; Motets with Double Text; Motets with Triple Text; Instrumental Motets; Clausula Mors & Motets with Triple Text STRV ▲ 33398 [DDD] (16.97)
Le Roman de fauvel *(14th cent satirical epic with music by Philippe de Vitry, et al.)* HMA ▲ 190994 (9.97)
Troubadours *(secular vocal music of the 12th century [Provençal])* HAM ▲ 90396 (17.97)
Troubadours HAM (40th Anniversary Edition) ▲ 94396 (12.97)

EARLY MUSIC

Clément Janequin Ensemble [cnd:Dominique Visse]

Une Fête Chez Rabelais: Chanson & Instrumental Pieces—features works by Compère *(Nous sommes de l'ordre de Saint Babouyn)*, la Fue *(Autant en emporte le vent regres; Puisqu'ainsi est; Je prens congies; A bien grant tort)*, Le Petit *(N'as tu poinct mis ton hault bonnet)*, Guiard *(Or oiez les introites de taverne)*, Primus *(Ce n'est pas trop)*, Willaert *(Dessus le marché darras)*, de Bussy *(Las il n'a nul mal)*, Clemens non Papa *(Une fillette bien gorriere; Imcessament suis triste et doloreux; Du laid tetin)*, D'Hesdin *(Ramonez moy ma cheminée)*, Josquin *(Scaramella)*, Pipelare *(Fors seulement)*, Certon *(La, la, la, je ne l'ose dire)*, Fresneau *(Souspir d'amours; Pensée de plaisir; La Fricassée)*, Coste *(Celle fillette a qui le tetin point)* HAM ▲ 901453 (17.97)

Fricasée parisienne: Renaissance French Chansons HMA ▲ 1901174 (9.97)

Collegium Pro Musica

Instrumental Music in Genoa in the 17th Century—features works by M. Bitti, A. Guerrieri, G.A. Guido, A. Stradella DYNC ▲ 75 [DDD] (16.97)

Collegium Terpsichore [cnd:Fritz Neumeyr]

Dance Music of the High Renaissance *(30 dances from the renaissance and early baroque periods)*—features works by Praetorius *(6 Dances from Terpsichore*; Gallairde de Monsieur Wustron; Galliarde de la guerre; Reprinse), Widmann *(5 Dances & Galliardes)*, Schein *(3 Suites from Banchetto Musicale*), Gervaise *(Branle de Bourgogne)*, Molinaro *(Ballo detto "Il Conte Orlando")*, Caroubel *(2 Courantes) (rec 1971 & 1973)* BOSK ▲ 118 [ADD] (15.97)

Collegium Vocale Cologne [cnd:Wolfgang Fromme]

Madrigals—features works by Gesualdo, Gibbons, Monteverdi, Morley, Weelkes, et al. COL 2-▲ 45622

Cologne Musica Antiqua [cnd:Reinhard Goebel]

Cologne Musica Antiqua—features works by Montéverdi, Farina, Rossi, Fontana, Marini, Buonamente PARC ▲ 415296-2 [ADD]

Compagnie Maître Guillaume

Si Pour T'Aymer: Danseries—features 21 sels of Renaissance dance music published by Pierre Phalèse II (1550-1629) PVY ▲ 797061 (16.97)

Completed Benko Consort [cnd:D. Benko]

Renaissance Pop—features Hungarian, German, French, Austrian, Dutch, Balkan, English & Italian music HUN ▲ 12575 (16.97)

Concert des Nations [cnd:Jordi Savall]

Suites d'Orchestre, 1650-1660—features works by Dumanoir, Mazuel, de la Voy, plus others FONT ▲ 9908 (18.97)

Concerto Palatino

North Italian Music for Cornetts & Trombones, 1580-1650—features works by Cavalli, G. Gabrieli, C. Gussago, Merulo, Palestrina, R. Trofeo, A. Trombetti, F. Usper, O. Vernizzi, L. Viadana ACCE ▲ 8861 [DDD] (17.97)

Sonate Concertate in Stil Moderno *(early 17th cent. Italian music for cornet and trombone ensemble by Dario Castello and Giuseppe Scarani)* ACCE ▲ 9058 [DDD] (17.97)

Concordia [cnd:Mark Levy]

Music for Mona Lisa, w. Robin Blaze (ct)—features works by A. Coppini *(Tanto à la donna mia)*, Josquin Desprez *(A l'heure que je vous p.x.)*, Tromboncino *(Hor che'l ciel e la terra; Vergine bella)*, J. Japart *(Amours amours amours)*, Compère *(Le grant désir)*, A. Busnois *(Je ne fay plus)*, Bruhier *(Latura tu)*, J. A. Dalza *(Pavana alla venetiana; Saltarello; Piva)*, H. Issac *(La morra)*, M. Cara *(Hor venduto la speranza)*, anon *(Saltarello el francosin; Rompeltier; Helas la fille Guillemin; Dit le burguygnon; Pavana el bisson; Gagliarda la traditora; Se mai per maraveglia; Petits reins; Hor oires un chanzon) [E,I] texts* MENO ▲ 1023 [DDD] (19.97)

Concordia Orch, I Fagiolini

All the King's Men—features works by Henry VIII *(Hélas Madame)*, Cornish *(A Robyn)*, Fairfax *(Paramese Tenor; Mese Tenor)*, van Wilder *(De vous servir)*, Alonso *(La tricotea)*, Anchieta *(Con amores, mi madre)*, da Flecha *(La Bomba)*, de Cabezón *(Diferencias sobre las vacas)*, del Encina *(Cucú, cucú)*, Vásquez *(Lágrimas de mi consuelo)* [attrib Mainerio] *(Ungarescha; Schiarazula maruzula)*, Desprez *(Comment peult avoir joye; Faulte d'argent)*, Gombert *(Amy souffrez)*, Richafort *(De mon triste deplaisir)*, le Petit *(Et la, la, la)*, L'héritier *(Jan, petiti Jan)*, Anon *(Claros y frescos rios; Serrana ¿donde dormistes?; Hey trolly lolly lo; Consort XXI; I love unloved; Madame d'amours; Pavana la gaiette; Tordion)* MENO ▲ 1012 [DDD] (19.97)

Consort of Musicke [cnd:Anthony Rooley]

Charming Strephon: A Celebration of the Life of John Wilmot, 2nd Earl of Rochester *(sels performed during the 350th birthday celebration of Wilmot)*, w. Emma Kirkby (sop), Andrew King (ten), David Thomas (bass), Anthony Rooley (lt), Stephen Divine (org/hpd)—features works by H. Lawes, W. Lawes, Blow, Weldon, Lanier, J. Hart, S. Ackeroyd, Grabu, R. King, Finger, Staggins, Draghi, Sandford *(rec Apr 1997)* ETC ▲ 1211 (17.97)

Concerto Delle Donne—features works by Carissimi, Luzzaschi, Marenzio, Monteverdi, Scarlatti, Strozzi DEHA ▲ 77154 [DDD] 77154

Lamento d'Arianna—features works by S. Bonini *(Lamento d'Arianna)*, F.C. Costa *(Pianto d'Arianna)*, C. Monteverdi *(Lamento d'Arianna a voce sola; Lamento d'Arianna a 5; Pianto della Madonna)*, C. Pari *(Il Lamento d'Arianna a 5)*, F.M. Rascarini *(Reciproco Amore)*, A. Il Verso *(Lasciatemi morire a 5) (rec 1983-84)* DEHA 2-▲ 77115 [ADD]

Consort of Viols [cnd:Alfred Deller], Schola Cantorum Basiliensis

William Byrd & His Age, w. August Wenzinger (cnd)—features works by Corkine *(What Booteth Love [arr Thurston Dart])*, Byrd *(Fant in g for Vls; Ye Sacred Muses [arr Fellowes]; Lullaby, My Sweet Little Baby [arr Fellowes]; Come, Pretty Babe [arr Peter le Huray & T. Dart])*, Ferrabosco II *(Fant in F & G for Vls)*, Whythorne *(Buy New Broom [arr Warlock])*, Nicholson *(In a Merry May Morn [arr Warlock])*, Parsons *(Pandolpho [arr Warlock])*, anon. *(My Sweet Little Darling [arr Fellowes]; Guichardo; Ah, Silly Poor Joas; O Death, Rock Me Asleep [all arr Warlock]) (rec Friends' Meeting House, Edgware Road, London, Feb 1956)* ORG ▲ 8101 [ADD] (13.97)

Consortium Hafniense

The King of Denmark's Delight *(instrumental & vocal music from the time of King Christian IV)*—features works by Brade *(Almain in G; Pavan & Galliard)*, Dowland *(The King of Denmark's Galliard; Mrs. Nichols' Almain; The Frog Galliard; Complaint; Lady Laiton's Almain; Pavan in C; The Earl of Essex's Galliard)*, Caroso *(Il canario)*, Fabricius *(La battaglia; Galliard)*, Pedersøn *(Pavan in d; Nu bede vi; Pavan in G; Min Sjael nu love)*, Hume *(The King of Denmark's Health; The King of Denmark's Delight)*, Howett *(Fantasia Graegorii)*, Anon. *(Greensleeves; Jeg saa to dejlig Roser; The Standing Masque; Al verdslig Pragt; Grimstock) (rec June 16-17, 1988)* DANR ▲ 307 [DDD]

Convivium Musicum [cnd:Sven Berger], Villanella Ensemble

Tugend und Untugend: German Secular Songs & Instrumental Music from the Time of Luther—features works by Isaac *(Carmen a 5; In meinem Sinn [3 versions]; Greiner zancker; Mein Freud allein; Ich stund an einem Morgen; La mi la sol; Las rauschen)*, Obrecht *(Stat ('tsaat) ein meskin)*, Senfl *(Will niemand singen; Ein Maidlein zue dem Brunnen ging; Dort oben auf dem Berge; Nun wollt ihr hören neue Mär'; Ich soll und müess ein'n Büehlen; Oho, so geb' der Mann; Es wollt ein Maidlein Wasser holn; Es wollt ein Frau zuem Weine gahn; Lamentatio; Ich stuend an einem Morgen; Albrecht mirs schwer; Ich weiss nicht was er ihr verhiess [2 versions])*, Hofhaimer *(Erst weis ich, was die Liebe ist; Greiner Zanner; Min ainigs A; Mein einigs A; Zucht, eer und lob; Zucht, eer und lob)*, Liederbuch *(Zenner greyner)*, Finck *(Greiner Zanner)*, Ammerbach *(Die Megdlein sind von Flandern)*, Bruck *(So trinken wir alle)*, Küffer *(Heth sold ein meisken garn om win)*, Meyer *(Bicinium germanicum)*, Rhaw *(Ich stuend an einem Morgen) (rec School of Music & Musicology, Gothenburg, May 12-15 & Sept 9-11, 1994)* NXIN ▲ 553352 [DDD] (5.97)

Currende Consort [cnd:Erik van Nevel], Capella Sancti Michaelis

A History of Flemish Polyphony—features works by Adrian Willaert, Philippe Rogier, Orlando de Lassus, Philippus De Monte, Nicolas Gombert, Isaac, Obrecht, De La Rue, Josquin Desprez, Ockeghem, Dufay, plus songs & dances from Flanders & related music EUFO 10-▲ 1160 [DDD] (134.97)

Currende Vocal Ensemble

Renaissance: polyfonie uit de Nederlanden—features works by Monte, Wert, Lassus *(rec Mar 13-16, 1986)* EUFO ▲ EUF 1104

Daedalus Ensemble

El Cancionero de la Catedral de Segovia *(selections from the Segovia Cathedral Song Book, compiled ca. 1500 in Spain)*—features works by Busnois, Juan del Encina, Hayne van Ghizeghem, Isaac, Obrecht, Francisco de la Torre, Johannes Tinctoris, Johannes Wreede, Anon. ACCE ▲ 9176 [DDD] (17.97)

Il Cantar Moderno *(18 Venetian and Neapolitan Songs of the 15th Century)* ACCE ▲ 9068 [DDD] (17.97)

Dasnoy, Evelyne (mez), André Vandeboshe (bar), Catherine Parmentier (lt)

Mirror of Voices—features works by Lassus, Adriaenssen, Manchicourt, Crequillon & Guyot de Chatelet DI ▲ 920398 [DDD] (5.97)

De Organographia, Gayle Stuwe Neuman, Philip Neuman, William Gavin

Music of the Ancient Greeks: Music from 500 BC-300 AD—performed on voice, kithara, aulos, pandoura, salpinx, syrinx, tympanon & other ancient Greek instrs PANN ▲ 1001 (17.97)

De Organographia, Oregon Renaissance Band

Carnevale: Carnival Songs & Dances & Festive Music from 16th Cent Italy PANN ▲ 1003 (17.97)

De Organographia, Oregon Renaissance Band [cnds:Gayle Neuman, Philip Neuman]

Carnevale!—features works by Azzaiolo *(Girometta, senza te)*, Lupacchino *(2 Bicinia; Sopra la battaglia)*, Tromboncino *(Ostinato)*, Cara *(O mia cieca)*, Tasso/Lupacchino *(Two Bicinia)*, Festa *(Amor, che mi consigli)*, Bendusi *(La falilela/ Galante)* Layolle *(Les Bourguignons)*, Mainerio *(L'arboscello ballo Furlano)*, Dufouilloux *(Horn call)*, plus L'amor, dona; Orsu, car' Signori; Canto di donne maestre; Canto dei sarti; Canto di lanzi sonatori; Gagliarda La Traditora; Ben venga maggio; Canto de' cardoni; La bella veriola; Era di maggio/Maggio valente; Canto de' savi; Alla cazza PANN ▲ PRCD1003 [DDD]

Deller, Alfred (ct)

17th & 18th Century Solo English Airs HAM ▲ 90215 (17.97)

The 3 Ravens: Elizabethan Folk & Minstrel Songs, w. Desmond Dupré (gtr/lt) includes the complete contents of "The Three Ravens," rec. 1955, and "Wraggle Taggle Gipsies," rec. 1956 VC ▲ 8026 (m) [ADD]

Deller, Alfred (ct), Wilfred Brown (ten), Gerald English (ten), Maurice Bevan (bar)

La Musique de Notre Dame *(New Age Music of the Middle Ages: From Chant to Harmony)*—features works by Pérotin *(Graduale, Viderunt omnes fines terrae; Graduale, Sederunt principes; Alleluja Nativitas)*, Chancelier *(Conductus, Dic Christi veritas)*, Machaut *(Messe de Notre Dame)*, anon. *(Alleluja Christus resurgens & Clausula, Mors; Conductus, Pater noster commiserans) (rec Jan 1961 & May 1964)* VC ▲ SVC 36 [AAD]

Deller Consort [cnd:Alfred Deller] [Eduard Melkus (vl), Alice Hoffner (vl), Gustav Leonhardt (b vl), Nicholas Harnoncourt (b vl)]

Deller Consort—features works by Machaut *(Messe de Notre Dame)*, Pérotin & Philippe Le Chancelier *(rec Reims Cathedral and in Notre Dame, Paris)* DEHA ▲ 77064 [ADD]

The English Madrigal School—features works by Morley *(Ho! Who Comes Here?; Sweet Nymph; Now Is the Month of Maying; In Dew of Roses; Shoot, False Love, I Care Not; Miraculous Love's Wounding!; Hark, Alleluia Cheerly; Arise, Get Up, My Dear; Leave This Tormenting; I Go before, My Darling; Say, Gentle Nymphs; Good Morrow, Fair Ladies; April Is in My Mistress' Face; Though Philomela Lost Her Love; Hard by a Crystal Fountain; Whither away, So Fast; I Follow, Lo, the Footing; O Grief!; When, Lo, by Break of Morning; Besides a Fountain; Fire! Fire! My Heart)*, Weelkes *(Cease Sorrows Now; To Shorten Winter's Sadness; O Care, Thou Wilt Despatch Me; The Ape, the Monkey and the Baboon; Strike It up, Tabor; On the Plains, Fairy Trains; All at Once Well Met; Young Cupid Hath Proclaimed; Thule, the Period of Cosmography)*, Edwards *(In Going to My Naked Bed; When Griping Griefs)*, Vautor *(Mother, I Will Have a Husband)*, Bartlett *(Of All the Birds That I Do Know)*, Bennet *(All Creatures Now Are Merry-Minded; Weep O Mine Eyes)*, Wilbye *(Oft Have I Vowed; Sweet Honey-Sucking Bees; Flora Gave Me Fairest Flowers; Lady, When I Behold; Adieu, Sweet Amaryllis)*, Ward *(Hope of My Heart)*, R. Johnson *(Defiled Is My Name; Enedicam Domino)*, Tallis *(Like As the Doleful Dove)*, Shepherd *(O Happy Dames)*, anon. *(The Bitter Sweet; The Happy Life; I Smile to See How You Devised) (rec Walthamstow Hall, London, July 1955 & July 1958)* VC (The Bach Guild) 2-▲ 2533 [ADD] (25.97)

Madrigal Masterpieces—features works by Byrd, Gesualdo, Janequin, Lassus, Marenzia, Monteverdi, Morley, Tomkins *(rec 1959)* VC (The Bach Guild) ▲ OVC 2000 [ADD]

Shakespeare Songs & Consort Music [E] HMA ▲ 190202 (9.97)

Deller Consort [cnd:Nikolaus Harnoncourt] [Eduard Melkus (vl), Alice Hoffner (vl), Gustav Leonhardt (b vl), Nicholas Harnoncourt (b vl)], Consort of Viols [Desmond Dupré (lt), Gustav Leonhardt (hpd), Alfred Deller (ct)]

Elizabethan & Jacobean Music - Airs & Instrumental Music of England—features works by Dowland *(Can She Forgive My Wrongs?; If My Complaints Could Passions Move; My Lady Hundson's Puffe; Air from Silent Night)*, Morley *(Air for 3 Viols)*, Bartlett *(Of All the Birds That I Do Know)*, Johnson *(Alman for Hpd)*, Jenkins *(Pavan for 4 Vls; Fantasia in C for 4 Vns)*, Campion *(I Care Not for These Ladies)*, Parsons *(Pandolpho)*, Farnaby *(Vars for Hpd on Up Tails All)* VC ▲ 8102 [ADD] (13.97)

Deller, Alfred (ct), Mark Deller (ct)

Folksongs *(13th-17th century)*, w. Desmond Dupré (lt/gtr) HMA ▲ 190226 (9.97)

Diabolus in Musica

La Chambre des Dames: Trouvere Love Songs & Polyphonies—features works by St. Louis *(L'autrier matin)*, de la Halle *(Li dous regars; A jointes matins; Hé Diex quant verrai; Trop désir; Diex comment porroie; Je muir, je muir; Harreu li maus d'amer; A Deiu commant)*, Brulé *(Les oisellons de mon païs)*, Muset *(Devers Chastelvilain)*, de Champagne *(Dex est ausi)*, Ferrières *(Quant la sesons)*, Lescurel *(Belle com loiaus amans)*, Coincy *(Royne celestre)*, plus anon/trad songs *(La quinte estampe royal; Tebor et Omnes; Ecce mundi; Fines amourettes; Hac in die; Virgo; Lasse, que deviendrai-gié; La prime estampie royal; Salve virgo)* STUD ▲ 2604 (18.97)

Manuscrits de Tours: 13th Century Feast Day Songs—features Circa Canit; O Martine,O Pie; Veni sancti spiritus; Virtus moritor; Hic est martinus; Ignis in rubo; O laudes debitas; O quam admiribilis vir; Micholaus inclitus; Alleluia, hic Martinus; Beata nobis gaudia; Salve virgo virginium; Ave presul gloriose; Gaude syon; Ave stella matutina; Agmina sacra; Honorem virginis; Processit in stipite; Deus pater fillium; Dominatrix ominum; Mittendus predicteur; O presul/o virtutis/sacerdotum; Mira christi clemencia; Martine presul optime STUD ▲ 2672 (18.97)

Dickey, Bruce (cornetto)

Virtuoso Solo Music for Cornetto, w. Stephen Stubbs (chit/vih), Erin Headley (vl), Andrew Lawrence-King (double hp/ Renaissance hp)—features works by Thomas Crecquillon, Fontana, Frescobaldi, A. Gabrieli, Tarquinio Merula, Palestrina, Cipriano da Rore ACCE ▲ 9173 [DDD] (17.97)

Discantus [cnd:Brigitte Lesne]

Campus Stellae *(12th cent. pilgrim songs venerating the tomb of St. James, patron saint of Spain)*—features Novus annus dies magnus; Ad superni regis decus; Dies ista celebris; Congaudeant catholici; Alleluia—Gratulemur et letemur; dies ista gaudium; Res est admirabilis; Plebs domini; Gregis pastor; Uterus hodie virginis flourit; Miri dies oritur; Cuncitipotens genitor Deus; Lilium floruit; Quam dilecta tabernacula; Rex immense; Clemens servulorum gemitus tuorum; Flore vernans gratie; Judicii signum OPUS ▲ 30102 (17.97)

Dame de Flors: Notre Dame School—features 12th & 13th century works from L'École Notre Dame OPUS ▲ 30175 (17.97)

Dolmetsch, Arnold (vir)

The Arnold Dolmetsch Years *(this series marks the 50th anniversary of the death of Arnold Dolmetsch (1858-1940) & "the first 100 years of the early music movement")*

Program 1, w. Wieland Kuijken (vl), Robert Kohnen (hpd)—features works by F. Couperin, Forqueray la père, Marais, Rameau IMPA ▲ 989 [DDD] (12.97)

Program 2, w. Frank Preuss (vn), Marguerite Dolmetsch (vl), Carl Dolmetsch (rec), Nigel Foster (hpd)—features works by Bach *(Violin Sonata, BWV.1015)*, Geminiani, Handel, Leclair IMPA ▲ 990 [DDD] (12.97)

Program 3, w. Jean-Charles François (rcr), Jeanne Dolmetsch (trb rcr), Marguerite Dolmetsch (vl), Nigel Foster (hpd), Kathleen Livingstone (sop), John Hancorn (bass), Jennifer Bate (org), et al.—features works by Arne *(Organ Concerto No. 4)*, Pepusch *(Quintet in F)*, Purcell *(Chaconne in F; Don Quixote—excerpt; Fairy Queen—excerpts)*, Woodcock *(Concerto No. 5 for 2 Sixth Flutes)* IMPA ▲ 995 [DDD]

Program 4, w. Carl Dolmetsch (rcr), François Dolmetsch (rcr), Marguerite Dolmetsch (rcr), Virginia Black (hpd), et al.—features works by Lorenzo Allegri *(Suite for 6 Recorders)*, Johann Friedrich Fasch *(Sonata in B♭)*, David Funck *(Suite in d for 4 Recorders)*, Luys de Milan *(Fantasia del Quarto Tono)*, Alonso Mudarra *(Fantasia que Contrahze la Harpa en la Manera de Ludovico)*, Luys de Navaraez *(La Cancion del Emperador—Mille Regretz)*, Giovanni Picchi *(Hungarian Suite for Harpsichord)*, D. Scarlatti *(Aria in d, K.32; Fugue, K.30)*, Thomas Tomkins *(Pavan in F for 5 Viols)*, Giovanni Maria Trabaci *(Gagliarda Prima "La Galante")* IMPA ▲ 1010 [DDD]

Douglass, David (vn), Paul O'Dette (lt), Andrew Lawrence-King (hp)

Apollo's Banquet: 17th Century Music from the Publications of John Playford HAM ▲ 907186 (17.97)

Doulce Mémoire Ensemble [cnd:Denis Raisin-Dadre]

Lorenzo il Magnifico: Trionfo di Bacco & Chants de Carnaval 1449-1492 ASTR ▲ 8626 (18.97)

Dowland Consort [cnd:Jakob Lindberg]

Heavenly Noise: English Music for Mixed Consort from the Golden Age—features works by Byrd, Campion, Dowland, Holborne, Hume, et al. BIS ▲ 451 [DDD] (17.97)

Dufay Collective

A Dance in the Garden of Mirth: Medieval Instrumental Music—features Istanpitta "Ghaetta"; La prime estampie real; La uitime estampie real; La seconde estampie royal; La tierche estampie roial; Danse; Retrove; Tortto—Salterello; La quinte estampie real; Istanpitta "Belicha"; Istanpitta "Isabella"; Salterello CHN (New Direction) ▲ 9320 [DDD] (16.97)

Miracles: 13th Century Spanish Songs in Praise of the Virgin Mary, w. Vivien Ellis (sop) CHN (New Direction) ▲ 9513 (16.97)

Miri It Is: Songs & Instrumental Music from Medieval England—features Merry it is while summer lasts; Miri it is (dance); Blessed be thou, queen of heaven; Edi beo thu (estampie); Formerly I knew no sorrow; Ductia; Bird on a briar; Estampie; O chosen bride of God; Beata viscera; Sanctus; Alleluya psallat; Ductia; Holy mother of grace; Sancta Mater graciae; Dance; Omnis caro peccaverat; Omnis caro (dance); Ductia; Summer is come CHN ▲ 9396 (16.97)

On the Banks of the Seine: Music of the Trouvères, w. Viven Ellis (sop), Jacob Heringman (lt)—features J'aloie l'autrier; Ses tres dous regars; C'est la fins; Prendès I garde; Pucelete/Je languis/Domino; A Paris/On parole/Frése nouvele; Les un pins; Volez vous que je vous chant; La septieme estampie Real; A Dieu commant amouretes; A jointes mains vous proi; Hé Dieus quant verrai; Tant con je vivrai; Onques n'amais; Fines Amouretes; La douçours; En ung vergier; Dame or sui traïs; Chanter voel par grant amour; Quant voi la flor nouvele; L'autre jour par un matin; Amor potest; Dieus soit en cheste maison; Je chevauchoie l'autrier CHN ▲ 9544 (16.97)

Early Music Consort [cnd:David Munrow]

Early Music Festival PLON (Double Deckers) 2-▲ 452967 (17.97)

▲ = CD ♦ = Enhanced CD △ = MD ▮ = Cassette Tape ▯ = DCC

Early Music Ensemble [cnd:Jany Renz]

Christesmas in Anglia Elektra/Nonesuch ▮ N5-71369

Eastman Brass Quintet [cnd:Florian Holland], Paris Instrumental Ensemble

Renaissance Brass Music—features works by Scheidt, Weelkes, William Simmes, Ferrabosco, Holborne, John O'Koever, Gibbons, G. Gabrielli, A. Gabrielli ALLO ▲ 8154 [ADD] ▮ 8154

Ebrel, Annie (sgr), Julie Murphy (sgr), Lillis O Laoire (sgr), Mairi Smith (sgr)

Celtic Tales & Tongues—features an anthology of Celtic music's roots presented by performers of "old style" singing IGO ▲ 209 (16.97)

Elyma Ensemble [cnd:Gabriel Garrido]

Gerusalemme Liberata: The Tears of Jerusalem—features works on the theme of Jerusalem by Monteverdi *(Combattimento di Tancredi e Clorinda; Sinf; Vattene pur, crudel; La tra 'l sangue e le morti; Poi ch'ella in sé tornò; Piagn'e sospira)*, Bernardi *(Sinf Prima à 6)*, Pietro de Negri *(L'Armida in stille recitativo)*, G. de Wert *(Vezzosi augelli; Qual musico gentil)*, S. d'India *(Forsennata gridava; La tra 'l sangue e le morti; Ma che? Squallido e oscuro)*, Eredi *(L'Armida del Tasso I-II & V-IX)*, Mazzocchi *(Chiudesti i lumi Armida)*, Marini *(Canzon VIII; Le Lagrime d'Erminia; La bella Erminia)*, Fiamengo *(Diologo di Sofronia e Olindo)*, G. B. Grillo *(Son Prima à 7)*, Cifra *(Era La Notte) (rec St. Martin Church, Sicily, Jul 1997) ([E,F,I] texts)* K617 2-▲ 7076 [DDD] (36.97)

Latin American Villancicos & Motets from the 1600s not advised of composers or selections SYM ▲ 5 [DDD]

Ensemble Alba Musica Kyo

Landini & His Time: 14th Century Italian Ars Nova—features works by Landini, de Perugia, da Bologna, da Firenze, and other anon. pieces CCL ▲ 5793 [DDD] (17.97)

Ensemble Alcatraz

Danse Royale *(French, Anglo-Norman & Latin songs & dances from the 13th century)*—features *(En Avril au tens pascour; La seconde estampe royal; S'onques nuls hoem; Flos pudicitie; DS 11:11; Danse Royale I; Si tost c'amis; Danse Royale II; El tens d'iver; Retrouve; Espris d'ire et d'amour; La prime estampe royal; La ultime estampe royal; La septieme estampe royal; Trop est mes maris jalos)* 75597 ▲ 79240 [DDD]

Visions & Miracles *(sacred Gallician & Latin songs from 13th century Spain)*—features *(Quen a Virgen ben servirá; Fontis in rivulum; Connoscudamente mostre miragres; Alavanca de Mudanza; Toda cousa que a Virgen; Gran deret; Ad honorem salvatoris; A Virgen mui groriosa)* NON ▲ 79180 [DDD] (16.97) 79180

Ensemble Concerto [cnd:Roberto Gini]

Strana Armonia D'Amore, Vol. 1: Arias, Madrigals & Canzonettas in Monteverdi's Time, w. Vincenzo Manno (ten), Rosario di Meglio (vn), Sabina Colonna Preti (vl), Paul Beier (archlt), Marco Fodella (chit), Maurizio Martelli (chit)—features works by G. Caccini, Rasi, Romano, Allegri, F. Caccini, Stefani STRV ▲ 33406 [DDD] (16.97)

Ensemble de Musique Ancienne Polyphonia Antiqua [cnd:Yves Esquieu]

Ultreia! *(a juxtaposition of musical pieces connected with the Galican pilgrimage to St. James of Compostella) (rec July 1982)* PVY ▲ 790042 [ADD] (16.97)

Ensemble Doulce Mémoire [cnd:Denis Raisin-Dadre]

Fricassées Lyonnaises—features works by Sandrin, Roquelay, Villiers, Lys, Fresneau, Lupi, Coste, Layolle, Celliers d'Hesdin, Bianchini & Clëreau ASTR ▲ 8567 (18.97)

Pierre Attaingnant, Chansons Nouvelles & Danceries—features works by Sermisy *(Au bois de deuil; Dont vient cela; Joyssance)*, Gervaise *(Pavane d'ell Estarpe; Allemande 4)*, Sandrin *(Puis que vivre en servitude)*, Jacotin *(Mary, je songay)*, Certon *(Je l'ay aimè)*, Cadéac *(Je suis deshériteé)*, De Mornable *(Vous qui voulez [chanson, pavene, gaillarde])*, Gosse *(Je file quant Dieu my donne)*, Courtois *(Si par souffrir)*, anon. *(Pavane 3; Gaillarde 4; Prélude; Pavane; Pavane 19 et Gaillarde; Basse dance 3; Sansserre; C'est grand plaisir)* ASTR ▲ 8545 (18.97)

Ensemble Kérylos [cnd:Annie Bélis]

Music from Ancient Greece—features Fanfare; Euripide, Oreste; Euripide, Iphigénie à Aulis; Hymnes Delphiques à Apollon; Anonymes de Bellermann; Eschyle, Ajax; Fragments Instrumentaux de Contrapollinopolis; Fragment d'Orestie; Seikilos, Chanson; Mesomède de Crète; Hymne Chrétienne d'Oxyrhynchus *(rec July 4-7, 1996)* K617 ▲ 7069 [DDD] (18.97)

Ensemble Lucidarium

Lo mio servente core—features Italian tradional & avant-garde music of Dante's time ED ▲ 13051 (7.97)

Troubadours & Minnesänger, En chantan m'aven a membrar ED ▲ 13079 (18.97)

Ensemble Lyrique Ibérique

Romances Judéo-Espagnoles—features Lavava i suspirava; Nani, nani; Ir me kyero; Kuando el rey Nimrod; Notches buenas; Durme durme mi alma donzeya; Mi suegra; Morenika a mi me yaman; A la una nasi yo; Skalerika de oro; Ven kerida, ven amada; La serena; O ke mueve mezes; Porke yorach blanka ninya, plus others ED ▲ 13017 (18.97)

Ensemble Organum [cnd:Marcel Pérès] [Gérard Lesne (ct), Dominique Vellard (ten), Josep Benet (ten), Josep Cabré (bar), Philippe Balloy (bar)]

Polyphonie aquitaine: 12th Century Aquitanian Polyphony from the Abbey of St. Martial de Limoges—features sels from the Matines de Noël HMA ▲ 1901134 [ADD] (9.97)

Ensemble Renaissance

Marco Polo-The Journey—features Anonymous *(Blue Mountains; Byzantine Chant; Chinese Ceremonial Music; Ghaetta; Girl Songs of Cyprus; Lamento di Tristano e rotta; Lauda novella; Manfredina e rotta; Persian-Arabian Dances; Saltarello; Saltarello II; Trotto)* ALSE ▲ 2003 (16.97)

Ensemble Weltgesang [cnd:Roberta Cristoni]

Primus ex Apostolis—features Dum paterfamilias; Como poden; Vos qui secuti; Stella nova; Kyrie; Ecce adest; Regi perennis; Beneditti laudati; Poys que dos reys; Madre e deus; plus other sels FON ▲ 9704 (13.97)

Estampie

A Chantar: Songs of Women—Courtly Love in the Middle Ages—features works by Machaut, Thibaut de Navarra, Wolkenstein, et al. CHR ▲ 74583 [DDD] (17.97)

Crusaders In Nomine Domini—sels unknown CHR ▲ 77183 (17.97)

Estampie [cnd:Graham Derrick]

Under the Greenwood Tree—features works by Vogelweide *(Palästinalied)*, Richard I, Coeur de Lion *(Ja nuls homs pris)*, Blondel de nesle *(A l'entrant d'este)*, R. de Vaquerias *(Kalenda Maya)*, Cornyshe *(Ah! Robin)*, Stoninges *(Browning My Dear)*, Gervaise *(Pavane:La Venissienne; Gaillarde)*, Playford *(Greenwood; Nottingham Castle; Green Goose Fair)*, Th. Simpson *(Ricercar on "Bonny Sweet Robin")*, Weelkes *(Robin Hood, Maid Marian & Little John Are Gone)*, plus anon pieces *(Novus miles sequitur; Estampie; Clap, clap par un matin s'en aloit Robin; The Wedding of Robin Hood; Under the Greenwood Tree; Sellegners Round; Greensleeves [2 versions]; Robin Hood & the Curtal Friar; Robin Hood & the Tanner; Robin Hood & Maid Marian; Sweet Angel of England; O Lusty May) (rec High Denton Farm, Ilkley, North Yorkshire, England, Apr 1995)* NXIN ▲ 8553442 [DDD] (5.97)

With Dances & Delight: 16th Century Music from England & Abroad—features works by Costa, Crecquillon, Dowland, dell Enzina, Finck, Kugelmann, Merulo, et al. [E,I,S,G] MER ▲ 84170 (16.97)

I Fagiolini

All the King's Horses *(knights, poets & patrons of the Renaissance courts)*, w. Concordia—features works by Janequin, Sandrin, Isaac, Senfl, Finck, Arcadelt, Cipriano de Rore, plus others MENO ▲ 1013 (19.97)

La Fenice, Maria-Cristina Kiehr (sop), John Elwes (ten), Ulrich Messthaler (bar)

L'heritage de Monteverdi, Vol. 2—features works by Grandi *(O vos omnes)*, Turini *(Son seconda)*, Cima *(O sacrum convivium; Son per cornette e trbn)*, Salvatore *(Durezze e ligature; Toccata per organo)*, Capello *(Dic mihi, sacratissima virgo)*, Sances *(Stabat mater dolorosa)*, Marini *(Madrigale spirituale)*, Piccinini *(Passacaglio)*, Mazzocchi *(Lagrime amare)*, Banchieri *(Mulier, cur ploras hic)*, Monteverdi *(Et resurrexit; Laudate Dominum)*, Graziani *(Regina coeli laetare)*, Cazzati *(Capriccio sopra 7 note)*, Grancini *(Exultate Christo adiutori nostro) (rec Eglise de Mormont, Nov 1995)* RICE ▲ 166148 (17.97)

Ferrara Ensemble [cnd:Crawford Young]

En Doulz Chastel de Pavie: Chansons from the Court of Visconti HAM ▲ 905241 (17.97)

Forse che si, forse che no: 15th Century Dance Music—features Verçeppe; Liondello; Pazienza; Cupido; Pellegrina; Voltati in ça Rosina; J'ay grant dolour; Tessara; Rostiboli gioioso; Anello; Giove; Pinzochera; Lauro; Venus; Foruna desperata; Alessandresca; Gelosia; Petit Riense; Spero; La figlia di Guielmo *(rec Oct 1989)* FMD ▲ 182 [DDD]

Fiati Virtuosi

De la Renaissance au Baroque—features works by Riccio *(Canzona La Finetta)*, Frescobaldi *(Canzona La Capriola; Canzona L'Altera; Canzona La Superba; Canzona La Nicolina)*, Taeggio *(Divisions sur Suzanne un jour)*, Salaverde *(Divisions sur Vestiva i colli)*, Bassano *(Divisions sur Ancor che col partire; Divisions sur Ancor che col partire; Divisions sur Frais et gaillard; Ricercata terza)*, Gabrieli *(Vars sur Frais et gaillard)*, Merula *(Canzona La Bersalina)*, Castello *(Son prima)* ANAL ▲ 29728

Figueras, Montserrat (sop), Capella Reial de Catalunya [cnd:Jordi Savall]

El Canto de la Sibila II FONT ▲ 9900 (18.97)

Fine Arts Brass Ensemble [Bryan Allen (tpt), Andy Culshaw (tpt), Stephen Roberts (hn), Simon Hogg (trbn), Richard Sandland (tuba)]

Music from the English Courts, w. Tristram Fry (perc)—features works by Handel *(Royal Fireworks Music)*, Dowland *(Flow My Tears; Fine Knacks for Ladies)*, Purcell *(Tpt Tunes & Airs; Son Tpt; Dido's Lament [from Dido & Aeneas])*, Locke *(Music for His Majesty's Sagbutts & Cornetts)*, Johnson *(Prince's Masque; The Merry Clerk; Comedian's Masque)*, Gibbons *(The Silver Swan; The Bee)*, Lanier *(Symphonia; The House Measure)*, Adson *(The Devil's Dance)*, King Henry VIII *(Pastime with Good Company) (rec All Saints Church Petersham, June 20-21, 1994)* NIMB ▲ 5546 [DDD] (16.97)

Fine Instruments Orch [cnd:Christodoulos Halaris]

Akritika: Odes of the Byzantine Empire Border-Guards—features 15 songs about the Greek border guards, symbolic of the ancient struggle of Greeks against Moslems AKR 2-▲ 1 (35.97)

Akritika, Vol. 2: Odes of the Byzantine Empire Border-Guards—features more songs about the Greek border guards AKR 2-▲ 2 (36.97)

Byzantine Maistores: Complete Works of the Greatest Byzantine Composers, Vol. 1—features 15 works by Manuel Chrysafis, reconstructed from medieval manuscripts OCRY 3-▲ 1 (53.97)

Byzantine Secular Classical Music—features 11 instrumental & vocal works reconstructed by Halaris from medieval manuscripts; includes an illustrated 100-page booklet ORA 3-▲ 1

Byzantine Secular Classical Music, Vol. 2—features 13 works reconstructed from medieval manuscripts ORA 3-▲ 2

Byzantine Secular Classical Music, Vol. 3—features 15 works reconstructed from medieval manuscripts ORA 3-▲ 3 (53.97)

Pandora: Music of the Post-Byzantine High Society, Vol. 1—features seven songs of love, youth, etc. for voices and instruments BYZ ▲ 1

Sympotika: Secular Music of Byzantine Banquets, Vol. 1—features seven songs and dances OSYM ▲ 1

Fleagle, John (sgr/gothic hp/lt/fid/sinfonia/bodhran)

World's Bliss: Medieval Songs of Love & Death, w. Shira Kammen (vielle/fid)—features Alysoun; Blow, Northerne Wynd; Da Day Dawn; Twa Corbies; Death & the Lady; Winter Wakeneth; Nou Shrinketh Rose; Doon da Rooth; O Speculum Spericum; The Hern; Maiden in the Moor; Worldes Blis; George Collins; Près de Paris; Nottamun Town; I Have a Yong Suster *(rec 1st & 2nd Church, Marlborough St., Boston, MA; Church of the Redeemer, Chestnut Hill, MA; July 27-28, 1995, Jan 25 & July 24-25, 1996)* ACTR ▲ 60103 [DDD] (16.97)

Florata [cnd:Tim Rayborn]

Far Away Lands: The Medeival Sephardic Heritage ASV ▲ 165 (16.97)

Folger Consort [Mark Bleeke (ten), Tina Chancey (fid/vn/vl/rcr), Robert Eisenstein (fid/vn/vl/rcr), Christopher Kendall (lt/hp/citole), Scott Reiss (rcr/perc/hackbrett), Tom Zajac (trbn/h-g/rcr/hp/ww/bagpipe)]

Alpine Airs—music of 15th-16th century Switzerland featuring works by Rudolf von Fenis-Neuenburg *(Minne gebiutet mir; Gewan ich ze Minnen)*, Rhau *(Der Appenzeller Jereyen)*, Sixtus Dietrich *(Elslin, liebes Elselin min; Omnes sitientes venite ad aquas; Sede a dextris; Fidelia omnia mandata ejus)*, Benedictus Apenzeller *(Buvons, ma comere; Le printemps facit florir; Morir d'aymer a dame si jolye; Gentilz galans, compaignons du raisin)*, Senfl *(Im Maien; Das Lang; Ich weiss ein' stolze Müllerin; Es taget vor dem Walde; Ach Elselein, liebes Elselein mein; Wann ich des Morgens früeh aufsteh'; Quodlibet:Es taget/Ach Elselein/Wann ich des Morgens; Es Wollt' ein Maidlein Wasser Hol'n; Ich weiss nit, was er ihr verhiess)*, plus anon/trad Swiss pieces *(Le Ranz des Vaches; Les aramaillis; Veni tote a la montagne; Por lo bin fitâ; L'yavait on yadz'; Célébrons en rond; A Medley of Minnesinger Tunes)* FOLG ▲ 9712 [DDD] (16.97)

Folger Consort [R. Eisenstein, C. Kendall, S. Reiss]

Carmina Burana & Other Spirited Songs from the German Middle Ages, w. M. Bleeke, T. Chancey—features works by Burana, Oswald Von Wolkenstein, Glogauer Liederbuch, Ludwig Sennfl FOLG ▲ BDCD 8901 [DAD]

Dance Songs of Renaissance England, w. M. Bleeke, T. Chancey, W. Gillespie, M. Springfels, Brent Wissick (vl)—features works by John Dowland, Anon., Phillip Rosseter, Richard Allison, Thomas Campion, Robert Parsons, Thomas Morley, Thomas Ford, Thomas Weelkes *(rec Jan 24, 1988)* FOLG ▲ BDCD 9004 [DDD]

A Distant Mirror: Music of the 14th Century & Shakespeare's Music DLS ▲ 1003 [AAD]

Divisions on an Ayre: Lute Songs & Instrumental Music circa 1600, w. W. Sharp (bar)—features works by John Dowland, Tobias Hume, Robert Johnson, Giovanni Cooperario, John Danyel, Thomas Morley, Orlando Gibbons, Anthony Holborne, Byrd/Morley, Michael Praetorius, Gilles Durant, Pierre Guedron, Annon., Gabriel Bataille, Giulio Caccini, Girolamo Frescobaldi, Giovanni Battista Fontana FOLG ▲ BDCD 9005 [DDD]

Of Kindly Lust & Love's Inspiring: Pastoral Music from Italy to Elizabethan England, w. D. Minter (cnd)—features works by Gastoldi *(A lieta vita; Tre balletti)*, Morley *(La coranto; Now is the month of Maying; Divisions on Amarilli; About the maypole; Now is the Gentle Seasons)*, Marenzio *(Ombrose e care selve)*, Holborne *(Pavan:Amareta; Galliard:Heigh ho holiday; Almaine)*, Palestrina *(Sound out my voice)*, di Lasso *(Susanna faire [from* Musica Transalpina*])*, Castello *(Son. for 2 Treble Instruments and Trombone)*, Caccini *(Amarilli mia bella)*, van Eyck *(Divisions on Amarilli)*, Coperarlo *(Suite)*, Bassano *(Ciprian's Rore's)*, Frescobaldi *(Canzona; Live not poor bloom)*, Johnson *(Care charming step)*, Frescobaldi *(Canzona detta La Diodata)*, Bateson *(Live not poor bloom)* FOLG ▲ 9308 (16.97)

La Fontegara Consort

Il Giardino dell'Amore: Instrumental Music in Europe from the Medieval & Renaissance Periods—features works by von der Vogelweide *(Palastinalied)*, de Ventadorn *(Con vei la lauzeta mover)*, de la Halle *(S'on me regard)*, de Machault *(Hocquetus David; Ma fin est mon commencement)*, Landini *(Occhi dolenti miei; Dolze meo drudo)*, anon. *(Los set Goyts; Mariam Matrem Virginem; Laudamus Virginem [all from El Llibre Vermell de Montserrat]; Beata Viscera; Dela a la riviere; Saltarello; Voltati ça Rosine; Estampie; Ductia)*, Ferrabosco *(Four note pavan)*, Dowland *(The Earl of Essex his Gaillard; Mr. G. Whitehead his Almand; King of Denmark his Galliard)*, Susato *(Pavana; Ronde Pass'et medio; Nachtanz)*, Praetorius *(Bransle de Montirande; Gagliarda; Branle double)*, Gabrieli *(Canzon prima à 5)* BONG ▲ 5532 [DDD] (16.97)

Frank, Susan Storey (sop), Julius Baker (fl), Sara Lambert Bloom (ob), et al.

Music from Cranberry Isles *(recordings made following performances at the Cranberry Isles music festival in Maine)*—features works by Bach, Gluck, Telemann, Vivaldi, et al. CENT ▲ 2084 (16.97)

Freiburg Spielleyt Ensemble

Nun grüss dich Gott, mein feine Krott: South German Composers around 1500—features works by S. Dietrich *(Nun grüss dich Gott; Nur nerrisch sinn)*, Senfl *(Die Brünnlein, die da fliessen; Mit Lust tritt ich an diesen Tanz)*, Newsidler *(Preambel & Welscher Tanz "Wascha Mesa")*, Moulu *(Ami souffre que le vous amie)*, Bruck/Senfl *(So trincken wir alle)*, Kotter *(Kochersperger Spanieler; Preamblum in fa)*, Widmann *(Der Floh)*, Laufenberg *(Ich weiss ein lieblich engelspil)*, Spoorer *(Frölich muss ich singen)*, H. Weck *(Hopper dancz)*, plus anon pieces *(Ich spring an disem ringe; Je m'y plains fort)* ARSM ▲ 1184 [DDD] (17.97)

O Fortuna: Luck & Misfortune in Songs & Texts of the Middle Ages ARSM ▲ 1181 (17.97)

Fretwork

In Nomine *(English music for viol consort)*—features works by Baldwin, Bull, Byrd, Cornysh, Ferrabosco, Johnson, Parsons, Preston, Tallis, Taverner, Tye AMON ▲ 29 [DDD] (16.97)

Gesualdo Consort

Early Music of the Netherlands, Vol. 1 (1400-1600), w. Ensemble Tragicomedia, Concerto Palatino members—features works by Fabri *(Ach Vlaendere vrie)*, de Binchois *(Nove cantum melody)*, Dufay *(Je ne vis onques la pareille)*, Obrecht *(Tstat een meskin; Mille quingentis)*, des Prez *(Ut Phebi radus; Kyrie)*, Agricola *(Credo Je ne vis onques)*, Brumel *(Tous les regretz)*, Appenzeller *(Buvons, ma comere)*, Clemens non Papa *(Psalm 31)*, Sweelinck *(Psalm 2)*, de Lassus *(Madonna mia, pieta [instrumental & vocal renditions])*, de Brouck *(Une Angelette; Pleurs et soupirs)*, de Rore *(Amor che col partire [instumental & vocal renditions])*, Utendal *(Tandem triumphans)*, Tollius *(Zefiro torna) (rec Dec 1988)* EMC ▲ 3987 [DDD] (19.97)

Gesualdo Consort [cnd:Gerald Place]

Madrigals & Motets from Renaissance Naples—features works by Gesualdo, Luzzaschi, Nenna, Nola & Stella ASVQ ▲ 6210 (10.97)

Gothic Voices [cnd:Christopher Page]

The Castle of Fair Welcome *(late 15th-cent. courtly songs)* [E,F] HYP ▲ 66194 [DDD] (17.97)

The Garden of Zephirus *(courtly songs of the early 15th century)* [F] HYP ▲ 66144 (17.97)

Missa Veterem hominem & Other 15th-century English Music ("Spirits of England & France, Vol. 5")—features Missa Veterem hominem; Sarum chant books hymns HYP ▲ 66919 (17.97)

The Spirits of England & France, Vol. 1, w. Pavlo Beznosiuk (medieval fid)—features works by Brolet *(He tres douce rossignol)*, Cooke *(Gloria)*, Machaut *(Ay mi! dame de valour)*, Matteo da Perugia *(Belle sans per)*, Perotinus *(Presul nostri temporis)*, Pykini *(Plaisance, or tost)*, anon. *(In Roma sonat gemitus; Le premier jor; Deduc, Syon, uberrimas; Virgo plena gratiae; Flos in monte cernitr; Crucifigat omnes; Beata nobis gaudia; Estampies; Ave Maria; Laus detur multipharia; Cred [Old Hall MS]; Quant la douce jouvencelle; En cest mois de May)* [F] HYP ▲ 66739 (17.97)

The Study of Love: French Songs & Motets of the 14th Century—features works by Machaut, Pycard, Solage [F] *(rec Apr-May 1992)* HYP ▲ 66619 [DDD]

The Voice in the Garden *(secular music from 15th and 16th century Spain)*—features works by Del Encina, Narvaez, de Peñalosa, de Modena, Enrique, Milan, Gabriel, Anonymous HYP ▲ 66653 (17.97)

La Grande Écurie et la Chambre du Roy [cnd:Jean-Claude Malgoire]

Dances of the Court & Villages *(16th century)* 34617 ▮ COL

Gruppo di Canto Ambrosiano [cnd:Luigi Benedetti]

Vernans Rosa—features transcriptions by Piero Damilano of melodies from Bobbio Monastery, 12-14th cent. STRV ▲ 31 (16.97)

Halaris, Christodoulos (cnd)

Eros Music, w. *(orch unknown)*—features ancient Greek folk songs and lullabies ORA ▲ 4013 [DDD]

Hallenser Madrigalists [cnd:Andreas Göpfert]

La Bella Ninfa: European Madrigals from around 1600—features works by Marenzio, Palestrina, Gesualdo, Janequin, Gibbons, Lassus, Bennet, Farmer, Arcadelt, Habler BER ▲ 9336 (10.97)

Harp Consort [cnd:Andrew Lawrence-King]

Ludus Danielis: The Play of Daniel DEHA ▲ 77395 [DDD] (16.97)

Les Haulz et les bas Ensemble

Gothic Winds—features works by H. de Libro Castro *(Virgo Dulcis)*, von Salzburg *(Das haizt dy trumpet & ich gut du blasen)*, Magister Grimace *(a l'Arme)*, Loyset *(Chose Loyset)*, Ciconia *(Regina gloriosa)*, Fabri *(Ach vlaendere vrie)*, Wolkenstein *(Kum liebster man)*, Japart *(3 filliez)*, Dufay *(Qui latiot in virgine)*, Ambrosio *(Petit reinse)*, Piacenza *(Anello)*, Ffranckes *(Quene note)*, plus anon 12-14th cent works *(Ballaam; Estampie; Retrove; Saltarello; Dal bel chastel' Bobik blazen; Auxci bonjoure delabonnestrenne; Le hault et la blas)* CHR ▲ 77193 [DDD] (17.97)

Hedos Ensemble [Hartmut Hein (bar), Bernhard Böhm (rcr/trns fl/bgp/Rauschpfeife), Jürgen Hübscher (renaissance lt/vih/perc), Michael Spengler (vl)]

Renaissance Love Songs from Germany, Spain, England & Italy—features works by L. Liederbuch *(Ich spring an diesem ringe; Der walt hat sich entlaubet [instrumental])*, S. Liederbuch *(Se hyn mein hercz)*, G. Liederbuch *(Ich sachs eins mals [instrumental]; Elslein, liebes Elselein)*, H. Sachs *(Der eyszapfen)*, H. Neusiedler *(Ein ser guter hoff tantz [instrumental])*, V. Hausmann *(Catkanei)*, M. Fuellana *(De los alamos)*, D. Ortiz *(Recercada primera sobre o felici occhi miei [instrumental]; Recercada ottava [instrumental]; Recercada sobre doulce memoire [instrumental])*, A. Mudarra *(Isabel)*, J. Dowland *(In Darkness Let Me Dwell; Now, O Now I Needs Must Part)*, T. Morley *(Whither Away So Fast? [instrumental])*, Anon *(The Cobbler's Jig [instrumental]; Budro, an Irish Dance [instrumental])*, F. Caroso *(Mascherada [instrumental]; Aria di Gran' Duc, Saltarello [instrumental])*, C. Bottegari *(Stanotte m'insognava; Donna vagh'e leggiadra)*, B. Tromboncino *(Per dolor mi bagno il viso)*, H. Vecchi *(So ben mi ch'ha bon tempo)*, anon *(Pase el agua; Vuestros ojos tienen d'amour; Der gestreifft Dantz/Gassenhauer [instrumental]; Huhner G'schrei [instrumental]) (rec St. Laurentius Church, Meeder/Coburg, July 16-20, 1995)* CPO ▲ 999388 [DDD] (14.97)

HelioTrope

The Romance of the Rose: Feminine Voices from Medieval France—features songs by the women troubadours from southern France KOCH ▲ 7103 [DDD] (16.97)

Hespèrion XX [cnd:Jordi Savall]

El barroco español: Spanish Secular Music, ca 1640-1700—features works by de Milanes *(Dexa la aljava)*, José Marín *(Aquella sierra nevada)*, Juan Hidalgo *(Peynándose estaba un olmo; Atiéna y da; Ay corazón amante; Con tanto respecto adoran; Ay que me rio de amor)*, Martín y Coll *(Diferencias sobre las Folias; La Chacona; Canarios)*, S. Durón *(Sosieguen descansen)*, Cabanilles *(Toccata; Gallarda)*, Juan del Vado *(No te embarques) (rec 1976)* VCL (Veritas) ▲ 61346 [ADD] (11.97)

El Cancionero de la Colombino: 1451-1506 *(music of Spain from the time of Columbus and the early years in the reign of the Catholic Kings)*—features mostly villancicos, from the library of Columbus's son ASTR ▲ 8763 (18.97)

El Cancionero de Palacio: 1474-1516 *(music of Spain at the time of the Catholic Kings)*—features works by Anchieta, Badajoz, Enzina, Gabriel, Millán, Román, et al. ASTR ▲ 8762 (18.97)

Elizabethan Consort Music 1558-1603—features works by Alberti, Parsons, Strogers, Taverner, White, Woodcock, anon AVOX ▲ 9804 (18.97)

Folias & Canarios—features works by Cabezón *(Folias)*, A. Mudarra *(Fantasia)*, Joan Cabanilles *(Tiento de falsas; Fantasia)*, G. Sanz *(Jàcaras; Canarios; Clarines y Tropetas)*, G. Kapsberger *(Arpegiatta; Canarios)*, G. Gorzanis *(Gallarda)*, Ortafà *(Si ay perdut mon saber)*, Ruiz de Ribadayaz *(Paradetas)*, Piccinini *(Toccata & Chiaccona)*, Correa de Arrauxo *(Todo el mundo en general)*, anon. *(Paduana del Re Saltarello; Con que la lavaré; El pare i la mare)* ASTR ▲ 8516 [DDD] (18.97)

Lope de Vega: Intermedios del Barroco Hispánico, w. Montserrat Figueras (sop)—features music of the Spanish theatre ca. 1580-1680 (music written for Lope de Vega *Comedias*, incl. selections by Cabanilles, Romero de Heredia & Correa de Arauxo) ASTR ▲ 8729 (18.97)

The Medinaceli Song Book: Music in the Kingdom of Castille During the Age of Philip II [Sp] *(compiled in the late 16th century)*—featuring works by Cabezón, Cébrian, F. Guerrero, P. Guerrero, G. de Morata, Mudarra, Anon. [Sp] [booklet w. Sp/F/G/E texts] ASTR ▲ 8764 [DDD] (18.97)

Moyen Âge & Renaissance *(sels from previous Harmonia Mundi releases)*—features works by Alfonso El Sabio *(Instrumental; Miragres fremosos faz por nos [w. La Capella Reial de Catalunya])*, Dufay *(Messe de "l'Homme arme" [Sanctus; w. La Capella Reial de Catalunya])*, Guerrero *(Trahe me post te, Virgo Maria à 5)*, C. Morales *(Missa Pro Defunctis à 5 [Introitus; w. La Capella Reial de Catalunya])*, Tye *(In Nomine à 5 My death)*, Orlandi Lassi *(Omnes de Saba vienient)*, Du Caurroy *(Vingthuictesme Fant sur 'Ad cornam agni providi')*, P. Guerrero *(Di perra mora)*, Enrique *(Buenas nuevas de alegría)*, Triana *(Dinos madre del donsel)*, Antonio de Cabezón *(Folias (Pavana con su glosa))*, Juan del Enzina *(Pues que jamás olvidaros)*, Cebrián *(Lágrimas de mi consuelo)*, anon *(Rondeau:La Trémouille; ¡Ay, que non ay!; Propiñan de Meylor; Tres morillas; Paduana del Re [Salterello]; Al alva venid; ¡Ay Jesús qué mal fraile!; Ta bonne grace; Bassedance I; Tordion 2)* FONT ▲ 9904 [DDD] (7.97)

Mvsicqve de Joye—features a selection of 26 instrumental ensemble works from the collection "Mvsicqve de Joye" [Joyous Music], published in Lyons ca. 1550: ricercari, branles, etc. ASTR ▲ 7724 [AAD] (18.97)

The Spirit of Gambo: English Consort & Viol Music FONT ▲ 9913 (16.97)

Hesperus [Rosa Lamoreaux (sop), Scott Reiss (rcr), Tina Chancey (vl/rebec/fid/rcr)]

I Love Lucette: French Theatrical Chansons, w. Howard Bass (lt), Jane Hershey (vl/rcr)—features works by Janequin, Sermisy, Attaingnant, et al. KOCH ▲ 7429 (16.97)

Hesperus [Tina Chancey (vielles/rebec/kamenji/lyra/rcr), Grant Herreid (lt/saz/psaltery/rcr), Scott Reiss (rcr/ham dlc/dombek/nakara)]

Neo-Medieval: Medieval Improvisations for a Postmodern Age—features works by Ciconia *(Una panthera; O Padua)*, Halle *(Tant que je vivrai)*, Lescurel *(Gracieusette)*, Senleches *(En attendant esperance)*, Machaut *(Ay, mi!; Dame, vostre doulz viaire; Se d'amer; Dame, se vous m'estes; Comment qu'a moi)*, anon *(Estampie; Istampita Manfredina; Chançoneta tedescha; Kyrie Cuthberte; Istampita chominciamento di gioia; Brid one brere; With ryght all me hert; Istampita Isabella; Pucelette; Crucifigat omnes; De ce que foul pense; Saltarello) (rec St. John's Episcopal Church, Ellicott City, MD, Aug 1996)* DORD ▲ 80155 [DDD] (13.97)

Unicorn: Medieval, Appalachian & World Musics in Fusion, w. Bruce Molsky (fid/gtr/banjo/voc)—features works by Moderne *(Bransles)*, Lescurel *(Gracieusette)*, Susato *(Allemande & Ronde)*, Edén *(Enhörningen [Unicorn])*, plus Say Old Man Can You Play the Fiddle; Cotton-eyed Joe; Shake it Down; Lady Gay; Red Rockin' Chair; Chicken Tree; Como Poden; Rhymer's Favorite; Contre le temps; Back Door Man; Captain Kidd; La Valse de Guedan; Herdsman's Tune; Lady Hamilton; Little Rabbit; Midnight on the Water; La Shymyze; La Bounette; Jenny on the Railroad *(rec Bias Studios, June 1996)* DORD ▲ 80157 [DDD] (13.97)

Hilliard Ensemble [cnd:Paul Hillier]

Codex Speciálník *(music from a Prague manuscript ca. 1500)*, w. D. James (alt), R. Covey-Crump (ten), J. Potter (ten), G. Jones (bass)—features works by Petrus de Grudencz *(Presulem ephebeatum; Paraneuma eructemus; Presidiorum erogatrix; Pneuma eucaristiarum/Veni vere illustrator/Dator eya/Paraclito tripudia)*, Johannes Touront *(Chorus iste)*, Gontrášek *(Bud' buohu chvála čest)*, Agricola *(O virens virginum)*, John Plummer *(Tota pulchra es)*, Josquin Desprez *(Ave Maria)*, anon *(Exordium quadruplate/Nate dei/Concrepet/Verbum caro; Tria sunt munera/Videntes stellam/Reges Tharsis; In natali domini; Sophia nascitur/O quam pulchra/Magi vindentes; Congaudemus pariter/En lux immensa; Magnum miraculum; Nobis est natus; Salve mater gracie; Christus iam surrexit/Terra tremuit/Angelus domini/Surrexit Christus; Terrigenarum plasmator;Pulcherrima rosa; Kyrie/Gloria/Credo/Sanctus [from Petite Camusette]; Ave pura tu peulla) (rec Gönningen City Church, Jan 1993)* ECM ▲ 21504 [DDD] (16.97)

Medieval English Music *(from the 14th & 15th centuries)* [E,L] HMA ▲ 1901106 (9.97)

Officium, w. D. James (alt), R. Covey-Crump (ten), J. Potter (ten), G. Jones (bass), J. Gabarek (sop/ten saxs)—features works by de Morales *(Parce mihi domine [from Officum defunctorium; performed three times])*, de La Rue *(O salutaris hostia)*, Perotinus *(Beata viscera)*, Dufay *(Ave maris stella)*, anon. *(Primo tempore; Sanctus; Regnantem sempiterna; Procedentem sponsum; Pulcherrima rosa; De spineto nata rosa; Credo; Virgo flagellatur; Oratio Ieremiae) (rec Sept 1993)* ECM ▲ 21525 (16.97) 21525

Popular Music from the Time of Henry VIII, w. New London Consort members—features O Lusty May; This Day Daws; Begone, Sweit Night; En Vray Amoure; O My Heart; Madame d'Amours; Consort Piece XX; Absent I Am; My Heartly Service; Hey Trolly Lolly Lo!; En Frolyk Weson; Be Peace! Ye Make Me Spill My Ale!; The Duke of Somersettes Dompe; Ah, Robin; I Love Unloved; Up I Arose in Verno Tempore; Puzzle Canon VI; And I Were a Maiden; England Be Glad SAGA ▲ 3357 [ADD] (14.97)

The Romantic Englishman—features works by Jonathan Battishill, William Beale, Julius Benedict, William Sterndale Bennett, Henry Bishop, John Goss, John Hatton, William Horsley, J.L. Molloy, Hubert Parry, R.L. de Pearsall, Thomas Phillips, Reginald Spofforth, John Stainer, Arthur Sullivan, T.F. Walmisley, Samuel Webbe DUO ▲ 89009

The Singing Club—features works by Ravenscroft, Lawes, Purcell, Arne, et al. HMA ▲ 1901153 (9.97)

Songs for a Tudor King, w. Judith Nelson (sop), David James (alt), Paul Elliott (ten), Leigh Nixon (ten), P. Hillier (bass)—features works by Fayrfax, Cornysh, Browne, Sheryngham, anon. SAGA ▲ 3378 [ADD] (14.97)

Sumer Is Icumen in: Medieval English Songs & Church Music [E,L] HAM ▲ 901154

Sweet Love, Sweet Hope *(songs from a 15th century Bodelian manuscript)*—features works by Dufay *(J'attendray tant qu'il vous playra; Quel fronte signorille in paradiso; Ce moys de may soyons lies et jouyeux; Je me complains piteusement; Ma belle dame souveraine; Navré je suis d'un art penetratif; Entre vois, gentils amoureux; Belle, veuilles moy retenir; Je veux chanter de cuer joyeux; Ce jour de l'an voudray joye mener; Par droit je puis bien complaindre et gemir)*, Rezon *(Il est temps que me retraye)*, Hasprois *(Ma doulce amor, je me doy bien complaindre)*, Brollo *(Nulx ne pourroit ymaginer)*, Malbecque *(Adieu vous di, mes seigneurs et amis; Quant de belle me parti; Dieu vous doinst bon jour)*, Paullet *(J'aim. Qui?)*, Brixiensis *(O spirito gentil, tu m'ay percosso)*, plus anon pieces *(Douce seperance my conforte tous jours; Or sus, mon cuer, vers ma dame t'encline) ([E,F] texts)* ISIS ▲ 30 [DDD] (16.97)

Hillier, Paul (bass)

Proensa *(Troubadour songs)*, w. Stephen Stubbs (lt/voc), Andrew Lawrence-King (hp/voc), Erin Headley (vielle) ECM ▲ 21368 [DDD] (16.97)

His Majesties Sagbutts & Cornetts

For His Majestys Sagbutts & Cornetts: English Music from Henry VIII to Charles II—features works by Henry VIII *(Bassedances)*, Alamire *(Bassedance T'Andernacken)*, Aston *(A Hornepype)*, Tye *(In nomine)*, Alwood *(In nomine II)*, Byrd *(In nomine V)*, Bull *(The Bull Masque; Fant)*, Coprario *(Fant; Gray's Inn the 1st)*, J. Bassano *(Fant No. 3)*, East *(When David Heard That Absalon Was Slain)*, A. Bassano *(Pavan & Galliard)*, Brade *(Cornish Dance; Scottish Dance)*, Locke *(Voluntaries in F, d & a)*, For His Majestys Sagbutts & Cornetts *(Pavan-Almand; Suite 1 in d; Suite 2 in F)*, anon *(The Trowmpettus; Hugh Ashton's Maske; The Queen's Masque; Irish Dance)* HYP ▲ 66894 (17.97)

His Majesties Sagbutts & Cornetts, Richard Wistreich (bass), Alistair Ross (org)

Music from 17th Century Germany—features works by Schein, Scheidt, Schütz, et al. MER ▲ 84096 (16.97)

L'Homme Armé

Musica a Firenze: The Time of Lorenzo the Magnificent *(14 songs reflecting life in Florenz under the Medicis)*—features works by Guillaume Dufay, Alessandro Coppini, Heinrich Isaac, Arnolfo Giliardi, Pintello & Rubinet, including Il carnasciale e la lauda (Carnival songs) *(rec Apr 1990)* CHR ▲ 77132 [DDD] (17.97)

Huelgas Ensemble [cnd:Paul van Nevel]

Codex las Huelgas *(music from 13th & 14th cent. Spain)*—features Ex illustri nata prosapia; Crucifigat omnes; O Maria maris stella; Ex agone sanguinis; Belial vocatur; Sanctus; Agnus Dei; Benedicamus Domino; Flavit auster; Eya mater; Quis dabit capiti; Casta catholica; Homo miserabilis [L] *(rec Oct 9-11, 1992)* COL ▲ 53341 [DDD] (16.97)

La Dissection d'un homme armé *(cycle of 6 15th-century masses after a Burgundian song)* COL (Vivarte) ▲ 45860 (16.97)

Febus Avant! Music at the Court of Gaston Febus, 1331-1391 COL (Vivarte) ▲ 48195 [DDD] (16.97)

In Morte di Madonna Laura: Madrigal Cycle after Texts of Petrarca, 1307-1374—features works by various Italian composers of the 16th century COL (Vivarte) ▲ 45942

Italia mia: Musical Imagination of the Renaissance *(16th-century Italian music)* COL (Vivarte) ▲ 48065 (16.97)

La Favola di Orfeo—features historic reconstruction of music by 4 composers for the 15th cent play La Favola di Orfeo COL (Seon) 2-▲ 60095 (14.97)

Matteo Flecha: Las Ensaladas *(Early Spanish Renaissance Music)* COL (Vivarte) ▲ 46699 (16.97)

Music from the Court of King Janus at Nicosia *(1374-1432)*—features Certes mout fu/Nous devons tresfort amer; Credo; Gloria; Je prens d'amour noriture; Je prens plaisir en une dame; Je sui trestout d'amour raimpli; Personet armonia; Sanctus in eternis/Sanctus et ingenitus; Si doulcement me fait amours/Nulz vrais amans; Si doulchement mon ceur je sens souspris *(rec Belgium, June 16-18, 1993)* COL (Vivarte) ▲ 53976 [DDD] (16.97)

Tears of Lisbon, w. Beatriz de Conceição, António Rocha—features 16th cent fado music COL ▲ 62256 (16.97)

Ibn Báya Ensemble

Musica Andalusi, w. Eduardo Paniagua, Omar Metiovi—features Qála Lí; Ya Wáhida Insád on Tab' Al-Istihlál; Gaybatuk; Akáml l-bhá Mawwál on Tab' Al-Istihlál; Indamá adá; Min Subayba; Gazálun samá Mawwál on Tab' Al-Hiyáz Al-Kabir & Tab' Raml Al-Máya COL ▲ 62262 (16.97)

In Canto Ensemble [Alexandrina Polo (sop), Toni Gubau (alt), Dolors Serra (trans fl), Jordi Comellas (rebec), Fernando Quiroga (vih), Jordi Reguant (positiv org)]

Musica ¡vanguardista! from the Court of Juan I, 1350-1396—features works by Cameraco *(Credo)*, Trebor *(Quant Joyne Cuer; Passerose de beauté; En Seumellant)*, Senleches *(Fuions de ci)*, Reyneau *(Va t'en mon cuer)*, anon *(Kyrie, "Rex Immensa Maiestatis"; Kyrie; Gloria; Kyrie, "O Virgo Sacrata Maria")* EAM ▲ 7474 [DDD] (16.97)

Indiana Univ Early Music Institute

Laude: Medieval Italian Spiritual Songs—features Laude novella; Plangiamo; Laudate la surrectione; Peccatrice, nominata FOCU ▲ 912 [AAD]

Invernizzi, Roberta (sop), Accademia Strumentale Italiana [cnd:Alberto Rasi]

O Dolce Vita Mia—features works by Lando *(Io Vivea Come Aquila)*, anon *(Canario; Pavana Detta La Battaglia; Pavana La Morte de la Ragione)*, Cambio *(La Morte di Marito; Non T'Arricordi Quando Me Dicevi)*, Rore *(Anchor Che Col Partire)*, Milano *(Ricercare e Fantasia; La Spagna)*, Ruffo *(Lieti, Felici Spirti; A Che Cercar gli Specchi; Gentil Mia Donna)*, Scandello *(Voria Che Tu Cantasse una Canzone)*, Modena *(Ricercare a 4)*, Cesena *(Non Posso Abbandonarte)*, Willaert *(O Dolce Vita Mia)*, Borrono *(Fant)*, Azzaiolo *(E Levai d'una Bella Mattina)* STRV ▲ 33396 [DDD] (16.97)

James, Ethan (h-g), Terra Nova Consort

Renaissance en Provence—features Traditional *(A la ciéuta de Betelèn; Adam e sa coumpagno; Ai proun coneigu; Ai! la bono fourtuno; Je sais, vierge Marie; La fe coumando do crèire; Lei Pastourèu; Li a proun de gènt; Li a quaucarèn que m'a fa pòu; Maire, lei campagno; Que disès, mei bon fraire?; Tout mon plus grand plaisir; Tu que cerques tei delice; Vènes lèu vèire la pièucello)* DOR ▲ 90269 [DDD] (16.97)

Clément Janequin Ensemble [cnd:Dominique Visse]

Canciones y Ensaladas: Songs & Instrumental Pieces of the Golden Age HAM ▲ 901627 (17.97)

Portrait—features works by Lassus, Regnard, de Castro, Le Jeune, de Bertrand, Le Petit, Gombert, de Sermisyde, L'Estocrat, Banchieri, Vasquez, Flecha, Janequin HAM ▲ 290868 (7.97)

Jehan de Channey Ensemble

Cantigas de Santa Maria—features Cantigas de Santa Maria (13th cent); Carmina Burana (12th cent) DPV ▲ 9128 (14.97)

Kalenda Maya

Medieval & Renaissance Songs & Dances from Spain, Italy, France & Germany *(1200-1550)* [period instrs] SIMX ▲ 1017 [DDD] (19.97)

Karasszon, Dezsö (org)

The Chants of the Reformation in Hungary, w. Debrecen College Cantus—features Antiphones, Psalms & Folk-hymns [Hun] HUN ▲ 12665 [DDD] (16.97)

Lancaster & Valois: French & English Music, ca. 1350-1420 HYP ▲ 66588 (17.97)

The Marriage of Heaven & Hell: Motets & Songs from 13th Century France HYP ▲ 66423 [DDD] (17.97)

The Medieval Romantics: French Songs & Motets, 1340-1440—features works by Dufay, Machaut, et al. HYP ▲ 66463 [DDD] (17.97)

A Song for Francesca: Music in Italy, 1330-1430—features works by Dufay, rossin, Haucourt, et al. HYP ▲ 66286 (17.97)

Kaslik Univ Musicological Institute Instrumental Ensemble Lebanon [cnd:Aida Chalhoub], Kaslik Univ Musicological Institute Chorus Lebanon

Mouwachah—features Arabo-Andalusian music from ca 711-1492 STUD ▲ 2669 (18.97)

King's Consort [cnd:Robert King]

Great Baroque Arias, Part I INMP ▲ 894 (12.97)

King's Consort [cnd:Robert King], King's Consort Choir

Lo Sposalizio—features works by G. Gabrieli, A. Gabrieli, plus others HYP 2-▲ 67048 (17.97)

King's Noyse [cnd:David Douglass]

Canzonetta: 16th Century Canzoni & Instrumental Dances, w. Ellen Hargis (sop), Paul O'Dette (lt)—includes works by Vecchi *(Saltarello detto Trivella; Fammi una conzonetta capriciosa; Non vo'pregare chi non m'ascolta; Fa una canzone senza note nere; Mostrav'in ciel)*, Banchieri *(La Guamina; L'Alcenagina sopra Vestiva i colli; La Pomponazza)*, Agostini *(all'arm', all' arm')*, Bottegari *(Sola soletta me ne vo)*, Willaert *(Io visans; O bene mio fam' uno favore)*, Rore *(Ancor che co'l partire [w. David Douglass (vn)]; S'eguale a la mia vogla)*, Bassano *(Divisions on "Frai et gaillard"; Divisions on "Onques amor")*, Crecquillon *(Onques amor; Content ou non)*; sels. from Chilesotti's & Bottegari's Lutebooks HAM ▲ 907127 (17.97)

Le Jardin de Mélodies: 16th Century French Dances & Songs, w. Ellen Hargis (sop), Paul O'Dette (lt) HAM ▲ 907194 (17.97)

The King's Delight: 17th Century Ballads for Voice & Violin Band—features works by Byrd *(Browning; Jog on [w. E. Hargis (soprano)])*, Praetorius *(Packington's Pound; Daphne)*, Whitfield *(Huntsuppe; The lovely northerne lasse [w. Hargis])*, Schultz *(Tantz)*, Scheidt *(O Nachbar Roland)*, Brade *(Dulcina; As att noone Dulcina rested [w. Hargis]; Grimstock; Robin is to the greenwood gone)*, Simpson *(Bonny sweet robin)*, Jack Pudding *(A light hears A jewell [w. Hargis]; Child Grove; Easter Thursday; The Begger Boy; Mr. Isaac's maggot; The little barley-corne [w. Hargis])*, anon. *(The king's delight; All in a Garden Green; Gathering peascods; Fortune my foe; Blew-cap for me [w. Hargis])* HAM ▲ 907101 (17.97)

Stravaganze: 17th Century Italian Songs & Dances, w. Andrew Lawrence-King (hp)—features works by Trabaci: *(Gagliarda terza sopra la mantoana; Gagliarda prima detta la galante; Consonanze stravaganti)*, Dell'Arpa *(Gagliarda)*, Monteverdi *(Non ha'l ciel cotanti lumi)*, Peri *(Qual cadavero spirante; O durezza di ferro; Un dì, soletto)*, Farina *(Pavana seconda)*, Vitali *(Se pur è ver)*, Zannetti *(Aria del gran Duca; Gagliarda di santino detto la muzza; La Bergamesca; Basso delle ninfe; Bassa fioiosa; Il Ceferino [all from Il Scolaro])*, Sabino *(Gagliarda falsa)*, Rovetta *(La Lagrime d'erminia)*, Castello *(Son 16 a 4)*, Gesualdo *(Gagliarda) (rec Campion Center, Boston, MA, Oct 17-19, 1994)* HAM ▲ 907159 (17.97)

Kirkby, Emma (sop), Robert White (bgp), Pavlo Beznosiuk (fid), Nick Bicat (perc), Gothic Voices [cnd:Christopher Page]

The Spirits of England & France, Vol. 2—features works by Adam de la Halle *(Assenés chi; Grievilier)*, Auderfroi *(Au novel tens pascor)*, Gace Brulé *(Cil qui d'amours; De bien amer grant joie atant; Desconfortez, plains de dolor; Quant define fueille et flor)*, Wibers Kaukesel *(Fins cures enamourés; Un chant novel)*, Gautier de Dargies *(La doce pensee)*, Ernous li Viele *(Por conforter mon corage)*, anon. *(Donna pos vos ay chausida; Amours m'art con fouc am flama; Quant voi la fleur nouvele; Estampies)* HYP ▲ 66773 (17.97)

984

▲ = CD ♦ = Enhanced CD △ = MD ▮ = Cassette Tape ▯ = DCC

Kithara [Shirley Rumsey (voc/lt/Renaissance gtr/cittern), J. Walters (Italianate triple hp), Susanna Pell (Renaissance b vl), W. Lyons (fls/rcr), D. Miller (thb/lt), C. Wilson (lt/Renaissance gtr/baroque gtr)]
Music Mediterranea: Music of the Italian & Spanish Renaissance—features works by Adiran Willaert *(A quand'a quand'haveva una vicina; O bene mio fam'uno favore)*, Gian D. da Mola *(Cingari simo venit'a giocare)*, Diego Ortiz *(La spagna; La gamba; O felici occhi miei)*, Melchiore de Barberiis *(Madonna qual certezza)*, Enríquez de Valderrábano *(Discantar sobre un punto)*, A. Valente *(Tenore del passo e mezo)*, Simone Molinaro *(Ballo detto il Conte Orlando e Saltarello)*, G. Picchi *(Ballo e Saltarello ongaro)*, A. Piccinini *(Chiaconna)*, Dosimo Bottegari *(Non si vedde giamai)*, G. Bassano *(Vestiva I colli)*, L. Rossi *(Passacaglia)*, J. Arañés *(Un sarao de la Chacona)*, anon. *(Riu, riu, riu; Recercar; D. vagh'e leggiadra; Folias)* CHN ▲ 562 [DDD] (16.97)

Koningsberger, Martin (bar), BRISK Recorder Quartet
Music of the Spheres: English Consort Songs of the Late 16th Century, w. Mike Fentross (lt)—features works by Byrd *(Elegy for Tallis; Elegy for Sidney; Fant à 4)*, plus works by Nicholson, Dowland, Strogers, Bennett, et al. GLOE ▲ 5163 (16.97)

Kreidler, Ute (sop)
In the Silo Warehouse, w. Russ Hodge (vl/fid/dilruba), Johannes Vogt (lt/gtr), Knut Rossler (sax)—early music & improvisations featuring works by Hildegard von Bingen, Sefardisch, Caccini, Narváez, plus other works BAYE ▲ 150021 (17.97)

Kühn Chamber Soloists [cnd:Pavel Kühn], Symposium Musicum
Torquato Tasso in the Music of His Contemporaries—features works by Gabrieli *(Le bella pargoletta)*, Gesualdo *(Se cosi dolce è il duolo; Non è questa la mano; Caro amoroso neo; Se taccio, il duol s'avanza)*, de Monte *(Al tuo vago pallore; In un bel bosco; Odi, filli, che tuona)*, Marenzio *(Vezzosi augelli infra le Verdi fronde)*, Monteverdi *(S'andasse amor a caccia; Ecco mormorar l'onde)*, Hassler *(Mentre la donna mia)*, Pallavicino *(Come vivrò nelle mie pene, amore)*, il Verso *(Voi bramate, ben mio)*, Cifra *(Chiudesti i lumi, armida il cielo)*, Falcone *(Sovra le Verdi chiome)*, Landi *(Se tu mi lasci)*, Nenna *(S'io taccio)*, Zanotti *(Giacea la mia virtu)*, plus more *(rec Apr 1995)* PANT ▲ 710377 [DDD] (16.97)

Kuijken, Wieland (vl), Sigiswald Kuijken (vn), Robert Kohnen (hpd)
Music for a Viol *(Fantasia, Duos, Divisions, etc.)*—features works by Simpson, Jenkins, Locke ACCE ▲ 68014 (17.97)

Kuijken, Sigiswald (vn), Wieland Kuijken (va), Gustav Leonhardt (hpd)
Music of Versailles—features works by d'Anglebert *(Prelude in d)*, Forqueray *(Suite in c)*, Marais *(La sonnerie de Ste. Geneviève; Tombea de M. de St.-Colombe)* DEHA ▲ 77145 [DDD]

Lacrimae Ensemble
Celeste Giglio: Flowers of 16th Century Italian Dance Music—features Courante; Celeste Giglio; Chiara Stella; Ballo fatto da sei Cavalieri; Il Bianco Fiore; Spagnoletta; Gagliarda detta la Lisfeltina di Santino; Gagliarda; La Battaglia; Villanella [2 versions]; La Volta; Improvs on La Folia; Bassa Toscana; Brando detto Alta Regina; Alta Mendozza; Ballo del Fiore/Branle du Chandelier *(rec Jan 1996)* ERAS ▲ 186 [DDD] (13.97)

Lamandier, Esther (voc/instrs)
Decameron *(14th-cent. Florentine songs)* ASTR ▲ 7706

Lane, Jennifer (mez), Timothy Burris (thb)
Lagrime Mie: Early Songs of Love & Torment—features works by Caccini *(Fortunato augellino; Chi mi confort'ahimè; Belle rose porporine; Amarilli, mia bella)*, Kapsberger *(Passamezzo; Toccata [both thb solo])*, d'India *(Cruda Amarilli; Piange madonna)*, Monteverdi *(Di misera Regina)*, Strozzi *(Lagrime Mie)*, Frescobaldi *(Così mi disprezzate; Ti lascio anima mia; Se l'aura spira) (rec St. Peter's Episcopal Church, New York City, Feb 27-28, 1996)* PGM ▲ 103 [DDD] (16.97)

Lesne, Brigitte (sgr/hp/perc)
Ave Eva: Songs of Womanhood from the 12th & 13th Centuries OPUS ▲ 30134 (17.97)

Little Consort [Lucia Meeuwsen (voc), Walter van Hauwe (rcrs), Toyohiko Satoh (lts), Kees Boeke (vls)]
Italian Chamber Music of the Seicento—features works by Caccini, van Eyck, Fontana, Frescobaldi, Monteverdi, Quagliati [I] CCL ▲ 2791 [DDD] (17.97)
Johannes Ciconia & His Time—features eleven ballades, madrigals, canons, etc., by Renaissance Dutch composer Johannes Ciconia & contemporaries CCL ▲ 290 [DDD] (17.97)
Little Consort with Frans Brüggen, w. Frans Brüggen (fl)—features works by Machaut *(S'onques douleureusement, "Lai de confort")* plus three anonymous Spanish, English & French pieces CCL ▲ 390 [DDD] (17.97)

Live Oak
The Art of Flemish Song in the Courts of Europe, w. Nancy Knowles (sop), Frank Wallace (bar/fl/vih)—features works by De La Rue, Josquin, Willaert, et al. CENT ▲ 2109 (16.97)

Live Oak & Company [Nancy Knowles (sop), Grant Herreid (ten/vih), Frank Wallace (bass/vih), Jane Hershey (vl)]
Lanterns of Fire: Love & the Mystic in Renaissance Spain—features works by D. Ortíz *(Recercadas 2 & 6)*, Juan de Antxieta *(Kyrie; Gloria; Sanctus; Agnus Dei [all from L'Homme Armé])*, Juan Vásquez *(¡A hermosa!; De dónde venís amores)*, San Juan de la Cruz *(Noche oscura; El pastorcico; Llama de amor viva)*, Alonso *(Niña, erguídeme los ojos)*, Moxica *(Dama, mi grande querer)*, Enrriquez de Valderrábano *(Diferencias [from Conde claros])*, Triana/Troya *(Juyzio fuerte/O ascondia verdad)*, Luys de Milán *(Fant 8)*, Mudarra/Desprez *(Pleni sunt coeli)*, P. de la Rue *(Vexilla regis/passio domini)*, María de San José *(¡Ay! nada me responde)*, T. L. de Victoria *(Caligaverunt oculi mei)*, Morales/M. de Fuenllana *(Et ressurexit [from L'Homme Armé)*, Ponce *(Alegría, alegría)*, Guerrero *(Dios inmortal)*, plus anon pieces *(Véante mis ojos [15th cent]; Con el viento; Templa, Bras, ese psalterio [both from Romances y Letras]; Mano a mano; Pase el agoa; Está la reina del cielo [all from Cancionero de Palacio]; Quien no sabe de penas [arr San Juan de la Cruz]; Tenebrae factae sunt; Dic nobis, Maria [from Cancionero de Colombina]) (rec Campion Center, Weston, MA, May 1995)* CENT ▲ 2316 [DDD] (16.97)

Loïnhdana Ensemble
Early Music at Wik *(twenty-eight 13th-16th cent. secular songs and dances)*—features works by Ludwig Senfl, Tielman Susato, et al. BIS ▲ 3 [ADD] (17.97)
The Four Seasons *(thirty-two 13th-17th cent. songs and dances)* BIS ▲ 75 [ADD] (17.97)
Woods, Women & Wine *(thirty-three 14th-17th cent. songs and dances)* BIS ▲ 120 [ADD] (17.97)

Loïnhdana Ensemble, Musica Antiqua, John Elwes (ten), André Isoir (org), Pierre Bardon (org)
Jewels of Early Music—features selections from Pierre Verany 785022, 787031, 787092, 790031 & 790043 *(rec 1982-86)* PVY ▲ 791051 [DDD] (16.97)

London Camerata
Music for Kings & Courtiers—features works by Coperario, Robert Johnson, Lawes, Bull, Frescobaldi, Castello, Caccini, anon. *(rec July 19-21, 1978)* SAGA ▲ 3367 [ADD]
Popular Music from the Time of Queen Elisabeth I—features works by R. Johnson *(Where the Bee Sucks)*, Cornysh *(Ah Robin)*, Dowland *(Sorrow, Stay; Can She Excuse My Wrongs?)*, Byrd *(Pavan & Gaillard, "Earl of Salisbury")*, Morley *(It Was a Lover & His Lass)*, Bull *(Les Buffons)*, Campion *(There Is a Garden in Her Face; Oft Have I Sighed)*, plus anon pieces *(All in a Garden Green; The 3 Ravens; Packington's Pound; The Wind & the Rain; Fortune, My Foe; Jouissance; Watkin's Ale; Heven & Erth; Good Fellows Must Go Learn to Dance)* SAGA ▲ 3352 [ADD] (14.97)
Sixteenth Century Music: The Muses' Garden for Delights—features music by Cara *(Non è tempo d'aspettare)*, Dalza *(Suite of Dances)*, Tromboncino *(Ave Maria; Poi che vole)*, da Mantua *(Urum bilirium)*, Henry VIII *(Pastime with Good Company)*, Cooper *(Farewell My Joy)*, Neusidler *(Preambel;Tantz Wascha mesa)*, Schlick *(Cupido hat im ie erdacht; Maria zart von edler Art)*, del Encina *(Ay triste que vengo)* & trad. anon. works SAGA ▲ 3392 (14.97)

London Early Music Consort [cnd:David Munrow]
The Art of Courtly Love—features works by Machaut, Dufay, Binchois, plus others *(rec 1976)* VCL (David Munrow Edition) 2-▲ 61284 (21.97)
The Art of the Netherlands, 1450-1520—features works by Josquin Desprez *(Scaramella va alla guerra; Allegez moy, doulce plaisant brunette; El grillo è buon cantore; Adieu mis amours; Credo super "De tous biens"; De profundis à 5; Benedicta es caelorum regina)*, H. Isaac *(Donna di dentro della tua casa; Missa la bassadanza [Agnus Dei])*, Ghizeghem *(Te tous beins plaine [4 versions])*, Brumel *(Du tout plongiet—Fors seulment l'attente; Missa et ecce terre motus [Gloria])*, Ghiselin *(Ghy syt die serste boven al)*, Barbireau *(En fröhlich wesen [attrib; 3 versions])*, Ockeghem *(Prenez sur moi vostre exemple amoureux; Intemerata Dei mater)*, Busnois *(Fortuna desperata [3 versions])*, Tinctoris *(Misse sine nomine [Kyrie])*, P. de la Rue *(Missa Ave Sanctissima Maria [Credo]; Ave sanctissima Maria [attrib])*, Obrecht *(Haec Deum caeli; Laudemus nunc Dominum)*, Compère *(O bone Jesu [attrib])*, Mouton *(Nesciens mater virgo virum)*, plus anon pieces *(Mijn morken gaf mij een jonck wijff; Guillaume se va chaufer; Inviolata integra et casta es Maria)* VCL (Veritas) ▲ 61334 [DDD] (21.97)
The Medieval Experience: Monks, Troubadours, Motets, Masses & Memorials—sels unknown PARC 4-▲ 49082 (26.97)
Monteverdi's Contemporaries—features works by Mainerio, Guami, Lappi, Priuli, Porta, Busatti, Donati, D'India & Grandi VCL (David Munrow Edition) ▲ 61288 (11.97)
Music of the Crusades *(12th & 13th century French music)* PLON (Jubilee) ▲ 30264 [ADD] (11.97)
Music of the Gothic Era *(excerpts from the now unavailable 3-LP set)* PARC ▲ 15292 [ADD] (16.97)
Pleasures of the Royal Court, w. Christopher Hogwood (kbd) 75597 ▲ 71326 [ADD]

London Early Music Group [cnd:James Tyler]
O Dolce Vita Mia: Italian Music of the High Renaissance 75597 ▲ 79029 [DDD]

London Musica Antiqua [cnd:Philip Thorby]
The Field of Cloth of Gold: A Celebration in Music of the Meeting in 1520 of Henry VIII of England & François I of France—features works by William Cornish, Henry VIII, Claude Gervaise, Jean Richefort, et al. AMON ▲ 51 [DDD] (16.97)

London Musica Reservata [cnd:Michael Morrow]
A Concert of Early Music, w. Jantina Noorman (mez)—features works by Morton *(Il sera pour vous conbatu/l'homme armé)*, Dunstable *(O Rosa bella)*, Azzaiolo *(Chi passa per sta strada)*, Senfl *(Es Taget vor dem Walde)*, Certon *(J'ay le rebours)*, Dalza *(Tastar de corde; Recercar)*, Vaqueiras *(Kalenda Maya)*, Sermisy *(Dont vient cela)*, Othmayr *(Mir ist ein schönst brauns Maidelein)*, Frye *(Tout a par moy)*, anon *(Pavana la bataille; L'homme armé; Galliard after Lavecha; Blame Not My Lute; Patrie pacis; Amor potest/ad amorem; Aime sospiri; Hoftanz und Hupfauff; Es Taget vor dem Walde; Belle qui tiens ma vie; Danse royale; Me Lykyth Ever; Amors, Amors; Tant apart; Saltarello) (rec Conway Hall, London, 1972) [F,L,E,I,G] texts* VC ▲ 96 [AAD] (13.97)
The Instruments of the Middle Ages & Renaissance, w. Martin Bookspan (nar), Jantina Noorman (sgr), John Dudley (sgr), Edgar Fleet (sgr), David Thomas (bass)—features a narrated presentation of the specific timbre, tonal range & unique qualities of each instrument, followed by an appropriate composition written for it [Bowed Strings, Plucked Strings, Wire-strung Instruments, Percussion, Winds, Brass & Keyboards] *(rec Conway Hall, London, June 28-July 9, 1972)* VC 2-▲ 8093 [ADD]

London Pro Musica [cnd:Bernard Thomas]
A Florentine Carnival: Festival of Music for Lorenzo d'Medici—features songs written for the May Carnival in 15th century Florence ICC ▲ 6701992 (8.97)
Gentil Madonna: Popular Music of the Italian Renaissance—features works by Azzaiolo *(Chi Passa Per Sta Strada; Girometta, Senza Te; Occhio non Fu; Vorrei Che Tu Cantassi; Gentil Madonna)*, Ortiz *(Passamezzo Moderno; Recercada Ottava)*, Da Nola *(Tre Ciechi Siamo; Medici Noi Siamo; Chi Chi Li Chi)*, Gabrieli *(Chi'nde Dar...la Bose)*, Festa *(L'ultimo di de maggio)*, Patavino *(Dilla da l'acqua)*, Pacoloni *(Padoana [Gentil Madonna]; Passamezzo-Padoana-Sltarello de Zorzi; La Gamba; Padoana della Zoppa)*, Bell'Haver *(Nu Serno Tre Vecchietti)*, anon *(Chi Passa Per Sta Strada; Saltarello [Zorzi]; Gagliarda [Gentil Madonna]; Pavana [Le Forze d'Ercole]; Pavana [El Todescho]; Gagliarda [La Rocha el Fuso])*, trad *(La Gamba)*, et al MKMT (Musick's Monument) ▲ 6500082 (16.97)

MacKillop, Rob (lt), William Taylor (hp)
Graysteil: Music from the Middle Ages & Renaissance in Scotland, w. Andy Hunter (sgr), Paul Rendall (ten)—features works by Carver *(Mass à 3 [Kyrie, Gloria, Credo, Sanctus & Benedictus, Agnus Dei])*, anon *(Orkney Wedding Song; Santcus: Voce vita; Hymn to St. Magnus, Earl of Orkney; Alleluya, Post partum; Lux et gloria; Ane lesson of 4 mynnymis; Canon The Fyvtent; Canon; Canon the Nyntene; Fantasie; Graysteil) (rec Rosslyn Chapel, Roslin, Scotland, Nov 1995)* DORD ▲ 80141 [DDD] (13.97)

Madrid Atrium Musicae [cnd:Gregorio Paniagua]
La Folia de la Spagna HAM ▲ 901050 (17.97)
Musique Arabo-Andalouse HAM ▲ 90389 (17.97)
Musique de la Grèce antique HMA ▲ 1901015 (9.97)
La Spagna BIS ▲ 163 (17.97) △ MD 163

Mala Punica [cnd:Pedro Memelsdorff]
Missa Cantilena—features missa cantilena based on secular songs from late 14th & 15th cent Italy ERAT ▲ 17069 (16.97)

Manno, Vincenzo (ten), Ensemble Concerto [cnd:Roberto Gini]
Strana Armonia d'Amore, Vol. 2, w. Sabina Colonna Preti (vl), Paul Beier (archlt), Marco Fodella (chit), Maurizio Martelli (chit), Roberto Gini (vl/hpd/org)—features works by Castaldi *(Fuor di noia; Hor che la notte; Vissi all'hor noiosa vita)*, Possenti *(E' questo il mio guidar l'onde)*, Ferrari *(Quando prendon riposo; Cielo, sia con tua pace; Che si pensa costei?; Voglio di vita uscire)*, Mazzocchi *(In braccio à Christo)*, Fontei *(Il pianto di erinna)*, Spighi *(Filli, tu posi) (rec July 1992)* STRV ▲ 33407 [DDD] (16.97)

Marc, Sébastien (rcr), Le Concert Français [cnd:P. Hantaï]
Maskes & Fantazies *(early 17th cent. consort music, mostly English)*—features works by J. Adson *(Adsonns maske)*, John Coperario *(Suite No. 9 in D; Suite No. 12 in d)*, R. Johnson *(The fairey masque; The first witches dance; The second witches dance; The nobleman)*, W. Lawes *(Musickes Handmaide, excerpt; Sellabrand)*, Matthew Locke *(Suite No. 6 in A)*, T. Tomkins *(Fancye for two to play)*, Johann Jakob Van Eyck *(Malle symen; Courante, of Harte diefje waerom zoo stil)*, Anon. *(Cuparaee or Graysin; Grays Inne masque; The Kinges mistresse; The ladies masque I; The furies; The goates masque; The nymphs dance; Sir Francis Bacon Masque I; The temple anticke I) (rec 1992)* ASTR ▲ 8504 [DDD]

Mare Balticum Ensemble
Music from the Time of the Royal Swedish Flagship Kronan *(original instrument performances of late 17th-century works)*—features works by Ahlenius, H. Albert, Albrici, Anonymous, Düben, Hake, Hammerschmiedt, A. Piccinini, Scheidt, Schmelzer, Vierdanck, Von Bibern KPT ▲ 32066 [DDD]

La Maurache
Bawdy Songs from the Time of Francis I & Henry IV—features works by Certon *(Ung Verd Galland)*, Clèreau *(Elle est d'andouille friande)*, Attaingnant *(Gaillarde; Le corps s'en va; Bransle de poictou)*, Janequin *(Un gros prieur; On dit que vous la voulés prendre; Ung jour colin)*, Arbeau *(Bransle du chandelier; Tourdion)*, Berchem *(Jehan de lagni)*, Petit *(Mon amy m'avait promis)*, Ballard *(Ballet; Bransles de village)*, De Sermisy *(En entrant en ung jardin)*, Susato *(Suite de danses)*, Praetorius *(Canarie; Irishe Ho-Hoane; Alman)*, Guedron *(À paris sul'petit pont)*, anon *(Der Winter; Faisons bonne chère)*, trad *(Le testament de l'âne; Le moine nicolas)* ARN ▲ 68344 [AAD] (16.97)
In Praise of Wine & the Vine: Songs & Dances from Rabelais to Henri IV—features interpretations of music from the Middle Ages and Renaissance using period documents and traditional instruments ARN ▲ 68248 [DDD] (16.97)
Musica Cathedralis: Chartres XIII siecle, w. Ensemble Fulbert, Maîtrise du Conservatoire de Chartres—features hymns, chansons, organ solos, chants, harp pieces, dances, motets from 13th-century France ARN 2-▲ 268428 (31.97)

Micrologus Ensemble
Landini & His Contemporaries *(14th cent. Florence)*—features works by Fiernze *(Quand'Amor; l' ò perduto l'albero)*, Landini *(Ochi dolenti mie; Abbonda di virtù)*, Gulielmus *(Mille merzé; Amore)*, Masi *(Come in sul fronte fu preso Narciso)*, Flrorentia *(De poni amor a me)*, anon. *(Salterello; La manfredina; Io son un pellegrin; Chosa non è che a sé tanto mi tiri; Giporte miebramant; Tre fontane; Salterello; Non posso far bucato che non piova)* OPUS ▲ 30112 (17.97)
O Yesu Dolce: 15th Century Italian Spiritual Songs OPUS ▲ 30169 (17.97)

Micrologus Ensemble Soloists, Hora Decima Singers
Laude Celestiniane—features 8 anon sels from the Medieval tradition of Aquila in the 14th & 15th centuries CNCE ▲ 2041 [DDD] (16.97)

Minstrelsy
Vieni o cara—features music from the Italian & English Baroque era LYR (Early Music) ▲ 8023 (16.97)

Montserrat Escolania [cnd:Franzjosef Maier], Tolz Boys' Choir, Collegium Aureum
Missa Salisburgensis DEHA ▲ 77050 [DDD] 77050

Mora Vocis
Mystery of Ancient Voices—features Alleluì posui adjutorium potentem electum de plebe mea; Stirps Jess, Mater Dei; Mane prima sabbatei, O natio naphandi generis, Conditio nature de fuit; Alleluia video celos apertos; Haec Dies; Alleluia post partum; Alleluia nativitas PVY ▲ 793101 [DDD]

Música Antigua de Albuquerque
A Rose of Swych Virtu: Reverence from the Renaissance & Middle Ages DORD ▲ 80104 [DDD] (13.97)

Musica Antiqua [cnd:Christian Mendoze]
Musica Antiqua, w. Christian Mendoze (rcr)—features works by Moderne, Morley, Holborne, Mainerio, d'Arras, Praetorius, Zanetti, Demantius & Vivaldi PVY ▲ 730073 (11.97)

Música Antigua de Albuquerque
The Sport of Love—features A. Agricola *(Pour voz plaisirs)*, Anonymous *(Blow thy horn, thou jolly hunter; Caccia 'Alla caccia su su'; Correno multi cani; Jägerhorn; Saltarello; Traditora; Trotto)*, Braconnier *(Amour me trocte par la pance)*, Certon *(Je ne fus jamais si ayse)*, Coppini *(Canto di uccellatori alle starne)*, Cornysh *(Blow thi horne hunter)*, Gherardello da Firenze *(Aquila bella; Tosta che l'alba)*, Henry VIII *(Pastime with Good Company)*, Jacopo da Bologna *(Vola el bel sparver)*, Janequin *(Chansons Nouvelles 19, Miii/77; Chansons Nouvelles 19, Miii/84)*, F. Landini *(Cosi pensoso; Lasso! di donna)*, Marle *(L'enfant Amour)*, Senfl *(Es jagt ein Jäger g'schwinde; Es taget vor dem Walde; Ich schell' mein Horn)*, O. Vecchi *(Son ben mi ch'ha)*, Verdelot *(I vostri acuti dardi)*, Waelrant *(Questa fera gentil)* DOR ▲ 93175 [DDD] (16.97)

Musica Antiqua Ensemble [cnd:Christian Mendoze]
Airs & Dances of Shakespeare's Time, w. John Elwes (ten), Stephen Stubbs (lt)—features works by Brade, Campion, Holborne, Johnson, Morley, Pilkington, Rosseter PVY ▲ 787092 [DDD] (16.97)
La Follia, w. Christian Mendoze (rcr)—features works by Bellinzani, Purcell, Telemann & Scarlatti PVY ▲ 730074 (11.97)

Musica Canterey Bamberg [cnd:Hermann Dechant]
Venetian Music at the Habsburg Court in the 17th Century—features works by Bertali, Buonamente, Neri, Priuli, Valentini DEHA ▲ 77086 [DDD]

Musica Fresca [cnd:Kveta Ciznerová]
Eros in Renaissance Music—features songs by Dowland, Vecchi, Lassus, Monteverdi, Janequin, Cabezón, plus others PANT ▲ 710528 (16.97)

COLLECTIONS

Musica Reservata

16th Century Italian & French Dance Music, w. Michael Morrow (cnd)—features 16th cent. dance music including *Al di dolce ben mio; La scarpa; Baxela un trato; La traditora; Fortuna d'un gran tempo; Che fa la ramacina; E si son; Dagdun vetusta; Piva; Gentil Madonna; Le forze d'Hercole; El marchese di Saluzzo; Occhio non fu; Giorgio; Zorzi; El colognese; Passamezzo & Gagliarda d'Italie; La Bataille; Dont vient cela; Belle, que tiens ma vie; Hoboeckendans; Tordion; Branle simple; La Mourisque; Cest a grant tort; tant que vivray; Au joli bois; J'amreoye mieus dormir seullette; Il estoit une fillette; Pourquoy donc; Le cuer est bon (rec Oct 1970 & July 1971)* BOSK ▲ 123 [ADD] (15.97)

Musicians of Swanne Alley

As I Went to Walsingham *(Elizabethan instrumental & vocal music)*—features works by Anon., Richard Allison, William Byrd, Edward Collarde, Anthony Holborne, John Johnson, Guillaume Tessier HAM ▲ 905192 (17.97)

Musicians of the Globe [cnd:Philip Pickett]

The Enchanted Island: Music for a Restoration "Tempest"—features works by Draghi, Humfrey, Locke, Purcell, plus others PPHI ▲ 456505 (16.97)

The Masque of Oberon *(all music for Ben Jonson's masque original or reconstructed by Peter Holman or Peter Downey)*—features works by A Bassano *(Almande 3; Pavana)*, J. Bassano *(Almande 16)*, R. Johnson *(Almande 5:The Princes Masque I; Almande 6:The Princes Masque II; Now My Cunning Lady, Moon; The Satyrs Dance; Seek You, Majesty, to Strike? [w. chorus by P. Holman]; The Fairies Dance; The 1st of the Princes; Nor Yet O You in This Night Blest; The 3rd of the Princes)*, H. Lübeck *(Fanfare [from Tpt Ensemble Son 53])*, E. Nelham *(Buzz, Quoth the Blue Fly)*, A. Ferrabosco II *(The Solemn Rites Are Well Begun [w. choruses by P. Holman]; Nay, Nay, You Must Not Stay; Gentle Knights; O Yet How Early & Before Her Time [both w. chorus by P. Holman]; Almande)*, A. Holborne *(Pavan; Coranto:The Fairie-round; Coranto:As It Fell on Holie Eve; 2 Galliards; Almaine:The Honie-suckle; Almaine:The Night Watch)*, M. Thomsen *(Fanfare [from Tpt Ensemble Son 34, "Meister Thomas Fideler"])*, anon *(2 Dulcina; Alman)*, P. Holman *(Melt Earth to Sea) (rec All Saints, Tooting, London, Nov 1994)* PPHI ▲ 446217 [DDD] (16.97)

Music from Shakespeare's Plays—features T. Morley *(It Was a Lover & His Lass; La Coranto; La Volta [set W. Byrd]; O Mistress Mine; Can She Excuse; The Frog Galliard; Go from My Window)*, R. Johnson *(Where the Bee Sucks, There Suck I; Full Fathom 5; Hark, Hark! The Lark; Get You Hence [both dubious])*, J. Wilson *(Take, O Take Those Lips Away)*, G. Farnaby *(Bonny Sweet Robin)*, R. Jones *(Farewell, Dear Love)*, J. Dowland *(Tarleton's Risurrectione)*, W. Byrd *(La Coranto; O Mistris Mine)*, anon *(Hollis Berrie; Daphne; My Robin is to the Greenwood Gone; Tickle My Toe; Kemp's Jig; Hold, Lingel, Hold; How Should I Your True Love Know; Walsingham; The Poor Soul Sat Sighing; Robin) (rec The Warehouse, Waterloo, London, Apr 1995)* PPHI ▲ 446687 [DDD] (16.97)

Nutmeg & Ginger: Spicey Ballade from Shakespeare's London PPHI ▲ 456507 (16.97)

Les Musiciens de Provence

Musique des Trouvères et Troubadours—features 24 instrumental selections; nine-member strings-flutes-reeds-brass-percussion ensemble *(rec 1973-81)* ARN ▲ 68064 [ADD] (16.97)

Popular Elizabethan Music—features Nutmigs & Ginger; The Batchelars Delight; Watkins Ale; Go from My Window; My Lord Willoghby's Welcome Home; My Sweet Little Darling; My Mistresse Is As Faire; A Round of 3 Country Dances in 1; Mall Simmes; Barrow Faustus Dreame; Monsieurs almain; Green Garters; The New Hunt Is up; Rogero; Bonnie Sweet Robin; Can She Excuse; Hackney; Where Griping Grief; Will You Buy a Fine Dog?; Galliard to Phillips Pavan; My Lord of Oxenfords Maske FOCU ▲ 933 [AAD] (16.97)

La Nef

The Garden of Earthly Delights—features works by Machaut *(Rose, liz, printemps, verdure; Comment qu'à moy lonteinne)*, Agricola *(Cave, Dominus videt)*, anon *(Ipse dixit; El Rey que tanto madruga; La Comida la mañana; Lunga Nahawend; Pesrev; En Këlohënu; Cave, Dominus videt; Todo bueno tengo; Pesrev; Mignonne, allons voir si la rose; Aurora; La Chançon des damnés; Deo confitemini; Aïdé; Cuando el Rey Nimrod; Kurdilicaz longa; Es la pasión de Jesus; Lamentos de las ánimas) (rec Saint-Alphonse-Rodriguez church, Lanaudière, Quebec, Apr 1993)* DORD ▲ 80135 [DDD] (13.97)

Montségur: The Tragedy of the Cathars—features Reis Gloriós Ov; El Fin'Amors [Beata viscera; La Tierche Estampie Royal; Quand vey la lauzeta mover; Lonc tems ai/Lo ferm voler]; Le Fléau [Alle Psalite/Reis Gloriós; Des Oge mais; La Quarte Estampie Royal; A chantarm'èr; La Septime Estampie Royal; La Seconde Estampie Royal; C'est la Fins/La Quinte Estampie Royal; Falsedatz et desmezura]; Consolamentum [Benedicite Parcite Nobis; Virgen, madre gloriósa; Jhesu Crist; Reis Gloriós]; Feux [Veni Sancte Spiritus] [all arr S. Bergeron] *(rec Quebec, May 1996)* DOR ▲ 90243 [DDD] (16.97)

Music for Joan the Mad, Spain, 1479-1555—features Songs of Exile *(Dame la mano; Una Matica de ruda; Poco le das; Dunula; Dame la Mano; El mi querido; Dolores tiene la Reina; Por allí pasó un cavallero; Los bilbilicos; Marcha sobre "Dame la mano")*, At Toledo, Seat of the Catholic Kings *(La Canela; Dios te salve, Maria; O Señor Dios; Triste España sin ventura; Alta/O Gloriosa Domina)*, Reconquest *(Acuérdate de Andalucía; Paséabase el Rey Moro; O Gloriaosa Domina; Levanta, Pascual!)*, Love & Death *(Mille regrets; Si je perdais mon amy; Adieu corage, adieu; De tous beien playne; Todas estas conciones; Con que la lavaré?)*, The New World *(L'Homme armé/Credo in umum Deum) (rec Notre-Dame de Bonsecours Church on L'Iselt-sur-mer, Quebec, Sept 1991)* DOR ▲ 80128 [DDD] (13.97)

New London Chamber Choir [cnd:James Wood]

The Brightest Heaven of Invention: Flemish Polyphony of the High Renaissance—features works by Antoine Brumel, Antoine Busnois, Dufay, Josquin, Jakob Obrecht, Johannes Regis AMON ▲ 56 [DDD] (16.97)

New London Collective [cnd:Philip Pickett]

Pilgrimage to Santiago—features vocal and instrumental music celebrating the journey to the shrine of St. James at the Cathedral of Santiago de Compostela in northern Spain PLOI 2-▲ 33148 [DDD] (32.97)

New London Consort [cnd:Philip Pickett] [Catherine Bott (sop), Michael George (bar), Philip Pickett (rcr), Pavlo Beznosiuk (vn), Mark Levy (vl), Jacob Heringman (cittern), Tom Finucane (lt), Lynda Sayce (bandora)]

Elizabethan & Jacobean Consort Music—features works by Morley, Byrd, Maynard, Brade, Jenkins, Lauder, Coleman, Holborne, Lupo, Campion, Melvill, anon HNLN ▲ 11 (16.97)

The Feast of Fools—features a program of medieval music for the religious ceremony The Feast of Fools, usually held on New Year's Day PLOI ▲ 33194 [DDD]

Music from the Time of Columbus—features sels from Historia Baetica; Cancionero Musical della Biblioteca Colombina; Cancionero Musical del Palacio HNLN ▲ 7 (16.97)

Sinners & Saints—features Dum pater familias; La Bouree; Gagliarda; Quen a Virgen ben servira; Bransles de Villages; Katerina collaudemus; La Scresa de' Pastori del Monte; Orientis Partibus; Volte; Stella Splendens; Tempus est iocondum; Ballo du Cigni; Bache, bene venis; Lux optata claruit; Ballet Incerti; Non e gran cause; Passo e mezzo/Saltarello Giorgio PLON (Ultimate) ▲ 48559 (16.97)

New Orleans Musica da Camera [cnd:Milton G. Scheuermann, Thaïs St. Julien]

The Cross of Red: Music of Love & War from the Time of the Crusades—features works by Guillaume IX *(Farai un vers de dreyt nien)*, Marcabru *(Pax in nomine Domine)*, Conon de Bethune *(Ah! Amors, com dure departie)*, Guiot de Dijon *(Chanterai por mon corage)*, Richard Coeur-de-Lion *(Ja nus hons pris)*, Blondel de Nesle *(Cuer Disirrous apaie)*, Raimbaut de Vaqueiras *(No m'agrad'iverns ni pascors)*, Thibaut de Navarre *(Seignor, sachiez)*, Walther von der Vogelweide *(Nu alerst lebe ich)*, anon *(Dum pater familias; Estampie; Parti de mal; Sexte estampie real; Ar ne kuth ich sorghe non; Bele doette; Sia laudato San Francesco) (rec De La Ronde Hall, Baton Rouge, LA, Jan 1996)* CENT ▲ 2373 [DDD] (16.97)

Satires, Desires & Excesses: Songs from the 13th Century Manuscript *(Carmina Burana)*—features selected songs including Deduc Syon; Ecce Torpet Probitas; Fas et Nefas Ambulant; Procurans Odium; Dic Christi Veritas/Bulla Fulminante; Flete Flenda; Crucifigat Omnes; Axe Phebus Aureo; Sic Mea Fata; Ave Nobilis; Temmpis Transit Gelidium; Exiit Diluculo Rustica Puella; Ich was ein Chint so wolgetan; Clauso Chronos; Hiemali Tempore; Bacche, Bene, Venies; Alte Clamat Epicurus; In Taberna CENT ▲ 2145 [DDD] (16.97)

New World Consort

Music from the Age of Discovery—features music grouped according to the time of various explorers, including: Columbus at the Court of Ferdinand & Isabella (works by Dalza, del Encina, P. de Escobar, Anon.); Samuel de Champlain a la Cour d'Henri IV (works by Chevallier, J. van Eyck, C. Gervaise, A. le Roy, Anon.); John Cabot—Citizen of Venice (works by J.A. Dalza, B. Donato, B. Tromboncino, Anon.); Queen Elizabeth & Her Master Mariners Raleigh, Drake & Gilbert (works by Hume, Johnson, Anon.) [Sp,F,E] MUVI (Musica Viva) ▲ 1044 [DDD] (16.97)

New World Renaissance Band

Live the Legend: Love Songs of the Renaissance—features works by Gastoldi *(La Sirena; Il Prigioniero)*, Senft *(Es Warb Ein Schöner Jüngling)*, Ms. of Benedictheuen *(In hac valle Florida)*, Playford *(Dissembling Love)*, Arbeau *(Belle qui tiens ma vie)*, Ronsard *(Mignone, allon vous si la roze)*, Rosseter *(What Then is Love but Mourning)*, A. Scott *(Depairt, Depairt)* NIW ▲ 1001 1001

La Tarentule *(17th and 18th century tarentellas)* HAM ▲ 90379 [DDD] (17.97)

Villancicos *(Popular Spanish songs of the 15th & 16th centuries)* HMA ▲ 1901025 (9.97)

New York Early Music Ensemble [cnd:Frederick Renz]

Istanpitta II, w. Glen Velez (perc) LYR (Early Music) ▲ 8022 (16.97)

The Play of Daniel *(rec Nov 1986)* FON ▲ 8809 [DDD] (13.97)

So Quick, So Hot, So Mad—features Whither runneth my sweetheart; Will you buy a fine dog?; Think'st thou to seduce me then; Can she excuse my wrongs; Cease mine (thine) eyes; Giles Farnaby's Dream; His Rest; Go to bed, sweet Muse; Musing my own self all alone; A toy:The dark is my delight; Of all the birds that I do know; I pray you, good Mother; Fantasia; I go before my darling; The Satyr's Masque; Pined I am and like to die; Peter's Pleasure—The Second Part of Peter; If thou long'st so much to learn; Away, call back what you have said; The Carman's Whistle; A Bellman's Song; So quick, so hot, so mad; Sweet Kate MUMA ▲ 67136 [AAD] (10.97)

New York Kammermusiker Double Reed Ensemble

A Renaissance Tour of Europe—features 40 works by 21 composers of Renaissance England, France, Flanders, Germany, Austria, Italy and Poland DOR ▲ 90133 [DDD] (16.97)

New York Pro Musica [cnd:Noah Greenberg]

The Play of Daniel & the Play of Herod MCA1 2-▲ 10102 [ADD]

New York Renaissance Band [cnd:Sally Logemann]

Country Capers *(music from John Playford's "The English Dancing Master")* ARA ▲ 6520

Newberry Consort [cnd:Mary Springfels]

Ay Amor! *(ca. 17th century Spanish Songs & Theatre Music)*—features works by B. De Selma y Salaverde, A. Falconiero, and J. Hidalgo HAM ▲ 907022

Newberry Consort [cnd:Mary Springfels], Marion Verbruggen (rcr), Paul O'Dette (lt)

The Golden Dream: 17th Century Music from the Low Countries—features works by Kempis *(Sinf in D; Sinf in g)*, Huygens *(Quare tristis es; Avertisti faciem; Erravi)*, Norcombe *(Divisions on a Theme)*, van den Hove *(Fant resonans)*, van Eyck *(Onse Vader)*, Schop *(Lachrime pavaen)*, Tarquinio Merula *(Ciaccona)*, Vallet *(Helas seigneur)*, Camphuysen *(Doulants lachrymae; Wanneer het hert)*, Coperario *(Fant a 3)*, Petersen *(Schriet niet meer)*, Gibbons *(Fant a 3)*, anon *(Je veux mon doux sauueur; En fin mon ame) (rec Troy Savings Bank Music Hall, Nov 1-3, 1993)* HAM ▲ 907123 (17.97)

Musick for Severall Friends, w. Drew Minter (ct), David Douglass (vn), Kevin Mason (thb/lt)—features instrumental works from mid-17th century England HAM ▲ 1907013 (9.97)

Secular Music of 15th Century Spain—features works by Belmonte/Cornago, Cornago/Ockeghem, Gijón, Heinrich Isaac, Juan de la Torre, Juan de Triana, Juan Urrede, Anon. [Sp] ((*see also* Composer Section, "Cornago")) HAM ▲ 907083

Wanderers' Voices *(Medieval cantigas & minnesang)* HAM ▲ 907082 (17.97)

Niederaltaich Scholars [cnd:Konrad Ruhland]

Ave Maris Stella: Life of the Virgin Mary in Plainsong—features Gregorian, baroque and 18th century selections, following the chronological order of events in Mary's life COL (Vivarte) ▲ 45861 (16.97)

Motets of the 17th Century—features works by Rupert Ignaz Mayr, Alberich Mazak, Philipp Jakob Rittler, Caspar Endres, Johann Heinrich Schmelzer, Benedikt Anton Aufschnaiter, Vinzenz Fux, Steffano Bernardi, Johann Stadlmayr, Johann Baptist Dolar, Alessandro Poglietti, Heinrich Ignaz Franz Biber, Andreas Hofer *(rec Apr 13-15, 1992)* COL ▲ 53117 [DDD] (16.97)

Oberlin, Russell (ct)

Music of the Middle Ages, Vol. 3, w. J. Ladone (lt)—features Las Cantigas de Santa Maria [sung in Galician] LYR ▲ 8003 [ADD] (16.97)

Music of the Middle Ages, Vol. 5: English Medieval Songs of the 12th & 13th Centuries, w. Seymour Barab (vl) LYR ▲ 8005 [ADD] (16.97)

Notre Dame Organa Leonius & Perotinus Magister *(12 cent.)*, w. C. Bressler (ten), D. Perry (ten), Seymour Barab (vl) LYR ▲ 8002 [ADD] (16.97)

Troubadour & Trouvere Songs *(12th & 13th cent.)*, w. Seymour Barab (vl) sels. unknown LYR ▲ 8001 [ADD] (16.97)

OP & PO Orch [cnd:Christodoulos Halaris]

Anthology of Byzantine Secular Music OANT ▲ 2 (16.97)

Corpus of Greek Music—features music of the Byzantine empire includes Sympotika, secular music of Byzantine banquets; Pandora, music of Post-Byzantine high society; Music of Ancient Greece; Music of Byzantine master composers Manouil Douks Chryssafis & Ioannis Koukouzelis OCOL 9-▲ 9 (161.97)

Hellenic Elegies—features elegies from Antiquity, the Middle-Ages & post-Byzantine periods ORM ▲ 4012

Medieval Greek Songs, Vol. 1 ORMS ▲ 1 (18.97)

Pandora: Music of the Post-Byzantine High Society, Vol. III—features My Strength is Exhausted; Kratima in 4th Plagal Mode; When Patience Reaches Its Limit; He, Who Does Not Observe the Terms; Kratima in 2nd Plagal Mode; When There Is Lightning in the Clouds, plus others ORA ▲ PAN 3 [DDD]

Organum Ensemble [cnd:Marcel Pérès]

Carmina Burana: The Passion Play *(13th Century)* HAM ▲ 901323 (35.97)

Chants de L'Église Milanaise *(Ambrosian plainsong)* HAM ▲ 901295

Codex Chantilly: Ballades et Rondeaux de L'Ars Subtilior HAM (Suite) ▲ 7901252 (12.97)

Laudario di Cortona—features very 1st religious songs written in the vernacular HAM ▲ 901582 (17.97)

12th Century Polyphony in Aquitaine *(St. Martial de Limoges)*—features excerpts from the Christmas Matins [L] HAM ▲ 901134 [ADD]

Orlando Consort [Robert Harre-Jones (alt), Charles Daniels (ten), Angus Smith (ten), Donald Grieg (bar)]

The Mystery of Notre Dame *(from the 13th cent Notre Dame School of Paris)*, w. Julian Clarkson (alt), Gerald Beatty (trb), Matthew Davies (trb), Benedict Durbin (trb), Dominic Walker (trb), Simon Berridge (ten), Stephen Charlesworth (bar), Charles Pott (bass), Michael McCarthy (bass)—features Etenim sederunt principes; Sederunt principes-Adiuva me domine; Alleluya-Video celos apertos; Video celos apertos [all for the Feast of St. Stephen]; Et valde mane una sabbatorum; Victimae paschali laudes; Terra tremuit; Pascha nostrum immolatus [all from Easter liturgy]; Benedicta-Virgo dei genitrix; Alleluya-Assumpta est Maria; Beata est Maria [all from the Feast of the Assumption of the Blessed Virgin Mary] *(rec St. Osdag Church, Mandelsloh (Neustadt), May 1996)* DEUT ▲ 453487 (16.97)

Orlando Consort

Philippe de Vitry & the Ars Nova: 14th Century Motets—features 19 motets by Vitry and his circle AMON ▲ 49 [DDD] (16.97)

Worcester Fragments: English Sacred Music of the Late Middle Ages—features Alleluya moduletur; O sponsa dei electa; Alleluya Nativitas; Sanctus; Ave virgo mater; Salve sancta parens; Thomas gemme Cantuarie primula; Super te Ierusalem; Munda Maria; Sponsa rectoris omnium; O Maria virgo pia; Candens crescit lilulium; Gloria; O quam glorifica; Fulget celestis curia; Senator regis curie; Inviolata integra mater; Dulciflua tua memoria; Virgo regalis; Puellare gremium; Beata viscera; Prolis eterne genitor; Lux polis refulgens aurea; De supernis sedibus; Quam admirabilis *(rec Mar 1992)* AMON ▲ 59 [DDD] (16.97)

Osnabrück Youth Choir

Llibre Vermell de Montserrat [The Red Book of Montserrat]: Medieval Pilgrim Songs from Spain *(rec Osnabrück Cathedral, May 1993)* RHI ▲ 79080 (15.97) 79080

Oxford Camerata [cnd:Jeremy Summerly]

The Early Music Collection—features works by White *(Lamentations [for 5 voices])*, Tallis *(Lamentations [1st & 2nd sets])*, Palestrina *(Lesson 1 for Maundy Thursday)*, Lassus *(Lessons 1 & 3 for Maundy Thursday)*, de Brito *(Lesson 1 for Good Friday)*, Ockeghem *(Intemerata Dei mater)*, attrib. Desprez *(Nunc dimittis)*, Morales *(Magnificat [Octavi toni])*, Lhéritier *(Surrexit pastor bonus)*, Rogier *(Laboravi in gemitu meo)*, Clemens *(Ego flos campi)*, Palestrina *(Si ignoras te)*, Lassus *(Lauda mater ecclesia)*, Victoria *(Vadam et circuibo)*, Byrd *(Laudibus in sanctis)*, King João IV of Portugal *(Crux fidelis)*, Palestrina *(Missa Papae Marcelli; Missa Aeterna Christi Munera) (rec Chapel of New College, Oxford, July 23-25, 1991)* † EARLY MUSIC COLLECTIONS:The Early Music Collection NXIN 4-▲ 504009 [DDD] (19.97)

Lamentations *(sacred Renaissance choral music)*—features works by R. White *(Lamentations for 5 Voices)*, T. Tallis *(Lamentations, sets 1 and 2)*, Giovanni Palestrina *(Lesson I for Maundy Thursday)*, Orlando de Lassus *(Lessons 1 and 3 for Maundy Thursday)*, Estêvao de Brito *(Lesson I for Good Friday) (rec 1991)* NXIN ▲ 550572 [DDD] (5.97)

Renaissance Masterpieces—features works by Ockeghem, Desprez, de Morales, Lhéritier, Rogier, Clemens, Palestrina, de Lassus, de Victoria, Byrd, King João IV of Portugal *(rec Apr 19-20, 1993)* NXIN ▲ 8.550843 [DDD]

Palladian Ensemble [Pamela Thorby (rcr), Rachel Podger (vn), Susanne Heinrich (vl), William Carter (thb/gtr)]

A Choice Collection: Music of Purcell's London—features works by Locke *(Broken Consort in D; Broken Consort in C)*, Matteis *(Sett of Ayres in F; Preludio in ostinatione; Andamento malinconico; Sett of Ayres in E)*, Baltzar *(John Come Kiss Me Now)*, Weldon *(Sett of Ayres in D)*, Blow *(Ground in g)*, Butler *(Vars on Callino Casturame)*, Banister *(Divisions on a Ground)*, anon *(Old Simon the King) (rec Fitcham Church, Leatherhead, Surrey, Mar 4-6, 1995)* HNLN ▲ 5041 (16.97)

Palladian Ensemble [Pamela Thorby (rcr), Rachel Podger (vn), Joanna Levine (vl/vc/vle), William Carter (thb/gtr)]

An Excess of Pleasure—features works by Uccellini *(Aria sopra la bergamasca)*, Matteis *(Aria spagnuola a due corde; Diverse bizzarie Sopra la Vecchia Sarabanda o pur Ciaccona; Andamento con divisione; Aria; Grave; Ground in D, la sol re per fa la mano [all from Ayres for the Vn]; Bizzarie all'imor Scozzeze [Ground after the Scotch Humour])*, Locke *(Broken Consort in D)*, Simpson *(Divisions on John Come Kiss Me Now)*, Blow *(Son in A)*, Marini *(Son)*, Geminiani *(Scots Airs)*, Purcell *(2 in 1 Upon a Ground) (rec Rosslyn Hill Chapel, Hampstead, Nov 4-6, 1992)* HNLN ▲ 5010 (16.97)

The Winged Lion—features works by Castello *(Son Duodecima)*, Vitali *(Ciaconna)*, Uccellini *(Son 4; Caporal Simon; La mia pedrina; Le scatola da gli agghi)*, Vivaldi *(Con in F, RV 100; Con in D, RV 84)*, Buonamente *(Gagliarda 2; Corrente 3 & 4; Brando 3 & 4; Avanti il Brando)*, Cavalli *(Canzon)*, de Murcia *(El Amor; La Jota)*, Turini *(Son a 3) (rec Nov 23-25, 1993)* HNLN ▲ 5015 (16.97)

PAN Ensemble

Ars Magis Subtiliter *(secular music, 10 songs and 5 instrumental pieces, from the late 14th-cent. Chantilly Codex)*—features works by Fransiscus Andrieu, Baude Cordier, Goscalch, Grimace, Machaut, P. des Molins, Solage, J. Suzay, J. Symonis, J. Vaillant [F] NALB ▲ 21 [DDD] (16.97) 21

The Island of St. Hylarion: Music of Cyprus, 1413-1422—features sixteen motets and secular songs from an early 15th cent. manuscript, marking a "brief but extraordinary flowering of western art music in Cyprus" [F, L] NALB ▲ 38 [DDD] (16.97)

Parley of Instruments [cnd:Peter Holman]

Hark! Hark! the Lark: Music for Shakespeare's Company, w. Catherine Bott (sop), Julia Gooding (sop), Joseph Cornwell (ten), Stephen Varcoe (bar) HYP ▲ 66836 (17.97)

986 ▲ = CD ♦ = Enhanced CD △ = MD ▮ = Cassette Tape ▯ = DCC

Parley of Instruments [cnd:Roy Goodman, Peter Holman], Baroque Orch, Baroque Choir, R. Holton (sop), R. Covey-Crump (ten), C. Daniels (ten), S. Birchall (bass)
Odes on the Death of Henry Purcell—features works by John Blow, Jeremiah Clarke, Godfrey Finger, Henry Hall, Thomas Morgan HYP ▲ 66578 [DDD] (18.97)

Parley of Instruments Renaissance Violin Consort [cnd:Peter Holman]
Musique of Violenze: Dances, Fantasia & Popular Tunes for Queen Elizabeth's Violin Band HYP ▲ 66929 (17.97)

Perceval Ensemble [cnd:Guy Robert]
La Cour du roi René: Chansons et Danses *(21 15th-century French, German and Italian songs and dances from the time of René of Anjou)*—features works by Binchois, Dufay, Josquin, et al. ARN ▲ 68104 [DDD] (16.97)
Manuscrit du roi (vers 1250): Trouvères & troubadours *(from the oldest & most important works of the courtly repertoire from the French manuscript of 844 A.D. of the Bibliotheque Nationale de Paris containing 600 chanson of the late 7th & early 8th centuries)* ARN ▲ 68225 [DDD] (16.97)
The Songs of Kings & Princes of the Middle Ages—features works by Thibaut IV, Count of Champagne and King of Navarre; Alfonso X el Sabio (Alfonso the Wise), King of Castille and Léon; Charles of Anjou, King of Naples; William VII, Count of Poitiers and IXth Duke of Aquitaine; Conon de Béthune, regent of the Empire of Constantinople; Richard I (Richard the Lion-Hearted) of England ARN ▲ 68031 [DDD] (16.97)

Perceval Ensemble, Sanacore Ensemble [cnd:Katia Caré]
The Ladies' Tournament—features ballads, rondos, motets & songs from the 12th & 13th centuries *(rec Sept 1996)* ARN ▲ 68350 [DDD] (16.97)

Philpot, Margaret (alt), Shirley Rumsey (vihs/lts/gtrs), Christopher Wilson (vihs/lts/gtrs)
From a Spanish Palace Songbook: Music from the Time of Columbus—features works by Anchieta, Badajoz, Capirola, Dalza, De La Torre, Del Encina, Gabriel, F. da Milano HYP ▲ 66454 [DDD] (17.97)

Piffaro
Canzoni e Danze: Wind Music from Renaissance Italy—sels unknown PARC ▲ 45883 (16.97)
Chansons et Danceries: French Renaissance Wind Music—sels unknown PARC ▲ 47107 (16.97)

Piffaro [cnd:Joan Kimball, Robert Wiemken]
Los Ministriles:Spanish Renaissance Wind Music—features works by Flecha *(La guerra)*, Dalza *(Calata ala spagnola)*, Narváez *(Fant del cuarto tono)*, Arañés *(Un sarao de la chacona)*, Torre *(Adorámoste, Señor)*, Encina *(¿Si habrá en este baldrés?)*, Guerrero *(untitled motet; Huyd, huyd, o çiegos amadores; Ojos claros y serenos)*, João IV of Portugal *(Crux fidelis)*, Cardoso *(Panis Angelicus)*, Rimonte *(De la piel de sus ovejas)*, Tavares *(Parce mihi)*, Mondéjar *(Sospiros pues que descansa)*, Mudarra *(Recuerde el alma dormida)*, Fernandes *(Pois con tanta graça)*, attrib Ortega *(Puesque me tienes, Miguel)*, anon *(Sencilla pastora (chacona ytaliana); Espanyoleta; Gayta; Alli in Midbar; Canario; Propiñán de Meylor; ¡Ay Jhesús, qué mal frayle!; ¡Yntolerable rrayo!; Villano; Paradetas; Baile a finale) (rec St. Osdag Church, Neustadt, Lower Saxony; June 1996)* DEUT ▲ 453441 [DDD] (16.97)

Pomerantz, L. (vocs/period dlc)
Jewels of the Sephardim, Vol. 1: Songs from Medieval Spain, w. P. Maund (perc), K. Higginson (rcr)—features El rey que tanto madruga; Dos amantes tengo; Nani, Nani; O! que mueve mezes; Durme, heremozo hijico; La rosa enflorece; Abrid, mi galanica; Abrid, mi galanica; Ay! Mancebo; Por la tu puerta yo pasí; El rey de Francia; Gerineldo SONG ▲ 1401 (16.97) 1401
Jewels of the Sephardim, Vol. 2: Wings of Time—The Sephardic Legacy of Multi-Cultural Medieval Spain, w. P. Maund (perc), K. Higginson (rcr), S. Kammen (vielle/rebec)—features Juicio de Solomon; Nacimiento de Moshe; Tres hermanicas eran; Instrumental I; Debajo del limon; Cuando yo en casa; Siete hijos tiene hanna; Desde hoy with Instrumental II; Katav Stav; Morena me Llaman; Esta Montaña d'enfrente; Instrumental III; Llami honrados; Alta es la luna; El dio alto; Instrumental IV; Scalerica de oro; Avday ziman SONG ▲ 1405 (16.97) 1405

Pomerium [cnd:Alexander Blachly]
Musical Book of Hours—features works by Dufay *(Bon jour, bon mois, bon an; Ave maris stella)*, Josquin Desprez *(In principio erat verbum; Inviolata, integra et casta; De profundis clamavi)*, Ockeghem *(Intemerata Dei mater)*, Busnoys *(Magnificat sexti toni)*, Penet *(Virgo prudentissima)*, Hygons *(Salve regina)*, Dunstable *(Veni sancte spiritus/Veni creator)*, Biteryng *(En Katerine solennia)*, plainchant *(Venit ad Petrum...caput) (rec Ascension Roman Catholic Church, New York, May 1997)* PARC ▲ 457586 [DDD] (16.97)

Pomerium Musices [cnd:Alexander Blachly]
Mannerist Revolution—features works by Gesualdo, Marenzio, Monteverdi, de Wert DOR ▲ 90154 [DDD] (16.97)

Prague Collegium Flauto Dolce [cnd:Jiří Kotouč]
Amore, Venere, Tersicore: Music of the XVIth & XVIIth Century—features works by Azzaiuolo, Dowland, Mainerio, Michna, Monteverdi & Praetorius NUO (Ancient Music) ▲ NUO 7271

Prague Rozmberk Consort [cnd:Frantisek Pok]
Renaissance Music at Princely Courts of Europe—features works by Holborn, Morley, Henry VIII, Dowland, Attaingnant, Gervaise, Certon, Jannequin, Sermisy, Praetorius, Franck, Dedekind, Gastoldi, Bendusi, Banchieri, Mainerio SUR ▲ SUP 3194

Prior, Maddy (voc), Carnival Band
Sing Lustily & with Good Courage: Gallery Hymns of the 18th & Early 19th Centuries—features 16 hymn settings by Anon., Arne, Croft, et al. [E] SAY ▲ 383 [DDD]

Pro Cantione Antiqua
Tears & Lamentations: Music from the Fairfax Manuscript & Henry VII's Book—features works by Whyte, Davy, Pygott, Sheryngham, Cornyshe, Browne & Banastir ASVQ ▲ 6151 [DDD] (10.97)

Purcell Consort of Voices [cnd:F. Harrison, E. Dobson, D. Smithers]
Now Make We Merthe, w. London Brass Ensemble, All Saints Boys' Choir—features medieval English lyrics, rounds & carols including *Sumer is icumen in [Perspice christicola]; Foweles in the firth; Edi be thu; Sainte Marie Virgine; Miri it is; Gabriel from heven-king; Stond wel, moder; Nowel, nowel/Owt of your sleep; Deo gracias Anglia/Owr king went forth; Pray for us thou Prince of Pes; Go hert, hurt with adversitee; This day day daws; A maske; Orientis partibus [Lux hodie]; Resonemus laudibus; Verbum caro; Verbum patris hodie; Lullay, lullow; Fulget hodie de l'espine; The borys hede; Verbum patris humanatur; Conditor fut le non-pareil; Dieus vous garde; Riu, riu chiu; Saltavan Ninfe; Est-ce Mars (rec May 1965, Dec 21-22, 1966 & June 24-26, 1969)* BOSK ▲ 121 [ADD] (10.97)

Ragin, Derek Lee (ct), Peter Croton (lt)
Italian Lute Songs—features works by Cosimo Bottegari *(selections from Arie e canzoni in musica di Cosimo Bottegari)*, Sigismondo D'India *(selections from Il primo libro di musiche da cantar solo)*, Girolamo Frescobaldi *(selections from Arie musicali)*, Francesco da Milano *(Ricercar)*, Alessandro Piccinini *(Toccata 24)*, Laurencini di Roma *(Praeludium; Courante)*, Philippe Verdelot *(selections from Intavolatura de li madrigali di Verdelotto da cantare et sonare nel lauto)*, Anon. *(3 Ricercari)* CCL ▲ 4092 [DDD] (17.97)

Ragossnig, Konrad (lt/gtr), Ulsamer Collegium
Dance Music of the Renaissance PARC ▲ 15294 [ADD]

Paul Rans Ensemble [P. Rans, P. Malfeyt, P. Strychers, P. van Loey]
Egidius waer bestu bleven: Gruuthuse Manuscript EUFO ▲ EUF 1170

Re, Bruno (b vl)
Bass Viol Suites, w. Robert Khonen (hpd)—features works by Boismortier, F. Couperin, Marais PVY ▲ 788012 [DDD]

Red Byrd, Rose Consort of Viols
Elizabethan Christmas Anthems—features works by Bull, Byrd, Gibbons, Holborne, Peerson, et al. AMON ▲ 46 [DDD] 46

Remnant, Mary (hp/psaltery/rcr/fid/organistrum/pipes/perc), Petronela Dittmer (sop/organistrum), Matthew Hart Dyke (tpt)
Music of the Age of Chivalry—features 12th-13th cent works *(Congaudentes celebremus; In exitu Israel; Novus miles sequitur; Jolittement; Worldes bliss ne last no throwe; Christus vincit; Fanfare; Santa Maria strela do dia; all psallite cum luya; Chose Tassin; Edi beo thu, heavene quene; Ma viele; Sumer is icumen in; Angelus ad Vigginem; Marionette douce; Byrd one brere; Cis chans veult boire; Maria muoter; Ad mortem festinamus; Fanfare; Ave Rex gentis Anglorum; In Gottes namen fehren wir; Lullay, lullay; Douce dame jolie; Trotto; Verbum caro factum est; Me lyketh ever the lenger the bet; Scibere proposui)* SALM (Music Treasury) ▲ 101 (14.97)

Renaissance Dance Band [John Tyson (rcr/pipe/tabor), Douglas Freundlich (lt), James Johnston (vn), Reinmar Seidler (vc), Jacqueline Schwab (vir)]
Renaissonics—features works by Caroso *(Furioso all'Italiana [Noblità di Dame]; Contrapasso Nuovo; Alta Vittoria; Celeste Giglio; Nido d'Amore; Spagnoletta Nuova)*, Negri *(Adda Felice [Le Grazie d'Amore])*, Phålese *(Pavane Lesquercarde; La Rocque Gaillarde; Pavane Ferrareze; Gaillard Ferrareze; Branles after Claude Gervaise [Premier Livre de Danseries])*, Lassus *(Susanne un Jour)*, Crequillon *(Petite Fleur) (rec Pamela Emerson's Music Room, Cambridge, MA, 1995)* TIT ▲ 232 [DDD] (16.97)

Renaissance Players [cnd:Winsome Evans]
Garland Dances—features C'est la fins; Prendes i garde; Estampie chemin; Vacillantis trutine [Carmina Burana, 108]; Bele emmelos; Li nouvianz tanz; Annualis mea [Carmina Burana, 168]; Voici le mai; Hyer matin a l'enjornee; Bele aielis par matin se leva; Main se levoit aaliz; Orientis partibus; Omittamus studia [Carmina Burana, 75]; Nobilitas ornata moribus WALC ▲ 8006 [DDD] (16.97)
Maria Morning Star: Cantigas de Santa Maria II WALC ▲ 8008 [DDD]
Mirror of Light: Cantigas de Santa Maria III WALC ▲ 8035 [DDD] (16.97)

Renaissance Players (cont.)
The Muses Gift—features works by Maro *(Copa Surisca; Copae Chorea)*, d'Arras *(Ce fut en mai)*, Pluckpayres *(Danse Vanse)*, Lemon/Pluckpares *(Ballata Limone)*, Vogelweide *(Nemt, frowe, disen kranz)*, anon *(Chançonetta Tedescha; L'homme armé; Veris ad imperia; A l'entrada del tens cl)*, Halle *(Bergeronette, douce baiselete; Danse de Robin et de Marion)*, Ekstein/Pluckpayres *(Dansse Juditha)*, Carmina Burana *(Virent prata hiemata; Chorea Venerea; Exiit diluculo rustiva puella; Nu gronet aver diu heide; Ecce gratum et optamum; Chorea Flora)* [Carmina Burana, 143] *(Ecce gratum et optatum; Chorea Flora)* WALC ▲ 8003 [DDD]
Songs for a Wise King—features Alfonso's Prologo; Rosa das rosas; Da que Deus mamou; Gran dereit e de seer; A Virgen que de Deus Madre; Santa Maria strela do dia; Assi pod'a Virgen; Quen quer que na Virgen fia; Como somos per conssello; Non sofre Santa Maria WALC ▲ 8007 [DDD] (16.97)

Restoration [Rosalind Salas (sop), Bronwen Pugh (baroque vn), Robert Petre (hpd)]
Musick Al'Italliana: Italian & English Music of the 17th Century—features works by Marini *(La Ponte; La Orlandia; Il Monteverde; La Caotorta)*, Monteverdi *(Laudate Dominum)*, Gibbons *(A Ground; The Italian Ground)*, Caccini *(Amarilli, Mia Bella)*, Philips *(Amarilli Vars)*, Byrd *(Fortune Vars)*, Matteis *(Suite in d)*, Carissimi *(Così Volete, Così Sarà)*, Purcell *(The Plaint)*, Handel *(Un'Alma Innamorata)*, anon *(Chi Passa; Fortune My Foe) (rec Aug 21-23, 1995)* MER ▲ 84316 [DDD] (16.97)

La Reverdie
Bestiarium: Animals & Nature in Medieval Music—features works by Jocopo da Bologna *(Oseletto selvaggio; Aquila altera/Creatura gentil/Uccei del Dio)*, Donato de Firenze *(l' fu' gia bianch'uccel' Lucida pecorella; L'aspido sordo)*, Landino *(Chosi pensoso)*, Giovanni di Firenze *(Con bracchi assai)*, Vaillant *(Par mentes foys)*, Wolkenstein *(Wolauff, gesell! wer jagen well; Ir alten weib frewt ew)*, anon/trad songs *(Ar Bleizi-mor; O tu qui servas; L'autrier jost'una sebissa; Chançonette/A la cheminée/Veritatem; Ich was ein chint so wolgetan; Na coire ar na sleibhtibh; Fuweles in the frith; Byrd one breré; Oseletto selvaggio; En ma forest) (rec Italy, May 1990)* CNTS ▲ 9601 [DDD] (18.97)

Ricercar Academy Orch [cnd:Pietro Busca]
La Rovattina—features canzonas & dances by Attaignant *(Bransie simple; Bransie gay; La Magdalena [basse dance]; Tourdion)*, Gervaise *(Almande; Bransie I & II; Bransie de champaigne I & II)*, Banchieri *(La Rovattina [canzone])*, Frescobaldi *(Canzone)*, Mainerio *(Pass'e mezzo [della Paganina]; Ballo furlano [L'arboscello]; Gagliarda [La lavandara])*, Byrd *(Pavane; Gaillard I & II)*, Susato *(Basse dance; Ronde; Gaillard; Pass'e mezzo e machtanz; La battoglia [Pavana])*, Aichinger *(Canzone)*, Praetorius *(Pass'e mezzo; Gagliarda; Balletto; Spagnoletta; Pavana di spagna; Volte)* STRV ▲ STV 33380 [DDD]

La Romanesca
Al Alva Venid *(15-16th century secular music)*—features works by Luys de Narvaez; Juan del Encina; Diego Ortiz; Alonso Mudarra; plus ohters GLSS ▲ 920203 (18.97)

La Rondinella [Alice Kosloski (alt), Paul Bensel (rcr/crumhorn/perc), Howard Bass (lt/gtr), Tina Chancey (trb vl/b vl/rebec/kamenj/lyra/rcr/perc)]
A Song of David: Music of the Sephardim & Renaissance Spain—features works by Flory Jagoda *(Pesah ala mano; El dia de Purim; Madre mia si mi muero; Yo hanino, tu hanina)*, Diego Ortiz *(Recercada segunda sobre "Douce memoire"; Recercada segunda)*, Juan Vasquez *(Zagaleja de lo verde)*, Luis de Narváez *(Canción del Emperador)*, Alonso Mudarra *(Fant. que contrahaze la harpa en la manera de Ludovico; Triste estava el rey David)*, Juan del Encina *(Ay triste, que vengo)*, Alonso Fernandes *(Tres morillas m'enamoran)*, Giacomo Fogliano *(L'amor, dona, ch'io te porto)*, Gulielmus Ebreo *(La bassa castiglia)*, trad. *(Triste está el rey David; Mizmor l'David; Buena semana; Mosé salió de Misrayim; Las hermanas, reina y cautiva; Il bastidor; Secretos quero descuvir; El rey por muncha madruga)*, anon. *(Jançu janto; Dime, robadora; Calabaça, no sé, buen amor; Yo me soy la morenica) (rec St. John's Episcopal Church, Ellicott City, MD, Sept 1994 & Jan 1995)* DOR ▲ 80130 [DDD] (13.97)

Rowallan Consort [Mhairi Lawson (sgr), Paul Rendall (sgr), Robert Phillips (lt), William Taylor (hp)]
Notes of Joy—features Come my Children, dere; Joy to the personne of my love; Canaries; A Port; A Daunces [Grein Greus ye Rasses]; I Long for Thy Virginitie; The Canaries; Defiled is My Name; In Nomine; Com Palefaced Death; The Lady Louthian's Lilte; Ladie Laudian's Lilte; My Ladie Laudian's Lilt; Lyk as the Lark; Lyk as the Dumb Solsequium; Depairte, Depairte; For Lov of 1; Ane Exempil of Tripla; Ane Lessone Upon the 1st Psalme; Ane Lessone Upon the 2nd Psalme; Gypsies Lilt; Corne Yairds; A Scots Tune [all are early Scottish tunes arr by Robert Phillips & William Taylor] *(rec Temple Record Studios, 1997)* TEMP ▲ COMD 2058

St. George's Canzona [cnd:John Sothcott]
A Medieval Banquet—features works by Machaut, Reuenthal, Landini & anon. ASVQ ▲ 6131 [DDD] (10.97)
Medieval Songs & Dances [F, I, Sp] CRD ▲ 3421 (17.97)
Merry It Is While Summer Lasts *(a collection of 12th/13th-cent. instrumental/vocal secular music from the Spring and Summer Festivals)* CRD ▲ 3412 [ADD] (17.97)

St. Peter's in the Loop Schola Cantorum
The Song of Angels—features works by Brahms *(Saint Raphael [setting of anon German folk hymn]; O Michael, Hear [arr from 17th cent German hymn])*, Colebault *(O angele Dei)*, Laudarino *(Exultando in Iesso Cristo)*, Lucario *(Angelis suis mandavit de te)*, Luis de Victoria *(Duo Seraphim)*, Nicholson *(Bell Peal)*, Verdelot *(Hymno dell' Arcangelo Raffaelo)*, Zelinski *(Stetit Angelus (II))*, plus In viam; In paradisum; Dixit autem Maria (all antiphons); Tibi Christe Splendor Patris (hymn); Terribilis est locus iste; Angelus Domini (both responsories); Ad celebres (sequence); Ingressus est; Stetit Angelus (I); Benedicite *(rec St. Pete's Roman Catholic Church "in the Loop", Aug 1996)* IMEG ▲ 534279 (16.97) 534279 (10.98)

Salomone Trio [Marie Costanza (sop), Carol Flamm (sop), Elissa Weiss (sop)]
Sacred & Profane, w. Adeline Sire (rcrs), Laura Liben (perc)—features works by ?Claudin *(Au pres de Vous; Il est en Vous)*, A. Brumel *(Vray Dieu d'Amors)*, S. Rossi *(Ele Moadei Adonai; Shir Hamaalot; Bar'chu)*, Bateson *(The Nightingale)*, Morley *(Though Philomena Lost Her Love)*, Weelkes *(Those Sweet Delightful Lillies)*, Youll *(While Joyful Springtime Lasteth)*, R. Johnson/J. Wilson *(Where the Bee Sucks)*, anon & trad *(Alleluya Psallat; Nas Mentes Senpre Teer; Alle, Psallita cum Luya; Pucelete-Je Languis-Domino; Le Grant Desir; Mais que ce Fust le Plaisir; Cuando el Rey Nimrod; Tu Madre cuando Te Parió; Scalerica de Oro; Mizmor l'David; Alli en el Midbar; Noches, Noches; Morena me Llaman/Morenica a mi me Llaman; Santa Maria Amar)* TIT ▲ 238 [DDD] (16.97)

Salzburg Bach Choir [cnd:Howard Arman], Innsbruck Wind Ensemble
Music at the Salzburg Court, Vol. 2: 1587-1612—features works by Agazzari, Leoni, Massaini, Stadlmayr and Vecchi DEHA ▲ 77157 [DDD]

Sator Musicæ [cnd:Roberto Meo]
Musicalis Scientia: Goliardic Songs of the Middle Ages—features Scampanio della festa; Nicholai Presulis Festum Celebremus; Cauda Ego Reus Confiteor Deo; Trois serors sor Rive Mer; Novus Miles Sequitur; Studentes/De Se Debent/Kyrie Eleison; Qualche frase dal Viderunt Omnes; Quant Define/Quant Repaire/Flos; Clausole su Manere; Ce Que/Certer Mout/Bone/ Manere; Dic Christi Veritas; Hac in Die Salutari; Ave Regina/Mater/Ite Missa Est; Roundellus Apollinis Eclipsatur; Musicalis Scientia; Scientie Laudabilis; Flores su Musicalis Scientia; Pantheon/Apollinis/Zodiacum Signis; Doctorum Principem/Melodia/Vir Mitis; Gaudeamus Igitur TACT ▲ 230201 (16.97)

SAVAE Vocal Ensemble, Eric Casillas (perc)
Native Angels: Musical Miracles From the New World IGO ▲ 204 (16.97)

Savall, Jordi (vl/cnd)
Ars Musicae: Portrait of Jordi Savall—features performances with Sophie Watillon (vl), Eunice Brandao (vl), Wieland Kuijken (vl) *(Purcell:Fant IX)*, Le Concert des Nations *(M.-A. Charpentier:Canticum ad Beatum Virginem Mariam [w. Montserrat Figueras (sop), Gérard Lesne (ct)]; Dumanoir:Ballet de Stockholm (sel); Purcell:The Prophetess [Dance of the Furies]; Handel:Royal Fireworks Music (ov); De Arriaga:Ov, Op. 1 [Nonetto]; Beethoven:Coriolan Ov [all w. Manfredo Kraemer (vn concertino)]; Bach:Art of the Fugue; Haydn:7 Last Words of Christ on the Cross [Evangelium Consummatum est & Son VI] [w. Rafael Raibo (spkr)])*, Anne Gallet (hpd), Hopkinson Smith (thb) *(Marais:Tombeau pour Mr. de Lully)*, Ton Koopman (hpd), Arianne Maurette (b vl) *(F. Couperin:Chaconne en Mi)*, La Capella Reial de Catalunya, Le Concert des Nations *(Mozart:Requiem [Agnus Dei] [w. Montserrat Figueras (sop)])*, Pedro Estevan (perc) *(Alfonso X:Rontundellus)*, La Capella Reial de Catalunya, Hespèrion XX *(Savall:Le sacre de Charles VII; C. de Morales:Officium defunctorum, in secundo nocturno; Victoria:Cantiga Beatae Virginis, Salve Regina à 8)*, Hespèrion XX *(Enzina:Pues que jamás olvidaros [w. Montserrat Figueras (sop), Francesc Garrigosa (ten), Lambert Climent (ten), Jordi Ricart (baryton)]; Scheidt:Paduan à 4 voc. Cantus IV; Castro:Desde las torres del alma [w. Montserrat Figueras (sop)]; Monteverdi:Vespro della Beata Vergina [w. Montserrat Figueras (sop), Maria Cristina Kiehr (sop), Elisabetta Tiso (sop), Patricia Vaccari (sop), Ulrike Wurdak (sop)])*, La Capella Reial de Catalunya *(Castellana:Sel [w. Montserrat Figueras (sop), Pedro Memelsdorff (fl), Andrew Lawrence-King (psalterion)]; Cererols:Missa pro defunctis [Hei mihi; w. Montserrat Figueras (sop), Maité Arruabarrena (sop), Lambert Climent (sgr), Joan Cabero (ten), Jordi Ricart (sgr), Josep Cabré (bar), Daniele Carnovich (bass)])*, Ton Koopman (hpd/org), Lorenz Dufschmid (vle), Rolf Lislevand (vih) *(D. Ortiz:Recercadas sobre tenores [Romanesca, passamezzo antiguo, passamezzo moderno])*, Sergi Casademunt (vl), Eunice Brandao (vl), Lorenz Duftschmid (vl) *(Correa de Arrauxo:Todo el mundo en general)*, Pedro Memelsdorff (fl), Andrew Lawrence-King (hp) *(El Cant dels ocells) (rec 1975-98)* FONT 2-▲ 9910 (17.97)

Schola Cantorum Basiliensis [cnd:Dominique Vellard, Wulf Arlt]
Codex Engelberg 314: Music of the Middle Ages DEHA ▲ 77185 [DDD]

Schola Hungarica
The Play of Daniel HUN ▲ 12457 [DDD] (16.97)

Schola Hungarica [cnd:László Dobszay, Janka Szendrei]
St. Elizabeth of Hungary: 2 Medieval Offices—features The Cambrai Office; The Central European Office *(rec Franciscan Church, Esztergom, 1995)* HUN ▲ 31605 [DDD] (16.97)

COLLECTIONS

Schreier, Peter (ten), Capella Fidicinia [cnd:Hans Grüss]
Music of the Reformation—features works by de Bruch, Ducis, Othmayr, Senfl & Walter [w. texts by Creuziger, Luther & Walter] BER ▲ 9120 (10.97)

Scottish Early Music Consort [cnd:Warwick Edwards]
Mary's Music—features 19 songs & dances from the time of Mary Queen of Scots CHN (Chaconne) ▲ 529 [DDD] (16.97)

Sequentia
Ancient Music for a Modern Age—features works by Von Bingen, Bishop Ato, anon. RCAV (Red Seal) ▲ 61868 (16.97) ▮ 61868
Aquitania: 12th Century Christmas Music from Aquitanian Monasteries—features Dulci dignum melodia; Mundo salus gracie; Clara sonnent organa; Noster cetus psallat letus; Virginis in gremio; Iudicii signum; Instrumentalstücke (2); Alleluia! Iustus ut palma florebit; Quam felix cubiculum; Uterus hodie; Iubilemus, exultemus; Descendit de celis; Guadia debita; De monte lapis scinditur; O Maria, Deu maire; Plebs domini DEHA ▲ 77383 [DDD] (16.97)
Dante & the Troubadours—features works by Aimeric de Peghuilhan *(En amour tob alques en que'm refraing)*, Bertran de Born *(Rassa, tan creis e monta e poia)*, Arnaut Daniel *(Lo ferm voler qu'el cor m'intra; Chanson do'ill mot son plan e prim)*, Folquet de Marseille *(Tant m'abellis l'amoros pessamens)*, Guiraut de Bornelh *(No posc sifrir c'a la dolor)*, Peire d'Alvernhe *(Dejosta'ls breus jorns e'ls loncs sers) (rec Abbaye de Fontevraud, France, Dec 4-7, 1993)* DEHA ▲ 77227 [DDD] (16.97)
[Editor's Note]: Also includes instrumental pieces based on melodies of Folquet de Marseille.
English Songs of the Middle Ages DEHA ▲ 77019 [DDD] ▮ 77019
Shining Light *(music from 12th century Aquitanian Monastaries)*—features Lux refulget; Verbum patris humanatur o o; Ora pro nobis beate Nicolae; Cantu miro summa laude; Instrumental pieces (3); Veri solis radius; Divinum stillant; Orienti Oriens; Per partum virginis; Congaudet hodie; Virga Jesse floruit; Senescente mundano filio; Radix Jesse castitatis lilium; Omnis curet homo; Benedicamus domino:Stirps Jesse florigeram; Resonemus hoc natali (I & II); Ad infantum triumphantum *(rec Church of the Campion Center, Weston, MA, Feb 1996)* DEHA ▲ 77370 [DDD] (16.97) 77370
Trouvères: Courtly Love Songs from Northern France, ca. 1175-1300 DEHA 2-▲ 77155 [DDD] (30.97)
Vox Iberica I: Sons of Thunder *(Codex Calixtinus)*—features 12th-cent. music for St. James the Apostle DEHA ▲ 77199
Vox Iberica II: Music from the Royal Convent of Las Huelgas de Burgos *(Codex las Huelgas)*—features 13th/14th cent. sacred music as was sung by the nuns of the Convent of Huelgas de Burgos DEHA ▲ 77238

Sequentia, Sons of Thunder
Visions from the Book—features Samson dux fortissime; A deserto veniens; Dolorum solatium; Liber generationis; O'onques non en liu s'asist; Omnis caro peccaverat; Syon egredere nunc de cubilibus *(rec Campion Center, Weston, MA, Nov 13-17, 1994)* DEHA ▲ 77347 [DDD] (16.97)

Simpson, Glenda (mez), Barry Mason (lt/baroque gtr/chit)
Now What Is Love? *(Aspects of Love in the 17th Century)*—features works by Gabriel Bataille, John Danyel, Dowland, Pierre Guédron, Robert Jones, Nichola Matteis, Etienne Moulinié, et al. AMON ▲ 50 [DDD] (16.97)

Sine Nomine Ensemble [Andrea Budgey (sop), Holly Cluett (sop), Jay Lambie (ten), Bryan Martin (bar), Bryan Martin (lt), Randall Rosenfeld (vielle/gittern/fl/rcr), Andrea Budgey (hp/rcr/darabukka)]
A Golden Treasury of Medieval Music—features works by Alfonso X "el Sabio" of Castile *(Quen quer que ten en desden [Cantiga 153])*, Dunstable *(Alma redemptoris mater)*, Muset *(Sire cuens, j'ai vielé)*, Solage *(Corps feminin)*, Binchois *(Je ne vis oncques la pareille)*, Wolkenstein *(Gesegnet sey die frucht)*, Suonhart (?) *(Petruslied: Unsar trohtin hat farsalt)*, Hildegard of Bingen *(Symphonia virginum: O dulcissime amator)*, anon *(Ex ejus tumba; Estampie; Rosa delectabilis; Regali ex progenie; Regalis exoritur; Peperit virgo; My Heartly Service; Conditor alme siderum; Saltarello; Io son un pellegrin; Titurel fragment: Sus lâgen sie unlange; Ad regnum epulentum; Nu bitt wir den heiligen geist; Ich bins erfreut; Der notter schwanctz; Cormacus scripsit) (rec Valley Recordings, Littleton-on-Severn, July 1995)* AMON (Golden Treasury) ▲ 63 (16.97)

Sinfonye [cnd:Stevie Wishart]
Bella Domna *(The Medieval Woman: Lover, Poet, Patroness and Saint)*—features 13th-14th cent. works by Martin Codax, La Comtesse de Die, Richart de Fournival, Anon. HYP ▲ 66283 [DDD] (17.97)
Cantigas de Santa Maria AL ▲ 110
Gabriel's Greeting *(medieval English Christmas music)*—features Gabriel, Sent from Heaven's King; Save Us, Star of Heaven; Miri It Is; Hail, Virgin of Virgins; Hail Mary, Virgin of Virgins; To the Boy Proceeding; Now Let the World Rejoice; So that Calamity Would Now End; Gabriel fram Evene King; an untitled instrumental piece; See, Wretched Man, and Judge—See, Wretched Man, and Consider—Winter; Estampie; Ther Is No Rose of Swych Vertu; Lolay, Lolay; Nowell, Nowell, Nowell!; This Is the Salutacyon Of the Angell Gabryell HYP ▲ 66685
Poder á Santa Maria, w. Vivien Ellis (sop), Equidad Barés (sgr), Paula Chateauneuf (sgr), Jim Denley (sgr)—features Ben Guarda Santa Maira; A Virgen Mui Groriosa; Poder á Santa Maria; Santa Maria Valed'ai sennor; Por nos Virgen Madre; Quantos Me Creveren Loaran; Os Que á Santa Maria; Sempr'a virgen Groriosa; Instrumental Improvisation; A Que Por Nos Salvar; *(O Que Mui Tarde ou Nunca; Ontra Toldalas Vertudes) (rec Cartuja de Santa Maria de Cazalla de la Sierra, Seville, Oct 1993)* AL ▲ 105 [DDD] (18.97)
The Sweet Look & the Loving Manner—features 12th-13th cent. love lyrics and chansons from medieval France HYP ▲ 66625 (17.97)

Sirinu [Sara Stowe (sop/org/perc), Matthew Spring (lt/h-g/lira da braccio/vl/gittern), Jon Banks (hp/sackbut/org/vl/perc), Henry Stobart (rcr/bgp/vl/shawm/pipe/tabor)]
The Cradle of the Renaissance *(Italian Music from the time of Leonardo da Vinci)*—features works by Cara, Agricola, Cornago, Giustiniani, Isaac, Poliziano, others HYP ▲ 66814 (17.97)

The Sixteen
A Renaissance Anthology—features works by Lotti, Palestrina, Allegri, Caldara, Gabrieli, Frescobaldi, Cavalli, Monteverdi & Lassus COC 2-▲ 7021 [DDD] (31.97)

Skeaping, Lucie (sgr), Douglas Wooton (sgr), Michael Brain (sgr), Roderick Skeaping (sgr), Charles Humphries (ct), Gareth Hancock (sgr), Rowen Frenner (sgr), Paul Robinson (sgr)
A Madrigal for All Seasons—features works by Weelkes *(To Shorten Winter's Sadness; On the Plains, Fairy Trains)*, Gibbons *(The Silver Swan)*, Farner *(Fair Phyllis I Saw Sitting Alone; A Little Pretty Bonny Lass)*, Dering *(Dear Love Be Not Unkind)*, Morley *(Since My Tears & Lamenting; April Is in My Mistress' Face; Sing We & Chant It; Say Gentle Nymphs)*, V. Galilei *(Bianco Fiori)*, Dowland *(Fine Knacks for Ladies; The Most Sacred Queen Elizabeth, Her Galliard; Weep You No More Sad Fountains; Say Love If Ever; Now, Oh Now)*, R. Johnson *(Have You Seen the Brighy Lilly Grow?; Tell Me Dearest, What Is Love?)*, R. Edwards *(In Going to My Naked Bed)*, Pilkington *(Amintas with His Phyllis Fair)*, Willbye *(Adieu, Sweet Amaryllis)*, Holborne *(Gaillard)*, Cornshire *(Ah, the Sighs)*, T. Ford *(There Is A Lady Sweet & Kind)*, T. Bateson *(If Love Be Blind)* SALM (Heritage) ▲ 201 [DDD] (14.97)

Skeaping, Roderick (vl/vn/rebec/voc), Robin Jeffery (lt/perc), Michael Brain (rcr/pipe/shawm), Jeremy Barlow (vir/org), Lucie Skeaping (voc/vn/rebec/rcr), Ian Gammie (vl/lt)
Music from the Tudor Age—features music from Tudor England by Henry VII *(Pastime with Good Company)*, Holborn *(Gaillard; Pavan; Gaillard; Nightwatch; The Honeisuckle; Dolent Depart; Heigh ho, Holiday)*, Morley *(Now Is the Month of Maying; Sing We & Chant It; Oh Mistress Mine)*, Ravenscroft *(The 3 Ravens)*, Bull *(Regina Gaillard)*, Valente *(Gaillard lombarda; Ballo lombarda)*, Ballet *(Greensleeves [from Lt Book])*, Byrd *(Earl of Salisbury's Pavan)*, Dowland *(Now Oh Now)*, trad *(Bransal; Tourdion [from Pierre Attaingnant collection, 1529]; Runden; Mohrentanz; Tourdion II; Mille Regrets [from Tielman Susato collection, 1551])* SALM (Music Treasury) ▲ 104 (14.97)

Sonus [Hazel Ketchum (voc/saz/chit/perc), James Carrier (rcr/shawm/hp/saz/tambourine), John Holenko (oud/saz), Geoff Cormier (perc)]
Echoes of Spain: Galician-Portuguese Music of the Middle Ages—features A que por muy gran Fermosa; Cantigas de amigo [Ondas do mare de Vigo, Mandad' ei comigo, Mia irmana fremosa, Ai Deus, Quantas sabedas amare amigo, Eno sagrado en Vigo, Ai ondas]; Muito domostrata; A Virgen que de Deus Madre; Fontis in rivulum; Senpre punnow muit' a Virgen; Ben pode Santa Maria; Quen a Virgen ben sevira; Pois que dos Reys Nostro Sennor; Ben per esta *(rec St. John's Epsicopal Church, Columbia, MD, May 22-24, 1996)* DORD ▲ 80154 [DDD] (13.97)

Sonus [James Carrier (shms/rcr/hp/saz/oud/psaltery/gemshn/perc), Hazel Ketchum (voc/saz/lt/perc), John Holenko (chit/saz/psaltery/oud/rcr/perc)]
Songs & Dances of the Middle Ages—features works by Alfonso X, Der Unverzagte, Wizlaw von Rügen, Carmina Burana No. 116, Walther von der Vogelweide, anon., Bernard de Ventadour, Colin Muset, Guillaume de Machaut, Giraut de Bornelh; 13th cent. French songs; 14th cent. Italian songs; Songs from the 14th cent. Spanish DOR ▲ 80109 [DDD] (13.97)

Studio of Early Music [cnd:Thomas Binkley]
Carmina Burana: The Benediktbeuren Manuscript, ca. 1300 TELC (Das alte Werke) 2-▲ 95521-2

Symposium Musicum [cnd:Miloslav Klement]
Music in Rudolphinian Prague: Instrumental Music at the Imperial Court—features works by Hassler *(Canzon duodecimi toni; Ricercar a 4)*, Otto *(4 Dance-Musics; Isabella)*, Haussmann *(2 Dance-Musics)*, Chilese *(Canzon a 8)*, de Monte *(Canzon a 4)*, Bonelli *(Canzoni e toccate)*, Orologio *(Intrada)*, Gussago *(2 canzones)*, Rossi *(Sinfonia grave—Gilliarda Massara)*, Frescobaldi *(Canzon a 8)*, Gabrieli *(Canzon quarta a 4; Canzon noni toni a 8) (rec Apr 1995)* PANT ▲ 811402 [DDD] (16.97)

Synaulia
Music From Ancient Rome, Vol. 1: Wind Instruments—features works composed & performed by Synaulia AMI ▲ 1396 (16.97)

Tallis Scholars [cnd:Peter Phillips]
Christmas Carols & Motets—features Angelus ad virginem; Nowell Sing We; There Is No Rose; Nowell: Dieu vous garde; Lullay: I Saw; Lully, lulla thou little tiney child; Lullaby; Settings of Ave Maria by Des Prés, Verdelot, Victoria; Es ist ein' Ros' entsprungen; Joseph lieber, Joseph mein; In dulci jubilo; Wachtet auf ruft uns die Stimme GIME ▲ 54910 [DDD] (16.97) ▮ 454910-4
Sarum Chant—features Missa in gallicantu; Christe Redemptor omnium; Veni, Redemptor gentium; Salvator mundi, Domine; A solis ortus cardine GIME ▲ 54917 [DDD] (16.97)

Tallis Scholars
Live in Oxford—features works by Obrecht *(Salve Regina)*, Josquin Desprez *(Gaude Virgo; Absalon fili mi)*, Taverner *(Gaude plurimum)*, Byrd *(Tribue, Domine)*, Tallis *(O sacrum convivium)*, Mundy *(Adolescentulus sum ego; Vox Patris caelestis)* GIME ▲ 454998 (16.97)
Silver: 25th Anniversary—features works by Allegri *(Miserere)*, Victoria *(Ave Maria for Double Choir)*, Palestrina *(Sicut lilium I)*, Josquin Desprez *(Praeter rerum seriem)*, Clemens *(Pater peccavi; Ego flos campi)*, Isaac *(Tota pulchra es)*, Rore *(Descendi in hortum meum)*, Lassus *(Alma Redemptoris Mater; Salve Regina; Ave Regina caelorum)*, Brumel *(Gloria [from Et ecce terrae motus])*, Sheppard *(Media vita)*, Tallis *(In manus tuas; O nata lux; Audivi vocem)*, White *(Exaudiat te)*, W. Cornysh (Jr.) *(Ah Robin; Salve Regina)*, Byrd *(Mass for 5 Voices)* GIME ▲ 454990 (17.97)

Terpsichore Ensemble
Birds & Harmony—features works by Bateson, Marenzio, Eccard, Dowland, Byrd, Janequin, Agricola, Monteverdi, plus others DI ▲ 920388 [DDD] (5.97)
Renaissance Vocal & Instrumental Music—features works by Anon., Attaingnant, Antoine de Bertrand, Guillaume de Costeley, Henning Dedekind, Constanzo Festa, Heinrich Finck, G. Gabrieli, Hassler, Henry VIII, Janequin, Josquin, Merulo, Morley, Obrecht, Paul Peuerl, Praetorius, Sermisy, Susato GALL ▲ CD 567 [ADD]

Theater of Voices [cnd:Paul Hillier]
Cantigas from the Court of Dom Dinis *(Devotional, satirical & courtly medieval love songs)*—features Porque ben Santa Maria sabe os seus dões dar; Par Deus, ai dona Leonor; Un cavalo non comeu; Non quer'eu donzela fea; Fois'o meu amigo a cas d'elrei; Quand'eu vejo las ondas; Muitas vezes volv'o demo; Sete cantigas d'amor de D. Dinis *(rec Skywalker Sound, Nicasio, CA, Feb 14-16, 1994)* HAM ▲ 907129 (17.97)

Theater of Voices members [Paul Hillier (ten), Andrew Lawrence-King (psaltery/hp/portative org)]
Chansons de Trouvères—features works by Gace Brulé *(Les oxelés de mon païx; A la douçor de la bele seson)*, Moniot d'Arras *(Ce fu en mai)*, Thibaut de Champagne *(Ausi conme unicorne sui; Deus est ensi conme li pellicanz; Chançon ferai, que talenz m'en est pris)*, Colin Muset *(En mai, quant li rossignolez)*, anon *(Volez vous que je vous chant; Quant voi la flor nouvele)* HAM ▲ 907184 (17.97)

Theatrum Instrumentorum
Carmina Burana—features 9 sels from the Medieval manuscript "Carmina Burana" AART ▲ 47511 (9.97)
Llibre Vermell de Montserrat (1399)—features Pilgrim songs & dances associated with the shrine to the Virgin of Montserrat, Spain, in the 14th cent. AART ▲ 47384 (9.97)

Tyler, James (lt/baroque gtr/mand), Nigel North (lt/thb/cittern), Douglas Wootton (lt/bandora), Jane Ryan (b vl)
Music of the Renaissance Virtuosi—features works by Vallet, Borrono, Corbetta, de Rore/Terzi, Allison, Bernia, Kapsperger, Piccinini, Ferrabosco, Castello, Dowland, anon. SAGA ▲ 3350 [ADD]

Unicorn Ensemble [cnd: Michael Posch]
The Black Madonna, w. Belinda Sykes (sgr), Bernhard Landauer (ct)—features Cuncti simus concanentes; Quant voi la flor novele; A Madre do que a bestia; Amours, ou trop tart me sui pris; Quant ay lomón consirat; Mariam, matrem Virginem; O Virgo splendens; Tanto son da gloriosa; Comencerai a fere un lai; Cantiga de Santa Maria No. 77/119; O Maria, maris stella; Los set gotxs *(rec W.A.R. Studio May 17-21, 1996) [E, L] text* NXIN ▲ 8554256 [DDD] (5.97)

Urrey, Frederick (ten), Ronn McFarlane (lt)
O Mistress Mine: A Collection of English Lute Songs—features 19 songs and 8 lute solos by Campion, Dowland, Morley, et al. DOR ▲ 90136 [DDD] (16.97)

Vallin, Marie-Claude (sop), Max van Egmond (bass), Lutz Kirchhof (renaissance lt)
Airs de Cour: French Court Music from the 17th Century—features 24 selections by Robert Ballard, Gabriel Bataille, et al. (6 for soprano & lute; 6 for baritone & lute; 6 for soprano, baritone & lute; 6 lute solos) COL (Vivarte) ▲ 48250 [DDD] (16.97)

Vellard, Dominique (ten), Emmanuel Bonnardot, Schola Cantorum Basiliensis
Nova Cantica: Latin Songs of the High Middle Ages DEHA ▲ 77196 [DDD]

Venance Fortunat Ensemble [cnd:Anne-Marie Deschamps]
Daniel—features music from the 12th Century Beauvais Manuscript [L, F, E] ED ▲ 13052 (7.97)
Miroir d'éternité—features motets & conductus of the 14th century including Parce virgo; Deus in adjutorium; Benedicta et cenerabilis es; Salve Regina; Solem justitae; Benedictus Dominus; Ecce jam; Haec Dies; plus 8 Motets & 2 Kyries *(rec Belgium, Oct 1996)* CYPR ▲ 3609 [DDD] (17.97)
Trouvères at the Court of Champagne—features works by Chrétien de Troyes, Gace Brulé, Guiot de Provins, Conon de Béthune, Raoul de Soissons, Gilles de Vieux-Maisons, Thibaut de Champagne, Gaultier de Coinci ED ▲ 13045 (19.97)

Venice Consort [cnd:Giovanni Toffano]
Musica Nova—features works by Willaert *(Ricercares I, X & XIV)*, Segni *(Ricercares III, IV, VI, VIII, IX, XI-XIII, XV, XVI, XIX)*, Benoist *(Ricercare VII)*, Golin *(Ricercare XVII)*, Parabosco *(Ricercare XVIII & XXI)*, Cavazzoni *(Ricercare XX)* TACT ▲ 540002 [DDD] (16.97)

Venice Consort [cnd:Giovanni Toffano], Accademia Strumentale Italiana
Cantar Alla Pavana—features works by Patavino *(Donne, venète al ballo)*, Cara *(Mentre io vo per questi boschi; Poi ch'al mio largo pianto; Per fugir la mia morte, alma mia speme; Doglia che non aguagli)*, Trombonicino *(Facto son per affanni ombra si oscura; Movesi 'l vecchiarel canuto e bianco; Sù, sù, leva, alza le ciglia; Occhi miei lassi, mentre ch'io vi giro; Aspicias utinam quae sit scribentis imago)*, Veneto *(Nel tempo che riveste il verde manto)*, Pesenti *(Quando lo pomo vien da lo pomaro)*, anon *(Da l'orto se ne vien la villanella; Tanto mi trovo, hay lasso, el cor piagato; Amor che fai; O vaghe montanine pastorelle; Se in me exstreme è l'ardor e 'l ghiaccio esstremo; Allhor che 'l verno dà loco a l'estade; Amor, da che convien che pur mi doglia; Nel dolce tempo de la prima etade; Sol del cor si pasce amore; Madonna i' non scio dir tante parole; Che sarà, che non sarà; Questo dolce mio dolore; Baco, Baco, santo idio; Dura passion che per amor soporto; Cossì esstrema è la doglia; Per ristor del corpo lasso; O dolce farfarela) (rec Villa Beatrice, Monte Gemola, Baone, Padova, Oct 1995)* TACT ▲ 520002 [DDD] (16.97)

Wallace, Frank (vih/bar)
Ay e Mi! *(16th cent. Spanish music for vihuela & voice)*—features works by Alonso, Fernandes, Francesco, Fuenllana, Milán, Mudarra, Narvaéz, Pisador, Valderábbano CENT ▲ 2112 (16.97)

Waverly Consort [cnd:Michael Jaffee]
Douce Dame: Music of Courtly Love from Medieval France & Italy—features works by de Machaut *(Douce dame jolie; Comment qu'a moy; Foys porter; Je sui aussi; Rose, liz, printemps)*, da Bologna *(Oselleto salvazo)*, Landini *(Ecco la primavera)*, Vaillant *(Par maintes foys)*, da Firenze *(Apposte messe)*, anon *(Lamento di Tristan; Rotta; Or sus, vous dormez trop; Istampita Isabella) (rec Vanguard's 23rd St. Studio, June 1973)* VC ▲ 8201 [ADD] (13.97)
1492: Music from the Age of Discovery ANGL ▲ 54506 (16.97)
Renaissance Favorites 37845 ▮ COL (10.98)

Weser-Renaissance Ensemble [cnd:M. Cordes]
The Spirit of the Renaissance—features Anonymous *(Lamentanza und Sprung)*, Attaingnant *(Pavane & Bransles)*, F. Desprez *(Iubilate Deo omnis terra à 4)*, Dulichius *(Gloria Patri qui creavit nos)*, H. Finck *(Ich stuend an einem Morgen)*, Greiter *(Ich stuend an einem Morgen)*, H. L. Hassler *(Iubilate Deo omnis terra)*, H. Isaac *(Ich stuend an einem Morgen; Introitus Omnis terra adoret te à 4)*, O. d. Lassus *(Deus qui sedes super thronum; Manus tuae Domine fecerunt me)*, L. Lechner *(Ach schwacher Geist; Ach Gott wie soll ich singen; Weil du dann wilt gen mir)*, Regnard *(Ach schwacher Geist; Ach Gott wie soll ich singen; Weil du dann wilt gen mir)*, Senfl *(Das Gläut zu Speyer; Ich stuend an einem Morgen)*, Stoltzer *(Melodia primi toni)*, Susato *(Pavane & Galliard)*, Willaert *(Dulces exuviae à 4)* CPO ▲ 999294 [DDD] (16.97)

Westminster Abbey Choir [cnd:Simon Preston]
Coronation Music for King James II (1685)—features works by John Blow, Henry Lawes, Purcell, William Child, William Turner PARC ▲ 419613-2 [DDD]
Sacred Works—features works by Palestrina, Allegri, Anerio, Nanino, Giovannielli PARC ▲ 15517 [DDD] (16.97)

The Whole Noyse [Stephen Escher (cnt/fl/rcr), Brian Howard (cnt/fl/rcr), Richard Van Hessel (fl/rcr/gittern), D. Sanford Stadtfeld (rcr), Herbert Myers (curtal fl/rcr/va/shm)]
Lo Splendore D'Italia—features works by Antegnati *(Canzon "La Moranda")*, Mortaro *(Canzon "La Mortara")*, Guami *(Canzon Decimanona; Canzon "La Guamina"; Canzon "La Todeschina")*, Frescobaldi *(Canzon Quinta)*, Ruffo *(Martin Minoit son Porceau au Marche; La Disperata; La gamba in Basso e Soprano)*, Bargnani *(Canzon Decimasesta)*, Zanetti *(Intrata del Marchese di Coravazza; Balletto; La sua Gagliardo; Il Bagaran; Il Canario; Gallaria d'amor el il suo Canaria)*, Gabrieli *(Canzon Prima)*, Mainerio *(Pass'e mezzo antico; Saltarello; Putta nera bello furlano; Ballo francese; Saltarello; schairazula marazula)*, Josquin Desprez *(De Tous Biens Playne)*, Isaac *(Palle, Palle; La Mi La Sol)*, Lapicida *(Tandernaken)*, Rore *(Clamabat Autumn Mulier)*, Corteccia *(Fammi pur Guerr'Amor)*, Taeggio *(Canzon "La Basgapera")*, Merulo *(Maria Virgo; Oh Se Quanto; Canzon Vigesimterza)*, anon. *(El Tutu; El Bisson; La Lavandara)* HEL ▲ 1011 (10.97)

Wistreich, Richard (voc), Robin Jeffrey (thb/baroque gtr)
The Musical Life of Samuel Pepys, w. chamber org & strs—features works by John Blow, Henry Lawes, Matthew Locke, et al. SAY ▲ 385 [DDD] (16.97)

▲ = CD ♦ = Enhanced CD △ = MD ▮ = Cassette Tape ▯ = DCC

Wöldike, Mogens (cnd)

Masterpieces of Music Before 1750: An Anthology of Music Examples from Gregorian Chant to J.S. Bach, Vol. 1: Gregorian Chant to the 16th Century, w. various Danish soloists & ensembles HAYD ▲ CD 7-9038

Masterpieces of Music Before 1750: An Anthology of Music Examples from Gregorian Chant to J.S. Bach, Vol. 2: The 16th & 17th Centuries, w. various Danish soloists & ensembles HAYD ▲ CD 7-9039

Masterpieces of Music Before 1750: An Anthology of Music Examples from Gregorian Chant to J.S. Bach, Vol. 3: The 17th & 18th Centuries, w. various Danish soloists & ensembles HAYD ▲ CD 7-9040

York Waits

The City Musicke: Wind Bands of Renaissance Europe, 1550-1600—features Intrada Decima; La Bataglia; T'Andernaken; Galliarde de la Guerre; Ohn Dich Müss Ich; Entré du Fol; Mille Regretz; Les Grands Douleurs; Allemande & Reprise; Le Joly Bois/Pour Quoy/Den Hoboecken Dans; Sans Roche; Mille Ducas; Les Quatre Bransles; Bergerette; Dont Vient Cela; Pass'e Mezzo della Paganina/La Parma/Ballo Anglese/Putta Nera Ballo Furlano; La Lavandara; Paduana & Gagliarda; L'Arboscello ballo furlano; Je suie aymé; La Rocque; Ick seg adieu; La Facca; D'eccelio; Pavane & Gaillarde; The Choise/Honie Suckle/The Fairie Round; Wilson's Wild Mistress Winter's Jump *(rec St. Botolph's Church, Bossall, 1993)* Brewhouse Music ▲ BHCD 9409 [DDD]

Old Christmas Return'd—features English, French, German and Flemish sacred and secular vocal and instrumental music from the 16th-17th centuries, music appropriate for the Christmas season, performed by this eight-member period instrument ensemble SAY ▲ 398 [DDD] 398

Zuchetto, Gérard (sgr)

Tensons e partimens de Trobairitz, Vol. 3 *(12th & 13th cent. troubadour songs)*, w. Katia Caré (sgr), Gisela Bellsolà (sgr), Patrice Brient (h-g/rebeck/voc), Guy Robert (medieval lt/oud/hp)—features Rosin digatz...; Na Lombarda; Amics, en gran cossirier...; Maria de Ventadorn; Isabella; Na Guillelma GALL ▲ 769 [DDD]

Troubador Songs of the 12th & 13th Centuries, w. Patrice Brient (h-g/rebeck/voc), Jacques Khoudir (perc)—features works by d'Orange, Vidal, Daniel, de Miraval GALL ▲ CD 529

Troubador Songs of the 12th & 13th Centuries, Vol. 2, w. Dominique Regef (rebec/israj/h-g), Jacques Khoudir (perc)—features works by de Miraval, Vidal, de Tolosa, Peirol GALL ▲ CD 684 [DDD]

Zurich Ancient Instrument Ensemble

Renaissance Dances 60036 ▮ COL (3.98)

EARLY MUSIC COLLECTIONS

Abondance—features performances by Das Neue Orch [cnd:Christoph Spering], Cologne Musicus Chorus *(R. Schumann:Der Rose Pilgerfahrt [2 versions])*, Concerto Italiano [cnd:Rinaldo Alessandrini] *(Monteverdi:Il Combattimento di Tancredi e Clorinda; Pergolesi:Stabat Mater [w. Sara Mingardo (cta), Gemma Bertagnolli (sop)]; A. Scarlatti: Stabat Mater [Juxta crucem tecum stare; w. Sara Mingardo (cta)])*, Discantus [cnd:Brigitte Lesne] *(Hildegard:Hortus deliciarum Herrad)*, Flanders Recorder Quartet *(Armonia di flauti)*, Cappella della Pietà de Turchini [cnd:Antonio Florio] *(Provenzale:Vespro)*, Alla Francesca *(Armes, amours)*, Musica Petropolitana *(Tessarini:Sinf in D)*, Micrologus *(Madre de Deus:Cantigas de Santa María [Ontre todales vertudes])*, Russian Patriarchate Choir *(Russian Christmas, Feast of the Nativity [All the angels exult])*, Olga Tverskaya (pno), Colin Lawson (cl), Alberto Grazzi (bn), Norbert Blume (va), Adrian Chandler (instr) *(Glinka:Trio Pathétique in d)*, Lina Mkrtchyan (cta), Evgeny Talisman (pno) *(Tchaikovsky:Do Not Ask Me)* OPUS ▲ 1008 [DDD] (5.97)

Angels, w. Concerto Soave, Ensemble Convivencia, Ensemble Lucidarum, Ensemble Venance Fortunat, La Fenice, Iberian Lyric Ensemble—features Stirps Jesse florigeram; Alleluia! in conspectu angelorum; Ex eius tumba; Huic Jacobo/Tristis est anima mea; Aucun vont souvent; Condicio; La prier de Daniel; Ave Stella Matutina; Quand le gril chante; Repicaba; Skalerika de oro; O Maria; Parasti cor meum; Usurpator Tiranno; Elle a voulu serviteur me nommer; Nigra sum *(budget priced)* ED ▲ 13050

Angels of Antiquity: Music from the Middle Ages to the Age of Enlightenment—features performances by Pomerium [cnd:Alexander Blachly] *(Busnois:Victime pascali; Missa O crux lignum triumphale [Kyrie]; Gesualdo:O vos omnes; Monteverdi:Ohimè, se tanto amate)*, Colin Tinley (vir) *(Gibbons:Ground in A; Bull:Why Ask You)*, Baltimore Consort *(My Heartly Service; Scotch Cap; Chardavoine:Mignonne, allons voir si la rose; Praetorius:Branle double; Branle de Montirande; Branle de la torche)*, Julianne Baird (sop), Ronn McFarlane (lt) *(Johnson:Have You Seen But a White Lily Grow; Morley:April is in My Mistress' Face)*, Julianne Baird (sop), Colin Tilney (hpd) *(Amarilli)*, La Rondinella *(Mizmor l'David; Ortiz:Recercada segunda; Puncha, puncha; Yo m'enamori)*, Apollo Ensemble [cnd:John Hsu] *(Haydn:Sym 42 [Finale: Scherzando e presto])*, Haydn Baryton Trio *(Haydn:Trio 52 in D [Menuet alla zoppa])*, Rob MacKillop (lts), William Taylor (clarsachs) *(Lux et gloria)*, Ronn McFarlane (lt) *(Ein welscher tantz Wascha mesa; Der hupff auff; Dowland:Lachrimae; Mrs. White's Nothing)*, Dorothea Röschmann (sop), Kevin McMillan (bar), Les Violons du Roy [cnd:Bernard Labadie] *(Bach:Cant 212)*, Colin Tilney (hpd) *(Frescobaldi:Corrente & Ciaccona)*, Altramar *(Saltarello Sancto Antonio)* DOR ▲ 90009 [DDD] (12.97)

The Art of Ornamentation in Early Music, w. Maureen Forrester (cta), Alfred Deller (ct), André Lardrot (ob), Jan Tomasow (vn), Anton Heiller (org/hpd), Igor Kipnis (hpd), Charles Mackerras (hpd), Gustav Leonhardt (hpd), Harold Lester (hpd), Deller Consort [cnd:Alfred Deller], Jaye Consort of Viols [cnd:Francis Baines], Vienna Baroque Players, Wenzinger Consort of Viols [cnd:August Wenzinger], Zagreb Solisti [cnd:Antonio Janigro], Ambrosian Singers [cnd:Denis Stevens], et al.—features works by Archilei, de Rore, Merulo, de Layolle, Hofhaimer, Sandrin, Parsons, Monteverdi, Boësset, Brewer, Corelli, Couperin, Marcello, Vivaldi, Handel, Nardini, Telemann, Quantz, Rameau, C.P.E. Bach, Gluck, anon *(rec Musikverein, Vienna, Nov 29-Dec 2, 1966)* VC 2-▲ 2537 (25.97)

Barocco Strumentale Italiano, Vol. 2—features works by Vivaldi, Torelli, Porpora, Geminiani, Pasquini, Platti, Bonporti, Lanzetti NUO (Ancient Music) ▲ 113

Bayeux Manuscript; 15th Century French Songs ED ▲ 13076 (18.97)

The Best of Millennium of Music, Volume 1—features works by Alfonso el Sabio *(Fror das frores [w. Ancient Music Group, Eduardo Paniagua (cnd)])*, Dering *(O vos omnes [w. Waverly Consort, Michael Jaffe (cnd)])*, Dufay *(Ave regina caelorum [w. Munich Capella Antiqua, Konrad Ruhland (cnd)])*, Festa *(Quis dabit oculis [w. Huelgas Ensemble, Paul van Nevel (cnd)])*, Gabrieli *(Nunc dimittis [w. E. Power Biggs (org), Gregg Smith Singers, Texas Boys Choir, Edward Tarr Brass Ensemble, Vittorio Negri (cnd)]; Canzona à 12 in echo [w. Philadelphia Brass Ensemble, Cleveland Brass Ensemble, Chicago Brass Ensemble])*, Gesualdo *(Moro, lasso, al mio duolo [w. Singers of Venosa, Robert Craft (cnd)]; Responsory:Tenebrae factae sunt [w. Westminster Abbey Choir, Martin Neary (cnd)])*, Gombert *(Tous les regretz [w. Huelgas Ensemble, Paul van Nevel (cnd)])*, Josquin Desprez *(Fanfare:Vive le roy [w. Columbia Brass Ensemble, Andrew Kazdin (cnd)]; Adieu mes amours [w. Munich Capella Antiqua, Konrad Ruhland (cnd)]; Qui habitat [w. Huelgas Ensemble, Paul van Nevel (cnd)])*, Lassus *(Providebam Dominum [w. Philadelphia Brass Ensemble])*, Merbecke *(The Booke of Common Praier Noter:Kyrie & Credo [w. Chapel of the General Theological Seminary of New York Mixed Choir, Harold W. Gilbert (cnd), Andrew Tietjen (org)])*, Monteverdi *(Vespro della Beata Vergine:Domine ad adjuvandum [w. Gregg Smith Singers, Texas Boys Choir of Fort Worth, Columbia Baroque Ensemble, Robert Craft (cnd)]; O Rosetta, che rosetta [w. Waverly Consort, Michael Jaffe (cnd)])*, anon *(Alleluia:Pascha nostrum [w. Schola Cantorum of Amsterdam Students, Wim van Gerven (cnd)]; Kyrie:Magnae Deus potentiae [w. Niederaltaich Scholaren Choralschola, Konrad Ruhland (cnd)]; Ave maris stella [w. Niederaltaich Scholaren, Konrad Ruhland (cnd)]; Conductus:Orientis partiphia [w. Waverly Consort, Michael & Kay Jaffe (cnds)]; Agincourt Hymn:Deo gratias Anglia [w. E. Power Biggs (org)]; Como la rosa en la güerta [w. Waverly Consort, Julianne Baird (sop)]; My lady careys dompe [w. Waverly Consort, Michael Jaffe (cnd)])*, plus Shakespeare *(As You Like It:Act II, Scene 7 [w. John Gielgud (speaker)])* VLEC ▲ VLEC 15023

The Best of the Millennium of Music, Volume 2—features works by M.-A. Charpentier *(Troisième O [w. Les Arts Florissants, William Christie (cnd)])*, Handel *(Pastoral Sym; He Shall Feed His Flock [both from Messiah; w. Les Arts Florissants, William Christie (cnd)])*, Hassler *(O Admirabile commercium [w. Ensemble Vocal Européen de la Chapelle Royale, Philippe Herreweghe (cnd)])*, Notker Balbullus *(Sequence:In natali domini [w. Ensemble Gilles Binchois, Dominique Vellard (cnd)])*, D. Read *(While Shepherds Watched [w. Theatre of Voices, Paul Hillier (cnd)])*, Schütz *(Der Engel sprach zu den Hirten [w. Academy of Ancient Music Orch & Chorus, Paul Goodwin (cnd)])*, Tallis *(Salvator mundi Domine [w. Deller Consort, Alfred Deller (cnd)])*, anon *(Communion for Advent:Beata viscera; Lullay, lullay:Als I lay on Yoolis Night; Novus annus adiit; Conductus:Salve mater salvatoris [all w. Anonymous 4]; Cant de la Sibilla [w. Barcelona Ars Musicae Ensemble, Enric Gispert (cnd)]; Alleluia:A newe werk; Ther is no rose of such vertu [both w. Hilliard Ensemble]; Gaudete, Gaudete, Christus natus est; In hoc anni circulo [both w. Theatre of Voices, Paul HIllier (cnd)]; Swete was the song the Virgine soong [arr T. Hammond; Coventry Carol [both w. Pro Arte Singers, Paul Hillier (cnd)])* VLEC ▲ 15024 (16.97)

Distant Voices—features Renaissance vocal music performances by Gabrieli Consort & Players [cnd:Paul McCreesh] *(Josquin DesPrez:Praeter rerum seriem; Palestrina:Sanctus; Agnus dei [both from Missa "Hodie Christus natus est"]; Victoria:O magnum mysterium; Gabrieli:Domine Deus meus a 6; Gregorian chant:Introit)*, Pomerium [cnd:Alexander Blachly] *(Dufay:Kyrie; Agnus Dei [both from Missa de St. Anthonii de Padua]; Nuper rosarum flores (motet))*, Orlando Consort *(Ockeghem:Kyrie; Sanctus [both from Missa "De plus en plus"])*, Regensburg Domspatzen [cnd:Hanns-Martin Schneidt] *(Monteverdi:Sanctus [from Missa in illo tempore; w. Hubert Gumz (positive org), Laurenzius Strehl (vn)])*, Westminster Abbey Choir [cnd:Simon Preston] *(Allegri:Miserere)* PPHI (Night Moods) ▲ 453907 [DDD/ADD] (11.97)

The Early Music Collection—features performances by Nova Schola Gregoriana [cnd:Alberto Turco] *(anon:Gregorian Chant for Good Friday [Responsorium Graduale])*, In Dulci Jubilo [cnd:Alberto Turco] *(anon:Gregorian Chant for Pentecost [Factus est repente])*, Rebecca Outram (sop) *(Hildegard of Bingen:O viridissima virga)*, Ensemble Unicorn *(anon Italian 14th Century:Chominciamento di gioia; Belicha; Saltarello 2)*, Oxford Camerata [cnd:Jeremy Summerly] *(Ockeghem:Intemerata Dei mater; Palestrina:Missa Papae Marcelli [Kyrie])*, Christopher Wilson (lt) *(Francesco da Milano:Fant [55])*, Joseph Payne (org) *(anon:La Bounette [Galliard from the Mulliner Book])*, Robert Parkins (org) *(anon:Entrada)*, Shirley Rumsey (vih) *(anon Spanish 16th Century:Guardame las vacas)*, Scholars of London *(Josquin:Faute d'argent)*, Shirley Rumsey (gtr) *(anon Spanish 16th Century:Conde Claros)*, Red Byrd, Rose Consort of Viols *(Byrd:Have Mercy upon Me, O God)*, Shirley Rumsey (voc/lt) *(Arcadelt:La Pastorella mia)*, Rose Consort of Viols *(Jenkins:Fant in c)*, Laurence Cummings (hpd) *(Louis Couperin:Suite in F [Gigue])* † EARLY MUSIC:Oxford Camerata NXIN 4-▲ 504009 [DDD] (19.97)

Gaudeamus Early Music Sampler, w. Great Consort, His Majesties Sagbutts & Cornetts, Rasumovsky String Quartet, Trio Sonnerie, Cappella Nova, Cardinall's Musick, Clerks' Group, Ex Cathedra, Gentlemen of the Chappell, Gonville & Caius College Choir Cambridge, et al.—features works by Carver, Couperin, Dowland, Duphly, Fayrfax, Finger, Gabrieli, Isaac, Jadin, Lassus Lawes, Leclair, Ludford, Marais, Monteverdi, Vivaldi, Wesley *(budget priced)* ASV ▲ 1002 (8.97)

The Glory of Early Music—features performances by Ensemble Unicorn *(Anon:Saltarello 3; Düdül; Nevestinko oro; Quinte estampie real; Saltarello 1; Lamento di Tristano-La Rotta; Dufay:J'ay mis nom cuer)*, Convivium Musicum, Ensemble Villanella *(Isaac:Carmen a 5; Las rauschen; Obrecht:Stat ('tsaat) ein meskin; Finck:So trinken wir alle; Bruck:Es ging ein Landsknecht; Senfl:Ich weiss nicht)*, Shirley Rumsey (lt) *(Anon:Guardame las vacas; Tomkins:Almain in F)*, Joseph Payne (org) *(Morton:Le souvenin; Mulliner Book [The Old Spagnoletta])*, Rose Consort of Viols, Red Byrd *(Byrd:Pavan, Galliard; Gibbons:Pavan; Lincoln's Inn Mask; Galliard; Fantasia of Four Parts; Tomkins:Almain in F; Jenkins: Newark Seidge [Pavan, Galliard])*, Wilson *(Franco Canova da Milano:Ricercar (13))* NXIN ▲ 8554064 [DDD] (5.97)

A Golden Treasury of Renaissance Music—features performances by London Musica Antiqua *(Henry VIII:En vray amour; Cornyshe:Adieu My Hertes Lust; Willaert:Basiez moi; Sermisy:Dont vient cela; anon:Consort Pieces; L'amour de moi; Gervaise:Pavane & Gaillard a'Angleterre)*, Fretwork *(Tye:In nomine à 5; Byrd:In nomine No. 4)*, York Waites *(anon:Watlins Ale; Anello; Mercantia; Tuba Gallicais; Morton:Le souvenir; Glogauer:In feurz hitz; Praetorius:Es ist ein ros entsprungen; Attaignant:Bransles de Champagne; Brumel:Nato canunt omnia; Obrecht:Den haghel ende ie calde snee; Encina:Todos los biennes del mundo)*, Musica Secreta *(Luzzaschi:Occhi del pinato moi; Strozzi:Amor dormiglione; Libertà)*, Paula Chanteneuf (chit) *(Piccinini:Toccata)*, New London Chamber Choir *(de la Rue:Missa pro defunctis)*, Francis Kelly (hp) *(Dufay:Je veuil chanter de ceur joyeux)*, Nigel North (vih) *(Mudarra:Fant que contrahaze la harpa en la mannera de Ludovico)* AMON ▲ 65 (16.97)

Guide des Instruments de la Renaissance, w. La Fenice, Ricercar Consort, Le Tourdion—features music from the 15th-17th centuries RICE 3-▲ 95001 (34.97)

A Handefull of Pleasant Delites—features E. Headley (vl), Circa 1500 Ensemble [cnd:N. Hadden] *(Anonymous:All in a Garden Grene; Fortune My Foe; Lancashire Pipes; Pavlett:Toye)*, E. Headley (fid/va da gamba), S. Player (gtr), M. Lawson (sop), Circa 1500 Ensemble [cnd:N. Hadden], J. Heringman (lt/cittern), N. Hadden (fl) *(Anonymous:Maid Will You Marrie?; Passymeasures(improv); The Lady Greensleeves; Turkeyloney-Lyke as the Dumb Solsequiem)*, E. Headley (va da gamba), M. Lawson (sop), Circa 1500 Ensemble [cnd:N. Hadden], V. Coode (va da gamba), J. Heringman (va da gamba) *(Alison:Our Father Which in Heaven Art; Anonymous:Lyke as the Lark)*, E. Headley (vl), M. Lawson (sop), Circa 1500 Ensemble [cnd:N. Hadden], N. Hadden (fl), L. Carolan (hpd) *(Anonymous:I Smile to See How You Devise)*, E. Headley (vl), Circa 1500 Ensemble [cnd:N. Hadden], L. Carolan (hpd) *(Anonymous:Tom O'Bedlam)*, E. Headley (fid), S. Player (gtr), Circa 1500 Ensemble [cnd:N. Hadden], V. Coode (va da gamba), J. Heringman (cittern), N. Hadden (fl), L. Carolan (hpd) *(Susato:Quarter Braules)*, S. Player (gtr), M. Lawson (sop), Circa 1500 Ensemble [cnd:N. Hadden], J. Heringman (lt), N. Hadden (fl) *(Anonymous:Garden So Green)*, S. Player (lt), N. Hadden (fl) *(Alison:Our Father Which in Heaven Art)*, M. Lawson (sop), Circa 1500 Ensemble [cnd:N. Hadden], J. Heringman (lt) *(Anonymous:What Mightie Motion)*, M. Lawson (sop), Circa 1500 Ensemble [cnd:N. Hadden] *(Anonymous:Taladh Chriosta)*, Circa 1500 Ensemble [cnd:N. Hadden], N. Hadden (fl) *(J. Dowland:Frog Galliard; Eyck:Fluyten Lust-Hof (sels) [Crimson Velvet; Een Schots lietjen; Onse vader])*, Circa 1500 Ensemble [cnd:N. Hadden], J. Heringman (lt) *(Anonymous:Grein Greus Ye Rasses-A Daunce; E. Collard:Ground)*, Circa 1500 Ensemble [cnd:N. Hadden], L. Carolan (hpd) *(Anonymous:Kypascie; Tallis:Jam lucis orto sidere)* ASV ▲ 163 [DDD] (16.97)

An Introduction to Early Music—features performances by Nova Schola Gregoriana [cnd:Alberto Turco] *(anon:Gregorian Chant for Good Friday [Responsorium Graduale])*, In Dulci Jubilo [cnd:Alberto Turco] *(anon:Gregorian Chant for Pentecost [from Factus est repente])*, Rebecca Outram (sop) *(Hildegard of Bingen:O viridissima virga)*, Ensemble Unicorn *(anon:Chominciamento di gioia; Belicha; Saltarello 2)*, Oxford Camerata [cnd:Jeremy Summerly] *(Ockeghem:Intemerata Dei mater; Palestrina:Missa Papae Marcelli [Kyrie])*, Christopher Wilson (lt) *(Milano:Fant No. 55)*, Joseph Payne (org) *(anon:Galliard; La Bounette [both from the Mulliner Book])*, Robert Parkins (org) *(anon:Entrada)*, Shirley Rumsey (vih/gtr/voice/lt) *(anon:Guardame las vacas; Conde Claros; Arcadelt:La Pastorella mia)*, Scholars of London *(Josquin:Faunte d'argent)*, Rose Consort of Vls *(Byrd:Have mercy upon me, O God [w. Red Byrd]; Jenkins:Fant in c)*, Laurence Cummings (hpd) *(Couperin:Suite in F [Gigue])* NXIN ▲ 551203 [DDD] (5.97)

Madre de Deus; Cantigas de Santa Maria OPUS ▲ 30225 (17.97)

Masterpieces of Music before 1750, Vol. 2—features an anthology of musical examples from Gregorian chant to J. S. Bach HAYD ▲ HSCD 9039

Masterpieces of Music before 1750, Vol. 3—features an anthology of musical examples from Gregorian chant to J. S. Bach HAYD ▲ HSCD 9040

A Medieval Journey—features performances by Sister Marie Keyrouz (voc) *(Byzantine Chant; Sacred Melchite Chant)*, Ensemble Organum [cnd:Marcel Pérès] *(Milanese, Roman & Mozarabic Chants; Cistercian chant; Polyphony in Aquitaine; Christmas Mass; Gradual of Eleanor of Brittany; Tournai Mass; Songs of Machaut, Landini, Guido, Baude Cordier; Ockeghem:Requiem)*, Deller Consort *(Gregorian Requiem Mass; Gallic Repertoire)*, Schola Hungarica *(Nativity Mass)*, Clemencic Consort [cnd:René Clemencic] *(Troubadours; Cantigas of Santa Maria; Carmina Burana [sels]; Le Roman de Fauvel [sels])*, Drew Minter (ct), Newberry Consort [cnd:Mary Springfels] *(Minnesänger)*, Anonymous 4 *(An English Lady Mass [Montpellier Manuscript])*, Hilliard Ensemble [cnd:Paul Hillier] *(English Sacred Music)*, Anonymous 4, Hilliard Ensemble, Newberry Consort *(Ciconia; English Carols & Motets; 15th Cent Spanish Instrumental Music)*, Paul O'Dette (lt) *(Marco Da l'Aquila:Lt Pieces)* HAM 6-▲ 290649 (52.97)

Médiévales de Québec *(music of the Renaissance & Middle Ages)*—features performances by Strada [cnd:Pierre Langevin] *(Bransle des chevaux; Saltarello; Skarazula Marazula; Lo paure satan & Er dei tripetas; Bransle de Poitou & d'Escosse; Ouadouni & Ourdouni souz shaya; Aï vist lo lop, lo rainard, la lebre; Chanconetta tedesca; Farandoulo; Rampaleda e corsa de la tarasca [all rec studio TRAM, Quebec, 1992 & 1995])*, Ensemble Anonymus [cnd:Claude Bernatchez] *(Nu al'erst; Ce fut en mai; Non sofre Santa Maria; Septime estampie réale; Ductiae; Es fur ein pawr; Ungaresca; Propiñan de Melyor; Basse danse [Jouyssance vous donneray] [all rec SISCOM Inc., 1982 & 1984])* ANAL ▲ 28003 [ADD]

Musica Humana, w. Françoise Atlan (mez), John Fleagle (ten/hp), Crawford Young (lt), Anonymous 4, Ensemble Discantus, Gilles Binchois Ensemble, Ensemble Organum, Gothic Voices, Greek Byzantine Choir, Hilliard Ensemble, Musica Nova, et al.—features Gaude Virgo Gratiosa; Salve Virgo Virginum [both from An English Ladymass]; Ave Maris Stella [from Repertory of the Women's Monastery of Las Huelgas]; Ex Sion [from The Creation & the Apocalypse]; Verses of the Great Complines [from Greek Orthodox & Grand Liturgy]; Requiem Aeternum [from Ockeghem Requiem]; Sanctus [from Machaut Notre-Dame Mass]; Amours, que vous ai meffait; Gli atti col dançar; Ave Virgo [from In Search of the Golden Fleece]; Ah, Gentil Jesu; An den Kozh Dall; Guerilla Song; Yavru, Yavru; Villemann og magnhild den underjoriske Klippekonsert; Durme, durme mi angelico ED ▲ 13047

Musica Sacra FONT ▲ 9916 (36.97)

Musical Europe in the Middle Ages: France, England & Spain, w. Barcelona Ars Musica [cnd:Enric Gispert], Clemencic Consort [cnd:René Clemencic], Hilliard Ensemble HMA 3-▲ 290859 (17.97)

Pathways of Renaissance Music: European Polyphony, 1480-1600 HAM (Special Boxed Sets) 5-▲ 2908016 (52.97)

Renaissance—features Collegium Vocale [cnd:P. Herreweghe], Hannover Boys' Choir [cnd:P. Herreweghe] *(O. d. Lassus:Moduli Quinis Vocibus (sels), Siii/112; Pater noster (sex vocum), Sxiii/77)*, Ensemble Polyphonique de France [cnd:C. Ravier] *(Janequin:Chansons Nouvelles 19, Miii/74)*, Hespèrion XX [cnd:J. Savall] *(Anonymous:Musicque de Ioye; A. d. Cabezón:Mvsicqve de Ioye; Costa:Mvsicqve de Ioye; Gervaise:Musicque de Ioye; Janequin:Mvsicqve de Ioye, Miii/77; Modena (Segni da):Musicque de Ioye; Mvsicqve de Ioye; Parabosco:Mvsicqve de Ioye; Roquelay:Mvsicqve de Ioye; Sandrin:Mvsicqve de Ioye, S 11; Willaert:Mvsicqve de Ioye)* ASTR 3-▲ 8608 (46.97)

To Drive the Dark Away; Traditional Songs & Dances for the Winter Solstice REVV ▲ 1098

A Treasury of Early Music: An Anthology of Masterworks of the Middle Ages, Renaissance & Baroque

Vol. 1: Music of the Middle Ages HAYD ▲ CD 7-9100

Vol. 2: Music of the Ars Nova & Renaissance HAYD ▲ CD 7-9101

Vol. 3: Music of the Renaissance & Baroque HAYD ▲ CD 7-9102

Vol. 4: Music of the Baroque HAYD ▲ CD 7-9103

EARLY MUSIC COLLECTIONS

Vous or la mort: Flemish Courtly Love Songs of the 15th Century, w. Guillemette Laurens (cant), Katelijne van Laethem (cant), Jan Caals (ten), Jan van Elsacker (ten), Erik van Nevel (ten), Job Boswinkel (bass), Erik van Nevel (cnd), Currende Consort, Capella Sancti Michaelis, Concerto Palatino—features works by Dufay *(Hé, compagnions; La belle se siet)*, Binchois *(Amours merchi; Triste plaisir de douloureuse joye)*, Agricola *(De tous bien plaine)*, Ockeghem *(Ma bouche rit)*, H. Isaac *(Alla battaglia; Es wolt ein Maegdlein; Ach, was will doch mein Herz; In meinem Sinn)*, Compère *(Vous me faites morir)*, Prioris *(Elle l'a pris)*, Obrecht *(Den haghel ende)*, de la Rue *(Il viendra le jour désire; Autant en emporte la vent)*, des Prez *(Douleur me bat; Plusieurs regrétz; Si l'avoye Marion; Ile fantazies de Joskin; Je ne me puis tenir d'aimer; Allegez moy; Adieu mes amours; A l'eure; Cueurs desolez) (rec Belgium, 1990 & 1994)* CNTS ▲ 9607 [DDD] (18.97)

Vox Aeterna, w. Hesperion XX [cnd:Jordi Savall]—features performances by La Capella Reial de Catalunya [cnd:Jordi Savall] *(C. Morales:Lecto II:Taedet animam meam vitae; Alfonso El Sabio:Pero cantigas de loor; Victoria:O Magnum mysterium à 4 [both w. Hespèrion XX]; Guerrero:Ave Maria à 8 [w. Montserrat Figueras (sop), Elisabetta Tiso (sop), Laurence Bonnal (cta), Paolo Costa (ct), Lambert Climent (ten), Francesc Garrigosa (ten), Jordi Ricart (bar), Daniele Carnovich (bass)]; Monteverdi:Hymnus:Ave maris stella à 8 [w. Montserrat Figueras (sop), Maria Cristina Kiehr (sop), Livio Picotti (ct), Guy de Mey (ten), Gerd Türk (ten), Paolo Fagotto (ten), Pietro Spagnoli (bar), Daniele Carnovich (bass), Padua Centro Music Antica Chorus]; Cererols:Missa pro Defunctis:Hei mihi à 7 [w. Montserrat Figueras (sop), Maïte Arruabarrena (sop), Joan Cabero (ten), Lambert Climent (ten), Josep Cabré (bar), Jordi Ricart (bar), Daniele Carnovich (bass)]; Mozart:Requiem, K.626 [Introitus Requiem Aeternam; w. Montserrat Figueras (sop), Le Concert des Nations]; anon:Sibil-la catalana [from El Cant de la Sibil-la I; w. Montserrat Figueras (sop)])*, Le Concert des Nations [cnd:Jordi Savall] *(Haydn:Les sept dernières paroles [Son 4 Largo; w. Rafael Taibo (nar)]; J. S. Bach:Air [from BWV 1068]; M.-A. Charpentier:Prélude pour Salve Regina à 3; Salve Regina à trois vois pareilles [both w. Gérard Lesne (ct), John Elwes (ten), Josep Cabré (bar)])*, Montserrat Figueras (sop), Maria Cristina Kiehr (sop), Kai Wessel (ct), Michael Behringer (org) *(Dufay:Veni Sancte spirito)* FONT ▲ 9902 [DDD] (16.97)

ELECTRONIC MUSIC

Anugama (syn)
Classic Fantasy II—features works by J.S. Bach *(Adagio; andante)*, Vivaldi *(Solo cantabile)*, Beethoven *(Son. No. 14 in c#, "Moonlight")*, Satie *(3 Gymnopédies)*, Mozart *(Trinklied)* NIG ▲ NGH 350 [ADD]

Baker, Joffrey Reid (syn)
Fantastic Favorites—features Beethoven *(Bagatelle in a, WoO 59; Ruinen von Athen (sels) [Turkish March])*, Boccherini *(Minuetto)*, J. Brahms *(Hungarian Dances Pno 4-Hands [No. 5 in g])*, Chaminade *(Flatterer)*, Chopin *(Waltzes Pno [No. 6 in D♭, Op. 64/1, "Minute"])*, Debussy *(Rêverie Pno)*, Ellmenreich *(Spinning Song)*, M. d. Falla *(Amor brujo (Ritual Fire Dance))*, L. M. Gottschalk *(Banjo, Op. 15)*, Gounod *(Ave Maria)*, Liszt *(Liebesträume, S.541)*, MacDowell *(Shadow Dance; To A Wild Rose)*, Mendelssohn (-Bartholdy) *(Lieder ohne Worte Pno [Book 6, No. 4 in C, Op. 67/4, Presto, "The Bee's Wedding"]; Rondo capriccioso, Op. 14)*, Moszkowski *(Pieces Pno, Op. 45 [Guitarre])*, W. A. Mozart *(Son 11 Pno, K.311/300i [3. Alla turca: allegretto])*, S. Prokofiev *(Love for 3 Oranges (march), Op. 33bis)*, S. Rachmaninoff *(Morceaux de fant, Op. 3)*, M. Ravel *(Pavane pour une infante défunte; Valse)*, Rimsky-Korsakov *(Tale of Tsar Saltan (orch sels) [Flight of the bumble-bee])*, Satie *(Gymnopédies [No. 1:Lent et douloureux])*, R. Schumann *(Kinderszenen Pno, Op. 15 [7. Träumerei])*, Sinding *(Pieces (6) Pno, Op. 32 [Rustles of Spring])* JRB ▲ 9004 [DDD]

Bayan, Michel (elec)
Best of Collage—features works by Saint Preux *(Dream of France)*, Morricone *(The Lady; Che Mai)*, Marcello *(Con Ob in d [Adagio & Presto])*, Kitaro *(Mirage; Winter God)*, Vangelis *(La Petit de la Mar)*, Rodrigo *(Concerto de Aranjuez)*, Martini *(Plaisir d'amour)*, Granados *(Vars on Spanish Dance 2)*, Bizet *(Aria [from Les Pêcheurs de Perles])*, Zamfir *(Rocking Chair)* Binaural Source-Audio Acoustical Collage ▲ X-22 [DDD]

Collage III: Scandinavian Fantasy—features Anticipating Winter; Winter Sym Part I; Christmastide; The Endless Tale; Midwinter Night; Summer Longing; Summer Herding; Winter Sym Part II; Legend of Joy Binaural Source-Audio Acoustical Collage ▲ X-15

Collage IV, w. Dorothy Larson (vc), Oren Fader (gtr), Arsen Tovmasian (hpd/pno/syn), Mark Wood (syn), Collage CO—features works by Jarre *(Equinox Part II)*, Kitaro *(Wind God; Mirage)*, Vangelis *(La Petit Fille de la Mar)*, Granados *(Spanish Dance 2 [plus vars])*, Sor *(Study in e)*, Tarrega *(Recuerdos de la Alhambra)*, Vivaldi *(Con in D [Allegro])* Binaural Source-Audio Acoustical Collage ▲ X-20 [DDD]

Collage V, w. Dorothy Larson (vc), Djivan Gasparyan (duduk), Oren Fader (gtr), Arsen Tovmasian (pno/syn), Yaron Gerschowsky (syn), Mark Wood (syn)—features works by Vangelis *(West Across the Ocean Sea; Ignacio [Part II-Lullaby])*, Martini *(Plaisir d'amore)*, Beethoven *(Son 14 Pno, "Moonlight")*, Bizet *(Aria [from Les Pêcheurs de perles])*, Satie *(Gymnopédie 1)*, Mozart *(Con Pno)*, trad *(Sister; Greensleeves)*, anon *(Spanish Romance)* Binaural Source-Audio Acoustical Collage ▲ X-21 [DDD]

Bayan, Michel (syn/tape/elec)
Collage I, w. Elada Chakoyan (voc), Paula Chang Bing (fl), Marcia Buttler (ob/bn), Oren Feder (gtr), David Labolte (syn), Lawrence (syn)—features works by Vangelis *(Sauvage; Antarctica)*, Morricone *(The Lady [La Dame aux Camelias]; Mystery [Vars on a theme from Le Professional])*, Marcello *(Inner Thoughts [Adagio from Con Ob in d])*, Saint Preux *(Summer [Un Ete]; Nocturne; Concert for Her; Confidence; Dream of France)*, Kitaro *(The Road in the Sky [Everlasting Road])* Binaural Source-Audio Acoustical Collage ▲ X-11

Collage II, w. Elada Chakoyan (voc), Paula Chang Bing (fl), Marcia Buttler (ob/bn), Oren Feder (gtr), David Labolte (syn), Lawrence (syn)—features works by Vangelis, Morricone, Wakeman, Zamfir, Marcello, Bach, Tarrega, Rodrigo Binaural Source-Audio Acoustical Collage ▲ X-13

Carlos, Wendy (elecs)
Digital Moonscapes COL ▲ 39340 39340

Secrets of Synthesis *(Electronic Orchestration from "Switched-On Bach" to "Digital Moonscapes")*, w. Wendy Carlos (nar)—features Analog timbres; Choral tone, vibrato, articulation; Vocal synthesis; Simple orchestration; etc. COL ▲ 42333

Switched-On Bach 2000 *(a completely new version of the 1960s CBS Records "Switched-On Bach" album; all selections newly performed and recorded)*—features Brandenburg Concerto No. 3; Jesu, joy of man's desiring; Toccata & Fugue in d; etc. TEL ▲ 80323 [DDD] (15.97) ▮

Switched-On Brandenburgs, Vol. 1—features works by Bach *(Brandenburg Concerti Nos. 1-3; Orchestral Suite No. 2 in b [excerpts]; 2-Part Inventions Nos. 12 & 13; Sheep May Safely Graze)* COL ▲ 42308 [AAD]

Switched-On Brandenburgs, Vol. 2—features works by Bach *(Brandenburg Concerti Nos. 4-6; Suite from the Anna Magdalena Notebook; "Little" Fugue in g, S.578)* COL ▲ 42309 [AAD]

Cope, David (elec)
Bach by Design: Experiments in Musical Intelligence—features compositions derived on Yamaha Disklavier in imitation of the composition styles of Bach, Mozart, Chopin, Brahms, Joplin, Bartók & Prokofiev CENT ▲ 2184 (16.97)

Classical Music Composed by Computer: Experiments in Musical Intelligence—Cope's computer compositions in performances by Mary Jane Cope (pno) *(Inventions (3) after Bach; Son after Beethoven; Mazurka, Op. 1/2 after Chopin; Another Rag after Joplin)*, Maria Ezerova (pno), Anatole Leikin (pno) *(Suite after Rachmaninoff)*, Randall Wong (male sop), Linda Burman-Hall (pno) *(Mozart (sels) after Mozart)*, David Cope (elec) *(Mozart in Bali after Mozart; Printemps after Stravinsky; Horizons after Cope) (rec Univ of CA Santa Cruz, 1994-96)* CENT ▲ 2329 [DDD] (16.97)

Dolat-Shahi, Dariush (elecs)
Garden of Butterflies Radius ▲ NPM RMD 01

Dorsey, Don (elecs)
Bachbusters *(music of J. S. Bach "as realized on digital and other authentic period synthesizers")*—features Italian Concerto, S.971; 2- & 3-Part Inventions, Nos. 1,8,10,12,15; Diverse Canons, S.1078; Toccata & Fugue in d, S.565; Jesu, Joy of Man's Desiring TEL ▲ 80123 [DDD] (15.97) ▮

Beethoven or Bust *(music of Beethoven "as realized on digital and other authentic period synthesizers")*—features Rage over a lost penny; Mixed Bagatelles; Moonlight Sonata; Various Variations; Presto from Piano Sonata No. 6; Six Ecossaises; Für Elise; Scherzo from Piano Sonata No. 18; Ode to Ludwig TEL ▲ 80153 [DDD] (15.97) ▮

Busted *("realized on digital and other authentic period synthesizers")*—features works by Bach *(Musette, BWV Anh.126; Cant 147 [Jesu, Joy of Man's Desiring]; Anna Magdalena Notebook [Menuet, BWV 114]; 2-Part Inventions 10 & 15; 3-Part Invention 8; Fugue, BWV 565)*, Beethoven *(Son 18 Pno [Scherzo]; Bagatelle Pno, WoO 8; Ecossaises (6) Pno, WoO 59; Sym 9 [Ode to Joy])*, Dorsey *(Ascent, Birthday Dimensions; Dimensions; Ode to Ludwig)*, Mozart *(Son 6 Pno [Allegro]; Eine kleine gigue, K.574; Eine Kleine Nachtmusik [Allegretto; Trio])*, plus *(Don Dorsey, Unplugged; Festival of Festivals)* TEL ▲ 80473 [DDD] (15.97)

Ensemble from the East, Trio Sparnaay/Kooistra/Abe
Musiana 95: Electroacoustic Music from Denmark & Japan, w. Hanne Andersen, Sofia Asunción Claro, Mari Kimura (hp/vn), Thomas Sandberg, Harry Sparnaay (b cl)—features works by Graugaard *(Tongues Enrobed)*, Kimura *(ECO II)*, Rai *(Sparkle; Transparency)*, Fukuda *(Jeux)*, Frounberg *(Los perfumes de la noche profunda)*, Matunuma *(A Song to Science)*, Kanding *(Subrisio Saltat)*, Matsuda *(Fragment)* CLSO ▲ 139 [DDD] (14.97)

First Avenue
Two Suns—features *(Gentle Riot; Still Life with Harem; Flutter-By Effect; Comets; Light Years from Marya's; Jesu. Joy of Amazing Grace [after Bach]; Newton's Idyl; Strange Attractors; Current Courante [after Bach]; Two Suns [w. Mieczyslaw Litwinsky])* NPT ▲ 60062 [DDD] (12.97)

Galindo, Guillermo (elec)
Kiyohime—features music for the Japanese legend Kiyohime Lumfissure ▲ *

Geisler, Kathy (elecs)
Six Concertos for Oboe & Virtual Orchestra—features works by Albinoni *(Con. a cinque in d for Oboe & Strings, Op. 9/2)*, Vivaldi *(Con. in F for Oboe, Strings & Continuo, R.455)*, Marcello *(Con. in d for Oboe & Strings)*, J.S. Bach *(Con. in A for Oboe d'amore & Strings)*, Telemann *(Con. in d for Oboe & Strings)*, Handel *(Con. in g for Oboe & Strings)* WETE ▲ 5167 [DDD]

21st Century Bach—features all-electronic realizations of 12 Cantata and Passion arias and chorales; using synthesized and sampled sounds, Geisler has rescored Bach's vocal music for harps, dulcimers, marimbas, and a wide variety of other real and imaginary instruments WETE ▲ 5160 [DDD] (16.97)

James, Bob (elec)
Keyboard Pieces on Synthesized Instruments COL ▲ 39540 [DDD] (9.97) 39540

Kamal (syn)
Classics for Love—features works by Gounod *(Mediation on Prelude in C from J.S. Bach's Das wohltemperiete Klavier)*, Beethoven *(Bagatelle, WoO 59, "Für Elise")*, Schubert *(Ave Maria, Op. 52/6 [performed twice])*, Gluck *(Reigen seliger Geister [from Orpheo ed Euridice])*, Schumann *(Träumerei [from Kinderscenen])*, J.S. Bach *(Jesu, J. of Man's Desiring; Brandenburg Con. No. 4, BWV 1049 [Andante])*, Mozart *(Divert. in D, K.136 [Andante])* NPT ▲ HGH 341 [DDD]

Levy, Al (kbd/elec/cmpt)
LFO Pops Orchestra *(collection of orchd pno works played on kbd, elec & computer)*—features works by Mozart *(Theme & 3 Vars; Allegro in F; Son 1 in C)*, Haydn *(Allegro in F; Little Dance in F)*, Grieg *(Waltz in a; Grandmother's Minuet; Sailor's Song)*, Schumann *(Arabesque; The Merry Farmer; First Loss; Of Foreign Lands & People; The Wild Horseman; Northern Song; The Reaper's Song; Soldier's March)*, Bach *(Minuet & Trio; Adagio in E♭; Minuet in G; Musette in D; Little Prelude in F)*, A. M. Bach *(Minuet in G)*, Beethoven *(Bagatelle; Ecossaise in G; Sonatina in F; Für Elise; Gertrude's Dream Waltz; Minuet in G; Son in G)*, Clementi *(Sonatina, Op. 36/1)*, Handel *(Gavotte; Gigue)*, Shostakovich *(March in C)*, Chopin *(Mazurkas, Opp. 7/2, 67/2, 68/3)*, Elmenreich *(Spinning Song)* LFO ▲ *

Mavrides, Anastasi (arr/syn)
Country Evening—features works by J.S. Bach *(Andante [from Brandenburg Concerto No. 2]; Prelude No. 1 [from Well-tempered Clavier]; Air [from Ov. No. 3 in D])*, Corelli *(Con. Grosso, Op. 6/8)*, Satie *(Gymnopedie No. 3)*, Vivaldi *(Con. for Lute)*, Mozart *(Con. in A for Cl; Con. No. 21 in C for Pno)*, Telemann *(Con. in D for Fl)*, Haydn *(Sonatina in C)*, Beethoven *(Son. quasi una Fant. [Moonlight Son.])* REM ▲ 67777-2 [DDD]

Mavrides, Anastasi (arr/syn), Manken Palmboom (kbd)
Country Morning—featuring works by J.S. Bach *(Son. No. 4 in C; Jesu, Joy of Man's Desiring [from Cant. No. 147]; Brandenburg Con. No.2; Ov. to Suite No. 2)*, Telemann *(Con. in D for Fl; Son. No. 5 in A)*, Handel *(Son. No. 3 in C; Con. Grosso, Op. 3/4)*, Vivaldi *(Spring [from The Four Seasons])*, Albinoni *(Con. in C for Ob, Op. 7/2)* REM ▲ 65555-2 [DDD]

Milesi, Piero (elecs), Daniel Bacalov (elecs)
La Camera Astratta [The Abstract Room] *(soundtrack for an Italian theatre production)*—features Astratta, Camera [Parts 1 & 2] Sequenza Ragazze [Parts 1 & 2], Sequenza Ragazzi, Acqua, Scirocco, Piccoli Sassi, Perdere Il Tempo CUNE ▲ 18

Plasma SO [cnd:Isao Tomita]
Back to the Earth *(Statue of Liberty centennial concert)*, w. Clamma Dale (sop), Nikolai Demidenko (pno), et al.—features works by Bach, Debussy, Dukas, Dvořák, Gershwin, Holst, Mahler, R. Strauss, Stravinsky, Wagner *(rec live, NYC, 1986)* RCA (Red Seal) ▲ 7717 [DDD] 7717

Firebird—features works by Stravinsky *(Firebird Suite)*, Mussorgsky *(A Night on Bare Mountain)*, Debussy *(Prelude to the Afternoon of a Faun)* RCAV ▲ 60578 [ADD] (10.97) 60578

Kosmos—features works by Bach, Grieg, Rodrigo, R. Strauss, Wagner, John Williams, et al. RCA ▲ 2616 [ADD] (10.97) 2616

Pictures at an Exhibition—features works by Mussorgsky RCAV ▲ 60576 [ADD] (10.97) 60576

Snowflakes Are Dancing—features works by Claude Debussy RCAV ▲ 60579 [ADD] (10.97) ▮ 60579

The Tomita Planets *(arr of Holst's "The Planets")* RCAV ▲ 60518 [ADD] (10.97) 60518

Tomita's Greatest Hits RCAV ▲ 5660 (16.97) ▮

Rockmore, Clara (elecs)
The Art of the Theremin: transcriptions—features works by Achron, Falla, Glazunov, Rachmaninoff, Ravel, Saint-Saëns, Stravinsky, Tchaikovsky, Wieniawski DLS ▲ 1014 [AAD]

Society of Composers Inc.
Potpurri *(works for chamber ensemble and electronic media)*—features works by Emmanuel Ghent *(Five Brass Voices)*, Leo Kraft *(Second Fantasy)*, Elliott Schwartz *(Reading Session)*, Victor Saucedo Tecayehuatzin *(Fluxions)*, John D. White *(Sonata for Cello & Piano)* CPS ▲ CPS 8609

watt
watt ever—features works by Wesley-Smith *(Dah Dit Dah Dah)*, Vine *(BBC Exercises [3]; Array)*, Drummond *(Sea, Frogs & Magpies)*, Franklin *(Rolling)*, Luca *(Opiate of the Masses Part II)*, Tony Hood *(Munyun)*, Knowles *(Therefore, I...)*, Fredericks *(Viable Alternative)*, Keenan *(Ex Terra)*, Jones *(Mandala)*, Knowles/Rue *(Heavy Industry)*, Monro *(Mandala 1086)*, Rue *(A Longer View)*, White *(Orchid)*, Douglas *(Homage a Bessemer)*, Schiemer/Leak *(Polyphonic Vars)*, watt *(The Rosella Sisters & the Rainbow Eel)* TALP 2-▲ TP 74 [DDD]

ELECTRONIC MUSIC COLLECTIONS

The Aerial: A Journal in Sound
(a series of new & experimental music, mainly electronic/computer, but also including improvisation, invented instruments, & text/sound poetry)

Number 1: Winter 1990—features composers' performances (unless noted) by David Moss (perc/voc) *(Language Linkage)*, Terry Setter (synclavier) *(Aphorism III; Like a Coat or a Mask)*, Christine Baczewska (voc/ukelele/perc) *(Day of the Dead)*, Richard Kostelanetz (elec) *(Murdoch and the Sufi [from Invocations])*, Rich Jensen (voc) *(Folly)*, Loren Mazzacan (elec gtr), Suzanne Langille (gtr/sgr) *(Haunted House)*, Steve Peters (bass rec/fiddle/voc) *(Idumea [composed by Ananias Davisson])*, Malcolm Goldstein (voc) *(qernerăq; our breath as bones)*, Elizabeth Was (voc/gourd gtr), Miekal And (voc/gourd sax) *(Burial Song)*, Jerry Hunt (elec) *(Babalon(string))*, Stuart Sherman (elec) *(Four Sound Pieces: Doors, Water, Click, Pin-Ball)*, Bern Porter (voc) *(The Last Acts of St. Fuckyou)* AERI ▲ AER 1 ▮ AER 1

Number 2: Spring 1990—features composers' performances (unless noted) by Aina Kemanis (voc), Sheilah Glover (voc) *(Poison Hotel [composed by Bob Davis & Jon Raskin])*, David Dunn (elec) *(Chaos & the Emergent Mind of the Pond)*, Jin Hi Kim (komungo/sampler) *(Komungo Permutations)*, Jeff Greinke (Javanese metallaphone/smpler/syn/voc) *(Road to Solo)*, Christopher Shultis (vib/pno interior/almglocken/bowls/wind gong) *(motion/less)*, Chris Cochrane (voc/drum machine), Pippin Barnett (drums) *(Santiago Penando Estas [composed by Violeta Parra])*, Sue Ann Harkey (voc/hp-gtr) *(In This the Year of the Snake)*, Art Baron (didjeridoo/conch shell), Scott Robinson (perc/voc/conch shell) *(Nautilus [composed by Annea Lockwood])*, LaDonna Smith (voc/syn), Davey Williams (gtr), Tom Cora (vc), Pippin Barnett (drums) *(Green Song)*, Hildegard Westerkamp *(Cricket Voice)* AERI ▲ AER 2 ▮ AER 2

Number 3: Spring 1991—features composers' performances (unless noted) by Ellen Fullman (long-string instr) *(Staggered Stasis)*, Marc Barreca (syn) *(Messier Crosses the Blue Line)*, Nicolas Collins (elec) *(Tobabo Fonio)*, Peter Cusack (gtr), Nicolas Collins (elec) *(Dandelion Clock)*, Tom Guralnick (ten/sop sax/elec) *(Over Time)*, Essential Music *(IV for Percussion [composed by Johanna Beyer])*, Guillermo Perich (va), David Bessinger (mar) *(Interface [composed by Zae Munn])*, Myra Melford (pno/perc), Marion Brandis (fl/ww) *(Three Interludes)*, William Hooker (perc) *(The Dream: Red)*, Lesli Dalaba *(Core Sample (Sylvan))* AERI ▲ AER 3

Number 4: Winter 1991—features composers' performances (unless noted) by Brenda Hutchinson (voc/bass drum) *(Eeeyah!)*, Peter Van Riper (metal strip) *(Heart)*, Erik Belgum (voc) *(Dick Tracy All over His Body)*, Leif Brush (elec) *(Terrain Instruments Are Activated)*, Elodie Lauten (voc/elec) *(Music for the Trine, Part IV)*, Elise Kermani (voc) *(Spiral)*, Anna Homler (voc), Steve Moshier (syn) *(Sirens)*, Joseph Weber (elec/voc) *(Transformation of the Brothers into the Sun and Moon)*, Patsy Rahn (voc/elec) *(Trojan Horse)*, Jeffrey Kreiger (elec vc) *(Come Window Golds Coming [composed by N. Sean William])* AERI ▲ AER 4

Number 5: Spring 1993—features composers' performances (unless noted) by Willem De Ridder (voc) *(Report)*, Helen Thorington (elec) *(In the Dark)*, Gustavo Matamoros (elec), Bob Gregory (voc) *(Portrait: Bob Gregory)*, Sarah Peebles (elec) *(Excerpts from Kai (revolving life))*, Sydney Davis (pno/tapes) *(Sydney Davis)*, Philip Corner (Korean cymbals/sounds) *(Gong/Ear)*, Richard Klein (voc), Mark Hosler (elec) *(Wildman)*, The Machine for Making Sense *(Changing the Subject)*, Derek Bailey (gtr/voc) *(In My Studio)* AERI ▲ AER 5 ▮ AER 5

Number 6: Winter 1995—features composers' performances (unless noted) by Carter Scholz (elec) *(Talus)*, Hal Rammel (elec) *(Afterthought (sonance in limbo))*, Ricardo Dal Farra (elec), Mats Gustafsson (ten sax) *(Zastock)*, Larry Polansky (elec) *(Study: Anna, the Long and Short of It)*, John Duesenberry (elec) *(Wave Break)*, Sharan Leventhal (vn), Nancy Zeltsman (mar) *(Levitation [composed by Robert Carl])*, Libby Van Cleve (ob) *(Zantippe's Rebuke [composed by Mary Jane Leach])*, Steven Dressler (kbds/strs/perc/cl/toy tpt) *(Woonsocket)*, Yat Kha [Albert Kuvesyn (Tuvan throat singing/instrs), Ivan Sokolovsky (kbd/perc)] *(Tundra's Ghosts/Wanderer's Charm)*, Frances White (elec) *(Walk Through Resonant Landscape)*, Ellen Band (elec) *(Railroad Gamelan)* AERI ▲ AER 6

▲ = CD ♦ = Enhanced CD △ = MD ▮ = Cassette Tape ▯ = DCC

Another Coast: Electronic Music from California—features works by Laetitia de Compiegne Sonami *(Pie Jesus - Sounds From Empty Spaces)*, Paul DeMarinis *(I Want You; Kokole)*, Paul Dresher *(Other Fire; Water Dreams)*, Maggi Payne *(Airwaves)*, Carl Stone *(Hop Ken; Wall Me Do)* MUA ▲ 276 [DDD]

CDCM Computer Music Series

(a series of new computer music works by composers affiliated with the Consortium to Distribute Computer Music)

Vol. 1 *see* Composer section under Austin, Clark, Hunt and Winsor CENT ▲ 2029 [DDD] (16.97)

Vol. 2 *see* Composer Section under Baitz, Bresnick, Lindroth, Rolnick and Teitelbaum CENT ▲ 2039 [DDD] (16.97)

Vol. 3 *see* Composer section under Brün, Martirano, Melby, Scaletti, Tipei, Wyatt CENT ▲ 2045 [DDD] (16.97)

Vol. 6 *see* Composer section under Appleton, Moravec, David Evan Jones & C. Wolff CENT ▲ 2052 [DDD] (16.97)

Vol. 7 *see* Composer section under Chadabe, Kabat, McLean, Oliveros, and Rolnick CENT ▲ 2047 [DDD] (16.97)

Vol. 8: Center for Computer Research in Music & Acoustics (CCRMA) at Stanford University,, w. Jefferson String Quartet—features works by Chris Chafe *(Quadro)*, Allan Schindler *(Tremor of Night & Day)*, David Jaffe *(Telegram to the President)*, Jonathan Berger *(Diptych)*, Dexter Morrill *(Quartet)* CENT ▲ 2091 [DDD] (16.97)

Vol. 9: ...musics, metaphors, machines...—features works by Austin, Keefe, McTee, Piekarski, Rogers, Waschka and Winsor CENT ▲ 2078 [DDD] (16.97)

Vol. 10: The Virtuoso in the Computer Age, 1 *see* Composer section under Austin, Braxton, Lansky, Melby and Rosenboom CENT ▲ 2110 [DDD] (16.97)

Vol. 11: The Virtuoso in the Computer Age, 2—features performances by Jon Appleton *(Appleton:Homenaje a Milanés for Synclavier Digital Music System)*, Percussion Group *(Austin:Life Pulse Prelude)*, Chris Chafe & Dexter Morrill *(Chafe & Morrill:Duo Improvisation for Celleto & Trumpet MIDI Systems)*, János Négyesy *(Loy:Blood from a Stone for Mathews Electric Violin & Interactive Computer Controlled System)*, A. La Berge *(Larry Polansky:And to rule...[Cantilliation Study #2] for Flute & Computer Music)*, Neil Rolnick *(Rolnick:The Persistence of the Clavé for Computer Music System)*, P. Barham & Y. Mayama-Livesay *(Waschka:Last Night for Alto Saxophone & Piano) (rec Dec 1991)* CENT ▲ 2133 [DDD] (16.97)

Vol. 12: Composers in the Computer Age *features works by R. Karpen, John Rahn, Diane Thome* CENT ▲ 2144 [DDD] (16.97)

Vol. 13: The Viruoso in the Computer Age—III *see* Composer section under Larry Austin, Joan La Barbara, Stephen Travis Pope, Laurie Spiegel CENT ▲ 2166 (16.97)

Vol. 14: The Virtuoso in the Computer Age, 4—features works by Slavatore Martirano, Allan Schindler, Douglas Scott, Morton Subotnick, Rodney Waschka II CENT ▲ 2170 [DDD] (16.97)

Vol. 15: Virtuoso in the Computer Age, 5,, w. Matthews/Boie Radio Drum & Radio Baton—features works by Jaffe/Schloss, Appleton, Rimbombo, Radunskaya, Austin CENT ▲ 2190 (16.97)

Vol. 16—features works by Austin, Matthews, Lippe, Chatham, plus works by Waschka & De Lisa CENT ▲ 2193 (16.97)

Vol. 17 Music from the Center for Contemporary Music at Mills College—features works by Bischoff *(The Glass Hand [1992])*, C. Brown *(Chain Reaction [1991])*, Erbe *(After a Day [1991])*, Payne *(Resonant Places [1992])*, Curran *(Animal Behavior [1992])*, Bischoff/Brown/Erbe/Payne *(CCM Flotsam [1993])* CENT ▲ 2195 [DDD] (16.97)

Vol. 20: Music From the University of Texas Electronic Music Studios—features works performed by Howard Frederics, Karl Korte, Jody Nagel, Russell Pinkston, Mark Schultz, Mark Wingate CENT ▲ 2245 (16.97)

Vol 21: The International Computer Music Association Commission Awards 1992-1993-—features works by Lippe, Mowitz, Rai, Vaggione CENT ▲ 2255 (16.97)

Desde al otro lado: Electro-acoustic Music from Latin America—features works by E. R. Miranda *(Electroacoustic Samba X)*, Elsa Justel *(Fy Mor)*, N. S. Eyzaguirre *(Chica Aruma)*, A. del Mónaco *(Syntagma (A))*, A. Russek *(Ohtzalan)*, Sergio Claros/ Oscar García *(Es Zas)*, Alejandro José *(Todo Es Uno)*, R. Dal Farra *(Ashram)* OOD ▲ 45 [DDD] (16.97)

The Devil's Staircase: Composer & Chaos *(music composed using algorithmic techniques based on theories of Chaos)*—features works by Degazio *(On Growth & Form)*, Ciamaga *(4 Micorclips)*, Celona *(Pacific Rims)*, Del Buono *(Night Voices)*, Foster *(Sheet Metal Music)*, Degazio *(Heatnoise)*, Free *(A Conversation with John Cage)* Soundprints ▲ SP 9302

Electro Accoustic Music III, w. Camilla Hoitenga (fl), William Buonocore (gtr), Maria Tegzes (sop), Jacques Linder (pno), Robert McCormick (perc)—features works by Saariaho, Karpen, J.C. Nelson, Dusman, Fuller, Risset NEU ▲ 45087 [DDD] (16.97)

Electro-Acoustic Music, Vol. 5—features works by Yuasa *(Projection Esemplastic for White Noise)*, Oliveros *(II of IV)*, Laske *(Treelink)*, Dusman *(And a Voice Was Heard in Rama)*, Hamman *(Topologies/Surfaces/Oblique Angles/Installed Parameters)*, Fuller *(Sherds of 5)*, DeLio *(Pine, Bamboo, Plum; "Because the...")* NEU ▲ 45092 [DDD] (16.97)

Experimental Tokyo—features composers' performances by Akira Iijima (elec) *(Pin-up You; Ice Water Cup)*, Akitsugu Maebayashi (elec) *(Swelling Fade-Out)*, Natsuki Emura (elec) *(24 Dots)*, Yuko Nexusó Kitamura (elec) *(Osaka)*, Satoru Wono (elec) *(Who Programs You)*, Horinori Murai (elec) *(Paralleled)*, Yasuhiro Ohtani (elec) *(Invisible Objects)* IEL ▲ IEL 0005

Exquisite Corpses from P.S. 122 *(30 improvisations recorded separately then mixed together)*, w. David Watson (shears/stick vn/gtr/tpt), Ageslaire Gignac (cta), Isabelle Marchand (sgr), Rafik Samman (bar), Sylvain Bergeron (sgr), Claire Gignac (rcr), Şylvain Bergeron (oud/psaltery/bells), Viviane LeBlanc (psaltery), Isabelle Marchand (bowed vielle), Angèle Laberge (hp), Eric Mercier (shawm/bgp), Rafik Samman (perc/oud), Vincent Dhavernas ¿What Next? ▲ WN 0002 [ADD]

From A to Z—features works by Dockstader *(Luna Park; Part Three from Apocalypse; Tango from Quatermass)*, Dresher *(Underground)*, Kasinskas *(The Rider)*, Lukasik *(Utamaro's Dreams)*, Pamela Z *(In Tymes of Olde)*, B. Imhoff & Pamela Z *(Obsession, Addiction & the Aristotelian Curve)*, Amirkhanian *(Vers Les Anges)*, Bimstein *(Garland Hirschi's Cows)* STKL ▲ 203 (16.97)

The Historical CD of Digital Sound Synthesis—features works by Guttman *(The Silver Scale; Pitch Variations)*, Pierce *(Stochatta; Vars in Timbre & Attack; Sea Sounds; 8 Tone Canon)*, Matthews *(Numerology; The 2nd Law; Bicycle Built for 2; Masquerades; International Lullaby)*, Lewin *(Studies Nos. 1 & 2)*, Tenney *(Dialogue)*, Ferretti *(Pipe & Drum; Trio)*, Randall *(Mudgett; Monologues for a Mass Murderer)*, Risset *(Sound examples of Introductory Catalogue of Computer Synthesized Sounds)* WER ▲ 2033 (19.97)

Imaginary Landscapes (New Electronic Music) *(works and excerpts from works by 15 American composers)*—features works by Maryanne Amacher, Nicolas Collins, Shelly Hirsch & David Weinstein, Ron Kuivila, Alvin Lucier, Christian Marclay, Gordon Monahan, Neil Rolnick, Laititia deCompiegne Sonami, Mark Trayle, David Tudor, "Blue" Gene Tyranny, Voice Crack 75597 ▲ 79235 ▮ 79235-4

Music from SEAMUS 1 [Society for Electro-Acoustic Music in the United States]—features works by James Mobberly *(Spontaneous Combustion [T. Timmons (sax)])*, James Phelps *(Chordlines)*, Anna Rubin *(Remembering [J. Kellock (sop), Karl Paulnack (pno)])*, Stephen David Beck *(Improvisation on Strange Attractors v1.0b [W. Ludwig (bn)])*, Bernardo Feldman *(Still Life)*, Kwok-ping John Chen *(Ring Shades [Heung-wing Lung (perc)])* SEAMUS ▲ EAM 9301

Music from SEAMUS 2 [Society for Electro-Acoustic Music in the United States]—features works by Scott Wyatt *(Time Mark [Glenn Schaft (perc)])*, Jeffery Haas *(Liaisons)*, Barry Schrader *(Barroco [Alissa Rhode (hpd)])*, Cort Lippe *(Paraptra)*, C. N. Mason *(Amaglam I [David Weber (ob)])*, George Todd *(Wordscapes)*, James Moberly *(Caution to the Winds [Richard Cass (pno)])* SEAMUS ▲ EAM 9401

Musique Méchanique: 'art is the technology of the soul'—[CD 1, European Trance] features performances by Popol Vuh *(Fricke:Aguirre)*, Eberhard Schoener *(Schoener:Mountain Music)*, Michael Hoenig *(Hoenig:Departure from the Northern Wasteland)*, Peter Michael Hamel *(Hamel:Apotheosis)*, ; [CD 2, Transcontinental Space] Michael Stearns *(Stearns:Labyrinth)*, Steve Roach, Kevin Braheny, Richard Burmer *(Roach, Braheny & Burmer:Western Spaces)*, Kevin Braheny *(Braheny:Desert Walkabout)*, Steve Roach *(Roach:A Circular Ceremony; Artifacts)*, David Parsons *(Parsons:Dakpa; Drilbu Ling)* CEHA 2-▲ 14102 (26.97)

Pioneers of Electronic Music—features Arel:Stereo Electronic Music No. 2; Davidovsky:Synchronisms No. 5; Luening:Low Speed; Invention in 12 Tones; Fantasy in Space; Moonflight; Luening/Ussachevsky:Incantation; Shields:Transformation of Ani; Smiley:Kolyosa; Ussachevsky:Sonic Contours; Piece for Tape Recorder; Computer Piece No. 1 CRI ▲ 611 [ADD] (16.97)

Radius #3: Transmissions from Broadcast Artists—features works by K. Kennedy *(Taking Steps)*, C. Migone *(Solar Plexus)*, C. Dumas *(Le spectacle des habile(i)tés)*, D. Lander *(Room)* ¿What Next? ▲ WN 0018

Radius #4: Transmissions from Broadcast Artists—features works by Hildegard Westerkamp *(Türen der Wahrnehmung)*, Darren Copeland *(Residence Elsewhere)*, Algojo) (Algojo [w. Alice Dumaine (voc), Hélène Genest (voc), Eugene Lee (voc), André Eric Lètourneau (voc)] *(Le nudisme n'est pas une menace pour l'industrie textile)*, R. Normandeau *(La chambre blanche [w. Gilles Laforce (voc), Jean-Pierre Matte (voc), Marie Claude Trépanier (voc), Marthe Turgeon (voc)])* ¿What Next? ▲ WN 0019

Roads to Chaos —*features works based upon theories of chaos mathematics by G. Ciamaga (Possible Spaces No. 2)*, H.-J. Florian *(Der Feigenbaum)*, R. Fein *(Saute de vent)*, B. Degazio *(Chaotic Etude No. 2; Ov for Tesla)*, K. Corey *(2-Part Invention No. 1)*, K. Mohr *(Excursion into the Jungle of Recursion)*, K. Essl *(Lexikon-Sonate)*, G. Monro *(Study in Dimension 1.245)*, J. Harley *(Song for Nobody)*, R. del Buono *(Cuban Dance)*, M. Guertner *(Fractude 7) (rec 1996)* Soundprints ▲ SP 9603 [DDD]

Sonic Circuits IV—features works by Harada *(Untitled 1)*, Claman *('70)*, Z *(Geekspeak)*, Ainger *(Dreaming Hills)*, Higham *(Duck Spindle Trilogy)*, Dhomont *(Lettre de Sarajevo)*, Belgum *(Life's Big Dream Home)*, Wadhams *(Harley)*, D. M. Schreier *(Exotic [short version])* INNO ▲ 113 [DDD] (14.97)

Transforms: The Nerve Events Project—features works by Greg Anderson *(Weeping Like a Bathtub)*, Ted Apel *(Venatian Division)*, T. Dimuzio *(Never Steven)*, Dave Douglas *(Balkanization)*, Yves Duboin *(Packed Like Eggs)*, T. Erbe *(Slimpering Toward Algoma)*, Doug Gourlay *(A Little Ditty)*, Mark Howell *(Greens)*, Iconoclast *(Damnation, Salvation)*, Henry Kaiser *(Nerve that Got)*, Judy Klein *(88" for Nick)*, Henry Lowengard *(Sublime Message No. 4)*, Steve MacLean *(Nerve 3 & 4)*, Robert Marsanyi *(Context)*, Bruno Meillier *(De tout pour faire un monde)*, Frank Pahl *(Columbus on Guadeloupe)*, Larry Polansky/Ray Guillette *(Four Voice Canon #8 (Nerve Canon))*, Neil Rolnick *(Nerve Us)*, Philip Strong *(Patent Pending)*, Jason Willett *(The Escape)* CUNE ▲ Cuneiform 55011

Women in Electronic Music - 1977—features performances by Johanna M. Beyer (elec), Electric Weasel Ensemble *(Beyer:Music of the Spheres)*, Annea Locwood (elec) *(Lockwood:World Rhythms)*, Pauline Oliveros (elec) *(Oliveros:Bye Bye Butterfly)*, Laurie Spiegel (elec) *(Spiegel:Appalachian Grove)*, Phil Loarie (voc), William Novak (voc), Danny Sofer (dr), Megan Roberts (elec) *(Roberts:I Could Sit Here All Day)*, Ruth Anderson (elec) *(R. Anderson:Points)*, Laurie Anderson (voc/ telephone/elec), Scott Johnson (tamboura) *(L. Anderson:New York Social Life)*, Laurie Anderson (voc/vn/elec), Scott Johnson (gtr/org) *(L. Anderson:Time To Go)* CRI ▲ 728 [ADD] (16.97)

FILM SOUNDTRACKS

Claude Bolling Big Band [cnd:Claude Bolling]

Cinemadreams—features works by Legrand/Demy *(The Young Girls of Rochefort)*, H. Mancini *(The Pink Panther)*, Jarre *(Lawrence of Arabia; Lara's Theme [from Doctor Zhivago])*, Joplin *(The Entertainer [from The Sting])*, Raksin/Mercer *(Laura)*, H. Hupfeld *(As Time Goes By [from Casablanca])*, Rota *(La Strada)*, Tiomkin/Washington *(High Noon)*, Huddleston/ Rinker *(Everybody Wants to Be a Cat [from The Aristocats])*, Bolling *(Borsalino)*, Bacharach/David *(Raindrops Keep Fallin' on My Head [from Butch Cassidy & the Sundance Kid])*, Lane/Harburg *(Old Devil Moon [from Finian's Rainbow])* MILA ▲ 35751 (16.97)

Boston Pops Orch [cnd:Arthur Fiedler]

Cinema Classics 7: Classical Music Made Famous in Films—features works by Verdi *(Il forza del destino:Ov [from J. de Florette]; La traviata [Dammi tu forza; from Pretty Woman])*, Tchaikovsky *(The Nutcracker [Waltz of the Flowers; from Fantasia]; Con in D for Vn, Op. 35 [Allegro vivacissimo; from Exposed])*, Schumann *(Con in a for Pno, Op. 54 [Allegro vivace; from Madame Sousatzka])*, A. Marcello *(Con in d for Ob [Adagio; from Anonimo Veneziano])*, Boccherini *(Qnt in E for Strs, G.275 [Minuetto; from The Lady Killers])*, Mozart *(Ave verum corpus, K.618 [from Lorenzo's Oil])*, Beethoven *(Trio No. 6 in B♭ for Pno, Vn & Vc, "Archduke," Op. 97 [Allegro moderato; from Swing Kids])* NXIN ▲ 551157 [DDD] (5.97)

Cinema Classics 8: Classical Music Made Famous in Films—features works by Wagner *(Tannhäuser:Ov [from Meeting Venus])*, Chopin *(Nocturne No. 2 in E♭, Op. 9/2 [from Man Trouble])*, Handel *(Xerxes [Largo; from Dangerous Liaisons])*, Satie *(Gymnopédie No. 1 [from My Dinner with André])*, Smetana *(Qt No. 1 in e for Strs [Allegro vivo-Appassionato; from Sneakers])*, Schubert *(Moment musical No. 2 [from Au revoir les enfants])*, Allegri *(Miserere [from Chariots of Fire])*, Mendelssohn *(Con No. 2 in d for Pno, Op. 40 [Adagio; from A Midsummer Night's Sex Comedy])*, Dukas *(L'apprenti sorcier [The Sorcerer's Apprentice; from Fantasia])* NXIN ▲ 551158 [DDD] (5.97)

Cinema Classics 9: Classical Music Made Famous in Films—features works by Mozart *(Il nozze di Figaro:Ov [from Trading Places])*, Chopin *(Waltz No. 15 in e, Op. posth. [from Sneakers])*, Tchaikovsky *(Con No. 1 in b♭, Op. 23 [Andantino semplice-Prestissimo; from The Music Lovers])*, Wagner *(Götterdämmerung [Siegfried's Death & Funeral March; from Excalibur])*, Verdi *(Il trovatore [Anvil Chorus; from A Night at the Opera])*, Beethoven *(Son No. 23 in f for Pno, "Appassionata" Op. 57 [Allegro assai; from Madame Sousatzka])*, Handel *(Water Music [Allegro-Andante; from Dead Poets Society])*, Ravel *(Son for Vn [Blues (Moderato); from Un coeur en hiver])*, J. S. Bach *(Partita No. 4 in D, BWV 828 [Courante; from Exposed])*, Beethoven *(Con No. 5 in E♭ for Pno, "Emperor," Op. 73 [Andante un poco mosso; from Picnic at Hanging Rock])*, Ponchielli *(La Gioconda [Dance of the Hours; from Fantasia])* NXIN ▲ 551159 [DDD] (5.97)

Boston Pops Orch [cnd:John Williams]

Space-taculars—features works by Williams *(Main Theme; Princess Leia [both from Star Wars]; The Asteroid Field; Yoda's Theme; The Imperial March [all from The Empire Strikes Back]; Parade of the Ewoks; Luke & Leia; Jabba the Hutt; The Forest Battle [all from Return of the Jedi]; The Flying Theme; Adventures on Earth [both from E.T.]; Suite [from Close Encounters of the 3rd Kind])*, Goldsmith *(Closing Title [from Aliens]; Main Title [from Star Trek, The Motion Picture])*, Courage *(Main Theme [from Star Trek, The TV Show])*, R. Strauss *(Thus Spake Zarathustra [from 2001, A Space Odyssey])* PPHI ▲ 46728 (16.97) ▮ 46728 (10.98)

Williams on Williams: The Classic Spielberg Scores—features music from E.T., Hook, Jurassic Park, Schindler's List, Raiders of the Lost Ark, 1941, Empire of the Sun, Jaws, Close Encounters of the 3rd Kind COL ▲ 68419 (16.97) △ SM 68419 ▮ 68419 (10.98)

Boston Pops Orch [cnd:Arthur Fiedler], Philadelphia Orch [cnd:Eugene Ormandy]

Blockbusters from the Movies—features works by Mendelssohn *(Wedding March [from A Midsummer Night's Dream in 4 Weddings & a Funeral])*, Handel *(Solomon [from Arrival of the Queen of Sheba in 4 Weddings & a Funeral])*, Rossini *(Largo al factotum [from Il barbieri di Siviglia in Mrs. Doubtfire]; William Tell Ov [in My Life])*, DiCapua *(O sole mio [in Only You])*, Mozart *(Eine kleine Nachtmusik [Allegro; in Ace Ventura: Pet Detective]; Sull'aria...Che soave zeffiretto [from Le nozze di Figaro in The Shawshank Redemption])*, Haydn *(Sym 104 [Minuet; in Prince of Tides])*, J. S. Bach *(Goldber Vars [Aria; in Silence of the Lambs])*, Catalani *(Ebben? Ne andrò lontano [from La Wally in Philadelphia])*, Giordano *(La mamma morta [from Andrea Chénier in Philadelphia])*, Stravinsky *(Lullaby [from The Firebird in Short Cuts])*, Tchaikovsky *(Love Theme [from Romeo & Juliet in Wayne's World])*, J. Strauss II *(Blue Danube Waltz [in Cool Runnings])*, Orff *(O fortuna [from Carmina Burana in The Doors])*, Verdi *(Libiamo ne' lieti calici [from La traviata in In the Line of Fire])* RCAV ▲ 68080 (10.97) ▮ 68080

Brandenburg PO [cnd:Manfred Rosenberg]

Original Motion Picture Scores—features works by Korngold *(The Adventures of Robin Hood)*, Rota *(The Godfather)*, Morricone *(Once Upon a Time in the West)*, Steiner *(Treasure of the Sierra Madre)*, North *(Spartacus)*, Rozsa *(Ben Hur)*, Goldsmith *(Masada)*, Jarre *(Lawrence of Arabia)*, Herrmann *(North by Northwest)* CAPO ▲ 10469 [DDD] (11.97)

Chertock, Michael (pno)

Cinematic Piano—features music from The Piano; Howard's End; Schindler's List; Frankie & Johnny; On Golden Pond; Cinema Paradiso; The Firm; E.T.; The Accompanist; Out of Africa; Love Story; Jennifer 8; My Dinner with Andre; Somewhere in Time; Casablanca TEL ▲ 80357 (15.97)

Palace of the Winds: At the Movies—features works by Silvestri *(Feather Theme [from Forrest Gump]; Main Theme from The Bodyguard)*, Menken *(Heaven's Light [from The Hunchback of Notre Dame])*, Ungar *(Ashokan Farewell [from The Civil War])*, Hirschfelder *(With God's Help, Shine)*, Rachmaninoff *(Prelude 2 in c#, Op. 3; Con 3 in d, Op. 30 [cadenza from Allegro man non tanto]; Prelude 15 in D♭, "Raindrop")*, T. Monk *(Round Midnight)*, Bacalov *(Main Theme [from Il Postino])*, Yared *(A Retreat; Read Me to Sleep; Palace of the Winds [all from The English Patient])*, Beethoven *(Son 14 Pno, "Moonlight" [Adagio Sostenuto], Für Elise)*, Niehaus/Eastwood *(Doe Eyes [from The Bridges of Madison County])*, Lloyd Webber *(Don't Cry For Me, Argentina)*, Snow *(Theme from X-Files)*, Lengrand *(Main Theme from Summer of '42)*, Eastwood *(Claudia's Theme [from Unforgiven]) (rec Chautauqua, NY, Feb 24-25, 1997)* TEL ▲ 80477 [DDD] (15.97)

Cincinnati Pops Orch [cnd:Erich Kunzel]

Beautiful Hollywood—features music from Forrest Gump *(Feather Theme [w. Steven Reineke (pno)])*, A River Runs Through It *(Main Theme [w. Julie Spangler (pno)])*, Rob Roy *(Robert & Mary [w. Eric Rigler (Celtic & Uillean pipes)])*, Jerry Maguire *(We Meet Again [w. Timothy Berens (gtr)])*, Legends of the Fall *(The Ludlows [w. Sylvia Mitchell (vn), Paul Patterson (vn), Julie Spangler (pno)])*, Evita *(You Must Love Me)*, The Bridges of Madison County *(Doe Eyes [w. Steven Reineke (pno)])*, Pocahontas *(Colors of the Wind)*, The Mission *(On Earth as It Is in Heaven [w. Christ Church Cathedral Chorus, Knox Presbyterian Chorus])*, Free Willy *(Whale Play; Farewell & Freedom)*, Forever Young *(Love Theme)*, Cinema Paradiso *(Love Theme [w. Michael Andres (a sax), Steven Reineke (pno)])*, Rudy *(Main Theme)*, Chaplin *(Main Theme)*, Grumpier Old Men *(End Credits)*, Bugsy *(Act of Faith [w. Philip Collins (flgl)])*, Schindler's List *(Main Theme [w. Alexander Kerr (vn)])*, Gettysburg *(Reunion & Finale [w. Timothy Berens (gtr)]) (rec Music Hall, Cincinnati, June 2-3 & Sept 9, 1996; Feb 8 & May 20-21, 1997)* TEL ▲ 80440 [DDD] (15.97)

Hollywood's Greatest Hits, Vol. 2—features works by North 2001: A Space Odyssey, Spartacus Rozsa Ben Hur Bernstein Ten Commandments Tiomkin Picnic Young Around the World in 80 days Kaper Mutiny on the Bounty Theodorakis Zorba the Greek Legrand Valley of the Dolls Previn Valley of the Dolls Barry Midnight Cowboy, Dances with Wolves Rota (The Godfather), Enya (Grand Canyon), J.N. Howard (Grand Canyon) TEL ▲ 80319 (15.97) ▮

Symphonic Star Trek—features works by Goldsmith *(Main Theme [from Star Trek:The Next Generation]; Main Theme [from Star Trek:Voyager]; Main Theme; The Klingon Battle [both from Star Trek:The Motion Picture]; A Busy Man [from Star Trek V:The Final Fontier])*, Eidelman *(End Title [from Star Trek VI:The Undiscovered Country])*, McCarthy *(Main Theme [from Star Trek:Deep Space 9]; End Title [from Star Trek:Generations])*, Rosenman *(Main Title [from Star Trek IV:The Voyage Home])*, Courage *(Main Theme [from Star Trek (original TV series)]; Suite [from The Menagerie (original TV pilot)])*, Horner *(Suite [from Star Trek II:The Wrath of Khan]; Main Theme [from Star Trek III:The Search for Spock])*, various sound fx *(Warp-One; The Destruction of Praxis & Its Aftermath; Starship Flyby; Alien Probe; Humpback Whale Song; Tribble Trouble; Bird-of-Prey Decloaking; Warp-Eight; Transporter; Nexus Energy Ribbon; The Borg) (rec Music Hall, Cincinnati, OH, 1983-95)* TEL ▲ 80383 (15.97)

City of Prague PO [cnd:Kenneth Alwyn]

Cinema's Classic Romances—features sels from the soundtracks to The English Patient; Emma; Sense & Sensibility; Much Ado About Nothing; Hamlet; Wuthering Heights; Romeo & Juliet; The Last of the Mohicans; Twelfth Night; Tess; Pride & Prejudice; Little Women; Far From the Maddening Crowd; Mrs. Dalloway SILC ▲ 6018 (16.97) 6018 (10.98)

FILM SOUNDTRACKS

Herrmann, Bernard (cnd)
Great Film Classics—features music from Citizen Kane; Jason & the Argonauts; The Snows of Kilimanjaro; The Devil & Daniel Webster; Jane Eyre; Mysterious Island PLON (Phase 4 Stereo) ▲ 48948 (11.97)

Hollywood Bowl Orch [cnd:John Mauceri]
Always & Forever: Movies' Greatest Love Songs—features works by Fain *(Love is a Many Splendored Thing)*, North *(Unchained)*, Goldsmith *(Forever Young)*, Puccini *(Room with a View)*, E. Bernstein *(The Age of Innocence)*, Morricone *(Cinema Paradiso)*, Barry *(Somewhere in Time)*, Bennett *(Four Weddings and a Funeral)*, Raskin & Mercer *(Laura)*, Warren & Friedhofer *(An Affair to Remember) (rec Hollywood, CA, Aug 9 & Sept 5, 1995)* † Herrmann:North by Northwest; Korngold:Escape Me Never; Newman:Wuthering Heights; Rózsa:Thief of Bagdad; Steiner:Now, Voyager; Waxman:Peyton Place PPHI ▲ 46681 [DDD] (16.97)
The Great Waltz—features works by J. Strauss & Tiomkin *(The Great Waltz)*, Ravel *(La Valse)*, Bennett *(Murder on the Orient Express)*, R. Strauss *(Der Rosenkavalier)*, Prokofiev *(Cincerella)*, Sondheim: *(A Little Night Music)*, L. Bernstein *(Candide) (rec Sony Studios, Culver City, CA, Jan 1993)* † Herrmann:The Snows of Kilimanjaro; Loewe:Gigi; Korngold:Prince & the Pauper; Rózsa:Madame Bovary; Steiner:Jezebel; Waxman:Hotel Berlin PPHI ▲ 38685 [DDD] 38685
Hollywood Dreams—features works by Schoenberg *(Fanfare for a Bowl Concert)*, Stravinsky *(Firebird Suite)*, L. Bernstein *(On the Waterfront)*, Stothart, Arlen & Harburg *(The Wizard of Oz)*, Prokofiev *(Semyon Kotko)*, Gore *(Defending Your Life)*, Barry *(Dances with Wolves) (rec Culver City, CA, Feb 1991)* † Korngold:Adventures of Robin Hood; Newman:20th Cent-Fox Fanfare; How to Marry a Millionaire; Rodgers:Carousel; Steiner:Gone with the Wind; Waxman:Place in the Sun; Williams:E.T. PPHI ▲ 32109 [DDD] 32109
Hollywood Nightmares—features works by Savino & Perry *(Phantom of the Opera)*, Stravinsky *(The Rite of Spring)*, Barry *(Body Heat)*, Goldsmith *(The Omen) (rec Culver City, CA, Sept 1993)* † Herrmann:Vertigo; Rózsa:Spellbound; Steiner:King Kong; Waxman:Sunset Boulevard; Dr. Jekyll & Mr. Hyde; Williams:Jurassic Park; Dracula PPHI ▲ 42425 [DDD]
Journey to the Stars: A Sci-Fi Fantasy Adventure—features works by Blomdahl *(Aniara)*, Goldsmith *(Star Trek V: The Final Frontier)*, Barron *(Forbidden Planet)*, Corigliano *(Altered States)*, R.Strauss *(Also Sprach Zarathustra)*, Ligeti *(Atmospheres)*, North *(2001: A Space Odyssey)*, Elfma *(Edward Scissorhands)*, Bliss *(Things to Come) (rec Hollywood, CA, July 11, Sept 20 & 22, 1994)* † Herrmann:Day the Earth Stood Still; Ligeti: Atmospheres; Waxman:Bride of Frankenstein; Williams:Witches of Eastwick; Star Wars PPHI ▲ 46403 (16.97)

Italian Solisti
I Solisti Italiani on Cinema—features works by Walton *(Henry V)*, Morricone *(Nuovo Cinema Paradiso)*, Donaggio *(De Palma Suite)*, Shostakovich *(sels from "The Gadfly", "Hamlet" & "5 Days & 5 Nights")*, Herrmann *(Psycho)*, Rossellini *(Le Sera Fiesolana)*, Vlad *(Romeo e Giulietta)*, Lavagnino *(Pocket Sym)* DNN ▲ 18004 [DDD] (16.97)

Lanza, Mario (ten)
Be My Love:Mario Lanza's Greatest Performances at MGM—features music from That Midnight Kiss [They Didn't Believe Me; Love is Music], The Toast of New Orleans [The Tina Linda; Be My Love; I'll Never Love You; Act I Finale [from Madama Butterfly]]; The Great Caruso [Celeste Aida [from Aida]; Ave Maria; Sxt [from Lucia di Lammermoor]; La Donna è mobile [from Rigoletto]; Vesti la giubba [from Pagliacci]]; Because You're Mine [Because you're Mine [2 versions]; All the Things You Are; Granada; Finale [from Cavalleria Rusticana]; Lord's Prayer]; The Student Prince [Serenade; Deep in my Heart, Dear; Beloved] RHI ▲ 72958 (16.97)

Michael Garson Ensemble
Screen Themes '93: The Best Film Scores of 1993—features music from Jurassic Park; Schindler's List; Indecent Propposal; The Fugitive; The Age of Innocence; Shadowlands; The Pelican Brief; The Piano; Bleu; Heaven & Earth; The Firm; Mrs. Doubtfire; Philadelphia; Sleepless in Seattle DTM ▲ 77009 (11.97) ▮ 77009 (5.98)

National PO
The Spectacular World of the Classic Film Scores—features music from The Five Studio Fanfares; Star Wars; Captain Blood; Now, Voyager; Gone with the Wind; Elizabeth & Essex, The Caine Mutiny; Citizen Kane; Knights of the Round Table; Objective Burma!; The Guns of Navarone; Julius Caesar; & others RCAV ▲ 2792 [ADD] (11.97) ▮ 2792

National PO [cnd:Charles Gerhardt]
Casablanca: Classic Film Scores for Humphrey Bogart RCAV ▲ 422 [ADD] (11.97) ▮ 422
Hollywood Screen Classics CHSK ▲ 71 (15.97)
Silver Screen Classics—features music from Gone with the Wind; Casablanca; Forever Amber; & others RCAV 4-▲ 60763 [ADD] 4- 60763
Themes from Academy Award Winners—features music from Star Wars; Tom Jones; Casablanca; Ben Hur; West Side Story; Lawrence of Arabia; Dr. Zhivago; Gone with the Wind RCAV ▲ 60966 [ADD] (11.97) ▮ 60966

National PO [cnd:Bernard Herrmann]
Great British Film Music—features music from Richard III; Things to Come; Anna Karenina; The Invaders; Oliver Twist; An Ideal Husband; Escape Me Never PLON (Phase 4 Stereo) ▲ 48954 (11.97)

Pasquier, Régis (vn), Lluís Claret (vc), Philippe Cassard (pno), Pierre Hantaï (hpd)
Colonel Chabert—features works by Beethoven *(Trio No. 4, Op. 70/1 "Ghost")*, Schumann *(Davidsbündlertänze, Op. 6/2 & 17; Symphonic Etudes, Op. 13, Var. 11)*, Mozart *(Trio in E♭, K.498 "Kegelstatt")*, D. Scarlatti *(Sons. K.322 & K.280)*, Schubert *(Son. in A, D.959)*, Rauber *(Marche Napoléonienne)* TRAV ▲ 1013
*[Editor's Note]*Original Soundtrack.

Perlman, Itzhak (vn), Pittsburgh SO [cnd:John Williams]
Cinema Serenade—features themes from The Color Purple, Il Postino, Age of Innocence, Far & Away, Four Horsemen of the Apocalypse, Sabrina, Out of Africa, Schindler's List, Cinema Paradiso; Tango (Por Una Cabeza) [from Scent of a Woman]; Papa, Can You Hear Me? [from Yentl]; I Will Wait for You [from The Umbrellas of Cherbourg]; Manha de Carnaval [from Black Orpheus] [arr J. Williams, E. Bernstein & A. Previn] COL ▲ 63005 (16.97) △ SM 63005 ▮ 63005 (10.98)

Prague PO [cnd:Nic Raine, Paul Bateman, Kenneth Alwyn], Crouch End Festival Choir [cnd:David Temple]
Cinema Choral Classics—features works by Orff *(O Fortuna [from Carmina Burana])*, Jarre *(Prelude & Birth of Christ [from Jesus of Nazareth])*, Barber *(Agnus Dei [from the Scarlett Letter])*, Goldsmith *(Never Surrender [from First Knight]; The Omen [suite])*, Silvestri *(The Abyss)*, Rozsa *(The Lord's Prayer [from King of Kings])*, Poledouris *(Riders of Doom [from Conan: The Barbarian])*, Morricone *(Ave Maria: Guarini; On Earth As It Is in Heaven [both from The Mission])*, Barry *(The Lion in Winter [suite])*, Vangelis *(1492: Conquest of Paradise)*, Nascimbene *(Funeral & Finale [from The Vikings])*, Doyle *(Non Nobis Domine [from Henry V])* SILC ▲ 6015 (16.97) 6015 (10.98)

Prague PO [cnd:Kenneth Alwyn, Paul Bateman, Nic Raine, Derek Wadsworth]
Hollywood Heroes—features works by E. Bernstein *(The Great Escape)*, Barry *(Dances with Wolves [John Dunbar Theme]; High Road to China [Waziri Village Attack & Escape]; Zulu [Main Title]; Out of Africa; Robin & Marion [Suite])*, Williams *(Raiders of the Lost Ark [March]; Born on the 4th of July [End Credits])*, Jarre *(Mad Max III: Beyond Thunderdome [Fanfare/I ain't Captain Walker])*, Tiomkin *(The Alamo [Ov])*, Rózsa *(El Cid [Ov])*, Fielding *(The Outlaw Josey Wales [The War is Over])*, Addison *(Torn Curtain [Main Title])*, Jones *(Cliffhanger [Suite])* SLTR ▲ 5009 (10.97)

Prague PO [cnd:Paul Bateman, Nic Raine, Kenneth Alwyn], Crouch End Festival Choir [cnd:David Temple]
Warriors of the Silver Screen—features works by Waxman *(Taras Bulba [suite]; Price Valiant [suite])*, J. Scott *(Anthony & Cleopatra [suite])*, Hadjidakis *(The 300 Spartans [march])*, Goldsmith *(First Knight Suite)*, Burwell *(Rob Roy)*, Moross *(The War Lord)*, Rozsa *(El Cid; The Thief of Bagdad [suite]; Ben-Hur [suite])*, Doyle *(Henry V Suite)*, North *(Spartacus)*, Barry *(The Last Valley)*, Horner *(Braveheart)*, Poledouris *(Conan the Barbarian)*, Herrmann *(Jason & the Argonauts)*, Nascimbene *(The Vikings [suite])* SIAM 2-▲ 1081 [DDD] (22.97)

Royal PO [cnd:Elmer Bernstein], Ambrosian Singers
Original Scores from the MGM Classics—features works by Forrest/Borodin *(Bridal Procession [from Kismet])*, Schwartz *(Dancing in the Dark [from The Band Wagon])*, Blane/Martin *(The Trolley Song [from Meet Me in St. Louis])*, Lerner/Loewe *(Titles & Fountain Scene; Waltz Sequence [both from Gigi]; The Heather on the Hill [from Brigadoon])*, Brown/Freed *(Singin' in the Rain [from Singin' in the Rain])*, Porter/Edens *(The Pirate Ballet [from The Pirate])*, Warren/Freed/Edens *(This Heart of Mine [from the Ziegfeld Follies])* CHN (7000) ▲ 7053 (13.97)

Royal PO Pops
Shows Orchestral—features works by Lloyd Webber & Hart *(Phantom of the Opera)*, Gershwin *(The Gershwin Songbook)*, Lloyd Webber & Rice *(Jesus Christ Superstar; Joseph & The Amazing Technicolor Dreamcoat)*, Lloyd Webber *(Aspects of Love)* HBOX 3-▲ 50 [DDD]

Royal PO Pops [cnd:John Scott]
Europe Goes to Hollywood—features music from The Godfather; Casablanca; Ben Hur; Gone with the Wind; Rebecca; The Adventures of Robin Hood; The Alamo; Citizen Kane Denon/PCM Digital ▲ DEN 75470

St. Petersburg PO [cnd:Georg Solti]
Anna Karenina—features works by Tchaikovsky *(Eugene Onegin [w. Galina Gorchakova (sop); Letter Scene]; Swan Lake [sels]; Sym 6 [sels]; Con Vn [w. Maxim Vengerov (vn); sels])*, Prokofiev *(Alexander Nevsky [w. St. Petersburg Chamber Choir; sels])*, Rachmaninoff *(All-Night Vigil (vespers) [Lord, Now Lettest Thou Thy Servant Depart; w. Vladimir Mastavoy (sgr), St. Petersburg Chamber Choir, Nikolai Korniev (cnd)])*, plus *(trad pieces & original score selections)* ELEC ▲ 92759 (17.97) 92759 (10.98)

Seattle SO
Bernard Herrmann: Fahrenheit 451—features works by Herrmann *(Fahrenheit 451; The Man in the Grey Flannel Suit; Tender Is the Night; & others)* VARE ▲ VSD 5551

Seattle SO [cnd:Cliff Eidelman]
Blood & Thunder—features music from Ben Hur; Captain from Castile; Cleopatra; The Wind & the Lion; North by Northwest; The 10 Commandments; Taras Bulba; Mutiny on the Bounty *(rec Seattle, WA, Sept 1994)* VARE ▲ VSD 5561
Hollywood '94—features music from Schindler's List; The Age of Innocence; & others VARE ▲ VSD 5531

Williams, John (cnd)
The Hollywood Sound, w. London SO—features music from Adventures of Robin Hood; Beauty & the Beast; Best Years of Our Lives; Dances with Wolves; Devil & Daniel Webster; E.T.; Godfather II; Jaws; Last Emperor; Lawrence of Arabia; Out of Africa; A Place in the Sun [w. Grover Washington Jr.]; Pocahontas; Spellbound; Star Wars; Wizard of Oz COL ▲ 62788 (16.97) ▮ 62788 (10.98)

FILM SOUNDTRACKS COLLECTIONS

Cannes Film Festival 50th Anniversary Album—features works by Constantin *(The 400 Blows [Générique & car de police])*, Rota/Ranieri *(La Dolce Vita [Main Theme])*, Croisille/Lai *(Un homme et une femme [Main Theme])*, Hancock *(Blow Up [Main Theme])*, Herrmann *(Taxi Driver [Main Theme])*, Argol *(Yol [The Island])*, Simjanovic *(When Father Was Away on Business [Odlazak Mase])*, Kneiper *(Wings of Desire [Die Kathedrale der Bücher])*, Piazzolla/Goyeneche *(Sur [Vuelvo al Sur])*, Zimmer *(A World Apart [Main Theme])* Lurie *(Mystery Train [Chaucer Street])*, Burwell *(Barton Fink [Typing Montage])*, Tiêt *(The Scent of Green Papaya [Estampe 1])*, Shore *(Crash [Main Theme])* MILA ▲ 35817

The Choir *(Original Soundtrack Recording from the Masterpiece Theater Presentation)*—features performances by Gloucester Cathedral Choir [cnd:David Briggs] *(Stanford:Magnificat in G; Mendelssohn:O, for the Wings of a Dove [all w. Anthony Way (trb)]; Tavener:Hymn to the Mother of God; Tallis:Salvator Mundi; Syrewicz:Main Theme & Ov; Glory; Britten:Jubilate Deo)*, English CO [cnd:David Willcocks], King's College Choir (Cambridge) *(Handel:Zadok the Priest)*, David Briggs (org) *(Syrewicz:Processional)*, Anthony Way (trb), Warsaw PO *(Syrewicz:The Roof; Panis Angelicus; Final Theme; Balloons; Franck:Panis Angelicus)*, Lucia Popp (sop), Brigitte Fassbaender (mez), Tom Krause (bar), Vienna Haydn Orch [cnd:István Kertész] *(Mozart:Trio [from Così fan tutte])*, Academy of St-Martin-in-the-Fields & Chorus [cnd:Neville Marriner] *(Handel:Hallelujah Chorus [from Messiah]; Syrewicz:Conspiracy)*, Anthony Way (trb) *(Wesley:Love One Another [from Blessed be the God & Father; w. James Hopkins (trb)]; Brahms:Cradle Song; Syrewicz:Betrayal) (rec Gloucester Cathedral, Polish Radio & TV Recording Studios, Warsaw & The Music Studio, BBC TV Centre Sept 1994-Feb 1995)* PLON ▲ 48165 (16.97)

Cinema Century—features music from 20th Century Fox Fanfare; City Lights; Bride of Frankenstein; Gone with the Wind; Stagecoach; Citizen Kane; Casablanca; Oliver Twist; Quo Vadis; Quiet Man; High & the Mighty; Searchers; Bridge on the River Kwai; Big Country; North by Northwest; Ben-Hur; Psycho; La Dolce Vita; Magnificent 7; Alamo; Pink Panther; Lawrence of Arabia; Great Escape; 633 Squardon; Zulu; Zorba the Greek; Doctor Zhivago; Born Free; Lion in Winter; Once upon a Time in the West; Where Eagles Dare; Midnight Cowboy; Wild Bunch; Godfather; Jaws; Rocky; Taxi Driver; Star Wars; Diva; Raiders of the Lost Ark; Chariots of Fire; Conan: The Barbarian; E.T.; Once upon a Time in America; Terminator; Witness; Out of Africa; Passage to India; Mission; Room with a View; Cimeno Paradiso; Ghost; Dances with Wolves; 1492: Conquest of Paradise; Unforgiven; Fugitive; Jurassic Park; Schindler's List SLTR 4-▲ 5006 (29.97) 5006 (27.98)

Cinema Choral Classics, w. Crouch End Festival Choir [cnd:David Temple], Prague PO [cnd:Nic Raine, Paul Bateman, Kenneth Alwyn]—features works by Barber *(Agnus Dei [in Henry V])*, Barry *(Suite for Choir & Orch [from The Lion in Winter])*, Doyle *(Non Nobis Domine [from Henry V])*, J. Goldsmith *(Never Surrender [from First Night]; The Omen (suite))*, Jarre *(The Birth of Christ [from Jesus of Nazareth])*, Morricone *(Ave Maria; & On Earth as it is in Heaven [from The Mission])*, Orff *(O Fortuna [from Carmina Burana])*, Poledouris *(Riders of Doom [from Conan: The Barbarian])*, Rozsa *(The Lord's Prayer [from King of Kings])*, Silverstri *(Theme [from The Abyss])*, Vangelis *(Theme [from 1492: Conquest of Paradise])* SILC ▲ 6015 (16.97) ▮ 6015 (10.98)

Cinema Classics: Classical Music Made Famous in Films—features works by R. Strauss, Puccini, Mahler, Barber, Bach, J. Strauss II, Mozart, Rossini, Wagner, Catalini, Pachelbel, Rachmaninoff, Albinoni, Sibelius, Mouret, Puccini, Gershwin, Mascagni, Handel, Orff, Verdi, Beethoven, Elgar, Berlioz, Lizst, Ravel, Mendelssohn NXIN 5-▲ 8.505019 [DDD]

Cinema Classics 1997—features works by Dvořák *(Rusalka [Polonaise])*, Chopin *(Mazurka 47, Op. 68/2; Polonaise 6, Op. 53)*, Bach *(Son in E♭, BWV 1031; Goldberg Vars, BWV 988 [Aria])*, Vivaldi *(Cons, Op. 8/1-4, "The Four Seasons" [Allegro non molto from Winter])*, Mozart *(Sym 25, K. 183 [Allegro con Brio]; Requiem [Lacrymosa])*, Schubert *(Qt 14 Strs, D. 810, "Death & the Maiden")*, Rachmaninoff *(Con 3 Pno [Allegro na non tanto])* NXIN ▲ 551181 [DDD] (5.97)

Cinema Classics 10: Classical Music Made Famous in Films—features music by Handel *(Solomon [Arrival of the Queen of Sheba; from Heartburn])*, Schubert *(Trio No. 2 in E♭ for Piano, Violin & Cello, K.929 [Andante con moto; from B. Lyndon])*, Mendelssohn *(Con. in e for Violin, Op. 64 [Andante-Allegro non troppo; from A Month in the Country])*, Marais *(Sonnerie de Sainte Geneviève du Mont de Paris [from Tous les matins du monde])*, Handel *(Con. No. 13 in F for Organ [Allegro; from Dangerous Liajsons])*, Elgar *(Sym. 1 in A♭, Op. 55 [Andante nobilmente e semplice; from Greystoke The Legend of Tarzan, Lord of the Apes])*, Chopin *(Prelude No. 2 in a, Op. 28 [from Autumn Sonata])*, Bach *(Mass in b, BWV 232 [Et resurrexit; from Man Trouble])*, Prokofiev *(Lieutenant Kijé [Troika; from Love & Death])*, Mozart *(Don Giovanni, K.527 [Il mio tesoro; from Kind Hearts & Coronets])*, Mussorgsky*(A Night on the Bare Mountain [from Fantasia])* NXIN ▲ 551160 [DDD] (5.97)

Cinema Classics 11: Classical Music Made Famous in Films—features works by Offenbach *(Can-Can [from Orpheus in the Underworld; in Peter's Friends])*, Bach *(Air [from Suite No. 3 in D, BWV 1068; in The Spy Who Loved Me]; Sarabande [from Suite No. 4 in E♭ for Vc, BWV 1010; in Autumn Sonata])*, Mozart *(Rondo [from Con. No. 2 in E♭ for Hn, K.417; in JFK])*, Puccini *(E lucevan le stelle [from Tosca; in Serpico])*, anon. *(Romance d'amour [in Forbidden Games])*, Delibes *(Viens Mallika...Dôme épais le jasmin [from Lakmé; in Someone to Watch Over Me])*, Beethoven *(Finale [from Son. No. 23 in f for Pno, Op. 57; in Hard Target])*, Canteloube *(Baïlèro [from Chants d'Auvergne; in Henry V])*, Mendelssohn *(Wedding March [from A Midsummer Night's Dream; in 4 Weddings & a Funeral])*, Giordano *(La mamma morta [from Andrea Chénier; in Philadelphia])*, Wagner *(Pilgrims' Chorus [from Tannhäuser; in Meeting Venus])* NXIN ▲ 551171 [DDD]

Cinema Classics 12: Classical Music Made Famous in Films—features works by Mozart *(Molto allegro [from Sym. No. 40 in g, K.550; in The Living Daylights]; Romance [from Eine kleine Nachtmusik, K.525; in Ace Ventura, Pet Detective])*, Schubert *(Ave Maria, D.839 [in Fantasia]; Andantino [from Pno Qnt. in A, D.667; in My Left Foot])*, Beethoven *(Für Elise [in Rosemary's Baby]; Adagio cantabile [from Son. No. 8 in c for Pno, Op. 13; in The Age of Innocence])*, Myers *(Cavatina [in The Deer Hunter])*, Flotow *(M'appari tutt' amor [from Martha; in The Grey Fox])*, Dvořák *(Song to the Moon [from Rusalka, Op. 114; in Driving Miss Daisy])*, Bach *(Sarabande [from Suite No. 5 in c for Cello, BWV 1011; in Cries & Whispers])*, Prokofiev *(Balcony Scene [from Romeo & Juliet; in The Turning Point])*, Shostakovich *(Allegro non troppo [from Sym. No. 5 in d, Op. 47; from Rollerball])* NXIN ▲ 8.551172 [DDD]

The Cinema Classics Collection, Vol. 1, w. David Buechner (pno), Angeles String Quartet, London SO, New Zealand SO, Phoenix SO—features works by E. Bernstein *(Magnificent 7)*, Rozsa *(Ov to a Sym Concert; March; Love Scene; Epilogue; Finale [all from El Cid])*, Waxman *(Rhap for Pno [from The Paradine Case])*, Moross *(Vars on a Waltz)*, Herrmann *(Devil & Daniel Webster Suite)*, Copland *(Red Pony)*, Korngold *(Allegro Moderato [from String Quartet])*, plus others KOCH ▲ 7604 (10.97)

Cinema Classics 1998: Classical Music Made Famous in Films—features works by Joh. Strauss (II) *(Blue Danube [in Titanic]; Frühlingsstimmen [in The Devil's Own])*, Rossini *(Guillaume Tell [Ov; in Brassed Off])*, Mozart *(Zauberflöte [Pamina's Aria; w. Elisabeth Norbert-Schulz (sop); in Face/Off])*, Donizetti *(Lucia di Lammermoor [Aria; w. Luba Orgonasova (sop); in 5th Element])*, Beethoven *(Son 8 Pno [Adagio; in The Lost World])*, Bach *(Air [in One Night Stand])*, Chopin *(Nocturne in f [in Peacemaker]; Son 2 Pno [March; in Paradise Road])*, Puccini *(Gianni Schicchi [O mio babbino caro; w.Miriam Gauci (sop); in G. I. Jane])*, Mendelssohn *(Hebrides Ov [in L. A. Confidential])* NXIN ▲ 8551182 [DDD] (5.97)

Classical Mob Hits—features various artists performing works featured in gangster movies by Rossini *(La Gazza Ladra [ov]; Il barbiere di Siviglia [ov])*, Boccherini *(Qnt in G, G.275 [Minuet])*, Bach *(Wir setzen uns und Tranen nieder)*, Mascagni *(Cavalleria Rusticana [intermezzo])*, Morricone *(Untouchables [Main Theme])*, Leoncavallo *(Vesti la guibba [from I Pagliacci])*, Donizetti *(Una furtiva lagrima [from L'Elisir d'amore])*, Bernstein *(On the Waterfront [Andante & presto barbaro])*, Puccini *(E lucevan le stelle [from Tosca])*, Joplin *(Entertainer)*, Rota *(Godfather Suite)* RCAV ▲ 68927 (10.97) ▮ 68927 (5.98)

Classics Go to the Movies
Vol. 1, w. Hungarian State Opera Orch, Vienna Strauss Orch, Jenö Jandó (pno), Plovdiv PO, Dresden PO, New Leipzig Bach Collegium Musicum, Budapest SO—features music from 2001: A Space Odyssey; Heat & Dust; Clockwork Orange; Ordinary People; Apocalypse Now LALI ▲ 15641 (3.97)
Vol. 2, w. Dresden PO, Budapest Festival Orch, Bulgarian Radio-TV SO, Bela Kovaks, Franz Liszt CO, Bruno Lazzaretti, Berlin RSO, Hungarian State Orch—features music from Gallipoli; Death in Venice; Excalibur; Out of Africa; 10 LALI ▲ 15642 (3.97)
Vol. 3, w. Hungarian State Orch, Lajos Meyer, Budapest Strings, Leonard Hokanson (pno), Carmerata Labacensis, Budapest SO, Prague Festival Orch—features music from Kramer vs. Kramer; The Music Lovers; & others LALI ▲ 15643 (3.97)
Vol. 4, w. Budapest SO, Budapest PO, Salzburg Mozarteum Orch, Christian Altenburger, Ernst Mayer-Schieming, German Bach Soloists, Sofia National Opera Orch—features music from Manhattan; Raging Bull; Nijinsky; & others LALI ▲ 15644 (3.97)
Vol. 5, w. Hannes Kästner (org), Salzburg Mozarteum Orch, Bavarian RSO, Ludovic Spiess (ten), Virginia Zeani (sop), Romanian Opera Orch, Romanian Radio-TV Studio Orch, Sofia PO, Budapest SO, Philharmonia Orch—features music from Amadeus; E La Nave Va; Ludwig; Breaking away; Moonstruck; & others LALI ▲ 15645 (3.97)

992 ▲ = CD ♦ = Enhanced CD △ = MD ▮ = Cassette Tape ▯ = DCC

Historic Organs of Connecticut—features performances on 15 historic organs by Joan Lippincott (org) *(Widor:Sym 6 Org [Allegro] D. Buck:Concert Vars on Star-Spangled Banner)*, David Dahl (org) *(Homilius:3 Chorales)*, Robert Barney (org) *(W. E. Thayer:Vars on a Russian Hymn)*, Margaret Irwin-Brandon (org) *(Bach:Chorale Prelude on "Ach Herr, mich armen Sünder"; Gherardeschi:Son Org [Rondo I])*, Bruce Stevens (org) *(Paine:Concert Vars on Star-Spangled Banner; Schumann:Canon in A♭; Parry:Toccata & Fugue, "Wanderer"; plus hymn:Holy Ghost, Dispel Our Sadness)*, Thomas Murray (org) *(Elgar:Enigma Vars [Nimrod]; Carillon)*, Charles Krigbaum (org) *(Reger:Fant & Fugue in d, Op. 135b; plus hymn:O God, Beneath Thy Guiding Hand)*, Christa Rakich (org) *(Wagner:Liebestod [from Tristan & Isolde]; E. L. Diemer:Sweet Story; All Things Bright & Beautiful; plus hymn:Amazing Grace)*, Lorenz Maycher (org) *(Dupré:Sketch in b♭, Op. 41/2)*, Ardyth Lohuis (org), Robert Murray (vn) *(H. H. A. Beach:Invocation, Op. 55)*, Timothy Edward Smith (org) *(P. Fletcher:Festival Toccata)*, Peter Sykes (org) *(Holst:Planets [Jupiter])*, R. Walden Moore (org) *(hymn:And Did Those Feet)*, Peter Stolzfus (org) *(Mulet:Tu es Petra)*, Victoria Wagner (org), Nancy Armstrong (sop) *(C. H. Work:Come Home, Father; Stanley:Voluntary III [Largo; Vivace])*, Rachelen Lein (org) *(J. C. Beckel:Opening Voluntary; plus hymn:Jerusalem, My Happy Home)*, Kevin Birch (org) *(Widor:Sym 2 Org [Prelude])*, Brian Jones (org) *(Viderø:Vars on "Built on a Rock")*, Leo Abbott (org) *(G. E. Whiting:Grand Son [Allegro con moto])*, Richard W. Hill (org) *(H. R. Shelley:Berceuse)*, Mark Bighley (org) *(Rinck:Vars on "Christus, der ist mein Leben")*, Stephen Long (org) *(Howells:4 Miniatures Org)*, John Cummins (org) *(Mendelssohn:Son 2; plus hymn:Praise the Lord, Ye Heav'ns Adore)*, Lynn Edwards (org) *(Walond:Voluntary, Op. 1/5; plus hymn:Lord of All Being, Throned Afar)*, Renea Waligora (org) *(Vierne:Postlude [from 24 Pieces in Free Style])*, Laraine Olson Waters (org) *(Lee Mitchell:Toccata on "Weinbergli")*, Dana Robinson (org), Paul Tegels (org) *(J. Christi. Bach:Duetto in F, Op. 18/6 [Allegro])*, John Ogasapian (org) *(C. P. E. Bach:Son in g [Adagio])*, William Aylesworth (org) *(Sowerby:In dulci jubilo; plus hymn:Praise My Soul The King)*, Rosalind Mohnsen (org) *(Liszt:St. Francis of Paola Walking on the Water)*, Glen Kime (org) *(Ives:Vars on America)*, Donald K. Fellows (org) *(Demessieux:Attende Domine; Hossana Filio David)*, Gregory Crowell (org) *(Foote:Meditation)*, Mark Dwyer (org) *(Howells:Psalm Prelude, Op. 32/1; plus hymn:All Praise to Thee)*, Will Headlee (org) *(Ahrens:Choralpartita on "Lobe den Herren")*, Marvin Mills (org) *(Conte:Pastorale)*, Kimberly Ann Hess (org) *(Sweelinck:Vars on "Puer Nobis Nascitur")*, Mark Brombaugh (org) *(Buxtehude:Toccata in d; plus hymn:New Songs of Celebration)* RAVN 4-▲ 94 [DDD] (62.97)

Historic Organs of Louisville—features performances by James Hammann (org) [St. Martin of Tours RCC, Louisville] *(Guilmant:Funeral March & Hymn of Seraphs; Son 1, Op. 42 [Finale])*, Lois Regenstein (org) [St. Mary's RCC, New Albany, IN] *(Clokey:Air "Little Red Lark"; Fireside Fancies; hymn:Lord Enthroned)*, Rosalind Mohnsen (org) [St. Frances Rome RCC, Louisville] *(Langlais:Canzona; Bonnet:Lied des Chrysanthèmes, Op. 3/1)*, Bruce Stevens (org) [Okolona Baptist, Louisville] *(Boély:Fant & Fugue in B♭; hymn:We Know that Christ is Raised)*, Kristin Gronning Farmer (org) [Ascencion RCC, Louisville] *(Grieg:Ases Tod [from Peer Gynt Suite 1])*, Michael R. Israel (org) [St. John's UCC, Madison, IN] *(Haydn:Andante; Arne:Organ Solo [from Con 1 Org])*, Susan Armstrong (org) [Windle Memorial Auditorium, Madison, IN] *(Hall/Kleinkauf:Johnson Rag)*, Peter V. Picerno (org) [St. Boniface RCC, Fulda, IN] *(Valeri:Son 4; Bossi:Ave Maria)*, Timothy J. Oliver (org) [St. John's Episcopal, Versailles] *(Thayer:Allegro Maestoso & Fugue on America)*, Lynn Thomson (org) [Pisgay Presbyterian, Woodford County] *(Correll:Homage to Persichetti)*, Theodore Rsinke (org) [St. Pius RCC, Troy, IN] *(Hovhaness:Dawn Hymn, Op. 138)*, Susan R. Werner Friesen (org) [Versailles Presbyterian, Versailles] *(Martin:Sunset to Sunrise)*, George Bozeman (org) [St. Mary Magdelen RCC, Louisville] *(Karg-Elert:O God, Thou Faithful God; Church Cantata)*, Ann Colbert Wade (org) [St. Anthony RCC, St. Anthony, IN] *(Cherwien:Hymn Interpret; hymn:Lord, Whose Love)*, Johnathan Crutchfield (org) [4th Ave Methodist, Louisville] *(C. P. E. Bach:Son V)*, Marilyn Kay Stulken (org) [St. Philip Neri RCC, Louisville] *(Benoit:Elevation, No. 30; Banchieri:Segundo Dialogo)*, Jane Edge (org) [First Baptist, Madison, IN] *(Rheinberger:Fughette on B-A-C-H; Monologue, Op. 162/1)*, Rachelein Lien (org) [St. Cecilia's RCC, Louisville] *(Lindsay:Homeward Bound; Oldroyd:Prayer)*, Mary Gifford (org) [DeHaven Baptist, LaGrange] *(Chaminade:Offertoire)*, John Courter (org) [Univ of Kentucky Conference Center, Lexington] *(Elgar:Chanson de Nuit, Op. 15/1; Massenet:Medetation [from Thaïs]; Wood:Prelude on Pisgah)*, Johnathan F. Oblander (org) [1st Church of Christ Scientist, Louisville] *(Mendelssohn:Son 4; Brahms:Fugue in A♭)*, Stephen Schnurr (org) [St. Anthony Medetation Center, Louisville] *(Williams:Prelude on Hyfrydol)*, Timothy Lee Baker (org) [Louisville Memorial Auditorium] *(Debussy:Prélude à l'après-midi d'un faune [arr Cellier]; Wagner:Ride of the Walküren [arr LeMare])*, John E. Cummins (org) [St. Peter's UCC, Louisville] *(Buck:Last Rose of Summer; hymn:O Praise Ye the Lord)*, Marsha W, Busey (org) [Clifton Baptist, Louisville] *(Callahan:Partita on Ein feste Burg; hymn:A Mighty Fortress Is Our God)*, Boyd M. Jones (org) [St. Andrew's Episcopal, Louisville] *(Saint-Saëns:Prelude & Fugue in E♭; Hindemith:Son 2; hymn:Sing Alleluia Forth)*, David Lang (org) [Monastary Church, Ferdinand, IN] *(Johnson:Tpt Tune)*, Phillip T. Hines, Jr. (org) [St. Joseph Proto-Catholic,Bardstown] *(Bellando:Grand March in B♭)*, Janet Hamilton (org) [Louisville Presbyterian Seminary] *(Kayser:Partita on Resonet in laudibus)*, F. Anthony Thurman (org) [St. Francis of Assisi RCC, Louisville] *(Robinson:Chorale-When in Our Music)* OHS 4-▲ 93 [DDD] (32.97)

Historic Organs of Milwaukee—features performances by Marilyn Stulken *(works by Guilmant, Wm. Selby)*, Bruce Stevens *(works by Louis Vierne)*, Bruce Bengtson *(works by Rheinberger)*, Jane Edge *(works by Arnold Dolmetsch, Horatio Parker)*, Michael Meyer, Frank Rippl *(works by Percy MacDonald)*, Susan Werner Friesen *(works by Francis S. Moore)*, Max Yount *(works by Elizabeth Stirling)*, Rosalin Mohnsen *(works by Karg-Elert)*, Theodore Reinke *(works by Reger)*, John Schwandt *(works by Paul Manz)*, Michael Hoerig *(works by Dom Paul Benoit, Benj. Carr, Guilmant)*, Stephen Cushman *(works by J.S. Bach)*, Ruth Tweeten *(works by Mendelssohn)*, Peter Press *(works by Reger)*, Gary Zwicky *(works by Robert Noehren)*, Lois Regestein *(works by Bartók, Sodermann)*, David Heller *(works by Brahms)*, Todd Miller *(works by Brahms, Dupré)*, Rev. Thomas Lijewski *(works by Vaughan Williams)*, Renea Waligora *(works by Louis Vierne)*, David Bohn *(works by Cherubim Schaefer)*, Mark Edwards *(works by Wm. Walond)*, John Panning *(works by Sassmannshausen)*, Thomas Murray *(works by Vierne, Wagner)* OHS 2-▲ OHS 90 [DDD]

Historic Organs of New Orleans, w. George Bozeman (org), James S. Darling (org), Jesse E. Eschbach (org), Gerald D. Frank (org), John Gearhart (org), James Hammann (org), Frederick Hohman (org), Lenora McCroskey (org), Mary Gifford Matthys (org), Lorenz Maycher (org), Donald Messer (org), J. Thomas Mitts (org), Rosalind Mohnsen (org), Marcus G. St. Julien (org), Gary John Savoie (org), Bruce Stevens (org), Carol Teti (org)—features works by Bach, Bingham, Boyce, Grobe, Guilmant, Handel, Hewitt, Karg-Elert, Lefébure-Wely, Micheelsen, Mozart, Paine, Parker, Perera, Reger, Rheinberger, Wesley, et al. *(rec 17 historic pipe organs, The Bayous to Natchez June 1989)* OHS 2-▲ OHS 89

Historic Organs of San Francisco—features works by Bingham, Bloch, Brahms, Handel, Langlais, Rheinberger, et al. *(rec OHS National Convention, June 1988)* OHS 2-▲ OHS 88 CD

The King of Instruments *(a Delos Records organ music sampler "a listener's guide to the art & science of recording the organ")*—features works by Bach, Buxtehude, Dupré, Duruflé, Gherardeschi, Lefebure-Wely, Messiaen, Rorem, Sowerby DLS ▲ 3503 [DDD]

March on!: Longwood Gardens Organ, Vol. 2—features works by Sousa *(The Washington Post March)*, Elgar *(Pomp & Circumstance March, No. 4; Pomp & Circumstance March, No. 1 [arr. Lemare/Stairs])*, Wagner *(Tannhäuser:Fest March)*, Gounod *(Funeral March of a Marionette)*, Coates *(Knightsbridge March)*, Prokofiev *(Love for 3 Oranges:March)*, Verdi *(Aida:Triumphal March)*, Guilmant *(Marche réligieuse on Handel's Lift up Your Heads)*, Medelssohn *(A Midsummer Night's Dream:Fairies March)*, Schubert *(Marche militaire, Op. 52/1)*, Parry *(The Birds:Bridal March [arr. Alcock])*, Clarke *(Prince of Denmark's March)* DTT ▲ 8901 ▮ DTR 8901

Old Swedish Organs—features performances by Rune Engsö (org) [Västra Eneby Church Org] *(Walther:Con in F del Sigr. Tomaso Albinoni, appropriato all'organo; Bach:4 Choralvorspiele; Ritter:Sonatina)* [Kuddby Chruch Org] *(Mendelssohn:Son No. 2 in c; Brahms:3 Choralvorspiele; Reger:Pastorale; Toccata in d)*, Hans Fagius (org) [Nysätra Church Org] *(Albrechtsberger:Prelude in d, Op. 3/4; Pachelbel:Partita on "Werde munter, mein Gemüte"; Bach:Wer nur den lieben Gott lässt walten; Lobt Gott, Ihr Christen allzugleich; Johnsen:Fugue in D)* [Lillkyrka Church Org] *(Mendelssohn:Andante in D; Nachspiel in D)* [Kungs-Husby Church Org] *(C.P.E. Bach:Son in a, W.70/4; Beethoven:3 Stücke für Spieluhr; Hummel:Andante in A♭)*, Rune Engsö (org) [Gammalkil Church Org] *(Toccata & Fugue in d, BWV 538; 3 Chorale Preludes; Vogler:2 Preludes; Krebs:Ach Gott! erhör mein Seufzen; Von Gott! will ich nicht lassen; Trio in c; Gheyn:Praeludium & Fugato in g)*, Lena Jacobson (org) [Virestad Org] *(Praetorius:Allein Gott inn der Höh sey Ehr; Buxtehude:Toccata Manual, BWV 164; Canzonet in C, BWV 167; Cantzon in G♭, BWV 173; Sivert:Puer natus in Bethlehem; Böhm:Preludio in g)* [Drottningholm Palace Chapel Org] *(Zachow:Praeludium in G; Zipoli:Pastorale; Zellbell:5 Preludes; Walther:Meinem Jesu lass ich nicht; Con del Sigr. Gentili appropriato all'Organo)* BIS 3-▲ 123 [AAD] (51.97)

The Organ: A Concise Illustrated Guide
HAM (Discovery) 2-▲ 595005 (35.97)

The Organ in Lorraine: Works by Composers of the Region from 1537 to the Present, w. Anne-Catherine Bucher (org), Michel Chapuis (org), Francois Menissier (org), Norbert Petry (org)—sels unknown [Organs of St. Etienne de Metz Cathedral, St. Maurice de Domgermain, St. Nicolas de la Croix aux Mines, St. Nicolas de Sarreguemines, Notre Dame de Verdun Cathedral] K617 2-▲ 7055 (36.97)

Romantic Recital—features performances by Bram Beekman (org) *(Rheinberger:Son 7 Org in f)*, Rinus Verhage (org) *(C. de Wolf:Canonisch voorspel over Psalm 84; S. de Lange, Sr.:Son über, "Sollt'ich meinem Gott nicht singen?")*, Kees van Eersel (org) *(Vaughan Williams:Rhosymedre; Willan:Chorale Prelude; Passacaglia & Fugue 2 in e)*, Mar van der Veer (org) *(Langlais:Suite Médiévale)* LDBG ▲ 59 [DDD] (17.97)

The Schiörlin Organ (1783) in Jonsered, w. Magnus Kjellson (org), Kimberly Marshall (org), Jacques van Oortmerssen (org), Mikael Wahlin (org), Elisabeth Yokota (org)—features works by C. P. E. Bach *(Fant & Fugue in c)*, Handel *(Con in F, Op. 4/2)*, Mozart *(Eine kleine Gigue)*, Haydn *(Son in D)*, Mendelssohn *(Andante mit Variationen in D)*, Frescobaldi *(Toccata, Canzona, Ricercar & Bergamasca ["Fiori Musicali"])*, Knecht *(Thema mit vier Veränderungen)*, Bach *(Kyrie, Gott Vater in Ewigkeit; Christe, aller Welt Trost; Kyrie, Gott heiliger Geist)*, Oortmerssen *(Improv on "Nun komm der heiden Heiland")*, Charpentier *(Noël)*, anon *(Daphne) (rec live, 1992 & 1995)* INTA ▲ 42

The Washington Organ Book *(6 organist/composers of the Washington, D.C. area perform their own compositions on the Great Organ in Washington National Cathedral)*—features works by Haig Mardirosian *(Fantasia/Improvisation Christ ist erstanden/Christus vincit)*, R. Grogan *(Variations on "Morning Song")*, Russell Woollen *(Meditation)*, Daniel E. Gawthrop *(Rodomontade)*, Lawrence P. Schreiber *(Cantilène pour Rampal)*, D. Major *(Concertino)* GOT ▲ 49059 [DDD] (17.97)

ORGAN, BRASS & PERCUSSION

Haselböck, Franz (org), Militärmusik Burgenland Wind Ensemble [cnd:Rudolf Schrumpf]
Intradas & Choral Settings for Organ & Brass—features works by Homilius, Krebs, Mösl, J.J. Schneider HANS ▲ 98.544 [AAD]

Houbart, François-Henri (org), Concert Arban
Great Heroic Pieces PVY (Favourites) ▲ 730015 [DDD] (11.97)

Houbart, François-Henri (org), Concert Arban Brass Quintet, Francis Petit (perc)
Brass & Organ at the Church of the Madeleine—features works by Dupré, Elgar, Fauré, Franck, Glazunov, Grieg, Karg-Elert, Liszt PVY ▲ 785096 [DDD]

Johnson, James (org), Eastman Brass
A Thousand Pearls—features works by Bach *(Christ lag in Todesbanden)*, Sweelinck *(A Thousand Pearls; Fant chromatica)*, Gabrieli *(Iam non dicam vos servos [trans J. Johnson]; Fugue on the 9th Tone; Canzon 1st Toni; Canzona per sonare 2; Canzon 7th Toni 2; Canzon 9th Toni)*, Frescobaldi *(Ricercare)*, Bonelli *(Toccata "Athalanta")*, Cornet *(Courante)*, Viviani *(Son 1 Trbn)*, Josquin des Prez *(Royal Fanfare)*, Bendusi *(Il stocco; Doi Stanchi; Chi non ha martello; Incognita [all from Opera Nova de Balli])*, Cabanilles *(Tiento on the 6th Tone)*, plus Gregorian Chant *(Haec dies...) (rec live, Abbey Chapel, Mt. Holyoke College, Apr 11, 1993)* Conch Classics ▲ CC-1

Lippincott, Joan (org), Philadelphia Brass [Brian Kuszyk (tpt), Lawrence Wright (tpt), Martin Webster (hn), John Ilika (trbn), Grant Moore II (tuba)]
Joan Lippincott & Philadelphia Brass—features works by Karg-Elert *(Marche Triomphale)*, R. Strauss *(Feierlicher Einzug)*, Campra *(Suite of Dances; Rigaudon)*, Lockwood *(Con for Org & Brass)*, Gigout *(Grand-choeur Dialogué)*, Pinkham *(Gloria for Brass & Org)*, Handel *(Royal Fireworks Music [w Kevin Rosenberry (tpt)])*, Dupré *(Poème héroïque [w Rosenberry])*, Widor *(Salvum fac populum tuum [w Rosenberry])* at the Org of Princeton Univ Chapel GOT ▲ 49072 [DDD] (16.97)

MacArthur, Frederick (org), Old South Brass [cnd:Roger Voisin]
The Old Brass Organ & Timpani—features works by Wagner *(The Ride of the Valkyries [arr. George Faxon])*, Karg-Elert *(Praise the Lord with Drums & Cymbals, Op. 101)*, Dupré *(Poème héroïque, Op. 33)*, N. Plummer Faxon *(Fanfare No. 2; Adagio from Miniature Suite for String Quartet; Toccata)*, Tchaikovsky *(1812 Ov. [arr. G. Faxon])*, Vierne *(Carillon de Westminster from Pièces de fantaisie, 3rd Suite, Op. 54 [arr. G. Faxon]; March triompale centenaire de Napoléon I, Op. 16)*, Perry *(Christos Patterakis)*, McKinley *(Hymn Tune Fant. on St. Clement)*, Chuckerbutty *(Fanfare)*, Elgar *(Pomp & Circumstance Military March No. 1, Op. 39 [arr. G. Faxon])*, Sousa *(The Stars & Strips Forever [arr. G. Faxon])* G. Faxon, arr. *(The Star-Spangled Banner; Auld Lang Syne)* PROO ▲ 7051 [DDD]

Murray, Michael (org), Empire Brass Quintet
Music for Organ, Brass & Percussion—features works by A. Campra, J. Clarke, M. Dupré, E. Gigout, Hovhaness, Karg-Elert, Monteverdi, Poulenc, Purcell, R. Strauss, Telemann TEL ▲ 80218 [DDD] (15.97) ▮

Obetz, John (org), Missouri Brass Quintet, Jon Donald (perc)
Festival of Organ & Brass—features works by C. F. Peeters *(Entrada festiva)*, Bach *(Nun danket alle Gott; Jesum nun sei gepreistet)*, G. Gabrieli *(Son Pian'e forte; Canzons on 9th & 12th Tones)*, Karg-Elert *(Marche triomphale)*, Purcell *(Music for the Funeral of Queen Mary)*, Praetorius *(In dulci jubilo)*, R. Strauss *(Feierlicher Einzug der Ritter des Johannitzordens)*, Pfautsch *(If thou but suffer God to guide thee)*, Widor *(Salvam fac populum tuum) (rec RLDS Peace Temple, Independence, MO, Dec 19-21, 1996)* RBW ▲ CD 008

Riedo, Paul (org), Dallas Wind Sym [cnd:F. Fennell]
Pomp & Pipes—features works by Karg-Elert *(Praise the Lord with Drums & Cymbals)*, Reed *(Allelujah! Laudamus Te)*, Gigout *(Grand Chorus in Dialogue)*, Wills *(The Vikings)*, Grainger *(The Power of Rome & the Christian Heart)*, Dupré *(Heroic Poem)*, Nelson *(Pebble Beach Sojourn)*, Widor *(Lord, Save Thy People)*, Weinberger *(Polka & Fugue [from* Schwanda the Bagpiper*]) (rec July 26-27, 1993)* Reference ▲ RR 58 [DDD]

PERCUSSION

Continuum Percussion Quartet
Continuum Percussion Quartet—features works by Bazelon, Cage, Harrison, Kurtz, Rouse, VerPlanck *(see Composer listings)* NWW ▲ 382 [AAD] (16.97)

Ensemble Bash [Richard Benjafield (perc), Chris Brannick (perc), Stephen Hiscock (perc), Andrew Martin (perc)]
Launch—features works by S. Copeland *(The Gene Pool)*, Daugherty *(Shaken Not Stirred)*, Ensemble Bash *(Dash Me Something)*, Garland *(Apple Blossom)*, N. Hayes *(Shining Through)*, O. Robinson *(Suite d'Lorenzo)*, Skempton *(Shiftwork)*, trad *(Kumpo (Senegalese Circumcision Drumming) [arr P. Bozie]) (rec Air Recording Studios, Lyndhurst Hall, Hampstead, England, Apr 24-28, 1995)* COL ▲ 69246 (16.97)

Gamelan Pacifica
Trance Gong—features works by Jakobsdottir/Keliehor/Fallat/Powell *(Small of My Back; Trance Gong)*, Morris *(Rain)*, Keliehor *(Peaches of Immortality)*, Powell *(Gending Erhu)*, Cage *(In a Landscape)* ¿What Next? ▲ WN 0016

Glennie, Evelyn (perc)
Drumming, w. Philip Smith (pno)—features works by Glennie *(Entrances; Sorbet Nos. 1 -7; Exits)*, Cauberghs *(Halasana)*, Sierra *(Bongo-O)*, Masson *(Prim)*, Lang *(The Anvil Chorus)*, Rzewski *(To the Earth)*, Zivkovic *(Pezzo da Concerto No. 1)*, Psathas *(Matre's Dance) (rec Whitfield Street Studios, London, Dec 11-15, 1994)* CAT ▲ 68195 [DDD] (16.97)
Her Greatest Hits—features Entrances; Halasana; Sorbet 1; Rhythm Song; My Spine; Slaugher on 10th Ave; The Swan; Sorbet 5; A Little Prayer; Eldorado; Sorbet 7; Black Key Study; Divert; Taps in Tempo; Born to Be Wild; Michi; Sorbet 4; Light in Darkness; Anvil Chorus; Rhap; Sorbet 3; Con solo Perc [1st movt]; Flight of the Bumble-Bee; Sorbet 6; Mar Spiritual; Hejre Kati; Maple Leaf Rag; Matre's Dance; Czardas; Oxygen RCAV (Red Seal) 2-▲ 47629 (16.97)
Light in Darkness—features works by Keiko Abe, Ross Edwards, Evelyn Glennie, John McLeod, Minoru Miki, Ney Rosauro, Toshimitsu Tanaka RCAV (Red Seal) ▲ 60557 [DDD] (16.97)
Rebounds: Concertos for Percussion, w. Scottish CO [cnd:Paul Daniel]—features works by Richard Rodney Bennett, Milhaud, Miyoshi, Rosauro *(see Composer Section for details)* RCAV (Red Seal) ▲ 61277 (16.97) 61277
Rhythm Song *(original works and popularized classics for marimba, timpani and other percussion instruments, with orchestra; arrangements by Christopher Palmer,et al.)*, w. National PO [cnd:Barry Wordsworth]—features works by Abe, Chopin, Fauré, Glennie, Joplin, Rimsky-Korsakov, et al. RCAV ▲ 60242 [DDD] (16.97) 60242

Horsholm Percussion [cnd:Ole Pedersen], Marimba Ensemble
Horsholm Percussion & Marimba Ensemble—features works by Bizet *(Carmen Suite [arr. Klaus-Dieter Zimmer])*, Rossini *(William Tell Fant. [arr. Gert Mortensen])*, Vittori Monti *(Czardas No. 1 [arr. Mogens Andersen])*, Joplin *(The Entertainer [arr. Lars Vinther])*, Arthur Frackenpohl *(Wooden Whirl)*, Chick Corea *(Spain [arr. Soran Monrad])*, Soran Monrad *(Joy Shuffle)*, Josef Zawinul *(Birdland [arr. Monrad])*, Randy Brecker *(Some Skunk Funk [arr. Monrad])* DANR ▲ 329

Kroumata Percussion Ensemble, Keiko Abe (perc)
Play Works for Marimba & Percussion (*see* Composer listings—Takemitsu, et al.) BIS ▲ 462 [DDD] (17.97)

Kuisma, Rainer (mar/vib)
Virtuoso Percussion Music, w. Norrköping SO [cnd:Jorma Pnula, Gustaf Sjökvist]—features works by Milhaud *(Con. for Marimba, Vibraphone & Orch.; Con. for Percussion & Small Orch.)*, Fissinger *(Suite for Marimba)*, Lemba *(Estonian Cradle Song for Marimba)*, Sibelius *(The Harp Player, Op. 34/8 for Vibraphone)*, Shostakovich *(Polka from The Golden Age for Marimba & Vibraphone)*, Bashmakov *(Quattro bagatelle for Flute & Percussion [w. Gunilla von Bahr])*, Kuisma *(Hommage à Béla Bartók)* BIS ▲ 149 [AAD] (17.97)

New Jersey Percussion Ensemble, R. DesRoches (perc)
New Jersey Percussion Ensemble, Desroches—features works by Colgrass, Cowell, Varèse, Wuorinen, et al. 75597 ▲ 79150

New Music Consort [cnd:Claire Heldrich, Madeleine Shapiro]
Pulse—features works by John Cage, John Cage & Lou Harrison, Henry Cowell, Lukas Foss, Harvey Sollberger *((see* Composer section for details)) NWW ▲ 80405 [AAD] (16.97)

Nexus
The Best of Nexus *(12 selections from various LP recordings made by Nexus in Canada between 1976 and 1989)*—features Kobina; Triplets; Xylophonia; etc. NEXU ▲ NEX 10251 [AAD/DDD]
Nexus Now *(5 compositions for percussion ensemble, 4 of which are by Nexus members)*—features works by Bob Becker, William Cahn, Robin Engelman, Toru Takemitsu, John Wyre NEXU ▲ NEX 10262 [DDD]

Nexus (cont.)

Nexus Plays the Novelty Music of George Hamilton Green *(featuring xylophone soloist Bob Becker; intricate, stylish arrangements by Nexus members Bob Becker and Bill Cahn of twelve lighthearted xylophone novelties by American xylophone virtuoso George Hamilton Green, 1893-1970)*—features Fluffy ruffles; Rajah; Frivolity; etc. NEXU ▲ NEX 10273 [DDD]

Origins *(7 fully-improvisational works, employing a total over 90 percussion instruments, recorded in real time with no overdubbing or added electronic sounds)* NEXU ▲ NEX 10295 [DDD]

Ragtime Concert, featuring xylophone soloist Bob Becker *(featuring xylophone soloist Bob Becker; arrangements by Nexus members Bob Becker and Bill Cahn for xylophone, four marimbas and other percussion instruments of eleven ragtime pieces, mostly composed by American xylophone virtuoso George Hamilton Green, 1893-1970; a 1976 direct-to-disc recording)* NEXU ▲ NEX 10284 [AAD]

The Story of Percussion in the Orchestra, w. Bill Moyers (nar), Rochester PO—features works by Beethoven, Britten, Lully, Mozart, Philidor, et al. NEXU ▲ NEX 10306 [DDD]

Toccata—features Kichari; Tongues; Reunion; Toccata [w. Eric Robertson (org)] *(rec live, 1995-96)* NEXU ▲ 10410 [DDD] (16.97)

O-Zone Percussion Group

Whiplash—features works by J.S. Bach *(Bourée [arr. Olmstead]; Prelude 22 [from Wohltemperierte Klavier, Book 2; arr. Peters])*, Tchaikovsky *(Scherzo from Sym. No. 4 [arr. Peters])*, Debussy *(La fille aux chevaux de lin [arr. Barton])*, Bizet *(Faradole [from L'Arlèsienne Suite No. 2; arr. Jeanne])*, Stamp *(Daybreak)*, Green *(Rainbow Ripples [w. Brian Tychinski (xyl); arr. Becker]; Log Cabin Blues [w. Marc Nelson (xylo)]; The Whistler [w. Greg Alico (xyl); arr. Becker])*, Bolcom *(The Graceful Ghost [arr. Smith])*, Billy Joel *(Root Beer Rag [w. Jeff Senley (xyl); arr. Holly])*, Levy *(Whiplash [arr. Snoeck])*, trad. *(Greensleeves [arr. Peters])* KLAV ▲ 77008 [DDD] (17.97)

Percussion Group The Hague

Irony—features works by Cage, Donatoni, Ford, Huber, Kondo, Reich *(see Composer section)* GLOE ▲ 5086 [DDD] (16.97)

Skin Hits—features works by Ron Ford, Maki Ishii, Iannis Xenakis *(see Composer section)*; plus 30 minutes of Sabar and Djembé Music (for percussion ensemble) from Senegal GLOE ▲ 5066 [DDD] (16.97)

The Wooden Branch—features works by John Cage *([Quartet])*, Ron Ford, Peter Smith, Katsuhiro Tsubonoh *(see Composer section)* plus 20 minutes of Timbala Music from Mozambique GLOE ▲ 5072 [DDD] (16.97)

Pluznick, Michael (perc)

Heat Beat, w. Derrick Jones (elec bass)—features Riding the Dragon; Buddha's Beat; Skywalking; Lion's Den; Percussion Discussion; Universal Roots; Havana Cabana; The Elder; Soulfire; Ju Ju Jump; Love Stomp; Village Fête WETE (Well-Tempered World) ▲ 5177 [DDD] (16.97)

Pugliese, Michael (perc)

Perkin' at Merkin *see* Composer section under Cage, Feldman, Xenakis, et al. *(rec in concert at Merkin Concert Hall NYC, Apr 4, 1989)* MODE ▲ 25

Rebello, Simone (perc)

Fascinating Rhythm, w. Edwards Jazz Quartet, Brittania Building Society Band [cnd:Howard Snell], Stewart Death (pno)—features works by Gershwin *(Fascinating Rhythm; Our Love Is Here to Stay [both w. Edwards Jazz Quartet; arr K. Edwards])*, J. Green *(Xylophonia [w. Brittania Building Society Brass Band; arr H. Snell])*, Smadbeck *(Rhythm Song)*, Mendelssohn *(Spinning Song [w Brittania Building Society Brass Band; arr H. Snell])*, Glentworth *(Blues for Gilbert)*, Oliveriar *(Tico Tico [w. Edwards Jazz Quartet, A. Grady (perc), S. Bentall (perc), G. Butvher (perc); arr K. Edwards])*, M. Edwards *(Rhapsodic Fant [w. Stewart Death (pno)])*, Lemmon *(Helter Skelter [w. Brittania Building Society Brass Band])*, Stout *(Mexican Dances for Mar (2))*, Bruer *(Happy Hammers [w .Edwards Jazz Quartet])*, G. H. Green *(Valse Brillante [w. Stewart Death (pno)])*, G. Richards *(Zimba Zimba [w. Brittania Building Society Brass Band])* DOY ▲ DOY 024 [DDD]

A Secret Place, w. Andrew Scott (a sax), Liz Gilliver (mar), Kalengo Percussion Ensemble, Eryl Roberts (perc), John Melbourne (perc), Chris Bastock (perc), Richard Dyson (perc)—features works by J. Rebello *(A Secret Place)*, Albéniz *(Leyenda [arr L. Maxey])*, Yuyama *(Divert for Mar & A Sax [w. Andrew Scott (a sax)])*, Molenhof *(Saturday's Child [w. Liz Gilliver (mar)])*, D. Mancini *(Suite for solo Drum Set & Perc Ensemble [w. Kalengo Percussion Ensemble, J. Melbourne (perc), E. Roberts (perc), C. Bastock (perc), R. Dyson (perc)])*, Stock *(Jupiter's Dance)*, Miki *(Marimba Spiritual [w. Kalengo Percussion Ensemble]) (rec Zion Institute, Manchester, 1995)* DOY ▲ DOY 040 [DDD]

Répercussion Ensemble

Repercussion—features works by Rachmaninoff, Bizet, Monti, Dvořák, Chopin, Ravel, Debussy, Vivaldi, Mussorgsky [all pieces arr for perc ensemble] ANAL ▲ 29719 (16.97)

Sadlo, Peter (perc)

Classic Percussion—features works by Keiko Abe, J.S. Bach, Siegfried Fink, Mark Glentworth, Peter Michael Hamel, Peter Sadlo, Reginald Smith Brindle, Toshimitsu Tanaka KSCH ▲ 310141 [DDD] (16.97)

Safri Duo [Morten Friis (perc), Uffe Savery (perc)]

Goldrush—features works by J.S. Bach *(Prelude & Fugue in C#)*, Mendelssohn *(Fugue No. 4 in f)*, Chopin *(Etude No. 4 in c#; Fantaisie-Impromptu in c#)*, Ravel *(Alborada del gracioso)*, Nøorgård *(Well-Tempered Percussionists)*, Barfoed *(Safricana)*, Wallin *(Twine)*, Veldhuis *(Goldrush) (rec Danish Radio Concert Hall, Feb 19-23, 1996)* CHN ▲ 9482 (16.97)

Samuels, Dave (vib/mar)

Synergy with Samuels—features works by R. Edwards *(Prelude & Dragonfly Dance)*, N. Westlake *(Malachite Glass)*, P. Sculthorpe *(From Jabiru Dreaming)*, Cage *(First Construction)*, Samuels *(Reconstructions; Night Rain; Square Corners)*, B. Ruyle *(#3)* TALP ▲ 30 [DDD] (18.97)

Slawson, Brian (perc)

Bach on Wood—features works by Bach, Handel, Pachelbel, Corelli, Vivaldi, et al. COL ▲ 39704 (9.97) 39704

Distant Drums COL ▲ 42333 [ADD]

Stensgaard, Kai (mar)

Marimba Classic—features works transcribed for solo marimba; *see* Composer section—Albéniz:Guitar Music; etc.) DANR ▲ DACOCD 304 [ADD]

Tharichen, Werner (timp)

Virtuoso Kettledrum Concertos, w. Berlin RSO [cnd:Uros Lajovic]—features works by Hertel, Tharichen, Anon. KSCH ▲ 311052 (16.97)

Walton, Sam (mar), Colin Currie (mar/vib/dr)

Striking A Balance, w. R. Michael (pno)—features J. S. Bach *(English Suites [No. 2, BWV 807])*, A. A. Corea *(Children's Songs [No. 1:Song to the Pharaoh Kings; No. 6:The Sky; No. 8:Pixieland Rag; No. 9:Children's Song #1])*, Emslie *(Hughs Chilled Red Snare Dr)*, Halt *(Marimbasonic)*, T. Ichiyanagi *(Paganini Personal)*, R. Michael *(Jazz Suite Vib [1. Latin; 2. Boogie])*, M. Ravel *(Alborada del gracioso)*, S. Reich *(Nagoya Mar)*, Rosauro *(Cenas Amerindias 1; Cenas Amerindias 2)* EMIC ▲ 72267 [DDD] (6.97)

Zeltsman, Nancy (mar)

Woodcuts—features works by Levitan *(Opening Day)*, T. *(Merlin)*, Piazzolla *(Tango Suite)*, Zeltsman *(Woodcuts)*, Kirgo *(November Mar)*, Morgan *(Pay No Attention to That Man Behind the Curtain)*, Aldridge *(From My Little Island)*, Vega *(Gypsy)*, Hedges *(Ragamuffin)* GMR ▲ 2043 (16.97)

PERCUSSION COLLECTIONS

Drums A' Plenty—features Drs A' Plenty; Dr Display; Precision in Perc; Dr Salute; Victory Drs; Windschi; Retreat Marches; It's a Long Way to Tipperary; San Lorenzo; Wandermarsch; Drumsticks for 2; Bedtime for Drs; Fascinating Drs; Moventa; St. Louis Blues; Massed Corps of Drs of the Guards Division; By Beat of Dr; The Sledgehammer Strikes Back; The Bass Dr BND ▲ 5072 [DDD]

The Percussion—features performances by Peter Sadlo (drum) *(Siegfried Fink:Intrada; Cadenza)*, Christian Roderburg (marimba) *(Keiko Abe:Dream of the Cherry Blossom)*, Peter Sadlo (percussion instruments) *(Rignald Smith Brindle:Orion M42)*, Werner Thärichen (timbals), Berlin RSO [cnd:V. Handley] *(Hertel:Poco adagio; Allegretto; Thärichen:Lento; Allegro moderato)*, Düsseldorf Percussion Ensemble *(Michael Denhoff:Bacchantische Tanzszenen)*, Peter Sadlo (vibraphone) *(Marc Glentworth:Blues for Gilbert)* KSCH ▲ 313412 [DDD] (16.97)

PIANO

Achatz, Dag (pno)

For Children—features works by Beethoven, Schumann, Debussy, Bartók, Villa-Lobos, Tchaikovsky *(rec Apr 30-May 1, 1980 & May 31, 1983)* BIS ▲ 158 [AAD/DDD] (17.97)

Afanassiev, Valery (pno)

Homages & Ecstasies—features works by Froberger *(Tombeau)*, Wagner *(Elsas Traum [from Lohengrin; arr Liszt]; Thema in A♭)*, Rachmaninoff *(Preludes, Op. 32/5 & 12)*, Scriabin *(Preludes, Op. 11/2, 4 & 10)*, Schumann *(Andantino di Clara Wieck)*, Grieg *(Lyric Pieces, Op. 43/1 & 2)*, Chopin *(Mazurka in f)*, Debussy *(Prélude 6 [from Book 1])*, Liszt *(Consolations 3 & 5)*, Tchaikovsky *(Barcarolle [from The Seasons])* DNN ▲ 18044 (16.97)

Agus, Ayke (pno)

Musical Momentos of Jascha Heifetz—features works by Albéniz, Bach/Rachmaninov, Mendelssohn, Schubert, et al. PROT ▲ PRCD 1108 [DDD]

Albert, Eugene d' (pno)

D'Albert—features works by Beethoven, Weber, Liszt, Brahms, D'Albert, Chopin, Schubert SYMP ▲ SYM 1046

The Recordings: 1911-30, w. Berlin RSO [cnd:Bruno Siedler-Winckler]—features works by d'Albert, Beethoven, Brahms, Chopin, Liszt, Schubert & Weber ENPL (Piano Library) ▲ 250 (13.97)

Aldrich, Ronnie (pno)

Adagio: 21 Great Melodies from the Classics, w. *(orch unknown)*—features works by Albinoni *(Adagio [arr Giazott])*, Khachaturian *(Adagio [from Spartactus; w chorus])*, Mozart *(Sym 40; Serenade; Theme [from Con 21 Pno]; Rondo alla turca)*, Massenet *(Méditation [from Thaïs])*, Schubert *(Serenade; Moment musical 3)*, Tchaikovsky *(None but the Lonely Heart)*, Rachmaninoff *(Vocalise)*, Offenbach *(Barcarolle [from Contes d'Hoffmann])*, Borodin *(Nocturne)*, Chopin *(Nocturne)*, J. S. Bach *(Air on the G string; Badineris [from Suite 2])*, Fauré *(Pavane [w Ladybirds])*, Satie *(Gymnopédie 1)*, Granados *(Andaluza [from Spanish Dance 5; w Ladybirds])*, Beethoven *(Adagio [from Son 8 Pno; w Ladybirds])*, Grieg *(Anitra's Dance [from Peer Gynt; w Ladybirds])* PLON ("Phase 4 Stereo") ▲ 44787 [ADD] (11.97)

Alieva, Adilia (pno)

Adilia Alieva Plays Piano—features works by Mendelssohn *(Vars. sérieuses, Op. 54)*, Villa-Lobos *(Prelude; Rhap.)*, Daetwyler *(Chants de l'Aurore)*, Kuliev *(Vars.; 2 Preludes)*, Gajiev *(Danse lente; Danse rapide; Ballade)*, Melikov *(7 Pieces)*, Dadashev *(Sonatina in C)*, Mustafa-Zade *(3 Preludes for Adilia Alieva)*, Mamedov *(Toccata [w. Baku Symphonic & Philharmonic Orch.; cond:Ramiz Melik-Aslanov])* GALL ▲ 707 [ADD]

Alpert, Pauline (pno)

Keyboard Wizards of the Gershwin Era, Vol. 1: Pauline Alpert—features works by Rimsky-Korsakov *(Song of India)*, Liszt *(Hungarian Rhap No. 2)*, Gershwin *(Fascinatin' Rhythm)*, Alpert, Rodgers & Hart, Youmans, Berlin, others *(rec 1927-44)* PHS ▲ 9201 [ADD] (17.97)

Armengaud, Jean-Pierre (pno)

Russian Avant-Garde Music—features works by Lourie, Scriabin, Roslavetz, Mossolov, Obouhov, Shostakovich NUO ▲ 7263

Backhaus, Wilhelm (pno)

A Journey in His Studio Recordings—features works by Beethoven, Bach, Liszt, Wagner, Chopin, Handel & Weber *(rec 1908-35)* ENPL (Piano Library) ▲ 229 (13.97)

Barere, Simon (pno)

Simon Barere at the Carnegie Hall, Vol. 1—features works by Bach, Schumann, Weber, Balakirev, Blumenfeld, Glazunov, Scriabin, Godowski, Rachmaninov APR ▲ APR 7008 [AAD]

Vol. 2—features works by Beethoven, Schumann, Liszt, Weber & Chopin APR ▲ APR 7009 [AAD]

Simon Barere: The Complete HMV Recordings (1936-36)—features works by Liszt, Balakirev, Blumenfeld, Glazunov, Scriabin, Godowski, Schumann & Chopin APR ▲ APR 7001 [AAD]

Bar-Illan, David (pno)

Recital—features works by Ben-Haim, Bernstein, Chopin, Moszkowski † Liszt:Piano Con. 1; Tchaikovsky:Piano Con. 2 *(see Composer section)* AUDO ▲ 72030 (16.97)

Bartók, Béla (pno)

Bartók at the Piano *(studio, broadcast and piano roll recordings by Bartók, ca 1920-1945)*—features works by Bartók *(Piano Music)*, Beethoven *(Violin Sonata No. 9)*, Debussy *(Sonata No. 3)*, Kodály *(Hungarian Folk Music)*, Liszt *(Années de pèlerinage, Book 3)*, D. Scarlatti *(Sonatas)* see Composer section for details HUN 6-▲ 12326 (m) [ADD]

Bärtschi, Werner (pno)

Werner Bärtschi-Live—features works by Bach, Beethoven, Chopin, Bärtschi, Janaçek, Franck *(rec Oct 19-23, 1988)* JEC ▲ JD 629-2 [ADD]

Bauer, Harold (pno)

The 1924-1928 Victor Recordings—features works by Bach/arr. Bauer, Bauer, Beethoven, Beethoven/arr, Bauer, Chopin, Durand, Gluck/arr. Saint-Saëns, Liszt, Rubinstein, Schubert, Schumann, Schutt BPS ▲ 7 [ADD]

The 1929 Victor & 1939 Schirmer Recordings—features works by Schumann, Brahms, J.S. Bach, Debussy, Handel, Scarlatti, Couperin, Schubert, Mendelssohn, Chopin BPS ▲ 9 [ADD]

Bayless, John (pno)

Bach Meets the Beatles *(improvisations on Beatles melodies in the style of Bach)* PRA ▲ 211 (14.97) ▮ 211 (10.98)

West Side Story Variations *(variations on songs from Leonard Bernstein's musical)* ANGL ▲ 54507 54507

Becker, Jörg (pno)

Sonate Facile—features works by J.C. Bach, Mozart, C.P.E. Bach, W.F. Bach, Dussek & Benda CAPO ▲ 10415 [DDD] (11.97)

Beedle, Helen (pno)

When the Galop Was the Rage, w. Jonathan Beedle (gtr/voc)—features works by Morant *(Wheatland Polka)*, Gottschalk *(The Dying Poet; The Dying Swan; The Banjo; Tournament Galop)*, Sloman *(The Ericsson Schottisch)*, Thalberg/Bishop *(Home Sweet Home)*, Moore *(Believe Me if All Those Endearing Young Charms)*, H. D. I. Webster/J. P. Webser *(Lorena)*, Root *(Battle Cry of Freedom)*, Foster *(Beautiful Dreamer)*, Root/Washburn *(The Vacant Chair)*, Thalberg *(The Last Rose of Summer)*, Work *(Marching through Georgia)*, Emmet *(Dixie's Land) (rec Spring House, PA)* Galop ▲ 01

Berkey, Jackson (pno)

Plays Beethoven, Debussy & Scriabin *see* Composer section: Beethoven—Piano Sonata No. 30; etc. AMG ▲ 381 [DDD] ▮ 381

Bernier, Sylvia (pno), Guy Penson (pno)

Musiques De Salon—features works by Gobbaerts *(Galop brillant [from Tramway])*, Eilenberg *(Gavotte Joséphine)*, Bachmann *(Impromptu-valse [from Les Sylphes])*, Stadeler *(Polka [from L'Éclat de rire])*, Hoffmann *(Sur l'eau; Chant du rossignol; Flocons de neige; L'Oiseau voyageur)*, Wachs *(Marche de concert [from Capricante])*, Burgmein *(Tramway-Galop)*, Gillet *(Pizzicati)*, Durand de Grau *(Galop brillant [from Les Clochettes])*, Wieniawski *(Berceuse)*, Kölling *(La Chasse au lion)*, Van Gael *(Marche indienne)*, Fischer *(3e Galop [from A travers bois])*, Ganz *(Grand galop de Concert [from Qui vive!])* RICE ▲ 147135 [ADD] (17.97)

Bessette, Louise (pno)

Louise Bessette—features works by Garant *(Cage d'oiseau)*, Tremblay *(Traçante)*, Saint-Marcoux *(Mandala II)*, Gagnon *(Jeux dans l'espace)*, Panneton *(Traits, Écart, Réparties)*, Cowell *(Exultation; Fabric; Advertisement; Tiger)*, Cage *(In a Landscape)*, Carter *(Night Fants)* SNE ▲ 553 (16.97)

Biret, Idil (pno)

Famous Piano Music—features works by Chopin *(Impromptu No. 4 in c#, Op. 66 "Fant-Impromptu"; Nocturne Nos. 2 & 8 in E♭ & D♭, Opp. 9/2 & 27/2; Waltzes Nos. 6 & 7 in D♭ & c#, Op. 64/1-2; Waltz No. 1 in E♭, Op. 18, "Grande valse brillante"; Son No. 2 in b♭ for Pno, Op. 35 [Marche funèbre]; Mazurka No. 5 in B♭, Op. 7/1; Polonaises Nos. 3 & 6 in A & A♭, Opp. 40/1 & 53; Prelude No. 15 in D♭, Op. 28/15 "Raindrop"; Etudes No. 3, 5 & 12 in E, G♭ & c, Op. 10/3, 5 & 12; Ballade No. 1 in g, Op. 23)* † PIANO:Thiollier, Francois-Joël; PIANO COLLECTIONS:Famous Piano Music NXIN 4-▲ 504010 [DDD] (19.97)

Biro, Sari (pno)

Sari Biro, w. Emmanuel Vardi (cnd) *(orch unknown)*—features works by Menotti *(Con in f)*, Weiner *(Concertino, Op. 15)*, Milhaud *(Con 2)*, Scarlatti, Mendelssohn, von Sauer & Pick-Mangiagalli *(rec Carnegie Hall, 1949)* PHS ▲ 9280 (17.97)

Blackwood, Easley (pno)

Radical Piano: Modernist Masterpieces from the 1st Half of the 20th Century—features works by Prokofiev *(Sarcasms, Op. 17)*, Stravinsky *(Son)*, Blackwood *(10 Experimental Pieces in Rhythm & Harmony)*, Berg *(Son, Op. 1)*, Neilsen *(3 Pieces, Op. 59)*, Alain *(Dans le rêve laissé par la ballade des pendus de Villon)*, Ives *(Study No. 20)*, Copland *(Pno Vars) (rec WFMT, Chicago, 1994-96)* CED ▲ 27 [DDD] (16.97)

Boegner, Michèle (pno)

Mon ami piano: 42 Pieces from Bach to Stravinsky—features works by Scarlatti *(Son Pastorale)*, Couperin *(Soeur monique)*, Bach *(Prélude & Fugue No. 6)*, Haydn *(Son No. 37)*, Clementi *(Son, Op. 26/3)*, Mozart *(Ah! Vous dirai-je, maman)*, Schumann *(Arabesque, Op. 18)*, Liszt *(Valse-Impromptu)*, Brahms *(Valse, Op. 39/2)*, Saint-Saëns *(Allegro appassionato, Op. 70)*, Debussy *(Clair de lune)*, Satie *(Croquis et agaceries d'un gros bohomme en bois)*, Ravel *(Jeux d'eau)*, Bartók *(6 danses populaires roumaines)*, Prokofiev *(Prélude [from 10 Pièces, Op. 12/7])*, Stravinsky *(Circus Polka)*, others ADES 2-▲ 203742 [AAD]

Bolcolm, William (pno)

Matthews & Scott: Pastimes & Piano Rags Elektra/Nonesuch ▮ 71299-4

Bollard, David (pno)

Songs of Sea & Sky, w. Nigel Westlake (cl)—features works by Sculthorpe, Sutherland, Edwards, Hyde, Isaacs, Banks TALP ▲ TP 4 [DDD]

Bordoni, Paolo (pno)
Piano Waltzes—features works by Chopin *(Waltz in E; Waltzes Op. 69/1 & 2)*, Zichy *(Valse d'Adèle)*, Liszt *(Valse d'Adèle [transcription])*, Schubert *(5 Waltzes, D.976, 949, 844, 980)*, Grieg *(Waltzes, Op. 12/2, 38/8, 47/1, 68/6)*, Debussy *(La plus que lente; Valse romantique)*, Godowsky *(Alt Wien)*, Ravel *(A la manière de Borodin; Valses nobles et sentimentales)* DVX ▲ 29310 [DDD] (16.97)

Borge, Victor (pno)
Victor Borge Live(!) *(a compilation of selections from Borge's mid-1950s albums "Comedy in Music" and "Caught in the Act"; includes the classic 'Phonetic Punctuation')* Sony Masterworks ▲ MDK 48482 (m) [ADD] ▮ MGT 48482

Brailowsky, Alexander (pno)
The Berlin Polydor Recordings, 1928-1934, Vol. 1 *see* Composer section—Chopin:Piano Concerto No. 1, etc. DANR 2-▲ 336 (m) [ADD]

The Berlin Polydor Recordings, 1928-1934, Vol. 2—features works by Debussy, Falla, Mendelssohn, Scarlatti/Tausig, Schubert/Leschetizky, Schubert/Tausig, Schumann, Scriabin, Weber † Liszt:Piano Concerto No. 1; etc. *(see Composer section)* DANR 2-▲ 338 (m) [ADD]

A Retrospective, Vol. 4—features works by Weber, Schumann, Liszt, Wagner, Schubert, Mendelssohn, Debussy, Scriabin, Falla, plus others *(rec 1928-34)* ENPL (Piano Library) ▲ 256 (13.97)

Brendel, Alfred (pno)
The Alfred Brendel Collection—features works by Chopin *(Andante Spianato, etc.)*, Liszt *(Hungarian Rhapsodies)*, Mozart *(Piano Concerti 9 & 14; Sonata in a, K.310, etc.)*, Schubert *(Sonatas D.840 & D.958, etc.)*, Schumann *(Fantasia in C & Symphonic Etudes)* see Composer section for details VC 6-▲ OVC 4015 and OVC 4023-4027 [ADD]

Burnett, Richard (pno)
A Golden Treasury of Historic Pianos—features works by Haydn *(Son 35 in A♭, H.XVI/43 [Moderato]; Son 60 in C, H.XVI/50 [Adagio]; Son in A, H.XVI/12)*, Field *(Nocturnes 1 & 11)*, Clementi *(Monferrinas (3) from Op. 49)*, Schubert *(Son, D.537 [Allegro quasi andantino])*, Verdi *(Romanza [w. Alan Hacker (cl), from Forza del Destino])*, Gottschalk *(Berecuse)*, Arne *(Fair Aurora [w. Canterbury Clerkes])*, Weber *(Son 4 Fl [Rondo vivace, w. Stephen Preston (fl)])*, Mozart *(Qt Pno in g [w. Solomon String Quartet members])*, Brahms *(Son 1, Op. 120 [Andante, w. Alan Hacker (cl)])*, Beethoven *(An die Hoffnung, Op. 32 [w. Ian Partridge (ten)])*, Mendelssohn *(Lieder ohne Worte, Opp. 62/6 & 67/4)* AMON ▲ 64 (16.97)

Busoni, Ferruccio (pno)
The Complete Recordings (1919-1922)—features works by Bach *(Prelude & Fugue in C)*, Bach/arr. Busoni *(Chorale Prelude, BWV.734)*, Beethoven/arr. Busoni *(Ecossaise, WoO.83)*, Chopin *(Études, Op. 10/5 (2 rec'gs)* and Op. 25/5; Nocturne, Op. 15/2; Prelude, Op. 28/7), Liszt *(Hungarian Rhapsody No. 13) see also* Composer section: Busoni—Piano Music and Spanish Rhapsody PHS ▲ 9347 (m) [AAD]

Cápová, Silvia (pno)
Piano Masterpieces—features works by Beethoven *(Für Elise)*, Chopin *(2 Études, 2 Preludes, etc.)*, Liszt *(Consolation No. 3 in D♭)*, Mendelssohn *(Barcarolle)*, Mozart *(Rondo alla turca)*, Rachmaninoff *(Prelude in c#, Op. 3/2)*, Schubert *(Moment musicaux No. 3 in f; Scherzo No. 1 in B♭)*, Schumann *(Das Abends, Aufschwung & Warum, Op. 12/1-3; Träumerei, Op. 15/7)*, Tchaikovsky *(Barcarolle [June], from The Seasons)* STRD ▲ 6020 [DDD] ▮ 6020

Caramia, Tony (pno)
Brass Knuckles: An Excursion into Contemporary Ragtime—features works by Tichenor *(Show Me Rag)*, Albright *(Morning Reveries [from Dream Rags])*, Albright/Bolcolm *(Brass Knuckles [from 3 Novelty Rags])*, Bolcolm *(Graceful Ghost; Dream Shadows [both from 3 Ghost Rags]; Serpent's Kiss [from Garden of Eden])*, Morath *(Golden Hours)*, Caramia *(Travelin' 2-step)*, Frost *(Olympic Stride Waltz; Nocturne; Satisfaction)*, Jenks *(Queen of Violets)*, Hodkinson *(Minnie-Rag)*, Putz *(Minimalist Rag)* ALBA ▲ 253 [DDD]

Chai-Hsio, Tsai (pno)
Children's Suite: Chinese Piano Music—features works by Shan-De *(Suite for Children)*, Wen-Yeh *(The Milky Way on July 7th; Fisherman's Song, Op. 56 [Capriccio]; Lion Dance at New Year)*, Moy *(Theme & Vars [from a Chinese Folk Song])*, Lam *(Flowers & Moonlight on a Spring River, Op. 12/2)*, Wen-Chung *(The Willows Are New)*, Tsang-Houei *(Romance No. 1; Cradle Song No. 2)*, Tcherepnin *(Homage to China No. 3; Kasperlspiel No. 4)*, Liuh-Ting *(Buffalo Boy's Flute) (rec Dec 1988)* THOR ▲ 2034 [ADD] (16.97)

Cherkassky, Shura (pno)
Last of the Great Piano Romantics, Vol. 1—features works by Godowsky, Balakirev, Rachmaninoff, Ravel, J. Strauss, Gould, de Falla, Daquin ASVQ ▲ 6096 [ADD] (10.97)

Piano Recital—features works by Mendelssohn *(Rondo capriccioso, Op. 14)*, Schumann *(Son. in f#, Op. 11)*, Berg *(Son., Op. 1)*, Debussy *(L'isle joyeuse)*, Stravinski *(3 movts. from Petrouchka)*, Poulenc *(Toccata) (rec Dec 5, 1963)* ERM ▲ 133

Chiu, Frederic (pno)
Piano Transcriptions—features works by Bach/arr. Busoni *(Three Organ Chorale Preludes)*, Bach/arr. Rachmaninoff *(Suite from the Partita in E for Violin)*, Schoenberg/arr. Busoni *(Klavierstück, Op. 11/2)*, Schubert/arr. Liszt *(Horch, horch die Lerche; Der Lindenbaum)*, Schubert/arr. Prokofiev *(Waltzes)*, Schubert/arr. Rachmaninoff *(The Brooklet [Wohin?])*, Schumann/arr. Liszt *(Frühlingsnacht)*, Joh. Strauss Jr./arr. Andrei Schulz-Evler *(Concert Arabesque on Themes of On the Beautiful Blue Danube)*, Wagner/arr. Liszt *(Liebestod from Tristan)* HAM ▲ 907054 (17.97)

Clemmow, Caroline (pno), Anthony Goldstone (pno)
The Virtuoso Piano Duo—features works by Brahms *(Son in f, Op. 34b)*, Chopin *(Rondo in C, Op. 73)*, Schütt *(Valse-Paraphrase, Op. 58/1)*, Philipp *(Caprice [en double notes])*, Chaminade *(La Sévillane, Op. 19)*, Sauer *(Die Spieluhr [The Musical Box])*, Gershwin *(Vars on "I Got Rhythm") (rec 1997)* OLY ▲ 626 [DDD] (16.97)

Cliburn, Van (pno)
My Favorite Encores—features works by Chopin *("Revolutionary" Etude, Op. 10/2; Nocturne in E, Op. 62/2; Scherzo No. 2, Op. 31)*, Debussy *(Clair de lune; l'Isle joyeuse; La plus que lente; Reflets dans l'eau; La fille aux cheveux de lin)*, Rachmaninoff *(Etude-tableau in e♭, Op. 39/5)*, Schumann/arr. Liszt *(Widmung)*, Scriabin *(Etude in d#, Op. 8/12)*, Szymanowski *(Etude in b♭, Op. 4/3)* RCAV (Gold Seal) ▲ 60726 [ADD] (10.97) ▮ 60726 (6.98)

A Romantic Collection—features works by Brahms *(Rhapsody in E♭, Op. 119/4)*, Granados *(The Maiden and the Nightingale)*, Liszt *(Consolation No. 3; Sonata in b)*, Rachmaninoff *(Prelude in g#, Op. 32/12)*, Ravel *(Pavane pour une infante défunte; Toccata from Tombeau de Couperin)*, Schumann *(Romance, Op. 28/2)*, Tchaikovsky *(Song of the Lark)* RCAV (Gold Seal) ▲ 60414 [ADD] (10.97) ▮ 60414 (6.98)

Coop, Jane (pno)
The Romantic Piano—features works by Brahms, Chopin, Debussy, Liszt, Mendelssohn, Rachmaninoff, Schumann *(see Piano Music entries under the respective composers in the Composer Section for full details)* MUVI (Musica Viva) ▲ 1015 [DDD] (16.97)

The Romantic Piano, Vol. 2—features works by Chopin *(Mazurka, Op. 50/3; Nouvelle études in f & A♭; Fant.-impromptu, Op. 66)*, Brahms *(Intermezzo, Op. 117/1; Capriccio, Op. 76/2)*, Liszt *(Sonetto 104 del Petrarca; Au bord d'une source)*, R. Schumann *(Zart und singend, Op. 6/14; Romance, Op. 28/2)*, Schubert *(Impromptu, Op. 90/2)*, Rachmaninoff *(Prelude, Op. 23/4)*, Mendelssohn *(Andante & rondo capriccioso, Op. 14)*, Ravel *(Pavane pour une infante défunte)*, Debussy *(La fille aux cheveux de lin; Feux d'artifice) (rec Glenn Gould Studio, CBC Toronto, Ontario, Apr 28-30, 1994)* CBC (Musica Viva) ▲ 1083 [DDD] (16.97)

Copeland, George (pno)
The Victor Solo Recordings—features works by Debussy, Satie, Milhaud, Bach, Albéniz, Turina, plus others *(rec 1933-38 & 1964)* PHS 2-▲ 10001 (33.97)

Cortot, Alfred (pno)
The Complete Acoustic Victor Recordings—features works by Weber *(Invitation to the Dance)*, Mendelssohn *(Scherzo in e; Rondo capriccioso)*, Chopin *(Études, Opp. 10/5 & 25/2, 3, 9 & 11; Impromptu in A♭; Grand Polonaise in E♭; Berceuse & Tarantella)*, Chopin/Liszt *(My Joys)*, Liszt *(Hungarian Rhap 2; La Laggeriezza; Paraphrase on Verdi's Rigoletto)*, Scriabin *(Etude in d#)*, Saint-Saëns *(Étude en forme de Valse)*, Fauré *(Romance in A♭; Berceuse [from Dolly])*, Debussy *(La Fille aux cheveaux du lin; Minstrels)*, Ravel *(Jeux d'eau)*, Albéniz *(Malagueña; Seguidilla; Triana)* Biddulph ▲ LHW 014/15

Cortot Plays Short Works—features works by Purcell *(Minuet; Siciliano)*, Vivaldi *(Con da Camera)*, Bach *(Arioso)*, Handel *(Harmonious Blacksmith)*, Schubert *(Litanei; Ländler (12))*, Brahms *(Wiegenlied)*, Albéniz *(Malagueña; Seguedillas; Sous le Palmier)*, Saint-Saëns *(Caprice en forme de Valse)*, Chopin *(Étude in A♭; Waltz in c#; Impromptu in F#; Ballade in g; Berceuse; My Joys)* Biddulph ▲ LHW 020

The Rarest 78s (1919-1947)—features works by Albéniz, Chopin, Liszt, Purcell, Saint-Saëns, Schumann, Scriabin MUA ▲ 615 (m) [AAD]

Victor Recordings (1919-1926)—features works by Brahms, Chopin, Debussy, Ravel, Saint-Saëns, Schubert PHS ▲ 9386 (m) [AAD] (17.97)

Costa, Sequeira (pno)
A Musical Snuff-Box: Sequeira Costa Plays Encores—features works by Seixas *(Son, in g)*, Daquin *(Le coucou)*, Chopin *(Etude No. 3 in E, Op. 10/3, "Chanson de l'adieu"; Waltz No. 13 in D♭, Op. 70/3)*, Schubert *(Ständchen, "Leise flehen meine lieder")*, Fauré *(Impromptu No. 2 in f, Op. 31)*, Debussy *(Arabesque No. 1)*, Ravel *(Borodin Waltz, "A la manière de...")*, Poulenc *(Mouvements perpétuels No. 1)*, Bortkievich *(Prelude No. 1, Op. 33/1)*, Henselt *(Si oiseau, Op. 2/6)*, Godowsky *(Triakontameron No. 11, "Alt wien")*, R. Strauss *(Ständchen)*, Moszkowski *(Etude de virtuosité No. 6 in F, Op. 72/6)*, Carreño *(Petite valse)*, Guarnieri *(Dansa negra)*, Villa-Lobos *(A lenda do caboclo)*, Levy *(Tango Brasileiro)*, Albéniz *(Tango in D, "España", Op. 165/2; Seguidillas, "Cantos de España", Op. 232/5)*, Mompou *(Cancion y danza No. 6)*, Liadow *(A Musical Snuff-Box, Op. 32)*, Prokofiev *(Waltz, Op. 96 [3 Pieces]) (rec Tamamura-machi Bunka Center, Japan, Nov 24, 1994)* CAMA ▲ 369 [DDD] (18.97)

Crossan, Jack Richard (pno)
The Bach Album *(see Composer section: Bach—Das Wohltemperierte Klavier)* Janus ▮ JAN 1109 (CrO2)

Crossan, Jack Richard (pno) (cont.)
Chopin's Nocturnes Nos. 1-19 *(digitally mastered, unedited single-take studio recordings; plus works by Scarlatti, Schumann & Paradies)* Janus 2-▮ JAN 1101-2 (CrO2)

Crossan in Recital *(digitally mastered, unedited single-take studio recordings)*—features works by Brahms *(2 Capriccios, Op. 76/2 & Op. 116/3)*, Chopin *(Sonata No. 2, Op. 35)*, Debussy *(Arabesque No. 1)*, Griffes *(The White Peacock)*, Mozart *(Rondo in a, K.511)*, Paradies *(Toccata)* Janus ▮ JAN 1108-1 (CrO2)

Crossan in Unique Live Performances *(digitally remastered, unedited recordings)*—features works by Rachmaninoff *(Rhapsody on a Theme by Pagainini (two-piano arrangement, performd by Crossan and Lilian Steuber)*, Bartók *(Allegro barbaro)*, Chopin *(Waltz in c#)*, Poldini *(Japanese Etude)*, Ravel *(Alborada del gracioso)*, Schubert *(Piano Sonata in a, D.784)* Janus ▮ JAN 1107-1 (CrO2)

Keyboard Excursions *(see "Harpsichord" section, above)*

Piano Masterworks, Vol. 1 *(digitally remastered, unedited live recordings)*—features works by Kohs *(Piano Variations)*, Schubert *(Valses nobles, Op. 77)*, Schumann *(Fantasia in C, Op. 17)*, Weber *(Perpetual motion)* Janus ▮ JAN 1102 (CrO2)

Piano Masterworks, Vol. 2 *(digitally remastered, unedited live recordings)*—features works by Bach, Chopin, Debussy, Franck, Mendelssohn, Scarlatti Janus ▮ JAN 1103 (CrO2)

Poulenc's Concerto for 2 Pianos & Orchestra plus solo piano selections by Chopin, Debussy, Charles Previn, Rachmaninoff, Schumann, Schubert Janus ▮ JAN 1104 (CrO2)

Crossan, Jack Richard (pno), Albert Dominguez (pno)
Great Piano Duos—features works by Copland/arr. Bernstein, Gershwin/arr. Crossan, Kohs, Rachmaninoff, Ravel, Saint-Saëns; plus solo piano selections by Chopin, Debussy, Schumann Janus ▮ JAN 1110 (CrO2)

Damerini, Massimiliano (pno)
Piano XX, Vol. 1—features G. Gershwin *(Waltzes Pno)*, C. Ives *(Three-Page Son)*, Janáček *(Son Oct 1, 1905 Pno)*, S. Rachmaninoff *(Études-tableaux Pno, Op. 33 [No. 8 in g])*, M. Ravel *(Valse)*, Scriabin *(Son 9 Pno, Op. 68)*, I. Stravinsky *(Cinq doigts)*, Szymanowski *(Metopes, Op. 29)* AART ▲ 47215 (9.97)

Darré, Jeanne-Marie (pno)
The Early Recordings, w. Paris Conservatory Orch [cnd:A. Cluytens], Colonne Concerts Orch [cnd:P. Paray]—features works by Chopin, Saint-Saëns, J. Strauss, J.S. Bach, Weber, Schumann, Mendelssohn, Liszt, Philipp, Rachmaninoff, Jaray-Janetschek *(rec 1922-47)* VAIA 2-▲ 1065 (m) [ADD] (31.97)

Davis, Ivan (pno)
The Wind Demon & Other 19th Century Piano Music—features works by Warren *(The Andes, Marche Di Bravoura)*, Bristow *(Dream Land, Op. 59)*, Grobe *(United States Grand Waltz, Op. 43)*, Hoffman *(In Memoriam L.M.G.; Dixiana [Caprice for Pno on the Popular Negro Minstrel's Melody Dixie's Land])*, Hopkins *(The Wind Demon, Op. 11)*, Heinrich *(Laurel Waltz [from The Elssler Dances])*, Gottschalk *(Romance)*, Fry *(Adieu [song for pno])*, Bartlett *(Grande Polka de Concert)*, Mason *(Silver Spring, Op. 6; A Pastoral Novellette) (rec Columbia Recording Studios, 30th Street, NYC)* NWW ▲ 80257 (16.97)

Deguchi, Tomoko (pno)
Syncopated Lady—features C. Barnett *(Syncopated Lady)*, J. Bohn *(Preludes (6))*, K. Carpenter *(Even Number of Odd Pieces)*, M. Davidson *(Etudes [Book I])*, Firant *(Shahrazad)*, R. Fleisher *(Secrets)*, C. B. Griffin *(Vernacular Dances)*, A. Kinney *(Son Pno)* CPS ▲ 8665 [DDD] (16.97)

Delgado, Imelda (pno)
Rediscovering...—features works by Schelling *(Nocturne a Ragusa)*, Dello Joio *(Son 3 Pno)*, Hosenpud *(Etude for the Left Hand)*, A. Khachaturian *(Poem)*, Scriabin *(Etudes, Op. 8/2,4 & 10)*, Prokofiev *(Visions Fugitives, Nos. 3, 4, 7, 14, 18 & 20)*, Castro *(Haciendo Nonito)*, Ginastera *(Danzas Argentinas (3))* BOST ▲ 1009 [DDD] (15.97)

Demidenko, Nikolai (pno)
Nikolai Demidenko Live at Wigmore Hall—features A. Berg *(Son Pno, Op. 1)*, Buxtehude *(Prelude & Fugue in d Org)*, Gubaidulina *(Chaconne Pno)*, J. Haydn *(Son in f Pno, H.XVII/6)*, Kalkbrenner *(Nocturne, Op. 129)*, Liszt *(Harmonies poétiques et religieuses, S.173 [No. 7, "Funérailles"]; Trans, Arrs & Paraphrases [Beethoven:An die ferne Geliebte [Op. 98], S.469 (arr 1849)])*, Mendelssohn (-Bartholdy) *(Fant Pno, Op. 28)*, D. Scarlatti *(Sons Kbd [K.11 in d; K.377 in b])*, F. Schubert *(Impromptus (4) Pno [No. 4 in A♭])*, R. Schumann *(Impromptus on a Theme by Clara Wieck, Op. 5)*, Voříšek *(Fant Pno, Op. 12)* HYP 2-▲ 22024 [DDD] (17.97)

Demus, Jörg (pno)
Jörg Demus—features works by Schubert, Schumann, Debussy & Bach *(rec Tokyo, 1988)* ITAL ▲ 48

Depass, Paul (pno)
Wrrnian Eorthe, w. Anne Conrad-Antoville (vc), Anthony C. Antoville (nar)—features works by Scriabin *(Études, Opp. 42/3-5 & 65/3)*, Rachmaninoff *(Prelude in d, Op. posth; Moment musicaux, Op. 16/2 in e♭)*, Chopin *(Étude in Double Sixths for Left Hand [arr Godowsky])*, Liszt *(Soirée de Vienna; Valse-caprice 4)*, Schumann *(Presto passionato, Op. 22)*, Saint-Saëns *(Danse macabre)*, Barber *(Ballade)*, Poulenc *(Presto in B♭)*, Conrad-Antoville *(Elegy of Existence to Extinction)* CRS ▲ CD 9763

Dohnányi, Ernst von (pno)
Ernö Dohnányi—features works by Mozart *(Son. No. 11 in A, K.331)*, Beethoven *(Son. No. 14 in c#, Op. 27/2, "Moonlight")*, Chopin *(Nocturne in B, Op. 62/1; Mazurka in C, Op. 56/2; Impromptu in F#, Op. 36)*, Liszt *(Consolation in D♭, R.12)*, Brahms *(Intermezzo in E)*, Dohnányi *(Rhaps. in f#; Pastorale; March from Humoresques, Op. 17/4)*, Schubert *(Valses nobles [arr. Dohnányi])* HUN ▲ 12085 (m) [ADD] (16.97)

Dorfmann, Ania (pno)
The Columbia Recordings, w. London SO [cnd:Walter Goehr]—features works by Mendelssohn *(Con 1 Pno)*, Weber, Chopin, et al. *(rec 1931-38)* PHS ▲ 10 (17.97)

Dutkiewicz, Andrzej (pno), Ewa Osinka (pno)
Twentieth Century Piano Music From Poland—features works by Borkowski *(Fragmenti for Piano)*, Dutkiewicz *(Suite for Piano)*, Kisielewski *(Danse Vive)*, Lutoslawski *(Bucolics for Piano)*, Malawski *(Tatra Triptych)*, Rudzinski *(Sonata)*, Serocki *(A Suite of Preludes)*, Szeligowsk *(Sonatina)*, Twardowski *(Little Sonata)* OLY ▲ 316 [AAD] (16.97)

Eden, Bracha (pno)
The World's Favorite Piano Music Vol. 1—features works by Bach, Beethoven, Brahms, Chopin, Dvořák, Granados, Liszt, Mendelssohn, Mozart, Prokofiev, Rubinstein, Schubert, Schumann 44510 ▮ COL

The World's Favorite Piano Music Vol. 2—features works by Brahms, Chopin, Debussy, Falla, Gershwin, Liszt, Mendelssohn, Prokofiev, Rachmaninoff, Tchaikovsky 44511 ▮ COL

The World's Favorite Piano Music Vol. 3—features works by Chopin, Daquin, Debussy, Grieg, Liszt, Ravel, Rubinstein, Satie, Sinding, Tchaikovsky 44512 ▮ COL

Eden, Bracha (pno), Alexander Tamir (pno)
Dances around the World—features works by Brahms, Debussy, Dvořák, Grieg, Moszkowski, Rachmaninoff, Rossini, Schubert PWK ▲ 1134 [DDD]

Dances round the World—features works by Brahms *(Hungarian Dances 4 & 6; Waltzes (4), Op. 39)*, Debussy *(Menuet & Ballet)*, Dvořák *(Slavonic Dances 6, 7 & 16)*, Grieg *(Norwegian Dances, Op. 35/2 & 3)*, Moszkowski *(Spanische Tänze, Op. 65/1 & 3)*, Schubert *(Valses sentimentales)*, plus S. Barber, Rachmaninoff, Rossini CACI ▲ 21.0020

Elson-Swarthout Duo [Margret Elson (pno), Elizabeth Swarthout (pno)]
20th Century American 4-Hand Piano Music—features works by Corigliano *(Gazebo Dances)*, Riegger *(The Cry)*, Persichetti *(Con)*, Levinson *(Morning Star)*, Polin *(Phantasmagoria)*, Shifrin *(The Modern Temper)*, Moss *(Omaggio)*, Riegger *(Evocation)* LARL ▲ 859 [DDD] (14.97)

Eskin, Virginia (pno)
Spring Beauties: The Ragtime Project—features works by Schuller *(Sand Point Rag)*, Laufer *(12 Note Rag)*, Zimmerman *(Lost & Found Rag)*, Kuss *(Jump Cut Rag)*, Merryman *(Dog Day Rag)*, Tenny *(Tangled Rag)*, Amlin *(South End Rag)*, Gilbert *(Rag Bag, Op. 19)*, Albright *(Nightmare Fant Rag; Behemoth 2-Step)*, Wheeler *(Calamity Rag; Fits & Starts Rag)*, Berlin/Snyder *(The Mysterious Rag-Characteristic Intermezzo)*, Dykstra *(Spring Beauties)*, Morath *(Anchoria Leland)*, Kozinski *(Maloney Rag)*, Zaimont *(Hesitation Rag)*, St. Clair *(Toccata Rag) (rec July 1997)* KOCH ▲ 7440 [DDD] (16.97)

Feghali, José (pno)
Valse Nobles—features works by Villa-Lobos *(Impressões seresteiras; Alma Brasileira; Valsa da dor)*, Nazareth *(Odeon; Escorregando; Brejeiro; Apanhei-te, Cavaquinho!)*, Lorenzo-Fernandez *(Valsa Surburbana)*, Ravel *(Valses nobles et sentimentales) (rec Aug 26-28, 1991)* KOSS ▲ 1018 [DDD] (17.97)

Feinberg, Alan (pno)
The American Romantic—features works by Beach, Gottschalk, Helps PRGO ▲ 430330-2 [DDD]

Fascinatin' Rhythm—features works by Gershwin *(Promenade)*, Cowell *(Woof I & II)*, Joplin *(Magnetic Rag)*, Waller *(Squeeze Me; Ain't Misbehavin')*, Grainger *(In Dahomey [Cakewalk Smasher])*, Wodehouse *(That Certain Feeling)*, Morton *(Mamanita)*, Nancarrow *(Player Piano Study No. 6)*, Johnson *(The Mule Walk)*, Gottschalk *(Columbia; Bamboula)*, Gershwin/Wild *(Fascinating Rhythm)* PRGO ▲ 44457 (16.97)

Fergus-Thompson, Gordon (pno)
Reverie—features works by Bach *(Jesu, joy of man's desiring; Wachet auf!)*, Brahms *(Intermezzo, Op. 118/2)*, Debussy *(Arabesque No. 1; Clair de lune; Rêverie)*, Glinka *(The Lark)*, Godowsky *(Alt Wien)*, Grieg *(Butterfly; Nocturne)*, Ravel *(Forlane; Pavane pour une infante défunte)*, Saint-Saëns *(The Swan)*, Schumann *(Arabesque; Träumerei)*, Scriabin *(Etude, Op. 42/4)* ASV ▲ 2066 (12.97)

Fessel, Erik (pno)
Danish Piano Music of the Golden Age DANR 2-▲ 434 (34.97)

PIANO

Fialkowska, Janina (pno)

La Jongleuse: Salon Pieces & Encores—features works by Moszkowski *(La jongleuse, Op. 52/4; Pantomime, Op. 77/8)*, Albéniz *(Navarra)*, Tausig *(Ungarische Zigeunerweisen)*, Henselt *(Etude, Op. 2/6)*, D. Scarlatti *(Son in G, K.427)*, Rosenthal *(Carnaval de Vienne)*, Chopin *(Waltz, Op. 64/2; Mazurka, Op. 59/1)*, Mendelssohn *(Spinnerlied, Op. 67/4)*, Grieg *(Butterfly, Op. 43/1; At the Cradle, Op. 68/5)*, Poulenc *(Intermezzo 3; Presto in B♭)*, Prokofiev *(Suggestion diabolique, Op. 4/4)*, Paderewski *(Nocturne, Op. 16/4)*, Bach *(Jesu, Joy of Man's Desiring [arr Myra Hess]) (rec Glenn Gould Studio, Toronto, July 31-Aug 2, 1996)* CBC ▲ 1114 [DDD] (16.97)

Fingerhut, Margaret (pno)

Russian Piano Music of the Mighty Handful—features works by Balakirev, Borodin, Cui, Mussorgsky & Rimsky-Korsakov CHN ▲ 8439 [DDD] (16.97)

Fiorentino, Sergio (pno)

Sergio Fiorentino in Germany—features works by Bach/Busoni *(Prelude & Fugue in D, BWV 532 [arr. Fiorentino])*, Beethoven *(Son 31 in A♭, Op. 110)*, Chopin *(Son No. 2 in b♭, Op. 35; Waltzes Nos. 1 in E♭, Op. 18 & 7 in c#, Op. 64/2)*, Scriabin *(Son No. 4 in F#, Op. 30)*, Schumann *(Fant in C, Op. 17)*, Liszt/Gounod *(Valse de l'opéra Faust, S.407)*, J. Strauss II/Tausig *(Man lebt nur einmal!)*, J. Strauss II/Godowsky *(Die Fledermaus)*, Tchaikovsky *(Waltz in A♭, Op. 40/8 [arr. Fiorentino])*, Brahms *(Liebesliederwalzer, Op. 52 [arr. Fiorentino]) (rec live, 1993)* APR 2-▲ 7036 [ADD] (38.97)

Firkušný, Rudolf (pno)

Vol 2:Czech Piano Music BN ▲ BN 2439/1

Fischer, Edwin (pno)

Edwin Fischer *(1931-1938 HMV recordings)*—features works by Bach/arr. Fischer *(Ricercar from A Musical Offering, arr. for piano & chamnber orchestra; rec. 1933)*, Bach/arr. Busoni *(Prelude & Fugue in E♭, "St. Anne"; rec. 1933)*, Beethoven *(Piano Sonata No. 31 in A♭, Op. 110; rec. 1938)*, Handel *(Chaconne in G; rec. 1931)*, Marcello/arr. Bach *(Adagio from Concerto No. 3 in d; rec. 1933)*, Mozart *(Piano Sonata No. 11 in A, K.331; rec. 1933)*, Schubert *(Impromptu in B♭, Op. 142/3; rec. 1938)* PHS ▲ 9481 (m) [AAD] (18.97)

Fleisher, Leon (pno)

Recital: Piano Works for the Left Hand—features works by Takacs, Saint-Saëns, Saxton, J.S. Bach, Blumenfeld, Scriabin, Godowsky *(rec June 21-24, 1992)* COL ▲ 48081 (16.97)

Foreman, Charles (pno)

Ballade—features works by Violet Archer, John Beckwith, Jean Coulthard, John Hawkins, Jacques Hètu, Oskar Morawetz *(rec 1984)* CTR ▲ CMC 1684 [DDD]

Frankl, Peter (pno)

The Hungarian Anthology—features works by Liszt *(Csárdás Macabre)*, Dohnanyi *(Gavotte & Musette)*, Kodaly *(7 Pieces for Piano, Op. 11)*, Bartok *(Dance Suite)*, Weiner *(3 Hungarian Rural Dances)*, Kurtag *(Plays & Games for Piano)*, Szollosy *(Paessaggio con morti)* ASV ▲ 860 (16.97)

Franzetti, Allison Brewster (pno)

South American Landscapes—features works by Piazolla, Mignone, Guarnieri, Guastavino, Ginastera, Villa-Lobos, Carlos Franzetti PREM ▲ 1036 [DDD] (16.97)

Freire, Nelson (pno)

In Recital—features works by Mozart, Chopin, Debussy, Villa-Lobos, Albéniz, Albéniz-Godowsky, Rachmaninoff *(rec Gusman Cultural Center, Miami, Florida, Dec 13, 1984)* AUDO ▲ 72023 (16.97)

Friedman, Ignaz (pno)

The Complete Solo Recordings: 1923-1936—features works by anon, Beethoven *(Son No. 14: comp master recording, plus alternate takes of movts 2 & 3)*, Chopin *(see Composer section under "Chopin: Pno Music" for listing of pieces)*, Dvořák, Friedman *(3 original works)*, Gaertner, Gluck, Grieg *(Pno Con, comp [w. Philippe Gaubert (cnd); rec 1928])*, Hummel, Liszt, Mendelssohn, Mittler, Moszkowski, Mozart, Paderewski, Rubinstein, Scarlatti, Schubert, Suk, Weber; plus "Friedman speaks on Chopin" & "Friedman speaks on Paderewski" (from 1940 New Zealand Radio transcription discs) PHS 4-▲ 2000 (m) [AAD] (66.97)

Piano Recital—features A. Dvořák *(Humoresques, Op. 101)*, I. Friedman *(Trans Pno [Paganini/Liszt/Busoni:La campanella [from Paganini's Concerto No. 2 for Violin]])*, J. N. Hummel *(Rondo Pno, Op. 11)*, Liszt *(Hungarian Rhaps, S.244 [No. 2 in c#])*, Moszkowski *(Serenata, Op. 15/1)*, W. A. Mozart *(Son 11 Pno, K.331/330i [Rondo alla turca])*, I. J. Paderewski *(Minuet, Op. 14/1)*, A. Rubinstein *(Romance in E♭, Op. 44)*, F. Schubert *(Marche militaire, D.733/1)*, C. M. Weber *(Invitation to the Dance Pno, J.260)* MTAL ▲ 48055 (6.97)

Gabrilowitsch, Ossip (pno)

The Complete Recordings 1923-29, w. Detroit SO [cnd:O. Gabrilowitsch], Flonzaley String Quartet, Harold Bauer (pno)—features works by Arenksy *(Suite 1, Op. 15; Près de la mer, Op. 52/4)*, Schütt *(Impromptu-Rococco)*, Gabrilowitsch *(Caprice)*, J. S. Bach *(Bouree)*, plus pno music by Grainger, Delibes, Glazunov, Gluck, Schumann, Moszkowski, Brahms, Tchiakovsky, Chabrier, Altschuler, plus others 9809 2-▲ 51

His Issued & Unissued Recordings (1923-1929)—features works by Schumann *(w. the Flonzaley String Quartet)*, Arensky *(w. Harold Bauer (rec.1929 issued version and a 1928 unissued recording])*, Scheutt *(w. Harold Bauer)*, Bach/arr. Saint-Saëns, Delibes, Gabrilowitsch, Glazunov, Gluck/arr. Brahms, Grainger, Moszkowski, Schumann VAIA ▲ 1018 (m) [ADD] (17.97)

Garzón, Maria (pno)

Piano Music of Spain—features works by Albéniz, Falla, Granados, Mompou, Soler, Yagüe ASV ▲ 798 [DDD]

Gaylord, Monica (pno)

Black Piano—features Coleridge-Taylor *(Valse-Suite Pno, Op. 71)*, Dett *(In the Bottoms)*, Ellington *(Come Sunday)*, U. Kay *(Inventions (3))*, O. Peterson *(Gentle Waltz)*, W. G. Still *(Traceries; Visions (3))*, H. Swanson *(Cuckoo Pno)*, Work, Jr. *(Big Bunch of Roses)* MUA ▲ 737 [DDD] (16.97)

Piano Music by William Grant Still & Other Black Composers—features works by Still *(3 Visions; 7 Traceries)*, Swanson *(The Cuckoo)*, Dett *(In the Bottoms)*, Kay *(3 Inventions in g, a & C)*, Work, Jr. *(Big Bunch of Roses)*, Peterson *(The Gentle Waltz [arr D. McErlain])*, Ellington *(Come Sunday [arr D. McErlain])*, Coleridge-Taylor *(Valse-Suite, Op. 71) (rec Studio 318, Toronto, Canada, 1992)* MUA ▲ 737 [DDD] (16.97)

Gierzod, Kazmierz (pno)

Polish Piano Works—features works by Podbielski *(Präludium)*, Oginski *(Polonaise)*, Chopin *(2 Polonaises; Nocturne, Op. 27/2)*, Paderewski *(Minuet, Op. 141; Melody, Op. 16/2; Krakowiak, Op. 14/6)*, Rozycki *(Ave Maria; Campo Santo; Dogaressa, Barcarolle; La mort de Beatrice Centi)*, Szymanowski *(Etude, Op. 4/3; Mazurka; Krakowiak; Oberek; Polonaise)*, Malawski *(Miniatures)* Binaural Source-Midas ▲ C-10

Gieseking, Walter (pno)

Broadcast Recitals, 1949-1951 *see* Composer section: Bach—English Suites; etc. MUA 4-▲ 743 [AAD]

A Retrospective, Vol. 1 *(1924-1940 Homochord, Parlophone and Columbia recordings, plus unissued live recordings from 1947-1956)*—features works by Poulenc *(Mouvements perpetuels)*, Debussy *(Deux Arabesques)*, Chopin *(Barcarolle)*, Beethoven *(Bagatelle Op. 33/1; Piano Sonatas 20 & 30)*, Bach *(Partita No. 1 in B♭—Prelude and Sarabande, Minuets & Gigue)*, Brahms *(Intermezzo in b♭ Op. 117/2)*, Scriabin *(Four Pieces Op. 51)*, Fauré *(Nocturne No. 4 in E♭, Op. 36)*, Brahms *(Capriccio in f#, Op. 76/1)*, Mendelssohn *(Andante & Rondo capriccioso)* PHS ▲ 9930 (m) [AAD] (17.97)

Vol. 2—features works by J.S. Bach, Falla, Chopin, Liszt, Beethoven, Scriabin *(rec 1931-51)* PHS ▲ 9011 [AAD] (17.97)

Gilels, Emil (pno)

Caregie Hall Recital, 1969—features works by J.S. Bach, Beethoven, Medtner, Prokofiev, Ravel, Chopin *(rec Feb 2, 1969)* MUA ▲ 773 [AAD] (16.97)

Emil Gilels Edition, Vols. 1-5—features works by Beethoven *(Sons 8, 14 & 29 Pno)*, Schubert *(Impromptu in f, D.935/1; Moments musicaux, D.780)*, Ravel *(Pavane pour une Infante défunte; Jeux d'eau)*, Medtner *(Son-reminiscenza in a, Op. 38/1)*, Chopin *(Etude in A♭, Op. posth; Etude in f, Op. 25/2; Con 1 Pno [w. K. Kondrashin (cnd), Moscow PO]; Ballade 1, Op. 23)*, Prokofiev *(Scherzo & March [from The Love for 3 Oranges, Op.33])*, Poulenc *(Concert champêtre in D [w. K. Kondrashin (cnd), Moscow PO])*, Mozart *(Son Pno, K.281; Vars (6) on "Salve tu, Domine", K.398; Vars (10) on "Unser dummer Pöbel meint", K.455; Fant in d, K.397; Son in a, K.310)*, Shostakovich *(Son 2 Pno, Op. 64)*, R. Schumann *(Arabeske, Op. 18)*, Scriabin *(Son 3 Pno; Preludes (5), Op. 74)* MELD 5-▲ 40116 [ADD] (33.97)

The First Russian Recordings—features works by Chopin, Liszt, Lully-Godowsky, Mendelssohn, Prokofiev & Schumann *(rec 1934-38)* ENPL (Piano Library) ▲ 235 (13.97)

Godowsky, Leopold (pno)

The Pianist's Pianist, Vol. 2—features works by Chopin, Mendelssohn, Liszt, Henselt, Rubinstein, Godowsky, Smith, Schubert, Bishop, Albeniz, Schutt, Rubinstein, Henselt, Sinding, Zeckwer, Lane, Verdi, Dohnanyi, Debussy APR ▲ APR 7011 [AAD]

Goldberg, Loretta (pno)

Tone over Tone—features works by George Boziwick, John Cage, Constance Cooper, John Eaton, Sorrel Hays, Mathew Rosenblum OPS1 ▲ OO 135

Goldstone, Anthony (pno)

The Britten Connection—features works by L. Berkeley, Bridge, Britten, Ireland, C. Matthews, R. Stevenson 6656 ▲ 526 [DDD]

Goldstone, Anthony (pno), Caroline Clemmow (pno)

Play Virtuoso Variations for Piano Duet—features works by Alkan, Beethoven, Franck, Schubert, Herzogenberg, Mendelssohn, Moscheles SYMP ▲ SYM 1037

Gould, Glenn (pno)

The Glenn Gould Edition *(The first ten releases plus a sampler disc, listed directly following, launch a two-year project which will encompass Gould's complete CBS Masterworks discography, including previously unissued studio recordings, the complete radio and television soundtracks that Gould recorded for the CBC, and live concert recordings from Toronto, Salzburg, Moscow and elsewhere)*

—features works by Bach *(Harpsichord Concerti 1-5 & 7; see Composer section)* COL 2-▲ 52591 (31.97)

—features works by Bach *(Goldberg Variations, etc.; see Composer section)* COL ▲ 52594 (16.97)

—features works by Beethoven *(Bagatelles & Vars; see Composer section)* COL 2-▲ 52646 (31.97)

—features works by Beethoven *(Cons for Pno (complete); see Composer section)* COL 3-▲ 52632 (47.97)

—features works by Beethoven *(Syms 5 & 6 (piano transcriptions); see Composer section)* COL ▲ 52636 (16.97)

—features works by Grieg *(Sonata,)*, Bizet & Sibelius *(see Composer section)* COL 2-▲ 52654 (31.97)

—features works by Hindemith *(5 Sonatas for Solo Brass Instruments & Piano; see Composer section)* COL 2-▲ 52671 (31.97)

—features works by Mozart *(Piano Concerto No. 24, etc.; see Composer section)* COL ▲ 52626 (16.97)

—features works by Strauss *(Piano Sonata, etc.; see Composer section)* COL 2-▲ 52657 (31.97)

Glenn Gould Legacy, Vol. 2 *(see COMPOSER section: Haydn:Sonatas, etc.)* COL 3-▲ 39036 (47.97)

Glenn Gould Plays Contemporary Music—features works by Anhalt, Morawetz, et al. *(see Composer section)* COL ▲ 52677 (16.97)

Images—features works by Bach *(Italian Con in F for Hpd, BWV 971; Invention in C for Hpd:2-Part, BWV 772; Invention in F for Hpd:2-Part, BWV 779; French Suite No. 2 in c for Hpd, BWV 813; Prelude & Fugue No. 1 in C for Hpd, BWV 846; Goldberg Vars for Hpd, BWV 988; Sinfs in g & b, BWV 797 & 801; Partita No. 1 in B♭ for Hpd, BWV 825; Prelude & Fugue in f# for Hpd, BWV 883; Toccata in g for Hpd, BWV 915)*, Brahms *(Rhap No. 1 for Pno, Op. 79)*, Gibbons *(Allemande [Italian Ground])*, Haydn *(Son in C for Pno, Hob. XVI:48 [Rondo. Presto])*, C. P. E. Bach *(Son in a, Wg.49 "Wurrenberg" [Allegro assai])*, Wagner *(Die Meistersinger von Nürnberg [Act 1 Prelude])*, Sibelius *(Sonatina No. 1 in f# for Pno, Op. 67 [Allegro moderato])*, Beethoven *(Con No. 5 in E♭ for Pno & Orch, Op. 73 "Emperor" [Rondo])*, Bizet *(Nocturne in F for Pno)*, R. Strauss *(Son in b for Pno, Op. 5 [Scherzo. Presto -Trio])*, Scriabin *(Deux morceaux, Op. 57 [Caresse dansée])*, Mozart *(Son No. 11 in A for Pno, K.331 [Alla Turca. Allegretto])*, Scarlatti *(Son in G, K.486)*, Prokofiev *(Son No. 7 in B♭ for Pno, Op. 83 [Allegro inquiero])* COL 2-▲ 62588 (23.97)

Thirty-Two Short Films about Glenn Gould *(motion picture soundtrack)*—features works by J.S. Bach *(Aria; Var. 19 [both from Goldberg Vars.]; Invention No. 13; Prelude [from English Suite No. 5]; Prelude No. 2; Prelude, Gigue [from English Suite No. 2]; Fugue No. 14; Sarabande [from French Suite No. 1]; Prelude in d; Prelude No. 1 in C; Contrapunctus 9)*, Beethoven *(Son. No. 13 [excerpt]; 32 Vars. on an Original Theme [excerpts]; Son. No. 17 [excerpt])*, Hindemith *(Son. No. 3 [excerpt])*, Prokofiev *(Son. No. 7 [excerpt])*, Schoenberg *(Suite for Piano [excerpt]; 6 Little Pieces [excerpt])*, Scriabin *(Desir [from 2 Pieces])*, Sibelius *(Sonatine for Piano [excerpt])*, R. Strauss *(Son. in b [excerpt])*, Wagner *(Prelude [from Tristan und Isolde; w. NBC SO (cond.:A. Toscanini)])* COL ▲ 46686 (16.97)

Grainger, Percy (pno)

Percy Grainger Plays *(1923-31 studio & 1948 live recordings)*—features works by Bach/Busoni, Bach/Liszt, Bach/Grainger, Chopin, Debussy, Grainger, Grieg, Schumann PHS ▲ 9957 (m) [AAD] (17.97)

Groote, Steven de (pno)

Van Cliburn International Piano Competition Retrospective Series, Vol. 1—features works by Haydn, Schubert, Chopin, Prokofiev VAIA ▲ 1145 [ADD] (16.97)

Grünfeld, Alfred (pno)

Alfred Grünfeld—features works by Bach *(Gavotte in d)*, Schubert *(Moment Musical, Op. 94/4; Impromptu, Op. 90/2)*, Chopin *(Mazurkas Opp. 67 & 334; Nocturne, Op. 32/2; Waltzes Opp. 34/2, 64/2 & post.)*, Schumann *(Vogel als Prophet; Traumerei; Schlummerlied)*, Brahms *(Capriccio, Op. 76/2; Waltzes, Op. 39/1-8 & 15)*, Grieg *(Schmetterling; Voglein; Sie Tanzt)*, Moszkowski *(Guitarre)*, Debussy *(Golliwog's Cakewalk)*, Korngold *(Wichtelmännchen)*, Goldmark *(Verloren)*, Wagner *(Liebestod arr. Liszt)*, J. Strauss (II) *(Frühlingstimmen Waltz arr. Grünfeld; Soirée de Vienne arr. Grünfeld)* POHS ▲ 9850 [AAD]

Grunschlag, Rosi (pno), Toni Grunschlag (pno)

Grunschlag & Grunschlag—features works by E. Bacon & O. Luening *(Coal Scuttle Blues)*, E. W. Ballou *(Sonata for 2 Pianos)*, N. Dello Joio *(Aria & Toccata for 2 Pianos)*, Hindemith *(Sonata for 2 Pianos)*, Martinu *(La Fantasie)*, Milhaud *(Les songes)*, R. Starer *(Sonata for 2 Pianos) (rec 1981 & 1991)* CRI ▲ 606 [ADD/DDD] (16.97)

Guller, Youra (pno)

The Art of Youra Guller, 1895-1980—features works by Albéniz, Bach, Balbastre, Chopin, Couperin, Daquin, Granados *(rec late 1970s)* NIMB ▲ 5030 (16.97)

Haddens [Frances Roots Hadden (pno), Richard Hadden (pno)]

Adventures in Music-Making: A Fresh Look at the Greats—features works by Bach *(Chorale Prelude, In Dir ist Freude; Vivace from Trio Sonata No. 2 for Organ, BWV 526)*, Gershwin *(Prelude No. 2)*, Milhaud *(Braziliera, from Scaramouche)*, Mozart *(Andante from 2-Piano Sonata K.448)*, Rachmaninoff *(Russian Easter & Tears, from 2-Piano Suite No. 1, Op. 5)*, Madeleine Dring *(Three Fantastic Variations on 'Lilliburlero,' for 2 Pianos)*, Frances Roots Hadden *(Fantasia on 'The Forgotten Factor'; Two Hundred Years, A Celebration:Bicentennial Suite)*, R. M. Hadden *(The Bells Must Ring!)*, W. L. Reed *(Prelude to 'Annie the Valiant')*, A. B. *(Jamaican Rhumba)*, Madeleine Dring *(Tarantelle)*, Benny Goodman *(Stomping at the Savoy)*, Morton Gould *(arrangement of Turkey in the Straw)*, Kay Kellogg *(arrangement of Dark Eyes)*, Ernesto Lecuona *(Gitanerias [Band of Gypsies])*, Alexandre Tansman *(Cakewalk, from Carnival Suite for 2 Pianos)* CMB ▲ 1065 [DDD]

Hall, Steven (pno)

Classic Piano—features works by J.S. Bach *(Chromatic Fant. & Fugue)*, D. Scarlatti *(Sons. in d, K.32 & d, K.141)*, Clementi *(Son. in f#, Op. 26/2)*, Beethoven *(Vars. in c)*, Mendelssohn *(Rondo Capriccioso, Op. 14)*, Chopin *(Ballade in f, Op. 52; Nocturne in D♭, Op. 27/2)*, Liszt *(Hungarian Rhap. No. 2) (rec Atlanta, GA, Dec 1988)* ACAD ▲ 20006 (16.97)

Hamelin, Marc-André (pno)

The Composer-Pianists—features works by Busoni *(Fant nach J. S. Bach)*, Feinberg *(Berceuse)*, plus Alkan, Godowsky, Hamelin, Medtner, Rachmaninoff, Scriabin, Sorabji HYP ▲ 67050 (17.97)

Marc-Andre Hamelin live at Wigmore Hall—features works by Beethoven/Alkan *(Con. 3 for Pno [1st movt.; w. Alkan's cadenza])*, Chopin/Balakirev *(Con. 1 for Pno [Romanza])*, Alkan *(3 grandes études, Op. 76)*, Busoni *(Sonatina 6 [Carmen Fant.])*, Godowsky *(Gardens of Buitenzorg)*, Medtner *(Danza festivo)* HYP ▲ 66765 (17.97)

Harris, Johana (pno)

Johana Harris: A Living Legacy *(two volumes—see COMPOSER section:Debussy:Children's Corner Suite, etc.)*

Haskil, Clara (pno)

Clara Haskil at the Ludwigsburg Festival—features works by Schumann *(Vars. on the Name "Abegg", Op. 1)*, Beethoven *(Son. No. 32 in c, Op. 111)*, Ravel *(Sonatina)*, D. Scarlatti, J.S. Bach & Debussy *(rec Apr 11, 1953)* MUA ▲ 859 [AAD] (17.97)

Clara Haskil in Ludwigsburg—features works by Bach *(Toccata in E, BWV 914)*, D. Scarlatti *(Sons in b, C & E♭)*, Beethoven *(Son 32 in c)*, Schumann *(A-B-E-G-G Vars)*, Debussy *(Studio-Etudes 7, "Pour les Degrés Chromatiques" & 10, "Pour les Sonoritèes")*, Ravel *(Sonatina in f#)* STRV ▲ 13602 [ADD] (12.97)

Heidsieck, Éric (pno)

Hommage à Rouget de Lisle—features La Marseillaise in the styles of Beethoven, Mozart, Bach, Handel, Schumann, Schubert, Chopin, Liszt, Mendelssohn, Brahms, Weber, Rachmaninoff, Grieg, Faure, Debussy, Couperin, Ravel, Stravinsky, Prokofiev AB ▲ 1404 (13.97)

Henry, Yves (pno)

Dou-Dou Piano—features 21 lullabies by Schumann, Chopin, Ravel, Liszt, Brahms, Stravinsky, Dutilleux, et al. ADES ▲ 604212

Herscovitch, Daniel (pno)

The Hands the Dream—features works by Hair *(Under Aldebaran; Seven Fleeting Glimpses)*, Whiticker *(The Hands the Dream)*, Vella *(Memory Pieces)*, Werder *(A Little Piano Music)*, Smalley *(Variations on a Theme of Chopin; Barcarolle)*, Kos *(Piano Sonata) (rec Dec 1990)* TALP ▲ TP 20 [DDD]

Hersh, Paul (pno), David Montgomery (pno)

Great Ragtime Classics 9543 ▮ RCA

Hess, Myra (pno)

A Cameo—features works by Mozart *(Con. No. 9 [w. Concertgebouw Orch. (cond.:Eduard van Beinem)])*, Bach *(Toccata in G; Jesu, J. of Man's Desiring [arr. Hess])*, D. Scarlatti *(selected Sons.)*, Chopin *(Nocturnes)*, Field *(Schwann)*, Beethoven *(Bagatelles)*, Brahms *(Kinderstücke) (rec 1928-50)* PHS ▲ 9114 [ADD] (17.97)

Dame Myra Hess—features works by Bach *(Jesu, Joy of Man's Desiring; Gigue in G; Prelude & Fugue in C#; Allegro in G)*, D. Scarlatti *(Sons Pno in C & c)*, Schubert *(Son Pno in A, D.664; Rosamunde [ballet music])*, Beethoven *(Bagatelle in B♭)*, Brahms *(Intermezzo in C; Capriccio in b)*, Schumann *(Vogel Als Prophet)*, Mendelssohn *(Duetto; Spinning Song)*, Palmgren *(Cradle Song)*, Ravel *(Pavane pour une infante defunte; Poissons d'or)*, Griffes *(The White Peacock)*, Falla *(Ritual Fire Dance)*, Debussy *(La fille aux cheveaux du lin)* BPS ▲ 24

Dame Myra Hess, Vol. 1 *(1928-37 Columbia recordings)*—features works by Bach *(Gigue from French Suite No. 5; Jesu, joy of man's desiring)*, Beethoven *(Cello Sonata in A, Op. 69; w. Emanuel Feuermann)*, Brahms *(Capriccio in b, Op. 76/2)*, Chopin *(Nocturne in f#, Op. 15/2)*, Debussy *(Poissons d'Or, from Images; La fille aux cheveux de lin & Minstrels, from Preludes Book 1)*, Dvořák *(Slavonic Dance in C, Op. 46/1; w. Hamilton Harty, 2nd piano)*, Mendelssohn *(Song without Words No. 18 in A♭, Op. 38/6)*, Schubert *(Sonata in A, D.664)* PHS ▲ 9462 (m) [AAD] (17.97)

▲ = CD ♦ = Enhanced CD △ = MD ▮ = Cassette Tape ▯ = DCC

Hinderas, Natalie (pno)

Piano Music by African-American Composers—features works by Arthur Cunningham, R. Nathaniel Dett, Talib Rasul Hakim, Thomas Kerr, Hale Smith, William Grant Still, George Walker, Olly Wilson, John Wesley Work III *(rec Sept-Oct 1970)* CRI ▲ 629 [ADD] (31.97)

Hobson, Ian (pno)

Hobson's Choice—features works by Grainger, Chopin, J.S. Bach, Mendelssohn, Tchaikovsky, Liszt, Rosenthal ARA ▲ 6639 [DDD] (16.97)

The London Piano School, Vol. 1 *see COMPOSER section: J. C. Bach, Burton, Busby, Clementi, Dussek, Wesley)* ARA ▲ 6594 (16.97)

Vol. 2: Romantic Pioneers *see COMPOSER section: Clementi, Cramer, Field, Pinto, Weber)* ARA ▲ 6595 (16.97)

Vol. 3: Early Victorian Masters *see COMPOSER section: Bennett, Chipp, Cramer, Moscheles, Wesley)* ARA ▲ 6596 (16.97)

Hofmann, Josef (pno)

The Complete Josef Hofmann, Vol. 1 *see COMPOSER section: Chopin—Concertos for Piano)* VAIA ▲ 1002 (m) [ADD] (17.97)

The Complete Josef Hofmann, Vol. 2—features performances by Curtis Institute Student Orchestra cond. by Fritz Reiner *(Brahms; Hofmann; Rubinstein; Chopin; Beethoven/arr Rubinstein; Mendelssohn; Moszkowski; Rachmaninoff)*, Curtis Institute Student Orchestra [cond.:Ignace Hilsberg] *(excerpts from a Carnegie Hall Concert of 3/24/45 (Chopin) (rec live, Metropolitan Opera House, New York City, Nov 28, 1937)* VAIA 2-▲ 1020 (m) [ADD] (31.97)

The Complete Josef Hofmann, Vol. 3—features works by Beethoven *(Moonlight Sonata, Op. 27/1 [1st movt])*, Chopin *(Valse in A♭, Op. 34/1; Valse in c#, Op. 64/2; Valse in e, Op. Post [2 versions]; Polonaise, Op. 40/1 [2 versions]; Impromptu No. 1, Op. 29; Fantasie-Impromptu, Op. 66; Berceuse, Op. 57; Chant Polonaise [arr Liszt], Nocturne, Op. 9/1)*, Dillon *(Birds at Dawn, Op. 20/2)*, Gluck *(Gavotte [arr Brahms])*, Grieg *(Papillon, Op. 43/1 [2 versions])*, Hofmann *(The Sanctuary)*, Liszt *(Liebestraum No. 3; Concert Etude No. 1; Venezia e Napoli—"Tarantella" [abridged])*, Mendelssohn *(Spinning Song, Op. 67/4 [2 versions]; Rondo Capriccioso, Op. 14 [abridged]; Spring Song, Op. 62/6 [2 versions]; Hunting Song, Op. 19/3 [2 versions])*, Moszkowski *(La Jongleuse; Caprice Espagnole, Op. 37 [abridged])*, Paderewski *(Minuet in G)*, Parker *(Valse Gracile)*, Rachmaninoff *(Prelude, Op. 23/2 [2 versions]; Prelude, Op. 23/5)*, Rubinstein *(Valse-caprice; Miniatures, Book 9, No. 7)*, Schubert *(Marche Militaire [arrTausig, 2 versions]; Der Erlkönig [arr Liszt, 2 versions])*, Schumann *(Fantasiestücke, Op. 12/3)*, Sternberg *(3rd Etude, Op. 120) (rec 1903 & 1912-1918)* VAIA 2-▲ 1036 [ADD] (31.97)

The Complete Josef Hofmann, Vol. 4—features works by Beethoven *(Turkish March [arr Rubinstein])*, Chopin *(Scherzo No. 1, Op. 20 [abridged]; Nocturne in f#, Op. 15/2; Waltz in c#; Polonaise in A, Op. 40/1; Chant Polonais, "My Joys" [arr Liszt])*, Gluck *(Gavotte [arr Brahms])*, Hofmann *(Nocturne [from* Mignonettes*])*, Liszt *(Concert Study No. 1, Paganini Etude No. 3, Hungarian Rhapsody No. 2 [2 versions, 1 abridged])*, Rachmaninoff *(Prelude in c#, Op. 3/2; Prelude in g, Op. 23/5)*, Rubinstein *(Melody in F, Op. 3/1)*, Scarlatti *(Pastorale & Capriccio [arr Tausig])*, Wagner *(Magic Fire Music [arr Brassin]) (rec 1922-23)* VAIA ▲ 1047 [ADD] (17.97)

The Complete Josef Hofmann, Vol. 5—features works by Hofmann *(Berceuse, Op. 20/5 [w. Efrem Zimbalist (vn); plus solo version]; Elegy)*, Chopin *(Waltzes, Opp. 18, 42 & 64/1; Nocturnes Opp. 9/2, 15/2 & 27/2; Polonaises, Opp. 40/1 & 74/1 & 12; Son 3, Op. 58 [Allegro maestoso]; Polonaise, Op. 40/1; Andante Spianato & Grande Polonaise, Op. 22; Berceuse, Op. 57)*, Beethoven *(Son 18, Op.31/3 [Scherzo])*, Mendelssohn *(Song Without Words, Op. 4/4; Rondo capriccioso, Op. 14)*, Liadov *(Musical Snuff Box)*, Weber *(Son 1, Op. 24 [Presto-Rondo])*, Liszt *(Liebestraum 3)*, Rachmaninoff *(Prelude, Op. 3/2)*, Prokofiev *(March, Op. 12/1)*, Debussy *(Clair de lune)*, Gluck *(Mélodie [from Orfeo et Euridice; arr Sgambati]) (rec 1935-48)* MRSN 2-▲ 52004 [ADD] (35.97)

Höjer, Olof (pno)

La Belle Inconnue - Forgotten Pearls from the Classical Era in Sweden MAP ▲ *

Horenstein, Jascha (pno)

Horenstein in Paris, w. French National Orch—features works by Haydn, Mahler [w. Marian Anderson (contralto)], Gluck [w. Marian Anderson (contralto)], Prokofiev; also includes Horenstein conducting Beethoven [American SO; rec. No. 9, 1960], Nielsen [w. Hallé Orch.; rec. Nov. 22, 1956] *(rec live, Paris, Nov 22, 1956)* MUA 2-▲ 784 [AAD] (32.97)

Horowitz, Vladimir (pno)

At the Met—features works by Scarlatti *(Sonatas L. 186, 118, 189, 494, 33, 224)*, Chopin *(Ballade, Op. 52; Waltz, Op. 69)*, Liszt, Rachm *(Prelude Op. 23, No. 5)*, Liszt *(Ballade 2 Pno)* RCAV (Gold Seal) ▲ 61416 (10.97) ▮ 61416

The Complete Masterworks Recordings, Vol. 1: The Studio Recordings 1962-63—features works by Beethoven *(Son. No. 8 in c, Op. 13)*, Chopin *(Études: in c, Op. 10/12; in c#, Op. 25/7; Son. No. 2 in b♭, Op. 35; Scherzo No. 1 in b, Op. 20)*, Debussy *(3 Préludes)*, Liszt *(Hungarian Rhap. No. 19 in d)*, Rachmaninoff *(Études-tableaux in C, Op. 33/2 & in e♭, Op. 39/5)*, D. Scarlatti *(Sons: in E, K.531; in A, K.322; in C, K.455)*, Scriabin *(Etudes: in c#, Op. 2/1; in d#, Op. 8/12; Poeme in F#, Op. 32/1)*, Schubert *(Impromptu in G♭, Op. 90/3)*, Schumann *(Arabeske in C, Op. 18; Kinderscenen, Op. 15; Toccata in C, Op. 7) (rec New York, Apr 18-May 14 & Nov 6-Dec 18, 1962, Nov 4 & 14, 1963)* COL 2-▲ 53457 [ADD] (31.97)

Vol. 3:The Historic Return Carnegie Hall 1965/The 1966 Concerts—features works by J.S. Bach, Schumann, Scriabin, Chopin, Debussy, Moszkowski, Mozart, Haydn, Liszt COL 3-▲ 53461 (47.97)

The Complete RCA Recordings *(22 CD set)*—features works by [Disc 1] Rachmaninoff *(Con. No. 3 [w. NY PO (cond.:Ormandy)])* [Disc 2] *(Horowitz at the Met (live);)* [Disc 3] *(Horowitz Plays Liszt;)* [Disc 4] *(Horowitz in London (live);)* [Disc 5] *(Horowitz Plays Chopin, Vol. 3;)* [Disc 6] *(Horowitz Plays Beethoven, Chopin, Dohnányi & Scarlatti;)* [Disc 7] Mussorgsky *(Pictures at an Exhibition)*, Scriabin, Tchaikovsky, Horowitz, Bizet, Rachmaninoff, Debussy & Sousa; [Disc 8] Brahms *(Con. No. 2 [w. NBC SO (cond.:Toscanini)])* [Disc 9] Schumann *(Kinderszenen)*, Liszt, Debussy, Fauré & Mendelssohn; [Disc 10] Beethoven, Haydn, Brahms, J.S. Bach, Scarlatti & Schumann; *([Disc 11] Mozart, Schubert, Czerny & Mendelssohn; [Disc 12] Mussorgsky (Pictures at an Exhibition)*, Tchaikovsky *(Con. No. 1 [w. NBC SO (cond.:Toscanini)])*; [Disc 13] Prokofiev, Barber & Kabalevsky; [Disc 14] Horowitz Plays Chopin, Vol. 2; [Disc 15] Horowitz Plays Beethoven Sonatas; [Disc 16] Beethoven *(Con. No. 5 [w. RCA Victor SO (cond.:Reiner)])*, Tchaikovsky *(Con. No. 1 [w. NBC SO (cond.:Toscanini)])*; [Disc 17] Horowitz Encores; [Disc 18] Rachmaninoff *(Con. No. 3 [w. RCA Victor SO (cond.:Reiner)])*; [Disc 19] Horowitz Plays Clementi; [Disc 20] Horowitz Plays Chopin, Vol. 1; [Disc 21] Horowitz Plays Schumann; [Disc 22] Horowitz Plays Scriabin) RCAV (Gold Seal) 22-▲ 61655 (204.97)

Discovered Treasures *(previously unreleased studio recordings, 1962-1972)*—features works by Bach-Busoni, Chopin, Clementi, Liszt, Medtner, Scarlatti, Scriabin COL ▲ 48093 [ADD] (10.98) ▮ 48093 (10.98)

Favorite Encores—features works by Chopin, Debussy, Horowitz *(Variations on Themes from Carmen)*, Moszkowski, Mozart, Rachmaninoff, D. Scarlatti, Schubert, Schumann, Scriabin COL ▲ 42305 [AAD] (16.97)

Horowitz at Home—features works by Mozart *(Son. in B♭, K.281; Adagio in b, K.540; Rondo in D, K.485)*, Schubert *(Moment musical in f, D.780/3)*, Liszt/Schubert *(Ständchen, D.957/4; Soirées de Vienne; Valses-Caprices Nos. 6 & 7)* DEUT ▲ 27772 [DDD] (11.97) ▮ 27772

Horowitz Encores *(1942-1951 mono rec'gs)*—features works by Sousa-Horowitz *(Stars & Stripes (arr pno))*, Bizet-Horowitz, Chopin, Debussy, Liszt, Liszt-Horowitz, Mendelssohn, Mendelssohn-Liszt-Horowitz, Moszkowski, Mozart, Rachmaninoff, Saint-Saëns-Liszt-Horowitz, Schumann RCAV (Gold Seal) ▲ 7755 (m) [ADD] (10.97) ▮ 7755

Horowitz the Poet *see COMPOSER Section: Schubert—Piano Sonata, D.960; Schumann—Kinderscenen)* 4236 ▲ 35025 [DDD]

In Moscow—features works by Scarlatti, Mozart, Rachmaninoff, Scriabin, Liszt, Liszt/Schubert, Chopin, Schumann, Moszkowski DEUT ▲ 19499 [DDD] (16.97) ▮ 19499

The Last Recording: Oct. 20-Nov. 1, 1989—features works by Chopin *(Études in e & A♭, Op. 25/1 & 5; Fantaisie-Impromptu, Op. 66; Mazurka in c, Op. 56/3; Nocturnes in E♭, Op. 55/2 & in B, Op. 62/1)*, Haydn *(Sonata in E♭, H.VXI:49)*, Liszt *(Praeludium from Weinen, Klagen, Sorgen, Zagen Variations)*, Wagner/arr. Liszt *(Isolde's Liebestod)* COL ▲ 45818 [DDD] △ SM 45818 [DDD]; ▮ 45818 (10.98)

Plays Bach, w. Nathan Milstein (vn)—features works by Beethoven *(Son 14 Pno, "Moonlight Son")*, Brahms *(Son 3 Vn)*, Haydn *(Son in E♭, H.XVI/52)*, Bach, Scarlatti, Schumann RCAV (Gold Seal) ▲ 60461 (m) [ADD] (10.97) 60461

A Portrait of Vladimir Horowitz—features works by Beethoven *(Piano Sonata No. 14)*, Chopin *(Piano Sonata No. 2)*, Horowitz *(Variations on Themes from Carmen)*, Moszkowski *(Etude in A♭, Op. 72/11)*, Mozart *(Piano Sonata in A, K.331)*, D. Scarlatti *(Sonatas in A, L.483 & in E, L.430)*, Schumann *(Traumerei)*, Scriabin *(Etude in d#, Op. 8/12) (rec 1962-72)* COL ▲ 44797 [ADD] (11.97) 44797

Recital—features works by Bach/Busoni, Mozart, Chopin, Schubert, Liszt, Schumann, Rachmaninoff, Scriabin, Moszkowski *(performances from the soundtrack of the CAMI Video film, "Vladimir Horowitz—The Last Romantic")* DEUT ▲ 19045 [DDD] (16.97)

The Solo European Recordings, Vol. 2—features works by D. Scarlatti *(Son in b, L.33; Son in G, L.487)*, Bach *(Chorale Prelude, "Nun fruet euch, lieben Christen gmein", BWV 734 [trans Busoni])*, Haydn *(Son Pno in E♭, H.XVI/52)*, Beethoven *(32 Vars on Original Theme, WoO 80)*, Schumann *(Presto apassionato in g; Arabeske, Op. 18; Traumes Wirren, Op. 12/7; Toccata, Op. 7)*, Debussy *(Etude XI, "Pour les arpèges composés")*, Poulenc *(L'Eventail de Jeanne [Pastourelle]; 3 Pièces Pno [Toccata])*, Rimsky-Korsakov *(Flight of the Bumblebee [arr Rachmaninoff])*, Stravinsky *(Danse Russe [from Petrouchka])*, Rachmaninoff *(Prelude in g, Op. 23/5)*, Prokofiev *(Toccata in C, Op. 11) (rec 1930-36)* APR ▲ 5517 [ADD] (18.97)

Solo Recordings 1928-36—features works by Bach, Beethoven, Bizet, Chopin, Debussy, Dohnanyi, Haydn, Horowitz, Liszt, Poulenc, Rachmaninoff, Rimsky-Korsakov, Scarlatti & Schumann PHS 2-▲ 9262 (33.97)

Studio Recordings, 1985—features works by Schumann, D. Scarlatti, Liszt, Scriabin, Schubert, Schubert/Tausig DEUT ▲ 19217 [DDD] (11.97) 19217

Horowitz, Vladimir (pno) (cont.)

Vladimir Horowitz—features works by J. S. Bach *(Chorale Prelude, BWV 734 [arr Busoni])*, D. Scarlatti *(Sons in b & G, K.87 & 125)*, Haydn *(Son in E♭, H.XVI/52)*, Beethoven *(Vars (32) in c [from Fant, Op. 80])*, R. Schumann *(Arabeske, Op. 18; Toccata in C, Op. 7; Traumes Wirren [from Fantasiestücke, Op. 12])*, Liszt *(Funérailles)*, Debussy *(Etude 11)*, Poulenc *(Pastourelle; Toccata)* MTAL ▲ 48005 (6.97)

Vladimir Horowitz—features works by Bach *(Chorale Prelude, "Nun freut euch, lieben Christen gmein", BWV 734 [trans Busoni])*, D. Scarlatti *(Son in b, K.87; Son in G, K.125)*, Haydn *(Son in E♭, H.XVI:52)*, Beethoven *(32 Vars in c [from Fant, Op. 80])*, Schumann *(Arabeske, Op. 18; Toccata in C, Op. 7; Traumes Wirren [Fantasiestücke, Op. 12/7])*, Liszt *(Funérailles [from Harmonies poétiques et religieuses])*, Debussy *(Étude No. 11, "Pour les arpèges composés")*, Poulenc *(Pastourelle [from L'éventail de Jeanne]; Toccata [from 3 Pièces]) (rec 1932-35)* MAGT ▲ 48005 [AAD]

Vladimir Horowitz—features works by Schumann *(Kinderscenen, Op. 15)*, Brahms *(Waltz in A♭, Op. 35/15)*, Chopin *(Barcarolle; 2 Mazurkas, Opp. 24/4 & 30/4; Nocturne in F#, Op. 15/2; Scherzo No. 3)*, Debussy *(Serenade for the doll)*, Fauré *(Impromptu No. 5, Op. 102)*, Liszt *(Stude No. 2 in E♭; Hungarian Rhapsody No. 6; Valse oubliée No. 1)*, Mendelssohn *(May breezes)* RCAV (Gold Seal) ▲ 60463 (10.97) 60463

Vladimir Horowitz—features works by Mussorgsky *(Pictures at an Exhibition)*, Bizet-Horowitz, Debussy, Horowitz, Prokofiev, Rachmaninoff, Scriabin, Sousa-Horowitz, Tchaikovsky RCAV (Gold Seal) ▲ 60526 (10.97) 60526

Vladimir Horowitz—features works by Scarlatti *(Sonatas K.531, 87, 380, 455, 322, 46)*, Tausig *(Capriccio in E)*, Beethoven *(Sonata No. 7)*, Chopin *(Mazurka No. 3, Op. 30; Nocturne Nos. 1, Opp. 27/72; Waltz Nos. 2, Opp. 34/64; Ballade No. 3, Op. 47)*, Dohnányi *(Capriccio in f)* RCAV (Gold Seal) ▲ 60986 (10.97) 60986

Vladimir Horowitz: The Complete Masterworks Recordings, 1962-73 *(thirteen volume box set)*—features works by [Vol. 1]—Chopin, Rachmaninoff, Schumann, Liszt; [Vol. 2]—D. Scarlatti, Beethoven, Schubert, Chopin, Debussy, Scriabin; [Vol. 3]—D. Scarlatti; [Vol. 4]—J.S. Bach, Schumann, Scriabin; [Vol. 5]—Chopin, Debussy, Scriabin, Moszkowski, Schumann, Mozart; [Vol. 6]—Chopin, Scriabin, Haydn, Schumann, Debussy, Liszt; [Vol. 7]—Chopin, D. Scarlatti, Schumann, Scriabin, Horowitz; [Vol. 8]—Clementi, J.S. Bach, D. Scarlatti, Haydn, Beethoven; [Vol. 9]—Beethoven; [Vol. 10]—Chopin; [Vol 11]—Chopin, Schumann; [Vol. 12]—Schubert, Liszt, Debussy, Mendelssohn; [Vol. 13]—Scriabin, Medtner, Rachmaninoff COL 13-▲ 53456 [ADD] (221.97)

Vladimir Horowitz: The Private Collection—features works by J.S. Bach *(Toccata in c)*, Clementi *(Sons. Opp. 36/1, 34/1 & 47/2)*, Mendelssohn *(Song without Words, Op. 67/3)*, Chopin *(Fant. in f; Polonaise No. 1 in c#; Mazurka No. 19 in b)*, Liszt *(Consolation No. 4 in D♭; Consolation No. 5 in E)*, Rachmaninoff *(Étude-tableau, Op. 39/7)* RCAV (Red Seal) ▲ 62643 (16.97)

Horszowski, Mieczyslav (pno)

The Horszowski Collection *(previously unpublished live recordings 1958-1983)*—features works by C.P.E. Bach *(rec. 1971 in Italy, mono)*, J.S. Bach *(rec. Dec. 3, 1983, New York, stereo)*, Beethoven *(rec. Jan. 28, 1958, Rome, mono; rec. March 17, 1982, Buffalo, New York, stereo)*, Chopin *(rec. May 22, 1973, Hayden Planetarium, New York, stereo; rec. March 17, 1982, Buffalo, stereo)*, Mozart *(rec. Dec. 13, 1969, Teatro La Pergola, Florence, mono)*, Schubert *(rec. 1971, Italy)* PHS 2-▲ 9979 (m/s) [AAD] (33.97)

Horszowski in Concert—features works by Bach, Beethoven, Chopin, Schumann, Villa-Lobos *(rec Comédie des Champs-Elysées June 1 & Oct 5, 1987)* Thésis ▲ THC 82008 [DDD]

In Recital at the Théâtre des Champs-Elysées—features works by Bach *(French Suite No. 6)*, Beethoven, Chopin, Schumann *(see* Composer section) *(rec Oct 8, 1989)* Thésis ▲ THC 82039 [DDD]

Hough, Stephen (pno)

My Favorite Things: Virtuoso Encores—features works by Chopin, Dohnányi, Friedman, Gabrilowitsch, Godowsky, Levitzki, MacDowell, Moszkowski, Paderewski, Palmgren, Quilter, Rosenthal, et al. MUMA ▲ 7046 [DDD]

The Piano Album—features J. S. Bach *(Sons & Partitas Vn [BWV 1002, Partita No. 1])*, Bizet *(Arlésienne (sels) [Adagietto])*, Czerny *(Vars brillantes, Op. 14)*, E. v. Dohnányi *(Capriccio, Op. 28; Fuchsia Tree)*, I. Friedman *(Music Box, Op. 33/3)*, Gabrilovich *(Caprice-Burlesque Pno; Melodie Pno in E)*, L. Godowsky *(Java Suite [The Gardens of Buitenzorg]; Triakontameron [No. 25:Erinnerungen])*, M. Levitzki *(Enchanted Nymph; Waltz in A♭, Op. 2)*, Liadov *(A Musical Snuff-Box, Op. 32)*, L. Liebermann *(Gargoyles, Op. 29)*, Liszt *(Trans, Arrs & Paraphrases [Chopin:Chants polonais No. 1 (Mädchens Wunsch) [Op. 74], S.480 (arr 1847-60)])*, MacDowell *(Fantasiestücke Pno, Op. 17 [02. Hexentanz])*, Moszkowski *(Caprice Espagnole, Op. 37; Serenata, Op. 15/1; Siciliano, Op. 42/2; Valse mignonne)*, I. J. Paderewski *(Humoresques, Op. 14 [1. Menuet célèbre in G]; Nocturne Pno, Op. 16/4)*, Palmgren *(En route, Op. 9)*, Quilter *(Elizabethan Lyrics, Op. 12 [Weep you no more]; Now Sleeps the Crimson Petal, Op. 3/2)*, J. Ravina *(Etude de style, Op. 40/1)*, Rebikov *(Musical Snuffbox)*, R. Rodgers *(King & I (sels) [March of the Siamese Children]; Sound of Music (sels) [My Favorite Things])*, M. Rosenthal *(Papillons)*, A. Rubinstein *(Melody in F, Op. 3/1)*, Saint-Saëns *(Cygne)*, Schlözer *(Etude Pno in A♭, Op. 1/2)*, R. Schumann *(Spanisches Liederspiel, Op. 74 [No. 10, Der Kontrebandiste])*, Tausig *(Ungarische Zigeunerweisen)*, Woodforde-Finden *(Indian Love Lyrics [Kashmiri Song; Till I Wake])* VCL 2-▲ 61498 [DDD] (11.97)

Howard, Leslie (pno)

Liszt at the Opera, Vol. IV—features works by Bellini *(Réminiscences des Puritans)*, Verdi *(Coro di festa & marcia funebre [from Don Carlos]; Salve Maria! [from Jérusalem])*, Wagner *(Chor der älteren Pilger [from Tannhäuser]; Am stillen Herd; Lied aus Die Meistersinger von Nürnberg)*, Donizetti *(Réminiscences de Lucrezia Borgia; Grande fantaisie I & II)*, Meyerbeer *(Réminiscences des Huguenots)*, Raff *(Andante finale; March [both from König Alfred])*, Mozart *(Song of the 2 Armed Men [from Die Zauberflöte])*, Auber *(Tyrolean Melody [from La Fiancée]; Tarantelle di bravura [from Masaniello])*, Bellini *(Intro & Polonaise [from I Puritani]; Grosse Concert-Fantasie [from Sonnambula])* HYP 2-▲ 67101 (35.97)

Rare Piano Encores—features works by Rossini, Mozart/Busoni, Gershwin, Reger, Grainger, Wagner, I. Friedman, Rachmaninoff, Bizet/Moszkowski, Rubinstein, Grieg, Bruckner, Liszt HYP ▲ 66090

Huang, Eileen (pno)

Chinese Piano Concertos, w. Hu Bing Xu (cnd), China Central PO, China Central Traditional Orch—features works by Xian Xing-Hi *(Yellow River Con)*, Xua Yan-Ju *(The Moon's Reflection over the 2nd Spring)*, Hsu Zuao-Ji *(Chinese Youth Con)*, plus 7 other ancient & modern Chinese works ASV ▲ 1031 (16.97)

Huybregts, Pierre (pno)

Spanish Piano Music *see Composer section—Mompou, et al.)* CENT ▲ 2026 [ADD] (16.97)

Hyman, Dick (pno), James Levine (pno)

Scott Joplin: Greatest Hits—features The Entertainer, The Easy Winners, Maple Leaf Rag, etc. RCAV ▲ 60842 (10.97) ▮ 60842 (5.98)

Iturbi, José (pno)

José Iturbi—features works by Mozart *(Con. No. 10 in E♭ for 2 Pianos [w. Amparo Iturbi, orch. unknown])*, D. Scarlatti, Beethoven, Albéniz, Granados, Lazar, Navarro & Paradies *(rec 1933-41)* PHS ▲ 9103 [ADD] (17.97)

José Iturbi—features works by Mozart *(Son 12 in F, K.332; Con 10 for 2 Pianos, K.365 [w. Amparo Itubi (pno)])*, D. Scarlatti *(Sons in C & b)*, Beethoven *(Andante in F, Op. 35)*, Albéniz *(Sevillana; Cordoba)*, Granados *(La Maja)*, Navarro *(Pequena)*, Lazar *(Marche funebre)* MTAL ▲ 48029 (6.97)

Ivaldi, Christian (pno), Noël Lee (pno)

Musique Américaine—features works for 2 pianos by Copland, Gershwin, Barber & Lee ARN ▲ 68375 (16.97)

Jacobs, Paul (pno)

Blues, Ballads & Rags—features works by Bolcolm, Copland, Rzewski, et al. 75597 ▲ 79006

Jandó, Jenö (pno)

Melody in F—features works by Brahms, Dvořák Grieg, Mendelssohn, Rubinstein, Sinding, Tchaikovsky LALI ▲ 15603 [DDD] (3.97)

Joyce, Eileen (pno)

Piano Recital—features E. D. Albert *(Scherzo in F#, Op.16/2)*, J. S. Bach *(Prelude & Fugue Hpd, BWV 894)*, E. von Dohnányi *(Rhaps, Op. 11)*, E. Grieg *(Lyric Pieces; Stimmungen, Op. 73)*, Liszt *(Études de concert (2), S.145; Études de concert (3), S.144)*, Palmgren *(En route, Op. 9)*, Paradies *(Toccata Hpd in A♭)*, S. Rachmaninoff *(Preludes Pno)*, Schlözer *(Etude Pno in A♭, Op. 1/2)*, C. Scott *(Danse Negre (1908); Lotus Land)*, Sinding *(Rustles of Spring)*, R. Strauss *(Ständchen, Op. 17/2)* TES ▲ 1174 (17.97)

Kalichstein, Joseph (pno)

Recital—features works by Schubert *(Allegretto in E♭ (No. 2 from Klavierstücke, D.946))*, Schumann *(Sonata No. 1 in f#, Op. 11)*, Schumann-Liszt *(Widmung)*, Schubert-Liszt *(Ständchen (from Schwanengesang))* AUDO ▲ 72028 (16.97)

Kapell, William (pno)

Kapell—features works by Khachaturian, Prokofiev & Liszt RCAV (Gold Seal:Legendary Performers) ▲ 60921 (10.97)

Kapell, William (pno) (cont.)

The William Kapell Edition—features works by Albéniz *(Evocación [from Iberia])*, Bach *(Partita 4 [Allemande]; Suite in a, BWV 818)*, Beethoven *(Con 2 Pno [w. Vladimir Golschmann (cnd), NBC SO])*, Brahms *(Intermezzo, Op. 16/6; Son 1 Va [w. William Primrose (va)]; Son 3 Vn [2nd movt; w. Jascha Heifetz (vn)])*, Chasins *(Pno Playtime, Nos. 1 & 4-6)*, Chopin *(Mazurkas, Opp. 6/2; 7/1 & 5; 17/2-4; 24/1 & 3; 30/3; 33/1, 3-4; 41/1-2; 50/2-3; 56/3; 59/1-2; 63/2-3; 67/2-4; 68/2-4; posth. in a, "Notre temps"; posth. in B♭; Nocturnes, Opp. 9/1 & 55/2; Polonaise-fant, Op. 61; Son 2 Pno [Marche funèbre]; Son 3 Pno [movts 1-2]; Waltz, Op. 18 in E♭)*, Copland *(Son Pno)*, Debussy *(Children's Corner)*, Liszt *(Hungarian Rhap 11; Mephisto Waltz 1; Sonetto del Petrarca No. 104 [from Années de pèlerinage 2])*, Khachaturian *(Con Pno [w. Serge Koussevitzky (cnd), Boston SO])*, Mendelssohn *(Lieder ohne Worte, Op. 67/4-5)*, Mozart *(Sons 10 Pno [1st movt]; Son 16 Pno [2nd movt])*, Mussorgsky *(Pictures at an Exhibition)*, R. Palmer *(Toccata ostinato)*, Prokofiev *(Con 3 Pno [w. Antal Dorati (cnd), Dallas SO])*, Rachmaninoff *(Con 2 Pno [w. William Steinberg (cnd), Robin Hood Dell SO]; Prelude in c#, Op. 3/2; Rhap on a Theme of Paganini, Op. 43 [w. Fritz Reiner (cnd), Robin Hood Dell SO]; Son Vc, Op. 19 [w. Edmund Kurtz (vc)])*, D. Scarlatti *(Son in E, K.380)*, Schubert *(German Dances, D.783/6-7; Impromptu, D.935/2; Ländler, D.734/1-2; Moment musicaux, D.780/3; Waltzes, D.145/2 & 365/26)*, Schumann *(Kinderszenen, Op. 15/1; Romance in F#, Op. 28/2)*, Shostakovich *(Preludes Pno, Op. 34/5, 10, 14 & 24) (rec 1944-53)* RCAV (Red Seal) 9-▲ 68442 (m) (122.97)

Kaplan Solomon, Nanette (pno)

Character Sketches: Solo Piano Works by 7 American Women—features works by Bond, León, Brockman, Schonthal, Walker, Richter, Zaimont LEON ▲ 334 [DDD]

Kasman, Yakov (pno), Aviram Reichert (pno)

10th Van Cliburn International Piano Competition: Yakov Kasman, Silver Medalist & Aviram Reichert, Bronze Medalist HAM ▲ 907219 (17.97)

Katchen, Julius (pno)

Julius Katchen PPHI (Great Pianists of the 20th Century) ▲ 456859 (22.97)

Katin, Peter (pno)

Piano Magic—features works by Chopin *(Fant. Impromptu; Polonaise in A♭)*, MacDowell *(To a Wild Rose)*, Tchaikovsky *(Chants sans paroles)*, Liszt *(Liebestraum No. 3)*, Schumann *(Traumerei)*, Beethoven *(Bagatelle, WoO 59, "Für Elise")* POS (The Orchid) ▲ 11001

Katsaris, Cyprien (pno)

Mozartiana *(piano transcriptions by Mozart)*—features works by Beethoven, Bizet, Czerny, Fischer, Gelinek, Katsaris, Kempff, Liszt, Thalberg COL ▲ 52551 [DDD]

Keene, Constance (pno)

Plays Familiar Favorites—features works by Albéniz/Godowsky, Chasins, Chopin, Chopin/Liszt, Gluck/Chasins, Griffes, Liszt, Mendelssohn, Rachmaninoff, Saint-Saëns/Godowsky, Schubert/Godowsky, Weinberger/Chasins PROT ▲ PRCD 1102 ▮ CSPR 169

Kikuchi, Yoko (pno)

Preludes—features works by Rachmaninoff *(Préludes, Opp. 3/2, 23/2 & 32/12)*, Prokofiev *(Prélude, Op. 12/7)*, Szymanowski *(Préludes (9), Op. 1)*, Ravel *(Prélude assez lent et très expressif)*, Debussy *(Préludes, Ce qu'a vu le vent d'Ouest; La fille aux chevaux de lin; Les fées d'exquises danseuses)*, Martin *(Préludes (8) Pno)*, Satie *(Véritables Préludes Flasques "pour un chien") (rec Brussels Conservatory Concert Hall, Nov 1995)* PAVA ▲ 7368 [DDD] (10.97)

Kissin, Evgeni (pno)

Carnegie Hall Debut Concert—features works by Chopin *(Waltz in c#, Op. 64/2)*, Liszt *(Libesträum No. 3; Rhapsodie espagnole, S.254; Transcendental Etude No. 10)*, Prokofiev *(Etude in c, Op. 2/3; Sonata No. 6 in A, Op. 82)*, Schumann-Liszt *(Song transcription, "Widmung")*, Schumann *(Symphonic Etudes, Op. 13; Variations on A-B-E-G-G, Op. 1) (rec live, Sept 1990)* RCAV (Red Seal) ▲ 60443 [DDD] (30.97) 60443

Carnegie Hall Debut Concert *(highlights, omitting the Chopin and Prokofiev sels)* RCAV (Red Seal) ▲ 61202 [DDD] (16.97) 61202 ▯ 09026-61202-5

Evgeny Kissin: A Musical Portrait *(a specially-priced CD only compilation of five piano concerto recordings)* see Composer section under Haydn, Mozart, Prokofiev, Rachmaninoff and Shostakovich RCAV (Red Seal) 2-▲ 60567 [DDD] (24.97)

The Kissin Collection—features works by Chopin *(Nocturnes 12 & 14; Son 3; Fant in f; Mazurkas 17, 20, 32, 34, 39, 40, 41 & 49; Scherzo 2; Waltz 14; Barcarolle)*, Bishop *(Home, Sweet Home)*, Schumann *(Arabesque in C, Op. 18; Etudes symphoniques, Op. 13)*, Scriabin *(Son 3)*, Liszt *(Hungarian Rhap 12)*, Bach *(Siciliano, BWV 1031)*, trad *(Auld Lang Syne) (rec live, 1986-88)* OLY 3-▲ 621 (16.97)

Kissin in Tokyo *(In recital at Suntory Hall, 5/12/87)*—features works by Prokofiev *(Son 6 Pno)*, Chopin, Liszt, Rachmaninoff, Scriabin, et al COL ▲ 45931 [DDD] (16.97) 45931

Klein, Elisabeth (pno)

Dance of the Bacchae, w. Ingrid Eriksen (pno), Ane Eriksen (rcrs)—features Nordic piano music by Pärt *(For Alena)*, Sonstevold *(Bagatelles (6))*, Holm *(Dance of the Bacchae)*, Wagner Smitt *(Ocean Depths)*, Leiviska *(Canto intima)*, Petersen *(Phant on a Fragment by Per Nørgård)*, Stromholm *(When Friends Meet)*, plus other sels CLSO ▲ 165 (14.97)

Klien, Walter (pno)

Walter Klien—features works by Beethoven *(Moonlight Sonata)*, plus 8 popular encore pieces by Debussy, Mendelssohn, Chopin, Schumann, Liszt, Brahms ALLO ▲ 8023 [ADD] ▮ 8023

Kokinos, Nelly (pno)

World's Favorite Piano—features works by Bach, Beethoven, Brahms, Chopin, Mendelssohn, Mozart, Scarlatti, Schubert, Schumann, Tchaikovsky RCAV ▲ 60936 (6.97) ▮ 60936

Kolassi, Irma (pno)

Volume 1—features works by Duparc, Fauré, Leguerney, Martini, Bizet, Hahn, Messager, Séverac, Koechlin, Dalcroze LYS 2-▲ 149 (30.97)

Kubalek, Antonin (pno)

Czech Miniature Masterpieces—features works by Suk, Dušek, Myslevičec, Vaňhal, Smetana, Dušik, Vořišek, Dvořák, Fibich, Janáček, Martinu, incl. 5 Preludes by Milan Kymlička (b. 1936) DOR ▲ 90121 [DDD] (16.97)

Labèque, Katia (pno), Marielle Labèque (pno)

Encore!—features works by Berio, J.S. Bach, Gershwin, Stravinsky, Brahms, Tchaikovsky, Bernstein, Joplin, Marie Jaell, Bartók, Schumann COL ▲ 48381 (16.97)

Love of Colours *(two-piano works in a jazz idiom; most arrangements by John McLaughlin)*—features works by Michel Camilo, Chick Corea, Miles Davis, Thelonious Monk, Martial Solal, et al. COL ▲ 47227 (9.97) △ SM 47227 47227

Landowska, Wanda (pno)

The Early Recordings—features works by Handel *(Harmonious Blacksmith)*, Bach *(Gavottes (2); Passepieds in e; Fant in c)*, D. Scarlatti *(Son in D)*, Rameau *(Rigadoun & Tambourin)*, Landowska *(Bourées d'Auvernge 1-2)*, Mozart *(Rondo alla Turca; Minuet; Son 9 Pno)*, Byrd *(Welsey's Wilde)*, Daquin *(Le Coucou)*, Couperin *(Le Roissignol en Amour)* BPS ▲ 16 (16.97)

Musique ancienne—features works by Byrd, Purcell, Rameau, Couperin, Daquin, Lully, Chambonniers, Pachelbel, Scarlatti, Francisque *(rec 1928-54)* PHS ▲ 9012 [AAD] (17.97)

Laredo, Ruth (pno)

My First Recital—features works by Bach *(Prelude No. 1 in C, BWV 846 [from The Well-Tempered Clavier, Book 1]; 2-Part Inventions Nos. 1 in C, BWV 772, 4 in d, BWV 775, 8 in F, BWV 779)*, Mozart *(Fant in d, K.397; Son in C, K.545)*, Beethoven *(Für Elise; Son in G, Op. 49/2)*, Chopin *(Waltzes in A, Op. 64/1 & in b, Op. 69/1; Grand Valse Brillant in A, Op. 18)*, Debussy *(The Girl With the Flaxen Hair [from Preludes, Book 1]; Clair de Lune [from Suite bergamasque])*, Schumann *(Kinderscenen, Op. 15 [sels])*, Prokofiev *(March [from Peter & the Wolf]) (rec Jan 3-4, 1990)* ESSY ▲ 1006 [DDD] (16.97)

My Second Recital—features works by Bach *(Jesu, Joy of Man's Desiring)*, Mozart *(Rondo alla turca [from Son in A, K.331])*, Beethoven *(Son in F#, Op. 78)*, Schumann *(Arabesque, Op. 18)*, Debussy *(Sarabande [from Pour le piano])*, Brahms *(Waltzes, Op. 39/2-5, 15; Intermezzo, Op. 117/1)*, Chopin *(Mazurka, Op. 6/1; Waltz, Op. 64/2; Nocturne, Op. 15/2)*, Tchaikovsky *(Humoresque [from Deux morceaux, Op. 10]; Natha-Valse [from 6 morceaux, Op. 51]; Barcarolle [from The Seasons, Op. 37b/6])*, Khachaturian *(Toccata (rec July 31-Aug 1, 1991)* ESSY ▲ 1026 [DDD] (16.97)

Laretei, Kabi (pno)

Exil: Home-Elsewhere *(music of composers who lived in exile)*—features works by Chopin, Bartók, Rachmaninoff, Hindemith, Martinů, Pärt, et al. PRPI ▲ 9113 (17.97)

Laria, Maria (pno)

Pianissimo—includes works by J. S. Bach *(Prelude & Fugue in F#)*, Chopin *(Études, Op. 10/5 & 12; Impromptu, Op. 36; Mazurkas, Opp. 17/4 & 24/4)*, Liszt *(Liebestraum)*, Prokofiev *(Son 3, Op. 28)* RANS ▲ 1307 (14.97)

Larrocha, Alicia de (pno)

Spanish Fireworks—features works by Albéniz, Falla, Granados, Mompou, Turina PLON ▲ 17795 [ADD] (11.97)

Lehrman, Leonard (pno)

Piano Music by Members of the Long Island Composer's Alliance—features Cory *(Crystals)*, H. Deutsch *(Quiet Times)*, L. Foss *(Prelude Pno in D)*, M. Gould *(Something to Do (sels))*, Hosza *(French Suite Pno)*, L. Kraft *(Short Pieces Pno)*, Lehrman *(Reineke Fuchs Suite)*, Mandelbaum *(Prelude Pno)*, Musolino *(Fugato & Extention Pno)*, Pleskow *(Untitled Pno)*, E. Siegmeister *(Festive March Pno)*, H. Smith *(Evocation Pno)*, Suny *(Brief Encounters)* CPS ▲ 8661

Leng Tan, Margaret (toy pno)

The Art of the Toy Piano features transcriptions of & original works by Beethoven *(Son 14 Pno, "Moonlight Son")*, Beatles *(Eleanor Rigby)*, Jed Distler *(3 Landscapes for Peter Wyer)*, Philip Glass *(Modern Love Waltz)*, Klucevsek *(Sweet Chinoiserie)*, D. Lang *(Miracle Ear)*, Montague *(Mirabella (tarantella))*, Mostel *(Furling Banner)*, Satie *(Gymnopédie No. 3)*, Toby Twining *(Bidaka; Nightmare Rag; Satie Blues)*, J. Wolfe *(East Broadway)* POIN ▲ 456345 (16.97)

Lester, Noel (pno)

Rags to Riches: An American Album—features works by Confrey *(Dizzy Fingers; Stumbling; Impromptu [from 3 Little Oddities]; Humorestless; Kitten on the Keys; High Hattin' [from African Suite])*, Joplin *(Maple Leaf Rag; Solace)*, Charles S. Johnson *(Dill Pickles)*, I. Berlin *(Alexander's Ragtime Band)*, Ohman *(Pno Pan)*, W. C. Handy *(Got No Mo' Home Dan a Dog)*, N. H. Brown *(The Doll Dance)*, Gershwin *(Rialto Ripples [arr W. Donaldson]; Do-Do-Do; Swanee; The Man I Love; Fascinating Rhythm; Do It Again; I'll Build a Stairway to Paradise; I Got Rhythm; Preludes [3] Pno)*, Copland *(The Cat & the Mouse)*, Eubie Blake *(The Baltimore Todolo)*, L. Alter *(Lopeziana)*, Mayerl *(Honky-Tonk)*, D. W. Guion *(The Harmonica Player; The Lonesome Whistler; Arkansas Traveler) (rec Univ of Maryland, Baltimore, Jan 1997)* ELAN ▲ 82296 [DDD]

Lester Roldan Duo [N. Lester (pno), N. Roland (pno)]

Music of the Americas, Lester/Roldan Duo—features works by Dello Joio, Guastavino, Codero, Benjamin, Copland, Aguirre CENT ▲ 2171 (16.97)

Levitzki, Mischa (pno)

His Rarest Recordings—features works by Gluck, Chopin, Paganini, Liszt, Moszkowski & Levitski *(rec 1923-29)* ENPL (Piano Library) ▲ 227 (13.97)

Mischa Levitzki: 1898-1941 *(1927-38 HMV/Victor recordings)*—features works by Beethoven/arr. d'Albert *(Ecossaise)*, Chopin *(Nocturne Op. 15/2; Polonaise in A♭, Op. 53; Scherzo No. 3, Op. 39; Waltz in G♭, Op. 70/1)*, Levitzki *(Arabesque valsante in a; Valse in A)*, Liszt *(Un sospiro; Hungarian Rhapsody No. 12; La Campanella)*, Mendelssohn *(Andante & Rondo capriccioso)*, Rubinstein *(Staccato Etude in C, Op. 23/2)*, Scarlatti *(Sonata in A, L.345)*, Schumann *(Sonata in g, Op. 22)* PHS ▲ 9962 (m) [AAD] (17.97)

Levy, Ernst (pno)

Forgotten Genius—features works by Beethoven, Liszt, Levy MRSN ▲ 52007 (17.97)

Lhévinne, Josef (pno), Rosina Lhévinne (pno)

Josef & rosina Lhévinne PPHI (Great Pianists of the 20th Century) ▲ 456889 (22.97)

Li, Bichuan (pno)

In Clara Wieck-Schumann's Circle—features works by Brahms, R. Schumann, Friedrich, Alwin, Marie Wieck, Bargiel, et al. WNR ▲ 49706 (17.97)

Lifchitz, Max (pno)

The American Collection—features works by T. Kramer *(Colors from a Changing Sky)*, Bassett *(Elaborations)*, Starer *(The Ideal Self)*, E. Bell *(Vars & Interludes)*, Crossman *(Gypsy Ballads)*, Wolpe *(Stehende Musik)*, Rands *(Espressioni [3])*, T. Whitman *(Romanza)*, Lebenbom *(Son Pno)*, Ogdon *(Pieces Pno [7])*, O. J. Garcia *(Images of Wood & Fire)* NSR 2-▲ 1014 [DDD] (15.97)

American Debuts: Piano Music by American Composers *(see Composer section—Franco, Mason, Stewart, Ziffrin, et al.)* NSR ▲ NS 1002 [DDD]

Contemporary Romantics: American Piano Music *(see Composer section—Pizer, Quilling, Schiffman, et al.)* NSR ▲ NS 1001 [DDD]

Max Lifchitz Plays American Piano Music—features works by, Elizabeth Bell:Night Music, Emma Lou Diemer:Encore *(Irwin Bazelon:Sonatina)*, Elizabeth Bell *(Elizabeth B)*, Emma Lou Diemer *(Emma L)*, Laura Greenberg *(Laura)*, Howard Quilling *(Howard Qu)*, Sherwood Shaffer *(Lines from Shelley)* VMM ▲ VMM 2002 [DDD]

Mexico: 100 Years of Piano Music—features works by R. Castro *(Nocturno; Vals Bluette; Suite Pno)*, Ponce *(Momento Doloroso; Preludio & Fuga para la mano izquierda)*, Chavez *(..de rosa en rosa..; Adelita y la Cucaracha; Sonatina)*, Moncayo *(Piezas (3))*, Moncada *(Costeña)*, Galindo *(Jaliscience)*, Halffter *(Laberinto)*, Renart *(Momentos (3))*, Enriquez *(Maxiena)*, Lavista *(Simurg)* NSR ▲ 1010 [DDD] (15.97)

Lill, John (pno), Cristina Ortiz (pno), J. L. Prats (pno)

The Heart of the Piano Concerto, w. London SO [cnd:J. Judd, W. Morris], Royal PO [cnd:L. Foster, E. Bátiz]—features works by Tchaikovsky *(Con. No. 1 [1st movt.])*, Schumann *(Con. in a [2nd movt.])*, Mozart *(Con. No. 1 [2nd movt.])*, Rachmaninoff *(Con. No. 2 [1st movt.])*, & others POS (The Orchid) ▲ 11012

Lindblom, Rolf (pno)

Quietude—features works by Fauré, Bach, Satie, Sjögren, et al. PRPI ▲ 9052 (17.97)

Lipatti, Dinu (pno)

Dinu Lipatti PPHI (Great Pianists of the 20th Century) ▲ 456892 (22.97)

Lortie, Louis (pno)

20th Century Original Piano Transcriptions *(see Composer section—Gershwin:Rhapsody in Blue; etc.)* CHN ▲ 8733 [DDD] (16.97)

Lympany, Moura (pno)

Best Loved Piano Classics *(see under "Classical Music Favorites" section above)*

Best Loved Piano Classics, Vol. 1—features works by Chopin *(Fant-impromptu, Op. 66; Études, Opp. 10/4 & 25/5)*, Brahms *(Waltz in A♭, Op. 39/15)*, Mozart *(Son 11 Pno, K.331 [Alla turca])*, Beethoven *(Minuet in C; Für Elise)*, Schumann *(Träumerai, Op. 15/7)*, Liszt *(Un sospiro)*, Dvořák *(Humoresque, Op. 101/7)*, MacDowell *(To a Wild Rose, Op. 51/1)*, Chaminade *(Automne, Op. 35/2)*, Debussy *(Clair de lune; Goliwogg's Cake Walk)*, Rachmaninoff *(Prelude, Op. 3/2)*, Rubenstein *(Melody in F, Op. 3/1)*, Granados *(The Maiden & the Nightingale)*, Falla *(Ritual Fire Dance)*, Albeniz *(Tango, Op. 165/2 [arr Godowsky])* CSER (Seraphim) ▲ 69590 (3.97)

Best Loved Piano Classics, Vol. 2—features works by Satie, Debussy, Chopin, Beethoven & others CSER (Seraphim) ▲ 69591 (3.97)

McCallum, Stephanie (pno)

Notations—features works by M. Henderson *(Cross Hatching)*, N. Butterley *(Uttering Joyous Leaves; L. Hargrave Flying Alone)*, P. Boulez *(Douze notations pour piano)*, C. Dench *(2 Phase Portraits)*, M. Sutherland *(Extension)*, K. Humble *(Arcade II)*, I. Xenakis *(Herma) (rec ABC Studio 200, ABC Ultimo Centre, Sydney, 1993)* TALP ▲ 37 [DDD] (18.97)

McDuffie, Margery (pno)

Piano Reflections: Encore Favorites—features works by Saint-Saëns *(Étude in forme de valse, Op. 52/6)*, Kreisler *(Liebeslied; Liebesfreud [both trans Rachmaninoff])*, Bach/Grainger *(Blithe Bells)*, Copland *(Hoe-Down [from Rodeo])*, Prokofiev *(Suggestion diabolique, Op. 4/4)*, Mozart *(Serenade [from Don Giovanni; trans Busoni])*, Grieg *(Ich liebe dich, Op. 41/3)*, Bizet *(Chanson bohème [from Carmen; trans Moszkowski])*, Fauré *(Barcarolle in A♭, Op. 44)*, I. Philipp *(Feux-follets, Op. 24/3, "Jack o' Lanterns")*, Liszt *(Concert Etude in D♭; Hungarian Rhap 6) (rec ACA Studios, Atlanta, GA, June-July 1996)* ACAD ▲ 20056 [DDD] (16.97)

MacGregor, Joanna (pno)

American Piano Classics *(20th century classical and jazz works)*—features works by Aaron Copland, Erroll Garner, George Gershwin, Charles Ives, Thelonious Monk, Conlon Nancarrow COC ▲ 1299 [DDD] (16.97)

McLachlan, Murray (pno)

Piano Music from Malta—features works by Camilleri *(3 Maltese Miniatures; 2 Canti; Leggenda; Etudes Book 3; 5 Maltese Dances)*, C. Pace *(The Lonely Valley; Impromptu)*, Isouard *(Son)*, Galea *(Maypole Dance & Cradle Song)*, A. Pace *(Tidwir)*, Azopardi *(Sonatina Pastorale)*, Buhagiar *(Il-Kitarra)*, Pirotta *(La Lyonnaise)* OLY ▲ 489 [DDD] (16.97)

Magaloff, Nikita (pno)

La Valse—features works by Chabrier, Chopin, Debussy, Godowsky, Kreisler/arr. Rachmaninoff, M. Levitzki, Liszt, Moszkowski, Schubert, Scriabin, Sibelius, Joh. Strauss, Weber/arr. Tausig DNN ▲ 77346 [DDD] (16.97)

The Waltz—features works by Moszkowski *(Valse, Op. 34/1)*, Sibelius *(Valse triste, Op. 44)*, Weber *(Aufforderung zum Tanz [from Invitation à la valse, Op. 65])*, Levitzki *(Arabesque valsante, Op. 6)*, Chopin *(Valse brillante, Op. 18)*, Schubert *(Valse)*, J. Strauss II *(Frühlingsstimmen [from Voix du printemps])*, Godowsky *(Alt-Wien)*, Chabrier *(Scherzo & valse)*, Debussy *(La plus que lente)*, Rachmaninoff *(Liebeslied [trans Kreisler])*, Scriabin *(Valse, Op. 38)*, Liszt *(Valse de faust)* ADES ▲ 204142 [DDD]

Markham, Richard (pno), David Nettle (pno)

Nettle & Markham in England—features works by Holst *(Jupiter [from The Planets])*, Grainger *(Country Gardens; Lisbon; The Brisk Young Sailor; The Lost Lady Found; Handel in the Strand; English Waltz)*, Walton *(Tango-Pasodoble; Popular Song; Old Sir Faulk; Swiss Yodeling Song; Polka [all from Facade])*, Coates *(By the Sleepy Lagoon)*, Vaughan Williams *(Fant on Greensleeves)*, Britten *(Mazurka Elegiaca, Op. 23/2)*, Carmichael *(Puppet Ov [from Puppet Show])*, Nicholas *(Quiet Peace No. 1)*, Dring *(Fantastic Var on Lilliburlero)*, Bridge *(Sally in Our Alley)*, Blake *(Slow Ragtime)*, Blade *(Folk Ballad)*, Gay *(The Lambeth Walk)*, Scott *(Lotus Land, Op. 47/1)*, Warlock *(Pavane [from Capriol Suite])* INMP (Classics) ▲ 6700172 (8.97)

Nettle & Markham in France—features works by Milhaud *(Vif, Modere & Brazileira [from Scaramouche])*, Fauré *(Berceuse [from Dolly Suite])*, Satie *(Gymnopedie No. 1 [arr Nettle & Markham])*, Chaminade *(Le Matin)*, Ibert *(Le Petit ane blanc [from Histoires])*, Bizet *(Marche [Trompette et tambour]; Berceuse [La Pouppe]; Impromptu [La Toupie]; Galop [Le Bal] [all from Jeux d'enfants])*, Poulenc *(Elegie; L'Embarquement pour cythere)*, Hahn *(Pour bercer un convalescent No. 2)*, Ravel *(Laideronnette, imperatrice des pagodes [from Ma mère l'oye])*, Inghelbrecht *(Sur le pont d'avignon [from La Nursery, Vol. 3])*, Saint-Saëns *(Fossiles; Le Cygne [both from Carnival of the Animals])*, Maio *(Souvenirs de mon oncle [arr Nettle & Markham])*, plus others IMAS (Masters) ▲ 6600142 (16.97)

Matsunaga, Kayako (pno)

Kayako Matsunaga: Pianist—features works by Xenakis *(Evryali)*, Tamaru *(Suishôren)*, Matsudaira *(Toy Box)*, Kanno *(A Cluster of Stars for Pno)*, Ichiyanagi *(Flowers Blooming in Summer for Hp & Pno [w. Atsuko Sato (hp)])*, Kang *(Sonate Bach)*, Matsunaga *(Meditation II)*, Crumb *(Processional)* VMM ▲ VMM 2014 [DDD]

▲ = CD ♦ = Enhanced CD △ = MD ▮ = Cassette Tape ▯ = DCC

Matsuya, Midori (pno)

Light Colored Album: Contemporary Japanese Piano Pieces—features works by Miyoshi *(Hommage [w. Saburo Ueki (vn), Akira Shirao (fl)])*, Hachimura *(Vision of Higanbana)*, Matsumura *(Deux berceuses à la grece)*, Takemitsu *(Pno Distance)*, Yoshimatsu *(Floral Dance; Apple Seed Dance; Interlude to Water; Invention for about 2 Voices; Ode to a Double Faced Man [all from Pleiades Dances])*, Sato *(Scenery with Tea Garden; Season of Yellow & Black; An August Lying to Rest; A Carpet of Bamboo Leaves Falling onto Northern Sea [all from Light Colored Album])*, Ogura *(Sonatina Pno) (rec 1993)* CAMA ▲ 318 [DDD] (17.97)

Mayorga, Lincoln (pno)

A Bouquet of Familiar Classics—features works by Beethoven *(Bagatelle [Für Elise], WoO 59)*, Chopin *(Prelude in A, Op. 28, No. 7; Waltz in c♯, Op. 64, No. 2; Polonaise in A♭, Op. 53; Prelude in c, Op. 28, No. 20; Valse brilliant in E♭, Op. 18; Nocturne in E♭, Op. 9, No. 2)*, Schubert *(Moment Musical No. 3 in f, D.780)*, Schumann *(Träumerei, Op. 15; Dedication [arr. Liszt])*, Brahms *(Waltz in A♭, Op. 53)*, Liszt *(Consolation No. 3 in D♭; Liebestraume No. 3 in A♭)*, J.S. Bach *(Jesu, Joy of Man's Desire [arr. Hess])*, Debussy *(La plus que lent; Clair de lune; Golliwogg's Cakewalk)*, Rachmaninoff *(Prelude in c♯, Op. 2, No. 3)*, Falla *(Ritual Fire Dance)*, Chaminade *(Scarf Dance)* TOWN ▲ 40 (17.97)

The Competition: Piano Solo Album—music from the motion picture played by the soundtrack artist featuring works by Chopin, D. Scarlatti, Brahms, Gottschalk, Scriabin, Schiffrin, Rachmaninoff, et al. TOWN ▲ 31 (17.97) ▮ 31

Sophisticated Innocence: American Novelty Piano Solos TOWN ▲ 35 (17.97)

Michelangeli, Arturo Benedetti (pno)

Arturo Benedetti Michelangeli, w. La Scala Orch [cnd:Antonio Pedrotti]; Swiss Romande Orch [cnd:Ernest Ansermet]—features works by Schumann *(Con Pno, Op. 54)*, Liszt *(Con 1 Pno)*, plus other works by Beethoven, Grieg & Vivaldi *(rec 1939-43)* ENT (Sirio) ▲ 530035 (13.97)

Arturo Benedetti Michelangeli—features works by Albéniz, Bach/Busoni, Beethoven, Brahms, Granados, Grieg, Mompou, D. Scarlatti EMIC ▲ 64490 (11.97)

Arturo Benedetti Michelangeli—features works by Liszt *(Con 1 Pno [w. Swiss Romande Orch, Ernst Ansermet (cnd)])*, Chopin *(Mazurka No. 47 on a; Scherzo No. 2 in b♭; Valse in A♭)*, plus Vivaldi [w. Swiss Romande Orch, Ernst Ansermet (cnd)], Debussy, Galuppi, Mascotti *(rec 1939; 1941; 1942)* MTAL ▲ 48050 (6.97)

The Complete First Recordings—features works by Liszt, Grieg, Schumann, Chopin, Beethoven, Vivaldi, Bach, Scarlatti *(rec 1939-42)* GRM2 2-▲ 78675 (25.97)

The Complete Studio & Live Recordings Including Fragments & Rarities—features works by Mozart *(Con 15)*, Grieg *(Con Pno)*, Schumann *(Con Pno)*, Liszt *(Con 1)*, Bach *(Italian Con)*, Beethoven *(Son 3 Pno)*, plus short pieces by Galuppi, Scarlatti, Tomeoni, Chopin, Grieg, Debussy, Granados, Albéniz, Mompou, Marescotti, Beethoven & Vivaldi *(rec 1939-47)* ENPL (Piano Library) 4-▲ 252 (51.97)

Moiseiwitsch, Benno (pno)

Benno Moiseiwitsch, Vol. 1—features works by Brahms *(Handel Vars.)*, Mendelssohn *(Con. No. 1 for Pno)*, Stravinsky *(Etude in F♯)*, Ravel *(Jeux d'eau)*, Wagner/Liszt *(Tannhauser Ov.)*, others PHS ▲ 9135 [ADD] (17.97)

A Centenary Celebration *(1928 & 1938-39 HMV rec'gs)*—features works by Godowsky, Medtner, Prokofiev; Beethoven *(Piano Concerto No. 5)*, Liszt *(Hungarian Fantasia)* see Composer Section for details *(rec 1928)* KOCH ▲ 7035

Moore, Lisa (pno)

Stroke—features works by Smetanin *(Stroke)*, Banks *(Commentary)*, Kats-Chernin *(Tast-En)*, Yu *(Impromptu)*, Ford *(A Kumquat for John Keats)*, Edwards *(Etymalong)*, Brophy *(Angelicon)*, Sculthorpe *(Djilile)*, Wesley-Smith *(Grey Beach)* TALP ▲ 40 [DDD]

Mornell, Adina (pno)

Deep Water, High Clouds: Tones & Tales of the Piano—features works by Beethoven, Mendelssohn, Ravel, Debussy, Janáček, Rachmaninoff KSCH ▲ 318352 (16.97)

Morrison, Jeannine (pno), Joanne Rogers (pno)

A Virtuoso Duo-Piano Showcase *(see Rogers)*

Moyer, Frederick (pno)

Rhapsody in Blue, etc.—features works by Schubert *(Impromptu in E♭, Op. 90/2)*, Beethoven *(Für Elise)*, Chopin *(Études in C & E, Op. 10/1 & 3; Scherzo e in c♯)*, Rubenstein *(Melody in F)*, Tchaikovsky *(October & November [both from The Seasons])*, Saint-Saëns *(The Swan [from Carnival of the Animals])*, Debussy *(Clair de Lune [from Suite Bergamesque])*, Grainger *(Irish Tune From Country Derry)*, A. von Henselt *(Preambles in E♭, C, c♯, F, d, E, G, A♭, E♭) (rec Roseholm Studios, New York)* Jupiter ▲ J 107

Muller, Dana (pno), Gary Steigerwalt (pno)

Muller & Steigerwalt—features works by Auric *(5 Bagatelles)*, Busoni *(Finlandische Volksweisen)*, Casella *(Pagine de guerra, Op. 25; Pupazzetti, Op. 27)*, Hindemith *(Sonata for Piano 4-Hands)*, Ravel *(La Valse)*, Schoenberg *(6 Pieces, Op. 19) (rec Aug-Sept 1991)* CENT ▲ 2127 [DDD] (16.97)

Müller, Dario (pno)

The American Indianists—features works by C.W. Cadman *(From the Land of the Sky-Blue Water)*, A. Farwell *(Navajo War Dance [from From Mesa and Plain]; Song of Peace [from Impressions of the Wa-Wan Ceremony of the Omahas, Op. 21])*, B. Fairchild *(The Song of Weasel Bear; The Song of Charging Thunder; The Elk's Song of the Forest; Song of White Robe; Siyaka's Dancing Song; The Song of the Eagle Shield; The Song of Shooter; The Song of Gray Hawk; The Song of the Buffalos; The Song of the Thunderbird Nation; Two Shields' Dance; The Song of the Wolf [from Some Indian Songs and Dances])*, H.F.B. Gilbert *(By the Arrow; In the Kutenal Country; The Night Scout; Signal Fire to the Mountain God [from Indian Scenes])*, H.W. Loomis *(Music of the Calumet; A Song of Sorrow; Around the Wigwam [from Lyrics of the Red Man])*, E. MacDowell *(Dirge [from Indian Suite, Op. 48])*, P.W. Orem *(American Indian Rhap.)*, C.S. Skilton *(Cheyenne War-Dance; Sioux Flute Serenade; Kikapoo Social Dance)*, G.T. Strong *(Une Jeune Indienne) (rec Lugano, Switzerland, Apr & Aug 1993)* MARC ▲ 8223715 [DDD] (14.97)

The American Indianists, Vol 2—features works by Cadman *(Thunderbird Suite; Idealized Indian Themes)*, Troyer *(Traditional Zuni Songs; Kiowa-Apache War Dance [w. V. Mininno (perc)])*, MacDowell *(Woodland Sketches; New England Idyls)*, Strickland *(Sun-Dance)*, Loomis *(Lyrics of the Red Man)*, Gilbert *(Indian Scenes)*, Farwell *(American Indian Melodies; Ichibuzzhi; From Mesa & Plain)*, Skilton *(Shawnee Indian Hunting Dance)* MARC ▲ 8223738 [DDD] (14.97)

Munro, Ian (pno)

Mere Bagatelles—features contemporary Australian piano music by Vine *(Bagatelles [5])*, Sculthorpe *(Simori)*, Lumsdaine *(Postcard Pieces [6])*, K. Humble *(Bagatelles [8])*, N. Butterly *(Arioso; Comment on a Popular Song; Il gubo)*, Munro *(Return; The Forest)*, E. Gyger *(Threshold)*, C. Bright *(Earth Flowering Time)*, A. Ghandar *(Bagatelles [4])*, Amanda Baker *(Bagatelles 1, 3 & 5)*, J. Woolrich *(Slow-Night-That Must Be Watched Away; Capricho; Procession; Little Pno Machine; The Gastrolater's Final Sacrifice; It Is Midnight; Promise & Unfoldment [all from Pianobooks, Vols. I & IV-VI])*, M. Wesley-Smith *(Waltz) (rec Newcastle Conservatorium Concert Hall, Jan 1996)* TALP ▲ 80 [DDD] (18.97)

A Patchwork of Shadows—features works by M. Williamson *(Son. No. 1 for Piano)*, G. Kerry *(Winter through Glass)*, K. Humble *(Son. Nos. 3 & 4 for Piano)*, P. Sculthorpe *(Nocturnal; Night Pieces)*, R. Smalley *(Vars. on a theme by Chopin)*, K. Parker *(4 Musical Sketches) (rec Llewellyn Hall, Canberra School of Music, Dec 1992)* TALP ▲ 58 [DDD] (18.97)

Nagy, Péter (pno)

Romantic Piano Favorites—features works by Delibes, Brahms, Mendelssohn, Liszt, Fauré, Schubert, Chopin, Granados, Rachmaninoff, Mozart, Elgar, Grieg, Ponchielli *(rec Apr 25-May 6, 1988)* NXIN ▲ 550216 [DDD] (5.97)

Romantic Piano Favorites, Vol. 2—features works by Beethoven *(Son. No. 14, "Moonlight")*, Mendelssohn *(Song without Words, Op. 102/3)*, Bizet *(Suite No. 1 [from* L'Arlesienne*])*, Schubert/Liszt *(Lelse flehen meine Lieder [from* Schwanengesang, D.957*])*, Tchaikovsky *(October)*, Offenbach *(Barcarolle)*, Chopin *(Prelude, Op. 28/15; Londonderry Air)*, Schubert *(Moment Musical)*, Mozart *(Son., K.310)*, Grieg *(Heimweh)*, Liszt *(Mephisto Waltz) (rec Sept 17-21, 1987)* NXIN ▲ 550053 [DDD] (5.97)

Vol. 4—features works by Sinding *(Rustle of Spring)*, Lange *(Edelweiss)*, Badarzewska-Baranowska *(The Maiden's Prayer)*, Chaminade *(The Flatterer)*, Mozart *(Adagio [from* Son. Piano,K.332*])*, Moszkowski *(Serenata, Op. 15)*, Tchaikovsky *(None but the Lonely Heart [from* Wilhelm Meister*])*, Rachmaninoff *(Vocalise)*, Chopin *(Waltz in c♯)*, Paderewski *(Mélodie in G)*, Debussy *(Clair de lune)*, Mendelssohn *(On Wings of Song)*, Dvořák *(Slavonic Dance No. 2) (rec Dec 1987-Jan 1988)* NXIN ▲ 550141 [DDD] (5.97)

Vol. 8—features works by Schubert *(The Trout; Moment musical)*, Kreisler *(Liebesfreud)*, Liszt *(Sonetto 123 del Petrarca)*, Mendelssohn *(Song without Words No. 20)*, Brahms *(Hungarian Dance No. 1)*, Gluck *(Orfeo e Euridice [Ballet])*, Beethoven *(Minuet in G)*, Godard *(Berceuse [from* Jocelyn*])*, Ellenberg *(Die Meuhle im Schwarzwald)*, Godowsky *(Night in Tanger)*, Rosas *(Über den Wellen)*, Chopin *(Waltz in e)*, Rachmaninoff *(Étude-tableau in e♭) (rec Sept 24-27, 1988)* NXIN ▲ 550217 [DDD] (5.97)

Vol. 10—features works by Mendelssohn *(Andante sostenuto [from* Song without Words No. 40*])*, Mozart *(Alla Turca; Adagio in b, K.540)*, Beethoven *(Rondo a capriccio)*, Grieg *(Evening in the Mountains)*, Chopin *(Waltz in A♭, Op. 42)*, Weber *(Son. No. 1 for Piano)*, Debussy *(L'Isle joyeuse)*, Tchaikovsky *(Chanson triste in g)*, Rachmaninoff *(Rhaps. on Theme of Paganini)*, Saint-Saëns *(Danse macabre, Op. 40) (rec Mar 18-26, 1988)* NXIN ▲ 550219 [DDD] (5.97)

Nakamatsu, Jon (pno)

10th Van Cliburn International Piano Competition: Jon Nakamatsu, Gold Medalist HAM ▲ 907218 (17.97)

Nero, Peter (pno)

Classic Connections *(pop/classical arr Nero for pno & orch)*, w. Rochester PO [cnd:Peter Nero]—features works by Leonard Bernstein, Vernon Duke, Duke Ellington, George Gershwin, Cole Porter, et al. PRA ▲ 576 [DDD] (14.97) 576 (10.98)

Newton, Molly (pno)

Winter—features works by Scarlatti *(Son Pno, K.119)*, J. S. Bach *(Sinf 15)*, Mozart *(Fant in D, K.397)*, Beethoven *(Bagatelle in g)*, Schumann *(Pleading Child; Perfectly Contented; Rememberance; At the Fireside; Little Cradle Song; Wintertime II; Fant Dance)*, Gade *(Christmas Bells; Boys Round; Dance of the Young Girls [all from Noël, Op. 36])*, Mendelssohn *(Sighing Wind)*, Stier *(I Died for Beauty)*, Fauré *(Clair de lune, Op. 46/2)*, Prokofiev *(Prélude, Op. 12/7)*, Tchaikovsky *(January; February)*, Debussy *(Footsteps in the Snow; The Snow Is Dancing)*, Bartók *(Rumanian Christmas Carols [sels])*, Busoni *(Christmas Night)*, Chopin *(Winter Wind) (rec 1995)* HALC ▲ HP 30106 [DDD]

Novacek, John (pno)

Classic Romance II—features works by Granados *(Spanish Dance 2, "Oriental")*, Chopin *(Ballade in g, Op. 23; Waltz in c♯, Op. 64/2; Nocturne in f♯, Op. 48/2)*, Debussy *(Clair de lune)*, Mendelssohn *(Song without Words, Op. 62/1)*, Schubert *(Impromptu in G♭; Serenade [arr Liszt])*, Ravel *(Jeux d'eau)*, Beethoven *(Für Elise)*, Verdi *(Rigoletto Paraphrase [arr Liszt])*, Rameau *(Gavotte & 6 Doubles)*, Scriabin *(Prelude for Left Hand, Op. 9/1)* FWIN ▲ 3006 (13.97)

Novarags—features works by John Novacek *(Intoxication; Recuperation; Schenectady; Melancholy drag; Full stride ahead; Back country rag; Novissong; Hog wild; Eubie Blake medley)*, Scott Joplin *(Gadiolus rag; Solace; Stoptime rag)*, J. Scott *(Efficiency rag; Kansas City rag)*, J. P. Johnson *(Daintiness rag)*, Luckey R.s *(Pork and beans)*, Joseph Lamb *(Top liner rag)*, John Novacek *(4th Street drag; Cockles; Waltzee; Ragamuffin; Rag Brillante [rags for piano & guitar, w. S. Novacek, guitar])*, Scott Joplin *(Paragon rag)* AMBA ▲ 1008 [DDD] (16.97) ▮ ARC 1008

Novaes, Guiomar (pno)

The Complete Victor 78s, 1919-1927—features works by Beethoven, Chopin, Gluck, Gottschalk, Liszt, Mendelsohn, Moszkowski, Paderewski, et al. MUA ▲ 702 (m) [AAD]

Guiomar Novaes, w. Vienna SO [cnd:Otto Klemperer]—features works by Beethoven *(Con 4 Pno)*, Chopin *(Con 2 Pno)*, Schumann *(Con Pno)*, Bach, Brahms, Gluck, Saint-Saëns *(rec 1950s & early 1960s)* VOXL 2-▲ 5501 [ADD] (9.97)

Nyiregyházi, Ervin (pno)

At the Opera—features 6 original operatic paraphrases for solo piano on Pagliacci, Eugen Onegin, Ballo in maschera, Otello, Trovatore, Rienzi, Lohengrin *(rec 1978)* VAIA ▲ 1003 (m) [ADD] (17.97)

O'Conor, John (pno)

Autumn Songs: Popular Works for Solo Piano—features works by R. Strauss *(Träumerei, Op. 9/4)*, Schumann *(Romance in F♯, Op. 28/2; Warum? [from Phantasiestücke, Op. 12])*, Debussy *(La fille aux cheveux de lin)*, Bach *(Prelude in C [from Well-Tempered Clavier, Book 1])*, Chopin *(Nocturne in c♯, Op. 27/1; Minute Waltz in D♭, Op. 64/1)*, Mozart *(Allegro [from Son in C, K.545])*, Grieg *(Andante molto [from Son in g, Op. 7])*, Rubinstein *(Melodie in F, Op. 3/1)*, Tchaikovsky *(Autumn Song)*, Mendelssohn *(Song Without Words in G, Op. 62/1; The Bee's Wedding, Op. 67/4)*, Daquin *(Le Coucou)*, Rimsky-Korsakov *(Flight of the Bumblebee)*, Durand *(Valse in E♭)*, Rachmaninoff *(Prelude in c♯, Op. 3/2)*, Liszt *(Consolation No. 3 in D♭)*, Gershwin *(Prelude No. 2) (rec Mechanics Hall, Worcester, MA, Feb 21-23, 1995)* TEL ▲ 80391 [DDD] (15.97)

Popular Works for Solo Piano—features works by Beethoven, Brahms, Chopin, Debussy, Grieg, MacDowell, Mendelssohn, Mozart, Rachmaninoff, Joachim Raff, Satie, Schumann, Scriabin, Sibelius TEL ▲ 80313 [DDD] (15.97)

Ogawa, Noriko (pno)

Just for Me: Noriko Agawa Plays Japanese Piano Music—features works by Taki *(Pieces (2) Pno)*, Mitsukuri *(Pieces (3) after the Flower)*, Sugawara *(Steam)*, Hashimoto *(Pieces (3) Pno)*, Kiyose *(Ryükyü Dances)*, Kanai *(Ryükyü Dances, "Maidens under the Moon")*, Hayasaka *(Autumn)*, Koyama *(Kagome-vars)*, Yashiro *(Nocturne)*, Nakata *(Variational Étude)*, Sakamoto *(Suite Pno; Just for Me) (rec Sweden, Dec 1996)* BIS ▲ 854 [DDD] (17.97)

Ogdon, John (pno)

John Ogdon—features works by Chopin *(Polonaise in A♭, Op. 53)*, Schubert *(Moment Musical 3)*, Mussorgsky *(The Old Castle)*, Ravel *(Laideronette Imperatrice des Pagodes; Pavane pour une infante defunte)*, Tchaikovsky *(Barcarolle, Op. 39/6)*, Debussy *(Son Fl Pno)*, Beethoven *(Bagatelle in a, "Für Elise")*, Mozart *(Rondo alla Turca)*, Mendelssohn *(Songs without Words)*, Brahms *(Rhap 2 in g, Op. 79)*, Satie *(Gymnopédie 1)* INMP (IMP Classics) ▲ 6701202 (8.97)

Okashiro, Chitose (pno)

Schumann Symphonic Etudes—features works by Schumann *(Symphonic Etudes, Op. 13 & Op.posth.; Arabesque, Op. 18)*, D. Scarlatti *(Son. in C, K.420)*, Mozart *(Son. in B♭, K.570)*, Chopin *(Etude in c, Op. 10/12)*, Scriabin *(Etude in c♯, Op. 42/5)*, Brahms *(Fant., Op. 116/6) (rec Academy of Arts & Letters, New York, Sept 23-24, 1993)* PPR ▲ PPR 224501 [DDD]

Olevsky, Estela (pno)

Piano Solos of Latin America—features works by Cervantes *(Danzas Cubanas)*, Ginastera *(Malambo; Milonga)*, Guastavino *(10 Preludios sobre temas de canciones populares argentinas)*, Villa-Lobos *(Alma brasileira [from Choros No. 5])*, Nazareth *(Escovado; Preigoso; Odeon)*, R. Stern *(Vars. on the Theme "Arrorró")*, Chávez *(Cake-Walk; Vals elegia)*, Copland *(El Salon Mexico [trans. Bernstein]) (rec Univ. of Mass., Amherst, July-Aug 1993)* CENT ▲ 2202 [DDD] (16.97)

Oppens, Ursula (pno)

Vol. 2—features works by Anthony Davis, John Harbison, Conlon Nancarrow, Tobias Picker, Frederic Rzewski *(see* Composer section) MUA ▲ 699 [DDD]

Oppitz, Gerhard (pno)

Nocturne—features works by Mozart *(Fant in d, K.397)*, Beethoven *(Rondo in G, Op. 51/2)*, Mendelssohn *(Frühlingslied [Spring Song] in A [from Lieder ohne Worte (Songs without Words), Op. 62])*, Chopin *(Prélude in c♯, Op. 45)*, Szymanowski *(Etude in b♭, Op. 4/3)*, Liszt *(Notturno No. 3 in A♭, "Liebestraum")*, Scriabin *(Etude in c♯, Op. 2/1)*, Rachmaninoff *(Prélude in c♯, Op. 3/2)*, Albéniz *(Mallorca, Barcarola, Op. 202)*, Falla *(Danza ritual del fuego [from El Amor bujo])*, Debussy *(La Cathédrale engloutie [from Préludes, Book 1])*, Fauré *(Nocturne No. 4 in E♭, Op. 36)*, Ravel *(Pavane pour une infante défunte) (rec Reitstadel, Neumarkt, Germany, July 24-26, 1993)* RCAV (Red Seal) ▲ 61968 [DDD]

Ortiz, Cristina (pno)

French Impressionist Piano—features works by Chabrier *(Danse villageoise)*, et al. *([see Composer Section for details])* 2371 ▲ 846 [DDD]

Pachmann, Vladimir de (pno)

Vladimir de Pachmann—features works by Brahms, Chopin, Liszt & Schumann *(rec 1911-16)* ENPL (Piano Library) ▲ 238 (13.97)

Paderewski, Ignace Jan (pno)

The Art of Paderewski, Vol. 1 *(1922-1938 recordings)*—features works by Beethoven, Haydn, Mozart, Paderewski, Schubert PHS ▲ 9499 (m) [AAD] (17.97)

Vol. 2 *(1911-1931 Victor recordings, and one 1938 radio broadcast selection)*—features works by Couperin, Liszt, Schelling, Sigismund Stojowski, Wagner (Liszt and Schelling transcriptions) PHS ▲ 9943 (m) [AAD] (17.97)

Vol. 3—features works by Schumann, Mendelssohn, Rubinstein, Debussy, Brahms & Strauss/Tausig *(rec 1911-30)* PHS ▲ 9109 [ADD] (17.97)

Ignace Jan Paderewski *(1922-31 Duo Art pno rolls)*—features works by Liszt *(Hungarian Rhaps 2 & 10; Grandes Etudes de Paganini [La Campanella])*, Schumann *(Nachtstück, Op. 23/4; Vogel als Prophet, Op. 82/7)*, Mendelssohn *(Spinning Song, Op. 67/4)*, Schubert *(Valse Caprice, Op. 67/6 [trans Liszt]; Impromptus, Op. 142/2 & 3)*, Beethoven *(Son 14)*, Wagner *(Isoldes Liebestod [from Tristan und Isolde; trans Liszt])*, Schelling *(Nocturne)* NIMB (Grand Piano) ▲ 8812 [DDD] (11.97)

Ignace Paderewski Plays Beethoven, Liszt, Schubert, Debussy, Vol. 1—features works by Beethoven *(Son., Op. 27/2)*, Schubert/Liszt *(Soirée de Vienna)*, Schubert *(Hark, Hark the Lark)*, Liszt *(Hungarian Rhaps. Nos. 2 & 10)*, Debussy *(Reflections in the Water)*, Mendelssohn *(Spinning Song)*, Wagner/Liszt *(Isoldes Love-Death)* KLAV ▲ KCD 11018 [ADD]

Paderewski RCAV (Gold Seal:Legendary Performers) ▲ 60923

Paperno, Dmitry (pno)

Uncommon Encores—features works by Albéniz, Bach-Siloti, Chopin, Glinka-Balakirev, Gluck-Sgambati, Hummel, Khachaturian, Liszt, Mendelssohn, Mompou, Mozart, Rachmaninoff, Scarlatti, Schumann-Levinson, Scriabin, Shchedrin CED ▲ 7 [DDD] (16.97)

Paratore, Anthony (pno), Joseph Paratore (pno)

Classic Romance—features works by Rachmaninoff *(A Night for Love)*, Saint-Saëns *(The Swan [from Carnival of the Animals])*, Fauré *(Pavane, Op. 50)*, Brahms *(Waltzes, Op. 39/2 & 15)*, Bach *(Jesu, Joy of Man's Desiring)*, Chopin *(Rondo in C, Op. 73)*, Scriabin *(Fant in a)*, Debussy *(Prélude à l'après-midi d'un faune)*, Ravel *(Boléro)* FWIN ▲ 3005 (13.97)

Classics to Broadway *(arrangements by the performers and others for piano duet)*—features works by Irving Berlin *(Song medley)*, Gershwin/arr. Grainger *(Fantasy on Themes from Porgy and Bess)*, Mozart/arr. Busoni *(Magic Flute overture)*, Joh. Strauss II/arr. Pierre Luboschutz *(Paraphrase on Themes from Die Fledermaus)*, Brahms, Falla, Saint-Saëns, Schubert KSCH ▲ 310115 [DDD] (16.97)

Variations for 4-Hands *(see Composer section: Beethoven—Variations, WoO 74; etc.)* KSCH ▲ 310088 [ADD]

Pekinel, Güher (pno), Süher Pekinel (pno)

Encores for 2 Pianos—features works by Liszt, Brahms, Milhaud, Poulenc, Lecuana, J.S. Bach, Lutoslawski, Rachmaninoff, J.C. Bach & Gershwin BER ▲ 1118 [DDD] (16.97)

Perahia, Murray (pno)

The Aldeburgh Recital—features works by Beethoven *(Variations in c)*, Liszt, Rachmaninoff, Schumann *(see* Composer section) COL ▲ 46437 [DDD] (16.97) 46437

Murray Perahia, w. Bavarian RSO [cnd:C. Davis], English CO [cnd:M. Perahia]—features B. Bartók *(Improvs on Hungarian Peasant Songs, Op. 20)*, Beethoven *(Vars (32) Pno, WoO 80)*, J. Brahms *(Rhaps (2) Pno, Op. 79 [No. 1 in b])*, Chopin *(Ballade 1 Pno, Op. 23)*, E. Grieg *(Con Pno, Op. 16)*, Liszt *(Consolations (6), S.172 [No. 3 in D])*, Mendelssohn (-Bartholdy) *(Vars sérieuses Pno, Op. 54)*, W. A. Mozart *(Con 25 Pno, K.503)*, D. Scarlatti *(Sons Kbd [Son No. 27 in b; Son No. 212 in A])*, F. Schubert *(Impromptus (4) [No. 3 in B♭])* PPHI (Great Pianists of the 20th Century) ▲ 456922 (22.97)

Perahia, Murray (pno) (cont.)

Murray Perahia: 25th Anniversary Edition—features works by D. Scarlatti *(Sons, K.27 & 212)*, Mozart *(German Dances, K.509; Adagio, K.540; Con 27 Pno [w. English CO [cnd:Murray Perahia]]*, Schubert *(Impromptu, D.899/4)*, Schumann *(Papillons, Op. 2)*, Chopin *(Ballade 1, Op. 23; Con 2 Pno [w. Israel PO [cnd:Zubin Mehta]]*, Liszt *(Gnomenreigen)*, Rachmaninoff *(Etudes-tableaux, Opp. 39/5 & 49/6)*, Bartók *(Suite Pno, Op. 14; Improvs on Hungarian Peasant Songs, Op. 20; Out of Doors, Sz.81)*, Berg *(Son Pno, Op. 1)*, Tippett *(Son 1 Pno)*, Beethoven *(Qt Pno Ww, Op. 16 [w. Neil Black (ob), Thea King (cl), Tony Halstead (hn), Graham Sheen (bn)]; Songs (5), Op. 40 [w. Peter Pears (ten)])*, Brahms *(Qt 1 Pno [w. Amadeus String Quartet members])* COL 4-▲ 63380 (47.97)

A Portrait of Murray Perahia *(see Composer section, Beethoven:Son 23 Pno, etc.) (rec 1975-83)* COL ▲ 42448 [AAD/DDD] (11.97) 42448

Petri, Egon (pno)

The Art of Egon Petri—features works by Bach, Beethoven, Busoni *(w. Carlo Bussotti)*, Chopin, Haydn, Gluck, Liszt, Medtner, Mozart, Schubert *(rec. 1954-62)* MUA 4-▲ 772 [AAD]

Egon Petri, w. London PO [cnd:Leslie Heward]—features Liszt *(Con 2 Pno)*, plus transcriptions & paraphrases from Gounod, Liszt, Paganini, Schubert, Verdi & Wagner *(rec 1929-38)* ENPL (Piano Library) ▲ 222 (13.97)

Egon Petri, Vol. 1 *(1929-1951 Columbia, HMV and private recordings)*—features works by Bach-Busoni *(Chromatic Fantasy and Fugue, 1951 private recording)*, Bach-Petri *(Menuet, rec. 1935)*, Beethoven *(Sonata No. 24, rec. 1936)*, Brahms *(Paganini Variations, rec. 1937)*, Gluck-Sgambati *(Orphée:Melodie, rec. 1936)*, Gounod-Liszt *(Faust Waltz Fantaisie, rec. 1936)*, Liszt *(Gnomenreigen, Mazeppa & Un sospiro, rec. 1929, 1935 & 1937)*, Schubert-Liszt *(Soirée de Vienne No. 6, rec. 1935; Die Forelle & Liebesbotschaft, 1948 recital recordings)* PHS ▲ 9916 (m) [AAD] (18.97)

His Recordings 1929-1942, Vol. 3—features works by Schubert/Tausig *(Andante & Vars.)*, Chopin *(Preludes, Op. 28)*, Franck *(Préludes, choral et fugue)*, Gluck/Sgambati *(Mélodie)*, J.S. Bach/Petri *(Menuet)*, J.S. Bach/Busoni *(Chorale Preludes; Ich ruf' zu dir, Herr Jesu Christ; Wachet auf, ruft uns die Stimme; Nun Freut euch, lieben Christen gemein)*, Busoni *(Fantasia after J.S. Bach; Serenade; An die Jugend No. 3; Sonatina No. 3; Sonatina No. 6; Indianisches Tagebuch; Albumblatt No. 3; Elegie No. 2)* APR 2-▲ 7027 [ADD] (38.97)

Pierce, Joshua (pno), Dorothy Jonas (pno)

Classically Broadway—features works by Leonard Bernstein *(Candide Overture; West Side Story medley)*, Richard Rodgers *(The Sound of Music medley; Waltz Medley; etc.)*, Andrew Lloyd Webber *(Memories, from Cats)*, Jerry Herman *(I Am What I Am, from La Cage aux Folles)*, Marvin Hamlisch *(A Chorus Line medley)* Kem-Disc ▲ * [DDD]

20th Century Romantic Music for 2 Pianos—features works by A. Benjamin *(Jamaican Rhumba)*, Bax *(The Poisoned Fountain)*, Britten *(Introduction & Rondo; Mazurka)*, Debussy/arr. Ravel *(Fêtes)*, Lutoslawski *(Variations on a Theme of Paganini)*, Rachmaninoff *(Symphonic Dances, Op. 45; Polka italienne; Prelude in c#, Op. 3/2; Russian Rhapsody)*, Saint-Saëns *(Danse macabre)* KOCH ▲ 7013 [DDD] (16.97)

Pivka, Marian (pno)

The Masterpiece Collection: Piano—features works by Chopin *(Waltzes, Opp. 64/1, 34/1; Prelude, Op. 28/25, "Raindrop"; Etude, Op. 10/12)*, Brahms *(Waltz in A♭, Op. 39/15)*, Beethoven *(Für Elise)*, Tchaikovsky *(Carnival; Autumn Song [both from The Seasons])*, Liszt *(Liebestraum No. 3; Consolation in E)*, Grieg *(To the Spring; Erotic [both from Lyric Pieces])*, Mendelssohn *(Spring Song; Song without Words, Op. 62/1)*, Schubert *(Moment Musical, Op. 94/3; Impromptu, Op. 142/2)*, Schumann *(Träumeri, Op. 15/7)*, Debussy *(Clair de Lune)* UNIN ▲ 8006 (5.97) 8006 (3.98)

Planté, Francis (pno)

Ricardo Viñes & Francis Planté—features works by Chopin, Gluck, Mendelssohn, Schumann, Boccherini & Berlioz *(rec 1928-36)* † PIANO:Viñes POHS ▲ 9857 [ADD] (17.97)

Pollack, Daniel (pno)

First Kiss: Romantic Piano Music for Love & Passion—features works by Liszt *(Consolation 3; Concert Etude in D♭ [Un sospiro])*, Ravel *(Pavane pour une infante défunte)*, Chopin *(Nocturne in D♭, Op. 27/2; Nocturne in c#, Op. posth)*, Debussy *(Girl with the Flaxen Hair; Arabesque 1)*, Schumann *(Carnaval, Op. 9 [Chiarina; Chopin]; Träumerei)*, Brahms *(Intermezzo, Op. 118/2)*, Scriabin *(Etude, Op. 2/1; Nocturne for Left-Hand, Op. 9/2)*, Rachmaninoff *(Prelude, Op. 32/12)*, Tchaikovsky *(The Seasons, Op. 37a [October])* FWIN ▲ 3002 (13.97)

Passionate Kiss: Romantic Piano Music—features works by Rachmaninoff *(Preludes, Opp. 3/2 & 23/4; Etude-Tableau,Op. 39/5)*, Debussy *(Reverie)*, Tchaikovsky *(The Seasons [June])*, Chopin *(Etudes, Opp. 10/3 & 25/7; Nocturne, Op. 9/2; Prelude, Op. 28/15)*, Szymanowski *(Etude, Op. 4/3)*, Beethoven *(Son 14 [1st movt])*, Mendelssohn *(Venetian Boat Song, Op. 30/6)*, Brahms *(Capriccio, Op. 76/1; Intermezzo, Op. 117/2)*, Grieg *(Lyric Suite [Notturno])* FWIN ▲ 3004 (13.97)

Ponti, Michael (pno)

Operatic Piano—features works by Grainger *(Paraphrase on Tchaikovsky's "Waltz of the Flowers")*, Liszt *(Operatic Paraphrases)*, Moszkowski *(Operatic Paraphrases of Bizet:Danse Bohème after "Carmen"; Offenbach:Barcarolle from "Tales of Hoffmann"; Wagner:Isolde's Death from "Tristan und Isolde," & Venusberg Bachanale, Paraphrase for Pno after Music of Wagner)*, Tausig *(Fantasy on Themes of Moniuszko's "Halka")*, Wagner *(Transcriptions)*, Thalberg *(Fantasy on Meyerbeer's "Huguenots")*, Meyerbeer *(Fantasy on "Robert")*, Brassin *(Magic Fire Music from Die Walküre)*, Pabst *(Concert Paraphrase on Tchaikovsky's Eugen Onegin) (rec 1970-75)* VB2 2-▲ 5047 [ADD]

Pöntinen, Roland (pno)

Evocation: Legendary Encores Played by Roland Pöntinen—features works by Chopin *(Grandes Valses Brillante in A♭ & a, Op. 34/1 & 2; Nocturne in B, Op. 32/1; Mazurka in a, Op. 17/4)*, Rachmaninoff *(Lilacs, Op. 21/5; Daisies, Op. 38/3)*, Granados *(Andaluza [Danzas españolas No. V]; Quejas ó la Maja y el Ruiseñor [from Goyescas])*, Weber *(Perpetuum Mobile)*, Moszkowski *(Étincelles, Op. 36/6)*, Handel *(Minuet in g [trans. Kempff])*, Falla *(Andaluza [from Cuatro piezas Españolas])*, Kreisler *(Liebesfreud [trans. Rachmaninoff])*, Tchaikovsky *(Lullaby [trans. Rachmaninoff])*, Albéniz *(Evocación [from Iberia, Book I]) (rec Gamla Musikaliska Akademi, Stockholm, Sweden, May 31-June 3, 1994)* BIS ▲ 661 [DDD] (17.97)

Music for a Rainy Day—features works by Chopin, Falla, Scriabin, Beethoven, Stenhammar, Schumann, Grieg, Wm. Seymer, Prokofiev, Debussy, Satie BIS ▲ 300 [DDD] (17.97)

Music for a Rainy Day 2—features works by Mendelssohn *(Rondo Capriccioso, Op. 14)*, Rachmaninoff *(Prelude in c#, Op. 3/2; Polka de V. R.)*, Liszt *(Valses oubliées 1 & 4; Nocturnes (3))*, Albéniz *(Tango español, Op. 164)*, Tausig *(Man lebt nur einmal)*, D. Scarlatti *(Son in f, L.118)*, Rubinstein *(Valse-Caprice in E♭)*, Ginastera *(Danza de la moza donosa)*, Debussy *(D'un cahier d'esquisses) (rec June 1997)* BIS ▲ 883 [DDD] (17.97)

Postolovskaya, Nina (pno)

Romantic Piano—features works by Debussy, Saint-Saëns, Chopin, Beethoven, Schubert, Brahms, Granados SGO ▲ 9310 [DDD] (16.97) ▮ 9310 (11.98)

Prokofiev, Sergei (pno)

Prokofiev Plays Prokofiev—features works by Prokofiev *(Toccata, Op. 11; Prelude, Op. 12/7; Tales of the Old Grandmother, Op. 31/3; Scherzo, Op. 12/10; Gavotte, Op. 12/2; Marche, Op. 12/1; Sarcasms, Op. 17/1 & 2; Rigaudon, Op. 12/2; Love for 3 Oranges [intermezzo])*, Mussorgsky *(Pictures at an Exhibition [Bydlo & Ballet])*, Glazunov *(Gavotte, Op. 49/3)*, Miaskovsky *(Grillen, Op. 25/1 & 6)*, Scriabin *(Prelude, Op. 45/5; Winged Poem, Op. 51/3)*, Rimsky-Korsakov *(Scheherazade [Fant. Arrangement from Symphonic Suite])* LALI ▲ 14203 (3.97)

Pugno, Raoul (pno)

The Complete 1903 Recordings—features works by Scarlatti; Handel; Weber; Chopin; Mendelssohn; Liszt; Bizet; Chabrier; Massenet; Saint-Saëns, plus more *(rec 1903)* ENPL (Piano Library) ▲ 218 (13.97)

His Complete Published Piano Solos (1903)—features works by Chabrier, Chopin, Handel, Liszt, Massenet, Mendelssohn, Pugno, Scarlatti, Weber; plus three songs, with contralto Maria Gay, by Bizet, Pugno, Saint-Saëns POHS ▲ 9836 (m) [AAD]

Queffélec, Anne (pno)

Satie: Piano Music (Vol. 1) VCL ▲ 59515 (16.97)

Quintana, Edison (pno)

Tango Nostalgia—features works by Piazzolla *(Rio Sena; Contrastes; Coral)*, Mores *(Taquito militar; Tanguera; Momento de tango)*, Gardel *(El día que me quieras)*, Ramírez *(Milonga uruguaya; Cajita de música criolla; Alfonsina y el mar)*, Nazareth *(Odeón; Tango brasilero)*, Rodríguez *(La cumparsita)*, Delfino *(Griseta)*, Lomuto *(Muñequita)*, Cobián *(Shusheta; La casita de mis viejos)*, Guastavino *(Preludio 1; El Patio)*, Bardi *(El gallo ciego)* URT ▲ 16

Rachmaninoff, Sergei (pno)

The Complete Recordings *(complete Victor recordings, featuring Rachmaninoff as soloist, chamber musician and conductor, programmed chronologically)*—features works by Rachmaninoff *(The Four Piano Concerti, Rhapsody on a Theme of Paganini, Symphony No. 3, Isle of the Dead, Vocalise, and Piano Music)*, Bach, Beethoven, Borodin, Chopin, Grieg, Handel, Liszt, Mendelssohn, Mozart, Paderewski, Rimsky-Korsakov, Schubert, Schumann, Scriabin, Tchaikovsky, et al. RCAV (Gold Seal) 10-▲ 61265 (102.97)

Piano Recital—features works by Chopin *(Waltzes (5) in E♭, D♭, c#, A♭ & b)*, Tchaikovsky *(Waltz in A♭; Troika en Traineaux [from Les Saisons])*, Beethoven *(Vars (32) in c)*, Schubert *(Impromptu in A♭)*, Mendelssohn *(Spinning Song Scherzo [from A Midsummer Night's Dream])*, Liszt *(Gnomenreigen [from Études de concert])*, plus Mussorgsky, Debussy, J. S. Bach, Bizet, Handel *(rec 1921-23; 1925; 1927; 1928; 1935; 1936)* MTAL ▲ 48036 (6.97)

The Romantic Composers—features works by Schubert, Liszt, Mendelssohn, Mussorgsky, Tchaikovsky, Rimsky-Korsakov, Borodin, Bizet, Saint-Saëns, Grieg *(rec 1919-42)* ENPL (Piano Library) ▲ 267 (13.97)

Sergei Rachmaninoff PPHI (Great Pianists of the 20th Century) ▲ 456943 (22.97)

Sergei Rachmaninoff in Concert—features works by Rachmaninoff *(Preludes, Opp. 3/2 & 23/5; Lilacs; Serenade, Op. 3/5; Mélodie, Op. 3/3; Etude tableau, Op. 39/4)*, Bach *(Sarabande in D)*, Chopin *(Nocturne, Op. 15/4; Maidens Wish, Op. 74; Scherzo, Op. 31)*, Bizet *(Minuet)*, Kreisler/Rachmaninoff *(Liebesfreud)*, Henselt *(Were I a Bird, Op. 2/6)*, Schubert *(Impromptu, Op. 90/4)*, Beethoven/Rubinstein *(Turkish, Op. 113)* KLAV ▲ 11008 [ADD]

Rangell, Andrew (pno)

A Recital of Intimate Works—features works by Sweelinck *(Vars on "Mein junges Leben hat ein End")*, Bach & Petri *(Menuett; Sheep May Safely Graze)*, Enescu *(Carillon Nocturne)*, Beethoven *(6 Bagatelles; Fuga; Adagio ma non troppo e molto espressivo [1st movt])*, Messiaen *(Les sons impalpables du rêve)*, Mozart *(Rondo in a)*, Froberger *(Ricercare VI, book of 1654) (rec Studio I, WGBH, Boston, Nov 1994 & Mar 1995)* DORD ▲ 80147 [DDD] (13.97)

Rasmussen, Kristian (pno)

Danish-American Composers—features works by Lornetzen *(Goldranken)*, Appledorn *(Contrasts)*, Germani *(Immotus)*, Hegaard *(Prelude 1)*, Beck *(Son 1 Pno)*, Lund *(Dialogues (5))*, Russo *(Toccatas 1 & 2)* CRSR ▲ 9664 (16.97)

Reding, Janine (pno), Henry Piette (pno)

Reding & Piette Play Works for 2 Pianos—features works by Alain, W.F. Bach, Brahms, Debussy, Milhaud, M. Poot, A. Tansman OLY ▲ 271 [AAD] (16.97)

Vol. 2—features works by Pasquini *(Son in d)*, Schumann *(Andante con variazioni)*, Stravinsky *(Con for 2 Pnos)*, Goossens *(Rhythmic Dance)*, Guarnieri *(Negro Dance)*, Tailleferre *(Jeux de plein)*, Martinů *(3 Czech Dances)* OLY ▲ 272 [AAD]

Renard, Rosita (pno)

Rosita Renard at Carnegie Hall *(w. rare 1928 recordings)*—features works by Bach *(Partita No. 1 in B♭)*, Mozart *(Sonata No. 15 in a, K.310; Rondo in D, K.485)*, Mendelssohn *(Variations sérieuses, Op. 54; Prelude in B♭, Op. 104, No. 1)*, Chopin *(Études, Op. 10, Nos. 2-4 & 11 & Op. 25, Nos.2-5 & 8; Mazurka in c#, Op. 30, No. 4; Mazurka in f#, Op. 59, No. 3; Prelude in A, Op. 28, No. 7; Nocturne in E♭, Op. 9, No. 2; Nocturne in F#, Op. 15, No. 2)*, Debussy *(Danse)*, Boccherini *(Minuet from Quintet, Op. 13, No. 5)*, Ravel *(Valses nobles et sentimentales)*, Beethoven *(Sonata No. 16 in G, Op. 31, No. 1)*, Strauss/Shulz-Evler *(Aragesque on Themes from The Beautiful Blue Danube)*, Santa Cruz *(Viñetas:Suite, Op. 8 [selections]) (rec live, Jan 19, 1949)* VAIA 2-▲ 1028 (m) [ADD] (31.97)

Richter, Sviatoslav (pno)

Concert Performances & Broadcasts, 1958-1976—features works by Beethoven *(w. Kiril Kondrashin)*, Chopin, Debussy, Mussorgsky, Prokofiev, Rachmaninoff, Schumann, Scriabin, Tchaikovsky MUA 3-▲ 775 [AAD]

In Memoriam: Legendary Recordings 1959-65—features works by J. S. Bach *(5 Preludes & Fugues [from Das wohltemperirte Clavier])*, Chopin *(Ballades, Opp. 47 & 52; Études, Op. 10/1 & 12; Polonaise-fant, Op. 61)*, Debussy *(Estampes; 3 Preludes [from Book 1])*, Haydn *(Son in g, H.XVI:44)*, Prokofiev *(Visions fugitives, Op. 22/3, 6 & 9)*, Rachmaninoff *(7 Preludes)*, Schubert *(Allegretto, D.915; Ländler in A)*, Schumann *(Vars on A-B-E-G-G, Op. 1)* DEUT (Two-Fers) 2-▲ 457667 (17.97)

Richter, Sviatoslav (pno) PPHI (Great Pianists of the 20th Century) ▲ 456946 (22.97)

Rische, Michael (pno)

Album des Six—features music by Auric, Honneger, Durey, Milhaud, Poulenc, Tailleferre KSCH ▲ 317692 (16.97)

Risler, Edouard Joseph (pno)

The Complete 1917 Pathé Recordings—features works by Daquin-Couperin, Rameau, Beethoven, Weber, Mendelssohn, Chopin, Liszt, Godard, Granados ENPL (Piano Library) ▲ 209 (13.97)

Rodriguez, Santiago (pno)

Music for Piano—features works by Ginastera, Albeniz, de Falla, Granados, Ruvo ELAN ▲ 2202 [DDD] (16.97)

Piano in Hollywood: The Classic Movie Concertos—features works by Addinsell *(Warsaw Con [from Dangerous Moonlight])*, Wildman *(Swedish Rhap [from Gypsy Fury])*, Rózsa *(Spellbound Con [from Spellbound])*, Bath *(Cornish Rhap [from Love Story])*, Gershwin *(New York Rhap [from Delicious])*, L. Stevens *(Con Pno [from Night Song])*, E. Ward *(Con Pno [from Phantom of the Opera; all w. William Hudson (cnd), Fairfax SO])*, S. Myers *(Cavatina [from The Deer Hunter]) (rec 1995)* ELAN ▲ 82268 [DDD] (16.97)

A Spanish Album—features works by de Falla, Soler, Turina, Lecuona ELAN ▲ 2206 [DDD]

Rogers, Joanne (pno), Jeannine Morrison (pno)

A Virtuoso Duo-Piano Showcase—features works by Duvernoy *(Feu roulant, Op. 256)*, von Dohnányi *(Suite en valse, Op. 39a)*, Stover *(Rag, Pastorale, & Carillon)*, Lutoslawski *(Vars. on a Theme by Paganini)*, Brahms *(Vars. on a Theme by Haydn, Op. 56b)*, Costa *(Flying Tigers) (rec Spivey Hall, Morrow, GA, June 8-9, 1993)* ACAD ▲ 20023 (16.97) ▮ CM 20023

Rosenberger, Carol (pno)

Night Moods—features works by Chopin, Debussy, Fauré, Granados, Griffes, Liszt DLS ▲ 3030 [DDD]

Perchance to Dream: A Lullaby Album for Children & Adults—features works by Bach, Beethoven, Brahms, Chopin, Fauré, Haydn, Kabalevsky, Mozart, Schubert, Schumann, Tchaikovsky DLS ▲ 3079 [DDD] ▮ CS-3079 (D)

Reveries—features works by Chopin *(Mazurka in a, Op. 17/4; Berceuse, Op. 57)*, Debussy *(Arabesque No. 1; Bruyères)*, Fauré *(Nocturne No. 8 in D♭, Op. 84)*, Griffes *(The Lake at Evening, Op. 5/1)*, Liszt *(Au lac de Wallenstadt; Sancta Dorothea; Consolation No. 3 in D♭)*, Ravel *(Pavane pour une infante défunte; Menuet from Le tombeau de Couperin)*, Schumann *(Romance in F#, Op. 28/2; Träumerei, from Kinderscenen)*, Haydn *(Andante from Sonata in A, H.XVI:12)*, Bach *(Sarabande from French Suite No. 5) (rec 1992)* DLS ▲ 3113 [DDD]

Singing on the Water: Piano Barcarolles—features works by Ravel: *(Une barque sur l'océan)*, Fauré *(Barcarolles No. 3 in G♭, Op. 42; No. 4 in A♭, Op. 44; No. 5 in f#, Op. 66; No. 6 in E♭, Op. 70; No. 8 in D♭, Op. 96)*, Bennett *(Barcarolle)*, Debussy *(L'isle joyeuse)*, Chopin *(Barcarolle, Op. 60)*, Rachmaninoff *(Barcarolle, Op. 10/3)*, Griffes *(Barcarolle, Op. 6/1)*, Diamond *(2 Barcarolles)*, Schubert/Liszt *(Auf dem Wasser zu singen) (rec 1st Congregational Church, Los Angeles, Dec 26-28, 1994)* DLS ▲ 3172 [DDD]

...Such Stuff as Dreams...—features works by Schumann *(Kinderszenen [About Faraway Lands & People])*, Kabalevsky *(Pieces (22) for Children [A Little Tale; Cradle Song; Dance on the Lawn])*, Schubert *(Impromptus, Op. 142/2 & 3)*, Bartók *(For Children [Nos. 3, "Lost Loves" & 26, "Rose Garden"])*, Mozart *(Son Pno, K.331; Son Pno, K.332 [Adagio])*, Beethoven *(Son Pno, Op. 109)*, Grieg *(Lyric Pieces, Op. 43/3)*, Ravel *(Sonatine [Menuet])*, Debussy *(La Fille aux cheveux de lin)*, Brahms *(Intermezzo, Op. 18/2; Waltzes, Op. 39/2 & 15)*, Satie *(Gymnopédie 1)*, Mendelssohn *(Lieder ohne Worte, Opp. 19/4, 67/1, 85/4 & 102/2) (rec First Congregational Church, Los Angeles, May 23-27, 1997)* DLS 2-▲ 3230 [DDD] (14.97)

Water Music of the Impressionists *(see Composer section, Debussy:Piano Music, et al.)* DLS ▲ 3006 [DDD]

Rosenthal, Moriz (pno)

Moriz Rosenthal, Vol. 2—features works by Chopin *(Mazurkas, Op. 33, Nos. 2 & 4, Op. 50 No. 2, Op.63, Nos. 1 & 3, Op. 67 No. 1; Preludes, Op. 28, Nos. 3, 6 & 7; Nocturnes, Op. 9, No. 2, Op. 27, No. 2; Valses, Op. 42, Op. 64, No. 3; Maiden's Wish)*, Liszt *(Hungarian Rhapsody No. 2; Liebestraum, No. 3; Maiden's Wish [after Chopin]; Soirée de Vienne, No. 6 [after Schubert])*, Albéniz *(Triana)*, Debussy *(Reflets dans l'eau)*, Liadov *(Tabatière à musique; Prelude, Op. 46, No. 1)*, Rosenthal *(Papillons)* PHS ▲ 9963 [AAD] (17.97)

Rubinstein, Artur (pno)

Artur Rubinstein—features works by Albéniz, Brahms, Chopin, Debussy, Granados *(rec 1928-33 for HMV)* PHS ▲ 9464 (m) [AAD] (17.97)

Arthur Rubinstein PPHI (Great Pianists of the 20th Century) ▲ 456955 (22.97)

Carnegie Hall Highlights—features works by Debussy, Szymanowski, Prokofiev, Villa-Lobos, Schumann, Albéniz *(rec 1961)* RCAV (Gold Seal) ▲ 61445 (10.97)

Highlights from the Rubinstein Collection—features works by Brahms, Chabrier, Chopin, Debussy, Falla, Poulenc, Schubert, Villa-Lobos RCAV (Gold Seal) ▲ 60211 [ADD] (10.97) ▮ 60211

In His Golden Years, Vol. 1—features works by Schubert *(Impromptu 4, D.899; Son 19 Pno, D.894)*, Chopin *(Waltz in A♭, Op. 34/1)*, Brahms *(Capriccio in b, Op. 76/2; Rhap in g, Op. 79/2)*, Albéniz *(Sevilla, Op. 47/3; Navarra)*, Debussy *(Prelude 10; Prelude [from Pour le piano])*, Ravel *(Forlane [from Le tombeau de Couperin])*, Falla *(Danse rituelle du feu [from El amor brujo])*, Liszt *(Liebestraum 3, Op. 62; Hungarian Rhap 10; Consolation 3)*, Rubinstein *(Valse caprice in E♭)*, Rachmaninoff *(Prelude in c#, Op. 3/2)*, Schumann *(Romanze, Op. 28/2) (rec 1928-37)* IN ▲ 1313 (m) [ADD] (14.97)

The Last Recital for Israel—featues works by Beethoven *(Son 23 Pno, "Appassionata")*, Chopin, Debussy, Schumann *(rec live, Ambassador College, California, Jan 15, 1975)* RCAV (Red Seal) ▲ 61160 (16.97) ▮ 61160 ▯ 09026-61160-5

Music of Spain—features works by Albéniz *(Córdoba; Evocación; Navarra; Sevilla, sevillanas)*, Falla *(Danza del molinaro; Danza del terror; Andaluza; Ritual Fire Dance; Nights in the Gardens of Spain [w. Golschmann, St. Louis SO])*, Granados *(Andaluza; The Maiden and the Nightingale)*, Mompou *(Cancións y Danzas Nos. 1 & 6)* RCAV (Gold Seal) ▲ 61261 (10.97)

Piano Greatest Hits, w. Boston SO, Chicago SO, RCA Victor SO—features works by Chopin *(Minute Waltz; Grand valse brillante; Waltz in c#)*, Grieg *(Con. in a)*, Mendelssohn *(Spinning Song)*, Beethoven *(Son. No. 8 in c, "Pathétique"; Son. No. 14 in c#, "Moonlight"; Con. No. 5 in E♭, "Emperor")*, Rachmaninoff *(Rhap. on a Theme of Paganini; Prelude in c#; Con. No. 2 in c)*, Mozart *(Con No. 21 in C, "Elvira Madigan")* RCAV ▲ 62662 (10.97) ▮ 62662 (5.98)

Rubinstein Favorites—features works by Schubert; Liszt; Chopin; Schumann; Brahms; Debussy; Rachmaninoff; Ravel; Falla; Albéniz, plus more ENT (Sirio) ▲ 530017 (13.97)

Rubinstein: Melody in F—features works by Sinding *(Rustle of Spring)*, Schumann *(Novelette)*, Mendelssohn *(Song without Words; Intermezzo in A, Op. 76/6; Intermezzo in a, Op. 76/7; Intermezzo in A, Op. 118/2, Intermezzo in e♭, Op. 118/6)*, Grieg *(Lyric Pieces, Opp. 12/1, 12/5, 43/1, 43/6, 54/4 & 65/6)*, Tchaikovsky *(Les Saisons, Op. 37b; Chants sans paroles, Op. 2/3)*, Rubinstein *(Melody in F, Op. 3/1)*, Dvorak *(Humoresquem Op. 101/7)* LALI ▲ 15603 (3.97)

Rudnytsky, Roman (pno)

Pianistic Portraits—features works by Rudnytsky, Talma, Rollin, Rachmaninoff, Liszt Dana Recording Project ▲ DRP 3 [DDD]

Ryabchikova, Tatyana (pno)

Gutzul Watercolors: Ukrainian Music of the 20th Century Sonora ▲ SO 22571

Saba, Geoffrey (pno)

Great Piano Transcriptions—features works by Percy Grainger, Walter Gieseking, Liszt, Moszkowski, Ravel INMP ▲ 858 [DDD]

1034 ▲ = CD ♦ = Enhanced CD △ = MD ▮ = Cassette Tape ▯ = DCC

Sack, Erna (pno)
Erna Sack—features works by Denza, Scotto, Czernik, Arditi, Strauss, Peccia, Petalozza, plus others LYS ▲ 2 (15.97)

Sainz, Liliana (pno), Jorge Bergaglio (pno)
Deux Pianos: Mozart, Ravel, Milhaud, Bartók, Guastavino, Piazzolla—features works by Mozart *(Son. in D for 2 Pianos, K.448/375a)*, Ravel *(La valse)*, Milhaud *(Scaramouche Suite for 2 Pianos, Op. 165b)*, Bartók *(Mikrokosmos [7 pieces])*, Guastavino *(2 Romances)*, Piazzolla *(Adios Nonino)* GALL ▲ 800 [ADD] (19.97)

Samaroff, Olga (pno)
Olga Samaroff: An American Virtuoso on the World Stage—features works by Beethoven, Chopin, Schumann, Brahms, Moszkowski, Debussy, Griffes, plus others PHS ▲ 9860 (17.97)

Samuel, Harold (pno)
The Art of Harold Samuel *(with the exception of the 1935 radio broadcast performance of the Brandenburg Concerto No. 5, all selections are from 1923-1932 HMV and Columbia recordings)*—features works by C.P.E. & J.C. Bach *(Sonata movements)*, J.S. Bach *(Chromatic Fantasy & Fugue; English Suite No. 2; Fantasia in c, BWV 906; Partitas 1 & 2, BWV 825/826; Four Preludes & Fugues from Das Wohltemperierte Klavier)*, Brahms, Clementi, Schubert; concerted works by J.S. Bach *(Violin Sonata No. 3 in E, BWV 1016—w. Isolde Menges, violin; Brandenburg Concerto No. 5—Frank Black [conductor], NBC Sym.; soloists Harold Samuel, piano, Joseph Stopak, violin & Arthur Lora, flute)* KOCH 2-▲ 7137

Sapellnikoff, Vassily (pno)
The Vocalion Recordings, 1923-27—features works by Tchaikovsky *(Con 1 Pno; Humoresque, Op. 10/2)*, Mendelssohn *(Scherzo, Op. 16/2)*, Schumann *(Traumeswirren, Op. 12/7)*, Liszt *(Valse-Impromptu; Gnomenreigen)*, Alabiev *(Le Rossignol)*, Wagner *(Spinnerlied [from Der Fliegende Holländer])*, Rubinstein *(Studio Staccato, Op. 23/2)*, Brahms *(Hungarian Dance No. 6; Mazurka No. 4)*, Liadov *(The Musical Snuff-Box, Op. 32)* ENPL (Piano Library) ▲ 212 (13.97)

Sauer, Emil von (pno)
The Complete Commercial Recordings 1923-41 MRSN ▲ 53002 (52.97)

Schäfer, Dirk (pno)
Dirk Schäfer—features works by Beethoven, Brahms, Chopin, Couperin, Handel, Henselt & Mozart *(rec 1924 & 1926)* PHS ▲ 9861 (17.97)

Schiller, Allan (pno)
Für Elise—features works by Albéniz, Beethoven, Chopin, Debussy, John Field. Grieg, Liszt, Mendelssohn, D. de Séverac ASVQ ▲ 6032 [ADD] (10.97)

Schnabel, Artur (pno)
Plays Bach & Brahms, Vol. 1 *(see Composer section: Bach—2-Harpsichord Concerto No. 2; Brahms—Piano Concerto No. 2)* PHS ▲ 9399 (m) [AAD] (18.97)

Schvartz, Haydée (pno)
Haydée Schvartz—features works by Pärt, John Cage, Scelsi, Kagel, Berio, Gandini, Valverde MODE ▲ 31 [DDD] (17.97)

Scioler, Victor (pno)
The Great Danish Pianist—features works by Liszt *(Con 1 Pno [w. Issay Dobrowen (cnd), Danish State RSO])*, Saint-Saëns *(Con 2 Pno [w. Nicolai Malko (cnd), Danish State RSO])*, Grieg *(Con Pno [w. Erik Tuxen (cnd), Danish State RSO])* plus solo works by Beethoven, D. Scarlatti, Chopin, Godowsky, Brahms, Sibelius, Rachmaninoff, Scriabin & Friedman DANR 2-▲ 491

Sevilla, Jean-Paul (pno)
Homage to Childhood—features works by Debussy, Grovlez, Ibert, Pierné, Prokofiev & Stravinsky DI 2-▲ 920169 [DDD] (11.97)

Shields, Roger (pno)
Piano Music in America, 1900-1945—features works by MacDowell, Griffes, Antheil, Cowell, Gershwin, Tom Turpin, Charles Hunter, Lamb, Joplin, Artie Matthews, James Scott, Robert Hampton, Gershwin & Donaldson, C. Luckyth Roberts, James Reese Europe, Blake, Carpenter, Thomson, Barber, Piston, Riegger, Ruggles, Ives, Harris, Sessions, Schuman, Copland VB3 3-▲ 3027 [ADD] (14.97)

Silverman, Robert (pno)
The Parlour Grand, Vol. 2: 18 Favorites From a Bygone Era—features works by Schubert *(Serenade [trans Liszt])*, Mendelssohn *(Spring Song, Op. 62/6)*, Albéniz *(Tango)*, Bridge *(Rosemary)*, Daquin *(Le coucou)*, Liadov *(The Musical Snuffbox)*, Gluck *(Melody—Dance of the Blessed Spirits)*, Pierné *(March of the Little Lead Soldiers)*, Godard *(Au matin)*, Chaminade *(Scarf Dance)*, Weber *(Invitation to the Dance)*, Godowsky *(Alt-Wien)*, Thomé*(Simple Aveu)*, Grainger *(Country Gardens)*, Badarszewska *(The Prayer Granted)*, Nevin *(Narcissus)*, Lavallée *(Le Papillon)*, Chopin *(Valse in c#)* MARQ ▲ 201 (16.97)

Skyrm, Susanne (pno)
Treasures of Iberian Keyboard Music—features works by Carvalho *(Allegro in D; Toccata in g)*, Albero *(Sons in g & G)*, Cordeiro de Silva *(Allegro in C)*, Seixas *(Sons in a, c & D)*, Larrañaga *(Son de quinto tono)*, Gomes de Silva *(Son in e)*, Baptista *(Son in g)*, Soler *(Son in G, R.45; Son in C, R.51; Son in c, R.100)* [Antunes fortepno, 1767] *(rec Univ of South Dakota, Vermillion, Aug 19-23, 1995)* MUA ▲ 985 [DDD] (16.97)

Society of Composers Inc.
View from the Keyboard—features works by Thomas Benjamin, Carlton Gamer, Arthur Digby Kurtz, John A. Lennon, Vincent McDermott, William Matthews, Edward Mattila, Raoul Pleskow, Hilary Tann CPS ▲ CPS 8606

Soerjadi, Wibi (pno)
A Touch of Romance—features works by Debussy *(Clair de lune)*, Chopin *(Nocturne in c#; Berceuse in D♭; Nocturne in E♭)*, Schubert *(Impromptu in A♭)*, Saint-Saëns/Godowsky *(Le Cygne)*, Liszt *(Liebestraum 3)*, Mendelssohn *(Songs without Words in E, A & A♭)*, Prokofiev *(Prelude in C)*, Rachmaninoff *(Prelude in d)*, Paderewski *(Menuet in G)*, Bach/Kempff *(Siciliano)*, Gluck/Sgambati *(Melody)*, Brahms *(Intermezzo in A)*, Ravel *(Pavane pour une infante défunte)* PPHI ▲ 454149 (16.97)

Sosa, Raoul (pno)
An Anthology for the Left Hand—features works by Bach *(Chaconne, BWV 1004 [trans Brahms]; Chromatic Fant & Fugue, BWV 903 [trans Sosa])*, Chopin *(Etudes, Op. 10/3-7 & 12 & Op. 25/1, 3, 10 & 12 [trans Godowsky])*, Moszkowski *(Etudes, Op. 92/1, 2, 4, 9, 11-12)*, Saint-Saëns *(Etudes, Op. 135/1-6)*, Scriabin *(Prelude & Nocturne, Op. 9)*, Lipatti *(Sonatina)*, Tisné *(Lac)*, Brenet *(Océanides)*, Ravel *(La valse) (rec 1992-95)* FL 2-▲ 23080 [DDD] (23.97)

Spada, Pietro (pno)
Piano Festival—features works by J. S. Bach *(In dir ist Freude [Choral BWV 675; trans F. Busoni])*, Scarlatti *(La Caccia [from Son Pno, K.159])*, Mozart *(Alla Turca [from Son Pno, K.331])*, Clementi *(Tocatta in B♭, Op. 13)*, Beethoven *(Für Elise)*, Mendelssohn *(Venetiansches Gondellied [from Lieder ohne Worte (No. 6)])*, Chopin *(Etude, Op. 10/3)*, Schumann *(Träumerei [from Kinderszenen])*, Liszt *(Liebstraum, R.211/3)*, Grieg *(To the Spring [from Lyric Pieces])*, Debussy *(Clair de lune)*, Rachmaninoff *(Prélude in c#, Op. 3/2)*, Falla *(Danza ritual del fuego)*, Prokofiev *(March [from The Love for 3 Oranges) (rec Roma, Italy, Apr 1984)* Arts ▲ 447198-2 [DDD]

Spring, Christian (pno)
Berceuses, Lullabies & Wiegenlieder—features works by Balakirev, Busoni, A. Casella, Chopin, Liszt, Vladimir Rébikov, Rolf Urs Ringger, A. Tansman, A. Tcherepnin, Pancho Vladigerov, Martin Wendel, Grieg, Henselt, Tchaikovsky, Brahms, Schumann, Suk, Villa-Lobos GALL ▲ CD 564 [DDD]
Music of Springtime—features works by Chopin, I. Friedman, H. Goetz, Grieg, Gruenberg, Mendelssohn, Milhaud, Reger, Schumann, Sinding, Suk, Tchaikovsky GALL ▲ CD 656 [DDD]

Stanczyk, Anna Maria (pno)
24 Classic Hits—features works by Mozart *(Alla Turca [Son No. 11 in A, K.331/300i])*, Beethoven *(Bagatelle in a, WoO 54, "Für Elise")*, Tchaikovsky *(Seasons, Op. 37b)*, Brahms *(Waltz in A♭, Op. 39/4)*, Rimsky-Korsakov *(Flight of the Bumblebee [from Tale of Tsar Saltan])*, Schumann *(Träumerei [from Kinderscenen, Op. 15])*, Boccherini *(Minuet [from Qnt for Strs, G.282 (op. 13)])*, Liszt *(Liebesträume, S.541/3)*, Liadov *(Musical Snuffbox, Op. 32)*, Saint-Saëns *(The Swan [from Carnival of the Animals])*, Daquin *(Le Coucou)*, Debussy *(Clair de lune)*, Schubert *(Moments musicaux in f, D.780/3)*, Chopin *(Waltz in D♭, Op. 64/1)*, Rachmaninoff *(Prelude in c#, Op. 3/2)*, Albéniz *(Tango [from España, Op. 165])*, Glinka *(The Lark [arr Balakirev])*, Bach *(Prelude in C [from Das wohltemperierte Klavier, Bk I])*, Dvořák *(Humoresque)*, Moniuszko *(The Spinner [trans Melcer])*, Satie *(Gymnopédie No. 1)*, Paderewski *(Minuet in G, Op. 14/1)*, Ogiński *(Polonaise in a, "A Farewell to Homeland")*, Badarzewska *(The Maiden's Prayer)* POLN ▲ ECD 060 [DDD]

Steiner, Karl (pno)
Music of the 2nd Generation of the 2nd Viennese School—features works by Schloss *(Son. for Pno; 12 Tone Suite; Suite for Fl & Pno; Impressions)*, Apostel *(Suite Concise, Op. 24; Sonatina Ritmica, Op. 5; 5 Songs for Low Voice & Pno, Op. 3; Kubiniana, Op. 13; 4 Little Pieces for Pno, Op. 31a)*, Jelinek *(Partita Canonica; Ein Spiegelkanon)*, Steuermann *(4 Pieces for Pno)*, Schoenberg *(Pno Piece, Op. 33b; 6 Little Pno Pieces, Op. 19)*, Berg *(Schliesse mir die Augen beide; Son., Op. 1)*, Rogers *(6 Short Preludes on a Tone Row)*, Webern *(Kinderstück)* CENT 2-▲ 2241 [ADD] (31.97)

Stevenson, Ronald (pno)
Cathedrals in Sound—features works by Bach-Busoni *(Chaconne)*, Chopin *(Nocturne in c; Prelude in c)*, Debussy *(La cathédrale egloutie)*, Liszt *(Abendglocken; Carillon])*, MacDowell *(In deep woods)*, Marek *(Tryptique)*, Sorabji *(Fantasiettina)*, Stevenson *(Heroic Song for Hugh MacDiarmid)* ALTA ▲ 9043

Stillman, Judith Lynn (pno)
Seasons Remembered 2, w. Toby Appel (va), John Deak (db), Eliot Porter (db), Diaz Trio [David Kim (vn), Roberto Diaz (va), Andrés Diaz (vc)], Lutz Rath (vc), Fenwick Smith (fl), Ruth Waterman (vn)—features works by Gluck, Niles, Vivaldi, J.S. Bach, Chaminade, Schumann, Scarlatti, Massenet, Mozart, Chopin, Beethoven, Haydn, Handel NOR ▲ 5 ▮ 5

Suková, Eva (pno)
Classical Piano Favorites—features works by Beethoven *(Son Pno, Op. 27/2, "Moonlight" [1st movt]; Für Elise)*, Tchaikovsky *(October; November [both from The Seasons]; Romance)*, Chopin *(Etude in E, Op. 10/3; Fant-Impromptu, Op. 66; Waltz in D♭, Op. 64/1, "Minute"; Waltz in e, Op.posth)*, Brahms *(Hungarian Dance 3)*, Mendelssohn *(Venetian Gondolier's Song; Prelude, Op. 28/15; Spring Song)*, Schubert *(Impromptu, Op. 90/4; Scherzo in B♭)*, Dvořák *(Humoresque)*, Liszt *(Liebestraume 3)* LYD ▲ 18023 [DDD] (2.97)

Szokolay, Balázs (pno)
The Romance Collection—features works by Mozart *(Rondo in D, K.485)*, Schubert *(Impromptu No. 3 in G♭)*, Weber *(Invitation to the Dance, J.260)*, Grieg *(Little Bird; Butterfly)*, Dvořák *(Humoresque, Op. 101)*, Schumann *(Bird as Prophet)*, Mendelssohn *(Hunting Song)*, Liszt *(Dream of Love No. 3)*, Chopin *(Fantasie-Impromptu in c#, Op. 66)*, Tchaikovsky *(Barcarolle)*, Fibich *(Poem)*, Gershwin *(3 Preludes)*, Rubinstein *(Melody in F)*, Bartók *(Romanian Folk Dances) (rec Italian Institute, Sept 9-11, 1987)* † FLUTE & HARP DUOS:Bálint, János; GUITAR:Garcia, Gerald; VIOLIN:Nishizaki, Takako NXIN 4-▲ 504005 [DDD] (19.97)
Romantic Piano Favorites, Vol. 5—features works by Scarlatti *(Son. in E, K.162)*, Boccherini *(Minuet in A)*, Schubert *(Marche militaire in D)*, Beethoven *(Bagatelle in a, "Für Elise")*, Schumann *(Album für die Jugend, Op. 68)*, Mendelssohn *(Venetian Boat Song)*, Grieg *(Wedding Day at Troldhaugen)*, Ravel *(Pavane pour une infante défunte)*, J. Strauss II *(Pizzicato-polka)*, Gossec *(Gavotte in D, "Rosine")*, Lehár *(Vilja Song)*, Debussy *(Arabesque in G)*, R. Strauss *(Serenade)*, Chopin *(Nocturne in E♭, Op. 9/2)*, Jessel *(Parade of the Tin Soldiers)*, Tchaikovsky *(Romance in f, Op. 5)*, Lange *(Der kleine Postillon)* (rec. Jan 20-28, 1988) NXIN ▲ 550168 [DDD] (5.97)
Romantic Piano Favorites, Vol. 6—features works by Haydn *(Fant. in C)*, Grieg *(Erotik)*, Schumann *(The Wild Horseman)*, Schubert *(Impromptu in A♭)*, Raff *(Cavatine)*, Mendelssohn *(Spinning Song)*, Kreisler *(Liebesleid)*, Rachmaninoff *(Prelude in c#)*, Chopin *(Barcarolle)*, Bartók *(For Children, Nos. 8, 13-16, 18-21, 25-26)*, Albéniz *(Sevilla)*, Schulz-Evler *(Concert arabesque)* (rec. Apr 25-June 30, 1988) NXIN ▲ 550215 [DDD] (5.97)

Tabe, Kyoko (pno)
Encore—features works by Griffes *(Fant. Pieces, Op. 6/3 [Scherzo])*, D. Scarlatti *(Son. in d, L.366)*, Mendelssohn/Liszt *(Auf Flügeln des Gesanges, S.547)*, Wagner/Liszt *(O du mein holder Abendstern, S.444 [from Tannhäuser])*, Balakirev *(Toccata in c#)*, Schubert *(Impromptu No. 3 in G♭, D.899)*, Liadov *(Barcarolle in F#, Op. 44)*, Liszt *(Liebesträume)*, Chopin *(Prelude in A♭, Op.posth.; Nocturne in c#, Op.posth.)*, Scriabin *(Etude in F#, Op. 42/3)*, Corea *(Children's Song No. 4)*, Grieg *(Carnival Scene [from Pictures from Life in the Country, Op. 19])*, Brahms *(Intermezzo in A, Op. 118/2)*, Schubert/Liszt *(Soirées de Vienne No. 6, S.427)*, Moszkowski *(Étincelles, Op. 36/6) (rec Swiss Radio DRS, Studio Zurich, May 9-12, 1994)* DNN ▲ 78928 [DDD] (16.97)

Taboloff, Gregory (pno)
Rare Russian Masterpieces—features works by Liadov *(Prelude, Op. 11/1)*, Rachmaninoff *(Melodie, Op. 3/3)*, Glazunov *(Prelude, Op. 59/1; Mazurka, Op. 25/3)*, Prokofiev *(March, Op. 12/1)*, Balakirev *(Rêverie in F)*, Liapunov *(Transcendental Etude, Op. 11/10, "Lezginka")*, Arensky *(Nocturne, Op. 36/3)*, Khachaturian *(Sabre Dance [arr. Lew Solin])*, Kallinikov *(Nocturne in f#)*, Kabalevsky *(Son. No. 3, Op. 45)*, Gretchaninov *(Plainte, Op. 3/1)*, Scriabin *(Prelude, Op. 11/14)* Better Music ▲ BMC 2001 [DDD]

Tarasov, Sergei (pno)
The Young Tarasov—features works by Brahms *(Variations on a Theme of Paganini)*, Liszt *(Mephisto Waltz No. 1)*, Rachmaninov *(Études Tableaux in c & e♭)*, Schubert *(Piano Sonata, D.664)*, Scriabin *(Fantasia in b)*, Tchaikovsky *(Dumka)* MCA1 ▲ 68018 [DDD] 68018

Tateno, Izumi (pno)
Finnish Piano Miniatures—features works by Sibelius, Merikanto, Melartin, Palmgren, Kuula, Kaski, Madetoja, Hannikainen, Linko, Klami *(rec Sept 18 & Dec 30, 1991)* ELEC 2-▲ 95870 [DDD]

Thiollier, François-Joël (pno)
Famous Piano Music—features works by Debussy *(Suite bergamasque; Nocturne; Danse bohémienne; Rêverie; Mazurka; Arabesque 1 in E; Arabesque 2 in G; Valse romantique; Ballade; Danse; Suite [Pour le piano]) (rec Temple Saint Marcel, Paris, Nov 28-Dec 1, 1994)* † PIANO:Biret, Idil; PIANO COLLECTIONS:Famous Piano Music NXIN 4-▲ 504010 [DDD] (19.97)

Tomšič, Dubravka (pno)
Favorite Encores—features works by Beethoven, Brahms, Chopin, Debussy, Grieg, Liszt, Rachmaninoff, Schumann, Sinding, Tchaikovsky STRD ▲ 6065 [DDD] ▮

Torok, Debra (pno)
Through & Within this Century Past—features works by Cheney Beach *(Les Rêves de Columbine, Op. 65 [No. 4])*, Griffes *(Fant Pieces, Op. 6 [Barcarolle; Notturno])*, Gershwin *(Impromptu in 2 Keys)*, Barber *(Interlude I [Adagio for Jeanne])*, Schuman *(3-Score Set)*, Muczynski *(Preludes, Op. 6)*, Bonds *(Troubled Water)*, Dello Joio *(Diversions [Preludio; Arietta; Caccia; Chorale; Giga])*, Lipkis *(Waltz-Fant)*, Saturen *(Son 2 Pno) (rec Recital Hall, Penn State Univ School of Music)* TACT ▲ 1001

Touyère, Raymond (pno)
Récital de Musique Française—features works of Dulphy *(La Forqueray)*, Dagincour *(La Couperin)*, Rameau *(La Triomphante; La Livri)*, Dandrieu *(Les Tourbillons; Les Tendres Reproches; La Lyre d'Orphée)*, Boismortier *(L'Indéterminée; La Caverneuse)*, Daquin *(La Mélodieuse)*, Couperin *(La Superbe ou la Forqueray; La Couperin; Les roseaux; L'Artiste; Les Idées Heureuses; Les Ondes; L'Art de Toucher le Clavecin (extraits)) (rec Eglise St-Paul à Genève, Mar 1974)* GALL ▲ 853 [ADD] (19.97)

Tryon, Valerie (pno)
The Joy of Piano—features works by Bach *(Siciliano)*, Liszt *(La campanella)*, Rimsky-Korsakov *(Flight of the Bumble Bee [arr. Rachmaninoff])*, Balakirev *(Islamey)*, Grieg *(At the Cradle; Wedding Day at Troldhaugen)*, MacDonnel *(To a Wild Rose)*, Chaminade *(Automne)*, Ravel *(Alborada del gracioso)*, Villa Lobos *(Plichinelle)*, Champagne *(Quadrilha Brasiliera)*, Glick *(Song; Caprice)*, Tremblay *(Trois huit)*, Hartwell *(Piece for Piano)*, Morel *(Deux études de sonorité)* (rec. Jan 27-29, 1992) CBC (Musica Viva) ▲ 1065 [DDD]

Tsachor, Uriel (pno)
The Simrock Story, Vol. 1—features works by Beethoven *(13 Vars on Dittersdorf's "Es war einmal ein alter Mann")*, Hiller *(Caprice in c#, Op. 4/2)*, Mendelssohn *(Songs Without Words)*, Brahms *(Fant, Op. 116)*, Brahms & Kirchner *(Transcriptions)*, Dvořák *(Lullaby in G; Caprice in g) (rec May 29-31)* DVX ▲ 29101 [DDD] (16.97)

Tureck, Rosalyn (pno)
Live at the Teatro Colón—features works by Bach *(Adiagio in G, BWV 968; Chromatic Fantasy; Partita No. 1, BWV 825; Goldberg Variation No. 29; Musette in D)*, Busoni *(Chaconne)*, Mendelssohn *(Songs Without Words, Op. 19, No. 1)*, Schubert *(Moments Musicaux)*, Brahms *(Variations and Fugue on a Theme by Handel, Op. 24)* see also individual composers *(rec live, Aug 14, 1992)* VAIA 2-▲ VAIA 1024-2 [DDD]

Tverskaya, Olga (pno)
Music at the Court of St. Petersburg, Vol. 1: Piano Music—features works by Field, Glinka, Hassler & Lizogub OPUS ▲ 30178 (17.97)

U Ko Ko (pno)
Burmese Piano—features works by U Ko Ko *(Mahn [Pride]; Shwei Thazin [Golden Thazin Flower]; Padauk Shweiwa [Golden Padauk Flower])*, Yan Nain Sein *(Chit Moe Gyi)*, YMB. Sayatin *(Oun Boun Chit [Secret Love])*, traditional *(Bóle; Tei tat; Bwé, Gandama Toung [Mountain Heavenly Flowers]; Tachin ghan, Sadan Aintha [Lake of the White Elephant]; Patt pyo, Htun Lin Hlyan Let [Bright & Sparkling]; Lei Twi Thankat, Ywe Nyi La [Song of Longing]; Myin Gin, Myan Myei Ne Zebu Boun; Yodaya, Mya Man Giri [Golden Mandalay]; id.; Nein We We; Yodaya, Pan Hey Won; Oh when the Saints) (rec Chapelle historique du Bon-Pasteur, Montréal)* UMM ▲ UMM 203

Utterback, Joe (pno)
Night & Day—features V. Duke *(I Can't Get Started with You)*, G. Gershwin *(Oh, Kay! (sels) [Someone to Watch over Me])*, M. Leonard *(Why Did I Choose You?)*, F. Loewe *(If Ever I Would Leave You)*, C. Porter *(Gay Divorce (sels) [Night& Day]; Mexican Hayride (sels) [I Love You])*, R. Rodgers *(Carousel (sels) [If I Loved You]; King & I (sels) [I Have Dreamed])*, Styne *(Just in Time; Make Someone Happy)*, Van Heusen *(Here's That Rainy Day)*, T. Waller *(Ain't Misbehavin'; Honeysuckle Rose)* CCOL ▲ 4220

Van Paassen, Marius (pno)
The Animal in 20th Century Piano Music *(solo piano works inspired by various creatures of nature)*—features works by Debussy, Granados, Messiaen, Ravel, Satie, Bernard van den Sigtenhorst Meyer, Stravinsky, Alexander Voormolen ATAC ▲ 8950 [DDD]

Vardi, Arie (pno)
Children's Corner—features works by Beethoven, J. S. Bach, Bartók, Debussy, Grieg, Hajdu, Mozart, Schumann PWK ▲ 1132 [DDD]

Vázonyi, Balint (pno)
13 Piano Reveries—features works by Mozart, Beethoven, Schubert, Schumann, Mendelssohn, Chopin, Brahms, Debussy, Paderewski ALLO ▲ 8038 [ADD] ▮ 8038

Verbit, Marthanne (pno)
Valentines—features works by Gershwin, Antheil, Diercks, Fennimore, Ornstein, Scott ALBA ▲ 71 [ADD] (16.97)

COLLECTIONS

Vered, Ilana (pno)
25 Virtuoso Etudes—features works by Debussy *(pour les Arpèges composés; pour les Degrés chormatiques [both from Etudes Book 2])*, Moszkowski *(Etudes Nos. 2 in g, 6 in F & 12 in A♭, Op. 72)*, Schumann *(7 Etudes [from Vars. on a Theme by Beethoven])*, Liszt *(Paganini Etude No. 6 in a)*, Chopin *(Etudes Nos. 3 in E, 4 in c#, 8 in F & 12 in c, Op. 10; Etudes Nos. 1 in A♭, 2 in f, 6 in g#, 7 in c# & 12 in c, Op. 25)*, Laderman *(Vered Etudes Nos. 1-3) (rec Music Hall, Tarrytown, NY, Feb 1992)* Connoisseur Society ▲ CD 4197

Viñes, Ricardo (pno), Francis Planté (pno)
Ricardo Viñes & Francis Planté—features works by D. Scarlatti, Gluck, Borodin, Albéniz, Turina, Debussy, Blancafort, Troiani, Lopez/Buchardo & Allende *(rec 1928-36)* † Piano:Planté POHS ▲ 9857 [ADD] (17.97)

Volkov, Oleg (pno)
All Russian—features works by Shostakovich *(Aphorisms, Op. 13)*, Scriabin *(5 Preludes; Son. No. 5 in F#, Op. 53)*, Borodin, Cui, Liadov, Rimsky-Korsakov BRIO ▲ 105 (16.97)
Live from Moscow—features works by Schubert *(Son. in a, Op. 164; Impromtu in A♭, Op. 90/4; Moment Musicaux in f, Op. 94/3)*, Prokofiev *(Sarcasms, Op. 17)*, Scriabin *(6 Preludes)*, Kreisler/Rachmaninoff *(Liebesleid; Liebesfreud)*, Liszt *(Gnomenreigen)*, Schumann *(Träumerei) (rec live, Tchaikovsky Concert Hall, Moscow, May 22, 1994)* BRIO ▲ 106 (16.97)

Volodos, Arcadi (pno)
Volodos: Piano Transcriptions—features works by Bizet *(Carmen Vars [after 1968 trans by Horowitz])*, Rachmaninoff *(Songs, Op. 4/2 [Utro] & Op. 21/9 [Melodiya] [both trans Volodos])*, Liszt *(Hungarian Rhap 2 [after trans Horowitz])*, Schubert *(Songs [Litanei; Aufenthalt; Liebesbotschaft; all trans Liszt])*, Rimsky-Korsakov *(Flight of the Bumblebee [trans Cziffra])*, Prokofiev *(Cinderella [Gavotte; Orientale; Valse; all trans Prokofiev])*, Tchaikovsky *(Sym 6 [Scherzo; trans Feinberg])*, Bach *(Trio Son 5 [Largo; trans Feinberg])*, Mozart *(Rondo alla turca [concert paraphrase from Son 11 Pno; trans Volodos]) (rec Snape Maltings Concert Hall, Snape, England & American Academy of Arts & Letters, New York, 1996)* COL ▲ 62691 [DDD] (16.97)

Walwyn, Karen (pno)
Dark Fires: 20th Century Music for Piano—features works by Dolores White *(Toccata)*, L. B. Alston *(Rhaps (3) Pno)*, T. Leon *(Ritual)*, Hale Smith *(Evocation)*, R. Dickerson *(Sonatina)*, Mumford *(Fragments from the Surrounding Evening)*, Hailstork *(Son 1 Pno)* ALBA ▲ 266 [DDD] (16.97)

Watkins, David (pno)
David Watkins at the Piano—features works by Ravel *(Pavane pour une infante défunte)*, Debussy *(Rêverie; Arabesque 1; Clair de Lune)*, Prokofiev *(Prélude in C, Op. 12/7)*, Rachmaninoff *(Préludes in c#, Op. 3/2 & in g, Op. 23/5)*, Chopin *(Nocturne in E♭, Op. 9/2; Waltzes in c#, Op. 64/2 & A♭, Op. 69/1)*, Beethoven *(Son 14 Pno [Adagio sostenuto])*, Brahms *(Intermezzo in A, Op. 118/2)*, Liszt *(Sonetto del Petrarca 104) (rec ACA Studio, Atlanta, GA, Aug 1996)* ACAD ▲ 20059 [DDD] (16.97)

Weber, Gustavo Rivero (pno)
Música Mexicana para Piano—features works by Carrasco *(Adiós; Mazurka No. 4)*, Serratos *(Waltz)*, Ponce *(Intermezzo; Romanza de Amor; Plenilunio; Scherzino Maya; Preludio Mexicano "Cuiden Su Vida"; Scherzino Mexicano; A Pesar de Todo [Danza para La Mano Izquierda])*, Elias *(Waltz)*, Armengol *(Preludio; Danzas Cubanas No. 1 "Recordando a Papá," No. 6 "Ayer y Hoy", No. 7, No. 15 "Baila Tristeza"; La Fr'as Montañas; Ay Amor, Amor...)* SPT ▲ 2 [DDD] (16.97)
Música Mexicana Para Piano, Vol. 3—features works by Ponce *(Valentina; Mazurka X; "La Vida Sonríe" XII Estudio de Concierto; Tema Mexicano Variado; Guateque; "Jarabe" X Estudio de Concierto; "Juventud" VII Estudio de Concierto)*, de Elías *(Adivinanza; Elegía)*, Villanueva *(Vals Poético)*, Armengol *(Danza Cubana No. 18; Nocturno a Ponce)*, Carrasco *(Melodía)*, Castro *(Vals Bluette) (rec Aug 1995)* SPT ▲ 3 [DDD]

Weiss, Liselotte (pno)
Liselotte Weiss—features works by Berg *(Son., Op. 1)*, Schoenberg *(6 kleine Klavierstücke, Op. 19)*, Eisler *(Son., Op. 1)*, Ravel *(Sonatina)*, Honegger *(3 Pièces)*, Granados *(Allegro de conceirto) (rec Apr 30-May 1, 1975)* BIS ▲ 23 [AAD] (17.97)

Wild, Earl (pno)
The Art of the Transcription—Live from Carnegie Hall—features works by Gluck-Sgambati, Rameau-Godowsky, Bach-Tausig, Wagner-Moszkowski, Rimsky-Korsakov-Rachmaninoff, Kreisler-Rachmaninoff, Mendelssohn-Rachmaninoff, Rossini-Thalberg, Chopin-Liszt, Tchaikovsky-Wild, Joh. Strauss-Schulz-Evler AUDO 2-▲ 72008 (16.97)
The Romantic Master: 13 Transcriptions for Solo Piano—features works by Tchaikovsky *(At the Ball; Dance of the 4 Swans [from Swan Lake]; Paraphrase on Sleeping Beauty)*, Chopin *(Largo [from Con No. 2 in f for Pno, Op. 21])*, Rachmaninoff *(Midsummer Nights)*, Mozart *(Serenade [from Don Giovanni])*, Handel *(Air & Vars [The Harmonious Blacksmith])*, Saint-Saëns *(Le rouet d'omphale)*, Kreisler *(Liebesleid)*, Fauré *(Improvisation on Après en rêve)*, Churchill *(Reminiscences of Snow White)*, J. Strauss *(1 Lives but Once)*, Bach/Wild *(Hommage à Poulenc)* COL ▲ 62036 (16.97)
Transcriptions—features works by Bach, Beethoven, Chopin, Paganini, Schubert, Schumann, Verdi, Wagner ONY 2-▲ 104 [DDD]
The Virtuosity of Earl Wild—features E. D. Albert *(Scherzo in F#, Op.16/2)*, Chopin *(Polonaise 6 Pno, "Heroic", Op. 53)*, E. v. Dohnányi *(Capriccio Pno, Op. 2/4; Capriccio Pno [from Op. 28/6])*, Liszt *(Études d'exécution transcendante (12), S.139 [No. 10, "Appassionata"; No. 2, "Fusées"; No. 7, "Eroica"]; Études d'exécution transcendante (6), S.140 [No. 3 in a♭ (La campanella); No. 4 in E (Arpeggio study); No. 5 in E (La chasse)]; Études de concert (2), S.145 [No. 1, "Waldesrauschen"]; Études de concert (3), S.144 [No. 2, "La leggierezza"]; Grand galop chromatique, S.219; Hungarian Rhaps, S.244 [No. 2 in c#; No. 4 in E♭; No. 12 in c#]; Mephisto Waltz 1 Pno, S.514; Polonaises (2) Pno, S.223 [No. 2 in E]; Trans, Arrs & Paraphrases [Wagner:Spinning Chorus (from Fliegende Holländer), S.440 (arr 1860); Verdi:Paraphrase de concert (from Rigoletto), S.434 (arr 1859)]; Valses oubliées (4), S.215 [No. 1])*, Mendelssohn (-Bartholdy) *(Spinning Song, Op.67/4)*, Moszkowski *(Étincelles, Op.36/6)*, F. Schubert *(Marche militaire, D.733/1)*, R. Schumann *(Liederkreis, Op. 39 [No. 12, Frühlingsnacht])*, P. Tchaikovsky *(Pieces (2) Pno, Op. 1 [Scherzo à la russe]; Swan Lake, Op. 20)* IVOR 2-▲ 70901 [DDD] (31.97)
The Virtuoso Piano *(Music from the Golden Age of the Keyboard)*—features works by Leopold Godowsky, Henri Herz, J.N. Hummel, Anton Rubinstein, Sigismond Thalberg; *(for a related release, see Composer section under "Liszt: Piano Music")* VC ▲ 4033 [ADD] (13.97)

Wilson, Catherine (pno)
Catherine Wilson & Friends: Classical Potpourri, w. Mark Skazinetsky (vn), Norman Hathaway (va), Jack Mendelsohn (vc), Joel Quarrington (db)—features works by Bach *(Preludium [from Cant 29])*, Chopin *(Etude in E, Op. 10/3)*, Gershwin *(3 Preludes for Pno)*, Wilson *(Knollwood Place)*, Falla *(Ritual Fire Dance [from El amor brujo])*, Ravel *(Pavane pour une infante défunte)*, Chaplin *(Charlie Chaplin Medley)*, Anderson *(Blue Tango)*, Satie *(3 Gymnopédies)*, Puccini *(O Mio Babbino Caro [from Gianni Schicchi])*, Beethoven *(Für Elise)*, Elgar *(Salut d'amour)*, Joplin *(Maple Leaf Rag)* DHR ▲ 71111 (12.97)
Catherine Wilson & Friends: 'W', w. Mark Skazinetsky (vn), Norman Hathaway (va), Jack Mendelsohn (vc), Joel Quarrington (db)—features works by Bach: *(Cant, BWV 29 [Preludium]; Con Hpd, BWV 1056 [Largo; both arr R. Wilkins for pno trio])*, Chopin *(Etude, Op. 10/3; Berceuse, Op. 57)*, Gershwin *(Preludes)*, Wilson *(Knollwood Place [arr R. Wilkins for pno trio])*, de Falla *(El Amor Brujo [Ritual Fire Dance; arr R. Wilkins for pno & strs])*, Chaplin *(Medley [arr R. Wilkins for pno & strs])*, Anderson *(Blue Tango [arr R. Wilkins for pno trio])*, Satie *(Gymnopédies)*, Kriesler *(Petit March Viennois [arr R. Wilkins for pno trio])*, Puccini *(O Mio Babbino Caro [from Gianni Schicchi; arr R. Wilkins for pno trio])*, Beethoven *(Bagatelle, WoO 59)*, Joplin *(Maple Leaf Rag [arr R. Wilkins for pno & strs]) (rec Humbercrest United Church & Glenn Gould Studio, Toronto, June 1995 & July 1996)* Aureole Classics ▲ AC 001 [DDD]

Winstin, Robert Ian (pno)
Piano Art—features works by Persichetti, Toch, Creston, Krenek, Lutoslawski, Foss, Casella, Rieti, Graves, Winstin *(rec Aug 18-21 1993)* E.R.M. ▲ ERM 6661 [DDD]
Winstin Sampler: A Fabulous Collection from 3 Albums—features works by Winstin, Gruber, Leontovich E.R.M. ▲ CCC 111 [ADD]

Yerlow, Stanley (pno)
Yerlow in Concert—features works by Scriabin, Beethoven, Chopin, Debussy, Gershwin, Strauss, Schumann, Liszt MAPR ▲ 1002 (16.97) ▮ 1002 (9.97)

Yost, Kelly (pno)
Piano Reflections: A Gentle Selection of Reflective Light Classics—features works by Saint-Saëns *(The Swan)*, Schumann *(Träumerei, Op. 15/7; Of Foreign Lands & People, Op. 15/1)*, Hardy *(Jennifer's Song)*, Bach *(Largo [from Con in f]; Prelude in C; Minuet in G [arr Yost])*, Clementi *(Andante [from Sonatina, Op. 36/1])*, Satie *(Gymnopédies Nos. 1 & 2)*, Chopin *(Largo in E♭; Prelude in A)*, Pachelbel *(Canon [arr Agay])*, Field *(Nocturne No. 1)*, Beethoven *(Adagio [from Son, Op. 13])*, Fauré *(Impromptu, Op. 34/3)*, Noona *(Reflections in the Rain)*, Haydn *(Arietta con variazioni)*, Gillock *(Last Spring)*, Brahms *(Waltz, Op. 39/15)*, Debussy *(Reverie)* CHAN ▲ 1684 1684
Roses & Solitude—features works by Massenet *(Méditation [from Thaïs])*, Liszt *(Consolation 3; Frühling)*, M. T. von Paradis/Kessler *(Sicilienne)*, M. Davies *(Farewell to Stromness)*, Rachmaninoff *(18th Var Rhap on Theme of Paganini)*, J. S. Bach *(Prelude in C#)*, Chopin *(Fant-Impromptu, Op. 66)*, Scriabin *(Album Leaf; Prelude, Op. 15/4)*, Hummel *(Polonaise, Op. 55)*, Rimsky-Korsakoff *(Romance in A♭)*, Tingley *(Reverie)*, Debussy *(Arabesque 1)*, Dvořák *(Silhouette, Op. 8/2)*, Valenti *(Nocturne 5)* CHAN ▲ 1696 1696

Zitterbart, Gerrit (pno)
What about This, Mr. Clementi?: A Comparison of Grand Pianos TACE ▲ TAC 34

PIANO COLLECTIONS

American Piano
Vol. 1, w. Alan Mandel (pno)—features works by V. Duke, M. Gould, A. North, E. Siegmeister *(see Composer section)* PREM ▲ 1013 [DDD] (16.97)
Vol. 2: Blue Voyage *(Music in the Grand Tradition)*, w. Ramon Salvatore (pno)—features works by Beach, Carpenter, Chadwick, Farwell, Foote, Foster, Paine, Riegger, Thomson *(see Composer section)* PREM ▲ 1019 [DDD] (16.97)
Vol. 3: Rags And Other Riches *(music composed from 1889-1976)*, w. Alan Mandel (pno)—features works by J. P. Sousa *(The Presidential Polonaise; Moonlight on the Potomac Waltzes)*, A. Matthews *(Past-Time Rags Nos. 1-5)*, R. Hampton *(Cataract Rag)*, J. Lamb *(Ragtime Nightingale; Reindeer [Rag-Time Two Step]; Bohemia [Rag])*, Z. Confrey *(Kitten on the Keys; Coaxing the Piano; Sport Model Encore)*, A. Ammons & P. Johnson *(Boogie-Woogie Man)*, P. Johnson *(Central Avenue Drag)*, M. Morath *(One for Amelia; The Golden Hours; One for Norma)*, D. Ashwander *(Astor Place Rag Waltz; Friday Night)* PREM ▲ 1021 [DDD] (16.97)
Vol. 4: Rhythmic Moments, w. Joseph Smith (pno)—features works by H. Arlen, B. Beiderbecke, D. Ellington, S. Foster, G. Gershwin, V. Herbert, J. P. Johnson, S. Joplin, O. Levant PREM ▲ 1028 [DDD] (16.97)

The Art of the Piano—features performances by Thérèse Dussaut (pno) *(Hadyn:Fant in C, H.XVII/4 [Presto])*, Jacqueline Robin (pno) *(Boëly:Moderato in D, Op. 50/4; Allegro in b♭, Op. 49/2; Gigue in a, Op. 54/11)*, Jean Martin (pno) *(Weber:Son 1 in C, Op. 24 [Adagio]; Schumann:Bunte Blätter, Op. 99; Brahms:Intermezzo II, Op. 117)*, Noël Lee (pno) *(Moscheles:Études in D♭ & G, Op. 95/3 & 7)*, Christian Ivaldi (pno) *(Mendelssohn:Son 1 in E, Op. 6 [Allegro con espressione])*, Chantal de Buchy (pno) *(Chopin:Nocturne in c; 3 Écossaises, Op. 72)*, Mélisande Chauveau (pno) *(Liszt:Étude de concert, "Bruissement de la forêt")* ARN ▲ 60390 [AAD] (13.97)

A Bouquet of Piano Music DNN ▲ 8080 [DDD] (12.97)

The Catalan Piano Tradition *(historic recordings by Spanish composers and performers, from cylinders and discs)*—features performances by Isaac Albéniz *(Three Improvisations, from cylinders ca. 1903)*, Enrique Granados *(Granados—Improvisation on "El Pelele"; Spanish Dances Nos. 7 & 10; Scarlatti/arr. Granados—Sonata No. 9 in B♭, after L.250; all from ca. 1912 Odeon 78s)*, Alicia de Larrocha *(Chopin—Nocturne Op. 32/1 & Waltz Op. 34/2; rec. 6/3/1932)*, Alicia de Larrocha accompanying soprano Conchita Badia *(Granados—Three Tonadillas; rec. in Barcelona in the 1960s)*, Joaquin Malats *(Chopin—Waltz in c#, Op. 64/2; Liszt—Hungarian Rhapsody No. 13; Malats—Serenata in F; Wagner/arr. Liszt—Isolde's Love Death; all from cylinders ca. 1903)*, Frank Marshall *(Norwegian Dance in A, Op. 35/2; ca. 1907 cylinder recording)*, Frank Marshall [accompanying contralto Conchita Supervia] *(Granados—Seven Tonadillas; rec. 11/1/32)* VAIA ▲ 1001 (m) [ADD] (17.97)
Chopin: Greatest Hits, w. Emanuel Ax (pno), Peter Serkin (pno), John Browning (pno), et. al.—features Minute Waltz, Revolutionary Etude, Piano Concerto No. 2; etc. RCAV ▲ 60830 (10.97) ▮ 60830 (5.98)

Classical Piano, Vol. 1—features works by Beethoven *(Son 14 Pno)*, Schumann *(Kinderszenen, Op. 15/1)*, Schubert *(Impromptu in E♭)*, Rachmaninoff *(Flight of the Bumble-Bee)*, Liszt *(Hungarian Rhap 2)*, Mendelssohn *(Spinner's Song, Op. 67/4)*, Mozart *(Son 15 Pno [Allegro])*, Grieg *(Morning Mood [from Peer Gynt])*, Debussy *(Arabesque 1)*, Grainger *(Irish Tune from Country Derry)*, Chopin *(Fant-impromptu, Op. 66; Nocturne, Op. 9/2; Waltz, Op. 64/2)*, Brahms *(Capriccio, Op. 76/2)* PUBM ▲ 1022 (4.97)

Classical Piano, Vol. 2—features works by Beethoven *(Son 8 Pno)*, Schumann *(Reverie, Op. 15/7)*, Mussorgsky *(Pictures at an Exhibition [Promenade])*, Rachmaninoff *(Prelude, Op. 3/2)*, Liszt *(Ave Maria)*, Mendelssohn *(Song of Spring, Op. 67/6)*, Mozart *(Son 11 Pno)*, Grieg *(March of the Dwarves, Op. 54/3)*, Debussy *(Le fille avec chevaux du lin [from Preludes, Book 1])*, Grainger *(Country Gardens)*, Bach *(Aria [from Goldberg Vars])*, Chopin *(Etude, Op. 10/5; Prelude, Op. 28/7; Waltz, Op. 64/1; Etude, Op. 10/12)* PUBM ▲ 1023 (4.97)

Classical Piano, Vol. 3—features works by Beethoven *(Für Elise)*, Tchaikovsky *(Ov; Russian Dance; Dance of the Reed Flutes; Dance of the Sugar-Plum Fairies; March [all from Nutcracker]; Old French Song, Op. 39/16)*, Schumann *(Soaring, Op. 12/2)*, Elgar *(Pomp & Crcumstance)*, Scarlatti *(Son, L.104)*, Mendelssohn *(Wedding March)*, Grieg *(Wedding Day at Troldhaugen, Op. 65/6)*, Debussy *(Claire de Lune)*, Chopin *(Polonaise, Op. 53; Prelude, Op. 28/4; Waltz in E, Op. posth)*, Sinding *(Rustles of Spring, Op. 32/3)*, Brahms *(Waltz, Op. 39/15)*, Boccherini *(Minuet)*, Bach *(French Suite 5 [Gavotte])* PUBM ▲ 1024 (4.97)

Early Romantic Piano Concerti—features performances by Felicja Blumenthal (pno), Prague New CO [cnd:Alberto Zedda] *(Clementi:Con Pno in C)*, Rena Kyriakou (pno), Berlin SO [cnd:C. A. Bünte] *(Field:Con No. 2 in A♭ for Pno & Orch, H.31)*, Martin Galling (pno), Berlin SO [cnd:C. A. Bünte] *(Hummel:Concertino in G for Small Orch, Op. 73)*, Akiko Sagara (pno), Luxembourg Radio Orch [cnd:Pierre Cao] *(Cramer:Con No. 5 in c for Pno, Op. 48)*, Michael Ponti (pno), Southwest German CO [cnd:Paul Angerer] *(Czerny:Divertissement de Concert, Op. 204)*, Maria Littauer (pno), Hamburg SO [cnd:Alois Springer] *(Ries:Con in c# for Pno, Op. 55) (rec 1968-69, 1972, 1974 & 1978)* VB2 2-▲ 5111

Ebony & Ivory: Gentle Classics for Piano—features performances by Tomsic Dubravka *(Beethoven's Piano Sonata No. 14 "Moonlight")*, Philippe Entremont *(Mozart's Piano Sonatas Nos. 11 & 15; Schubert's Quintet in A for Piano & Strings, D.667 "Trout" [w. soloists of the Vienna CO]; Dvořák's Quintet for Piano & Strings "Dumka" [w. soloists of the Vienna CO])*, Russell Sherman *(Schubert's Preludes for Pinao, Op. 28)*, James Tocco *(Copland's Music from Our Town:Our Town Story, Conversation at the Soda Fountain & The Resting Place on the Hill)*, John Arpin *(Joplin's Pleasant Moments)* REFF ▲ RD 6118

Famous Piano Music—features performances by Jenö Jandó (pno) *(Schubert:Impromptu in A♭, D.935, Op. 142/2; Mozart:Son No. 11 in A for Pno, K.331 [Alla turca]; Schumann:Träumerei [from Kinderszenen, Op. 15])*, Idil Biret (pno) *(Chopin:Etude in E, Op. 10/3; Nocturne in E♭, Op. 9/2; Prelude No. 15 in D♭, Op. 28, "Raindrop"; Rachmaninov:Prélude in c#, Op. 3/2)*, Balázs Szokolay (pno) *(Beethoven:Bagatelle in a, WoO 59 "Für Elise"; Andante in F, WoO 57 "Andante favori"; Brahms:Waltz in A♭, Op. 39/15; Mendelssohn:Spring Song in A, Op. 62/6 [from Songs Without Words]; Liszt:Liebestraum No. 3 in A♭, Op. 62, S.541/3; Schubert:Impromptu in G♭, Op. 90, D.899/3; Albéniz:Tango in D, Dvořák:Humoresque in G♭, Op. 101/8; Saint-Saëns:The Swan [from Carnival of the Animals]; Rubinstein:Melodie in F, Op. 3, no.1; Boccherini:String Quintet in E, G.275 [Minuet]; Kreisler:Liebesleid; Caprice Viennois, Op. 2; Paderewski:Minuet in G, Op. 14/1; Grieg:Wedding Day at Troldhaugen, Op. 65/6; Drdla:Souvenir in D; Gossec:Gavotte "Rosine" in D; Lehár:Vilja Song [from The Merry Widow]; Fibich:Poème, Op. 41/6; Jessel:Parade of the Tin Soldiers)*, Ilona Prunyi (pno) *(Tchaikovsky:June:Barcarolle [from The Seasons, Op. 37b]; Romance in f, Op. 5; Chanson triste in g, Op. 40/2)*, Klára Körmendi (pno) *(Debussy:Clair de lune [from Suite bergamasque]; Satie:Gymnopédie 3)*, Péter Nagy (pno) *(Baranowska:The Maiden's Prayer; Beethoven:Minuet in G, WoO 10/6; Sinding:Rustle of Spring, Op. 22/3; Lance:Edelweiss; Elgar:Salut d'amour, Op. 12)*, Péter Szokolay (pno) *(Offenbach:Barcarolle [from Tales of Hoffman]; Tchaikovsky:None but the Lonely Heart, Op. 6/6; Mendelssohn:On Wings of Song, Op. 34/2)* † PIANO:Biret, Idil; PIANO:Thiollier, Francois-Joël NXIN 4-▲ 504010 [DDD] (19.97)

Favorite Piano, w. Daniel Adni (pno),A. Brownridge (pno), J. Février (pno), M. Lympany (pno), J. Ogdon (pno), G. Tacchino (pno)—features works by Chopin *(Waltz, Op. 64/1, "Minute"; Fant.-Impromptu, Op. 66; Nocturne 2, Op. 9/2)*, Beethoven *(Für Elise, WoO 10; Son. 14, Op. 27/2)*, Rachmaninoff *(Prelude, Op. 3/2)*, Grieg *(Wedding Day at Troldhaugen)*, Schubert *(Marche militaire, D.733)*, Sinding *(Rustle of Spring, Op. 32/3)*, Mozart *(Rondo alla Turca, K.331)*, Debussy *(La Fille aux Cheveux de Lin; Claire de Lune)*, Satie *(Gymnopédie 1)*, Liszt *(Liebstraum 3)*, Chaminade *("Autumn", Op. 35)*, Falla *(Ritual Fire Dance [from El Amor brujo])*, Albéniz/Godowsky *(Tango, Op. 165/2)*, Grainger *(Country Gardens)* CFP ▲ 4622 [ADD/DDD] (12.97)

Favourite Piano Concertos, Vol. 1, w. Alfred Brendel (pno), Clara Haskil (pno), Byron Janis (pno), Sviatoslav Richter (pno), Academy of St. Martin in the Fields, Lamoureux Concert Orch, London SO, London PO, Minneapolis SO, Antal Dorati (cnd), Bernard Haitink (cnd), Kyrill Kondrashin (cnd), Igor Markevich (cnd), Neville Marriner (cnd)—features works by Chopin *(Con 2 Pno, Op. 21)*, Liszt *(Con 1 Pno, S.124)*, Mozart *(Con 21 Pno, K.467)*, plus Beethoven, Rachmaninoff PPHI (Duo) 2-▲ 462176 (17.97)

Favorite Piano Concertos, Vol. 2, w. Martha Argerich (pno), Misha Dichter (pno), Stephen Kovacevich (pno), Colin Davis (cnd), Kyrill Kondrashin (cnd), Neville Marriner (cnd), Bavarian RSO, BBC SO, London SO, Philharmonia Orch—features works by Addinsell, Brahms, Grieg, Schumann, Tchaikovsky PPHI (Duo) 2-▲ 462182 (17.97)

French 4-Hand Piano Music—features performances by Walter Klien & Beatriz Klien *(Bizet:Jeux d'enfants; Ravel:Ma mère l'oye; Debussy:En blanc et noir; Petite Suite; Épigraphes antiques Fauré:Dolly Suite, Op. 56)*, Farnk Glazer & R. Deas *(Satie:Trois Morceaux en forme de poire; En habit de cheval)*, Marylène Dosse & Annie Petit *(Saint-Saëns:March interalliée, Op. 155; Caprice arabe, Op. 96; Milhaud:Scaramouche)*, Walter Klien & Rena Kyriakou *(Chabrier:Trois valses romantiques; Corège burlesque; Souvenirs de Munich)* VB2 2-▲ 5078 [ADD]

Für Elise—features performances by Jenö Jandó *(Mozart:Alla turca [from Son. No. 11 in A for Pno, K.331]; Schubert:Impromptu in A♭, Op. 142/2; Schumann:Träumerei [from Kinderszenen, Op. 15])*, Idil Biret *(Chopin:Etude in E, Op. 10/3; Nocturne in E♭, Op. 9/2; Prelude No. 15 in D♭, Op. 28 [Raindrop]; Rachmaninoff:Prélude in c#, Op. 3/2)*, Balázs Szokolay *(Albéniz:Tango in D; Beethoven:Andante in F, WoO 57 [Antante favori]; Bagatelle in a, WoO 59, "Für Elise"; Brahms:Waltz in A♭, Op. 39/15; Liszt:Liebestraum No. 3 in A♭, Op. 62/3; Mendelssohn:Spring Song in A [from Songs without Words], Op. 62/6; Schubert:Impromptu in G♭, Op. 90/3)*, Ilona Prunyi *(Tchaikovsky:June: Barcarolle [from The Seasons, Op. 37b]; Romance in f, Op. 5)*, Klára Körmendi *(Debussy:Clair de lune [from Suite bergamasque]; Satie: No. 3 Gymnopédie)* NXIN ▲ 550647 [DDD] (5.97)

Für Elise—features performances by Ashkenazy, Schiff, Lupu, Bolet, de Larrocha, et al. PLON ▲ 17751 [DDD]

The Grand Piano Era, w. Harold Bauer (pno), Ferruccio Busoni (pno), Ignaz Friedman (pno), Percy Grainger (pno), Josef Hofmann (pno), Frederic Lamond (pno), Nikolai Medtner (pno), Ignaz Jan Paderewski (pno)—features works by Liszt, Chopin, Moszkowski, Paderewski, Bach, Medtner, Friedman, Schumann, Stanford & Grainger NIMB ▲ 8801 (11.97)

▲ = CD ♦ = Enhanced CD △ = MD ▮ = Cassette Tape ▯ = DCC

Great Composers at the Keyboard

Busoni, Ferruccio: Piano Roll Recordings (1915-1925)—features works by Bach *(Chaconne [from Partita No. 2 for Vn, BWV 1004; trans Busoni])*, Liszt *(Etude d'Execution No. 5; Grand Etude de Paganini No. 5; Polonaise No. 2)*, Chopin *(Preludes, Op. 28)* FON (Historical Piano) ▲ 9013 [DDD] (13.97)

Joplin, Gershwin, Berlin, Whiteman—features performances by S. Joplin *(Joplin:Maple Leaf Rag; Magnetic Rag; Cascades; Somethin' Doin'; Weeping Willow; Frog Legs Rag; Handy:Ole Miss' Rag)*, G. Gershwin *(Grant:Arrah Go on I'm Gonna Go Back to Oregon; Kern:The Land Where the Good Songs Go [w. R. Erlebach (pno)]; Shilkret:Make Believe; Gershwin:So Am I [from Lady Be Good]; Tee-Oodle-Um-Bum-Bo [from La-La-Lucille]; Rhap in Blue [arr Gershwin for solo pno])*, P. Ohman *(Gershwin:Oh Gee! Oh Joy! [from Rosalie]; Berlin:What Does It Matter?)*, F. Rich *(Gershwin:Fascinatin' Rhythm; Oh, Lady Be Good [both from Lady Be Good])*, C. Merring *(Berlin:A Russian Lullaby)*, F. Milne *(Berlin:How Deep Is the Ocean; Lady of the Evening [from Music Box Revue; w. R. Erlebach (pno)]; A Pretty Girl Is Like a Melody; Whiteman:Play That Song of India Again [w. R. Erlebach (pno)])* FON (Historical Piano) ▲ 9016 [DDD] (13.97)

Prokofiev, Sergei, Alfredo Casella & Georges Enescu: Piano Roll Recordings—features performances by S. Prokofiev *(Prokofiev:Fant on Themes from Rimsky-Korsakov's "Scheherazade"; March, Op. 21/1; Love of 3 Oranges:Intermezzo & March; Tales of the Old Grandmother, Op. 31/3; Toccata, Op. 11; Rachmaninoff:Prelude, Op. 23/5; Scriabin:Prelude, Op. 45/3; Winged Poem, Op. 51/3; Mussorgsky:Pictures at an Exhibition:Byldo; Promenade, the Old Castle)*, A. Casella *(Casella:Baracola, Op. 15; Berceuse triste, Op. 14)*, G. Enescu *(Sarasate:Zigeunerweisen; Enescu:Adagio, Op. 3/3)* FON (Historical Piano) ▲ 9015 [DDD] (13.97)

Saint-Saëns, Camille, Maurice Ravel & Enrique Granados: Piano Roll Recordings—features performances by C. Saint-Saëns *(Chopin:Impromptu, Op. 36; Saint-Saëns:Improv on "Samson & Dalilah"; Valse Mignonne, Op. 104; Mazurca 3, Op. 66)*, M. Ravel *(Ravel:Le gibet No. 2 [from Gaspard de la nuit]; Miriors No. 5, "La vallée des cloches")*, E. Granados *(Granados:Danzas españolas, Nos. 2, 5, 7 & 10; El pelele; Quejas, o la maja y el ruiseñor [both from Goyescas]; Rêverie; Imrpov on themes of V. Jota)* FON (Historical Piano) ▲ 9014 [DDD] (13.97)

Great Composers Play Their Own Works—features Grieg *(Butterfly)*, Mahler *(Funeral March [trans from Sym 5])*, Scriabin *(Désir)*, Saint-Saëns *(Rapsodie d'Auvergne; Valse mignonne)*, R. Strauss *(Intermezzo; Dance of the 7 Veils [trans from Salome])*, Reger *(Intermezzo in E♭; Silhouette in f#)*, Ravel *(Sonatine in f# [2nd movt])*, Debussy *(D'un cahier d'esquisses; La soirée dans Grenade)* [original Welte-Mignon pno rolls] *(rec 1905-14)* INTC ▲ 860855 (13.97)

Great Pianists Box Set No. 1
PPHI (Great Pianists of the 20th Century) ▲ 462731 (228.97)

Great Pianists Box Set No. 2
PPHI (Great Pianists of the 20th Century) ▲ 462732 (228.97)

Great Pianists: Complete Guide
PPHI (Great Pianists of the 20th Century) ▲ 462699 (11.97)

Great Pianists of the Golden Era
(piano roll recordings)

Backhaus, Wilhelm: Piano Roll Recordings (1923-1926)—features works by Mozart *(Serenade [from Don Giovanni; trans Backhaus])*, Mendelssohn *(Con 1 Pno [arr Backhaus for solo pno])*, Brahms *(Vars on a theme of Paganini)*, Schumann *(Vidmung [trans Liszt])*, R. Strauss *(Ständchen, Op. 17/2 [trans Backhaus])*, Kreisler *(Liebeslied No. 2 [trans Rachmaninoff])*, Smetana *(Caprice Bohemian in F)*, Delibes *(Waltz [from Naïla; trans E. Dohnanyi])*, Pick-Mangiagalli *(La danse d'Olaf)* FON (Historical Piano) ▲ 9011 [DDD] (13.97)

Cortot, Alfred & Vladimir Horowitz: Piano Roll Recordings by Cortot (1919-1927) & Horowitz (1928-1940)—features works by Beethoven *(Carmen Variations; Waltz in fVianna da Motta, Saint-Saïns, Hoffman, Debussy, Busoni, D'Albert, Landowska, Ravel, Grunfield, Paderewski)*, V. Horowitz *(Saint-Saëns:Danse Macabre [trans Liszt]; Schubert:Liebesbotschaft [trans Liszt]; Rachmaninoff:Prélude, Op. 32/1; Horowitz:Carmen Vars; Valse in f)* FON (Historical Piano) ▲ 9012 [DDD] (13.97)

Friedman, Ignaz: Duo-Art Piano Roll Recordings (1921-1929)—features works by Alyabiev *(Nightingale [trans Liszt])*, Chopin *(Nocturnes, Op. 37/1 & 62/1; Polonaise, Op. 71/2)*, Liszt *(Hungarian Rhap No. 14 [arr Friedman]; Grand Etude de Paganini No. 3 [arr Busoni]; Reminiscences de Don Juan [abbreviated & arr Friedman])*, Moszkowski *(Serenata, Op. 15/1 [arr pno])*, Joh. Strauss II *(Blue Danube, Op. 314)* FON (Historical Piano) ▲ 9010 [DDD] (13.97)

Lamond, Frederic: Piano Roll Recordings (1923-1929)—features works by Beethoven *(Pno Son No. 32 in c, Op. 111 [1st & 2nd movts])*, Liszt *(Gnomenreigen; Un sospiro)*, Rossini *(Cuius animam [from Stabat Mater; trans Liszt for pno])*, Joh. Strauss II *(Frühlingsstimmen)*, Tchaikovsky *(Sym 5 [2nd movt; trans for pno])*, C. M. Weber *(Freischütz:Ov [arr Lamond for pno])* FON (Historical Piano) ▲ 9006 [DDD] (13.97)

Paderewski, Ignace Jan: Piano Roll Recordings (1919-1927)—features works by Beethoven *(Pno Son No. 14, "Moonlight Son")*, Chopin *(Etudes, Opp. 10/5 & 25/9; Valse, Op. 42; Polonaise, Op. 40/1; Mazurka, Op. 17/4; Scherzo, Op. 39/3; Ballade, Op. 47/3; The Maiden's Wish, Op. 74/1 [trans Liszt])*, Liszt *(Hungarian Rhap No. 10)*, Schubert *(Impromptu, Op. 142/2; Hark, Hark the Lark [trans Liszt])*, Schumann *(Waldscenen, Op. 82/7, "Vogel als Prophet")*, Wagner *(Isolde's Liebestod [trans Liszt])* FON (Historical Piano) ▲ 9009 [DDD] (13.97)

Rubinstein, Artur, Leopold Godowsky & Wanda Landowska: Piano Roll Recordings—features performances by A. Rubinstein *(Chopin:Polonaise, Op. 44; Ballade No. 3, Op. 47; Debussy:Danse; Prokofiev:Suggestion diabolique; Rimsky-Korsakov:Le coq d'or (sels))*, L. Godowsky *(Chopin:Nocturne, Op. 9/2; Ballade No. 1, Op. 23; Henselt:Berceuse)*, W. Landowska *(Mozart: Son 15 Pno; Lanner:Valses Viennoises [trans Landowska])* FON (Historical Piano) ▲ 9008 [DDD] (13.97)

Siloti, Alexander & Arthur Friedheim: Piano Roll Recordings—features performances by A. Siloti *(Bach:Chorale Prelude in e for Org [trans Szanto]; Liadov:Goolenki [Cradle Song; arr Silot]; Liszt:Harmonies poétiques et religieuses No. 3, "Benediction"; Schubert:Wandererfantasie, D.760)*, A. Friedheim *(Gottschalk:Banjo, Op. 82; Liszt:Legendes Nos. 1 & 2; Années de pèlerinage, 3rd year, No. 4, "Les jeux d'eaux"; Grande etudes de Paganini, Nos. 1 & 3; Etudes d'execution, No. 11, "Harmonies du soir")* FON (Historical Piano) ▲ 9007 [DDD] (13.97)

Great Pianists on Piano Rolls—features performances by Grieg, Stavenhagen, Pachman, Vianna da Motta, Saint-Saïns, Hoffman, Debussy, Busoni, D'Albert, Landowska, Ravel, Grunfield, Paderewski PHG ▲ 5027 [ADD] (14.97)

Great Piano Music—features works by Debussy *(Claire de Lune)*, Schumann *(Kinderszenen)*, Chopin *(Nocturne in g)*, Liszt *(Consolation in E)*, plus others PUBM (Majestic) ▲ PMO 1031

Great Romantic Piano Sonatas, w. various artists—features performances by Rafael Orozco *(Chopin:Son. No. 2 in b♭, Op. 35; Liszt:Son. in d, "Sonetto 104 del Petrarca")*, Dinorah Varsi *(Schumann:Son. No. 2 in g, Op. 22)*, Ingrid Haebler *(Schubert:Son in B♭, D.960)*, Paul Crossley *(Tchaikovsky:Son. in G, Op. 37)*, Jean Louis Steuermann *(Scriabin:Son. No. 4, Op. 30)* PPHI 2-▲ 42617 (17.97)

Keyboard Wizards of the Gershwin Era, Vol. 4, w. Zez Confrey (pno)—features works by Confrey *(Poor Buttermilk; All Muddled up; Nickel in the Spot; Kitten on the Keys)*, Williams, Donaldson, Cantor & Caesar *(rec 1921-43)* PHS ▲ 9204 (17.97)

Keyboard Wizards of the Gershwin Era, Vol. 5, w. Felix Arndt (pno), Mike Bernard (pno), Roy Bargy (pno), Frank Banta (pno), Rube Bloom (pno)—features works by Arndt, Bernard, Bargy, Banta, Bloom, et al. *(rec 1912-28)* PHS ▲ 9205 (17.97)

Keyboard Wizards of the Gershwin Era, Vol. 6, w. Vee Lawnhurst (pno), Constance Mering (pno), Muriel Pollock (pno)—features works by Bloom, Barnes, Gensler & Simon, Berlin, Arndt, et al. *(rec 1926-34)* PHS ▲ 9206 (17.97)

Keyboard Wizards of the Gershwin Era, Vol. 7, w. Raie da Costa (pno)—features works by da Costa, Strauss, Mayerl, Turk & Ahlert, Bernatzky & Stolz, et al. *(rec 1928-34)* PHS ▲ 9207 (17.97)

Largo I *(a collection of baroque to modern piano works and excerpts, all recordings under license from Decca)*, w. Vladimir Ashkenazy (pno), Alfred Brendel (pno), Alicia de Larrocha (pno), Julius Katchen (pno), András Schiff (pno), Ilana Vered (pno), et al.—features works by Bach/Hess, Beethoven, Brahms, Chopin, Messiaen, Mompou, Mozart, Schubert, Schumann, Scriabin CEHA ▲ 35509 2-▮ 35509 (16.98)

Largo II, w. Vladimir Ashkenazy (pno), Alfred Brendel (pno), Alicia de Larrocha (pno), Julius Katchen (pno), András Schiff (pno), Ilana Vered (pno), et al.—features works by Bach/Hess, Beethoven, Brahms, Chopin, Messiaen, Mompou, Mozart, Schubert, Schumann, Scriabin CEHA ▲ 19504-2 ▮ 19504-4

Legendary Piano Duos—features H. Bauer (pno), O. Gabrilovich (pno) *(Arensky:Suite 1 for 2 Pnos, Op. 15 [Valse]; F. Schubert:Marche militaire, D.733 [No. 1])*, H. Bauer (pno), M. Hess (pno) *(G. Pierné:March of the Little Lead Soldiers, Op. 28)*, W. Damrosch (pno), P. Damrosch (pno) *(M. Ravel:Ma mère l'oye [3. Laideronette, Impératrice des Pagodes; 4. Les Entretiens de la Belle et de la Bête])*, I. Friedman (pno) *(F. Schubert:Marches héroïques, D.602 [No. 3 in D])*, P. Grainger (pno), R. Leopold (pno) *(Delius:North Country Sketches)*, P. Grainger (pno), C. Scott (pno) *(C. Scott:Sym Dances [No. 1, "Old English Dance"])*, J. Lambert (pno), N. Reisenberg (pno) *(Litolff:Con Symphonique 4, Op. 102 [Scherzo])*, T. Lerner (pno), V. Shavits (pno) *(Liszt:Con pathétique Pnos, S.258)* KLAV ▲ 11095 [ADD] (18.97)

The Magic of the Piano—features performances by Maria-João Pires *(Schumann:Rêverie [from Scenes From Childhood, Op. 15]; Einsame Blumen [from Forest Scenes, Op. 82]; Schubert:Impromptus in G♭, Op. 90/3 & in A♭, Op. 90/4; Beethoven:Adagio sostenuto [from Son No. 14, Op. 27/2]; Chopin:Waltzes Nos. 6 & 9, Opp. 64/1 & 69/1)*, François-René Duchable *(Chopin:Preludes No. 3 in G & No. 6 in b; Impromptu No. 1 in A♭, Op. 29; Ballade No. 2 in F, Op. 38)*, Viktoria Postnikova *(Tchaikovsky:Valse [Douze morceaux de difficulté moyenne, Op. 40]; 6 Morceaux, Op. 19 [Nocturne])*, Michel Dalberto *(Brahms:Andante non troppo e con molta espressione in B♭ [from Intermezzo No. 2, Op. 117])*, Anne Queffelec *(Liszt:Liebestraum [No. 3])*, Pierre Barbizet *(Chabrier:10 pièces pittoresques [Idylle])* ERAT ▲ 94692 (9.97)

Moonlight: Classics for a New Age—features performances by Peter Dickson (pno) *(Satie:Gymnopédie 1)*, Kathryn Stott (pno) *(Fauré:Nocturne 8; Chopin:Contredanse)*, Andrew Wilde (pno) *(J. S. Bach:Jesu, Joy of Man's Desiring; Scriabin:Etude in c#, Op. 2/1)*, Gerhard Oppitz (pno) *(Schumann:Traümerei; Grieg:I Love You; Love; Liszt:Consolation No. 5)*, Rudolf Firkušný (pno) *(Janáček:In the Mist; In Tears; Our Evenings)*, Catherine Collard (pno) *(Debussy:The Girl with the Flaxen Hair)*, Alexis Weissenberg (pno) *(Rachmaninoff:Prelude in g, Op. 32/5)*, Barry Douglas (pno) *(Tchaikovsky:Baracole No. 6 [from the Seasons])*, Jörg Demus (pno) *(Beethoven:Adagio sostenuto [from Son 14])*, Robert Leonardy (pno) *(Liszt:Liebestraum No. 3)* RCAV (Gold Seal) ▲ 68354 [DDD] (10.97) 68354

The New Golden Era—features performances by Abrams Chasins (pno), Shura Cherkassky (pno), Robert Goldsand (pno) & Vladimir Horowitz (pno) NIMB ▲ 8811 [DDD] (11.97)

Piano for Dummies EMIC (Classical Music for Dummies) ♦ CDU 66403

The Piano G & T's: Recordings from the Gramophone & Typewriter Era (1900-07), Vol. 1—features performances by Alfred Grünfeld (pno) *(Chopin:Mazurka in b, Op. 33/4; Schubert:Ballettmusik [from Rosamunde]; Wohin? [both arr Grünfeld]; Grünfeld:Serenade in B, Op. 32; Etude à la tarentella, Op. 47/3; Mazurka, Op. 51; Hungarian Fant, Op. 55; Valse mignone, Op. 51/4; Romance in D♭, Op. 42; Strauss II:Frühlingsstimmenwalzer, Op. 410)*, Natalia Janotha (pno) *(Chopin:Fugue in a; Mendelssohn:Song without Words, Op. 67/4; Janotha:Polish Carillion; Gavotte impériale)*, Raoul Pugno (pno) *(Handel:Gavottte & Vars; Scarlatti:Son in A, L.495; Pugno:Impromptu valse; Valse lente; Chopin:Waltz in A♭, Op. 34/1; Nocturne in F#, Op. 15/2; Impromptu in A♭, Op. 29; Berecuse in D♭, Op. 57; Marche funèbre; Mendelssohn:Song without Words, Op. 67/4; Scherzo in e, Op. 16/2; Massenet:Valse folle; Chabrier:Scherzo-valse) (rec 1900-07)* APR ▲ 5531 (m) [ADD] (19.97)

Piano Rarities from the Husum Festival, w. Anton Kuerti (pno), Ina Peeken (pno), Michael Struck (pno), Jeffrey Swann (pno), Marie-Catherine Girod (pno), Kathryn Scott (pno), Yuri Martinov (pno), Roberto Capello (pno)—features works by H. Goetz, Witte, Hahn, Debussy, Dohnányi, Alexandrov, Schubert, Liszt Danacord ▲ DAN 489

Polish Piano Music, w. Teresa Rutkowska (pno), Marian Brokowski (pno), Maria Nosowska (pno), Baroara Halska (pno)—features works by Chopin, Pankiewicz, Brzezinski, Rozycki, Kamienski, Lutoslawski, Gorecki, Twardowski OLY ▲ 394 [AAD]

The Pupils of Liszt *(recordings, 1912-1941, by students of Franz Liszt)*—features performances by Conrad Ansorge [1862-1930] *(works by Chopin/Liszt, Schumann)*, Eugene D'Albert [1864-1932] *(Beethoven, Brahms, Carreño, D'Albert, Liszt)*, José Vianna Da Motta [1868-1948] *(Liszt)*, Arthur Friedheim [1859-1932] *(Chopin, Liszt)*, Arthur de Greef [1862-1940] *(Grieg)*, Frederic Lamond [1868-1948] *(Beethoven, Glinka/Balakirev, Liszt)*, Moriz Rosenthal [1862-1946] *(Chopin, Joh. Strauss)*, Emil von Sauer [1862-1942] *(Beethoven/Rubinstein, Chopin, Liszt, Mendelssohn, Sauer)*, Josef Weiss [1864-1945] *(Beethoven, Liszt)* PHS 2-▲ 9972 (m) [AAD] (33.97)

Rarities of Piano Music at Schloss von Husum

1989—features performances by R. Smith *(Alkan)*, M. Ponti *(Rachmaninoff)*, M. Hamelin *(Chopin/Godowsky, Confrey)*, J. DeBeenhouwer *(H. von Sahr)*, H. Milne *(W.S. Bennett, Medtner)*, J. Lusada *(Bizet, Fauré)*, I. Biret *(Fauré)*, P. Froundjian *(Fauré/Grainger, Palmgren)*, B. Bloch *(Glinka/Balakirey, Tchaikovsky/Pletnjov)*, R.M. Klaas *(Liszt)*, D. Berman *(Gluck/Chasins, Gershwin/Wild)* (rec. Aug 19-26, 1989) DANR ▲ 349 [AAD]

1990—features performances by I. Shukow *(Scriabin)*, C. Tanski *(Clementi, Liszt)*, J. Weber *(Liszt, Schubert/Godowsky)*, M. Hamelin *(Chopin/Godowsky, Prokofiev)*, B. Koehlen *(Janácek)*, B. Forsberg *(Mankell, Medtner)*, G.D. Madge *(Godowsky)*, A. Simon *(Albeniz/Godowsky) (rec Aug 12-25, 1990)* DANR ▲ 379

1991—features performances by H. Milne *(Busoni, Siloti, Medtner)*, A. Ljubimov *(Glinka)*, K. Lessing *(Rimski-Korsakov, Strasfogel)*, D. Amato *(Scott)*, S. Speidel *(Erdmann) (rec Aug 19-20 & Sept 14, 1991)* DANR ▲ 389 [DDD]

Relaxing Piano—features works by Beethoven *(Adagio Sostenuto [from Son No. 14, Op. 27/2]; Adagio Cantabile [from Son No. 13])*, Chopin *(Nocturne No. 2 in E♭, Op. 9/2; Tristesse [from Étude in E, Op. 10/3]; Romance [from Con. No. 1 in e, Op. 11])*, Mozart *(Andante [from Con No. 21 in C, K.467])*, Debussy *(Clair de Lune; La fille aux cheveux de lin)*, Tchaikovsky *(Andantino Semplice [from Con No. 1 in b♭, Op. 23])*, Liszt *(Liebestraum No. 3 in A♭)*, Schumann *(Träumerei [from Scenes from Childhood])*, Ravel *(Adagio Assai [from Con in G])*, Satie *(Gymnopédie No. 1)*, Rachmaninoff *(Rhap on a Theme of Paganini, Op. 43 [18th Var])* CFP (Relaxing) ▲ 4662 (12.97)

The Romantic Piano Concerto, Vol. 1, w. P. Lane (pno), BBC Scottish SO [cnd:J. Maksymiuk] *see* Composer section under Moszkowski & Paderewski HYP ▲ 66452 [DDD] (17.97)

The Romantic Piano Concerto, Vol. 2, w. N. Demidenko (pno), BBC Scottish SO [cnd:J. Maksymiuk] *see* Composer section under Medtner HYP ▲ 66580 [DDD] (17.97)

The Romantic Piano Concerto, Vol. 7—features performances by Roland Keller, Berlin SO [cnd.:Siegfried Kohler] *(Weber:Con. No. 1 in C, Op. 11; Con. No. 2 in E♭, Op. 32)*, Jerome Rose, Luxembourg Radio Orch. [cnd.:Pierre Cao] *(Volkmann:Konzertstück, Op. 42)*, Michael Ponti *(Berwald:Con. No. 1 in D; Alkan:Con. da camera No. 2 in c# [w. Southwest German CO (cond.:Paul Angerer)]; Schumann:Introduction & Allegro appassionata in G, Op. 92 [w. Luxembourg Radio Orch. (cond.:Louis de Froment)]; Raff:Ode to Spring, Op. 76 [w.Hamburg SO (cond.:Richard Kapp)] Liszt:Totentanz [w. Berlin SO (cond.:Volker Schmidt-Gertenbach)])* VB2 2-▲ 5098 [ADD] (9.97)

Romantic Piano Favorites, Vol. 1, w. Balázs Szokolay (pno)—features works by Bartók, Chopin, Dvořák, Fibich, Gershwin, Grieg, Liszt, Mendelssohn, Mozart, Rubinstein, Schubert, Schumann, Tchaikovsky, Weber NXIN ▲ 550052 [DDD] (5.97)

Romantic Piano Music—featuring performances by M. Bácher, I. Rohmann, A. Drescher, I. Pogorelich, Jenö Jando, Dieter Goldman, Maurizio Pollini, Sandor Falvai, Evelyne Dubourg *(music by Beethoven, Schubert, Schumann, Chopin & Liszt)* LALI ▲ 15052 [DDD] (3.97)

Romantic Rarities, Vol. 2: An Anthology of Rare Recordings From the Golden Age of Pianism—features performances by Ignaz Friedman *(Chopin)*, Simon Baere *(Liszt, Chopin, Scarlatti, Scriabin)*, Mischa Levitzky *(Gluck-Sgambati, Chopin, Moszkowski, Liszt, Levitzky, Tchaikovsky)*, Vladimir Horowitz *(Scarlatti-Tausig, Liszt, Chopin, Debussy, Dohnányi, Horowitz)* APR ▲ APR 7014 [AAD]

Russian Piano School—[Vol. 1] features performances by Alexander Goldenweiser *(Rachmaninoff:Suite 2 [w. Grigori Ginzburg (pno)]; works by Tchaikovsky, Arensky, Borodin, Medtner & Goldenweiser)* [Vol. 2] Heinrich Neuhaus *(Mozart:Son. for 2 Pnos, K.448 [w. Stanislav Neuhaus]; Debussy:8 Preludes; Prokofiev:Visions fugitives)* [Vol. 3] Samuil Feinberg *(Bach:4 Chorale Preludes [arr. Feinberg]; Mozart:Sons. K.282 & K.576; Fant. & Fugue, K.394; Vars. on an Allegretto, K.500)* [Vol. 4] Maria Yudina *(Stravinsky:Serenade; Bartók:sels. from Mikrokosmos; Hindemith:Son. 3; Berg:Son.; Krenek: Son. No. 2)* [Vol. 5] Vladimir Sofronitzky [2 disc set, rec. live] *(Mozart:Fant. K.475; Schubert:Impromptus Nos. 3 & 4; Schumann:Son. No. 1; Chopin:2 Nocturnes; Scherzos Nos. 1 & 2; Rachmaninoff:Moments musicaux Nos. 2 & 5; Scriabin:Son. No. 4; Prokofiev:4 Grandmother's Tales)* [Vol. 6] Sviatoslav Richter *(Bach:Italian Con.; Fant. & Fugue in A; Haydn:Son. 50; Chopin:Ballades Nos. 1 & 2; Beethoven:Son. No. 12)* [Vol. 7] Emil Gilels *(Bach/Busoni:Prelude & Fugue in D; Beethoven:Vars. on an Original Theme, WoO 80; Weber:Son. No. 2; Liszt:Rhapsodie espagnole; Prokofiev:sels. from Visions Fugitives)* [Vol. 8] Lazar Bermen *(Liszt)* [Vol. 9] Mikhail Pletnev *(Tchaikovsky/Pletnev:sels. from The Nutcracker; Shchedrin/Pletnev:Prelude & Horse Race from Anna Karenina; Prokofiev:Son. 7; Mozart:Son. K.570)* [Vol. 10] Evgeny Kissin *(works by Rachmaninoff & Scriabin; Prokofiev:sels. from Visions fugitives; Kissin:2 Inventions)* MELD 11-▲ 25172 [ADD/DDD] (60.97)

Russian Piano School *(each disc focuses on one pianist's performances)*—features Yelena Bekman-Shcherbina (pno) *(Balakirev:The Lark; Au Jardin; Titov:Waltzes; Liszt:Nightingale; Rubinstein:Barcarolle; Waltzes; Glinka:Souvenir de Mazurka; Tchaikovsky:Scherzo humoristique in D; Liadov:Mazurkas; Glazunov:Etude in E, Op. 31/3; Arensky:Ruisseau dans la forêt; Etude in F#; Scriabin:Preludes; Waltz; Rachmaninoff:Prelude; Etude-Tableaux in E♭)*, Grigory Ginsburg (pno) *(Liszt:Fant on 2 Themes from Mozart; Reminiscences; Paraphrase Verdi; Trans Waltz Gounod; Ginsburg:Trans Largo Rossini)*, Lev Oborin (pno) *(Beethoven:Son No. 31 in A♭, Op. 110; Chopin:Son No. 3 in b, Op. 58; Brahms:Pieces (4), Op. 119; Scriabin:Son No. 2 in g#, Op. 19)*, Maria Grinberg (pno) *(Seixas:Menuet in f; Toccata in f; Soler:Son No. 12 in F#; Son No. 2 in c#; Son No. 11 in g; D. Scarlatti:Son in f, K.69; Son in A, K.113; Son in c, K.11; Son in c, K.22; Mozart:Fant in c, K.396; Schumann:Bunte Blätter, Op. 99; 3 Little Pieces; 5 Album Leaves; Brahms:Vars Schumann; Waltzes)*, Tatiana Nikolayeva (pno) *(Schumann:Romances (3), Op. 28; Vars on Original Theme in E♭; Prokofiev:Son No. 8 in B♭, Op. 84; Peter & the Wolf)*, Igor Zhukov (pno) *(J.S. Bach:Passacaglia in c, BWV 582; Schumann:Waldszenen, Op. 82; Tchaikovsky:Souvenir de Hapsal, Op. 2; Rachmaninoff:Barcarolle in g, Op. 10/3; Prokofiev:Children's Music, Op. 65)*, Vladimir Ashkenazy (pno) *(Chopin:Etudes, Opp. 10 & 25; Liszt:Mephisto Waltz No. 1)*, Eliso Virsaladze (pno) *(Chopin:Son No. 3 in b, Op. 58; Ballade No. 3 in A♭, Op. 47; Mazurkas 21 & 23; Waltzes 2 & 9; Polonaise-Fant No. 7 in A♭, Op. 61; Nocturne No. 8 in D♭, Op. 27/2; Polonaise No. 6 in A♭, Op. 53)*, Edvard Syomin (pno) *(Godowsky:Renaissance; Künstlerleben; Chopin:Souvenir de Paganini; Berceuse in D♭, Op. 57; Stanchinsky:Preludes (8); Medtner:Fairy Tales, Op. 20; Eiges:Son-Toccata No. 4 in f#/E, Op. 15; Albéniz:Navarra; Tango in D, Op. 165/2; Busoni:Chamber Fant Bizet)*, Yekaterina Ervy-Novitskaya (pno) *(Prokofiev:Sarcasms, Op. 17; Son No. 5 in C, Op. 38/135; Visions fugitives, Op. 22; Romeo & Juliet, Op. 75)* MELD 10-▲ 33230 (m) [ADD]

Timeless Kiss: The Best Romantic Piano Music, w. Anthony Paratore (pno), Joseph Paratore (pno), Daniel Pollack (pno), John Novacek (pno) FWIN ▲ 3007 (13.97)

25 Piano Favorites—features performances by Michael Ponti (pno), Prague SO [cnd:Richard Kapp] *(Tchaikovsky:Pno Con No. 1 in b♭ [Intro])*, Walter Klein (pno) *(Brahms:Rhap in g; Mozart:Son No. 15 in C for Pno [Allegro]; Liszt:Liebestraum)*, Balint Vaszonyi (pno) *(Schubert:Moment Musical No. 2; Debussy:Clair de lune; Paderewski:Menuett; Chopin:Etude in E; Beethoven:Minuet in G)*, Rudolf Firkusny (pno) *(Dvorak:Humoresque No. 7)*, Peter Frankl (pno) *(Debussy:Prelude "La Fille aux cheveux de lin"; Reverie; Schumann:from Kinderszenen [Von fremden Ländern und Menschen])*, Leonard Hokanson (pno) *(Grieg:Butterfly [from Lyrical Pieces]; Rubinstein:Melody in F; Mozart:Son No. 11 in A)*, Norman Krieger (pno) *(Chopin:Etude in c)*, Maria Tipo (pno) *(Scarlatti:Sonata in E)*, Sylvia Capova (pno) *(Rachmaninoff:Prelude in c#)*, Grant Johannesen (pno) *(Chopin:"Military" Polonaise)*, Shoshana Rudiakov (pno) *(Scriabin:Etude No. 12, Op. 8)*, Dubravka Tomsic (pno), Ljubljana SO [cnd:Anton Nanut] *(Rachmaninoff:Rhap on a Theme by Paganini [Var No. 18])*, Alfred Brendel (pno), Vienna Volk Opera Orch [cnd:Wilfried Besttcher] *(Mozart:Con No. 20 in d for Pno [Romance])*, Guiomar Novaes (pno) *(Chopin:Waltz in D♭)*, Eugene List (pno), Berlin SO [cnd:Samuel Adler] *(Gershwin:Rhapsody in Blue [Finale])* VCC (25 Favorites) ▲ 8818 ▮ 8818

PIANO COLLECTIONS

Van Cliburn International Piano Competition Retrospective Series, Vol. 2—features performances by Steven de Groote (pno), Alexander Toradze (pno), Jeffrey Swann (pno) *(works by Chopin, Bartók, Liszt, Stravinsky, Schumann (rec live, 1977)* VAIA ▲ 1146 [ADD] (16.97)

Van Cliburn International Piano Competition Retrospective Series, Vol. 3—features performances by Cristina Ortiz (pno), Minoru Nojima (pno), Mark Wescott (pno) *(works by Brahms, Chopin, Ravel, Lorenzo-Fernandez, Bartók, Scarlatti, Schubert, Keats (rec live, 1969)* VAIA ▲ 1147 [ADD] (16.97)

Van Cliburn International Retrospective, Vol. 2—features performances by Steven de Groote *(Chopin:Scherzo Pno, Op. 39; Bartók:Out of Doors [1st & 4th movt]; Barber:Ballade)*, Alexander Toradze *(Liszt:Vars Pno, S.179; Stravinsky:Pétrouchka)*, Jeffrey Swann *(Schumann:Fant Pno) (rec 1977)* VAIA ▲ 1146 [ADD] (16.97)

Van Cliburn International Retrospective, Vol. 3—features performances by Cristina Ortiz (pno) *(Lorenzo-Fernandez:Brazilian Suite 2; Brahms:Intermezzo, Op. 118/6; Chopin:Nocturne in e; Ravel:Gaspard de la nuit [Scarbo])*, Minoru Nojima (pno) *(Liszt:Transcendental Etudes [Feux Follets]; Dello-Joio:Capriccio; Bartók:Son)*, Mark Westcott (pno) *(D. Scarlatti:Son in D; Schubert:Son in b♭, D.960 [1st movt]; D. Keats:Son [4th movt]) (rec 1969)* VAIA ▲ 1147 [ADD] (16.97)

Van Cliburn International Retrospective, Vol. 4—features performances by Ralph Votapek *(MacDowell:Son 2 Pno; Brahms:Pieces Pno, Op. 118/1-3; Copland:Son Pno)*, Nicolai Petrov *(Scarlatti:Sons in A & G Pno; MacDowell:Son 3 Pno)*, Radu Lupu *(Prokofiev:Con 2 Pno) (rec 1962 & 1966)* VAIA ▲ 1156 [ADD] (16.97)

Van Cliburn International Retrospective, Vol. 5—features performances by José Feghali *(Haydn:Allegro [from Son Pno, H.XVI/52]; Chopin:Fant; Scherzos, Op. 20/1)*, Philippe Bianconi *(Prokofiev:Son 3 Pno; Ravel:Noctuelles [from Miroirs]; Liszt:Mephisto Waltz 1 Pno)*, Barry Douglas *(Beethoven:Allegro molto e con brio [from Son 4 Pno]; Liszt:Après une lecture de Dante [from Dante Son]) (rec 1985)* VAIA ▲ 1157 [ADD] (16.97)

Van Cliburn International Retrospective, Vol. 6—features performances by Alexei Sultanov *(Haydn:Son Pno, H.XVI/49 [1st movt]; Mozart:Son 10 Pno [2nd & 3rd movts]; Chopin:Scherzo 2 Pno, Op. 31)*, José Carlos Cocarelli *(Brahms:Son 3 Pno [1st, 3rd & 5th movts]; Barber:Son Pno [Fuga])*, Benedetto Lupo *(Schumann:Son 2 Pno; Liszt:Études transcendante, S.139 [Wilde Jagd]) (rec 1989)* VAIA ▲ 1158 [ADD] (16.97)

View from the Keyboard—features performances by Judith Bokor (pno) *(V. McDermott:Magic Ground)*, Leonard Mastrogiacomo (pno), Norma Mastrogiacomo (pno) *(Wm. Matthews:Ferns)*, Carole Ross (pno) *(Mattila:Little Arrays (6))*, Robert Fakazerly (pno) *(T. Benjamin:That Old Second-Viennese-School Rag)*, Susan Grace (pno) *(C. Gamer:Pno Raga Music)*, Donna Coleman (pno) *(John A. Lennon:Death Angel)*, Pola Baytelman (pno) *(H. Tann:Doppelgänger)*, David Holzman (pno) *(Pleskow:Caprice)*, Bynell Figler (pno) *(A. D. Kurtz:Preludes (6) on Ostinato Basses & Ornamentations)* CPS (Society of Composers, Inc, No. 1) ▲ 8606 [DDD]

RECORDER

Antwerp Recorder Consort
Antwerp Recorder Consort—features works by Ortiz *(Recercadas 2 & 4 sobre Doulce Memorie; Recercarada 8)*, Scheidt *(Galliard Battaglia)*, Susato *(Pavane & Gaillarde sur la Bataille)*, Diomedes *(Fant Cromatica)*, Dowland *(Lachrimae Antiquae Pavan; The Earle of Essex Gaillard; Captain Digorie Piper his Gaillard; Sir Henry Umpton's Funeral)*, Rosenmüller *(Sinf sesta)*, Purcell *(Fant upon 1 Note)*, Serocki *(Arrs)*, plus anon 16th cent works *(Istampia Tre Fontane; T'Andernaeken; La Spagna; Lamento di Tristano)* ECCO ▲ 8007 (10.97)

Capriole Ensemble
De la musique à voir...—features works by D. Becker *(Suite in 3 Movts in C)*, Schickhardt *(Con 2 in d)*, Telemann *(Con in e)*, Pezel *(Son Abella)*, Mainerio *(Danses de la Renaissance)*, Vivaldi *(Con in D, Op. 10/3)*, Saux *(Qt in F for Rcrs)*, Cooke *(Suite in 6 Movts)* SNE ▲ 576 (16.97)

Clemencic, René (rcr)
Flûte à bec, Luth et Giutare, w. András Kecskés (lt/gtr)—features works by Telemann, Bach, Handel, Dowland & Van Eyck HAM ▲ 90427 (17.97)
Plays 21 Recorders *(Renaissance & Baroque music)* HMA ▲ 190384 (9.97)

Flanders Recorder Quartet [Bart Spanhove (rcr), Geert Van Gele (rcr), Joris Van Goethem (rcr), Paul van Loey (rcr)]
The Nations—features works by Dornel, Bach, Scheidt, de Cabezon, Isaac, Hacquart, Farina, Merula, Paradizo, Baldwin & Byrd DI ▲ 920191 [DDD] (5.97)

Flanders Recorder Quartet [A. Breukink (rcr), K. Rooman (rcr), G. Van Gele (rcr), B. Spanhove (rcr)]
Armonia di Flauti, w. P. Van Heyghen (rcr)—features J. S. Bach *(Art of the Fugue (sels), BWV 1080 [Contrapunctus No. 1; Contrapunctus No. 9; Contrapunctus No. 18]; Cant 29, BWV 29 [Sinfonia]; Fant & Fugue Org, BWV 542)*, Ciconia *(Abane missa celitus; Ut te per omnes)*, Hirose *(Idyll)*, Holborne *(Fruit of Love; Heigh Ho Holiday; Heres Patemus; Muy Linda; Night-Watch)*, H. Isaac *(A la Bataglia)*, Susato *(Pavane La Battaille)*, Van Landeghem *(Turkish Bumble-Bee Rondo)*, Vivaldi *(Cons Vn(s), Strs, Op. 3/1-12 [No. 8 in a])* OPUS ▲ 30201 [DDD] (17.97)

La Fontegara Amsterdam [Saskia Coolen (rcr), Peter Holtslag (rcr), Hans Tol (rcr)]
Common Grounds—features works by anon. *(Estampie; Llibre Vermell)*, Isaac *(J'ay pris amours; La morra; O Venus bant; Tart ara)*, Eccles *(Divisions upon a ground)*, Bevin *(Browning)*, Corelli/Marais/Scarlatti *(La Follia [arr. La Fontegara Amsterdam])*, Baldwine *(Browning)*, Brumel *(Tandernaken)*, Ruffo *(La Disperata)*, Lapicida *(Tandernaken)*, Ruffo/Merula/Marini *(La Gamba) (rec Utrecht, Dec 1993)* GLOE ▲ 5112 [DDD] (16.97)
17th Century Italian Recorder Music—features works by Buonamente, Cesare, Corradini, Farina, Fontana, Frescobaldi, Merula, Riccio, Uccellini GLOE ▲ 5065 [DDD] (16.97)

Il Giardino Armonico Ensemble
Italian Recorder Sonatas—features works by Barsanti *(Sonata in D, Op. 1/2)*, Corelli *("La Follia," Op. 5/12; Sonatas in F & d, Op. 5/4 & 5)*, Geminiani *(Sonata in e)*, Veracini *(Sonata No. 6 in a)* NUO ▲ 6789 [DDD]

Hamon, Pierre (rcr)
Lucente Stella: Middle Ages to the 20th Century—features Lai du chèvrefeuille; Lucente stella; Belicha; Mes cuers est emprisonnés; Nota; In pro; Fragmente; Tels rit au main; Non perch' i' speri, donna; Chominciamento di gioia; Black Intention; Chant du papillon OPUS ▲ 30122 (17.97)

Harvey, Richard (rcr)
The Genteel Companion, w. Monica Huggett (vn), Sarah Cunningham (vl), Mark Caudle (vc), et al.—features works by Croft, Dalla Casa, van Eyck, Finger, Handel, Leclair, Vivaldi & anon ASV ▲ 117 (16.97)

Hauwe, Walter van (rcr)
Blockflutes 3: The Early 17th Century, w. Toyohiko Satoh (lt)—features works by Bassano, Castello, Eccles, van Eyck, Finger, Frescobaldi, Schop, Tollett, Virgiliano CCL ▲ 3392 [DDD] (17.97)
Ladder of Escape 3 *(Vol. 3 in a series of portraits of musicians in search of a "Ladder of Escape" from the limitations of their instruments)*—features works by Andriessen, Berio, Debussy, Stravinsky, van Hauwe, Varèse, et al. ATAC ▲ 8847

Husenbeth, Barbara (rcr)
French Music for Recorder, w. Monica Schwamberger (vl), Gottfried Bach (hpd)—features works by Dieupart, F. Couperin, Danican-Philidor, Hervelois, Hotteterre ENTE ▲ 98 (10.97)

Kristensen, Helle (rcr)
Nocturnal Birds—features works by Vivaldi *(Cons Rcr, Op. 10/2-3 [w. Con Strumenti])*, Thommessen *(The Blockbird)*, Crowl *(Revoada)*, Rasmussen *(Fuhlaljómur)*, Nakanishi *(Uguisu)*, Borup-Jørgensen *(Chant d'oiseaux, Op. 82)*, Hänshcke *(Bird of the Night)*, Nørgård *(Heyday's Night [w. Jane Odriozola (vc), Claus Borch (hpd)])*, M. Christensen *(Birds of a Winter Night)*, plus anon piece *(The Bird Fancier's Delight (1717))* PLAL ▲ PACD 97 [DDD]

Mendoze, Christian (rcr)
Six Venetian Concerti, w. Cologne CO—features works by Locatelli, Sammartini, Vivaldi PVY ▲ 787093 [DDD] (16.97)
Sonatas for Recorder & Basso Continuo—features works by Bach, Corelli, Handel, Telemann, Vivaldi PVY ▲ 787023 [DDD] (16.97)

Musica Dolce Recorder Quintet
English Consort Music—features works by Brade, Byrd, Holborne, Simpson, Michael East, Alfonso Ferrabosco II, Robert Philips BIS ▲ 305 [DDD] (17.97)
From Byrd to Birds—features works by de Boismortier *(Con. for 5 Tenor Recorders in d)*, Scheidt *(Cantus XXVIII)*, Woodcock *(Browning Fantasy)*, Byrd *(Fantasia:The Leeves Be Green)*, Lyne *(Three Epigrams)*, Pergament *(Little Suite for 2 Recorders)*, Hindemith *(Trio: Der Plöner Musiktag)*, Warlock *(Capriol Suite)*, Prins Gustaf *(Varsang)*, Schubert *(Marche militaire)*, Meacham *(American Patrol)*, Jim Henson *(Mupparna)* (rec. 1976 & 1990) BIS ▲ 57 [ADD/DDD] (17.97)

Pehrsson, Claes (rcr)
The Artistry of Clas Pehrsson, w. Solveig Faringer (sop), Cecilia Peijel (gtr), Jörgen Rörby (lt)—features works by Francesco da Milano *(Ricercare)*, Dowland *(Lacrimae Pavan)*, Ferrabosco *(Pavane)*, Telemann *(Son in C)*, Handel *(Son in a)*, van Eyck *(Pieces (3) Rcr)*, Ortiz *(Recercadas (3) Rcr & Gtr)*, Certon *(Biblical Settings (4))*, Machaut *(Plus dure; Ballad)*, Dufay *(Vergina bella)*, plus anon/trad pieces *(Dulcissima Maria; Motett; Flos filius eius; Greensleeves)* BIS ▲ 135 [AAD] (17.97)
Clas Pehrsson—features works by Fontana *(Son. Prima [w. B. Ericson (cello) & A. Öhrwall (piano)])*, Barsanti *(Son. in c [w. B. Ericson & A. Öhrwall])*, Telemann *(Son. in e [w. B. Ericson & A. Öhrwall]; Trio Son. [w. K. Ottesen (cello) & T. Andersen (theorbo)])*, Van Eyck *(Comagain; Fantasia en echo; O Heiligh Zalighj)*, Castello *(Son. Prima [w. T. Schuback (harpsichord)])*, Frescobaldi *(Toccata [w. T. Schuback & M. Wieslander (organ)]; Canzona [w. T. Schuback]) (rec 1976 & 1982)* BIS ▲ 48 [AAD] (17.97)

Pehrsson, Claas (rcr) (cont.)
17th Century Italian & English Music for Recorder & Lute, w. Jakob Lindberg (lt)—features works by Selma y Salaverde, Melii, Montalbano, Bassano, Castello, Piccinini, Parcham, Purcell, Pepusch, G. Finger, W. Croft, Anon. BIS ▲ 266 (17.97)

Pro Arte Recorder Ensemble
The Recorder: 4 Centuries of Recorder Music—features works by El Sabio, Josquin Desprez, Henry VIII, Garvalse, Van Eyck, Finer, Marcello, Couperin, et al. LYR (Early Music) ▲ 8030 [ADD] (16.97)

Steinmann, Conrad (rcr)
Italian Concert, w. London Baroque—features works by F. Mancini *(Sons 13 & 14)*, A. Scarlatti *(Son 21; Son in a)*, Corelli *(Son a tre, WoO 8)*, Colista *(Son IV in D)* CLAV ▲ 8912 [DDD]

Stivín, Jiří (rcr)
My Youth Is Over, w. Václav Uhlír (org/hpd)—features works by Stivín *(Variaces I-VII)*, Frescobaldi *(Conzona seconda detta la Bernardinia; Canzona quarta detta La Donatina; Canzona terza detta la Lucchesina; Canzona per 4 flauti)*, Cima *(Son 2)*, Riccio *(Canzona La Rubina; Canzona)*, Quagliati *(Toccata)*, Rossi *(Son sopra l' aria di Ruggiero)*, van Eyck *(Pavane Lachrymae)*, Castello *(Son Prima)*, Selma y Salaverde *(Canzona)*, Sweelinck *(Mein junges Leben hat ein End)*, anon *(Cupararee or Grays In; The Standing Masque; The Nymphs Dance; The 1st Witches Dance) (rec Studio PAST, Hradec Králové, 1996)* SUR ▲ 3341 [DDD]

Tyson, John (rcr)
Something for Recorder & Strings, w. Frances Conover Fitch (hpd), Jane Starkman (vn), Katheryn Shaw (vn), Jann Cosart (va), Alice Robbins (vc), Tom Coleman (db)—features works by Vivaldi, de Boismortier, Cooke, Hovhaness & Lovenstein TIT ▲ 169 [DDD]

Verbruggen, Marion (rcr)
German Baroque Chamber Music VII, w. Flanders Recorder Quartet—features works by Schein, Scheidt, Hassler, Rosenmüller, plus others RICE ▲ 206432 (17.97)

Vienna Recorder Ensemble
Musik der Renaissance—features works by Anon., Cabézon, A. Gabrieli, G. Gabrieli, Isaac, Josquin, Praetorius, Rossi, Senfl, Tasso, Widmann TUD ▲ 719 (16.97)

RECORDER COLLECTIONS

The Recorder—features performances by Karl Stangenberg *(Handel, Schickhardt, Schultze, Baston)*, Michael McCraw *(Graun)*, René Clemencic *(Telemann, Quantz)* KSCH ▲ 313432 [DDD] (16.97)

SAXOPHONE

Accademia Saxophone Quartet [Gaetano Di Bacco (s sax), Enzo Filippetti (a sax), Giuseppe Berardini (t sax), Fabrizio Paoletti (bar sax)]
Allegro Scherzando—features works by Piazzolla *(Adios Nonino; Oblivion; Libertango)*, Morricone *(C'era una volta in America)*, Rota *(Amarcord; Otto e 1/2)*, Weill *(Kleine Dreigroschenmusik [all arr Accademia Sax Qt])*, V. Monti *(Czardas [arr Di Bacco])*, A. Romero *(Qt latinamericano)*, Rossini *(Rossini...per quattro [suite of Rossini themes arr G. Di Bacco]) (rec Rome, Dec 1997)* DYNC ▲ 188 [DDD] (16.97)

Amherst Saxophone Quartet
Mozart to Modern—features works by Eubie Blake *(Jassamine Lane)*, Blake/Guarnieri *(Eubie Dubie)*, Lukas Foss *(Saxophone Quartet)*, Gershwin *(Lullaby)*, Mozart *(Piano Quintet, K.452 trans. for saxophones)* MCA1 ▲ 10055 [DDD] 10055

Bensmann, Detlef (sax)
Saxophone & Piano, w. Michael Rische (pno)—features works for by Paul Dessau *(Suite, 1935)*, Dietrich Erdmann *(Akzente, 1989)*, Isao Matsushita *(Atoll II, 1982)*, Milhaud *(Scaramouche)*, Ravel *(Five o-clock Foxtrot; Pièce en forme de habanera)*, Erwin Schulhoff *(Hot-Sonate, 1930)* KSCH ▲ 310071 [ADD] (17.97)
Saxophone & Piano, Vol. 2, w. Michael Rische (pno)—features works by Dubois, Jolivet, Schulhoff, Macha, Heiden, Rische, Raphael, Denissov & Thomys KSCH ▲ 364302 (16.97)

Berlin Saxophone Quartet [Detlef Bensmann (sax), Klaus Kreczmarsky (sax), Christof Griese (sax), Friedemann Graef (sax)]
Berlin Saxophone Quartet—features works by Singelée, Pierné, Debussy, Schaeuble, Graef, Agnesens, Kröll KSCH ▲ 313142 [DDD] (17.97)

Bluefield, D. (sax), Chris Bank (sax)
Clazzual Sax—features works by Beethoven *(Sonata No. 8)*, Borodin *(Polevetzian Dance No. 1)*, Brahms *(Waltz in B)*, Chopin *(Prelude No. 4 in e)*, Cuccini *(Amarilli Mia Bella)*, Fauré *(Chanson d'Amour)*, Rachmaninoff *(Piano Concerto No. 2)*, Ravel *(Pavane for a Dead Princess)*, Tchaikovsky *(Waltz of the Flowers)*, Wagner *(Evening Star)*, *([all arr. Bluefield for sax])* 84166 ▲ 1002

Borioli, Orazio (sax)
Music for Saxophone, w. Cesarini (pno)—features works by Granados, Ibert, Ravel, et al. GALL ▲ CD 516

Bornkamp, Arno (sax)
Works for Saxophone & Piano *(see Composer section—Creston, Denisov, et al.)* GLOE ▲ 5032 [DDD] (16.97)

Brodie, Paul (sax)
The Golden Age of the Saxophone, w. Myriam Schechter (pno)—features popular and light classical music MUVI (Musica Viva) ▲ 1005 [ADD] (16.97)

Chicago Saxophone Quartet [Wayne Richard (sax), Paul Bro (sax), Roger Birkeland (sax), James Kaspryzyk (sax)]
Chicago Saxophone Quartet—features works by S. Barab, M. W. Karlins, D. Scarlatti, I. Albeniz, G. Gershwin, S. Joplin, C. Debussy, G. Briegel, M. Shrude, J. River *(rec Apr-May 1989)* CENT ▲ 2086 [DDD] (16.97)

Danovitch, Gerald (sax), Saxophone Quartet
The Gerald Danovitch Saxophone Quartet—features works by Bach, Françaix, Gershwin, Gibbons, Joplin, Mozart, Paquito d'Rivera, Rossini MUVI (Musica Viva) ▲ 1018 [DDD] (16.97)

Delangle, Claude (sax)
The Japanese Saxophone, w. Odile Delangle (pno), Jean Geoffroy (perc)—features works by Natsuda *(West, or Evening in Autumn)*, Nodaïra *(Arabesque 3)*, Taïra *(Pénombre 4)*, Hosokawa *(Vertical Time Study 2)*, Tanada *(Mysterious Morning 3)*, Takemitsu *(Distance)*, Tanaka *(Night Bird)*, Yuasa *(Not I but the Wind)* BIS ▲ 890 [DDD] (17.97)

Duo Portejoie-Lagarde [Philippe Portejoie (sax), Frédéric Lagarde (pno)]
Dedicaces, w. Fuzako Kondo (mez), Sylvie Hue (cl)—features works by Laferriere, Boutry, Dubois, Gasparian & Margoni PVY ▲ 796111 (16.97)

East Coast Saxophone Quartet [Dale Underwood (s sax), Charlie Young (a sax), Timothy Roberts (t sax), Audrey Cupples (b sax)]
Americana Suite—features music by Rossini *(William Tell Ov [arr Art Gault])*, Mascagni *(Intermezzo [from Cavalliera rusticana; arr Robert C. Jones])*, Niehaus *(Rondolette; Jazz Mosaics No. 2)*, Brahms *(Hungarian Dance No. 5 [arr Robert C. Jones]; Vars on a Theme by Sweelinck [arr Ramon Ricker])*, Sousa *(Manhattan Beach; Stars & Stripes Forever [both arr Art Gault])*, J.S. Bach *(2 Preludes [arr Richard Fote])*, Purcell *(Abdelazer Suite; Annie Laurie; Boston Harbor; What Shall We Do with a Drunken Sailor? [all arr John C. Worley])*, plus *(Americana Suite-Hello, My Baby; By the Beautiful Sea; Shenandoah; Little Brown Jug; Memories; Oh, Susana; Take Me out to the Ballgame [arr Ralph Martino]; Christmas Jazz Favorites No. 2 [arr Lennie Niehaus]) (rec Omega Studios, Rockville, MD, Sept 1994)* OPEN ▲ 25 [DDD] (16.97)

Empire Saxophone Quartet
Escape to the Center—features works by Handel *(Arrival of the Queen of Sheba)*, Françaix *(Petit Quatuor for Saxophones)*, J. S. Bach *(Aria; Bandinerie)*, Gershwin *(Rialto Ripples)*, Wilson *(Escape to the Center)*, Dubois *(Qt Saxes)*, Marshall *(Goldrush Suite)*, Beethoven *(Allegro Molto Quasi Presto)*, Williams *(That's A-Plenty)* OPEN ▲ 32 [DDD] (16.97)

Fairer Sax
Diversions with the Fairer Sax—features works by Bach, Byrd, Handel, Scott Hayden & Scott Joplin, Praetorius, Schubert † Dubois; Gardner; Harvey; Patterson *(see Composer section)* SAY ▲ 365 [DDD] (16.97) ▌CSDL 365 (D)

Goldsbury, Mack (saxes/fl)
Sunday's Symphony *(symphonic improvs on jazz themes)*, w. Andreas Bottcher (org) QUER ▲ 9807 (18.97)

Gwozdz, Lawrence (sax)
An American Tribute to Sigurd Rascher—features works by Wirth *(Jephthah [w. Lois Leventhal (pno), Michael Reimer (s sax)]; Beyond These Hills [w. David Evenson (pno)])*, Russell *(Particles [w. Leventhal])*, Cowell *(Air & Scherzo [w. Leventhal])*, Still *(Romance [w. Leventhal])*, J.D. Lamb *(3 Antique Dances)*, Husa *(Élegie et rondeau [w. Evenson])*, Worley *(Son. [w. Evenson]) (rec Mannoni Performing Arts Center, Univ. of Southern Mississippi, Dec 20-22, 1993 & Jan 9 & 18, 1994)* CRYS ▲ 652 (15.97)

1038

▲ = CD ♦ = Enhanced CD △ = MD ▌ = Cassette Tape ▯ = DCC

Gwozdz, Lawrence (sax) (cont.)
Rascher International, w. S. Hass (sax), L. Leventhal (pno)—features E. Dressel *(Partita A Sax)*, Eisenmann *(Nevermore, Op. 28)*, Fournes *(Piece Sax)*, P. Grainger *(Folk Song Settings [Molly on the Shore])*, E. v. Koch *(Birthday Music)*, Massenet *(Méditation from Thaïs)*, Osterc *(Son A Sax)*, H. Purcell *(Bourrées Hpd)*, Sasamori *(Vars on Taki's 'Kojo no Tsuki')* ALBA ▲ 289 [DDD] (16.97)

Harle, John (sax)
John Harle's Saxophone Songbook—features works by Birtwistle *(Nick & Dinah's Love Song)*, Corea *(Children's Songs)*, Debussy *(Sphinx)*, Dowland *(Lachrymae)*, Johnson *(Where the Bee Sucks)*, Nyman *(The Ariel Songs)*, Prokofiev *(Melodies)*, Rachmaninoff *(Vocalise)* UNIC ▲ 9160 (19.97)
Saxophone Concertos, w. Academy of St. Martin in the Fields [cnd:Neville Marriner]—features works by Debussy, Glazunov, Heath, Ibert, et al. *(see Composer section for details)* EMIC ▲ 54301 (16.97)

Kelly, John-Edward (sax)
John-Edward Kelly, w. B. Versteegh (pno)—features works by Karkoff *(Sonatina for Saxophone & Piano)*, Badings *(La Malinconia)*, Maros *(Undulation)*, Glaser *(Allegro, Cadenza & Adagio)*, Macha *(Plač Saxofonu)*, Von Knorr *(Sonate for Alto Saxophone)* 40101 ▲ 31805

Kientzy, Daniel (sax)
The Romanian Saxophone, w. various orchs—features works by Marbe, Niculescu and Vieru *(see Composer section)* OLY (Explorer) ▲ 410 [AAD] (16.97)

Klock, Lynn (sax)
Vintage Flora, w. Nadine Shank (pno)—features works by P. Creston *(Sonata for Alto Saxophone & Piano, Op. 19)*, P.e Maurice *(Tableaux de Provence)*, Lawson Lunde *(Sonata for Alto Saxophone & Piano)*, Karel Husa *(Elegie et Rondeau)*, R. Schumann *(Three Romances)* OPEN ▲ 7 (16.97)

Lulloff, Joseph (sax)
Interplay, w. Philip Hosford (pno)—features works by Ruggiero, Poulenc & Vaughan Williams CCL ▲ 10497 (17.97)

Marsalis, Branford (s sax)
Romances for Saxophone *(orchd & arr Michel Colombier)*, w. English CO [cnd:Andrew Litton]—features works by M. Colombier, Debussy, Fauré, Mussorgsky, Rachmaninoff, Ravel, Satie, Stravinsky, Villa-Lobos COL ▲ 42122 (9.97) ▮ 42122 (5.98)

Mauk, Steven (s sax)
Classical Bouquet: Music for Soprano Saxophone & Piano, w. Mary Ann Covert (pno)—features works by Bach *(Sonata in E♭, BWV 1031)*, Mozart *(Oboe Concerto in C, K.314)*, Ravel *(Pièce en forme de habanera)*, Villa-Lobos *(Fantasia)*, Giovanni Platti *(Sonata in G, Op. 3)*, C. Rochester Young *(Sonata)* OPEN ▲ OL 008
Distances within Me: Contemporary Classics for Alto Saxophone, w. S. Mauk (a sax), Mary Ann Covert (pno)—features works by Alfred Desenclos *(Prélue, Cadence et Finale)*, John A. Lennon *(Distances Within Me)*, P. Hindemith *(Sonata)*, Ned Rorem *(Picnic on the Marne)*, Gregory Yasinitsky *(Sixth Sense)* OPEN ▲ OL 012

Mauk, Steven (t sax)
Tenor Excursions, w. Mary Ann Covert (pno)—features works by Hartley *(Son.; Poem)*, Debussy *(Beau Soir)*, Pasquale *(Son.)*, Vivaldi *(Son. No. 6 in g, Op. 13a)*, Weiner *(Etude)*, Chopin *(Largo, Op. 65)*, Duckworth *(Pitt County Excursions)*, Schmidt *(Sonatina)*, Singelée *(Adagio et Rondo) (rec Walter Ford Hall Auditorium, Ithaca College, Ithaca, New York, June 1-3, 1993)* OPEN ▲ 19 [DDD] (16.97)

Mule, Marcel (sax)
"Le Patron" of the Saxophone, w. Guy Chauvet (ten), G. Charon (sgr), F. l'Homme (sgr), P. Romby (sgr), Eugène Bozza (cnd), Francis Cébron (cnd), Philippe Gaubert (cnd), *(orchs unknown)*, Joseph Benvenutti (pno), Marcel Gaveau (pno), Marthe Pellas-Lenom (pno), François Combelle (sax)—features works by Rameau/Mule *(Gavotte)*, Roelens *(Pavane et Menuet Vif)*, Fonse/Marie *(La Tryolienne)*, Forêt *(Patres)*, Genin/Combelle *(Vars sur Marlborogh)*, Demersseman *(Le Carnival de Venise)*, Vellones *(Con [Andante]; Valse Chromatique)*, Glazounov *(Quatuor Theme & Scherzo)*, Bolzoni *(Menuetto)*, Françaix *(Serenade Comique)*, Ibert *(Concertino de Camera)*, Pierné *(Canzonetta)*, Ravel/Mule *(Pièce en Forme de Habanera)*, Drigo/Auer *(Les Millions d'Arléquin [Serenade])*, Combelle *(Esquisse)*, Bozza *(Concertino; Scherzo)*, Albeniz *(Sevilla)*, Clérisse *(Cache-Cache) (rec 1930-40)* CLCL ▲ 13 [AAD] (17.97)

New Danish Saxophone Quartet
Contemporary Works for Saxophone Quartet—features works by F.C. Hansen *(A la memoire de Dali)*, J. Hendze *(Beauty of the Beast)*, B. Lorentz *(Lines)*, I. Nørholm *(Patchwork in Pink)*, K. Roikjer *(Divertimento)*, H.P.S. Teglbjaerg *(Skel)* KPT ▲ 32051 [DDD]

Perconti, Bill (sax)
Duo I point 5—features works by Thomys *(Minatury w Róznych Stylach for Saxophone & Piano [w. J. March])*, Noda *(Improvisation III for solo Alto Saxophone)*, Hovhaness *(Suite for Saxophone & Guitar, Op. 129 [w. J. Reid])*, Massias *(Suite monodique for solo Saxophone)*, J. Grant *(Duo I point 5 for Saxophone & Tape)*, Bozza *(Improvisation et Caprice for solo Saxophone)*, Gershwin *(Three-quarter Blues [arr. Perconti]; Promenade [arr. Perconti])* CRYS ▲ 653 (15.97)

Pittel, Harvey (sax)
Bach & Noodles, w. Gabor Rejto (vc), Levering Rothfuss (pno), Anton Nel (pno)—features works by Bach *(Son No. 2 for Fl [arr. John Rodby])*, Rimsky-Korsakov *(Flight of the Bumblebee)*, Rachmaninoff *(Vocalise, Op. 34/14)*, J. Dorsey *(Oodles of Noodles)*, Demersseman *(Carnival of Venice)*, Del Tredici *(Acrostic Song [from Final Alice])*, Wiedoeft *(Saxophobia; Valse Yvonne)*, Bozza *(Caprice)*, Bonneau *(Caprice en Forme de Valse)*, Paganini *(Moto Perpetuo)*, Milhaud *(Scaramouche Suite)* CRYS ▲ 654 (15.97)
Saxophone Quartet, w. Shelly Manne (dr), Monty Budwig (bass)—features works by Bach, Glazunov, et al. CRYS ▮ 155
Trio, w. Julian Fifer (vc), Levering Rothfuss (pno)—features works by Creston, Villa-Lobos, Ellington, et al. CRYS ▮ 157

Potts, Leo (sax)
Two Sides, w. Jack Reidling (pno)—features works by Lunde *(Son. No. 1, Op. 12)*, Bruno *(Encore)*, Reidling *(Pophalgric Bint; Caprice)*, Colombier *(Emmanuel)*, Higgins *(Suite)*, Pierce *(3 Street Scenes)*, Morley *(Kehaar's Theme [from Watership Down])*, J.S. Bach *(Son. No. 4 for Fl [arr. Sharon Davis]) (rec North Hollywood, CA, Nov 20-21, 1994)* CMB ▲ 1075 [ADD]

Rahbari, Sohre (a sax)
Saxophone & Orchestra, w. Brussels BRTN PO [cnd:Alexander Rahbari]—features works by Debussy *(Rapsodie for Saxophone & Orchestra)*, Glazunov *(Concerto for Saxophone, Flute & Strings)*, Ibert *(Concertino da camera for Saxophone & 11 Instruments)*, Milhaud *(Scaramouche Suite)*, Mussorgsky *(The Old Castle, from Pictures at an Exhibition)*, Sohre Rahbari *(Japanese Improvisation for Solo Saxophone)* MARC ▲ *

Rorive, Jean-Pierre (a sax/s sax)
Famous Adagios: Saxophone & Organ, Vol. 4, w. André Lamproye (org)—features works by Marcello *(Adagio)*, Schubert *(Ave Maria)*, Gounod *(Ave Maria)*, Albinoni *(Adagio)*, Fauré *(Après un rêve)*, Handel *(Largo)*, Bach *(Aria)*, Mozart *(Ave verum)*, Raff, Schubert, Binge, Vivaldi PAVA ▲ 7333 (10.97)

Rorive, Jean-Pierre (sax)
Saxophone & Organ, Vol. 3, w. J. Hermans (org)—features works by Espejo *(Andantino)*, Bozza *(Aria)*, Rorive *(Novummonasterium)*, Schumann *(Träumerei)*, Matot *(Spleen [arr Rorive])*, J.S. Bach *(English Suite No. 3 [Gavotte])*, Albinoni *(Con. Saint-Marc)*, Lamproye *(Hommage à Saint-Hadelin)*, Purcell *(Son. in D for Trumpet)*, Surzynski *(Capriccio in f)*, plus *(N. des pauvres)* PAVA ▲ 7320 [DDD]

Rorive, Jean-Pierre (sax), André Lamproye (org)
Rêveries: Saxophone & Organ V—features works by Charpentier *(Prélude au Te Deum)*, Elgar *(Largamente [from Pomp & Circumstance])*, Saint-Saëns *(Le Cygne)*, Franck *(Prélude)*, Fauré *(Pie Jesu [from Requiem])*, Bach *(3 Menuets [from Petit livre de clavecin d'Anna Magdalena]; Badinerie de la Suite No. 2; Aria [from L'Oratorio de Noël]; Bist Du bei mir; Louré de la suite en ré pour vc; Gavottes [from Suite in D])*, Baiwir *(Planète océan [from Seasong])*, Vivaldi *(Largo [from l'Hiver des quatre saisons]; Adagio du concerto en la mineur pour vn)*, Grieg *(Solvejgs Lied [from Peer Gynt])*, Satie *(Gymnopédies Nos. 1 & 3)*, Clarke *(Tpt tune)*, Rachmaninoff *(Vocalise)*, Bozza *(Chanson à bercer)*, Cimarosa *(Larghetto du con en do mineur pour ob)*, Rorive *(Novummonasterium) (rec 1996)* PAVA ▲ 7364 [DDD] (10.97)

Rossi, Jamal (sax)
Caprice: Solos for Saxophone—features works by Paganini *(Caprice, Op. 1/24 [arr Rossi])*, Couf *(Intro., Dance & Furioso)*, Bonneau *(Caprice en forme de valse)*, Bach *(Suite No. 1 for Vc, BWV 1007 [arr Ramon Ricker])*, Hartley *(Petite Suite)*, Noda *(Improvisation I)*, Debussy *(Syrinx [arr Michael Reid])*, Persichetti *(Parable XI, Op. 123)*, Maurice *(Volio)*, Tull *(Threnody)*, Bozza *(Improvisation et Caprice) (rec Walter B. Ford Hall Auditorium, Ithaca College, NY, May 21-22 & Oct 15-16, 1993)* OPEN ▲ 16 [DDD] (16.97)

Rousseau, Eugène (sax)
Saxophone Colors, w. Hans Graf (pno)—features works by Bach, Debussy, Feld, Gershwin, Heiden, Orrego-Salas, Villa-Lobos DLS ▲ 1007 [AAD]

Saexophones [Marco Falaschi (s sax), Alda Dalle Lucche (cta sax), Sandro Tani (t sax), Roberto Frati (br sax)]
From Gesualdo to Sting—features works by Gesualdo *(Moro lasso al mio duolo)*, Gervaise *(Bransle Gay)*, Byrd *(Pavane for the Earl of Salisbury)*, Praetorius *(Courante & Springdance)*, Frescobaldi *(Se l'aura spira)*, Bach *(Bourrées [from Suite in C])*, Mozart *(Divertimento, K.138 [Andante])*, Gounod *(Marcia funebre d'una marionetta)*, Fauré *(Pavane, Op. 50)*, Gershwin *(Visit)*, Shostakovich *(Lyrical Waltz, Polka & Hurdy-Gurdy [from Dances of the Dolls])*, Piazzolla *(Night Club 1960)*, Lennon & McCartney *(Yesterday)*, Sting *(Moon over Bourbon Street) (rec 1995)* AMI ▲ 996 [DDD]

Sampen, John (elec sax)
The Electric Saxophone—features works by Tower *(Wings)*, Cage *(Four⁵)*, Ussachevsky *(Mimicry)*, Shrude *(Drifting over a Red Place)*, Furman *(Music for Alto Sax & Tape)*, Bunce *(Waterwings)*, Mobberly *(Spontaneous Combustion)* CPS ▲ 8636 [DDD] (16.97)

Saxology Saxophone Quartet
The Sax: Centenary Collection—features works by Absil *(3 Pieces for Quartet)*, Bozza *(Andante & Scherzo)*, Clérisse *(Serenade mélancolique)*, Debussy, Françiax, Ibert, Dubois, Ravel & Vellones ASV ▲ 2090 [DDD] (12.97)

Saxpak
Saxomania—features works by Grieg *(Holberg Prelude)*, Mozart *(Le nozze di Figaro [Ov])*, Debussy *(The Girl with the Flaxen Hair)*, Grainger *(Shepherd's Hey)*, plus Portrait of a Flirt, Sophisticated Lady, Liza, I'll Remember April, 12th Street Rag, Candlelights, Holiday for Strings, String of Pearls, Saxophobia, Westminster Waltz, I'm Old Fashioned, 4 Brothers, Promenade, Czardas, Perfidia, Lover Man, The Continental, Turkey in the Straw, Nola, Yankee Doodle ASV ▲ 2106 (12.97)

Tse, Kenneth (sax/a sax)
Kenneth Tse Plays Bernstein, Morosco, Benson, w. K. Miller (pno)—features W. Benson *(Con for A Sax [Aeolian Song]; Concertino for A Sax)*, L. Bernstein *(West Side Story (sels) [America; Somewhere; Tonight])*, J. Feld *(Son for A Sax [1. Allegro ritmico; 2. Adagio, "Bells of Liberty"; 3. Allegro vivo; 4. Allegro con fuoco])*, Heiden *(Solo A Sax)*, W. Kaufmann *(Meditation)*, Morosco *(Blue Caprice)*, Muczynski *(Son for A Sax & Piano, Op. 29 [1. Andante maestoso; 2. Allegro energico]; Son for Sax, Op. 29)* CRYS ▲ 656 (15.97)

Underwood, Dale (sax)
Classic Pastiche—features worksby R. Muczynski *(Sonata, Op. 29)*, Jeanine Rueff *(Chanson et Passepied)*, Wolfgang Jacob *(Sonata)*, P. Lantier *(Sicilienne)*, Fisher Tull *(Sarabande and Gigue)*, Henri Eccles *(Sonata)*, Maurice Whitney *(Introducton and Samba)*, G.F. Handel *(Sonata No. 3)* OPEN ▲ OL 009
Soliloquy, w. Texas Tech Univ Wind Ensemble [cnd:James Sudduth]—features works by Claude Smith, Paul Creston, Sammy Nestico, Urban Carvalho, Maurice Whitney, Clare Grundman, Elliot del Borgo OPEN ▲ OL 013

West Coast Saxophone Quartet [Phil Sobel (s sax), Leo Potts (a sax), Mark Costner (t sax), Chris Bleth (bar sax)]
All the Sax You've Ever Dreamed Of—features works by Mozart *(Qt 8 Strs [4th movt; arr Jack Reiding])*, Villa-Lobos *(Bachiana brasileira 5 [arr Mauro Bruno])*, Wyle *(Memoirs; Spanish Dance Suite; Wet Bar Rag)*, Debussy *(La Plus que lente)*, Hammerstein & Kern *(All the Things You Are [arr George Wyle])*, Kessler *(Light & Easy [w. Evan Diner (dr)])*, Niehaus *(Jazz Vignettes [w. Evan Diner (dr)])*, Rose *(Dance of the Spanish Onion [arr Mauro Bruno])*, Baker *(Ballons)*, Satie *(Gymnopédie 1 [arr Mauro Bruno])*, Garcia *(Miniature Sym for Sax)* CMB ▲ 1045 [DDD] (16.97)

Wiedoeft, Rudy (sax)
Rudy Wiedoeft: Kreisler of the Saxophone—features works by Wiedoeft *(Sax Serene [w. Percival Mackey's Band]; Saxarella; Dans l'Orient [both w. F. Banta (pno)]; Valse Vanité; Saxema; Valse Erica; [all w. studio orch]; Valse Mazanetta; Sax-O-Phun; Song of the Volga Boatman; Llewellyn-Waltz [all w. Oscar Levant (pno)]; Valse Marylin [w. J. Shilkret (pno)]; Rubenola [w. C. Robison (gtr); arr Frey])*, Cooke/Browne *(That Moaning Sax Rag [w. Brown Brothers])*, Drdla *(Souvenir)*, Yradier *(La Paloma)*, Beethoven *(Minuet in G [arr Wiedoeft])*, Dawes *(Melody)*, Drigo *(Serenade "Les Millions d'Arlequin" [all w. Oscar Levant (pno)])*, Rosebrook *(Sax Fant [w. studio orch])*, Hager/Ring *(Danse-Hongroise [w. F. Banta (pno)]; Gloria [w. L. Briers (pno)])*, Gabriel-Marie *(Serenade Badine)*, Tchaikovsky *(Melodie [both w. Oscar Levant (pno)])*, Nevin *(Narcissus [w. Wiedoeft Sax Sextet]) (rec 1920-27)* CLCL ▲ 18 [ADD] (17.97)

Wolford, Dale (a sax/s sax)
More Than Sax: Baroque, Blues & Beyond, w. Stephanie Friedman (mez), Ivan Rosenblum (pno)—features works by Ravel *(Pièce en forme de Habanera)*, Heider *(Son. in Jazz)*, Rosenblum *(Shtetl Voices [song cycle; poems by E. Leider; w. S. Friedman (mezzo-soprano)])*, Buel *(Reflections on Raga Todi)*, Bach *(Son. in f)*, Wirth *(Lullaby)*, Negro spiritual *(City Called Heaven) (rec Belmont, CA & Richmond, CA, Aug 17-20, 1993 & Jan 28, 1994)* Gliddon ▲ GP 001 [DDD]

STRING ENSEMBLE

Allegra String Quartet
Baroque n' Beatles n' Bach—features works by Lennon/McCartney *(I Want to Hold Your Hand; Yesterday/Eleanor Rigby)*, Ellington *(I Don't Get around Much Anymore)*, Gershwin *(Summertime [from Porgy & Bess])*, Debussy *(Clair de Lune)*, Dréjac *(Under Paris Skies)*, Albéniz *(Spanish Dance)*, Telemann *(Con Va:Allegro)*, Pachelbel *(Canon in D)*, Foster *(I Dream of Jeanie)*, I. Anderson *(The Syncopated Clock)*, Auric *(The Song from Moulin Rouge)*, McBroom *(The Rose)*, Andrée *(Ceylon Tango)*, Heuberger *(Im chambre separée)*, Handel *(Arrival of the Queen of Sheba)*, Ellington/Mills/Bigard *(Mood Indigo)*, Mozart *(Presto, K.157)* [all arr for str qt] Black Bear ▲ BBR 6006

Arcado String Trio [Mark Feldman (vn), Ernst Reijseger (vc), Mark Dresser (db)]
Live in Europe—features Harkening; Xanax; Armadillo; Lanette; Ediiface; Biruta; Behind the Myth AVAK ▲ 58 (21.97)

Arditti String Quartet [Irvine Arditti (vn), David Alberman (vn), Garth Knox (va), Rohan de Saram (vc)]
From Italy—features string quartets by Maderna, Berio, Scelsi, Bussotti, Scodanibbio, Donatoni, Stroppa, Castiglioni, Melchiore, Sciarrino DISQ ▲ 782042 (36.97)
From Vienna—features works by Amy, Berio, Birtwistle, Boulez, Denisov, Gielen, Halffter, Kurtág, Krauze, Liebermann, Ligeti, Messiaen, Miroglio, Pärt, Pousseur, Rihm, Schnittke & Zendler DISQ ▲ 782027 (18.97)
[Editor's Note]: All written for Arditti String Qt. & dedicated to Alfred Schlee.
1974—Arditti Quartet—1994—features works by Schoenberg *(Qt. for Strings, Op. 10, Weihnachtsmusik [sels.])*, Kurtág *(Officium breve in memoriam A. Szervásky, Op. 28)*, Kagel *(Streichquartett II)*, Lachenmann *(Tanzsuite mit Deutschlandslied)*, Dusapin *(Time Zones)*, Webern *(5 Pieces, Op. 5)*, Ferneyhough *(Adagissimo)*, Nono *(Fragmente-Stille, An Diotima)*, Xenakis *(Tetras)*, Mâche *(Eridan)*, Rihm *(Im Innerstern)*, Birtwistle *(Movt.)*, Carter *(Elegy)* DISQ ▲ 782070 (7.97)
U.S.A.—features Conlon Nancarrow *(Qt 1 Strs)*, Carter *(Elegy)*, Ives *(Scherzo)*, Jay Alan Yim *(Autumn Rhythm)*, Feldman *(Structures)*, Lucier *(Fragments)*, L. Young *(On Remembering a Naiad)*, Cage *(4)* DISQ ▲ 782010 [DDD] (18.97)

Babayaga String Quartet
Blue Rosin—features Yore Da Best; Fax It to Me; Ceilidh; House of Spirits; Little Linda; Fiddlehead Shuffle; Devil Bemused; Blue Rosin; Time After Time; Grand Central; I Got It Bad SKYL ▲ 9502

Borodin String Quartet [M. Kopelman (vn), A. Abramenkov (vn), D. Shebalin (va), V. Berlinsky (vc)]
Russian Miniatures—features works by Borodin, Prokofiev, Tchaikovsky, Rachmaninoff, Stravinsky, Shostakovich & others TELC ▲ 94572-2

Brodsky String Quartet [Michael Thomas (vn), Ian Belton (vn), Paul Cassidy (va), Jacquelin Thomas (vc)]
Brodsky Unlimited—features works by Brubeck, Copland, Debussy, Elgar, Falla, Gershwin, Prokofiev, Ravel, Shostakovich, et al. ELEC ▲ 46015

Budapest Strings [cnd:Károly Botvay]
Classical Favorites for Strings: Nocturnes, Songs, Arias & Etudes—features transcriptions of works by Chopin, De Curtis, Mendelssohn, Sarasate, et al. LALI ▲ 14039 [DDD] (3.97)
Classical Favorites for Strings: Songs, Romances & Dances—features transcriptions of works by Brahms, Grieg, Schubert, et al. LALI ▲ 14040 [DDD] (3.97)
Serenade—features works by Dvořák *(Humoresque, Op. 101/7; Waltz, Op. 54/1; Songs My Mother Taught Me)*, Rubinstein *(Melody, Op. 3/1)*, Schubert *(Ave Maria, D. 839; Moment musical; Serenade)*, Boccherini *(Minuet)*, Brahms *(Waltz, Op. 39/15)*, Beethoven *(Minuet)*, Grieg *(I Love You)*, Mozart *(Alla turca)*, Svendsen *(Romance, Op. 26)*, Mendelssohn *(Spring Song)*, Schumann *(Traumerei)*, Gounod *(Ave Maria)* LALI ▲ 15505 (3.97)

Busch String Quartet [Adolf Busch (vn), Gösta Andreasson (vn), Karl Doktor (va), Hermann Busch (vc)]
Great Violinists, Vol. 5—features works by Corelli, Bach, Tartini, Gossec, Hofstetter, Mozart, Schubert, Verdi, Brahms, Kreisler SYMP ▲ SYM 1109

Camilli String Quartet
Garden Song—features works by Boccherini *(Minuetto in E)*, Mozart *(Qt Strs in B♭ [Minuetto]; Eine kleine Nachtmusik [Allegro]; Qt Strs in D [Andante])*, Haydn *(Qt Strs in F [Serenade]; Qt Strs in D [Allegro Moderato]; Qt Strs in g [Finale])*, Borodin *(Qt 2 Strs in D [Notturno])*, Tchaikovsky *(Qt 1 Strs in D [Andante Cantabile])*, Mendelssohn *(Qt Strs in E♭ [Canzonetta])*, Glazunov *(5 Novelettes [Valse])* SGO ▲ 9617 [DDD] (16.97)

Concordia
Crye: Viol Music from England's Golden Age—features works by Holborne *(Pavana Ploravit; The Teares of the Muses)*, Tye *(Crye; Rachell's Weepings)*, Sumarte *(Lachrimae)*, Hume *(Captain Hume's Lamentations; I Am Melancholy)*, Stonings *(Miserere)*, Tallis *(Felix namque)*, Johnson *(A Knell of Johnson)*, Weelkes *(Lachrimae Pavan)*, Lawes *(Consort Set in c)* MENO ▲ 1020 [DDD] (19.97)

Conjunto Ibérico Cello Octet [cnd:Elias Arizcuren]
Conjunto Ibérico—features works by Pablo, Marco, Turina, Halffter CCL ▲ 11597 (17.97)
French Music—features works by Xenakis, Boulez, Tisné, Thomassin, Looten CCL ▲ 11798 (17.97)

Double-Cordes Duo [Jean-Pierre Nouhaud (vc), Marie Nouhaud (db)]
Départ—features works by Boismortier *(Son in g Vc & Bc [rev Hugo Ruf])*, Benda *(Son in F VI & Bc [arr Jörg Baumann])*, Pleyel *(Theme & Vars [arr Jörg Baumann & Klaus Stoll])*, Caix d'Hervelois *(Suite 2 VI & Bc [arr Double-Cordes])*, Rossini *(Duet Vc & Db:Allegro Final)*, Double-Cordes Duo *(Poursuite; Sidéral; L'esprit de Feu; Tandem)* Integral ▲ INT 529462 [DDD]

COLLECTIONS

STRING ENSEMBLE

Emerson String Quartet
The Great Romantic Quartets—features works by Borodin *(Qt. No. 2)*, Brahms *(Qt. No. 1)*, Debussy *(Qt. for Strings)*, Dvořák *(Qt. No. 12)*, Ravel *(Qt. in F)*, Schumann *(Qt. No. 3)*, Smetana *(Qt. No. 1 in e)*, Tchaikovsky *(Qt. 1)* BOMR 4-▲ 21-7526 [DDD] 3-▮ 11-7525 (D)

La Gamba Freiburg
Ricercari, Capricci e Fantasie a tre—features works by Guami *(Recercars 3 & 8)*, Ruffo *(El Chioco; La Brava; Il Capriccioso; La Disperata; La Sol Fa Re Mi; La Gamba in Basso & Sop; La Gamba in Ten; El Pietoso; La Piva)*, Lasso *(La Sol Fa Re Mi; Fant)*, Willaert *(Ricercars 1, 6 & 7)*, Agricola *(A les regrets; L'homme banni; Cecus non judicat de coloribus)*, Bassano *(Fants I-V)*, Monteverdi *(Canzonettas I-V)*, Conforti *(Ricercar del secondo tono) (rec May 1996)* ARSM ▲ 1168 [DDD] (17.97)

Hampton String Quartet
What If Mozart Wrote Born to Be Wild *('60s rock hits played in the styles of various classical composers)* RCAV (Red Seal) ▲ 7803 [DDD] (16.97) ▮ 7803
What If Mozart Wrote Have Yourself a Merry Little Christmas *(traditional carols in the styles of Bach, Beethoven, Chopin, Debussy, and Mozart)* RCAV ▲ 60246 [DDD] ▮ 60246
What If Mozart Wrote I Saw Mommy Kissing Santa Claus RCAV ▲ 60120 [DDD] ▮ 60120
What If Mozart Wrote Roll over Beethoven *('50s r&b pop hits played in the styles of Beethoven, Debussy, Mozart, Pachelbel, et al.)* RCAV (Red Seal) ▲ 6675 [DDD] 6675

Holloway, John (vn), Andrew Manze (vn), Stanley Ritchie (vn)
Pachelbel Canon (original version) & Other 17th Century Music for 3 Violins, w. John Toll (hpd/org), Nigel North (thb), Mary Springfels (vl) HAM (Suite) ▲ 7907091 (12.97)

Joachim String Quartet
Quatuors Concertants—features works by Boulogne, Cambini, Gossec & Jadin KSCH ▲ 364112 (16.97)

Kocian String Quartet
Select Encores for String Quartet—features works by Dvořák, Mozart, Borodin, Beethoven, Shostakovich, Suk, Puccini, Tchaikovsky, Kalivoda & Krejci BONT ▲ 120 (10.97)

Kohon String Quartet [Harold Kohon (vn), Isadora Kohon (vn), Eugenie Dengel (va), W. Ted Hoyle (vc)]
American String Quartets, 1900-1950—features works by W. Schuman, Hanson, Thomson, Gershwin, Sessions, Ives, Piston, Copland VB2 2-▲ 5090 [ADD] (9.97)

Kronos Quartet [David Harrington (vn), John Sherba (vn), Hank Dutt (va), Joan Jeanrenaud (vc)]
Africa *(in new works by seven African composers, all commissioned by Kronos, with musical elements from Ghana, Morocco, Nubia, Zimbwabwe, Gambia and South Africa, Kronos is joined by African string instruments, drums & gospel choir)* 75597 ▲ 79275 ▮ 79275-4
Early Music—features works by Machaut *(Kyrie I; Kyrie II & III [both w. Marja Mutru (harm)])*, Partch *(Studies (2) [w. Marja Mutru (harm)])*, Pärt *(Psalom)*, Lamb *(Langdans efter Byfans Mats [w. David Lamb (bgp)])*, Dowland *(Lachrymae Antiquae [w. Wu Man (zhong ruan da rua)])*, Cage *(Totem Ancestor; Quod Libet)*, Hildegard *(O Virtus Sapientie)*, Tye *(Rachael's Weepinge; Farewell My Good 1)*, Kassia *(Using the Apostate Tyrant...)*, Hardin *(Moondog) (Synchrony 2)*, Perotin *(Viderunt Omnes)*, Purcell *(Fant 4-Part)*, Body *(Long-Ge)*, Schnittke (Collected Songs), plus *(Brudmarsch frä Östa [w. Olov Johansson (nyckelharpa)]; Uleg-Khem [w. Throatsingers of Tuva])* Nonesuch ▲ 79457
Kronos Quartet: The "Singles"—features works by K. Volans *(Hunting: Gathering)*, A. Piazzolla *(5 Tango Sensations)*, W. Lutoslawski *(Str Qt)* 75597 3-▲ 79253 3-▮ 79253/5-4
Kronos Released, 1985-95—features works by S. Barber *(Adagio)*, Crumb *(God-music [from Black Angels])*, Daugherty *(Elvis Everywhere)*, P. Glass *(Str Qt 5 [3rd movt])*, Górecki *(Arioso [from Quasi una Fant])*, Hendrix *(Purple Haze)*, S. Johnson *(It Raged [from How It Happens—The Voice of I.F. Stone])*, Johnston *(Str Qt 4 (Amazing Grace))*, Maraire *(Mai Nozipo (Mother Nozipo))*, Pärt *(Fratres)*, Maraire, A. Piazzolla *(Asleep [from 5 Tango Sensations])*, Reich *(America—Before the War [from Different Trains])*, T. Riley *(excerpt from The Ecstasy [from Salome Dances for Peace])*, R. Scott *(Dinner Music for a Pack of Hungry Cannibals)*, Tahmizyan *(A Cool Wind Is Blowing)* NON ▲ 79394 (19.97) 79394
Short Stories—features works by Sharp *(Digital)*, W. Dixon *(Spoonful [arr S. Mackey])*, Oswald *(Spectre)*, Zorn *(Cat O'Nine Tails)*, Cowell *(Qt Euphometric)*, Mackey *(Physical Property)*, Scott Johnson *(How It Happens [Soliloquy; w. I. F. Stone (nar)])*, Gubaidulina *(Qt 2 Strs)*, Pandit Pran Nath *(Aba kee tayk hamaree [It Is My Turn, Oh Lord]) (rec 1990-92)* NON ▲ 79310 (16.97) 79310
White Man Sleeps: Music of Ornette Coleman—features Lonely Woman; Charles Ives—Scherzo:Holding Your Own † Bartók:Qt No. 3; etc. *(see Composer section)* 75597 ▲ 79163 [DDD] ▮ 79163-4 (D)
Winter Was Hard—features works by Sallinen *(Winter Was Hard [arr Kronos Quartet; w. Earl L. Miller (reed org), Elizabeth Appling (cnd), San Francisco Girls Chorus])*, Riley *(Salome Dances for Peace [Half-Wolf Dances Mad in Moonlight])*, Pärt *(Fratres [arr Thomas Höfer for str qt])*, Webern *(Bagatelles (6), Op. 9)*, Zorn/Kronos Qt/Marclay/Hiromi *(Forbidden Fruit [w. Ohata Hiromi (voc), Christian Marclay (turntables)])*, Lurie *(Bella by Barlight)*, Piazzolla *(Four, for Tango)*, Schnittke *(Qt 3 Strs)*, Barber *(Adagio)*, plus trad piece *(A Door Is Ajar)* NON ▲ 79181 [DDD] (16.97) 79181

Pierlot, Philippe (b vl), François Fernandez (vn), Hidemi Suzuki (vc), Ricercar Consort
Defense de la Basse Viole contre les Enterprises du Violon et les Pretentions du Violoncelle [Defense of the Bass Viol against the Enterprise of the Violin & the Pretension of the Cello]—features works by Morel, Marais, Cappus, Dolle, D'Hervelois, Dornel, Duval, Rebel, Leclair, Corrette, Boismortier, Masse, Barriere & Canavas RICE 3-▲ 93005 (34.97)

Prima Carezza
Extase—features Tango Torero; Kinderparade; Extase; Max und Moritz; Spanischer Zigeunertanz; Radiomarsch; Florentinermarsch; Majarska; Illusion; Liebling der Frauen; Blauer Himmel; La trioletta; Rote Rosen; Amerikanische Vision; Alta Kameraden; Neopolitanisches Ständchen; Pizzicato Waltz TUD ▲ 795 [DDD]

Sejong Soloists
Sejong Soloists—features works by Arensky, Shostakovich, Stravinsky & Tchaikovsky SSCL ▲ 13 (16.97)

Smetana String Quartet
The 50th Anniversary of the Smetana Quartet—features works by Smetana *(Qts Nos. 1 in e [From My Life] & 2 in d for Strs)*, Janáček: *(Qts Nos. 1 [Kreutzer Son] & 2 [Intimate Letters] for Strs)*, Jaroch *(Qt No. 2 for Strs)*, Dvořák *(Qt No. 12 in F for Strs, Op. 96 [American])*, Suk *(Qt No. 1 in B♭ for Strs, Op. 11)*, Novák *(Qt No. 2 in D for Strs, Op. 35)*, Mozart *(Qts Nos. 15 in d, K.421 & 17 in B♭, K.458 [The Hunt] for Strs)*, Beethoven *(Qts No. 12 in E♭, Op. 127, No. 14 in c#, Op. 131 & No. 15 in a, Op. 132 for Strs; Grosse Fuge, Op. 133)* SUR 6-▲ 76 [AAD/DDD]

Da Sonar Ensemble [Chantal Rémillard, Christine Moran, Margaret Little, Susie Napper, Sylvain Bergeron, Réjean Poirier]
A Tre Violini—features works by Gabrielli, Marini, Fontana, Uccellini, Schmelzer, Purcell, Dornel, Boismortier, Telemann, Pachelbel *(rec Feb 1993)* UMM ▲ 304 (16.97)

Stubner, Heidi (vn), Mela Tenenbaum (vn), John Dexter (va), Roger Shell (vc)
Greatest Hits for String Quartet, w. Daniel Goldberg (cl), Theodore Mook (vc), Ricardo Cobo (gtr), Michael Hinton (perc)—features works by Haydn *(Qt Strs, Op. 3/5 [Andante cantabile])*, Boccherini *(Qnt Strs, Op. 13/5 [Minuetto]; Qnt Gtr, G.448 [Fandango])*, Mozart *(Qnt Cl, K.581 [Larghetto])*, Schubert *(Qt 13 Strs, D.804 [Andante])*, Mendelssohn *(Qt 3 Strs, Op.44/1 [Andante espressivo ma con moto])*, Borodin *(Qt 2 Strs [Nocturne-Andante];)*, Tchaikovsky *(Qt 1 Strs, Op. 11 [Andante cantabile])*, Dvořák *(Qt 12 Strs, Op. 96 [Finale-Vivace ma non troppo])*, plus more *(rec St. Paul's Evangelical Lutheran Church, Jersey City, NJ, May 19 & July 2, 1993)* ESSY ▲ 1036 [DDD] (16.97)

Venice String Quartet [Andrea Vio (vn), Alberto Bassiston (vn), Luca Morassutti (va), Angelo Zanin (vc)]
Fun Time with the String Quartet—features works by Thomas-Mifune *(Comic Str Qt on Beethoven's Sym 5; Chromatic Syncopations)*, Chaplin *(Theme from Limelight)*, Shostakovich *(Golden Age, Op. 22 [Allegretto])*, Rachmaninoff *(Vocalise, Op. 34/14 [arr Thorp])*, Heidrich *(Happy Birthday Vars)*, Gershwin *(Lullaby)*, Pachelbel *(Canon)*, Razek *(Cat's Serenade [trans Thomas-Mifune])*, Kern *(Smoke Gets in Your Eyes)*, Porter *(Anything Goes [arr Thorp])*, Elgar *(Salut d'amour [arr Donald Faser]) (rec Sept 1997)* DYNC ▲ 195 [DDD] (16.97)

Violines Concierto Universal
Romantica y Apasianado—features Estrelita; Nocturne; Playas de Ensueno; Fiesta para Cuerdas; El Tren; Valses Americanos; Potpourri Tchaikovsky; Potpourri Mexicanos; Involvidable; Potpourri Juan Gabriel; plus other sels GLMU ▲ 8317 (10.97)

STRING ENSEMBLE COLLECTIONS

The String Quartet in Sweden: A Cavalcade of Its History, w. Barkel String Quartet, Stockholm String Quartet, Garaguly String Quartet, Kyndel String Quartet, Ivan Ericson String Quartet, Grünfarb String Quartet, Skůne String Quartet, Hälsingborg String Quartet, Gothenburg String Quartet, Galli String Quartet, Kjellström String Quartet, Föllinger-Hedberg String Quartet *(rec before 1951)* CAPA 5-▲ 21506 [AAD/ADD] (79.97)

Trusler, John (vn), John Underwood (va), Galina Solodchin (vn), Jonathan Williams (vc)
Favourite Encores for String Quartet—features E. Bloch *(Night)*, Borodin *(Qt 2 Strs)*, F. Bridge *(Cherry Ripe; Sally in Our Alley)*, A. Dvořák *(Waltzes Strs, Op. 54)*, J. Haydn *(Qts (6) Strs, Op. 33)*, F. Kreisler *(Qt Strs)*, Mendelssohn (-Bartholdy) *(Qt 1 Strs, Op. 12)*, G. Puccini *(Crisantemi)*, J. Suk *(Meditation, Op. 35a)*, P. Tchaikovsky *(Qt 1 Strs, Op. 11)*, H. Wolf *(Italian Serenade Str Qt)* HYP ▲ 55002 (9.97)

TROMBONE

Allessi, Joseph (trbn), Blair Bollinger (trbn), Scott A. Hartman (trbn), Mark H. Lawrence (trbn)
Four of a Kind: Music for Trombone Quartet—features works by Bach, Beethoven, Debussy, D. Dondayne, Haydn, H. Isaac, A.-C. Jobim, Mendelssohn, Scheidt, K. Serocki, Verdi, Webern SUMM ▲ 123 [DDD] (16.97) ▮

Ashworth, T. (trbn)
Solo Pro: Contest Music for Trombone, w. T. Lichtmann (cnd)—features works by Jacob *(Trombone Concerto)*, Alexander von Kreisler *(Sonatina)*, P. V. de la Nux *(Concertpiece)*, Hasse *(Hasse Suite)*, Wagenseil *(Concerto for Trombone)*, Bennie Beach *(Suite for Trombone)*, Clifford Barnes *(Arioso & Caprice)*, Fauré *(Après un rêve)*, J.S. Bach *(Musette)*, Forrest Buchtel *(Beau Brummel)* SUMM ▮ SMT 105

Barron, Ronald (trbn)
All American Trombone, w. Fredrik Wanger (pno), Harvard Univ Wind Ensemble, Atlantic Brass Quintet—features works by Goldstein *(Colloquy for Trbn)*, Wilder *(Son forTrbn)*, Bernstein *(Elegy for Mippy II)*, Willey *(3 Pieces for Trbn & Pno)*, Clarke *(Bride of the Waves [arr Joseph Foley])*, Pryor *(Thoughts of Love [arr Joseph Foley]; Annie Laurie [arr Richard Schumann] (rec Sanders Theater, Harvard Univ; Symphony Hall, Boston; Morse Auditorium, Boston Univ, Nov 7 & Dec 8-9, 1995, Jan 3 & 14, 1996)* Boston Brass ▲ BB 1003
Hindemith on Trombone *(see Composer section: Hindemith—Trauermusik; etc.)* Boston Brass ▲ BB 1002CD ▮ BB 1002CT
In The Family, w. Marianne Gedigian (fl), Ann Hobson Pilot (hp), Douglas Yeo (trbn), Edwin Barker (bass), Thomas Gauger (perc)—features works by Shapero *(In The Family)*, Shostakovich *(8 Preludes, Op 34 [arr Douglas Yeo])*, Campo *(Commedie, Op. 42)*, Vaughan-Williams *(6 Studies in English Folksong [adapted for trbn by Ronald Barron])*, Small *(Conversation)*, Kellaway *(Esque) (rec Morse Auditorium, Boston Univ, Dec 1995)* Boston Brass ▲ BB 1004
Le Trombone français—features works by Berghmanns, Boutry, Defaye, Guilmant, Ropartz, Saint-Saëns, Salzedo *(rec Jan 1976)* Boston Brass ▮ BB 1001

Berlin Trombone Quintet
Berlin Trombone Quintet *(14 classical and popular selections)*—features works by Beethoven, Handel, Joplin, Khachaturian, Lennon-McCartney, et al. KSCH ▲ 310089 [DDD] (16.97)
Vol. 2: Music For Festive Occasions—features works by Bach, Brahms, F. Couperin, Franz Gruber, Handel, Paul Peuerl, Johann Christoph Pezelius KSCH ▲ 312062 [DDD] (16.97)

Bonvin, Dany (trbn), 13 Étoiles Brass Band
Trombone Festival *(see Composer section under Daetwyler, Langford, Newsome & Voegelin)* GALL ▲ CD 474 [ADD]

Clark, Stanley (trbn)
Contrasts, w. Avis Romm (pno) J.S. Bach, Johann Ernst Galliard, Mozart, Telemann, Eugène Bozza, Jacques Casterede, Enrique Crespo, Frank Martin, Sammy Nestico EBS ▲ 6023 [DDD] (18.97)

Danish Concert Band [cnd:Jørgen Misser Jensen]
Trombone Concepts—features works by Rimsky-Korsakov *(Con. for Trbn & Military Band)*, Simons *(Atlantic Zephyrs)*, Guilmant *(Morceau Symphonique, Op. 88)*, McDunn/Christensen *(Trbn Concepts)*, von Koch *(Monoloque No. 8 for solo Trbn)*, Jocob *(Concetino)*, Pryor *(Thoughts of Love)*, Bozza *(Ballade for Trbn, Op. 62)*, Lohmann *(Bavarian Polka)*, Saint-Saëns *(Cavatine for Trbn & Pno, Op. 144) (rec Brønby Strand Church, 1994)* ROND ▲ 8349

Hass, Simone de (trbn)
In the Pipeline *(contemporary Australian chamber music & improvisations)*, w. Daryl Pratt (perc), Phil Treloar (perc)—features works by Haan *(Autumn Collage)*, Treloar *(Integrations I)*, Pratt *(Sock Bop a Dop)*, plus improvs *(Blues Part I; re:sounds; Shifting Energies; Song; Response; Reflections; Sometimes, Mirrors...; Blues Part II) (rec 1993)* TALP ▲ 95 [DDD] (18.97)

Johansen, Niels-Ole Bo (trbn)
Trombone & Organ Music, w. Ulrik Spang-Hanssen (org)—features works by Holst *(Duo Concertante for Trombone & Organ)*, Ropartz, Guilmant, Elgar, Vaughan Williams, Liszt, Eben CLSO ▲ 122 (14.97)

Knaub, Donald (b trbn)
Donald Knaub, w. Rex Woods (pno)—features works by Gordon Jacob *(Cameos)*, Frigyes Hidas *(Rhapsody)*, Donald Grantham *(Sonata in One Movement)*, Mahler *(Songs of a Wayfarer)* CRYS ▮ 680

Lawrence, Mark (trbn)
Trombonology, w. Robin Sutherland (pno)—features works by Defaÿ *(Danses (2) pour Trombone et Piano)*, F. Strauss *(Nocturno)*, Martin *(Ballade for Trombone & Piano)*, Albinoni *(Con in d for Oboe & Piano, Op. 9/2 [arr. Lawrence])*, Marcello *(Son No. 3 for Cello & Piano [arr. Schulz])*, Massenet *(Meditation from Thaïs for Violin & Piano)*, Arnold *(Fant for Trombone)*, Castérède *(Sonatine pour Trombone & Piano)*, Dorsey *(Trombonology for Trombone & Piano) (rec Little Bridges Hall, Claremont College, Pomona, CA)* DNC ▲ 1012 [DDD] (16.97)

Lindberg, Christian (trbn)
The Burlesque Trombone, w. R. Pöntinen (pno)—features L. Bernstein *(Elegy for Mippy II)*, Casterede *(Sonatine Trbn)*, Chopin *(Waltzes Pno [No. 6 in D♭, Op. 64/1, "Minute"])*, J. Defaye *(Danses Trbn)*, Dutilleux *(Choral, Cadence et Fugato)*, J. Jacobsen *(Son Serioso)*, R. Pöntinen *(Camera per Trombone e Fortepiano)*, Rabe *(Basta for Trombone Solo)*, Serocki *(Sonatina na puzon i fortepian)* BIS ▲ 318 [DDD] (17.97)
The Burlesque Trombone & Romantic Trombone Concertos, w. Roland Pöntinen (pno), Bamberg SO [cnd:Leif Segerstam]—features works by Rabe, Serocki, Bernstein, Defaye, Casterede, Dutilleux, Chopin, Jacobsen, Pöntinen, Ropartz, Mercandante, Saint-Saëns, Gaubert, Jongen, Stojowski, Alfvén, Weber BIS (BIS Twins) 2-▲ 318/378 (17.97)
The Criminal Trombone, w. Roland Pöntinen (pno)—features works by Albinoni, Rossini, Vivaldi, et al. BIS ▲ 328 (17.97)
The Romantic Trombone, w. Roland Pöntinen (pno)—features works by Ropartz, Mercadante, Saint-Saëns, P. Gaubert, Jongen, S. Stojowski, Alfvén, Weber BIS ▲ 298 (17.97)
The Russian Trombone, w. Roland Pöntinen (pno)—features works by Edison Denisov, Viktor Ewald, Alexander Goedicke, and German Okunev; arrangements by Lindberg of music by Prokofiev, and Tchaikovsky BIS ▲ 478 [DDD] (17.97)
The Sacred Trombone, w. Gunnar Idenstam (org)—features works by Petr Eben, Anders Hillborg, Franz Liszt, Gardner Read, Jan Sandström, Alfred Schnittke BIS ▲ 488 [DDD] (17.97)
The Solitary Trombone *(see Composer section—Berio, Cage, Eliasson, Kagel, Stockhausen, Xenakis)* BIS ▲ 388 [DDD] (17.97)
Songs for Sunset, w. Per Lundberg (pno)—features works by Massenet *(Méditation from Thaïs)*, Debussy *(La plus que lente; La fille aux chevaux de lin; Rêverie)*, Saint-Saëns *(Le Cygne)*, Chaplin *(The Terry Theme [from Limelight]; Smile [from Modern Times])*, Grieg *(To Spring, Op. 43/6)*, Schubert *(Serenade)*, Mendelssohn *(Auf Flügeln des Gesanges, Op. 43/2)*, Glazunov *(Chant du Ménestrel, Op. 71)*, Fauré *(Après un rêve)*, Elgar *(Salut d'amour, Op. 12)*, Sandström *(SÅng till Lotta)*, Tchaikovsky *(Lied der Mignon:Nur wer die Sehnsucht kennt, Op. 6/6)*, Rachmaninoff *(Son Vc, Op. 19:Adagio; Vocalise, Op. 34/14) (rec 1996)* BIS ▲ 808 [DDD] (17.97)
10 Year Jubilee—features works by Rimsky-Korsakov, Saint-Saëns, Jacobsen, Giazotto, Larsson, David, Xenakis, Prokofiev, Hillborg, Sandstrom, Joseph I, Schnittke, Anonymous, Ligeti, Lutoslawski, Lindbergh & Berio *(rec 1983, 1985-88 & 1990-93)* BIS ▲ 638 [DDD] (17.97)
Trombone & Voice in the Hapsburg Empire *(18th century music arr for trbn, voc, vc, org & strs)*, w. Monica Groop (mez)—features works by Joseph I, Emperor of Austria *(Alme ingrate)*, Johann Ernst Eberlin *(Der verlorene Sohn; Sigismundus)*, L. Mozart *(Agnus Dei)*, Johann Georg Zechner *(Aria Solemnus; Vota Quinquagenalia)*, Johann Georg Albrechtsberger *(Aria de Passione Domine)*, Georg Reutter *(Alma Redemptoris No. 5; Salve Regina)*, Georg Christoph Wagenseil *(Memoriam from Confitebor) (rec 1992)* BIS ▲ 548 [DDD] (17.97)
Trombone Odyssey: 20th Century Landmarks for Trombone & Orchestra, w. Swedish RSO [cnd:Leif Segerstam] (*see* Composer section under Bloch, Martin, Sandström & Serocki) BIS ▲ 538 [DDD] (17.97)
The Virtuoso Trombone, w. Roland Pöntinen (pno)—features works by Berio *(Sequenza V)*, Hindemith *(Son Trbn)*, plus Rimsky-Korsakov, Sulek, Martin, Monti, Kreisler, Pryor BIS ▲ 258 (17.97)
The Winter Trombone *(see Composer section—Larsson, Milhaud, et al.)* BIS ▲ 348 [DDD] (17.97)

Los Angeles PO Trombone Ensemble, Moravian Trombone Choir of Downey
Music for All Seasons: Moravian Trombones—features works by Antes *(3 Chorales)*, Cruse *(3 Sons.)*, anon. *(Communion Hymn; Moravian Funeral Chorales; The Liturgical Year; Moravian Chorale Cycle)*, Rachmaninoff *(Ave Maria)*, Gregor *(Hosanna)*, Lotti *(Crucifixus)*, Forsyth *(Solemn intrada)*, J.S. Bach *(Break forth O Beauteous Heavenly Light)*, anon. & trad. *(Hosanna; O come, Immanuel; All the World Gives Praises; How Shall I Meet My Savior?; To Us a Child Is Born this Night; Once He Came in Blessing; O Come All Ye Faithful; Angels We Have Heard on High; hark the Herald Angels Sing; Prague; Ride on in Majesty; Go to Dark Gethsemane; Christians Dismiss Your Fear; The Day of Resurrection; Wurttemberg Gesangbuch; Jesus Christ Is Risen Today; Lyra Davidica; Christ unto Us Has Left an Example)* CRYS ▲ 220 (15.97)

Pryor, Arthur (trbn)
Trombone Soloist of the Sousa Band, w. Sousa Band, Pryor Band—features Blue Bells of Scotland; Intermezzo-Forever; We Won't Go Home until Morning; Stay in Your Own Back Yard; Parisian Melodies; Message of the Violet [from Prince of Pilsen]; Little Nell; Cujus Animam; Inflammatus [both from Stabat Mater]; My Old Kentucky Home; The Patriot-Polka; Love's Enchantment; The Holy City; One Sweetly Solemn Thought; Congo Love Song [from Nancy Brown]; Non e Ver; Love Thoughts Waltz; The Low Back'd Car; Navajo; Dearie [from Sgt. Brue]; Celeste Aida [from Aida]; Come Down from the Big Fig Tree; Oh, Dry Those Tears; Pagliacci sel; Love Me & World is Mine; Polka Fantastic *(rec 1897-1911)* CRYS ▲ CD 451 ▮

▲ = CD ♦ = Enhanced CD △ = MD ▮ = Cassette Tape ▯ = DCC

Ruffo, Titta (bar)

The Best of Titta Ruffo, w. various orchs—features arias from Don Giovanni, Un ballo in maschera, Otello, Nabucco, Tosca, La forza del destino, Il barbiere di Siviglia, Rigoletto, Ernani, Falstaff & La Gioconda *(rec 1912-29)* GRM2 ▲ 78518 [ADD] (13.97)

In His Vocal Prime, 1907-1922—features arias from Faust, Martha, Rigoletto, Don Giovanni, Otello, Falstaff, Hamlet, Thaïs, C. & Pagliacci PHS ▲ 9088 [ADD] (18.97)

Ruffo NIMB (Prima Voce) ▲ 7810 (m) [ADD] (11.97)

Titta Ruffo Edition *(44 arias & 26 songs)* (rec. 1912-29 for Victor) PRE (Lebendige Vergangenheit) 3-▲ 89303 (m) [AAD] (47.97)

Titta Ruffo, Vol. 1 PHS (The Titta Ruffo Edition) 2-▲ 9212 (33.97)

Titta Ruffo, Vol. 2 PHS (The Titta Ruffo Edition) 2-▲ 9213 (33.97)

Titta Ruffo, Vol. 3 PHS (The Titta Ruffo Edition) 2-▲ 9214 (33.97)

Russell, Anna (sop)

The Anna Russell Album—features Introduction to the Concert; How to Write your own Gilbert & Sullivan Opera; The Ring of the Nibelungs; Canto dolciamente pipo; etc. COL ▲ 47252 (9.97) ▮ 47252 (5.98)

Rydén, Susanne (sop)

Bella Madre De'Fiori: Italian Baroque Arias PROE ▲ 2 (17.97)

Ryhänen, Jaakko (bass)

Summer Night, w. Tapiola Sinfonietta [cnd:Seppo Hovi]—features works by Kuula *(Morning Song; Autumn Mood)*, Sibelius *(Driftwood; The Song of the Spider; Musette)*, Merikanto *(At Sea; The Thunderbird; To Life; The Vallinkorva Song; Lake Ladoga)*, Kilpinen *(Summer Night)*, Palmgren *(Cinderella Waltz; Illusion)*, Luolajan-Mikkola *(Wedding Dance)*, Sonninen *(A Song of Happiness)*, Hovi *(Sad Lake)*, Willebrand *(Like the Glow of Evening Slowly Fading)*, trad *(Ballad of Vestmanviiki [arr Sallinen])* [Fin] *(rec Aug 1996)* 64157 ▲ 16885 [DDD]

Salminen, Matti (bass)

Opera Arias, w. Lahti SO [cnd:Eri Klas]—features 14 arias from Fidelio, Entführung aus dem Serail, Zauberflöte, Bohème, Barbiere di Siviglia, Schweigsame Frau, Eugen Onegin, Don Carlo, Macbeth, Simon Boccanegra, Fliegende Holländer BIS ▲ 520 [DDD] (17.97)

Salters, Stephen (bar)

Stephen Salters, Baritone, w. Sheila Kibbe (pno)—features works by Ravel *(Don Quichotte a Dulcinee)*, Duparc *(Songs)*, Brahms *(Songs)*, Schubert *(Songs)*, Schumann *(Songs)*, R. Strauss *(Songs)*, plus trad spirituals *(He's Got the Whole World in His Hands; Didn't It Rain; Lit'l Boy; Sweet Little Jesus Boy; The Deceivers; Ride up in the Chariot)* CYPR ▲ 9602 (17.97)

Sammarco, Mario (bar)

Mario Sammarco—features works by Mozart, Donizetti, Verdi, Meyerbeer, Thomas, Ponchielli, Giordano, Leoncavallo, Franchetti, Cilea, Wolf-Ferrari & others *(rec 1905-11)* PRE (Lebendige Vergangenheit) ▲ 89100 [AAD] (16.97)

Sargon, Merja (sop)

Our Musical Past, Vol. 1: A Concert for Brass Band, Voice & Piano, w. Bernard Rose (pno)—features Ah! May the Red Rose Live Always, Old Memories, Upon a Summer's Day, La Fontaine & Scots Wha Hae, etc.) OMP ▲ 101 [ADD]

Sayão, Bidù (sop)

Opera Arias & Brazilian Folk Songs—features works by Villa-Lobos *(Aria-Cantilena [from Bachiana brasileira 5; w Leonard Rose (vc), Heitor Villa-Lobos (cnd)])*, Gounod *(Je veux vivre [from Roméo et Juliette; w Erich Leinsdorf (cnd), Columbia SO]; Roi de Thulé; Jewel Song [both from Faust, Act III; w Fausto Cleva (cnd), Metropolitan Opera Orch])*, Massenet *(Je suis encore tout étourdie; Adieu, notre petite table [both from Manon, Acts I & II; w Fausto Cleva (cnd), Metropolitan Opera Orch]; Restons ici... Voyons, Manon [from Manon, Act I; w Pietro Cimara (cnd), Metropolitan Opera Orch]; Obéissons [from Manon, Act III; w Erich Leinsdorf (cnd), Columbia SO])*, Hahn *(Si mes vers avaient des ailes [w Paul Breisach (cnd), Columbia Concert Orch])*, Duparc *(Chanson triste [w Paul Breisach (cnd), Columbia Concert Orch])*, Debussy *(L'Année en vain chasse [from L'Enfant prodigue; w Paul Breisach (cnd), Columbia Concert Orch]; De fleurs [w Milne Charnley (pno)])*, Ravel *(Toi, le coeur de la rose [from L'Enfant et les sortilèges; w Milne Charnley (pno)])*, Koechlin *(Si tu le veux [w Milne Charnley (pno)])*, Moret *(Le Nelumbo [w Milne Charnley (pno)])*, Braga *(Nigue, Nigue, Ninhas; Capim di Pranta; O'Kinimba; São-João-da Ra-Rão; Engenho Noval; A Casinha pequenina; Meu boi barroso; Ogund varêrê [all arrs of traditional Brazilian folk songs; w Milne Charnley (pno)])* *(rec 1941-50)* COL (Masterworks Heritage) ▲ 62355 (12.97)

Rarities, w. Gaetano Merola (cnd), Donald Vorhees (cnd)—features works by Bizet *(Je dis que rien ne m'epouvante [from Carmen])*, Costa *(Canto da saudade; Cisnes; O luar da minha terra)*, Donizetti *(Quanto amore [from L'Elisir d'amore; w. Italo Tajo (bass)])*, Flotow *(The Last Rose of Summer [from Martha])*, Gomes *(C'era una volta un principe; Gentile di cuore [both from Il Guarany])*, Gounod *(Je veux vivre; Va! je t'ai pardonné [w. Jussi Björling (ten)] [both from Roméo et Juliette])*, Mascagni *(Son pochi piori [from L'Amico Fritz])*, Massenet *(Voyons, Manon; Adieu, notre petite table [both from Manon])*, Netto *(Canção da felicidade; Cantiga)*, Puccini *(In quelle trine morbide [from Manon Lescaut]; Donde lieta uscì [from La Bohème])*, arr Braga *(A casinha pequenina)* VAIA ▲ 1171 (m) [ADD] (16.97)

Schade, Michael (ten), Russell Braun (bar)

Soirée Française, w. Canadian Opera Company Orch [cnd:Richard Bradshaw]—features works by Bizet *(C'est toi!...Au fond du temple saint [from Les Pêcheurs de perles])*, Massenet *(Aux troupes du Sultan...Promesse de mon avenir [from Le Roi de Lahore]; A-t-il dit vrai?...Solitaire sur ma terrasse [from Cléopâtre]; En fermant les yeux... [from Manon])*, Lalo *(Puisqu'on ne peut fléchir...Vainement ma bien-aimée [from Le Roi d'Ys])*, Gounod *(Ai-je deviné?...Puis-je oublier, ô ma Glycère [from Sappho])*, Thomas *(Où suis-je? [from Le songe d'une nuit d'été]; O vin, dissipe la tristesse... [from Hamlet])*, Donizetti *(Léonor viens...Léonor, mon amour brave [from La favorita])*, Auber *(Mais j'aperçois Pietro...Mieux vaut mourir [from La muette de Portici])*, Paer *(Ah! quel bonheur de pressentir...Pour imiter son seducteur [from Le Maître de chapelle])*, Méhul *(Vainement Pharaon...Champs paternels [from Le Légende de Joseph en Egypte])*, Rossini *(Moment fatal [from Moïse et Pharaon])* *(rec Massey Hall, Toronto, Ontario, Oct 20 & 23-24, 1996)* SMS (SM 5000) ▲ 5174 [DDD] (16.97)

Scheidl, Theodor (bar)

Theodor Scheidl—features works by Marschner *(An jenem Tag [from Hans Heiling])*, Kreutzer *(Die Nacht ist schön [from Das Nachtlager von Granada])*, Lortzing *(Es wohnt an Seegestade [from Undine])*, Wagner *(Versank ich jetzt [from Der fliegende Holländer; w. Elisabeth Ohms (sgr)]; Was duftet doch der Flieder [from Die Meistersinger von Nürnberg]; Des Weihgefässes göttlicher Gehalt [from Parsifal])*, Verdi *(Für dein Glück [from Un ballo in maschera]; Och glaube an einen Gott [from Otello]; Vernehmt ihr? [from Il trovatore; w. Hedwig von Debička (sop)])*, Meyerbeer *(Dir, o Königin; Hei, Adamstor [both from L'Africaine])*, Leoncavallo *(Was gibts? [from Pagliacci; w. Hedwig von Debička (sop)])*, Weinberger *(Ich bin der Schwanda; Wie kann ich denn vergessen [both from Schwanda der Dudelsackpfeifer])*, plus 2 Viennese songs: Wia si der Weaner 'n Himmel vorstellt; 's wird schöne Maderln geb'n *(rec 1927-30)* PRE (Lebendige Vergangenheit) ▲ 89156 (16.97)

Schiøtz, Aksel (ten)

Aksel Schiøtz Sings Nielsen, Reesen, Agerby, Heise—features songs by Nielsen, Reesen, Agerby & Heise *(rec 1938-41)* PHS ▲ 9140 [ADD] (17.97)

Classic Schiøtz—features Schumann *(Dichterliebe)*, plus songs by Dowland, Grieg, arias by Bach, Buztehude, Handel, Mozart PHS ▲ 9254 (17.97)

Schipa, Tito (ten)

Ave Schipa: Recordings of 1913-1942—features arias from L'Amico Fritz, La Boheme, Manon, Faust, Lucia di Lammermoor, L'Arlesiana, Cavalleria Rusticana, Tosca, Don Pasquale, I Pagliacci, Luisa Miller, Werther, plus selected songs and two recordings sung in English PHS ▲ 9017 [AAD] (17.97)

Best Victor & HMV Recordings—features V. Bellini *(Sonnambula (sels))*, Cilea *(Arlesiana (sels))*, Donizetti *(Don Pasquale (sels); Elisir d'amore (sels))*, Flotow *(Martha (sels))*, C. W. Gluck *(Orfeo ed Euridice (sels))*, G. F. Handel *(Serse (sels))*, P. Mascagni *(Amico Fritz (sels))*, Massenet *(Werther (sels))*, W. A. Mozart *(Don Giovanni (sels))*, G. Rossini *(Barbiere di Siviglia (sels))*, A. Thomas *(Mignon (sels))*, Verdi *(Luisa Miller (sels); Rigoletto (sels))* ENT (Vocal Archives) ▲ 1175 (13.97)

The Early Recordings from HMV & Pathé Records—features works by Mascagni *(O Lola; Viva il vino [both from Cavalleria Rusticana])*, Ponchielli *(Cielo e mar! [from La Gioconda])*, Puccini *(Recondita armonia [2 versions]; E lucevan le stelle [2 versions; both from Tosca]; Che gelida manina [from La bohème])*, Donizetti *(Tu che a Dio [from Lucia di Lammermoor])*, Verdi *(Elle mi fu rapita; Questa o quella; La donna è mobile [all from Rigoletto]; Libiamo nei lieti calici [from La traviata])*, Gounod *(Salve dimora [from Faust])*, Massenet *(Ah! dispar vision! [from Manon])*, Leoncavallo *(Ed ora io mi domando [from Zazà]; O Colombina [from Pagliacci])*, Rossini *(Ecco, ridente in cielo [from Il barbiere di Siviglia])* *(rec 1913-19)* IN ▲ 1320 (m) [ADD] (14.97)

The Early Years: Complete Gramophone & Pathé Recordings *(rec 1913-21)* MRSN ▲ 52008 (35.97)

The 1st Recordings, 1913-19—features works by Mascagni *(O Lola; Viva il Vino [from Cavalleria Rusticana])*, Ponchielli *(Cielo e Mar [from La Gioconda])*, Puccini *(Recondita Armonia; E Lucevan le Stelle [from Tosca]; Che Gelida Manina [from La Bohème])*, Donizetti *(Tu Che a Dio Spiegasti l'Ali [from Lucia di Lammermoor])*, Verdi *(Ella Mi Fu Rapita...Parmi Veder Le Lacrime; Questa o Quella; La donna è mobile [all from Rigoletto]; Libiamo nei Lieti Calici [from La Traviata])*, Gounod *(Salve Dimora Casta e Pura [from Faust])*, Massenet *(Ah! Dispar Vision [from Manon])*, Leoncavallo *(Ed Ora Io Mi Domando [from Zazà]; O Colombina [from Pagliacci])*, Rossini *(Ecco Ridente in Cielo [from Il Barbiere di Siviglia])* VOCA (Vocal Archives) ▲ 1130 (13.97)

Le Grandi Voci Italiana, Vol. 7—features arias from works by Donizetti *(Lucia di Lammermoor)*, Verdi *(La traviata; Rigoletto)*, Gounod *(Faust)*, Ponchielli *(La Gioconda)*, Massenet *(Manon; Werther)*, Puccini *(La Bohème; Tosca)*, Rossini *(Il barbiere di Siviglia)*, Thomas *(Mignon)*, Flotow *(Martha)*, Handel *(Xerxes)*, Mozart *(Don Giovanni)* *(rec 1913-27)* CECL ▲ 515

Schipa, Tito (ten) (cont.)

In Neapolitan Song—features works by Buzzi-Peccia *(Mal d'amore)*, Falvo *(Guapparia; Dicitencello vuje!)*, Tagliaferri *(Piscatore' e Pusilleco; Mandulinata a Napule)*, Barthélemy *(Pesca d'ammore)*, di Capua *(O sole mio; I'te vurria vasà)*, Nutile *(Mamma mia, che vò' sape?)*, Tosti *('A vucchella; Marechiare; Ideale; L'alba separa dalla luce l'ombra)*, Benelli *(Ninna-nanna)*, Valente *(Torna!)*, Gambardella *(O marenariello; Serenata a Surriento; Comme facette mammeta?)*, Sadero *(Fa la nana bambin)*, de Curtis *(Senza nisciuno; Tu, ca nun chiagne!)*, Costa *(Era de maggio)*, Mario *(Canzone appassiunata)*, trad *(Vieni sul mar!)* *(rec 1925-38)* NIMB (Prima Voce) ▲ 7887 [ADD] (11.97)

Neopolitan Songs—features Torna a surriento; Surdate; Voce e notte; Passione; 'O Marenariello; Marchiare; 'A Canzone d'e stelle; Napule ca nun more; 'A vucchella; Core'ngrato; Era de Maggio; Comme facette Mammeta; Serenata a Surriento; Canzone appassiunata; Mandulinata a Napule; Sincerita; Napulitanta; 'O balcone e Napule *(rec 1927-46)* RICE ▲ 205852 (m) [AAD] (17.97)

New York Farewell Recital, w. Albert Carlo Amato (pno)—features works by Scarlatti, Schubert, Tosti, et al. *(and six arias from L'Arlesiana, Don Pasquale, Elisir d'amore, Martha, Semele & Werther),)* *(rec Nov 1962)* SRON ▲ SRO 817-1 [ADD]

Opera Arias, w. Toti dal Monte (sop), Mafalda Favero (sop)—features 18 arias from works by Mascagni *(L'amico Fritz)*, Gluck *(Orfeo ed Eurydice)*, Puccini *(Tosca; La Bohème)*, Massenet *(Manon; Werther)*, Cilea *(L'Arlesiana)*, Ponchielli *(La Gioconda)*, Donizetti *(L'elisir d'amore; Don Pasquale; Lucia di Lammermoor)*, Mozart *(Don Giovanni)*, plus others OPIT ▲ 54510 (6.97)

Rare Recordings 1918-1957 PHS 2-▲ 9988 (m) [AAD] (33.97)

The Romance of Spain—features works by Buzzi-Peccia, Guaracha, Falla, Huarte, Schipa, Ponce, Rodriguez, Freire, Alvarez, Barrera, Roig, Amadori, Lara, Longas, Palacios, Fuentes, Oteo, Padilla, Michelena, Serrano, Ray, Herbert PHS ▲ 9183 (17.97)

Schipa in Song—features works by Scarlatti *(Son tutto duolo; Le Violette; Sento nel cor)*, Pergolesi *(Nina)*, Handel *(Ombra mai fu [from Serse])*, Gluck *(Che faro senza Euridice [from Orfeo ed Euridice])*, Donaudy *(O del mio amato ben)*, Liszt *(Liebestraum)*, Sibella *(La Farfalletta & La Girometta)*, Palomero *(Princesita)*, Barrera *(Granadinas [from Emigrantes])*, Blasco *(La Partida)*, Arniches *(Cancion Hungara [from Alma de Dios])*, Oteo *(Mi viejo amor)*, Ponce *(A la orilla de un palmar)*, Palacios *(Cancion Andaluza [from A. Granada])*, Perez *(Ay-ay-ay [from Guyana])*, Anton *(A la luz de la luna)*, Guaracha *(Los Rumberos)*, Falla *(Jota [from Siete canciones populares españolas])*, Badet *(En effeuillant la Marguerite)*, Rimsky-Korsakov *(Aimant la rose, le rossignol)* NIMB ▲ 7870 [ADD] (11.97)

Tito Schipa *(1889-1965)*—features arias from L'Arlesiana, Don Pasquale, Elisir d'amore, Lucia, Martha, Pagliacci, L'Amico fritz, Cavalleria rusticana, Manon, Werther, Barbiere di Sivglia, Mignon, Luisa Miller, Rigoletto *(rec 1913-37)* NIMB (Prima Voce) ▲ 7813 (m) [ADD] (11.97)

Tito Schipa—features arias by Handel, Gluck, Mozart, Rossini, Donizetti, Thomas, Flotow, Verdi, Gounod, Ponchielli, Massenet, Puccini, Mascagni, Cilea & Giordano *(rec 1913-38)* PHG (Great Voices) 2-▲ PHG 5092

Tito Schipa—features arias from Sonnambula, L'Elisir d'amore, Serse, Pagliacci, Manon, Werther, Don Giovanni, Barber of Seville, Rigoletto, Traviata; plus various songs RCAV (Gold Seal) ▲ 7969 (m) [ADD] (10.97) ▮ 7969

Tito Schipa (1889-1965), w. Lucrezia Bori (sop), Amelita Galli-Curci (sop)—features works by Mozart *(Dalla sua pace; Il mio tesoro intanto [both from Don Giovanni])*, Rossini *(Ecco ridente in cielo; Se il mio nome [both from Il barbiere di Siviglia])*, Donizetti *(Adina, credimi; Una furtiva lagrima [both from L'elisir d'amore]; Una vergin, un angiol del Dio [from La favorita]; Sogno soave e casto; Tornami a dir che m'ami [both from Don Pasquale])*, Flotow *(M'appari tutt'amor [from Martha])*, Verdi *(Questa o quella; È il sol dell'anima; Parmi veder le lagrime; La donna è mobile [all from Rigoletto]; Quando le sere al placido [from Luisa Miller]; Un di felice, etera; Parigi, o cara [both from La traviata])*, Delibes *(Fant aux divins mensonges [from Lakmé])*, Massenet *(Pourquoi me réveiller? [from Werther]; Chiudo gli occhi [from Manon])*, Leoncavallo *(O Colombina [from Pagliacci])*, Cilea *(È la solita storia [from L'Arlesiana])*, Puccini *(Sono andati? [from La bohème])* [F,I] *(rec 1925-28)* PRE (Lebendige Vergangenheit) ▲ 89160 (m) [AAD] (16.97)

Tito Schipa II, w. Carlo Sabajno (cnd), E. Bervily (cnd)—features works by Donizetti *(Una furtiva lagrima [from L'Elisir d'amore])*, Benelli *(Ninna-Nanna)*, Schipa *(Luntananza amara; Scrivenno a Mammema)*, Ochoa/Longàs *(Gitana)*, Sadero *(Fa la nanna, bambin)*, Fiore/Valente *(Nun é Carmela mia!)*, Tagliaferri *(Mandulinata a Napule)*, Murolo/Tagliaferri *('A canzone d'e stelle)*, Scarlatti *(Sento nel core)*, Gluck *(Che farò senza Euridice [from Orfeo ed Euridice])*, D'Andrea/Schipa *(Sei tu)*, Trevisan/Schipa *(Catina)*, Martini *(Plaisir d'amour)*, Rimsky-Korsakov *(Aimant la rose, le rossignol)*, Barbieri/De Curtis *(Senza nisciuno)*, Vento/Valente *(Torna!)*, Fusco/Falvo *(Dicitencello vuje)*, Russo/Di Capua *(I te vurria vasà)*, Ochoa/Schipa *(Adnaluza)*, Simons/Moises *(El manisero)*, Caldieri/Caslar *(Canto per te; Quando?)* *(rec 1929-32)* PRE (Lebendige Vergangenheit) ▲ 89171 (m) [AAD]

Tito Schipa in Berlin, w. Michael Raucheisen (pno), F. Marschalek (cnd) Berlin Radio Orch—features arias & songs by Verdi, Cilea, Tosti, Scarlatti, Sodero, Pergolesi, De Curtis, Barthelemy & others *(rec 1939 & 1942)* GRM2 ▲ 78684 (13.97)

Tito Schipa In Concert 1939-1959 *(21 songs and arias, from four concerts)*—features 13 songs from two June 1939 Berlin recitals, w. piano accompanist Michael Raucheisen *(selections by Barthelemy, De Curtis, Pergolesi, Scarlatti, Sodero, Tosti)*, two arias from a 1942 concert with the Berlin Radio Orchestra cond. by F. Marschalek *(L'Arlesiana—E la solita storia del pastor; Rigoletto—Parmi veder le lagrime)*, six songs from a concert at Volendam, 10/31/59, w. piano accompanist Frans Beeldsnijder *(selections by Barthelemy, Bixio, Lacalle, Palacios, Tosti)* EKLR ▲ 10

Tito Schipa in Concert—features live recs 1955-1964; 1962 interview *(rec Milan, Moscow, Washington, New York)* EKLR ▲ 57

Tito Schipa in Opera & Song—features works by Leoncavallo *(Serenata d'Arlecchino [from I Pagliacci])*, Donizetti *(Sogno soave e casto; Com'è gentil; Tornami a dir [w. Toti dal Monte (sop); all from Don Pasquale]; Una furativa lagrima [from L'Elisir d'amore])*, Bellini *(Prendi, l'anel ti dono [w. Toti dal Monte (sop); from La Sonnambula])*, Mozart *(Dalla sua pace; Il mio tesoro [both from Don Giovanni])*, Verdi *(Questa o quella; E il sol dell'anima [w. Amelita Galli-Curci (sop); both from Rigoletto])*, Rossini *(Se il mio nome [from Il barbiere di Siviglia])*, Massenet *(Il sogno [from Manon]; Pourquoi me réviller? [from Werther])*, Delibes *(Fant aux divins mensonges [from Lakmé])*, Gluck *(Che farò senza Euridice [from Orfeo ed Euridice])*, A. Scarlatti *(Sento nel core; Le violette; Son tutta duolo)*, Tosti *('A Vucchella; Marechiare)*, Padilla *(Princesita)*, Benelli *(Ninna-nanna)*, Lacalle *(Amapola)* *(rec 1925-39)* MECL ▲ 437 (m) (17.97)

Tito Schipa, Vol. 1—features works by Delibes, Donizetti, Flotow, Handel, Leoncavallo, Massenet, Rossini, Thomas, Verdi, et al. PHS ▲ 9322 (m) [AAD] (17.97)

Tito Schipa, Vol. 2—features Sonnambula, Don Pasquale, Favorita, Lucia di Lammermoor, Manon, Werther, Don Giovanni, Bohème, Mignon, Rigoletto; plus 8 Neapolitan & art songs by Costa *(rec 1924-1934)* PHS ▲ 9364 (m) [AAD] (17.97)

Schlick, Barbara (sop)

Ave Maria: Famous Arias & Choruses, w. Paul Kuentz Orch [cnd:Paul Kuentz]—features works by Schubert, Vivaldi, Bach, Cherubini, Mozart, Cimarosa, Fauré, Handel, et al. PVY ▲ 730086 (11.97)

Schlusnus, Heinrich (bar)

Heinrich Schlusnus—features works by Mozart, Abt, Rossini, Verdi, Meyerbeer, Bizet, Offenbach, Tchaikovsky, Puccini *(rec 1921-25)* PRE (Lebendige Vergangenheit) ▲ 89110 [AAD] (16.97)

Heinrich Schlusnus Liederalbum, w. Franz Rupp (pno/org), Hermann Weigert (cnd), Alois Melichar (cnd), Berlin State Opera Orch—features works by Beethoven, Schubert, Schumann, Mendelssohn, Brahms, Wolf, R. Strauss, Wetzel, Graener, Giordani, Handel, Liszt, Mussorgsky, Weingartner, Hermann *(rec 1930-34)* PRE 2-▲ 89205 [ADD] (31.97)

Heinrich Schlusnus Liederalbum, Vol. 2—features songs by Beethoven, Schubert, Schumann, Loewe, Liszt, Gretchinoff, Tchaikovsky, Wolf & R. Strauss *(rec 1934-38)* PRE 2-▲ 89206 [ADD] (31.97)

Heinrich Schlusnus Liederalbum, Vol. 3—features works by Beethoven, Schubert, Schumann, Brahms, Wolf, Strauss, Schillings, Lothar, Vollerthun, Grabert & Schoeck *(rec 1925-31)* PRE 2-▲ 89216 [AAD] (31.97)

Heinrich Schlusnus: Opera Arias *(1888-1952)*—features arias by Bizet, Borodin, Leoncavallo, Lortzing, Márschner, Tchaikovsky, Verdi, Wagner *(rec 1932-38)* PRE (Lebendige Vergangenheit) ▲ 89006 (m) [AAD] (16.97)

Opera Arias & Scenes—features sels. from operas by Verdi *(Rigoletto; Il Trovatore; La Traviata)*, Rossini *(Otello; Il Barbiere di Siviglia)*, Mozart *(Don Giovanni)*, Wagner *(Tannhäuser)*, others *(rec 1927-43)* PRE 2-▲ 89212 [AAD] (31.97)

Schmidt, Joseph (ten)

Film Soundtracks—features sels from German & English films & radio-broadcasts *(rec 1930's)* KSCH 2-▲ 317932 (31.97)

Joseph Schmidt *(see above this section under "Moore, Grace & Josef Schmidt")*

Joseph Schmidt *(previously unpublished live recordings, 1930-1937; 21 opera and operetta arias, 2 songs)*, w. Berlin RSO [cnd:Rudolf Hindemith, Bruno Seidler-Winkler, Hermann Scherchen, Fritz Stiedry, Max von Schillings], unknown orchestra [cnd:Idris Lewis], General Motors SO, General Motors Sym Chorus [cnd:Ernö Rapée, José Iturbi, Oscar Straus], Helen Gleason (sop), Maria Jeritza (sop), Grace Moore (sop) KSCH ▲ 312572 [ADD] (16.97)

Opera Arias—features works by Mozart *(Dies Bildnis ist bezaubernd schön [from Die Zauberflöte])*, Donizetti *(Una furtiva lagrima [from L'Elisir d'amore])*, Smetana *(Komm, mein Söhnchen, auf ein Wort...Weiss ich doch eine, die hat Dukaten [from The Bartared Bride])*, Meyerbeer *(Land so wunderbar/O paradis [from L'Africaine])*, Verdi *(Questa o quella; Ach wie so trügerisch/La Donna è mobile [both from Rigoletto]; Einsam steh ich und verlassen; Dass nur für mich dein Herz erbebt [both from Il Trovatore]; Ach, ihres Auges Zauberblick [from La Traviata]; Doch heisst dich auch ein Pflichtgebot [from Un ballo in maschera])*, Adam *(Freunde, vernehmet die Geschichte [from Le Postillon de Lonjumeau])*, Puccini *(Wie eiskalt ist dies Händchen; Kokett ist dieses Mädchen [both from La Bohème]; Wie sich die Bilder gleichen; Und es blitzten di Sterne; Nur deinetwegen woll't ich noch nicht sterben [all from Tosca]; Nun sind es sechs Monate; Für sie, für sie allein—Lasset sie glauben, dass ich in die Welt zog [both from La Fnaciulla del West]; Non piangere, Liù; Nessun dorma [both from Turnadot])*, anon. *(Recha, als Gott dich einst zur Tochter mir gegeben [from La Juive])* BLAG ▲ 103004 [ADD] (14.97)

Religious Songs & Arias—features arias from Tosca, Faust, Eugen Onegin, El Cid, Manon & Die Tote Stadt; selected religious songs *(rec 1929-34)* PRE ▲ 90145 [AAD] (16.97)

COLLECTIONS 1075

Schmidt, Joseph (ten) (cont.)

To The Memory—features works by Donizetti, Verdi, Puccini, Leoncavallo, Flotow, Korngold, Meyerbeer, Adam, Massenet, Lehár, J. Strauss II, Rossini, plus others — VOCA (Vocal Archives) ▲ 1152 (13.97)

Das Zauberlied—features Musica probita; Marechiare; Lolita; Mal d'amore; La Paloma; O sole mio; Mattinata; Vorrei morire; Nina; Zigeunerlied; Canzonetta; Tausendmal du; Du sollst der Kaiser meiner Seele sein; Das Zauberlied; Emigrant; Heimatland; Ein Lied geht um die Welt; Wenn du jung bist, gehört dir die Welt; Ein Stern fällt vom Himmel; Heut' ist der schönste Tag in meinem Leben; Es wird im Leben dir mehr genommen als gegeben; Liebe kleine Frau, ich muss dir was gesteh'n; Wiener Bonbons *(rec 1929-30 & 1932)* — BLAG ▲ 103001 [ADD] (14.97)

Schmithüsen, Ingrid (sgr)

Silhouetten, Vol. 2: European Folksongs, w. Thomas Palm (pno)—features folksong arrangements by Britten *(The trees they grow so high; The Ash Grove; The Miller of Dee; Oliver Cromwell; Come you not from Newcastle; The Brisk Young Widow)*, Schoenberg *(Der Mai tritt ein mit Freuden; Es gingen zwei Gespielen gut; Mein Herz ist mir gemenget; Mein Herz in steten Treuen)*, Falla *(Canciones populaires españolas (7))*, Janáček *(Moravian Dances (5))*, Bartók *(Dorfszenen (5))*, Ravel *(Mélodies populaires grecques)*, Brahms *(Deutsche Volkslieder (4))* — CANT ▲ 1022 (17.97)

Schneider, Mary (sgr)

Yodeling the Classics, w. Sydney International Orch [cnd:Tommy Tycho]—features arrs of popular classical melodies including William Tell Ov; Carmen Ov; Can-Can Ov; Skater's Waltz Yodel; Sanctuary of the Heart; Czardas; Cl Polka Yodel; Toselli's Serenade; A Heart That's Free; Merry Widow Waltz; Schön Rosmarin; Brahms Lullaby Yodel; Mozart's Cradle Song; Largo Lullaby Yodel; Tritsch Tratsch Polka Yodel; Beethoven's Minuet Yodel; Washington Post; Sempre Fidelis; Liberty Bell; Blaze Away — 70630 ▲ 24935

Schock, Rudolf (ten)

Rudolf Schock, w. Berlin German Opera Orch [cnd:W. Schüchter], Berlin Orch [cnd:W. Schüchter], Berlin PO [cnd:J. Keilberth], FFB Orch [cnd:W. Schmidt-Boelcke], E. Grümmer (sop), J. Hammond (sop), North German RSO [cnd:W. Schüchter], Northwest German PO [cnd:W. Schüchter], Philharmonia Orch [cnd:I. Dobrowen], Berlin City Opera Chorus [cnd:W. Schüchter], Berlin German Opera Chorus [cnd:R. Kempe], St. Hedwig's Cathedral Choir [cnd:R. Kempe], L. Clam (ten), A. Hendriks (ten), H. Kraus (ten), M. Schmidt (ten), H. Wilhelm (ten), F. Frantz (bass), G. Frick (bass), R. Koffmane (bass), A. Metternich (bass), G. Neidlinger (bass), H. Pick (bass), W. Stoll (bass)—features A. Adam *(Postillon de Lunjumeau (sels) [Mes amis, écoutez l'histoire])*, Giordano *(Andrea Chénier (sels) [Vicino a te s'acqueta])*, Künneke *(Vetter aus Dingsda (sels) [Ich bin nur ein armer Wandergesell'])*, F. Lehár *(Friederike (sels) [O Mädchen, mein Mädchen]; Land des Lächelns (sels) [Dein ist mein ganzes Herz]; Lustige Witwe (sels) [O Vaterland...Da geh' ich zu Maxim])*, P. Mascagni *(Amico Fritz (sels) [Suzel, buon dì (Cherry duet)])*, W. A. Mozart *(Entführung aus dem Serail (sels) [Wenn der Freude Tränen fliessen]; Zauberflöte (sels) [Dies Bildnis ist bezaubernd schön])*, J. Offenbach *(Contes d'Hoffmann (sels) [Il était une fois à la cour d'Eisenach (Legend of Kleinsach)])*, G. Puccini *(Turandot (sels) [Nessun dorma])*, R. Wagner *(Lohengrin (sels) [In fernem Land, unnahbar euren Schritten; Mein lieber Schwan]; Meistersinger (sels) [Am stillen Herd; Morgenlich leuchtend (Prize Song)])*, C. M. Weber *(Freischütz (sels) [Nein, länger trag' ich nicht die Qualen...Durch die Wälder, durch die Auen])* — EMIC (Heroes) ▲ 66811 (m) [ADD] (11.97)

16 Operetta Arias—features works by Kálmán, Lehár, Offenbach, Joh. Strauss, et al. [G] — Acanta ▲ 43480

12 Opera & Operetta Arias—features works by Jan Brandts Buys, Cornelius, Korngold, Lortzing, Mozart, Weber [G] — Acanta ▲ 13553

Schöffler, Paul (b-bar)

Paul Schöffler, w. Bayreuth Festival Orch [cnd:Hermann Abendroth]; Great Opera Orchestra [cnd:Wilhelm Loibner]; London PO [cnd:Karl Rankl]; London SO [cnd:Karl Rankl]; Vienna PO [cnd:Karl Böhm]; Bayreuth Festival Chorus—features works by Mozart *(Der Prozess schon gewonnen [from Le nozze di Figaro])*, Beethoven *(Ha! welch' ein Augenblick! [from Fidelio])*, Wagner *(O du mein holder Abendstern [from Tannhäuser]; Was duftet doch der Flieder; Gut'n Abend, Meister; Wahn! Wahn ! Überall Wahn!; Verachtet mir die Meister nicht [all from Die Meistersinger von Nürnberg]; Leb' wohl, du kühnes, herrliches Kind [from Die Walküre])*, Verdi *(Credo in un Dio crudel; Era la notte [both from Otello]) (rec 1943-50)* — PRE (Lebendige Vergangenheit) ▲ 90325 [AAD] (16.97)

Scholl, Andreas (ct)

English Folksongs & Lute Songs, w. Andreas Martin (lt)—features The 3 Ravens; Waly, Waly; I Will Give My Love an Apple; Barbara Allen; Lord Rendall & Lute Songs by Dowland, Campion — HAM ▲ 901603 (17.97)

Kantate, w. Basel Consort, Concerto di Viole—features I. Albertini *(Son 4 Vn)*, J. C. Bach *(Ach, dass ich Wassers genug hätte)*, Buxtehude *(Fried- und Freudenreiche Hinfarth, BuxWV 76; Jubilate Domino, omnis terra, BuxWV 64)*, P. H. Erlebach *(Wer sich dem Himmel übergeben)*, Legrenzi *(Son Quinta a quattro)*, G. Rovetta *(Ach, Herr, lass deine lieben Engelein)*, H. Schütz *(Herzlich lieb hab' ich dich, O Herr; Kleine geistliche Konzerte (sels) [O Jesu, nomen dulce, SWV 308 (No. 3)]; Was hast du verwirket, SWV 307)*, Tunder *(Salve mi Jesus)* — HAM ▲ 901651 (17.97)

Schöne, Lotte (sop)

The Art of Lotta Sch(uml)one—features works by Mozart, Meyerbeer, J. Strauss, Puccini, Zeller, Nicolai Suppe, Schubert, Verdi, Massenet, Millocker, Jones *(rec 1924-31)* — PRE 2-▲ 89224 (31.97)

Lotte Schöne & Richard Tauber In Operetta *(9 solo arias by Schöne, 1924-25 Odeon acoustics; 11 solo arias by Tauber, 1924-32 Odeon recordings)*—features Schöne singing arias from *(Der arme Jonathan [Millöcker]; Cagliostro in Wien, Die Fledermaus, Indigo und die Vierzig Räuber, Die lustige Krieg [Joh. Strauss]; Die schöne Galathea [Suppé]; Der Obersteiger, Der Vogelhändler [Zeller])* † VOCAL:Tauber — NIMB (Prima Voce) ▲ 7833 [ADD] (11.97)

Schorr, Friedrich (b-bar)

Friedrich Schorr *(1889-1953)*—features arias from Fidelio, Huguenots, Don Giovanni, Zauberflöte, Fliegende Holländer, Meistersinger, Tannhäuser, Walküre, Euryanthe rec. 1921-1922 for Grammophon) — PRE (Lebendige Vergangenheit) ▲ 89052 (m) [AAD] (16.97)

Schreier, Peter (ten)

Music for Tenor & Lute, w. Konrad Ragossnig (lt) — CAPO ▲ 10047 [DDD]

Schumann, Elisabeth (sop)

Arias & Songs—features works by Mozart *(arias from Nozze di Figaro, Don Giovanni, Re pastore; Alleluia, from "Exsultate, jubilate")*, Bach *(arias from St. Matthew Passion, Cantata No. 159)*, songs by Handel, Strauss, Marx, Flies, Mozart, Mahler, Schumann rec. 1926-30, from HMV 78 rpm discs) — PRE (Lebendige Vergangenheit) ▲ 89031 (m) [AAD] (16.97)

The Complete Edison & Polydor Recordings—features works by Mozart, plus others *(rec 1915-23)* — ROMO ▲ 81028 (17.97)

Elisabeth Schumann, w. orch—features songs by Benatzky, Marx, Reger, Schubert, Sieckzynski, Josef Strauss, Richard Strauss; *(arias from Joshua [Handel], Der Opernball [Heuberger], Der Obersteiger [Zeller], Der Vogelhändler [Zeller], Der Fremdenführer [Ziehrer], Der Landstreicher [Ziehrer])* (rec. 1927-38 for HMV) — PHS ▲ 9398 (m) [AAD] (18.97)

Songs, Lieder & Cantatas—features works by Bach, Handel, Haydn, Mozart, Schubert, R. Schumann, R. Strauss & Wolf *(rec 1927-30)* — VOCA (Vocal Archives) ▲ 1153 (13.97)

Schumann-Heink, Ernestine (cta)

The Complete Zonophone, Columbia & Victor Recordings—features works by Wagner, Donizetti, Schubert, Brahms, plus others *(rec 1900-08)* — ROMO 2-▲ 81029 (35.97)

The 1943 Broadcasts—features works by Brahms, Gruber, McFayden, Wagner, Schumann, Lang, Tchaikovsky, Cadman, Grieg, Lieurance, R. Strauss, Foster, Bond, Handel, Gluck, Mozart, & Meyerbeer [E,G] *(rec 1943)* — BLAG ▲ 103006 (14.97)

Schumann-Heink — NIMB (Prima Voce) ▲ 7811 (m) [ADD] (11.97)

The Stanford Archive Series—features works by Arditi *(Leggero Invisible)*, Mehrkens *(Wie ein Grüssen)*, Schubert *(Der Tod und das Mädchen; Die Forelle; Der Erlkönig)*, Wagner *(Weiche, Wotan [from Das Rheingold]; Gerechter Gott! [from Rienzi]; Traüme: Gedichte Wesendonck Lieder; Höre mit Sinn [from Götterdämmerung])*, Meyerbeer *(O prêtres de Baal; Il va venir; Ah, mon fils [from Le Prophete])*, Millöcker *(I und mei Bua)*, Donizetti *(Il segreto per essere felice [from Lucrezia Borgia])*, Mozart *(Parto, parto ma tu ben mio [from La Clemenza di Tito])*, Gounod *(O ma lyre immortelle [from Sapho])*, Schumann *(Liederkreis 5 [from Mondnacht)*, Hermann *(Barbchen; Schlafliedchen)*, Saint-Saëns *(Sieh, mein Herz; Die Sonne, sie lachte [from Samson und Dalila])*, Raff *(Sei still)*, Ronald *(Down in the Forest [from A Cycle of Life])*, Rubinstein *(Der Wanderers Nachlied)*, Delibes *(Bonjour, Suzon)*, Grieg *(Moderen Synger; Im Kahn)*, Brahms *(Wiegenlied; Sapphische Ode)*, Loewe *(Das Erkennen)*, Foster *(Old Black Joe)*, R. Strauss *(Traum durch die Dämmerung)*, Manahan *(Shepherd's Love)*, Huerter *(Pirate Dreams)*, Grueber *(Stille Nacht, heilige Nacht [2 versions])*, Humperdinck *(Weihnachten)*, Elgar *(Land of Hope & Glory)*, Carpenter *(The Home Road)*, J. S. Smith *(Star Spangled Banner)*, Weatherly*(Danny Boy)*, Hildach *(Der Lenz)*, Nevin *(Rosary)*, Mendelssohn *(And He Journeyed; But the Lord Is Mindful of His Own [from St. Paul])*, O'Hara *(There Is No Death)*, Bach *(My Heart Ever Faithful [from Cant 68])*, Esenwein-Pasternack *(Taps) [rec 1900-35]* — DLS 2-▲ 5503 [ADD] (20.97)

Schwarz, Joseph (bar)

Joseph Schwarz *(1880-1926)*—features eleven Verdi arias *(from Ballo in maschera, Otello, Rigoletto, Traviata & Trovatore [incl. four with soprano Claire Dux])*, four arias by Meyerbeer, Offenbach & Rossini,), two songs *(Lewandowski-Rosenfeld—Kol nidre; Liszt—O komm' im Traum)* rec. 1916-18 for Gramophone) — PRE (Lebendige Vergangenheit) ▲ 89033 (m) [AAD] (16.97)

Schwarzkopf, Elisabeth (sop)

Elisabeth Schwarzkopf—features arias from Arabella, Ariadne auf Naxos, The Bartered Bride, Così fan tutte, Don Giovanni, Fidelio, Die Fledermaus, Der Freischütz, Lohengrin, Der Opernball, Der Rosenkavalier — EMIC (Diva) ▲ 65577 (11.97)

The Elisabeth Schwarzkopf Album—features songs by Arne, Beethoven, Brahms, Gluck, Leveridge, Loewe, Mozart, Rameau, Reger, Rossini, Sammartini, Schubert, R. Strauss, Zilcher *(Rokoko-Suite, Op. 65)*, et al. — Acanta ▲ 43801

Farewell Recital, w. Geoffrey Parsons (pno)—features works by Schubert, Wolf, Liszt, Mahler, plus others *(rec Concertgebouw, Amsterdam, Feb 8, 1977)* — BELV ▲ 7002 (14.97)

Schwarzkopf, Elisabeth (sop) (cont.)

Lieder Recital, w. Gerald Moore (pno)—features works by Bach *(Bist du bei mir)*, Pergolesi *(Se tu m'ami, se tu sospiri)*, Handel *(Care selve [Atalanta])*, Gluck *(Einem Bach, der fliebt [die Pilger von Mekka])*, Beethoven *(Wonne der Wehmut, Op. 83 No. 1)*, Schubert *(An Sylvia, D.891; Ungeduld, D.795 No. 7; Romanze aus "Rosamund", D.797; Die Vögel, D.691; Die Einsame, D.800; Vediquato adoro, D.510)*, Wolf *(Lied der mignon; Philine; Nachzauber Die zigeunerin)*, Strauss *(Ruhe meine Seele, Op. 27 No. 1; Wiegenlied, Op. 41 No. 1; Schlectes Wetter, Op. 69 No. 5; Hat's gesagt, bliebt's nicht dabei, Op. 36 No. 3)*, Mozart *(Warnung, K.433 [416c])*, Schumann *(Der Nubaum, Op. 25/3) (rec Aug 7, 1956)* — EMIC ▲ 66084 (11.97)

Recital, w. Geoffrey Parsons (pno)—features 19 songs by Mozart, Schubert, Schumann, Wolf & Wolf-Ferrari (rec. live, from a Swiss-Italian Radio 2 broadcast Oct 6, 1967) — ERM ▲ 109 [ADD]

Sings Operetta, w. Philharmonia Orch, Philharmonia Chorus [cnd:O. Ackermann]—features arias from Der Opernball, Der Vogelhändler, Der Obersteiger, Der Zarewitsch, Der Graf von Luxemburg, Giuditta, Casanova, Die Dubarry, Boccaccio [G] — EMIC ▲ 47284 (16.97)

Scola, Vincenza la (ten)

Vincenzo La Scola, w. Paola Molinari (pno)—features works by Stradella [attrib] *(Pietà Signore)*, Mascagni *(Ave Maria)*, Verdi *(Ah, la paterna mano [from Macbeth]; De' miei bollenti spiriti [from La traviata]; Quando le sere al placido [from Luisa Miller]; In solitaria stanza; L'Esule)*, Tosti *(Non t'amo più; Marechiare)*, Cilea *(È la solita stroria del pastore [from L'Arlesiana])*, Respighi *(L'ultima ebbrezza; Ballata)*, Sorozabal *(No puede ser [from La Tabernera del Puerto])*, Cardillo *(Core 'ngrato) (rec Apr 15, 1996)* — BONG ▲ 2520 [DDD] (16.97)

Scotto, Renata (sop)

Renata Scotto—features arias from La Straniera [Bellini], Elisir d'amore, Lucia di Lammermoor, I Lombardi, Requiem Mass [Verdi], Traviata — MEMO (Great Voices) 2-▲ 4291 (m) [ADD]

Scotto, Renata (sop), José Carreras (ten)

Great Operatic Scenes—features duets from Butterfly, I Lombardi, Traviata (rec. live 1973-74) — LCD ▲ 150 (m) [AAD] (13.97)

Scotto, Renata (sop), Giulietta Simionato (mez)

Renata Scotto & Giulietta Simionato—features arias from La sonnambula; Don Pasquale; La traviata; The Pearl Fishers; Lodoletta; Il barbiere di Siviglia; La cenerentola; Il matrimonio segreto; Aida; Cavalleria rusticana — CECL (Classic Collection) ▲ 111

Seefried, Irmgard (sop)

Arias & Songs, w. Gerald Moore (pno), Hermann von Nordberg (pno), Wilhelm Schmidt (pno), London Mozart Players [cnd:Harry Blech]—features works by Mozart, Flies, Brahms, Schubert & Wolf — TES ▲ 1026 [ADD] (17.97)

Segal, Miriam Hayward (sop)

Ave Maria, w. K. Bower (pno), Miriam Keough (hp)—features *Ave Maria* set by Coates, Turina, Liddle, Reger, Franck, Verdi, Mascagni & Bruch — SYMP ▲ 1175 [DDD] (17.97)

Seinemeyer, Meta (sop)

The Art of Meta Seinemeyer—features arias & songs by Bizet, Mascagni, Strauss, Giordano, Puccini, Verdi, Offenbach, Weber, Ponchielli, Mozart, Wagner, Schubert, Gounod, Humperdinck, Liszt, Rubenstein, Weingartner *(rec 1920-29)* — PRE 4-▲ 89402 (63.97)

Opera Arias & Duets *(historic recordings)*, w. Berlin State Opera Orch [cnd:Frieder Weissmann]—features selections from Andrea Chénier, Bohème, Madama Butterfly, Manon Lescaut, The Czar's Bride, Aida, Ballo in maschera, Don Carlos, Otello; *(()* rec. 1926-29, from Parlophon 78 rpm discs) — PRE (Lebendige Vergangenheit) ▲ 89029 (m) [AAD] (16.97)

Sembrich, Marcella (sop)

Her Recordings From 1903-1919—features arias by Verdi, Rossini, Handel, Thomas, Bellini & Mozart, plus other songs *(rec 1903-19)* — VOCA (Vocal Archives) ▲ 1139 (13.97)

Marcella Sembrich (1858-1935), w. A. Scotti (bar), E. De Gogorza (sgr)—features Arditi *(Parla Walz)*, M. Arne *(The Lass with the Delicate Air)*, V. Bellini *(Norma (sels); Sonnambula (sels))*, H. Bishop *(Home Sweet Home)*, Donizetti *(Don Pasquale (sels); Lucia di Lammermoor (sels))*, Flotow *(Martha (sels))*, R. Hahn *(Si mes vers avaient des ailes!)*, Moniuszko *(Halka (sels))*, G. Rossini *(Barbiere di Siviglia (sels); Semiramide (sels))*, F. Schubert *(Schöne Müllerin, D.795)*, Strauss (II) *(Frühlingsstimmen, Op. 410)*, A. Thomas *(Hamlet (sels))*, Traditional *(Comin' Thro' the Rye)*, Verdi *(Ernani (sels); Rigoletto (sels); Traviata (sels); Vespri siciliani (sels))*, Viardot *(Aime-moi)* — NIMB (Prima Voce) ▲ 7901 [ADD] (11.97)

The Victor Recordings *(rec 1904-08)* — ROMO ▲ 81026 (35.97)

The Victor Recordings (1908-19) — ROMO ▲ 81027 (35.97)

Serra, Luciana (sop)

Luciana Serra—features arias by Rossini *(La cambiale di matrimonio:Come tacer...Vorrei spiegarvi il giubilo)*, Bellini *(I Puritani:Qui la voce sua soave)*, Donizetti *(Linda di Chamounix:Ah, tardai troppo)*, Verdi *(I Masnadieri:Dall'infame banchetto m'involai)*, Thomas *(Hamlet:A vox jeux, mes amis)*, Meyerbeer *(Dinorah:Me voice...Ombre légère)* (rec. June 1993) — FONI ▲ 23 [DDD] (16.97)

Opera Arias, w. Bruno Campanella, Carlo Felice Cellario, various orchs & choruses—feature arias by Donizetti *(from Don Pasquale, Figlia di regimmento, Gianni di Parigi)*, Rossini *(from Barber of Seville)* [I] (rec. live 1987-89) — NUO ▲ 6820 [DDD] (16.97)

Shalyapin, Fiodor (bar)

Fiodor Shalyapin—features songs by Solokov *(Tempest Rages)*, Slonov *(Ah Thou Red Sun; A Word of Farewell)*, Manykin-Nevstruev *(Song of the Needy Pilgrim)*, Korganov *(Elegy)*, Glazunov *(Bacchanal Song)*, Malashkin *(Oh, Could I in Song Tell Tomorrow)*, Keneman *(When the King Went to War)*, Lishin *(She Laughed)*, plus Russian folk songs *(I Have Worn My Eyes Out; Sweet Night; From under the Oak, from under the Elm; Tale of Tsar Ivan Vasilyevich; The Mother-in-Law Had 7 Sons-in-Law)*, Ukranian folk songs *(On the Meadow; The Green Oak-Tree; A Big Mosquito) (rec 1902-34)* — RD (Talents of Russia) ▲ 16004 [ADD] (16.97)

Russia & Fiodor Ivanovich Shalyapin—features The Tail of the Il'ya Murometz; The Sun Rises & Sets; Down on the Mother Volga; The Legend of the 12 Brigands; Lutchinushka [The Little Birch Spinter]; Eh You, Van'ka; They Don't Let Masha; Down the Peterskaya; Black Eyes; Farewell to Thee, My Joy [Siberian prisoners' song]; From Behind the Island to the Midstream; It's Not Autumnal Drizzle; Hey, Ukhnem; Rise, Red Sun; The Oak Cudgel *(rec 1910-34)* — RD (Russian Vocal School) ▲ 16003 (16.97)

Sheridan, Margaret (sop)

Rich & Rare: The Voice of Margaret Sheridan, w. Aureliano Pertile (ten), Renato Zanelli (ten), Hubert Greenslade (pno), Carlo Sabajno (cnd), La Scala Orch, Queen's Hall Orch—features works by Puccini *(Tu tu amore [from Manon Lescaut]; Si, mi Chiamano Mimi [from La bohème]; Ancora un passo; Un bel di vedremo; E questo; Bimba dagli occhi miei [all from Madama Butterfly])*, Verdi *(Gia nella notte denza; Ave Maria [both from Otello])*, Giordano *(Vicino a te, La nostra morte [from Andrea Chenier])*, Claribel *(Come Back to Erin)*, Moore *(Believe Me if All Those Endearing Young Charms; Has Sorrow Thy Young Days Shaded?; Rich & Rare)*, Balfe *(I Dreamt I Dwelt in Marble Halls)*, Hughes *(The Lovers Curse) (rec 1926-29)* — TM ▲ 100

Shin, Young Ok (sop)

Ave Maria, w. Owen Hughes (trb), English CO [cnd:Uriel Segal], London Voices [cnd:Terry Edwards]—features works by Bach *(Schafe k'nnen sicher weiden; Jauchzet Gott in allen Landen)*, Mozart *(Laudate Dominum; Alleluia; Et incarnatus est)*, Franck *(Panis Angelicus)*, Fauré *(Pie Jesu)*, Schubert *(Ave Maria)*, Gounod *(Ave Maria; O divin rèdempteur)*, Nah *(The Lord Is My Shepherd)*, Webber *(Pie Jesu)*, Handel *(Let the Bright Seraphim)*, Malotte *(The Lord's Prayer)*, plus Amazing Grace *(rec St. Jude on the Hill, London, July 1996)* — SSCL ▲ 17 (16.97)

A Dream, w. Warren Jones (pno)—features works by Handel *(Arias [from Rinaldo; Giulio Cesare; Alcina])*, Bellini *(4 Songs)*, Rossini *(3 Songs)*, Fauré *(Après un rêve)*, Duparc *(Chanson triste; Extase)*, Liszt *(Comment, disaient-ils; Oh! Quand le dors)*, Rachmaninoff *(3 Songs)* — SSCL ▲ 25 (16.97)

Shumskaya, Yelizaveta (sop)

Yelisaveta Shumskaya: Russian Vocal School—features performances w. V. Gnutov (cnd), N. Osipov State Russian Folk Orch *(You, My Spaciousness; What Did I Meet You For, Darling [both Russian Folk Songs]; Varlamov:The Red Sarafan; Diubuk:Don't Scold Me, Dear)*, S. Stuchevski (pno) *(Guriliov:The Swallow Circles; Glinka:The Northern Star; Taneyev:In the Invisible Haze)*, N. Valter (pno) *(Glinka:The Bird-Cherry Tree in Blossom)*, V. Nebolsin (cnd), Bolshoi Theater Orch *(Glinka:Cavatina & Rondo of Antonida [from A Life for the Tsar]; Rimsky-Korsakov:Aria of the Snow Maiden [from The Snow Maiden])*, N. Golovanov (cnd), Bolshoi Theater Orch *(Rimsky-Korsakov:Lullaby of Volkhova [from Sadko])*, N. Golovanov (cnd), Radioinformation Committee Grand SO *(Rimsky-Korsakov:Aria of Marfa [from The Bride for the Tsar])*, G. Orentilkher (pno) *(Tchaikovsky:It is Painful & Sweet)*, M. Zhukov (cnd), Bolshoi Theater Orch *(Tchaikovsky:Tatiana's letter scene [from Eugene Onegin]) (rec 1948-63)* — RD ▲ 16005 [AAD]

▲ = CD ♦ = Enhanced CD △ = MD ▮ = Cassette Tape ▯ = DCC

Siems, Margarethe (sop)

Königlische Sächische Hofopernsängerin, w. G. Förstel (sop), M. Nast (sop), E. v. Osten (sop), D. Zádor (bar), D. Aranyi (sgr)—features Alyabiev *(The Nightingale)*, V. Bellini *(Norma (sels) [Mira, o Norma])*, Delibes *(Lakmé (sels) [Là-bas dans la forêt plus sombre])*, Donizetti *(Fille du régiment (sels) [Chacun le sait]; Lucia di Lammermoor (sels) [Ah! Verranno a te; Spargi d'amaro pianto (Mad Scene); Soffriva nel pianto; Spargi d'amaro pianto (Mad Scene); Spargi d'amaro pianto (Mad Scene)])*, Flotow *(Martha (sels) [Letzte Rose (ballad)])*, Meyerbeer *(Dinorah (sels) [Ombre légère, qui suis mes pas]; Huguenots (sels) [Si j'étais coquette; O beau pays de la Touraine!; A ce mot seul s'anime])*, W. A. Mozart *(Nozze di Figaro (sels) [Deh vieni, non tardar, o gioja bella])*, O. Nicolai *(Lustigen Weiber von Windsor (sels) [Non eilt herbei])*, G. Rossini *(Guillaume Tell (sels) [Doux aveu!])*, R. Strauss *(Rosenkavalier (sels) [Kann mich auch als an ein Mädel erinnern; Mit ihren Augen voll Tränen; Ist ein Traum; Marie Thérès'...Hab' mir's gelobt; Mir ist die Ehre widerfahren; Mit ihren Augen voll Tränen; Marie Thérès'...Hab' mir's gelobt; Ist ein Traum])*, Strauss (II) *(Frühlingsstimmen, Op. 410)*, A. Thomas *(Mignon (sels) [Je suis Titania (polonaise)])*, Verdi *(Aida (sels) [O cieli azzurri; O patria mia]; Traviata (sels) [Ah fors'è lui quest'anima; Ah fors'è lui quest'anima]; Trovatore (sels) [D'amor sull'ali rosee; D'amor sull'ali rosee])* SYMP 2-▲ 1227 (34.97)

Margarethe Siems, Soprano (1879-1952), w. Gertrude Förstel (sop), Minnie Nast (sop), Eva van der Osten (sop), Desider Aranyi (ten), Desider Zador (bar)—features works by Rossini *(Ah! Doux aveau [from Guillaume Tell])*, Proch *(Variationen)*, Delibes *(Là-bas, dans le forêt [from Lakmé])*, Verdi *(Ah! fors' à lui [2 versions; from La traviata]; D'amor sull'ali rosee [2 versions; from Il trovatore]; O patria mia; O cieli azzuri [both from Aida])*, Donizetti *(Soffriva nel pianto; Mad Scene; Cadenza from Mad Scene [2 versions]; Verranno a te [all from Lucia di Lammermoor]; Chacum le sait, chacun le dit [from La Fille du Regiment])*, Thomas *(Je suis Titania [from Mignon])*, Meyerbeer *(Ah! si j'étais coquette; O beau pays [both from Les Huguenots]; Ombre légère que suis mes pas [from Dinorah])*, Alabiev *(Die Nachtigall)*, Bellini *(Mira o Norma [from Norma])*, Flotow *(Die letzte Rose [from Martha])*, Mozart *(Deh vieni, non tardar [from Le nozze di Figaro])*, Joh. Strauss (II) *(Frühlingstimmen Walzer)*, Nicolai *(Nun eilt herbei [from Die lustigen Weiber von Windsor])*, R. Strauss *(Kann mich auch an ein Mädel erinnern; Mit ihren Augen voll [2 versions]; Hab' mirs gelobt [2 versions]; Ist ein Traum [2 versions]; Mir ist die Ehre [all w. Thomas Beechem (cnd), Royal Opera House Covent Garden Orch; all from Der Rosenkavalier]) (rec 1903-11)* SYMP 2-▲ 1227 (m) [ADD] (34.97)

Siepi, Cesare (bass)

Cesare Siepi, w. Arturo Basile (cnd), Alfredo Simonetto (cnd), Franco Capuano (cnd), Gabriele Santini (cnd), Turin RAI SO—features selections from Verdi *(I vespri siciliani; Don Carlos; Nabucco; Ernani)*, Mozart *(Don Giovanni)*, Bellini *(La Sonnambula)*, Rossini *(L'Italiana in Algeri; Il barbiere di Siviglia)*, Boito *(Mefistofele)*, Puccini *(La Bohème) (rec Torino, 1955)* CECL (Classic Collections) ▲ 107

Cesare Siepi: Recital (1947-1957)—features arias from operas by Mozart *(Don Giovanni)*, Rossini *(L'Italiana in Algeri; Il Barbiere di Saviglia)*, Bellini *(La Somnambula)*, Verdi *(Nabucco; Ernani; I Vespri Siciliani; Simone Boccanegra; Don Carlos)*, Meyerbeer *(Robert Le Diable; Les Huguenots)*, Halévy *(La Juive)*, Gounod *(Faust)*, Boito *(Mefistofele)*, Gomes *(Salvator Rosa)*, Ponchielli *(La Gioconda)* MYTO ▲ 93591 (17.97)

Sills, Beverly (sop)

The Art of Beverly Sills—features works by Bellini, Donizetti, Heuberger, Massenet, Meyerbeer, Mozart, Offenbach, Rossini, R. Strauss, Verdi EMIC ▲ 64425

Opera Arias—features works by Mozart *(Ruhe sanft [from Zaide]; Martern allen Arten [from Die Entführung aus dem Serail])*, Donizetti *(Ah, tardai troppo [from Linda di Chamounix]; Prendi, per me sei libero [from L'Elisir d'amore]; Il dolce suono; Ardon gli incensi; Spargi d'amaro [all from Lucia di Lammermoor])*, Charpentier *(Depuis le jour [from Louise])*, Bellini *(Eccomi in lieta vesta [from I Capuleti])*, Meyerbeer *(Ombre légère qui suis mes pas [from Dinorah])*, Verdi *(Suarta è la notte; Tutto sprezzo [both from Ernani])*, Gounod *(Je yeux vivre dans le rêve [from Roméo & Juliette]) (rec 1968 & 1971)* ARKA (Great Interpreters) ▲ 804 [ADD]

Welcome to Vienna, w. London PO [cnd:Julius Rudel]—features works by Korngold, Heuberger, Lehár, Sieczynski, Joh. Strauss EMIC ▲ 64424

Sills, Beverly (sop), Plácido Domingo (ten)

Great Scenes—features sels. from Roberto Devereux, Manon, Contes d'Hoffmann, Il Tabarro, Traviata (Rec. live, 1965-71) LCD ▲ * [ADD]

Simándy, József (ten)

József Simándy, Tenor, w. Hungarian State Opera Orch, Budapest PO—features works by Mozart *(Dies Bildnis ist [from Die Zauberflöte])*, Beethoven *(Gott! welch! Dunkel hier! [from Fidelio])*, Halévy *(Rachel guand du Signeur [from La Juive])*, Erkel *(O végre egy pár nyugodt pillanat; Mily boldogság, hogy mellettem vagy végre [w. Júlia Orosz (sop); both from Hunyadi László]; Lett volna vak e szem; Mint számüzött, ki vándorol [both from Bánk bán])*, Verdi *(La donna è mobile [from Rigoletto]; Ah! si bien, mio; Di quella pira [w. Hungarian State Opera Male Chorus; both from Il trovatore]; Se quel guerrier io fossil [from Aida]; Niun me tema [from Otello])*, Wagner *(Morgenlich leuchtend [from Die Meistersinger von Nürnberg])*, Puccini *(Recondita armonia [from Tosca]; Nessun dorma [from Turandot])* HUN (Great Hungarian Voices) ▲ 31726 [AAD] (16.97)

Simionato, Giulietta (mez), Giuseppe di Stefano (ten)

The Martini & Rossi Concerts, Vol. 15, w. Milan RAI Orch, Milan RAI Chorus [cnd:Nino Sanzogno]—features arias from Rossini *(L'Italiana in Algeri; Tancredi; Il barbiere di Siviglia; La Cenerentola)*, Verdi *(Un ballo in Maschera)*, Giordano *(Andrea Chénier)*, Puccini *(Turandot)* Maristella *(rec Nov 26, 1956)* INM ▲ 5015

Skovhus, Bo (bar)

Arias, w. English National Opera Orch [cnd:J. Conlon]—features B. Britten *(Billy Budd (sels) [Look! Through the port...And farewell to ye, old Rights o' Man!])*, Gounod *(Faust (sels) [Avant de quitter])*, Korngold *(Tote Stadt (sels) [Da Ihr befehlet, Königin ... Mein Sehnen, mein Wähnen])*, Massenet *(Werther (sels) [Pourquoi me réveiller?])*, P. Tchaikovsky *(Eugene Onegin (sels) [Vy mne pisali; Can this really be the same Tatiana? [Užel' ta samaja Tat'jana]; Queen of Spades (sels) [Vy tak pečal'ny, dorogaja ... Ja vas ljublju])*, A. Thomas *(Hamlet (sels) [Spectre infernal!; C'est en croyant revoir; O vin, dissipe la tristesse (Brindisi); J'ai pu frapper le misérable ... Être ou ne pas être; La fatigue alourdit mes pas; Come une pâle fleur])*, Verdi *(Don Carlos (sels) [C'est moi Carlos!])*, R. Wagner *(Tannhäuser (sels) [Blick' ich umher in diesem edlen Kreise; Wie Todesahnung Dämm'rung deckt die Lande...O du, mein holder Abendstern])* COL ▲ 60035 [DDD] (16.97)

Slezak, Leo (ten)

Lebendige Vergangenheit—features arias by Mozart, Boieldieu, Meyerbeer, Halevy, Gounod, Bizet, Delibes, Wagner, Verdi, Goldmark, Puccini *(rec 1905 & 1907)* PRE ▲ 89136 (16.97)

Leo Slezak, w. various pno accompanists—features works by Rossini, Verdi, Mascagni, Leoncavallo, Puccini, Giordano, Gounod, Massenet, Halévy, Meyerbeer, Mozart, Goldmark, Wagner, Grieg, Schumann, Schubert *(rec 1903-23)* PHS 2-▲ 9299 (33.97)

Leo Slézak Sings—features Disc One—13 Schubert lieder; 12 songs by Brahms, Schumann, Richard Strauss & Hugo Wolf; Disc Two—2 songs by Hildach & Loewe; 10 arias from La juive, Pagliacci, Othello, Lohengrin, Meistersinger, Tannhäuser [G] (piano accompaniment in songs by Heinrich Schacker and Michael Raucheisen; orchestral accompaniment in arias by Manfred Gurlitt, Berlin State Opera Orch.) *(rec 1928-29 for Grammophon)* PRE (Lebendige Vergangenheit) ▲ 89203 (m) [AAD] (16.97)

Opera Arias & Duets—features arias from La muette de Portici [Auber], Die Königin von Saba, Roméo et Juliette, La juive (w. bass Wilhelm Hesch), Les huguenots (w. soprano Elsa Bland), Le prophête, William Tell (w. baritone Leopold Demuth), Ballo in maschera, Ernani, Rigoletto, Trovatore, Lohengrin, Euryanthe (rec. 1905-08 from G & T 78 rpm discs) PRE (Lebendige Vergangenheit) ▲ 89020 (m) [AAD] (16.97)

Smirnov, Dmitri (ten)

Dmitri Smirnov—features arias from Les Huguenots, Les pêcheurs de perles, Carmen, Rigoletto, Il Tabarro, Russlan & Ludmilla, Russalka, E. Onengin, B. Godunov, Sorotschinsky Fair, Prince Igor, May Night, Sadko & Queen of Spades *(rec 1912-24)* PHS ▲ 9106 [ADD] (17.97)

Dmitri Smirnov—features arias & songs by Boïto, Gretchaninoff, Mascagni, Massenet, Puccini, Rachmaninoff, Rimsky-Korsakov, Rossini, Tchaikovsky, Verdi & Wagner PHS ▲ 9241 (17.97)

Il Mito dell'opera—features works by Rossini *(Se il mio nome [from Il barbiere di Siviglia])*, Donizetti *(Una furtiva lacrima [from L'elisir d'amore]; Spirito gentil [from La favorita])*, Verdi *(Questa o quella; La donna è mobile [both from Rigoletto]; De' mei bollento spiriti [from La traviata])*, Boito *(Giunto sul passo estremo [from Mefistofele])*, Mascagni *(Brindisi [from Cavalleria rusticana])*, Bizet *(Mi par d'udire ancor [from Les Pêcheurs de perles])*, Massenet *(Sogno; Ah dispar vision (2 versions) [all from Manon]; Pourquoi me réveiller [from Werther])*, Puccini *(Che gelida manina [from La Bohème]; E lucevan le stelle; Recondita armonia [both from Tosca])*, Tchaikovsky *(Lenski's Aria, Act II [from Eugene Onegin])*, Rimsky-Korsakov *(Canzione Indu [from Sadko])*, Rachmaninoff *(Lilla; Dietro la mia finestra)*, Freire *(Ay ay ay)* BONG ▲ 1144 [ADD] (16.97)

Söderström, Elisabeth (sop)

Örhängen, w. Håkan Sund (pno), Claas Pehrsson (rcr)—features 7 Scandinavian folksongs & 11 songs by Tauro, Davidson, Wennerberg, Norlén, Olrog, Söderlundh [Sw] *(rec June 15-18, 1981)* BIS ▲ 187 [AAD] (17.97)

Swedish Songs SWES ▲ 1017

Söderström, Elisabeth (sop), Kerstin Meyer (mez)

Elisabeth Söderström & Kerstin Meyer, w. Jan Eyron (pno)—features works by Kodály, Tchaikovsky, Dvořák, Purcell, Wennerberg, Geijer, Rossini *(rec Nov 1-3, 1974)* BIS ▲ 17 [AAD] (17.97)

Solari, Cristy (ten)

Cristy Solari—features works by Rossini *(Se il mio nome saper voi bramate [from Il Barbiere di Siviglia])*, Donizetti *(Quanto è bella; Una furtiva lacrima [both from L'elisir d'amore]; Di pescatore ignobile [from Lucrezia Borgia]; Tu che a Dio [from Lucia di Lammermoor]; Una vergine, un angiol di Dio; Spirito gentil; Pietoso al par del nume [all from La Favorita]; Se tanto in ira agli uomini [from Linda di Chamounix]; Sogno soave e casto; Cercherò lontana terra; Com'è gentil [all from Don Pasquale])*, Bellini *(A te o cara; Credeasi, misera! [both from I Puritani])*, Flotow *(M'apparì [from Marta])*, Verdi *(Quando le sere al placido [from Luisa Miller])*, Thomas *(Addio Mignon; Ah! non credevi tu [both from Mignon])*, Massenet *(Ah! non mi ridestar [from Werther])*, Losso/Valerio/Frati *(Fra mille donne tu)*, Barczi/Tibor/Marf *(Cosa ne hai fatto del mio cuore?)*, Hollaender/Zorro *(Dimmi ancora che mi vuoi bene)*, Bracchi/Stothart/Ward *(Provincialina)*, Galdieri/Derewitsky *(Fascino)* BONG ▲ 1090 [ADD] (16.97)

Sotkilava, Zurab (ten)

Russian Vocal School—features works by Y. Feldman *(Coachman, Don't Drive the Horses!)*, Potskhverashvili *(Indi-Mindi)*, Chubinishvili *(She Didn't Bestow a Kiss)*, Arakishvili *(I Will Look at You)*, Varlamov *(Snowstorm)* [all w. USSR State SO, All-Union Radio-TV Great Choir, D. Kitayenko (cnd)], Rachmaninoff *(Sing Not to Me, Beautiful Maiden; Spring Waters)*, Rimsky-Korsakov *(Sadko)*, Tchaikovsky *(Queen of Spades (sels))*, plus trad & folk songs *(Evening Chimes; Encircled by the Steppe; The Bell Thunders Monotonously; For You Alone)* [all w. All-Union Radio-TV Great SO, V. Fedoseyev (cnd)] RD (Talents of Russia) ▲ 16013 [ADD] (16.97)

Russian Vocal School: Zurab Sotkilava, Vol. 1, w. *(various orchs & cnds)*—features works by Tirindelli *(O, Spring)*, Tosti *(Charm; Serenade; April)*, Gastaldoni *(Forbidden Melody)*, Mario *(Distant Santa Lucia)*, Curtis *(I Love You So)*, Verdi *(Duet by Azucena & Manrico [from Il trovatore, w. I. Arkhipova (sop)]; Duet by Otello & Iago [w. O. Klenov (bass)]; Otello's Death Scene [both from Otello]; Rodrigo & Carlos' scene [from Don Carlos, w. V. Redkin])*, Mascagni *(Duet by Santuzza & Turiddu [w. T. Tatishvili]; Turiddu's Song [both from Cavalleria rusticana]) (rec 1983-90)* RD (Talents of Russia) ▲ RCD 16014 [ADD]

Russian Vocal School: Zurab Sotkilava, Vol. 2, w. USSR State Academic SO [cnd:O. Taktakishvili], Rustavi Male Vocal & Instrumental Ensemble—features works by Tchaikovsky *(Pimpinella; Crazy Nights)*, Rachmaninoff *(Dream)*, Bizet *(Jose's Aria [from Carmen])*, Paisiello *(Baron Calloandro's Aria [from La Molinara])*, Giordano *(Andrea's Improv [from Andrea Chénier])*, Verdi *(Otello's Death Scene [from Otello]; Manrico's Aria [from Il trovatore])*, Mario *(Distant Santa Lucia)*, Taktaishvili *(Mingrelian Songs (suite))*, plus trad Georgian folk song *(Sisatura) (rec Moscow Conservatory Great Hall, May 4, 1974)* RD (Talents of Russia) ▲ 16016 [ADD] (16.97)

Spani, Hina (sop)

Hina Spani—features arias by Rossini, Verdi, Wagner, Gounod, Massenet, Leoncavallo, Mascagni, Catalani & Puccini PHS ▲ 9196 (17.97)

Hina Spani *(1896-1969)*, w. La Scala Orch [cnd:Carlo Sabajno], double quintet [cnd:Gino Nastrucci]—features songs by Buchardo, Ugarte *(rec 1927-30 for HMV)* PRE (Lebendige Vergangenheit) ▲ 89037 (m) [AAD] (16.97)

Sperry, Paul (ten)

Paul Sperry Sings American Cycles & Sets, w. Irma Vallecillo-Gray (pno)—features works by R. Beaser, L. Gruenberg, L.A. Smith, R. Wilson, L. Talma, C. Berg ALBA ▲ 58 [DDD] (16.97)

Paul Sperry Sings an American Sampler: From Billings to Bolcom, w. Irma Vallecillo-Gray (pno)—features works by Talma, Wm. Schuman, Weisgall, Morten Lauridsen, Weill, Celius Dougherty, Ben Weber, Bolcom, J. Duke, Flanagan, Carter, Cowell, Musto, Beaser, Rorem, Barber, Griffes, Billings, Foster, Warren Swenson, Maury Yeston ALBA ▲ 81 [DDD] (16.97)

Paul Sperry Sings Romantic American Songs, w. Irma Vallecillo-Gray (pno)—features 37 American art songs by Paul Bowles, Theodore Chanler, Arthur Farwell, Richard Hundley, Virgil Thomson ALBA ▲ 43 [ADD] (16.97)

Songs of an Innocent Age, w. Irma Vallecillo-Gray (pno)—features works by Cadman, Loomis, Ayres, Paine, Sousa, Nevin, Martel, Clough-Leighter, Foote, Chadwick, Gilbert, Beach, Carpenter, McDowell, Griffes, Ives, Bond, Buck ALBA ▲ 34 [ADD]

Stade, Frederica von (mez)

Portrait of Frederica von Stade COL ▲ 39315 (16.97) 39315

Simple Gifts, w. Mormon Tabernacle Choir, Utah SO [cnd:Joseph Silverstein], John Longhurst (org)—features sacred & secular music by Bernstein, Canteloube, Copland, Gluck, Hall, Handel, Mendelssohn, Mozart, Puccini, Schubert, Vaughan Williams PLON ▲ 36284 [DDD] (16.97)

Songs of the Cat *("classically inspired tunes, specially tailored by Garrison Keillor for cats and those who adore them")*, w. Garrison Keillor (spkr) RCAV ▲ 61161 [DDD] ▮ 61161

Voyage à Paris, w. Martin Katz (pno)—features works by Poulenc *(La courte paille; Hotel; Voyage à Paris; C'est ainsi que tu es; Fêtes galantes; A sa guitare)*, Satie *(3 Mélodies)*, Debussy *(Ariettes oubliées; Fêtes galantes)*, Honegger *(Petit cours de morale)*, Ravel *(5 mélodies populaires grecques)*, Messiaen *(3 mélodies)* RCAV (Red Seal) ▲ 62711 (16.97)

Stark, Paulina (sop)

American-Jewish Art Songs, w. Nadine Shank (pno)—features works by L. Bernstein, Castelnuovo-Tedesco, Julius Chajes, Herbert Fromm, Miriam Gideon, Max Helfman, Richard Neumann, Robert Stern, Lazar Weiner CENT ▲ 2108 (16.97)

Stavad, Hanne (cta)

Vol 1: Contemporary Danish Song Composers DANR ▲ 438 (17.97)

Vol 2: A Recital of Music DANR ▲ 439 (17.97)

Steber, Eleanor (sop)

Eleanor Steber—features arias from Carmen, Louise, Faust, Roméo et Juliette, Abduction from the Seraglio, Magic Flute, Marriage of Figaro, Madama Butterfly, Ernani, Traviata; and two songs, by Bachelet and Duparc RCAV (Gold Seal) ▲ 60521 [ADD] 60521

The Eleanor Steber Collections, Vol. 1—features works by Debussy *(Air de Lia [from L'enfant prodigue])*, Flotow *(The Last Rose of Summer [from Martha])*, Bland *(Carry Me Back to Old Virginny)*, Verdi *(Ernani, involami [from Ernani]; Libiamo, ne'lieti calici; Ah, fors'è lui...Sempre libera; Parigi, o cara...Gran Dio! Morir sì giovine [all from La Traviata])*, Leoncavallo *(Decidi il mio destin [from I Pagliacci])*, Rossini *(Una voce poco fa [from Barbiere di Siviglia]; Inflammatus [from Stabat Mater])*, Thomas *(Je suis Titania [from Mignon])*, Massenet *(Il est doux, il est bon [from Hérodiade])*, Puccini *(Mi chiamano Mimì [from La Bohème]; Signore, ascolta! [from Turandot]; O mio babbino caro [from Gianni Schicchi])*, plus trad. *(Danny Boy) (rec 1938-51)* VAIA ▲ 1072 (16.97)

Eleanor Steber in Concert 1956-1958 *(complete Carnegie Hall concert of October 10, 1958, plus excerpts from a 1956 recital; piano accompaniment by Edwin Bitcliffe)*—features works by Barber *(Knoxville)*, Berlioz *(Nuits d'été)* arias from Puritani, Louise, Entführung aus dem Serail, Exsultate jubilate, Idomeneo, Madama Butterfly, Tosca, Frau ohne Schatten, Ernani Canteloube, Copland, Menotti, Schubert, Strauss, Wolf, et al. VAIA 2-▲ 1005 (m) [ADD] (31.97)

Her First Recordings, w. Armand Tokatyan (ten), Lucielle Browning (mez), Pino Bontempi (sgr), Annamary Dickey (sgr), George Cehanovsky (bar), Lorenzo Alvary ((bass), Arthur Kent (bar), Raoul Jobin (ten), Norman Cordon (bass)—features works by Puccini *(Madama Butterfly; La Bohème)*, Gounod *(Faust) (rec May 30-31, June 17 & 25-26, 1940)* VAIA ▲ 1023 (m) [ADD] (17.97)

Steber, Eleanor (sop), Milldred Miller (mez), John McCollum (ten), Donald Gramm (b-bar)

Love's Secrets & Other Songs By American Composers, w. Edwin Biltcliffe (pno), Richard Cumming (pno)—features works by Diamond *(David Mourns for Absalom; Brigid's Song [both w. Mildred Miller & Edwin Biltcliffe])*, Persichetti *(Sonatina to Hans Christian [w. Mildred Miller & Edwin Biltcliffe])*, Luening *(The Divine Image; Love's Secret [both w. Mildred Miller, Edwin Biltcliffe])*, Fine *(Polaroli; The Frog & the Snake [both w. Mildred Miller & Edwin Biltcliffe])*, Flanagan *(Valentine to Sherwood Anderson; Send Home My Long Strayed Eyes [both w. Mildred Miller & Edwin Biltcliffe])*, Rorem *(Bedlam [w. Mildred Miller & Edwin Bilcliffe]; Alleluia [w. Eleanor Steber & Edwin Biltcliffe])*, Ives *(General William Booth Enters Heaven [w. Donald Gramm & Richard Cumming])*, Moore *(Come Away Death [w. Donald Gramm & Richard Cumming]; Death Be Not Proud [w. Eleanor Steber & Edwin Biltcliffe])*, Beeson *(Clavanistic Evensong [w. Donald Gramm & Richard Cumming])*, Bowles *(Blue Mountain Ballads [w. Donald Gramm & Richard Cumming])*, Edmunds *(The Drummer; The Faucon [both w. Donald Gramm & Richard Cumming])*, Carpenter *(Looking Glass River; Jazz Boys [both w. Donald Gramm & Richard Cumming])*, Bacon *(Songs (4) from Emily Dickinson It's All I Have To Bring; So Bashful; To Make a Prairie; And This of All My Hopes [w. Eleanor Steber & Edwin Biltcliffe])*, Barber *(Nuvoletta [w. Eleanor Steber & Edwin Biltcliffe])*, Bergsma *(Lullee, Lullay [w. Eleanor Steber & Edwin Biltcliffe])*, Griffes *(Waikiki [w. Eleanor Steber & Edwin Biltcliffe])*, La Montaine *(Stopping by Woods on a Snowy Evening [w. Eleanor Steber & Edwin Biltcliffe])*, Thomson *(The Tiger [w. Eleanor Steber & Edwin Biltcliffe])*, MacDowell *(The Sea [w. John McCollum & Edwin Biltcliffe])*, Chanler *(The Rose; I Rise When You Enter [both w. John McCollum & Edwin Biltcliffe])*, Copland *(Dirge in the Woods [w. John McCollum & Edwin Biltcliffe])*, Ward *(Sorrow of Mydath [w. John McCollum & Edwin Biltcliffe])*, Gruen *(3 by e. e. cummings [w. John McCollum & Edwin Biltcliffe])*, Pinkham *(Slow, Slow, Fresh Fount [w. John McCollum & Edwin Biltcliffe])*, Weber *(Mourn! Mourn! [w. John McCollum & Edwin Biltcliffe])*, Cowell *(The Donkey [w. John McCollum & Edwin Biltcliffe])* VB2 (The American Composers) 2-▲ 5129

Stefano, Giuseppe di (ten)

Chicago 1950 *(10 solo arias & 8 duets)*, w. Bidù Sayão (sop), Renata Tebaldi (sop), Chicago Radio Orch [cnd:Gaetano Merola]—features selections from Lucia di Lammermoor *(3 duets with Sayão)*, Martha, Faust, Le Cid, Gioconda, Bohème *(solo aria and one duet with Sayão)*, Madama Butterfly *(4 duets with Tebaldi)*, Tosca, Rigoletto; plus 4 duets with Mafalda Favero from Manon *(w. Antonio Guarnieri, La Scala Orch., rec. live 3/15/47, Milan)* MYTO ▲ 92467 [ADD] (17.97)

Stefano, Giuseppe di (ten) (cont.)

Giuseppe di Stefano: The Early Years—features works by Cilea *(E' la solita storia del pastore [from L'Arlesiana])*, Mascagni *(Ed anche Beppe amò [from L'amico fritz])*, Puccini *(E lucevan le stelle [from Tosca]; Che gelida manina [from La Bohème]; Hai ben ragione; Perché, gli hai chiesto...Vorrei tenerti [both from Il Tabarro])*, Donizetti *(Una furtiva lacrima; Voglio dire...lo stupendo elisir; La rà, la rà, la lera; Adina, credimi; Venti scudi [all from L'eslisir d'amore])*, Massenet *(Sogno [from Manon]; Pourquoi me réveiller [from Werther]; Elegie)*, Bizet *(Mi par d'udir ancora [from I pescatori di perle])*, Denza *(Si vous l'avez compris)*, Bixio *(Ninna nanna della vita)*, Cottrau *(Santa Lucia)*, Gastaldon *(Musica proibita)*, Mario *(Santa Lucia Luntana)*, De Curtis *(Torna a surriento)* BONG ▲ 1141 [ADD] (16.97)

Grandi Voci: Giuseppe di Stefano *(performs arias from French and Italian operas)*—features works by Giordano, Puccini, Massanet, Bizet, Gounod, Donizetti, Ponchielli, Verdi & Boito *(rec 1955-59)* PLON ▲ 40403 [ADD] (11.97)

Italian Songs PLON ▲ 17794 (11.97)

Liederabend, w. Rudolf Bibl (pno)—features songs by Bellini, Verdi, Fauré, Bizet, Berlioz, Favara, Tosti, Curtis & Cardillo *(rec Vienna, June 22, 1968)* KSCH ▲ 318332 (16.97)

Neapolitan Songs, w. G. M. Guarino (cnd) EMIC ▲ 47838 (16.97)

Neapolitan Songs, Vol. 1—features O sole mio; Marechiare; Dicitencello vuje; Tu, ca nun chiagne!; I'te vurria vasa!; Core'ngrato; Torna a Surriento; Silenzio cantatore; Chiove; O paese d'o sole; Santa Lucia luntana; Maria, Mari'!; E pallume; Fenesta che lucive; 'Na sera 'e maggio; Voc'e notte!; Auntunno; Santa Lucia; Senza nisciuno; Piscatore e pusilecco; O Marianiello *(rec 1953 & 1957)* TES ▲ 1097 (m) (17.97)

Neapolitan Songs, Vol. 2—features Funiculà, funiculì; Luna nova; Mamma mia, che vo' sape?; Torna!; Carmela; Guapparia; Mandulinata a Napule; I' m'arricordo 'e Napule; Pecchè?; Anima 'e core; Me so'mbriacato 'e sole; Vurria; Lolita; Ideale; L'ultiima canzone; Aprile; Luna d'este; La Serenata; Mattinata; Non t'amo più; Maila; Chanson de l'adieu; 'A Vucchella; Musica Probita *(rec 1960)* TES ▲ 1098 (17.97)

1944: His 1st Recordings—features arias from L'Arlesiana, L'amico fritz, Tosca, La Bohème, L'elisir d'amore, Manon, I Pescatori di Perle, Werther; plus songs by Massenet, Denza, Bixio-Cherubini, Cottrau, Gastaldon, Mario, De Curtis GRM2 ▲ 78635 (13.97)

Il Nostro Concerto—features Il Cielo in una Stanza; Il Mondo; Concerto d'Autunno; Io Che Amo Solo Te; Noi; Amore Scusami; plus others REPL ▲ 8007 (13.97)

O sole mio *(12 Neapolitan songs)* REPL ▲ 4038

Torna a Surriento: Italian Songs PLON (Jubilee) ▲ 17794 [ADD] (11.97)

Various Albums with Maria Callas *(see above under "Callas, Maria & Giuseppe Di Stefano")*

Voce 'e notte *(12 Neapolitan songs)* REPL ▲ 4032

The Young Giuseppe Di Stefano *(rec Lausanne, London & New York, 1944-56)* TES ▲ 1096 (17.97)

Stella, Antonietta (sop), Fiorenza Cossotto (mez), Mario del Monaco (ten)

The Martini & Rossi Concerts, Vol. 31 INM ▲ 5031 (16.97)

Stewart, Thomas (bar)

Songs of Gambling & the Sea—features works by Dougherty *(Sea Chanties)*, Niles *(Gambler Songs)*, Barber *(Dover Beach; [plus works by Ives, Foster, Moore, Copland, Giannini & others])* *(rec 1959-78)* VAIA ▲ 1122 [ADD] (16.97)

Stich-Randall, Teresa (sop)

Teresa Stich-Randall, w. Hans Rosbaud (pno)—features works by Mozart, Schubert, Brahms, R. Strauss, Debussy, Schumann *(rec July 31, 1956)* MEMV ▲ 262008 (m) [ADD]

Stich-Randall, Teresa (sop), Sesto Bruscantini (b-bar)

The Martini & Rossi Concerts, Vol. 27, w. Turin RAI SO [cnd:Mario Rossi]—features arias from Cimarosa *(Les Astuzie femminili)*, Mozart *(Il ratto dal Serraglio; Le nozze de Figaro; Così fan tutte; Don Giovanni)*, Rossini *(Il barbiere di Siviglia)*, Verdi *(Ernani)* INM ▲ 5027 [ADD] (16.97)

Stignani, Ebe (mez)

Ebe Stignani—features arias from Serse; Norma; Alceste; Orfeo ed Euridice; Semiramide; Il trovatore; Don Carlo; Samson et Dalila CECL (Classic Collection) ▲ 115 [ADD]

Opera Arias *(from Cetra 78 rpm discs)*, w. Turin EIAR SO—features arias from Norma, La favorita, Linda di Chamounix, Alceste [Gluck], Orfeo ed Euridice [Gluck], L'amico Fritz, Mignon, Semiramide, Samson et Delila, Ballo in maschera, Don Carlos, Forza del destino, Trovatore *(rec 1937-41)* PRE (Lebendige Vergangenheit) ▲ 89014 (m) [AAD] (16.97)

Stignani, Ebe (mez), Magda Olivero (sop), Salvatore Gioia (ten), Giuseppe di Stefano (ten)

The Martini & Rossi Concerts, Vol. 24, w. Milan RAI SO [cnd:Ferruccio Scaglia]—features works by Verdi *(Un giorno dolce nel core; Più che i vezzi e lo splendore [both from Oberto, Conte di San Bonifacio])*, Puccini *(Nessun dorma [from Turandot]; In quelle trine morbide [from Manon Lescaut])*, Saint-Saëns *(S'apre per te il mio cor [from Samson et Dalila])*, Donizetti *(Ah, mio ben [from La favorita]; Una furtiva lacrima [from L'elisir d'amore])*, Massenet *(En fermant les yeux [from Manon])*, Catalani *(Ebben ne andrò lontana [from La Wally])*, Cilea *(È la solita storia del pastore [from L'Arlesiana])* *(rec 1952 & 1958)* INM ▲ 5024 [ADD] (16.97)

Stignani, Ebe (mez), Nicola Rossi-Lemeni (bass)

The Martini & Rossi Concerts, Vol. 13, w. Milan RAI SO [cnd:Angelo Questa]—features selections from Verdi *(Nabucco; Ernani; Il trovatore)*, Gluck *(Orfeo ed Euridice)*, Mozart *(Le nozze di Figaro)*, Cilea *(Adriana Lecouvreur)*, Monleone *(Cavalleria Rusticana)*, others *(rec Jan 31, 1955)* INM ▲ 5013 (16.97)

Stoffel, David (b-bar)

Songs with a Touch of Bass, w. Milton Masciadri (db), Ivan Frazier (pno)—features music by Tchaikovsky *(None but the Lonely Heart; Pilgrim's Song)*, Lully *(Air de Caron)*, Barber *(Sure on This Shining Night)*, Mozart *(Per questa bella mano)*, Durante *(Danza, Danza, Fanciulla Gentile)*, Falconieri *(O Bellissimi Capelli)*, Tosti *(La Serenata)*, Foster *(Beautiful Dreamer; I Dream of Jeannie with the Light Brown Hair [both arr Sid Haton])*, Vogel *(Of Celebration)*, Lehmann *(As Then the Tulip)*, Head *(Money, Oh! [arr Sid Haton])*, plus trad songs *(Shenandoah [arr Sid Haton]; Deep River; Simple Gifts [both arr Copland/Hulsberg]; Danny Boy [arr Sid Haton])* *(rec Central Presbyterian Church, Athens, GA 1995)* ACAD ▲ 20030 (16.97)

Storojev, Nikita (bass)

Kalinka: Popular Russian Songs, w. David Ashkenazy (pno)—features Coachman, Do Not Speed; Strains of a Waltz; My Love Lies in a Tower; The Street; Two Guitars; I Dreamt of a Garden in Bridal Attire; Song of the Peddler; Bright is the Night; Kalinka; I Met You; Down the Peterskaya Road; I Loved You; Dark Eyes; Shine On, shine On, O Star of Mine; Song of the Coachman; Song of the Volga Boatmen; Down the Long Road; Listen to Me; No, It's Not You; Evening Bells [R; all arr D. Ashkenazy for bass & pno] CHN (Enchant) ▲ 7067 (13.97)

Stracciari, Riccardo (bar)

Great Operatic Recordings, Vol. 1—features arias from works by Mozart *(Don Giovanni)*, Rossini *(Il barbiere di Siviglia)*, Meyerbeer *(Dinorah)*, Donizetti *(La favorita; Lucia di Lammermoor)*, Verdi *(Nabucco; Ernani; Rigoletto; La traviata; Il trovatore; La forza del destino; Otello)*, Wagner *(Tannhäuser)*, Leoncavallo *(Pagliacci)*, Catalani *(La Wally)*, Puccini *(Tosca)*, Giordano *(Andrea Chénier)* *(rec 1917-28)* VOCA (Vocal Archives) ▲ 23600 (13.97)

Portrait of a Baritone—features Berlioz *(Damnation de Faust (sels))*, Gounod *(Faust (sels))*, Leoncavallo *(Zazà (sels))*, Massenet *(Roi de Lahore (sels))*, Meyerbeer *(Africaine (sels))*, G. Puccini *(Tosca (sels))*, G. Rossini *(Barbiere di Siviglia (sels))*, A. Thomas *(Hamlet (sels))*, Verdi *(Ballo in maschera (sels); Nabucco (sels); Otello (sels); Rigoletto (sels))* GRM2 ▲ 78927 (11.97)

Recital: 5 Arias & 5 Songs—features arias from La Wally, L'Africaine, Zaza, Nabucco, plus Aprile; Agnus Dei; Ideale; Nina; Occhi di Fata † Rossini:Barbiere di Siviglia (complete opera) MMO 2-▲ 30276/77

Riccardo Stracciari—features works by Gounod, Verdi, Rossini, Giordano, Mascagni, Donizetti, Berlioz, Meyerbeer, De Curtis *(rec 1917-28)* PHS ▲ 9178 [ADD] (17.97)

Riccardo Stracciari *(1875-1955) (Columbia recordings)*—features arias from Damnation de Faust, Lucia di Lammermoor, Pagliacci, Il re di Lahore [Massenet], L'Africana, Dinorah, Gioconda, Tosca, Barbiere di Siviglia, Nabucco, Otello, Tannhäuser plus one song by Di Capua *(O sole mio)* *(rec 1925)* PRE (Lebendige Vergangenheit) ▲ 89003 (m) [AAD] (16.97)

Streich, Rita (sop)

Waltzes & Arias, w. Berlin RSO [cnd:Kurt Gaebel], Berlin RIAS SO [cnd:Kurt Gaebel]—features works by Alabiev *(Die Nachtigall)*, Arditi *(Il bacio; Parla-Walzer)*, Czernik *(Chi sa?)*, Delibes *(Les Filles de Cadix)*, Dell'Acqua *(Villanelle)*, Dvořák *(Lied an den Mond [from Rusalka])*, Flotow *(Last Rose of Summer)*, Godard *(Wiegenlied [from Jocelyn])*, Marchesi *(La folletta)*, Meyerbeer *(Schattentanz [from Dinorah])*, Saint-Saëns *(Le Rossignol et la rose)*, Joh. Strauss (II) *(Draussen in Sievering; Frühlingsstimmen, Op. 410)*, Josef Strauss *(Dorfschwalben aus Österreich, Op. 164)*, Suppé *(Ha' ich nur deine Liebe [from Boccaccio])*, Verdi *(Lo spazzacamino)* *(rec Jesus-Christus Church, Berlin, Feb 1955 & May 1958)* DEUT (The Originals) ▲ 457729 [ADD] (11.97)

Strienz, Wilhelm (bass)

Wilhelm Strienz—features selections from Mozart *(Die Zauberflöte; Die Entführung aus dem Serail)*, Lortzing *(Der Wildshütz; Der Waffenschmied)*, Flotow *(Martha)*, Cornelius *(Der Barbier von Bagdad)*, Smetana *(The Bartered Bride)*, Verdi *(I Vespri Siciliani; Simon Boccanegra; Don Carlos)*, Tchaikovsky *(Eugen Onegin)*, Mussorgsky *(Boris Godunov)* *(rec 1935-40)* PRE (Lebendige Vergangenheit) ▲ 89089 [AAD] (16.97)

Stutzmann, Nathalie (cta)

Pergolesi, w. Elizabeth Norberg-Schulz (sop), Hanover Band, Roy Goodman (org)—features Stabat Mater & Salve Regina RCAV (Red Seal) ▲ 61215

Šubrtová, Milada (sop)

Operatic Recital, w. Prague National Theater Orch [cnd:Z. Chalabala], Prague Opera Orchestra [cnd:L. Šíp], Prague RSO [cnd:F. Dyk], Prague Smetana Theatre Orchestra [cnd:J. Tichý], I. Mixová (mez), I. Žídek (ten), B. Blachut (ten)—features Blodek *(In the Well)*, G. Charpentier *(Louise (sels))*, A. Dvořák *(Rusalka (sels))*, J. B. Foerster *(Eva (sels), Op. 50)*, W. A. Mozart *(Don Giovanni (sels))*, J. Offenbach *(Contes d'Hoffmann (sels))*, Ryba *(O Lovely Nightengale)*, Smetana *(Devil's Wall; Libuše (sels))*, P. Tchaikovsky *(Queen of Spades (sels))*, Verdi *(Ballo in maschera (sels); Traviata (sels))* SUR ▲ 3409 [AAD/ADD] (10.97)

Suddaby, Elsie (sop)

The Lass with the Delicate Air, Vol. 2, w. Madame Adami (pno), Gerald Moore (pno), Reginald Paul (pno), John Barbirolli (cnd), Thomas Beecham (cnd), Lawrence Collingwood (cnd), Malcolm Sargent (cnd) *(various orchs)*—features works by Bach, Handel, Purcell, Schubert, Beethoven, plus others *(rec 1924-49)* AMPH ▲ 140 (16.97)

Supervia, Conchita (mez)

Conchita Supervia *(1895-1936)*, w. Angelo Albergoni (cnd)—features arias, duets & ensembles from Carmen, Hansel und Gretel, Nozze di Figaro, Barbiere di Sivigla, La Cenerentola, Samson et Dalila, Rosenkavalier *(rec 1927-28)* PRE (Lebendige Vergangenheit) ▲ 89023 (m) [AAD] (16.97)

Conchita Supervia, Vol. 1—features works by Pergolesi or V. Ciampi, Paisiello, Delibes, Lehár, Joaquín Valverde, Albeníz, Granados, Falla, Turina, Nin, Osman Perez-Freire *(rec 1930-32)* PHS ▲ 9975 [ADD] (18.97)

Opera & Zarzuela—features arias from works by Mozart *(Le nozze di Figaro)*, Rossini *(Il barbiere di Siviglia; La Cenerentola)*, Bizet *(Carmen)*, Saint-Saëns *(Samson et Dalila)*, plus songs from Las Hijas del Zebedeo; El Huésped del Sevillano; Flor de España; El Mal de Amores and others *(rec 1927-32)* VOCA (Vocal Archives) ▲ 1164 (13.97)

Supervia in Opera & Song *(Odeon recordings)*—features excerpts from Carmen (G. Micheletti [Don José], A. Vavon [Mercédès], A. Bernadet [Frasquita], G. Cloëz, Orchestra); La Algería del Batallón; Faust; El Mal de Amores; Barbiere di Siviglia; Cenerentola; Italiana in Algeri; Samson et Dalila; Mignon plus songs by Falla *(Canciones populares españolas—w. Frank Marshall, piano; rec. 1930)*, Delibes, Baldomir, de Yradier, Joaquin Valverde *(rec 1927-32)* NIMB (Prima Voce) 2-▲ 7836 [ADD] (13.97)

The Unknown Supervia *(rare operatic excerpts, plus rare and little-known songs in Catalan, Spanish, French and Italian)*—features areas from Damnation de Faust, Faust, Werther, Mignon and 21 songs *(rec 1929-34)* PHS ▲ 9969 (m) [AAD] (17.97)

Sutherland, Joan (sop)

The Age of Bel Canto, w. London PO, London SO [cnd:Richard Bonynge]—features works by Bellini, Bononcini, Donizetti, Handel, Mozart, Rossini, Verdi, Weber, et al. PLON (Opera Gala) ▲ 21881 [ADD]

The Art of the Prima Donna PLON 2-▲ 25493 [ADD] (22.97)

The Art of the Prima Donna, w. Royal Opera House Orch [cnd:Francesco Molinari-Pradelli], Royal Opera House Chorus PLON (The Classic Sound) ▲ 452298 (22.97)

BBC Recitals, w. Richard Bonynge (pno) *(rec 1958-61)* BELV ▲ 7005 (14.97)

Coloratura Spectacular—features arias from Attila, La fille du régiment, Magic Flute, I puritani, La sonnambula, etc. PPHI ▲ 17814 [ADD]

Grandi Voci: Joan Sutherland—features works by Bellini *(Norma:Sediziose voci; Casta diva; Ah! Bello e me ritorna; I puritani:Chi la voce sua soave; Vien, diletto)*, Verdi *(Atila:Santo di patria; Alloe che i forti corrono; Da te questo or m'e concesso; Ernani:Surta e la notte; Ernani, Ernani,involami; I vespri siciliani:Merce, dilette amiche)*, Donizetti *(Lucia di Lammermoor:Il dolce suono mi colpi di sua voce!; Ancor non giunse!; Regnava nel silenzio; Linda di Chamounix:Ah! non tradai troppo; O luce di quest'anima)* *(rec 1959-60)* PLON ▲ 40404 [ADD]

Greatest Hits—features arias from Faust, Lakmé, Lucia, Norma, etc. PLON (Jubilee) ▲ 17780 [ADD] (11.97)

The Greatest Hits PLON (Opera Gala) ▲ 458209 (11.97)

Home Sweet Home, w. Richard Bonynge (cnd), New Philharmonia Orch, Ambrosian Light Opera Chorus PLON ▲ 25048 [ADD]

Operetta Gala, w. Richard Bonynge (cnd), New Philharmonia Orch, Swiss Romande Orch, Ambrosian Light Opera Chorus—features arias by Lehár, Offenbach, Strauss, et al. PLON (Opera Gala) ▲ 21880 [ADD]

Romantic French Arias, w. Richard Bonynge (cnd), Swiss Romande Orch, Geneva Grand Théâter Chorus—features arias by Bizet, Charpentier, Gounod, Meyerbeer, Offenbach, et al. PLON (Opera Gala) ▲ 21879 [ADD]

Verdi, Bellini, & Donizetti Arias PLON ▲ 21305 [ADD]

Sutherland, Joan (sop), Marilyn Horne (mez), Luciano Pavarotti (ten)

Live from Lincoln Center PLON 2-▲ 17587 [DDD] (16.97)

Sutherland, Joan (sop), Luciano Pavarotti (ten)

Operatic Duets—features sels from Traviata, Sonnambula, Linda di Chamounix, Otello, Aida PPHI ▲ 58 58

Operatic Duets—features sels from Elisir d'amore, Fille du régiment, Maria Stuarda, Puritani, Rigoletto, etc. PPHI (Opera Gala) ▲ 21894 [ADD]

Sved, Alexander (bar)

Il Mito Dell'Opera—features works by Verdi *(Pari siamo; Figlia...mio padre; Deh non parlare al misero; Veglia, o donna, questo fiore; Cortigiani, vil razza dannata; Ah! solo per me l'infamia; Si, vendetta; Chi e mai, chi e qui in sua vece [all from* Rigoletto*]; Quest'assisa [from* Aida*]; Alla vita [from* Un ballo in maschero*]; Era la notte [from* Otello*])*, Rossini *(Resta immobilie [from* Guillaume Tell*])*, Puccini *(Tre schirri, una carrozza; Tarda e la notte; La povera mia cena [all from* Tosca*])*, Wagner *(O du, mein holder [from* Tannhäuser*])*, Gounod *(Avant de quitter [from* Faust*])* BONG ▲ 1081 (16.97)

Swenson, Ruth Ann (sop)

I Carry Your Heart, w. Warren Jones (pno), Charles Neidich (cl)—features works by Cavalli *(Speranze; Vaghe stelle)*, Bellini *(Vaga luna; Almen se non poss'io)*, Rossini *(L'invito; La promessa)*, Verdi *(La seduzione; Stornello)*, Schubert *(Der Hirt auf dem Felsen)*, Hahn *(Si mes vers avaient des ailes; L'heure exquise)*, Obradors *(Con amores, la mi madre; Del cabello más sutil)*, Bachelet *(Chère nuit)*, Duke *(Little Elegy; Aubade; The Bird; I Carry Your Heart)* EMIC ▲ 56158 (16.97)

Sykes, Jubilant (bar)

Jubilant, w. Wesley Holland (sgr), Gary Murphy (sgr), Terence Blanchard (tpt), David McKelvy (hmc), David Low (vc), Don Vappie (gtr), Reginald Veal (elec bass), Troy Davis (dr), Mulgrew Miller (pno)—features works by Rufus *(Mary, Did You Know?)*, Knapp *(Blessed Assurance)*, plus trad spirituals *(Fix Me, Jesus; Go Down, Moses; They Led My Lord Away; If I Got My Ticket; Deep River; How I Got Over; A City Called Heaven; Let Us Break Bread Together; At the Cross; Give Me Jesus; Live a-Humble; Were You There? [all arr Terence Blanchard])* *(rec Los Angeles, May 26-30, 1997)* COL ▲ 63294 (16.97) 63294 (10.98)

Székely, Mihály (bass)

Great Hungarian Voices: Mihály Székely—features works by Mozart *(Wer ein Liebchen hat gefunden; Ha! Wie will ich triumphieren [both from Entführung aus dem Serail]; Madamina, il catologo à questo; O statua gentilissima [both from Don Giovanni]; O Isis und Osiris; In diesen heil'gen Hallen [both from Die Zauberflöte])*, Rossini *(La calunnia [from Barbiere di Siviglia])*, Verdi *(Il lacerato spirito [from Simon Boccanegra]; Ella giammai m'amò; Il Grand Inquisitor [both from Don Carlo])*, Tchaikovsky *(Lyubvi vse vozrasti pokorni [from Eugene Onegin])*, Borodin *(Darogi Knyaz [from Prince Igor])*, Mussorgsky *(Dostig ya vishey vlasti [from Boris Godunov])*, R. Strauss *(Da lieg' ich! Was einem Kavalier [from Der Rosenkavalier])* [G, Hun] *(rec 1953-62)* HUN ▲ 31615 [AAD] (16.97)

Taccani, Giuseppe (ten)

Giuseppe Taccani (1885-1959)—features works by Donizetti *(Hai tradito il cielo [from Lucia di Lammermoor])*, Verdi *(Ah! si, bien mio; Deserto sulla terra; Di quella pira [all from Il trovatore]; Le minacie, i ieri accenti [from La forza del destino]; Questa o quella; Ella mi fu rapita; La donna è mobile [all from Rigoletto])*, Bizet *(Il fior che avevi a me tu dato; Sei tu? Son io! [both from Carmen])*, Puccini *(Donna non vidi mai; Ah! Manon mi tradisce; Guardate pazzo son [all from Manon Lescaut])*, Ponchielli *(Cielo e mar [from La Gioconda])*, Giordano *(Un di all'azzurro spazio [from Andrea Chenier])*, Mascagni *(Quando fanciulla ancora; Ombra secreta [both from Gugliemo Ratcliff]; S'è spento il Sol [from Silvano])*, Leoncavallo *(Vesti la giubba [from Pagliacci])*, Franchetti *(Studenti, udite [from Germania])* [I] *(rec 1909-28)* PRE (Lebendige Vergangenheit) ▲ 89173 (m) [AAD]

Taddei, Giuseppe (bar)

Arias & Duets (1974-1986), w. P. Domingo (ten), L. Pavarotti (ten), et al., Vienna State Opera Orch [var. cnd]—features sels. from L'Elisir d'amore, Nozze di Figaro, Tosca, Cenerentola, Luisa Miller, Otello, Traviata [I] Acanta ▲ 49402

Giuseppe Taddei, w. Arturo Basile (cnd), Fernando Previtali (cnd), Angelo Questa (cnd), RAI SO—features selections from Meyerbeer *(L'Africaine)*, Giordano *(Andrea Chenier)*, Mozart *(Don Giovanni; Le nozze di Figaro)*, Massenet *(Hérodiade)*, Verdi *(Falstaff; Otello; Rigoletto)*, Puccini *(La fanciulla del west)*, Rossini *(Il barbiere di Siviglia)* Guglielmo Tell *(rec 1955)* FONI (Classic Collection) ▲ 109

Sings Arias & Neapolitan Songs, w. various orchs—features 8 arias from Puritani, L'Arlesiana, Adriana Lecouvreur, Favorita, Andrea Chénier, Ballo in maschera, Don Carlos, Vespri siciliani; and 10 Neapolitan songs [I] PRE ▲ 90020 (m) [AAD] (16.97)

Tagliabue, Carlo (bar)

Carlo Tagliabue, w. Margherita Carosio (sop), Rosetta Noli (sop), Galliano Masini (ten), Orch of the Opera Italiana [cnd:Umberto Berrettoni], Orch Sinfonica dell'EIAR [cnd:Ugo Tansini, Gino Marinuzzi], Royal Opera House Orch, Covent Garden [cnd:Franco Patanè]—features works by Donizetti *(Appressati Lucia [from Lucia di Lammermoor])*, Rossini *(Dunque io son [from Il barbiere di Siviglia])*, Verdi *(Il balen del suo sorriso [from Il trovatore]; Pari siamo; Corigiani vil razza dannata; Ah! solo per me l'infamia [all from Rigoletto]; Pura siccome un angelo; Di Provenza il mar [both from La traviata]; Al tradimento; Fratello...Don Carlo voi vivente [both from La forza del destino])*, Gounod *(Dio possente, Dio d'amor [from Faust])*, Ponchielli *(Pescator, affonda l'esca [from La Gioconda])* *(rec 1939-50)* PRE (Lebendige Vergangenheit) ▲ 89139 (16.97)

Tagliabue, Carlo (bar) (cont.)

Carlo Tagliabue *(11 arias & 2 songs)*, w. Margherita Carosio (sop), Ettore Bergamaschi (ten), Zinka Milanov (sop), Bruna Castagna (mez), Frederick Jagel (ten), Norman Cordon (bass), Renata Tebaldi (sop), Alfredo Colella (bass) *(rec in studio and live, 1928-51)* BONG ▲ 1070 [ADD] (16.97)

Carlo Tagliabue: Opera Arias *(1898-1978) (historic recordings)*—features arias from Puritani, Barber of Seville, Ballo in maschera, Ernani, Otello, Rigoletto, Trovatore, Tannhauser, etc. PRE (Lebendige Vergangenheit) ▲ 89015 (m) [AAD] (16.97)

Great Voices: Carlo Tagliabue—features arias by Bellini, Bizet, Donizetti, Gounod, Leoncavallo, Ponchielli, Rossini & Verdi PHG ▲ 5069 (14.97)

Tagliavini, Ferruccio (ten)

Ferruccio Tagliavini Edition, Vol. 1—features arias by Rossini, Bellini, Verdi, Flotow, Massenet, Puccini, Mascagni, Cilea *(rec 1941-55)* FONI ▲ 143

Ferruccio Tagliavini (1913-1995), w. Italian Radio Orch [cnd:Ugo Tansini], RCA Victor Orch [cnd:Antál Dorati, Jean Paul Morel]—features works by Rossini *(Ecco ridente in cielo [from Il barbiere di Siviglia])*, Bellini *(Prendi l'anel ti dono [from La sonnambula])*, Donizetti *(Una furtiva lagrima [from L'elisir d'amore])*, Verdi *(Ella mi fu rapita [from Rigoletto]; La mia letizia infondere [from I Lombardi]; Dal labbro il canto [from Falstaff])*, Thomas *(Addio Mignon! [from Mignon])*, Meyerbeer *(Mi batte il cor [from L'Africana])*, Massenet *(En ferment les yeux [from Manon]; Pourquoi me réveiller? [from Werther])*, Mascagni *(Suzel, buon di; Ed anche Beppe amò [both from L'Amico Fritz])*, Puccini *(Che gelida manina; Addio dolce svegliare [both from La Bohème]; E lucevan le stelle; Recondita armonia; O dolci mani [all from Tosca])*, Cilea *(E la storita storia [from L'Arlesiana])*, Wolf-Ferrari *(Lucieta ce un bel nome [from I quattro resteghi])* [I] *(rec 1940-47)* PRE (Lebendige Vergangenheit) ▲ 89163 (m) [AAD] (16.97)

The Cetra Recordings, 1940-43—features works by Donizetti *(Una Furtiva Lagrima [from L'elisir d'amore])*, Bellini *(Prendi, l'Anel Ti Dono [from La Sonnambula])*, Thomas *(Addio Mignon [from Mignon])*, Verdi *(Parmi Veder le Lacrime [from Rigoletto]; Dal Labbro il Canto [from Falstaff])*, Massenet *(Chiudo gli Occhi [from Manon])*, Puccini *(Che Gelida Manina & Dunque è Proprio Finita [from La Bohème]; Recondita Armonia & e Lucevan le Stelle [from Tosca])*, Cilea *(E' la Solita Storia del Pastore [from L'Arlesiana])*, Wolf-Ferrari *(Lucieta è un Bel Nome [from I Quattro Rusteghi])*, Mascagni *(Suzel, Buon Di [L'amico fritz])* VOCA (Vocal Archives) ▲ 1131 (13.97)

The Early Operatic Recordings 1940-43, w. EIAR Orch [cnd:Ugo Tansini] CENT ▲ 2164 (16.97)

Ferruccio Tagliavini—features arias from Rigoletto; Un ballo in maschera; Il barbiere di Siviglia; La sonnambula; Martha; Mefistofele; L'amico Fritz; Werther; La Bohème; Tosca; Madama Butterfly; L'arlesiana CECL (Italia) ▲ 105

Ferruccio Tagliavini in Opera, w. Turin EIAR SO [cnd:Ugo Tansini]—features works by Mascagni *(Suzel, buon di; Ed anché Beppe amo..O amore [both from L'Amico Fritz])*, Cilea *(E la solita storia [from L'Arlesiana])*, Verdi *(Ella mi fu rapita [from Rigoletto]; Dal labbro il canto [from Falstaff]; La mia letzia infondere [from I Lombardi])*, Rossini *(Ecco ridente in cielo [from Il barbiere di Siviglia])*, Donizetti *(Una furtiva lagrima [from L'Elisir d'amore])*, Bellini *(Prendi, l'anel ti dono [from La Sonnambula])*, Puccini *(Che gelida manina; Dunque proprio finita [both from La Bohème]; Recondita armonia; E lucevan le stelle; O dolci mani [all from Tosca])*, Thomas *(Addio Mignon [from Mignon])*, Massenet *(O dolce incanto [from Manon])*, Wolf-Ferrari *(Lucieta xe un bel nome [from Il quattro Rusteghi])* MECL ▲ 439 [ADD] (17.97)

Recital, 1941-1950—features arias by Rossini, Bellini, Donizetti, von Flotow, Verdi, Meyerbeer, Massenet, Mascagni *(w. Pia Tassinari [soprano])*, Giordano, Puccini, Cilea, Wolf-Ferrari MYTO ▲ 93382 (17.97)

Recital—features 20 sels from works by Wolf-Ferrari *(I quatro rusteghi)*, Donizetti *(Lucia di Lammermoor; L'elisir d'amore)*, Meyerbeer *(L'Africana)*, Verdi *(Rigoletto; Falstaff)*, Puccini *(Tosca)*, Massenet *(Manon)*, Bellini *(La sonnambula)*, Flotow *(Martha)*, Rossini *(Il barbiere di Siviglia)*, plus others including duet w. Pia Tassinari (sop) OPIT ▲ 54508 (6.97)

Talley, Marion (sop)

The Vocal Artistry of Marion Talley, w. various accompanists—features works by J. Strauss II *(Tales from the Vienna Woods)*, Rossini *(Una voce poco fa [from Il barbiere di Siviglia])*, Verdi *(Caro nome [from Rigoletto]; Bella figlia dell'amore [from Rigoletto; w. Jeanne Gordon (sgr), Beniamino Gigli (ten), Giuseppe de Luca (bar)])*, Thomas *(Je suis Titania [from Mignon])*, Offenbach *(Les oiseaux dans la charmille [from Les Contes d'Hoffmann])*, Bellini *(Ah, non credea mirarti ; Ah! non giunge [both from La sonnambula])*, Donizetti *(Lucia, perdona...Verranno a te [from Lucia di Lammermoor; w. Beniamino Gigli (ten)])*, Bishop *(Lo, Here the Gentle Lark)*, Eckert *(Swiss Echo Song)*, Benedict *(The Wren)*, Glazunov *(La Primavera d'Or)*, Lecuona *(Siboney)*, Harker *(How Beautiful Upon the Mountains)*, Ambrose *(One Sweetly Solemn Thought [w. Louise Homer (cta)])*, Hawthorne *(Whispering Hope [w. Louise Homer (cta)])*, anon *(Comin' Thro' the Rye) (rec 1923-38)* CMB (Historical) ▲ 1080 [ADD]

Tamagno, Francesco (ten)

The Complete Recordings (1903-04), w. pno accompaniment—features works by Verdi *(Otello:Esultate (2 versions); Niun mi tema (3 versions); Ora e per sempre addio (3 versions); Trovatore:Deserto sulla terra; Di quella pira (2 versions))*, Giordano *(Andrea Chénier:Un dì all'azzurro spazio (2 versions))*, Rossini *(Guglielmo Tell:O muto asil (2 versions); Corriamo, corriamo (2 versions); arias from Le prophète, Hérodiade, Samson et Dalila)* POHS ▲ 9846 (m) [AAD] (17.97)

Francesco Tamagno—features arias by Verdi, Meyerbeer, Rossini, Saint-Saëns, Massenet & Giordano *(rec 1903-04)* CECL ▲ 512 (16.97)

Francesco Tamagno—features works by Verdi *(Esultate [4 takes]; Ora e per sempre [4 takes]; Niun mi tema [4 takes] [all from Otello]; Deserto sulla terra; Di quella pira [2 takes] [both from Il Trovatore])*, Giordano *(Un di all'azzuro [4 takes; from Andrea Chénier])*, Meyerbeer *(Sopra Berta l'amor mio [2 takes]; Re del ciel [3 takes] [both from Le Prophète])*, Massenet *(Adieu donc, vains objets [2 takes]; Quand nos jours [2 takes] [both from Hérodiade]; O casto fior [from Le Roi de Lahore])*, Saint-Saëns *(Figli miei [2 takes; from Samson et Dalila])*, Rossini *(O muto asil [2 takes]; Corriam, corriam [2 takes] [both from Guillaume Tell])*, Lara *(Dei del patrio suol [from Messaline])*, Filippi *(Perchè? [Romance]) (rec 1903-04)* SYMP 2-▲ 1186 (34.97)

Tassinari, Pia (sop), Virginia Zeani (sop), Ferruccio Tagliavini (ten), Nicola Rossi Lemeni (bass)

The Martini & Rossi Concerts, Vol. 28, w. Milan RAI SO [cnd:A. Paoletti], Turin RAI SO [cnd:F. Vernizzi]—features arias from Donizetti *(L'elisir d'amore; Anna Bolena)*, Flotow *(Martha)*, Giordano *(Fedora)*, Massenet *(Manon)*, Cilea *(Adriana Lecouvreur)*, Massenet *(Erodiade)* INM ▲ 5028 [ADD] (16.97)

Pia Tassinari—features arias from Le nozze di Figaro; La Bohème; Manon; Mignon; L'amico Fritz; Carmen; Marta; plus others CECL (Classic Collection) ▲ 117 [ADD] (13.97)

Tauber, Richard (ten)

The Acoustic Lieder Recordings (1919-1926)—features twenty-one songs by Grieg, Schubert, Schumann, Loewe, Hildach, Massenet, Mendelssohn, Radecke, Wagner (9 w. orchestra, 12 w. piano) PHS ▲ 9901 (m) [AAD] (18.97)

Arias & Duets, w. Lotte Lehmann (sop), Elisabeth Rethberg (sop), et al.—features arias & duets from Martha; Eugene Onegin; Der Rosenkavalier; Carmen; Tosca; Madame Butterfly; Der Troubadour; Barber of Seville; Mignon; Aida; Die Zauberflote *(rec 1919-26)* PRE 2-▲ PRE 89219

Lotte Schöne & Richard Tauber in Operetta *(11 solo arias by Tauber, 1924-32 Odeon recordings [5 acoustics & 6 electrics]; 9 solo arias by Schöne, 1924-25 Odeon acoustics)*—features Tauber singing arias by Berté, Kálmán, Lehár, Nessler, Joh. Strauss † VOCAL:Lotte Schöne NIMB (Prima Voce) ▲ 7833 [ADD] (11.97)

My Heart & I—features Serenade (Frasquita); You Are My Heart's Delight; Ha wie in meiner Seele; Red Rose; Ave Maria; Thine Is My Heart; To Music; Don't Ask Me Why; Don't Be Cross; I'll See You Again; Im chambre separée; One Day When We Were Young; I'm in Love with Vienna; One Night of Love; Sympathy; Waltz of My Heart; Can I Forget You?; Long Ago & Far Away; All The Things You Are; Rosalie; In the Still of the Night; Vienna, City of My Dreams; Love, Here Is My Heart; Fascination; Indian Summer; plus other sels HADA 2-▲ 52250

My Heart's Delight: Operetta Gems & Songs of Romance *(rec 1928-43)* ASVQ ▲ 5146 [ADD] (12.97)

My Love for You—features My Love for You; The English Rose; Love Everlasting; Can I Forget You; The World Is Waiting For the Sunrise; I Know of 2 Bright Eyes; Sympathy; At the Balalaika; Rosalie; Intermezzo; So Deep Is the Night; Caprice Viennois; Liebestraum; Angels Guard Thee; Elégie; Love's Last Word Is Spoken; My Heart & I; Jealousy; Little Grey Home in the West; Starlight Serenade; Girls Were Made to Love & Kiss; Die Fledermaus [Finale to Act 2] MECL ▲ 433 (17.97)

Only a Rose—features Serenade; Un peu d'amour [A Little Love, A Little Kiss]; Rose Marie; Lover Come Back to Me; Für dich allein [For You Alone]; Simple Little Melody; 1 Alone; 1 Day When We Were Young; Waltz of My Heart; 1 Night of Love; Marchera [A Love Song of Old Mexico]; Only a Rose; All the Things You Are; Sweethearts; Kiss Me Again; Will You Remember; Sleepy Lagoon; You Mean the World to Me [Du bist die Welt für mich]; Your Love Could Be Everything to Me; Rosen aus dem Süden [Roses From the South]; Wien, du Stadt meiner Träume [Vienna, City of My Dreams]; Dein ist mein ganzes Herz [You Are My Heart's Delight] MECL ▲ 421 [AAD] (17.97)

Rarities (1929-29)—features works by Kálmán, Lehár, Schubert, Schumann, O. Straus, Joh. Strauss, Sr., Joh. Strauss II, Tauber, Wagner & Weber VOCA (Vocal Archives) ▲ 1142 (13.97)

Richard Tauber, w. Percy Kahn (pno), *(orch unknown)* [cnd:Karl Alwin, Henry Geehl, Walter Goehr, Ernst Hauke, Frieder Weissmann]—features works by Mozart *(O wie ängstlich [from Die Entführung aus dem Serail]; Dies Bildnis ist bezaubernd schön [from Die Zauberflöte]; Dalla sua pace; Il mio tesoro [both from Don Giovanni])*, Haydn *(In native worth [from The Creation])*, Méhul *(Mein Vaterland [from Joseph in Ägypten])*, Weber *(Durch die Wälder, durch die Auen [from Der Freischütz])*, Bizet *(La fleur que tu m'avais jetée [from Carmen])*, Offenbach *(Es war einmal am Hofe von Eisenack; Ha, wie in meiner Seele [both from Les Contes d'Hoffman])*, d'Albert *(Wie ich nun gestern Abend in der Hütte liege; Mein Leben wagt ich drum [both from Tiefland])*, Kienzl *(Lug' Dursel, lug'; Zu Strassburg auf der Schanz' [both from Der Kuhreigen]; Selig sind, die Verfolgung leiden [from Der Evangelimann])*, R. Strauss *(Heimliche Aufforderung; Morgen!; Traum durch die Dämmerung; Ständchen; Allerseelen; Ich trage meine Minne) (rec 1928-46)* PRE (Lebendige Vergangenheit) ▲ 89144 (16.97)

Tauber, Richard (ten) (cont.)

Richard Tauber In Concert 1937-1947—features sels. from four Fall 1937 Carnegie Hall recital broadcasts, w. orchestra cond. by Erno Rapée & Vladimir Golschmann *(14 arias and songs by Bizet, Gounod, Grieg, Kálmán, Lehár, Liszt, Leoncavallo, Massenet, Joh. Strauss, Thomas)*, sels. from five 1945-6 BBC concerts, w. accompanists Percy Kahn (piano) and the George Melachrino Orch. *(21 arias and songs by Bowen, Grieg, Handel, Hartley, Herbert, Kálmán, Kienzl, Lehár, May, Murray, Sharp, O. Straus, Schubert, Schumann, Tauber, Tchaikovsky, Zeller)*, w. Maria Cebotari, Josep Krips, Royal Opera House Orch., rec. live 9/27/47, Covent Garden *(three arias from Don Giovanni: Ma quel mai; Dalla sua pace; Il mio tessoro)* EKLR 2-▲ 5

Richard Tauber In Concert—features arias from Carmen, Land Without Music [Oscar Straus], The Chocolate Soldier [Oscar Straus], Lohengrin & Freischütz, and *Rosen aus dem suden* by Joh. Strauss; plus four songs and operetta arias (rec'g dates not indicated) by Friml, German, Tauber, Tosti *(rec from Netherlands Radio, July 18, 1939)* † Smetana:The Bartered Bride (*see* Composer section) SRON 2-▲ SRO 830-2 [ADD]

Richard Tauber: Operatic Arias—features works by Mozart, Wagner, Tchaikovsky, Verdi, Puccini, Flotow, D'Albert, Leoncavallo, others *(rec 1923-39)* PHS ▲ 9145 [ADD] (17.97)

Richard Tauber Sings Lieder: 12 German Folk Songs, w. Mischa Spoliansky (pno) [G] (see Composer section, Schubert:Winterreise (selections); Schumann:Songs *(rec 1926)* PHS ▲ 9370 (m) [AAD] (17.97)

The Singing Dream—features operetta arias & duets *(rec 1927-34 from Parlophone/Odeon 78 rpm discs)* PHS ▲ 9444 (m) [AAD] (17.97)

Sings German Folk Songs—features Ach, wie ist's möglich dann; Du, du liegst mir im Herzen; Im Wald und auf der Heide; In einem kühlen Grunde; Morgen muss ich fort von hier; Kommt a Vogerl geflogen; Der Mai ist gekommen; Ich wiss nicht, was soll es bedeuten; Alle Tage ist kein Sonntag; ja, grün ist die Heide; Verloren; Herzblatt am Lindenbaum; Rose im Schnee; Schäferlied; Husarenlied; Auf Feldwache; Vergissmeinnicht, du Blümlein blau; Tausendschönchen; Der Tauber; Der Dragoner; Verschütt; Liebe kleine Nachtigall; Gute Nacht, mein holdes, süsses Mädchen; Ich hab' amal a Räuscherl g'habt; Aus der Jugendzeit; Deine Mutter bleibt immer bei dir; Wandern, ach wandern; Still wie die Nacht, tief wie das Meer *(rec 1926-35)* BLAG ▲ 103002 [ADD] (14.97)

Sings Light Music of the '20s & '30s, w. orch [G] rec. 1920-35) PHS ▲ 9416 (m) [AAD] (17.97)

Tauber in Opera—features arias from Carmen, Der Evangelimann, Die Tote Stadt, Undine, Don Giovanni, Zauberflöte, Contes d'Hoffmann, Bohème, Butterfly, Tosca, Turandot, The Bartered Bride, Rosenkavalier, Eugen Onegin, Trovatore, Meistersinger, Walküre [G] *(rec 1920-28 for Odeon)* NIMB (Prima Voce) ▲ 7830 [ADD] (11.97) 7830

Vienna, City of My Dreams—features sels from Land without Music; Heart's Desire; Frederica; Blossom Time; plus Santa Lucia; The Swan; Tales from the Vienna Woods; Plaisir d'amore; I Love Thee; Creation's Hymn; Netherland Hymn; Silent Night, Holy Night; plus other sels HADA ▲ 189

The Voice of Romance—features 1 Night of Love; Lover Come Back to Me; Roses of Picardy; Smilin' Through; Only a Rose; Sweethearts; All the Things You Are; Sleepy Lagoon; Because; Begin the Beguine; Waltz Song [from Merry Widow]; plus others PRSM ▲ 113 (6.97)

You Are My Heart's Delight—features works by Lehár, Kalman, Zeller, J. Strauss, Hueberger, Tauber, *(plus the song Vienna, City of My Dreams) (rec 1927-42)* PEFL ▲ 7042 [AAD] (17.97)

Tebaldi, Renata (sop)

The Early Recordings (1949-1952), w. Alberto Erede (cnd), St. Cecilia Academy Orch Rome, Swiss Romande Orch—features arias from Faust, Bohème, Madama Butterfly, Manon Lescaut, Tosca, Aida, Trovatore PPHI (Historic) ▲ 25989 [ADD]

The Farewell Tour - Moscow 1975, w. Eduardo Müller (pno)—features works by Beethoven *(Ah, perfido!)*, Bellini *(Malinconia, ninfa gentile; Vanne, o rosa fortunata)*, Buzzi-Peccia *(Serenatella veneziana; Lolita)*, De Curtis *(Non ti scordar di me)*, Donizetti *(Me voglio fa' 'na casa)*, Gluck *(O del mio dolçe ardor [from Paride ed Elena])*, Paradisi *(M'ha presa alla sua ragna)*, Parisotti *(Se tu m'ami [attrib Pergolesi])*, Puccini *(E l'uccellino; In quelle trine morbide [from Manon Lescaut]; O mio babbino caro [from Gianni Schicchi]; Sì, mi chiamano Mimi [from La Bohème]; Un bel dì vedremo [from Madama Butterfly])*, Rossini *(La promessa)*, A. Scarlatti *(O, cessate di piagarmi)*, Tosti *('A vucchella)*, Verdi *(Stornello; In solitaria stanza)*, Zandonai *L'assiuolo) (rec live, Moscow, Oct 13, 1975)* VAIA ▲ 1164 [ADD] (16.97)

Grandi Voci: Renata Tebaldi—features opera arias by Puccini, Verdi, Giordano, Catalani, Cilea & Boito *(rec 1954-55, 1957-59, 1962 & 1968)* PLON ▲ 40408 [ADD] (11.97)

La Leggendaria Tebaldi: A 40th Anniversary Tribute—features arias & songs by Verdi *(Tacea la notte placida [from Il trovatore; rec. Jan. 22, 1966]; Son giunta!...Madre, pietosa vergine; Pace, pace mio Dio [both from La forza del destino; rec. June 16, 1953]; Ritorna vincitor! [from Aida; rec. Jan. 22, 1966]; Teneste la promessa...Addio del passato [from La traviata; rec. May 28, 1952]; Ave Maria [from Otello; rec. Jan. 7, 1954]; O fatidica foresta [from Giovanna d'Arco; rec. Mar. 26, 1951])*, Puccini *(In quelle trine morbide; Sola, perduta, abbandonata! [both from Manon Lescaut; rec. Jan 22, 1966 & Nov. 29, 1954]; Si, mi chimano Mimi; Donde lieta usci [both from La bohème; Nov. 29, 1954 & Apr. 8, 1959]; Un bel di [from Madama Butterfly; rec. Oct. 15, 1950]; Vissi d'arte [from Tosca; rec. June 30, 1955]; O mio babbino caro [from Gianni Schicchi; rec. Jan. 22, 1966])*, Mascagni *(Voi lo sapete [from Cavalleria rusticana; rec. Dec. 15, 1966])*, Ponchielli *(Suicidio! [from La Gioconda; rec. Jan. 7, 1968])*, Tchaikovsky *(Letter Scene [from Eugene Onegin; abridged; I; rec. Nov. 10, 1956])*, Tosti *(A vuchella [rec. Dec. 15, 1966])* LCD ▲ * [ADD]

The New York Farewell Recital, w. Martin Katz (pno) *(rec Feb 19, 1976)* VAIA ▲ 1116 (m) (17.97)

A Portrait of the Artist, 1949-1958—features 13 arias from Mefistofele, La Wally, Louise, Adriana Lecouvreur, Andrea Chénier, L'Amico fritz, Bohème, Madama Butterfly, Manon Lescaut, Stabat Mater [Rossini], Otello, Traviata; one song (Turina—Poema en forma de canciones) LCD ▲ 115 (m) [AAD]

Renata Tebaldi—features arias from La traviata; Aida; Otello; Le nozze di Figaro; Mefistofele; La Wally; La Bohème; Andrea Chénier CECL (Italia) ▲ 102

Renata Tebaldi—features arias from Adriana Lecouvreur; Otello; Trovatore; La Wally; etc. PLON ▲ 21312 [ADD] (11.97)

Renata Tebaldi alla Scala, w. Martin Katz (pno)—features works by A. Scarlatti, Paradisi, Gluck, Pergolesi, Rossini, Bellini, Verdi, Donizetti, Beethoven, Puccini, Zandonai, Buzzi Peccia, Mascagni, Massenet, Schubert, Curtis *(rec May 20, 1974)* MYTO ▲ 943105 (17.97)

Renata Tebaldi in Concert, w. Milan RAI Orch [cnd:Nino Sanzogno]—features four arias from Lodoletta, Suor Angelica, William Tell, Otello *(rec Nov 30, 1953)* † Boito:Mefistofele (*see* Composer section under Boito) SRON 2-▲ SRO 824-2 [ADD]

La Tebaldi *(aria collection)* PLON 2-▲ 30481 [ADD] (19.97)

A Tebaldi Festival, w. New Philharmonia Orch [cnds:Anton Guadagno, Richard Bonynge], Monte Carlo National Opera Orch [cnd:Fausto Cleva]—features Wagner *(Salve d'amor, recinto eletto!; O! Vergin santa, deh! Mi ascolta! [both from Tannhäuser]; Sola ne' miei prim' anni...Cinto d'usebergo e maglia [from Lohengrin]; Dolce e calmo [from Tristan und Isolde])*, Bizet *(Ella vien! ella vien!...E' l'amour uno strano augello; Quadri! Picche! [both from Carmen])*, Saint-Saëns *(Sansone, anelante d'amore...Amor! I miei fini proteggi; S'apre per te il mio cor [both from Samson et Dalila])*, Massenet *(Ebben! Lo degg'io...Addio, o nostro picciol desco; Ahimè! L'auge!...la tua non è la mano che mi tocca? [both from Manon])*, Verdi *(Ritona vincitor! [from Aida]; Ben io t'invenni...Anch'io dischiuso...Salgo già del trono [from Nabucco]; O don fatale [from Don Carlo])*, Puccini *(Quando me n'vo [from La Bohème])*, Bellini *(Sediziose voci...Casta diva [from Norma]; O rendetemi la speme...Qui la voce sua soave...Vien, diletto [from I Puritani]; Oh! Se una volta sola...Ah! Non credea mirarti [from La sonnambula])*, Rossini *(La regata veneziana [from Les soirées musicales])*, Lara *(Granada)*, Ponce *(Estrellita)*, Cardillo *(Catarì, Catarì)*, Tosti *('A vucchella)*, De Curtis *(Non ti scordar di me)*, Rodgers *(If I Loved You [from Carousel])* PLON 2-▲ 452456 (22.97)

The Martini & Rossi Concerts, Vol. 12, w. Fedora Barbieri (mez), Cesare Valletti (ten) *(rec 1951 & 1953)* INM ▲ 5012 (16.97)

Tebaldi, Renata (sop), Giacinto Prandelli (ten)

The Martini & Rossi Concerts, Vol. 23, w. Rome RAI Orch [cnd:Arturo Basile], Milan RAI SO [cnd:Nino Sanzogno]—features works by Ambrose *(Ah, non credevi tu [from Mignon])*, Puccini *(O mio babbino caro [from Gianni Schicchi]; E lucean le stelle [from Tosca]; Sola, perduta, abbandonata [from Manon Lescaut])*, Massenet *(Ah! non mi ridestar [from Werther]; Addio, O nostro picciol desco [from Manon])*, Meyerbeer *(O Paradiso [from L'Africaine])*, Verdi *(Ritorna vincitor [from Aida])*, Rossini *(Selva opaca [from Guillaume Tell]) (rec 1953 & 1961)* INM ▲ 5023 [ADD] (16.97)

Te Kanawa, Kiri (sop)

Ave Maria—features sacred & devotional songs by Handel, Gounod, Mozart, Mendelssohn, Franck, et al. PPHI ▲ 12629 [DDD] (11.97) ▮ 12629 (7.98) ▯ 412629-5

Blue Skies, w. Nelson Riddle Orch PLON ▲ 14666 [DDD] (16.97)

Christmas with Kiri, w. Carl Davis, Philharmonia Orch, London Voices PLON ▲ 14632 [DDD] (16.97)

Come to the Fair (Danny Boy & Other British Folksongs) EMIC ▲ 47080 [DDD] (16.97)

French Opera Arias, w. Royal Opera Orch [cnd:Jeffrey Tate]—features arias by Berlioz, Bizet, Charpentier, Debussy, Gluck, Massenet, Offenbach, Verdi EMIC ▲ 49863 [DDD] (16.97) 49863

Heart to Heart *(pop songs, incl. seven duets with fellow New Zealander Malcolm McNeill; guitar-bass-drums-keyboard accompaniment)* ANGL ▲ 54299 (16.97) 54299

Italian Opera Arias, w. London SO [cnd:M. W. Chung] EMIC ▲ 54062 (16.97) 54062

Kiri!: Her Greatest Hits—features performances w. London SO [cond.:S. Barlow] *(Charpentier:Depuis le jour [from* Louise*]; Korngold:Marietta Lied zur Laute [from* Die tote Stadt*]; Mozart:Porgi amor [from* Le nozze di Figaro*]; R. Strauss:Befriet, Op. 39/4; Puccini:O soave fanciulla [w. D. O'Niell (tenor)]; Si, Mi chiamano Mimi [both from* La bohème*]; O mi babbino caro [from* Gianni Schicchi*]; Rogers & Hammerstein:You'll Never Walk Alone [w. LSO Chorus; from* Carousel*]; Climb Ev'ry Mountain [w. LSO Chorus; from* The Sound of Music*]; Lloyd Webber:With One Look [from* Sunset Boulevard*]; Hermann:Salaambo's Aria [from* Citizen Kane*]; Bernstein:Somewhere [from* West Side Story*]; Herbert:Art Is Calling for Me [from* The Enchantress*])*, w. A. Previn & Previn Trio *(Weill:It Never Was You; McCoy:Why Don't You Do Right?)*, w. Waihirere Maori Group *(Hine e hine [Lullaby]; Tahi nei taru kino [Action song])* PLON ▲ 43600 [DDD] (16.97) ▮ 43600

Te Kanawa, Kiri (sop) (cont.)

Kiri on Broadway—features Broadway hits from Lerner & Loewe, Sondheim/Bernstein, Weill/Nash, Rodgers & Hart, Rodgers & Hammerstein, Cole Porter PLON ▲ 40280 (16.97) 40280

The Kiri Selection ANGL ▲ 54530 (17.97) 54530

Kiri Sings Kern, w. London Sinfonietta [cnd:John McGlinn]—features music by Jerome Kern *(The folks who live on the hill; I'm old fashioned; The way you look tonight; The song is you; Smoke gets in your eyes; All through the day; The last time I saw Paris; A fine romance; Yesterdays; All the things you are; Bill; Long ago & far away; Look for the silver lining; Can't help lovin' dat man)* ANGL ▲ 54527 (17.97) 54527

Kiri Te Kanawa—features arias from Adriana Lecouvreur, Andrea Chenier, La Damnation de Faust, Eugene Onegin, La forza del Destino, Hérodiade, Iphigénie en Tauride, Louise, Manon, Pagliacci, Der Rosenkavalier, Suor Angelica EMIC (Diva) ▲ 65578 (11.97)

A Portrait of Kiri Te Kanawa—features arias from Hansel and Gretel, Don Giovanni, Gianni Schicchi, Tosca, Traviata [w. various orchestras]; songs by R. Strauss, Schubert, Schumann, Fauré, Walton [w. Richard Amner (piano)] COL ▲ 39208 (16.97) 39208

Songs of Inspiration, w. Julius Rudel, Utah SO, Mormon Tabernacle Choir—features songs by Joh. Strauss II/arr. Benatzky, Gounod, Verdi, Mendelssohn, Beethoven, Bach/Gounod, Mascagni, Franck, Rodgers & Hammerstein, Robertson, Bishop PLON ▲ 25431 [DDD] (16.97)

The Young Kiri (Early Recordings, 1964-70), w. various orchs—features arias, Maori folk songs, and popular songs PPHI 2-▲ 30325 [ADD]

Telese, Maryanne (sop), Arthur Woodley (b-bar)

Let My Song Fill Your Heart: A Remembrance of the American Concert Song, w. Peter Howard (pno), Joseph Smith (pno)—features works by Charles *(Let My Song Fill Your Heart; And So, Goodbye)*, Firestone *(If I Could Tell You; In My Garden)*, Logan *(Pale Moon)*, Mana-Zucca *(Nichavo!; I Love Life)*, Speaks *(Morning)*, Malotte *(My Friend)*, Herbert *(When Knighthood was in Flower)*, Fox *(The Hills of Home)*, Guion *(All Day on the Prairie; Ride, Cowboy, Ride)*, Ball *(Love Me & the World is Mine)*, Beach *(Mine Be the Lips!)*, Homer *(Sing to Me, Sing)*, Homer *(Sing to Me, Sing)*, Penn *(Smilin' Through)*, Jacobs-Bond *(Just A-Wearyin' for You)*, Hageman *(Miranda)*, Edwards *(By the Bend of the River)*, Nevin *(Slumber Song)*, Friml *(L'Amour-Toujours-L'Amour)*, Strickland *(I Remember)*, Speaks *(On the Road to Mandalay)* PREM ▲ 1002 (16.97)

Terfel, Bryn (b-bar)

Opera Arias, w. Metropolitan Opera Orch [cnd:James Levine]—features arias by Mozart *(Non piùandrai [from Nozze di Figaro]; Madamina, il catalogo è questa; Deh! vieni alla finestra [both from Don Giovanni]; Rivolgete a lui lo sguardo [from Cosi fan tutti]; Der Vogelfänger bin ich ja [from Zauberflöte])*, Wagner *(Wie Todesahnung; O du mein holder Abendstern [from Tannhäuser]; Die Frist ist um [from Flying Dutchman])*, Offenbach *(Allez! Pour te livrer combat; Scintille, diamant [both from Contes d'Hoffman])*, Gounod *(Vous qui faites l'endormie [from Faust])*, Borodin *(No sleep, no rest [from Prince Igor])*, Donizetti *(Bella siccome un angelo [from Don Pasquale])*, Rossini *(Miei rampolli femminini [from Cenerentola])*, Verdi *(Perfidi! All'angelo caontra me v'unite!, Pietà, rispetto, amore [both from MacBeth]; Ehi! paggio; L'Onore! Ladri [from Falstaff])* DEUT ▲ 4458862 [DDD]

Teschemacher, Margarete (sop)

Margarete Teschemacher (1903-1959), w. various Berlin orchs, Karl Böhm (cnd), Hanns Udo Müller (cnd), Bruno Seidler-Winkler (cnd), Fritz Zaun (cnd)—features arias by Lortzing *(Der Waffenschmied—Er schläft)*, Mozart *(Marriage of Figaro—Nur zu flüchtig; Wenn die anften Abendlüfte, w. Irma Beilke)*, R. Strauss *(Arabella—Aber der Richtige, wenn's einen gibt, w. Irma Beilke; Das war sehr gut, Mandryka; Daphne—O wie gerne blieb ich bei dir; Wind...spiele mit mir)*, Verdi *(Don Carlos—Du, im irdischen Wahn)*, Wagner *(Lohengrin—Einsam in trüben Tagen; Das süsse Lied verhallt, w. Marcel Wittrisch; Wesendonck Songs—Der Engel; Träume)*, Weber *(Der Freischütz—Und ob die Wolke sie verhülle; Oberon—Ozean, du Ungeheuer) (rec 1933-39 HMV recordings)* PRE (Lebendige Vergangenheit) ▲ 89049 (m) [AAD] (16.97)

Tetrazzini, Luisa (sop)

The Complete Known Recordings [1903-1922] *(96 recordings: for HMV, 1908-1913; Victor, 1911-1922; Zonofono, 1903-1905)* PHS 5-▲ 9220 (m) [AAD] (82.97)

The Complete Zonophone & Victor Recordings—features arias from Lakme, Dinorah, Mignon, La sonnambula, La traviata, Il trovatore, Rigoletto, La forza del destino, I vespri siciliani, plus others *(rec 1904, 1911-20)* ROMO 2-▲ 81025 (35.97)

Great Italian Voices, Vol. 4: Luisa Tetrazzini, Part 1—features arias by Mozart, Rossini, Donizetti, Bellini, Verdi *(rec 1907-14)* CECL ▲ 509 (13.97)

Tetrazzini *(rec 1908-14)* NIMB (Prima Voce) ▲ 7808 (m) [ADD] (11.97)

Tetrazzini, Vol. 2, w. Cleofonte Campanini (pno), Percy Pitt (cnd), Walter B. Rogers (cnd)—features works by Bellini *(Vien diletto [from I Puritani]; Come per me sereno...Sovra il sen; Ah! non credea mirarti; Ah! non giunge [all from La sonnambula])*, David *(Charmant oiseau [from La perle du Brésil])*, Donizetti *(O luce di quest' anima [from Linda di Chamounix])*, Tosti *(Aprile)*, Rossini *(Bel raggio lusinghier [from Semiramide]; Una voce poco fa [from Il barbiere di Siviglia])*, Grieg *(Solveig's Song [from Peer Gynt, Op. 23/1])*, Gounod *(Je veux vivre dans ce rêve; Je veux vivre dans ce rêve [both from Romeo et Juliette])*, Bizet *(Je dis que rien ne m' épouvante [from Carmen])*, Meyerbeer *(Ombra leggiera [from Dinorah]; O, beau pays...A ce mot [from Les Huguenots])*, Braga *(La Serenata)*, Benedict *(Carnevale di Venezia)*, Verdi *(D'amor sull' ali rosee [from Il trovatore]; Ah! fors' è lui...Sempre libera [from La traviata]) (rec 1904-14)* NIMB (Prima Voce) ▲ 7891 [ADD] (11.97)

Teyte, Maggie (sop)

Maggie Teyte: In Concert—features arias and concert pieces by Gretry *(Rose chérie)*, De Severac *(Si l'on avait l'audace)*, Britten *(Quand j'étais chez mon père)*, Fauré *(Songs from La Chanson d'Eve)*, Debussy *(Pelléas and Mélisande [sels.])*, Britten *(Les Illuminations, Op. 18)*, Hahn *(Si mes vers avaient des ailes)*, R. Strauss *(Salome [sels.]) (rec 1935 & 1948)* VAIA ▲ 1066 (m) [ADD] (31.97)

Maggie Teyte Live (1934-1948)—features arias and songs by Debussy, Giordani, Hageman, Messager, Mozart, Offenbach, Puccini, Russell, Tchaikovsky, trad. *(rec mostly from USA radio broadcasts, 1945-48)* † Massenet:Manon (selections: *see Composer section*) PHS ▲ 9326 (m) [AAD] (17.97)

Thill, Georges (ten)

Georges Thill—features 11 arias (all sung in French) from Cantata No. 65 [Bach], Damnation de Faust, Carmen, Roméo et Juliette, Hérodiade, Werther, Bohème, Sadko, Traviata, Lohengrin; 8 songs by Fauré; 2 songs by Gounod & Trad. (Le rêve passe) *(rec 1925-36 for Columbia)* PHS ▲ 9947 (m) [AAD] (17.97)

Georges Thill (1897-1984)—features works by Gluck *(Unis dès ma plus tendre enfance [from Iphigine en Tauride])*, Berlioz *(Nature immense [from La Damnation de Faust])*, Wagner *(Aux bords lointains [from Lohengrin]; O glaive promis par mon père [from Die Walküre]; Une arme seule et sûre [from Parsifal])*, Gounod *(Salut! Demeure chaste et pure [from Faust]; Anges du paradis [from Mireille])*, Massenet *(Ne pouvant réprimer les élans de la foi [from Herodiade]; Et je sais votre nom [from Manon]; J'aurais sur ma poitrine [from Werther])*, Reyer *(Le bruit des chants [from Sigurd])*, Verdi *(Je suis aimé de toi [from La traviata]; Comme la plume au vent [from Rigoletto])*, Leoncavallo *(Avec moi, vrai, tenter ce jeu; Pauvre Paillasse [both from Paillasse])*, Puccini *(Le ciel luisait d'étoiles [from Tosca]; Ne pleure plus Liu; Nessun dorma [both from Turandot])*, Giordano *(Un di all'azzurro spazio [from Andrea Chenier])* [F] *(rec 1927-35)* PRE (Lebendige Vergangenheit) ▲ 89168 (m) [AAD]

Georges Thill, Tenor—features arias from Rigoletto; La Traviata; Faust; Pagliacci; Andrea Chenier; Turandot BONG (Il Mito dell'Opera) ▲ 1145 (16.97)

L'Incomparable Georges Thill—features Ne pouvant réprimer [from Hérodiade]; Céleste Aida [from Aida]; Rachel, quand du Seigneur [from La Juive]; Bannis la crainte et les alarmes [from Alceste]; O noble lame étincelante [from Le Cid]; Plus blanche que la blanche hermine [from Les Huguenots]; Pauvre Paillasse [from Paillasse]; Aux bords lointains [from Lohengrin]; Je suis aimé de toi [from La traviata]; Asile héréditaire [from Guillaume Tell]; Vainement Pharaon [from Joseph]; Ah! qu'il est loin mon pays [from Sapho]; Ah! lève-toi soleil [from Romeo et Juliette]; J'aimais ma vieille maison grise [from Fortunio]; Adieu forêt profonde [from L'Attaque du moulin] FORL ▲ 16727 (16.97)

King of the French Tenors *(18 arias by Cherubini, Delibes, Gluck, Gounod, Massenet, Meyerbeer, Verdi, Wagner, et al.; recording dates and source material not indicated)* MMO ▲ 30190

Thomas, John Charles (bar)

An American Classic *(22 songs, spirituals and operetta arias; Victor recordings, 1931-1941)* NIMB (Prima Voce) ▲ 7838 (m) [AAD] (11.97)

Home on the Range—features 13 selections with orchestra, rec. 1923-39—Trees; If you only knew; The heart bow'd down; Mother o' mine; At dawning; In the gloaming; Smilin' through; Nichavo; Rolling down to Rio; My message; Nocturne; Home on the range; Bendemeer's stream; 8 selections with keyboard accompaniment by Carroll Hollister, rec. 1933-41—The green-eyed dragon; Sailormen; The Lord's prayer; Just for today; The ballad of Lord Randall; When children pray; O Men from the fields; Tell me the story of Jesus *(rec 1923-41 for HMV, Victor, Vocalion & Brunswick)* PHS ▲ 9977 [AAD] (17.97)

Thompson, Jeanette (sop)

Negro Spirituals, w. Ieper Chamber Choir, David Miller (pno) PAVA ▲ 7267 [DDD] (10.97)

Thorborg, Kerstin (mez)

Kerstin Thorborg—features works by Gluck, Bizet, Saint-Saëns, Wagner, Schubert, Brahms & Wolf *(rec 1933-40)* PRE (Lebendige Vegangenheit) ▲ 89084 [AAD] (16.97)

Tibbett, Lawrence (bar)

The Best of Lawrence Tibbett *(17 songs) (rec 1927-35)* PHS ▲ 9307 (m) [AAD] (17.97)

Tibbett, Lawrence (bar) (cont.)

From Broadway to Hollywood—features 9 songs from *Porgy and Bess* (with Helen Jepson); 4 songs from the 1930 MGM film *The Rogue Song*; 2 songs from the 1931 MGM film *The Prodigal*; one aria each from the American operas *Merry Mount* by Howard Hanson and *Emperor Jones* by Louis Gruenberg; 3 Spirituals (De glory road, Goin' home, Old Black Joe) *(rec 1927-36)* NIMB ▲ 7881 [ADD] (11.97)

Lawrence Tibbett—features arias from Carmen, Faust, Pagliacci, Tosca, Barber of Seville, Ballo in maschera, Falstaff, Simon Boccanegra, Walküre; songs by Gershwin, Hanson, Gruenberg RCAV (Gold Seal) ▲ 7808 (m) [ADD] (10.97) 7808

Lawrence Tibbett: His Rarities & Famous Performances on Radio, Films & Records (1930-43)—features arias from Il barbiere di Siviglia; Otello; Carmen; I Pagliacci; Faust; Boris Godunov; sels. from The White Dove; & songs: And Love Was Born; Life is a Dream; A Cuban Love Song; Edward; Love Comes Like a Bird on the Wind; others RY (The Radio Years) ▲ 29 (m) (16.97)

Lawrence Tibbett on Stage—features arias from works by Rossini *(Il barbiere di Siviglia)*, Verdi *(Un ballo in maschera; Simon Boccanegra; Otello; Falstaff)*, Wagner *(Die Walküre)*, Gounod *(Faust)*, Bizet *(Carmen)*, Puccini *(Tosca)*, Leoncavallo *(Pagliacci)*, Offenbach *(Les Contes d'Hoffmann)*, Mussorgsky *(Song of the Flea) (rec 1926-39)* VOCA (Vocal Archives) ▲ 1161 (13.97)

The Stanford Archive Series: Lawrence Tibbett—features works by Bizet *(Votre toast [from Carmen])*, Leoncavallo *(Si può?/Un nido de memori; Vesta la giubba [both from Pagliacci])*, Rossini *(Largo al factotum [from Il barbiere di Siviglia])*, Kipling/Speaks *(On the Road to Mandalay)*, J. Wolf *(De Glory Road; Hallelujah Ryhthm [w. Andrew Smallens (cnd)])*, Hughes/Carpenter *(Shake Your Brown Feet, Honey)*, Bradley/Hughes *(The Packet Boat/The Roustabout [w. Stewart Wille (pno)])*, Hammerstein/Kern *(Ol' Man River [w. Stewart Wille (pno); from Showboat])*, Sommervell *(A Kingdom by the Sea [w. Stewart Wille (pno)])*, Stokes/Hanson *('Tis an Earth Defiled [w. W. Pelletier (cnd), Metropolitan Opera Orch; from Merry Mount])*, Handel *(Defend Her! Heaven [from Theodora])*, Hoare/Riego *(A Star Was His Candle [w. Stewart Wille (pno)])*, Fauré *(The Crucifix [w. R. Crooks (ten), Mark Andrews (org)])*, Loewe *(Edward, Op. 1/1 [w. S. Wille (pno)])*, Key/Smith *(Star Spangled Banner)*, Pacius *(Suomen laulu [w. K. Flagstad (sop), L. Melchoir (ten), Eugene Goosens (cnd); arr Frank Black])*, Verdi *(Pari Siamo; Povero Rigoletto [both from Rigoletto]; Inaffia l'ugola; Vanne, la tua meta già vedo; Era la notte [all from Otello]; Il balen del suo sorriso [from Il trovatore]; Mio figlio! [from La traviata])*, Wagner *(Als du im kühnem Sangel Wie Todesahnung Dämmrung [both w. A. Bodanzky (cnd), from Tannhäuser])*, Gounod *(Bouons! Trinquons!; Merci da ta chanson [w. Alfred Newman (cnd); from Faust])*, Dietz/Schwartz *(Amigo; My Little Mule Wagon; Under Your Spell [all from Under Your Spell])*, plus trad/spirituals *(De Glory Road; Travelin' to de Grave) (rec 1928-40)* DLS 2-▲ 5500 (m) (20.97)

Tibbett in Opera—features 13 arias from Carmen, Faust, Pagliacci, Tosca, Ballo in maschera, Barbiere di Siviglia, Otello, Rigoletto, Simon Boccanegra, Tannhäuser, Walküre *(rec 1926-39 for Victor)* NIMB (Prima Voce) ▲ 7825 [ADD] (11.97)

Tokatyan, Armand (ten)

Armand Tokatyan (1894-1960), w. Eleanor Steber (sop), Lucille Browning (mez), Jean Dickensen (sgr), Annamary Dickey (sgr), George Cehanovsky (bar), Leonard Warren (bar), Norman Cordon (bass), Pino Bontempi (sgr)—features works by Gounod *(Salut! demure chaste et pure; Il se fait tard [both from Faust])*, Massenet *(Ay, fuyez, douce image [from Manon])*, Bizet *(Il fior che avevi a me tu dato [from Carmen])*, Giordano *(Un di all'azzurro spazio [from Andrea Chenier])*, Puccini *(Ch'ella mi creda libero [from La fanciulla del West]; Che gelida manina; O soave fanciulla; Addio, dolce svegliare [all from La Bohème]; Bimba degli occhi pieni di malia [from Madame Butterfly])*, Buzzi-Peccia *(Lolita)*, Tosti *(L'ultima canzone)*, Verdi *(Questa o quella [from Rigoletto]; Libiamo ne' lieti calici; Praigi, o cara, noi lasceremo [both from La traviata])* [I] *(rec 1923-40)* PRE (Lebendige Vergangenheit) ▲ 89170 (m) [AAD]

Tokody, Ilona (sop)

Live in Tokyo, w. Masahiro Saitoh (pno)—features works by Tosti, Durante, Bellini, Mascagni, Bartók, Massenet, Poulenc, Guastavino, Ponce, Alfano, Puccini, Grever *(rec Apr 20, 1991)* LINO ▲ 7243

A Portrait of the Artist—features sels. from Bánk Bán [Erkel], La Juive, Bohème, Manon Lescaut, Forza del Destino SRON ▲ SRO 823-1 [ADD]

Portrait of the Artist *(11 arias & 4 songs)* features arias from Risurrezione [Alfano], Norma, Mefistofele, La Wally, Shulamis [Goldfaden], Székely fonó [Kodály], Zazà, Cavalleria rusticana, Bohème, Gianni Schicchi, Madama Butterfly; songs by Grever, Massenet, Tosti *(rec live, 1991-92)* VAIA ▲ 1009 [ADD/DDD] (17.97)

Tomowa-Sintow, Anna (sop)

Famous Opera Arias, w. Munich Radio Orch [cnd:Peter Sommer] features sels. from Adriana Lecouvreur, Andrea Chénier, Così fan tutte, Manon Lescaut, Turandot, Adriane auf Naxos, Daphne, Ballo, Ernani, Tannhäuser, Freischütz [G,I] ORF ▲ 106841 [DDD] (18.97)

Toppin, Louise (sop), Bill Brown (ten)

Songs of Illumination, w. Howard Watkins (pno), Vivian Taylor (pno)—features works by Hale Smith *(Jesus Lay Your Head in the Window)*, C. Nickerson *(Gué, Gué solangae)*, Kerr *(Git on Board)*, Hailstork *(Song of Ruth)*, Newby *(His Eye Is on the Sparrow)*, Swanson *(Goodnight)*, Banfield *(A New Song)*, Simpson-Curenton *(Lord I Don't Feel Nowadays Tired)*, T. J. Anderson *(Songs of Illumination) (rec 1995-96)* CENT ▲ 2375 [DDD] (16.97)

Torntoft, Preben (trb)

Danish Songs, w. pno accompaniment—features 20 songs by Carl Nielsen, C.E.F. Weyse, et al., sung in Danish; no texts *(rec 1951-53)* DANR ▲ 347 (m) [ADD]

Torre, Manuel (sgr)

Historical Flamenco Recordings—features Tientos, Soleares, Seguiriyas, Peteneras AL 2-▲ 203 (36.97)

Tracht, Avery (ten)

The Jewish Palette, w. Herman Rouw (pno), Jules van Hessen (cnd), *(ensemble unknown)*—features works by D. Goldstein *(V'shamroe; Kaddish and Avot)*, Sulzer *(Mi Adir)*, Alter *(R'tzei)*, Lewandowski *(K'dusha; V'al y'dei/Zacharti lach; Ki K'shimcha)*, Weill *(Kiddush)*, B. Steinberg *(Shiru Ladonai; Hashkivenu)*, Halévy *(Min Hametzar)*, Katchko *(Acheinu)*, Russotto *(Kol Nidrei)*, Binder *(Adonai Ro'i)*, Janowski *(Sim Shalom) (rec Amsterdam, May 1996)* ERAS ▲ 195 [DDD] (13.97)

Traubel, Helen (sop)

Helen Traubel in Concert—features works by Wagner *(Einsam in trüben Tagen [from Lohengrin]; Brunnhilde's Battle Cry; Du bist der Lenz [both from Walküre]; Tristan und Isolde [sels])*, Beethoven *(Egmont [sels])*, Brahms *(Wiegenlied [sels])*, Rodgers *(Oklahoma [sels]) (plus songs from Monteux, Steinberg, Wallenstein, Walter, Pelletier; Traubel interview) (rec 1941-46)* EKLR ▲ 56 (16.97)

Helen Traubel Rarities on Radio—features Just the Way You Look Tonight; Whethter By Day; Adios Grenada; Oh What a Beautiful Morning; I'm Wearin' Away Jean; Yours is My Heart Alone; The Lost Chord; Ave Maria [by Bach-Gounod]; The Lord's Prayer; Greensleeves; The Lonesome Road; Divinité du Styx; Stout-Hearted Men *(rec 1937-44)* RY (The Radio Years) ▲ 10 (m) (16.97)

Trawińska-Moroz, Urszula (sop)

Bel Canto, w. Polish Radio-TV Orch [cnd:Jan Pruszak, Wlodzimierz Kamirski]—features works by Delibes *(Lakmé aria [from Lakmé, Act III])*, Verdi *(Gildy aria [from Rigoletto, Act II]; Violetty aria [from Traviata, Act I])*, Donizetti *(Cavatina Lindy [from Lidna di Chamounix, Act I])*, Rossini *(Cavatina Rozyny [from Il Barbiere di Siviglia, Act I])*, Gounod *(Walc Julii [from Roméo et Juliette, Act I])*, Puccini *(Walc Musetty [from La Bohéme, Act III])*, Moniuszko *(Dumka Zosi [from Flis])*, Zerbin *(Con for Voice & Orchestra)* POLN ▲ ECD 063

Tucci, Gabriella (sop), Giuseppe Taddei (bar)

The Martini & Rossi Concerts, Vol. 29, w. Turin RAI SO [cnd:Arturo Basile]—features arias from Donizetti *(Linda di Chamounix; La favorita)*, Verdi *(Il trovatore; Otello)*, Mozart *(Don Giovanni)*, Puccini *(Suor angelica)*, Cilea *(Adriana Lecouvreur)*, Massenet *(Erodiade)* INM ▲ 5029 [ADD] (16.97)

Tucker, Richard (ten)

Richard Tucker In Recital, w. pno accompaniment—features arias from Pecheurs de perles, L'Arlesiana, L'Elisir d'amore, Floridante [Handel], Cavalleria Rusticana, Joseph [Méhul], L'Africana, Euridice [Peri], Tosca, Turandot, Luisa Miller; plus 12 Italian, Jewish & Traditional Songs *(rec New York recitals, 1972 & 1974)* HRE ▲ 1003-1 [ADD]

Tullio, Eileen di (sop)

The Art of Eileen di Tullio—features works by Mozart *(Et Incarnatus Est; Exultate Jubilate; Ach Ich Liebte)*, Handel *(Care Selve)*, R. Strauss *(Die Verschwiegenen; Die Nacht; Mohnblumen; Heimkehr; Amor)*, Sergius Kagen *(I'm Nobody)*, Rimsky-Korsakov *(The Rose Enslaves the Nightingale)*, Rachmaninoff *(Here Beauty Dwells)*, Meyerbeer *(Aria; Shadow Song)*, Debussy *(Voici que le Printemps; Green)*, Liszt *(O Quand Je Dors)*, Poulenc *(Air Vif; A Sa Guitare)*, Donizetti *(Romance [Il Faut Partir])*, Milhaud *(Tais-Toi Babillarde)*, Moore *(Dearest mama, I am writing)*, Saint-Saëns *(Vocalise)*, anon. *(Shepherd Thy Demeanour Vary)* LCD ▲ 196 (13.97)

Turner, Richard (ten)

Voices That Are Gone: Songs from Victorian America, w. Anne Beetem (pno)—features Daisy Bell; Love's Old Sweet Song; The Flying Trapeze; The Lost Chord; Jean; Beautiful Dreamer; Please Let Me Sleep; The Voices That Are Gone; Danny Deever; Because; My Wife Is A Most Knowing Woman; The Holy City; Come Home Father; Come into the Garden; Maude; Grandfather's Clock; The Last Rose of Summer; Stars & Stripes Forever Corvus ▲ RT 1196

Upshaw, Dawn (sop)

The Girl with Orange Lips *(songs for solo voice and chamber ensemble)*—features works by Maurice Delage *(Quatre poèmes hindous)*, Falla *(Psyché)*, Earl Kim *(Where grief slumbers)*, Ravel *(Trois poèmes de Mallarmé)*, Stravinsky *(Three Japanese Lyrics; Two Poems of Constantin Bal'mont)* 75597 ▲ 79262 ▮ 79262-4 AW

1080 ▲ = CD ♦ = Enhanced CD △ = MD ▮ = Cassette Tape ▯ = DCC

VOCAL

Upshaw, Dawn (sop) (cont.)
White Moon: Songs to Morpheus—features works by Warlock *(Sleep [w. Margo Garrett (pno)])*, Handel *(Alceste [Gentle Morpheus; w. Orpheus CO])*, Monteverdi *(L'incoronazione di Poppea [Oblivion Soave; w. Sérgio Assad (gtr), Odair Assad (gtr)])*, R. C. Seeger *(White Moon [w. Margo Garrett (pno)])*, Schwantner *(2 Poems of Agueda Pizarro [Black Anemones; w. Margo Garrett (pno)])*, Dowland *(Weep You No More, Sad Fountains [w. S. Assad (gtr)])*, Villa-Lobos *(Bachianas brasileiras 5 [Aria])*, Crumb *(Night of the 4 Moons [w. Susan Rotholz (a fl/pic), David Starobin (banjo), Eric Bartlett (elec vc), James Baker (perc)])*, Purcell *(The Fairy Queen [See, Even Night; w. Sérgio Assad (gtr), Odair Assad (gtr)]) (rec The Hit Factory, New York, June 1995)* NON ▲ 79364 (16.97)

Urbanová, Eva (sop)
Opera Arias, w. Prague SO [cnd:Jiří Bělohlávek]—features arias from *Aida, Un ballo in maschera, La forza del destino, Don Carlos, Tosca, Norma & Don Giovanni* SUR ▲ 111851 [DDD]

Vaduva, Leontina (sop)
Opera Arias, w. Plácido Domingo (cnd), Philharmonia Orch—features works by Gounod *(Ah! Je veux vivre; Dieu! Quel frisson court dans mes [both from Roméo & Juliette]; Heureux petit berger; Le Désert de la Crau; Voici la vaste plaine et le désert de feu [all from Mireille])*, Massenet *(Restons ici, puisqu'il le faut; Adieu, notre petite table [both from Manon])*, Bizet *(Me violà seule dans la nuit [from Les Pêcheurs des perles])*, Donizetti *(Quel guardo il cavaliere [from Don Pasquale])*, Rossini *(Di piacer mi balza il cor [from La gazza ladra])*, Verdi *(E strano...Ah, fors'è lui; Teneste la promessa [both from La traviata])*, Puccini *(O mio babbino caro [from Gianni Schicchi])*, Leoncavallo *(Qual fiamma avea nel guardo! [from Pagliacci])*, Dendrino *(Această melodie...Te iubsec [from Lăsați-mă să cînt])* [E,F,I,Romanian] *(rec Lyndhurst Hall, London, Jun-Aug 1997)* EMIC ▲ 56584 [DDD] (16.97)

Valdengo, Giuseppe (bar)
Giuseppe Valdengo, Vol. 2—features works by Donizetti *(Cruda, funesta smania [from Lucia di Lammermoor]; O Lisbona alfin ti miro [from San Sebastiano])*, Rossini *(Largo al factotum; All'idea di quel metallo [both from Il barbiere di Siviglia]; Resta immobile [from Guglielmo Tell])*, Mozart *(Hai già vinto la causa; Non più andrai [from Le nozze di Figaro]; Deh vieni alla finestra [from Don Giovanni])*, Giordano *(Nemico della patria [from Andrea Chenier])*, Massenet *(O casto fior [from Il Re di Lahore])*, Tosti *(L'Ultima canzone; La serenata; A' vucchella; La mia canzone; Ideale; Occhi di fata; Chitarra abruzzese)*; Bixio *(Rondine al nido)*, De Leva *(Canta il mare) (rec 1946-55)* BONG (Il Mito della'Opera) ▲ 1085 (16.97)

Valente, Alessandro (ten)
Alessandro Valente—features arias & songs by Leoncavallo, Puccini, Wolf-Ferrari, Giordano, Verdi, Meyerbeer, Bizet, Mascagni *(rec 1927-30)* PRE (Lebendige Vergangenheit) ▲ 89126 (16.97)

Valletti, Cesare (ten)
Cesare Valletti—features arias from Sonnambula, Lucia di Lammermoor, Manon, Werther, Don Giovanni, Barbiere di Siviglia, Italiana in Algeri, Betulia Liberata, Traviata *(rec live, 1954-60)* MEMO (Great Voices) 2-▲ 4191 (m)

Vallin, Ninon (sop)
The Complete Pathé-Art Recordings *(rec 1927-29)* MRSN 2-▲ 52006 (35.97)
Opera & Mélodie *(17 arias & songs)*, w. various orchs & pno accompaniment—features arias from Carmen, Pêcheurs de perles, Louise, Le Roi d'Ys, Hérodiade, Fortunio [Messager]; songs by Balakirev, Bemberg, Chabrier, Debussy, Duparc, Fauré *(rec 1927-38 from Odéon, Pathé & Columb)* PHS ▲ 9948 (m) [AAD] (18.97)

Van Dam, José (b-bar)
Le Chant d'un Maître—features works by Donizetti *(Vieni, la mia vendetta [from Lucrezia Borgia])*, Mahler *(Revelge [from Des Knaben Wunderhorn]; Ich bin der Welt abhanden gekommen; Um Mitternacht [both from Rückert-Lieder]; Wenn dein Mütterlein [from Kindertotenlieder])*, Mozart *(Madamina! Il catalogo; Deh, vieni vieni alla finestra [both from Don Giovanni]; Der Vogelfänger bin ich ja...[from Die Zauberflöte]; Hai Già vinta la causa [from Le nozze di Figaro]; Mentre ti lascio, O Figlia [aria, K.513])*, Leoncavallo *(Si può [from Pagliacci])*, Puccini *(Vecchia zimmara, senti...[from La Bohème])*, Rossini *(La calunnia è un venticello [from Il barbiere di Siviglia])*, Verdi *(Cortigiani, vil razza damnata [from Rigoletto])*, Wagner *(O du mein holder Abendstern [from Tannhäuser])*, plus others FORL 2-▲ 302269 (31.97)
Les grands airs italiens, w. Loire PO [cnd:Marc Soustrot]—features music from I Pagliacci; La boheme; Guillaume Tell; Barbiere di Siviglia; Lucrezia Borgia; Mefistofele; Nabucco; Attila; Don Carlos; Rigoletto; Andrea Chenier FORL ▲ 16681 [DDD] (16.97)

Vane, Kyra (sop)
Kyra Vayne—features works by Borodin, Verdi, Gluck, Boito, Tchaikovsky, Spontini, Puccini, Schubert, Glière, Gretchaninoff, Mussorgsky & Rachmaninoff PRE (Lebendige Vergangenheit) ▲ 89996 [AAD] (16.97)

Varcoe, Stephen (bass)
If There Were Dreams to Sell: English Orchestral Songs, w. City of London Sinfonia [cnd:Richard Hickox] *(see* Composer listings under Butterworth, Elgar, Finzi, Ireland, Quilter and Vaughan Williams) CHN ▲ 8743 [DDD] (16.97)
La Procession: 80 Years of French Song (1839-1919), w. Graham Johnson (pno)—features works by Auric, Bizet, Chabrier, Chausson, Debussy, Delibes, Duparc, Durey, Fauré, Franck, Gounod, Hahn, Honegger, Lalo, Liszt, Marchetti, Massenet, Messager, Ravel, Saint-Saëns, Satie [F] HYP ▲ 66248 [DDD]

Vargas, Ramón (ten)
Canzoni italiane, w. Roberto Negri (pno)—features works by Bellini *(Vaga luna)*, Cordillo & Cordiferro-Fields *(Core'ngrato)*, De Crescenzo & Sica *(Rondine al nido)*, De Curtis *(Autunno; A'Vucchella)*, Falvo *(Dicitencello vuie!)*, Gastaldon *(Musica proibita)*, Grever *(Muñequita linda; Despedida)*, Leoncavallo *(Mattinata)*, Nacho *(Borrichita)*, Nardella *(Chiove)*, Ponce *(Lejos de ti)*, A. Scarlatti *(Già il sole dal Gange)*, Tosti *(Ideale)*, anon *(Fenesta che lucive)* LALI ▲ 14307 (3.97)

Varjabed, David (bar)
Operatic Arias & Neapolitan Songs *(all sels arr Melik Mavisakalian, w. Kevork Adjemian & Yervant Erkanian)*, w. Yerevan RSO [cnd:Rafael Mangasarian], Yerevan String Orch [cnd:Kevork Adjemian]—features works by Verdi *(Cortigiani, vil razza dannata [from Rigoletto]; Tutto è deserto/Il balen del suo sorriso [from Il trovatore]; Alzati/Eri tu che macchiavi quell 'anima [from Un ballo in maschera]; Di provenza il mar [from La traviata])*, Rossini *(Largo al factotum [from Il barbiere di Siviglia])*, Gounod *(Avant de quitter ces lieux [from Faust])*, Mozart *(Deh vieni alla finestra; Finch'han dal vino [from Don Giovanni]; Se vuol ballare, Non più andrai [from Le nozze di Figaro])*, Tchookhadjian *(I desire [from Arshag II])*, di Capua *(O sole mio)*, Mario *(Santa Lucia luntana)*, de Curtis *(Non ti scordar di me; Senza nisciuno; Torna a Surriento)*, Falvo *(Dicitencello vuie)*, Lara *(Granada)*, Gastaldon *(Musica Prohibita)*, Tosti *(A Vucchella)*, d'Hardelot *(Because)* DHR ▲ 71121 [AAD] (11.97)

Vayne, Kyra (sop)
Kyra Vayne, Vol. 2—features songs & arias by Tchaikovsky, Kotchetov, Gretchaninov, Vasilenko, Mussorgsky, Szymanowski, Berlioz, Wagner, Puccini, Provost, Lehár, Bach, Gounod, J. Strauss *(rec 1945-64)* PRE (Lebendige Vergangenheit) ▲ 89993 (16.97)
Kyra Vayne in Opera & Concert—features works by Spontini *(Vestale [sels])*, Verdi *(Trovatore [sels])*, Puccini *(Tosca [sels])*, Mussorgsky *(Songs)*, Prokofiev *(Songs)*, Foley *(Songs) (plus others) (rec 1946)* EKRP ▲ 16

Vázquez, Encarnación (mez)
Cuando Dos, w. Jaime Márquez (gtr)—features works by Revueltas *(5 Songs for Children)*, Falla *(7 Popular Spanish Songs)*, Guastavino *(5 Songs)*, Moreno *(2 Songs)*, Echevarria *(Cuando dos)* URT ▲ 13

Verrett, Shirley (mez)
Great Operatic Duets *(see above under "Caballé, Montserrat & Shirley Verrett")*
Shirley Verrett in Opera—features works by Gluck *(Amour, viens rendre [from Orfeo ed Eurydice])*, Donizetti *(Sposa a Percy [from Anna Bolena]; Fia dunque vero [from La favorita])*, Berlioz *(Premiers transports [from Roméo et Juliette]; D'amour l'arente flamme [from La damnation de Faust])*, Gounod *(Ou suis-je [from Sapho])*, Massenet *(Letter Scene [from Werther])*, Saint-Saëns *(Mon coeur s'ouvre a ta voix [from Samson et Dalila])*, Verdi *(Lasciatelo ch'ei vada [from La forza del destino]; Re dell'abisso affrettati [from Un ballo in maschera])* RCAV (Gold Seal) ▲ 61457 (10.97)

Vickers, Jon (ten)
Canadian Art Songs, w. Richard Woitach (pno)—features works by S. I. Glick *(2 Landscapes)*, Somers *(3 Songs to Words by Whitman)*, Coulthard *(6 Mediaeval Love Songs)*, G. Ridout *(Folk Songs of Eastern Canada)*, Beckwith *(5 Lyrics of the T'ang Dynasty)*, B. Naylor *(Speaking from the Snow)*, Morawetz *(Piping Down the Valleys Wild; Love the Jocund Dance; Land of Dreams) ([E,F] texts)* 2381 ▲ 6398 [DDD]
Italian Opera Arias, w. Rome Opera Orch [cnd.:Tullio Serafin]—features 12 arias from Ponchielli, Flotow, Verdi, Cilea, Leoncavallo, Giordano, Puccini *(rec Rome, July 1961)* VAIA ▲ 1016 [AAD] (17.97)
Live Performances 1961-1970—features arias & scenes from Fidelio *(w. Rysanek, Tozzi, Berry, K. Böhm, San Francisco Opera 1968)*, Carmen *(w. Grace Bumbry, Karajan, Vienna State Opera 1966 & 1967)*, Medea [Cherubini] *(w. Callas, Cossotto, Schippers, La Scala 1961)*, Otello *(five scenes—w. Freni, Davies, Glossop, Karajan, Vienna State Opera 1970)*, Walküre *(41 minutes of excerpts—w. Janowitz, Talvela, Karajan, Berlin PO 1967)* MEMO 2-▲ 4394 (m) [ADD]

Vidal, Elisabeth (sop)
Romances & Songs about Birds, w. S. Manoff (pno), Philippe Bernold (fl)—features works by Debussy *(Mélodies)*, Benedict *(La gitane et l'oiseau)*, Saint-Saëns *(La libellule; Le rossignol et la rose)*, David *(Air de Lora)*, Beydts *(Chansons pour les oiseaux)*, Longas *(Le rossignol et l'Emperuer)*, Rosenthal *(Trois précieuses)* VAL ▲ 4707

Viglione-Borghese, Domenico (b-bar)
Domenico Viglione Borghese—features works by Verdi *(Pari salmo; Cortigiani, vil razza dannata [both from Rigoletto]; Tace la notte...deserto sulla terra [from Il trovatore]; Solenne in quest'ora [from La forza del destino]; Di Napatale gole [from Aida]; Credo in un Dio crudel [from Otello])*, Marchetti *(A'miei revali cedere [from Ruy Blas])*, Bizet *(Con voi ber [from Carmen])*, Ponchielli *(O Monumento; Pescatore, affonda l'esca [both from La gioconda])*, Massenet *(Vision fugitiva [from Herodïade]; Ecco dunque l'orribile citta [from Thaïs])*, Puccini *(Anima santa della figlia mia [from Le villi]; Tarda è la notte [from Tosca])*, Mascagni *(Il cavallo scalpita [from Cavalleria rusticana])*, Leoncavallo *(Si può? [from Pagliacci]; Zaza, piccola zingara [from Zaza])*, Catalani *(Sei tu che domandasti la mia mano; L'Hagenbach qui? [both from La Wally])*, Giordano *(Son sessant'anni; Un di m'era di gioia [both from Andrea Chenier])*, Franchetti *(Ferito, prigionier [from Germania])* BONG (Il mito dell'opera) ▲ 1146 [ADD] (31.97)

Vodička, Leo Marian (ten)
Famous Italian Canzonettas, w. Prague RSO [cnd:Oliver Dohnányi]—features O Sole Mio; Non ti scordar di me; Torna a Surriento; Nina; Santa Lucia; Caro Mio Bien; Viene sul Mar; plus others BONT ▲ 82 (10.97)

Voldby, Leni (mez)
This Is Denmark, w. Inke Kessler (pno)—features 16 Danish songs with music by Svenningsen *(rec Dec 1990)* DANR ▲ DACOCD 377 [DDD]

Völker, Franz (ten)
Franz Völker Sings Lieder—features works by Mozart, Schubert, Schumann, Loewe, Wolf, Brahms & R. Strauss *(rec 1927-41)* PRE ▲ 89997 [ADD] (16.97)
Franz Völker, Vol. 2—features arias from The Magic Flute, Der Freischütz, Fidelio, La juive, Rienzi, Der fliegende Holländer, Tannhäuser, Die Walküre, Otello, I Pagliacci, Dalibor & Tiefland *(rec 1933-41)* PRE ▲ 89070 [ADD] (16.97)
In the Kingdom of Operettas—features arias by Lehár, Strauss, Eyssler, Zeller, Benatzky, Hollaender, Millocker, Friml *(rec 1927-38)* PRE 2-▲ 89221 (31.97)
Opera Arias, w. Berlin State Opera Orch [var. cnds]—features sels. from Rienzi, Fliegende Holländer, Lohengrin, Meistersinger, La juive, L'Africaine, Trovatore, Aida, Otello, Pagliacci PRE (Lebendige Vergangenheit) ▲ 89005 (m) [AAD] (16.97)

Wächter, Eberhard (bar)
Eberhard Wächter, w. Berlin RSO [cnd:Gustav König], Munich PO [cnd:Ferdinand Leitner], Bamberg SO [cnd:Ferdinand Leitner]—features works by Gluck *(Ihr, die ihr mich verfolgt; Die Ruhe kehret mir zurück [both from Iphigenie in Tauride])*, Donizetti *(Leonare, meine Krone [from La favorita])*, Kreutzer *(Ein Schütz bin ich [from Das Nachtlager in Grenada])*, Nicolai *(In einem Waschkorb? [from Die lustigen Weiber von Windsor])*, Wagner *(Blick' ich umher in deisem edlen Kreise; Wie Todesahnung Dämm'rung deckt die Lande [both from Tannhäuser])*, Gounod *(Da ich nun verlassen soll; Schnell hierher [both from Margarethe]; Avant de quitter ces lieux; Par ici, par ici, mes amis! [both from Faust])*, Humperdinck *(Verdorben! Gestorben! [from Königskinder])*, Leoncavallo *(Nedda-Silvio! Zu dieser Stunde [w. Anny Schlem (mez); from Pagliacci])* [G,F] *(rec 1955-57)* PRE ▲ 90346 (m) [ADD] (16.97)

Wagner, Lauren (sop)
American Song Recital, w. Fred Weldy (pno)—features works by Richard Hundley, Bernstein, Urquart, Lari Laitman, Paul Bowles, John Corigliano, John Duke, Richard Thomas, John Musto, William Bolcom, Gershwin CCL ▲ 5293 [DDD] (17.97)

Walker, Norman (bass)
A Portrait of Norman Walker, w. Joan Cross (sop), Alfred Deller (ct), Webster Booth (ten), Richard Lewis (ten), Malcolm Sargent (cnd)—features works by Handel *(I Rage, I Melt, I Burn...O Ruddier Than the Cherry [from Acis & Galatea]; I Feel the Deity Within...Arm, Arm, Ye Brave [from Judas Maccabaeus]; Why Do the Nations; The Trumpet Shall Sound [both from Messiah])*, Haydn *(And God Said; Now Heav'n in Fullest Glory [both from Die Schöpfung])*, Elgar *(Jesu! By That Shuddering Dread [from The Dream of Gerontius])*, Holbrooke *(Sea King's Song [from Dylan]; Noden's Song [from Children of Don])*, Gounod *(Then Leave Her [from Faust])*, Purcell *(What, What Can Be Done?)*, Mozart *(O Isis & Osiris [from Die Zauberflöte]; Ah My Pretty Brace of Fellows [from Die Entführung aus dem Serail])* [E] *(rec 1928-54)* DLAB ▲ 7021 [ADD]

Walker, Sarah (mez)
Cabaret Songs, w. Roger Vignoles (pno)—features works by Britten, Coward, Dankworth, Duke, Gershwin, Ives, Mallory *(rec live 1982 & 1988)* MER ▲ 84167
Dreams and Fancies (Favorite Songs in English)—features works by Bridge, Clarke, Delius, Dunhill, Gibbs, Gurney, Head, Hoiby, Howells, Ireland, Nelson, Quilter, Stanford, Sullivan, Vaughan Williams, Warlock CRD ▲ 3473 [DDD] (17.97)
The Sea *(see Allen, Thomas above)*
Shakespeare's Kingdom [E,F,G] HYP ▲ 66136 (17.97)

Warren, Leonard (bar)
His First Recordings (1940), w. Wilfrid Pelletier (cnd)—features ten arias and scenes from Carmen, Pagliacci, Aida [w. Rose Bampton], Rigoletto [w. Jean Dickenson], Armand Tokatyan, et al., Traviata [w. Eleanor Steber] *(rec Town Hall, New York City and Academy of Music, Philadelphia, May-June 1940)* VAIA ▲ 1017 (m) [ADD] (17.97)
Leonard Warren, w. Jan Peerce (ten), RCA Victor Orch [cnd:Jean-Paul Morel, Wilfred Pelletier, William Tarrasch, Frieder Weissman], Robert Shaw Chorale—features works by Verdi *(Il balen del suo sorriso; Qual suono...Per me ora fatale [both from Il trovatore]; Pari siamo; Cortigiani, vil razza dannata [both from Rigoletto]; Invano Alvaro [from La forza del destino]; Eri tu che macchiavi [from Un ballo in maschera]; Credo in un Dio crudel [from Otello]; È sogno? o realtà? [from Falstaff])*, Ponchielli *(O monumento; Pescator, affonda l'esca [both from La Gioconda])*, Gounod *(Avant de quitter ces lieux [from Faust])*, Offenbach *(Scintille diamant [from Les Contes d'Hoffman])*, Bizet *(Votre toast, je peux vous le rendre [from Carmen])*, Rossini *(Largo al factotum [from Il barbiere di Siviglia])*, Leoncavallo *(Si può? [from Pagliacci]) (rec 1941-47)* PRE (Lebendige Vergangenheit) ▲ 89145
Live Radio Broadcasts (1940-1958)—features 14 arias from Andrea Chénier, Gioconda, Barbiere di Siviglia, Aida, Falstaff, Otello, Simon Boccanegra, Traviata BIM (Biographies in Music) ▲ 707 (m) (13.97)
On Tour in Russia, w. William Sektberg (pno)—features arias and songs by Bach, Beethoven, Bizet, Bridge, Fauré, Giordano, Gounod, Griffes, Handel, Leoncavallo, Ravel, Tosti, Verdi, et al. RCAV (Gold Seal) ▲ 7807 (m) [ADD] (10.97) 7807
Recital, 1941-1947—features arias from operas by Rossini, Verdi, Ponchielli, Bizet, Gounod, Offenbach & Leoncavallo MYTO ▲ 93593 (17.97)

Weikl, Bernd (bar)
Opera & Operetta Arias features sels. from Tiefland [d'Albert], Zar und Zimmermann [Lortzing], Hans Heiling [Märschner], Der Vampyr [Märschner], Feuersnot [R. Strauss], Meistersinger, Tannhäuser, Euryanthe [G] Acanta ▲ 43266
Operetta Recital, w. Austrian Radio Orch, Austrian Radio Chorus [cnd:Kurt Eichhorn]—features 15 arias by Eysler, Kálmán, Lehár, Lincke, Millöcker, Stolz, O. Straus, Joh. Strauss, Zeller, et al. ORF ▲ 77831 (18.97)

Weir, Scot (ten)
Frei, aber Einsam, Vol. 2: Friends of Schumann & Their Music, w. T. A. Körber (pno)—features Baroni (-Cavalcabò) *(Schäfers Klagelied)*, F. David *(Tanz, Op. 30/4)*, A. Dietrich *(Mit dem blauen Federhute; Still weht die Nacht, Op. 10/5)*, N. W. Gade *(Spring Flowers (3), Op. 2b)*, S. Heller *(Nähe des Geliebten)*, F. v. Hiller *(Mignon, Op. 129/3; Nähe des Geliebten, Op. 129/1; Wanderers Nachtlied, Op. 129/11)*, J. Joachim *(Ich habe im Traum geweint)*, T. Kirchner *(Songs, Op. 1)*, O. Lorenz *(Mignon Lied)*, Mendelssohn (-Bartholdy) *(Das Waldschloss; Ferne, Op. 9/9; Frage, Op. 9/1; Gondellied; Pagenlied, Op. posth.)*, Mendelssohn (-Hensel) *(Ach, die Augen sind es wieder; Fichtenbaum und Palme; O Traum der Jugend; Warum sind denn die Rosen so Blass?)*, R. Schumann *(Gesanges Erwachen; Gesänge, Op. 142; Klavierstücke, Op. 85; Lieder und Gesänge, Op. 127)*, Schunke *(Gretchen am Spinnrad)*, L. Spohr *(Mignon's Lied, Op. 37/1; Songs (6), Op. 41)*, Taubert *(Heindenröslein, Op. 5/2)* TACE ▲ 39
Frei Aber Einsam-Vol. 3 The Friends of Robert Schumann & their Music, w. T. A. Körber (pno)—features W. S. Bennett *(Diversions (3), Op. 17; Millstream; Songs (6), Op. 23; Songs (6), Op. 35)*, J. Brahms *(Intermezzos (3) Pno, Op. 117; Songs (6), Op. 85)*, F. David *(Elegie, Op. 30/8; Tarantelle, Op. 30/20)*, Henselt *(Rhapsody in f)*, F. v. Hiller *(Mitternacht, Op. 129/9)*, Liszt *(Albumblatt Pno in A, S.166)*, C. Reinecke *(Liebst du um Schönheit, Op. 5/6; Lied, Op. 5/3; Romanze)*, Rietz *(Du bist die Ruh)*, C. Schumann *(Ihr Bildnis; Liebst du um Schönheit, Op. 12/4; Sie liebten sich beide, Op. 13/2; Volkslied)*, R. Schumann *(Gedichte, Op. 35; Romanzen und Balladen, Op. 64; Variationen über ein Nocturne von Chopin)* TACE ▲ 48
Schöne Welt, wo bist du?, w. Till Korber (pno)—German songs EIGE ▲ EIG 0150

Welitsch, Ljuba (sop)

Unforgettable Recitals: Ljuba Welitsch—features performances w. Wilhelm Furtwängler (cnd), Vienna PO *(Mozart:Ma qual mai s'offre...Fuggi, crudele, fuggi!; Don Ottavio, son morta...Or sai chi l'onore; Crudele? Ah no, mio bene [all from Don Giovanni; rec. Salzburg, 1950])*, James Robertson (cnd), BBC SO *(Mozart:Sagt, holde Frauen [from Le nozze di Figaro]; Weber:Wie nahte mir der Schlummer [from Der Freischütz]; Smetana:Endlich allein, allein mit mir [from Die Verkaufte Braut] [all rec. London, 1948])*, Joseph Nelles (pno) *(Schumann:Widmung; Der Nussbaum; Mondnacht; Schubert:Die junge Nonne; Die Forelle; Die Liebesbotschaft; Brahms:Von ewger Liebe; Mondnacht; Meine Liebe ist grün [all rec. London, 1949])*, Richard Kraus (cnd), Monaco RSO *(Dvořák:Du liber Mond [from Rusalka; rec. Munich, 1949])*, Vittorio Gui (cnd), Royal PO *(Verdi:Morrò, ma prima in grazia [from Un ballo in maschera; rec. Edinburgh, 1949])*, Ramon Vinay (ten—Radamès), Robert Merrill (bar—Amonasro), Emil Cooper (cnd), Metropolitan Orch *(Verdi:Quì Radames verrà; O cieli azzurri; Cielo! Mio padre!; Su, dunque sorgete; Pur ti riveggo, mia dolce Aida; Fuggiam gli ardori inospiti; Di Napata le gole [all from Aida; rec. New York, 1950])*, Meinhard von Zallinger (cnd), Vienna RSO *(Puccini:Wer errät Dorettens Liebestraum; Das Geld, immer nur das Geld [both from La Rondine; rec. Vienna, 1955])*, Musica Leggera Orch *(Puccini:Quando men vo soletta [from La bohème; rec. Vienna, 1952])*, James Robertson (cnd), BBC SO *(Puccini:Vissi d'arte [from Tosca; rec. London, 1948])*, Thomas Beecham (cnd), Royal PO *(R. Strauss:Ich kann nicht sitzen und ins Dunkel starren [from Elektra; rec. London, 1947])*, Fritz Reiner (cnd), Metropolitan Opera House Orch & Chorus *(R. Strauss:In dein Haar bin ich verliebt, Jochanaan [from Salome; rec. New York, 1952])*, Hans Müller Kray (cnd), RSO *(R. Strauss:Ah! Du wolltest mich nicht deinen Mund küssen lassen [from Salome; rec. Stüttgart, 1955])* MELO 2-▲ 204004 [ADD]

White, Robert (ten)

Sure on This Shining Night: The Romantic Song in America, w. Samuel Sanders (pno)—features works by Chanler *(The Children; These, My Ophelia)*, Beach *(The Year's at the Spring)*, Chadwick *(When Stars Are in the Quiet Skies)*, W. Schuman *(Orpheus with His Lute)*, Ives *(The Side Show; The Collection)*, Corigliano *(Song to the Witch of the Cloisters)*, Barber *(Sure on This Shining Night)*, V. Thomson *(Sigh No More, Ladies)*, Korngold *(Come away, Death)*, Hindemith *(On Hearing 'The Last Rose of Summer'; Echo)*, Firestone *(If I Could Tell You)*, Malotte *(The Lord's Prayer)*, Copland *(Nature, the Gentlest Mother)*, Ewazen *(The Tiger)*, Bolcom *(Never More Will the Wind)*, Rorem *(Little Elegy)*, Romberg *(One Alone)*, Hageman *(Do Not Go, My Love)*, Marder *(To a Stranger)*, E. Charles *(When I Have Sung My Songs)*, Griffes *(An Old Song Re-sung)*, H. Parker *(June Night)*, Musto *(Triolet)*, Friml *(Rose Marie)*, V. Herbert *(Ah! Sweet Mystery of Life)* HYP ▲ 66920 (17.97)

With a Song in My Heart, w. Yo-Yo Ma (vc), Dick Hyman (pno), National PO [cnd:Ivor Bolton, Charles Gerhardt]—features works by Handel, Beethoven, Von Weber, Foster, Berlin, et al. SGLI 3-▲ 1 [ADD/DDD] (30.97)

White, Willard (bass)

10 American Spirituals, w. Graeme McNaught (pno)—features Go down, Moses; I couldn' hear nobody pray; Were you there when they crucified my Lord?; When I lay my burden down; Steal away to Jesus; In the mornin'; Gospel train; Swing low, sweet chariot; Deep river; Ev'ry time I feel de spirit); 3 Folk Songs from Barbados and Jamaica *(Linstead Market; Cordelia Brown; Murder in the market)*; Copland—Old American Songs (Sets 1 & 2) CHN ▲ 8960 [DDD] (16.97)

Wiegold, Mary (sop)

Mary Wiegold's Songbook, w. Composers Ensemble—features works by Dowland, Judith Weir, Colin Matthews, Simon Bainbridge, Howard Skempton, Harrison Birtwistle, Philip Wilby, Keith Tippett, John Woolrich, Dominic Muldowney, Sally Beamish, Bayan Northcott, David Bedford, Michael Nyman NMC ▲ NMC 3 [DDD]

Wiest, Gregory (ten)

Time Marches On: More Modern American Songs, w. Oresta Cybriwsky (pno)—features works by N. Mathews *(Songs of the Poet)*, Wallach *(Up into the silence)*, C. Field *(Yeats Songs [3])*, E. Austin *(A Birthday Bouquet)*, S. Wilcox *(Facing the Moon)*, P. A. Epstein *(BirdSongs)*, Perera *(Songs from Sleep Now)* CPS ▲ 8646 [DDD] (16.97)

Wildbrunn, Helene (sop)

Helene Wildbrunn—features works by Gluck, Mozart, Beethoven, Weber, Verdi, Wagner, Ponchielli, Mascagni & Puccini *(rec 1919-24)* PRE (Lebendige Vergangenheit) ▲ 89097 [AAD] (16.97)

Wilton, Ebba (sop)

The Danish Nightingale—features songs by Donizetti, Dupuy, Weyse, Heise, Schubert, Henriques, Flotow, Mozart, Rossini PONT ▲ 5111 (19.97)

Wittrisch, Marcel (ten)

Marcel Wittrisch: Opera Arias *(1901-1955)*—features arias by Bizet, Cornelius, Delibes, Leoncavallo, Mascagni, Meyerbeer, Offenbach, Puccini, Rossini, Verdi *(rec 1931-36)* PRE (Lebendige Vergangenheit) ▲ 89024 (m) [AAD] (16.97)

The Voice of Romance, w. Berlin State Opera Orch—features works by Verdi, Strauss, Bizet, Millöcker, Meyerbeer, Wagner, Smetana, Kienzl, Flowtow *(rec 1930-38)* PHS ▲ 9256 (17.97)

Wright, Patricia (sop)

Jane Austen Songs *(14 popular selections from the more than 200 songs that survive in Jane Austen's personal music collection)*, w. Jon Gillaspie (pno) [E] PHS ▲ 9613 [DDD] (17.97)

Serenata: Songs by Italian Opera Composers, w. David Vine (pno)—features works by Bellini, Verdi, Donizetti, Rossini, Puccini, Mascagni ATOL ▲ 9803 (18.97)

Wunderlich, Fritz (ten)

Arias, Lieder & Popular Songs *(budget-priced; includes family photos, and notes by Eva Wunderlich)*—features works by Bizet, Handel, Lortzing, Mozart, Schubert, Schumann, Tchaikovsky, Verdi, et al. DEUT 5-▲ 35145 (33.97)

Fritz Wunderlich's Last Concert, w. Hubert Giesen (pno)—features works by Schumann *(Dichterliebe, Op. 48 (complete))* and three individual songs by Schubert and Schumann; plus 12 songs by Beethoven and Schubert from a Salzburg recital, 8/19/65 *(rec Edinburgh, Sept 17, 1966)* MYTO ▲ 89011 (m) [ADD] (17.97)

The Great German Tenor EMIC 3-▲ 62993 (20.97)

The Legendary Voice of Fritz Wunderlich—features operetta arias from Giuditta, Der Zarewitsch, Das Land des Lächelns, Die Rose von Stambul, Die Fledermaus, Gräfin Mariza, Der Vogelhändler, et al. Acanta ▲ CD 43567

Münich Sunday Concerts 1961-66—features works by Mozart *(Ich baue ganz auf deine Stärke [from Entfürung aus dem Serail]; Nur ihrem Frieden; Il mio tesoro [both from Don Giovanni]; Dies Bildnis ist bezaubernd schön [from Zauberflöte])*, Rossini *(Strahlt suf mich der Glanz des Goldes [from Il barbiere di Siviglia]; Warum schlägt so rasch mein Herz [from Cenerantola])*, Donizetti *(Nun drang aus ihrem Herzen [from Liebestrank])*, Tchaikovsky *(Wohin seid ihr entschwinden [from Eugene Onegin])*, Verdi *(Lungi da lei-Dei miei bollenti spriti; O, lass uns fliehen [both from La traviata])*, Puccini *(Wie eiskalt ist dies Händschen [from La Bohème]; Mädschen, in deinen Augen liegt ein Zauber [from Madama Butterfly])*, Leoncavallo *(Mattinata)* [G] *(rec 1961-66)* ORFE ▲ 445961 (m) [ADD] (16.97)

Opera & Operetta Arias—features arias from Fidelio, Barbier von Bagdad [Cornelius], Der Kuhreigen [Kienzl], Undine [Lortzing], Waffenschmied [Lortzing], Zauberflöte, Zaide, Fierabras [Schubert] [G] Acanta ▲ 43267

Young, Thomas (ten)

Clair de Lune & Sister Moon, w. Jay Leonhart (bass), Mike Renzi (pno), Grady Tate (dr)—features works by Fauré *(En Sourdine; Au Bord de L'eau; Mandoline; Clair de lune; Automne; Prison)*, Rodgers *(I Have Dreamed)*, G. Wood *(My One & Only Love)*, Sondheim *(Pretty Women)*, Sting *(Sister Moon)*, E. Drake *(It Was a Very Good Year)*, B. Strayhorn *(Lush Life) (rec Nola Recording Studio, NYC, Oct 21 & 23, 1996)* ORC ▲ 104 (16.97)

Zaepffel, Alain (ct)

Dramatic Laments, w. Eugène Ferre (lt), Les Elements Ensemble of Viols—features works by Dowland, Hume, Byrd, plus others ADES ▲ 243722

Zanelli, Renato (ten)

Renato Zanelli—features works by Donizetti, Verdi, Planquette, Catalani, Leoncavallo, Luzzi, Friere, Nitke, Gastaldon, Ferri, Alvarez, Tirindelli, Padilla, Tosti, Di Chiara, Giordano, Bizet *(rec 1919-29)* PHS ▲ 9028 [AAD] (18.97)

Zeani, Virginia (sop)

Il mito dell'opera—features arias from Donizetti *(Maria di Rohan)*, Verdi *(Rigoletto; La traviata; Aida)*, Boito *(Mefistofele)*, Massenet *(Thaïs)*, Puccini *(La Bohème; Tosca)*, Cilea *(Adriana Lecouvreur)* BONG ▲ 1112 (16.97)

Virginia Zeani, w. various Italian orchs—features nine arias from Puritani, Anna Bolena, Elisir d'amore, Lucia di Lammermoor, La Vadova allegra [Lehár], Aida, Don Carlos, Forza del destino; and one song, "Vilja" *(rec live, 1957-69)* BONG ▲ 1060 [ADD] (16.97)

Zenatello, Giovanni (ten)

The Collected Recordings, Vol. 1—features over 90 sels. *(rec 1903 & 1905-11)* PHS 4-▲ 9073 [AAD] (67.97)

Giovanni Zenatello (1876-1949), w. Rosario Bourdon (cnd), Carlo Sabajno (cnd)—features 14 arias from Carmen, Andrea Chénier, Pagliacci, Manon Lescaut, Tosca, Ballo in maschera, Otello *(rec 1926-30 for HMV)* PRE (Lebendige Vergangenheit) ▲ 89038 (m) [AAD] (16.97)

La Grandi Voci Italiana, Vol. 8—features arias from works by Donizetti *(Lucia di Lammermoor)*, Verdi *(La traviata; Un ballo in maschera; Aida; Otello)*, Wagner *(Die Meistersinger von Nürnberg)*, Gounod *(Faust)*, Ponchielli *(La Gioconda)*, Saint-Saëns *(Samson et Dalila)*, Boito *(Mefistofele)*, Puccini *(Manon Lescaut) (rec 1903-08)* CECL ▲ 518 (13.97)

The Harold Wayne Collection, Vol. 17: The Fonotipia Recordings—features arias & scenes from Aida *(Celeste Aida; La, tra foreste; Gia i sacerdoti; O terra addio)*, Otello *(Niun mi tema; Gia nella notte densa; Ora e per sempre addio sante memorie; Si pel ciel; Dio mi potevi; Niun mi tema)*, Ruy Blas *(O dolce volutta)*, & La Gioconda *(Enzo Grimaldo; Cielo e mar; Duetto finale [Act 2]; Dal carcere m'hai tratto) (rec 1908-10)* SYMP ▲ 1148 (17.97)

The Harold Wayne Collection, Vol. 19: G. Zenatello—The Fonotipia Recordings—features arias & scenes from L. di Lammermoor, Norma, Mephistofele, Germania, La Figlia di Jorio, Andrea Chénier, I maestri cantori, Gli Ugonotti, Faust, Sansone e Dalila & Il Guarany; Songs by Rosa, Denza & Rotoli *(rec 1906-12)* SYMP ▲ 1168 (17.97)

The Tenor, Vol. 1—features arias from Un ballo in maschera; Manon Lescaut; Otello; La traviata; Carmen; La Gioconda; Mefistofele; La Bohème; Faust; Tosca; Pagliacci; Aida; La forza del destino; Il trovatore; La fanciulla del West VOCA (Vocal Archives) ▲ 1136 (13.97)

Žídek, Ivo (ten)

Ivo Žídek Operatic Recital, w. Prague National Theater Orch—features his best known arias SUR ▲ 3189

Zilani, Alessandro (ten)

Alessandro Zilani (1906-1977), w. Maria Caniglia (sop), Gina Cigna (sop), Mafalda Favero (sop), Augusta Oltrabella (sop), Berlin State Opera Orch [cnd:Bruno Siedler-Winkler], La Scala Orch [cnd:Giuseppe Antonicelli, Franco Ghione, Alberto Erede, Dino Olivieri]—features works by Boieldieu *(Vieni mio tesoro [from La dama bianca])*, Wagner *(Mai devi domandarmi [from Lohengrin])*, Giordano *(Amor ti vieta; Vedi, io piango [both from Fedora])*, Puccini *(Donna non vidi mai [from Manon Lescaut]; Che gelida manina; O soave fanciulla [both from La Bohème]; Bimba dagli occhi [from Madama Butterfly]; Ch'ella mi creda libero [from La fanciulla del West]; Non piangere liù; Nessun dorma [both from Turandot])*, Zandonai *(Benvenuto, signore mio cognato [from Francesca da Rimini])*, Denza *(Funiculi' funicula)*, Borgmann-Beckmann *(Königin der Liebe)*, Mascagni *(Serenata)* [I] *(rec 1935-36)* PRE (Lebendige Vergangenheit) ▲ 89165 (m) [AAD] (16.97)

Zinetti, Giuseppina (sop)

Opera Arias—features selections from works by Bizet *(Carmen)*, Verdi *(Ballo in maschera)*, Thomas *(Mignon)*, Ponchielli *(Gioconda)*, Gluck *(Orfeo ed Euridice)*, Saint-Saëns *(Samson et Dalila)*, Donizetti *(Favorita)* MNER ▲ 52 (14.97)

Zouves, Maria (sop)

With Flowers Crowned, w. Peter Lingen (gtr), John Goodin (mand), Jessica Paul (pno), Carol Hester (fl)—features works by Hadzidakis *(Somewhere My Love Exists; It Happened in Athens; Never on Sunday; Tired Young Man)*, Kalomiris *(The Temple; Hello, Roses & Flowers)*, Lambelet *(The River/Jasmine; With Flowers Crowned)*, Ravel *(Greek Folk Songs (5))*, Theodorakis *(I Planted a Heart; The Heartache)*, Xarhakos *(Bouzouki Interlude [from Stou Othona ta Xronia]; Barcarole; Place Another Plate on the Table; A Better Day for Us)*, Zoras *(The Flute; The Gypsy) (rec Center for Faith & Life, Luther College, Decorah, IA)* VAIA ▲ 1167 [DDD] (16.97)

VOCAL COLLECTIONS

A Capella—features performances by United States Naval Academy Men's Glee Club [cnd:John Talley] *(Hassler:Cantate Domino; Victoria:O Vos Omnes; Shepherd:Christ Rising Again; Grechaninov:Credo; Ippolitov-Ivanov:Bless the Lord O My Soul; Beibl:Ave Maria; Sprenkle:To Him that Lov'd; Behold the Mountain; I to the Hills; plus trad songs Anchors Aweigh; A Capital Ship; Spanish Ladies; Boston Harbor; Star Spangled Banner; America the Beautiful; Didn't My Lord Deliver Daniel; Steal Away; Ain'a that Good News)*, United States Naval Academy Barbershop Quartet *(The Java Jive; Chord Busters' March; Alexander's Rag Time Band)*, The Skivs *(The Lion Sleeps; Cupid)*, Those Guys *(Banana Boat Song; The Bluest Eyes of Texas; Under the Boardwalk)* Richardson ▲ 3297700202

The Age of Bel Canto, w. Joan Sutherland (sop), Marilyn Horne (mez), Richard Conrad (bar), London SO [cnd:Richard Bonynge], London Sym Chorus PLON (The Classic Sound) ▲ 48594 (22.97)

The American Opera Singer—features performances by Anna Moffo (sop), Roberta Peters (sop), Leontine Price (sop), Beverly Sills (sop), Eleanor Steber (sop), Dawn Upshaw (sop), Carol Vaness (sop), Deborah Voight (sop), Marilyn Horne (mez), Frederica von Stade (mez), Shirley Verrett (mez), Marian Anderson (cta), Enrico Caruso (ten), Ben Heppner (ten), Jan Peerce (ten), Richard Tucker (ten), Robert Merrill (bar), Sherill Milnes (bar), Leonard Warren (bar), Samuel Ramey (bass), et al. RCAV (Red Seal) 2-▲ 68921 (16.97)

American Prima Donnas—features arias & American ballads by Bernadette Antoine (sop), Dorothy Maynor (sop), Grace Moore (sop), Rosa Ponselle (sop), Thelma Votipka (mez), MacDonald (sgr), McCormic (sgr), Namara (sgr) EKLR ▲ 46 (16.97)

American Singers, Vol. 1, w. Louise Homer (cta), Paul Althouse (ten), Lucy Isabelle Marsh (sgr), Carolina White (sgr), Clarence Whitehill (sgr)—features sels from works by Cilea *(Adriana Lecouvreur)*, Mussorgsky *(Boris Godunov)*, Verdi *(Aida)*, Wagner *(Parsifal)*, Bizet *(Carmen)*, Joh. Strauss II *(Fledermaus)*, Meyerbeer *(Roberto le diable) (plus others)* IRCC ▲ 810 (16.97)

American Singers, Vol. 2, w. Carolina Lazzari (sgr), Queena Mario (sgr), Mario Chamlee (ten), Richard Bonelli (sgr) *(rec 1917-1936)* IRCC ▲ 811 (16.97)

American Singers, Vol. 3, w. Bessie Abott (sgr), Eleanora de Cisneros (sgr), George Hamlin (sgr), Henri Scott (sgr)—features sels from works by Verdi *(Rigoletto; Vespri siciliani)*, Wagner *(Walküre)*, Meyerbeer *(Huguenots), (plus others)* IRCC ▲ 816 (16.97)

Amor: Opera's Great Love Songs, w. Montserrat Caballé (sop), Mirella Freni (sop), Joan Sutherland (sop), Kiri Te Kanawa (sop), Renata Tebaldi (sop), Marilyn Horne (mez), José Carreras (ten), Franco Corelli (ten), Plácido Domingo (ten), Luciano Pavarotti (ten) PLON (Opera Gala) ▲ 458201 (11.97)

Amore: The Great Italian Love Arias, w. Kiri Te Kanawa (sop), Luciano Pavarotti (ten), Eva Martón (sop), et. al.—features works by Puccini, Verdi, Cilea, Donizetti, Flotow, Giordano, Leoncavallo COL ▲ 45747 (9.97) ▮ 45747 (5.98)

Angel's Visits—features performances of Victorian American songs by Harmoneion Singers [cnd:Neely Bruce], L. Skrobacs (pno) *(Webster:Sweet By & By; Willie's Grave [w. R. Murcell (bar)]; Woodbury:We Are Happy Now, Dear Mother; Lowry:Shall We Know Each Other There? [w. J. Pierce (sop), R. Taylor (mez)]; Buck:Rock of Ages [w. M. Stewart (sop)]; J. N. S:Oh, You Must Be a Lover of the Lord [w. H. Crook (ten), R. Murcel (bar)]; Pratt:Put My Little Shoes Away [w. R. Taylor (mez)]; Fischer:I Love to Tell the Story [w. R. Taylor (mez), R. Murcell (bar)]; Hicks:The Last Hymn [w. R. Taylor (mez), R. Murcell (bar)]; Dadmun:The Babe of Bethlehem)*, Lawrence Skrobacs (pno) *(White:Trusting [w. K. Battle (sop), C. Ryam (ten)]; Melnotte:Angel's Visits [w. K. Battle (sop)]; anon:Flee as a Bird [w. R. Taylor (mez)])* NWW ▲ 80220 (16.97)

Aria: A Passion for Opera—features performances by M. Callas (sop) *(Bizet:Quand je vous aimerai?...L'amour [from Carmen]; Bellini:Casta diva [from Norma])*, M. Caballé (sop) *(Puccini:Un bel dì vedremo [from Madama Butterfly]; Vissi d'arte [from Tosca])*, F. Corelli (ten) *(Leoncavallo:Recitar!...Vesti la giubba [from I Pagliacci]; Puccini:Nessun dorma [from Turandot]; Verdi:Di quella pira [from Il trovatore])*, P. Domingo (ten) *(Puccini:E Lucevan le stelle [from Tosca])*, M. Freni (sop) *(Puccini:O mio babbino caro [from Gianni Schicchi]; Chi il bel sogno di Doretta [from La Rondine]; Charpentier:Depuis le jour [from Louise])*, T. Gobbi (bar) *(Rossini:Largo al factotum [from Il Barbiere di Siviglia])*, A. Kraus (ten) *(Verdi:La donna è mobile [from Rigoletto])*, G. di Stefano (ten) *(Puccini:Avete torto! [from Gianni Schicchi])*, N. Gedda (ten) *(Donizetti:Una furtiva lagrima [from L'elisir d'amore])*, M. Mesplé (sop), D. Millet (sop) *(Delibes:Flower Duet [from Lakme])* EMIC ▲ 65163 (11.97) ▮ 65163 (7.98)

Arias, Duets & Trios from Operas—features performances by Arleen Augér (sop), Gundula Janowitz (sop), Tatiana Troyanos (mez), Nicolai Gedda (ten) BELV 2-▲ 7212 (28.97)

Aria III: A Passion for Opera—features performances by José Carreras (ten) *(Verdi:Celeste Aida [w. Herbert von Karajan (cnd), Vienna PO; from Aida]; Bizet:La fleur que tu m'avais jetée [w. Jacques Delacôte (cnd), Royal Opera House Orch; from Carmen]; Puccini:Non piangere, Liù [w. Alain Lombard (cnd), Strasbourg PO; from Turandot])*, Alfredo Kraus (ten) *(Gounod:Ah, lève-toi soleil [w. Michel Plasson (cnd), Toulouse Capitole Orch; from Roméo et Juliette]; Mozart:Un aura amarosa [w. Julius Redel (cnd), Philharmonia Orch; from Così fan tutte]; Verdi:De' miei bollenti spiriti [w. Riccardo Muti (cnd), Philharmonia Orch; from La traviata])*, Montserrat Caballé (sop) *(Boito:L'altra notte in fondo al mare [w. Julius Redel (cnd), London SO; from Mefistofele]; Puccini:Se come voi piccina [w. Charles Mackerras (cnd), London SO; from Le Villi]; Verdi:Pace, pace mio Dio [w. Anton Guadagno (cnd), Royal PO; from La forza del destino])*, Nicolai Gedda (ten) *(Massenet:Pourquoi me réveiller [w. Georges Prêtre (cnd), Orchestre de Paris; from Werther]; Verdi:Di' te se fedele [w. Giuseppe Pantané (cnd), Royal Opera House Orch; from Un ballo en maschera]; Thomas:Elle ne croyait [w. Georges Prêtre (cnd), French National RSO; from Mignon])*, Victoria de los Angeles (sop) *(Rossini:Una voce poco fa [w. Vittorio Gui (cnd), Royal PO; from Il barbiere di Siviglia])*, Franco Corelli (ten) *(Cilea:L'anima ho stanca [w. Franco Ferraris (cnd), Philharmonia Orch; from Adriana Lecouvreur])*, Maria Callas (sop) *(Ponchielli:Suicidio [w. Antonino Votto (cnd), La Scala Orch; from La Gioconda])*, Luigi Alva (ten) *(Mozart:Dalla sua pace [w. Carlo Maria Giulini (cnd), Philharmonia Orch; from Don Giovanni])*, Elisabeth Schwarzkopf (sop) *(Mozart:Porgi amor [w. Carlo Maria Giulini (cnd), Philharmonia Orch; from Le nozze di Figaro])* EMIC ▲ 66752 (11.97)

Aria: Une sélection de Radio-Canada: A CBC Records Collection—features performances by Maureen Forrester (cta), Brian Priestman (cnd), Vienna Radio Orch *(Handel:Frondi tenere...Ombra mai fù [from Serse])*, Manon Feubel (sop), Jacques Lacombe (cnd), Laval SO *(Puccini:Chi il bel sogno [from La Rondine])*, Ben Heppner (ten), Andrew Davis (cnd), Toronto SO *(Strauss:Di rigori armato il seno [from Rosenkavalier]; In Syriens Glut [from Die Liebe der Danae])*, Judith Forst (mez), Mario Bernardi (cnd), Vancouver SO *(Bellini:Deh! Tu bell'anima [from I Capuleti e i Montecchi])*, Richard Margison (ten), Richard Bradshaw (cnd), Canadian Opera Company Orch *(Giordano:Come un bel dì di maggio [from Andrea Chénier])*, Louis Quilico (bar), Uri Mayer (cnd), Edmonton SO *(Verdi:Cortigiani, vil razza dannata [from Rigoletto])*, Lyne Fortin (sop), Richard Margison (ten), Simon Streatfield (cnd), Quebec SO *(Massenet:Et je sais votre nom...nous vivrons à Paris...tous les deux [from Manon])*, Tracy Dahl (sop), Mario Bernardi (cnd), Calgary PO *(Donizetti:Chacun le sait [from La fille du régiment])*, Gaétan Laperrière (bar), Gilles Bellemare (cnd), Trois-Rivières SO *(Donizetti:Bella siccome un angelo [from Don Pasquale])*, Lois Marshall (sop), Thomas Beecham (cnd), Royal PO *(Mozart:Ach ich liebte, war so glücklich [from Die Entführung aus dem Serail])*, Linda Maguire (mez), Alan Curtis (cnd), Tafelmusik Baroque Orch *(Handel:Barbaro! t'odio a morte [from Floridante])*, Wendy Nielsen (sop), Anita Krause (mez), Richard Margison (ten), Gary Relyea (b-bar), Richard Bradshaw (cnd), Canadian Opera Company Orch, Canadian Opera Company Chorus *(Rossini:Dal tuo stellato soglio [from Mosè in Egitto])*, Mark DuBois (ten), Raffi Armenian (cnd), Kitchener-Waterloo SO *(Verdi:Lunge da lei...De' miei bollenti spiriti [from La traviata])*, Ermanno Mauro (ten), Uri Mayer (cnd), Edmonton SO *(Leoncavallo:Recitar!...Vesti la giubba [from Pagliacci])*, Joanne Kolomyjec (sop), Mario Bernardi (cnd), Calgary PO *(Rimsky-Korsakov:Spi, moy krasavitsa [from A May Night])*, Allan Monk (bar), Mario Bernardi (cnd), Calgary PO *(Tchaikovsky:Postoite, ma odno mgnovenye! [from Queen of Spades]*, Michèle Boucher (sop), Raffi Armenian (cnd), Kitchener-Waterloo SO *(Kálman:Höre ich Zigeunergeigen [from Gräfin Mariza])*, Joanne Kolomyjec (sop), Mark DuBois (ten), Raffi Armenian (cnd), Kitchener-Waterloo SO *(Kálman:Tanzen möcht ich [from Die Csárdásfürstin])* SMS ▲ 97 [DDD] (12.97)

The Art of the Savoyard *(collection of singers who worked personally w. Gilbert & Sullivan singing Gilbert & Sullivan)*—features performances by R. Temple (bar) *(A more humane Mikado [from The Mikado; rec Sept 1902]; I am a pirate king [from The Pirates of Penzance; rec 1903])*, Courtice Pounds (sgr) *(When a pullet is plump [from Chu Chin Chow; rec 1916])*, Isabel Jay (sop) *(Poor wand'ring one [from the Pirates of Penzance; rec 1904])*, Rutland Barrington (sgr) *(The moody mariner [rec 1905])*, Scott Russell (sgr) *(Would you know the kind of maid [from Princess Ida; rec Nov 21, 1900]; A tenor all singers above [from Utopia Limited; rec Nov 21, 1900]; Drinking song [from The Rose of Persia; rec Nov 21, 1900])*, Ruth Vincent (sgr) *(Waltz song [from Taylor/German's Tom Jones; rec 1915])*, Henry Lytton (bar) *(None shall part us [from Iolanthe; rec June 1902]; Imagination; The Yeoman of England [both from Hood/German's Merrie England; rec June & May 1902]; The curate's song [from The Sorcerer; rec May 1902])*, Walter Passmore (bar) *(My name is John Wellington Wells [from The Sorcerer; rec Dec 19, 1900]; If you're anxious for to shine [from Patience; rec Dec 19, 1900); As some day it may happen; On a tree by a river [both from The Mikado; both rec 1908])*, R. Evett (sgr) *(Is life a boon?; Free'd from his fetters grim [both from The Yeoman of the Guard; both rec 1907])*, Ilka von Palmay (sgr) *(Butterfly (folk song) [rec 1903])*, Amy Augarde (sgr) *(I'm called Little Buttercup [from HMS Pinafore; rec 1907])*, C. H. Workman (bar) *(Major-General's song [from The Pirates of Penzance; rec 1910]; If you give me your attention; Whene'er I spoke [both from Princess Ida; rec 1910 & 1912]; I have a song [w. Elsie Spain (sop)]; I've jibe & joke; A private buffoon [all from The Yeoman of the Guard; rec 1910, 1912 & 1910]; First you're born [from Utopia Limited; rec 1912])*, A. Sullivan *(Address to T. A. Edison [rec 1888 from private cylider made at Edison's behest])* PHS ▲ 9991 [AAD] (17.97)

Ave Maria—features works by J.S. Bach, Handel, Schubert, Liszt, Bizet & Weber CFP ▲ 4616 [ADD] (12.97)

Ave Maria—features works by J.S. Bach, Berlioz, Brahms, Gounod, Handel, Mozart, Rossini, Verdi PLON (Jubilee) ▲ 25016 [DDD/ADD]

Ave Maria, w. Bozena-Sieradzka Betley (sop), Wieslaw Ochman (ten), Leonard Mróz (bass), Marian Sawa (org)—features 16 versions of Ave Maria by Gounod, Schubert, Donizetti, Doss, Luzzi, Saint-Saëns, Bottazzo, Auer, Mascagni, Nowakowski, Katski, Chlondowski, Maklakiewicz, Raczkowski, Sawa POLN ▲ ECD 049 [DDD]

Ave Maria: Sacred Arias & Choruses, w. Failoni CO Budapest, Hungarian Radio Chorus [cnd:Mátyás Antál], Ingrid Kertesi (sop), Budapest Camerata [cnd:László Kovács], Jószsef Mukk (ten), Scholars Baroque Ensemble, Anna de Mauro (mez), Priti Coles (sop), Camerata Cassovia, Kosice Teachers' Choir [cnd:Johannes Wildner], Lisa Beckley (sop), Colm Carey (org), Oxford Camerata [cnd:Jeremy Summerly]—features works by J.S. Bach *(Jesu bleibet meine Freude [from Cantata, BWV 147]; Bist du bei mir, BWV 508 [from Anna Magdalena Bach Notebook])*, J.S. Bach/Gounod *(Ave Maria)*, Beethoven *(Die Ehre Gottes aus der Natur [from 6 Songs, Op. 48])*, Bizet *(Agnus Dei)*, Donizetti *(Ave Maria)*, Fauré *(Pie Jesu [from Requiem])*, Franck *(Panis Angelicus)*, Giordani *(Caro mio ben)*, Handel *(Hallelujah Chorus [from Messiah]; Lascia ch'io pianga [from Rinaldo]; Ombra mai fù [Largo; from Serse])*, Mozart *(Ave verum corpus, K.618; Excultate, jubilate, K.165; Laudate Dominum [from Vesperae Solennes de Confessore, K.339])*, Schubert *(Ave Maria, D.839)* NXIN ▲ 8553751 [DDD] (5.97)

Bel Canto—features performances by Brigitte Fassbaender (mez) *(Gluck:Che faro senza Euridice)*, Kurt Moll (bass) *(Mozart:Solche hergelauf'ne Laffen)*, Edita Gruberová (sop) *(Cherubini:E tu, che ma me divin prometti il destino; Dell'acqua:Villanelle)*, Anna Tomowa-Sintow (sop) *(Weber:Und ob die Wolke sie verhülle)*, Lucia Aliberti (sop) *(Bellini:Ah! non credea mirarti)*, Agnes Baltsa (mez) *(Mercadante:Ah si, mie care)*, Maria Dragoni (sop) *(Verdi:Timor di me?)*, Carlo Bergonzi (ten), Dietrich Fischer-Dieskau (bar) *(Verdi:Talor vedeste in mano; Bizet:Au fond du temple saint)*, Grace Bumbry (mez) *(Ponchielli:Suicido)*, Marjana Lipovšek (mez) *(Saint-Saëns:Mon coeur d'ouver á ta voix)*, Bernd Weikl (bar) *(Millöcker:Dunkelrote Rosen)*, Franco Bonisolli (ten) *(Rossini:La danza)* ORF ▲ 321931 [DDD] (18.97)

Berlin Gala: Songs of Love & Desire DEUT ▲ 459555 (16.97)

Berlin 1930: Songs & Chansons *(9 German & French cabaret songs)*—features performances by Marlene Dietrich (sgr), Curt Bois, et al. *(rec 1929-31)* † Kurt Weill's Threepenny Opera TELC ▲ 2025 [ADD] (16.97)

The Best of Opera, Vol. 1, w. various artists—features works by Verdi *(Ov [from La forza del destino]; Libiamo ne'lieti calici [from La traviata]; Bella figlia dell'amore [from Rigoletto]; Va, pensiero [from Nabucco])*, Puccini *(E lucevan le stelle [from Tosca]; O mio babbino caro [from Gianni Schicchi]; Bimba dagli occhi [from Madama Butterfly]; Sì. Mi chiamano Mimì [from La Bohème]; Nessun dorma [from Turandot])*, Dvořák *(O, Silver Moon [from Rusalka])*, Bizet *(Au fond du temple saint [from Les pêcheurs de perles]; Votre Toast [from Carmen])*, Leoncavallo *(Recitar!...Vesti la giubba [from Pagliacci])*, Mascagni *(Intermezzo [from Cavalleria Rusticana])*, Wagner *(Beglückt darf nun dich [from Tannhäuser])*, Mozart *(Der Hölle Rache [from Die Zauberflöte])* NXIN ▲ 553166 [DDD] (5.97)

Best of Tenors, w. Luigi Alva (ten), Francisco Araiza (ten), Carlo Bergonzi (ten), Giuseppe Campora (ten), José Carreras (ten), Franco Corelli (ten), Plácido Domingo (ten), Nicolai Gedda (ten), Alfredo Kraus (ten), Richard Lewis (ten), Carlo del Monte (ten), Luciano Pavarotti (ten), Rudolf Schock (ten), Jon Vickers (ten), Fritz Wunderlich (ten)—features arias from Turandot; Tosca; L'elisir d'amore; Così fan tutte; La favorita; Lohengrin; Der Freischütz; La traviata; Le Roi D'Ys; Martha; L'Amico Fritz; Carmen; La Bohème; Macbeth; Rigoletto; La fanciulla del West ROYA ▲ 70029 (10.97)

Bitter Ballads: Ancient & Modern Poetry Sung to Medieval & Traditional Melodies HAM ▲ 907204 (17.97)

Björling Family: 4 Singing Brothers & 2 Ladies—features performances by Jussi Björling (ten) *(Eklöf:Morgon; Sjöberg:Tonerna; Puccini:Che Gelida Manina [from La Bohème]; Donna Non Vidi Mai [from Manon Lescaut]; Bizet:La Fleur que tu m'avais jetée [from Carmen]; Gounod:Ange Adorable [from Roméo et Juliette; w. Hjördis Schymberg (sop)]; Mascagni:Mamma!...Quel Vino [from Cavalleria Rusticana])*, Gösta Björling (sgr) *(Randel:Jag Sjunger Och Dansar; Kraus:O Gudar Styrken Mig; Smetana:My...My...Mother Dear [from The Bartered Bride]; Donizetti:Chi Mi Frena [from Lucia di Lammermoor; w. Eva Prytz (sop), Bette Wermine-Björling (sop), Erik Saedén (bar), Kim Borg (bass), Arne Wirén (sgr)]; Bizet:Au fond du temple saint [from Les Pêcheurs de perles; w. Erik Saedén (bar)]; Tosti:Addio)*, Olle Björling (sgr) *(Gustaf:I Rosens Doft; trad:Tantis Serenad)*, Karl Björling (sgr) *(Wiklund:En Dalmastrall)*, Anna-Lisa Björling (sop) *(Puccini:O Mio Babbino Caro [from Gianni Schicchi])*, Bette Wermine-Björling (mez) *(Saint-Saëns:Mon coeur s'souvre à ta voix [from Samson et Dalila])*, Juvenile Trio [Jussi Björling (ten), Gösta Björling (sgr), Olle Björling (sgr)] *(trad:Sommarglädje)*, Adult Trio [Jussi Björling (ten), Gösta Björling (sgr), Olle Björling (sgr)] *(trad:Sommarglädje)* BLUB ▲ 66 [ADD] (18.97)

Jussi Björling Memorial Concert, w. Birgit Nilsson (sop), Nicolai Gedda (ten), Giuseppe di Stefano (ten), Gösta Winbergh (ten), James McCracken (bar), Robert Merrill (bar), Rolf Björling (sgr), plus others SWES ▲ SCD 1056

Broadway, w. Ethel Merman (sgr), Judy Holliday (sgr), Dick Van Dyke (sgr), Doris Day (sgr), Topol (sgr), Mary Martin (sgr), Jill Haworth (sgr), William Warfield (sgr), et al.—features sels from Oklahoma; Fiddler on the Roof; West Side Story; Sound of Music; My Fair Lady; Annie; Music Man; Cabaret; Gypsy; Showboat; Phantom of the Opera; plus others COL (Greatest Hits) ▲ 62365 (9.97) ▮ 62365 (5.98)

Brother, Can You Spare A Dime?: The Roots Of American Song—features performances by Roland Hayes (ten), John Payne (bar), Evelyn Dove (sop), Edna Thomas (mez), Jules Bledsoe (bass), George Dosher (bass) *(rec 1924-39)* PHS ▲ 9484 (m) [AAD] (17.97)

Canta pe' mé: Caruso, Gigli & Schipa Sing the Best of the Neapolitan Songs, w. Enrico Caruso (ten), Beniamino Gigli (ten), Tito Schipa (ten)—features Fenesta ca lucive; O sole mio; A vucchella; Canta pe' mé; Tu ca nin chiagne; Tiempo antico; Manella mia; Tarantella sincera; Sultanto a te; Come facette mammeta; Napule; I' te vurria vasà; Era de Maggio; Voce è notte; Dicitencello vuie; Maria, Marì; Funiculì, Funiculà; Mandulinata a Napule; Quanno 'a femmena vo'; Santa Lucia luntana; Mamma mia che vo' sape *(rec 1910-40)* VOCA (Vocal Archives) ▲ 1140 (13.97)

Canti di Palermo e Napoli—features performances by Simone Alaimo (b-bar) *(U Cavadduzzu di Villabati; Abballati; La cuperta arraccamata; Apuzza nica; Ciuri ciuri; La favula di cola Pisci; Carnasicalata dei Pulcinelli; Comu si li cugghreu li beddi pira; E vui durmiti ancora; La pampina di l'aliva; Mi votu e mi rivotu; Si maritau Rosa; U sciccareddu; Vitti 'na crozza; Sicilia bedda)*, Vittoria Mazzoni (sgr) *(Fenesta che lucive; A vucchella; Lo ninno mio; U passairello; Te voglio bene assaje; Luna nova; Mmiez' o ggrano; Era de Maggio; Fenesta vascia; Zompa 'llari 'lira; N'ata gioventù; La palummella; Silenzio cantatore; Polamina 'e notte; Ve voglio fa na casa)* AG 2-▲ 41 [DDD] (18.97)

The Carlo Felice in Genoa: A Century of Great Voices, Vol. 3 *(rec 1906-34)* PHG ▲ 5075 (14.97)

The Carlo Felice in Genoa: A Century of Great Voices, Vol. 4 *(rec 1903-41)* PHG ▲ 5076 (14.97)

The Carlo Felice in Genoa: A Century of Great Voices, Vol. 5—features performances by Giannina Arangi-Lombardi (sop), Maria Caniglia (sop), Giuseppina Cobelli (sop), Olga de Franco (sop), Toti dal Monte (sop), Augusta Oltrabella (sop), Rosetta Pampanini (sop), Hina Spani (sop), Ines Alfani Tellini (sop), Maria Capuana (mez), Irene Minghini-Cattaneo (mez), Vera Amerighi Rutili (sgr), Giovanni Breviario (ten), Lionello Cecil (ten), Alessandro Granda (ten), Giovanni Manurita (ten), Luigi Marini (ten), Galliano Masini (ten), Antonio Melandri (ten), John O' Sullivan (ten), Nino Piccaluga (ten), Cristy Solari (ten), Armando Borgioli (bar), Antonio Righetti (bass), Isidoro Fagoaga (sgr), Carmelo Maugeri (sgr), Alexander Vesselowsky (sgr) *(rec 1925-41)* PHG ▲ 5077 (14.97)

The Carlo Felice in Genoa: A Century of Great Voices, Vol. 6, w. Gina Cigna (sop), Bidù Sayão (sop), Ebe Stignani (mez), Maria Carbone (sgr), Dino Borgioli (ten), Francesco Merli (ten), Gino Bechi (bar), Giacomo Rimini (bar), Tancredi Pasero (bass), Ettore Parmeggiani (sgr), plus others—features arias by Puccini, Verdi, Cimarosa, Mascagni, Rossini, Zandonai, Donizetti, Wagner, Gounod, plus others *(rec 1914-46)* PHG ▲ 5078 (14.97)

The Carlo Felice in Genoa: A Century of Great Voices, Vol. 7 *(rec 1912-46)* PRE ▲ 5079 (16.97)

The Carlo Felice in Genoa: A Century of Great Voices, Vol. 8 *(rec 1924-46)* PHG ▲ 5080 (14.97)

The Castrato Voice & the Old School, 1899-1913—features performances by Suzanne Adams (sop), Emma Albani (sop), Sigrid Arnoldson (sop), Nellie Melba (sop), Adelina Patti (sop), Marcella Sembrich (sop), Luisa Tetrazzini (sop), Lillian Blauvelt (sgr), Emma Earnes (sgr), Alessandro Moreschi (sgr), Ellen Beach Yaw (sgr) VOCA (Vocal Archives) 2-▲ 2100 (26.97)

The Castrato Voice & the First Divas—features performances by Alessandro Moreschi (castrato) *(Rossini:Crucifixus [from Petite Messe Sollennelle]; Mozart:Ave Verum Corpus, K.618; Voi che sapete [from Le nozze di Figaro]; Palestrina:Cruda mia nemica; Bach/Gounod:Ave Maria)*, Adelina Patti (sop) *(Mozart:Batti, batti, o bel Massetto [from Don Giovanni]; Gounod:Ah! je ris [from Faust]; Arditi:Il bacio; Bach/Gounod:Ave Maria; Bellini:Ah, non credea mirarti [from La sonnambula]; Casta Diva [from Norma]; Thomas:Connais-tu le pays? [from Mignon]; Tosti:Serenata)*, Amma Albani (sop) *(Chaminade:L'Eté)*, Marcella Sembrich (sop) *(Bellini:Qui la voce [from I Puritani]; Mozart:Sull'aria...Soave zeffiretto [from Le nozze di Figaro]; Schubert:Wohin?; Hahn:Si mes vers)*, Nellie Melba (sop) *(Puccini:Si, mi chiamano Mimi [from La bohème]; Vissi d'arte [from Tosca]; Verdi:Ah! fors'é lui...Sempre libera [from La traviata]; Mozart:Voi che sapete [from Le nozze di Figaro]) (rec 1902-08)* MNER ▲ 73 (m) [ADD] (14.97)

Celebrated Italian Singers Perform Italian Songs—features performances by Muzio (sop), Ponselle (sop), Tetrazzini (sop), Caruso (ten), Corelli (ten), Lucia (ten), Martinelli (ten), Pertile (ten), Schipa (ten), Battistini (bar), Stracciari (bar), et al. *(rec 1906-44)* PHG ▲ 5035 [ADD] (14.97)

A Century Of Voices at the Teatro Carlo Felice di Genova

Vol. 1—features performances by Antonio Aramburo (ten), Vittorio Arimondi (bass), Teresa Arkel (sop), Maria Barrientos (sop), Giuseppe Bellantoni (bar), Gemma Bellincioni (sop), Vincenzo Bettoni (bass), Ramon Blanchart (sgr), Alessandro Bonci (ten), Giuseppe Borgatti (ten), Icilio Calleja (sgr), Emma Carelli (sop), Enrico Caruso (ten), Lina Cavalieri (sgr), Emilia Corsi (sop), Antonio Cotogni (bar), Giuseppe Danise (sgr), Hericlea Darclée (sgr), Ines De Frate (sgr), Giuseppe De Luca (bar), Maria De Macchi (sgr), Giovanni Battista De Negri (ten), Maria Farneti (sop), Cesira Ferrani (sgr), Cesare Formichi (bar), Edoardo Garbin (ten), Eugenio Giraldoni (bar), Fiorello Giraud (ten), Virginia Guerrini (sgr), Giuseppe Kaschmann (bar), Hipólito Lazaro (ten), Oreste Luppi (bass), Giovanni Martinelli (ten), Victor Maurel (bar), Nellie Melba (sop), Luigi Montesanto (bar), Francesco Navarrini (bass), Giuseppe Pacini (bar), José Palet (ten), Angelica Pandolfini (sop), Antonio Paoli (ten), Taurino Parvis (bar), Emilio Perea (sgr), Antonio Pini-Corsi (bar), Regina Pinkert (sop), Amelia Pinto (sop), Titta Ruffo (bar), Giannina Russ (sop), Piero Schiavazzi (ten), Francesco Signorini (sgr), Adelina Stehle (sop), Rosina Storchio (sop), Riccardo Stracciari (bar), Francesco Tamagno (ten), Fernando Valero (ten), Elvino Ventura (ten), Domenico Viglione-Borghese (bar), Francisco Viñas (ten), Nicla Zerola (sgr) *(rec 1901-62)* MEMO 2-▲ 4408 (m)

Vol. 2—features performances by Carmelo Alabiso (sgr), Roberto d'Alessio (ten), Ernesto Badini (bar), Attilio Barbieri (sgr), Amedeo Bassi (ten), Ettore Bergamaschi (ten), Gabriella Besanzoni (mez), Augusto Beuf (bar), Aurora Buades (mez), Eugenia Burzio (sop), Giorgina Caprile (sgr), Mercedes Capsir (sop), Margherita Carosio (sop), Elvira Casazza (mez), Irene Minghini Cattaneo (mez), Ersilde Cervi-Caroli (sop), Francesco Cigada (bar), Luigi Cilla (ten), Pablo Civil (ten), Giulio Crimi (sgr), Gilda dalla Rizza (sop), Nazzareno De Angelis (bass), Fernando De Lucia (ten), Bernardo De Muro (ten), Octave Dua (ten), Guerrina Fabbri (sgr), Benvenuto Franci (bar), Nicola Fusati (ten), Carlo Galeffi (bar), Emilio Ghirardini (bar), Beniamino Gigli (ten), Rinaldo Grazzi (sgr), Giovanni Inghilleri (bar), Giuseppe Krismer (sgr), Aroldo Lindi (ten), Francesco Merli (ten), Gaston Micheletti (ten), Angelo Minghetti (sgr), Enrico Molinari (bar), Toti dal Monte (sop), Claudia Muzio (sop), Giuseppe Nessi (ten), Iva Pacetti (sop), Graciela Pareto (sop), Tancredi Pasero (bass), Piero Pauli (ten), Aureliano Pertile (ten), Tina Poli-Randaccio (sop), Luigi Rossi Morelli (sgr), Adelaide Saraceni (sop), Bianca Scacciati (sop), Margaret Sheridan (sop), Mariano Stabile (bar), Conchita Supervia (mez), Giuseppe Taccani (ten), Carlo Tagliabue (bar), Gino Vanelli (bar), Ismaele Voltolini (sgr), Maria Zamboni (sop), Giovanni Zenatello (ten) *(rec 1903-53)* MEMO 2-▲ 4475 (m) [AAD]

The Champions of Opera—features performances of arias by José Carreras (ten) *(Leoncavallo:Pagliacci; Mascagni:Cavalleria rusticana; Puccini:Turandot; Verdi:Don Carlos)*, Plácido Domingo (ten) *(Puccini:Tosca; Verdi:Aida; Un ballo in maschera; Ernani; La forza del destino; Otello)*, Luciano Pavarotti (ten) *(Mascagni:L'amico Fritz; Verdi:Requiem Mass)* EMPD ▲ 70024 (8.97)

Chime Again, Beautiful Bells: The Historic Countertenor—features performances by Hatherley Clarke, Frank Colman, Frank Coombs, Charles Hawkins, Richard José, Ben Millett, Will Oakland, Manuel Romain *(rec 1906-32)* POHS ▲ 9848 (m) [AAD] (18.97)

Classic Love Duets—features performances by Emma Luart (sop), Gaston Micheletti (ten) *(The Tales of Hoffman)*, Ninon Vallin (sop), Miguel Villabella (ten) *(Massenet:Manon)*, Margarethe Teschemacher (sop), Marcel Wittrisch (ten) *(Meyerbeer:Les Huguenots)*, Toti dal Monte (sop), Tito Schipa (ten) *(Bellini:La Sonnambula)*, Erna Berger (sop), Julius Patzak (ten) *(Verdi:Rigoletto)*, Elisabeth Rethberg (sop), Giacomo Lauri-Volpi (ten) *(Verdi:La traviata)*, Licia Albanese (sop), Beniamino Gigli (ten) *(Verdi:Aida)*, Malfalda Fevero (sop), Alessandro Ziliani (ten) *(Puccini:Madama Butterfly)*, Hina Spani (sop), Apollo Granforte (bar) *(Leoncavallo:I Pagliacci)*, Rosetta Pampanini (sop), Dino Borgioli (ten) *(Mascagni:L'amico Fritz)*, Margaret Sheridan (sop), Aureliano Pertile (ten) *(Giordano:Andrea Chenier)* MECL ▲ 430 (17.97)

A Companion CD to Nigel Douglas' Book: Legendary Voices—features performances by Luisa Tetrazzini (sop), Enrico Caruso (ten), Rosa Ponselle (sop), Tito Schipa (ten), Giuseppe de Luca (bar), Eva Turner (sop), Alfred Piccaver (ten), Ezio Pinza (bass), Alexander Kipnis (bass), Lotte Lehmann (sop), Kirsten Flagstad (sop), Jussi Björling (ten), Tito Gobbi (bar), Fritz Wunderlich (ten) NIMB ▲ 7851 (11.97)

The Complete Adelina Patti & Victor Maurel, w. Adelina Patti (sop), Victor Maurel (bar) MRSN 2-▲ 52011 (35.97)

Covent Garden: An Early History on Record—features performances by Caruso (ten) *(Questa o quella [from Rigoletto])*, Chaliapin (bass) *(Prayer & Death [from Boris])*, Emmy Destinn (sop) *(Con onor muore [from Butterfly])*, Flagstad (sop), Melchior (ten) *(Love Duet [from Tristan])*, Johanna Gadski (sop) *(Fliegt heim ihr Raben [from Götterdämmerung])*, Gigli (ten) *(Si, fui soldato [from Andrea Chénier])*, Lehmann (sop), Schumann (sop), Oiczewska (mez) *(Maria Theres [from Rosenkavalier])*, McCormack (ten) *(De miei bollenti spiriti [from Traviata])*, Melba (sop) *(The Jewel Song [from Faust])*, Schorr (b-bar) *(Was duftet doch der Flieder [from Meistersinger])*, Supervia (mez) *(Les tringles des sistres [from Carmen])*, Tauber (ten) *(Dalla sua pace [from Don Giovanni])*, Tetrazzini (sop) *(Quando rapita [from Lucia])*, Tibbett (bar) *(Te Deum [from Tosca])*, Eva Turner (sop) *(Vissi d'arte [from Tosca])*, Renato Zanelli (ten) *(Ora e per sempre [from Otello]) (rec 1904-39)* NIMB (Prima Voce) ▲ 7819 [ADD] (11.97)

Covent Garden On Record: A History, Vol. 1: 1870-1904 *(recordings by John Steane)*—features performances by Sigrid Arnoldson (sop), Gemma Bellincioni (sop), Emma Calvé (sop), Emma Eames (sop), Johanna Gadski (sop), Lilli Lehmann (sop), Felia Litvinne (sop), Nellie Melba (sop), Adelina Patti (sop), Regina Pinkert (sop), Gianina Russ (sop), Marcella Sembrich (sop), Olive Fremstad (cta), Louise Homer (cta), Ernestine Schumann-Heink (cta), Albert Alvarez (ten), Giuseppe Anselmi (ten), Alessandro Bonci (ten), Enrico Caruso (ten), Fernando De Lucia (ten), Francesco Marconi (ten), Emile Scaramberg (ten), Francesco Tamagno (ten), Fernando Valero (ten), Francesco Vignas (ten), Mario Ancona (bar), Mattia Battistini (bar), Theodor Bertram (bar), Francesco D'Andrade (bar), Jean Lassalle (bar), Victor Maurel (bar), Antonio Pini-Corsi (bar), Maurice Renaud (bar), Tita Ruffo (bar), Antonio Scotti (bar), Anton Van Rooy (bar), Edouard De Reszke (bass), Pedro Gailhard (bass), Marcel Journet (bass), Francesco Navarini (bass), Pol Plançon (bass) *(rec Covent Garden Royal Opera House, 1902-20)* PHS 3-▲ 9923 (m) [AAD] (50.97)

Covent Garden On Record: A History, Vol. 2 PHS 3-▲ 9924 (m) [AAD] (50.97)

Covent Garden On Record: A History, Vol. 3: 1910-1925—features recordings by Florence Austral (sop), Gilda Dalla Rizza (sop), Toti dal Monte (sop), Louise Edvina (sop), Maria Jeritza (sop), Melanie Kurt (sop), Lotte Lehmann (sop), Frida Leider (sop), Miriam Licette (sop), Lydia Lipkowska (sop), Gota Ljungberg (sop), Nellie Melba (sop), Claudia Muzio (sop), Graziella Pareto (sop), Elisabeth Rethberg (sop), Elisabeth Schumann (sop), Margaret Sheridan (sop), Margerete Siems (sop), Eva Turner (sop), Clara Butt (cta), Edna Thornton (cta), Dino Borgioli (ten), Miguel Fleta (ten), Paul Franz (ten), Joseph Hislop (ten), Giacomo Lauri-Volpi (ten), Giovanni Martinelli (ten), Lauritz Melchior (ten), Aureliano Pertile (ten), Alfred Piccaver (ten), Jacques Urlus (ten), Walter Widdop (ten), Giovanni Zenatello (ten), John Brownlee (bar), Giuseppe De Luca (bar), Benvenuto Franci (bar), Dinh Gilly (bar), Richard Mayr (bar), Dennis Noble (bar), Friedrich Schorr (bar), Antonio Scotti (bar), Norman Allin (bass), Feodor Chaliapin (bass), Adamo Didur (bass), Lev Sibiriakov (bass) *(rec Covent Garden Royal Opera House, 1907-32)* PHS 3-▲ 9925 (m) [AAD] (50.97)

Covent Garden On Record: A History, Vol. 4: 1926-1939—features performances by Maria Caniglia (sop), Joan Cross (sop), Kirsten Flagstad (sop), Fanny Heldy (sop), Maria Ivogün (sop), Lotte Lehmann (sop), Frida Leider (sop), Tiana Lemnitz (sop), Carmen Melis (sop), Grace Moore (sop), Maria Nemeth (sop), Lina Pagliughi (sop), Rosetta Pampanini (sop), Lisa Perli (sop), Rosa Ponselle (sop), Elisabeth Rethberg (sop), Lotte Schoene (sop), Elisabeth Schumann (sop), Clara Butt (cta), Irene Minghini-Cattaneo (cta), Conchita Supervia (mez), Edna Thornton (cta), Fernand Ansseau (ten), Dino Borgioli (ten), Antonio Cortis (ten), Beniamino Gigli (ten), Joseph Hislop (ten), Giacomo Lauri-Volpi (ten), Giovanni Martinelli (ten), Lauritz Melchior (ten), Heddle Nash (ten), Aureliano Pertile (ten), Torsten Ralf (ten), Helge Roswaenge (ten), Richard Tauber (ten), Georges Thille (ten), Walter Widdop (ten), Giovanni Zenatello (ten), Rudolf Bockelmann (bar), Giovanni Inghilleri (bar), Herbert Janssen (bar), Mariano Stabile (bar), Lawrence Tibbett (bar), Renato Zanelli (bar), Ivar Andresen (bass), Feodor Chaliapin (bass), Alexander Kipnis (bass), Ezio Pinza (bass) *(rec 1919-41)* PHS 3-▲ 9926 (m) [AAD] (50.97)

Creators' Records: World Premieres, 1877-1903—features performances by Gemma Bellincioni (sop), Celestina Boninsegna (sop), Georgette Bréjean-Silver (sop), Emma Calvé (sop), Rose Caron (sop), Cesira Ferrani (sop), Mary Garden (sop), Nellie Melba (sop), Angelica Pandolfini (sop), Amelia Pinto (sop), Rosina Storchio (sop), Marie Delna (cta), Medea Mei-Figner (cta), Giuseppe Anselmi (ten), Enrico Caruso (ten), Ben Davies (ten), Francesco Daddi (ten), Fernando De Lucia (ten), Emilio De Marchi (ten), Nicolai Figner (ten), Edoardo Garbin (ten), Edward Lloyd (ten), Joseph O'Mara (ten), Gaetano Pini-Corsi (ten), Francesco Tamagno (ten), Ernst Van Dyck (ten), Ferruccio Corradetti (bar), Giuseppe de Luca (bar), Jean Lassalle (bar), Victor Maurel (bar), Giuseppe Pacini (bar), Maurice Renaud (bar), Mario Sammarco (bar), Richard Temple (bar); arias by Herman Bemberg *(from Elaine)*, Alfred Bruneau *(from L'Attaque du Moulin)*, Alfred Cellier *(from Doris)*, Cilea *(from Adriana Lecouvreur)*, Debussy *(from Pelléas et Mélisande)*, Alphonse Duvernoy *(from Helle)*, Franchetti *(from Germania)*, Giordano *(from Andrea Chénier, Fedora & Siberia)*, Leoncavallo *(from La bohème, Pagliacci & Zaza)*, Mascagni *(from L'amico Fritz, Cavalleria Rusticana, Gugliemo Ratcliff, Iris & Le maschere)*, Massenet *(from Manon, Le Roi de Lahore, Sapho & Werther)*, Eduard Napravnik *(from Dubrowski)*, Puccini *(from La bohème, Manon Lescaut & Tosca)*, Ernest Reyer *(from Sigurd)*, Charles Silver *(from La Belle au bois dormant)*, Charles Stanford *(from Shamus O'Brien)*, Arthur Sullivan *(from The Martyr of Antioch, The Mikado & The Pirates of Penzance)*, Tchaikovsky *(from The Queen of Spades)*, Verdi *(from Falstaff & Otello) (rec 1900-17)* SRON 2-▲ SRO 818-2 (m) [ADD]

Crimes of Passion: Opera's Bloodiest Crimes—features performances by Mirella Freni (sop), Luciano Pavarotti (ten), Vienna PO [cnd:H. von Karajan] *(Puccini:Con onor muore...tu? Piccolo iddio [from Madama Butterfly]),* Julia Varady (sop), Ida Bormida (mez), Luciano Pavarotti (ten), National PO, London Opera Chorus [cnd:G. Gavazzeni] *(Mascagni:Turiddu's Farewell [from Cavalleria Rusticana]),* Kiri Te Kanawa (sop), Leo Nucci (bar), National PO [cnd:G. Solti] *(Puccini:Io tenni la promessa [from Tosca]),* Kiri Te Kanawa (sop), Piero de Palma (ten), Paul Hudson (bass), National PO, Welsh National Opera [cnd:G. Solti] *(Puccini:Come e lunga l'attesa!; Presto, su! Mario! [both from Tosca]),* Mirella Freni (sop), Vincenzo Bello (ten), Luciano Pavarotti (ten), Lorenzo Saccomoni (bar), Ingvar Wixell (bar), National PO, London Opera Chorus [cnd:G. Patane] *(Leoncavallo:No! Pagliaccio non son [from Pagliacci]),* Tatiana Troyanos (mez), Plácido Domingo (ten), London PO, John Alldis Choir [cnd:G. Solti] *(Bizet:C'est toi! C'est Moi! [from Carmen]),* June Anderson (sop), Shirley Verrett (mez), Nicolai Ghiaurov (bass), Bologna Teatro Comunale Orch & Chorus [cnd:R. Chailly] *(Verdi:Ah, piu non ragiono [from Rigoletto]),* Birgit Nilsson (sop), Vienna PO [cnd:G. Solti] *(R. Strauss:Ah! Du wolltest mich nicht deinen Mund küssen lassen, Jokanaan! [from Salome]),* Kiri Te Kanawa (sop), Elzbieta Ardam (mez), Luciano Pavarotti (ten), Anthony Rolfe Johnson (ten), Leo Nucci (bar), Dmitri Kavrekos (bass), Chicago SO [cnd:G. Solti] *(Verdi:Ave Maria, piena di grazia; Otello compare; Diceste questa sera le vostre preci?; Aprite! Aprite!; Niun mi tema [all from Otello])* PPHI ▲ 44863 ▮ 44863

Czech Opera Highlights, w. various artists—features sels from The Bartered Bride, Rusalka, The Brandenburgers in Bohemia, The Devil's Wall, The Kiss, The 2 Widows, Jacobin; Dalibor & Libuse SUR ▲ 112220 [DDD]

Divas

Vol. 1: 1906-1935—features performances by Amelita Galli-Curci (sop), Frieda Hempel (sop), Nina Koshetz (sop), Lotte Lehmann (sop), Nellie Melba (sop), Claudia Muzio (sop), Maria Nemeth (sop), Eidé Norena (sop), Adelina Patti (sop), Rosa Ponselle (sop), Luisa Tetrazzini (sop), Eva Turner (sop) NIMB (Prima Voce) ▲ 7802 [ADD] (11.97)

Vol. 2: 1909-1940—features performances by Geraldine Farrar (sop), Mafalda Favero (sop), Kirsten Flagstad (sop), Amelita Galli-Curci (sop), Mabel Garrison (sop), Alma Gluck (sop), Frieda Hempel (sop), Maria Ivogün (sop), Nina Koshetz (sop), Selma Kurz (sop), Frida Leider (sop), Eidé Norena (sop), Rosa Ponselle (sop), Lotte Schöne (sop), Maggie Teyte (sop), Ninon Vallin (sop), Sigrid Onegin (cta) NIMB (Prima Voce) ▲ 7818 [ADD] (11.97)

Divas: 1917-1939—features performances by Amelita Galli-Curci (sop), Eidé Norena (sop), Rosa Ponselle (sop) NIMB (Prima Voce) 3-▲ 1795 [ADD] (34.97)

Divas in Song: Marylin Horne, a 60th Birthday Celebration, w. Montserrat Caballé (sop), H. Donath (sop), R. Fleming (sop), R. A. Swenson (sop), F. von Stade (mez), S. Ramey (bass), J. Levine (cnd), M. Katz (pno), W. Jones (pno), K. Donath (pno), Manuel Burgueras (pno)—features works by Britten *(Let the Florid Music Praise),* Strauss *(Ständchen; Zueignung; Voci di primavera),* Rachmaninoff *(Vocalise),* Duke *(The Bird),* Schubert *(Der Musensohn),* Turina *(Cantares),* Mahler *(Lob des hohen Verstands),* Brahms *(Von ewiger Liebe),* Schoenberg *(Arie von der Spiegel von Arkadien),* Foster *(If You've Only Got a Moustache),* Monstsalvage *(Vocalise),* Lehár *(Vilja-Lied; Dein ist mein ganzes Herz),* Kander *(A Letter from Sulivan Ballou),* Martini *(Plasir d'amour),* Rodgers *(Oh, What a Beautiful Morning),* Kern *(Ol' Man River),* Bolcolm *(Amor),* Copland *(At the River)* RCAV (Red Seal) ▲ 62547 (16.97)

Divine Sopranos—features performances by D. Upshaw (sop) *(Haydn:On Mighty Wings [from Die Schöpfung; rec May 2 & 4-5, 1992]),* Sylvia McNair (sop) *(Rachmaninoff:Vocalise [rec Feb 16-17, 1992]; Handel:Rejoice Greatly [from Messiah; rec Dec 18-20, 1983]),* J. Blegen (sop) *(Fauré:Pie Jesu [from Requiem; rec Nov 25, 1985]; Orff:In Truttina [from Carmina Burana; rec Nov 16-18, 1980]),* E. Ameling (sop) *(Berlioz:Absence [from Les Nuits d'Été; rec Mar 21, 1983]),* A. Augér (sop) *(Strauss:Im Abendrot [from 4 Last Songs; rec Nov 22-23, 25 & 28, 1988]; Brahms:Ihr habt nun Traurigkeit [from Ein deutsches Requiem; rec Nov 5-7, 1983]),* D. Upshaw (sop), P. Jensen (sop) *(Vivaldi:Laudamus Te [from Gloria; rec Dec 18-20, 1988]),* B. Hendricks (sop) *(Mozart:Ach, ich fühl's [from Die Zauberflöte; rec July 13-22, 1991]),* Diane Soviero (sop) *(Catalani:Ebben?...Ne Andrò Lontano [from La Wally; rec Mar 12, 1990]),* F. von Stade (sop) *(Rodgers:My Favorite Things [from The Sound of Music; rec Dec 13-14, 1987]),* M. McLaughlin (sop) *(Sullivan:Yum-Yum's Song [from The Mikado; rec Sept 2-4, 1991]),* K. Battle (sop) *(Mahler:Sym 2, "Resurrection" [movt 5; w. M. Forrester (cta); rec Oct 10 & 12, 1982])* TEL ▲ 80407 [DDD] (15.97)

Don't Give the Name a Bad Place: Types & Stereotypes in American Musical Theater, 1870-1900—features performances by Lois Winter (sop), Rose Marie Jun (alt), Max Morath (ten), Phil Olsen (ten), Charles Magruder (bass), Dick Hyman (pno/cnd) *(Braham/Harrigan:The Babies on Our Block; Maggie Murphy's Home; John Riley's Always Dry; Paddy Duffy's Cart; Hang the Mulligan Banner Up),* Danny Barker (bar), Dick Hyman (pno) *(Bland:De Golden Wedding; Cook:Darktown Is Out Tonight; Bland:Tell 'Em I'll Be There [all w. Bobby Floyd (ten), Ralph Fields (ten), Bernard Knee (bar), Charles Magruder (bass)]; Udall/Kennett:Stay in Your Own Back Yard; Fagan:My Gal Is a High-born Lady),* Clifford Jackson (ten), Dick Hyman (pno) *(Williams:The German 5th; Cat Song [or Can Anyvone Tell Vere Dot Cat is Gone?]; Don't Give de Name a Bad Blace [all w. Alan Sokoloff (ten), Raph Fields (ten), Bernard Knee (bar), Charles Magruder (bass)]; Schwartz/Jerome:Rip van Winkle Was a Lucky Man) (rec Columbia Recording Studios, NYC)* NWW ▲ 80265 (16.97)

Drottningholms Court Theatre, 1922-1992, w. various artists—features performances of excerpts from operas by Handel, Gluck, Paisiello, Mozart, Haydn, Scarlatti, Purcell, Cimarosa, Donizetti, Rossini, Monteverdi & Cavalli CAPA ▲ 21512 [AAD/ADD] (16.97)

Duets & Arias from Italian Operas, w. G. Aragall (ten), E. Tumagian (bar), A. Rahbari (cnd), Czech-Slovak RSO Bratislava—features works by Verdi *(Invano Alvaro; Solenne in quest'ora [both from Forza del destino]; Pari siamo!; Cortigiani, vil razza dannata [both from Rigoletto]; E lui...Dio, che nell'alma [from Don Carlo]),* Mascagni *(Prelude; A voi tutti salute [both from Cavalleria Rusticana]),* Donizetti *(Venti scudi [from L'elisir d'amore]),* Ponchielli *(Scene & Duet [from La Gioconda]),* Leoncavallo *(Si puo? Si puo? [from I Pagliacci])* NXIN ▲ 550684 [DDD] (5.97)

Early Recordings—features Berlin State Opera Orch [cnd:B. Seidler-Winkler], H. Roswaenge (ten) *(A. Adam:Postillon de Lonjumeau (sels) [Mes amis, écoutez l'histoire]),* G. Farrar (sop) *(G. Puccini:Madama Butterfly (sels) [Un bel dì vedremo]),* L. Lehmann (sop) *(R. Wagner:Walküre (sels) [Der Männer Sippe sass hier im Saal]),* N. Melba (sop) *(G. Charpentier:Louise (sels) [Depuis le jour]),* C. Muzio (sop) *(Boito:Mefistofele (sels) [L'altra notte]),* A. Nezhdanova (sop) *(M. Glinka:Life for the Tsar (sels) [I do not grieve]),* E. Norena (sop) *(G. F. Handel:Atalanta (sels) [Care selve, ombre beate]),* RCA SO [cnd:R. Shaw], M. Anderson (cta) *(J. S. Bach:Cant 81),* L. Tetrazzini (sop) *(V. Bellini:Sonnambula (sels) F[Ah, non giunge]),* S. Onegin (cta) *(Donizetti:Lucrezia Borgia (sels) [Il segreto per esser felici (Brindisi)]),* E. Caruso (ten) *(Boito:Mefistofele (sels) [Dai campi, dai prati; Giunto sul passo estremo]; Denza:Non t'amo più; Donizetti:Elisir d'amore (sels) [Una furtiva lagrima]; Franchetti:Germania (sels) [Studenti, udite; Ah vieni qui...No, non chiuder; Studenti, udite; Ah vieni qui...No, non chiuder]; U. Giordano:Fedora (sels) [Amor ti vieta]; Leoncavallo:Mattinata; Pagliacci (sels) [Recitar!... Vesti la giubba; Recitar!... Vesti la giubba]; P. Mascagni:Cavalleria rusticana (sels) [O Lola (Siciliana); O Lola (Siciliana)]; Iris (sels) [Apri la tua finestra]; Massenet:Manon (sels) [En fermant les yeux]; Meyerbeer:Huguenots (sels) [Ah, quel spectacle; Plus blanche que la blanche hermine]; Ponchielli:Gioconda (sels) [Cielo e mar!; Cielo e mar!]; G. Puccini:Tosca (sels) [Recondita armonia; E lucevan le stelle; E lucevan le stelle; E lucevan le stelle]; Verdi:Aida (sels) [Celeste Aida; Celeste Aida]; Rigoletto (sels) [La donna è mobile; Questa o quella] [w. F. Lapitino (hp)]),* E. Caruso (ten) *(Bizet:Pêcheurs de perles (sels) [Je crois entendre encore; Je crois entendre encore] [w. S. Cottone (pno)]),* M. Fleta (ten) *(G. Puccini:Tosca (sels) [E lucevan le stelle; E lucevan le stelle; E lucevan le stelle]),* T. Schipa (ten) *(Massenet:Werther (sels) [O nature, pleine de grâce]),* D. Smirnov (ten) *(Bizet:Pêcheurs de perles (sels) [Je crois entendre encore; Je crois entendre encore] [w. S. Cottone (pno)]),* R. Tauber (ten) *(W. A. Mozart:Don Giovanni (sels) [Dalla sua pace]),* P. Amato (bar) *(Leoncavallo:Pagliacci (sels) [Si può? (Prologue)] [w. F. Lapitino (hp)]),* M. Battistini (bar) *(Verdi:Ballo in maschera (sels) [Eri tu che macchiavi quell'anima]),* G. d. Luca (bar) *(V. Bellini:Puritani (sels) [Ah! per sempre]),* F. Chaliapin (bass) *(A. Rubinstein:Persian Songs, Op. 34),* M. Journet (bass) *(Massenet:Cléopâtra (sels) [Air de la Lettre])* NIMB 2-▲ 7900 [ADD] (11.97)

Echoes of the Temple: Cantors in Prayer & Folksong, w. Gershon Sirota (cant), Pierre Pinchik (cant), Samuel Vigoda (cant), Joseph Rosenblatt (cant), Arthur Tracy (cant), et al. *(rec 1914-36)* PHS ▲ 9126 [ADD] (17.97)

18 Tenors d'Expression Française—features works by Auber, Bizet, Chaminade, Gounod, Grétry, Halévy, Méhul, Massenet, Reyer, Saint-Saëns, Verdi; sung by Léon Escalaïs (ten), Emile Scaramberg (ten), Lucien Muratore (ten), Leon Campagnola (ten), Paul Franz (ten), Emile Marcelin (ten), Charles Friant (ten), Joseph Rogatchewsky (ten), Edmond Rambaud (ten), Miguel Villabella (ten), David Devriès (ten), Gaston Micheletti (ten), Fernand Ansseau (ten), Georges Thill (ten), René Verdière (ten), Cesar Vezzani (ten), René Maison (ten), José Luccioni (ten) *(rec 1905-35)* MMO ▲ 30377

Emile Berliner's Gramophone: The Earliest Discs (1888-1901) SYMP ▲ SYM 1058 (m)

The Era of Adelina Patti—features performances by Adelina Patti (sop) *(Yradier:La Calesera; Mozart:Batti batti [from Don Giovanni]; Voi che sapete [from Le nozze di Figaro]; Bellini:Ah, non credea [from La sonnambula]; Hook:'Twas within a Mile o' Edinboro Town; Bishop:Home Sweet Home),* Victor Maurel (bar) *(Verdi:Quand' ero paggio [from Falstaff]; Mozart:Deh vieni alla finestra [from Don Giovanni]),* Pol Plançon (bass) *(Verdi:Je dormirai dans mon manteau régal [from Don Carlos]; Adam:Arrétons-nous ici [from Le Chalet]),* Emma Eames (sop) *(Tosti:Dopo),* Lucien Fugère (bar) *(Rameau:Le tambourin; Gluck:C'est un torrent impétueux [from Les pèlerins de la mecque]),* Francisco Vignas (sgr) *(Meyerbeer:Sopra Berta [from Le Prophète]),* Emma Calvé (sop) *(Bizet:Habanera [from Carmen]),* Maurice Renaud (bar) *(Massenet:Vision fugitive [from Hérodiade]; Gounod:Le soir),* Fernando de Lucia (ten) *(Massenet:Il sogno [from Manon]; Rossini:Ah! qual colpo [from Il barbiere di Siviglia]),* Francesco Tamagno (ten) *(Massenet:Quand nos jours [from Hérodiade]),* Nellie Melba (sop) *(Thomas:Des larmes de la nuit [from Hamlet]; Donizetti:Ardon gl'incensi [from Lucia]),* Félia Litvinne (sop) *(Wagner:Elsa's Dream [from Lohengrin]),*Wilhelm Hesch (bass) *(Wagner:Das schöne Fest [from Die Meistersinger]),* Lillian Nordica (sgr) *(Erkel:Ah rebéges [from Hunyadi László]; R. Strauss:Serenade),* Mario Ancona (sgr) *(Donizetti:A tanto amor [from La favorita]; Verdi:Era la none [from Otello]),* Edouard de Reszke (bass) *(Flotow:Porter Song [from Martha]),* Marcella Sembrich (sop) *(Bellini:Qui la voce sua soave [from I Puritani]),* Francesco Marconi (ten) *(Donizetti:Di pescatore [from Lucrezia Borgia]),* Mattia Battistini (bar) *(Mozart:Fin ch'han dal vino [from Don Giovanni]; Verdi:Oh, de'verd'anni miei [from Ernani]; Gomes:Senza tetto [from Il Guarany]),* Lilli Lehmann (sop) *(Mozart:Heil'ge Quelle [from Le nozze di Figaro]),* Charles Santley (sgr) *(Hatton:Simon the cellarer)* NIMB 2-▲ NI 7840 [ADD]

Essential Opera—features performances by Freni (sop), Te Kanawa (sop), Sutherland (sop), Carreras (ten), Pavarotti (ten), Domingo (ten), et al. PLON ▲ 33822 [ADD/DDD] (16.97) ▮ 433822-4

Essential Opera, Vol. 2—features performances by K. Te Kanawa (sop), M. Caballé (sop), J. Sutherland (sop), C. Bartoli (mez), L. Pavarotti (ten), P. Domingo (ten), J. Carreras (ten), et al. performing Wagner *(Ride of the Valkyries [from* Die Walküre*),* Bizet *(Habanera l'amour est un oiseau rebelle [from* Carmen*]; C'est toi...Au fond du temple sait [from* Les pêcheurs de perles*),* Mozart *(Non più andrai; Dovo sono [both from* Le nozze di Figaro*]; Soave si il vento [from* Così fan tutte*]; Là ci darem la mano [from* Don Giovanni*]; Der Vogelfänger bin ich ja [from* Die Zauberflöte*]),* Puccini *(Humming chorus [from* Madama Butterfly*]; Signore, ascolta [from* Turnadot*]; E lucevan le stelle [from* Tosca*]; Si, mi chiamano Mimi [from* La bohème*]),* Verdi *(Un di felice [from* La traviata*]; La donna è mobile [from* Rigoletto*]),* Leoncavallo *(Rectiar!...Vesti la giubba [from* I Pagliacci*]),* Rossini *(Il sono docile [from* Il barbiere di Siviglia*]),* Cilea *(Lamento di Federico [from* L'Arlesiana*]),* Delibes *(Dôme épais le jasmin [from* Lakmé*]),* Gounod *(Soldier's Chorus [from* Faust*])* PLON ▲ 40947 [ADD/DDD] (16.97) ▮ 440947-4

The Essential 3 Tenors, w. José Carreras (ten), Plácido Domingo (ten), Luciano Pavarotti (ten) RCAV (Gold Seal) ▲ 21273 [ADD] (10.97) 21273 (6.98)

Estrada: Russian Gypsy Singers—features works by Maria Komarova, M.A. Karinskaya, Elena Khorvat, Dorianna Masha, Pola Negri, Varya Panina, Nadezhda Plevitskaya, Natalia Tamara, Anastasia Vilatzeva *(rec St. Petersburg, Moscow, London 1905-31)* PHS ▲ 9960 (m) [AAD] (17.97)

Famous Basses of the Past—features performances by Feodor Chaliapin (bass), Marcel Journet (bass), Alexander Kipnis (bass), Ezio Pinza (bass), Pol Plançon & others *(rec 1906-47)* PRE ▲ 89991 (16.97)

Famous German Baritones of the Past—features performances by Theodor Scheidl (bar) *(Lortzing:Es wohnt am Seegestade [from Undine]),* Emil Schipper (bar) *(Gluck:O Artemis [from Iphigenie in Aulis]),* Wilhelm Rode (bar) *(Meyerbeer:Hei, Adamastor! [from L'Africaine]),* Michael Böhnen (bass) *(Brüll:Wie anders war es [from Das goldene Kreuz]),* Heinrich Schlusnus (bar) *(Wagner:Als du in kühnem Sange [from Tannhäuser]),* Rudolf Bockelmann (b-bar) *(Bizet:Euren Toast kann ich wohl erwidern [from Carmen]),* Heinrich Rehkemper (bar) *(Lortzing:Heiterkeit und Fröhlichkeit [from Der Wildschütz]),* Herbert Janssen (bar) *(Lortzing:Sonst spielt ich mit Zepter [from Zar und Zimmermann]),* Hans Reinmar (bar) *(Verdi:Adel, Plebejer, Genuas Volk [from Simon Boccanegra]),* Hans Hermann Nissen (bass) *(Meyerbeer:Dir, Königin, bin ich ergeben [from L'Africaine]),* Mathieu Ahlersmeyer (bar) *(Offenbach:Leuchte, heller Spiegel [from Les Contes d'Hoffmann]),* Karl Hammes (bar) *(Weinberger:Wie kann ich denn vergessen [from Schwanda der Dudelsackpfeifer]),* Willi Domgraf-Fassbaender (bar) *(Mozart:Ach öffnet eure Augen [from Le nozze di Figaro]),* Paul Schöffler (b-bar) *(Gounod:Hör mich jetzt an, Margarethe [from Faust]),* Karl Schmitt-Walter (bar) *(Mozart:Horch auf dem Klang der Zither [from Don Giovanni]),* Gerhard Hüsch (bar) *(Mozart:Mädchen, dass ihr's treibt mit allen [from Così fan tutte]),* Arno Schellenberg (bar) *(Thomas:O Wein, zerstreue uns're Sorgen [from Hamlet]),* Josef Herrmann (bar) *(Marschner:An jenem Tag [from Hans Heiling]),* Hans Wocke (bar) *(Kreutzer:Ein Schütz bin ich [from Das Nachtlager in Granada]),* Hans Hotter (b-bar) *(Verdi:Zur Nachtzeit war es [from Otello]),* Erich Kunz (bar) *(Mozart:Ein Mädchen oder Weibchen [from Die Zauberflöte])* [G] *(rec 1928-47)* PRE ▲ 89967 (m) (16.97)

Famous Italian Baritones—features performances by Antonio Magini-Coletti, Mattia Battistini, Mario Ancona, Antonio Scotti, Mario Sammarco, Riccardo Stracciari, Giuseppe De Luca, Titta Ruffo, Domenico Viglione Borghese, Pasquale Amato, Carlo Galeffi, Enrico Molinari, Cesare Formichi, Giuseppe Danise,), Apollo Granforte, Luigi Montesanto, Mariano Stabile, Benvenuto Franci, Mario Basiola, Carlo Tagliabue, Gino Bechi, Tito Gobbi, Giuseppe Taddei *(rec 1906-51)* PRE ▲ 89995 [AAD] (16.97)

Famous Love Duets, Vol. 2, w. Gianna d'Angelo (sop), Montserrat Caballé (sop), Maria Callas (sop), Renata Scotto (sop), Beverly Sills (sop), Renata Tebaldi (sop), José Carreras (ten), Mario del Monaco (ten), Giuseppe di Stefano (ten), Plácido Domingo (ten), Luciano Pavarotti (ten), et al.—features arias from operas by Puccini *(Madama Butterfly; La Bohème; Tosca),* Verdi *(Rigoletto; Il Trovatore; La Traviata),* Massenet *(Manon),* Donizetti *(Maria Stuarda)* ENT (Documents) ▲ 999 (13.97)

Famous Operatic Arias, w. *(aritists unknown)*—features selections from Faust; Prince Igor; Rigoletto; Tosca; La traviata; Don Carlos; Eugene Onegin GRFM ▲ 290 (10.97)

Famous Tenors of the Past—features performances by Enrico Caruso (ten) *(Donizetti:Spirto gentil [from La favorita]),* Leo Slezak (ten) *(Weber:Unter blüh'nden Mandelbäumen [from Euryanthe]),* Giovanni Zenatello (ten) *(Verdi:Ora per sempre addio [from Otello]),* Bernardo de Muro (ten) *(Giordano:Si, fui soldato [from Andrea Chénier]),* Alfred Piccaver (ten) *(Gounod:Ach, gehe auf [from Roméo et Juliette]),* Giovanni Martinelli (ten) *(Giordano:Amor ti vieta [from Fedora]),* Aureliano Pertile (ten) *(Verdi:Ah, si ben mio coll'essere [from Il trovatore]),* Francesco Merli (ten) *(Puccini:Donna non vidi mai [from Manon Lescaut]),* Hipólito Lázaro (ten) *(Puccini:Ch'ella mi creda libera [from La fanciulla del West]),* Tito Schipa (ten) *(Donizetti:Sogno soave e casto [from Don Pasquale]),* Fernand Ansseau (ten) *(Bizet:La fleur que tu m'avais jetée [from Carmen]),* Beniamino Gigli (ten) *(Mascagni:Viva il vino spumeggiante [from Cavalleria rusticana]),* Lauritz Melchoir (ten) *(Wagner:Inbrunst im Herzen [from Tannhäuser]),* Tino Pattiera (ten) *(Puccini:Recondita armonia [from Tosca]),* Joseph Rogatchewsky (ten) *(Massenet:Pourquoi me réveiller [from Werther]),* Dino Borgioli (ten) *(Mascagni:O amore, o bella luce [from L'amico Fritz]),* Antonio Cortis (ten) *(Giordano:Io non ho armata ancor [from Andrea Chénier]),* Richard Tauber (ten) *(Offenbach:Es war einmal am Hofe von Eisenack [from Les Contes d'Hoffman]),* Nino Ederle (ten) *(Thomas:Ah! non credevi tu [from Mignon]),* Giacomo Lauri Volpi (ten) *(Bellini:Meco all'altar di Venere [from Norma]),* Miguel Fleta (ten) *(Verdi:Celeste Aida [from Aida]),* Koloman von Pataky (ten) *(Nicolai:Horch, die Lerche singt im Hain [from Die lustigen Weiber von Windsor]),* Georges Thill (ten) *(Meyerbeer:O Paradis sorti de l'onde [from L'Africaine]),* Helge Rosvaenge (ten) *(Weber:Seit frühster Jugend in Kampf und Streit [from Oberon]),* Giuseppe Lugo (ten) *(Puccini:Che gelida manina [from La Bohème]),* Julius Patzak (ten) *(Smetana:Es muss gelingen [from The Bartered Bride]),* Franz Völker (ten) *(Wagner:Morgenlich leuchtend [from Die Meistersinger von Nürnberg]),* Ivan Kozlovsky (ten) *(Tchaikovsky:Faint echo of my youth [from Eugene Onegin]),* Richard Crooks (ten) *(Rimsky-Korsakov:Chanson hindoue [from Sadko]),* Torsten Ralf (ten) *(Wagner:Fanget an! [from Die Meistersinger von Nürnberg]),* Andre d'Arkor (ten) *(Boieldieu:Viens, gentille dame [from La dame blanche]),* Enzo de Muro Lomanto (ten) *(Verdi:Parmi veder le lagrime [from Rigoletto]),* Max Lorenz (ten) *(Wagner:Schmeide, mein Hammer, ein hartes Schwert [from Siegfried]),* Jan Kiepura (ten) *(Flotow:Ach, so fromm [from Martha]),* Sergei Lemeshev (ten) *(Napravnik:Give me oblivion [from Dubrovsky]),* Charles Kullmann (ten) *(R. Strauss:Di rigori armato il seno [from Der Rosenkavalier]),* Georgi Nelepp (ten) *(Tchaikovsky:Her name is unknown to me [from Queen of Spades]),* Set Svanholm (ten) *(Wagner:Höchstes Vertrau'n [from Lohengrin]),* Marcel Wittrisch (ten) *(Moniuszko:Rauschen hör' ich Tannen leise [from Halka]),* Mario Filippeschi (ten) *(Puccini:Addio fiorito asil [from Madama Butterfly]),* Peter Anders (ten) *(Mozart:Konstanze, dich wiederzusehen [from Die Entführung aus dem Serail]),* Anton Dermota (ten) *(Massenet:Ich schloss die Augen [from Manon]),* Jussi Björling (ten) *(Rossini:Cujus animam [from Stabat Mater]),* Ferruccio Tagliavini (ten) *(Puccini:E lucevan le stelle [from Tosca]) (rec 1906-47)* PRE 2-▲ 89229 (31.97)

Favorite Italian Opera—features performances by Renata Tebaldi *(Gianni Schicchi—O mio babbino; La Rondine—Sogno di Doretta),* Anita Cerquetti *(Norma—Casta diva),* Maria Chiara *(La Wally—Ebben?...Ne andrò lontana),* Fiorenza Cossotto *(La Favorita—O mio Fernando),* Giulietta Simionato *(Cenerentola—Nacqui all'affano...Non più mesta),* Luciano Pavarotti *(Bohème—Si, michiamano Mimi; Turandot—Nessun dorma; Rigoletto—La donna è mobile),* Mario Del Monaco *(Pacgiliacci—Vesti la giubba),* Giuseppe Di Stefano *(L'Elisir d'amore—Una furtiva lagrima; Aida—Celeste Aida),* Bruno Prevedi *(Fedora—Amor ti vieta),* Franco Corelli *(Tosca—E lucevan le stelle),* Ettore Bastianini *(Barber of Seville—Largo al factotum),* Ambrosian Singers *(Nabucco—Va, pensiero),* Academy of St. Cecilia Chorus *(Madama Butterfly—Humming Chorus)* PPHI (Opera Gala) ▲ 21895 [ADD]

Favourite Opera—features performances by Maria Callas, Joan Sutherland, Mirella Freni & Victoria de los Angeles (sopranos), Luciano Pavarotti, Placido Domingo, Carlo del Monte, Charles Craig & Nicolai Gedda (tenors), & others *(selections from Carmen, The Pearl Fishers, Don Giovanni, Manon Lescaut, Tosca, Nabucco, La bohème, Rigoletto, La traviata, Il trovatore, L'amico Fritz, Turandot, Les contes d'Hoffmann, Die Zauberflöte, Il barbiere di Siviglia & Faust)* CFP ▲ 4602 [ADD] (12.97)

Finnish Vocal Music—features performances by Taru Valjakka (sop), Jorma Hynninen (bar), w. Ralf Gothóni (pno) [E,Fin,G] *(solo bar song cycles by Yrjö Kilpinen (Spielmannslieder),* Einojuhani Rautavaara *(3 Sonnets of Shakespeare),* & Erkki Salmenhaara *(Kolme japanilaista laulua, "3 Japanese Songs");* 8 solo bar songs by Erik Bergman, Erkki Melartin, & Selim Palmgren; solo sop song cycles by Ilkka Kuusisto *(Suomalainen vieraanvara, "Finnish Husbandry"),* & Tauno Pylkkanen *(Kuoleman joutsen, "The Swan of Death");* 5 solo sop songs by Leevi Madetoja) BIS ▲ 88 [AAD] (17.97)

The 1st Plácido Domingo International Voice Competition Gala Concert—features performances by P. Domingo (ten) *(Meyerbeer:Pays merveilleux...ô paradis [from L'Africaine]; Sorozabel:No puede ser! [from La tabernera del puerto]),* Inva Mula-Tchako (sop) *(Bellini:Qui la voce sua soave [from I Puritani]),* Nina Stemme (sop) *(Catalani:Ebben? Ne andrò lontana [from La Wally]),* Domingo (ten) & Kwangchul Youn (bass) *(Gounod:Mais ce Dieu...Me voici!...A moi les plaisirs [from Faust]),* Aïnhoa Arteta (sop) *(Massenet:Obéissons quand leur voix appelle [from Manon]),* Domingo (ten) & Mula-Tchako (sop) *(Donizetti:Caro elisir, sei mio [from L'elisir d'amore]),* Domingo (ten) & Stemme (sop) *(Verdi:Già nella notte densa [from Otello]),* Domingo (ten), Stemme (sop) & Youn (bass) *(Verdi:È quest'ancora...Non imprecare, umiliati [from La forza del destino]),* Arteta (sop) & Domingo (ten) *(Penella:Me llamabas, Rafaeliyo? [from El gato montés]; Puccini:O soave fanciulla [from La bohème]),* Youn (bass) & Mula-Tchako (sop) *(Mozart:Là ci darem la mano [from Don Giovanni]),* Stemme (sop) & Arteta (sop) *(Mozart:Che soave zeffiretto [from Le nozze di Figaro]),* Domingo (ten), Mula-Tchako (sop), Stemme (sop), Arteta (sop) & Youn (bass) *(Verdi:Libiamo, nei lieti calici [from La traviata]) (rec Opéra de Paris-Bastille Nov 20-21, 1993)* COL ▲ 46691 [DDD] (16.97)

Five Mystical Songs, Five Tudor Portraits, A Choral Suite HYP ▲ 55004 (9.97)

The Flowering of English Song—features performances by Elen Phillips (sop), Philip Frohnmayer (bar), w. Logan Skelton (pno) *(solo songs & duets by Balfe, Bax, Besly, Bridge, German, Holst, Ireland, Somerville, Vaughan Williams)* CENT ▲ 2075 [DDD] (16.97)

▲ = CD ♦ = Enhanced CD △ = MD ▮ = Cassette Tape ▯ = DCC

VOCAL COLLECTIONS

Flowering of Vocal Music in America, 1767-1823, w. Susan Belling (sop), Cynthia Clarey (sop), Barbara Wallace (sop), Debra Vanderlinde (sop), Evelyn Petros (sop), D'Anna Fortunato (mez), Charles Bressler (ten), Richard Anderson (bar), James Tyeska (bar), Joseph McKee (bass), Cynthia Otis (hp), Leonard Raver (org), Harriet Wingreen (pno), Regis Iandiorio (vn), New World SO—features works by Dencke *(Meine Seele erhebet dem Herrn; Gehet in dem Geruch seines Bräutigams-Names)*, Müller *(Mein Heiland geht ins Leiden)*, Michael *(Ich bin in meinem Geiste)*, Peter *(Leite mich in deiner Wahrheit)*, Herbst *(Abide in Me; See Him; And Thou Shalt Know It; How Greatly Doth My Soul Rejoice; Thanks Be to Thee)*, Heinrich *(Philanthropy)*, Carr *(Mary; Soldier, Rest!; Hymn to the Virgin; Blanche of Devan; Alice Brand; Coronach [all from The Lady of the Lake])*, Shaw *(There's Nothing True but Heav'n)*, Jackson *(The Dying Christian to his Soul)* NWW ▲ 80467 (29.97)

41 Golden Opera Treasures, w. Pamela Bori (sop), Amelita Galli-Curci (sop), G. A. Lombardi (sop), Claudia Muzio (sop), Rosa Ponselle (sop), Meta Seinemeyer (sop), Vallin (sop), Conchita Supervia (mez), Jussi Björling (ten), Enrico Caruso (ten), Beniamino Gigli (ten), Josef Schmidt (ten), Tito Schipa (ten), Richard Tauber (ten)—features arias by Bizet, Gounod, Leoncavallo, Puccini, Mascagni, Massenet, Mozart, Rossini, Verdi, Wagner EMPD 2-▲ 70367 (10.97)

Four American Baritones of the Past—features performances by John Charles Thomas (bar) *(Massenet:Vision fugitive; Salomé! Demande au prisonnier [both from Hérodiade]; Giordano:Nemico della Patria [from Andrea Chénier]; Verdi:Credo in un Dio crudel [from Otello]; Leoncavallo:Zazà, piccolo zingara [from Zazà])*, Lawrence Tibbett (bar) *(Rossini:Largo al factotum [from Il barbiere di Siviglia]; Verdi:Eri tu che macchiavi [from Un ballo in maschera]; Gruenberg:O Lord!..Standin' in the need of prayer [from Emperor Jones]; Hanson:O, 'tis an earth defiled [from Merry Mount])*, Leonard Warren (bar) *(Verdi:Contigiani, vil razza dannata [from Rigoletto]; Il balen del suo sorriso; Qual suono...Per me ora fatale [both from Il trovatore]; Leoncavallo:Si può? [from I Pagliacci])*, Robert Merrill (bar) *(Verdi:Di Provenza il mar [from La traviata]; Meyerbeer:Adamastor, re delle acque profonde [from L'Africana]; Thomas:O vin, dissipe la tristesse [from Hamlet]; Bizet:Votre toast, je peux vous le rendre [from Carmen]) (rec 1934-47)* PRE ▲ 89957 (m)

Four Austrian Sopranos of the Past—features performances by Berta Kiurina (sop) *(Mozart:Ihr, die ihr Triebe des Herzens [from Le nozze di Figaro]; Gounod:Ha, welch Glück [from Faust]; Bizet:Ich sprach, dass ich furchlos mich fühle [from Carmen]; Puccini:Eines Tages seh'n wir [from Madame Butterfly]; Prinzessin, die Liebe [from Turandot])*, Luise Helletsgruber (sop) *(Mozart:Ich weiss nicht was ich tue [from Le nozze di Figaro]; Leoncavallo:Wie die Vöglein schweben [from Pagliacci]; Puccini:Man nennt mich Mimi; Will ich allein [both from La bohème]; Höre mich an, Herr [from Turandot])*, Maria Reining (sop) *(Mozart:Und Sussana kommt nicht [from Le nozze di Figaro]; Wagner:Der Männer Sippe sass hier im Saal [from Die Walküre]; Einsam in trüben Tagen; Euch Lüften, die mein Klagen [both from Lohengrin])*, Hilde Konetzni (sop) *(Wagner:Dich, teure Halle, grüss ich wieder; Allmächt'ge Jungfrau [both from Tannhäuser]; Weber:Wie nahte mir der Schlummer [from Der Freischütz]; R. Strauss:Da geht er hin [from Der Rosenkavalier])* [G] *(rec 1927-44)* PRE ▲ 89973 (m) (16.97)

Four Dramatic Sopranos of the Past—features performances by Elisabeth Ohms (sop) *(Beethoven:Abscheulicher, wo eilst du hin? [from Fidelio]; Wagner:Versank ich jetzt [from Der fliegende Holländer]; R. Strauss:Kann mich auch ein Mädel [from Der Rosenkavalier])*, Gertrud Bindernagel (sop) *(Weber:Ozean, du Ungeheuer! [from Oberon]; Wagner:Mild und leise [from Tristan & Isolde]; Verdi:Als Sieger kehre heim! [from Aida])*, Marta Fuchs (sop) *(Wagner:Traft ihr das Schiff [from Der fliegende Holländer]; Nun zäume dein Ross; War es so schmählich was ihr verbrach? [both from Die Walküre])*, Anny Konetzni (sop) *(Wagner:Dein Werk? [from Tristan & Isolde]; Starke Scheite schichtet mir dort [from Götterdämmerung]; R. Strauss:Bald aber naht ein Bote [from Adrianne auf Naxos])* [G] *(rec 1929-41)* PRE ▲ 89987 (m) (16.97)

Four Famous Baritones of the Past—features performances by Carlo Drago Hržić (bar) *(Delibes:Lakmé, es schweift dein Blick [from Lakmé]; Korngold:Mein Sehnen, mein Wähnen [from Tote Stadt]; Tchaikovsky:Als du zum Gatten mich erkoren [from Queen of Spades]; Thomas:O Wein, zerstreu' uns're Sorgen [from Hamlet]; Verdi:Ihr holden Jünglingsträume [from Ernani])*, Celestino Sarobe (bar), Julius Prüwer (cnd), Berlin German Opera Orch *(Leoncavallo:Si può? [from Pagliacci]; Meyerbeer:Figlia di regi [from L'Africana]; Verdi:Di Provenza il mar [from Traviata]; Credo in un Dio crudel [from Otello])*, Alexander Sved (bar), Clemens Krauss (cnd), Berlin German Opera Orch *(Verdi:Pari siamo; Cortigiani, vil razza dannata [both from Rigoletto]; Sieh meiner hellen Tränen Flut [w. Viorica Ursuleac (sop); from Trovatore]; Für dein Glück; Du allein hast dies Herz mir entwendet [both from Ballo in maschera])*, Umberto Urbano (bar), Manfred Gurlitt (cnd), Berlin German Opera Orch *(Rossini: Largo al factotum [from Barbiere di Siviglia]; Tosti: L'ultima canzone; Verdi: Il balen del suo sorriso [from Trovatore]; Per me giunto è il di supremo [from Donb Carlo]; Era la notte [from Otello]) (rec 1928-36)* PRE (Lebendige Vergangenheit) ▲ 89974 (m) (16.97)

Four Famous Basses of the Past—features performances by Marcel Journet (bass) *(Mozart:Madamina! Il catalogo è questo [from Don Giovanni]; Rossini:Pro peccatis [from Stabat Mater]; Massenet:Fleurissait une Rose [from Le Jongleur de Notre Dame]; Charpentier:Reste, repose-toi! [from Louise])*, Nazzareno de Angelis (bass) *(Meyerbeer:Suore che riposate [from Roberto il Diavolo]; Verdi:Sperate o figli; Tu sul labbro dei veggenti [both from Nabucco]; Halévy:Voi che del Dio vivente [from La Juive]; Boito:Ave Signor [from Mefistofele])*, Ezio Pinza (bass) *(Bellini:Ite sul colle, o Druidi! [from Norma]; Thomas:Le Tambour-Major tout galonné d'or [from La Caïd]; Verdi:O tu, Palermo [from I vespri siciliani]; Dormirò sol nel manto mio regal [from Don Carlos]; Puccini:Vecchia zimarra [from La Bohème])*, Tancredi Pasero (bass) *(Verdi:Il mio sangue, la vita darei [from Luisa Miller]; A te l'estremo addio [from Simon Boccanegra]; Confutatis maledictis [from Requiem Mass]; Boito:Son lo spirito che nega; Ecco il mondo [both from Mefistofele]) (rec 1926-44)* PRE ▲ 89990 (16.97)

Four Famous Contraltos of the Past—features performances by Emmi Leisner (cta) *(Gluck:Wehklagend irr' ich so; Ach, ich habe sie verloren [both from Orfeo ed Euridice]; Handel:Ombra mai fù [from Serse]; Wagner:Einsam wachend [from Tristan und Isolde]; Bizet:Ja, die Liebe hat bunte Flügel [from Carmen])*, Sigrid Onegin (cta) *(Donizetti:Il segreto per esser felici [from Lucrezia Borgia]; O mio Fernando [from La favorita]; Verdi:O don fatale [from Don Carlos]; Meyerbeer:Ah! mon fils; O prêtres de Baal [both from Le Prophète])*, Karin Branzell (mez) *(Verdi:Lodernde Flammen [from Il trovatore]; König des Abgrunds [from Un ballo in maschera]; Bizet:Wenn dir die Karten einmal bitt'res Unheil künden [from Carmen]; Saint-Saëns:Sieh', mein Herz erschliesset sich [from Samson et Dalila]; Wagner:Weiche, Wotan, weiche [from Das Rheingold])*, Rosette Anday (cta) *(Wagner:Seit er von dir geschieden [from Götterdämmerung]; Bizet:Draussen am Wall von Sevilla [from Carmen]; Saint-Saëns:Printemps qui commence; Amour! viens aider ma Faiblesse [both from Samson et Dalila]) (rec 1927-29)* PRE ▲ 89985 (16.97)

Four Famous French Sopranos—features performances by Ninon Vallin (sop) *(Massenet:Il est doux, il est bon [from Herodiade]; Adieu, notre petite table; Obéissons quand leur voix appelle [both from Manon]; Charpentier:Depuis le jour [from Louise])*, Lily Pons (sop) *(Meyerbeer:Ombre légère [from Dinorah]; Thomas:Je suis Titania [from Mignon]; Rimsky-Korsakov:Hymne au soleil [from Le Coq d'Or]; Ponce:Estrellita)*, Janine Micheau (sop) *(Thomas:A vos jeux... [from Hamlet]; R. Strauss:Grossmächtige Prinzessin [from Ariadne auf Naxos])*, Mado Robin (sop) *(Mozart:O zitt're nicht, mein lieber Sohn; Der Hölle Rache [both from Die Zauberflöte]; Gallini:Chason bohème; Fevrier:L'Oiseau; Benedict:La Gitane et L'Oiseau) (rec 1928-43)* PRE ▲ 89951 (m)

Four Famous German Baritones—features performances by Herbert Janssen (bar) *(Lortzing:Du lässt mich kalt von hinnen scheiden [from Der Waffenschmeid]; Sonst spielt ich mit Zepter [from Zar und Zimmermann]; Gounod:Da ich nun verlassen soll; Höre mich jetzt an, Margarethe! [both from Faust]; Wagner:Blick' ich umher [from Tannhäuser])*, Karl Hammes (bar) *(Wagner:O du mein holder Abendstern [from Tannhäuser]; Weinberger:Ich bin der Schwanda; Wie kann ich denn vergessen [both from Schwanda der Dudelsackpfeifer]; Korngold:Mein Sehnen, mein Wähnen [from Die tote Stadt])*, Gerhard Hüsch (bar) *(Nicolai:In einem Waschkorb? [from Die lustigen Weiber von Windsor; w. Eugen Fuchs (bar)]; Gumbert:An des Rheines grünen Ufern; Lortzing:Nun ist's vollbracht [from Undine]; Humperdinck:Besenbinderlied [from Hänsel und Gretel]; Verdorben, gestorben [from Königskinder])*, Hans Wocke (bar) *(Kreutzer:Ein Schütz bin ich [from Das Nachtlager in Granada]; Lortzing:Es wohnt am Seegestade [from Undine]; Wie freundlich strahlt [from Der Wildschütz]; Rossini:Ich bin das Faktotum [from Il barbiere di Siviglia]) (rec 1928-43)* PRE ▲ 89978

Four Famous German Baritones—features performances by Theodor Schiedl (bar) *(Marschner:An jenem Tag [from Hans Heiling]; Meyerbeer:Dir, o Königin [from L'Africaine]; Wagner:Was duftet doch der Flieder [from Die Meistersinger von Nürnberg]; Des Weihgefässes göttlicher Gehalt [from Parsifal])*, Emil Schipper (bar) *(Gluck:O Artemis [from Iphigenie in Aulis]; Wagner:O König, trugbetöre Fürsten [from Lohengrin]; Verdi:Gleich sind wir bewede [from Rigoletto]; Gounod:Höre mich jetzt an, Margarethe [from Faust])*, Michael Böhnen (bass) *(Mozart:Will einst das Gräflein; Dort vergiss leises Fleh'n [both from Le nozze di Figaro]; Brüll:Bom bom bom, trarara; Wie anders war es [both from Das goldene Kreuz]; Wagner:Jerum! Jerum! [w. Emmy Bettendorf (sop), Carl Martin Öhmann (ten), Leo Schützendorf (sgr); from Die Meistersinger von Nürnberg])*, Wilhelm Rode (bar) *(Boito:Ich, der Geist, der stets verneinet [from Mefistofele]; Meyerbeer:Hei, Adamstor [from L'Africaine]; Bizet:Euren Toast kann ich wohl erwidern [from Carmen]; Verdi:Ich glaube an einen grausamen Gott [from Otello]; Puccini:Drei Häscher mit einem Wagen [from Tosca])* [G] *(rec 1926-30)* PRE ▲ 89969 (m) (16.97)

Four Famous German Sopranos—features performances by Elisabeth Rethberg (sop) *(Wagner:Dich, teure Halle [from Tannhäuser]; Einsam in trüben Tagen [from Lohengrin]; Verdi:Ritorna vincitor!; O patria mia [both from Aida]; Meyerbeer:Leb' wohl, freundlich Gestade [from L'Africaine])*, Maria Müller (sop) *(Weber:Wie nahte mir der Schlummer [from Der Freischütz]; Wagner:Zurück von ihm! [from Tannhäuser]; Das süsse Lied verhallt [from Lohengrin])*, Tiana Lemnitz (sop) *(Weber:Und ob die Wolke sie verhülle [from Der Freischütz]; Wagner:Allmächt'ge Jungfrau [from Tannhäuser]; Euch Lüften, die mein Klagen [from Lohengrin]; Verdi:Sie sass voll Leide auf öder Heide [from Otello])*, Margarete Teschmacher (sop) *(Weber:Ozean, du Ungeheuer! [from Oberon]; Smetana:Endlich allein! [from The Bartered Bride]; Puccini:Bald sind wir auf der Höh' [from Madame Butterfly]; Nur der Schönheit weiht' ich mein Leben [from Tosca])* [G,I] *(rec 1927-43)* PRE ▲ 89971 (m) (16.97)

Four Famous Italian Baritones—features performances by Mario Basiola (bar) *(Rossini:Largo al factotum [from Il barbiere di Siviglia]; Donizetti:A tanto amor [from La favorita]; Ponchielli:Roaccogli e calma [from Il Figliol prodigo]; Massenet:Vision fuggitiva [from Erodiade])*, Carlo Tagliabue (bar) *(Verdi:Pari siamo [from Rigoletto]; Il balen del suo sorriso [from Il trovatore]; Eri tu che macchiavi [from Un ballo in maschera]; Leoncavallo:Si può? [from Pagliacci])*, Gino Bechi (bar) *(Verdi:Oh! de' verd'anni miei [from Ernani]; Cortigiani vil razza dannata [from Rigoletto]; Credo in un Dio crudel [from Otello]; Giordano:Nemico della patria [from Andrea Chénier]; Catalani:T'amo ben io [from La Wally])*, Tito Gobbi (bar) *(Mozart:Deh vieni alla finestra [from Don Giovanni]; Cilea:Come due tizzi accesi [from L'Arlesiana]; Leoncavallo:Buona Zazà del mio buon tempo; Zazà, piccola zingara [both from Zazà]; Puccini:Minnie dalla mia casa son partito [from La fanciulla del West]) (rec 1935-42)* PRE ▲ 89988 (16.97)

Four Famous Italian Baritones—features performances by Mariano Stabile (bar) *(Verdi:L'ononre, ladri; Signore, v'assista il cielo!; Ehi, taverniere...Mondo ladro! [all from Falstaff])*, Antenore Reali (bar) *(Ponchielli:Enzo Grimaldo [from La Gioconda]; Leoncavallo:Si può? [from Pagliacci]; Giordano:Nemico della Patria [from Andrea Chénier]; Cilea:Come due tizzi accesi [from L'Arlesiana]; Leoncavallo:Zazà, piccola zingara [from Zazà])*, Carlo Tagliabue (bar) *(Bellini:Or dove fuggo io mai [from I puritani]; Verdi:Oh de' verd'anni miei [from Ernani]; Credo in un Dio crudel [from Otello]; Ponchielli:Pescator, affonda l'esca [from La Gioconda])*, Paolo Silveri (bar) *(Rossini:Largo al factotum [from Il barbiere di Siviglia]; Verdi:Cortigani, cil razza dannata [from Rigoletto]; Di Provenza il mar [from La traviata]; Gounod:Dio possente, Dio d'amor [from Faust]) (rec 1942-48)* Preiser ▲ PRE 89955 (m)

Four Famous Italian Basses—features performances by Luciano Neroni (bass) *(Donizetti:Dalle stanze ove Lucia [from Lucia di Lammermoor]; Bellini:Suoni la tromba [from I Puritani]; Verdi:Il lacerato spirito [from Simon Boccanegra]; Gomes:Si sposo, di padre [from Salvator Rosa])*, Giulio Neri (bass) *(Boito:Ave Signor; Son lo spirito che nega; Popoli! e secreto [all from Mefistofele])*, Italo Tajo (bass) *(Mozart:La vendetta [from Le nozze di Figaro]; Rossini:La calumnia [from Il barbiere di Sivigia]; Verdi:Come dal ciel precipita [from Macbeth]; Gounod:Vous qui faites l'endormie [from Faust]; Puccini:Vecchia zimarra [from La bohème])*, Cesare Siepi (bass) *(Bellini:Vi ravviso o luoghi ameni [from La sonnambula]; Verdi:Ella giammai m'amò [from Don Carlo]; O tu Palermo [from I vespri siciliani]; Ponchielli:Si, morir elle dè [from La Gioconda]) (rec 1939-52)* PRE ▲ 89960 (m)

Four Famous Italian Mezzo-Sopranos—features performances by Irene Minghini-Cattaneo (mez) *(Donizetti:O mio Fernando [from La favorita]; Verdi:Condotta ell'era in ceppi [from Il trovatore]; Re dell'abisso [from Un ballo in maschera]; Ponchielli:L'amo come il fulgor del creato [from La Gioconda])*, Gianna Pederzini (mez) *(Mozart:Voi che sapete [from Le nozze di Figaro]; Rossini:Cruda sorte, amor tiranno; Per lui che adoro [both from L'Italiana in Algeri]; Bizet:Quadri! Picche!; Presso il bastion di Siviglia [both from Carmen])*, Ebe Stignani (mez) *(Rossini:Ah! quel giorno ognor rammento [from Semiramide]; Donizetti:Per sua madre andrò una figlia [from Linda di Chamounix]; Verdi;Stride la vampa [from Il trovatore]; O don fatale [from Don Carlos]; Saint-Saëns:Amor! i miei sini proteggi [from Samson et Dalila])*, Cloë Elmo (mez) *(Ponchielli:Stella del marinar [from La Gioconda]; Giordano:O grandi occhi lucenti [from Fedora]; Cilea:O vagabonda stella d'Oriente; Io son sua per l'amore [both from Adriana Lecouvereur]; Massenet:Vi scrivo qui dalla stanzetta mia [from Werther])* [I] *(rec 1930-42)* PRE ▲ 89954 (m)

Four Famous Italian Sopranos—features performances by Augusta Oltrabella (sop) *(Mascagni:Un dì ero piccina [from Iris]; Puccini:Donde lieta usci [from La bohème]; Senza mamma [from Suor Angelica]; Verdi:Addio del passato [from La traviata]; Boito:Spunta l'aurora pallida [from Mefistofele])*, Mafalda Favero (sop) *(Puccini:In quelle trine morbide [from Manon Lescaut]; Signore, ascolta! [from Turandot]; Mascagni:Flammen, perdonami [from Lodoletta]; Verdi:Ave Maria [from Otello]; Mozart:Vedrai carino [from Don Giovanni])*, Pia Tassinari (sop) *(Gounod:Come vorrei saper...I gran Signori sol [from Faust]; Mascagni:Son pochi fiori; Non mi resta che il pianto [both from L'Amico Fritz]; Massenet:M'ha scritto che m'ama [from Werther])*, Magda Olivero (sop) *(Boito:L'altra notte in fondo al mare [from Mefistofele]; Puccini:Si, mi chiammano Mimi [from La bohème]; Vissi d'arte [from Tosca]; Cilea:Io son l'umile ancella; Poveri fiori [both from Adriana Lecouvreur]) (rec 1933-41)* PRE ▲ 89961 (m) (16.97)

Four Famous Met-Tenors of the Past, w. Columbia Opera Orch [cnd:Sylvan Levin, Frieder Weissmann, Jean Paul Morel, Erich Leinsdorf] RCA Victor Orch [cnd:Wilfred Pelletier]—features performances by Jan Peerce (ten) *(Verdi:Parmi veder le lagrime [from Rigoletto]; Ai nostri monti [from Il trovatore]; De' miei bollenti spiriti [from La traviata]; Me se m'è forza perderti [from Un ballo in maschera])*, Jussi Björling (ten) *(Gounod:Salut, demure chaste et pure [from Faust]; Bizet:La fleur que tu m'avais jetée [from Carmen]; Verdi:Ah, si, bien mio; Di quella pira [both from Il trovatore]; Puccini:Che gelida manina [from La bohème])*, Richard Tucker (ten) *(Halévy:Rachel, quand du Seigneur [from La Juive]; Bizet:Je crois entendre encore [from Les Pêcheurs des Perles]; Meyerbeer:O Paradiso! [from L'Africaine]; Ponchielli:Cielo e mar [from La Gioconda])*, Ramon Vinay (ten) *(Puccini:Perchè chiuso? [from Tosca]; Bizet:C'est toi? [from Carmen]) (rec 1936-47)* PRE ▲ 89952 (m)

Four Famous Mezzos of the Past—features performances by Gertrud Rünger (sop) *(Verdi:Dieser Fleck da kommt immer wieder [from Macbeth]; Dass nocheinmal sie erschiene; In unsre Heimat kehren wir wieder [both from Il trovatore; w. Julius Patzak (ten)]; Welch ein Verhängnis war das Geschenk [from Don Carlos])*, Friedel Beckmann (mez) *(Gluck:Ach, ich habe sie verloren [from Orfeo ed Euridice]; Endlich soll mir erblühen [from Paride ed Elena]; Goetz:Die Kraft versagt [from Der widerspenstigen Zähmung]; Thomas:Ihr Schwalben in den Lüften [from Mignon; w. Arno Schellenberg (bar)])*, Elisabeth Höngen (cta) *(Bizet:Ja, die Liebe hat bunte Flügel [from Carmen]; Draussen am Wall von Sevilla [from Carmen; w. Torsten Ralf (ten)]; Wenn dir die Karten einmal bitt'res Unheil künden [from Carmen; w. Elfriede Troetschel (sop), Helena Rott (mez)]; R. Strauss:Mit ihren Augen voll Tränen; Ist ein Traum [both from Der Rosenkavalier; w. Esther Réthy (sop)])*, Georgine van Milinkovic (mez) *(Verdi:König des Abgrunds zeige dich [from Un ballo in maschera]; Wagner:In seiner Blüte bleicht mein Leben [from Rienzi]; Weiche, Wotan, weiche [from Das Rheingold]; Einsam wachend [from Tristan und Isolde]; Kienzl:O schöne Jugendtage [from Der Evangelimann]) (rec 1935-43)* PRE ▲ 89977 (16.97)

Four Famous Mezzo-Sopranos of the Past—features performances by Jennie Tourel (mez) *(Rossini:Una voce poco fa [from Il barbiere di Siviglia]; Cruda sorte! [from L'Italiana in Algeri]; Bel raggio lusinghier [from Semiramide]; Nacqui all'affanno [from La Cenerentola])*, Gladys Swarthout (mez) *(Bizet:L'amour est un oiseaux rebelle [from Carmen]; Thomas:Connais-tu le pays?; Je connais un pauvre enfant [both from Mignon]; Gounod:Qui fais-tu [from Roméo et Juliette])*, Risë Stevens (mez) *(Mozart:Non so più; Voi che sapete [both from Le nozze di Figaro]; Donizetti:O mio Fernando [from La favorita]; Meyerbeer:Ah! mon fils [from Le Prophète]; Tchaikovsky:Adieum forêts [from Jeanne d'Arc])*, Blanche Thebom (mez) *(Wagner:So ist es denn aus mit den ewigen Göttern [from Die Walküre]; Seit er von dir geschieden [from Götterdämmerung]; Einsam wachend [from Tristan & Isolde]) (rec 1942-46)* PRE ▲ 89958 (m)

Four Famous Sopranos of the Past—features performances by Viorica Ursuleac (sop) *(R. Strauss:Es gibt ein Reich [from Ariadne auf Naxos]; Hab' mir's gelobt [from Der Rosenkavalier]; Puccini:Nur der Schönheit weiht' ich mein Leben [from Tosca]; In diesem Schlosse [from Turandot])*, Hildegarde Ranczak (sop) *(Verdi:Der Tod sei mir willkommen [from Un ballo in maschera]; Als Sieger kehre heim [from Aida]; Gegrüsst seist du, Maria [from Otello]; Puccini:Man nennt mich jetzt nur Mimi [from La bohème])*, Helena Braun (sop) *(Beethoven:Abscheulicher, wo eilst du hin? [from Fidelio]; Wagner:Mild und leise [from Tristan & Isolde]; Ewig war, ewig bin ich [from Siegfried])*, Trude Eipperle (sop) *(Weber:Leise, leise, fromme Weise; Und ob die Wolke sie verhülle [both from Der Freischütz]; Wagner:Dich, teure Halle; Allmäct'ge Jungfrau [both from Tannhäuser])* [G] *(rec 1932-48)* PRE ▲ 89953 (m)

Four Famous Sopranos of the Past—features performances by Gitta Alpar (sop) *(Ah! fors è lui [from La traviata]; Meyerbeer;Du leichter Schatten bleib' mir zur Seite [from Dinorah]; Delibes:Saht ihr des Paria Tochter [from Lakmé])*, Jarmila Novotná (sop) *(Offenbach:Belle nuit, o nuit d'amour; Elle a fui, la tourterelle [both from Les contes d'Hoffmann]; Smetana:Cradle Songs [from Hubička]; Dvořák:Songs my mother taught me; Humoreske; Fibich:Poèm)*, Maria Cebotari (sop) *(Puccini:Man nennt mich jetzt nur Mimi [from La bohème]; Leoncavallo:Wie die Vöglein schweben [from Pagliacci]; Alabieff:Die Nachtigall; Rachmaninoff:O schönes Mädchen; Arditi:Il Bacio)*, Esther Réthy (sop) *(Puccini:Will ich allein des Abends in Paris [from La Bohème]; Väterchen, teures höre [from Gianni Schicchi]; Lehár:Bin verliebt [from Schön ist die Welt]; Hör' ich Cymbalklänge [from Zigeunerliebe]; Einer wird kommen [from Der Zarewitsch]; Wien du bist das Herz der Welt)* [G,I] *(rec 1930-45)* PRE ▲ 89956 (m)

Four Famous Sopranos of the Past—features performances by Frida Leider (sop) *(Gluck:Ah! si la liberté [from Armide]; Mozart:Or sai chi l'onore [from Don Giovanni]; Beethoven:Abscheulicher, wo eilst du hin? [from Fidelio])*, Barbara Kemp (sop) *(R. Strauss:Kann mich auch an ein Mädel erinnern; Die Zeit, die ist ein sonderbar Ding; Ich weiss auch nix [all from Der Rosenkavalier]; Bizet;Du bist's? Ich bin's! [from Carmen])*, Delia Reinhardt (sop) *(Weber:Wie nahte mir der Schlummer [from Der Freischütz]; Wagner:O Sachs! Mein Freund [from Die Meistersinger von Nürnberg]; Der Männer Sippe sass hier im Saal; Du bist der Lenz [both from Die Walküre])*, Göta Ljungberg (sop) *(R. Strauss:Ah! Du wollest mich nicht deinen Mund [from Salome]; Mascagni:Als euer Sohn einst fortzog [from Cavalleria rusticana]; Puccini:Nur der Schönheit weiht' ich mein Leben [from Tosca]; Eines Tages seh'n wir [from Madame Butterfly])* [G] *(rec 1927-30)* PRE ▲ 89959 (m)

Four Famous Sopranos of the Past—features performances by Lotte Schöne (sop) *(Nicolai:Nun eilt herbei [from Die lustigen Weiber von Windsor]; Massenet:Leb' wohl, mein liebes leines Tischchen; Folget dem Ruf, so lieblich zu hören [both from Manon]; Puccini:Done lieta usci [from La Bohème]; Rossini:L'invito)*, Fritzi Jokl (sop) *(Rossini:Frag' ich mein beklomm'nes Herz [from Il barbiere di Siviglia]; Meyerbeer:Ihr edlen Herr'n allhier [from Les Huguenots]; Donizetti:Ich kenn' den tiefen Zauber [from Don Pasquale]; Flotow:Seid meiner Wonne stille Zeugen [from Alessandro Stradella])*, Irene Eisinger (sop) *(Mozart:Schmäle, schmäle, lieber Junge; Wenn du fein fromm bist [both from Don Giovanni]; Weber:Kommt ein schlanker Bursch gegangen [from Der Freischütz]; Auber:Welches Glück, ich atme freier [from Fra Diavolo]; Puccini:Will ich allein des Abends [from La Bohème]; Väterchen, teures, höre [from Gianni Schicchi])*, Luise Szabó (sop) *(Mozart:O zittre nicht, mein leiber Sohn; Der Hölle Rache kocht in meinem Herzen [both from Die Zauberflöte]; Ach, ich liebte [from Die Entführung aus dem Serail]; Verdi:Teuer Name, dessen Klang [from Rigoletto])* [G,I] *(rec 1924-31)* PRE ▲ 89966 (m) (16.97)

COLLECTIONS

COLLECTIONS 1085

VOCAL COLLECTIONS

Four Famous Sopranos of the Past—features performances by Erna Sack (sop) *(Rossini:Frag ich mein beklommnen Herz [from Il barbiere di Siviglia]; Weber:Einst träumte meiner sel'gen Base [from Der Freischütz]; Flotow:Den Teuren zu versöhnen [from Martha]; Arditi:Parla! Waltz)*, Erna Berger (sop) *(Donezetti:Tirolienne [from La fille du regiment]; Flotow:Letzte Rose [from Martha]; Auber:Welches Glück, ich atme freier [from Fra Diavolo]; Bizet:Es hing die Nacht [from Les Pêcheurs des Perles]; Puccini:Eines Tages seh'n wir [from Madame Butterfly]; Grieg:Solveigs Lied [from Peer Gynt])*, Miliza Korjus (sop) *(Meyerbeer:Du leichter Schatten folgst meinen Schritten [from Dinorah]; Offenbach:Phöbus stolz im Sonnenwagen [from Les Contes d'Hoffmann]; Gounod:Holde Nachtigall [from Mirelle]; Verdi:Mercè, dilette amiche [from I Vespri Siciliani]; Arditi:Il Bacio)*, Adele Kern (sop) *(Mozart:Durch Zärtlichkeit und Schmeicheln [from Die Entführung aus dem Serail]; Beethoven:O wär' ich schon mit dir vereint [from Fidelio]; Meyerbeer:Ihr edlen Herrn allhier [from Les Huguenots]; Verdi:Lasst ab mit Fragen [from Un ballo in maschera]; Puccini:Will ich allein das Abends [from La Bohème]) (rec 1929-35)* PRE ▲ 89976 (m) (16.97)

Four Famous Wagnerian Baritones—features performances by Rudolf Bockelmann (bar) *(Jerum! Jerum!; Verachtet mir die Meister nicht [both w. Berlin State Opera Orch, Clemens Schmalstich (cnd); both from Die Meistersinger von Nürnberg]; Kenntest du mich, kühner Spross [w. London SO, Albert Coates (cnd); from Siegfried])*, Hans Hermann Nissen (bar) *(Die Frist ist um [from Der fliegende Holländer]; Abendlich strahlt der Sonne Auge [from Das Rheingold]; Auf wolkigen Höh'n wohnen die Götter [from Siegfried] [all w. German Opera House Orch, Bruno Seidler-Winkler (cnd)]; Euch macht ihr's leicht [w. Saxon State Opera Orch, Karl Böhm (cnd); from Die Meistersinger von Nürnberg])*, Josef Herrmann (bar) *(Was duftet doch der Flieder [w. Saxon State Opera Orch, Karl Böhm (cnd); from Die Meistersinger von Nürnberg]; Leb' wohl, du kühnes, herrliches Kind [w. Vienna PO, Rudolf Moralt (cnd); from Die Walküre])*, Joel Berglund (bar) *(Blick' ich umher; Wie Todesahnung Dämm'rung [both w. (orch unknown)*, Leo Blech (cnd); both from Tannhäuser]; Wahn! Wahn! [w. Stockholm Royal Orch, Nils Grevillius (cnd); from Die Meistersinger von Nürnberg]) PRE ▲ 89982 (16.97)

Four Famous Wagnerian Basses—features performances by Ivar Andrésen (bass) *(Ein furchtbares Verbrechen ward begangen [w. (cnd & orch unknown); from Tannhäuser]; Nun höret mich...Mein Herr und Gott [w. Eduard Habich (bass), Berlin State Opera Orch, Frieder Weissmann (cnd); from Lohengrin]; Kurwenal! Hör!...Tot denn alles [w. Genia Guszalewicz (sop), Marcel Noë (bar), Eduard Habich (bass), Berlin State Opera Orch, Leo Blech (cnd); from Tristan und Isolde]; Titurel, der fromme Held [w. Berlin State Opera Orch, Leo Blech (cnd); from Parsifal])*, Emanuel List (bass) *(Hier sitz' ich zur Wacht; Hoiho! Hoihohoho! Ihr Gibichsmannen [both w. Berlin State Opera Orch Eduard Mörike (cnd); both from Götterdämmerung])*, Alexander Kipnis (bass) *(Das schöne Fest [w. Berlin State Opera Orch, Erich Orthmann (cnd); from Die Meistersinger von Nürnberg]; So ward es uns verhiessen [w. Fritz Wolff (ten), Bayreuth Festival Orch, Siegfried Wagner (cnd); from Parsifal])*, Josef von Manowarda (bass) *(Tatest du 's wirklich? [from Tristan und Isolde]; Gott grüss' euch, liebe Männer von Brabant! [from Lohengrin] [both w. Vienna SO, Hans Weissbach (cnd)]) (rec 1927-40)* PRE ▲ 89983 (16.97)

Four Famous Wagnerian Heroines—features performances by Frida Leider (sop), Berlin State Opera Orch [cnd:Leo Blech] *(Doch nun von Tristan! [w. Elfriede Marherr-Wagner (mez); from Tristan und Isolde]; War es so schmählich [w. Friedrich Schorr (bar); from Die Walküre])*, Frida Leider (sop), London SO [cnd:John Barbirolli] *(Ich sah das Kind an seiner Mutter Brust [from Parsifal])*, Nanny Larsen-Todsen (sop), Berlin State Opera Orch *(Traft ihr das Schiff [w. Frieder Weissmann (cnd); from Der fliegende Holländer]; Ewig war ich [w. Eduard Mörike (cnd); from Siegfried]; Starke Scheite schichtet mir dort [w. Frieder Weissmann (cnd); from Götterdämmerung])*, Kirsten Flagstad (sop), Victor SO [cnd:Hans Lange] *(Allmächt'ge Jungfrau hör' mein Fleh'n! [from Tannhäuser]; Hojotohoh! hojotohoh! heiaha! [from Die Walküre]; Mild und leise [from Tristan und Isolde])*, Helen Traubel (sop), Victor SO [cnd:Charles O'Connell] *(Dich, teure Halle [from Tannhäuser])*, Helen Traubel (sop), New York Phil SO [cnd:Artur Rodzinski] *(Einsam in trüben Tagen [from Lohengrin])*, Helen Traubel (sop), Metropolitan Opera Orch [cnd:Ernst Knoch] *(Du bist der Lenz; Fort denn eile [both from Die Walküre]) (rec 1927-45)* PRE ▲ 89984 (16.97)

Four Famous Wagnerian Tenors—features performances by Lauritz Melchoir (ten) *(Allmächt'ger Vater, blick' herab [from Rienzi]; Dir töne Lob! [from Tannhäuser] [both w. London SO, John Barbirolli (cnd)]; Dass der mein Vater nicht ist [w. London SO, Albert Coates (cnd); from Siegfried]; Wie sie selig [w. London SO, Robert Heger (cnd); from Tristan und Isolde])*, Max Lorenz (ten) *(Erstehe, hohe Roma, neu! [w. Vienna PO, Rudolf Moralt (cnd); from Rienzi]; Inbrunst im Herzen [from Tannhäuser]; Ein Schwert verhiess mir der Vater [from Die Walküre] [both w. Berlin State Opera Orch, Bruno Seidler-Winkler (cnd)])*, Torsten Ralf (ten) *(Das süsse Lied verhalt [w. Tiana Lemnitz (sop), Berlin State Opera Orch, Bruno Seidler-Winkler (cnd); from Lohengrin]; Fanget an! [from Die Meistersinger von Nürnberg]; Winterstürme wichen dem Wonnemond [from Die Walküre] [both w. Berlin State Opera Orch, Hans Udo Müller (cnd)])*, Set Svanholm (ten) *(Höchstes Vertrau'n; In fernem Land [both from Lohengrin]; Am stillen Herd; Morgenlich leuchtend [both from Die Meistersinger von Nürnberg] [all w. RCA Victor Orch, Frieder Weissman (cnd)])* PRE ▲ 89981 (16.97)

Four German Basses of the Past—features performances by Ludwig Hoffman (bass) *(Mozart:O Isis und Osiris; In diesen heil'gen Hallen [both from Die Zauberflöte]; Wagner:Mein Herr und Gott [from Lohengrin]; Lortzing:Auch ich war ein Jüngling [from Der Waffenschmied]; Im Wein ist Wahrheit nur allein [from Undine; w. Albert Peters (ten)])*, Hellmut Schweebs (bass) *(Mozart:Schöne Donna [from Don Juan]; Verdi:Knie nieder am Kreuz [from La forza del destino; w. Margarete Teschemacher (sop)])*, Wilhelm Schirp (bass) *(Wagner:Mögst du mein Kind [from Der fliegende Holländer]; Flotow:Lasst mich euch fragen [from Martha]; Smetana:Komm, mein Söhnchen [from The Bartered Bride; w. Peter Anders (ten)]; Tchaikovsky:Ein jeder kennt die Lieb' [from Eugene Onegin])*, Josef Greindl (bass) *(Wagner:Gott grüss' euch, liebe Männer [from Lohengrin]; Das schöne Fest [from Die Meistersinger von Nürnberg]; Verdi:Sie hat mich nie geliebt [from Don Carlos]; Der alte Mann verfluchte mich [from Rigoletto; w. Heinrich Schlusnus (bar)]) (rec 1929-44)* PRE ▲ 89980

Four German Basses of the Past, w. Bavarian State Opera Orch [cnd:Heinrich Hollreiser], Berlin German Opera Orch [cnd:Artur Gother], London PO [cnd:Thomas Beecham], Sächsische Staatskapelle [cnd:Karl Elmendorff, Kurt Striegler], Leipzig Gewandhaus Orch [cnd:Franz Konwitschny]—features performances by Georg Hann (bass) *(Mozart:O Isis und Osiris; In diesen heil'gen Hallen [both from Die Zauberflöte]; Rossini:Die Verleumdung [from Il barbiere di Siviglia]; Wagner:Mögst du, mein Kind [from Der fliegende Holländer]; Mein Herr und Gott [from Lohengrin])*, Ludwig Weber (bass) *(Wagner:Hier sitz'ich zur Wacht; Hoiho! Hoihohoho! [w. Herbert Janssen (bar); both from Götterdämmerung])*, Gottlob Frick (bass) *(Mozart:Hab'verstanden, gnäd'ger Herr [from Don Giovanni]; Wagner:Tod denn alles [from Tristan & Isolde]; Wolf:Wer ist da? [w. Margarete Teschemacher (sop), Josef Herrmann (bar); from Der Corregidor]; Orff:O hätt' ich meiner Tochter [from Die Kluge])*, Kurt Böhme (bass) *(Mozart:Schöne Donna, dies genaue Register [from Don Giovanni]; Wagner:Durch Sturm und bösen Wind [from Der fliegende Holländer]; Verdi:Das ist nicht möglich [from Luisa Miller])* [G] *(rec 1936-50)* PRE ▲ 89968 (m) (16.97)

Four German Contraltos of the Past—features performances by Luise Willer (mez) *(Verdi:Lodernde Flammen; Die Hände in schweren Ketten [both from Il trovatore]; Bizet:Draussen am Wall von Sevilla [from Carmen]; Saint-Saëns:Sieh, mein Herz erschliesset sich [from Samson et Dalila])*, Eva Liebenberg (cta) *(Gluck:Ach, ich habe sie verloren [from Orfeo ed Euridice]; Handel:Es blaut die Nacht [from Giulio Cesare in Egitto]; Dank sei dir, Herr; Wagner:Einsam wachend [from Tristan und Isolde])*, Maria Olszewska (cta) *(Handel:Lascia ch'io pianga [from Rinaldo]; Bizet:Ja, die Liebe hat bunte Flügel [from Carmen]; Lasst seh'n, was für mich übrig blieb [from Carmen; w. Genia Guszalewicz (sop); Else Knepel (sgr)]; Saint-Saëns:Printemps qui commence [from Samson et Dalila])*, Margarete Klose (mez) *(Gluck:Ihr Götter ew'ger Nacht [from Alceste]; O del mio dolce ardor [from Paride ed Elena]; Verdi:In uns're Heimat kehren wir wieder [from Il trovatore; w. Marcel Wittrisch (ten)]; König des Abgrunds, zeige dich [from Un ballo in maschera]; Verhängnisvoll war das Geschenk [from Don Carlos]) (rec 1927-38)* PRE ▲ 89979

Four German Sopranos of the Past—features performances by Käte Heidersbach (sop) *(Mozart:Hör mein Flehn, o Gott der Liebe [from Le nozze di Figaro]; Ach, ich fühl's [from Die Zauberflöte]; Weber:Wie? was? Entsetzen! [from Der Freischütz]; Wagner:O Fürstin! [from Tannhäuser])*, Emmy Bettendorf (sop) *(Wagner:Traft ihr das Schiff [from Der fliegende Holländer]; Ortrud! wo bist du? [from Lohengrin]; Verdi:Wohl war euch das Los der Waffen feindlich [from Aida])*, Else Gentner-Fischer (sop) *(Beethoven:Komm, Hoffnung [from Fidelio]; Verdi:Ich seh dich wieder, meine Aida [from Aida])*, Margarete Bäumer (sop) *(Mozart:Du kennst nun den Frevler [from Don Giovanni]; Wagner:Siegmund! Sieh' auf mich! [from Die Walküre])* [G] *(rec 1927-32)* PRE ▲ 89964 (m) (16.97)

Four Golden Tenors of the Past—features performances by Giovanni Martinelli (ten) *(Verdi:Se quel guerrier io fossi...Celeste Aida [from Aida]; Giordano:Un di all'azzurro spazio; Come un bel di di maggio [both from Andrea Chénier]; Amor ti vieta di non amar [from Fedora]; Puccini:Che gelida manina [from La Bohème])*, Aureliano Pertile (ten) *(Verdi:Ah! si, bien mio; Di quella pira [both from Il trovatore]; Quando le sere al placido [from Luisa Miller]; O tu, che in segno agli Angeli [from La forza del destino]; Leoncavallo:Recitar...Vesti la giubba [from Pagliacci])*, Beniamino Gigli (ten) *(Donizetti:Tombe degli ave miei [from Lucia di Lammermoor]; Verdi:De' miei bollenti spiriti [from La traviata]; Meyerbeer:O Paradiso! [from L'Africaine]; Ponchielli:Cielo e mar [from La Gioconda]; Boito:Dai campi, dai prati [from Mefistofele])*, Giacomo Lauri-Volpi (ten) *(Bellini:Meco all'altar di Venere [from Norma]; Meyerbeer:Bianca al par di neve alpina [from Les Huguenots]; Gounod:Salut! demure chaste et pure [from Faust]; Bizet:La fleur que te n'avais jetée [from Carmen]; Puccini:È lucevan le stelle [from Tosca]) (rec 1926-30)* PRE ▲ 89972 (m) (16.97)

Four Great Divas—features arias performed by Montserrat Caballé (sop) *(Bellini:Il pirata; Giordano:Andrea Chenier; Puccini:Manon Lescaut; Turandot)*, Maria Callas (sop) *(Donizetti:L'elisir d'amore; Rossini:La Cenerentola)*, Mirella Freni (sop) *(Bellini:I Puritani; Gounod:Faust; Puccini:Madama Butterfly)*, Anna Moffo (sop) *(Bellini:La sonnambula; Rossini:Il barbiere di Siviglia; Verdi:Rigoletto; La traviata)* EMPD ▲ 70261 (8.97)

Four Italian Baritones of the Past—features performances by Enrico Molinari (bar) *(Rossini:Largo al factotum [from Il barbiere di Siviglia]; Verdi:O vecchio cor, che batti; Questa dunque è l'iniqua mercede [both from I due Foscari]; Wagner:Allor che tu coll'estro; O tu cell'astro incantator [both from Tannhäuser])*, Carlo Galeffi (bar) *(Verdi:Cortigiani, vil razza dannata; Compiuto pur quanto [both from Rigoletto]; Ciel, mio padre! [from Aida]; Mascagni:E sempre il vecchio andazzo [from Gugliemo Ratcliff])*, Mariano Stabile (bar) *(Mozart:Deh, vieni alla finestra [from Don Giovanni]; Non più andrai [from Le nozze di Figaro]; Verdi:Inaffia l'ugola! [from Otello]; L'onore! Ladri!; Alfin t'ho colto [both from Falstaff])*, Benvenuto Franci (bar) *(Rossini:Resta immobile [from Gugliemo Tell]; Qual voce! Come! [from Il trovatore]; Quest'assisa che io vesto [from Aida]; Meyerbeer:Adamastor, re delle acque profonde; Averla tanto amato [both from L'Africana]) (rec 1926-29)* PRE ▲ 89962 (m)

Four Scandinavian Tenors of the Past—features performances by Björn Talén (ten) *(Mozart:Dies Bildnis ist bezaubernd schön [from Die Zauberflöte]; Cornelius:Vor deinem Fenster [from Der Barbier von Bagdad]; Verdi:Ich lieb' ihn ja noch immer [from Aida; w. Karin Branzell (mez)]; Offenbach:Es war einmal am Hofe von Eisenack [from Les Contes d'Hoffman])*, Carl Martin Oehmann (ten) *(Wagner:Am stillen Herd; Morgenlich leuchtend [both from Die Meistersinger von Nürnberg]; Mein lieber Schwan [from Lohengrin]; Verdi:Jeder Knabe kann mein Schwert mir entreissen [from Otello]; Giordano:Gleich einem Frühlingsabend [from Andrea Chénier])*, Gunnar Graarud (ten) *(Wagner:O König, das kann ich dir nicht sagen [from Tristan und Isolde]; Winterstürme wichen dem Wonnemond; Siegmund heiss' ich [both from Die Walküre]; Kienzl:Des Lebens ganzer Leidenskelch [from Der Evangelimann])*, Torsten Ralf (ten) *(Verdi:Bei des Himmels ehernem Dache; Gott, warum hast du gehäuft dieses Elend? [both from Otello]; Puccini:Lasset sie glauben [from La fanciulla del West]; d'Albert:Zwei Vaterunser bet' ich; Schau her, das ist ein Taler [both from Tiefland]) (rec 1926-42)* PRE ▲ 89986 (16.97)

From Bourbon Street to Paradise: The French Opera House of New Orleans & its Singers, 1859-1919—features performances by Adelina Patti (sop) *(Yradier:La Calesera (sels))*, Henri Albers (bar) *(Gounod:Sur le flot qui vous entraine [from Cinq Mars])*, Ameline Talexis (sop) *(Meyerbeer:Septour [from L'Africaine; w. Georges Régis (ten), Billot (sgr), Dubois(sgr), Lise Landouzy (sgr), Lauger-Dubois (sgr), Rigaux (sgr)])*, Françis Mézy (bar) *(Rossini:Sois immobile [from Guillaume Tell])*, Jean Vallier (bass) *(Halévy:Si la rigueur [from La Juive])*, Georges Régis (ten) *(Thomas:Adieu, Mignon, courage; Elle ne croyait pas [both from Mignon])*, Fernand Baer (bass) *(Saint-Saëns:Anne, ma bien-aimée [from Henri VIII])*, Lillian Nordica (sop) *(Erkel:Ah! rebegés [from Hunyady Lśló])*, Florencio Constantino (ten) *(Adorables tourments [w. E. Caruso (ten), R. Barthélemy (sgr)])*, Alice Nielsen (sop) *(Verdi:E il sol dell' anima [from Rigoletto; w.Florencio Constantino (ten)])*, Andrés Perello de Segurola (bass) *(Donizetti:Vieni la mia vendetta [from Lucrezia Borgia]*, Francis Nuibo (ten) *(Gounod:Anges du Paradis [from Mireille])*, Albert Huberty (bass) *(Paladilhe:Pauvre martyr obscur [from Patrie]; Flégier:Le Cor)*, Léon Escalaïs (ten) *(Verdi:Supplice infâme [from Le Trouvére; Meyerbeer:Sicilienne [from Robert le Diable])*, Lucette Korsoff (sop) *(Massenet:Je suis encore toute étourdie; Fabliau [both from Manon])*, Auguste Affre (ten) *(Massenet:Ah! parais, astre de mon ciel])* VAIA ▲ 1153 (m) [ADD] (16.97)

Gala Lirica—features performances by Giacomo Aragall, Teresa Berganza, Montserrat Caballé, José Carreras, Placido Domingo, Alfredo Kraus, Pedro Lavirgen, Pilar Lorengar, Juan Pons (soloists), Orquesta Sinfonica de Seville *(Gimenez:La torre del oro (orchestral prelude); & opera arias by Barbieri, Bizet, Catalani, Donizetti, Massenet, Puccini, Rossini, Serrano, Sorozobal, Verdi) (rec Seville, Spain May 10, 1995)* RCAV (Red Seal) ▲ 61191 (16.97) ▮ 61191 ▯ 09026-61191-5

Gentil Madonna: A Vision of the Italian Renaissance—features performances by Anita Biltoo (sop), Kevin Smith (alt), John Potter (ten), Charles Daniels (ten), Richard Wistreich (bass), London Pro Musica [cnd:B. Thomas] UNIT ▲ UNI 88004 [DDD]

The Glory of Italy: Jewels of Italian Song—features performances by Alessandro Ziliani, Rosa Ponselle, Dino Borgioli, Hina Spani, Tito Schipa, Ezio Pinza, Enrico Caruso, Mario Chamlee, Claudio Muzio, Alessandro Valente, Giacomo Lauri-Volpi, Dusolina Giannini, Riccardo Stracciari, Tino Pattiera, Beniamino Gigli MECL ▲ 420 [AAD] (17.97)

Golden Opera—features performances by Bergonzi, Corelli, Crespin, Horne, Milnes, Pavarotti, Popp, Sutherland, and Tebaldi *(sels from Aida; Butterfly; Carmen; Lakmé; Nabucco; Rigoletto; Tosca; Traviata; La Wally; etc.)* PLON ▲ 21322 [ADD] (11.97)

The Golden Treasury of Immortal Singers, w. Enrico Caruso (ten), Beniamino Gigli (ten), John McCormack (ten), Tito Schipa (ten), Richard Tauber (ten), Nelson Eddy (bar), John Charles Thomas (bar), Lawrence Tibbett (bar), Paul Robeson (b-bar), Feodor Chaliapin (bass), Ezio Pinza (bass)—features arias from Carmen; Aida; Rigoletto; Don Giovanni; L'elisir d'amore; Das Land des Lächelns; plus others; also trad songs from Italy, England, USA HADA ▲ 200

Grand Bulgarian Voices, Vol. 3: Great Arias from Russian Operas—features performance by Nicolai Ghiaurov (bass) *(Borodin:Air de Galitzky [from Prince Igor:Act 1/Scene 1]; Tchaikovsky:Air de Grémine [from Eugene Onegin:Act 3/Scene 1] [both w. Bulgarian RSO]; Rachmaninoff:Scène Près du Berceau [w. Blagovesta Karnobatlova (sgr), Plovdiv PO; from Aleko]; Mussorgsky:Scène et Monologue de Boris & Prière et Mort de Boris [w. Sofia PO; from Boris Godunov:Acts 2 & 4])*, Alexandrina Milcheva (mez) *(Glinka:Air de Vanya [from Ivan Soussanine:Act 3]; Mussorgsky:Air de Marfa [from La Khovanshchina] [both w. Bulgarian RSO])*, Pavel Kourchoumov (ten) *(Rachmaninoff:Romance du Tzigane [w. Bulgarian RSO; from Aleko])*, Dimiter Petkov (bass) *(Rachmaninoff:Romance du Vieux Tzigane [w. Plovdiv PO; from Aleko])* FORL ▲ 16743 [ADD] (16.97)

I Grandi Concerti—features performances by Bonaldo Giaiotti *(arias from Verdi:Macbeth & Simon Boccanegra; Boito:Mefistofele; Rossini:Il barbiere di Siviglia [w. New Jersey Opera Orch, Alfredo Silipigni (cnd)])*, Montserrat Caballé *(arias from Donizetti:Lucrezia Borgia; Rossini:La donna del lago; Verdi:Aroldo; Puccini:Manon Lescaut [w. New Jersey Opera Orch, Alfredo Silipigni (cnd)])*, Franco Corelli *(Verdi:Macbeth; Massenet:Le Cid; Meyerbeer:L'Africana; Tosti:A vuchella [w. New Jersey Opera Orch, Alfredo Silipigni (cnd)]; Verdi:Rigoletto; Giordano:Andrea Chenier; Meyerbeer:L'Africana; Puccini:La Bohème & La Fanciulla del west; Massenet:Le Cid; Di Capua:I'te vurria vasaà; O sole mio; Core 'ngrato; Tu ch'ha non chiagne; A vuchella [w. NHK Symphony Orch, Alberto Ventura (cnd)])*, Montserrat Caballé & Franco Corelli [w. New Jersey Opera Orch, Alfredo Silipigni (cnd)] *(aria from Giordano:Andrea Chenier)*, Montserrat Caballé [w. Philadelphia Orch, Seiji Ozawa (cnd)] *(arias from Donizetti:Anna Bolena & Roberto Devereux)*, Gianfranco Cecchele [w. Philadelphia Orch, Seiji Ozawa (cnd)] *(arias from Puccini:Turandot & Verdi:Un ballo in maschera)*, Montserrat Caballé & Gianfranco Cecchele [w. Philadelphia Orch, Seiji Ozawa (cnd)] *(aria from Verdi:Aida) (rec 1967-71)* MELO 2-▲ 28051 [ADD] (32.97)

The Great Baritones: The Italian Tradition—features performances by Mattia Battistini (bar), Gino Bechi (bar), Carlo Galeffi (bar), Apollo Granforte (bar), Giuseppe De Luca (bar), Titta Ruffo (bar), Riccardo Stracciari (bar), Carlo Tagliabue (bar) *(rec 1906-45)* PHG 2-▲ 5084 (28.97)

The Great Baritones: The Italian Tradition (1906-1946)—features performances by Mattia Battistini *(6 arias from Don Sebastiano [Donizetti], La Favorita, Don Giovanni, Amleto [Thomas], Ballo in maschera, Ernani)*, Gino Bechi *(aria from Don Carlos)*, Giuseppe De Luca *(6 arias from Puritani, Faust, Herodiade, Nozze di Figaro, William Tell, Don Carlos)*, Carlo Galeffi *(5 arias from Aida, Ballo in maschera, Rigoletto, Trovatore)*, Apollo Granforte *(4 arias from Otello, Rigoletto, Traviata, Trovatore)*, Titta Ruffo *(2 arias from L'Africana and Gioconda)*, Riccardo Stracciari *(7 arias from Lucia di Lammermoor, Gioconda, Barbiere di Siviglia, Nabucco, Otello, Tannhäuser)*, Carlo Tagliabue *(5 arias from Carmen, Pescatori di perle, Pagliacci, Forza del destino) (rec 1906-46)* MEMO 2-▲ 4434 [ADD]

The Great Cantors—features performances by tenors Berele Chagy, Mordechai Hershman, David Roitmann, Joseph Rosenblatt and Gershon Sirota, and baritones Hermann Fleishmann, Zevulun Kwartin and Salomo Pinkasovicz *(rec 1908-28)* PHS ▲ 9285 (m) [AAD] (17.97)

Great Love Duets, w. Erna Berger (sop), Miliza Korjus (sop), Lotte Lehmann (sop), Frida Leider (sop), Charles Kullman (ten), Lauritz Melchior (ten), Helge Roswaenge (ten), Tito Schipa (ten), Richard Tauber (ten), et al. PHS ▲ 9217 (17.97)

Great Love Duets—features performances by Corelli, Cossutta, Freni, Pavarotti, Price, Sutherland, and Tebaldi *(excerpts from Bohème; Butterfly; Manon; etc.)* PLON ▲ 21308 [ADD/DDD]

Great Operatic Arias , w. Barry Banks (ten), Mary Plazas (sop), Bruce Ford (ten), Philharmonia Orch [cnd:D. Parry], Geoffrey Mitchell Choir [cnd:D. Parry]—features Bizet *(Jolie fille de Perth (sels) [A la voix d'un amant fidèle])*, Delibes *(Lakmé (sels) [Lakmé! c'est toi; Ah! c'est l'amour endormi])*, Donizetti *(Elisir d'amore (sels) [Una furtiva lagrime])*, Flotow *(Martha (sels) [Ach so fromm])*, G. F. Handel *(Semele (sels) [Where'er you walk])*, Lalo *(Roi d'Ys (sels) [Vainement ma bien aimée])*, W. A. Mozart *(Entführung aus dem Serail (sels) [Constanze! Constanze! O wie ängstlich])*, Rimsky-Korsakov *(Sadko (sels) [Song of the Indian Guest])*, G. Rossini *(Armida (sels) [Come l'aurette placide]; Barbiere di Siviglia (sels) [Cessa di più resistere])*, Verdi *(Falstaff (sels) [Dal labbro il canto])* CHN ▲ 3006 [DDD] (13.97)

Great Operatic Duets—features performances by Bergonzi, Freni, Horne, Ludwig, del Monaco, Sutherland, et al. *(excerpts from Don Carlo; Lakmé; Lammermoor; etc.)* PLON ▲ 21314 [ADD] (11.97)

Great Operatic Duets—features performances by Joan Sutherland, Kiri Te Kanawa, Montserrat Caballé, Margaret Price, Agnes Baltsa, Luciano Pavarotti, José Carreras, Giacomo Aragall *(duets from Norma, Gioconda, Manon Lescaut, Tosca, Ballo in maschera, Otello, Traviata)* PLON ▲ 30724 [DDD]

Great Singers at La Scala—features performances by V. Maurel (baritone) *(Veri:Era la notte [from Otello; rec. 1904])*, F. Tamagno (tenor) *(Rossini:O muto asil...Corriam, voliam [from Guillaume Tell; rec. 1903])*, F. Navarrini (bass) *(Verdi:A te l'estremo addio...Il lacerato spirito [from Simon Boccanegra; rec.1907])*, Mattia Battistini (baritone) *(Meyerbeer:Averla tanto amata [from L'Africana; rec.1912])*, Nelli Melba (soprano) *(Verdi:Caro nome [from Rigoletto; rec. 1907])*, F. de Lucia (tenor) *(Mascagni:Apri la tua finestra [from Iris; rec. 1920])*, Rosina Storchio (soprano) *(Donizetti: Quel guardo il cavaliere...So anch'io la virtu magica [from Don Pasquale; rec. 1905])*, A. Bonci (tenor) *(Puccini:Che gelida manina [from La bohème; rec. 1905])*, Eugenia Burzio (soprano) & G. de L. (baritone) *(Ponchiella:Cosi mantieni il patto?...Ebbrezza! Delirio! [from La Gioconda; rec. 1907])*, Celestina Boninsegna (soprano), w. G. Valls (tenor) *(Verdi:Fuggiam gli ardori inospiti [from Aida; rec. 1904])*, R. Stracciari (baritone) *(Verdi:Cortigiani, vil razza dannata [from Rigoletto; rec. 1917])*, M. Gay (contralto) *(Gounod:Je veux vivre dans ce rêve [from Roméo et Juliette; rec. 1922])*, B. de Muro (tenor) *(Mascagni:Tu ch'odi lo mio grido [from Isabeau; rec.1912])*, Gilda Dalla Rizza (soprano) *(Verdi:Addio del passato [from La traviata; rec. 1922])*, Toti Dal Monet (soprano) *(Rossini:Una voce poco fa [Il barbiere di Siviglia; rec. 1924])*, Ezio Pinza (bass) *(Donizetti:Dalla stanza ove Lucia [from Lucia di Lammermoor; rec. 1923])*, Miguel Fleta (tenor) *(Bizet:La fleur que tu m'avais jetée [from Carmen; I; rec. 1922])* NIMB ▲ 7858 [ADD] (11.97)

Great Singers at the Berlin State Opera: Recordings from 1925-39 *(recordings of singers from the pre-war years of the great opera houses of Berlin: the Staatsoper Unter den Linden, the Kroll Opera & the Berlin City Opera)*—features performances by sopranos Margherita Perras, Erna Berger, Tiana Lemnitz, Frieda Leider, Maria Cebotari, Lotte Schnöne; tenors Marcel Wittrisch, Helge Roswaenge, Franz Völker, Max Lorenz, Gino Sinimberghi; baritones Willi Domgraf-Fassbaender, Friedrich Schorr, Heinrich Schlusnus; bass Alexander Kipnis *(works by Mozart, Beethoven, Wagner, Verdi, Humperdinck, R. Strauss & Puccini)* NIMB ▲ 7848 [ADD] (11.97)

▲ = CD ♦ = Enhanced CD △ = MD ▮ = Cassette Tape ▯ = DCC

Great Singers at the Gran Teatro del Liceo—features performances by Maria Gay (mez), Giovanni Zenatello (ten) *(Bizet:Jamais Carmen ne cédra [from Carmen])*, Tito Schipa (ten) *(Verdi:La donna è mobile [from Rigoletto])*, Conchita Supervia (mez) *(Thomas:Connais-tu le pays? [from Mignon])*, Mercedes Capsir (sop) *(Verdi:E strano...Ah, fors è lui...Sempre libera [from La Traviata; w. Lionello Cecil (ten)])*, Apollo Granforte (bar) *(Verdi:Il balen del suo sorriso...Per me ora fatale [from Il Trovatore; w. Guglielmo Masini (bass)])*, Lauritz Melchoir (bar/ten) *(Wagner:Und drauf Isolde...Wie so selig [from Tristan und Isolde])*, Hina Spani (sop) *(Wagner:Einsam in trüben Tagen [from Lohengrin])*, Miguel Fleta (ten) *(Arrieta:Se fue la ingrata...Feliz morada [from Marina; w. Emilio Sagi-Baba (bar)])*, Elvira de Hidalgo (sop) *(Meyerbeer:Ombre Légère [from Dinorah])*, Hipólito Lázaro (ten) *(Verdi:Se quel guerrier io fossi...Celeste Aida [from Aida])*, Titta Ruffo (bar) *(Thomas:Ombre chère, ombre vengereuse [from Hamlet])*, Graziella Pareto (sop) *(Bellini:Ah! non credea mirarti [from La Sonnambula])*, José Palet (ten) *(Verdi:Parmi veder le lagrime [from Rigoletto])*, Riccardo Stracciari (bar) *(Rossini:Largo al factotum [from Il barbiere di Siviglia])*, Maria Barrientos (sop) *(Rossini:Una voce poco fa [from Il barbiere di Siviglia])*, Mattia Battistini (bar) *(Donizetti:Son cifre di Riccardo...Bella e di sol vestita [from Maria di Rohan])*, Francisco Viñas (ten) *(Mascheroni:Ecco mia giovinezza [from Lorenza])* NIMB ▲ 7869 [ADD] (11.97)

Great Singers at the Mariinsky Theater, w. Olympia Boronat (sop), Eugenia Bronskaya (sop), Elena Katulskaya (sop), Maria Kovalenko (sop), Lidia Lipkovskaya (sop), Antonina Nezhdanova (sop), Evgenia Popello-Davidova (mez), Evgenia Zbrueva (cta), Andrei Labinsky (ten), Eugene Vitting (ten), David Yuzhin (ten), Dimitri Smirnov (ten), Leonid Sobinov (ten), Mikhail Karakash (bar), Vladimir Kastorsky (bass) NIMB (Prima Voce) ▲ 7865 (11.97)

Great Singers at the Opera Houses of Europe, w. Nellie Melba (sop), Enrico Caruso (ten), Lauritz Melchior (ten), Francesco Tamagno (ten), Victor Maurel (bar), Alexander Kipnis (bass), et al.—features performances from Covent Garden, La Scala, Berlin State Opera NIMB (Prima Voce) 3-▲ 1783 (34.97)

Great Singers in Moscow, w. Antonina Nezhdanova (sop), Nicolai Figner (ten), Dmitri Smirnov (ten), Feodor Chaliapin (bass), et al. *(rec 1901-13)* NIMB (Prima Voce) ▲ 7876 (11.97)

Great Singers in New York—features performances by Enrico Caruso *(Mascagni:Addio alla madre from Cavalleria rusticana [rec. 1913])*, Emmy Destinn *(Ponchielli:Suicidio from La gioconda [rec. 1914])*, José Mardones *(Verdi:Vieni, o Levità from Nabucco [rec. 1923])*, Margarete Matzenauer *(Donizetti:O mio Fernando from La favorita [rec. 1912])*, Giuseppe de Luca *(Mozart:Se vuol ballare from Le nozze di Figaro [rec. 1917])*, Pasquale Amato *(Rossini:Largo al factotum from Il barbiere di Siviglia [rec. 1911])*, Geraldine Farrar *(Gounod:Je veux vivre dans ce rêve from Romeo et Juliette [rec. 1911])*, Dimitri Smirnov *(Gounod:Cavatina...Ah! lève-toi soleil from Romeo et Juliette [R; rec. 1909])*, Frances Alda *(Puccini:Donde lieta usci from La bohème [rec. 1914])*, Alma Gluck *(Leoncavallo:Ballatella from Pagliacci [rec. 1911])*, Alessandro Bonci *(Thomas:Adieu, Mignon from Mignon [I; rec. 1908])*, Johanna Gadski *(Wagner:Euch Lüften die mein Klagen from Lohengrin [rec. 1912])*, Marcel Journet *(Flotow:Chi mi dirà from Marta [rec. 1912])*, Adamo Didur *(Rossini:La clunnia è un venticello from Il barbiere di Siviglia [rec. 1908])*, Louise Homer *(Gluck:Fatal divinita from Alceste [rec. 1911])*, Nellie Melba *(Verdi:Ah, fors' è lui from La traviata [rec. 1910])*, Antonio Scotti *(Verdi:Quand' ero paggio from Falstaff [rec. 1909])*, Emma Eames *(Bember:La chanson des baisers [rec. 1908])*, Ernestine Schumann-Heink *(Donizetti:Brindisi from Lucrezia Borgia [rec. 1906])*, Pol Plançon *(Thomas:De son coeur from Mignon [I; rec. 1908])*, Marcella Sembrich *(Donizetti:O luce di quest' anima from Linda di Chamounix [rec. 1908])*,) NIMB (Prima Voce) ▲ 7855 [ADD] (11.97)

Great Singers of the Bayreuth Festival, w. Emmy Destinn (sop), Lily Hafgren (sop), Frida Leider (sop), Karin Branzell (mez), Emmi Leisner (cta), Sigrid Onegin (cta), Heinrich Hensel (ten), Ernst Kraus (ten), Max Lorenz (ten), Lauritz Melchior (ten), Franz Völker (ten), Leopold Demuth (bar), Theodor Scheidl (bar), Hans Hotter (b-bar), Friedrich Schorr (b-bar), Walter Soomer (b-bar), Michael Böhnen (bass), Paul Knupfer (bass), Josef von Manowarda (bass), Richard Mayr (bass) *(rec 1907-28)* VOCA (Vocal Archives) 2-▲ 1148 (25.97)

Great Singers Sing Tosti—features performances by Emma Eames (sop), Geraldine Farrar (sop), Nellie Melba (sop), Rosa Ponselle (sop), Luisa Tetrazzini (sop), Giuseppe Anselmi (ten), Enrico Caruso (ten), Beniamino Gigli (ten), John McCormack (ten), Tito Schipa (ten), Victor Maurel (bar), Titta Ruffa (bar), Antonio Scotti (bar), Ezio Pinza (bass), Moreschi (sgr), Pasquariello (sgr) VOCA (Vocal Archives) ▲ 1138 (13.97)

Great Singers: 1907-1938—features performances by Anderson, Caruso, Galli-Curci, Gigli, Lauri-Volpi, McCormack, Muzio, Ponselle, Schipa, Schumann-Heink, Stracciari, Supervia, Tauber, Tetrazzini, Tibbett, Turner
NIMB (Prima Voce) ▲ 7801 (m) [ADD] (11.97) 7801
Great Singers, Vol. 2 NIMB (Prima Voce) ▲ 7812 (m) [ADD] (11.97) 7812

Great Soprano Arias—features performances by Crespin, Tebaldi, Sutherland, Jones, Suliotis, Chiara—arias from Boheme, Tosca, Faust, Aida, Gianni Schicchi, La Wally PLON (Weekend Classics) ▲ 30412 [AAD] ■ 30412

Great Soprano Cabalettas—features performances by Caballé, Callas, Cerquetti, Chiara, Cruz-Romo, Deutekom, Freni, Milanov, Olivero, Pons, Price, Ricciarelli, Robin, Sills, Souliotis, Stella, Sutherland, Tebaldi, Verrett, Von Stade, Zeani *(works by Bellini, Donizetti, Meyerbeer, Rossini and Verdi) (rec 1940-88)* LCD ▲ 161 (m) [ADD]

Great Sopranos of Our Time, w. Maria Callas (sop), Joan Sutherland (sop), Renata Scotto (sop), Montserrat Caballé (sop), Elisabeth Schwarzkopf (sop), Victoria de los Angeles (sop), Mirella Freni (sop), Ileana Cotrubas (sop), Edita Gruberová (sop)—features arias from operas by Verdi *(Aida)*, Donizetti *(Lucia di Lammermoor)*, Bizet *(The Pearl Fishers)*, Rossini *(Il barbiere di Siviglia)*, Puccini *(La Bohème; Madame Butterfly)*, Delibes *(Lakmé)*, Mozart *(Così Fan Tutte; Don Giovanni)* CFP ▲ 9519 [ADD]

Great Sopranos of Our Time, w. various orchs—features performances by Caballé, Callas, Cotrubas, Freni, Gruberova, Schwarzkopf, Scotto, Sutherland, de los Angeles *(arias from Madama Butterfly, Così fan tutte, Don Giovanni, Lakmé, Barbiere di Siviglia, Bohème, Lucia di Lammermoor, Pêcheurs de perles, Aida)* EMIC (Eminence) ▲ 62040 (11.97)

The Great Sopranos of the Fifties & the Sixties: The Italian Tradition—features performances by Magda Olivero, Anita Cerquetti, Renata Tebaldi, Maria Callas, Rosanna Carteri, Leyla Gencer, Anna Moffo *(rec 1958-63)* ENT (Documents) 2-▲ 957 [ADD] (26.97)

Great Voices of the Century, w. Povla Frijsh (sop), Elena Gerhardt (sop), Lotte Lehmann (sop), Gerald Moore (pno)—features works by Koechlin, Georges, Tchaikovsky, Grieg, Fauré, Křička, Cui, Schubert [all sung by Povla Frijsh], Brahms, Schubert, Wolf [all sung by Elena Gerhardt], Bach, Brahms, Schubert, Schumann [all sung by Lotte Lehmann] *(rec 1929-39)* SANC ▲ 1 [ADD] (17.97)

Great Voices of the Century in Opera & Operetta in Europe in the 1920's & 30's—features performances by Erna Berger (sop) *(Weber:Non paventar mia vita; Come tradir potrei [w. Johannes Schüller (cnd), Berlin State Opera Orch])*, Friedrich Schorr (bar) *(Wagner:Fliedermonolog [w. Leo Blech (cnd), Berlin State Opera Orch, from Die Meistersinger von Nürnberg])*, Michael Bohnen (bass) *(J. Strauss II:Im Rausch der Gemuse [w. Emmy Sturn (sop)]; Als ich zum ersten Mal dich sah [w. Anni Frind (sop), Trude Lieske (sop), Anny Ahlers (sop), both w. Ernst Hauke (cnd), Berlin Great Theatre Orch, both from Cassanova])*, Irene Jessner (sop) *(Lehár:Melodrama & Aria; Weingartner:Liebesliefer, Op. 16/2; Stucken:O komm mit mir in die Frühlingsnacht [all w. Bruno Reibold (cnd), RCA Victor SO])*, Armin Weltner (bass) *(Weber:Die Freischütz (abridged) [w. E. Marherr (sop), T. de Garmo (sop), H. Klust (sop), F. Soot (ten), A. Reiss (ten), D. Ernster (bass), E. Kandl (bass), W. Henke (nar), H. Weigert (cnd), Berlin State Opera Orch, Berlin State Opera Chorus]) (rec 1927-40)* SANC ▲ 6 [ADD] (17.97)

Great Voices of the Century: Recorded Rarities 1—features performances by Kirsten Flagstad (sop) *(Franz:Im Herbst, Op. 17/6; Schubert:Im Abendrot, D.690 [both w. Edwin McArthur (pno)])*, Helen Traubel (sop) *(R. Strauss:Ruhe, meine seele, Op. 27/1; Schubert:Wiegenlied, Op. 105/2 [both w. Coenraad V. Bos (pno)])*, Florence Austral (sop) *(Verdi:Ritorna Vincitor [from Aida]; R. Strauss:Cäcilie, Op. 27/2; Traum durch die Dämmerung, Op. 29/1 [both w. Percy Khan (pno)])*, Marjorie Lawrence (sop) *(Wagner:Beünnhilde-Valkyries Scene (Act III.1) [from Die Walküre; w. M. P. Coppola (cnd), Pasedeloup Orch, Troupe des Walkyries de l'Opéra])*, Hulda Lashanka (sop) *(Mendelssohn:Ich Wollt' meine Lieb, Op. 63/1; Abschiedslied der Zugvögel, Op. 63/2; Gruss, Op. 63/3; Herbstlied, Op. 63/4; Abendlied; Sonntagsmorgen, Op. 77/1; Wasserfahrt; Lied aus 'Ruy blas' [all w. Kirsten Thorborg (cta), George Schick (pno)])*, Kersten Thorborg (cta) *(Hahn:Paysage; Si mes vers avaient des ailes [both w. Leo Rosenek (pno)]; Reger:Mariä Wiegenlied, Op. 76/52; Lundvik:Summer Breezes [w. Leo Rosenek (pno)]) (rec 1928-45)* SANC ▲ 7 [ADD] (17.97)

Great Voices of the Century: Recorded Rarities 2—features performances by Dusolina Giannini (sop) *(Verdi:Ritorna vincitor; O patria mia [both from Aida])*, Donald Dickinson (bar) *(Verdi:Pre me giunto è il di supremo [w. Robert Armbruster (cnd), Victor SO, from Aida])*, Frances Alda (sop) *(Puccini:In quelle trini morbide; L'ora, o tirsi è vaga e bella [both from Manon Lescaut])*, Bruna Castagna (cta) *(Thomas:Gavotte [w. W. Pelletier (cnd), Victor SO, from Mignon])*, Jeanne Gordon (cta) *(Bizet:Séguedille [from Carmen])*, Barbara Kemp (cta) *(Bizet:Final Scene [w. Tino Pattiera (ten), Frieder Weissmann (cnd), Berlin State Opera Orch, from Carmen])*, Ursula van Diemen (sop) *(Mozart:Laudate Dominum [from Vesperae solennes de confessore]; Mendelssohn:Ace Maria [both w. Siegfried Ochs (cnd), Berlin PO, Berlin Phil Choir, from Loreley])*, Lotte Leonard (sop) *(Bach:Cant 68; Haydn:Nun beut die Flur das frische Grün [both w. Freider Weissmann (cnd), Berlin State Opera Orch, from Schöpfung]) (rec 1925-40)* SANC ▲ 8 [ADD] (17.97)

Great Voices of the Century Sing Exotica—features performances by Elisabeth Schumann (sop) *(Was I'hab; Taubert:Der Vogel im Wald [w. K. Alwin (cnd)])*, Lucrezia Bori (sop) *(El jilguerito con Pico de Oro; Aria de Acis & Galatea [w. George Copeland (pno)])*, Conchita Supervia (mez) *(Pel Teu Amor; Grieg:Le Printemps, Op. 26/4)*, Margarete Matzenauer (cta) *(Perguntales a las Estrellas; La Golondrina)*, Frances Alda (sop) *(Waiata Maori; A Maori Lullaby [both w. Frank LaForge (pno)])*, Eide Norena (sop) *(Grieg:Fra Monte Pincio, Op. 39/1; Spring, Op. 33/2; The First Meeting, Op. 21/1; Lie:Snow [all w. Piero Coppola (cnd)])*, Maggie Teyte (sop) *(Messager:Petite Dinde, ah quel outrage; Ma foi, venir de Provence [both from Véronique]; Offenbach:Tu n'es pas beau; tu n'es pas riche [from La Périchole])*, Miliza Korjus (sop) *(Delibes:Les Filles de Cadiz; Die Nachtigall [w. Johannes Müller (cnd)])*, Irene Jessner (sop) *(Rimsky-Korsakov:May Night; Tchaikovsky:It's Near Midnight [from Queen of Spades, w. Bruno Reibold (cnd), RCA Victor SO]) (rec 1925-42)* SANC ▲ 5 [ADD] (17.97)

Great Voices of the 50s *(boxed set, also available singly)*—features performances by Kirsten Flagstad (sop) *(Wagner:Wesendonck Songs [w. Hans Knappertsbusch (cnd), Vienna PO])*, Kathleen Ferrier (cta) *(Mahler:Songs from Rückert [w. Bruno Walter (cnd), Vienna PO])*, Lisa della Casa (sop) *(R. Strauss:4 Last Songs [w. Karl Böhm (cnd), Vienna PO]; 4 Lieder [w. Karl Hudez (pno)])*, Suzanne Danco (sop) *(Ravel:Poèmes de Mallarme; Shéhérazade [both w. Ernest Ansermet (cnd), Swiss Romande Orch])*, Irma Kolassi (mez) *(Chausson:Poème de l'amour et de la mer [w. Louis de Froment (cnd), London PO])*, Janine Micheau (sop), Janine Collard (mez) *(Debussy:La Damoiselle élue [w. Jean Fournet (cnd), Paris Conservatory Société des Concerts Orch])*, Mado Robin (sop) *(Bellini:Son Vergin Vezzosa; Qui La Voce [both from I puritani]; Come Per Me Sereno...Sovra Il Sen; Ah! Non Credea...Ah! Non Giunge [both from La sonnambula]; Arditi:Il Bacio; Proch:Theme & Vars; dell'Acqua:Villanelle; Alabiev:Le Rossignol [all w. Anatole Fistoulari (cnd), London PO])*, Julius Patzak (ten) *(Offenbach:Wohlan, nur Mut und Vertrauen; Die Legende von klein Zaches [both from Les Contes d'Hoffmann]; Beethoven:Gott! welch' Dunkel hier [from Fidelio] [all w. Rudolf Moralt (cnd), Karl Böhm (cnd), Vienna PO])*, Hilde Gueden (sop) *(Mozart:L'Amero [from Il rè pastore]; Exsultate, jubilate [both w. Alberto Erede (cnd), Vienna PO])*, Ljuba Welitsch (sop) *(Tchaikovsky:Ich muss am Fenster lehnen; Es geht auf Mitternacht [both from Queen of Spades]; Verdi:Ma Dall'Arido Stelo Divulsa; Morro, Ma Prima in Grazia [both from Un ballo in maschera]; Lehár:Lied und Csardas [from Zigeunerliebe]; Vilja Lied [from Die lustige Witwe]; Einer wird kommen [from Der Zarewitsch]; Millocker:Ich schenk' mein Herz [from Die Dubarry] [all w. Rudolf Moralt (cnd), Vienna State Opera Orch])*, Paul Schoeffler (b-bar) *(Mozart:Non piu andrai [from Le nozze di Figaro]; Wagner:Wotan's Farewell & Magic Fire Music [from Die Walküre] [both w. Rudolf Moralt (cnd), Karl Böhm (cnd), Vienna PO])*, Inge Borkh (sop) *(Weber:Ocean! Du Ungeheurer [from Oberon]; R. Strauss:Closing Scene [from Salome] [both w. Josef Krips (cnd), Vienna PO])*, Ettore Bastianini (bar) *(Rossini:Largo al factotum [from Il barbiere di Siviglia]; Verdi:Morir!...Urna fatale [from La forza del destino] [both w. Alberto Erede (cnd), Francesco Molinari-Pradelli (cnd), St. Cecilia Academy Orch Rome, Florence Maggio Musicale Orch])*, Renata Tebaldi (sop) *(Mozart:Dove Sono [from Le nozze di Figaro]; Catalani:Me mai dunque [from La Wally]; Mascagni:Flammen, perdonami [from Lodoletta]; Refice:Per amor di Gesu [from Cecilia] [all w. Alberto Erede (cnd), St. Cecilia Academy Orch Rome])*, Renata Tebaldi (sop), Giulietta Simionato (mez), Ettore Bastianini (bar) *(Saint-Saëns:S'Apre per te il mio cor [from Samson et Dalila]; Tchaikovsky:Tatyana's Letter Scene [from Eugene Onegin]; Mascagni:Voi lo sapete [from Cavalleria rusticana]; Mozart:Voi che sapete [from Le nozze di Figaro]; Giordano:Nemico della patria [from Andrea Chenier]; Boito:L'Altra notte [from Mefistofele]; Ponchielli:E' un anatema [from La Gioconda] [all w. Georg Solti (cnd), Chicago Lyric Opera Orch])* PLON 5-▲ 455295 (57.97)

Great Voices of the 50s, Vol 1 *(see Composer section under Mahler, R. Strauss, Wagner)* PLON ▲ 448150 (11.97)

Great Voices of the 50s, Vol 2 *(see Composer section under Chausson, Debussy, Ravel)* PLON ▲ 448151 (11.97)

Great Voices of the 50s, Vol 3—features performances by Mado Robin (sop) *(Bellini:Son Vergin Vezzosa; Qui La Voce [both from I puritani]; Come Per Me Sereno...Sovra Il Sen; Ah! Non Credea...Ah! Non Giunge [both from La sonnambula]; Arditi:Il Bacio; Proch:Theme & Vars; dell'Acqua:Villanelle; Alabiev:Le Rossignol [all w. Anatole Fistoulari (cnd), London PO])*, Julius Patzak (ten) *(Offenbach:Wohlan, nur Mut und Vertrauen; Die Legende von klein Zaches [both from Les Contes d'Hoffmann]; Beethoven:Gott! welch' Dunkel hier [from Fidelio] [all w. Rudolf Moralt (cnd), Karl Böhm (cnd), Vienna PO])*, Hilde Gueden (sop) *(Mozart:L'Amero [from Il rè pastore]; Exsultate, jubilate [both w. Alberto Erede (cnd), Vienna PO])* PLON ▲ 448152 (11.97)

Great Voices of the 50s, Vol 4—features performances by Ljuba Welitsch (sop) *(Tchaikovsky:Ich muss am Fenster lehnen; Es geht auf Mitternacht [both from Queen of Spades]; Verdi:Ma Dall'Arido Stelo Divulsa; Morro, Ma Prima in Grazia [both from Un ballo in maschera]; Lehár:Lied und Csardas [from Zigeunerliebe]; Vilja Lied [from Die lustige Witwe]; Einer wird kommen [from Der Zarewitsch]; Millocker:Ich schenk' mein Herz [from Die Dubarry] [all w. Rudolf Moralt (cnd), Vienna State Opera Orch])*, Paul Schoeffler (b-bar) *(Mozart:Non piu andrai [from Le nozze di Figaro]; Wagner:Wotan's Farewell & Magic Fire Music [from Die Walküre] [both w. Rudolf Moralt (cnd), Karl Böhm (cnd), Vienna PO])*, Inge Borkh (sop) *(Weber:Ocean! Du Ungeheurer [from Oberon]; R. Strauss:Closing Scene [from Salome] [both w. Josef Krips (cnd), Vienna PO])* PLON ▲ 448153 (11.97)

Great Voices of the 50s, Vol 5—features performances by Ettore Bastianini (bar) *(Rossini:Largo al factotum [from Il barbiere di Siviglia]; Verdi:Morir!...Urna fatale [from La forza del destino] [both w. Alberto Erede (cnd), Francesco Molinari-Pradelli (cnd), St. Cecilia Academy Orch Rome, Florence Maggio Musicale Orch])*, Renata Tebaldi (sop) *(Mozart:Dove Sono [from Le nozze di Figaro]; Catalani:Me mai dunque [from La Wally]; Mascagni:Flammen, perdonami [from Lodoletta]; Refice:Per amor di Gesu [from Cecilia] [all w. Alberto Erede (cnd), St. Cecilia Academy Orch Rome])*, Renata Tebaldi (sop), Giulietta Simionato (mez), Ettore Bastianini (bar) *(Saint-Saëns:S'Apre per te il mio cor [from Samson et Dalila]; Tchaikovsky:Tatyana's Letter Scene [from Eugene Onegin]; Mascagni:Voi lo sapete [from Cavalleria rusticana]; Mozart:Voi che sapete [from Le nozze di Figaro]; Giordano:Nemico della patria [from Andrea Chenier]; Boito:L'Altra notte [from Mefistofele]; Ponchielli:E' un anatema [from La Gioconda] [all w. Georg Solti (cnd), Chicago Lyric Opera Orch])* PLON ▲ 448154 (11.97)

Great Voices of the Vienna State Opera—features performances by Margit Angerer (sop), Selma Kurz (sop), Jarmila Novotna (sop), Margherita Perras (sop), Lea Piltti (sop), Elisabeth Schumann (sop), Helene Wildbrunn (sop), Maria Olszewska (cta), Trajahn Grosavescu (ten), Charles Kullman (ten), Koloman von Pataky (ten), Leo Slezak (ten), Karl Hammes (bar), Wilhelm Röde (bar), others sels. unknown PRE 4-▲ 89401 [AAD] (63.97)

The Greatest Opera Show on Earth—features works by Bizet *(Prelude [w. London PO]; L'Amour est un Oiseau Rebelle [w. Tatiana Troyanos (mez)]; Flower Song [w. Plácido Domingo (ten)]; Toreador Song [w. José Van Dam (b-bar), Tatiana Troyanos (mez)] [all from Carmen; all w. Georg Solti (cnd)]; C'est toi [from Les Pêcheurs de perles; w. Gregory Cross (ten), Gino Quilico (bar), Charles Dutoit (cnd)])*, Catalani *(Ebben?...Ne Andro Lontana [from La Wally; w. Angela Gheorghiu (sop), John Mauceri (cnd)])*, Delibes *(Flower Duet [w. Joan Sutherland (sop), Jane Berbié (mez), Richard Bonynge (cnd)])*, Donizetti *(Una Furtiva Lagrima [from L'elisir d'amore; w. Roberto Alagna (ten), Evelino Pidò (cnd)])*, Dvořák *(Song to the Moon [from Rusalka; w. Renée Fleming (sop), Georg Solti (cnd)])*, Giordano *(Amor Ti Vieta [from Fedora; w. Jussi Björling (ten), Alberto Erede (cnd)])*, Gounod *(Soldiers' Chorus [from Faust; w. Ambrosian Opera Chorus, Richard Bonynge (cnd)])*, Leoncavallo *(Vesti la Giubba [from Pagliacci; w. Luciano Pavarotti (ten), Patané (cnd)]; Mattinata [w. Bocelli (sgr), Leone Magiera (cnd)])*, Mascagni *(Intermezzo [from Cavalleria Rusticana; w. Gianandrea Gavazzeni (cnd)])*, Massenet *(Donna non vidi Mai [from Manon Lescaut; w. Jose Carreras (ten), Riccardo Chailly (cnd)])*, Mozart *(Dove Sono [w. Kiri Te Kanawa (sop), Georg Solti (cnd)]; Voi Che Sapete [w. Cecilia Bartoli (mez), Fischer (cnd)] [both from Le nozze di Figaro]; La Ci Darem la Mano [w. Lucia Popp (sop), Tom Krause (bar), Kertesz (cnd)]; Champagne Aria [w. Bryn Terfel (b-bar), Georg Solti (cnd)] [both from Don Giovanni]; Soave sia il Vento [from Così fan tutte; w. Renée Fleming (sop), Anne Sofie von Otter (mez), Georg Solti (cnd)])*, Offenbach *(Belle Nuit [from Les Contes d'Hoffmann; w. Joan Sutherland (sop), Richard Bonynge (cnd)])*, Puccini *(Che Gelida Manina [w. Luciano Pavarotti (ten), Herbert von Karajan (cnd)]; O Soave Fanciulla [w. Mirella Freni (sop), Luciano Pavarotti (ten), Herbert von Karajan (cnd)]; Si, Mi Chiamano Mimi [w. Angela Gheorghiu (sop), John Mauceri (cnd)] [all from La Bohème]; Humming Chorus; Un Bel di [w. Mirella Freni (sop)]; Love Duet [w. Mirella Freni (sop), Luciano Pavarotti (ten)] [all from Madama Butterfly; all w. Herbert von Karajan (cnd)]; E Lucevan le stelle [w. Plácido Domingo (ten), Zubin Mehta (cnd)]; Vissi d'Arte [w. Kiri Te Kanawa (sop), Georg Solti (cnd)] [both from Tosca]; Signore, Ascolta! [w. Montserrat Caballé (sop)]; Nessun Dorma [w. Luciano Pavarotti (ten)] [both from Turandot; both w. Zubin Mehta (cnd)]; O Mio Babbino Caro [from Gianni Schicchi; w. Renata Tebaldi (sop), Lamberto Gardelli (cnd)])*, Rossini *(Largo al Factotum [from Il barbiere di Siviglia; w. Leo Nucci (bar), Patané (cnd)])*, Verdi *(Libiamo, Ne'Lieti Calici [from La traviata; w. Luciano Pavarotti (ten), Joan Sutherland (sop)]; Va Pensiero [from Nabucco; w. Georg Solti (cnd)]; La Donna e Mobile [from Rigoletto; w. Luciano Pavarotti (ten), Richard Bonynge (cnd)]; Di Quella Pira [from Il trovatore; w. Luciano Pavarotti (ten), Joan Sutherland (sop), Richard Bonynge (cnd)])*, Wagner *(Bridal Chorus [from Lohengrin]; Ride of the Valkyries [from Die Walküre] [both w. Georg Solti (cnd)])*, plus *Anvil Chorus [w. Chicago SO, Georg Solti (cnd)]* PLON (Double Decker) 2-▲ 458118 (17.97)

Greatest Voices of Bolshoi—features performances by Pavel Lisistan (bar) *(Tchaikovsky:Yeletsky's Aria [from Queen of Spades; w. A. Melik-Pashayev (cnd), Bolshoi Theatre Orch])*, Vera Firssova (sop) *(Rimsky-Korsakov:Oskana's Aria [from Christmas Eve; w. E. Svetlanov (cnd), Bolshoi Theatre Orch])*, Ivan Petrov (bass) *(Tchaikovsky:King Rene's Aria [from Iolantha; w. V. Nebolssin (cnd), Bolshoi Theatre Orch])*, Galina Vishnevskaya (sop) *(Verdi:Lenora'a Aria [from Forza del destino; w. B. Khaikin (cnd), Bolshoi Theatre Orch])*, Zurab Andzhaparidze (ten) *(Tchaikovsky:Hermann's Aria (scene 1) [from Queen of Spades; w. B. Khaikin (cnd), Bolshoi Theatre Orch])*, Tamara Milashkina (sop) *(Tchaikovsky:Kuma's Aria (act 4) [from Sorceress; w. M. Ermler (cnd), Bolshoi Theatre Orch])*, Vladimir Atlantov (ten) *(Borodin:Vladimir's recitative & Cavatina [from Prince Igor; w. M. Ermler (cnd), Bolshoi Theatre Orch])*, Bela Rudenko (sop) *(Delibes:Scene & Legend (Bell Song) [from Lakmé; w. O. Ryabov (cnd), Bolshoi Theatre Orch])*, Irina Arkhipova (mez) *(Saint-Saëns:Dalila's Aria (act 2) [from Samson & Delila; w. V. Pyavko (ten—Samson), M. Ermler (cnd), Bolshoi Theatre Orch])*, Yuri Mazurok (bar) *(Tchaikovsky:Mazeppa's Aria (act 2) [from Mazeppa; w. M. Ermler (cnd), Bolshoi Theatre Orch])*, Elena Obraztsova (mez) *(Mussorgsky:Marina'a Aria (act 3) [from Boris Godunov; w. M. Ermler (cnd), Bolshoi Theatre Orch])*, Evegny Nesterenko (bass) *(Glinka:Susanin's Aria & Scene (act 4) [from Life for the Tsar; W. M. Ermler (cnd), Bolshoi Theatre Orch])*, Valeriya Barssova (sop) *(Rimsky-Korsakov:Snogourotchka's Aria & Prologue [from Snow Maiden; w. V. Nebolssin (cnd), Bolshoi Theatre Orch])*, Alexander Pirogov (bass) *(Borodin:Galitsky's Recitative & Scene (act 1) [from Prince Igor; w. A. Melik-Pashayev (cnd), Bolshoi Theatre Orch & Chorus])*, Xenia Derzhinskaya (sop) *(Tchaikovsky:Lisa's Scene & Aria; Duet of Lisa & Hermann (scene 6) [from Queen of Spades; w. N. Khanayev (ten—Hermann), S. Samossud (cnd), Bolshoi Theatre Orch])*, Maxim Mikhailov (bass) *(Borodin:Konchak's Aria (act 2) [from Prince Igor; w. V. Nebolssin (cnd), Bolshoi Theatre Orch])*, Georgi Nelepp (ten) *(Verstovsky:Toropka's Song [from Askold's Tomb; w. V. Smirnov (cnd), USSR Radio Large SO])*, Mark Reisen (bass) *(Mussorgsky:Pimen's Monologue (act 1) [from Boris Godunov; w. V. Nebolssin (cnd), Bolshoi Theatre Orch])*, Sergei Lemeshov (ten) *(Tchaikovsky:Lenski's Aria (act 2) [from Eugene Onegin; w. S. Sakharov (cnd)]; Rimsky-Korsakov:Song of the Indian Guest [from Sadko; w. V. Nebolssin (cnd), both w. Bolshoi Theatre Orch])*, Natalia Speiller (sop) *(Iolantha'a Aria [from Iolantha; w. S. Sakharov (cnd), Bolshoi Theatre Orch])*, Ivan Kozlovsky (ten) *(Mussorgsky:Simpleton's Scene [from Boris Godunov; w. M. Ippolitov-Ivanov (cnd)]; Rimsky-Korsakov:Cavatina of Tsar Benedict (act 3) [from Snow Maiden; w. E. Svetlanov (cnd), both w. Bolshoi Theatre Orch])*, Antonina Nezhdanova (sop) *(Glinka:Antonida's Romance (act 3) [from Life for the Tsar; w. I. Arkadiev (cnd), Gramophone Company Orch])*, Grigori Pirogov (bar) *(Verstovsky:Aria of the Unknown [from Askold's Tomb; w. Pathe Company Orch])*, Leonid Sobinov (ten) *(Wagner:Lohengrin's Farewell [from Lohengrin; w. B. Seidler-Winkler (cnd), Gramophone Company Orch])*, Feodor Chaliapin (bass) *(Massenet:Don Quichotte's Death Scene [from Don Quichotte; w. R. Bourdon (cnd), Bolshoi Theatre Orch])*, Nadezhda Obukhova (mez) *(Borodin:Konchakovna's Cavatina (act 2) [from Prince Igor; w. A. Melik-Pashayv (cnd), Bolshoi Theatre Orch & Chorus])* MELD 2-▲ 39505 [ADD]

The Harold Wayne Collection

Vol. 1—features performances by Giovanni Gravina, Guierrina Fabbri, Giovanni Battista de Negri, Giuseppe Kaschmann, Fanny Toresella, Leopoldo Signoretti SYMP ▲ SYM 1065

Vol. 2—features performances by Francesco Marconi (tenor) and Antonio Cotogni (baritone), w. Bice Mililotti, Maria Galvany, Nestore della Torre SYMP ▲ SYM 1069

Vol. 3—features performances by Francesco Marconi, Angelica Pandolfini, Fernando Valero, Eugenio Giraldoni, Giovanni Zenatello, Gemma Bellincioni, Fiorello Giraud SYMP ▲ SYM 1073

Vol. 4—features performances by Cesira Ferrani (soprano), Fiorello Giraud (tenor) SYMP ▲ SYM 1077

Vol. 5—features performances by Sophie Sedlmair & Emilie Feuge (sopranos), Hermann Winkelmann, Otto Briesemeister, Hans Breuer & Alfred von Bary (tenors), Theodor Bertram (baritone), and Clarence Whitehill (bass-baritone) (rec Bayreuth 1904) SYMP ▲ SYM 1081

Vol. 6—features performances by Anna von Mildenburg, Sophie Sedlmair & Lola Beeth (sopranos), Marianne Brandt (contralto), Hans Buff-Giessen & Gustav Walter (tenors), and Karl Scheidemantel (baritone) (rec Dresden, Vienna, Berlin 1902-07) SYMP ▲ SYM 1085

Vol. 7—features performances by Mary Garden, Emma Albani & Frances Saville (sopranos), Joseph O'Mara (tenor), and David Bispham & Sir Charles Santley (baritones) SYMP ▲ SYM 1093

Vol. 8—features performances by Suzanne Adams & Emma Calve (sopranos), Anton Van Rooy, Antonio Scotti & Maurice Renaud (baritones), and Pol Plançon (bass) SYMP ▲ SYM 1100

Vol. 9—features performances by Felia Litvinne (soprano) and Victor Maurel (baritone) (rec 1902-03) SYMP ▲ SYM 1101

Vol. 10 (rec St. Petersburg, Moscow) SYMP ▲ SYM 1105

Vol. 11—features performances by Emma Carelli & Amelia Pinto (sopranos) and Giuseppe De Luca (baritone) SYMP ▲ SYM 1111

Vol. 12—features performances by D. Juzhin (tenor) (Bleichmann:Spring Song; Verdi:Di quella pira [from Il trovatore]; Gounod:Cavatina [from Romeo et Juliette]; Vrangel:Your ardent image attracted me), L.N. Brangina (contralto) (I still love him madly), A. Labinsky (tenor) (Glinka:North Star), M. Emskaya (soprano) (Gounod:Il m'aime [from Faust]), G. Morskoj (tenor) (Plotnikov:The sweet fragrance of lilies; Davidov:Leave me; Rimsky-Korsakov:Maid of Pskov; Sing little cuckoo, in the dark forest; Dlussky:Romance; Cui:I remember the evening), M.A. Max (baritone) (Verdi:Infelice, e tuo credivi [from Ernani]), A.M. Davydov (Leoncavallo:Vesti la giubba [from I Pagliacci]), I.V. Tartakoff (baritone) (Bizet:Votre toast [from Carmen]; Cui:The statue of Tarasakoe Selo), J. Korolewicz-Waydowa (soprano) (Moiuszko:Like the shrub in the whirlwind; If I were the morning sun [from Halka]; If someone mentions to me [from Hrabina]; Reverie [from Flis]; Zosa's song [from Widma]; Przaniczka, pionska), S. Bogucki (baritone) (Maximus' aria [from Lalka]), K. Czosnowska (soprano) (Swedish folk song), A. Didur (bass) (Gall:Hidden love), J. Bochnicek (tenor) (Jen Jeste chvilku s tebou deiti), J. Martapoura (soprano) (Thomas:O vin, dissippe la tristesse [from Hamlet]), C. Mastio (soprano) (Sombre fotět), D. Aranyi (tenor) (Mascagni:Leb'wehl [from Cavalleria Rusticana]; Verdi:Ständchen [from Il trovatore]), R. Chalia (soprano) (Gounod:Le parlate d'amor [from Faust]; Bishop:Home, sweet home), Nikolaj Seversky (Zeller:Shepherd's waltz [Der Obersteiger], Nightingale's song [from Vogelhändler]; I adore you [trad. gypsy romance])) (rec 1901 & 1904) SYMP ▲ SYM 1112

Vol. 13—features performances by Russ, Pacini, Barrientos, Stehle, Pinkert, Brejean (sopranos), Parsi-Pettinella (contralto), Luppi (bass), et al. (rec Milan, Paris, Berlin 1904-08) SYMP ▲ SYM 1113

Vol. 14—features performances by Léon Escalais (tenor), w. Luppi, Magini-Coletti, Talexis, Algos, Coradetti, Masotti, Sala (rec Milan 1905-06) SYMP ▲ SYM 1126

Vol. 21: The Paris Fonotipias—features performances by J.-F. Delmas (Berlioz:Voici des roses [from La damnation de Faust]; Wagner:Les adieux de Wotan [from Die Walküre]; Gounod:Le Soir; Schumann:Les deux grandiers; Meyerbeer:Benediction [from Les Huguenots]; Paladilhe:Aire du pauvre martyre [from Patrie]), P. Gailhaud (Gounod:Serenade [from Faust]; Yradier:La Paloma; Meyerbeer:Hollah Matelots [from L'Africaine]), R. Caron (Gounod:Prières; Duvernoy:Hellé-Cantilène; Reyer:Sigurd-Des présents de Gunther), E. van Dyck (Schumann:Ich grolle nicht [Dichterlieb]; Frühlingsnacht; Wagner:Frühlingslied [from Die Walküre]; Nicolai (Ein Blömken), L. David (Thomas:Elle ne croyait pas [from Mignon]; Bourgeois:La Veritable Manola; Bizet:Grand Air [from Carmen]), V. Capoul (Godard/ Capoul:Jocelyn-Berceuse), M. de Reszke (Gounod:Au Rossignol), A. Adini (Braga:La Serenata), Aramis (Massenet:Il est doux [from Herodiade]; De Lara (Le champs de pavots), G. Brejean-Silver (Sempre libera [from La traviata]) (rec 1904-05) SYMP ▲ 1172 (17.97)

Vol. 22: The Paris Fonotipias Part 2—features performances by Brejean-Silver (Caro nome [from Rigolleto]; On m'apelle Mimi [from La bohème]), Cornubert (Hilda! Vierge au pale sourire [from Sigurd]; Chanson du printemps [from Die Walküre]; Les vers d'Ossian [from Werther]; Entree de Raoul [from Les Huguenots]; Grand Air [from L'Africana]; Ah fuyez douce image [from Manon]; Scene du tombeau [from Romeo et Juliette]; Grand Air [from Les Huguenots]), Scaramberg (Grand air [from Romeo et Juliette]; Grand air [from Manon]; Grand Air [from La reine de Saba]; Grand Air [from Carmen]; Ah! respirons [from Lohengrin]; Grand Air [from Werther]; Comme la plume [from Rigoletto]; Sicilienne [from Cavalleria rusticana]; Entree de Sigurd [from Sigurd]; Air de Loris [from Fedora]), Litvinne (Voi lo sapete [from Cavalleria rusticana]; Reve d'Elsa [from Lohengrin]) (rec 1904-05) SYMP ▲ 1173 (17.97)

Vol. 26—features performances by Léon David (ten) (Thomas:Elle ne croyait pas [from Mignon]; Massenet:Pourquoi me réveiller [from Werther]; Rossini:Des rayons de l'aurore [from Il barbiere di Siviglia]; Massenet:Ah! fuyez, douce image [from Manon]), Jean Lassalle (bar) (Chaminade:Amour d'automne; Massenet:Si tu veux mignonne; Chant Provençal; Fontenailles:Les deux coeurs; Pierné:Le sais-tu bien?), Louise Bérat (sgr) (Hahn:Le pays du rêve), Edmond Clément (ten) (Rossini:Des rayons [from Il barbiere di Siviglia]; Gounod:Ah! lève-toi, soleil [from Roméo et Juliette]; Massenet:Ah! fuyez, douce image [from Manon]), Blanche Deschamps-Jéhin (sgr) (Verdi:La flamme brille [Le Trouvère]; Saint-Saëns:Printemps qui commence; Mon coeur s'ouvre [both from Samson et Dalila]; Meyerbeer:Ah! mon fils [from Le Prophète] [all w. Léon Jéhin (cnd), Monte-Carlo Orch]), Léon Melchissédec (bar) (Meyerbeer:Fille des rois; Adamastor, roi des vagues [both from L'Africaine]; Verdi:Oui, c'etait toi [from Le Bal Masqué]; O mes maîtres [from Rigoletto]; Mozart:Sérénade [from Don Juan]; Gounod:Air de Capulet [from Roméo et Juliette]), Emile Scaramberg (ten) (Meyerbeer:Plus blanche [from Les Huguenots]) SYMP ▲ 1191 (17.97)

Vol. 28—features performances by Giuseppe de Luca (bar) (Wagner:O tu, bell'astro [from Tannhäuser]; Gounod:Dio possente [from Faust]; Ponchielli:O monumento; Cosi mantieni...Ebbrezza! Delirio! [w. Eugenia Burzio (sop); both from Faust]; Tchaikovsky:Se all'equal di vaghi augelli [2 versions; from La Dama di Picche]; Massenet:O casto flor [from Il re di Lahore]; Visione fuggitiva [from Erodiade]; Leoncavallo:Buona Zazà del mio buon tempo; Zazà, piccola zingara [both from Zazà]; Franchetti:Ferito prigionier [from Germania]; Denza:Occhi di fati; Tosti:Ideale; de Leva:Pastorale-Nu zampugnaro; Impressioni Campestri-E voi passate nel vial; Morlacci:Sereneta-Brilla la luna; Rotoli:La mia bandiera; de Luca:Dolce Madonna; Fasolo:Lungi è amor; Ruggi:I Due ciabatini [w. Ferruccio Corradetti (bar)]), Giuseppe Segura-Talien (bar) (Meyerbeer:Sei vendicata assai [from Dinorah]; Verdi:Pari siamo [from Rigoletto]), Giuseppe Bellantoni (bar) (Pacini:Di sua voce il suon giungea; Un'Errnni [both from Saffo]) (rec Milan, 1905-10) SYMP ▲ 1198 (17.97)

Vol. 29—features performances by Giuseppe Borgatti (ten), Icilio Calleja (ten), Edoardo Garbin (ten), Mario Gilion (ten), Fernando Carpi (sgr), Romano Ciaroff-Cerini (sgr) SYMP ▲ 1199 (m) [AAD] (17.97)

Vol. 31—features performances by Francisco Vignas (ten) (Meyerbeer:Sopra Berta, l'amor mio [from Le Prophète]; O paradiso [from L'Africaine]; Wagner:Da voi lontano [from Lohengrin]; Dell'alba tinto [from Meistersinger von Nürnburg]; Verdi:Celeste Aida; Pur ti reveggo [both from Aida]; Ore e per sempre addio [from Otello]; Ponchielli:Cielo e mar! [from La Gioconda]; Mascheroni:Ecco mia giovinezza [from Lorenza]; Gastaldon:Donna Clara; Guetary:Mi Niña; Maria; Amadei:Si ti dicessi; Mandeno:La Partida), Amedeo Bassi (ten) (Giordano:Amor ti vieta [from Fedora]; Orride steppe [from Siberia]; Canzone Guerresca; D'Erlanger:Stanotte ho fatto un sogno [from Tess]), Alessandro Bonci (ten) (Donizetti:Spirito gentil [from La Favorita]; Verdi:Ah fede negar potessi [from Luisa Miller]; Bizet:Mi par d'udir [from Les Pêcheurs des perles]) (rec 1905-08) SYMP ▲ 1224 (m) [AAD] (17.97)

Hidden Gems of 19th Century Italian Opera, w. various artists—features arias from operas by Donizetti, Salieri, Mercandante, Bellini, Rossini & Leoncavallo NUO ▲ 110 [DDD]

Historic Baritones: The French School (Cylinder and disc rec'gs)—features performances by Maximilien-Nicolas Bouvet, 1854-1943; Jean-Baptiste Fauré, 1830-1914; Lucien Fugere, 1848-1935; Alexis Ghasne, 1868-19??; Jean Lassalle, 1847-1909; Victor Maurel, 1848-1923; Leon Melchissidec, 1843-1925; Jean Note, 1859-1922; Jean Perier, 1869-1954; Maurice Renaud, 1861-1933; Gabriel Soulacroix, 1853-1905 (rec 1900-12) SYMP ▲ SYM 1089

The Hugo Wolf Society Recordings, Vol. 1—features performances by A. Trianti (soprano), E. Gerhardt (mezzo-soprano), J. McCormack (tenor), H. Janssen (baritone), G. Hüsch (baritone), F. Schorr (bass-baritone), A. Kipnis (bass) (rec 1931-32) PHS 2-▲ 9075 [AAD] (34.97)

I Grandi Dell'Opera: The Glory of the Past, w. Margherita Carosio (sop), Amelita Galli-Curci (sop), Toti dal Monte (sop), Lina Pagliughi (sop), Enrico Caruso (ten), Giacomo Lauri-Volpi (ten), Aureliano Pertile (ten), Tito Schipa (ten), Francesco Tamagno (ten), Titta Ruffo (bar), Riccardo Stracciari (bar), Tancredi Pasero (bass), Ezio Pinza (bass)—features 21 arias from La favorita; Il barbiere di Siviglia; Aida; Rigoletto; Andrea Chenier; Ernani; La sonnambula; Guillaume Tell; Manon; Robert il Diavolo; Werther; plus others OPIT ▲ 54511 (6.97)

If Music Be the Food of Love, w. Emma Kirkby (sop), John Mark Ainsley (ten), Ian Partridge (ten), James Bowman (ct), Paul Esswood (ct), Michael George (bass)—features works by Morley (My Bonnie Lass), Ford (There Is a Lady), Handel (Wher'er You Walk), Farmer (Fair Phyllis), Linley (Tomorrow Is St. Valentine's Day), Peerson (The Primrose), Lassus (O, occhi, manza mia Girometta, senza te), Monteverdi (Non è di gentil core), Gastoldi (Viver lieto voglio), Azzaiolo (Gentil Madonna), Purcell (When I Am Laid in Earth; If Music Be the Food of Love), Gibbons (The Silver Swan), Negri (Torneo amoroso), Greaves (Come Away Sweet Love), Wert (Vezzosi augelli), Wilbye (Adieu Sweet Amaryllis), anon (Greensleeves), plus others INMP ▲ 6801052 (16.97)

Immortal Voices Of The Vienna Opera—features performances by Maria Jeritza (sop), Anny Konetzni (sop), Hilde Konetzni (sop), Lotte Lehmann (sop), Maria Nemeth (sop), Elisabeth Schumann (sop), Rosette Anday (cta), Maria Olszewska (cta), Jan Kiepura (ten), Koloman von Pataky (ten), Alfred Piccaver (ten), Helge Roswaenge (ten), Leo Slezak (ten), Richard Tauber (ten), Franz Völker (ten), Hans Hermann Nissen (bar), Wilhelm Rode (bar), Emil Schipper (bar), Alexander Sved (bar), Alexander Kipnis (bass), Richard Mayr (bass) (rec 1926-39) PRE (Lebendige Vergangenheit) ▲ 89999 (m) (16.97)

In Concert—features performances by Ruggero Raimondi (bass) (Duparc:L'Invitation au voyage; Le Manoir de Rosemonde; Tosti:L'Ultima canzone; Malìa; Mussorgsky:La pulce; Rossini:La Calunnia [from Il Barbiere di Siviglia]), Vincenzo La Scola (ten) (Bellini:Vaga luna che inargenti; Ma rendi pur contento; Puccini:Mentìa l'avviso; Sole e amore; Avanti Urania!; Tosti:A' vucchella; L'alba separa dalla luce l'ombra; Giordano:Amor ti vieta [from Fedora]), Luciana Serra (sop) (Rossini:La fioraia fiorentina; Una voce poco fa [from Il Barbiere di Siviglia]; Donizetti:La corrispondenza amorosa; Nè ornerà la bruna chioma) (rec Bologne Community Theater, May 3, 1994) BONG ▲ 2517 [DDD] (16.97)

International Tchaikovsky Competition, Vol. 3: The Great Vocalists—features performances by Jane Marsh (sop) (Tchaikovsky:Lullaby in a Storm, Op. 16/1), Symon Estes (bass) (Verdi:Otello [Act 1]; Mozart:Don Giovanni [Act 1]; Tchaikovsky:Gremin's Aria [from Eugene Onegin]; Not a Word, O My Friend, Op. 6/2), Elena Obraztsova (mez) (Saint-Saëns:Amour viens alder ma faiblesse [from Samson et Dalila]; Bizet:Habanera [from Carmen]; Shaporin:Invocation, Op. 10/4), Evegni Nesterenko (bass) (Borodin:Konchak's Aria [from Prince Igor]; Rachmaninoff:Aleko's Cavatina [from Aleko]; Sviridov:Soldier's Homecoming), Peter Dvorsky (ten) (Dvořák:Oh, What a Perfect Golden Dream), Dolora Zajick (sop) (Mascagni:Voi lo sapete [from Cavalleria rusticana]), Nina Rautio (sop) (Slominsky:Stuffy Hop; Russian folksong:Always I'm Walking Alone, along My Cell) MELD ▲ 52961 (6.97)

It Ain't over 'til She Sings (from CBS Masterworks opera recordings of the '60s, '70s & '80s)—features performances by Caballé (Tristan:Isoldes Liebestod), Cotrubas (Forza del destino:Pace, pace, mio Dio), Eileen Farrell (Götterdämmerung:Brünhilde's Immolation Scene), Eva Marton (Gioconda:Suicidio!; Bohème:Donde lieta; Madama Butterfly:Tu, tu, piccolo iddio), Ricciarelli (Turandot:Tu, che di gel sei cinta), Scotto (Manon Lescaut:Sola, perduta, abbandonata; Suor Angelica:Senza mama, o bimbo, tu sei morto; Otello:Ave Maria), Te Kanawa (Don Giovanni:In quali eccessi...Mi tradi; Trovatore:Timor di me...d'amor sull'ali rosee), Lucia Valenti Terrani (Cenerentola:Non più mesta accanto al fuoco) COL Masterworks ▲ 46288 [AAD] (9.97) 46288

Italian Baritones of the "Acoustic Era" (1904-1924)—features performances by Ernesto Badini (2 arias [from Faust & Hamlet]), Giuseppe Bellantoni (2 arias [from La Favorita & Herodiade]), Francesco Maria Bonini (4 arias [from Rolando di Berlino (Leoncavallo), Forza del destino, Rigoletto]), Giuseppe Campanari (Tirindelli:Song), Ferruccio Corradetti (3 arias [from Elisir d'amore (Donizetti) & Jone (Petrella)]; Robaudi:Song; Trindelli:Song), Luigi Montesanto (2 arias [from Aida & Forza del destino]), Taurino Parvis (aria [from Marchetti:Ruy Blas]; Gastaldon:2 Songs), Gaetano Viviani (2 arias [from Carmen & Forza del destino]) BONG ▲ 1043 [AAD] (16.97)

Italian Sopranos of the Beginnings of the 20th Century (1900-09)—features performances by Adelina Patti (sop) (Arditi:Il bacio [w. Landon Ronald (pno)]; Mozart:Voi che sapete [from Le nozze di Figaro]; Batti, batti o bel Masetto [from Don Giovanni]; Gounod:Air des bijoux [from Faust]; Bellini:Casta diva [from Norma]; Ah, non credea mirarti [from La sonnambula; w. Alfredo Barili (pno)]), Emma Albani (sop) (Chaminade:L'eté), Ines de Frate (sop) (Donizetti:M'odi, ah! m'odi [from Lucrezia Borgia]), Ada Adini (sop) (Massenet:Celui dont la parole [from Hérodiade]), Fanny Torresella (sop) (De Beriot:Prendi, per me sei libero), Medea Mei-Figner (sop) (Tchaikovsky:It Is Midnight [from Queen of Spades]), Elena Teodorini (sop) (Donizetti:M'odi, ah! m'odi [from Lucrezia Borgia]), Cesira Ferrani (sop) (Puccini:Sì, mi chiamano Mimì [from La Bohème]), Gemma Bellincioni (sop) (Bizet:En vain pour éviter [from Carmen]), Olimpia Boronat (sop) (Gianelli:E lo sapevi [from Olga]), Teresa Arkel (sop) (Boito:Spunta l'aurora pallida [from Mefistofele; w. Salvatore Cottone (pno)]), Maria De Macchi (sop) (Donizetti:Di qual soavi lacrime [from Poliuto]), Angelica Pandolfini (sop) (Godard:Chanson d'Estelle [w. Salvatore Cottone (pno)]), Luisa Tetrazzini (sop) (Donizetti:Splendon le sacre faci; Regnava nel silenzio...Quando rapita in estasi [both from Lucia di Lammermoor]; Rossini:Una voce poco fa [from Il Barbiere di Siviglia]; Verdi:Saper vorreste [from Un ballo in maschera] [all w. Albert Fransella (fl), Percy Pitt (cnd)]) MNER ▲ 33 (m) [ADD] (14.97)

The Italian Tenor from Caruso to Zenatello—features performances by Enrico Caruso (ten), Bassi (ten), Schiavazzi (ten), Ventura (ten), Giovanni Zenatello (ten) (rec 1903-13) MNER ▲ 53 (14.97)

Last Singing Despot CAPA ▲ 21586 (63.97)

Legendary Baritones—features performances by Lucien Fugère (Massenet:Legende de la sauge [from Le Jongleur de Notre Dame; rec 1928]), Victor Maurel (Tosti:Au temps du grand roi [rec 1907]), Antonio Magini-Coletti (Verdi:Quand' ero paggio [from Falstaff; w. Elsa Petri (sop); rec 1906]), Mattia Battistini (Verdi:Di Provenza il mar, il suol... [from La traviata; rec 1911]), Mario Ancona (Verdi:Eri tu [from Un ballo in maschera; rec 1907]), Maurice Renaud (Massenet:Promesse de mon avenir [from Le Roi de Lahore; rec 1906]), Eugenio Giraldoni (Verdi:Dio crudel [from Otello; rec 1905]), Riccardo Stracciari (Puccini:Già, mi dicon venal [from Tosca; rec 1910]), Giuseppe de Luca (from Verdi:O, de' verd' anni miei [from Ernani; rec 1916]), Titta Ruffo (Verdi:L'onore! Ladri! [from Falstaff; rec 1921]), Pasquale Amato (Verdi:O vecchio cor, che batti [from I Due Foscari; rec 1913]), Joseph Schwarz (Wagner:O du, mein holder Abendstern [from Tannhäuser; rec ca 1918]), Heinrich Schlusnus (Marschner:An jenem Tag [from Hans Heiling; rec 1917]), Renato Zanelli (Leoncavallo:Zazà piccola zingara [from Zazà; rec 1919]), Carlo Galeffi (Verdi:Pari siamo [from Rigoletto; rec 1926]), John Charles Thomas (Giordano:Nemico della patria [from Andrea Chénier; rec 1939]), Lawrence Tibitt (Rossini:Largo al factotum [from Il barbiere de Siviglia; rec 1930]), Gerhard Hüsch (Lortzing:Wie freundlich strahlt [from Der Wildschütz; rec 1928]), Igor Gorin (Verdi:Dagli immortali vertici [from Attila; rec 1941) NIMB ▲ 7867 [ADD] (11.97)

The Legendary Singers at Lindenoper Berlin (1927-1945), w. Gitta Alpar (sop), Erna Berger (sop), Tiana Lemnitz (sop), Maria Müller (sop), Margarete Klose (mez), Peter Anders (ten), Max Lorenz (ten), Walther Ludwig (ten), Lauritz Melchior (ten), Rudolf Schock (ten), Franz Völker (ten), Willi Domgraf-Fassbaender (bar), Karl Schmitt-Walter (bar), Friedrich Schorr (b-bar), Josef Greindl (bass), Alexander Kipnis (bass)—features works by Mozart (Dies Bildnis ist bezaubernd schön; Der Hölle Rache kocht in meinem Herzen; Die Vogelfänger bin ich ja [all from Die Zauberflöte]; Welch ein Geschick... Ha! Du sollest für mich sterben [from Die Entführung aus dem Serail]; Nun vergiss leises Fleh'n [from Le nozze di Figaro]), Mussorgsky (Die höchste Macht ist mein [from Boris Godunov]), Wagner (Allmächtiger Vater, blick herab [from Rienzi]; Dich, teure Halle, grüss' ich wieder [from Tannhäuser]; Mögst du, mein Kind, den fremden Mann willkommen heissen [from Der fliegende Holländer]; Das süsse Lied verhallt [from Lohengrin]; Einsam wachend in der Nacht [from Tristan und Isolde]; Den Weg, den es zeigte [from Siegfried]) (rec 1927, 1937 & 1941-45) MNER ▲ 21 [ADD] (14.97)

Legendary Singers in Rare Live Performances—features performances by Kirsten Flagstad (sop), Maria Jeritza (sop), Margarete Matzenauer (mez), Marian Anderson (cta), Ernestine Schumann-Heink (cta), Lauritz Melchoir (ten), Albrecht Sack (ten), Richard Tauber (ten), Amand Tokatyan (ten), Schmidt (sgr) (rec 1934-40) EKLR ▲ 36 (17.97)

Legendary Tenors—features performances by Francesco Tamagno (ten) (Verdi:Esultate!; Niun mi tenia [both from Otello]), Dmitri Smirnov (ten) (Tchaikovsky:Lenski's Aria [from Eugene Onegin]), Alessandro Bonci (ten) (Verdi:Ah fede negar potessi...Quando le sere al placido [from Luisa Miller]), Edmond Clément (ten) (Massenet:En fermant les yeux [from Manon]), Leo Slezak (ten) (Goldmark:Magische Töne [from Die Königin von Saba]), Enrico Caruso (ten) (Verdi:Ora e per sempre addio [from Otello]), Leonid Sobinov (ten) (Rimsky-Korsakov:Sleep, My Beauty [from May Night]), Giacomo Lauri-Volpi (ten) (Ideale [from Tosti]), Aureliano Pertile (ten) (Mascagni:O Lola [from Cavalleria Rusticana]), Giovanni Martinelli (ten) (Leoncavallo:E un riso gentil [from Zazà]), Julius Patzak (ten) (Thomas:Adieu, Mignon [from Mignon]), Helge Roswaenge (ten) (Flotow:Ach, so fromm [from Martha]), Lauritz Melchoir (ten) (Wagner:Winter stürme wichen dem Wonne mond [from Die Walküre]), Richard Tauber (ten) (Mozart:Il mio tesoro [from Don Giovanni]), David Devries (ten) (Boïeldieu:Rêverie de Georges Brown [from La dame blanche]), Georges Thill (ten) (Massenet:Ah! fuyez douce image [from Manon]), Beniamino Gigli (ten) (Leoncavallo:No! Pagliaccio non son [from Pagliacci]), Renato Zanelli (ten) (Giordano:Un dì, all' azzurro spazio [from Andrea Chénier]), Jussi Björling (ten) (Puccini:Nessun dorma [from Turandot]), Tito Schipa (ten) (Massenet:Io non so...O Natura [from Werther]) NIMB ▲ 7856 [ADD] (11.97)

Legendary Voices, w. Kirsten Flagstad (sop), Lotte Lehmann (sop), Rosa Ponselle (sop), Luisa Tetrazzini (sop), Eva Turner (sop), Jussi Björling (ten), Enrico Caruso (ten), Alfred Piccaver (ten), Tito Schipa (ten), Fritz Wunderlich (ten), Tito Gobbi (bar), Giuseppe de Luca (bar), Alexander Kipnis (bass), Ezio Pinza (bass)—features works by Bellini, Gomez, Puccini, Herbert, Thomas, Verdi, Mascagni, Mozart, Schubert, Schumann, Wagner, Ponchielli, Millöcker, Cilea, Tchaikovsky NIMB (Prima Voce) ▲ 7851 (11.97)

Legends Of Opera In Live Performance—features performances by Richard Bonelli, Gladys Swarthout (Don Giovanni [La ci darem la mano; 1937]), Mary Garden (My bonnie Jeannie; 1946), Beniamino Gigli (Puritani [A te o cara; 1934]), Gigli & Marion Talley (Lucia [Act 1 duet; 1927]), Maria Jeritza & Franz Volker w. Clemens Krauss (Walküre [Todesverkundiging (sel); 1933]), Alexander Kipnis (Don Carlo [Ella giammai m'amo; 1943]), Frieda Leider (Walküre (sels); 1938), Germaine Lubin (Tristan [Liebestod; Bayreuth 1938]), Margaret Matzenauer (Aida [L'abborita rivale; 1943]), Rosa Ponselle (Aida [Ritorna vincitor; 1936]), Ponselle & John Charles Thomas (Old folks at home; 1952), Rosa Raisa (Plaisir d'amour; 1927), Stella Roman (Die tote Stadt [Marietta's Lied; 1938]), Richard Tauber (Lohengrin [In fernem land; 1946]) LCD ▲ * (m) [ADD]

Live from Carnegie Hall, Jan. 7, 1973, w. R. Merrill (bar), R. Tucker (ten)—features works by Ponchielli (La Gioconda), Meyerbeer (L'Africana), Mozart (Don Giovanni; Le nozze di Figaro), Leoncavallo (Zaza), Verdi (Otello; I Vespri Siciliani; La traviata; La Forza del Destino), Bizet (Les pecheurs du perles), Donizetti (L'Elisir d'Amore), Mascagni (Cavalleria Rusticana), Giordano (Andrea Chenier), Bock-Hartnick (Fiddler on the Roof), Goldfadden-Secunda (Roshinkes mit Mandlen)) (rec Carnegie Hall, NYC Jan 7, 1973) TELC 2-▲ 93706

Mad About Opera—features performances by June Anderson, Agnes Baltsa, Teresa Berganza, José Carreras, Placido Domingo, Mirella Freni, Jerry Hadley, Thomas Hampson, Sylvia McNair, Jessye Norman, Luciano Pavarotti, Samuel Ramey, Cheryl Studer, Kiri Te Kanawa, Dawn Upshaw, Anne Sofie Von Otter (sels from Candide, Carmen, Don Giovanni, Marriage of Figaro, Bohème, Butterfly, Barber of Seville, Aida, & others) DEUT ▲ 37636 (6.97) ▮ 437636-4 GH

1088

▲ = CD ♦ = Enhanced CD △ = MD ▮ = Cassette Tape ▯ = DCC

Mario Basiola & Giovanni Inghilleri—features performances by Mario Basiola (bar) *(Rossini:Largo al Factotum [from Il barbiere di Siviglia]; Donizetti:A tanto amor [from La favorita]; Verdi:Il balen del suo sorriso [from Il trovatore]; Gounod:Avant de quitter ces lieux [from Faust]; Massenet:O casto fidor [from Il re di Lahore]; Vision fuggitiva [from Herodiade]; Ponchielli:Era dessa...Raccogli e calma [from Il figliuol prodigo]; Pescator, affonda l'asca [from La Gioconda]; Leoncavallo:Prologo; Ah! se la!..credea che te ne fossi andato [w. Iva Pacetti (sop); both from I Pagliacci]; Cilea:Come due tizzi accesi [from L'Arlesiana])*, Giovanni Inghilleri (bar) *(Verdi:La vedremo, o veglio audace [from Ernani]; Il balen del suo sorriso [from Il trovatore]; Di Provenza [from La traviata]; Eri tu [from Un ballo in maschera]; Leoncavallo:Prologue [from Pagliacci]; Puccini:Nulla! Silenzio [from Il tabarro]; O Mimi, tu più non torni [from La Bohème]; Giordano:Son sessant'anni [from Andrea Chénier]) (rec 1926-35)* BONG ▲ 1151 [ADD] (16.97)

Mezzo-Soprano Greatest Hits—features performances by Marilyn Horne (mez) *(Handel:Vivi, tiranno! [from Rodelinda]; Meyerbeer:Non, non, non...vous n'avez jamais [from Les Huguenots])*, Frederica von Stade (mez) *(Offenbach:Amours divins [from La Belle Hélène])*, Vesselina Kasarova (mez) *(Rossini:Una voce poco fa [from Il barbiere di Siviglia]; Nacqui all'affanno e al pianto [from La Cenerentola]; Mozart:Non so più cosa son; Voi che sapete [both from Le nozze di Figaro])*, Shirley Verrett (mez) *(Saint-Saëns:Mon coeur s'ouvre à ta voix [from Samson et Dalila]; Verdi:Re dell'abiso affretatti [from Un ballo in maschera]; Donizetti:Fia dunque vero; O Mio Fernando [both from La favorita])*, Risë Stevens (mez) *(Bizet:L'amour est un oiseaux rebelle; Prés des remparts de Séville [both from Carmen]; Gluck:Che farò senza Euridice [from Orfeo ed Eurydice])*, Rosalind Elias (mez) *(Berlioz:Premier transports que nul n'oublie [from Roméo et Juliette]; Verdi:Stride la vampa [from Il trovatore])* RCAV (Greatest Hits) ▲ 63340 (10.97) ■ 63340 (5.98)

The Minstrel Boy: Irish Singers of Great Renown—features performances by Barbara Mullen (sop) 1914-1979 *(5 1940-41 HMV recordings; w. Ivor Newton (pno), Gerald Moore (pno))*; Delia Murphy (sop) b. 1903 *(1939 Regal-Zono recording; w. Arthur Darley (gtr))*; Margaret Burke Sheridan (sop) 1889-1958 *(2 1928 HMV recordings; w. Gerald Moore (pno))*; Tom Burke (ten) 1890-1969 *(unpublished 1927 Columbia recording, w. pno; 1934 Imperial recording, w. Foster Richardson (bar) & orch)*; Cavan O'Connor (ten) born ca 1900 *(1940 Rex recording; w. orch)*; Denis O'Neil (ten) *(2 1931 Edison Bell recordings, w. orch—Eileen Oge)*; Denis O'Sullivan (ten) 1868-1908 *(2 1906 Favorite recordings, 1 w. orch, 1 w. pno)*; William F. Watt (ten) born ca 1895 *(1928 Columbia recording; w. pno)*; J.C. Doyle (bar) *(1924 Edison Bell Winner recording; w. orch)*; Harry Plunket Greene (bar) 1865-1936 *(1 1909 Gramophone Co & 2 1933 Columbia recordings, all w. pno)*; Robert Irwin (bar) b. 1900 *(2 1940 HMV recordings, w. Gerald Moore (pno))*; James McCafferty (bar) *(2 1930 & 1932 HMV & Decca recordings, w. Molly Brannigan (pno))*; Patrick Colbert (bass) 1897-1971 *(1934 Parlophone recording; w. orch) (rec 1906-41)*
PHS ▲ 9989 (m) [AAD] (17.97)

More Legendary Voices, w. Maria Callas (sop), Maria Jeritza (sop), Claudia Muzio (sop), Elisabeth Schumann (sop), Conchita Supervia (mez), Kathleen Ferrier (cta), Beniamino Gigli (ten), John McCormack (ten), Lauritz Melchior (ten), Richard Tauber (ten), Titta Ruffo (bar), Feodor Chaliapin (bass)—features works by Lake, Marshall, Handel, Leoncavallo, Korngold, Giordano, Bizet, Lehár, Mozart, Zeller, Massenet, Saint-Saëns, Boito, Wagner, Bellini, anon
NIMB (Prima Voce) ▲ 7864 (11.97)

The Most Famous Opera Arias—features performances by Anna Moffo (sop) *(Verdi:Caro nome [from Rigoletto]; Rossini:Una voce poco fà [from Il barbiere di Siviglia] [both w. Colin Davis (cnd), Philharmonia Orch])*, Alfredo Kraus (ten) *(Verdi:La donna é mobile [from Rigoletto; w. Julius Rudel (cnd), Philharmonia Orch])*, Ghena Dimitrova (sop) *(Puccini:O mio babbino caro [from Gianni Schicchi]; Un bel dì, vedremo [from Madama Butterfly]; Vissi d'arte, vissi d'amore [from Tosca] [all w. Anton Guadagno (cnd), Philharmonia Orch]; Catalani:Ebben? Ne andrò lontano [from La Wally; w. Lamberto Gardelli (cnd), Munich RSO])*, Elena Obraztsova (mez) *(Bizet:La voila...L'amour est oiseau rebelle [from Carmen]; Saint-Saëns:Mon coeur s'ouvre à ta voix [from Samson et Dalila] [both w. Giuseppe Patané (cnd), Philharmonia Orch])*, Agnes Baltsa (mez) *(Gluck:Che farò senza Euridice [from Orfeo ed Euridice; w. Riccardo Muti (cnd), Philharmonia Orch])*, Edita Gruberova (sop) *(Gounod:Ah! je veux vivre [from Roméo et Juliette]; Delibes:Ou va la jeune indoue? [from Lakmé] [both w. Gustav Kuhn (cnd), Munich RSO])*, Lucia Popp (sop) *(Mozart:Voi che sapete che cosa è amor [from Le nozze di Figaro; w. Leonard Slatkin (cnd), Munich RSO]; Mozart:Die Hölle Rache kocht in meinem Herzen [from Die Zauberflöte; w. Bernard Haitink (cnd), Bavarian RSO])* Placido Domingo (ten) *(Verdi:Celesta Aida [from Aida; w. Riccardo Muti (cnd), New Philharmonia Orch])*, Nicolai Gedda (ten) *(Puccini:Che gelida manina [from La Bohème; w. Thomas Schippers (cnd), Rome Opera Orch])*
EMIC (Encore) ▲ 68306 [ADD/DDD] (3.97)

The Movies Go to the Opera ANGL ▲ 69596 (11.97) 69596

Nessun Dorma: 20 Great Tenor Arias, w. Giacomo Aragall (ten), Carlo Bergonzi (ten), Jussi Björling (ten), José Carreras (ten), Franco Corelli (ten), Plácido Domingo (ten), René Kollo (ten), Mario del Monaco (ten), Luciano Pavarotti (ten), Giuseppe di Stefano (ten) PLON (Opera Gala) ▲ 458215 (11.97)

A 1940's Radio Hour, Vol. 1—features performances by Eileen Farrel (sop) *(Halévy:Il va venir [from La Juive])*, Juan Pons (bar), Gino Bonelli (sgr) *(Donizetti:Soffriva nel pianto [from Lucia de Lammermoor])*, Licia Albanese (sop) *(Mascagni:Voi lo sapete [from Cavalleria rusticana]; Puccini:Perchè chiuso? [from Tosca; w. Jan Peerce (ten)])*, Gladys Swarthout (mez) *(Alfano:Dieu de grace [from Resurrection]), (plus others)* IRCC ▲ 806 (16.97)

A 1940's Radio Hour, Vol. 2—features performances by Regina Resnik (mez) *(Verdi:Vieni! t'affretta [from Macbeth])*, Helen Traubel (sop) *(Masagni:Voi lo sapete [from Cavalleria Rusticana])*, Bidù Sayão (sop) *(Donizetti:Prendi per me [from L'Elisir d'amore])*, Mario Lanza (ten), Tennyson (sgr) *(Verdi:Già nella notte densa [from Otello])*, Lawrence Tibbet (bar), Moore (sgr) *(Puccini:Tosca [sel from Act 2])*, Eileen Farrell (sop) *(Verdi:La Forza del Destino [Aria]), (plus others)* IRCC ▲ 807

A 1940's Radio Hour, Vol. 3, w. Rose Bampton (sop), Erna Berger (sop), Eleanor Steber (sop), Risë Stevens (mez), Ferruccio Tagliavini (ten), Arthur Kent (bar), Carlos Guichandut (sgr)—features sels from works by Verdi *(Forza del destino; Trovatore)*, Leoncavallo *(Pagilacci)*, Bizet *(Carmen)*, R. Strauss *(Rosenkavalier)*, Puccini *(Bohème)* IRCC ▲ 809 (16.97)

1921-1929: La Scala of Toscanini—features performances by Toti dal Monte (sop), Claudio Muzio (sop), Bianca Scacciati (sop), Giacomo Lauri-Volpi (ten), Aureliano Pertile (ten), Miguel Fleta (ten), Francesco Merli (ten), Carlo Galeffi (bar), Riccardo Stracciari (bar), Mariano Stabile (bar), Tancredo Pasero (b-bar), Marcel Journet (bass), Ezio Pinza (bass)
GRM2 ▲ 78508 [ADD] (13.97)

O Sole Mio: Song of Italy by Five Famous Tenors of the Past—features performances by Beniamino Gigli (ten) *(di Capua:O Sole Mio; de Curtis:Torna a Surriento; Ti voglio tanto bene; Bixio:La canzone dell'Amore; Ninna nanna della vita; Tosti:La Serenata; [all w. Dino Oliveri (cnd)]; Veroli:Casarella [w. Vito Carnevali (cnd)]; Mario:Santa Lucia Luntana [w. Nathaniel Shirket (cnd)])*, Joseph Schmidt (ten) *(Biscardi:L'ariatella; Tosti:Penso; Addio; Tagliaferri:Piscatore è pusilleco; Nun me sceta; Cottrau:Santa Lucia [all w. Otto Dobrindt (cnd)]; di Capua:Maria, Mari; O Sole Mio [both w. Felix Günther (cnd), Fritz Brunner Salon Orch])*, Luigi Infantino (ten), Alberto Erede (cnd), Royal PO *(Falvo:Dicitencello vuje)*, Jussi Björling (ten), Nils Grevillius (cnd) *(Tosti:Ideale; L'alba sepera dalla luce d'ombra [w. Stockholm Concerts Association Orch]; Leoncavallo:Mattinata; di Capua:O Sole Mio)*, Giuseppe di Stefano (ten), Alberto Erede (cnd), New London Opera Orch *(Favara:A la Barcillunisa; Cantu a Timinu)* [l] *(rec 1926-49)* EMIC ▲ 66863 (m) [ADD] (11.97)

Old Chelsea—features performances by Jacob Bray, Nancy Gibbs, Mary Fenton, Richard Tauber, Nancy Brown & Carol Lynn *(rec May 7, 1943)*.† Tauber BBC recital featuring arias by Lalo & Weber & songs by Grieg (rec 1947) EKLR ▲ 22

On the Muse's Isle
ATMM ▲ 22133 (14.97)

Opera Arias—features performances by Cotrubas, Te Kanawa, Scotto, Domingo, et al.—arias from Bohème, Tosca, Otello, Rigoletto, etc. COL (Essential Classics) ▲ 46548 [ADD] (7.97) ■ 46548 (3.98)

The Opera Collection, Vol. 2—features performances by Callas, Dimitrov, Caballé, Pavarotti, De Los Angeles, Bastin, Rhodes, Blanc, Mesplé, Sills, Schwarzkopf, Crespin, Behrens, Fischer-Dieskau EMIC 2-▲ 69131 (13.97)

Opera Festival—features performances by Berganza, Popp, Migenes, Donath, Arroyo, Bumbry, Guerrero, Aragall, Domingo, Araiza, Cappuccilli, Prey, Weikl, Ricciarelli, Kollo, Kabaivanska, Bonisolli, Bier, w. various orchs *(sels from Carmen, Louise, Roméo et Juliette, Bohème, Madama Butterfly, Tosca, L'Elisir d'amore, El Huesped del Sevillano, Tosca, Pagliacci, Barber of Seville, Don Carlos, Andrea Chénier, Trovatore)* Acanta ▲ 43808

Opera for Pleasure:Duets—features V. d. Angeles (sop), Rome Opera Orch [cnd:T. Serafin], C. d. Monte (ten) *(Verdi:Traviata (sels) [Parigi, o cara noi lasceremo])*, Bavarian RSO [cnd:B. Haitink], B. Lindner (sop), W. Brendel (bar) *(W. A. Mozart:Zauberflöte (sels) [Papagena! Papageno!])*, Bavarian RSO [cnd:J. Tate], B. Bonney (sop), A. v. Otter (mez) *(Humperdinck:Hänsel und Gretel (sels) [Brüderchen, komm' tanz mit mir (Dance Duet)])*, M. Caballé (sop), Philharmonia Orch [cnd:R. Muti], J. Carreras (ten) *(P. Mascagni:Cavalleria rusticana (sels) [No, no, Turiddu, rimani])*, M. Callas (sop), Paris Opera Orch [cnd:G. Prêtre], N. Gedda (ten) *(Bizet:Carmen (sels) [Près des remparts de Séville (Séguidille)])*, M. Freni (sop), Royal Opera House Covent Garden Orch [cnd:G. Gavazzeni], L. Pavarotti (ten) *(P. Mascagni:Amico Fritz (sels) [Suzel, buon dì (Cherry duet)])*, M. Freni (sop), Philharmonia Orch [cnd:R. Muti], N. Gedda (ten) *(Donizetti:Don Pasquale (sels) [Tornami a dir])*, R. Grist (sop), Rome Opera Orch [cnd:F. Molinari-Pradelli], N. Gedda (ten) *(Verdi:Rigoletto (sels) [E il sol dell'anima])*, E. Gruberova (sop), Royal PO [cnd:N. Rescigno], A. Kraus (ten) *(Donizetti:Lucia di Lammermoor (sels) [Lucia perdona; Ah! Verranno a te])*, National PO [cnd:J. Levine], A. Kraus (ten), S. Milnes (bar) *(G. Puccini:Bohème (sels) [O Mimi, tu più non torni])*, Philharmonia Orch [cnd:A. Galliera], L. Alva (ten), T. Gobbi (bar) *(G. Rossini:Barbiere di Siviglia (sels) [All'idea di quel metallo])*, Rome Opera Orch [cnd:J. Barbirolli], R. Scotto (sop), C. Bergonzi (ten) *(G. Puccini:Madama Butterfly (sels) [Vogliatemi bene])*, Rome Opera Orch [cnd:T. Schippers], G. Simionato (mez), F. Corelli (ten) *(Verdi:Trovatore (sels) [Se m'ami ancor])*, Royal Opera House Covent Garden Orch [cnd:C. Giulini], P. Domingo (ten), S. Milnes (bar) *(Verdi:Don Carlos (sels) [Ascolta!...Dio, che nell'alma infondere amor])* CFP ▲ 72510 [ADD/DDD] (10.97)

Opera Goes to the Movies, w. Plácido Domingo (ten), Roberta Peters (sop), Leontyne Price (sop), et al.—features opera highlights from hit films *Fatal Attraction, Godfather III, Moonstruck, Prizzi's Honor, et al.*
RCAV ▲ 60841 (10.97) ■ 60841 (5.98)

Opera in Chicago, Vol. 1—features performances by E. Mason (sop) *(Mendelssohn:Oh, for the wings of a dove; Flotow:The last rose of summer [from* Martha*]; Gounod:Air des bijoux [from* Faust*]; Puccini (Ancora un passo; Un bel di vedremo [from* Madama Butterfly*]; Cadman:Far off I hear a lover's flute; Woodford/Finden:Kashmiri Song; Strickland:Dreamin' Time; Tosti:Serenade; Good-bye)*, M. Garden (sop) *(Debussy:L'ombre des arbres; Verdi:Ah! fors'è lui [from* La traviata*]; Massenet:Liberté [from* Le Jongleur de Notre Dame*]; Il est doux [from* Herodiade*]; Charpentier:Depuis le jour [from* Louise*]; Gretchaninov:Over the Steppe; Bizet:En vain pour inviter [from* Carmen*])* SYMP ▲ 1136 (17.97)

Opera in Chicago, Vol. 2—features performances by Rosa Raisa (sop) *(Meyerbeer:In grembo a me [from L'Africaine]; Bellini:Casta diva...Ah! bello a me ritorna [from Norma]; Verdi:Miserere [from Il trovatore; w. Giulio Crimi (ten)]; Bolero [from Les vêpres Siciliennes]; Pace, mio dio [from La forza del destino]; O terra addio [from Aida; w. Giulio Crimi (ten)]; Ave Maria [from Otello])*, Virgilio Lazzari (bass) *(Rossini:La calunnia [from Il Barbiere di Siviglia]; Verdi:Il lacerato spirito [from Simon Boccanegra]; Gounod:Dio dell'or [from Faust]; Puccini:Vecchia zimarra [from La Bohème])*, Mario Chamlee (ten) *(Donizetti:Un afurativa lagrima [from L'Elisir d'amore]; Puccini:E lucevan le stelle [from Tosca])*, Cyrena van Gordon (mez) *(Donizetti:O mio Fernando [from La favorita]; Verdi:Stride la vampa [from Il trovatore])*, Giacomo Rimini (bar) *(Thomas:Brindisi [from Hamlet]; Verdi:Alla vita [from Un ballo in maschera]; Giordano:Canzonetta russa [from Fedora])*, Carolina Lazzari (mez) *(Saint-Saëns:Amor, viens aider; Mon coeur s'ourve [both from Samson et Dalila])*, Giulio Crimi (ten) *(Leoncavallo:O mio piccolo tavolo [from Zaza])*, Armand Tokatyan (ten) *(Mascagni:Siciliana [from Cavalleria rusticana]; Giordano:Amor ti vieta [from Fedora]) (rec Chicago, 1919-27)* SYMP ▲ 1200 (17.97)

The Opera Lover's Broadway: Great Voices Sing Broadway's Greatest Hits, w. Vienna PO [cnd:Herbert von Karajan], New Philharmonia Orch [cnd:Richard Bonynge], Roland Shaw Orch, London SO [cnd:John Mauceri], Nelson Riddle & His Orch, London Festival Orch [cnd:Robert Sharples]—features performances by Birgit Nilsson (sop) *(I Could Have Danced All Night [from My Fair Lady])*, Cesare Siepi (bass) *(So In Love; Wunderbar [both from Kiss Me Kate])*, Joan Sutherland (sop) *(Make Believe [from Show Boat])*, George London (b-bar) *(Ol' Man River [from Show Boat])*, Kiri Te Kanawa (sop) *(Wouldn't it Be Lovely [from My Fair Lady]; I Didn't Know What Time It Was [from Too Many Girls]; I Feel Pretty; One Hand, One Heart [w. José Carreras]; Somewhere [all from West Side Story]; Speak Low [from One Touch of Venus])*, Eileen Farrell (sop) *(If I Loved You [from Carousel])*, José Carreras (ten) *(Maria; Tonight [both from West Side Story])*, Robert Merrill (bar), Molly Picon (sgr) *(You'll Never Walk Alone [from Carousel])* PLON ▲ 48282 (16.97) ■

Opera Stars Sing on Radio, Vol. 1: Unpublished Broadcasts from the Fourties, w. Dusolina Giannini (sop), Helen Traubel (sop), Gladys Swarthout (cta), Richard Crooks (ten), Lauritz Melchoir (ten), Robert Merrill (bar), Lawrence Tibbett (bar), Ezio Pinza (bass)—features works by Romberg *(Drinking Song & Golden Days [from The Student Prince]; When You Walk in the Room [from Up in Central Park]; The Song of the Vagabonds [from The Vagabond King])*, J. Strauss (II) *(You & Your [from Die Fledermaus]; Iris)* [Negro Spiritual] *(Deep River)*, Bond *(A Perfect Day; When Children Play)*, Grieg *(A Dream; Ich liebe dich)*, Glover *(Rose of Tralee)*, Bach-Gounod *(Ave maria)*, Dvořák *(Songs My Mother Taught Me; The Year That Was Spring)*, Fernandez *(Cielito lindo)*, Denza *(Funiculi, Funicula)*, Bizet *(Près des remparts de Séville [from Carmen])*, Wagner *(In fernem Land [from Lohengrin])*, Saint-Saëns *(Amour viens aider ma faiblesse [from Samson et Dalila])*, Verdi *(Urna fatale [from La forza del destino])*, Mozart *(Bravo, signor Padrone...se vuol ballare [from Le nozze di Figaro])*
RY (The Radio Years) ▲ 11 (16.97)

Opera Stoppers—features performances by Marilyn Horne, Kiri Te Kanawa, Barbara Cook, Renata Scotto, Luciano Pavarotti, Richard Tucker, Ruggiero Raimondi, Leon Nucci *(arias from Bohème, Butterfly, Tosca, Turandot, Rigoletto, Traviata, etc.)* COL Masterworks ▲ 46577 (9.97) ■ 46577 (5.98)

Opera's Greatest Drinking Songs & Other Intoxicating Melodies, w. various artists—features works by Verdi *(Brindisi [La Traviata]; Anvil Chorus [from Il trovatore]; La donna è mobile [from Rigoletto]; Holá, holá, holá [from La forza del destino]; Inaffia l'ugola! [from Otello])*, Flotow *(Lasst mich euch fragen [from Martha])*, Romberg *(Drink, Drink, Drink [from the Student Prince])*, Mascagni *(Intanto, amici [from Cavalleria rusticana])*, Bizet *(Votre toast [from Carmen])*, Orff *(In taberna quando sumus [from Carmina Burana])*, Massenet *(Vous parlez de Péril [from Chérubin])*, Mahler *(Der Trunkene im Frühling [from Das Lied von der Erde])*, J. Strass II *(Stoss an! [from Wiener Blut]; Solch ein Wirsthaus lob ich mir [from Nacht in Venedig]; O Fledermaus, Champagne hat's verschuldet [from Die Fledermaus])*, Donizetti *(Il segreto per esser felici [from Lucrezia Borgia])*, Weber *(Hier im ird'schen Jammertal [from Der Freischütz])*, Berlioz *(Song of the Rat [from La Damnation de Faust])*, Mozart *(Finch'han dal vino [from Don Giovanni])*, Brahms *(Tafellied)*, Smetana *(Welch Gottesgabe ist das Bier [from The Bartered Bride])*, trad *(What Shall We Do with the Drunken Sailor)* RCAV (Red Seal) ▲ 68095 (10.97) ■ 68095

Opera's Greatest Duets—features performances by L. Price (sop), P. Domingo (ten) *(Verdi:Gia nella notte [from Otello])*, Domingo (ten), S. Milnes (bar) *(Bizet:Au fond du temple saint [from Les pêcheurs des perles])*, R. Elias (mez), R. Tucker (ten) *(Verdi:Se m'ami ancor...Ai nostri nomi [from Il trovotore] & more)* RCAV (Red Seal) ▲ 62699 (10.97) ■ 62699 (9.98)

Opera's Greatest Fathers, w. Piero Cappuccilli (bar), Cornell MacNeil (bar), Robert Merrill (bar), Sherrill Milnes (bar), Theo Adam (b-bar), Siegmund Nimsgern (b-bar), Matthias Hölle (bass), Martti Talvela (bass)—features arias from Rigoletto; Simon Boccanegra; La traviata; Die Walküre; La juive; Luisa Miller; I vespri siciliani; Fidelio; Le nozze de Figaro; Die Zauberflöte; Guillaume Tell RCAV (Gold Seal) ▲ 63189 (10.97)

Opera's Greatest Love Songs—features performances by Placido Domingo (ten) *(Flowtow:Martha [M'appari]; Gounod: Roméo et Juliette [L'amour! L'amour!])*, Anna Moffo (sop) *(works by Puccini, Verdi)*, Jussi Björling (ten) *(works by Verdi)*, Montserrat Caballé (sop) *(works by Verdi)*, Luciano Pavarotti (ten) *(works by Puccini)*, Richard Tucker (ten) *(works by Puccini)*, Dawn Upshaw (sop) *(works by Massenet)*, Eric Tappy (ten) *(works by Mozart)*, Margaret Price (sop) *(works by Puccini)*, Luciano Pavarotti (ten) *(works by Puccini)*, Leontyne Price (sop) *(works by Wagner)*
RCAV (Red Seal) ▲ 61886 (10.97) ■ 61886 (9.98)

Opera's Greatest Moments—features performances by Teresa Berganza *(Carmen:Habañera)*, Björling & Merrill *(Pearl Fishers:Au fond du temple)*, Caballé *(Bohème:Mi chiamano Mimi)*, Cotrubas *(Zauberflöte:Ach, ich fühl's)*, Domingo *(Elisir d'amore:Una furtiva lagrima; Pagliacci:Vesti la giubba)*, Helen Donath *(Gianni Schicchi:O mio babbino caro)*, Ben Heppner *(Turandot:Nessun dorma)*, Dmitri Hvorostovsky *(Pique Dame:Yeletsky's Aria)*, Alfredo Kraus *(Rigoletto:La donna è mobile)*, Mario Lanza *(Aida:Celeste Aida)*, Eva Martón *(La Wally:Ebben, ne andrò lontana)*, Robert Merrill *(Barber of Seville:Largo al factotum)*, Anna Moffo & Richard Tucker *(Traviata:Brindisi)*, Jessye Norman *(Walküre:Du bist der Lenz)*, Leontyne Price *(Madama Butterfly:Un bel di; Forza del destino:Pace, pace, mio Dio)*, Julia Varady *(Marriage of Figaro:Dove sono)*
RCAV (Red Seal) ▲ 61440 (10.97) ■ 61440 (9.98)

Opera's Greatest Mothers, w. Montserrat Caballé (sop), Leontyne Price (sop), Zdzislawa Donat (sop), Fiorenza Cossotto (mez), Gwendolyn Killebrew (mez), Cornelia Kallisch (cta)—features arias from Norma; Lucrezia Borgia; Die Zauberflöte; Madama Butterfly; Il trovatore; Suor Angelica; Un ballo in maschera; Dialogues des Carmelites; Andrea Chenier; Le nozze de Figaro; Mefistofele RCAV (Gold Seal) ▲ 63188 (10.97)

The Original Tenors: Caruso, Gigli, Björling—features opera arias from Faust; Il trovatore; Carmen; La fancuilla del West; Carmen; L'Africaine; Les Pêcheurs de perles; & songs by Tosti, Bixio, Sjoberg, Di Capua, plus others PRSM ▲ 38 (6.97)

Popular Musicals—features Club Orch [cnd:H. Lewis], Club Chorus [cnd:H. Lewis], G. Baker (voc) *(Bizet:Carmen (sels) [Votre toast (Toreador's Song)])*, London Sinfonietta [cnd:J. McGlinn], Ambrosian Chorus [cnd:J. McGlinn] *(G. Gershwin:Capitol Revue (sels) [Swanee])*, London Sinfonietta [cnd:J. McGlinn], London Sinfonietta Chorus [cnd:J. McGlinn] *(H. Warren:Gold Diggers of 1933 (sels) [The Gold Diggers' Song (We're in the Money)])*, London Sinfonietta [cnd:J. McGlinn], T. Stratas (voc) *(J. Kern:Show Boat (sels) [Bill])*, London Sinfonietta [cnd:J. McGlinn], J. Barstow (voc), T. Hampson (voc) *(C. Porter:Kiss Me, Kate (sels) [Wunderbar])*, London Sinfonietta [cnd:J. McGlinn], T. Hampson (voc) *(I. Berlin:Annie Get Your Gun (sels) [The Girl That I Marry])*, London Sinfonietta [cnd:J. McGlinn], Ambrosian Chorus [cnd:J. McGlinn], G. Dvorsky (voc), R. Luker (voc) *(Youmans:No, No, Nanette (sels) [Tea for Two])*, London Sinfonietta [cnd:J. McGlinn], London Sinfonietta Chorus [cnd:J. McGlinn], B. Barrett (voc), D. S. Gravitte (voc) *(H. Warren:Forty-Second Street (sels) [Forty-Second Street])*, London Sinfonietta [cnd:J. McGlinn], K. Colson (voc) *(K. Weill:Knickerbocker Holiday (sels) [15. September Song])*, London Sinfonietta [cnd:J. McGlinn], B. Barrett (voc), R. Luker (voc) *(A. Schwartz:Band Wagon (sels) [Dancing in the Dark])*, London Sinfonietta [cnd:J. McGlinn], London Sinfonietta Chorus [cnd:J. McGlinn], B. Barrett (voc), S. Chandler (voc), D. Engel (voc), D. S. Gravitte (voc), A. Morrison (voc), L. Raben (voc) *(H. Warren:Gold Diggers of 1935 (sels) [Lullaby of Broadway])*, Monte Carlo PO [cnd:J. McGlinn], L. Wilson (voc) *(L. Bernstein:West Side Story (sels) [Maria]; Schönberg:Misérables (sels) [Empty Chairs at Empty Tables])*, Ambrosian Chorus, G. Dvorsky (voc), C. Groenendaal (voc), J. Lehman (voc), R. Luker (voc) *(J. Kern:Very Warm For May (sels) [All the things you are])*, K. Criswell (voc), London Sinfonietta [cnd:J. McGlinn], T. Hampson (voc) *(I. Berlin:Annie Get Your Gun (sels) [They Say It's Wonderful])* EMIC ▲ 72117 [DDD] (6.97)

Prima Voce Party, w. Amelita Galli-Curci (sop), Miliza Korjus (sop), Nellie Melba (sop), Rosa Ponselle (sop), Elisabeth Schumann (sop), Margaret Teyte (sop), Enrico Caruso (ten), Hugues Cuénod (ten), Beniamino Gigli (ten), John McCormack (ten), Tito Schipa (ten), Richard Tauber (ten), Paul Robeson (b-bar), Alexander Kipnis (bass), et al.
NIMB (Prima Voce) ▲ 7839 (11.97)

Prima Voce Sampler—features performances by J. Björling (ten) *(Puccini:Nessun Dorma [from* Turandot*])*, G. Lauri-Volpi (ten) *(Verdi:Solenne in quest'ora [from* La forza del destino*])*, K. Flagstad (sop) *(Wagner:Ho-jo-to-ho [from* Die Walküre*])*, R. Ponselle (sop) *(Puccini:Vissi d'arte [from* Tosca*])*, E. Caruso (ten) *(Verdi:Bella figlia dell'amore [from* Rigoletto*])*, E. Destinn (sop) *(Ponchielli:Suicidio [from* La Gioconda*])*, V. Maurel (bar) *(Verdi:Quand'ero paggio [from* Falstaff*])*, F. Tamagno (ten) *(Verdi:Esultate! [from* Otello*])*, C. Supervia (mez) *(Bizet:Les tringles des sistres tintaient [from* Carmen*])*, J. McCormack (ten) *(Norah O'Neale [traditional Irish])*, F. Hempel (sop) *(Mangold:Zweigesang)*, E. Berger (sop), T. Lemnitz (sop) *(R. Strauss:Ist ein Traum, kann nicht wirklich sein [from* Der Rosenkavalier*]) (rec 1903-44)* NIMB ▲ 1430 [ADD] (6.97)

Puccini Favorites—features performances by Renata Tebaldi, Renata Tebaldi, Carlo Bergonzi, Renato Cesari, Cesare Siepi & Ettore Bastianini, Leona Mitchell, Bruno Prevedi, Renata Tebaldi & Carlo Bergonzi, Maria Chiara, George London & Piero de Palma, Joan Sutherland, James McCracken, Felicia Weathers, Renata Tebaldi, Mario del Monaco, Nicola Zaccaria, Fernando Corena & Mario Carlin, Giuseppe di Stefano, Humming Chorus PLON ▲ 36295 (6.97)

VOCAL COLLECTIONS

Queen Elisabeth of Belgium International Competition—features performances by Stephen Salters (sgr) [*Donizetti:*Come Paride vezzoso {from *L'elisir d'amore*}], Hindemith:Here I Coffin That Slowly Passes; Respighi:Notte; *Bellini:*O dove fuggo...Ah! Per sempre {from *I Puritani*}], Ana Camelia Stefanescu (sgr) [*Bellini:*Care compagne...Come per me serena {from *La Sonnambula*}], Haydn:Es bringe...Nun beut die Flur {from *Die Schöpfung*}, Boesmans:Seasons' Dream; Menotti:Hello, Margaret, It's You? {from *The Telephone*}], Eleni Matos (sgr) [*Tchaikovsky:*Da tchas nastal {from *Maid of Orleans*}]; Verdi:Liber scriptus {from *Requiem*}, Mahler:Ich hab' ein glühend Messer; Dvořák:Pie Jesu {from *Requiem*}], Mariana Zvetkova (sgr) [*Rachmaninoff:*Vesenniye vodi {from *Tyutchev*}; Puccini:Sola, perduta, abbandonata {from *Manon Lescaut*}], Ray Wade (sgr) [*Bach:*Deposuit potentes {from *Magnificat*}; Mozart:Konstanze, Konstanze {from *Die Entführung aus dem Serail*}], Anja Vincken (sgr) [*Bizet:*C'est des contrebandiers...Je dis que rien ne m'épouvante {from *Carmen*}] (rec Royal Conservatory of Music & Palais des Beaux-Arts, Brussels, May 14-24, 1996) CYPR ▲ 9601 [DDD] (17.97)

Queens of the Night—w. Yovanka Marville (hpd), Luca Antoniotti (org), Raoul Esmerode (perc)—features works by Corelli, Handel, Scheidt, Pachelbel, Albinoni, Mozart, Puccini, Schubert, Tchaikovsky, Chopin, Bizet, Bovet GALL ▲ CD 658 [ADD]

Rare Italian Tenors—features performances by Francesco Signorini (ten) [*Rossini:*O muto asil del pianto {from *Guglielmo Tell*}], Amedeo Bassi (ten) [*Giordano:*Amor ti vieta {from *Fedora*}], Giorgina Caprile (sgr) [*Cilea:*La dolcissima effige {from *Adriana Lecouvreur*}], Emilio Perea (ten) [*Giordano:*No, non pensarci più {from *Marcella*}], Nicola Zerola (ten) [*Verdi:*Nun mi tema {from *Otello*}], Fernando Capri (ten) [*Rossini:*All'idea di quel metallo {w.Riccardo Stracciari (bar)}; Se il mio nome {both from *Il barbiere di Siviglia*}], Edoardo Ferrari-Fontana (ten) [*Wagner:*Noto Regina e a me chiuso {from *Tristan & Isolde*}], Leoncavallo:Vesti la giubba {from *Pagliacci*}], Aristodemo Giorgini (ten) [*Bellini:*A te o cara {from *I Puritani*}], Ulysses Lappas (ten) [*Giordano:*Come un bel dì di maggio {from *Andrea Chenier*}], Icilio Calleja (ten) [*Puccini:*Ch'ella mi creda {from *La fanciulla de West*}], Rinaldo Grassi (ten) [*Puccini:*Donna non vidi mai {from *Manon Lescaut*}], Giuseppe Taccani (ten) [*Mascagni:*Ombra esecrata {from *Guglielmo Ratcliff*}], Giulio Crimi (ten) [*Leoncavallo:*O mio cocciolo tavolo {from *Zazà*}], Hipolito Lazaro (ten) [*Bellini:*Vieni tra queste braccia {from *I Puritani*}], Verdi:Questa o quella {from *Rigoletto*}] (rec 1905-24) MNER ▲ 71 (m) [ADD] (14.97)

Russian Religious Singing, Vol. 3—features works by Glinka (Cherubic song), Mussorgsky (The angel said), Balakirev (The Prophets inspired by Heaven), Tchaikovsky (Happy is the man), Kalinnikov (Who sing unto Thee), Taneev (In the celestial church), Rimsky-Korsakov (The Lord is risen), Liadov (Glory to God), Ippolitov-Ivanov (This day all people; My soul doth), Rachmaninoff (Mother of God; We sing unto thee; Peaceful Light; Great Doxology) RUSS ▲ 288095

Singers of Russia, 1900-1917: Sergei Levik & His Contemporaries—features performances by Sergei Levik (sgr) [*Rubinstein:*Do Not Weep, Oh Child; Accursed World {both from *The Demon*}], Oscar Kamionsky (bar) [*Tchaikovsky:*Night], Nicolai Shevelev (bar) [*Rimsky-Korsakov:*All is Quiet in the Camp {from *Khovanshchina*}], Lev Sibiriakov (bass) [*Rubinstein:*I Am He Whom You Heard {from *The Demon*}], Alexander Davidov (ten) [*Tchaikovsky:*Forgive Me, Bright Celestial Visions {from *Eugen Onegin*}], Lev Klementieff (sgr) [*Rubinstein:*Ah! mon sort {from *Nero*}], Dmitri Smirnoff (ten) [*Rachmaninoff:*Romance of the Young Gypsy {from *Aleko*}], Nicolai Figner (ten) [*Tchaikovsky:*Before God & Thee {from *Oprichnik*}], Félia Litvinne (sop) [*Gounod:*Seigneur, daignez permettre {from *Faust*}], Maria Kuznetsova (sop) [*Glinka:*O My Ratmir! {from *Ruslan & Ludmilla*}], Georges Baklanoff (bass) [*Verdi:*Credo in un dio crudel {from *Otello*}], Lidya Lipkowska (sop) [*Verdi:*Cara nome {from *Rigoletto*}], Ivan Gryzunov (sgr) [*Rimsky-Korsakov:*O Beautiful Town {from *Sadko*}], Vasili Damaev (sgr) [*Rimsky-Korsakov:*Sing, Little Cuckoo {from *Maid of Pskov*}], Antonina Nezhdanova (sop) [*Taubert:*Der Vogel im Walde], Ivan Yershov (sgr) [*Meyerbeer:*Roi du ciel & Pour Bertha {from *Le Prophète*}], Leonid Sobinov (ten) [*Tchaikovsky:*I Love You Olga {from *Eugen Onegin*}, Vladimir Kastorsky (bass) [*Glinka:*O Say, Ye Fields! {from *Ruslan & Ludmilla*}], Joachim Tartakov (bar) [*Rubinstein:*Der Asra}], Eugene Vitting (sgr) [*Bizet:*La fleur que tu m'avais jetée {from *Carmen*}], Andrei Labinsky (ten) [*Lassena:*But This Was a Dream], Feodor Chaliapin (bass) [*Boito:*Prologue {from *Mefistofele*}], Alexander Moszhukhin (sgr) [*Engel:*The Stonemason] SYMP ▲ 1151 [AAD] (17.97)

Songfest—features performances by Canta Sonare [*cond:*Robert Newell] [*Newell:*New London Street Cries], Robert Maher (bar), Steven Eldridge (pno) [*W. Penn:*A Cornfield in July; The River], Nicole Philibosian (sop), Crispin Campbell (vc), Michael Coonrod (pno) [*S. Hurley:*Wind River Songs], Melinda Liebermann (sop), Christine Witthoeft (pno) [*Scheidel-Austin:*5 Sonnets from the Portuguese], Trio Santa Fe [*A. Schmitz:*4 Songs from Green Lotus Maid}], Lori Berg (sopher), Mary Jeanne Van Appledorn (M.J. Van Appledorn:Freedom of Youth] CPS ▲ 8618 (16.97)

Songs & Lieder, w. Elly Ameling (sop), Victoria de los Angeles (sop), Helen Donath (sop), Jessye Norman (sop), Lucia Popp (sop), Margaret Price (sop), Elisabeth Schwarzkopf (sop), Janet Baker (mez), Christa Ludwig (mez), Frederica von Stade (mez), Olaf Bär (bar), Dietrich Fischer-Dieskau (bar), Boris Christoff (bass), Jean-Philippe Collard (pno), Jörg Demus (pno), Klaus Donath (pno), Irwin Gage (pno), Gerald Moore (pno), Geoffrey Parsons (pno), Wolfgang Sawallisch (pno), John Barbirolli (cnd), Rafael Frühbeck de Burgos (cnd), Georges Prêtre (cnd)—features works by Beethoven, Berlioz, Brahms, Duparc, Fauré, Grieg, Mahler, Mendelssohn, Montsalvatge, Mozart, Saint-Saëns, Schubert, Schumann, R. Strauss, Tchaikovsky, Wagner SIMP 2-▲ 70329 (10.97)

Songs of France, w. Claire Croiza (sop), Madeleine Grey (sop), Yvonne Printemps (sop)—features works by Canteloube, Ravel, de Bréville, Hahn, Poulenc, Moussorgsky (rec 1929-35) PHS ▲ 13 (17.97)

Songs Of The Civil War—features performances by Bonnie Hamilton (sop), John Aler (ten), Alan Baker (bar), The Harmoneion Singers, Lawrence Skrobacs (pno), Tony Randall (narr) NWW ▲ 202 [ADD] (16.97) 202 (9.98)

The Sopranos: The Greatest Opera Arias Performed by 6 Divas, w. Maria Callas (sop), Joan Sutherland (sop), Leontyne Price (sop), Birgit Nilsson (sop), Renata Tebaldi (sop), Montserrat Caballé (sop)—features arias from La forza del destino; La traviata; Tosca; Die Walküre; Gianni Schicchi; Die Zauberflöte; Don Giovanni; Il barbiere di Siviglia; Norma; La Gioconda; plus others PRSM ▲ 47 (6.97)

Souvenirs from Verismo Opera, Vol. 1, w. Lucrezia Bori (sop), Carmen Melis (sop), Piero Pauli (ten), Giovanni Zentatello (ten), Pasquale Amato (bar), plus others—features sels from works by Franchetti (*Germania; La Figlia di Iorio*), Mascagni (*Iris*), D'Erlanger (*Tess*) IRCC ▲ 812 (16.97)

Souvenirs from Verismo Opera, Vol. 2, w. John McCormack (ten), Bernardo de Muro (ten), dalla Rizza (sgr), Giuseppe de Luca (bar), Kirby-Lunn (sgr), Melis (sgr), plus others—features sels from works by Wolf-Ferrari (*Gioielli della Madonna*), Virgilio (*Jana*), Mascagni (*Isabeau*) (rec 1905-30) IRCC ▲ 813 (16.97)

Souvenirs of 19th Century Italian Opera, w. Celestina Boninsegna (sop), Bidú Sayão (sop), Pasquale Amato (bar), et al.—features sels from works by Apolloni (*L'Ebreo*), Ruggi (*Due Ciabattini* {w. *Giuseppe De Luca (bar)*}), Faccio (*Amleto*), Ponchielli (*Promessi Sposi; Lina*) IRCC ▲ 808 (16.97)

Souvenirs of Opera & Song, Vol. 2 (*Pathé & Edison recordings*)—features performances by Celestina Boninsegna (sop), Freida Hempel (sop), Margarethe Matzenauer (sgr), Lucien Muratore (ten), Alice Verlet (sgr), Jacques Urlus (sgr) IRCC ▲ 814 (16.97)

Souvenirs of Rare French Opera—features performances by Léon Escalais (ten), Renau (sgr) [*DeLara:*Messalin {Arias}]; Reyer:Sigurd {Arias}], Fernand Ansseau (ten), [*Massenet:*Ariane {sels}; Roma {sels}; Saint-Saëns:Les Barbares {sels}]; Février:Monna Vanna {sels}] (rec 1903-40) IRCC ▲ 802 (16.97)

Stars of English Opera: Volume 4—features orch unknown, J. Cross (sop) [*G. Puccini:*Bohème {sels} [Mi chiamano Mimi]; Madama Butterfly {sels} [Un bel di vedremo]], A. Alsop (sop), Boyd Neel String Orch [cnd:B. Neel] [*G. F. Handel:*Semele {sels} [O Sleep! Why dost thou leave me]], F. Austral (sop), London SO [cnd:L. Collingwood] [*L. Spohr:*Zemire und Azor {sels} [Rose wie bist du erquicked mit]], J. Hammond (sop), Philharmonia Orch [cnd:W. Susskind], H. Nash (ten) [*Leoncavallo:*Pagliacci {sels} [O Colombina]], Liverpool PO [cnd:M. Sargent], G. Ripley (mez) [*Saint-Saëns:*Samson et Dalila {sels} [Printemps qui commence]], London SO [cnd:M. Carner], M. Langdon (bass) [*C. M. Weber:*Euryanthe {sels} [Wo berg' ich mich]], London SO [cnd:A. Erede], T. Ferendinos (voc) [*Donizetti:*Elisir d'amore {sels} [Una furtiva lagrima], Massenet:Manon {sels} [C'est un rêve]], London SO [cnd:M. Carner], D. Barsham (trb), N. Lumsden (bass) [*Mussorgsky:*Boris Godunov {sels} [Nursery scene]], Philharmonia Orch [cnd:W. Braithwaite], R. Llewellyn (bar) [*R. Wagner:*Tannhäuser {sels} [O du mein holder Abendstern]], Royal Opera House Orch [cnd:S. Robinson], T. Ferendinos (voc) [*Flotow:*Martha {sels} [Ach so fromm (M'appari tutt'amor)]], Royal PO [cnd:L. Collingwood], O. Kraus (bar) [*Smetana:*Libuše {sels} [Již pane slunce {The sun is blazing}]], Sadler's Wells Opera Orch [cnd:V. Tausky], J. Johnston (ten) [*Verdi:*Rigoletto {sels} [La donna è mobile]], M. Brunskill (mez) [*Saint-Saëns:*Samson et Dalila {sels} [Mon coeur s'ouvre à ta voix]], A. Young (ten) [*W. A. Mozart:*Clemenza di Tito {sels} [Se all' impero, amici Dei]] DLAB ▲ 7030 [ADD] (17.97)

The Stars of the Warsaw Opera House: The Unknown Recordings—features performances by Salomea Kruszelnicka (sop) [*Moniuszko:*Gdyby rannym slonkiem {from *Halka*}; Puccini:Un bel di vedremo {from *Madama Butterfly*}], Janina Korolewicz (sop) [*Orefice:*Duet {from *Chopin*}], Moniuszko:O mój dziadku {from *Countess*}; Gounod:Ah je ris {from *Faust*}; Halevy:On nadejsc ma {from *La Juive*}], Helena Zboinska-Ruszkowska (sop) [*Wagner:*Das süsse Lied wehalt {from *Lohengrin*}; w. S. Gruszynski (cnd)]; Verdi:Addio del passato {from *La forza del destino*}]; Moniuszko:O moi makienki {both w. *B. Szulc (cnd)*}, Warsaw Opera Orch {from *Halka*}], Ada Sari (sop) [*Adam:*Vars on Mozart's "Ah, vous dirai-je maman"; Donizetti:Quando rapita in estasi; Il dolce suono {both from *Lucia di Lammermoor*}; Rossini:Una voce poco fa {from *Barbiere di Siviglia*}; Verdi:È strano e strano {from *Traviata*}; Delibes:Dov'è l'Indiana Bruna {from *Lakmé*}], Waclaw Brzezinski (bar) [*Moniuszko:*Polonaise {from *Haunted Castle*}; Thomas:Brindisi {w. *Warsaw Opera Orch, from *Hamlet*}]; Verdi:O sommo Carlo {w. *Warsaw Opera Orch, Warsaw Opera Chorus, from *Ernani*}], Eugeniusz Mossakowski (bar) [*Verdi:*Pari Siamo {from *Rigoletto*}; Gounod:Avant de quitter ces lieux {both w. *Warsaw Opera Orch, from *Faust*}], Adam Ostrowski (bass) [*Moniuszko:*Ensign's Aria {from *Countess*}; Glinka:The Night Review], Aleksander Michalowski (pno) [*Moniuszko:*O moscivi mi panowie {from *Halka*}]; Gounod:Jesli twój uczuć prostych {from *Faust*}]; Flotow:Dobra to dziewczyna lecz nie cos dla mnie {from *Marta*}]; Boito:Strano tyjto del Calos {w. *Giovanni Zenatello (ten), from *Mefistofele*}]; Gounod:Idziesz dzis żegnam cię {from *Faust*}]; Halevy:Voi che de Dio {from *Juive*}], Tadeusz Orda (bass) [*Mussorgsky:*Boris Monologue, Act II {w. *Warsaw Opera Orch, from *Boris Godunov*}] (rec 1902-27) MNER 2-▲ 49 (m) [ADD] (28.97)

La Storia dell'Opera—features performances by Fritz Wunderlich (ten) [*Handel:*Serse], Rita Gorr (mez) [*Gluck:*Orfeo ed Euridice], Walter Berry (bass) [*Mozart:*Die Zauberflöte], Renata Tebaldi (sop) [*Catalani:*La Wally], Maria Callas (sop) [*Puccini:*Tosca], et al † OPERA & ORATORIO CHORUSES & OVERTURES COLLECTIONS:Storia dell'Opera SMP 2-▲ 850504 (25.97)

Sweet & Low: Ten Great Mezzos & Contraltos—features performances by Mary Garden (sop), Nina Koshetz (sop), Maria Gay (mez), Helene Jung (mez), Irene Minghini-Cattaneo (mez), Maartje Offers (mez), Conchita Supervia (mez), Clara Butt (cta), Louise Homer (cta), Sigrid Onegin (cta), Gladys Knight (cta) PHS ▲ 9247 (17.97)

Tears from Heaven—features performances by Angela Maria Blasi (sop) [*Mozart:*Introitus {from *Requiem*, K.626; w. *C. Davis (cnd), Bavarian RSO & Chorus*}], Kathleen Battle (sop) [*Brahms:*Ihr habt nun Traurigkeit {from *Deutsches Requiem; w. J. Levine (cnd), Chicago SO*}]; J. S. Bach:Cantata 202 {w. *J. Levine (cnd)*}], Jard van Nes (cta) [*J. S. Bach:*Erbarme dich {from *St. Matthew Passion*; w. *E. von Huttenberg (cnd), Munich Bach Collegium*}], Nathalie Stutzmann (cta) [*Pergolesi:*Mater Dolorosa {w. *R. Goodman (cnd), Hanover Band*}]; Vivaldi:Stabat Mater {w. *V. Spivakov (cnd), Moscow Virtuosi*}], Trinity College Cambridge Choir [*Allegri:*Miserere mei Deus]; Parry:Jerusalem], Camilla Otaki (sop), Fauré:Pie Jesu {from *Requiem*; w. *R. Marlow (cnd), London Music*}], London Voices [*Mozart:*Ave verum corpus {w. *C.-P. Flor (cnd), Philharmonia Orch*}], Leontyne Price (sop), Janet Baker (sop) [*Verdi:*Recordare {from *Missa de Requiem*; w. *G. Solti (cnd), Chicago SO*}], Plácido Domingo (ten) [*Bizet:*Agnus Dei; Franck:Panis Angelicus; Bach/Gounod:Ave Maria {all w. *H. Froschauer (cnd), Vienna Sym*}], Bavarian RSO & Chorus [cnd:W. Sawallisch], Schumann:Requiem aeternam {from *Requiem*}], Brahms:Ruf zur Maria], Montserrat Caballé (sop) [*Rossini:*Inflammatus et accensus {from *Stabat Mater*; w. *C. F. Cillario (cnd), RCA Italian Orch*}], Musica Sacra [cnd:R. Westenburg] [*Schütz:*Selig sind die Toten], R. Thompson:Alleluia], Bryn Terfel (b-bar) [*Brahms:*Herr, lehre doch mich {from *Deutsches Requiem*; w. *C. Davis (cnd), Bavarian RSO & Chorus*}], Lucia Popp (sop) [*Mozart:*Laudate Dominum; Exultate, Jubilate; Schubert:Ave Maria; {all w. *K. Eichhorn (cnd), Bavarian RSO*}], St. Hedwigs Cathedral Choir [cnd:R. Bader] [*Haydn:*Stimmt an die Saiten {from *Schöpfung*}], John Mark Ainsley (ten) [*Handel:*Comfort Ye; Ev'ry Valley {both from *Messiah*; w. *M. Stephenson (cnd), London Music*}], King's Singers [*Josquin Desprez:*O virgo virginum], Yvonne Kenny (sop) [*Mozart:*Agnus Dei Dona Nobis Pacem {from *Krönungsmesse*; w. *C.-P. Flor (cnd), Philharmonia Orch, London Voices*}], Brigitte Fassbaender (mez) [*Rossini:*Agnus Dei {from *Petit messe solennelle*; w. *W. Sawallisch (cnd), Munich Vocalists*}], Elisabeth Norberg-Schulz (sop) [*Gounod:*Gloria {from *Messe solennelle*; w. *E. von Guttenberg (cnd), Bamberg SO & Chorus*}], Mario Lanza (ten) [*Malotte:*The Lord's Prayer {w. *R. Sinatra (cnd), Jeff Alexander Chorus*}] RCAV (Red Seal) 2-▲ 88606 [ADD] (16.97)

Ten Top Mezzos—features performances by Cecilia Bartoli, Frederica von Stade, Regina Resnik, J. Baker, Agnes Baltsa, Christa Ludwig, Fiorenza Cossotto, Grace Bumbry, Teresa Berganza, Marilyn Horne PLON ▲ 36462 [ADD/DDD] (11.97)

Ten Top Sopranos—features performances by Mirella Freni, Kathleen Battle, Kiri Te Kanawa, Jessye Norman, Birgit Nilsson, Régine Crespin, Leontyne Price, Renata Tebaldi, Montserrat Caballé, Joan Sutherland PLON ▲ 36461 [ADD/DDD] (11.97)

Ten Top Tenors—features performances by Luciano Pavarotti, Giacomo Aragall, Franco Corelli, Carlo Bergonzi, José Carreras, Jon Vickers, Mario del Monaco, Jussi Björling, Giuseppe di Stefano, Placido Domingo PLON ▲ 36463 [ADD/DDD] (11.97)

Ten Top Tenors II—features performances by Luciano Pavarotti [*Rossini:*Non mi lasciare {from *Guglielmo Tell*}], Carlo Bergonzi [*Verdi:*La vita e un inferno {from *La forza del destino*}], Mario del Monaco [*Verdi:*Nuin mi tema {from *Otello*}], Giuseppe di Stefano [*Giordano:*Colpito qui m'avete {from *Andrea Chenier*}], Plácido Domingo [*Wagner:*In fernem Land {from *Lohengrin*}], René Kollo [*Wagner:*Morgenlich leuchtend {from *Die Meistersinger*}], Franco Corelli [*Gounod:*Quel trouble inconnu {from *Faust*}], Fritz Wunderlich [*Bach:*O Schmerz! Hier zittert {from *Matthew's Passion*}], Jussi Björling [*Lehár:*Dein ist mein ganzes Herz], José Carreras [*Lara:*Granada] PLON ▲ 43379 (11.97)

Tenors: 1904-1937—features performances by Enrico Caruso, John McCormack, Giuseppe Anselmi and Tito Scipa NIMB (Prima Voce) 3-▲ 1794 [ADD] (34.97)

Tenors Greatest Hits—features performances by Luciano Pavarotti (ten), Plácido Domingo (ten), José Carreras (ten)—features works by Puccini, Bizet, Verdi, Flotow, Donizetti, Leoncavallo, Sorozabal & Tchaikovsky RCAV ▲ 62709 (10.97) 62709 (5.98)

Tenors: In the Grand Tradition—features performances by N. Gedda [*Bizet:*Je crois entendre encore {from *Les pêcheurs de perles*}], J. Björling [*Gounod:*Ah! lève-toi, soleil {from *Roméo et Juliette*}]; Puccini:Che gelida manina {from *La bohème*}], Offenbach:Au mont l. trois déesses {from *La Belle Hélène*}], Beniamino Gigli [*Lalo:*Puisqu'on ne peut me fléchir...Vainemnet, ma bien-aimée {from *Le roi d'Ys*}], Cilea:È la solita storia del pastor {from *L'Arlesiana*}]; Giordano:Amor ti vieta {from *Fedora*}], L. Alva [*Mozart:*Dalla sua pace {from *Don Giovanni*}]; Rossini:Ecco, ridente in cielo {from *Il barbiere di Siviglia*}], G. di Stefano [*Thomas:*Addio, M. from *Mignon*}]; Puccini:Non piangere, Liu {from *Turandot*}]; Ch'ella mi creda libero {from *La fanciulla del West*}], Franco Corelli [*Puccini:*Donna non vidi mai {from *Manon Lescaut*}]; Giordano:Come un bel di di Maggio {from *A. Chenier*}], F. Tagliavini [*Donizetti:*Una furtiva lagrima {from *L'Elisir d'amore*}], R. Tucker [*Verdi:*Se quel guerriero io fossi!...Celeste Aida {from *Aida*}], F. Wunderlich [*Lehár:*Dein ist mein gazes Herz {from *Das Land des Lächelns*}], C. Bergonzi [*Puccini:*Dammi i colori...Recondita armonia; E lucevan le stelle {both from *Tosca*}], L. Pavarotti [*Mascagni:*O amore, obelle ikia per una or fissa {from *L'Amico Fritz*}] EMIC ▲ 65431 (11.97) 65431 (9.98)

The Tenors: Paris 1998, w. J. Carreras (ten), P. Domingo (ten), L. Pavarotti (ten), L'Orch de Paris [cnd:James Levine]—features arias & songs [arr & orchd Lalo Schifrin] (rec live, Paris, July 10, 1998) ATL ▲ 83110 (19.97) ▼ 83110 (14.98)

The 30 Tenors—features performances by Francesco Tamagno (ten) [*Verdi:*Esultate {from *Otello*}], Léon Escalaïs (ten) [*Verdi:*Je veux encore entendre {from *Jérusalem*}], Fernando de Lucia (ten) [*Verdi:*Un di felice, eterea {from *La traviata*}], Ivan Ershov (ten) [*Meyerbeer:*Roi du ciel {from *Le Prophète*}], Alessandro Bonci (ten) [*Donizetti:*Cercherò lontana terra {from *Don Pasquale*}], Leonid Sobinov (ten) [*Arensky:*My Heart Trembles {from *Raphael*}], Enrico Caruso (ten) [*Verdi:*Di quella pira {from *Il trovatore*}], Leo Slezak (ten) [*Goldmark:*Magische Töne {from *Die Königin von Saba*}], Giovanni Zenatello (ten) [*Denza:*Veni], Giuseppe Anselmi (ten) [*Verdi:*Quando le sere al placido {from *Luisa Miller*}], Bernardo de Muro (ten) [*Puccini:*Or son sei mesi {from *Fanciulla del West*}], Alfred Piccaver (ten) [*Giordano:*Amor ti vieta {from *Fedora*}], John McCormack (ten) [*Verdi:*Che vi sembra {from *Manon Lescaut*}], Giordano:Come un bel dì di Maggio {from *A. Chenier*}], Aureliano Pertile (ten) [*Cilea:*La dolcissima effige {from *Adriana Lecouvreur*}], Francesco Merli (ten) [*Puccini:*Nol pazzo son! {from *Manon Lescaut*}], Tito Schipa (ten) [*Donizetti:*Sogno soave e casto {from *Don Pasquale*}], Tom Burke (ten) [*Leoncavallo:*Vesti la giubba {from *Pagliacci*}], Beniamino Gigli (ten) [*Verdi:*La donna e mobile {from *Rigoletto*}], Lauritz Melchoir (ten) [*Wagner:*Wintersturme wichen {from *Die Walküre*}], Richard Tauber (ten) [*Kienzl:*Selig sind die Verfolgung leiden {from *Evangelimann*}], Antonio Cortis (ten) [*Puccini:*Nessun dorma {from *Turandot*}], Walter Widdop (ten) [*Handel:*Thou Shalt Break Them in Pieces {from *Messiah*}], Giacomo Lauri-Volpi (ten) [*Bellini:*Meco all'altar di venere {from *Norma*}], Miguel Fleta (ten) [*Puccini:*E lucevan le stelle {from *Tosca*}], Helge Rosavenge (ten) [*Weber:*Du, der diesa Prüfung schickt {from *Oberon*}], Georges Thill (ten) [*Massenet:*Ah! qu'il est loin mon pays! {from *Sapho*}], Sergei Lemeshev (ten) [*Rimsky-Korsakov:*The Sun Descends {from *May Night*}], Joseph Schmidt (ten) [*Flotow:*Ach so fromm {from *Martha*}], Jussi Bjørling (ten) [*Offenbach:*Au Mont Ida {from *La Belle Hélène*}] (rec 1903-40) SYMP ▲ 1209 (17.97)

Three Edison Tenors, w. Luciano Pavarotti (ten), Alessandro Bonci (ten), Jose Mojica (ten) MRSN ▲ 51002 (17.97)

Three Historic Tenors "In Concert": Gigli - Tauber - Caruso—features performances by Gigli (arias—from *Andrea Chénier, L'Africana*; songs—Funiculi funicula, Marta, Quanno a femmena vo, Rondine al nido, Tango in D), Tauber (arias—from *Land of Smiles, Tosca, Turandot, Traviata, Der Vogelhändler*; songs—Ballade, Melody in F, Plaisir d'amour), Caruso (arias—from *Tosca*; songs—Core 'ngrato, Lolita, Mattinata, O sole mio, Santa Lucia, Vieni sul mar) (rec 1904-33) PEFL (Flapper) ▲ 9776 (m) [AAD] (17.97)

Three Tenors—features performances by Enrico Caruso (ten) [*Puccini:*Che gelida manina {from *La bohème*}], Prelude & Siciliana {from *Cavalleria Rusticana*}; w. *A. Buesst (cnd), British National Opera Company Orch*}], Elégie {from *Massenet*; w. *Mischa Elman (vn), Percy Kahn (pno)*}], Bella Figlia {from *Rigoletto*}], Vesti la Giubba {from *Pagliacci*}], M'appari {from *Marta*}], Richard Crooks (ten) [*Una furtiva lagrima {from *L'elisir d'amore*}; Il mio tessoro {from *Don Giovanni*}]; Preislied {from *Die Meistersinger*}]; Recondita Armonia {from *Tosca*; w. *C. Schmalstich (cnd), Berlin State Opera Orch*}], Walter Widdop (ten) [*In Distant Land {from *Lohengrin*}], Daylight is Fading Away {from *Prince Igor*}], Lend Me Your Aid {from *Queen of Sheba*}], I Know of 2 Bright Eyes {w. *Percy Kahn (pno)*}], Traum auf der Dämmerung {w. *Josephine Lee*}] GSE ▲ 785052 (16.97)

The Three Tenors—features performances by José Carreras (ten) [*Oh! Feder negar potessi...quando le sere al placido...l'ara, o'havido agram mari; De miei bollenti spiriti; Dammi I colori...recondita armonia; Questa o quella; Scena della borsa; De miei bollenti spiriti; Forse la soglia attinse; Addio fioriti asil; Dovunque al mondo; Di tu se fedele; La rivedra nell'estasi; E lucevan le stelle; Rondita armonia; Mercello, finalmente*], Placido Domingo (ten) [*Dammi I colori...recondita armonia; Di quella pira; De miei bollenti spiriti; Recitar...vesti la giubba; Brindisi: Intanto amici...a voi tutti salute...viva il vino spumeggaiante; Hai ben ragione; Lunga da lei; Ingemisco; E lucevan le stelle; Siciliana: O Iola!; Che gelida manina*], Luciano Pavarotti (ten) [*Nessun dorma; Oh meschina! Oh fato orrendo! Giusto cielo ah! Rispondete!; Ola chi sei che ardisci aggirarti furtivo in queste mura? Soltoi ad un sol mio...Biolo mille a puniriti avrei; Padre mio caro padre, della natura al suo autor; Ha inseparabile...E il sol dell'anima; Ella mi fu rapita...parma veder le lacrime; Un de ben sen rammentovi...bella figlia dell'amore; Parpet'! Crudele; La donna e mobile; Kyrie Eleison; Non sono in vena...chi e la?; Oh di cappello, generosi amici; Non salvo, alfia son salvo; Scena e concertante finale; Dunque a proprio finita; Oh! Feda negar potessi agli occhi miei...; La mia canzon d'amor... VLMK 3-▲ 1041 (13.97)

Three Tenors: Björling - Gigli - Tauber (rec 1936-39) MECL (Great Voices of the Century) ▲ 409 [ADD] (17.97)

The Three Tenors in Concert—features works by Cilea (Il lamento di Federico), Meyerbeer (O paradis), Puccini (Recondita armonia; E lucevan le stelle; Nessun dorma), Lehár (Dein ist mein ganzes Herz), de Crescenzo (Rondine al nido), Cardillo (Core 'ngrato), de Curtis (Torna a Surriento), Lara (Granada), Sorozabal (No puede ser), Giordano (L'improvviso), Bernstein/Sondheim (Maria/Tonight), D'Annibale (O paese d' 'o sole), Lloyd Weber (Memory), Filiberto (Caminito), Louigny (La Vie en rose), Leoncavallo (Mattinata), Sieczynski (Wien, Wien, nur du allein), Lacalle (Amapola), di Capua (O sole mio) (Cielito lindo; Ochi tchornye); encores (O sole mio; Nessun dorma) PLON ▲ 44000 (19.97)

Three Tenors of the Century—features performances by E. Caruso, J. McCormack & Beniamino Gigli (rec 1907-23) ASLE ▲ 5137 [ADD] (12.97) ▼ 5137 (7.98)

1090   ▲ = CD   ♦ = Enhanced CD   △ = MD   ▬ = Cassette Tape   □ = DCC

Three Tenors: Their First 78 RPM Disc, w. Mario del Monaco (ten), Giuseppe di Stefano (ten), Ferruccio Tagliavini (ten)—features arias from works by Puccini (Turandot; Tosca; La fanciulla del West), Wagner (Lohengrin), Giordano (Andrea Chénier), Meyerbeer (L'Africaine), Cilea (L'Arlesiana), Verdi (La traviata), Massenet (Manon), Thomas (Mignon), Bizet (Les Pêcheurs de perles), plus Sicilian folksongs & others (rec 1947-48) VOCA (Vocal Archives) ▲ 1168 (13.97)

To Music: Isobel Baille & Kathleen Ferrier, w. Gerald Moore (pno)—features performances by Isobel Baille (sop) (Stript of Their Green Our Groves Appear; I Saw That You Were Grown So High; Arne:O Ravishing Delight; Where the Bee Sucks; Schubert:To Music; Grieg:With a Waterlilly; Brahms:Sister Dear; Scott:Think on Me; trad:O Can Ye Sew Cushions; O Whistle an' I'll Come to You), Kathleen Ferrier (mez) (Handel:Come to Me, Soothing Sleep; Spring Is Coming [both arr Somervell]; M. Greene:I Will Lay Me Down in Peace; O Praise the Lord [all arr Roper]; Gluck:What Is Life [from Orfeo ed Euridice]; Elgar:My Work Is Done; Brahms:Constancy; Sweetheart), Isobel Baille (sop) & Kathleen Ferrier (mez) (Purcell:Sound the Trumpet; Let Us Wander, Not Unseen; Shepherd, Shepherd, Leave Decoying; Mendelssohn:Greeting; I Would That My Love) (rec 1941-45) APR 2-▲ 5544 [ADD] (18.97)

Top Twenty Operatic Scenes & Arias—features performances by R. Stracciari (Rossini:Larg al factotum [from Il barbiere di Siviglia]), N. Vallin & M. Sibelle (Offenbach:Bell nuit, ô nuit d'amour [from Les contes d'Hoffmann]), L. Pons (Verdi:Caro nome [from Rigoletto]), M. Fleta (Verdi:La donna é mobile [from Rigoletto]), A. Pertile (Verdi:Se quel guirrier...Celeste Aida [from Aida]), C. Muzio (Puccini:Vissi d'Arte [from Tosca]), B. Gigli (Puccini:Che gelida manina [from La bohème]), G. Ljungberg (Puccini:Un bel di [from Madama Butterfly]), A. Valente (Puccini:Nessun dorma [from Turandot]), J. Hammond (Puccini:O mio babbino caro [from Gianni Schicchi]), A. Piccaver (Puccini:E lucevan le stelle [from Tosca]), R. Pampanini (Catalani:Ebben?...Ne andro lontana [from La Wally]), G. Martinelli (Leoncavallo:Recitar!...Vesti la giubba [from I Pagliacci]), L. Tibbett (Bizet:Votre toast [from Carmen]), E. Caruso (Bizet:La fluer que tu m'avais jetée [from Carmen]), B. Gigli & G. de Luca (Bizet:O fond du Temple saint [from Les pécheurs de perles]), C. Supervia (Mozart:Voi che sapete [from Le nozze di Figaro]), E. Pinza (Mozart:Finch'han dal vino [from Don Giovanni]), H. Rosvaenge (Wagner:Morgenlich leuchtend [from Die Meistersinger von Nürnberg]), P. Anders (Flotow:Ach so fromm [from Martha]) MECL ▲ 423 [AAD] (17.97)

Treasures of the French Voices: The Bass—features performances by Pedro Gailhard (bass) (Gounod:Vous qui faites l'endormie [from Faust]), Pol Plançon (bass) (Godard:Embarquez-vous?; Thomas:Enfant chérie des dames, des grisettes (3 versions) [from Le Caïd]; Berlioz:Devant la maison; Voici les roses [both from Damnation de Faust]; Gounod:Allons! Jeunes gens [from Roméo & Juliette]; Le veau d'or (2 versions); Vous qui faites l'endormie (2 versions) [both from Faust]; Au brit des lourds marteaux [from Philémon & Baucis]; Adam:Vallons de l'Helvétie [from Le Chalet]; Meyerbeer:En chasse [from Le Pardon de Ploërmel]; Nonnes qui reposez [from Robert le Diable]; Verdi:Ou je suis...Je dormerai dans mon manteau royal [from Don Carlos]), Jean-François Delmas (bass) (Bizet:Quand la flamme de l'amour [from La Jolie de Perth]), Juste Nivette (bass) (Meyerbeer:Valse infernale [from Robert le Diable]), Marcel Journet (bass) (Gounod:Sous les pieds [from La Reine de Saba]; Meyerbeer:Du rendez-vous...Le bonheur [w. Edward Clément (ten); from Robert le Diable]; Bizet:Au fond du temple saint [from Les Pêcheurs de Perles]) (rec 1902-13) MNER ▲ 45 (m) [ADD] (14.97)

Trust in Me: The Old America on the Air—features performances by Connie Boswell (sgr), Joan Crawford (sgr), Dinah Shore (sgr), Nat King Cole (sgr), Bing Crosby (sgr), Al Jolson (sgr), Louis Jordan (sgr), Dick Powell (sgr), Frank Sinatra (sgr) (rec 1924-44) RY (Radio Years) ▲ 82 (16.97)

20th Century Voices in America—features performances by Jan de Gaetani (sop) (Rochberg:Tableaux [Sound Pictures from "The Silver Talons of Piero Kostrov"] for Sop & 11 Players [w. Richard Wernick (cnd), Penn Contemporary Players]), Elizabeth Suderburg (sop) (Crumb:Madrigals [Books 1-4; w. Robert Suderburg (cnd), Contemporary Group]), Rosalind Rees (sop) (Carter:Tell Me Where is Fancy Bred for Voice & Gtr; W. Schuman:Orpheus with his Lute for Voice & Gtr; Imbrie:Tell Me Where is Fancy Bred for Voice, Cl & Gtr [w. Richard Wagner (cl)]; Blumenfeld:Rilke for Voice & Gtr; Gregg Smith:Steps for Voice & Gtr; Kolb:The Sentences for Voice & Gtr [all w. David Starobin (gtr)]; Cage:The Wonderful Widow of 18 Springs for Voice & Pno [w. David Starobin (pno)]), Gloria Davy (sop) (Ran:O, The Chimneys for Mez, Fl, Cl, Vc, Perc & Pno [w. Shulamit Ran (pno), Robert Johnson (cnd), New York Philomusica Chamber Ensemble]), Phyllis Bryn-Julson (sop) (Rochberg:Qt No. 2 for Sop & Str Qt [w. Concord String Quartet]) (rec 1972-76) Vox Box 2-▲ CDX 5145

20 Great Basses Sing Great Arias—features performances by Pol Plançon (bass), Feodor Chaliapin (bass), Peter Dawson (bass), Mark Reizen (bass), Ezio Pinza (bass), Alexander Kipnis (bass), Ivar Andresen (bass), Marcel Jounet (bass), Salvatore Baccaloni (bass), Paul Knüpfer (bass), Emmanuel List (bass), Richard Mayr (bass), plus others (rec 1905-42) PHS ▲ 9122 [ADD] (17.97)

20 Great Sopranos Sing 20 Great Soprano Arias—features performances by Frieda Hempel, Amelita Galli-Curci, Toti dal Monte, Adelina Patti, Lotte Lehmann, Luisa Tetrazzini, Selma Kurz, Ninon Vallin, Kirsten Flagstad, Rosa Ponselle, Elisabeth Schumann, Conchita Supervia, Emma Calvé, Lilian Pons, Elisabeth Rethberg, Lucrezia Bori, Dame Nellie Melba, Meta Seinemeyer, Geraldine Farrar and Joan Hammond (rec 1902-42) PHS ▲ 9039 [AAD] (18.97)

20 Great Tenors Sing 20 Great Tenor Arias—features performances by Richard Tauber, John McCormack, Julius Patzak, Fernando de Lucia, Tito Schipa, Alfred Piccaver, Allesandro Bonci, Jan Kiepura, Joseph Hislop, Beniamino Gigli, Giovanni Zenatello, Lauritz Melchior, Enrico Caruso, Georges Thill, Richard Crooks, Francesco Tamagno, Giovanni Martinelli, Heddle Nash, Jussi Bjorling, Allesandro Valente (rec 1903-39) PHS ▲ 9040 [AAD] (17.97)

The Ultimate Aria Collection—features performances by Maria Callas (sop) (Bizet:Quand je vous aimerai? [w. Georges Prêtre (cnd), French National Opera Theater Orch; from Carmen]; Bellini:Casta diva [w. Tullio Serafin (cnd), La Scala Orch; from Norma]; Gluck:J'ai perdu mon Eurydice [w. Georges Prêtre (cnd), French National RSO; from Orphée ed Eurydice]; Cilea:Ecco: respiro appena [w. Tullio Serafin (cnd), Philharmonia Orch; from Adriana Lecouvreur]; Ponchielli:Suicido [w. Antonio Votto (cnd), La Scala Orch; from La Gioconda]), Franco Corelli (ten) (Verdi:Di quella pira [w. Thomas Schippers (cnd), Rome Opera Theater Orch; from Il trovatore]; Leoncavallo:Reitar!..Vesti la giubba [w. Lovro von Matačić (cnd), La Scala Orch; from I Pagliacci]; Puccini:Nessun dorma [w. Francesco Molinari-Pradelli (cnd), Rome Opera Theater Orch; from Turandot]; Recondita Armonia [from Tosca]; Cilea:L'anima ho stanca [from Adriana Lecouvreur]; Ponchielli:Cielo e mar [all w. Franco Ferraris (cnd); from La Gioconda]), Montserrat Caballé (sop) (Puccini:Un bel di vedremo [from Madama Butterfly]; Vissi d'arte [from Tosca]; Si, mi chiamano Mimi [from La Bohème]; In quelle trine morbide [from Manon Lescaut]; Se come voi piccina [from Le Villi; all w. Charles Mackerras (cnd), London SO]; Verdi:Pace, pace mio Dio [w. Anton Guadango (cnd), Royal PO; from La forza del destino]; Boito:L'altra notte in fondo al mare [w. Julius Rudel (cnd), London SO; from Mefistofele]), Nicolai Gedda (ten) (Donizetti:Una furtiva lagrima; Quanto è bella, quanto è cara! [both w. Francesco Molinari-Pradelli (cnd), Rome Opera Theater Orch; both from L'Elisir d'amore]; Thomas:Elle ne croyait pas dans sa candeur naïve [from Mignon]; Lalo:Puisqu'on ne peut [both w. Georges Prêtre (cnd), French National RSO; from Le Roi d'Ys]; Verdi:Di' tu se fedele [w. Giuseppe Patané (cnd), Royal Opera House Covent Garden Orch; from Un ballo in maschera]; Massenet:Toute mon âme est là [w. Georges Prêtre (cnd), Orch de Paris; from Werther]), Riccardo Muti (cnd), La Scala Orch, La Scala Chorus (Verdi:Va pensiero (Hebrew Slaves' Chorus) [from Nabucco]), Mirella Freni (sop) (Puccini:O mio babbino caro [from Gianni Schicchi]; Chi il bel sogno di Doretta [from La Rondine; both w. Leone Magiera (cnd)]; Signore, ascolta [from Turandot]; Charpentier:Depuis le jour [from Louise; both w. Franco Ferraris (cnd), Rome Opera Theater Orch]), Alfredo Kraus (ten) (Verdi:La donna è mobile [from Rigoletto]; Mozart:Un aura amorosa [from Così fan tutte; both w. Julius Redel (cnd), Philharmonia Orch]; Gounod:L'amour, l'amour...Ah, lève-toi soleil! [w. Michel Plasson (cnd), Toulouse Capitole Orch; from Roméo et Juliette]), Tito Gobbi (bar), Alceo Galliera (cnd), Philharmonia Orch (Rossini:Largo al factotum [from Il barbiere di Siviglia]), Mady Mesplé (sop), Danielle Millet (sop), Alain Lombard (cnd), Paris Opéra-Comique Orch (Delibes:Flower Duet [from Lakmé]), Giuseppe di Stefano (ten), La Scala Orch (Puccini:Avete torto! [from Gianni Schicchi]; Che gelida manina [from La Bohème; both w. Antonio Votto (cnd)]; Donna non vidi mai [w. Tullio Serafin (cnd); from Manon Lescaut]), Plácido Domingo (ten) (Puccini:E lucevan le stelle [w. James Levine (cnd), Philharmonia Orch; from Tosca]; Boito:Dai campi, dai prati [w. Julius Rudel (cnd), London SO; from Mefistofele]), Renato Bruson (bar), Riccardo Muti (cnd), Philharmonia Orch (Verdi:Di Provenza il mar [from La traviata]), Luciano Pavarotti (ten), Gianandrea Gavazzeni (cnd), Royal Opera House Covent Garden Orch (Mascagni:O amore, o bella luce del core [from L'Amico Fritz]), Fiorenza Cossotto (mez), Carlo Maria Giulini (cnd), Philharmonia Orch (Mozart:Voi che aspete [from Le nozze di Figaro]), Elena Obraztsova (mez), Giuseppe Patané (cnd), Philharmonia Orch (Saint-Saëns:Mon coeur s'ourve à ta voix [from Samson et Dalila]), Fritz Wunderlich (ten), Hans Müller-Kray (cnd), Bavarian State Opera Orch (Handel:Ombra mai fu [from Serse]), Victoria de los Angeles (sop) (Catalani:Ebben? ne andrò lontana [w. Giuseppe Morelli (cnd), Rome Opera Theater Orch; from La Wally]; Rossini:Una voce poco fa [w. Vittorio Gui (cnd), Royal PO; from Il barbiere di Siviglia]), José Carreras (ten) (Verdi:Celeste Aida [w. Herbert von Karajan (cnd), Vienna PO; from Aida]; Bizet:La fleur que tu m'avais jetée [w. Jacques Delacôte (cnd), Royal Opera House Orch; from Carmen]; Puccini:Non piangere, Liù [w. Alain Lombard (cnd), Strausborg PO; from Turandot]), Luigi Alva (ten), Carlo Maria Giulini (cnd), Philharmonia Orch (Mozart:Dalla sua pace [from Don Giovanni]), Alfredo Kraus (ten), Riccardo Muti (cnd), Philharmonia Orch (Verdi:De' miei bollenti spiriti [from La traviata]), Elisabeth Schwarzkopf (sop), Carlo Maria Giulini (cnd), Philharmonia Orch (Mozart:Porgi amor [from Le nozze di Figaro]) (rec 1955-92) EMIC 3-▲ 66884 (m/s) [ADD/DDD] (31.97)

The Ultimate Divas Album—features arias from works by Bellini (Norma [w. Joan Sutherland]), Bizet (Carmen [w. Tatiana Troyanos]), Catalani (La Wally [w. Renata Tebaldi]), Giordano (Andrea Chénier [w. Montserrat Caballé]), Mozart (Le nozze di Figaro [w. Kiri Te Kanawa, Frederica von Stade]; Die Zauberflöte [w. Sumi Jo]; Die Entführung aus dem Serail [w. Kathleen Battle]), Ponchielli (La Gioconda [w. Zinka Milanov]), Puccini (Madama Butterfly [w. Mirella Freni]), Rossini (Cenerentola [w. Cecilia Bartoli]; L'italiana in Algeri [w. Marilyn Horne]), Verdi (La Traviata [w. Angela Gheorghiu]; Tosca [w. Leontyne Price]; Otello [w. Renée Fleming]), Wagner (Die Walküre [w. Kirsten Flagstad]; Tristan und Isolde [w. Birgit Nilsson]) PLON ▲ 460596 (16.97)

The Ultimate Opera Collection, w. Venice Solisti, James Conlon (cnd), Armin Jordan (cnd), Raymond Leppard (cnd), Alain Lombard (cnd), Lorin Maazel (cnd), Claudio Scimone (cnd), London PO, Lyon Opera Orch, et al.—features performances by Julia Migenes, Ruggero Raimondi (Carmen), Luca Canonici (L'Elisir d'amore), Janet Baker (Orfeo et Euridice), Giacomo Aragall; Rhine Opera Chorus; Montserrat Caballé (Faust), Marilyn Horne (Rinaldo; Serse), Plácido Domingo (Pagliacci; Turandot; Aida), Kiri Te Kanawa & Frederica Von Stade (Così fan tutte), Sumi Jo (Magic Flute), Barbara Hendricks; José Carreras (Bohème) ERAT ▲ 45797 (16.97) ▮ 45797

The Ultimate Opera Queen—features arias by Puccini (Vissi d'arte [from Tosca, w Leontyne Price (sop), Rome Opera Orch [cnd:Oliviero de Fabritiis]]; Un Bel dì [from Madama Butterfly, w Anna Moffo (sop), Rome Opera Orch [cnd:Erich Leinsdorf]]; Signore, ascolta! [from Turandot, w Renata Tebaldi (sop), Rome Opera Orch [cnd:Erich Leinsdorf]]), Bellini (Casta diva [from Norma, w. Montserrat Caballé (sop), London PO [cnd:Carlo Felice Cillario], Ambrosian Opera Chorus]), Rossini (Una Voce poco fa [from Il Barbiere di Siviglia, w. Roberta Peters (sop), Metropolitan Opera Orch [cnd:Erich Leinsdorf]]), Verdi (Gualtier Maldè...Caro nome [from Rigoletto, w. Anna Moffo (sop), RCA Italiana Opera Orch [cnd:Georg Solti]]; O patria mia; Ritorna vincitor! [both from Aida, w. Leontyne Price (sop), Rome Opera Orch [cnd:Oliviero de Fabritiis]]; E strano...Afors è lui...Follie!; Teneste la promessa [both from La Traviata, w. Anna Moffo (sop), Rome Opera Orch [cnd:Fernando Previtali]]; Pace, pace mio dio [from La Forza del destino, w. Leontyne Price (sop), RCA Italiana Opera Orch [cnd:Thomas Schippers]]), Catalani (Ebben?...Ne andrò lontano [from La Wally, w. Eva Marton (sop), Munich RSO [cnd:Pinchas Steinberg]]), Mozart (Crudele?...Non mi dir [from Don Giovanni, w. Margaret Price (sop), English CO]), Cilèa (Io son l'umile ancella [from Adriana Lecouvreur, w. Leontyne Price (sop), RCA Italiana Opera Orch [cnd:Francesco Molinari-Pradelli]]) RCAV (Red Seal) ▲ 68540 [ADD/DDD] (10.97) 68540

Vienna Opera Favorites of the Past—features performances by Hilde Güden (sop), Josef Krips (cnd), London SO (Mozart:Non so più cosa son), Erich Kunz (bar), Herbert von Karajan (cnd), Vienna PO (Mozart:Non più andrai), Irmgard Seefried (sop), Herbert von Karajan (cnd), Vienna PO (Mozart:Giunse alfin il momento [all from Le nozze di Figaro]), Maria Cebotari (sop), Herbert von Karajan (cnd), Vienna PO (Mozart:Or sai chi l'onore), Anton Dermota (ten), Rudolf Moralt (cnd), Vienna PO (Mozart:Nur ihrem Frieden [both from Don Giovanni]), Herbert Alsen (bass), Rudolf Moralt (cnd), Vienna PO (Mozart:Solche hergelaufnen Laffen [from Die Entführung aus dem Serail]), Max Lorenz (ten), Karl Elmendorff (cnd), Saxon State Orch (Wagner:Ein Schwert verhiess mir der Vater), Maria Renning (sop), Artur Rother (cnd), Berlin RSO (Wagner:Der Männer Sippe sass hier am Saal), Hans Hotter (b-bar), Heinrich Hollreiser (cnd), Bavarian State Opera Orch (Wagner:Leb' wohl, du kühnes, herrliches Kind [all from Die Walküre]), Set Svanholm (ten), Frieder Weissmann (cnd), RCA Victor Orch (Wagner:Am stillen Herd), Paul Schöffler (b-bar), Karl Böhm (cnd), Vienna PO (Wagner:Was duftet doch der Flieder [both from Die Meistersinger von Nürnberg]), Elisabeth Höngen (cta), Erwin Baltzer (cnd), Vienna Opera Orch (Verdi:Verhängisvoll war das Geschenk [from Don Carlos]), Ljuba Welitsch (sop), Josef Krips (cnd), Philharmonia Orch (Verdi:Ritorna vincitor! [from Aida]), Helge Roswaenge (ten), Hanns Steinkopf (cnd), Berlin RSO (Puccini:Keiner schlafe [from Turandot]), Hilde Konetzni (sop), Herbert von Karajan (cnd), Vienna PO (R. Strauss:Kann mich auch an ein Mädel erinnern), Luise Willer (mez), Ludwig Weber (bass) (R. Strauss:Herr Cavalier! [both from Der Rosenkavalier]) (rec 1942-47) PRE ▲ 90345 (m) (16.97)

Vocalises

EMIC ▲ 56565 (16.97)

Voices From Lindenoper on Radio, w. Gitta Alpar (sop), Erna Berger (sop), Tiana Lemnitz (sop), Maria Müller (sop), Margarete Klose (mez), Peter Anders (ten), Max Lorenz (ten), Lauritz Melchior (ten), Franz Völker (ten), Friedrich Schorr (b-bar), Joseph Greindl (bass), Alexander Kipnis (bass) (rec 1927-45) RY (The Radio Years) ▲ 76 (16.97)

The Voices of Living Stereo, Vol. 1—features performances by Leontyne Price, Robert Merrill, Anna Moffo, Jussi Björling, Zinka Milanov, Risë Stevens, Roberta Peters, Giorgio Tozzi, Jan Peerce, Renata Tebaldi, Leonard Warren, Birgit Nilsson, Richard Tucker, & others; w. Herbert von Karajan, Erich Leinsdorf, Pierre Monteux, Dimitri Mitropolous, Arturo Basile, Tullio Serafin RCAV (Living Stereo) ▲ 62689 (10.97) ▮ 62689

The Voices of Living Stereo, Vol. 2, w. Eileen Farrell (sop), Birgit Nilsson (sop), Roberta Peters (sop), Leontyne Price (sop), Galina Vishnevskaya (sop), Rosalind Elias (mez), Shirley Verrett (mez), Marian Anderson (cta), Maureen Forrester (cta), Sergio Franchi (ten), Mario Lanza (ten), Richard Lewis (ten), Jan Peerce (ten), Cesare Valletti (ten), Alexander Dedyukhin (pno), Franz Rupp (pno), Leo Taubman (pno), George Trovillo (pno), Charles Wadsworth (pno), Boston Pops Orch [cnd:Arthur Fiedler], Boston SO [cnd:Charles Munch], Chicago SO [cnd:Fritz Reiner], RCA Victor Orch, RCA Victor Chorus [cnd:Warner Bass]—features works by Grieg (Solvejg's Song [from Peer Gynt]), Mahler (Der Trunkene im Frühling [from Das Lied von der Erde]; In diesem Wetter [from Kindertotenlieder]), Schubert (Ave Maria), Falvo (Dicitencello vuie), Berlioz (Premiers transports que nul n'oublie! [from Roméo et Juliette]; Le Spectre de la rose [from Les Nuits d'été]), Debussy (Apparition), A. Scarlatti (Caldo sangue), Wagner (Träume), Rachmaninoff (O Cease Thy Singing, Maiden Fair, Op. 4/4), Vian (Luna rossa), Montsalvatge (Canción de cuna para dormir a un negrito), trad (Kol Nidrei; He's Got the Whole World in His Hands) (rec Boston, Chicago, New York & Rome, 1957-64) RCAV (Living Stereo) ▲ 68167 [ADD] (10.97) 68167

Voices of the Czar: The Old Recordigs 1902-1916—features performances by Alma Fohrström (sop) (Alabiev:Solovei), Nina Friede (sop) (Gounod:Que fais-tu blanche tourtourelle [from Roméo & Juliette]), Marie Michailova (sop) (Glinka:I Look into Empty Fields [from A Life for the Czar]), Anastasia Vialtzeva (sop) (Vrangel:Oh! What a Glorious Night), Antonina Nezhdanova (sop) (Rimsky-Korsakov:Hymn to the Sun [from Le Coq d'or]), Maria Kouznetsova (sop) (Massenet:Je ne suis que faiblesse.. [from Manon]), Lydia Lipkowska (sop) (Tchaikovsky:Why Have I Not Known This Before? [from Iolanta]), Natalia Yuzina (sop) (Serov:I Put on My Garments [from Judith]), Eugenia Bronskaya (sop) (Verdi:E' stranto...Ah! fors'è lui [from Traviata]), Marianne Tcherkasskaya (sop) (Glinka:O my Ratmir [from Russlan & Ludmilla]), Nina Koshetz (sop) (Tchaikovsky:Lullaby), Eugenia Zbrujeva (mez) (Glinka:I Do Not Grieve about That [from A Life for the Czar]), Vera Pertova-Zvanceva (mez) (Tchaikovsky:Farewell to the Forests [from Maid of Orleans]; Je crains de parler la nuit [from Pique Dame]), Klaudia Tugarinova (mez) (Gounod:Faites-lui mes aveux [from Faust]), Elisaveta Peterenko (mez) (Gounod:Que fais-tu blanche tourtourelle [from Roméo & Juliette]) (rec 1902-16) MNER ▲ 48 (m) [ADD] (14.97)

Von der Königlichen Hofoper zur Staatsoper Unter den Linden—features works by D'Albert (Nun hab ich nichts als Dich mehr auf der Welt [from Tiefland; w. Violetta de Strozzi (sgr), Max Roth (sgr)]), Bellini (Casta diva [from Norma; w. Lilli Lehmann (sop)]), Bizet (Euren Toast kann ich wohl erwidern [w. Karl Armster (sgr)]; Liebst du mich treu und innig..Du bist's? [w. Margarete Klose (mez), Marcel Wittrisch (ten), Walther Grossmann (bass), Susanne Fischer (cta), Therese Gerson (sop)] [both from Carmen]), Cherubini (Segne, Gottheit, mein Bestreben [from Les Deux journées; w. Benno Ziegler (bar)]), Donizetti (Um stets heiter und glücklich zu leben [from Lucrezia Borgia; w. Ernestine Schumann-Heink (cta)]; O süsse Nacht im Mai durchwacht [from Don Pasquale; w. Gino Sinimberghi (ten)]), Flotow (Ach, so fromm [from Martha; w. Richard Tauber (ten)]), Gluck (O du, die mir einst Hilfe gab [from Iphigénie en Tauride [w. Zinaida Jurjewskaja (sgr)]), Gounod (Es ist schon spät [w. Geraldine Farrar (sop), Karl Jörn (ten)]; Ja, das Gold regiert die Welt [w. Ludwig Hofmann (bass)] [both from Faust]), Leoncavallo (Nein, bin Bajazzo nicht bloss [from Bajazzo; w. Josef Mann (ten)]), Lortzing (Du lässt mich kalt von hinnen scheiden [from Der Waffenschmied; w. Herbert Janssen (bar)]), Meyerbeer (Ach, mein Sohn, Segen dir [from Le Prophète; w. Marianne Brandt (sop)]; Dir, o Königin [from L'Africaine; w. Baptist Hoffmann (sgr)]), Mozart (Dies Bildnis ist bezaubernd schön [w. Peter Anders (ten)]; Ach, ich fühl's, es ist verschwunden [w. Käte Heidersbach (sop)]; O Isis und Osiris [w. Paul Knüpfer (bass)]; Der Hölle Rache kocht in meinem Herzen [w. Gitta Alpar (sop)]; Bei Männern, welche Liebe fühlen [w. Margherita Perras (sop), Gerhard Hüsch (bar)] [all from Die Zauberflöte]; Ich baue ganz auf deine Stäre [from Die Entführung aus dem Serail; w. Hermann Jadlower (ten)]; So lang hab ich geschmachtet [w. Lola Artôt de Padilla (sgr), Franz Egénieff (sgr)]; Heil'ge Quelle reiner Treibe [w. Lilly Hafgren (sop)]; Und Sie konnten warten...Süsse Rache [w. Alexander Kipnis (bass), Else Ruziczka (mez)]; Nun vergiss leises Fleh'n [w. Willi Domgraf-Fassbaender (bass)]; Wenn die sanften Abendlüfte [w. Viorica Ursuleac (sop), Erna Berger (sop)] [all from Le nozze di Figaro]), Mussorgsky (Ach, ich ersticke [from Boris Godunov; w. Leo Schützendorf (sgr)]), Offenbach (Sie entfloh, die Taube so minnig [from Les Contes d'Hoffmann; w. Emmy Bettendorf (sop)]), Puccini (Man nennt mich jetzt Mimi [w. Maria Cebotari (sop)]; Will ich allein [w. Carla Spletter (sop)]; O du süssestes Mädchen [w. Hedwig von Debitzka (sop), Helge Roswaenge (ten)] [all from La Bohème]; Wie sich die Bilder gleichen [w. Tino Pattiera (ten)]; Mit deinen Augen, den wundersamen [w. Mafalda Salvatini (sop), Björn Talén (ten)] [both from Tosca]), Saint-Saëns (O Liebe, meinen Hass steh' zur Seite [from Samson et Dalila; w. Marie Goetze (sgr)]), Joh. Strauss (II) (Dieser Anstand, so manierlich [w. Emilie Herzog (sop), Robert Philipp (sgr)]; Spiel' ich die Unschuld vom Lande [w. Marie Dietrich (sop)] [both from Die Fledermaus]), Verdi (Dieser Fleck da kommt immer wieder [from Macbeth; w. Gertrud Rünger (sop)]; Vernehmt ihr? [w. Frida Leider (sop), Heinrich Schlusnus (bar)]; In deines Kerkers tiefe Nacht [w. Barbara Kemp (sop)]; Lodernde Flamme [w. Emmi Leisner (cta)] [all from Il trovatore]; Wenn das Kraut, wie die Seherin kündet [w. Vera Schwarz (sop)]; Für dein Glück und für dein Leben [w. Theodor Scheidl (bar)]; König des Abgrunds, zeige dich [w. Karin Branzell (mez)] [all from Un ballo in maschera]; Bald kommt Radames [from Aida; w. Gertrud Bindernagel (sop)]; So hold, so reizend und engelsmild [from La traviata; w. Frieda Hempel (sop), Franz Naval (ten)]; Ach! Gott für mich nur erflehe ich [from Rigoletto; w. Claire Dux (sop), Joseph Schwaz (bar)]; Ich glaube an einen grausamen Gott [from Otello; w. Michael Böhnen (bass)]; Noch hegt mich der geliebte Ort [from La forza del destino; w. Hilde Scheppan (sop)]; Sie hat mich nie geliebt [from Don Carlos; w. Josef von Manowarda (bass)]), Wagner (War es so schmählich was ich verbrach [w. Marta Fuchs (sop)]; Der Männer Sippe sass hier im Saal [w. Delia Reinhardt (sgr)]; Siegmund heiss' ich [w. Rudolf Berger (ten)]; So ist es denn aus mit den ewigen Göttern [w. Margarete Arndt-Ober (mez)]; Winterstürme wichen dem Wonnemond [w. Walther Kirchhoff (ten)] [all from Die Walküre]; Fanget an [w. Set Svanholm (ten)]; Verachtet mir die Meister nicht [w. Friedrich Schorr (b-bar)]; Das schöne Fest [w. Josef Greindl (bass)] [all from Die Meistersinger]; Dir töne Lob [2 versions; w. Max Lorenz (ten); w. Francis Maclennan (ten)]; Dich teure Halle, grüss' ich wieder [w. Maria Müller (sop)]; Als du in kühnem Sange uns bestrittest [w. Cornelis Bronsgeest (bar)] [all from Tannhäuser]; Atmest du nicht mit mir die süssen Düfte [3 versions; w. Fritz Wolff (ten); w. Wilhelm Grüning (ten); w. Robert Hutt (ten)]; Das süsse Lied verhallt [w. Emmy Destinn (sop), Ernst Kraus (ten)]; Du Ärmste kannst wohl nie ermessen [w. Erna Denera (sgr), Thila Plaichinger (sgr)]; Dank, König, dir [w. Jaro Prohaska (bar)]; In fernem Land [w. Ludwig Suthaus (ten)] [all from Lohengrin]; Die Wunde? Wo? Lass sie mich heilen [w. Göta Ljungberg (sop)]; Mild und leise [w. Paula Buchner (sop)] [both from Tristan und Isolde]; Hier sitz' ich zur Wacht [w. Emanuel List (bass)]; Brünnhilde! Heilige Braut [w. Fritz Soot (ten)]; Starke Scheite schichtet mir dort [w. Anny Konetzni (sop)] [all from Götterdämmerung]; Ewig war ich [w. Helene Wildbrunn (sop)]; Das ist nun der Liebe schlimmer Lohn! [w. Julius Lieban (bar)] [both from Siegfried]; Vollendet das ewige Werk [w. Hermann Bachmann (bar)]; Abendlich strahlt der Sonne Auge [w. Rudolf Bockelmann (b-bar)] [both from Das Rheingold]; Traft ihr das Schiff [w. Melanie Kurt (sop)]; Auf hohem Felsen lag ich [w. Franz Völker (ten), Irmgard Langhammer (sop)] [both from Der fliegende Holländer]), Weber (Und ob die Wolke sie verhülle [from Der Freischütz; w. Tiana Lemnitz (sop)]) (rec 1905-46) PRE 4-▲ 89403 (m) (63.97)

VOCAL COLLECTIONS

Where Home Is: Life in 19th Century Cincinnati—features performances of 19th century songs by Harmoneion Singers [cnd:John Miner] (*Root:Where Home Is* [w. P. Basquin (harm)]; *Larcom/Pease:Ho! for Kansas*; *Grannis/Root:Old Canoe* [w. P. Basquin (harm)]; *Holman:Wake Up, Jake* [w. C. Jackson (bar), P. Basquin (pno)]; *Bliss:Sounds of the Singing School* [w. P. Basquin (pno)]; *Fillmore:Ohio*; *Blessed Bible*; *Henry: Murray:Who'll Buy?*; *Firmament* [w. J. Aler (ten)]; trad:*Sweet Home*], Clifford Jackson (bar), Peter Basquin (pno) (*Morris/Russell:A Life in the West*; *Howard:You Never Miss the Water 'till the Well Runs Dry*), Peter Basquin (pno) (*Peters:Old Rosin the Bow*; *Frankfort Belle*; *Murray:Galop*)
NWW ▲ 80251 (16.97)

The William Cullen Bryant Bicentennial Concert—features performances by Lenora Eve (mez), Leonard Lehrman (pno) (*Becky Dale:Summer Wind* [w. Akmal Parwez (bar)]; *Frederick Frahm:The Future Life*), Helene Williams (sop), Leonard Lehrman (pno) (*Matthew Marullo:Mutation*; *George Selbst:The Death of the Flowers*), Janis Sabatino Hills (sop), Leonard Lehrman (pno) (*Abram Plum:Mutation*; *Anne Watson Born:November*), Judi Silvano:*The Nature of Life*; Herbert Feldman:*A Song for New Year's Eve* [w. Christine Sabatino Dunleavy (sop)]; Akmal Parwez (bar) (*Harriette Slack Richardson:Yet I Smile More* [w. Leonard Lehrman (pno)]; *Joseph Pehrson:Thanatopsis* [w. Patricia Leland Rudoff (vn), Joseph Pehrson (pno)]), Christine Sabatino Dunleavy (sop), Leonard Lehrman (pno) (*Akmal Parwez:Song of the Prairies*), Ronald Edwards (ten), Leonard Lehrman (pno) (*Leo Kraft:Oct. 1864* [My Autumn Walk]) (rec Bryant Library, NYC)
CPS ▲ 8623 (16.97)

The World of Singing, Vol. 2: Singers of Imperial Russia, w. Nina Koshetz (sop), Evgenia Zbrueva (cta), Nicolai Figner (ten), Feodor Chaliapin (bass), Nina Friede (sgr), Maria Kouznetsova (sgr), Anastasia Vialtzeva (sgr)
VOCA (Vocal Archives) 2-▲ 2102 (26.97)

The World of Singing, Vol. 3: The Italian School, Part 1: The Italian Tenors before World War I (1902-13), w. Antonio Aramburo (ten), Alessandro Bonci (ten), Giuseppe Borgatti (ten), Enrico Caruso (ten), Edoardo Garbin (ten), Fiorello Giraud (ten), Fernando de Lucia (ten), Francesco Marconi (ten), Giovanni Battista de Negri (ten), Antonio Paoli (ten), Francesco Tamagno (ten), Fernando Valero (ten)
VOCA (Vocal Archives) 3-▲ 2104 (39.97)

The World of Singing, Vol. 4: The Italian School Part 1: Tenors before World War I, Book 2—features performances by Carlo Albani (ten), Amedeo Bassi (ten), Giuseppe Borgatti (ten), Enrico Caruso (ten), Florencio Costantino (ten), Edoardo Garbin (ten), Fiorello Giraud (ten), Antonio Paoli (ten), Piero Schivazzi (ten), Elvino Ventura (ten), Giovanni Zenatello (ten)
VOCA (Vocal Archives) 3-▲ 2107 (39.97)

The World of Singing, Vol. 5: The Polish School, Part 1: Sopranos & Mezzo-Sopranos, w. Ewa Bandoska-Turska (sop), Jadwiga Debicka (sop), Janina Korolewicz-Waydowa (sop), Salomea Kruszelnicka (sop), Helena Lipowska (sop), Maria Mokrzycka (sop), Matylda Polinska-Lewicka (sop), Ada Sari (sop), Marcella Sembrich (sop), Helena Zboinska-Ruszkowska (sop), Maria Olczewska (mez), Wanda Werminska (mez)
VOCA (Vocal Archives) 3-▲ 2110 (38.97)

The World of Singing, Vol. 6: The French School Part 1: Basses (1897-1913), w. Hypolite Belhomme (bar), Jean-François Delmas (b-bar), Paul Amonier (bass), Hector Dufranne (bass), Pedro Gailhard (bass), Marcel Journet (bass), Juste Nivette (bass), Pol Plançon (bass), Edouard de Reszke (bass)
VOCA (Vocal Archives) ▲ 2113 (38.97)

The World of Singing, Vol. 7: The Polish School, Part I: Tenors, Baritones, Basses (Book 2)—features performances by Wiktor Bregy (ten), Adam Dobosz (ten), Ignacy Dygas (ten), Stanislaw Gruszczynski (ten), Tadeusz Leliwa (ten), Jozef Mann (ten), Waclaw Brzezinski (bar), Eugeniusz Mossakowski (bar), Adam Didur (bass), Aleksander Michalowski (bass), Tadeusz Orda (bass), Adam Ostrowski (bass) (rec 1902-30)
VOCA (Vocal Archives) 3-▲ 2116 (38.97)

The World of Singing, Vol. 8: The Italian School: Tenors before & after World War I, w. Giuseppe Anselmi (ten), Giovanni Zenatello (ten), et al.—features arias from Don Giovanni; Il barbiere di Siviglia; L'elisir d'amore; Lucrezia Borgia; Lucia di Lammermoor; La favorita; Don Pasquale; Il Duca d'Alba; Luisa Miller; Rigoletto; Aida & Manon
VOCA (Vocal Archives) 3-▲ 2119 (38.97)

The World of Singing, Vol. 9: The Italian School, Part 2: Tenors before & during World War I, Book 1—features performances by Giovanni Martinelli (ten) (arias from *Tosca*, *Aida*, *Il trovatore*, *Ernani*, *Rigoletto*, *L'Africaine & others*), Tito Schipa (ten) (arias from *Cavalleria rusticana*, *La Gioconda*, *Lucia di Lammermoor*, *Faust & others*), Bernardo de Muro (ten) (arias from *Andrea Chénier*, *Isabeau*, *Carmen* & *La fanciulla del West*) (rec 1912-28)
VOCA (Vocal Archives) 3-▲ 2122 (38.97)

Zürcher Liederbuch 1986 und Lieder von Othmar Schoeck—features performances by Graf, Widmer, Gehri, Otto, Gähwiller, Som, Jakobi, Haefliger, Gohl, Boesch, Wyttenbach, Schoeck, Fervers, Fueter, Derungs, Gierè (works by Schoeck, Boesch, Wettstein, Jordi, Haselbach, Derungs, Irman)
JEC 2-▲ JD 270/1-2 (ADD)

VOCAL ENSEMBLE

A Sei Voci
Salve Regina: Musiques festives mariales du grégorien au 17ème siècle, w. Jean Boyer (org)—features works by Croce (*Magnificat Quarti Toni*), Morales (*Jubilate Deo*), Raquet (*Fant sur Regina Coeli*), Gabrieli (*Beata Es Virgo*), Dufay (*Alma Redemptoris Mater*), Bruna (*Tiento Sobre la Letania de la Virgen*), Guerrero (*Ave Virgo Sanctissima*), Frescobaldi (*Ricercar*), Correa De Arauxo (*Canto llano de la Immaculada Conception*), Titelouze (*Magnificat du 8ème ton*), anon (*Gaudeamus*; *Regina Coeli*; *Salve Regina*)
ACCO ▲ 205072 [DDD]

Akademia Vocal Ensemble
Motets from Johann to Johann Sebastian Bach, w. La Fenice Instrumental Ensemble [cnd:Françoise Lasserre]—features motets by members of the Bach family, including Hans, Johann, Johann Michael, Johann Christoph, Johann Sebastian, Wilhelm Friedrich Ernst, et al.
PVY ▲ 797111 (16.97)

Alderson, Ann (sgr), Richard Alderson (sgr), Stacy Kowalczyk (sgr), Carey Lovett (sgr)
Catholic Classics, Vol. 1—features How Great Thou Art; Blest Are They; Hail Mary, Gentle Woman; Eat This Bread; You Are Near; Make Me a Channel of Your Peace (Prayer of St. Francis); On Eagle's Wings; Sing With All the Saints in Glory; We Remember; I Am the Bread of Life
GA ▲ 375 (16.97)

Duodena Cantitans
Mirabile Mysterium, w. Capella Rudolphina—features music from the time of Holy Roman Emperor Rudolph II
SUR ▲ 192

Canzone Choir
The Danish Song Treasury, Vol. 3—features 22 Danish songs from the 16th & 17th, trad. & romantic pops
KPT ▲ 32155 [DDD]

Canzone Choir [cnd:Frans Rasmussen]
The Danish Song Treasury, Vol. 4—features I Danmark Er Jeg Født; Vi Sletternes Sønner; Vor Sol Er Bleven Kold; Lystyldt Morgen; Den Grøonne, Søode Vår; Han Kommer Med Sommer; Du Kaere Blide Danske Baek; Jeg Ved En Laerkerede; Alle Mine Laengsler; I Skyggen Vi Vanke; Laer Mig, Nattens Stjerne; Snart Er Natten Svenden; Morgendug, Der Sagte Baever; Som Dybest Brønd; Solen Er Så Rød, Mor; Sig Naermer Tiden, Da Jeg MA Vaek
KPT ▲ 32230

Canzone Vocal Ensemble [cnd:Frans Rasmussen]
Danish Folk Ballads—features 18 sels arr by various Danish composers
KPT ▲ 32268

La Capella Reial de Catalunya Vocal Ensemble [cnd:Jordi Savall]
El Cançoner del Duc de Calàbria—features 17 sels from the songbook of Ferdinand of Aragon, Duke of Calàbria
ASTR ▲ 8582 (18.97)

Clare College Choir Cambridge [cnd:John Rutter] Clare College Orch
Carols from Clare College Cambridge
EMIC ▲ CDM 69950

Daughters of St. Paul
A Little Love—features People of God, Prayer of St. Francis, They'll Know We Are Christians, O Taste and See, To Jesus Heart All Burning/O Lord I Am Not Worthy, Spirit of God, Put a Little Love in Your Heart, How Deep the Riches, O Sacrum Convivium, How Can I Keep from Singing, I Love You Lord, Do Right, People Need the Lord, Count It All Joy, O Salutaris/Tantum Ergo, On Holy Ground
St. Paul Books & Media ▲ 4472-X ▮ 4473-1

Dufay Collective
Johnny, Cock Thy Beaver—features works by Playford (*Indian Queen/Of Noble Race Was Shinkin* [from *The English Dancing Master*]; *A Moriscо*; *Goddesses/Jamaica*; *The Waits*; *Ham House/Half Hannikin*; *Pell Mell*; *On the Cold Ground*; *Glory of the Sun*; *Kettledrum*; *Paul's Wharf*; *Sat. Night & Sun Morn*; *Johnny, Cock Thy Beaver*), Dowland (*My Lord Wilobies Welcome Home*), T. Simpson (*Bonny Sweet Robin*), Farnaby (*Mal Sims*; *Muscadin*; *A Maske*; *The Old Spagnoletta*), Ravenscroft (*The 3 Ravens*; *New Oysters*; *Jolly Shepherd*; *A Wooing song of a Yeoman of Kent's Sonne*; *Come, Follow Me*; *Of All the Birds*), C. Simpson (*Divisions for 2 Bass Vls*), Anonymous (*Daphne*; *Fortune My Foe*; *Bonny Sweet Robin*; *The Clothiers Song*) (rec Forde Abbey, Sept 7-9, 1995)
CHN ▲ 9446 (16.97)

Hilliard Ensemble [David James (ct), Rogers Covey-Crump (ten), John Potter (ten), Gordon Jones (bar)]
A Hilliard Songbook: New Music for Voices—features works by Guy (*Un coup de dés* [w Barry Guy (db)]), Fulkerson (*Only*), Moody (*Endechas y Canciones*; *Canticum Canticorum I*), Hellawell (*The Hilliard Songbook*), P. Robinson (*Incantation*), Tormis (*Kullervo's Message*), Gregorian (*Adoro te devote*), MacMillan (*...here in hiding...*), Pärt (*And One of the Pharisees...*; *Summa*), Liddle (*Whale Paint*), Metcalf (*Music for the Star of the Sea*), Finnissy (*Stabant autem iuxta crucem*), Casken (*Sharp Thorne*) (rec 1995-96)
ECM 2-▲ 21614 [DDD] (30.97)

Elmer Iseler Singers [cnd:Lydia Adams, Howard Cable, Elmer Iseler]
The Maple Leaf Forever, w. Carolynne Godin (mez), Vladimir Radian (ten), Sandra Fan (hp), Russell Hartenberger (perc), True North Brass (The Maple Leaf Forever; Red River Valley; Farewell to Nova Scotia; Sioux Lullaby; Song for Canada; plus others
ODRE ▲ 9314 (16.97)

King's Singers
America, w. English CO [cnd:C. Davis]
EMIC ▲ 49701 (16.97) 49701
Madrigal History
EMIC ▲ 69837 (11.97)
My Spirit Sang All Day—features works by Parry, Stanford, Elgar, Vaughan Williams, Holst, Bridge, Grainger, Moeran, Rubbra, Finzi, & others
EMIC ▲ 49765 (16.97) 49764
New Day
EMIC ▲ 49564 (16.97) 49564

Lionheart [Jeffrey Johnson (ten), Lawrence Lipnik (ct), Kurt-Owen Richards (bass), John Olund (sgr), Richard Porterfield (sgr), Stephen Rosser (sgr)]
My Fayre Ladye: Tudor Songs & Chant
NIMB ▲ 5512 [DDD] (16.97)

Measure for Measure [cnd:Leonard Ricciotto]
Measure for Measure at Orchestra Hall—features works by Praetorius (*Sing Dem Herrn*), Sullivan (*The Lost Chord*), Palmgren (*Sing, Maiden, Sing*, arr James Porter (bar)]), Fauré (*Cantique de Jean Racine* [w. Adam Riccinto (vc)]), Barber (*I Hear An Army*), Pfautsch (*Go & Tell John*), Sweelinck (*Hodie Christus Natus Est*), Shaw (*La Virgen Lava Panales* [w. William Condon (ten)]; *Run To The Manger*), Smith (*The Star-Spangled Banner*), anon (*How Still & Tiny* [arr Mishkin]; *Do You Hear What I Hear?* [arr Simeone]; *Shenandoah* [arr Erb]; *Waitin' For The Dawn of Peace* [arr Jeffers]; *Down In The Valley* [arr Mead]; *Joshua* [arr Sells]; *Sometimes I Feel Like a Motherless Child* [arr Heath; w. Bernard Moner (bar)]; *River In Judea* [arr Leavitt]; *Shadrack* [arr Casey]; *Whistle, Maggie, Whistle* [arr Stocker])
Binaural Source-Measure for Measure ▲ C-24

Opus Angelicum [John Touhey (nar), Stephen Tilton (ct), Julian Stocker (ten), William Lee (ten), Roland Robertson (bar), John Rowlands-Pritchard (bass)]
The Seeds of Love: Collecting English Folk Music (English folk songs, collected by Cecil Sharp & the English Folk-Song Society, in original versions and arrangements by composers and Opus Angelicum; plus readings from the Folk-Song Society Journal)—features Hal an Tow; The Padstow Morning [both arr P. T. Nardone]; I Sowed the Seeds of Love; Dives & Lazarus; Bushes & Briars; Our Captain Calls All Hands/He Who Would Valiant Be; The Ploughboy's Dream/O Little Town of Bethlehem; High Germany [all arr Vaughan Williams]; Lord Randel; The Gypsy Laddie; The Water Is Wide; The Coal-black Smith; The Turtle Dove; Cold Blows the Wind Tonight; Brigg Fair [arr Grainger]; The Cutty Wren; John Barleycorn; Banks of Green Willow [arr Butterworth/Chenery]; Sailor's Chanties [collected by H. E. Piggott]; 6 Chanties (rec John Wood Chapel, Prior Park, Bath, July 1997)
HER ▲ 216 [DDD] (18.97)

Quink
English Madrigals—features works by Morley, Pilkington, Tomkins, Bateson, Byrd, Farmer, Wilbye, Weelkes (rec Dec 1991-Jan 1997)
TEL ▲ 80328 [DDD] (15.97)

St. Petersburg Vocal Ensemble
Aleko—features works by Gretchaninoff (*Lobe den Herren, meine Seele*), Archangelski (*Selig ist am Tage des Gerichts*; *Selig ist der Mann*; *Stärke mich, o Herr, im Gebet*), Degtiarow (*Es freut sich jedes Geschöpf*), Tschesnokow (*Seit meiner Jugend*; *Dir singen wir*; *Selig ist der Mann*), Bortnjanski (*Dich, o Herr Herrn*), Balakirev (*Prophetenlied*), Glisovic (*Kunstkopfumgang*), trad (*Mit uns ist Gott*; *Ein Unglück ist geschehen*; *Dubinuschka*; *Im dunklen Wald*; *Die Mondnacht*; *Der rote Sarafan*) (rec live, Nov 16, 1994)
Binaural Source-Abandone ▲ C-21

St. Quirinus Chorkreis Rosenheim [G. Hamberger, I. Hamberger, L. Hamberger, K. Ginthör, T. Hamberger, H. Huber]
Beautiful Marian Songs (rec Feb 1983)
CALG ▲ CAL 50807 [DAD]

Schola Cantorum Basiliensis [cnd:Rudolf Lutz]
Lamentationes, w. St. Gallen String Orch—features works by Reger (*O Mensch bewein dein' Sünde gross*), Shostakovich (*Requiem for Str Orch, Op. 144a*), Franck (*Choral in b*), anon chants (*Crucem Tuam adoramus Domine*; *Crux Fidélis, inter omnes Arbor una nobilis*; *De profundis clamávi ad te, Domine*; *Impropérium expectávit cormeum*; *Christus factus est pro nobis*) (rec St. Mangen Church, St. Gallen, Switzerland)
GILD ▲ 7123 [DDD] (16.97)

Singer Pur
Nordic Vocal Music—features works by Stenhammar (*I Seraillets Have*), H. Parkman (*Sonnet 147*; *Madrigal*), Fougstedt (*Tiga blott*), Rautavaara (*Nattvarden*; *Kvällen stundar*), Lindberg (*Visa om Torn Erik*; *Shall I Compare Thee*), Sarmanto (*Iltarukous*), Tauro (*Höstvisa*), Peterson-Berger (*Till rosorna*), Långbacka (*Karkoff* (*Lek*), Kruse (*Vanitas*), Kverno (*Corpus Christi Carol*), Mellnäs (*NAgon gäng*; *Vinternam*), Wikander (*A Lullaby Nung Lijjekonvalje*), B. Hansson (*Som när handen*), Perder (*Jämtländsk Folkvisa*), Hermodsson (*Visa till färö*) (rec Apr 1997)
ARSM ▲ 1208 [DDD] (17.97)

Skaraborg Vocal Ensemble
The Top Ten of Sweden's Great Power Period, w. Jakob Lindberg (lt)—features the ten most popular melodies from 17th century Sweden
PRPI ▲ 9083 (17.97)

Souvenirs de Venise [Felicity Lott (sop), Ann Murray (mez), Anthony Rolfe Johnson (ten), Richard Jackson (bar)]
The Songmakers' Almanac, w. Graham Johnson (pno), et al.—features works by Beethoven, Fauré, Glinka, Gounod, Hahn, Jensen, Massenet, Mendelssohn, Rossini, Schubert, Taneyev
HYP ▲ 66112 [DDD] (17.97)

3 Counter-Tenors [Pascal Bertin (ct), Andreas Scholl (ct), Dominique Visse (ct)]
The 3 Countertenors—features works by Di Capua (*O Sole mio*), Bizet (*Habañera* [from *Carmen*]), Massenet (*Pleurez, mes yeux* [from *Le Cid*]), Bernstein (*Maria* [from *West Side Story*]), Saint-Saëns (*Mon heart at Thy Sweet Voice* [from *Samson & Dalila*]), Scholl (*White as Lilies*), Offenbach (*Je suis grise* [from *La Périchole*]), Paul Anka (*My Way*), Donizetti (*Una furtiva lagrima* [from *L'Elisir d'amore*])
HAM ▲ 901552 (14.97) ▮

WEDDING MUSIC

Bowyer, Kevin (org)
For Weddings—features 23 sels from the Oxford Book of Wedding Music Chichester Cathedral org
NIMB ▲ 7712 (11.97)

Budapest Strauss Ensemble [cnd:István Bogár]
Wedding Celebrations—features works by Ivanovici (*Bavarian Ländler*; *Donauwellen* [waltz]), Offenbach (*La vie parisienne* [2 versions, polka & cancan]), Pazeller (*Souvenir de Herkulesbad*), Schrammel (*Wien bleibt Wien* [march]), Johann Strauss I (*Radetzky-Marsch, Op. 228*), Johann Strauss II (*Figaro-Polka française, Op. 320*; *Einzugs-Marsch from Der Zigeunerbaron*]; *Böhmisch-Polka*, *Spanischer Tanz* [from *Die Fledermaus*], *Annen-Polka-française*, Op. 117; *Wein, Weib und Gesang* [waltz], Op. 333), J. Strauss (*Frauenherz, Op. 166*; *Flora, Op. 54*), J.F. Wagner (*Tyrolean Woodcutters' March*) (rec Apr 5-7, 1993)
NXIN ▲ 550900 [DDD] (5.97)
Wedding Music, w. B. Hoch (org)—features works by Mendelssohn, Wagner, Schubert, Widor, Boëllmann, Clarke, Gounod, Handel, Purcell, Albinoni, Vivaldi, Bach, J. Strauss Jr. (rec 1992)
NXIN ▲ 550790 [DDD] (5.97)

Florida Symphonic Pops Orch [cnd:Mark Azzolina], Lyn Larsen (org)
A Bride's Book—features works by PART ONE: 'The Traditional Wedding"—music by Purcell (*Trumpet Voluntary*), Campra (*Rigaudon*), Schubert (*Ave Maria*), Mouret (*Rondeau* [Masterpiece Theatre Theme]), Wagner (*Bridal Chorus from Lohengrin*), Malotte (*The Lord's Prayer*), Bach (*Now thank we all our God*), Mendelssohn (*Wedding March from A Midsummer Night's Dream*), Clarke (*Trumpet Tune*); PART TWO: "The Contemporary Wedding"—Wind beneath my wings; And I love her; One hand, one heart; Bridal Chorus from Lohengrin; The Wedding Song; Endless love; Wedding March from A Midsummer Night's Dream (all selections in Part One are solo organ performances, except for "Ave Maria" which is orchestral; all selections in Part Two are played by orchestra—this is a 'Digital Surround Sound' recording)
PRA ▲ 564 [DDD] (14.97) 564 (10.98)

Florida Symphonic Pops Orch [cnd:Mark Azzolina], Lyn Larsen (org), St. Louis Brass
Wedding Day—features works by PART ONE: 'The Traditional Wedding"—music by Purcell (*Trumpet Voluntary*), Campra (*Rigaudon*), Grieg (*I love thee*; *Erotik*), Mouret (*Rondeau* [Masterpiece Theatre Theme]), Wagner (*Bridal Chorus from Lohengrin*), Malotte (*The Lord's Prayer*), Bach (*Now thank we all our God*; *Jesu, joy of man's desiring*), Stanley (*Trumpet tune*), Mendelssohn (*Wedding March from A Midsummer Night's Dream*); PART TWO: "The Contemporary Wedding"—Wind beneath my wings; We've only just begun; One hand, one heart; Bridal Chorus from Lohengrin; The Wedding Song; Endless love; Wedding March from A Midsummer Night's Dream
PRA ▲ 569 [DDD] (14.97) 569 (10.98)

Richard Hayman SO [cnd:Richard Hayman]
I Love You Truly—features works by Bach (*Aria*), Pachelbel (*Arrival of the Guests*, *Canon & Gigue*) Hawaiian Wedding Song, Ich liebe dich, I Love You Truly, Norwegian Bridal Procession, Suite de Symphonies, Trumpet Prelude, Wedding Dance, Wedding Day at Troldhaugen, Wedding March, Wedding March from Lohengrin
NXIN ▲ 8.990019 [DDD]

Philharmonic Wedding Ensemble
Everybody's Favorite Wedding Music (19 selections designed to take the bride, groom and wedding party through every step of the ceremony and reception: 1) Prelude: Music for the Arrival of the Guests; 2) The Ceremony: Processional; 3) Music for the Reception: Songs of Love, and More Songs of Love; 4) Recessional), w. Bert Lucarelli (obo), Marnie Nixon (sop), John Cullum (bar)
ESX ▲ 7050 (9.97) ▮ 7050

▲ = CD   ♦ = Enhanced CD   △ = MD   ▮ = Cassette Tape   □ = DCC